P9-CBP-945

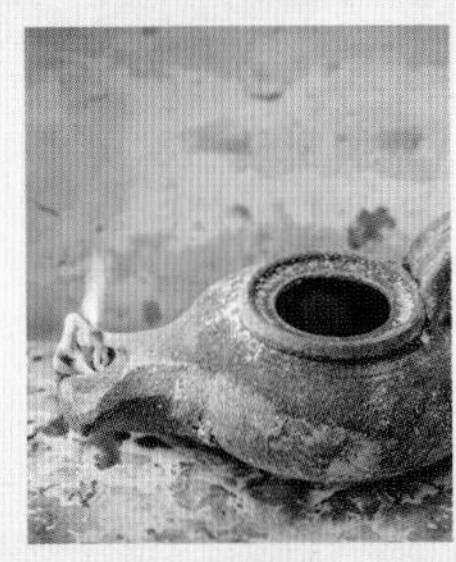

THE HOLY BIBLE

YOUR WORD IS A LAMP FOR MY FEET,
A LIGHT ON MY PATH.
— PSALM 119:105 —

PRESENTED TO:

BY:

ON:

NEW INTERNATIONAL VERSION

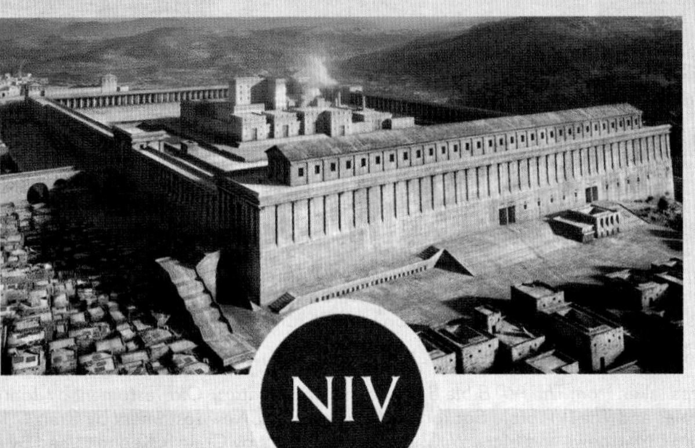

NIV

CULTURAL BACKGROUNDS STUDY BIBLE

Bringing to Life the Ancient World of Scripture

ZONDERVAN®

Published by Zondervan
Grand Rapids, Michigan, USA

www.zondervan.com

Library of Congress Catalog Card Number 2015955619

Printed in China

N120712

---

17 18 19 20 21 22 23 24 25 /DSC/ 15 14 13 12 11 10 9 8 7 6 5 4 3

A portion of the purchase price of your NIV® Bible is provided to Biblica so together we support the mission of *Transforming lives through God's Word.*

Biblica provides God's Word to people through translation, publishing and Bible engagement in Africa, Asia Pacific, Europe, Latin America, Middle East, and North America. Through its worldwide reach, Biblica engages people with God's Word so that their lives are transformed through a relationship with Jesus Christ.

Quick Start Guide

to the *NIV Cultural Backgrounds Study Bible*

"Even though the Bible was written *for* us, it wasn't written *to* us. When we take our Western, modern culture and impose it on the text, we're putting in meaning that wasn't there, and we're missing the meaning that the text has."

—*Dr. John H. Walton*

"Sometimes people get frustrated with the Bible because the difficult figures of speech and the images and the customs they read about seem foreign to them. But when we explain those, then we open up the text of the Bible in a fresh, new way to understand what the text of the Bible is really addressing. Ultimately, everything in the Bible was written in particular times and cultures. So even though everything in it is for all time, not everything in it is for all circumstances. The better we understand the circumstances a passage originally addressed, the more confidently we can reapply its message to appropriate circumstances today."

—*Dr. Craig S. Keener*

Welcome to the *NIV Cultural Backgrounds Study Bible*. You have in your hands a comprehensive, multiuse tool that has been designed specifically to enhance your understanding of and appreciation for the cultural backgrounds that form the footings on which the foundation of God's Word is built.

About the *NIV Cultural Backgrounds Study Bible*

This study Bible has been purpose-built to do one thing: to increase your understanding of the cultural nuances behind the text of God's Word so that your study experience, and your knowledge of the realities *behind* the ideas in the text, is enriched and expanded.

This study Bible contains the full text of the New International Version of the Bible along with a library of study features designed to help you more completely grasp what the text is saying. These notes introduce and explain a wide variety of information on the Biblical text, providing deeper insights for individuals who are ready to devote themselves to serious study of the text.

What Help Do These Study Features Offer?

Each of the features in the *NIV Cultural Backgrounds Study Bible* has been developed with the goal of allowing readers to immerse themselves in the culture, the literature, the geography and the everyday life of the people to whom the Bible was originally written.

- Book Introductions answer questions about who wrote the books of the Bible, to whom, and when, as well as informing readers about the larger cultural and political context in which a book was written. In the Old Testament, dates of writing and specific authorship for each book are less clear than in the New Testament, where such information is marginally less controversial, although still debated. That's why the Old Testament introductions include "Key Concepts" and the New Testament Introductions include "Quick Glance" information to help readers orient themselves.
- The Old Testament includes a helpful chart that explains the nuances of meaning contained in Hebrew words that don't have exact equivalents in English. That chart is called "Hebrew to English Translation Chart," and can be found on p. xix.

- Also included before the Old Testament is a helpful article entitled, “Major Background Issues from the Ancient Near East” (p. xxxix) that is a must-read before you begin your OT study.
- The New Testament includes a reference feature entitled “Key New Testament Terms” (p. 1584) that is designed to help clarify and further define the cultural contexts behind these terms. It’s included as a background feature to define and explain terms that often repeat in the New Testament notes.
- The NIV Center-column Cross Reference system aids in deeper study of the Bible’s themes, language and concepts by leading readers to related passages on the same or similar themes.
- Over 10,000 study notes have been placed close to the text that they amplify and explain. These have been designed to provide the reader with a deep and rich understanding of the nuances that the original readers and hearers of the Bible would have intuitively understood. They focus on the land, the literature, and the political and cultural contexts that the Bible’s authors lived in, and emphasize how the people of Israel were both influenced by, as well as how they were called to be different from, their surrounding culture.
- Full-color in-text maps, charts and diagrams, along with some 320 essays, summarize and explain important background information and ideas from Scripture.
- Front and end matter features include author information, an author’s introduction with helpful questions and answers about this Bible, more information on the NIV translation itself (in the NIV Preface), and many other helpful study tools.
- The NIV Concordance is a tool designed to help readers who remember a key word or phrase in a passage to locate the verses they are looking for. Words and names are listed alphabetically, along with their more significant verse references.
- Color maps at the end of this study Bible complement the color maps in the interior of the Bible to help readers to visualize the geographic context of what they are studying.

Please take a few minutes to familiarize yourself with these features as you begin your study. We’re confident that as you expand your understanding of the social, economic, literary and political culture in which the Bible was written over the course of many centuries, that your understanding of and love for God’s Word will increase all the more.

—The authors and editors
NIV Cultural Backgrounds Study Bible

Table of Contents

Charts

Maps

Author Introduction

to the *NIV Cultural Backgrounds Study Bible*

Editor's Note: This study Bible draws on the contributions of various scholars. The Old Testament (OT) comprises three-quarters of the Bible, and to provide study notes and articles on this body of work, Dr. John Walton has drawn on the works of various contributors, including his own work, in the *Zondervan Bible Backgrounds Commentary: Old Testament*. Also drawing on a range of research, Dr. Craig Keener, author of *The IVP Bible Background Commentary: New Testament*, authored most NT notes, but others contributed some sidebars and "Quick Glance" notes.

Both scholars have published heavily documented works that support the sort of background that is provided here on a more accessible level. Both have been studying, writing and lecturing around the world about the field of the Bible's cultural backgrounds for the duration of their decades-long careers as academics.

For whom has this study Bible been designed?

This study Bible is for those who want more out of the study of the Bible than they can get by just reading the text on their own. The notes, illustrations, charts and other study tools offer content for understanding that goes beyond most study Bibles. It is for the reader who isn't content with being told what they should understand from the text, or with being given what they could figure out on their own. It is for the reader who already understands the importance of reading in context and seeing each book of the Bible as a whole. It is for the reader who is serious about the Bible itself, but has not had advanced training in the world in which the message of the Bible first came alive.

Can't I read and understand the Bible just from the text itself?

Study Bibles often focus on helping readers apply the Bible to daily life. To be sure, applying the Bible to daily life is very important. Yet those who read the Bible enough can glean most principles from the Bible directly. After all, God's story in the Bible is designed to be understood by children. As Jesus said, "I praise you, Father, Lord of heaven and earth, because you have hidden these things from the wise and learned, and revealed them to little children" (Mt 11:25), and "Truly I tell you, unless you change and become like little children, you will never enter the kingdom of heaven" (Mt 18:3). Hearing God's personal challenge from the Bible itself is more direct than hearing a challenge from someone else's comments. Spiritual life comes from God's Word itself.

The complication is the gulf between the world of the Bible and the modern reader's world. The problem is normally not that the modern reader doesn't know their own world; it's that the reader is not familiar with the world of the Bible. It is here that a study Bible can help most by explaining the language, literature and culture of the Bible.

How does this study Bible differ from others that are available?

What these notes supply is background — the missing pieces of information that the Biblical writers did not need to state explicitly because their original audiences intuitively knew them. Understanding these nuances help the reader "hear" the Bible in a way much closer to the way the Bible's first audience heard it. Although the best study Bibles today include some background, this study Bible is unique in the massive wealth of background that it provides.

How will understanding the Bible's cultural background improve my faith walk?

There is no such thing as a story or a teaching that doesn't have a cultural setting. That is not to say that a story or teaching is not *relevant* for another setting, but to remember that it comes to us from a particular place and in a particular language. God sent his Son Jesus Christ in the flesh, in a specific home, nation, town and era. Likewise, God didn't send the Bible as a transcultural feeling or impression, but gave it to us through the experiences that real people had in real historical situations. This Bible's notes are meant to help readers hear and visualize the story closer to the way it was originally written, so they can get to know the people and places in the Bible more on their own terms.

Readers from different cultures bring a range of experiences and insights to their Bible reading. The place where we come together, however, is when we read God's Word in the concrete framework in which he gave it. It is especially when we hear the message in its authentic, original cultural setting that we can reapply it afresh for our own different settings most fully, because we understand what issues were really being addressed. You should keep this purpose in mind as you read the notes.

Please tell me more about the notes in this Bible.

The study tools in this Bible are not meant to tell the reader everything about the Biblical text—especially not what will be self-evident from the context. They do not always tell readers what is most important or what applies most directly to life, because these are points that mature readers can learn to do on their own. What they do is equip readers to study the Bible more on its own terms so they can discover its most valuable treasures for themselves.

Not every proposed background is equally relevant or certain, though the authors of the study notes have tried to screen out the least relevant and least certain proposals. New discoveries, especially in archaeology, also periodically invite us to revise older views, but the vast information available already allows us to affirm much Biblical background with full confidence.

How can we know for sure what the Bible's ancient culture was like?

As a result of the recovery of over a million texts from the ancient world and a century of persistent research by scholars, we are now in a position to add significant nuances to our understanding of the life and thought of those who lived in Israel in Bible times. The end result is a more thorough and comprehensive understanding of the text.

Through understanding the background, we can better understand why people spoke and acted the ways they did and can better identify with them. Besides helping us understand the world in which people in the Bible lived, study of ancient texts from the cultures in the Biblical world can provide information that we really need to understand the Biblical material. If, as readers, we are isolated from the cultural background of the Bible, we might be inclined to think that the ideas in the Biblical text have no anchors in time and culture.

How was Israelite culture shaped by its surrounding culture?

Though the Bible is unique in its inspiration, we find that God often communicated *through* culture rather than in total isolation from it. Becoming aware of this continuity with the ancient and classical worlds can help us see these ideas in a larger context. God was replacing his people's views of God with a better one, but he was not replacing all of their culture.

Even when a Biblical text persuasively corrects its contemporary culture, we must be aware of how the text interacts with then-current thinking and literature. The Biblical text formulated its discussion in relation to the thinking found in the ancient literature. It would be no surprise, then, if areas of similarity should be found. This is far different from the contention that Israelite literature is simply derivative mythology. There is a great distance between borrowing from a particular piece of literature and resonating with the larger culture that has itself been influenced by its literatures.

Can you provide a modern example of this?

When Americans speak of the philosophy of "eat, drink and be merry, for tomorrow we die," they are resonating with an idea that has penetrated society over thousands of years rather than simply borrowing from the writings of Epicurus. In a similar way, an observer from the distant future would fail to understand American culture of the 21st century if they did not understand the foundations of individualism, personal rights or consumerism (just to name a few of the influences). To offer a more specific example: a reader in the distant future would need some historical background to understand a familiar American question from the early twenty-first century: "Where were you on 9/11?" The question assumes a shared understanding of background that the asker does not bother to state.

Successful interpreters must try to understand the cultural background of the Bible just as successful missionaries must learn the culture, language and worldview of the people they are trying to reach. This is the rationale for us to study the Bible in light its cultural context. What we would contend, then, is that comparative work has three goals in mind:

1. We study the *history* of the Biblical world as a means of recovering knowledge of the events that shaped the lives of people in the ancient world.
2. We study *archaeology* as a means of recovering the lifestyle reflected in the material culture of the ancient world.
3. We study the *literature* of the ancient world as a means of penetrating the heart and soul of the people who inhabited that world.

These goals are at the heart of comparative studies and will help us understand the Bible better.

How do we understand the Bible — a book that billions have turned to over multiple centuries and many cultures — as literature in its ancient context?

Readers today approach very differently such different sorts of writings as satire, news reports or a declaration of war. Knowing how a work was intended is an important key for understanding it. It should therefore be no surprise that the inspired authors adapted genres (literary types) that already existed in the larger culture; otherwise the first audiences would not have known what these works were meant for. Whether we are looking at wisdom literature, hymnic literature, historical literature, legal literature or the letters in the NT, we find generous doses of both similarities to and differences from the Biblical text and the literature of the time.

Understanding the genre of a piece of literature is necessary if we want to more fully understand the author's intentions. Since perceiving an author's intentions is essential to our theological interpretation of a text, we recognize that understanding genre contributes to legitimate theological interpretation. Some genres will operate differently in the ancient world than do the most similar genres in our own culture so we must become familiar with the mechanics of the genres represented in the ancient Near East and the Greco-Roman world.

In light of all of this, we can logically concluded that without the guidance of comparative studies, readers in cultures removed from the ancient world are bound to misinterpret the text at some points.

But why is the study of cultural backgrounds so important?

This field of research is important because grasping the original audience's perspective helps us understand the setting to which the inspired authors communicated their message.

A text is a complex of ideas linked by threads of writing. Each phrase and each word communicates by the ideas and thoughts that they will trigger in the reader or hearer. Biblical writers normally could take for granted that their audiences shared their language and culture; some matters, therefore, they assumed rather than stated. But what happens when later readers from different cultures approach these texts? As each person hears or reads the text, the message takes for granted underlying gaps that need to be filled with meaning by the audience. (To use a previous example, in a message today, we might take for granted that our audience understands the term "9/11.") Interpreters have the task of filling in those gaps, and when we are interpreting authoritative texts, it is theologically essential that we fill them appropriately.

This approach is critical to practical application, because information from the original culture often fills those gaps in ways different from those we might guess, and these differences can sometimes yield quite theological insights. As readers who are interested in understanding the text's message, we should value comparative studies that highlight conceptual issues intended to illumine the cultural dynamics behind the text.

Another importance to cultural backgrounds, then, is that by becoming aware of the ways that ancient people thought, we can see the differences between them and us. If we know nothing of the ancient world, we will be inclined to impose our own culture and worldview on the Biblical text. This will always be detrimental to our understanding.

What do I need to know before I begin?

Readers should carefully weigh how to use information in our notes, which we have deliberately kept concise. Information present may show contrasts as well as similarities. Here are therefore some principles to consider when comparing Biblical texts with their ancient contexts:

1. Both cultural similarities and cultural differences must be considered.
2. Similarities may suggest a common cultural heritage rather than borrowing from a specific piece of literature.
3. It is common to find similarities at the surface but differences at the conceptual level or vice versa.
4. All elements of the text must be understood in their own context as accurately as possible before cross-cultural comparisons are made.
5. Proximity in time, geography and spheres of cultural contact all increase the possibility of interaction leading to influence.
6. A case for literary borrowing can rarely be made and requires identification of likely channels of transmission.
7. Similar functions may be performed by different genres in different cultures.
8. When literary or cultural elements are borrowed they may in turn be transformed into something quite different.
9. A single culture will rarely be monolithic, either in a contemporary cross-section or in consideration of a passage of time.
10. Specificity in marking dates for events in the ancient world is inherently debatable. There was no universal cultural reference point with which the ancients could mark time (such as our dates BC and AD). Different cultures used different historical reference points when marking time, so that even when researchers find recorded dates in ancient cultural literature or on artifacts, these can rarely be cited as definitive. The differences in dates for specific events in the Old Testament notes reflect this reality as various contributors reflect their own assessments. The earlier the time period, the more tenuous the dating becomes.
11. Cultural terms in the text of the notes (e.g., use of the term "Palestine" in the Old Testament, which refers to the larger region in which the Hebrew people lived), do not refer to current political realities unless the notes indicate as such.

For more information, please see the article "Major Background Issues from the Ancient Near East," p. xxxix.

—John H. Walton and Craig S. Keener

ACKNOWLEDGMENTS

The editors would like to thank the following individuals and institutions for their contributions to the editorial and composition stages of the *NIV Cultural Backgrounds Study Bible*.

Editors of the *Zondervan Illustrated Bible Backgrounds Commentary, Old Testament*

David W. Baker
Daniel Block
Daniel Bodi
Eugene E. Carpenter
Mark W. Chavalas
R. Dennis Cole
Izak Cornelius
Paul W. Ferris, Jr.
Roy E. Gane
Duane Garrett
Richard S. Hess
John W. Hilber
Andrew E. Hill
Kenneth G. Hoglund
Philip S. Johnston
V. Phillips Long
Tremper Longman III
Ernest C. Lucas
Frederick J. Mabie
Dale W. Manor
Daniel M. Master
Victor H. Matthews
Alan R. Millard
John Monson
Iain Provan
Simon Sherwin
J. Glen Taylor
Anthony Tomasino
Steven Voth
Bruce Wells
Edwin M. Yamauchi

Other Content Providers

- InterVarsity Press for their permission to use portions of the *IVP Bible Background Commentary* for both the Old and New Testaments
- HarperCollins Christian Publishing and Gordon Conwell Theological Seminary for their permission to use twenty-four articles in the New Testament from the *NIV Archaeological Study Bible*

NIV Cultural Backgrounds Study Bible Editorial and Composition Team

- Natalie J. Block, content editor
- Nancy Erickson, Hebrew editor
- John R. Greco, New Testament theological reviewer
- Sherri Hoffman, Matthew Van Zomeren and Nancy Wilson, page composition
- Ron Huizinga, art director
- Peachtree Editorial and Proofreading Service
- Holly Lynne Smith, Old Testament theological reviewer
- Thinkpen Design, cover and interior design
- Michael Vander Klipp, editor
- Jonathan Walton, editorial assistant and illustrator
- Kim Walton and Kim Tanner, visual editors

About the Authors

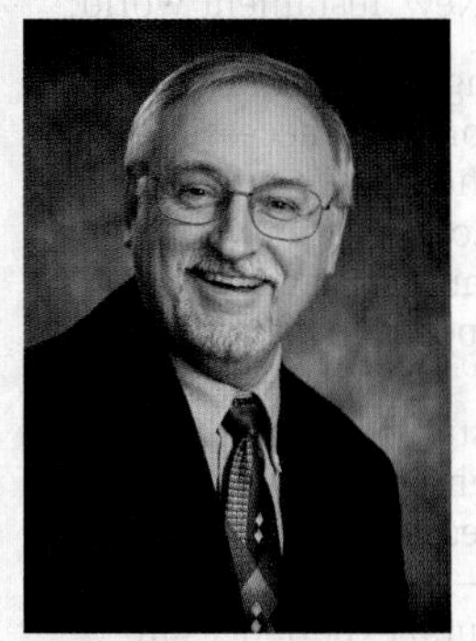

John H. Walton, Old Testament Editor

Ph.D. 1981 Hebrew and Cognate Studies, Hebrew Union College-Jewish Institute of Religion, Cincinnati, Ohio.

M.A. 1975 Biblical Studies: Old Testament; Wheaton Graduate School

A.B. 1974 Economics/Accounting, Muhlenberg College, Allentown, PA

Dr. John H. Walton is Professor of Old Testament at Wheaton College, Wheaton, IL, where he has been a professor since 2001. Dr. Walton came to Wheaton after a 20-year career as a professor at Moody Bible Institute in Chicago. He has written extensively on the backgrounds of the Old Testament, and has travelled the world lecturing about this field of study.

His publications include *Lost World of Adam and Eve* (IVP: 2015); *Lost World of Scripture* (IVP: 2013) with Brent Sandy; *Job, NIV Application Commentary* (Zondervan: 2012); *Genesis 1 as Ancient Cosmology* (Eisenbrauns: 2011); *The Zondervan Illustrated Bible Backgrounds Commentary: Old Testament* (General Editor, Zondervan, 2009); *The Lost World of Genesis One: Ancient Cosmology and the Origins Debate* (IVP, 2009); *Jonah* (Expositor's Bible Commentary, Zondervan: 2008); *Ancient Near Eastern Thought and the Old Testament* (Baker: 2006); and *Old Testament Today* (Zondervan: 2004).

Dr. Walton summarizes his chosen path of study in this way:

> "It was in my college years that I encountered a book by Joseph Free, a former Wheaton professor, called Archaeology and Bible History. It was apologetic in focus but brought to my attention the tremendous impact that archaeology and cultural background studies could have on our understanding of the Old Testament. It was in the very year that I read that book that I made the decision to pursue Old Testament studies as a vocational discipline. Instead of training to be an archaeologist, I determined to focus my attention on studies comparing the culture and literature of the Bible and the ancient Near East.
>
> "I have never lost my fascination with this subject. But comparative studies only provide one of the means by which I try to get people excited about the Old Testament. I am saddened by how little exposure to and understanding of the Old Testament many Christians have, but I am passionate in doing whatever I can do to remedy this spiritual and theological loss."

Craig S. Keener, New Testament Editor

Ph.D., Duke University, 1991

M.A., M.Div., Assemblies of God Theological Seminary, 1985, 1987

B.A., Central Bible College / Evangel University, 1982

Dr. Craig S. Keener is the F.M. and Ada Thompson professor of Biblical Studies at Asbury Seminary, Wilmore, KY. Before coming to Asbury in July 2011, Dr. Keener was professor of New Testament at Palmer Theological Seminary of Eastern University, where he taught for 15 years; before that time he was professor at Hood Theological Seminary. Craig is a sought-after speaker, writer and lecturer on the subject of New Testament cultural backgrounds.

Craig has authored 17 books, five of which have won book awards in *Christianity Today*. His *IVP Bible Background Commentary: New Testament* (1993), now in its 2nd revised edition (2014), has sold more than half a million copies (including editions in several languages, more than fifty thousand copies in Korean). His recent books include *Acts: An Exegetical Commentary* (4 vols., 4500 pages; Baker Academic, 2012 – 2015); *Miracles: The Credibility of the New Testament Accounts* (2 vols., Baker Academic, 2011); *The Historical Jesus of the Gospels* (Eerdmans, 2009); *The Gospel of Matthew: A Socio-Rhetorical Commentary* (Eerdmans, 2009); *Romans* (Cascade, 2009); *1 – 2 Corinthians* (Cambridge, 2005); *The Gospel of John: A Commentary* (2 vols., Hendrickson/ Baker Academic, 2003).

Dr. Keener describes the origins of his interest in the cultures of the New Testament world:

> "Not everyone is called to spend their professional career studying the cultural settings of the Bible, but some of us are called to bring this information in an accessible way to the body of Christ, as in this Bible. I've been studying the Bible's cultural settings since the beginning of my undergraduate work. But the Lord was preparing me for this field of study even before my conversion. Even as an early teenager I was reading the works of Plato and Tacitus, the Roman historian, and spent time studying many different ancient sources.
>
> "After my conversion I said to myself, 'No, I don't need to study any of these sources. I'm just going to read the Bible. The Bible is good enough on its own.' But the more I read the Bible, often 40 chapters a day, the more I realized that the authors took for granted some information that their first readers knew — information that I didn't have without studying background. Additionally, cross-cultural experiences in Africa, Asia and Latin America have helped me to think more cross-culturally. Both in preaching and teaching contexts, I have found that understanding the culture of the Bible helps my hearers understand the Biblical text more concretely and accurately."

PREFACE

The goal of the New International Version (NIV) is to enable English-speaking people from around the world to read and hear God's eternal Word in their own language. Our work as translators is motivated by our conviction that the Bible is God's Word in written form. We believe that the Bible contains the divine answer to the deepest needs of humanity, sheds unique light on our path in a dark world and sets forth the way to our eternal well-being. Out of these deep convictions, we have sought to recreate as far as possible the experience of the original audience — blending transparency to the original text with accessibility for the millions of English speakers around the world. We have prioritized accuracy, clarity and literary quality with the goal of creating a translation suitable for public and private reading, evangelism, teaching, preaching, memorizing and liturgical use. We have also sought to preserve a measure of continuity with the long tradition of translating the Scriptures into English.

The complete NIV Bible was first published in 1978. It was a completely new translation made by over a hundred scholars working directly from the best available Hebrew, Aramaic and Greek texts. The translators came from the United States, Great Britain, Canada, Australia and New Zealand, giving the translation an international scope. They were from many denominations and churches — including Anglican, Assemblies of God, Baptist, Brethren, Christian Reformed, Church of Christ, Evangelical Covenant, Evangelical Free, Lutheran, Mennonite, Methodist, Nazarene, Presbyterian, Wesleyan and others. This breadth of denominational and theological perspective helped to safeguard the translation from sectarian bias. For these reasons, and by the grace of God, the NIV has gained a wide readership in all parts of the English-speaking world.

The work of translating the Bible is never finished. As good as they are, English translations must be regularly updated so that they will continue to communicate accurately the meaning of God's Word. Updates are needed in order to reflect the latest developments in our understanding of the biblical world and its languages and to keep pace with changes in English usage. Recognizing, then, that the NIV would retain its ability to communicate God's Word accurately only if it were regularly updated, the original translators established the Committee on Bible Translation (CBT). The Committee is a self-perpetuating group of biblical scholars charged with keeping abreast of advances in biblical scholarship and changes in English and issuing periodic updates to the NIV. The CBT is an independent, self-governing body and has sole responsibility for the NIV text. The Committee mirrors the original group of translators in its diverse international and denominational makeup and in its unifying commitment to the Bible as God's inspired Word.

In obedience to its mandate, the Committee has issued periodic updates to the NIV. An initial revision was released in 1984. A more thorough revision process was completed in 2005, resulting in the separately published TNIV. The updated NIV you now have in your hands builds on both the original NIV and the TNIV and represents the latest effort of the Committee to articulate God's unchanging Word in the way the original authors might have said it had they been speaking in English to the global English-speaking audience today.

Translation Philosophy

The Committee's translating work has been governed by three widely accepted principles about the way people use words and about the way we understand them.

First, the meaning of words is determined by the way that users of the language actually use them at any given time. For the biblical languages, therefore, the Committee utilizes the best and most recent scholarship on the way Hebrew, Aramaic and Greek words were being used in biblical times. At the same time, the Committee carefully studies the state of modern English. Good translation is like good communication: one must know the target audience so that the appropriate choices can be made about which English words to use to represent the original words of Scripture. From its inception, the NIV has had as its target the general English-speaking population all over the world, the "International" in its title reflecting this concern. The aim of the Committee is to put the Scriptures into natural English that will communicate effectively with the broadest possible audience of English speakers.

Modern technology has enhanced the Committee's ability to choose the right English words to convey the meaning of the original text. The

Abbreviations

General

c	*century*
c.	*about, approximately*
cf.	*compare, confer*
ch., chs.	*chapter, chapters*
e.g.	*for example*
etc.	*and so on*
i.e.	*that is*
KJV	*King James (Authorized) Version*
lit.	*literally, literal*
NT	*New Testament*
OT	*Old Testament*
p., pp.	*page, pages*
v., vv.	*verse, verses (in the chapter being commented on)*

Standard abbreviations of month names are also sometimes used, as well as a few other common abbreviations.

The Old Testament

Genesis	Ge
Exodus	Ex
Leviticus	Lev
Numbers	Nu
Deuteronomy	Dt
Joshua	Jos
Judges	Jdg
Ruth	Ru
1 Samuel	1Sa
2 Samuel	2Sa
1 Kings	1Ki
2 Kings	2Ki
1 Chronicles	1Ch
2 Chronicles	2Ch
Ezra	Ezr
Nehemiah	Ne
Esther	Est
Job	Job
Psalms	Ps
Proverbs	Pr
Ecclesiastes	Ecc
Song of Songs	SS
Isaiah	Isa
Jeremiah	Jer
Lamentations	La
Ezekiel	Eze
Daniel	Da
Hosea	Hos
Joel	Joel
Amos	Am
Obadiah	Ob
Jonah	Jnh
Micah	Mic
Nahum	Na
Habakkuk	Hab
Zephaniah	Zep
Haggai	Hag
Zechariah	Zec
Malachi	Mal

The New Testament

Matthew	Mt
Mark	Mk
Luke	Lk
John	Jn
Acts	Ac
Romans	Ro
1 Corinthians	1Co
2 Corinthians	2Co
Galatians	Gal
Ephesians	Eph
Philippians	Php
Colossians	Col
1 Thessalonians	1Th
2 Thessalonians	2Th
1 Timothy	1Ti
2 Timothy	2Ti
Titus	Titus
Philemon	Phm
Hebrews	Heb
James	Jas
1 Peter	1Pe
2 Peter	2Pe
1 John	1Jn
2 John	2Jn
3 John	3Jn
Jude	Jude
Revelation	Rev

throughout. The Masoretic Text tradition contains marginal notations that offer variant readings. These have sometimes been followed instead of the text itself. Because such instances involve variants within the Masoretic tradition, they have not been indicated in the textual notes. In a few cases, words in the basic consonantal text have been divided differently than in the Masoretic Text. Such cases are usually indicated in the textual footnotes. The Dead Sea Scrolls contain biblical texts that represent an earlier stage of the transmission of the Hebrew text. They have been consulted, as have been the Samaritan Pentateuch and the ancient scribal traditions concerning deliberate textual changes. The translators also consulted the more important early versions. Readings from these versions, the Dead Sea Scrolls and the scribal traditions were occasionally followed where the Masoretic Text seemed doubtful and where accepted principles of textual criticism showed that one or more of these textual witnesses appeared to provide the correct reading. In rare cases, the translators have emended the Hebrew text where it appears to have become corrupted at an even earlier stage of its transmission. These departures from the Masoretic Text are also indicated in the textual footnotes. Sometimes the vowel indicators (which are later additions to the basic consonantal text) found in the Masoretic Text did not, in the judgment of the translators, represent the correct vowels for the original text. Accordingly, some words have been read with a different set of vowels. These instances are usually not indicated in the footnotes.

The Greek text used in translating the New Testament has been an eclectic one, based on the latest editions of the Nestle-Aland/United Bible Societies' Greek New Testament. The translators have made their choices among the variant readings in accordance with widely accepted principles of New Testament textual criticism. Footnotes call attention to places where uncertainty remains.

The New Testament authors, writing in Greek, often quote the Old Testament from its ancient Greek version, the Septuagint. This is one reason why some of the Old Testament quotations in the NIV New Testament are not identical to the corresponding passages in the NIV Old Testament. Such quotations in the New Testament are indicated with the footnote "(see Septuagint)."

Footnotes and Formatting

Footnotes in this version are of several kinds, most of which need no explanation. Those giving alternative translations begin with "Or" and generally introduce the alternative with the last word preceding it in the text, except when it is a single-word alternative. When poetry is quoted in a footnote a slash mark indicates a line division.

It should be noted that references to diseases, minerals, flora and fauna, architectural details, clothing, jewelry, musical instruments and other articles cannot always be identified with precision. Also, linear measurements and measures of capacity can only be approximated (see the Table of Weights and Measures). Although *Selah*, used mainly in the Psalms, is probably a musical term, its meaning is uncertain. Since it may interrupt reading and distract the reader, this word has not been kept in the English text, but every occurrence has been signaled by a footnote.

As an aid to the reader, sectional headings have been inserted. They are not to be regarded as part of the biblical text and are not intended for oral reading. It is the Committee's hope that these headings may prove more helpful to the reader than the traditional chapter divisions, which were introduced long after the Bible was written.

Sometimes the chapter and/or verse numbering in English translations of the Old Testament differs from that found in published Hebrew texts. This is particularly the case in the Psalms, where the traditional titles are included in the Hebrew verse numbering. Such differences are indicated in the footnotes at the bottom of the page. In the New Testament, verse numbers that marked off portions of the traditional English text not supported by the best Greek manuscripts now appear in brackets, with a footnote indicating the text that has been omitted (see, for example, Matthew 17:[21]).

Mark 16:9 – 20 and John 7:53 — 8:11, although long accorded virtually equal status with the rest of the Gospels in which they stand, have a questionable standing in the textual history of the New Testament, as noted in the bracketed annotations with which they are set off. A different typeface has been chosen for these passages to indicate their uncertain status.

Basic formatting of the text, such as lining the poetry, paragraphing (both prose and poetry), setting up of (administrative-like) lists, indenting letters and lengthy prayers within narratives and the insertion of sectional headings, has been the work of the Committee. However, the choice between single-column and double-column formats has been left to the publishers. Also the issuing of "red-letter" editions is a publisher's choice — one that the Committee does not endorse.

The Committee has again been reminded that every human effort is flawed — including this revision of the NIV. We trust, however, that many will find in it an improved representation of the Word of God, through which they hear his call to faith in our Lord Jesus Christ and to service in his kingdom. We offer this version of the Bible to him in whose name and for whose glory it has been made.

The Committee on Bible Translation

field of computational linguistics harnesses the power of computers to provide broadly applicable and current data about the state of the language. Translators can now access huge databases of modern English to better understand the current meaning and usage of key words. The Committee utilized this resource in preparing the 2011 edition of the NIV. An area of especially rapid and significant change in English is the way certain nouns and pronouns are used to refer to human beings. The Committee therefore requested experts in computational linguistics at Collins Dictionaries to pose some key questions about this usage to its database of English—the largest in the world, with over 4.4 billion words, gathered from several English-speaking countries and including both spoken and written English. (The Collins Study, called "The Development and Use of Gender Language in Contemporary English," can be accessed at *http://www.thenivbible.com/about-the-niv/about-the-2011-edition/*.) The study revealed that the most popular words to describe the human race in modern U.S. English were "humanity," "man" and "mankind." The Committee then used this data in the updated NIV, choosing from among these three words (and occasionally others also) depending on the context.

A related issue creates a larger problem for modern translations: the move away from using the third-person masculine singular pronouns—"he/him/his"—to refer to men and women equally. This usage does persist in some forms of English, and this revision therefore occasionally uses these pronouns in a generic sense. But the tendency, recognized in day-to-day usage and confirmed by the Collins study, is away from the generic use of "he," "him" and "his." In recognition of this shift in language and in an effort to translate into the natural English that people are actually using, this revision of the NIV generally uses other constructions when the biblical text is plainly addressed to men and women equally. The reader will encounter especially frequently a "they," "their" or "them" to express a generic singular idea. Thus, for instance, Mark 8:36 reads: "What good is it for someone to gain the whole world, yet forfeit their soul?" This generic use of the "distributive" or "singular" "they/them/their" has been used for many centuries by respected writers of English and has now become established as standard English, spoken and written, all over the world.

A second linguistic principle that feeds into the Committee's translation work is that meaning is found not in individual words, as vital as they are, but in larger clusters: phrases, clauses, sentences, discourses. Translation is not, as many people think, a matter of word substitution: English word *x* in place of Hebrew word *y*. Translators must first determine the meaning of the words of the biblical languages in the context of the passage and then select English words that accurately communicate that meaning to modern listeners and readers. This means that accurate translation will not always reflect the exact structure of the original language. To be sure, there is debate over the degree to which translators should try to preserve the "form" of the original text in English. From the beginning, the NIV has taken a mediating position on this issue. The manual produced when the translation that became the NIV was first being planned states: "If the Greek or Hebrew syntax has a good parallel in modern English, it should be used. But if there is no good parallel, the English syntax appropriate to the meaning of the original is to be chosen." It is fine, in other words, to carry over the form of the biblical languages into English—but not at the expense of natural expression. The principle that meaning resides in larger clusters of words means that the Committee has not insisted on a "word-for-word" approach to translation. We certainly believe that every word of Scripture is inspired by God and therefore to be carefully studied to determine what God is saying to us. It is for this reason that the Committee labors over every single word of the original texts, working hard to determine how each of those words contributes to what the text is saying. Ultimately, however, it is how these individual words function in combination with other words that determines meaning.

A third linguistic principle guiding the Committee in its translation work is the recognition that words have a spectrum of meaning. It is popular to define a word by using another word, or "gloss," to substitute for it. This substitute word is then sometimes called the "literal" meaning of a word. In fact, however, words have a range of possible meanings. Those meanings will vary depending on the context, and words in one language will usually not occupy the same semantic range as words in another language. The Committee therefore studies each original word of Scripture in its context to identify its meaning in a particular verse and then chooses an appropriate English word (or phrase) to represent it. It is impossible, then, to translate any given Hebrew, Aramaic or Greek word with the same English word all the time. The Committee does try to translate related occurrences of a word in the original languages with the same English word in order to preserve the connection for the English reader. But the Committee generally privileges clear natural meaning over a concern with consistency in rendering particular words.

Textual Basis

For the Old Testament the standard Hebrew text, the Masoretic Text as published in the latest edition of *Biblia Hebraica*, has been used

HEBREW TO ENGLISH TRANSLATION CHART

Description of Meaning of Hebrew Words That Have No Exact Equivalent in English

One of the constant challenges of exegesis involves the understanding of words. Most Bible readers are dependent on translations and so must be content to interpret the text based on what words the translators of their Bibles have chosen. Even readers who compare translations or consult commentaries can sometimes fall short of finding answers to their questions.

What readers do not often recognize is that even translators work with significant limitations. No ancient lexicon exists that offers explanations of the meanings of words by those who spoke classical Hebrew. We have traditions, sometimes ancient ones such as the translation offered in the Greek Septuagint; we have comments made by Medieval Rabbinic grammarians whose expertise was substantial; and, of course, we have the multitude of translations that exist today as an outpouring of scholarly attention. With all of that said, the fact is that we only perceive the meanings of Hebrew words by their usage, not from following some ancient academic repository of lexicography.

Finally, modern readers and translators face the problem that some Hebrew words that scholars understand well enough still pose problems because there is no English word that corresponds sufficiently to capture the breadth of nuance that the Hebrew word contains. Many of these are significant words pregnant with important nuances. The following list deals with a number of the Hebrew words that fall into this category; also included at the end of the chart are three English terms that require further explanation.

Transliteration and Goodrick/ Kohlenberger #	Hebrew	NIV	Select Key Verses
br' (1343)	ברא	create	Ge 1:1
This sort of creative act often entails giving something a role, purpose or function in an ordered system. Its emphasis is therefore on God acting with purpose and giving things a purpose rather than on simple materiality.			
ḥesed (2876)	חֶסֶד	unfailing love, kindness, mercy	Ge 19:19; Ex 15:13; 20:6; 34:6; Jos 2:12; Ru 1:8; 2Sa 7:15; 9:7; Ps 23:6; 100:5; 136; Pr 19:22; Isa 54:8; Da 1:9; Hos 6:6; Mic 6:8
Acting to fulfill an obligation formal or informal, stated and agreed upon or inherent in the normal expectations of human interaction or protocol. Conforming to an understood expectation and therefore addressing propriety.			
qādôš (7705, 7727, 7731)	קָדוֹשׁ	holy, holiness, consecrate, holy place	Ex 3:5; 19:6; 29:37; Lev 11:44; 19:2; Dt 7:6; Jos 24:19; 1Sa 2:2; 1Ki 6:16; 2Ki 19:22; Ps 48:1; 99:3–9; Isa 6:3; Isa 43; Hab 2:20; Zec 14:20
Situated in the divine realm. This is a conferred status; not something that can be pursued and achieved. God is holy and he conferred that holy status on Israel so that he could remain living among them. God's presence brought benefits and relationship, but Israel's failure to take their status into account when considering their behavior brought consequences. That status could not be gained or lost, but Yahweh's presence could be.			
šālôm (8934)	שָׁלֹם	peace	Ps 34:14; Isa 9:6; 26:3
Though war or conflict can result in the absence of *šālôm*, true *šālôm* is not so much the absence of war or conflict, but the absence of fear and anxiety.			

Transliteration and Goodrick/ Kohlenberger #	Hebrew	NIV	Select Key Verses
qn' (7861, 7863)	קנא	jealous	Ge 37:11; Nu 25:13; Dt 32:21; 2Ki 19:31; Ps 69:9; SS 8:6; Isa 9:7; Eze 39:25; Zec 8:2
Expression of proprietary rights with exclusivistic implications. When someone belongs to someone else it is expected others will recognize that and respect those rights. The basis of “belonging” is not economic (e.g., a possession) but is relational.			
tôʿēbâ (9359)	תּוֹעֵבָה	abomination	Ge 46:34; Lev 18:22 – 30; Dt 14:3; 18:12; 32:16; Pr 13:19; 29:27
Counterproductive to order. When God’s sense of order is involved, *tôʿēbâ* indicates something that is contrary to holy status; it describes what is contrary to the inherent sense of order reflected in one’s inclinations or conventions and is therefore a description that is relative to the one who experiences the sense of revulsion.			
ʿārûm (6874)	עָרוּם	crafty	Ge 3:1; Job 5:12; Pr 12:16, 23; 13:16; 14:8, 15,18; 22:3
People who are *ʿārûm* conceal what they feel and what they know. They esteem knowledge and plan how to use it in achieving their objectives; they do not believe everything they hear; they know how to avoid trouble and punishment. In sum, they are shrewd and calculating, willing to bend and torture the limits of acceptable behavior but not to cross the line into illegality. They may be unpleasant and purposely misleading in speech but are not out-and-out liars. They know how to read people and situations and how to turn their readings to advantage. A keen wit and a rapier tongue are their tools. (Z. Zevit, *What Really Happened in the Garden of Eden*, 163). The term is therefore not intrinsically pejorative but can be manifested in negative ways.			
tardēmâ (8101, 9554)	תַּרְדֵּמָה	deep sleep	Ge 2:21; 15:12; Jdg 4:21; 1Sa 26:12; Da 10:9; Jnh 1:5
In such a sleep one is either (a) unaware of threatening circumstances, or (b) prepared to receive a vision.			
hebel (2039)	הֶבֶל	meaningless	throughout Ecclesiastes
The opposite of self-fulfillment; not able to give “meaning to life.”			
ʿalmâ (6625)	עַלְמָה	virgin (young woman)	Isa 7:14
A woman who has not yet given birth (thus an *ʿalma* can be pregnant). A woman ceases to be an *ʿalmâ* when she becomes a mother. It pertains to family status, not sexual status (see *bĕtûlâ*).			
ʿśh (6913)	עשׂה	do, make (plus many other translations)	Often in Ge 1; Ge 2:2 – 3; 3:21; Ex 20:8 – 11; Am 5:8
Indicates a role in causation, but does not specify whether direct or indirect; could be mediated or not; could involve material or not. Often involves supervising, commissioning or delegating. Can pertain to providing or preparing.			
nwḥ (5663)	נוח	rest	Ex 20:11 (as a reflection on Ge 2:1 – 2, which does not use this word); Dt 12:10; Jos 1:13 – 15; 21:44; Ps 132:7 – 14
Can pertain to relaxation or refreshment, but more often refers to experiencing stability, security and equilibrium — everything as it ought to be. God’s rest is associated with his presence in the temple and his rule of the cosmos. Rest is the opposite of unrest and when God rests he is not disengaging, but engaging.			

<table>
<tr><th>Transliteration and Goodrick/ Kohlenberger #</th><th>Hebrew</th><th>NIV</th><th>Select Key Verses</th></tr>
<tr><td>ṭôb/ ra' (3201/8273)</td><td>טוֹב/ רַע</td><td>good/evil</td><td>Often in Ge 1; Ge 2:9; 2:18; Ps 34:8; 118:1; Isa 31:2; 45:7; Eze 14:21</td></tr>
<tr><td colspan="4">"Good" refers to everything functioning in the way that it should. It does not refer to perfection, but to what is best from an optimal perspective. "Evil" can refer to wickedness, but it can be broadly used to refer to a variety of negative actions or results. Neither of these terms is essentially moral in nature, though they often are used in moral contexts. So, for example, God can be described as doing either (Ecc 7:14).</td></tr>
<tr><td>'iṣṣābôn (6779)</td><td>עִצָּבוֹן</td><td>pains, painful toil</td><td>Ge 3:16; 3:19; 5:29</td></tr>
<tr><td colspan="4">These are the only three occurrences of this word. The latter two give insufficient information to determine whether it refers to physical pain or psychological anxiety. Other words derived from the same root could refer to either. In Ge 3:16 it refers specifically to conception (despite the NIV's more general "pains in childbearing"). Since conception did not involve physical pain but was fraught with anxiety in the ancient world (because a woman was not fully secure in the family until she conceived), the translation "anxiety" captures the nuance better. Ge 5:29 indicates that this word is one aspect of what interferes with rest.</td></tr>
<tr><td>tĕšûqâ (9592)</td><td>תְּשׁוּקָה</td><td>desire</td><td>Ge 3:16; 4:7; SS 7:11</td></tr>
<tr><td colspan="4">These are the only three occurrences of this word. Since they refer to very different types of desire, we should infer that the word itself is more general than specific. It can be used to refer to any natural instinct, and only the context can specify which sort of instinct is intended.</td></tr>
<tr><td>ṣela' (7521)</td><td>צֵלָע</td><td>rib, side</td><td>Ge 2:21–22; often in Ex chs. 25–27, 1Ki 6 and Eze 41</td></tr>
<tr><td colspan="4">Only in Ge 2 does it refer to anatomy. Most frequently it refers to two sides of something (e.g., altar, temple), but can also refer to planks or beams in a construction. In Ge 2 this word would therefore more likely refer to one of Adam's sides being taken rather than an individual rib (with NIV note).</td></tr>
<tr><td>'rr/qll (826/7837)</td><td>ערר/ קלל</td><td>curse</td><td>'rr Ge 3:14, 17; 4:11; 5:29; 9:25; 12:3
qll Ge 8:21; 12:3; Ex 21:17; Lev 20:9; 24:15</td></tr>
<tr><td colspan="4">'rr refers not to a magical hex but to something more like banishment, specifically removing someone or something from the protection of God. God is almost always the subject of this verb, and is never the direct object of the verb. qll pertains to belittling someone and can refer to anything from insult to blasphemy. People are usually the subject of this verb. It basically means invoking words of power against someone and ranges from expressing contempt to putting a curse on someone. So Ge 12:3 should be understood as saying that the one who invokes words of power (qll) against Israel will be removed from God's protection and favor ('rr).</td></tr>
<tr><td>bĕtûlâ (1435)</td><td>בְּתוּלָה</td><td>virgin</td><td>Ge 24:16; Ex 22:16; Est 2; Job 31:1</td></tr>
<tr><td colspan="4">Describes a woman who is still under the authority of her father rather than a husband. A woman ceases to be a bĕtûlâ when she becomes a wife. This is not specifically a term referring to sexual experience but rather to social status. Hebrew had no term of classifying a woman by sexual status (they had to use a phrase like, "she had not yet known a man"). See 'almâ.</td></tr>
<tr><td>'ôlām (6409)</td><td>עוֹלָם</td><td>forever, everlasting</td><td>Ge 3:22; 17:7–8; 48:4; Ex 12:17; Dt 32:40; Jos 14:9; 1Sa 2:30; 2Sa 7:13–16; 1Ki 10:9; Ps 136; Isa 40:28</td></tr>
<tr><td colspan="4">When qualified by context this word can refer to something or someone eternal, but that sense is not carried inherently by the word. Its basic meaning pertains to an enduring quality or an open-ended situation that is sustained in perpetuity.</td></tr>
</table>

<table>
<tr><th>Transliteration and Goodrick/ Kohlenberger #</th><th>Hebrew</th><th>NIV</th><th>Select Key Verses</th></tr>
<tr><td>nš' (5958)</td><td>נשׁא</td><td>deceive</td><td>Ge 3:13; 2Ki 18:29; 19:10; Jer 4:10; 37:9; 49:16</td></tr>
<tr><td colspan="4">Several different Hebrew words are translated “deceive” in the Old Testament. This one is used when the person being accused of deceiving does not know that the information they are conveying is false.</td></tr>
<tr><td>hištāḥăwôt (2556)</td><td>הִשְׁתַּחֲוֹת</td><td>worship, bow down</td><td>Ge 18:2; 22:5; 23:12; 24:48; 49:8; Ex 20:5; 23:24; Dt 5:9; Jos 5:14; 1Sa 24:8; Est 3:2</td></tr>
<tr><td colspan="4">Worship is one of the activities that accompany this posture, but in the end it is a position of the body intended to show respect, not the activity of worship. It is never used as a posture for prayer.</td></tr>
<tr><td>rûaḥ (8120)</td><td>רוּחַ</td><td>spirit, wind, breath</td><td>Ge 1:2; 7:15; Ex 10:13; 15:8; Nu 11:25; Dt 34:9; Jdg 6:34; 11:29; 14:6; 1Sa 16:14; 2Ki 2:15 – 16; Ps 51:10 – 12; Ecc 3:19 – 21; Eze 8:3</td></tr>
<tr><td colspan="4">Given its use that covers all three of these English words, it is likely that it does not strictly refer to any of them. All three are somewhat ethereal and unseen, yet the word conveys something having a noticeable effect (picked up even in Jesus’ comment in Jn 3:8). It is never used in the Old Testament to refer to the third person of the Trinity (even the Spirit of the Lord was not recognized in context as a person of the godhead) though some of the occurrences can today be recognized as reflecting the involvement of the Holy Spirit. The spirit in a person is given by God; it energizes one’s life and returns to God at death.</td></tr>
<tr><td>nepeš (5883)</td><td>נֶפֶשׁ</td><td>life, soul, self</td><td>Ge 1:30;</td></tr>
<tr><td colspan="4">In Israelite thinking, a person does not have a nepeš; he or she is a nepeš. The word does not refer to a “soul” in anything like the platonic or even theological sense. It is the nepeš that goes to the netherworld whereas the rûaḥ returns to God who gave it. It pertains to a human’s personal identity.</td></tr>
<tr><td>'ōhēl mô'ēd (185 + 4595)
miškān (5438)</td><td>אֹהֶל מוֹעֵד
מִשְׁכָּן</td><td>tent of meeting
tabernacle</td><td>'ōhēl mô'ēd Ex 27:21; 29 – 30; 33:7; Lev 1 – 8; 16 – 17
miškān Ex 25 – 40</td></tr>
<tr><td colspan="4">miškān refers to the sanctuary as the place of Yahweh’s presence; it is his home and his throne room. 'ōhēl mô'ēd refers to the sanctuary as the place where people meet with God; it is his audience chamber and it focuses on communication and relationship. The 'ōhēl mô'ēd exists before the miškān is constructed, but once the miškān is constructed, it serves also as the 'ōhēl mô'ēd.</td></tr>
<tr><td>kippēr (4105)</td><td>כִּפֵּר</td><td>atonement</td><td>Ex 29 – 30; Lev 4 – 5; 16; Isa 6:7</td></tr>
<tr><td colspan="4">It is common to hear that this verb basically means “to cover,” but that interpretation is based on a false association with a homonym. It most often refers to a ritual act (generally using blood) designed to remove the effects of sin from the sanctuary. It does not remove the sin from the person (Heb 10:4), but cleanses the sanctuary so that Yahweh can continue to dwell there. In this way it serves as a ritual disinfectant. In contrast, “atonement” (the English technical theological term) speaks of paying the penalty for sin; that is done by the animal that is put to death. Kippēr is closer in concept to the English technical theological term “justification” (but of a location, not of an individual).</td></tr>
</table>

<table>
<tr><th>Transliteration and Goodrick/ Kohlenberger #</th><th>Hebrew</th><th>NIV</th><th>Select Key Verses</th></tr>
<tr><td>ḥṭʾ (2627)</td><td>חטא</td><td>sin</td><td>Ge 20:6; Jos 7:11; Jdg 11:27; 1Sa 2:25; Job 1:22; Ps 51:4–7</td></tr>
<tr><td colspan="4">It is not uncommon to encounter the statement that "sin" in the Old Testament means "missing the mark." It is true that this verb can refer to failing to achieve an objective (Pr 8:36; Isa 65:20) and once is even used for slingers who do not miss their target (Jdg 20:16). There is no reason, however, to think of these uses as reflecting the "original" meaning of the word that is translated "sin." This verb simply means "to sin" and is not necessarily limited to the idea of missing a mark or failing to achieve an objective. Sin can be seen as a threat to relationship with God — it results in alienation because offense has been committed against God. In this case, the translation "sin" is straightforward, but the more "in-depth" explanations sometimes offered can be misleading.</td></tr>
<tr><td>ḥaṭṭʾāt (2633)</td><td>חַטָּאת</td><td>sin offering</td><td>Lev 4–9</td></tr>
<tr><td colspan="4">Since this word is built from the same root as the word for "sin" it has traditionally been rendered "sin offering," but that rendering fails to capture the essence of this ritual. This sacrifice is called for when anything that is insufficiently pure or holy infringes on sacred space. The profane has encroached on the holy; the presence of impurity defiles sacred space and must be removed (kippēr) through appropriate procedures.</td></tr>
<tr><td>ʾāšām (871)</td><td>אָשָׁם</td><td>guilt offering</td><td>Lev 5, 14</td></tr>
<tr><td colspan="4">Guilt has little to do with this ritual. Instead of the profane encroaching on the sacred, this sacrifice is called for when the sacred is appropriated for profane use — that is, when something which is restricted to use in sacred space or belongs to Yahweh is removed from sacred space or never delivered (as in a vowed animal).</td></tr>
<tr><td>śāṭān (8476–7)</td><td>שָׂטָן</td><td>satan, adversary</td><td>Nu 22:22; 1Ki 11:23–25; 1Ch 21:1; Job 1–2; Ps 109:20; Zec 3:1–2</td></tr>
<tr><td colspan="4">As a verb this can refer to any being who plays a role as adversary, opponent or challenger — whether in service to God or acting contrary to his plan and people. It is not essentially a role that is inherently morally deficient or evil (the angel of the Lord takes this role at one point). As a noun it can refer to either human or heavenly beings. Capitalizing the word is misleading since Hebrew has no capital letters and since the designation of this being typically uses the definite article, thus indicating that it is not a personal name. Furthermore, OT Israel had not yet developed a concept of "the devil" and the NT never indicates that any of these passages refer to the devil.</td></tr>
<tr><td>yrʾ (3707, 3710–11)</td><td>ירא</td><td>fear</td><td>Ge 3:10; 15:1; 32:7; Ex 1:17; Lev 19:3; Dt 10:20; Job 1:9; 28:28; Pr 1:7</td></tr>
<tr><td colspan="4">This verb (and associated substantive) has broad usage with either people or God as the direct object. In the latter cases, it can refer to being afraid of God (particularly of his anger or judgment when sin has been committed). Translation problems arise from the misunderstanding that is created when the word serves as a positive and necessary response to God, a nuance not expressed by the English word "fear." It refers to holding God (and occasionally humans of authority) in high esteem and therefore treating them with respect. That respect can at times be motivated by the consequences of failure to do so, but in the end it should operate independently of consequences. "Fear" of the Lord accords God his proper place and role and is a response to his authority. By way of example: When someone today works with radioactive material, there is potential danger in the interaction that they need to respect.</td></tr>
</table>

<table>
<tr><th>Transliteration and Goodrick/ Kohlenberger #</th><th>Hebrew</th><th>NIV</th><th>Select Key Verses</th></tr>
<tr><td>ḥōkmâ (2683)</td><td>חָכְמָה</td><td>wisdom</td><td>Ex 28:3; Dt 34:9; 1Ki 4:29 – 34; 2Ch 1:10 – 12; Job 12:13; 28:28; Ps 104:24; 111:10; Pr 1:7; 2:6; 8:12; Isa 11:2; Jer 9:23</td></tr>
<tr><td colspan="4">This concept in Hebrew has a different focus than the English word. It does not pertain to intelligence or common sense (though both of those could be expressions of ḥōkmâ). Ḥōkmâ is intimately connected with the concept of order. Wisdom is the pursuit of order and Yahweh is the source and center of both. Ḥōkmâ perceives what constitutes order and pursues, preserves, promotes and practices order in every area of life. Relationship with God is primary, but ḥōkmâ seeks order in family relationships, response to civil authorities, making good choices, controlling one's tongue, etc.</td></tr>
<tr><td>māšîaḥ (5431)</td><td>מָשִׁיחַ</td><td>Messiah, anointed</td><td>Lev 4:3; 1Sa 2:10; 16:6; 24:6 – 10, Ps 2:2; 18:50; 89:38; 132:10; Isa 45:1; Da 9:25 – 26; Hab 3:13</td></tr>
<tr><td colspan="4">Capitalizing this word creates confusion. It can refer to anyone who is anointed to a position of authority. Anointing someone is a visual indicator for their endowment with the spirit of God. It is used only four times in the prophets (once to refer to the Persian king Cyrus) and it is not until the intertestamental period that it comes to be used as a technical term for the future, ideal, Davidic king. Most occurrences in the OT use it to refer to the kings in the Davidic line. Though Jesus fulfills this role, the OT authors were not aware that he was the one of whom they spoke.</td></tr>
<tr><td>ṣedeq (7404 – 7)</td><td>צֶדֶק</td><td>righteous(ness)</td><td>Ge 6:9; 15:6; 18:23; Job 9:2; 27:6; Ps 33:5; Eze 18:5</td></tr>
<tr><td colspan="4">This word should not be read as the NT technical theological term for the status of righteousness that no one can achieve. In fact, though it can be used as a description of Yahweh (e.g., Ps 119:137), a high percentage of its uses describe people. It can describe integrity, honesty or innocence as it represents a certain relative standing in society. It is expected of God's people and is achievable to a large degree.</td></tr>
<tr><td>mišpaṭ (5477)</td><td>מִשְׁפָּט</td><td>justice</td><td>Ge 18:19; Ex 21:1; 23:6; 28:30; Lev 19:15; Dt 1:17; 16:19</td></tr>
<tr><td colspan="4">This term is sometimes paired with ṣedeqâ ("righteousness"), combining to express one's social responsibility toward others (pursuing mišpaṭ) and one's responsibility toward God (ṣedeqâ). This word can also be used to refer to judicial decisions that are made and to certain types of regulations, rights and even customs. Yahweh is viewed as the source of mišpaṭ and he is pleased when his people are characterized by it; his laws and ways are just, and he does not pervert justice, but it is not a word that describes an attribute of people or God. The word pertains to what one does (cf. Jer 22:3); not what one is. God himself is never described as "just."</td></tr>
<tr><td>ḥerem (3049, 3051)</td><td>חֵרֶם</td><td>devoted (to destruction)</td><td>Lev 27:21, 28 – 29; Nu 18:14; Dt 7:2, 26; 20:17; Jos 6:17 – 21; 7:1 – 15; often in 1Sa 15</td></tr>
<tr><td colspan="4">No English word even approximates the wide range of meaning of this Hebrew term: from its description of things devoted to the Lord, to the instruction regarding enemies and their cities. Unlike qādôš where something is identified as belonging to the divine realm, ḥerem refers to something as no longer eligible for use in the human realm (see them compared in Lev 27:21), except on occasion by priests (Nu 18:14). Its focus is not on destruction per se; instead, destruction is one of the possible ways of putting something beyond human use. A city so designated cannot be resettled; an object so designated must be burned or given to the sanctuary; a person so designated cannot be taken into possession by another human. The main point is that such a city needs to be returned to God with no inhabitants (whether they are killed or driven away). None shall survive in the city or from the battle. Decreeing ḥerem is not the same as calling for the death of all, so the "destruction" element is misleading. God repeatedly says that he will "drive out" the inhabitants before them, not that he will annihilate them.</td></tr>
</table>

<table>
<tr><th>Transliteration and Goodrick/ Kohlenberger #</th><th>Hebrew</th><th>NIV</th><th>Select Key Verses</th></tr>
<tr><td>ʾhb (170, 173)

śnʾ (8533-4)</td><td>אהב

שׂנא</td><td>love

hate</td><td>ʾhb Ge 22:2; 24:67; 25:28; 29:20, 30; Ex 20:6; Dt 4:37; 21:16; Jdg 14:16; 1Sa 16:21; 18:1 – 3; 2Sa 1:26; 1Ki 5:1; 11:1; Est 2:17; Ecc 3:8; Jer 2:25; Hos 2:5; Mal 1:2
śnʾ Ge 26:27; 29:33; Ex 20:5; Dt 21:17; 22:13; Pr 19:7; Mal 1:3; 2:16</td></tr>
<tr><td colspan="4">Though these terms can carry emotion or sentiment, they pertain primarily to either being in relationship or not. They can refer to preference and favor or the opposite. They can also refer to political alliances and the formal aspects of marriages.</td></tr>
<tr><td>rāqîaʿ (8385)</td><td>רָקִיעַ</td><td>vault</td><td>Ge 1:6 – 8, 14 – 20; Eze 1:22 – 26</td></tr>
<tr><td colspan="4">Going back to the KJV translation of “firmament,” this word was understood to refer to the solid sky — a standard element of ancient cosmic geography. In more recent times “expanse” was favored in an attempt to bridge the gap between science and Scripture. Some translations have now returned to words like “vault” and “dome” to reflect the ancient thinking believed to stand behind this word. The ancient Israelites unquestionably understood the sky to be a solid dome, but uncertainty remains as to whether rāqîaʿ is the Hebrew word that refers to the dome (other stronger candidates exist). “Expanse” may not be far off if we think of the space inside the dome (rather than in modern terms of an atmosphere) since it separates waters above from waters below (rather than heaven and earth). Also note that the sun, moon and stars are said to be in the rāqîaʿ.</td></tr>
<tr><td>šōpēṭ (9149)</td><td>שׁוֹפֵט</td><td>judge</td><td>Ex 18; Jdg 2:16 – 18; 1Sa 7:6</td></tr>
<tr><td colspan="4">A label used to refer to someone who helped establish justice. In some cases such officials were engaged in deciding cases, but in the period of the Israel’s judges, they filled military roles bringing about justice for the people of Israel who were oppressed by enemies.</td></tr>
<tr><td>plʾ (7098-7099)</td><td>פלא</td><td>wonderful, miracles</td><td>Ge 18:14; Ex 3:20; Dt 30:11; Jdg 6:13; 2Ch 2:9; Job 42:3; Ps 139:14; Pr 30:18; Isa 9:6; 28:29; Jer 32:17</td></tr>
<tr><td colspan="4">Israelites had no category for “natural” so they likewise had no category “supernatural.” Consequently “miracles” would not be an appropriate translation (since that English word pertains to phenomena without natural explanation). At the same time, they believed that some issues and levels of understanding were beyond human capacity to grasp. “Incomprehensible” captures it fairly well, with the additional nuance that it is incomprehensible because it is something characteristic of deity: not for frail mortals to expect to understand.</td></tr>
<tr><td>ʾôt (253)</td><td>אות</td><td>sign</td><td>Ge 1:14; 4:15; 9:12; Ex 3:12; 4:8 – 17; 12:13; Dt 6:8; Isa 7:11, 14; 8:18; Jer 32:20 – 21; Eze 20:12</td></tr>
<tr><td colspan="4">“Sign(s)” is an adequate translation as long as it is understood that something does not have to be miraculous in order to qualify for being so designated. A sign demonstrates God’s power, ability to deliver, love for his people, faithfulness to the covenant, etc. It indicates God’s actions, though we should recognize that Israel understood that God acted through both what we call “natural” events and those that we label supernatural.</td></tr>
<tr><td>zkr (2349)</td><td>זכר</td><td>remember</td><td>Ge 8:1; 9:15 – 16; 19:29; Ex 2:24; 20:8; Ps 25:6 – 7</td></tr>
<tr><td colspan="4">Remembering, and the corresponding forgetting, often do not have to do with memory per se, but with attention. zkr means to give attention to someone or something: to act on their behalf, especially when God is doing the remembering.</td></tr>
</table>

Transliteration and Goodrick/ Kohlenberger #	Hebrew	NIV	Select Key Verses
tāmîm (9459)	תָּמִים	without defect, blameless, perfect	Ge 6:9; 17:1; Lev 1:3; Dt 18:13; Ps 18:30; 19:7
Refers most often to the idea that animals for sacrifice are without defect. As a description of a person, it describes them as blameless — having no obvious faults or besetting sins. God's laws and ways are so described, but this is never used as an attribute descriptor of God himself. He expects this quality in sacrifices offered to him and in the lives of his people.			
'mn (586)	אמן	believe, trust	Ge 15:6; 45:26; Ex 4:1–9; Nu 14:11; 20:12; Jnh 3:5
Involves more trusting than reflecting a belief system. Believing that what someone says is true (affirming the truth of the testimony) falls somewhat short of "believing in them." English uses "believe in" to express metaphysical commitments affirming that someone or something exists and thus accepting all the implications of that. *'mn* is not used that way. In other forms *'mn* pertains to being trustworthy or reliable.			
slḥ (6142)	סלח	forgive	Ex 34:9; Lev 4–5; Nu 14:19–20; 1Ki 8:30–39; Ps 103:3
This is a relational term not a judicial one, so it does not pertain to exoneration or absolution. It is used in the sacrificial system to express that the person who has offered a sacrifice has done what was necessary to be welcomed back into fellowship with and relationship to God. The concern of Israelites was that their sinful behavior may cause God to abandon his sanctuary. Forgiveness was the assurance from God that access to his presence was restored.			
'ebed (6269)	עֶבֶד	slave, servant	Ge 9:25; 14:15; 19:19; 40:20; Ex 21:2; 32:13; Lev 25:39, 44; 26:13; Dt 5:15; 1Sa 16:17; 2Sa 3:22; 1Ki 9:22; Job 1:8; Est 1:3; Isa 20:3; 52:13; 53:11
'ebed is an appropriate designation for a slave, but also for a servant or even a high-ranking royal administrator. Slavery in ancient Israel and in the ancient world as a whole showed little similarity to the ethnic dehumanization that is characteristic of the slavery of American history. Some of the distinctions result from Israel being a communal society; others point to the reasons for slavery (e.g., managing debt in an agricultural society).			
tôrâ (9368)	תּוֹרָה	law, regulations, instruction	Ge 26:5; Ex 18:16, 20; 24:12; Lev 6:9; 13:59; Dt 4:44; 17:18; 27:8; 30:10; 31:9; Jos 1:7–8; 8:32; 1Ki 2:3; 2Ki 22:8; Ezr 7:10; Neh 8–9; Ps 1:2; 19:7; 78:1; 119:174; Pr 1:8; 13:14; 31:26; Jer 31:33; Mal 2:8; 4:4
Too often when we think of "law" in English we think of formal, statutory legislation and/or codified, prescribed behavior. The ancient world and Israel were more inclined to think in terms of instruction from an authority figure that became accepted as foundational for societal expectation and obligation. Informal aspects of behavior such as customs, mores and taboos would all be included. In ancient Israel the *tôrâ* offered instruction in wisdom for understanding how Israel was to live out its holy calling. It helped them understand how to live so that Yahweh could continue to dwell among them.			

Transliteration and Goodrick/ Kohlenberger #	Hebrew	NIV	Select Key Verses
gô'ēl (1457)	גּוֹאֵל	redeemer; kinsman redeemer; avenger	Lev 25–27; Nu 35; Ru 2:20; 4:1–8; Job 19:25; Ps 19:14; 107:2; Isa 41:14; 44:6–24; 48:20
"Redeem" has become a technical theological term in Christian usage to refer to the work of Christ on our behalf, but we must be careful not to import that meaning into the Hebrew Bible. In the OT, the *gô'ēl* is one who carries out family obligations to get a family member out of trouble or protect the family interests. It may require a man to marry his deceased brother's widow to make sure the deceased has a descendant. It may involve making sure that allotted land remains in the family. It may require revenging the death of a family member. When God takes this role he is responding as a father to the plight of his children to get them out of some trouble (rarely understood in the OT as the problem of sin that needs to be resolved). In Job 19:25, for example, the *gô'ēl* that he looks for is the one who will come to his aid by demonstrating that Job does not deserve what he has been experiencing. In other words, Job is not looking for someone to redeem him from his sins, but to demonstrate that he doesn't have any. His redemption would then be his vindication from wrongdoing.			
ṭâmē' (3238)	טָמֵא	unclean	*ṭâmē'* Lev 5:2; 7:19–21; 11; 15:2, 25–33; Jos 22:19; 2Ch 23:19; Isa 6:5; 52:1; Hag 2:13–14
ṭâhôr (3196)	טָהוֹר	pure, clean	*ṭâhôr* Ge 7:2, 8; Lev 13:13–41; Ps 12:6; 51:10; Pr 30:12
These terms do not have to do with hygiene. Outside of ritual texts these refer to something that is polluted or unpolluted (e.g., gold of a certain quality), but most uses are in ritual texts and refer to ceremonial defilement or lack of it. Uncleanness can be caused by sin, but often simply represents a breach in propriety.			

Prophet: A prophet is not a fortune teller. He or she is more involved in prognosticating than in predicting. Prophets served as champions of the covenant by being mouthpieces for God. They proclaimed God's plan whether in reference to the past, the present or the future. Prophetic oracles were more interested in revealing God than in revealing the future.

Priest: Though priests performed rituals and instructed people in the fine points of the Torah, those only encompass a few of their tasks rather than circumscribing their identity. Above all, priests had the responsibility to preserve the sanctity of sacred space. Yahweh was living in their midst and his presence needed to be preserved at any cost. The priests were experts not only on Torah, but on holiness. People needed to receive instruction in holiness and in the rituals required to preserve it so that God's presence would not be lost. The priests therefore provided continued access to God's presence and revelation from God to assure ongoing relationship.

King: Modern ideas about kingship are distorted when we think of European history. Kings in the ancient world were believed to be conceived by the gods, chosen by the gods, sponsored by the gods and directed by the gods. They were accountable to the gods and were the link between heaven and earth.

ANCIENT TEXTS RELATING TO THE OLD TESTAMENT

Major representative examples of ancient Near Eastern non-Biblical documents that provide parallels to or shed light on various Old Testament passages

TITLE	ORIGIN	DESCRIPTION
AMARNA LETTERS	**Canaanite Akkadian** *Fourteenth century BC*	Hundreds of letters, written primarily by Canaanite scribes, illuminate social, political and religious relationships between Canaan and Egypt during the reigns of Amunhotep III and Akhenaten.
AMENEMOPE'S WISDOM	**Egyptian** *Late second millennium BC*	Thirty chapters of wisdom instruction are similar to Pr 22:17—24:22 and provide the closest external parallels to OT Wisdom Literature.
ATRAHASIS EPIC	**Akkadian** *Early second millennium BC*	A cosmological epic depicts creation and early human history, including the flood (cf. Ge 1–9).
BABYLONIAN THEODICY	**Akkadian** *Early first millennium BC*	A sufferer and his friend dialogue with each other (cf. Job).
CYRUS CYLINDER	**Akkadian** *Sixth century BC*	King Cyrus of Persia records the conquest of Babylon (cf. Da 5:30; 6:28) and boasts of his generous policies toward his new subjects and their gods.

Cyrus Cylinder, a cuneiform text that describes Cyrus's (Persian ruler 559–530 BC) capture of Babylon in 539 BC. Cyrus allowed the Jews to return from Babylonia and rebuild the temple in Jerusalem (2 Ch 36:23; Ezr 1:2–4; 7:1–5).

Kim Walton, courtesy of the British Museum

Gezer Calendar—one of the earliest examples of Hebrew writing—highlights the agricultural seasons in Israel.

© 1995 Phoenix Data Systems

TITLE	ORIGIN	DESCRIPTION
DEAD SEA SCROLLS	**Hebrew, Aramaic, Greek** *Third century BC to first century AD*	Several hundred scrolls and fragments include the oldest copies of OT books and passages.
EBLA TABLETS	**Sumerian, Eblaite** *Mid-third millennium BC*	Thousands of commercial, legal, literary and epistolary texts describe the cultural vitality and political power of a pre-patriarchal civilization in northern Syria.
ELEPHANTINE PAPYRI	**Aramaic** *Late fifth century BC*	Contracts and letters document life among Jews who fled to southern Egypt after Jerusalem was destroyed in 586 BC.
ENUMA ELISH	**Akkadian** *Second millennium BC*	Marduk, the Babylonian god of cosmic order, is elevated to the supreme position in the pantheon. The seven-tablet epic contains an account of creation (cf. Ge 1–2).
GEZER CALENDAR	**Hebrew** *Tenth century BC*	A schoolboy from west-central Israel describes the seasons, crops and farming activity of the agricultural year.
GILGAMESH EPIC	**Akkadian** *Early second millennium BC*	Gilgamesh, ruler of Uruk, experiences numerous adventures, including a meeting with Utnapishtim, the only survivor of a great deluge (cf. Ge 6–9).
HAMMURAPI'S CODE	**Akkadian** *Eighteenth century BC*	Together with similar law codes that preceded and followed it, the Code of Hammurapi exhibits close parallels to numerous passages in the Mosaic legislation of the OT.

ANCIENT TEXTS RELATING TO THE OLD TESTAMENT (CONT.)

Major representative examples of ancient Near Eastern non-Biblical documents that provide parallels to or shed light on various Old Testament passages

TITLE	ORIGIN	DESCRIPTION
HYMN TO THE ATEN	**Egyptian** *Fourteenth century BC*	The poem praises the beneficence and universality of the sun in language somewhat similar to that used in Ps 104.
ISHTAR'S DESCENT	**Akkadian** *First millennium BC*	The goddess Ishtar temporarily descends to the netherworld, which is pictured in terms reminiscent of OT descriptions of Sheol.
JEHOIACHIN'S RATION DOCKETS	**Akkadian** *Early sixth century BC*	Brief texts from the reign of Nebuchadnezzar II refer to rations allotted to Judah's exiled king Jehoiachin and his sons (cf. 2Ki 25:27–30).
KING LISTS	**Sumerian** *Early second millennium BC*	The reigns of Sumerian kings before the flood are described as lasting for thousands of years, reminding us of the longevity of the preflood patriarchs in Ge 5.
LACHISH LETTERS (OSTRACA)	**Hebrew** *Early sixth century BC*	Inscriptions on pottery fragments vividly portray the desperate days preceding the Babylonian siege of Jerusalem in 588–586 BC (cf. Jer 34:7).
LAMENTATION OVER THE DESTRUCTION OF UR	**Sumerian** *Early second millennium BC*	The poem mourns the destruction of the city of Ur at the hands of the Elamites (cf. the OT book of Lamentations).
LUDLUL BEL NEMEQI	**Akkadian** *Late second millennium BC*	A suffering Babylonian nobleman describes his distress in terms faintly reminiscent of the experiences of Job.
MARI TABLETS	**Akkadian** *Eighteenth century BC*	Letters and administrative texts provide detailed information regarding customs, language and personal names that reflect the culture of the OT patriarchs.
MERNEPTAH STELE	**Egyptian** *Thirteenth century BC*	Pharaoh Merneptah figuratively describes his victory over various peoples in western Asia, including "Israel."
MESHA STELE (MOABITE STONE)	**Moabite** *Ninth century BC*	Mesha, king of Moab (see 2Ki 3:4 and note on 1:1), rebels against a successor of Israel's king Omri.

Mesha Stele (Moabite Stone), a Moabite inscription (c. 840–820 BC), recounts the exploits of Mesha, king of Moab (2 Ki 3:4).

Z. Radovan/www.BibleLandPictures.com

Sennacherib's Prism was discovered among the ruins of Nineveh, the ancient capital of the Assyrian Empire. It contains the annals of Sennacherib, the Assyrian king who besieged Jerusalem in 701 BC during the reign of King Hezekiah.

© 1995 Phoenix Data Systems

ANCIENT TEXTS RELATING TO THE OLD TESTAMENT (CONT.)

Major representative examples of ancient Near Eastern non-Biblical documents that provide parallels to or shed light on various Old Testament passages		
TITLE	**ORIGIN**	**DESCRIPTION**
MURASHU TABLETS	**Akkadian** *Fifth century BC*	Commercial documents describe financial transactions engaged in by Murashu and Sons, a Babylonian firm that did business with Jews and other exiles.
MURSILIS'S TREATY WITH DUPPI-TESSUB	**Hittite** *Mid-second millennium BC*	King Mursilis imposes a suzerainty treaty on King Duppi-Tessub. The literary outline of this and other Hittite treaties is strikingly paralleled in OT covenants established by God with his people.
NABONIDUS CHRONICLE	**Akkadian** *Mid-sixth century BC*	The account describes the absence of King Nabonidus from Babylon. His son Belshazzar is therefore the regent in charge of the kingdom (cf. Da 5:29–30).
NEBUCHADNEZZAR CHRONICLE	**Akkadian** *Early sixth century BC*	A chronicle from the reign of Nebuchadnezzar II includes the Babylonian account of the siege of Jerusalem in 597 BC (see 2Ki 24:10–17).
NUZI TABLETS	**Akkadian** *Mid-second millennium BC*	Adoption, birthright sale and other legal documents graphically illustrate OT patriarchal customs current centuries earlier.
PESSIMISTIC DIALOGUE	**Akkadian** *Early first millennium BC*	A master and his servant discuss the pros and cons of various activities (cf. Ecc 1–2).
RAS SHAMRA TABLETS	**Ugaritic** *Fifteenth–fourteenth centuries BC*	Canaanite deities and rulers experience adventures in epics that enrich our understanding of Canaanite mythology and religion and of OT poetry.
SARGON LEGEND	**Akkadian** *First millennium BC*	Sargon I (the Great), ruler of Akkad in the late third millennium BC, claims to have been rescued as an infant from a reed basket found floating in a river (cf. Ex 2).
SARGON'S DISPLAY INSCRIPTION	**Akkadian** *Eighth century BC*	Sargon II takes credit for the conquest of Samaria in 722/721 BC and states that he captured and exiled 27,290 Israelites.
SENNACHERIB'S PRISM	**Akkadian** *Early seventh century BC*	Sennacherib vividly describes his siege of Jerusalem in 701 BC, making Hezekiah a prisoner in his own royal city (but cf. 2Ki 19:35–37).
SEVEN LEAN YEARS TRADITION	**Egyptian** *Second century BC*	Egypt experiences seven years of low Niles and famine, which, by a contractual agreement between Pharaoh Djoser (twenty-eighth century BC) and a god, will be followed by prosperity (cf. Ge 41).
SHALMANESER'S BLACK OBELISK	**Akkadian** *Ninth century BC*	Israel's king Jehu presents tribute to Assyria's king Shalmaneser III. Additional Assyrian and Babylonian texts refer to other kings of Israel and Judah.
SHISHAK'S GEOGRAPHICAL LIST	**Egyptian** *Tenth century BC*	Pharaoh Shishak lists the cities that he captured or made tributary during his campaign in Judah and Israel (cf. 1Ki 14:25–26 and note on 14:25).
SILOAM INSCRIPTION	**Hebrew** *Late eighth century BC*	A Judahite workman describes the construction of an underground conduit to guarantee Jerusalem's water supply during Hezekiah's reign (cf. 2Ki 20:20; 2Ch 32:30).
SINUHE'S STORY	**Egyptian** *Twentieth–nineteenth centuries BC*	An Egyptian official of the Twelfth Dynasty goes into voluntary exile in Aram (Syria) and Canaan during the OT patriarchal period.
TALE OF TWO BROTHERS	**Egyptian** *Thirteenth century BC*	A young man rejects the amorous advances of his older brother's wife (cf. Ge 39).
WENAMUN'S JOURNEY	**Egyptian** *Eleventh century BC*	An official of the temple of Amun at Thebes in Egypt is sent to Byblos in Canaan to buy lumber for the ceremonial barge of his god.

Old Testament Chronology

Creation	Fall	Flood	Babel
Ge 1–2	Ge 3	Ge 6–9	Ge 11
?	?	?	?

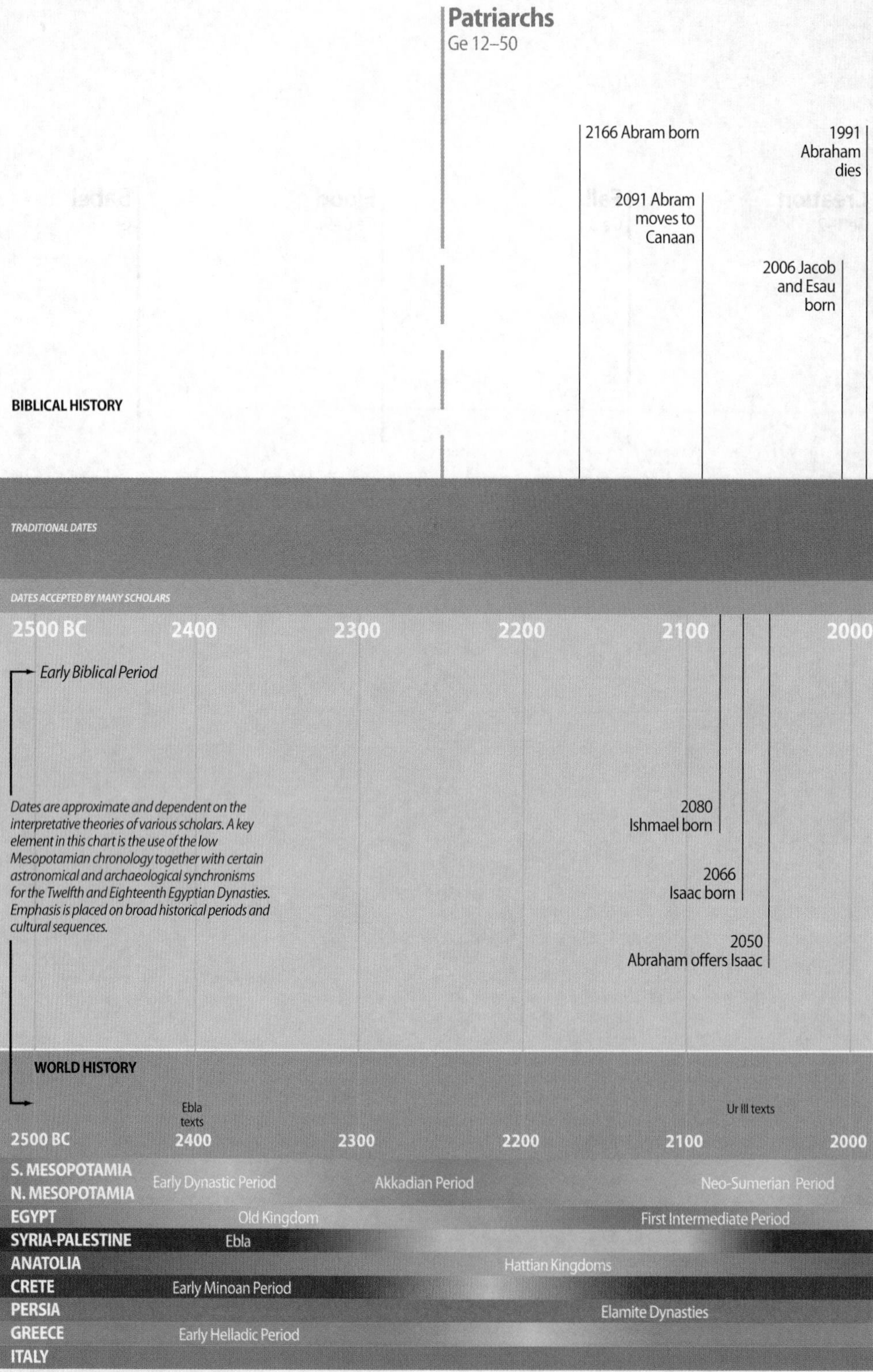
Patriarchs
Ge 12–50
2166 Abram born
1991 Abraham dies
2091 Abram moves to Canaan
2006 Jacob and Esau born
BIBLICAL HISTORY
TRADITIONAL DATES
DATES ACCEPTED BY MANY SCHOLARS
2500 BC
2400
2300
2200
2100
2000
Early Biblical Period
Dates are approximate and dependent on the interpretative theories of various scholars. A key element in this chart is the use of the low Mesopotamian chronology together with certain astronomical and archaeological synchronisms for the Twelfth and Eighteenth Egyptian Dynasties. Emphasis is placed on broad historical periods and cultural sequences.
2080 Ishmael born
2066 Isaac born
2050 Abraham offers Isaac
WORLD HISTORY
Ebla texts
Ur III texts
2500 BC
2400
2300
2200
2100
2000
S. MESOPOTAMIA
N. MESOPOTAMIA
Early Dynastic Period
Akkadian Period
Neo-Sumerian Period
EGYPT
Old Kingdom
First Intermediate Period
SYRIA-PALESTINE
Ebla
ANATOLIA
Hattian Kingdoms
CRETE
Early Minoan Period
PERSIA
Elamite Dynasties
GREECE
Early Helladic Period
ITALY

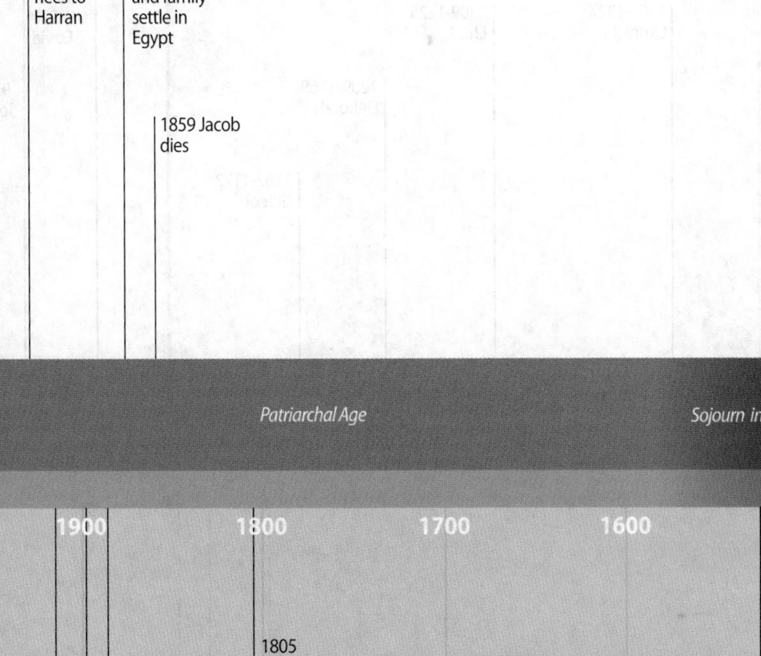

Cappadocian texts | Mari texts | Hammurapi texts

1900 | 1800 | 1700 | 1600 | 1500 BC

Isin-Larsa Period | Old Babylonian Period

Middle Kingdom | Second Intermediate (Hyksos) Period | New Kingdom

Amorite Period | Hyksos Period | Late Canaanite Period

Hittite Old Kingdom

Middle Minoan Period

Middle Helladic Period

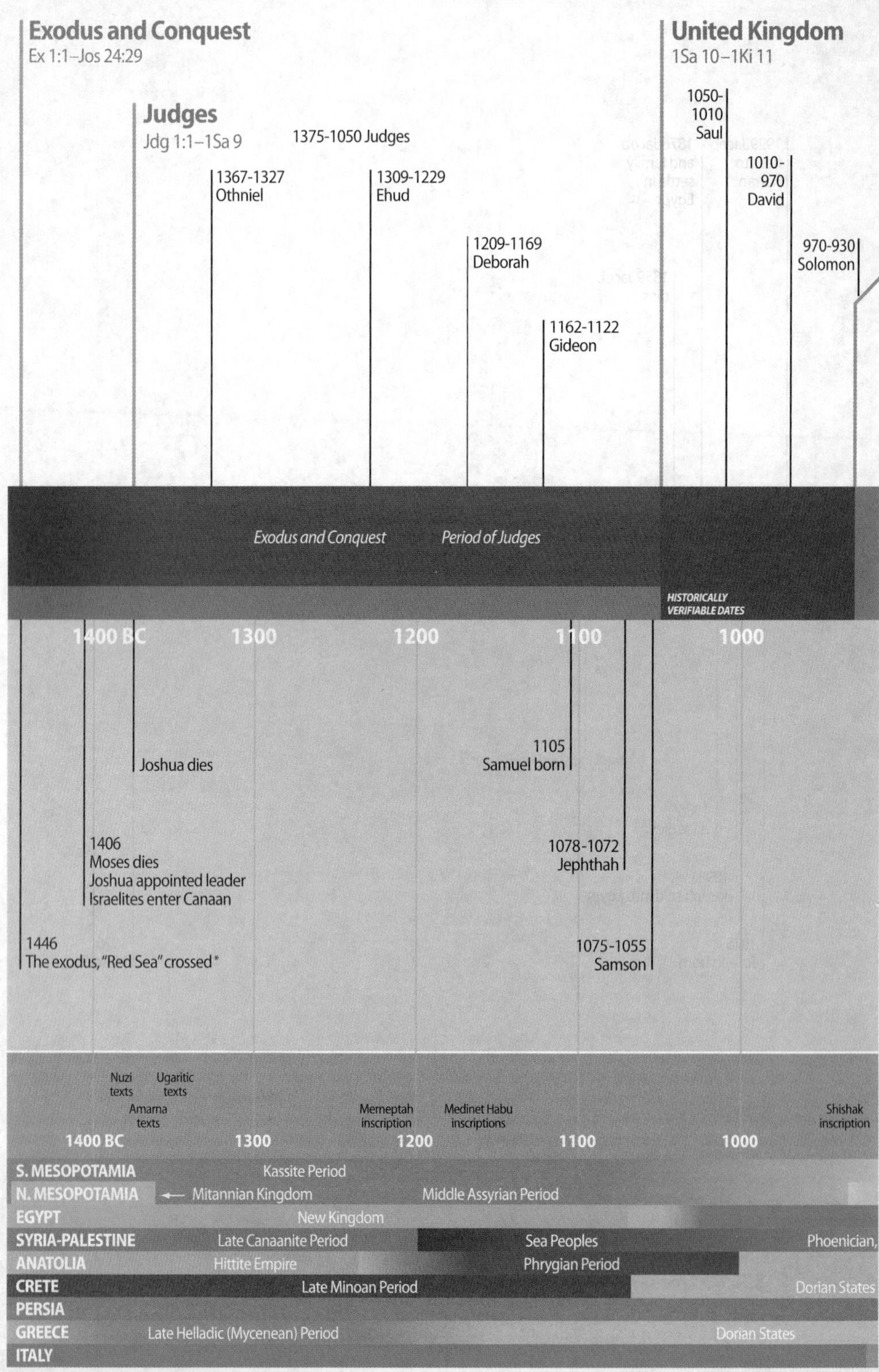

*This date and earlier dates in this timeline are based on an earlier Exodus dating, which is only one of the alternative dating options. See "The Timing of the Exodus," pp. 118–119.

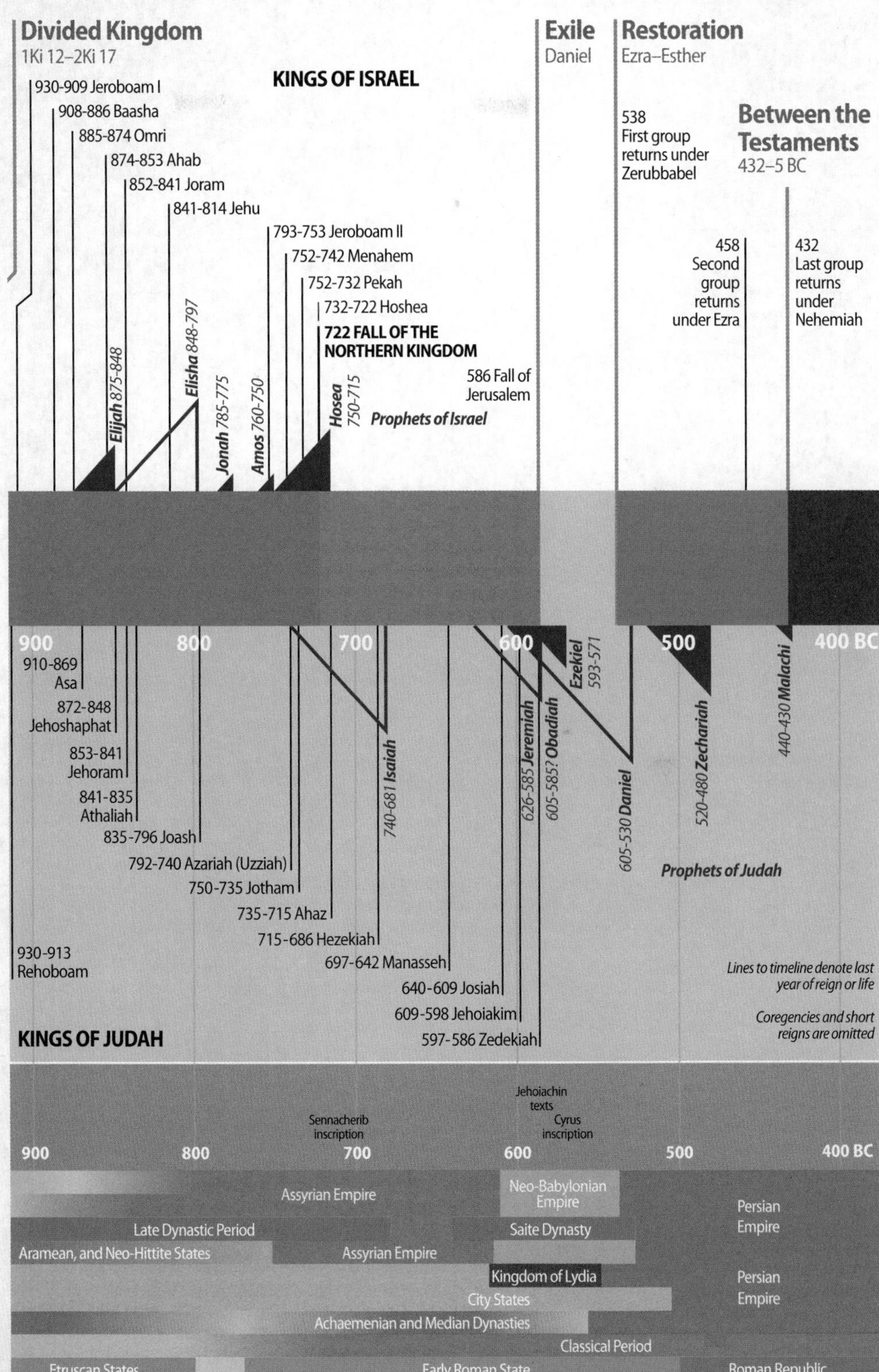
Divided Kingdom
1Ki 12–2Ki 17
KINGS OF ISRAEL
930-909 Jeroboam I
908-886 Baasha
885-874 Omri
874-853 Ahab
852-841 Joram
841-814 Jehu
793-753 Jeroboam II
752-742 Menahem
752-732 Pekah
732-722 Hoshea
722 FALL OF THE NORTHERN KINGDOM
Elijah 875-848
Elisha 848-797
Jonah 785-775
Amos 760-750
Hosea 750-715
Prophets of Israel
586 Fall of Jerusalem
Exile
Daniel
Restoration
Ezra–Esther
538 First group returns under Zerubbabel
Between the Testaments
432–5 BC
458 Second group returns under Ezra
432 Last group returns under Nehemiah
900
800
700
600
500
400 BC
910-869 Asa
872-848 Jehoshaphat
853-841 Jehoram
841-835 Athaliah
835-796 Joash
792-740 Azariah (Uzziah)
750-735 Jotham
735-715 Ahaz
715-686 Hezekiah
697-642 Manasseh
640-609 Josiah
609-598 Jehoiakim
597-586 Zedekiah
930-913 Rehoboam
KINGS OF JUDAH
740-681 Isaiah
626-585 Jeremiah
605-585? Obadiah
Ezekiel 593-571
605-530 Daniel
520-480 Zechariah
440-430 Malachi
Prophets of Judah
Lines to timeline denote last year of reign or life
Coregencies and short reigns are omitted
Jehoiachin texts
Sennacherib inscription
Cyrus inscription
900
800
700
600
500
400 BC
Assyrian Empire
Neo-Babylonian Empire
Persian Empire
Late Dynastic Period
Saite Dynasty
Aramean, and Neo-Hittite States
Assyrian Empire
Kingdom of Lydia
Persian Empire
City States
Achaemenian and Median Dynasties
Classical Period
Etruscan States
Early Roman State
Roman Republic

Old Testament

Major Background Issues from the Ancient Near East

To think about the ancient world, we can use the metaphor of a cultural river that flowed through the societies and thoughts of the peoples and nations of the ancient Near East. Israel was immersed in that cultural river; it was embedded in that conceptual world. Sometimes God gave revelation that drew them out, as Moses from the Nile, and distinguished them; but we should generally think of them in this cultural river. Sometimes they were simply floating on its currents; sometimes they veered out of the currents and stood apart. At other times they swam resolutely upstream against those currents.

The twelve issues identified below describe major currents in this metaphorical ancient cultural river. Israel's relationship to those currents varies case by case. Importantly, however, as modern readers, we have no familiarity with that river at all. Our cultural river is very different. Whether Israel was floating or swimming, as we read through the Old Testament we must recognize that they were in a different river than we are. To interpret the Old Testament well, we must try to dip into their cultural river.

1. *The "Great Symbiosis."* People in the ancient world believed that the gods had made people as slave laborers because they were tired of growing their own food and taking care of their own needs. People cared for the gods (who lived an opulent, pampered lifestyle including food, drink, clothing, housing, etc.) and in turn, the gods took care of the people (because they had vested interests in doing so). Thus there was a codependent relationship of mutual need. This provides the context for understanding temples, rituals, worship, and religious obligation in the ancient world. Israel is called to a far different way of thinking, as Yahweh has no needs.

2. *Presence of God in Sacred Space.* This is an extension of the previous item. People in the ancient world highly desired that their god to take up residence among them. It was important for the god so they could be pampered, and important for the people so that they could receive blessing. The presence of the god created sacred space that had to be respected and honored. Limited access and purity requirements were taken very seriously. Combined with the Great Symbiosis, this shows why all religion in the ancient world was local. Only those who lived in the vicinity of the temple could be engaged in caring for the gods. And the gods would only be interested in providing for and protecting those who could take care of him/her. It is not that the gods were powerless beyond their local area; rather, they were disinterested in other places. Their needs were all that mattered. Israel took its sacred space very seriously, but Yahweh was a very different sort of God.

3. *Gods in Community.* The polytheism of the ancient world was not just a matter of numbers. In the ancient world identity was found in one's community rather than in one's individuality. Like people, gods found their identity in relationship to the group to which they belonged. Each god had a constellation of attributes, just as people have different skills and abilities. As in human communities, the community of the gods called for hierarchy. So the pantheon of the gods was characterized by a hierarchy (cosmic gods, national gods, city patrons, clan deities, ancestral deities) and by differentiation (according to their jurisdiction, manifestations and attributes). Given this cultural reality, we can surmise that it was very difficult for the Israelites to adjust to a single God spanning all levels of hierarchy and all categories of jurisdiction.

continued on next page

4. *Revelation and Manifestation of Deities.* The gods in the ancient word were generally believed to not be forthcoming—that is, they were not believed to reveal themselves broadly (with exceptions in responding to divinatory inquiries). Consequently, one could never be sure exactly what the god expected from people (except to be pampered). Whenever something went wrong, people in the ancient world would assume that they had somehow offended a petty deity. Even though the gods did not reveal themselves or their expectation, they did manifest themselves in diverse ways. The sun, moon, planets and stars, for example, were all considered manifestations of various gods. The most important manifestation of the deity was in the image, which was commissioned by the god, manufactured from the finest of materials with the help of the god, and then ritually energized so that the essence of the god took up residence in the image. The image was not the god, but a manifestation of the god, and therefore it was capable of serving as mediator for the presence of the deity, for the care of the deity and for the worship given the deity. The Israelites were to have no such mediators—no man-made image could accomplish such things and Yahweh had no needs to be met through the image.

5. *Spirit world.* In the ancient world the reality of spiritual beings extended beyond the gods themselves. Other classes of spirit beings included chaos creatures, demons, servants of the gods, and spirits of deceased humans. These beings were generally not considered to be morally flawed or evil. Sometimes their intrinsic nature just wreaked havoc. Some could serve apotropaic functions whereas others were more inclined to devour. None of this fits in to how we think about demons today as evil fallen angels. The Old Testament lacks demons almost entirely and considers chaos creatures less free of Yahweh's control.

6. *Natural versus Supernatural.* Today we are inclined to separate our understanding of events and phenomena into the categories of "natural" or "supernatural," the former of these two being the result of natural laws and explainable as natural cause and effect; the latter being acts of God beyond scientific explanation. In the ancient world there was no such classification system. Nothing would have been considered purely natural with God/the gods uninvolved. They would not speak of miracles (i.e., supernatural occurrences), but rather of signs and wonders that were manifestations of God's power. Israel was very much like the rest of the ancient world in this regard.

7. *Deep Reality.* Corresponding to the previous point, in the ancient world people did not circumscribe reality within the category of historical events. Today it is not uncommon for us to think that reality is defined by events: we ask ourselves, "Did it really happen?" In the ancient world people considered events as a small slice of a reality that transcended events of history. What we call their mythology was more real to them than their history. When ancient people talked about events, they often found the most significant reality in what God/the gods had done, not in what people had done. We misunderstand when we think of mythology as made-up stories about gods that did not exist and therefore treat them as fairy tales. Ancient Israel's thinking was very similar to the ancient world in this regard.

8. *Creation and Order.* Since we modern readers tend to be materially focused, when we think of creation and origins we think in material terms. In the ancient world people were much more inclined to think of creation not so much as manufacturing the material cosmos, but of establishing order in the cosmos and making it function with a particular purpose in mind. Gods were the source of order; wisdom was the pursuit of order; creation was the establishment of order. Israelites would have thought about the cosmos and God's creative work in similar terms, but, of course, Yahweh was the Creator.

9. *Religion and Magic.* Religion and magic were not different categories in the ancient world and it is not possible to separate them from one another. Magic entailed the exercise of power (in spells, hexes, exorcisms, sorcery, necromancy, etc.) but operated primarily on the power associated with the name of a person and the name

continued on next page

of a deity. A god's name could be invoked either for effective exercise of power over another person, or for summoning or commanding the god himself. Divination was understood to provide access to information about what the gods were doing (signaled in the stars, terrestrial occurrences, dreams, entrails of sacrificed animals, and in many other indicators). Israelites were forbidden to practice most forms of divination and were not to use God's name to attempt to control him.

10. *Death and Memory.* In the ancient world people viewed community as extending beyond the world of the living. When someone died, the deceased joined the group of ancestors in the netherworld, yet also remained in the community of those still alive — remembered by them and in most instances, receiving care from them (in the form meals to the dead). Burial customs reflected these beliefs: people believed that improper burial (or no burial) would make it impossible for the dead to join the community of ancestors and would therefore leave them homeless, uncared for, and very unhappy (as well as prone to haunt the living). As to the concern to be remembered, people would strive throughout their lives to make a name for themselves (defined as doing anything that would cause them to be remembered). Having children was the most important way of doing this. To die childless was to die with little hope of being remembered, which in turn would have a severely negative impact on their existence in the netherworld. Israel thought in very similar ways.

11. *Identity in Community.* In stark contrast to Westerners who find their main identity in themselves as individuals, in the ancient world people found their identity in their community. It was in this sort of context that arranged marriages made sense and levirate marriage would be important. In such a community context, religion was a family choice, not an individual choice. Families worshiped gods within their family circle, so that a woman who married into another clan naturally adopted the gods of that clan. Legal cases related to clan identities and judgment could target the whole communal group rather than just one individual. Guilt and blessing both operated on a communal level. Israel's perspectives were very much the same.

12. *Retribution Principle.* People believed that the righteous would prosper and the wicked would suffer. This led to the belief that if one pleased the gods (took care of them well), one would receive their blessing; if one didn't, the gods would be angry and lash out. Such a belief led people to conclude that if someone was prospering, they must be doing well by the gods; if they were suffering, they must have done something to anger the gods and as such should be shunned. In the ancient world this was applied not only to the level of the individual but also to the level of the community, clan or family. This particular belief can be problematic for the modern Bible reader because some of the psalms and proverbs seem to affirm this principle. A full reading of the Bible, however, especially from the book of Job, nuances this principle. ◆

OLD TESTAMENT

THE TORAH

GOD ESTABLISHES HIS COVENANT

Introduction to the Torah

A wide array of literature from the ancient Near East provides information that is helpful for interpreting the Pentateuch. Ancient Near Eastern mythology reflects ideas about creation. Though ancient texts provide accounts of creation from Mesopotamia and Egypt and in the process provide insight into the creator deities and their roles (which are far different from what we find in the Bible), they also provide important information concerning how the ancients thought about the cosmos (which is often very similar to what we find in the Bible).

The patriarchal narratives can be read against the background of family archives from the ancient Near East that explain customs and legal traditions that are unlike our modern traditions in many ways. The religious practices and beliefs of the patriarchs can be investigated in comparison to the ancient world. Though these practices and beliefs were rooted in the ancient world, God was also gradually drawing them out of their familiar ways of thinking. At the same time, we would be mistaken to think that Abraham's theology was the same as ours.

Ritual descriptions can be illuminated by ritual texts available in wide variety. Covenant documents in the Pentateuch can be read in light of treaties between countries. Laws can be compared to a variety of law collections dating from the second millennium BC. Such comparison can not only focus on the form or content of the individual laws but, more important, it can expand to a study of the source of law and the literary functions of law collections. How did people in the ancient world think about such collections of laws? These collections certainly did not have the same role as our legislative literature does today. All of these studies show us that God communicated to Israel within the cultural context of their world.

Historical and archaeological studies can provide background information to help understand the situation in Canaan during the patriarchal period and try to resolve basic questions such as the historical setting of Israel's slavery in Egypt and the date of the exodus. Of particular importance are all of the archaeological studies trying to bring further understanding to the Egyptian backdrop of these events.

Sociological studies can comment on the concept of sacred space and the variety of institutions that existed in a society to manage sacred space — from priests to sanctuaries to rituals. Additional studies in religion also help us understand some of the ways that God called the people of Israel to be distinct from the people around them. As we learn about the ancient perception of deity and the way that perception is reflected in ancient Near Eastern ideas about pantheons, images, divination and magic, we can understand more clearly some of what Israel was to guard against.

What eventually is included in the books of Exodus through Deuteronomy identifies Moses as the authority figure from whom the material derives, and there is no reason to doubt the centrality of his role. At the same time, communication in the ancient world was primarily oral, since these were hearing-dominant cultures. Writing was known and conducted largely by the specialists (scribes), but scribes primarily produced documents rather than what we call books. The scribes themselves were not authors; they preserved the words of authority figures such as Moses. We don't know when scribal archives of this sort of document would have been compiled into the books as we know them today. ◆

THE TORAH

GENESIS

Date and Author

We have no certain information about the authorship of Genesis, though early Biblical tradition views Moses as having a significant role in transmitting and perhaps even formulating the traditions preserved in the book. The oral nature of ancient culture may suggest that actual written forms of the traditions came much later, though whenever they were produced, they maintained their connectedness to the authority figures, such as Moses, who were instrumental. Regardless of the date of the final writing, the text largely preserves its mid-second-millennium BC context and perspective.

KEY CONCEPTS

- The covenant is God's program of revelation.
- The focus of creation is the establishment and maintenance of order and operation.
- The stories in the Bible are stories about God.

Literary Setting

Literary genres have rules and conventions by which they operate. Communication is jeopardized if we do not understand the parameters of the genre of the literature we are reading. How confusing it would be if we were reading a mystery in which the author gave every appearance of writing a biography! But at the same time, the features that indicate whether a literary work is a mystery or biography are to some extent culturally determined. The reason that genre categories work is that the categories represent a consensus of expectation among the readers.

When we approach a book like Genesis, we must be aware of what genres we will be encountering. But just as important, we must adjust our expectations so that we will come to those genres understanding the ancient conventions attached to that genre rather than imposing our own genre conventions on their literature.

Genesis contains cosmogony texts, i.e., texts that deal with the origins of key aspects of the cosmos. It also contains genealogies (e.g., chs. 5; 11; 36), founders' or ancestors' narratives (e.g., chs. 12 – 35), destiny proclamations (i.e., formal blessings and/or curses from father to son, e.g., chs. 9; 27; 49), conflict tales (e.g., chs. 4; 6 – 7; 11; 19; 34), battle accounts (e.g., ch. 14), and a narrative about the rise of a courtier from humble beginnings to a position of power (chs. 40 – 45). Some of these are unparalleled in the ancient world, and even when possible parallels exist, significant differences lead us to proceed with caution. ◆

The Beginning

1 In the beginning[a] God created the
heavens and the earth.[b] 2 Now the
earth was formless and empty,[c] darkness was over the surface of the deep,
and the Spirit of God[d] was hovering
over the waters.
3 And God said,[e] "Let there be light," and

1:1 [a] Jn 1:1-2 [b] Job 38:4; Ps 90:2; Isa 42:5; 44:24; 45:12, 18; Ac 17:24; Heb 11:3; Rev 4:11 **1:2** [c] Jer 4:23 [d] Ps 104:30 **1:3** [e] Ps 33:6, 9; 148:5; Heb 11:3

1:1 *In the beginning.* In the OT "beginning" refers to a preliminary period of time rather than the first in a series of events. In English, we might refer to such an initial period as "the primordial period." This leads us to conclude that the "beginning" is a way of talking about the seven-day *period* rather than a *point* in time prior to the seven days. **1:2** *formless and empty.* Prior to creation the Egyptian texts talk about the "nonexistent." In their thinking this nonexistent realm continues to be present in the sea, in the dark night sky, and even in the desert—places without role or function (see the article "Creation and Existence," p. 4). In the Egyptian precreation state of nonexistence there are two elements: primeval waters and total darkness. In Hebrew, "formless" (*tohu*) is also used to refer to the desert (e.g., Dt 32:10). In general it designates a situation in which positive values such as purpose and worth are lacking. As a result, it is more appropriate to translate "without function" rather than "without form," the idea being similar to the Egyptian "nonexistent." This is also apparent in Jer 4:23, where the same pair of Hebrew terms is used to describe a nonfunctional, nonproductive state. *deep.* Hebrew *tehom*; it refers to the primordial or primeval sea. In the precreation period it covered everything. In creation it was pushed out to the edges of the cosmos, where it was restrained by God's power. There it is identified as the cosmic waters of chaos that can be brought back at any moment if deity requires its services. Although the Hebrew word is the cognate of the Babylonian *tamtu/Tiamat*, it is not personified as a being associated with chaos, nor can it be considered a depersonification or demythologization that is dependent on the ancient Near Eastern texts. It is simply used to describe the "precosmic condition." **1:3** *Let there be light.* As God calls the cosmos into existence, it is important to remember that it is a functional

GENESIS 1:1

Creation and Existence

If creation is the act of bringing something into existence, we must ask what constituted existence in the ancient world. In our culture, we consider existence to be either material (i.e., having molecules/taking up space and extending to energy and subatomic particles) or experiential (e.g., abstractions such as love or time). Those definitions, however, are culturally determined. By contrast, in the ancient world something existed when it had a function—a role to play.

In Mesopotamia one way to accomplish this was to name something, because a name designated a thing's function or role. Thus, in the Babylonian creation account, bringing the cosmos into existence begins "When on high no name was given in heaven, nor below was the netherworld called by name ... When no gods at all had been brought forth, none called by names, none destinies ordained, then were the gods formed." In Egyptian accounts existence was associated with something having been differentiated. The god Atum is conceptualized as the primordial monad—the singularity embodying all the potential of the cosmos, from whom all things were separated and thereby created. The Genesis account includes both of these concepts as God separates and names.

The actual Hebrew verb "create" (*bara*) also focuses our attention in this direction. In the Bible, only God can perform this action of bringing something into existence. What is even more intriguing is that the objects of this verb point consistently toward its connection to functional existence rather than material existence; e.g., God "creates" fire, cloud, destruction, calamity, darkness, righteousness and purity. This is much like the ancient Near Eastern way of thinking that it was more important to determine who controlled functions rather than who/what gave something its physical form. In the ancient world something was created when it was given a function. In the ancient world, the cosmos is less like a machine, more like a kingdom. ◆

there was light.[f] 4God saw that the
light was good, and he separated the
light from the darkness. 5God called
the light "day," and the darkness he
called "night."[g] And there was evening, and there was morning — the
first day.
6 And God said, "Let there be a vault[h] between the waters to separate water
from water." 7So God made the vault
and separated the water under the
vault from the water above it.[i] And it
was so. 8God called the vault "sky."
And there was evening, and there
was morning — the second day.
9 And God said, "Let the water under the
sky be gathered to one place,[j] and let
dry ground appear." And it was so.
10God called the dry ground "land,"
and the gathered waters he called
"seas." And God saw that it was
good.
11Then God said, "Let the land produce vegetation:[k] seed-bearing plants
and trees on the land that bear fruit
with seed in it, according to their various kinds." And it was so. 12The land
produced vegetation: plants bearing
seed according to their kinds and
trees bearing fruit with seed in it according to their kinds. And God saw
that it was good. 13And there was evening, and there was morning — the
third day.
14 And God said, "Let there be lights[l] in
the vault of the sky to separate the
day from the night, and let them
serve as signs[m] to mark sacred
times,[n] and days and years, 15and let
them be lights in the vault of the sky
to give light on the earth." And it was
so. 16God made two great lights — the
greater light to govern[o] the day and
the lesser light to govern[p] the night.
He also made the stars.[q] 17God set
them in the vault of the sky to give
light on the earth, 18to govern the day
and the night,[r] and to separate light
from darkness. And God saw that it
was good. 19And there was evening,
and there was morning — the fourth
day.
20 And God said, "Let the water teem
with living creatures, and let birds
fly above the earth across the vault of
the sky." 21So God created the great
creatures of the sea and every living
thing with which the water teems and
that moves about in it,[s] according to
their kinds, and every winged bird
according to its kind. And God saw
that it was good. 22God blessed them
and said, "Be fruitful and increase
in number and fill the water in the

1:3 [f] 2Co 4:6* **1:5** [g] Ps 74:16 **1:6** [h] Jer 10:12 **1:7** [i] Job 38:8-11, 16; Ps 148:4 **1:9** [j] Job 38:8-11; Ps 104:6-9; Pr 8:29; Jer 5:22; 2Pe 3:5 **1:11** [k] Ps 65:9-13; 104:14 **1:14** [l] Ps 74:16 [m] Jer 10:2 [n] Ps 104:19 **1:16** [o] Ps 136:8 [p] Ps 136:9 [q] Job 38:7, 31-32; Ps 8:3; Isa 40:26 **1:18** [r] Jer 33:20, 25 **1:21** [s] Ps 104:25-26

existence, not necessarily a physical existence (see the article "Creation and Existence," p. 4). In this case, though we think of light as a having physical properties, the ancients did not think in those terms. They also did not think of all light as coming from the sun. "Daylight" was not caused by "sunlight"; although the sun, moon and stars were bearers of light, daylight was present even when these were hidden by clouds or an eclipse. Light was not considered something physical in the ancient world; rather, it was a phenomenon. Here in Genesis, light is identified with alternating periods of day and night. Since light is called "day" and darkness is called "night" (v. 5), the text indicates that the functional focus is time.

1:6 *a vault.* See the article "The 'Vault' and 'Water Above,'" p. 6.

1:9 *dry ground.* Nonexistence for the Egyptians was not wiped out in the acts of creation, but was pushed to the outer limits of the cosmos. Consequently their literature speaks of the primeval hillock that emerged from the primeval waters. Temples were sometimes understood as containing the original primeval hillock in the center of their sacred space. Mesopotamian literature does not speak much of the emergence of the land, but there is discussion of the collection of the waters to their appropriate place. In this feature, then, Genesis shows more similarity to Egyptian literature. It was common in the ancient world to think of the earth as a single continent in the shape of a flat disc. Likewise in Genesis, the waters are all gathered into one place, and land appears, presumably in one place.

1:11 *vegetation.* The indication that the land produces vegetation is not a statement about the land being involved in creation. What is being created by God is a function whereby the land regularly and characteristically produces vegetation — the principle of fecundity whereby agriculture can exist and food can be grown.

1:14 *signs.* The Hebrew word used for "sign" has a cognate in Akkadian that is used for omens, but the Hebrew has a more neutral sense. The author has emptied the elements of the cosmos of their more personal traits, as he did with the description of the precosmic condition; the sun, moon, etc. are not depicted as gods as they are in Near Eastern literature.

1:21 *creatures of the sea.* In the mythologies of the ancient Near East a variety of terrible creatures inhabited the sea, and these are occasionally associated with the threatening forces of chaos that need to be defeated and harnessed by creator deities. The OT also refers to a number of different cosmic sea creatures (e.g., Ps 74:13 – 15; Isa 27:1). In Ps 74:13 – 14 the sea creature (Hebrew *tannin*) is portrayed with multiple heads and is parallel to Leviathan. This depiction of battle is also seen in Isa 51:9, where *tannin*, like "Rahab," is defeated. Unlike the ancient Near East creation texts, though, Genesis shows no indication of a battle — only that *tannin* is created.

This is the first use of the verb *bara* ("created") since v. 1, perhaps emphasizing that *tannin* is not some primeval chaos monster that must be overcome, but a creature being given its role (see the article "Creation and Existence," p. 4) just like everything else in creation. Yet it ought to be viewed as a cosmic creature rather than a marine specimen. The passages in which the word may refer to zoological specimens (Ex 7:9 – 10; Dt 32:33; Ps 91:13) indicate a land creature or amphibian, not a sea creature as here.

GENESIS 1:6–7

THE "VAULT" AND "WATER ABOVE"

The Hebrew *raqia* ("vault") is of unspecified material, but in at least one text it refers to something solid (cf. Eze 1:25–26). It is the boundary between heaven and earth, and its main function is to hold back the water above. Some mountains are identified as intersecting the sky and perhaps holding it up. Mesopotamian literature at times suggests some sort of skin, but also speaks of the various levels of heaven having pavements, the most visible one being blue. Heaven and earth were kept in place by cables held by the gods.

In Egyptian iconography the sky is represented by the goddess Nut, whose body arched over the land. The Israelites portray no god, living or dead, as the sky, but their cosmic geography saw the sky as having a composition and role similar to what can be seen across the ancient Near East. We know from Ex 24:10 that they shared the idea of a pavement in God's abode—and it is even of sapphire as in the Mesopotamian texts.

Intertestamental and rabbinic speculation sometimes focused on the material that the vault was made of and how thick it was. The church fathers likewise were united in their belief that the vault was solid. Though it may be surprising for modern minds to learn, the testimony of historical evidence shows that most people in the ancient world believed the sky was solid. The idea that it's not is a thoroughly modern notion.

Pictorial representations throughout the ancient Near East portray waters above and below, which demonstrates that this was a common feature of ancient cosmic geography. In Mesopotamia the god Marduk assigns guards to keep the heavenly waters from flooding the earth. In Egyptian texts, the sun-god's barque travels from horizon to horizon across a heavenly ocean. In the OT, the heavenly waters are sometimes called the *mabbul*, above which Yahweh is enthroned (Ps 29:10) and which are released in the time of Noah (Ge 7:10).

The concept of heavenly waters is the natural deduction to be drawn from the experience of precipitation. If moisture comes from the sky, there must be moisture up there. Thus the sky becomes the pivotal phenomenon associated with weather.

continued on next page

seas, and let the birds increase on the
earth."[t] 23 And there was evening, and
there was morning—the fifth day.
24 And God said, "Let the land produce living creatures according to their kinds:
the livestock, the creatures that move
along the ground, and the wild animals, each according to its kind."
And it was so. 25 God made the wild
animals[u] according to their kinds, the
livestock according to their kinds,
and all the creatures that move along
the ground according to their kinds.
And God saw that it was good.
26 Then God said, "Let us[v] make
mankind in our image,[w] in our likeness, so that they may rule[x] over the
fish in the sea and the birds in the
sky, over the livestock and all the
wild animals,[a] and over all the creatures that move along the ground."

27 So God created mankind in his own
image,[y]
in the image of God he created them;
male and female[z] he created them.

28 God blessed them and said to
them, "Be fruitful and increase in
number; fill the earth[a] and subdue it.
Rule over the fish in the sea and the

1:22 [t] ver 28; Ge 8:17 **1:25** [u] Jer 27:5 **1:26** [v] Ps 100:3 [w] Ge 9:6; Jas 3:9 [x] Ps 8:6-8 **1:27** [y] 1Co 11:7 [z] Ge 5:2; Mt 19:4*; Mk 10:6* **1:28** [a] Ge 9:1,7; Lev 26:9

[a] *26* Probable reading of the original Hebrew text (see Syriac); Masoretic Text *the earth*

1:28 *Be fruitful and increase in number.* Contrary to concerns about overpopulation that are evident in early Mesopotamian literature, in Genesis God desires that people multiply without restriction—they may fill the earth. In contrast, in the Akkadian Atrahasis epic, the gods are distressed because, with the multiplica-

Mesopotamian imagery refers to "breasts of heaven," through which rain comes. Ugaritic texts use the symbolism of the clouds serving as buckets to deliver the rain. The OT refers to gates in the sky through which precipitation comes as "windows" used only for rain, not for the celestial bodies (e.g., Ge 7:11; 8:2; 2Ki 7:2,19). Job 38:22 also poetically speaks of storehouses for snow and hail. All precipitation (including dew, see Pr 3:19 – 20) comes from above, and thus weather is regulated by the sky.

It should also be noted that an alternative interpretation of the Hebrew word *raqia* is that it refers to the living space created by the separation of the waters. In this case, a different Hebrew word refers to the vault. ◆

In Egyptian iconography the sky is represented by the goddess Nut, whose body arched over the land.

Wikimedia Commons

birds in the sky and over every living
creature that moves on the ground."
29 Then God said, "I give you every seed-bearing plant on the face of
the whole earth and every tree that
has fruit with seed in it. They will be
yours for food.[b] 30 And to all the beasts
of the earth and all the birds in the sky
and all the creatures that move along
the ground — everything that has the
breath of life in it — I give every green
plant for food.[c]" And it was so.
31 God saw all that he had made,[d]
and it was very good.[e] And there was
evening, and there was morning —
the sixth day.

1:29 [b] Ps 104:14
1:30 [c] Ps 104:14,27; 145:15
1:31 [d] Ps 104:24 [e] 1Ti 4:4

tion of people, problems and "noise" also increase. The gods therefore send plagues, famine and drought to counteract the population explosion. *subdue it. Rule over.* The characterization of humans being made in the image of God and the functions listed here reflect a royal role for people since these descriptions would most frequently be applied to kings (see the article "Image and Likeness," p. 8). They are given the responsibility of bringing order to their world. Again, this is in stark contrast to the role of humanity in the ancient Near East, where they are created to serve. Here we see the attribution to all people what was the sole prerogative of the king in the rest of the ancient Near East.
1:29 *yours for food.* When people are created in other ancient Near East narratives, it is for the purpose of performing all the menial tasks necessary for providing food for the gods. God as the one providing food for people, rather than the other way around, is not absent from those other ancient Near East accounts, but the theme occupies a more central role here in Genesis (cf. also 2:8 – 9, where God planted a garden for food).

GENESIS 1:26

IMAGE AND LIKENESS

Throughout the ancient Near East, an image was believed to contain the essence of that which it represented. That essence equipped the image to carry out its function. In Egyptian literature, there is one occurrence of people in general having been created in the image of deity, but it is generally the king who is spoken of in such terms. The image is the source of his power and prerogative.

In Mesopotamia there are three categories of significance. (1) As in Egypt, the king is occasionally described as being in the image of deity. (2) An idol contained the image of the deity. (3) Monuments featuring the image of a king were set up in territories he had conquered. In an image, it was not physical likeness that was important, but a more abstract, idealized representation of identity relating to the office/role and the value connected to the image. When Assyrian king Esarhaddon is referred to as "the perfect likeness of the god," it is his qualities and his attributes that are under discussion. The image of the god did the god's work on the earth.

The Biblical view is similar as people were created in the image of God, embodying his qualities and doing his work. They are symbols of his presence and act on his behalf as his representatives. The two words used in the text differ in nuance. "Image" refers to the something that contains the "essence" of something else, while "likeness" is more connected to "substance," expressing a resemblance at some level. ◆

2 Thus the heavens and the earth
were completed in all their vast array.
2 By the seventh day God had finished
the work he had been doing; so on
the seventh day he rested from all his
work.[f] 3 Then God blessed the seventh
day and made it holy,[g] because on it
he rested from all the work of creating that he had done.

Adam and Eve

4 This is the account of the heavens and
the earth when they were created, when the
LORD God made the earth and the heavens.
5 Now no shrub had yet appeared on the
earth[a] and no plant had yet sprung up,[h]
for the LORD God had not sent rain on the
earth[i] and there was no one to work the
ground, 6 but streams[b] came up from the
earth and watered the whole surface of
the ground. 7 Then the LORD God formed
a man[c] from the dust[j] of the ground[k] and
breathed into his nostrils the breath[l] of
life,[m] and the man became a living being.[n]

2:2 [f] Ex 20:11; 31:17; Heb 4:4* **2:3** [g] Lev 23:3; Isa 58:13 **2:5** [h] Ge 1:11 [i] Ps 65:9-10 **2:7** [j] Ge 3:19 [k] Ps 103:14 [l] Job 33:4 [m] Ac 17:25 [n] 1Co 15:45*

[a] 5 Or *land;* also in verse 6 [b] 6 Or *mist* [c] 7 The Hebrew for *man (adam)* sounds like and may be related to the Hebrew for *ground (adamah);* it is also the name *Adam* (see verse 20).

2:5 *no plant.* The description of an inchoate condition on the earth is paralleled in part by descriptions of a primeval condition in some ancient Near Eastern texts. Unlike Genesis, these texts consider the primeval condition of humans to be primitive and uncivilized. Like the ancient Near East, however, Genesis begins with a time when no irrigation or planting strategies were being carried out by people. In the ancient Near East this resulted in no offerings for the gods. In Genesis God plants the garden and puts people in it. The similarities show the common idea that creation accounts proceed from an unordered, nonfunctional beginning through an ordering process. It does not mean that God had not yet produced any plants.

2:7 *formed a man from the dust.* The creation of humans from dust is similar to what is found in ancient Near Eastern mythology. In Mesopotamia, physical elements from the gods such as blood and flesh are mixed with clay, while in Egypt it is tears or breath. Genesis, by contrast, represents the divine element in human beings as seen in the image of God and the breath of life (closer to Egyptian than Mesopotamian thinking).

In the rest of the ancient Near East the creation of people focuses on archetypal and often corporate elements. Ge 1:26–27 could be viewed as corporate and generic rather than individual. Here in ch. 2 there are archetypal elements that are identifiable. Man is made from the dust, and since he will also return to dust (3:19), all people can be seen as created from the dust (see Ps 103:14). The creation of Eve from Adam's side (Ge 2:21–23) likewise expresses a relationship between man and woman that permeates the race. In these Adam and Eve are archetypes representing all of humanity in their creation, just

[8]Now the LORD God had planted a garden in the east, in Eden;[o] and there he put
the man he had formed. [9]The LORD God
made all kinds of trees grow out of the
ground—trees that were pleasing to the
eye and good for food. In the middle of the
garden were the tree of life[p] and the tree of
the knowledge of good and evil.[q]

2:8 [o]Ge 3:23,24; Isa 51:3
2:9 [p]Ge 3:22, 24; Rev 2:7; 22:2,14,19 [q]Eze 47:12

as they do in their sin and their destiny (death) in ch. 3. Their function as archetypes does not suggest that they are not historical individuals; it only suggests that they function more importantly as representatives of the race.
2:8 *a garden ... in Eden.* Verse 10 indicates that we should understand the garden as adjoining Eden because the water flows "from Eden" and waters the garden. The garden adjoins God's residence in the same way that a garden of the palace adjoins the palace. Eden is the source of the waters and the residence of God. The text describes a situation that was well known in the ancient world: a sacred spot featuring a spring with an adjoining, well-watered park. The word "garden" here should not make us think of vegetables or even necessarily flowers. Public gardens or a "country garden" convey the idea more accurately as indicating a park with careful landscaping, pools, watercourses, and paths winding among fruit trees and shade trees. Such arboretums, sometimes even containing animals of various sorts, were a common feature of palace complexes in the ancient world.
2:9 *the tree of life.* In Pr 3:16–18 the tree of life offers an extension of life, which suggests rejuvenating qualities. In the Gilgamesh Epic there is a rejuvenating plant that grows at the bottom of the cosmic river. In the Story of Adapa, the hero is offered food by the god Anu that is eventually identified as "food of life" and "water of life." He refuses to partake, having been told it was food of death. Thus humankind is prevented from joining the gods in immortality. In Egyptian literature, Amun-Re is the god who created the tree of life, but no further information is given. *the tree of the knowledge of good and evil.* Nothing is known of this tree from any of the traditions of the ancient Near East. In the Gilgamesh Epic, the primitive Enkidu becomes wise (possessing reason), not by eating the fruit of a tree, but by engaging in sexual intercourse with a prostitute who was sent to entice and capture him.

GENESIS 2:2

REST

The concept of divine rest is prominent in ancient Near Eastern literature. Deity's rest is achieved in a temple, generally as a result of order having been established. The rest, while it represents *disengagement* from any process of establishing order (whether through conflict with other deities or not), is more importantly an expression of *engagement* as the deity takes his place at the helm to maintain an ordered, secure and stable cosmos. The following aspects of divine rest can be found in literature of the ancient Near East:

1. The divine rest can be disturbed by rebellion.
2. The divine rest is achieved after conflict.
3. The divine rest is achieved after order-bringing acts of creation.
4. The divine rest is achieved in the temple.
5. The divine rest is achieved in part by creating people to work in their place and on their behalf.
6. The divine rest is characterized by ongoing control and stability.

Only point 3 is transparent in Genesis, though points 4 and 6 can also be defended. Given the connection between temple and rest in the ancient Near East, it becomes natural to see the Biblical creation of the cosmos as being configured in temple-building and dedication terms; the seven-day creation account culminating in divine rest should be understood as somehow parallel to the building of temples for divine rest. This course of analogy and logic results in the understanding that Ge 1 is framed in terms of the creation of a cosmic temple in which Yahweh takes up his repose. The seven days are comparable to seven-day temple dedications at the end of which the deity takes up his rest in the temple.

The temple on earth was considered only a type of the larger, archetypal cosmic

continued on next page

temple, and there are many images and symbols that evoke the relationship between temple and cosmos. The temple is considered the center of the cosmos and is itself a microcosmos. In Egypt the temple contained within its sacred precincts a representation of the original primeval hillock that emerged from the cosmic waters. In Mesopotamia, the primary imagery of the temple was that it was the center of the cosmos. In Syro-Palestine, the temple is the architectural embodiment of the cosmic mountain. This concept is represented in Ugaritic literature as well as in the Bible, where Mount Zion is understood as the mountain of the Lord (e.g., Ps 48) and the place where his temple, a representation of Eden, was built. In Isa 66:1 the Lord indicated: "Heaven is my throne, and the earth is my footstool. Where is the house you will build for me? Where will my resting place be?" Here God indicates that the man-made temple cannot be considered the true temple (cf. 1Ki 8:27). It is only a micro-scale representation of the cosmic temple. Ps 78:69 communicates a similar idea by indicating that the temple was built on the model of the cosmos. Ideas like these are also found in literature from Mesopotamia that compares temples to the heavens and the earth and gives them a cosmic location and function. It is evident, then, that Israel and her neighbors viewed the cosmos in temple terms and viewed the temple as a model of the cosmos or the cosmic temple.

If the cosmos is being ordered as sacred space, then it is possible that a cosmological text could adopt the language of temple-building and temple-dedication. In a temple construction project, the structure would be built, and the furniture and trappings would be made in preparation for the moment when all was ready for the dedication of the temple. On this occasion, often a seven-day celebration, the functions of the temple were declared, the furniture and hangings were put in place, the priests installed, and the appropriate sacrifices made to initiate the temple's operation. Somewhere in the process, the image of the deity was brought into the temple to take up his repose. On the basis of all of this, Ge 1 can be viewed as using the metaphor of temple-dedication as it portrays God's creation (= making functional/operational) of his cosmos (which is his temple, Isa 66:1). The main connection, however, is the rest motif, for rest is the principal function of a temple, and a temple is always where deity finds rest. ◆

[10]A river watering the garden flowed
from Eden; from there it was separated
into four headwaters. [11]The name of the
first is the Pishon; it winds through the
entire land of Havilah, where there is gold.
[12](The gold of that land is good; aromatic resin[a] and onyx are also there.) [13]The
name of the second river is the Gihon; it
winds through the entire land of Cush.[b]
[14]The name of the third river is the Tigris;[r]

2:14 [r] Da 10:4

[a] *12* Or *good; pearls* [b] *13* Possibly southeast Mesopotamia

2:10–14 Most scholars would place Eden in or near the northern end of the Persian Gulf, based on the locations of the Tigris and Euphrates Rivers. The distinction "in the east" (v. 8) merely indicates Mesopotamia, and is typical of primordial narratives. The flow of the rivers and the uncertainty of the location of the Pishon and Gihon (see note on vv. 11–13) has caused some to look near the source of the Tigris and Euphrates and some scholars have identified two other major rivers in that area that might qualify. In such a mountainous region the garden would be in an elevated valley, though for some, the imagery of a well-watered garden where humans do no work and life springs up without cultivation is more suited to the marshy areas around the Persian Gulf.

2:10 *four headwaters.* Genesis uses a familiar picture of fertile waters flowing from the seat of deity. In Egyptian depictions two or four rivers flow out of the mouth of Nun, who represents the cosmic abyss. An ivory inlaid plaque from Assyria shows a central divine figure with four rivers flowing from him in four directions. He is flanked by two trees, and standing next to each tree is a winged guardian. It should also be noted that the idea of rivers flowing from the holy place is found not only in ch. 2 (which portrays Eden as the Most Holy Place) but also in Ezekiel's temple (Eze 47:1). The picture is of a mighty spring that gushes out from Eden and is channeled through the garden for irrigation purposes. All of these channels then serve as headwaters, for the four rivers flow out in various directions as the waters exit the garden.

2:11–13 *Pishon ... Gihon.* Attempts to identify these two rivers include: canals, other rivers of Mesopotamia (Balikh, Diyala, Zab, etc.), other rivers outside of Meso-

it runs along the east side of Ashur. And
the fourth river is the Euphrates.
[15]The LORD God took the man and put
him in the Garden of Eden to work it and
take care of it. [16]And the LORD God commanded the man, "You are free to eat from
any tree in the garden; [17]but you must not
eat from the tree of the knowledge of good
and evil, for when you eat from it you will
certainly die."[s]
[18]The LORD God said, "It is not good for
the man to be alone. I will make a helper
suitable for him."[t]
[19]Now the LORD God had formed out of
the ground all the wild animals[u] and all
the birds in the sky. He brought them to
the man to see what he would name them;
and whatever the man called each living
creature,[v] that was its name. [20]So the man
gave names to all the livestock, the birds
in the sky and all the wild animals.
But for Adam[a] no suitable helper was
found. [21]So the LORD God caused the man
to fall into a deep sleep; and while he was
sleeping, he took one of the man's ribs[b]
and then closed up the place with flesh.
[22]Then the LORD God made a woman from
the rib[c][w] he had taken out of the man, and
he brought her to the man.

2:17 [s]Dt 30:15, 19; Ro 5:12; 6:23; Jas 1:15 **2:18** [t]1Co 11:9 **2:19** [u]Ps 8:7 [v]Ge 1:24 **2:22** [w]1Co 11:8, 9, 12

2:23 [x]Ge 29:14; Eph 5:28-30 **2:24** [y]Mal 2:15 [z]Mt 19:5*; Mk 10:7-8*; 1Co 6:16*; Eph 5:31* **2:25** [a]Ge 3:7, 10-11 **3:1** [b]2Co 11:3; Rev 12:9; 20:2 **3:4** [c]Jn 8:44; 2Co 11:3 **3:5** [d]Isa 14:14; Eze 28:2

[23]The man said,

"This is now bone of my bones
and flesh of my flesh;[x]
she shall be called 'woman,'
for she was taken out of man."

[24]That is why a man leaves his father and
mother and is united[y] to his wife, and they
become one flesh.[z]
[25]Adam and his wife were both naked,[a]
and they felt no shame.

The Fall

3 Now the serpent[b] was more crafty
than any of the wild animals the LORD
God had made. He said to the woman,
"Did God really say, 'You must not eat
from any tree in the garden'?"
[2]The woman said to the serpent, "We may
eat fruit from the trees in the garden, [3]but
God did say, 'You must not eat fruit from
the tree that is in the middle of the garden,
and you must not touch it, or you will die.'"
[4]"You will not certainly die," the serpent
said to the woman.[c] [5]"For God knows that
when you eat from it your eyes will be
opened, and you will be like God,[d] knowing good and evil."

[a] 20 Or *the man* [b] 21 Or *took part of the man's side* [c] 22 Or *part*

potamia (e.g., Nile, Indus, Ganges), or larger bodies such as the Persian Gulf or the Red Sea. Recent investigations have attempted to identify the Pishon as a major river that dried up in antiquity. This possibility emerges from the analysis of sand patterns and satellite photography, which have revealed an old riverbed running northeast through Saudi Arabia from the Hijaz mountains near Medina (which contains one of the richest gold mines in the region) to the Persian Gulf in Kuwait, near the mouth of the Tigris and Euphrates Rivers. As mentioned in note on vv. 10–14, others have identified the Pishon and Gihon as rivers in the area of Urartu. A final suggestion is that the Pishon and Gihon refer to the encircling cosmic waters. None of these options may be adopted with any confidence, though some are more plausible than others.

2:15 *to work it and take care of it.* In the rest of the ancient world it was believed that humans had been created to serve the needs of the gods; the gods had grown tired of the drudgery of providing for themselves. In Genesis people also serve God but not by meeting his needs.

When people are assigned their function here, priestly terms are used in contrast to the royal functions given in 1:28–29. In the rest of the ancient Near East, caring for the needs of the gods was also a priestly function. In the OT, the priestly function involved maintaining the status of sacred space and providing for the proper worship and obedience to God's requirements.

2:20 *names.* Names were not given randomly in the ancient world. A name may identify the essential nature of the creature, so that giving a name may be an act of assigning the function that creature will have. In Mesopotamia the assigning of function is referred to as the decreeing of destiny. Decreeing destiny by giving a name is an act of authority. In the ancient world, when a king conquered another country, the king he put on the throne was given a new name. In other cases, the giving of a name is an act of discernment in which the name is determined by the circumstances. In either case, Adam's naming of the animals is his first step in subduing and ruling (see 1:28 and note). He is fulfilling the role that he had by virtue of being in God's image (see the article "Image and Likeness," p. 8), but it also leads him to realize that among the animals there is no social equal to share his function and place.

2:22 *rib.* In Genesis the woman was built from the side (Hebrew *tsela*) of the man (see NIV text note on v. 21). The Hebrew word is usually architectural, and is used anatomically only here in the OT. In Akkadian, the cognate term *tsela* is also both architectural and anatomical. Its anatomical uses generally refer not just to bone, but to bones and flesh (cf. v. 23).

2:24 *leaves ... united ... one flesh.* The text establishes a "flesh-line," which is stronger than a bloodline and causes the man to seek her out. Woman is recognized as being of the same essence as man and therefore of serving as his ally in sacred space.

2:25 *naked.* In Genesis the nakedness of the humans does not appear to be a negative comment, though it is contrasted through wordplay to the craftiness of the serpent in the next verse (3:1), so it may refer to a relative naïveté. In contrast, ancient Near Eastern texts indicate that the primeval nakedness of people is a sign of a primitive, uncivilized condition. When Enkidu is civilized in the Gilgamesh Epic, he is clothed by the woman who civilizes him. The Sumerian text Ewe and Wheat opens with a description of primeval humans who are clearly primitive, and the text apparently considers that a negative. In this way there are similarities in how Genesis and the Mesopotamian texts describe early humankind, but there is a contrasting assessment of how their condition should be interpreted.

3:5 *be like God.* One can imagine a variety of ways in which people might desire or strive to "be like God"—some commendable, others inappropriately ambitious or subversive.

GENESIS 3:1

The Serpent

In the Gilgamesh Epic, after Gilgamesh acquires the magical plant that will rejuvenate him, it is stolen by a snake. In the Story of Adapa, one of the guardians of Anu's palace, where Adapa is offered the food of life, is serpent-shaped or accompanied by horned serpents, and he is the guardian of the demons who live in the netherworld. In Egypt, the serpent was associated with both death and wisdom. The Genesis account draws on both aspects in the wisdom dialogue between the serpent and Eve and with the introduction of death after the expulsion from Eden.

Many Egyptian gods, especially the primeval gods, were represented in serpent form. Wadjit, a lower Egyptian deity, was considered the protector of the pharaoh and is represented by the *uraeus* serpent on his crown. The earth-god Geb had a serpent's head. The snake-god Apophis was considered the enemy of order. In addition, the idea that animals in general, and serpents in particular, could communicate with humans is common in Egyptian literature. Serpents in Egypt are also connected with occult wisdom. The *ureaus* is sometimes invoked as a magician.

Because of the NT and the development of Christian theology, it is most common for people today immediately to think of Satan as the serpent in Ge 3, but the Israelites never made that connection. We cannot recover what Adam and Eve would have thought about the serpent, but the ancient Near Eastern literature gives us an idea of some of the images that came to mind for the Israelites living in their time and culture. Foremost is the association of the serpent with life and death. Likewise the serpent is wise, is connected with disorder, and can be the enemy of God—perspectives that are meaningful in this context. ◆

6 When the woman saw that the fruit of
the tree was good for food and pleasing to
the eye, and also desirable[e] for gaining wisdom, she took some and ate it. She also
gave some to her husband, who was with
her, and he ate it.[f]
7 Then the eyes of both of
them were opened, and they realized they
were naked; so they sewed fig leaves together and made coverings for themselves.
8 Then the man and his wife heard the
sound of the LORD God as he was walking[g] in the garden in the cool of the day,
and they hid[h] from the LORD God among
the trees of the garden.
9 But the LORD God
called to the man, "Where are you?"
10 He answered, "I heard you in the garden, and I was afraid because I was naked; so I hid."
11 And he said, "Who told you that you
were naked? Have you eaten from the tree
that I commanded you not to eat from?"
12 The man said, "The woman you put
here with me—she gave me some fruit
from the tree, and I ate it."
13 Then the LORD God said to the woman,
"What is this you have done?"

3:6 [e] Jas 1:14-15; 1Jn 2:16 [f] 1Ti 2:14 **3:8** [g] Dt 23:14 [h] Job 31:33; Ps 139:7-12; Jer 23:24

The aspiration targeted here is in the category of wisdom, a defensibly laudable pursuit. In the ancient Near East godlikeness pertains to the categories of splendor (Enkidu became handsome like a god) or immortality (Gilgamesh, Adapa). It is interesting that Gilgamesh and Adapa both encounter a snake figure and Enkidu achieves his godlikeness through a woman (who also gives him understanding). Gilgamesh and Adapa fail to achieve immortality, both through an inability to eat the necessary food.

These examples show that in the ancient world it was common for people to meditate on ways in which people succeeded and failed in becoming like deity. At the same time the differences are significant. In Genesis disobedience figures prominently, and the category of godlikeness is distinct. Furthermore, the consequences of the attempt differ. Adam and Eve do achieve a level of godlikeness (like Enkidu), but with significant negative repercussions. At the same time they lose their access to immortality (like Gilgamesh and Adapa) and also suffer in their lost relationship with God, which is not an issue in any of the others. This is then an excellent example of how the comparison between the Bible and the ancient Near East shows a similar landscape but with important variations in the essential nature of the issue.

The woman said, "The serpent deceived
me,[i] and I ate."
[14]So the LORD God said to the serpent,
"Because you have done this,

"Cursed[j] are you above all livestock
and all wild animals!
You will crawl on your belly
and you will eat dust[k]
all the days of your life.
[15]And I will put enmity
between you and the woman,
and between your offspring[a][l] and
hers;[m]
he will crush[b] your head,[n]
and you will strike his heel."

[16]To the woman he said,

"I will make your pains in childbearing
very severe;
with painful labor you will give birth
to children.
Your desire will be for your husband,
and he will rule over you.[o]"

[17]To Adam he said, "Because you listened to your wife and ate fruit from the
tree about which I commanded you, 'You
must not eat from it,'

"Cursed[p] is the ground because of
you;
through painful toil you will eat
food from it
all the days of your life.[q]
[18]It will produce thorns and thistles for
you,
and you will eat the plants of the
field.[r]
[19]By the sweat of your brow
you will eat your food[s]
until you return to the ground,
since from it you were taken;
for dust you are
and to dust you will return."[t]

[20]Adam[c] named his wife Eve,[d] because
she would become the mother of all the
living.
[21]The LORD God made garments of skin
for Adam and his wife and clothed them.
[22]And the LORD God said, "The man has
now become like one of us, knowing good
and evil. He must not be allowed to reach
out his hand and take also from the tree
of life[u] and eat, and live forever." [23]So the
LORD God banished him from the Garden
of Eden[v] to work the ground[w] from which
he had been taken. [24]After he drove the
man out, he placed on the east side[e] of the
Garden of Eden cherubim[x] and a flaming
sword[y] flashing back and forth to guard
the way to the tree of life.[z]

Cain and Abel

4 Adam[c] made love to his wife Eve, and
she became pregnant and gave birth to
Cain.[f] She said, "With the help of the LORD
I have brought forth[g] a man." [2]Later she
gave birth to his brother Abel.[a]
Now Abel kept flocks, and Cain worked
the soil. [3]In the course of time Cain brought
some of the fruits of the soil as an offering

3:13 [i] 2Co 11:3; 1Ti 2:14 **3:14** [j] Dt 28:15-20 [k] Isa 65:25; Mic 7:17 **3:15** [l] Jn 8:44; Ac 13:10; 1Jn 3:8 [m] Isa 7:14; Mt 1:23; Rev 12:17 [n] Ro 16:20; Heb 2:14 **3:16** [o] 1Co 11:3; Eph 5:22 **3:17** [p] Ge 5:29; Ro 8:20-22 [q] Job 5:7; 14:1; Ecc 2:23 **3:18** [r] Ps 104:14 **3:19** [s] 2Th 3:10 [t] Ge 2:7; Ps 90:3; 104:29; Ecc 12:7 **3:22** [u] Rev 22:14 **3:23** [v] Ge 2:8 [w] Ge 4:2 **3:24** [x] Ex 25:18-22 [y] Ps 104:4 [z] Ge 2:9 **4:2** [a] Lk 11:51

[a] *15* Or *seed* [b] *15* Or *strike* [c] *20,1* Or *The man* [d] *20* *Eve* probably means *living.* [e] *24* Or *placed in front* [f] *1* *Cain* sounds like the Hebrew for *brought forth* or *acquired.* [g] *1* Or *have acquired*

3:14 *God said to the serpent, "... Cursed are you."* The Egyptian Pyramid Texts were designed to aid the pharaohs of the Old Kingdom on their journey to the afterlife. Among the over 700 utterances are several dozen spells and curses on snakes that may impede the king's progress. These utterances contain phrases that are reminiscent of the curse on the serpent in ch. 3. *crawl on your belly.* This statement is paralleled by frequent spells in the Egyptian Pyramid Texts that call on snakes to lie down, fall down, get down, or crawl away. Another spell says that he should "go with your face on the path." These suggest that when God tells the serpent that he will crawl on his belly, there is no suggestion that the serpent had legs that he now loses. Instead, he is going to be docile rather than in an attack position. The serpent on its belly is nonthreatening, while the one reared up is protecting or attacking. *eat dust.* Not a comment about the actual diet of snakes but likely a reference to their habitat. Again the Pyramid Texts show some similarity as they attempt to banish the serpent to the dust. The serpent is a creature of the netherworld (that is why the pharaoh encounters it on his journey), and denizens of the netherworld were typically portrayed as eating dust. There is no suggestion that the Israelites are borrowing from the Pyramid Texts, only that these texts help us determine how someone in the ancient Near East might understand such words and phrases.
3:23 *banished.* In the ancient Near East there is no time when "sin" begins; no point when humanity moves from a positive relationship with deity into a worse position; no sense of people once being in sacred space but then banished. It was common in the ancient world to portray "before" and "after" pictures with regard to human death and the relationship between God and humanity, but Genesis identifies different elements in the portrayal and reflects a different theology.
3:24 *cherubim.* Cherubs are a class of supernatural creature generally functioning as guardians and typically portrayed in beast form rather than human form. They can be four-footed or upright. In cases where it can be determined, they appear to be composite (i.e., having characteristics of various beasts the way griffins or sphinxes did in other literatures).
4:3 *fruits of the soil.* There is intrinsically no problem with Cain bringing produce as a gift to God. The Hebrew word used for his sacrifice (*minhah*) is one that describes the kind of offering outlined in Lev 2, which is normally something other than an animal sacrifice. It was likewise common throughout the rest of the ancient world to offer food offerings from what was grown. Genesis does not record God asking for these sacrifices, though he approved of the practice as a means of expressing thanks. Gratitude would not be expressed when the gift is given grudgingly, as was possibly the case with Cain (see Heb 11:4, which contrasts Abel's sacrifice offered in faith with Cain's gift).

to the LORD.[b] 4And Abel also brought an offering — fat portions[c] from some of the firstborn of his flock.[d] The LORD looked with favor on Abel and his offering,[e] 5but on Cain and his offering he did not look with favor. So Cain was very angry, and his face was downcast.

6Then the LORD said to Cain, "Why are you angry? Why is your face downcast? 7If you do what is right, will you not be accepted? But if you do not do what is right, sin is crouching at your door;[f] it desires to have you, but you must rule over it.[g]"

8Now Cain said to his brother Abel, "Let's go out to the field."[a] While they were in the field, Cain attacked his brother Abel and killed him.[h]

9Then the LORD said to Cain, "Where is your brother Abel?"

"I don't know," he replied. "Am I my brother's keeper?"

10The LORD said, "What have you done? Listen! Your brother's blood cries out to me from the ground.[i] 11Now you are under a curse and driven from the ground, which opened its mouth to receive your brother's blood from your hand. 12When you work the ground, it will no longer yield its crops for you. You will be a restless wanderer on the earth."

13Cain said to the LORD, "My punishment is more than I can bear. 14Today you are driving me from the land, and I will be hidden from your presence;[j] I will be a restless wanderer on the earth, and whoever finds me will kill me."[k]

15But the LORD said to him, "Not so[b]; anyone who kills Cain[l] will suffer vengeance seven times over.[m]" Then the LORD put a mark on Cain so that no one who found him would kill him. 16So Cain went out from the LORD's presence and lived in the land of Nod,[c] east of Eden.[n]

17Cain made love to his wife, and she became pregnant and gave birth to Enoch. Cain was then building a city, and he named it after his son[o] Enoch. 18To Enoch was born Irad, and Irad was the father of Mehujael, and Mehujael was the father of Methushael, and Methushael was the father of Lamech.

19Lamech married two women, one named Adah and the other Zillah. 20Adah gave birth to Jabal; he was the father of those who live in tents and raise livestock. 21His brother's name was Jubal; he was the father of all who play stringed instruments and pipes. 22Zillah also had a son, Tubal-Cain, who forged all kinds of tools out of[d] bronze and iron. Tubal-Cain's sister was Naamah.

23Lamech said to his wives,

"Adah and Zillah, listen to me;
  wives of Lamech, hear my words.
I have killed[p] a man for wounding me,
  a young man for injuring me.
24If Cain is avenged[q] seven times,[r]
  then Lamech seventy-seven times."

4:3 [b] Nu 18:12 **4:4** [c] Lev 3:16 [d] Ex 13:2, 12 [e] Heb 11:4 **4:7** [f] Nu 32:23 [g] Ro 6:16 **4:8** [h] Mt 23:35; 1Jn 3:12 **4:10** [i] Ge 9:5; Nu 35:33; Heb 12:24; Rev 6:9-10 **4:14** [j] 2Ki 17:18; Ps 51:11; 139:7-12; Jer 7:15; 52:3 [k] Ge 9:6; Nu 35:19, 21, 27, 33
4:15 [l] Eze 9:4, 6 [m] ver 24; Ps 79:12 **4:16** [n] Ge 2:8 **4:17** [o] Ps 49:11 **4:23** [p] Ex 20:13; Lev 19:18 **4:24** [q] Dt 32:35 [r] ver 15

[a] 8 Samaritan Pentateuch, Septuagint, Vulgate and Syriac; Masoretic Text does not have *"Let's go out to the field."* [b] 15 Septuagint, Vulgate and Syriac; Hebrew *Very well* [c] 16 *Nod* means *wandering* (see verses 12 and 14). [d] 22 Or *who instructed all who work in*

4:7 *sin is crouching at your door.* Recent commentators have preferred seeing the participle "crouching" (Hebrew *robes*) as a reference to a well-known Mesopotamian demon (*rabisu*) who lingers around doorways. "Sin" is then portrayed as a doorway demon waiting for its victim to cross the threshold. From the Old Babylonian period on in Mesopotamia, such demons were considered evil and were thought to ambush their victims.

4:12 *wanderer.* In Mesopotamian thinking the ideal lifestyle is urban. Civilized life in the city is the gift of the gods and highly valued. Agricultural and pastoral activities are part of the urban landscape and are foundational to the success of the city. In this way of thinking, nomadic groups are considered uncivilized and a threat to society. The motif of the wild man living out in the steppe country among the animals is represented by Enkidu in the Gilgamesh Epic and is an archetype for these despised and feared people.

An interesting contrast here in Genesis is that the categories are set up differently. As in Mesopotamia, Cain's status as a wanderer marks him as undesirable. But this wandering is in contrast to being a farmer rather than to being a city dweller. In fact, it is within his line that the arts of civilization are developed (vv. 17 – 22).

4:14 *whoever finds me will kill me.* Blood feuding between clans is not a foreign concept. In the ancient world it was typically the business of the clan to avenge the death of one of its members. This concept is represented in Biblical law — e.g., cities of refuge and the avenger of blood (Nu 35; Dt 19:1 – 14) — as well as in the ancient Near East. Cain's comment assumes that Abel has an extended family who might seek revenge.

4:15 *mark.* The Hebrew word does not indicate a tattoo or mutilation, but rather a mark of divine protection similar to that placed on the foreheads of innocents in Eze 9:4 – 6. It may be an external marking to serve as an indicator to others, or it might represent a sign from God to Cain that he will not be harmed.

4:17 *building a city.* According to Mesopotamian tradition, the first city built was Eridu (remarkably similar to the name Irad, see v. 18). Within this tradition, city building was a divine enterprise. It was an enterprise related to, and a part of, creation, since creation involved the establishment of the world as they knew it — not only in terms of the physical cosmos, but also the civilized aspect of the social and economic world. In contrast, Genesis sees city building in purely human terms.

4:20 *live in tents and raise livestock.* Describes the pastoralist, who had to keep herds and flocks moving to a variety of water sources and grazing lands. This refers not to an achievement (e.g., domestication) but to a lifestyle. Just as Mesopotamians believed cities and kingship to have originated with the gods, so did pastoralism, agriculture and other lifestyles. In contrast, Genesis sees them as human developments.

25Adam made love to his wife again,
and she gave birth to a son and named
him Seth,[a][s] saying, "God has granted me
another child in place of Abel, since Cain
killed him."[t] 26Seth also had a son, and he
named him Enosh.

At that time people began to call on[b] the
name of the LORD.[u]

4:25 [s] Ge 5:3 [t] ver 8 **4:26** [u] Ge 12:8; 1Ki 18:24; Ps 116:17; Joel 2:32; Zep 3:9; Ac 2:21; 1Co 1:2
5:1 [v] Ge 1:27; Eph 4:24; Col 3:10

From Adam to Noah

5 This is the written account of Adam's
family line.

When God created mankind, he made
them in the likeness of God.[v] 2He created

[a] *25 Seth* probably means *granted.* [b] *26* Or *to proclaim*

4:26 *call on the name of the LORD.* Just as there is no implication that only Cain's line had cities and the arts of civilization, so the text does not imply that only the line of Seth called on the name of the Lord. About a dozen times in the OT people are said to call on the name of the Lord — generally either calling for help in connection with a ritual or invoking God's presence at a cultic site. Eventually humans sought to procure the presence of God through establishing cultic places and performing rituals there, but here there is no indication of these trappings. Thus it seems that people began to invoke the Lord's presence (the presence that was lost at the fall). This verse, then, represents the beginning of religion.

GENESIS 4:26

THE NAME OF GOD

The personal name "Yahweh" (NIV "LORD") is used frequently throughout Genesis. The patriarchs address God by that name, and God identifies himself by that name. But a problem surfaces in Exodus: At the burning bush Moses asks what name he should give for the God who is sending him — even though God has already identified himself as the God of Abraham, Isaac and Jacob (Ex 3:6 – 13). In Ex 3:15, the name Yahweh (NIV "LORD") is introduced and it seems to some interpreters that God is giving a new name not previously revealed.

The situation is made more confusing in Ex 6:2 – 3, where God says to Moses, "I am the LORD [Yahweh]. I appeared to Abraham, to Isaac and to Jacob as God Almighty [El-Shaddai], but by my name the LORD [Yahweh], I did not make myself fully known to them." Verses such as these have led some to postulate that the occurrence of Yahweh in the patriarchal narratives is simply the work of the editor of Genesis, showing the continuity between the patriarchs and later Israel.

The fact that Genesis takes its final form no earlier than the time of Moses has allowed some conservative scholars to be content with viewing the references to Yahweh in the patriarchal narratives as purposeful intrusion. To them, the name of Yahweh was added in appropriate places to affirm that the patriarchs really did worship the same God as the Israelites, though they called him by a different name. This may be acceptable in some cases, but it does not explain the passages in which God is presented as identifying himself as Yahweh.

In Ex 3:13, Moses is not looking to fill an information gap concerning God's identity, but rather, is asking which previously known epithet is most appropriate to use. In Ex 3:15, God explains that the epithet Yahweh (NIV "LORD") is the appropriate one. In Ex 6:3 God explains that El-Shaddai (NIV "God Almighty") was the epithet most appropriately connected with how God interacted with the patriarchs and what he accomplished for them. They did not experience firsthand the significance of the epithet Yahweh, which was connected to the longer-term promises of God, specifically the land. In other words, it is not that the patriarchs were ignorant of the name Yahweh, but the epithet El-Shaddai was appropriate for the aspects of the covenant they experienced. The name Yahweh was one of many epithets they used to refer to their God, but it was not the primary one in their usage or understanding. ◆

them male and female[w] and blessed them.
And he named them "Mankind"[a] when
they were created.
3 When Adam had lived 130 years, he
had a son in his own likeness, in his own
image;[x] and he named him Seth. 4 After
Seth was born, Adam lived 800 years and
had other sons and daughters. 5 Altogether,
Adam lived a total of 930 years, and then
he died.[y]
6 When Seth had lived 105 years, he became the father[b] of Enosh. 7 After he became the father of Enosh, Seth lived 807
years and had other sons and daughters.
8 Altogether, Seth lived a total of 912 years,
and then he died.

5:2 [w] Ge 1:27; Mt 19:4; Mk 10:6; Gal 3:28
5:3 [x] Ge 1:26; 1Co 15:49
5:5 [y] Ge 3:19

9 When Enosh had lived 90 years, he became the father of Kenan. 10 After he became the father of Kenan, Enosh lived 815
years and had other sons and daughters.
11 Altogether, Enosh lived a total of 905
years, and then he died.
12 When Kenan had lived 70 years, he
became the father of Mahalalel. 13 After
he became the father of Mahalalel, Kenan
lived 840 years and had other sons and
daughters. 14 Altogether, Kenan lived a total of 910 years, and then he died.
15 When Mahalalel had lived 65 years, he
became the father of Jared. 16 After he be-

[a] 2 Hebrew *adam* [b] 6 *Father* may mean *ancestor*; also in verses 7-26.

GENESIS 5

Genealogies

Mesopotamian genealogies are mostly royal, mostly linear (one line of descent, such as Ge 5) as opposed to segmented (containing more than one line of descent, such as Ge 10), and rarely more than three or four generations deep. Fluidity occurs primarily in telescoping (i.e., eliminating names), though some rearrangement of the order of the ancestors may be detected in the king lists. Egyptian sources (mostly from the Persian and Hellenistic periods) preserve long linear genealogies, sometimes extending 15 to 20 generations, often connecting to priestly lines. Fluidity is also evident only in telescoping within these genealogies. Comparing Biblical genealogies to one another shows that often several generations are skipped. Thus, a genealogy's purpose is apparently not to represent every generation, as our modern family trees attempt to do. Genealogies represent continuity and relationship and are often used for purposes of power and prestige. Genealogies are sometimes formatted to suit a literary purpose. Thus, e.g., the genealogies between Adam and Noah, and Noah and Abraham, are each set up to contain ten members with the last having three sons.

If the long lives in the antediluvian world (cf. Methuselah, 969 years) seem amazing to us, we will be utterly astounded by the length of reign credited to antediluvian kings in the Sumerian King List:

Alulim	28,800 years
Alalgar	36,000 years
Enmenluanna	43,200 years
Enmengalanna	28,800 years
Dumuzi	36,000 years
Ensipazianna	28,800 years
Enmeduranna	21,000 years
Uburtutu	18,600 years

Eight kings compile 241,200 years between them. The Sumerian King List uses the standard Sumerian sexagesimal system. If the notation is read with decimal values rather than sexagesimal values, the numbers are in the same range as the Biblical numbers, and the totals of the lists are nearly identical. ◆

came the father of Jared, Mahalalel lived
830 years and had other sons and daughters. 17 Altogether, Mahalalel lived a total of
895 years, and then he died.
18 When Jared had lived 162 years, he
became the father of Enoch.[z] 19 After he
became the father of Enoch, Jared lived
800 years and had other sons and daughters. 20 Altogether, Jared lived a total of 962
years, and then he died.
21 When Enoch had lived 65 years, he became the father of Methuselah. 22 After he
became the father of Methuselah, Enoch
walked faithfully with God[a] 300 years
and had other sons and daughters. 23 Altogether, Enoch lived a total of 365 years.
24 Enoch walked faithfully with God;[b] then
he was no more, because God took him
away.[c]
25 When Methuselah had lived 187
years, he became the father of Lamech.
26 After he became the father of Lamech,
Methuselah lived 782 years and had other
sons and daughters. 27 Altogether, Methuselah lived a total of 969 years, and then
he died.

5:18 [z] Jude 1:14
5:22 [a] ver 24; Ge 6:9; 17:1; 48:15; Mic 6:8; Mal 2:6
5:24 [b] ver 22 [c] 2Ki 2:1, 11; Heb 11:5

28 When Lamech had lived 182 years,
he had a son. 29 He named him Noah[a]
and said, "He will comfort us in the labor
and painful toil of our hands caused by
the ground the LORD has cursed.[d]" 30 After
Noah was born, Lamech lived 595 years
and had other sons and daughters. 31 Altogether, Lamech lived a total of 777 years,
and then he died.
32 After Noah was 500 years old, he became the father of Shem, Ham and Japheth.

Wickedness in the World

6 When human beings began to increase
in number on the earth[e] and daughters were born to them, 2 the sons of God
saw that the daughters of humans were
beautiful, and they married any of them
they chose. 3 Then the LORD said, "My Spirit will not contend with[b] humans forever,[f]
for they are mortal[c];[g] their days will be a
hundred and twenty years."

5:29 [d] Ge 3:17; Ro 8:20
6:1 [e] Ge 1:28
6:3 [f] Isa 57:16 [g] Ps 78:39

[a] 29 *Noah* sounds like the Hebrew for *comfort.*
[b] 3 Or *My spirit will not remain in* [c] 3 Or *corrupt*

5:24 *Enoch ... was no more, because God took him away.* The idea of humans being taken to heaven is known in the ancient world outside of the Bible, but not in the way that would develop in Christian theology. First is the example of Utuabzu, the seventh of the renowned sages (just as Enoch is the seventh from Adam, vv. 3–18). Second are characters such as Etana and Adapa, who both ascend to heaven under different circumstances. Notable is the fact that their ascensions are passing experiences rather than changes in status and therefore are not in the same category as Enoch.

As a further observation, we should note that Genesis does not indicate where Enoch was taken, so we should not necessarily assume ascension to heaven. Utnapishtim (the survivor of the flood in the Gilgamesh Epic) was a favorite of the gods and was also "taken" so that he did not experience death. But he was taken neither to heaven nor to the netherworld, but to a faraway, inaccessible place "at the mouth of the rivers" (Gilgamesh Epic, 11.205–6). None of these offer transparent explanation of Enoch's experience, but they show a variety of possibilities to be considered that otherwise would not be recognized. As a result of his piety ("walking with God"), Enoch was "taken" as an alternative to dying, the stated fate of all others in the genealogy.

6:2 *sons of God.* Royal titles of the ancient Near East regularly suggested the divine descent of kings, even outside Egypt's context of deified kings. This idea of divine descent was a rhetorical expression of the divine election and legitimization of the king and is typical in royal inscriptions. Throughout the Biblical period it was part of the royal prerogative to claim divine heritage. Thus the title "son of God" can be identified as a royal motif both in the Bible and outside of it. Gilgamesh is portrayed as two-thirds god and one-third man (Gilgamesh Epic, 1.48) and "flesh of the gods" (Gilgamesh Epic, 9.49). Nevertheless, though it is common for kings to be portrayed as having divine parentage, there is no precedent for ancient kings as a group being referred to as "sons of god." This keeps open the possibility that this title could refer to royal elites, though a reference to members of the heavenly council (cf. Job 1:6) certainly cannot be ruled out. *married any of them they chose.* There are no examples from Akkadian or Northwest Semitic mythological texts of divine beings marrying or cohabiting with human women, so it would be difficult to make the claim, as some do, that this account is a vestige of ancient mythology. There are examples of kings claiming mixed ancestry of gods and humans (see "sons of God" above in this note), but that is a different concept. If the "sons of God" are viewed as kings, the question remains as to what offense they are committing here. Polygamy has always been a weak candidate since the OT does not condemn it. Promiscuity is likewise an unlikely explanation since the Hebrew text describes the situation using the standard idiom for marriage ("taking wives"). An alternate understanding may be found in a practice noted in the Gilgamesh Epic as the prime example of Gilgamesh's tyranny, namely, his exercising the right of the first night with a new bride: "He will couple with the wife-to-be, he first of all, the bridegroom after" (Gilgamesh Epic, Old Babylonian version, v.159–60). This practice accommodates the marriage terminology, and in Gilgamesh it is clearly both oppressive and offensive behavior. The remaining problem is that this practice is infrequently attested in ancient literature. Nonetheless, in the Gilgamesh Epic it is clear.

6:3 *a hundred and twenty years.* A Sumerian folktale speaks of 120 years as an ideal human lifespan. Speculation suggests that this number derives not from observation but from abstraction within the Sumerian mathematical system. (It is clearly not a fixed boundary, as a woman who died in 1997 lived for 122 years). The idea that deity governs lifespan is reflected in Mesopotamia in the Gilgamesh Epic as the hero continues his quest for immortality. In the Egyptian "Book of the Dead" the god Thoth reports to the creator-god Atum: "You shall not witness wrongdoing, you shall not suffer it! Shorten their years, cut short their months, because they have done hidden damage to all that you have made." This is the same Atum who in the beginning floated in Nun, the

4The Nephilim[h] were on the earth in
those days—and also afterward—when
the sons of God went to the daughters of
humans and had children by them. They
were the heroes of old, men of renown.
5The LORD saw how great the wickedness of the human race had become on
the earth, and that every inclination of
the thoughts of the human heart was only
evil all the time.[i] 6The LORD regretted[j] that
he had made human beings on the earth,
and his heart was deeply troubled. 7So the
LORD said, "I will wipe from the face of the
earth the human race I have created—and
with them the animals, the birds and the
creatures that move along the ground—
for I regret that I have made them." 8But
Noah found favor in the eyes of the LORD.[k]

Noah and the Flood

9This is the account of Noah and his
family.

Noah was a righteous man, blameless
among the people of his time,[l] and he
walked faithfully with God.[m] 10Noah had
three sons: Shem, Ham and Japheth.[n]
11Now the earth was corrupt in God's
sight and was full of violence.[o] 12God saw
how corrupt the earth had become, for all
the people on earth had corrupted their
ways.[p] 13So God said to Noah, "I am going
to put an end to all people, for the earth
is filled with violence because of them.
I am surely going to destroy both them
and the earth.[q] 14So make yourself an ark
of cypress[a] wood;[r] make rooms in it and
coat it with pitch[s] inside and out. 15This
is how you are to build it: The ark is to
be three hundred cubits long, fifty cubits
wide and thirty cubits high.[b] 16Make a roof
for it, leaving below the roof an opening
one cubit[c] high all around.[d] Put a door in
the side of the ark and make lower, middle and upper decks. 17I am going to bring
floodwaters on the earth to destroy all life
under the heavens, every creature that has
the breath of life in it. Everything on earth
will perish.[t] 18But I will establish my covenant with you,[u] and you will enter the
ark[v]—you and your sons and your wife
and your sons' wives with you. 19You are
to bring into the ark two of all living creatures, male and female, to keep them alive
with you. 20Two[w] of every kind of bird, of
every kind of animal and of every kind of
creature that moves along the ground will
come to you to be kept alive. 21You are to
take every kind of food that is to be eaten
and store it away as food for you and for
them."
22Noah did everything just as God commanded him.[x]

7 The LORD then said to Noah, "Go into
the ark, you and your whole family,[y]
because I have found you righteous[z] in
this generation. 2Take with you seven pairs
of every kind of clean[a] animal, a male
and its mate, and one pair of every kind
of unclean animal, a male and its mate,

6:4 [h] Nu 13:33 **6:5** [i] Ge 8:21; Ps 14:1-3 **6:6** [j] 1Sa 15:11, 35; Isa 63:10 **6:8** [k] Ge 19:19; Ex 33:12, 13, 17; Lk 1:30; Ac 7:46 **6:9** [l] Ge 7:1; Eze 14:14, 20; Heb 11:7; 2Pe 2:5 [m] Ge 5:22 **6:10** [n] Ge 5:32 **6:11** [o] Eze 7:23; 8:17 **6:12** [p] Ps 14:1-3 **6:13** [q] ver 17; Eze 7:2-3 **6:14** [r] Heb 11:7; 1Pe 3:20 [s] Ex 2:3

6:17 [t] Ge 7:4, 21-23; 2Pe 2:5 **6:18** [u] Ge 9:9-16 [v] Ge 7:1, 7, 13 **6:20** [w] Ge 7:15 **6:22** [x] Ge 7:5, 9, 16 **7:1** [y] Mt 24:38 [z] Ge 6:9; Eze 14:14 **7:2** [a] ver 8; Ge 8:20; Lev 10:10; 11:1-47

[a] *14* The meaning of the Hebrew for this word is uncertain. [b] *15* That is, about 450 feet long, 75 feet wide and 45 feet high or about 135 meters long, 23 meters wide and 14 meters high [c] *16* That is, about 18 inches or about 45 centimeters [d] *16* The meaning of the Hebrew for this clause is uncertain.

primeval ocean. In this way the first two references to the Spirit of God in Genesis (here; 1:2) both have parallels to the role of Atum in Egyptian texts. One key difference is that Atum is identified as the creator-God in the Egyptian texts, while in Genesis, God (*Elohim*) and not the Spirit of God (*ruah Elohim*) is the Creator.

6:4 *Nephilim.* They occur only here and in Nu 13:33. The text presents them not as the offspring of the union, but as contemporaries. The fact that they are also around after the flood indicates that the label is not ethnic. Analysis of the meaning of the designation has been unsuccessful in identifying this group. The latter part of the verse indicates that they are heroic figures, perhaps of the sort exemplified by Gilgamesh, who is described as possessing heroism (Gilgamesh Epic, 1.30) and as being tall, magnificent, and terrible (Gilgamesh Epic, 1.37). He has a six-cubit (nine-foot or 2.7-meter) stride (Gilgamesh Epic, 1.57) and is 11 cubits (16.5 feet or 5 meters) tall (Hittite version of Gilgamesh Epic, 1.8).

A more specific interpretation suggests that the Nephilim ought to be identified as the ancient sages (the *apkallu*). The *apkallu* were considered semidivine (one of their number, Adapa, is called the "son of [the god] Ea"). They likewise marry human women, creating mixed classes. After the flood, the sages are considered of human descent and are called the *ummianu*. These individuals, unlike their predecessors, are more infamous than famous (though only in general terms, e.g., "angered Adad").

The *apkallu* and the *ummianu*, were indeed heroic figures of old. This makes sense of the terminology here. This view is additionally attractive in that in Genesis this section is in close proximity to the account of the flood, which is also recorded in the context of the *apkallu*. Though some similarities are evident, the term "Nephilim" remains unexplained, as does their connection to the inhabitants of the land in Nu 13:33.

7:2 *clean animal.* This is the only hint that the category of "clean" animals existed prior to Sinai. Here it is not a designation pertaining to diet since the eating of meat was ostensibly not permitted until after the flood (cf. 9:3). No distinction between clean and unclean animals is made anywhere else in the ancient Near East. Nevertheless, the designation "clean" could refer to the acceptability of the animal for sacrifice (one could infer that this is how Noah used them). On this count, every temple and culture had its regulations about which animals could be offered and which could not.

When we remember that sacrifices in the rest of the ancient Near East were considered meals for the nourishment of the gods, the decision about acceptable and unacceptable animals would have been based on what was considered edible or delectable. In Egypt, wild animals such as wild cattle, antelope, gazelle, and ibex were

3 and also seven pairs of every kind of bird, male and female, to keep their various kinds alive throughout the earth. 4 Seven days from now I will send rain on the earth for forty days and forty nights, and I will wipe from the face of the earth every living creature I have made."

5 And Noah did all that the LORD commanded him.[b]

6 Noah was six hundred years old when the floodwaters came on the earth. 7 And Noah and his sons and his wife and his sons' wives entered the ark to escape the waters of the flood. 8 Pairs of clean and unclean animals, of birds and of all creatures that move along the ground, 9 male and female, came to Noah and entered the ark, as God had commanded Noah. 10 And after the seven days the floodwaters came on the earth.

11 In the six hundredth year of Noah's life, on the seventeenth day of the second month — on that day all the springs of the great deep[c] burst forth, and the floodgates of the heavens[d] were opened. 12 And rain fell on the earth forty days and forty nights.[e]

13 On that very day Noah and his sons, Shem, Ham and Japheth, together with his wife and the wives of his three sons, entered the ark. 14 They had with them every wild animal according to its kind, all livestock according to their kinds, every creature that moves along the ground according to its kind and every bird according to its kind, everything with wings. 15 Pairs of all creatures that have the breath of life in them came to Noah and entered the ark.[f] 16 The animals going in were male and female of every living thing, as God had commanded Noah. Then the LORD shut him in.

17 For forty days[g] the flood kept coming on the earth, and as the waters increased they lifted the ark high above the earth. 18 The waters rose and increased greatly on the earth, and the ark floated on the surface of the water. 19 They rose greatly on the earth, and all the high mountains under the entire heavens were covered.[h] 20 The waters rose and covered the mountains to a depth of more than fifteen cubits.[a,b] 21 Every living thing that moved on land perished — birds, livestock, wild animals, all the creatures that swarm over the earth, and all mankind.[i] 22 Everything on dry land that had the breath of life[j] in its nostrils died. 23 Every living thing on the face of the earth was wiped out; people and animals and the creatures that move along the ground and the birds were wiped from the earth.[k] Only Noah was left, and those with him in the ark.[l]

24 The waters flooded the earth for a hundred and fifty days.[m]

8 But God remembered[n] Noah and all the wild animals and the livestock that were with him in the ark, and he sent a wind over the earth,[o] and the waters receded. 2 Now the springs of the deep and the floodgates of the heavens[p] had been closed, and the rain had stopped falling from the sky. 3 The water receded steadily from the earth. At the end of the hundred and fifty days the water had gone down, 4 and on the seventeenth day of the seventh month the ark came to rest on the mountains of Ararat. 5 The waters continued to recede until the tenth month, and on the first day of the tenth month the tops of the mountains became visible.

6 After forty days Noah opened a window he had made in the ark 7 and sent out a raven, and it kept flying back and forth until the water had dried up from the earth. 8 Then he sent out a dove to see if the water had receded from the surface of the ground. 9 But the dove could find nowhere to perch because there was water over all the surface of the earth; so it returned to Noah in the ark. He reached out his hand and took the dove and brought it back to himself in the ark. 10 He waited seven more days and again sent out the dove from the ark. 11 When the dove returned to him in the evening, there in its beak was a freshly plucked olive leaf!

7:5 [b] Ge 6:22
7:11 [c] Eze 26:19 [d] Ge 8:2
7:12 [e] ver 4
7:15 [f] Ge 6:19
7:17 [g] ver 4
7:19 [h] Ps 104:6

7:21 [i] Ge 6:7, 13
7:22 [j] Ge 1:30
7:23 [k] Mt 24:39; Lk 17:27; 1Pe 3:20; 2Pe 2:5 [l] Heb 11:7
7:24 [m] Ge 8:3
8:1 [n] Ge 9:15; 19:29; Ex 2:24; 1Sa 1:11, 19 [o] Ex 14:21
8:2 [p] Ge 7:11

a 20 That is, about 23 feet or about 6.8 meters
b 20 Or *rose more than fifteen cubits, and the mountains were covered*

favored for sacrifice, while sheep and goats were largely avoided. Other cultures favored domesticated animals in their sacrificial practices, mostly ungulates such as sheep, goats and cattle. Finally, among the birds, doves and pigeons are the most widely attested sacrificial types. Many of these were recognized as appropriate in the broader ancient Near Eastern world.

7:11 *springs ... floodgates.* These are terms from the contemporary understanding of cosmic geography (see the article "Cosmic Geography," p. 836). The Hebrew word translated "deep" (*tehom*) in this verse is the same Hebrew word used in 1:2. It refers to the great cosmic ocean that not only surrounds the land, but is that on which the land floats (cf. Ps 24:1 – 2). This is what 1:7 calls "the water under the vault." The "springs" were considered the entry points of these waters to the earth. The "floodgates," or the windows of heaven, were the comparable entry points for the waters above the earth that are held back by the sky. These allowed rain to fall. In ch. 1 separating these waters and then inserting the dry land between them remedied the initial watery condition. In the flood, the restraints on these cosmic waters were lifted and the cosmos was returned to its nonfunctional watery state.

8:11 *olive leaf.* Olive trees are difficult to kill, and they resprout easily. They do not mind rocky soil and grow

Then Noah knew that the water had receded from the earth. 12He waited seven
more days and sent the dove out again,
but this time it did not return to him.
13By the first day of the first month of
Noah's six hundred and first year, the
water had dried up from the earth. Noah
then removed the covering from the ark
and saw that the surface of the ground
was dry. 14By the twenty-seventh day of
the second month the earth was completely dry.
15Then God said to Noah, 16"Come out
of the ark, you and your wife and your
sons and their wives.[q] 17Bring out every
kind of living creature that is with you—

8:16 [q] Ge 7:13

best on hillsides, but not in high elevations. The olive leaf brought by the dove gives Noah an indication that the lower elevations have drained and that vegetation is once again sprouting.

GENESIS 6–8

The Flood

Beginning centuries before the book of Genesis took shape, the story of a massive, destructive flood was circulating in written form in Mesopotamia. As the tale was read—or, more often, recounted through long centuries of family and community gatherings—transformations occurred that shaped the details of its telling to the culture of the audience. Like Nathaniel Hawthorne adapting the myths of classical Greece to his nineteenth-century audience in the *Wonder Book*, or Walt Disney reshaping the Arabian Nights in *Aladdin*, ancient audiences interpreted the epic event to reflect their own particular worldview.

Comparing the versions is more important for telling us about the cultures in which they were preserved than for helping us reconstruct a trail of literary evolution. Whether the Bible is related to the ancient Near Eastern material through exchange of literary or oral traditions, the similarities make it difficult to dissociate them. Most telling is the fact that both include the episode of sending out the birds to determine when it was safe to leave the ark.

The earliest flood account is in Sumerian and recounts the story of Ziusudra. The oldest Babylonian account is found in the Atrahasis epic, dating to early in the second millennium BC. The most well-known version from Mesopotamia is imbedded in the famous Gilgamesh Epic. There it is presented as the explanation for how Utnapishtim (the flood hero) gained eternal life (which Gilgamesh was seeking). These three flood accounts are stages in a single tradition as the similarities clearly indicate.

In the Biblical flood story God is distressed with the behavior of the people whom he has created (Ge 6:5–7). In the monotheistic setting of Genesis, it is his decision alone to send the flood and to preserve Noah and his family alive. He is portrayed as resigned to this course of action, which is sadly the only appropriate response. The Mesopotamian versions derive from a polytheistic culture and therefore portray the gods deliberating in a council. The decision to send the flood is portrayed as a reaction of angry frustration. As the story progresses the gods are duplicitous, shortsighted, and absorbed in petty squabbles.

Genesis documents the downward slide of humanity from the idyllic garden to the chaotic anarchy that introduces the flood story (2:4—6:7). Violence has become an incorrigible way of life, and the waters are sent as an act of justice. The Atrahasis epic preserves most clearly the reasons for the flood in the Mesopotamian tradition. People had been created to do the work that the gods were tired of doing. But the growing population and the inevitable internal strife that resulted had made even more work for the gods, for people were constantly disturbing them with their troubles, demands

continued on next page

the birds, the animals, and all the creatures that move along the ground — so
they can multiply on the earth and be
fruitful and increase in number on it."[r]
18 So Noah came out, together with his
sons and his wife and his sons' wives.
19 All the animals and all the creatures that
move along the ground and all the birds —
everything that moves on land — came out
of the ark, one kind after another.
20 Then Noah built an altar to the LORD[s]
and, taking some of all the clean animals
and clean[t] birds, he sacrificed burnt offerings[u] on it. 21 The LORD smelled the pleasing aroma[v] and said in his heart: "Never
again will I curse the ground[w] because of

8:17 [r] Ge 1:22
8:20 [s] Ge 12:7-8; 13:18; 22:9 [t] Ge 7:8; Lev 11:1-47 [u] Ge 22:2, 13; Ex 10:25
8:21 [v] Lev 1:9, 13; 2Co 2:15 [w] Ge 3:17

8:21 *pleasing aroma.* The contrast between the Biblical and ancient Near Eastern accounts is more distinct on this point than on any other (see the article "The Flood," p. 20). In the Gilgamesh Epic the gods have apparently

and requests. All of this is captured as the "noise" of humankind that led the gods to embark on a course of total destruction.

Noah attracts God's attention as one who should not share in the fate of the rest of the population (6:8). Special provision is therefore made for him to be spared. Mesopotamian accounts agree among themselves that the plan of the gods was that no one should survive. Despite the fact that they were sworn to secrecy concerning the plans of the assembly, one of their number, Ea, successfully carried out a scheme so that his favorite human would learn of the coming flood. He then instructed him secretly how to keep his knowledge hidden from the gods and the rest of the people and survive the seven days of the flood. His boat resembled a temple and saved not just his family, but also various skilled workmen so that the arts of civilization could be preserved.

When Noah disembarked from the ark, he offered a sacrifice of thanksgiving and received covenant promises that God would preserve a certain order in the cosmos rather than oppose the chaos of human sin by means of flooding waters (8:18 – 22). When the Mesopotamian flood heroes emerged, they offered a sacrifice of appeasement to calm the anger of the gods. The gods had forgotten how much they were dependent on humans to supply them with food (sacrifices) and gathered around hungrily, wondering how such a foolish decision (the flood) could have been made. The hero is grudgingly granted eternal life by the head of the gods, who remains miffed that word of the flood leaked out.

The most well-known Mesopotamian version of the flood is imbedded in the famous Gilgamesh Epic.

The flood stories from the ancient Near East and from around the world offer persuasive evidence that a flood of significant magnitude occurred and was remembered. The accounts from the ancient Near East are closest to the Biblical account and help us see how the Israelites would have understood the whole event differently than their neighbors. ◆

humans, even though[a] every inclination of
the human heart is evil from childhood.[x]
And never again will I destroy all living
creatures,[y] as I have done.

22 "As long as the earth endures,
seedtime and harvest,
cold and heat,
summer and winter,
day and night
will never cease."[z]

God's Covenant With Noah

9 Then God blessed Noah and his sons,
saying to them, "Be fruitful and increase in number and fill the earth.[a] 2 The
fear and dread of you will fall on all the
beasts of the earth, and on all the birds
in the sky, on every creature that moves
along the ground, and on all the fish in the
sea; they are given into your hands. 3 Everything that lives and moves about will
be food for you.[b] Just as I gave you the
green plants, I now give you everything.
4 "But you must not eat meat that has its
lifeblood still in it.[c] 5 And for your lifeblood
I will surely demand an accounting. I will
demand an accounting from every animal.[d] And from each human being, too, I
will demand an accounting for the life of
another human being.[e]

6 "Whoever sheds human blood,
by humans shall their blood be shed;[f]
for in the image of God[g]
has God made mankind.

7 As for you, be fruitful and increase in
number; multiply on the earth and increase upon it."[h]
8 Then God said to Noah and to his sons
with him: 9 "I now establish my covenant
with you[i] and with your descendants after
you 10 and with every living creature that
was with you—the birds, the livestock and
all the wild animals, all those that came out
of the ark with you—every living creature
on earth. 11 I establish my covenant[j] with
you: Never again will all life be destroyed
by the waters of a flood; never again will
there be a flood to destroy the earth.[k]"
12 And God said, "This is the sign of the
covenant[l] I am making between me and
you and every living creature with you, a
covenant for all generations to come: 13 I
have set my rainbow in the clouds, and it
will be the sign of the covenant between
me and the earth. 14 Whenever I bring
clouds over the earth and the rainbow appears in the clouds, 15 I will remember my
covenant[m] between me and you and all
living creatures of every kind. Never again
will the waters become a flood to destroy
all life. 16 Whenever the rainbow appears in
the clouds, I will see it and remember the
everlasting covenant[n] between God and all
living creatures of every kind on the earth."
17 So God said to Noah, "This is the sign
of the covenant[o] I have established between me and all life on the earth."

The Sons of Noah

18 The sons of Noah who came out of the
ark were Shem, Ham and Japheth. (Ham
was the father of Canaan.)[p] 19 These were
the three sons of Noah, and from them
came the people who were scattered over
the whole earth.[q]
20 Noah, a man of the soil, proceeded[b] to
plant a vineyard. 21 When he drank some
of its wine, he became drunk and lay

8:21 [x] Ge 6:5; Ps 51:5; Jer 17:9 [y] Ge 9:11, 15; Isa 54:9 **8:22** [z] Ge 1:14; Jer 33:20, 25 **9:1** [a] Ge 1:22 **9:3** [b] Ge 1:29 **9:4** [c] Lev 3:17; 17:10-14; Dt 12:16, 23-25; 1Sa 14:33 **9:5** [d] Ex 21:28-32 [e] Ge 4:10 **9:6** [f] Ge 4:14; Ex 21:12, 14; Lev 24:17; Mt 26:52 [g] Ge 1:26 **9:7** [h] Ge 1:22 **9:9** [i] Ge 6:18 **9:11** [j] ver 16; Isa 24:5 [k] Ge 8:21; Isa 54:9 **9:12** [l] ver 17; Ge 17:11 **9:15** [m] Ex 2:24; Lev 26:42, 45; Dt 7:9; Eze 16:60 **9:16** [n] ver 11; Ge 17:7, 13, 19; 2Sa 7:13; 23:5 **9:17** [o] ver 12; Ge 17:11 **9:18** [p] ver 25-27; Ge 10:6, 15 **9:19** [q] Ge 10:32

[a] 21 Or *humans, for* [b] 20 Or *soil, was the first*

neglected to realize that with all humans destroyed, no one will be left to give them sacrifices. Without sacrifices they are deprived of their sustenance. Consequently, when the sacrifice is offered after the survivors disembark from the boat, "the gods smelled the sweet savour, the gods gathered like flies around the sacrificer" (Gilgamesh Epic, 11.161–63). Both the Gilgamesh Epic and Genesis refer to the aroma/savor of the sacrifice, but the portrayal offered of deity is far different. In the Gilgamesh Epic this represents the gods' needs and exposes their shortsightedness. It functions to appease their anger. In Genesis it represents God's pleasure in the creatures he has made and the resulting commitment not to destroy them.

9:3 *food for you.* In Mesopotamia the motif of the wild man includes that he lives in the wild with the animals and eats grass. This is also part of the description of human existence in general before they become civilized. Here in Genesis the provision for eating meat is not connected with the development of civilization (ch. 4) but with the restatement of the blessing. In general in the ancient world meat was a delicacy, eaten only on special occasions in connection with cultic activities. Meat was more regularly part of the palace fare, and Egyptian reliefs and paintings portray the butchering process.

9:6 Exacting punishment for murder is not reserved for deity but is placed under the purview of human judicial systems here, whether they are located in courts or in clans. This verse may well mark the beginning of judicial responsibility that is eventually evidenced in the compilations of sample verdicts (such as those found on the Hammurapi Stele) throughout the ancient Near East. These compendia demonstrate that the kings and societies of the ancient world took their judicial responsibilities seriously. Many of these indicate that capital punishment was common in cases of homicide, though often lesser penalties were exacted depending on the social status of both the perpetrator and the victim.

9:8 *covenant.* An agreement between two parties containing stipulations for one or both. In this case, God takes the stipulations on himself, rather than imposing them on Noah. Unlike the later Abrahamic covenant, this covenant does not entail a new phase of revelation, and is made with "every living creature" (v. 10), not just people (v. 9).

9:20–27 In the history of interpretation of this passage, a number of alternatives have been suggested for explaining the offense committed by Ham, especially in

MAJOR COVENANTS IN THE OLD TESTAMENT

COVENANTS	REFERENCE	TYPE	PARTICIPANT	DESCRIPTION
Noahic	Ge 9:8–17	Royal Grant	Made with righteous (6:9) Noah (and his descendants and every living thing on earth—all life that is subject to human jurisdiction)	An unconditional divine promise never to destroy all earthly life with some natural catastrophe, the covenant "sign" (9:13,17) being the rainbow in the storm cloud
Abrahamic A	Ge 15:9–21	Royal (land) Grant	Made with "righteous" (his faith was "credited . . . to him as righteousness," v. 6) Abram (and his descendants, v. 16)	An unconditional divine promise to fulfill the grant of the land; a self-maledictory oath symbolically enacted it (v. 17; see the article "Ratifying the Covenant," p. 42)
Abrahamic B	Ge 17	Suzerain-vassal	Made with Abraham as patriarchal head of his household	A conditional divine pledge to be Abraham's God and the God of his descendants (cf. "as for me," v. 4; "as for you," v. 9); the condition: total consecration to the Lord as symbolized by circumcision
Sinaitic	Ex 19–24	Suzerain-vassal	Made with Israel as the descendants of Abraham, Isaac and Jacob and as the people the Lord had redeemed from bondage to an earthly power	A conditional divine pledge to be Israel's God (as the protector and the guarantor of Israel's blessed destiny); the condition: Israel's total consecration to the Lord as his people (his kingdom) who live by his rule and serve his purposes in history
Phinehas	Nu 25:10–13	Royal Grant	Made with the zealous priest Phinehas	An unconditional divine promise to maintain the family of Phinehas in a "lasting priesthood" (v. 13; implicitly a pledge to Israel to provide it forever with a faithful priesthood)
Davidic	2Sa 7:5–16	Royal Grant	Made with faithful King David after his devotion to God as Israel's king and the Lord's anointed vassal had come to special expression (v. 2)	An unconditional divine promise to establish and maintain the Davidic dynasty on the throne of Israel (implicitly a pledge to Israel) to provide the nation forever with a godly king like David and through that dynasty to do what he had done through David—bring Israel into rest in the promised land (1Ki 4:20–21; 5:3–4)
New	Jer 31:31–34	Royal Grant	Promised to rebellious Israel as the people are about to be expelled from the promised land in actualization of the most severe covenant curse (Lev 26:27–39; Dt 28:36–37, 45–68)	An unconditional divine promise to unfaithful Israel to forgive the people's sins and establish his relationship with his people on a new basis by writing his law "on their hearts" (v. 33)—a covenant of pure grace

MAJOR TYPES OF ROYAL COVENANTS/TREATIES IN THE ANCIENT NEAR EAST

ROYAL GRANT (UNCONDITIONAL)	PARITY	SUZERAIN-VASSAL (CONDITIONAL)
A king's grant (of land or some other benefit) to a loyal servant for faithful or exceptional service. The grant was normally perpetual and unconditional, but the servant's heirs benefited from it only as they continued their father's loyalty and service. (cf. 1Sa 8:14; 22:7; 27:6; Est 8:1.)	A covenant between equals, binding them to mutual friendship or at least to mutual respect for each other's spheres and interests. Participants called each other "brother." (cf. Ge 21:27; 26:31; 31:44–54; 1Ki 5:12; 15:19; 20:32–34; Am 1:9.)	A covenant regulating the relationship between a great king and one of his subject kings. The great king claimed absolute right of sovereignty, demanded total loyalty and service (the vassal must "love" his suzerain) and pledged protection of the subject's realm and dynasty, conditional on the vassal's faithfulness and loyalty to him. The vassal pledged absolute loyalty to his suzerain—whatever service his suzerain demanded—and exclusive reliance on the suzerain's protection. Participants called each other "lord" and "servant" or "father" and "son." (cf. Jos 9:6,8; Eze 17:13–18; Hos 12:1.)

Commitments made in these covenants were accompanied by self-maledictory oaths (made orally, ceremonially or both). The gods were called on to witness the covenants and implement the curses of the oaths if the covenants were violated.

uncovered inside his tent. 22Ham, the father of Canaan, saw his father naked and
told his two brothers outside. 23But Shem
and Japheth took a garment and laid it
across their shoulders; then they walked
in backward and covered their father's
naked body. Their faces were turned the
other way so that they would not see their
father naked.

24When Noah awoke from his wine and
found out what his youngest son had done
to him, 25he said,

> "Cursed be Canaan![r]
> The lowest of slaves
> will he be to his brothers.[s]"

26He also said,

> "Praise be to the LORD, the God of
> Shem!
> May Canaan be the slave of Shem.
> 27May God extend Japheth's[a] territory;
> may Japheth live in the tents of
> Shem,
> and may Canaan be the slave of
> Japheth."

28After the flood Noah lived 350 years.
29Noah lived a total of 950 years, and then
he died.

The Table of Nations

10 This is the account[t] of Shem, Ham
and Japheth, Noah's sons, who
themselves had sons after the flood.

9:25 [r]ver 18 [s]Ge 25:23; Jos 9:23
10:1 [t]Ge 2:4

The Japhethites

10:2-5pp — 1Ch 1:5-7

2The sons[b] of Japheth:
Gomer,[u] Magog,[v] Madai, Javan, Tubal,[w] Meshek and Tiras.
3The sons of Gomer:
Ashkenaz,[x] Riphath and Togarmah.[y]
4The sons of Javan:
Elishah, Tarshish,[z] the Kittites and
the Rodanites.[c] 5(From these the
maritime peoples spread out into
their territories by their clans within their nations, each with its own
language.)

The Hamites

10:6-20pp — 1Ch 1:8-16

6The sons of Ham:
Cush, Egypt, Put and Canaan.[a]
7The sons of Cush:
Seba, Havilah, Sabtah, Raamah
and Sabteka.
The sons of Raamah:
Sheba and Dedan.

8Cush was the father[d] of Nimrod, who
became a mighty warrior on the earth. 9He

10:2 [u]Eze 38:6 [v]Eze 38:2; Rev 20:8 [w]Isa 66:19
10:3 [x]Jer 51:27 [y]Eze 27:14; 38:6
10:4 [z]Eze 27:12,25; Jnh 1:3
10:6 [a]ver 15; Ge 9:18

[a] 27 *Japheth* sounds like the Hebrew for *extend.*
[b] 2 *Sons* may mean *descendants* or *successors* or *nations*; also in verses 3, 4, 6, 7, 20-23, 29 and 31.
[c] 4 Some manuscripts of the Masoretic Text and Samaritan Pentateuch (see also Septuagint and 1 Chron. 1:7); most manuscripts of the Masoretic Text *Dodanites*
[d] 8 *Father* may mean *ancestor* or *predecessor* or *founder*; also in verses 13, 15, 24 and 26.

---

light of the severe curse (on Canaan!) that results. The options of "voyeurism" and paternal (homosexual) incest have little support from the ancient Near East regardless of the case that might be made for them in the Biblical text. The option of castration was offered in rabbinic literature and has one supporting text from ancient mythology that portrays a son castrating his father (both deities) in an attempt to usurp his position. Another option that can be supported conceptually from the ancient Near East is that Ham committed incest with his mother in an attempt to usurp the authority of the family from his father (cf. Reuben in Ge 35:22 and Absalom in 2Sa 16:21 – 22), or in an attempt to provide for additional offspring in a depopulated world (cf. Lot's daughters in Ge 19:30 – 38). The idea of usurping someone's authority by taking his wife is attested in royal contexts in an Akkadian text from Ugarit. None of this information offers clarification of Ham's behavior, but it does alert us to a number of alternatives that we otherwise might not have recognized.

10:2 – 29 This passage is called the table of nations. The list of the sons of Shem, Ham and Japheth contains 70 names, a number that stood for totality and completion. More important, the concept of 70 nations is offered as the design of God. Nevertheless, the list is certainly not complete in its presentation of the descendants of Noah and his sons. The author penetrated selectively into various lines in order to achieve that final number.

This group of 70 does not reflect the perspective of Noah's descendants in the third or fourth generation; rather, it is Israel's perspective at the time of the author. Note that there is no discussion of anyone outside the known world of the ancient Near East in the middle of the second millennium BC. The text only seeks to account for the groups the Israelites were aware of and does not hint at a world beyond the ancient Near East. In other words, the author has not attempted to provide a comprehensive list of all people(s) descended from the sons of Noah. Instead, he has addressed how all the known peoples and nations of his day are related to the sons of Noah.

10:8 – 12 Attempts to identify Nimrod with some historical or literary figure from the ancient world have been many, including an Assyrian king (Tukulti-Ninurta I, end of the thirteenth century BC) or the Assyrian god Ninurta, a warrior and hunter of myriad mythical creatures. An Assyrian poem from the end of the second millennium BC epitomizes an Assyrian king (thought to be Tiglath-Pileser I) as a great hunter, but the piece is an extended metaphor using the language of hunting to describe the conquests of the king. It cannot be ruled out that this is also the case in the description of Nimrod, since hunting is a metaphor for royal conquest from earliest times. For example, the royal mace head of Mesilim, king of Kish in the twenty-sixth century BC, is decorated with six intertwined lions around its circumference. The identification of the hunter as a royal metaphor would offer an explanation of why v. 9 includes "before the LORD"; it would indicate that his conquests had divine support. The royal lion hunt was considered a cultic act. "King of Kish" (notice the similarity

was a mighty hunter before the LORD; that
is why it is said, "Like Nimrod, a mighty
hunter before the LORD." 10 The first centers of his kingdom were Babylon,[b] Uruk,
Akkad and Kalneh, in[a] Shinar.[b][c] 11 From
that land he went to Assyria,[d] where he
built Nineveh,[e] Rehoboth Ir,[c] Calah 12 and
Resen, which is between Nineveh and Calah—which is the great city.

13 Egypt was the father of
the Ludites, Anamites, Lehabites,
Naphtuhites, 14 Pathrusites, Kaslu-
hites (from whom the Philistines[f]
came) and Caphtorites.
15 Canaan[g] was the father of
Sidon[h] his firstborn,[d] and of the
Hittites,[i] 16 Jebusites,[j] Amorites,
Girgashites, 17 Hivites, Arkites, Sinites, 18 Arvadites, Zemarites and
Hamathites.

Later the Canaanite[k] clans scattered
19 and the borders of Canaan[l] reached from
Sidon[m] toward Gerar as far as Gaza, and
then toward Sodom, Gomorrah, Admah
and Zeboyim, as far as Lasha.
20 These are the sons of Ham by their
clans and languages, in their territories
and nations.

The Semites
10:21-31pp — Ge 11:10-27; 1Ch 1:17-27

21 Sons were also born to Shem, whose
older brother was[e] Japheth; Shem was the
ancestor of all the sons of Eber.[n]
22 The sons of Shem:
Elam,[o] Ashur, Arphaxad,[p] Lud and
Aram.
23 The sons of Aram:
Uz,[q] Hul, Gether and Meshek.[f]
24 Arphaxad was the father of[g] Shelah,
and Shelah the father of Eber.[r]
25 Two sons were born to Eber:
One was named Peleg,[h] because in
his time the earth was divided; his
brother was named Joktan.
26 Joktan was the father of
Almodad, Sheleph, Hazarmaveth,
Jerah, 27 Hadoram, Uzal, Diklah,
28 Obal, Abimael, Sheba, 29 Ophir,
Havilah and Jobab. All these were
sons of Joktan.

30 The region where they lived stretched
from Mesha toward Sephar, in the eastern
hill country.
31 These are the sons of Shem by their
clans and languages, in their territories
and nations.

32 These are the clans of Noah's sons,[s]
according to their lines of descent,
within their nations. From these the nations spread out over the earth[t] after the
flood.

10:10 [b] Ge 11:9 [c] Ge 11:2 **10:11** [d] Ps 83:8; Mic 5:6 [e] Jnh 1:2; 4:11; Na 1:1 **10:14** [f] Ge 21:32, 34; 26:1, 8 **10:15** [g] ver 6; Ge 9:18 [h] Eze 28:21 [i] Ge 23:3, 20 **10:16** [j] 1Ch 11:4 **10:18** [k] Ge 12:6; Ex 13:11 **10:19** [l] Ge 11:31; 13:12; 17:8 [m] ver 15 **10:21** [n] ver 24; Nu 24:24 **10:22** [o] Jer 49:34 [p] Lk 3:36 **10:23** [q] Job 1:1 **10:24** [r] ver 21 **10:32** [s] ver 1 [t] Ge 9:19

[a] *10* Or *Uruk and Akkad—all of them in* [b] *10* That is, Babylonia [c] *11* Or *Nineveh with its city squares* [d] *15* Or *of the Sidonians, the foremost* [e] *21* Or *Shem, the older brother of* [f] *23* See Septuagint and 1 Chron. 1:17; Hebrew *Mash.* [g] *24* Hebrew; Septuagint *father of Cainan, and Cainan was the father of* [h] *25* *Peleg* means *division.*

between Kish and Cush) was a title that indicated some level of rule over a hegemony in the first half of the third millennium BC.

The description of Nimrod positions him at the head of an empire. Only three major empires are known prior to the time of Moses: the Old Akkadian Empire (2335–2218 BC), the Third Dynasty of Ur (2112–2004), and the Old Babylonian Empire ruled by Hammurapi (1792–1750). If Nimrod is to be identified as a historical individual of early history, he must be connected to one of these. Scholars have argued for the following:

1. Sargon (Dynasty of Akkad): Some records indicate military activity on the upper Tigris (Gasur = Nuzi and Assur, and his son built a temple at Nineveh), but little associates Sargon with the cities named in Genesis. Sargon built up Akkad and made it his capital city. Nothing in contemporary records connects him with "Babylon."

2. Shulgi (Ur III Dynasty): Shulgi praises himself as a hunter in his poems, and in his inscriptions he regularly refers to himself as the mighty man or mighty hero. The core area of his political control was in southern Mesopotamia, but his capital was at Ur, not Babylon. His records make no mention of Babylon, though a late chronicle suggests that he despoiled Esagila, the temple of Marduk in Babylon. If this is true, there is even more distinction between him and Nimrod since the latter rules at Babylon. Shulgi also extended his empire from the south to the north, including some cities of Assyria. Extension to the upper Tigris involved cities that paid taxes (as far north as Assur) and allied cities, which included Nineveh, but there was little military control of these regions. There is no name for Shulgi that makes sense of Nimrod.

3. Hammurapi (Old Babylonian Dynasty): Here we finally find a ruler of an empire whose center is Babylon. He campaigned north on the Tigris, but did not control the Assyrian region and is not referred to as a "hunter." The fact that he often identified himself as "king of the Mardu" gives a possible connection to the name Nimrod, since a variety of prefixes or determinatives could combine an N with Mardu, though none of them is attested in his inscriptions.

None of these names offers a close match to the description of Nimrod. Perhaps future finds will reveal an earlier empire and king that will better fit the data.

10:10 *Babylon.* Babylon is first mentioned (in passing) in contemporary records in the twenty-third century BC. References to it remain occasional and suggest no great significance until the First Dynasty of Babylon (first half of the second millennium BC), when the predecessors to Hammurapi make it their capital. From that time on it becomes legendary as the seat of culture and religion in Mesopotamia. Archaeologically, excavations can only recover data as far back as the First Dynasty of Babylon because the water table shifted and destroyed all earlier layers. We therefore know nothing of the history of Babylon's founding from either extra-Biblical literary or archaeological records.

The Historical Setting of Genesis

Mesopotamia: Sumer Through Old Babylonia

Sumerians. It is not possible at this time to put Ge 1 – 11 into a specific place in the historical record. Our history of the ancient Near East begins in earnest after writing has been invented, and the earliest civilization known to us in the historical record is that of the Sumerians. This culture dominated southern Mesopotamia for over 500 years during the first half of the third millennium BC (2900 – 2350 BC), known as the Early Dynastic Period. The Sumerians have become known through the excavation of several of their principal cities, which include Eridu, Uruk and Ur. The Sumerians are credited with many of the important developments in civilization, including the foundations of mathematics, astronomy, law and medicine. Urbanization is also first witnessed among the Sumerians. By the time of Abraham, the Sumerians no longer dominate the ancient Near East politically, but their culture continues to influence the region. Other cultures replace them in the political arena but benefit from the advances they made.

Dynasty of Akkad. In the middle of the twenty-fourth century BC, the Sumerian culture was overrun by the formation of an empire under the kingship of Sargon I, who established his capital at Akkad. He ruled all of southern Mesopotamia and ranged eastward into Elam and northwest to the Mediterranean on campaigns of a military and economic nature. The empire lasted for almost 150 years before being apparently overthrown by the Gutians (a barbaric people from the Zagros Mountains east of the Tigris), though other factors, including internal dissent, may have contributed to the downfall.

Ur III. Of the next century little is known as more than 20 Gutian kings succeeded one another. Just before 2100 BC, the city of Ur took control of southern Mesopotamia under the kingship of Ur-Nammu, and for the next century there was a Sumerian renaissance in what has been called the Ur III period. It is difficult to ascertain the limits of territorial control of the Ur III kings, though the territory does not seem to have been as extensive as that of the dynasty of Akkad. Under Ur-Nammu's son Shulgi, the region enjoyed almost a half century of peace. Decline and fall came late in the twenty-first century BC through the infiltration of the Amorites and the increased aggression of the Elamites to the east. The Elamites finally overthrew the city.

It is against this backdrop of history that the OT patriarchs emerge. Some have pictured Abraham as leaving the sophisticated Ur that was the center of the powerful Ur III period to settle in the unknown wilderness of Canaan, but that involves both chronological and geographic speculation. By the highest chronology (i.e., the earliest dates attributed to him), Abraham probably would have traveled from Ur to Harran during the reign of Ur-Nammu, but many scholars are inclined to place Abraham in the later Isin-Larsa period or even the Old Babylonian period. From a geographic standpoint it is difficult to be sure that the Ur mentioned in the Bible is the famous city in southern Mesopotamia (see note on 11:28). All this makes it impossible to give a precise background of Abraham.

The Ur III period ended in southern Mesopotamia as the last king of Ur, Ibbi-Sin, lost the support of one city after another and was finally overthrown by the Elamites, who lived just east of the Tigris. In the ensuing two centuries (c. 2000 – 1800 BC),

continued on next page

power was again returned to city-states that controlled more local areas. Isin, Larsa, Eshnunna, Lagash, Mari, Assur and Babylon all served as major political centers.

Old Babylonian Period. Thanks substantially to the royal archives from the town of Mari, the eighteenth century BC has become thoroughly documented. As the century opened there was an uneasy balance of power among four cities: Larsa ruled by Rim-Sin, Mari ruled by Yahdun-Lim (and later, Zimri-Lim), Assur ruled by Shamshi-Adad I, and Babylon ruled by Hammurapi. Through a generation of political intrigue and diplomatic strategy, Hammurapi eventually emerged to establish the prominence of the first dynasty of Babylon.

The Old Babylonian period covered the time from the fall of the Ur III dynasty (c. 2000 BC) to the fall of the first dynasty of Babylon (just after 1600 BC). This is the period during which most of the narratives in Ge 12–50 occur. The rulers of the first dynasty of Babylon were Amorites. The Amorites had been coming into Mesopotamia as early as the Ur III period, at first being fought as enemies, then gradually taking their place within the society of the Near East. With the accession of Hammurapi to the throne, they reached the height of success. Despite his impressive military accomplishments, Hammurapi is most widely known today for his collection of laws.

ERAS OF MESOPOTAMIAN HISTORY (ROUND DATES)	
Early Dynastic Period	2900–2350 BC
Dynasty of Akkad	2350–2200 BC
Ur III Empire	2100–2000 BC
Old Babylonian Period	2000–1600 BC

ERAS OF EGYPTIAN HISTORY (ROUND DATES)	
Old Kingdom	3100–2200 BC
First Intermediate Period	2200–2050 BC
Middle Kingdom	2050–1720 BC
Second Intermediate Period	1720–1550 BC
Hyksos	1650–1550 BC

The first dynasty of Babylon extends for more than a century beyond the time of Hammurapi, though decline began soon after his death and continued unabated, culminating in the Hittite sack of Babylon in 1595 BC. This was nothing more than an incursion on the part of the Hittites, but it dealt the final blow to the Amorite dynasty, opening the doors of power for another group, the Kassites.

Palestine: Middle Bronze Age

Abraham entered the Palestine region during the Middle Bronze Age (2200–1550 BC), which was dominated by scattered city-states, much as Mesopotamia had been, though Palestine was not as densely populated or as extensively urbanized as Mesopotamia. The period began about the time of the fall of the dynasty of Akkad in Mesopotamia (c. 2200 BC) and extended until about 1500 BC (plus or minus 50 years, depending on the theories followed). In Syria there were power centers at Yamhad, Qatna, Alalakh and Mari, and the coastal centers of Ugarit and Byblos seemed to be already thriving.

In Palestine only Hazor is mentioned in prominence. Contemporary records from Palestine are scarce, though the Egyptian *Story of Sinuhe* has Middle Bronze Age Palestine as a backdrop and therefore offers general information. Lists of cities in Palestine are also given in the Egyptian texts. Most are otherwise unknown, though Jerusalem and Shechem are mentioned. As the period progresses there is more and more contact with Egypt and extensive caravan travel between Egypt and Palestine.

Egypt: Old and Middle Kingdoms

Roughly concurrent to the Early Dynastic period in Mesopotamia was the formative Old Kingdom period in Egypt, which permanently shaped Egypt both politically and culturally. This was the age of the great pyramids. During Egypt's Sixth Dynasty, contemporary with the dynasty of Akkad in Mesopotamia, disintegration became

continued on next page

evident. From the mid-twenty-second century BC until about 2000 BC, Egypt was plunged into a dark period known as the First Intermediate Period, which was characterized by disunity and at times by practical anarchy. Order was finally restored when Mentuhotep reunited Egypt, and Amenemhet I founded the Twelfth Dynasty, beginning a period of more than two centuries of prosperous growth and development.

The Twelfth Dynasty developed extensive trade relations with Syro-Palestine and is the most likely period for initial contacts between Egypt and the Hebrew patriarchs. By the most conservative estimates, Sesostris III would have been the pharaoh who elevated Joseph to his high administrative post. Others are more inclined to place the emigration of the Israelites to Egypt during the time of the Hyksos. The Hyksos were Semitic peoples who began moving into Egypt (particularly the delta region in the north) as early as the First Intermediate Period. As the Thirteenth Dynasty ushered in a gradual decline, the reins of power eventually fell to the Hyksos (whether by conquest, coup or consent is still indeterminable), who then controlled Egypt from about the middle of the eighteenth century BC to the middle of the sixteenth century BC. It was during this time that the Israelites began to prosper and multiply in the delta region, waiting for the covenant promises to be fulfilled. ◆

TABLE OF NATIONS

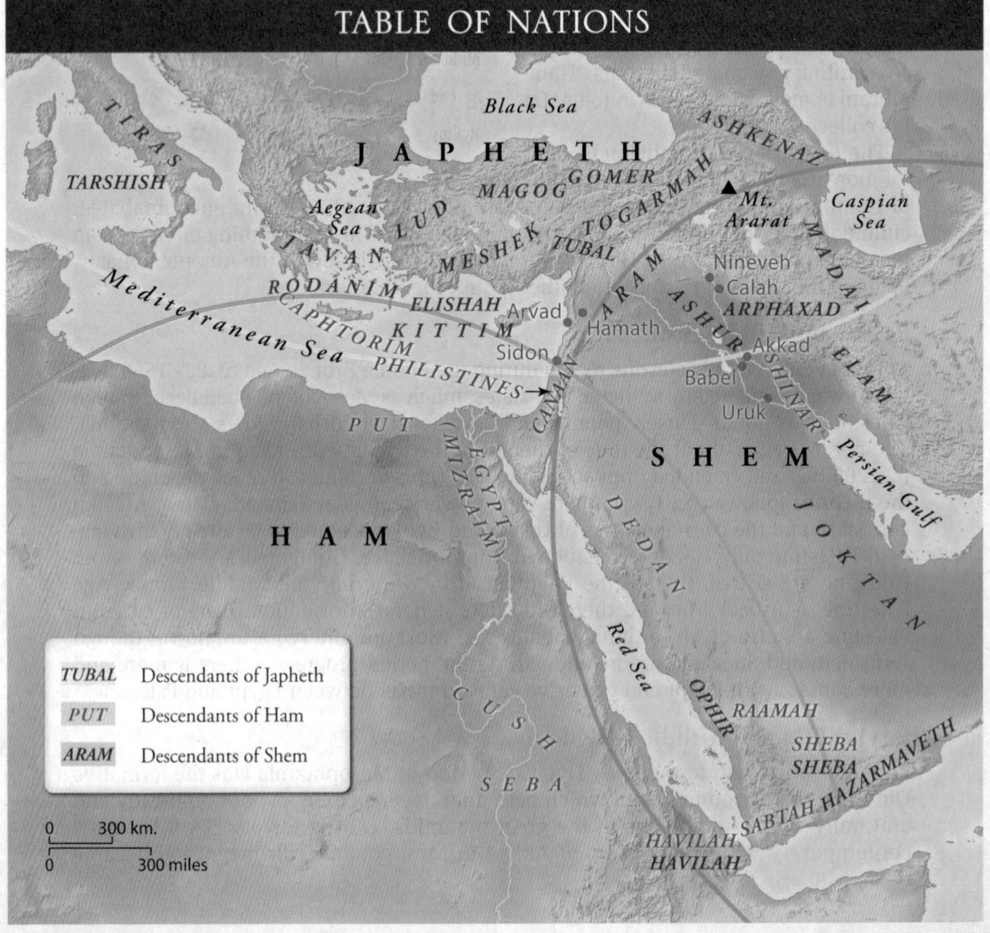

The Tower of Babel

11 Now the whole world had one language and a common speech. 2As
people moved eastward,[a] they found a
plain in Shinar[b][u] and settled there.
3They said to each other, "Come, let's
make bricks[v] and bake them thoroughly."
They used brick instead of stone, and tar[w]
for mortar. 4Then they said, "Come, let us
build ourselves a city, with a tower that
reaches to the heavens,[x] so that we may
make a name[y] for ourselves; otherwise we
will be scattered over the face of the whole
earth."[z]
5But the LORD came down[a] to see the
city and the tower the people were building. 6The LORD said, "If as one people
speaking the same language they have begun to do this, then nothing they plan to
do will be impossible for them. 7Come, let
us[b] go down and confuse their language
so they will not understand each other."[c]
8So the LORD scattered them from there
over all the earth,[d] and they stopped building the city. 9That is why it was called Babel[c][e]—because there the LORD confused
the language of the whole world. From

11:2 [u] Ge 10:10 **11:3** [v] Ex 1:14 [w] Ge 14:10 **11:4** [x] Dt 1:28; 9:1 [y] Ge 6:4 [z] Dt 4:27 **11:5** [a] ver 7; Ge 18:21; Ex 3:8; 19:11, 18, 20 **11:7** [b] Ge 1:26 [c] Ge 42:23 **11:8** [d] Ge 9:19; Lk 1:51 **11:9** [e] Ge 10:10

[a] 2 Or *from the east*; or *in the east* [b] 2 That is, Babylonia [c] 9 That is, Babylon; *Babel* sounds like the Hebrew for *confused*.

11:1 *one language.* A Sumerian epic entitled *Enmerkar and the Lord of Aratta* speaks of a time when there was only harmony among people and "the whole universe in unison spoke to Enlil in one tongue." Speech was then changed and "contention" was brought into it. Nothing else in this account parallels the tower of Babel, but it indicates that confusion of language by deity was a known theme in the ancient world.

11:2 *moved eastward.* Geological and hydrological studies and migration patterns discernible from the fourth and third millennia BC suggest that there was a drying out of the southern alluvial plain as the Persian Gulf receded and a corresponding population movement into that plain toward the end of the fourth millennium BC. This period, known as the Uruk Phase, features technological advances in urbanization, architecture, technology and language that correspond to elements referred to in v. 3 (see note). *Shinar.* The Hebrew term (*shinar*) refers to the area that ancient Near Eastern texts refer to as Sumer. It covered the southern part of the Tigris-Euphrates River basin as far north as Sippar, where the rivers converge in the area of modern southern Iraq. Major cities of the region included Kish, Nippur, Shuruppak, Girsu, Uruk, Eridu and Ur. This is the area where urbanization developed and is the heartland of Mesopotamian civilization.

11:3 *make bricks and bake them.* Stone is not readily available in the alluvial plain of southern Mesopotamia, so a logical economical choice is to use brick—there is plenty of mud. Mud brick, however, is not durable, so it was a great technological development to discover that baking the brick made it as durable as stone. This was still an expensive process, since the kilns had to be fueled. As a result, mud brick was used as much as possible, with baked brick used only for outer shells of important buildings or where waterproofing was desirable. No baked bricks have been found earlier than the Uruk period (latter part of the fourth millennium BC).

11:4 *a city, with a tower.* One single architectural feature dominated the landscape of early Mesopotamian cities: towers known as ziggurats (see the article "Ziggurats," p. 30). In the earliest stages of urbanization, the city was not designed for the private sector. People did not live in the city. Instead, it was comprised of the public buildings, such as administrative buildings, and granaries, which were mostly connected with the temple. Consequently, the city was, in effect, a temple complex. *reaches to the heavens.* Throughout Mesopotamian literature, almost every occurrence of the expression describing a building "with its head in the heavens" refers to a temple with a ziggurat (see the article "Ziggurats," p. 30). It is this language, along with the indication that God "came down" (v. 5), that gives textual confirmation that the tower is a ziggurat. This would have been transparent to the ancient reader. In keeping with the negative results of the project here, the reader of Genesis will find a few of the omens in the *Shumma Alu* series remarkable: "If a city lifts its head to the midst of heaven, that city will be abandoned" (1.15), and "If a city rises like a mountain peak to the midst of heaven, that city will be turned to a ruin" (1.16). Yet Mesopotamian cities were regularly built on high ground, with the temple on the highest ground. The wording of these omens understood in the context of the omen series is essentially about exceeding natural boundaries to the effect that a city can overreach itself to rival sacred structures and thus bring about its own destruction. *make a name.* The ancient world placed immense value on the sense of continuity from one generation to another. In some cultures a person's continued comfort in the afterlife was dependent on care from descendants in the land of the living. The details often involved memorial meals and various regular mortuary rites, but more important for this passage, they provided opportunity for the name of the deceased to be spoken. There is continued life and vitality as long as one is remembered. The building of monuments could also contribute to the desirable end result, as could achievements and adventures of various sorts. The important point here is that the desire to make a name in the ancient world is common to all. The more people who remember one's name, the more secure is one's existence in the afterlife. While there is nothing inherently evil or sinful in the desire to be remembered (e.g., God promises to "make your name great" for Abraham in 12:2 and David in 2Sa 7:9), this desire may become obsessive or motivate evil or sinful behavior. *scattered.* The fear of scattering is directly related (both syntactically and conceptually) to the previously stated desire to make a name. Remembrance takes place in the vicinity of the burial ground. Descendants who move away (as Abraham does in ch. 12) cut the ties of continuity between the past and the present. Though some have considered this desire not to scatter as disobedience to the blessing in 1:28, it must be recognized that the blessing does not relate to scattering, only to filling—far different issues. God scattered them, not because it was wrong for them to be together, but because their desire to retain continuity was causing them to launch flawed strategies.

11:5 *the LORD came down.* Precisely the reason the tower was built—for God to come down (see the article "Ziggurats," p. 30). Unfortunately, rather than being pleased to take up his residence among the people, God finds it an occasion for counteraction. Rather than being pleased at the convenience, he is distressed by the pagan concepts inherent in the nature of the ziggurat.

GENESIS 11:4

ZIGGURATS

Though they may resemble pyramids in appearance, ziggurats are nothing like them in function. Ziggurats have no inside. The structure was framed in mud brick, and then the core was packed with fill dirt. The facade was then completed with kiln-fired brick. Ziggurats were dedicated to particular deities. Any given deity may have several ziggurats dedicated to him or her in different cities. Furthermore, a given city may have several ziggurats, though the main one was associated with the patron deity of the city. Archaeologists have discovered nearly 30 ziggurats in the general region, and texts mention several others. The main architectural feature is the stairway or ramp that leads to the top. There was a small room at the top where a bed was made and a table set for the deity. Ziggurats range in size from 60 feet (18 meters) per side to almost 200 feet (60 meters) per side.

Most important is the function of the ziggurat. The ziggurat did not play a role in any of the rituals known to us from Mesopotamia. If known literature were our only guide, we would conclude that common people did not use the ziggurat for anything. It was sacred space and was strictly off-limits to profane use. Though the structure at the top was designed to accommodate the god, it was not a temple where people would go to worship. In fact, the ziggurat was typically accompanied by an adjoining temple near its base, where the worship did take place.

The best indication of the function of zig-

Stele of Nebuchadnezzar looking at the design of Babylon's ziggurat, Etemenanki, Babylon, 604–562 BC. Many also believe the Tower of Babel was a ziggurat.

The Schøyen Collection, Oslo and London, MS 2063, www.schoyencollection.com

continued on next page

there the LORD scattered them over the
face of the whole earth.

From Shem to Abram

11:10-27pp — Ge 10:21-31; 1Ch 1:17-27

10 This is the account of Shem's family
line.

Two years after the flood, when Shem
was 100 years old, he became the father[a]
of Arphaxad. 11 And after he became the
father of Arphaxad, Shem lived 500 years
and had other sons and daughters.

12 When Arphaxad had lived 35 years, he
became the father of Shelah.[f] 13 And after
he became the father of Shelah, Arphaxad
lived 403 years and had other sons and
daughters.[b]

11:12 [f] Lk 3:35

[a] 10 *Father* may mean *ancestor*; also in verses 11-25.
[b] 12,13 Hebrew; Septuagint (see also Luke 3:35, 36 and note at Gen. 10:24) *35 years, he became the father of Cainan. 13 And after he became the father of Cainan, Arphaxad lived 430 years and had other sons and daughters, and then he died. When Cainan had lived 130 years, he became the father of Shelah. And after he became the father of Shelah, Cainan lived 330 years and had other sons and daughters*

gurats comes from the names that are given to them. For instance, the name of the ziggurat at Babylon, *Etemenanki*, means "temple of the foundation of heaven and earth." One at Larsa means "temple that links heaven and earth." Most significant is the name of the ziggurat at Sippar, "temple of the stairway to pure heaven." The word translated "stairway" in this last example is used in the mythology as the means by which the messenger of the gods moved between heaven, earth, and the netherworld. As a result of these data, we can conclude that the ziggurat was a structure built to support the stairway. This stairway was a visual representation of that which was believed to be used by the gods to travel from one realm to another. It was solely for the convenience of the gods and was maintained in order to provide the deity with amenities and to make possible his descent into his temple.

At the top of the ziggurat was the gate of the gods, the entrance into their heavenly abode; adjoining the tower was the temple, where hopefully the god would descend to receive the gifts and worship of his people.

In summary, the project is a temple complex featuring a ziggurat, which was designed to make it convenient for the god to come down to his temple, receive their worship, and bless his people. The key for understanding the tower of Babel is to realize that the tower was not built so that people could ascend to heaven, but so that deity could descend to earth. ◆

14 When Shelah had lived 30 years, he
became the father of Eber. 15 And after he
became the father of Eber, Shelah lived 403
years and had other sons and daughters.

16 When Eber had lived 34 years, he became the father of Peleg. 17 And after he
became the father of Peleg, Eber lived 430
years and had other sons and daughters.

18 When Peleg had lived 30 years, he
became the father of Reu. 19 And after he
became the father of Reu, Peleg lived 209
years and had other sons and daughters.

20 When Reu had lived 32 years, he became the father of Serug.[g] 21 And after he
became the father of Serug, Reu lived 207
years and had other sons and daughters.

22 When Serug had lived 30 years, he became the father of Nahor. 23 And after he
became the father of Nahor, Serug lived
200 years and had other sons and daughters.

24 When Nahor had lived 29 years, he
became the father of Terah.[h] 25 And after
he became the father of Terah, Nahor lived
119 years and had other sons and daughters.

11:20 [g] Lk 3:35
11:24 [h] Lk 3:34

[26]After Terah had lived 70 years, he became the father of Abram,[i] Nahor[j] and Haran.

Abram's Family

[27]This is the account of Terah's family line.

Terah became the father of Abram, Nahor and Haran. And Haran became the father of Lot.[k] [28]While his father Terah was still alive, Haran died in Ur of the Chaldeans,[l] in the land of his birth. [29]Abram and Nahor both married. The name of Abram's wife was Sarai,[m] and the name of Nahor's wife was Milkah;[n] she was the daughter of Haran, the father of both Milkah and

11:26 [i]Lk 3:34 [j]Jos 24:2
11:27 [k]ver 31; Ge 12:4; 14:12; 19:1; 2Pe 2:7
11:28 [l]ver 31; Ge 15:7
11:29 [m]Ge 17:15 [n]Ge 22:20

11:28 *Ur of the Chaldeans.* The city of Ur in southern Mesopotamia is well known in the literature of the ancient Near East, particularly prominent over the latter half of the third millennium BC. A temple already stood there in the late fourth millennium BC and its ziggurat (completed later) is the best preserved from ancient Mesopotamia. An early empire with Ur as its capital existed for about a century at the end of the third millennium BC founded by Ur-Nammu and solidified by his successor, Shulgi.

By some chronological schemes Abraham's time in Ur and Harran coincide with the empire phase. Some have deduced that Abraham was an urbane socialite in this grand center of civilization and that Yahweh's call required a substantial change in lifestyle. Even if it were true that Abraham was born in this highly civilized city, however, we cannot necessarily conclude that he was a city dweller. Ur had its share of herdsmen and farmers as any city did.

Controversy still remains as to why Genesis adds "of the Chaldeans." Unfortunately we know little about the history of the Chaldeans at this period. During the mid-first millennium BC the Chaldeans ruled in southern Mesopotamia (Nebuchadnezzar), and consequently the Chaldeans are associated with Babylon by the prophets Isaiah, Jeremiah and Ezekiel. But prior to this period, the earliest substantial reference to the Chaldeans is in the ninth-century BC inscriptions of Shalmaneser III, when the Chaldeans are located southeast of Babylon near Elam.

A vague, earlier reference is in the campaign inscriptions of Ashurnasirpal II, where the Chaldeans are referred to in passing. Their mention in Job 1:17 suggests that they

GENESIS 11

Cosmic History and Mythology

Defining the term "mythology" is treacherous. Many formal definitions have been offered, and beyond those, one can find a wide variety of popular conceptions that impede fruitful discussion. Rather than offer yet another definition, it is more productive to identify the function of mythological literature. The mythology of the ancient world encapsulated contemporary thinking about how the world worked and how it came to work that way. It features the gods prominently because the ancients found the answers to their questions about the world in the divine realm. If we describe mythology functionally in this way, we can conclude that our modern mythology is what we call science. That is our culture's way of encapsulating how the world works and how it came to work that way. Contrary to the divine orientation of the ancients, our scientific worldview is naturalistic and empiricist.

Genesis functions in Israelite society the same way that science functions in our culture and the same way that mythology functioned in the rest of the ancient world. Genesis offers an alternative encapsulation of how the world worked and how it came to work that way. Like the rest of the ancient world, it has a divine orientation rather than a naturalistic/empiricist one as is common today. But its view of the situation in the divine realm also makes it distinct from the mythology of the ancient world.

Consequently, studying the mythological literature of the ancient world can help us, whose cultural worldview tends toward empiricism, to make adjustments as we try to understand how a nonempiricist worldview works. The result is that we can be drawn out of the restricted perspectives that come most naturally to us. This is the value of the mythological literature for the study of the Bible. ◆

Iskah. 30Now Sarai was childless because
she was not able to conceive.[o]
31Terah took his son Abram, his grandson Lot son of Haran, and his daughter-
in-law Sarai, the wife of his son Abram,
and together they set out from Ur of the
Chaldeans[p] to go to Canaan.[q] But when
they came to Harran, they settled there.
32Terah lived 205 years, and he died in
Harran.

The Call of Abram

12 The LORD had said to Abram, "Go
from your country, your people and
your father's household to the land I will
show you.[r]

2"I will make you into a great nation,[s]
and I will bless you;[t]
I will make your name great,
and you will be a blessing.[a]
3I will bless those who bless you,
and whoever curses you I will
curse;[u]
and all peoples on earth
will be blessed through you.[v]"[b]

4So Abram went, as the LORD had told
him; and Lot went with him. Abram was
seventy-five years old when he set out
from Harran.[w] 5He took his wife Sarai, his
nephew Lot, all the possessions they had
accumulated and the people[x] they had acquired in Harran, and they set out for the
land of Canaan, and they arrived there.
6Abram traveled through the land[y] as
far as the site of the great tree of Moreh[z]
at Shechem. At that time the Canaanites[a]
were in the land. 7The LORD appeared to
Abram[b] and said, "To your offspring[c] I will
give this land."[c] So he built an altar there
to the LORD,[d] who had appeared to him.
8From there he went on toward the hills
east of Bethel[e] and pitched his tent, with
Bethel on the west and Ai on the east.
There he built an altar to the LORD and
called on the name of the LORD.

11:30 [o]Ge 16:1; 18:11 **11:31** [p]Ge 15:7; Ne 9:7; Ac 7:4 [q]Ge 10:19 **12:1** [r]Ac 7:3*; Heb 11:8 **12:2** [s]Ge 15:5; 17:2, 4; 18:18; 22:17; Dt 26:5 [t]Ge 24:1, 35 **12:3** [u]Ge 27:29; Ex 23:22; Nu 24:9 [v]Ge 18:18; 22:18; 26:4; Ac 3:25; Gal 3:8* **12:4** [w]Ge 11:31 **12:5** [x]Ge 14:14; 17:23 **12:6** [y]Heb 11:9 [z]Ge 35:4; Dt 11:30 [a]Ge 10:18 **12:7** [b]Ge 17:1; 18:1; Ex 6:3 [c]Ge 13:15, 17; 15:18; 17:8; Ps 105:9-11 [d]Ge 13:4 **12:8** [e]Ge 13:3

[a] 2 Or *be seen as blessed* [b] 3 Or *earth / will use your name in blessings* (see 48:20) [c] 7 Or *seed*

were nomadic raiders at some point in their history, but it does not help locate them geographically.

Suspicion arises concerning the identification of Abraham's Ur as the famous city in the south because the move to Harran does not seem a logical one from there. The distance is at least 700 miles (1,125 kilometers), and Harran is well off the beaten track for someone traveling to Canaan. If a town were 80 miles (125 kilometers) out of the way (especially traveling on foot), it would hardly be considered on the way. This geographic problem leads some to consider alternatives, and the literature of the ancient Near East preserves numerous other town names with some similarity to Ur. However, since the only Chaldeans we know of are from the south, the designation "of the Chaldeans" in relationship to Ur must be considered a later explanation placed in the text to help readers who were no longer familiar with the location of the town.

11:30 *Sarai ... was not able to conceive.* Barrenness was considered a judgment from God in the ancient world. Ancient peoples did not yet understand the physiology associated with fertilization. They viewed the woman as a receptacle for male seed. Rather than supplying an egg to be fertilized, the woman was seen simply as an incubator for the child. Therefore, if man provided the seed at the proper time (they understood that timing was in relation to menstruation) and nothing came of it, the woman was seen to be a faulty incubator. But this defect would not be seen as simply a physical problem, since no illness, symptom or condition was simply physical. Deity was responsible for creation in the womb, and deity was the one who opened the womb.

Sarai's barrenness would have potentially resulted in a fragile marriage (since failure to deliver children to the family was the most common cause of divorce), in societal shame (since her condition would appear to be the result of having angered a god so that she was therefore unable to fulfill her societal role), and in an uncertainty for the afterlife (since descendants were believed to sustain the deceased in the netherworld). In Abraham and Sarai's case, it also presented quite an obstacle to the covenant promise of having many descendants (12:2; 15:5).

12:1–3 God's covenant with Abram targets the most essential elements of identity in the value system of the ancient Near East. Land was connected to one's survival, livelihood and political identity. Family linked the past, present and future, offering one's most basic sense of identity (more so than self). Inheritance fixed one's place in the family and ensured that the generations past would be remembered in the present and future. When Abram gave up his place in his father's household, he forfeited his security. He was putting his survival, his identity, his future and his security in the hands of the Lord.

12:1 *Go from your country, your people and your father's household.* One reason God may ask Abram to leave these behind is because it is in these three connections that one related to deity. The gods one worshiped tended to be national or city gods ("country"), the clan god ("people"), or ancestral gods, i.e., ancestors who have taken a place in the divine world ("father's household"). As Yahweh severed the ties Abram would have had with other deities, he then filled the resulting void as the only God Abram would need.

12:2 *great nation.* This offer is unique in the ancient world. One can certainly find offers by deities to make someone king and to prosper their line — or even a promise that a particular individual would have many offspring. But the prospect that an individual would grow into a great nation is not broached in any other extant literature from the ancient world.

12:6 *great tree of Moreh.* No hint is given that trees themselves were worshiped, but notable trees became places where various sacred rituals were performed. The significance given to certain trees in the Biblical text suggests that they designated sacred space (cf. 13:18; 35:4,8; Dt 11:30; Jdg 4:5; 6:11; 9:37). Note the eventual indictment of the Israelites that they set up sacred stones and Asherah poles "under every spreading tree" (2Ki 17:10). *Moreh.* The name given to the oak here has been interpreted as suggesting that oracular information was gained here (Moreh means "teacher"). Of all of the divination procedures known from the ancient world, there is no suggestion of trees used as divinatory mechanisms; thus, we conclude that the tree had significance as a locale rather than as a mechanism.

12:8 *altar.* Usually thought of as raised platforms used for offering sacrifices; here, however, there is no mention of sacrifices. Furthermore, sacrifices usually take place in

GENESIS 12:1 – 3

Patriarchal Religion

Around 2000 BC, when the Abraham stories should probably be placed, an interesting development was taking place in Mesopotamia — the rise of the concept of a "personal God." In this period people began to see themselves in a personal relationship with a family god who undertook the divine sponsorship of the family. As a result, most family worship was directed to this god with the expectation that protection and guidance would be provided. When someone sensed that a god had taken his family under his protective wing, the expression used is that they had "acquired a god."

In Mesopotamia this god came to be known as the "god of the father(s)" — a description also used in Genesis (Ge 26:24; 28:13; 31:5,29,42,53; 32:9; 43:23; 46:1 – 3; 50:17; cf. the plural in Ex 3:13 – 16). A personal god was not viewed as the only god, but was the god most directly involved with the family and the one that was the focus of most of the routine religious activity. Devotion to this deity was extended in the family from generation to generation, and as such was inherited rather than chosen. Though the major gods could on occasion serve as a personal god, more typically a personal god was a lower-echelon deity in terms of rank within the pantheon. Only in Israel did a personal God eventually become the God of a nation.

The Biblical text is clear on the point that Abram comes from a family that is not monotheistic (cf. Jos 24:2,14). We must assume that he was brought up sharing the polytheistic beliefs of the ancient world. In this type of system the gods are connected with the forces of nature and show themselves through natural phenomena. These gods do not reveal their natures or give any idea of what will bring their favor or wrath. They are worshiped by being flattered, cajoled, humored and appeased. Manipulation is the operative term. They are gods with needs made in the image of human beings. One of the main reasons God makes a covenant with Abram is in order to reveal what he is really like — to correct the false view of deity that people have developed. But this is projected to take place in stages, not all at once.

The Lord, Yahweh, is not portrayed as a god whom Abram already worshiped. It is interesting, then, that God does not give him a doctrinal statement or require rituals or issue demands when he appears to Abram; he makes an offer. Yahweh does not tell Abram that he is the only god there is, and he does not ask him to stop worshiping the gods his family is worshiping. God does not tell him to get rid of his idols, nor does he proclaim a coming Messiah or salvation. Instead, God says that he has something to give Abram if Abram is willing to give up some things first.

It is possible that Abram first views Yahweh as a "personal god" who is willing to become his "divine sponsor." The Lord provides for Abram and protects him, while obedience and loyalty are expected in return. One major difference, however, is that our clearest picture of the personal god in Mesopotamia comes from the many laments that are offered as individuals seek favors from the deity or complain about his neglect of them. There is no hint of this in Abram's approach to Yahweh. Abram maintains an elevated view of deity that is much more characteristic of the overall Biblical view of deity than it is of the Mesopotamian perspective.

Though we have no indication that Yahweh explained or demanded a monotheistic belief or that Abram responded with one, it is clear that the worship of Yahweh dominated Abram's religious experience. By making a break with his land, his family and his inheritance, Abram is also breaking all of his religious ties, since deities are associated with geographic, political and ethnic divisions. In his new land, Abram does not have any territorial gods; as a new people he does not bring any family gods (though Rachel attempts to when she leaves); having left his country he does not have any national or city gods. It is Yahweh who fills this void, becoming "the God of Abraham, Isaac and Jacob" (Ex 3:16; cf. Ex 3:6,15). ◆

GENESIS 12:1–3

THE COVENANT

Though the agreement between the Lord and Abram is not termed a "covenant" until Ge 15:18, the first articulation of the general terms of the covenant occurs in Ge 12:1–3. The monotheistic worship of Yahweh is a clear distinctive for Israel in contrast to the peoples of the ancient world, but more distinctive still is the covenant relationship between God and people. Israel's self-identity, her view of history, her belief in her destiny, her understanding of the attributes of God (e.g., as holy and faithful), her understanding of her obligations to God (articulated in the *torah*), and the basis of the prophetic institution all derive directly from the covenant.

In each of those areas, despite the existence of similarities with the rest of the ancient world, the Abrahamic covenant marks the departure and underlies the uniqueness of Israel. In the ancient world gods may have been viewed as personal gods who undertook the protection of the family, but they did not make covenants. ◆

9Then Abram set out and continued toward the Negev.[f]

Abram in Egypt

12:10-20Ref — Ge 20:1-18; 26:1-11

10Now there was a famine in the land,
and Abram went down to Egypt to live
there for a while because the famine was
severe. 11As he was about to enter Egypt,
he said to his wife Sarai, "I know what
a beautiful woman you are. 12When the
Egyptians see you, they will say, 'This is
his wife.' Then they will kill me but will let
you live. 13Say you are my sister,[g] so that I

12:9 [f]Ge 13:1,3
12:13 [g]Ge 20:2; 26:7

the vicinity of a temple and are serviced by a priesthood. No ancient Near Eastern document refers to altars used for anything other than sacrifices in the presence of deity; sacrifices were pointless if not offered where a deity was believed to be present. In fact, the only sacrifice by Abram described in the text is the near sacrifice of Isaac (ch. 22). If Abram was not using the altar for sacrifice in a place where God's presence was established, what was he using it for? One option: as a land claim marker. This use of "altar" is attested in the OT in Jos 22:26–28, but nothing in Genesis indicates this function. We are told only that Abram "called on the name of the LORD" at the place of the altars he built here and in 13:4. *called on the name of the LORD.* Can be understood as invoking God's presence, thus anticipating God's presence rather than assuming it. Support for this interpretation is that several of Abraham's altars are built at potentially sacred sites (trees, v. 6; 13:18; hills, here).
12:10 *famine.* In the Negev rainfall is minimal (averaging 4–12 inches [10–30 centimeters] per year), thus making the availability of grazing lands and subsistence agriculture fragile and vulnerable to climatic whims. Water is supplied to the region by wells, and even the rain that does fall does not easily support agriculture. Modern archaeologists and geologists have found evidence of a massive 300-year drought cycle that occurred during the end of the third millennium BC and the beginning of the second millennium BC — one of the time periods to which Abraham is dated. *Egypt.* Recourse there in time of famine in Canaan was not unusual because the food supply in Canaan depended on rainfall, while the food supply in Egypt depended on the flooding of the Nile. The text offers no identification of the pharaoh at this time. By the earliest chronology for Abraham, the pharaoh of ch. 12 would have been one of the kings of the "First Intermediate Period" that preceded the Middle Kingdom (perhaps Inyotef II). Many are more comfortable locating Abraham and his immediate descendants in the first quarter of the second millennium BC, which coincides with the Middle Kingdom. Little is known of this period in Egyptian history, and it is difficult to date the patriarchs with any precision or confidence.
12:11 *beautiful woman.* Sarai was 65 when she and Abram left Harran; perhaps several years have gone by, so we can estimate her age at 70. The compliment cannot simply be attributed to a doting husband, for the text indicates that the Egyptians share this opinion (vv. 14–15). What is not clear is which features lead to this assessment. In 41:2 the cows of pharaoh's dream are described by this same Hebrew term (translated "sleek"), where it conveys robust healthiness — fine specimens. We need not think that every culture is as superficial as our modern culture in their assessments of beauty. A woman in the ancient world could be attractive either as showing good potential for childbearing or as a tool for political alliance. Neither of these seems appropriate for Sarai, however, for she is clearly not entering childbearing years, and there is no political alliance that makes it attractive to marry her; however, we should not assume that Sarah has miraculously attained the beauty of youth. Her dignity, bearing or countenance could all create the impression of a striking woman.
12:13 *Say you are my sister.* This is the first of three narratives

ABRAM'S TRAVELS

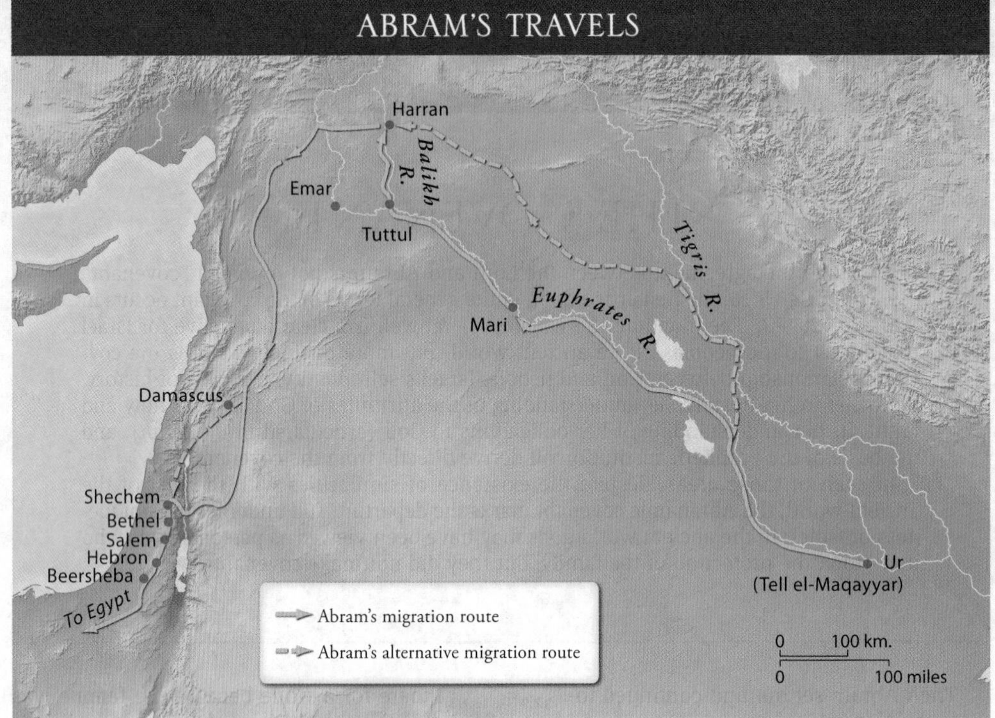

will be treated well for your sake and my
life will be spared because of you."
14When Abram came to Egypt, the Egyptians saw that Sarai was a very beautiful
woman. 15And when Pharaoh's officials
saw her, they praised her to Pharaoh, and
she was taken into his palace. 16He treated
Abram well for her sake, and Abram acquired sheep and cattle, male and female
donkeys, male and female servants, and
camels.
17But the LORD inflicted serious diseases
on Pharaoh and his household[h] because
of Abram's wife Sarai. 18So Pharaoh summoned Abram. "What have you done to
me?"[i] he said. "Why didn't you tell me she
was your wife? 19Why did you say, 'She
is my sister,' so that I took her to be my
wife? Now then, here is your wife. Take
her and go!" 20Then Pharaoh gave orders
about Abram to his men, and they sent
him on his way, with his wife and everything he had.

12:17 [h] 1Ch 16:21 **12:18** [i] Ge 20:9; 26:10

Abram and Lot Separate

13 So Abram went up from Egypt to
the Negev,[j] with his wife and everything he had, and Lot went with him.
2Abram had become very wealthy in livestock and in silver and gold.
3From the Negev he went from place to
place until he came to Bethel,[k] to the place
between Bethel and Ai where his tent had
been earlier 4and where he had first built

13:1 [j] Ge 12:9 **13:3** [k] Ge 12:8

---

in which a patriarch attempts to identify his wife as his sister to avoid problems with the power establishment of the region (see also 20:1 – 18; 26:1 – 11). Interpreters have proposed many ingenious explanations for this behavior. One that was popular for several decades suggested that the wife's status would be elevated if her husband also adopted her as a sister. Others have argued that if the wife posed as a sister, the patriarch would be viewed as a party to negotiate with rather than as an obstacle to be eliminated. Many of the proposed theories have the underlying motivation to save Abram's reputation. Unfortunately, at present we remain ignorant of what sociological realities commended this course of action to Abram. The Israelite audience undoubtedly knew what advantage was to be gained from the ruse, so there was no need for the author to explain it. For our part, we accomplish nothing by devising solutions designed to either vindicate or vitiate Abram.

12:17 *diseases.* The terminology here is as general as it can possibly be. With no symptoms being given, it is impossible to speculate on what these diseases may have been. In the ancient world, with no knowledge of epidemiology, parasites, viruses, bacteria or any of the diagnostic tools of modern medicine, people believed disease had its source in the supernatural realm. Treatment focused on the symptoms and combined herbal remedies with magical potions and incantation rituals. Prognoses could offer hope for healing most confidently if an offense against deity could be identified and appeasement effected. Extensive catalogs of symptoms and treatments are available in medical texts from Mesopotamia.

INTEGRATED CHRONOLOGY OF THE PATRIARCHS

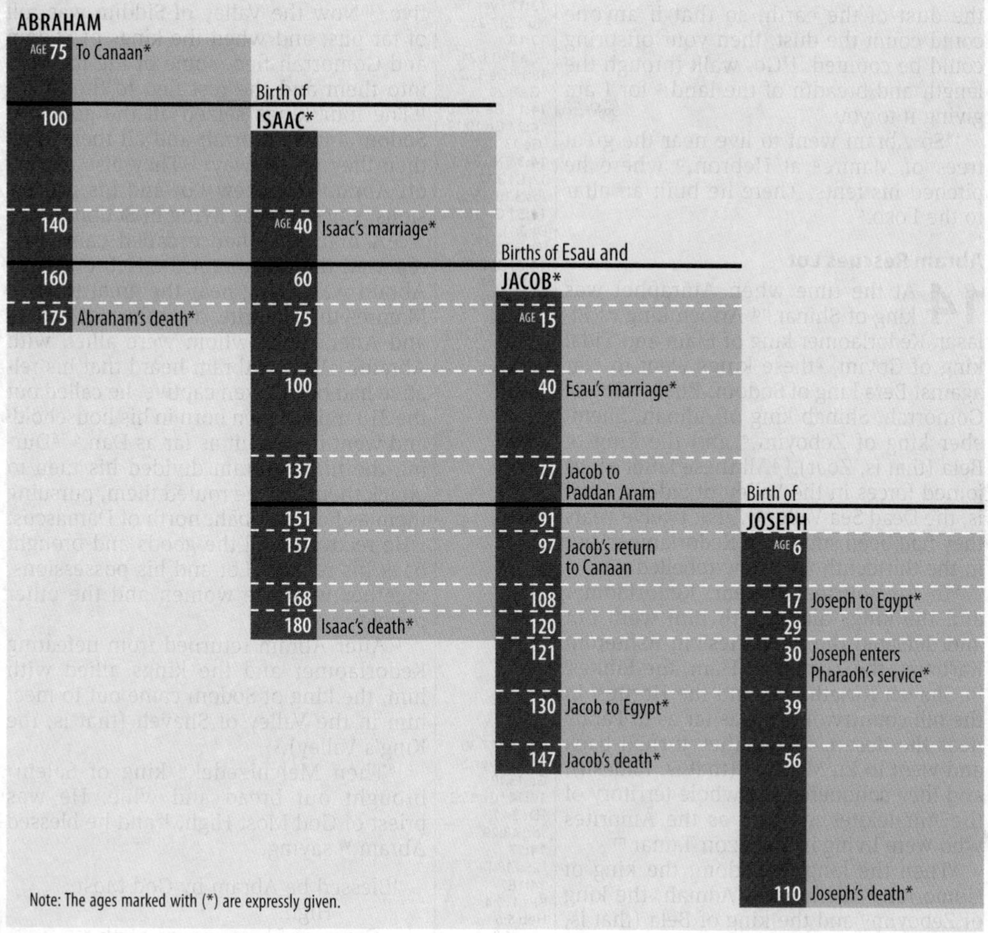

an altar.[l] There Abram called on the name
of the LORD.
5Now Lot, who was moving about with
Abram, also had flocks and herds and
tents. 6But the land could not support
them while they stayed together, for their
possessions were so great that they were
not able to stay together.[m] 7And quarreling[n] arose between Abram's herders and
Lot's. The Canaanites and Perizzites were
also living in the land[o] at that time.
8So Abram said to Lot, "Let's not have
any quarreling between you and me,[p] or
between your herders and mine, for we
are close relatives.[q] 9Is not the whole land
before you? Let's part company. If you go
to the left, I'll go to the right; if you go to
the right, I'll go to the left."

13:4 [l]Ge 12:7 **13:6** [m]Ge 36:7 **13:7** [n]Ge 26:20, 21 [o]Ge 12:6 **13:8** [p]Pr 15:18; 20:3 [q]Ps 133:1
13:10 [r]Ge 19:22, 30 [s]Ge 2:8-10; Isa 51:3 [t]Ge 14:8; 19:17-29 **13:12** [u]Ge 19:17, 25, 29 [v]Ge 14:12 **13:13** [w]Ge 18:20; Eze 16:49-50; 2Pe 2:8 **13:14** [x]Ge 28:14; Dt 3:27

10Lot looked around and saw that the
whole plain of the Jordan toward Zoar[r]
was well watered, like the garden of the
LORD,[s] like the land of Egypt. (This was
before the LORD destroyed Sodom and
Gomorrah.)[t] 11So Lot chose for himself
the whole plain of the Jordan and set
out toward the east. The two men parted company: 12Abram lived in the land of
Canaan, while Lot lived among the cities
of the plain[u] and pitched his tents near
Sodom.[v] 13Now the people of Sodom were
wicked and were sinning greatly against
the LORD.[w]
14The LORD said to Abram after Lot
had parted from him, "Look around from
where you are, to the north and south, to
the east and west.[x] 15All the land that you

13:10 *plain of the Jordan.* The Jordan Valley is at a considerably lower elevation than the hill country and has a more stable climate. The area features lush vegetation and is therefore attractive. It is difficult to determine how the plain of the Jordan relates to the "cities of the plain" (v. 12) since we still cannot identify the location of those cities with any certainty (see the article "Genesis 14 and Ancient History," p. 40).

see I will give to you and your offspring[a] forever.[y] 16I will make your offspring like the dust of the earth, so that if anyone could count the dust, then your offspring could be counted. 17Go, walk through the length and breadth of the land,[z] for I am giving it to you."

18So Abram went to live near the great trees of Mamre[a] at Hebron,[b] where he pitched his tents. There he built an altar to the LORD.[c]

Abram Rescues Lot

14 At the time when Amraphel was king of Shinar,[b][d] Arioch king of Ellasar, Kedorlaomer king of Elam and Tidal king of Goyim, 2these kings went to war against Bera king of Sodom, Birsha king of Gomorrah, Shinab king of Admah, Shemeber king of Zeboyim,[e] and the king of Bela (that is, Zoar).[f] 3All these latter kings joined forces in the Valley of Siddim (that is, the Dead Sea Valley[g]). 4For twelve years they had been subject to Kedorlaomer, but in the thirteenth year they rebelled.

5In the fourteenth year, Kedorlaomer and the kings allied with him went out and defeated the Rephaites[h] in Ashteroth Karnaim, the Zuzites in Ham, the Emites[i] in Shaveh Kiriathaim 6and the Horites[j] in the hill country of Seir,[k] as far as El Paran[l] near the desert. 7Then they turned back and went to En Mishpat (that is, Kadesh), and they conquered the whole territory of the Amalekites, as well as the Amorites who were living in Hazezon Tamar.[m]

8Then the king of Sodom, the king of Gomorrah,[n] the king of Admah, the king of Zeboyim[o] and the king of Bela (that is, Zoar) marched out and drew up their battle lines in the Valley of Siddim 9against Kedorlaomer king of Elam, Tidal king of Goyim, Amraphel king of Shinar and Arioch king of Ellasar—four kings against five. 10Now the Valley of Siddim was full of tar pits, and when the kings of Sodom and Gomorrah fled, some of the men fell into them and the rest fled to the hills.[p] 11The four kings seized all the goods of Sodom and Gomorrah and all their food; then they went away. 12They also carried off Abram's nephew Lot and his possessions, since he was living in Sodom.

13A man who had escaped came and reported this to Abram the Hebrew. Now Abram was living near the great trees of Mamre[q] the Amorite, a brother[c] of Eshkol and Aner, all of whom were allied with Abram. 14When Abram heard that his relative had been taken captive, he called out the 318 trained men born in his household[r] and went in pursuit as far as Dan.[s] 15During the night Abram divided his men to attack them and he routed them, pursuing them as far as Hobah, north of Damascus. 16He recovered all the goods and brought back his relative Lot and his possessions, together with the women and the other people.

17After Abram returned from defeating Kedorlaomer and the kings allied with him, the king of Sodom came out to meet him in the Valley of Shaveh (that is, the King's Valley).[t]

18Then Melchizedek[u] king of Salem[v] brought out bread and wine. He was priest of God Most High, 19and he blessed Abram,[w] saying,

> "Blessed be Abram by God Most
> High,
> Creator of heaven and earth.[x]

13:15 [y] Ge 12:7; Gal 3:16* **13:17** [z] ver 15; Nu 13:17-25 **13:18** [a] Ge 14:13,24; 18:1 [b] Ge 35:27 [c] Ge 8:20 **14:1** [d] Ge 10:10 **14:2** [e] Ge 10:19 [f] Ge 13:10 **14:3** [g] Nu 34:3, 12; Dt 3:17; Jos 3:16; 15:2,5 **14:5** [h] Ge 15:20; Dt 2:11,20 [i] Dt 2:10 **14:6** [j] Dt 2:12, 22 [k] Dt 2:1,5, 22 [l] Ge 21:21; Nu 10:12 **14:7** [m] 2Ch 20:2 **14:8** [n] Ge 13:10; 19:17-29 [o] Dt 29:23 **14:10** [p] Ge 19:17,30 **14:13** [q] ver 24; Ge 13:18 **14:14** [r] Ge 15:3 [s] Dt 34:1; Jdg 18:29 **14:17** [t] 2Sa 18:18 **14:18** [u] Ps 110:4; Heb 5:6 [v] Ps 76:2; Heb 7:2 **14:19** [w] Heb 7:6 [x] ver 22

[a] 15 Or *seed*; also in verse 16 [b] 1 That is, Babylonia; also in verse 9 [c] 13 Or *a relative*; or *an ally*

13:17 *I am giving it to you.* It is common for the Biblical covenants to be compared to political treaties in the ancient Near East. These treaties formed relationships between political entities that required loyalty from the vassal and offered protection from the suzerain. The formal documents that articulate the covenant between Yahweh and Israel compare favorably in form and function to these treaties (see the article "Treaty Formats," p. 303). The covenant with Abram, however, seems different. Rather, it is better to compare this covenant with ancient land grants. In the ancient Near East ruling elites commonly made land grants to their faithful vassals. While the form of treaties and land grants overlap considerably, the important difference is that the treaty is a document that imposes obligation on the vassal, while the royal grant represents an obligation of the suzerain. Abram would have easily recognized what is transpiring here, and it will be formally confirmed and ratified in ch. 15.

14:13 *Hebrew.* The designation of Abram as a "Hebrew" may reflect a social status more than an ethnic identity. The term is usually used in the Bible to identify Israelites to foreigners (39:14–17; Ex 2:11; 1Sa 4:6; Jnh 1:9). As a social status it seems to have referred to dispossessed or disenfranchised peoples. This is the usage of a similar-sounding term throughout a wide range of ancient texts (often transliterated *habiru*, more accurately, *Apiru*, referring to various people groups throughout the second millennium BC). At times the label implies an "outsider" status and that the people are unsettled or even lawless renegades. Other times they are refugees or political opponents. In the Amarna texts they sometimes serve as mercenaries. The term cannot be considered as a reference to ethnic Israelites, but it is possible that ethnic Israelites (and here, Abram) are being classified socially as *Apiru*.

14:18 *Melchizedek king of Salem.* If we base our analysis solely on information from this chapter, Melchizedek is a city-state king of Canaanite, Amorite or Hurrian extraction, and apparently one of the chief petty kings of the region. His city is Salem, generally considered to be Jerusalem (cf. Ps 76:2). Archaeological finds, though scant, attest to the fact that Jerusalem is settled at this period. The city is mentioned in extra-Biblical literature as early as the Egyptian execration texts from around 1900 BC.

[20]And praise be to God Most High,[y]
who delivered your enemies into
your hand."

Then Abram gave him a tenth of everything.[z]

[21]The king of Sodom said to Abram, "Give me the people and keep the goods for yourself."

[22]But Abram said to the king of Sodom, "With raised hand[a] I have sworn an oath to the LORD, God Most High, Creator of heaven and earth,[b] [23]that I will accept nothing belonging to you,[c] not even a thread or the strap of a sandal, so that you will never be able to say, 'I made Abram rich.' [24]I will accept nothing but what my men have eaten and the share that belongs to the men who went with me — to Aner, Eshkol and Mamre. Let them have their share."

14:20 [y]Ge 24:27 [z]Ge 28:22; Dt 26:12; Heb 7:4 **14:22** [a]Ex 6:8; Da 12:7; Rev 10:5-6 [b]ver 19 **14:23** [c]2Ki 5:16

15:1 [d]Da 10:1 [e]Ge 21:17; 26:24; 46:3; 2Ki 6:16; Ps 27:1; Isa 41:10, 13-14 [f]Dt 33:29; 2Sa 22:3, 31; Ps 3:3

The LORD's Covenant With Abram

15 After this, the word of the LORD came to Abram[d] in a vision:

"Do not be afraid,[e] Abram.
I am your shield,[af]
your very great reward.[b]"

[a] 1 Or *sovereign* [b] 1 Or *shield; / your reward will be very great*

Melchizedek makes a brief appearance in Ps 110:4, where the idealized Davidic king is identified as also having priestly credentials "in the order of Melchizedek." Once we get to the intertestamental period, Melchizedek becomes a much more intriguing figure. The Hasmoneans, seeking to establish a Messianic dimension to their rule in the second century BC, justified their priestly-royal prerogatives by reference to Melchizedek. This practice was continued by the Sadducees. In the Dead Sea Scrolls Melchizedek has become the subject of much speculative interpretation. He is depicted as a heavenly redeemer figure, a leader of the forces of light, who brings release to the captives and reigns during the Messianic age. He is the heavenly high priest to whom archangels make expiation for the sins of ignorance of the righteous.

When we get to Heb 7, all of this Jewish tradition is mixed into consideration of Melchizedek. The author of Hebrews is not drawing his information on Melchizedek solely from the OT; he is also interacting with the traditions known to his audience. It is the Jewish profile of Melchizedek, not just the canonical profile, that informs his comparison. As a result, there is nothing in Hebrews or anywhere else to suggest that we need to believe that Melchizedek in the context of Ge 14 was anything other than the Canaanite king he is depicted to be. The fact that he combined the roles of priest and king (as many did in the ancient world) in Jerusalem was sufficient to establish the precedent of a royal priesthood in Jerusalem that was adopted by the Davidic dynasty and therefore came into the Messianic profile.

bread and wine. It is unclear whether these are shared by all of Abram's men or just in council between Melchizedek and the victorious commander(s). It would seem to be meager fare if the latter were the case. Abram's success has signaled the possibility of a major shift of power in the region, and it appears that Melchizedek is taking the opportunity of the army's return to explore what ambitions or loyalties Abram might have. It was common for a meal to be shared when treaty negotiations were being finalized, but generally meat was part of the meal as sacrifices were made in association with oaths to the respective deities. *God Most High.* A translation of El Elyon, a compound divine name/title. El is well-known as the chief Canaanite god in Ugaritic and Phoenician literature, but it is sufficiently generic to use for any high God. Though Hebrew regularly uses the plural form *Elohim* for the God of Israel, El is also sometimes used. Consequently, El could refer to either a Canaanite deity or to Abram's God. The epithet Elyon (*elyon*) is used parallel to the Canaanite El as well as of Baal, but El Elyon never occurs as a compound in Ugaritic texts. No evidence of Elyon as an independent deity is found until the writings of Philo (first century AD). Since El Elyon can designate a Canaanite god, we have no reason to think of Melchizedek as a worshiper of Yahweh or even as monotheistic. It is Abram who identifies El Elyon as Yahweh.

14:20 *a tenth.* Tithing (giving "a tenth") is known in the ancient Near East and in the OT in a variety of contexts. Evidence from the ancient Near East occurs as early as about 2000 BC, where the obligatory tithe is in goods given to the temples. In this period there is also reference to a tithe assessed by the palace. Ugaritic texts attest to grain payment tithes to the royal storehouses being made from villages rather than individuals. No texts suggest a tithe of booty taken in battle.

The question, then, is whether this tithe was paid to Melchizedek in his role as priest (thereby indirectly to the god El Elyon) or in his role as king (tribute and acknowledgment of his political position). Hittite treaties did not require vassals fighting on the suzerain's behalf to give the suzerain a share of their "take," but allowed them to keep captives and booty (though the land remained in the possession of the suzerain). In light of all of this information, Abram's payment of a tithe to Melchizedek stands as unique both in the Bible and the ancient Near East.

14:23 *accept nothing.* Though it seems likely that the armies of the East did not traverse the territory west of the Jordan, they had come into possession of much land in the region by virtue of conquest. Abram's defeat of them would have theoretically given him possession of that land, however its boundaries would be drawn. This right has suddenly made him a political power to be reckoned with and explains Melchizedek's overtures. Abram, instead of exerting his newfound political leverage, relinquishes any and all claims to the land, claiming that he is under oath to Yahweh (who he identifies with El Elyon) not to profit from military action. This claim may have prompted the formation of a document to formalize the terms, which may in turn have served as the source for the material in this chapter.

15:1 *vision.* Visions may be either visual or auditory and are not the same as dreams in that one does not have to be asleep to experience a vision. God used visions to communicate to people; they constitute a more aggressive form of communication than dreams. In contrast to this one, visions in the OT were typically given to prophets in order to communicate oracles or messages that were to be delivered to the people. They may involve natural or supernatural settings, and the individual having the vision may be either an observer or a participant. Besides the category of "dream" in the ancient Near East, there are "waking dreams," but these are the dreams one has when half-awake in the morning, not like Biblical visions. The closest things to Biblical visions are the oracular

GENESIS 14:1 – 17

Genesis 14 and Ancient History

Genesis 14 theoretically offers the best chance of placing the patriarchal narratives in the framework of the ancient Near East historically and chronologically. Unfortunately, details continue to give a mixed picture and connections elude us.

None of the kings of the East mentioned in 14:1 is clearly attested in ancient literature. The issues concerning their identities are as follows:

Amraphel king of Shinar. Amraphel is a Semitic name that has many possible connections to names known from the ancient Near East. Both the "Amar" element and the "*a-p-l*" element occur in personal names. Shinar refers to the southern Mesopotamian plains, better known as Sumer (see note on 11:2). During the early part of the second millennium BC southern Mesopotamia was characterized by independent city-states.

Arioch king of Ellasar. One name from the second millennium BC similar to this one is Zimri-Lim's subordinate, Arriwuk, from the eighteenth-century BC Mari archives. A city named Ilan-Sura is also known from those texts in the vicinity of Shubat-Enlil north of Mari, though it does not seem prominent enough to figure here. Others have noticed the vague similarity to Larsa, a prominent city-state in Mesopotamia during the first half of the second millennium BC.

Kedorlaomer king of Elam. Kedorlaomer appears to be the head of the coalition. The first part of the name is a common element in Elamite royal names (compare Kutir-Nahhunte, who ruled during the Old Babylonian period in the eighteenth century BC. Nahhunte is the name of an Elamite deity, as is Lagamar (represented in the Hebrew *Laomer*). Though the two elements of Kedorlaomer (= *Kutir-Lagamar) are thus attested as authentic, so far that combination is not known among Elamite royal names. Elam is the usual name for the region that in this period comprised all the land east of Mesopotamia from the Caspian Sea to the Persian Gulf (modern Iran). In the first several centuries of the second millennium BC Elam was involved in international politics in Mesopotamia and the West, but no information suggests the Elamites controlled any section of Palestine.

Tidal king of Goyim. Goyim (Hebrew "nations") is the most vague, but is generally associated by commentators with the Hittites (located in the eastern section of present-day Turkey), mostly because the king's name (Tidal) is easily associated with Tudhaliya, the common Hittite royal name. The earliest occurrence of this name for a ruler, however, is about 1400 BC, far too late to match this context. Furthermore, the names of the Hittite kings as early as the mid-eighteenth century BC are known, and none of them bears any resemblance to Tidal.

As a reference to a group of people, Goyim could be handled in a number of different ways. One option is that it reflects how the population of Anatolia called themselves: "peoples" from the land of Hatti. A second option is that it should be considered a way to refer to a coalition of "barbaric" peoples, like the Akkadian designation "Umman Manda," a term associated with the Gutians who overran Mesopotamia at the end of the dynasty of Akkad toward the end of the third millennium BC. "Umman Manda" continues to be used as a reference to enemies of the Hittites and the Babylonians in the mid-second millennium BC. The trouble with this interpretation is that the Umman Manda would not likely be involved in a large, formal coalition of nations. None of these options offers clarification of this king's identity.

While there were many periods in the first half of the second millennium BC when the Elamites were closely associated with powers in Mesopotamia, it is more difficult to bring the Hittites into the picture (and, it should be noted, we are not even sure the

continued on next page

Hittites are involved here). We do know that Assyrian merchants had a trading colony in the Hittite region, and one of the key trade items was tin from Elam. But there is no indication of joint military ventures.

Early Hittite history is sketchy as well, and we have little information about where they came from or precisely when they moved into Anatolia. None of the known empires or major military coalitions from Mesopotamia is known to have made forays into the southern Levant (Canaan) at any time during the second millennium BC.

Likewise, even the "cities of the plain" (Ge 13:12) themselves are not yet attested. The association of Sodom and Gomorrah with Zoar (14:2,8) and the bitumen pits in "the Valley of Siddim" (14:10) both point to the southern end of the Dead Sea as the most likely location of these cities. Arguments for their identification with the north end are based on the distance to travel from Hebron (18 miles [30 kilometers] versus 40 miles [65 kilometers] to the southern location) and the mention of the "plain of the Jordan" in Ge 13:11. The southern location enjoys stronger Biblical support as well as the support of earliest extra-Biblical traditions.

There are five sites of Early Bronze Age cities on the southeast plain of the Dead Sea; these demonstrate that fairly large populations existed there in the third millennium BC. From north to south they are Bab edh-Dhra (Sodom?), Numeira (Gomorrah?), Safi (Zoar), Feifa and Khanazir — with the last being about 20 miles (32 kilometers) from the first. Only Bab edh-Dhra and Numeira have been excavated extensively, and the destruction of these cities (by fire) has been set by archaeologists at about 2350 BC, seemingly too early for Abraham, though chronological reckoning of this period is difficult.

The route described in Ge 14:5 – 10 represents a straightforward march through the land going south on the main route through Transjordan to Tamar and from there north to the cities of the plain in the vicinity of the Dead Sea. Ashteroth (14:5) was the capital of the region just east of the Sea of Galilee and was the home to people known as the Rephaim. Little is known of the Rephaim as an ethnic group, though the same term is used in other places both in and out of the Bible as a reference to the heroic dead. Zuzites, Emites and Horites (14:5 – 6), judging by the cities identified with them, are the inhabitants of Transjordan in the regions eventually occupied by the Ammonites, Moabites and Edomites, respectively (see notes on Dt 2:10,11). Ham is located in northern Gilead, and Shaveh, also known as Kiriathaim, was in Reubenite territory when the land was divided among the tribes (Jos 13:19).

El Paran (Ge 14:6) should probably be equated with Elath at the tip of the Gulf of Aqaba. The Amalekites are engaged at Kadesh Barnea, i.e., En Mishpat (14:7), located in the northeastern Sinai peninsula near the southwestern extremity of Canaan (about 50 miles [80 kilometers] southwest of Beersheba). It is identified with Wadi el-Ain near Ain el-Qudeirat and boasts one of the most productive water sources in the region in its oasis. Finally, the Amorites are met at Hazezon Tamar (14:7). 2Ch 20:2 identifies it with En Gedi, halfway up the western shore of the Dead Sea. The association with En Gedi is problematic if the cities of the plain are along the southeastern rim of the Dead Sea, since the itinerary then requires significant retracing of steps. No known routes travel the western bank of the Dead Sea to En Gedi.

It is difficult to imagine what route would have taken the armies of the east through Dan (Ge 14:14) if they were traveling from the cities of the plain. The only route that would take them through Dan proceeds north along the spine of hills through Jerusalem, Shechem and Hazor — and there is no indication that they went that far west or had any reason to do so. Thus, it was most likely Abram and his allies who traveled the route through Dan, rather than the armies, as they tried to cut off the armies traveling by the King's Highway. Dan is mentioned not as the place where Abram catches them, but as a marker that he is leaving the land. The only other alternative is to maintain that the whole region was different at this time before the destruction in the region in Ge 19.

Consequently, though many authentic features characterize this narrative, no ready links to the known history are currently possible. ◆

2But Abram said, "Sovereign LORD, what can you give me since I remain childless[g] and the one who will inherit[a] my estate is Eliezer of Damascus?" 3And Abram said, "You have given me no children; so a servant[h] in my household will be my heir."
4Then the word of the LORD came to him: "This man will not be your heir, but a son who is your own flesh and blood will be your heir.[i]" 5He took him outside and said, "Look up at the sky and count the stars[j]—if indeed you can count them."

15:2 [g] Ac 7:5 **15:3** [h] Ge 24:2, 34 **15:4** [i] Gal 4:28 **15:5** [j] Ps 147:4; Jer 33:22

[a] *2* The meaning of the Hebrew for this phrase is uncertain.

decisions seen when in a semicomatose state or trance. The idea of "seeing an oracular decision" makes sense both in the context of this chapter (where Abram asks an oracular question, v. 8) and in the context of the prophets (where messages emerge from the vision). As in the OT, these visions are distinct from dreams but can be communicated in dreams.

15:3 *no children … a servant … will be my heir.* Besides today's practice in which children are adopted to provide for the child, ancient Near Eastern practice sometimes

GENESIS 15:9–21

RATIFYING THE COVENANT

Controversy remains about what kind of ceremony is carried out in Ge 15:9–21. What/whom do the pieces represent (possibilities: sacrifice for oath, God if he reneges, nations already as good as dead, Israelites in slavery)? Whom do the birds of prey represent (nations seeking to seize available land, e.g., Ge 14, or to plunder Israel)? Whom do the implements represent (God and/or Abram)?

These issues cannot currently be resolved, but a few observations can help identify some of the possible connections with the ancient world. Before we look at the options, a word is in order about what this is not.

1. It is *not a sacrifice*. There is no altar, no offering of the animals to deity and no ritual with the carcasses, the meat or the blood.
2. It is *not divination*. The entrails are not examined and no meal is offered to deity.
3. It is *not an incantation*. No words are spoken to accompany the ritual and no efficacy is sought—Abram is asleep.

The remaining options are based on where animals are ritually slaughtered in the ancient world when it is not for the purposes of sacrifice, divination or incantation.

Option 1: A covenant ceremony or, more specifically, a royal land grant ceremony. In this case the animals typically are understood as substituting for the participants or proclaiming a self-curse if the stipulations are violated. Examples of the slaughter of animals in such ceremonies but not for sacrificial purposes are numerous. In tablets from Alalakh, the throat of a lamb is slit in connection to a deed executed between Abba-El and Yarimlim. In a Mari text, the head of a donkey is cut off when sealing a formal agreement. In an Aramaic treaty of Sefire, a calf is cut in two with the explicit statement that such will be the fate of the one who breaks the treaty. In Neo-Assyrian literature, the head of a spring lamb is cut off in a treaty between Ashurnirari V and Mati'ilu, not for sacrifice but explicitly as an example of punishment. The strength of these examples lies in the contextual connection to covenant. The weakness is that only one animal is killed in these examples, and there is no passing through the pieces and no torch and firepot. Furthermore, there are significant limitations regarding the efficacy of a divine self-curse.

Option 2: Purification. The "torch" (Ge 15:17) is a portable, handheld object for bringing light. The "smoking firepot" (15:17) can refer to a number of different vessels used to heat things (e.g., an oven for food, a kiln for pottery). Here the two items are generally assumed to be associated with God, but need not be symbolic

continued on next page

Then he said to him, "So shall your offspring[a] be."[k]
6 Abram believed the LORD, and he credited it to him as righteousness.[l]
7 He also said to him, "I am the LORD, who
brought you out of Ur of the Chaldeans to
give you this land to take possession of it."

15:5 [k]Ge 12:2; 22:17; Ex 32:13; Ro 4:18*; Heb 11:12 **15:6** [l]Ps 106:31; Ro 4:3*, 20-24*; Gal 3:6*; Jas 2:23* **15:8** [m]Lk 1:18

8 But Abram said, "Sovereign LORD, how
can I know[m] that I will gain possession
of it?"
9 So the LORD said to him, "Bring me a
heifer, a goat and a ram, each three years

[a] 5 Or *seed*

involved adopting an adult for the purpose of providing for the parents. Through adoption the parents vouchsafed an heir to keep property and possessions intact and procured someone to care for them in old age. In these cases at times a trusted slave was adopted as a son. Despite the attestation of this practice, information is lacking here to suggest that Abram has actually adopted Eliezer. Another possibility is that Abram simply sees this as his only option at the moment.

representations of him. These implements are occasionally used symbolically to represent deities in ancient Near Eastern literature, but usually sun-gods (e.g., Shamash) or fire-gods (e.g., Girru/Gibil). Gibil and Kusu are often invoked together as divine torch and censer in a wide range of cultic ceremonies for purification. Abram would have probably been familiar with the role of Gibil and Kusu in purification rituals, so that function would be plausibly communicated to him by the presence of these implements. Yet in a purification role, neither the torch nor the censer ever pass between the pieces of cut-up animals in the literature available to us. Further weakness is in the fact that Yahweh doesn't need purification and Abram is a spectator, not a participant, so neither does he. In the Mesopotamian Hymn to Gibil (the torch), the god purifies the objects used in the ritual, but the only objects in the ritual in Ge 15 are the dead animals, and it is difficult to understand why they would need to be purified.

Option 3: Confirming signs related to the promise of what will be done to the nations. In incantations seeking to rid a person of the consequences of offense, the torch and oven are two in a series of objects that can serve as confirmatory signs. This same incantation series also occasionally speaks of the person who is swearing an oath in connection with their participation in the incantation as holding an implement of light and/or heat. The strength of this option is that it fits best the context of land promise. The problem is that it offers little connection to the cutting up of the animals. The parts of the animals would refer to the nations to be dispossessed.

The only example of ritual participants passing between the pieces of several cut-up animals occurs in a Hittite military ritual. In response to their army's defeat, several animals are cut in half (goat, puppy, piglet — as well as a human), and the army passes through the parts on their way to sprinkling themselves with water from the river to purify themselves; the idea is that this will ensure a better outcome next time. As with Achan's story in Jos 7, they fear that some offense of the soldiers has caused them to be defeated. The obvious problem is that the context of the Hittite ritual has no similarity to the context in Ge 15.

In summary, the torch and censer figure frequently in a variety of Mesopotamian ritual contexts, and multiple examples can be found of rituals that involve passing through the pieces of a single animal — but these two elements never occur together. There are plenty of examples of oaths with division of animals, but never passing through the pieces. There are plenty of examples with self-curse, but never by a deity. It is therefore difficult to combine all of the elements from the context of Ge 15 into a bona fide ritual assemblage.

The context refers to a "covenant" (15:18), and therefore an oath (by Yahweh) could easily be involved. If there is purification, it would have to be purification of the ritual or its setting, for neither Abram nor Yahweh require purification. Since the pieces cannot represent self-curse, the only other ready option is that they represent the nations, but it is hard to imagine in that case what the force of the ritual is. ◆

old, along with a dove and a young pigeon."
10 Abram brought all these to him, cut
them in two and arranged the halves opposite each other;[n] the birds, however, he
did not cut in half.[o] 11 Then birds of prey
came down on the carcasses, but Abram
drove them away.
12 As the sun was setting, Abram fell into
a deep sleep,[p] and a thick and dreadful
darkness came over him. 13 Then the LORD
said to him, "Know for certain that for four
hundred years[q] your descendants will be
strangers in a country not their own and
that they will be enslaved[r] and mistreated
there. 14 But I will punish the nation they
serve as slaves, and afterward they will
come out[s] with great possessions.[t] 15 You,
however, will go to your ancestors in peace
and be buried at a good old age.[u] 16 In the
fourth generation your descendants will
come back here, for the sin of the Amorites[v] has not yet reached its full measure."
17 When the sun had set and darkness
had fallen, a smoking firepot with a blazing torch appeared and passed between
the pieces.[w] 18 On that day the LORD made
a covenant with Abram and said, "To your
descendants I give this land,[x] from the
Wadi[a] of Egypt[y] to the great river, the Euphrates— 19 the land of the Kenites, Ken-
izzites, Kadmonites, 20 Hittites, Perizzites,
Rephaites, 21 Amorites, Canaanites, Girgashites and Jebusites."

Hagar and Ishmael

16 Now Sarai, Abram's wife, had
borne him no children.[z] But she
had an Egyptian slave[a] named Hagar; 2 so

15:10 [n] ver 17; Jer 34:18 [o] Lev 1:17 **15:12** [p] Ge 2:21 **15:13** [q] ver 16; Ex 12:40; Ac 7:6, 17 [r] Ex 1:11 **15:14** [s] Ac 7:7* [t] Ex 12:32-38 **15:15** [u] Ge 25:8 **15:16** [v] 1Ki 21:26 **15:17** [w] ver 10 **15:18** [x] Ge 12:7 [y] Nu 34:5 **16:1** [z] Ge 11:30; Gal 4:24-25 [a] Ge 21:9

16:2 [b] Ge 30:3-4, 9-10 **16:3** [c] Ge 12:5 **16:5** [d] Ge 31:53 **16:7** [e] Ge 21:17; 22:11, 15; 31:11 [f] Ge 20:1 **16:10** [g] Ge 13:16; 17:20

she said to Abram, "The LORD has kept me
from having children. Go, sleep with my
slave; perhaps I can build a family through
her."[b]
Abram agreed to what Sarai said. 3 So
after Abram had been living in Canaan[c]
ten years, Sarai his wife took her Egyptian
slave Hagar and gave her to her husband
to be his wife. 4 He slept with Hagar, and
she conceived.
When she knew she was pregnant, she
began to despise her mistress. 5 Then Sarai
said to Abram, "You are responsible for
the wrong I am suffering. I put my slave in
your arms, and now that she knows she is
pregnant, she despises me. May the LORD
judge between you and me."[d]
6 "Your slave is in your hands," Abram
said. "Do with her whatever you think
best." Then Sarai mistreated Hagar; so she
fled from her.
7 The angel of the LORD[e] found Hagar
near a spring in the desert; it was the
spring that is beside the road to Shur.[f]
8 And he said, "Hagar, slave of Sarai,
where have you come from, and where
are you going?"
"I'm running away from my mistress Sarai," she answered.
9 Then the angel of the LORD told her,
"Go back to your mistress and submit to
her." 10 The angel added, "I will increase
your descendants so much that they will
be too numerous to count."[g]
11 The angel of the LORD also said to her:

"You are now pregnant
and you will give birth to a son.

[a] 18 Or *river*

16:2 *build a family through her.* The solution proposed by Sarai is not as shocking or outlandish as it would seem to us today. In the ancient world, barrenness was a catastrophe (see note on 11:30) because one of the primary roles of the family was to produce the next generation. The survival of the family line was of the highest value, and it depended on producing progeny. Whatever threat a second wife might pose to harmony in the family paled in comparison to the necessity of an heir being produced.

Marriage contracts of the ancient world, therefore, anticipated the possibility of barrenness and at times specifically dictated a course of action. Solutions ranged from serial monogamy (divorcing the barren wife to take another, presumably fertile, bride), to polygyny (taking a second wife of equal status), to polycoity (the addition of handmaids or concubines for the purpose of producing an heir), to adoption. The third option is the one pursued here; this attempted remedy is consistent with contemporary practice as a strategy for heirship. This option was often more attractive because if the wife were divorced, there would be an economic impact on the family (she took her marriage fund/dowry with her). Concubines bring no dowry, only their fertility, to the family.

A marriage contract from the town of Nuzi a few centuries after the patriarchal period illustrates the practice: "If Gilimninu bears children, Shennima shall not take another wife. But if Gilimninu fails to bear children, Gilimninu shall get for Shennima a woman from the Lullu country (a slave girl) as concubine. In that case, Gilimninu herself shall have authority over the offspring." An Old Assyrian marriage contract closer to the time of the patriarchs reflects a similar solution to infertility. It is therefore plausible that Sarai is simply invoking the terms of their marriage contract.

16:7 *angel of the LORD.* In the ancient world direct communication between important parties was a rarity. Diplomatic and political exchange normally required the use of an intermediary, whose function was similar to that of ambassadors today. The messenger who served as the intermediary was a fully vested representative of the party he represented. He spoke for that party and with the authority of that party. He was accorded the same treatment as that party would enjoy were he there in person. While this was standard protocol, there was no confusion about the person's identity. This explains how the angel in this chapter can comfortably use the first person to convey what God will do (v. 10). When official words are spoken by the representative, everyone understands that he is not speaking for himself but is merely conveying the words, opinions, policies and decisions of his liege. So in

You shall name him Ishmael,[a]
for the LORD has heard of your
misery.[h]
12He will be a wild donkey of a man;
his hand will be against everyone
and everyone's hand against him,
and he will live in hostility
toward[b] all his brothers.[i]"

13She gave this name to the LORD who
spoke to her: "You are the God who sees
me," for she said, "I have now seen[c] the
One who sees me."[j] 14That is why the well
was called Beer Lahai Roi[d]; it is still there,
between Kadesh and Bered.
15So Hagar bore Abram a son,[k] and
Abram gave the name Ishmael to the son
she had borne. 16Abram was eighty-six
years old when Hagar bore him Ishmael.

The Covenant of Circumcision

17 When Abram was ninety-nine years
old, the LORD appeared to him and
said, "I am God Almighty[e];[l] walk before me
faithfully and be blameless.[m] 2Then I will
make my covenant between me and you[n]
and will greatly increase your numbers."
3Abram fell facedown, and God said
to him, 4"As for me, this is my covenant
with you:[o] You will be the father of many
nations.[p] 5No longer will you be called
Abram[f]; your name will be Abraham,[g][q] for
I have made you a father of many nations.[r]
6I will make you very fruitful;[s] I will make
nations of you, and kings will come from
you.[t] 7I will establish my covenant as an
everlasting covenant between me and you
and your descendants after you for the generations to come, to be your God[u] and the
God of your descendants after you.[v] 8The
whole land of Canaan,[w] where you now reside as a foreigner,[x] I will give as an everlasting possession to you and your descendants after you;[y] and I will be their God."

9Then God said to Abraham, "As for
you, you must keep my covenant, you and
your descendants after you for the generations to come. 10This is my covenant
with you and your descendants after you,
the covenant you are to keep: Every male
among you shall be circumcised.[z] 11You are
to undergo circumcision,[a] and it will be the
sign of the covenant[b] between me and you.
12For the generations to come every male
among you who is eight days old must be
circumcised,[c] including those born in your
household or bought with money from a
foreigner—those who are not your offspring. 13Whether born in your household
or bought with your money, they must be
circumcised. My covenant in your flesh is
to be an everlasting covenant. 14Any uncircumcised male, who has not been circumcised in the flesh, will be cut off from
his people;[d] he has broken my covenant."
15God also said to Abraham, "As for
Sarai your wife, you are no longer to call
her Sarai; her name will be Sarah. 16I will
bless her and will surely give you a son by
her.[e] I will bless her so that she will be the
mother of nations;[f] kings of peoples will
come from her."
17Abraham fell facedown; he laughed[g]
and said to himself, "Will a son be born
to a man a hundred years old? Will Sarah
bear a child at the age of ninety?" 18And
Abraham said to God, "If only Ishmael
might live under your blessing!"
19Then God said, "Yes, but your wife Sarah will bear you a son,[h] and you will call
him Isaac.[h] I will establish my covenant
with him[i] as an everlasting covenant for
his descendants after him. 20And as for

16:11 [h] Ex 2:24; 3:7,9 **16:12** [i] Ge 25:18 **16:13** [j] Ge 32:30 **16:15** [k] Gal 4:22 **17:1** [l] Ge 28:3; Ex 6:3 [m] Dt 18:13 **17:2** [n] Ge 15:18 **17:4** [o] Ge 15:18 [p] ver 16; Ge 12:2; 35:11; 48:19 **17:5** [q] ver 15; Ne 9:7 [r] Ro 4:17* **17:6** [s] Ge 35:11 [t] Mt 1:6 **17:7** [u] Ex 29:45, 46 [v] Ro 9:8; Gal 3:16 **17:8** [w] Ps 105:9, 11 [x] Ge 23:4; 28:4; Ex 6:4 [y] Ge 12:7 **17:10** [z] ver 23; Ge 21:4; Jn 7:22; Ac 7:8; Ro 4:11 **17:11** [a] Ex 12:48; Dt 10:16 [b] Ro 4:11 **17:12** [c] Lev 12:3; Lk 2:21 **17:14** [d] Ex 4:24-26 **17:16** [e] Ge 18:10 [f] Ge 35:11; Gal 4:31 **17:17** [g] Ge 18:12; 21:6 **17:19** [h] Ge 18:14; 21:2 [i] Ge 26:3

[a] *11 Ishmael* means *God hears.* [b] *12* Or *live to the east / of* [c] *13* Or *seen the back of* [d] *14 Beer Lahai Roi* means *well of the Living One who sees me.* [e] *1* Hebrew *El-Shaddai* [f] *5 Abram* means *exalted father.* [g] *5 Abraham* probably means *father of many.* [h] *19 Isaac* means *he laughs.*

Ugaritic literature when Baal sends messengers to Mot, the messengers use first-person forms of speech. Such usage indicates that the messengers are not only envoys of the god, but actually embody the power of the deity who sent them.

17:1 *God Almighty.* Translates the epithet El-Shaddai. Much controversy surrounds the meaning of the name El-Shaddai. One Ugaritic text refers to "El of the field" (*il sh*) while Akkadian refers to the "Lord of the Mountain/Steppe" (*belu shadu*), though these may be descriptions rather than divine epithets. The only extra-Biblical use of the divine epithet occurs in the Balaam text of Deir Alla, where the *shdyn* are the beings of the heavenly council.

17:5 *Abraham.* Personal names in the ancient world provided much more than a moniker. Sometimes they preserved recognition of a distinguishing characteristic or reflected circumstances at the time of the person's birth. Often they made statements about deity (e.g., Isaiah = Yahweh saves). Names generally offered information, at some level, about the person's identity and in a variety of ways names were believed to be intertwined with a person's destiny (see note on 2:20). Knowing a person's name created a relationship with that person—i.e., the person was further known by knowing the name. Knowing a person's name also provided potential power over that person, most radically when used in spells or hexes. The naming of a person was one of the most dramatic impositions of authority over another individual. Since the name of a person was believed to be intertwined with their destiny, to name a person meant that you controlled their identity and directed their destiny. In this verse, it is not that God is demonstrating his authority over Abram (though the fact that he can change his name is not insignificant), but more important, he is designating Abram's destiny—to be the father of a multitude. The name Abram meant "the father is exalted." Reference to "father" (*ab*) in personal names usually indicated veneration of an ancestor, so this name looked to the past. His new name Abraham designates him as the significant ancestor as it looks to future generations yet to be born.

GENESIS 17:9 – 14

CIRCUMCISION

Circumcision is well-known in the ancient Near East from as early as the fourth millennium BC, though the details of its practice and its significance vary from culture to culture. Circumcision was practiced in the ancient Near East by many peoples. The Egyptians practiced circumcision as early as the third millennium BC. West Semitic peoples, Israelites, Ammonites, Moabites and Edomites performed circumcision. Eastern Semitic peoples did not (e.g., Assyrians, Babylonians, Akkadians) — nor did the Philistines, an Aegean or Greek people. Anthropological studies have suggested that the rite always has to do with at least one of four basic themes: fertility, virility, maturity and genealogy. Study of Egyptian mummies demonstrates that the surgical technique in Egypt differed from that used by the Israelites; while the Hebrews amputated the prepuce of the penis, the Egyptians merely incised the foreskin and so exposed the glans penis. Egyptians were not circumcised as children, but in either prenuptial or puberty rites. The common denominator, however, is that it appears to be a rite of passage, giving new identity to the one circumcised and incorporating him into a particular group.

Evidence from the Levant comes as early as bronze figurines from the Amuq Valley (Tell el-Judeideh) from the early third millennium BC. An ivory figurine from Megiddo from the mid-second millennium BC shows Canaanite prisoners who are circumcised. Southern Mesopotamia shows no evidence of the practice, nor is any Akkadian term known for the practice. The absence of such evidence is significant since Assyrian and Babylonian medical texts are available in abundance. Abraham is therefore aware of the practice from living in Canaan and visiting Egypt rather than from his roots in Mesopotamia. Since Ishmael is 13 years old at this time, Abraham may even have been wondering whether it was a practice that would characterize this new family of his. In Ge 17 circumcision is retained as a rite of passage, but one associated with identity in the covenant.

In light of today's concerns with gender issues, some have wondered why the sign of the covenant should be something that marks only males. Two cultural issues may offer an explanation: patrilineal descent and identity in the community. (1) The concept

continued on next page

Ishmael, I have heard you: I will surely
bless him; I will make him fruitful and
will greatly increase his numbers.[j] He will
be the father of twelve rulers,[k] and I will
make him into a great nation.[l] 21 But my
covenant I will establish with Isaac, whom
Sarah will bear to you by this time next
year."[m] 22 When he had finished speaking
with Abraham, God went up from him.
23 On that very day Abraham took his son
Ishmael and all those born in his household or bought with his money, every male
in his household, and circumcised them, as
God told him. 24 Abraham was ninety-nine
years old when he was circumcised,[n] 25 and
his son Ishmael was thirteen; 26 Abraham
and his son Ishmael were both circumcised
on that very day. 27 And every male in Abraham's household, including those born in his household or bought from a foreigner, was circumcised with him.

17:20 [j] Ge 16:10 [k] Ge 25:12-16 [l] Ge 21:18 **17:21** [m] Ge 21:2 **17:24** [n] Ro 4:11

The Three Visitors

18 The Lord appeared to Abraham near the great trees of Mamre[o] while he was sitting at the entrance to his tent in the heat of the day. 2 Abraham
looked up and saw three men[p] standing nearby. When he saw them, he hurried from the entrance of his tent to meet them and bowed low to the ground.
3 He said, "If I have found favor in your
eyes, my lord,[a] do not pass your servant
by. 4 Let a little water be brought, and then

18:1 [o] Ge 13:18; 14:13 **18:2** [p] ver 16, 22; Ge 32:24; Jos 5:13; Jdg 13:6-11; Heb 13:2

[a] 3 Or *eyes, Lord*

of patrilineal descent resulted in males being considered the representatives of the clan and the ones through whom clan identity was preserved (as, e.g., the wife took on the tribal and clan identity of her husband). (2) Individuals found their identity more in the clan and the community than in a concept of self. Decisions and commitments were made by the family and clan more than by the individual. The rite of passage represented in circumcision marked each male as entering a clan committed to the covenant, a commitment that he would then have the responsibility to maintain. If this logic holds, circumcision would not focus on individual participation in the covenant as much as on continuing communal participation. The community is structured around patrilineal descent, so the sign on the males marks the corporate commitment of the clan from generation to generation. ◆

Relief in the tomb of Ankhmahor at Saqqara depicting a priest performing a ritual circumcision.

Wikimedia Commons/Science Museum, London, Wellcome Images, CC BY 4.0

you may all wash your feet[q] and rest under this tree. 5Let me get you something to
eat,[r] so you can be refreshed and then go
on your way — now that you have come to
your servant."
"Very well," they answered, "do as you
say."

6So Abraham hurried into the tent to
Sarah. "Quick," he said, "get three seahs[a]
of the finest flour and knead it and bake
some bread."
7Then he ran to the herd and selected

18:4 [q] Ge 19:2; 43:24
18:5 [r] Jdg 13:15

[a] 6 That is, probably about 36 pounds or about 16 kilograms

18:5 Abraham's hospitality includes the offering of protection (shade), the necessary amenities (foot washing), and a generous provision of food and drink. Custom mandated such hospitality from a host when travelers passed through since public accommodation was scarce and the climate threatening. In towns taverns might provide lodging, and there were occasionally strategically located caravansaries, but in many regions one could not expect to find these whenever one needed to eat or sleep. Travelers were welcomed as a ready source of news.

In ancient Near Eastern literature humans occasionally encounter the gods, but rarely the messengers of the gods. In the Ugaritic Legend of 'Aqhat, Dan'el offers hospitality to the representative of the gods, Kothar-wa-Hasis (himself also a god), when the representative comes traveling through town, by having his wife prepare a meal of cooked lamb.

18:6 *three seahs.* About 36 pounds (16 kilograms); the amount reflects Abraham's generosity. *finest flour.* The terminology here indicates that this flour is from wheat rather than from barley and therefore of higher quality. In Mesopotamia, 36 pounds (16 kilograms) of barley

a choice, tender calf and gave it to a servant, who hurried to prepare it. 8He then
brought some curds and milk and the calf
that had been prepared, and set these before them.[s] While they ate, he stood near
them under a tree.
9"Where is your wife Sarah?" they asked
him.
"There, in the tent," he said.
10Then one of them said, "I will surely
return to you about this time next year,
and Sarah your wife will have a son."[t]
Now Sarah was listening at the entrance to the tent, which was behind him.
11Abraham and Sarah were already very
old,[u] and Sarah was past the age of childbearing.[v] 12So Sarah laughed[w] to herself as
she thought, "After I am worn out and my
lord[x] is old, will I now have this pleasure?"
13Then the LORD said to Abraham, "Why
did Sarah laugh and say, 'Will I really have
a child, now that I am old?' 14Is anything
too hard for the LORD?[y] I will return to you
at the appointed time next year, and Sarah
will have a son."
15Sarah was afraid, so she lied and said,
"I did not laugh."
But he said, "Yes, you did laugh."

18:8 [s]Ge 19:3
18:10 [t]Ro 9:9*
18:11 [u]Ge 17:17 [v]Ro 4:19
18:12 [w]Ge 17:17; 21:6 [x]1Pe 3:6
18:14 [y]Jer 32:17, 27; Zec 8:6; Mt 19:26; Lk 1:37; Ro 4:21
18:17 [z]Am 3:7 [a]Ge 19:24
18:18 [b]Gal 3:8*
18:19 [c]Dt 4:9-10; 6:7 [d]Jos 24:15; Eph 6:4
18:21 [e]Ge 11:5
18:22 [f]Ge 19:1

Abraham Pleads for Sodom

16When the men got up to leave, they
looked down toward Sodom, and Abraham walked along with them to see them
on their way. 17Then the LORD said, "Shall
I hide from Abraham[z] what I am about to
do?[a] 18Abraham will surely become a great
and powerful nation,[b] and all nations on
earth will be blessed through him.[a] 19For
I have chosen him, so that he will direct
his children[c] and his household after him
to keep the way of the LORD[d] by doing
what is right and just, so that the LORD
will bring about for Abraham what he has
promised him."
20Then the LORD said, "The outcry
against Sodom and Gomorrah is so great
and their sin so grievous 21that I will go
down[e] and see if what they have done is
as bad as the outcry that has reached me.
If not, I will know."
22The men turned away and went toward Sodom,[f] but Abraham remained
standing before the LORD.[b] 23Then Abraham approached him and said: "Will you

[a] 18 Or *will use his name in blessings* (see 48:20)
[b] 22 Masoretic Text; an ancient Hebrew scribal tradition *but the LORD remained standing before Abraham*

represented rations for a month for an adult. This amount of flour would have probably made up to 60 loaves of bread. In the end, however, we don't know how many people the food is serving. The text only mentions Abraham, Sarah and the three guests, but we learned earlier that Abraham has a large household (12:16; 14:14), and perhaps some of his most trusted servants join him for a meal with the travelers. *bake some bread.* This bread would have been baked in an oven of pottery that probably used animal dung as fuel.

18:7 *choice, tender calf.* The offer of fresh meat is extremely generous since it is not a normal component in their daily diet.

18:9 *Where is your wife Sarah?* It could be inferred from the angel's question that it was unusual for Sarah not to be there—either in a serving capacity or joining them in the meal (there is no evidence of women eating separately in the ancient world). It could also be inferred from Abraham's curt response ("there, in the tent") that this was not just the circumstance of the moment and that she could be sent for. These are not necessary inferences, but there is a possibility that something is indicated here that was transparent to the Israelite reader, yet elusive to us. That is, it is possible that Sarah has had to retreat to the tent and is now confined there—that she has suddenly, much to her shock and consternation, become "indisposed." Menstruation rendered a woman unclean in the ancient world and would have prohibited her from social contact and from food preparation and serving. The text specifically indicates that she had already gone through menopause (v. 11), but if she were to bear a child, her period would need to restart. The timing would have to be precise here. In v. 6 Abraham asked Sarah to bake some bread, an activity often forbidden to menstruating women in Abraham's time, so at that point her period had not begun. Yet she would not be confined to her tent unless she actually had her period. If this is the issue, she experienced the onset of her period as dinner is being served. We know even from the Biblical narratives that menstruating women were at times confined to their tents (cf. 31:34–35). This view is also attested in the ancient Near East. Though somewhat speculative, this line of thinking would explain why the announcement that Sarah would bear a child is introduced by a question concerning Sarah's whereabouts, leading the somewhat embarrassed Abraham to offer the euphemistic explanation that she is "in the tent" as a way of explaining that she is indisposed (note our modern euphemism, "it's that time of the month"). One could almost imagine a transitional, "Indeed, and that is just the beginning ..." It would have constituted a remarkable sign of the resumption of her fertility.

18:23 *Will you sweep away the righteous with the wicked?* In the ancient world people tended to find their identity not as individuals, but in the family, clan or city of which they were a part. Consequently, it was not unusual for good fortune or ill fortune to be experienced on the communal level. The crimes of one member of the group could often lead to the consequences being experienced by all, for they constituted an organic whole. Yet at times a discerning judge needed to impose punishment on discrete individuals rather than on the larger group. This is particularly the case when the group in question extended beyond clan boundaries. Examples of such a concern occur in a few places in ancient Near Eastern literature. In the Hittite Prayer of Mursili, the king prays: "Whoever is a cause of rage and anger to the gods, and whoever is not respectful to the gods, let not the good ones perish with the evil ones. Whether it is a single town, a single house, or a single person, O gods, destroy only that one!" Likewise in the Gilgamesh Epic, after the flood, the god Ea reprimands the god Enlil with the exhortation that in the future he "punish the sinner for his sin, punish the criminal for his crime" rather than bringing widespread destruction. Abraham is making a similar plea on behalf of the cities of the plain.

sweep away the righteous with the wicked?[g] 24What if there are fifty righteous people in the city? Will you really sweep it away and not spare[a] the place for the sake of the fifty righteous people in it?[h] 25Far be it from you to do such a thing — to kill the righteous with the wicked, treating the righteous and the wicked alike. Far be it from you! Will not the Judge of all the earth do right?"[i]

26The LORD said, "If I find fifty righteous people in the city of Sodom, I will spare the whole place for their sake.[j]"

27Then Abraham spoke up again: "Now that I have been so bold as to speak to the Lord, though I am nothing but dust and ashes,[k] 28what if the number of the righteous is five less than fifty? Will you destroy the whole city for lack of five people?"

"If I find forty-five there," he said, "I will not destroy it."

29Once again he spoke to him, "What if only forty are found there?"

He said, "For the sake of forty, I will not do it."

30Then he said, "May the Lord not be angry, but let me speak. What if only thirty can be found there?"

He answered, "I will not do it if I find thirty there."

31Abraham said, "Now that I have been so bold as to speak to the Lord, what if only twenty can be found there?"

He said, "For the sake of twenty, I will not destroy it."

32Then he said, "May the Lord not be angry, but let me speak just once more.[l] What if only ten can be found there?"

He answered, "For the sake of ten,[m] I will not destroy it."

33When the LORD had finished speaking with Abraham, he left, and Abraham returned home.

Sodom and Gomorrah Destroyed

19 The two angels arrived at Sodom[n] in the evening, and Lot was sitting in the gateway of the city.[o] When he saw them, he got up to meet them and bowed down with his face to the ground. 2"My lords," he said, "please turn aside to your servant's house. You can wash your feet[p] and spend the night and then go on your way early in the morning."

"No," they answered, "we will spend the night in the square."

3But he insisted so strongly that they did go with him and entered his house. He prepared a meal for them, baking bread without yeast, and they ate.[q] 4Before they had gone to bed, all the men from every part of the city of Sodom — both young and old — surrounded the house. 5They called to Lot, "Where are the men who came to you tonight? Bring them out to us so that we can have sex with them."[r]

6Lot went outside to meet them[s] and shut the door behind him 7and said, "No, my friends. Don't do this wicked thing.

18:23 [g] Nu 16:22 **18:24** [h] Jer 5:1 **18:25** [i] Job 8:3, 20; Ps 58:11; 94:2; Isa 3:10-11; Ro 3:6 **18:26** [j] Jer 5:1 **18:27** [k] Ge 2:7; 3:19; Job 30:19; 42:6

18:32 [l] Jdg 6:39 [m] Jer 5:1 **19:1** [n] Ge 18:22 [o] Ge 18:1 **19:2** [p] Ge 18:4; Lk 7:44 **19:3** [q] Ge 18:6 **19:5** [r] Jdg 19:22; Isa 3:9; Ro 1:24-27 **19:6** [s] Jdg 19:23

[a] 24 Or *forgive;* also in verse 26

19:1 *gateway of the city.* The central public gate was a place of assembly, business and legal transactions (cf. Am 5:15). Impressive flagstone pavement was used to garnish the gate at Tell Dan. Offerings during festivals were sometimes presented at city gates to honor the gods at the *Zukru* festival at Emar. In this case the name of the gate was the Gate of the Upright Stones (for the storm-god and Hebat, his consort). The gate area constituted special space in the ancient Near East that separated the city from tilled ground; hence, it was the center of many religions and social activities. At Megiddo over 400 people could gather just outside its central gate.

Lot's presence at the gate is neither casual nor incidental. At the gate formal activities took place. Public decisions were made, cases heard, business transacted, and visitors processed or registered according to the conventions of the city. Lot's presence in the gate was undoubtedly related to some of these activities. We have no reason to think that Lot was alone in the gateway, yet he was the one who interacted with the messengers. Perhaps security in the city had been heightened in the aftermath of the invasion in ch. 14 so that they were on the watch for the infiltration of possible spies reconnoitering the city (cf. the spies who go to Jericho in Jos 2). In this view Lot's intention in taking the visitors in not only fulfilled the obligations of hospitality, but also placed them under guard.

19:4 *all the men.* Though the designation "all" can be hyperbolic, the addition of the merism "both young and old" indicates widespread participation. It is unlikely, though, that every single member of the male population is present, for Lot's sons-in-law do not seem to be there.

19:5 *have sex with them.* Perhaps one of the most developed alternative interpretations to the Hebrew here is the contention that when the men say they want to "know" the visitors, they are expressing distrust in Lot's ability to protect the city from spies and they want to "interrogate" the men. Lot identifies this intention as "wicked" (v. 7) because interrogations in the ancient world were typically not gentle. In this view Lot offers his daughters as hostages to be held as warranty that he has the situation well in hand. The most devastating problem to this position is that in Hebrew, when the verb "to know" (*yada*) has a personal direct object (i.e., to know someone), it always has a sexual innuendo.

19:7 *wicked thing.* The text does not discuss what social norms are being broken. The sin of the Sodomites is self-evident and multileveled, blatant and unambiguous. The standard is not the later Mosaic Law but civilized behavior regulated by laws in every city and country. There is nothing subtle or secretive about their behavior. No inhibitions interfere with their threats of violence or demands to indulge their lust. The last thing anyone in the reading audience would be expected to do would be to come to the defense of Sodom or try to make excuses for their behavior. The text also makes it clear that the wicked behavior was not isolated (see note on v. 4). The intentions

The paved gateway at Dan featured a canopied platform where either the king or the image of the god stood. Lined up beside it were stone benches where the elders would have sat and business of the city would have been conducted (Ge 19:1).

[8]Look, I have two daughters who have
never slept with a man. Let me bring them
out to you, and you can do what you like
with them. But don't do anything to these
men, for they have come under the protection of my roof."[t]
[9]"Get out of our way," they replied.
"This fellow came here as a foreigner, and
now he wants to play the judge![u] We'll
treat you worse than them." They kept
bringing pressure on Lot and moved forward to break down the door.
[10]But the men inside reached out and
pulled Lot back into the house and shut
the door. [11]Then they struck the men who
were at the door of the house, young and
old, with blindness[v] so that they could not
find the door.
[12]The two men said to Lot, "Do you
have anyone else here—sons-in-law, sons
or daughters, or anyone else in the city
who belongs to you?[w] Get them out of
here, [13]because we are going to destroy
this place. The outcry to the LORD against
its people is so great that he has sent us
to destroy it."[x]
[14]So Lot went out and spoke to his sons-
in-law, who were pledged to marry[a] his
daughters. He said, "Hurry and get out
of this place, because the LORD is about

19:8 [t]Jdg 19:24 **19:9** [u]Ex 2:14; Ac 7:27 **19:11** [v]Dt 28:28-29; 2Ki 6:18; Ac 13:11 **19:12** [w]Ge 7:1 **19:13** [x]1Ch 21:15

[a] *14* Or *were married to*

of the men of the city have traditionally seemed clear enough, but recent interpreters have suggested various alternatives (see note on v. 5).

19:8 *I have two daughters … do what you like with them.* Lot's response to the demand of the men is startling. Was he really offering his daughters to be gang-raped and probably murdered? An alternative is that his suggestion implied a more subtle, "I would as soon have you violate my family members as violate those whom I have taken in and offered hospitality!" It would be like sarcastically saying to a mortgage company, "Why don't you just take the clothes off my children's backs and the food off their plates?" Such a comment is not suggesting they will really do that. If this is the correct reading, Lot's offer of his daughters was intended to prick the conscience of the mob. Just as they would (hopefully) not consider treating a citizen's daughters in this way, so the same inhibitions should protect Lot's guests. The mob refused to be placated or dissuaded from its intentions and indicated it is even willing to treat Lot with the same violence.

19:11 *blindness.* The Hebrew word here is used elsewhere only for the Aramean army at Dothan (2Ki 6:18). It is a term related to an Akkadian word for day or night blindness. This rare Akkadian word is used only in medical texts apparently referring to a corneal disease. As a judgment of the gods, blindness can be found in the Ugaritic Legend of 'Aqhat. Dan'el curses three towns near where his son 'Aqhat has been slain with the words, "May Baal strike you blind" (cf. Dt 28:28).

to destroy the city![y]" But his sons-in-law thought he was joking.[z]

15 With the coming of dawn, the angels urged Lot, saying, "Hurry! Take your wife and your two daughters who are here, or you will be swept away[a] when the city is punished.[b]"

16 When he hesitated, the men grasped his hand and the hands of his wife and of his two daughters and led them safely out of the city, for the LORD was merciful to them. 17 As soon as they had brought them out, one of them said, "Flee for your lives![c] Don't look back,[d] and don't stop anywhere in the plain! Flee to the mountains or you will be swept away!"

18 But Lot said to them, "No, my lords,*[a]* please! 19 Your*[b]* servant has found favor in your*[b]* eyes, and you*[b]* have shown great kindness to me in sparing my life. But I can't flee to the mountains; this disaster will overtake me, and I'll die. 20 Look, here is a town near enough to run to, and it is small. Let me flee to it—it is very small, isn't it? Then my life will be spared."

21 He said to him, "Very well, I will grant this request too; I will not overthrow the town you speak of. 22 But flee there quickly, because I cannot do anything until you reach it." (That is why the town was called Zoar.*[c]*)

23 By the time Lot reached Zoar, the sun had risen over the land. 24 Then the LORD rained down burning sulfur on Sodom and Gomorrah[e]—from the LORD out of the heavens.[f] 25 Thus he overthrew those cities and the entire plain, destroying all those living in the cities—and also the vegetation in the land.[g] 26 But Lot's wife looked back,[h] and she became a pillar of salt.[i]

27 Early the next morning Abraham got up and returned to the place where he had stood before the LORD.[j] 28 He looked down toward Sodom and Gomorrah, toward all the land of the plain, and he saw dense smoke rising from the land, like smoke from a furnace.[k]

29 So when God destroyed the cities of the plain, he remembered Abraham, and he brought Lot out of the catastrophe[l] that overthrew the cities where Lot had lived.

Lot and His Daughters

30 Lot and his two daughters left Zoar and settled in the mountains,[m] for he was afraid to stay in Zoar. He and his two daughters lived in a cave. 31 One day the older daughter said to the younger, "Our father is old, and there is no man around here to give us children—as is the custom all over the earth. 32 Let's get our father to drink wine and then sleep with him and preserve our family line through our father."

33 That night they got their father to drink wine, and the older daughter went in and slept with him. He was not aware of it when she lay down or when she got up.

34 The next day the older daughter said to the younger, "Last night I slept with my father. Let's get him to drink wine again tonight, and you go in and sleep with him so we can preserve our family line through our father." 35 So they got their father to drink wine that night also, and the younger daughter went in and slept with him. Again he was not aware of it when she lay down or when she got up.

19:14 [y] Nu 16:21 [z] Ex 9:21; Lk 17:28 **19:15** [a] Nu 16:26 [b] Rev 18:4 **19:17** [c] Jer 48:6 [d] ver 26 **19:24** [e] Dt 29:23; Isa 1:9; 13:19 [f] Lk 17:29; 2Pe 2:6; Jude 7 **19:25** [g] Ps 107:34; Eze 16:48 **19:26** [h] ver 17 [i] Lk 17:32 **19:27** [j] Ge 18:22 **19:28** [k] Rev 9:2; 18:9 **19:29** [l] 2Pe 2:7 **19:30** [m] ver 19

a 18 Or *No, Lord;* or *No, my lord* *b* 19 The Hebrew is singular. *c* 22 *Zoar* means *small.*

19:17 *Don't look back . . . !* The angel's prohibition did not concern looking at the destruction. After all, people standing on the walls of Zoar would have been able to watch the carnage take place. We should notice that when the angel gave the instructions not to look back, it was placed between two other commands. If the prohibition was not concerned with seeing the destruction, it seems the three commands form a sequence: (1) Get out of here; (2) don't turn back; (3) don't stop before reaching your destination. The verb "look" must therefore have idiomatic value. The implication is that Lot's wife returned to Sodom. In this interpretation the command of the angel is broken not by glancing over one's shoulder and seeing what should not be seen, but in directing attention back and returning to the city (see note on v. 26).

19:24 *rained down burning sulfur.* The scene is one of divine retribution, and brimstone appears here and elsewhere as an agent of purification and divine wrath on the wicked (Ps 11:6; Eze 38:22). One can only speculate about the actual manner of this destruction, but perhaps the combustion of natural tars and sulfur deposits and the release of noxious gases during an earthquake form part of the story (Dt 29:23). The mineral salts of the region include sodium, potash, magnesium, calcium chlorides, and bromide. An earthquake in the area could easily have ignited these chemicals, causing them to rain down on the victims of the destruction.

19:26 *Lot's wife . . . became a pillar of salt.* This need not be seen as an arbitrary and instantaneous transformation. The destruction is described in terms of the burning sulfur (brimstone) and fire that God "rained down" on the cities (v. 24; see note). Since the destruction did not begin until Lot and his daughters reached Zoar (vv. 23–24), we should assume that Lot's wife did not simply glance back, but returned to the city and was swept up in the destruction like everyone else in the cities (cf. Lk 17:28–32). Many "pillars of salt" would have littered the streets.

19:30 *left Zoar and settled in the mountains.* Perhaps Lot saw that Zoar was just as bad as Sodom, or perhaps he was fearful that the angels would change their mind and destroy the city anyway (without forewarning this time).

19:31–34 The five cities of the plain were the only cities in the region. It most likely seemed to Lot's daughters that they were the last people on earth. Even so, the audience would not have needed prompting to recognize their action as reprehensible. Incest is already viewed in negative terms in the ancient world. The Mosaic Law is not the first to condemn it; there are, e.g., a number of paragraphs treating incest in Hammurapi's laws. Lot is exonerated in that the daughters realize they have to get him drunk first.

36So both of Lot's daughters became
pregnant by their father. 37The older
daughter had a son, and she named him
Moab[a]; he is the father of the Moabites[n] of
today. 38The younger daughter also had a
son, and she named him Ben-Ammi[b]; he
is the father of the Ammonites[c][o] of today.

Abraham and Abimelek

20:1-18Ref — Ge 12:10-20; 26:1-11

20 Now Abraham moved on from
there[p] into the region of the Negev
and lived between Kadesh and Shur. For a
while he stayed in Gerar,[q] 2and there Abraham said of his wife Sarah, "She is my
sister.[r]" Then Abimelek king of Gerar sent
for Sarah and took her.[s]
3But God came to Abimelek in a dream[t]
one night and said to him, "You are as
good as dead because of the woman you
have taken; she is a married woman."[u]
4Now Abimelek had not gone near her,
so he said, "Lord, will you destroy an innocent nation?[v] 5Did he not say to me,
'She is my sister,' and didn't she also say,
'He is my brother'? I have done this with a
clear conscience and clean hands."
6Then God said to him in the dream,
"Yes, I know you did this with a clear
conscience, and so I have kept[w] you from
sinning against me. That is why I did not
let you touch her. 7Now return the man's
wife, for he is a prophet, and he will pray
for you[x] and you will live. But if you do
not return her, you may be sure that you
and all who belong to you will die."
8Early the next morning Abimelek summoned all his officials, and when he told
them all that had happened, they were
very much afraid. 9Then Abimelek called
Abraham in and said, "What have you
done to us? How have I wronged you that
you have brought such great guilt upon
me and my kingdom? You have done
things to me that should never be done.[y]"
10And Abimelek asked Abraham, "What
was your reason for doing this?"
11Abraham replied, "I said to myself,
'There is surely no fear of God[z] in this
place, and they will kill me because of my
wife.'[a] 12Besides, she really is my sister, the
daughter of my father though not of my
mother; and she became my wife. 13And
when God had me wander from my father's household, I said to her, 'This is how
you can show your love to me: Everywhere
we go, say of me, "He is my brother."'"
14Then Abimelek brought sheep and cattle and male and female slaves and gave
them to Abraham,[b] and he returned Sarah
his wife to him. 15And Abimelek said, "My
land is before you; live wherever you like."[c]

19:37 [n] Dt 2:9
19:38 [o] Dt 2:19
20:1 [p] Ge 18:1 [q] Ge 26:1,6,17
20:2 [r] ver 12; Ge 12:13; 26:7 [s] Ge 12:15
20:3 [t] Job 33:15; Mt 27:19 [u] Ps 105:14
20:4 [v] Ge 18:25
20:6 [w] 1Sa 25:26,34
20:7 [x] ver 17; 1Sa 7:5; Job 42:8
20:9 [y] Ge 12:18; 26:10; 34:7
20:11 [z] Ge 42:18; Ps 36:1 [a] Ge 12:12; 26:7
20:14 [b] Ge 12:16
20:15 [c] Ge 13:9

[a] 37 *Moab* sounds like the Hebrew for *from father.*
[b] 38 *Ben-Ammi* means *son of my father's people.*
[c] 38 Hebrew *Bene-Ammon*

19:37–38 *Moabites ... Ammonites.* They historically occupied the regions east of the Jordan River from the Jabbok River in the north to Wadi Zered (= el-Hesa) in the south. The latter is the wadi by which Zoar is located. The northern border of Moab was traditionally the Arnon, but it frequently extended its border north to the Wadi Heshban. If the southern locations of the cities are correct, the three northernmost cities of the plain were then in traditionally Moabite territory, while the two southern ones were in what was to become Edomite territory. The fact that one would expect to find the cities of the plain closer to Ammonite territory would be another point in favor of a more northern location for the cities.

Both Amon and Moab were enemies of Israel for most of their history. It is unlikely that they were literally the descendants of the incestuous relationship between Lot and his daughters (cf. Dt 2:9, Ps 83:5–8); it is possible that this account is included as a political or ethnic slur. Another interpretation may be that the Moabites and Ammonites owe their existence, not to incestuous acts, but to Abraham. As the offspring of Lot, they are related to Abraham; but since Lot is a nephew, these are not among the many nations of whom Abraham is the father. Still, the text indicates that Lot is spared because the Lord remembers Abraham by acting favorably toward him. The Moabites and Ammonites only receive this chance to exist because the Lord has remembered Abraham. This gives the audience of Moses insight into the status of those who live around the land they are entering.

20:2 *She is my sister.* The wife-as-sister motif appears here again, but there are significant differences from ch. 12. Here there is no famine to suggest God's abandonment, nor is Gerar outside the land. Most significant, unlike the prior occasion when Sarah was barren, Sarah is now fertile and the promised son is to be born within the year. Sarah is not obviously pregnant, or she would not have been taken and the ruse would not have been attempted. If Sarah spends even one night in Abimelek's embrace, the paternity of the child to be born would be in question. In ch. 12 Abraham was in danger of losing his wife. In ch. 20 he is in danger of losing claim to his heir, since he would not definitively be the father.

20:7 *prophet ... pray.* The connection between prayer and prophets is not transparent. In the ancient world, prophets gave messages from deity because they were reputed to have a seat in the heavenly council where decisions of judgment and destiny were made. This privileged seat also gave a prophet the ability to effectuate a curse or remove it (cf. 1Ki 13:4–6, which included prayer as part of the prophet's procedure). Their messages comprised the announcement of the decisions of the heavenly council. The intercessory role of the prophet was therefore found in the opportunity he or she had to bring issues to the council table for discussion and to serve as advocate for the earthly party. Then, as spokesperson for the council and deity, he or she would announce the verdict in the form of a prophetic message. Such information was typically given by prophetic message, usually derived from a divination setting (note Balaam's procedures in Nu 22–24). *will pray ... will live.* The Hebrew verbs describing Abraham's anticipated action are modal ("he *may* pray for you, so that you *may* live"). No guarantee is offered of either, though if there is no restoration the death sentence is certain. In this context, however, there is no hint of divination.

16To Sarah he said, "I am giving your
brother a thousand shekels[a] of silver. This
is to cover the offense against you before
all who are with you; you are completely
vindicated."
17Then Abraham prayed to God,[d] and
God healed Abimelek, his wife and his female slaves so they could have children
again, 18for the LORD had kept all the wom-
en in Abimelek's household from conceiving because of Abraham's wife Sarah.[e]

The Birth of Isaac

21 Now the LORD was gracious to Sarah[f]
as he had said, and the LORD did for
Sarah what he had promised.[g] 2Sarah became pregnant and bore a son[h] to Abraham
in his old age,[i] at the very time God had
promised him. 3Abraham gave the name
Isaac[b][j] to the son Sarah bore him. 4When
his son Isaac was eight days old, Abraham
circumcised him,[k] as God commanded him.
5Abraham was a hundred years old when
his son Isaac was born to him.
6Sarah said, "God has brought me
laughter,[l] and everyone who hears about
this will laugh with me." 7And she added,
"Who would have said to Abraham that
Sarah would nurse children? Yet I have
borne him a son in his old age."

Hagar and Ishmael Sent Away

8The child grew and was weaned, and
on the day Isaac was weaned Abraham
held a great feast. 9But Sarah saw that the
son whom Hagar the Egyptian had borne
to Abraham[m] was mocking,[n] 10and she
said to Abraham, "Get rid of that slave
woman and her son, for that woman's son
will never share in the inheritance with
my son Isaac."[o]
11The matter distressed Abraham greatly because it concerned his son.[p] 12But
God said to him, "Do not be so distressed
about the boy and your slave woman. Listen to whatever Sarah tells you, because it
is through Isaac that your offspring[c] will
be reckoned.[q] 13I will make the son of the
slave into a nation[r] also, because he is
your offspring."
14Early the next morning Abraham took
some food and a skin of water and gave
them to Hagar. He set them on her shoulders and then sent her off with the boy.
She went on her way and wandered in the
Desert of Beersheba.[s]
15When the water in the skin was gone,
she put the boy under one of the bushes.
16Then she went off and sat down about a
bowshot away, for she thought, "I cannot
watch the boy die." And as she sat there,
she[d] began to sob.
17God heard the boy crying,[t] and the angel of God called to Hagar from heaven
and said to her, "What is the matter, Hagar? Do not be afraid; God has heard the
boy crying as he lies there. 18Lift the boy
up and take him by the hand, for I will
make him into a great nation.[u]"
19Then God opened her eyes[v] and she saw
a well of water. So she went and filled the
skin with water and gave the boy a drink.
20God was with the boy[w] as he grew up.
He lived in the desert and became an archer. 21While he was living in the Desert
of Paran, his mother got a wife for him[x]
from Egypt.

The Treaty at Beersheba

22At that time Abimelek and Phicol the
commander of his forces said to Abraham,

20:17 [d] Job 42:9
20:18 [e] Ge 12:17
21:1 [f] 1Sa 2:21 [g] Ge 8:1; 17:16, 21; Gal 4:23
21:2 [h] Ge 17:19 [i] Gal 4:22; Heb 11:11
21:3 [j] Ge 17:19
21:4 [k] Ge 17:10, 12; Ac 7:8
21:6 [l] Ge 17:17; Isa 54:1
21:9 [m] Ge 16:15 [n] Gal 4:29
21:10 [o] Gal 4:30*
21:11 [p] Ge 17:18
21:12 [q] Ro 9:7*; Heb 11:18*
21:13 [r] ver 18
21:14 [s] ver 31, 32
21:17 [t] Ex 3:7
21:18 [u] ver 13
21:19 [v] Nu 22:31
21:20 [w] Ge 26:3, 24; 28:15; 39:2, 21, 23
21:21 [x] Ge 24:4, 38

[a] 16 That is, about 25 pounds or about 12 kilograms
[b] 3 *Isaac* means *he laughs.* [c] 12 Or *seed*
[d] 16 Hebrew; Septuagint *the child*

20:16 *I am giving your brother … you are completely vindicated.* Abimelek's payment to Abraham and Sarah is like a reverse bride price. A bride price was paid by the groom to the family of the bride as surety that the marriage would take place. Here the payment moves the same direction, but the woman is moving the opposite direction—from the would-be husband back to the family. Rather than a bride price, it is a restitution payment restoring the woman to her family intact. The text is clear, however, that this is more than a social transaction when Abimelek indicates that by this payment she is vindicated. *a thousand shekels of silver.* An exorbitant amount. We encounter the same number in the Ugaritic poem "The Betrothal of Yarikh and Nikkal-Ib," in which 1,000 shekels of silver was part of the bride price paid among the gods, along with 10,000 shekels of gold and precious stones. In weight it equals about 25 pounds (12 kilograms) of silver; in value it was more than a worker could expect to make in a lifetime (common wage earners were paid ten shekels per year). The king's generous payment is multifunctional. It is his guarantee that Sarah has been untouched, a fee to Abraham for his intercessory role, and an appeasement of the deity who has virtually cut off all fertility in his family (vv. 17–18).

21:10 *Get rid of that slave woman.* Hagar's status in the household of Abraham created friction. Her initial status as Sarah's handmaiden was altered when Sarah chose her as one to give an heir to Abraham—i.e., when she became not just a concubine (whose children would not have the status of a legitimate heir) but a wife. A concubine had no dowry and her children were slaves in the household, not legitimate heirs. She could be sold and did not have to be divorced. But with a handmaiden given as a wife, as Hagar was, all this changed. Consequently a dual claim of authority was established. A woman of Hagar's status could be expelled, but not by either husband or wife alone, and she could not be sold. Her son had the status of a legitimate heir, and she would generally have to be divorced. By sending her away, both Hagar's and Ishmael's claims were being dissolved. This meant that Hagar was being given her freedom as well as being divorced (see note on v. 14).

21:14 *sent her off.* The Hebrew verb used is the verb for divorce (cf. Mal 2:16).

"God is with you in everything you do.
23Now swear[y] to me here before God that
you will not deal falsely with me or my
children or my descendants. Show to me
and the country where you now reside
as a foreigner the same kindness I have
shown to you."
24Abraham said, "I swear it."
25Then Abraham complained to Abimelek about a well of water that Abimelek's
servants had seized.[z] 26But Abimelek said,
"I don't know who has done this. You
did not tell me, and I heard about it only
today."
27So Abraham brought sheep and cattle
and gave them to Abimelek, and the two
men made a treaty.[a] 28Abraham set apart
seven ewe lambs from the flock, 29and
Abimelek asked Abraham, "What is the
meaning of these seven ewe lambs you
have set apart by themselves?"
30He replied, "Accept these seven lambs
from my hand as a witness[b] that I dug this
well."
31So that place was called Beersheba,[a][c]
because the two men swore an oath there.
32After the treaty had been made at Beersheba, Abimelek and Phicol the commander of his forces returned to the land
of the Philistines. 33Abraham planted a
tamarisk tree in Beersheba, and there he
called on the name of the LORD,[d] the Eternal God.[e] 34And Abraham stayed in the
land of the Philistines for a long time.

Abraham Tested

22 Some time later God tested[f] Abraham. He said to him, "Abraham!"
"Here I am," he replied.
2Then God said, "Take your son[g], your
only son, whom you love — Isaac — and
go to the region of Moriah.[h] Sacrifice him
there as a burnt offering on a mountain I
will show you."
3Early the next morning Abraham got
up and loaded his donkey. He took with
him two of his servants and his son Isaac.
When he had cut enough wood for the
burnt offering, he set out for the place
God had told him about. 4On the third day
Abraham looked up and saw the place
in the distance. 5He said to his servants,
"Stay here with the donkey while I and the
boy go over there. We will worship and
then we will come back to you."
6Abraham took the wood for the burnt
offering and placed it on his son Isaac,[i]
and he himself carried the fire and the
knife. As the two of them went on together, 7Isaac spoke up and said to his father
Abraham, "Father?"
"Yes, my son?" Abraham replied.

21:23 [y] ver 31; Jos 2:12 **21:25** [z] Ge 26:15, 18, 20-22 **21:27** [a] Ge 26:28, 31 **21:30** [b] Ge 31:44, 47, 48, 50, 52 **21:31** [c] Ge 26:33 **21:33** [d] Ge 4:26 [e] Dt 33:27 **22:1** [f] Dt 8:2, 16; Heb 11:17; Jas 1:12-13 **22:2** [g] ver 12, 16; Jn 3:16; Heb 11:17; 1Jn 4:9 [h] 2Ch 3:1 **22:6** [i] Jn 19:17

[a] *31* Beersheba can mean *well of seven* and *well of the oath.*

21:25 *well.* The region of Beersheba had limited rainfall, so the water supply was largely provided through wells. Water rights in such ecological situations were established by contracts, as in vv. 27 – 32. That such discussion could become important for international relations is evidenced by some correspondence between Rim-Sin of Larsa and the king of Eshnunna in the Old Babylonian period, where water rights are under dispute and negotiations take place. Well technology required sufficient knowledge of hydrology to identify the location of aquifers and the ability to dig down to them, but also sufficient knowledge of well-building technology, including the construction of a lining to stabilize the shaft and prevent seepage from the sides. The significant amount of labor necessary for such an undertaking makes it obvious why the rights to this water supply would be worth fighting over.

21:32 *Philistines.* Known from the time of the judges and the early monarchy, they did not come into the region and occupy this territory until around 1200 BC — much later than the time of Abraham and likewise later than the time of Moses. The first known mention of the Philistines outside the Bible is in the records of Ramesses III (1182 – 1151 BC). They were one of the tribes of the Sea Peoples who eventually settled in five city-states along the southern coast of Canaan. Abimelek is a Semitic name, and as "king of Gerar" he matches nothing that is known of the Philistine profile. While it is not impossible that this story represents contact with an earlier group of Philistines who settle the area prior to the Sea Peoples, this may simply be an anachronistic use of the name Philistines for the area rather than an ethnic identification of the people whom Abraham encounters.

21:33 *the Eternal God.* Hebrew *El Olam*, the enduring God, which depicts God as responsible for the grand scheme of things. He is the God of the long term.

22:2 *Moriah.* Since the journey takes two to three days (v. 4), the location of Moriah is within a radius of 40 miles (65 kilometers) of Beersheba. This circle reaches from Kadesh Barnea in the south to Jerusalem in the north, and from the Dead Sea to the Mediterranean coast. The only other reference to Moriah is in 2Ch 3:1, which identifies it as the site of the temple in Jerusalem, but it makes no mention of Abraham or this incident. Abraham appears to be familiar with the place, and since he takes firewood with him, presumably he knows that wood is not available in the region (v. 3). In contrast, the wooded hills around Jerusalem would have provided ample firewood for the sacrifice. Furthermore, if the site were Jerusalem, we would expect it to be designated "Salem" (as in 14:18; see note there). Consequently we cannot be certain that the Moriah of Ge 22:2 and the Moriah of 2Ch 3:1 refer to the same place. *Sacrifice him.* God's demand that Abraham offer Isaac is unlike anything in the ancient world. Child sacrifices would have been carried out soon after birth and would have been associated either with fertility rituals or foundation offerings to secure protection for the home. Contemporary literary sources outside of the Bible that refer to child sacrifice or even human sacrifice are virtually nonexistent. The prohibition against child sacrifice in the Pentateuch (e.g., Lev 18:21) demonstrates that it was sometimes practiced, but none of the potential ritual contexts are pertinent to Ge 22. Human sacrifice may have been carried out in extreme circumstances, but there are no dire conditions here. Undoubtedly Abraham would not have considered this command of God commonplace.

"The fire and wood are here," Isaac
said, "but where is the lamb[j] for the burnt
offering?"
8 Abraham answered, "God himself will
provide the lamb for the burnt offering,
my son." And the two of them went on
together.
9 When they reached the place God had
told him about, Abraham built an altar
there and arranged the wood on it. He
bound his son Isaac and laid him on the altar,[k] on top of the wood. 10 Then he reached
out his hand and took the knife to slay his
son. 11 But the angel of the LORD called out
to him from heaven, "Abraham! Abraham!"
"Here I am," he replied.
12 "Do not lay a hand on the boy," he
said. "Do not do anything to him. Now
I know that you fear God,[l] because you
have not withheld from me your son, your
only son.[m]"
13 Abraham looked up and there in a
thicket he saw a ram[a] caught by its horns.
He went over and took the ram and sacrificed it as a burnt offering instead of his
son.[n] 14 So Abraham called that place The
LORD Will Provide. And to this day it is
said, "On the mountain of the LORD it will
be provided.[o]"
15 The angel of the LORD called to Abraham from heaven a second time 16 and
said, "I swear by myself,[p] declares the
LORD, that because you have done this
and have not withheld your son, your
only son, 17 I will surely bless you and
make your descendants[q] as numerous as
the stars in the sky[r] and as the sand on
the seashore.[s] Your descendants will take
possession of the cities of their enemies,[t]
18 and through your offspring[b] all nations
on earth will be blessed,[c][u] because you
have obeyed me."[v]

22:7 [j] Lev 1:10
22:9 [k] Heb 11:17-19; Jas 2:21
22:12 [l] 1Sa 15:22; Jas 2:21-22 [m] ver 2; Jn 3:16
22:13 [n] Ro 8:32
22:14 [o] ver 8
22:16 [p] Lk 1:73; Heb 6:13
22:17 [q] Heb 6:14* [r] Ge 15:5 [s] Ge 26:24; 32:12 [t] Ge 24:60
22:18 [u] Ge 12:2, 3; Ac 3:25*; Gal 3:8* [v] ver 10

[a] 13 Many manuscripts of the Masoretic Text, Samaritan Pentateuch, Septuagint and Syriac; most manuscripts of the Masoretic Text *a ram behind him* [b] 18 Or *seed* [c] 18 Or *and all nations on earth will use the name of your offspring in blessings* (see 48:20)

22:13 *sacrificed it as a burnt offering instead of his son.* Though animal substitution is clear enough in the OT (e.g., firstborn substitution, Passover), the idea of an animal being sacrificed as a substitute for a human being is not as common in the ancient world as might be expected. In the cultures in which animal sacrifice was practiced, the people often simply provide a lavish meal for the deity, at times with the participation of the officiates and the worshipers. The theory that the animal takes the place of the person whose offenses are thereby vicariously expiated is a different matter (and it should be noted that even in Ge 22 no offense is identified as a reason for the sacrifice). When rituals from the ancient world do involve animal substitution, it is typically in the context of magic—i.e., that through ritual the disease, impurity, evil spirit or spell might be transferred to the animal, which was then slaughtered, thus bringing relief to the human.

GENESIS 22:14

"THE LORD WILL PROVIDE"

When Abraham names this place, he affirms that God is superintending the flow of events. This is to be read as complimentary to the name given to God in Ge 21:33 (see note there). Here the designation of the place recognizes Yahweh as God of the short term, caring for the needs of the moment. This is an important point to make in the context of the ancient Near East. In the polytheism of Abraham's day, national and cosmic deities handled the long-term kinds of issues that concerned the stability of the world and national destiny. Other deities were more involved in the daily life of the people. These patron (city, ancestral) deities were believed to have the bulk of the impact in the life of the individual. We must remember that God has still not presented to Abraham the tenets of monotheism either on the practical level (the sole object of worship) or on the philosophical level (no other god exists). Nevertheless, in the names attributed to God, Abraham is moving in that direction. He has now recognized that this covenant God of his is not just a replacement for one of the standard categories of deity. He is filling all the roles of deity. We can hardly begin to understand how revolutionary this was. ◆

19Then Abraham returned to his servants,
and they set off together for Beersheba.
And Abraham stayed in Beersheba.

Nahor's Sons

20Some time later Abraham was told,
"Milkah is also a mother; she has borne
sons to your brother Nahor:[w] 21Uz the firstborn, Buz his brother, Kemuel (the father
of Aram), 22Kesed, Hazo, Pildash, Jidlaph
and Bethuel." 23Bethuel became the father
of Rebekah.[x] Milkah bore these eight sons
to Abraham's brother Nahor. 24His concubine, whose name was Reumah, also had
sons: Tebah, Gaham, Tahash and Maakah.

The Death of Sarah

23 Sarah lived to be a hundred and
twenty-seven years old. 2She died
at Kiriath Arba[y] (that is, Hebron)[z] in the
land of Canaan, and Abraham went to
mourn for Sarah and to weep over her.
3Then Abraham rose from beside his
dead wife and spoke to the Hittites.[a] He
said, 4"I am a foreigner and stranger[a]
among you. Sell me some property for a
burial site here so I can bury my dead."
5The Hittites replied to Abraham, 6"Sir,
listen to us. You are a mighty prince[b]
among us. Bury your dead in the choicest
of our tombs. None of us will refuse you
his tomb for burying your dead."
7Then Abraham rose and bowed down
before the people of the land, the Hittites.
8He said to them, "If you are willing to
let me bury my dead, then listen to me
and intercede with Ephron son of Zohar[c]
on my behalf 9so he will sell me the cave
of Machpelah, which belongs to him and
is at the end of his field. Ask him to sell
it to me for the full price as a burial site
among you."
10Ephron the Hittite was sitting among
his people and he replied to Abraham in
the hearing of all the Hittites who had
come to the gate[d] of his city. 11"No, my
lord," he said. "Listen to me; I give[b][e] you
the field, and I give[b] you the cave that is
in it. I give[b] it to you in the presence of my
people. Bury your dead."
12Again Abraham bowed down before
the people of the land 13and he said to
Ephron in their hearing, "Listen to me, if
you will. I will pay the price of the field.
Accept it from me so I can bury my dead
there."
14Ephron answered Abraham, 15"Listen
to me, my lord; the land is worth four hundred shekels[c] of silver,[f] but what is that
between you and me? Bury your dead."
16Abraham agreed to Ephron's terms
and weighed out for him the price he had
named in the hearing of the Hittites: four
hundred shekels of silver,[g] according to
the weight current among the merchants.
17So Ephron's field in Machpelah near
Mamre[h]—both the field and the cave in it,
and all the trees within the borders of the
field—was deeded 18to Abraham as his
property in the presence of all the Hittites
who had come to the gate of the city. 19Af-
terward Abraham buried his wife Sarah in
the cave in the field of Machpelah near
Mamre (which is at Hebron) in the land
of Canaan. 20So the field and the cave in

22:20 [w]Ge 11:29 **22:23** [x]Ge 24:15 **23:2** [y]Jos 14:15 [z]ver 19; Ge 13:18 **23:4** [a]Ge 17:8; 1Ch 29:15; Ps 105:12; Heb 11:9, 13 **23:6** [b]Ge 14:14-16; 24:35 **23:8** [c]Ge 25:9 **23:10** [d]Ge 34:20-24; Ru 4:4 **23:11** [e]2Sa 24:23 **23:15** [f]Eze 45:12 **23:16** [g]Jer 32:9; Zec 11:12 **23:17** [h]Ge 25:9; 49:30-32; 50:13; Ac 7:16

[a] 3 Or *the descendants of Heth*; also in verses 5, 7, 10, 16, 18 and 20 [b] 11 Or *sell* [c] 15 That is, about 10 pounds or about 4.6 kilograms

23:3 *Hittites.* The terminology in this chapter identifies these people as the "sons of Heth" throughout, except for "the Hitti" in v. 10 (NIV "the Hittite"). In 10:15 the Hittites are descendants of Canaan and listed among largely Semitic peoples. Outside of the Bible, the most well-known Hittites were Indo-European peoples who inhabited central Anatolia in the middle of the second millennium BC. After the collapse of that empire around 1200 BC, remnants of the civilization persevered in northern Syria. The term "Hittites" for the Anatolian peoples derives from their association with the land of Hatti, not only in their own texts but also in Ugaritic, Egyptian and Akkadian texts. The Indo-European "Hittites" (speaking Nesite) gained prominence over the original Hattian inhabitants beginning about 2000 BC. The OT probably makes no reference to the Nesite Hittites of the empire age. The Anatolian people referred to as "Hittites" should more precisely be referred to as "Hattians" or "Nesites" (referring to land and language, respectively); these should not be confused with the Semitic Hethites/Hittites of Genesis.
23:4 *burial site.* The negotiations here are not concerned with the rights to dig a hole and mark a grave. Contemporary burial practices favored rock-cut or cave tombs, which were meant to accommodate the clan through generations. Bodies would be laid out on rock shelves until nothing remained but the bones, at which point the bones would either be cleared to the back of the tomb or relocated into a container of some sort to make room for another body. The use of family tombs may partially explain the use of the phrase "gathered to his people" (25:8). Deceased ancestors were honored through a variety of practices that did not stop after burial. These practices made it desirable for tombs to be in proximity to somewhat permanent settlements.
23:9 *sell it to me for the full price.* Abraham negotiates for the long term. If he had been willing to accept the land on a grant basis, the land could have been reclaimed in a later generation or in hard times.
23:15 *four hundred shekels of silver.* A significant amount of money. It equals about 10 pounds (4.6 kilograms) of silver, but its value can be assessed by the fact that the average wage was 10 shekels of silver per year. Having said this, it is still not determinable whether the price is fair, exorbitant or a bargain because the text does not indicate the size of the parcel of land. It is much less than what Omri paid for the much larger site of Samaria (150 pounds [68 kilograms] or 6,000 shekels of silver; see NIV text note on 1Ki 16:24), and it is not comparable to what David paid for the site of the temple (15 pounds [6.9 kilograms] or 600 shekels of *gold*; see NIV text note on 1Ch 21:25).

it were deeded[i] to Abraham by the Hittites
as a burial site.

Isaac and Rebekah

24 Abraham was now very old, and
the LORD had blessed him in ev-
ery way.[j] 2He said to the senior servant
in his household, the one in charge of all
that he had,[k] "Put your hand under my
thigh.[l] 3I want you to swear by the LORD,
the God of heaven and the God of earth,[m]
that you will not get a wife for my son[n]
from the daughters of the Canaanites,[o]
among whom I am living, 4but will go to
my country and my own relatives[p] and get
a wife for my son Isaac."
5The servant asked him, "What if the
woman is unwilling to come back with me
to this land? Shall I then take your son
back to the country you came from?"
6"Make sure that you do not take my son
back there," Abraham said. 7"The LORD,
the God of heaven, who brought me out of
my father's household and my native land
and who spoke to me and promised me
on oath, saying, 'To your offspring[a][q] I will
give this land'[r]—he will send his angel
before you[s] so that you can get a wife for
my son from there. 8If the woman is unwilling to come back with you, then you
will be released from this oath of mine.
Only do not take my son back there." 9So
the servant put his hand under the thigh[t]
of his master Abraham and swore an oath
to him concerning this matter.
10Then the servant left, taking with him
ten of his master's camels loaded with all
kinds of good things from his master. He
set out for Aram Naharaim[b] and made his
way to the town of Nahor. 11He had the
camels kneel down near the well[u] outside
the town; it was toward evening, the time
the women go out to draw water.[v]
12Then he prayed, "LORD, God of my
master Abraham,[w] make me successful
today, and show kindness to my master
Abraham. 13See, I am standing beside this
spring, and the daughters of the townspeople are coming out to draw water.
14May it be that when I say to a young
woman, 'Please let down your jar that I
may have a drink,' and she says, 'Drink,
and I'll water your camels too'—let her be
the one you have chosen for your servant
Isaac. By this I will know[x] that you have
shown kindness to my master."
15Before he had finished praying,[y] Rebekah[z] came out with her jar on her
shoulder. She was the daughter of Bethuel son of Milkah,[a] who was the wife of
Abraham's brother Nahor.[b] 16The woman
was very beautiful,[c] a virgin; no man had
ever slept with her. She went down to the
spring, filled her jar and came up again.
17The servant hurried to meet her and
said, "Please give me a little water from
your jar."
18"Drink,[d] my lord," she said, and
quickly lowered the jar to her hands and
gave him a drink.
19After she had given him a drink, she
said, "I'll draw water for your camels too,[e]
until they have had enough to drink." 20So

23:20 [i]Jer 32:10
24:1 [j]ver 35
24:2 [k]Ge 39:4-6 [l]ver 9; Ge 47:29
24:3 [m]Ge 14:19 [n]Ge 28:1; Dt 7:3 [o]Ge 10:15-19
24:4 [p]Ge 12:1; 28:2
24:7 [q]Gal 3:16* [r]Ge 12:7; 13:15 [s]Ex 23:20,23
24:9 [t]ver 2
24:11 [u]Ex 2:15 [v]ver 13; 1Sa 9:11
24:12 [w]ver 27,42, 48; Ge 26:24; Ex 3:6,15,16
24:14 [x]Jdg 6:17,37
24:15 [y]ver 45 [z]Ge 22:23 [a]Ge 22:20 [b]Ge 11:29
24:16 [c]Ge 26:7
24:18 [d]ver 14
24:19 [e]ver 14

[a] 7 Or *seed* [b] 10 That is, Northwest Mesopotamia

24:2 *under my thigh.* It is possible that the oath is sworn on the genitals of Abraham, which would then be understood to be binding even if Abraham should die. None of this can be confirmed, however, because the text offers no explanation and no parallels have been found in the ancient Near East.

24:4 *go to my country and my own relatives and get a wife for my son Isaac.* In the ancient world it was common to restrict or at least prefer marriage within the social group, a practice called endogamy. Endogamy is particularly significant in social contexts that emphasize inheritance. In this way the lineage is isolated for purposes of social status and property ownership. In Israel the concerns are ethnic because the land was promised to Abraham and his family and he is avoiding assimilation with the people in the land. At this point in history, no one else shares Abraham's beliefs or worships "the God of Abraham" (31:53)—at least as far as we know; certainly Laban and his family do not, so this is not a matter of marrying within the faith. We must keep in mind that Abraham's relatives are no more monotheistic than the Canaanites. They are not worshipers of Yahweh. Abraham was called out of a polytheistic setting. The proscription here is concerned about ethnic separation.

24:14 *May it be that when I say.* In seeking guidance from God, the servant uses a strategy much like that used for seeking oracles in the ancient world. In an oracle a binary question (i.e., yes/no) was put to deity and then a device of some sort was used as a means by which the deity could give an answer. In the ancient world the device often used was either casting lots or employing a divination priest to perform extispicy (the investigation of the entrails of sacrificed animals for positive or negative signs). In Israel the high priest used the Urim and Thummim as a way of conducting such an oracular procedure. Since Abraham's servant has no lots to cast and has no immediate access to specialized professionals, he has to improvise. He therefore resorts to using his current surroundings to devise an oracle. When this procedure is used, it is typical that a highly irregular occurrence designates "yes" and the normal turn of events designates "no," with the expectation that God will thereby communicate his answer. Here the question is whether the girl whom the servant approaches is the chosen mate for Isaac. The designated indicator of a "yes" answer is if the girl offers to do far beyond what human nature or the conventions of hospitality would dictate, specifically, to water all his camels when he asks only for a drink for himself. Such an unusual offer would serve as evidence that deity was overriding all natural instinct and social etiquette. For similar mechanistic oracles, see Jdg 6:36–40; 1Sa 6:7–12.

24:19 *I'll draw water for your camels too.* If the servant's camels had gone several days without water, they could potentially drink up to 25 gallons (almost 100 liters) each.

she quickly emptied her jar into the trough, ran back to the well to draw more water, and drew enough for all his camels. 21 Without saying a word, the man watched her closely to learn whether or not the LORD had made his journey successful.[f]

22 When the camels had finished drinking, the man took out a gold nose ring[g] weighing a beka[a] and two gold bracelets weighing ten shekels.[b] 23 Then he asked, "Whose daughter are you? Please tell me, is there room in your father's house for us to spend the night?"

24 She answered him, "I am the daughter of Bethuel, the son that Milkah bore to Nahor.[h]" 25 And she added, "We have plenty of straw and fodder, as well as room for you to spend the night."

26 Then the man bowed down and worshiped the LORD,[i] 27 saying, "Praise be to the LORD,[j] the God of my master Abraham, who has not abandoned his kindness and faithfulness[k] to my master. As for me, the LORD has led me on the journey[l] to the house of my master's relatives."[m]

28 The young woman ran and told her mother's household about these things. 29 Now Rebekah had a brother named Laban,[n] and he hurried out to the man at the spring. 30 As soon as he had seen the nose ring, and the bracelets on his sister's arms, and had heard Rebekah tell what the man said to her, he went out to the man and found him standing by the camels near the spring. 31 "Come, you who are blessed by the LORD,"[o] he said. "Why are you standing out here? I have prepared the house and a place for the camels."

32 So the man went to the house, and the camels were unloaded. Straw and fodder were brought for the camels, and water for him and his men to wash their feet.[p] 33 Then food was set before him, but he said, "I will not eat until I have told you what I have to say."

"Then tell us," Laban said.

34 So he said, "I am Abraham's servant. 35 The LORD has blessed my master abundantly,[q] and he has become wealthy. He has given him sheep and cattle, silver and gold, male and female servants, and camels and donkeys.[r] 36 My master's wife Sarah has borne him a son in her old age,[s] and he has given him everything he owns.[t] 37 And my master made me swear an oath, and said, 'You must not get a wife for my son from the daughters of the Canaanites, in whose land I live,[u] 38 but go to my father's family and to my own clan, and get a wife for my son.'[v]

39 "Then I asked my master, 'What if the woman will not come back with me?'[w]

40 "He replied, 'The LORD, before whom I have walked faithfully, will send his angel with you[x] and make your journey a success, so that you can get a wife for my son from my own clan and from my father's family. 41 You will be released from my oath if, when you go to my clan, they refuse to give her to you—then you will be released from my oath.'[y]

42 "When I came to the spring today, I said, 'LORD, God of my master Abraham, if you will, please grant success[z] to the journey on which I have come. 43 See, I am standing beside this spring.[a] If a young woman comes out to draw water and I say to her, "Please let me drink a little water from your jar,"[b] 44 and if she says to me, "Drink, and I'll draw water for your camels too," let her be the one the LORD has chosen for my master's son.'

45 "Before I finished praying in my heart,[c] Rebekah came out, with her jar on her shoulder.[d] She went down to the spring and drew water, and I said to her, 'Please give me a drink.'[e]

46 "She quickly lowered her jar from her shoulder and said, 'Drink, and I'll water your camels too.'[f] So I drank, and she watered the camels also.

47 "I asked her, 'Whose daughter are you?'[g]

"She said, 'The daughter of Bethuel son of Nahor, whom Milkah bore to him.'[h]

"Then I put the ring in her nose and the bracelets on her arms,[i] 48 and I bowed down and worshiped the LORD.[j] I praised the LORD, the God of my master Abraham, who had led me on the right road to get the granddaughter of my master's brother for his son.[k] 49 Now if you will show kindness and faithfulness[l] to my master, tell me; and if not, tell me, so I may know which way to turn."

50 Laban and Bethuel answered, "This is from the LORD;[m] we can say nothing to you one way or the other.[n] 51 Here is Rebekah; take her and go, and let her become the wife of your master's son, as the LORD has directed."

52 When Abraham's servant heard what they said, he bowed down to the ground

a 22 That is, about 1/5 ounce or about 5.7 grams
b 22 That is, about 4 ounces or about 115 grams

24:21 [f] ver 12 **24:22** [g] ver 47 **24:24** [h] ver 15 **24:26** [i] ver 48, 52; Ex 4:31 **24:27** [j] Ex 18:10; Ru 4:14; 1Sa 25:32 [k] ver 49; Ge 32:10; Ps 98:3 [l] ver 21 [m] ver 12, 48 **24:29** [n] ver 4; Ge 29:5, 12, 13 **24:31** [o] Ge 26:29; Ru 3:10; Ps 115:15 **24:32** [p] Ge 43:24; Jdg 19:21 **24:35** [q] ver 1 [r] Ge 13:2 **24:36** [s] Ge 21:2, 10 [t] Ge 25:5 **24:37** [u] ver 3 **24:38** [v] ver 4 **24:39** [w] ver 5 **24:40** [x] ver 7 **24:41** [y] ver 8 **24:42** [z] ver 12 **24:43** [a] ver 13 [b] ver 14 **24:45** [c] 1Sa 1:13 [d] ver 15 [e] ver 17 **24:46** [f] ver 18-19 **24:47** [g] ver 23 [h] ver 24 [i] Eze 16:11-12 **24:48** [j] ver 26 [k] ver 27 **24:49** [l] Ge 47:29; Jos 2:14 **24:50** [m] Ps 118:23 [n] Ge 31:7, 24, 29, 42

Given the standard size of the vessels used to draw water, this would mean that Rebekah would have to draw eight to ten jars for each camel, thus requiring nearly a hundred trips from the well—several hours of work. Since it was already almost evening when the scene opens (v. 11), it is sensible to conclude that the camels may have been watered more recently and would have required considerably less water than that. But Rebekah would not have known the current needs of the camels, so the offer remains impressive and extraordinary.

before the LORD.[o] 53Then the servant
brought out gold and silver jewelry and
articles of clothing and gave them to Rebekah; he also gave costly gifts[p] to her
brother and to her mother. 54Then he and
the men who were with him ate and drank
and spent the night there.

When they got up the next morning, he
said, "Send me on my way[q] to my master."

55But her brother and her mother replied, "Let the young woman remain with
us ten days or so; then you[a] may go."
56But he said to them, "Do not detain
me, now that the LORD has granted success
to my journey. Send me on my way so I
may go to my master."

24:52 [o] ver 26 24:53 [p] ver 10, 22 24:54 [q] ver 56, 59

[a] 55 Or *she*

GENESIS 24:50 – 54

Marriage Contracts

In addition to the nose ring and bracelets initially presented in Ge 24:22, the remainder of the bride price is summarized here. Marriage customs included an exchange of wealth between the families with several purposes. The *marriage price* indicated here is given from the groom's family to the bride's family. This transfer is part of the socioeconomic system of provision and should not be thought of as purchase of chattel. In Sumerian sources, one form of bride wealth (*nigmussa*) is made up primarily of foodstuffs presented just before the wedding feast. This type of gift would have been an impractical option for Abraham's servant because of the long trip. Provision of foodstuff by the family brings to mind our modern practice of the groom's parents bearing the responsibility for the rehearsal dinner and the bride's family bearing the responsibility for the reception. A less common form (*nigdea*) sometimes includes precious objects and is presented when the agreement is made between the families. The latter is more likely represented here.

The transfer often took place in two parts: a small "down payment" offered as surety that the wedding would take place, with the remainder changing hands shortly before the wedding. These two stages are approximated in Ge 24:22,53. In the Nuzi texts of the mid-second millennium BC, bride prices averaged 30 to 40 shekels of silver, or three to four years of average income.

The *dowry* was given by the bride's family to the bride (a transaction from father to daughter, not between families per se) and represented her inheritance from the family since she typically did not inherit land. Movable property and valuables were common dowry items. Its function was to provide for the support of the woman should the husband die, desert or divorce her. At times, part of the dowry remained the personal property of the wife, but whatever its disposition, it could not be sold without her consent. In like manner, however, she was not free to dispose of it. If it were not used to support her at some stage in life, it would become part of the inheritance of her children. The dowry of Rebekah is not detailed, though her nurse may have been part of it (24:59).

It is neither typical nor necessary for the woman to be consulted with regard to marriage arrangements by the family (24:57), though certainly the ones to be married were known to express their opinions or even exercise choice through various legitimate and less-than-legitimate options. It should be noted here, however, that it is possible that Rebekah's opinion is only asked when the question concerns the unusual circumstance of her being so quickly and completely removed from the potential protection provided by her family. Until a woman conceived and bore a child to her new family, her status within the family was tenuous, and the proximity of her father's family would have been a strong motivator for her husband not to mistreat her or discard her. ◆

57Then they said, "Let's call the young woman and ask her about it." 58So they called Rebekah and asked her, "Will you go with this man?"

"I will go," she said.

59So they sent their sister Rebekah on her way, along with her nurse[r] and Abraham's servant and his men. 60And they blessed Rebekah and said to her,

"Our sister, may you increase
to thousands upon thousands;[s]
may your offspring possess
the cities of their enemies."[t]

61Then Rebekah and her attendants got ready and mounted the camels and went back with the man. So the servant took Rebekah and left.

62Now Isaac had come from Beer Lahai Roi,[u] for he was living in the Negev.[v] 63He went out to the field one evening to meditate,[aw] and as he looked up, he saw camels approaching. 64Rebekah also looked up and saw Isaac. She got down from her camel 65and asked the servant, "Who is that man in the field coming to meet us?"

"He is my master," the servant answered. So she took her veil and covered herself.

66Then the servant told Isaac all he had done. 67Isaac brought her into the tent of his mother Sarah, and he married Rebekah.[x] So she became his wife, and he loved her;[y] and Isaac was comforted after his mother's death.[z]

The Death of Abraham

25:1-4pp — 1Ch 1:32-33

25 Abraham had taken another wife, whose name was Keturah. 2She bore him Zimran, Jokshan, Medan, Midian, Ishbak and Shuah.[a] 3Jokshan was the father of Sheba and Dedan; the descendants of Dedan were the Ashurites, the Letushites and the Leummites. 4The sons of Midian were Ephah, Epher, Hanok, Abida and Eldaah. All these were descendants of Keturah.

5Abraham left everything he owned to Isaac.[b] 6But while he was still living, he gave gifts to the sons of his concubines[c] and sent them away from his son Isaac[d] to the land of the east.

7Abraham lived a hundred and seventy-five years. 8Then Abraham breathed his last and died at a good old age,[e] an old man and full of years; and he was gathered to his people.[f] 9His sons Isaac and Ishmael buried him[g] in the cave of Machpelah near Mamre, in the field of Ephron son of Zohar the Hittite,[h] 10the field Abraham had bought from the Hittites.[bi] There Abraham was buried with his wife Sarah. 11After Abraham's death, God blessed his son Isaac, who then lived near Beer Lahai Roi.[j]

Ishmael's Sons

25:12-16pp — 1Ch 1:29-31

12This is the account of the family line of Abraham's son Ishmael, whom Sarah's slave, Hagar[k] the Egyptian, bore to Abraham.[l]

13These are the names of the sons of Ishmael, listed in the order of their birth: Nebaioth the firstborn of Ishmael, Kedar, Adbeel, Mibsam, 14Mishma, Dumah, Massa, 15Hadad, Tema, Jetur, Naphish and Kedemah. 16These were the sons of Ishmael, and these are the names of the twelve

24:59 [r]Ge 35:8
24:60 [s]Ge 17:16 [t]Ge 22:17
24:62 [u]Ge 16:14; 25:11 [v]Ge 20:1
24:63 [w]Ps 1:2; 77:12; 119:15, 27,48,97,148; 143:5; 145:5
24:67 [x]Ge 25:20 [y]Ge 29:18,20 [z]Ge 23:1-2
25:2 [a]1Ch 1:32, 33
25:5 [b]Ge 24:36
25:6 [c]Ge 22:24 [d]Ge 21:10,14
25:8 [e]Ge 15:15 [f]ver 17; Ge 35:29; 49:29,33
25:9 [g]Ge 35:29 [h]Ge 50:13
25:10 [i]Ge 23:16
25:11 [j]Ge 16:14
25:12 [k]Ge 16:1 [l]Ge 16:15

[a] *63* The meaning of the Hebrew for this word is uncertain. [b] *10* Or *the descendants of Heth*

24:65 *veil.* Veils were used in a variety of ways in different cultures and different times, but they always signified something of the woman's status. Some veils might cover only the hair (a scarf or turban), while others covered the lower part of the face. More common, the veil in the ancient Near East covered both hair and lower face. These were not sheer or gauzy. In the Middle Assyrian laws, married women or concubines were not to appear in public without face and head veiled, whereas veils were prohibited to prostitutes and slave girls. In the Code of Hammurapi, the betrothed wears a veil. In texts from the ancient Near East, veils are most often mentioned in connection with marriage, as here. It is more usual, however, that the husband veils the wife-to-be in a legal act. In a Mari text from about the time of the patriarchs, when the king's legal emissaries bring a bride from her country to be presented to the king, her future husband, it is the emissaries who cover her with a particular garment.

24:67 *tent of his mother.* Sarah's status was mistress of the household, and her tent would have been empty since her death (23:1 – 2). By taking Rebekah into his mother's tent, Isaac demonstrates that she is now the mistress of the household.

25:6 *sons of his concubines.* The children of concubines did not have the status of legitimate heirs. A concubine typically brought no dowry and her children had the status of servants or slaves in the household. They were part of the inheritance rather than recipients of it. *sent them away.* Thus removing them from any presumed position of privilege; yet at the same time he gives them freedom and gifts. Gifts of movable property (rather than land) would be a typical procedure used to consolidate the chief heir's inheritance. For Abraham to provide this for these sons is unusual generosity.

25:8 *gathered to his people.* This expression finds its roots in ancient views about burial and afterlife. Both the practice of burials in family tombs and the view of continuing social relationships in the afterlife retain the concept of the ancestors as a distinguishable group. One's place in the family of deceased ancestors was just as central to one's identity as one's place in the family in the land of the living. The living family honored the deceased both individually and corporately through a variety of practices that did not stop after burial.

25:13 *sons of Ishmael.* The Ishmaelites — i.e., the peoples descended from Ishmael — are mentioned infrequently

tribal rulers[m] according to their settlements and camps. 17Ishmael lived a hundred and thirty-seven years. He breathed
his last and died, and he was gathered to
his people.[n] 18His descendants settled in
the area from Havilah to Shur, near the
eastern border of Egypt, as you go toward
Ashur. And they lived in hostility toward[a]
all the tribes related to them.[o]

Jacob and Esau

19This is the account of the family line
of Abraham's son Isaac.

Abraham became the father of Isaac,
20and Isaac was forty years old[p] when he
married Rebekah[q] daughter of Bethuel the
Aramean from Paddan Aram[b] and sister of
Laban[r] the Aramean.
21Isaac prayed to the LORD on behalf of
his wife, because she was childless. The
LORD answered his prayer,[s] and his wife
Rebekah became pregnant. 22The babies
jostled each other within her, and she
said, "Why is this happening to me?" So
she went to inquire of the LORD.[t]
23The LORD said to her,

"Two nations[u] are in your womb,
and two peoples from within you
will be separated;
one people will be stronger than the
other,
and the older will serve the younger."[v]

24When the time came for her to give
birth, there were twin boys in her womb.
25The first to come out was red, and his
whole body was like a hairy garment;[w]
so they named him Esau.[c] 26After this, his
brother came out, with his hand grasping
Esau's heel;[x] so he was named Jacob.[d][y]
Isaac was sixty years old when Rebekah
gave birth to them.
27The boys grew up, and Esau became
a skillful hunter, a man of the open country,[z] while Jacob was content to stay at
home among the tents. 28Isaac, who had a
taste for wild game,[a] loved Esau, but Rebekah loved Jacob.[b]
29Once when Jacob was cooking some
stew, Esau came in from the open country,
famished. 30He said to Jacob, "Quick, let
me have some of that red stew! I'm famished!" (That is why he was also called
Edom.[e])
31Jacob replied, "First sell me your
birthright."
32"Look, I am about to die," Esau said.
"What good is the birthright to me?"
33But Jacob said, "Swear to me first." So
he swore an oath to him, selling his birthright[c] to Jacob.
34Then Jacob gave Esau some bread and

25:16 [m]Ge 17:20 **25:17** [n]ver 8 **25:18** [o]Ge 16:12 **25:20** [p]ver 26; Ge 26:34 [q]Ge 24:67 [r]Ge 24:29 **25:21** [s]1Ch 5:20; 2Ch 33:13; Ezr 8:23; Ps 127:3; Ro 9:10 **25:22** [t]1Sa 9:9; 10:22 **25:23** [u]Ge 17:4 [v]Ge 27:29, 40; Mal 1:3; Ro 9:11-12* **25:25** [w]Ge 27:11 **25:26** [x]Hos 12:3 [y]Ge 27:36 **25:27** [z]Ge 27:3, 5 **25:28** [a]Ge 27:19 [b]Ge 27:6 **25:33** [c]Ge 27:36; Heb 12:16

[a] 18 Or *lived to the east of* [b] 20 That is, Northwest Mesopotamia [c] 25 *Esau* may mean *hairy.*
[d] 26 *Jacob* means *he grasps the heel,* a Hebrew idiom for *he deceives.* [e] 30 *Edom* means *red.*

in Scripture and are absent entirely from the ancient Near Eastern literature. Besides the genealogical listing (here; 1Ch 1:29 – 31) and the reference to groups associated with the Midianites (Ge 37:25 – 28; 39:1; Jdg 8:24) and with a wide array of Israel's enemies (Ps 83:6), individual Ishmaelites are only mentioned in connection with Esau's wives (Ge 28:9; 36:3) and David's administration (1Ch 2:17; 27:30). The Ishmaelites are never identified with a group designated in the OT as "Arabs" — a term that refers to various tribes who inhabit the area of the Arabian peninsula. The term "Arab" is not a tribal term. "Arab" takes on its modern sense only after the rise of Islam in the seventh century AD, at which point it is still not a tribal reference, but a combination of geographic, linguistic and religious identity. Modern Muslims are not descended from Ishmael, nor do they share common biological descent from Muhammad. Moreover, even the prophet of Islam himself did not claim descent from Ishmael. We have no record of what became of the Ishmaelites after the time of David and have no basis for seeing their survival in any known group in the later OT period, and certainly not today.

25:22 *inquire of the LORD.* At times this phrase can refer to dependence upon the Lord rather than on other entities for aid (e.g., gods, foreign nations, as in Isa 31:1; Jer 10:21). At other times it refers to the formal act of asking for an oracle from Yahweh through an official prophet (e.g., 1Ki 22:8; 2Ki 22:13,18). The latter must be the preferred option here because the result of her inquiry is an oracle (v. 23). Usually an oracle is delivered by a prophet or priest, and in the ancient world at large is mediated by a diviner. The statement that "she went" suggests travel to a sanctuary, though if she visited a prophet, they are not always associated with a sanctuary. Whatever the source of the oracle, this statement features the same laconic silence about the details as Laban's divination (30:27) and the role of the household gods (31:34). All of these derive from Laban's family and indicate the continuation of standard ancient Near Eastern religious practices that are preserved by that side of the family. Yet Yahweh showed some level of tolerance for the slow progress and here was willing to communicate through whatever specialist Rebekah consulted. During the time of Moses, God likewise communicated through the foreign prophet Balaam.

25:29 *Jacob was cooking some stew.* In a large household such as Isaac's, one would expect servants to do such work. Most likely this exchange takes place at a shepherd camp, where Jacob has traveled to graze the flocks (cf. 37:2,12 – 17). We need not picture Jacob out on his own camping or at home doing kitchen detail. Most realistic is a setting in which Jacob is in charge of a group of herders at a grazing site. When Esau stumbles into the camp, there may have been many servants and hired help around, but Jacob is the one who sees the opportunity and takes charge.

25:32 *I am about to die.* Esau is a skilled hunter (v. 27). Is he truly on the brink of starvation, or is he simply using careless hyperbole? The Hebrew word translated "die" can be used either to describe being famished or experiencing life-endangering hunger. Giving Esau the benefit of the doubt, we may accept that he believes that hunger threatens his life. Nevertheless, the original reading audience would react to Esau's blunt statement with horror, regardless of how extreme his circumstances.

GENESIS 25:31

Inheritance Rights and Birthrights

The privilege of the firstborn in inheritance is referred to as "primogeniture." Primogeniture was not universally practiced in the ancient world, but it was a sort of default position. Sufficient numbers of examples exist of either a younger son having the privileges or of the estate being equally divided to demonstrate that a variety of arrangements was possible. Primogeniture functioned in the ancient Near East, but not everywhere, nor was it, if present, always observed. In the Code of Hammurapi (section 165) other divisions of property are allowed. In Lipit Ishtar's laws the inheritance goes equally to the children of two wives; in the Code of Hammurapi the first wife's firstborn receives a preferential share. Thus the ancient provenance and some shared features of Israel's law are evident.

At Mari a legal decision granted a double portion to the natural firstborn son; at Nuzi (fifteenth century BC) the same provision was followed. At Alalakh on the Orontes a father was aware of but did not have to recognize the law of primogeniture in his will. He could designate a first son for inheritance purposes. Primogeniture was recognized at Emar, where the son received an "extra share." Each son first claimed a bride price from the inheritance. A daughter could rarely be an equal heir with the sons in Mesopotamia.

In Egypt by the Middle Kingdom the law of primogeniture could be disregarded by the dying person; property could be willed to a brother. In the New Kingdom era the oldest son was the expected heir, but the entire family or an appointed trustee could become the heir. In the Tale of Sinuhe, a fugitive Egyptian in Canaan, upon departing from Egypt, turned over all of his possessions to his family, both men and property to be given to his firstborn son.

In Neo-Babylonian laws the sons of a first wife received two-thirds of the inheritance, while the sons of the second wife received one-third. Sons who were different in status might fare differently, since sons of the first and main wife could receive the major inheritance. Among sons, in a Middle Assyrian law the oldest son inherited the largest portion; the rest of the inheritance was divided according to set instructions. In some cases the kind of property to be divided up determined how it could be distributed.

The birthright consists of the material inheritance. The firstborn usually received a greater share from the father because he was expected to become the paterfamilias, having ultimate responsibility for all members of the extended family (e.g., mother, unwed sisters) as well as for the continuing care of the deceased. With this greater responsibility came greater resources. When Jacob negotiates to purchase the birthright in Ge 25:29–34, it is not clear whether the additional responsibilities come along with that or not. It is likely that this incident involves only the extra share of the inheritance, while leadership in the clan is given in Ge 27. ◆

some lentil stew. He ate and drank, and
then got up and left.

So Esau despised his birthright.

Isaac and Abimelek

26:1-11Ref — Ge 12:10-20; 20:1-18

26 Now there was a famine in the
land[d] — besides the previous famine in Abraham's time — and Isaac went
to Abimelek king of the Philistines in Gerar.[e] 2 The LORD appeared[f] to Isaac and
said, "Do not go down to Egypt; live in
the land where I tell you to live.[g] 3 Stay
in this land for a while,[h] and I will be
with you and will bless you.[i] For to you
and your descendants I will give all these
lands[j] and will confirm the oath I swore
to your father Abraham. 4 I will make your
descendants as numerous as the stars in
the sky[k] and will give them all these lands,
and through your offspring[a] all nations on
earth will be blessed,[b][l] 5 because Abraham
obeyed me[m] and did everything I required
of him, keeping my commands, my decrees and my instructions." 6 So Isaac
stayed in Gerar.
7 When the men of that place asked him
about his wife, he said, "She is my sister,[n]" because he was afraid to say, "She
is my wife." He thought, "The men of this
place might kill me on account of Rebekah, because she is beautiful."
8 When Isaac had been there a long time,
Abimelek king of the Philistines looked
down from a window and saw Isaac ca-
ressing his wife Rebekah. 9 So Abimelek
summoned Isaac and said, "She is really
your wife! Why did you say, 'She is my
sister'?"

Isaac answered him, "Because I thought
I might lose my life on account of her."
10 Then Abimelek said, "What is this you
have done to us?[o] One of the men might
well have slept with your wife, and you
would have brought guilt upon us."
11 So Abimelek gave orders to all the people: "Anyone who harms[p] this man or his
wife shall surely be put to death."
12 Isaac planted crops in that land and
the same year reaped a hundredfold, because the LORD blessed him.[q] 13 The man
became rich, and his wealth continued
to grow until he became very wealthy.[r]
14 He had so many flocks and herds and
servants[s] that the Philistines envied him.[t]
15 So all the wells[u] that his father's servants
had dug in the time of his father Abraham, the Philistines stopped up,[v] filling
them with earth.
16 Then Abimelek said to Isaac, "Move
away from us; you have become too powerful for us.[w]"
17 So Isaac moved away from there and
encamped in the Valley of Gerar, where
he settled. 18 Isaac reopened the wells[x]
that had been dug in the time of his father Abraham, which the Philistines had
stopped up after Abraham died, and he
gave them the same names his father had
given them.
19 Isaac's servants dug in the valley and
discovered a well of fresh water there.
20 But the herders of Gerar quarreled with
those of Isaac and said, "The water is
ours!"[y] So he named the well Esek,[c] because they disputed with him. 21 Then they
dug another well, but they quarreled over
that one also; so he named it Sitnah.[d]
22 He moved on from there and dug another well, and no one quarreled over it.
He named it Rehoboth,[e] saying, "Now the
LORD has given us room and we will flourish[z] in the land."
23 From there he went up to Beersheba.
24 That night the LORD appeared to him and
said, "I am the God of your father Abraham.[a] Do not be afraid,[b] for I am with
you; I will bless you and will increase the
number of your descendants[c] for the sake
of my servant Abraham."[d]
25 Isaac built an altar[e] there and called
on the name of the LORD. There he pitched
his tent, and there his servants dug a well.
26 Meanwhile, Abimelek had come to
him from Gerar, with Ahuzzath his personal adviser and Phicol the commander
of his forces.[f] 27 Isaac asked them, "Why

26:1 [d] Ge 12:10 [e] Ge 20:1 **26:2** [f] Ge 12:7; 17:1; 18:1 [g] Ge 12:1 **26:3** [h] Ge 20:1; 28:15 [i] Ge 12:2; 22:16-18 [j] Ge 12:7; 13:15; 15:18 **26:4** [k] Ge 15:5; 22:17; Ex 32:13 [l] Ge 12:3; 22:18; Gal 3:8 **26:5** [m] Ge 22:16 **26:7** [n] Ge 12:13; 20:2, 12; Pr 29:25 **26:10** [o] Ge 20:9 **26:11** [p] Ps 105:15 **26:12** [q] ver 3; Job 42:12 **26:13** [r] Pr 10:22 **26:14** [s] Ge 24:36 [t] Ge 37:11 **26:15** [u] Ge 21:30 [v] Ge 21:25 **26:16** [w] Ex 1:9 **26:18** [x] Ge 21:30 **26:20** [y] Ge 21:25 **26:22** [z] Ge 17:6; Ex 1:7 **26:24** [a] Ge 24:12; Ex 3:6 [b] Ge 15:1 [c] ver 4 [d] Ge 17:7 **26:25** [e] Ge 12:7, 8; 13:4, 18; Ps 116:17 **26:26** [f] Ge 21:22

[a] 4 Or *seed* [b] 4 Or *and all nations on earth will use the name of your offspring in blessings* (see 48:20) [c] 20 *Esek* means *dispute.* [d] 21 *Sitnah* means *opposition.* [e] 22 *Rehoboth* means *room.*

26:1 *Abimelek king of the Philistines.* In 20:2 Abimelek is referred to only as the "king of Gerar," but he is located in "the land of the Philistines" (21:32). *king.* This is not as lofty a title as may be assumed since even the rulers of small cities in a city-state system (as this is) are referred to in that way. *Philistines.* See note on 21:32.

26:7 – 11 Although similar to the incidents in 12:10 – 20; 20:1 – 18, the differences between those passages and this one is how the scene unfolds. Isaac's rationale for the ruse is the same as Abraham's, but Rebekah is not actually taken by the ruler as Sarah had been on both occasions. Discovery of the ruse does not occur through divine revelation or because of plagues, but through a chance glimpse of Isaac's intimate interaction with Rebekah. We can note, therefore, a decreasing danger in the three accounts. Pharaoh actually took Sarah into his palace (12:15), which probably implies that he had relations with her. Abimelek sent for Sarah but did not have relations with her (20:2,4). In the case of Rebekah, Abimelek never even sent for her. Also, as a result of the incident, Pharaoh sends Abraham away (12:20); Abimelek gives gifts and freedom in the land to Abraham (20:14 – 16); and Abimelek gives protection to Isaac (26:11).

have you come to me, since you were hostile to me and sent me away?[g]"
28They answered, "We saw clearly
that the LORD was with you;[h] so we said,
'There ought to be a sworn agreement between us'—between us and you. Let us
make a treaty with you 29that you will do
us no harm, just as we did not harm you
but always treated you well and sent you
away peacefully. And now you are blessed
by the LORD."[i]
30Isaac then made a feast[j] for them, and
they ate and drank. 31Early the next morning the men swore an oath[k] to each other.
Then Isaac sent them on their way, and
they went away peacefully.
32That day Isaac's servants came and
told him about the well they had dug.
They said, "We've found water!" 33He
called it Shibah,[a] and to this day the name
of the town has been Beersheba.[b][l]

Jacob Takes Esau's Blessing

34When Esau was forty years old,[m] he
married Judith daughter of Beeri the Hittite, and also Basemath daughter of Elon
the Hittite.[n] 35They were a source of grief
to Isaac and Rebekah.[o]
27 When Isaac was old and his eyes
were so weak that he could no lon-
ger see,[p] he called for Esau his older son[q]
and said to him, "My son."
"Here I am," he answered.
2Isaac said, "I am now an old man and
don't know the day of my death.[r] 3Now
then, get your equipment—your quiver
and bow—and go out to the open country[s] to hunt some wild game for me. 4Pre-
pare me the kind of tasty food I like and
bring it to me to eat, so that I may give you
my blessing[t] before I die."
5Now Rebekah was listening as Isaac
spoke to his son Esau. When Esau left for
the open country to hunt game and bring
it back, 6Rebekah said to her son Jacob,[u]
"Look, I overheard your father say to your
brother Esau, 7'Bring me some game and
prepare me some tasty food to eat, so that
I may give you my blessing in the presence
of the LORD before I die.' 8Now, my son, listen carefully and do what I tell you:[v] 9Go
out to the flock and bring me two choice
young goats, so I can prepare some tasty
food for your father, just the way he likes
it. 10Then take it to your father to eat, so
that he may give you his blessing before
he dies."
11Jacob said to Rebekah his mother, "But
my brother Esau is a hairy man[w] while I
have smooth skin. 12What if my father
touches me?[x] I would appear to be tricking him and would bring down a curse on
myself rather than a blessing."
13His mother said to him, "My son, let
the curse fall on me.[y] Just do what I say;[z]
go and get them for me."
14So he went and got them and brought
them to his mother, and she prepared
some tasty food, just the way his father
liked it. 15Then Rebekah took the best
clothes[a] of Esau her older son, which she
had in the house, and put them on her
younger son Jacob. 16She also covered his
hands and the smooth part of his neck
with the goatskins. 17Then she handed to
her son Jacob the tasty food and the bread
she had made.
18He went to his father and said, "My
father."
"Yes, my son," he answered. "Who is it?"
19Jacob said to his father, "I am Esau
your firstborn. I have done as you told me.
Please sit up and eat some of my game,
so that you may give me your blessing."[b]
20Isaac asked his son, "How did you
find it so quickly, my son?"
"The LORD your God gave me success,[c]"
he replied.

26:27 [g] ver 16 **26:28** [h] Ge 21:22 **26:29** [i] Ge 24:31; Ps 115:15 **26:30** [j] Ge 19:3 **26:31** [k] Ge 21:31 **26:33** [l] Ge 21:14 **26:34** [m] Ge 25:20 [n] Ge 28:9; 36:2 **26:35** [o] Ge 27:46 **27:1** [p] Ge 48:10; 1Sa 3:2 [q] Ge 25:25 **27:2** [r] Ge 47:29 **27:3** [s] Ge 25:27 **27:4** [t] ver 10, 25, 31; Ge 49:28; Dt 33:1; Heb 11:20 **27:6** [u] Ge 25:28

27:8 [v] ver 13, 43 **27:11** [w] Ge 25:25 **27:12** [x] ver 22 **27:13** [y] Mt 27:25 [z] ver 8 **27:15** [a] ver 27 **27:19** [b] ver 4 **27:20** [c] Ge 24:12

[a] 33 *Shibah* can mean *oath* or *seven.* [b] 33 *Beersheba* can mean *well of the oath* and *well of seven.*

27:4 *give you my blessing.* This blessing is one that transfers the leadership of the clan to the next generation. If the inheritance remained undivided for some time (which was common), the privileged son (usually the firstborn) was designated the administrator of the estate. The administrator had significant control of the estate. His roles included presiding at sacrificial meals celebrated by the family, supervising burials and funerary rites, and serving as guardian-redeemer. Jacob (and Rebekah on his behalf) would desire this because it was also in the administrator's hands to approve the timing for the division of the inheritance. If Esau were the administrator, he could presumably delay the division indefinitely and thus deprive Jacob of the advantage of the double share of the inheritance. The blessing also served as a proclamation of the destiny of the sons. It was not accorded the same status as a prophecy from God (note Isaac's use of the first person in v. 37: "I have made him"), but it still was an exercise of authority believed to be binding through the very speaking of the words. This is why Isaac could not take it back even though it became clear that he had been tricked. It was clearly a celebratory occasion since Isaac asks for the preparation of a special meal, but as such it is odd that the whole household was not asked to be present, both as co-celebrants and as witnesses to the legal transaction. It is not hard to imagine, however, that when political issues of favoritism are involved, there is an inclination to be secretive.

27:11 – 13 Rebekah responded to Jacob's fear of a curse by appropriating any curse that may have resulted onto herself. Can she do that? Blessings are nontransferable, so curses would be the same. In this case, Rebekah was likely referring to the consequence of the curse rather than the curse itself. Since deity was the enforcer of the curse, she was acknowledging that she has forced Jacob to deceive his father and ensured that the deity will target her instead.

21 Then Isaac said to Jacob, "Come near
so I can touch you,[d] my son, to know
whether you really are my son Esau or not."
22 Jacob went close to his father Isaac,
who touched him and said, "The voice is
the voice of Jacob, but the hands are the
hands of Esau." 23 He did not recognize
him, for his hands were hairy like those
of his brother Esau;[e] so he proceeded to
bless him. 24 "Are you really my son Esau?"
he asked.
"I am," he replied.
25 Then he said, "My son, bring me some
of your game to eat, so that I may give you
my blessing."[f]
Jacob brought it to him and he ate;
and he brought some wine and he drank.
26 Then his father Isaac said to him, "Come
here, my son, and kiss me."
27 So he went to him and kissed him[g].
When Isaac caught the smell of his
clothes,[h] he blessed him and said,

"Ah, the smell of my son
is like the smell of a field
that the LORD has blessed.[i]
28 May God give you heaven's dew[j]
and earth's richness[k]—
an abundance of grain and new wine.[l]
29 May nations serve you
and peoples bow down to you.[m]
Be lord over your brothers,
and may the sons of your mother
bow down to you.[n]
May those who curse you be cursed
and those who bless you be
blessed.[o]"

30 After Isaac finished blessing him, and
Jacob had scarcely left his father's presence, his brother Esau came in from hunting. 31 He too prepared some tasty food
and brought it to his father. Then he said
to him, "My father, please sit up and eat
some of my game, so that you may give
me your blessing."[p]
32 His father Isaac asked him, "Who are
you?"[q]
"I am your son," he answered, "your
firstborn, Esau."
33 Isaac trembled violently and said,
"Who was it, then, that hunted game and
brought it to me? I ate it just before you
came and I blessed him—and indeed he
will be blessed![r]"
34 When Esau heard his father's words,
he burst out with a loud and bitter cry[s]
and said to his father, "Bless me—me too,
my father!"

27:21 [d] ver 12
27:23 [e] ver 16
27:25 [f] ver 4
27:27 [g] Heb 11:20 [h] SS 4:11 [i] Ps 65:9-13
27:28 [j] Dt 33:13 [k] ver 39 [l] Ge 45:18; Nu 18:12; Dt 33:28
27:29 [m] Isa 45:14, 23; 49:7, 23 [n] Ge 9:25; 25:23; 37:7 [o] Ge 12:3; Nu 24:9; Zep 2:8
27:31 [p] ver 4
27:32 [q] ver 18
27:33 [r] ver 29; Ge 28:3, 4; Ro 11:29
27:34 [s] Heb 12:17
27:35 [t] Jer 9:4; 12:6
27:36 [u] Ge 25:26 [v] Ge 25:33
27:37 [w] ver 28
27:38 [x] Heb 12:17
27:39 [y] ver 28
27:40 [z] 2Sa 8:14 [a] Ge 25:23 [b] 2Ki 8:20-22
27:41 [c] Ge 37:4 [d] Ge 32:11 [e] Ge 50:4, 10 [f] Ob 1:10
27:43 [g] ver 8 [h] Ge 24:29 [i] Ge 11:31
27:44 [j] Ge 31:38, 41
27:45 [k] ver 35
27:46 [l] Ge 26:35
28:1 [m] Ge 24:3
28:2 [n] Ge 25:20

35 But he said, "Your brother came deceitfully[t] and took your blessing."
36 Esau said, "Isn't he rightly named
Jacob[a]?[u] This is the second time he has
taken advantage of me: He took my birthright,[v] and now he's taken my blessing!"
Then he asked, "Haven't you reserved any
blessing for me?"
37 Isaac answered Esau, "I have made
him lord over you and have made all his
relatives his servants, and I have sustained
him with grain and new wine.[w] So what
can I possibly do for you, my son?"
38 Esau said to his father, "Do you have
only one blessing, my father? Bless me
too, my father!" Then Esau wept aloud.[x]
39 His father Isaac answered him,

"Your dwelling will be
away from the earth's richness,
away from the dew[y] of heaven above.
40 You will live by the sword
and you will serve[z] your brother.[a]
But when you grow restless,
you will throw his yoke
from off your neck.[b]"

41 Esau held a grudge[c] against Jacob[d] because of the blessing his father had giv-
en him. He said to himself, "The days of
mourning[e] for my father are near; then I
will kill my brother Jacob."[f]
42 When Rebekah was told what her older
son Esau had said, she sent for her younger
son Jacob and said to him, "Your brother
Esau is planning to avenge himself by killing you. 43 Now then, my son, do what I
say:[g] Flee at once to my brother Laban[h] in
Harran.[i] 44 Stay with him for a while[j] until
your brother's fury subsides. 45 When your
brother is no longer angry with you and
forgets what you did to him,[k] I'll send word
for you to come back from there. Why
should I lose both of you in one day?"
46 Then Rebekah said to Isaac, "I'm disgusted with living because of these Hittite
women. If Jacob takes a wife from among
the women of this land, from Hittite wom-
en like these, my life will not be worth
living."[l]

28 So Isaac called for Jacob and
blessed him. Then he command-
ed him: "Do not marry a Canaanite woman.[m] 2 Go at once to Paddan Aram,[b] to the
house of your mother's father Bethuel.[n]
Take a wife for yourself there, from among

[a] 36 *Jacob* means *he grasps the heel*, a Hebrew idiom for *he takes advantage of* or *he deceives*. [b] 2 That is, Northwest Mesopotamia; also in verses 5, 6 and 7

28:2 *Go … Take a wife … from among the daughters of … your mother's brother.* Just as Abraham insisted that Isaac marry someone from outside the land (24:2–4), Isaac expresses the same desire for Jacob. In addition to echoing the past generation, this served as a tacit condemnation of Esau's marriage (26:34–35). Why was Isaac prohibited from leaving the land, yet Jacob was encouraged to do so? The difference lies in the fact that if Isaac

the daughters of Laban, your mother's
brother. 3 May God Almighty[a][o] bless you
and make you fruitful[p] and increase your
numbers until you become a community of peoples. 4 May he give you and your
descendants the blessing given to Abraham,[q] so that you may take possession of
the land where you now reside as a foreigner,[r] the land God gave to Abraham."
5 Then Isaac sent Jacob on his way, and
he went to Paddan Aram,[s] to Laban son
of Bethuel the Aramean, the brother of
Rebekah,[t] who was the mother of Jacob
and Esau.
6 Now Esau learned that Isaac had
blessed Jacob and had sent him to Paddan Aram to take a wife from there, and
that when he blessed him he commanded him, "Do not marry a Canaanite woman,"[u] 7 and that Jacob had obeyed his father and mother and had gone to Paddan
Aram. 8 Esau then realized how displeasing the Canaanite women[v] were to his father Isaac;[w] 9 so he went to Ishmael and
married Mahalath, the sister of Nebaioth[x]
and daughter of Ishmael son of Abraham,
in addition to the wives he already had.[y]

Jacob's Dream at Bethel

10 Jacob left Beersheba and set out for
Harran.[z] 11 When he reached a certain
place, he stopped for the night because
the sun had set. Taking one of the stones
there, he put it under his head and lay
down to sleep. 12 He had a dream[a] in
which he saw a stairway resting on the
earth, with its top reaching to heaven,
and the angels of God were ascending
and descending on it.[b] 13 There above it[b]
stood the LORD,[c] and he said: "I am the
LORD, the God of your father Abraham
and the God of Isaac.[d] I will give you
and your descendants the land[e] on which
you are lying. 14 Your descendants will be
like the dust of the earth, and you[f] will
spread out to the west and to the east, to
the north and to the south.[g] All peoples
on earth will be blessed through you and
your offspring.[c][h] 15 I am with you[i] and will
watch over you[j] wherever you go, and I
will bring you back to this land. I will not
leave you[k] until I have done what I have
promised you."[l]
16 When Jacob awoke from his sleep, he
thought, "Surely the LORD is in this place,
and I was not aware of it." 17 He was afraid
and said, "How awesome is this place![m]
This is none other than the house of God;
this is the gate of heaven."
18 Early the next morning Jacob took
the stone he had placed under his head
and set it up as a pillar[n] and poured oil on
top of it.[o] 19 He called that place Bethel,[d]
though the city used to be called Luz.[p]
20 Then Jacob made a vow,[q] saying, "If
God will be with me and will watch over
me[r] on this journey I am taking and will
give me food to eat and clothes to wear
21 so that I return safely[s] to my father's
household, then the LORD[e] will be my God[t]
22 and[f] this stone that I have set up as a
pillar will be God's house,[u] and of all that
you give me I will give you a tenth.[v]"

28:3 [o] Ge 17:1 [p] Ge 17:6 **28:4** [q] Ge 12:2, 3 [r] Ge 17:8 **28:5** [s] Hos 12:12 [t] Ge 24:29 **28:6** [u] ver 1 **28:8** [v] Ge 24:3 [w] Ge 26:35 **28:9** [x] Ge 25:13 [y] Ge 26:34 **28:10** [z] Ge 11:31 **28:12** [a] Ge 20:3 [b] Jn 1:51 **28:13** [c] Ge 12:7; 35:7, 9; 48:3 [d] Ge 26:24 [e] Ge 13:15; 35:12 **28:14** [f] Ge 26:4 [g] Ge 13:14 [h] Ge 12:3; 18:18; 22:18; Gal 3:8 **28:15** [i] Ge 26:3; 48:21 [j] Nu 6:24; Ps 121:5, 7-8 [k] Dt 31:6, 8 [l] Nu 23:19 **28:17** [m] Ex 3:5; Jos 5:15 **28:18** [n] Ge 35:14 [o] Lev 8:11 **28:19** [p] Jdg 1:23, 26 **28:20** [q] Ge 31:13; Jdg 11:30; 2Sa 15:8 [r] ver 15 **28:21** [s] Jdg 11:31 [t] Dt 26:17 **28:22** [u] Ge 35:7, 14 [v] Ge 14:20; Lev 27:30

[a] 3 Hebrew *El-Shaddai* [b] 13 Or *There beside him* [c] 14 Or *will use your name and the name of your offspring in blessings* (see 48:20) [d] 19 *Bethel* means *house of God.* [e] 20,21 Or *Since God . . . father's household, the LORD* [f] 21,22 Or *household, and the LORD will be my God,* 22 *then*

left and Abraham subsequently died, no heir of the family would be left to safeguard the land by their presence. But when Jacob left, Isaac and Esau were still there to maintain the claim. Abraham and Sarah's graves were also there. The jeopardy that Isaac and Jacob face has to do with the survival of the family. Jacob is therefore sent from the land to save his life (v. 5).

28:18 *set it up as a pillar.* In the ancient world, cult symbols (such as the pillar set up here) are abundantly observable. These standing stones could at times be deified (i.e., considered to contain the essence of a deity). Others were believed to represent ancestral spirits, whereas others could simply stand as memorials of treaties or special events (notice the 12 stone pillars set up by Moses in Ex 24:4–8). In the context here the standing stone may well have been intended to mark where the presence of God was manifest in Jacob's vision. Jacob had slept in what is in effect the antechamber of a temple and had seen the stairway leading to the gate of heaven (the inner chamber) with the messengers coming and going from the Lord's presence; therefore, he set up a standing stone either to mark the "Most Holy Place" (at the top of the stairway) or the place where Yahweh stood ("above" or "beside" the stairway, see v. 13 and NIV text note there). Alternatively, the standing stone could have functioned as a commemoration of the covenant agreement and Jacob's response in a vow.

28:20 *made a vow.* Vows in the ancient world generally involved a request made of deity with a promise of a gift in return when the request is fulfilled. The request often concerned protection or provision, and the gift was typically a sacrifice or a donation to the sanctuary of the deity. The details in this chapter conform to that pattern. God has promised protection, provision and return to the land, so Jacob made those the condition of his proffered gift—a tithe ("a tenth," v. 22) of all that he acquires during his absence.

28:22 *a tenth.* Wealth and possession in the ancient world were not based on money, so Jacob expected to gain flocks and herds. Though tithes could at times be a form of taxation, this tithe was not imposed on Jacob. Gifts related to vows were usually given to the temple (whether by means of sacrifice or donation), but in this case it would have had to be by sacrifice because donations were to be handed over to temple administrators, and there is no formal temple here. Jacob returned to Bethel to fulfill his vow in ch. 35, and presumably animals were sacrificed at that time (though the text does not say so). Jacob built an altar (35:1), but no further information is given.

GENESIS 28:10–22

Stairway to Heaven

From the fact that the messengers of God appeared passing between the realms in Jacob's dream, it is clear that he was viewing a portal to heaven. Such portals are envisioned as stairways (as opposed to ladders) in ancient mythology (see the article "Ziggurats," p. 30). They are also architecturally represented in the ziggurats of ancient Mesopotamia, which were built to provide the stairway for the gods to come down and be worshiped in their temples. Jacob did not see a ziggurat, but the stairway portal between heaven and earth that ziggurats were designed to provide. These portals were considered sacred space. The link between heaven and earth provided passage for the deity from the gate of his heavenly temple-palace to the sacred space marked out on earth for his presence and worship. Such places were marked with temples once their location had been revealed to people living in the area.

When kings sought to build temples to particular deities, they sought the deity's direction to identify such a sacred place. Thus, the "house of God" (Ge 28:17)—usually referring to a temple (in v. 17 Jacob identified a sacred space but there was no temple yet built to mark the spot)—is linked along with the "gate of heaven" (v. 17) to the entry to the heavenly abode of deity.

There is a continuum in space between the heavenly dwelling and the earthly one such that they are not simply considered mirror images or paired structures, but in the sense that they are more like the upstairs and downstairs of the same building. Yet it is even more than that as the earthly temple can be thought of as actually existing in the heavenly realm. The temple is a place in both worlds, just as the grave is a place both on earth and in the netherworld.

Some temples featured a stairway from the antechamber up to the central cella (the temple's inner sanctum) where the deity dwelt, indicating perhaps that the deity's heavenly dwelling was there in the middle of the earthly temple. If this is so, the "gate of heaven" could be considered the entryway to the temple's inner sanctum (whether at the bottom of the stairway or at the top).

We should not imagine that the angels Jacob saw were marching in procession down and up the stairway as often pictured in art. Rather he saw messengers (= angels) going off on missions and returning from delivering their messages. ◆

Jacob Arrives in Paddan Aram

29 Then Jacob continued on his journey and came to the land of the
eastern peoples.[w] 2There he saw a well
in the open country, with three flocks of
sheep lying near it because the flocks were
watered from that well. The stone over the
mouth of the well was large. 3When all
the flocks were gathered there, the shepherds would roll the stone away from the
well's mouth and water the sheep. Then
they would return the stone to its place
over the mouth of the well.

29:1 [w] Jdg 6:3, 33

29:4 [x] Ge 28:10

4Jacob asked the shepherds, "My brothers, where are you from?"
"We're from Harran,[x]" they replied.
5He said to them, "Do you know Laban,
Nahor's grandson?"
"Yes, we know him," they answered.
6Then Jacob asked them, "Is he well?"
"Yes, he is," they said, "and here comes
his daughter Rachel with the sheep."
7"Look," he said, "the sun is still high; it is
not time for the flocks to be gathered. Water
the sheep and take them back to pasture."
8"We can't," they replied, "until all the

29:8 *We can't . . . until all the flocks are gathered . . . Then we will water the sheep.* Herding contracts in the ancient world were critical to assure the fair distribution of resources that were the foundation for survival. Grazing land and water were often in limited supply. Legal agreements existed between herdsmen and the livestock owners whose

flocks are gathered and the stone has been
rolled away from the mouth of the well.
Then we will water the sheep."
9While he was still talking with them,
Rachel came with her father's sheep,[y] for
she was a shepherd. 10When Jacob saw
Rachel daughter of his uncle Laban, and
Laban's sheep, he went over and rolled
the stone away from the mouth of the well
and watered his uncle's sheep.[z] 11Then
Jacob kissed Rachel and began to weep
aloud.[a] 12He had told Rachel that he was a
relative[b] of her father and a son of Rebekah. So she ran and told her father.[c]
13As soon as Laban[d] heard the news
about Jacob, his sister's son, he hurried to meet him. He embraced him and
kissed him and brought him to his home,
and there Jacob told him all these things.
14Then Laban said to him, "You are my
own flesh and blood."[e]

Jacob Marries Leah and Rachel

After Jacob had stayed with him for a
whole month, 15Laban said to him, "Just
because you are a relative of mine, should
you work for me for nothing? Tell me what
your wages should be."
16Now Laban had two daughters; the
name of the older was Leah, and the
name of the younger was Rachel. 17Leah
had weak[a] eyes, but Rachel had a lovely
figure and was beautiful. 18Jacob was in
love with Rachel and said, "I'll work for
you seven years in return for your younger
daughter Rachel."[f]
19Laban said, "It's better that I give her
to you than to some other man. Stay here
with me." 20So Jacob served seven years
to get Rachel, but they seemed like only
a few days to him because of his love for
her.[g]
21Then Jacob said to Laban, "Give me
my wife. My time is completed, and I want
to make love to her.[h]"
22So Laban brought together all the people of the place and gave a feast.[i] 23But
when evening came, he took his daughter
Leah and brought her to Jacob, and Jacob made love to her. 24And Laban gave
his servant Zilpah to his daughter as her
attendant.
25When morning came, there was Leah!
So Jacob said to Laban, "What is this you
have done to me?[j] I served you for Rachel,
didn't I? Why have you deceived me?[k]"
26Laban replied, "It is not our custom

29:9 [y] Ex 2:16 **29:10** [z] Ex 2:17 **29:11** [a] Ge 33:4 **29:12** [b] Ge 13:8; 14:14, 16 [c] Ge 24:28 **29:13** [d] Ge 24:29 **29:14** [e] Ge 2:23; Jdg 9:2; 2Sa 19:12-13

29:18 [f] Hos 12:12 **29:20** [g] SS 8:7; Hos 12:12 **29:21** [h] Jdg 15:1 **29:22** [i] Jdg 14:10; Jn 2:1-2 **29:25** [j] Ge 12:18 [k] Ge 27:36

[a] 17 Or *delicate*

animals they cared for since they all shared responsibility for the welfare of the herds and flocks. Legal agreements also presumably existed among livestock owners who shared resources. The latter sort of contract is not well represented in the extant literature, and it is that sort that is probably the basis for this scene at the well, though there may have been more of an informal agreement here. Herdsmen typically operated outside of urban areas, but often in symbiosis with the sedentary population. It is not unusual to find groups that are part-time farmers and part-time herdsmen. In this passage the herds are being kept in close proximity to the settlement. These groups are not nomadic in lifestyle, but do their herding in an orbit around the settled areas.

29:14 *You are my own flesh and blood.* This initial statement by Laban shows some similarity to terminology used in adoption literature. It is possible that Laban is proposing taking Jacob into partnership, which suggests that Jacob will have some prospects for inheritance. A month later, however, Laban acts as if no such deal has ever been made—or he legally repudiates the arrangement, which he can do (see v. 15 and note).

29:15 *Just because you are a relative of mine, should you work for me for nothing?* In this proposal the entire relationship is restructured (see note on v. 14) in that Jacob is considered as doing "work-for-hire" as an employee rather than enjoying a share in the property as a family partner.

29:18 *seven years.* The groom and his family traditionally provided a contribution to the bride wealth often referred to as the bride price (see the article "Marriage Contracts," p. 59). Jacob has brought no wealth with him (the inheritance he will eventually gain as heir to Isaac has not yet been divided), so the agreement is reached that his seven years' labor will serve in lieu of a bride price. Since bride prices averaged around 30 to 40 shekels of silver in the mid-second millennium BC Nuzi, and since Jacob's work would normally pay about a shekel per month, the substitution of seven years of Jacob's labor for the bride price results in about twice the normal going rate for brides. Perhaps Laban can take advantage of Jacob because Jacob, being penniless and moonstruck, is in a poor bargaining position.

29:22 *gave a feast.* According to ancient customs marriage was celebrated as a joyful business transaction between families rather than as a civil or sacred ceremony. Though the personal feelings of the couple were not immaterial, legal, economic and social issues were predominant in the institution. The marriage did not take place in the vicinity of sacred space, nor did religious personnel officiate. No vows were made in the name of deity and there was certainly no sacramental aspect to the institution. The agreement was often struck years before the marriage took place and initiated a period termed "inchoate marriage." When the agreed time came, a feast marked the culmination of the agreement after which the marriage was consummated (often within the family compound of the bride's parents). It was not unusual for the wife to continue living with her family as the husband made conjugal visits for several months until the woman conceived. Her pregnancy was the signal that the time was right for her to move into the household of her new husband.

29:26 *It is not our custom.* The Code of Hammurapi (section 160) stipulates a penalty for failing to deliver the bride for whom the bride-price has been received. The very existence of the law indicates that this breach sometimes occurred, though there it specifies that the woman had been given to another man. Laban deflects any accusation of breach of contract by claiming custom as support for his action. Little evidence can substantiate Laban's claim of custom on the basis of ancient Near Eastern documents.

here to give the younger daughter in marriage before the older one. 27 Finish this daughter's bridal week;[l] then we will give you the younger one also, in return for another seven years of work."

28 And Jacob did so. He finished the week with Leah, and then Laban gave him his daughter Rachel to be his wife. 29 Laban gave his servant Bilhah[m] to his daughter Rachel as her attendant.[n] 30 Jacob made love to Rachel also, and his love for Rachel was greater than his love for Leah.[o] And he worked for Laban another seven years.[p]

Jacob's Children

31 When the LORD saw that Leah was not loved,[q] he enabled her to conceive,[r] but Rachel remained childless. 32 Leah became pregnant and gave birth to a son. She named him Reuben,[a] for she said, "It is because the LORD has seen my misery.[s] Surely my husband will love me now."

33 She conceived again, and when she gave birth to a son she said, "Because the LORD heard that I am not loved, he gave me this one too." So she named him Simeon.[b][t]

34 Again she conceived, and when she gave birth to a son she said, "Now at last my husband will become attached to me,[u] because I have borne him three sons." So he was named Levi.[c][v]

35 She conceived again, and when she gave birth to a son she said, "This time I will praise the LORD." So she named him Judah.[d][w] Then she stopped having children.

30 When Rachel saw that she was not bearing Jacob any children,[x] she became jealous of her sister.[y] So she said to Jacob, "Give me children, or I'll die!"

2 Jacob became angry with her and said, "Am I in the place of God, who has kept you from having children?"[z]

3 Then she said, "Here is Bilhah, my servant. Sleep with her so that she can bear children for me and I too can build a family through her."[a]

4 So she gave him her servant Bilhah as a wife.[b] Jacob slept with her,[c] 5 and she became pregnant and bore him a son. 6 Then Rachel said, "God has vindicated me;[d] he has listened to my plea and given me a son." Because of this she named him Dan.[e][e]

29:27 [l] Jdg 14:12
29:29 [m] Ge 30:3 [n] Ge 16:1
29:30 [o] ver 16 [p] Ge 31:41
29:31 [q] Dt 21:15-17 [r] Ge 11:30; 30:1; Ps 127:3
29:32 [s] Ge 16:11; 31:42; Ex 4:31; Dt 26:7; Ps 25:18
29:33 [t] Ge 34:25; 49:5
29:34 [u] Ge 30:20; 1Sa 1:2-4 [v] Ge 49:5-7
29:35 [w] Ge 49:8; Mt 1:2-3
30:1 [x] Ge 29:31; 1Sa 1:5-6 [y] Lev 18:18
30:2 [z] Ge 16:2; 20:18; 29:31
30:3 [a] Ge 16:2
30:4 [b] ver 9, 18 [c] Ge 16:3-4
30:6 [d] Ps 35:24; 43:1; La 3:59 [e] Ge 49:16-17
30:8 [f] Hos 12:3-4 [g] Ge 49:21
30:9 [h] ver 4
30:11 [i] Ge 49:19
30:13 [j] Ps 127:3 [k] Pr 31:28; Lk 1:48 [l] Ge 49:20
30:14 [m] SS 7:13
30:15 [n] Nu 16:9, 13
30:17 [o] Ge 25:21
30:18 [p] Ge 49:14
30:20 [q] Ge 35:23; 49:13; Mt 4:13
30:22 [r] Ge 8:1; 1Sa 1:19-20 [s] Ge 29:31

7 Rachel's servant Bilhah conceived again and bore Jacob a second son. 8 Then Rachel said, "I have had a great struggle with my sister, and I have won."[f] So she named him Naphtali.[f][g]

9 When Leah saw that she had stopped having children, she took her servant Zilpah and gave her to Jacob as a wife.[h] 10 Leah's servant Zilpah bore Jacob a son. 11 Then Leah said, "What good fortune!"[g] So she named him Gad.[h][i]

12 Leah's servant Zilpah bore Jacob a second son. 13 Then Leah said, "How happy I am! The women will call me[j] happy."[k] So she named him Asher.[i][l]

14 During wheat harvest, Reuben went out into the fields and found some mandrake plants,[m] which he brought to his mother Leah. Rachel said to Leah, "Please give me some of your son's mandrakes."

15 But she said to her, "Wasn't it enough[n] that you took away my husband? Will you take my son's mandrakes too?"

"Very well," Rachel said, "he can sleep with you tonight in return for your son's mandrakes."

16 So when Jacob came in from the fields that evening, Leah went out to meet him. "You must sleep with me," she said. "I have hired you with my son's mandrakes." So he slept with her that night.

17 God listened to Leah,[o] and she became pregnant and bore Jacob a fifth son. 18 Then Leah said, "God has rewarded me for giving my servant to my husband." So she named him Issachar.[j][p]

19 Leah conceived again and bore Jacob a sixth son. 20 Then Leah said, "God has presented me with a precious gift. This time my husband will treat me with honor, because I have borne him six sons." So she named him Zebulun.[k][q]

21 Some time later she gave birth to a daughter and named her Dinah.

22 Then God remembered Rachel;[r] he listened to her and enabled her to conceive.[s]

[a] 32 *Reuben* sounds like the Hebrew for *he has seen my misery*; the name means *see, a son.* [b] 33 *Simeon* probably means *one who hears.* [c] 34 *Levi* sounds like and may be derived from the Hebrew for *attached.* [d] 35 *Judah* sounds like and may be derived from the Hebrew for *praise.* [e] 6 *Dan* here means *he has vindicated.* [f] 8 *Naphtali* means *my struggle.* [g] 11 Or *"A troop is coming!"* [h] 11 *Gad* can mean *good fortune* or *a troop.* [i] 13 *Asher* means *happy.* [j] 18 *Issachar* sounds like the Hebrew for *reward.* [k] 20 *Zebulun* probably means *honor.*

30:14 *mandrake plants.* The usual identification of this plant is *Mandragora*, frequently believed in the ancient and classical world to possess magical properties, primarily as an aphrodisiac (see SS 7:13) with the power to make a barren woman conceive. In Egypt it appears to be the aroma that had the erotic powers. Modern study has confirmed that the fruit is a sedative, narcotic and purgative. Unusual characteristics include that the shape of the roots is often reminiscent of the human form and that the plant shines in the dark. Yet there remains some question whether the identification with the fruit in this passage as *Mandragora* is correct since that plant is not known to grow in Mesopotamia.

23She became pregnant and gave birth to
a son[t] and said, "God has taken away my
disgrace."[u] 24She named him Joseph,[a][v]
and said, "May the LORD add to me another son."[w]

Jacob's Flocks Increase

25After Rachel gave birth to Joseph, Jacob said to Laban, "Send me on my way[x]
so I can go back to my own homeland.
26Give me my wives and children, for
whom I have served you,[y] and I will be on
my way. You know how much work I've
done for you."
27But Laban said to him, "If I have
found favor in your eyes, please stay. I
have learned by divination that the LORD
has blessed me because of you."[z] 28He
added, "Name your wages,[a] and I will pay
them."
29Jacob said to him, "You know how I
have worked for you[b] and how your livestock has fared under my care.[c] 30The little
you had before I came has increased greatly, and the LORD has blessed you wherever I have been. But now, when may I do
something for my own household?[d]"
31"What shall I give you?" he asked.
"Don't give me anything," Jacob replied. "But if you will do this one thing for
me, I will go on tending your flocks and
watching over them: 32Let me go through
all your flocks today and remove from
them every speckled or spotted sheep, every dark-colored lamb and every spotted
or speckled goat.[e] They will be my wages.
33And my honesty will testify for me in the
future, whenever you check on the wages
you have paid me. Any goat in my possession that is not speckled or spotted, or
any lamb that is not dark-colored, will be
considered stolen."
34"Agreed," said Laban. "Let it be as you
have said." 35That same day he removed
all the male goats that were streaked or
spotted, and all the speckled or spotted female goats (all that had white on
them) and all the dark-colored lambs, and
he placed them in the care of his sons.[f]
36Then he put a three-day journey between
himself and Jacob, while Jacob continued
to tend the rest of Laban's flocks.
37Jacob, however, took fresh-cut branches from poplar, almond and plane trees
and made white stripes on them by peel-
ing the bark and exposing the white inner
wood of the branches. 38Then he placed
the peeled branches in all the watering
troughs, so that they would be directly
in front of the flocks when they came to
drink. When the flocks were in heat and
came to drink, 39they mated in front of
the branches. And they bore young that
were streaked or speckled or spotted.
40Jacob set apart the young of the flock
by themselves, but made the rest face the
streaked and dark-colored animals that
belonged to Laban. Thus he made separate flocks for himself and did not put
them with Laban's animals. 41Whenever
the stronger females were in heat, Jacob
would place the branches in the troughs
in front of the animals so they would
mate near the branches, 42but if the animals were weak, he would not place them
there. So the weak animals went to Laban
and the strong ones to Jacob. 43In this way
the man grew exceedingly prosperous and

30:23 [t] ver 6 [u] Isa 4:1; Lk 1:25 **30:24** [v] Ge 35:24; 37:2; 39:1; 49:22-26 [w] Ge 35:17 **30:25** [x] Ge 24:54 **30:26** [y] Ge 29:20,30; Hos 12:12 **30:27** [z] Ge 26:24; 39:3,5 **30:28** [a] Ge 29:15 **30:29** [b] Ge 31:6 [c] Ge 31:38-40 **30:30** [d] 1Ti 5:8 **30:32** [e] Ge 31:8,12 **30:35** [f] Ge 31:1

[a] 24 *Joseph* means *may he add.*

30:25 *After Rachel gave birth.* A woman's status in the marriage is not fully attained until she bears a son. In some contracts from the second millennium BC, a time limit is set after which she can be divorced should an heir not be provided. Prior to Joseph's birth, it would have been inappropriate for Jacob to leave with Rachel since her status would be more secure with family in the area.

30:27 *learned by divination.* The details of the divination are not given here, so we do not know what sort of specialist Laban consulted (if any) or what class of divination was used. Divination is divided into categories labeled "inspired" (divine communication using a human intermediary, e.g., prophecy, dreams) or "deductive" (divine communication through events and phenomena, either provoked situations, such as lots or extispicy using animal entrails, or passive, such as celestial observation). Given Laban's report of the result of the divination, it is most likely that he consulted an expert in extispicy. In this procedure, a binary (yes/no) question is posed and then the specialist slaughters an animal and examines the entrails (usually the liver) for indications that their experience dictates as being positive or negative. To get the information Laban conveys, he must have asked whether Jacob's God was the one bringing prosperity.

30:32 *They will be my wages.* Shepherds' wages in the ancient Near East were usually the by-products of the herd (mostly a percentage of the wool and milk). Sometimes the shepherd would also get to keep a percentage of the new births. The percentage is not often stated in the texts, but one text from Ischali indicates that the shepherd was allowed to keep 20 percent. Rather than using a percentage, Jacob requests that his share be those that are marked in their coloring. The Awassi fat-tailed sheep was most common in the region and was usually white. Goats were typically black. Deviations from these norms were relatively uncommon and would certainly have been less than 20 percent in normal circumstances.

30:38 *placed the peeled branches in all the watering troughs.* In vv. 41 – 42 Jacob shows some knowledge of breeding by favoring the stronger animals. The principle of "like breeds like" is common in pastoral societies worldwide. But his use of the visual aids in the water troughs indicates, unsurprisingly, that he also is bound to the superstitions of the day. No evidences have yet been found in the ancient Near East of the procedure used by Jacob, or of similar ones, based on the premise that what the animal sees will influence the lambs.

came to own large flocks, and female and
male servants, and camels and donkeys.[g]

Jacob Flees From Laban

31 Jacob heard that Laban's sons
were saying, "Jacob has taken everything our father owned and has gained
all this wealth from what belonged to our
father." 2And Jacob noticed that Laban's
attitude toward him was not what it had
been.
3Then the LORD said to Jacob, "Go back[h]
to the land of your fathers and to your relatives, and I will be with you."[i]
4So Jacob sent word to Rachel and Leah
to come out to the fields where his flocks
were. 5He said to them, "I see that your
father's attitude toward me is not what it
was before, but the God of my father has
been with me.[j] 6You know that I've worked
for your father with all my strength,[k] 7yet
your father has cheated me by changing
my wages ten times.[l] However, God has
not allowed him to harm me.[m] 8If he said,
'The speckled ones will be your wages,'
then all the flocks gave birth to speckled
young; and if he said, 'The streaked ones
will be your wages,'[n] then all the flocks
bore streaked young. 9So God has taken
away your father's livestock and has given
them to me.[o]
10"In breeding season I once had a
dream in which I looked up and saw
that the male goats mating with the flock
were streaked, speckled or spotted. 11The
angel of God[p] said to me in the dream,
'Jacob.' I answered, 'Here I am.' 12And he
said, 'Look up and see that all the male
goats mating with the flock are streaked,
speckled or spotted, for I have seen all
that Laban has been doing to you.[q] 13I am
the God of Bethel,[r] where you anointed a
pillar and where you made a vow to me.
Now leave this land at once and go back
to your native land.[s]' "
14Then Rachel and Leah replied, "Do we
still have any share in the inheritance of
our father's estate? 15Does he not regard
us as foreigners? Not only has he sold us,
but he has used up what was paid for us.[t]
16Surely all the wealth that God took away
from our father belongs to us and our children. So do whatever God has told you."
17Then Jacob put his children and his
wives on camels, 18and he drove all his
livestock ahead of him, along with all
the goods he had accumulated in Paddan
Aram,[a] to go to his father Isaac[u] in the
land of Canaan.[v]
19When Laban had gone to shear his
sheep, Rachel stole her father's household gods.[w] 20Moreover, Jacob deceived[x]
Laban the Aramean by not telling him he
was running away.[y] 21So he fled with all
he had, crossed the Euphrates River, and
headed for the hill country of Gilead.[z]

Laban Pursues Jacob

22On the third day Laban was told that
Jacob had fled. 23Taking his relatives with
him, he pursued Jacob for seven days and
caught up with him in the hill country of
Gilead. 24Then God came to Laban the

30:43 [g] ver 30; Ge 12:16; 13:2; 24:35; 26:13-14
31:3 [h] ver 13; Ge 32:9 [i] Ge 21:22; 26:3; 28:15
31:5 [j] Ge 21:22; 26:3
31:6 [k] Ge 30:29
31:7 [l] ver 41; Job 19:3 [m] ver 52; Ps 37:28; 105:14
31:8 [n] Ge 30:32
31:9 [o] ver 1, 16; Ge 30:42
31:11 [p] Ge 16:7; 48:16
31:12 [q] Ex 3:7
31:13 [r] Ge 28:10-22 [s] ver 3; Ge 32:9
31:15 [t] Ge 29:20
31:18 [u] Ge 35:27 [v] Ge 10:19
31:19 [w] ver 30, 32, 34-35; Ge 35:2; Jdg 17:5; 1Sa 19:13; Hos 3:4
31:20 [x] Ge 27:36 [y] ver 27
31:21 [z] Ge 37:25

[a] *18* That is, Northwest Mesopotamia

31:15 *Does he not regard us as foreigners?* The bride price paid by the groom was often transferred to the bride as an indirect dowry. As such it became part of a financial reserve for her that served as an insurance policy of sorts. This claim of Leah and Rachel suggests that they had neither direct nor indirect dowry (their share of the inheritance); therefore, no financial security would have been provided by staying in the region of their family. The value of Jacob's 14 years of labor had apparently never been assigned to their present or future holdings. Laban alone profited from Jacob's labor, meaning that he had, in effect, simply sold his daughters.

31:23 *pursued Jacob for seven days.* The site of Mizpah (where Laban caught up to Jacob) is not known, but from Harran to the northern end of the hill country of Gilead is approximately 350 miles (565 kilometers). To reach there in ten days (a three-day head start plus seven days for Laban's travel, vv. 22–23), Jacob must travel 35 miles (55 kilometers) a day, an incredible rate; caravans usually managed 23 miles (37 kilometers) at most. Sheep and goats could neither achieve nor maintain that pace (see 33:13), and women and children would likewise slow down the speed of travel. Given the circumstances, Jacob could not expect to make more than ten miles (16 kilometers) per day. This has led even conservative commentators to suspect that we are reading something wrong. Whenever the Biblical text refers to a journey (Hebrew *derek*) of a particular number of days, the number is one, three or seven, suggesting the possibility that the expression is idiomatic rather than precise. Yet that does not solve all the problems, because if Jacob travels at a rate of only ten miles (16 kilometers) per day, one would expect Laban to catch him long before he arrives at the hill country of Gilead. Laban can perhaps travel 20 miles (32 kilometers) per day, in which case he could have caught Jacob after only three days, about 65 miles (100 kilometers) from Harran, soon after he crossed the Euphrates at Til-Barsib. Certainly the results will be different if one assumes that Jacob is traveling faster or Laban slower, but the numbers we have used (10 and 20 miles [16 kilometers and 32 kilometers], respectively) are the most defensible. If Jacob is traveling 12 or 13 miles (20 or 21 kilometers) per day, and Laban is traveling 17 miles (27 kilometers), Laban would catch Jacob after about seven days (as the text seems to suggest), but they would only be about 110 miles (175 kilometers) from Harran. That would put them somewhere near Ebla, still only one-third of the way to the hill country of Gilead. The only conceivable solution at the moment that explains Laban's not catching up to Jacob before the hill country of Gilead is to assume that it takes Laban a week or ten days to prepare for the trip before he can set out and that he cannot travel very fast (after all, he is over 150 years old at this point).

GENESIS 31:19

HOUSEHOLD GODS

Household gods (*teraphim*) were images that represented deceased ancestors in order to venerate them. There are a variety of opinions about the *teraphim*, and there probably were various practices with regard to whether these ancestors were worshiped or considered to even have quasi-divine status. Minimally, ancestor images provided a focus for rites related to the care of the dead and also were at times used in divination.

In some of the archives from the mid-second millennium BC, legal documents allow us to see how the family gods figured in the inheritance. At Nuzi, several texts indicate that the principal heir received the family gods. In texts from Emar one document suggests that the household gods were not to be given to a man outside the family. In Ge 31, Rachel would have no right to this portion of the inheritance, nor would Jacob. Laban is logically distressed over this breach of inheritance practices as well as concerned that the care of the ancestors will be jeopardized by the loss of the images. We can therefore conclude that Rachel's interest in the *teraphim* has more to do with family and inheritance than with the issue of worshiping other gods. The spirits of the ancestors were not substitute deities, though some uses of them were certainly proscribed in ideal Yahwism as it eventually took shape.

When women married, it was customary for them to transfer their loyalty to the gods of their husband rather than exercise any individual freedom to choose their own God. Wives were automatically by marriage bound to the god of the husband. In most cases, because of endogamy, the god of her fathers would be the same as the god of her husband, because people in the same geographic location, and especially people in the same clan, tended to worship the same deities. ◆

Protective figurine, Iraq, 900–612 BC.

Kim Walton. The Oriental Institute Museum, University of Chicago.

Aramean in a dream at night and said to
him,[a] "Be careful not to say anything to
Jacob, either good or bad."[b]
25 Jacob had pitched his tent in the hill
country of Gilead when Laban overtook
him, and Laban and his relatives camped
there too. 26 Then Laban said to Jacob,
"What have you done? You've deceived
me,[c] and you've carried off my daughters
like captives in war.[d] 27 Why did you run
off secretly and deceive me? Why didn't
you tell me, so I could send you away
with joy and singing to the music of timbrels[e] and harps?[f] 28 You didn't even let me

31:24 [a] Ge 20:3; Job 33:15 [b] Ge 24:50
31:26 [c] Ge 27:36 [d] 1Sa 30:2-3
31:27 [e] Ex 15:20 [f] Ge 4:21
31:28 [g] ver 55
31:29 [h] ver 7 [i] ver 53
31:30 [j] ver 19; Jdg 18:24
31:32 [k] Ge 44:9

kiss my grandchildren and my daughters
goodbye.[g] You have done a foolish thing.
29 I have the power to harm you;[h] but last
night the God of your father[i] said to me,
'Be careful not to say anything to Jacob,
either good or bad.' 30 Now you have gone
off because you longed to return to your
father's household. But why did you steal
my gods?[j]"
31 Jacob answered Laban, "I was afraid,
because I thought you would take your
daughters away from me by force. 32 But
if you find anyone who has your gods,
that person shall not live.[k] In the presence

of our relatives, see for yourself whether
there is anything of yours here with me;
and if so, take it." Now Jacob did not
know that Rachel had stolen the gods.
33 So Laban went into Jacob's tent and
into Leah's tent and into the tent of the
two female servants, but he found nothing. After he came out of Leah's tent, he
entered Rachel's tent. 34 Now Rachel had
taken the household gods and put them
inside her camel's saddle and was sitting
on them. Laban searched[l] through everything in the tent but found nothing.
35 Rachel said to her father, "Don't be
angry, my lord, that I cannot stand up in
your presence;[m] I'm having my period."
So he searched but could not find the
household gods.
36 Jacob was angry and took Laban to
task. "What is my crime?" he asked Laban. "How have I wronged you that you
hunt me down? 37 Now that you have
searched through all my goods, what have
you found that belongs to your household? Put it here in front of your relatives[n]
and mine, and let them judge between the
two of us.
38 "I have been with you for twenty years
now. Your sheep and goats have not mis-
carried, nor have I eaten rams from your
flocks. 39 I did not bring you animals torn
by wild beasts; I bore the loss myself.
And you demanded payment from me
for whatever was stolen by day or night.[o]
40 This was my situation: The heat consumed me in the daytime and the cold at
night, and sleep fled from my eyes. 41 It
was like this for the twenty years I was
in your household. I worked for you fourteen years for your two daughters[p] and six
years for your flocks, and you changed my
wages ten times.[q] 42 If the God of my father,[r] the God of Abraham and the Fear of
Isaac,[s] had not been with me,[t] you would
surely have sent me away empty-handed.
But God has seen my hardship and the toil
of my hands,[u] and last night he rebuked
you."
43 Laban answered Jacob, "The wom-
en are my daughters, the children are my
children, and the flocks are my flocks. All
you see is mine. Yet what can I do today
about these daughters of mine, or about
the children they have borne? 44 Come
now, let's make a covenant,[v] you and I,
and let it serve as a witness between us."[w]
45 So Jacob took a stone and set it up as
a pillar.[x] 46 He said to his relatives, "Gather some stones." So they took stones and
piled them in a heap, and they ate there by
the heap. 47 Laban called it Jegar Sahadutha, and Jacob called it Galeed.[a]
48 Laban said, "This heap is a witness
between you and me today." That is why
it was called Galeed. 49 It was also called
Mizpah,[b][y] because he said, "May the LORD
keep watch between you and me when we
are away from each other. 50 If you mistreat
my daughters or if you take any wives besides my daughters, even though no one is
with us, remember that God is a witness[z]
between you and me."
51 Laban also said to Jacob, "Here is this
heap, and here is this pillar[a] I have set up
between you and me. 52 This heap is a witness, and this pillar is a witness,[b] that I
will not go past this heap to your side to
harm you and that you will not go past this
heap and pillar to my side to harm me.[c]

31:34 [l] ver 37; Ge 44:12 **31:35** [m] Ex 20:12; Lev 19:3,32 **31:37** [n] ver 23 **31:39** [o] Ex 22:13 **31:41** [p] Ge 29:30 [q] ver 7 **31:42** [r] ver 5; Ex 3:15; 1Ch 12:17 [s] ver 53; Isa 8:13 [t] Ps 124:1-2 [u] Ge 29:32 **31:44** [v] Ge 21:27; 26:28 [w] Jos 24:27 **31:45** [x] Ge 28:18 **31:49** [y] Jdg 11:29; 1Sa 7:5-6 **31:50** [z] Jer 29:23; 42:5 **31:51** [a] Ge 28:18 **31:52** [b] Ge 21:30 [c] ver 7; Ge 26:29

[a] *47* The Aramaic *Jegar Sahadutha* and the Hebrew *Galeed* both mean *witness heap.* [b] *49* *Mizpah* means *watchtower.*

31:35 *having my period.* In the ancient world menstruation was a mysterious thing. Blood was often connected to impurity, and since impurity was contagious, menstruating women were typically isolated, and there was some reluctance to touch them or even be near them. In some cultures, the monthly bleeding made one vulnerable to demonic attack—she was considered a woman under taboo (see note on 18:9). Any of these aspects of belief would have made Laban reticent to search Rachel's tent too carefully.

31:48 *This heap is a witness.* In v. 45 Jacob responds to the suggestion of a covenant by setting up a pillar, after which a heap of stones is gathered. The agreement is then marked ceremonially by a communal meal and the formal proclamation of stipulations and an oath. The pillar (see note on 28:18) serves two purposes here: to commemorate the covenant and to mark a territorial boundary (v. 52). Jacob's obligation concerns the treatment of his wives, Laban's daughters. He agrees not to take other wives (vv. 50–53), an act that would potentially lower the status of Leah and Rachel in Jacob's family. This sort of clause is also found in marriage contracts from the town of Nuzi in the mid-second millennium. There it appears that marriage contracts were typically drawn up only when there were unusual circumstances that called for a document to protect the rights of the groom, the legal status of the wife, or the property rights of children.

31:49 *May the LORD keep watch.* It is not unusual today to hear this intoned by a minister as the benediction to the congregation at the end of a service or even to find it inscribed on wedding rings. In using it this way, we show our misunderstanding of the words. Here in Genesis they express suspicion. Laban does not trust Jacob, and Jacob does not trust Laban. They both regret that they will have no means to keep an eye on one another and prevent mischief-making, so they commend one another to the watchful eye of deity. A paraphrase is "I don't trust you out of my sight, but since I can no longer personally hold you accountable, may God do so." It is hardly a sentiment that one would want on a wedding ring, and although a minister may feel that way about a congregation, it is not in good taste to express it so unequivocally.

31:50 *take any wives besides my daughters.* Jacob's taking of other wives would potentially lower the status of Leah and Rachel in Jacob's family. Hence he promises their father (in v. 53) that he will not do so.

53 May the God of Abraham[d] and the God
of Nahor, the God of their father, judge between us."[e]
So Jacob took an oath[f] in the name of
the Fear of his father Isaac.[g] 54 He offered a
sacrifice there in the hill country and invited his relatives to a meal. After they had
eaten, they spent the night there.
55 Early the next morning Laban kissed
his grandchildren and his daughters[h] and
blessed them. Then he left and returned
home.[a][i]

Jacob Prepares to Meet Esau

32 [b] Jacob also went on his way,
and the angels of God[j] met him.
2 When Jacob saw them, he said, "This
is the camp of God!"[k] So he named that
place Mahanaim.[c][l]
3 Jacob sent messengers ahead of him to
his brother Esau[m] in the land of Seir, the
country of Edom.[n] 4 He instructed them:
"This is what you are to say to my lord
Esau: 'Your servant Jacob says, I have
been staying with Laban and have remained there till now. 5 I have cattle and
donkeys, sheep and goats, male and female servants.[o] Now I am sending this
message to my lord, that I may find favor
in your eyes.[p]' "
6 When the messengers returned to Jacob, they said, "We went to your brother
Esau, and now he is coming to meet you,
and four hundred men are with him."[q]
7 In great fear[r] and distress Jacob divided the people who were with him into
two groups,[d] and the flocks and herds
and camels as well. 8 He thought, "If Esau
comes and attacks one group,[e] the group[e]
that is left may escape."
9 Then Jacob prayed, "O God of my father Abraham, God of my father Isaac,[s]
LORD, you who said to me, 'Go back to
your country and your relatives, and I
will make you prosper,'[t] 10 I am unworthy
of all the kindness and faithfulness[u] you

31:53 [d] Ge 28:13 [e] Ge 16:5 [f] Ge 21:23,27 [g] ver 42 **31:55** [h] ver 28 [i] Ge 18:33; 30:25 **32:1** [j] Ge 16:11; 2Ki 6:16-17; Ps 34:7; 91:11; Heb 1:14 **32:2** [k] Ge 28:17 [l] 2Sa 2:8,29 **32:3** [m] Ge 27:41-42 [n] Ge 25:30; 36:8,9

32:5 [o] Ge 12:16; 30:43 [p] Ge 33:8, 10,15 **32:6** [q] Ge 33:1 **32:7** [r] ver 11 **32:9** [s] Ge 28:13; 31:42 [t] Ge 31:13 **32:10** [u] Ge 24:27

[a] *55* In Hebrew texts this verse (31:55) is numbered 32:1. [b] In Hebrew texts 32:1-32 is numbered 32:2-33. [c] *2* *Mahanaim* means *two camps.* [d] *7* Or *camps* [e] *8* Or *camp*

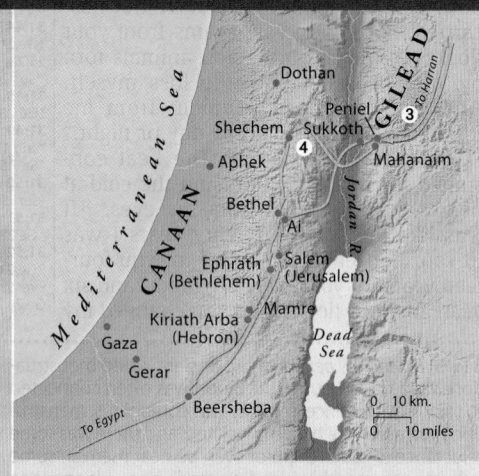

JACOB'S JOURNEYS

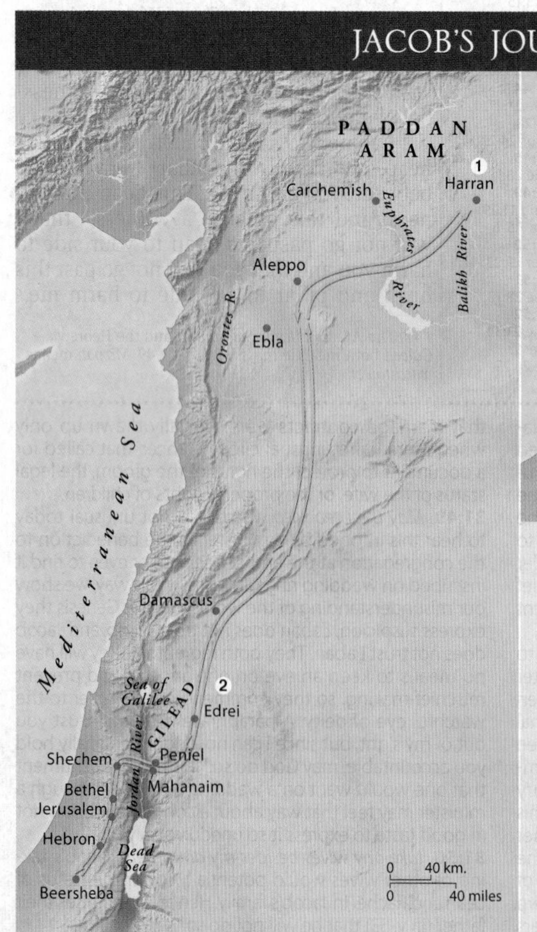

1 The Euphrates-Balikh River basin was Jacob's destination as he fled from Esau, ultimately reaching the home of his maternal uncle (Laban) near Harran.

2 Jacob's lengthy sojourn ended in a dispute with Laban and another flight—this time back to Canaan. His route likely took him toward Aleppo, then to Damascus and Edrei before reaching Peniel on the Jabbok River.

3 He and his dependents reached the hill country of Gilead before their caravan was overtaken by Laban. The covenant at Mizpah was celebrated on one of the hills later used as a border station between Aramean and Israelite territories.

4 Jacob lingered at Sukkoth, entered Canaan and proceeded to Shechem, where he erected an altar to the Lord.

have shown your servant. I had only my
staff when I crossed this Jordan, but now
I have become two camps. 11 Save me, I
pray, from the hand of my brother Esau,
for I am afraid he will come and attack
me,[v] and also the mothers with their children.[w] 12 But you have said, 'I will surely
make you prosper and will make your descendants like the sand[x] of the sea, which
cannot be counted.[y]' "
13 He spent the night there, and from
what he had with him he selected a gift[z]
for his brother Esau: 14 two hundred female
goats and twenty male goats, two hundred
ewes and twenty rams, 15 thirty female
camels with their young, forty cows and
ten bulls, and twenty female donkeys and
ten male donkeys. 16 He put them in the
care of his servants, each herd by itself,
and said to his servants, "Go ahead of me,
and keep some space between the herds."
17 He instructed the one in the lead:
"When my brother Esau meets you and
asks, 'Who do you belong to, and where
are you going, and who owns all these animals in front of you?' 18 then you are to
say, 'They belong to your servant[a] Jacob.
They are a gift sent to my lord Esau, and
he is coming behind us.' "
19 He also instructed the second, the
third and all the others who followed the
herds: "You are to say the same thing to
Esau when you meet him. 20 And be sure
to say, 'Your servant Jacob is coming behind us.' " For he thought, "I will pacify him with these gifts I am sending on
ahead; later, when I see him, perhaps he
will receive me."[b] 21 So Jacob's gifts went
on ahead of him, but he himself spent the
night in the camp.

32:11 [v]Ps 59:2 [w]Ge 27:41 **32:12** [x]Ge 22:17 [y]Ge 28:13-15; Hos 1:10; Ro 9:27 **32:13** [z]Ge 43:11, 15, 25, 26; Pr 18:16 **32:18** [a]Ge 18:3 **32:20** [b]Ge 33:10; Pr 21:14 **32:22** [c]Dt 2:37; 3:16; Jos 12:2 **32:24** [d]Ge 18:2 **32:25** [e]ver 32

Jacob Wrestles With God

22 That night Jacob got up and took his
two wives, his two female servants and
his eleven sons and crossed the ford of
the Jabbok.[c] 23 After he had sent them
across the stream, he sent over all his possessions. 24 So Jacob was left alone, and
a man[d] wrestled with him till daybreak.
25 When the man saw that he could not
overpower him, he touched the socket of
Jacob's hip[e] so that his hip was wrenched
as he wrestled with the man. 26 Then the
man said, "Let me go, for it is daybreak."

32:13 *a gift.* It serves several functions, but above all it indicates to Esau that Jacob is not interested in taking anything that Esau may have inherited.

32:14–15 This gift is generous. It is larger than many towns would have been able to pay in tribute to conquering kings even at later dates. If Esau or his men had plunder on their mind, it saves them the trouble and makes the trip worth their time and effort. Assyrian sources contain numerous lists of plunder collected in their conquests.

32:24 *wrestled with him till daybreak.* Jacob was 97 years old at this point, so he could hardly be considered a challenge to an angel in physical terms. When the text tells us that Jacob's opponent could not overcome him (v. 25), it is not suggesting that Jacob was physically besting the man. The ease with which he inflicted physical damage on Jacob indicates that any ability must have been in the spiritual arena, not the physical one.

One tale from Hittite literature has some intriguing features in the context of a ritual to honor the gods Teshub and Hebat. The goddess speaks something to the king and begins to depart or at least states an intention to do so. The next section has some familiarity:

> The king (answers), "Come back!"
> The goddess (says) as follows: "If I come back, will you in whatever manner—(such as) with horses and chariots—(strive to) prevail over me?
> The king (says) as follows, "I shall (strive to) prevail over you."
> The goddess (says) as follows, ["Make (then) a wish."]
> The king (says) as follows, "Give me life, health, sons (and) daughters in the future, [(strong weapons)], and put my enemies under my feet."

Clearly, there is no actual combat here. Common features include only that the human being detains the deity, conveys his intention to prevail, and requests a blessing. The most important common motif to be recognized here is in the human risk in initiating a confrontation (though it never becomes physical) with a divine representative in order to gain audience and receive a blessing. Jacob and the Hittite king were both pursuing the same sort of goal. The Hittite text has been identified as a rite designed to ensure that the gods give powers to the king.

32:25 The "socket" of Jacob's "hip" is "touched" and as a result is "wrenched" or, more likely, torn or ruptured. Consequently, Jacob limps (v. 31). The Hebrew word for "hip" is the same word translated "thigh" in Ge 24:2,9. In that context there is no mention of the "socket"; instead, Abraham's servant places his hand "under" the thigh. The Hebrew word translated "thigh/hip" usually refers to flesh or muscle rather than the pelvic bone. It is possible that the Hebrew word refers to the groin area. Verse 31 says that in the morning Jacob is limping—it does not say that he has a limp for the rest of his life. If there were only the description of the injury, a blow to the groin area causing a rupture of the testicles would make the most sense of the language used here, as opposed to a dislocation of the hip joint. Until more linguistic information comes to light, the precise interpretation must remain obscure.

32:26 *Then the man said, "Let me go, for it is daybreak."* Three factors to observe—this encounter took place by a river (v. 22), the stranger could be interpreted as fearing daylight, and Jacob clearly believed the wrestler was a supernatural being—together led to a multitude of ingenious mythological explanations about the stranger's concerns and his nature based on literature from much later times. On the basis of anthropological folklore and Greco-Roman literature, it has been proposed that it was a river demon or a guardian of the fords, a creature of the night who attacked Jacob. The data relevant to comparative studies, however, should not be sought in such literature. It is much more difficult to find in the literature of the ancient Near East examples of river-gods and supernatural

But Jacob replied, "I will not let you go
unless you bless me."[f]
27The man asked him, "What is your
name?"
"Jacob," he answered.
28Then the man said, "Your name will
no longer be Jacob, but Israel,[a][g] because
you have struggled with God and with humans and have overcome."
29Jacob said, "Please tell me your
name."[h]
But he replied, "Why do you ask my
name?"[i] Then he blessed[j] him there.
30So Jacob called the place Peniel,[b] saying, "It is because I saw God face to face,[k]
and yet my life was spared."
31The sun rose above him as he passed
Peniel,[c] and he was limping because of his
hip. 32Therefore to this day the Israelites
do not eat the tendon attached to the socket of the hip, because the socket of Jacob's
hip was touched near the tendon.

Jacob Meets Esau

33 Jacob looked up and there was
Esau, coming with his four hundred men;[l] so he divided the children
among Leah, Rachel and the two female
servants. 2He put the female servants
and their children in front, Leah and her
children next, and Rachel and Joseph in
the rear. 3He himself went on ahead and
bowed down to the ground[m] seven times
as he approached his brother.
4But Esau ran to meet Jacob and embraced him; he threw his arms around
his neck and kissed him. And they wept.[n]
5Then Esau looked up and saw the women
and children. "Who are these with you?"
he asked.
Jacob answered, "They are the children
God has graciously given your servant.[o]"
6Then the female servants and their
children approached and bowed down.
7Next, Leah and her children came and
bowed down. Last of all came Joseph and
Rachel, and they too bowed down.
8Esau asked, "What's the meaning of all
these flocks and herds I met?"[p]
"To find favor in your eyes, my lord,"[q]
he said.
9But Esau said, "I already have plenty,
my brother. Keep what you have for yourself."
10"No, please!" said Jacob. "If I have
found favor in your eyes, accept this gift
from me. For to see your face is like seeing the face of God,[r] now that you have
received me favorably.[s] 11Please accept the
present[t] that was brought to you, for God
has been gracious to me[u] and I have all I
need." And because Jacob insisted, Esau
accepted it.
12Then Esau said, "Let us be on our
way; I'll accompany you."
13But Jacob said to him, "My lord
knows that the children are tender and
that I must care for the ewes and cows
that are nursing their young. If they are
driven hard just one day, all the animals
will die. 14So let my lord go on ahead of
his servant, while I move along slowly at
the pace of the flocks and herds before me
and the pace of the children, until I come
to my lord in Seir.[v]"
15Esau said, "Then let me leave some of
my men with you."
"But why do that?" Jacob asked. "Just
let me find favor in the eyes of my lord."[w]
16So that day Esau started on his way
back to Seir. 17Jacob, however, went to
Sukkoth,[x] where he built a place for himself and made shelters for his livestock.
That is why the place is called Sukkoth.[d]
18After Jacob came from Paddan Aram,[e][y]
he arrived safely at the city of Shechem[z]
in Canaan and camped within sight of the
city. 19For a hundred pieces of silver,[f] he
bought from the sons of Hamor, the father
of Shechem,[a] the plot of ground[b] where he
pitched his tent. 20There he set up an altar
and called it El Elohe Israel.[g]

32:26 [f] Hos 12:4
32:28 [g] Ge 17:5; 35:10; 1Ki 18:31
32:29 [h] Jdg 13:17 [i] Jdg 13:18 [j] Ge 35:9
32:30 [k] Ge 16:13; Ex 24:11; Nu 12:8; Jdg 6:22; 13:22
33:1 [l] Ge 32:6
33:3 [m] Ge 18:2; 42:6
33:4 [n] Ge 45:14-15
33:5 [o] Ge 48:9; Ps 127:3; Isa 8:18
33:8 [p] Ge 32:14-16 [q] Ge 24:9; 32:5
33:10 [r] Ge 16:13 [s] Ge 32:20
33:11 [t] 1Sa 25:27 [u] Ge 30:43
33:14 [v] Ge 32:3
33:15 [w] Ge 34:11; 47:25; Ru 2:13
33:17 [x] Jos 13:27; Jdg 8:5,6,8,14-16; Ps 60:6
33:18 [y] Ge 25:20; 28:2 [z] Jos 24:1; Jdg 9:1
33:19 [a] Jos 24:32 [b] Jn 4:5

[a] *28 Israel* probably means *he struggles with God.* [b] *30 Peniel* means *face of God.* [c] *31* Hebrew *Penuel,* a variant of *Peniel* [d] *17 Sukkoth* means *shelters.* [e] *18* That is, Northwest Mesopotamia [f] *19* Hebrew *hundred kesitahs;* a kesitah was a unit of money of unknown weight and value. [g] *20 El Elohe Israel* can mean *El is the God of Israel* or *mighty is the God of Israel.*

beings who cannot be seen in the light of day. There is no shortage of river-gods in the literature of ancient Mesopotamia and Syria and they can be antagonistic, but the idea of these gods attacking humans to prevent their crossing is not attested in the ancient Near East.

At the end of the episode, Jacob designates the individual as *elohim.* This word usually is a designation for deity but can be used for any supernatural being. The clearest statement comes from Hos 12:4, where the prophet indicates that Jacob struggled with an angel. Since an angel can legitimately be referred to either as a "man" [v. 24; cf. Da 10:5] or as *elohim* [cf. Ps 8:5, see NIV text note], Hosea does not contradict either of the statements in Genesis, so it offers the most acceptable solution.

33:3 *bowed down to the ground seven times.* This practice is attested protocol used when a vassal has an audience with his superior. Most notably, the petty city-state kings of Canaan speak of themselves acting this way toward the Egyptian pharaoh in the Amarna letters (mid-second millennium BC).

33:19 *pieces of silver.* The monetary unit referred to here (*qesitah*) has not been identified. It occurs elsewhere only in Jos 24:32 (a reference back to this passage) and Job 42:11. Neither archaeology nor extra-Biblical literature provides further information. One possibility is that these pieces are not shaped like coins but take some other form. In Egypt at this time rings of silver (known as *shat*) were used for exchange.

GENESIS 32:1 – 21

JACOB'S STRATEGY

Jacob decided that it was best to inform Esau of his return. He probably assumed that his father had died by now, whereupon Esau had come into the entire inheritance, Jacob's status or whereabouts having been undetermined. In Jacob's initial communication, he made three basic points.

1. "I have been staying with Laban and have remained there till now" (Ge 32:4). This implied that he had not been hiding, avoiding Esau, or sneaking around behind his back.
2. "I have cattle and donkeys, sheep and goats, male and female servants" (Ge 32:5). This implied that Jacob was not coming to take anything of Esau's or trick him out of anything he had acquired.
3. "I am sending this message ... that I may find favor in your eyes" (Ge 32:5). This implied that Jacob was hoping they could put their past behind them.

This was a good start and a worthy gesture that Jacob reasonably expected would succeed. But the answer he received made him ill at ease in its ambiguity, for Esau was coming to meet him with 400 men, and it was unclear whether or not his intentions were friendly.

Jacob's gift was sufficient for Esau to get a good start on a herding operation of his own or, probably more to the point, to reward any mercenaries in his employ who may have been anticipating plunder. In addition to seeking Esau's favor as a response to his generosity, Jacob planned three strategic advantages.

1. The five distinct groups of animals arriving in succession would wear down the military readiness of Esau's band. If they were planning an ambush, they would have to set it up each time a group arrived. When they discovered that Jacob was not in the group, they would all have gathered again and proceeded on their way. After five times it was unlikely that they would be as alert for combat as they might have been at first. By that time Esau and his men would probably have given up the idea of an ambush altogether.
2. As the gifts arrived, Esau became more and more encumbered in his travel. The animals would have forced him to move more slowly and would have made his band much noisier. It would be difficult to take Jacob by surprise given the unavoidable cacophony of the livestock.
3. As Jacob's servants brought gifts, they joined the march of Esau's band. Esau's military tactics would have been less effective if he had to cope with members of Jacob's household mixed in among his own retinue of soldiers. ◆

Dinah and the Shechemites

34 Now Dinah,[c] the daughter Leah
had borne to Jacob, went out to
visit the women of the land. [2]When Shechem son of Hamor the Hivite, the ruler of
that area, saw her, he took her and raped
her. [3]His heart was drawn to Dinah daughter of Jacob; he loved the young woman
and spoke tenderly to her. [4]And Shechem
said to his father Hamor, "Get me this girl
as my wife."
[5]When Jacob heard that his daughter

34:1 [c] Ge 30:21

34:2 *took her and raped her.* In societies in which marriages were arranged with economic and sociological goals in mind, the couple did not always have an opportunity to pursue their love interests. One way around the problem of parents' unwillingness to accept their children's preference for a spouse was to bypass the process and engage in consensual intercourse. Whether this expression of interest was only on the part of the

Dinah had been defiled, his sons were in the fields with his livestock; so he did nothing about it until they came home.

6Then Shechem's father Hamor went out to talk with Jacob.[d] 7Meanwhile, Jacob's sons had come in from the fields as soon as they heard what had happened. They were shocked and furious, because Shechem had done an outrageous thing in[a] Israel[e] by sleeping with Jacob's daughter—a thing that should not be done.[f]

8But Hamor said to them, "My son Shechem has his heart set on your daughter. Please give her to him as his wife. 9Intermarry with us; give us your daughters and take our daughters for yourselves. 10You can settle among us;[g] the land is open to you.[h] Live in it, trade[b] in it,[i] and acquire property in it."

11Then Shechem said to Dinah's father and brothers, "Let me find favor in your eyes, and I will give you whatever you ask. 12Make the price for the bride[j] and the gift I am to bring as great as you like, and I'll pay whatever you ask me. Only give me the young woman as my wife."

13Because their sister Dinah had been defiled, Jacob's sons replied deceitfully as they spoke to Shechem and his father Hamor. 14They said to them, "We can't do such a thing; we can't give our sister to a man who is not circumcised.[k] That would be a disgrace to us. 15We will enter into an agreement with you on one condition only: that you become like us by circumcising all your males.[l] 16Then we will give you our daughters and take your daughters for ourselves. We'll settle among you and become one people with you. 17But if you will not agree to be circumcised, we'll take our sister and go."

18Their proposal seemed good to Hamor and his son Shechem. 19The young man, who was the most honored of all his father's family, lost no time in doing what they said, because he was delighted with Jacob's daughter.[m] 20So Hamor and his son Shechem went to the gate of their city[n] to speak to the men of their city. 21"These men are friendly toward us," they said. "Let them live in our land and trade in it; the land has plenty of room for them. We can marry their daughters and they can marry ours. 22But the men will agree to live with us as one people only on the condition that our males be circumcised, as they themselves are. 23Won't their livestock, their property and all their other animals become ours? So let us agree to their terms, and they will settle among us."

24All the men who went out of the city gate[o] agreed with Hamor and his son Shechem, and every male in the city was circumcised.

25Three days later, while all of them were still in pain, two of Jacob's sons, Simeon and Levi, Dinah's brothers, took their swords[p] and attacked the unsuspecting city, killing every male.[q] 26They put Hamor and his son Shechem to the sword and took Dinah from Shechem's house and left. 27The sons of Jacob came upon the dead bodies and looted the city where[c] their sister had been defiled. 28They seized their flocks and herds and donkeys and everything else of theirs in the city and out in the fields. 29They carried off all their wealth and all their women and children, taking as plunder everything in the houses.

30Then Jacob said to Simeon and Levi, "You have brought trouble on me by making me obnoxious[r] to the Canaanites and Perizzites, the people living in this land.[s] We are few in number,[t] and if they join forces against me and attack me, I and my household will be destroyed."

31But they replied, "Should he have treated our sister like a prostitute?"

Jacob Returns to Bethel

35 Then God said to Jacob, "Go up to Bethel[u] and settle there, and build an altar there to God, who appeared to you when you were fleeing from your brother Esau."[v]

2So Jacob said to his household[w] and to all who were with him, "Get rid of the foreign gods[x] you have with you, and purify

34:6 [d] Jdg 14:2-5
34:7 [e] Dt 22:21; Jdg 20:6; 2Sa 13:12 [f] Jos 7:15
34:10 [g] Ge 47:6, 27 [h] Ge 13:9; 20:15 [i] Ge 42:34
34:12 [j] Ex 22:16; Dt 22:29; 1Sa 18:25
34:14 [k] Ge 17:14; Jdg 14:3
34:15 [l] Ex 12:48
34:19 [m] ver 3
34:20 [n] Ru 4:1; 2Sa 15:2
34:24 [o] Ge 23:10
34:25 [p] Ge 49:5 [q] Ge 49:7
34:30 [r] Ex 5:21; 1Sa 13:4 [s] Ge 13:7 [t] Ge 46:27; 1Ch 16:19; Ps 105:12
35:1 [u] Ge 28:19 [v] Ge 27:43
35:2 [w] Ge 18:19; Jos 24:15 [x] Ge 31:19

[a] 7 Or *against* [b] 10 Or *move about freely*; also in verse 21 [c] 27 Or *because*

would-be husband, in which case it would be termed "rape," or involved a mutual decision of engaging in consensual sex, the result is similar: the parents would generally have to go ahead with allowing the marriage. Both Ex 22:16–17 and Dt 22:28–29 include regulations to address this situation. It was also regulated in ancient Near Eastern law. Whether Dinah had been raped or virtually "eloped," the family was undeniably shamed by the incident. A rape would certainly be tragic and devastating to Dinah and the family. But if Dinah were in any way involved in the decision, the family would be shamed not only by Shechem's act, but also by Dinah's lack of respect for the family.

34:29 *plunder.* Beyond the slaughter of the entire male population, the brothers took all the women and children as well as all the goods in the city as plunder. Presumably the brothers rationalized their conduct by insisting that such is the mandated bride price for the violation of their sister. Nevertheless, the level of brutality is incomprehensible and far exceeds the justifiable retribution for the crime of the city's prince.

35:2 *Get rid of the foreign gods.* In order to fulfill the vow made to Yahweh in 28:20–22, Jacob commanded several activities, each with ritual significance. Jacob's vow had included not only the payment of a tithe, but the promise that Yahweh would be his God. Consequently,

yourselves and change your clothes.[y]
3 Then come, let us go up to Bethel, where
I will build an altar to God, who answered
me in the day of my distress[z] and who has
been with me wherever I have gone.[a]" 4 So
they gave Jacob all the foreign gods they
had and the rings in their ears, and Jacob
buried them under the oak at Shechem.[b]
5 Then they set out, and the terror of God[c]
fell on the towns all around them so that
no one pursued them.

6 Jacob and all the people with him
came to Luz[d] (that is, Bethel) in the land
of Canaan. 7 There he built an altar, and he
called the place El Bethel,[a] because it was
there that God revealed himself to him[e]
when he was fleeing from his brother.

8 Now Deborah, Rebekah's nurse,[f] died
and was buried under the oak outside
Bethel. So it was named Allon Bakuth.[b]

9 After Jacob returned from Paddan
Aram,[c] God appeared to him again and
blessed him.[g] 10 God said to him, "Your
name is Jacob,[d] but you will no longer be
called Jacob; your name will be Israel.[e]"[h]
So he named him Israel.

11 And God said to him, "I am God Almighty[f];[i] be fruitful and increase in number. A nation[j] and a community of nations
will come from you, and kings will be
among your descendants.[k] 12 The land I
gave to Abraham and Isaac I also give to
you, and I will give this land to your descendants after you.[l]"[m] 13 Then God went
up from him[n] at the place where he had
talked with him.

14 Jacob set up a stone pillar at the place
where God had talked with him, and he
poured out a drink offering on it; he also
poured oil on it.[o] 15 Jacob called the place
where God had talked with him Bethel.[g][p]

The Deaths of Rachel and Isaac

35:23-26pp — 1Ch 2:1-2

16 Then they moved on from Bethel.
While they were still some distance from
Ephrath, Rachel began to give birth and
had great difficulty. 17 And as she was having great difficulty in childbirth, the midwife said to her, "Don't despair, for you
have another son."[q] 18 As she breathed her
last — for she was dying — she named her
son Ben-Oni.[h] But his father named him
Benjamin.[i]

19 So Rachel died and was buried on
the way to Ephrath (that is, Bethlehem[r]).
20 Over her tomb Jacob set up a pillar,
and to this day that pillar marks Rachel's
tomb.[s]

35:2 [y]Ex 19:10, 14
35:3 [z]Ge 32:7 [a]Ge 28:15,20-22; 31:3,42
35:4 [b]Jos 24:25-26
35:5 [c]Ex 15:16; 23:27; Jos 2:9
35:6 [d]Ge 28:19; 48:3
35:7 [e]Ge 28:13
35:8 [f]Ge 24:59
35:9 [g]Ge 32:29
35:10 [h]Ge 17:5
35:11 [i]Ge 17:1; Ex 6:3 [j]Ge 28:3; 48:4 [k]Ge 17:6
35:12 [l]Ge 13:15; 28:13 [m]Ge 12:7; 26:3
35:13 [n]Ge 17:22
35:14 [o]Ge 28:18
35:15 [p]Ge 28:19
35:17 [q]Ge 30:24
35:19 [r]Ge 48:7; Ru 1:1,19; Mic 5:2; Mt 2:16
35:20 [s]1Sa 10:2

[a] 7 *El Bethel* means *God of Bethel.* [b] 8 *Allon Bakuth* means *oak of weeping.* [c] 9 That is, Northwest Mesopotamia; also in verse 26 [d] 10 *Jacob* means *he grasps the heel,* a Hebrew idiom for *he deceives.* [e] 10 *Israel* probably means *he struggles with God.* [f] 11 Hebrew *El-Shaddai* [g] 15 *Bethel* means *house of God.* [h] 18 *Ben-Oni* means *son of my trouble.* [i] 18 *Benjamin* means *son of my right hand.*

he instructed his household to bury all the foreign gods (v. 4), the presence of which was indicative of divided loyalty. Burial was one of the approved methods of discarding images. These were not the household gods Rachel brought with her, for those were not strictly divine images but images of the ancestors (see the article "Household Gods," p. 72). Instead, the buried images were most likely ones plundered from the town of Shechem. This is the first instance in Genesis of disposing of other gods. There has been little discussion thus far in Genesis about the issue of other gods and no clear call to monotheistic belief or practice. But here Jacob makes a statement by his actions. *purify yourselves and change your clothes.* Purification was a normal preparation for ritual activity. Those officiating in rituals often had outfits befitting their position, from the elaborate garments of priests and kings to the linen of assistants. But here the celebrants were directed to change clothes. Some ritual texts, especially those involving the king, portray him putting on clean garments for a ritual. For many celebrants, however, the issue may not be what they are changing into, but what they are changing out of. When work or other activity has sullied one's clothing, it is appropriate to change clothes in order to avoid ritual impurity. For Jacob's entourage, this may have been necessitated simply to eliminate the dirt and grime of travel with all the animals, but it could also refer to the residue of the recent massacre at Shechem.

35:4 *the rings in their ears.* The earrings referred to were closely related to the images. Commentators commonly suggest, though tentatively, that earrings in their shape or symbolism may have been quasi-representations of deity themselves. However, archaeology thus far attests no earrings in the shape of deity, but it is speculated that crescent-shaped earrings may have been symbolic representations of the moon-god. Many images in the ancient Near East were adorned with earrings, so in this phrase the pronoun "their" could point to the gods, not to Jacob's household; i.e., as they disposed of the images, they should not hold back the earrings from the images for themselves.

35:16,19 *Ephrath.* See note on v. 20.

35:20 *Rachel's tomb.* The text, geography and traditions all complicate its precise location. Jacob was traveling south from Bethel (v. 16) to arrive eventually in Hebron (v. 27). Specifically they were on the way to Ephrath/Bethlehem (cf. 48:7) and had not yet arrived at Migdal Eder (35:19 – 21). They were therefore following the main north-south road through the central hill country. From Bethel to Bethlehem is just under 20 miles (32 kilometers) (going through Jerusalem). In 1Sa 10:2 Rachel's tomb is identified as being at Zelzah on the border of Benjamin (cf. Jer 31:15, which has been interpreted to suggest it was near Ramah, just east of Gibeon, more in the middle of Benjamite territory). Jerusalem is on Benjamin's southern border with Judah. Zelzah is unknown other than this reference.

Part of the confusion occurs because the term "Ephrath" (vv. 16,19) has multiple references (cf. 1Ch 2:50 – 51). Besides its association with Bethlehem (see Mic 5:2), it can refer to people from the tribe of Ephraim. The traditional tomb of Rachel today, located outside Bethlehem, does not fit these details. One last wild card is the location of Migdal Eder (v. 21), which unfortunately is unknown, but it may not have helped since it could have been some distance from Rachel's tomb, just not as far as Hebron.

21 Israel moved on again and pitched his
tent beyond Migdal Eder. 22 While Israel
was living in that region, Reuben went in
and slept with his father's concubine[t] Bilhah,[u] and Israel heard of it.

Jacob had twelve sons:

23 The sons of Leah:
Reuben the firstborn[v] of Jacob,
Simeon, Levi, Judah,[w] Issachar and
Zebulun.[x]

24 The sons of Rachel:
Joseph[y] and Benjamin.[z]

25 The sons of Rachel's servant Bilhah:
Dan and Naphtali.[a]

26 The sons of Leah's servant Zilpah:
Gad[b] and Asher.[c]

These were the sons of Jacob, who were
born to him in Paddan Aram.

27 Jacob came home to his father Isaac
in Mamre,[d] near Kiriath Arba[e] (that is,
Hebron), where Abraham and Isaac had
stayed. 28 Isaac lived a hundred and eighty
years.[f] 29 Then he breathed his last and
died and was gathered to his people,[g] old
and full of years.[h] And his sons Esau and
Jacob buried him.[i]

35:22 [t] Ge 49:4; 1Ch 5:1 [u] Ge 29:29; Lev 18:8 **35:23** [v] Ge 46:8 [w] Ge 29:35 [x] Ge 30:20 **35:24** [y] Ge 30:24 [z] ver 18 **35:25** [a] Ge 30:8 **35:26** [b] Ge 30:11 [c] Ge 30:13 **35:27** [d] Ge 13:18; 18:1 [e] Jos 14:15 **35:28** [f] Ge 25:7, 20 **35:29** [g] Ge 25:8; 49:33 [h] Ge 15:15 [i] Ge 25:9 **36:1** [j] Ge 25:30 **36:2** [k] Ge 28:8-9 [l] Ge 26:34 [m] ver 25

Esau's Descendants

36:10-14pp — 1Ch 1:35-37
36:20-28pp — 1Ch 1:38-42

36 This is the account of the family
line of Esau (that is, Edom).[j]

2 Esau took his wives from the
women of Canaan:[k] Adah daughter
of Elon the Hittite,[l] and Oholibamah
daughter of Anah[m] and granddaughter of Zibeon the Hivite — 3 also Basemath daughter of Ishmael and sister
of Nebaioth.

36:4 [n] 1Ch 1:35 **36:6** [o] Ge 12:5 **36:7** [p] Ge 13:6; 17:8; 28:4 **36:8** [q] Dt 2:4 [r] Ge 32:3 **36:11** [s] ver 15-16; Job 2:11 [t] Am 1:12; Hab 3:3 **36:12** [u] Ex 17:8, 16; Nu 24:20; 1Sa 15:2 [v] ver 16

4 Adah bore Eliphaz to Esau, Basemath bore Reuel,[n] 5 and Oholibamah
bore Jeush, Jalam and Korah. These
were the sons of Esau, who were
born to him in Canaan.

6 Esau took his wives and sons and
daughters and all the members of his
household, as well as his livestock
and all his other animals and all the
goods he had acquired in Canaan,[o]
and moved to a land some distance
from his brother Jacob. 7 Their possessions were too great for them to
remain together; the land where they
were staying could not support them
both because of their livestock.[p] 8 So
Esau[q] (that is, Edom) settled in the
hill country of Seir.[r]

9 This is the account of the family line of
Esau the father of the Edomites in the hill
country of Seir.

10 These are the names of Esau's sons:
Eliphaz, the son of Esau's wife
Adah, and Reuel, the son of Esau's
wife Basemath.

11 The sons of Eliphaz:[s]
Teman,[t] Omar, Zepho, Gatam and
Kenaz.

12 Esau's son Eliphaz also had a concubine named Timna, who bore
him Amalek.[u] These were grandsons of Esau's wife Adah.[v]

13 The sons of Reuel:
Nahath, Zerah, Shammah and
Mizzah. These were grandsons of
Esau's wife Basemath.

14 The sons of Esau's wife Oholibamah
daughter of Anah and granddaughter
of Zibeon, whom she bore to Esau:
Jeush, Jalam and Korah.

Given all of this information, it is most logical to locate Rachel's tomb somewhere along the road from Bethel to Jerusalem, but it is difficult to be more precise.

35:22 *slept with his father's concubine.* Though this is technically an incestuous act, the offense here was treated more as social usurpation than as sexual immorality. Possession of the concubines that belonged to the head of the clan was presumably a sign of leadership in the clan. When the father died, the care and ownership of the concubines (as part of his property) passed to the next head of the clan. To seize ownership of the concubines prior to the father's death would be then seen as an act of subversion and disrespect (comparable to seizing land or herds), but would not be unusual if succession to clan leadership were contested. In this context, Reuben's offense against his father circumvented proper succession procedures and implies that his father was powerless. Beyond clan leadership, Reuben's act was not necessarily to secure his own position in the clan, but by treating Bilhah (Rachel's servant) this way, it assured that Leah would assume the place of principal wife (since Rachel had just died). In this sense it was an offense against Bilhah, but again, not just in a sexual sense, but by an act intended to undermine her status in the clan.

36:9 *Esau the father of the Edomites.* Esau's descendants lived in Seir (a region between the Dead Sea and the Gulf of Aqaba) and formed, with other elements, the tiny tribal kingdom of Edom. Edom was sparsely settled and virtually no Late Bronze Age (1400 – 1200 BC) settlements are present. However, people did inhabit the region during the Late Bronze Age, for Egyptian records from about the thirteenth to the tenth centuries BC (Rameses I – III; Merneptah) first mention this territory/people and groups of Shasu (nomads) from Edom/Seir. Shasu parallels Seir in these texts; these nomads are a major part of Edom's population.

Travel and commerce existed between Egypt and Edom very early. Inhabitants of Edom were probably tent dwellers as well as pastoralists in some sense. Later references to them come from Assyrians and Babylonians. Adadnirari III of Assyria (810 – 783 BC) was the first one to deal with Edom as a vassal state. Tiglath-Pileser III (744 – 727 BC) subjugated Edom. Nabonidus nearly destroyed Edom in about 550 BC (Mal 1:1 – 3), but it grew healthy under Persian rule.

[15]These were the chiefs[w] among Esau's descendants:
The sons of Eliphaz the firstborn of Esau:
Chiefs Teman,[x] Omar, Zepho, Kenaz, [16]Korah,[a] Gatam and Amalek. These were the chiefs descended from Eliphaz in Edom; they were grandsons of Adah.[y]
[17]The sons of Esau's son Reuel:[z]
Chiefs Nahath, Zerah, Shammah and Mizzah. These were the chiefs descended from Reuel in Edom; they were grandsons of Esau's wife Basemath.
[18]The sons of Esau's wife Oholibamah:
Chiefs Jeush, Jalam and Korah. These were the chiefs descended from Esau's wife Oholibamah daughter of Anah.

[19]These were the sons of Esau (that is, Edom),[a] and these were their chiefs.

[20]These were the sons of Seir the Horite,[b] who were living in the region:
Lotan, Shobal, Zibeon, Anah, [21]Dishon, Ezer and Dishan. These sons of Seir in Edom were Horite chiefs.
[22]The sons of Lotan:
Hori and Homam.[b] Timna was Lotan's sister.
[23]The sons of Shobal:
Alvan, Manahath, Ebal, Shepho and Onam.
[24]The sons of Zibeon:
Aiah and Anah. This is the Anah who discovered the hot springs[c] in the desert while he was grazing the donkeys of his father Zibeon.
[25]The children of Anah:
Dishon and Oholibamah daughter of Anah.
[26]The sons of Dishon[d]:
Hemdan, Eshban, Ithran and Keran.
[27]The sons of Ezer:
Bilhan, Zaavan and Akan.
[28]The sons of Dishan:
Uz and Aran.
[29]These were the Horite chiefs:
Lotan, Shobal, Zibeon, Anah, [30]Dishon, Ezer and Dishan. These were the Horite chiefs, according to their divisions, in the land of Seir.

The Rulers of Edom

36:31-43pp — 1Ch 1:43-54

[31]These were the kings who reigned in Edom before any Israelite king[c] reigned:
[32]Bela son of Beor became king of Edom. His city was named Dinhabah.
[33]When Bela died, Jobab son of Zerah from Bozrah[d] succeeded him as king.
[34]When Jobab died, Husham from the land of the Temanites[e] succeeded him as king.
[35]When Husham died, Hadad son of Bedad, who defeated Midian in the country of Moab,[f] succeeded him as king. His city was named Avith.
[36]When Hadad died, Samlah from Masrekah succeeded him as king.
[37]When Samlah died, Shaul from Rehoboth on the river succeeded him as king.
[38]When Shaul died, Baal-Hanan son of Akbor succeeded him as king.
[39]When Baal-Hanan son of Akbor died, Hadad[e] succeeded him as king. His city was named Pau, and his wife's name was Mehetabel daughter of Matred, the daughter of Me-Zahab.

[40]These were the chiefs descended from Esau, by name, according to their clans and regions:
Timna, Alvah, Jetheth, [41]Oholibamah, Elah, Pinon, [42]Kenaz, Teman, Mibzar, [43]Magdiel and Iram. These were the chiefs of Edom, according to their settlements in the land they occupied.

This is the family line of Esau, the father of the Edomites.

Joseph's Dreams

37 Jacob lived in the land where his father had stayed,[g] the land of Canaan.[h]

[2]This is the account of Jacob's family line.

Joseph, a young man of seventeen, was tending the flocks[i] with his brothers, the sons of Bilhah[j] and the sons of Zilpah,[k] his father's wives, and he brought their father a bad report[l] about them.

[3]Now Israel loved Joseph more than any of his other sons,[m] because he had

36:15 [w]Ex 15:15 [x]Job 2:11 **36:16** [y]ver 12 **36:17** [z]1Ch 1:37 **36:19** [a]Ge 25:30 **36:20** [b]Ge 14:6; Dt 2:12, 22; 1Ch 1:38 **36:31** [c]Ge 17:6; 1Ch 1:43 **36:33** [d]Jer 49:13, 22 **36:34** [e]Eze 25:13 **36:35** [f]Ge 19:37; Nu 22:1; Dt 1:5; Ru 1:1,6 **37:1** [g]Ge 17:8 [h]Ge 10:19 **37:2** [i]Ps 78:71 [j]Ge 35:25 [k]Ge 35:26 [l]1Sa 2:24 **37:3** [m]Ge 25:28

[a] *16* Masoretic Text; Samaritan Pentateuch (also verse 11 and 1 Chron. 1:36) does not have *Korah.*
[b] *22* Hebrew *Hemam,* a variant of *Homam* (see 1 Chron. 1:39)
[c] *24* Vulgate; Syriac *discovered water;* the meaning of the Hebrew for this word is uncertain.
[d] *26* Hebrew *Dishan,* a variant of *Dishon*
[e] *39* Many manuscripts of the Masoretic Text, Samaritan Pentateuch and Syriac (see also 1 Chron. 1:50); most manuscripts of the Masoretic Text *Hadar*

37:3 *ornate robe.* An Egyptian tomb painting from the nineteenth century BC depicts a troupe of Semitic merchants coming down to Egypt. Some of the men are wearing colorful knee-length, sleeveless garments. We do not know whether this was the type of garment Jacob gave Joseph, but it gives an idea of the fashions of the general period. A fresco from Mari (eighteenth century BC) portrays priests dressed in garments made of rectangular

been born to him in his old age;[n] and he
made an ornate[a] robe[o] for him. 4When his
brothers saw that their father loved him
more than any of them, they hated him[p]
and could not speak a kind word to him.
5Joseph had a dream,[q] and when he
told it to his brothers, they hated him all
the more. 6He said to them, "Listen to this
dream I had: 7We were binding sheaves of
grain out in the field when suddenly my
sheaf rose and stood upright, while your
sheaves gathered around mine and bowed
down to it."[r]
8His brothers said to him, "Do you intend to reign over us? Will you actually rule us?"[s] And they hated him all the
more because of his dream and what he
had said.
9Then he had another dream, and he
told it to his brothers. "Listen," he said, "I
had another dream, and this time the sun
and moon and eleven stars were bowing
down to me."
10When he told his father as well as his
brothers,[t] his father rebuked him and said,
"What is this dream you had? Will your
mother and I and your brothers actually
come and bow down to the ground before
you?"[u] 11His brothers were jealous of him,[v]
but his father kept the matter in mind.[w]

37:3 [n] Ge 44:20 [o] 2Sa 13:18-19 **37:4** [p] Ge 27:41; 49:22-23; Ac 7:9 **37:5** [q] Ge 20:3; 28:12 **37:7** [r] Ge 42:6, 9; 43:26, 28; 44:14; 50:18 **37:8** [s] Ge 49:26 **37:10** [t] ver 5 [u] ver 7; Ge 27:29 **37:11** [v] Ac 7:9 [w] Lk 2:19, 51

Joseph Sold by His Brothers

12Now his brothers had gone to graze
their father's flocks near Shechem, 13and
Israel said to Joseph, "As you know, your
brothers are grazing the flocks near Shechem. Come, I am going to send you to
them."
"Very well," he replied.
14So he said to him, "Go and see if all
is well with your brothers and with the
flocks, and bring word back to me." Then
he sent him off from the Valley of Hebron.[x]
When Joseph arrived at Shechem, 15a
man found him wandering around in the
fields and asked him, "What are you looking for?"
16He replied, "I'm looking for my brothers. Can you tell me where they are grazing their flocks?"
17"They have moved on from here," the
man answered. "I heard them say, 'Let's
go to Dothan.'[y]"
So Joseph went after his brothers and
found them near Dothan. 18But they saw
him in the distance, and before he reached
them, they plotted to kill him.[z]
19"Here comes that dreamer!" they said
to each other. 20"Come now, let's kill him

37:14 [x] Ge 13:18; 35:27 **37:17** [y] 2Ki 6:13 **37:18** [z] 1Sa 19:1; Mk 14:1; Ac 23:12

[a] 3 The meaning of the Hebrew for this word is uncertain; also in verses 23 and 32.

pieces of cloth of various colors sewn together into a long strip that is then wrapped around the body seven or eight turns from the ankles up to the chest and then draped over one shoulder.

Various types of clothing communicated rank and status in society. In the ancient world the fabrics, ornamentation, colors, length and hem all played a role in indicating the position of the wearer. Undoubtedly Joseph's coat designated authority as well as favor, but little more can be said because the Hebrew word for "ornate" occurs only here (also in vv. 23,32) and in the passage describing Tamar's cloak (2Sa 13:18,19). No cognates from comparative Semitic languages offer any confident clarification. The traditional interpretation of a coat of many colors goes back to the Greek and Latin translations of the OT (though now abandoned in many scholarly circles). Most commentators favor something more along the line of a full-length coat or a long-sleeved coat, reflected in Aquila's Greek translation in the second century AD.

37:5 *Joseph had a dream.* The ancients believed dreams derived from the divine realm and were therefore taken seriously. Dreams of a rise to power, like the ones Joseph had, are known in the ancient Near East, notably one by Sargon, king of Akkad, half a millennium earlier than Joseph. Sargon, cupbearer to King Ur-Zababa, recounts to the king his dream in which the king was drowned in a river of blood unleashed by a gigantic vision of Inanna:

> There was a single young woman [the goddess Inanna],
> she was high as the heavens, she was broad as the earth,
> She was firmly set as the base of a wall.
> For me, she drowned you in a great [river] of blood.

Ur-Zababa's advisors reinterpreted the dream to suggest that it was Sargon who was going to die rather than the king. This demonstrates how even fairly transparent dreams could be reinterpreted to suit the desires of one party or another. Joseph's dream indicated not the death of his brothers, but simply their subordination to him. There was nothing in the dream that led them to consider that Joseph's eventual prominence would extend beyond the confines of the family, for only his family members bowed down to him in the dream. It would not have occurred to any of them that Joseph would rise to the position of second-in-command of a dominant world power.

Both in Sargon's and Joseph's dreams the dreamer's life was put in jeopardy as those who would have been supplanted in his rise to authority sought to prevent the fulfillment of that dream by eliminating the one marked for ascendancy. Of course, there is no reason to think of literary dependence here, only to observe the common motifs that reflect widespread human experience.

A curious feature of the second dream (vv. 9–10) is the symbolic presence of Joseph's mother and all 11 brothers. This is odd in that his mother had previously died giving birth to her second son. The inclusion of Joseph's parents is of significance here, because it indicates that the message of the dream did not just suggest that Joseph would be first among his brothers (in which case it would be similar to the patriarchal blessings found in 9:26; 27:29), but that Joseph would rise to prominence in the entire ancestral line, superseding his parents in significance. This justifies the inclusion of family members living or dead. Another option is that—since Joseph was still less than ten years old when his mother died, and therefore Rachel's handmaid, Bilhah, had been a surrogate mother to Joseph and Benjamin—the dream perhaps referred to Bilhah.

and throw him into one of these cisterns[a]
and say that a ferocious animal devoured
him. Then we'll see what comes of his
dreams."[b]
21 When Reuben heard this, he tried to
rescue him from their hands. "Let's not
take his life," he said.[c] 22 "Don't shed any
blood. Throw him into this cistern here in
the wilderness, but don't lay a hand on
him." Reuben said this to rescue him from
them and take him back to his father.
23 So when Joseph came to his brothers,
they stripped him of his robe — the ornate
robe he was wearing — 24 and they took
him and threw him into the cistern.[d] The
cistern was empty; there was no water in it.
25 As they sat down to eat their meal,
they looked up and saw a caravan of Ishmaelites coming from Gilead. Their camels were loaded with spices, balm and
myrrh,[e] and they were on their way to
take them down to Egypt.[f]
26 Judah said to his brothers, "What will
we gain if we kill our brother and cover
up his blood?[g] 27 Come, let's sell him to the
Ishmaelites and not lay our hands on him;
after all, he is our brother,[h] our own flesh
and blood." His brothers agreed.
28 So when the Midianite[i] merchants
came by, his brothers pulled Joseph up
out of the cistern and sold him for twenty
shekels[a] of silver to the Ishmaelites, who
took him to Egypt.[j]
29 When Reuben returned to the cistern
and saw that Joseph was not there, he tore
his clothes.[k] 30 He went back to his brothers and said, "The boy isn't there! Where
can I turn now?"[l]
31 Then they got Joseph's robe,[m] slaughtered a goat and dipped the robe in the
blood. 32 They took the ornate robe back
to their father and said, "We found this.
Examine it to see whether it is your son's
robe."
33 He recognized it and said, "It is my
son's robe! Some ferocious animal[n] has
devoured him. Joseph has surely been
torn to pieces."[o]
34 Then Jacob tore his clothes,[p] put on
sackcloth[q] and mourned for his son many
days.[r] 35 All his sons and daughters came
to comfort him, but he refused to be comforted. "No," he said, "I will continue to
mourn until I join my son in the grave.[s]"
So his father wept for him.
36 Meanwhile, the Midianites[b] sold Joseph in Egypt to Potiphar, one of Pharaoh's officials, the captain of the guard.[t]

37:20 [a] Jer 38:6, 9 [b] Ge 50:20 **37:21** [c] Ge 42:22 **37:24** [d] Jer 41:7 **37:25** [e] Ge 43:11 [f] ver 28 **37:26** [g] ver 20; Ge 4:10 **37:27** [h] Ge 42:21 **37:28** [i] Ge 25:2; Jdg 6:1-3 [j] Ge 45:4-5; Ps 105:17; Ac 7:9 **37:29** [k] ver 34; Ge 44:13; Job 1:20 **37:30** [l] ver 22; Ge 42:13, 36 **37:31** [m] ver 3, 23 **37:33** [n] ver 20 [o] Ge 44:20, 28 **37:34** [p] ver 29 [q] 2Sa 3:31 [r] Ge 50:3, 10, 11 **37:35** [s] Ge 42:38; 44:22, 29, 31 **37:36** [t] Ge 39:1 **38:2** [u] 1Ch 2:3 **38:3** [v] ver 6; Ge 46:12; Nu 26:19 **38:7** [w] ver 10; Ge 46:12; 1Ch 2:3

Judah and Tamar

38 At that time, Judah left his brothers and went down to stay with a
man of Adullam named Hirah. 2 There Judah met the daughter of a Canaanite man
named Shua.[u] He married her and made
love to her; 3 she became pregnant and
gave birth to a son, who was named Er.[v]
4 She conceived again and gave birth to a
son and named him Onan. 5 She gave birth
to still another son and named him Shelah.
It was at Kezib that she gave birth to him.
6 Judah got a wife for Er, his firstborn,
and her name was Tamar. 7 But Er, Judah's
firstborn, was wicked in the LORD's sight;
so the LORD put him to death.[w]
8 Then Judah said to Onan, "Sleep with
your brother's wife and fulfill your duty

[a] *28* That is, about 8 ounces or about 230 grams
[b] *36* Samaritan Pentateuch, Septuagint, Vulgate and Syriac (see also verse 28); Masoretic Text *Medanites*

37:20 *cisterns.* Where wells could not be dug and precipitation was sufficient, cisterns were constructed to catch rain and runoff during the wet season to provide some supply for the dry season. The area of Dothan averages 24 – 28 inches (60 – 70 centimeters) of rainfall annually; thus, if 20 percent of the runoff from a half-acre (one-hectare) field could be caught and stored, about 5,000 sheep could be supplied with water for the year. As one can imagine, water collected in cisterns easily became stagnant. It was not unusual for dry cisterns to be miry at the bottom, because the runoff would carry sediment. But if it were maintained for constant use, it would have been cleaned out regularly. The region of Dothan features limestone, which is porous, and thus cisterns were coated on the inside with plaster (a procedure documented in the Early Bronze and Middle Bronze periods [e.g., at Taanach and Megiddo, respectively]) to prevent absorption of the water.

37:25 *caravan of Ishmaelites.* The text refers to both Ishmaelites and Midianites, kinfolk both descended from Abraham (Midianites through Keturah, 25:1 – 2; Ishmaelites through Hagar, 16:15). The forebears of these two peoples were half brothers to one another (and to Isaac), and uncles to Jacob; thus, these traders are second or third cousins to Joseph and his brothers. Both clans occupied the Arabian Desert region. *spices, balm and myrrh.* The goods that the caravan was transporting were common commodities for trade. Myrrh was imported from southern Arabia and must have come by caravan up the Incense Road, which traversed the west coast of Arabia to the King's Highway, which led north-south through Transjordan (east of the Jordan Valley) to Damascus. Perhaps the Ishmaelites purchased this myrrh and other spices from the Arabian caravans passing through Gilead on the King's Highway and then added to their shipment some of the balm that was native to that region to make their trip down to Egypt.

37:28 *twenty shekels of silver.* The going rate for a slave in the mid-second millennium BC. Examples from Hammurapi, Mari, and a variety of Old Babylonian documents support this. In contrast, prices in southern Mesopotamia about 2000 BC were 10 shekels and by the time of Nuzi and Ugarit (fourteenth and thirteenth centuries BC) the price was more like 30 shekels. By the time we get into the first millennium BC, the going rate was 50 shekels, and by the Persian period, 80 to 100 shekels was common.

38:8 *fulfill your duty to her as a brother-in-law.* The custom of levirate marriage mandated that if a man died without

to her as a brother-in-law to raise up offspring for your brother."[x] 9But Onan knew
that the child would not be his; so whenever he slept with his brother's wife, he
spilled his semen on the ground to keep
from providing offspring for his brother.
10What he did was wicked in the LORD's
sight; so the LORD put him to death also.[y]
11Judah then said to his daughter-in-law
Tamar, "Live as a widow in your father's
household until my son Shelah grows
up."[z] For he thought, "He may die too,
just like his brothers." So Tamar went to
live in her father's household.
12After a long time Judah's wife, the
daughter of Shua, died. When Judah had
recovered from his grief, he went up to
Timnah,[a] to the men who were shearing
his sheep, and his friend Hirah the Adullamite went with him.
13When Tamar was told, "Your father-
in-law is on his way to Timnah to shear
his sheep," 14she took off her widow's
clothes, covered herself with a veil to disguise herself, and then sat down at the entrance to Enaim, which is on the road to
Timnah. For she saw that, though Shelah[b]
had now grown up, she had not been giv-
en to him as his wife.
15When Judah saw her, he thought
she was a prostitute, for she had covered
her face. 16Not realizing that she was his
daughter-in-law,[c] he went over to her by
the roadside and said, "Come now, let me
sleep with you."
"And what will you give me to sleep
with you?" she asked.
17"I'll send you a young goat[d] from my
flock," he said.
"Will you give me something as a
pledge[e] until you send it?" she asked.
18He said, "What pledge should I give
you?"
"Your seal[f] and its cord, and the staff
in your hand," she answered. So he gave
them to her and slept with her, and she

38:8 [x] Dt 25:5-6; Mt 22:24-28 **38:10** [y] Ge 46:12; Dt 25:7-10 **38:11** [z] Ru 1:13 **38:12** [a] ver 14; Jos 15:10,57 **38:14** [b] ver 11 **38:16** [c] Lev 18:15; 20:12 **38:17** [d] Eze 16:33 [e] ver 20 **38:18** [f] ver 25

a male heir, a relative was to sire a son with the widow on his behalf. See the article "Levirate Marriage," p. 85.

38:9 *spilled his semen on the ground.* This does not refer to masturbation, as is occasionally suggested. It rather refers to the practice of ejaculating outside the woman's body ("withdrawal") as a means to avoid impregnation. Interestingly, while masturbation is not forbidden in the Bible, a negative confession in the Egyptian "Book of the Dead" proclaims, "I have not masturbated."

38:11 *Live as a widow.* A widow without children was a woman without legal, economic or social status—a woman without a household. Judah here relegates Tamar (through his continuing authority over her) to the protection of her father's household. This is unusual in that a dowry would have been initially paid by her father precisely for the purpose of supporting her in a situation such as this. It is unlikely that her father would have had any legal obligation to support her.

38:14 *widow's clothes.* Would be sufficiently distinctive to mark Tamar's station, but our sources are inadequate for determining what these clothes looked like.

38:15 *prostitute.* Sheep-shearing time was payday, and the income windfall, the celebratory atmosphere, and the isolation of the men from the family compound all were conducive to the activity of prostitutes. Prostitution in the ancient world can be divided into a number of different categories, and there is some dispute concerning the labels and descriptions.

Particularly debatable is what is called "sacred prostitution" (in which the proceeds go the temple) and "cultic prostitution" (which is performed as a rite of fertility). The latter is only attested in relation to the tightly regulated sacred marriage rites and was not engaged in by the public at large. It is not legitimately labeled "prostitution." With regard to the former, though undoubtedly secular prostitutes might congregate around the temple (especially at festival times), evidence is lacking for the temples profiting from or organizing prostitution (though Dt 23:18 makes it clear that such a practice did exist).

Some groups of women in the Old Babylonian period (1800–1600) e.g., the *naditu* and *qadishtu*, were regulated by codes and identified with male deities; their sexuality was controlled by either celibacy or marriage. These were often associated with temples. Other groups (e.g., the *harimtu*) were associated with female deities, had no regulating codes, and were uncontrolled sexually. The latter typically operated from the tavern and acted for pay.

Tamar is referred to by two separate terms in this chapter. In v. 15 Judah considered her a *zonah*, the normal Hebrew word for "prostitute" (used also in v. 24). He reached this conclusion not because her face was veiled (that detail is given to explain why he did not recognize her—usually prostitutes were unveiled), but because she had stationed herself by the road as a prostitute would. But when Judah sent his friend to look for her, the friend inquired concerning the *qedeshah* (vv. 21–22, NIV "shrine prostitute").

This latter term is used only two other times in the OT (Dt 23:18; Hos 4:14). Ugaritic texts list women similarly labeled (*qdsh*) among the temple personnel, and Akkadian literature attests those who were dedicated for life to serve the temple with a cognate term (*qadishtu*). These shrine functionaries were not by definition prostitutes—they had other, legitimate roles. But in practice, it may not have been uncommon for them to engage in prostitution. By inquiring after the *qedeshah* Judah's friend concealed the specifics in ambiguity—there may have been a number of reasons a gift would be brought to a shrine functionary.

38:18 *seal … cord … staff.* In the ancient world legal identification was not by signature or specially assigned numbers as today. The seal was the most common form of identification. In Mesopotamia inscribed cylinders were used (and often worn around the neck), whereas in the rest of the ancient world scarab or stamp seals were carved in intaglio on disk-shaped bits of stone (the size of a small coin), usually decorated with some sort of simple picture and occasionally with the individual's name and/or position. These were often pierced so as to be worn somewhere on the body, often around the neck on a cord, probably referred to in this verse. Stamp seals are attested as early as the seventh-millennium BC Neolithic period. Cylinder seals made their appearance in the early fourth millennium BC. The staff that Judah left with Tamar must have also been distinctive and capable of identifying the owner. One possibility is that it was a staff that designated the head of the family (cf. Nu 17:2). Akkadian

GENESIS 38:6 – 11

Levirate Marriage

A number of possible motives or anticipated results may underlie this custom, and the issue is still disputed. Alternative and not unrelated possibilities include provision of an heir, protection of the family holdings and/or dowry, or caring for the widow. Information from the ancient Near East comes from family documents from Emar as well as Hittite laws and Middle Assyrian laws.

Care for the widow cannot be seen as the sole motive, for then the legislation would simply mandate that the dead husband's family care for her. It is also unlikely that the retention and benefit of the dowry was the sole motivation, for then the new husband (the brother) would have much to gain and would hardly view the task as an unpleasant duty. The primary beneficiary of the practice must therefore be considered to be the dead husband rather than the surviving family. However, it is not simply for the memory of the dead husband that an heir must be born, but so that the deceased might be provided with an heir to his estate. If the land has been forfeited, the relative must redeem it for the widow and then produce an heir to whom to pass it.

It should be pointed out that the law pertains when brothers are living together (cf. Dt 25:5). This refers to a situation in which the inheritance has not yet been divided. In such a case, if one brother dies, each of the others would receive a larger share. Three circumstances call for the invoking of the levirate rule: (1) the father is alive and the brothers are still living in his house; (2) the father is dead but the inheritance has not yet been divided; (3) the land has been alienated and the levir must redeem it.

None of the ancient Near Eastern material reflects identical circumstances, but shows that concern for the central issues was shared across the ancient world.

Levirate marriage was practiced at Ugarit, at least at the royal level of society (c. 1345 – 1336 BC), with reference to the childless Arhalba and his brother Niqmepa. Hittite laws and possibly laws at Nuzi recognized this marriage practice. In Hittite law a widowed wife could, if necessary, marry her brother-in-law, her father-in-law, or the son of her brother-in-law.

In some Hittite and Assyrian laws the issue is not whether the deceased had sons, but rather the need to support the widow in whom the father had a large investment through the bride price. More recent textual finds from Emar emphasize the desire of legislation like this to keep property within the family. Concern for the preservation of seed and inheritance is found late into the time of Ptolemy II Philadelphus (273/272 BC).

In the more ancient Middle Assyrian laws the wife of a son who died could be given by the son's father to another of his sons, even if the other son were betrothed to someone else but not yet married. But if the father of that betrothed daughter did not agree to this, the father of the deceased son could still proceed as planned and give the betrothed bride to his son. Or he could withdraw from the entire process. If a betrothed daughter died before the marriage, her father could give his prospective son-in-law another daughter, or the betrothed groom could withdraw.

If a wife's husband died while they were living in her father's house, if she had borne no children, her father-in-law could marry her to the son of his choice, or she could be given in marriage by her father to her father-in-law. This option was not permitted in Israel (cf. Ge 38:26). If her husband and father-in-law both died, she became a widow and was free to do as she pleased. If the wife had borne children, she was free to live in a house for her and her son in her father's household. ◆

became pregnant by him. 19 After she left, she took off her veil and put on her widow's clothes[g] again.

20 Meanwhile Judah sent the young goat by his friend the Adullamite in order to get his pledge back from the woman, but he did not find her. 21 He asked the men who lived there, "Where is the shrine prostitute[h] who was beside the road at Enaim?"

"There hasn't been any shrine prostitute here," they said.

22 So he went back to Judah and said, "I didn't find her. Besides, the men who lived there said, 'There hasn't been any shrine prostitute here.'"

23 Then Judah said, "Let her keep what she has, or we will become a laughingstock. After all, I did send her this young goat, but you didn't find her."

24 About three months later Judah was told, "Your daughter-in-law Tamar is guilty of prostitution, and as a result she is now pregnant."

Judah said, "Bring her out and have her burned to death!"[i]

25 As she was being brought out, she sent a message to her father-in-law. "I am pregnant by the man who owns these," she said. And she added, "See if you recognize whose seal and cord and staff these are."[j]

26 Judah recognized them and said, "She is more righteous than I,[k] since I wouldn't give her to my son Shelah.[l]" And he did not sleep with her again.

27 When the time came for her to give birth, there were twin boys in her womb.[m] 28 As she was giving birth, one of them put out his hand; so the midwife took a scarlet thread and tied it on his wrist and said, "This one came out first." 29 But when he drew back his hand, his brother came out, and she said, "So this is how you have broken out!" And he was named Perez.[a][n] 30 Then his brother, who had the scarlet thread on his wrist, came out. And he was named Zerah.[b][o]

Joseph and Potiphar's Wife

39 Now Joseph had been taken down to Egypt. Potiphar, an Egyptian who was one of Pharaoh's officials, the captain of the guard,[p] bought him from the Ishmaelites who had taken him there.[q]

2 The LORD was with Joseph[r] so that he prospered, and he lived in the house of his Egyptian master. 3 When his master saw that the LORD was with him[s] and that the LORD gave him success in everything he did,[t] 4 Joseph found favor in his eyes and became his attendant. Potiphar put him in charge of his household, and he entrusted to his care everything he owned.[u] 5 From the time he put him in charge of his household and of all that he owned, the LORD blessed the household of the Egyptian because of Joseph.[v] The blessing of the LORD was on everything Potiphar had, both in the house and in the field. 6 So Potiphar left everything he had in Joseph's care; with Joseph in charge, he did not concern himself with anything except the food he ate.

Now Joseph was well-built and handsome,[w] 7 and after a while his master's wife took notice of Joseph and said, "Come to bed with me!"[x]

8 But he refused.[y] "With me in charge," he told her, "my master does not concern himself with anything in the house; everything he owns he has entrusted to my care. 9 No one is greater in this house than I am.[z] My master has withheld nothing from me except you, because you are his wife. How then could I do such a wicked thing and sin against God?"[a] 10 And though she spoke to Joseph day after day, he refused to go to bed with her or even be with her.

11 One day he went into the house to attend to his duties, and none of the household servants was inside. 12 She caught him by his cloak[b] and said, "Come to bed with me!" But he left his cloak in her hand and ran out of the house.

13 When she saw that he had left his cloak in her hand and had run out of the house, 14 she called her household servants. "Look," she said to them, "this Hebrew has been brought to us to make sport of us! He came in here to sleep with me, but I screamed.[c] 15 When he heard me scream for help, he left his cloak beside me and ran out of the house."

16 She kept his cloak beside her until his master came home. 17 Then she told

38:19 [g] ver 14 **38:21** [h] Lev 19:29; Hos 4:14 **38:24** [i] Lev 21:9; Dt 22:21, 22 **38:25** [j] ver 18 **38:26** [k] 1Sa 24:17 [l] ver 11 **38:27** [m] Ge 25:24 **38:29** [n] Ge 46:12; Nu 26:20, 21; Ru 4:12, 18; 1Ch 2:4; Mt 1:3 **38:30** [o] 1Ch 2:4 **39:1** [p] Ge 37:36 [q] Ge 37:25; Ps 105:17 **39:2** [r] Ge 21:20, 22; Ac 7:9 **39:3** [s] Ge 21:22; 26:28 [t] Ps 1:3 **39:4** [u] ver 8, 22; Ge 24:2 **39:5** [v] Ge 26:24; 30:27 **39:6** [w] 1Sa 16:12 **39:7** [x] 2Sa 13:11; Pr 7:15-18 **39:8** [y] Pr 6:23-24 **39:9** [z] Ge 41:33, 40 [a] Ge 20:6; 42:18; 2Sa 12:13 **39:12** [b] Pr 7:13 **39:14** [c] Dt 22:24, 27

[a] 29 *Perez* means *breaking out.* [b] 30 *Zerah* can mean *scarlet* or *brightness.*

hattu is used for the scepter of a king, but also for the shepherd's staff and the staff that serves as the insignia of office for important people. It seems that the top of the staff was often engraved.

38:24 *have her burned to death!* It was a fact of life and society that sometimes widows were forced into (either regular or occasional) prostitution in order to live. Yet it was still unacceptable behavior and was punished severely. The punishment of burning is rare and reserved for the most serious of sexual crimes (cf. Lev 20:14; 21:9 for the only other Biblical occurrences). In ancient Near Eastern legal texts, burning is likewise a rare punishment, but used in similar circumstances: for a *naditu* (see note on v. 15) who opens a tavern or enters a tavern to drink beer, and for incest with one's mother. This was a most serious punishment since it probably precluded proper burial.

him this story:[d] "That Hebrew slave you
brought us came to me to make sport of
me. 18 But as soon as I screamed for help,
he left his cloak beside me and ran out of
the house."
19 When his master heard the story his
wife told him, saying, "This is how your
slave treated me," he burned with anger.[e]
20 Joseph's master took him and put him in
prison,[f] the place where the king's prisoners were confined.
But while Joseph was there in the prison,
21 the LORD was with him; he showed him
kindness and granted him favor in the eyes
of the prison warden.[g] 22 So the warden put
Joseph in charge of all those held in the
prison, and he was made responsible for all
that was done there.[h] 23 The warden paid no
attention to anything under Joseph's care,
because the LORD was with Joseph and
gave him success in whatever he did.[i]

The Cupbearer and the Baker

40 Some time later, the cupbearer[j]
and the baker of the king of Egypt
offended their master, the king of Egypt.
2 Pharaoh was angry[k] with his two officials, the chief cupbearer and the chief
baker, 3 and put them in custody in the
house of the captain of the guard,[l] in the
same prison where Joseph was confined.
4 The captain of the guard assigned them
to Joseph,[m] and he attended them.
After they had been in custody for some
time, 5 each of the two men — the cupbearer and the baker of the king of Egypt, who
were being held in prison — had a dream
the same night, and each dream had a
meaning of its own.[n]

6 When Joseph came to them the next
morning, he saw that they were dejected.
7 So he asked Pharaoh's officials who were
in custody with him in his master's house,
"Why do you look so sad today?"[o]
8 "We both had dreams," they answered,
"but there is no one to interpret them."[p]
Then Joseph said to them, "Do not interpretations belong to God?[q] Tell me your
dreams."
9 So the chief cupbearer told Joseph his
dream. He said to him, "In my dream I
saw a vine in front of me, 10 and on the
vine were three branches. As soon as it
budded, it blossomed, and its clusters ripened into grapes. 11 Pharaoh's cup was in
my hand, and I took the grapes, squeezed
them into Pharaoh's cup and put the cup
in his hand."
12 "This is what it means,[r]" Joseph said
to him. "The three branches are three
days. 13 Within three days Pharaoh will lift
up your head and restore you to your position, and you will put Pharaoh's cup in
his hand, just as you used to do when you
were his cupbearer. 14 But when all goes
well with you, remember me[s] and show
me kindness;[t] mention me to Pharaoh and
get me out of this prison. 15 I was forcibly
carried off from the land of the Hebrews,[u]
and even here I have done nothing to deserve being put in a dungeon."
16 When the chief baker saw that Joseph
had given a favorable interpretation, he
said to Joseph, "I too had a dream: On my
head were three baskets of bread.[a] 17 In the
top basket were all kinds of baked goods

39:17 [d] Ex 23:1, 7; Ps 101:5 **39:19** [e] Pr 6:34 **39:20** [f] Ge 40:3; Ps 105:18 **39:21** [g] Ex 3:21 **39:22** [h] ver 4 **39:23** [i] ver 3 **40:1** [j] Ne 1:11 **40:2** [k] Pr 16:14, 15 **40:3** [l] Ge 39:20 **40:4** [m] Ge 39:4 **40:5** [n] Ge 41:11 **40:7** [o] Ne 2:2 **40:8** [p] Ge 41:8, 15 [q] Ge 41:16; Da 2:22, 28, 47 **40:12** [r] Ge 41:12, 15, 25; Da 2:36; 4:19 **40:14** [s] Lk 23:42 [t] Jos 2:12; 1Sa 20:14, 42; 1Ki 2:7 **40:15** [u] Ge 37:26-28

[a] 16 Or *three wicker baskets*

39:20 *where the king's prisoners were confined.* Jails were not common in the ancient world since imprisonment was not a standard punishment for crimes. If Potiphar truly believed that Joseph, his slave, was guilty of sexually assaulting his wife, execution would have been the swift and normal response. Instead, Joseph was confined where political prisoners were kept to await trial, judgment or execution. Since Potiphar was referred to as the "captain of the guard" (v. 1) and later Joseph met Pharaoh's other officials in the house of the captain of the guard (40:3), it appears that Joseph was detained under Potiphar's supervision and was there again given authority. In other words, Joseph was transferred to another part of Potiphar's house. That does not mean that his imprisonment was a farce, but it suggests that Potiphar's anger may well have been directed toward his wife and that after an adequate show of indignation, Joseph was gradually moved into a position of authority once again.

40:2 *the chief cupbearer and the chief baker.* Though these titles may in part be ceremonial, these two men had overall responsibility for what was served to the king. The potential for assassination attempts through the king's food and drink was real and constant, so these officials not only needed to be incorruptible themselves, but also had to be able to hire people above reproach and identify attempts at infiltration of the staff by enemies of the king. The text is silent concerning their offense, but since both were responsible for meals it seems logical to speculate that the king may have gotten sick from a meal.

40:5 *each dream had a meaning of its own.* Dreams were considered important vehicles of divine communication in the ancient world (see note on 37:5). Trained specialists interpreted the dreams of important people and paying customers using "dream books," compiled both in Egypt and Mesopotamia. These books were consulted for the meaning of symbols in dreams. The Egyptian books typically indicate that a particular element in the dream is good or bad. Mesopotamian dream books offer ritual remedies. The specialists depended on this literature because the gods did not reveal the interpretation of the dreams. Joseph, however, has no knowledge of the "science" and no access to the literature; he relies on God for the interpretation of the dream. The interpretation he offers nevertheless uses principles well known from the literature. For instance, the idea that the number of items indicates the number of days/years (vv. 12,18) has precedent in the literature. The symbols in these dreams are similar to some of those found in the dream books. A full goblet (v. 11), e.g., is indicative of having a name and offspring. Carrying fruit on one's head (cf. v. 16) is indicative of sorrow.

Painting in the tomb of Qenamun, West Thebes, depicts bakers mixing, kneading dough and filling bread molds. The chief baker (Ge 40:2) would have overseen these types of activities.

Werner Forman Archive/E. Strouhal/Glow Images

for Pharaoh, but the birds were eating
them out of the basket on my head."
18"This is what it means," Joseph said.
"The three baskets are three days.[v] 19With-
in three days Pharaoh will lift off your
head[w] and impale your body on a pole.
And the birds will eat away your flesh."
20Now the third day was Pharaoh's birth-
day,[x] and he gave a feast for all his officials.[y]
He lifted up the heads of the chief cupbearer and the chief baker in the presence of his
officials: 21He restored the chief cupbearer
to his position, so that he once again put
the cup into Pharaoh's hand[z]— 22but he
impaled the chief baker,[a] just as Joseph had
said to them in his interpretation.[b]
23The chief cupbearer, however, did not
remember Joseph; he forgot him.[c]

40:18 [v] ver 12
40:19 [w] ver 13
40:20 [x] Mt 14:6-10 [y] Mk 6:21
40:21 [z] ver 13
40:22 [a] ver 19 [b] Ps 105:19
40:23 [c] Job 19:14; Ecc 9:15

40:20 *Pharaoh's birthday.* No evidence for celebrations surrounding the birthday of a pharaoh is known until the first millennium BC. The day of birth may refer to the anniversary of his accession or coronation as king (cf. Ps 2:7), for which there is evidence as early as the Sixth Dynasty (second half of the third millennium).

40:22 *impaled the chief baker.* The Hebrew verb used here refers to being hanged. Hanging in the ancient world was generally not a means of execution, but an additional indignity in the treatment of a corpse. The corpse would be hung in some way (often impaled on a stick) to be devoured by insects, birds, and animals of prey. Here the execution was carried out by beheading (v. 19; cf. 1Sa 31:9–10) and then the body was hung out to be devoured.

Pharaoh's Dreams

41 When two full years had passed,
Pharaoh had a dream:[d] He was
standing by the Nile, 2when out of the river
there came up seven cows, sleek and fat,[e]
and they grazed among the reeds.[f] 3After
them, seven other cows, ugly and gaunt,
came up out of the Nile and stood beside
those on the riverbank. 4And the cows
that were ugly and gaunt ate up the sev-
en sleek, fat cows. Then Pharaoh woke up.
5He fell asleep again and had a second dream: Seven heads of grain, healthy
and good, were growing on a single stalk.
6After them, seven other heads of grain
sprouted—thin and scorched by the east
wind. 7The thin heads of grain swallowed
up the seven healthy, full heads. Then
Pharaoh woke up; it had been a dream.
8In the morning his mind was troubled,[g]
so he sent for all the magicians[h] and wise
men of Egypt. Pharaoh told them his
dreams, but no one could interpret them
for him.
9Then the chief cupbearer said to Pharaoh, "Today I am reminded of my shortcomings. 10Pharaoh was once angry with
his servants,[i] and he imprisoned me and
the chief baker in the house of the captain
of the guard.[j] 11Each of us had a dream the
same night, and each dream had a meaning of its own.[k] 12Now a young Hebrew
was there with us, a servant of the captain of the guard. We told him our dreams,
and he interpreted them for us, giving each
man the interpretation of his dream.[l] 13And
things turned out exactly as he interpreted
them to us: I was restored to my position,
and the other man was impaled.[m]"
14So Pharaoh sent for Joseph, and he
was quickly brought from the dungeon.[n]
When he had shaved and changed his
clothes, he came before Pharaoh.
15Pharaoh said to Joseph, "I had a
dream, and no one can interpret it. But
I have heard it said of you that when you
hear a dream you can interpret it."[o]
16"I cannot do it," Joseph replied to
Pharaoh, "but God will give Pharaoh the
answer he desires."[p]
17Then Pharaoh said to Joseph, "In my
dream I was standing on the bank of the
Nile, 18when out of the river there came up
seven cows, fat and sleek, and they grazed

41:1 [d] Ge 20:3 **41:2** [e] ver 26 [f] Isa 19:6 **41:8** [g] Da 2:1, 3; 4:5, 19 [h] Ex 7:11, 22; Da 1:20; 2:2, 27; 4:7

41:10 [i] Ge 40:2 [j] Ge 39:20 **41:11** [k] Ge 40:5 **41:12** [l] Ge 40:12 **41:13** [m] Ge 40:22 **41:14** [n] Ps 105:20; Da 2:25 **41:15** [o] Da 5:16 **41:16** [p] Ge 40:8; Da 2:30; Ac 3:12; 2Co 3:5

41:1 *Pharaoh.* It is impossible (given the insufficient data) to identify the pharaoh of the Joseph story, who throughout is simply called "Pharaoh." The term "Pharaoh" (= "great house") originally referred to the palace and is not attested as a designation for the king of Egypt until the fifteenth century BC. Even then, for the next 500 years or so it was not used with the name of the king, but stood alone as here and in Exodus. It is not until the tenth century BC that it is used in combination with a personal name. The general chronology locates Joseph in the period known as the Middle Kingdom (first quarter of second millennium BC) or the Second Intermediate Period (second quarter of the second millennium BC). Those who feel that a precise chronology can be derived from the Biblical record place Joseph in the reign of Amenemhet II or Senusret (Sesostris) II or III. *a dream.* A king's dream is always of special import, and he customarily employed dream specialists to interpret the dream and offer advice as to how to proceed. It was of particular importance if a dream were repeated, and a number of examples are known from the literature. Just as Pharaoh had a double dream here, Gudea, king of Lagash (around 2000 BC), had a double dream concerning the building of a temple. In a Mari letter, the king is warned twice (given to someone else on consecutive nights) that he should not rebuild a temple in Terqa. In the Gilgamesh Epic at the end of tablet 1, Gilgamesh has a double dream about his upcoming encounter with Enkidu. In tablet 4 he has a sequence of five dreams concerning the upcoming encounter with the guardian, Huwawa. In the Babylonian "Poem of the Righteous Sufferer" (*Ludlul bel Nemeqi*), the sufferer receives three dreams informing him that he has been cleansed from his offense. In these examples multiple dreams give warning (Mari), inform concerning the future (Gilgamesh), and offer absolution ("Righteous Sufferer"). Pharaoh's dreams contain the first two of these.

41:8 *magicians and wise men.* "Magicians" (*hartummim*) is a technical term that refers to the specialists centered in the "House of Life," where the dream interpretation manuals were stored and studied. This term is constructed from an Egyptian title referring to a chief lector priest (*hry-tp hry-hb*). This same term is used in late (Ptolemaic) literature to describe Imhotep, the famous Egyptian architect from the Third Dynasty (middle of the third millennium BC) who was also the high priest of Heliopolis. Another famous Egyptian lector priest was the prophet Neferti, who rehearses the troubled times of the First Intermediate Period at the end of the third millennium BC.

Egyptians, like the Mesopotamians and Hittites, had guilds of magicians whose tasks included both medicinal procedures and oneiromancy (divination based upon dreams). They used exorcism to frighten away gods and demons, and used incantations and curses to transfer evil to or from someone or somewhere. Thousands of texts have been discovered containing protection spells, as well as objects such as amulets, dolls, incantation bowls and figurines (and the recipes to create them), which were used in magical rituals. Mesopotamians distinguished between "black" (harmful) and "white" (helpful) magic, and thus practitioners were divided into "sorcerers" and "magicians"/"wise men," respectively, but Egyptians did not draw this distinction. Although their primary task was medical, Egyptian magicians sometimes employed a less respectful manner toward the gods, including spells to help a soul escape the underworld as seen in the "Book of the Dead."

It is unusual in Egypt for Pharaoh to be in need of a dream interpreter. Pharaoh was considered divine, so when the gods communicated with him through dreams, the meaning should have been obvious.

41:14 *shaved.* As Egyptian monuments certify, male Egyptians were characteristically clean-shaven and at times shaved their heads as well (bald or close-cropped), though they would then at times wear wigs made of human hair. The text here is unclear concerning the extent to which Joseph was shaved.

among the reeds. 19 After them, seven other
cows came up — scrawny and very ugly and
lean. I had never seen such ugly cows in all
the land of Egypt. 20 The lean, ugly cows ate
up the seven fat cows that came up first.
21 But even after they ate them, no one could
tell that they had done so; they looked just
as ugly as before. Then I woke up.

22 "In my dream I saw seven heads of
grain, full and good, growing on a single stalk. 23 After them, seven other
heads sprouted — withered and thin and
scorched by the east wind. 24 The thin
heads of grain swallowed up the seven
good heads. I told this to the magicians,
but none of them could explain it to me.[q]"

25 Then Joseph said to Pharaoh, "The
dreams of Pharaoh are one and the same.
God has revealed to Pharaoh what he is
about to do.[r] 26 The seven good cows[s] are
seven years, and the seven good heads of
grain are seven years; it is one and the
same dream. 27 The seven lean, ugly cows
that came up afterward are seven years,
and so are the seven worthless heads of
grain scorched by the east wind: They are
seven years of famine.[t]

28 "It is just as I said to Pharaoh: God
has shown Pharaoh what he is about to
do. 29 Seven years of great abundance[u]
are coming throughout the land of Egypt,
30 but seven years of famine[v] will follow
them. Then all the abundance in Egypt
will be forgotten, and the famine will ravage the land.[w] 31 The abundance in the
land will not be remembered, because the
famine that follows it will be so severe.
32 The reason the dream was given to Pharaoh in two forms is that the matter has
been firmly decided[x] by God, and God will
do it soon.

33 "And now let Pharaoh look for a discerning and wise man[y] and put him in
charge of the land of Egypt. 34 Let Pharaoh
appoint commissioners over the land to
take a fifth[z] of the harvest of Egypt during the seven years of abundance.[a] 35 They
should collect all the food of these good
years that are coming and store up the
grain under the authority of Pharaoh, to
be kept in the cities for food.[b] 36 This food
should be held in reserve for the country, to be used during the seven years of
famine that will come upon Egypt,[c] so
that the country may not be ruined by the
famine."

37 The plan seemed good to Pharaoh and
to all his officials.[d] 38 So Pharaoh asked
them, "Can we find anyone like this man,
one in whom is the spirit of God[a]?"[e]

39 Then Pharaoh said to Joseph, "Since
God has made all this known to you, there
is no one so discerning and wise as you.
40 You shall be in charge of my palace, and
all my people are to submit to your orders.[f] Only with respect to the throne will
I be greater than you."

Joseph in Charge of Egypt

41 So Pharaoh said to Joseph, "I hereby put you in charge of the whole land

41:24 [q] ver 8
41:25 [r] Da 2:45
41:26 [s] ver 2
41:27 [t] Ge 12:10; 2Ki 8:1
41:29 [u] ver 47
41:30 [v] ver 54; Ge 47:13 [w] ver 56
41:32 [x] Nu 23:19; Isa 46:10-11
41:33 [y] ver 39
41:34 [z] 1Sa 8:15 [a] ver 48
41:35 [b] ver 48
41:36 [c] ver 56
41:37 [d] Ge 45:16
41:38 [e] Nu 27:18; Job 32:8; Da 4:8-9, 18; 5:11, 14
41:40 [f] Ps 105:21-22; Ac 7:10

[a] 38 Or *of the gods*

41:27 *seven years of famine.* Extended famines were known in Egypt. If the nineteenth century BC is the time period of Joseph, it may be of interest that there is evidence of massive irrigation projects in the Faiyum area designed to reclaim additional land for farming (probably during the reign of Senusret II). It might also be noted that during the reign of Amenemhet III around 1800 BC, a number of years show record high levels of the Nile during the inundation (reaching as high as 16 feet [5 meters]), but in succeeding years it declined markedly so that ten years later it was only 1.5 feet (0.5 meters). Either of these events could conceivably be related to the system suggested and administered by Joseph, though there is no conclusive evidence to support such a connection.

41:34 *appoint commissioners.* In Egypt as well as in the rest of the ancient Near East, incantations were generally used to avoid the negative consequences portended by dreams. Here, in contrast, Joseph offers a strategy to counteract the effect of the dream. In the nineteenth century BC, Senusret III is known for reducing the power of the nomarchs (provincial governors) to restore a more centralized government. In the process a new "bureau of the vizier" and a new bureaucracy were established involving new commissioners. Again, there is no evidence to associate this with Joseph, but it demonstrates that periodic modifications in the bureaucracy were not uncommon.

41:40 *in charge of my palace.* Pharaoh's initial appointment gives Joseph authority in the palace based on the recognition of the Spirit of God in Joseph (v. 38). The combination of insight (indicated by the dream interpretation) and wisdom (indicated by the proposed strategy) were sufficient to conclude that Joseph enjoyed divine favor — a good reason to keep him close to the throne.

In Egyptian documents, the administrative second-in-command over Egypt is the vizier, known as the "Overseer of the Royal Estates." Joseph's new role, however, may not be quite as lofty as that. There are other posts that could make the claim of being second-in-command in the area of their responsibility. This is similar to a company today that has a President and CEO, and a staff of vice presidents: Vice President of Production, Vice President of Marketing, Vice President of Legal, etc. Each of these individuals could legitimately claim to be second-in-command in his or her particular area and to be set in charge of the entire company in the area of his or her jurisdiction. Similarly, numerous Egyptian nobles could serve in offices and bear titles that identified them as second only to Pharaoh. Such titles include "Great Favorite of the Lord of the Two Lands" and "Foremost Among His Courtiers."

One of the most appropriate known titles that describes Joseph's duties is "Overseer of the Granaries of Upper and Lower Egypt." It is not unusual to find accounts of officials who were elevated from lowly status to high positions of authority.

41:41 *in charge of the whole land of Egypt.* Joseph is given authority that is neither municipal nor regional.

of Egypt."[g] 42Then Pharaoh took his signet ring[h] from his finger and put it on Joseph's finger. He dressed him in robes of
fine linen and put a gold chain around his
neck.[i] 43He had him ride in a chariot as his
second-in-command,[a] and people shouted
before him, "Make way[b]!"[j] Thus he put
him in charge of the whole land of Egypt.
44Then Pharaoh said to Joseph, "I am
Pharaoh, but without your word no one
will lift hand or foot in all Egypt."[k] 45Phar-
aoh gave Joseph the name Zaphenath-Pa-
neah and gave him Asenath daughter of
Potiphera, priest of On,[c] to be his wife.[l]
And Joseph went throughout the land of
Egypt.
46Joseph was thirty years old[m] when he
entered the service[n] of Pharaoh king of
Egypt. And Joseph went out from Pharaoh's presence and traveled throughout
Egypt. 47During the seven years of abundance the land produced plentifully. 48Jo-
seph collected all the food produced in
those seven years of abundance in Egypt
and stored it in the cities. In each city he
put the food grown in the fields surrounding it. 49Joseph stored up huge quantities
of grain, like the sand of the sea; it was
so much that he stopped keeping records
because it was beyond measure.
50Before the years of famine came, two
sons were born to Joseph by Asenath
daughter of Potiphera, priest of On.[o] 51Jo-
seph named his firstborn[p] Manasseh[d] and
said, "It is because God has made me
forget all my trouble and all my father's
household." 52The second son he named
Ephraim[e][q] and said, "It is because God
has made me fruitful[r] in the land of my
suffering."
53The seven years of abundance in Egypt
came to an end, 54and the seven years of
famine began,[s] just as Joseph had said.
There was famine in all the other lands,
but in the whole land of Egypt there was
food. 55When all Egypt began to feel the
famine,[t] the people cried to Pharaoh for
food. Then Pharaoh told all the Egyptians,
"Go to Joseph and do what he tells you."[u]
56When the famine had spread over
the whole country, Joseph opened all the
storehouses and sold grain to the Egyptians, for the famine[v] was severe throughout Egypt. 57And all the world came to
Egypt to buy grain from Joseph,[w] because
the famine was severe everywhere.

41:41 [g] Ge 42:6; Da 6:3 **41:42** [h] Est 3:10 [i] Da 5:7,16,29 **41:43** [j] Est 6:9 **41:44** [k] Ps 105:22 **41:45** [l] ver 50; Ge 46:20,27 **41:46** [m] Ge 37:2 [n] 1Sa 16:21; Da 1:19 **41:50** [o] Ge 46:20; 48:5 **41:51** [p] Ge 48:14, 18,20 **41:52** [q] Ge 48:1, 5; 50:23 [r] Ge 17:6; 28:3; 49:22 **41:54** [s] ver 30; Ps 105:11; Ac 7:11 **41:55** [t] Dt 32:24 [u] ver 41 **41:56** [v] Ge 12:10 **41:57** [w] Ge 42:5; 47:15 **42:1** [x] Ac 7:12 **42:2** [y] Ge 43:8 **42:4** [z] ver 38 **42:5** [a] Ge 41:57 [b] Ge 12:10; Ac 7:11 **42:6** [c] Ge 41:41 [d] Ge 37:7-10 **42:7** [e] ver 30 **42:8** [f] Ge 37:2 **42:9** [g] Ge 37:7

Joseph's Brothers Go to Egypt

42 When Jacob learned that there was
grain in Egypt,[x] he said to his sons,
"Why do you just keep looking at each
other?" 2He continued, "I have heard that
there is grain in Egypt. Go down there and
buy some for us, so that we may live and
not die."[y]
3Then ten of Joseph's brothers went
down to buy grain from Egypt. 4But Jacob
did not send Benjamin, Joseph's brother,
with the others, because he was afraid
that harm might come to him.[z] 5So Israel's
sons were among those who went to buy
grain,[a] for there was famine in the land of
Canaan also.[b]
6Now Joseph was the governor of the
land,[c] the person who sold grain to all
its people. So when Joseph's brothers arrived, they bowed down to him with their
faces to the ground.[d] 7As soon as Joseph
saw his brothers, he recognized them, but
he pretended to be a stranger and spoke
harshly to them.[e] "Where do you come
from?" he asked.
"From the land of Canaan," they replied, "to buy food."
8Although Joseph recognized his brothers, they did not recognize him.[f] 9Then he
remembered his dreams[g] about them and
said to them, "You are spies! You have
come to see where our land is unprotect-
ed."

[a] 43 Or *in the chariot of his second-in-command*; or *in his second chariot* [b] 43 Or *Bow down* [c] 45 That is, Heliopolis; also in verse 50 [d] 51 *Manasseh* sounds like and may be derived from the Hebrew for *forget.* [e] 52 *Ephraim* sounds like the Hebrew for *twice fruitful.*

41:42–43 The signet ring allows Joseph to make decisions and authorize them in the name of Pharaoh. The clothing, jewelry and transportation all designate his high station.

41:45 Joseph's renaming and his marriage into a priestly family give him a new identity as an Egyptian noble. *On.* This city (reflecting Egyptian *Iunu*) is later known as Heliopolis and is one of the most revered of Egypt's ancient cities (along with Memphis and Thebes). It is located just north of modern Cairo at the base of the Nile delta.

42:9 *You are spies!* Semites/Asiatics were often distrusted by the Egyptians, so this is not an unusual charge. The Egyptians referred to them by various epithets such as "sand dwellers" and "throat slitters" and considered them wild and uncivilized.

But for what purpose would they be spying on Egypt? It is not likely that the Egyptians feared invasion from Canaan, though they may have been wary of limited raids. Since we use the word "spy" mostly for military intelligence, an alternate translation here might be "scouts." Economic motives would be more logical than military ones. Fields and storehouses could be plundered. What might ostensibly be a request for grain could serve as a guise for discovering what supplies of grain existed and how they might be ransacked. Reflections on the First Intermediate Period (last century and a half of the third millennium BC) in works such as the Instructions of Merikare and the Prophecy of Neferti reveal the social unrest caused by unruly foreign elements infiltrating Egyptian society. The result was increased attention to fortification of the Nile delta during the Middle Kingdom period (2100–1800 BC).

10“No, my lord,” they answered. “Your
servants have come to buy food. 11We are
all the sons of one man. Your servants are
honest men, not spies.”
12“No!” he said to them. “You have
come to see where our land is unprotect-
ed.”
13But they replied, “Your servants were
twelve brothers, the sons of one man, who
lives in the land of Canaan. The youngest is now with our father, and one is no
more.”[h]
14Joseph said to them, “It is just as I told
you: You are spies! 15And this is how you
will be tested: As surely as Pharaoh lives,[i]
you will not leave this place unless your
youngest brother comes here. 16Send one
of your number to get your brother; the
rest of you will be kept in prison, so that
your words may be tested to see if you
are telling the truth.[j] If you are not, then
as surely as Pharaoh lives, you are spies!”
17And he put them all in custody[k] for three
days.
18On the third day, Joseph said to them,
“Do this and you will live, for I fear God:[l]
19If you are honest men, let one of your
brothers stay here in prison, while the rest
of you go and take grain back for your
starving households. 20But you must bring
your youngest brother to me,[m] so that
your words may be verified and that you
may not die.” This they proceeded to do.
21They said to one another, “Surely we
are being punished because of our brother.[n] We saw how distressed he was when
he pleaded with us for his life, but we
would not listen; that's why this distress[o]
has come on us.”
22Reuben replied, “Didn't I tell you not
to sin against the boy?[p] But you wouldn't
listen! Now we must give an accounting[q]
for his blood.”[r] 23They did not realize that
Joseph could understand them, since he
was using an interpreter.
24He turned away from them and began
to weep, but then came back and spoke
to them again. He had Simeon taken from
them and bound before their eyes.[s]
25Joseph gave orders to fill their bags
with grain,[t] to put each man's silver back
in his sack,[u] and to give them provisions
for their journey.[v] After this was done for
them, 26they loaded their grain on their
donkeys and left.
27At the place where they stopped for
the night one of them opened his sack to
get feed for his donkey, and he saw his silver in the mouth of his sack.[w] 28“My silver
has been returned,” he said to his brothers. “Here it is in my sack.”
Their hearts sank and they turned to
each other trembling and said, “What is
this that God has done to us?”[x]
29When they came to their father Jacob
in the land of Canaan, they told him all
that had happened to them. They said,
30“The man who is lord over the land
spoke harshly to us[y] and treated us as
though we were spying on the land. 31But
we said to him, ‘We are honest men; we
are not spies.[z] 32We were twelve brothers,
sons of one father. One is no more, and
the youngest is now with our father in Canaan.’
33“Then the man who is lord over the
land said to us, ‘This is how I will know
whether you are honest men: Leave one
of your brothers here with me, and take
food for your starving households and go.[a]
34But bring your youngest brother to me
so I will know that you are not spies but
honest men. Then I will give your brother back to you, and you can trade[a] in the
land.[b]’ ”
35As they were emptying their sacks,
there in each man's sack was his pouch of
silver! When they and their father saw the
money pouches, they were frightened.[c]
36Their father Jacob said to them, “You
have deprived me of my children. Joseph
is no more and Simeon is no more, and
now you want to take Benjamin.[d] Everything is against me!”
37Then Reuben said to his father, “You
may put both of my sons to death if I do
not bring him back to you. Entrust him to
my care, and I will bring him back.”
38But Jacob said, “My son will not go
down there with you; his brother is dead[e]
and he is the only one left. If harm comes
to him[f] on the journey you are taking,
you will bring my gray head down to the
grave[g] in sorrow.[h]”

The Second Journey to Egypt

43 Now the famine was still severe in
the land.[i] 2So when they had eaten
all the grain they had brought from Egypt,
their father said to them, “Go back and
buy us a little more food.”
3But Judah said to him, “The man
warned us solemnly, ‘You will not see
my face again unless your brother is with

42:13 [h] Ge 37:30, 33; 44:20 **42:15** [i] 1Sa 17:55 **42:16** [j] ver 11 **42:17** [k] Ge 40:4 **42:18** [l] Ge 20:11; Lev 25:43 **42:20** [m] ver 15, 34; Ge 43:5; 44:23 **42:21** [n] Ge 37:26-28 [o] Hos 5:15 **42:22** [p] Ge 37:21-22 [q] Ge 9:5 [r] 1Ki 2:32; 2Ch 24:22; Ps 9:12 **42:24** [s] ver 13; Ge 43:14, 23; 45:14-15 **42:25** [t] Ge 43:2 [u] Ge 44:1, 8 [v] Ro 12:17, 20-21 **42:27** [w] Ge 43:21-22 **42:28** [x] Ge 43:23 **42:30** [y] ver 7 **42:31** [z] ver 11 **42:33** [a] ver 19, 20 **42:34** [b] Ge 34:10 **42:35** [c] Ge 43:12, 15, 18 **42:36** [d] Ge 43:14 **42:38** [e] Ge 37:33 [f] ver 4 [g] Ge 37:35 [h] Ge 44:29, 34 **43:1** [i] Ge 12:10; 41:56-57

[a] 34 Or *move about freely*

42:25 *each man's silver.* In supplying each of the brothers with both the grain and their silver, Joseph confirmed the accusation that they were scouts, intent on stealing grain (see previous note). Frequently we might see trade in grain or herds (rather than silver), but Jacob's family had no grain, and the herds were difficult to transport. It is no surprise, then, that they brought silver with which to trade.

you.'[j] 4If you will send our brother along with us, we will go down and buy food for you. 5But if you will not send him, we will not go down, because the man said to us, 'You will not see my face again unless your brother is with you.[k]' "

6Israel asked, "Why did you bring this trouble on me by telling the man you had another brother?"

7They replied, "The man questioned us closely about ourselves and our family. 'Is your father still living?'[l] he asked us. 'Do you have another brother?'[m] We simply answered his questions. How were we to know he would say, 'Bring your brother down here'?"

8Then Judah said to Israel his father, "Send the boy along with me and we will go at once, so that we and you and our children may live and not die.[n] 9I myself will guarantee his safety; you can hold me personally responsible for him. If I do not bring him back to you and set him here before you, I will bear the blame before you all my life.[o] 10As it is, if we had not delayed, we could have gone and returned twice."

11Then their father Israel said to them, "If it must be, then do this: Put some of the best products of the land in your bags and take them down to the man as a gift[p]—a little balm[q] and a little honey, some spices[r] and myrrh, some pistachio nuts and almonds. 12Take double the amount of silver with you, for you must return the silver that was put back into the mouths of your sacks.[s] Perhaps it was a mistake. 13Take your brother also and go back to the man at once. 14And may God Almighty[a][t] grant you mercy before the man so that he will let your other brother and Benjamin come back with you.[u] As for me, if I am bereaved, I am bereaved."[v]

15So the men took the gifts and double the amount of silver, and Benjamin also. They hurried[w] down to Egypt and presented themselves[x] to Joseph. 16When Joseph saw Benjamin with them, he said to the steward of his house,[y] "Take these men to my house, slaughter an animal and prepare a meal;[z] they are to eat with me at noon."

17The man did as Joseph told him and took the men to Joseph's house. 18Now the men were frightened[a] when they were taken to his house. They thought, "We were brought here because of the silver that was put back into our sacks the first time. He wants to attack us and overpower us and seize us as slaves and take our donkeys."

19So they went up to Joseph's steward and spoke to him at the entrance to the house. 20"We beg your pardon, our lord," they said, "we came down here the first time to buy food.[b] 21But at the place where we stopped for the night we opened our sacks and each of us found his silver—the exact weight—in the mouth of his sack. So we have brought it back with us.[c] 22We have also brought additional silver with us to buy food. We don't know who put our silver in our sacks."

23"It's all right," he said. "Don't be afraid. Your God, the God of your father, has given you treasure in your sacks;[d] I received your silver." Then he brought Simeon out to them.[e]

24The steward took the men into Joseph's house,[f] gave them water to wash their feet[g] and provided fodder for their donkeys. 25They prepared their gifts for Joseph's arrival at noon, because they had heard that they were to eat there.

26When Joseph came home, they presented to him the gifts[h] they had brought into the house, and they bowed down before him to the ground.[i] 27He asked them how they were, and then he said, "How is your aged father you told me about? Is he still living?"[j]

28They replied, "Your servant our father is still alive and well." And they bowed down, prostrating themselves before him.[k]

29As he looked about and saw his brother Benjamin, his own mother's son, he asked, "Is this your youngest brother, the one you told me about?"[l] And he said, "God be gracious to you,[m] my son." 30Deeply moved[n] at the sight of his brother, Joseph hurried out and looked for a place to weep. He went into his private room and wept[o] there.

31After he had washed his face, he came out and, controlling himself,[p] said, "Serve the food."

32They served him by himself, the brothers by themselves, and the Egyptians who ate with him by themselves, because Egyptians could not eat with Hebrews,[q] for that is detestable to Egyptians.[r] 33The men had been seated before him in the order of their ages, from the firstborn to the youngest; and they looked at each other in astonishment. 34When portions were served to them from Joseph's table, Benjamin's portion was five times as much as anyone else's.[s] So they feasted and drank freely with him.

A Silver Cup in a Sack

44 Now Joseph gave these instructions to the steward of his house: "Fill the men's sacks with as much food as they can carry, and put each man's silver in the mouth of his sack.[t] 2Then put my

43:3 [j] Ge 42:15; 44:23 **43:5** [k] Ge 42:15; 2Sa 3:13 **43:7** [l] ver 27 [m] Ge 42:13 **43:8** [n] Ge 42:2; Ps 33:18-19 **43:9** [o] Ge 42:37; 44:32; Phm 1:18-19 **43:11** [p] Ge 32:20; Pr 18:16 [q] Ge 37:25; Jer 8:22 [r] 1Ki 10:2 **43:12** [s] Ge 42:25 **43:14** [t] Ge 17:1; 28:3; 35:11 [u] Ge 42:24 [v] Est 4:16 **43:15** [w] Ge 45:9,13 [x] Ge 47:2,7 **43:16** [y] Ge 44:1,4,12 [z] ver 31; Lk 15:23 **43:18** [a] Ge 42:35 **43:20** [b] Ge 42:3 **43:21** [c] ver 15; Ge 42:27,35 **43:23** [d] Ge 42:28 [e] Ge 42:24 **43:24** [f] ver 16 [g] Ge 18:4; 24:32 **43:26** [h] Mt 2:11 [i] Ge 37:7,10 **43:27** [j] ver 7 **43:28** [k] Ge 37:7 **43:29** [l] Ge 42:13 [m] Nu 6:25; Ps 67:1 **43:30** [n] Jn 11:33,38 [o] Ge 42:24; 45:2,14,15; 46:29 **43:31** [p] Ge 45:1 **43:32** [q] Gal 2:12 [r] Ge 46:34; Ex 8:26 **43:34** [s] Ge 37:3; 45:22 **44:1** [t] Ge 42:25

[a] 14 Hebrew *El-Shaddai*

cup, the silver one, in the mouth of the
youngest one's sack, along with the silver
for his grain." And he did as Joseph said.
3As morning dawned, the men were
sent on their way with their donkeys.
4They had not gone far from the city when
Joseph said to his steward, "Go after those
men at once, and when you catch up with
them, say to them, 'Why have you repaid
good with evil?[u] 5Isn't this the cup my
master drinks from and also uses for divination?[v] This is a wicked thing you have
done.' "
6When he caught up with them, he repeated these words to them. 7But they
said to him, "Why does my lord say such
things? Far be it from your servants to do
anything like that! 8We even brought back
to you from the land of Canaan the silver we found inside the mouths of our
sacks.[w] So why would we steal silver or
gold from your master's house? 9If any of
your servants is found to have it, he will
die;[x] and the rest of us will become my
lord's slaves."
10"Very well, then," he said, "let it be as
you say. Whoever is found to have it will
become my slave; the rest of you will be
free from blame."
11Each of them quickly lowered his sack
to the ground and opened it. 12Then the
steward proceeded to search, beginning
with the oldest and ending with the youngest. And the cup was found in Benjamin's
sack.[y] 13At this, they tore their clothes.[z]
Then they all loaded their donkeys and returned to the city.
14Joseph was still in the house when Judah and his brothers came in, and they
threw themselves to the ground before
him.[a] 15Joseph said to them, "What is this
you have done? Don't you know that a
man like me can find things out by divination?[b]"
16"What can we say to my lord?" Judah
replied. "What can we say? How can we
prove our innocence? God has uncovered
your servants' guilt. We are now my lord's
slaves[c]—we ourselves and the one who
was found to have the cup.[d]"
17But Joseph said, "Far be it from me to
do such a thing! Only the man who was
found to have the cup will become my
slave. The rest of you, go back to your father in peace."
18Then Judah went up to him and said:
"Pardon your servant, my lord, let me
speak a word to my lord. Do not be angry[e]
with your servant, though you are equal to
Pharaoh himself. 19My lord asked his servants, 'Do you have a father or a brother?'[f]
20And we answered, 'We have an aged father, and there is a young son born to him
in his old age.[g] His brother is dead,[h] and
he is the only one of his mother's sons
left, and his father loves him.'[i]
21"Then you said to your servants,
'Bring him down to me so I can see him
for myself.'[j] 22And we said to my lord, 'The
boy cannot leave his father; if he leaves
him, his father will die.'[k] 23But you told
your servants, 'Unless your youngest
brother comes down with you, you will
not see my face again.'[l] 24When we went
back to your servant my father, we told
him what my lord had said.
25"Then our father said, 'Go back and
buy a little more food.'[m] 26But we said,
'We cannot go down. Only if our youngest
brother is with us will we go. We cannot
see the man's face unless our youngest
brother is with us.'
27"Your servant my father said to us,
'You know that my wife bore me two
sons.[n] 28One of them went away from me,
and I said, "He has surely been torn to
pieces."[o] And I have not seen him since.
29If you take this one from me too and
harm comes to him, you will bring my
gray head down to the grave in misery.'[p]
30"So now, if the boy is not with us
when I go back to your servant my father, and if my father, whose life is closely
bound up with the boy's life,[q] 31sees that
the boy isn't there, he will die. Your servants will bring the gray head of our father down to the grave in sorrow. 32Your
servant guaranteed the boy's safety to my
father. I said, 'If I do not bring him back to
you, I will bear the blame before you, my
father, all my life!'[r]
33"Now then, please let your servant remain here as my lord's slave[s] in place of
the boy,[t] and let the boy return with his
brothers. 34How can I go back to my father if the boy is not with me? No! Do not
let me see the misery that would come on
my father."[u]

Joseph Makes Himself Known

45 Then Joseph could no longer control himself[v] before all his attendants, and he cried out, "Have everyone
leave my presence!" So there was no

44:4 [u] Ps 35:12 **44:5** [v] Ge 30:27; Dt 18:10-14 **44:8** [w] Ge 42:25; 43:21 **44:9** [x] Ge 31:32 **44:12** [y] ver 2 **44:13** [z] Ge 37:29; Nu 14:6; 2Sa 1:11 **44:14** [a] Ge 37:7, 10 **44:15** [b] ver 5; Ge 30:27 **44:16** [c] ver 9; Ge 43:18 [d] ver 2

44:18 [e] Ge 18:30; Ex 32:22 **44:19** [f] Ge 43:7 **44:20** [g] Ge 37:3 [h] Ge 37:33 [i] Ge 42:13 **44:21** [j] Ge 42:15 **44:22** [k] Ge 37:35 **44:23** [l] Ge 43:5 **44:25** [m] Ge 43:2 **44:27** [n] Ge 46:19 **44:28** [o] Ge 37:33 **44:29** [p] Ge 42:38 **44:30** [q] 1Sa 18:1 **44:32** [r] Ge 43:9 **44:33** [s] Ge 43:18 [t] Jn 15:13 **44:34** [u] Est 8:6 **45:1** [v] Ge 43:31

44:5 *cup ... for divination.* The idea that a cup was used for divination suggests that divination took place by observing liquids poured into the cup (either the shapes of oil on water or the ripples of the water, to name a few techniques known from Mesopotamia). Little is known of these techniques in Egyptian practice. Divination was a means of acquiring information. It is of interest that Joseph acquired information by means of the cup, not by pouring liquid into it, but by using it to test his brothers, thus using observation at a different level.

one with Joseph when he made himself
known to his brothers. 2And he wept[w] so
loudly that the Egyptians heard him, and
Pharaoh's household heard about it.[x]
3Joseph said to his brothers, "I am Joseph! Is my father still living?"[y] But his
brothers were not able to answer him,[z] because they were terrified at his presence.
4Then Joseph said to his brothers,
"Come close to me." When they had done
so, he said, "I am your brother Joseph,
the one you sold into Egypt![a] 5And now,
do not be distressed[b] and do not be angry
with yourselves for selling me here,[c] because it was to save lives that God sent me
ahead of you.[d] 6For two years now there
has been famine in the land, and for the
next five years there will be no plowing
and reaping. 7But God sent me ahead of
you to preserve for you a remnant[e] on
earth and to save your lives by a great deliverance.[a][f]
8"So then, it was not you who sent me
here, but God. He made me father[g] to
Pharaoh, lord of his entire household and
ruler of all Egypt.[h] 9Now hurry back to my
father and say to him, 'This is what your
son Joseph says: God has made me lord
of all Egypt. Come down to me; don't delay.[i] 10You shall live in the region of Goshen[j] and be near me—you, your children and grandchildren, your flocks and
herds, and all you have. 11I will provide for
you there,[k] because five years of famine
are still to come. Otherwise you and your
household and all who belong to you will
become destitute.'
12"You can see for yourselves, and so
can my brother Benjamin, that it is really I
who am speaking to you. 13Tell my father
about all the honor accorded me in Egypt
and about everything you have seen. And
bring my father down here quickly.[l]"
14Then he threw his arms around his
brother Benjamin and wept, and Benjamin
embraced him, weeping. 15And he kissed[m]
all his brothers and wept over them. Afterward his brothers talked with him.[n]
16When the news reached Pharaoh's
palace that Joseph's brothers had come,[o]
Pharaoh and all his officials were pleased.
17Pharaoh said to Joseph, "Tell your brothers, 'Do this: Load your animals and return to the land of Canaan, 18and bring
your father and your families back to me. I
will give you the best of the land of Egypt[p]
and you can enjoy the fat of the land.'[q]
19"You are also directed to tell them, 'Do
this: Take some carts[r] from Egypt for your
children and your wives, and get your father and come. 20Never mind about your
belongings, because the best of all Egypt
will be yours.' "
21So the sons of Israel did this. Joseph
gave them carts, as Pharaoh had commanded, and he also gave them provisions for their journey.[s] 22To each of them
he gave new clothing, but to Benjamin he
gave three hundred shekels[b] of silver and
five sets of clothes.[t] 23And this is what he
sent to his father: ten donkeys loaded with
the best things of Egypt, and ten female
donkeys loaded with grain and bread and
other provisions for his journey. 24Then he
sent his brothers away, and as they were
leaving he said to them, "Don't quarrel on
the way!"[u]
25So they went up out of Egypt and
came to their father Jacob in the land of
Canaan. 26They told him, "Joseph is still
alive! In fact, he is ruler of all Egypt."
Jacob was stunned; he did not believe
them.[v] 27But when they told him everything Joseph had said to them, and when
he saw the carts[w] Joseph had sent to carry
him back, the spirit of their father Jacob
revived. 28And Israel said, "I'm convinced!
My son Joseph is still alive. I will go and
see him before I die."

Jacob Goes to Egypt

46 So Israel set out with all that was
his, and when he reached Beershe-
ba,[x] he offered sacrifices to the God of his
father Isaac.[y]
2And God spoke to Israel in a vision at
night[z] and said, "Jacob! Jacob!"
"Here I am,"[a] he replied.
3"I am God, the God of your father,"[b]
he said. "Do not be afraid to go down to
Egypt, for I will make you into a great
nation[c] there.[d] 4I will go down to Egypt
with you, and I will surely bring you back
again.[e] And Joseph's own hand will close
your eyes.[f]"
5Then Jacob left Beersheba, and Israel's

[a] 7 Or *save you as a great band of survivors* [b] 22 That is, about 7 1/2 pounds or about 3.5 kilograms

45:2 [w] Ge 29:11 [x] ver 16; Ge 46:29 **45:3** [y] Ac 7:13 [z] ver 15 **45:4** [a] Ge 37:28 **45:5** [b] Ge 42:21 [c] Ge 42:22 [d] ver 7-8; Ge 50:20; Ps 105:17 **45:7** [e] 2Ki 19:4, 30,31; Isa 10:20,21; Mic 4:7; Zep 2:7 [f] Ex 15:2; Est 4:14; Isa 25:9 **45:8** [g] Jdg 17:10 [h] Ge 41:41 **45:9** [i] Ge 43:10 **45:10** [j] Ge 46:28,34; 47:1 **45:11** [k] Ge 47:12 **45:13** [l] Ac 7:14 **45:15** [m] Lk 15:20 [n] ver 3 **45:16** [o] Ac 7:13 **45:18** [p] Ge 27:28; 46:34; 47:6, 11, 27; Nu 18:12,29 [q] Ps 37:19 **45:19** [r] Ge 46:5 **45:21** [s] Ge 42:25 **45:22** [t] Ge 37:3; 43:34 **45:24** [u] Ge 42:21-22 **45:26** [v] Ge 44:28 **45:27** [w] ver 19 **46:1** [x] Ge 21:14; 28:10 [y] Ge 26:24; 28:13; 31:42 **46:2** [z] Ge 15:1; Job 33:14-15 [a] Ge 22:1; 31:11 **46:3** [b] Ge 28:13 [c] Ge 12:2; Dt 26:5 [d] Ex 1:7 **46:4** [e] Ge 28:15; 48:21; Ex 3:8 [f] Ge 50:1,24

45:8 *father to Pharaoh.* The Egyptian title *it-ntr* ("father of the god") refers to a variety of officials and priests. Since Pharaoh was considered divine, it is likely that "father to Pharaoh" carries a similar connotation of advisor.
45:10 *region of Goshen.* In Egyptian texts the heaviest concentrations of Semites occur in the eastern delta region closest to Canaan. This corresponds to the Biblical texts in which the region of Goshen is equated to the "district of Rameses" (47:11), which is certainly in the delta region. In the early chapters of Exodus, this is the location of the Israelite labors in towns such as Pithom and Rameses. The region is bounded by the branches of the Nile delta on the west and the series of lakes from the Mediterranean down to the Red Sea on the east. Crossing east to west through the center of it is the Wadi Tumilat.

sons took their father Jacob and their children and their wives in the carts[g] that Pharaoh had sent to transport him. 6So Jacob
and all his offspring went to Egypt,[h] taking
with them their livestock and the possessions they had acquired in Canaan. 7Jacob
brought with him to Egypt his sons and
grandsons and his daughters and granddaughters — all his offspring.[i]

8These are the names of the sons of Israel[j] (Jacob and his descendants) who went
to Egypt:

Reuben the firstborn of Jacob.
9The sons of Reuben:[k]
Hanok, Pallu, Hezron and Karmi.
10The sons of Simeon:[l]
Jemuel,[m] Jamin, Ohad, Jakin, Zohar and Shaul the son of a Canaanite woman.
11The sons of Levi:[n]
Gershon, Kohath and Merari.
12The sons of Judah:[o]
Er, Onan, Shelah, Perez and Zerah
(but Er and Onan had died in the
land of Canaan).
The sons of Perez:[p]
Hezron and Hamul.
13The sons of Issachar:[q]
Tola, Puah,[a r] Jashub[b] and Shimron.
14The sons of Zebulun:[s]
Sered, Elon and Jahleel.

15These were the sons Leah bore to Jacob in Paddan Aram,[c] besides his daughter
Dinah. These sons and daughters of his
were thirty-three in all.

16The sons of Gad:[t]
Zephon,[d u] Haggi, Shuni, Ezbon,
Eri, Arodi and Areli.
17The sons of Asher:[v]
Imnah, Ishvah, Ishvi and Beriah.
Their sister was Serah.
The sons of Beriah:
Heber and Malkiel.

18These were the children born to Jacob
by Zilpah,[w] whom Laban had given to his
daughter Leah[x] — sixteen in all.

19The sons of Jacob's wife Rachel:
Joseph and Benjamin.[y] 20In Egypt,
Manasseh[z] and Ephraim[a] were
born to Joseph by Asenath daughter of Potiphera, priest of On.[e]

46:5 [g] Ge 45:19
46:6 [h] Dt 26:5; Jos 24:4; Ps 105:23; Isa 52:4; Ac 7:15
46:7 [i] Ge 45:10
46:8 [j] Ex 1:1; Nu 26:4
46:9 [k] 1Ch 5:3
46:10 [l] Ge 29:33; Nu 26:14 [m] Ex 6:15
46:11 [n] Ge 29:34; Nu 3:17
46:12 [o] Ge 29:35 [p] 1Ch 2:5; Mt 1:3
46:13 [q] Ge 30:18 [r] 1Ch 7:1
46:14 [s] Ge 30:20
46:16 [t] Ge 30:11 [u] Nu 26:15
46:17 [v] Ge 30:13; 1Ch 7:30-31
46:18 [w] Ge 30:10 [x] Ge 29:24
46:19 [y] Ge 44:27
46:20 [z] Ge 41:51 [a] Ge 41:52
46:21 [b] Nu 26:38-41; 1Ch 7:6-12; 8:1
46:25 [c] Ge 30:8 [d] Ge 29:29
46:26 [e] ver 5-7; Ex 1:5; Dt 10:22
46:27 [f] Ac 7:14
46:28 [g] Ge 45:10
46:29 [h] Ge 45:14-15; Lk 15:20
46:31 [i] Ge 47:1
46:33 [j] Ge 47:3

21The sons of Benjamin:[b]
Bela, Beker, Ashbel, Gera, Naaman,
Ehi, Rosh, Muppim, Huppim and
Ard.

22These were the sons of Rachel who
were born to Jacob — fourteen in all.

23The son of Dan:
Hushim.
24The sons of Naphtali:
Jahziel, Guni, Jezer and Shillem.

25These were the sons born to Jacob
by Bilhah,[c] whom Laban had given to his
daughter Rachel[d] — seven in all.

26All those who went to Egypt with Jacob — those who were his direct descendants, not counting his sons' wives —
numbered sixty-six persons.[e] 27With the
two sons[f] who had been born to Joseph
in Egypt, the members of Jacob's family,
which went to Egypt, were seventy[g] in all.[f]

28Now Jacob sent Judah ahead of him to
Joseph to get directions to Goshen.[g] When
they arrived in the region of Goshen, 29Jo-
seph had his chariot made ready and
went to Goshen to meet his father Israel.
As soon as Joseph appeared before him,
he threw his arms around his father[h] and
wept for a long time.[h]

30Israel said to Joseph, "Now I am ready
to die, since I have seen for myself that
you are still alive."

31Then Joseph said to his brothers and
to his father's household, "I will go up
and speak to Pharaoh and will say to him,
'My brothers and my father's household,
who were living in the land of Canaan,
have come to me.[i] 32The men are shepherds; they tend livestock, and they have
brought along their flocks and herds and
everything they own.' 33When Pharaoh
calls you in and asks, 'What is your occupation?'[j] 34you should answer, 'Your
servants have tended livestock from our
boyhood on, just as our fathers did.' Then

[a] *13* Samaritan Pentateuch and Syriac (see also 1 Chron. 7:1); Masoretic Text *Puvah* [b] *13* Samaritan Pentateuch and some Septuagint manuscripts (see also Num. 26:24 and 1 Chron. 7:1); Masoretic Text *Iob* [c] *15* That is, Northwest Mesopotamia [d] *16* Samaritan Pentateuch and Septuagint (see also Num. 26:15); Masoretic Text *Ziphion* [e] *20* That is, Heliopolis [f] *27* Hebrew; Septuagint *the nine children* [g] *27* Hebrew (see also Exodus 1:5 and note); Septuagint (see also Acts 7:14) *seventy-five* [h] *29* Hebrew *around him*

46:34 *all shepherds are detestable to the Egyptians.* By identifying themselves as shepherds, Jacob's clan offers assurance that they are not coming to take Egyptian farmland or get involved in politics. Flocks and herds were kept by Egyptians during all periods and were used for meat, milk, and wool or hides, as well as for some sacrifices (more cattle than sheep and goats). They are depicted in reliefs, models and tomb paintings, remains are found in excavation, and deities were associated with the ram and the cow (but not sheep or goats) — all demonstrating the pervasive penetration of these animals into Egyptian culture. In contrast, sheep and goats do not figure prominently in fables, metaphors or personal names, which indicates that they were considered rather common.

It is difficult to ascertain whether shepherds were detested because of their associations with foreigners, with a low status in society, or with sheep and goats as

Egyptian painting at Beni Hasan of man with goats. Many depictions of flocks and herds have been discovered, demonstrating the pervasive penetration of these animals into Egyptian culture. It is difficult to ascertain whether shepherds were detested (Ge 46:34) because of their associations with foreigners, with a low status in society, or with sheep and goats as inferior animals that threatened farm land.

you will be allowed to settle in the region of Goshen,[k] for all shepherds are detestable to the Egyptians.[l]"

47 Joseph went and told Pharaoh, "My father and brothers, with their flocks and herds and everything they own, have come from the land of Canaan and are now in Goshen."[m] 2He chose five of his brothers and presented them before Pharaoh.

3Pharaoh asked the brothers, "What is your occupation?"[n]

"Your servants are shepherds," they replied to Pharaoh, "just as our fathers were." 4They also said to him, "We have come to live here for a while,[o] because the famine is severe in Canaan[p] and your servants' flocks have no pasture. So now, please let your servants settle in Goshen."[q]

5Pharaoh said to Joseph, "Your father and your brothers have come to you, 6and the land of Egypt is before you; settle your father and your brothers in the best part of the land.[r] Let them live in Goshen. And if you know of any among them with special ability,[s] put them in charge of my own livestock."

7Then Joseph brought his father Jacob in and presented him before Pharaoh. After Jacob blessed[a] Pharaoh,[t] 8Pharaoh asked him, "How old are you?"

9And Jacob said to Pharaoh, "The years of my pilgrimage are a hundred and thirty.[u] My years have been few and difficult,[v] and they do not equal the years of the pilgrimage of my fathers.[w]" 10Then Jacob blessed[b] Pharaoh[x] and went out from his presence.

11So Joseph settled his father and his brothers in Egypt and gave them property in the best part of the land, the district of Rameses,[y] as Pharaoh directed. 12Joseph also provided his father and his brothers and all his father's household with food, according to the number of their children.[z]

Joseph and the Famine

13There was no food, however, in the whole region because the famine was severe; both Egypt and Canaan wasted away because of the famine.[a] 14Joseph collected all the money that was to be found in Egypt and Canaan in payment for the grain they were buying, and he brought it to Pharaoh's palace.[b] 15When the money of the people of Egypt and Canaan was gone, all Egypt came to Joseph and said, "Give us food. Why should we die before your eyes?[c] Our money is all gone."

16"Then bring your livestock," said Joseph. "I will sell you food in exchange for your livestock, since your money is gone."

[a] 7 Or *greeted* [b] 10 Or *said farewell to*

46:34 [k]Ge 45:10 [l]Ge 43:32; Ex 8:26
47:1 [m]Ge 46:31
47:3 [n]Ge 46:33
47:4 [o]Ge 15:13; Dt 26:5 [p]Ge 43:1 [q]Ge 46:34
47:6 [r]Ge 45:18 [s]Ex 18:21,25
47:7 [t]ver 10; 2Sa 14:22
47:9 [u]Ge 25:7 [v]Heb 11:9,13 [w]Ge 35:28
47:10 [x]ver 7
47:11 [y]Ex 1:11; 12:37
47:12 [z]Ge 45:11
47:13 [a]Ge 41:30; Ac 7:11
47:14 [b]Ge 41:56
47:15 [c]ver 19; Ex 16:3

inferior animals that threatened farm land. Extant Egyptian records offer no insight on this.

47:11 *district of Rameses.* At this period Rameses was not a common name and no city was yet so named. The pharaohs with the names Rameses do not come along until the thirteenth century BC. It is logical to conclude that this geographic name is supplied at a later period. The city of Rameses, Pi-Ramesse, is eventually going to be located at Qantir/Avaris (Tell ed-Dab'a, which has been extensively excavated and provides much evidence of a Semitic population that lived there). The site was founded in the Twelfth Dynasty (1963–1786 BC), the most likely setting for Joseph. Despite the growing Syro-Palestinian population of this town over the next several centuries, no remains permit the identification of descendants of Abraham. The material culture is Canaanite and the religious practices show a syncretism of Canaanite and Egyptian elements.

17So they brought their livestock to Joseph, and he gave them food in exchange
for their horses,[d] their sheep and goats,
their cattle and donkeys. And he brought
them through that year with food in exchange for all their livestock.
18When that year was over, they came
to him the following year and said, "We
cannot hide from our lord the fact that
since our money is gone and our livestock belongs to you, there is nothing left
for our lord except our bodies and our
land. 19Why should we perish before your
eyes — we and our land as well? Buy us
and our land in exchange for food, and we
with our land will be in bondage to Pharaoh. Give us seed so that we may live and
not die, and that the land may not become
desolate."
20So Joseph bought all the land in Egypt
for Pharaoh. The Egyptians, one and all,
sold their fields, because the famine was
too severe for them. The land became
Pharaoh's, 21and Joseph reduced the people to servitude,[a] from one end of Egypt to
the other. 22However, he did not buy the
land of the priests, because they received
a regular allotment from Pharaoh and had
food enough from the allotment[e] Pharaoh
gave them. That is why they did not sell
their land.
23Joseph said to the people, "Now that
I have bought you and your land today
for Pharaoh, here is seed for you so you
can plant the ground. 24But when the crop
comes in, give a fifth[f] of it to Pharaoh. The
other four-fifths you may keep as seed for
the fields and as food for yourselves and
your households and your children."
25"You have saved our lives," they said.
"May we find favor in the eyes of our
lord;[g] we will be in bondage to Pharaoh."
26So Joseph established it as a law concerning land in Egypt — still in force today — that a fifth of the produce belongs
to Pharaoh. It was only the land of the
priests that did not become Pharaoh's.[h]
27Now the Israelites settled in Egypt in
the region of Goshen. They acquired property there and were fruitful and increased
greatly in number.[i]
28Jacob lived in Egypt[j] seventeen years,
and the years of his life were a hundred
and forty-seven. 29When the time drew
near for Israel to die,[k] he called for his
son Joseph and said to him, "If I have
found favor in your eyes, put your hand
under my thigh[l] and promise that you will
show me kindness and faithfulness.[m] Do
not bury me in Egypt, 30but when I rest
with my fathers, carry me out of Egypt and
bury me where they are buried."[n]
"I will do as you say," he said.
31"Swear to me,"[o] he said. Then Joseph
swore to him,[p] and Israel worshiped as he
leaned on the top of his staff.[bq]

Manasseh and Ephraim

48 Some time later Joseph was told,
"Your father is ill." So he took his
two sons Manasseh and Ephraim[r] along
with him. 2When Jacob was told, "Your
son Joseph has come to you," Israel rallied
his strength and sat up on the bed.
3Jacob said to Joseph, "God Almighty[c]
appeared to me at Luz[s] in the land of Ca-

47:17 [d]Ex 14:9 **47:22** [e]Dt 14:28-29; Ezr 7:24 **47:24** [f]Ge 41:34 **47:25** [g]Ge 32:5 **47:26** [h]ver 22 **47:27** [i]Ge 17:6; 46:3; Ex 1:7 **47:28** [j]Ps 105:23 **47:29** [k]Dt 31:14 [l]Ge 24:2 [m]Ge 24:49 **47:30** [n]Ge 49:29-32; 50:5,13; Ac 7:15-16 **47:31** [o]Ge 21:23 [p]Ge 24:3 [q]Heb 11:21 *fn;* 1Ki 1:47 **48:1** [r]Ge 41:52 **48:3** [s]Ge 28:19

[a] *21* Samaritan Pentateuch and Septuagint (see also Vulgate); Masoretic Text *and he moved the people into the cities* [b] *31* Or *Israel bowed down at the head of his bed* [c] *3* Hebrew *El-Shaddai*

47:19 *Buy us and our land.* Joseph's policy suggests a shift from privately owned property to centralized ownership of property worked by tenant farmers. The Middle Kingdom and Early New Kingdom (2100 – 1500 BC) evidence large tracts of crown property administered by government officials. In this way centralization is in evidence as is the state-run redistributive economy. In the New Kingdom, much land gradually came under control of the temples. In that period, there was no longer any private property, but only personal rights to the use of property granted in trust for a land-owning institution such as the crown or temple.

Though it may appear as if Joseph's policies were economically repressive, hard times require hard solutions. The text documents the sequence of how the people were impoverished by the famine (not by the government). First they spent all their money buying food, then they traded away their livestock, and finally they gave up their land and worked as tenant farmers. Their rent for the land was 20 percent of the produce — a lower than normal percentage in the ancient world. This was a progressive tax in that it was proportioned according to income. Theoretically, then, a prosperous farmer could have rebuilt his wealth when the famine ended, though it is not clear whether he would have been allowed to buy back the land. This turned Egypt into a state in which all the wealth was centralized in the government. Despite the personal hardship and servitude that resulted, the people were grateful for their lives.

47:22 *priests ... received a regular allotment from Pharaoh.* Priests did not need to grow their own food, and therefore shortages did not drive them to sell their land. Instead, temples, like the kings, were owners of land and benefited from renting out the land to be farmed by laborers. Temple ownership of land is well documented in Egypt of all periods, but became extensive by the mid-second millennium BC.

47:29 *Do not bury me in Egypt.* Jacob's sentiment reflects the extent to which he is tied to the land of Canaan, as it looks to both past and future. Since the ancestral burial ground is in Canaan, he will "rest with [his] fathers" (v. 30) by being buried with them, thus actualizing his solidarity with them. One's burial place also serves as the focus for any ongoing care and remembrance after death. The request to be buried in Canaan thus serves as an indication that he sees the future of his descendants as connected to the covenant land — a statement of faith in God's promise to bring his family back there.

naan, and there he blessed me[t] 4and said
to me, 'I am going to make you fruitful
and increase your numbers.[u] I will make
you a community of peoples, and I will
give this land as an everlasting possession
to your descendants after you.'
5"Now then, your two sons born to you
in Egypt[v] before I came to you here will be
reckoned as mine; Ephraim and Manasseh
will be mine,[w] just as Reuben and Simeon
are mine. 6Any children born to you after
them will be yours; in the territory they
inherit they will be reckoned under the
names of their brothers. 7As I was returning from Paddan,[a] to my sorrow Rachel
died in the land of Canaan while we were
still on the way, a little distance from Ephrath. So I buried her there beside the road
to Ephrath" (that is, Bethlehem).[x]
8When Israel saw the sons of Joseph, he
asked, "Who are these?"
9"They are the sons God has given me
here,"[y] Joseph said to his father.
Then Israel said, "Bring them to me so I
may bless[z] them."
10Now Israel's eyes were failing because
of old age, and he could hardly see.[a] So
Joseph brought his sons close to him, and
his father kissed them[b] and embraced
them.
11Israel said to Joseph, "I never expected
to see your face again, and now God has
allowed me to see your children too."[c]
12Then Joseph removed them from Israel's knees and bowed down with his face
to the ground. 13And Joseph took both of
them, Ephraim on his right toward Israel's
left hand and Manasseh on his left toward
Israel's right hand,[d] and brought them
close to him. 14But Israel reached out his
right hand and put it on Ephraim's head,
though he was the younger, and crossing
his arms, he put his left hand on Manasseh's head, even though Manasseh was
the firstborn.[e]
15Then he blessed[f] Joseph and said,

"May the God before whom my fathers
Abraham and Isaac walked
faithfully,
the God who has been my shepherd[g]
all my life to this day,
16the Angel who has delivered me from
all harm
—may he bless these boys.[h]
May they be called by my name
and the names of my fathers
Abraham and Isaac,[i]
and may they increase greatly
on the earth."

17When Joseph saw his father placing
his right hand on Ephraim's head[j] he was
displeased; so he took hold of his father's
hand to move it from Ephraim's head to
Manasseh's head. 18Joseph said to him,
"No, my father, this one is the firstborn;
put your right hand on his head."
19But his father refused and said, "I
know, my son, I know. He too will become
a people, and he too will become great.[k]
Nevertheless, his younger brother will be
greater than he,[l] and his descendants will
become a group of nations." 20He blessed
them that day and said,

"In your[b] name will Israel pronounce
this blessing:
'May God make you like Ephraim[m]
and Manasseh.[n]'"

So he put Ephraim ahead of Manasseh.
21Then Israel said to Joseph, "I am
about to die, but God will be with you[c][o]
and take you[c] back to the land of your[c] fathers.[p] 22And to you I give one more ridge
of land[d][q] than to your brothers,[r] the ridge
I took from the Amorites with my sword
and my bow."

Jacob Blesses His Sons

49:1-28Ref — Dt 33:1-29

49 Then Jacob called for his sons and
said: "Gather around so I can tell
you what will happen to you in days to
come.[s]

2"Assemble and listen, sons of Jacob;
listen to your father Israel.[t]
3"Reuben, you are my firstborn,[u]
my might, the first sign of my
strength,[v]

48:3 [t]Ge 28:13; 35:9-12 **48:4** [u]Ge 17:6 **48:5** [v]Ge 41:50-52; 46:20 [w]1Ch 5:1; Jos 14:4 **48:7** [x]Ge 35:19 **48:9** [y]Ge 33:5 [z]Ge 27:4 **48:10** [a]Ge 27:1 [b]Ge 27:27 **48:11** [c]Ge 50:23; Ps 128:6 **48:13** [d]Ps 110:1 **48:14** [e]Ge 41:51 **48:15** [f]Ge 17:1 [g]Ge 49:24 **48:16** [h]Heb 11:21 [i]Ge 28:13 **48:17** [j]ver 14 **48:19** [k]Ge 17:20 [l]Ge 25:23 **48:20** [m]Nu 2:18 [n]Nu 2:20; Ru 4:11 **48:21** [o]Ge 26:3; 46:4 [p]Ge 28:13; 50:24 **48:22** [q]Jos 24:32; Jn 4:5 [r]Ge 37:8 **49:1** [s]Nu 24:14; Jer 23:20 **49:2** [t]Ps 34:11 **49:3** [u]Ge 29:32 [v]Dt 21:17; Ps 78:51

[a] *7* That is, Northwest Mesopotamia
[b] *20* The Hebrew is singular. [c] *21* The Hebrew is plural. [d] *22* The Hebrew for *ridge of land* is identical with the place name Shechem.

48:22 *ridge of land ... I took from the Amorites with my sword and my bow.* The Hebrew word *shekam* (NIV "ridge of land"; NIV text note, Septuagint, the pre-Christian Greek translation of the OT) refers to the conquest of Shechem by Simeon and Levi (34:25 – 29). Jacob did not approve of this act and was not proud of it, but it was irreversible and undeniable. The land was therefore his to give, since it was taken in his name and by his clan. This justifies Jacob's use of the first person ("I took").

49:1 *what will happen to you in days to come.* As was typical of patriarchal pronouncements, Jacob made statements concerning the future destiny of his sons. These were not prophecy, for they were not given in the name of deity. They forecasted the future. Like a weather forecaster or an economic forecaster, Jacob identified his expectations derived from observed indicators that were considered reliable and thus could be interpreted with a high level of probability. Words had power in the ancient world, and the very speaking of them, especially by some-one in authority, was taken seriously.

excelling in honor, excelling in
power.
4 Turbulent as the waters,[w] you will no
longer excel,
for you went up onto your father's
bed,
onto my couch and defiled it.[x]

5 "Simeon and Levi are brothers —
their swords[a] are weapons of
violence.[y]
6 Let me not enter their council,
let me not join their assembly,[z]
for they have killed men in their anger[a]
and hamstrung oxen as they pleased.
7 Cursed be their anger, so fierce,
and their fury, so cruel!
I will scatter them in Jacob
and disperse them in Israel.[b]

8 "Judah,[b] your brothers will praise you;
your hand will be on the neck of
your enemies;
your father's sons will bow down to
you.[c]
9 You are a lion's[d] cub, Judah;[e]
you return from the prey, my son.
Like a lion he crouches and lies down,
like a lioness — who dares to rouse
him?
10 The scepter will not depart from
Judah,[f]
nor the ruler's staff from between
his feet,[c]
until he to whom it belongs[d] shall
come
and the obedience of the nations
shall be his.[g]
11 He will tether his donkey to a vine,
his colt to the choicest branch;
he will wash his garments in wine,
his robes in the blood of grapes.
12 His eyes will be darker than wine,
his teeth whiter than milk.[e]

13 "Zebulun[h] will live by the seashore
and become a haven for ships;
his border will extend toward Sidon.

14 "Issachar[i] is a rawboned[f] donkey
lying down among the sheep pens.[g]
15 When he sees how good is his resting
place
and how pleasant is his land,
he will bend his shoulder to the
burden
and submit to forced labor.

49:4 [w] Isa 57:20 [x] Ge 35:22; Dt 27:20 **49:5** [y] Ge 34:25; Pr 4:17 **49:6** [z] Pr 1:15; Eph 5:11 [a] Ge 34:26 **49:7** [b] Jos 19:1, 9; 21:1-42 **49:8** [c] Dt 33:7; 1Ch 5:2 **49:9** [d] Nu 24:9; Eze 19:5; Mic 5:8 [e] Rev 5:5 **49:10** [f] Nu 24:17, 19; Ps 60:7 [g] Ps 2:9; Isa 42:1, 4 **49:13** [h] Ge 30:20; Dt 33:18-19; Jos 19:10-11 **49:14** [i] Ge 30:18

[a] *5* The meaning of the Hebrew for this word is uncertain. [b] *8 Judah* sounds like and may be derived from the Hebrew for *praise.* [c] *10* Or *from his descendants* [d] *10* Or *to whom tribute belongs*; the meaning of the Hebrew for this phrase is uncertain. [e] *12* Or *will be dull from wine, / his teeth white from milk* [f] *14* Or *strong* [g] *14* Or *the campfires*; or *the saddlebags*

49:7 *I will scatter them in Jacob and disperse them in Israel.* The tribes of Simeon and Levi were to be dispersed (not the individuals, of course), deprived of clearly identified land as a consequence of their violence in Shechem (ch. 34). This represents virtual disinheritance. Simeon is eventually assigned villages scattered in Judah's territory (Jos 19:1 – 9) and Levi, though having no claim to land, serves its priestly function from the bases known as the Levitical cities, which were distributed among the tribal territories (Nu 35).

49:8 *your father's sons will bow down to you.* This is the legal transfer of clan leadership to Judah. Though Joseph received the double portion of the inheritance (since Ephraim and Manasseh both inherited shares among Jacob's sons; see ch. 48), Judah would be the administrator of the undivided inheritance.

49:9 *Like a lion.* Lion imagery is common in the ancient Near East. There are lion/lioness cults in Egypt, particularly associated with On, where Joseph's in-laws were from. More important, the lion is used in Egypt as the symbol of the king. In Mesopotamia the lion is most often associated with the goddess Ishtar. The god Nergal carries a lion scepter, and numerous other gods are described using lion metaphors. The lion as a royal metaphor as well as an animal for the royal hunt is more familiar in Mesopotamia from the later Neo-Assyrian period, though it is not absent from the earlier periods. In these contexts, the image that the metaphor presents is one of fierceness, cruelty and power. This imagery has its focus on the male lion, which is prevalent in the art of the Levant. In contrast, rather than representing an immediate threat, the imagery associated with Judah invokes quiet power at rest, but a power that's not to be trifled with as both the cub and lioness are included.

49:11 *wash his garments in wine.* This imagery is suggestive of Judah's descendants having the blue/purple/red clothing often associated with royalty, though that coloring is usually achieved through the processing of murex snails (an expensive process because of the large number of snails needed to produce the dye).

The earliest written records concerning dyeing are from Nuzi in the mid-second millennium BC. The earliest evidence of the use of the snail for purple dye comes from seventeenth-century BC Crete. That suggests that at the time of the patriarchs, that technology for dyeing was unknown, yet dyeing itself was known because Egyptian tomb paintings show clothing with color patterns.

Prior to the discovery of murex-snail purple, might wine have been used for dyeing? Would red/purple have been associated with royalty? Royal women in the tomb of Ur from the end of the third millennium BC wore red-colored clothing, but no evidence suggests that wine was used for dyeing, though its staining effect would have been well recognized since wine was filtered through linen cloth.

49:13 *haven for ships.* Seafaring took place primarily from the north, where there were natural harbors. The difficulty with this verse is that Zebulun, to our knowledge, never had territory adjacent to the sea. The tribal allotment given him was in western lower Galilee, entirely landlocked, and 65 miles (100 kilometers) from Sidon. This would actually be a more appropriate description of the territory allotted to Asher, which stretched along the coast from Akko to Tyre. These apparent discrepancies suggest that this blessing does not reflect a later description of the territories as they existed after the conquest. There is no known period when Zebulun controlled the coastal regions.

16 "Dan[a][j] will provide justice for his
people
as one of the tribes of Israel.
17 Dan[k] will be a snake by the roadside,
a viper along the path,
that bites the horse's heels
so that its rider tumbles backward.

18 "I look for your deliverance, LORD.[l]

19 "Gad[b][m] will be attacked by a band of
raiders,
but he will attack them at their heels.

20 "Asher's[n] food will be rich;
he will provide delicacies fit for a king.

21 "Naphtali[o] is a doe set free
that bears beautiful fawns.[c]

22 "Joseph[p] is a fruitful vine,
a fruitful vine near a spring,
whose branches climb over a wall.[d]
23 With bitterness archers attacked him;
they shot at him with hostility.[q]
24 But his bow remained steady,
his strong arms[r] stayed[e] limber,
because of the hand of the Mighty One
of Jacob,[s]
because of the Shepherd, the Rock of
Israel,[t]
25 because of your father's God,[u] who
helps you,
because of the Almighty,[f] who
blesses you
with blessings of the skies above,
blessings of the deep springs below,[v]
blessings of the breast and womb.
26 Your father's blessings are greater
than the blessings of the ancient
mountains,
than[g] the bounty of the age-old hills.
Let all these rest on the head of
Joseph,
on the brow of the prince among[h]
his brothers.[w]

27 "Benjamin[x] is a ravenous wolf;
in the morning he devours the prey,
in the evening he divides the
plunder."

28 All these are the twelve tribes of Israel, and this is what their father said to
them when he blessed them, giving each
the blessing appropriate to him.

The Death of Jacob

29 Then he gave them these instructions:[y] "I am about to be gathered to my
people.[z] Bury me with my fathers[a] in the
cave in the field of Ephron the Hittite,
30 the cave in the field of Machpelah,[b] near
Mamre in Canaan, which Abraham bought
along with the field[c] as a burial place from
Ephron the Hittite. 31 There Abraham[d] and
his wife Sarah[e] were buried, there Isaac
and his wife Rebekah[f] were buried, and
there I buried Leah. 32 The field and the
cave in it were bought from the Hittites.[i]"
33 When Jacob had finished giving instructions to his sons, he drew his feet up
into the bed, breathed his last and was
gathered to his people.[g]

50 Joseph threw himself on his father and wept over him and kissed
him.[h] 2 Then Joseph directed the physicians in his service to embalm his father
Israel. So the physicians embalmed him,[i]
3 taking a full forty days, for that was the
time required for embalming. And the
Egyptians mourned for him seventy days.[j]
4 When the days of mourning had
passed, Joseph said to Pharaoh's court,
"If I have found favor in your eyes, speak
to Pharaoh for me. Tell him, 5 'My father
made me swear an oath[k] and said, "I am
about to die; bury me in the tomb I dug
for myself[l] in the land of Canaan."[m] Now
let me go up and bury my father; then I
will return.' "
6 Pharaoh said, "Go up and bury your
father, as he made you swear to do."
7 So Joseph went up to bury his father. All Pharaoh's officials accompanied
him—the dignitaries of his court and all
the dignitaries of Egypt— 8 besides all the
members of Joseph's household and his
brothers and those belonging to his father's household. Only their children and
their flocks and herds were left in Goshen.
9 Chariots and horsemen[j] also went up
with him. It was a very large company.
10 When they reached the threshing floor
of Atad, near the Jordan, they lamented
loudly and bitterly;[n] and there Joseph
observed a seven-day period[o] of mourning for his father. 11 When the Canaanites
who lived there saw the mourning at the
threshing floor of Atad, they said, "The
Egyptians are holding a solemn ceremony
of mourning." That is why that place near
the Jordan is called Abel Mizraim.[k]

49:16 [j] Ge 30:6; Dt 33:22; Jdg 18:26-27 **49:17** [k] Jdg 18:27 **49:18** [l] Ps 119:166, 174 **49:19** [m] Ge 30:11; Dt 33:20; 1Ch 5:18 **49:20** [n] Ge 30:13; Dt 33:24 **49:21** [o] Ge 30:8; Dt 33:23 **49:22** [p] Ge 30:24; Dt 33:13-17 **49:23** [q] Ge 37:24 **49:24** [r] Ps 18:34 [s] Ps 132:2, 5; Isa 1:24; 41:10 [t] Isa 28:16 **49:25** [u] Ge 28:13 [v] Ge 27:28 **49:26** [w] Dt 33:15-16 **49:27** [x] Ge 35:18; Jdg 20:12-13 **49:29** [y] Ge 50:16 [z] Ge 25:8 [a] Ge 15:15; 47:30; 50:13 **49:30** [b] Ge 23:9 [c] Ge 23:20 **49:31** [d] Ge 25:9 [e] Ge 23:19 [f] Ge 35:29 **49:33** [g] ver 29; Ge 25:8; Ac 7:15 **50:1** [h] Ge 46:4 **50:2** [i] ver 26; 2Ch 16:14 **50:3** [j] Ge 37:34; Nu 20:29; Dt 34:8 **50:5** [k] Ge 47:31 [l] 2Ch 16:14; Isa 22:16 [m] Ge 47:31 **50:10** [n] 2Sa 1:17; Ac 8:2 [o] 1Sa 31:13; Job 2:13

[a] *16* Dan here means *he provides justice.* [b] *19* Gad sounds like the Hebrew for *attack* and also for *band of raiders.* [c] *21* Or *free; / he utters beautiful words* [d] *22* Or *Joseph is a wild colt, / a wild colt near a spring, / a wild donkey on a terraced hill* [e] *23,24* Or *archers will attack . . . will shoot . . . will remain . . . will stay* [f] *25* Hebrew *Shaddai* [g] *26* Or *of my progenitors, / as great as* [h] *26* Or *of the one separated from* [i] *32* Or *the descendants of Heth* [j] *9* Or *charioteers* [k] *11* *Abel Mizraim* means *mourning of the Egyptians.*

50:2 *directed the physicians . . . to embalm his father.* Jacob's embalming took 40 days (see the article "Embalming," p. 102), and he was mourned for 70 days (v. 3).

50:11 *Abel Mizraim.* Its location is unknown, and it is difficult to understand why a procession from Egypt to Hebron should bring them anywhere near the Jordan.

12So Jacob's sons did as he had commanded them: 13They carried him to the
land of Canaan and buried him in the cave
in the field of Machpelah, near Mamre,
which Abraham had bought along with
the field[p] as a burial place from Ephron
the Hittite. 14After burying his father, Joseph returned to Egypt, together with his
brothers and all the others who had gone
with him to bury his father.

50:13 [p]Ge 23:20; Ac 7:16
50:15 [q]Ge 37:28; 42:21-22

Joseph Reassures His Brothers

15When Joseph's brothers saw that
their father was dead, they said, "What
if Joseph holds a grudge against us and
pays us back for all the wrongs we did to
him?"[q] 16So they sent word to Joseph, saying, "Your father left these instructions before he died: 17'This is what you are to say
to Joseph: I ask you to forgive your brothers the sins and the wrongs they commit-

GENESIS 50:2

EMBALMING

Embalming served to preserve the body of the deceased, but in Egypt the reason for doing so involved significant theology. They preserved the body so that it could be reinhabited by the spirit (*ka*) in the afterlife. Nothing in the text suggests that Joseph or his family had adopted the complex afterlife theology of ancient Egypt with its emphasis on rituals, spells and other sorts of magic.

The physicians referred to (Ge 50:2) are probably mortuary priests, who were the experts in the techniques of embalming as they prepared the body not only physically for the grave, but also spiritually for the afterlife. Evidence of embalming goes back to about 2600 BC. The principal agent used in the embalming process is natron, which served to dry out the body after the important viscera (internal organs) were removed. This dehydration process took about 40 days. The viscera were packed in natron individually and eventually replaced in the body.

Meanwhile the body was washed out with spiced wine, and after the process was over, it was anointed with oils and gum resins. As the body was wrapped in linen, protective amulets were included at various places. As a final step a liquid resin was poured over the whole body.

Although it was common practice in Egypt (for any who could afford it), embalming of Israelites is found only in this chapter. The fact that the bodies of Jacob and Joseph are embalmed (Ge 50:2,26) may suggest the desire of the Israelites to soothe the feelings of the Egyptians, but it also serves the purpose of preserving their bodies for later burial in Canaan. ◆

Funerary stele of the "servant of Osiris." Ankh-Hapy depicts Anubis preparing a mummy for burial, Memphis, 525–500 BC.

Kim Walton. The Vatican Museum.

THE TRIBES OF ISRAEL

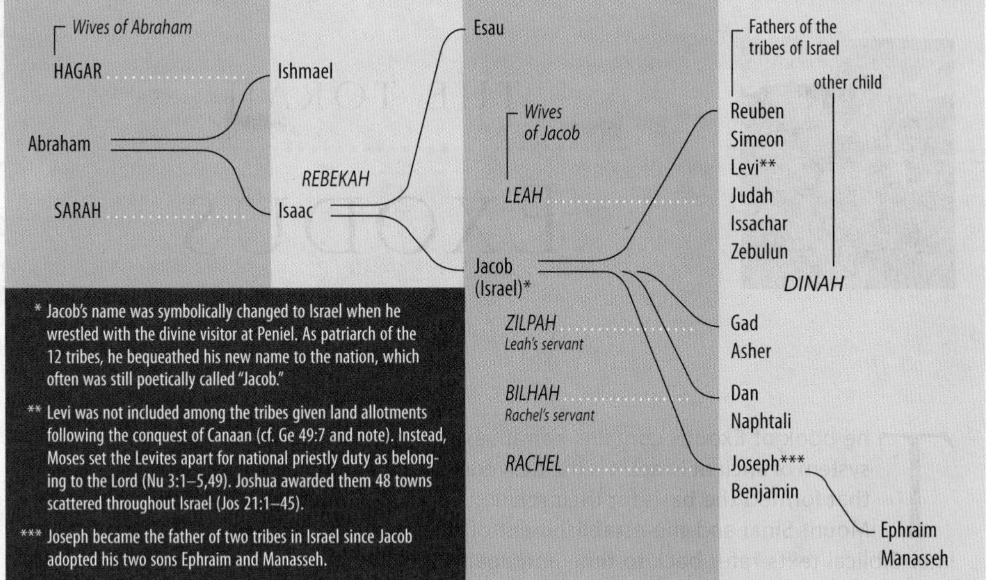
Wives of Abraham
HAGAR
Ishmael
Abraham
SARAH
Isaac
REBEKAH
Esau
Wives of Jacob
LEAH
Jacob (Israel)*
ZILPAH
Leah's servant
BILHAH
Rachel's servant
RACHEL
Fathers of the tribes of Israel
other child
Reuben
Simeon
Levi**
Judah
Issachar
Zebulun
DINAH
Gad
Asher
Dan
Naphtali
Joseph***
Benjamin
Ephraim
Manasseh
* Jacob's name was symbolically changed to Israel when he wrestled with the divine visitor at Peniel. As patriarch of the 12 tribes, he bequeathed his new name to the nation, which often was still poetically called "Jacob."
** Levi was not included among the tribes given land allotments following the conquest of Canaan (cf. Ge 49:7 and note). Instead, Moses set the Levites apart for national priestly duty as belonging to the Lord (Nu 3:1–5,49). Joshua awarded them 48 towns scattered throughout Israel (Jos 21:1–45).
*** Joseph became the father of two tribes in Israel since Jacob adopted his two sons Ephraim and Manasseh.

ted in treating you so badly.' Now please
forgive the sins of the servants of the God
of your father." When their message came
to him, Joseph wept.
[18]His brothers then came and threw
themselves down before him.[r] "We are
your slaves,"[s] they said.
[19]But Joseph said to them, "Don't be
afraid. Am I in the place of God?[t] [20]You
intended to harm me,[u] but God intended[v]
it for good[w] to accomplish what is now
being done, the saving of many lives.[x] [21]So
then, don't be afraid. I will provide for you
and your children.[y]" And he reassured
them and spoke kindly to them.

The Death of Joseph

[22]Joseph stayed in Egypt, along with all
his father's family. He lived a hundred and
ten years[z] [23]and saw the third generation[a]
of Ephraim's children. Also the children
of Makir[b] son of Manasseh were placed at
birth on Joseph's knees.[a]
[24]Then Joseph said to his brothers, "I
am about to die.[c] But God will surely come
to your aid[d] and take you up out of this
land to the land[e] he promised on oath to
Abraham, Isaac and Jacob."[f] [25]And Joseph made the Israelites swear an oath
and said, "God will surely come to your
aid, and then you must carry my bones up
from this place."[g]
[26]So Joseph died at the age of a hundred
and ten. And after they embalmed him,[h]
he was placed in a coffin in Egypt.

[a] 23 That is, were counted as his

50:18 [r]Ge 37:7 [s]Ge 43:18 **50:19** [t]Ro 12:19; Heb 10:30 **50:20** [u]Ge 37:20 [v]Mic 4:11-12 [w]Ro 8:28 [x]Ge 45:5 **50:21** [y]Ge 45:11; 47:12 **50:22** [z]Ge 25:7; Jos 24:29 **50:23** [a]Job 42:16 [b]Nu 32:39,40 **50:24** [c]Ge 48:21 [d]Ex 3:16-17 [e]Ge 15:14 [f]Ge 12:7; 26:3; 28:13; 35:12 **50:25** [g]Ge 47:29-30; Ex 13:19; Jos 24:32; Heb 11:22 **50:26** [h]ver 2

50:22 *a hundred and ten years.* This was considered the ideal life span for an Egyptian, despite the fact that examination of mummies has demonstrated that the average life expectancy in Egypt was between 40 and 50.

THE TORAH

EXODUS

The book of Exodus contains narratives that became foundational for the belief system of ancient Israel. It is the deliverance of the Israelites from Egypt (chs. 1 – 15) that formed the basis for their relationship with God. It is the series of events at Mount Sinai and the establishment of the covenant there (chs. 19 – 24; 34) that later Biblical texts refer back to time and again. The specific ideas and the theological message of this book played an especially integral role in ancient Israel's identity and self-understanding.

Historical Setting

The historical setting for the book of Exodus is essentially unknown. The book describes events that led to the escape of the ancient Israelites from Egypt, but a specific time period during which events such as these might have taken place cannot be determined with certainty. Suggestions have been made (see the article "Historicity of the Exodus," p. 116), and some accord better with the available evidence than others. The book of Exodus, however, yields too little information to establish a precise and convincing historical framework. The best one can do is to ascertain a broad time period into which the text attempts to place its narrated events.

Many scholars believe that the book of Exodus places the events it recounts in a time period that fits best within the second half of the second millennium BC. In Egypt, this period of time is known as the New Kingdom (1550 – 1069 BC), whereas in the Levant it corresponds to the Late Bronze Age (1550 – 1200 BC, though some extend the period to 1150) and the first part of the Iron Age (referred to as Iron I, 1200 – 1000 BC).

While Semitic slaves had been in Egypt for some time, it was during the New Kingdom that their numbers increased significantly. Building projects — tombs, monuments, temples — also grew until they reached unprecedented levels during the reign of Rameses II. Thus, Egypt's control of Palestine, its increasing numbers of Semitic slaves and its swiftly growing construction efforts combine to make the New Kingdom an attractive option as a backdrop for many of the narratives in the book of Exodus.

KEY CONCEPTS

- The law is part of God's revelation of himself; giving it is an act of grace.
- God's presence comes on his terms and in his time.
- Deliverance is God's business — and his alone.
- "Then you will know that I am the LORD your God" (Ex 6:7).

Types of Literature

The book of Exodus contains an array of literary forms. The grand saga describing the Israelites' miraculous escape from enslavement in Egypt may best be described as epic narrative. In addition to the Ten Commandments, the book contains a long list of legal provisions; thus, the genre of law must be considered. The section concerning the construction of the tabernacle is an example of the ancient Near Eastern literary form used to describe the building of sacred shrines. There are also ritual instructions in the latter part of the book that lay out the elaborate ceremonies required to consecrate Aaron and his sons as priests. Other ancient Near Eastern societies utilized each of these literary forms as well. The nature of these forms or genres and how they were used must function as key elements in any background analysis of Biblical texts. Thus, literary considerations are, at times, equally important as are the historical and cultural aspects of the ancient world in shedding light on the text of Exodus. ◆

The Israelites Oppressed

1 These are the names of the sons of Israel[a] who went to Egypt with Jacob, each
with his family: [2]Reuben, Simeon, Levi
and Judah; [3]Issachar, Zebulun and Benjamin; [4]Dan and Naphtali; Gad and Asher.
[5]The descendants of Jacob numbered seventy[a] in all;[b] Joseph was already in Egypt.
[6]Now Joseph and all his brothers and
all that generation died,[c] [7]but the Israelites were exceedingly fruitful; they multiplied greatly, increased in numbers[d] and
became so numerous that the land was
filled with them.
[8]Then a new king, to whom Joseph
meant nothing, came to power in Egypt.
[9]"Look," he said to his people, "the Israelites have become far too numerous[e] for
us. [10]Come, we must deal shrewdly[f] with
them or they will become even more numerous and, if war breaks out, will join
our enemies, fight against us and leave the
country."[g]
[11]So they put slave masters[h] over them
to oppress them with forced labor,[i] and
they built Pithom and Rameses[j] as store
cities[k] for Pharaoh. [12]But the more they
were oppressed, the more they multiplied and spread; so the Egyptians came
to dread the Israelites [13]and worked them
ruthlessly.[l] [14]They made their lives bitter
with harsh labor in brick and mortar and
with all kinds of work in the fields; in all
their harsh labor the Egyptians worked
them ruthlessly.[m]
[15]The king of Egypt said to the Hebrew
midwives, whose names were Shiphrah

1:1 [a]Ge 46:8 **1:5** [b]Ge 46:26 **1:6** [c]Ge 50:26 **1:7** [d]Ge 46:3; Dt 26:5; Ac 7:17 **1:9** [e]Ps 105:24-25 **1:10** [f]Ps 83:3 [g]Ac 7:17-19 **1:11** [h]Ex 3:7 [i]Ge 15:13; Ex 2:11; 5:4; 6:6-7 [j]Ge 47:11 [k]1Ki 9:19; 2Ch 8:4 **1:13** [l]Dt 4:20 **1:14** [m]Ex 2:23; 6:9; Nu 20:15; Ps 81:6; Ac 7:19

[a] 5 Masoretic Text (see also Gen. 46:27); Dead Sea Scrolls and Septuagint (see also Acts 7:14 and note at Gen. 46:27) *seventy-five*

1:1 *Egypt.* Ancient Egypt stretched from the Mediterranean Sea south along the Nile River and was divided—conceptually and sometimes politically—between Upper Egypt in the south (the Nile valley) and Lower Egypt (the Nile delta) in the north. *each with his family.* There is ample evidence that Semitic peoples (from Syria and Palestine) entered the Nile delta region for a variety of reasons. Obtaining food for themselves and their herds during times of famine was one of them. A well-known Egyptian text from around 1200 BC contains a letter that mentions a group of Semitic nomads or Bedouin (Egyptian *shasu*) coming into Egypt. These Bedouin were mainly shepherds and their families who periodically roamed along the borders of Egypt looking for better pastures for their herds. These *shasu* were coming from the Sinai Desert, east of Egypt. They entered at one of the border checkpoints set up by the Egyptian military. While the *shasu* mentioned are probably not Israelites, the text does show that it was not unusual for nomadic Semites to enter Egypt at this time, especially along the eastern border of the Delta.

1:8 *to whom Joseph meant nothing.* Scholars have tried to determine what this statement means in terms of Egyptian history. One idea relates to the people known as the Hyksos. The Hyksos were Semitic foreigners in Egypt who took over and ruled Lower Egypt (which includes the Nile delta) for about 100 years (c. 1630–1530 BC). They were eventually ousted by Egyptians who had retained power over Upper Egypt.

In light of the Hyksos rule in Egypt and their eventual demise, at least two inferences are possible with respect to the Biblical text. First, it seems reasonable to identify the period of Hyksos rule as a period of time when a person from, perhaps, another Semitic group could have risen to an extraordinarily high position within the governmental hierarchy, as the story of Joseph in the book of Genesis describes. Presumably, the Hyksos were sympathetic to other Semites and amenable to sharing some political power with them. Second, it is conceivable that the defeat of the Hyksos and the return of indigenous Egyptian rule to Lower Egypt form the background for this verse in Exodus. The Hebrews—and any Semitic persons for that matter—would have come under great suspicion after the Egyptians had just retaken their Nile delta from the despised Hyksos. Thus, it is likely that a Semitic group that had been shown special favor by the Hyksos would have fallen out of favor under the new Egyptian king.

Inferences regarding the Israelites in particular must remain tentative. If there were Israelites living in or near Avaris (the very region from which the Bible indicates the Israelites left Egypt), their material remains would be indistinguishable from those left by other Semitic groups. Thus, some of the so-called Hyksos archaeological evidence in this region may be Israelite, though there is as yet no reliable means by which to establish this.

1:10 *our enemies.* If they are the Hyksos, this would place events in the period when they were being driven from the land. *leave the country.* The Egyptians, it seems, wanted to keep the Israelites around for economic reasons.

1:11 *forced labor.* Not infrequent in engineering and construction projects of the ancient world. Common people might be forced to work without pay for a percentage of the year, effectively paying their time as a form of taxation. Other laborers included prisoners of war. When building projects became too ambitious and expensive for these to be sufficient, vulnerable groups of people would be targeted for forced labor. It is possible to imagine Semitic slaves, even Hebrew slaves, as part of those conscripted. *Pithom and Rameses.* These names probably refer to locations near the eastern edge of the Nile delta. *Pithom.* Likely the Hebrew rendering of the Egyptian phrase "House of (the god) Atum," and it perhaps refers to Tell el-Retabeh, which was an important military point on Egypt's eastern border during the time of Rameses II. *Rameses.* Named after Rameses II, who reigned more than 60 years in the mid-1200s BC; called Pi-Ramesse ("House of Rameses") in Egyptian—identified today as Tell ed-Dab'a—where significant remains of a Semitic settlement have been excavated. The building projects of Rameses II surpassed those of all other pharaohs and required a massive labor force.

1:14 *harsh labor in brick and mortar.* Brick making was a filthy and miserable job. Intensive brick making was needed to support the large-scale building projects in Egypt (requiring literally millions of bricks), particularly at sites like Pi-Ramesse (see previous note).

1:15 *Hebrew.* The term has linguistic connections to the term *Apiru*, used in a number of ancient texts. It occurs frequently, e.g., in the approximately 380 tablets discovered at the site of el-Amarna, about 150 miles (240 kilometers) south of Cairo. Most of these tablets come from the mid-fourteenth century BC and are letters that were written by local rulers in Syria and Palestine to the Egyp-

EXODUS 1:8

Egyptian Kings of the New Kingdom

An Egyptian priest named Manetho, who lived during the 200s BC, attempted to divide Egyptian history as he saw it into sections or dynasties. He did this based on groups of kings who, in his view, shared important kinship, political or geographic ties. He numbered each dynasty, and the New Kingdom includes the Eighteenth, Nineteenth, and Twentieth Dynasties. Overlapping dates can be explained by coregencies (two rulers sharing power). ◆

EIGHTEENTH DYNASTY			
Ahmose	1550–1525 BC	Thutmose IV	1400–1390 BC
Amenhotep I	1525–1504 BC	Amenhotep III	1390–1352 BC
Thutmose I	1504–1492 BC	Amenhotep IV/Akhenaten	1352–1336 BC
Thutmose II	1492–1479 BC	Neferneferuaten	1338–1336 BC
Thutmose III	1479–1425 BC	Tutankhamun	1336–1327 BC
Queen Hatshepsut	1473–1458 BC	Ay	1327–1323 BC
Amenhotep II	1427–1400 BC	Horemheb	1323–1295 BC

NINETEENTH DYNASTY			
Rameses I	1295–1294 BC	Amenmesses	1203–1200 BC
Seti I	1294–1279 BC	Seti II	1200–1194 BC
Rameses II	1279–1213 BC	Saptah	1194–1188 BC
Merneptah	1213–1203 BC	Queen Tausret	1188–1186 BC

TWENTIETH DYNASTY			
Sethnakht	1186–1184 BC	Rameses VII	1136–1129 BC
Rameses III	1184–1153 BC	Rameses VIII	1129–1126 BC
Rameses IV	1153–1147 BC	Rameses IX	1126–1108 BC
Rameses V	1147–1143 BC	Rameses X	1108–1099 BC
Rameses VI	1143–1136 BC	Rameses XI	1099–1069 BC

and Puah, 16“When you are helping the
Hebrew women during childbirth on the
delivery stool, if you see that the baby is a
boy, kill him; but if it is a girl, let her live.”
17The midwives, however, feared[n] God and
did not do what the king of Egypt had told
them to do;[o] they let the boys live. 18Then
the king of Egypt summoned the midwives
and asked them, “Why have you done
this? Why have you let the boys live?”

19The midwives answered Pharaoh,
“Hebrew women are not like Egyptian
women; they are vigorous and give birth
before the midwives arrive.”[p]

20So God was kind to the midwives[q] and
the people increased and became even
more numerous. 21And because the midwives feared God, he gave them families[r]
of their own.

22Then Pharaoh gave this order to all his
people: “Every Hebrew boy that is born
you must throw into the Nile, but let every
girl live.”[s]

The Birth of Moses

2 Now a man of the tribe of Levi married
a Levite woman,[t] 2and she became
pregnant and gave birth to a son. When
she saw that he was a fine child, she hid
him for three months.[u] 3But when she
could hide him no longer, she got a papyrus basket[a] for him and coated it with tar
and pitch. Then she placed the child in it
and put it among the reeds along the bank
of the Nile. 4His sister[v] stood at a distance
to see what would happen to him.

5Then Pharaoh's daughter went down
to the Nile to bathe, and her attendants
were walking along the riverbank.[w] She
saw the basket among the reeds and sent
her female slave to get it. 6She opened it
and saw the baby. He was crying, and she
felt sorry for him. “This is one of the Hebrew babies,” she said.

7Then his sister asked Pharaoh's daughter, “Shall I go and get one of the Hebrew
women to nurse the baby for you?”

8“Yes, go,” she answered. So the girl
went and got the baby's mother. 9Phar-
aoh's daughter said to her, “Take this baby
and nurse him for me, and I will pay you.”
So the woman took the baby and nursed
him. 10When the child grew older, she took
him to Pharaoh's daughter and he became
her son. She named him Moses,[b] saying,
“I drew him out of the water.”

1:17 [n] ver 21; Pr 16:6 [o] Da 3:16-18; Ac 4:18-20; 5:29 **1:19** [p] Jos 2:4-6; 2Sa 17:20 **1:20** [q] ver 12; Pr 11:18; Isa 3:10 **1:21** [r] 1Sa 2:35; 2Sa 7:11,27-29; 1Ki 11:38 **1:22** [s] Ac 7:19 **2:1** [t] Ex 6:20; Nu 26:59 **2:2** [u] Ac 7:20; Heb 11:23 **2:4** [v] Ex 15:20; Nu 26:59 **2:5** [w] Ex 7:15; 8:20

[a] 3 The Hebrew can also mean *ark*, as in Gen. 6:14.
[b] 10 *Moses* sounds like the Hebrew for *draw out.*

---

tian king who had established his capital at this site. Egypt had loose control of Syria and Palestine during this period. The letters speak disparagingly of the Apiru people. For example, Abdi-Hepa, the local ruler in Jerusalem, wrote with the dire news: "The land of the king has gone over to the Apiru. And now, in addition to this, a town belonging to Jerusalem, Bit-Ninurta by name, a town belonging to the king, has gone over to the men of Qiltu. May the king listen to Abdi-Hepa, your servant, and send archers to restore the land of the king to the king. If there are no archers, the land of the king will go over to the Apiru!" The Apiru may refer to groups of people who were social outcasts, did not own property, often resorted to banditry, and threatened the status quo for settled people. Those viewed as outsiders or foreigners were also often labeled as Apiru. Before forming the nation of Israel, most likely the Hebrews were viewed in this way. A Hebrew could certainly have been called an Apiru, though not every Apiru was a Hebrew. Note that while "Hebrew" is primarily an ethnic designation, "Apiru" is strictly a social one. *Shiphrah and Puah.* An Egyptian papyrus from around the year 1700 BC presents a list of 95 household servants. Over half the names are Semitic. One is Shiphrah, who is designated as a weaver of fine linen. This woman is clearly not the one referred to in the Biblical text, but this Semitic name (meaning "fair, beautiful") appears to have been known in Egypt.

1:16 *delivery stool.* Women in the ancient world would give birth in a crouching or kneeling position. Stools, stones or bricks could be used to support the mother's weight during this process.

2:3 *she placed the child in it.* The baby's mother abandoned her child in hopes of saving him. This is reminiscent of a theme—an abandoned or exposed child who is rescued and eventually grows up to perform some heroic deed—that turns up in a wide variety of other literature. The story closest to the Exodus account is the Legend of Sargon from Mesopotamia, which tells of the rise to power of a Mesopotamian king from around 2300 BC. Like Moses' mother, Sargon's mother places her baby in a reed basket, seals it and sets it adrift on a river. Like Moses, Sargon is then taken from the water by the one who eventually adopts him.

Evidence suggests that it was not uncommon for a child to be abandoned. Reasons for this practice are not entirely clear, although families often had great difficulties finding enough food for the members they already had. We do know that abandoned children who were then later adopted could receive names that referred to their abandonment—e.g., Ha-pi-kalbi ("He-of-the-dog's-mouth") and Naru-eriba ("The-river-has-compensated-me"). By means of this traumatic event, the Biblical text hints to the reader regarding the kind of future in store for this child. Moses has "hero" written all over him.

2:9 *nurse him for me.* Both Egyptian and Mesopotamian records, mostly from the second millennium BC, indicate that a woman could have the occupation of wet nurse (a woman who breast-feeds another woman's child). They were often employed after the adoption of an abandoned child and were typically paid with basic provisions such as food and clothing. The standard period of time for a wet nurse was about three years.

2:10 *took him to Pharaoh's daughter.* As a child of Pharaoh's court, Moses would perhaps have had access to education (literature, scribal arts, warfare, rhetoric), but this is not a certainty. There is no evidence that the particular daughter of Pharaoh who rescued Moses had a position of power or influence. Harem children existed in every court. Children of influential wives would be trained for administrative positions, but others may have had much lower status and fewer opportunities and advantages. We simply are not given enough information to

Moses Flees to Midian

11 One day, after Moses had grown up, he
went out to where his own people[x] were
and watched them at their hard labor. He
saw an Egyptian beating a Hebrew, one of
his own people. 12 Looking this way and that
and seeing no one, he killed the Egyptian
and hid him in the sand. 13 The next day he
went out and saw two Hebrews fighting.
He asked the one in the wrong, "Why are
you hitting your fellow Hebrew?"[y]

14 The man said, "Who made you ruler and judge over us?[z] Are you thinking
of killing me as you killed the Egyptian?"
Then Moses was afraid and thought,
"What I did must have become known."

15 When Pharaoh heard of this, he tried
to kill Moses, but Moses fled from Pharaoh
and went to live in Midian,[a] where he sat
down by a well. 16 Now a priest of Midian[b] had seven daughters, and they came
to draw water[c] and fill the troughs to water their father's flock. 17 Some shepherds
came along and drove them away, but Moses got up and came to their rescue and
watered their flock.[d]

18 When the girls returned to Reuel[e] their
father, he asked them, "Why have you returned so early today?"

19 They answered, "An Egyptian rescued
us from the shepherds. He even drew water for us and watered the flock."

20 "And where is he?" Reuel asked his
daughters. "Why did you leave him? Invite him to have something to eat."[f]

21 Moses agreed to stay with the man,
who gave his daughter Zipporah[g] to Moses in marriage. 22 Zipporah gave birth to
a son, and Moses named him Gershom,[a]
saying, "I have become a foreigner[h] in a
foreign land."

23 During that long period,[i] the king of
Egypt died. The Israelites groaned in their
slavery and cried out, and their cry[j] for
help because of their slavery went up to
God. 24 God heard their groaning and he
remembered his covenant[k] with Abraham, with Isaac and with Jacob. 25 So
God looked on the Israelites and was concerned[l] about them.

Moses and the Burning Bush

3 Now Moses was tending the flock of
Jethro[m] his father-in-law, the priest of
Midian, and he led the flock to the far side
of the wilderness and came to Horeb,[n]

2:11 [x] Ac 7:23; Heb 11:24-26 **2:13** [y] Ac 7:26 **2:14** [z] Ac 7:27* **2:15** [a] Ac 7:29; Heb 11:27 **2:16** [b] Ex 3:1 [c] Ge 24:11 **2:17** [d] Ge 29:10 **2:18** [e] Nu 10:29

2:20 [f] Ge 31:54 **2:21** [g] Ex 18:2 **2:22** [h] Ex 18:3-4; Heb 11:13 **2:23** [i] Ac 7:30 [j] Ex 3:7,9; Dt 26:7; Jas 5:4 **2:24** [k] Ex 6:5; Ps 105:10,42 **2:25** [l] Ex 3:7; 4:31 **3:1** [m] Ex 2:18 [n] 1Ki 19:8

[a] *22 Gershom* sounds like the Hebrew for *a foreigner there.*

reach confident conclusions. *Moses.* Frequently used in Egyptian names, e.g., Ahmose, Thutmose and Rameses. Its basic meaning is "to father" or "to be fathered (born)." For example, Thutmose probably means "the god Thoth is born," or perhaps "the god Thoth has fathered" or "born of the god Thoth." In this case, Moses' name, then, is really just a half-name: "born of …" Alternatively, the Egyptian word *ms* means "boy," so she may have simply called him "boy." In any event, the name fits the narrative and is suitably left as it is, since it sounds like the Hebrew word for "to pull out, retrieve"—in this case, from the water.

2:11 *beating.* The Hebrew word here is the same as the one for "killed" in v. 12, so the word can refer to a fatal beating, depending on the context. Beating slaves was certainly not uncommon or illegal in the ancient world. Even killing a slave was not a serious crime. When a person caused the death of another's slave—in this case, the taskmaster may have killed one of Pharaoh's slaves—the perpetrator typically only had to pay a fine to compensate the victim's owner for the loss of labor. Here the taskmaster would have had Pharaoh's authority to beat the slave and may not, therefore, have been culpable of any wrongdoing. Thus, Moses' reaction is severe—especially if the slave did not die—but understandable in light of his relation to the one beaten.

2:15 *he tried to kill Moses.* There is virtually no evidence from ancient Egypt regarding the treatment of homicide. Egypt certainly had the death penalty, however, since participants in an unsuccessful coup during the reign of Rameses III (1186–1155 BC) were executed. Apparently, a minor queen and her supporters had wanted to dethrone Rameses and make her son king. The Egyptian justice system had no qualms about imposing the death penalty on those guilty of murder. In this case, the Egyptian king is interested not only in justice but also in revenge. Since one from his own court has violated the system for enforcing his authority, Pharaoh is out to kill Moses not only to ensure that the latter receives what he deserves but also to make clear that violations of Pharaoh's authority will be dealt with severely. *Midian.* This area is probably located in northwestern Arabia, just to the east of the Gulf of Elath (Aqaba). This area raises an interesting possibility when one considers that it is here where Moses for the first time encounters Yahweh (the Israelite name for God; see the article "God's Name," p. 112). This region is referred to as the "Land of the Shasu"—*shasu* refers to Bedouin shepherds (see note on 1:1)—in two Egyptian texts found in ancient Nubia (modern Sudan) from approximately 1400 BC. These texts mention "*Yhw* (in) the land of the Shasu." This *Yhw* is most likely a form of Yahweh and represents a location possibly based on the Israelite name for God. This may support the conclusion that some people in that region may have been worshiping Yahweh at this time. In fact, the Biblical text may be trying to depict Moses' eventual father-in-law, called a priest in v. 16, as a worshiper of Yahweh. That he lives in this region and has flocks that need shepherding certainly qualifies him and his family as *shasu.* All that is missing is an explicit reference to his worship of Yahweh, though this may come in 18:10–11. The Midianites were descended from Abraham through Keturah (Ge 25:1–2).

3:1 *Horeb, the mountain of God.* Horeb (Hebrew "wasteland, desert") is specifically referred to as the "mountain of God" only here and in 1Ki 19:8. In Ex 24:13–16 the "mountain of God" is given the name "Sinai." That one particular mountain is referred to as God's mountain is intriguing. Ancient Near Eastern deities often had their dwelling place on a mountain. In the mythology of Ugarit in Syria, e.g., Baal had his palatial abode on Mount Zaphon (Jebel el-Aqra in western Syria), about 25 miles (40 kilometers) north of Ugarit.

One reason the people of Israel left Egypt was to come to this abode of God to worship him (v. 12). In fact, when

the mountain[o] of God. 2 There the angel
of the LORD[p] appeared to him in flames
of fire from within a bush.[q] Moses saw
that though the bush was on fire it did
not burn up. 3 So Moses thought, "I will go
over and see this strange sight — why the
bush does not burn up."
4 When the LORD saw that he had gone
over to look, God called to him from within the bush, "Moses! Moses!"
And Moses said, "Here I am."
5 "Do not come any closer," God said.
"Take off your sandals, for the place where
you are standing is holy ground."[r] 6 Then
he said, "I am the God of your father,[a] the
God of Abraham, the God of Isaac and the
God of Jacob."[s] At this, Moses hid his face,
because he was afraid to look at God.
7 The LORD said, "I have indeed seen
the misery of my people in Egypt. I have
heard them crying out because of their
slave drivers, and I am concerned[t] about
their suffering. 8 So I have come down[u] to
rescue them from the hand of the Egyptians and to bring them up out of that
land into a good and spacious land, a
land flowing with milk and honey[v] — the
home of the Canaanites, Hittites, Amorites, Perizzites, Hivites and Jebusites.[w]
9 And now the cry of the Israelites has
reached me, and I have seen the way
the Egyptians are oppressing[x] them. 10 So
now, go. I am sending you to Pharaoh
to bring my people the Israelites out of
Egypt."[y]
11 But Moses said to God, "Who am I[z]
that I should go to Pharaoh and bring the
Israelites out of Egypt?"
12 And God said, "I will be with you.[a]
And this will be the sign to you that it
is I who have sent you: When you have
brought the people out of Egypt, you[b] will
worship God on this mountain."
13 Moses said to God, "Suppose I go to
the Israelites and say to them, 'The God of
your fathers has sent me to you,' and they
ask me, 'What is his name?' Then what
shall I tell them?"
14 God said to Moses, "I AM WHO I AM.[c]

3:1 [o] Ex 18:5
3:2 [p] Ge 16:7 [q] Dt 33:16; Mk 12:26; Ac 7:30
3:5 [r] Ge 28:17; Jos 5:15; Ac 7:33*
3:6 [s] Ex 4:5; Mt 22:32*; Mk 12:26*; Lk 20:37*; Ac 7:32*
3:7 [t] Ex 2:25
3:8 [u] Ge 50:24 [v] ver 17; Ex 13:5; Dt 1:25 [w] Ge 15:18-21
3:9 [x] Ex 1:14; 2:23
3:10 [y] Mic 6:4
3:11 [z] Ex 6:12, 30; 1Sa 18:18
3:12 [a] Ge 31:3; Jos 1:5; Ro 8:31

[a] *6* Masoretic Text; Samaritan Pentateuch (see Acts 7:32) *fathers* [b] *12* The Hebrew is plural. [c] *14* Or *I WILL BE WHAT I WILL BE*

they arrive at the mountain, Yahweh states, "I ... brought you to myself" (19:4). Yahweh then leaves this dwelling place and travels with the people in the tabernacle — a portable dwelling place (40:34–38).

This understanding accords with the idea that there were already worshipers of Yahweh in the area of Midian (the general vicinity of Horeb) before Moses arrived (see note on 2:15). It would not be out of place, then, for some Israelites to have believed that *the*, or perhaps *a*, dwelling place of God was in this location.

3:2 *the angel of the LORD.* In the ancient world it was rare for heads of state to communicate directly. Diplomatic and political exchange required the use of an intermediary messenger, who was a fully vested representative of the party he represented, speaking for that party and with the authority of that party, and receiving the same treatment that party would enjoy if he were there in person. Still, there was no confusion about the messenger's identity. Gifts given belonged to the represented party, and there was an expectation that words spoken would be reported in accurate detail as if spoken directly to the individual being represented. When the messenger spoke official words, he was not speaking for himself but for his patron. In the same way, the angel of the Lord is a messenger endowed with the authority of Yahweh. When the messenger is speaking, it is the Lord speaking.

3:5 *Take off your sandals.* Some depictions of religious rituals from the ancient Near East show worshipers going barefoot before their gods. Also, in ancient Egypt it seems to have been unacceptable to wear sandals in the presence of the king, even if he should be wearing them. Thus, this act is probably symbolic for Moses; it shows respect for sacred space ("holy ground") or subservience to God. Others have suggested that it may simply have been a matter of not tracking dirt — perhaps representative of that which is unclean — into the holy presence of God.

3:8 *flowing with milk and honey.* Evokes the image of a prosperous land. The Egyptian *Story of Sinuhe* (from the early second millennium BC) also describes the land of Canaan as prosperous: "It was a wonderful land called Yaa. There were cultivated figs in it and grapes, and more wine than water. Its honey was abundant, and its olive trees numerous. On its trees were all varieties of fruit. There were barley and emmer, and there was no end to all varieties of cattle." But the land seems not to have been consistently prosperous; several Biblical texts refer to famine in Canaan (Ge 12:10; 26:1; 43:1). Biblical texts describe the blessing of Yahweh as the determining factor. When he wished for there to be prosperity, there was. Ugaritic texts present a similar perspective: When there was divine blessing — in their case, from Baal — then "the heavens rain oil, / the wadis run with honey." In Sumerian literature, Gilgamesh, Enkidu and the Netherworld indicates that the destiny of stillborn children in the netherworld is to play at a table of gold and silver laden with honey and ghee, showing that these were symbols of prosperity.

Regarding the kind of prosperity, the Biblical expression probably does not refer to the most common forms of agriculture, such as the cultivation of grains. Rather, the "milk" most likely refers to animal husbandry and the use of animal by-products for food and clothing. Sheep were important for their wool and meat, but goats may have been more important. They provide twice as much milk as sheep, and their hair and hides could be used for tents, clothing, carpets, and even satchels for holding liquids. The "honey" refers to horticulture — the cultivation of fruits and vegetables. "Honey" in Israel is more commonly the syrup from grapes and dates than the substance produced by bees.

Given the mountainous and arid landscape of much of Canaan, it would be difficult for a society to rely strictly on agricultural crops. Herding and horticulture were essential. Still, to the casual observer, the lush environs of Egypt's fertile delta appeared far more inviting than Canaan (cf. 16:3; especially Nu 16:13, where Israelites call Egypt a "land flowing with milk and honey"). Moreover, parts of Canaan were indeed verdant compared to the nearby desert.

This is what you are to say to the Israelites: 'I AM[b] has sent me to you.' "
15God also said to Moses, "Say to the
Israelites, 'The LORD,[a] the God of your fathers — the God of Abraham, the God of
Isaac and the God of Jacob — has sent me
to you.'

"This is my name[c] forever,
the name you shall call me
from generation to generation.

16"Go, assemble the elders[d] of Israel and
say to them, 'The LORD, the God of your
fathers — the God of Abraham, Isaac and
Jacob — appeared to me and said: I have
watched over you and have seen what has
been done to you in Egypt. 17And I have
promised to bring you up out of your misery in Egypt[e] into the land of the Canaanites, Hittites, Amorites, Perizzites, Hivites
and Jebusites — a land flowing with milk
and honey.'
18"The elders of Israel will listen[f] to you.
Then you and the elders are to go to the
king of Egypt and say to him, 'The LORD,
the God of the Hebrews, has met with us.
Let us take a three-day journey into the
wilderness to offer sacrifices[g] to the LORD
our God.' 19But I know that the king of
Egypt will not let you go unless a mighty
hand[h] compels him. 20So I will stretch out
my hand[i] and strike the Egyptians with all
the wonders[j] that I will perform among
them. After that, he will let you go.[k]
21"And I will make the Egyptians favorably disposed[l] toward this people, so that
when you leave you will not go empty-
handed.[m] 22Every woman is to ask her
neighbor and any woman living in her
house for articles of silver and gold[n] and
for clothing, which you will put on your
sons and daughters. And so you will plunder[o] the Egyptians."

3:14 [b] Ex 6:2-3; Jn 8:58; Heb 13:8
3:15 [c] Ps 135:13; Hos 12:5
3:16 [d] Ex 4:29
3:17 [e] Ge 15:16; Jos 24:11
3:18 [f] Ex 4:1,8, 31 [g] Ex 5:1,3
3:19 [h] Ex 4:21; 5:2
3:20 [i] Ex 6:1,6; 9:15 [j] Dt 6:22; Ne 9:10; Ac 7:36 [k] Ex 12:31-33
3:21 [l] Ex 12:36 [m] Ps 105:37
3:22 [n] Ex 11:2 [o] Eze 39:10

Signs for Moses

4 Moses answered, "What if they do not
believe me or listen[p] to me and say,
'The LORD did not appear to you'?"
2Then the LORD said to him, "What is
that in your hand?"
"A staff,"[q] he replied.
3The LORD said, "Throw it on the
ground."
Moses threw it on the ground and it became a snake, and he ran from it. 4Then
the LORD said to him, "Reach out your
hand and take it by the tail." So Moses
reached out and took hold of the snake
and it turned back into a staff in his hand.
5"This," said the LORD, "is so that they
may believe[r] that the LORD, the God of
their fathers — the God of Abraham, the
God of Isaac and the God of Jacob — has
appeared to you."
6Then the LORD said, "Put your hand inside your cloak." So Moses put his hand
into his cloak, and when he took it out,
the skin was leprous[b] — it had become as
white as snow.[s]
7"Now put it back into your cloak," he
said. So Moses put his hand back into his
cloak, and when he took it out, it was restored,[t] like the rest of his flesh.
8Then the LORD said, "If they do not believe you or pay attention to the first sign,
they may believe the second. 9But if they
do not believe these two signs or listen to
you, take some water from the Nile and
pour it on the dry ground. The water you
take from the river will become blood[u] on
the ground."
10Moses said to the LORD, "Pardon your
servant, Lord. I have never been eloquent,

4:1 [p] Ex 3:18; 6:30
4:2 [q] ver 17,20
4:5 [r] Ex 19:9
4:6 [s] Nu 12:10; 2Ki 5:1,27
4:7 [t] Nu 12:13-15; Dt 32:39; 2Ki 5:14; Mt 8:3
4:9 [u] Ex 7:17-21

[a] *15* The Hebrew for *LORD* sounds like and may be related to the Hebrew for *I AM* in verse 14.
[b] *6* The Hebrew word for *leprous* was used for various diseases affecting the skin.

4:3 *it became a snake.* Tales even from the modern era have been told of an Egyptian magical act in which a snake becomes as stiff as a staff. One account refers to "both a snake and a crocodile thrown by hypnotism into the condition of rigidity in which they could be held up as rods by the tip of the tail." The sign given to Moses was the opposite, which raises the possibility that the sign was intended as an obvious reversal of Egyptian magic.

4:6 *leprous.* Exactly what the Hebrew term for "leprous" means is uncertain. Gerhard Henrik Armauer Hansen, a Norwegian physician, in the 1860s discovered the organism that he named *Mycobacterium leprae* — the bacterium that causes what today is known as leprosy or Hansen's disease. There is little evidence, however, that this disease existed to any substantial degree in the ancient Near East. Examinations of skeletal remains from both Egypt and Israel show little evidence of the bone deformities typically caused by leprosy; the earliest indication of true leprosy in Egypt dates to the early Christian period. The Hebrew term *metsoraat,* often translated as "leprosy," most likely refers to changes in the skin that result from any number of dermatological conditions (e.g., psoriasis, eczema), fungal infections (e.g., ringworm), or other causes.

Here Moses' hand is said to be "as snow." This could refer either to color (white) or to texture (flaky), though the latter is more likely, in light of other Biblical texts referring to *metsoraat.* Ancient Mesopotamians also had names for skin diseases that have been translated into English as "leprosy." Like the Israelites, they feared these diseases. Some texts use this disease to curse wrongdoers: "May Sîn, great lord, fill him with leprosy and may he bed down like a wild ass outside the city." A court case at ancient Nuzi (c. 1400 BC) cites testimony of one man to another, "You are filled with 'leprosy' [*epqu*]. Do not come near me." Thus, the condition of Moses' hand, whatever it was, is meant to startle and repulse any observer and even Moses himself, though he cannot run from this as he had from the snake (v. 3).

EXODUS 3:13–15

God's Name

God's statement "I AM WHO I AM" (Ex 3:14) is essentially in answer to the question, "What is your name?" God's initial answer seems evasive. He is hinting at the real answer, though, since the Hebrew words for "I am" sound a bit like "Yahweh," the name finally revealed in Ex 3:15 ("the LORD"). Two aspects of how divine names were utilized in ancient Egypt may relate to this revelation of God's name.

First, ancient Egyptians believed in a close relationship between the name of a deity and the deity itself—i.e., the name of a god could reveal part of the essential nature of that god. In Egyptian texts that refer to different but important names for the same deity, the names are often associated with particular actions or characteristics, and the words used tend to sound similar to the names with which they are associated. One can say there is wordplay between the action or characteristic and the name.

For example, one text says, "You are complete [*km*] and great [*wr*] in your name of Bitter Lake [*Km wr*] ... See you are great and round [*šn*] in (your name of) Ocean [*Šn wr*]." One can discern a similar wordplay at work in Ex 3:14. The action God refers to is that of being or existing. The wordplay consists in that the statement "I AM" comes from the Hebrew consonants *h-y-h*, while the name in Ex 3:15 contains the consonants *y-h-w-h*. Both words come from the same verbal root, and the linguistic connection would be immediately clear to an ancient listener or reader. It is not that God's name is actually "I am" but that "Yahweh" reveals something about the essence of who God is—an essence that relates to the concept of being and to the idea of one who brings others into being.

A second aspect of divine names in Egypt may be relevant. Deities sometimes had secret names, and special power was granted to those who knew them. Certain Egyptian magical texts (e.g., the Harris Magical Papyrus) give instructions on how to use the words of a god and thereby wield a degree of that god's power.

It would have been unusual in the ancient Near East for a deity quickly and easily to reveal his name (e.g., Ge 32:29); this may be part of the reason for the delayed answer here in Ex 3. Nevertheless, Yahweh's name is not meant to be kept secret, and it is vitally important for Moses to have this knowledge. He is to speak Yahweh's words (6:29), wield his power (7:17) and function like Yahweh to both his brother Aaron (4:16) and to Pharaoh (7:1).

To this day, no one knows for sure how to pronounce the name of God—at least not as the ancient Israelites would have pronounced it. There are four consonants in the name—sometimes called the Tetragrammaton ("four-letter word"): *y-h-w-h*. The vowels are the tricky part. Hebrew is generally written without vowels. In the second half of the first millennium AD, some Jewish scribes began adding small marks to Biblical manuscripts in order to indicate how the vowel sounds of each word should

continued on next page

neither in the past nor since you have
spoken to your servant. I am slow of
speech and tongue."[v]
11 The LORD said to him, "Who gave human beings their mouths? Who makes
them deaf or mute? Who gives them sight
or makes them blind?[w] Is it not I, the
LORD? 12 Now go; I will help you speak and
will teach you what to say."[x]

4:10 [v] Ex 6:12; Jer 1:6 **4:11** [w] Ps 94:9; Mt 11:5 **4:12** [x] Isa 50:4; Jer 1:9; Mt 10:19-20; Mk 13:11; Lk 12:12; 21:14-15 **4:14** [y] ver 27 **4:15** [z] Nu 23:5, 12,16

13 But Moses said, "Pardon your servant,
Lord. Please send someone else."
14 Then the LORD's anger burned against
Moses and he said, "What about your
brother, Aaron the Levite? I know he can
speak well. He is already on his way to
meet[y] you, and he will be glad to see you.
15 You shall speak to him and put words in
his mouth;[z] I will help both of you speak

be pronounced. They treated the name of God, however, differently from other words. It had long been customary in Jewish tradition *not* to pronounce the name Yahweh. Instead of saying "Yahweh," people would often say "*Adonay*," which means "my Lord" (and has led to "the LORD" as the traditional rendering of Yahweh in the English Bible). In order to remind readers to say "*Adonay*" instead of "Yahweh," the scribes added the marks for the vowel sounds of *Adonay* to the consonants for Yahweh in their manuscripts. Pronouncing the consonants of *yhwh* with the vowels of *adonay* produces the well-known "Jehovah," which is certainly *not* the right pronunciation.

What, then, were the original vowels in God's name? Ultimately, we do not know. During the period of the divided kingdom, the name may have been pronounced something like "Yau," with the "au" forming a diphthong rather than two separate syllables. Evidence from classical Hebrew (found in both Biblical and non-Biblical texts) and certain Greek renderings of the name, however, have led scholars generally to believe that "Yahweh" was the way in which the name eventually came to be pronounced.

The Tetragrammaton in one of the Dead Sea Scrolls and in a modern scroll, with the vowel sounds of Adonay added.
Wikimedia Commons

More significant is the *meaning* of the name Yahweh. For this there has been a wide range of suggestions: "Truly He!"; "My One"; "He Who Is"; "He Who Brings into Being"; "He Who Storms." One of the best suggestions is that the name is a shortened form of a longer name, Yahweh Sabaoth (often rendered in English as "the LORD of Hosts" or "the LORD Almighty"; see, e.g., 2Sa 6:2). The word "Yahweh" itself is most likely a verb. Many other shortened names from the ancient Near East are verb forms, which is exactly what Yahweh appears to be. It comes from the Hebrew verb meaning "to be." But if the first vowel really is an *a*-vowel, then the verb likely has a causative sense: "to cause to be." Thus, a fairly literal translation of Yahweh Sabaoth would be "He Who Causes the Hosts (of Heaven) to Be." In general, then, the name refers to the One who creates or brings into being. ◆

and will teach you what to do. 16He will
speak to the people for you, and it will be
as if he were your mouth[a] and as if you
were God to him. 17But take this staff[b] in
your hand so you can perform the signs[c]
with it."

4:16 [a] Ex 7:1-2
4:17 [b] ver 2
[c] Ex 7:9-21

Moses Returns to Egypt

18Then Moses went back to Jethro his
father-in-law and said to him, "Let me return to my own people in Egypt to see if
any of them are still alive."
Jethro said, "Go, and I wish you well."

4:17 *this staff.* It becomes the symbol of God's presence and power. Moses never uses it in connection with incantations, and so it is distinguished from an instrument of magic. Magic is employed to manipulate deity; Moses

19Now the LORD had said to Moses in
Midian, "Go back to Egypt, for all those
who wanted to kill[d] you are dead.[e]" 20So
Moses took his wife and sons, put them on
a donkey and started back to Egypt. And
he took the staff[f] of God in his hand.
21The LORD said to Moses, "When you
return to Egypt, see that you perform before Pharaoh all the wonders[g] I have given
you the power to do. But I will harden his
heart[h] so that he will not let the people
go. 22Then say to Pharaoh, 'This is what
the LORD says: Israel is my firstborn son,[i]
23and I told you, "Let my son go,[j] so he
may worship me." But you refused to let
him go; so I will kill your firstborn son.' "[k]
24At a lodging place on the way, the LORD
met Moses[a] and was about to kill[l] him.
25But Zipporah took a flint knife, cut off
her son's foreskin[m] and touched Moses'
feet with it.[b] "Surely you are a bridegroom
of blood to me," she said. 26So the LORD let
him alone. (At that time she said "bridegroom of blood," referring to circumcision.)

4:19 [d]Ex 2:15 [e]Ex 2:23
4:20 [f]Ex 17:9; Nu 20:8-9,11
4:21 [g]Ex 3:19,20 [h]Ex 7:3,13; 9:12,35; 14:4,8; Dt 2:30; Isa 63:17; Jn 12:40; Ro 9:18
4:22 [i]Isa 63:16; 64:8; Jer 31:9; Hos 11:1; Ro 9:4
4:23 [j]Ex 5:1; 7:16 [k]Ex 11:5; 12:12,29
4:24 [l]Nu 22:22
4:25 [m]Ge 17:14; Jos 5:2,3
4:27 [n]Ex 3:1 [o]ver 14
4:28 [p]ver 8-9,16
4:29 [q]Ex 3:16
4:31 [r]ver 8; Ex 3:18 [s]Ex 2:25
5:1 [t]Ex 3:18

27The LORD said to Aaron, "Go into the
wilderness to meet Moses." So he met Moses at the mountain[n] of God and kissed[o]
him. 28Then Moses told Aaron everything
the LORD had sent him to say,[p] and also
about all the signs he had commanded
him to perform.
29Moses and Aaron brought together all
the elders[q] of the Israelites, 30and Aaron
told them everything the LORD had said to
Moses. He also performed the signs before the people, 31and they believed.[r] And
when they heard that the LORD was concerned[s] about them and had seen their
misery, they bowed down and worshiped.

Bricks Without Straw

5 Afterward Moses and Aaron went to
Pharaoh and said, "This is what the
LORD, the God of Israel, says: 'Let my people go, so that they may hold a festival[t] to
me in the wilderness.' "

[a] 24 Hebrew *him* [b] 25 The meaning of the Hebrew for this clause is uncertain.

only uses the staff this way in one incident (Nu 20), for which he is severely punished.

4:24 *was about to kill him.* Yahweh appears intent on killing Moses, the one he has just commissioned as the deliverer of the Israelites. If Yahweh felt compelled to punish Moses for the latter's murder of an Egyptian taskmaster (2:12), it seems odd that he would wait until now. In other Biblical texts, those who are guilty of accidental or unintentional homicide may flee to so-called cities of refuge or asylum (21:13; Nu 35:9–34; Dt 19:1–13; Jos 20:1–9). This affords them protection from the relatives of the victim who are likely to seek revenge, and they must remain in their chosen city of refuge until the death of the high priest (Nu 35:28; Jos 20:6).

By analogy Moses' flight to Midian could be seen as an effort to seek asylum. That there was justification for Moses' killing of the Egyptian is debatable, but it may have counted as a crime of passion or an appropriate act of revenge for the killing of Israelites. In this way, Moses qualifies for leniency and thus for the chance at asylum. He then remains in Midian until he is told, "All those who wanted to kill you are dead" (v. 19). This suggests that Moses is now free to leave his place of asylum and make his return. Yet Yahweh still attacks him. The idea may be that, even though Moses is free in a legal sense to return, he still carries about on his person a kind of spiritual or religious pollution as a result of the homicide—a pollution that must be purged. In the case of homicide, the pollution is referred to by the Hebrew word *dam* ("blood"); the perpetrator has been contaminated by the victim's blood.

This notion of blood contamination turns up in ancient Greece and Mesopotamia as well. An Assyrian text from the mid-600s BC declares that the perpetrator of a homicide must make a payment (what is really a ransom for his own life) to the victim's family and in so doing "wash the blood away." A text from Mari (c. 1800 BC) refers to a "criminal who is polluted with that blood (shed in murder)." In ch. 4, Yahweh cannot allow Moses to emerge from his place of asylum unless the contamination is purged.

4:25 *bridegroom of blood.* Zipporah's act of circumcision is important. It appears to function as the expiation—purging, atonement—for the guilt, pollution or "blood" that Moses is still carrying around and on account of which Yahweh attacks him. It is hard to say, however, exactly how circumcision accomplishes this expiation. There is a Phoenician myth in which the god Kronos circumcises himself and thereby seems to halt an impending catastrophe sent by another god. "At the occurrence of a fatal plague, Kronos immolated his only son to his father Ouranos and circumcised himself, forcing the allies who were with him to do the same." This myth reflects a belief that circumcision could quell divine wrath.

If some such similar belief is at work here, the problem then becomes why Moses himself is not the one circumcised. In light of both Egyptian and Hebrew customs, though, he likely already is circumcised and thus cannot be physically circumcised again. Thus, the touching of his son's bloody foreskin to Moses' own genitalia (the Hebrew word for "feet" [v. 25] can be euphemistic for male sex organs) may have functioned as a symbolic circumcision and produced the required expiatory effect.

In light of all this, Zipporah's comment about "a bridegroom of blood" probably contains a pair of double meanings. First, Moses is a bridegroom of blood because he still possesses the blood or pollution that resulted from his homicide, but also because of the bloody circumcision that Zipporah performs. The other double meaning comes from the Hebrew word for "bridegroom" (*hatan*). The verb form of this word in both Hebrew and Arabic means "to become a relative by means of marriage." But the etymology of this word leads to another verb that means "to circumcise." By the word "bridegroom," then, Zipporah refers both to a bridegroom and to a circumcised one. This suggests that Moses is indeed circumcised, albeit symbolically, by her act. In the end, the circumcision cleanses Moses and thereby appeases Yahweh's anger.

5:1 *hold a festival to me in the wilderness.* Mesopotamian and Egyptian societies both had numerous festivals tied to particular times of their civil calendar. The Hittites too had festivals that were held monthly or yearly, while others, such as the Festival of the Sickle or the Festival of Cutting Grapes, took place in connection with events of the agricultural year (civil and agricultural calendars did

2Pharaoh said, "Who is the LORD,[u] that
I should obey him and let Israel go? I do
not know the LORD and I will not let Israel go."[v]
3Then they said, "The God of the Hebrews has met with us. Now let us take a
three-day journey into the wilderness to
offer sacrifices to the LORD our God, or he
may strike us with plagues[w] or with the
sword."
4But the king of Egypt said, "Moses
and Aaron, why are you taking the people away from their labor?[x] Get back to
your work!" 5Then Pharaoh said, "Look,
the people of the land are now numerous,[y]
and you are stopping them from working."
6That same day Pharaoh gave this order to the slave drivers and overseers in
charge of the people: 7"You are no longer
to supply the people with straw for making bricks; let them go and gather their
own straw. 8But require them to make the
same number of bricks as before; don't reduce the quota. They are lazy; that is why
they are crying out, 'Let us go and sacrifice to our God.' 9Make the work harder
for the people so that they keep working
and pay no attention to lies."
10Then the slave drivers and the overseers went out and said to the people,
"This is what Pharaoh says: 'I will not
give you any more straw. 11Go and get
your own straw wherever you can find it,
but your work will not be reduced at all.'"
12So the people scattered all over Egypt to
gather stubble to use for straw. 13The slave
drivers kept pressing them, saying, "Complete the work required of you for each
day, just as when you had straw." 14And
Pharaoh's slave drivers beat the Israelite
overseers they had appointed,[z] demanding, "Why haven't you met your quota of
bricks yesterday or today, as before?"
15Then the Israelite overseers went and
appealed to Pharaoh: "Why have you
treated your servants this way? 16Your
servants are given no straw, yet we are
told, 'Make bricks!' Your servants are being beaten, but the fault is with your own
people."
17Pharaoh said, "Lazy, that's what you
are—lazy![a] That is why you keep saying, 'Let us go and sacrifice to the LORD.'
18Now get to work. You will not be given
any straw, yet you must produce your full
quota of bricks."
19The Israelite overseers realized they
were in trouble when they were told, "You
are not to reduce the number of bricks required of you for each day." 20When they
left Pharaoh, they found Moses and Aaron waiting to meet them, 21and they said,
"May the LORD look on you and judge you!
You have made us obnoxious[b] to Pharaoh
and his officials and have put a sword in
their hand to kill us."[c]

God Promises Deliverance

22Moses returned to the LORD and said,
"Why, Lord, why have you brought trouble on this people?[d] Is this why you sent
me? 23Ever since I went to Pharaoh to
speak in your name, he has brought trouble on this people, and you have not rescued[e] your people at all."

6 Then the LORD said to Moses, "Now
you will see what I will do to Pharaoh:
Because of my mighty hand[f] he will let
them go;[g] because of my mighty hand he
will drive them out of his country."[h]

5:2 [u] 2Ki 18:35; Job 21:15 [v] Ex 3:19 **5:3** [w] Ex 3:18 **5:4** [x] Ex 1:11 **5:5** [y] Ex 1:7,9 **5:14** [z] Isa 10:24 **5:17** [a] ver 8 **5:21** [b] Ge 34:30 [c] Ex 14:11 **5:22** [d] Nu 11:11 **5:23** [e] Jer 4:10 **6:1** [f] Ex 3:19 [g] Ex 3:20 [h] Ex 12:31, 33,39

not always match). In almost every case, a festival connected with a particular deity took place at that deity's place of residence—at its temple or wherever the priests happened to place its statue. Perhaps the Israelites could not hold a festival to their God in Egypt because his place of residence was the "mountain of God" in "the desert."

5:2 *I do not know the LORD.* It is not that the Egyptian king is unfamiliar with deities worshiped by Semitic peoples. The Egyptians knew well and even venerated a number of Semitic deities. Baal, e.g., was highly revered. The Egyptian king was at times said to be "great in power like Baal over foreign lands" or to have a "roar like that of Baal in heaven." Perhaps Pharaoh here is saying that he has never heard of Yahweh. But his statement more likely means a refusal to acknowledge Yahweh as one worthy of his attention.

5:11 *get your own straw.* Straw was a crucial ingredient in mud bricks to hold the materials firmly together. Even in modern Egypt, bricks have often been made of soil, water and what is known in Arabic as *tibn*—essentially the same term as the Hebrew word for straw (*teben*). Without straw, more bricks would fail, and quotas would be more difficult to meet.

5:14 *quota of bricks.* The Louvre Leather Scroll, an Egyptian text from the reign of Rameses II, contains a list of brick quotas assigned to individual workers and how many bricks each worker delivered. The relevant portion of the text begins: "The great Stable of Rameses II, Life Prosperity and Health! Amenemhat son of Kuroy—bricks, 2000: delivered, 150; delivered, 150; delivered, 165, delivered, 185; delivered, 170; total, 820. Wepwawetmose son of Huy—bricks, 2000: delivered, 100; delivered, 350; delivered, 180; delivered, 320; total, 950." Of the approximately 35 workers listed, not one met his quota of bricks. To what degree this caused problems for the building project or to what degree these workers may have been punished is not disclosed.

5:17 *Lazy.* Time off from work for worship was not unheard of in Egypt. A collection of texts has been preserved from the New Kingdom site of Deir el-Medina, where many Egyptian workers were stationed in order to construct and decorate royal tombs. Records list workers who were absent for a variety of reasons, including participation in religious rituals and festivities.

6:1 *my mighty hand.* This phrase can just as easily be translated "my strong arm." The "hand of the LORD" or "his hand" is a Biblical and ancient Near Eastern expression. In Akkadian literature it often refers to the punishing, destructive or threatening hand of a particular god. The poor sufferer

2God also said to Moses, "I am the LORD.
3I appeared to Abraham, to Isaac and to Jacob as God Almighty,[a][i] but by my name[j] the
LORD[b][k] I did not make myself fully known
to them. 4I also established my covenant[l]
with them to give them the land of Canaan,
where they resided as foreigners.[m] 5More-
over, I have heard the groaning[n] of the Israelites, whom the Egyptians are enslaving,
and I have remembered my covenant.
6"Therefore, say to the Israelites: 'I am
the LORD, and I will bring you out from

6:3 [i] Ge 17:1 [j] Ps 68:4; 83:18; Isa 52:6 [k] Ex 3:14 **6:4** [l] Ge 15:18 [m] Ge 28:4,13 **6:5** [n] Ex 2:23

[a] 3 Hebrew *El-Shaddai* [b] 3 See note at 3:15.

in that literature who utters the line "I Will Praise the Lord of Wisdom" can complain of his god that "heavy was his hand [upon me], I could not bear it." In Biblical texts this phrase stood for the power/might of Israel's God (3:20; 9:15; Dt 3:24; 7:8). In Egyptian documents (annals, historical texts, oracles and prophecies) the expressions "hand of Pharaoh" or "strong arm of Pharaoh" were metaphors for the power/might of Egypt (3:8; 18:9). The equivalent expression "outstretched arm" (v. 6; Dt 4:34; 11:2) was often used in and even combined with the "mighty hand" of the LORD (Dt 4:34; 5:15; 7:19; 9:29; 11:2; 26:8).

These terms are found ubiquitously in Egyptian literature since Pharaoh was known as "lord of the strong arm" (Neb Khopesh). Rameses II affirmed that his god Seth had made Rameses' arm "mighty to the height of heaven and [his] strength to the width of the earth!" The Hittite king Mursili conquered the enemy "with [his strong] arm." These idioms were also used in Canaan as evidenced by the Amarna letters.

6:2 *I am the LORD.* Other ancient Near Eastern texts also record deities speaking in this way, although such statements are not common in Egyptian texts. Part of the Sphinx Stele from the time of Thutmose IV states: "See me, look at me, my son Thutmose. I am thy father, Harmakhis-Kepri-Re-Atum, I shall give thee my kingdom upon earth." Assyrian texts from the 600s BC ascribe the following statements to the goddess Ishtar: "I am the great divine lady, I am the goddess Ishtar of Arbela, who will destroy your enemies from before your feet ... I am Ishtar of Arbela. I shall lie in wait for your enemies"; "I am Ishtar of Arbela, O Esarhaddon, king of Assyria. In the cities of Ashur, Nineveh, Calah, protracted days ... unto [you] shall

EXODUS 6:2 – 8

HISTORICITY OF THE EXODUS

Decisive proof for the historicity of any event is virtually unattainable. Events can be shown to be *possible*, *plausible* or even *probable*, depending on the nature and amount of evidence supporting them. But they cannot be *proved* in any ultimate sense.

Little historical evidence offers corroboration of an escape of slaves from Egypt on the order of the large-scale exodus described in the Bible. There is one aspect of the Biblical narrative, however, that has a fair amount of circumstantial evidence in its favor: the enslavement of Israelites in Egypt. This evidence, apart from the Biblical text itself, is sufficient to argue for the *plausibility* of this event. The Egyptians used a particular term, often translated "Asiatics," to refer to Semitic people groups. This term typically applied to those who hailed from the regions of western Asia, such as Syria and Palestine, and it could easily have been used of Israelites. Asiatics entered Egypt by one of several means: as prisoners of war; as part of tribute payments from Asiatic rulers to the Egyptian king; as victims of slave trade; as merchants on business trips to conduct trade and related activities; and as hungry people in search of food and water for themselves and their flocks. The first three ways usually led to enslavement, often at the hands of official institutions, such as the palace, the temple or the military.

Many scholars believe that the book of Exodus places the events it recounts in a time period that fits best within the second half of the second millennium BC. In Egypt, this is known as the New Kingdom (1550 – 1069 BC). For the area of Syria and Palestine in western Asia, this time period includes the Late Bronze Age (c. 1550 – 1200 BC) and the first part of the Iron Age (referred to as Iron I, 1200 – 1000 BC).

In Palestine it is in the Iron I period that remains of a distinctly Israelite character begin to appear and continue to predominate throughout the Iron II period (1000 – 586 BC; in 586 BC Jerusalem and much of Judah were overrun by the

continued on next page

under the yoke of the Egyptians. I will
free you from being slaves to them, and
I will redeem[o] you with an outstretched
arm[p] and with mighty acts of judgment. 7I
will take you as my own people, and I will
be your God.[q] Then you will know[r] that I
am the LORD your God, who brought you
out from under the yoke of the Egyptians.
8And I will bring you to the land[s] I swore
with uplifted hand[t] to give to Abraham, to
Isaac and to Jacob.[u] I will give it to you as
a possession. I am the LORD.' "
9Moses reported this to the Israelites,
but they did not listen to him because of
their discouragement and harsh labor.
10Then the LORD said to Moses, 11"Go,

6:6 [o] Dt 7:8; 1Ch 17:21 [p] Dt 26:8 **6:7** [q] Dt 4:20; 2Sa 7:24 [r] Ex 16:12; Isa 41:20 **6:8** [s] Ge 15:18; 26:3 [t] Ge 14:22 [u] Ps 136:21-22

I grant." Such "I am" statements seem mainly associated with assertions of a deity's power and authority. King Esarhaddon of Assyria can rest assured that he will enjoy long life and see his enemies defeated, because Ishtar has confirmed her declaration: "I am Ishtar of Arbela." For its part, the Biblical text insists that all involved in this situation in Egypt acknowledge ("know") who Yahweh is and accept his power and authority, even though Pharaoh fails to acknowledge any of this (5:2). Moreover, the driving force behind Israel's deliverance from Egypt is to build in them an unwavering conviction: "Then you will know that I am the LORD your God" (6:7). The Egyptians too are not left out of this equation: "And the Egyptians will know that I am the LORD" (7:5). Exodus repeatedly stresses this kind of knowing (7:17; 8:10; 10:2; 14:4,18).

6:7 *take you as my own people.* This expression comes from contract law. It is the classical expression of the covenantal (or "contractual," since the Hebrew *berit* can be translated "covenant" or "contract") relationship between Yahweh and the Israelites. They will be his people, and he will be their God. The statement is lit. "I take [*laqah*] you to myself as a people." The forming of a marriage relationship is also expressed in this way: "Aaron took [*laqah*] Elisheba ... to himself as a wife" (lit. translation of v. 23).

Adoption also provides a helpful analogy. In Mesopotamia, adoption was often expressed by "take" (Akkadian *lequ*, cognate with Hebrew *laqah*) in conjunction with the expression "as a son" or "as a daughter." For example, section 186 of the Code of Hammurapi begins: "If a man takes a young child as a son ..." Here Yahweh says that he will

Babylonians). Any departure of Israelites from Egypt would presumably have taken place before this settlement process begins, and there are no compelling reasons to consider time periods prior to the New Kingdom in Egypt and the Late Bronze Age in Palestine. Moreover, in Palestine, the transition from the Late Bronze to the Iron Age is primarily one from Egyptian domination to a marked absence of Egyptian control.

It was during the New Kingdom that Egypt's imperialistic ambitions grew. One of its early kings, Amenhotep I, led Egypt to renewed military success in Nubia (modern Sudan) to the south, and his kingdom began to reap economic benefits. Later, during the reign of Thutmose III, Egypt expanded its power into Syria and Palestine, subjecting a number of city-states to its control. This provided Egypt with access to a variety of raw materials, an important source of human labor from prisoners of war, military spoils and tribute payments from vassal rulers. Such rewards motivated subsequent kings to continue to exert control over Syria and Palestine. An archive of letters from the site of el-Amarna (see note on Ex 1:15) amply attests to this.

Much of the evidence for Asiatic slaves in Egypt comes from the New Kingdom. Beginning with Thutmose III in the 1400s BC, Egyptian kings brought back unprecedented numbers of Asiatic slaves from their military campaigns into Syria and Palestine. From the 1300s BC, the Amarna letters (see note on Ex 1:15) show a fairly active slave trade between Palestine and Egypt. Kings from the 1200s BC, such as Seti I and Rameses II, continued forays into Palestine, capturing large numbers of prisoners. ◆

The Beth Shean Stele of Egyptian King Seti I, c. 1289 – 1278 BC, notes his military campaign into Palestine and capture of a large numbers of prisoners.

Steven Voth

EXODUS 6:13

The Timing of the Exodus

The two major candidates for the date of the exodus are the fifteenth century BC and the thirteenth century BC. Biblical information supporting the fifteenth century BC includes a calculation from numbers given in 1Ki 6:1 and Jdg 11:26, and the requisite time necessary for an extended period in Midian before Pharaoh dies (40 years) and another extended period of time in the wilderness before entering Canaan (40 years). The former may require a long-lived pharaoh for the oppression (e.g., Thutmose III). If the long-lived pharaoh were Rameses II (thirteenth century BC) there is not enough time for Israel to be in the wilderness before Rameses' successor, Merneptah, says that Israel is in the land.

Biblical information supporting the thirteenth-century BC date includes the fact that one of the cities the Israelites are working on is named Rameses (Ex 1:11). It is far-fetched to think that the Israelites were building a city named Rameses two centuries before there even *was* a Rameses.

Each of these pieces of Biblical information, however, can be mitigated without casting aspersions on the credibility of the Bible. First, numbers in the ancient world sometimes took on a schematic, rhetorical sense. If that is how the speakers meant them, that would be how we should read them. We cannot assume that it is just a matter of "doing the math." Second, when Moses is told that those who wanted to kill him were dead (Ex 4:19), that does not mean that they had just died. Therefore a long-lived pharaoh (over 40 years) is not necessary. Third, the reference to the city of Rameses in the Biblical text could easily be an updated name. The city named

continued on next page

tell Pharaoh king of Egypt to let the Israelites go out of his country."

[12]But Moses said to the LORD, "If the Israelites will not listen to me, why would Pharaoh listen to me, since I speak with faltering lips[a]?"[v]

Family Record of Moses and Aaron

[13]Now the LORD spoke to Moses and Aaron about the Israelites and Pharaoh king of Egypt, and he commanded them to bring the Israelites out of Egypt.

6:12 [v] ver 30; Ex 4:10; Jer 1:6
6:14 [w] Ge 46:9
6:15 [x] Ge 46:10; 1Ch 4:24

[14]These were the heads of their families[b]:[w]

The sons of Reuben the firstborn son of Israel were Hanok and Pallu, Hezron and Karmi. These were the clans of Reuben.

[15]The sons of Simeon[x] were Jemuel, Jamin, Ohad, Jakin, Zohar and

[a] *12* Hebrew *I am uncircumcised of lips*; also in verse 30
[b] *14* The Hebrew for *families* here and in verse 25 refers to units larger than clans.

"take" the Israelites "as [his] own people." One can say he adopts them.

Adoption functions for at least three purposes: (1) to provide a secure way to care for orphans, abandoned children and children from families in distress; (2) to provide children for couples with none of their own; and (3) to provide an heir for an individual or a couple. Yahweh's "adoption" of the Israelites fulfills at least two of these purposes. First, Biblical texts liken the Israelites to an abandoned child and refer to them, collectively, as Yahweh's son (Eze 16:4–5; Hos 11:1). Second, Israel is called "the people of his inheritance" (Dt 4:20), and the land of Canaan is "the good land the LORD your God is giving you as your inheritance" (Dt 4:21). The practice of adoption may have provided an important context for ancient Israel's understanding of its relationship with Yahweh.

6:12 *I speak with faltering lips.* Lit. "I am uncircumcised of lips." Biblical texts speak of two other body parts that one would not ordinarily think of as being uncircumcised: the ear (Jer 6:10) and the heart (Lev 26:41; Dt 10:16; 30:6; Jer 4:4; 9:26; Eze 44:7,9). These passages do not refer to physical malfunction, but rather imperviousness to the divine word. Moses is here no longer speaking of himself as "slow of speech and tongue" (4:10); he is referring to something entirely different. It is not a physical disability that he has in mind but a moral one. He is acutely aware of his lack of success so far with both Pharaoh and the Israelites. Moses' statement implies that he believes his

Rameses is located at what is today Tell ed-Dab'a. Rameses rebuilt it as his capital, but it had formerly been built as the Hyksos capital, Avaris. If the exodus was in the fifteenth century BC, the Israelites were building Avaris and later scribes put the more recent name, Rameses, in the text as it was being copied.

Consequently, the Bible does not give the answer. Unfortunately, neither do ancient texts. The most important evidence is provided by the so-called Merneptah Stele, also referred to as the Israel Stele. This monument contains an inscription regarding a military campaign that the Egyptian king Merneptah apparently led into Syria and Palestine around 1210 BC. It refers to several sites that Merneptah claims to have conquered, including "Israel." This is the earliest non-Biblical historical reference to Israel, and suggests that any Israelite departure from Egypt would have had to take place in the first half of the thirteenth century BC at the latest to allow for a generation in the wilderness and time for Israel to get somewhat settled. Beyond this stele, no Egyptian document mentions Israel either in slavery or escaping.

From fourteenth-century BC Egypt (i.e., between the two proposed dates of the exodus), letters from the city of Amarna document the political situation that existed in Canaan. We learn that the city-states of Canaan were being threatened by people they referred to as Apiru, renegade groups of disenfranchised people. In those texts, some of the major cities are the same as in the book of Joshua (e.g., Jerusalem), but some that are prominent are largely absent from Joshua (e.g., Shechem, where the Israelites seem to be able to go with impunity). Others that are prominent in Joshua are totally absent from the Amarna correspondence (e.g., Jericho). It cannot be determined whether the Amarna period is after the exodus and the Israelites are among the Apiru who are causing trouble, or whether the exodus is after the Amarna period and others have paved the way for Israel's entrance into the land.

Another possible source of information to make a determination would be the excavations at the sites involved in the conquest. Unfortunately, the information from excavations does not offer solid evidence for either of the proposed dates. ◆

Shaul the son of a Canaanite woman.
These were the clans of Simeon.
16 These were the names of the sons
of Levi according to their records:
Gershon,[y] Kohath and Merari.[z] Levi
lived 137 years.
17 The sons of Gershon, by clans,
were Libni and Shimei.[a]
18 The sons of Kohath were Amram,
Izhar, Hebron and Uzziel.[b] Kohath
lived 133 years.
19 The sons of Merari were Mahli
and Mushi.[c]

These were the clans of Levi according to their records.
20 Amram married his father's sister
Jochebed, who bore him Aaron and
Moses.[d] Amram lived 137 years.
21 The sons of Izhar[e] were Korah,
Nepheg and Zikri.

6:16 [y] Ge 46:11 [z] Nu 3:17
6:17 [a] 1Ch 6:17
6:18 [b] 1Ch 6:2, 18
6:19 [c] Nu 3:20, 33; 1Ch 6:19; 23:21
6:20 [d] Ex 2:1-2; Nu 26:59
6:21 [e] 1Ch 6:38
6:22 [f] Lev 10:4; Nu 3:30
6:23 [g] Ru 4:19, 20 [h] Lev 10:1 [i] Nu 3:2, 32 [j] Nu 26:60
6:24 [k] Nu 26:11
6:25 [l] Nu 25:7, 11; Jos 24:33; Ps 106:30
6:26 [m] Ex 7:4; 12:17, 41, 51

22 The sons of Uzziel were Mishael,
Elzaphan[f] and Sithri.
23 Aaron married Elisheba, daughter of Amminadab[g] and sister of Nahshon, and she bore him Nadab and
Abihu,[h] Eleazar[i] and Ithamar.[j]
24 The sons of Korah[k] were Assir, Elkanah and Abiasaph. These were the
Korahite clans.
25 Eleazar son of Aaron married one
of the daughters of Putiel, and she
bore him Phinehas.[l]

These were the heads of the Levite families, clan by clan.

26 It was this Aaron and Moses to whom
the LORD said, "Bring the Israelites out of
Egypt by their divisions."[m] 27 They were
the ones who spoke to Pharaoh king of

mouth is no longer a clean, free and open channel for Yahweh's words.

This focus on the mouth and lips may relate to the so-called mouth-washing rituals in Mesopotamia, which were to purify a person or object in order to come into contact with a divine presence. For objects, after the washing, the mouth was "opened"—a necessary step in the process of transforming the statue into a god. Clearly, preparing the mouth was critical for preparing the entire person or object for divine contact (cf. Isa 6:5).

Egypt about bringing the Israelites out of Egypt — this same Moses and Aaron.

Aaron to Speak for Moses

28 Now when the LORD spoke to Moses in Egypt, 29 he said to him, "I am the LORD.[n] Tell Pharaoh king of Egypt everything I tell you."

30 But Moses said to the LORD, "Since I speak with faltering lips,[o] why would Pharaoh listen to me?"

7 Then the LORD said to Moses, "See, I have made you like God[p] to Pharaoh, and your brother Aaron will be your prophet. 2 You are to say everything I command you, and your brother Aaron is to tell Pharaoh to let the Israelites go out of his country. 3 But I will harden Pharaoh's heart,[q] and though I multiply my signs and wonders in Egypt, 4 he will not listen[r] to you. Then I will lay my hand on Egypt and with mighty acts of judgment[s] I will bring out my divisions, my people the Israelites. 5 And the Egyptians will know that I am the LORD[t] when I stretch out my hand[u] against Egypt and bring the Israelites out of it."

6 Moses and Aaron did just as the LORD commanded[v] them. 7 Moses was eighty years old[w] and Aaron eighty-three when they spoke to Pharaoh.

Aaron's Staff Becomes a Snake

8 The LORD said to Moses and Aaron, 9 "When Pharaoh says to you, 'Perform a miracle,[x]' then say to Aaron, 'Take your staff and throw it down before Pharaoh,' and it will become a snake."[y]

10 So Moses and Aaron went to Pharaoh and did just as the LORD commanded. Aaron threw his staff down in front of Pharaoh and his officials, and it became a snake. 11 Pharaoh then summoned wise men and sorcerers, and the Egyptian magicians[z] also did the same things by their secret arts:[a] 12 Each one threw down his staff and it became a snake. But Aaron's staff swallowed up their staffs. 13 Yet Pharaoh's heart[b] became hard and he would not listen to them, just as the LORD had said.

The Plague of Blood

14 Then the LORD said to Moses, "Pharaoh's heart is unyielding;[c] he refuses to let the people go. 15 Go to Pharaoh in the morning as he goes out to the river. Confront him on the bank of the Nile, and take in your hand the staff that was changed into a snake. 16 Then say to him, 'The LORD, the God of the Hebrews, has sent me to say to you: Let my people go, so that they may worship[d] me in the wilderness. But until now you have not listened. 17 This is what the LORD says: By this you will know that I am the LORD:[e] With the staff that is in my hand I will strike the water of the Nile, and it will be changed into blood.[f] 18 The fish in the Nile will die, and the river will stink; the Egyptians will not be able to drink its water.' "[g]

6:29 [n] ver 11; Ex 7:2
6:30 [o] ver 12; Ex 4:10
7:1 [p] Ex 4:16
7:3 [q] Ex 4:21; 11:9
7:4 [r] Ex 11:9 [s] Ex 3:20; 6:6
7:5 [t] ver 17; Ex 8:19,22 [u] Ex 3:20
7:6 [v] ver 2
7:7 [w] Dt 31:2; 34:7; Ac 7:23,30
7:9 [x] Isa 7:11; Jn 2:18 [y] Ex 4:2-5
7:11 [z] Ge 41:8; 2Ti 3:8 [a] ver 22; Ex 8:7,18
7:13 [b] Ex 4:21
7:14 [c] Ex 8:15,32; 10:1,20,27
7:16 [d] Ex 3:18; 5:1,3
7:17 [e] Ex 5:2 [f] Ex 4:9; Rev 11:6; 16:4
7:18 [g] ver 21,24

7:10 *snake.* The Hebrew word here is different from the one used in 4:3. The Hebrew word here can refer to a sea-monster, dragon, crocodile or snake. The purpose of this event is also different. The sign with Moses' staff was for the Israelite elders. They saw it and, initially, believed Moses (4:30 – 31). The sign with Aaron's staff is for Pharaoh and his officials and demonstrates what appears to be an assault on Egyptian ideology. If Aaron's staff did indeed become a snake, then its devouring of the magicians' snakes, on the one hand, demonstrates an overpowering of the magicians and even a commandeering of their own abilities and expertise.

On the other hand, it could also serve as an attack on the snake as a symbol of Egyptian power. It is hard to know, though, whether Aaron's staff was supposed to become a snake that the Egyptians feared and despised or one that they worshiped. In ancient Egypt various preternatural beings (deities, demons, etc.) took the form of a snake; e.g., Apophis was an evil serpent and a great enemy of the sun-god Re. In Egyptian mythology, he regularly attacked the sun-god and, unless regularly defeated, could impede or even halt the sun-god's orbit and thus bring disaster for human life on earth. Another important snake-deity was the goddess Wadjit. She functioned as the protective and representative deity of Lower Egypt, the delta region. She was normally portrayed as an up-reared cobra — referred to as a uraeus — ready to strike. Wadjit was represented by the uraeus adorning the Egyptian king's headdress. Having the cobra just above the king's forehead was meant to bring protection to Pharaoh and terror to his enemies. The inscription commemorating Rameses II's victory at Qadesh over the Hittites (c. 1275 BC) also refers to Wadjit. Rameses speaks of how he entered the fray and fought ferociously, with his "uraeus-serpent" beating back his enemies and spitting "fiery flame" into the faces of his enemies. The uraeus on the king's head imbued him with the mystical force by which he maintained order in Egypt and even the entire world; no uraeus meant no power.

The episode with Aaron's staff makes a more effective attack on Egyptian ideology if the snake is one like the king's uraeus rather than an evil creature like Apophis. If so, this narrative is another instance when the Biblical text takes a power symbol, crucial within the Egyptian worldview, and attempts to reverse its power and make it advantageous for the Israelites.

7:11 *magicians.* The Hebrew term appears related to an Egyptian word often used to refer to theological specialists in ancient Egypt who studied their culture's sacred literature and knew an array of secret charms, spells and rituals. They were often said to be associated with the "House of Life," a special section in some Egyptian temples that housed ritual and magic texts said to be inspired by the sun-god. They would have practiced "sympathetic magic," based on the idea that there is an association between an object and that which it symbolizes. Magic tapped into the cosmic forces that held creation together and could be used offensively or defensively by human or divine practitioners to command gods and spirits. Magical wands are also known from ancient Egypt, used mainly to ward off evil power and illness. Whether these Egyptian magicians here use such wands ("staffs") is not clear.

19The LORD said to Moses, "Tell Aaron, 'Take your staff and stretch out your
hand[h] over the waters of Egypt—over the
streams and canals, over the ponds and
all the reservoirs—and they will turn to
blood.' Blood will be everywhere in Egypt,
even in vessels[a] of wood and stone."
20Moses and Aaron did just as the LORD
had commanded. He raised his staff in the
presence of Pharaoh and his officials and
struck the water of the Nile,[i] and all the
water was changed into blood.[j] 21The fish
in the Nile died, and the river smelled so
bad that the Egyptians could not drink its
water. Blood was everywhere in Egypt.
22But the Egyptian magicians did the
same things by their secret arts,[k] and Pharaoh's heart became hard; he would not listen to Moses and Aaron, just as the LORD
had said. 23Instead, he turned and went
into his palace, and did not take even this
to heart. 24And all the Egyptians dug along
the Nile to get drinking water, because
they could not drink the water of the river.

The Plague of Frogs

25Seven days passed after the LORD struck
8[b] the Nile. 1Then the LORD said to Moses, "Go to Pharaoh and say to him,
'This is what the LORD says: Let my people
go, so that they may worship[l] me. 2If you
refuse to let them go, I will send a plague
of frogs on your whole country. 3The Nile
will teem with frogs. They will come up
into your palace and your bedroom and
onto your bed, into the houses of your officials and on your people,[m] and into your
ovens and kneading troughs. 4The frogs
will come up on you and your people and
all your officials.' "

7:19 [h] Ex 8:5-6, 16; 9:22; 10:12, 21; 14:21 **7:20** [i] Ex 17:5 [j] Ps 78:44; 105:29 **7:22** [k] ver 11 **8:1** [l] Ex 3:12, 18; 4:23 **8:3** [m] Ex 10:6

8:5 [n] Ex 7:19 **8:6** [o] Ps 78:45; 105:30 **8:7** [p] Ex 7:11 **8:8** [q] ver 28; Ex 9:28; 10:17 [r] ver 25 **8:10** [s] Ex 9:14; Dt 4:35; 33:26; 2Sa 7:22; 1Ch 17:20; Ps 86:8; Isa 46:9; Jer 10:6 **8:15** [t] Ex 7:14

5Then the LORD said to Moses, "Tell Aaron, 'Stretch out your hand with your staff[n]
over the streams and canals and ponds, and
make frogs come up on the land of Egypt.' "
6So Aaron stretched out his hand over
the waters of Egypt, and the frogs[o] came
up and covered the land. 7But the magicians did the same things by their secret
arts;[p] they also made frogs come up on the
land of Egypt.
8Pharaoh summoned Moses and Aaron
and said, "Pray[q] to the LORD to take the
frogs away from me and my people, and I
will let your people go to offer sacrifices[r]
to the LORD."
9Moses said to Pharaoh, "I leave to you
the honor of setting the time for me to
pray for you and your officials and your
people that you and your houses may be
rid of the frogs, except for those that remain in the Nile."
10"Tomorrow," Pharaoh said.
Moses replied, "It will be as you say, so
that you may know there is no one like the
LORD our God.[s] 11The frogs will leave you
and your houses, your officials and your
people; they will remain only in the Nile."
12After Moses and Aaron left Pharaoh,
Moses cried out to the LORD about the
frogs he had brought on Pharaoh. 13And
the LORD did what Moses asked. The frogs
died in the houses, in the courtyards and
in the fields. 14They were piled into heaps,
and the land reeked of them. 15But when
Pharaoh saw that there was relief, he
hardened his heart[t] and would not listen
to Moses and Aaron, just as the LORD had
said.

[a] 19 Or *even on their idols* [b] In Hebrew texts 8:1-4 is numbered 7:26-29, and 8:5-32 is numbered 8:1-28.

7:20 *water was changed into blood.* This is usually considered the first of the ten plagues that Yahweh sends against Egypt. Within ancient Near Eastern societies, this event would have signified national calamity, the invasion of chaos and even a divine curse on the land. In Egypt, e.g., it was Pharaoh's responsibility to maintain a state of proper order and justice, referred to as *maat.* In a sense, Egyptian religion with all its beliefs and practices was designed to restore *maat* to Egypt and preserve it as fully as possible. As titular and functional head of his religion, the Egyptian king was expected to protect his land against the forces of chaos, disorder and injustice. The Admonitions of Ipuwer (c. 2000 BC) uses a variety of verbal imagery to describe what chaos in the land would look like.

In the Sumerian myth Inanna and Shu-kale-tuda, the goddess Inanna is sleeping and, unbeknownst to her, is raped by a gardener. Upon awaking and discovering what has happened, Inanna inflicts three plagues on the land; the third is the turning of all water to blood. Another Sumerian myth, The Exaltation of Inanna, refers to a land that has failed to worship Inanna: "In the mountain where homage is withheld from you vegetation is accursed. Its grand entrance you have reduced to ashes. Blood rises in its rivers for you, its people have naught to drink." Thus, for the Nile and its canals to be turned to blood meant that chaos had crossed Egypt's borders, that Pharaoh had failed in his duty, and that a divine power was at work against them.

8:3 *The Nile will teem with frogs.* Some scholars see a direct cause-and-effect relationship between the plague of blood and this plague of frogs. If the Nile, never in short supply of frogs, were to become uninhabitable, where else would the frogs go but up onto the land? This is speculative at best. Another idea is that this plague is one more attack on Egyptian ideology, with the frog-goddess Heqt as its particular target. Heqt was a giver of life. As the consort of Khnum, a creator-god, she assisted in the creation of infants. In a Middle Kingdom (c. 2055–1650 BC) tale, she and others serve with Isis at the birth of three kings. Later, she develops a special association with childbirth and becomes a kind of patron goddess of midwives.

Egyptians did not, however, associate every common frog with the goddess. If there is symbolic meaning in the account of this plague, it may simply be to point out the inability of Pharaoh and the Egyptian gods to maintain proper order. First the water is ruined, and now the frogs are out of control. The disorder is taking different forms.

The Plague of Gnats

[16]Then the LORD said to Moses, "Tell
Aaron, 'Stretch out your staff and strike
the dust of the ground,' and throughout the
land of Egypt the dust will become gnats."
[17]They did this, and when Aaron stretched
out his hand with the staff and struck the
dust of the ground, gnats[u] came on people
and animals. All the dust throughout the
land of Egypt became gnats. [18]But when
the magicians[v] tried to produce gnats by
their secret arts,[w] they could not.
Since the gnats were on people and animals everywhere, [19]the magicians said to
Pharaoh, "This is the finger[x] of God." But
Pharaoh's heart was hard and he would
not listen, just as the LORD had said.

The Plague of Flies

[20]Then the LORD said to Moses, "Get up
early in the morning[y] and confront Pharaoh as he goes to the river and say to him,
'This is what the LORD says: Let my people
go, so that they may worship[z] me. [21]If you
do not let my people go, I will send swarms
of flies on you and your officials, on your

8:17 [u]Ps 105:31 **8:18** [v]Ex 9:11; Da 5:8 [w]Ex 7:11 **8:19** [x]Ex 7:5; 10:7; Ps 8:3; Lk 11:20 **8:20** [y]Ex 7:15; 9:13 [z]ver 1; Ex 3:18

8:19 *finger of God.* For the ancient Egyptians, the concept of the "finger" of a deity represented something dangerous and powerful that could bring about good or evil. The "finger of Seth" was feared for the harm it had done to the god Horus, while the "finger of Thoth" was praised for the threat it posed to the evil Apophis. By attributing this statement to the Egyptian magicians, the Biblical text presents an admission on their part that they are powerless in the face of one whom they perceive to be a hostile deity. They now recognize that they and their land are under divine attack.

This same phrase occurs in 31:18 but in a different context. There, the two tablets of stone that record God's covenant with the Israelites are said to be "inscribed by the finger of God." The verse clearly does not imply a hostile threat but still seems to invoke the image of a potent and mystical God. Thus, "finger" is probably a symbol for power and ability.

EXODUS 7:14—11:10

Interpreting the Plagues

The first six plagues could be explained as disasters in a progression of events, each of which naturally resulted from one of the plagues before it.

Blood. According to some theories, the water did not change into actual blood. Instead, it took on the appearance of blood. This could have been caused by flagellates (single-cell organisms living in water) flowing down the Nile from Ethiopia. Certain types of flagellates made the river water appear red and, because they upset the balance of oxygen in the water, killed the fish.

Frogs. Frogs were already abundant along the banks of the Nile, but with the changes in the river due to the flagellates, many more came up onto the land. Their sudden death (Ex 8:13) was caused by anthrax, contracted from the piles of rotting fish.

Gnats. These came to feast on the rotting fish and frogs and possibly spread one of the diseases mentioned later in Exodus.

Flies. Biting flies appeared for the same reason as the gnats and later spread disease from animals to humans, thereby causing the plague of boils.

Livestock Plague. This would be anthrax, spread by the frogs and possibly the gnats.

Boils. Anthrax has symptoms similar to boils and is spread to humans by the flies.

The next three plagues can be recognized as coming from the general climatic condition.

Hail. Violent thunderstorms occur in Egypt during the time when barley and flax are harvested (9:31).

Locusts. Large swarms of invading locusts are not unknown in the Middle East and northern Africa.

Darkness. This plague may have been a desert sandstorm, not uncommon in Egypt during the spring, perhaps about six months after the time when the first plague occurred.

continued on next page

people and into your houses. The houses of
the Egyptians will be full of flies; even the
ground will be covered with them.
22“ ‘But on that day I will deal differently
with the land of Goshen, where my people
live;[a] no swarms of flies will be there, so
that you will know[b] that I, the LORD, am
in this land. 23 I will make a distinction[a]
between my people and your people. This
sign will occur tomorrow.’ ”
24 And the LORD did this. Dense swarms
of flies poured into Pharaoh’s palace and
into the houses of his officials; throughout
Egypt the land was ruined by the flies.[c]
25 Then Pharaoh summoned[d] Moses and
Aaron and said, “Go, sacrifice to your God
here in the land.”
26 But Moses said, “That would not be
right. The sacrifices we offer the LORD
our God would be detestable to the Egyptians.[e] And if we offer sacrifices that are
detestable in their eyes, will they not stone
us? 27 We must take a three-day journey
into the wilderness to offer sacrifices[f] to
the LORD our God, as he commands us.”
28 Pharaoh said, “I will let you go to offer sacrifices to the LORD your God in the
wilderness, but you must not go very far.
Now pray[g] for me.”
29 Moses answered, “As soon as I leave
you, I will pray to the LORD, and tomorrow the flies will leave Pharaoh and his
officials and his people. Only let Pharaoh
be sure that he does not act deceitfully[h]
again by not letting the people go to offer
sacrifices to the LORD.”
30 Then Moses left Pharaoh and prayed to
the LORD,[i] 31 and the LORD did what Moses
asked. The flies left Pharaoh and his officials and his people; not a fly remained.
32 But this time also Pharaoh hardened his
heart[j] and would not let the people go.

8:22 [a] Ex 9:4,6, 26; 10:23; 11:7 [b] Ex 7:5; 9:29 **8:24** [c] Ps 78:45; 105:31 **8:25** [d] ver 8; Ex 9:27 **8:26** [e] Ge 43:32; 46:34
8:27 [f] Ex 3:18 **8:28** [g] ver 8; Ex 9:28; 1Ki 13:6 **8:29** [h] ver 15 **8:30** [i] ver 12 **8:32** [j] ver 8, 15; Ex 4:21

[a] 23 Septuagint and Vulgate; Hebrew *will put a deliverance*

Though Exodus is silent on any direct connection between the different plagues, we realize that in the ancient world people did not think in terms of natural cause and effect. Divinities were behind everything that happened—especially events of this magnitude and impact. The point of the text is theological and symbolic (defeat of the gods of Egypt), and the extent to which God used natural phenomena to serve his purposes is not disclosed.

Each event is presented as unexpected and unbelievable. The idea of naturally occurring disasters may have some merit, but there is little in the plagues stories themselves to move the reader in that direction. Even those who maintain this position must acknowledge the miraculous nature of the plagues in terms of timing, prior announcement, discrimination between Israelites and Egyptians, and severity.

Another popular idea about the plagues is that each one was directed at a particular Egyptian deity. Ex 12:12 states: “I will bring judgment on all the gods of Egypt” (though this refers primarily, and perhaps only, to the last plague). The ancient Egyptians had numerous deities—nearly 1,500 throughout their recorded history. Many deities could take the form of more than one animal or creature. If one were to look hard enough, one should eventually be able to find a deity or two whose significance and symbolism could, conceivably, serve as the object of an attack by each plague account.

For example, the god Hapi was associated with the inundation of the Nile, which was crucial for ensuring good crops. Perhaps the first plague was directed at him. It is difficult, though, to find deities for all the plagues that, together, make a convincing case. With the third and fourth plagues, e.g., one suggestion is that the god Khepri, usually portrayed as a scarab beetle, is under attack. But there is little consensus regarding even which insects are in view here, and any correlation with Khepri is inexact. In the end, no consistent linking of the plagues with Egyptian deities is discernible. To be sure, there are a number of points at which the Biblical text does seem to be directed at the Egyptian belief system, but each instance must be examined on its own merits.

Ultimately, the plagues are symbolic of chaos, and they overthrow the right ordering of life so prized by the Egyptians. Announced by Moses, chaos is turning up everywhere in Egypt, and Pharaoh is powerless to stop it. ◆

The Plague on Livestock

9 Then the LORD said to Moses, "Go to
Pharaoh and say to him, 'This is what
the LORD, the God of the Hebrews, says:
"Let my people go, so that they may worship[k] me." 2If you refuse to let them go and
continue to hold them back, 3the hand[l] of
the LORD will bring a terrible plague on
your livestock in the field — on your horses, donkeys and camels and on your cattle,
sheep and goats. 4But the LORD will make
a distinction between the livestock of Israel and that of Egypt,[m] so that no animal
belonging to the Israelites will die.' "
5The LORD set a time and said, "Tomorrow the LORD will do this in the land."
6And the next day the LORD did it: All the
livestock[n] of the Egyptians died,[o] but not
one animal belonging to the Israelites died.
7Pharaoh investigated and found that not

9:1 [k] Ex 8:1
9:3 [l] Ex 7:4
9:4 [m] ver 26; Ex 8:22
9:6 [n] ver 19-21; Ex 11:5 [o] Ps 78:48-50

9:3 *plague.* The Hebrew word used here (*deber*) means "plague" in the medieval sense: a disease of epidemic proportions that is sure to bring death. Jer 21:6 states: "I will strike down those who live in this city — both man and beast — and they will die of a terrible plague [*deber*]." Some interpret this word to mean bubonic plague. Since ancient Near Eastern texts, including Biblical texts, do not differentiate precisely between diseases, this term likely

EXODUS 8:15

The Hardening of Pharaoh's Heart

Scholars tend to agree that the meaning of this and similar expressions probably find their background in Egyptian terminology and beliefs. But there is disagreement as to which aspect of Egyptian culture provides this background. One view relates the concept of a hard heart to the judgment that ancient Egyptians believed would take place in the afterlife. Much of this belief is revealed in the document known as the "Book of the Dead." A portion of this text describes the judgment scene at which the heart of the deceased is weighed on a scale to determine if it is heavier than the feather that represents the Egyptian conception of what is right and just. If not, the deceased is granted great favor in the afterlife. If it is, the creature Ammit (also known as the "Devouress" or "Swallower") will consume the deceased. The Biblical expressions about a hard or strong heart, according to this view, are actually about a heavy heart. Each time the text says that Pharaoh's heart grows hard or strong, it means that his heart grows heavier; i.e., he becomes more and more guilty when compared to the standard of what is right. At times, Yahweh is said to be the one to "harden" the heart of Pharaoh, which refers to Yahweh's judging Pharaoh to be guilty of wrongdoing, even though ancient Egyptians believed their king could do no wrong.

There is another view, however, that points to Egyptian expressions that appear to be the functional equivalents of the Biblical language. One of these, which means lit. "heavy-hearted," is often used of those who have great self-control and are able to refrain from speaking rashly. The expression could be translated "levelheaded." Another expression means "stouthearted" and refers to those who have great courage and determination. Perhaps, then, the Biblical text is attempting to use these expressions in a way that Egyptian texts most certainly would not. Whereas the latter speak positively of a heart that grows hard, heavy or strong, the Exodus passages use this language to render a severe critique of the Egyptian king. In fact, the Biblical text may be offering a caustic satire on these Egyptian ideas. By strengthening Pharaoh's heart, Yahweh is giving the king exactly what he wants — stoutheartedness, a concept highly prized by the Egyptians. In this case, however, getting what he wants leads Pharaoh and his land straight to disaster. On the other hand, it is generally not Yahweh who "makes heavy" Pharaoh's heart. It is instead Pharaoh himself who heaps the guilt of

continued on next page

even one of the animals of the Israelites
had died. Yet his heart was unyielding and
he would not let the people go.[p]

The Plague of Boils

8 Then the LORD said to Moses and Aaron, "Take handfuls of soot from a furnace
and have Moses toss it into the air in the
presence of Pharaoh. 9 It will become fine
dust over the whole land of Egypt, and
festering boils[q] will break out on people
and animals throughout the land."
10 So they took soot from a furnace and
stood before Pharaoh. Moses tossed it
into the air, and festering boils broke out
on people and animals. 11 The magicians[r]

9:7 [p] Ex 7:14; 8:32
9:9 [q] Dt 28:27, 35; Rev 16:2
9:11 [r] Ex 8:18

refers to a number of different illnesses. Nevertheless, any disease referred to by this term would probably have been deadly and widespread (Eze 14:19).

9:10 *boils.* Again (see previous note), it is hard to say what type of condition is meant here. The term *shehin* is often translated as "boil," "ulcer" or "sore." Words from other languages that are related to this term mean "to burn" (Ugaritic *shhn*) and "to become hot" (Akkadian *shahanu*). Some have wondered if this condition is equivalent to "Nile sores," a condition dubbed so by British travelers who contracted them while in the region. A skin disease of this type is representative of divine disapproval and punishment. A number of Neo-Assyrian treaties call for the gods to curse future treaty breakers with a skin disease

wrongdoing — assuming this is the import of a heavy heart — on himself and thereby dooms himself to punishment.

Both views have some evidence in their favor. The second view connects the Hebrew phrases to Egyptian terminology that is indeed similar. None of this terminology occurs in the accounts of the judgment scene involving the weighing of the heart. Nevertheless, the first view seems able to explain the "hardening" process in a way that fits with the tendency of Exodus to condemn Pharaoh and his actions.

Whatever the case might be, we need to recall that God's hardening of Pharaoh's heart is not what is bringing Pharaoh under judgment — he has already come under judgment, as have the people and gods of Egypt. This act is only a means of giving them what they have so richly earned. ◆

The Weighing of the Heart ritual from the papyrus of the scribe Hunefer, Thebes, early Nineteeth Dynasty, about 1280 BC.

Kim Walton. The British Museum.

could not stand before Moses because of the boils that were on them and on all the Egyptians. 12But the LORD hardened Pharaoh's heart[s] and he would not listen to Moses and Aaron, just as the LORD had said to Moses.

The Plague of Hail

13Then the LORD said to Moses, "Get up early in the morning, confront Pharaoh and say to him, 'This is what the LORD, the God of the Hebrews, says: Let my people go, so that they may worship[t] me, 14or this time I will send the full force of my plagues against you and against your officials and your people, so you may know[u] that there is no one like[v] me in all the earth. 15For by now I could have stretched out my hand and struck you and your people[w] with a plague that would have wiped you off the earth. 16But I have raised you up[a] for this very purpose,[x] that I might show you my power[y] and that my name might be proclaimed in all the earth. 17You still set yourself against my people and will not let them go. 18Therefore, at this time tomorrow I will send the worst hailstorm[z] that has ever fallen on Egypt, from the day it was founded till now.[a] 19Give an order now to bring your livestock and everything you have in the field to a place of shelter, because the hail will fall on every person and animal that has not been brought in and is still out in the field, and they will die.' "

20Those officials of Pharaoh who feared[b] the word of the LORD hurried to bring their slaves and their livestock inside. 21But those who ignored the word of the LORD left their slaves and livestock in the field.

22Then the LORD said to Moses, "Stretch out your hand toward the sky so that hail will fall all over Egypt—on people and animals and on everything growing in the fields of Egypt." 23When Moses stretched out his staff toward the sky, the LORD sent thunder[c] and hail,[d] and lightning flashed down to the ground. So the LORD rained hail on the land of Egypt; 24hail fell and lightning flashed back and forth. It was the worst storm in all the land of Egypt since it had become a nation. 25Throughout Egypt hail struck everything in the fields—both people and animals; it beat down everything growing in the fields and stripped every tree.[e] 26The only place it did not hail was the land of Goshen,[f] where the Israelites were.[g]

27Then Pharaoh summoned Moses and Aaron. "This time I have sinned,"[h] he said to them. "The LORD is in the right,[i] and I and my people are in the wrong. 28Pray[j] to the LORD, for we have had enough thunder and hail. I will let you go;[k] you don't have to stay any longer."

29Moses replied, "When I have gone out of the city, I will spread out my hands[l] in prayer to the LORD. The thunder will stop and there will be no more hail, so you may know that the earth[m] is the LORD's. 30But I know that you and your officials still do not fear the LORD God."

31(The flax and barley[n] were destroyed, since the barley had headed and the flax was in bloom. 32The wheat and spelt, however, were not destroyed, because they ripen later.)

33Then Moses left Pharaoh and went out of the city. He spread out his hands toward the LORD; the thunder and hail stopped, and the rain no longer poured down on the land. 34When Pharaoh saw that the rain and hail and thunder had stopped, he sinned again: He and his officials hardened their hearts. 35So Pharaoh's heart[o] was hard and he would not let the Israelites go, just as the LORD had said through Moses.

The Plague of Locusts

10 Then the LORD said to Moses, "Go to Pharaoh, for I have hardened his heart[p] and the hearts of his officials so that I may perform these signs[q] of mine among them 2that you may tell your children[r] and grandchildren how I dealt harsh-

9:12 [s]Ex 4:21
9:13 [t]Ex 8:20
9:14 [u]Ex 8:10 [v]2Sa 7:22; 1Ch 17:20; Ps 86:8; Isa 46:9; Jer 10:6
9:15 [w]Ex 3:20
9:16 [x]Pr 16:4 [y]Ro 9:17*
9:18 [z]ver 23 [a]ver 24
9:20 [b]Pr 13:13
9:23 [c]Ps 18:13 [d]Jos 10:11; Ps 78:47; 105:32; Isa 30:30; Eze 38:22; Rev 8:7; 16:21
9:25 [e]Ps 105:32-33
9:26 [f]ver 4 [g]Ex 8:22; 10:23; 11:7; 12:13
9:27 [h]Ex 10:16 [i]2Ch 12:6; Ps 129:4; La 1:18
9:28 [j]Ex 10:17 [k]Ex 8:8
9:29 [l]1Ki 8:22, 38; Ps 143:6; Isa 1:15 [m]Ex 19:5; Ps 24:1; 1Co 10:26
9:31 [n]Ru 1:22; 2:23
9:35 [o]Ex 4:21
10:1 [p]Ex 4:21 [q]Ex 7:3
10:2 [r]Ex 12:26-27; 13:8, 14; Dt 4:9; Ps 44:1; 78:4,5; Joel 1:3

[a] 16 Or *have spared you*

---

often translated as "leprosy." This is another of the divinely orchestrated calamities for the Egyptians.

9:23 *staff.* Moses' staff is the same as the staff of God. A variety of ancient Near Eastern texts make use of the idea that a deity can bestow his staff upon a favored individual; e.g., the king of Mari (in eastern Syria), Zimri-Lim (c. 1780–1758 BC), is said to receive the staff of the god Addu, which Addu used to slay the great enemy Sea. Sennacherib (c. 700 BC) says that the god Assur "placed in [his] hand the just scepter that extends the realm, the merciless staff for the destruction of enemies."

The Egyptian king also received a divine staff that symbolized his power and rule over the land. The staff here presents a direct challenge to Pharaoh's rule. One theme running throughout Exodus is that Yahweh, not Pharaoh, is the legitimate ruler, even within the borders of Egypt. Thus, the staff in Moses' hand is the genuine article; the one in Pharaoh's hand is fake and powerless.

9:31 *flax and barley.* According to 13:4, the Israelites left Egypt in the March-April time frame. This verse probably indicates a time in February for the plague of hail, since flax and barley in Egypt are typically harvested in late February or early March. This text reflects some knowledge of the Egyptian agricultural calendar. In Palestine, barley is not harvested until April. If the narrative had placed the plague at that time, there would not have been enough time left in the narrative to include both the subsequent plagues and the exodus from Egypt.

ly with the Egyptians and how I performed my signs among them, and that you may know that I am the LORD."

3So Moses and Aaron went to Pharaoh and said to him, "This is what the LORD, the God of the Hebrews, says: 'How long will you refuse to humble[s] yourself before me? Let my people go, so that they may worship me. 4If you refuse to let them go, I will bring locusts[t] into your country tomorrow. 5They will cover the face of the ground so that it cannot be seen. They will devour what little you have left[u] after the hail, including every tree that is growing in your fields. 6They will fill your houses and those of all your officials and all the Egyptians — something neither your parents nor your ancestors have ever seen from the day they settled in this land till now.'" Then Moses turned and left Pharaoh.

7Pharaoh's officials said to him, "How long will this man be a snare[v] to us? Let the people go, so that they may worship the LORD their God. Do you not yet realize that Egypt is ruined?"[w]

8Then Moses and Aaron were brought back to Pharaoh. "Go, worship[x] the LORD your God," he said. "But tell me who will be going."

9Moses answered, "We will go with our young and our old, with our sons and our daughters, and with our flocks and herds, because we are to celebrate a festival to the LORD."

10Pharaoh said, "The LORD be with you — if I let you go, along with your women and children! Clearly you are bent on evil.[a] 11No! Have only the men go and worship the LORD, since that's what you have been asking for." Then Moses and Aaron were driven out of Pharaoh's presence.

12And the LORD said to Moses, "Stretch out your hand[y] over Egypt so that locusts swarm over the land and devour everything growing in the fields, everything left by the hail."

13So Moses stretched out his staff over Egypt, and the LORD made an east wind blow across the land all that day and all that night. By morning the wind had brought the locusts;[z] 14they invaded all Egypt and settled down in every area of the country in great numbers. Never before had there been such a plague of locusts,[a] nor will there ever be again. 15They covered all the ground until it was black. They devoured[b] all that was left after the hail — everything growing in the fields and the fruit on the trees. Nothing green remained on tree or plant in all the land of Egypt.

16Pharaoh quickly summoned Moses and Aaron and said, "I have sinned[c] against the LORD your God and against you. 17Now forgive my sin once more and pray[d] to the LORD your God to take this deadly plague away from me."

18Moses then left Pharaoh and prayed to the LORD.[e] 19And the LORD changed the wind to a very strong west wind, which caught up the locusts and carried them into the Red Sea.[b] Not a locust was left anywhere in Egypt. 20But the LORD hardened Pharaoh's heart,[f] and he would not let the Israelites go.

The Plague of Darkness

21Then the LORD said to Moses, "Stretch out your hand toward the sky so that darkness[g] spreads over Egypt — darkness that can be felt." 22So Moses stretched out his hand toward the sky, and total darkness[h]

10:3 [s] 1Ki 21:29; Jas 4:10; 1Pe 5:6
10:4 [t] Rev 9:3
10:5 [u] Ex 9:32; Joel 1:4
10:7 [v] Ex 23:33; Jos 23:13; 1Sa 18:21; Ecc 7:26 [w] Ex 8:19
10:8 [x] Ex 8:8
10:12 [y] Ex 7:19
10:13 [z] Ps 105:34
10:14 [a] Ps 78:46; Joel 2:1-11,25
10:15 [b] ver 5; Ps 105:34-35
10:16 [c] Ex 9:27
10:17 [d] Ex 8:8
10:18 [e] Ex 8:30
10:20 [f] Ex 4:21; 11:10
10:21 [g] Dt 28:29
10:22 [h] Ps 105:28; Rev 16:10

[a] *10* Or *Be careful, trouble is in store for you!* [b] *19* Or *the Sea of Reeds*

10:4 *locusts.* The societies of the ancient Near East viewed invading locusts as a clear sign of divine outrage and punishment (cf. Am 4:9). A number of texts from Mesopotamia and Syria refer to locust swarms as a divine curse; e.g., in the vassal treaties of the Neo-Assyrian king Esarhaddon (c. 670 BC) comes this curse for those who violate their oath to the gods: "May Adad, the canal inspector of heaven and earth, put an end [to vegetation] in your land, may he avoid your meadows and hit your land with a severe destructive downpour, may locusts, which diminish the (produce) of the land, [devour] your crops." Ex 10 is again stressing how many of Yahweh's actions against the Egyptians come from what are perceived as the standard repertoire of the angry god, who wishes to inflict pain and agony on those who oppose him.

10:21 *darkness that can be felt.* This wording suggests the presence of something airborne such as the *khamsin* dust storms, which are well-known in the Middle East. Three days is typical for the duration of this kind of storm, most likely between March and May. Such storms would not usually bring total darkness, so this one is extreme.

10:22 *total darkness.* From the perspective of the Egyptians, the absence of sunlight had profound meaning. They believed that the regular circling of the sun-god in the sky meant his blessing on Egypt. Any interruption in that cycle spelled disaster. Thus, this text seems to be targeting the sun-god, probably the most venerated deity in Egypt.

Throughout Egyptian history, the sun was worshiped as a manifestation of various deities, such as Atum, Re, Amun and Amun-Re. Pharaoh was also associated with the sun. Despite this ambiguity, the narrative of Exodus is once again claiming utter powerlessness for the king and the gods of Egypt. Moreover, darkness frequently turns up in Biblical texts as a symbol of judgment (Isa 8:22; Joel 2:2; Zep 1:15). Here, the Egyptian life force has been extinguished. For them, at this juncture in the narrative, the favor (or, at least, efficacy) of their gods has vanished. The wrath of the Hebrew deity has reached its most intense stage yet. Creation has been undone. Chaos has returned.

covered all Egypt for three days. 23No one could see anyone else or move about for three days. Yet all the Israelites had light in the places where they lived.[i]

24Then Pharaoh summoned Moses and said, "Go, worship the LORD. Even your women and children[j] may go with you; only leave your flocks and herds behind."

25But Moses said, "You must allow us to have sacrifices and burnt offerings to present to the LORD our God. 26Our livestock too must go with us; not a hoof is to be left behind. We have to use some of them in worshiping the LORD our God, and until we get there we will not know what we are to use to worship the LORD."

27But the LORD hardened Pharaoh's heart,[k] and he was not willing to let them go. 28Pharaoh said to Moses, "Get out of my sight! Make sure you do not appear before me again! The day you see my face you will die."

29"Just as you say," Moses replied. "I will never appear[l] before you again."

The Plague on the Firstborn

11 Now the LORD had said to Moses, "I will bring one more plague on Pharaoh and on Egypt. After that, he will let you go from here, and when he does, he will drive you out completely. 2Tell the people that men and women alike are to ask their neighbors for articles of silver and gold."[m] 3(The LORD made the Egyptians favorably disposed toward the people, and Moses himself was highly regarded[n] in Egypt by Pharaoh's officials and by the people.)

4So Moses said, "This is what the LORD says: 'About midnight[o] I will go throughout Egypt. 5Every firstborn[p] son in Egypt will die, from the firstborn son of Pharaoh, who sits on the throne, to the firstborn son of the female slave, who is at her hand mill, and all the firstborn of the cattle as well. 6There will be loud wailing[q] throughout Egypt—worse than there has ever been or ever will be again. 7But among the Israelites not a dog will bark at any person or animal.' Then you will know that the LORD makes a distinction[r] between Egypt and Israel. 8All these officials of yours will come to me, bowing down before me and saying, 'Go,[s] you and all the people who follow you!' After that I will leave." Then Moses, hot with anger, left Pharaoh.

9The LORD had said to Moses, "Pharaoh will refuse to listen[t] to you—so that my wonders may be multiplied in Egypt." 10Moses and Aaron performed all these wonders before Pharaoh, but the LORD hardened Pharaoh's heart,[u] and he would not let the Israelites go out of his country.

The Passover and the Festival of Unleavened Bread

12:14-20pp — Lev 23:4-8; Nu 28:16-25; Dt 16:1-8

12 The LORD said to Moses and Aaron in Egypt, 2"This month is to be for you the first month,[v] the first month of your year. 3Tell the whole community of Israel that on the tenth day of this month each man is to take a lamb[a] for his family, one for each household. 4If any household is too small for a whole lamb, they must share one with their nearest neighbor, having taken into account the number of people there are. You are to determine the amount of lamb needed in accordance with what each person will eat. 5The animals you choose must be year-old males without defect,[w] and you may take them from the sheep or the goats. 6Take care of them until the fourteenth day of

10:23 [i]Ex 8:22 **10:24** [j]ver 8-10 **10:27** [k]ver 20; Ex 4:21 **10:29** [l]Heb 11:27 **11:2** [m]Ex 3:21, 22 **11:3** [n]Dt 34:11 **11:4** [o]Ex 12:29 **11:5** [p]Ex 4:23; Ps 78:51

11:6 [q]Ex 12:30 **11:7** [r]Ex 8:22 **11:8** [s]Ex 12:31-33 **11:9** [t]Ex 7:4 **11:10** [u]Ex 4:21; 10:20,27 **12:2** [v]Ex 13:4; Dt 16:1 **12:5** [w]Lev 22:18-21; Heb 9:14

[a] 3 The Hebrew word can mean *lamb* or *kid*; also in verse 4.

12:2 *first month of your year.* The commemoration of Rosh Hashanah, the Jewish New Year, takes place today in the fall. Biblical texts, however, are ambiguous regarding when the new year begins. This verse places it in the spring. Jer 36:22 speaks of the ninth month as being in the winter, indicating that the first month comes in the spring. 2Ki 25:8 concurs, stating that the destruction of Jerusalem by the Babylonians took place in the fifth month (the summer, probably late July), again placing the first month in the spring.

But there are also hints that the new year began in the fall. In 2Ki 22:3, e.g., King Josiah orders repairs on the temple "in the eighteenth year of his reign." Subsequent to this order, a number of events transpire. Then, 2Ki 23:23 states that Passover was celebrated "in the eighteenth year of King Josiah." According to Ex 12:1,3 Passover was to begin on the tenth day of the first month. The only way for Josiah's order and this Passover celebration both to occur in his eighteenth year—if the first day of the year was in the spring and Passover was celebrated on the tenth day of the year—is for all of the intervening events to have occurred within ten days, the first ten days of Josiah's eighteenth year. This seems unlikely. Thus, this narrative may be assuming that the new year came in the fall.

Exodus itself has two verses that seem to assume a change of years in the fall (23:16; 34:22). In addition, there is the so-called Gezer Calendar—a small, inscribed limestone tablet discovered at Gezer and probably dating to the late tenth century BC. The inscription is a brief explanation (a bit like a riddle, since the months are not named) of the months of the year as they relate to agricultural production. Its year begins in the fall.

Even in later Judaism, there is disagreement about the calendar. One way to solve the problem is to assume more than one "New Year's Day." Perhaps there was a new year's celebration based on the agricultural calendar and one tied to a religious calendar. Some indication of this dual-calendar system comes through in later rabbinic literature.

EXODUS 12

PASSOVER

Any reading of the accounts of the major festivals in the OT suggests that at least some of them incorporated elements of harvest festivals that were later historicized—i.e., given an association with some historical event and thereafter tied to that event though often retaining some of the original harvest associations. It would therefore not be unusual if some roots to the Passover antedated the events recorded in Exodus. If so, the "institution" of Passover refers to its institution in association with a historical event.

Certain elements in the Passover suggest that at its roots may be a nomadic herdsmen's ritual in which they sought both protection from demonic attack as they moved to summer pasture and fertility for the herds in the new breeding season. Note how the observance is centered in the family (therefore not necessitating proximity to a sanctuary) and requires no altar (no animal is offered to deity) or priestly personnel. The blood on the doorpost purifies one's house and thus prepares it for Yahweh's presence and protection from the slaughtering angel. In this regard, it is evident that the verb *psh* has its meaning of "protect" (as seen clearly in Isa 31:5) rather than "pass over." Blood is used, for instance, in Mesopotamian *namburbi* rituals, in which it is smeared on the door and keyhole to protect a house from spirit invasion.

The existence of such roots is plausible enough, though the details of its practice and function can only be speculated since no specific predecessors are known. Blood as an apotropaic device and ritual animal substitution are both known, but a spring nomadic ritual for protection and fertility of the herd is unattested in the ancient Near East. ◆

the month,[x] when all the members of the
community of Israel must slaughter them
at twilight.[y] 7Then they are to take some of
the blood and put it on the sides and tops
of the doorframes of the houses where
they eat the lambs. 8That same night[z] they
are to eat the meat roasted[a] over the fire,
along with bitter herbs,[b] and bread made
without yeast.[c] 9Do not eat the meat raw
or boiled in water, but roast it over a fire—
with the head, legs and internal organs.
10Do not leave any of it till morning;[d] if
some is left till morning, you must burn it.
11This is how you are to eat it: with your
cloak tucked into your belt, your sandals
on your feet and your staff in your hand.
Eat it in haste;[e] it is the LORD's Passover.[f]
12"On that same night I will pass
through[g] Egypt and strike down every
firstborn of both people and animals, and
I will bring judgment on all the gods[h] of
Egypt. I am the LORD.[i] 13The blood will be
a sign for you on the houses where you
are, and when I see the blood, I will pass
over you. No destructive plague will touch
you when I strike Egypt.

12:6 [x] Lev 23:5; Nu 9:1-3,5, 11 [y] Ex 16:12; Dt 16:4,6
12:8 [z] Ex 34:25; Nu 9:12 [a] Dt 16:7 [b] Nu 9:11 [c] Dt 16:3-4; 1Co 5:8
12:10 [d] Ex 23:18; 34:25
12:11 [e] Dt 16:3 [f] ver 13,21,27, 43; Dt 16:1
12:12 [g] Ex 11:4; Am 5:17 [h] Nu 33:4 [i] Ex 6:2
12:14 [j] Ex 13:9 [k] ver 17,24; Ex 13:5,10; 2Ki 23:21
12:15 [l] Ex 13:6-7; 23:15; 34:18; Lev 23:6; Dt 16:3 [m] Ge 17:14; Nu 9:13
12:17 [n] ver 41; Ex 13:3
12:18 [o] ver 2; Lev 23:5-8; Nu 28:16-25

14"This is a day you are to commemorate;[j] for the generations to come you shall
celebrate it as a festival to the LORD—a
lasting ordinance.[k] 15For seven days you
are to eat bread made without yeast.[l] On
the first day remove the yeast from your
houses, for whoever eats anything with
yeast in it from the first day through the
seventh must be cut off[m] from Israel. 16On
the first day hold a sacred assembly, and
another one on the seventh day. Do no
work at all on these days, except to prepare food for everyone to eat; that is all
you may do.
17"Celebrate the Festival of Unleavened
Bread, because it was on this very day that
I brought your divisions out of Egypt.[n]
Celebrate this day as a lasting ordinance
for the generations to come. 18In the first
month[o] you are to eat bread made without
yeast, from the evening of the fourteenth
day until the evening of the twenty-first
day. 19For seven days no yeast is to be
found in your houses. And anyone, whether foreigner or native-born, who eats anything with yeast in it must be cut off from

the community of Israel. 20 Eat nothing
made with yeast. Wherever you live, you
must eat unleavened bread."
21 Then Moses summoned all the elders
of Israel and said to them, "Go at once
and select the animals for your families
and slaughter the Passover[p] lamb. 22 Take
a bunch of hyssop, dip it into the blood
in the basin and put some of the blood[q]
on the top and on both sides of the doorframe. None of you shall go out of the
door of your house until morning. 23 When
the LORD goes through the land to strike
down the Egyptians, he will see the blood[r]
on the top and sides of the doorframe and
will pass over[s] that doorway, and he will
not permit the destroyer[t] to enter your
houses and strike you down.
24 "Obey these instructions as a lasting
ordinance for you and your descendants.
25 When you enter the land that the LORD
will give you as he promised, observe this
ceremony. 26 And when your children[u] ask
you, 'What does this ceremony mean to
you?' 27 then tell them, 'It is the Passover[v]
sacrifice to the LORD, who passed over the
houses of the Israelites in Egypt and spared
our homes when he struck down the Egyptians.'" Then the people bowed down and
worshiped.[w] 28 The Israelites did just what
the LORD commanded Moses and Aaron.
29 At midnight[x] the LORD struck down all

12:21 [p] ver 11; Mk 14:12-16 **12:22** [q] ver 7; Heb 11:28 **12:23** [r] Rev 7:3 [s] ver 13
[t] 1Co 10:10; Heb 11:28 **12:26** [u] Ex 10:2; 13:8, 14-15; Jos 4:6 **12:27** [v] ver 11 [w] Ex 4:31 **12:29** [x] Ex 11:4

12:23 *destroyer.* In Mesopotamia the demon Lamashtu was responsible for the death of children, while Namtar was responsible for plague. Egyptians likewise believed in demons that threatened life and health. The destroyer here is not operating independently of deity, but as an instrument of God's judgment. That is often also the case in Mesopotamia. Demons themselves were often viewed as having no independent will, so they could be randomly destructive.

HEBREW CALENDAR AND SELECTED EVENTS

NUMBER OF MONTH		HEBREW NAME	MODERN EQUIVALENT	BIBLICAL REFERENCES	AGRICULTURE	FESTIVALS**
1 Sacred sequence begins	7	**Aviv; Nisan**	March–April	Ex 12:2; 13:4; 23:15; 34:18; Dt 16:1; Ne 2:1; Est 3:7	Spring (latter) rains; barley and flax harvest begins	Passover; Unleavened Bread; Firstfruits
2	8	**Ziv (Iyyar)***	April–May	1Ki 6:1,37	Barley harvest; dry season begins	
3	9	**Sivan**	May–June	Est 8:9	Wheat harvest	Pentecost (Weeks)
4	10	**(Tammuz)***	June–July		Tending vines	
5	11	**(Av)***	July–August		Ripening of grapes, figs and olives	
6	12	**Elul**	August–September	Ne 6:15	Processing grapes, figs and olives	
7	1 Civil sequence	**Ethanim (Tishri)***	September–October	1Ki 8:2	Autumn (early) rains begin; plowing	Trumpets; Day of Atonement; Tabernacles (Booths)
8	2	**Bul (Marcheshvan)***	October–November	1Ki 6:38	Sowing of wheat and barley	
9	3	**Kislev**	November–December	Ne 1:1; Zec 7:1	Winter rains begin (snow in some areas)	Hanukkah ("Dedication")
10	4	**Tebeth**	December–January	Est 2:16		
11	5	**Shebat**	January–February	Zec 1:7		
12	6	**Adar**	February–March	Ezr 6:15; Est 3:7,13; 8:12; 9:1,15,17,19,21	Almond trees bloom; citrus fruit harvest	Purim
		(Adar Sheni)*— Second Adar	This intercalary month was added about every three years so the lunar calendar would correspond to the solar year.			

*Names of months in parentheses are not in the Bible. **For more information on the festivals, see chart, p. 222 and the article "Festivals," p. 220.

the firstborn[y] in Egypt, from the firstborn of
Pharaoh, who sat on the throne, to the firstborn of the prisoner, who was in the dungeon, and the firstborn of all the livestock[z]
as well. 30 Pharaoh and all his officials and all
the Egyptians got up during the night, and
there was loud wailing[a] in Egypt, for there
was not a house without someone dead.

The Exodus

31 During the night Pharaoh summoned
Moses and Aaron and said, "Up! Leave my
people, you and the Israelites! Go, worship[b] the LORD as you have requested.
32 Take your flocks and herds,[c] as you have
said, and go. And also bless me."
33 The Egyptians urged the people to
hurry and leave[d] the country. "For otherwise," they said, "we will all die!" 34 So
the people took their dough before the
yeast was added, and carried it on their
shoulders in kneading troughs wrapped
in clothing. 35 The Israelites did as Moses
instructed and asked the Egyptians for articles of silver and gold[e] and for clothing.
36 The LORD had made the Egyptians favorably disposed toward the people, and they
gave them what they asked for; so they
plundered[f] the Egyptians.
37 The Israelites journeyed from Rameses
to Sukkoth.[g] There were about six hundred
thousand men[h] on foot, besides women and
children. 38 Many other people[i] went up with
them, and also large droves of livestock,
both flocks and herds. 39 With the dough
the Israelites had brought from Egypt, they
baked loaves of unleavened bread. The
dough was without yeast because they had
been driven out[j] of Egypt and did not have
time to prepare food for themselves.
40 Now the length of time the Israelite
people lived in Egypt[a] was 430 years.[k]
41 At the end of the 430 years, to the very
day, all the LORD's divisions[l] left Egypt.[m]
42 Because the LORD kept vigil that night to
bring them out of Egypt, on this night all
the Israelites are to keep vigil to honor the
LORD for the generations to come.[n]

Passover Restrictions

43 The LORD said to Moses and Aaron,
"These are the regulations for the Passover meal:[o]
"No foreigner[p] may eat it. 44 Any slave
you have bought may eat it after you have
circumcised[q] him, 45 but a temporary resident or a hired worker[r] may not eat it.
46 "It must be eaten inside the house; take
none of the meat outside the house. Do not
break any of the bones.[s] 47 The whole community of Israel must celebrate it.
48 "A foreigner residing among you who
wants to celebrate the LORD's Passover
must have all the males in his household
circumcised; then he may take part like
one born in the land.[t] No uncircumcised
male may eat it. 49 The same law applies
both to the native-born and to the foreigner[u] residing among you."
50 All the Israelites did just what the LORD
had commanded Moses and Aaron. 51 And
on that very day the LORD brought the Israelites out of Egypt by their divisions.[v]

Consecration of the Firstborn

13 The LORD said to Moses, 2 "Consecrate to me every firstborn male.[w]
The first offspring of every womb among
the Israelites belongs to me, whether human or animal."
3 Then Moses said to the people, "Commemorate this day, the day you came out
of Egypt, out of the land of slavery, because the LORD brought you out of it with
a mighty hand.[x] Eat nothing containing
yeast.[y] 4 Today, in the month of Aviv,[z] you
are leaving. 5 When the LORD brings you
into the land of the Canaanites, Hittites,
Amorites, Hivites and Jebusites[a] — the
land he swore to your ancestors to give
you, a land flowing with milk and honey — you are to observe this ceremony[b]
in this month: 6 For seven days eat bread
made without yeast and on the seventh
day hold a festival[c] to the LORD. 7 Eat unleavened bread during those seven days;
nothing with yeast in it is to be seen
among you, nor shall any yeast be seen
anywhere within your borders. 8 On that
day tell your son,[d] 'I do this because of
what the LORD did for me when I came out
of Egypt.' 9 This observance will be for you
like a sign on your hand and a reminder
on your forehead[e] that this law of the LORD
is to be on your lips. For the LORD brought
you out of Egypt with his mighty hand.
10 You must keep this ordinance[f] at the appointed time year after year.

[a] 40 Masoretic Text; Samaritan Pentateuch and Septuagint *Egypt and Canaan*

12:29 [y] Ex 4:23; Ps 78:51 [z] Ex 9:6
12:30 [a] Ex 11:6
12:31 [b] Ex 8:8
12:32 [c] Ex 10:9, 26
12:33 [d] Ps 105:38
12:35 [e] Ex 3:22
12:36 [f] Ex 3:22
12:37 [g] Nu 33:3-5 [h] Ex 38:26; Nu 1:46; 11:13, 21
12:38 [i] Nu 11:4
12:39 [j] ver 31-33; Ex 6:1; 11:1
12:40 [k] Ge 15:13; Ac 7:6; Gal 3:17
12:41 [l] ver 17; Ex 6:26 [m] Ex 3:10
12:42 [n] Ex 13:10; Dt 16:1,6
12:43 [o] ver 11 [p] ver 48; Nu 9:14
12:44 [q] Ge 17:12-13
12:45 [r] Lev 22:10
12:46 [s] Nu 9:12; Jn 19:36*
12:48 [t] Nu 9:14
12:49 [u] Nu 15:15-16, 29; Gal 3:28
12:51 [v] ver 41; Ex 6:26
13:2 [w] ver 12, 13, 15; Ex 22:29; Nu 3:13; Dt 15:19; Lk 2:23*
13:3 [x] Ex 3:20; 6:1 [y] Ex 12:19
13:4 [z] Ex 12:2
13:5 [a] Ex 3:8 [b] Ex 12:25-26
13:6 [c] Ex 12:15-20
13:8 [d] ver 14; Ex 10:2; Ps 78:5-6
13:9 [e] ver 16; Dt 6:8; 11:18
13:10 [f] Ex 12:24-25

12:36 *plundered the Egyptians.* The silver and gold items taken were some of the most valuable of the Egyptians' possessions. Moreover, these events took place in the spring, when it was customary for Egyptian kings, particularly those of the New Kingdom, to send out messengers (and accompanying armies) in order to collect tribute payments from the smaller political entities (e.g., city-states) outside Egypt. In a sense, then, springtime was the time the Egyptians officially plundered their subject peoples. Once again, the Biblical text turns the tables on an Egyptian custom. This time, the Egyptians are the ones exploited and forced to pay.

12:37 *six hundred thousand men.* See the article "Numbers in Numbers," p. 235.

[11]"After the LORD brings you into the
land of the Canaanites and gives it to you,
as he promised on oath to you and your
ancestors, [12]you are to give over to the
LORD the first offspring of every womb. All
the firstborn males of your livestock belong to the LORD.[g] [13]Redeem with a lamb
every firstborn donkey, but if you do not
redeem it, break its neck.[h] Redeem every
firstborn among your sons.[i]
[14]"In days to come, when your son[j] asks
you, 'What does this mean?' say to him,
'With a mighty hand the LORD brought us
out of Egypt, out of the land of slavery.[k]
[15]When Pharaoh stubbornly refused to let
us go, the LORD killed the firstborn of both

13:12 [g]Lev 27:26; Lk 2:23* **13:13** [h]Ex 34:20 [i]Nu 18:15 **13:14** [j]Ex 10:2; 12:26-27; Dt 6:20 [k]ver 3,9

13:15 *redeem each of my firstborn sons.* Redemption in the ancient Near East usually involved a specific purpose. Often a man who had taken on debt and could not pay it off was forced to sell himself or one of his family members to the creditor as a debt-slave. No actual "sale" took place, but the person was transferred into the possession of the creditor. The "sale price" was understood to be a loan, which the debtor had already received and was now unable to repay. Redemption occurred when the debtor or one of his family members eventually acquired the means to pay off the debt and thereby retrieve the debt-slave from the creditor. To redeem a person was, in a sense, the act of buying the person back from the creditor, often at the same price (the amount of the loan) at which the person was "sold."

Perhaps the Israelites believed they owed a debt to Yahweh for their deliverance from Egypt. The means of this deliverance is explicit: "the LORD killed the firstborn of both people and animals in Egypt." The Israelites were

EXODUS 13:18

THE RED SEA

The Hebrew phrase translated "Red Sea" is *yam sup*; it is not clear to which body of water this phrase refers. The term *sup* in Hebrew means "reed(s)"; it is among the *sup* that Moses' mother placed the waterproof basket that served as his hiding place shortly after his birth (Ex 2:3). Perhaps, then, the *yam sup* is not the Red Sea but a body of water known as the "Sea of Reeds." However, the Septuagint, the pre-Christian Greek translation of the OT, translates *yam sup* with a Greek phrase that means "Red Sea." This term refers, depending on context, to three potential areas: the Gulf of Aqaba (Nu 21:4), the Gulf of Suez (Nu 33:10–11), or the place where Israel crossed or encountered the "*yam sup*." Most scholars today believe the Hebrew text intends a body of water around which reeds grew in abundance—perhaps one of the lakes found north of the Gulf of Suez. Others still opt for the Red Sea, the large body of water south of the Sinai peninsula that runs between Egypt and Arabia.

Among those who reject the Red Sea, at least four main possibilities stand out. The first is Lake Menzaleh, located in the northeast corner of the Nile delta along the Mediterranean coast. About 30 miles (48 kilometers) to the south were the Balah Lakes, most of which were drained during the construction of the Suez Canal. A smaller lake south of the Balah Lakes is Lake Timsah. Finally, the Bitter Lakes are located even farther south. All of these bodies of water were situated along ancient Egypt's eastern border, where it meets the Sinai peninsula, between the Mediterranean Sea in the north and the Gulf of Suez in the south.

A strong case can be made in favor of the Balah Lakes. First, Ex 14:2 indicates that the Israelites made a turn to the north (they were to "turn back") after having traveled in a southeasterly direction. This would have taken them away from Lake Timsah and the Bitter Lakes, since they were still north of both, and toward the Balah Lakes. Second, Egyptian literary sources seem to indicate that the *yam sup* lay in fairly close proximity to the site of Tjaru; of the four major possibilities, Tjaru is closest to the Balah Lakes. Third, Abu Sefeh, the modern Arabic name for a site probably located on the edge of the Balah Lakes in ancient times, may be related linguistically to the

continued on next page

people and animals in Egypt. This is why
I sacrifice to the LORD the first male offspring of every womb and redeem each of
my firstborn sons.'[l] [16]And it will be like a
sign on your hand and a symbol on your
forehead[m] that the LORD brought us out of
Egypt with his mighty hand."

Crossing the Sea

[17]When Pharaoh let the people go, God
did not lead them on the road through the
Philistine country, though that was shorter. For God said, "If they face war, they
might change their minds and return to
Egypt."[n] [18]So God led[o] the people around
by the desert road toward the Red Sea.[a]
The Israelites went up out of Egypt ready
for battle.[p]
[19]Moses took the bones of Joseph[q] with
him because Joseph had made the Israelites

13:15 [l] Ex 12:29 **13:16** [m] ver 9 **13:17** [n] Ex 14:11; Nu 14:1-4; Dt 17:16 **13:18** [o] Ps 136:16 [p] Jos 1:14 **13:19** [q] Jos 24:32; Ac 7:16

[a] *18* Or *the Sea of Reeds*

given, in a sense, all the firstborn of Egypt as the purchase price of their freedom, and they now owed to Yahweh their own firstborn, both "people and animals." The animals they could pay directly through sacrifice. Their sons too belonged to Yahweh by right, but the Israelites were offered a way to buy back their sons from Yahweh. By sacrificing a lamb, an Israelite family could "redeem" their firstborn son.

13:17 *road through the Philistine country.* For quite some time, scholars have considered this road probably to refer to a road that in ancient Egypt was known as the "Ways of Horus" and later as the *Via Maris* ("Way of the Sea"). This

Egyptian term from which Hebrew *yam sup* comes. Ultimately, the evidence is inconclusive, but it is unlikely to be the Red Sea because the Israelites were not that far south and they would have no reason to travel along the western shore of the Red Sea if they were trying to get to Sinai. ◆

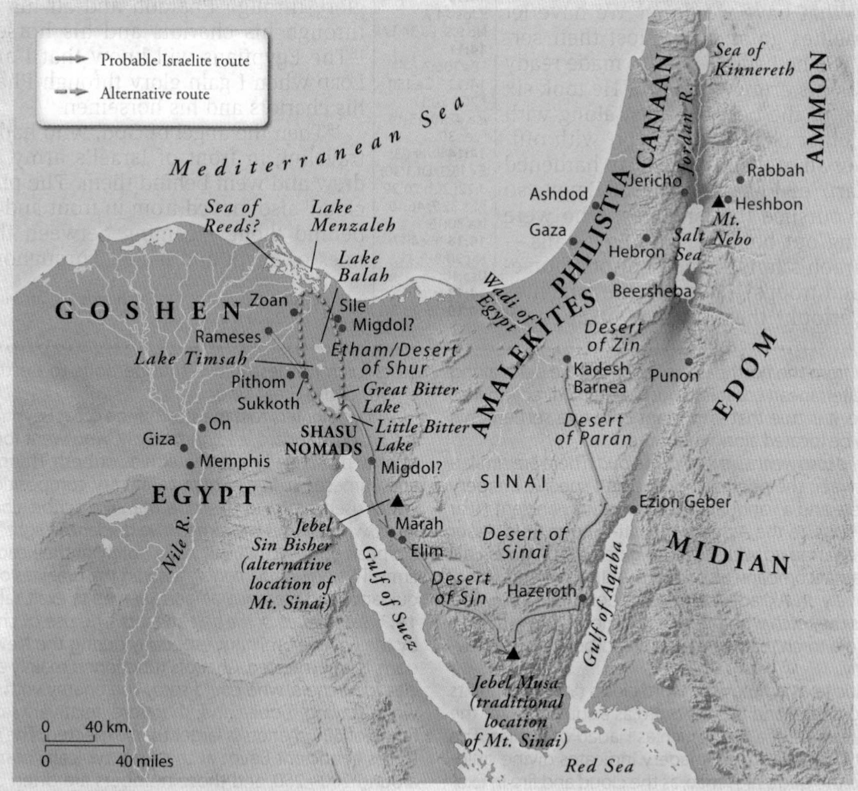

Possible locations of the Red Sea.

swear an oath. He had said, “God will surely come to your aid, and then you must carry my bones up with you from this place.”[a][r]
20 After leaving Sukkoth they camped at
Etham on the edge of the desert.[s] 21 By day
the LORD went ahead of them in a pillar of
cloud[t] to guide them on their way and by
night in a pillar of fire to give them light,
so that they could travel by day or night.
22 Neither the pillar of cloud by day nor the
pillar of fire by night left its place in front
of the people.

14 Then the LORD said to Moses, 2 “Tell
the Israelites to turn back and encamp near Pi Hahiroth, between Migdol[u]
and the sea. They are to encamp by the
sea, directly opposite Baal Zephon. 3 Pharaoh will think, ‘The Israelites are wandering around the land in confusion, hemmed
in by the desert.’ 4 And I will harden Pharaoh’s heart,[v] and he will pursue them. But
I will gain glory[w] for myself through Pharaoh and all his army, and the Egyptians
will know that I am the LORD.”[x] So the Israelites did this.
5 When the king of Egypt was told that
the people had fled, Pharaoh and his officials changed their minds about them and
said, “What have we done? We have let
the Israelites go and have lost their services!” 6 So he had his chariot made ready
and took his army with him. 7 He took six
hundred of the best chariots, along with
all the other chariots of Egypt, with officers over all of them. 8 The LORD hardened
the heart[y] of Pharaoh king of Egypt, so
that he pursued the Israelites, who were
marching out boldly.[z] 9 The Egyptians—
all Pharaoh’s horses and chariots, horsemen[b] and troops—pursued the Israelites
and overtook[a] them as they camped by
the sea near Pi Hahiroth, opposite Baal
Zephon.
10 As Pharaoh approached, the Israelites
looked up, and there were the Egyptians,
marching after them. They were terrified
and cried[b] out to the LORD. 11 They said
to Moses, “Was it because there were no
graves in Egypt that you brought us to the
desert to die?[c] What have you done to us
by bringing us out of Egypt? 12 Didn’t we
say to you in Egypt, ‘Leave us alone; let us
serve the Egyptians’? It would have been
better for us to serve the Egyptians than to
die in the desert!”
13 Moses answered the people, “Do not
be afraid.[d] Stand firm and you will see[e]
the deliverance the LORD will bring you today. The Egyptians you see today you will
never see[f] again. 14 The LORD will fight[g] for
you; you need only to be still.”[h]
15 Then the LORD said to Moses, “Why
are you crying out to me? Tell the Israelites to move on. 16 Raise your staff[i] and
stretch out your hand over the sea to divide the water[j] so that the Israelites can
go through the sea on dry ground. 17 I will
harden the hearts of the Egyptians so that
they will go in after them.[k] And I will gain
glory through Pharaoh and all his army,
through his chariots and his horsemen.
18 The Egyptians will know that I am the
LORD when I gain glory through Pharaoh,
his chariots and his horsemen.”
19 Then the angel of God, who had been
traveling in front of Israel’s army, withdrew and went behind them. The pillar of
cloud[l] also moved from in front and stood
behind them, 20 coming between the armies of Egypt and Israel. Throughout the

13:19 [r] Ge 50:24-25 **13:20** [s] Nu 33:6 **13:21** [t] Ex 14:19, 24; 33:9-10; Nu 9:16; Dt 1:33; Ne 9:12, 19; Ps 78:14; 99:7; 105:39; Isa 4:5; 1Co 10:1 **14:2** [u] Nu 33:7; Jer 44:1 **14:4** [v] Ex 4:21 [w] Ro 9:17, 22-23 [x] Ex 7:5 **14:8** [y] ver 4; Ex 11:10 [z] Nu 33:3; Ac 13:17 **14:9** [a] Ex 15:9 **14:10** [b] Jos 24:7; Ne 9:9; Ps 34:17 **14:11** [c] Ps 106:7-8 **14:13** [d] Ge 15:1 [e] 2Ch 20:17; Isa 41:10, 13-14 [f] ver 30 **14:14** [g] ver 25; Ex 15:3; Dt 1:30; 3:22; 2Ch 20:29 [h] Ps 37:7; 46:10; Isa 30:15 **14:16** [i] Ex 4:17; Nu 20:8-9, 11 [j] Isa 10:26 **14:17** [k] ver 4 **14:19** [l] Ex 13:21

a 19 See Gen. 50:25. *b* 9 Or *charioteers*; also in verses 17, 18, 23, 26 and 28

road ran from the northeastern region of the delta along the Mediterranean coast in a northeasterly direction into Palestine. It is true that important Philistine settlements came to be located along this route.

13:21 *the LORD went ... in a pillar of cloud.* There are similarities between the poetic language and specific imagery given here and a vanguard motif in various ancient Near Eastern texts. In the Assyrian Tukulti-Ninurta Epic, Assur leads the vanguard with devouring flame. The gods Enlil and Adad accompany also with burning fire and flood, respectively. In Akkadian texts Erra designates the god Ishum as the torch who precedes and leads the others as a fire and a torch that went ahead and behind the heavenly army.

Ugaritic texts employ the word cloud (*'nn*) in contexts featuring deities and use the word as a substitute for the name/presence of a deity, such as Hadad or Athirat. The cloud at Ugarit as storm imagery indicates divine guidance and the god's presence, as the cloud and fire in Exodus designate the Lord. Ugaritic texts depict messengers of fire of the god Yamm, who appear like two flames of fire. A light accompanies Baal. The god Shapshu serves as the luminary of the gods. The storm-god of the Hittites casts forth his destructive thunderbolts to destroy the enemy of the Great King.

Ancient writers told the story of the great Egyptian god Amon, his standard leading the way, who went forth in a mighty presence before the armies of both Thutmose III and Rameses III. In an Egyptian literary composition, the writer used simile to describe the wise scribe, choice of heart, who uses his wisdom to give guidance ("light") to the Egyptian troops (c. 1280 BC) as a "torch" at the head of the army. This powerful imagery assured the Israelites of God's guidance and presence, as it also served to exalt Yahweh.

14:7 *six hundred of the best chariots.* The use of chariotry by the Egyptian military, especially during the New Kingdom, is well attested. Chariots functioned mainly as vehicles for archers, who could spray the enemy with arrows while staying mobile and, therefore, relatively safe. The figure of 600 chariots is larger than expected. The chariot forces in ancient Egypt at this time typically numbered around 200–250, and those numbers are often considered inflated. Nevertheless, the Egyptian account of their battle against the Hittites at Qadesh lists the Hittite chariot force at 2,500 though that is perhaps an exaggeration to magnify their victory.

night the cloud brought darkness to the
one side and light to the other side; so neither went near the other all night long.
21Then Moses stretched out his hand
over the sea, and all that night the LORD
drove the sea back with a strong east
wind[m] and turned it into dry land. The
waters were divided,[n] 22and the Israelites
went through the sea on dry ground,[o] with
a wall of water on their right and on their
left.
23The Egyptians pursued them, and all
Pharaoh's horses and chariots and horsemen followed them into the sea. 24During
the last watch of the night the LORD looked
down from the pillar of fire and cloud[p] at
the Egyptian army and threw it into confusion. 25He jammed[a] the wheels of their
chariots so that they had difficulty driving.
And the Egyptians said, "Let's get away
from the Israelites! The LORD is fighting[q]
for them against Egypt."
26Then the LORD said to Moses, "Stretch
out your hand over the sea so that the
waters may flow back over the Egyptians
and their chariots and horsemen." 27Mo-
ses stretched out his hand over the sea,
and at daybreak the sea went back to its
place.[r] The Egyptians were fleeing toward[b]
it, and the LORD swept them into the sea.[s]
28The water flowed back and covered the
chariots and horsemen — the entire army
of Pharaoh that had followed the Israelites
into the sea. Not one of them survived.
29But the Israelites went through the sea
on dry ground,[t] with a wall of water on
their right and on their left. 30That day the
LORD saved[u] Israel from the hands of the
Egyptians, and Israel saw the Egyptians
lying dead on the shore. 31And when the
Israelites saw the mighty hand of the LORD
displayed against the Egyptians, the people feared the LORD and put their trust[v] in
him and in Moses his servant.

The Song of Moses and Miriam

15 Then Moses and the Israelites sang
this song[w] to the LORD:

"I will sing[x] to the LORD,
  for he is highly exalted.
Both horse and driver
  he has hurled into the sea.

2"The LORD is my strength[y] and my
  defense[c];
  he has become my salvation.[z]
He is my God,[a] and I will praise him,
  my father's God, and I will exalt[b]
    him.
3The LORD is a warrior;[c]
  the LORD is his name.[d]
4Pharaoh's chariots and his army[e]
  he has hurled into the sea.
The best of Pharaoh's officers
  are drowned in the Red Sea.[d]
5The deep waters have covered them;
  they sank to the depths like a stone.[f]
6Your right hand,[g] LORD,
  was majestic in power.
Your right hand, LORD,
  shattered the enemy.

14:21 [m]Ex 15:8 [n]Ps 74:13; 114:5; Isa 63:12 **14:22** [o]Ex 15:19; Ne 9:11; Ps 66:6; Heb 11:29 **14:24** [p]Ex 13:21 **14:25** [q]ver 14 **14:27** [r]Jos 4:18 [s]Ex 15:1,21; Ps 78:53; 106:11 **14:29** [t]ver 22 **14:30** [u]Ps 106:8, 10,21 **14:31** [v]Ps 106:12; Jn 2:11 **15:1** [w]Rev 15:3 [x]Ps 106:12 **15:2** [y]Ps 59:17 [z]Ps 18:2, 46; Isa 12:2; Hab 3:18 [a]Ge 28:21 [b]Ex 3:6, 15-16; Isa 25:1 **15:3** [c]Ex 14:14; Ps 24:8; Rev 19:11 [d]Ex 6:2-3, 7-8; Ps 83:18 **15:4** [e]Ex 14:6-7 **15:5** [f]ver 10; Ne 9:11 **15:6** [g]Ps 118:15

[a] *25* See Samaritan Pentateuch, Septuagint and Syriac; Masoretic Text *removed* [b] *27* Or *from* [c] *2* Or *song* [d] *4* Or *the Sea of Reeds*; also in verse 22

14:20 *cloud brought darkness.* The motif of the warrior deity who aids his people at crucial moments in battle against their enemies occurs frequently in ancient Near Eastern literature. Here, Yahweh sends a cloud so dense that it functions as an impenetrable — by sight or movement — barrier between the Egyptians and the Israelites. Records of the military exploits of the Hittite king Mursili report a similar phenomenon:

- Storm god came to his aid
- Rained all night
- Enemy could not see camp
- Storm god sent cloud
- Cloud went before troops
- Thus provided deliverance and guidance

It was not uncommon in military reports to speak of advantageous circumstances in terms of divine intervention and aid. If one group found itself on the successful end of a skirmish, it credited its own god or gods and often spoke of the deity as if he had arranged all aspects of the natural order in order to ensure a triumphant outcome.

15:1 *the Israelites sang.* The text does not reveal who composed the song, but the distinct possibility exists that it was authored by one or more of the women. Ancient Israelite culture seems to have developed a significant musical tradition. Rhythm (as opposed to melody) was probably the music's dominant feature, and women may have had a crucial role in creating and performing this type of music. Women are the only ones explicitly mentioned in Biblical texts as using the "timbrel" (cf. v. 20). Moreover, clay figurines from Iron Age Israel that depict musicians show all percussionists to be women.

It also stands to reason that victory songs, like the one here, would come from women, since they are the ones who most likely sang songs as the men returned home from battle.

15:6 *shattered the enemy.* Significantly, the drowning of the Egyptian army is celebrated in terms of smashing and shattering. This statement is reminiscent of how a particular set of Egyptian inscriptions, known as Execration Texts, was used. These inscriptions were incised on stone, wood and clay objects, which were often shaped to represent a foreign ruler. Many have been found on pottery bowls as well. The objects and their accompanying inscriptions apparently played an important role in Egyptian curse rituals. Though it is not clear that all such rituals involved the use of objects like these, there is evidence that formal cursing of enemies was practiced in Egypt throughout much of the second and third millennia BC. Most of the objects bearing inscriptions, however, seem to date to a more narrow period of time — generally the first half of the second millennium BC.

The inscriptions themselves contain the names of various local rulers in Syria and Palestine and often conclude

[7]"In the greatness of your majesty
you threw down those who opposed
you.
You unleashed your burning anger;[h]
it consumed them like stubble.
[8]By the blast of your nostrils[i]
the waters piled up.[j]
The surging waters stood up like a
wall;[k]
the deep waters congealed in the
heart of the sea.
[9]The enemy boasted,
'I will pursue,[l] I will overtake
them.
I will divide the spoils;[m]
I will gorge myself on them.
I will draw my sword
and my hand will destroy them.'
[10]But you blew with your breath,
and the sea covered them.
They sank like lead
in the mighty waters.[n]
[11]Who among the gods
is like you,[o] LORD?
Who is like you —
majestic in holiness,[p]
awesome in glory,[q]
working wonders?
[12]"You stretch out your right hand,
and the earth swallows your
enemies.
[13]In your unfailing love you will lead[r]
the people you have redeemed.
In your strength you will guide
them
to your holy dwelling.[s]

15:7 [h]Ps 78:49-50 **15:8** [i]Ex 14:21 [j]Ps 78:13 [k]Ex 14:22 **15:9** [l]Ex 14:5-9 [m]Jdg 5:30; Isa 53:12 **15:10** [n]ver 5; Ex 14:27-28 **15:11** [o]Ex 8:10; Dt 3:24; Ps 77:13 [p]Isa 6:3; Rev 4:8 [q]Ps 8:1 **15:13** [r]Ne 9:12; Ps 77:20 [s]Ps 78:54

15:14 [t]Dt 2:25 **15:15** [u]Ge 36:15 [v]Nu 22:3 [w]Jos 5:1 **15:16** [x]Ex 23:27; Jos 2:9 [y]1Sa 25:37 [z]Ps 74:2 **15:17** [a]Ps 44:2 [b]Ps 78:54,68 **15:19** [c]Ex 14:28 [d]Ex 14:22 **15:20** [e]Nu 26:59 [f]Jdg 4:4 [g]Jdg 11:34; 1Sa 18:6; Ps 30:11; 150:4

[14]The nations will hear and tremble;[t]
anguish will grip the people of
Philistia.
[15]The chiefs[u] of Edom will be terrified,
the leaders of Moab will be seized
with trembling,[v]
the people[a] of Canaan will melt[w] away;
[16]terror[x] and dread will fall on them.
By the power of your arm
they will be as still as a stone[y] —
until your people pass by, LORD,
until the people you bought[b][z]
pass by.
[17]You will bring them in and plant[a] them
on the mountain[b] of your
inheritance —
the place, LORD, you made for your
dwelling,
the sanctuary, Lord, your hands
established.
[18]"The LORD reigns
for ever and ever."

[19]When Pharaoh's horses, chariots and
horsemen[c] went into the sea,[c] the LORD
brought the waters of the sea back over
them, but the Israelites walked through
the sea on dry ground.[d] [20]Then Miriam[e]
the prophet,[f] Aaron's sister, took a timbrel
in her hand, and all the women followed
her, with timbrels and dancing.[g] [21]Miriam
sang to them:

"Sing to the LORD,
for he is highly exalted.

[a] 15 Or *rulers* [b] 16 Or *created* [c] 19 Or *charioteers*

with a summary reference to anyone "who may rebel, who may plot, who may fight, who may talk of fighting, or who may talk of rebelling." A curse formula was then pronounced over the object, and the object was smashed to depict the fulfillment of the curse and the hoped-for destruction of the targeted enemy. The wording of this verse in Exodus may be alluding to this type of symbolic action. Although the narrative speaks of drowning, the song describes the destruction of Yahweh's enemies in terms that would have offended ancient Egyptian sensibilities, since it reverses the roles and presents Egypt as the shattered enemy.

15:12 *the earth swallows.* This is a common Hebrew idiom for death, but also may bring to mind the Egyptian conception of the punishment that awaits wrongdoers in the afterlife. Those who are, at the postmortem judgment, found guilty of wrongdoing and thus unworthy of a blissful afterlife are eaten by a beast known as the "Devouress" or "Swallower" (see the article "The Hardening of Pharaoh's Heart," p. 124). By stating that the Egyptians have been swallowed up, the Biblical text reminds them of the one fate every ancient Egyptian hoped to avoid.

15:14 *Philistia.* This may be an anachronism; i.e., it may come from a time later than the purported time of the exodus. The Philistines probably did not settle in the area until the early twelfth century BC. They came from the area of Crete and Greece (i.e., the region around the Aegean Sea). A massive upheaval in that area (the exact causes of which are unknown) seems to have led to large numbers of people, including the Philistines, moving east into Syria and Palestine. An Egyptian inscription from around 1190 BC commemorates the Egyptians' victory over "those who came on the sea" (often referred to as the Sea Peoples). Included in this category are the "Philistines, Tjeker, Shekelesh, Denye(n), and Weshesh." Although the inscription boasts of a decisive Egyptian victory, most likely the Egyptians did little more than keep the invading Sea Peoples at bay and maintain the security of their borders.

15:18 *The LORD reigns.* Yahweh is not portrayed as a mythical king at the head of a divine pantheon, having subdued the cosmos and defeated the other gods, as Baal in Ugaritic literature. Rather, he rules in the historical realm over a historical people.

15:20 *Miriam the prophet.* Two other women prophets are mentioned in the OT: Deborah (Jdg 4:4) and Huldah (2Ki 22:14). It is not completely unexpected, then, to encounter a reference here to a female prophet. Other ancient Near Eastern societies also accorded prophetic ability to women. The city-state of Mari, located in eastern Syria along the Euphrates River, provides some of the best examples. A number of the texts from Mari, which date to the first half of the eighteenth century BC, refer to women who offer prophetic utterances, primarily concerning the king of Mari, Zimri-Lim, and his prospects for the future.

Both horse and driver
he has hurled into the sea."[h]

The Waters of Marah and Elim

22Then Moses led Israel from the Red
Sea and they went into the Desert of Shur.
For three days they traveled in the desert
without finding water. 23When they came
to Marah, they could not drink its water
because it was bitter. (That is why the
place is called Marah.[a][i]) 24So the people
grumbled[j] against Moses, saying, "What
are we to drink?"
25Then Moses cried out[k] to the LORD,
and the LORD showed him a piece of wood.
He threw it into the water, and the water
became fit to drink.

15:21 [h] ver 1; Ex 14:27
15:23 [i] Nu 33:8
15:24 [j] Ex 14:12; 16:2
15:25 [k] Ex 14:10

[a] 23 *Marah* means *bitter.*

EXODUS 15:1 – 21

Yahweh's Victory

There are parallels between the description of Yahweh's victory in Ex 15 and the victory of Baal recorded in Ugaritic literature. In the latter, the terrible and monstrous character "Sea" demands that the high god El hand Baal over to him as a prisoner. El complies. Later, the craftsman-god Kothar fashions two mighty clubs with which Baal defeats Sea. El then grants Baal a palatial residence on Mount Zaphon, in part because he has proved his superiority in the divine council with his defeat of Sea. In Exodus, Yahweh too shows his mastery over the sea. By means of the victory won there, Yahweh receives praise as the greatest among the gods.

Ex 15:11 contains a straightforward rhetorical question with "no one" as the obvious answer. After the victory, Yahweh and the people he has rescued head for the "mountain of God" (3:1), the place where Moses was told that he and the people would worship God (3:12). This may be what is meant by the "mountain of your inheritance—the place, LORD, you made for your dwelling" (15:17). Baal wins a victory *over* Sea and then settles on his mountain; Yahweh's victory *with* the sea is followed by travel to his mountain.

In light of this, it is interesting to note the combination of the two miraculous crossings for the Israelites: crossing a sea in Exodus (ch. 15) and crossing a river in Joshua (Jos 3). Baal's victory over Sea is described in this fashion:

Sea fell,
He sank to earth
His joints trembled,
His frame collapsed
Baal destroyed,
Drank Sea!
He finished off Judge River.

In the Ugaritic poem, "Judge River" is a common nickname for Sea. Any god who claims superiority must surely demonstrate victory over Sea/River. This is also evident in the Babylonian creation myth *Enuma Elish.* Marduk proves his superiority by defeating Tiamat, the watery sea goddess/monster. Yahweh's demonstration of his ability to control deftly both sea and river may be reminiscent of this idea. He shows their complete submission to him.

In contrast to ancient Near Eastern sources, the sea in Exodus is a body of water, not a supernatural being, and his enemies are human rather than cosmic or divine. Nonetheless, Yahweh's triumph over the combination of sea and river holds important theological implications for the Israelites and functions as a significant part of their basis for exalting Yahweh above all other purported deities. ◆

There the LORD issued a ruling and instruction for them and put them to the test.[l] 26He said, "If you listen carefully to the LORD your God and do what is right in his eyes, if you pay attention to his commands and keep all his decrees,[m] I will not bring on you any of the diseases[n] I brought on the Egyptians, for I am the LORD, who heals[o] you."

27Then they came to Elim, where there were twelve springs and seventy palm trees, and they camped[p] there near the water.

Manna and Quail

16 The whole Israelite community set out from Elim and came to the Desert of Sin,[q] which is between Elim and Sinai, on the fifteenth day of the second month after they had come out of Egypt. 2In the desert the whole community grumbled[r] against Moses and Aaron. 3The Israelites said to them, "If only we had died by the LORD's hand in Egypt![s] There we sat around pots of meat and ate all the food[t] we wanted, but you have brought us out into this desert to starve this entire assembly to death."

4Then the LORD said to Moses, "I will rain down bread from heaven[u] for you. The people are to go out each day and gather enough for that day. In this way I will test them and see whether they will follow my instructions. 5On the sixth day they are to prepare what they bring in, and that is to be twice[v] as much as they gather on the other days."

6So Moses and Aaron said to all the Israelites, "In the evening you will know that it was the LORD who brought you out of Egypt,[w] 7and in the morning you will see the glory[x] of the LORD, because he has heard your grumbling[y] against him. Who are we, that you should grumble against us?"[z] 8Moses also said, "You will know that it was the LORD when he gives you meat to eat in the evening and all the bread you want in the morning, because he has heard your grumbling against him. Who are we? You are not grumbling against us, but against the LORD."[a]

9Then Moses told Aaron, "Say to the entire Israelite community, 'Come before the LORD, for he has heard your grumbling.' "

10While Aaron was speaking to the whole Israelite community, they looked toward the desert, and there was the glory[b] of the LORD appearing in the cloud.[c]

11The LORD said to Moses, 12"I have heard the grumbling[d] of the Israelites. Tell them, 'At twilight you will eat meat, and in the morning you will be filled with bread. Then you will know that I am the LORD your God.' "

15:25 [l] Jdg 3:4
15:26 [m] Dt 7:12 [n] Dt 28:27, 58-60 [o] Ex 23:25-26
15:27 [p] Nu 33:9
16:1 [q] Nu 33:11, 12
16:2 [r] Ex 14:11; 15:24; 1Co 10:10
16:3 [s] Ex 17:3 [t] Nu 11:4, 34
16:4 [u] Dt 8:3; Jn 6:31*
16:5 [v] ver 22
16:6 [w] Ex 6:6
16:7 [x] ver 10; Isa 35:2; 40:5 [y] ver 12; Nu 14:2, 27, 28 [z] Nu 16:11
16:8 [a] 1Sa 8:7; Ro 13:2
16:10 [b] ver 7; Nu 16:19 [c] Ex 13:21; 1Ki 8:10
16:12 [d] ver 7
16:13 [e] Nu 11:31; Ps 78:27-28; 105:40 [f] Nu 11:9
16:14 [g] ver 31; Nu 11:7-9; Ps 105:40
16:15 [h] ver 4; Jn 6:31
16:16 [i] ver 32, 36
16:18 [j] 2Co 8:15*
16:19 [k] ver 23; Ex 12:10; 23:18
16:22 [l] ver 5 [m] Ex 34:31
16:23 [n] Ge 2:3; Ex 20:8; 23:12; Lev 23:3
16:26 [o] Ex 20:9-10
16:28 [p] 2Ki 17:14; Ps 78:10; 106:13

13That evening quail[e] came and covered the camp, and in the morning there was a layer of dew[f] around the camp. 14When the dew was gone, thin flakes like frost[g] on the ground appeared on the desert floor. 15When the Israelites saw it, they said to each other, "What is it?" For they did not know what it was.

Moses said to them, "It is the bread[h] the LORD has given you to eat. 16This is what the LORD has commanded: 'Everyone is to gather as much as they need. Take an omer[a][i] for each person you have in your tent.' "

17The Israelites did as they were told; some gathered much, some little. 18And when they measured it by the omer, the one who gathered much did not have too much, and the one who gathered little did not have too little.[j] Everyone had gathered just as much as they needed.

19Then Moses said to them, "No one is to keep any of it until morning."[k]

20However, some of them paid no attention to Moses; they kept part of it until morning, but it was full of maggots and began to smell. So Moses was angry with them.

21Each morning everyone gathered as much as they needed, and when the sun grew hot, it melted away. 22On the sixth day, they gathered twice[l] as much — two omers[b] for each person — and the leaders of the community[m] came and reported this to Moses. 23He said to them, "This is what the LORD commanded: 'Tomorrow is to be a day of sabbath rest, a holy sabbath[n] to the LORD. So bake what you want to bake and boil what you want to boil. Save whatever is left and keep it until morning.' "

24So they saved it until morning, as Moses commanded, and it did not stink or get maggots in it. 25"Eat it today," Moses said, "because today is a sabbath to the LORD. You will not find any of it on the ground today. 26Six days you are to gather it, but on the seventh day, the Sabbath,[o] there will not be any."

27Nevertheless, some of the people went out on the seventh day to gather it, but they found none. 28Then the LORD said to Moses, "How long will you[c] refuse to keep my commands[p] and my instructions? 29Bear in mind that the LORD has given you the Sabbath; that is why on the sixth day he gives you bread for two days. Everyone is to stay where they are on the seventh day; no one is to go out." 30So the people rested on the seventh day.

a *16* That is, possibly about 3 pounds or about 1.4 kilograms; also in verses 18, 32, 33 and 36 *b* *22* That is, possibly about 6 pounds or about 2.8 kilograms *c* *28* The Hebrew is plural.

31The people of Israel called the bread
manna.[a][q] It was white like coriander seed
and tasted like wafers made with honey.
32Moses said, "This is what the LORD has
commanded: 'Take an omer of manna and
keep it for the generations to come, so
they can see the bread I gave you to eat
in the wilderness when I brought you out
of Egypt.' "
33So Moses said to Aaron, "Take a jar
and put an omer of manna[r] in it. Then
place it before the LORD to be kept for the
generations to come."
34As the LORD commanded Moses, Aaron put the manna with the tablets of the
covenant law,[s] so that it might be preserved. 35The Israelites ate manna[t] forty
years,[u] until they came to a land that was
settled; they ate manna until they reached
the border of Canaan.[v]
36(An omer is one-tenth of an ephah.)

Water From the Rock

17 The whole Israelite community
set out from the Desert of Sin,[w]
traveling from place to place as the LORD
commanded. They camped at Rephidim,
but there was no water[x] for the people to
drink. 2So they quarreled with Moses and
said, "Give us water[y] to drink."
Moses replied, "Why do you quarrel
with me? Why do you put the LORD to the
test?"[z]
3But the people were thirsty for water
there, and they grumbled[a] against Moses.
They said, "Why did you bring us up out
of Egypt to make us and our children and
livestock die of thirst?"
4Then Moses cried out to the LORD,
"What am I to do with these people? They
are almost ready to stone[b] me."
5The LORD answered Moses, "Go out in
front of the people. Take with you some of
the elders of Israel and take in your hand
the staff with which you struck the Nile,[c]
and go. 6I will stand there before you by
the rock at Horeb. Strike the rock, and
water[d] will come out of it for the people
to drink." So Moses did this in the sight
of the elders of Israel. 7And he called the
place Massah[b] and Meribah[c][e] because the
Israelites quarreled and because they tested the LORD saying, "Is the LORD among
us or not?"

The Amalekites Defeated

8The Amalekites[f] came and attacked
the Israelites at Rephidim. 9Moses said to
Joshua, "Choose some of our men and go
out to fight the Amalekites. Tomorrow I
will stand on top of the hill with the staff[g]
of God in my hands."
10So Joshua fought the Amalekites as
Moses had ordered, and Moses, Aaron and
Hur[h] went to the top of the hill. 11As long
as Moses held up his hands, the Israelites
were winning,[i] but whenever he lowered
his hands, the Amalekites were winning.
12When Moses' hands grew tired, they
took a stone and put it under him and he
sat on it. Aaron and Hur held his hands
up — one on one side, one on the other —
so that his hands remained steady till sunset. 13So Joshua overcame the Amalekite
army with the sword.
14Then the LORD said to Moses, "Write[j]
this on a scroll as something to be remembered and make sure that Joshua hears
it, because I will completely blot out the
name of Amalek[k] from under heaven."
15Moses built an altar and called it The
LORD is my Banner. 16He said, "Because
hands were lifted up against[d] the throne of
the LORD,[e] the LORD will be at war against
the Amalekites from generation to generation."

Jethro Visits Moses

18 Now Jethro, the priest of Midian[l]
and father-in-law of Moses, heard
of everything God had done for Moses and
for his people Israel, and how the LORD
had brought Israel out of Egypt.
2After Moses had sent away his wife
Zipporah,[m] his father-in-law Jethro received her 3and her two sons.[n] One son

16:31 [q]Nu 11:7-9 16:33 [r]Heb 9:4 16:34 [s]Ex 25:16, 21,22; 40:20; Nu 17:4,10 16:35 [t]Jn 6:31, 49 [u]Ne 9:21 [v]Jos 5:12 17:1 [w]Ex 16:1 [x]Nu 33:14 17:2 [y]Nu 20:2 [z]Dt 6:16; Ps 78:18,41; 1Co 10:9 17:3 [a]Ex 15:24; 16:2-3 17:4 [b]Nu 14:10; 1Sa 30:6 17:5 [c]Ex 7:20 17:6 [d]Nu 20:11; Ps 114:8; 1Co 10:4

17:7 [e]Nu 20:13, 24; Ps 81:7 17:8 [f]Ge 36:12; Dt 25:17-19 17:9 [g]Ex 4:17 17:10 [h]Ex 24:14 17:11 [i]Jas 5:16 17:14 [j]Ex 24:4; 34:27; Nu 33:2 [k]1Sa 15:3; 30:17-18 18:1 [l]Ex 2:16; 3:1 18:2 [m]Ex 2:21; 4:25 18:3 [n]Ex 4:20; Ac 7:29

[a] 31 *Manna* sounds like the Hebrew for *What is it?* (see verse 15). [b] 7 *Massah* means *testing.* [c] 7 *Meribah* means *quarreling.* [d] 16 Or *to* [e] 16 The meaning of the Hebrew for this clause is uncertain.

16:31 *called the bread manna.* See note on Nu 11:7.
17:6 *the rock at Horeb.* Elsewhere, Horeb is called the "mountain of God" (3:1; 18:5). Hence, the water flows from God's mountain, the place of God's presence. This idea may have religious or even cosmic implications. In Ugaritic literature, the god El is said to reside at "the Sources of the Two Floods / In the midst of the headwaters of the Two Oceans." He is also said to have his abode on a mountain that would appear to be Mount Amanus. These two places probably refer to the same location. In the ancient world waters typically flow from sacred space.
17:8 *Amalekites.* See note on Nu 13:29.
17:11 *held up his hands.* The reason for Moses' gesture has long puzzled scholars. It could be a smiting or warlike gesture, similar to what Joshua does with his javelin in Jos 8:18. It could be symbolic of prayer, beseeching Yahweh for victory, although Moses, uncharacteristically, does not explicitly seek help or guidance from Yahweh here. One possible clue comes in the name for the altar in v. 15: "The LORD is my Banner." The word "banner" (*nes*) refers to a battle standard, flag or insignia that leads an army into war. Perhaps Moses' raised arms are symbolic of raising Yahweh, their "banner" of military strength and power. With the banner raised, the army prevails.
18:1 *priest of Midian.* See note on vv. 9–12.

EXODUS 17:14

LITERACY

Little is known about the extent of literacy among the ancient Israelites and other Near Eastern societies. For the most part, only scribes, certain religious and governmental officials, and some wealthy businessmen, along with other elite persons, could read and write beyond the basics. Possibly those with lower socioeconomic standing would have had basic literary training, but the evidence for this is small.

The invention of writing appears to have occurred in Egypt and Mesopotamia at about the same time — the late fourth millennium BC — but neither of those writing systems is alphabetic like ancient Hebrew. One must presume that some predecessor of ancient Hebrew, a Northwest Semitic language, is the language that the Biblical text is referring to in Ex 17:14, since the writing is to be preserved for future reference. Ancient Hebrew itself and most other alphabetic languages (including modern languages such as English) all appear to derive from the same alphabet — likely a Semitic invention in the first half of the second millennium BC. Recent discoveries of primitive alphabetic inscriptions in Egypt have raised the possibility that the alphabet was developed by Semitic peoples living there as early as 1800 BC.

In assessing literacy rates for ancient Israel, one must consider both Biblical and epigraphic evidence, and little assessment can be done for periods prior to the Iron Age (begins about 1200 BC). Nothing that is recognizable as Hebrew appears before this time period. From the Late Bronze Age come nearly 400 Amarna letters (fourteenth century BC), written mostly by scribes living in Syria and Palestine, but these are in Akkadian (an East Semitic language), though they do contain some West Semitic features. Apart from those, however, there are only about 20 texts that have survived from Palestine. These date to the general time period covered by the Late Bronze Age (1550 – 1200 BC) and seem to reflect a Northwest Semitic language, but this language is not Hebrew.

continued on next page

was named Gershom,[a] for Moses said,
"I have become a foreigner in a foreign
land";[o] 4and the other was named Eliezer,[b][p] for he said, "My father's God was
my helper; he saved me from the sword
of Pharaoh."
5Jethro, Moses' father-in-law, together
with Moses' sons and wife, came to him
in the wilderness, where he was camped
near the mountain[q] of God. 6Jethro had
sent word to him, "I, your father-in-law
Jethro, am coming to you with your wife
and her two sons."
7So Moses went out to meet his father-
in-law and bowed down[r] and kissed[s] him.
They greeted each other and then went
into the tent. 8Moses told his father-in-
law about everything the LORD had done
to Pharaoh and the Egyptians for Israel's
sake and about all the hardships they had
met along the way and how the LORD had
saved[t] them.
9Jethro was delighted to hear about all
the good things the LORD had done for Israel in rescuing them from the hand of
the Egyptians. 10He said, "Praise be to the

18:3 [o] Ex 2:22
18:4 [p] 1Ch 23:15
18:5 [q] Ex 3:1
18:7 [r] Ge 43:28 [s] Ge 29:13
18:8 [t] Ex 15:6, 16; Ps 81:7

[a] 3 *Gershom* sounds like the Hebrew for *a foreigner there.* [b] 4 *Eliezer* means *my God is helper.*

18:7 *bowed down.* A standard greeting and act of respect toward one of higher social standing. *kissed him.* A kiss on the cheek is a greeting of friendship. This is the only instance where both bowing and kissing are recorded together.
18:9 – 12 Jethro is identified as a "priest of Midian" (v. 1) rather than a priest of a particular god. Priests were not necessarily affiliated with only one god, and there is no evidence that Jethro was a monotheist or that he converted to monotheism. Polytheism allows for the recognition of the relative strengths of deities, especially in the face of a display of power. There is no reason to believe that Jethro would not have acknowledged the power of other gods when manifested as well.

It is not until the Iron Age that actual Hebrew inscriptions turn up. This evidence, in combination with Biblical references to writing, however, still does not indicate widespread literacy among ancient Israelites. There is insufficient evidence for the kind of educational and economic systems that typically promote the growth of literacy in human societies. While ancient Israel may have had a higher rate of literacy than some other Near Eastern societies — one estimate for ancient Egypt is a literacy rate of 1 percent — still only a small percentage of the population could actually read and write.

Someone with the kind of background that the text describes for Moses would probably have been literate, and the Biblical text attributes to Moses the ability both to read (Ex 24:7) and to write (17:11) in a language that the Israelites can understand. We do not know what specific language would have been spoken by Israelites coming out of Egypt toward the end of the Late Bronze Age. To suppose they spoke some type of Northwest Semitic dialect is not unreasonable, but it almost certainly was not the kind of Hebrew we find in the Bible, a dialect of Northwest Semitic that did not fully develop until later. Thus, anything written down in the Late Bronze Age or the early Iron Age and preserved in Biblical texts has been updated for presentation in the kind of classical Hebrew found in Biblical manuscripts. ◆

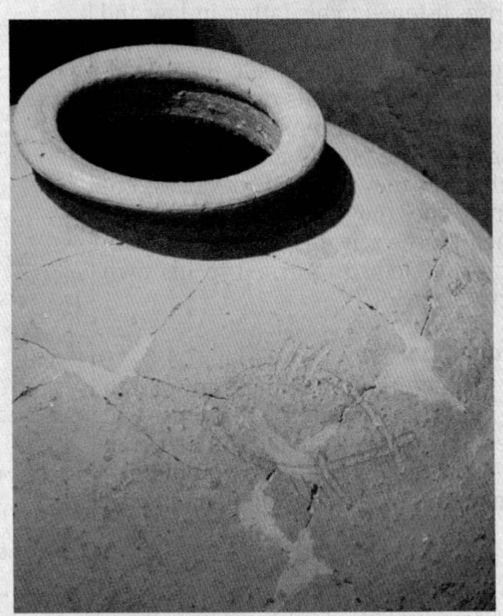

Sixteenth-century BC storage jar from Dan (Middle Bronze II) with proto-Canaanite writing.

LORD,[u] who rescued you from the hand of
the Egyptians and of Pharaoh, and who
rescued the people from the hand of the
Egyptians. 11 Now I know that the LORD is
greater than all other gods,[v] for he did this
to those who had treated Israel arrogantly."[w] 12 Then Jethro, Moses' father-in-law,
brought a burnt offering and other sacrifices to God, and Aaron came with all the
elders of Israel to eat a meal with Moses'
father-in-law in the presence[x] of God.

13 The next day Moses took his seat to
serve as judge for the people, and they
stood around him from morning till evening. 14 When his father-in-law saw all that
Moses was doing for the people, he said,
"What is this you are doing for the people?
Why do you alone sit as judge, while all
these people stand around you from morning till evening?"

15 Moses answered him, "Because the
people come to me to seek God's will.[y]
16 Whenever they have a dispute, it is
brought to me, and I decide between the
parties and inform them of God's decrees
and instructions."[z]

17 Moses' father-in-law replied, "What
you are doing is not good. 18 You and these
people who come to you will only wear
yourselves out. The work is too heavy for
you; you cannot handle it alone.[a] 19 Listen
now to me and I will give you some advice, and may God be with you.[b] You must
be the people's representative before God
and bring their disputes[c] to him. 20 Teach
them his decrees and instructions,[d] and
show them the way they are to live[e] and
how they are to behave.[f] 21 But select capable men[g] from all the people — men who
fear God, trustworthy men who hate dishonest gain[h] — and appoint them as officials[i] over thousands, hundreds, fifties and

18:10 [u] Ge 14:20; Ps 68:19-20
18:11 [v] Ex 12:12; 15:11; 2Ch 2:5 [w] Lk 1:51
18:12 [x] Dt 12:7
18:15 [y] Nu 9:6, 8; Dt 17:8-13
18:16 [z] Lev 24:12
18:18 [a] Nu 11:11, 14, 17
18:19 [b] Ex 3:12 [c] Nu 27:5
18:20 [d] Dt 5:1 [e] Ps 143:8 [f] Dt 1:18
18:21 [g] Ac 6:3 [h] Dt 16:19; Ps 15:5; Eze 18:8 [i] Dt 1:13, 15; 2Ch 19:5-10

tens. 22 Have them serve as judges for the
people at all times, but have them bring
every difficult case[j] to you; the simple cases they can decide themselves. That will
make your load lighter, because they will
share[k] it with you. 23 If you do this and God
so commands, you will be able to stand
the strain, and all these people will go
home satisfied."
24 Moses listened to his father-in-law and
did everything he said. 25 He chose capable
men from all Israel and made them leaders of the people, officials over thousands,
hundreds, fifties and tens.[l] 26 They served
as judges for the people at all times. The
difficult cases they brought to Moses, but
the simple ones they decided themselves.[m]
27 Then Moses sent his father-in-law on
his way, and Jethro returned to his own
country.[n]

At Mount Sinai

19 On the first day of the third month
after the Israelites left Egypt — on
that very day — they came to the Desert of
Sinai. 2 After they set out from Rephidim,[o]
they entered the Desert of Sinai, and Israel
camped there in the desert in front of the
mountain.[p]
3 Then Moses went up to God, and the
LORD called[q] to him from the mountain
and said, "This is what you are to say to
the descendants of Jacob and what you
are to tell the people of Israel: 4 'You yourselves have seen what I did to Egypt,[r] and
how I carried you on eagles' wings[s] and
brought you to myself. 5 Now if you obey
me fully[t] and keep my covenant,[u] then
out of all nations you will be my treasured
possession.[v] Although the whole earth[w] is
mine, 6 you[a] will be for me a kingdom of
priests[x] and a holy nation.'[y] These are the
words you are to speak to the Israelites."
7 So Moses went back and summoned
the elders of the people and set before
them all the words the LORD had commanded him to speak. 8 The people all responded together, "We will do everything
the LORD has said."[z] So Moses brought
their answer back to the LORD.
9 The LORD said to Moses, "I am going to
come to you in a dense cloud,[a] so that the
people will hear me speaking[b] with you
and will always put their trust in you."
Then Moses told the LORD what the people had said.
10 And the LORD said to Moses, "Go to

18:22 [j] Dt 1:17-18 [k] Nu 11:17 **18:25** [l] Dt 1:13-15 **18:26** [m] ver 22 **18:27** [n] Nu 10:29-30 **19:2** [o] Ex 17:1 [p] Ex 3:1 **19:3** [q] Ex 3:4; Ac 7:38 **19:4** [r] Dt 29:2 [s] Isa 63:9 **19:5** [t] Ex 15:26 [u] Dt 5:2 [v] Dt 14:2; Ps 135:4 [w] Ex 9:29; Dt 10:14 **19:6** [x] 1Pe 2:5 [y] Dt 7:6; 26:19; Isa 62:12 **19:8** [z] Ex 24:3, 7; Dt 5:27 **19:9** [a] ver 16; Ex 24:15-16 [b] Dt 4:12, 36

[a] 5,6 Or *possession, for the whole earth is mine.* 6 *You*

18:22 *judges.* Israel's judicial framework, though not always the laws themselves per se or the motivations for the laws, was fairly common in the ancient Near East. Three spheres of government "housed" the constitutional and administrative law: the divine (gods, king and dynasty), state and local authorities. Outside of Israel the king was at the top of the pyramid in constitutional and administrative law and judicial procedures. Kingship originated from the gods and was passed on to the king, who could claim to be ruler of the world and as such could promulgate laws. He was ultimately the head of any legislative group and acted as supreme judge, who especially (in theory at least) championed the cause of the widow, the orphan, the poor and the oppressed. There was typically some kind of central administration as well as provincial or city-state administrative structures. The courts recognized the king as supreme judge along with supportive royal judges under him, and there were evidently local judges as well.

In Mesopotamia levels of the judicial system are evident. A town assembly of elders was established. Then additional local, temple or royal officials could get involved, often serving as witnesses. The parties involved in a case represented themselves, for there were no lawyers or professionals involved.

In Egypt the king and his royal staff administered justice and ruled the land. The king derived his authority from the gods. Egyptian law codes have not been uncovered, though royal decrees and edicts have been. But references in ancient writings imply that such laws did exist, at least to some extent. There were "judges" and supporting court personnel, members of a scribal class who functioned as "quasi-lawyers," and court and legal procedure that functioned in rudimentary form. Justice was available to the poor as well as the rich. Some persons (judges) were charged to see that "law" (*maat*) was used to the good of all humanity.

We have records of Hittite instructions to officers in the thirteenth century BC (Tudhalias IV). Officers are classified as commanders of thousands, designated as majors, and so on. Officers in the military served as judges. The king, however, was the one who gave out the commands and instructions. Extremely difficult cases for the various judges could be refused; justice was to be passed in all cases to those involved, with no partiality shown for the rich or the poor. In Egypt similar actions are recorded in a fourteenth-century BC stele of Horemheb, where we read that he sought out men of integrity and excellent character to serve as judges.

18:24 – 26 Jethro advised Moses to establish a hierarchy with himself at the top, where a king would be in a monarchy. Moses' nominees could handle civil matters, while those matters that needed to be brought before God would be handled through Moses. This separated the "religious" from the "civil" aspects of the judicial process as is similar to the system found in Egypt, where Pharaoh appointed a vizier entitled "prophet of Ma'at" (the goddess of truth and justice) to sit in judgment. In contrast, among the Hittites, the king served in the highest court, which was also a court of appeals. He was the steward of the Land of Hatti under the creator storm-god, who owned the land, just as Yahweh owned the land in Israel. This king also served as the chief priest of the gods.

19:4 *eagles' wings.* The bird in question is probably a griffin vulture. While Biblical reference books report that these birds carry their young when they are weary of flying or catch them as they fall from early flights, naturalists have been unable to confirm this behavior. If the metaphor does concern a vulture, the statement may be political in nature. In Egypt the vulture-goddess, Nekhbet, is the protector of Pharaoh. Yahweh may be using this imagery to connote his protection of the Israelites.

EXODUS 19:5

COVENANTS

One of the most crucial concepts to understanding ancient Israelite religion and the theology of the OT is that of the covenant. The Hebrew word for covenant (*berit*) essentially means a binding legal agreement (contract) and can refer to agreements in a wide variety of contexts, including personal (Ge 31:44), familial (1Sa 20:16; Mal 2:14), business (Jer 34:8–10) and international settings (Jos 9:6; 1Ki 15:19). Other ancient Near Eastern societies utilized the same sorts of agreements, a number of which have survived to this day. The covenant established at Sinai between Yahweh and the Israelites is both like and unlike these more ordinary agreements that were necessary for the effective functioning of those societies.

There are several similarities. Like legal agreements of the day, the covenant at Sinai carried with it obligations for both parties. To "keep" the covenant for the Israelites meant obeying the laws — their covenantal obligations — set forth in Ex 20–23. In Ex 24:7 we hear of "the Book of the Covenant," which likely refers to a written record of these obligations. Yahweh also had obligations, namely, to treat the Israelites as his own people, as his "treasured possession" (19:5).

At a more specific level, many scholars have understood the Sinai covenant to find its closest parallel in one particular type of "contract" — namely, international treaties from the ancient Near East typically called a "suzerainty treaty" or a "vassal treaty," because it was concluded between a superior state (suzerain) and an inferior state (vassal). A number of such treaties have been preserved from the Hittite Empire (mid-second millennium BC) in Anatolia (modern-day Turkey) and from the Neo-Assyrian Empire (early to mid-first millennium BC) based in northern Mesopotamia. While both Hittite and Assyrian texts offer parallels to the Biblical idea of covenant, the Hittite treaties have often been the focal point of comparison. Similarities can also be found with ancient land contracts (for Yahweh has promised a land to them). In this way we can see that the covenant takes a legal form that would have been familiar to the Israelites.

Important differences, however, must not be overlooked. Typically, both parties to a contract, treaty or similar legal agreement could expect to benefit from their commitment. It is not at all clear that the Biblical text wants its readers to believe that Yahweh will receive some benefit from this relationship with the Israelites that he would not otherwise be able to obtain. The text speaks of great benefit awaiting the Israelites for their consistent obedience to their covenantal obligations. For Yahweh's part, his actions do not appear to be based in self-interest but in a willingness to be gracious and to extend freely his blessing. It must also be stressed that no treaty or contract from the ancient Near East provides a precise match for the Sinai covenant. There is no evidence of an agreement between a deity and a people group in these terms.

Thus, all parallels are inexact. Israel's relationship with Yahweh — at least in the form it takes — is unique. Exactly why the relationship takes the form of a covenant is difficult to say. Nevertheless, a number of the implications of having a covenantal relationship with their God would have been clear to many Israelites, since it mirrored, at least in some respects, several types of relationships they already knew well. ◆

the people and consecrate[c] them today
and tomorrow. Have them wash their
clothes[d] 11and be ready by the third day,[e]
because on that day the LORD will come
down on Mount Sinai in the sight of
all the people. 12Put limits for the people around the mountain and tell them,
'Be careful that you do not approach the
mountain or touch the foot of it. Whoever touches the mountain is to be put to
death. 13They are to be stoned[f] or shot
with arrows; not a hand is to be laid on
them. No person or animal shall be permitted to live.' Only when the ram's horn
sounds a long blast may they approach
the mountain."
14After Moses had gone down the mountain to the people, he consecrated them,
and they washed their clothes. 15Then he
said to the people, "Prepare yourselves for
the third day. Abstain from sexual relations."
16On the morning of the third day there
was thunder and lightning, with a thick
cloud over the mountain, and a very loud
trumpet blast.[g] Everyone in the camp
trembled.[h] 17Then Moses led the people
out of the camp to meet with God, and

19:10 [c]Lev 11:44; Heb 10:22 [d]Ge 35:2 **19:11** [e]ver 16 **19:13** [f]Heb 12:20* **19:16** [g]Heb 12:18-19; Rev 4:1 [h]Heb 12:21

EXODUS 19:11

Mount Sinai

Exodus 19:11 is the first use of the exact phrase "Mount Sinai" in the Bible. Its precise geographic location has been the subject of great debate and probably still remains unknown despite a number of attempts since antiquity to identify it. Traditionally, Mount Sinai has been identified with a mountain known as Jebel Musa (Arabic for "Mountain of Moses"). Saint Catherine's Monastery sits at the foot of this mountain and for centuries has welcomed visitors who believe they are visiting the very ground that Moses trod. Jebel Musa rises 7,500 feet (2,285 meters) in the southern part of the Sinai peninsula, which probably derives its name from the traditions that placed the famous mountain there. Early Christian writings show that Jebel Musa was believed to be Mount Sinai as early as the middle of the fourth century AD. But this means that the earliest evidence for this belief comes over 1,500 years after any possible journey of the Israelites to this mountain.

Older traditions actually point to an entirely different location for Mount Sinai. There is evidence from Biblical and other ancient texts that Mount Sinai was not located anywhere in the Sinai peninsula but was thought to be in northwest Arabia, slightly to the east of the Gulf of Aqaba. This would place the mountain in the region referred to as Midian. To begin with, Moses was in or near Midian when he came to "Horeb, the mountain of God" (Ex 3:1), often identified as Mount Sinai. In addition, Moses was to bring the Israelites back to "this mountain" (3:12) in or near Midian, in order for the people to worship God there. This is what happens in Ex 19, where the mountain is called "Mount Sinai" (19:11).

Ex 18 may also suggest that the mountain is in the vicinity of Midian, since Jethro, called the "priest of Midian" (3:1), visits Moses when the latter is camped with the Israelites at Mount Sinai. In light of this, some have speculated that a mountain known as Jebel al-Lawz, the tallest mountain in the region of ancient Midian, may be the correct identification of Mount Sinai. Nevertheless, though the core region of Midian may be in northwest Arabia, the Midianites were wandering peoples not rooted in one geographic location.

Non-Biblical texts also support Midian as the location of the mountain. The translators of the Septuagint, the pre-Christian Greek translation of the OT (done in the last two centuries before Christ), refer to Midian and Mount Sinai in a way that shows they likely believed Mount Sinai was in northwest Arabia rather than in the Sinai

continued on next page

they stood at the foot of the mountain.
[18]Mount Sinai was covered with smoke,[i]
because the LORD descended on it in fire.[j]
The smoke billowed up from it like smoke
from a furnace,[k] and the whole mountain[a]
trembled[l] violently. [19]As the sound of the
trumpet grew louder and louder, Moses
spoke and the voice[m] of God answered[n]
him.[b]

[20]The LORD descended to the top of
Mount Sinai and called Moses to the top
of the mountain. So Moses went up [21]and
the LORD said to him, "Go down and warn
the people so they do not force their way
through to see[o] the LORD and many of
them perish. [22]Even the priests, who approach[p] the LORD, must consecrate themselves, or the LORD will break out against
them."[q]

[23]Moses said to the LORD, "The people
cannot come up Mount Sinai, because you
yourself warned us, 'Put limits[r] around the
mountain and set it apart as holy.' "

[24]The LORD replied, "Go down and
bring Aaron[s] up with you. But the priests

19:18 [i]Ps 104:32 [j]Ex 3:2; 24:17; Dt 4:11; 2Ch 7:1; Ps 18:8; Heb 12:18 [k]Ge 19:28 [l]Jdg 5:5; Ps 68:8; Jer 4:24 **19:19** [m]Ne 9:13 [n]Ps 81:7 **19:21** [o]Ex 3:5; 1Sa 6:19 **19:22** [p]Lev 10:3 [q]2Sa 6:7 **19:23** [r]ver 12 **19:24** [s]Ex 24:1,9

[a] *18* Most Hebrew manuscripts; a few Hebrew manuscripts and Septuagint *and all the people*
[b] *19* Or *and God answered him with thunder*

peninsula. Other Jewish writers before, during and after the time of Jesus, such as Demetrius the Chronographer, Philo of Alexandria and Josephus, placed Mount Sinai in the region of Midian. Paul himself refers to "Mount Sinai in Arabia" (Gal 4:25). It is not entirely clear, though, whether Paul's "Arabia" meant only what we know today as the Arabian peninsula or whether it included a broader region encompassing the Sinai peninsula as well. Still, the evidence for northwest Arabia as the location of Mount Sinai substantially predates the evidence for Jebel Musa. Nevertheless, problems exist, such as the fact that Moses requests of Pharaoh that they be allowed to "take a three-day journey into the wilderness" (Ex 5:3), presumably to Mount Sinai.

Even if Midian is the region where the Biblical authors believed Mount Sinai to be, however, we still do not know whether Jebel al-Lawz is the correct identification. There is no clear evidence to tell us which mountain is the right one. The region of Midian lies in modern Saudi Arabia and is currently closed to archaeological excavation. Whether such work would provide further data to help clarify the issue remains to be seen. ◆

Jebel Musa, the traditional location of Mt. Sinai.

and the people must not force their way
through to come up to the LORD, or he will
break out against them."
25 So Moses went down to the people
and told them.

The Ten Commandments

20:1-17pp — Dt 5:6-21

20 And God spoke all these words:
2 "I am the LORD your God, who
brought you out of Egypt, out of
the land of slavery.[t]
3 "You shall have no other gods before[a] me.[u]
4 "You shall not make for yourself an
image[v] in the form of anything
in heaven above or on the earth
beneath or in the waters below.
5 You shall not bow down to them
or worship[w] them; for I, the LORD
your God, am a jealous God,[x]
punishing the children for the
sin of the parents to the third and
fourth generation[y] of those who
hate me, 6 but showing love to a
thousand[z] generations of those
who love me and keep my commandments.
7 "You shall not misuse the name of the
LORD your God, for the LORD will
not hold anyone guiltless who
misuses his name.[a]
8 "Remember the Sabbath[b] day by
keeping it holy. 9 Six days you

20:2 [t] Ex 13:3 **20:3** [u] Dt 6:14; Jer 35:15 **20:4** [v] Lev 26:1; Dt 4:15-19, 23; 27:15 **20:5** [w] Isa 44:15, 17, 19 [x] Ex 34:14; Dt 4:24 [y] Nu 14:18; Jer 32:18 **20:6** [z] Dt 7:9 **20:7** [a] Lev 19:12; Mt 5:33 **20:8** [b] Ex 31:13-16; Lev 26:2

[a] 3 Or *besides*

20:3 The Hebrew wording of this verse is ambiguous. This could be an assertion of either monotheism or henotheism (also termed monolatry). Practitioners of a henotheistic religion believe in and worship one deity, but they do not deny the possible existence of other deities. If this verse reflects a henotheistic perspective, then this call is for the Israelites to devote their worship exclusively to Yahweh, while accepting the possibility that other gods could legitimately be worshiped by non-Israelites (see note on Dt 5:7).

In another way of thinking, it is possible for this verse to be understood as proceeding from monotheistic belief. The reference to "no other gods *before* me" (emphasis added) may be an attempt to counteract belief in a divine assembly. To have no other gods in the presence of Yahweh implies that he is, in a sense, an assembly unto himself. In this case, "before" means "in front of," as it often does, a reference to spatial arrangement rather than hierarchy or priority. God consults with no other divine beings, and since the latter are thus removed from the divine decision-making process, it makes little sense to consider them as gods. Later Biblical texts (e.g., Isa 44) are more recognizably and dogmatically monotheistic.

Ancient Near Eastern societies were, of course, polytheistic. Throughout Israelite history, this type of religious perspective impacted Israelite religion to varying degrees, particularly regarding the god Baal. Baal was an important deity in several societies located near Israel (e.g., Ugarit, Phoenicia), and there is evidence, from the Bible and elsewhere, that he was worshiped at times by Israelites. Engravings that depict Baal and that come from the period of the divided monarchy have been discovered at several sites in Israel. Clearly, the Israelites did not consistently follow the principle set forth in this command. This is part of what led to the outrage of later Biblical prophets and authors.

20:4 *an image in the form of anything.* Since the previous commandment (v. 3) has already disallowed other gods, the images here are images of Yahweh. This commandment is not a restriction on art but is concerned with cultic practice. The prohibition concerns display and power. Images of deity were believed to be the places where the presence of the deity was specially manifest, actually embodying to an extent the essence of the god. Likewise, the image could be cared for in order to meet the needs of the deity. These images mediated the presence of god, the revelation of god, and worship to god. The issue here is not the image per se but the accompanying worldview and conception of deity that is inconsistent with the way Yahweh has revealed himself.

20:5 *third and fourth generation.* This statement likely refers to the punishment of an entire household, not to punishment of children yet to be born. There are Biblical examples of entire households (including wives, sons and daughters, and young children) receiving punishment for acts of wrongdoing committed primarily by the male heads of those households (e.g., Nu 16:25 – 33; Jos 7:24 – 26). It was not uncommon in the ancient world to have three or even four generations living in the same household.

A young woman typically entered marriage in her early teens, shortly after she began menstruating, in order to ensure as many productive childbearing years as possible. If her groom had not yet inherited a portion of his father's estate, she would live with her husband's family and be under her father-in-law's authority. She would likely give birth shortly after the marriage, and, if the infant survived, the three generations lived together for quite some time.

20:7 *misuse the name.* Based on this verse, it has been traditional for many Jews to avoid ever saying the name "Yahweh," saying instead "*Adonay*" ("lord, master") or "*ha-Shem*" ("the Name"). Complete nonuse of the name precluded any misuse. One interpretation of this is that it prohibits the use of the Lord's name in ways that treat it as powerless (casual use in profanity, blasphemous use, false oaths). Alternatively, and more importantly, the prohibition could target behavior that is well aware of the power of the name and seeks to exploit it for personal gain or advantage. This would include the use of the divine name in magical spells and hexes (against others or against the deity), or speaking something in God's name that is contrary to what he has said. It could be understood as a form of what today we call identity theft. In the NT the Lord's Prayer addresses this same issue (see Mt 6:9; Lk 11:2).

20:8 *Remember the Sabbath.* The hallowing of the seventh day — even the use of a seven-day week — was unique in Israel within the broader ancient Near Eastern world. Calendars and most measurements of time were based on the lunar or the solar cycle; the seven-day week is based on neither. Still, a period of seven days seems to have had special significance.

Several examples can be cited. Gudea, the ruler of the Mesopotamian city of Lagash (end of the third millennium BC), held a seven-day dedicatory festival after completing the temple for his god Ningirsu. In the Gilgamesh Epic, Utnapishtim (the Noah-like figure in the story) builds his ark in seven days and experiences six

EXODUS 20

Ancient Laws, Scripture and Modern Issues

The laws in the Bible reflect in large measure the way ancient societies were structured. God's revelation speaks into that context. The laws in the Bible do not seek to restructure society, but to affect how people live and think in the societal structure that they have. The laws do not seek to transform a patriarchal society into an egalitarian one. They do not seek to abolish slavery. They do not promote a democratic society over a monarchy. They do not endorse clan solidarity over individualism. The laws of the Bible seek to transform how people live in whatever sort of society they find themselves. No societal structure is flawless; it is always subject to the nature of the people who are part of it.

Consequently, when we look at the laws of the Bible, we are not looking for the picture of a perfect society nor should we think that God is endorsing such a society. We will find that the shape of Israelite society is often very much like those of her neighbors, but we should be attentive to the ways that the Bible goes further to protect the rights and dignity of those who might be vulnerable. In this way the Bible can pioneer new moral ground even while being situated in the familiar social structures of the ancient world. Primarily, however, it is instructing Israel about what is required for them to preserve the sanctity of sacred space. When legal passages are considered, we should identify both their similarities and differences to the ancient Near Eastern world. Doing so demonstrates that while the Biblical laws describe a society very much rooted in the ancient world, God calls his people to higher standards. The areas of commonality do not suggest that the Bible has borrowed from the legal literature of the ancient world; only that God addressed their society as it was, but sought to show them a pathway to holy living within that framework. ◆

shall labor and do all your work,[c]
10 but the seventh day is a sabbath to the LORD your God. On it
you shall not do any work, neither you, nor your son or daughter, nor your male or female servant, nor your animals, nor any
foreigner residing in your towns.
11 For in six days the LORD made
the heavens and the earth, the
sea, and all that is in them, but
he rested[d] on the seventh day.
Therefore the LORD blessed the
Sabbath day and made it holy.
12 "Honor your father and your mother,[e]
so that you may live long in the
land the LORD your God is giving
you.

20:9 [c] Ex 34:21; Lk 13:14
20:11 [d] Ge 2:2
20:12 [e] Mt 15:4*; Mk 7:10*; Eph 6:2

straight days of rain, but then it ceases on the seventh. The Ugaritic Baal Cycle describes a six-day cleansing by fire of Baal's palace, which ceases on the seventh. Each of these examples has religious significance. The Israelite practice, as a recognition of God's rest and therefore his control and rule of the ordered cosmos, has its closest functional parallel in the ancient Near Eastern New Year festivals commemorating and reenacting the enthronement of the deity. Israel's commemoration takes place weekly rather than annually.

While the law in Exodus also carries religious overtones, it includes a humanitarian component, allowing rest for everyone at all levels of society.

20:12 *Honor your father and your mother.* In the ancient world the only institution for the support of the elderly was the family. Most ancient readers would have understood this at the very least as an admonition to care for one's elderly parents, though other forms of honor would not be excluded. Minimally this would have included the supply of provisions for subsistence. Mesopotamian texts typically refer to rations for three items that ancient Near Eastern societies regarded as basic necessities: barley, wool and oil. Barley was most important. The idea of supporting one's aging parents accords well with the last half of v. 12. If a son, e.g., supports his parents as they grow older and thereby helps to extend their lifetimes, he can reasonably expect to receive similarly beneficent treatment in his twilight years.

Beyond those basics, the children would be expected

13 “You shall not murder.[f]
14 “You shall not commit adultery.[g]
15 “You shall not steal.[h]
16 “You shall not give false testimony
against your neighbor.[i]
17 “You shall not covet[j] your neighbor’s
house. You shall not covet your
neighbor’s wife, or his male or
female servant, his ox or donkey,
or anything that belongs to your
neighbor.”

18 When the people saw the thunder and
lightning and heard the trumpet[k] and saw
the mountain in smoke, they trembled
with fear. They stayed at a distance 19 and
said to Moses, “Speak to us yourself and
we will listen. But do not have God speak
to us or we will die.”[l]
20 Moses said to the people, “Do not be
afraid. God has come to test you, so that
the fear[m] of God will be with you to keep
you from sinning.”[n]
21 The people remained at a distance,
while Moses approached the thick darkness[o] where God was.

20:13 [f] Mt 5:21*; Ro 13:9* **20:14** [g] Mt 19:18* **20:15** [h] Lev 19:11, 13; Mt 19:18* **20:16** [i] Ex 23:1, 7; Mt 19:18* **20:17** [j] Ro 7:7*; 13:9*; Eph 5:3 **20:18** [k] Ex 19:16-19; Heb 12:18-19 **20:19** [l] Dt 5:5, 23-27; Gal 3:19 **20:20** [m] Dt 4:10; Isa 8:13 [n] Pr 16:6 **20:21** [o] Dt 5:22

---

to carry on the family and clan traditions, including the worship and maintenance of the family gods. The gods would subsequently continue to bring prosperity to the family. For the Israelites honoring their parents in this way meant maintaining loyalty to the covenant that would result in their continued possession of the land.

20:13 *murder.* The term used takes a person as both its subject and object and specifically refers to homicide, meaning this verse cannot easily be brought into discussions of pacifism, capital punishment or vegetarianism. Explicit prohibitions of homicide occur in a number of other ancient Near Eastern legal texts, and they often distinguish between intentional and unintentional homicide. This verse does not make explicit any such distinction, though other Biblical texts do (Nu 35:16–28; Dt 19:4–7). If this verse should be read in light of that distinction, then the command refers only to intentional homicide.

But even within the category of intentional homicide, a distinction can be made between intentional killing deemed lawful and that which is deemed unlawful. According to both Biblical and other ancient Near Eastern law codes, the former includes acts of self-defense (22:2), killing in war (Dt 20:13) and the execution of certain lawbreakers (kidnappers in Ex 21:16; murderers in Nu 35:20–21; adulterers in Dt 22:22). Most instances of unlawful killing mentioned in law codes and trial records involve the intentional murder of one’s fellow citizen when there is no legal justification for the death.

20:14 *adultery.* Biblical texts (e.g., Lev 20:10; Dt 22:22) reveal that the death penalty could be imposed on those found guilty of committing adultery. In the ancient Near East, adultery was considered an act of sexual relations between a married woman and any man not her husband. Married men could have sex with single women and either not be subject to any penalty (in the case of prostitutes or their own female slaves) or be subject to a penalty much less severe than those for adultery (Dt 22:28–29).

There seem to be at least two reasons for an ancient society’s desire to control sexual behavior. First, certain sexual acts brought about a change in legal status. It was often the act of sexual consummation that established a couple as fully married. Sleeping with the wives and concubines of a deceased monarch demonstrated that the successor had made the transition from heir apparent to king. Such changes in status had to be regulated. Second, a man needed to know that the offspring of his wife were indeed his own children. He particularly needed to know who his sons were, because they would be his legitimate heirs. It is this concern that is the most likely motivating force behind rules concerning adultery in the ancient Near East.

Ancient societies viewed acts of adultery as wrongs against the husband of the woman involved. This meant that the husband had the right to determine the penalty for his adulterous wife and her lover. He could not, however, pardon his wife and punish her lover. The same seems to have been true in ancient Israel. The husband had the right to determine the penalty, and he was free to choose a penalty other than death. For instance, Jer 3:8 indicates that divorce was one of the lesser penalties a husband could impose on his adulterous wife. The Babylonians, Assyrians and Hittites permitted the husband to exact punishment or to give clemency to his wife. Pardon for the wife meant pardon for the man as well.

This sin, sometimes referred to as the “great sin,” angered the gods. Adultery was an “abomination” to Marduk in Babylon and considered a breach of trust, abandonment and a failure of reciprocation. In Hittite law the husband could kill his wife and paramour (if caught in the act) and go free. In Assyrian law the husband could effect castration, disfigurement or death on the guilty parties.

20:15 *steal.* This prohibition was directed against a wide variety of thefts in the ancient Near East, including kidnapping (cf. Ge 37:22–28; Dt 22:1–4; 24:7). Common “stealing” of property or robbery is in view also and includes theft from sanctuary, state, an ordinary citizen or a business. In the Code of Hammurapi, death is most often prescribed. This could be avoided in some cases if the thief had the means to do so. In other cases a fine was permitted.

The Middle Assyrian Laws (c. 1100–400 BC) on theft call for a variety of punishments depending on the parties involved. Punishments included death, waiver of punishment or horrible disfigurements. Hittite laws treat a variety of thefts of animals and related actions. Ordinary theft called for restitution, as did most other types of theft.

20:16 *false testimony.* Some have interpreted this verse as a prohibition on lying in general. This is not the case. The Hebrew terms used here have forensic connotations; i.e., they relate to the proceedings of a trial court. Furthermore, the language here points to a particular type of false statement: false accusation. This prohibition is about wrongful prosecution, specifically coming before a court to initiate a trial and wrongfully accuse another person.

Provisions in the Code of Hammurapi also deal with false testimony. Two of these address false accusation (the same issue as here). Two others address false statements given by third-party witnesses—those who are neither the accuser nor the defendant in the trial. These provisions set forth a particular type of punishment for both types of wrongdoing. They say that the false accuser/witness should be punished with the same punishment that the defendant in the trial would have received if the court had found him guilty. Other Biblical texts (22:7–9; Dt 19:16–21) call for this same type of punishment for those who falsely accuse another person. There are no Biblical texts, however, that explicitly require this punishment for nonparty witnesses.

20:17 *covet.* This commandment prohibits an internal

Idols and Altars

22Then the LORD said to Moses, "Tell the
Israelites this: 'You have seen for yourselves that I have spoken to you from
heaven:[p] 23Do not make any gods to be
alongside me;[q] do not make for yourselves
gods of silver or gods of gold.[r]
24" 'Make an altar of earth for me and
sacrifice on it your burnt offerings and fellowship offerings, your sheep and goats
and your cattle. Wherever I cause my
name[s] to be honored, I will come to you
and bless[t] you. 25If you make an altar of
stones for me, do not build it with dressed
stones, for you will defile it if you use a
tool[u] on it. 26And do not go up to my altar on steps, or your private parts may be
exposed.'

21 "These are the laws[v] you are to set
before them:

Hebrew Servants

21:2-6pp — Dt 15:12-18
21:2-11Ref — Lev 25:39-55

2"If you buy a Hebrew servant, he is to
serve you for six years. But in the seventh
year, he shall go free,[w] without paying
anything. 3If he comes alone, he is to go
free alone; but if he has a wife when he
comes, she is to go with him. 4If his master gives him a wife and she bears him
sons or daughters, the woman and her
children shall belong to her master, and
only the man shall go free.
5"But if the servant declares, 'I love
my master and my wife and children and
do not want to go free,'[x] 6then his master must take him before the judges.[a][y] He
shall take him to the door or the doorpost
and pierce his ear with an awl. Then he
will be his servant for life.[z]
7"If a man sells his daughter as a servant, she is not to go free as male servants
do. 8If she does not please the master who
has selected her for himself,[b] he must let
her be redeemed. He has no right to sell
her to foreigners, because he has broken faith with her. 9If he selects her for
his son, he must grant her the rights of
a daughter. 10If he marries another woman, he must not deprive the first one of
her food, clothing and marital rights.[a] 11If
he does not provide her with these three
things, she is to go free, without any payment of money.

Personal Injuries

12"Anyone who strikes a person with a
fatal blow is to be put to death.[b] 13Howev-
er, if it is not done intentionally, but God
lets it happen, they are to flee to a place[c]

20:22 [p]Ne 9:13
20:23 [q]ver 3 [r]Ex 32:4, 8, 31
20:24 [s]Dt 12:5; 16:6, 11; 2Ch 6:6 [t]Ge 12:2
20:25 [u]Dt 27:5-6
21:1 [v]Dt 4:14
21:2 [w]Jer 34:8, 14
21:5 [x]Dt 15:16
21:6 [y]Ex 22:8-9 [z]Ne 5:5
21:10 [a]1Co 7:3-5
21:12 [b]Ge 9:6; Mt 26:52
21:13 [c]Nu 35:10-34; Dt 19:2-13; Jos 20:9; 1Sa 24:4, 10, 18

[a] 6 Or *before God* [b] 8 Or *master so that he does not choose her*

---

motivation or condition that desires (*hmd*, stimulated by vision) what a person is prohibited from having, the wife of another man. A different word is used (*wh*, inner need) to prohibit taking of things. The verb *hmd* in this context has the connotation of "to appropriate" as well. The phrase "covet this city" occurs in a Phoenician text.

The phrase "his land [field]" is coupled with house and is used in legal documents in the ancient Near East, especially at Ugarit. In an Egyptian document recording the negative confessions of a deceased person, the deceased denies that he had been covetous. The fabled wise Egyptian Ptahhotep denounced covetousness as a deadly vice. In the Ramesside era the covetous person was considered a fool and covetousness a sin. Neither a poor man's possessions nor a nobleman's wealth were to be coveted.

The Eloquent Peasant of Egypt expected a leader to be free from covetousness, and a covetous person would not enjoy success. One's own house should fill all of one's needs. The inwardness of these admonitions is paramount, for the heart was regarded as "the god who dwells in man." This central concept seems to be absent from Mesopotamian law; there is an emphasis on the act of appropriation, which was condemned. In ancient wisdom literature, "coveting murders" is an abomination to the gods Ninurta and Enlil.

21:2 *a Hebrew servant ... is to serve you for six years.* See note on Lev 25:39.

21:4 *only the man shall go free.* When a free man gave a wife to another man who owed him something, certain conditions applied to that marriage. The man in the inferior position was often a pledge (one who worked as a servant, not a slave, and whose services functioned as security or collateral for a debt that was owed) or a debt-slave, as here in Exodus. Typically, the pledge or debt-slave could take his wife—and any children she had borne him—only by satisfying particular requirements.

The record of a contract from the city of Emar (probably thirteenth century BC) presents an example of such a situation. The pledge in this case may take his wife and children with him when he leaves the service of his creditor, but only if he abides by the basic agreement set forth in the contract. When this document addresses the possibility that the pledge might renege on his commitment to abide by the contract, then the pledge "will have no claim to his wife and children." This law in Exodus may be establishing what was standard procedure in these types of situations; modifications were probably allowed if clearly established in a contractual agreement.

21:8 *let her be redeemed.* It was standard procedure to allow debt-slaves to be redeemed (see v. 2; 13:15). But in this case, the daughter has been sold into debt-slavery with the understanding that she will become the concubine of her master (the creditor). If the master does makes her his concubine, redemption appears to be disallowed. Why is it resurrected if she displeases him and he decides not to make her his concubine? The Code of Hammurapi (sections 146–147) indicates that a slave concubine who bore children had certain protections that ordinary slaves (even debt-slaves) did not. If the daughter does not become the master's concubine, she loses the chance to gain these extra protections, and thus the right of redemption is revived.

21:12 *put to death.* See note on Lev 24:17.

I will designate. 14But if anyone schemes and kills someone deliberately,[d] that person is to be taken from my altar and put to death.[e]

15"Anyone who attacks[a] their father or mother is to be put to death.

16"Anyone who kidnaps someone is to be put to death,[f] whether the victim has been sold[g] or is still in the kidnapper's possession.

17"Anyone who curses their father or mother is to be put to death.[h]

18"If people quarrel and one person hits another with a stone or with their fist[b] and the victim does not die but is confined to bed, 19the one who struck the blow will not be held liable if the other can get up and walk around outside with a staff; however, the guilty party must pay the injured person for any loss of time and see that the victim is completely healed.

20"Anyone who beats their male or female slave with a rod must be punished if the slave dies as a direct result, 21but they are not to be punished if the slave recovers after a day or two, since the slave is their property.[i]

22"If people are fighting and hit a pregnant woman and she gives birth prematurely[c] but there is no serious injury, the offender must be fined whatever the woman's husband demands[j] and the court allows. 23But if there is serious injury, you are to take life for life,[k] 24eye for eye, tooth for tooth,[l] hand for hand, foot for foot, 25burn for burn, wound for wound, bruise for bruise.

26"An owner who hits a male or female slave in the eye and destroys it must let the slave go free to compensate for the eye. 27And an owner who knocks out the tooth of a male or female slave must let the slave go free to compensate for the tooth.

28"If a bull gores a man or woman to death, the bull is to be stoned to death,[m] and its meat must not be eaten. But the owner of the bull will not be held responsible. 29If, however, the bull has had the habit of goring and the owner has been warned but has not kept it penned up and it kills a man or woman, the bull is to be stoned and its owner also is to be put to death. 30However, if payment is demanded, the owner may redeem his life by the payment of whatever is demanded.[n] 31This law also applies if the bull gores a son or daughter. 32If the bull gores a male or female slave, the owner must pay thirty shekels[d][o] of silver to the master of the slave, and the bull is to be stoned to death.

33"If anyone uncovers a pit or digs one and fails to cover it and an ox or a donkey falls into it, 34the one who opened the pit must pay the owner for the loss and take the dead animal in exchange.

35"If anyone's bull injures someone else's bull and it dies, the two parties

21:14 [d] Heb 10:26 [e] Dt 19:11-12; 1Ki 2:28-34 **21:16** [f] Ex 22:4; Dt 24:7 [g] Ge 37:28 **21:17** [h] Lev 20:9-10; Mt 15:4*; Mk 7:10* **21:21** [i] Lev 25:44-46 **21:22** [j] ver 30; Dt 22:18-19 **21:23** [k] Lev 24:19; Dt 19:21 **21:24** [l] Mt 5:38* **21:28** [m] ver 32; Ge 9:5 **21:30** [n] ver 22; Nu 35:31 **21:32** [o] Zec 11:12-13; Mt 26:15; 27:3,9

[a] 15 Or *kills* [b] 18 Or *with a tool* [c] 22 Or *she has a miscarriage* [d] 32 That is, about 12 ounces or about 345 grams

21:18 *If people quarrel.* One of Hammurapi's laws states that the one who struck the blow must pay the physician, who, presumably, was summoned to help care for the one injured. This may be what is meant by "and see that the victim is completely healed" in v. 19.

21:20 *beats their male or female slave with a rod.* One of Hammurapi's laws stipulates a punishment for a man who beats to death a distrainee (someone forcibly detained by the creditor in order to coerce the debtor to pay) in his possession. The creditor could treat the distrainee poorly but could not kill or sell the person. If the distrainee dies because of a beating by the creditor, the punishment is as follows: If the distrainee was the debtor's son, then the creditor's son is to be killed; if the distrainee was a slave, then the creditor must pay 20 shekels of silver; in either case, the debt is canceled. If this law in Exodus has in view a debt-slave, then a similar punishment may be intended here.

21:22 There are two possible understandings of this verse, both having to do with who sustains serious injury—the fetus or the mother. Ancient Near Eastern parallels to this law suggest the mother is in view. Four other law codes address the issue of a man's striking a pregnant woman and causing her to miscarry. All stipulate monetary penalties that the assailant must pay in order to compensate the family for the loss of the child. Three of these codes go on to consider what to do if the woman is killed by the blow. In two, the man who struck the blow is to be killed. In another, the daughter of the man is killed, since the law assumes that he struck the pregnant daughter of another man. Only once is the death of the fetus linked to a death penalty: If the husband of the victimized woman has no sons and the fetus is male, the perpetrator is to be killed. In light of the provisions in these other codes, it seems likely that this law in Exodus follows their general pattern. The law calls for a fine in this verse, probably as compensation for the fetus. It then addresses possible "serious injury" to the woman. If she dies, the perpetrator dies—"life for life" (v. 23). Otherwise, the perpetrator will suffer a punishment similar to that inflicted on the woman (vv. 24–25).

21:24 *eye for eye.* See note on Lev 24:20.

21:31 *a son or daughter.* An important principle of most ancient Near Eastern legal systems was that of vicarious punishment. For instance, if a man (a free citizen who was the head of his household) were to kill the son of another man (another free citizen and head of household), the man himself—the actual murderer—would not be subject to the death penalty. Rather, it is his son who could be put to death (see, e.g., the Code of Hammurapi, sections 229–230). Because it was the son within the other household who was the victim, it is the one with the same status or rank in the first household who receives the punishment vicariously—as a substitute for the real perpetrator. This reflects a society in which clan identity is more important than individual identity. Scholars disagree as to whether this law in Exodus rejects or accepts the principle of vicarious punishment. The wording in Exodus provides too little clarity to decide. Other Biblical texts, however, do indeed appear to reject the principle (Dt 24:16; Eze 18).

are to sell the live one and divide both
the money and the dead animal equally.
36However, if it was known that the bull
had the habit of goring, yet the owner did
not keep it penned up, the owner must
pay, animal for animal, and take the dead
animal in exchange.

Protection of Property

22[a] "Whoever steals an ox or a sheep
and slaughters it or sells it must
pay back[p] five head of cattle for the ox and
four sheep for the sheep.
2"If a thief is caught breaking in[q] at
night and is struck a fatal blow, the defender is not guilty of bloodshed;[r] 3but if
it happens after sunrise, the defender is
guilty of bloodshed.
"Anyone who steals must certainly
make restitution, but if they have nothing,
they must be sold[s] to pay for their theft.
4If the stolen animal is found alive in their
possession—whether ox or donkey or
sheep—they must pay back double.[t]
5"If anyone grazes their livestock in a
field or vineyard and lets them stray and
they graze in someone else's field, the offender must make restitution from the best
of their own field or vineyard.
6"If a fire breaks out and spreads into
thornbushes so that it burns shocks of
grain or standing grain or the whole field,
the one who started the fire must make
restitution.
7"If anyone gives a neighbor silver or
goods for safekeeping and they are stolen
from the neighbor's house, the thief, if
caught, must pay back double.[u] 8But if the
thief is not found, the owner of the house
must appear before the judges,[v] and they
must[b] determine whether the owner of the
house has laid hands on the other person's
property. 9In all cases of illegal possession
of an ox, a donkey, a sheep, a garment, or
any other lost property about which somebody says, 'This is mine,' both parties are
to bring their cases before the judges.[c][w]
The one whom the judges declare[d] guilty
must pay back double to the other.
10"If anyone gives a donkey, an ox, a
sheep or any other animal to their neighbor for safekeeping and it dies or is injured
or is taken away while no one is looking,
11the issue between them will be settled
by the taking of an oath[x] before the LORD
that the neighbor did not lay hands on the
other person's property. The owner is to
accept this, and no restitution is required.
12But if the animal was stolen from the
neighbor, restitution must be made to the
owner. 13If it was torn to pieces by a wild
animal, the neighbor shall bring in the
remains as evidence and shall not be required to pay for the torn animal.[y]
14"If anyone borrows an animal from
their neighbor and it is injured or dies
while the owner is not present, they must
make restitution. 15But if the owner is with
the animal, the borrower will not have to
pay. If the animal was hired, the money
paid for the hire covers the loss.

22:1 [p] 2Sa 12:6; Pr 6:31; Lk 19:8 **22:2** [q] Mt 6:19-20; 24:43 [r] Nu 35:27 **22:3** [s] Ex 21:2; Mt 18:25 **22:4** [t] Ge 43:12 **22:7** [u] ver 4 **22:8** [v] Ex 21:6; Dt 17:8-9; 19:17 **22:9** [w] ver 28; Dt 25:1 **22:11** [x] Heb 6:16 **22:13** [y] Ge 31:39

[a] In Hebrew texts 22:1 is numbered 21:37, and 22:2-31 is numbered 22:1-30. [b] 8 Or *before God, and he will* [c] 9 Or *before God* [d] 9 Or *whom God declares*

22:3 *after sunrise.* The same type of legal logic shows up in the Laws of Eshnunna, 12–13, where a thief caught in another's field or house at night can lawfully be killed by the latter.
22:7 *silver or goods for safekeeping.* See note on Lev 6:2.
22:9 *pay back double.* This verse establishes the general principle on which the situation in the previous verse is based. Whenever there is disagreement between the depositor and the receiver about goods that may or may not have been deposited, the case is to be decided by a judicial oracle (see the article "Divine Verdict," p. 152). If the receiver is declared guilty, he has most likely committed wrongdoing by appropriating the deposited goods for himself, and perhaps he has denied that the depositor ever gave him anything. But if the depositor is declared guilty, it means either he never deposited any goods in the first place and now claims that certain goods, which actually belong to the receiver, are his, or he has asked to be returned to him more goods than he originally deposited and is accusing the receiver of cheating him.

Interestingly, the penalty for the depositor in Exodus matches that of the receiver, if the latter should be found guilty. The reason is that if the depositor (or would-be depositor) is guilty, what he is guilty of is false accusation. He has brought against the receiver criminal charges, which the judicial oracle has clearly refuted. In much of ancient Near Eastern law and in a later Biblical text (Dt 19:16–21), false accusers are to be punished with the same penalty that the defendant in the trial would have received if the accusation had turned out to be true; hence, the matching penalty.
22:11 *an oath before the LORD.* Rather than a receiver of a deposit in general, the issue here is a receiver who has been given an animal for safekeeping—i.e., a person has been hired to perform the duties of a shepherd or herdsman. This law establishes the limits on the shepherd's liability for the loss of or any injury to the animal. Verse 12 states that theft of the animal requires the shepherd to compensate the owner for the latter's loss. Verse 13 releases the shepherd from any liability if an animal predator attacks and kills the animal in his keeping.

In other situations—death, injury, loss (with, presumably, no conclusive evidence of theft)—the shepherd is allowed to take an "oath before the LORD." This is the suprarational procedure known as the judicial oath (see the article "Divine Verdict," p. 152). The shepherd swears, invoking the name of Yahweh, that he is not the cause of the death, injury or loss. In short, he swears to his innocence. Taking the oath is decisive here: "The owner is to accept this." Numerous Mesopotamian trial records refer to this type of oath and make clear that the one who takes the court-ordered judicial oath is guaranteed to win the case.

EXODUS 22:8 – 11

Divine Verdict

The phrase "appear before the judges" in Ex 22:8 can also be translated "appear before God." The word translated as "judges/God" is *Elohim,* a common designation for God. While "judges" might be a possible translation in Ex 22:8, the most natural reading is to understand it as referring to God. When the text indicates that the receiver of the goods (the "owner of the house" [22:8]) is to appear before God, it has in view a particular method for resolving the dispute at hand, namely, what scholars call suprarational procedures. These are procedures that go beyond the pale of rational evidence, such as testimony, physical evidence or documentary evidence, by appealing directly to divinity to settle the matter.

There are three basic categories of suprarational methods used for resolving legal disputes: the judicial oath, the judicial ordeal and the judicial oracle. Only one party to a trial could take the *judicial oath.* If that party did so, the court granted that party victory in the case and felt confident that divine power would punish the oath-taker, if the latter had sworn falsely, with greater severity than any legal penalty might (see note on 20:7).

The most common version of the *judicial ordeal* was the river ordeal, popular in Mesopotamia. In such cases, Mesopotamian courts allowed the river god to render the verdict. If the party undergoing the ordeal sank, the person was guilty; if not, the person was innocent.

What appears most common in ancient Egypt and Israel was the *judicial oracle.* Here too the case is offered directly to the deity for a verdict, but not by means of an ordeal. Thus, this law regarding deposit in Ex 22:8 is calling for a judicial oracle to decide the case (see note on 18:22). Ex 22:8 says that God will decide whether one person "has laid his hands on the other person's property." According to Ex 22:9, the one whom God finds guilty must pay damages ("pay back double"). ◆

Social Responsibility

16 "If a man seduces a virgin[z] who is not
pledged to be married and sleeps with her,
he must pay the bride-price, and she shall
be his wife. 17 If her father absolutely refuses to give her to him, he must still pay the
bride-price for virgins.
18 "Do not allow a sorceress[a] to live.
19 "Anyone who has sexual relations
with an animal[b] is to be put to death.
20 "Whoever sacrifices to any god other
than the LORD must be destroyed.[a][c]

21 "Do not mistreat or oppress a foreigner,[d] for you were foreigners[e] in Egypt.
22 "Do not take advantage of the widow
or the fatherless.[f] 23 If you do and they cry
out[g] to me, I will certainly hear their cry.[h]
24 My anger will be aroused, and I will kill
you with the sword; your wives will become widows and your children fatherless.[i]

22:16 [z]Dt 22:28 **22:18** [a]Lev 20:27; Dt 18:11; 1Sa 28:3 **22:19** [b]Lev 18:23; Dt 27:21 **22:20** [c]Dt 17:2-5 **22:21** [d]Lev 19:33 [e]Dt 10:19 **22:22** [f]Dt 24:6, 10, 12, 17

[a] *20* The Hebrew term refers to the irrevocable giving over of things or persons to the LORD, often by totally destroying them.

22:23 [g]Lk 18:7 [h]Dt 15:9; Ps 18:6 **22:24** [i]Ps 69:24; 109:9

22:16 *seduces a virgin.* Here the term "seduces" implies that the woman has given her consent. Another important element in this law is the status of the woman. She is not married and is "not pledged to be married." If she were married or pledged to be married, then for a man—other than the one to whom she is pledged—to have sex with her constitutes adultery. Thus, what is mentioned here is what we call premarital sex. The law here does not forbid premarital sex but attempts to regulate it. *he must pay the bride-price.* Part of the reason for the payment of a monetary fine is to compensate the father for losing his opportunity to obtain a full bride-price for his virgin daughter. But now that the man has paid a bride-price (and a rather high one), the father may, if he chooses, allow his daughter to marry him. He can also refuse for this to happen. Even if he refuses, though, he still receives the payment from the man, since he may not be able to marry his daughter off in the future.
22:22 *widow or the fatherless.* See note on Dt 10:18.

25 “If you lend money to one of my people among you who is needy, do not treat it like a business deal; charge no interest.[j] 26 If you take your neighbor’s cloak as a pledge,[k] return it by sunset, 27 because that cloak is the only covering your neighbor has. What else can they sleep in? When they cry out to me, I will hear, for I am compassionate.[l]

28 “Do not blaspheme God[a][m] or curse the ruler of your people.[n]

29 “Do not hold back offerings[o] from your granaries or your vats.[b]

“You must give me the firstborn of your sons.[p] 30 Do the same with your cattle and your sheep.[q] Let them stay with their mothers for seven days, but give them to me on the eighth day.[r]

31 “You are to be my holy people.[s] So do not eat the meat of an animal torn by wild beasts;[t] throw it to the dogs.

Laws of Justice and Mercy

23 “Do not spread false reports.[u] Do not help a guilty person by being a malicious witness.[v]

2 “Do not follow the crowd in doing wrong. When you give testimony in a lawsuit, do not pervert justice[w] by siding with the crowd, 3 and do not show favoritism to a poor person in a lawsuit.

4 “If you come across your enemy’s ox or donkey wandering off, be sure to return it.[x] 5 If you see the donkey[y] of someone who hates you fallen down under its load, do not leave it there; be sure you help them with it.

6 “Do not deny justice[z] to your poor people in their lawsuits. 7 Have nothing to do with a false charge[a] and do not put an innocent or honest person to death, for I will not acquit the guilty.

8 “Do not accept a bribe,[b] for a bribe blinds those who see and twists the words of the innocent.

9 “Do not oppress a foreigner;[c] you yourselves know how it feels to be foreigners, because you were foreigners in Egypt.

Sabbath Laws

10 “For six years you are to sow your fields and harvest the crops, 11 but during the seventh year let the land lie unplowed and unused. Then the poor among your people may get food from it, and the wild animals may eat what is left. Do the same with your vineyard and your olive grove.

12 “Six days do your work,[d] but on the seventh day do not work, so that your ox and your donkey may rest, and so that the slave born in your household and the foreigner living among you may be refreshed.

13 “Be careful[e] to do everything I have said to you. Do not invoke the names of other gods; do not let them be heard on your lips.

The Three Annual Festivals

14 “Three times[f] a year you are to celebrate a festival to me.

15 “Celebrate the Festival of Unleavened Bread;[g] for seven days eat bread made without yeast, as I commanded you. Do this at the appointed time in the month of Aviv, for in that month you came out of Egypt.

“No one is to appear before me empty-handed.[h]

16 “Celebrate the Festival of Harvest with the firstfruits[i] of the crops you sow in your field.

“Celebrate the Festival of Ingathering at the end of the year, when you gather in your crops from the field.[j]

17 “Three times[k] a year all the men are to appear before the Sovereign LORD.

18 “Do not offer the blood of a sacrifice to me along with anything containing yeast.[l]

22:25 [j] Lev 25:35-37; Dt 23:20; Ps 15:5 **22:26** [k] Dt 24:6 **22:27** [l] Ex 34:6 **22:28** [m] Lev 24:11, 16 [n] Ecc 10:20; Ac 23:5* **22:29** [o] Ex 23:15, 16, 19 [p] Ex 13:2 **22:30** [q] Ex 13:12; Dt 15:19 [r] Lev 22:27 **22:31** [s] Lev 19:2 [t] Eze 4:14 **23:1** [u] Ex 20:16; Ps 101:5 [v] Ps 35:11; Ac 6:11 **23:2** [w] Dt 16:19 **23:4** [x] Dt 22:1-3 **23:5** [y] Dt 22:4 **23:6** [z] ver 2 **23:7** [a] Eph 4:25 **23:8** [b] Dt 10:17; 16:19; Pr 15:27 **23:9** [c] Ex 22:21 **23:12** [d] Ex 20:9 **23:13** [e] 1Ti 4:16 **23:14** [f] Ex 34:23, 24 **23:15** [g] Ex 12:17 [h] Ex 34:20 **23:16** [i] Ex 34:22 [j] Dt 16:13 **23:17** [k] Dt 16:16 **23:18** [l] Ex 34:25

[a] 28 Or *Do not revile the judges* [b] 29 The meaning of the Hebrew for this phrase is uncertain.

23:3 *do not show favoritism.* This statement is reminiscent of sayings that come from ancient Near Eastern wisdom literature. In addition to the laws that are part of the Sinai covenant, Exodus includes these statements that, at first glance, appear to be more at home in Proverbs. What this wisdom material can do, however, is to help clarify the nature of the entire block of stipulations in Ex 21 – 23. While the Biblical text certainly seems to make the rules in these chapters obligatory for the Israelites, it also points toward a particular interest in the spirit, as well as the letter, of the law.

Wisdom literature is typically interested in general guidelines that individuals should bear in mind and apply as they make daily decisions that affect the direction of their lives. The legal material in Exodus also points beyond itself to principles of living and decision making that are about more than simply ensuring that a rule has not been violated. They are about a commitment to living as part of a community that has a special relationship with Yahweh and that pursues a lifestyle in keeping with that relationship.

23:14 – 16 The three festivals mentioned here are to be held at set times during the Israelite year. These are, presumably, the same three times per year when “all the men are to appear before the Sovereign LORD” (v. 17). The times designated for the festivals are tied to agricultural activities and especially to harvest times. Each festival, while having its own particular religious focus, also celebrates the material provision of Yahweh for the Israelites.

23:15 *Festival of Unleavened Bread.* Celebrated in the spring at the time of the barley harvest. It is referred to as a seven-day festival here in Exodus. Evidence for regularized, seven-day festivals from other ancient Near Eastern societies is meager, but texts from the Late Bronze Age site of Emar in Syria do attest to such festivals.

23:16 *Festival of Harvest.* Also called the “Festival of Weeks”; occurs in the late spring or early summer, which coincides with the wheat harvest. *Festival of Ingathering.* Also called the “Festival of Tabernacles” or “Booths”; comes when summer fruit is harvested.

"The fat of my festival offerings must
not be kept until morning.[m]
19 "Bring the best of the firstfruits[n] of
your soil to the house of the LORD your
God.
"Do not cook a young goat in its mother's milk.[o]

God's Angel to Prepare the Way

20 "See, I am sending an angel[p] ahead
of you to guard you along the way and to
bring you to the place I have prepared.[q]
21 Pay attention to him and listen[r] to what
he says. Do not rebel against him; he will
not forgive your rebellion,[s] since my Name
is in him. 22 If you listen carefully to what
he says and do all that I say, I will be an
enemy[t] to your enemies and will oppose
those who oppose you. 23 My angel will go
ahead of you and bring you into the land
of the Amorites, Hittites, Perizzites, Canaanites, Hivites and Jebusites,[u] and I will
wipe them out. 24 Do not bow down before
their gods or worship[v] them or follow their
practices.[w] You must demolish[x] them and
break their sacred stones to pieces. 25 Worship the LORD your God,[y] and his blessing[z]
will be on your food and water. I will take
away sickness[a] from among you, 26 and
none will miscarry or be barren[b] in your
land. I will give you a full life span.[c]
27 "I will send my terror[d] ahead of you
and throw into confusion[e] every nation
you encounter. I will make all your enemies turn their backs and run. 28 I will
send the hornet[f] ahead of you to drive
the Hivites, Canaanites and Hittites out of
your way. 29 But I will not drive them out
in a single year, because the land would
become desolate and the wild animals[g]
too numerous for you. 30 Little by little I
will drive them out before you, until you
have increased enough to take possession
of the land.
31 "I will establish your borders from the
Red Sea[a] to the Mediterranean Sea,[b] and
from the desert to the Euphrates River.[h] I
will give into your hands the people who
live in the land, and you will drive them
out[i] before you. 32 Do not make a covenant[j]
with them or with their gods. 33 Do not let
them live in your land or they will cause
you to sin against me, because the worship of their gods will certainly be a snare[k]
to you."

The Covenant Confirmed

24 Then the LORD said to Moses,
"Come up to the LORD, you and
Aaron, Nadab and Abihu,[l] and seventy
of the elders[m] of Israel. You are to worship at a distance, 2 but Moses alone is to
approach the LORD; the others must not
come near. And the people may not come
up with him."
3 When Moses went and told the people all the LORD's words and laws, they
responded with one voice, "Everything
the LORD has said we will do."[n] 4 Moses
then wrote[o] down everything the LORD had
said.
He got up early the next morning and
built an altar at the foot of the mountain
and set up twelve stone pillars[p] representing the twelve tribes of Israel. 5 Then he
sent young Israelite men, and they offered
burnt offerings and sacrificed young bulls
as fellowship offerings to the LORD. 6 Moses
took half of the blood[q] and put it in bowls,
and the other half he splashed against the
altar. 7 Then he took the Book of the Covenant[r] and read it to the people. They responded, "We will do everything the LORD
has said; we will obey."
8 Moses then took the blood, sprinkled it
on the people and said, "This is the blood
of the covenant[s] that the LORD has made
with you in accordance with all these
words."
9 Moses and Aaron, Nadab and Abihu,
and the seventy elders[t] of Israel went up
10 and saw[u] the God of Israel. Under his
feet was something like a pavement made
of lapis lazuli,[v] as bright blue as the sky.[w]
11 But God did not raise his hand against
these leaders of the Israelites; they saw[x]
God, and they ate and drank.
12 The LORD said to Moses, "Come up to
me on the mountain and stay here, and I
will give you the tablets of stone[y] with the
law and commandments I have written for
their instruction."
13 Then Moses set out with Joshua[z] his
aide, and Moses went up on the moun-

[a] 31 Or *the Sea of Reeds* [b] 31 Hebrew *to the Sea of the Philistines*

23:18 [m] Dt 16:4 **23:19** [n] Ex 22:29; Dt 26:2, 10 [o] Dt 14:21 **23:20** [p] Ex 14:19; 32:34 [q] Ex 15:17 **23:21** [r] Nu 14:11; Dt 18:19 [s] Ps 78:8, 40, 56 **23:22** [t] Ge 12:3; Dt 30:7 **23:23** [u] ver 20; Jos 24:8, 11 **23:24** [v] Ex 20:5 [w] Dt 12:30-31 [x] Ex 34:13; Nu 33:52 **23:25** [y] Dt 6:13; Mt 4:10 [z] Dt 7:12-15; 28:1-14 [a] Ex 15:26 **23:26** [b] Dt 7:14; Mal 3:11 [c] Job 5:26 **23:27** [d] Ex 15:14; Dt 2:25 [e] Dt 7:23 **23:28** [f] Dt 7:20; Jos 24:12 **23:29** [g] Dt 7:22 **23:31** [h] Ge 15:18 [i] Jos 21:44; 24:12, 18 **23:32** [j] Ex 34:12; Dt 7:2

23:33 [k] Dt 7:16; Ps 106:36 **24:1** [l] Ex 6:23; Lev 10:1-2 [m] Nu 11:16 **24:3** [n] Ex 19:8; Dt 5:27 **24:4** [o] Dt 31:9 [p] Ge 28:18 **24:6** [q] Heb 9:18 **24:7** [r] Heb 9:19 **24:8** [s] Heb 9:20*; 1Pe 1:2 **24:9** [t] ver 1 **24:10** [u] Mt 17:2; Jn 1:18; 6:46 [v] Eze 1:26 [w] Rev 4:3 **24:11** [x] Ge 32:30; Ex 19:21 **24:12** [y] Ex 32:15-16 **24:13** [z] Ex 17:9

23:19 *mother's milk.* See note on Dt 14:21.
23:28 *hornet.* This may be a form of divine terror like the plagues in Egypt. Assyrian and Egyptian sources portray deity as a winged disc flying ahead of the army to terrorize the enemy before engagement. The Hebrew word *tsirah* ("hornet") may also be a pun on the word *mitsrayim* ("Egypt") in reference to the Egyptian military campaigns weakening the Canaanite forces in the area at this time.
24:8 *took the blood, sprinkled it on the people.* While the purpose of this sprinkling is not entirely clear, we can infer some aspects of its significance. The blood may have created a connection between the people and the sacrificed animals. In a sense, the people are now part of what has been offered to Yahweh. The blood also seems to make binding the people's commitment to abide by the obligations that the agreement places on them. Their submitting to the sprinkling may be compared to signing a contract today.

tain[a] of God. 14He said to the elders, "Wait
here for us until we come back to you.
Aaron and Hur are with you, and anyone
involved in a dispute can go to them."
15When Moses went up on the moun-
tain, the cloud[b] covered it, 16and the glory[c]
of the LORD settled on Mount Sinai. For
six days the cloud covered the mountain,
and on the seventh day the LORD called
to Moses from within the cloud.[d] 17To the
Israelites the glory of the LORD looked like
a consuming fire[e] on top of the mountain.
18Then Moses entered the cloud as he went
on up the mountain. And he stayed on the
mountain forty[f] days and forty nights.[g]

Offerings for the Tabernacle

25:1-7pp — Ex 35:4-9

25 The LORD said to Moses, 2"Tell the
Israelites to bring me an offering.
You are to receive the offering for me from
everyone whose heart prompts[h] them to
give. 3These are the offerings you are to receive from them: gold, silver and bronze;
4blue, purple and scarlet yarn and fine
linen; goat hair; 5ram skins dyed red and
another type of durable leather[a]; acacia
wood; 6olive oil[i] for the light; spices for
the anointing oil and for the fragrant incense; 7and onyx stones and other gems
to be mounted on the ephod[j] and breastpiece.[k]
8"Then have them make a sanctuary[l] for
me, and I will dwell[m] among them. 9Make
this tabernacle and all its furnishings exactly like the pattern[n] I will show you.

The Ark

25:10-20pp — Ex 37:1-9

10"Have them make an ark[b][o] of acacia
wood — two and a half cubits long, a cubit and a half wide, and a cubit and a half
high.[c] 11Overlay it with pure gold, both
inside and out, and make a gold molding around it. 12Cast four gold rings for it
and fasten them to its four feet, with two
rings on one side and two rings on the
other. 13Then make poles of acacia wood
and overlay them with gold. 14Insert the
poles into the rings on the sides of the ark
to carry it. 15The poles are to remain in
the rings of this ark; they are not to be
removed.[p] 16Then put in the ark the tablets of the covenant law,[q] which I will give
you.

24:13 [a] Ex 3:1 **24:15** [b] Ex 19:9 **24:16** [c] Ex 16:10 [d] Ps 99:7 **24:17** [e] Ex 3:2; Dt 4:36; Heb 12:18, 29 **24:18** [f] Dt 9:9 [g] Ex 34:28 **25:2** [h] Ex 35:21; 1Ch 29:5, 7, 9; Ezr 2:68; 2Co 8:11-12; 9:7 **25:6** [i] Ex 27:20; 30:22-32 **25:7** [j] Ex 28:4, 6-14 [k] Ex 28:15-30 **25:8** [l] Ex 36:1-5; Heb 9:1-2 [m] Ex 29:45; 1Ki 6:13; 2Co 6:16; Rev 21:3 **25:9** [n] ver 40; Ac 7:44; Heb 8:5 **25:10** [o] Dt 10:1-5; Heb 9:4 **25:15** [p] 1Ki 8:8 **25:16** [q] Dt 31:26; Heb 9:4

[a] *5* Possibly the hides of large aquatic mammals
[b] *10* That is, a chest [c] *10* That is, about 3 3/4 feet long and 2 1/4 feet wide and high or about 1.1 meters long and 68 centimeters wide and high; similarly in verse 17

25:4 *blue, purple and scarlet yarn.* The dyeing of this fabric would have been a costly and labor-intensive process. Many thousands of murex snails would have been required to produce the amount of material described in Exodus. Scarlet dye probably came from the eggs of an insect that fed on oak trees.

25:8 *I will dwell among them.* Sacred space — space set aside for inhabitation by a deity — was important in all ancient Near Eastern societies. It was the place where heaven met earth and had to be treated accordingly. What we call temples are typically referred to as the "house" of a deity: house of Nabu, house of Shamash, house of Yahweh. These houses served partly as a visible reminder to the members of a society that their patron god or goddess was present with them. Their main purpose in the ancient world was to care for the deity with clothing and food (presenting offerings to the deity), with a focus on the divine statue living inside. The presence of the deity made the space sacred.

25:9 *pattern.* There is debate on the Hebrew word for "pattern" (*tabnit*). One possibility is that the item shown to Moses is actually supposed to represent Yahweh's dwelling place in the heavens. This is, then, the pattern for the tabernacle, which becomes the earthly counterpart to the heavenly residence. The other possibility is that the text refers simply to a scale model of the structure that Moses is commanded to build.

Several ancient Near Eastern texts seem to support this second option. These documents refer to instances of divine intervention when models of or plans for religious objects are revealed to those responsible for building them. The models appear to have no connection to heavenly counterparts. In one Middle Babylonian document, a clay model of the statue of the god Shamash was miraculously discovered on the banks of the Euphrates River; it showed how the statue was to look and what clothing was to adorn it. This was important since these items had been missing for many years. With the model in hand, the Babylonian king had a new statue and new clothing made. With regard to temples in particular, a famous statue of Gudea, governor of Lagash about 2000 BC, portrays him with a ground plan of a temple on his lap.

25:10 A cubit is the measure from the tip of the middle finger to the elbow. Comparison of the reported length of the Siloam tunnel that Hezekiah built in Jerusalem at 1,200 cubits with its actual length of 1,732.6 feet (528 meters) yields an estimation for the cubit as 17.5 – 18 inches (44 – 46 centimeters).

25:16 *ark.* This was the most holy of all the items in the tabernacle, for it marked the location of the divine presence (v. 22). It is referred to numerous times in Exodus as the "ark of the covenant law" (v. 22; 26:33,34; 30:6,26; 31:7; 39:35; 40:3,5,21), because of the deposit of "the tablets of the covenant law" within it. The Hebrew word *edut* (sometimes translated "testimony") is a synonym of *berit* and should thus be understood to mean "covenant." What is to be placed within the ark, then, is most likely the written record (perhaps the "tablets of stone" in 24:12) of the covenantal agreement that Yahweh has made with the Israelites.

Disagreement exists, however, about whether the Israelites viewed the ark as Yahweh's throne or as his footstool (with the wings of the cherubim then functioning as his seat or throne [see vv. 18 – 22]). Extra-Biblical evidence tends to favor the latter view; e.g., the records of some international treaties, similar to the covenant between Yahweh and the Israelites, were deposited into box-like containers, which were then placed at the feet of deities. Further support for this conception comes from Biblical texts such as 1Ch 28:2, where David says, "I had it in my

17“Make an atonement cover[r] of pure
gold — two and a half cubits long and a
cubit and a half wide. 18And make two
cherubim out of hammered gold at the
ends of the cover. 19Make one cherub on
one end and the second cherub on the other; make the cherubim of one piece with
the cover, at the two ends. 20The cherubim
are to have their wings spread upward,
overshadowing[s] the cover with them. The
cherubim are to face each other, looking
toward the cover. 21Place the cover on top
of the ark[t] and put in the ark the tablets
of the covenant law[u] that I will give you.
22There, above the cover between the two
cherubim[v] that are over the ark of the covenant law, I will meet[w] with you and give
you all my commands for the Israelites.

The Table

25:23-29pp — Ex 37:10-16

23“Make a table[x] of acacia wood — two
cubits long, a cubit wide and a cubit and
a half high.[a] 24Overlay it with pure gold
and make a gold molding around it. 25Also
make around it a rim a handbreadth[b] wide
and put a gold molding on the rim. 26Make
four gold rings for the table and fasten
them to the four corners, where the four
legs are. 27The rings are to be close to the
rim to hold the poles used in carrying the
table. 28Make the poles of acacia wood,
overlay them with gold and carry the table with them. 29And make its plates and
dishes of pure gold, as well as its pitchers and bowls for the pouring out of offerings.[y] 30Put the bread of the Presence[z]
on this table to be before me at all times.

The Lampstand

25:31-39pp — Ex 37:17-24

31“Make a lampstand[a] of pure gold.
Hammer out its base and shaft, and make
its flowerlike cups, buds and blossoms of
one piece with them. 32Six branches are to
extend from the sides of the lampstand —
three on one side and three on the other.
33Three cups shaped like almond flowers
with buds and blossoms are to be on one
branch, three on the next branch, and the
same for all six branches extending from
the lampstand. 34And on the lampstand
there are to be four cups shaped like almond flowers with buds and blossoms.
35One bud shall be under the first pair of
branches extending from the lampstand,
a second bud under the second pair, and
a third bud under the third pair — six
branches in all. 36The buds and branches
shall all be of one piece with the lampstand, hammered out of pure gold.
37“Then make its seven lamps[b] and set
them up on it so that they light the space
in front of it. 38Its wick trimmers and trays
are to be of pure gold. 39A talent[c] of pure
gold is to be used for the lampstand and

25:17 [r] Ro 3:25 **25:20** [s] 1Ki 8:7; 1Ch 28:18; Heb 9:5 **25:21** [t] Ex 26:34 [u] ver 16 **25:22** [v] Nu 7:89; 1Sa 4:4; 2Sa 6:2; 2Ki 19:15; Ps 80:1; Isa 37:16 [w] Ex 29:42-43 **25:23** [x] Heb 9:2 **25:29** [y] Nu 4:7 **25:30** [z] Lev 24:5-9 **25:31** [a] 1Ki 7:49; Zec 4:2; Heb 9:2; Rev 1:12 **25:37** [b] Ex 27:21; Lev 24:3-4; Nu 8:2

[a] *23* That is, about 3 feet long, 1 1/2 feet wide and 2 1/4 feet high or about 90 centimeters long, 45 centimeters wide and 68 centimeters high [b] *25* That is, about 3 inches or about 7.5 centimeters [c] *39* That is, about 75 pounds or about 34 kilograms

heart to build a house as a place of rest for the ark of the covenant of the LORD, for the footstool of our God.”

25:18 *cherubim.* These sculpted creatures are most likely winged sphinxes known from a number of other sites throughout the ancient Near East (see note on Ge 3:24). Such composite creatures have been found in temples and shrines and are often arranged as if guarding the entrance. Their purpose seems to have been protective — to prevent, perhaps only symbolically, unauthorized individuals from entering space where they were not allowed. In the Exodus tabernacle, the creatures seem to function as protectors of Yahweh's presence. They are the last barrier between any possible human entrant and the divine presence. It is not out in front of them but “between” them, says Yahweh, that “I will meet with you and give you all my commands for the Israelites” (v. 22). It is therefore also significant that winged composite creatures are found flanking the thrones of kings in the ancient world. For a physical description of cherubim, see Eze 10.

25:30 *bread of the Presence.* It is not clear whether this enigmatic phrase symbolizes the presence of Yahweh or whether there must be bread in or near the presence of Yahweh — a presence located within the Most Holy Place. A temple or shrine in the ancient world typically had as one of its chief purposes to feed the deity who was worshiped there. Large quantities of food were thus kept in temples and placed in front of a divine statue; specifically, the laying out of bread before a god is attested in Egypt, Mesopotamia and Anatolia. But this seems unlikely as the reason for the “bread of the Presence.” Nothing is said here about the bread being for Yahweh's consumption. Moreover, bread used as food for a god or goddess was prepared on a daily basis; but according to Lev 24:8 – 9, new bread for the tabernacle table is set out once per week — every Sabbath — and is eventually to be eaten by Aaron and his sons. It may have been placed “before” Yahweh as a token or symbolic offering and only then used as food by the priests.

25:31 – 40 Lampstands with a range of similarities to the one described here are known from the ancient Near East and the Mediterranean world. Some depictions of such lampstands show them in the presence of deities, who are seated on a winged sphinx as if on a throne, much as the divine presence hovers over the ark in the tabernacle. Many of the terms that describe items on the lampstand (e.g., flowers, buds, blossoms), along with the extended branches described in vv. 32 – 33, lead one to believe that the lampstand is meant to represent a tree. This tree of light recalls the tree of life of Ge 2:17; 3:22 – 24, a common life motif in Mesopotamian texts and iconography; it is crafted with seven tiers, symbolic of God's perfect presence and life illumination. Mesopotamia and Egypt offer no evidence of lampstands in cultic contexts, but the motif of vase altars with trees on them in worship scenes is extant in the iconography from the earliest periods. In later periods palm branches are replaced with conical fires, at times with seven flames.

all these accessories. 40See that you make them according to the pattern[c] shown you on the mountain.

The Tabernacle

26:1-37pp — Ex 36:8-38

26 "Make the tabernacle with ten curtains of finely twisted linen and blue, purple and scarlet yarn, with cherubim woven into them by a skilled worker. 2All the curtains are to be the same size — twenty-eight cubits long and four cubits wide.[a] 3Join five of the curtains together, and do the same with the other five. 4Make loops of blue material along the edge of the end curtain in one set, and do the same with the end curtain in the other set. 5Make fifty loops on one curtain and fifty loops on the end curtain of the other set, with the loops opposite each other. 6Then make fifty gold clasps and use them to fasten the curtains together so that the tabernacle is a unit.

7"Make curtains of goat hair for the tent over the tabernacle — eleven altogether. 8All eleven curtains are to be the same size — thirty cubits long and four cubits wide.[b] 9Join five of the curtains together into one set and the other six into another set. Fold the sixth curtain double at the front of the tent. 10Make fifty loops along the edge of the end curtain in one set and also along the edge of the end curtain in the other set. 11Then make fifty bronze clasps and put them in the loops to fasten the tent together as a unit. 12As for the additional length of the tent curtains, the half curtain that is left over is to hang down at the rear of the tabernacle. 13The tent curtains will be a cubit[c] longer on both sides; what is left will hang over the sides of the tabernacle so as to cover it. 14Make for the tent a covering of ram skins dyed red, and over that a covering of the other durable leather.[d][d]

15"Make upright frames of acacia wood for the tabernacle. 16Each frame is to be ten cubits long and a cubit and a half wide,[e] 17with two projections set parallel to each other. Make all the frames of the tabernacle in this way. 18Make twenty frames for the south side of the tabernacle 19and make forty silver bases to go under them — two bases for each frame, one under each projection. 20For the other side, the north side of the tabernacle, make twenty frames 21and forty silver bases — two under each frame. 22Make six frames for the far end, that is, the west end of the tabernacle, 23and make two frames for the corners at the far end. 24At these two corners they must be double from the bottom all the way to the top and fitted into a single ring; both shall be like that. 25So there will be eight frames and sixteen silver bases — two under each frame.

26"Also make crossbars of acacia wood: five for the frames on one side of the tabernacle, 27five for those on the other side, and five for the frames on the west, at the far end of the tabernacle. 28The center crossbar is to extend from end to end at the middle of the frames. 29Overlay the frames with gold and make gold rings to hold the crossbars. Also overlay the crossbars with gold.

30"Set up the tabernacle according to the plan[e] shown you on the mountain.

31"Make a curtain[f] of blue, purple and scarlet yarn and finely twisted linen, with cherubim[g] woven into it by a skilled worker. 32Hang it with gold hooks on four posts of acacia wood overlaid with gold and standing on four silver bases. 33Hang the curtain from the clasps and place the ark of the covenant law behind the curtain.[h] The curtain will separate the Holy Place from the Most Holy Place.[i] 34Put the atonement cover[j] on the ark of the covenant law in the Most Holy Place. 35Place the table[k] outside the curtain on the north side of the tabernacle and put the lampstand[l] opposite it on the south side.

36"For the entrance to the tent make a curtain of blue, purple and scarlet yarn and finely twisted linen — the work of an embroiderer. 37Make gold hooks for this curtain and five posts of acacia wood overlaid with gold. And cast five bronze bases for them.

The Altar of Burnt Offering

27:1-8pp — Ex 38:1-7

27 "Build an altar[m] of acacia wood, three cubits[f] high; it is to be square, five cubits long and five cubits

25:40 [c] Ex 26:30; Nu 8:4; Ac 7:44; Heb 8:5*
26:14 [d] Ex 36:19; Nu 4:25
26:30 [e] Ex 25:9, 40; Ac 7:44; Heb 8:5
26:31 [f] 2Ch 3:14; Mt 27:51; Heb 9:3 [g] Ex 36:35
26:33 [h] Ex 40:3, 21; Lev 16:2 [i] Heb 9:2-3
26:34 [j] Ex 25:21; 40:20; Heb 9:5
26:35 [k] Heb 9:2 [l] Ex 40:22, 24
27:1 [m] Eze 43:13

[a] *2* That is, about 42 feet long and 6 feet wide or about 13 meters long and 1.8 meters wide [b] *8* That is, about 45 feet long and 6 feet wide or about 13.5 meters long and 1.8 meters wide [c] *13* That is, about 18 inches or about 45 centimeters [d] *14* Possibly the hides of large aquatic mammals (see 25:5) [e] *16* That is, about 15 feet long and 2 1/4 feet wide or about 4.5 meters long and 68 centimeters wide [f] *1* That is, about 4 1/2 feet or about 1.4 meters

26:14 *durable leather.* Identification of this material has baffled scholars for years. Suggestions have included skin of badgers, seals, porpoises, narwhals and even unicorns. Some have opted for the dugong, a marine mammal known to live in the Red Sea. The Hebrew terminology here is simply not clear and may not be referring to any kind of animal. What is probably a more plausible suggestion is that reference is being made to the color of the material that is to cover the inner section of the tabernacle. The Hebrew term in question, then, may indicate a color on the order of orange or red.

27:1 *an altar of acacia wood.* This altar stands approximately

EXODUS 26 – 27

THE TABERNACLE

The instructions in Ex 27:9 – 13 for the outer section of the tabernacle specify a structure 50 cubits wide and 100 cubits long (roughly 75 feet by 150 feet [23 meters by 46 meters]). The inner section was approximately 16 feet by 48 feet (25 meters by 75 meters). Its height was a remarkable 10 cubits (15 feet or 24 meters) (Ex 26:16).

Most buildings in that part of the ancient world had some open space that was enclosed but unroofed. This made easier certain activities such as cooking large amounts of food and caring for animals. The purpose of this courtyard probably included similar activities, since the altar for burnt offerings is there, but it may also have allowed ordinary Israelites to enter the general precinct of the tabernacle and still be protected, by means of the enclosure around the Holy Place, from any dangers associated with drawing too near the location of the divine presence.

The inner section or Holy Place contained yet another room called the "Most Holy Place" (Ex 26:33) and is often referred to as the "Holy of Holies." This makes the tabernacle a tripartite structure: the outer section or "courtyard" (27:9), the inner section or "Holy Place" (26:33), and the "Most Holy Place" (26:33). The arrangement of religious structures in this way was not unusual in the ancient Near East. For instance, the temple uncovered at Arad (southern Israel) is dated to the divided monarchy. It consisted of a forecourt, main hall and Holy of Holies. Outside of Israel in Syria to the north, temples have been excavated at Tel Tayinat and at Ain Dara that feature this tripartite structure. The most likely purpose of this arrangement was to establish a hierarchy of space, with a progression toward space that was more holy and thus more restricted. This prevented those unfit for direct contact with the divine from trespassing within the space inhabited by the presence of Yahweh.

Another parallel to this three-part division comes from Egyptian reliefs depicting the military encampment of Rameses II during the battle of Qadesh. The inner section consists of the king's reception tent, which contained, at the west end, the pharaoh's private area and throne room. As the divine commander of the Egyptian military, Pharaoh was deserving of this specialized tent-shrine for his travels. For the Israelites,

continued on next page

wide.[a] 2Make a horn[n] at each of the four
corners, so that the horns and the altar are of one piece, and overlay the altar with bronze. 3Make all its utensils of
bronze — its pots to remove the ashes,
and its shovels, sprinkling bowls, meat
forks and firepans. 4Make a grating for
it, a bronze network, and make a bronze
ring at each of the four corners of the network. 5Put it under the ledge of the altar
so that it is halfway up the altar. 6Make
poles of acacia wood for the altar and
overlay them with bronze. 7The poles
are to be inserted into the rings so they
will be on two sides of the altar when it
is carried. 8Make the altar hollow, out of
boards. It is to be made just as you were
shown[o] on the mountain.

27:2 [n] Ps 118:27
27:8 [o] Ex 25:9, 40

[a] *1* That is, about 7 1/2 feet or about 2.3 meters long and wide

4.5 feet (1.4 meters) tall with a square top roughly 7.5 feet by 7.5 feet (2.3 meters by 2.3 meters). Most altars discovered by archaeologists are smaller than the one described here, though the stone horned altar at Beersheba is about the same height with the top surface being a little more than 5 feet (8 meters) square, and the mud brick and fieldstone altar at Arad is also about the same height and a little more than 8 feet (about 13 meters) square on the top. Typically altars in ancient Syria, Palestine and nearby regions were made of dirt or stone. Intriguingly, this altar consists primarily of wood overlaid with bronze (v. 2) — otherwise undocumented in archaeological finds or in literary descriptions. The burning coals and animal parts would come in contact with the grate (vv. 5 – 6) rather than with the overlaid wood. The melting point of bronze is about 1750°F (950°C), higher than most wood fires.

27:2 *Make a horn.* See note on 30:2.

the tabernacle was the tent-shrine for Yahweh, their commander and the one who was to lead them to their ultimate destination.

Finally, an important parallel comes from Ugaritic literature. The chief god of the pantheon at Ugarit was El. His dwelling place is frequently said to be a tent, and the Ugaritic term *mshkn* occurs in several texts with reference to his abode. This term corresponds to the Hebrew *mishkan* ("tabernacle"). Thus, portable tent-shrines for deities existed in several ancient Near Eastern societies.

Because of the theophany at Mount Sinai, the tabernacle was critically important for the Israelites. The visible manifestation of Yahweh and the establishment of his covenant with them at the mountain marked that spot as holy—a place where the Israelites had encountered the divine. But this location was not to be their permanent dwelling place. The tabernacle was the place where the encounter with the divine could take place on a regular basis. It would house, as it were, the holiness of the Mount Sinai experience and the very presence of Yahweh as they traveled to the promised land. ◆

Artist's recreation of the Tabernacle.

The Courtyard

27:9-19pp — Ex 38:9-20

9"Make a courtyard for the tabernacle.
The south side shall be a hundred cubits[a] long and is to have curtains of finely twisted linen, 10with twenty posts and
twenty bronze bases and with silver hooks
and bands on the posts. 11The north side
shall also be a hundred cubits long and is
to have curtains, with twenty posts and
twenty bronze bases and with silver hooks
and bands on the posts.
12"The west end of the courtyard shall
be fifty cubits[b] wide and have curtains,
with ten posts and ten bases. 13On the
east end, toward the sunrise, the courtyard shall also be fifty cubits wide. 14Cur-
tains fifteen cubits[c] long are to be on one
side of the entrance, with three posts and
three bases, 15and curtains fifteen cubits
long are to be on the other side, with three
posts and three bases.
16"For the entrance to the courtyard,
provide a curtain twenty cubits[d] long, of
blue, purple and scarlet yarn and finely
twisted linen—the work of an embroiderer—with four posts and four bases. 17All
the posts around the courtyard are to have
silver bands and hooks, and bronze bases.
18The courtyard shall be a hundred cubits
long and fifty cubits wide,[e] with curtains
of finely twisted linen five cubits[f] high,

[a] *9* That is, about 150 feet or about 45 meters; also in verse 11 [b] *12* That is, about 75 feet or about 23 meters; also in verse 13 [c] *14* That is, about 23 feet or about 6.8 meters; also in verse 15 [d] *16* That is, about 30 feet or about 9 meters [e] *18* That is, about 150 feet long and 75 feet wide or about 45 meters long and 23 meters wide [f] *18* That is, about 7 1/2 feet or about 2.3 meters

TABERNACLE FURNISHINGS

The furnishings of the tabernacle have deep roots in both the symbolism of the ancient world and in the symbolism from the garden of Eden. Likely reconstructions of the furnishings are based on the detailed descriptions and precise measurements recorded in Exodus 25–40. (The bronze basin is not shown here.)

1 ARK OF THE COVENANT

The ark of the covenant compares with the roughly contemporary shrine and funerary furniture of Tutankhamun (c. 1300 BC), which, along with the Nimrud and Samaria ivories from a later period, have been used to guide the graphic interpretation of the text. Both sources show the conventional way of depicting extreme reverence, with facing winged guardians shielding a sacred place.

2 INCENSE ALTAR

3 LAMPSTAND

The traditional form of the lampstand is not attested archaeologically until much later.

4 TABLE

The table holding the bread of the Presence was made of wood overlaid with thin sheets of gold. All of the objects were portable and were fitted with rings and carrying poles, practices typical of Egyptian ritual processions as early as the Old Kingdom period (c. 2715–2640 BC).

5 BRONZE ALTAR

The altar of burnt offering was made of wood overlaid with bronze. The size, five cubits square and three cubits high, matches that of an altar found at Arad from the time of Solomon.

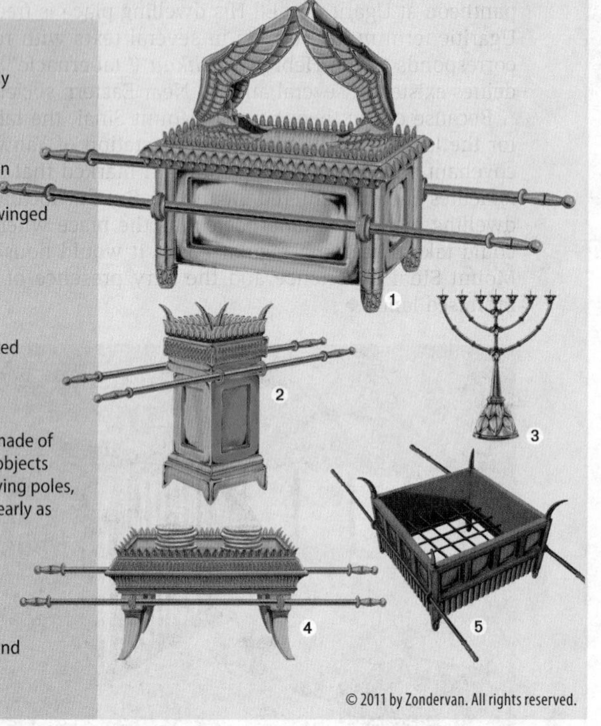

and with bronze bases. 19All the other articles used in the service of the tabernacle,
whatever their function, including all the
tent pegs for it and those for the courtyard,
are to be of bronze.

Oil for the Lampstand

27:20-21pp — Lev 24:1-3

20"Command the Israelites to bring you
clear oil of pressed olives for the light so
that the lamps may be kept burning. 21In the
tent of meeting,[p] outside the curtain that
shields the ark of the covenant law,[q] Aaron
and his sons are to keep the lamps[r] burning
before the LORD from evening till morning.
This is to be a lasting ordinance[s] among the
Israelites for the generations to come.

The Priestly Garments

28 "Have Aaron[t] your brother brought
to you from among the Israelites,
along with his sons Nadab and Abihu, Eleazar and Ithamar, so they may serve me
as priests.[u] 2Make sacred garments[v] for
your brother Aaron to give him dignity
and honor. 3Tell all the skilled workers[w]
to whom I have given wisdom[x] in such
matters that they are to make garments
for Aaron, for his consecration, so he may
serve me as priest. 4These are the garments they are to make: a breastpiece,[y] an
ephod, a robe,[z] a woven tunic,[a] a turban
and a sash. They are to make these sacred garments for your brother Aaron and
his sons, so they may serve me as priests.
5Have them use gold, and blue, purple and
scarlet yarn, and fine linen.

The Ephod

28:6-14pp — Ex 39:2-7

6"Make the ephod of gold, and of blue,
purple and scarlet yarn, and of finely
twisted linen — the work of skilled hands.
7It is to have two shoulder pieces attached

27:21 [p]Ex 28:43 [q]Ex 26:31, 33 [r]Ex 25:37; 30:8; 1Sa 3:3; 2Ch 13:11 [s]Ex 29:9; Lev 3:17; 16:34; Nu 18:23; 19:21 **28:1** [t]Heb 5:4 [u]Nu 18:1-7; Heb 5:1 **28:2** [v]Ex 29:5, 29; 31:10; 39:1; Lev 8:7-9,30 **28:3** [w]Ex 31:6; 36:1 [x]Ex 31:3 **28:4** [y]ver 15-30 [z]ver 31-35 [a]ver 39

28:6-8 This description portrays the ephod as a rather expensive piece of clothing, given the material of which it consists. A similar garment appears to be mentioned in Old Assyrian texts (the term is *epattu*) and in a few documents from Ugarit (*ipd* in Ugaritic). Based on the Biblical account and some possibly related Egyptian portrayals,

to two of its corners, so it can be fastened.
8Its skillfully woven waistband is to be like
it — of one piece with the ephod and made
with gold, and with blue, purple and scarlet yarn, and with finely twisted linen.
9"Take two onyx stones and engrave on
them the names of the sons of Israel 10in
the order of their birth — six names on one
stone and the remaining six on the other.
11Engrave the names of the sons of Israel
on the two stones the way a gem cutter
engraves a seal. Then mount the stones in
gold filigree settings 12and fasten them on
the shoulder pieces of the ephod as memorial stones for the sons of Israel. Aaron
is to bear the names on his shoulders as
a memorial before the LORD. 13Make gold
filigree settings 14and two braided chains
of pure gold, like a rope, and attach the
chains to the settings.

The Breastpiece

28:15-28pp — Ex 39:8-21

15"Fashion a breastpiece for making decisions — the work of skilled hands. Make it
like the ephod: of gold, and of blue, purple
and scarlet yarn, and of finely twisted lin-
en. 16It is to be square — a span[a] long and
a span wide — and folded double. 17Then
mount four rows of precious stones on it.
The first row shall be carnelian, chrysolite
and beryl; 18the second row shall be turquoise, lapis lazuli and emerald; 19the third
row shall be jacinth, agate and amethyst;
20the fourth row shall be topaz, onyx and
jasper.[b] Mount them in gold filigree settings. 21There are to be twelve stones, one
for each of the names of the sons of Israel,
each engraved like a seal with the name of
one of the twelve tribes.
22"For the breastpiece make braided
chains of pure gold, like a rope. 23Make
two gold rings for it and fasten them to
two corners of the breastpiece. 24Fasten the
two gold chains to the rings at the corners
of the breastpiece, 25and the other ends of
the chains to the two settings, attaching
them to the shoulder pieces of the ephod
at the front. 26Make two gold rings and attach them to the other two corners of the
breastpiece on the inside edge next to the
ephod. 27Make two more gold rings and
attach them to the bottom of the shoulder
pieces on the front of the ephod, close to
the seam just above the waistband of the
ephod. 28The rings of the breastpiece are
to be tied to the rings of the ephod with
blue cord, connecting it to the waistband,
so that the breastpiece will not swing out
from the ephod.
29"Whenever Aaron enters the Holy
Place,[b] he will bear the names of the sons
of Israel over his heart on the breastpiece
of decision as a continuing memorial before the LORD. 30Also put the Urim and
the Thummim[c] in the breastpiece, so they
may be over Aaron's heart whenever he
enters the presence of the LORD. Thus Aaron will always bear the means of making
decisions for the Israelites over his heart
before the LORD.

Other Priestly Garments

28:31-43pp — Ex 39:22-31

31"Make the robe of the ephod entirely
of blue cloth, 32with an opening for the
head in its center. There shall be a woven
edge like a collar[c] around this opening, so
that it will not tear. 33Make pomegranates
of blue, purple and scarlet yarn around the
hem of the robe, with gold bells between
them. 34The gold bells and the pomegranates are to alternate around the hem of the
robe. 35Aaron must wear it when he ministers. The sound of the bells will be heard
when he enters the Holy Place before the
LORD and when he comes out, so that he
will not die.
36"Make a plate of pure gold and engrave on it as on a seal: HOLY TO THE LORD.[d]
37Fasten a blue cord to it to attach it to
the turban; it is to be on the front of the
turban. 38It will be on Aaron's forehead,
and he will bear the guilt[e] involved in the

28:29 [b] ver 12 **28:30** [c] Lev 8:8; Nu 27:21; Dt 33:8; Ezr 2:63; Ne 7:65 **28:36** [d] Zec 14:20 **28:38** [e] Lev 10:17; 22:9,16; Nu 18:1; Heb 9:28; 1Pe 2:24

[a] *16* That is, about 9 inches or about 23 centimeters
[b] *20* The precise identification of some of these precious stones is uncertain. [c] *32* The meaning of the Hebrew for this word is uncertain.

the ephod was probably like an apron that wrapped around the body from the waist down.

28:11 *engraves a seal.* Legal documents frequently have seal impressions. After the document was drawn up, an individual pressed or rolled his stone seal onto a portion of clay affixed to the document, thereby leaving his insignia on the document and making it officially his.

28:15 *breastpiece for making decisions.* This covered the pectoral area of the high priest and was also made of costly material. Scholars have attempted to identify parallels to this piece, though there is little consensus. One possible artifact comes from Byblos along the Phoenician coast and dates to the 1700s BC. It is a type of vest with a front piece for the chest and cords to be strapped around the back. It has 11 precious or semiprecious stones affixed to the outer edge and contains Egyptian artwork or an imitation thereof. This may have been worn by a Phoenician king, who also functioned as a priest. The inclusion of the stones is especially intriguing, although their arrangement differs from those described in vv. 17 – 21. While some scholars have dismissed the relevance of this piece from Byblos, it nevertheless points to the idea that the priestly clothing in the Bible was probably not devised from scratch, as it were. Rather, priestly garments were reminiscent of what some Israelites would already have known to be religiously significant apparel. The reference to decision making is probably an allusion to the Urim and Thummim (see the article "Urim and Thummim," p. 162).

sacred gifts the Israelites consecrate, whatever their gifts may be. It will be on Aaron's forehead continually so that they will
be acceptable to the LORD.
39“Weave the tunic of fine linen and
make the turban of fine linen. The sash is
to be the work of an embroiderer. 40Make
tunics, sashes and caps for Aaron's sons[f]
to give them dignity and honor. 41After
you put these clothes on your brother Aaron and his sons, anoint[g] and ordain them.
Consecrate them so they may serve me as
priests.[h]
42“Make linen undergarments[i] as a covering for the body, reaching from the waist
to the thigh. 43Aaron and his sons must
wear them whenever they enter the tent
of meeting[j] or approach the altar to minister in the Holy Place, so that they will not
incur guilt and die.[k]
“This is to be a lasting ordinance[l] for
Aaron and his descendants.

28:40 [f] ver 4; Ex 39:41 **28:41** [g] Ex 29:7; Lev 10:7 [h] Ex 29:7-9; 30:30; 40:15; Lev 8:1-36; Heb 7:28 **28:42** [i] Lev 6:10; 16:4, 23; Eze 44:18 **28:43** [j] Ex 27:21 [k] Ex 20:26 [l] Lev 17:7

Consecration of the Priests

29:1-37pp — Lev 8:1-36

29 “This is what you are to do to consecrate them, so they may serve me
as priests: Take a young bull and two rams
without defect. 2And from the finest wheat
flour make round loaves without yeast,

29:1 *serve me as priests.* If prophets are individuals who spoke messages from God to humans, priests are those who operated in the opposite direction: representing the people before God. While the priests here are said to possess the equipment necessary to receive messages from Yahweh, their primary role was that of an intermediary on behalf of the people. For Yahweh to be their God and for there to be proper worship, the people needed religious officials who could make contact with Yahweh and provide the necessary worship and service to Yahweh within

EXODUS 28:30

URIM AND THUMMIM

No description of these objects is present in the text, but later traditions suggest that they were markers used in casting lots (cf. Ex 28:30; Nu 27:21; 1Sa 14:37–41). There is no negative character attached to Urim and Thummim as there is to other divinatory practice. Neither are they mentioned in passages describing non-Israelite rituals or worship.

Divination by lots is known in the ancient Near East. Babylonian oracular texts preserve the answers given to yes-no questions. In a procedure known from Mesopotamia called psephomancy, a yes-no question would be posed and a stone drawn out; whether the stone was light or dark would determine a positive or negative response. “Urim” is the Hebrew word for “lights” and may represent the white stone.

The closest parallel to Urim and Thummim comes from an incantation ritual text from Assur. The Assyrian ritual process is clearly one of divination by using a black stone (hematite) and a white stone (alabaster). The will of seven gods is sought by lifting up one of these stones.

In order to perceive that will, Shamash, the god of oracles, is addressed, offerings are made and two stones are put into the hem of the ritualist's garment to be retrieved at the right time. The ritualist writes the names of seven gods on the ground and then lifts up a stone; a judgment is rendered and a revelation given, if the god so desires (yes). If no revelation or judgment is received, a stone of no desire (no) is given. It is not stated explicitly which stone stands for desirable/not desirable, but based on other ancient Near Eastern divination texts, white is probably the “yes” stone, black the “no” stone.

Evidently the ritualist repeats the process three times to confirm the answer given, as was somewhat common in rituals. The process involved, the stones involved (light, truth), the binary options available, the technical terms used, the option of no answer, the drawing of stones from a garment, and the types of questions addressed all suggest that the Urim and Thummim and this process may be related. ◆

thick loaves without yeast and with olive oil mixed in, and thin loaves without yeast and brushed with olive oil.[m] 3Put them in a basket and present them along with the bull and the two rams. 4Then bring Aaron and his sons to the entrance to the tent of meeting and wash them with water.[n] 5Take the garments[o] and dress Aaron with the tunic, the robe of the ephod, the ephod itself and the breastpiece. Fasten the ephod on him by its skillfully woven waistband.[p] 6Put the turban on his head and attach the sacred emblem[q] to the turban. 7Take the anointing oil[r] and anoint him by pouring it on his head. 8Bring his sons and dress them in tunics 9and fasten caps on them. Then tie sashes on Aaron and his sons.[a][s] The priesthood is theirs by a lasting ordinance.[t]

"Then you shall ordain Aaron and his sons.

10"Bring the bull to the front of the tent of meeting, and Aaron and his sons shall lay their hands on its head. 11Slaughter it in the LORD's presence at the entrance to the tent of meeting. 12Take some of the bull's blood and put it on the horns[u] of the altar with your finger, and pour out the rest of it at the base of the altar. 13Then take all the fat[v] on the internal organs, the long lobe of the liver, and both kidneys with the fat on them, and burn them on the altar. 14But burn the bull's flesh and its hide and its intestines outside the camp.[w] It is a sin offering.[b]

15"Take one of the rams, and Aaron and his sons shall lay their hands on its head. 16Slaughter it and take the blood and splash it against the sides of the altar. 17Cut the ram into pieces and wash the internal organs and the legs, putting them with the head and the other pieces. 18Then burn the entire ram on the altar. It is a burnt offering to the LORD, a pleasing aroma,[x] a food offering presented to the LORD.

19"Take the other ram,[y] and Aaron and his sons shall lay their hands on its head. 20Slaughter it, take some of its blood and put it on the lobes of the right ears of Aaron and his sons, on the thumbs of their right hands, and on the big toes of their right feet. Then splash blood against the sides of the altar. 21And take some blood[z] from the altar and some of the anointing oil[a] and sprinkle it on Aaron and his garments and on his sons and their garments. Then he and his sons and their garments will be consecrated.[b]

22"Take from this ram the fat, the fat tail, the fat on the internal organs, the long lobe of the liver, both kidneys with the fat on them, and the right thigh. (This is the ram for the ordination.) 23From the basket of bread made without yeast, which is before the LORD, take one round loaf, one thick loaf with olive oil mixed in, and one thin loaf. 24Put all these in the hands of Aaron and his sons and have them wave them before the LORD as a wave offering.[c] 25Then take them from their hands and burn them on the altar along with the burnt offering for a pleasing aroma to the LORD, a food offering presented to the LORD. 26After you take the breast of the ram for Aaron's ordination, wave it before the LORD as a wave offering, and it will be your share.[d]

27"Consecrate those parts of the ordination ram that belong to Aaron and his sons:[e] the breast that was waved and the thigh that was presented. 28This is always to be the perpetual share from the Israelites for Aaron and his sons. It is the contribution the Israelites are to make to the LORD from their fellowship offerings.[f]

29"Aaron's sacred garments will belong to his descendants so that they can be anointed and ordained in them.[g] 30The son[h] who succeeds him as priest and comes to the tent of meeting to minister in the Holy Place is to wear them seven days.

31"Take the ram for the ordination and cook the meat in a sacred place. 32At the entrance to the tent of meeting, Aaron and his sons are to eat the meat of the ram and the bread[i] that is in the basket. 33They are to eat these offerings by which atonement was made for their ordination and consecration. But no one else may eat[j] them, because they are sacred. 34And if any of the meat of the ordination ram or any bread is left over till morning,[k] burn it up. It must not be eaten, because it is sacred.

35"Do for Aaron and his sons everything I have commanded you, taking seven days to ordain them. 36Sacrifice a bull each day[l] as a sin offering to make atonement. Purify the altar by making atonement for it, and anoint it to consecrate[m] it. 37For seven days make atonement for the altar and consecrate it. Then the altar will be most holy, and whatever touches it will be holy.[n]

38"This is what you are to offer on the altar regularly each day:[o] two lambs a year old. 39Offer one in the morning and the other at twilight.[p] 40With the first lamb

29:2 [m] Lev 2:1, 4; 6:19-23
29:4 [n] Ex 40:12; Heb 10:22
29:5 [o] Ex 28:2; Lev 8:7 [p] Ex 28:8
29:6 [q] Lev 8:9
29:7 [r] Ex 30:25, 30, 31; Lev 8:12; 21:10; Nu 35:25; Ps 133:2
29:9 [s] Ex 28:40 [t] Ex 40:15; Nu 3:10; 18:7; 25:13; Dt 18:5
29:12 [u] Ex 27:2
29:13 [v] Lev 3:3, 5, 9
29:14 [w] Lev 4:11-12, 21; Heb 13:11
29:18 [x] Ge 8:21
29:19 [y] ver 3
29:21 [z] Heb 9:22 [a] Ex 30:25, 31 [b] ver 1
29:24 [c] Lev 7:30
29:26 [d] Lev 7:31-34
29:27 [e] Lev 7:31, 34; Dt 18:3
29:28 [f] Lev 10:15
29:29 [g] Nu 20:26, 28
29:30 [h] Nu 20:28
29:32 [i] Mt 12:4
29:33 [j] Lev 10:14; 22:10, 13
29:34 [k] Ex 12:10
29:36 [l] Heb 10:11 [m] Ex 40:10
29:37 [n] Ex 30:28-29; 40:10; Mt 23:19
29:38 [o] Nu 28:3-8; 1Ch 16:40; Da 12:11
29:39 [p] Eze 46:13-15

[a] 9 Hebrew; Septuagint *on them* [b] 14 Or *purification offering*; also in verse 36

his place of residence (the tabernacle). While prophets were often reformers and individualistic, priests were more institutionalized and associated with long-standing traditions. The priests serving in the tabernacle were engaged in all aspects involved with mediating access to sacred space for the people.

offer a tenth of an ephah[a] of the finest flour mixed with a quarter of a hin[b] of oil from pressed olives, and a quarter of a hin of wine as a drink offering. 41 Sacrifice the other lamb at twilight with the same grain offering and its drink offering as in the morning—a pleasing aroma, a food offering presented to the LORD.

42 "For the generations to come[q] this burnt offering is to be made regularly at the entrance to the tent of meeting, before the LORD. There I will meet you and speak to you;[r] 43 there also I will meet with the Israelites, and the place will be consecrated by my glory.[s]

44 "So I will consecrate the tent of meeting and the altar and will consecrate Aaron and his sons to serve me as priests.[t] 45 Then I will dwell[u] among the Israelites and be their God.[v] 46 They will know that I am the LORD their God, who brought them out of Egypt so that I might dwell among them. I am the LORD their God.[w]

The Altar of Incense

30:1-5pp — Ex 37:25-28

30 "Make an altar[x] of acacia wood for burning incense.[y] 2 It is to be square, a cubit long and a cubit wide, and two cubits high[c]—its horns[z] of one piece with it. 3 Overlay the top and all the sides and the horns with pure gold, and make a gold molding around it. 4 Make two gold rings for the altar below the molding—two on each of the opposite sides—to hold the poles used to carry it. 5 Make the poles of acacia wood and overlay them with gold. 6 Put the altar in front of the curtain that shields the ark of the covenant law—before the atonement cover[a] that is over the tablets of the covenant law—where I will meet with you.

7 "Aaron must burn fragrant incense[b] on the altar every morning when he tends the lamps. 8 He must burn incense again when he lights the lamps at twilight so incense will burn regularly before the LORD for the generations to come. 9 Do not offer on this altar any other incense[c] or any burnt offering or grain offering, and do not pour a drink offering on it. 10 Once a year Aaron shall make atonement[d] on its horns. This annual atonement must be made with the blood of the atoning sin offering[d] for the generations to come. It is most holy to the LORD."

Atonement Money

11 Then the LORD said to Moses, 12 "When you take a census[e] of the Israelites to count them, each one must pay the LORD a ransom[f] for his life at the time he is counted. Then no plague[g] will come on them when you number them. 13 Each one who crosses over to those already counted is to give a half shekel,[e] according to the sanctuary shekel,[h] which weighs twenty gerahs. This half shekel is an offering to the LORD. 14 All who cross over, those twenty years old or more, are to give an offering to the LORD. 15 The rich are not to give more than a half shekel and the poor are not to give less[i] when you make the offering to the LORD to atone for your lives. 16 Receive the atonement money from the Israelites and use it for the service of the tent of meeting.[j] It will be a memorial for the Israelites before the LORD, making atonement for your lives."

Basin for Washing

17 Then the LORD said to Moses, 18 "Make a bronze basin,[k] with its bronze stand, for washing. Place it between the tent of meeting and the altar, and put water in it. 19 Aaron and his sons are to wash their hands and feet[l] with water[m] from it. 20 Whenever they enter the tent of meeting, they shall wash with water so that they will not die. Also, when they approach the altar to minister by presenting a food offering to the LORD, 21 they shall wash their hands and feet so that they will not die. This is to be a lasting ordinance[n] for Aaron

29:42 [q] Ex 30:8 [r] Ex 25:22 **29:43** [s] 1Ki 8:11 **29:44** [t] Lev 21:15 **29:45** [u] Ex 25:8; Lev 26:12; Zec 2:10; Jn 14:17 [v] 2Co 6:16; Rev 21:3 **29:46** [w] Ex 20:2 **30:1** [x] Ex 37:25 [y] Rev 8:3 **30:2** [z] Ex 27:2 **30:6** [a] Ex 25:22; 26:34 **30:7** [b] ver 34-35; Ex 27:21; 1Sa 2:28 **30:9** [c] Lev 10:1

30:10 [d] Lev 16:18-19,30 **30:12** [e] Ex 38:25; Nu 1:2,49; 2Sa 24:1 [f] Nu 31:50; Mt 20:28 [g] 2Sa 24:13 **30:13** [h] Nu 3:47; Mt 17:24 **30:15** [i] Pr 22:2; Eph 6:9 **30:16** [j] Ex 38:25-28 **30:18** [k] Ex 38:8; 40:7,30 **30:19** [l] Ex 40:31-32; Isa 52:11 [m] Ps 26:6 **30:21** [n] Ex 27:21; 28:43

[a] *40* That is, probably about 3 1/2 pounds or about 1.6 kilograms [b] *40* That is, probably about 1 quart or about 1 liter [c] *2* That is, about 1 1/2 feet long and wide and 3 feet high or about 45 centimeters long and wide and 90 centimeters high [d] *10* Or *purification offering* [e] *13* That is, about 1/5 ounce or about 5.8 grams; also in verse 15

29:40 *ephah.* See NIV text note. *hin.* Evidence for liquid measurements in preexilic Israel is murky. Estimates of modern equivalents for units like the hin have varied among scholars over the years (see NIV text note for one option). One of the most detailed studies to date estimates that the hin is equal to approximately 6 liters, making the amount called for here the equivalent of about 1.5 liters.

30:2 *horns of one piece with it.* Archaeologists have discovered four-horned incense altars at various sites throughout Palestine, including Philistine and Israelite sites. This particular altar style appears to have Late Bronze Age antecedents that take the shape of models of towers made of clay. Some of these clay models are close to 4 feet (6.5 meters) tall with a rectangular base slightly over 1 foot (30 centimeters) square. At the top of these model towers, the corners slope upward to form points as if on a turret. Offerings were burned on the tops of these models as a way to imitate the longstanding practice, in some ancient Near Eastern societies, of performing religious rituals and presenting burned sacrifices on the rooftops of houses. Perhaps the Israelite horned altar is an offshoot of this tradition, with the top of the altar shaped to represent the roof of a shrine and to accommodate the symbolism of sending up incense to Yahweh from the highest point on the shrine.

EXODUS 29

CONSECRATION

Exodus 29:10 begins a lengthy set of instructions regarding the ceremonies that had to be performed in order to "consecrate" (Ex 29:1; lit. "make holy") Aaron and his sons as priests. Modern readers may wonder at the elaborate and often bloody details of the rituals described here. Ancient readers would have puzzled much less over the details, in part because of previous experiences with such rites, but also because they understood the nature of what was taking place. In order to serve as a priest, a person had to be prepared for contact with that which was holy — the sacred realm, the world of the divine.

Ancient Israelite society operated on the understanding that there were three distinct categories or states in which persons (and objects) could find themselves: the state of uncleanness, the state of cleanness and the state of holiness. Yahweh inhabited the last, and animals unfit to eat inhabited the first. Persons could move between being clean and unclean, depending on what they had recently been doing, eating, touching, etc. Persons in a state of uncleanness were not allowed to approach anyone or anything deemed holy. Even persons who believed themselves to be in a state of cleanness could suffer dire consequences for coming into contact with that which was holy without authorization (e.g., 2Sa 6:6–7).

One of the goals of Yahweh's covenant with the Israelites was to make of them a "holy nation" (Ex 19:6). But this would not happen in an instant, and for the time being only the priests were to be made holy. The consecration of priests thus was a process fraught with peril. The transfer of a human being from the world of the ordinary — the world of the profane, where things and people were either only clean or unclean — to the world of the holy was not to be approached carelessly. While the significance of all the ritual actions described is not clear to us, what is clear is that this type of transfer process required time and ritual precision. Similarly elaborate rituals accompanied the installation of religious functionaries in other ancient Near Eastern societies. The Israelites were no exception in the attention they gave to the proper consecration of their priests.

The placing of blood and oil on Aaron and his sons (29:7,20–21) assist in consecrating them — transferring them into the realm of the sacred and making them fit for service to Yahweh. What is unclear is how blood and oil bring this about. An interesting parallel turns up from Emar in a text about the celebration of the *Zukru* festival, which can be characterized as a celebration of the new year. At one point during the ceremonies, a set of stones is to be rubbed with oil and blood. This may also be an act of consecration, but the type of stones involved and the precise nature of the act are obscure. Nevertheless, the combination of oil and blood seems to have held important religious significance in other ancient Near Eastern societies and may relate to ceremonies where people and objects must cross the sometimes dangerous chasm between the sacred and profane. ◆

and his descendants for the generations to come."

Anointing Oil

[22]Then the LORD said to Moses, [23]"Take
the following fine spices: 500 shekels[a] of
liquid myrrh,[o] half as much (that is, 250
shekels) of fragrant cinnamon, 250 shekels[b] of fragrant calamus, [24]500 shekels of
cassia[p] — all according to the sanctuary
shekel — and a hin[c] of olive oil. [25]Make
these into a sacred anointing oil, a fragrant

30:23 [o]Ge 37:25
30:24 [p]Ps 45:8

[a] 23 That is, about 12 1/2 pounds or about 5.8 kilograms; also in verse 24 [b] 23 That is, about 6 1/4 pounds or about 2.9 kilograms [c] 24 That is, probably about 1 gallon or about 3.8 liters

blend, the work of a perfumer.[q] It will be the sacred anointing oil.[r] 26Then use it to anoint[s] the tent of meeting, the ark of the covenant law, 27the table and all its articles, the lampstand and its accessories, the altar of incense, 28the altar of burnt offering and all its utensils, and the basin with its stand. 29You shall consecrate them so they will be most holy, and whatever touches them will be holy.[t]

30"Anoint Aaron and his sons and consecrate[u] them so they may serve me as priests. 31Say to the Israelites, 'This is to be my sacred anointing oil for the generations to come. 32Do not pour it on anyone else's body and do not make any other oil using the same formula. It is sacred, and you are to consider it sacred.[v] 33Whoever makes perfume like it and puts it on anyone other than a priest must be cut off[w] from their people.' "

Incense

34Then the LORD said to Moses, "Take fragrant spices—gum resin, onycha and galbanum—and pure frankincense, all in equal amounts, 35and make a fragrant blend of incense, the work of a perfumer.[x] It is to be salted and pure and sacred. 36Grind some of it to powder and place it in front of the ark of the covenant law in the tent of meeting, where I will meet with you. It shall be most holy[y] to you. 37Do not make any incense with this formula for yourselves; consider it holy[z] to the LORD. 38Whoever makes incense like it to enjoy its fragrance must be cut off[a] from their people."

Bezalel and Oholiab

31:2-6pp — Ex 35:30-35

31 Then the LORD said to Moses, 2"See, I have chosen Bezalel[b] son of Uri, the son of Hur, of the tribe of Judah, 3and I have filled him with the Spirit of God, with wisdom, with understanding, with knowledge and with all kinds of skills[c]—4to make artistic designs for work in gold, silver and bronze, 5to cut and set stones, to work in wood, and to engage in all kinds of crafts. 6Moreover, I have appointed Oholiab son of Ahisamak, of the tribe of Dan, to help him. Also I have given ability to all the skilled workers to make everything I have commanded you: 7the tent of meeting,[d] the ark of the covenant law[e] with the atonement cover[f] on it, and all the other furnishings of the tent— 8the table[g] and its articles, the pure gold lampstand[h] and all its accessories, the altar of incense, 9the altar of burnt offering and all its utensils, the basin with its stand— 10and also the woven garments[i], both the sacred garments for Aaron the priest and the garments for his sons when they serve as priests, 11and the anointing oil[j] and fragrant incense for the Holy Place. They are to make them just as I commanded you."

The Sabbath

12Then the LORD said to Moses, 13"Say to the Israelites, 'You must observe my Sabbaths.[k] This will be a sign[l] between me and you for the generations to come, so you may know that I am the LORD, who makes you holy.[m]

14" 'Observe the Sabbath, because it is holy to you. Anyone who desecrates it is to be put to death;[n] those who do any work on that day must be cut off from their people. 15For six days work[o] is to be done, but the seventh day is a day of sabbath rest,[p] holy to the LORD. Whoever does any work on the Sabbath day is to be put to death. 16The Israelites are to observe the Sabbath, celebrating it for the generations to come as a lasting covenant. 17It will be a sign[q] between me and the Israelites forever, for in six days the LORD made the heavens and the earth, and on the seventh day he rested and was refreshed.[r]' "

18When the LORD finished speaking to Moses on Mount Sinai, he gave him the two tablets of the covenant law, the tablets of stone[s] inscribed by the finger of God.[t]

The Golden Calf

32 When the people saw that Moses was so long in coming down from the mountain,[u] they gathered around Aaron and said, "Come, make us gods[a] who will go before us. As for this fellow Moses who brought us up out of Egypt, we don't know what has happened to him."[v]

2Aaron answered them, "Take off the gold earrings[w] that your wives, your sons and your daughters are wearing, and bring them to me." 3So all the people took off their earrings and brought them to Aaron. 4He took what they handed him and made it into an idol cast in the shape of a calf,[x] fashioning it with a tool. Then they

30:25 [q] Ex 37:29 [r] Ex 40:9 **30:26** [s] Ex 40:9; Lev 8:10; Nu 7:1 **30:29** [t] Ex 29:37 **30:30** [u] Ex 29:7; Lev 8:2, 12, 30 **30:32** [v] ver 25, 37 **30:33** [w] ver 38; Ge 17:14 **30:35** [x] ver 25 **30:36** [y] ver 32; Ex 29:37; Lev 2:3 **30:37** [z] ver 32 **30:38** [a] ver 33 **31:2** [b] Ex 36:1, 2; 1Ch 2:20 **31:3** [c] 1Ki 7:14 **31:7** [d] Ex 36:8-38 [e] Ex 37:1-5 [f] Ex 37:6 **31:8** [g] Ex 37:10-16 [h] Ex 37:17-24 **31:10** [i] Ex 28:2; 39:1, 41 **31:11** [j] Ex 30:22-32 **31:13** [k] Ex 20:8; Lev 19:3, 30 [l] Eze 20:12, 20 [m] Lev 11:44 **31:14** [n] Nu 15:32-36 **31:15** [o] Ex 20:8-11 [p] Ge 2:3; Ex 16:23 **31:17** [q] ver 13 [r] Ge 2:2-3 **31:18** [s] Ex 24:12 [t] Ex 32:15-16; 34:1, 28; Dt 4:13; 5:22 **32:1** [u] Ex 24:18; Dt 9:9-12 [v] Ac 7:40* **32:2** [w] Ex 35:22 **32:4** [x] Dt 9:16; Ne 9:18; Ps 106:19; Ac 7:41

[a] 1 Or *a god;* also in verses 23 and 31

31:18 *finger of God.* See note on 8:19.

32:4 *These are your gods.* What is uncertain here is whether the golden calf is being introduced as connected to the same God they have been worshiping or whether it is related to a new god(s). The translation "this is your god" is equally justifiable because the Hebrew word for "God/god" is *Elohim* and can be taken as either singular or plural. The Hebrew pronoun for "these" is indeed plural, but this could simply be the result of grammatical agreement with *Elohim,* which is grammatically plural. Thus, this statement may indeed have only one god in view.

EXODUS 32

THE GOLDEN CALF

Our understanding of the golden calf can benefit from an understanding of the iconography of the ancient world. From the ancient Near East (mostly from the Late Bronze Age), there are pictures of gods standing atop various animals, especially lions and bulls, as well as atop composite creatures. Moreover, there are depictions of bovines (these are generally from the Iron Age) — most likely bulls — that have no rider whatsoever. In the first set of images, the animal clearly functions as the seat or pedestal for the deity. In the second, there is no deity, which may raise possibilities for understanding the use of the golden calf here.

One idea is that the calf is still the pedestal, but this time of an invisible deity. The ark within the tabernacle functioned as a seat or footstool (see note on Ex 25:16) for the divine presence without any object to represent that presence. Perhaps, then, the golden calf functioned similarly. Or perhaps the calf is more in the nature of an emblem or symbol that stands in for the deity. The worship is still directed toward Yahweh (note the festival to Yahweh proclaimed by Aaron in 32:5), but it makes use of a representative, one that embodies Yahweh's power and protection and brings reassurance to the people with Moses absent. Regardless of how one interprets the calf, the worship in which the people engage angers Yahweh, in all likelihood because it violates the prohibition on making images (20:4), which they are supposed to know and to which they have already agreed. In this sense, the calf functions more to replace the absent Moses as a mediator than to replace Yahweh as the one who delivered them from Egypt. ◆

Basalt stele of god Adad on a bull with a thunderbolt in hand, c. 744 – 727 BC. This sort of image shows the animal functioning as the seat or pedestal for the deity, which gives some idea as to how the Golden Calf was possibly used and understood.

Wikimedia Commons/Rama, CC BY-SA 2.0 FR

said, "These are your gods,[a] Israel, who
brought you up out of Egypt."
5 When Aaron saw this, he built an altar in front of the calf and announced,
"Tomorrow there will be a festival[y] to the
LORD." 6 So the next day the people rose
early and sacrificed burnt offerings and
presented fellowship offerings.[z] Afterward
they sat down to eat and drink and got up
to indulge in revelry.[a]

32:5 [y] Lev 23:2, 37; 2Ki 10:20
32:6 [z] Nu 25:2; Ac 7:41 [a] ver 17-19; 1Co 10:7*

[a] 4 Or *This is your god*; also in verse 8

32:6 *indulge in revelry.* This is a notoriously difficult phrase to interpret. The most basic meaning of the Hebrew verbal root used here (*shq*) is "to laugh" (e.g., Ge 17:17). Some forms of this verb can also indicate joking (Ge 19:14), teasing (Ge 39:14), amusement (Jdg 16:25), and perhaps sexual fondling (Ge 26:8). One suggestion for the way in which the verb is used here is "to amuse oneself wildly," though the precise nature of such amusement

7 Then the LORD said to Moses, "Go down, because your people, whom you brought up out of Egypt,[b] have become corrupt.[c] 8 They have been quick to turn away from what I commanded them and have made themselves an idol[d] cast in the shape of a calf. They have bowed down to it and sacrificed[e] to it and have said, 'These are your gods, Israel, who brought you up out of Egypt.'[f]

9 "I have seen these people," the LORD said to Moses, "and they are a stiff-necked[g] people. 10 Now leave me alone so that my anger may burn against them and that I may destroy them. Then I will make you into a great nation."[h]

11 But Moses sought the favor[i] of the LORD his God. "LORD," he said, "why should your anger burn against your people, whom you brought out of Egypt with great power and a mighty hand?[j] 12 Why should the Egyptians say, 'It was with evil intent that he brought them out, to kill them in the mountains and to wipe them off the face of the earth'?[k] Turn from your fierce anger; relent and do not bring disaster on your people. 13 Remember[l] your servants Abraham, Isaac and Israel, to whom you swore by your own self:[m] 'I will make your descendants as numerous as the stars[n] in the sky and I will give your descendants all this land[o] I promised them, and it will be their inheritance forever.'" 14 Then the LORD relented[p] and did not bring on his people the disaster he had threatened.

15 Moses turned and went down the mountain with the two tablets of the covenant law[q] in his hands.[r] They were inscribed on both sides, front and back. 16 The tablets were the work of God; the writing was the writing of God, engraved on the tablets.[s]

17 When Joshua heard the noise of the people shouting, he said to Moses, "There is the sound of war in the camp."

18 Moses replied:

"It is not the sound of victory,
it is not the sound of defeat;
it is the sound of singing that I
hear."

19 When Moses approached the camp and saw the calf[t] and the dancing, his anger burned and he threw the tablets out of his hands, breaking them to pieces[u] at the foot of the mountain. 20 And he took the calf the people had made and burned it in the fire; then he ground it to powder, scattered it on the water[v] and made the Israelites drink it.

21 He said to Aaron, "What did these people do to you, that you led them into such great sin?"

22 "Do not be angry, my lord," Aaron answered. "You know how prone these people are to evil.[w] 23 They said to me, 'Make us gods who will go before us. As for this fellow Moses who brought us up out of Egypt, we don't know what has happened to him.'[x] 24 So I told them, 'Whoever has any gold jewelry, take it off.' Then they gave me the gold, and I threw it into the fire, and out came this calf!"[y]

25 Moses saw that the people were running wild and that Aaron had let them get

32:7 [b] ver 4, 11 [c] Ge 6:11-12; Dt 9:12 **32:8** [d] Ex 20:4 [e] Ex 22:20 [f] 1Ki 12:28 **32:9** [g] Ex 33:3, 5; 34:9; Isa 48:4; Ac 7:51 **32:10** [h] Nu 14:12; Dt 9:14 **32:11** [i] Dt 9:18 [j] Dt 9:26 **32:12** [k] Nu 14:13-16; Dt 9:28 **32:13** [l] Ex 2:24 [m] Ge 22:16; Heb 6:13 [n] Ge 15:5; 26:4 [o] Ge 12:7 **32:14** [p] 2Sa 24:16; Ps 106:45
32:15 [q] Ex 31:18 [r] Dt 9:15 **32:16** [s] Ex 31:18 **32:19** [t] Dt 9:16 [u] Dt 9:17 **32:20** [v] Dt 9:21 **32:22** [w] Dt 9:24 **32:23** [x] ver 1 **32:24** [y] ver 4

is not at all clear. Since the calf may be symbolic of the power that delivered the people from slavery in Egypt, perhaps the term simply refers to the idea of celebration—the kind of celebration that often ensues following a stunning military victory.

The bull as a symbol of military prowess was common throughout ancient Near Eastern societies, including Mesopotamia, Syria and Egypt. With Moses apparently having disappeared, the people need another tangible sign of their connection to Yahweh, their mighty deliverer. He is their warrior, their conquering hero, and a celebration of him would not be out of place.

32:19 *breaking them to pieces.* This may describe an outburst of anger on Moses' part, but the implications of breaking the tablets go beyond that. To smash tablets recording a legal agreement signifies the annulment of that agreement. The Biblical text never makes clear precisely what is written on the tablets. We do know from 24:12 that they contain the "law and commandments." The latter were directly related to the covenant established between Yahweh and the Israelites and contained the essence of the Israelites' obligations—what they were required to do to fulfill their end of the contract. For Moses to smash them is to declare unequivocally that the agreement is broken. Israel's recent action constitutes a violation of the agreement.

As mentioned previously (see the article "Covenants," p. 143), the covenant in Exodus is modeled after the standard legal agreements or contracts of that day. In Mesopotamia, such agreements were typically recorded on clay tablets. The legal act that declared the end or invalidation of the agreement often included breaking the tablet. The Israelites' violation of the covenant and Moses' invalidation of the agreement by breaking the tablets make necessary a renewal of the covenant, which comes in ch. 34.

32:20 It is difficult to determine if this verse portrays a literal description. The actions of Moses may be patterned after actions considered standard in any description of the destruction of a hated and despised deity or divine symbol. In the Baal Cycle from Ugarit, the goddess Anat sets out to destroy the god Mot. When she finally catches him, she grinds him to dust and sows it in a field, where it is eaten by birds. Anat's actions convey, with literary flourish, the complete destruction of Mot. Perhaps Moses' actions are stylized in similar fashion. Anat casts the leftover particles of Mot into a field; Moses strews the dust in the water. The birds, unwittingly, devour the last of Mot; the Israelites drink the last bits of the idol. Literal or not, it is the utter end of the image of the young bull.

out of control and so become a laughingstock to their enemies. 26So he stood at the entrance to the camp and said, "Whoever is for the LORD, come to me." And all the Levites rallied to him.

27Then he said to them, "This is what the LORD, the God of Israel, says: 'Each man strap a sword to his side. Go back and forth through the camp from one end to the other, each killing his brother and friend and neighbor.' "[z] 28The Levites did as Moses commanded, and that day about three thousand of the people died. 29Then Moses said, "You have been set apart to the LORD today, for you were against your own sons and brothers, and he has blessed you this day."

30The next day Moses said to the people, "You have committed a great sin.[a] But now I will go up to the LORD; perhaps I can make atonement[b] for your sin."

31So Moses went back to the LORD and said, "Oh, what a great sin these people have committed![c] They have made themselves gods of gold.[d] 32But now, please forgive their sin—but if not, then blot me[e] out of the book[f] you have written."

33The LORD replied to Moses, "Whoever has sinned against me I will blot out[g] of my book. 34Now go, lead the people to the place[h] I spoke of, and my angel[i] will go before you. However, when the time comes for me to punish,[j] I will punish them for their sin."

35And the LORD struck the people with a plague because of what they did with the calf[k] Aaron had made.

33 Then the LORD said to Moses, "Leave this place, you and the people you brought up out of Egypt, and go up to the land I promised on oath to Abraham, Isaac and Jacob, saying, 'I will give it to your descendants.'[l] 2I will send an angel[m] before you and drive out the Canaanites, Amorites, Hittites, Perizzites, Hivites and Jebusites.[n] 3Go up to the land flowing with milk and honey.[o] But I will not go with you, because you are a stiff-necked[p] people and I might destroy[q] you on the way."

4When the people heard these distressing words, they began to mourn[r] and no one put on any ornaments. 5For the LORD had said to Moses, "Tell the Israelites, 'You are a stiff-necked people. If I were to go with you even for a moment, I might destroy you. Now take off your ornaments and I will decide what to do with you.' " 6So the Israelites stripped off their ornaments at Mount Horeb.

The Tent of Meeting

7Now Moses used to take a tent and pitch it outside the camp some distance away, calling it the "tent of meeting."[s] Anyone inquiring of the LORD would go to the tent of meeting outside the camp. 8And whenever Moses went out to the tent, all the people rose and stood at the entrances to their tents,[t] watching Moses until he entered the tent. 9As Moses went into the tent, the pillar of cloud[u] would come down and stay at the entrance, while the LORD spoke[v] with Moses. 10Whenever the people saw the pillar of cloud standing at the entrance to the tent, they all stood and worshiped, each at the entrance to their tent. 11The LORD would speak to Moses face to face,[w] as one speaks to a friend. Then Moses would return to the camp, but his young aide Joshua son of Nun did not leave the tent.

32:27 [z]Nu 25:3,5; Dt 33:9
32:30 [a]1Sa 12:20 [b]Lev 1:4; Nu 25:13
32:31 [c]Dt 9:18 [d]Ex 20:23
32:32 [e]Ro 9:3 [f]Ps 69:28; Da 12:1; Php 4:3; Rev 3:5; 21:27
32:33 [g]Dt 29:20; Ps 9:5
32:34 [h]Ex 3:17 [i]Ex 23:20 [j]Dt 32:35; Ps 99:8; Ro 2:5-6
32:35 [k]ver 4
33:1 [l]Ge 12:7
33:2 [m]Ex 32:34 [n]Ex 23:27-31; Jos 24:11
33:3 [o]Ex 3:8 [p]Ex 32:9 [q]Ex 32:10
33:4 [r]Nu 14:39
33:7 [s]Ex 29:42-43
33:8 [t]Nu 16:27
33:9 [u]Ex 13:21 [v]Ex 31:18; Ps 99:7
33:11 [w]Nu 12:8; Dt 34:10

32:32 *book you have written.* The idea that deities kept written records that related to human activity is prevalent throughout the ancient Near East, particularly in Mesopotamia. Such books or records are referred to in both Sumerian and Akkadian texts and fall essentially into two categories: (1) "tablets of destiny" or "tablets of life" and (2) tablets that record human behavior. The book referred to by Moses in this verse is most likely one of the first type. In v. 33, Yahweh speaks of blotting "out of [his] book" those who have sinned against him, and the punishments that occur in vv. 28,35 are death. Inhabitants of the ancient world hoped that the heavenly books of destiny/life designated long life for them. To be removed from the book would lead to certain death. Thus, Moses is saying that he would prefer to die on the spot if Yahweh refuses to forgive the people as a collective group for their violation of Yahweh's law.

33:7 *tent of meeting.* Apparently, because of the illegitimate worship practiced in ch. 32, a separate tent is erected *outside* the camp. Yahweh will meet with Moses there. He will not come inside the camp because, as the text points out, Yahweh is angry and prone to wreak havoc on the people if he is in their midst (v. 5). Here in v. 7, the structure in question goes by the term "tent of meeting," a term used also of the tabernacle (e.g., 40:34). The tent here in v. 7, though, does not perform the equivalent function of the tabernacle. There is no indication that this particular tent will house the presence of Yahweh, since no rituals are performed to purify the tent and make it fit for the divine presence. A possible parallel comes from the Mesopotamian celebration of the *akitu* festival. In Babylonia, the celebration of this festival merged with the New Year celebration and was marked by the procession of Marduk outside the city to a small structure where he would dwell for several days. During this time, prayers were offered in the hopes that Marduk would restrain his anger and bless his people. His regular dwelling, the temple, underwent a ritual purification during his absence. The highlight of the festival came with the procession of the god back to the city and to his proper residence. The Mesopotamian parallel is imprecise, but the removal of the divine presence from the camp or the city was significant in both instances. It undoubtedly meant that the first priority was doing all that was necessary to ensure the deity's return to dwell securely among his people.

Moses and the Glory of the LORD

12Moses said to the LORD, "You have
been telling me, 'Lead these people,'[x] but
you have not let me know whom you will
send with me. You have said, 'I know you
by name[y] and you have found favor with
me.' 13If you are pleased with me, teach
me your ways[z] so I may know you and
continue to find favor with you. Remember that this nation is your people."[a]
14The LORD replied, "My Presence[b] will
go with you, and I will give you rest."[c]
15Then Moses said to him, "If your Presence does not go with us, do not send us
up from here. 16How will anyone know
that you are pleased with me and with
your people unless you go with us?[d] What
else will distinguish me and your people
from all the other people on the face of
the earth?"[e]
17And the LORD said to Moses, "I will do
the very thing you have asked, because I
am pleased with you and I know you by
name."
18Then Moses said, "Now show me your
glory."
19And the LORD said, "I will cause all my
goodness to pass in front of you, and I will
proclaim my name, the LORD, in your presence. I will have mercy on whom I will
have mercy, and I will have compassion
on whom I will have compassion.[f] 20But,"
he said, "you cannot see my face, for no
one may see[g] me and live."
21Then the LORD said, "There is a place
near me where you may stand on a rock.
22When my glory passes by, I will put you
in a cleft in the rock and cover you with
my hand[h] until I have passed by. 23Then I
will remove my hand and you will see my
back; but my face must not be seen."

The New Stone Tablets

34 The LORD said to Moses, "Chisel
out two stone tablets like the first
ones, and I will write on them the words
that were on the first tablets,[i] which you
broke.[j] 2Be ready in the morning, and then
come up on Mount Sinai.[k] Present yourself to me there on top of the mountain.
3No one is to come with you or be seen
anywhere on the mountain;[l] not even the
flocks and herds may graze in front of the
mountain."
4So Moses chiseled out two stone tablets like the first ones and went up Mount
Sinai early in the morning, as the LORD
had commanded him; and he carried the
two stone tablets in his hands. 5Then the
LORD came down in the cloud and stood
there with him and proclaimed his name,
the LORD.[m] 6And he passed in front of Moses, proclaiming, "The LORD, the LORD, the
compassionate[n] and gracious God, slow
to anger,[o] abounding in love[p] and faithfulness,[q] 7maintaining love to thousands,[r]
and forgiving wickedness, rebellion and
sin.[s] Yet he does not leave the guilty unpunished;[t] he punishes the children and
their children for the sin of the parents to
the third and fourth generation."
8Moses bowed to the ground at once
and worshiped. 9"Lord," he said, "if I have
found favor in your eyes, then let the Lord
go with us.[u] Although this is a stiff-necked
people, forgive our wickedness and our
sin, and take us as your inheritance."[v]
10Then the LORD said: "I am making a
covenant[w] with you. Before all your people I will do wonders never before done
in any nation in all the world.[x] The people you live among will see how awesome
is the work that I, the LORD, will do for
you. 11Obey what I command you today. I
will drive out before you the Amorites, Canaanites, Hittites, Perizzites, Hivites and
Jebusites.[y] 12Be careful not to make a treaty with those who live in the land where
you are going, or they will be a snare[z]
among you. 13Break down their altars,
smash their sacred stones and cut down
their Asherah poles.[a a] 14Do not worship
any other god,[b] for the LORD, whose name
is Jealous, is a jealous God.[c]

[a] *13* That is, wooden symbols of the goddess Asherah

33:12 [x] Ex 3:10 [y] ver 17; Jn 10:14-15; 2Ti 2:19 **33:13** [z] Ps 25:4; 86:11; 119:33 [a] Ex 34:9; Dt 9:26, 29 **33:14** [b] Isa 63:9 [c] Jos 21:44; 22:4 **33:16** [d] Nu 14:14 [e] Ex 34:10 **33:19** [f] Ro 9:15* **33:20** [g] Ge 32:30; Isa 6:5 **33:22** [h] Ps 91:4 **34:1** [i] Dt 10:2, 4 [j] Ex 32:19

34:2 [k] Ex 19:11 **34:3** [l] Ex 19:12-13, 21 **34:5** [m] Ex 33:19 **34:6** [n] Ps 86:15 [o] Nu 14:18; Ro 2:4 [p] Ne 9:17; Ps 103:8; Joel 2:13 [q] Ps 108:4 **34:7** [r] Ex 20:6 [s] Ps 103:3; 130:4, 8; Da 9:9; 1Jn 1:9 [t] Job 10:14; Na 1:3 **34:9** [u] Ex 33:15 [v] Ps 33:12 **34:10** [w] Dt 5:2-3 [x] Ex 33:16; Dt 4:32 **34:11** [y] Ex 33:2 **34:12** [z] Ex 23:32-33 **34:13** [a] Ex 23:24; Dt 12:3; 2Ki 18:4 **34:14** [b] Ex 20:3 [c] Ex 20:5; Dt 4:24

34:6 *The LORD, the LORD.* This repetition of Yahweh's name is followed by a list of attributes that focus on his love and compassion. This was not uncommon in descriptions of deities in the ancient world. Examples abound of gods or goddesses (and even kings) who are described in lengthy lists of epithets or titles that refer to their character traits or special activities. The epilogue to the Code of Hammurapi, e.g., mentions a dozen deities, after whose names are listed various epithets. With its focus on love, this description of Yahweh seems in contrast with the portrayal of Yahweh in chs. 32 – 33, when he was ready, at the very least, to sever ties with the disobedient Israelites. This proclamation to Moses, then, may be emphasizing that Yahweh's anger has now subsided and the people may expect to be back on good terms with him again.

34:13 *Asherah poles.* The goddess Asherah was worshiped under various names in ancient Near Eastern societies, and she apparently had followers in some parts of ancient Israel. Other Biblical texts condemn Asherah worship (Dt 7:5; 12:3; 2Ki 21:7); the goddess may also have been referred to as the "Queen of Heaven" (Jer 7:18). An eighth-century BC ink inscription on a pottery jar, discovered at Kuntillet Ajrud, a site in the northern Sinai region, refers to a blessing offered in the name of "Yahweh and his Asherah." This may suggest an aberrant ancient Israelite belief in a goddess wife of Yahweh, and this type of belief and the practices associated with it may be the target of commands like this one and those in Deuteronomy.

It is unlikely that the "poles" referred to in this verse are images of the goddess; rather, they are probably religious

15“Be careful not to make a treaty with
those who live in the land; for when they
prostitute[d] themselves to their gods and
sacrifice to them, they will invite you and
you will eat their sacrifices.[e] 16And when
you choose some of their daughters as
wives[f] for your sons and those daughters
prostitute themselves to their gods,[g] they
will lead your sons to do the same.
17“Do not make any idols.[h]
18“Celebrate the Festival of Unleavened
Bread.[i] For seven days eat bread made without yeast,[j] as I commanded you. Do this at
the appointed time in the month of Aviv,[k]
for in that month you came out of Egypt.
19“The first offspring[l] of every womb
belongs to me, including all the firstborn
males of your livestock, whether from
herd or flock. 20Redeem the firstborn donkey with a lamb, but if you do not redeem
it, break its neck.[m] Redeem all your firstborn sons.
“No one is to appear before me empty-handed.[n]
21“Six days you shall labor, but on the
seventh day you shall rest;[o] even during
the plowing season and harvest you must
rest.
22“Celebrate the Festival of Weeks with
the firstfruits of the wheat harvest, and the
Festival of Ingathering[p] at the turn of the
year.[a] 23Three times[q] a year all your men
are to appear before the Sovereign LORD,
the God of Israel. 24I will drive out nations[r]
before you and enlarge your territory, and
no one will covet your land when you go
up three times each year to appear before
the LORD your God.
25“Do not offer the blood of a sacrifice to
me along with anything containing yeast,[s]
and do not let any of the sacrifice from the
Passover Festival remain until morning.[t]
26“Bring the best of the firstfruits of your
soil to the house of the LORD your God.
“Do not cook a young goat in its mother’s milk.”[u]
27Then the LORD said to Moses, “Write[v]
down these words, for in accordance with
these words I have made a covenant with
you and with Israel.” 28Moses was there
with the LORD forty days and forty nights[w]
without eating bread or drinking water.
And he wrote on the tablets[x] the words of
the covenant—the Ten Commandments.[y]

34:15 [d] Jdg 2:17 [e] Nu 25:2; 1Co 8:4 **34:16** [f] Dt 7:3 [g] 1Ki 11:4 **34:17** [h] Ex 32:8 **34:18** [i] Ex 12:17 [j] Ex 12:15 [k] Ex 12:2 **34:19** [l] Ex 13:2 **34:20** [m] Ex 13:13, 15 [n] Ex 23:15; Dt 16:16 **34:21** [o] Ex 20:9; Lk 13:14 **34:22** [p] Ex 23:16 **34:23** [q] Ex 23:14 **34:24** [r] Ex 23:28; 33:2; Ps 78:55 **34:25** [s] Ex 23:18 [t] Ex 12:8, 10 **34:26** [u] Ex 23:19 **34:27** [v] Ex 17:14; 24:4 **34:28** [w] Ge 7:4; Ex 24:18; Mt 4:2 [x] ver 1; Ex 31:18 [y] Dt 4:13; 10:4

34:29 [z] Ex 32:15 [a] Ps 34:5; Mt 17:2; 2Co 3:7, 13 **34:32** [b] Ex 24:3 **34:33** [c] 2Co 3:13 **35:1** [d] Ex 34:32 **35:2** [e] Ex 20:9-10; 34:21; Lev 23:3 **35:3** [f] Ex 16:23

The Radiant Face of Moses

29When Moses came down from Mount
Sinai with the two tablets of the covenant
law in his hands,[z] he was not aware that
his face was radiant[a] because he had spoken with the LORD. 30When Aaron and all
the Israelites saw Moses, his face was radiant, and they were afraid to come near
him. 31But Moses called to them; so Aaron
and all the leaders of the community came
back to him, and he spoke to them. 32Af-
terward all the Israelites came near him,
and he gave them all the commands[b] the
LORD had given him on Mount Sinai.
33When Moses finished speaking to
them, he put a veil[c] over his face. 34But
whenever he entered the LORD’s presence
to speak with him, he removed the veil
until he came out. And when he came out
and told the Israelites what he had been
commanded, 35they saw that his face was
radiant. Then Moses would put the veil
back over his face until he went in to
speak with the LORD.

Sabbath Regulations

35 Moses assembled the whole Israelite community and said to them,
“These are the things the LORD has commanded[d] you to do: 2For six days, work is
to be done, but the seventh day shall be
your holy day, a day of sabbath[e] rest to
the LORD. Whoever does any work on it
is to be put to death. 3Do not light a fire
in any of your dwellings on the Sabbath
day.[f]”

Materials for the Tabernacle

35:4-9pp — Ex 25:1-7
35:10-19pp — Ex 39:32-41

4Moses said to the whole Israelite community, “This is what the LORD has commanded: 5From what you have, take an
offering for the LORD. Everyone who is
willing is to bring to the LORD an offering
of gold, silver and bronze; 6blue, purple
and scarlet yarn and fine linen; goat hair;
7ram skins dyed red and another type of
durable leather[b]; acacia wood; 8olive oil
for the light; spices for the anointing oil
and for the fragrant incense; 9and onyx

[a] *22* That is, in the autumn [b] *7* Possibly the hides of large aquatic mammals; also in verse 23

objects used in rituals associated with Asherah worship or perhaps with non-Yahwistic fertility rites in general.
34:28 *the Ten Commandments.* Lit. “the ten words.” This is the first time this phrase occurs in Exodus. The list in Ex 20 that we normally associate with the Ten Commandments is simply called “these words” (20:1). Moreover, these two lists differ substantially. Ex 20 contains several essentially noncultic provisions (e.g., commandments related to murder, adultery, theft, false accusation, coveting), which tie it to some degree to the content of the ancient Near Eastern law codes. The provisions in Ex 34, by contrast, seem to have no connection to the law code tradition since they reflect a much more cultic focus. They center on laws related to proper worship and ritual and, as part of the covenant that must be created because of the annulment of the first covenant, may possess this focus because of the failings in the area of worship so clearly demonstrated in the episode of the golden calf.

EXODUS 34:29

Moses' Horns

Despite the many English translations that refer to radiance or brightness emanating from the face of Moses, it is not clear what the Hebrew text means to say. Literally, Ex 34:29 says, "The skin of his face *qaran*." The main reason why many English translations refer to brilliance is that several ancient translations do so: the Septuagint, the pre-Christian Greek translation of the OT (done two centuries before Christ), the Peshitta (the Syriac translation probably completed by the fourth or fifth century AD), and the Targums (the Aramaic translations of OT books that originated during the first few centuries BC and continued to develop throughout the first millennium AD).

The most basic meaning of the Hebrew word *qaran* is "to have horns." Iconography, notably the representation of Moses by Michelangelo, portrays Moses with horns protruding from his head. This interpretation is not so far-fetched as one might think. Besides the surface meaning of the Hebrew, horns are a prevalent symbol of divinity throughout Mesopotamian art (though the focus of the Biblical text is on his face, not the top of his head).

Somewhat more convincing is an interpretation that attempts to combine the concepts of horns and light. The basis for this comes from a series of astronomical texts from ancient Babylonia known as *Enuma Anu Enlil*, and the way in which these texts use the Sumerian word *si*. At one point the text states: "If the sun's horn (*si*) fades and the moon is dark, there will be deaths; (*explanation*:) in the evening watch, the moon is having an eclipse (and in this context,) *si* means 'horn,' and *si* means 'shine'. . . ." The Exodus passage may thus be referring to "horns" of light radiating from Moses' face (similar to a halo expressed using vectors rather than a circle). This would be similar to a phenomenon labeled *melammu* in ancient Near Eastern texts that pertains to the brilliant glow of light from the gods (and kings) sometimes portrayed as rays of light that look a bit like horns. ◆

A lamassu (Mesopotamian celestial being) with horns on its helmet, c. 721 – 705 BC. Horns are a prevalent symbol of divinity throughout Mesopotamian art. It is possible that Moses' encounter had left him with horns or "horns of light" radiating from his face (Ex 34:29).

Kim Walton. The Oriental Institute Museum, the University of Chicago.

stones and other gems to be mounted on
the ephod and breastpiece.
10"All who are skilled among you are
to come and make everything the LORD
has commanded:[g] 11the tabernacle[h] with
its tent and its covering, clasps, frames,
crossbars, posts and bases; 12the ark[i] with
its poles and the atonement cover and the
curtain that shields it; 13the table[j] with its
poles and all its articles and the bread of
the Presence; 14the lampstand[k] that is for
light with its accessories, lamps and oil for
the light; 15the altar[l] of incense with its
poles, the anointing oil[m] and the fragrant
incense;[n] the curtain for the doorway at
the entrance to the tabernacle; 16the altar[o]
of burnt offering with its bronze grating,
its poles and all its utensils; the bronze
basin with its stand; 17the curtains of the
courtyard with its posts and bases, and the
curtain for the entrance to the courtyard;[p]
18the tent pegs for the tabernacle and for
the courtyard, and their ropes; 19the woven garments worn for ministering in the
sanctuary—both the sacred garments[q] for
Aaron the priest and the garments for his
sons when they serve as priests."
20Then the whole Israelite community
withdrew from Moses' presence, 21and everyone who was willing and whose heart
moved them came and brought an offering to the LORD for the work on the tent
of meeting, for all its service, and for the
sacred garments. 22All who were willing,
men and women alike, came and brought
gold jewelry of all kinds: brooches, earrings, rings and ornaments. They all presented their gold as a wave offering to the
LORD. 23Everyone who had blue, purple
or scarlet yarn[r] or fine linen, or goat hair,
ram skins dyed red or the other durable
leather brought them. 24Those presenting
an offering of silver or bronze brought it
as an offering to the LORD, and everyone
who had acacia wood for any part of the
work brought it. 25Every skilled woman[s]
spun with her hands and brought what
she had spun—blue, purple or scarlet
yarn or fine linen. 26And all the women
who were willing and had the skill spun
the goat hair. 27The leaders[t] brought onyx
stones and other gems to be mounted on
the ephod and breastpiece. 28They also
brought spices and olive oil for the light
and for the anointing oil and for the fragrant incense.[u] 29All the Israelite men and
women who were willing[v] brought to the
LORD freewill offerings[w] for all the work
the LORD through Moses had commanded
them to do.

Bezalel and Oholiab

35:30-35pp — Ex 31:2-6

30Then Moses said to the Israelites, "See,
the LORD has chosen Bezalel son of Uri,
the son of Hur, of the tribe of Judah, 31and
he has filled him with the Spirit of God,
with wisdom, with understanding, with
knowledge and with all kinds of skills[x]—
32to make artistic designs for work in gold,
silver and bronze, 33to cut and set stones,
to work in wood and to engage in all kinds
of artistic crafts. 34And he has given both
him and Oholiab[y] son of Ahisamak, of the
tribe of Dan, the ability to teach[z] others.
35He has filled them with skill to do all
kinds of work[a] as engravers, designers,
embroiderers in blue, purple and scarlet
yarn and fine linen, and weavers—all of
them skilled workers and design-
36
ers. 1So Bezalel, Oholiab and every
skilled person[b] to whom the LORD has giv-
en skill and ability to know how to carry
out all the work of constructing the sanctuary[c] are to do the work just as the LORD
has commanded."
2Then Moses summoned Bezalel[d] and
Oholiab[e] and every skilled person to whom
the LORD had given ability and who was
willing[f] to come and do the work. 3They
received from Moses all the offerings[g] the
Israelites had brought to carry out the
work of constructing the sanctuary. And
the people continued to bring freewill offerings morning after morning. 4So all the
skilled workers who were doing all the
work on the sanctuary left what they were
doing 5and said to Moses, "The people are
bringing more than enough[h] for doing the
work the LORD commanded to be done."
6Then Moses gave an order and they
sent this word throughout the camp: "No
man or woman is to make anything else
as an offering for the sanctuary." And so
the people were restrained from bringing
more, 7because what they already had was
more[i] than enough to do all the work.

The Tabernacle

36:8-38pp — Ex 26:1-37

8All those who were skilled among the
workers made the tabernacle with ten

35:10 [g] Ex 31:6 **35:11** [h] Ex 26:1-37 **35:12** [i] Ex 25:10-22 **35:13** [j] Ex 25:23-30; Lev 24:5-6 **35:14** [k] Ex 25:31 **35:15** [l] Ex 30:1-6 [m] Ex 30:25 [n] Ex 30:34-38 **35:16** [o] Ex 27:1-8 **35:17** [p] Ex 27:9 **35:19** [q] Ex 28:2; 31:10; 39:1 **35:23** [r] 1Ch 29:8 **35:25** [s] Ex 28:3 **35:27** [t] 1Ch 29:6; Ezr 2:68 **35:28** [u] Ex 25:6 **35:29** [v] ver 21; 1Ch 29:9 [w] ver 4-9; Ex 25:1-7; 36:3; 2Ki 12:4 **35:31** [x] ver 35; 2Ch 2:7,14 **35:34** [y] Ex 31:6 [z] 2Ch 2:14 **35:35** [a] ver 31; Ex 31:3,6; 1Ki 7:14 **36:1** [b] Ex 28:3 [c] Ex 25:8 **36:2** [d] Ex 31:2 [e] Ex 31:6 [f] Ex 25:2; 35:21, 26; 1Ch 29:5 **36:3** [g] Ex 35:29 **36:5** [h] 2Ch 24:14; 31:10; 2Co 8:2-3 **36:7** [i] 1Ki 7:47

36:8 *made the tabernacle.* Chs. 35–40 recount the fulfillment of the instructions given to Moses in chs. 25–31. Much of this fulfillment section repeats or restates passages from the instructions section. One plausible explanation is that the entire section in Exodus devoted to the tabernacle (chs. 25–31; 35–40) is based, in part, on a particular literary pattern for describing the building of divinely sanctioned shrines in the ancient Near East. One feature of this pattern was its requirement that the building be described after an account of the preparations and before the dedication ceremonies.

curtains of finely twisted linen and blue, purple and scarlet yarn, with cherubim woven into them by expert hands. 9All the curtains were the same size—twenty-eight cubits long and four cubits wide.[a] 10They joined five of the curtains together and did the same with the other five. 11Then they made loops of blue material along the edge of the end curtain in one set, and the same was done with the end curtain in the other set. 12They also made fifty loops on one curtain and fifty loops on the end curtain of the other set, with the loops opposite each other. 13Then they made fifty gold clasps and used them to fasten the two sets of curtains together so that the tabernacle was a unit.[j]

14They made curtains of goat hair for the tent over the tabernacle—eleven altogether. 15All eleven curtains were the same size—thirty cubits long and four cubits wide.[b] 16They joined five of the curtains into one set and the other six into another set. 17Then they made fifty loops along the edge of the end curtain in one set and also along the edge of the end curtain in the other set. 18They made fifty bronze clasps to fasten the tent together as a unit.[k] 19Then they made for the tent a covering of ram skins dyed red, and over that a covering of the other durable leather.[c]

20They made upright frames of acacia wood for the tabernacle. 21Each frame was ten cubits long and a cubit and a half wide,[d] 22with two projections set parallel to each other. They made all the frames of the tabernacle in this way. 23They made twenty frames for the south side of the tabernacle 24and made forty silver bases to go under them—two bases for each frame, one under each projection. 25For the other side, the north side of the tabernacle, they made twenty frames 26and forty silver bases—two under each frame. 27They made six frames for the far end, that is, the west end of the tabernacle, 28and two frames were made for the corners of the tabernacle at the far end. 29At these two corners the frames were double from the bottom all the way to the top and fitted into a single ring; both were made alike. 30So there were eight frames and sixteen silver bases—two under each frame.

31They also made crossbars of acacia wood: five for the frames on one side of the tabernacle, 32five for those on the other side, and five for the frames on the west, at the far end of the tabernacle. 33They made the center crossbar so that it extended from end to end at the middle of the frames. 34They overlaid the frames with gold and made gold rings to hold the crossbars. They also overlaid the crossbars with gold.

35They made the curtain[l] of blue, purple and scarlet yarn and finely twisted linen, with cherubim woven into it by a skilled worker. 36They made four posts of acacia wood for it and overlaid them with gold. They made gold hooks for them and cast their four silver bases. 37For the entrance to the tent they made a curtain of blue, purple and scarlet yarn and finely twisted linen—the work of an embroiderer;[m] 38and they made five posts with hooks for them. They overlaid the tops of the posts and their bands with gold and made their five bases of bronze.

The Ark

37:1-9pp — Ex 25:10-20

37 Bezalel[n] made the ark[o] of acacia wood—two and a half cubits long, a cubit and a half wide, and a cubit and a half high.[e] 2He overlaid it with pure gold,[p] both inside and out, and made a gold molding around it. 3He cast four gold rings for it and fastened them to its four feet, with two rings on one side and two rings on the other. 4Then he made poles of acacia wood and overlaid them with gold. 5And he inserted the poles into the rings on the sides of the ark to carry it.

6He made the atonement cover[q] of pure gold—two and a half cubits long and a cubit and a half wide. 7Then he made two cherubim[r] out of hammered gold at the ends of the cover. 8He made one cherub on one end and the second cherub on the other; at the two ends he made them of one piece with the cover. 9The cherubim had their wings spread upward, overshadowing[s] the cover with them. The cherubim faced each other, looking toward the cover.[t]

The Table

37:10-16pp — Ex 25:23-29

10They[f] made the table[u] of acacia wood—two cubits long, a cubit wide and a cubit and a half high.[g] 11Then they overlaid it with pure gold[v] and made a gold molding around it. 12They also made around it a rim a handbreadth[h] wide and put a gold molding on the rim. 13They cast four gold rings for the table and fastened

36:13 [j] ver 18
36:18 [k] ver 13
36:35 [l] Ex 39:38; Mt 27:51; Lk 23:45; Heb 9:3
36:37 [m] Ex 27:16
37:1 [n] Ex 31:2 [o] Ex 30:6; 39:35; Dt 10:3
37:2 [p] ver 11,26
37:6 [q] Ex 26:34; 31:7; Heb 9:5
37:7 [r] Eze 41:18
37:9 [s] Heb 9:5 [t] Dt 10:3
37:10 [u] Heb 9:2
37:11 [v] ver 2

[a] *9* That is, about 42 feet long and 6 feet wide or about 13 meters long and 1.8 meters wide [b] *15* That is, about 45 feet long and 6 feet wide or about 14 meters long and 1.8 meters wide [c] *19* Possibly the hides of large aquatic mammals (see 35:7) [d] *21* That is, about 15 feet long and 2 1/4 feet wide or about 4.5 meters long and 68 centimeters wide [e] *1* That is, about 3 3/4 feet long and 2 1/4 feet wide and high or about 1.1 meters long and 68 centimeters wide and high; similarly in verse 6 [f] *10* Or *He*; also in verses 11-29 [g] *10* That is, about 3 feet long, 1 1/2 feet wide and 2 1/4 feet high or about 90 centimeters long, 45 centimeters wide and 68 centimeters high [h] *12* That is, about 3 inches or about 7.5 centimeters

them to the four corners, where the four legs were. 14The rings[w] were put close to the rim to hold the poles used in carrying the table. 15The poles for carrying the table were made of acacia wood and were overlaid with gold. 16And they made from pure gold the articles for the table—its plates and dishes and bowls and its pitchers for the pouring out of drink offerings.

The Lampstand

37:17-24pp — Ex 25:31-39

17They made the lampstand[x] of pure gold. They hammered out its base and shaft, and made its flowerlike cups, buds and blossoms of one piece with them. 18Six branches extended from the sides of the lampstand—three on one side and three on the other. 19Three cups shaped like almond flowers with buds and blossoms were on one branch, three on the next branch and the same for all six branches extending from the lampstand. 20And on the lampstand were four cups shaped like almond flowers with buds and blossoms. 21One bud was under the first pair of branches extending from the lampstand, a second bud under the second pair, and a third bud under the third pair—six branches in all. 22The buds and the branches were all of one piece with the lampstand, hammered out of pure gold.[y]

23They made its seven lamps,[z] as well as its wick trimmers and trays, of pure gold. 24They made the lampstand and all its accessories from one talent[a] of pure gold.

The Altar of Incense

37:25-28pp — Ex 30:1-5

25They made the altar of incense[a] out of acacia wood. It was square, a cubit long and a cubit wide and two cubits high[b]—its horns[b] of one piece with it. 26They overlaid the top and all the sides and the horns with pure gold, and made a gold molding around it. 27They made two gold rings[c] below the molding—two on each of the opposite sides—to hold the poles used to carry it. 28They made the poles of acacia wood and overlaid them with gold.[d]

29They also made the sacred anointing oil[e] and the pure, fragrant incense[f]—the work of a perfumer.

37:14 [w] ver 27 **37:17** [x] Heb 9:2; Rev 1:12 **37:22** [y] ver 17; Nu 8:4 **37:23** [z] Ex 40:4, 25 **37:25** [a] Ex 30:34-36; Lk 1:11; Heb 9:4; Rev 8:3 [b] Ex 27:2; Rev 9:13 **37:27** [c] ver 14 **37:28** [d] Ex 25:13 **37:29** [e] Ex 31:11 [f] Ex 30:1, 25; 39:38 **38:2** [g] 2Ch 1:5 **38:3** [h] Ex 31:9 **38:8** [i] Ex 30:18; 40:7 [j] Dt 23:17; 1Sa 2:22; 1Ki 14:24

The Altar of Burnt Offering

38:1-7pp — Ex 27:1-8

38 They[c] built the altar of burnt offering of acacia wood, three cubits[d] high; it was square, five cubits long and five cubits wide.[e] 2They made a horn at each of the four corners, so that the horns and the altar were of one piece, and they overlaid the altar with bronze.[g] 3They made all its utensils[h] of bronze—its pots, shovels, sprinkling bowls, meat forks and firepans. 4They made a grating for the altar, a bronze network, to be under its ledge, halfway up the altar. 5They cast bronze rings to hold the poles for the four corners of the bronze grating. 6They made the poles of acacia wood and overlaid them with bronze. 7They inserted the poles into the rings so they would be on the sides of the altar for carrying it. They made it hollow, out of boards.

The Basin for Washing

8They made the bronze basin[i] and its bronze stand from the mirrors of the women[j] who served at the entrance to the tent of meeting.

The Courtyard

38:9-20pp — Ex 27:9-19

9Next they made the courtyard. The south side was a hundred cubits[f] long and had curtains of finely twisted linen, 10with twenty posts and twenty bronze bases, and with silver hooks and bands on the posts. 11The north side was also a hundred cubits long and had twenty posts and twenty bronze bases, with silver hooks and bands on the posts.

12The west end was fifty cubits[g] wide and had curtains, with ten posts and ten

[a] *24* That is, about 75 pounds or about 34 kilograms
[b] *25* That is, about 1 1/2 feet long and wide and 3 feet high or about 45 centimeters long and wide and 90 centimeters high
[c] *1* Or *He*; also in verses 2-9
[d] *1* That is, about 4 1/2 feet or about 1.4 meters
[e] *1* That is, about 7 1/2 feet or about 2.3 meters long and wide
[f] *9* That is, about 150 feet or about 45 meters
[g] *12* That is, about 75 feet or about 23 meters

38:8 *women who served at the entrance.* Unlike much of the rest of Ex 35–40, this verse contains information not already given in Ex 25–31. Women could serve in a variety of capacities at a sacred shrine. Some temples maintained large estates, operated economic ventures, and thus employed women to provide labor in the form of agricultural and weaving work. Some women served as devotees of a particular deity and lived, often as celibates, within the precinct of that deity's shrine. Others held what was essentially the status of slave and served the temple to which they were attached; some speculate that such women could have been hired out as prostitutes to generate income for the temple.

Exodus offers no clear indication regarding the precise role these women played in the life of the tabernacle, though it seems unlikely that their service was economic in nature. Since we know that women in other societies were involved in the basic operations and upkeep of religious shrines, it is reasonable to assume that Exodus is speaking of similar functions here, though it may be hinting that they remained at the door of the shrine because they were not allowed to enter within it.

bases, with silver hooks and bands on the
posts. 13The east end, toward the sunrise,
was also fifty cubits wide. 14Curtains fifteen cubits[a] long were on one side of the
entrance, with three posts and three bases, 15and curtains fifteen cubits long were
on the other side of the entrance to the
courtyard, with three posts and three bases. 16All the curtains around the courtyard
were of finely twisted linen. 17The bases
for the posts were bronze. The hooks and
bands on the posts were silver, and their
tops were overlaid with silver; so all the
posts of the courtyard had silver bands.
18The curtain for the entrance to the
courtyard was made of blue, purple and
scarlet yarn and finely twisted linen—the
work of an embroiderer. It was twenty
cubits[b] long and, like the curtains of the
courtyard, five cubits[c] high, 19with four
posts and four bronze bases. Their hooks
and bands were silver, and their tops were
overlaid with silver. 20All the tent pegs[k]
of the tabernacle and of the surrounding
courtyard were bronze.

The Materials Used

21These are the amounts of the materials used for the tabernacle, the tabernacle
of the covenant law,[l] which were recorded
at Moses' command by the Levites under
the direction of Ithamar[m] son of Aaron,
the priest. 22(Bezalel[n] son of Uri, the son
of Hur, of the tribe of Judah, made everything the LORD commanded Moses; 23with
him was Oholiab[o] son of Ahisamak, of the
tribe of Dan—an engraver and designer,
and an embroiderer in blue, purple and
scarlet yarn and fine linen.) 24The total
amount of the gold from the wave offering
used for all the work on the sanctuary[p]
was 29 talents and 730 shekels,[d] according
to the sanctuary shekel.[q]
25The silver obtained from those of the
community who were counted in the census[r] was 100 talents[e] and 1,775 shekels,[f]
according to the sanctuary shekel—26one
beka per person,[s] that is, half a shekel,[g]
according to the sanctuary shekel,[t] from
everyone who had crossed over to those
counted, twenty years old or more,[u] a total
of 603,550 men.[v] 27The 100 talents of silver
were used to cast the bases[w] for the sanctuary and for the curtain—100 bases from
the 100 talents, one talent for each base.
28They used the 1,775 shekels to make the
hooks for the posts, to overlay the tops of
the posts, and to make their bands.
29The bronze from the wave offering
was 70 talents and 2,400 shekels.[h] 30They
used it to make the bases for the entrance
to the tent of meeting, the bronze altar
with its bronze grating and all its utensils,
31the bases for the surrounding courtyard
and those for its entrance and all the tent
pegs for the tabernacle and those for the
surrounding courtyard.

The Priestly Garments

39 From the blue, purple and scarlet
yarn[x] they made woven garments
for ministering in the sanctuary.[y] They
also made sacred garments[z] for Aaron, as
the LORD commanded Moses.

The Ephod

39:2-7pp — Ex 28:6-14

2They[i] made the ephod of gold, and
of blue, purple and scarlet yarn, and of
finely twisted linen. 3They hammered out
thin sheets of gold and cut strands to be
worked into the blue, purple and scarlet
yarn and fine linen—the work of skilled
hands. 4They made shoulder pieces for the
ephod, which were attached to two of its
corners, so it could be fastened. 5Its skillfully woven waistband was like it—of one
piece with the ephod and made with gold,
and with blue, purple and scarlet yarn,
and with finely twisted linen, as the LORD
commanded Moses.
6They mounted the onyx stones in gold
filigree settings and engraved them like a
seal with the names of the sons of Israel.
7Then they fastened them on the shoulder
pieces of the ephod as memorial[a] stones
for the sons of Israel, as the LORD commanded Moses.

The Breastpiece

39:8-21pp — Ex 28:15-28

8They fashioned the breastpiece[b]—the
work of a skilled craftsman. They made it
like the ephod: of gold, and of blue, purple and scarlet yarn, and of finely twisted
linen. 9It was square—a span[j] long and

38:20 [k]Ex 35:18 **38:21** [l]Nu 1:50, 53; 8:24; 9:15; 10:11; 17:7; 1Ch 23:32; 2Ch 24:6; Ac 7:44; Rev 15:5 [m]Nu 4:28,33 **38:22** [n]Ex 31:2 **38:23** [o]Ex 31:6 **38:24** [p]Ex 30:16 [q]Ex 30:13; Lev 27:25; Nu 3:47; 18:16 **38:25** [r]Ex 30:12 **38:26** [s]Ex 30:12 [t]Ex 30:13 [u]Ex 30:14 [v]Ex 12:37; Nu 1:46 **38:27** [w]Ex 26:19

39:1 [x]Ex 35:23 [y]Ex 35:19 [z]ver 41; Ex 28:2 **39:7** [a]Lev 24:7; Jos 4:7 **39:8** [b]Lev 8:8

[a] *14* That is, about 22 feet or about 6.8 meters
[b] *18* That is, about 30 feet or about 9 meters
[c] *18* That is, about 7 1/2 feet or about 2.3 meters
[d] *24* The weight of the gold was a little over a ton or about 1 metric ton.
[e] *25* That is, about 3 3/4 tons or about 3.4 metric tons; also in verse 27
[f] *25* That is, about 44 pounds or about 20 kilograms; also in verse 28
[g] *26* That is, about 1/5 ounce or about 5.7 grams
[h] *29* The weight of the bronze was about 2 1/2 tons or about 2.4 metric tons.
[i] *2* Or *He*; also in verses 7, 8 and 22
[j] *9* That is, about 9 inches or about 23 centimeters

39:3 *thin sheets of gold.* The Egyptians were well-known for their ability to cover items of wood in a layer of thin gold. A number of objects from the famous tomb of the Egyptian king Tutankhamun are remarkable attestations to this skill. This verse, then, may be referring to a method of gilding that was derived from an originally Egyptian practice.

a span wide—and folded double. 10Then they mounted four rows of precious stones on it. The first row was carnelian, chrysolite and beryl; 11the second row was turquoise, lapis lazuli and emerald; 12the third row was jacinth, agate and amethyst; 13the fourth row was topaz, onyx and jasper.[a] They were mounted in gold filigree settings. 14There were twelve stones, one for each of the names of the sons of Israel, each engraved like a seal with the name of one of the twelve tribes.[c]

15For the breastpiece they made braided chains of pure gold, like a rope. 16They made two gold filigree settings and two gold rings, and fastened the rings to two of the corners of the breastpiece. 17They fastened the two gold chains to the rings at the corners of the breastpiece, 18and the other ends of the chains to the two settings, attaching them to the shoulder pieces of the ephod at the front. 19They made two gold rings and attached them to the other two corners of the breastpiece on the inside edge next to the ephod. 20Then they made two more gold rings and attached them to the bottom of the shoulder pieces on the front of the ephod, close to the seam just above the waistband of the ephod. 21They tied the rings of the breastpiece to the rings of the ephod with blue cord, connecting it to the waistband so that the breastpiece would not swing out from the ephod—as the LORD commanded Moses.

Other Priestly Garments

39:22-31pp — Ex 28:31-43

22They made the robe of the ephod entirely of blue cloth—the work of a weaver— 23with an opening in the center of the robe like the opening of a collar,[b] and a band around this opening, so that it would not tear. 24They made pomegranates of blue, purple and scarlet yarn and finely twisted linen around the hem of the robe. 25And they made bells of pure gold and attached them around the hem between the pomegranates. 26The bells and pomegranates alternated around the hem of the robe to be worn for ministering, as the LORD commanded Moses.

27For Aaron and his sons, they made tunics of fine linen[d]—the work of a weaver— 28and the turban[e] of fine linen, the linen caps and the undergarments of finely twisted linen. 29The sash was made of finely twisted linen and blue, purple and scarlet yarn—the work of an embroiderer—as the LORD commanded Moses.

30They made the plate, the sacred emblem, out of pure gold and engraved on it, like an inscription on a seal: HOLY TO THE LORD. 31Then they fastened a blue cord to it to attach it to the turban, as the LORD commanded Moses.

Moses Inspects the Tabernacle

39:32-41pp — Ex 35:10-19

32So all the work on the tabernacle, the tent of meeting, was completed. The Israelites did everything just as the LORD commanded Moses.[f] 33Then they brought the tabernacle to Moses: the tent and all its furnishings, its clasps, frames, crossbars, posts and bases; 34the covering of ram skins dyed red and the covering of another durable leather[c] and the shielding curtain; 35the ark of the covenant law[g] with its poles and the atonement cover; 36the table with all its articles and the bread of the Presence; 37the pure gold lampstand[h] with its row of lamps and all its accessories, and the olive oil for the light; 38the gold altar,[i] the anointing oil, the fragrant incense, and the curtain[j] for the entrance to the tent; 39the bronze altar with its bronze grating, its poles and all its utensils; the basin with its stand; 40the curtains of the courtyard with its posts and bases, and the curtain for the entrance to the courtyard;[k] the ropes and tent pegs for the courtyard; all the furnishings for the tabernacle, the tent of meeting; 41and the woven garments worn for ministering in the sanctuary, both the sacred garments for Aaron the priest and the garments for his sons when serving as priests.

42The Israelites had done all the work just as the LORD had commanded Moses.[l] 43Moses inspected the work and saw that they had done it just as the LORD had commanded. So Moses blessed[m] them.

Setting Up the Tabernacle

40 Then the LORD said to Moses: 2"Set up the tabernacle, the tent of meeting,[n] on the first day of the first month.[o] 3Place the ark[p] of the covenant law in it and shield the ark with the curtain. 4Bring in the table and set out what belongs on it.[q] Then bring in the lampstand[r] and set

39:14 [c]Rev 21:12
39:27 [d]Lev 6:10
39:28 [e]Ex 28:4
39:32 [f]ver 42-43; Ex 25:9
39:35 [g]Ex 30:6
39:37 [h]Ex 25:31
39:38 [i]Ex 30:1-10 [j]Ex 36:35
39:40 [k]Ex 27:9-19
39:42 [l]Ex 25:9
39:43 [m]Lev 9:22, 23; Nu 6:23-27; 2Sa 6:18; 1Ki 8:14, 55; 2Ch 30:27
40:2 [n]Nu 1:1 [o]ver 17; Ex 12:2
40:3 [p]ver 21; Nu 4:5; Ex 26:33
40:4 [q]Ex 25:30 [r]ver 22-25; Ex 26:35

[a] 13 The precise identification of some of these precious stones is uncertain. [b] 23 The meaning of the Hebrew for this word is uncertain. [c] 34 Possibly the hides of large aquatic mammals

39:27 *fine linen.* Linen has already been mentioned a number of times in the instructions for and the construction of the tabernacle. The linen here, though, is for the priestly garments. This material was considered to be of a high quality and was known for its white color. The art of weaving is well documented and depicted in Egypt, and the Biblical text may be referring to a method of performing this craft that originated there.

EXODUS 40:34 – 38

GLORY

Several instances throughout Exodus (e.g., Ex 16:10; 34:5) have made clear that the visible manifestation of Yahweh's presence often occurs in the form of a cloud. Since the Israelites conceived of Yahweh as invisible, they needed a visible entity — a reminder or symbol that could be seen by the human eye — to reassure them that Yahweh was indeed present with them. That visible entity is often referred to in the OT as the "glory" (*kabod*) of Yahweh. Isa 40:5, e.g., states that it is the "glory of the LORD" that "all people will see."

Once the construction and arrangement of the tabernacle in Exodus is complete, the glory of Yahweh, in the form of a cloud, so fills the place that Moses is unable even to enter it (Ex 40:35). It seems, therefore, to have been more than something that could merely be seen; it could be sensed in other ways. At one point in Exodus, the "glory" is called a "consuming fire" (24:17). The glory of Yahweh was reassuring and fear-inspiring all at the same time.

This is reminiscent of the Mesopotamian concept of *melammu* ("radiance, supernatural awe-inspiring sheen") — a quality that gods and goddesses possessed and one that they could bestow on humans, typically royalty, and take back again if they so desired. In fact, anything that was imbued with divine power and presence was believed to possess *melammu*. On the one hand, it was a blessing, for it was considered part of what gave legitimacy to a king and his rule; on the other hand, it was a terror that could overwhelm and decimate one who had become the enemy of the gods.

Seal impression depicting emanating rays may indicate the figure on the right is the sun god or could be the *melammu* (divine glow).

Kim Walton. The Oriental Institute Museum, the University of Chicago.

Yahweh's glory was also dual in nature, bringing reassurance to some, terror to others, and probably equal parts of both to most. This recalls Moses' close encounter with Yahweh in Ex 33, when Moses asked to see Yahweh's "glory" (33:18). When he is granted this request, Yahweh descends, stands before him, and proclaims both his love and loyalty and his willingness to punish. Throughout the Exodus narrative, Moses himself has experienced both aspects of Yahweh's presence — the providential deliverance of the Israelites and yet an angry Yahweh threatening to annihilate his people. It is this glory, as both cloud and fire, that, as Exodus comes to a close, is always "in the sight of all the Israelites" (40:38), ever reminding them of God's presence and their covenantal obligation to obey him. ◆

THE TORAH

LEVITICUS

Leviticus, the central book of the Pentateuch, deals with the areas of ritual worship and religious, criminal and civil law, which were central to the cultural life and governance of all ancient Near Eastern societies and generated a vast quantity of preserved texts and objects. We will find similar ritual procedures, infrastructure, terminology and concepts, as well as similar approaches to law in terms of literary context, formulation, reasoning and content between Israelite and surrounding cultures. It is abundantly clear that Leviticus was meant to communicate with and address the needs of real people in the context of their ancient Near Eastern culture, which contained a number of positive elements worthy to be affirmed and continued. At the same time, we recognize crucial differences that highlight and give depth perspective to the uniqueness of Israel's God and his timeless message through Leviticus, which was countercultural in important respects.

KEY CONCEPTS

- Ritual impurity is not the same as sin, but either can restrict access to God's presence.
- Holiness distinguishes God from people and God's people from other people.
- Sacred space must be defined and preserved (the job of priests).
- Sacrifice is a mechanism to allow people to pray to God, thank God, preserve sacred space for God and be in relationship with God.

Historical Setting

According to the narrative framework of the Pentateuch, God gave the legislation of Leviticus to Israel through Moses in the Sinai Desert during the first month of the second year after the Israelites exited from slavery in Egypt, before they moved on toward the land of Canaan (compare Ex 40:17 and Nu 1:1). Within the framework of Biblical chronology, this was during the second half of the second millennium BC.

Literary Setting

Some major features of Leviticus relate to similar aspects of other ancient Near Eastern texts.

1. Divine speech in a narrative setting. Compare, e.g., the Sumerian Cylinder A of Gudea, which extensively quotes the deities Ningirsu and Nanshe regarding construction of the Eninnu temple in Lagash.
2. Instructions for performance of rituals and festivals. Compare the Ugaritic Rites for the Vintage.

up its lamps. 5Place the gold altar[s] of incense in front of the ark of the covenant
law and put the curtain at the entrance to
the tabernacle.
6"Place the altar of burnt offering in
front of the entrance to the tabernacle, the
tent of meeting; 7place the basin[t] between
the tent of meeting and the altar and put
water in it. 8Set up the courtyard around it
and put the curtain at the entrance to the
courtyard.
9"Take the anointing oil and anoint[u] the
tabernacle and everything in it; consecrate
it and all its furnishings, and it will be
holy. 10Then anoint the altar of burnt offering and all its utensils; consecrate[v] the
altar, and it will be most holy. 11Anoint the
basin and its stand and consecrate them.
12"Bring Aaron and his sons to the entrance to the tent of meeting and wash
them with water.[w] 13Then dress Aaron in
the sacred garments,[x] anoint him and consecrate[y] him so he may serve me as priest.
14Bring his sons and dress them in tunics.
15Anoint them just as you anointed their
father, so they may serve me as priests.
Their anointing will be to a priesthood
that will continue throughout their generations.[z]" 16Moses did everything just as
the LORD commanded him.
17So the tabernacle[a] was set up on the
first day of the first month[b] in the second
year. 18When Moses set up the tabernacle, he put the bases in place, erected the
frames, inserted the crossbars and set up
the posts. 19Then he spread the tent over
the tabernacle and put the covering over
the tent, as the LORD commanded him.
20He took the tablets of the covenant
law[c] and placed them in the ark, attached
the poles to the ark and put the atonement
cover over it. 21Then he brought the ark
into the tabernacle and hung the shielding
curtain[d] and shielded the ark of the covenant law, as the LORD commanded him.
22Moses placed the table[e] in the tent of
meeting on the north side of the tabernacle outside the curtain 23and set out the
bread[f] on it before the LORD, as the LORD
commanded him.
24He placed the lampstand[g] in the tent
of meeting opposite the table on the south
side of the tabernacle 25and set up the
lamps[h] before the LORD, as the LORD commanded him.
26Moses placed the gold altar[i] in the tent
of meeting in front of the curtain 27and
burned fragrant incense on it, as the LORD
commanded[j] him.
28Then he put up the curtain[k] at the entrance to the tabernacle. 29He set the altar of burnt offering near the entrance to
the tabernacle, the tent of meeting, and
offered on it burnt offerings and grain offerings,[l] as the LORD commanded him.
30He placed the basin[m] between the tent
of meeting and the altar and put water in
it for washing, 31and Moses and Aaron and
his sons used it to wash their hands and
feet. 32They washed whenever they entered the tent of meeting or approached
the altar,[n] as the LORD commanded Moses.
33Then Moses set up the courtyard[o]
around the tabernacle and altar and put up
the curtain[p] at the entrance to the courtyard. And so Moses finished the work.

The Glory of the LORD

34Then the cloud[q] covered the tent of
meeting, and the glory of the LORD filled
the tabernacle. 35Moses could not enter
the tent of meeting because the cloud had
settled on it, and the glory of the LORD
filled the tabernacle.[r]
36In all the travels of the Israelites,
whenever the cloud lifted from above the
tabernacle, they would set out;[s] 37but if the
cloud did not lift, they did not set out—
until the day it lifted. 38So the cloud[t] of the
LORD was over the tabernacle by day, and
fire was in the cloud by night, in the sight
of all the Israelites during all their travels.

40:5 [s] ver 26; Ex 30:1 **40:7** [t] ver 30; Ex 30:18 **40:9** [u] Ex 30:26; Lev 8:10 **40:10** [v] Ex 29:36 **40:12** [w] Lev 8:1-13 **40:13** [x] Ex 28:41 [y] Lev 8:12 **40:15** [z] Ex 29:9; Nu 25:13 **40:17** [a] Nu 7:1 [b] ver 2 **40:20** [c] Ex 16:34; 25:16; Dt 10:5; 1Ki 8:9; Heb 9:4 **40:21** [d] Ex 26:33 **40:22** [e] Ex 26:35 **40:23** [f] ver 4 **40:24** [g] Ex 26:35 **40:25** [h] ver 4; Ex 25:37 **40:26** [i] ver 5; Ex 30:6 **40:27** [j] Ex 30:7 **40:28** [k] Ex 26:36 **40:29** [l] ver 6; Ex 29:38-42 **40:30** [m] ver 7 **40:32** [n] Ex 30:20 **40:33** [o] Ex 27:9 [p] ver 8 **40:34** [q] Nu 9:15-23; 1Ki 8:12 **40:35** [r] 1Ki 8:11; 2Ch 5:13-14 **40:36** [s] Nu 9:17-23; 10:13; Ne 9:19 **40:38** [t] Ex 13:21; Nu 9:15; 1Co 10:1

3. Rules for priests and other persons regarding their treatment of sacred things. Compare the Hittite "Instructions to Priests and Temple Officials."
4. Laws grouped by topic. Compare the Hittite and Mesopotamian law collections.
5. Blessings and curses after laws (ch. 26). Compare the epilogues to the Laws of Lipit-Ishtar and the Code of Hammurapi. ◆

The Burnt Offering

1 The LORD called to Moses[a] and spoke to
him from the tent of meeting.[b] He said,
2"Speak to the Israelites and say to them:
'When anyone among you brings an offering to the LORD, bring as your offering an
animal from either the herd or the flock.[c]
3" 'If the offering is a burnt offering from
the herd, you are to offer a male without
defect.[d] You must present it at the entrance
to the tent[e] of meeting so that it will be
acceptable to the LORD. 4You are to lay
your hand on the head[f] of the burnt offering, and it will be accepted on your behalf
to make atonement[g] for you. 5You are to
slaughter[h] the young bull before the LORD,
and then Aaron's sons the priests shall
bring the blood and splash it against the
sides of the altar[i] at the entrance to the tent
of meeting. 6You are to skin[j] the burnt offering and cut it into pieces. 7The sons of
Aaron the priest are to put fire on the altar and arrange wood[k] on the fire. 8Then
Aaron's sons the priests shall arrange the
pieces, including the head and the fat,[l] on
the wood that is burning on the altar. 9You
are to wash the internal organs and the legs
with water, and the priest is to burn all of
it on the altar.[m] It is a burnt offering, a food
offering, an aroma pleasing to the LORD.[n]

1:1 [a]Ex 19:3; 25:22 [b]Nu 7:89 **1:2** [c]Lev 22:18-19 **1:3** [d]Ex 12:5; Dt 15:21; Heb 9:14; 1Pe 1:19 [e]Lev 17:9 **1:4** [f]Ex 29:10, 15; Lev 3:2 [g]2Ch 29:23-24 **1:5** [h]Lev 3:2, 8 [i]Heb 12:24; 1Pe 1:2 **1:6** [j]Lev 7:8 **1:7** [k]Lev 6:12 **1:8** [l]ver 12 **1:9** [m]Ex 29:18 [n]ver 13; Ge 8:21; Nu 15:8-10; Eph 5:2

1:3 *burnt offering.* This category of sacrifice, in which all edible material was burned, served as a basic and general gift and was meant to invoke the deity (cf. Ge 8:20; Nu 23). At least one was offered each day on behalf of the people of Israel, and festivals and ceremonies would include them as well. Burnt offerings were practiced by other ancient Syro-Palestinian peoples, whose rituals were closest to those of the Israelites. They were also performed in Anatolia, but apparently not in Egypt or Mesopotamia. In Ugaritic literature, where words for several kinds of outwardly similar (but by no means identical) sacrifices parallel Hebrew terms, burnt offerings are often coupled with well-being offerings ("peace" or "fellowship" offerings; see notes on Lev 3:1,11), as they are in the Bible (e.g., Ex 20:24). So we see that Israelite sacrifice was not an isolated phenomenon. There have been many theories as to what purpose animal sacrifice was to serve. In some cultures it was seen as caring for the deity by providing food (see the article "Great Symbiosis," p. 186). Others saw the sacrifice as a gift to please or request aid from the god. Still others saw the sacrifice as a means of entering into relationship. The earliest Sumerian literature indicates that sacrifice was used as a means of allowing meat consumption, as the process of sharing meat with the deity allowed them to slaughter the animal for food. In Assyria and Babylon, animals were sacrificially slaughtered in order to obtain the entrails, which were used for divination. *from the herd.* In ch. 1, objects of sacrifice are logically presented in descending order of size and value. Similarly, a third-century BC Punic sacrificial tariff (the so-called Marseilles Tariff from Carthage) lists fees for priestly officiation in descending order, corresponding to the decreasing sizes of the sacrificial animals. *male.* Male animals were both expendable and valuable. Many females were required to sustain the herd by bearing young, but only a few males were necessary. On the other hand, strong males were desirable because their genetics would be reflected in a large portion of the herd.

1:4 *lay your hand on the head.* In Hittite ritual, this gesture appears to carry the same function of identifying the owner as the one who is giving the sacrifice, perhaps analogous to the signature on a letter. Even though the priest "delivers" the offering, this gesture signifies that the offering comes from the one who "signed" it. *make atonement.* The Hebrew word (*kipper*) refers to the removal of ritual impurity. Most scholars now agree that "atonement" ("reconciliation") is a poor translation of the concept on either a ritual or theological level. In the past, it was common for scholars to connect *kipper* with Arabic *kafara* ("cover") and to interpret a ritual accomplishing *kipper* as "covering sin" (see Ge 3:6–7; Zec 3:3–5). In the context of purification offerings ("sin offerings"), though, *kipper* followed by the Hebrew preposition *min* ("from") denotes removal rather than covering. Furthermore, the grammatical object of *kipper* in Hebrew is generally neither the sin nor the person, but a holy object such as the ark or the altar (e.g., Ex 29:36). Finally, in a number of cases this process is necessary even though no sin has been committed. Therefore, recent scholars prefer the terminology of "purification" or "purgation" (in this case, of the altar) on behalf of the individual whose ritual impurity (caused by sin or otherwise) has tarnished it. The ritual, like a disinfectant, is usually remedial, but can be preventative as well, and usually (but not always) uses blood as the reagent. The decontamination process renders the offender "clean" and paves the way for reconciliation, but the actual word *kipper* refers to the decontamination process, not its final results. The idea of removal is also present in the Akkadian cognate *kuppuru.* In ritual or medical usage, this term usually denotes a physical wiping that is directly applied to persons or things from which evil is removed, though this and other examples from the ancient Near East are usually magical in nature (see the article "Magic," p. 326).

1:5 *bring the blood and splash it.* Blood represented life (17:11). The idea that blood contained the essence of life is evidenced in the use of blood (of a slain deity) to create the first people in Mesopotamian cosmogony. By contrast to the Israelite ritual system, in which blood was intentionally and meaningfully applied in various ways (splashing, sprinkling, daubing, etc.) to objects, areas and persons, Mesopotamian and Ugaritic cults lacked such ritual use of blood. In some ancient cultures (Hittite, Greek), blood could be used for libations to underworld deities, conveyed to them by means of ritual holes in the ground. One ritual, involved in establishing a new Hittite temple for the "Goddess of the Night," purified the new deity and temple by bloodying the golden image, the wall and all the implements of the deity. A Greek ritual for purification from homicide called for the slaughtering of a piglet over the head of the person undergoing purification, followed by the rinsing off the blood. In another Greek purification ritual, officials carried a piglet around the city square in Athens, then slaughtered it, sprayed its blood over the seats, and discarded the carcass. These practices somewhat resembled Israelite purification ("sin") offerings, the blood of which was used to purify persons, objects and places (see notes on 4:3,35; 16:14). Unlike the Greek purifications, Israelite sacrifices applied blood to part of the sanctuary/temple of their deity, such as an altar. *splash it against the sides of the altar.* A symbolic means of applying the death of the animal to the purging of any contamination that might interfere with the function of the sacrifice. See note on v. 4.

1:9 *food offering.* The Hebrew term *ishsheh* derives from the word for "fire" (*esh*). Weakening this idea, *ishsheh* can refer to food portions that are eaten rather than burned

10 " 'If the offering is a burnt offering
from the flock, from either the sheep or
the goats,[o] you are to offer a male without
defect. 11 You are to slaughter it at the north
side of the altar before the LORD, and Aaron's sons the priests shall splash its blood
against the sides of the altar.[p] 12 You are
to cut it into pieces, and the priest shall

1:10 [o] ver 3; Ex 12:5
1:11 [p] ver 5

(Dt 18:1), and it also is never used of purification ("sin") offerings, which are always burned. However, scholars have found an alternative in an Ugaritic cognate (the same word in another language) that means "gift." This concept fits the Biblical contexts well: An offering is given to God, whether it is burned or not, but the purification ("sin") offering (where *ishsheh* is not used) is not a gift because it is a mandatory token payment of "debt." *an aroma pleasing to the LORD.* Other ancient Near Eastern peoples also viewed deities as favorably disposed to the smell of incense and offerings. But whereas Israel's deity does not need human food (Ps 50:12–13), other nations' gods were thought to be dependent on such sustenance. In the Ugaritic Baal Cycle, when the god Ilu sees the goddess

LEVITICUS 1

Ancient Law Codes and Leviticus

Leviticus has an almost limitless amount of parallels with ancient Near Eastern documents and sources, some surprisingly close. Here we find, e.g., similar ritual procedures, infrastructure, terminology and concepts, as well as similar approaches to law in terms of literary context, formulation, reasoning and content. It is abundantly clear that Leviticus was meant to communicate with and address the needs of real people in the context of their ancient Near Eastern culture, which contained a number of positive elements worthy to be affirmed and continued. At the same time, we will recognize crucial differences that highlight and give depth and perspective to the unique nature of Israel's God.

While there are some narrative portions in Leviticus (1:1; 8:1—10:20; 24:10–23), the book is mostly a collection of laws. In terms of content, laws in the latter part of Leviticus (the so-called Holiness Code [chs. 17 or 18 to 26 or 27]) thematically overlap Mesopotamian and Hittite law collections in the criminal law categories of sexual offenses, dishonesty and injustice (including lying and stealing), murder and assault, and the civil law categories of property ownership, slavery and debt. The laws of Leviticus were stipulations given to Israel by the superior party (God) in a covenant/treaty formulation, as shown by inclusion of covenant blessings and curses near the end of the book. In this sense the overall literary function of Leviticus is equivalent to that of ancient Near Eastern treaty documents (see the article "Decrees and Laws," p. 301) rather than law codes.

The term "code" is a misnomer, since neither these codes nor the ones in the Bible fit the definition of a modern law code. First, all are far from comprehensive in scope and omit a number of topics one might expect in a law code. Second, their content more closely resembles case law than legislation. Most of the provisions in the codes present possible cases—usually beginning with "if"—and then give a ruling for that case. Third, scholarship on the ancient Near Eastern codes is now generally agreed that the primary purpose of these written collections was not to establish law in their respective societies but was by and large propagandistic—to justify and legitimize the rule of the king who authorized the compilation of the code, or to promote the legal wisdom of the king and to influence the rulings of local judges. Therefore, it seems that the primary motivation to compile ancient Near Eastern codes in written form had more to do with politics than with law.

For example, the laws in Exodus that deal with goring by an ox (or bull) are

continued on next page

remarkably similar to the Laws of Eshnunna and the Code of Hammurapi. The closest parallel between Biblical law and other ancient Near Eastern codes occurs with Ex 21:35 and LE (Law of Eshnunna) 53. The latter states: "If an ox gores another ox and thus causes its death, the two ox-owners shall divide the value of the living ox and the carcass of the dead ox." What stands out, however, is that, even though the issue of the goring ox occurs in some detail in several law codes, there is no mention of any such case in the thousands of trial-related records from the ancient Near East. This suggests that ancient Near Eastern law codes were not concerned only with legal issues that might arise in daily life. They also seem to include legal problems and cases that were more academic in nature and that allowed certain legal principles to be expressed, even if the details had little to do with the problems people encountered on a regular basis. A similar understanding can be applied to Biblical law collections, such as the Covenant Code in Ex 21 – 23, the Holiness Code in Lev 17 – 27, and the Deuteronomic Code in Dt 12 – 26. Primarily religious rather than legal considerations led to the incorporation of these codes into the Biblical texts. In this written form, moreover, they represented for the ancient Israelites obligations based more in religious belief than in legislative activity, though it is likely that they also provide important insight into the legal systems of Israel and Judah.

So we see that many of the Biblical regulations and rituals had precedent in the ancient world. In this way it can be seen that God used familiar ways of thinking to guide the Israelites, even as he was giving them some new ways to think and distinguishing them as his own special people. ◆

Hittite law code tablet, Hattuša, Hittite Empire, thirteenth century BC. The instructions to priests and temple officials is very similar to those in Leviticus.

arrange them, including the head and the
fat, on the wood that is burning on the altar. 13You are to wash the internal organs
and the legs with water, and the priest is
to bring all of them and burn them on the
altar. It is a burnt offering, a food offering,
an aroma pleasing to the LORD.
14" 'If the offering to the LORD is a burnt
offering of birds, you are to offer a dove or
a young pigeon.[q] 15The priest shall bring it

1:14 [q] Ge 15:9; Lev 5:7; Lk 2:24

Atiratu coming to him, he says to her, "Are you really hungry (because) you've been wandering?" In the Babylonian Atrahasis epic, the gods suffer from hunger and thirst during the great flood because there are no humans to offer them sacrifices. Therefore, when Atrahasis (the Noah-like figure) subsequently offers his sacrifice, the gods smell the offering (cf. Ge 8:20 – 21), and they crowd around like flies. Unlike Yahweh, they enjoy the smell because it promises an end to their hunger. In a Hittite prayer, King Mursili II pointedly uses the gods' need for food as an argument to plead that they remove a plague from his land, lest they suffer because of a lack of humans to serve them.

to the altar, wring off the head and burn it
on the altar; its blood shall be drained out
on the side of the altar.[r] 16He is to remove
the crop and the feathers[a] and throw them
down east of the altar where the ashes[s] are.
17He shall tear it open by the wings, not
dividing it completely,[t] and then the priest
shall burn it on the wood[u] that is burning
on the altar. It is a burnt offering, a food
offering, an aroma pleasing to the LORD.

The Grain Offering

2 " 'When anyone brings a grain offering[v] to the LORD, their offering is to be
of the finest flour. They are to pour olive
oil[w] on it, put incense on it 2and take it to
Aaron's sons the priests. The priest shall
take a handful of the flour[x] and oil, together with all the incense,[y] and burn this as
a memorial[b] portion[z] on the altar, a food
offering, an aroma pleasing to the LORD.
3The rest of the grain offering belongs to
Aaron and his sons;[a] it is a most holy part
of the food offerings presented to the LORD.
4" 'If you bring a grain offering baked
in an oven, it is to consist of the finest
flour: either thick loaves made without
yeast and with olive oil mixed in or thin
loaves made without yeast and brushed
with olive oil.[b] 5If your grain offering is
prepared on a griddle, it is to be made of
the finest flour mixed with oil, and without yeast. 6Crumble it and pour oil on it;
it is a grain offering. 7If your grain offering
is cooked in a pan,[c] it is to be made of the
finest flour and some olive oil. 8Bring the
grain offering made of these things to the
LORD; present it to the priest, who shall
take it to the altar. 9He shall take out the
memorial portion[d] from the grain offering
and burn it on the altar as a food offering,
an aroma pleasing to the LORD.[e] 10The rest
of the grain offering belongs to Aaron and
his sons;[f] it is a most holy part of the food
offerings presented to the LORD.
11" 'Every grain offering you bring to the
LORD must be made without yeast,[g] for
you are not to burn any yeast or honey
in a food offering presented to the LORD.
12You may bring them to the LORD as an
offering of the firstfruits,[h] but they are not
to be offered on the altar as a pleasing aroma. 13Season all your grain offerings with
salt. Do not leave the salt of the covenant[i]
of your God out of your grain offerings;
add salt to all your offerings.
14" 'If you bring a grain offering of firstfruits[j] to the LORD, offer crushed heads of
new grain roasted in the fire. 15Put oil and
incense on it; it is a grain offering. 16The
priest shall burn the memorial portion[k]
of the crushed grain and the oil, together
with all the incense, as a food offering presented to the LORD.

The Fellowship Offering

3 " 'If your offering is a fellowship offering,[l] and you offer an animal from the
herd, whether male or female, you are to

1:15 [r] Lev 5:9 **1:16** [s] Lev 6:10 **1:17** [t] Ge 15:10 [u] Lev 5:8 **2:1** [v] Lev 6:14-18 [w] Nu 15:4 **2:2** [x] Lev 5:11 [y] Lev 6:15; Isa 66:3 [z] ver 9, 16; Lev 5:12; 6:15; 24:7; Ac 10:4 **2:3** [a] ver 10; Lev 6:16; 10:12, 13 **2:4** [b] Ex 29:2 **2:7** [c] Lev 7:9 **2:9** [d] ver 2 [e] Ex 29:18; Lev 6:15 **2:10** [f] ver 3 **2:11** [g] Ex 23:18; 34:25; Lev 6:16 **2:12** [h] Lev 7:13; 23:10 **2:13** [i] Nu 18:19; Eze 43:24 **2:14** [j] Lev 23:10 **2:16** [k] ver 2 **3:1** [l] Lev 7:11-34

[a] 16 Or *crop with its contents*; the meaning of the Hebrew for this word is uncertain.
[b] 2 Or *representative*; also in verses 9 and 16

2:1 *grain offering.* Throughout the ancient Near East, people frequently presented sacrifices consisting of grain, which was a staple in their diet. While grain offerings could be independent (as in ch. 2), they were often served with drinks as accompaniments to animal sacrifices (Nu 15). Thus, on the fifth day of the Hittite Ninth Year Festival of Telipinu, the god was to be offered choice meat portions (of 10 bovines and 200 sheep!), plus thick breads and drink offerings (see note on Lev 7:7).

2:11 *you are not to burn any yeast or honey.* The reason for excluding yeast from the altar was mostly that leavening involves a kind of decay through fermentation. Along the same lines, honey (most likely syrup from fruit, not the by-product of bees) was banned from the altar because of its susceptibility to fermentation. Fermentation was associated with death and therefore excluded.

Non-Israelite peoples frequently offered honey to their gods. Thus in Assyria and Anatolia, honey (along with other liquids, such as oil and wine) could be poured into a ritual hole in the ground as a libation for an underworld deity. The final ritual of the fifth day of the Babylonian New Year Festival of Spring was a burnt offering to celestial gods that included honey, along with ghee (clarified butter) and oil.

2:13 *salt of the covenant of your God.* Salt was the finest preservative in antiquity, and it symbolized permanence and preservation. Salt was probably used in the covenant ceremony in which Israel celebrated its unbreakable covenant with God. The salt that accompanied many Israelite sacrifices was used physically in the seasoning of the elements, but it also symbolically contributed to the quality of the covenant relationship between humanity and God. In antiquity, parties who shared salt (here the Lord and the Israelites) were united by mutual obligations. Thus, a letter from Neo-Babylonia refers to a tribe's covenantal allies as those who "tasted the salt of the Jakin tribe." Similarly, the Greeks salted their covenantal meals, and in Ezr 4:14 those who tasted the salt (the literal Hebrew) of the Persian king's palace were bound to loyalty to him.

Since human allies establishing a covenant would commonly share a meal featuring salted meat, it made sense for the salt in Israelite sacrifices to serve as a reminder of the covenant between God and Israel. Because salt was employed as a preservative, its use in a covenantal context also emphasized the expectation that the covenant would last for a long time, a meaning attached to salt in Babylonian, Persian, Arabic and Greek covenant contexts. Because salt inhibits the leavening action of yeast, which represented rebellion, salt could additionally stand for that which prevented rebellion. An additional explanation for the appropriateness of salt in connection with the covenant is found in its association with agricultural infertility: In a Hittite treaty, the testator pronounces a curse: if the treaty is broken, "may he and his family and his lands, like salt that has no seed, likewise have no progeny."

3:1 *fellowship offering.* The Hebrew term for this kind of

LEVITICUS 2:9

Great Symbiosis

In the ancient Near Eastern world, people believed that the gods were initially quite content to live without human beings. The gods had created the cosmos for themselves, built cities and lived together in community. As time went on, however, they grew tired of feeding themselves, making clothes for themselves and building houses for themselves. Digging ditches for irrigation to grow crops was heavy labor.

They therefore decided to create humans as a slave labor force. The responsibility of humans was to care for the gods in every way. Rituals provided food and drink for the gods. Temples provided housing. The gods then became dependent on people to provide the luxury to which they were accustomed and which they deserved. In turn, the gods would provide for the people (so the people could provide for them) and protect the people who were caring for them. This defined the codependent relationship between the gods and humans in the ancient world. It was a need-based system and comprised the religious responsibilities that people had.

Besides the rituals and the temple building, the gods were interested in maintaining justice among the people, but not because the gods were inherently just or because of any sense of ethical right and wrong. Rather, the gods understood that if society was plagued by lawlessness, violence and disorder, the people would not be at liberty to carry out their ritual obligations. Thus there was a symbiotic relationship between gods and people (which may be called the "Great Symbiosis"), which was maintained for a smoothly operating ritual system, designed to keep the gods happy.

The difference in Israel was that even though they offered sacrifices to Yahweh, Yahweh did not need these sacrifices as food. In his covenant with Israel he promised to provide for his people and to take care of them, much like other gods did. However, what he required of them was not care and feeding, but covenant fidelity. We could therefore say that the Great Symbiosis was replaced in Israel by the Covenant Symbiosis. ◆

present before the LORD an animal without
defect.[m] 2You are to lay your hand on the
head[n] of your offering and slaughter it[o] at
the entrance to the tent of meeting. Then
Aaron's sons the priests shall splash the
blood against the sides of the altar. 3From
the fellowship offering you are to bring a
food offering to the LORD: the internal organs and all the fat[p] that is connected to
them, 4both kidneys with the fat on them
near the loins, and the long lobe of the liver, which you will remove with the kidneys. 5Then Aaron's sons[q] are to burn it on
the altar on top of the burnt offering[r] that
is lying on the burning wood; it is a food
offering, an aroma pleasing to the LORD.
6" 'If you offer an animal from the flock
as a fellowship offering[s] to the LORD, you
are to offer a male or female without defect. 7If you offer a lamb, you are to present it before the LORD,[t] 8lay your hand on
its head and slaughter it[u] in front of the
tent of meeting. Then Aaron's sons shall
splash its blood against the sides of the altar. 9From the fellowship offering you are
to bring a food offering to the LORD: its fat,

3:1 [m]Lev 1:3; 22:21 **3:2** [n]Ex 29:10, 15 [o]Lev 1:5 **3:3** [p]Ex 29:13 **3:5** [q]Lev 7:29-34 [r]Ex 29:13,38-42 **3:6** [s]ver 1 **3:7** [t]Lev 17:8-9 **3:8** [u]ver 2; Lev 1:5

sacrifice is from the same root as the well-known word for "well-being/peace" (*shalom*) and is better understood as "well-being offering." A sacrifice designated by a noun from the same Semitic root appears frequently in Ugaritic ritual texts, especially in tandem with burnt offerings (see note on 1:3). The chief difference between a fellowship offering and a burnt offering was that in a fellowship offering the offerers (and others with whom they could share) ate meat from their own well-being offerings as sacred meals shared with their deity; in a burnt offering the offerers were not permitted to partake of the offering.
3:4 *fat.* "Suet" is the layer of fat around the internal organs. It is inedible and easily removed. Mesopotamians did not include suet in their sacrifices, but many other cultures did.
3:9 *fat tail.* When a flock animal is offered, the "fat tail"

the entire fat tail cut off close to the backbone, the internal organs and all the fat
that is connected to them, 10both kidneys
with the fat on them near the loins, and
the long lobe of the liver, which you will
remove with the kidneys. 11The priest shall
burn them on the altar[v] as a food offering[w]
presented to the LORD.
12" 'If your offering is a goat, you are
to present it before the LORD, 13lay your
hand on its head and slaughter it in front
of the tent of meeting. Then Aaron's sons
shall splash[x] its blood against the sides of
the altar. 14From what you offer you are to
present this food offering to the LORD: the
internal organs and all the fat that is connected to them, 15both kidneys with the fat
on them near the loins, and the long lobe
of the liver, which you will remove with
the kidneys. 16The priest shall burn them
on the altar as a food offering, a pleasing
aroma. All the fat is the LORD's.[y]
17" 'This is a lasting ordinance for the
generations to come,[z] wherever you live:
You must not eat any fat or any blood.[a]' "

The Sin Offering

4 The LORD said to Moses, 2"Say to the
Israelites: 'When anyone sins unintentionally[b] and does what is forbidden in
any of the LORD's commands —
3" 'If the anointed priest sins, bringing
guilt on the people, he must bring to the
LORD a young bull[c] without defect as a sin
offering[a][d] for the sin he has committed.
4He is to present the bull at the entrance
to the tent of meeting before the LORD.[e]
He is to lay his hand on its head and
slaughter it there before the LORD. 5Then
the anointed priest shall take some of the
bull's blood[f] and carry it into the tent of
meeting. 6He is to dip his finger into the
blood and sprinkle some of it seven times
before the LORD, in front of the curtain of
the sanctuary. 7The priest shall then put
some of the blood on the horns of the altar of fragrant incense that is before the
LORD in the tent of meeting. The rest of
the bull's blood he shall pour out at the
base of the altar[g] of burnt offering[h] at the
entrance to the tent of meeting. 8He shall
remove all the fat[i] from the bull of the
sin offering — all the fat that is connected to the internal organs, 9both kidneys
with the fat on them near the loins, and
the long lobe of the liver, which he will
remove with the kidneys[j] — 10just as the
fat is removed from the ox[b] sacrificed as a
fellowship offering. Then the priest shall

3:11 [v] ver 5 [w] ver 16; Lev 21:6,17 **3:13** [x] Ex 24:6 **3:16** [y] 1Sa 2:16 **3:17** [z] Lev 6:18; 17:7 [a] Ge 9:4; Lev 7:25-26; 17:10-16; Dt 12:16; Ac 15:20 **4:2** [b] Lev 5:15-18; Ps 19:12; Heb 9:7
4:3 [c] ver 14; Ps 66:15 [d] Lev 9:2-22; Heb 9:13-14 **4:4** [e] Lev 1:3 **4:5** [f] Lev 16:14 **4:7** [g] ver 34; Lev 8:15 [h] ver 18,30; Lev 5:9; 9:9; 16:18 **4:8** [i] Lev 3:3-5 **4:9** [j] Lev 3:4

[a] *3* Or *purification offering*; here and throughout this chapter [b] *10* The Hebrew word can refer to either male or female.

is included in the sacrifice. Sheep of this region had long (4–5 feet, or 1.2–1.5 meters) tails weighing up to 50 pounds (23 kilograms).

3:11 *food offering.* Offerings presented to the Lord at the outer altar are called the "food" of God (21:8; Nu 28:2). Non-Israelite peoples also offered food, but they regarded their deities as needing to consume it (see note on Lev 1:9). As part of the daily care and feeding of the gods, Egyptians, Hittites and Babylonians regularly placed various kinds of food and drink on tables or stands before idols in their temples. In Hittite cults, consumption of bread offered to a deity could be symbolized by breaking it. In Egypt, care of the gods included not only feeding them, but also washing and clothing their idols and even providing them with painted makeup. See the article "Great Symbiosis," p. 186.

To complicate matters, many ancient Near Easterners believed that dead people continued to live on in divine form. This meant that those living were required to provide food and drink for these powerful and potentially dangerous spirits, lest they return from the grave hungry, thirsty and angry (see note on Dt 5:16).

In contrast, while Yahweh accepted food to affirm that he dwelt among them, he did not need it for nourishment (Ps 50:12–13). Therefore, the food was burned up so that he only received the smoke.

4:2 *sins unintentionally.* In the ancient Near East, deities were believed to possess superhuman powers of perception and to hold human beings accountable for their faulty actions, whether or not they knew that they had done wrong. Therefore a person could suffer evil consequences without knowing why. One Egyptian prayer asks a god for mercy: "Visit not my many offenses upon me, I am one ignorant of himself. I am a mindless man, who all day follows his mouth, like an ox after grass." This kind of uncertainty was compounded by the difficulty of discerning what deities wanted and expected from humans. One Mesopotamian "righteous sufferer" expressed this problem: "I wish I knew that these things were pleasing to a god! What seems good to one's self could be an offense to a god. What in one's own heart seems abominable could be good to one's god!"

Such uncertainty demanded a solution. Besides knowing which sacrifices, incantations or magical rituals to perform in order to appease deities or otherwise turn away evil (which could originate from the gods themselves or from demons), priests often practiced divination to sort out the variables, such as why the gods reacted as they did and what would placate them. In Israel, divination was unnecessary, because several factors greatly simplified reconciliation with the Lord: (1) In monotheism there was no need to determine which deity to approach. (2) Sin that required a ritual remedy was defined as violation of a command that the Lord had explicitly communicated to the Israelites. (3) Israelites who committed inadvertent wrongs (results of either accident or ignorance) were liable for presenting purification ("sin") offerings only when they came to know what they had done wrong (vv. 14,23,28; but see note on 5:17). (4) A limited number of ritual types (burnt, purification ["sin"], and reparation ["guilt"] offerings) were prescribed to remedy a wide range of offenses.

4:3 *sin offering.* This sacrifice was necessary when someone's actions or status resulted in something that was sacred becoming exposed to impurity. This sacrifice purified offerers (throughout the year) or parts of the sanctuary (at its consecration and on the Day of Atonement) from moral faults, or from physical ritual impurities, which were not sins in the moral sense (12:6–8; 14:19). Thus, the

burn them on the altar of burnt offering.
11But the hide of the bull and all its flesh,
as well as the head and legs, the internal
organs and the intestines[k]— 12that is, all
the rest of the bull—he must take outside
the camp[l] to a place ceremonially clean,[m]
where the ashes are thrown, and burn it
there in a wood fire on the ash heap.

13" 'If the whole Israelite community sins unintentionally[n] and does what
is forbidden in any of the LORD's commands, even though the community is
unaware of the matter, when they realize
their guilt 14and the sin they committed
becomes known, the assembly must bring
a young bull[o] as a sin offering[p] and present it before the tent of meeting. 15The
elders of the community are to lay their
hands on the bull's head[q] before the LORD,
and the bull shall be slaughtered before
the LORD. 16Then the anointed priest is to
take some of the bull's blood[r] into the tent
of meeting. 17He shall dip his finger into
the blood and sprinkle it before the LORD[s]
seven times in front of the curtain. 18He
is to put some of the blood on the horns
of the altar that is before the LORD[t] in the
tent of meeting. The rest of the blood he
shall pour out at the base of the altar of
burnt offering at the entrance to the tent
of meeting. 19He shall remove all the fat[u]
from it and burn it on the altar, 20and do
with this bull just as he did with the bull
for the sin offering. In this way the priest
will make atonement[v] for the community,
and they will be forgiven.[w] 21Then he shall

4:11 [k]Ex 29:14; Lev 9:11; Nu 19:5 **4:12** [l]Heb 13:11 [m]Lev 6:11 **4:13** [n]ver 2; Lev 5:2-4, 17; Nu 15:24-26 **4:14** [o]ver 3 [p]ver 23, 28 **4:15** [q]Lev 1:4; 8:14, 22; Nu 8:10 **4:16** [r]ver 5 **4:17** [s]ver 6 **4:18** [t]ver 7 **4:19** [u]ver 8 **4:20** [v]Heb 10:10-12 [w]Nu 15:25

name of the sacrifice is better translated "purification offering" (see NIV text note). The procedure was unique in requiring application of blood to the horns of the outer altar or the incense altar. This ritual has no close parallel outside Israel (cf. note on 1:5).

4:12 *burn it there in a wood fire on the ash heap.* There is no indication that remnants of Israelite purification ("sin") offerings were regarded as having absorbed dangerous demonic impurity. By contrast, a Hittite law warns: "If anyone performs a purification ritual on a person, he shall dispose of the remnants (of the ritual) in the incineration dumps. But if he disposes of them in someone's house, it is sorcery (and) a case for the king." The offering is burned so that none of it benefits the human offerers.

OLD TESTAMENT SACRIFICES

SACRIFICE	OT REFERENCES	ELEMENTS	PURPOSE
Burnt Offering	Lev 1; 6:8–13; 8:18–21; 16:24	Bull, ram or male bird (dove or young pigeon for the poor); wholly consumed; no defect	Voluntary act of worship; atonement for unintentional sin in general; expression of devotion, commitment and complete surrender to God
Grain Offering	Lev 2; 6:14–23	Grain, finest flour, olive oil, incense, baked bread (cakes or wafers), salt; no yeast or honey; accompanied burnt offering and fellowship offering (along with drink offering)	Voluntary act of worship; recognition of God's goodness and provisions; devotion to God
Fellowship Offering	Lev 3; 7:11–34	Any animal without defect from herd or flock; variety of breads	Voluntary act of worship; thanksgiving and fellowship (it included a communal meal)
Sin Offering	Lev 4:1—5:13; 6:24–30; 8:14–17; 16:3–22	1. Young bull: for high priest and congregation 2. Male goat: for leader 3. Female goat or lamb: for common person 4. Dove or pigeon: for the poor 5. Tenth of an ephah of finest flour: for the very poor	Mandatory atonement for specific unintentional sin; confession of sin; forgiveness of sin; cleansing from defilement
Guilt Offering	Lev 5:14—6:7; 7:1–6	Ram	Mandatory atonement for unintentional sin requiring restitution; cleansing from defilement; make restitution; pay 20 percent fine

When more than one kind of offering was presented (as in Nu 7:13–17), the procedure was usually as follows: (1) sin offering or guilt offering, (2) burnt offering, (3) fellowship offering and grain offering (along with a drink offering). This sequence furnishes part of the spiritual significance of the sacrificial system. First, sin had to be dealt with (sin offering or guilt offering). Second, the worshipers committed themselves completely to God (burnt offering and grain offering). Third, fellowship or communion between the Lord, the priest and the worshiper (fellowship offering) was established. To state it another way, there were sacrifices of expiation (sin offerings and guilt offerings), consecration (burnt offerings and grain offerings) and communion (fellowship offerings—these included vow offerings, thank offerings and freewill offerings).

take the bull outside the camp and burn it
as he burned the first bull. This is the sin
offering for the community.[x]
22 " 'When a leader[y] sins unintentionally[z] and does what is forbidden in any
of the commands of the LORD his God,
when he realizes his guilt 23 and the sin he
has committed becomes known, he must
bring as his offering a male goat without
defect. 24 He is to lay his hand on the goat's
head and slaughter it at the place where
the burnt offering is slaughtered before
the LORD. It is a sin offering. 25 Then the
priest shall take some of the blood of the
sin offering with his finger and put it on
the horns of the altar of burnt offering and
pour out the rest of the blood at the base
of the altar.[a] 26 He shall burn all the fat on
the altar as he burned the fat of the fellowship offering. In this way the priest will
make atonement for the leader's sin, and
he will be forgiven.[b]
27 " 'If any member of the community
sins unintentionally[c] and does what is forbidden in any of the LORD's commands,
when they realize their guilt 28 and the sin
they have committed becomes known,
they must bring as their offering[d] for the
sin they committed a female goat[e] without
defect. 29 They are to lay their hand on the
head[f] of the sin offering[g] and slaughter it
at the place of the burnt offering. 30 Then
the priest is to take some of the blood with
his finger and put it on the horns of the altar of burnt offering[h] and pour out the rest
of the blood at the base of the altar. 31 They
shall remove all the fat, just as the fat is
removed from the fellowship offering, and
the priest shall burn it on the altar as an
aroma pleasing to the LORD.[i] In this way
the priest will make atonement for them,
and they will be forgiven.
32 " 'If someone brings a lamb as their sin
offering, they are to bring a female without defect.[j] 33 They are to lay their hand on
its head and slaughter it for a sin offering
at the place where the burnt offering is
slaughtered.[k] 34 Then the priest shall take
some of the blood of the sin offering with
his finger and put it on the horns of the altar of burnt offering and pour out the rest
of the blood at the base of the altar.[l] 35 They
shall remove all the fat, just as the fat is
removed from the lamb of the fellowship
offering, and the priest shall burn it on the
altar[m] on top of the food offerings presented to the LORD. In this way the priest will
make atonement for them for the sin they
have committed, and they will be forgiven.

5 " 'If anyone sins because they do not
speak up when they hear a public
charge to testify[n] regarding something
they have seen or learned about, they will
be held responsible.[o]
2 " 'If anyone becomes aware that they
are guilty—if they unwittingly touch anything ceremonially unclean (whether the
carcass of an unclean animal, wild or domestic, or of any unclean creature that
moves along the ground)[p] and they are
unaware that they have become unclean,
but then they come to realize their guilt;
3 or if they touch human uncleanness[q]
(anything that would make them unclean)
even though they are unaware of it, but
then they learn of it and realize their guilt;
4 or if anyone thoughtlessly takes an oath[r]
to do anything, whether good or evil (in
any matter one might carelessly swear
about) even though they are unaware of it,
but then they learn of it and realize their
guilt— 5 when anyone becomes aware that
they are guilty in any of these matters,
they must confess[s] in what way they have

4:21 [x] Lev 16:5, 15 **4:22** [y] Nu 31:13 [z] ver 2 **4:25** [a] ver 7, 18, 30, 34; Lev 9:9 **4:26** [b] Lev 5:10 **4:27** [c] ver 2; Nu 15:27 **4:28** [d] ver 23 [e] ver 3 **4:29** [f] ver 4, 24 [g] Lev 1:4 **4:30** [h] ver 7 **4:31** [i] Ge 8:21

4:32 [j] ver 28 **4:33** [k] ver 29 **4:34** [l] ver 7 **4:35** [m] ver 26, 31 **5:1** [n] Pr 29:24 [o] ver 17 **5:2** [p] Lev 11:11, 24-40; Dt 14:8 **5:3** [q] Nu 19:11-16 **5:4** [r] Nu 30:6, 8 **5:5** [s] Lev 16:21; 26:40; Nu 5:7; Pr 28:13

4:35 *forgiven.* The intended result of the purification ("sin") offering is forgiveness. Only God can forgive (the Hebrew verb used here never has humans as the subject) and forgiveness does not rule out punishment (cf. Nu 14:9–24). The one who brings the offering seeks reconciliation—i.e., restoration of relationship—not pardon from punishment.

5:1 *public charge to testify.* In the ancient Near East, it was common for heralds to make public proclamations and summons. For example, the Code of Hammurapi reads: "If a man should harbor a fugitive slave or slave woman of either the palace or of a commoner in his house and not bring him out at the herald's public proclamation, that householder shall be killed." The procedure was similar in Israel, where compliance of witnesses, whose negligence could easily go undetected by human beings, was enforced by the deity. Following discovery of a crime, an imprecation invoking divine punishment would be pronounced on anyone who had knowledge but did not come forward. Serving as a witness against a member of one's community could be uncomfortable or even hazardous. Thus the early Mesopotamian Shuruppak composition advises: "Do not loiter about where there is a dispute. Do not appear as a witness in a dispute" (cf. Pr 26:17). In Lev 5 the concession of amnesty through a purification ("sin") offering for the deliberate sin of failure to respond to a binding summons to testify would encourage reticent witnesses to speak up even though they have delayed. *they will be held responsible.* The idiom here indicates that "they will bear their culpability." Culpability is viewed as a burden that inevitably leads to punishment, unless or until someone takes it away. To illustrate the concept that a higher authority requires the punishment of the culpable, compare the Turin Judicial Papyrus regarding judgment on conspirators against Pharaoh Ramses III: "And they examined them; they found them guilty; they caused that their punishment overtake them; their crimes seized them." Here the judges are human, but in ch. 5 it is God who sees to it that culpability bears its fruit, even if the guilty party is not apprehended by other human beings.

5:5 *confess.* Confession is necessary here because the faults in question are not inadvertent but have been

sinned. 6As a penalty for the sin they have committed, they must bring to the LORD a female lamb or goat from the flock as a sin offering[a];[t] and the priest shall make atonement for them for their sin.

7" 'Anyone who cannot afford[u] a lamb is to bring two doves or two young pigeons to the LORD as a penalty for their sin—one for a sin offering and the other for a burnt offering. 8They are to bring them to the priest, who shall first offer the one for the sin offering. He is to wring its head from its neck,[v] not dividing it completely,[w] 9and is to splash some of the blood of the sin offering against the side of the altar; the rest of the blood must be drained out at the base of the altar.[x] It is a sin offering. 10The priest shall then offer the other as a burnt offering in the prescribed way[y] and make atonement for them for the sin they have committed, and they will be forgiven.[z]

11" 'If, however, they cannot afford two doves or two young pigeons, they are to bring as an offering for their sin a tenth of an ephah[b] of the finest flour[a] for a sin offering. They must not put olive oil or incense on it, because it is a sin offering. 12They are to bring it to the priest, who shall take a handful of it as a memorial[c] portion and burn it on the altar on top of the food offerings presented to the LORD. It is a sin offering. 13In this way the priest will make atonement[b] for them for any of these sins they have committed, and they will be forgiven. The rest of the offering will belong to the priest,[c] as in the case of the grain offering.' "

5:6 [t]Lev 4:28 **5:7** [u]Lev 12:8; 14:21 **5:8** [v]Lev 1:15 [w]Lev 1:17 **5:9** [x]Lev 4:7, 18 **5:10** [y]Lev 1:14-17 [z]Lev 4:26 **5:11** [a]Lev 2:1 **5:13** [b]Lev 4:26 [c]Lev 2:3

The Guilt Offering

14The LORD said to Moses: 15"When anyone is unfaithful to the LORD by sinning unintentionally in regard to any of the LORD's holy things, they are to bring to the LORD as a penalty[d] a ram[e] from the flock, one without defect and of the proper value in silver, according to the sanctuary shekel.[d][f] It is a guilt offering. 16They must make restitution[g] for what they have failed to do in regard to the holy things, pay an additional penalty of a fifth of its value[h] and give it all to the priest. The priest will make atonement for them with the ram as a guilt offering, and they will be forgiven.

17"If anyone sins and does what is forbidden in any of the LORD's commands, even though they do not know it,[i] they are guilty and will be held responsible. 18They are to bring to the priest as a guilt offering a ram from the flock, one without defect and of the proper value. In this way the priest will make atonement for them for the wrong they have committed unintentionally, and they will be forgiven.[j] 19It is a guilt offering; they have been guilty of[e] wrongdoing against the LORD."

6[f] The LORD said to Moses: 2"If anyone sins and is unfaithful to the LORD[k] by deceiving a neighbor[l] about something entrusted to them or left in their care[m] or

5:15 [d]Lev 22:14 [e]Nu 5:8 [f]Ex 30:13 **5:16** [g]Lev 6:4 [h]Lev 22:14; Nu 5:7 **5:17** [i]ver 15; Lev 4:2 **5:18** [j]ver 15 **6:2** [k]Nu 5:6; Ac 5:4; Col 3:9 [l]Pr 24:28 [m]Ex 22:7

[a] *6* Or *purification offering*; here and throughout this chapter [b] *11* That is, probably about 3 1/2 pounds or about 1.6 kilograms [c] *12* Or *representative* [d] *15* That is, about 2/5 ounce or about 12 grams [e] *19* Or *offering; atonement has been made for their* [f] In Hebrew texts 6:1-7 is numbered 5:20-26, and 6:8-30 is numbered 6:1-23.

hidden deliberately (v. 1) or were the result of forgetfulness (vv. 2–4). Other ancient Near Eastern peoples were also keenly aware that confession was a vital part of restoration. A Sumerian poem of confession and reconciliation shows several important points of contact with Biblical teaching regarding the sinful nature of the present human condition, need for recognition of sins, distinctions between sins in terms of whether they are recognized/visible or forgotten, and the value of sincere (rather than artful) confession and supplication in gaining reconciliation with the deity so that joy rather than punishment results (cf. Ps 51).

5:15 *sinning unintentionally in regard to any of the LORD's holy things.* Respect for holy things, such as gifts dedicated to a deity (cf. Nu 18), was basic to all ancient Near Eastern religion. The Hittite document "Instructions to Priests and Temple Officials" takes pains to specify and prohibit several categories of sacrilege, including temple personnel appropriating sacrificial portions that are not theirs or taking dedicated things from the temple for their families, and farmers cheating gods out of property or delaying presentation of dedicated offerings. At one point the document warns: "You may steal it from a man, but you cannot steal it from a god. It (is) a sin for you."

5:17 *even though they do not know it, they are guilty.* Here the reparation ("guilt") offering addresses the problem of suspected but unidentified sin, which could constitute sacrilege and lead to adverse consequences, regardless of intention. A prayer of Ashurbanipal expresses similar uncertainty: "[Through a misdeed] which I am or am not aware of, I have become weak!" Notice that circumstances indicate divine disfavor. Similarly, one ancient writer recorded that when the Anatolian deity Telipinu became angry, he disappeared and took fertility with him until ritual appeased him. Unlike other ancient Near Eastern people, when an Israelite could identify no particular sin but was led by circumstances to suspect that he/she was no longer enjoying divine favor, there was only one deity to approach and only one kind of sacrifice to offer (see note on 4:2).

6:2 *entrusted to them or left in their care.* Verses 1–7 deal with cases of sacrilege that involve fraud: misuses of the divine name by swearing falsely in order to avoid human detection of an act that takes advantage of another person. In the ancient Near East, oaths were used to resolve disputes when other evidence was insufficient (see the article "Divine Verdict," p. 152). One person (the depositor) has deposited goods with another (the receiver) until such time as the first person will require the goods again. The Code of Hammurapi considers what to do in a variety of situations: if the receiver lies and claims no deposit was ever made; if the depositor claims a deposit was made but has no witnesses to prove it; if the deposited goods are taken by a thief (the law says the receiver must compen-

about something stolen, or if they cheat their neighbor, 3or if they find lost property and lie about it,[n] or if they swear falsely about any such sin that people may commit— 4when they sin in any of these ways and realize their guilt, they must return[o] what they have stolen or taken by extortion, or what was entrusted to them, or the lost property they found, 5or whatever it was they swore falsely about. They must make restitution[p] in full, add a fifth of the value to it and give it all to the owner on the day they present their guilt offering.[q] 6And as a penalty they must bring to the priest, that is, to the LORD, their guilt offering,[r] a ram from the flock, one without defect and of the proper value. 7In this way the priest will make atonement[s] for them before the LORD, and they will be forgiven for any of the things they did that made them guilty."

The Burnt Offering

8The LORD said to Moses: 9"Give Aaron and his sons this command: 'These are the regulations for the burnt offering: The burnt offering is to remain on the altar hearth throughout the night, till morning, and the fire must be kept burning on the altar. 10The priest shall then put on his linen clothes, with linen undergarments next to his body,[t] and shall remove the ashes of the burnt offering that the fire has consumed on the altar and place them beside the altar. 11Then he is to take off these clothes and put on others, and carry the ashes outside the camp to a place that is ceremonially clean.[u] 12The fire on the altar must be kept burning; it must not go out. Every morning the priest is to add firewood and arrange the burnt offering on the fire and burn the fat of the fellowship offerings on it. 13The fire must be kept burning on the altar continuously; it must not go out.

The Grain Offering

14" 'These are the regulations for the grain offering:[v] Aaron's sons are to bring it before the LORD, in front of the altar. 15The priest is to take a handful of the finest flour and some olive oil, together with all the incense on the grain offering,[w] and burn the memorial[a] portion[x] on the altar as an aroma pleasing to the LORD. 16Aaron and his sons[y] shall eat the rest[z] of it, but it is to be eaten without yeast[a] in the sanctuary area;[b] they are to eat it in the courtyard of the tent of meeting. 17It must not be baked with yeast; I have given it as their share of the food offerings presented to me. Like the sin offering[b] and the guilt offering, it is most holy.[c] 18Any male descendant of Aaron may eat it.[d] For all generations to come it is his perpetual share of the food offerings presented to the LORD. Whatever touches them will become holy.[c][e]' "

19The LORD also said to Moses, 20"This is the offering Aaron and his sons are to bring to the LORD on the day he[d] is anointed: a tenth of an ephah[e][f] of the finest flour as a regular grain offering,[g] half of it in the morning and half in the evening. 21It must be prepared with oil on a griddle;[h] bring it well-mixed and present the grain offering broken[f] in pieces as an aroma pleasing to the LORD. 22The son who is to succeed him as anointed priest shall prepare it. It is the LORD's perpetual share and is to be burned completely. 23Every grain offering of a priest shall be burned completely; it must not be eaten."

The Sin Offering

24The LORD said to Moses, 25"Say to Aaron and his sons: 'These are the regulations for the sin offering: The sin offering is to be slaughtered before the LORD[i] in the place[j] the burnt offering is slaughtered; it is most holy. 26The priest who offers it shall eat it; it is to be eaten in the sanctuary area,[k] in the courtyard[l] of the tent of meeting. 27Whatever touches any of the flesh will become holy,[m] and if any of the blood is spattered on a garment, you must wash it in the sanctuary area. 28The clay pot[n] the meat is cooked in must be broken; but if it is cooked in a bronze pot, the pot is to be scoured and rinsed with water. 29Any male in a priest's family may eat it;[o] it is most holy.[p] 30But any sin offering whose blood is brought into the tent of meeting to make atonement in the Holy Place[q] must not be eaten; it must be burned up.[r]

The Guilt Offering

7 " 'These are the regulations for the guilt offering,[s] which is most holy: 2The guilt offering is to be slaughtered in the place where the burnt offering is

6:3 [n] Dt 22:1-3
6:4 [o] Lk 19:8
6:5 [p] Nu 5:7 [q] Lev 5:15
6:6 [r] Lev 5:15
6:7 [s] Lev 4:26
6:10 [t] Ex 28:39-42, 43; 39:28
6:11 [u] Lev 4:12
6:14 [v] Lev 2:1; 15:4
6:15 [w] Lev 2:9 [x] Lev 2:2
6:16 [y] Lev 2:3 [z] Eze 44:29 [a] Lev 2:11 [b] Lev 10:13
6:17 [c] ver 29; Ex 40:10; Nu 18:9, 10
6:18 [d] ver 29; Nu 18:9-10 [e] ver 27
6:20 [f] Ex 16:36 [g] Ex 29:2
6:21 [h] Lev 2:5
6:25 [i] Lev 1:3 [j] Lev 1:5, 11
6:26 [k] ver 16 [l] Lev 10:17-18
6:27 [m] Ex 29:37
6:28 [n] Lev 11:33; 15:12
6:29 [o] ver 18 [p] ver 17
6:30 [q] Lev 4:18 [r] Lev 4:12
7:1 [s] Lev 5:14-6:7

[a] *15* Or *representative* [b] *17* Or *purification offering*; also in verses 25 and 30 [c] *18* Or *Whoever touches them must be holy*; similarly in verse 27 [d] *20* Or *each* [e] *20* That is, probably about 3 1/2 pounds or about 1.6 kilograms [f] *21* The meaning of the Hebrew for this word is uncertain.

sate the depositor for the stolen goods); and if the depositor lies and claims his goods have gone missing when, in fact, they have not.

6:9 *the fire must be kept burning on the altar.* The Hittite "Instructions to Priests and Temple Officials" also regulate fire at the residence of a deity; however, the concern is the opposite: to put the fire out at night so that it does not burn down the temple.

slaughtered, and its blood is to be splashed
against the sides of the altar. 3 All its fat[t]
shall be offered: the fat tail and the fat that
covers the internal organs, 4 both kidneys
with the fat on them near the loins, and
the long lobe of the liver, which is to be removed with the kidneys. 5 The priest shall
burn them on the altar as a food offering
presented to the LORD. It is a guilt offering.
6 Any male in a priest's family may eat it,[u]
but it must be eaten in the sanctuary area;
it is most holy.[v]
7 " 'The same law applies to both the sin
offering[a] and the guilt offering: They belong to the priest[w] who makes atonement
with them. 8 The priest who offers a burnt
offering for anyone may keep its hide for
himself. 9 Every grain offering baked in an
oven or cooked in a pan or on a griddle[x]
belongs to the priest who offers it, 10 and
every grain offering, whether mixed with
olive oil or dry, belongs equally to all the
sons of Aaron.

The Fellowship Offering

11 " 'These are the regulations for the fellowship offering anyone may present to
the LORD:
12 " 'If they offer it as an expression of
thankfulness, then along with this thank
offering[y] they are to offer thick loaves
made without yeast and with olive oil
mixed in, thin loaves[z] made without yeast
and brushed with oil, and thick loaves of
the finest flour well-kneaded and with oil
mixed in. 13 Along with their fellowship
offering of thanksgiving they are to present an offering with thick loaves of bread
made with yeast.[a] 14 They are to bring one
of each kind as an offering, a contribution
to the LORD; it belongs to the priest who
splashes the blood of the fellowship offering against the altar. 15 The meat of their
fellowship offering of thanksgiving must
be eaten on the day it is offered; they must
leave none of it till morning.[b]
16 " 'If, however, their offering is the result of a vow or is a freewill offering, the
sacrifice shall be eaten on the day they offer it, but anything left over may be eaten
on the next day.[c] 17 Any meat of the sacrifice left over till the third day must be
burned up. 18 If any meat of the fellowship
offering is eaten on the third day, the one
who offered it will not be accepted.[d] It will
not be reckoned[e] to their credit, for it has
become impure; the person who eats any
of it will be held responsible.
19 " 'Meat that touches anything ceremonially unclean must not be eaten; it must
be burned up. As for other meat, anyone
ceremonially clean may eat it. 20 But if anyone who is unclean eats any meat of the
fellowship offering belonging to the LORD,

7:3 [t] Ex 29:13; Lev 3:4,9 **7:6** [u] Lev 6:18; Nu 18:9-10 [v] Lev 2:3 **7:7** [w] Lev 6:17, 26; 1Co 9:13 **7:9** [x] Lev 2:5 **7:12** [y] ver 13, 15 [z] Lev 2:4; Nu 6:15

7:13 [a] Lev 23:17; Am 4:5 **7:15** [b] Lev 22:30 **7:16** [c] Lev 19:5-8 **7:18** [d] Lev 19:7 [e] Nu 18:27

[a] 7 Or *purification offering*; also in verse 37

7:7 *They belong to the priest who makes atonement with them.* In ancient Near Eastern religious cultures, it was common for priests to eat portions of food that had been dedicated to deities (see note on Nu 18:9). Thus on the fourth day of the Hittite Ninth Year Festival of Telipinu, the priests ate sacrificial meat that had been presented to the god Telipinu.

The Hittite "Instructions to Priests and Temple Officials" stipulate that all sacrificial food and drink must first be offered to the god. Then the priests and their family members consume it on the same day if possible, but if necessary, they may have up to three days (cf. vv. 16 – 17, which give a two-day limit). Some Hittite food or drink items were permitted only to priests and some was to be consumed within the sacred precincts (as the food in v. 6; 6:16,26; 24:9). While such Hittite procedures showed important similarities to Israelite ritual practice, the key difference is that Yahweh had no need of food for sustenance.

The animals offered by individuals as purification ("sin") offerings were specified according to one's rank within Israelite society. The reparation ("guilt") offering, brought on account of a violation of someone's property or an inadvertent break of a covenant stipulation, usually consisted of a ram (or its equivalent in silver shekels), plus a penalty of one-fifth the value of the animal (vv. 1 – 10; 5:14 – 19). The sacrificial process included the ritual slaughtering of the animal, the deposition of the drained blood on the altar or its sides, the burning of assigned portions such as the fat and entrails on the large bronze altar, and the setting aside and consumption of priestly portions. In keeping with v. 6; 6:29, only the males among the priests and their families were permitted to consume these "most holy" of offerings.

Besides edible portions, the hide of an animal was valuable and could serve as payment for an officiating priest both in Israelite (v. 8) and Emar (Syria) ritual systems. The Punic Marseilles Tariff not only regulated distribution of dedicated items among priests and offerers; it set monetary fees for some offerings in proportion to the size of the animals.

7:12 *expression of thankfulness.* Gratitude or a vow (v. 16) could also motivate non-Israelites to make offerings to their deities. For example, the Phoenician king Yehawmilk gave works of art to his goddess to express gratitude for her favor. The Aramean king Bir-Hadad set up a stele "for his lord Melqart, to whom he made a vow and who heard his voice." Here fulfillment of a votive obligation is also an expression of gratitude.

7:16 *vow.* See previous note.

7:20 *they must be cut off from their people.* This terminal penalty for very serious sin (cf. Nu 15:30 – 31) is administered by God himself and denies the offender an afterlife, most likely through extirpation of his line of descendants. It therefore makes sense that a wrongdoer could be put to death and "cut off" as well (see Lev 20:2 – 3).

Non-Israelites also referred to loss of posterity as a form of punishment. The Hittite "Instructions to Priests and Temple Officials" warn of the consequences for anyone who neglects to properly extinguish the fire on the hearth, thereby causing the temple to burn down: "He who commits this sin will perish along with his descendants. Of those in the temple none will be left living. They will perish together with their descendants."

they must be cut off from their people.[f] 21Anyone who touches something unclean[g]—whether human uncleanness or an unclean animal or any unclean creature that moves along the ground[a]—and then eats any of the meat of the fellowship offering belonging to the LORD must be cut off from their people.' "

Eating Fat and Blood Forbidden

22The LORD said to Moses, 23"Say to the Israelites: 'Do not eat any of the fat of cattle, sheep or goats.[h] 24The fat of an animal found dead or torn by wild animals[i] may be used for any other purpose, but you must not eat it. 25Anyone who eats the fat of an animal from which a food offering may be[b] presented to the LORD must be cut off from their people. 26And wherever you live, you must not eat the blood[j] of any bird or animal. 27Anyone who eats blood[k] must be cut off from their people.' "

The Priests' Share

28The LORD said to Moses, 29"Say to the Israelites: 'Anyone who brings a fellowship offering to the LORD is to bring part of it as their sacrifice to the LORD. 30With their own hands they are to present the food offering to the LORD; they are to bring the fat, together with the breast, and wave the breast before the LORD as a wave offering.[l] 31The priest shall burn the fat on the altar, but the breast belongs to Aaron and his sons.[m] 32You are to give the right thigh of your fellowship offerings to the priest as a contribution.[n] 33The son of Aaron who offers the blood and the fat of the fellowship offering shall have the right thigh as his share. 34From the fellowship offerings of the Israelites, I have taken the breast that is waved and the thigh[o] that is presented and have given them to Aaron the priest and his sons[p] as their perpetual share from the Israelites.' "

35This is the portion of the food offerings presented to the LORD that were allotted to Aaron and his sons on the day they were presented to serve the LORD as priests. 36On the day they were anointed,[q] the LORD commanded that the Israelites give this to them as their perpetual share for the generations to come.

37These, then, are the regulations for the burnt offering,[r] the grain offering,[s] the sin offering, the guilt offering, the ordination offering[t] and the fellowship offering, 38which the LORD gave Moses at Mount Sinai in the Desert of Sinai on the day he commanded the Israelites to bring their offerings to the LORD.[u]

The Ordination of Aaron and His Sons

8:1-36pp — Ex 29:1-37

8 The LORD said to Moses, 2"Bring Aaron and his sons, their garments, the anointing oil,[v] the bull for the sin offering,[c] the two rams and the basket containing bread made without yeast,[w] 3and gather the entire assembly[x] at the entrance to the tent of meeting." 4Moses did as the LORD commanded him, and the assembly gathered at the entrance to the tent of meeting.

5Moses said to the assembly, "This is what the LORD has commanded to be done." 6Then Moses brought Aaron and his sons forward and washed them with water.[y] 7He put the tunic on Aaron, tied

7:20 [f] Lev 22:3-7
7:21 [g] Lev 5:2; 11:24,28
7:23 [h] Lev 3:17; 17:13-14
7:24 [i] Ex 22:31
7:26 [j] Ge 9:4
7:27 [k] Lev 17:10-24; Ac 15:20,29
7:30 [l] Ex 29:24; Nu 6:20
7:31 [m] ver 34
7:32 [n] ver 34; Lev 9:21; Nu 6:20
7:34 [o] Lev 10:15; [p] Ex 29:27; Nu 18:18-19
7:36 [q] Ex 40:13, 15; Lev 8:12,30
7:37 [r] Lev 6:9; [s] Lev 6:14; [t] ver 1,11
7:38 [u] Lev 1:2
8:2 [v] Ex 30:23-25,30; [w] Ex 29:2-3
8:3 [x] Nu 8:9
8:6 [y] Ex 29:4; 30:19; Ps 26:6; Ac 22:16; 1Co 6:11; Eph 5:26

[a] *21* A few Hebrew manuscripts, Samaritan Pentateuch, Syriac and Targum (see 5:2); most Hebrew manuscripts *any unclean, detestable thing* [b] *25* Or *offering is* [c] *2* Or *purification offering*; also in verse 14

7:30 *wave offering.* The Hebrew word translated "wave offering" denotes a type of offering that is lifted up toward the heavens in presentation and dedication to God and then lowered into the hands of the priest. This practice is evidenced in Egyptian and Mesopotamian ritual offerings pictured on monuments, steles and plaques. Often the breast or right thigh of the animal was uplifted as a wave offering. In Israel, the wave offering was associated with the peace offering (here; v. 34; 23:20), the consecration of the priests (8:29; Ex 29:27), the dedication of the Levites (Nu 8:11 – 13,21), and the purification ritual for Nazirites (Nu 6:19 – 20).

In Lev 10:15, the thigh of the heave (elevation) offering and the breast of the wave (side to side) offering were ordained as gifts for the Aaronic priesthood. Grain and oil offerings were also presented in such fashion, as with the consecration of the priests (8:27; Ex 29:23 – 24), cleansing ritual for lepers (Lev 14:12,21,24) and the sheaf of grain and two loaves for the Festival of Weeks (23:15,17). The transference ritual of up and down, forward and backward movement signified that the offering was moving from its temporary owner to its ultimate owner, God.

8:2 *Bring Aaron and his sons.* Preparing the Israelite sanctuary and its priesthood for their sacred function was an elaborate week-long procedure that purified and sanctified them by ritual agents such as water, anointing oil and sacrificial blood. Non-Israelites also used rituals to consecrate objects and persons. For example, establishing a satellite temple as a new place of worship for the Hittite Goddess of the Night was a seven-day process (five days for the old temple and two days for the new temple) that included purification of new sancta with blood on the last day (see note on 1:5).

All ancient Near Eastern religious systems employed cultic officials of various hierarchical levels to promote positive human interactions with deities by administering and maintaining temples, protecting boundaries of the sacred sphere, performing rituals, seeking to ascertain the divine will through oracles or divination, and leading corporate worship, such as through the performance of festivals. These were weighty responsibilities, so priests at the top of the hierarchy were invested with great power and prestige, and inducting such a person into office often required an elaborate process.

the sash around him, clothed him with the robe and put the ephod on him. He also fastened the ephod with a decorative waistband, which he tied around him.[z] 8He placed the breastpiece on him and put the Urim and Thummim[a] in the breastpiece. 9Then he placed the turban on Aaron's head and set the gold plate, the sacred emblem,[b] on the front of it, as the LORD commanded Moses.

10Then Moses took the anointing oil[c] and anointed[d] the tabernacle and everything in it, and so consecrated them. 11He sprinkled some of the oil on the altar seven times, anointing the altar and all its utensils and the basin with its stand, to consecrate them.[e] 12He poured some of the anointing oil on Aaron's head and anointed[f] him to consecrate him.[g] 13Then he brought Aaron's sons forward, put tunics on them, tied sashes around them and fastened caps on them, as the LORD commanded Moses.

14He then presented the bull[h] for the sin offering,[i] and Aaron and his sons laid their hands on its head. 15Moses slaughtered the bull and took some of the blood, and with his finger he put it on all the horns of the altar[j] to purify the altar.[k] He poured out the rest of the blood at the base of the altar. So he consecrated it to make atonement for it.[l] 16Moses also took all the fat around the internal organs, the long lobe of the liver, and both kidneys and their fat, and burned it on the altar. 17But the bull with its hide and its flesh and its intestines[m] he burned up outside the camp,[n] as the LORD commanded Moses.

18He then presented the ram[o] for the burnt offering, and Aaron and his sons laid their hands on its head. 19Then Moses slaughtered the ram and splashed the blood against the sides of the altar. 20He cut the ram into pieces and burned the head, the pieces and the fat. 21He washed the internal organs and the legs with water and burned the whole ram on the altar. It was a burnt offering, a pleasing aroma, a food offering presented to the LORD, as the LORD commanded Moses.

22He then presented the other ram, the ram for the ordination,[p] and Aaron and his sons laid their hands on its head. 23Moses slaughtered the ram and took some of its blood and put it on the lobe of Aaron's right ear, on the thumb of his right hand and on the big toe of his right foot. 24Moses also brought Aaron's sons forward and put some of the blood on the lobes of their right ears, on the thumbs of their right hands and on the big toes of their right feet. Then he splashed blood against the sides of the altar.[q] 25After that, he took the fat, the fat tail, all the fat around the internal organs, the long lobe of the liver, both kidneys and their fat and the right thigh. 26And from the basket of bread made without yeast, which was before the LORD, he took one thick loaf, one thick loaf with olive oil mixed in, and one thin loaf, and he put these on the fat portions and on the right thigh. 27He put all these in the hands of Aaron and his sons, and they waved them before the LORD as a wave offering. 28Then Moses took them from their hands and burned them on the altar on top of the burnt offering as an ordination offering, a pleasing aroma, a food offering presented to the LORD. 29Moses also took the breast, which was his share of the ordination ram,[r] and waved it before the LORD as a wave offering, as the LORD commanded Moses.

30Then Moses took some of the anointing oil and some of the blood from the altar and sprinkled them on Aaron and his garments[s] and on his sons and their garments. So he consecrated[t] Aaron and his garments and his sons and their garments.

31Moses then said to Aaron and his sons, "Cook the meat at the entrance to the tent of meeting and eat it there with the bread from the basket of ordination offerings, as I was commanded: 'Aaron and his sons are to eat it.' 32Then burn up the rest of the meat and the bread. 33Do not leave the entrance to the tent of meeting for seven days, until the days of your ordination are completed, for your ordination will last seven days. 34What has been done today was commanded by the LORD[u] to make atonement for you. 35You must stay at the entrance to the tent of meeting day and night for seven days and do what the LORD requires,[v] so you will not die; for that is what I have been commanded."

8:7 [z] Ex 28:4
8:8 [a] Ex 28:30
8:9 [b] Ex 28:36
8:10 [c] ver 2 [d] Ex 30:26
8:11 [e] Ex 30:29
8:12 [f] Lev 21:10, 12 [g] Ex 30:30
8:14 [h] Lev 4:3 [i] Ps 66:15; Eze 43:19
8:15 [j] Lev 4:7 [k] Heb 9:22 [l] Eze 43:20
8:17 [m] Lev 4:11 [n] Lev 4:12
8:18 [o] ver 2
8:22 [p] ver 2
8:24 [q] Heb 9:18-22
8:29 [r] Lev 7:31-34
8:30 [s] Ex 28:2 [t] Nu 3:3
8:34 [u] Heb 7:16
8:35 [v] Nu 3:7; 9:19; Dt 11:1; 1Ki 2:3; Eze 48:11

8:10 *anointing oil.* In order to symbolize divine designation for leadership positions that involved special contracts/covenants with Yahweh, Israelites anointed individuals to change their status to that of priest or king. Elsewhere in the ancient Near East, symbolic anointing of persons could accompany business contracts, marriages, liberations of slaves, and vassal treaties, and they typically represented the obligation and a conditional curse that would take effect if the party that received the oil were to break the treaty. Outside Israel, anointing could also represent elevation of status, including elevation to priesthood.

8:22 *ordination.* The Hebrew word here is derived from the idiom for "to ordain," which, translated word-for-word, is "to fill the hand" (see v. 33). The Akkadian cognate expression illuminates the meaning of the idiom: It can refer to authorization for a particular official role, which could be symbolized by filling one's hand with the relevant tool or insignia, such as a scepter for a king.

36So Aaron and his sons did everything
the LORD commanded through Moses.

The Priests Begin Their Ministry

9 On the eighth day[w] Moses summoned
Aaron and his sons and the elders of
Israel. 2He said to Aaron, "Take a bull calf
for your sin offering[a] and a ram for your
burnt offering, both without defect, and
present them before the LORD. 3Then say
to the Israelites: 'Take a male goat for a sin
offering, a calf and a lamb — both a year
old and without defect — for a burnt offering, 4and an ox[b] and a ram for a fellowship offering to sacrifice before the LORD,
together with a grain offering mixed with
olive oil. For today the LORD will appear
to you.[x]' "
5They took the things Moses commanded to the front of the tent of meeting, and
the entire assembly came near and stood
before the LORD. 6Then Moses said, "This
is what the LORD has commanded you to
do, so that the glory of the LORD[y] may appear to you."
7Moses said to Aaron, "Come to the
altar and sacrifice your sin offering and
your burnt offering and make atonement
for yourself and the people; sacrifice the
offering that is for the people and make
atonement for them, as the LORD has commanded.[z]"
8So Aaron came to the altar and slaughtered the calf as a sin offering[a] for himself.
9His sons brought the blood to him,[b] and
he dipped his finger into the blood and
put it on the horns of the altar; the rest of
the blood he poured out at the base of the
altar.[c] 10On the altar he burned the fat, the
kidneys and the long lobe of the liver from
the sin offering, as the LORD commanded
Moses; 11the flesh and the hide[d] he burned
up outside the camp.[e]
12Then he slaughtered the burnt offering. His sons handed him the blood, and
he splashed it against the sides of the altar. 13They handed him the burnt offering
piece by piece, including the head, and he
burned them on the altar.[f] 14He washed
the internal organs and the legs and
burned them on top of the burnt offering
on the altar.
15Aaron then brought the offering that
was for the people.[g] He took the goat for
the people's sin offering and slaughtered
it and offered it for a sin offering as he did
with the first one.
16He brought the burnt offering and offered it in the prescribed way.[h] 17He also
brought the grain offering, took a handful
of it and burned it on the altar in addition
to the morning's burnt offering.[i]
18He slaughtered the ox and the ram
as the fellowship offering for the people.[j]
His sons handed him the blood, and he
splashed it against the sides of the altar.
19But the fat portions of the ox and the
ram — the fat tail, the layer of fat, the
kidneys and the long lobe of the liver —
20these they laid on the breasts, and then
Aaron burned the fat on the altar. 21Aaron
waved the breasts and the right thigh before the LORD as a wave offering,[k] as Moses commanded.
22Then Aaron lifted his hands toward
the people and blessed them.[l] And having
sacrificed the sin offering, the burnt offering and the fellowship offering, he stepped
down.
23Moses and Aaron then went into the
tent of meeting. When they came out, they
blessed the people; and the glory of the
LORD[m] appeared to all the people. 24Fire[n]
came out from the presence of the LORD
and consumed the burnt offering and the
fat portions on the altar. And when all the
people saw it, they shouted for joy and fell
facedown.[o]

The Death of Nadab and Abihu

10 Aaron's sons Nadab and Abihu[p]
took their censers, put fire in them[q]
and added incense; and they offered unauthorized fire before the LORD, contrary
to his command.[r] 2So fire came out from

9:1 [w] Eze 43:27 **9:4** [x] Ex 29:43 **9:6** [y] ver 23; Ex 24:16 **9:7** [z] Heb 5:1, 3; 7:27 **9:8** [a] Lev 4:1-12 **9:9** [b] ver 12, 18 [c] Lev 4:7 **9:11** [d] Lev 4:11 [e] Lev 4:12; 8:17 **9:13** [f] Lev 1:8 **9:15** [g] Lev 4:27-31 **9:16** [h] Lev 1:1-13 **9:17** [i] Lev 2:1-2; 3:5 **9:18** [j] Lev 3:1-11 **9:21** [k] Ex 29:24, 26; Lev 7:30-34 **9:22** [l] Nu 6:23; Dt 21:5; Lk 24:50 **9:23** [m] ver 6 **9:24** [n] Jdg 6:21; 2Ch 7:1 [o] 1Ki 18:39 **10:1** [p] Ex 24:1; Nu 3:2-4; 26:61 [q] Lev 16:12 [r] Ex 30:9

[a] 2 Or *purification offering*; here and throughout this chapter [b] 4 The Hebrew word can refer to either male or female; also in verses 18 and 19.

9:23 *the glory of the LORD appeared.* When Aaron and his sons initiated the ritual system by performing their first priestly officiation, Yahweh's glory appeared, and he consumed the sacrifices with fire to complete his acceptance of the sanctuary. Compare the Sumerian Cylinder B of the ruler Gudea, which describes the initiation festivities for when the god Ningirsu and his consort Baba, as represented by their idols, were settled into their new temple. Their entrance was accompanied by offerings, as well as purification and divination procedures. Gudea presented "housewarming gifts" to the divine couple (cf. Nu 7), prepared a banquet for Ningirsu, and offered animal sacrifices.

10:1 *unauthorized fire.* Burning incense as an offering to a deity had to be done correctly. Thus, in the daily ritual in the temple of the god Amun-Re at Karnak (Egypt), the high priest was obliged to follow a detailed protocol: reciting spells for striking the fire, taking the censer, placing the incense bowl on the censer arm, putting incense on the flame and advancing to the sacred place. Aaron's sons had the right idea (incense should be in the air to serve as a screen between the people and the divine presence), but their ritual execution was flawed. The ritual mistake of Aaron's two sons was burning incense to Yahweh with "unauthorized fire," which apparently refers to live coals from a fire other than that which God himself had just lit on the altar in the courtyard (9:24; cf. 16:12; Nu 16:46). These coals brought impurity into contact with

the presence of the LORD and consumed them,[s] and they died before the LORD. 3Moses then said to Aaron, "This is what the LORD spoke of when he said:

"'Among those who approach me[t]
I will be proved holy;[u]
in the sight of all the people
I will be honored.[v]'"

Aaron remained silent.

4Moses summoned Mishael and Elzaphan,[w] sons of Aaron's uncle Uzziel,[x] and said to them, "Come here; carry your cousins outside the camp,[y] away from the front of the sanctuary." 5So they came and carried them, still in their tunics,[z] outside the camp, as Moses ordered.

6Then Moses said to Aaron and his sons Eleazar and Ithamar, "Do not let your hair become unkempt[a][a] and do not tear your clothes, or you will die and the LORD will be angry with the whole community.[b] But your relatives, all the Israelites, may mourn for those the LORD has destroyed by fire. 7Do not leave the entrance to the tent of meeting or you will die, because the LORD's anointing oil[c] is on you." So they did as Moses said.

8Then the LORD said to Aaron, 9"You and your sons are not to drink wine[d] or other fermented drink[e] whenever you go into the tent of meeting, or you will die. This is a lasting ordinance for the generations to come, 10so that you can distinguish between the holy and the common, between the unclean and the clean,[f] 11and so you can teach[g] the Israelites all the decrees the LORD has given them through Moses.[h]"

12Moses said to Aaron and his remaining sons, Eleazar and Ithamar, "Take the grain offering left over from the food offerings prepared without yeast and presented to the LORD and eat it beside the altar,[i] for it is most holy. 13Eat it in the sanctuary area, because it is your share and your sons' share of the food offerings presented to the LORD; for so I have been commanded. 14But you and your sons and your daughters may eat the breast that was waved and the thigh that was presented. Eat them in a ceremonially clean place;[j] they have been given to you and your children as your share of the Israelites' fellowship offerings. 15The thigh[k] that was presented and the breast that was waved must be brought with the fat portions of the food offerings, to be waved before the LORD as a wave offering. This will be the perpetual share for you and your children, as the LORD has commanded."

16When Moses inquired about the goat of the sin offering[b][l] and found that it had been burned up, he was angry with Eleazar and Ithamar, Aaron's remaining sons, and asked, 17"Why didn't you eat the sin offering[m] in the sanctuary area? It is most holy; it was given to you to take away the guilt of the community by making atonement for them before the LORD. 18Since its blood was not taken into the Holy Place,[n] you should have eaten the goat in the sanctuary area, as I commanded."

19Aaron replied to Moses, "Today they sacrificed their sin offering and their burnt offering[o] before the LORD, but such things as this have happened to me. Would the LORD have been pleased if I had eaten the sin offering today?" 20When Moses heard this, he was satisfied.

Clean and Unclean Food

11:1-23pp — Dt 14:3-20

11 The LORD said to Moses and Aaron, 2"Say to the Israelites: 'Of all the animals that live on land, these are the ones you may eat:[p] 3You may eat any

[a] 6 Or *Do not uncover your heads* [b] 16 Or *purification offering*; also in verses 17 and 19

10:2 s Nu 3:4; 16:35; 26:61 **10:3** t Ex 19:22 u Ex 30:29; Lev 21:6; Eze 28:22 v Isa 49:3 **10:4** w Ex 6:22 x Ex 6:18 y Ac 5:6,9,10 **10:5** z Lev 8:13 **10:6** a Lev 21:10 b Nu 1:53; 16:22; Jos 7:1; 22:18; 2Sa 24:1 **10:7** c Ex 28:41; Lev 21:12 **10:9** d Hos 4:11 e Pr 20:1; Isa 28:7; Eze 44:21; Lk 1:15; Eph 5:18; 1Ti 3:3; Titus 1:7 **10:10** f Lev 11:47; 20:25; Eze 22:26 **10:11** g Mal 2:7 h Dt 24:8 **10:12** i Lev 6:14-18; 21:22 **10:14** j Ex 29:24, 26-27; Lev 7:31, 34; Nu 18:11 **10:15** k Lev 7:34 **10:16** l Lev 9:3 **10:17** m Lev 6:24-30 **10:18** n Lev 6:26, 30 **10:19** o Lev 9:12 **11:2** p Ac 10:12-14

the divine presence, with dramatic and tragic results—the natural result of impurity coming into contact with God's presence.

10:6 *Do not let your hair become unkempt and do not tear your clothes.* Forbidden here (see also 21:10–12) are ancient Near Eastern mourning customs that would have adversely affected the purity status of Aaron and his surviving sons. See note on Nu 14:6.

10:9 *You and your sons are not to drink wine.* All over the ancient Near East, wine and beer were regularly served to the gods with their sacrificial meals. The idea that deities could become intoxicated by such beverages is reflected in Ugaritic mythology and in the Babylonian epic of creation (*Enuma Elish*), where partying gods make a momentous decision to exalt Marduk above other gods while they are "under the influence." There is some evidence in extra-Biblical literature of ritual intoxication among the priests (see also Isa 28:7).

The Hittite "Instructions to Priests and Temple Officials" recognize that drunken priests could cause disturbance or quarreling, or could disrupt a festival. Rather than directly restricting alcohol use, however, these instructions mandate beating as punishment for obnoxious behavior and warn priests that they are accountable for proper performance of festivals, which implies the need for mental clarity.

10:17 *eat the sin offering.* The purification ("sin") offering absorbs the impurities that it was presented to remedy. When a great deal is absorbed, the offering is burnt (see note on 4:12), but on most occasions the priest's eating of the offering is part of the purification process. Aaron's reluctance to eat the offering may be caused by the presence of the corpses of his sons (v. 2), which add dangerous levels of impurity.

11:2 *these are the ones you may eat.* From the rather extensive taxonomy of animals in this chapter (cf. Dt 14), a modern reader could gain the impression that meat constituted a substantial portion of the ancient diet. However,

LEVITICUS 11

Unclean Food

Leviticus 11 does not provide an explicit rationale for its division of animals into clean/permitted versus unclean/forbidden categories.

Interpreters have proposed a wide variety of possible rationales, including effects on human physical health, reflection of societal values (i.e., based on what is "normal" for each category), analogy to God's holy sacrificial "diet" (i.e., what God can "eat" by means of sacrifice, people can eat), the need to teach reverence for the sanctity of life by limiting animal slaughter, and the concept that nonpermitted animals depart from the creation ideal of life in that they are associated with death in various ways (e.g., those that burrow in the ground or are predators). Any of the last three of these rationales are persuasive insofar as they can be understood in relation to the reason given in Lev 11 for this dietary legislation as a whole: that even Israel's diet should distinguish them from others as they live out the holy status conferred on them by God. ◆

animal that has a divided hoof and that
chews the cud.
4"'There are some that only chew the
cud or only have a divided hoof, but you
must not eat them. The camel, though it
chews the cud, does not have a divided
hoof; it is ceremonially unclean for you.
5The hyrax, though it chews the cud, does
not have a divided hoof; it is unclean for
you. 6The rabbit, though it chews the cud,
does not have a divided hoof; it is unclean
for you. 7And the pig,[q] though it has a divided hoof, does not chew the cud; it is
unclean for you. 8You must not eat their
meat or touch their carcasses; they are unclean for you.[r]

11:7 [q] Isa 65:4; 66:3, 17 **11:8** [r] Isa 52:11; Heb 9:10

such was not the case. Meat was primarily eaten in relation to sacrifices.

There were also restrictions on diet in ancient Egypt and Mesopotamia, but these were unrelated to each other or to the Biblical ones, and unlike the latter, they did not comprise overall dietary systems. In Egypt restrictions were localized, and generally in each geographic area they dealt with only one species that was prohibited for a religious reason; e.g., it was forbidden to eat a cow where the principal god was Hathor, who takes the form of a bovine (cf. the sacred cow in India). Mesopotamians were supposed to avoid particular activities at certain times, which could include eating some kinds of animals on specific days of the month. They were also to avoid violating taboos, which in some cases could involve eating food reserved for deities.

11:7 *the pig ... is unclean for you.* Of all animals in Israel's environment, only the pig has cloven hooves but does not chew cud. The rules in ch. 11 implicitly single out the pig for exclusion from the holy Israelite diet. Why Israel was not to eat pigs is unclear. Some level of Egyptian society considered pigs unclean. The god Seth injured Horus's eye, transformed himself into a black pig/boar, and injured it further. The god Re healed the eye and then pronounced the pig an abomination (*bwt*) for Horus's sake. This pronouncement explained why, according to the gods, the pig was an abomination to Horus. The concept became a part of Egyptian culture, though pork was eaten in Egypt by at least the lower classes of the land, and it was a staple of the working class at Amarna in the Egyptian New Kingdom. Pigs do not tolerate arid conditions, so Israel would certainly not have herded pigs through the Sinai Desert.

In the ancient Near East the pig was cheap, contemptible and, evidently, not eaten in rituals. Pigs were a part of Hittite rituals that were tied to gods of the netherworld, and they were considered unclean. Thus, sacrificing a pig may be synonymous with sacrificing to demons or the dead. In such a sacrifice, the offerer received none of the meat. Pigs could also be utilized in nonsacrificial rites of purification, including symbolic/magical elimination of impurity or plague (see note on 1:5). A pig could be sacrificed to settle a domestic quarrel. Mesopotamian religion rarely used pigs as food or as sacrifices. In general it was unclean and "not fit for a temple ... an offense to all the gods." Pigs, along with dogs, were regarded with contempt in the ancient Near East because of their roles as scavengers. The Hittite "Instructions to Priests and Temple Officials" warn against letting a pig or dog into rooms containing sacred bread. A Mesopotamian saying goes: "The pig is unholy [...] bespattering his backside, Making the streets smell ... polluting the houses."

The pig and wild boar were probably used in Canaanite and/or Syrian rituals, and it is possible that the Israelites did not use them partly because of a connection with these nearby pagan nations. There is no definite evidence in Palestine for a cultic use of pigs in the Bronze Age (3500 – 1200 BC). In the Middle Bronze Age

9" 'Of all the creatures living in the water of the seas and the streams you may
eat any that have fins and scales. 10 But all
creatures in the seas or streams that do
not have fins and scales—whether among
all the swarming things or among all the
other living creatures in the water—you
are to regard as unclean.[s] 11 And since you
are to regard them as unclean, you must
not eat their meat; you must regard their
carcasses as unclean. 12 Anything living
in the water that does not have fins and
scales is to be regarded as unclean by you.

13" 'These are the birds you are to regard
as unclean and not eat because they are
unclean: the eagle,[a] the vulture, the black
vulture, 14 the red kite, any kind of black
kite, 15 any kind of raven, 16 the horned
owl, the screech owl, the gull, any kind of
hawk, 17 the little owl, the cormorant, the
great owl, 18 the white owl, the desert owl,
the osprey, 19 the stork, any kind of heron,
the hoopoe and the bat.

20" 'All flying insects that walk on all
fours are to be regarded as unclean by
you.[t] 21 There are, however, some flying insects that walk on all fours that you may
eat: those that have jointed legs for hop-
ping on the ground. 22 Of these you may
eat any kind of locust,[u] katydid, cricket or
grasshopper. 23 But all other flying insects
that have four legs you are to regard as
unclean.

24" 'You will make yourselves unclean
by these; whoever touches their carcasses will be unclean till evening. 25 Whoever
picks up one of their carcasses must wash
their clothes,[v] and they will be unclean till
evening.[w]

26" 'Every animal that does not have a
divided hoof or that does not chew the
cud is unclean for you; whoever touches
the carcass of any of them will be unclean.
27 Of all the animals that walk on all fours,
those that walk on their paws are unclean
for you; whoever touches their carcasses
will be unclean till evening. 28 Anyone who
picks up their carcasses must wash their
clothes, and they will be unclean till evening. These animals are unclean for you.

29" 'Of the animals that move along the
ground, these are unclean for you: the
weasel, the rat,[x] any kind of great lizard,
30 the gecko, the monitor lizard, the wall
lizard, the skink and the chameleon. 31 Of
all those that move along the ground, these
are unclean for you. Whoever touches
them when they are dead will be unclean
till evening. 32 When one of them dies and
falls on something, that article, whatever
its use, will be unclean, whether it is made
of wood, cloth, hide or sackcloth.[y] Put it
in water; it will be unclean till evening,
and then it will be clean. 33 If one of them
falls into a clay pot, everything in it will
be unclean, and you must break the pot.[z]
34 Any food you are allowed to eat that
has come into contact with water from
any such pot is unclean, and any liquid
that is drunk from such a pot is unclean.
35 Anything that one of their carcasses falls
on becomes unclean; an oven or cooking
pot must be broken up. They are unclean,
and you are to regard them as unclean. 36 A
spring, however, or a cistern for collecting water remains clean, but anyone who
touches one of these carcasses is unclean.
37 If a carcass falls on any seeds that are to
be planted, they remain clean. 38 But if water has been put on the seed and a carcass
falls on it, it is unclean for you.

39" 'If an animal that you are allowed to
eat dies, anyone who touches its carcass
will be unclean till evening. 40 Anyone who
eats some of its carcass must wash their
clothes, and they will be unclean till evening.[a] Anyone who picks up the carcass
must wash their clothes, and they will be
unclean till evening.

41" 'Every creature that moves along the
ground is to be regarded as unclean; it is
not to be eaten. 42 You are not to eat any
creature that moves along the ground,
whether it moves on its belly or walks on
all fours or on many feet; it is unclean.
43 Do not defile yourselves by any of these
creatures.[b] Do not make yourselves unclean by means of them or be made unclean by them. 44 I am the LORD your God;[c]
consecrate yourselves[d] and be holy,[e] because I am holy.[f] Do not make yourselves

11:10 [s] Lev 7:18 **11:20** [t] Ac 10:14 **11:22** [u] Mt 3:4; Mk 1:6 **11:25** [v] Lev 14:8, 47; 15:5 [w] ver 40; Nu 31:24 **11:29** [x] Isa 66:17 **11:32** [y] Lev 15:12 **11:33** [z] Lev 6:28; 15:12 **11:40** [a] Lev 17:15; 22:8; Eze 44:31 **11:43** [b] Lev 20:25 **11:44** [c] Ex 6:2, 7; Isa 43:3; 51:15 [d] Lev 20:7 [e] Ex 19:6 [f] Lev 19:2; Ps 99:3; Eph 1:4; 1Th 4:7; 1Pe 1:15, 16*

[a] *13* The precise identification of some of the birds, insects and animals in this chapter is uncertain.

(c. 2000–1550 BC) in Syria and the Holy Land pig remains decrease near cities, especially large cities, but remains are found in rural areas.

Nevertheless, texts and archaeological remains (especially bones) in Egypt and Mesopotamia, as well as Syria-Palestine and North Africa, confirm that pigs were commonly raised for food by non-Israelites. Philistines living on or near coastal areas herded pigs, but the herding and eating of pigs were basically taboo in the highlands of Canaan where Israel settled. The herding and production of pigs actually competed with more productive and profitable agricultural activities. Perhaps this also helps to explain the Biblical prohibition.

11:25 *wash their clothes, and they will be unclean till evening.* Ablutions with water for ritual purification were also practiced outside Israel. In a Sumerian inscription, Gudea prepares to offer a sacrifice by bathing before dressing. While the concept of evening-ending impurity appears to be unique to Israel, a Ugaritic text views sunset as a boundary for another ritual category: "At the descent of the sun, the day is profane. At the setting of the sun, the king is profane."

unclean by any creature that moves along
the ground. 45I am the LORD, who brought
you up out of Egypt[g] to be your God;[h]
therefore be holy, because I am holy.[i]
46" 'These are the regulations concerning animals, birds, every living thing that
moves about in the water and every creature that moves along the ground. 47You
must distinguish between the unclean and
the clean, between living creatures that
may be eaten and those that may not be
eaten.[j] ' "

Purification After Childbirth

12 The LORD said to Moses, 2"Say to the
Israelites: 'A woman who becomes
pregnant and gives birth to a son will be
ceremonially unclean for seven days, just
as she is unclean during her monthly period.[k] 3On the eighth day the boy is to be
circumcised.[l] 4Then the woman must wait
thirty-three days to be purified from her
bleeding. She must not touch anything sacred or go to the sanctuary until the days
of her purification are over. 5If she gives
birth to a daughter, for two weeks the
woman will be unclean, as during her period. Then she must wait sixty-six days to
be purified from her bleeding.
6" 'When the days of her purification for
a son or daughter are over,[m] she is to bring
to the priest at the entrance to the tent of
meeting a year-old lamb[n] for a burnt offering and a young pigeon or a dove for a
sin offering.[a][o] 7He shall offer them before
the LORD to make atonement for her, and
then she will be ceremonially clean from
her flow of blood.
" 'These are the regulations for the woman who gives birth to a boy or a girl. 8But
if she cannot afford a lamb, she is to bring
two doves or two young pigeons,[p] one for
a burnt offering and the other for a sin offering.[q] In this way the priest will make
atonement for her, and she will be clean.[r] ' "

11:45 [g] Lev 25:38, 55; Ex 6:7; 20:2 [h] Ge 17:7 [i] Ex 19:6; 1Pe 1:16* **11:47** [j] Lev 10:10 **12:2** [k] Lev 15:19; 18:19 **12:3** [l] Ge 17:12; Lk 1:59; 2:21 **12:6** [m] Lk 2:22 [n] Ex 29:38; Lev 23:12; Nu 6:12, 14; 7:15 [o] Lev 5:7 **12:8** [p] Ge 15:9; Lev 14:22 [q] Lev 5:7; Lk 2:22-24* [r] Lev 4:26 **13:2** [s] ver 10, 19, 28, 43 [t] ver 4, 38, 39; Lev 14:56 [u] ver 3, 9, 15; Ex 4:6; Lev 14:3, 32; Nu 5:2; Dt 24:8 [v] Dt 24:8 **13:3** [w] ver 8, 11, 20, 30; Lev 21:1; Nu 9:6 **13:4** [x] ver 2 [y] ver 5, 21, 26, 33, 46; Lev 14:38; Nu 12:14, 15; Dt 24:9 **13:5** [z] Lev 14:9 [a] ver 27, 32, 34, 51 **13:6** [b] ver 13, 17, 23, 28, 34; Mt 8:3; Lk 5:12-14 [c] Lev 11:25 [d] Lev 11:25; 14:8, 9, 20, 48; 15:8; Nu 8:7 **13:7** [e] Lk 5:14

Regulations About Defiling Skin Diseases

13 The LORD said to Moses and Aaron,
2"When anyone has a swelling[s] or a
rash or a shiny spot[t] on their skin that may
be a defiling skin disease,[b][u] they must be
brought to Aaron the priest[v] or to one of
his sons[c] who is a priest. 3The priest is to
examine the sore on the skin, and if the
hair in the sore has turned white and the
sore appears to be more than skin deep, it
is a defiling skin disease. When the priest
examines that person, he shall pronounce
them ceremonially unclean.[w] 4If the shiny
spot[x] on the skin is white but does not
appear to be more than skin deep and the
hair in it has not turned white, the priest
is to isolate the affected person for seven
days.[y] 5On the seventh day[z] the priest is
to examine them,[a] and if he sees that the
sore is unchanged and has not spread in
the skin, he is to isolate them for another
seven days. 6On the seventh day the priest
is to examine them again, and if the sore
has faded and has not spread in the skin,
the priest shall pronounce them clean;[b]
it is only a rash. They must wash their
clothes,[c] and they will be clean.[d] 7But if
the rash does spread in their skin after
they have shown themselves to the priest
to be pronounced clean, they must appear
before the priest again.[e] 8The priest is to
examine that person, and if the rash has
spread in the skin, he shall pronounce
them unclean; it is a defiling skin disease.

[a] *6* Or *purification offering*; also in verse 8 [b] *2* The Hebrew word for *defiling skin disease*, traditionally translated "leprosy," was used for various diseases affecting the skin; here and throughout verses 3-46. [c] *2* Or *descendants*

12:2 *ceremonially unclean for seven days.* Throughout history, many cultures all over the world have treated genital discharges, including those involved in menstruation and childbirth, as causing ritual impurity (see notes on ch. 15). A Hittite birth ritual text requires a sacrifice on the seventh day after birth and says that a male infant is pure by the age of three months, but a female is pure at four months. As in ch. 12, there is a weeklong initial period of impurity, and purification of a girl takes longer (cf. vv. 4–5). One possible reason why a daughter requires a longer time for purification is that a daughter often has a slight vaginal discharge at birth, making both mother and daughter unclean. We can observe that whereas the Hittite process has to do with the baby's impurity, Leviticus is concerned with that of the mother. Also, the Hittite sacrifice is offered at the end of the first week, but Israelite sacrifices come after the entire period of purification.

12:7 *atonement.* See note on 1:4. This case makes it clear that the "sin offering" is more accurately a purification ritual, since no sin is involved here.

13:2 *a defiling skin disease.* A more descriptive rendering is "a scaly skin condition." Here the issue regarding a scaly (with lesions) skin disease is not infection/contagion in the sense that it would make other people physically sick. Rather, the concern is with protection of the sphere of holiness, centered at the sanctuary, from defilement by ritual impurity.

The maladies lumped in chs. 13–14 under the heading of scale disease cannot be simply equated with modern "leprosy" (i.e., Hansen's disease). The Hebrew term applies to a complex of conditions, including some that resemble psoriasis and vitiligo, just as Hippocrates used Greek *lepra* for several skin diseases (see note on Ex 4:6). In Leviticus, scale disease is not restricted to just human beings, but could also affect a house (see note on Lev 14:34). In some instances, white discoloration of skin or hair could be a factor among others that was symptomatic of the impure affliction. For a similar dim view of white discolorations, compare Mesopotamian omens. Hansen's disease was little known in the ancient Near East prior to the time of Alexander, though there is one Assyrian medical text that describes symptoms that may well be Hansen's disease.

9“When anyone has a defiling skin disease, they must be brought to the priest.
10The priest is to examine them, and if
there is a white swelling in the skin that
has turned the hair white and if there is
raw flesh in the swelling, 11it is a chronic skin disease[f] and the priest shall pronounce them unclean. He is not to isolate
them, because they are already unclean.
12“If the disease breaks out all over their
skin and, so far as the priest can see, it
covers all the skin of the affected person
from head to foot, 13the priest is to examine them, and if the disease has covered
their whole body, he shall pronounce them
clean. Since it has all turned white, they are
clean. 14But whenever raw flesh appears
on them, they will be unclean. 15When
the priest sees the raw flesh, he shall pronounce them unclean. The raw flesh is unclean; they have a defiling disease.[g] 16If the
raw flesh changes and turns white, they
must go to the priest. 17The priest is to examine them, and if the sores have turned
white, the priest shall pronounce the affected person clean;[h] then they will be clean.
18“When someone has a boil[i] on their
skin and it heals, 19and in the place where
the boil was, a white swelling or reddish-white[j] spot[k] appears, they must present themselves to the priest. 20The priest
is to examine it, and if it appears to be
more than skin deep and the hair in it has
turned white, the priest shall pronounce
that person unclean. It is a defiling skin
disease[l] that has broken out where the boil
was. 21But if, when the priest examines it,
there is no white hair in it and it is not
more than skin deep and has faded, then
the priest is to isolate them for seven days.
22If it is spreading in the skin, the priest
shall pronounce them unclean; it is a defiling disease. 23But if the spot is unchanged
and has not spread, it is only a scar from
the boil, and the priest shall pronounce
them clean.[m]
24“When someone has a burn on their
skin and a reddish-white or white spot appears in the raw flesh of the burn, 25the
priest is to examine the spot, and if the
hair in it has turned white, and it appears
to be more than skin deep, it is a defiling
disease that has broken out in the burn.
The priest shall pronounce them unclean;
it is a defiling skin disease.[n] 26But if the
priest examines it and there is no white
hair in the spot and if it is not more than
skin deep and has faded, then the priest is
to isolate them for seven days.[o] 27On the
seventh day the priest is to examine that
person,[p] and if it is spreading in the skin,
the priest shall pronounce them unclean;
it is a defiling skin disease. 28If, however,
the spot is unchanged and has not spread
in the skin but has faded, it is a swelling
from the burn, and the priest shall pronounce them clean; it is only a scar from
the burn.[q]
29“If a man or woman has a sore on
their head[r] or chin, 30the priest is to examine the sore, and if it appears to be more
than skin deep and the hair in it is yellow
and thin, the priest shall pronounce them
unclean; it is a defiling skin disease on the
head or chin. 31But if, when the priest examines the sore, it does not seem to be
more than skin deep and there is no black
hair in it, then the priest is to isolate the
affected person for seven days.[s] 32On the
seventh day the priest is to examine the
sore,[t] and if it has not spread and there is
no yellow hair in it and it does not appear
to be more than skin deep, 33then the man
or woman must shave themselves, except
for the affected area, and the priest is to
keep them isolated another seven days.
34On the seventh day the priest is to examine the sore,[u] and if it has not spread
in the skin and appears to be no more
than skin deep, the priest shall pronounce
them clean. They must wash their clothes,
and they will be clean.[v] 35But if the sore
does spread in the skin after they are pronounced clean, 36the priest is to examine
them, and if he finds that the sore has
spread in the skin, he does not need to
look for yellow hair; they are unclean.[w]
37If, however, the sore is unchanged so far
as the priest can see, and if black hair has
grown in it, the affected person is healed.
They are clean, and the priest shall pronounce them clean.
38“When a man or woman has white
spots on the skin, 39the priest is to examine them, and if the spots are dull white, it
is a harmless rash that has broken out on
the skin; they are clean.
40“A man who has lost his hair and is
bald[x] is clean. 41If he has lost his hair from
the front of his scalp and has a bald forehead, he is clean. 42But if he has a reddish-white sore on his bald head or forehead, it is a defiling disease breaking out
on his head or forehead. 43The priest is to
examine him, and if the swollen sore on
his head or forehead is reddish-white like
a defiling skin disease, 44the man is diseased and is unclean. The priest shall pronounce him unclean because of the sore
on his head.
45“Anyone with such a defiling disease
must wear torn clothes,[y] let their hair be
unkempt,[a] cover the lower part of their
face[z] and cry out, ‘Unclean! Unclean!’[a]

[a] 45 Or *clothes, uncover their head*

13:11 [f] Ex 4:6; Lev 14:8; Nu 12:10; Mt 8:2
13:15 [g] ver 2
13:17 [h] ver 6
13:18 [i] Ex 9:9
13:19 [j] ver 24, 42; Lev 14:37 [k] ver 2
13:20 [l] ver 2
13:23 [m] ver 6
13:25 [n] ver 11
13:26 [o] ver 4
13:27 [p] ver 5
13:28 [q] ver 2
13:29 [r] ver 43, 44
13:31 [s] ver 4
13:32 [t] ver 5
13:34 [u] ver 5 [v] Lev 11:25
13:36 [w] ver 30
13:40 [x] Lev 21:5; 2Ki 2:23; Isa 3:24; 15:2; 22:12; Eze 27:31; 29:18; Am 8:10; Mic 1:16
13:45 [y] Lev 10:6 [z] Eze 24:17, 22; Mic 3:7 [a] Lev 5:2; La 4:15; Lk 17:12

46 As long as they have the disease they remain unclean. They must live alone; they must live outside the camp.[b]

Regulations About Defiling Molds

47 "As for any fabric that is spoiled with a defiling mold—any woolen or linen clothing, 48 any woven or knitted material of linen or wool, any leather or anything made of leather— 49 if the affected area in the fabric, the leather, the woven or knitted material, or any leather article, is greenish or reddish, it is a defiling mold and must be shown to the priest.[c] 50 The priest is to examine the affected area[d] and isolate the article for seven days. 51 On the seventh day he is to examine it,[e] and if the mold has spread in the fabric, the woven or knitted material, or the leather, whatever its use, it is a persistent defiling mold; the article is unclean.[f] 52 He must burn the fabric, the woven or knitted material of wool or linen, or any leather article that has been spoiled; because the defiling mold is persistent, the article must be burned.[g]

53 "But if, when the priest examines it, the mold has not spread in the fabric, the woven or knitted material, or the leather article, 54 he shall order that the spoiled article be washed. Then he is to isolate it for another seven days. 55 After the article has been washed, the priest is to examine it again, and if the mold has not changed its appearance, even though it has not spread, it is unclean. Burn it, no matter which side of the fabric has been spoiled. 56 If, when the priest examines it, the mold has faded after the article has been washed, he is to tear the spoiled part out of the fabric, the leather, or the woven or knitted material. 57 But if it reappears in the fabric, in the woven or knitted material, or in the leather article, it is a spreading mold; whatever has the mold must be burned. 58 Any fabric, woven or knitted material, or any leather article that has been washed and is rid of the mold, must be washed again. Then it will be clean."

59 These are the regulations concerning defiling molds in woolen or linen clothing, woven or knitted material, or any leather article, for pronouncing them clean or unclean.

Cleansing From Defiling Skin Diseases

14 The LORD said to Moses, 2 "These are the regulations for any diseased person at the time of their ceremonial cleansing, when they are brought to the priest:[h] 3 The priest is to go outside the camp and examine them.[i] If they have been healed of their defiling skin disease,[a] 4 the priest shall order that two live clean birds and some cedar wood, scarlet yarn and hyssop be brought for the person to be cleansed.[j] 5 Then the priest shall order that one of the birds be killed over fresh water in a clay pot. 6 He is then to take the live bird and dip it, together with the cedar wood, the scarlet yarn and the hyssop, into the blood of the bird that was killed over the fresh water.[k] 7 Seven times he shall sprinkle[l] the one to be cleansed of the defiling disease, and then pronounce them clean. After that, he is to release the live bird in the open fields.

8 "The person to be cleansed must wash their clothes,[m] shave off all their hair and bathe with water;[n] then they will be ceremonially clean.[o] After this they may come into the camp,[p] but they must stay outside their tent for seven days. 9 On the seventh day they must shave off all their hair; they must shave their head, their beard, their eyebrows and the rest of their hair. They must wash their clothes and bathe themselves with water, and they will be clean.

13:46 [b] Nu 5:1-4; 12:14; 2Ki 7:3; 15:5; Lk 17:12 **13:49** [c] Mk 1:44 **13:50** [d] Eze 44:23 **13:51** [e] ver 5 [f] Lev 14:44 **13:52** [g] ver 55, 57

14:2 [h] Mt 8:2-4; Mk 1:40-44; Lk 5:12-14; 17:14 **14:3** [i] Lev 13:46 **14:4** [j] ver 6, 49, 51, 52; Nu 19:6; Ps 51:7 **14:6** [k] ver 4 **14:7** [l] 2Ki 5:10, 14; Isa 52:15; Eze 36:25 **14:8** [m] Lev 11:25; 13:6 [n] ver 9 [o] ver 20 [p] Nu 5:2, 3; 12:14, 15; 2Ch 26:21

[a] 3 The Hebrew word for *defiling skin disease,* traditionally translated "leprosy," was used for various diseases affecting the skin; also in verses 7, 32, 54 and 57.

13:46 *they must live outside the camp.* Some Mesopotamian curses also speak of ostracizing persons afflicted with scale disease (see previous note). Compare the Babylonian rule in which cultic functionaries who became ritually impure by purging the Ezida cella of the god Nabu on the fifth day of the Babylonian New Year Festival of Spring were required to remain outside the city of Babylon for the duration of the festival.

14:4 *two live clean birds.* This elimination ritual symbolically transfers ritual impurity from the recovered person to the living bird by means of the blood of the (other) slain bird, in which (along with water) the living bird is dipped. Then the living bird is set free and carries the impurity away. Birds were also used in Anatolian and Mesopotamian elimination rituals. A Hittite ritual to remove evil mandates the dispatch of a goat (cf. 16:21–22) and the release of an eagle and a hawk.

In a Mesopotamian *namburbi* ritual to get rid of evil portended by a bird (in an omen), a male and female partridge are obtained. The patient raises them with his hands and recites an incantation before the sun-god Shamash that includes a request that the evil be distanced from the patient. Upon completion of the rite, the male bird is released to the east, before the sun-god. Unlike the Biblical ritual, the freed bird does not receive a transfer of impurity, but by its physical form represents the evil (cf. Nu 21:6–9).

14:5 *fresh water.* Hittites and Babylonians also regarded fresh flowing water, such as rivers, as superior sources for purification. On the fourth day of the Ninth Year Festival of Telipinu, Hittites would take images of Telipinu and other gods, plus a cult pedestal, to a river and wash them. During the Babylonian New Year Festival, the high priest is to bathe in water from the Tigris and Euphrates Rivers (see note on 16:4).

[10]“On the eighth day[q] they must bring
two male lambs and one ewe lamb a
year old, each without defect, along with
three-tenths of an ephah[a] of the finest
flour mixed with olive oil for a grain offering,[r] and one log[b] of oil.[s] [11]The priest who
pronounces them clean shall present both
the one to be cleansed and their offerings
before the LORD at the entrance to the tent
of meeting.
[12]“Then the priest is to take one of the
male lambs and offer it as a guilt offering,[t]
along with the log of oil; he shall wave
them before the LORD as a wave offering.[u]
[13]He is to slaughter the lamb in the sanctuary area[v] where the sin offering[c] and the
burnt offering are slaughtered. Like the sin
offering, the guilt offering belongs to the
priest;[w] it is most holy. [14]The priest is to
take some of the blood of the guilt offering
and put it on the lobe of the right ear of
the one to be cleansed, on the thumb of

14:10 [q]Mt 8:4; Mk 1:44; Lk 5:14 [r]Lev 2:1 [s]ver 12, 15, 21, 24
14:12 [t]Lev 5:18; 6:6-7 [u]Ex 29:24
14:13 [v]Ex 29:11 [w]Lev 6:24-30; 7:7

[a] *10* That is, probably about 11 pounds or about 5 kilograms [b] *10* That is, about 1/3 quart or about 0.3 liter; also in verses 12, 15, 21 and 24 [c] *13* Or *purification offering;* also in verses 19, 22 and 31

LEVITICUS 14:8

ZONES OF PURITY IN THE CAMP OF ISRAEL

The full sanctuary of ancient Israel consisted of concentric zones based on degrees of purity (sometimes referred to as the “sacred compass”): (1) The inner zone was the ark of Yahweh in the Most Holy Place, (2) extending outward to the priestly court within the curtains of the Holy Place, (3) then to the realm of the priests and three clans of Levites, (4) moving to the four triads of the tribes of Israel, and then (5) outside the camp of the holy where unclean persons were designated during their term of impurity. In the ancient world the temple complex was likewise a sacred zone, presumably possessing increasing sanctity as one moved toward the center. Each zone had its own rules of purity and accessibility (zone 1, 2: most holy place/antechamber, chs. 1 – 17; zone 3: courtyard, chs. 8 – 10; zone 4: camp, chs. 11 – 15). ◆

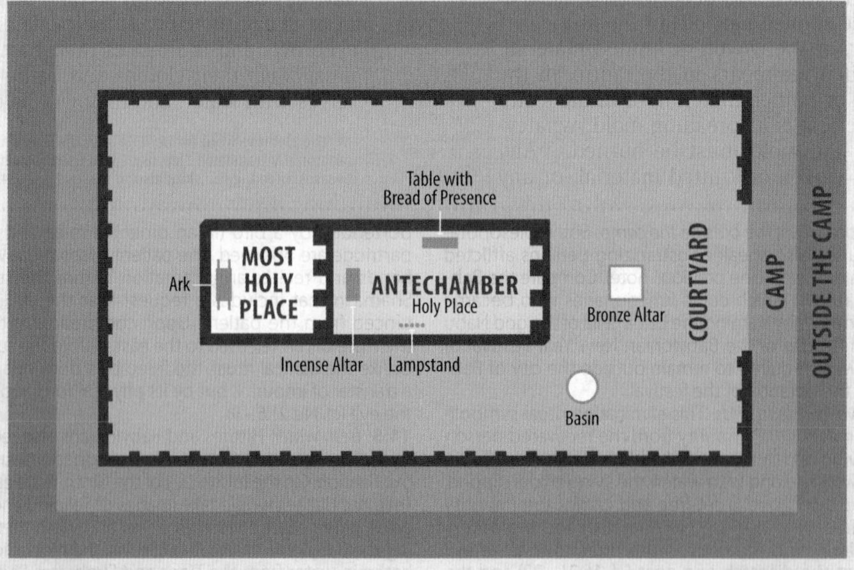

their right hand and on the big toe of their
right foot.[x] 15 The priest shall then take
some of the log of oil, pour it in the palm
of his own left hand, 16 dip his right fore-
finger into the oil in his palm, and with his
finger sprinkle some of it before the LORD
seven times. 17 The priest is to put some of
the oil remaining in his palm on the lobe
of the right ear of the one to be cleansed,
on the thumb of their right hand and on
the big toe of their right foot, on top of the
blood of the guilt offering. 18 The rest of the
oil in his palm the priest shall put on the
head of the one to be cleansed and make
atonement for them before the LORD.
19 "Then the priest is to sacrifice the sin
offering and make atonement for the one
to be cleansed from their uncleanness. After that, the priest shall slaughter the burnt
offering 20 and offer it on the altar, together
with the grain offering, and make atonement for them, and they will be clean.[y]
21 "If, however, they are poor[z] and cannot afford these,[a] they must take one male
lamb as a guilt offering to be waved to
make atonement for them, together with
a tenth of an ephah[a] of the finest flour
mixed with olive oil for a grain offering,
a log of oil, 22 and two doves or two young
pigeons,[b] such as they can afford, one for
a sin offering and the other for a burnt
offering.
23 "On the eighth day they must bring
them for their cleansing to the priest at the
entrance to the tent of meeting, before the
LORD.[c] 24 The priest is to take the lamb for
the guilt offering,[d] together with the log
of oil,[e] and wave them before the LORD as
a wave offering.[f] 25 He shall slaughter the
lamb for the guilt offering and take some
of its blood and put it on the lobe of the
right ear of the one to be cleansed, on the
thumb of their right hand and on the big
toe of their right foot.[g] 26 The priest is to
pour some of the oil into the palm of his
own left hand,[h] 27 and with his right fore-
finger sprinkle some of the oil from his
palm seven times before the LORD. 28 Some
of the oil in his palm he is to put on the
same places he put the blood of the guilt
offering—on the lobe of the right ear of
the one to be cleansed, on the thumb of
their right hand and on the big toe of their
right foot. 29 The rest of the oil in his palm
the priest shall put on the head of the one
to be cleansed, to make atonement for
them before the LORD.[i] 30 Then he shall
sacrifice the doves or the young pigeons,
such as the person can afford,[j] 31 one as a
sin offering and the other as a burnt offering,[k] together with the grain offering. In
this way the priest will make atonement
before the LORD on behalf of the one to be
cleansed.[l]"
32 These are the regulations for anyone
who has a defiling skin disease[m] and who
cannot afford the regular offerings[n] for
their cleansing.

Cleansing From Defiling Molds

33 The LORD said to Moses and Aaron,
34 "When you enter the land of Canaan,[o]
which I am giving you as your possession,[p] and I put a spreading mold in a
house in that land, 35 the owner of the
house must go and tell the priest, 'I have
seen something that looks like a defiling
mold in my house.' 36 The priest is to order
the house to be emptied before he goes
in to examine the mold, so that nothing
in the house will be pronounced unclean.
After this the priest is to go in and inspect
the house. 37 He is to examine the mold on
the walls, and if it has greenish or reddish[q] depressions that appear to be deeper
than the surface of the wall, 38 the priest
shall go out the doorway of the house and
close it up for seven days.[r] 39 On the seventh day[s] the priest shall return to inspect
the house. If the mold has spread on the
walls, 40 he is to order that the contaminated stones be torn out and thrown into
an unclean place outside the town.[t] 41 He
must have all the inside walls of the house

14:14 [x] Ex 29:20; Lev 8:23
14:20 [y] ver 8
14:21 [z] Lev 5:7; 12:8 [a] ver 22, 32
14:22 [b] Lev 5:7
14:23 [c] ver 10, 11
14:24 [d] Nu 6:14 [e] ver 10 [f] ver 12
14:25 [g] ver 14; Ex 29:20
14:26 [h] ver 15
14:29 [i] ver 18
14:30 [j] Lev 5:7
14:31 [k] ver 22; Lev 5:7; 15:15, 30 [l] ver 18, 19
14:32 [m] Lev 13:2 [n] ver 21
14:34 [o] Ge 12:5; Ex 6:4; Nu 13:2 [p] Ge 17:8; 48:4; Nu 27:12; 32:22; Dt 3:27; 7:1; 32:49
14:37 [q] Lev 13:19
14:38 [r] Lev 13:4
14:39 [s] Lev 13:5
14:40 [t] ver 45

[a] *21* That is, probably about 3 1/2 pounds or about 1.6 kilograms

14:34 *a spreading mold in a house.* In Mesopotamia, fungus in the walls of a house could be a good or bad omen. Black fungus portended brisk trade and wealth at that address, but green and red fungi (cf. v. 37) were ominous: "The master of the house will die, dispersal of the man's house." By contrast, while fungus in an Israelite house could generate the need to replace some of its material and ritually purify it—or (in a worst case scenario) could lead to its condemnation and demolition—the problem was limited to the structure of the house (as opposed to something in it) and did not indicate other kinds of dangers for future inhabitants.

In contrast, an Anatolian ritual invokes underworld deities to come up, take evils (impurity, perjury, bloodshed, curse, threat, tears, sin, quarrel and/or gossip) haunting a house and transport them back down into the nether regions. At the end of the process, safe disposal of the ritual paraphernalia takes place out in the steppe country. In terms of the nature of evils remedied, deities involved and procedures implemented, the Anatolian ritual differs greatly from Israelite purification of a fungous house. However, there are some strikingly specific points of contact: use of water ("water of cleansing"—cf. Nu 8:7; 19:9; spring water—cf. Lev 14:51), the number seven (drawing water and pouring it out; cf. seven days in vv. 38–39), red wool (cf. v. 49), contact of a slain animal with water (but libating a lamb before slaughtering it, unlike v. 50), and slaughter of birds (but cooked for sacrifice, unlike vv. 50–52).

scraped and the material that is scraped off dumped into an unclean place outside the town. 42 Then they are to take other stones to replace these and take new clay and plaster the house.

43 "If the defiling mold reappears in the house after the stones have been torn out and the house scraped and plastered, 44 the priest is to go and examine it and, if the mold has spread in the house, it is a persistent defiling mold; the house is unclean.[u] 45 It must be torn down—its stones, timbers and all the plaster—and taken out of the town to an unclean place.

46 "Anyone who goes into the house while it is closed up will be unclean till evening.[v] 47 Anyone who sleeps or eats in the house must wash their clothes.[w]

48 "But if the priest comes to examine it and the mold has not spread after the house has been plastered, he shall pronounce the house clean,[x] because the defiling mold is gone. 49 To purify the house he is to take two birds and some cedar wood, scarlet yarn and hyssop.[y] 50 He shall kill one of the birds over fresh water in a clay pot.[z] 51 Then he is to take the cedar wood, the hyssop,[a] the scarlet yarn and the live bird, dip them into the blood of the dead bird and the fresh water, and sprinkle the house seven times.[b] 52 He shall purify the house with the bird's blood, the fresh water, the live bird, the cedar wood, the hyssop and the scarlet yarn. 53 Then he is to release the live bird in the open fields[c] outside the town. In this way he will make atonement for the house, and it will be clean.[d]"

54 These are the regulations for any defiling skin disease,[e] for a sore, 55 for defiling molds[f] in fabric or in a house, 56 and for a swelling, a rash or a shiny spot,[g] 57 to determine when something is clean or unclean.

These are the regulations for defiling skin diseases and defiling molds.[h]

Discharges Causing Uncleanness

15 The LORD said to Moses and Aaron, 2 "Speak to the Israelites and say to them: 'When any man has an unusual bodily discharge,[i] such a discharge is unclean. 3 Whether it continues flowing from his body or is blocked, it will make him unclean. This is how his discharge will bring about uncleanness:

4 " 'Any bed the man with a discharge lies on will be unclean, and anything he sits on will be unclean. 5 Anyone who touches his bed must wash their clothes[j] and bathe with water,[k] and they will be unclean till evening.[l] 6 Whoever sits on anything that the man with a discharge sat on must wash their clothes and bathe with water, and they will be unclean till evening.

7 " 'Whoever touches the man[m] who has a discharge[n] must wash their clothes and bathe with water, and they will be unclean till evening.

8 " 'If the man with the discharge spits[o] on anyone who is clean, they must wash their clothes and bathe with water, and they will be unclean till evening.

9 " 'Everything the man sits on when riding will be unclean, 10 and whoever touches any of the things that were under him will be unclean till evening; whoever picks up those things[p] must wash their clothes and bathe with water, and they will be unclean till evening.

11 " 'Anyone the man with a discharge touches without rinsing his hands with water must wash their clothes and bathe with water, and they will be unclean till evening.

12 " 'A clay pot[q] that the man touches must be broken, and any wooden article[r] is to be rinsed with water.

13 " 'When a man is cleansed from his discharge, he is to count off seven days[s] for his ceremonial cleansing; he must wash his clothes and bathe himself with fresh water, and he will be clean.[t] 14 On the eighth day he must take two doves or two young pigeons[u] and come before the LORD to the entrance to the tent of meeting and give them to the priest. 15 The priest is to sacrifice them, the one for a sin offering[a][v] and the other for a burnt offering.[w] In this way he will make atonement before the LORD for the man because of his discharge.[x]

16 " 'When a man has an emission of semen,[y] he must bathe his whole body with

14:44 [u] Lev 13:51
14:46 [v] Lev 11:24
14:47 [w] Lev 11:25
14:48 [x] Lev 13:6
14:49 [y] ver 4; 1Ki 4:33; ver 4
14:50 [z] ver 5
14:51 [a] ver 6; Ps 51:7 [b] ver 4, 7
14:53 [c] ver 7 [d] ver 20
14:54 [e] Lev 13:2, 30
14:55 [f] Lev 13:47-52
14:56 [g] Lev 13:2
14:57 [h] Lev 10:10
15:2 [i] ver 16, 32; Lev 22:4; Nu 5:2; 2Sa 3:29; Mt 9:20
15:5 [j] Lev 11:25 [k] Lev 14:8 [l] Lev 11:24
15:7 [m] ver 19; Lev 22:5 [n] ver 16; Lev 22:4
15:8 [o] Nu 12:14
15:10 [p] Nu 19:10
15:12 [q] Lev 6:28 [r] Lev 11:32
15:13 [s] Lev 8:33 [t] ver 5
15:14 [u] Lev 14:22
15:15 [v] Lev 5:7 [w] Lev 14:31 [x] Lev 14:18, 19
15:16 [y] ver 2; Lev 22:4; Dt 23:10

[a] *15* Or *purification offering;* also in verse 30

15:2 *an unusual bodily discharge.* The male impurity stems from an abnormal urethral discharge that could consist of pus or excessive mucus and which could be caused by gonorrhea or infectious urinary bilharzia, an ailment known to have been a problem in antiquity. The abnormal female condition in vv. 25–30 has to do with a chronic vaginal discharge of blood, which arises from a disorder of the uterus.

15:10 *whoever touches any of the things that were under him will be unclean.* A discharge from the genitals directly contaminated objects underneath, such as a bed or chair, which would secondarily contaminate anyone else who touched them. A Mesopotamian incantation also speaks of secondary contamination by sleeping on the bed, sitting in the chair, eating at the table, or drinking from the cup of an accursed person.

15:16 *emission of semen.* A Mesopotamian omen says: "If a man ejaculates in his dream and is spattered with his

DISEASE TRANSMISSION IN THE ANCIENT WORLD

Though no knowledge of germs existed in the ancient world, medical documents show that ancient peoples had some basic knowledge of contagion and therefore sometimes practiced quarantine. Nevertheless, they did not understand the sources of disease. God did not give the Israelites any advanced information in that regard. The rest of the ancient world believed that some diseases were demon induced, and it is possible that Israel shared that viewpoint, though the Bible does nothing to encourage it, nor does it show evidence of such a belief. Treatment of disease in the ancient Near East included exorcistic rites, herbal remedies, magical remedies or some combination of those. ◆

water, and he will be unclean till evening.[z]
17 Any clothing or leather that has semen
on it must be washed with water, and it
will be unclean till evening. 18 When a
man has sexual relations with a woman
and there is an emission of semen,[a] both
of them must bathe with water, and they
will be unclean till evening.
19 " 'When a woman has her regular flow
of blood, the impurity of her monthly period[b] will last seven days, and anyone who
touches her will be unclean till evening.
20 " 'Anything she lies on during her period will be unclean, and anything she sits
on will be unclean. 21 Anyone who touches
her bed will be unclean; they must wash
their clothes and bathe with water, and
they will be unclean till evening.[c] 22 Anyone who touches anything she sits on will
be unclean; they must wash their clothes
and bathe with water, and they will be unclean till evening. 23 Whether it is the bed
or anything she was sitting on, when anyone touches it, they will be unclean till
evening.
24 " 'If a man has sexual relations with
her and her monthly flow[d] touches him,
he will be unclean for seven days; any bed
he lies on will be unclean.
25 " 'When a woman has a discharge of
blood for many days at a time other than
her monthly period[e] or has a discharge
that continues beyond her period, she
will be unclean as long as she has the discharge, just as in the days of her period.
26 Any bed she lies on while her discharge
continues will be unclean, as is her bed
during her monthly period, and anything
she sits on will be unclean, as during her
period. 27 Anyone who touches them will
be unclean; they must wash their clothes
and bathe with water, and they will be unclean till evening.
28 " 'When she is cleansed from her discharge, she must count off seven days,
and after that she will be ceremonially
clean. 29 On the eighth day she must take
two doves or two young pigeons[f] and
bring them to the priest at the entrance to
the tent of meeting. 30 The priest is to sacrifice one for a sin offering and the other for
a burnt offering. In this way he will make
atonement for her before the LORD for the
uncleanness of her discharge.[g]

15:16 [z] ver 5; Dt 23:11 **15:18** [a] 1Sa 21:4 **15:19** [b] ver 24; Lev 12:2 **15:21** [c] ver 27 **15:24** [d] ver 19; Lev 12:2; 18:19; 20:18; Eze 18:6 **15:25** [e] Mt 9:20; Mk 5:25; Lk 8:43 **15:29** [f] Lev 14:22 **15:30** [g] Lev 5:10; 14:20,31; 18:19; 2Sa 11:4; Mk 5:25; Lk 8:43

semen—that man will find riches; he will have financial gain." But in the Israelite religious system, any seminal discharge, including nocturnal emission (Dt 23:11), generated ritual impurity. Nevertheless, this impurity simply disqualified a person from coming in contact with holy things. There was no acknowledgment of the belief held by some ancient people (such as Hittites) that nocturnal emissions indicated sexual relations with spirits, even with deceased family members.

An Israelite who engaged in sexual relations was barred from entering the sacred precincts of the sanctuary until evening. The situation was similar for Egyptians, but differed in other religious cultures, where ritualized sex flourished. The Hittite "Instructions to Priests and Temple Officials" prohibit cultic functionaries from defiling sancta (on pain of death for a kind of intentional violation; cf. Lev 22:9) by approaching sacrificial loaves and libation vessels without bathing after sexual intercourse, but that is all. There is no waiting period and no prohibition of sexual activity elsewhere in the temple precincts.

31"'You must keep the Israelites separate from things that make them unclean,
so they will not die in their uncleanness
for defiling my dwelling place,[a][h] which is
among them.'"

32These are the regulations for a man
with a discharge, for anyone made unclean by an emission of semen,[i] 33for a
woman in her monthly period, for a man
or a woman with a discharge, and for a
man who has sexual relations with a
woman who is ceremonially unclean.[j]

The Day of Atonement

16:2-34pp — Lev 23:26-32; Nu 29:7-11

16 The LORD spoke to Moses after the
death of the two sons of Aaron who
died when they approached the LORD.[k]
2The LORD said to Moses: "Tell your brother Aaron that he is not to come whenever
he chooses[l] into the Most Holy Place[m] behind the curtain in front of the atonement
cover on the ark, or else he will die. For I
will appear[n] in the cloud[o] over the atonement cover.

3"This is how Aaron is to enter the Most
Holy Place:[p] He must first bring a young
bull for a sin offering[b] and a ram for a
burnt offering. 4He is to put on the sacred
linen tunic, with linen undergarments
next to his body; he is to tie the linen sash
around him and put on the linen turban.[q]
These are sacred garments;[r] so he must
bathe himself with water[s] before he puts
them on. 5From the Israelite community[t]
he is to take two male goats[u] for a sin offering and a ram for a burnt offering.

6"Aaron is to offer the bull for his own
sin offering to make atonement for himself and his household.[v] 7Then he is to
take the two goats and present them before the LORD at the entrance to the tent
of meeting. 8He is to cast lots for the two
goats — one lot for the LORD and the other
for the scapegoat.[c] 9Aaron shall bring the
goat whose lot falls to the LORD and sacrifice it for a sin offering. 10But the goat
chosen by lot as the scapegoat shall be
presented alive before the LORD to be used
for making atonement[w] by sending it into
the wilderness as a scapegoat.

11"Aaron shall bring the bull for his own
sin offering to make atonement for himself
and his household,[x] and he is to slaughter

15:31 [h] Lev 20:3; Nu 5:3; 19:13, 20; 2Sa 15:25; 2Ki 21:7; Ps 33:14; 74:7; 76:2; Eze 5:11; 23:38
15:32 [i] ver 2
15:33 [j] ver 19, 24, 25
16:1 [k] Lev 10:1
16:2 [l] Ex 30:10; Heb 9:7 [m] Heb 9:25; 10:19 [n] Ex 25:22 [o] Ex 40:34
16:3 [p] Heb 9:24, 25
16:4 [q] Ex 28:39 [r] Ex 28:42 [s] ver 24; Heb 10:22
16:5 [t] Lev 4:13-21 [u] 2Ch 29:23
16:6 [v] Lev 9:7; Heb 5:3; 7:27; 9:7, 12
16:10 [w] Isa 53:4-10; Ro 3:25; 1Jn 2:2
16:11 [x] Heb 7:27; 9:7

[a] 31 Or *my tabernacle* [b] 3 Or *purification offering;* here and throughout this chapter [c] 8 The meaning of the Hebrew for this word is uncertain; also in verses 10 and 26.

16:2 *into the Most Holy Place.* By contrast to the Israelite high priest, who was permitted to enter the inner apartment of the sanctuary only once per year, other ancient Near Eastern priests were required to enter the inner sanctums of their temples every day in order to care for and "feed" (images of) their gods. Even such daily access was restricted to authorized persons. Ancient Near Eastern temples were not places of public worship like our churches or synagogues today because they were regarded as possessing or containing sanctity that had to be guarded against profanation or defilement (see note on Nu 18:1). *behind the curtain.* The Israelite sanctuary had three curtains: a screen (Hebrew *masak*) at the entrance to the court, another screen (also called a *masak*) at the entrance to the outer sanctum, and an inner curtain (Hebrew *paroket*; see the article "The Tabernacle," p. 158). In this verse the Hebrew word is *paroket,* which only denotes the curtain that formed the boundary of the inner sanctum by separating the two apartments of the tabernacle. This special usage agrees with the fact that the Akkadian cognate *parakku* refers to a defined sacred space around the presence of a deity (or divine symbol/image). The Israelite sanctuary was not unique in having such a curtain; a Mesopotamian omen refers to "the linen curtain of a temple (in front of the cult statue)." The function of such curtains was to shield the sacred image (or in Israel, the ark) from profane visibility. *atonement cover.* The Hebrew (*kapporet*) is also translated "mercy seat," but all translations are speculative. The term refers to the solid plate or sheet on top of the ark, described in Ex 25:17. One suggestion is that *kapporet* comes from an Egyptian cognate, which refers to a place to rest one's feet. Since the ark is seen as a footstool for God (see 1Ch 28:2), this would fit well.

16:4 *he must bathe himself with water.* Non-Israelites also purified themselves with water before engaging in ritual activity. In a Sumerian inscription, the ruler Gudea prepares to offer a sacrifice to his god Ningirsu by bathing before dressing. In Babylon, during the New Year Festival of Spring (= Akitu Festival), the high priest was to do the following: "On the 5th day of the month *Nisannu,* during the final four hours of the night, the High Priest arises and bathes in the waters of the Tigris and Euphrates rivers." By washing with water from these special sources, which also provided water for later sprinkling the temple to remove ritual impurity, the high priest attained a degree of ritual purity necessary for subsequent officiation, which involved entering the presence of the high god Bel (= Marduk) and his consort (see note on 22:3 – 9).

16:10 *making atonement by sending it into the wilderness as a scapegoat.* Azazel's nonsacrificial "tote" goat (NIV "scapegoat") served as a ritual "garbage truck" to purge the Israelite community of desecration through a process of transfer and disposal of impurity from the sanctuary. Other ancient Near Eastern rituals included transfer and disposal. The Hittite Ambazzi and Huwarlu rituals closely parallel the Israelite ritual in that they used live animals as bearers of the evil and lack the motif of substitution. The "Ritual of Ambazzi" to rid people of "evil sickness" and "evil tension" goes as follows:

- Wraps some tin a on a bowstring
- Puts it against right foot and right hand of participant
- Puts the tin on a mouse
- Incantation to indicate transfer of offense
- Mouse charged to carry offense far away
- God to drive mouse away
- Goat is promised to god as meal
- Offerings then presented

Unlike the Biblical ritual, in this description a deity is entreated (by words and sacrifice) for help in getting rid of the animal bearing the evil.

the bull for his own sin offering. 12He is to
take a censer full of burning coals[y] from
the altar before the LORD and two handfuls
of finely ground fragrant incense[z] and take
them behind the curtain. 13He is to put the
incense on the fire before the LORD, and
the smoke of the incense will conceal the
atonement cover above the tablets of the
covenant law, so that he will not die.[a] 14He
is to take some of the bull's blood[b] and
with his finger sprinkle it on the front of
the atonement cover; then he shall sprinkle some of it with his finger seven times
before the atonement cover.[c]

15"He shall then slaughter the goat for
the sin offering for the people[d] and take
its blood behind the curtain[e] and do with
it as he did with the bull's blood: He shall
sprinkle it on the atonement cover and in
front of it. 16In this way he will make atonement[f] for the Most Holy Place because of
the uncleanness and rebellion of the Israelites, whatever their sins have been. He
is to do the same for the tent of meeting,
which is among them in the midst of their
uncleanness. 17No one is to be in the tent
of meeting from the time Aaron goes in to
make atonement in the Most Holy Place

16:12 [y] Lev 10:1 [z] Ex 30:34-38 **16:13** [a] Ex 28:43; Lev 22:9 **16:14** [b] Lev 4:5; Heb 9:7,13,25 [c] Lev 4:6 **16:15** [d] Heb 9:7,12 [e] Heb 9:3 **16:16** [f] Ex 29:36

16:14 *take some of the bull's blood.* On the Day of Atonement, the high priest purged (Hebrew *kipper*—usually rendered "atone") the three major consecrated components of the sanctuary—the inner sanctum, outer sanctum and outer altar—on behalf of the priests and nonpriests by applying blood of special purification ("sin") offerings (bull and goat), to parts of them (see vv. 14–19,20,33).

Non-Israelite peoples also periodically cleansed their sacred precincts and/or sacred objects contained in them, but they generally used substances other than blood (see note on 1:5). The Sumerian Nanshe Hymn mentions purification of the temple belonging to the goddess Nanshe: "her house Sirara where water is sprinkled." On the fourth day of the Hittite Ninth Year Festival of Telipinu, images of several deities (including the god Telipinu) and a cult pedestal were ceremonially transported on a cart from Telipinu's temple to a river, in which they were washed.

Like purgation of the Israelite sanctuary, purification of the Babylonian temple precincts on the fifth day of the New Year (or Akitu) Festival of Spring was also a three-stage process: purgation of the god Marduk's great Esagila temple complex as a whole by sprinkling water, sounding a copper bell, and carrying around a censer and torch inside the temple; this was followed by two purifications of the Ezida guest cella of the god Nabu. The first purification of the Ezida included not only sprinkling holy water and carrying a censer and torch, but also smearing the doors with cedar oil and wiping (Akkadian *kuppuru*, cognate to Hebrew *kipper*) the cella with the decapitated carcass of a ram. The second purification of the Ezida involved setting up a kind of canopy called "the Golden Heaven" and reciting an incantation calling on the gods to exorcise demons from the temple (see note on v. 10).

Notice that whereas the Israelite sanctuary was cleansed from physical ritual impurities and moral faults caused by the people throughout the year (v. 16), the goal of purging Babylonian holy places was to remove impurity caused by the presence of demons. It was not unusual in the ancient Near East to have elimination rites similar to the Israelite Day of Atonement. Other ancient peoples sometimes used blood and sometimes used an animal to carry away the impurity or offense.

LEVITICUS 16:10

AZAZEL

Though still contested on many fronts, *'az'azel* is likely a spirit being of some sort. The demonic interpretation becomes prominent in Hellenistic Jewish literature (e.g., the book of Enoch). It is designated as having a living area (desert), not as having power, not as bringing plague or illness, not as intimidating, and not the object of incantation. In elimination rituals in the ancient world, the animal used to carry the offense is not a sacrifice to the demon; it is slaughtered so that the offense dies with it. Rites of elimination do not view the killed animal as being sacrificed because no part of it is given to deity—in fact, it could not be a gift to deity because it is tainted with the evil that has been transferred to it. Another option is that Azazel has been stripped of personality and is just a place of disposal, specifically a place of disorder—where all offense belongs. If Azazel is a spirit, it is not one that is viewed as having any responsibility for the sin having been committed, nor for the offense received by means of the goat. ◆

until he comes out, having made atonement for himself, his household and the
whole community of Israel.
18“Then he shall come out to the altar[g]
that is before the LORD and make atonement for it. He shall take some of the
bull’s blood and some of the goat’s blood
and put it on all the horns of the altar.[h]
19He shall sprinkle some of the blood on
it with his finger seven times to cleanse it
and to consecrate it from the uncleanness
of the Israelites.[i]
20“When Aaron has finished making
atonement for the Most Holy Place, the
tent of meeting and the altar, he shall
bring forward the live goat. 21He is to lay
both hands on the head of the live goat
and confess[j] over it all the wickedness and
rebellion of the Israelites — all their sins —
and put them on the goat’s head. He shall
send the goat away into the wilderness
in the care of someone appointed for the
task. 22The goat will carry on itself all their
sins[k] to a remote place; and the man shall
release it in the wilderness.
23“Then Aaron is to go into the tent of
meeting and take off the linen garments
he put on before he entered the Most
Holy Place, and he is to leave them there.[l]
24He shall bathe himself with water in the
sanctuary area and put on his regular garments.[m] Then he shall come out and sacrifice the burnt offering for himself and
the burnt offering for the people, to make
atonement for himself and for the people.
25He shall also burn the fat of the sin offering on the altar.
26“The man who releases the goat as
a scapegoat must wash his clothes[n] and
bathe himself with water; afterward he
may come into the camp. 27The bull and
the goat for the sin offerings, whose blood
was brought into the Most Holy Place to
make atonement, must be taken outside
the camp;[o] their hides, flesh and intestines are to be burned up. 28The man who
burns them must wash his clothes and
bathe himself with water; afterward he
may come into the camp.
29“This is to be a lasting ordinance
for you: On the tenth day of the seventh
month you must deny yourselves[a][p] and
not do any work — whether native-born
or a foreigner residing among you — 30be-
cause on this day atonement will be made
for you, to cleanse you. Then, before the
LORD, you will be clean from all your sins.[q]
31It is a day of sabbath rest, and you must
deny yourselves;[r] it is a lasting ordinance.
32The priest who is anointed and ordained
to succeed his father as high priest is to
make atonement. He is to put on the sacred linen garments[s] 33and make atonement for the Most Holy Place, for the tent
of meeting and the altar, and for the priests
and all the members of the community.[t]
34“This is to be a lasting ordinance for
you: Atonement is to be made once a
year[u] for all the sins of the Israelites.”
And it was done, as the LORD commanded Moses.

Eating Blood Forbidden

17 The LORD said to Moses, 2“Speak to
Aaron and his sons and to all the Israelites and say to them: ‘This is what the
LORD has commanded: 3Any Israelite who
sacrifices an ox,[b] a lamb or a goat in the
camp or outside of it 4instead of bringing
it to the entrance to the tent of meeting

16:18 [g] Lev 4:7 [h] Lev 4:25 **16:19** [i] Eze 43:20 **16:21** [j] Lev 5:5 **16:22** [k] Isa 53:12 **16:23** [l] Eze 42:14; 44:19 **16:24** [m] ver 3-5 **16:26** [n] Lev 11:25 **16:27** [o] Lev 4:12, 21; Heb 13:11 **16:29** [p] Lev 23:27, 32; Nu 29:7; Isa 58:3 **16:30** [q] Jer 33:8; Eph 5:26 **16:31** [r] Isa 58:3, 5 **16:32** [s] ver 4; Nu 20:26, 28 **16:33** [t] ver 11, 16-18 **16:34** [u] Heb 9:7, 25

[a] 29 Or *must fast*; also in verse 31 [b] 3 The Hebrew word can refer to either male or female.

16:26,28 *must wash his clothes and bathe himself with water.* The need for this purification implies that such an assistant was contaminated by contact with the purification (“sin”) offering carcasses, which had indirectly absorbed evils as ritual “sponges” when blood from the same animals was directly applied to the sanctuary. Somewhat similarly, Babylonian functionaries slaughtered a ram, directly wiped (*kuppuru*) Nabu’s Ezida shrine with the carcass to absorb impurity (cf. previous note) and disposed of the ritual “sponge,” consisting of the ram’s body, by throwing it and the ram’s head in the river. Consequently, these functionaries became ritually impure, as indicated by the fact that they were required to remain outside Babylon for the remainder of the New Year Festival of Spring, i.e., from days 5 to 12 of the month Nisannu.
16:29 *On the tenth day of the seventh month you must deny yourselves.* Once a year on the Day of Atonement, all Israelites were to physically deny themselves by fasting and participating in related customs, such as wearing sackcloth (cf. Ezr 8:21; Ps 35:13; Isa 58:3,5), and to abstain from work (see Lev 16:31). In these ways they would demonstrate their humble loyalty to the Lord at the time when his sanctuary was purged of their impurities and sins. If they willfully neglected to participate in the practice of self-denial or to keep Sabbath on this day, he would reject and terminally punish them (23:29 – 30). In that sense, the Day of Atonement was Israel’s judgment day. Notice that every fiftieth year, the Day of Atonement marked New Year’s Day for the beginning of the Jubilee Year (25:9 – 13), which brought judgment in the additional sense of legal deliverance from negative effects of insolvency.

Written centuries before Leviticus, the Sumerian Nanshe Hymn (c. 2100 – 2000 BC) also expresses the concept that human beings would be annually judged by their deity. The hymn describes a New Year celebration at which the goddess Nanshe is portrayed as holding a yearly review of persons economically dependent on her temple. Depending on whether they were faithful in observing her ritual and ethical standards throughout the year and in coming to her temple to participate at the New Year, she would renew or terminate their contracts.
17:3 – 4 Domestic animals suitable for sacrifice could only be slaughtered in the tabernacle. This prohibition would prevent the sacrifice of these animals to other gods or as appeasement to underworld deities. The crime here is participation in illicit rituals.

to present it as an offering to the LORD in
front of the tabernacle of the LORD[v]—that
person shall be considered guilty of bloodshed; they have shed blood and must be
cut off from their people.[w] 5This is so the
Israelites will bring to the LORD the sacrifices they are now making in the open fields.
They must bring them to the priest, that
is, to the LORD, at the entrance to the tent
of meeting and sacrifice them as fellowship offerings. 6The priest is to splash the
blood against the altar of the LORD[x] at the
entrance to the tent of meeting and burn
the fat as an aroma pleasing to the LORD.[y]
7They must no longer offer any of their
sacrifices to the goat idols[a][z] to whom they
prostitute themselves.[a] This is to be a lasting ordinance for them and for the generations to come.'
8"Say to them: 'Any Israelite or any foreigner residing among them who offers a
burnt offering or sacrifice 9and does not
bring it to the entrance to the tent of meeting[b] to sacrifice it to the LORD must be cut
off from the people of Israel.
10" 'I will set my face against any Israelite
or any foreigner residing among them who
eats blood,[c] and I will cut them off from the
people. 11For the life of a creature is in the
blood,[d] and I have given it to you to make
atonement for yourselves on the altar; it is
the blood that makes atonement for one's
life.[b][e] 12Therefore I say to the Israelites,
"None of you may eat blood, nor may any
foreigner residing among you eat blood."
13" 'Any Israelite or any foreigner residing among you who hunts any animal or
bird that may be eaten must drain out the
blood and cover it with earth,[f] 14because
the life of every creature is its blood. That
is why I have said to the Israelites, "You
must not eat the blood of any creature, because the life of every creature is its blood;
anyone who eats it must be cut off."[g]
15" 'Anyone, whether native-born or foreigner, who eats anything found dead or
torn by wild animals[h] must wash their
clothes and bathe with water, and they

17:4 [v] Dt 12:5-21 [w] Ge 17:14 **17:6** [x] Lev 3:2 [y] Nu 18:17 **17:7** [z] Ex 22:20; 2Ch 11:15 [a] Ex 32:8; 34:15; Dt 32:17; 1Co 10:20 **17:9** [b] ver 4 **17:10** [c] Ge 9:4; Lev 3:17; Dt 12:16, 23; 1Sa 14:33 **17:11** [d] ver 14; Ge 9:4 [e] Heb 9:22 **17:13** [f] Lev 7:26; Dt 12:16 **17:14** [g] ver 11; Ge 9:4 **17:15** [h] Ex 22:31; Dt 14:21

18:2 [i] Ex 6:7; Lev 11:44; Eze 20:5 **18:3** [j] ver 24-30; Ex 23:24; Lev 20:23 **18:4** [k] ver 2 **18:5** [l] Eze 20:11; Ro 10:5*; Gal 3:12* **18:7** [m] Lev 20:11 [n] Eze 22:10 **18:8** [o] 1Co 5:1 [p] Lev 20:11 **18:9** [q] Lev 20:17 **18:12** [r] Lev 20:19 **18:14** [s] Lev 20:20

will be ceremonially unclean till evening;
then they will be clean. 16But if they do
not wash their clothes and bathe themselves, they will be held responsible.' "

Unlawful Sexual Relations

18 The LORD said to Moses, 2"Speak to
the Israelites and say to them: 'I am
the LORD your God.[i] 3You must not do as
they do in Egypt, where you used to live,
and you must not do as they do in the land
of Canaan, where I am bringing you. Do
not follow their practices.[j] 4You must obey
my laws and be careful to follow my decrees. I am the LORD your God.[k] 5Keep my
decrees and laws, for the person who obeys
them will live by them.[l] I am the LORD.
6" 'No one is to approach any close relative to have sexual relations. I am the LORD.
7" 'Do not dishonor your father[m] by having sexual relations with your mother.[n]
She is your mother; do not have relations
with her.
8" 'Do not have sexual relations with
your father's wife;[o] that would dishonor
your father.[p]
9" 'Do not have sexual relations with
your sister,[q] either your father's daughter
or your mother's daughter, whether she
was born in the same home or elsewhere.
10" 'Do not have sexual relations with
your son's daughter or your daughter's
daughter; that would dishonor you.
11" 'Do not have sexual relations with
the daughter of your father's wife, born to
your father; she is your sister.
12" 'Do not have sexual relations with
your father's sister;[r] she is your father's
close relative.
13" 'Do not have sexual relations with
your mother's sister, because she is your
mother's close relative.
14" 'Do not dishonor your father's brother by approaching his wife to have sexual
relations; she is your aunt.[s]
15" 'Do not have sexual relations with

[a] 7 Or *the demons* [b] 11 Or *atonement by the life in the blood*

17:7 *goat idols.* These goat idols (Hebrew *sheirim*) appear to be objects of worship, receiving sacrifices, which would make them unlike any demons in Mesopotamia (which do not have any associated temples, cult or priests and do *not* receive sacrifices). Though it is not uncommon to translate the term "goat-gods" or "satyrs," there is no indication that these are composite creatures. The word occurs many other times to refer simply to domesticated goats. The case cannot be made that we must consider these to be "demons" just because they fit into what we see in the ancient Near East; they most definitively do not, for not a single aspect matches up with demons from Mesopotamia. They are being treated in the category of gods even though the sacrifices they receive are illegitimate, which puts them in the same category as foreign gods. Given the connections between goats, uninhabited country, demons, and the underworld, we can better understand why ch. 17 would emphasize proper use of blood on the Lord's altar.

18:6 Genesis recounts incest between Lot and his daughters (Ge 19:30–38) and between Reuben and Bilhah, his father's concubine (Ge 35:22; 49:4). Incest was common in families of Egyptian pharaohs for the purpose of concentrating power. In ancient Persia, marriages of men to their sisters, daughters or even mothers were regarded as acts of piety. However, most ancient societies discouraged incest. The Babylonian Code of Hammurapi and the Hittite laws viewed some sexual liaisons in ways that are paralleled in Lev 18; 20 (see the article "Sanctioned Relationships in the Ancient Near East," p. 210).

LEVITICUS 18

Sanctioned Relationships in the Ancient Near East

Here are some points of comparison between Leviticus and the Hittite laws:

1. The Hittite laws explicitly label sexual relations between a man and his daughter or son "an unpermitted sexual pairing." These cases are not specified in Leviticus but are covered, along with the case of a full sister, by the general principle that "no one is to approach any close relative to have sexual relations" (Lev 18:6).
2. The Hittite laws forbid sexual union of a man with his brother's wife only while his brother is alive and mandate: "If a man has a wife, and the man dies, his brother shall take his widow as wife. (If the brother dies) his father shall take her. When afterward his father dies, his (i.e., the father's) brother shall take the woman whom he had." This is like levirate (brother-in-law) marriage in Dt 25:5 – 10, which is more restricted in that it applies only if the widow has no son and does not provide for the event that her brother-in-law subsequently dies. However, in Ge 38 Tamar tricks her father-in-law into impregnating her after his son has died.
3. In the Hittite laws, a man is not permitted to sexually approach his wife's daughter. If he is married to a daughter, he may not sexually approach her mother or sister. However, "if a man's wife dies, [he may take her] sister [as his wife.] It is not an offense." This cluster of provisions would include the situation addressed in Lev 18:18 — "Do not take your wife's sister as a rival wife." Some have argued that "sister" here broadly refers to any other woman, so that this is a blanket prohibition of polygamy. But the immediately preceding context is incest, and in the parallel Hittite legislation "sister" is obviously used narrowly and literally within the immediate family, along with "daughter" and "mother."
4. The Hittite laws introduce a subjective element not present in Leviticus: a man's knowledge of relationships between women. If he "sleeps with free sisters who

continued on next page

your daughter-in-law.[t] She is your son's wife; do not have relations with her.

16 " 'Do not have sexual relations with your brother's wife;[u] that would dishonor your brother.

17 " 'Do not have sexual relations with both a woman and her daughter.[v] Do not have sexual relations with either her son's daughter or her daughter's daughter; they are her close relatives. That is wickedness.

18 " 'Do not take your wife's sister as a rival wife and have sexual relations with her while your wife is living.

19 " 'Do not approach a woman to have sexual relations during the uncleanness of her monthly period.[w]

20 " 'Do not have sexual relations with your neighbor's wife[x] and defile yourself with her.

21 " 'Do not give any of your children[y] to be sacrificed to Molek,[z] for you must not profane the name of your God.[a] I am the LORD.

22 " 'Do not have sexual relations with a

18:15 [t] Lev 20:12 **18:16** [u] Lev 20:21 **18:17** [v] Lev 20:14 **18:19** [w] Lev 15:24; 20:18 **18:20** [x] Ex 20:14; Lev 20:10; Mt 5:27, 28; 1Co 6:9; Heb 13:4 **18:21** [y] Dt 12:31 [z] Lev 20:2-5 [a] Lev 19:12; 21:6; Eze 36:20

18:22 There is plenty of evidence for homosexuality and bestiality in the ancient Near East. A Mesopotamian omen (concerned with results rather than morality) prognosticates: "If a man has anal sex with a man of equal status — that man will be foremost among his brothers and colleagues." However, the Middle Assyr-

have the same mother and with their mother—one in one country and the other in another, it is not an offense." But if this occurs in the same place and he knows that the women are related, "it is an unpermitted sexual pairing."
5. Unlike Lev 18 and Lev 20, the Hittite laws include permitted liaisons, cover situations in which male relatives sleep with the same woman, and address cases involving slaves or prostitutes, in which cases incest standards are lowered. ◆

RELATIONSHIP TO A MAN	LEV 18	LEV 20	CODE OF HAMMURAPI	HITTITE LAWS
Mother	Forbidden		Forbidden	Forbidden
Daughter	Implicitly forbidden		Forbidden	Forbidden
Son	Implicitly forbidden			Forbidden
Full sister	Implicitly forbidden			
Father's wife	Forbidden	Forbidden	Forbidden if she was the principal wife who had borne children	Forbidden with step-mother only while father is alive
Half sister				
Grandchild	Forbidden			
Step-sister	Forbidden			
Aunt	Forbidden		Forbidden	
Daughter-in-law	Forbidden	Forbidden	Forbidden	
Brother's wife	Forbidden	Forbidden		Forbidden only while brother is alive
Woman + her daughter or mother	Forbidden	Forbidden		Forbidden if he is married to one or the other
Woman + her granddaughter	Forbidden			
Sister of wife while wife is alive	Forbidden to marry			Forbidden

man as one does with a woman;[b] that is detestable.
23"'Do not have sexual relations with an animal and defile yourself with it. A woman must not present herself to an animal to have sexual relations with it; that is a perversion.[c]
24"'Do not defile yourselves in any of these ways, because this is how the nations that I am going to drive out before you[d] became defiled.[e] 25Even the land was defiled; so I punished it for its sin,[f] and the land vomited out its inhabitants.[g]
26But you must keep my decrees and my laws. The native-born and the foreigners

18:22 [b]Lev 20:13; Dt 23:18; Ro 1:27 **18:23** [c]Ex 22:19; Lev 20:15; Dt 27:21 **18:24** [d]ver 3, 27,30 [e]Dt 18:12 **18:25** [f]Lev 20:23; Dt 9:5; 18:12 [g]ver 28; Lev 20:22

ian laws have a different attitude, which is closer to that of Leviticus: "If a man sodomizes his comrade and they prove the charges against him and find him guilty, they shall sodomize him and they shall turn him into a eunuch." In harmony with this negative assessment, a confession of righteousness in the Egyptian "Book of the Dead" affirms: "I have not copulated with a boy." Both homosexuality and bestiality were practiced in the context of ritual or magic in the ancient Near East. The latter particularly occurred in Ugarit, but was banned in Hittite laws (see note on v. 23).

18:23 *Do not have sexual relations with an animal.* Unlike the Bible, Ugaritic mythology describes bestiality by deities. When the deity Motu threatens Balu (Baal) with death, the latter seeks to guarantee himself a form of afterlife through progeny by repeatedly copulating with

residing among you must not do any of
these detestable things, 27for all these
things were done by the people who lived
in the land before you, and the land became defiled. 28And if you defile the land,
it will vomit you out as it vomited out the
nations that were before you.
29“ ‘Everyone who does any of these detestable things — such persons must be
cut off from their people. 30Keep my requirements[h] and do not follow any of the
detestable customs that were practiced before you came and do not defile yourselves
with them. I am the LORD your God.[i] ’ ”

Various Laws

19 The LORD said to Moses, 2“Speak
to the entire assembly of Israel and
say to them: ‘Be holy because I, the LORD
your God, am holy.[j]
3“ ‘Each of you must respect your mother and father,[k] and you must observe my
Sabbaths. I am the LORD your God.[l]
4“ ‘Do not turn to idols or make metal
gods for yourselves.[m] I am the LORD your
God.
5“ ‘When you sacrifice a fellowship offering to the LORD, sacrifice it in such a
way that it will be accepted on your behalf. 6It shall be eaten on the day you sacrifice it or on the next day; anything left
over until the third day must be burned
up. 7If any of it is eaten on the third day, it
is impure and will not be accepted. 8Who-
ever eats it will be held responsible because they have desecrated what is holy to
the LORD; they must be cut off from their
people.
9“ ‘When you reap the harvest of your
land, do not reap to the very edges of your
field or gather the gleanings of your harvest.[n] 10Do not go over your vineyard a
second time or pick up the grapes that
have fallen. Leave them for the poor and
the foreigner. I am the LORD your God.
11“ ‘Do not steal.[o]
“ ‘Do not lie.[p]
“ ‘Do not deceive one another.
12“ ‘Do not swear falsely by my name[q]
and so profane the name of your God. I
am the LORD.
13“ ‘Do not defraud or rob your neighbor.[r]
“ ‘Do not hold back the wages of a hired
worker overnight.[s]
14“ ‘Do not curse the deaf or put a stumbling block in front of the blind,[t] but fear
your God. I am the LORD.
15“ ‘Do not pervert justice;[u] do not show
partiality[v] to the poor or favoritism to the
great, but judge your neighbor fairly.
16“ ‘Do not go about spreading slander[w]
among your people.
“ ‘Do not do anything that endangers
your neighbor’s life.[x] I am the LORD.

18:30 [h] Dt 11:1 [i] ver 2 **19:2** [j] 1Pe 1:16*; Lev 11:44 **19:3** [k] Ex 20:12 [l] Lev 11:44 **19:4** [m] Ex 20:4, 23; 34:17; Lev 26:1; Ps 96:5; 115:4-7 **19:9** [n] Lev 23:10, 22; Dt 24:19-22 **19:11** [o] Ex 20:15 [p] Eph 4:25 **19:12** [q] Ex 20:7; Mt 5:33 **19:13** [r] Ex 22:15, 25-27 [s] Dt 24:15; Jas 5:4 **19:14** [t] Dt 27:18 **19:15** [u] Ex 23:2, 6 [v] Dt 1:17 **19:16** [w] Ps 15:3; Eze 22:9 [x] Ex 23:7

---

a cow, which conceives and bears him a son. This is not so surprising because mixed beings were common in the realm of the gods (see notes on 19:19; Eze 1:5,10) throughout the ancient Near East.

The Hittite laws condemn to death a person who engages in bestiality with certain kinds of animals (a cow, sheep, pig, dog) unless the king grants him mercy, which may also be extended to the animal. Even if the monarch hears his case, the offender may not personally appear before him lest the king be (secondarily) defiled.

19:2 *Be holy because I, the LORD your God, am holy.* The Egyptian “Instruction of Amenemope” presents the divine standard as unattainable for human beings as it contrasts the perfection of God as over against human failures. The Law (Torah) provides the Israelites with instructions that will enable them to live in close proximity to a holy God and to preserve the purity and sanctity of sacred space. They have been conferred a holy status and are expected to conduct themselves in a way that is fitting to that status. They are able to meet these requirements, though it is not easy. The instructions also provide a means by which failures can be addressed so that God can remain present among them. Compare the Sumerian Nanshe Hymn, according to which temple dependents are judged by their faithfulness (or lack thereof) to the personal cultic and ethical standards of the goddess.

19:4 *Do not turn to idols.* Ancient Near Eastern peoples regarded their deities as powerful living beings, but they worshiped gods through idols identified with them, which were believed to somehow partake of and reflect the divine essence (see note on Ex 20:4).

19:10 In fertility cults the portion left would have been an offering to the gods of the ground; here it becomes a means to care for the poor (see Ru 2). Texts from Nuzi suggest a similar practice among the Hurrians.

19:15 *Do not pervert justice.* Throughout the ancient Near East, justice was a high priority and rulers prided themselves on carrying out their god-given responsibility to protect weaker members of society from oppression (cf. Ex 22:22). The Sumerian king Uruinimgina of Lagash (c. 2351 – 2342 BC) appears to have pioneered a long tradition of social justice in the ancient Near East by establishing the first-known systematic legal reforms. Later laws and hymns echoed the ideals that Uruinimgina expressed as follows: “A citizen of Lagash living in debt, (or) who had been condemned to its prison for impost, hunger, robbery, (or) murder — their freedom he established. Uruinimgina made a compact with the divine Nin-Girsu that the powerful man would not oppress the orphan (or) widow.” Human justice and mercy were thought to reflect attributes of divinities, such as the sun-god (Šamaš/Utu), who was the patron of justice. Although at this point in their history Israel had no royal mediator (see note on Dt 5:27), they were still expected to reflect their deity’s attributes of justice and mercy in their society.

19:16 *Do not go about spreading slander.* Ancient Near Eastern texts similarly discourage slander of various kinds. The Egyptian “Instruction of Amenemope” admonishes: “Guard your tongue from harmful speech, / Then you will be loved by others ... / Do not shout “crime” against a man, / When the cause of (his) flight is hidden.” In an Old Aramaic inscription, King Panammuwa boasts that he did away with war and slander (lit. “sword and tongue”) from his father’s house. At Nuzi, the penalty for slander

17“ ‘Do not hate a fellow Israelite in your
heart.[y] Rebuke your neighbor frankly[z] so
you will not share in their guilt.
18“ ‘Do not seek revenge[a] or bear a
grudge[b] against anyone among your people, but love your neighbor as yourself.[c] I
am the LORD.
19“ ‘Keep my decrees.
“ ‘Do not mate different kinds of animals.
“ ‘Do not plant your field with two kinds
of seed.[d]
“ ‘Do not wear clothing woven of two
kinds of material.[e]
20“ ‘If a man sleeps with a female slave
who is promised to another man but who
has not been ransomed or given her freedom, there must be due punishment.[a] Yet
they are not to be put to death, because
she had not been freed. 21The man, however, must bring a ram to the entrance to
the tent of meeting for a guilt offering to
the LORD.[f] 22With the ram of the guilt offering the priest is to make atonement for
him before the LORD for the sin he has
committed, and his sin will be forgiven.

19:17 [y] 1Jn 2:9; 3:15 [z] Mt 18:15; Lk 17:3
19:18 [a] Ro 12:19 [b] Ps 103:9 [c] Mt 5:43*; 19:16*; 22:39*; Mk 12:31*; Lk 10:27*; Jn 13:34; Ro 13:9*; Gal 5:14*; Jas 2:8*
19:19 [d] Dt 22:9 [e] Dt 22:11
19:21 [f] Lev 5:15
19:24 [g] Pr 3:9
19:26 [h] Lev 17:10 [i] Dt 18:10
19:27 [j] Lev 21:5
19:29 [k] Dt 23:18

23“ ‘When you enter the land and plant
any kind of fruit tree, regard its fruit as forbidden.[b] For three years you are to consider it forbidden[b]; it must not be eaten. 24In
the fourth year all its fruit will be holy,[g]
an offering of praise to the LORD. 25But in
the fifth year you may eat its fruit. In this
way your harvest will be increased. I am
the LORD your God.
26“ ‘Do not eat any meat with the blood
still in it.[h]
“ ‘Do not practice divination or seek
omens.[i]
27“ ‘Do not cut the hair at the sides of
your head or clip off the edges of your
beard.[j]
28“ ‘Do not cut your bodies for the dead
or put tattoo marks on yourselves. I am
the LORD.
29“ ‘Do not degrade your daughter by
making her a prostitute,[k] or the land will
turn to prostitution and be filled with
wickedness.

[a] *20* Or *be an inquiry* [b] *23* Hebrew *uncircumcised*

was payment of one ox. In the Middle Assyrian Laws, a man who goes around spreading baseless rumors or falsely claims in a public quarrel that someone sodomized another man is punished with 50 blows, service to the king, a humiliating haircut and a fine of 3,600 shekels of lead.

19:18 *love your neighbor as yourself.* Such an attitude is illustrated by the covenanted love between David and Jonathan, who "loved [David] as himself" (1Sa 18:3). Similar loyal love is described in a treaty between the Hittite king Tudhaliya IV and Kurunta of Tarhuntassa. Lev 19:34 extends the command to demonstrate such love to the resident alien, who is to be treated like a native citizen. Similarly, a Mesopotamian treaty text from Alalakh provides that "[if people of my land] enter your land to preserve themselves from starvation, you must protect them and you must feed them like (citizens of) your land." In these sorts of examples it can be seen that "love" does not refer to an emotion or sentiment, but to service, consideration and preferential treatment.

19:19 *Do not mate different kinds of animals.* In ancient Near Eastern art and literature, mixed beings are prevalent in the superhuman sphere of gods and demons (cf. Eze 1:5–11; see note on Lev 18:23). In Mesopotamia, demons, monsters and minor protective deities were depicted as bulls and lions with human heads, lion-centaurs, snake-dragons, goat-fish, bird-men, scorpion-people, and so on. *two kinds of seed.* In Israel mixtures belonged to the sacred realm: the yield resulting from planting two kinds of seed in a vineyard would become holy and therefore forfeited to sacred ownership by the sanctuary (Dt 22:9). *two kinds of material.* In Israel fabric of mixed wool and linen was reserved for parts of the tabernacle, high priest's garments, and belts of ordinary priests (Ex 26:1,31; 28:6,15; 39:29).

19:20 *not to be put to death, because she had not been freed.* The violation does not call for the death penalty, as it would if the woman possessed the power of consent belonging to a free woman (Dt 22:23–24), provided that an inquest confirms her status, along with determining the amount of compensation due to her owner (Lev 6:4–5). Compare the Mesopotamian Laws of Ur-Nammu and Laws of Eshnunna, according to which a man who deflowers a slave woman must pay her owner.

19:26 *Do not eat any meat with the blood still in it.* This idea carries the more precise sense of "You shall not eat over the blood." This is not simply a reiteration of the command to abstain from eating meat (not including fish) from which the blood is not drained out at the time of slaughter (17:10–14; cf. Ge 9:4; Ac 15:20,29). The prohibition in this verse appears related to the rest of the same verse, which forbids various kinds of divination (not including "sorcery"). Because we know that some ancient peoples poured blood into the ground as libations to underworld deities (see notes on Lev 1:5; 17:7), the prohibition of eating *over* the blood was presumably designed to prevent Israelites from associating with some pagan practice, such as a form of divination that consulted ancestral spirits (cf. vv. 27–28; Dt 14:1–2; Jer 48:37; Eze 33:25; see the article "Balaam," p. 268).

19:28 *Do not cut your bodies for the dead.* Lacerating oneself in mourning was a heightened expression of sorrow (Jer 16:6; 41:5). In the Ugaritic Baal Cycle, when the chief god Ilu (El) learns that Balu (Baal) is dead, he goes into paroxysms of grief that emphasize the magnitude of the catastrophe: "He pours dirt of mourning on his head, dust of humiliation on his cranium, for clothing, he is covered with a girded garment. With a stone he scratches incisions on (his) skin, with a razor he cuts cheeks and chin. He harrows his upper arms, plows (his) chest like a garden, harrows (his) back like a (garden in a) valley." In the Aqhat Legend professional mourners cut or possibly bruise their skin. An Akkadian text from Ugarit describes persons who lacerate themselves on behalf of a dying righteous person. *tattoo marks.* Unlike the first part of the verse, tattoos are not associated with mourning rites. The use of tattoos is evidenced from early in the Biblical period. Some Egyptian mummies display them. Many simply feature geometric patterns but some have portrayals of gods or are the names of gods. They were at times used to mark someone's loyalty to a particular god. In Mesopotamia most known tattoos are

[30]" 'Observe my Sabbaths and have reverence for my sanctuary. I am the LORD.[l]
[31]" 'Do not turn to mediums or seek out
spiritists,[m] for you will be defiled by them.
I am the LORD your God.
[32]" 'Stand up in the presence of the
aged, show respect for the elderly[n] and revere your God. I am the LORD.

[33]" 'When a foreigner resides among
you in your land, do not mistreat them.
[34]The foreigner residing among you must
be treated as your native-born.[o] Love them
as yourself, for you were foreigners in
Egypt.[p] I am the LORD your God.
[35]" 'Do not use dishonest standards
when measuring length, weight or quanti-

19:30 [l] Lev 26:2 **19:31** [m] Lev 20:6; Isa 8:19 **19:32** [n] 1Ti 5:1 **19:34** [o] Ex 12:48 [p] Dt 10:19

slave markings, though there are also known examples of priests receiving marks to designate the god they serve. It can therefore be concluded that tattoos are likely banned not just because of what they do to the body, but because of what they communicate about a relationship to deity.

19:31 *mediums ... spiritists.* See the article "Magic," p. 326.

19:35 *Do not use dishonest standards.* Honesty through use of standard weights and measures was a common topic in ancient Near Eastern literature. In the Egyptian "Book of the Dead," an Egyptian claims innocence: "I have

LEVITICUS 19:35–36

WEIGHTS AND MEASURES

Throughout the ancient world, there were different standards for different types of shekels. This, along with other factors, leads to some uncertainty in the attempt to identify the modern equivalence of ancient measures for weight. During the Late Bronze Age, e.g., the shekel from Ugarit was about 20 percent heavier than the shekel from Ashdod. Moreover, the Ashdod shekel was probably equivalent to the weight designated by the Hebrew *pim* (1Sa 13:21), which itself seems to have been equal to about two-thirds of an Israelite shekel. This makes the Israelite shekel heavier than other shekel standards in the West Semitic world.

Some archaeological evidence (mainly small weights) points to a shekel standard in Israel that falls between 0.39 and 0.46 ounces (between 11 and 13 grams); some have opted for 0.4 ounces (11.4 grams) as the modern equivalent of this shekel. Small artifacts marked with the Hebrew letters *bq* ("beka") are equal in weight to about 0.2 ounces (6 grams). That the beka weight is the same as a half shekel (cf. Ex 38:26) indicates that the sanctuary shekel does indeed fall into the range of the 0.39–0.46 ounce (11–13 gram) standard. In most cases, payments of the type mentioned here were made in silver based on the weight (number of shekels) required.

Based on Biblical texts and archaeological finds, the table below lists the units of measurement for weight used in ancient Israel. They are listed from lightest to heaviest. The modern equivalents are based on the assumption that one shekel is approximately 0.4 ounces or 12 grams. ◆

UNIT	TEXTS	ANCIENT EQUIVALENT	MODERN EQUIVALENT
gerah	Ex 30:13; Lev 27:25; Nu 3:47; 18:16; Eze 45:12		0.02 ounces (0.6 gram)
beka	Ge 24:22; Ex 38:26	10 gerahs; half shekel	0.2 ounces (6 grams)
pim	1Sa 13:21	two-thirds shekel	0.28 ounces (8 grams)
shekel	e.g., Ex 21:32; 30:13,15,24; 38:24,25,26,29	2 bekas	0.42 ounces (12 grams)
mina	1Ki 10:17; Ezr 2:69; Ne 7:70,71; Eze 45:12	50 shekels	1.32 pounds (0.6 kg)
talent	e.g., Ex 25:39; 37:24; 38:24,25,27,29	3,000 shekels	79.3 pounds (36 kg)
daric	1Ch 29:7; Ezr 2:69, 8:27; Ne 7:70–72		0.33 ounce (8.4 grams)

ty. 36Use honest scales and honest weights,
an honest ephah[a] and an honest hin.[b][q] I
am the LORD your God, who brought you
out of Egypt.
37" 'Keep all my decrees and all my laws
and follow them. I am the LORD.' "

Punishments for Sin

20 The LORD said to Moses, 2"Say to
the Israelites: 'Any Israelite or any
foreigner residing in Israel who sacrifices
any of his children to Molek is to be put
to death. The members of the community
are to stone him. 3I myself will set my face
against him and will cut him off from his
people; for by sacrificing his children to
Molek, he has defiled my sanctuary[r] and
profaned my holy name.[s] 4If the members
of the community close their eyes when
that man sacrifices one of his children to
Molek and if they fail to put him to death,[t]
5I myself will set my face against him and
his family and will cut them off from their
people together with all who follow him in
prostituting themselves to Molek.
6" 'I will set my face against anyone who
turns to mediums and spiritists to prostitute themselves by following them, and I
will cut them off from their people.[u]
7" 'Consecrate yourselves and be holy,[v]
because I am the LORD your God. 8Keep
my decrees and follow them. I am the
LORD, who makes you holy.[w]
9" 'Anyone who curses their father or
mother[x] is to be put to death.[y] Because
they have cursed their father or mother,
their blood will be on their own head.[z]
10" 'If a man commits adultery with another man's wife[a]—with the wife of his
neighbor—both the adulterer and the
adulteress are to be put to death.
11" 'If a man has sexual relations with
his father's wife, he has dishonored his father.[b] Both the man and the woman are
to be put to death; their blood will be on
their own heads.
12" 'If a man has sexual relations with
his daughter-in-law,[c] both of them are to
be put to death. What they have done is
a perversion; their blood will be on their
own heads.
13" 'If a man has sexual relations with a
man as one does with a woman, both of
them have done what is detestable.[d] They
are to be put to death; their blood will be
on their own heads.
14" 'If a man marries both a woman and
her mother,[e] it is wicked. Both he and
they must be burned in the fire, so that no
wickedness will be among you.[f]
15" 'If a man has sexual relations with an
animal,[g] he is to be put to death, and you
must kill the animal.
16" 'If a woman approaches an animal
to have sexual relations with it, kill both
the woman and the animal. They are to be
put to death; their blood will be on their
own heads.
17" 'If a man marries his sister[h], the
daughter of either his father or his mother, and they have sexual relations, it is a
disgrace. They are to be publicly removed
from their people. He has dishonored his
sister and will be held responsible.
18" 'If a man has sexual relations with
a woman during her monthly period,[i] he
has exposed the source of her flow, and
she has also uncovered it. Both of them
are to be cut off from their people.
19" 'Do not have sexual relations with
the sister of either your mother or your
father,[j] for that would dishonor a close relative; both of you would be held responsible.
20" 'If a man has sexual relations with
his aunt,[k] he has dishonored his uncle.
They will be held responsible; they will
die childless.
21" 'If a man marries his brother's wife,[l]
it is an act of impurity; he has dishonored
his brother. They will be childless.
22" 'Keep all my decrees and laws and
follow them, so that the land[m] where I
am bringing you to live may not vomit
you out. 23You must not live according to
the customs of the nations[n] I am going to
drive out before you.[o] Because they did
all these things, I abhorred them. 24But I
said to you, "You will possess their land;
I will give it to you as an inheritance, a
land flowing with milk and honey."[p] I am
the LORD your God, who has set you apart
from the nations.[q]

19:36 [q] Dt 25:13-15 **20:3** [r] Lev 15:31 [s] Lev 18:21 **20:4** [t] Dt 17:2-5 **20:6** [u] Lev 19:31 **20:7** [v] Eph 1:4; 1Pe 1:16* **20:8** [w] Ex 31:13 **20:9** [x] Dt 27:16 [y] Ex 21:17; Mt 15:4*; Mk 7:10* [z] ver 11; 2Sa 1:16 **20:10** [a] Ex 20:14; Dt 5:18; 22:22 **20:11** [b] Lev 18:7; Dt 27:23 **20:12** [c] Lev 18:15 **20:13** [d] Lev 18:22 **20:14** [e] Lev 18:17 [f] Dt 27:23 **20:15** [g] Lev 18:23 **20:17** [h] Lev 18:9 **20:18** [i] Lev 15:24; 18:19 **20:19** [j] Lev 18:12-13 **20:20** [k] Lev 18:14 **20:21** [l] Lev 18:16 **20:22** [m] Lev 18:25-28 **20:23** [n] Lev 18:3 [o] Lev 18:24, 27,30 **20:24** [p] Ex 3:8; 13:5; 33:3 [q] Ex 33:16

[a] *36* An ephah was a dry measure having the capacity of about 3/5 of a bushel or about 22 liters. [b] *36* A hin was a liquid measure having the capacity of about 1 gallon or about 3.8 liters.

not added to the weight of the balance. I have not tampered with the plummet of the scales." The Code of Hammurapi requires standardization for repayment of debts and for purchases. The Egyptian "Instruction of Amenemope" provides a reminder of accountability to divine power: "Do not move the scales nor alter the weights, / Nor diminish the fractions of the measure … / Do not make for yourself deficient weights, / They are rich in grief through the might of god."

20:2 *sacrifices … his children to Molek.* It is possible, or even likely, that this refers to human sacrifice (for some qualifications, see notes on Ge 22:2; Dt 12:30), which involved passing one's child through fire as part of Syro-Palestinian worship of the underworld god Molek. In addition to terminally condemning anyone who engages in this practice, ch. 20 condemns anyone who tolerates a Molek worshiper.

LEVITICUS 20

PENALTIES FOR SEXUAL OFFENSES IN BIBLICAL AND MESOPOTAMIAN LAW

There are common principles for determining penalties in Biblical and Mesopotamian laws concerning adultery and other sexual offenses. The basic factors determining classification of cases are the woman's status (married/betrothed, unbetrothed, or slave) and her intention (consenting, seduced, or forced). Mesopotamian law treated premeditated adultery as a crime punishable by death, as in Biblical law. However, the Mesopotamians had a more subjective and variable approach to other kinds of cases. There were distinctions between degrees of adultery, depending on degrees of intention, with circumstances affecting the severity of penalties. An adulteress who had not premeditated the act was under her husband's jurisdiction, and whatever punishment he decided for her was also meted out to her paramour. Circumstances, such as the location and/or reaction of the woman (Dt 22:23–27; Middle Assyrian Laws 23; cf. Hittite Laws 197), could help to reveal the woman's intention.

BIBLICAL LAW

OFFENDER(S)	OFFENSE	PENALTY	REFERENCE
Man and married woman	Adultery	Death	Lev 20:10; Dt 22:22
Man and betrothed woman	Adultery	Death	Dt 22:23–24
Priest's daughter	Promiscuity	Burned	Lev 21:9
Bride	Promiscuity (not virgin)	Death	Dt 22:20–21
Man	Rape of betrothed woman	Death	Dt 22:25–27
Man	Rape of unbetrothed woman	50 shekels, forced marriage, no right of divorce	Dt 22:28–29
Man	Seduction of unbetrothed woman	Bride-price, forced marriage at discretion of father	Ex 22:15–16

continued on next page

25" 'You must therefore make a distinction between clean and unclean animals and between unclean and clean birds.[r] Do not defile yourselves by any animal or bird or anything that moves along the ground—those that I have set apart as unclean for you. 26You are to be holy to me because I, the LORD, am holy,[s] and I have set you apart from the nations to be my own.
27" 'A man or woman who is a medium or spiritist among you must be put to death.[t] You are to stone them; their blood will be on their own heads.' "

20:25 [r]Lev 11:1-47; Dt 14:3-21 **20:26** [s]Lev 19:2 **20:27** [t]Lev 19:31 **21:1** [u]Eze 44:25

Rules for Priests

21 The LORD said to Moses, "Speak to the priests, the sons of Aaron, and say to them: 'A priest must not make himself ceremonially unclean for any of his people who die,[u] 2except for a close rela-

21:1 *A priest must not make himself ceremonially unclean.* Uncleanness was not always avoidable, and often the cause of uncleanness was not something that would be considered sinful, including sexual or disease-related impurities, or impurity resulting from contact with a corpse. Although a matter of etiquette rather than ethics,

However, a slave woman was legally incapable of consent and therefore not accountable for her intention (Lev 19:20).

A man who violated the right of a husband/fiancé committed a criminal action. But one who wronged the father of an unbetrothed woman or the owner of a slave was required to pay civil compensation. The marital status of men involved in illicit sex was not relevant for classification of cases, because ancient Near Eastern society tolerated polygamy. Thus, there was a double standard: a married man could have more than one sexual partner at a time, but this was strictly forbidden for a married woman.

The offense category of promiscuity/harlotry is unique to Biblical law. This offense involves consenting immorality by a woman living in her father's house, which disgraces him. If she is the daughter of a priest, whose reputation for holiness is crucial, she suffers the most severe punishment: burning (see Lev 21:9; see also Ge 38:24), probably after death by stoning (cf. Jos 7:25). See note on Dt 22:22. ◆

MESOPOTAMIAN LAW

OFFENDER(S)	OFFENSE	PENALTY	REFERENCE*
Man and married woman	Premeditated adultery and the man knows the woman is married	Death	MAL 13
Married woman	Premeditated adultery	Death	LU 4; LE 28; CH 133b
Man and married woman	Adultery in the act	Death or according to husband	MAL 15
Married woman	Seduces to adultery	According to husband	MAL 16
Man and married woman	Adultery	According to husband	CH 129; MAL 14,23a
Married woman	Adultery as consent to rape	According to husband	MAL 23c
Unbetrothed woman	Consenting to sex	According to father	MAL 56
Man	Rape of married woman	Death	MAL 12,23b–c
Man	Rape of betrothed woman	Death	LE 26; CH 130
Man	Rape of seducing married woman	According to husband	MAL 16
Man	Rape of unbetrothed woman	Price of a virgin, taking rapist's wife, forced marriage at discretion of father, no right of divorce	MAL 55
Man	Deflowering virgin slave woman	Payment to owner	LU 5; LE 31

* LE = Laws of Eshnunna; CH = Code of Hammurapi; LU = Laws of Ur-Nammu; MAL = Middle Assyrian Laws

tive, such as his mother or father, his son
or daughter, his brother, 3or an unmarried
sister who is dependent on him since she
has no husband — for her he may make
himself unclean. 4He must not make himself unclean for people related to him by
marriage,[a] and so defile himself.
5" 'Priests must not shave their heads or
shave off the edges of their beards[v] or cut
their bodies.[w] 6They must be holy to their
God and must not profane the name of
their God.[x] Because they present the food
offerings to the LORD,[y] the food of their
God, they are to be holy.
7" 'They must not marry women defiled by prostitution or divorced from

21:5 [v] Eze 44:20
[w] Lev 19:28; Dt 14:1
21:6 [x] Lev 18:21
[y] Lev 3:11

[a] 4 Or *unclean as a leader among his people*

the purpose of this mandate was to protect the sanctuary and those who officiated in it from that which was inappropriate. Ancient Near Eastern priests were also required to be ritually pure — through avoiding impurities or undergoing purification rituals — before approaching their deities.

21:7 *defiled by prostitution.* Implies flagrant, repeated offenses. *divorced.* The priest was denied the right to

their husbands,[z] because priests are holy
to their God.[a] 8Regard them as holy,[b] because they offer up the food of your God.
Consider them holy, because I the LORD
am holy—I who make you holy.
9“ ‘If a priest’s daughter defiles herself
by becoming a prostitute, she disgraces
her father; she must be burned in the fire.[c]
10“ ‘The high priest, the one among his
brothers who has had the anointing oil
poured on his head and who has been
ordained to wear the priestly garments,[d]
must not let his hair become unkempt[a]
or tear his clothes.[e] 11He must not enter a
place where there is a dead body.[f] He must
not make himself unclean,[g] even for his
father or mother, 12nor leave the sanctuary
of his God or desecrate it, because he has
been dedicated by the anointing oil[h] of his
God. I am the LORD.
13“ ‘The woman he marries must be a
virgin.[i] 14He must not marry a widow, a
divorced woman, or a woman defiled by
prostitution, but only a virgin from his
own people, 15so that he will not defile his
offspring among his people. I am the LORD,
who makes him holy.’ ”
16The LORD said to Moses, 17“Say to Aaron: ‘For the generations to come none of
your descendants who has a defect may
come near to offer the food of his God.[j]
18No man who has any defect[k] may come
near: no man who is blind or lame, disfigured or deformed; 19no man with a crippled foot or hand, 20or who is a hunchback or a dwarf, or who has any eye
defect, or who has festering or running
sores or damaged testicles.[l] 21No descendant of Aaron the priest who has any defect is to come near to present the food
offerings to the LORD. He has a defect; he
must not come near to offer the food of his
God. 22He may eat the most holy food of
his God,[m] as well as the holy food; 23yet
because of his defect, he must not go near
the curtain or approach the altar, and so
desecrate my sanctuary. I am the LORD,
who makes them holy.’ ”
24So Moses told this to Aaron and his
sons and to all the Israelites.

22 The LORD said to Moses, 2“Tell Aaron and his sons to treat with respect the sacred offerings the Israelites
consecrate to me, so they will not profane
my holy name. I am the LORD.
3“Say to them: ‘For the generations to
come, if any of your descendants is ceremonially unclean and yet comes near the
sacred offerings that the Israelites consecrate to the LORD, that person must be cut
off from my presence.[n] I am the LORD.
4“ ‘If a descendant of Aaron has a defiling skin disease[b] or a bodily discharge,[o]
he may not eat the sacred offerings until
he is cleansed. He will also be unclean if
he touches something defiled by a corpse[p]
or by anyone who has an emission of semen, 5or if he touches any crawling thing[q]
that makes him unclean, or any person[r]
who makes him unclean, whatever the
uncleanness may be. 6The one who touches any such thing will be unclean till evening. He must not eat any of the sacred offerings unless he has bathed himself with
water. 7When the sun goes down, he will
be clean, and after that he may eat the sacred offerings, for they are his food.[s] 8He
must not eat anything found dead[t] or torn
by wild animals,[u] and so become unclean[v]
through it. I am the LORD.
9“ ‘The priests are to perform my service
in such a way that they do not become
guilty and die[w] for treating it with contempt. I am the LORD, who makes them
holy.
10“ ‘No one outside a priest’s family may
eat the sacred offering, nor may the guest
of a priest or his hired worker eat it. 11But
if a priest buys a slave with money, or if
slaves are born in his household, they may
eat his food.[x] 12If a priest’s daughter marries anyone other than a priest, she may
not eat any of the sacred contributions.
13But if a priest’s daughter becomes a widow or is divorced, yet has no children, and
she returns to live in her father’s household as in her youth, she may eat her father’s food. No unauthorized person, however, may eat it.
14“ ‘Anyone who eats a sacred offering
by mistake must make restitution to the
priest for the offering and add a fifth of the
value[y] to it. 15The priests must not dese-

21:7 [z] ver 13,14 [a] Eze 44:22 **21:8** [b] ver 6 **21:9** [c] Ge 38:24; Lev 19:29 **21:10** [d] Lev 16:32 [e] Lev 10:6 **21:11** [f] Nu 19:11,13,14 [g] Lev 19:28 **21:12** [h] Ex 29:6-7; Lev 10:7 **21:13** [i] Eze 44:22 **21:17** [j] ver 6 **21:18** [k] Lev 22:19-25 **21:20** [l] Dt 23:1; Isa 56:3 **21:22** [m] 1Co 9:13

22:3 [n] Lev 7:20,21; Nu 19:13 **22:4** [o] Lev 14:1-32; 15:2-15 [p] Lev 11:24-28,39 **22:5** [q] Lev 11:24-28,43 [r] Lev 15:7 **22:7** [s] Nu 18:11 **22:8** [t] Lev 11:39 [u] Ex 22:31; Lev 17:15 [v] Lev 11:40 **22:9** [w] ver 16; Ex 28:43 **22:11** [x] Ge 17:13; Ex 12:44 **22:14** [y] Lev 5:15

[a] *10* Or *not uncover his head* [b] *4* The Hebrew word for *defiling skin disease,* traditionally translated “leprosy,” was used for various diseases affecting the skin.

marry a divorced woman, most likely because the principal charge against a woman in a divorce was infidelity.
21:17 *none … who has a defect may come near to offer.* Respect for the deity required that his priestly servants be free from physical defects, just as animals offered to him were not to be defective (22:17–25). This includes birth defects and disfiguration caused by accident or disease. Hittite ritual rules also excluded persons with physical disabilities from intimate access to deity in sacred precincts. Even though he could not approach the altar, the disabled priest in these cultures was still allowed his share of the priestly portion of the sacrifice.
22:3–9 The altar and those who served it were required to maintain strict purity and cleanness. One Hittite text contains a long list of instructions for maintaining ritual purity and cleansing the priest or temple in the case of contamination, which is similar to that found in ch. 22, but adds the prohibition that anyone who has had sexual

crate the sacred offerings the Israelites present to the LORD[z] 16 by allowing them to
eat the sacred offerings and so bring upon
them guilt requiring payment.[a] I am the
LORD, who makes them holy.' "

Unacceptable Sacrifices

17 The LORD said to Moses, 18 "Speak to
Aaron and his sons and to all the Israelites
and say to them: 'If any of you — whether an Israelite or a foreigner residing in Israel — presents a gift[b] for a burnt offering
to the LORD, either to fulfill a vow or as a
freewill offering, 19 you must present a male
without defect[c] from the cattle, sheep or
goats in order that it may be accepted on
your behalf. 20 Do not bring anything with a
defect,[d] because it will not be accepted on
your behalf. 21 When anyone brings from
the herd or flock a fellowship offering[e] to
the LORD to fulfill a special vow or as a
freewill offering, it must be without defect
or blemish to be acceptable. 22 Do not offer
to the LORD the blind, the injured or the
maimed, or anything with warts or festering or running sores. Do not place any of
these on the altar as a food offering presented to the LORD. 23 You may, however,
present as a freewill offering an ox[a] or a
sheep that is deformed or stunted, but it
will not be accepted in fulfillment of a vow.
24 You must not offer to the LORD an animal
whose testicles are bruised, crushed, torn
or cut.[f] You must not do this in your own
land, 25 and you must not accept such animals from the hand of a foreigner and offer
them as the food of your God.[g] They will
not be accepted on your behalf, because
they are deformed and have defects.' "

26 The LORD said to Moses, 27 "When
a calf, a lamb or a goat is born, it is to
remain with its mother for seven days.[h]
From the eighth day on, it will be acceptable as a food offering presented to the
LORD. 28 Do not slaughter a cow or a sheep
and its young on the same day.[i]

29 "When you sacrifice a thank offering[j] to the LORD, sacrifice it in such a way
that it will be accepted on your behalf. 30 It
must be eaten that same day; leave none
of it till morning.[k] I am the LORD.

31 "Keep[l] my commands and follow them.
I am the LORD. 32 Do not profane my holy

22:15 [z] Nu 18:32 **22:16** [a] ver 9 **22:18** [b] Lev 1:2 **22:19** [c] Lev 1:3 **22:20** [d] Dt 15:21; 17:1; Mal 1:8, 14; Heb 9:14; 1Pe 1:19 **22:21** [e] Lev 3:6; Nu 15:3, 8 **22:24** [f] Lev 21:20 **22:25** [g] Lev 21:6 **22:27** [h] Ex 22:30 **22:28** [i] Dt 22:6, 7 **22:29** [j] Lev 7:12; Ps 107:22 **22:30** [k] Lev 7:15 **22:31** [l] Dt 4:2, 40; Ps 105:45

22:32 [m] Lev 18:21 [n] Lev 10:3 **22:33** [o] Lev 11:45 **23:2** [p] ver 4, 37, 44; Nu 29:39 [q] ver 21, 27 **23:3** [r] Ex 20:9 [s] Ex 20:10; 31:13-17; Lev 19:3; Dt 5:13; Heb 4:9, 10 **23:5** [t] Ex 12:18-19; Nu 28:16-17; Dt 16:1-8 **23:7** [u] ver 3, 8 **23:10** [v] Ex 23:16, 19; 34:26 **23:11** [w] Ex 29:24 **23:13** [x] Lev 2:14-16; 6:20

name,[m] for I must be acknowledged as
holy by the Israelites.[n] I am the LORD, who
made you holy 33 and who brought you out
of Egypt to be your God.[o] I am the LORD."

The Appointed Festivals

23 The LORD said to Moses, 2 "Speak
to the Israelites and say to them:
'These are my appointed festivals,[p] the appointed festivals of the LORD, which you
are to proclaim as sacred assemblies.[q]

The Sabbath

3 " 'There are six days when you may
work,[r] but the seventh day is a day of sabbath rest,[s] a day of sacred assembly. You
are not to do any work; wherever you live,
it is a sabbath to the LORD.

The Passover and the Festival of Unleavened Bread

23:4-8pp — Ex 12:14-20; Nu 28:16-25; Dt 16:1-8

4 " 'These are the LORD's appointed festivals, the sacred assemblies you are to
proclaim at their appointed times: 5 The
LORD's Passover begins at twilight on the
fourteenth day of the first month.[t] 6 On
the fifteenth day of that month the LORD's
Festival of Unleavened Bread begins; for
seven days you must eat bread made without yeast. 7 On the first day hold a sacred
assembly[u] and do no regular work. 8 For
seven days present a food offering to the
LORD. And on the seventh day hold a sacred assembly and do no regular work.' "

Offering the Firstfruits

9 The LORD said to Moses, 10 "Speak to
the Israelites and say to them: 'When you
enter the land I am going to give you and
you reap its harvest, bring to the priest a
sheaf[v] of the first grain you harvest. 11 He
is to wave the sheaf before the LORD[w] so it
will be accepted on your behalf; the priest
is to wave it on the day after the Sabbath.
12 On the day you wave the sheaf, you must
sacrifice as a burnt offering to the LORD a
lamb a year old without defect, 13 together
with its grain offering[x] of two-tenths of an
ephah[b] of the finest flour mixed with olive

[a] *23* The Hebrew word can refer to either male or female. [b] *13* That is, probably about 7 pounds or about 3.2 kilograms; also in verse 17

relations with a horse or mule could not become a priest, specifying an additional means to acquire uncleanness.
22:21 *it must be without defect or blemish to be acceptable.* Following the same principle centuries earlier, Gudea of Lagash sacrificed to his god Ningirsu, "properly arranging perfect ox and perfect he-goat." Cheating the Lord by sacrificing defective animals (except for some defects allowed in freewill offerings, see v. 23) was forbidden (cf. Mal 1:6 – 14). This ruled out the substitution of defective animals for acceptable ones previously designated as sacrifices. Like Malachi, the Hittite "Instructions to Priests and Temple Officials" warn that the deity holds people accountable for such cheating.
22:28 The regulation that a mother and her young not be offered on the same day provided some protection to those with just a few animals who might otherwise have been forced to decimate their herds.

LEVITICUS 23

FESTIVALS

Numbers 28–29 complements the liturgical calendar of Lev 23 by specifying communal sacrifices to be performed regularly every day, weekly on the seventh-day Sabbath, monthly at New Moons, and yearly at the various annual festivals (see note on Nu 28:2). Aside from the Sabbath, a practice unique to Israel, other peoples had similar ritual cycles. At Ugarit there were regular daily sacrifices, New Moon sacrifices and annual festivals, and Hittite cult inventories specify daily offerings and festivals.

Although the Israelites, Babylonians and Hittites had different ritual and theological systems, they shared some basic concepts concerning the timetable of obligations toward their deities. Even from earliest times, ancient Near Eastern people were very religious, and nowhere is this more evident than in their splendid array of cyclical festivals, which were often lengthy. For example, the *Zukru* festival to all the gods of Emar lasted seven days. Hittite festival texts, the largest attested genre of extant Hittite literature, preserve memory of some extraordinarily elaborate Hittite festivals (AN.TAH.ŠUM and *nuntarriyšhaš*) that lasted for several weeks and apparently involved royal tours/pilgrimages to cultic centers around the empire.

Outside Israel, festivals often commemorated events related to the activities of the gods. For example, the Babylonian New Year Festival included celebration of Marduk's elevation to supremacy over the gods. Fertility was a major festival theme, and some narratives about deities, such as the death of Baal in the fall and his revival in the spring (Canaanite), were related to renewal of agricultural cycles.

As with Israelite festivals (especially Firstfruits, Weeks and Tabernacles/Booths), cyclical holy days and sacrifices of other peoples could punctuate the agricultural calendar at crucial points, such as harvest time. This was because agricultural bounty, which was crucial for survival and well-being, was regarded as dependent on the favor of deities. Thus, there were yearly celebrations of the grape harvest at the temple of Baal in Ugarit. Festivals could also include purification of holy places and objects (see note on Lev 16:14). But non-Israelite festivals did not explicitly commemorate historical deliverance of a people by their deity as did some Israelite sacred times, such as Passover-Unleavened Bread and Tabernacle/Booths. ◆

oil—a food offering presented to the LORD,
a pleasing aroma—and its drink offering
of a quarter of a hin[a] of wine. 14You must
not eat any bread, or roasted or new grain,
until the very day you bring this offering
to your God.[y] This is to be a lasting ordinance for the generations to come,[z] wherever you live.

The Festival of Weeks

23:15-22pp — Nu 28:26-31; Dt 16:9-12

15"'From the day after the Sabbath, the
day you brought the sheaf of the wave offering, count off seven full weeks. 16Count
off fifty days up to the day after the seventh Sabbath,[a] and then present an offering of new grain to the LORD. 17From wherever you live, bring two loaves made of
two-tenths of an ephah of the finest flour,
baked with yeast, as a wave offering of
firstfruits[b] to the LORD. 18Present with this
bread seven male lambs, each a year old
and without defect, one young bull and
two rams. They will be a burnt offering
to the LORD, together with their grain offerings and drink offerings—a food offering, an aroma pleasing to the LORD.
19Then sacrifice one male goat for a sin
offering[b] and two lambs, each a year old,
for a fellowship offering. 20The priest is to
wave the two lambs before the LORD as a
wave offering, together with the bread of

23:14 [y]Ex 34:26 [z]Nu 15:21 **23:16** [a]Nu 28:26; Ac 2:1 **23:17** [b]Ex 34:22; Lev 2:12

[a] *13* That is, about 1 quart or about 1 liter [b] *19* Or *purification offering*

the firstfruits. They are a sacred offering to the LORD for the priest. 21 On that same day you are to proclaim a sacred assembly[c] and do no regular work.[d] This is to be a lasting ordinance for the generations to come, wherever you live.

22 " 'When you reap the harvest[e] of your land, do not reap to the very edges of your field or gather the gleanings of your harvest.[f] Leave them for the poor and for the foreigner residing among you. I am the LORD your God.' "

The Festival of Trumpets

23:23-25pp — Nu 29:1-6

23 The LORD said to Moses, 24 "Say to the Israelites: 'On the first day of the seventh month you are to have a day of sabbath rest, a sacred assembly commemorated with trumpet blasts.[g] 25 Do no regular work,[h] but present a food offering to the LORD.' "

The Day of Atonement

23:26-32pp — Lev 16:2-34; Nu 29:7-11

26 The LORD said to Moses, 27 "The tenth day of this seventh month[i] is the Day of Atonement.[j] Hold a sacred assembly[k] and deny yourselves,[a] and present a food offering to the LORD. 28 Do not do any work on that day, because it is the Day of Atonement, when atonement is made for you before the LORD your God. 29 Those who do not deny themselves on that day must be cut off from their people.[l] 30 I will destroy from among their people[m] anyone who does any work on that day. 31 You shall do no work at all. This is to be a lasting ordinance for the generations to come, wherever you live. 32 It is a day of sabbath rest for you, and you must deny yourselves. From the evening of the ninth day of the month until the following evening you are to observe your sabbath."

The Festival of Tabernacles

23:33-43pp — Nu 29:12-39; Dt 16:13-17

33 The LORD said to Moses, 34 "Say to the Israelites: 'On the fifteenth day of the seventh month the LORD's Festival of Tabernacles[n] begins, and it lasts for seven days. 35 The first day is a sacred assembly; do no regular work. 36 For seven days present food offerings to the LORD, and on the eighth day hold a sacred assembly[o] and present a food offering to the LORD. It is the closing special assembly; do no regular work.

37 (" 'These are the LORD's appointed festivals, which you are to proclaim as sacred assemblies for bringing food offerings to the LORD — the burnt offerings and grain offerings, sacrifices and drink offerings[p] required for each day. 38 These offerings are in addition to those for the LORD's Sabbaths[q] and[b] in addition to your gifts and whatever you have vowed and all the freewill offerings you give to the LORD.)

39 " 'So beginning with the fifteenth day of the seventh month, after you have gathered the crops of the land, celebrate the festival to the LORD for seven days;[r] the first day is a day of sabbath rest, and the eighth day also is a day of sabbath rest. 40 On the first day you are to take branches from luxuriant trees — from palms, willows and other leafy trees[s] — and rejoice before the LORD your God for seven days. 41 Celebrate this as a festival to the LORD for seven days each year. This is to be a lasting ordinance for the generations to come; celebrate it in the seventh month. 42 Live in temporary shelters[t] for seven days: All native-born Israelites are to live in such shelters 43 so your descendants will know[u] that I had the Israelites live in temporary shelters when I brought them out of Egypt. I am the LORD your God.' "

44 So Moses announced to the Israelites the appointed festivals of the LORD.

Olive Oil and Bread Set Before the LORD

24:1-3pp — Ex 27:20-21

24 The LORD said to Moses, 2 "Command the Israelites to bring you clear oil of pressed olives for the light so that the lamps may be kept burning continually. 3 Outside the curtain that shields the ark of the covenant law in the tent of meeting, Aaron is to tend the lamps before the LORD from evening till morning, continually. This is to be a lasting ordinance for the generations to come. 4 The lamps on the pure gold lampstand[v] before the LORD must be tended continually.

23:21 [c] ver 2 [d] ver 3 **23:22** [e] Lev 19:9 [f] Lev 19:10; Dt 24:19-21; Ru 2:15 **23:24** [g] Lev 25:9; Nu 10:9, 10; 29:1 **23:25** [h] ver 21 **23:27** [i] Lev 16:29 [j] Ex 30:10 [k] Nu 29:7 **23:29** [l] Ge 17:14; Nu 5:2 **23:30** [m] Lev 20:3 **23:34** [n] Ex 23:16; Dt 16:13; Ezr 3:4; Ne 8:14; Zec 14:16; Jn 7:2 **23:36** [o] 2Ch 7:9; Ne 8:18; Jn 7:37 **23:37** [p] ver 2, 4 **23:38** [q] Eze 45:17 **23:39** [r] Ex 23:16; Dt 16:13 **23:40** [s] Ne 8:14-17 **23:42** [t] Ne 8:14-16 **23:43** [u] Dt 31:13; Ps 78:5 **24:4** [v] Ex 25:31; 31:8

[a] 27 Or *and fast*; similarly in verses 29 and 32
[b] 38 Or *These festivals are in addition to the LORD's Sabbaths, and these offerings are*

23:24 *On the first day of the seventh month.* The first month of the Israelite calendar is Nisan in the spring (see Ex 12:2). However, in post-Biblical tradition the first day of the seventh month (Tishri) has become *Rosh Hashanah* ("New Year"). This is not a contradiction. In antiquity, a group of people could have more than one New Year's Day to mark half years that commenced with events such as equinoxes, or to initiate different kinds of full years that overlapped each other (cf. a modern-day fiscal year beginning July 1). Once Jewish tradition came to regard the first day of the seventh month as New Year's Day, it was a short step to view it, along with the Day of Atonement, as a day of judgment (see, e.g., in the Mishnah see *Rosh Hashanah* 1:2) in harmony with ancient Near Eastern traditions that placed judgment in the framework of New Year celebrations (see note on 16:29).

OLD TESTAMENT FESTIVALS AND OTHER SACRED DAYS

NAME	OLD TESTAMENT REFERENCES	OLD TESTAMENT TIME	MODERN EQUIVALENT
Sabbath	Ex 20:8–11; 31:12–17; Lev 23:3; Dt 5:12–15	7th day	Same
Sabbath Year	Ex 23:10–11; Lev 25:1–7	7th year	Same
Year of Jubilee	Lev 25:8–55; 27:17–24; Nu 36:4	50th year	Same
Passover	Ex 12:1–14; Lev 23:5; Nu 9:1–14; 28:16; Dt 16:1–3a,4b–7	1st month (Aviv) 14	March – April
Unleavened Bread	Ex 12:15–20; 13:3–10; 23:15; 34:18; Lev 23:6–8; Nu 28:17–25; Dt 16:3b,4a,8	1st month (Aviv) 15–21	March – April
Firstfruits	Lev 23:9–14	1st month (Aviv) 16	March – April
Weeks (Pentecost) (Harvest)	Ex 23:16a; 34:22a; Lev 23:15–21; Nu 28:26–31; Dt 16:9–12	3rd month (Sivan) 6	May – June
Trumpets (later: Rosh Hashanah–New Year's Day)	Lev 23:23–25; Nu 29:1–6	7th month (Tishri) 1	September – October
Day of Atonement (Yom Kippur)	Lev 16; 23:26–32; Nu 29:7–11	7th month (Tishri) 10	September – October
Tabernacles (Booths) (Ingathering)	Ex 23:16b; 34:22b; Lev 23:33–36a,39–43; Nu 29:12–34; Dt 16:13–15; Zec 14:16–19	7th month (Tishri) 15–21	September – October
Sacred Assembly	Lev 23:36b; Nu 29:35–38	7th month (Tishri) 22	September – October
Purim	Est 9:18–32	12th month (Adar) 14,15	February – March

On Kislev 25 (mid-December) Hanukkah, the Festival of Dedication or Festival of Lights, commemorated the purification of the temple and altar in the Maccabean period (165/64 BC). This festival is mentioned in Jn 10:22 (see note there).

5 "Take the finest flour and bake twelve
loaves of bread,[w] using two-tenths of an
ephah[a] for each loaf. 6 Arrange them in two
stacks, six in each stack, on the table of
pure gold[x] before the LORD. 7 By each stack
put some pure incense as a memorial[b] portion[y] to represent the bread and to be a
food offering presented to the LORD. 8 This
bread is to be set out before the LORD regularly,[z] Sabbath after Sabbath,[a] on behalf
of the Israelites, as a lasting covenant. 9 It
belongs to Aaron and his sons,[b] who are to
eat it in the sanctuary area, because it is a
most holy part of their perpetual share of
the food offerings presented to the LORD."

A Blasphemer Put to Death

10 Now the son of an Israelite mother and
an Egyptian father went out among the Israelites, and a fight broke out in the camp
between him and an Israelite. 11 The son of
the Israelite woman blasphemed the Name[c]
with a curse; so they brought him to Moses.
(His mother's name was Shelomith, the

24:5 [w] Ex 25:30 **24:6** [x] Ex 25:23-30; 1Ki 7:48 **24:7** [y] Lev 2:2 **24:8** [z] Nu 4:7; 1Ch 9:32; 2Ch 2:4 [a] Mt 12:5 **24:9** [b] Lev 8:31; Mt 12:4; Mk 2:26; Lk 6:4 **24:11** [c] Ex 3:15

[a] 5 That is, probably about 7 pounds or about 3.2 kilograms [b] 7 Or *representative*

24:8 *Sabbath after Sabbath ... as a lasting covenant.* Compare Ex 31:16, where Sabbath signifies a "lasting covenant" between the Lord and the Israelites, whom he makes holy (Ex 31:13), because God created the heavens and earth and rested on the seventh day, a day he made holy (Ex 31:17; see Ge 1 – 2). A Syrian amulet bears a Phoenician inscription that expresses some parallel motifs: "Ashur has made an eternal covenant with us. He has made (a covenant) with us, along with all the sons of 'El and the leaders of the council of all the Holy Ones, with a covenant of the Heavens and Eternal Earth, with an oath of Bal."
24:11 *blasphemed the Name with a curse.* In the ancient Near East, deities and their names were regarded as holy. The Egyptian "Great Hymn to Osiris" praises the god: "Holy and splendid is his name." Speaking evil of a deity or blaspheming his/her name (cf. Ex 22:28) was a serious offense, as shown by harsh Assyrian punishments on blasphemers, including cutting their tongues and having them skinned alive. In a Syrian treaty between Ebla and Abarsal, one who committed treason by blaspheming his own king, gods and country could be put to death. A negative confession in the Egyptian "Book of the Dead" declares, "I have not reviled a god ... I have not cursed a god."

DESCRIPTION	PURPOSE	NEW TESTAMENT REFERENCES
Day of rest; no work	Rest for people and animals	Mt 12:1–14; 28:1; Lk 4:16; Jn 5:9–10; Ac 13:42; Col 2:16; Heb 4:1–11
Year of rest; fallow fields	Rest for land	
Canceled debts; liberation of slaves and indentured servants; land returned to original family owners	Help for poor; stabilize society	
Slaying and eating a lamb, together with bitter herbs and bread made without yeast, in every household	Remember Israel's deliverance from Egypt	Mt 26:17; Mk 14:12–26; Jn 2:13; 11:55; 1Co 5:7; Heb 11:28
Eating bread made without yeast; holding several assemblies; making designated offerings	Remember how the Lord brought the Israelites out of Egypt in haste	Mk 14:1; Ac 12:3; 1Co 5:6–8
Presenting a sheaf of the first of the barley harvest as a wave offering; making a burnt offering and a grain offering	Recognize the Lord's bounty in the land	Ro 8:23; 1Co 15:20–23
A festival of joy; mandatory and voluntary offerings, including the firstfruits of the wheat harvest	Show joy and thankfulness for the Lord's blessing of harvest	Ac 2:1–4; 20:16; 1Co 16:8
An assembly on a day of rest commemorated with trumpet blasts and sacrifices	Present Israel before the Lord for his favor	
A day of rest, fasting and sacrifices of atonement for priests and people and atonement for the tabernacle and altar	Atone for the sins of priests and people and purify the Holy Place	Ro 3:24–26; Heb 9:7; 10:3,19–22
A week of celebration for the harvest; living in booths (temporary shelters) and offering sacrifices	Memorialize the journey from Egypt to Canaan; give thanks for the productivity of Canaan	Jn 7:2,37
A day of convocation, rest and offering sacrifices	Commemorate the closing of the cycle of festivals	
A day of joy and feasting and giving presents	Remind the Israelites of their national deliverance in the time of Esther	

In addition, New Moon feasts were prescribed (see Nu 28:11–15; 1 Sa 20:5; Ps 81:3; Isa 1:13–14 and notes; see also 1Ch 23:31; Ezr 3:5; Ne 10:33; Hos 5:7; Am 8:5; Col 2:16).

daughter of Dibri the Danite.) 12 They put
him in custody until the will of the LORD
should be made clear to them.[d]
13 Then the LORD said to Moses: 14 "Take
the blasphemer outside the camp. All
those who heard him are to lay their
hands on his head, and the entire assembly is to stone him.[e] 15 Say to the Israelites: 'Anyone who curses their God[f] will
be held responsible; 16 anyone who blasphemes the name of the LORD is to be put
to death.[g] The entire assembly must stone
them. Whether foreigner or native-born,
when they blaspheme the Name they are
to be put to death.
17 " 'Anyone who takes the life of a human being is to be put to death.[h] 18 Anyone
who takes the life of someone's animal

24:12 [d] Ex 18:16; Nu 15:34 **24:14** [e] Lev 20:27; Dt 13:9; 17:5,7; 21:21 **24:15** [f] Ex 22:28 **24:16** [g] 1Ki 21:10,13; Mt 26:66 **24:17** [h] Ge 9:6; Ex 21:12; Nu 35:30-31; Dt 27:24

24:14 *stone him.* In the Bible, stoning is a common way for the community to execute someone guilty of a crime against it, perhaps so that no one individual would be responsible for the death of the offender. Outside the Bible, various modes of execution are attested (e.g., drowning, impaling and burning); stoning is present in some non-Israelite texts, such as the Syrian "Hadad Inscription," but it is rare.

24:17 Outside Israel, a person who committed homicide could receive capital punishment, as in the Mesopotamian Laws of Ur-Nammu. Alternatively, he could be forced to give up one or more persons who belonged to him (Hittite Laws). If a death occurred during a brawl, the penalty was a monetary fine (Laws of Eshnunna, Code of Hammurapi). According to the Hittite king Telipinu, it was up to the heir of a murdered person to decide whether the murderer would die or pay. The death penalty for those who committed intentional homicide seems uniformly allowed in the ancient Near East. However, the death penalty was not usually mandatory; it simply represented the fullest extent of the law. Convicted murderers could, in some cases, make a payment that functioned as a ransom for their life. The text of one Neo-Assyrian document states that the perpetrator will, instead of making a monetary payment, give a person (perhaps from his household) to the son of the victim. Here, the ransom takes the place of the death penalty. In Israel, on the other hand, a person who takes the life of another forfeits his own right to live, and there is no alternative to capital punishment.

24:18 *make restitution.* Law collections outside the Bible present similar remedies. For death of an animal or such

must make restitution[i] — life for life.
19Anyone who injures their neighbor is to
be injured in the same manner: 20fracture
for fracture, eye for eye, tooth for tooth.[j]
The one who has inflicted the injury must
suffer the same injury. 21Whoever kills an
animal must make restitution, but whoever kills a human being is to be put to
death.[k] 22You are to have the same law for
the foreigner[l] and the native-born.[m] I am
the LORD your God.' "

23Then Moses spoke to the Israelites,
and they took the blasphemer outside the
camp and stoned him. The Israelites did as
the LORD commanded Moses.

The Sabbath Year

25 The LORD said to Moses at Mount
Sinai, 2"Speak to the Israelites and
say to them: 'When you enter the land I
am going to give you, the land itself must
observe a sabbath to the LORD. 3For six
years sow your fields, and for six years
prune your vineyards and gather their
crops.[n] 4But in the seventh year the land
is to have a year of sabbath rest, a sabbath to the LORD. Do not sow your fields or
prune your vineyards. 5Do not reap what
grows of itself or harvest the grapes of
your untended vines. The land is to have
a year of rest. 6Whatever the land yields
during the sabbath year[o] will be food for
you — for yourself, your male and female
servants, and the hired worker and temporary resident who live among you, 7as well
as for your livestock and the wild animals
in your land. Whatever the land produces
may be eaten.

The Year of Jubilee

25:8-38Ref — Dt 15:1-11
25:39-55Ref — Ex 21:2-11; Dt 15:12-18

8" 'Count off seven sabbath years — sev-
en times seven years — so that the seven
sabbath years amount to a period of for-
ty-nine years. 9Then have the trumpet[p]
sounded everywhere on the tenth day of
the seventh month; on the Day of Atonement sound the trumpet throughout your
land. 10Consecrate the fiftieth year and
proclaim liberty[q] throughout the land to
all its inhabitants. It shall be a jubilee[r] for

24:18 [i] ver 21
24:20 [j] Ex 21:24; Mt 5:38*
24:21 [k] ver 17
24:22 [l] Ex 12:49 [m] Nu 9:14; 15:16
25:3 [n] Ex 23:10
25:6 [o] ver 20
25:9 [p] Lev 23:24
25:10 [q] Isa 61:1; Jer 34:8, 15, 17; Lk 4:19 [r] Nu 36:4

serious injury to an ox that it is unusable, the Code of Hammurapi stipulates replacement with an animal of comparable value. For other permanent injuries, money payments suffice. The Hittite Laws mandate money payments for death or permanent injuries to animals.

24:20 *eye for eye.* The principle of "an eye for an eye" also shows up in the Code of Hammurapi. This type of punishment, which tries to mirror the injury committed, is known as talionic retribution, and it constituted a basic principle of ancient Near Eastern law. Part of its purpose was to deter potential wrongdoers and to ensure that they would be punished appropriately. Another purpose, though, was to ensure that punishments did not go too far. If a man gouges out the eye of another, his eye can be gouged out, but his ear cannot also be cut off. The system may still seem cruel to modern readers, but this was one way in the ancient world to put limits on punishment. In their time, retaliatory punishments administered by civil courts were a major advance for the cause of justice, in that they curbed unlimited retribution and ensured that rich and poor were treated in a way that affected them equally.

These talionic penalties thus constituted for ancient Near Eastern legal systems the maximum penalty for a given crime. It was also possible for lesser punishments to be imposed. For instance, in the Law of Eshnunna, the penalty for the loss of an eye does not call for the assailant's eye to be put out; rather, it stipulates a 60-shekel fine. It is probable that most, if not all, ancient Near Eastern societies allowed for such lesser penalties (usually monetary fines). Statements like "eye for eye" thus declare the most severe punishment allowed by law.

25:2 *the land itself must observe a sabbath.* This concept will be most clearly understood when we recognize that the issue of "rest" in the Bible does not have "relaxation" as its focus. It is more basically involved with recognition that God is the source and center of order, and that he, not our own effort, is the one who provides to satisfy our needs. The land sabbatical enforces the same point, since God is the one who is responsible for the fertility of the fields. For that reason, the Israelites are still allowed to eat "whatever the land yields" (v. 6) — i.e., what God provides in growth.

The practical benefit derived from resting the land is the preservation of the soil's fertility; large areas of Mesopotamia were abandoned due to high sodium levels in the soil caused by irrigation. Ugaritic texts also feature a seven-year agricultural calendar that allowed portions of the field to "rest" each year (a practice we now call "crop rotation").

25:10 *liberty.* The Hebrew word here is *deror* (see also Isa 61:1; Jer 34:8). It is related to the Akkadian word *anduraru*, which refers to various kinds of release, including remission of commercial debts and manumission of private slaves. Especially near the beginnings of their reigns, several Mesopotamian kings proclaimed releases similar to the Biblical Jubilee, in that they provided relief for debtors and return of land and persons pledged, sold, or enslaved in direct consequence of debt. The purpose of such legislation was to restore some economic and social equilibrium. The main unique feature of the Israelite Jubilee release was its regular recurrence, which gave it predictability and independence from the arbitrary will of an absolute human ruler. Also, whereas exceptions to releases in Mesopotamia could be specified by royal edicts or by contracts, the Israelite Jubilee was designed to benefit all Israelites (but not non-Israelites, vv. 44–46). *to your family property and to your own clan.* Basic to the Israelite economic system was the concept that God was the ultimate owner of all land and granted to each family an inalienable right to use (but not permanently sell) a piece of agricultural real estate. This right was based on the premise of the covenant land grant. Some Ugaritic real estate documents show similar concern for permanence of land grants, though not on the basis of a covenant relationship with a god. In Egypt, the pharaoh, who was regarded as divine, was the overall owner of land and assigned it to his subjects. Whatever the situation for commoners may have been in actual practice, an Egyptian treatise on kingship recognized the ideal of free people with use of their

you; each of you is to return to your family property and to your own clan. 11The fiftieth year shall be a jubilee for you; do not sow and do not reap what grows of itself or harvest the untended vines. 12For it is a jubilee and is to be holy for you; eat only what is taken directly from the fields.

13" 'In this Year of Jubilee[s] everyone is to return to their own property.

14" 'If you sell land to any of your own people or buy land from them, do not take advantage of each other.[t] 15You are to buy from your own people on the basis of the number of years[u] since the Jubilee. And they are to sell to you on the basis of the number of years left for harvesting crops. 16When the years are many, you are to increase the price, and when the years are few, you are to decrease the price,[v] because what is really being sold to you is the number of crops. 17Do not take advantage of each other,[w] but fear your God.[x] I am the LORD your God.[y]

18" 'Follow my decrees and be careful to obey my laws, and you will live safely in the land.[z] 19Then the land will yield its fruit,[a] and you will eat your fill and live there in safety. 20You may ask, "What will we eat in the seventh year[b] if we do not plant or harvest our crops?" 21I will send you such a blessing[c] in the sixth year that the land will yield enough for three years. 22While you plant during the eighth year, you will eat from the old crop and will continue to eat from it until the harvest of the ninth year comes in.[d]

23" 'The land must not be sold permanently, because the land is mine[e] and you reside in my land as foreigners[f] and strangers. 24Throughout the land that you hold as a possession, you must provide for the redemption of the land.

25" 'If one of your fellow Israelites becomes poor and sells some of their property, their nearest relative[g] is to come and redeem[h] what they have sold. 26If, however, there is no one to redeem it for them but later on they prosper and acquire sufficient means to redeem it themselves, 27they are to determine the value for the years since they sold it and refund the balance to the one to whom they sold it; they can then go back to their own property. 28But if they do not acquire the means to repay, what was sold will remain in the possession of the buyer until the Year of Jubilee. It will be returned in the Jubilee, and they can then go back to their property.[i]

29" 'Anyone who sells a house in a walled city retains the right of redemption a full year after its sale. During that time the seller may redeem it. 30If it is not redeemed before a full year has passed, the house in the walled city shall belong permanently to the buyer and the buyer's descendants. It is not to be returned in the Jubilee. 31But houses in villages without walls around them are to be considered as belonging to the open country. They can be redeemed, and they are to be returned in the Jubilee.

32" 'The Levites always have the right to redeem their houses in the Levitical towns,[j] which they possess. 33So the property of the Levites is redeemable—that is, a house sold in any town they hold—and is to be returned in the Jubilee, because the houses in the towns of the Levites are their property among the Israelites. 34But the pastureland belonging to their towns must not be sold; it is their permanent possession.[k]

35" 'If any of your fellow Israelites become poor[l] and are unable to support themselves among you, help them[m] as you would a foreigner and stranger, so they can continue to live among you. 36Do not take interest[n] or any profit from them, but fear your God, so that they may continue to live among you. 37You must not lend them money at interest or sell them food at a profit. 38I am the LORD your God, who brought you out of Egypt to give you the land of Canaan and to be your God.[o]

39" 'If any of your fellow Israelites become poor and sell themselves to you, do

25:13 [s] ver 10 **25:14** [t] Lev 19:13; 1Sa 12:3,4 **25:15** [u] Lev 27:18,23 **25:16** [v] ver 27, 51,52 **25:17** [w] Pr 22:22; Jer 7:5, 6; 1Th 4:6 [x] Lev 19:14 [y] Lev 19:32 **25:18** [z] Lev 26:4,5; Dt 12:10; Ps 4:8; Jer 23:6 **25:19** [a] Lev 26:4 **25:20** [b] ver 4 **25:21** [c] Dt 28:8, 12; Hag 2:19; Mal 3:10 **25:22** [d] Lev 26:10 **25:23** [e] Ex 19:5 [f] Ge 23:4; 1Ch 29:15; Ps 39:12; Heb 11:13; 1Pe 2:11 **25:25** [g] Ru 2:20; Jer 32:7 [h] Lev 27:13,19, 31; Ru 4:4

25:28 [i] ver 10 **25:32** [j] Nu 35:1-8; Jos 21:2 **25:34** [k] Nu 35:2-5 **25:35** [l] Dt 24:14, 15 [m] Dt 15:8; Ps 37:21,26; Lk 6:35 **25:36** [n] Ex 22:25; Dt 23:19-20 **25:38** [o] Ge 17:7; Lev 11:45

own land; such people were more likely to be contented, unified and loyal than they would have been had their situation been otherwise. Unlike Israel and Egypt, Mesopotamia lacked a unified system of land ownership.

25:25 *their nearest relative is to come and redeem what they have sold.* The Laws of Eshnunna contain the provision: "If a man becomes impoverished and then sells his house, whenever the buyer offers it for sale, the owner of the house shall have the right to redeem it." Lev 25 provides a higher level of protection for the original owner: an Israelite can redeem his ancestral property anytime, not just when the other party decides to put it up for sale, and even if he is unable to redeem it, his kinsman should step in to keep the property in the extended family (cf. Ru 4:1–12; Jer 32:6–15).

25:36 *Do not take interest or any profit from them.* Agreements to pay interest were common in the ancient Near East, but the need to prevent exploitation was well recognized. The Code of Hammurapi limits the amount of interest that can be charged and cancels interest payments for any year in which a farmer's crop is devastated by an "act of god" (storm, flood, drought). So, as in Israelite law, a creditor was to show mercy to (rather than receive profit from) an individual beset by unfortunate circumstances.

25:39 *fellow Israelites ... sell themselves.* If an Israelite farmer fell on hard times, he would have no way to support himself and could be forced into slavery, along with his family members, whether by selling himself (and them) or by being seized as collateral for a debt in default. Other ancient Near Easterners could fall into slavery for

not make them work as slaves.[p] 40They
are to be treated as hired workers or temporary residents among you; they are to
work for you until the Year of Jubilee.
41Then they and their children are to be
released, and they will go back to their
own clans and to the property[q] of their
ancestors. 42Because the Israelites are my
servants, whom I brought out of Egypt,
they must not be sold as slaves. 43Do not
rule over them ruthlessly,[r] but fear your
God.
44" 'Your male and female slaves are to
come from the nations around you; from
them you may buy slaves. 45You may also
buy some of the temporary residents living among you and members of their clans
born in your country, and they will become your property. 46You can bequeath
them to your children as inherited property and can make them slaves for life, but
you must not rule over your fellow Israelites ruthlessly.
47" 'If a foreigner residing among you
becomes rich and any of your fellow Israelites become poor and sell themselves
to the foreigner or to a member of the foreigner's clan, 48they retain the right of redemption after they have sold themselves.
One of their relatives[s] may redeem them:
49An uncle or a cousin or any blood relative in their clan may redeem them. Or
if they prosper,[t] they may redeem themselves. 50They and their buyer are to
count the time from the year they sold
themselves up to the Year of Jubilee. The
price for their release is to be based on the
rate paid to a hired worker[u] for that number of years. 51If many years remain, they
must pay for their redemption a larger
share of the price paid for them. 52If only
a few years remain until the Year of Jubilee, they are to compute that and pay for
their redemption accordingly. 53They are
to be treated as workers hired from year
to year; you must see to it that those to
whom they owe service do not rule over
them ruthlessly.
54" 'Even if someone is not redeemed
in any of these ways, they and their children are to be released in the Year of Jubilee, 55for the Israelites belong to me as
servants. They are my servants, whom I
brought out of Egypt. I am the LORD your
God.

Reward for Obedience

26 " 'Do not make idols[v] or set up an
image or a sacred stone[w] for yourselves, and do not place a carved stone[x] in
your land to bow down before it. I am the
LORD your God.
2" 'Observe my Sabbaths and have reverence for my sanctuary.[y] I am the LORD.
3" 'If you follow my decrees and are
careful to obey[z] my commands, 4I will

25:39 [p] Ex 21:2; Dt 15:12; 1Ki 9:22 **25:41** [q] ver 28 **25:43** [r] Ex 1:13; Eze 34:4; Col 4:1 **25:48** [s] Ne 5:5 **25:49** [t] ver 26

25:50 [u] Job 7:1; Isa 16:14; 21:16 **26:1** [v] Ex 20:4; Lev 19:4; Dt 5:8 [w] Ex 23:24 [x] Nu 33:52 **26:2** [y] Lev 19:30 **26:3** [z] Dt 7:12; 11:13,22; 28:1,9

similar reasons, as well as through defeat in warfare (Dt 20:10–11; 2Sa 12:31).

In Babylonia, debt-slaves were theoretically to be kept in bondage until the debt had been worked off. In practice, however, unless they were redeemed, they remained in the possession of the creditor as long as they lived. The Code of Hammurapi remedied this grim scenario by limiting the service of a wife and children to three years. Ex 21 and Dt 15 went further, extending amnesty to the debtor himself and limiting service to six years, regardless of the size of the debt. Lev 25 adds crucial elements: An insolvent Israelite forced to sell his land is to be treated as a hired worker, and release of such servants is coordinated with release of their land, which is essential for their independent survival. When the man was finally able to repay the debt, along with any interest charges, he could redeem his family member(s) from slavery. If he sold himself into slavery, a relative, such as a brother, might try to redeem him. Redemption of persons was also practiced in Mesopotamia.

In Israel, then, the institution of slavery was not the result of bigotry or ethnic exploitation. It was an economic relief structure designed to deal with insolvency and its related threat to life and welfare that was all too common in an agrarian society. It was supposed to reflect compassion, not oppression. This does not mean, however, that it was always successful or that it was somehow a God-approved institution. God's interaction with Israel was rarely designed to replace one shape of society with another. God was concerned that, whatever the shape of their social institutions, people should live out the holy status they had been given in association with a holy God.

26:1 *sacred stone.* At Bethel, Jacob set up a stone as a pillar to mark the place of his dream and dedicated it to God by pouring oil on it (Ge 28:18). From very early times, other ancient Near Eastern people also set up religious standing stones, called *matstsebot* in Hebrew. For example, in the Negev and Sinai deserts, archaeologist Uzi Avner has identified and documented many prehistoric sites that contain such stone pillars. Avner has demonstrated that some of these *matstsebot* represented groups of deities, just as groups of gods were depicted in sculpture throughout the ancient Near East. *Matstsebot* and idols differed in that the former represented divine presence more loosely did than cult images. These standing stones did mark places where the presence of the god could be invoked. It is therefore no wonder that Israelite law prohibited their use. However, while Jacob earlier set up his stone as a sacred *matstsebah* to mark the spot where the Lord had appeared to him (Ge 28:16–22; 31:13), there is no hint that he regarded the stone as an object of worship. *do not place a carved stone in your land to bow down before it.* Because this kind of idolatrous practice is attested only here in the Bible, its nature remains obscure. However, comparison with an Assyrian text has led one scholar to propose that the "carved stone" is a stone slab placed in the ground, possibly in a doorway, decorated with engraved divine symbols. A supplicant would bow down upon the stone, enabling him to kiss the ground in order to have a wish granted. The engraved divine symbols would constitute connection to worship of other gods and therefore be forbidden.

26:3–46 These blessings and curses conclude the treaty between God (as the superior party) and Israel recorded

send you rain[a] in its season, and the
ground will yield its crops and the trees
their fruit.[b] 5Your threshing will continue
until grape harvest and the grape harvest
will continue until planting, and you will
eat all the food you want[c] and live in safety in your land.[d]
6“ ‘I will grant peace in the land,[e] and
you will lie down[f] and no one will make
you afraid.[g] I will remove wild beasts[h]
from the land, and the sword will not
pass through your country. 7You will pursue your enemies, and they will fall by
the sword before you. 8Five of you will
chase a hundred, and a hundred of you
will chase ten thousand, and your enemies
will fall by the sword before you.[i]
9“ ‘I will look on you with favor and
make you fruitful and increase your numbers,[j] and I will keep my covenant[k] with
you. 10You will still be eating last year’s
harvest when you will have to move it out
to make room for the new.[l] 11I will put my
dwelling place[a][m] among you, and I will not
abhor you. 12I will walk[n] among you and
be your God, and you will be my people.[o]
13I am the LORD your God, who brought
you out of Egypt so that you would no
longer be slaves to the Egyptians; I broke
the bars of your yoke[p] and enabled you to
walk with heads held high.

Punishment for Disobedience

14“ ‘But if you will not listen to me and
carry out all these commands,[q] 15and if
you reject my decrees and abhor my laws
and fail to carry out all my commands and
so violate my covenant, 16then I will do
this to you: I will bring on you sudden terror, wasting diseases and fever[r] that will
destroy your sight and sap your strength.[s]
You will plant seed in vain, because your
enemies will eat it.[t] 17I will set my face[u]
against you so that you will be defeated by your enemies; those who hate you
will rule over you,[v] and you will flee even
when no one is pursuing you.[w]
18“ ‘If after all this you will not listen to
me, I will punish you for your sins seven
times over.[x] 19I will break down your stubborn pride[y] and make the sky above you
like iron and the ground beneath you like
bronze.[z] 20Your strength will be spent in
vain,[a] because your soil will not yield its
crops, nor will the trees of your land yield
their fruit.[b]
21“ ‘If you remain hostile toward me
and refuse to listen to me, I will multiply
your afflictions seven times over,[c] as your
sins deserve. 22I will send wild animals[d]
against you, and they will rob you of your
children, destroy your cattle and make you
so few in number that your roads will be
deserted.
23“ ‘If in spite of these things you do
not accept my correction[e] but continue to
be hostile toward me, 24I myself will be
hostile toward you and will afflict you for
your sins seven times over. 25And I will
bring the sword on you to avenge the
breaking of the covenant. When you withdraw into your cities, I will send a plague[f]
among you, and you will be given into enemy hands. 26When I cut off your supply

[a] 11 Or *my tabernacle*

26:4 [a] Dt 11:14 [b] Ps 67:6
26:5 [c] Dt 11:15; Joel 2:19, 26; Am 9:13 [d] Lev 25:18
26:6 [e] Ps 29:11; 85:8; 147:14 [f] Ps 4:8 [g] Zep 3:13 [h] ver 22
26:8 [i] Dt 32:30; Jos 23:10
26:9 [j] Ge 17:6; Ne 9:23 [k] Ge 17:7
26:10 [l] Lev 25:22
26:11 [m] Ex 25:8; Ps 76:2; Eze 37:27
26:12 [n] Ge 3:8 [o] 2Co 6:16*
26:13 [p] Eze 34:27
26:14 [q] Dt 28:15-68; Mal 2:2
26:16 [r] Dt 28:22, 35 [s] 1Sa 2:33 [t] Job 31:8
26:17 [u] Lev 17:10 [v] Ps 106:41 [w] ver 36, 37; Dt 28:7, 25; Ps 53:5
26:18 [x] ver 21
26:19 [y] Isa 25:11 [z] Dt 28:23
26:20 [a] Ps 127:1; Isa 17:11 [b] Dt 11:17
26:21 [c] ver 18
26:22 [d] Dt 32:24
26:23 [e] Jer 2:30; 5:3
26:25 [f] Nu 14:12; Eze 5:17

in Exodus – Leviticus (cf. Dt 27 – 28). In the ancient Near East, blessings and curses could be appended to a law collection in order to encourage obedience. See the article “Decrees and Laws,” p. 301.

26:7 *You will pursue your enemies.* In the ancient world, military protection and victory were crucial benefits commonly sought from deities. In the inscription of Zakkur, king of Hamath, the god Balshamayn encourages the ruler: “Do not be afraid! Since I have made [you king, I will stand] beside you. I will save you from all [these kings who] have besieged you.” Mesha, king of Moab, claims that his god, Chemosh, has provided military guidance, deliverance and victory for the Moabites (against Israel). Divine protection that is explicitly conditional on obedience to treaty stipulations, as in Lev 26, also appears in the Hittite treaty between Mursili and Duppi-Teshub.

26:17 *I will set my face against you.* The negative impact of divine displeasure was keenly felt throughout the ancient Near East. Thus, King Mesha viewed the anger of Chemosh against his land of Moab as the cause of its earlier subjugation to Israel. An Egyptian complaint links violation of divine plans to resultant chaos and suffering. In the ancient Near East, people believed that if a god was neglected or offended, he would be more likely simply to abandon individual people or a group, leaving them vulnerable to demonic attack. In contrast, in Israel, if God was neglected or offended, he promised to himself carry out judgment.

26:19 *the sky … like iron and the ground … like bronze.* The basic idea of this conditional curse is that heaven would bar any rain from getting through to earth; consequently, the land would dry up and become hard like metal. Dt 28:23 reverses the metals. Likewise, curses in the succession treaty of the Assyrian king Esarhaddon call on the gods to “make your ground like iron (so that) nothing can sprout from it. Just as rain does not fall from a brazen heaven, so may rain and dew not come upon your fields and meadows.” This imagery of an iron or brazen sky reflects the belief of ancient Near Eastern people that a solid sky held back waters above.

26:25 *I will send a plague among you.* Compare a prayer of Mursili II, in which the king assumes that a lethal plague on his Hittite people is vengeance from the gods because his father killed a man. In the epilogue to the Code of Hammurapi, a curse on any who disrespect the royal pronouncements calls on the goddess Ninkarrak to “cause a grievous malady to break out upon his limbs, an evil demonic disease.” In the Babylonian context, the plague is carried out by a demon.

26:26 *ten women will be able to bake your bread in one oven.* This formula can be compared to the Tel Fakhariyah Inscription (c. 850 – 25 BC), the Sefire Treaty (c. 760 – 40 BC),

of bread,[g] ten women will be able to bake
your bread in one oven, and they will dole
out the bread by weight. You will eat, but
you will not be satisfied.
27“ ‘If in spite of this you still do not listen to me but continue to be hostile toward me, 28then in my anger I will be hostile toward you, and I myself will punish
you for your sins seven times over. 29You
will eat the flesh of your sons and the
flesh of your daughters.[h] 30I will destroy
your high places,[i] cut down your incense
altars[j] and pile your dead bodies[a] on the
lifeless forms of your idols,[k] and I will abhor you. 31I will turn your cities into ruins and lay waste your sanctuaries,[l] and I
will take no delight in the pleasing aroma
of your offerings. 32I myself will lay waste
the land,[m] so that your enemies who live
there will be appalled. 33I will scatter you
among the nations[n] and will draw out my
sword and pursue you. Your land will be
laid waste, and your cities will lie in ruins. 34Then the land will enjoy its sabbath
years all the time that it lies desolate and
you are in the country of your enemies;[o]
then the land will rest and enjoy its sabbaths. 35All the time that it lies desolate,
the land will have the rest it did not have
during the sabbaths you lived in it.
36“ ‘As for those of you who are left, I
will make their hearts so fearful in the
lands of their enemies that the sound of
a windblown leaf will put them to flight.[p]
They will run as though fleeing from the
sword, and they will fall, even though no
one is pursuing them. 37They will stumble
over one another as though fleeing from
the sword, even though no one is pursuing them. So you will not be able to stand
before your enemies.[q] 38You will perish
among the nations; the land of your enemies will devour you.[r] 39Those of you who
are left will waste away in the lands of
their enemies because of their sins; also
because of their ancestors' sins they will
waste away.[s]
40“ ‘But if they will confess their sins
and the sins of their ancestors[t]—their unfaithfulness and their hostility toward me,
41which made me hostile toward them so
that I sent them into the land of their enemies—then when their uncircumcised
hearts[u] are humbled and they pay for
their sin, 42I will remember my covenant
with Jacob[v] and my covenant with Isaac[w]
and my covenant with Abraham, and I
will remember the land. 43For the land
will be deserted by them and will enjoy
its sabbaths while it lies desolate without
them. They will pay for their sins because
they rejected my laws and abhorred my
decrees. 44Yet in spite of this, when they
are in the land of their enemies, I will
not reject them or abhor[x] them so as to
destroy them completely,[y] breaking my
covenant[z] with them. I am the LORD their
God. 45But for their sake I will remember[a]
the covenant with their ancestors whom I
brought out of Egypt[b] in the sight of the
nations to be their God. I am the LORD.' ”
46These are the decrees, the laws and
the regulations that the LORD established
at Mount Sinai between himself and the
Israelites through Moses.[c]

Redeeming What Is the LORD's

27 The LORD said to Moses, 2“Speak to
the Israelites and say to them: 'If
anyone makes a special vow[d] to dedicate
a person to the LORD by giving the equiv-

26:26 [g]Ps 105:16; Isa 3:1; Mic 6:14 **26:29** [h]Dt 28:53 **26:30** [i]2Ch 34:3; Eze 6:3 [j]Eze 6:6 [k]Eze 6:13 **26:31** [l]Ps 74:3-7 **26:32** [m]Jer 9:11 **26:33** [n]Dt 4:27; Eze 12:15; 20:23; Zec 7:14 **26:34** [o]ver 43; 2Ch 36:21 **26:36** [p]Eze 21:7 **26:37** [q]Jos 7:12 **26:38** [r]Dt 4:26 **26:39** [s]Eze 4:17 **26:40** [t]Jer 3:12-15; Lk 15:18; 1Jn 1:9 **26:41** [u]Eze 44:7,9; Ac 7:51 **26:42** [v]Ge 22:15-18; 28:15 [w]Ge 26:5 **26:44** [x]Ro 11:2 [y]Dt 4:31; Jer 30:11 [z]Jer 33:26 **26:45** [a]Ge 17:7 [b]Ex 6:8; Lev 25:38 **26:46** [c]Lev 7:38; 27:34 **27:2** [d]Nu 6:2

[a] 30 Or *your funeral offerings*

---

and the Bukan Inscription (c. 725–700 BC)—all of which emphasize a scarcity of grain by speaking of multiple women baking bread in one oven.

26:29 Ancient Near Easterners turned to cannibalism only as a desperate last resort to prevent imminent starvation (cf. 2Ki 6:24–30). Frightful curses of cannibalism also show up in Dt 28:53–57 and in Assyrian treaties of Esarhaddon.

27:2 *a special vow.* An Israelite could give such a votive offering to the Lord either (1) in hope of a future divine blessing or (2) in fulfillment of a promise to present the offering after a divine favor has been bestowed. Both kinds of voluntary agreements with deities—before or after divine blessings—have parallels elsewhere in the ancient Near East. As an example of the first type, a royal votive inscription of the Mesopotamian king Ibbi-Sin was originally carved on a sculpture of an animal that he dedicated to the deity Nanna "for the sake of his (Ibbi-Sin's) (long) life." A Hittite conditional promise to give a votive offering of the second type reads as follows:

> [The queen] made the following vow [on behalf of] the royal prince, the king of Išuwa: "If the prince recovers from this illness, I will [...] and I will give to the deity on behalf of the prince, the king of Išuwa, a sword, a dagger(?), and one silver ZI-ornament of unspecified weight."

Vows in the ancient world entailed a gift to be given to the deity (generally a ritual offering with or without an object of some sort). They differed from an oath, which was a promise made in the name of deity to do something. *to dedicate a person to the LORD.* In the ancient Near East, votive objects were various kinds of valuable items that worshipers of deities transferred to their sacred realm. They were often sculptures or replicas of items used in daily life and were often inscribed with prayers. Here in Lev 27, the votive object is the monetary work valuation of a person who would otherwise be literally pledged to service at the sanctuary, as Samuel was (1Sa 1:11,25–28; 2:11). Related to the vow of a human being's work valuation is a situation in which a wealthy person vows to present a deity with a multiple of another person's weight in precious metal. In an Ugaritic epic, King Kirta vows to give the goddess Atiratu double the weight of Princess Hurraya in silver and triple her weight in gold if he succeeds in taking

alent value, 3set the value of a male between the ages of twenty and sixty at fifty
shekels[a] of silver, according to the sanctuary shekel[b];[e] 4for a female, set her value at
thirty shekels[c]; 5for a person between the
ages of five and twenty, set the value of a
male at twenty shekels[d] and of a female
at ten shekels[e]; 6for a person between one
month and five years, set the value of a
male at five shekels[f][f] of silver and that of
a female at three shekels[g] of silver; 7for
a person sixty years old or more, set the
value of a male at fifteen shekels[h] and of
a female at ten shekels. 8If anyone making
the vow is too poor to pay[g] the specified
amount, the person being dedicated is to
be presented to the priest, who will set the
value[h] according to what the one making
the vow can afford.
9“ ‘If what they vowed is an animal that
is acceptable as an offering to the LORD,
such an animal given to the LORD becomes
holy. 10They must not exchange it or substitute a good one for a bad one, or a bad
one for a good one;[i] if they should substitute one animal for another, both it and
the substitute become holy. 11If what they
vowed is a ceremonially unclean animal—
one that is not acceptable as an offering to
the LORD—the animal must be presented
to the priest, 12who will judge its quality
as good or bad. Whatever value the priest
then sets, that is what it will be. 13If the
owner wishes to redeem[j] the animal, a
fifth must be added to its value.
14“ ‘If anyone dedicates their house as
something holy to the LORD, the priest will
judge its quality as good or bad. Whatever value the priest then sets, so it will
remain. 15If the one who dedicates their
house wishes to redeem it,[k] they must
add a fifth to its value, and the house will
again become theirs.
16“ ‘If anyone dedicates to the LORD part
of their family land, its value is to be set
according to the amount of seed required
for it—fifty shekels of silver to a homer[i] of
barley seed. 17If they dedicate a field during the Year of Jubilee, the value that has
been set remains. 18But if they dedicate a
field after the Jubilee, the priest will determine the value according to the number of
years that remain[l] until the next Year of Jubilee, and its set value will be reduced. 19If
the one who dedicates the field wishes to
redeem it, they must add a fifth to its value, and the field will again become theirs.
20If, however, they do not redeem the field,
or if they have sold it to someone else, it
can never be redeemed. 21When the field
is released in the Jubilee,[m] it will become
holy, like a field devoted to the LORD;[n] it
will become priestly property.
22“ ‘If anyone dedicates to the LORD a
field they have bought, which is not part
of their family land, 23the priest will determine its value up to the Year of Jubilee,
and the owner must pay its value on that
day as something holy to the LORD. 24In
the Year of Jubilee the field will revert to
the person from whom it was bought,[o] the
one whose land it was. 25Every value is to
be set according to the sanctuary shekel,[p]
twenty gerahs[q] to the shekel.
26“ ‘No one, however, may dedicate the
firstborn of an animal, since the firstborn
already belongs to the LORD;[r] whether an
ox[j] or a sheep, it is the LORD’s. 27If it is one
of the unclean animals,[s] it may be bought
back at its set value, adding a fifth of the
value to it. If it is not redeemed, it is to be
sold at its set value.
28“ ‘But nothing that a person owns and
devotes[k][t] to the LORD—whether a human

27:3 [e] Ex 30:13; Nu 3:47; 18:16 **27:6** [f] Nu 18:16 **27:8** [g] Lev 5:11 [h] ver 12, 14 **27:10** [i] ver 33 **27:13** [j] ver 15, 19; Lev 25:25 **27:15** [k] ver 13, 20 **27:18** [l] Lev 25:15 **27:21** [m] Lev 25:10 [n] ver 28; Nu 18:14; Eze 44:29 **27:24** [o] Lev 25:28 **27:25** [p] Ex 30:13; Nu 18:16 [q] Nu 3:47; Eze 45:12 **27:26** [r] Ex 13:2, 12 **27:27** [s] ver 11 **27:28** [t] Nu 18:14; Jos 6:17-19

[a] *3* That is, about 1 1/4 pounds or about 575 grams; also in verse 16 [b] *3* That is, about 2/5 ounce or about 12 grams; also in verse 25 [c] *4* That is, about 12 ounces or about 345 grams [d] *5* That is, about 8 ounces or about 230 grams [e] *5* That is, about 4 ounces or about 115 grams; also in verse 7 [f] *6* That is, about 2 ounces or about 58 grams [g] *6* That is, about 1 1/4 ounces or about 35 grams [h] *7* That is, about 6 ounces or about 175 grams [i] *16* That is, probably about 300 pounds or about 135 kilograms [j] *26* The Hebrew word can refer to either male or female. [k] *28* The Hebrew term refers to the irrevocable giving over of things or persons to the LORD.

her as his wife. Compare the post-Biblical Jewish text in the Mishnah, in *Arak* 5:1, which tells how a mother vowed her daughter’s weight in gold and paid it at Jerusalem.

27:3 *the value of a male between the ages of twenty and sixty at fifty shekels of silver.* This expensive valuation of a man in the prime of life (2Ki 15:20; cf. annual wage in Jdg 17:10) would have been reasonable as the price of a male adult slave in Mesopotamia. However, unlike slave prices, the fixed scale here does not fluctuate over time according to market conditions and treats individuals equally by not taking variable factors (e.g., a particular person’s strength or speed) into account, which would affect actual productivity.

27:10 *must not exchange it or substitute.* The Hittite “Instructions to Priests and Temple Officials” forbid cheating the deity by exchanging high-quality animals for inferior ones. The present verse goes further by categorically ruling out any substitution, including even an exchange that could be regarded as upgrading the value: “a good one for a bad one, or a bad one for a good one.” Therefore, there can be no justification based on rationalizing relative values.

27:28 *nothing that a person owns and devotes to the LORD ... may be sold or redeemed.* The paramount type of offering for Yahweh and the sanctuary was called the *herem* or “devoted” offering. Anything presented as *herem* could not be redeemed via payment or substitution. All such material reverted to the priests, whether a field, personal property, animal or human. The totality of the *herem* of the fields or flocks was granted to the priests, and unclean animals not sacrificed or consumed or humans could be used in the service of the sanctuary.

being or an animal or family land — may
be sold or redeemed; everything so devoted is most holy to the LORD.
29 " 'No person devoted to destruction[a]
may be ransomed; they are to be put to
death.
30 " 'A tithe[u] of everything from the land,
whether grain from the soil or fruit from
the trees, belongs to the LORD; it is holy
to the LORD. 31 Whoever would redeem any
of their tithe must add a fifth of the value
to it. 32 Every tithe of the herd and flock —
every tenth animal that passes under the
shepherd's rod[v] — will be holy to the LORD.
33 No one may pick out the good from the
bad or make any substitution.[w] If anyone
does make a substitution, both the animal
and its substitute become holy and cannot
be redeemed.' "

34 These are the commands the LORD
gave Moses at Mount Sinai for the Israelites.[x]

27:30 [u]Ge 28:22; 2Ch 31:6; Mal 3:8
27:32 [v]Jer 33:13; Eze 20:37
27:33 [w]ver 10
27:34 [x]Lev 26:46; Dt 4:5

[a] 29 The Hebrew term refers to the irrevocable giving over of things or persons to the LORD, often by totally destroying them.

THE TORAH

NUMBERS

Geographic Setting

The book of Numbers contains three geographic settings, providing a thematic and theological program for the book. The Desert of Sinai (Nu 1:1 — 10:10) is where the Israelites who had departed from Egypt spent almost a year encamped at the base of Mount Sinai, the mountain of God. There Moses and the Israelites encountered God, received the gift of the law, constructed the tabernacle and its holy furnishings, and prepared for the journey through the wilderness to the promised land. The final location was the plains of Moab, across the Jordan River from Jericho (Nu 22:1 — 36:13), where the second generation of Israelites was prepared for the conquest of their promised inheritance in the land of Canaan. The Israelites journeyed for more than 38 years through several rugged wilderness regions between Mount Sinai and the plains of Moab (the second setting: chs. 10:11 — 21:35).

KEY CONCEPTS

- Some generations fail and lose benefits and privileges, but God faithfully offers new opportunities for faithfulness.
- Submission to God and trust in his plan and provision are essential to God's people.

Historical Setting

Archaeologists and historians date the Israelite wilderness sojourn to the middle or latter part of the Late Bronze Age (1550 – 1200 BC) in the ancient Near East. The world of Egypt, the eastern Mediterranean and Mesopotamia experienced dramatic political and territorial transitions during this era. Egypt would conquer the lands of Canaan and beyond under the Eighteenth Dynasty kings Thutmose I and Thutmose III, but Egyptian power would diminish under the reign of Amenhotep IV/Akhenaton. During the fifteenth century BC, Egypt exacted extensive political and economic control over the region extending to the Hittite border to the north. Yet in the fourteenth century BC, as the Amarna letters reflect, the Egyptians experienced a significant loss of power among loyal Canaanite puppet-kings due to invasions from the Hapiru, Shasu and other marauding bands. Then the Nineteenth Dynasty kings Seti I and Ramses II restored the Egyptian hegemony over much of Canaan, having established a boundary with the Hittites at Qadesh on the Orontes River.

The importance of this information is that whatever the specific dates of these events (see the article "Historicity of the Exodus," p. 116), God delivered the Israelites from Egypt during the reign of a powerful pharaoh who oversaw a vast empire that stretched through much of the land of Canaan. The wilderness sojourn in the Sinai wilderness as described in the book of Numbers came at a time when Egyptian focus was on maintaining the lucrative trade routes through northern Sinai and into Canaan. The southern two-thirds of the Sinai region was less in focus during this era. Thus the Israelites' experiences with God were less likely to be impacted by the imperial pursuits of her former taskmasters. ◆

The Census

1 The LORD spoke to Moses in the tent
of meeting[a] in the Desert of Sinai[b] on
the first day of the second month[c] of the
second year after the Israelites came out
of Egypt. He said: 2"Take a census[d] of the
whole Israelite community by their clans
and families, listing every man by name,
one by one. 3You and Aaron are to count
according to their divisions all the men in
Israel who are twenty years old or more[e]
and able to serve in the army. 4One man
from each tribe, each of them the head of
his family,[f] is to help you.[g] 5These are the
names of the men who are to assist you:

from Reuben,[h] Elizur son of Shedeur;
6 from Simeon, Shelumiel son of Zurishaddai;
7 from Judah,[i] Nahshon son of Amminadab;[j]
8 from Issachar,[k] Nethanel son of Zuar;
9 from Zebulun,[l] Eliab son of Helon;
10 from the sons of Joseph:
from Ephraim,[m] Elishama son of Ammihud;
from Manasseh, Gamaliel son of Pedahzur;
11 from Benjamin, Abidan son of Gideoni;
12 from Dan,[n] Ahiezer son of Ammishaddai;
13 from Asher,[o] Pagiel son of Okran;
14 from Gad, Eliasaph son of Deuel;[p]
15 from Naphtali,[q] Ahira son of Enan."

16These were the men appointed from
the community, the leaders[r] of their ancestral tribes. They were the heads of the
clans of Israel.[s]
17Moses and Aaron took these men
whose names had been specified, 18and
they called the whole community together
on the first day of the second month.[t] The
people registered their ancestry[u] by their
clans and families, and the men twenty
years old or more were listed by name,
one by one, 19as the LORD commanded Moses. And so he counted them in the Desert
of Sinai:

20 From the descendants of Reuben[v] the firstborn son of Israel:
All the men twenty years old or more who were able to serve in the army were listed by name, one by one, according to the records of their clans and families. 21The number from the tribe of Reuben was 46,500.

22 From the descendants of Simeon:[w]
All the men twenty years old or more who were able to serve in the army were counted and listed by name, one by one, according to the records of their clans and families. 23The number from the tribe of Simeon was 59,300.

24 From the descendants of Gad:[x]
All the men twenty years old or more who were able to serve in the army were listed by name, according to the records of their clans and families. 25The number from the tribe of Gad was 45,650.

26 From the descendants of Judah:[y]
All the men twenty years old or more who were able to serve in the army were listed by name, according to the records of their clans and families. 27The number from the tribe of Judah was 74,600.

28 From the descendants of Issachar:[z]
All the men twenty years old or more who were able to serve in the army were listed by name, according to the records of their clans and families. 29The number from the tribe of Issachar was 54,400.

30 From the descendants of Zebulun:[a]
All the men twenty years old or more who were able to serve in the army were listed by name, according to

1:1 [a] Ex 40:2 [b] Ex 19:1 [c] Ex 40:17 **1:2** [d] Ex 30:11-16; Nu 26:2 **1:3** [e] Ex 30:14 **1:4** [f] ver 16 [g] Ex 18:21; Dt 1:15 **1:5** [h] Ge 29:32; Dt 33:6; Rev 7:5 **1:7** [i] Ge 29:35; Ps 78:68 [j] Ru 4:20; 1Ch 2:10; Lk 3:32 **1:8** [k] Ge 30:18 **1:9** [l] ver 30 **1:10** [m] ver 32 **1:12** [n] ver 38 **1:13** [o] ver 40 **1:14** [p] Nu 2:14 **1:15** [q] ver 42 **1:16** [r] Ex 18:25 [s] ver 4; Ex 18:21; Nu 7:2 **1:18** [t] ver 1 [u] Ezr 2:59; Heb 7:3 **1:20** [v] Nu 26:5-11; Rev 7:5 **1:22** [w] Nu 26:12-14; Rev 7:7 **1:24** [x] Ge 30:11; Nu 26:15-18; Rev 7:5 **1:26** [y] Ge 29:35; Nu 26:19-22; Mt 1:2; Rev 7:5 **1:28** [z] Nu 26:23-25; Rev 7:7 **1:30** [a] Nu 26:26-27; Rev 7:8

1:1 *tent of meeting.* See note on Ex 33:7. *Sinai.* See the article "Mount Sinai," p. 144. *first day of the second month of the second year.* This chronological statement places the military conscription census during a New Moon feast, a year and two weeks after the exodus, which took place on fourteenth of Aviv (= Nisan), the first month. A comparison with Ex 40 reveals that the tabernacle had been up for a month and the people had been camped at Sinai for nearly a year.
1:2 *Take a census.* A census for military conscription purposes was common in the Bible and texts of the ancient Near East (cf. ch. 26; 2Sa 24:1–17; 1Ch 21:1–17). In numerous other cases, a simple total of the military conscripted for battle is given. The census involved a head count—the idiomatic Hebrew terminology reads lit. "lift up the head" and "every male by their skulls"—of capable military men, age 20 years and up.

A troop census before going to battle was common in the warfare plans of ancient Sumer, Akkad and Assyria. Sargon of Akkad (c. 2350 BC) had an army of 5,400 who dined at his table after victories in Amurru. His son and heir to the throne fought with armies of 10,000 or more. In terms of the sizes of armies conquered, Shalmaneser I (c. 1275–1245 BC) claims to have slaughtered 14,400 Hittites and Ahlamu troops. Numbers may at times be exaggerated depending on the type of document; e.g., it would not be unusual for an inscription to inflate the number of enemy casualties.
1:3 *twenty years old or more.* Twenty years of age was the accepted age of full maturity in the Bible for military conscription (cf. 26:2; 2Ch 25:5), even though marriage often took place in a young man's late teens.

the records of their clans and families. 31The number from the tribe of
Zebulun was 57,400.

32 From the sons of Joseph:
From the descendants of Ephraim:[b]
All the men twenty years old or
more who were able to serve in the
army were listed by name, according to the records of their clans and
families. 33The number from the
tribe of Ephraim was 40,500.

34 From the descendants of Manasseh:[c]
All the men twenty years old or
more who were able to serve in the
army were listed by name, according to the records of their clans and
families. 35The number from the
tribe of Manasseh was 32,200.

36 From the descendants of Benjamin:[d]
All the men twenty years old or
more who were able to serve in the
army were listed by name, according to the records of their clans and
families. 37The number from the
tribe of Benjamin was 35,400.

38 From the descendants of Dan:[e]
All the men twenty years old or
more who were able to serve in the
army were listed by name, according to the records of their clans and
families. 39The number from the
tribe of Dan was 62,700.

40 From the descendants of Asher:[f]
All the men twenty years old or
more who were able to serve in the
army were listed by name, according to the records of their clans and
families. 41The number from the
tribe of Asher was 41,500.

42 From the descendants of Naphtali:[g]
All the men twenty years old or
more who were able to serve in the
army were listed by name, according to the records of their clans and
families. 43The number from the
tribe of Naphtali was 53,400.

44These were the men counted by Moses
and Aaron[h] and the twelve leaders of Israel, each one representing his family. 45All
the Israelites twenty years old or more
who were able to serve in Israel's army
were counted according to their families.
46The total number was 603,550.[i]
47The ancestral tribe of the Levites,[j]
however, was not counted[k] along with
the others. 48The LORD had said to Moses:
49"You must not count the tribe of Levi or
include them in the census of the other
Israelites. 50Instead, appoint the Levites to
be in charge of the tabernacle of the covenant law[l] — over all its furnishings and
everything belonging to it. They are to carry the tabernacle and all its furnishings;
they are to take care of it and encamp
around it. 51Whenever the tabernacle is to
move, the Levites are to take it down, and
whenever the tabernacle is to be set up,
the Levites shall do it.[m] Anyone else who
approaches it is to be put to death. 52The
Israelites are to set up their tents by divisions, each of them in their own camp
under their standard.[n] 53The Levites, however, are to set up their tents around the
tabernacle of the covenant law so that my
wrath will not fall[o] on the Israelite community. The Levites are to be responsible
for the care of the tabernacle of the covenant law.[p]"
54The Israelites did all this just as the
LORD commanded Moses.

The Arrangement of the Tribal Camps

2 The LORD said to Moses and Aaron:
2"The Israelites are to camp around
the tent of meeting some distance from it,
each of them under their standard[q] and
holding the banners of their family."

3On the east, toward the sunrise,
the divisions of the camp of Judah
are to encamp under their standard.
The leader of the people of Judah is
Nahshon son of Amminadab.[r] 4His division numbers 74,600.
5The tribe of Issachar will camp
next to them. The leader of the people
of Issachar is Nethanel son of Zuar.[s]
6His division numbers 54,400.
7The tribe of Zebulun will be next.

1:32 [b] Nu 26:35-37
1:34 [c] Nu 26:28-34; Rev 7:6
1:36 [d] Nu 26:38-41; 2Ch 17:17; Rev 7:8
1:38 [e] Ge 30:6; Nu 26:42-43
1:40 [f] Nu 26:44-47; Rev 7:6
1:42 [g] Nu 26:48-50; Rev 7:6
1:44 [h] Nu 26:64
1:46 [i] Ex 12:37; 38:26; Nu 2:32; 26:51
1:47 [j] Nu 2:33; 26:57 [k] Nu 4:3, 49
1:50 [l] Ex 38:21; Ac 7:44
1:51 [m] Nu 3:38; 4:1-33
1:52 [n] Nu 2:2; Ps 20:5
1:53 [o] Lev 10:6; Nu 16:46; 18:5 [p] Nu 18:2-4
2:2 [q] Nu 1:52; Ps 74:4; Isa 31:9
2:3 [r] Nu 10:14; Ru 4:20; 1Ch 2:10
2:5 [s] Nu 1:8

1:47 – 51 The three clans of the Levites are not counted in the military conscription census because of their noncombatant role. Priests in ancient Near Eastern societies were similarly not required to carry arms in battle but served to carry symbols of the national deity(s) into battle and do other nonfighting functions. Though the Levites are not technically priests — that position is restricted to those in the direct line of Aaron — they perform duties similar to those in the priestly circles of ancient Ugarit, Mari, Emar, Assyria and Babylon.

The duty of the Levites is to restrict access to the tabernacle. Ancient sanctuaries were not public worship centers but residences of deity. In Hittite and Mari texts the priests also served as guards. In Babylon the temple was believed to be guarded by demons or protective spirits.

1:52 *standard.* Comparison of the Hebrew *degel* with the usage of Akkadian terms *dagalu* and *diglu* in the second millennium BC suggests that this is something that was seen (e.g., a banner or flag) and served as an identity feature for the given tribal troop unit. In later Hebrew and Aramaic this term refers to a military troop unit of a thousand men who lived together with their families and functioned as a legal and economic entity.

NUMBERS 1:46

Numbers in Numbers

The large numbers in Exodus and Numbers have long posed problems for interpreters. With an able militia of over 600,000 and an additional population of 22,273 Levites, the total population of Israel coming out of Egypt would have easily exceeded two million (cf. Ex 12:37; 38:26; Nu 11:21). Internal evidence from the Bible and external data both cause considerable difficulty in accepting these figures at face value. The numbering of the Levites at 22,000 for the redemption of the firstborn of Israel's males (well over 603,550 [Nu 1:46], if firstborn males under age 20 are included) would mean that the average Israelite woman bore more than 27 males, plus females. In the OT the largest number of males born to a single male (Jacob) is 12, and they were through multiple wives and concubines (Ge 29:31 — 30:22; 35:18,22 - 36). Dt 7:1 describes "seven nations larger and stronger than you [Israel]" in the promised land, whom the Lord would drive out from before the Israelites. If Israel were two million, this figure would yield an aggregate population of Canaan of 15 - 20 million, far more than the modern population of the region. The optimum estimates of the total population of the region in the Late Bronze Age and Iron I period that have come as a result of archaeological surveys and demographic distribution studies come to less than one million.

Thus, evangelical scholars have suggested several possible solutions: (1) The figures represent hyperbole to show the fulfillment of God's promise to make a nation through Abraham that would be as numerous as the stars in the heavens (Ge 13:16; 15:5). (2) Comparison of this military census with those of Assyrian and Babylonian military conscription texts suggests that such figures were used to demonstrate the power of ancient kings in their conquest annals (see note on Ex 14:7). (3) The Hebrew term translated "thousand" (*elep*) has been taken to mean "military unit" (vocalized *'allup*, from the same Semitic root); hence the total would be 598 units yielding a total militia of 5,550 combat-ready soldiers in Nu 1 and 5,730 men in 596 units in the second census of Nu 26.

Another possibility is that an epic narrative such as this was expected, by the literati of the ancient world, to use numbers for their rhetorical value — i.e., for stylistic effect — rather than to communicate mathematical precision, especially regarding the numbers of the protagonist's army. In the Kirta epic from Ugarit, the main character, Kirta, leads an army of three million men, and many of the epic's features (e.g., religious rituals and sacrifices, a journey interrupted by a stopover at a sacred site) show similarities to those of the exodus story. This Ugaritic work has clearly put its numbers to use as rhetorical devices. It is certainly plausible to conclude that the Biblical text has as well, as long as we consider that the ancient reader would have recognized this as a rhetorical device. ◆

The leader of the people of Zebulun
is Eliab son of Helon.[t] [8]His division
numbers 57,400.

[9]All the men assigned to the camp
of Judah, according to their divisions,
number 186,400. They will set out
first.[u]

[10]On the south will be the divisions
of the camp of Reuben under their
standard. The leader of the people
of Reuben is Elizur son of Shedeur.[v]
[11]His division numbers 46,500.

[12]The tribe of Simeon will camp
next to them. The leader of the people of Simeon is Shelumiel son of Zurishaddai.[w] [13]His division numbers
59,300.

[14]The tribe of Gad will be next.
The leader of the people of Gad is

2:7 [t]Nu 1:9
2:9 [u]Nu 10:14
2:10 [v]Nu 1:5
2:12 [w]Nu 1:6

ENCAMPMENT OF THE TRIBES OF ISRAEL

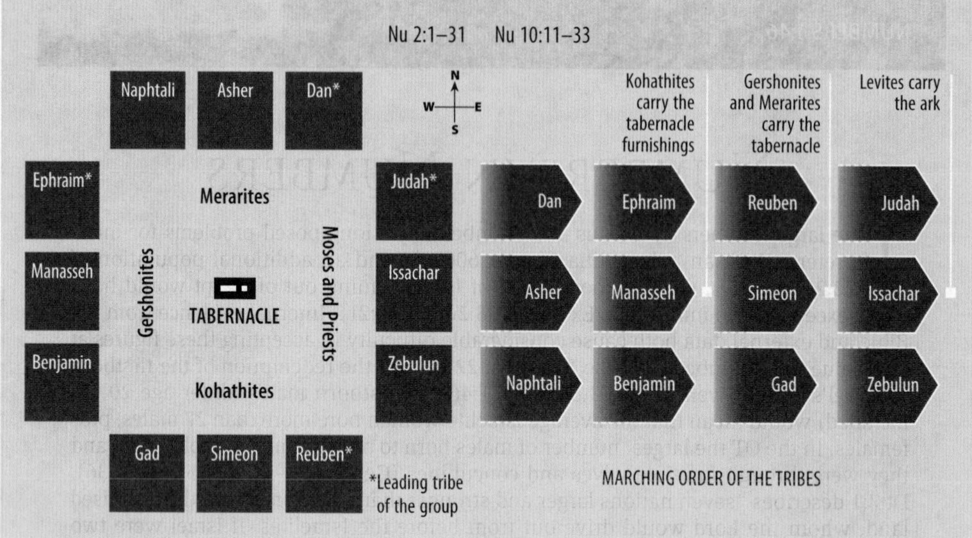

Eliasaph son of Deuel.[a x] 15His division numbers 45,650.
16All the men assigned to the camp
of Reuben,[y] according to their divisions, number 151,450. They will set
out second.
17Then the tent of meeting and the
camp of the Levites[z] will set out in
the middle of the camps. They will
set out in the same order as they encamp, each in their own place under
their standard.
18On the west will be the divisions
of the camp of Ephraim[a] under their
standard. The leader of the people of
Ephraim is Elishama son of Ammihud.[b] 19His division numbers 40,500.
20The tribe of Manasseh will be
next to them. The leader of the people of Manasseh is Gamaliel son of
Pedahzur.[c] 21His division numbers
32,200.
22The tribe of Benjamin will be
next. The leader of the people of
Benjamin is Abidan son of Gideoni.[d]
23His division numbers 35,400.
24All the men assigned to the camp
of Ephraim,[e] according to their divisions, number 108,100. They will set
out third.[f]
25On the north will be the divisions of the camp of Dan under their
standard. The leader of the people of
Dan is Ahiezer son of Ammishaddai.[g]
26His division numbers 62,700.
27The tribe of Asher will camp next
to them. The leader of the people of
Asher is Pagiel son of Okran.[h] 28His
division numbers 41,500.
29The tribe of Naphtali will be next.
The leader of the people of Naphtali
is Ahira son of Enan.[i] 30His division
numbers 53,400.
31All the men assigned to the camp
of Dan number 157,600. They will set
out last,[j] under their standards.
32These are the Israelites, counted
according to their families. All the
men in the camps, by their divisions,
number 603,550.[k] 33The Levites, however, were not counted[l] along with
the other Israelites, as the LORD commanded Moses.
34So the Israelites did everything the
LORD commanded Moses; that is the way
they encamped under their standards, and
that is the way they set out, each of them
with their clan and family.

The Levites

3 This is the account of the family of
Aaron and Moses[m] at the time the
LORD spoke to Moses at Mount Sinai.
2The names of the sons of Aaron were

2:14 [x] Nu 1:14
2:16 [y] Nu 10:18
2:17 [z] Nu 1:53; 10:21
2:18 [a] Ge 48:20; Jer 31:18-20 [b] Nu 1:10
2:20 [c] Nu 1:10
2:22 [d] Nu 1:11; Ps 68:27
2:24 [e] Nu 10:22 [f] Ps 80:2
2:25 [g] Nu 1:12
2:27 [h] Nu 1:13
2:29 [i] Nu 1:15
2:31 [j] Nu 10:25
2:32 [k] Ex 38:26; Nu 1:46
2:33 [l] Nu 1:47; 26:57-62
3:1 [m] Ex 6:27

[a] *14* Many manuscripts of the Masoretic Text, Samaritan Pentateuch and Vulgate (see also 1:14); most manuscripts of the Masoretic Text *Reuel*

3:1 *the account of the family.* See the article "Genealogies," p. 16.

3:2 *firstborn.* See the article "Inheritance Rights and Birthrights," p. 62.

Nadab the firstborn and Abihu, Eleazar and Ithamar.[n] 3 Those were the names of Aaron's sons, the anointed priests,[o] who were ordained to serve as priests. 4 Nadab and Abihu, however, died before the LORD[p] when they made an offering with unauthorized fire before him in the Desert of Sinai.[q] They had no sons, so Eleazar and Ithamar served as priests during the lifetime of their father Aaron.[r]

5 The LORD said to Moses, 6 "Bring the tribe of Levi[s] and present them to Aaron the priest to assist him.[t] 7 They are to perform duties for him and for the whole community at the tent of meeting by doing the work[u] of the tabernacle. 8 They are to take care of all the furnishings of the tent of meeting, fulfilling the obligations of the Israelites by doing the work of the tabernacle. 9 Give the Levites to Aaron and his sons;[v] they are the Israelites who are to be given wholly to him.[a] 10 Appoint Aaron and his sons to serve as priests;[w] anyone else who approaches the sanctuary is to be put to death."[x]

11 The LORD also said to Moses, 12 "I have taken the Levites[y] from among the Israelites in place of the first male offspring[z] of every Israelite woman. The Levites are mine,[a] 13 for all the firstborn are mine.[b] When I struck down all the firstborn in Egypt, I set apart for myself every firstborn in Israel, whether human or animal. They are to be mine. I am the LORD."

14 The LORD said to Moses in the Desert of Sinai, 15 "Count[c] the Levites by their families and clans. Count every male a month old or more."[d] 16 So Moses counted them, as he was commanded by the word of the LORD.

17 These were the names of the sons of Levi:[e]

Gershon, Kohath and Merari.[f]

18 These were the names of the Gershonite clans:

Libni and Shimei.[g]

19 The Kohathite clans:

Amram, Izhar, Hebron and Uzziel.[h]

20 The Merarite clans:[i]

Mahli and Mushi.[j]

These were the Levite clans, according to their families.

21 To Gershon belonged the clans of the Libnites and Shimeites;[k] these were the Gershonite clans. 22 The number of all the males a month old or more who were counted was 7,500. 23 The Gershonite clans were to camp on the west, behind the tabernacle. 24 The leader of the families of the Gershonites was Eliasaph son of Lael. 25 At the tent of meeting the Gershonites were responsible for the care of the tabernacle[l] and tent, its coverings,[m] the curtain at the entrance[n] to the tent of meeting, 26 the curtains of the courtyard[o], the curtain at the entrance to the courtyard surrounding the tabernacle and altar, and the ropes[p] — and everything related to their use.

27 To Kohath belonged the clans of the Amramites, Izharites, Hebronites and Uzzielites;[q] these were the Kohathite clans. 28 The number of all the males a month old or more was 8,600.[b] The Kohathites were responsible for the care of the sanctuary. 29 The Kohathite clans were to camp on the south side[r] of the tabernacle. 30 The leader of the families of the Kohathite clans was Elizaphan son of Uzziel. 31 They were responsible for the care of the ark,[s] the table,[t] the lampstand,[u] the altars,[v] the articles of the sanctuary used in ministering, the curtain,[w] and everything related to their use.[x] 32 The chief leader of the Levites was Eleazar son of Aaron, the priest. He was appointed over those who were responsible for the care of the sanctuary.

33 To Merari belonged the clans of the Mahlites and the Mushites;[y] these were the Merarite clans. 34 The number of all the males a month old or more who were counted was 6,200. 35 The leader of the families of the Merarite clans was Zuriel son of Abihail; they were to camp on the north side of the tabernacle.[z] 36 The Merarites were appointed[a] to take care of the frames of the tabernacle, its crossbars, posts, bases, all its equipment, and everything related to their use, 37 as well as the posts of the surrounding courtyard with their bases, tent pegs and ropes.

3:2 [n] Ex 6:23; Nu 26:60 **3:3** [o] Ex 28:41 **3:4** [p] Lev 10:2 [q] Lev 10:1 [r] 1Ch 24:1 **3:6** [s] Dt 10:8; 31:9; 1Ch 15:2 [t] Nu 8:6-22; 18:1-7; 2Ch 29:11 **3:7** [u] Lev 8:35; Nu 1:50 **3:9** [v] Nu 8:19; 18:6 **3:10** [w] Ex 29:9 [x] Nu 1:51 **3:12** [y] Mal 2:4 [z] ver 41; Nu 8:16, 18 [a] Ex 13:2 **3:13** [b] Ex 13:12 **3:15** [c] ver 39 [d] Nu 26:62 **3:17** [e] Ge 46:11 [f] Ex 6:16 **3:18** [g] Ex 6:17 **3:19** [h] Ex 6:18 **3:20** [i] Ge 46:11 [j] Ex 6:19 **3:21** [k] Ex 6:17 **3:25** [l] Ex 25:9 [m] Ex 26:14 [n] Ex 26:36; Nu 4:25 **3:26** [o] Ex 27:9 [p] Ex 35:18 **3:27** [q] 1Ch 26:23 **3:29** [r] Nu 1:53 **3:31** [s] Ex 25:10-22 [t] Ex 25:23 [u] Ex 25:31 [v] Ex 27:1; 30:1 [w] Ex 26:33 [x] Nu 4:15 **3:33** [y] Ex 6:19 **3:35** [z] Nu 1:53; 2:25 **3:36** [a] Nu 4:32

[a] *9* Most manuscripts of the Masoretic Text; some manuscripts of the Masoretic Text, Samaritan Pentateuch and Septuagint (see also 8:16) *to me* [b] *28* Hebrew; some Septuagint manuscripts *8,300*

3:10 *put to death.* The Levites served as guardians of the sanctuary, functioning as a lightning rod for the fiery wrath of God against potential encroachment on the sanctuary. Elsewhere human and divine guardians were positioned to prevent violation of temples and cities; e.g., gargoyles and various creatures in Egypt and Mesopotamia (symbols of divine entities) were positioned at the entrances to temples. Priests at Mari on the Euphrates and at the Hittite capital of Hattusas performed nighttime guard duty, for which improper performance of duty was punishable by death.

3:12 *The Levites are mine.* Rather than having individual clan rights of primogeniture for maintaining the sanctuary and ancestral worship, Israel had an entire tribe dedicated to the proper worship of God. In the exodus event, the Lord commanded that every firstborn male from among humans and animals be dedicated or sacrificed to the Lord as a sign of faithfulness (Ex 13:1 – 16). The Levites became the substitute for the firstborn males of Israel.

38 Moses and Aaron and his sons were to camp to the east[b] of the tabernacle, toward the sunrise, in front of the tent of meeting.[c] They were responsible for the care of the sanctuary[d] on behalf of the Israelites. Anyone else who approached the sanctuary was to be put to death.[e]

39 The total number of Levites counted at the LORD's command by Moses and Aaron according to their clans, including every male a month old or more, was 22,000.[f]

40 The LORD said to Moses, "Count all the firstborn Israelite males who are a month old or more[g] and make a list of their names. 41 Take the Levites for me in place of all the firstborn of the Israelites,[h] and the livestock of the Levites in place of all the firstborn of the livestock of the Israelites. I am the LORD."

42 So Moses counted all the firstborn of the Israelites, as the LORD commanded him. 43 The total number of firstborn males a month old or more, listed by name, was 22,273.[i]

44 The LORD also said to Moses, 45 "Take the Levites in place of all the firstborn of Israel, and the livestock of the Levites in place of their livestock. The Levites are to be mine. I am the LORD. 46 To redeem[j] the 273 firstborn Israelites who exceed the number of the Levites, 47 collect five shekels[a][k] for each one, according to the sanctuary shekel,[l] which weighs twenty gerahs.[m] 48 Give the money for the redemption of the additional Israelites to Aaron and his sons."

49 So Moses collected the redemption money from those who exceeded the number redeemed by the Levites. 50 From the firstborn of the Israelites he collected silver weighing 1,365 shekels,[b][n] according to the sanctuary shekel. 51 Moses gave the redemption money to Aaron and his sons, as he was commanded by the word of the LORD.

The Kohathites

4 The LORD said to Moses and Aaron: 2 "Take a census[o] of the Kohathite branch of the Levites by their clans and families. 3 Count all the men from thirty to fifty years of age[p] who come to serve in the work at the tent of meeting.

4 "This is the work of the Kohathites at the tent of meeting: the care of the most holy things.[q] 5 When the camp is to move, Aaron and his sons are to go in and take down the shielding curtain[r] and put it over the ark of the covenant law.[s] 6 Then they are to cover the curtain with a durable leather,[c] spread a cloth of solid blue over that and put the poles[t] in place.

7 "Over the table of the Presence[u] they are to spread a blue cloth and put on it the plates, dishes and bowls, and the jars for drink offerings; the bread that is continually there[v] is to remain on it. 8 They are to spread a scarlet cloth over them, cover that with the durable leather and put the poles in place.

9 "They are to take a blue cloth and cover the lampstand that is for light, together with its lamps, its wick trimmers and trays,[w] and all its jars for the olive oil used to supply it. 10 Then they are to wrap it and all its accessories in a covering of the durable leather and put it on a carrying frame.

11 "Over the gold altar[x] they are to spread a blue cloth and cover that with the durable leather and put the poles in place.

12 "They are to take all the articles used for ministering in the sanctuary, wrap them in a blue cloth, cover that with the durable leather and put them on a carrying frame.

13 "They are to remove the ashes from the bronze altar[y] and spread a purple cloth over it. 14 Then they are to place on it all the utensils used for ministering at the altar, including the firepans, meat forks,[z] shovels and sprinkling bowls.[a] Over it they are to spread a covering of the durable leather and put the poles[b] in place.

15 "After Aaron and his sons have finished covering the holy furnishings and all the holy articles, and when the camp is ready to move, only then are the Kohathites to come and do the carrying.[c] But they must not touch the holy things or they will die.[d] The Kohathites are to carry those things that are in the tent of meeting.

16 "Eleazar[e] son of Aaron, the priest, is to have charge of the oil for the light,[f] the fragrant incense, the regular grain offering[g] and the anointing oil. He is to be in charge of the entire tabernacle and everything in it, including its holy furnishings and articles."

17 The LORD said to Moses and Aaron, 18 "See that the Kohathite tribal clans are not destroyed from among the Levites. 19 So that they may live and not die when they come near the most holy things,[h] do this for them: Aaron and his sons are to go into the sanctuary and assign to each man his work and what he is to carry. 20 But the Kohathites must not go in to look[i] at the holy things, even for a moment, or they will die."

3:38 [b] Nu 2:3 [c] Nu 1:53 [d] ver 7; Nu 18:5 [e] ver 10; Nu 1:51 **3:39** [f] Nu 26:62 **3:40** [g] ver 15 **3:41** [h] ver 12 **3:43** [i] ver 39 **3:46** [j] Ex 13:13; Nu 18:15 **3:47** [k] Lev 27:6 [l] Ex 30:13 [m] Lev 27:25 **3:50** [n] ver 46-48 **4:2** [o] Ex 30:12 **4:3** [p] ver 23; Nu 8:25; 1Ch 23:3,24,27; Ezr 3:8 **4:4** [q] ver 19 **4:5** [r] Ex 26:31,33 [s] Ex 25:10,16

4:6 [t] Ex 25:13-15; 1Ki 8:7; 2Ch 5:8 **4:7** [u] Ex 25:23,29; Lev 24:6 [v] Ex 25:30 **4:9** [w] Ex 25:31,37,38 **4:11** [x] Ex 30:1 **4:13** [y] Ex 27:1-8 **4:14** [z] 2Ch 4:16 [a] Jer 52:18 [b] Ex 27:6 **4:15** [c] Nu 7:9 [d] Nu 1:51; 2Sa 6:6,7 **4:16** [e] Lev 10:6 [f] Ex 25:6 [g] Ex 29:41; Lev 6:14-23 **4:19** [h] ver 15 **4:20** [i] Ex 19:21; 1Sa 6:19

[a] *47* That is, about 2 ounces or about 58 grams
[b] *50* That is, about 35 pounds or about 16 kilograms
[c] *6* Possibly the hides of large aquatic mammals; also in verses 8, 10, 11, 12, 14 and 25

3:48 *money for the redemption.* See note on Ex 13:15.

4:6 *durable leather.* See note on Ex 26:14.

The Gershonites

21 The LORD said to Moses, 22 "Take a census also of the Gershonites by their families and clans. 23 Count all the men from thirty to fifty years of age[j] who come to serve in the work at the tent of meeting.

24 "This is the service of the Gershonite clans in their carrying and their other work: 25 They are to carry the curtains of the tabernacle,[k] that is, the tent of meeting,[l] its covering[m] and its outer covering of durable leather, the curtains for the entrance to the tent of meeting, 26 the curtains of the courtyard surrounding the tabernacle and altar, the curtain for the entrance to the courtyard, the ropes and all the equipment used in the service of the tent. The Gershonites are to do all that needs to be done with these things. 27 All their service, whether carrying or doing other work, is to be done under the direction of Aaron and his sons. You shall assign to them as their responsibility all they are to carry. 28 This is the service of the Gershonite clans[n] at the tent of meeting. Their duties are to be under the direction of Ithamar son of Aaron, the priest.

The Merarites

29 "Count the Merarites by their clans and families.[o] 30 Count all the men from thirty to fifty years of age who come to serve in the work at the tent of meeting. 31 As part of all their service at the tent, they are to carry the frames of the tabernacle, its crossbars, posts and bases,[p] 32 as well as the posts of the surrounding courtyard with their bases, tent pegs, ropes, all their equipment and everything related to their use. Assign to each man the specific things he is to carry. 33 This is the service of the Merarite clans as they work at the tent of meeting under the direction of Ithamar son of Aaron, the priest."

The Numbering of the Levite Clans

34 Moses, Aaron and the leaders of the community counted the Kohathites[q] by their clans and families. 35 All the men from thirty to fifty years of age who came to serve in the work at the tent of meeting, 36 counted by clans, were 2,750. 37 This was the total of all those in the Kohathite clans[r] who served at the tent of meeting. Moses and Aaron counted them according to the LORD's command through Moses.

38 The Gershonites[s] were counted by their clans and families. 39 All the men from thirty to fifty years of age who came to serve in the work at the tent of meeting, 40 counted by their clans and families, were 2,630. 41 This was the total of those in the Gershonite clans who served at the tent of meeting. Moses and Aaron counted them according to the LORD's command.

42 The Merarites were counted by their clans and families. 43 All the men from thirty to fifty years of age who came to serve in the work at the tent of meeting, 44 counted by their clans, were 3,200. 45 This was the total of those in the Merarite clans.[t] Moses and Aaron counted them according to the LORD's command through Moses.

46 So Moses, Aaron and the leaders of Israel counted all the Levites by their clans and families. 47 All the men from thirty to fifty years of age[u] who came to do the work of serving and carrying the tent of meeting 48 numbered 8,580.[v] 49 At the LORD's command through Moses, each was assigned his work and told what to carry.

Thus they were counted,[w] as the LORD commanded Moses.

The Purity of the Camp

5 The LORD said to Moses, 2 "Command the Israelites to send away from the camp anyone who has a defiling skin disease[a][x] or a discharge[y] of any kind, or who is ceremonially unclean[z] because of a dead body. 3 Send away male and female alike; send them outside the camp so they will not defile their camp, where I dwell among them.[a]" 4 The Israelites did so; they sent them outside the camp. They did just as the LORD had instructed Moses.

Restitution for Wrongs

5 The LORD said to Moses, 6 "Say to the Israelites: 'Any man or woman who wrongs another in any way[b] and so is unfaithful[b] to the LORD is guilty[c] 7 and must confess[d] the sin they have committed. They must make full restitution[e] for the wrong they have done, add a fifth of the value to it and give it all to the person they have

4:23 [j] ver 3; 1Ch 23:3,24,27 **4:25** [k] Ex 27:10-18; Nu 3:26 [l] Nu 3:25 [m] Ex 26:14 **4:28** [n] Nu 7:7 **4:29** [o] Ge 46:11 **4:31** [p] Nu 3:36 **4:34** [q] ver 2 **4:37** [r] Nu 3:27

4:38 [s] Ge 46:11 **4:45** [t] ver 29 **4:47** [u] ver 3 **4:48** [v] Nu 3:39 **4:49** [w] Nu 1:47 **5:2** [x] Lev 13:46 [y] Lev 15:2; Mt 9:20 [z] Lev 13:3; Nu 9:6-10 **5:3** [a] Lev 26:12; Nu 35:34; 2Co 6:16 **5:6** [b] Lev 6:2 [c] Lev 5:14-6:7 **5:7** [d] Lev 5:5; 26:40; Jos 7:19; Lk 19:8 [e] Lev 6:5

[a] 2 The Hebrew word for *defiling skin disease,* traditionally translated "leprosy," was used for various diseases affecting the skin. [b] 6 Or *woman who commits any wrong common to mankind*

5:1–4 The sacred camp of Israel has been numbered and organized with concentric circles of holiness; the priests and Levites constituted the first level of human presence in proximity to the sanctuary (the tent of meeting). The 12 tribes encamped symmetrically around the central sanctuary and its attendants constituted the second level of human presence in the camp. Now the next level of the encampment is described in terms of relative cultic isolation on the perimeter of the camp of those with various impurities.

5:2 *defiling skin disease.* See note on Ex 4:6. *ceremonially unclean.* See note on Lev 21:1.

5:7 *full restitution.* The sanctity of the community applies to economic relationships, whereby monetary compensation

wronged. 8But if that person has no close
relative to whom restitution can be made
for the wrong, the restitution belongs to
the LORD and must be given to the priest,
along with the ram with which atonement
is made for the wrongdoer.[f] 9All the sacred contributions the Israelites bring to a
priest will belong to him.[g] 10Sacred things
belong to their owners, but what they give
to the priest will belong to the priest.[h]' "

The Test for an Unfaithful Wife

11Then the LORD said to Moses, 12"Speak
to the Israelites and say to them: 'If a
man's wife goes astray[i] and is unfaithful
to him 13so that another man has sexual
relations with her,[j] and this is hidden from
her husband and her impurity is undetected (since there is no witness against her
and she has not been caught in the act),
14and if feelings of jealousy[k] come over
her husband and he suspects his wife and
she is impure—or if he is jealous and suspects her even though she is not impure—
15then he is to take his wife to the priest.
He must also take an offering of a tenth of
an ephah[a][l] of barley flour[m] on her behalf.
He must not pour olive oil on it or put incense on it, because it is a grain offering
for jealousy, a reminder-offering[n] to draw
attention to wrongdoing.
16" 'The priest shall bring her and have
her stand before the LORD. 17Then he shall
take some holy water in a clay jar and put
some dust from the tabernacle floor into
the water. 18After the priest has had the
woman stand before the LORD, he shall
loosen her hair[o] and place in her hands
the reminder-offering, the grain offering
for jealousy, while he himself holds the
bitter water that brings a curse. 19Then the
priest shall put the woman under oath and
say to her, "If no other man has had sexual
relations with you and you have not gone
astray[p] and become impure while married
to your husband, may this bitter water
that brings a curse not harm you. 20But
if you have gone astray[q] while married to
your husband and you have made yourself
impure by having sexual relations with a
man other than your husband"— 21here
the priest is to put the woman under this
curse[r]—"may the LORD cause you to become a curse[b] among your people when
he makes your womb miscarry and your
abdomen swell. 22May this water[s] that
brings a curse[t] enter your body so that
your abdomen swells or your womb mis-
carries."
" 'Then the woman is to say, "Amen. So
be it.[u]"
23" 'The priest is to write these curses
on a scroll[v] and then wash them off into
the bitter water. 24He shall make the woman drink the bitter water that brings a
curse, and this water that brings a curse
and causes bitter suffering will enter her.
25The priest is to take from her hands the
grain offering for jealousy, wave it before
the LORD[w] and bring it to the altar. 26The

5:8 [f]Lev 6:6, 7; 7:7
5:9 [g]Lev 6:17; 7:6-14
5:10 [h]Lev 10:13
5:12 [i]Ex 20:14
5:13 [j]Lev 18:20; 20:10
5:14 [k]Pr 6:34; SS 8:6
5:15 [l]Ex 16:36 [m]Lev 6:20 [n]Eze 29:16
5:18 [o]Lev 10:6; 1Co 11:6
5:19 [p]ver 12, 29
5:20 [q]ver 12
5:21 [r]Jos 6:26; 1Sa 14:24; Ne 10:29
5:22 [s]Ps 109:18 [t]ver 18 [u]Dt 27:15
5:23 [v]Jer 45:1
5:25 [w]Lev 8:27

[a] *15* That is, probably about 3 1/2 pounds or about 1.6 kilograms [b] *21* That is, may he cause your name to be used in cursing (see Jer. 29:22); or, may others see that you are cursed; similarly in verse 27.

for fraud or extortion between individuals provides stability and justice in society. By comparison, the Code of Hammurapi called for restitution penalties ranging from one-sixth of the value to 100 percent of the value in addition to the principal amount of the damage incurred for defrauding another person under oath. For example, if a person deposited gold or silver with another person in the presence of witnesses and later denied the transaction, the witnesses would be called to testify on behalf of the depositor, and the repayment would then be double the original amount (Lev 6:1–7).

5:11–31 This particular case concerns a woman suspected by her husband of having an adulterous affair. In Mesopotamian law, as well as Biblical law, if a man or a woman was caught having intercourse with another's spouse, they were both executed. Two laws from the Code of Hammurapi relate to cases of suspected but unobserved adultery. One contains a trial by ordeal, in which the woman is thrown to the divine realm of the river gods: "If a citizen charges a woman with adultery, but has no evidence, then she is to be tried by ordeal in the river to restore the honor of her husband. If she survives she must pay a fine." Another focuses on false accusation by a husband, whereby the woman must simply swear an oath of innocence: "If a citizen falsely accuses his wife of adultery, and she swears an oath of innocence before the divine patron of her household, then she may return home." In both cases ultimate adjudication is rendered into the hands of the divine. See the article "Penalties for Sexual Offenses in Biblical and Mesopotamian Law," p. 216, for a comparison of Biblical and ancient Near Eastern policies concerning sexual offenses.

5:15 *barley flour.* The *shurpu* purification ritual from Assur of the Middle Babylonian Period (c. 1350–1050 BC) used flour in relation to a variety of misdemeanors, including a case in which a man had intercourse with a neighbor's wife (2.48). A "magic circle of flour" was placed around a brazier, then wiped over the offender in an atonement (*ukappar*) ritual. This act was accompanied by several sympathetic magic rituals involving onions, dates, matting and wool, which were then thrown into the brazier's fire with some of the flour.

5:18 *loosen her hair.* The unbinding of one's hair was a sign of mourning or disgrace (Lev 10:6; 13:45; 21:10). In ancient Greek literature, the loosening of the hair was a sign of one's unmarried state or a potential sign of freedom, including sexual immorality and eroticism, but similar customs are not evident in the ancient Near East.

5:24 *drink the bitter water.* From the archives of Mari comes a case in which a water potion made with dirt from the gate of the city is consumed by the accused and then is followed by an oath before the gods. Water mixed with dust may not be bitter to the physical taste, which would normally be alkaline, but bitter in terms of the potential distress and bitterness of the life situation being tried.

priest is then to take a handful of the grain offering as a memorial[a] offering and burn it on the altar; after that, he is to have the woman drink the water. 27 If she has made herself impure and been unfaithful to her husband, this will be the result: When she is made to drink the water that brings a curse and causes bitter suffering, it will enter her, her abdomen will swell and her womb will miscarry, and she will become a curse.[x] 28 If, however, the woman has not made herself impure, but is clean, she will be cleared of guilt and will be able to have children.

29 " 'This, then, is the law of jealousy when a woman goes astray[y] and makes herself impure while married to her husband, 30 or when feelings of jealousy come over a man because he suspects his wife. The priest is to have her stand before the LORD and is to apply this entire law to her. 31 The husband will be innocent of any wrongdoing, but the woman will bear the consequences[z] of her sin.' "

The Nazirite

6 The LORD said to Moses, 2 "Speak to the Israelites and say to them: 'If a man or woman wants to make a special vow[a], a vow of dedication to the LORD as a Nazirite,[b] 3 they must abstain from wine[c] and other fermented drink and must not drink vinegar[d] made from wine or other fermented drink. They must not drink grape juice or eat grapes or raisins. 4 As long as they remain under their Nazirite vow, they must not eat anything that comes from the grapevine, not even the seeds or skins.

5 " 'During the entire period of their Nazirite vow, no razor[e] may be used on their head.[f] They must be holy until the period of their dedication to the LORD is over; they must let their hair grow long.

6 " 'Throughout the period of their dedication to the LORD, the Nazirite must not go near a dead body.[g] 7 Even if their own father or mother or brother or sister dies, they must not make themselves ceremonially unclean[h] on account of them, because the symbol of their dedication to God is on their head. 8 Throughout the period of their dedication, they are consecrated to the LORD.

9 " 'If someone dies suddenly in the Nazirite's presence, thus defiling the hair that symbolizes their dedication,[i] they must shave their head on the seventh day—the day of their cleansing.[j] 10 Then on the eighth day they must bring two doves or two young pigeons[k] to the priest at the entrance to the tent of meeting. 11 The priest is to offer one as a sin offering[b] and the other as a burnt offering[l] to make atonement[m] for the Nazirite because they sinned by being in the presence of the dead body. That same day they are to consecrate their head again. 12 They must rededicate themselves to the LORD for the same period of dedication and must bring a year-old male lamb as a guilt offering. The previous days do not count, because they became defiled during their period of dedication.

13 " 'Now this is the law of the Nazirite when the period of their dedication is over.[n] They are to be brought to the entrance to the tent of meeting. 14 There they are to present their offerings to the LORD: a year-old male lamb without defect for a burnt offering, a year-old ewe lamb without defect for a sin offering,[o] a ram without defect for a fellowship offering, 15 together with their grain offerings and drink offerings,[p] and a basket of bread made with the finest flour and without yeast—thick loaves with olive oil mixed in, and thin loaves brushed with olive oil.[q]

16 " 'The priest is to present all these before the LORD and make the sin offering and the burnt offering. 17 He is to present the basket of unleavened bread and is to sacrifice the ram as a fellowship offering to the LORD, together with its grain offering and drink offering.

18 " 'Then at the entrance to the tent of meeting, the Nazirite must shave off the hair that symbolizes their dedication.[r] They are to take the hair and put it in the fire that is under the sacrifice of the fellowship offering.

19 " 'After the Nazirite has shaved off the hair that symbolizes their dedication, the priest is to place in their hands a boiled shoulder of the ram, and one thick loaf and one thin loaf from the basket, both made without yeast. 20 The priest shall then wave these before the LORD as a wave offering; they are holy and belong to the

5:27 [x] Isa 43:28; 65:15; Jer 26:6; 29:18; 42:18; 44:12,22; Zec 8:13 **5:29** [y] ver 19 **5:31** [z] Lev 5:1; 20:17 **6:2** [a] Ge 28:20; Ac 21:23 [b] Jdg 13:5; 16:17; Am 2:11,12 **6:3** [c] Lk 1:15 [d] Ru 2:14; Ps 69:21; Pr 10:26 **6:5** [e] Ps 52:2; 57:4; 59:7; Isa 7:20; Eze 5:1 [f] 1Sa 1:11 **6:6** [g] Lev 21:1-3; Nu 19:11-22 **6:7** [h] Nu 9:6 **6:9** [i] ver 18 [j] Lev 14:9 **6:10** [k] Lev 5:7; 14:22 **6:11** [l] Ge 8:20 [m] Ex 29:36 **6:13** [n] Ac 21:26 **6:14** [o] Lev 14:10; Nu 15:27 **6:15** [p] Nu 15:1-7 [q] Ex 29:2; Lev 2:4 **6:18** [r] ver 9; Ac 21:24

[a] *26* Or *representative* [b] *11* Or *purification offering*; also in verses 14 and 16

6:19 *boiled shoulder of the ram.* Normally the breast and the upper portion of the right hind leg were reserved for priestly consumption (Lev 7:30–35). A similar practice seems apparent in Egyptian, Mesopotamian and Hittite texts and murals in which the right thigh was the choice portion for presentation to various deities. The boiling of sacrifices is known from pre-Israelite Lachish and premonarchical Shiloh (1Sa 2:13–14).

6:20 *wave offering.* To wave or, more likely, to elevate an offering before Yahweh is a ritual act signifying the transfer of the ownership of the offering from the offerer to Yahweh (see note on Lev 7:30).

priest, together with the breast that was waved and the thigh that was presented. After that, the Nazirite may drink wine.[s]

21 " 'This is the law of the Nazirite who vows offerings to the LORD in accordance with their dedication, in addition to whatever else they can afford. They must fulfill the vows they have made, according to the law of the Nazirite.' "

6:20 [s]Ecc 9:7 6:23 [t]Dt 21:5; 1Ch 23:13 6:24 [u]Dt 28:3-6; Ps 28:9 [v]1Sa 2:9; Ps 17:8 6:25 [w]Job 29:24; Ps 31:16; 80:3; 119:135 [x]Ge 43:29; Ps 25:16; 86:16

The Priestly Blessing

22 The LORD said to Moses, 23 "Tell Aaron and his sons, 'This is how you are to bless[t] the Israelites. Say to them:

24 " ' "The LORD bless you[u]
and keep you;[v]
25 the LORD make his face shine on you[w]
and be gracious to you;[x]

6:24–26 A phylactery containing two silver scrolls the size of two small cigarettes, on which were written two versions of the priestly blessing, was found in a sixth-century BC burial site (Ketef Hinnom) near Jerusalem. Both inscriptions contain additional appellations to YHWH as "the restorer and rock" and as "the warrior and the rebuker of evil." These texts had been used as amulets either while these individuals were alive or as burial pendants. The text on the larger one is nearly identical to this passage; an abbreviated version of the second and third blessings is written on the smaller. Containing the oldest attestation to the Tetragrammaton (YHWH = Yahweh) in Jerusalem, these texts indicate the authenticity and antiquity of this "priestly benediction." Its text became a standardized liturgical form no later than the end of the preexilic period. Ancient Near Eastern texts from the second millennium BC contain parallels to the themes of divine countenance, the lifting up of the face, and the blessing of well-being (*shalom*).

6:25 *the LORD make his face shine on you.* The metaphor portraying God's face as light shining on his people occurs in numerous Biblical (Ps 44:3; 80:3) and extra-Biblical texts. This imagery occurs in several Mesopotamian and Ugaritic contexts, in which the gods bestow gifts and extend mercy to individuals or nations. An Egyptian text from the First Intermediate Period (c. 2134–2040 BC) has a Letter

NUMBERS 6:1–21

NAZIRITES

Vows among ancient Near Eastern cultures from Mesopotamia, Anatolia and the Levant reflect the following pattern: (1) The vow grows out of a situation of need or distress. (2) The vow is made by a human to the gods. (3) The vow is generally conditional in nature. (4) A responsive votive offering is made publicly at a cultic place at the conclusion of the vow conditions.

Restrictions for the Nazirite are more stringent than those for the priest; the priest need only refrain from fermented beverage during his period of service in the sanctuary (Lev 10:9). A Nazirite must abstain from all vineyard products at all times, defined in detail down to the grape hulls, pits and even the vines.

In Nu 6:3 the intoxicant beverages are listed as "wine" (*yayin*) and "other fermented drink" (*shekar*). Wine was the most common form of grape beverage, produced in the late summer and early fall in ancient Israel in winepress installations and then stored in subterranean bell-shaped caves for fermentation.

The "other fermented drink" (*shekar*) has historically been translated as "beer"—a common Mesopotamian and Egyptian beverage made from barley known from inscriptions and carved or painted murals—or as "strong drink" (a grape by-product such as brandy). *Shekar* had an alcohol content of 20–60 percent in comparison to wine's 12–14 percent. The emphasis here is total abstinence from anything associated with the vineyard, lending support to the interpretation of *shekar* as an intoxicating beverage produced from vineyard produce. However, it is not drunkenness that is the issue here, but rather grape drinks or products of any sort.

The visible distinctiveness of allowing the hair to grow long and remain uncut for the duration of the vow (Nu 6:5) set the Nazirite apart from societal norms. In Mesopotamian and Mediterranean law codes, hair played a significant role in ritual and legal practices. In the Code of Hammurapi, cutting one's hair was a form of

continued on next page

26 the LORD turn his face[y] toward you
and give you peace.[z]"'
27 "So they will put my name[a] on the Israelites, and I will bless them."

Offerings at the Dedication of the Tabernacle

7 When Moses finished setting up the
tabernacle,[b] he anointed and consecrated it and all its furnishings.[c] He also
anointed and consecrated the altar and
all its utensils.[d] 2 Then the leaders of Israel,[e] the heads of families who were the
tribal leaders in charge of those who were
counted, made offerings. 3 They brought as
their gifts before the LORD six covered carts
and twelve oxen — an ox from each leader
and a cart from every two. These they presented before the tabernacle.
4 The LORD said to Moses, 5 "Accept these
from them, that they may be used in the
work at the tent of meeting. Give them to
the Levites as each man's work requires."
6 So Moses took the carts and oxen and
gave them to the Levites. 7 He gave two
carts and four oxen to the Gershonites,[f]
as their work required, 8 and he gave four
carts and eight oxen to the Merarites,[g] as
their work required. They were all under

6:26 [y] Ps 4:6; 44:3 [z] Ps 29:11; 37:11,37; Jn 14:27
6:27 [a] Dt 28:10; 2Sa 7:23; 2Ch 7:14; Ne 9:10; Jer 25:29
7:1 [b] Ex 40:17 [c] Ex 40:9 [d] ver 84,88; Ex 40:10
7:2 [e] Nu 1:5-16
7:7 [f] Nu 4:24-26,28
7:8 [g] Nu 4:31-33

to the Dead inscribed on a tubular jar stand: "You live for (me), The Great One shall praise you, and the face of the Great God will be gracious over you; he will give you pure bread with his two hands." While this text somewhat parallels the priestly blessing in form and content, its broader context is significantly different insofar as it focuses on petitioning the deceased father for assistance in producing a male heir.

6:27 *they will put my name on the Israelites.* Placing the name of a deity on a place or a people asserted the claim of deity and established his presence.

punishment and humiliation for bringing a false accusation against another man's wife in matters of property.

Touching or even coming into close proximity with a corpse was a common means of ritual contamination (6:6 – 8). To maintain the sanctity of a vow, a Nazirite could not participate in the standard ritual mourning for the dead, even a member of one's own family. Nu 6:9 – 12 provides for accidental contamination, whereby the Nazirite removes the outward symbol of identification by shaving the hair and offering it to Yahweh at the conclusion of the period of uncleanness (6:18). Restriction also included the Levitically prohibited participation in ritual associated with the cult of the dead. The story of Samson implies that the restriction also applied to animal corpses since he withheld from his parents the knowledge that the honey he presented them was gathered from the carcass of a lion he had killed with his bare hands (Jdg 14:5 – 9). ◆

Fresco from the tomb of Nahat Beni-Amon, fourteenth century BC. On the right of the pictures, people are collecting grapes, on the left others are pressing grapes. While wine production was common in Israel, a Nazirite vowed to abstain from all vineyard products at all times.

Z. Radovan/www.BibleLandPictures.com

the direction of Ithamar son of Aaron, the
priest. 9But Moses did not give any to the
Kohathites, because they were to carry on
their shoulders[h] the holy things, for which
they were responsible.
10When the altar was anointed,[i] the
leaders brought their offerings for its dedication[j] and presented them before the
altar. 11For the LORD had said to Moses,
"Each day one leader is to bring his offering for the dedication of the altar."

12The one who brought his offering on the
first day was Nahshon son of Amminadab
of the tribe of Judah.

13His offering was one silver plate
weighing a hundred and thirty shekels[a] and one silver sprinkling bowl
weighing seventy shekels,[b] both according to the sanctuary shekel,[k] each
filled with the finest flour mixed with
olive oil as a grain offering;[l] 14one gold
dish weighing ten shekels,[c] filled with
incense;[m] 15one young bull,[n] one ram
and one male lamb a year old for a
burnt offering;[o] 16one male goat for
a sin offering[d];[p] 17and two oxen, five
rams, five male goats and five male
lambs a year old to be sacrificed as a
fellowship offering.[q] This was the offering of Nahshon son of Amminadab.[r]

18On the second day Nethanel son of
Zuar,[s] the leader of Issachar, brought his
offering.

19The offering he brought was one
silver plate weighing a hundred and
thirty shekels and one silver sprinkling bowl weighing seventy shekels, both according to the sanctuary
shekel, each filled with the finest
flour mixed with olive oil as a grain
offering; 20one gold dish[t] weighing
ten shekels, filled with incense; 21one
young bull, one ram and one male
lamb a year old for a burnt offering;
22one male goat for a sin offering;
23and two oxen, five rams, five male
goats and five male lambs a year old
to be sacrificed as a fellowship offering. This was the offering of Nethanel
son of Zuar.

24On the third day, Eliab son of Helon,[u] the
leader of the people of Zebulun, brought
his offering.

25His offering was one silver plate
weighing a hundred and thirty shekels and one silver sprinkling bowl
weighing seventy shekels, both according to the sanctuary shekel, each
filled with the finest flour mixed with
olive oil as a grain offering; 26one gold
dish weighing ten shekels, filled with
incense; 27one young bull, one ram
and one male lamb a year old for a
burnt offering; 28one male goat for
a sin offering; 29and two oxen, five
rams, five male goats and five male
lambs a year old to be sacrificed as a
fellowship offering. This was the offering of Eliab son of Helon.

30On the fourth day Elizur son of Shedeur,[v] the leader of the people of Reuben,
brought his offering.

31His offering was one silver plate
weighing a hundred and thirty shekels and one silver sprinkling bowl
weighing seventy shekels, both according to the sanctuary shekel, each
filled with the finest flour mixed
with olive oil as a grain offering;
32one gold dish weighing ten shekels, filled with incense; 33one young
bull, one ram and one male lamb a
year old for a burnt offering; 34one
male goat for a sin offering; 35and
two oxen, five rams, five male goats
and five male lambs a year old to be
sacrificed as a fellowship offering.
This was the offering of Elizur son
of Shedeur.

36On the fifth day Shelumiel son of Zurishaddai,[w] the leader of the people of Simeon, brought his offering.

37His offering was one silver plate
weighing a hundred and thirty shekels
and one silver sprinkling bowl weighing seventy shekels, both according to
the sanctuary shekel, each filled with
the finest flour mixed with olive oil
as a grain offering; 38one gold dish
weighing ten shekels, filled with incense; 39one young bull, one ram and
one male lamb a year old for a burnt
offering; 40one male goat for a sin offering; 41and two oxen, five rams, five
male goats and five male lambs a year
old to be sacrificed as a fellowship offering. This was the offering of Shelumiel son of Zurishaddai.

7:9 [h] Nu 4:15
7:10 [i] ver 1 [j] 2Ch 7:9
7:13 [k] Ex 30:13; Nu 3:47 [l] Lev 2:1
7:14 [m] Ex 30:34
7:15 [n] Ex 24:5; 29:3; Nu 28:11 [o] Lev 1:3
7:16 [p] Lev 4:3, 23
7:17 [q] Lev 3:1 [r] Nu 1:7
7:18 [s] Nu 1:8
7:20 [t] ver 14
7:24 [u] Nu 1:9
7:30 [v] Nu 1:5
7:36 [w] Nu 1:6

[a] *13* That is, about 3 1/4 pounds or about 1.5 kilograms; also elsewhere in this chapter [b] *13* That is, about 1 3/4 pounds or about 800 grams; also elsewhere in this chapter [c] *14* That is, about 4 ounces or about 115 grams; also elsewhere in this chapter [d] *16* Or *purification offering*; also elsewhere in this chapter

7:12–83 The pattern of enumeration here reflects an administrative record following the traditional pattern of temple records of the ancient Near East. The repetitive nature of the material may be primarily theological, to emphasize that every tribe has an equal stake in the worship of God and that each is fully committed to the support of the tabernacle and its priesthood.

42 On the sixth day Eliasaph son of Deuel,[x]
the leader of the people of Gad, brought
his offering.
43 His offering was one silver plate
weighing a hundred and thirty shekels and one silver sprinkling bowl
weighing seventy shekels, both according to the sanctuary shekel, each
filled with the finest flour mixed with
olive oil as a grain offering; 44 one gold
dish weighing ten shekels, filled with
incense; 45 one young bull, one ram
and one male lamb a year old for a
burnt offering; 46 one male goat for
a sin offering; 47 and two oxen, five
rams, five male goats and five male
lambs a year old to be sacrificed as a
fellowship offering. This was the offering of Eliasaph son of Deuel.

48 On the seventh day Elishama son of Ammihud,[y] the leader of the people of Ephraim, brought his offering.
49 His offering was one silver plate
weighing a hundred and thirty shekels and one silver sprinkling bowl
weighing seventy shekels, both according to the sanctuary shekel, each
filled with the finest flour mixed with
olive oil as a grain offering; 50 one gold
dish weighing ten shekels, filled with
incense; 51 one young bull, one ram
and one male lamb a year old for a
burnt offering; 52 one male goat for
a sin offering; 53 and two oxen, five
rams, five male goats and five male
lambs a year old to be sacrificed as a
fellowship offering. This was the offering of Elishama son of Ammihud.[z]

54 On the eighth day Gamaliel son of Pedahzur,[a] the leader of the people of Manasseh, brought his offering.
55 His offering was one silver plate
weighing a hundred and thirty shekels and one silver sprinkling bowl
weighing seventy shekels, both according to the sanctuary shekel, each
filled with the finest flour mixed with
olive oil as a grain offering; 56 one gold
dish weighing ten shekels, filled with
incense; 57 one young bull, one ram
and one male lamb a year old for a
burnt offering; 58 one male goat for
a sin offering; 59 and two oxen, five
rams, five male goats and five male
lambs a year old to be sacrificed as a
fellowship offering. This was the offering of Gamaliel son of Pedahzur.

60 On the ninth day Abidan son of Gideoni,[b] the leader of the people of Benjamin,
brought his offering.
61 His offering was one silver plate
weighing a hundred and thirty shekels and one silver sprinkling bowl
weighing seventy shekels, both according to the sanctuary shekel, each
filled with the finest flour mixed with
olive oil as a grain offering; 62 one gold
dish weighing ten shekels, filled with
incense; 63 one young bull, one ram
and one male lamb a year old for a
burnt offering; 64 one male goat for
a sin offering; 65 and two oxen, five
rams, five male goats and five male
lambs a year old to be sacrificed as a
fellowship offering. This was the offering of Abidan son of Gideoni.

66 On the tenth day Ahiezer son of Ammishaddai,[c] the leader of the people of Dan,
brought his offering.
67 His offering was one silver plate
weighing a hundred and thirty shekels and one silver sprinkling bowl
weighing seventy shekels, both according to the sanctuary shekel, each
filled with the finest flour mixed with
olive oil as a grain offering; 68 one
gold dish weighing ten shekels, filled
with incense; 69 one young bull, one
ram and one male lamb a year old
for a burnt offering; 70 one male goat
for a sin offering; 71 and two oxen, five
rams, five male goats and five male
lambs a year old to be sacrificed as a
fellowship offering. This was the offering of Ahiezer son of Ammishaddai.

72 On the eleventh day Pagiel son of Okran,[d] the leader of the people of Asher,
brought his offering.
73 His offering was one silver plate
weighing a hundred and thirty shekels and one silver sprinkling bowl
weighing seventy shekels, both according to the sanctuary shekel, each
filled with the finest flour mixed with
olive oil as a grain offering; 74 one gold
dish weighing ten shekels, filled with
incense; 75 one young bull, one ram
and one male lamb a year old for a
burnt offering; 76 one male goat for
a sin offering; 77 and two oxen, five
rams, five male goats and five male
lambs a year old to be sacrificed as a
fellowship offering. This was the offering of Pagiel son of Okran.

78 On the twelfth day Ahira son of Enan,[e]
the leader of the people of Naphtali,
brought his offering.
79 His offering was one silver plate
weighing a hundred and thirty shekels
and one silver sprinkling bowl weighing seventy shekels, both according to

7:42 [x] Nu 1:14
7:48 [y] Nu 1:10
7:53 [z] Nu 1:10
7:54 [a] Nu 1:10; 2:20
7:60 [b] Nu 1:11
7:66 [c] Nu 1:12; 2:25
7:72 [d] Nu 1:13
7:78 [e] Nu 1:15; 2:29

the sanctuary shekel, each filled with the finest flour mixed with olive oil as a grain offering; 80one gold dish weighing ten shekels, filled with incense; 81one young bull, one ram and one male lamb a year old for a burnt offering; 82one male goat for a sin offering; 83and two oxen, five rams, five male goats and five male lambs a year old to be sacrificed as a fellowship offering. This was the offering of Ahira son of Enan.

84These were the offerings of the Israelite leaders for the dedication of the altar when it was anointed:[f] twelve silver plates, twelve silver sprinkling bowls[g] and twelve gold dishes.[h] 85Each silver plate weighed a hundred and thirty shekels, and each sprinkling bowl seventy shekels. Altogether, the silver dishes weighed two thousand four hundred shekels,[a] according to the sanctuary shekel. 86The twelve gold dishes filled with incense weighed ten shekels each, according to the sanctuary shekel. Altogether, the gold dishes weighed a hundred and twenty shekels.[b] 87The total number of animals for the burnt offering came to twelve young bulls, twelve rams and twelve male lambs a year old, together with their grain offering. Twelve male goats were used for the sin offering. 88The total number of animals for the sacrifice of the fellowship offering came to twenty-four oxen, sixty rams, sixty male goats and sixty male lambs a year old. These were the offerings for the dedication of the altar after it was anointed.[i]

89When Moses entered the tent of meeting to speak with the LORD,[j] he heard the voice speaking to him from between the two cherubim above the atonement cover[k] on the ark of the covenant law. In this way the LORD spoke to him.

Setting Up the Lamps

8 The LORD said to Moses, 2"Speak to Aaron and say to him, 'When you set up the lamps, see that all seven light up the area in front of the lampstand.[l]' "

3Aaron did so; he set up the lamps so that they faced forward on the lampstand, just as the LORD commanded Moses. 4This is how the lampstand was made: It was made of hammered gold[m]—from its base to its blossoms. The lampstand was made exactly like the pattern[n] the LORD had shown Moses.

The Setting Apart of the Levites

5The LORD said to Moses: 6"Take the Levites from among all the Israelites and make them ceremonially clean.[o] 7To purify them, do this: Sprinkle the water of cleansing[p] on them; then have them shave their whole bodies[q] and wash their clothes.[r] And so they will purify themselves. 8Have them take a young bull with its grain offering of the finest flour mixed with olive oil;[s] then you are to take a second young bull for a sin offering.[c] 9Bring the Levites to the front of the tent of meeting[t] and assemble the whole Israelite community.[u] 10You are to bring the Levites before the LORD, and the Israelites are to lay their hands on them.[v] 11Aaron is to present the Levites before the LORD as a wave offering[w] from the Israelites, so that they may be ready to do the work of the LORD.

12"Then the Levites are to lay their hands on the heads of the bulls,[x] using one for a sin offering to the LORD and the other for a burnt offering, to make atonement[y] for the Levites. 13Have the Levites stand in front of Aaron and his sons and then present them as a wave offering to the LORD. 14In this way you are to set the Levites apart from the other Israelites, and the Levites will be mine.[z]

15"After you have purified the Levites and presented them as a wave offering,[a] they are to come to do their work at the tent of meeting. 16They are the Israelites who are to be given wholly to me. I have taken them as my own in place of the firstborn, the first male offspring[b] from every Israelite woman. 17Every firstborn male in Israel, whether human or animal,[c] is mine. When I struck down all the firstborn in Egypt, I set them apart for myself.[d] 18And I have taken the Levites in place of all the

7:84 [f] ver 1, 10 [g] Nu 4:14 [h] ver 14 **7:88** [i] ver 1, 10 **7:89** [j] Ex 25:21, 22; 33:9, 11 [k] Ps 80:1; 99:1 **8:2** [l] Ex 25:37; Lev 24:2, 4 **8:4** [m] Ex 25:18, 36; 25:18 [n] Ex 25:9 **8:6** [o] Lev 22:2; Isa 1:16; 52:11 **8:7** [p] Nu 19:9, 17 [q] Lev 14:9; Dt 21:12 [r] Lev 14:8 **8:8** [s] Lev 2:1; Nu 15:8-10 **8:9** [t] Ex 40:12 [u] Lev 8:3 **8:10** [v] Ac 6:6 **8:11** [w] Lev 7:30 **8:12** [x] Ex 29:10 [y] Ex 29:36 **8:14** [z] Nu 3:12 **8:15** [a] Ex 29:24 **8:16** [b] Nu 3:12 **8:17** [c] Ex 4:23 [d] Ex 13:2; Lk 2:23

[a] *85* That is, about 60 pounds or about 28 kilograms
[b] *86* That is, about 3 pounds or about 1.4 kilograms
[c] *8* Or *purification offering*; also in verse 12

8:2 *lampstand.* See note on Ex 25:31–40.

8:7 *shave their whole bodies.* Egyptian priests shaved their bodies every three days as a means of purification. The purification ritual sequence of shaving, bathing and washing (clothes) was also practiced among Mesopotamian cultures; e.g., the high priestess at Emar was shaved in preparation for her installation.

The cleansing process ensured ritual purification, so that a level of holiness could be maintained for those in service for the Lord. A slightly higher level of holiness was maintained for the priests who received new clothes when they were consecrated for service (Lev 8:12–13). Recent study suggests that shaving was one way to designate a temporary change in status.

8:10,12 *lay their hands on.* See note on Lev 1:4.

8:18 *Levites in place of all the firstborn sons.* See note on 3:12. The firstborn of all people and animals, and the first of the harvest, belonged to Yahweh. In Mesopotamia it was common to give the choicest products to the gods, whether "firstfruits" or firstborn animals, but there is no indication of firstborn sons being regularly consecrated.

firstborn sons in Israel.[e] 19From among all
the Israelites, I have given the Levites as
gifts to Aaron and his sons[f] to do the work
at the tent of meeting on behalf of the Israelites[g] and to make atonement for them[h]
so that no plague will strike the Israelites
when they go near the sanctuary."
20Moses, Aaron and the whole Israelite
community did with the Levites just as the
LORD commanded Moses. 21The Levites purified themselves and washed their clothes.[i]
Then Aaron presented them as a wave offering before the LORD and made atonement
for them to purify them.[j] 22After that, the
Levites came to do their work at the tent
of meeting under the supervision of Aaron
and his sons. They did with the Levites just
as the LORD commanded Moses.
23The LORD said to Moses, 24"This applies to the Levites: Men twenty-five years
old or more[k] shall come to take part in
the work at the tent of meeting,[l] 25but at
the age of fifty, they must retire from their
regular service and work no longer. 26They
may assist their brothers in performing
their duties at the tent of meeting, but they
themselves must not do the work. This,
then, is how you are to assign the responsibilities of the Levites."

The Passover

9 The LORD spoke to Moses in the Desert of Sinai in the first month[m] of the
second year after they came out of Egypt.[n]
He said, 2"Have the Israelites celebrate the
Passover at the appointed time. 3Celebrate
it at the appointed time, at twilight on the
fourteenth day of this month, in accordance with all its rules and regulations.[o]"
4So Moses told the Israelites to celebrate
the Passover, 5and they did so in the Desert
of Sinai at twilight on the fourteenth day of
the first month.[p] The Israelites did everything just as the LORD commanded Moses.
6But some of them could not celebrate
the Passover on that day because they
were ceremonially unclean[q] on account of
a dead body. So they came to Moses and
Aaron[r] that same day 7and said to Moses,
"We have become unclean because of a
dead body, but why should we be kept
from presenting the LORD's offering with
the other Israelites at the appointed time?"
8Moses answered them, "Wait until I
find out what the LORD commands concerning you."[s]
9Then the LORD said to Moses, 10"Tell the
Israelites: 'When any of you or your descendants are unclean because of a dead
body or are away on a journey, they are
still to celebrate[t] the LORD's Passover, 11but
they are to do it on the fourteenth day of
the second month at twilight. They are to
eat the lamb, together with unleavened
bread and bitter herbs.[u] 12They must not
leave any of it till morning[v] or break any of
its bones.[w] When they celebrate the Passover, they must follow all the regulations.
13But if anyone who is ceremonially clean
and not on a journey fails to celebrate the
Passover, they must be cut off from their
people[x] for not presenting the LORD's offering at the appointed time. They will bear
the consequences of their sin.
14" 'A foreigner[y] residing among you is
also to celebrate the LORD's Passover in
accordance with its rules and regulations.
You must have the same regulations for
both the foreigner and the native-born.' "

The Cloud Above the Tabernacle

15On the day the tabernacle, the tent of
the covenant law, was set up, the cloud[z]
covered it. From evening till morning
the cloud above the tabernacle looked
like fire.[a] 16That is how it continued to
be; the cloud covered it, and at night it
looked like fire. 17Whenever the cloud lifted from above the tent, the Israelites set
out; wherever the cloud settled, the Israelites encamped.[b] 18At the LORD's command
the Israelites set out, and at his command
they encamped. As long as the cloud
stayed over the tabernacle, they remained
in camp. 19When the cloud remained over
the tabernacle a long time, the Israelites
obeyed the LORD's order and did not set
out. 20Sometimes the cloud was over the
tabernacle only a few days; at the LORD's
command they would encamp, and then at
his command they would set out. 21Some-
times the cloud stayed only from evening
till morning, and when it lifted in the
morning, they set out. Whether by day or
by night, whenever the cloud lifted, they
set out. 22Whether the cloud stayed over
the tabernacle for two days or a month
or a year, the Israelites would remain in
camp and not set out; but when it lifted,
they would set out. 23At the LORD's command they encamped, and at the LORD's
command they set out. They obeyed the
LORD's order, in accordance with his command through Moses.

The Silver Trumpets

10 The LORD said to Moses: 2"Make
two trumpets[c] of hammered silver,
and use them for calling the community[d]
together and for having the camps set out.

8:18 [e] Nu 3:12
8:19 [f] Nu 3:9 [g] Nu 1:53 [h] Nu 16:46
8:21 [i] ver 7 [j] ver 12
8:24 [k] 1Ch 23:3 [l] Ex 38:21; Nu 4:3
9:1 [m] Ex 40:2 [n] Nu 1:1
9:3 [o] Ex 12:2-11,43-49; Lev 23:5-8; Dt 16:1-8
9:5 [p] Ex 12:1-13; Jos 5:10
9:6 [q] Lev 5:3 [r] Ex 18:15; Nu 27:2
9:8 [s] Ex 18:15; Nu 27:5,21; Ps 85:8
9:10 [t] 2Ch 30:2
9:11 [u] Ex 12:8
9:12 [v] Ex 12:10, 43 [w] Ex 12:46; Jn 19:36*
9:13 [x] Ge 17:14; Ex 12:15
9:14 [y] Ex 12:48, 49
9:15 [z] Ex 40:34 [a] Ex 13:21
9:17 [b] Ex 40:36-38; Nu 10:11, 12; 1Co 10:1
10:2 [c] Ne 12:35; Ps 47:5 [d] Jer 4:5, 19; 6:1; Hos 5:8; Joel 2:1, 15; Am 3:6

9:2 *Passover.* See the article "Passover," p. 129.
9:15 *cloud.* See the article "Glory," p. 178.
10:2 *trumpets of hammered silver.* The silver trumpets are
to be distinguished from the ram's horn in function as

3When both are sounded, the whole community is to assemble before you at the
entrance to the tent of meeting. 4If only
one is sounded, the leaders[e]—the heads of
the clans of Israel—are to assemble before
you. 5When a trumpet blast is sounded,
the tribes camping on the east are to set
out.[f] 6At the sounding of a second blast,
the camps on the south are to set out.[g] The
blast will be the signal for setting out. 7To
gather the assembly, blow the trumpets,[h]
but not with the signal for setting out.[i]
8"The sons of Aaron, the priests, are to
blow the trumpets. This is to be a lasting
ordinance for you and the generations to
come.[j] 9When you go into battle in your
own land against an enemy who is oppressing you,[k] sound a blast on the trumpets. Then you will be remembered[l] by the
LORD your God and rescued from your enemies.[m] 10Also at your times of rejoicing—
your appointed festivals and New Moon
feasts[n]—you are to sound the trumpets[o]
over your burnt offerings and fellowship
offerings, and they will be a memorial for
you before your God. I am the LORD your
God."

The Israelites Leave Sinai

11On the twentieth day of the second
month of the second year,[p] the cloud lifted[q] from above the tabernacle of the covenant law. 12Then the Israelites set out
from the Desert of Sinai and traveled from
place to place until the cloud came to rest
in the Desert of Paran. 13They set out, this
first time, at the LORD's command through
Moses.[r]
14The divisions of the camp of Judah
went first, under their standard.[s] Nahshon son of Amminadab[t] was in command. 15Nethanel son of Zuar was over
the division of the tribe of Issachar, 16and
Eliab son of Helon was over the division of
the tribe of Zebulun. 17Then the tabernacle
was taken down, and the Gershonites and
Merarites, who carried it, set out.[u]
18The divisions of the camp of Reuben
went next, under their standard.[v] Elizur
son of Shedeur was in command. 19Shelu-
miel son of Zurishaddai was over the division of the tribe of Simeon, 20and Eliasaph
son of Deuel was over the division of the
tribe of Gad. 21Then the Kohathites set out,
carrying the holy things.[w] The tabernacle
was to be set up before they arrived.[x]
22The divisions of the camp of Ephraim[y]
went next, under their standard. Elishama
son of Ammihud was in command. 23Ga-
maliel son of Pedahzur was over the division of the tribe of Manasseh, 24and Abidan son of Gideoni was over the division
of the tribe of Benjamin.
25Finally, as the rear guard[z] for all the
units, the divisions of the camp of Dan set
out under their standard. Ahiezer son of
Ammishaddai was in command. 26Pagiel
son of Okran was over the division of the
tribe of Asher, 27and Ahira son of Enan
was over the division of the tribe of Naphtali. 28This was the order of march for the
Israelite divisions as they set out.
29Now Moses said to Hobab[a] son of
Reuel[b] the Midianite, Moses' father-in-
law,[c] "We are setting out for the place
about which the LORD said, 'I will give it
to you.'[d] Come with us and we will treat
you well, for the LORD has promised good
things to Israel."
30He answered, "No, I will not go;[e] I am
going back to my own land and my own
people."
31But Moses said, "Please do not leave
us. You know where we should camp in
the wilderness, and you can be our eyes.[f]
32If you come with us, we will share with
you[g] whatever good things the LORD
gives us.[h]"

10:4 [e] Ex 18:21; Nu 1:16; 7:2 **10:5** [f] ver 14 **10:6** [g] ver 18 **10:7** [h] Eze 33:3; Joel 2:1 [i] 1Co 14:8 **10:8** [j] Nu 31:6 **10:9** [k] Jdg 2:18; 6:9; 1Sa 10:18; Ps 106:42 [l] Ge 8:1 [m] Ps 106:4 **10:10** [n] Ps 81:3 [o] Lev 23:24 **10:11** [p] Ex 40:17 [q] Nu 9:17 **10:13** [r] Dt 1:6 **10:14** [s] Nu 2:3-9 [t] Nu 1:7

10:17 [u] Nu 4:21-32 **10:18** [v] Nu 2:10-16 **10:21** [w] Nu 4:20 [x] ver 17 **10:22** [y] Nu 2:24 **10:25** [z] Nu 2:31; Jos 6:9 **10:29** [a] Jdg 4:11 [b] Ex 2:18 [c] Ex 3:1 [d] Ge 12:7 **10:30** [e] Mt 21:29 **10:31** [f] Job 29:15 **10:32** [g] Dt 10:18 [h] Ps 22:27-31; 67:5-7

well as appearance. The ram's horn announced the Day of Atonement throughout the land (Lev 25:9) and was used in the marching around Jericho (Jos 6:2–21). The bright pitch of the silver trumpet called the people to march through the wilderness and was blown by Phinehas in the battle against Midian (Nu 31:6).

These trumpets were likely styled after those known from Egypt during the Late Bronze Age, examples of which were found in King Tutankhamun's tomb. These instruments were about 2 feet (0.6 meters) long with narrow tubes; when blown in certain patterns they emitted a bright and piercing sound that communicated clearly to the people the desired intent. In Egypt they were used both in cultic and military contexts.

10:5–7 The trumpets were blown with varying tones and lengths of blast. The two trumpets were likely of slightly different size, producing varying tones so that both could be distinguished. In terms of length of blast, the short blast alerted the camps to break camp and begin a journey (vv. 5–6); the long blast called the assemblies together (vv. 3–4,7).

10:8 Only the Aaronic priests are to blow the silver trumpets.

10:10 Whole burnt offerings for consecration and atonement, and peace offerings for community celebration, are accompanied by the long blast of the silver trumpets during the pilgrimage festivals of Passover, Weeks and Tabernacles, and during the monthly New Moon rites.

10:29 *Hobab son of Reuel.* Some suggest the dual names Reuel (Ex 2:18) and Jethro (father of Zipporah, Ex 3:1) may refer to variant patriarchal clan leaders of this tier of the Midianites, with the patriarchal clan founder named "Reuel" and the actual father-in-law of Moses named "Jethro." Others suggest Jethro and Reuel are the same person, since dual names are common in Bronze Age texts from Mesopotamia and the Levant. *father-in-law.* The Hebrew *hoten* can mean "brother-in-law" or "father-in-law" (Ex 3:1).

NUMBERS 10:12

Geography of the Wilderness

The geographic parameters of this initial movement are the Sinai and Paran Deserts. According to 33:16–18, the Israelites camped at Taberah (11:3), Kibroth Hattaavah (11:34–35), and Hazeroth (12:16) on their way to the Paran Desert, the parameters of which are difficult to outline. No cartographic mapping remains from this period to identify these regions. From the Biblical data Paran was west of Midian and east of Egypt, extending from some point north or northeast of Mount Sinai—north toward Kadesh Barnea and east to the Arabah.

Kadesh is associated with both the Paran and Zin Deserts. Paran seems to encompass a broader geographic area, which included in its northeast quadrant the Desert of Zin, more narrowly defined by the Nahal Zin and its water drainage basin. Hence, the text shifts from the general Paran Desert region (10:17; 13:26) to a context in which greater specificity is needed, as in the listing of the itinerary of the spies (13:21) and later the rebellion of Moses (20:1–13; 27:14). Paran's relationship to Midian is confirmed later in history when the Edomite king Hadad fled from Solomon to Egypt via Midian and Paran (1Ki 11:18). Most of the 40 years of wilderness sojourn were spent in the Paran-Zin Desert region. See map 3 at the end of the Bible. ◆

Kadesh Barnea, an oasis in eastern Sinai and the southern boundary of Canaan.

Z. Radovan/www.BibleLandPictures.com

33 So they set out[i] from the mountain of the LORD and traveled for three days. The ark of the covenant of the LORD[j] went before them during those three days to find them a place to rest. 34 The cloud of the LORD was over them by day when they set out from the camp.[k]

35 Whenever the ark set out, Moses said,

"Rise up, LORD!
May your enemies be scattered;[l]
may your foes flee before you.[m]"

36 Whenever it came to rest, he said,

"Return,[n] LORD,
to the countless thousands of
Israel.[o]"

Fire From the LORD

11 Now the people complained about their hardships in the hearing of the LORD, and when he heard them his anger was aroused. Then fire from the LORD burned among them[p] and consumed some of the outskirts of the camp. 2 When the people cried out to Moses, he prayed to the LORD[q] and the fire died down. 3 So that place was called Taberah,[a][r] because fire from the LORD had burned among them.

Quail From the LORD

4 The rabble with them began to crave other food,[s] and again the Israelites started wailing[t] and said, "If only we had meat to eat! 5 We remember the fish we ate in Egypt at no cost—also the cucumbers, melons, leeks, onions and garlic.[u] 6 But now we have lost our appetite; we never see anything but this manna!"

7 The manna was like coriander seed[v] and looked like resin.[w] 8 The people went around gathering it, and then ground it in a hand mill or crushed it in a mortar. They cooked it in a pot or made it into loaves. And it tasted like something made with olive oil. 9 When the dew[x] settled on the camp at night, the manna also came down.

10 Moses heard the people of every family wailing at the entrance to their tents. The LORD became exceedingly angry, and Moses was troubled. 11 He asked the LORD, "Why have you brought this trouble on your servant? What have I done to displease you that you put the burden of all these people on me?[y] 12 Did I conceive all these people? Did I give them birth? Why do you tell me to carry them in my arms, as a nurse carries an infant,[z] to the land you promised on oath to their ancestors?[a] 13 Where can I get meat for all these people?[b] They keep wailing to me, 'Give us meat to eat!' 14 I cannot carry all these people by myself; the burden is too heavy for me.[c] 15 If this is how you are going to treat me, please go ahead and kill me[d]—if I have found favor in your eyes—and do not let me face my own ruin."

16 The LORD said to Moses: "Bring me seventy of Israel's elders who are known to you

10:33 [i] ver 12; Dt 1:33 [j] Jos 3:3 **10:34** [k] Nu 9:15-23 **10:35** [l] Ps 68:1 [m] Dt 7:10; 32:41; Ps 68:2; Isa 17:12-14 **10:36** [n] Isa 63:17 [o] Dt 1:10 **11:1** [p] Lev 10:2 **11:2** [q] Nu 21:7 **11:3** [r] Dt 9:22 **11:4** [s] Ex 12:38 [t] Ps 78:18; 1Co 10:6 **11:5** [u] Ex 16:3 **11:7** [v] Ex 16:31 [w] Ge 2:12 **11:9** [x] Ex 16:13 **11:11** [y] Ex 5:22 **11:12** [z] Isa 40:11; 49:23 [a] Ex 13:5 **11:13** [b] Jn 6:5-9 **11:14** [c] Ex 18:18 **11:15** [d] Ex 32:32; 1Ki 19:4; Jnh 4:3

[a] 3 *Taberah* means *burning.*

10:33 *three days ... three days.* The Battle Song of the Ark is preceded by a dual chronological marker about the first stage in the movement of Yahweh's cloud the distance of a three-day journey (i.e., about 35–45 miles [55–70 kilometers]). This journey is reminiscent of Moses' request to Pharaoh to allow the Israelites to journey three days into the wilderness to worship their God (Ex 8:27).

11:3 *Taberah.* Means "burning," which refers to the form of fiery judgment that often comes by means of lightning, though the mode of igniting the fire is not specified. This form of judgment parallels that which was meted out against Nadab and Abihu (Lev 10:1–3), though that fire came out from the tabernacle. Natural disasters such as those caused by lightning were considered acts of divine judgment by people of the ancient Near East, even cases of fire caused by lightning in sacred precincts such as the Esagila in Babylon or the Assur Temple in Assyria. Fire was considered a divine quality that gave light to the people and fire for cooking sacred meals. The fiery judgment of the gods could be summoned by a diviner to bring down destruction upon one's enemies.

11:4 *meat.* Meat was available in Israel's livestock and herds, but those were reserved for festive occasions and their supply of milk products. Their desire for "flesh" leads to their recollection of their more substantial diet in Egypt (v. 5).

11:5 Goshen in the eastern Nile delta was the breadbasket of Egypt, lush with vegetation and abounding with natural and man-made canals, whose waters teemed with fish and were replete with nutrients for abundant crop production. The foods listed here are among the most commonly grown in the region. Several of these are represented in Egyptian tomb murals. All require ample amounts of water for irrigation.

11:7 *manna.* Its precise identification with known agricultural products of ancient or modern times is somewhat tentative. The association with coriander seed is likely an indicator of its taste, since that seed is used for flavoring (similar to sesame or poppy seeds), in which case "manna" may refer to a variety of small seeds produced by desert plants. Generally manna has been associated with a byproduct of the tamarisk tree found in northern Arabia, but this material is only available for a few months of the year and only where Tamarisk trees are present; further, the yield of this product is far lower than the half pound (227 grams) per person per day reported in the text. Israelites would have believed that every provision came from God regardless of whether we might be able to offer "natural" explanations. To date no "natural" explanation has been identified and perhaps never will be.

Eating at the king's table and tasting "the food of the gods" was part of the culture of the ancient Near East. In the last Babylonian era of 900–705 BC, an already old tradition is recorded concerning Adadnirari III that permitted the kings to eat "remnants" of divine meals offered to the gods. Perhaps the analog here is one of a royal, priestly nation, each and every person receiving food from the table of the Great King.

as leaders and officials among the people.
Have them come to the tent of meeting,
that they may stand there with you. 17 I will
come down and speak with you there, and
I will take some of the power of the Spirit
that is on you and put it on them.[e] They will
share the burden of the people with you so
that you will not have to carry it alone.[f]
18 "Tell the people: 'Consecrate yourselves[g] in preparation for tomorrow, when
you will eat meat. The LORD heard you
when you wailed,[h] "If only we had meat to
eat! We were better off in Egypt!"[i] Now the
LORD will give you meat, and you will eat
it. 19 You will not eat it for just one day, or
two days, or five, ten or twenty days, 20 but
for a whole month—until it comes out of
your nostrils and you loathe it[j]—because
you have rejected the LORD,[k] who is among
you, and have wailed before him, saying,
"Why did we ever leave Egypt?"'"
21 But Moses said, "Here I am among
six hundred thousand men[l] on foot, and
you say, 'I will give them meat to eat for a
whole month!' 22 Would they have enough
if flocks and herds were slaughtered for
them? Would they have enough if all the
fish in the sea were caught for them?"[m]
23 The LORD answered Moses, "Is the
LORD's arm too short?[n] Now you will see
whether or not what I say will come true
for you.[o]"
24 So Moses went out and told the people what the LORD had said. He brought
together seventy of their elders and had
them stand around the tent. 25 Then the
LORD came down in the cloud[p] and spoke
with him,[q] and he took some of the power
of the Spirit[r] that was on him and put it on
the seventy elders.[s] When the Spirit rested
on them, they prophesied[t]—but did not
do so again.
26 However, two men, whose names
were Eldad and Medad, had remained in
the camp. They were listed among the elders, but did not go out to the tent. Yet
the Spirit also rested on them, and they
prophesied in the camp. 27 A young man
ran and told Moses, "Eldad and Medad are
prophesying in the camp."
28 Joshua son of Nun, who had been Moses' aide[u] since youth, spoke up and said,
"Moses, my lord, stop them!"[v]
29 But Moses replied, "Are you jealous for
my sake? I wish that all the LORD's people
were prophets[w] and that the LORD would
put his Spirit on them!" 30 Then Moses and
the elders of Israel returned to the camp.
31 Now a wind went out from the LORD
and drove quail[x] in from the sea. It scattered them up to two cubits[a] deep all
around the camp, as far as a day's walk in
any direction. 32 All that day and night and
all the next day the people went out and
gathered quail. No one gathered less than
ten homers.[b] Then they spread them out
all around the camp. 33 But while the meat
was still between their teeth[y] and before it
could be consumed, the anger of the LORD
burned against the people, and he struck
them with a severe plague.[z] 34 Therefore
the place was named Kibroth Hattaavah,[c][a]
because there they buried the people who
had craved other food.
35 From Kibroth Hattaavah the people
traveled to Hazeroth[b] and stayed there.

11:17 [e] ver 25, 29; 1Sa 10:6; 2Ki 2:9, 15; Joel 2:28 [f] Ex 18:18 **11:18** [g] Ex 19:10 [h] Ex 16:7 [i] ver 5; Ac 7:39 **11:20** [j] Ps 78:29; 106:14, 15 [k] Jos 24:27; 1Sa 10:19 **11:21** [l] Ex 12:37 **11:22** [m] Mt 15:33 **11:23** [n] Isa 50:2; 59:1 [o] Nu 23:19; Eze 12:25; 24:14 **11:25** [p] Nu 12:5 [q] ver 17 [r] 1Sa 10:6 [s] Ac 2:17 [t] 1Sa 10:10 **11:28** [u] Ex 33:11; Jos 1:1 [v] Mk 9:38-40 **11:29** [w] 1Co 14:5 **11:31** [x] Ex 16:13; Ps 78:26-28 **11:33** [y] Ps 78:30 [z] Ps 106:15 **11:34** [a] Dt 9:22 **11:35** [b] Nu 33:17

[a] *31* That is, about 3 feet or about 90 centimeters [b] *32* That is, possibly about 1 3/4 tons or about 1.6 metric tons [c] *34 Kibroth Hattaavah* means *graves of craving.*

11:25 *prophesied.* Though Israelite prophecy generally did not involve ecstasy, the context and the Hebrew terminology suggest that the elders are having ecstatic experiences. Ecstatic prophets are known from the texts at Mari and Babylon, where they were called *mahhu* (or *muhhum*; female *muhhutum*) and function as one category of divination personnel. The *mahhu* would go into a frenzied trance and speak utterances believed to be derived from gods or goddesses like Ishtar, Nergal or Adad. These "prophets" (or better, "diviners") were sometimes considered madmen because of their abnormal behavior.

11:31–32 An east wind and a south wind descend on the camp with provision of meat. Writers through history have described the movement of quail (genus *coturnix coturnix* or *coturnix vulgaris*) across the Sinai, generally northward in the spring (as here) and southward in the fall. Fowling using low-slung nets is known from several Egyptian tomb murals, including those of Kagemmi at Saqqarah dating to the Sixth Dynasty (twenty-fourth–twenty-second century BC). Israelite fowling with nets is mentioned in Hos 7:12.

The fourteenth-century Arab writer Al-Qazwini described the fowling activity of the people El-Arish in the north coastal Sinai. Arabs are known to have caught between one and two million quail in the autumn migration of these small birds. The extraordinary quantity of quail in the Biblical account is swept in "from the sea" (probably from the Gulf of Aqaba if the wind is from the east), and then downward toward the encampment of Israel.

The magnitude of the quail is measured in three ways. (1) Breadth: a day's journey in each direction (about 12–15 miles or 20–25 kilometers, hence an area of more than 400 square miles or 650 square kilometers). (2) Height: 2 cubits (3 feet or about a meter) above the ground, referring either to the height of the birds' flight or the depth of the piles of quail. (3) Quantity: over a two-day period each person gathers at least ten homers, a volume estimated at between 38 and 65 bushels (between 1,350 and 2,300 liters). Some of the birds are eaten right away, while most of them are spread out around the camp, presumably for drying the meat in the hot sun after cleaning and salting them.

11:35 *Kibroth Hattaavah ... Hazeroth.* The location of these sites is conjecture and dependent on the location of Mount Sinai (see the article "Mount Sinai," p. 144). If Mount Sinai is Jebel Musa, then Hazeroth may be associated with the Wadi Hudeirat region, 40 miles (65 kilometers) northeast of Jebel Musa. If Mount Sinai is located at Jebel

Relief of a fowler's snare. It is possible the Israelites gathered the quail (11:31) in low-slung nets such as these.

Kim Walton. The Art Institute of Chicago.

Miriam and Aaron Oppose Moses

12 Miriam and Aaron began to talk
against Moses because of his Cushite wife,[c] for he had married a Cushite.
2"Has the LORD spoken only through Moses?" they asked. "Hasn't he also spoken
through us?"[d] And the LORD heard this.[e]
3(Now Moses was a very humble man,[f]
more humble than anyone else on the face
of the earth.)
4At once the LORD said to Moses, Aaron
and Miriam, "Come out to the tent of meeting, all three of you." So the three of them
went out. 5Then the LORD came down in a
pillar of cloud;[g] he stood at the entrance
to the tent and summoned Aaron and Miriam. When the two of them stepped forward, 6he said, "Listen to my words:

"When there is a prophet among you,
I, the LORD, reveal myself to them in visions,[h]
I speak to them in dreams.[i]
7But this is not true of my servant Moses;[j]
he is faithful in all my house.[k]
8With him I speak face to face,
clearly and not in riddles;[l]
he sees the form of the LORD.[m]
Why then were you not afraid
to speak against my servant Moses?"

9The anger of the LORD burned against
them, and he left them.[n]
10When the cloud lifted from above the
tent, Miriam's skin was leprous[a]—it became as white as snow.[o] Aaron turned
toward her and saw that she had a defiling skin disease,[p] 11and he said to Moses,
"Please, my lord, I ask you not to hold
against us the sin we have so foolish-
ly committed.[q] 12Do not let her be like a
stillborn infant coming from its mother's
womb with its flesh half eaten away."

12:1 [c]Ex 2:21 **12:2** [d]Nu 16:3 [e]Nu 11:1 **12:3** [f]Mt 11:29 **12:5** [g]Nu 11:25 **12:6** [h]Ge 15:1; 46:2 [i]Ge 31:10; 1Ki 3:5; Heb 1:1 **12:7** [j]Jos 1:1-2; Ps 105:26 [k]Heb 3:2,5 **12:8** [l]Dt 34:10 [m]Ex 20:4; Ps 17:15 **12:9** [n]Ge 17:22 **12:10** [o]Ex 4:6; Dt 24:9 [p]2Ki 5:1,27 **12:11** [q]2Sa 19:19; 24:10

[a] *10* The Hebrew for *leprous* was used for various diseases affecting the skin.

Sin Bisher, then Kibroth Hattaavah and Hazeroth may be situated along the route eastward across the central Sinai region toward Elath and Mount Seir.

12:1 *Cushite wife.* "Cush" has a few possible identifications: (1) On the basis of Ge 2:13; 10:6; Ps 68:31; Isa 18:1, Cush, the first son of Ham, is identified with Nubia in modern Sudan, bordering ancient Egypt on the south. If this connection is assumed, Moses' Cushite wife would be a woman other than Zipporah, his Midianite wife from the clan of Jethro. Some have suggested that Zipporah died and the Cushite wife is of a recent marriage. (2) The synonymous parallel lines in Hab 3:7 suggest an association of Cushan with the Midianites, giving credence to the identity of the Cushite woman with Zipporah. (3) The term Cushite may refer to a distinguishable physiological trait, such as that of the deeply tanned Midianites from northwest Arabia.

Ethnic purity was an important issue in ancient Israel; note the commands to drive out and/or annihilate the Canaanites from the promised land (33:51–56). The Pentateuch, however, contains explicit instructions that there was to be one code of law for the native Israelite and the sojourning foreigners in their midst. In 9:14, non-Israelites living among the Israelites could even celebrate the Passover if they did so according to the statutes related to its commemoration, including circumcision as an indicator of that individual's coming under the covenant relationship with the God of Israel (Ex 12:48–49; cf. Nu 15:14–16,29; Lev 24:22). It would seem, then, that Miriam's complaint against Moses on the basis of ethnicity is not necessarily the real reason for her objections.

12:10 *leprous.* See note on Ex 4:6

13 So Moses cried out to the LORD,
"Please, God, heal her![r]"
14 The LORD replied to Moses, "If her father had spit in her face,[s] would she not
have been in disgrace for seven days? Confine her outside the camp[t] for seven days;
after that she can be brought back." 15 So
Miriam was confined outside the camp for
seven days, and the people did not move
on till she was brought back.
16 After that, the people left Hazeroth[u]
and encamped in the Desert of Paran.

Exploring Canaan

13 The LORD said to Moses, 2 "Send
some men to explore[v] the land of
Canaan, which I am giving to the Israelites. From each ancestral tribe send one
of its leaders."
3 So at the LORD's command Moses sent
them out from the Desert of Paran. All of
them were leaders of the Israelites. 4 These
are their names:

from the tribe of Reuben, Shammua son of Zakkur;
5 from the tribe of Simeon, Shaphat son of Hori;
6 from the tribe of Judah, Caleb son of Jephunneh;[w]
7 from the tribe of Issachar, Igal son of Joseph;
8 from the tribe of Ephraim, Hoshea son of Nun;
9 from the tribe of Benjamin, Palti son of Raphu;
10 from the tribe of Zebulun, Gaddiel son of Sodi;
11 from the tribe of Manasseh (a tribe of Joseph), Gaddi son of Susi;
12 from the tribe of Dan, Ammiel son of Gemalli;
13 from the tribe of Asher, Sethur son of Michael;
14 from the tribe of Naphtali, Nahbi son of Vophsi;
15 from the tribe of Gad, Geuel son of Maki.

16 These are the names of the men Moses
sent to explore the land. (Moses gave Hoshea son of Nun[x] the name Joshua.)[y]
17 When Moses sent them to explore Canaan, he said, "Go up through the Negev[z]
and on into the hill country.[a] 18 See what
the land is like and whether the people
who live there are strong or weak, few or
many. 19 What kind of land do they live in?
Is it good or bad? What kind of towns do
they live in? Are they unwalled or fortified? 20 How is the soil? Is it fertile or poor?
Are there trees in it or not? Do your best to
bring back some of the fruit of the land.[b]"
(It was the season for the first ripe grapes.)
21 So they went up and explored the land
from the Desert of Zin[c] as far as Rehob,[d]
toward Lebo Hamath.[e] 22 They went up
through the Negev and came to Hebron,
where Ahiman, Sheshai and Talmai,[f] the
descendants of Anak,[g] lived. (Hebron
had been built seven years before Zoan in
Egypt.)[h] 23 When they reached the Valley
of Eshkol,[a] they cut off a branch bearing a
single cluster of grapes. Two of them carried it on a pole between them, along with

12:13 [r] Isa 30:26; Jer 17:14 **12:14** [s] Dt 25:9; Job 17:6; 30:9-10; Isa 50:6 [t] Lev 13:46; Nu 5:2-3 **12:16** [u] Nu 11:35 **13:2** [v] Dt 1:22 **13:6** [w] ver 30; Nu 14:6, 24; 34:19; Jdg 1:12-15 **13:16** [x] ver 8 [y] Dt 32:44 **13:17** [z] Ge 12:9 [a] Jdg 1:9 **13:20** [b] Dt 1:25 **13:21** [c] Nu 20:1; 27:14; 33:36; Jos 15:1 [d] Jos 19:28 [e] Jos 13:5 **13:22** [f] Jos 15:14 [g] Jos 15:13 [h] Ps 78:12, 43; Isa 19:11, 13

[a] 23 *Eshkol* means *cluster*; also in verse 24.

13:20 *grapes.* This is the time of the first harvest of the vineyards, hence late summer or early fall, several months after the departure from Mount Sinai in early spring.

13:21–22 *Desert of Zin ... Rehob ... Lebo Hamath.* The 12 Israelite men launched their exploration of the land from the Paran Desert (see the article "Geography of the Wilderness," p. 249). They reached as far north as Rehob of Lebo Hamath in southeast Lebanon. The scouts headed north through the hill country regions later known as Judah, Samaria and Galilee, starting in the Negev and going as far north as Lebo Hamath. See notes on vv. 21,22 below.

13:21 *Desert of Zin.* The Desert of Zin was the region of the drainage basin around the Nahal Zin, an expanse westward on a line from just south of the Dead Sea that includes the wilderness, as well as Kadesh Barnea to the west (v. 26). *Rehob.* The exact location of this Rehob is unknown, though the region of Lebo Hamath suggests a site in southern Lebanon, such as Beth Rehob near Tel Dan on the southern flank of Mount Hermon. *Lebo Hamath.* Has been identified with modern Lebweh on the Orontes River, on the southern border of the ancient kingdom of Hamath and about 14 miles (22 kilometers) north-northeast of Baalbek. Lebo is recounted as a city on the northern border of the promised land (34:7–8) and later of the Israelite kingdom of David and Solomon (1Ki 8:65).

13:22 *Negev.* Hebrew for "south"; it refers to the dry southland. In the OT, the Negev region stretched south from Hebron (Qiryath Arba) into the Desert of Zin (e.g., 21:1; 33:40; Ge 12:9; 13:3; 20:1; 24:62); in modern geography the term denotes the region from the Arad and Beersheba region south to Elath on the Gulf of Aqaba. *Hebron.* Formerly known as Qiryath Arba, is located about 20 miles (32 kilometers) south of Jerusalem in the central hill country. It must have been a prominent city at this time because of its comparison here with the Egyptian stronghold of Zoan. Hebron is said to have been fortified seven years before Zoan. *Ahiman, Sheshai and Talmai.* The ancestors of the Hebronites. These names are Semitic in origin, reflecting the fact that the inhabitants of the land spoke a Semitic dialect. *Anak.* The name is associated with a people feared for their great size and military prowess; it may also be associated with the ethnic phrase *Iy-anaq* found among the Egyptian Execration Texts of the early second millennium BC. Verse 33 in the Septuagint, the pre-Christian Greek translation of the OT, translates the term as "giants," and they were associated with the Rephaim in Dt 2:11 (see note there; cf. also Dt 9:2). Remnants of these giants survived into the time of the judges and the beginning of the Israelite monarchy. No extra-Biblical reference to Anak exists, but an Egyptian letter from the thirteenth century BC describes warriors in Canaan that are 9 feet

some pomegranates and figs. 24 That place was called the Valley of Eshkol because of the cluster of grapes the Israelites cut off there. 25 At the end of forty days they returned from exploring the land.

Report on the Exploration

26 They came back to Moses and Aaron and the whole Israelite community at Kadesh in the Desert of Paran. There they reported to them[i] and to the whole assembly and showed them the fruit of the land. 27 They gave Moses this account: "We went into the land to which you sent us, and it does flow with milk and honey![j] Here is its fruit.[k] 28 But the people who live there are powerful, and the cities are fortified and very large.[l] We even saw descendants of Anak there. 29 The Amalekites live in the Negev; the Hittites, Jebusites and Amorites live in the hill country; and the Canaanites live near the sea and along the Jordan."

30 Then Caleb silenced the people before Moses and said, "We should go up and take possession of the land, for we can certainly do it."

31 But the men who had gone up with him said, "We can't attack those people; they are stronger than we are."[m] 32 And they spread among the Israelites a bad report[n] about the land they had explored. They said, "The land we explored devours[o] those living in it. All the people we saw there are of great size.[p] 33 We saw the Nephilim[q] there (the descendants of Anak[r] come from the Nephilim). We seemed like grasshoppers in our own eyes, and we looked the same to them."

The People Rebel

14 That night all the members of the community raised their voices and wept aloud. 2 All the Israelites grumbled against Moses and Aaron, and the whole assembly said to them, "If only we had died in Egypt! Or in this wilderness![s] 3 Why is the LORD bringing us to this land only to let us fall by the sword? Our wives and children will be taken as plunder. Wouldn't it be better for us to go back to Egypt?" 4 And they said to each other, "We should choose a leader and go back to Egypt.[t]"

13:26 [i] Nu 32:8 **13:27** [j] Ex 3:8 [k] Dt 1:25 **13:28** [l] Dt 1:28; 9:1,2 **13:31** [m] Dt 1:28; 9:1; Jos 14:8 **13:32** [n] Nu 14:36,37 [o] Eze 36:13,14 [p] Am 2:9 **13:33** [q] Ge 6:4 [r] Dt 1:28 **14:2** [s] Nu 11:1 **14:4** [t] Ne 9:17

(2.7 meters) tall. *Zoan.* Located in the eastern Nile delta. This name is the equivalent of the Egyptian Djanet, which was vocalized by the Greeks as Tanis, long identified with the modern site of San el-Hagar.

13:25 *forty days.* The scouts' 40-day exploration of the land accords with the approximate time such a journey would have taken on foot. The number 40 is often used in the Bible for an indefinite period in excess of a month. Having trekked from the Desert of Zin all the way to Lebo Hamath and back again means they would have covered 350–500 miles (550–800 kilometers) while reconnoitering the hill country and valleys. According to the annals of the campaigns of Thutmose III and Rameses II, a day's journey was approximately 12–15 miles (20–25 kilometers).

13:26 *Kadesh in the Desert of Paran.* Kadesh (Barnea) is usually identified with Ain el-Qudeirat in the upper reaches of the Desert of Zin, about 50 miles (80 kilometers) southwest of Beersheba. The springs there produce a volume of about 40 cubic meters (about 1,412 cubic feet) of water per hour. Pottery remains suggest this spring area was often the stopping point for nomadic groups since the late Neolithic period through the Bronze Ages. An Israelite fortress was constructed there in the tenth century BC and destroyed by the Babylonians in 586 BC. The spies' report concludes with a listing of the various Semitic and non-Semitic tribes living throughout the country (v. 29).

13:27 *flow with milk and honey.* See note on Ex 3:8. This classic description of the abundance of certain natural resources in Canaan (e.g., Ex 3:8,17; 13:5; 33:3; Lev 20:24; Dt 6:3; 11:9) is echoed in the Egyptian travel account the *Story of Sinuhe*, in which the princely emissary describes the land of Yaa.

13:29 *Amalekites.* A seminomadic tribe descended from Abraham through Esau (Ge 36:12); their origins were in the region of Edom, and they ranged throughout the southern Levant, from North Sinai to the hill country of Samaria. Hormah (Tel Masos in the Negev) may have been one of their cities (14:45; cf. Ge 36:16; Jdg 12:15; 1Sa 15:7). No reference is found to the Amalekites in ancient Near Eastern documents. *Hittites.* See note on Ge 23:3. *Jebusites.* A non-Semitic clan living in Jerusalem during the Middle Bronze through Iron I periods (2000–1000 BC); they controlled the city through most of the early history of Israel until the time of David (see Jos 15:8,63; 18:16; Jdg 1:8,21; 2Sa 5:6–9). They are unknown outside the Bible, and scholars have suggested they may have been a subclan of the Perizzites or related to the Hurrians. The table of nations in Ge 10:2–29 lists the Jebusites as descendants of Canaan (Ge 10:16). *Amorites.* The term "Amorite" can refer in general to a number of the ethnic groups inhabiting the Levant, including areas known today as Syria, Lebanon, Jordan, Israel and Palestine. It may also refer more specifically to an ethnic descendant of Palestine as delineated in Ge 10:16. Referred to as the Amurru ("Amorites" or "westerners") in Akkadian records at Mari and the Martu in Sumerian texts of the third and second millennia BC, some of this people group established city-states in Syria, while others were more nomadic, migrating southeast into southern Sumer and southwest into the Levant. Egyptian records describe their territory as extending from the Negev (see note on v. 22) to the heights of Lebanon. *Canaanites.* See the article "The Canaanites," p. 294. Aside from being the name of Ham's son in Ge 9, the designation of "Canaan" may derive from the Akkadian *kinannu* ("red purple"), based on the production of red-to-purple dyes produced along coastal regions of Lebanon from the abundant murex shells found there. Other scholars point to the Semitic root *k-n-* meaning "to bend, be subdued." The earliest reference to "Canaan" in extra-Biblical texts comes from the eighteenth century BC in Mari.

13:33 *Nephilim.* See note on Ge 6:4. Referring to the descendants of Anak as Nephilim was designed to instill fear in the hearts of the Israelites in the face of their enemies, to make them feel like grasshoppers. Grasshoppers were the smallest of edible creatures permitted for Israelite consumption (Lev 11:22).

5Then Moses and Aaron fell facedown[u] in front of the whole Israelite assembly gathered there. 6Joshua son of Nun and Caleb son of Jephunneh, who were among those who had explored the land, tore their clothes 7and said to the entire Israelite assembly, "The land we passed through and explored is exceedingly good.[v] 8If the LORD is pleased with us,[w] he will lead us into that land, a land flowing with milk and honey,[x] and will give it to us. 9Only do not rebel[y] against the LORD. And do not be afraid of the people of the land,[z] because we will devour them. Their protection is gone, but the LORD is with us. Do not be afraid of them."

10But the whole assembly talked about stoning[a] them. Then the glory of the LORD[b] appeared at the tent of meeting to all the Israelites. 11The LORD said to Moses, "How long will these people treat me with contempt? How long will they refuse to believe in me,[c] in spite of all the signs I have performed among them? 12I will strike them down with a plague and destroy them, but I will make you into a nation[d] greater and stronger than they."

13Moses said to the LORD, "Then the Egyptians will hear about it! By your power you brought these people up from among them.[e] 14And they will tell the inhabitants of this land about it. They have already heard[f] that you, LORD, are with these people and that you, LORD, have been seen face to face, that your cloud stays over them, and that you go before them in a pillar of cloud by day and a pillar of fire by night.[g] 15If you put all these people to death, leaving none alive, the nations who have heard this report about you will say, 16'The LORD was not able to bring these people into the land he promised them on oath, so he slaughtered them in the wilderness.'[h]

17"Now may the Lord's strength be displayed, just as you have declared: 18'The LORD is slow to anger, abounding in love and forgiving sin and rebellion.[i] Yet he does not leave the guilty unpunished; he punishes the children for the sin of the parents to the third and fourth generation.'[j] 19In accordance with your great love, forgive[k] the sin of these people,[l] just as you have pardoned them from the time they left Egypt until now."[m]

20The LORD replied, "I have forgiven them,[n] as you asked. 21Nevertheless, as surely as I live[o] and as surely as the glory of the LORD fills the whole earth,[p] 22not one of those who saw my glory and the signs I performed in Egypt and in the wilderness but who disobeyed me and tested me ten times[q]— 23not one of them will ever see the land I promised on oath[r] to their ancestors. No one who has treated me with contempt will ever see it.[s] 24But because my servant Caleb has a different spirit and follows me wholeheartedly,[t] I will bring him into the land he went to, and his descendants will inherit it.[u] 25Since the Amalekites and the Canaanites are living in the valleys, turn[v] back tomorrow and set out toward the desert along the route to the Red Sea.[a]"

26The LORD said to Moses and Aaron: 27"How long will this wicked community grumble against me? I have heard the complaints of these grumbling Israelites.[w] 28So tell them, 'As surely as I live,[x] declares the LORD, I will do to you the very thing I heard you say: 29In this wilderness your bodies will fall[y]—every one of you twenty years old or more[z] who was counted in the census and who has grumbled against me. 30Not one of you will enter the land I swore with uplifted hand to make your home, except Caleb son of Jephunneh and Joshua son of Nun. 31As for your children that you said would be taken as plunder, I will bring them in to enjoy the land you have rejected.[a] 32But as for you, your bodies will fall[b] in this wilderness. 33Your children will be shepherds here for forty years, suffering for your unfaithfulness, until the last of your bodies lies in the wilderness. 34For forty years—one year for each of the forty days you explored the land[c]—you will suffer for your sins and know what it is like to have me against you.' 35I, the LORD, have spoken, and I will surely do these things[d] to this whole wicked community, which has banded together

[a] 25 Or *the Sea of Reeds*

14:5 [u] Nu 16:4, 22, 45 **14:7** [v] Nu 13:27; Dt 1:25 **14:8** [w] Dt 10:15 [x] Nu 13:27 **14:9** [y] Dt 1:26; 9:7, 23, 24 [z] Dt 1:21; 7:18; 20:1 **14:10** [a] Ex 17:4 [b] Lev 9:23 **14:11** [c] Ps 78:22; 106:24 **14:12** [d] Ex 32:10 **14:13** [e] Ex 32:11-14; Ps 106:23 **14:14** [f] Ex 15:14 [g] Ex 13:21 **14:16** [h] Jos 7:7 **14:18** [i] Ex 34:6; Ps 145:8; Jnh 4:2 [j] Ex 20:5 **14:19** [k] Ex 34:9 [l] Ps 106:45 [m] Ps 78:38 **14:20** [n] Ps 106:23; Mic 7:18-20 **14:21** [o] Dt 32:40; Isa 49:18 [p] Ps 72:19; Isa 6:3; Hab 2:14 **14:22** [q] Ex 14:11; 32:1; 1Co 10:5 **14:23** [r] Nu 32:11 [s] Heb 3:18 **14:24** [t] ver 6-9; Jos 14:8, 14 [u] Nu 32:12 **14:25** [v] Dt 1:40 **14:27** [w] Ex 16:12 **14:28** [x] ver 21 **14:29** [y] Nu 26:65 [z] Nu 1:45 **14:31** [a] Ps 106:24 **14:32** [b] 1Co 10:5 **14:34** [c] Nu 13:25 **14:35** [d] Nu 23:19

14:6 *tore their clothes.* A form of self-debasing lament in the OT; widely practiced in the ancient Near East when mourning for the dead, expressing sorrow over disease or plague, or prefacing a prophetic lament of judgment against an individual or nation.

14:13–14 Everyone in the ancient Near East believed in the patronage of gods, whether for cities or professions (Marduk for Babylon, Thoth for scribes, etc.). Clans had their divine patrons as well, and individuals connected to deities whom they thought of as their "personal gods." This meant that when a people went to war, their gods fought alongside them. The god(s) of the losing side were discredited and often abandoned by their worshipers. If Yahweh were to destroy the Israelites, it might be interpreted as a failure on Yahweh's part to fulfill his duties as their patron.

14:25 *the route to the Red Sea.* The "Way of the Red Sea Wilderness" was the trade route connecting to Ezion Geber on the Gulf of Aqaba/Elath from Kadesh Barnea through the Desert of Zin and the southern Arabah. A second leg of the route then extended westward across the central Sinai peninsula toward Egypt.

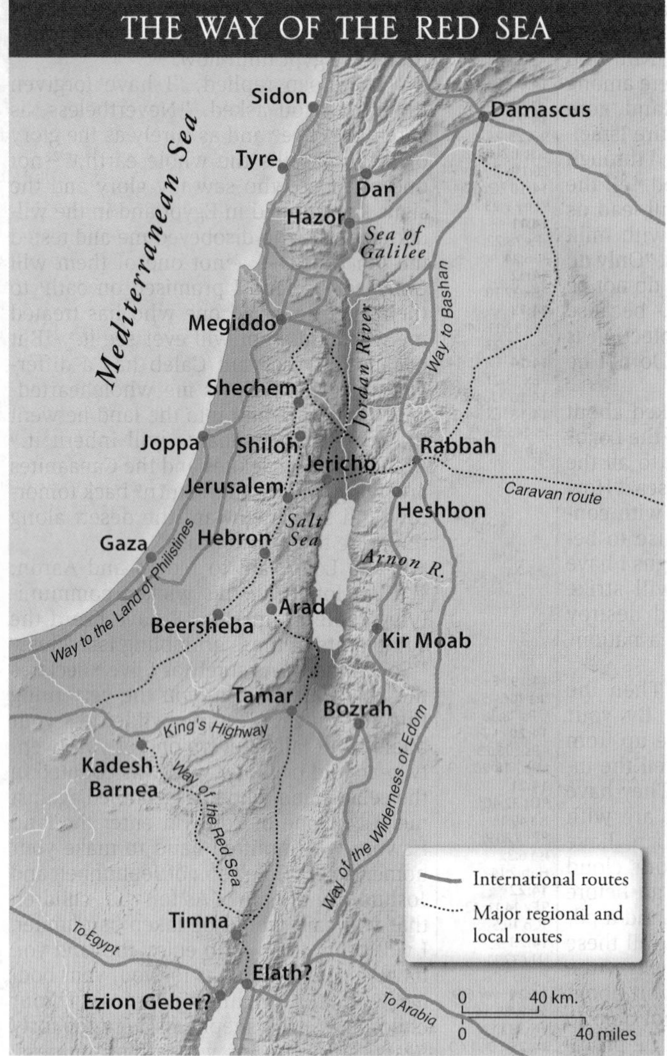

against me. They will meet their end in
this wilderness; here they will die."
36So the men Moses had sent[e] to explore
the land, who returned and made the
whole community grumble against him by
spreading a bad report[f] about it — 37these
men who were responsible for spreading
the bad report[g] about the land were struck
down and died of a plague[h] before the
LORD. 38Of the men who went to explore
the land, only Joshua son of Nun and Caleb son of Jephunneh survived.[i]
39When Moses reported this to all the
Israelites, they mourned[j] bitterly. 40Early the next morning they set out for the highest point in the hill country,
saying, "Now we are ready
to go up to the land the LORD
promised. Surely we have
sinned![k]"
41But Moses said, "Why
are you disobeying the
LORD's command? This will
not succeed![l] 42Do not go up,
because the LORD is not with
you. You will be defeated by
your enemies,[m] 43for the Amalekites and the Canaanites
will face you there. Because
you have turned away from
the LORD, he will not be with
you and you will fall by the
sword."
44Nevertheless, in their
presumption they went up[n]
toward the highest point in
the hill country, though neither Moses nor the ark of the
LORD's covenant moved from
the camp.[o] 45Then the Amalekites and the Canaanites
who lived in that hill country came down and attacked
them and beat them down all
the way to Hormah.[p]

14:36 [e]Nu 13:4-16 [f]Nu 13:32 **14:37** [g]1Co 10:10 [h]Nu 16:49 **14:38** [i]Jos 14:6 **14:39** [j]Ex 33:4 **14:40** [k]Dt 1:41 **14:41** [l]2Ch 24:20 **14:42** [m]Dt 1:42 **14:44** [n]Dt 1:43 [o]Nu 31:6 **14:45** [p]Nu 21:3;

Supplementary Offerings

15 The LORD said to Moses, 2"Speak to the Israelites and say to them: 'After you enter the land I am
giving you[q] as a home 3and
you present to the LORD food
offerings from the herd or the
flock,[r] as an aroma pleasing
to the LORD[s] — whether burnt offerings[t]
or sacrifices, for special vows or freewill
offerings[u] or festival offerings[v] — 4then
the person who brings an offering shall
present to the LORD a grain offering[w] of
a tenth of an ephah[a] of the finest flour
mixed with a quarter of a hin[b] of olive oil.

[a] 4 That is, probably about 3 1/2 pounds or about 1.6 kilograms [b] 4 That is, about 1 quart or about 1 liter; also in verse 5

Dt 1:44; Jdg 1:17 **15:2** [q]Lev 23:10 **15:3** [r]Lev 1:2 [s]ver 24; Ge 8:21; Ex 29:18 [t]Nu 28:19,27 [u]Lev 22:18,21; Ezr 1:4 [v]Lev 23:1-44 **15:4** [w]Lev 2:1; 6:14

15:3 *food offerings.* The "fellowship" (or "peace") offering, the "special" (i.e., "vow") offering, and the "freewill" offering were offerings of the communion type, in which certain portions of animals were offered to God as a savory aroma, and the remaining were consumed by the priests and the offerer in the communal setting of the tabernacle or temple. Hence, the totality of the Israelite community engaged in a corporate meal that celebrated the unity of the community of faith. *an aroma pleasing to the LORD.* Unlike the descriptions noted in Mesopotamian ritual texts, which depict the gods as consuming the sacrifices as necessary to their survival, God's pleasure in the Israel-

5With each lamb for the burnt offering or the sacrifice, prepare a quarter of a hin of wine[x] as a drink offering.

6“ ‘With a ram[y] prepare a grain offering[z] of two-tenths of an ephah[a] of the finest flour mixed with a third of a hin[b] of olive oil,[a] 7and a third of a hin of wine as a drink offering. Offer it as an aroma pleasing to the LORD.

8“ ‘When you prepare a young bull as a burnt offering or sacrifice, for a special vow or a fellowship offering[b] to the LORD, 9bring with the bull a grain offering of three-tenths of an ephah[c][c] of the finest flour mixed with half a hin[d] of olive oil, 10and also bring half a hin of wine as a drink offering. This will be a food offering, an aroma pleasing to the LORD. 11Each bull or ram, each lamb or young goat, is to be prepared in this manner. 12Do this for each one, for as many as you prepare.

13“ ‘Everyone who is native-born[d] must do these things in this way when they present a food offering as an aroma pleasing to the LORD. 14For the generations to come, whenever a foreigner or anyone else living among you presents a food offering as an aroma pleasing to the LORD, they must do exactly as you do. 15The community is to have the same rules for you and for the foreigner residing among you; this is a lasting ordinance for the generations to come.[e] You and the foreigner shall be the same before the LORD: 16The same laws and regulations will apply both to you and to the foreigner residing among you.[f]’ ”

17The LORD said to Moses, 18“Speak to the Israelites and say to them: ‘When you enter the land to which I am taking you 19and you eat the food of the land,[g] present a portion as an offering to the LORD. 20Present a loaf from the first of your ground meal[h] and present it as an offering from the threshing floor.[i] 21Throughout the generations to come you are to give this offering to the LORD from the first of your ground meal.[j]

Offerings for Unintentional Sins

22“ ‘Now if you as a community unintentionally fail to keep any of these commands the LORD gave Moses[k]— 23any of the LORD's commands to you through him, from the day the LORD gave them and continuing through the generations to come— 24and if this is done unintentionally without the community being aware of it,[l] then the whole community is to offer a young bull for a burnt offering[m] as an aroma pleasing to the LORD, along with its prescribed grain offering and drink offering, and a male goat for a sin offering.[e][n] 25The priest is to make atonement for the whole Israelite community, and they will be forgiven,[o] for it was not intentional and they have presented to the LORD for their wrong a food offering and a sin offering. 26The whole Israelite community and the foreigners residing among them will be forgiven, because all the people were involved in the unintentional wrong.[p]

27“ ‘But if just one person sins unintentionally,[q] that person must bring a year-old female goat for a sin offering. 28The priest is to make atonement before the LORD for the one who erred by sinning unintentionally, and when atonement has been made, that person will be forgiven.[r] 29One and the same law applies to everyone who sins unintentionally, whether a native-born Israelite or a foreigner residing among you.

30“ ‘But anyone who sins defiantly,[s] whether native-born or foreigner,[t] blasphemes the LORD and must be cut off from the people of Israel. 31Because they have

15:5 [x] Nu 28:7, 14
15:6 [y] Lev 5:15 [z] Nu 28:12 [a] Eze 46:14
15:8 [b] Lev 1:3; 3:1
15:9 [c] Lev 14:10
15:13 [d] Lev 16:29
15:15 [e] ver 29; Nu 9:14
15:16 [f] Nu 9:14
15:19 [g] Jos 5:11, 12
15:20 [h] Ex 34:26; Lev 23:14; Dt 26:2, 10 [i] Lev 2:14
15:21 [j] Ro 11:16
15:22 [k] Lev 4:2
15:24 [l] Lev 5:15 [m] Lev 4:14 [n] Lev 4:3
15:25 [o] Lev 4:20; Ro 3:25; Heb 2:17
15:26 [p] ver 24
15:27 [q] Lev 4:27
15:28 [r] Lev 4:35
15:30 [s] Nu 14:40-44; Dt 1:43; 17:13; Ps 19:13 [t] ver 14

[a] *6* That is, probably about 7 pounds or about 3.2 kilograms [b] *6* That is, about 1 1/3 quarts or about 1.3 liters; also in verse 7 [c] *9* That is, probably about 11 pounds or about 5 kilograms [d] *9* That is, about 2 quarts or about 1.9 liters; also in verse 10 [e] *24* Or *purification offering*; also in verses 25 and 27

ite sacrifices is described in anthropomorphic terms of a pleasing aroma that ascends in the smoke into the invisible realm of the heavenly abode.

15:20 *the first of your ground meal.* During the spring harvest of barley and wheat (the season of Passover, Unleavened Bread and Weeks), the grain firstfruit offering was presented to God. Even the mundane daily practice of kneading dough for making bread was a time of worship and celebration of God's benevolence and faithfulness. The first or choicest dough made from the first coarsely ground flour of the season was set aside for honoring God. Bread was the essential food staple, and hence a sacred sacrifice was rendered back to God as the giver of life and the provider of grain from which the bread was made. Similarly, wine and grapes from the vineyard, olive oil and olives from the orchard, and fruit juices from the fall fruit harvest were offered to God. According to 18:11 – 16, all firstfruits and products brought to Yahweh were supplied to the priests.

15:30 *sins defiantly.* The raised right hand with the outstretched arm was a common symbol of strength and power in ancient Near Eastern literature and iconography. The sinner with a high hand feels no guilt; thus, the offense is not sacrificially expiable. Such a defiant person must suffer the ultimate of judgment: being "cut off." *blasphemes.* This is the only occurrence of the Hebrew word translated "to blaspheme" and it means to taunt or revile God such as to deny his authority. This act represents defiance of the law and is so dangerous to the community that it necessitates the perpetrator being "cut off." *cut off.* Hebrew *karat*; it was reserved for the most heinous or sacrilegious offenses. This may involve capital punishment but probably implies divine punishment by the elimination of the family line. A Babylonian text from the sixth

despised the LORD's word and broken his
commands,[u] they must surely be cut off;
their guilt remains on them.[v]' "

The Sabbath-Breaker Put to Death

32While the Israelites were in the wilderness, a man was found gathering wood
on the Sabbath day.[w] 33Those who found
him gathering wood brought him to Moses
and Aaron and the whole assembly, 34and
they kept him in custody, because it was
not clear what should be done to him.[x]
35Then the LORD said to Moses, "The man
must die.[y] The whole assembly must stone
him outside the camp."[z] 36So the assembly
took him outside the camp and stoned him
to death, as the LORD commanded Moses.

Tassels on Garments

37The LORD said to Moses, 38"Speak to
the Israelites and say to them: 'Throughout the generations to come you are to
make tassels on the corners of your garments,[a] with a blue cord on each tassel.
39You will have these tassels to look at and
so you will remember[b] all the commands
of the LORD, that you may obey them and
not prostitute yourselves by chasing after the lusts of your own hearts and eyes.
40Then you will remember to obey all my
commands and will be consecrated to
your God.[c] 41I am the LORD your God, who
brought you out of Egypt to be your God.
I am the LORD your God.' "

15:31 [u] 2Sa 12:9; Ps 119:126; Pr 13:13 [v] Lev 5:1; Eze 18:20 **15:32** [w] Ex 31:14, 15; 35:2, 3 **15:34** [x] Nu 9:8 **15:35** [y] Ex 31:14, 15; Dt 21:21 [z] Lev 20:2; 24:14; Ac 7:58 **15:38** [a] Dt 22:12; Mt 23:5 **15:39** [b] Dt 4:23; 6:12; Ps 73:27 **15:40** [c] Lev 11:44; Ro 12:1; Col 1:22; 1Pe 1:15

Korah, Dathan and Abiram

16 Korah[d] son of Izhar, the son of Kohath, the son of Levi, and certain
Reubenites—Dathan and Abiram, sons of
Eliab,[e] and On son of Peleth—became insolent[a] 2and rose up against Moses. With
them were 250 Israelite men, well-known
community leaders who had been appointed members of the council.[f] 3They
came as a group to oppose Moses and Aaron[g] and said to them, "You have gone too
far! The whole community is holy,[h] every
one of them, and the LORD is with them.[i]
Why then do you set yourselves above the
LORD's assembly?"[j]
4When Moses heard this, he fell facedown.[k] 5Then he said to Korah and all his
followers: "In the morning the LORD will
show who belongs to him and who is
holy,[l] and he will have that person come
near him. The man he chooses[m] he will
cause to come near him. 6You, Korah, and
all your followers are to do this: Take censers 7and tomorrow put burning coals and
incense in them before the LORD. The man
the LORD chooses will be the one who is
holy. You Levites have gone too far!"

16:1 [d] Jude 1:11 [e] Nu 26:8; Dt 11:6 **16:2** [f] Nu 1:16; 26:9 **16:3** [g] ver 7; Ps 106:16 [h] Ex 19:6 [i] Nu 14:14 [j] Nu 12:2 **16:4** [k] Nu 14:5 **16:5** [l] Lev 10:3; 2Ti 2:19* [m] Nu 17:5; Ps 65:4

[a] 1 Or *Peleth—took men*

century BC charges king Nabonidus with failing to recognize the authority of Marduk; the god abandoned the city and allowed it to fall to the Persians. In the OT, five categories of infractions in which the *karat* was meted out are identifiable: (1) violation of sacred time, as in the neglect of certain holy days; (2) violation of sacred substance, such as in the consumption of blood; (3) neglect of purification ritual, such as circumcision; (4) illicit worship, such as idolatry or sorcery; and (5) illicit sexual activity, such as incest or bestiality.

15:32–36 This provides a legal etiology concerning the seriousness of the Sabbath regulations and provides a precedent for future violations. Detention of the culprit is temporary until God provides the proper punishment, which is stoning. Executions must be performed outside the camp to prevent contamination from the corpse.

15:38 *tassels.* In the ancient Near East, special garments were made for priests and royalty that identified them within their communities and to the outside world. Several images of garments with corded fringes are found on the statue of Puzur-Ishtar, governor of Mari in the late third millennium BC, on depictions of Asiatics in the tomb of the Egyptian Khnumhotep II in the nineteenth century BC, and in later Neo-Assyrian murals. Tassels were attached to the outer garment used by Israelite men. Both men and women wore an outer cloak and wrapped it around their bodies or draped it over the shoulder. A belt secured it to protect a person from inclement weather. It functioned as a cover during the night and was considered valuable enough to secure a debt (Ex 22:26–27; Dt 24:10–13). The Black Obelisk (c. 820 BC) contains a picture of King Jehu of Israel with a fringed outer garment laid over his left shoulder.

16:1 *Reubenites ... sons of Eliab.* In tribal and clan-structured societies of the ancient Near East, the position of leadership often fell on the eldest son of the family patriarch. The men of Reuben, Jacob's firstborn, sought to claim what they perceived as their rightful positions in Israel, thereby usurping the role of Moses. Rivalries between kinship groups (in this case the Reubenites versus Moses, a Levite) are common in tribal confederations. In this loose political structure, loyalties to smaller kinship groups often supersede loyalty to the larger group. This mixed loyalty remains problematic even into the monarchy (2Sa 20:1–2; 1Ki 12:16–17).

As the Reubenites desire to supplant Moses, so Korah wants to supplant Aaron. Korah's lineage is traced back fully through three major figures in the Levitical line. As a Kohathite, Korah was among the favored clan of the Levites whose responsibility was to transport the sacred furnishings of the tabernacle after being packed by the Aaronic priests (4:1–20; cf. Ex 6:16–25). All priests are Levites, but not all Levites are priests. The priests are the descendants of Aaron and actually performed the rituals in the sacred areas. Although the Levites are members of the priestly caste, they have less power and privilege than the designated Aaronic priests. Korah is attempting to claim this distinct status for himself.

16:6 *censers.* Censers for incense were pans or shallow bowls at the end of long handles (Lev 10:1). These pans carried hot coals on which incense could be sprinkled, creating a savory aroma. Such censers are believed to have originated in Egypt, where they were used in the performance of apotropaic magic for driving away evil deities or demonic forces by waving them in a ritual manner.

16:7 *incense.* Often burned on small incense altars or

8Moses also said to Korah, "Now listen, you Levites! 9Isn't it enough for you
that the God of Israel has separated you
from the rest of the Israelite community
and brought you near himself to do the
work at the LORD's tabernacle and to stand
before the community and minister to
them?[n] 10He has brought you and all your
fellow Levites near himself, but now you
are trying to get the priesthood too.[o] 11It
is against the LORD that you and all your
followers have banded together. Who is
Aaron that you should grumble[p] against
him?[q]"

12Then Moses summoned Dathan and
Abiram, the sons of Eliab. But they said,
"We will not come! 13Isn't it enough that
you have brought us up out of a land flowing with milk and honey to kill us in the
wilderness?[r] And now you also want to
lord it over us![s] 14Moreover, you haven't
brought us into a land flowing with milk
and honey[t] or given us an inheritance of
fields and vineyards.[u] Do you want to treat
these men like slaves[a]?[v] No, we will not
come!"

15Then Moses became very angry and
said to the LORD, "Do not accept their offering. I have not taken so much as a donkey[w] from them, nor have I wronged any
of them."

16Moses said to Korah, "You and all
your followers are to appear before the
LORD tomorrow—you and they and Aaron.[x] 17Each man is to take his censer and
put incense in it—250 censers in all—and
present it before the LORD. You and Aaron are to present your censers also." 18So
each of them took his censer, put burning
coals and incense in it, and stood with Moses and Aaron at the entrance to the tent
of meeting. 19When Korah had gathered all
his followers in opposition to them[y] at the
entrance to the tent of meeting, the glory
of the LORD[z] appeared to the entire assem-

16:9 [n] Nu 3:6; Dt 10:8 **16:10** [o] Nu 3:10; 18:7 **16:11** [p] 1Co 10:10 [q] Ex 16:7 **16:13** [r] Nu 14:2 [s] Ac 7:27,35 **16:14** [t] Lev 20:24 [u] Ex 22:5; 23:11; Nu 20:5 [v] Jdg 16:21; 1Sa 11:2 **16:15** [w] 1Sa 12:3 **16:16** [x] ver 6 **16:19** [y] ver 42 [z] Ex 16:7; Nu 14:10; 20:6

16:21 [a] Ex 32:10 **16:22** [b] Nu 14:5 [c] Nu 27:16; Job 12:10; Heb 12:9 [d] Ge 18:23 **16:26** [e] Isa 52:11 [f] Ge 19:15 **16:28** [g] Ex 3:12; Jn 5:36; 6:38 **16:29** [h] Ecc 3:19 **16:30** [i] ver 33; Ps 55:15 **16:31** [j] Mic 1:3-4 **16:32** [k] Nu 26:11; Dt 11:6; Ps 106:17

bly. 20The LORD said to Moses and Aaron,
21"Separate yourselves from this assembly
so I can put an end to them at once."[a]

22But Moses and Aaron fell facedown[b]
and cried out, "O God, the God who gives
breath to all living things,[c] will you be angry with the entire assembly when only
one man sins?"[d]

23Then the LORD said to Moses, 24"Say to
the assembly, 'Move away from the tents
of Korah, Dathan and Abiram.'"

25Moses got up and went to Dathan and
Abiram, and the elders of Israel followed
him. 26He warned the assembly, "Move
back from the tents of these wicked men![e]
Do not touch anything belonging to them,
or you will be swept away[f] because of all
their sins." 27So they moved away from the
tents of Korah, Dathan and Abiram. Dathan and Abiram had come out and were
standing with their wives, children and
little ones at the entrances to their tents.

28Then Moses said, "This is how you
will know that the LORD has sent me[g] to
do all these things and that it was not my
idea: 29If these men die a natural death
and suffer the fate of all mankind, then
the LORD has not sent me.[h] 30But if the
LORD brings about something totally new,
and the earth opens its mouth and swallows them, with everything that belongs
to them, and they go down alive into the
realm of the dead,[i] then you will know
that these men have treated the LORD with
contempt."

31As soon as he finished saying all this,
the ground under them split apart[j] 32and
the earth opened its mouth and swallowed
them[k] and their households, and all those
associated with Korah, together with their
possessions. 33They went down alive into
the realm of the dead, with everything
they owned; the earth closed over them,

[a] 14 Or *to deceive these men*; Hebrew *Will you gouge out the eyes of these men*

---

cultic stands made of bronze, stone or ceramics. In ancient Near Eastern cultic contexts, incense was often offered to pacify or appease the wrath of gods and goddesses and to soothe their spirits. Incense enhanced the sweet-smelling aroma of burning sacrifices that ascended into the heavens, symbolically entering into the nostrils of God (or the gods) (cf., e.g., Lev 1:9,13,17; 2:2,9,11; 3:5,16). Incense was produced from the sap, bark, roots and fruits of a variety of trees and shrubs, especially from East Africa and Arabia. *The man the LORD chooses.* Moses orchestrates a test, ordering the followers of Korah to burn incense before God. This was the exclusive prerogative of the priests and could be dangerous for anyone, priest or not (cf. Lev 10:1–2), who did it improperly.

16:33 *the realm of the dead.* The grave (Sheol) at this point in Israel's history was perceived to be a shadowy, unknown realm of the dead—the netherworld of both good and evil where one was gathered to one's ancestors at death. Normally, one placed a dead person in a cave or man-made tomb, where the body slowly deteriorated. Later the bones of the deceased were added or gathered to those of one's ancestors in the ancestral burial site. But in this incident the bodies of the rebels (and perhaps their families as well as their possessions) plummeted into a gaping abyss, which soon closed over them with collapsed dirt and rock from the desert terrain. The second census informs us that Korah's fate was the same as that of Dathan and Abiram (26:10).

Sheol is described as opening its mouth to receive the dead (Pr 1:12; Isa 5:14; Hab 2:5) in a manner parallel to the Canaanite god Mot. In the Baal Cycle, the champion deity admonishes his emissaries to Mot to beware "lest he put you in his mouth like a lamb, and crush you like a kid in his jaws." Later Baal himself was mortally wounded and descended into the belly of Mot; Mot "stretched out his tongue to the stars, Baal entered his innards, he

and they perished and were gone from the community. [34]At their cries, all the Israelites around them fled, shouting, "The earth is going to swallow us too!"

[35]And fire came out from the LORD[l] and consumed[m] the 250 men who were offering the incense.

[36]The LORD said to Moses, [37]"Tell Eleazar son of Aaron, the priest, to remove the censers from the charred remains and scatter the coals some distance away, for the censers are holy— [38]the censers of the men who sinned at the cost of their lives.[n] Hammer the censers into sheets to overlay the altar, for they were presented before the LORD and have become holy. Let them be a sign[o] to the Israelites."

[39]So Eleazar the priest collected the bronze censers brought by those who had been burned to death, and he had them hammered out to overlay the altar, [40]as the LORD directed him through Moses. This was to remind the Israelites that no one except a descendant of Aaron should come to burn incense[p] before the LORD,[q] or he would become like Korah and his followers.[r]

[41]The next day the whole Israelite community grumbled against Moses and Aaron. "You have killed the LORD's people," they said.

[42]But when the assembly gathered in opposition[s] to Moses and Aaron and turned toward the tent of meeting, suddenly the cloud covered it and the glory of the LORD appeared. [43]Then Moses and Aaron went to the front of the tent of meeting, [44]and the LORD said to Moses, [45]"Get away from this assembly so I can put an end to them at once." And they fell facedown.

[46]Then Moses said to Aaron, "Take your censer and put incense in it, along with burning coals from the altar, and hurry to the assembly[t] to make atonement[u] for them. Wrath has come out from the LORD; the plague[v] has started." [47]So Aaron did as Moses said, and ran into the midst of the assembly. The plague had already started among the people,[w] but Aaron offered the incense and made atonement for them. [48]He stood between the living and the dead, and the plague stopped.[x] [49]But 14,700 people died from the plague, in addition to those who had died because of Korah.[y] [50]Then Aaron returned to Moses at the entrance to the tent of meeting, for the plague had stopped.[a]

The Budding of Aaron's Staff

17 [b] The LORD said to Moses, [2]"Speak to the Israelites and get twelve staffs from them, one from the leader of each of their ancestral tribes. Write the name of each man on his staff. [3]On the staff of Levi write Aaron's name,[z] for there must be one staff for the head of each ancestral tribe. [4]Place them in the tent of meeting in front of the ark of the covenant law,[a] where I meet with you.[b] [5]The staff belonging to the man I choose[c] will sprout, and I will rid myself of this constant grumbling against you by the Israelites."

[6]So Moses spoke to the Israelites, and their leaders gave him twelve staffs, one for the leader of each of their ancestral tribes, and Aaron's staff was among them. [7]Moses placed the staffs before the LORD in the tent of the covenant law.[d]

[8]The next day Moses entered the tent and saw that Aaron's staff, which represented the tribe of Levi, had not only sprouted but had budded, blossomed and produced almonds.[e] [9]Then Moses brought out all the staffs from the LORD's presence to all the Israelites. They looked at them, and each of the leaders took his own staff.

[10]The LORD said to Moses, "Put back Aaron's staff in front of the ark of the covenant law, to be kept as a sign to the rebellious.[f] This will put an end to their grumbling against me, so that they will

16:35 [l]Nu 11:1-3; 26:10 [m]Lev 10:2
16:38 [n]Pr 20:2 [o]Nu 26:10; Eze 14:8; 2Pe 2:6
16:40 [p]Ex 30:7-10; Nu 1:51 [q]2Ch 26:18 [r]Nu 3:10
16:42 [s]ver 19; Nu 20:6
16:46 [t]Lev 10:6 [u]Nu 18:5; 25:13; Dt 9:22 [v]Nu 8:19; Ps 106:29
16:47 [w]Nu 25:6-8
16:48 [x]Nu 25:8; Ps 106:30
16:49 [y]ver 32
17:3 [z]Nu 1:3
17:4 [a]ver 7 [b]Ex 25:22
17:5 [c]Nu 16:5
17:7 [d]Ex 38:21; Ac 7:44
17:8 [e]Eze 17:24; Heb 9:4
17:10 [f]Dt 9:24

[a] *50* In Hebrew texts 16:36-50 is numbered 17:1-15.
[b] In Hebrew texts 17:1-13 is numbered 17:16-28.

descended into his mouth." Here the realm of Sheol and the dead is under the sovereign power of Israel's God; since Moses pronounces the curse prior to the event, no one can mistake the judgment as circumstantial.

16:46–47 This plague is a visitation of the destroyer angel who had destroyed the firstborn of Egypt. Aaron burns incense in an attempt to avert God's wrath, a remedy similar to the blood on the doorposts in Ex 12:7. Although blood sacrifice is more common, incense burned by an authorized priest can expiate sin and guard against God's anger. Aaron's walking among the dead is extraordinary, since priests are normally not allowed to come into contact with corpses, and demonstrates the desperate measures required by the situation.

17:2 *staff.* The official symbol of the tribal chieftain; in Babylonia and Egypt it often was designed so as to signify its owner (see Ge 38:18). The Hebrew *matteh* means both "tribe" and "staff/scepter" and hence carried some representation of the tribe's identity. In this context the names were inscribed for unmistakable identification.

The use of wood articles to discern the will of the gods is well documented in the ancient Near East, wherein the wooden symbols of Asherah, Astarte or Ishtar are used in fertility rites. Even in Egypt Asherah was combined with Hathor during the Nineteenth Dynasty (the twelfth century BC) and represented as a nude figure standing on a lion and holding snakes and flowers. In the Ugaritic "Incantation Against Sorcery," Baal uses his staff to drive off a man's accuser into the underworld. Such cultic practices were forbidden and condemned elsewhere in the OT; the event here is not to be repeated and is not part of a cultic ritual, and cannot be confused with the divination practices condemned in Hos 4:12.

not die.” 11Moses did just as the LORD commanded him.
12The Israelites said to Moses, “We will
die! We are lost, we are all lost![g] 13Any-
one who even comes near the tabernacle
of the LORD will die.[h] Are we all going to
die?”

Duties of Priests and Levites

18 The LORD said to Aaron, “You, your
sons and your family are to bear
the responsibility for offenses connected with the sanctuary,[i] and you and your
sons alone are to bear the responsibility
for offenses connected with the priesthood. 2Bring your fellow Levites from your
ancestral tribe to join you and assist you
when you and your sons minister[j] before
the tent of the covenant law. 3They are to
be responsible to you and are to perform
all the duties of the tent,[k] but they must
not go near the furnishings of the sanctuary or the altar. Otherwise both they and
you will die.[l] 4They are to join you and
be responsible for the care of the tent of
meeting — all the work at the tent — and
no one else may come near where you are.
5“You are to be responsible for the care
of the sanctuary and the altar,[m] so that my
wrath will not fall on the Israelites again.
6I myself have selected your fellow Levites
from among the Israelites as a gift to you,[n]
dedicated to the LORD to do the work at the
tent of meeting. 7But only you and your
sons may serve as priests in connection
with everything at the altar and inside the
curtain.[o] I am giving you the service of
the priesthood as a gift.[p] Anyone else who
comes near the sanctuary is to be put to
death.[q]”

Offerings for Priests and Levites

8Then the LORD said to Aaron, “I myself have put you in charge of the offerings presented to me; all the holy offerings the Israelites give me I give to you
and your sons as your portion, your perpetual share.[r] 9You are to have the part of
the most holy offerings that is kept from
the fire. From all the gifts they bring me
as most holy offerings, whether grain[s] or
sin[a][t] or guilt offerings,[u] that part belongs
to you and your sons. 10Eat it as something
most holy; every male shall eat it.[v] You
must regard it as holy.
11“This also is yours: whatever is set
aside from the gifts of all the wave offerings[w] of the Israelites. I give this to you
and your sons and daughters as your perpetual share. Everyone in your household
who is ceremonially clean[x] may eat it.
12“I give you all the finest olive oil and
all the finest new wine and grain they give
the LORD as the firstfruits of their harvest.[y]
13All the land’s firstfruits that they bring to
the LORD will be yours.[z] Everyone in your
household who is ceremonially clean may
eat it.
14“Everything in Israel that is devoted[b]
to the LORD[a] is yours. 15The first offspring
of every womb, both human and animal,

[a] 9 Or *purification* [b] 14 The Hebrew term refers to the irrevocable giving over of things or persons to the LORD.

17:12 [g] Isa 6:5
17:13 [h] Nu 1:51
18:1 [i] Ex 28:38
18:2 [j] Nu 3:10
18:3 [k] Nu 1:51
[l] ver 7; Nu 4:15
18:5
[m] Nu 16:46
18:6 [n] Nu 3:9
18:7
[o] Heb 9:3,6
[p] ver 20; Ex 29:9
[q] Nu 3:10
18:8 [r] Lev 6:16; 7:6,31-34,36
18:9 [s] Lev 2:1
[t] Lev 6:25
[u] Lev 5:15; 7:7
18:10 [v] Lev 6:16
18:11
[w] Ex 29:26
[x] Lev 22:1-16
18:12
[y] Ex 23:19; Ne 10:35
18:13
[z] Ex 22:29; 23:19
18:14
[a] Lev 27:28

18:1 *offenses connected with the sanctuary.* This phrase should be read as “infractions against the purity of the sanctuary.” Impurity was an external force that attached itself to a person. Ridding oneself of this foreign force was the primary purpose of expiation. The priests and Levites provided a layer of security for the nation as a holy and undefiled people and defined its prophetic destiny as God’s people in the midst of a defiled world. Encroachment by any outside or unauthorized person on the holy objects was punishable by death. Priests were also culpable of violating the sanctity of the Holy Place if they allowed an unauthorized person within its defined sacred space. The priests themselves were prohibited from going beyond the curtain and entering the Most Holy Place; only the high priest was permitted to enter that sanctum on the Day of Atonement.
18:3 *they must not go near.* The full sanctuary of ancient Israel consisted of concentric zones of holiness. Each zone had its own rules of purity and accessibility. See the article “Zones of Purity in the Camp of Israel,” p. 202.
18:9 *most holy offerings.* The priestly tribute is divided into two levels of sanctity. The holiest of the offerings, to be consumed only by the priests, were made up of the people’s dedicated offerings presented at the sanctuary — grain offerings, plus sin (purification) and guilt (reparation) offerings (Lev 4:1 – 35; 5:14 – 19; 7:1 – 10). The grain offering (Lev 2:1 – 13; 6:14 – 23) was an unleavened mixture of fine flour, oil and incense. A memorial portion was burned on the altar as a sweet aroma to Yahweh, with the remainder eaten by the Aaronic priests (see note on Lev 7:7).
18:11 *wave offerings.* See note on Lev 7:30.
18:12 *firstfruits.* The three plant products specified here were the cream of the crop — the very finest of the olive oil, wine and grain. These first processed offerings were distinguished from the normal firstfruit offerings of the first ripe olives, grapes and grain (Lev 2:14). The first yields of what was produced from oil from the olive crushing vats, newly pressed wine and freshly ground flour were to be returned to Yahweh, the owner and giver of all produce. The quality of the produce offered was deemed as the best or choicest of the crops. As the fat of any animal sacrificed or slaughtered was not to be consumed, the fat of the produce from field, orchard or vineyard was also not to be eaten but was to be devoted to Yahweh.

Later in the history of the Israelite kingdoms, prophets such as Hosea illustrated the nation’s unfaithfulness using the imagery of abused firstfruits of the fig season that went to Baal Peor instead of Yahweh (Hos 9:10). Offering the firstfruits to deity was standard practice in the ancient Near East.
18:14 *devoted to the LORD.* See note on Lev 27:28
18:15 *first offspring … firstborn.* The second part of the tribute list for the priests related to firstborn animals and

that is offered to the LORD is yours.[b] But
you must redeem[c] every firstborn son and
every firstborn male of unclean animals.[d]
16When they are a month old, you must
redeem them at the redemption price set
at five shekels[a][e] of silver, according to the
sanctuary shekel,[f] which weighs twenty
gerahs.

17"But you must not redeem the firstborn of a cow, a sheep or a goat; they are
holy.[g] Splash their blood[h] against the altar
and burn their fat as a food offering, an
aroma pleasing to the LORD. 18Their meat is
to be yours, just as the breast of the wave
offering[i] and the right thigh are yours.
19Whatever is set aside from the holy offerings the Israelites present to the LORD I
give to you and your sons and daughters
as your perpetual share. It is an everlasting
covenant of salt[j] before the LORD for both
you and your offspring."

20The LORD said to Aaron, "You will
have no inheritance in their land, nor will
you have any share among them;[k] I am
your share and your inheritance[l] among
the Israelites.

21"I give to the Levites all the tithes[m] in
Israel as their inheritance[n] in return for
the work they do while serving at the tent
of meeting. 22From now on the Israelites
must not go near the tent of meeting, or
they will bear the consequences of their
sin and will die.[o] 23It is the Levites who
are to do the work at the tent of meeting
and bear the responsibility for any offenses they commit against it. This is a lasting ordinance for the generations to come.
They will receive no inheritance[p] among
the Israelites. 24Instead, I give to the Levites as their inheritance the tithes that
the Israelites present as an offering to the
LORD. That is why I said concerning them:
'They will have no inheritance among the
Israelites.' "

25The LORD said to Moses, 26"Speak to
the Levites and say to them: 'When you
receive from the Israelites the tithe I give
you[q] as your inheritance, you must present
a tenth of that tithe as the LORD's offering.[r]
27Your offering will be reckoned to you as
grain from the threshing floor or juice from
the winepress. 28In this way you also will
present an offering to the LORD from all the
tithes[s] you receive from the Israelites. From
these tithes you must give the LORD's portion to Aaron the priest. 29You must present as the LORD's portion the best and holiest part of everything given to you.'

30"Say to the Levites: 'When you present the best part, it will be reckoned to
you as the product of the threshing floor
or the winepress.[t] 31You and your households may eat the rest of it anywhere, for
it is your wages for your work at the tent
of meeting. 32By presenting the best part[u]
of it you will not be guilty in this matter;
then you will not defile the holy offerings[v]
of the Israelites, and you will not die.' "

The Water of Cleansing

19 The LORD said to Moses and Aaron: 2"This is a requirement of the
law that the LORD has commanded: Tell

18:15 [b] Ex 13:2 [c] Nu 3:46 [d] Ex 13:13 **18:16** [e] Lev 27:6 [f] Ex 30:13 **18:17** [g] Dt 15:19 [h] Lev 3:2 **18:18** [i] Lev 7:30 **18:19** [j] Lev 2:13; 2Ch 13:5 **18:20** [k] Dt 12:12 [l] Dt 10:9; 14:27; 18:1-2; Jos 13:33; Eze 44:28 **18:21** [m] Dt 14:22; Mal 3:8 [n] Lev 27:30-33; Heb 7:5 **18:22** [o] Lev 22:9; Nu 1:51 **18:23** [p] ver 20 **18:26** [q] ver 21 [r] Ne 10:38 **18:28** [s] Mal 3:8 **18:30** [t] ver 27 **18:32** [u] Lev 22:15 [v] Lev 19:8

[a] *16* That is, about 2 ounces or about 58 grams

humans brought to the sanctuary for offering or dedication. The firstborn offspring were the first male issue from the womb of its mother, whether human or animal. Animals defined by the law as clean, such as cattle, sheep and goats, were offered as sacrifices. *redeem.* Since humans could not be sacrificed physically, nor could unclean animals, a redemption price was set by which a substitutionary value was rendered to the priesthood. According to Ex 34:19 the unclean donkey could be redeemed with a lamb, otherwise its neck was to be broken. Other unclean animals are not discussed, probably since they were of little use to the priesthood or the average Israelite. The process of human and animal redemption had a didactic purpose of reminding the Israelites of their redemption from Egypt, an object lesson of history rehearsed in every generation so the people would not forget the Lord's benevolence and the heavy price paid for their deliverance to freedom and blessing. No practices comparable to these have yet been found in the ancient Near East.

18:19 *covenant of salt.* See note on Lev 2:13.

18:21 *tithes.* See note on Ge 14:20. The concept of tithing is known from ancient Near Eastern sources in the Levant and Mesopotamia. Not only were agricultural goods tithed, but also various commodities such as metals and goods produced by craftsmen. Ugaritic texts evidence a royal temple structure in which contributions to the sanctuary could be used by royalty. A kind of royal priesthood is evidenced in the account of Melchizedek in Ge 14:18–24.

In Babylon of the sixth century BC, cattle contributed as tithes were branded for the temple treasuries, and other goods were earmarked on storage jars and other receptacles. In the Iron II Israelite kingdom period goods collected for the royal provision were inscribed with the term *lmlk* ("for the king"). Whether some of these may have been dedicated for the temple stores is unknown, but there is little doubt that some means of identifying the tithed goods was employed during the First Temple period.

18:27 *grain ... juice.* These were two key agricultural products to be set aside by the Levites for their tithe: the best grain from the threshing floor and the finest juice from the wine vat. From the painted wall murals of Egypt to the hewn murals of the Hittites in central and eastern Anatolia and the Assyrians of Mesopotamia, the activities and products of grain processing and wine production were esteemed as sacred aspects of human endeavor in utilizing these gifts from the gods. Rites associated with bread and wine held significant places in ancient cultic activities, as they did in ancient Israel. Cultic activities were associated with threshing floors and winepresses, as well as olive presses. In Numbers particular attention is given to the bread, oil and wine accompaniments to a number of animal sacrifices.

19:2 *red heifer.* The process begins with the selection of

the Israelites to bring you a red heifer[w] without defect or blemish[x] and that has never been under a yoke.[y] 3Give it to Eleazar[z] the priest; it is to be taken outside the camp[a] and slaughtered in his presence. 4Then Eleazar the priest is to take some of its blood on his finger and sprinkle[b] it seven times toward the front of the tent of meeting. 5While he watches, the heifer is to be burned — its hide, flesh, blood and intestines.[c] 6The priest is to take some cedar wood, hyssop[d] and scarlet wool[e] and throw them onto the burning heifer. 7After that, the priest must wash his clothes and bathe himself with water.[f] He may then come into the camp, but he will be ceremonially unclean till evening. 8The man who burns it must also wash his clothes and bathe with water, and he too will be unclean till evening.

9"A man who is clean shall gather up the ashes of the heifer[g] and put them in a ceremonially clean place outside the camp. They are to be kept by the Israelite community for use in the water of cleansing;[h] it is for purification from sin. 10The man who gathers up the ashes of the heifer must also wash his clothes, and he too will be unclean till evening. This will be a lasting ordinance both for the Israelites and for the foreigners residing among them.

11"Whoever touches a human corpse[i] will be unclean for seven days.[j] 12They must purify themselves with the water on the third day and on the seventh day;[k] then they will be clean. But if they do not purify themselves on the third and seventh days, they will not be clean. 13If they fail to purify themselves after touching a human corpse,[l] they defile the LORD's tabernacle.[m] They must be cut off from Israel.[n] Because the water of cleansing has not been sprinkled on them, they are unclean;[o] their uncleanness remains on them.

14"This is the law that applies when a person dies in a tent: Anyone who enters the tent and anyone who is in it will be unclean for seven days, 15and every open container without a lid fastened on it will be unclean.

19:2 [w] Ge 15:9; Heb 9:13 [x] Lev 22:19-25 [y] Dt 21:3; 1Sa 6:7
19:3 [z] Nu 3:4 [a] Lev 4:12,21; Heb 13:11
19:4 [b] Lev 4:17
19:5 [c] Ex 29:14
19:6 [d] ver 18; Ps 51:7 [e] Lev 14:4
19:7 [f] Lev 11:25; 16:26,28; 22:6
19:9 [g] Heb 9:13 [h] ver 13; Nu 8:7
19:11 [i] Lev 21:1; Nu 5:2 [j] Nu 31:19
19:12 [k] ver 19; Nu 31:19
19:13 [l] Lev 20:3 [m] Lev 15:31; 2Ch 36:14 [n] Lev 7:20; 22:3 [o] Hag 2:13

a quality red cow (a roan or reddish-brown color) that is unblemished and has never been harnessed with a yoke. In that the cow has never been yoked for any physical task, it is probably young and strong. Elsewhere a bull is sacrificed as a sin offering for the high priest and his family (Lev 4:3 – 12; 16:6,11) or for the community as a whole (Lev 4:13 – 21), and so the female is specified here. The cow offers the maximum potential yield of purification ashes so the ritual need not be repeated often. The redness of the cow reflects the color of blood, as do the other sacrificial elements burned with the cow: red cedar wood, scarlet wool and hyssop (see v. 6 and note).

19:6 *cedar wood, hyssop and scarlet wool.* The use of reddish materials along with other colored elements in ritual sanctification is echoed in texts from the Assyrian holy city of Ashur, known as "The Ritual Followed by the Kalš-Priest When Covering the Temple Kettle-Drum." The assembly and sanctification of the bronze kettle-drum was accompanied by "cypress, one-half pound [0.23 kilograms] of sweet-smelling reed ... of roses, ten shekels of aromatic annuba ... two qa-measures of wine ... one-half qa-measure of cedar sap ... white ... cloth, one red ... cloth ... pounds of wool ... seven pounds [3.2 kilograms] of blue wool," as well as other materials. *hyssop.* Probably not the Greek *hyssopos* (from which the English name was derived) since it is not native to this region. Perhaps it is marjoram, sage or thyme, the leaves of which are very absorbent.

19:7 *wash his clothes and bathe himself with water.* The priest (Eleazar) who carries out the slaughtering and sprinkling, the assistant who burns the cow (v. 8), and the one who gathers and stores the ashes (v. 10) are each rendered unclean by touching this purification (sin) offering. But this is a lesser state of uncleanness than one who touches a dead body. After taking the prescribed ritual bath, they are permitted to reenter the camp and remain unclean only until evening. Hittite and Ugaritic ritual texts prescribe the wearing of clean clothes and taking ritual baths for both kings and priests, especially to prepare for ceremonial and festival days.

19:10 *foreigners residing among them.* In future generations this purification (sin) offering and ritual becomes one of the more commonly applied purification (sin) offerings because of the continual potentiality of becoming unclean through the death of someone in the family, of a neighbor or of a sojourner in the land. The ritual guidelines apply to both the native Israelite and to resident non-Israelites. The openness of Israelite ritual law to resident non-Israelites who desire to identify with the community of faith stands in contrast to some other religious practices in the ancient Near East. Hittite temple ritual prohibited foreigners from bringing anything to the gods or even approaching them.

19:11,14,16 *seven days.* The time period of the impurity is the common maximum length for persons who have become unclean. Yet with some forms of impurity, such as contact with the red cow during the preparation process, one is rendered impure only until sundown (v. 7). The attention to death impurity stands in contrast to the prevalent cults of the dead in the ancient Near East, where ritual practice shows no concept of contracting contamination or impurity from a corpse, but a notable Babylonian text evidences a seven-day period of isolation for one who comes in contact with the "dust from a place of mourning." The ritual includes reciting a *namburbi* incantation to protect from evil, offering libations to the god Shamash, taking a ritual bath and changing clothes, after which the offender remains secluded in his house for seven days.

The cult of the dead consisted of elaborate rituals on behalf of dead family members in order to assure life in the hereafter and placate the gods of death and the underworld. This process began with funerary rites of the deceased family member and continued well after the initial event. Mesopotamian texts from Mari (eighteenth century BC) prescribed offerings for the dead four times a year, in which the name of the dead person was invoked, food presented and a water libation rendered.

19:13 *cut off.* See note on Lev 7:20.

16 “Anyone out in the open who touches someone who has been killed with a
sword or someone who has died a natural
death,[p] or anyone who touches a human
bone or a grave,[q] will be unclean for sev-
en days.
17 “For the unclean person, put some ashes[r] from the burned purification offering
into a jar and pour fresh water over them.
18 Then a man who is ceremonially clean is
to take some hyssop,[s] dip it in the water
and sprinkle the tent and all the furnishings
and the people who were there. He must
also sprinkle anyone who has touched a
human bone or a grave or anyone who has
been killed or anyone who has died a natural death. 19 The man who is clean is to
sprinkle those who are unclean on the third
and seventh days, and on the seventh day
he is to purify them.[t] Those who are being
cleansed must wash their clothes and bathe
with water, and that evening they will be
clean. 20 But if those who are unclean do
not purify themselves, they must be cut off
from the community, because they have
defiled the sanctuary of the LORD. The water of cleansing has not been sprinkled on
them, and they are unclean. 21 This is a lasting ordinance for them.
“The man who sprinkles the water of
cleansing must also wash his clothes, and
anyone who touches the water of cleansing will be unclean till evening. 22 Anything that an unclean[u] person touches becomes unclean, and anyone who touches
it becomes unclean till evening.”

Water From the Rock

20 In the first month the whole Israelite community arrived at the Desert
of Zin,[v] and they stayed at Kadesh.[w] There
Miriam[x] died and was buried.
2 Now there was no water for the community,[y] and the people gathered in opposition[z] to Moses and Aaron. 3 They
quarreled[a] with Moses and said, “If only
we had died when our brothers fell dead
before the LORD![b] 4 Why did you bring
the LORD’s community into this wilderness, that we and our livestock should die
here?[c] 5 Why did you bring us up out of
Egypt to this terrible place? It has no grain
or figs, grapevines or pomegranates.[d] And
there is no water to drink!”
6 Moses and Aaron went from the assembly to the entrance to the tent of meeting
and fell facedown,[e] and the glory of the
LORD[f] appeared to them. 7 The LORD said to
Moses, 8 “Take the staff,[g] and you and your
brother Aaron gather the assembly together. Speak to that rock before their eyes and
it will pour out its water.[h] You will bring
water out of the rock for the community
so they and their livestock can drink.”
9 So Moses took the staff from the LORD’s
presence,[i] just as he commanded him. 10 He
and Aaron gathered the assembly together in front of the rock and Moses said to
them, “Listen, you rebels, must we bring
you water out of this rock?”[j] 11 Then Moses
raised his arm and struck the rock twice
with his staff. Water[k] gushed out, and the
community and their livestock drank.
12 But the LORD said to Moses and Aaron,
“Because you did not trust in me enough
to honor me as holy[l] in the sight of the Israelites, you will not bring this community
into the land I give them.”[m]
13 These were the waters of Meribah,[a][n]
where the Israelites quarreled[o] with the
LORD and where he was proved holy
among them.

Edom Denies Israel Passage

14 Moses sent messengers from Kadesh[p]
to the king of Edom,[q] saying:
“This is what your brother Israel
says: You know[r] about all the hard-

19:16 [p] Nu 31:19 [q] Mt 23:27 **19:17** [r] ver 9 **19:18** [s] ver 6 **19:19** [t] Eze 36:25; Heb 10:22 **19:22** [u] Lev 5:2; Hag 2:13, 14 **20:1** [v] Nu 13:21 [w] Nu 33:36 [x] Ex 15:20 **20:2** [y] Ex 17:1 [z] Nu 16:19 **20:3** [a] Ex 17:2 [b] Nu 14:2; 16:31-35 **20:4** [c] Ex 14:11; 17:3; Nu 14:3; 16:13 **20:5** [d] Nu 16:14 **20:6** [e] Nu 14:5 [f] Nu 16:19 **20:8** [g] Ex 4:17, 20 [h] Ex 17:6; Isa 43:20 **20:9** [i] Nu 17:10 **20:10** [j] Ps 106:32, 33 **20:11** [k] Ex 17:6; Dt 8:15; Ps 78:16; Isa 48:2; 1Co 10:4 **20:12** [l] Nu 27:14 [m] ver 24; Dt 1:37; 3:27 **20:13** [n] Ex 17:7 [o] Dt 33:8; Ps 95:8; 106:32 **20:14** [p] Jdg 11:16-17 [q] Dt 2:4 [r] Jos 2:11; 9:9

[a] *13 Meribah* means *quarreling.*

20:8–11 The actions of Moses have been examined against the backdrop of Egyptian and Mesopotamian magicians and diviners as well as in the context of the nature of God as seen in the Pentateuch. Magical acts in the ancient world were usually performed after appropriate sacrifices were made, ritual actions performed and incantations recited. In these ways, Moses' behavior here would not have looked or sounded like that of the Egyptian lector priests (the magicians that he faced during the plagues, see notes on Ge 41:8; Ex 7:11). Nevertheless, Moses' words (v. 10) and actions (v. 11) were tantamount to those of an idolatrous pagan magician, ascribing miraculous, almost God-like, powers to himself and Aaron.
20:8 *Take the staff.* The staff was taken from the Lord's presence, implying this is the staff of Aaron that budded, blossomed and produced almonds in the divine confirmation of his priestly authority after the Korah rebellion (ch. 17). It was kept before the ark of the covenant law as a sign to any future grumbling rebels so that their murmuring might be summarily dismissed (17:10).
20:11 *Water gushed out.* No parallel accounts exist in the ancient Near East of deities providing water in this way. While geographers and Biblical interpreters have written of the extensive aquifers that exist beneath the surface of the sedimentary rock strata of the Sinai peninsula, aquifers would not normally provide nearly enough water to care for the needs of a group the size of the Israelites.
20:14–17 The message to the king of Edom follows classical Hebrew epistolary form and protocol. The content has all the earmarks of ancient Near Eastern diplomatic correspondence usually delivered by royal messengers.
20:14 *king.* The Hebrew term (*melek*) may range from a reference to internationally acclaimed kings of Egypt, Assyria, Babylon or Persia of the ninth to fifth centuries BC to simply the rulers of lesser towns such as Sodom and Gomorrah (Ge 14:2) or Jericho, Ai, Jerusalem, Yarmuth,

ships that have come on us. 15Our
ancestors went down into Egypt,[s]
and we lived there many years.[t] The
Egyptians mistreated[u] us and our
ancestors, 16but when we cried out
to the LORD, he heard our cry[v] and
sent an angel[w] and brought us out of
Egypt.

“Now we are here at Kadesh, a
town on the edge of your territory. 17Please let us pass through your
country. We will not go through any
field or vineyard, or drink water
from any well. We will travel along
the King’s Highway and not turn to
the right or to the left until we have
passed through your territory.[x]”

18But Edom answered:

“You may not pass through here; if
you try, we will march out and attack
you with the sword.”

19The Israelites replied:

“We will go along the main road,
and if we or our livestock[y] drink any
of your water, we will pay for it.[z] We
only want to pass through on foot—
nothing else.”

20Again they answered:

“You may not pass through.”

Then Edom came out against them with
a large and powerful army. 21Since Edom
refused to let them go through their territory, Israel turned away from them.[a]

The Death of Aaron

22The whole Israelite community set
out from Kadesh and came to Mount
Hor.[b] 23At Mount Hor, near the border of
Edom,[c] the LORD said to Moses and Aaron,
24“Aaron will be gathered to his people.[d]
He will not enter the land I give the Israelites, because both of you rebelled against
my command[e] at the waters of Meribah.
25Get Aaron and his son Eleazar and take
them up Mount Hor.[f] 26Remove Aaron’s
garments and put them on his son Eleazar,
for Aaron will be gathered to his people;[g]
he will die there.”

27Moses did as the LORD commanded:
They went up Mount Hor in the sight of
the whole community. 28Moses removed
Aaron’s garments and put them on his
son Eleazar.[h] And Aaron died there[i] on
top of the mountain. Then Moses and Eleazar came down from the mountain, 29and
when the whole community learned that
Aaron had died, all the Israelites mourned
for him[j] thirty days.

Arad Destroyed

21 When the Canaanite king of Arad,[k]
who lived in the Negev,[l] heard that
Israel was coming along the road to Ath-
arim, he attacked the Israelites and captured some of them. 2Then Israel made
this vow to the LORD: “If you will deliver
these people into our hands, we will totally destroy[a] their cities.” 3The LORD listened
to Israel’s plea and gave the Canaanites
over to them. They completely destroyed
them and their towns; so the place was
named Hormah.[b]

The Bronze Snake

4They traveled from Mount Hor[m] along
the route to the Red Sea,[c] to go around

20:15 [s] Ge 46:6 [t] Ge 15:13; Ex 12:40 [u] Ex 1:11; Dt 26:6 **20:16** [v] Ex 2:23; 3:7 [w] Ex 14:19 **20:17** [x] Nu 21:22 **20:19** [y] Ex 12:38 [z] Dt 2:6,28 **20:21** [a] Dt 2:8; Jdg 11:18 **20:22** [b] Nu 33:37 **20:23** [c] Nu 33:37 **20:24** [d] Ge 25:8 [e] ver 10 **20:25** [f] Nu 33:38 **20:26** [g] ver 24 **20:28** [h] Ex 29:29 [i] Nu 33:38; Dt 10:6; 32:50 **20:29** [j] Dt 34:8 **21:1** [k] Nu 33:40; Jos 12:14 [l] Jdg 1:9,16 **21:4** [m] Nu 20:22

[a] 2 The Hebrew term refers to the irrevocable giving over of things or persons to the LORD, often by totally destroying them; also in verse 3. [b] 3 *Hormah* means *destruction.* [c] 4 Or *the Sea of Reeds*

Lachish and Debir of the period of the Israelite conquest (Jos 10:1—12:24). *Edom.* See note on Ge 36:9. Edom seems to have been organized under chieftains at this time, the head of which may have been designated broadly as a king.
20:17 The Israelites promise to respect Edomite dominion. Israel will not be a burden to Edom or disturb their agricultural activities. *not go through any field or vineyard.* The seasonal description indicates springtime, and the grain fields are near harvest time. Thus it is important to assure the Edomites that their crops will not be trampled or scavenged. *water from any well.* Water rights were of great concern in the ancient Near East (as they are even today). The Israelites will presumably bring their own water from Kadesh during their passage of perhaps two days through the Edomite highlands. *King’s Highway.* This famous north-south trade route connected the Damascus trade center with Arabia, Sinai and Egypt via a route through the Transjordan tablelands and the southern mountains, paralleling the Arabah on the eastern side. Egyptian kings such as Thutmose III passed along this road in their conquests of Transjordan and the eastern Levant. From southern Arabia caravanners brought the highly prized commodities of incense, spices, perfumes and precious jewels, as well as copper from the Sinai and the Desert of Paran.
20:19 *We will go along the main road.* The attempt at diplomatic correspondence carries alternative stipulations, the only part of which is preserved in v. 19. Israel again avows to ascend into the mountainous territory of Edom by the most direct route, the “main road” used by trade caravans and military troops. The suggestion of payment for safe passage is in keeping with ancient Near Eastern protocol, as often tolls were exacted from trade caravans traversing the regions of Mesopotamia and the Levant. Thus, this is not an unusual request, though the strong-handed military response to the second appeal is unusual (v. 20).
20:26 *gathered to his people.* See note on Ge 25:8. This phrase conveys the idea of being reunited with one’s ancestral families in Sheol, the place of the dead (see note on 16:33). Being left unburied or “ungathered” was viewed as an ignominious end of life (cf. Jer 8:2; see note on Dt 21:23).

Edom. But the people grew impatient on
the way;[n] 5they spoke against God[o] and
against Moses, and said, "Why have you
brought us up out of Egypt to die in the
wilderness?[p] There is no bread! There is no
water! And we detest this miserable food!"[q]
6Then the LORD sent venomous snakes[r]
among them; they bit the people and many
Israelites died.[s] 7The people came to Moses[t] and said, "We sinned when we spoke
against the LORD and against you. Pray that
the LORD[u] will take the snakes away from
us." So Moses prayed[v] for the people.
8The LORD said to Moses, "Make a snake
and put it up on a pole;[w] anyone who is
bitten can look at it and live." 9So Moses
made a bronze snake[x] and put it up on
a pole. Then when anyone was bitten by
a snake and looked at the bronze snake,
they lived.[y]

The Journey to Moab

10The Israelites moved on and camped
at Oboth.[z] 11Then they set out from Oboth
and camped in Iye Abarim, in the wilderness that faces Moab[a] toward the sunrise.
12From there they moved on and camped
in the Zered Valley.[b] 13They set out from
there and camped alongside the Arnon[c],
which is in the wilderness extending into
Amorite territory. The Arnon is the border
of Moab, between Moab and the Amorites.
14That is why the Book of the Wars of the
LORD says:

> ". . . Zahab[a] in Suphah and the ravines,
> the Arnon 15and[b] the slopes of the
> ravines
> that lead to the settlement of Ar[d]
> and lie along the border of Moab."

16From there they continued on to Beer,[e]
the well where the LORD said to Moses,
"Gather the people together and I will give
them water."
17Then Israel sang this song:[f]

> "Spring up, O well!
> Sing about it,
> 18about the well that the princes dug,
> that the nobles of the people sank—
> the nobles with scepters and staffs."

Then they went from the wilderness to
Mattanah, 19from Mattanah to Nahaliel,
from Nahaliel to Bamoth, 20and from Bamoth to the valley in Moab where the top
of Pisgah overlooks the wasteland.

Defeat of Sihon and Og

21Israel sent messengers to say to Sihon[g]
king of the Amorites:

> 22"Let us pass through your coun-
> try. We will not turn aside into any
> field or vineyard, or drink water from
> any well. We will travel along the
> King's Highway until we have passed
> through your territory.[h]"

23But Sihon would not let Israel pass
through his territory.[i] He mustered his entire army and marched out into the wilderness against Israel. When he reached
Jahaz,[j] he fought with Israel. 24Israel, however, put him to the sword[k] and took over
his land from the Arnon to the Jabbok,
but only as far as the Ammonites,[l] because
their border was fortified. 25Israel captured
all the cities of the Amorites[m] and occupied them, including Heshbon and all its
surrounding settlements. 26Heshbon was
the city of Sihon[n] king of the Amorites,
who had fought against the former king of

21:4 [n] Dt 2:8; Jdg 11:18 **21:5** [o] Ps 78:19 [p] Nu 14:2,3 [q] Nu 11:6 **21:6** [r] Dt 8:15; Jer 8:17 [s] 1Co 10:9 **21:7** [t] Ps 78:34; Hos 5:15 [u] Ex 8:8; Ac 8:24 [v] Nu 11:2 **21:8** [w] Jn 3:14 **21:9** [x] 2Ki 18:4 [y] Jn 3:14-15 **21:10** [z] Nu 33:43 **21:11** [a] Nu 33:44 **21:12** [b] Dt 2:13, 14 **21:13** [c] Nu 22:36; Jdg 11:13, 18 **21:15** [d] ver 28; Dt 2:9, 18 **21:16** [e] Jdg 9:21 **21:17** [f] Ex 15:1 **21:21** [g] Dt 1:4; 2:26-27; Jdg 11:19-21 **21:22** [h] Nu 20:17 **21:23** [i] Nu 20:21 [j] Dt 2:32; Jdg 11:20 **21:24** [k] Dt 2:33; Ps 135:10-11; Am 2:9 [l] Dt 2:37 **21:25** [m] Nu 13:29; Jdg 10:11; Am 2:10 **21:26** [n] Dt 29:7; Ps 135:11

[a] 14 Septuagint; Hebrew *Waheb* [b] 14,15 Or *"I have been given from Suphah and the ravines / of the Arnon* 15*to*

21:6 *venomous snakes.* "Venomous" (*serapim,* "burning") may refer to the burning pain from the lethal injection of venom through the serpents' fangs or to a species of snake whose bite caused a burning sensation. The carpet viper (*Echis carinatus* or *Echis coleratus*) is a highly poisonous viper known from Africa and the Middle East—thus a likely candidate. Other suggestions include the puff adder and sand viper, neither of which is as lethal as the carpet viper.

21:8 *Make a snake and put it up on a pole.* The function of the image resembles a form of homeopathic and apotropaic ritual, whereby a votive form of the source of the disease (homeopathic element) is used in a ritual to ward off evil (apotropaism)—here, death from snake bite.

The use of a copper or bronze serpent in a worship context was found in the excavated remains of a temple to Hathor. Temple remains from the later Midianite occupation included a 5-inch-long (12.7-centimeter-long) copper snake with a gilded head, representative of some deity in the local cult. A coiled copper snake form that was about 8 inches (20 centimeters) long was excavated at Tel Mevorakh in the northern Sharon Plain, dating to the Late Bronze Age. Some Egyptians wore miniature models of serpents as amulets in order to prevent snakebites.

21:14 *Book of the Wars of the LORD.* This document is not preserved, but probably consisted of victory songs and tales of the deeds of Yahweh and the leaders of Israel. This book, along with the Book of Jashar (Jos 10:13; 2Sa 1:18), indicates that the composition of the Biblical narrative was based at least in part on cultural memories.

21:21 *sent messengers.* Diplomatic envoys were sent to negotiate passage northward along the King's Highway in the Transjordan highlands and then westward down the hillsides to the shores of the Jordan River. *Amorites.* A large ethnic group that formed in Upper Mesopotamia near the end of the Early Bronze Age and extended westward to the Mediterranean coastlands (see note on 13:29). Sometimes "Amorite" is used generically in the Bible as a reference to the population of Canaan.

21:22 *field or vineyard . . . well.* See notes on 20:17,19. *King's Highway.* See note on 20:17.

Moab and had taken from him all his land
as far as the Arnon.
27That is why the poets say:

"Come to Heshbon and let it be rebuilt;
let Sihon's city be restored.

28"Fire went out from Heshbon,
a blaze from the city of Sihon.[o]
It consumed Ar[p] of Moab,
the citizens of Arnon's heights.[q]
29Woe to you, Moab![r]
You are destroyed, people of
Chemosh![s]
He has given up his sons as fugitives[t]
and his daughters as captives[u]
to Sihon king of the Amorites.

30"But we have overthrown them;
Heshbon's dominion has been
destroyed all the way to Dibon.[v]
We have demolished them as far as
Nophah,
which extends to Medeba."

31So Israel settled in the land of the Amorites.
32After Moses had sent spies to Jazer,[w]
the Israelites captured its surrounding settlements and drove out the Amorites who
were there. 33Then they turned and went
up along the road toward Bashan[x,y] and
Og king of Bashan and his whole army
marched out to meet them in battle at
Edrei.[z]
34The LORD said to Moses, "Do not be
afraid of him, for I have delivered him into
your hands, along with his whole army
and his land. Do to him what you did to
Sihon king of the Amorites, who reigned
in Heshbon.[a]"
35So they struck him down, together
with his sons and his whole army, leaving
them no survivors. And they took possession of his land.

Balak Summons Balaam

22 Then the Israelites traveled to the
plains of Moab and camped along
the Jordan across from Jericho.[b]
2Now Balak son of Zippor[c] saw all that
Israel had done to the Amorites, 3and
Moab was terrified because there were
so many people. Indeed, Moab was filled
with dread[d] because of the Israelites.
4The Moabites said to the elders of Midian, "This horde is going to lick up everything around us, as an ox licks up the
grass of the field."
So Balak son of Zippor, who was king
of Moab at that time, 5sent messengers to
summon Balaam son of Beor,[e] who was
at Pethor, near the Euphrates River, in his
native land. Balak said:

21:28 [o] Jer 48:45 [p] ver 15 [q] Nu 22:41; Isa 15:2 **21:29** [r] Isa 25:10; Jer 48:46 [s] Jdg 11:24; 1Ki 11:7,33; 2Ki 23:13; Jer 48:7, 46 [t] Isa 15:5 [u] Isa 16:2 **21:30** [v] Nu 32:3; Isa 15:2; Jer 48:18,22 **21:32** [w] Nu 32:1,3,35; Jer 48:32 **21:33** [x] Dt 3:3 [y] Dt 3:4 [z] Dt 1:4; 3:1,10; Jos 13:12,31 **21:34** [a] Dt 3:2 **22:1** [b] Nu 33:48 **22:2** [c] Jdg 11:25 **22:3** [d] Ex 15:15 **22:5** [e] Dt 23:4; Jos 13:22; 24:9; Ne 13:2; Mic 6:5; 2Pe 2:15

21:29 *Chemosh.* First appears among the deities at Ebla about 2600 – 2250 BC and is associated with production of mud brick. He is mentioned 12 times in the Mesha Stele, including in the appellation Ashtar-Chemosh, as the god who enabled Mesha to break the yoke of Israel's domination and recapture and rebuild a number of his cities, including Jahaz (l.19; cf. Nu 21:23), Dibon (l.21; also Dibon Gad in Nu 33:45 – 46), Beth Diblathiam (l.30; cf. Nu 33:46 – 47), and Medeba (l.30; cf. Nu 21:30). Heshbon is not preserved in the Mesha inscription, though it remained a vital city of this period in Moab's history.

As national god of Moab, Chemosh stood in opposition to Yahweh as Moab did against Israel. His cult is similar to Yahweh's and he too was credited with providing victory in battle and land to his people. This may indicate that the expectations placed on gods by their people were similar from one nation to another.

21:33 *Bashan.* Situated east-northeast of the Sea of Galilee and north of the Yarmuk River. The modern Golan area in Israel covers some of this territory, but in ancient times Bashan extended to Mount Hermon in the north and to the Yarmuk River in the south, and was bounded on the west by the Jordan Valley and on the east by the great eastern desert. It was lush and fertile and noted for its rich grazing lands. Ashtaroth, Og's capital, was due east of Galilee on one of the tributaries of the Yarmuk River. It was mentioned in Egyptian, Assyrian and possibly Ugaritic texts and is designated as Tell Ashtarah today.

22:1 *plains of Moab.* This area is the broad plain between the Transjordan highlands and the Jordan River, extending about 10 miles (16 kilometers) from just north of the Dead Sea. From this locale the campaign into the promised land of Canaan will be launched.

22:2 *Balak.* Unknown outside the Bible, he is called a "king of Moab" (v. 4), meaning he was the titular head of an emerging tribal confederation (one of several groups in Transjordan, such as the Edomites and Ammonites). Territorial borders of these clans were not well defined until the Iron Age (beginning around 1200 BC), when classical Moab extended from the Wadi Zered border on the south with the Edomites to the Arnon River gorge on the north, and from the Dead Sea on the west to the desert on the east.

22:3 *Moab.* See note on Dt 2:9.

22:4 *elders of Midian.* The Midianites have their origins in northern Arabia and southern Transjordan; they were descendants of Abraham and Keturah (Ge 25:1 – 6). Their loose-knit, seminomadic culture carried them from Arabia to Sinai and Egypt (10:29; Ex 2:15 – 22); occasionally they made forays into Canaan as traders (Ge 37:25 – 36) and as invaders (Jdg 6:1 – 6). In this narrative a group of Midianite elders (note that no king is cited) joins the emissaries from Balak in enlisting the services of Balaam to curse Israel.

22:5 *Pethor, near the Euphrates River.* Pethor is likely Pitru, situated 13 miles (21 kilometers) south of Carchemish on the Sajur River tributary west of the Euphrates River. Pitru is cited in the annals of Shalmaneser III (859 – 824 BC), and earlier a Pedru is mentioned in the annals of Thutmose III (c. 1467 BC). The distance from Pethor to Moab exceeded 400 miles (650 kilometers), making each leg of the journey by the emissaries and Balaam a 20- to 25-day trek. *in his native land.* This phrase is probably better rendered "in the land of Amaw," a region west of the Euphrates possibly mentioned in Egyptian and Mari inscriptions.

"A people has come out of Egypt;
they cover the face of the land and
have settled next to me. 6Now come
and put a curse[f] on these people, because they are too powerful for me.
Perhaps then I will be able to defeat
them and drive them out of the land.
For I know that whoever you bless
is blessed, and whoever you curse is
cursed."

22:6 [f] ver 12, 17; Nu 23:7, 11,13

22:6 *curse.* Ancient Near Eastern texts recount the power of diviners, magicians and sorcerers to discern, intervene and even manipulate the will of the gods through divination, special sacrificial rituals such as extispicy (ritual reading of a liver or other entrails), and incantations aimed at blessing or cursing an individual or group, forecasting the future, and advising kings and other leaders.

The reading of omens through the observation of various aspects of nature was considered a skilled science.

NUMBERS 22

BALAAM

Ancient Near Eastern cuneiform texts from Mari, Babylon and Anatolia illustrate the roles of prophets and diviners in society during the Bronze and Iron Ages. These experts plied their skills in addressing matters that were of concern to kings and chieftains in the ancient world.

Was Balaam a prophet, diviner or sorcerer? In the OT certain forms of divination were permissible while other forms, especially sorcery, were condemned. Sorcery, punishable by death (Ex 22:18; Lev 19:26; 20:27; Dt 18:10), used black magic, incantations, necromancy or manipulation of deity so as to effect change in the course of events set forth by God (or the gods). In the ancient Near East such a practice was predicated on the belief that the will of the gods and goddesses of one's pantheon could be manipulated by human activity so that they would change their minds and accomplish the desired response. Certain forms of sorcery, such as casting evil spells, sought someone's death. Divination attempts to forecast the future, but magic/sorcery goes further by attempting to alter the future through occult means.

Forms of divination that sought answers from the Lord, such as legitimate prophecy and the Urim and Thummim worn by the high priest (see Ex 28:30 and the article "Urim and Thummim," p. 162), were permitted for Israel, but divination that failed to trust in God's knowledge and wisdom by resorting to other sources was forbidden (see Lev 19:31; 20:6; Dt 18:10–12). Necromancy (divination by consulting the dead) was especially serious and punishable by death (Lev 20:27) because it claimed to bring up underworld spirits by what amounted to a kind of sorcery (1Sa 28:13–15). Sorcery, which purported to draw on superhuman power apart from that of God and thereby denied his exclusive sovereignty, was a capital crime (Ex 22:18).

Outside Israel, divination was ubiquitous. In fact, cuneiform tablets preserved from ancient Babylonia include more omen texts than any other genre of literature. Divination manifested itself in many forms and with a wide variety of techniques. Omens could be derived from practically anything, such as oil patterns on water, patterns of incense smoke, flight patterns of birds, positions of heavenly bodies (astrology), casting lots, dreams and characteristics of organs (especially the liver) in the body of a slaughtered animal.

Among Israel's neighbors, divination was regarded as indispensable for ascertaining the thinking of the gods and to make crucial decisions in time of war (cf. Eze 21:21). Some forms of sorcery, such as exorcising demons, countering black magic and using magic against enemy nations, were also viewed as legitimate. On the other hand, black magic to harm others belonging to one's own society was a serious crime in Anatolia and a capital offense in Mesopotamia and Egypt.

continued on next page

7The elders of Moab and Midian left,
taking with them the fee for divination.[g]
When they came to Balaam, they told him
what Balak had said.
8"Spend the night here," Balaam said to
them, "and I will report back to you with
the answer the LORD gives me.[h]" So the
Moabite officials stayed with him.
9God came to Balaam[i] and asked,[j] "Who
are these men with you?"

22:7 [g]Nu 23:23; 24:1
22:8 [h]ver 19
22:9 [i]Ge 20:3 [j]ver 20

Glossaries of omens and detailed lists of animals and objects and their potential use in divination are found among the texts of the Hittites, Babylonians, Assyrians, Egyptians and other peoples. Knowledge of the ways, workings and occasional whims of the divine and the skill of cajoling these deities into bringing beneficial or detrimental results was a highly prized craft.

22:7 *fee for divination.* This Hebrew phrase describes the men "carrying divination in their hands," which various scholars have translated as a divination fee, divination

Although Balaam uses sacrificial rituals to obtain God's answer, he cannot merely be considered a diviner. Divination is reserved for cultic personnel who examine sacrificial animals or natural phenomena, while Balaam seems to have direct communication with God and speaks oracles to Balak. This is the typical form of prophetic address and is found in the later OT (Isaiah, Jeremiah, etc.), but also in the Mari texts originating several centuries prior to Balaam. Prophecy was considered one form of divination.

Prophecy in the ancient Near Eastern style was well developed by the time Israel appears on the scene. In the Old Babylonian era and the late second millennium BC at Emar, Egypt and Byblos, prophetic activity included assertions about the future by "the ancients." So it goes for Syria, Palestine, Hamath and Jordan in the first part of the first millennium BC. From the Neo-Assyrian era of Esarhaddon and Ashurbanipal (seventh century BC) oracles/prophecies are extant. Some touch on Esarhaddon's rise to power or Assurbanipal's rise to kingship as well as his wars. Bel declares to Esarhaddon, "I will deliver all the countries into your hands."

Prophets spoke of victory, healing or death, and wise counsel, and they gave consultation. Kings could be warned, though rarely, about their actions or words. Prophets sometimes warned kings of Assyria, Mari and Egypt concerning their sins (cf. Da 4:24).

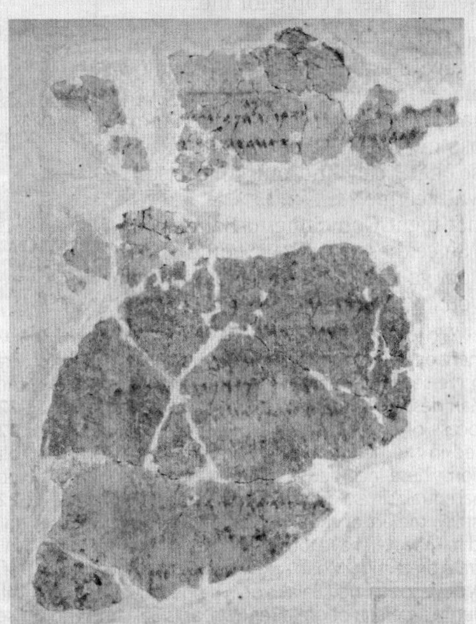

Deir 'Alla Inscription, c. 840–760 BC, which mentions Bala'am, son of Be'or.

Inscriptions from Deir Alla were uncovered that recount the activities of a Balaam son of Beor. They are written in red and black ink on a plastered wall or stele, possibly in a temple. The fragmented plaster sections have been pieced together into 12 combinations, only two of which are substantial enough to conjecture a translation. Though Combinations I and II have a number of gaps, several conclusions can be drawn from the contents. One Balaam son of Beor, described as a "seer of the gods," has a frightening night vision that he shares with his colleagues in the midst of his fasting and grief. He foretells a period of drought and darkness, of mourning and death, in which the natural order is upended. ◆

10 Balaam said to God, "Balak son of Zippor, king of Moab, sent me this message:
11 'A people that has come out of Egypt covers the face of the land. Now come and
put a curse on them for me. Perhaps then
I will be able to fight them and drive them
away.' "
12 But God said to Balaam, "Do not go
with them. You must not put a curse on
those people, because they are blessed.[k]"
13 The next morning Balaam got up and
said to Balak's officials, "Go back to your
own country, for the LORD has refused to
let me go with you."
14 So the Moabite officials returned to
Balak and said, "Balaam refused to come
with us."
15 Then Balak sent other officials, more
numerous and more distinguished than
the first. 16 They came to Balaam and said:

> "This is what Balak son of Zip-
> por says: Do not let anything keep
> you from coming to me, 17 because I
> will reward you handsomely[l] and do
> whatever you say. Come and put a
> curse[m] on these people for me."

18 But Balaam answered them, "Even if
Balak gave me all the silver and gold in
his palace, I could not do anything great
or small to go beyond the command of
the LORD my God.[n] 19 Now spend the night
here so that I can find out what else the
LORD will tell me.[o]"
20 That night God came to Balaam[p] and
said, "Since these men have come to summon you, go with them, but do only what
I tell you."[q]

22:12 [k] Ge 12:2; 22:17; Nu 23:20 **22:17** [l] ver 37; Nu 24:11 [m] ver 6 **22:18** [n] ver 38; Nu 23:12, 26; 24:13; 1Ki 22:14; 2Ch 18:13; Jer 42:4 **22:19** [o] ver 8 **22:20** [p] Ge 20:3 [q] ver 35, 38; Nu 23:5, 12, 16, 26; 24:13; 2Ch 18:13

22:22 [r] Ex 4:14 [s] Ge 16:7; Ex 23:20; Jdg 13:3, 6, 13 **22:23** [t] Jos 5:13 [u] ver 25, 27 **22:27** [v] Nu 11:1; Jas 1:19 **22:28** [w] 2Pe 2:16 [x] ver 32 **22:29** [y] Dt 25:4; Pr 12:10; 27:23-27; Mt 15:19 **22:31** [z] Ge 21:19

Balaam's Donkey

21 Balaam got up in the morning, saddled
his donkey and went with the Moabite officials. 22 But God was very angry[r] when
he went, and the angel of the LORD[s] stood
in the road to oppose him. Balaam was
riding on his donkey, and his two servants
were with him. 23 When the donkey saw
the angel of the LORD standing in the road
with a drawn sword[t] in his hand, it turned
off the road into a field. Balaam beat it[u] to
get it back on the road.
24 Then the angel of the LORD stood in a
narrow path through the vineyards, with
walls on both sides. 25 When the donkey
saw the angel of the LORD, it pressed close
to the wall, crushing Balaam's foot against
it. So he beat the donkey again.
26 Then the angel of the LORD moved on
ahead and stood in a narrow place where
there was no room to turn, either to the
right or to the left. 27 When the donkey saw
the angel of the LORD, it lay down under
Balaam, and he was angry[v] and beat it
with his staff. 28 Then the LORD opened the
donkey's mouth,[w] and it said to Balaam,
"What have I done to you to make you
beat me these three times?[x]"
29 Balaam answered the donkey, "You
have made a fool of me! If only I had a
sword in my hand, I would kill you right
now.[y]"
30 The donkey said to Balaam, "Am I not
your own donkey, which you have always
ridden, to this day? Have I been in the
habit of doing this to you?"
"No," he said.
31 Then the LORD opened Balaam's eyes,[z]

---

equipment or an idiom describing the emissaries of Balak as men "versed in divination." Several parallel contexts from Mari describe situations in which objects used in the process of divination were presented, dispatched and used in the negotiation with the recipient of the divination. These included such items as clay models of intestinal entrails, livers or other parts used in the practice of extispicy, the art of ritual dissection. The equipment referred to may well have included baked clay models of the entrails predicting Moab's downfall. Fear of the Israelites may have so alarmed Balak's own trained diviners that they sought a person of great renown, as is Balaam, who might exercise his expertise in allaying Moab's potential destruction by cursing Israel.

22:18 *the LORD my God.* There is no reason to think that Balaam (the Mesopotamian prophet who spoke in the name of many gods) served Yahweh exclusively. The familiar language may indicate that he is aware of Israel's God at least by reputation (cf. Rahab in Jos 2:9 – 11) or that he refers to any god in this personal manner to demonstrate prophetic authority.

22:21 – 35 Three times (vv. 22 – 23, 24 – 25, 26 – 27) Balaam's female donkey observes the angel of the Lord in a manner more perceptive than that of the renowned seer of the gods. The vineyard scene (vv. 24 – 25) indicates that the theophany took place in the arable highlands of Transjordan, probably between Damascus and Rabbah Ammon.

22:22 *the angel of the LORD.* See note on Ex 3:2.

22:24 *walls.* Piles of stones gathered from the area for planting were used to create boundaries between neighboring vineyards.

22:28 *opened the donkey's mouth.* Tales of talking animals in the ancient world often contain warning, irony or satire. In the Egyptian Story of Two Brothers, a cow advises one of the brothers to flee because his brother was seeking to kill him with a lance. From the Aramaic Words of Ahiqar (seventh century BC) comes a conversation between a lion, a leopard, a bear and a goat, each representing a human characteristic in facing the struggles of life before the gods.

Interpretation of this Biblical event has given rise to two general options: (1) God gave the animal the power of speech similar to how he empowered Ezekiel to speak after a prolonged period of silence (Eze 3:27; 33:22); (2) the donkey's normal braying was heightened such that it was perceived and interpreted by Balaam in a human manner. The scene is replete with irony in that the donkey is more perceptive of God and is able to speak God's word in a manner superior to the internationally renowned expert. Balaam is reminded that he will only be allowed to speak what Yahweh, God of Israel, permits him to speak.

and he saw the angel of the LORD standing
in the road with his sword drawn. So he
bowed low and fell facedown.
32 The angel of the LORD asked him,
"Why have you beaten your donkey these
three times? I have come here to oppose
you because your path is a reckless one
before me.[a] 33 The donkey saw me and
turned away from me these three times. If
it had not turned away, I would certainly
have killed you by now,[a] but I would have
spared it."
34 Balaam said to the angel of the LORD,
"I have sinned.[b] I did not realize you were
standing in the road to oppose me. Now if
you are displeased, I will go back."
35 The angel of the LORD said to Balaam,
"Go with the men, but speak only what
I tell you." So Balaam went with Balak's
officials.
36 When Balak heard that Balaam was
coming, he went out to meet him at the
Moabite town on the Arnon[c] border, at the
edge of his territory. 37 Balak said to Balaam, "Did I not send you an urgent summons? Why didn't you come to me? Am I
really not able to reward you?"
38 "Well, I have come to you now," Balaam replied. "But I can't say whatever I
please. I must speak only what God puts
in my mouth."[d]
39 Then Balaam went with Balak to Kiriath Huzoth. 40 Balak sacrificed cattle and
sheep,[e] and gave some to Balaam and the
officials who were with him. 41 The next
morning Balak took Balaam up to Bamoth
Baal,[f] and from there he could see the outskirts of the Israelite camp.[g]

Balaam's First Message

23 Balaam said, "Build me seven altars here, and prepare seven bulls
and seven rams[h] for me." 2 Balak did as
Balaam said, and the two of them offered
a bull and a ram on each altar.[i]
3 Then Balaam said to Balak, "Stay here
beside your offering while I go aside. Perhaps the LORD will come to meet with me.[j]
Whatever he reveals to me I will tell you."
Then he went off to a barren height.
4 God met with him,[k] and Balaam said,
"I have prepared seven altars, and on each
altar I have offered a bull and a ram."
5 The LORD put a word in Balaam's
mouth[l] and said, "Go back to Balak and
give him this word."[m]
6 So he went back to him and found him
standing beside his offering, with all the
Moabite officials.[n] 7 Then Balaam[o] spoke
his message:[p]

"Balak brought me from Aram,
    the king of Moab from the eastern
        mountains.
'Come,' he said, 'curse Jacob for me;
    come, denounce Israel.'[q]
8 How can I curse
    those whom God has not cursed?[r]
How can I denounce
    those whom the LORD has not
        denounced?
9 From the rocky peaks I see them,
    from the heights I view them.
I see a people who live apart
    and do not consider themselves one
        of the nations.[s]
10 Who can count the dust of Jacob[t]
    or number even a fourth of Israel?
Let me die the death of the righteous,[u]
    and may my final end be like theirs![v]"

11 Balak said to Balaam, "What have you
done to me? I brought you to curse my
enemies, but you have done nothing but
bless them!"[w]
12 He answered, "Must I not speak what
the LORD puts in my mouth?"[x]

Balaam's Second Message

13 Then Balak said to him, "Come with
me to another place where you can see

22:33 [a] ver 29 **22:34** [b] Ge 39:9; Nu 14:40; 1Sa 15:24, 30; 2Sa 12:13; 24:10; Job 33:27; Ps 51:4 **22:36** [c] Nu 21:13 **22:38** [d] Nu 23:5, 16, 26 **22:40** [e] Nu 23:1, 14, 29; Eze 45:23 **22:41** [f] Nu 21:28 [g] Nu 23:13 **23:1** [h] Nu 22:40 **23:2** [i] ver 14, 30

23:3 [j] ver 15 **23:4** [k] ver 16 **23:5** [l] Dt 18:18; Jer 1:9 [m] Nu 22:20 **23:6** [n] ver 17 **23:7** [o] Nu 22:5 [p] ver 18; Nu 24:3, 21 [q] Nu 22:6; Dt 23:4 **23:8** [r] Nu 22:12 **23:9** [s] Ex 33:16; Dt 32:8; 33:28 **23:10** [t] Ge 13:16 [u] Ps 116:15; Isa 57:1 [v] Ps 37:37 **23:11** [w] Nu 24:10; Ne 13:2 **23:12** [x] Nu 22:20, 38

[a] *32* The meaning of the Hebrew for this clause is uncertain.

22:41 *Bamoth Baal.* A cultic center dedicated to a primary deity of the region (Baal, the champion of creation in the mythology of Ugarit). Balak apparently thinks that Yahweh, God of Israel, might be more apt to be manipulated from there. Bamoth ("high places") is found in several compound names in the OT, but does not occur as a topographic name anywhere but in Moab.

23:1 *seven altars.* Multiple altars are not attested elsewhere in the OT, though the number seven denotes completeness or fulfillment. The importance of the number seven is reflected in the days of creation, the sanctity of the Sabbath, the sprinkling of the blood of the sin offerings on the Day of Atonement (*Yom Kippur*) and the series of sevens in the NT book of Revelation. A parallel use of seven is found in a Babylonian text in which a worshiper is instructed to "erect seven altars before Ea, Shamash, and Marduk, to set up seven censers of cypress, and then pour out [as a libation offering] the blood of seven sheep."

23:2 *a bull and a ram.* In ancient Near Eastern culture, the bull and ram were the most prized of animals and the obligatory sacrifices for persons from the upper echelon of society. These animals are also a regular part of special offerings in the Canaanite-type culture at Ugarit in the mid-second millennium BC. For a divination context, this is a large offering reflecting the importance of the situation—a king acting on behalf of his people in an international crisis. Usually a sacrifice performed in connection with divination required just one animal whose entrails were then examined for an answer. Here Balaam offers the sacrifices in order to try to induce Yahweh to deliver prophecy through him.

23:3 *Stay here beside your offering.* Here the king himself acts on behalf of the Moabite people, performing a priestly role not uncommon among Northwest Semitic people.

them; you will not see them all but only
the outskirts of their camp. And from
there, curse them for me." 14So he took
him to the field of Zophim on the top of
Pisgah, and there he built seven altars and
offered a bull and a ram on each altar.[y]
15Balaam said to Balak, "Stay here beside your offering while I meet with him
over there."
16The LORD met with Balaam and put a
word in his mouth[z] and said, "Go back to
Balak and give him this word."
17So he went to him and found him
standing beside his offering, with the Moabite officials. Balak asked him, "What did
the LORD say?"
18Then he spoke his message:

"Arise, Balak, and listen;
hear me, son of Zippor.
19 God is not human,[a] that he should lie,
not a human being, that he should
change his mind.[b]
Does he speak and then not act?
Does he promise and not fulfill?
20 I have received a command to bless;
he has blessed,[c] and I cannot change
it.[d]

21 "No misfortune is seen in Jacob,[e]
no misery observed[*a*] in Israel.[f]
The LORD their God is with them;[g]
the shout of the King[h] is among
them.
22 God brought them out of Egypt;[i]
they have the strength of a wild ox.[j]
23 There is no divination against[*b*] Jacob,
no evil omens[k] against[*b*] Israel.
It will now be said of Jacob
and of Israel, 'See what God has
done!'
24 The people rise like a lioness;[l]
they rouse themselves like a lion[m]
that does not rest till it devours its prey
and drinks the blood of its victims."

25Then Balak said to Balaam, "Neither
curse them at all nor bless them at all!"

23:14 [y]ver 2
23:16 [z]Nu 22:38
23:19 [a]Isa 55:9; Hos 11:9 [b]1Sa 15:29; Mal 3:6; Titus 1:2; Jas 1:17
23:20 [c]Ge 22:17; Nu 22:12 [d]Isa 43:13
23:21 [e]Ps 32:2, 5; Ro 4:7-8 [f]Isa 40:2; Jer 50:20 [g]Ex 29:45, 46; Ps 145:18 [h]Dt 33:5; Ps 89:15-18
23:22 [i]Nu 24:8 [j]Dt 33:17; Job 39:9
23:23 [k]Nu 24:1; Jos 13:22
23:24 [l]Na 2:11 [m]Ge 49:9

26Balaam answered, "Did I not tell you I
must do whatever the LORD says?"

Balaam's Third Message

27Then Balak said to Balaam, "Come, let
me take you to another place.[n] Perhaps it
will please God to let you curse them for
me from there." 28And Balak took Balaam to
the top of Peor,[o] overlooking the wasteland.
29Balaam said, "Build me seven altars
here, and prepare seven bulls and seven
rams for me." 30Balak did as Balaam had
said, and offered a bull and a ram on each
altar.

24 Now when Balaam saw that it
pleased the LORD to bless Israel, he
did not resort to divination[p] as at other
times, but turned his face toward the wilderness.[q] 2When Balaam looked out and
saw Israel encamped tribe by tribe, the
Spirit of God came on him[r] 3and he spoke
his message:

"The prophecy of Balaam son of Beor,
the prophecy of one whose eye sees
clearly,
4 the prophecy of one who hears the
words of God,[s]
who sees a vision from the
Almighty,[*c*][t]
who falls prostrate, and whose eyes
are opened:

5 "How beautiful are your tents, Jacob,
your dwelling places, Israel!
6 "Like valleys they spread out,
like gardens beside a river,
like aloes[u] planted by the LORD,
like cedars beside the waters.[v]
7 Water will flow from their buckets;
their seed will have abundant water.

"Their king will be greater than Agag;[w]
their kingdom will be exalted.[x]

[*a*] *21* Or *He has not looked on Jacob's offenses / or on the wrongs found* [*b*] *23* Or *in* [*c*] *4* Hebrew *Shaddai*; also in verse 16

23:27 [n]ver 13
23:28 [o]Ps 106:28
24:1 [p]Nu 23:23 [q]Nu 23:28
24:2 [r]Nu 11:25, 26; 1Sa 10:10; 19:20; 2Ch 15:1
24:4 [s]Nu 22:20 [t]Ge 15:1
24:6 [u]Ps 45:8 [v]Ps 1:3; 104:16
24:7 [w]2Sa 15:8 [x]2Sa 5:12; 1Ch 14:2; Ps 145:11-13

23:19 *change his mind.* Unlike the gods of Mesopotamia, who were often whimsical and malleable, Israel's God was unchangeable and therefore of incomparable integrity. Mesopotamian gods were believed to be capable of exploiting the ambiguity of omens to their pleasure. Ishtar, a principal Mesopotamian goddess, is known for possessing paradoxical, and at times mutually exclusive, traits. *change.* Here it denotes making idle or deceptive promises or failing to follow through on one's word.
23:22 *strength of a wild ox.* Israel's strength was totally in God; by his power Israel is compared to a ravaging wild ox. Hammurapi of Babylon declared himself to be like "the fiery wild ox who gores the foe." Ancient Near Eastern deities were often depicted as horned bulls or as humans with the head and/or horns of a bull. Baal is depicted as wearing the horns of a bull or wild ox in a sculptural relief from Ugarit.

23:23 *no divination against Jacob.* Israel did not need augurs, sorcerers, diviners or magicians; in fact, these were condemned. (Augury included reading cloud patterns, bird movements and other activities in the skies.) Israel's defense came from no such activity, nor could such powers be used effectively against Israel. God would use a pagan diviner to communicate divine revelation for the purpose of blessing those whom Balaam had been expected to condemn.
24:7 *Agag.* He ruled the Amalekites (see note on 13:29) at the time of King Saul (1Sa 15:8). The Amalekites were Israel's greatest enemy during Moses' lifetime, having been routed by Israel soon after the exodus (Ex 17:8–16). The Amalekites defeated Israel after Israel rejected the gift of the land (Nu 14:43–45). Agag seems to have been a dynastic name among the Amalekites, and this oracle depicts a future victory in the exaltation of Israel.

8 "God brought them out of Egypt;
they have the strength of a wild ox.
They devour hostile nations
and break their bones in pieces;[y]
with their arrows they pierce them.[z]
9 Like a lion they crouch and lie down,
like a lioness[a] — who dares to rouse them?
"May those who bless you be blessed
and those who curse you be cursed!"[b]

10 Then Balak's anger burned against Balaam. He struck his hands together[c] and
said to him, "I summoned you to curse
my enemies, but you have blessed them[d]
these three times.[e] 11 Now leave at once
and go home! I said I would reward you
handsomely,[f] but the LORD has kept you
from being rewarded."
12 Balaam answered Balak, "Did I not tell
the messengers you sent me,[g] 13 'Even if
Balak gave me all the silver and gold in
his palace, I could not do anything of my
own accord, good or bad, to go beyond
the command of the LORD[h] — and I must
say only what the LORD says'?[i] 14 Now I am
going back to my people, but come, let me
warn you of what this people will do to
your people in days to come."[j]

Balaam's Fourth Message

15 Then he spoke his message:

"The prophecy of Balaam son of Beor,
the prophecy of one whose eye sees clearly,
16 the prophecy of one who hears the words of God,
who has knowledge from the Most High,
who sees a vision from the Almighty,
who falls prostrate, and whose eyes are opened:

17 "I see him, but not now;
I behold him, but not near.[k]
A star will come out of Jacob;[l]
a scepter will rise out of Israel.[m]
He will crush the foreheads of Moab,[n]
the skulls[a] of[b] all the people of Sheth.[c]
18 Edom[o] will be conquered;
Seir, his enemy, will be conquered,
but Israel will grow strong.
19 A ruler will come out of Jacob[p]
and destroy the survivors of the city."

Balaam's Fifth Message

20 Then Balaam saw Amalek[q] and spoke his message:

"Amalek was first among the nations,
but their end will be utter destruction."

Balaam's Sixth Message

21 Then he saw the Kenites[r] and spoke his message:

"Your dwelling place is secure,
your nest is set in a rock;
22 yet you Kenites will be destroyed
when Ashur[s] takes you captive."

Balaam's Seventh Message

23 Then he spoke his message:

"Alas! Who can live when God does this?[d]
24 Ships will come from the shores of Cyprus;[t]
they will subdue Ashur and Eber,[u]
but they too will come to ruin.[v]"

24:8 [y] Ps 2:9; Jer 50: 17 [z] Ps 45:5 **24:9** [a] Ge 49:9; Nu 23:24 [b] Ge 12:3 **24:10** [c] Eze 21:14 [d] Nu 23:11 [e] Ne 13:2 **24:11** [f] Nu 22:17 **24:12** [g] Nu 22:18 **24:13** [h] Nu 22:18 [i] Nu 22:20 **24:14** [j] Ge 49:1; Nu 31:8, 16; Da 2:28; Mic 6:5

24:17 [k] Rev 1:7 [l] Mt 2:2 [m] Ge 49:10 [n] Nu 21:29; Isa 15:1-16:14 **24:18** [o] Am 9:12 **24:19** [p] Ge 49:10; Mic 5:2 **24:20** [q] Ex 17:14 **24:21** [r] Ge 15:19 **24:22** [s] Ge 10:22 **24:24** [t] Ge 10:4 [u] Ge 10:21 [v] ver 20

[a] *17* Samaritan Pentateuch (see also Jer. 48:45); the meaning of the word in the Masoretic Text is uncertain. [b] *17* Or possibly *Moab, / batter* [c] *17* Or *all the noisy boasters* [d] *23* Masoretic Text; with a different word division of the Hebrew *The people from the islands will gather from the north.*

24:10 *struck his hands together.* Fierce clapping of the hands was a sign of derision or defiance (Job 27:23; 34:37; La 2:15). The same meaning is evident in Esarhaddon's Prism Inscription, where the gesture accompanies mourning in response to what he calls the wicked behavior of his father.
24:17 *star.* It is difficult to document the star being used as a symbol or metaphor for kingship in ancient Near Eastern literature. In later literature, this passage served as a basis for the star used on the coinage of Alexander Jannaeus (103 – 76 BC) to elevate the status of his kingship. Rabbi Akiba in the second century AD proclaimed Simon bar Kosiba to be Bar Kokhba ("son of the star"), thereby claiming fulfillment of this Messianic passage. *scepter.* Symbolized royal power in both heavenly and earthly realms, as seen in royal monuments of the ancient Near East in iconographic and epigraphic forms. Thutmose III subdues his captives with his scepter in a relief from the temple of Amon at Karnak.
24:22 *Kenites.* A nomadic clan living in the eastern Sinai region; their roots are traced Biblically to the descendants of Cain and are associated with metallurgical craftsmanship (Ge 4:17 – 22). In Jdg 1:16 the association is made between the Kenites and Moses' in-laws (the Midianites), the descendants of whom settled in the Negev near Arad. Later Kenites are found living as far north as the territory of Naphtali (cf. 10:29 – 32; Ex 2:11 — 3:1; 18:1 – 5; Jdg 4:17; 5:24 – 27). The present text notes a group of Kenites who, like some Midianites, become enemies of Israel and are eventually subdued. *Ashur.* Probably refers not to the later Assyrian Empire of the ninth to seventh centuries BC, or even the Middle Assyrian peoples of the Late Bronze Age, who seldom ventured west of the Euphrates. Rather, this denotes the relatively unknown Ashurites, a nomadic group of the Negev region mentioned in Ge 25:3,18; Ps 83:8. They were descendants of Abraham and his concubine Keturah.
24:24 *Cyprus.* In several OT passages the term is used generically for the islands of the Mediterranean and their inhabitants (Jer 2:10; Da 11:30). The inhabitants of Cyprus — also called Kittiyim in ancient literature after Cyprus's major city Kition — mentioned in the Arad

25Then Balaam[w] got up and returned
home, and Balak went his own way.

Moab Seduces Israel

25 While Israel was staying in
Shittim,[x] the men began to indulge
in sexual immorality[y] with Moabite wom-
en,[z] 2who invited them to the sacrifices[a]
to their gods.[b] The people ate the sacrificial meal and bowed down before these
gods. 3So Israel yoked themselves to the
Baal of Peor.[c] And the LORD's anger burned
against them.
4The LORD said to Moses, "Take all the
leaders of these people, kill them and expose them in broad daylight before the
LORD,[d] so that the LORD's fierce anger[e] may
turn away from Israel."
5So Moses said to Israel's judges, "Each
of you must put to death[f] those of your
people who have yoked themselves to the
Baal of Peor."
6Then an Israelite man brought into the
camp a Midianite woman right before the
eyes of Moses and the whole assembly of
Israel while they were weeping at the entrance to the tent of meeting. 7When Phinehas son of Eleazar, the son of Aaron, the
priest, saw this, he left the assembly, took
a spear in his hand 8and followed the Israelite into the tent. He drove the spear
into both of them, right through the Israelite man and into the woman's stomach. Then the plague against the Israelites

24:25 [w]Nu 31:8
25:1 [x]Jos 2:1; Mic 6:5 [y]1Co 10:8; Rev 2:14 [z]Nu 31:16
25:2 [a]Ex 34:15 [b]Ex 20:5; Dt 32:38; 1Co 10:20
25:3 [c]Ps 106:28; Hos 9:10
25:4 [d]Dt 4:3 [e]Dt 13:17
25:5 [f]Ex 32:27
25:8 [g]Nu 16:46-48; Ps 106:30
25:9 [h]Nu 14:37; 1Co 10:8 [i]Nu 31:16
25:11 [j]Ps 106:30 [k]Ex 20:5; Dt 32:16, 21; Ps 78:58
25:12 [l]Isa 54:10; Eze 34:25; Mal 2:4, 5
25:13 [m]Ex 29:9 [n]Nu 16:46
25:15 [o]ver 18 [p]Nu 31:8; Jos 13:21
25:17 [q]Nu 31:1-3
25:18 [r]Nu 31:16
26:2 [s]Ex 30:11-16; 38:25-26; Nu 1:2

was stopped;[g] 9but those who died in the
plague[h] numbered 24,000.[i]
10The LORD said to Moses, 11"Phinehas
son of Eleazar, the son of Aaron, the priest,
has turned my anger away from the Israelites.[j] Since he was as zealous for my hon-
or[k] among them as I am, I did not put an
end to them in my zeal. 12Therefore tell him
I am making my covenant of peace[l] with
him. 13He and his descendants will have a
covenant of a lasting priesthood,[m] because
he was zealous for the honor of his God
and made atonement[n] for the Israelites."
14The name of the Israelite who was
killed with the Midianite woman was Zimri son of Salu, the leader of a Simeonite
family. 15And the name of the Midianite
woman who was put to death was Kozbi[o]
daughter of Zur, a tribal chief of a Midianite family.[p]
16The LORD said to Moses, 17"Treat the
Midianites[q] as enemies and kill them.
18They treated you as enemies when they
deceived you in the Peor incident[r] involving their sister Kozbi, the daughter of a
Midianite leader, the woman who was
killed when the plague came as a result of
that incident."

The Second Census

26 After the plague the LORD said to
Moses and Eleazar son of Aaron,
the priest, 2"Take a census[s] of the whole
Israelite community by families—all those

inscriptions are probably Greek and Cypriot mercenaries serving in the Judean army in border fortresses. During the Hellenistic age "Kittim" became a byword for the arch-enemies of God, a prominent motif in the Qumran scrolls in reference to the Greeks and then the Romans.

25:3 *Baal of Peor.* This is the first occurrence in the Hebrew Bible of the god Baal, who becomes the primary antagonist to Yahweh for the hearts of the Israelites. In the latter half of the Late Bronze Age, Baal was emerging as one of the major operative deities in Canaan. From Ugaritic texts Baal was the agent of the creative order, who with his consort Anath defeated the forces of evil, namely, Yamm (Sea), Mot (Death) and Lotan (Leviathan, "Sea Monster").

Baal was a lesser-known deity in Mesopotamia during the Early Bronze Age and in the beginning of the Middle Bronze (patriarchal) period (2200–1550 BC). His first appearance as a prominent deity in Canaan surfaces in Hyksos-period texts from Egypt in the latter half of the Middle Bronze Age (c. 1720–1570 BC). The Egyptians bemoaned the fact that the "foreign rulers" from the land of the Hurru and Retenu were not worshipers of Amon-Re, but of a god called Baal-hazor, which they associated with their god Seth. With the emergence of the classical Canaanites in the southern Levant, apparently a mix of Northwest Semitic peoples and some non-Semitic elements such as the Hurrians and Hittites, came the emergence of Baal as a primary deity in the cults of the land.

25:4 *Take all the leaders of these people, kill them and expose them in broad daylight before the LORD.* Lit. "Take all the leaders of the people and impale them to Yahweh before the sun." That is, Moses must round up all the tribal leaders, those representatives of the people who presumably should have either prevented the idolatrous activities or carried out the punishment of the guilty members of their tribes, and execute them by impaling them on poles so that their bodies hang out in broad daylight. The term "impale" is a rare Hebrew verb that has been variously translated as "kill, execute, impale, dismember." The instructions given to Moses are severe but necessary to accomplish the purging of the sins of the people.

Exposure to the elements usually followed this form of execution, as with Saul's sons (2Sa 21:8–13). Such public exposure was reserved for only the most heinous of crimes in ancient Israel and Mesopotamia. Later Assyrian sculptural relief murals depict rebellious vassals impaled on poles and left for public viewing, presumably to deter further insurrection. That the guilty parties were to be executed as "unto Yahweh" means that they were rendered unto Yahweh in order to expiate the divine wrath as evidenced in the plague.

25:6 *brought into the camp.* The offense here is probably not a violation of ethnic purity (since exogamy is allowed under certain circumstances), but rather something involving ritual intercourse. Alternatively, the intercourse could involve a ritual tied to the cult of the dead, perhaps an appeasement ritual regarding the plague in v. 3, where the "camp" in question is the ancestral spirits.

25:8,9 *plague.* This is not the word used for the ten plagues in Exodus, but it is the same word for plague that is used in Nu 14:37; 16:46–50. It is some sort of epidemic.

25:9 *24,000.* May be 24 clans rather than 24,000 people since the Hebrew words are nearly identical.

twenty years old or more who are able to
serve in the army[t] of Israel." 3So on the
plains of Moab[u] by the Jordan across from
Jericho,[v] Moses and Eleazar the priest
spoke with them and said, 4"Take a census of the men twenty years old or more,
as the LORD commanded Moses."

These were the Israelites who came out
of Egypt:

5The descendants of Reuben, the firstborn
son of Israel, were:
 through Hanok,[w] the Hanokite clan;
 through Pallu,[x] the Palluite clan;
6through Hezron, the Hezronite clan;
 through Karmi, the Karmite clan.
7These were the clans of Reuben; those
numbered were 43,730.

8The son of Pallu was Eliab, 9and the
sons of Eliab[y] were Nemuel, Dathan
and Abiram. The same Dathan and Abiram were the community[z] officials who
rebelled against Moses and Aaron and
were among Korah's followers when they
rebelled against the LORD.[a] 10The earth
opened its mouth and swallowed them
along with Korah, whose followers died
when the fire devoured the 250 men. And
they served as a warning sign.[b] 11The line
of Korah,[c] however, did not die out.[d]

12The descendants of Simeon by their
clans were:
 through Nemuel, the Nemuelite clan;
 through Jamin,[e] the Jaminite clan;
 through Jakin, the Jakinite clan;
13through Zerah,[f] the Zerahite clan;
 through Shaul, the Shaulite clan.
14These were the clans of Simeon; those
numbered were 22,200.[g]

15The descendants of Gad by their clans
were:
 through Zephon,[h] the Zephonite clan;
 through Haggi, the Haggite clan;
 through Shuni, the Shunite clan;
16through Ozni, the Oznite clan;
 through Eri, the Erite clan;
17through Arodi,[a] the Arodite clan;
 through Areli, the Arelite clan.
18These were the clans of Gad;[i] those numbered were 40,500.

19Er and Onan were sons of Judah, but
they died[j] in Canaan.
20The descendants of Judah by their clans
were:
 through Shelah,[k] the Shelanite clan;
 through Perez, the Perezite clan;
 through Zerah, the Zerahite clan.[l]
21The descendants of Perez were:
 through Hezron,[m] the Hezronite clan;
 through Hamul, the Hamulite clan.
22These were the clans of Judah;[n] those
numbered were 76,500.

23The descendants of Issachar by their
clans were:
 through Tola,[o] the Tolaite clan;
 through Puah, the Puite[b] clan;
24through Jashub,[p] the Jashubite clan;
 through Shimron, the Shimronite clan.
25These were the clans of Issachar;[q] those
numbered were 64,300.

26The descendants of Zebulun by their
clans were:
 through Sered, the Seredite clan;
 through Elon, the Elonite clan;
 through Jahleel, the Jahleelite clan.
27These were the clans of Zebulun;[r] those
numbered were 60,500.

28The descendants of Joseph by their clans
through Manasseh and Ephraim were:

29The descendants of Manasseh:
 through Makir,[s] the Makirite clan
  (Makir was the father of Gilead[t]);
 through Gilead, the Gileadite clan.
30These were the descendants of Gilead:
  through Iezer,[u] the Iezerite clan;
  through Helek, the Helekite clan;
31through Asriel, the Asrielite clan;
  through Shechem, the Shechemite clan;
32through Shemida, the Shemidaite clan;
  through Hepher, the Hepherite clan.
33(Zelophehad[v] son of Hepher had
  no sons; he had only daughters,
  whose names were Mahlah, Noah,
  Hoglah, Milkah and Tirzah.)[w]
34These were the clans of Manasseh; those
numbered were 52,700.[x]

35These were the descendants of Ephraim
by their clans:

26:2 [t]Nu 1:3 **26:3** [u]Nu 33:48 [v]Nu 22:1 **26:5** [w]Ge 46:9 [x]1Ch 5:3 **26:9** [y]Nu 16:1 [z]Nu 1:16 [a]Nu 16:2 **26:10** [b]Nu 16:35, 38 **26:11** [c]Ex 6:24 [d]Nu 16:33; Dt 24:16 **26:12** [e]1Ch 4:24 **26:13** [f]Ge 46:10 **26:14** [g]Nu 1:23 **26:15** [h]Ge 46:16 **26:18** [i]Nu 1:25; Jos 13:24-28 **26:19** [j]Ge 38:2-10; 46:12 **26:20** [k]1Ch 2:3 [l]Jos 7:17 **26:21** [m]Ru 4:19; 1Ch 2:9 **26:22** [n]Nu 1:27 **26:23** [o]Ge 46:13; 1Ch 7:1 **26:24** [p]Ge 46:13 **26:25** [q]Nu 1:29 **26:27** [r]Nu 1:31 **26:29** [s]Jos 17:1 [t]Jdg 11:1 **26:30** [u]Jos 17:2; Jdg 6:11 **26:33** [v]Nu 27:1 [w]Nu 36:11 **26:34** [x]Nu 1:35

[a] *17* Samaritan Pentateuch and Syriac (see also Gen. 46:16); Masoretic Text *Arod* [b] *23* Samaritan Pentateuch, Septuagint, Vulgate and Syriac (see also 1 Chron. 7:1); Masoretic Text *through Puvah, the Punite*

26:4 *Israelites who came out of Egypt.* This second census of Israel's military provides genealogical information not listed in the first census (in ch. 1; see the article "Genealogies," p. 16). Lists of successive kings of Sumer, Assyria and Babylon were common among the cuneiform texts excavated at Nineveh and Babylon. The genealogical census lists in Numbers connect the second generation of Israelites with the first generation, whom God delivered from Egypt. The familial relationships also form the basis for the land distribution by lot noted in vv. 52–56; 33:53–54.

through Shuthelah, the Shuthelahite
clan;
through Beker, the Bekerite clan;
through Tahan, the Tahanite clan.
36 These were the descendants of Shuthelah:
through Eran, the Eranite clan.
37 These were the clans of Ephraim;[y] those
numbered were 32,500.

These were the descendants of Joseph by
their clans.

38 The descendants of Benjamin[z] by their
clans were:
through Bela, the Belaite clan;
through Ashbel, the Ashbelite clan;
through Ahiram, the Ahiramite clan;
39 through Shupham,[a] the Shuphamite
clan;
through Hupham, the Huphamite clan.
40 The descendants of Bela through Ard[a]
and Naaman were:
through Ard,[b] the Ardite clan;
through Naaman, the Naamite
clan.
41 These were the clans of Benjamin;[b]
those numbered were 45,600.

42 These were the descendants of Dan by
their clans:
through Shuham,[c] the Shuhamite
clan.
These were the clans of Dan: 43 All of them
were Shuhamite clans; and those numbered were 64,400.

44 The descendants of Asher by their clans
were:
through Imnah, the Imnite clan;
through Ishvi, the Ishvite clan;
through Beriah, the Beriite clan;
45 and through the descendants of Beriah:
through Heber, the Heberite clan;
through Malkiel, the Malkielite
clan.
46 (Asher had a daughter named Serah.)
47 These were the clans of Asher;[d] those
numbered were 53,400.

48 The descendants of Naphtali[e] by their
clans were:
through Jahzeel, the Jahzeelite clan;
through Guni, the Gunite clan;

26:37 [y] Nu 1:33
26:38 [z] Ge 46:21; 1Ch 7:6
26:40 [a] Ge 46:21; 1Ch 8:3
26:41 [b] Nu 1:37
26:42 [c] Ge 46:23
26:47 [d] Nu 1:41
26:48 [e] Ge 46:24; 1Ch 7:13
26:50 [f] Nu 1:43
26:51 [g] Ex 12:37; 38:26; Nu 1:46; 11:21
26:53 [h] Jos 11:23; 14:1; Eze 45:8
26:54 [i] Nu 33:54
26:55 [j] Nu 34:14
26:57 [k] Ge 46:11; Ex 6:16-19
26:58 [l] Ex 6:20
26:59 [m] Ex 2:1 [n] Ex 6:20
26:60 [o] Nu 3:2
26:61 [p] Lev 10:1-2 [q] Nu 3:4
26:62 [r] Nu 3:39

49 through Jezer, the Jezerite clan;
through Shillem, the Shillemite clan.
50 These were the clans of Naphtali;[f] those
numbered were 45,400.

51 The total number of the men of Israel
was 601,730.[g]

52 The LORD said to Moses, 53 "The land
is to be allotted to them as an inheritance
based on the number of names.[h] 54 To a
larger group give a larger inheritance, and
to a smaller group a smaller one; each
is to receive its inheritance according to
the number[i] of those listed. 55 Be sure that
the land is distributed by lot.[j] What each
group inherits will be according to the
names for its ancestral tribe. 56 Each inheritance is to be distributed by lot among the
larger and smaller groups."

57 These were the Levites[k] who were counted by their clans:
through Gershon, the Gershonite
clan;
through Kohath, the Kohathite clan;
through Merari, the Merarite clan.
58 These also were Levite clans:
the Libnite clan,
the Hebronite clan,
the Mahlite clan,
the Mushite clan,
the Korahite clan.
(Kohath was the forefather of Amram;[l] 59 the name of Amram's wife
was Jochebed,[m] a descendant of
Levi, who was born to the Levites[c]
in Egypt. To Amram she bore Aaron,
Moses[n] and their sister Miriam. 60 Aaron was the father of Nadab and Abihu, Eleazar and Ithamar.[o] 61 But Nadab and Abihu[p] died when they made
an offering before the LORD with unauthorized fire.)[q]

62 All the male Levites a month old or
more numbered 23,000.[r] They were not

[a] *39* A few manuscripts of the Masoretic Text, Samaritan Pentateuch, Vulgate and Syriac (see also Septuagint); most manuscripts of the Masoretic Text *Shephupham*
[b] *40* Samaritan Pentateuch and Vulgate (see also Septuagint); Masoretic Text does not have *through Ard.*
[c] *59* Or *Jochebed, a daughter of Levi, who was born to Levi*

26:51 *601,730.* See the article "Numbers in Numbers," p. 235. If one takes the interpretation of *elep* ("thousand") as "troop, clan," the second census total is 596 troops, totaling 5,730 men (an additional 180 men).
26:55 *distributed by lot.* The antiquity of this directive is echoed in the practice of census taking in the ancient Near East of the second millennium BC. Census taking for military and land distribution purposes is known from the royal archives of Mari dating to the nineteenth century BC. The principle of proportion is described in explicit terms — greater territory for larger tribes, smaller portions for the less populated tribes. Clan apportionment is assumed under the aegis of their ancestral tribe.

The proportional distribution takes into consideration the percentage of arable land available or accessible by clearing or irrigation. Joshua will later challenge tribes to harvest forested areas for ample farming acreage (Jos 17:17 – 18). The second principle governing land allocation is that of providential probability. The Lord oversees the tossing of the lots and thereby brings his decision to pass. Distribution of land for tribal inheritance follows this method; the assigned inheritance is to remain within the tribal family for posterity.

counted[s] along with the other Israelites
because they received no inheritance[t]
among them.[u]

63These are the ones counted by Moses
and Eleazar the priest when they counted the Israelites on the plains of Moab[v]
by the Jordan across from Jericho. 64Not
one of them was among those counted[w]
by Moses and Aaron the priest when they
counted the Israelites in the Desert of Sinai. 65For the LORD had told those Israelites
they would surely die in the wilderness,[x]
and not one of them was left except Caleb son of Jephunneh and Joshua son of
Nun.[y]

Zelophehad's Daughters

27:1-11pp — Nu 36:1-12

27 The daughters of Zelophehad[z] son
of Hepher,[a] the son of Gilead, the
son of Makir,[b] the son of Manasseh, belonged to the clans of Manasseh son of
Joseph. The names of the daughters were
Mahlah, Noah, Hoglah, Milkah and Tirzah. They came forward 2and stood before Moses, Eleazar the priest, the leaders
and the whole assembly at the entrance to
the tent of meeting and said, 3"Our father
died in the wilderness.[c] He was not among
Korah's followers, who banded together against the LORD,[d] but he died for his
own sin and left no sons.[e] 4Why should
our father's name disappear from his clan
because he had no son? Give us property
among our father's relatives."

5So Moses brought their case[f] before
the LORD,[g] 6and the LORD said to him,
7"What Zelophehad's daughters are saying is right. You must certainly give them
property as an inheritance[h] among their
father's relatives and give their father's inheritance to them.[i]

8"Say to the Israelites, 'If a man dies
and leaves no son, give his inheritance
to his daughter. 9If he has no daughter,
give his inheritance to his brothers. 10If
he has no brothers, give his inheritance
to his father's brothers. 11If his father had
no brothers, give his inheritance to the
nearest relative in his clan, that he may
possess it. This is to have the force of law[j]
for the Israelites, as the LORD commanded
Moses.' "

Joshua to Succeed Moses

12Then the LORD said to Moses, "Go up
this mountain in the Abarim Range[k] and
see the land[l] I have given the Israelites.
13After you have seen it, you too will be
gathered to your people,[m] as your brother Aaron[n] was, 14for when the community rebelled at the waters in the Desert of
Zin, both of you disobeyed my command
to honor me as holy[o] before their eyes."
(These were the waters of Meribah[p] Kadesh, in the Desert of Zin.)

15Moses said to the LORD, 16"May the
LORD, the God who gives breath to all living things,[q] appoint someone over this
community 17to go out and come in before them, one who will lead them out and
bring them in, so the LORD's people will
not be like sheep without a shepherd."[r]

18So the LORD said to Moses, "Take Joshua son of Nun, a man in whom is the spirit of leadership,[a][s] and lay your hand on
him.[t] 19Have him stand before Eleazar the

26:62 [s] Nu 1:47 [t] Nu 18:23 [u] Nu 2:33; Dt 10:9 **26:63** [v] ver 3 **26:64** [w] Nu 14:29; Dt 2:14-15; Heb 3:17 **26:65** [x] Nu 14:28; 1Co 10:5 [y] Jos 14:6-10 **27:1** [z] Nu 26:33 [a] Jos 17:2,3 [b] Nu 36:1 **27:3** [c] Nu 26:65 [d] Nu 16:2 [e] Nu 26:33 **27:5** [f] Ex 18:19 [g] Nu 9:8 **27:7** [h] Job 42:15 [i] Jos 17:4 **27:11** [j] Nu 35:29 **27:12** [k] Nu 33:47; Jer 22:20 [l] Dt 3:23-27; 32:48-52 **27:13** [m] Nu 31:2 [n] Nu 20:28 **27:14** [o] Nu 20:12 [p] Ex 17:7; Dt 32:51; Ps 106:32 **27:16** [q] Nu 16:22 **27:17** [r] Dt 31:2; 1Ki 22:17; Eze 34:5; Zec 10:2; Mt 9:36; Mk 6:34 **27:18** [s] Ge 41:38; Nu 11:25-29 [t] ver 23; Dt 34:9

[a] 18 Or *the Spirit*

27:1 *daughters of Zelophehad.* In the two census tallies only male descendants are registered. If a man dies without a male heir, a male relative will redeem the land so that the territory remains within the clan. The levirate land responsibilities are outlined in Lev 25:23 – 28 for cases in which land is sold to pay one's debts, and in the Year of Jubilee land debts are fully restored (Lev 25:8 – 17).

The account in vv. 1 – 11 provides an example of the development of casuistic legislation early in Israelite history. (1) The specific case is presented at the entrance to the tent of meeting (vv. 1 – 4). (2) Appeal is made to divine legislative authority (v. 5). (3) A precedent-setting decision is issued, accompanied by derived principles (vv. 6 – 11). Zelophehad "died for his own sin" (v. 3) without a rightful male heir through which his family would receive its share in the allotment of the land. The concern shared by his daughters was that their family would be passed over in the apportionment and thus their name would be forgotten in posterity (v. 4).

The potential disappearance of one's family name is a matter of grave concern, often associated with divine judgment leading to societal abandonment. The entreaty within the clan allotment derives from the principles set forth in 26:52 – 56. Thus the daughters of Zelophehad desire status and inheritance rights within the Makirite clan of Manasseh. Later the Makirites receive an inheritance in the Gilead region of Transjordan (32:39 – 42).

Parallels to female inheritance in the Pentateuch occur in ancient Near Eastern texts from several countries. Ancient Sumerian law from Nippur and the decrees of Gudea of Lagash (c. 2150 BC) allowed a woman to inherit property when there were no sons. Z. Ben-Barak cites numerous other cases from Babylon, Nuzi and elsewhere, including one from sixth-century BC Athens that stipulated that the woman marry within the family. Egyptian laws seem to develop progressively from the Middle to New Kingdom periods, moving from a case in which a woman's husband has provided for her in his will to a general case in which a woman received one-third of an estate. Verses 1 – 11 establish the legal rights of women within the sphere of property law with respect to possession and inheritance.

27:18 *the spirit.* Nothing in the OT text suggests that this is the Holy Spirit, the third person of the Trinity; neither is it the Spirit of God that comes on the OT prophets; rather it is Joshua's God-given skills as a leader (hence the NIV "spirit of leadership"). The recognition of empowerment by God becomes the criterion by which political authority

priest and the entire assembly and commission him[u] in their presence.[v] 20 Give
him some of your authority so the whole
Israelite community will obey him.[w] 21 He
is to stand before Eleazar the priest, who
will obtain decisions for him by inquiring[x]
of the Urim[y] before the LORD. At his command he and the entire community of the
Israelites will go out, and at his command
they will come in."

22 Moses did as the LORD commanded
him. He took Joshua and had him stand
before Eleazar the priest and the whole assembly. 23 Then he laid his hands on him
and commissioned him, as the LORD instructed through Moses.

Daily Offerings

28 The LORD said to Moses, 2 "Give this
command to the Israelites and say
to them: 'Make sure that you present to
me at the appointed time my food[z] offerings, as an aroma pleasing to me.' 3 Say to
them: 'This is the food offering you are to
present to the LORD: two lambs a year old
without defect, as a regular burnt offering
each day.[a] 4 Offer one lamb in the morning
and the other at twilight, 5 together with a
grain offering of a tenth of an ephah[a] of
the finest flour mixed with a quarter of
a hin[b] of oil[b] from pressed olives. 6 This
is the regular burnt offering instituted at
Mount Sinai[c] as a pleasing aroma, a food
offering presented to the LORD. 7 The accompanying drink offering[d] is to be a
quarter of a hin of fermented drink with
each lamb. Pour out the drink offering to
the LORD at the sanctuary.[e] 8 Offer the second lamb at twilight, along with the same
kind of grain offering and drink offering
that you offer in the morning. This is a
food offering, an aroma pleasing to the
LORD.[f]

Sabbath Offerings

9 " 'On the Sabbath[g] day, make an offering of two lambs a year old without defect,
together with its drink offering and a grain
offering of two-tenths of an ephah[c][h] of the
finest flour mixed with olive oil. 10 This is
the burnt offering for every Sabbath, in
addition to the regular burnt offering[i] and
its drink offering.

Monthly Offerings

11 " 'On the first of every month,[j] present
to the LORD a burnt offering of two young
bulls, one ram and seven male lambs
a year old, all without defect.[k] 12 With
each bull there is to be a grain offering[l]
of three-tenths of an ephah[d][m] of the finest flour mixed with oil; with the ram, a
grain offering of two-tenths of an ephah of
the finest flour mixed with oil; 13 and with

27:19 [u] Dt 3:28; 31:14,23 [v] Dt 31:7 **27:20** [w] Jos 1:16,17 **27:21** [x] Jos 9:14 [y] Ex 28:30 **28:2** [z] Lev 3:11 **28:3** [a] Ex 29:38 **28:5** [b] Lev 2:1; Nu 15:4 **28:6** [c] Ex 19:3 **28:7** [d] Ex 29:41 [e] Lev 3:7 **28:8** [f] Lev 1:9 **28:9** [g] Ex 20:10 [h] Lev 23:13 **28:10** [i] ver 3 **28:11** [j] Nu 10:10 [k] Lev 1:3 **28:12** [l] Nu 15:6 [m] Nu 15:9

[a] *5* That is, probably about 3 1/2 pounds or about 1.6 kilograms; also in verses 13, 21 and 29 [b] *5* That is, about 1 quart or about 1 liter; also in verses 7 and 14 [c] *9* That is, probably about 7 pounds or about 3.2 kilograms; also in verses 12, 20 and 28 [d] *12* That is, probably about 11 pounds or about 5 kilograms; also in verses 20 and 28

is recognized by the tribes. *lay your hand on him.* The divine selection of Joshua son of Nun to succeed Moses is conveyed via the laying on of hands—the means of officially transferring authority from one leader to another. Among the rock-cut tombs of El-Amarna in Egypt of the fourteenth century BC is a scene depicting the pharaoh conferring authority to his officials by extending his hands over their heads.

27:21 *Urim.* See the article "Urim and Thummim," p. 162.

28:2 *appointed time.* Most ancient Near Eastern cultures held annual agricultural festivals celebrating the gifts of the gods and goddesses in the flocks, herds and grain in the spring, and wine and oil in the fall. From Ugarit comes the annual fall festival for the offering of new wine, and perhaps other cyclical festivals as well. In the Hittite "Instructions to Priests and Temple Officials," the firstfruits of animals and grain were presented "for the pleasure of the gods." In texts from Emar of Upper Mesopotamia a six-month ritual calendar is outlined, beginning with the *Zukru* festival in the fall month of Zarati and extending to the spring. During the Emar rituals, sacrifices of sheep, grain (bread) and beer (strong drink) are listed.

The Israelite cycle of holy days combine the agricultural calendar with celebrations of God's dynamic acts in history. Daily, monthly and annual offerings are prescribed for purification and atonement, consecration, and celebration in the covenant relationship between God and his people. The Gezer Calendar delineates eight periods in the 12-month cycle for various harvest periods in ancient Israel, beginning with the fall harvest of the olive orchards.

28:7 *fermented drink.* The addition of one-fourth hin of strong drink (*shekar*, see the article "Nazirites," p. 242) completes the collection of agricultural products that combine to produce a savory smell when consumed by fire. Wine and other fermented liquids were considered special gifts from God (or the gods) in the ancient Near East and thus were to be reciprocated as part of the array of sacrifices.

28:11 *On the first of every month.* Lunar calendars dominate the time-reckoning measurements in the ancient Near East, and the New Moon feast held an important place in the cycle of religious observances. In northern Mesopotamia the moon-god Suen (Sin) was honored, and in Emar the New Moon of Dagan was celebrated by drinking wine and burning birds. Ram's horns and/or trumpets were sounded over the burnt offerings (10:10; Ps 81:3) on *Rosh Hodesh* (the first day of the month), and commerce was suspended (Am 8:5).

During the eighth century BC, this celebration and other rituals became contemptible in the eyes of Yahweh because of social injustice and religious idolatry in the nation (Isa 1:13; Hos 2:11). The lunar month set the sequence of the annual holy days and festivals (e.g., "on the first day of the seventh month"[Lev 23:24]). The sizable quantity of sacrificial elements offered on this day bespeaks the status of the holiday for the Israelite community.

each lamb, a grain offering[n] of a tenth of
an ephah of the finest flour mixed with
oil. This is for a burnt offering, a pleasing aroma, a food offering presented to
the LORD. 14With each bull there is to be
a drink offering[o] of half a hin[a] of wine;
with the ram, a third of a hin[b]; and with
each lamb, a quarter of a hin. This is the
monthly burnt offering to be made at each
new moon[p] during the year. 15Besides the
regular burnt offering[q] with its drink offering, one male goat is to be presented to
the LORD as a sin offering.[c][r]

The Passover

28:16-25pp — Ex 12:14-20; Lev 23:4-8; Dt 16:1-8

16" 'On the fourteenth day of the first
month the LORD's Passover[s] is to be held.
17On the fifteenth day of this month
there is to be a festival; for seven days[t]
eat bread made without yeast.[u] 18On the
first day hold a sacred assembly and do
no regular work.[v] 19Present to the LORD
a food offering consisting of a burnt offering of two young bulls, one ram and
seven male lambs a year old, all without
defect. 20With each bull offer a grain offering of three-tenths of an ephah[w] of the
finest flour mixed with oil; with the ram,
two-tenths; 21and with each of the seven
lambs, one-tenth. 22Include one male goat
as a sin offering[x] to make atonement for
you.[y] 23Offer these in addition to the regular morning burnt offering. 24In this way
present the food offering every day for sev-
en days as an aroma pleasing to the LORD;
it is to be offered in addition to the regular
burnt offering and its drink offering. 25On
the seventh day hold a sacred assembly
and do no regular work.

The Festival of Weeks

28:26-31pp — Lev 23:15-22; Dt 16:9-12

26" 'On the day of firstfruits,[z] when you
present to the LORD an offering of new
grain during the Festival of Weeks,[a] hold a
sacred assembly and do no regular work.[b]
27Present a burnt offering of two young
bulls, one ram and seven male lambs a
year old as an aroma pleasing to the LORD.
28With each bull there is to be a grain offering of three-tenths of an ephah of the
finest flour mixed with oil; with the ram,
two-tenths; 29and with each of the seven
lambs, one-tenth.[c] 30Include one male goat
to make atonement for you. 31Offer these
together with their drink offerings, in addition to the regular burnt offering[d] and
its grain offering. Be sure the animals are
without defect.

The Festival of Trumpets

29:1-6pp — Lev 23:23-25

29 " 'On the first day of the seventh
month hold a sacred assembly
and do no regular work.[e] It is a day for
you to sound the trumpets. 2As an aroma
pleasing to the LORD,[f] offer a burnt offering of one young bull, one ram and sev-
en male lambs a year old, all without defect.[g] 3With the bull offer a grain offering
of three-tenths of an ephah[d] of the finest
flour mixed with olive oil; with the ram,
two-tenths[e]; 4and with each of the seven
lambs, one-tenth.[f] 5Include one male goat[h]
as a sin offering[g] to make atonement for
you. 6These are in addition to the monthly[i]
and daily burnt offerings[j] with their grain
offerings and drink offerings as specified.
They are food offerings presented to the
LORD, a pleasing aroma.

The Day of Atonement

29:7-11pp — Lev 16:2-34; 23:26-32

7" 'On the tenth day of this seventh
month hold a sacred assembly. You must
deny yourselves[h][k] and do no work.[l] 8Pre-
sent as an aroma pleasing to the LORD a
burnt offering of one young bull, one ram
and seven male lambs a year old, all without defect. 9With the bull offer a grain offering[m] of three-tenths of an ephah of the
finest flour mixed with oil; with the ram,
two-tenths; 10and with each of the sev-
en lambs, one-tenth.[n] 11Include one male
goat as a sin offering, in addition to the

28:13 [n] Lev 6:14 **28:14** [o] Nu 15:7 [p] Ezr 3:5 **28:15** [q] ver 3, 23, 24 [r] Lev 4:3 **28:16** [s] Ex 12:6, 18; Lev 23:5; Dt 16:1 **28:17** [t] Ex 12:19 [u] Ex 23:15; 34:18; Lev 23:6; Dt 16:3-8 **28:18** [v] Ex 12:16; Lev 23:7 **28:20** [w] Lev 14:10 **28:22** [x] Ro 8:3 [y] Nu 15:28 **28:26** [z] Ex 34:22 [a] Ex 23:16 [b] ver 18; Dt 16:10

28:29 [c] ver 13 **28:31** [d] ver 3, 19 **29:1** [e] Lev 23:24 **29:2** [f] Nu 28:2 [g] Nu 28:3 **29:5** [h] Nu 28:15 **29:6** [i] Nu 28:11 [j] Nu 28:3 **29:7** [k] Ac 27:9 [l] Ex 31:15; Lev 16:29; 23:26-32 **29:9** [m] ver 3, 18 **29:10** [n] Nu 28:13

[a] 14 That is, about 2 quarts or about 1.9 liters
[b] 14 That is, about 1 1/3 quarts or about 1.3 liters
[c] 15 Or *purification offering*; also in verse 22
[d] 3 That is, probably about 11 pounds or about 5 kilograms; also in verses 9 and 14
[e] 3 That is, probably about 7 pounds or about 3.2 kilograms; also in verses 9 and 14
[f] 4 That is, probably about 3 1/2 pounds or about 1.6 kilograms; also in verses 10 and 15
[g] 5 Or *purification offering*; also elsewhere in this chapter
[h] 7 Or *must fast*

28:26 *Festival of Weeks.* Originally called the Festival of Harvest (Ex 23:16), the Festival of *Shavuoth* (Weeks) celebrated the completion of the grain harvest season begun at Passover/Unleavened Bread. The early barley harvest bore a direct connection to the end of the wheat harvest by the counting of the omer grain offering during the 50-day period. The celebration also included the offering of two portions of new grain baked with yeast as a sign of the fullness of God's blessing in comparison to the earlier week-long consumption of unleavened bread, the sign of poverty and affliction (Lev 23:15–22; Dt 16:3). *Shavuoth* included a goat for a sin (purification) offering and was also designated as a Sabbath. The timing of the two festivals in the first and third months led to the association of *Shavuoth* with the giving of the law on Mount Sinai (Ex 19:1). Unlike most holy days, this festival was not connected to the lunar calendar cycle. For the Messianic Qumran sectarians, the festival was the most important of their solar calendar year and given the name "Feast of the Renewal of the Covenant."

sin offering for atonement and the regular
burnt offering[o] with its grain offering, and
their drink offerings.

The Festival of Tabernacles
29:12-39pp — Lev 23:33-43; Dt 16:13-17

12“ ‘On the fifteenth day of the seventh[p]
month,[q] hold a sacred assembly and do
no regular work. Celebrate a festival to the
LORD for seven days. 13Present as an aroma
pleasing to the LORD a food offering consisting of a burnt offering of thirteen young
bulls, two rams and fourteen male lambs
a year old, all without defect. 14With each
of the thirteen bulls offer a grain offering[r]
of three-tenths of an ephah of the finest
flour mixed with oil; with each of the two
rams, two-tenths; 15and with each of the
fourteen lambs, one-tenth. 16Include one
male goat as a sin offering, in addition to
the regular burnt offering with its grain offering and drink offering.[s]
17“ ‘On the second day[t] offer twelve
young bulls, two rams and fourteen male
lambs a year old, all without defect.[u]
18With the bulls, rams and lambs, offer
their grain offerings[v] and drink offerings[w]
according to the number specified.[x] 19In-
clude one male goat as a sin offering,[y] in
addition to the regular burnt offering with
its grain offering, and their drink offerings.
20“ ‘On the third day offer eleven bulls,
two rams and fourteen male lambs a year
old, all without defect.[z] 21With the bulls,
rams and lambs, offer their grain offerings
and drink offerings according to the number specified.[a] 22Include one male goat as
a sin offering, in addition to the regular
burnt offering with its grain offering and
drink offering.
23“ ‘On the fourth day offer ten bulls,
two rams and fourteen male lambs a year
old, all without defect. 24With the bulls,
rams and lambs, offer their grain offerings
and drink offerings according to the number specified. 25Include one male goat as
a sin offering, in addition to the regular
burnt offering with its grain offering and
drink offering.
26“ ‘On the fifth day offer nine bulls, two
rams and fourteen male lambs a year old,
all without defect. 27With the bulls, rams
and lambs, offer their grain offerings and
drink offerings according to the number
specified. 28Include one male goat as a sin
offering, in addition to the regular burnt
offering with its grain offering and drink
offering.
29“ ‘On the sixth day offer eight bulls, two
rams and fourteen male lambs a year old, all
without defect. 30With the bulls, rams and
lambs, offer their grain offerings and drink
offerings according to the number specified.
31Include one male goat as a sin offering, in
addition to the regular burnt offering with
its grain offering and drink offering.
32“ ‘On the seventh day offer seven
bulls, two rams and fourteen male lambs
a year old, all without defect. 33With the
bulls, rams and lambs, offer their grain
offerings and drink offerings according to
the number specified. 34Include one male
goat as a sin offering, in addition to the
regular burnt offering with its grain offering and drink offering.
35“ ‘On the eighth day hold a closing
special assembly[b] and do no regular work.
36Present as an aroma pleasing to the
LORD[c] a food offering consisting of a burnt
offering of one bull, one ram and seven
male lambs a year old,[d] all without defect.
37With the bull, the ram and the lambs, offer their grain offerings and drink offerings
according to the number specified. 38In-
clude one male goat as a sin offering, in
addition to the regular burnt offering with
its grain offering and drink offering.
39“ ‘In addition to what you vow[e] and
your freewill offerings, offer these to the
LORD at your appointed festivals:[f] your
burnt offerings,[g] grain offerings, drink offerings and fellowship offerings.’ ”
40Moses told the Israelites all that the
LORD commanded him.[a]

Vows

30[b] Moses said to the heads of the
tribes of Israel:[h] “This is what the
LORD commands: 2When a man makes a
vow to the LORD or takes an oath to ob-

[a] 40 In Hebrew texts this verse (29:40) is numbered 30:1. [b] In Hebrew texts 30:1-16 is numbered 30:2-17.

29:11 [o] Lev 16:3; Nu 28:3
29:12 [p] 1Ki 8:2 [q] Lev 23:24
29:14 [r] ver 3
29:16 [s] ver 6
29:17 [t] Lev 23:36 [u] Nu 28:3
29:18 [v] ver 9 [w] Nu 28:7 [x] Nu 15:4-12
29:19 [y] Nu 28:15
29:20 [z] ver 17
29:21 [a] ver 18
29:35 [b] Lev 23:36
29:36 [c] Lev 1:9 [d] ver 2
29:39 [e] Nu 6:2 [f] Lev 23:2 [g] Lev 1:3; 1Ch 23:31; 2Ch 31:3
30:1 [h] Nu 1:4

29:12 *On the fifteenth day of the seventh month.* This was the Festival of Tabernacles (*Sukkot*). The *sukkah* was a hut or tent constructed during the wilderness period to protect from the elements of the desert. First called the Festival of Ingathering (Ex 23:16b), the celebration commemorated God's provision in the fall harvest of the vegetable crops, vineyards and olive orchards.

Such a celebration was common among ancient Near Eastern cultures, such as the Emar *Zukru* ("remembrance") rituals on the eighth and fifteenth days of the seventh month of Zarati. When the Israelites settled the promised land, they were to imitate their ancestors by building a *sukkah* adjacent to their home and live in it during the seven days of the festival (Lev 23:39–43) to remind them of God's protection and provision during the 40-year sojourn. The association of *Sukkot* with the exodus from Egypt provided a continuation of the salvation-redemption-providence-preservation motifs of Passover, Unleavened Bread and Pentecost.

There are more animals sacrificed during this festival than during any other festival: 71 bulls, 15 rams, 105 lambs, and 8 goats, with accompanying food and drink offerings.

30:2 *When a man makes a vow.* Vows were binding on

ligate himself by a pledge, he must not
break his word but must do everything he
said.[i]
3 “When a young woman still living in
her father’s household makes a vow to
the LORD or obligates herself by a pledge
4 and her father hears about her vow or
pledge but says nothing to her, then all her
vows and every pledge by which she obligated herself will stand.[j] 5 But if her father
forbids her when he hears about it, none
of her vows or the pledges by which she
obligated herself will stand; the LORD will
release her because her father has forbidden her.
6 “If she marries after she makes a vow[k]
or after her lips utter a rash promise by
which she obligates herself 7 and her
husband hears about it but says nothing
to her, then her vows or the pledges by
which she obligated herself will stand.
8 But if her husband[l] forbids her when he
hears about it, he nullifies the vow that
obligates her or the rash promise by which
she obligates herself, and the LORD will release her.
9 “Any vow or obligation taken by a widow or divorced woman will be binding on
her.
10 “If a woman living with her husband makes a vow or obligates herself by
a pledge under oath 11 and her husband
hears about it but says nothing to her and
does not forbid her, then all her vows or
the pledges by which she obligated herself will stand. 12 But if her husband nullifies them when he hears about them, then
none of the vows or pledges that came
from her lips will stand.[m] Her husband
has nullified them, and the LORD will release her. 13 Her husband may confirm or
nullify any vow she makes or any sworn
pledge to deny herself.[a] 14 But if her husband says nothing to her about it from day
to day, then he confirms all her vows or
the pledges binding on her. He confirms
them by saying nothing to her when he
hears about them. 15 If, however, he nullifies them some time after he hears about
them, then he must bear the consequences of her wrongdoing.”
16 These are the regulations the LORD
gave Moses concerning relationships between a man and his wife, and between a
father and his young daughter still living
at home.

Vengeance on the Midianites

31 The LORD said to Moses, 2 “Take
vengeance on the Midianites[n] for
the Israelites. After that, you will be gathered to your people.[o]”
3 So Moses said to the people, “Arm
some of your men to go to war against
the Midianites so that they may carry out
the LORD’s vengeance[p] on them. 4 Send
into battle a thousand men from each of
the tribes of Israel.” 5 So twelve thousand
men armed for battle, a thousand from
each tribe, were supplied from the clans

30:2 [i] Dt 23:21-23; Jdg 11:35; Job 22:27; Ps 22:25; 50:14; 116:14; Pr 20:25; Ecc 5:4,5; Jnh 1:16 **30:4** [j] ver 7 **30:6** [k] Lev 5:4 **30:8** [l] Ge 3:16 **30:12** [m] Eph 5:22; Col 3:18 **31:2** [n] Ge 25:2 [o] Nu 20:26; 27:13 **31:3** [p] Jdg 11:36; 1Sa 24:12; 2Sa 4:8; 22:48; Ps 94:1; 149:7

[a] 13 Or *to fast*

all community members, with special exceptions for women. Making vows was voluntary, but anyone who did so or swore an oath in an obligatory relationship had to fulfill that commitment. Vows involved a verbal act of commitment to a task or to consecration of oneself or one’s property to the Lord; sacrificial offerings were part of the obligation, and in the case of the Nazirite also an oath of abstinence. Biblical vows were made only to deity, intensifying the solemnity of the pledge. To break a vow in which God’s name had been evoked was to profane that name (see Lev 27).

Vows to the gods for favors were common in the ancient Near East in requests for victory in battle, healing, deliverance, childlessness or the love of a woman. The recitation of a vow was often inscribed on a stele. Examples include those made by kings and other worshipers in Mesopotamia, Ugarit and Aram. In the New Kingdom of Egypt, several prayers of the poor reflect vows to praise the god Ptah in response to his beneficent acts.

30:9 *widow or divorced woman.* A woman no longer under the patriarchal authority of her father or her husband, whether by his death or by divorce, possessed the same status and responsibility of a man with regard to vows and obligations. Independent women were afforded a significant position in Israelite society, being permitted to buy and sell property, negotiate contracts, operate businesses, and make vows and pledges (cf Pr 31:10–31 for similar activities by a married woman).

30:10 *a woman living with her husband.* Vows that might be detrimental to the woman, her husband or the husband-wife relationship could be annulled by the husband. Special considerations were given to the circumstances and time sequence of when the wife took a vow or oath, when the husband was apprised of the commitment, and when and how he responded to the information. Childlessness was a common concern in the Bible and the ancient Near East (e.g., Hannah in 1Sa 1:11; the mother of Samson in Jdg 13:1–23), and that would be a common focus of a woman’s vow. In Mesopotamia severe childhood disease or mortality is deemed the result of unpaid vows.

31:3 *vengeance.* The action against the Midianites is sometimes compared to the way that the Israelites were supposed to treat the peoples of the land in the time of Joshua, but the same term *herem* (see the article “Divine War,” p. 365) is not used here. Unlike Joshua’s actions against the Canaanites, here a specific offense serves as the backdrop, and it is that offense that is the basis for vengeance. The actions of the Canaanites are not acts of vengeance. Here plunder can be taken and even some of the people can be assimilated. This bears more resemblance to how Israel was instructed to treat the people and cities who were not inside the land that Yahweh was giving to them (Dt 20:10–15).

of Israel. 6Moses sent them into battle,
a thousand from each tribe, along with
Phinehas son of Eleazar, the priest, who
took with him articles from the sanctuary[q]
and the trumpets[r] for signaling.
7They fought against Midian, as the
LORD commanded Moses, and killed every
man.[s] 8Among their victims were Evi, Rekem, Zur, Hur and Reba[t]—the five kings
of Midian.[u] They also killed Balaam son of
Beor with the sword.[v] 9The Israelites captured the Midianite women and children
and took all the Midianite herds, flocks
and goods as plunder. 10They burned all
the towns where the Midianites had settled, as well as all their camps.[w] 11They
took all the plunder and spoils, including
the people and animals,[x] 12and brought
the captives, spoils and plunder to Moses and Eleazar the priest and the Israelite
assembly[y] at their camp on the plains of
Moab, by the Jordan across from Jericho.
13Moses, Eleazar the priest and all the
leaders of the community went to meet
them outside the camp. 14Moses was angry with the officers of the army[z]—the
commanders of thousands and commanders of hundreds—who returned from the
battle.
15"Have you allowed all the women to
live?" he asked them. 16"They were the
ones who followed Balaam's advice[a] and
enticed the Israelites to be unfaithful to
the LORD in the Peor incident,[b] so that a
plague struck the LORD's people. 17Now
kill all the boys. And kill every woman
who has slept with a man,[c] 18but save for
yourselves every girl who has never slept
with a man.
19"Anyone who has killed someone or
touched someone who was killed[d] must
stay outside the camp seven days. On the
third and seventh days you must purify
yourselves[e] and your captives. 20Purify every garment[f] as well as everything made of
leather, goat hair or wood."
21Then Eleazar the priest said to the soldiers who had gone into battle, "This is
what is required by the law that the LORD
gave Moses: 22Gold, silver, bronze, iron,[g]
tin, lead 23and anything else that can withstand fire must be put through the fire,[h]
and then it will be clean. But it must also
be purified with the water of cleansing.[i]
And whatever cannot withstand fire must
be put through that water. 24On the seventh day wash your clothes and you will
be clean.[j] Then you may come into the
camp."

Dividing the Spoils

25The LORD said to Moses, 26"You and
Eleazar the priest and the family heads
of the community are to count all the
people[k] and animals that were captured.
27Divide[l] the spoils equally between the
soldiers who took part in the battle and
the rest of the community. 28From the soldiers who fought in the battle, set apart
as tribute for the LORD[m] one out of ev-

31:6 [q] Nu 14:44 [r] Nu 10:9 **31:7** [s] Dt 20:13; Jdg 21:11; 1Ki 11:15,16 **31:8** [t] Jos 13:21 [u] Nu 25:15 [v] Jos 13:22 **31:10** [w] Ge 25:16; 1Ch 6:54; Ps 69:25; Eze 25:4 **31:11** [x] Dt 20:14 **31:12** [y] Nu 27:2 **31:14** [z] ver 48; Ex 18:21; Dt 1:15 **31:16** [a] 2Pe 2:15; Rev 2:14 [b] Nu 25:1-9 **31:17** [c] Dt 7:2; 20:16-18; Jdg 21:11 **31:19** [d] Nu 19:16 [e] Nu 19:12 **31:20** [f] Nu 19:19 **31:22** [g] Jos 6:19; 22:8 **31:23** [h] 1Co 3:13 [i] Nu 19:9,17 **31:24** [j] Lev 11:25 **31:26** [k] Nu 1:19 **31:27** [l] Jos 22:8; 1Sa 30:24 **31:28** [m] Nu 18:21

31:6 *articles from the sanctuary.* Scholars have debated which holy implements may have been taken from the sanctuary into battle. Some have suggested the ark of the covenant law, but it seems that if the ark of the covenant law were intended by this phrase, it would have been mentioned as when the Israelites tried to use it against the Philistines in the battle of Aphek-Ebenezer (1Sa 4:3–11). Others suggest these vessels were the Urim and Thummim, but this is unlikely since they were kept by the high priest. More likely these are the signal trumpets, which were kept in the sanctuary for their regular cultic usage and for waging battle (see notes on 10:2,5–7,8).
31:8 *Evi, Rekem, Zur, Hur and Reba.* The names of the five kings are recounted again in the same order in the battle summary of Jos 13:21, where they are called "Midianite chiefs" and "princes allied with Sihon." The precise political relationships among the Amorites, Moabites and Midianites remain somewhat nebulous. These Midianite chieftains may have been subject to Sihon prior to the defeat of the Amorites and then gained their independence through the earlier Israelite victory. *Zur.* The father of Kozbi, the Midianite woman killed by Phinehas along with her Israelite paramour, Zimri son of Salu (25:14–15). Zur and Zimri are both regarded as patriarchal clan leaders. *kings.* See note on 20:14.
31:19 *purify yourselves.* The purpose of holy war was the eradication of all impure elements from the geographic region or ethnic territory placed under the ban. Coming on the heels of an idolatrous and adulterous affair at Baal Peor involving Israelite and non-Israelite participants, a cleansing of the camp was needed for the sanctity and purity of the community. The violence of war brings death and a state of ritual impurity through contact with the dead.
31:22–23 *Gold, silver ... put through the fire.* This new ordinance has to do with the purification of metallic products by means of fire because they can withstand the high temperatures. Perishable goods such as glass beads, clothing, wood, leather, animals and other organic commodities are to be purified with water, probably through washing, and then put through the waters of purification made from fresh water and the ashes of the red cow (see ch. 19).
31:27 *Divide the spoils equally.* This instruction for distributing the spoils of war among the community members sets the standard for the coming campaigns in the promised land. In many other marauding cultures of the ancient Near East, the warriors retained whatever goods or persons they captured during and after battle, with certain portions being allocated to the king and his court and other portions rewarded to the priesthoods of the patron deity of that people.
31:28 *tribute.* The Hebrew term (*mekes*) occurs three times in this chapter but nowhere else in the Hebrew Bible. This term is attested in Ugaritic (*mekes*) and Akkadian (*miksu*) and occurs often in later rabbinic sources. The tradition in Abraham's day was a tithe of 10 percent presented to the temple priesthood, as he did with the spoils of war confiscated from the battle against the four kings of Mesopotamia (Ge 14).

ery five hundred, whether people, cattle, donkeys or sheep. 29 Take this tribute from their half share and give it to Eleazar the priest as the LORD's part. 30 From the Israelites' half, select one out of every fifty, whether people, cattle, donkeys, sheep or other animals. Give them to the Levites, who are responsible for the care of the LORD's tabernacle.[n]" 31 So Moses and Eleazar the priest did as the LORD commanded Moses.

32 The plunder remaining from the spoils that the soldiers took was 675,000 sheep, 33 72,000 cattle, 34 61,000 donkeys 35 and 32,000 women who had never slept with a man.

36 The half share of those who fought in the battle was:

> 337,500 sheep, 37 of which the tribute for the LORD[o] was 675;
> 38 36,000 cattle, of which the tribute for the LORD was 72;
> 39 30,500 donkeys, of which the tribute for the LORD was 61;
> 40 16,000 people, of whom the tribute for the LORD was 32.

41 Moses gave the tribute to Eleazar the priest as the LORD's part,[p] as the LORD commanded Moses.

42 The half belonging to the Israelites, which Moses set apart from that of the fighting men— 43 the community's half—was 337,500 sheep, 44 36,000 cattle, 45 30,500 donkeys 46 and 16,000 people. 47 From the Israelites' half, Moses selected one out of every fifty people and animals, as the LORD commanded him, and gave them to the Levites, who were responsible for the care of the LORD's tabernacle.

48 Then the officers who were over the units of the army—the commanders of thousands and commanders of hundreds—went to Moses 49 and said to him, "Your servants have counted the soldiers under our command, and not one is missing.[q] 50 So we have brought as an offering to the LORD the gold articles each of us acquired—armlets, bracelets, signet rings, earrings and necklaces—to make atonement for ourselves[r] before the LORD."

51 Moses and Eleazar the priest accepted from them the gold—all the crafted articles. 52 All the gold from the commanders of thousands and commanders of hundreds that Moses and Eleazar presented as a gift to the LORD weighed 16,750 shekels.[a] 53 Each soldier had taken plunder[s] for himself. 54 Moses and Eleazar the priest accepted the gold from the commanders of thousands and commanders of hundreds and brought it into the tent of meeting as a memorial[t] for the Israelites before the LORD.

The Transjordan Tribes

32 The Reubenites and Gadites, who had very large herds and flocks, saw that the lands of Jazer[u] and Gilead were suitable for livestock.[v] 2 So they came to Moses and Eleazar the priest and to the leaders of the community, and

31:30 [n] Nu 3:7; 18:3 **31:37** [o] ver 38-41 **31:41** [p] Nu 5:9; 18:8

31:49 [q] Jer 23:4 **31:50** [r] Ex 30:16 **31:53** [s] Dt 20:14 **31:54** [t] Ex 28:12 **32:1** [u] Nu 21:32 [v] Ex 12:38

[a] *52* That is, about 420 pounds or about 190 kilograms

31:32–35 These totals are much higher than those confiscated in the campaign of Thutmose III of Egypt (c. 1460 BC) during his campaign against Megiddo and other northern Canaanite cities. The Karnak temple account lists plunder of 1,929 cattle, 2,000 goats, 20,500 sheep and 2,503 slaves (men, women and children), along with a variety of physical objects such as gold bowls and ebony statues. In ancient cultures, numbers were sometimes more than mere quantities—numbers could have rhetorical value.

31:52 *16,750 shekels.* The amount of the gold offered by Israel's commanders on behalf of their troops exceeds the minimal requirement of one-half shekel per person, a ransom of some 6,000 shekels, or about 2,500 ounces (71,000 grams), which equals 158 pounds (71 kilograms) of gold. Instead, they present nearly three times the minimal amount, with a combined weight of the armlets, bracelets, signet rings, earrings and necklaces totaling 16,750 shekels, or about 7,000 ounces (200,000 grams), which equals 440 pounds (200 kilograms) of gold.

This much gold seems phenomenal considering the seminomadic nature of the Midianites, and it is important to keep in mind that numbers can be chosen for rhetorical value rather than as reports of actual quantities. Yet they traveled the caravan routes into Arabia and beyond, by which such wealth could have come, and adornment in gold is still prized today among Bedouins. Samples of such wealth occasionally find their way into burials. Note the excavation of Tel Beth Shean, in which material goods from a child burial from the Middle Bronze II (Hyksos) period (c. 1700 BC) include an ornate white alabaster vase, four gold earrings and a gold ring with an etched amethyst mounted on it with gold thread.

32:1 *lands of Jazer and Gilead.* Having journeyed through the more arid regions south of the Arnon (such as Edom and Moab), the Gadites and Reubenites observe how the more northern region of Gilead is more fertile with highland grassy regions for grazing, and with valleys and hillsides suitable for grain and fruit orchards. *Jazer.* An arable region northwest of Amman, generally associated with the area around Khirbet Jazzir, located about 10 miles (16 kilometers) west-northwest of Amman and 12 miles (20 kilometers) south of the Jabbok River. *Gilead.* Extended through the Transjordan highlands from the Bashan and Golan regions in the north to the Jabbok River in the south, rising to more than 4,000 feet (1,200 meters) in elevation. Rivers such as the Yarmuk, Jabesh, Jabbok and their tributaries, as well as the numerous springs in the region, provide ample water supply for humans and animals alike. Gilead is perhaps *gld* mentioned in the texts from Ugarit, and *ga-ala[a]-(za)* of Akkadian texts of Tiglath-Pileser III, a possible reference to Ramoth Gilead bordered on the north by the Arameans.

said, 3“Ataroth,[w] Dibon, Jazer,
Nimrah,[x] Heshbon, Elealeh,[y]
Sebam, Nebo and Beon[z] —
4the land the LORD subdued[a]
before the people of Israel —
are suitable for livestock,[b]
and your servants have livestock. 5If we have found favor in your eyes,” they said,
“let this land be given to your
servants as our possession.
Do not make us cross the Jordan.”

6Moses said to the Gad-
ites and Reubenites, “Should
your fellow Israelites go to
war while you sit here? 7Why
do you discourage the Is-
raelites from crossing over
into the land the LORD has
given them?[c] 8This is what
your fathers did when I sent
them from Kadesh Barnea
to look over the land.[d] 9Af-
ter they went up to the Valley of Eshkol[e] and viewed
the land, they discouraged
the Israelites from entering
the land the LORD had giv-
en them. 10The LORD’s anger
was aroused[f] that day and he
swore this oath: 11‘Because
they have not followed me
wholeheartedly, not one of
those who were twenty years
old or more[g] when they came
up out of Egypt will see the
land I promised on oath[h] to
Abraham, Isaac and Jacob[i] —
12not one except Caleb son of
Jephunneh the Kenizzite and Joshua son
of Nun, for they followed the LORD wholeheartedly.’[j] 13The LORD’s anger burned
against Israel[k] and he made them wander in the wilderness forty years, until the
whole generation of those who had done
evil in his sight was gone.[l]

14“And here you are, a brood of sinners,
standing in the place of your fathers and
making the LORD even more angry with Israel.[m] 15If you turn away from following
him, he will again leave all this people in
the wilderness, and you will be the cause
of their destruction.[n]”

16Then they came up to him and said,
“We would like to build pens here for our
livestock[o] and cities for our women and
children. 17But we will arm ourselves for
battle[a] and go ahead of the Israelites[p] until we have brought them to their place.[q]
Meanwhile our women and children will
live in fortified cities, for protection from
the inhabitants of the land. 18We will not
return to our homes until each of the Israelites has received their inheritance.[r] 19We

LANDS OF JAZER AND GILEAD

32:3 [w] ver 34 [x] ver 36 [y] ver 37; Isa 15:4; 16:9; Jer 48:34 [z] ver 38; Jos 13:17; Eze 25:9 **32:4** [a] Nu 21:34 [b] Ex 12:38 **32:7** [c] Nu 13:27-14:4 **32:8** [d] Nu 13:3, 26; Dt 1:19-25 **32:9** [e] Nu 13:23; Dt 1:24 **32:10** [f] Nu 11:1 **32:11** [g] Ex 30:14 [h] Nu 14:23 [i] Nu 14:28-30

[a] *17* Septuagint; Hebrew *will be quick to arm ourselves*

32:12 [j] Nu 14:24, 30; Dt 1:36; Ps 63:8 **32:13** [k] Ex 4:14 [l] Nu 14:28-35; 26:64, 65 **32:14** [m] ver 10; Dt 1:34; Ps 78:59 **32:15** [n] Dt 30:17-18; 2Ch 7:20 **32:16** [o] Ex 12:38; Dt 3:19 **32:17** [p] Jos 4:12, 13 [q] Nu 22:4; Dt 3:20 **32:18** [r] Jos 22:1-4

32:3 – 5 After the list of the cities conquered from the Amorites (v. 3) and an acclamation that Yahweh their God was responsible for granting them the victory (v. 4), the Gadites and Reubenites make a request of Moses and Israel’s other leaders (v. 5). A similar entreaty for a land grant in proper protocol format is found in diplomatic correspondence of the ancient Near East, including the basic letter writing language found in the Lachish, Arad and Samaritan ostraca.

32:16 *pens.* The Hebrew (*gidrot tson*) means “stone pens for sheep” or simply “sheepfolds.” They are perhaps the V-shaped stone enclosures found in Transjordan and the Arabah for protecting sheep, goats and cattle during times of danger.

will not receive any inheritance with them
on the other side of the Jordan, because
our inheritance has come to us on the east
side of the Jordan."[s]
20 Then Moses said to them, "If you will
do this — if you will arm yourselves before
the LORD for battle[t] 21 and if all of you who
are armed cross over the Jordan before
the LORD until he has driven his enemies
out before him — 22 then when the land
is subdued before the LORD, you may return[u] and be free from your obligation to
the LORD and to Israel. And this land will
be your possession before the LORD.[v]
23 "But if you fail to do this, you will be
sinning against the LORD; and you may
be sure that your sin will find you out.[w]
24 Build cities for your women and children, and pens for your flocks,[x] but do
what you have promised.[y]"
25 The Gadites and Reubenites said to
Moses, "We your servants will do as our
lord commands. 26 Our children and wives,
our flocks and herds will remain here in
the cities of Gilead.[z] 27 But your servants,
every man who is armed for battle, will
cross over to fight before the LORD, just as
our lord says."
28 Then Moses gave orders about them[a]
to Eleazar the priest and Joshua son of
Nun and to the family heads of the Israelite
tribes. 29 He said to them, "If the Gadites and
Reubenites, every man armed for battle,
cross over the Jordan with you before the
LORD, then when the land is subdued before
you, you must give them the land of Gilead as their possession. 30 But if they do not
cross over with you armed, they must accept their possession with you in Canaan."
31 The Gadites and Reubenites answered,
"Your servants will do what the LORD has
said.[b] 32 We will cross over before the LORD
into Canaan armed, but the property we
inherit will be on this side of the Jordan."
33 Then Moses gave to the Gadites,[c] the
Reubenites and the half-tribe of Manasseh
son of Joseph the kingdom of Sihon king
of the Amorites[d] and the kingdom of Og
king of Bashan — the whole land with its
cities and the territory around them.[e]
34 The Gadites built up Dibon, Ataroth,
Aroer,[f] 35 Atroth Shophan, Jazer,[g] Jogbehah, 36 Beth Nimrah[h] and Beth Haran as
fortified cities, and built pens for their
flocks. 37 And the Reubenites rebuilt Heshbon, Elealeh and Kiriathaim, 38 as well as
Nebo[i] and Baal Meon (these names were
changed) and Sibmah. They gave names
to the cities they rebuilt.
39 The descendants of Makir[j] son of Manasseh went to Gilead, captured it and
drove out the Amorites who were there.
40 So Moses gave Gilead to the Makirites,[k]
the descendants of Manasseh, and they
settled there. 41 Jair, a descendant of Manasseh, captured their settlements and
called them Havvoth Jair.[a][l] 42 And Nobah
captured Kenath and its surrounding settlements and called it Nobah after himself.[m]

Stages in Israel's Journey

33 Here are the stages in the journey of the Israelites when they
came out of Egypt[n] by divisions under the
leadership of Moses and Aaron.[o] 2 At the
LORD's command Moses recorded the stages in their journey. This is their journey
by stages:

3 The Israelites set out from Rameses on the fifteenth day of the first
month, the day after the Passover.[p]
They marched out defiantly[q] in full
view of all the Egyptians, 4 who were
burying all their firstborn, whom the
LORD had struck down among them;
for the LORD had brought judgment
on their gods.[r]

[a] 41 Or *them the settlements of Jair*

32:19 [s] Jos 12:1 **32:20** [t] Dt 3:18 **32:22** [u] Jos 22:4 [v] Dt 3:18-20 **32:23** [w] Ge 4:7; 44:16; Isa 59:12 **32:24** [x] ver 1, 16 [y] Nu 30:2 **32:26** [z] Jos 1:14 **32:28** [a] Dt 3:18-20; Jos 1:13 **32:31** [b] ver 29 **32:33** [c] Jos 13:24-28; 1Sa 13:7 [d] Dt 2:26 [e] Nu 21:24; Jos 12:6 **32:34** [f] Dt 2:36; Jdg 11:26 **32:35** [g] ver 3 **32:36** [h] ver 3 **32:38** [i] ver 3; Isa 15:2; Jer 48:1,22 **32:39** [j] Ge 50:23 **32:40** [k] Dt 3:15; Jos 17:1 **32:41** [l] Dt 3:14; Jos 13:30; Jdg 10:4; 1Ch 2:23 **32:42** [m] 2Sa 18:18; Ps 49:11 **33:1** [n] Mic 6:4 [o] Ps 77:20 **33:3** [p] Ex 13:4 [q] Ex 14:8 **33:4** [r] Ex 12:12

32:20 *If you will do this.* The compromise proposed by the Gadites and Reubenites is structured as a covenant with stipulations in the formula of blessing and curse: "If you do X, then you will have Y blessing; but if you do not do X, then Z curse will come to you." The covenant between the tribes of Gad and Reuben and the other ten tribes has Moses as the mediator and Yahweh as the witness and guarantor of the commitment made by the two tribes.
32:34 – 36 The Gadites are allocated land grants in the southern part of the former kingdom of Sihon of the Amorites, most of which are cited in v. 3. Gad shares its northern border with the half-tribe of Manasseh. The cities listed for Gad in the OT suggest a narrow strip of land in the Jordan River plain extending from the Jabbok River to the Sea of Galilee. Aroer (modern-day Arair) was located on the King's Highway, just north of the Arnon River. The Gadite cities are detailed in Jos 13:24 – 28.
32:37 – 38 The Reubenites receive the area and cities generally allocated south of those belonging to Gad. Among the cities is Heshbon, the former capital of Sihon's Amorite kingdom.
32:39 – 42 The allocation to the half-tribe of Manasseh is generally north of Gad, extending from the region of Gilead into Bashan and the Golan.
33:1 – 49 The list of the stages of Israel's departures and encampments from Rameses in Egypt to the plains of Moab stands in the tradition of itineraries of ancient Near Eastern kings in their travels and conquests. This compares with the Late Bronze Age itineraries of Thutmose III from Karnak, which were both military and economic expeditions that included topographic, geographic and toponymic information. Later in the ninth and eighth centuries BC, Assyrian kings such as Shalmaneser III and Tiglath-Pileser III listed cities and geographic features in their conquest annals.

[5]The Israelites left Rameses and camped at Sukkoth.[s]

[6]They left Sukkoth and camped at Etham, on the edge of the desert.[t]

[7]They left Etham, turned back to Pi Hahiroth, to the east of Baal Zephon,[u] and camped near Migdol.[v]

[8]They left Pi Hahiroth[a] and passed through the sea[w] into the desert, and when they had traveled for three days in the Desert of Etham, they camped at Marah.[x]

[9]They left Marah and went to Elim, where there were twelve springs and seventy palm trees, and they camped[y] there.

[10]They left Elim and camped by the Red Sea.[b]

[11]They left the Red Sea and camped in the Desert of Sin.[z]

[12]They left the Desert of Sin and camped at Dophkah.

[13]They left Dophkah and camped at Alush.

[14]They left Alush and camped at Rephidim, where there was no water for the people to drink.

[15]They left Rephidim[a] and camped in the Desert of Sinai.[b]

[16]They left the Desert of Sinai and camped at Kibroth Hattaavah.[c]

[17]They left Kibroth Hattaavah and camped at Hazeroth.[d]

[18]They left Hazeroth and camped at Rithmah.

[19]They left Rithmah and camped at Rimmon Perez.

[20]They left Rimmon Perez and camped at Libnah.[e]

[21]They left Libnah and camped at Rissah.

[22]They left Rissah and camped at Kehelathah.

[23]They left Kehelathah and camped at Mount Shepher.

[24]They left Mount Shepher and camped at Haradah.

[25]They left Haradah and camped at Makheloth.

[26]They left Makheloth and camped at Tahath.

[27]They left Tahath and camped at Terah.

[28]They left Terah and camped at Mithkah.

[29]They left Mithkah and camped at Hashmonah.

[30]They left Hashmonah and camped at Moseroth.[f]

[31]They left Moseroth and camped at Bene Jaakan.

[32]They left Bene Jaakan and camped at Hor Haggidgad.

[33]They left Hor Haggidgad and camped at Jotbathah.[g]

[34]They left Jotbathah and camped at Abronah.

[35]They left Abronah and camped at Ezion Geber.[h]

[36]They left Ezion Geber and camped at Kadesh, in the Desert of Zin.[i]

[37]They left Kadesh and camped at Mount Hor,[j] on the border of Edom.[k]
[38]At the LORD's command Aaron the priest went up Mount Hor, where he died[l] on the first day of the fifth month of the fortieth year after the Israelites came out of Egypt.[m]
[39]Aaron was a hundred and twenty-three years old when he died on Mount Hor.

[40]The Canaanite king of Arad,[n] who lived in the Negev of Canaan, heard that the Israelites were coming.

[41]They left Mount Hor and camped at Zalmonah.

[42]They left Zalmonah and camped at Punon.

[43]They left Punon and camped at Oboth.[o]

[44]They left Oboth and camped at Iye Abarim, on the border of Moab.[p]

[45]They left Iye Abarim and camped at Dibon Gad.

[46]They left Dibon Gad and camped at Almon Diblathaim.

[47]They left Almon Diblathaim and camped in the mountains of Abarim,[q] near Nebo.

[48]They left the mountains of Abarim and camped on the plains of Moab by the Jordan across from Jericho.[r]
[49]There on the plains of Moab they camped along the Jordan from Beth Jeshimoth to Abel Shittim.[s]

[50]On the plains of Moab by the Jordan across from Jericho the LORD said to Moses,
[51]"Speak to the Israelites and say to them: 'When you cross the Jordan into Canaan,[t]
[52]drive out all the inhabitants of the land before you. Destroy all their carved

33:5 [s] Ex 12:37
33:6 [t] Ex 13:20
33:7 [u] Ex 14:9 [v] Ex 14:2
33:8 [w] Ex 14:22 [x] Ex 15:23
33:9 [y] Ex 15:27
33:11 [z] Ex 16:1
33:15 [a] Ex 17:1 [b] Ex 19:1
33:16 [c] Nu 11:34
33:17 [d] Nu 11:35
33:20 [e] Jos 10:29
33:30 [f] Dt 10:6
33:33 [g] Dt 10:7
33:35 [h] Dt 2:8; 1Ki 9:26; 22:48
33:36 [i] Nu 20:1
33:37 [j] Nu 20:22 [k] Nu 20:16; 21:4
33:38 [l] Dt 10:6 [m] Nu 20:25-28
33:40 [n] Nu 21:1
33:43 [o] Nu 21:10
33:44 [p] Nu 21:11
33:47 [q] Nu 27:12
33:48 [r] Nu 22:1
33:49 [s] Nu 25:1
33:51 [t] Jos 3:17

[a] 8 Many manuscripts of the Masoretic Text, Samaritan Pentateuch and Vulgate; most manuscripts of the Masoretic Text *left from before Hahiroth* [b] 10 Or *the Sea of Reeds*; also in verse 11

33:52 *cast idols.* Molten cast images of deities are those in which clay or molten metal, such as copper or bronze, was poured into a pottery mold forming the shape of the deity. Numerous deity forms and their molds have been uncovered in excavations throughout Israel/Palestine. *high places.* Translates the Hebrew *bamot,* which may or may not refer to an elevated site or structure. With the variety of usage in the OT, a generic phrase such as "sacred site" or "cultic installation" may better render this kind of worship center. Such a site may include (1) an

images and their cast idols, and demolish
all their high places.[u] 53Take possession of
the land and settle in it, for I have given
you the land to possess.[v] 54Distribute the
land by lot, according to your clans.[w] To a
larger group give a larger inheritance, and
to a smaller group a smaller one. Whatever falls to them by lot will be theirs.
Distribute it according to your ancestral
tribes.
55" 'But if you do not drive out the inhabitants of the land, those you allow to
remain will become barbs in your eyes
and thorns[x] in your sides. They will give
you trouble in the land where you will
live. 56And then I will do to you what I
plan to do to them.' "

Boundaries of Canaan

34 The LORD said to Moses, 2"Command the Israelites and say to
them: 'When you enter Canaan, the land
that will be allotted to you as an inheritance[y] is to have these boundaries:[z]

3" 'Your southern side will include some
of the Desert of Zin[a] along the border of
Edom. Your southern boundary will start
in the east from the southern end of the
Dead Sea,[b] 4cross south of Scorpion Pass,[c]
continue on to Zin and go south of Kadesh
Barnea.[d] Then it will go to Hazar Addar
and over to Azmon, 5where it will turn,
join the Wadi of Egypt[e] and end at the
Mediterranean Sea.
6" 'Your western boundary will be the
coast of the Mediterranean Sea. This will
be your boundary on the west.
7" 'For your northern boundary,[f] run a
line from the Mediterranean Sea to Mount
Hor 8and from Mount Hor to Lebo Hamath.[g] Then the boundary will go to Zedad, 9continue to Ziphron and end at Hazar Enan. This will be your boundary on
the north.
10" 'For your eastern boundary, run a
line from Hazar Enan to Shepham. 11The
boundary will go down from Shepham to
Riblah[h] on the east side of Ain and continue along the slopes east of the Sea of Galilee.[a][i] 12Then the boundary will go down
along the Jordan and end at the Dead Sea.
" 'This will be your land, with its boundaries on every side.' "
13Moses commanded the Israelites: "Assign this land by lot as an inheritance.[j]
The LORD has ordered that it be given to
the nine and a half tribes, 14because the
families of the tribe of Reuben, the tribe of
Gad and the half-tribe of Manasseh have
received their inheritance.[k] 15These two
and a half tribes have received their inheritance east of the Jordan across from
Jericho, toward the sunrise."
16The LORD said to Moses, 17"These are
the names of the men who are to assign
the land for you as an inheritance: Eleazar the priest and Joshua[l] son of Nun.
18And appoint one leader from each tribe
to help[m] assign the land. 19These are their
names:

Caleb[n] son of Jephunneh,
from the tribe of Judah;[o]
20Shemuel son of Ammihud,
from the tribe of Simeon;[p]
21Elidad son of Kislon,
from the tribe of Benjamin;[q]
22Bukki son of Jogli,
the leader from the tribe of Dan;
23Hanniel son of Ephod,
the leader from the tribe of Manasseh son of Joseph;
24Kemuel son of Shiphtan,
the leader from the tribe of Ephraim son of Joseph;
25Elizaphan son of Parnak,
the leader from the tribe of Zebulun;
26Paltiel son of Azzan,
the leader from the tribe of Issachar;
27Ahihud son of Shelomi,
the leader from the tribe of Asher;[r]
28Pedahel son of Ammihud,
the leader from the tribe of Naphtali."

29These are the men the LORD commanded to assign the inheritance to the
Israelites in the land of Canaan.

Towns for the Levites

35 On the plains of Moab by the Jordan across from Jericho, the LORD
said to Moses, 2"Command the Israelites
to give the Levites towns to live in[s] from
the inheritance the Israelites will possess.
And give them pasturelands around the

[a] 11 Hebrew *Kinnereth*

33:52 [u] Ex 23:24; 34:13; Lev 26:1; Dt 7:2, 5; 12:3; Jos 11:12; Ps 106:34-36
33:53 [v] Dt 11:31; Jos 21:43
33:54 [w] Nu 26:54
33:55 [x] Jos 23:13; Jdg 2:3; Ps 106:36
34:2 [y] Ge 17:8; Dt 1:7-8; Ps 78:54-55 [z] Eze 47:15
34:3 [a] Jos 15:1-3 [b] Ge 14:3
34:4 [c] Jos 15:3 [d] Nu 32:8
34:5 [e] Ge 15:18; Jos 15:4
34:7 [f] Eze 47:15-17
34:8 [g] Nu 13:21; Jos 13:5
34:11 [h] 2Ki 23:33; Jer 39:5 [i] Dt 3:17; Jos 11:2; 13:27
34:13 [j] Jos 14:1-5
34:14 [k] Nu 32:33; Jos 14:3
34:17 [l] Jos 14:1
34:18 [m] Nu 1:4, 16
34:19 [n] Nu 26:65 [o] Ge 29:35; Dt 33:7
34:20 [p] Ge 49:5
34:21 [q] Ge 49:27; Ps 68:27
34:27 [r] Nu 1:40
35:2 [s] Lev 25:32-34; Jos 14:3, 4

---

altar on which animal, grain, vegetable, incense or other product is rendered to the deity; (2) cultic symbols and/or figurines; (3) standing stones (*matstsebot*); or (4) other cultic instruments.

34:2 *Canaan.* A definable geographic entity in Egyptian lists of names of cities and regions as early as the fifteenth century BC, since Egypt controlled much of Canaan (Retenu) during the Eighteenth and Nineteenth Dynasties (mid-second millennium BC). Though the detailed borders are not as explicitly demarcated in the Egyptian records of the Late Bronze and Early Iron Ages, the cities and towns listed in both sets of documents encompass substantially the same region.

35:2 – 15 Limited portions of land on the perimeter of 48 cities were prescribed for Levite use in pasturage and farming, including the six cities of refuge. Parallel to the

towns. 3Then they will have towns to live in and pasturelands for the cattle they own and all their other animals.

4"The pasturelands around the towns that you give the Levites will extend a thousand cubits[a] from the town wall. 5Outside the town, measure two thousand cubits[b] on the east side, two thousand on the south side, two thousand on the west and two thousand on the north, with the town in the center. They will have this area as pastureland for the towns.

Cities of Refuge

35:6-34Ref — Dt 4:41-43; 19:1-14; Jos 20:1-9

6"Six of the towns you give the Levites will be cities of refuge, to which a person who has killed someone may flee.[t] In addition, give them forty-two other towns. 7In all you must give the Levites forty-eight towns, together with their pasturelands. 8The towns you give the Levites from the land the Israelites possess are to be given in proportion to the inheritance of each tribe: Take many towns from a tribe that has many, but few from one that has few."[u]

9Then the LORD said to Moses: 10"Speak to the Israelites and say to them: 'When you cross the Jordan into Canaan,[v] 11select some towns to be your cities of refuge, to which a person who has killed someone[w] accidentally[x] may flee. 12They will be places of refuge from the avenger,[y] so that anyone accused of murder may not die before they stand trial before the assembly. 13These six towns you give will be your cities of refuge. 14Give three on this side of the Jordan and three in Canaan as cities of refuge. 15These six towns will be a place of refuge for Israelites and for foreigners residing among them, so that anyone who has killed another accidentally can flee there.

16" 'If anyone strikes someone a fatal blow with an iron object, that person is a murderer; the murderer is to be put to death.[z] 17Or if anyone is holding a stone and strikes someone a fatal blow with it, that person is a murderer; the murderer is to be put to death. 18Or if anyone is holding a wooden object and strikes someone a fatal blow with it, that person is a murderer; the murderer is to be put to death. 19The avenger of blood shall put the murderer to death; when the avenger comes upon the murderer, the avenger shall put the murderer to death.[a] 20If anyone with malice aforethought shoves another or throws something at them intentionally[b] so that they die 21or if out of enmity one person hits another with their fist so that the other dies, that person is to be put to death; that person is a murderer. The avenger of blood shall put the murderer to death when they meet.

22" 'But if without enmity someone suddenly pushes another or throws something

35:6 [t] Jos 20:7-9; 21:3,13 **35:8** [u] Nu 26:54; 33:54; Jos 21:1-42 **35:10** [v] Jos 20:2 **35:11** [w] ver 22-25 [x] Ex 21:13; Dt 19:1-13 **35:12** [y] Dt 19:6; Jos 20:3 **35:16** [z] Ex 21:12; Lev 24:17 **35:19** [a] ver 21 **35:20** [b] Ge 4:8; Ex 21:14; Dt 19:11; 2Sa 3:27; 20:10

[a] *4* That is, about 1,500 feet or about 450 meters
[b] *5* That is, about 3,000 feet or about 900 meters

encampment of the priests and Levites around the tabernacle during the wilderness journey (ch. 2), the Levites provided a constant visible presence among the 12 tribes to remind them of the need for holiness and righteousness as God's people. This distribution parallels the Eighteenth Dynasty of Egyptian administration of Canaan in which royal land grants were made, administered by the priesthood. These fortified cities collected tribute from the region, providing wealth to the priesthood in Egypt.

Instead of being granted a designated portion of the land, the Levites' inheritance is Yahweh himself (18:20). The Levitical pasturelands around the grant cities are to extend outward 1,000 cubits (about 1,500 feet or 450 meters) from the wall of the city, and the territory is described as 2,000 cubits (about 3,000 feet or 900 meters) on each of the sides. Levite presence facilitates the rendering of the tithes by the Israelites (18:21 – 24,30 – 32) to the Lord. The Levite land grants are primarily for pasturing animals, not for crop production (Jos 21:11 – 12). On the specific areas where the Kohathites, Gershonites and Merarites lived, see Jos 21.

35:11 *cities of refuge.* Six cities were set aside to provide refuge for a person who caused the accidental death of someone else (cf. Dt 4:41 – 43). The accused was to flee to the appointed city immediately after committing the act to be afforded the opportunity for refuge from a potential avenger of blood. For the names and placement of these six cities, three on each side of the Jordan River and all somewhat equidistant from each other, see Jos 20:7 – 8.

35:12 *the avenger.* The avenger (Hebrew *goel*; cf. "avenger of blood "in vv. 19 – 27) is the same term used of the "guardian-redeemer" in Ru 2:20; 4:3,6; he is someone who "redeems" property or persons from another. In Lev 25:33 *gaal* denotes the redemption of property of the Levites that has been sold, and in Lev 25:47 – 54 it relates to the redemption by a relative of persons sold into slavery. The "avenger of blood" (vv. 19 – 27) was a relative who redeemed the lost life of a relative by exacting the life of the murderer. The responsibility to carry out this judgment fell to the nearest surviving relative (father, then eldest brother and on down the line). The city of refuge provided a safe haven for the accused until the community had opportunity to discover the nature of the crime and determine whether murder or manslaughter had been committed.

35:16 – 29 Case laws governing murder and manslaughter are stated in a formula of option, with the first set of laws governing murder and the avenging adjudication by the avenger of blood (vv. 16 – 21), and with the second set of laws governing manslaughter and the responsibilities of the community in such cases (vv. 22 – 29).

35:22 – 28 According to Jos 20:4, one seeking asylum was to appear at the entrance to the city gate, where the city's elders and judges heard and settled a variety of judicial cases. If the case was determined to be accidental, the Levitical city would offer asylum and sanctuary. The sending of a person convicted of manslaughter "back to the city of refuge" (v. 25) suggests that the trial took place just

NUMBERS 34:2 – 12

CANAAN'S BORDERS

The natural western boundary is the Mediterranean Sea (v. 6). A stormy body of water in the fall, winter and early parts of spring — and often unpredictable even in the summer — all ancient peoples respected it. In Ugaritic mythology the sea was believed to be the abode of an often malevolent deity Yamm and his associate, the great sea serpent Litan (perhaps Leviathan of the OT). The western border extends along the shoreline from the Wadi/Brook of Egypt in the south (v. 5) to a point west of Mount Hor (v. 7) and Lebo Hamath (v. 8). These coastal plain regions were occupied by the Philistines (south of the Yarkon River) and various Sea Peoples and Phoenicians during the Iron I and Iron II periods; they were under Israelite control only briefly during the reigns of David and Solomon. All these borders reflect the ideal territorial limits for the land of Israel, but they were not fully realized until the time of David and Solomon (2Sa 8:1 – 18; 10:1 – 19; 2Ch 18:1 — 20:3). ◆

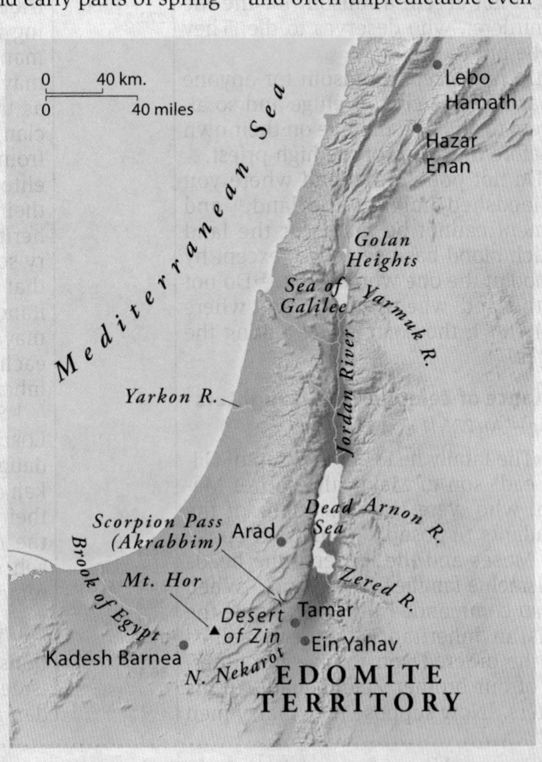

Territorial boundaries of the land.

at them unintentionally[c] 23or, without seeing them, drops on them a stone heavy
enough to kill them, and they die, then
since that other person was not an enemy
and no harm was intended, 24the assembly[d] must judge between the accused and
the avenger of blood according to these
regulations. 25The assembly must protect the one accused of murder from the
avenger of blood and send the accused
back to the city of refuge to which they
fled. The accused must stay there until the
death of the high priest, who was anointed
with the holy oil.[e]

26"'But if the accused ever goes outside
the limits of the city of refuge to which
they fled 27and the avenger of blood finds
them outside the city, the avenger of blood
may kill the accused without being guilty
of murder. 28The accused must stay in the

35:22 [c] ver 11; Ex 21:13 **35:24** [d] ver 12; Jos 20:6 **35:25** [e] Ex 29:7

outside the city walls, whereby also a person convicted of murder could be rendered readily to the avenger of blood for execution. One convicted of manslaughter had to remain in the city of refuge until the death of the high priest (vv. 25,28), which marked the end of an era in Israelite cultic history, similar to the ancient practice of a king or governor granting amnesty or pardon to convicted felons. In effect the death of the accused individual or the high priest ransomed the death of the victim.

city of refuge until the death of the high
priest; only after the death of the high
priest may they return to their own property.
29“ ‘This is to have the force of law[f] for
you throughout the generations to come,
wherever you live.
30“ ‘Anyone who kills a person is to be
put to death as a murderer only on the
testimony of witnesses. But no one is to
be put to death on the testimony of only
one witness.[g]
31“ ‘Do not accept a ransom for the life
of a murderer, who deserves to die. They
are to be put to death.
32“ ‘Do not accept a ransom for anyone
who has fled to a city of refuge and so allow them to go back and live on their own
land before the death of the high priest.
33“ ‘Do not pollute the land where you
are. Bloodshed pollutes the land,[h] and
atonement cannot be made for the land
on which blood has been shed, except by
the blood of the one who shed it. 34Do not
defile the land[i] where you live and where
I dwell,[j] for I, the LORD, dwell among the
Israelites.’ ”

Inheritance of Zelophehad’s Daughters

36:1-12pp — Nu 27:1-11

36 The family heads of the clan of Gilead[k] son of Makir, the son of Manasseh, who were from the clans of the
descendants of Joseph, came and spoke
before Moses and the leaders,[l] the heads
of the Israelite families. 2They said, “When
the LORD commanded my lord to give the
land as an inheritance to the Israelites
by lot, he ordered you to give the inheritance of our brother Zelophehad[m] to his
daughters. 3Now suppose they marry men
from other Israelite tribes; then their inheritance will be taken from our ancestral
inheritance and added to that of the tribe
they marry into. And so part of the inheritance allotted to us will be taken away.
4When the Year of Jubilee[n] for the Israelites comes, their inheritance will be added
to that of the tribe into which they marry,
and their property will be taken from the
tribal inheritance of our ancestors.”
5Then at the LORD’s command Moses
gave this order to the Israelites: “What the
tribe of the descendants of Joseph is saying is right. 6This is what the LORD commands for Zelophehad’s daughters: They
may marry anyone they please as long
as they marry within their father’s tribal
clan. 7No inheritance[o] in Israel is to pass
from one tribe to another, for every Israelite shall keep the tribal inheritance of
their ancestors. 8Every daughter who inherits land in any Israelite tribe must marry someone in her father’s tribal clan,[p] so
that every Israelite will possess the inheritance of their ancestors. 9No inheritance
may pass from one tribe to another, for
each Israelite tribe is to keep the land it
inherits.”
10So Zelophehad’s daughters did as the
LORD commanded Moses. 11Zelophehad’s
daughters — Mahlah, Tirzah, Hoglah, Milkah and Noah[q] — married their cousins on
their father’s side. 12They married within
the clans of the descendants of Manasseh son of Joseph, and their inheritance
remained in their father’s tribe and clan.
13These are the commands and regulations the LORD gave through Moses[r] to the
Israelites on the plains of Moab by the Jordan across from Jericho.[s]

35:29 [f]Nu 27:11
35:30 [g]ver 16; Dt 17:6; 19:15; Mt 18:16; Jn 7:51; 2Co 13:1; Heb 10:28
35:33 [h]Ge 9:6; Ps 106:38; Mic 4:11
35:34 [i]Lev 18:24, 25 [j]Ex 29:45
36:1 [k]Nu 26:29 [l]Nu 27:2
36:2 [m]Nu 26:33; 27:1, 7
36:4 [n]Lev 25:10
36:7 [o]1Ki 21:3
36:8 [p]1Ch 23:22
36:11 [q]Nu 26:33; 27:1
36:13 [r]Lev 26:46; 27:34 [s]Nu 22:1

35:30 No one could be executed on the basis of a single witness to a crime; a minimum of two witnesses was necessary for conviction of a capital crime. This is consistent with cases delineated in Deuteronomy as well as ancient Near Eastern law collections, such as the Code of Hammurapi. Bribery, ransom or other forms of compensation for the death of a human being were strictly prohibited, whether the death was murder or manslaughter.

36:1 – 12 The particular concern of the larger Gileadite clan is the possible loss of land to another Israelite tribe should the daughters of Zelophehad marry outside the tribe of Manasseh. Under the Lord’s direction, Zelophehad’s daughters were granted territorial inheritance rights, thereby setting a legal precedent that the land should remain within the family or tribe. The Gileadite leaders brought to the judicial proceedings the other legal precedent of the Lord’s direction for the distribution of tribal territory by lot, and territorial sovereignty of each tribe was to be maintained.

With these two precedents on the judicial table, the Gileadites presented their case in two parts before Moses and the Israelite leadership for a legal decision. First was the question of one of the daughters of Zelophehad marrying outside the tribe of Manasseh, in which case the property would accrue to the husband’s tribe, thereby violating tribal territorial sovereignty. Tribal sovereignty was maintained by requiring Zelophehad’s daughters to marry within the tribal clan. This decision settled a potential conflict within property laws related to the Year of Jubilee, during which property reverted to its original tribal or clan owner and indentured slaves were emancipated (Lev 25:13 – 55). Since the Jubilee statutes applied only to purchased property and not to inherited property, this case set a precedent for future potential litigation.

THE TORAH

DEUTERONOMY

Historical Setting

Three powerful speeches by Moses 40 years after the Lord had delivered Israel from Egypt are preserved in the book of Deuteronomy. The people had spent 40 years in the wilderness of the Sinai peninsula, including a year at Mount Sinai, where God made a covenant with his people. Moses' exposition of the Sinai covenant occurred in the plains of Moab, which is just north-northeast of the northern tip of the Dead Sea and on the eastern side of the Jordan River. Moses viewed the future extent of Israel's promised inheritance from Mount Nebo.

At this time Egypt was weakening but still ruled the ancient Near East. The pharaohs stopped major expeditions into the land of Canaan, which now allowed Israel a providential opportunity to gain a foothold in the land. The larger historical-cultural context for Israel's experiences with Egypt was the New Kingdom period (c. 1550 – 1069 BC, Dynasties Eighteen through Twenty). For more specific discussion of the date of the exodus, see the article "Historicity of the Exodus," p. 116. It certainly took place before the reign of Pharaoh Merneptah (1213 – 1203 BC), who erected a stele in western Thebes that records many of his victories. In a small section, Merneptah mentions Israel as a people already in Canaan in 1209 BC. While Merneptah claims to have wiped out the seed of Israel, ironically his stele is the earliest extra-Biblical witness to Israel's presence in the land of Canaan.

KEY CONCEPTS

- One God, one people, one sanctuary and one law.
- God's law impacts every area of life, and all law is rooted in the Ten Commandments.
- Obedience is only the beginning of what is expected of God's people — he wants his people to be in relationship with him.
- God's people are to love him.

Literary Setting

Deuteronomy shares many affinities with literature from the ancient Near East. The most evident is its relationship to the various law collections that have been recovered. These collections have come from as early as 2000 BC and before, e.g., the Sumerian Laws of Ur-Nammu (2064 – 2046 BC), the Laws of Lipit-Ishtar (1875 – 1864 BC), the Old Babylonian Laws of Eshnunna (c. 1850 BC), and the Code of Hammurapi (1792 – 1750 BC). The OT contains both similarities and differences with these collections in subcategories of types of laws, e.g., case law, apodictic law, laws involving curses, motive clauses, etc. Whether showing similarities or differences, comparison can give us a good idea of how society was ordered in the ancient world.

Deuteronomy also displays a form and structure that reflects a close affinity with suzerain-vassal treaties in the ancient world. Such parallels offer evidence that God's communication with Israel did not take place in a vacuum. He used familiar literary forms to communicate what ends up being a remarkably unique relationship with his people. The curses and blessings of Deuteronomy reflect similarities to ancient Near Eastern traditions of such literature reaching back as far as the third millennium BC. The book of Deuteronomy celebrates covenant renewal. If Israel were to claim and retain the land promised to them, they would have to maintain this covenant. But more important, they will need to keep the law and be faithful to the covenant so that God's presence will continue to be evident among them. ◆

The Command to Leave Horeb

1 These are the words Moses spoke to
all Israel in the wilderness east of the
Jordan—that is, in the Arabah—opposite
Suph, between Paran and Tophel, Laban,
Hazeroth and Dizahab. 2 (It takes eleven
days to go from Horeb[a] to Kadesh Barnea[b]
by the Mount Seir road.)
3 In the fortieth year,[c] on the first day of
the eleventh month, Moses proclaimed[d] to
the Israelites all that the LORD had commanded him concerning them. 4 This was
after he had defeated Sihon[e] king of the
Amorites, who reigned in Heshbon,[f] and
at Edrei had defeated Og[g] king of Bashan,
who reigned in Ashtaroth.
5 East of the Jordan in the territory of
Moab, Moses began to expound this law,
saying:
6 The LORD our God said to us[h] at Horeb,[i] "You have stayed long enough at this
mountain. 7 Break camp and advance into
the hill country of the Amorites; go to all
the neighboring peoples in the Arabah, in
the mountains, in the western foothills, in
the Negev[j] and along the coast, to the land
of the Canaanites and to Lebanon,[k] as far
as the great river, the Euphrates. 8 See, I
have given you this land. Go in and take
possession of the land the LORD swore[l] he
would give to your fathers—to Abraham,
Isaac and Jacob—and to their descendants after them."

The Appointment of Leaders

9 At that time I said to you, "You are too
heavy a burden for me to carry alone.[m]
10 The LORD your God has increased your
numbers so that today you are as numerous[n] as the stars in the sky.[o] 11 May the LORD,
the God of your ancestors, increase you a
thousand times and bless you as he has
promised![p] 12 But how can I bear your problems and your burdens and your disputes
all by myself? 13 Choose some wise, understanding and respected men[q] from each of
your tribes, and I will set them over you."
14 You answered me, "What you propose
to do is good."

1:2 [a] Ex 3:1 [b] Nu 13:26; Dt 9:23
1:3 [c] Nu 33:38 [d] Dt 4:1-2
1:4 [e] Nu 21:21-26 [f] Nu 21:25 [g] Nu 21:33-35; Jos 13:12
1:6 [h] Nu 10:13 [i] Ex 3:1
1:7 [j] Jos 10:40 [k] Dt 11:24
1:8 [l] Ge 12:7; 15:18; 17:7-8; 26:4; 28:13
1:9 [m] Ex 18:18
1:10 [n] Ge 15:5 [o] Dt 10:22; 28:62
1:11 [p] Ge 22:17; Ex 32:13
1:13 [q] Ex 18:21

1:1 *wilderness east of the Jordan.* This area is in the Arabah, along the Jordan rift valley, bounded by the Dead Sea to the north and the Gulf of Aqaba to the south. The author's list of geographic locations here seems to reflect an itinerary (see Nu 33 for a schematized itinerary), including locations where the words of Moses were delivered before, during, and after Sinai—words that are now to be expounded on the plains of Moab.

1:2 *Kadesh.* The name means "holy place." It lay on the southern boundary of Canaan and later served as a southern boundary marker of Judah. It was about 50 miles (80 kilometers) southwest of Beersheba in the Desert of Zin, and about 170 miles or 275 kilometers (an 11-day journey) from Jebel Musa, the traditional site of Horeb. At least two significant trade routes ran through this area.

The Israelites did not encamp en masse at this spot for 40 years. They had been barred from the land of Canaan and sentenced to wander in this desert area. The archaeological evidence indicates that they would need to move about in this area in order to obtain sufficient sustenance to live. They probably returned often to Kadesh, using it as a base camp. The Israelites left no definitive evidence of their wanderings in the vicinity, but this is not surprising given their use of mobile tents instead of more permanent architecture.

1:3 *In the fortieth year.* Ancient chronology had no fixed points for dating purposes. Events were related to various key events (e.g., see Am 1:1 and the dating formula "before the earthquake"). The exodus marked the birth of the people of Israel as a nation and the proclamation of the Torah; these words in Deuteronomy took place in the 40th year after Israel came out of Egypt, whether in the fifteenth century or thirteenth century BC (see the article "The Timing of the Exodus," p. 118). *eleventh month.* Tebet in Israel's calendar, which overlaps with our modern December-January.

1:4 *Sihon ... Og.* See Nu 21:21–35.

1:7 *the hill country of the Amorites.* This description of Palestine recalls the description of the land given in Ge 15:18–21. Palestine divided into four longitudinal regions running north-south: (1) a coastal plain that stretched from beyond the northern city of Tyre south along the Mediterranean Sea to the Wadi of Egypt (Wadi el-Arish); (2) a central mountain range that ran north from the Negev beyond Upper Galilee into Lebanon and was crossed only by the Jezreel Valley near Megiddo; (3) a Jordan rift valley (Arabah) that ran from the southern end of the Sea of Galilee south to the Gulf of Aqaba; and (4) a Transjordanian mountain range that rose parallel to and east of the Jordan rift valley (see v. 25). At the time the Israelites entered Palestine, the Amorites occupied much of the Transjordanian mountain area just north of the Arnon River. Historically they had lived on both sides of the Jordan in the hill country (Nu 13:29). Thus, either the entire land of Canaan may be in mind here or only the Transjordanian hill country. *the Arabah.* Referred to the eastern edge of the Dead Sea and the Jordan rift valley that ran up to the Sea of Galilee. *the mountains.* Evidently referred to the central hill country running along the western side of the Jordan rift valley and up to the southern end of the Sea of Galilee and into Upper Galilee. *the western foothills.* The "Shephelah" were the low-lying areas of the central mountain range that extended down to the Mediterranean coastal plain. *the Negev.* Served as the southern border of Judah; it was essentially desert and extended east from Beersheba to the southern end of the Dead Sea and west to Gaza near the coast. Its southern extensions merged with the highlands of the Sinai peninsula and reached to the Gulf of Aqaba. Its eastern border was the Arabah, which ran from the Dead Sea to the Gulf of Aqaba. *the land of the Canaanites.* Stretched at various times from the Wadi of Egypt (Wadi el-Arish) to Lebo Hamath north of Damascus. Strong textual evidence indicates that there was both a geographic area called Canaan and a people there who were called "Canaanites," earlier possessors of the geographic area (see the article "The Canaanites," p. 294). *Lebanon.* Ran parallel to the Phoenician coast; it indicates a northeast boundary of the land. The northwestern branch of the Euphrates River served as the northeastern border of the area. Similar clichés for boundary markers were common in the ancient Near East, e. g., "from the Euphrates to the great sea where the sun sets."

DEUTERONOMY 1:7

THE CANAANITES

Genesis 12:6 has at times been interpreted as suggesting that at the time of the author or editor of Genesis, Canaanites were no longer living in the land. The Hebrew particle used here, however, is not usually used to indicate a situation that existed at one point but not any longer. The background question here, nevertheless, is through which periods were Canaanites in the land?

It must first be noted that there is some question whether "Canaanite" is more properly understood as an ethnic designation or as a geographic designation. Recent studies have leaned toward the latter, understanding the term as referring to the multi-ethnic people living in the region at this time who shared a common culture. While not without support, this interpretation is problematic in regard to the Biblical text. When the Pentateuch and Joshua refer to the inhabitants of the land, many groups are mentioned alongside the Canaanites (see, e.g., Ge 15:21; Ex 3:8; Dt 7:1; Jos 9:1); thus "Canaanites" does not appear as a word for just anyone living within the geographic boundaries of Canaan.

Nevertheless, assuming an ethnic identification, we have no information about where they may have come from or when they entered the land. Early in the Iron Age (beginning about 1200 BC), the Canaanites disappear from both the written and archaeological records. They are displaced by the Philistines as the great enemy of Israel and are not among the enemies fought by Saul or David, and there is only a brief mention in the reign of Solomon (1Ki 9:16). As a result, the time when "the Canaanites were in the land" is roughly equivalent to the second millennium BC.

The city of Ugarit is located just north of the Canaanite boundaries, and the beliefs of those in Ugarit probably reflect much of the life and times of the Canaanites. Based on hundreds of cuneiform documents found at ancient Ugarit near the Syrian coast, we catch at least some glimpses about these people.

The Canaanite worldview(s) included a cult of the dead, the worship of many gods, especially El (the high god) and Baal. Female goddesses abounded (e.g., Anat, Asherah). Many high places, sacred prostitutes, and possibly Molek cults (potentially involving human sacrifice) are evidenced. The Canaanites or West Semitic peoples developed the alphabet much earlier than previously thought and greatly influenced not only Israel's history but several other areas as well. ◆

15So I took[r] the leading men of your
tribes, wise and respected men, and appointed them to have authority over
you—as commanders of thousands, of
hundreds, of fifties and of tens and as tribal officials. 16And I charged your judges
at that time, "Hear the disputes between
your people and judge fairly,[s] whether the
case is between two Israelites or between
an Israelite and a foreigner residing among
you.[t] 17Do not show partiality[u] in judging;
hear both small and great alike. Do not be
afraid of anyone,[v] for judgment belongs to
God. Bring me any case too hard for you,
and I will hear it."[w] 18And at that time I
told you everything you were to do.

1:15 [r]Ex 18:25 **1:16** [s]Dt 16:18; Jn 7:24 [t]Lev 24:22 **1:17** [u]Lev 19:15; Dt 16:19; Pr 24:23; Jas 2:1 [v]2Ch 19:6 [w]Ex 18:26 **1:19** [x]Dt 8:15; Jer 2:2,6 [y]ver 2; Nu 13:26

Spies Sent Out

19Then, as the LORD our God commanded us, we set out from Horeb and went
toward the hill country of the Amorites
through all that vast and dreadful wilderness[x] that you have seen, and so we
reached Kadesh Barnea.[y] 20Then I said to
you, "You have reached the hill country
of the Amorites, which the LORD our God
is giving us. 21See, the LORD your God has
given you the land. Go up and take pos-

1:16 *judges.* See note on Ex 18:22.

session of it as the LORD, the God of your
ancestors, told you. Do not be afraid;[z] do
not be discouraged."

22Then all of you came to me and said,
"Let us send men ahead to spy out the
land for us and bring back a report about
the route we are to take and the towns we
will come to."

23The idea seemed good to me; so I selected[a] twelve of you, one man from each
tribe. 24They left and went up into the hill
country, and came to the Valley of Eshkol[b] and explored it. 25Taking with them
some of the fruit of the land, they brought
it down to us and reported,[c] "It is a good
land that the LORD our God is giving us."

Rebellion Against the LORD

26But you were unwilling to go up;[d] you
rebelled against the command of the LORD
your God. 27You grumbled[e] in your tents
and said, "The LORD hates us; so he brought
us out of Egypt to deliver us into the hands
of the Amorites to destroy us. 28Where can
we go? Our brothers have made our hearts
melt in fear. They say, 'The people are
stronger and taller[f] than we are; the cities
are large, with walls up to the sky. We even
saw the Anakites[g] there.'"

29Then I said to you, "Do not be terrified; do not be afraid of them. 30The LORD
your God, who is going before you, will
fight[h] for you, as he did for you in Egypt,
before your very eyes, 31and in the wilderness. There you saw how the LORD
your God carried[i] you, as a father carries
his son, all the way you went until you
reached this place."

32In spite of this, you did not trust[j] in
the LORD your God, 33who went ahead of
you on your journey, in fire by night and
in a cloud by day,[k] to search[l] out places
for you to camp and to show you the way
you should go.

34When the LORD heard what you said,
he was angry and solemnly swore:[m] 35"No
one from this evil generation shall see the
good land[n] I swore to give your ancestors,
36except Caleb son of Jephunneh. He will
see it, and I will give him and his descendants the land he set his feet on, because
he followed the LORD wholeheartedly.[o]"

37Because of you the LORD became angry[p] with me also and said, "You shall not
enter[q] it, either. 38But your assistant, Joshua[r] son of Nun, will enter it. Encourage[s]
him, because he will lead[t] Israel to inherit
it. 39And the little ones that you said would
be taken captive,[u] your children who do
not yet know[v] good from bad—they will
enter the land. I will give it to them and
they will take possession of it. 40But as for
you, turn around and set out toward the
desert along the route to the Red Sea.[a][w]"

41Then you replied, "We have sinned
against the LORD. We will go up and fight,
as the LORD our God commanded us."
So every one of you put on his weapons,
thinking it easy to go up into the hill country.

42But the LORD said to me, "Tell them,
'Do not go up and fight, because I will not
be with you. You will be defeated by your
enemies.'"[x]

43So I told you, but you would not listen.
You rebelled against the LORD's command

1:21 [z] Jos 1:6, 9, 18 **1:23** [a] Nu 13:1-3 **1:24** [b] Nu 13:21-25 **1:25** [c] Nu 13:27 **1:26** [d] Nu 14:1-4 **1:27** [e] Dt 9:28; Ps 106:25 **1:28** [f] Nu 13:32 [g] Nu 13:33; Dt 9:1-3 **1:30** [h] Ex 14:14; Dt 3:22; Ne 4:20 **1:31** [i] Dt 32:10-12; Isa 46:3-4; 63:9; Hos 11:3; Ac 13:18 **1:32** [j] Ps 106:24; Jude 1:5 **1:33** [k] Ex 13:21; Ps 78:14 [l] Nu 10:33 **1:34** [m] Nu 14:23, 28-30 **1:35** [n] Ps 95:11 **1:36** [o] Nu 14:24; Jos 14:9 **1:37** [p] Dt 3:26; 4:21 [q] Nu 20:12 **1:38** [r] Nu 14:30 [s] Dt 31:7 [t] Dt 3:28 **1:39** [u] Nu 14:3 [v] Isa 7:15-16 **1:40** [w] Nu 14:25 **1:42** [x] Nu 14:41-43

[a] 40 Or *the Sea of Reeds*

1:25 *It is a good land that the LORD ... is giving us.* The land in general was well-endowed with agricultural potential, but it was not rich in natural resources, although the Dead Sea provided some salt and bitumen, and small amounts of iron have been found. Some turquoise is present in the Negev. Large desert areas were neither fruitful nor fertile. Certain regions were suited to produce wine, grain and olive oil in abundance (see 7:13; Ge 27:28); some regions, such as Gilead, were capable of sustaining cattle, flocks and herds in great numbers. The Mediterranean coastal area, the Sea of Galilee and the Jordan River provided an abundance of fish. Other features of the land offered many challenges to its inhabitants. Drought, disease or locusts could destroy the produce of an entire year or more. The land featured a diversity of topography and climatic conditions that were, and are, hardly equaled anywhere else on earth. Agricultural activity varied with the seasons of the year, the geography of the land and the yearly rainfall. The central mountain regions favored pastoral pursuits; the lower, broader valleys and plains provided productive farming areas. Agrarian activity produced wheat and barley (April, June), fruits of various kinds (summer) and grapes and olives (late summer, early fall). From these raw materials bread, wine and oil were produced. Heavy summer dew made the cultivation of cucumbers, melons and grapes possible. Legumes such as lentils, fava beans and chickpeas were produced along with onions, leeks and garlic. The pastoralists raised cattle, sheep and goats, from which wool, hair, milk and meat came. Farmers terraced the narrow slopes of the mountainous regions and could cultivate trees (olive, date palms, pomegranates, fig and sycamore) and vines.

1:28 *Anakites.* See note on Nu 13:22.

1:33 *fire ... cloud.* See note on Ex 13:21.

1:40 *the Red Sea.* See the article "The Red Sea," p. 132.

1:41 *We have sinned.* Israel's collective confession of guilt here and in v. 45 (cf. Ex 33:6; Lev 16) is also found in the extra-Biblical world—especially in Mesopotamia, where laments reveal that people attributed the destruction of their cities to divine displeasure. Confession of sin and laments by individuals, including kings, are well represented, and there are analogues in lamentations, psalms and individual laments found in the OT.

The Hittite king Mursili II performs a confessional in which he presents not only his own sins but the sins of his people, of his father, and of his own court officials. At Ugarit, sacrifices were presented to regain one's virtue or to atone for offensive behavior or words. Communal laments over Sumer and specific city-states such as Ur, Eridu, Nippur and Uruk were recorded, as were personal laments.

and in your arrogance you marched up into the hill country. 44The Amorites who lived in those hills came out against you; they chased you like a swarm of bees[y] and beat you down from Seir all the way to Hormah. 45You came back and wept before the LORD, but he paid no attention to your weeping and turned a deaf ear to you. 46And so you stayed in Kadesh[z] many days — all the time you spent there.

Wanderings in the Wilderness

2 Then we turned back and set out toward the wilderness along the route to the Red Sea,[a][a] as the LORD had directed me. For a long time we made our way around the hill country of Seir.

2Then the LORD said to me, 3"You have made your way around this hill country long enough; now turn north. 4Give the people these orders:[b] 'You are about to pass through the territory of your relatives the descendants of Esau, who live in Seir. They will be afraid of you, but be very careful. 5Do not provoke them to war, for I will not give you any of their land, not even enough to put your foot on. I have given Esau the hill country of Seir as his own.[c] 6You are to pay them in silver for the food you eat and the water you drink.' "

7The LORD your God has blessed you in all the work of your hands. He has watched[d] over your journey through this vast wilderness. These forty years the LORD your God has been with you, and you have not lacked anything.

8So we went on past our relatives the descendants of Esau, who live in Seir. We turned from the Arabah road, which comes up from Elath and Ezion Geber,[e] and traveled along the desert road of Moab.[f]

9Then the LORD said to me, "Do not harass the Moabites or provoke them to war, for I will not give you any part of their land. I have given Ar[g] to the descendants of Lot[h] as a possession."

10(The Emites[i] used to live there — a people strong and numerous, and as tall as the Anakites.[j] 11Like the Anakites, they too were considered Rephaites, but the Moab-

1:44 [y] Ps 118:12 **1:46** [z] Nu 20:1; Jdg 11:17 **2:1** [a] Nu 21:4 **2:4** [b] Nu 20:14-21 **2:5** [c] Ge 36:8; Jos 24:4 **2:7** [d] Dt 8:2-4 **2:8** [e] 1Ki 9:26 [f] Jdg 11:18 **2:9** [g] Nu 21:15 [h] Ge 19:36-38 **2:10** [i] Ge 14:5 [j] Nu 13:22, 33

[a] 1 Or *the Sea of Reeds*

2:1 *the wilderness along the route to the Red Sea ... around the hill country of Seir.* Israel's retreat took them back through the Desert of Paran west of the Arabah leading down to the modern Gulf of Aqaba (here designated as the "Red Sea"). They traveled from the northwest area of the mountains in Seir southeast to the Gulf of Aqaba, and later ranged throughout the western and southern borders of Seir (Edom) for 38 years (cf. v. 7).
2:3 *now turn north.* Israel now traveled from Kadesh Barnea east across the Arabah into Seir by the Wadi Murra and Varb es-Sultan, where the Edomites lived. At Punon or Wadi Ghurveir they caught a road coming from the Gulf of Aqaba. They then turned northeast to complete their trek around central Edom and headed north on the eastern fringes of Edom and Moab.
2:6 *pay them in silver for the food you eat.* The Israelites had little that they could use for barter, but they were not supposed to just take food, so silver payment is mandated. *silver.* The preferred medium of payment also in the time of the divided monarchy. But the use of silver (usually), gold or electrum (alloy of gold and silver) goes back to the eighteenth century BC. The Late Bronze Age to Iron Age II (1400–600 BC) reveals silver as a medium of exchange. Often scrap pieces were weighed out in a balance pan and balanced by a stone weight(s) in another pan attached to a balance beam. Long before coins (silver ingots were used as coinage in some Neo-Hittite city-states in the eighth century BC), pieces of silver (or gold or copper) properly weighed served as payment for various commodities. These mediums of exchange existed alongside the standard means of exchange, such as bartering, in Canaan, Assyria, Babylonia and Egypt (cf. Ex 21:32; Jos 7:21). Weights were carefully monitored to prevent cheating (see note on Lev 19:35).
2:8 *descendants of Esau.* See note on Ge 36:9.
2:9 *Moabites.* See note on Ge 19:37–38. The kingdom of Moab, which featured a tribal organization rather than "statehood" per se, had a significant population and presence during the Late Bronze Age (1550–1200 BC), including scarce traces east of the Dead Sea. Moab is mentioned in Egyptian texts from the time of Rameses II (c. 1270 BC), and a Moabite king may be represented in a stele from the Late Bronze Age (the Balu'a Stele from Wadi el-Mujib). Dibon, one of Moab's capital cities, existed in 1270 BC. References from Ebla (twenty-fifth century BC) and from southern Moab (tenth to ninth century BC) mention the chief Moabite god Chemosh. The deity name also appears in the ritual texts at Ugarit (fourteenth century BC) and is present in Eblaite theophoric names, such as the city-name Carchemish (Kar-Kamish). Mesha, a Moabite king, is identified on the Mesha Stele/Moabite Stone (c. 830 BC) found at Dibon (cf. 2Ki 3). Babylon crippled Moab in 582–581 BC, but it seems to have limped into Hellenistic times. By the time of Rome, Ammon, Moab and Edom had dissolved. *Ar.* May refer to a city, an area or to all of Moab. Here and in v. 29 the word refers to a region or to the entire land of Moab.
2:10 *Emites.* Unknown outside the OT, they were physically huge in stature, much like the Rephaites (Rephaim) and Anakites (Anakim). *Anakites.* See note on Nu 13:22. They, like the Emites, were considered Rephaites (see next note). The Ammonites dispossessed the Rephaites, whom they named the Zamzummites (see note on v. 20). Hence, the basic stock of giants in these areas were called Emites by the Moabites (v. 11), but Zamzummites by the Ammonites (v. 20), and were all huge like the Anakites.
2:11 *Rephaites.* A race of giants, indigenous to Bashan, they were a powerful people at one time, but at the time Israel was entering Canaan there was only a remnant left. Og, a king of Bashan, was one of the last (Jos 12:4). The Rephaites also inhabited Moabite territory. While they originated as an ethnic group, they became a people and a nation that exercised power from Mount Hermon as far as Moab.

The term "Rephaim" also refers to spirits of the dead, especially spirits of kings and heroes of old, perhaps chariot warriors. Ugaritic literature indicates that certain rites were held for the Rephaim of the land (earth), and

ites called them Emites. 12 Horites used to
live in Seir, but the descendants of Esau
drove them out. They destroyed the Horites from before them and settled in their
place, just as Israel did[k] in the land the
LORD gave them as their possession.)
13 And the LORD said, "Now get up and
cross the Zered Valley." So we crossed the
valley.
14 Thirty-eight years passed from the
time we left Kadesh Barnea[l] until we
crossed the Zered Valley. By then, that
entire generation[m] of fighting men had
perished from the camp, as the LORD had
sworn to them.[n] 15 The LORD's hand was
against them until he had completely eliminated[o] them from the camp.
16 Now when the last of these fighting
men among the people had died, 17 the
LORD said to me, 18 "Today you are to pass
by the region of Moab at Ar. 19 When you
come to the Ammonites,[p] do not harass
them or provoke them to war, for I will not
give you possession of any land belonging
to the Ammonites. I have given it as a possession to the descendants of Lot.[q]"

2:12 [k] ver 22 **2:14** [l] Nu 13:26 [m] Nu 14:29-35 [n] Dt 1:34-35 **2:15** [o] Ps 106:26 **2:19** [p] Ge 19:38 [q] ver 9

20 (That too was considered a land of the
Rephaites, who used to live there; but the
Ammonites called them Zamzummites.
21 They were a people strong and numerous, and as tall as the Anakites.[r] The LORD
destroyed them from before the Ammonites, who drove them out and settled in
their place. 22 The LORD had done the same
for the descendants of Esau, who lived in
Seir,[s] when he destroyed the Horites from
before them. They drove them out and
have lived in their place to this day. 23 And
as for the Avvites[t] who lived in villages as
far as Gaza, the Caphtorites[u] coming out
from Caphtor[a][v] destroyed them and settled
in their place.)

Defeat of Sihon King of Heshbon

24 "Set out now and cross the Arnon
Gorge.[w] See, I have given into your hand
Sihon the Amorite, king of Heshbon, and
his country. Begin to take possession of it
and engage him in battle. 25 This very day
I will begin to put the terror[x] and fear[y] of

2:21 [r] ver 10 **2:22** [s] Ge 36:8 **2:23** [t] Jos 13:3 [u] Ge 10:14 [v] Am 9:7 **2:24** [w] Nu 21:13-14; Jdg 11:13, 18 **2:25** [x] Dt 11:25 [y] Jos 2:9, 11

[a] *23* That is, Crete

the term applies to heroes who were considered divine. The term "Rephaim" used for spirits of the elite dead is also found in Phoenician and Punic-Latin texts/inscriptions. The sarcophagus inscriptions of Tabnit use the term to describe the "shades/spirits" of the common person. The OT refers to the spirits of "the dead" as *repaim* (Ps 88:11 – 12; Isa 14:9; 26:14,19; see also Pr 2:18; 9:18; 21:16).

2:12 *Horites.* Inhabited the territory of Seir. Some scholars have closely tied them to the Hurrians, a non-Semitic people, located in various places, such as Mitanni, Syria, Anatolia and Canaan. The Hurrians around Canaan spread there from territory east of the Tigris River in Mesopotamia. The identification of the Horites with the Hurrians is still held by some, but other scholars recently strongly disavow it, asserting that the resemblance of names is only incidental. The name "Horites" may be derived from Hebrew *hor* ("cave") and, hence, may refer to mountainous cave dwellers in the regions of Seir. Both the geology and geography of the region would support this theory. See note on 7:1 ("Hivites").

2:15 *The LORD's hand.* See note on Ex 6:1.

2:19 *Ammonites.* Related to the Israelites through Lot (see Ge 19:38), so the Lord gave them territory in Transjordan, from the Arnon River to the Jabbok River, covering a north-south distance of about 39 miles (65 kilometers). Archaeological material from the Early Bronze (3100 – 2650 BC), Middle Bronze (1800 – 1650 BC), and Late Bronze (1500 – 1200 BC) Ages testify to the Ammonites as a people. The national god Molek is mentioned in texts at Ebla (twenty-fifth century BC) and also at Ugarit, where he is equated to the god Rapiu. Ugaritic texts and Egyptian texts mention the city of Ashtarot, an earlier cultic location for the worship of Molek/Rapiu. The capital city was Rabbah (modern Amman). There is sufficient evidence at Transjordanian sites to suggest that the Iron Age Ammonites were continuous from the Late Bronze Age people.

From the reign of Tiglath-Pileser III, the Neo-Assyrian annals refer to the Land of Benammanu and the House of Ammon. Ammonite kings are known from Assyrian records kept by kings, including Shalmaneser III (853 BC, Qarqar), Sennacherib (704 – 681 BC) and Esarhaddon (680 – 669 BC). The Ammonites, as a mini-power, ceased to exist in c. 582/581 BC, when the Babylonians defeated them. However, they continued to play minor but troublesome roles in Israel's history into the second century BC.

2:20 *Zamzummites.* The same as "Zuzites" in Ge 14:5. Rephaites (shades, ghosts), Emim (frightful ones) and Zuzites all indicate dread or discomfort surrounding their appearance (see note on v. 11). The Septuagint, the pre-Christian Greek translation of the OT, renders "Zamzummites" as "mighty ones," an even closer fit to the other two words.

2:23 *Avvites.* Lived south of the key Philistine city of Gaza, both before and after the conquest of Canaan (see Jos 13:3). It is possible that they were a part of the displaced Sea Peoples who landed in or migrated to this area. Some scholars tie the Avvites to the Hyksos settlements that were followed later by the Aegean Sea Peoples. *villages.* The dwellings (Hebrew *hatserim*) of the Avvites are understood to have been small unwalled villages or even seminomadic tent encampments. *Caphtorites.* May have been a part of the Philistines at an early stage (see Jer 47:4; Am 9:7). They came from Crete rather than Cyprus, as some have argued. Caphtor (Hebrew *kaptor*) is equivalent to ancient Kaptara (Crete), and was significant before the Philistines were in the region. Mari texts from the second millennium BC mention a king of Hagor who sent gifts to Kaptara. Egyptian texts mention *kefl(i)u*, a variant of Kaptara.

2:24 *Arnon Gorge.* A perennial stream that opens into the east side of the Dead Sea almost opposite En Gedi. It is about 30 miles (48 kilometers) long, with breathtaking canyon views. It once served as a heavily fortified border area of Ammon and of Moab (see 3:12,16; Jdg 11:18 – 19). It also functioned as the southern border of the tribe of Reuben. *Sihon ... king of Heshbon.* He was also king of the Amorites (see Nu 21:21 – 31). Nu 21:27 celebrates the takeover of Heshbon from Sihon and Israel's subsequent rebuilding of it.

2:25 *terror and fear of you.* In Egyptian literature, the terror of Amun, god of Egypt, overwhelmed the enemy. Hittite,

you on all the nations under heaven. They
will hear reports of you and will tremble[z]
and be in anguish because of you."
26 From the Desert of Kedemoth I sent
messengers to Sihon king of Heshbon offering peace and saying, 27 "Let us pass
through your country. We will stay on the
main road; we will not turn aside to the
right or to the left.[a] 28 Sell us food to eat
and water to drink for their price in silver.
Only let us pass through on foot[b]— 29 as
the descendants of Esau, who live in Seir,
and the Moabites, who live in Ar, did for
us — until we cross the Jordan into the
land the LORD our God is giving us." 30 But
Sihon king of Heshbon refused to let us
pass through. For the LORD[c] your God had
made his spirit stubborn[d] and his heart
obstinate in order to give him into your
hands, as he has now done.
31 The LORD said to me, "See, I have begun to deliver Sihon and his country over
to you. Now begin to conquer and possess
his land."[e]
32 When Sihon and all his army came
out to meet us in battle[f] at Jahaz, 33 the
LORD our God delivered him over to us
and we struck him down,[g] together with
his sons and his whole army. 34 At that
time we took all his towns and completely destroyed[a][h] them — men, women and
children. We left no survivors. 35 But the
livestock and the plunder from the towns
we had captured we carried off for ourselves. 36 From Aroer[i] on the rim of the
Arnon Gorge, and from the town in the
gorge, even as far as Gilead, not one town
was too strong for us. The LORD our God
gave[j] us all of them. 37 But in accordance
with the command of the LORD our God,[k]
you did not encroach on any of the land
of the Ammonites,[l] neither the land along
the course of the Jabbok[m] nor that around
the towns in the hills.

Defeat of Og King of Bashan

3 Next we turned and went up along the
road toward Bashan, and Og king of
Bashan with his whole army marched out
to meet us in battle at Edrei.[n] 2 The LORD
said to me, "Do not be afraid[o] of him, for I
have delivered him into your hands, along
with his whole army and his land. Do to
him what you did to Sihon king of the Amorites, who reigned in Heshbon."
3 So the LORD our God also gave into our
hands Og king of Bashan and all his army.
We struck them down, leaving no survivors.[p] 4 At that time we took all his cities.
There was not one of the sixty cities that
we did not take from them — the whole
region of Argob, Og's kingdom in Bashan.[q]
5 All these cities were fortified with high
walls and with gates and bars, and there
were also a great many unwalled villages. 6 We completely destroyed[a] them, as
we had done with Sihon king of Heshbon,
destroying[a][r] every city — men, women and
children. 7 But all the livestock and the
plunder from their cities we carried off for
ourselves.
8 So at that time we took from these two
kings of the Amorites the territory east of
the Jordan, from the Arnon Gorge as far
as Mount Hermon. 9 (Hermon is called Sirion[s] by the Sidonians; the Amorites call
it Senir.)[t] 10 We took all the towns on the
plateau, and all Gilead, and all Bashan as
far as Salekah[u] and Edrei, towns of Og's

2:25 [z]Ex 15:14-16 **2:27** [a]Nu 21:21-22 **2:28** [b]Nu 20:19 **2:30** [c]Jos 11:20 [d]Ex 4:21; Nu 21:23; Ro 9:18 **2:31** [e]Dt 1:8 **2:32** [f]Nu 21:23 **2:33** [g]Dt 29:7 **2:34** [h]Dt 3:6; 7:2 **2:36** [i]Dt 3:12; 4:48; Jos 13:9 [j]Ps 44:3 **2:37** [k]ver 18-19 [l]Nu 21:24 [m]Ge 32:22; Dt 3:16 **3:1** [n]Nu 21:33 **3:2** [o]Nu 21:34 **3:3** [p]Nu 21:35 **3:4** [q]1Ki 4:13 **3:6** [r]Dt 2:24,34 **3:9** [s]Dt 4:48; Ps 29:6 [t]1Ch 5:23 **3:10** [u]Jos 13:11

[a] *34,6* The Hebrew term refers to the irrevocable giving over of things or persons to the LORD, often by totally destroying them.

Assyrian and Babylonian texts feature divine warriors and armies who struck fear into the enemy. The king led the army in the Old Babylonian era, but he was amply supported by the gods, whose will was discerned through diviners. In the Middle Babylonian eras and throughout the Assyrian epochs, the divine hosts helped to overwhelm the enemy. These gods accompanied and supported their troops. A similar situation functioned in Hittite military activity.

2:34 *completely destroyed them.* This agrees with the mandate to devote things to destruction (Hebrew *herem*) in the OT, especially during times of war. To violate this mandate was a serious offense, punishable by death. *Herem* was practiced elsewhere in the ancient Near East; e.g., King Mesha of Moab seized the city of Nebo from Israel and devoted all in it to destruction in the name of his god, Ashtar-Chemosh. Hittite texts give evidence of conquered towns being totally obliterated, but also testify to the practice of designating them as sacred to a god, not by having a temple built, but by being treated as taboo.

3:1 *Bashan.* See note on Nu 21:33.

3:4 *Argob.* Refers to a confederation of cities within the larger Bashan area or to a region to the east of the Jordan.

3:5 *All these cities were fortified.* Fortified cities were a feature of the culture of Mesopotamia, Aram/Syria, Canaan and Egypt across the millennia in the ancient Near East. The multiplication of cities in ancient Mesopotamia created competition between them, and they became heavily fortified for protection and security purposes as early as 2800 BC, as siege warfare became ever more a part of life. Palaces housed the political and military machinery of the cities, and arsenals were located near city walls.

In the Levant, military fortifications developed rapidly (e.g., at Megiddo, Jericho, Taanach, Arad and Ai), and walls, buttresses, bastions, glacis, gates and towers proliferated. The same was true for Egypt, although archaeological remains are fewer. In the early and middle second millennium BC, powerful fortified cities appeared in Syria and Canaan. Moats were often a part of Middle Bronze Age fortifications (c. 1800 – 1550 BC). They appear in pictures and are mentioned in texts of the Late Bronze Age and Iron Age II. Ramparts were constructed on one or both sides of massive walls, perhaps to hinder an attacking enemy. City gates were constructed to serve as a vital part of these fortified cities.

kingdom in Bashan. 11 (Og king of Bashan was the last of the Rephaites.[v] His bed was decorated with iron and was more than nine cubits long and four cubits wide.[a] It is still in Rabbah[w] of the Ammonites.)

Division of the Land

12 Of the land that we took over at that time, I gave the Reubenites and the Gadites the territory north of Aroer[x] by the Arnon Gorge, including half the hill country of Gilead, together with its towns. 13 The rest of Gilead and also all of Bashan, the kingdom of Og, I gave to the half-tribe of Manasseh. (The whole region of Argob in Bashan used to be known as a land of the Rephaites. 14 Jair,[y] a descendant of Manasseh, took the whole region of Argob as far as the border of the Geshurites and the Maakathites; it was named after him, so that to this day Bashan is called Havvoth Jair.[b]) 15 And I gave Gilead to Makir.[z] 16 But to the Reubenites and the Gadites I gave the territory extending from Gilead down to the Arnon Gorge (the middle of the gorge being the border) and out to the Jabbok River,[a] which is the border of the Ammonites. 17 Its western border was the Jordan in the Arabah, from Kinnereth[b] to the Sea of the Arabah (that is, the Dead Sea[c]), below the slopes of Pisgah.

18 I commanded you at that time: "The LORD your God has given you this land to take possession of it. But all your able-bodied men, armed for battle, must cross over ahead of the other Israelites.[d] 19 However, your wives, your children and your livestock (I know you have much livestock) may stay in the towns I have given you, 20 until the LORD gives rest to your fellow Israelites as he has to you, and they too have taken over the land that the LORD your God is giving them across the Jordan. After that, each of you may go back to the possession I have given you."

Moses Forbidden to Cross the Jordan

21 At that time I commanded Joshua: "You have seen with your own eyes all that the LORD your God has done to these two kings. The LORD will do the same to all the kingdoms over there where you are going. 22 Do not be afraid[e] of them; the LORD your God himself will fight[f] for you."

23 At that time I pleaded with the LORD: 24 "Sovereign LORD, you have begun to show to your servant your greatness[g] and your strong hand. For what god[h] is there in heaven or on earth who can do the deeds and mighty works[i] you do?[j] 25 Let me go over and see the good land[k] beyond the Jordan—that fine hill country and Lebanon."

26 But because of you the LORD was angry[l] with me and would not listen to me. "That is enough," the LORD said. "Do not speak to me anymore about this matter. 27 Go up to the top of Pisgah and look west and north and south and east. Look at the land with your own eyes, since you are not going to cross this Jordan.[m] 28 But commission[n] Joshua, and encourage and strengthen him, for he will lead this people across[o] and will cause them to inherit the land that you will see." 29 So we stayed in the valley near Beth Peor.[p]

Obedience Commanded

4 Now, Israel, hear the decrees and laws I am about to teach you. Follow them so that you may live[q] and may go in and take possession of the land the LORD, the God of

3:11 [v] Ge 14:5 [w] 2Sa 12:26; Jer 49:2
3:12 [x] Nu 32:32-38; Dt 2:36; Jos 13:8-13
3:14 [y] Nu 32:41; 1Ch 2:22
3:15 [z] Nu 32:39-40
3:16 [a] Nu 21:24
3:17 [b] Nu 34:11; Jos 13:27 [c] Ge 14:3; Jos 12:3
3:18 [d] Nu 32:17
3:22 [e] Dt 1:29 [f] Ex 14:14; Dt 20:4
3:24 [g] Dt 11:2 [h] Ex 15:11; Ps 86:8 [i] Ps 71:16, 19 [j] 2Sa 7:22
3:25 [k] Dt 4:22
3:26 [l] Dt 1:37; 31:2
3:27 [m] Nu 27:12
3:28 [n] Nu 27:18-23 [o] Dt 31:3, 23
3:29 [p] Dt 4:46; 34:6
4:1 [q] Dt 5:33; 8:1; 16:20; 30:15-20; Eze 20:11; Ro 10:5

[a] *11* That is, about 14 feet long and 6 feet wide or about 4 meters long and 1.8 meters wide [b] *14* Or *called the settlements of Jair*

3:11 *bed.* Huge objects such as this bedstead (sometimes translated "sarcophagus") and the giant sword of Goliath were kept as memorials that recalled these ancient giants (1Sa 21:9), along with the victory the Lord gave Israel over them. The bed was not necessarily made of solid iron (iron was a precious metal in the Bronze Age), but might simply have been decorated or overlaid with it. The bed is the same size as Marduk's bed in the temple Esagila at Babylon, and may have been used for reclining rather than sleeping. A Neo-Assyrian relief of Ashurbanipal pictures the king reclining on a magnificent couch.
3:14 *Geshurites.* Inhabited a tiny kingdom of Arameans north-northeast of the Sea of Kinnereth (i.e., Sea of Galilee). Gilead was at their southern border, Bashan was on their eastern boundary, and Mount Hermon was to the north of them (Jos 13:11). Their relationship to Israel was ambivalent. Some of their cities were taken by Manasseh, but later recovered (1Ch 2:22–33). David took a Geshurite wife, Maakah, from whom Absalom was born (2Sa 3:3). *Maakathites.* A small Aramean kingdom south of Mount Hermon whose land went to the half-tribe of Manasseh (Jos 12:5; 13:11). They lived north of the Geshurites, northeast of the Sea of Kinnereth (i.e., the Sea of Galilee), west of the Jordan rift valley. The Maakathites had a checkered relationship with King David, but eventually became his vassals (2Sa 10:6; 1Ch 19:7).
3:17 *Kinnereth.* Refers to the Sea of Galilee. The name indicates the shape of a lyre, a musical instrument, which the lake resembles. *the Sea of the Arabah.* Refers to the Dead (Salt) Sea.
4:1 *the decrees and laws I am about to teach you.* The basic stipulations in the Sinai covenant, as it forms the framework for Deuteronomy, are found in ch. 4 and fit into the ancient Near Eastern pattern of treaties between 1400–1200 BC (see the article "Decrees and Laws," p. 301). Ch. 4 introduces basic stipulations and accompanying exhortations. While the form of the covenant between Israel and their God has many ancient Near Eastern analogues, the enactment of a covenant between a god and that god's people featuring divinely imparted laws in even subsequent promulgations and revisions has not, so far, been evidenced in detail (see the article "Ancient Law Codes and Leviticus," p. 183). The extent and depth to which covenant, history and law are combined is not matched in the ancient Near Eastern

your ancestors, is giving you. 2Do not add[r]
to what I command you and do not subtract from it, but keep the commands of the
LORD your God that I give you.
3You saw with your own eyes what the
LORD did at Baal Peor.[s] The LORD your God
destroyed from among you everyone who
followed the Baal of Peor, 4but all of you
who held fast to the LORD your God are
still alive today.
5See, I have taught you decrees and laws
as the LORD my God commanded me, so
that you may follow them in the land you
are entering to take possession of it. 6Ob-
serve them carefully, for this will show your
wisdom[t] and understanding to the nations,
who will hear about all these decrees and
say, "Surely this great nation is a wise and
understanding people."[u] 7What other nation is so great[v] as to have their gods near[w]
them the way the LORD our God is near us
whenever we pray to him? 8And what other
nation is so great as to have such righteous
decrees and laws as this body of laws I am
setting before you today?
9Only be careful,[x] and watch yourselves
closely so that you do not forget the things
your eyes have seen or let them fade from
your heart as long as you live. Teach[y]
them to your children[z] and to their children after them. 10Remember the day you
stood before the LORD your God at Horeb,[a]
when he said to me, "Assemble the people before me to hear my words so that
they may learn to revere me as long as
they live in the land and may teach them
to their children." 11You came near and
stood at the foot of the mountain while
it blazed with fire[b] to the very heavens,
with black clouds and deep darkness.
12Then the LORD spoke[c] to you out of the
fire. You heard the sound of words but saw
no form; there was only a voice. 13He declared to you his covenant,[d] the Ten Commandments,[e] which he commanded you
to follow and then wrote them on two
stone tablets. 14And the LORD directed me
at that time to teach you the decrees and
laws you are to follow in the land that you
are crossing the Jordan to possess.

Idolatry Forbidden

15You saw no form[f] of any kind the day
the LORD spoke to you at Horeb out of the
fire. Therefore watch yourselves very carefully,[g] 16so that you do not become corrupt and make for yourselves an idol,[h] an
image of any shape, whether formed like
a man or a woman, 17or like any animal
on earth or any bird that flies in the air,
18or like any creature that moves along the
ground or any fish in the waters below.
19And when you look up to the sky and
see the sun,[i] the moon and the stars — all
the heavenly array[j] — do not be enticed
into bowing down to them and worshiping
things the LORD your God has apportioned
to all the nations under heaven. 20But as
for you, the LORD took you and brought
you out of the iron-smelting furnace,[k] out

4:2 [r] Dt 12:32; Jos 1:7; Rev 22:18-19
4:3 [s] Nu 25:1-9; Ps 106:28
4:6 [t] Dt 30:19-20; Ps 19:7; Pr 1:7 [u] Job 28:28
4:7 [v] 2Sa 7:23 [w] Ps 46:1; Isa 55:6
4:9 [x] Pr 4:23 [y] Ge 18:19; Eph 6:4 [z] Ps 78:5-6
4:10 [a] Ex 19:9, 16
4:11 [b] Ex 19:18; Heb 12:18-19
4:12 [c] Ex 20:22; Dt 5:4,22
4:13 [d] Dt 9:9, 11 [e] Ex 24:12; 31:18; 34:28
4:15 [f] Isa 40:18 [g] Jos 23:11
4:16 [h] Ex 20:4-5; 32:7; Dt 5:8; Ro 1:23
4:19 [i] Dt 17:3; Job 31:26 [j] 2Ki 17:16; 21:3; Ro 1:25
4:20 [k] 1Ki 8:51; Jer 11:4

materials. *the God of your ancestors.* This is a key OT concept within Israel's worldview (cf. 1:11,21; Ex 3:13–16; see the article "Patriarchal Religion," p. 34). Similar terminology is also found in the Mari documents, and kings of the cities of Aleppo and Qatna use the phrase. The phrase implied that the god would be passed on from father to sons, sons to grandsons, and so on. Interestingly, the god named on a family seal served to identify the family rather than an individual person. The father's seal passed on in the family bore the name of the father's god. Family gods tended to stay in the family (e.g., Adad). This practice is traceable back to 2500 BC. This does not mean, however, that the power or jurisdiction of a family god was exclusive to the particular family. On the contrary, these gods were thought to be effective beyond the boundaries of the family, as was Israel's God.

4:2 *Do not add … do not subtract.* This "canonical formula" (cf. 13:1–3) is common in ancient Near Eastern treaty literature. It is found especially in Egyptian scribal guidelines and in Assyrian literature from the reign of Esarhaddon as a warning against changing any part of a covenant/treaty. Hammurapi included this charge in his epilogue and called down curses on anyone who would change his laws, and the same language occurs in the prologue/epilogue of the Lipit-Ishtar law code.

4:3 *Baal Peor.* Both a geographic location and a major deity of the Moabites, Midianites and Ammonites. The name "Baal" as used here refers to a local manifestation of the Canaanite god Baal, a fertility/weather god (see note on Nu 25:3).

4:5 *I have taught you decrees and laws … so that you may follow them.* The creation and collection of law(s) in the ancient Near East was, as here, considered proof of wisdom in those collections and clearly stated as such. Hammurapi asserted that his laws would be an object of splendor to the wise man, and he threatened those who did not heed them with curses and with dispersion. The various laws of the different nations reflected their character and culture in some basic national worldviews (e.g., polytheism versus monotheism). Underlying axioms to some extent were imbedded and emphasized in the laws (see the article "Ancient Laws, Scripture and Modern Issues," p. 147).

4:10 *Horeb.* Refers to Sinai once in Deuteronomy (1:6), but elsewhere it refers to a desert region called Horeb. See the article "Mount Sinai," p. 144, for discussion as to the location of Horeb/Sinai.

4:13 *two stone tablets.* Judging from legal practices in the ancient world, Moses was probably given two copies, not one document spread over two tablets. Although probably larger than clay tablets would have been, a stone tablet could hold 15–20 lines and still fit in the palm of the hand.

4:15 *no form.* See notes on 5:8; Ex 20:4.

4:20 *iron-smelting furnace.* Modern cast iron is made in a blast furnace, which was unknown in the ancient world. Iron heated beyond 1100°C (2012°F) becomes soft and spongy, able to be forged. Carbon from the charcoal fuel assists the chemical process. While the furnace can be used as a symbol of oppression, here it is a creative force. As the smelting furnace transforms malleable ore into a hardened, usable product, so the exodus transformed Israel into God's covenant people.

of Egypt, to be the people of his inheritance,[l] as you now are.
21 The LORD was angry with me[m] because of you, and he solemnly swore that
I would not cross the Jordan and enter
the good land the LORD your God is giving
you as your inheritance. 22 I will die in this
land; I will not cross the Jordan; but you
are about to cross over and take possession of that good land.[n] 23 Be careful not
to forget the covenant[o] of the LORD your
God that he made with you; do not make
for yourselves an idol[p] in the form of anything the LORD your God has forbidden.

4:20 [l] Ex 19:5; Dt 9:29
4:21 [m] Nu 20:12; Dt 1:37
4:22 [n] Dt 3:25
4:23 [o] ver 9, 16 [p] Ex 20:4

DEUTERONOMY 4:1

DECREES AND LAWS

Deuteronomy shares many affinities with literature from the ancient Near East. The most evident is its relationship to the various collections of legal sayings that have been recovered. These collections have come from as early as 2000 BC and before — e.g., Sumerian Laws of Ur-Nammu (2064 – 2046 BC), the Laws of Lipit-Ishtar (1875 – 1864 BC), Old Babylonian Laws from Eshnunna (c. 1850 BC), and the Code of Hammurapi king of Babylon (1792 – 1750 BC). The OT contains both similarities with and differences from these collections in subcategories of types of laws, such as case law, apodictic law, laws involving curses, motive clauses, etc.

Deuteronomy also displays a form/structure similar to ancient Near Eastern suzerain-vassal treaties. Israel's laws shared both in the literary tradition of the laws, treaties and covenants in the ancient Near East, and, to a lesser but still notable extent, in its content and legal presentations.

There are many other types of parallels in Deuteronomy that set it squarely within its ancient Near Eastern cultural context. Oaths were a common feature of ancient Near Eastern covenantal documents (cf. Dt 29:19). The poetry of Dt 32 – 33 reflects poetic features, style and theological themes found in the literature of Ugarit (Ras Shamra) near the Mediterranean coast. Curses and blessings similar to those found in Deuteronomy show up in other ancient Near Eastern literature reaching back to the third millennium BC. The centrality of love for the suzerain and among the Great Kings of the Near East, expressed in religious ritual and covenantal and literary documents, reflects the supreme commandment of love for the Lord and for one's fellow human being in Deuteronomy.

Deuteronomy celebrates covenant renewal, specifically the renewal of the covenant at Sinai (see Exodus and Leviticus). If Israel is to claim and retain the land promised to them, they must maintain this covenant. The covenant is renewed again in Jos 24. In each case, the call to worship and to commitment is paramount; in each case the form and content of the covenantal renewals reflect ancient Near Eastern suzerain-vassal treaty/covenant patterns with necessary changes made to fit special circumstances. ◆

The Hammurapi Stele, c. 1760 BC.

24For the LORD your God is a consuming fire,[q] a jealous God.

25After you have had children and grandchildren and have lived in the land a long time—if you then become corrupt and make any kind of idol, doing evil[r] in the eyes of the LORD your God and arousing his anger, 26I call the heavens and the earth as witnesses against you[s] this day that you will quickly perish from the land that you are crossing the Jordan to possess. You will not live there long but will certainly be destroyed. 27The LORD will scatter[t] you among the peoples, and only a few of you will survive among the nations to which the LORD will drive you. 28There you will worship man-made gods[u] of wood and stone, which cannot see or hear or eat or smell.[v] 29But if from there you seek[w] the LORD your God, you will find him if you seek him with all your heart[x] and with all your soul.[y] 30When you are in distress and all these things have happened to you, then in later days[z] you will return to the LORD your God and obey him. 31For the LORD your God is a merciful[a] God; he will not abandon or destroy you or forget the covenant with your ancestors, which he confirmed to them by oath.

The LORD Is God

32Ask[b] now about the former days, long before your time, from the day God created human beings on the earth;[c] ask from one end of the heavens to the other.[d] Has anything so great as this ever happened, or has anything like it ever been heard of? 33Has any other people heard the voice of God[a] speaking out of fire, as you have, and lived?[e] 34Has any god ever tried to take for himself one nation out of another nation,[f] by testings, by signs[g] and wonders,[h] by war, by a mighty hand and an outstretched arm,[i] or by great and awesome deeds,[j] like all the things the LORD your God did for you in Egypt before your very eyes?

35You were shown these things so that you might know that the LORD is God; besides him there is no other.[k] 36From heaven he made you hear his voice[l] to discipline you. On earth he showed you his great fire, and you heard his words from out of the fire. 37Because he loved[m] your ancestors and chose their descendants after them, he brought you out of Egypt by his Presence and his great strength,[n] 38to drive out before you nations greater and stronger than you and to bring you into their land to give it to you for your inheritance,[o] as it is today.

39Acknowledge and take to heart this day that the LORD is God in heaven above and on the earth below. There is no other.[p] 40Keep[q] his decrees and commands, which I am giving you today, so that it may go well[r] with you and your children after you and that you may live long[s] in the land the LORD your God gives you for all time.

Cities of Refuge

4:41-43Ref — Nu 35:6-34; Dt 19:1-14; Jos 20:1-9

41Then Moses set aside three cities east of the Jordan, 42to which anyone who had

[a] 33 Or *of a god*

4:24 [q] Ex 24:17; Dt 9:3; Heb 12:29
4:25 [r] 2Ki 17:2, 17
4:26 [s] Dt 30:18-19; Isa 1:2; Mic 6:2
4:27 [t] Lev 26:33; Dt 28:36, 64; Ne 1:8
4:28 [u] Dt 28:36, 64; 1Sa 26:19; Jer 16:13 [v] Ps 115:4-8; 135:15-18
4:29 [w] 2Ch 15:4; Isa 55:6 [x] Jer 29:13 [y] Dt 30:1-3, 10
4:30 [z] Dt 31:29; Jer 23:20; Hos 3:5
4:31 [a] 2Ch 30:9; Ne 9:31; Ps 116:5; Jnh 4:2
4:32 [b] Dt 32:7; Job 8:8 [c] Ge 1:27 [d] Mt 24:31
4:33 [e] Ex 20:22; Dt 5:24-26
4:34 [f] Ex 6:6 [g] Ex 7:3 [h] Dt 7:19; 26:8 [i] Ex 13:3 [j] Dt 34:12
4:35 [k] Dt 32:39; 1Sa 2:2; Isa 45:5, 18
4:36 [l] Ex 19:9, 19
4:37 [m] Dt 10:15 [n] Ex 13:3, 9, 14
4:38 [o] Dt 7:1; 9:5
4:39 [p] ver 35; Jos 2:11
4:40 [q] Lev 22:31; Dt 5:33 [r] Dt 5:16 [s] Dt 6:3, 18; Eph 6:2-3

4:24 *consuming fire.* This designation of God (cf. Ex 24:17) indicates his propensity to consume that which is dross or unholy in his presence or to consume his enemies, as the phrase "like a fire consuming" is used in a ninth-century BC Phoenician text (where the beard and hand of the enemy were burned). Ancient Near Eastern gods were believed to rain down fire on the earth just as Yahweh had at Sodom and Gomorrah. The goddess Inanna destroyed covenant breakers during the time of Sargon I (2329–2274 BC). Foreign rebels were subdued by thunderbolts from a Hittite god or goddess, such as the sun-goddess of Arinna in the time of Mursili II (c. 1325 BC). In Akkadian texts, Assur sends biting flames, and a burning flame comes from Enlil. The Mesopotamian god Nergal, a warrior-god and god of plagues, carried a fiery-like glance that consumed enemies in battle. Ishkur, a storm-god in Mesopotamia, radiated lightning as a weapon. *jealous God.* In English, the adjective "jealous" usually indicates a petty form of envy (one of the deadly vices) and, in the context of a relationship, usually connotes paranoia and overbearing possessiveness. As such, some are inclined to think that this description contrasts with the Lord's character as merciful and compassionate (cf. v. 31). However, the covenantal ceremonies have features of a marriage celebration, and the covenant itself entails an exclusive relationship reminiscent of marriage. The "jealous" attribute of Yahweh reflects a desire to protect and preserve that relationship. No similar description of other gods in the ancient Near East has been found. This makes sense because gods in the ancient Near East were not thought to establish the same sorts of relationships with people.

4:26 *I call the heavens and the earth as witnesses.* A "swearing of oaths by heaven and earth" occurs in the Eridu Genesis text (1600 BC). Some Akkadian political decrees from Ugarit called the heaven and earth as gods to be witnesses to treaties. An Aramaic treaty (c. 900 BC) employs this phraseology in the presence of both political deities and "Heaven and Earth the (Abysmal) Springs and Sources and Day and Night." The invocation of the heaven and earth as witnesses was an ancient custom in covenants from Sefire and in Hittite treaties. The heavens and earth are called as witnesses against covenant offenders. This is a common feature paralleled in ancient Near Eastern treaties and covenants.

4:27 *The LORD will scatter you among the peoples.* Exile and dispersion was a reality for many peoples in the ancient Near East long before this assertion in Deuteronomy. This way of dealing with whole peoples occurred at Mari (1800/1700 BC), among the Hittites (sixteenth and fourteenth centuries BC) and in Egypt (fifteenth, thirteenth and twelfth centuries BC).

DEUTERONOMY 4:13

Treaty Formats and Biblical Covenants

Covenantal thinking and documents constituted a vital component of ancient Near Eastern culture and functioned in manifold ways. The Bronze Age (3500 – 1200 BC) produced many treaties. The treaty between Hattusili/Rameses II (c. 1280 BC) displays a treaty form and model that fits well the treaty form at Sinai (Ex 19 – 24) and its various renewals in Deuteronomy (Dt 1 – 28) and Joshua (Jos 24). While legitimate points of comparison are also evident in Neo-Assyrian treaties in the first millennium BC, the cultural, historical and literary connections of the covenant at Sinai, as reiterated in Deuteronomy, are most closely connected with the Late Bronze covenants. Those from the Iron Age and later lack either a preamble or blessings, as well as some technical vocabulary found in earlier documents. ◆

Order of Sections in Hittite Treaties (Second Millennium)

	DESCRIPTION	EX – LEV	DT	JOS 24
Introduction of Speaker	Identifying author and his right to proclaim treaty	Ex 20:1	1:1 – 5	Vv. 1 – 2
Historical Prologue	Survey of past relationship between parties	Ex 20:2	1:6–3:29	Vv. 2 – 13
Stipulations	Listing of obligations	Decalogue 20:1 – 17 Covenant Code 20:22 – 23:19 Ritual 34:10 – 26 Lev 1 – 25	Chs. 4 – 26	Vv. 14 – 25
Statement Concerning Document	Storage and public reading instructions	Ex 25:16?	27:2 – 3	V. 26
Witness	Usually identifying the gods who are called to witness the oath	Lev 26:1 – 33	Ch. 28	V. 20
Curses and Blessings	How deity will respond to adherence to or violation of treaty	Lev 26:1 – 33	Ch. 28	V. 20

killed a person could flee if they had unintentionally killed a neighbor without malice aforethought. They could flee into one
of these cities and save their life. [43]The
cities were these: Bezer in the wilderness
plateau, for the Reubenites; Ramoth in Gilead, for the Gadites; and Golan in Bashan,
for the Manassites.

Introduction to the Law

[44]This is the law Moses set before the
Israelites. [45]These are the stipulations, decrees and laws Moses gave them when
they came out of Egypt [46]and were in the
valley near Beth Peor east of the Jordan,
in the land of Sihon[t] king of the Amorites,
who reigned in Heshbon and was defeated
by Moses and the Israelites as they came
out of Egypt. [47]They took possession of his
land and the land of Og king of Bashan,
the two Amorite kings east of the Jordan.
[48]This land extended from Aroer[u] on the
rim of the Arnon Gorge to Mount Sirion[a][v]
(that is, Hermon), [49]and included all the
Arabah east of the Jordan, as far as the
Dead Sea,[b] below the slopes of Pisgah.

4:46 [t] Nu 21:26; Dt 3:29 **4:48** [u] Dt 2:36 [v] Dt 3:9

[a] *48* Syriac (see also 3:9); Hebrew *Siyon* [b] *49* Hebrew *the Sea of the Arabah*

The Ten Commandments

5:6-21pp — Ex 20:1-17

5 Moses summoned all Israel and said:
Hear, Israel, the decrees and laws I declare in your hearing today. Learn them
and be sure to follow them. 2The LORD our
God made a covenant[w] with us at Horeb.
3It was not with our ancestors[a] that the
LORD made this covenant, but with us,
with all of us who are alive here today.[x]
4The LORD spoke[y] to you face to face out
of the fire on the mountain. 5(At that time
I stood between[z] the LORD and you to declare to you the word of the LORD, because
you were afraid[a] of the fire and did not go
up the mountain.) And he said:

6"I am the LORD your God, who
brought you out of Egypt, out of
the land of slavery.
7"You shall have no other gods before[b] me.
8"You shall not make for yourself an
image in the form of anything
in heaven above or on the earth
beneath or in the waters below.
9You shall not bow down to them
or worship them; for I, the LORD
your God, am a jealous God,
punishing the children for the
sin of the parents to the third and
fourth generation of those who
hate me,[b] 10but showing love to
a thousand generations of those
who love me and keep my commandments.[c]
11"You shall not misuse the name of the
LORD your God, for the LORD will
not hold anyone guiltless who
misuses his name.[d]
12"Observe the Sabbath day by keeping it holy,[e] as the LORD your
God has commanded you. 13Six
days you shall labor and do all
your work, 14but the seventh
day[f] is a sabbath to the LORD
your God. On it you shall not do
any work, neither you, nor your
son or daughter, nor your male
or female servant, nor your ox,
your donkey or any of your animals, nor any foreigner residing in your towns, so that your
male and female servants may
rest, as you do. 15Remember that
you were slaves in Egypt and
that the LORD your God brought
you out of there with a mighty
hand and an outstretched arm.[g]
Therefore the LORD your God has
commanded you to observe the
Sabbath day.

5:2 [w] Ex 19:5 **5:3** [x] Heb 8:9 **5:4** [y] Dt 4:12, 33,36 **5:5** [z] Gal 3:19 [a] Ex 20:18,21 **5:9** [b] Ex 34:7 **5:10** [c] Jer 32:18 **5:11** [d] Lev 19:12; Mt 5:33-37 **5:12** [e] Ex 20:8 **5:14** [f] Ge 2:2; Heb 4:4 **5:15** [g] Dt 4:34

[a] 3 Or *not only with our parents* [b] 7 Or *besides*

5:6 – 21 No concentrated collection of laws from the ancient Near East matches this crystallization of "ten words," the Decalogue. These commands are apodictic (saying what one should and should not do) in form and state unequivocal prescriptions and proscriptions, but they do not define the penalties for breaking them. Ancient Near Eastern law collections do not feature this type of law, but rather use, like most Biblical law, case law (casuistic law, which says what the verdict will be when certain crimes are committed).

Covenantal and treaty stipulations, on the other hand, featured apodictic law, indicating that these "ten words" of instructions were to function as part of a covenant (see the article "Covenants," p. 143). Apodictic formulations are also found in the wisdom literature of the ancient Near East, and in Israel divinely given wisdom often centers around the instructions of the Ten Commandments and the larger Torah. Apodictic instruction is used in the Instructions of Shuruppak (2600 – 1100 BC): "Do not steal something; do not kill yourself"; in Instructions of Ur-Ninurta: The god-fearing man "keeps ... swearing away from his house"; and in Egyptian literature: "Do not set your heart on wealth."

5:6 *I am the LORD your God, who brought you ... out of the land of slavery.* This assertion identifies Yahweh as the liberator of Israel. It parallels the preambles found in many ancient Near Eastern covenants and treaties, especially those involving the Hittites and their vassals (c. 1400 – 1200 BC). The Great King Suppiluliuma says in his preamble that he has "taken you, Aziru, as my subject" (cf. v. 9).

5:7 *have no other gods before me.* See note on Ex 20:3. The exclusivity of Yahweh is vaguely paralleled in other ancient Near Eastern treaty texts, but in the form of an allegiance of the human vassal to his human suzerain and the suzerain's many gods — not to just one god, as in Israel.

5:8 *You shall not make ... an image in the form of anything.* See note on Ex 20:4. The power of art forms to carry religious messages and to communicate ideology, class status, etc. was utilized abundantly in the ancient Near East. More relevantly, images often served a cultic function.

Yahweh's form was never revealed to Israel (cf. 4:15). An Egyptian papyrus at Thebes from the close of the reign of Rameses II asserts that Amun's real appearance was unknown even to the other gods, for Amun (meaning "hidden") hid himself from them. Even though Yahweh's form was likewise hidden from the Israelites, he revealed himself to them through words.

5:9 *third and fourth generation.* Though this extension of guilt applies primarily to the living generations of descendants (see note on Ex 20:5), examples also exist of ramifications continuing further in time. During the reign of the Hittite king Mursili II (1339 – 1306 BC), a devastating plague ravaged his land. The king believed that his father Suppiluliuma had "sinned" against the word of a storm-god, breaking covenant and angering the storm-god. The plague rendered divine retribution for that fault. Mursili II admits *his own* guilt as a result of his father's failures, praying that the pestilence will cease: "It is only too true, however, that the father's sin falls upon the son. So my father's sin has fallen upon me." In so acting Mursili both confesses his father's sin and his *own* sin even though he had "not sinned in any respect."

5:11 *You shall not misuse the name of the LORD your God.* See note on Ex 20:7.

5:12 *Observe the Sabbath day.* See note on Ex 20:8.

16 "Honor your father and your mother,[h]
as the LORD your God has commanded you, so that you may live long[i] and that it may go well with you in the land the LORD your God is giving you.
17 "You shall not murder.[j]
18 "You shall not commit adultery.[k]
19 "You shall not steal.
20 "You shall not give false testimony against your neighbor.
21 "You shall not covet your neighbor's wife. You shall not set your desire on your neighbor's house or land, his male or female servant, his ox or donkey, or anything that belongs to your neighbor."[l]

22 These are the commandments the
LORD proclaimed in a loud voice to your
whole assembly there on the mountain
from out of the fire, the cloud and the
deep darkness; and he added nothing
more. Then he wrote them on two stone
tablets[m] and gave them to me.
23 When you heard the voice out of the
darkness, while the mountain was ablaze
with fire, all the leaders of your tribes and
your elders came to me. 24 And you said,
"The LORD our God has shown us his glory and his majesty, and we have heard his
voice from the fire. Today we have seen
that a person can live even if God speaks
with them.[n] 25 But now, why should we die?
This great fire will consume us, and we will
die if we hear the voice of the LORD our God
any longer.[o] 26 For what mortal has ever
heard the voice of the living God speaking
out of fire, as we have, and survived?[p] 27 Go
near and listen to all that the LORD our God
says. Then tell us whatever the LORD our
God tells you. We will listen and obey."
28 The LORD heard you when you spoke
to me, and the LORD said to me, "I have
heard what this people said to you. Everything they said was good.[q] 29 Oh, that their
hearts would be inclined to fear me[r] and
keep all my commands[s] always, so that it
might go well with them and their children forever![t]
30 "Go, tell them to return to their tents.
31 But you stay here[u] with me so that I may
give you all the commands, decrees and
laws you are to teach them to follow in the
land I am giving them to possess."

5:16 [h] Ex 20:12; Lev 19:3; Dt 27:16; Eph 6:2-3*; Col 3:20 [i] Dt 4:40 **5:17** [j] Mt 5:21-22* **5:18** [k] Mt 5:27-30; Lk 18:20*; Jas 2:11* **5:21** [l] Ro 7:7*; 13:9* **5:22** [m] Ex 24:12; 31:18; Dt 4:13

5:24 [n] Ex 19:19 **5:25** [o] Dt 18:16 **5:26** [p] Dt 4:33 **5:28** [q] Dt 18:17 **5:29** [r] Ps 81:8, 13 [s] Dt 11:1; Isa 48:18 [t] Dt 4:1,40 **5:31** [u] Ex 24:12

5:16 *Honor your father and your mother.* See note on Ex 20:12. In Scripture, this is the first commandment with a promise: "so that you may live long" (here; cf. v. 33; 11:9; 17:20; 22:7). Among other ancient Near Eastern peoples, this reward was often connected to faithful service to a god or gods. Agbar, an Assyrian priest of the god Sin, asserts from his grave that because he did righteousness in life, demonstrating faithful service to Sakar, his god had prolonged his life, such that he lived to see the fourth generation of his descendants. In a vassal treaty of Esarhaddon (680–669 BC), old age was to be withheld from a covenant breaker.

In the ancient Near East the honor due to parents extended beyond their life through the ongoing care of the dead. In Israel, ancestor worship or cults were prohibited, but in most areas of the ancient Near East an honorable son, usually the oldest son, was to present regular offerings to the ancestors, especially his own father. After the death of a father, the oldest son became the head of the family. Daughters normally did not attain this position (see the article "Inheritance Rights and Birthrights," p. 62). In Israel, the honor due to parents has a definitively covenant context and pertains to accepting and passing on the Torah.

5:17 *murder.* See note on Ex 20:13.
5:18 *adultery.* See note on Ex 20:14.
5:19 *steal.* See note on Ex 20:15.
5:20 *give false testimony.* See note on Ex 20:16.
5:21 *covet.* See note on Ex 20:17. A treaty between Assyrians in that area and their Anatolian trading partners (early second millennium BC) imposes a number of obligations that include requirements to follow certain business practices, to hand over any persons responsible for the death of an Assyrian, and to compensate Assyrian merchants for any thefts they might suffer in Anatolian territory. The treaty goes on to state: "You shall not covet a fine house, a fine slave, a fine slave woman, a fine field, or a fine orchard belonging to any Assyrian, and you will not take any of these by force and hand them over to your own subjects/servants." This treaty seems to confirm that it is not out of place for the issue of coveting to be included in a list of stipulations. It also points to the idea that the concern behind coveting is the illegal acts of confiscation that it can motivate. All of the items in the treaty—house, slave, slave woman and field—also appear in Deuteronomy, suggesting that the concerns of society in Israel were of the same sort that is evident throughout the ancient world.
5:22 *two stone tablets.* See note on 4:13.
5:24 *we have heard his voice from the fire.* See note on Ex 13:21.
5:27 *tell us whatever the LORD our God tells you.* On the one hand, Moses plays a typical ancient Near Eastern role as a covenant mediator, chosen by a god and/or a people. On the other hand, his role and the Lord's role are uniquely adapted to the Lord's covenant with his people. It was customary to seek out the proper sacred officials of the temple or other sacred precincts in the ancient Near East so that a relevant answer could be given to a concerned inquirer. The will of the deity was revealed in this way. Pharaoh Akhenaten was believed to be a mediator of his god's will in a unique sense, one that approaches Moses' position. *We will listen and obey.* In the ancient Near East, the people involved in covenant/treaty processes and ceremonies were to pledge and respond at the conclusion of the covenant or treaty ceremony. Responses were to be from the whole heart in words expressing a treaty commitment and conclusion. In an eighth-century BC Aramaic treaty made between Bar-gahdayah, king of KTK, and Matihdel of Arpad, the words "you do swear" appear; they also appear in vassal treaties of Esarhaddon. One of his treaties with a vassal includes a loyalty oath involving words, lips and heart. The same can be said of a Hittite text that contains ratification responses concerning Hatti and Hurrians represented by their king Kurtiwaza. Those pledging were to assert in essence, as the Israelites did at Sinai, "We will listen and obey."

32 So be careful to do what the LORD your
God has commanded you; do not turn
aside to the right or to the left.[v] 33 Walk in
obedience to all that the LORD your God
has commanded you,[w] so that you may
live and prosper and prolong your days[x]
in the land that you will possess.

Love the LORD Your God

6 These are the commands, decrees and
laws the LORD your God directed me to
teach you to observe in the land that you
are crossing the Jordan to possess, 2 so that
you, your children and their children after
them may fear[y] the LORD your God as long
as you live by keeping all his decrees and
commands that I give you, and so that you
may enjoy long life. 3 Hear, Israel, and be
careful to obey so that it may go well with
you and that you may increase greatly[z] in
a land flowing with milk and honey,[a] just
as the LORD, the God of your ancestors,
promised you.

4 Hear, O Israel: The LORD our God, the
LORD is one.[a][b] 5 Love[c] the LORD your God
with all your heart and with all your soul
and with all your strength.[d] 6 These commandments that I give you today are to be
on your hearts.[e] 7 Impress them on your
children. Talk about them when you sit at
home and when you walk along the road,

5:32 [v] Dt 17:11, 20; 28:14; Jos 1:7; 23:6; Pr 4:27 **5:33** [w] Jer 7:23 [x] Dt 4:40 **6:2** [y] Ex 20:20; Dt 10:12-13 **6:3** [z] Dt 5:33 [a] Ex 3:8 **6:4** [b] Mk 12:29*; 1Co 8:4 **6:5** [c] Mt 22:37*; Mk 12:30*; Lk 10:27* [d] Dt 10:12 **6:6** [e] Dt 11:18

[a] 4 Or *The LORD our God is one LORD;* or *The LORD is our God, the LORD is one;* or *The LORD is our God, the LORD alone*

6:3 *flowing with milk and honey.* This phrase occurs often (e.g., 11:9; 26:9,15; 27:3; 31:20; cf. Ex 3:8; Lev 20:24; Nu 13:27). It is closely paralleled in Ugaritic poetry: "The heavens fat did rain, / The wadis flow with honey!" Milk and fat are mentioned as a blessed feature of the world ordered by Enki, who determined Sumer's destiny. This hyperbolic metaphoric phrase stresses both the richness of Canaan and the special favor God has bestowed on it as the dwelling place for his people.

6:4 *the LORD is one.* The claim that a deity is one or alone, as made by Enlil and Baal, relates to the supremacy of that god's rule. In this sense, it may be a sociological more than a metaphysical statement. See the article "Monotheism, Monolatry and Henotheism," p. 308. Another possibility is that this statement demands a unified view of Yahweh, in contrast to the views of other ancient Near Eastern peoples who would have many different shrines celebrating or emphasizing a different perspective or aspect of their gods. For example, in Mesopotamia, Ishtar of Arbela was conceived quite differently from Ishtar of Uruk. This kind of division was not unknown in Israel, as inscriptions refer to "Yahweh of Samaria" and "Yahweh of Teman"; however, in the Bible, such divisions are condemned.

6:5 *Love the LORD your God with all your heart.* "Love" in the context of a treaty refers to amicable and loyal international relationships. The Great King, the suzerain, in a suzerain-vassal treaty in the ancient Near East expected his vassal to love him, not merely in a legal way, but with fervor and emotional commitment. Correspondence between the great kings of that era is replete with expressions of love toward one another. Kings of Egypt, Babylon, Assyria, Hatti and Mitanni exude mutual brotherhood, loyalty and love to one another. In Hittite parlance the vassal and his lord were to love each other as they loved themselves. Love unto death, the greatest love, was expected toward the suzerain from the vassal. Furthermore, those surrounding the king (e.g., Esarhaddon, Ashurbanipal) were to love the king as they loved their own lives. The vassal was to hate the enemy of his lord and the lord was to hate the enemy of his vassal. The subjects of the king were to love him.

There are rare instances when an individual is admonished to love a deity, but in general the gods of the ancient Near East did not expect love from their worshipers. The concept of the heart is central to the theological anthropology of the ancient Near East. In a hymn to Aten, the pharaoh says, "Thou art in *my heart* and there is no other that knows thee." In Egypt the heart was nothing less than "the god who dwells in man." The heart itself dwelt in its shrine. A righteous Egyptian worshiper was said "to hold Amun in his heart."

Israel's love for Yahweh, though not lacking in emotional commitment, was also an expression of loyalty and faithfulness. This provides a distinction from the ancient Near East since in a polytheistic system gods did not expect worshipers to be exclusively devoted to them.

6:6 *on your hearts.* The heart, as the seat of reason and cognitive functions, is by far the most important bodily organ mentioned in the OT. In Ugaritic literature the heart is often paired with the liver as the internal organs facilitating joy and laughter. In the Memphite theology of Egypt, the heart of the god Ptah functions both as a center of conceptual thinking and feeling through the senses. The heart is paired with the tongue and the control of all limbs. The heart gathers information from all of the senses, while the tongue repeats what the heart formulates.

Putting words on one's heart and soul is expressed in loyalty oaths of the ancient Near East, as in Hittite treaties of Mursili II and oaths of allegiance to Assyrian king Esarhaddon. In an intimate didactic wisdom text (c. 900–500 BC), a father, Ka-nakht, instructs his son to give ear to his words, "to put them in their heart." The heart of the pharaoh was the key to his thinking and behavior and is mentioned hundreds of time in ancient Egyptian literature.

6:7 *Impress them on your children.* The inculcation of moral principles and wisdom in youth was practiced widely in the ancient Near East. In Egypt, teaching and instruction were used from at least 2500 BC up until the time of the Ptolemies (c. 300 BC). Rules of conduct and learning were prepared for sons. From moral issues to royal protocol, children were trained in the home or in the king's palace. Order, truth and justice were important.

In Mesopotamia, Sumerian literature includes the advice of a father to his son. Several famous works of a didactic nature come from Mesopotamia. Repetition by mouth, copying texts and strict discipline (the rod!) were the main pedagogical means of "impressing" a desired curriculum on a student or child. This was done both in the home and in any place of learning available.

Covenantal conditions and stipulations were passed on so that following generations would know and pursue them diligently—and, of course, for political purposes. Esarhaddon declared a curse on anyone who would not pass on the traditions and conditions of his vassal treaties: "If you . . . do not transmit it to your sons who will live after this treaty . . ." He continues, "May your sons and grandsons because of this fear, in the future, your god Assur and your lord, the crown prince designate Assurbanipal."

when you lie down and when you get
up.[f] 8Tie them as symbols on your hands
and bind them on your foreheads.[g] 9Write
them on the doorframes of your houses
and on your gates.[h]
10When the LORD your God brings you
into the land he swore to your fathers, to
Abraham, Isaac and Jacob, to give you—a
land with large, flourishing cities you did
not build,[i] 11houses filled with all kinds
of good things you did not provide, wells
you did not dig, and vineyards and olive
groves you did not plant—then when you
eat and are satisfied,[j] 12be careful that you
do not forget the LORD, who brought you
out of Egypt, out of the land of slavery.
13Fear the LORD[k] your God, serve him
only[l] and take your oaths in his name.
14Do not follow other gods, the gods of the
peoples around you; 15for the LORD your

6:7 [f] Dt 4:9; 11:19; Eph 6:4 **6:8** [g] Ex 13:9, 16; Dt 11:18 **6:9** [h] Dt 11:20 **6:10** [i] Jos 24:13 **6:11** [j] Dt 8:10 **6:13** [k] Dt 10:20 [l] Mt 4:10*; Lk 4:8*

6:8 *Tie them as symbols on your hands and bind them on your foreheads.* Examples of symbols of power worn on the forehead can be seen as something as common as a pharaoh's crown. The Egyptian pharaoh wore a uraeus, a protective serpent figurine, on his forehead, a symbol also worn by the Egyptian gods in artistic depictions. In Egypt, during the New Kingdom era, children wore cylindrical amulets containing strips of papyrus. Inscriptions on the tiny papyrus strips protected them from various dangers. No ambiance of magic surrounded an Israelite's display of God's law; this symbol reminded them to follow the covenant stipulations; nevertheless, it is reminiscent of practices known from the ancient world. Unfortunately, we have no evidence by which to suggest what the Israelite practice would have actually looked like.

6:9 *Write them on the doorframes of your houses and on your gates.* Doorposts or doorframes seem to be related to Akkadian *manzazu* ("stand, position, door, socket"). Silver plaques written in ancient Hebrew script have been unearthed (eighth or seventh century BC). All types of materials and writing surfaces were used to display important written materials, including silver amulets in Egypt. These amulets were fastened to a person's arm, hand or neck, and bore important messages. Many people who wore them would not have been able to read them, but they were aware of the important information they contained.

Plastered walls and doorways, more germane to this Biblical text, were used at Kuntillet Ajrud (eighth century BC). Gates of cities also provided exposure for important notices. Papyrus, stone, copper, bronze, arrowheads, clay seals, waxed wood boards and leather—all of these were employed in writing. These materials and the inscriptions on them provided an opportunity to tie a person to a god who protected them and whom they wanted to constantly revere; they also served as a memorial sign in the presence of the deity.

6:10 *large, flourishing cities.* In many cases these "cities" were taken over, not built for the first time. This was common in the ancient Near East, where whole peoples and nations could be uprooted and their land and cities taken over by intruders or conquerors.

6:11 *houses.* A typical Israelite house may have featured (1) two, three or four rooms, (2) three rooms formed by rows of longitudinal pillars that created a central large room, and (3) a back room or broad room for storage. Small, open windows were left in the walls, and ceramic lamps or flax wicks (using olive oil for fuel) created artificial light in the house. The door pivoted in sockets, and the lintel over the doorframe was supported by two doorposts, with a single block of stone for the threshold. Wooden bolts and tumble locks were used in the doors of palaces, temples, granaries, storage facilities and domestic houses. Houses supported by pillars always had roofs. In some cases stairs led up to the roof. The "typical" four-room pillared Israelite house has been found outside of Israel and may have been simply a common Canaanite house, not an innovation by the Israelites. *wells.* Some translate this Hebrew word (*borot*) as "cisterns"—i.e., artificial reservoirs of water that were normally hewn out of bedrock. They were used from ancient times, as far back as the sixth millennium BC. Wells at Lachish, Tell Sheva, existed in Biblical times. Water shafts were connected to springs at Hazor, Megiddo, Gibeon and Jerusalem. Over 100 wells were located at the Philistine city of Ashkelon. Pools were constructed around wells for watering animals.

6:13 *take your oaths in his name.* Oaths were common in ancient Near Eastern treaties. This fact appears in the essentials of its literary form, namely, the promulgation of terms of the treaty or covenant and some adumbration of an oath in the list of gods invoked as witnesses or in the curses or blessings. The enactment of the curses or blessings was dependent on the fidelity or infidelity of the covenantal parties to the oath.

Oaths were a part of treaties and covenants from the earliest times in Sumer and Elam (third millennium BC), Mesopotamia, Ebla, Mari, Hatti, Syria (seventeenth century BC) and Assyria. Oaths were sworn in Akkadian to the life of the king or to the life of a god, also in Egypt, and in the Canaanite-Phoenician milieu. Soldiers took solemn oaths to serve the king, the nation and its gods. To break this oath could lead to death, abject humility and shaming.

Though Israel inherited the land and cities of the Canaanites, they were not to inherit their gods. One way to demonstrate rejection of these gods was to refuse to take oaths in their name, thus denying their power.

6:14 *Do not follow ... the gods of the peoples around you.* All the nations around Israel had multiple gods, and Israel's great sin was that she whored after the gods of Canaan (Jdg 2:17). El was the head of the Canaanite pantheon, and he had a consort, Asherah (Athirat). As father of the pantheon, he was perceived as rather distant from the common worshiper and even from the priests. The god Baal, however, was believed to be in touch with the people and the one through whom the forces of nature were controlled. He was recognized under other names, such as Hadad and Dagan, and he manifested himself in various locations, taking to himself the name of each location (e.g., Baal Peor, Baal Berith, Baal Zebul). Baal achieved hegemony among the other gods in Canaan, such as El, Yamm (Sea), Nahar (River), Mot (Death) and Anat (Baal's sister). Rain was thought to be Baal's semen, which "impregnated" the earth; Asherah, his wife, was the goddess of fertility.

The other neighbors of Israel delighted in their multiplicity of gods: Ammonites (Milkom, the chief god, plus nine others); Moabites (Chemosh/Kemosh and Ashtar-Chemosh, both mentioned in the Moabite Stone); Edom (Qaws, the chief god; Baa, Hadad, and an unnamed goddess); Byblos (Baal Shemayin, the chief deity; Baal Dor, Baal, Ba'alat gbl ["lady of Byblos"]); Sidon (Eshmun, Astarte, Resheph, Rehaim); Tyre (Melqart). The list goes on for Sarepta and Ugarit (at least three goddesses). A divine council of gods was thought to function in most areas. Chthonic deities (earth/underworld gods) were also common at Ebla, Ugarit and some Transjordanian areas.

DEUTERONOMY 6:4

MONOTHEISM, MONOLATRY AND HENOTHEISM

Several scholars in different fields of expertise have recently demonstrated that monotheism in a recognizable form, practical and conceptual, existed at least as early as the fifteenth to fourteenth centuries BC. In Egypt, a hymn to Amun (c. 1500/1400 BC) presents Amun as "creator" of the other gods. Approximately a century later, the pharaoh Akhenaten attempted to establish the sun-god Aten as the only god, demoting all other Egyptian gods to non-god status.

Egyptian religion in general rejected Akhenaten's attempt to deny the reality of a multiplicity of deities, but ultimately accepted an approach according to which the multiplicity of deities reflected various forms and manifestations of the one single transcendent god. Amun was the "apogee of religious thought in ancient Egypt. He was the fashioner of himself who formed his own body, the first creator who was never born, without parallel and who oversees all."

From our distance in history, it is difficult to discern whether ancient people were practicing monotheism (in which only one God is believed to exist), henotheism (in which one god among many is chosen for focus of worship) or monolatry (in which only one god among many is believed to be worthy of worship). A variety of these may be present at the same time in any given culture — even in Israel, considering that unorthodox syncretism was always present. ◆

Akhenaten, Nefertiti and three of their daughters. New Kingdom, Eighteenth Dynasty, c. 1350 BC. The pharaoh Akhenaten attempted to establish the sun-god Aten as the only god, demoting all other Egyptian gods to non-god status.

Kim Walton. The Neues Museum, Berlin.

God[m], who is among you, is a jealous God and his anger will burn against you, and he will destroy you from the face of the land. 16 Do not put the LORD your God to the test[n] as you did at Massah. 17 Be sure to keep the commands of the LORD your God and the stipulations and decrees he has given you.[o] 18 Do what is right and good in the LORD's sight, so that it may go well[p] with you and you may go in and take over the good land the LORD promised on oath to your ancestors, 19 thrusting out all your enemies before you, as the LORD said.

20 In the future, when your son asks you,[q] "What is the meaning of the stipulations, decrees and laws the LORD our God has commanded you?" 21 tell him: "We were slaves of Pharaoh in Egypt, but the LORD brought us out of Egypt with a mighty hand. 22 Before our eyes the LORD sent signs and wonders—great and terrible—on Egypt and Pharaoh and his whole household. 23 But he brought us out from there to bring us in and give us the land he promised on oath to our ancestors. 24 The LORD commanded us to obey all these decrees and to fear the LORD our God,[r] so that we might always prosper and be kept alive, as is the case today.[s] 25 And if we are careful to obey all this law before the LORD our God, as he has commanded us, that will be our righteousness.[t]"

6:15 [m] Dt 4:24 **6:16** [n] Ex 17:7; Mt 4:7*; Lk 4:12* **6:17** [o] Dt 11:22; Ps 119:4 **6:18** [p] Dt 4:40 **6:20** [q] Ex 13:14 **6:24** [r] Dt 10:12; Jer 32:39 [s] Ps 41:2 **6:25** [t] Dt 24:13; Ro 10:3,5

Driving Out the Nations

7 When the LORD your God brings you into the land you are entering to possess and drives out before you many nations[u]—the Hittites, Girgashites, Amorites, Canaanites, Perizzites, Hivites and Jebusites, seven nations larger and stronger than you— 2 and when the LORD your God has delivered them over to you and you have defeated them, then you must destroy them totally.[a] Make no treaty[v] with them, and show them no mercy.[w] 3 Do not intermarry with them.[x] Do not give your daughters to their sons or take their daughters for your sons, 4 for they will turn your children away from following me to serve other gods, and the LORD's anger will burn against you and will quickly destroy[y] you. 5 This is what you are to do to them: Break down their altars, smash their sacred stones, cut down their Asherah poles[b] and burn their idols in the fire.[z] 6 For you are a people holy[a] to the LORD your God.[b] The LORD your God has chosen[c] you out of all the peoples on the face of the earth to be his people, his treasured possession.

7:1 [u] Dt 31:3; Ac 13:19 **7:2** [v] Ex 23:32 [w] Dt 13:8 **7:3** [x] Ex 34:15-16; Ezr 9:2 **7:4** [y] Dt 6:15 **7:5** [z] Ex 23:24; Dt 12:2-3 **7:6** [a] Ex 19:5-6; 1Pe 2:9 [b] Ps 50:5; Jer 2:3 [c] Dt 14:2

[a] *2* The Hebrew term refers to the irrevocable giving over of things or persons to the LORD, often by totally destroying them; also in verse 26. [b] *5* That is, wooden symbols of the goddess Asherah; here and elsewhere in Deuteronomy

7:1 *Hittites.* The New Kingdom of Hatti, a people who inhabited and ruled in the area of Anatolia and Syria, began under Tudhaliya I (c. 1430–1410 BC) and expanded until Hattusili III (c. 1239). They concluded a treaty with Egypt in the 21st year of Rameses II. The Hittite Empire lasted from about 1239 to 1180 BC. The Hittites vied with Egypt for rule over Canaan and southern Syria, especially the area around Kedesh on the Orontes. They immigrated throughout Syria, spread south into upper Canaan, and adapted to Canaanite life and culture. There is only circumstantial evidence for Hittites in Canaan in the Late Bronze Age (c. 1600–1200). The migration of the Sea Peoples undoubtedly swept many people along with it or before it into Canaan in about 1220–1200 BC or earlier, including Hittites, but this movement is later than the conquest of Canaan by the Israelites. Tribes of Hittites could have been migrating into the region earlier, or alternatively, these Hittites could be related to those in Ge 23. *Girgashites.* A subgroup of Canaanites. They descended from Ham (Ge 10:15–16). At Ugarit the name Girgash and the phrase "son of Grgs" are present, suggesting that the name was at least known in early Israel. Some suggest they came from Asia Minor. *Amorites.* See notes on 1:7; Nu 13:29. *Canaanites.* See note on 1:7; see also the article "The Canaanites," p. 294. *Perizzites.* In the OT, the Perizzites are located in the hill country of northern Canaan (Jos 11:3). Additional references suggest other areas farther south and certain regions of Carmel. Archaeologists and philologists are divided over whether they were Hurrians or a subgroup of Amorites. The personal name Perissi or Perizzi (Hurrian) describes an envoy from the land of Mitanni (in northern Mesopotamia) in both cuneiform and Egyptian texts. *Hivites.* Some scholars connect the Hivites to the Luwians from the area of Cilicia; others identify the Hivites with the Horites/Hurrians (cf. 2:12,22). They were found as far south as Edom/Seir. *Jebusites.* The Jebusites were located in the hill country of Canaan and inhabited Jerusalem in the twelfth to eleventh centuries BC. Their origin is obscure except for circumstantial Biblical evidence, which suggests (weakly) that they were from the land of the Hittites. Some scholars continue to tie them to the Hurrians and note the similarities between worship in Jerusalem and the rituals of the Hittites/Hurrians. The Amarna letters contain the name of a king of Jerusalem, Abdi-Hepa, who reasonably could have been a Jebusite. Only under David, who took over Jerusalem for Israel, were these people finally conquered.

7:2 *destroy them totally.* See note on 2:34.

7:5 *altars...sacred stones...Asherah poles.* Standing stones, altars and symbols (poles, trees, figures) of Asherah were part of the furnishings of the cults and rituals in Canaan from 1200 to 930 BC, as were idols/images. The Asherahs (sacred symbols) represented the female aspect of deity.

At Ugarit, the goddess Athirat is presented as the wife of El, head of the pantheon. In Mesopotamia (c. 1830–1531 BC) the female deity Ashratum seems to be equivalent to Ugaritic Athirat. The name of the goddess Asherah appears in kings' names at Amurru. The word "Asherah" also denoted a symbolic tree or pole. In Egypt the goddess Qdsh parallels Asherah/Athirat/Ashratum, especially since this name for Asherah is found at Ugarit. Ashertu, a Hittite goddess, certainly represents Asherah of the Bible as well. From about 750 BC and 800 BC, respectively, we have references to "asherah of YHWH" from Kuntillet Ajrud (about 40 miles [65 kilometers] south of Kadesh Barnea) and from Khirbet el-Qom (nine miles [14 kilometers] west of Hebron).

7:6 *treasured possession.* The Hebrew word (*segullah*)

7The LORD did not set his affection on
you and choose you because you were
more numerous than other peoples, for
you were the fewest of all peoples.[d] 8But
it was because the LORD loved[e] you and
kept the oath he swore[f] to your ancestors
that he brought you out with a mighty
hand and redeemed you from the land of
slavery,[g] from the power of Pharaoh king
of Egypt. 9Know therefore that the LORD
your God is God;[h] he is the faithful God,[i]
keeping his covenant of love[j] to a thousand generations of those who love him
and keep his commandments. 10But

those who hate him he will repay to
their face by destruction;
he will not be slow to repay to their
face those who hate him.

11Therefore, take care to follow the commands, decrees and laws I give you today.
12If you pay attention to these laws
and are careful to follow them, then the
LORD your God will keep his covenant
of love with you, as he swore to your
ancestors.[k] 13He will love you and bless
you[l] and increase your numbers. He will
bless the fruit of your womb, the crops of
your land—your grain, new wine and olive oil—the calves of your herds and the
lambs of your flocks in the land he swore
to your ancestors to give you.[m] 14You will
be blessed more than any other people;
none of your men or women will be childless, nor will any of your livestock be
without young.[n] 15The LORD will keep you
free from every disease.[o] He will not inflict
on you the horrible diseases you knew in
Egypt, but he will inflict them on all who
hate you. 16You must destroy all the peoples the LORD your God gives over to you.
Do not look on them with pity[p] and do not
serve their gods, for that will be a snare[q]
to you.
17You may say to yourselves, "These
nations are stronger than we are. How
can we drive them out?[r]" 18But do not be
afraid[s] of them; remember well what the
LORD your God did to Pharaoh and to all
Egypt.[t] 19You saw with your own eyes the
great trials, the signs and wonders, the
mighty hand and outstretched arm, with
which the LORD your God brought you
out. The LORD your God will do the same
to all the peoples you now fear.[u] 20More-
over, the LORD your God will send the hornet[v] among them until even the survivors
who hide from you have perished. 21Do
not be terrified by them, for the LORD your
God, who is among you,[w] is a great and
awesome God.[x] 22The LORD your God will
drive out those nations before you, little
by little.[y] You will not be allowed to eliminate them all at once, or the wild animals
will multiply around you. 23But the LORD
your God will deliver them over to you,
throwing them into great confusion until they are destroyed. 24He will give their
kings into your hand, and you will wipe
out their names from under heaven. No
one will be able to stand up against you;[z]
you will destroy them. 25The images of
their gods you are to burn[a] in the fire. Do
not covet[b] the silver and gold on them,

7:7 [d] Dt 10:22 **7:8** [e] Dt 10:15 [f] Ex 32:13 [g] Ex 13:14 **7:9** [h] Dt 4:35 [i] 1Co 1:9; 2Ti 2:13 [j] Ne 1:5; Da 9:4 **7:12** [k] Lev 26:3-13; Dt 28:1-14; Ps 105:8-9 **7:13** [l] Jn 14:21 [m] Dt 28:4 **7:14** [n] Ex 23:26 **7:15** [o] Ex 15:26

7:16 [p] ver 2; Ex 23:33 [q] Jdg 8:27 **7:17** [r] Nu 33:53 **7:18** [s] Dt 31:6 [t] Ps 105:5 **7:19** [u] Dt 4:34 **7:20** [v] Ex 23:28; Jos 24:12 **7:21** [w] Jos 3:10 [x] Dt 10:17; Ne 9:32 **7:22** [y] Ex 23:28-30 **7:24** [z] Jos 23:9 **7:25** [a] Ex 32:20; 1Ch 14:12 [b] Jos 7:21

used to describe Israel as God's "treasured possession" is used eight times in the OT. This term occurs in the ancient Near East from the first part of the second millennium BC, with cognates in Akkadian and Ugaritic. This word and its cognates designate someone as a special personal possession of his god. In Hittite texts, the word refers to a special position of status for the king at Ugarit based upon a covenant relationship with Hatti. In the Bible, its meaning shades over into "beloved" and thus singles out Israel before Yahweh.

7:8 *because the LORD loved you and kept the oath.* The Lord's love for Israel justifies her special place before him. This concept has some partial analogues in ancient Near Eastern literature. Whole cities such as Babylon fall within this purview, for the Babylonian creation account justifies and proclaims Babylon as the favored of Marduk. Individuals who were portrayed as enjoying a chosen status, among others, included Hattusili III of Hatti and Nabonidus of Babylon. But in Israel this relationship extends beyond the king or a city to a chosen people.

7:15 *diseases.* The sicknesses and medicines of Egypt were a part of Israel's historical memory (cf. Ex 15:26). These diseases are described amply in many ancient Near Eastern texts (see the article "Disease Transmission in the Ancient World," p. 205). The etiology of disease in Egypt traced many illnesses to internal decay; hence, the use of purgatives and enemas was common. Defecation was a process and product that was watched carefully. Hygienic processes were prescribed and followed to thwart possible diseases. Diseases or conditions that were certainly present included dental problems (attrition and cavities), broken bones, bone cancer, arthritis, obesity, baldness and, less certainly, smallpox, polio and malaria. Epidemics occurred because of poor sanitation. From a study of Egyptian art, dwarfism, hunchback, clubfeet, hernias and emaciation were the result of poor health conditions in the ancient world. Persons rarely lived beyond 40 or 50 years. "Drugs" made from vegetables, animals and minerals constituted an Egyptian pharmacopoeia.

7:20 *hornet.* See note on Ex 23:28.

7:23–24 *the LORD . . . will deliver them over to you . . . you will destroy them.* The statement that Yahweh is giving Israel's enemies into Israel's power ("hand," v. 24), often so that Israel can "wipe [them] out" (Hebrew *abad*, v. 24), occurs many times in Deuteronomy. This divine activity on behalf of Israel parallels other ancient Near Eastern literature. In the Amarna letters, a king of Mitanni tells Amenhotep III (c. 1403–1364 BC) that Teshub (a god of Mitanni) has given his enemies into his hand so that he may destroy them. Nebuchadnezzar asserts that Marduk has given many peoples into his hand and he has subdued them. The same divine activity in history is attributed to the sun-goddess of Arinna on behalf of a Hittite king, Mursili I (1330–1295 BC).

and do not take it for yourselves, or you
will be ensnared[c] by it, for it is detestable[d]
to the LORD your God. 26Do not bring a
detestable thing into your house or you,
like it, will be set apart for destruction.[e]
Regard it as vile and utterly detest it, for it
is set apart for destruction.

Do Not Forget the LORD

8 Be careful to follow every command I
am giving you today, so that you may
live[f] and increase and may enter and possess the land the LORD promised on oath to
your ancestors. 2Remember how the LORD
your God led[g] you all the way in the wilderness these forty years, to humble and
test you in order to know what was in your
heart, whether or not you would keep his
commands. 3He humbled you, causing
you to hunger and then feeding you with
manna,[h] which neither you nor your ancestors had known, to teach you that man
does not live on bread alone but on every
word that comes from the mouth of the
LORD.[i] 4Your clothes did not wear out and
your feet did not swell during these forty
years.[j] 5Know then in your heart that as a
man disciplines his son, so the LORD your
God disciplines you.[k]
6Observe the commands of the LORD
your God, walking in obedience to him
and revering him.[l] 7For the LORD your God
is bringing you into a good land—a land
with brooks, streams, and deep springs
gushing out into the valleys and hills;[m] 8a
land with wheat and barley, vines and fig
trees, pomegranates, olive oil and honey;
9a land where bread will not be scarce and
you will lack nothing; a land where the
rocks are iron and you can dig copper out
of the hills.
10When you have eaten and are satisfied,[n] praise the LORD your God for the
good land he has given you. 11Be careful
that you do not forget the LORD your God,
failing to observe his commands, his laws
and his decrees that I am giving you this
day. 12Otherwise, when you eat and are
satisfied, when you build fine houses and
settle down,[o] 13and when your herds and
flocks grow large and your silver and gold
increase and all you have is multiplied,
14then your heart will become proud and
you will forget[p] the LORD your God, who
brought you out of Egypt, out of the land
of slavery. 15He led you through the vast
and dreadful wilderness,[q] that thirsty and
waterless land, with its venomous snakes[r]
and scorpions. He brought you water
out of hard rock.[s] 16He gave you manna
to eat in the wilderness, something your
ancestors had never known,[t] to humble
and test you so that in the end it might
go well with you. 17You may say to yourself,[u] "My power and the strength of my
hands have produced this wealth for me."
18But remember the LORD your God, for it
is he who gives you the ability to produce
wealth,[v] and so confirms his covenant,
which he swore to your ancestors, as it
is today.
19If you ever forget the LORD your God
and follow other gods and worship and
bow down to them, I testify against you
today that you will surely be destroyed.[w]
20Like the nations the LORD destroyed before you, so you will be destroyed for not
obeying the LORD your God.

7:25 [c] Jdg 8:27 [d] Dt 17:1 **7:26** [e] Lev 27:28-29 **8:1** [f] Dt 4:1 **8:2** [g] Am 2:10 **8:3** [h] Ex 16:12, 14, 35 [i] Ex 16:2-3; Mt 4:4*; Lk 4:4* **8:4** [j] Dt 29:5; Ne 9:21 **8:5** [k] 2Sa 7:14; Pr 3:11-12; Heb 12:5-11; Rev 3:19 **8:6** [l] Dt 5:33 **8:7** [m] Dt 11:9-12 **8:10** [n] Dt 6:10-12 **8:12** [o] Hos 13:6 **8:14** [p] Ps 106:21 **8:15** [q] Jer 2:6 [r] Nu 21:6 [s] Nu 20:11; Ps 78:15; 114:8 **8:16** [t] Ex 16:15 **8:17** [u] Dt 9:4, 7, 24 **8:18** [v] Pr 10:22; Hos 2:8 **8:19** [w] Dt 4:26; 30:18

8:3 *feeding you with manna.* See the note on Nu 11:7.
8:8–9 *a land with wheat and barley, vines and fig trees … bread.* The description of the land in these verses is the same sort of description typically used in ancient land grants. Certain political ancient Near Eastern covenants contained a land grant description with features as are found here, but it is also found in treaties. The essential difference between political treaties and land grant treaties was that in the latter the master obligated himself freely to the vassal or grantee. In the former the vassal was obligated to his master. The land grant is held in perpetuity even if the vassal breaks faith and the stipulations of the grant. His descendants retain the land/property granted. The historical prologues of political treaties could contain land grant features that included careful descriptions of the land in question. The land is described similarly in the Egyptian story of Sinuhe (c. 1960 BC), a fugitive from Egypt residing in the land of Canaan. He describes the land as "a good land" producing figs, grapes, abundance of wine, honey, olives, fruit trees, barley, and emmer, and it was full of cattle. The land flowed with an abundance of milk.
8:8 *wheat and barley.* A failure of barley and wheat was a major disaster in time of drought to an agricultural community. When this crop flourished, the god of the nation was given credit. In a good year wheat and barley were produced in abundance by the latter spring rains. A school boy's writing exercise, the Gezer Calendar, contains a record of the months of barley and wheat planting.
8:9 *a land where the rocks are iron … dig copper out of the hills.* Copper and iron were found in the Arabah, especially from the Dead Sea to the Gulf of Aqaba and possibly in Transjordan. This expression reveals the author's view of the geographic extent of the promised land. Copper was the first metal used in the ancient world and was mined deep in the ground in the Beersheba Valley as far back as the fourth millennium BC. Copper metallurgy was practiced in Arad, but most of the metal objects found there came from an earlier period. Copper ores were also used at Timna, on the eastern border of the Arabah. Tin (10 percent) and copper (80 percent) were combined to produce bronze. The ancient sources of tin are uncertain. Iron was, however, scarce in Canaan. Small amounts of surface iron ore deposits have been found north of the Jabbok River. Significant deposits of iron were found at several other places, such as the Ajlun Hills, and ironsmith shops were located in Tell Deir Allah (near where the Jabbok and Jordan Rivers meet) and Tell Qasile (near Tel Aviv). Because of the high temperature needed, it was not possible to produce cast iron in the period of the OT.

Not Because of Israel's Righteousness

9 Hear, Israel: You are now about to cross the Jordan to go in and dispossess nations greater and stronger than you,[x] with large cities that have walls up to the sky.[y] 2 The people are strong and tall — Anakites! You know about them and have heard it said: "Who can stand up against the Anakites?"[z] 3 But be assured today that the LORD your God is the one who goes across ahead of you[a] like a devouring fire.[b] He will destroy them; he will subdue them before you. And you will drive them out and annihilate them quickly,[c] as the LORD has promised you.

4 After the LORD your God has driven them out before you, do not say to yourself,[d] "The LORD has brought me here to take possession of this land because of my righteousness." No, it is on account of the wickedness of these nations[e] that the LORD is going to drive them out before you. 5 It is not because of your righteousness or your integrity[f] that you are going in to take possession of their land; but on account of the wickedness of these nations, the LORD your God will drive them out before you, to accomplish what he swore[g] to your fathers, to Abraham, Isaac and Jacob. 6 Understand, then, that it is not because of your righteousness that the LORD your God is giving you this good land to possess, for you are a stiff-necked people.[h]

The Golden Calf

7 Remember this and never forget how you aroused the anger of the LORD your God in the wilderness. From the day you left Egypt until you arrived here, you have been rebellious against the LORD. 8 At Horeb you aroused the LORD's wrath so that he was angry enough to destroy you.[i] 9 When I went up on the mountain to receive the tablets of stone, the tablets of the covenant that the LORD had made with you, I stayed on the mountain forty days and forty nights; I ate no bread and drank no water.[j] 10 The LORD gave me two stone tablets inscribed by the finger of God.[k] On them were all the commandments the LORD proclaimed to you on the mountain out of the fire, on the day of the assembly.

11 At the end of the forty days and forty nights, the LORD gave me the two stone tablets, the tablets of the covenant. 12 Then the LORD told me, "Go down from here at once, because your people whom you brought out of Egypt have become corrupt.[l] They have turned away quickly[m] from what I commanded them and have made an idol for themselves."

13 And the LORD said to me, "I have seen this people[n], and they are a stiff-necked people indeed! 14 Let me alone,[o] so that I may destroy them and blot out[p] their name from under heaven. And I will make you into a nation stronger and more numerous than they."

15 So I turned and went down from the mountain while it was ablaze with fire. And the two tablets of the covenant were in my hands.[q] 16 When I looked, I saw that you had sinned against the LORD your God; you had made for yourselves an idol cast in the shape of a calf.[r] You had turned aside quickly from the way that the LORD had commanded you. 17 So I took the two tablets and threw them out of my hands, breaking them to pieces before your eyes.

18 Then once again I fell[s] prostrate before the LORD for forty days and forty nights; I ate no bread and drank no water, because of all the sin you had committed, doing what was evil in the LORD's sight and so arousing his anger. 19 I feared the anger and wrath of the LORD, for he was angry enough with you to destroy you.[t] But again the LORD listened to me.[u] 20 And the LORD was angry enough with Aaron to destroy him, but at that time I prayed for Aaron too. 21 Also I took that sinful thing of yours, the calf you had made, and burned it in the fire. Then I crushed it and ground it to powder as fine as dust and threw the dust into a stream that flowed down the mountain.[v]

22 You also made the LORD angry at Taberah,[w] at Massah[x] and at Kibroth Hattaavah.[y]

23 And when the LORD sent you out from Kadesh Barnea, he said, "Go up and take possession of the land I have given you." But you rebelled against the command of the LORD your God. You did not trust[z] him or obey him. 24 You have been rebellious against the LORD ever since I have known you.[a]

25 I lay prostrate before the LORD those forty days and forty nights because the LORD had said he would destroy you.[b] 26 I

9:1 [x] Dt 4:38; 11:23,31 [y] Dt 1:28
9:2 [z] Nu 13:22, 28,32-33
9:3 [a] Dt 31:3; Jos 3:11 [b] Dt 4:24; Heb 12:29 [c] Ex 23:31; Dt 7:23-24
9:4 [d] Dt 8:17 [e] Lev 18:21,24-30; Dt 18:9-14
9:5 [f] Titus 3:5 [g] Ge 12:7; 13:15; 15:7; 17:8; 26:4
9:6 [h] ver 13; Ex 32:9; Dt 31:27
9:8 [i] Ex 32:7-10; Ps 106:19
9:9 [j] Ex 24:12, 15, 18; 34:28
9:10 [k] Ex 31:18; Dt 4:13
9:12 [l] Ex 32:7-8; Dt 31:29 [m] Jdg 2:17
9:13 [n] ver 6; Ex 32:9; Dt 10:16
9:14 [o] Ex 32:10 [p] Nu 14:12; Dt 29:20
9:15 [q] Ex 19:18; 32:15
9:16 [r] Ex 32:19
9:18 [s] Ex 34:28
9:19 [t] Ex 32:10-11, 14 [u] Dt 10:10
9:21 [v] Ex 32:20
9:22 [w] Nu 11:3 [x] Ex 17:7 [y] Nu 11:34
9:23 [z] Ps 106:24
9:24 [a] ver 7; Dt 31:27
9:25 [b] ver 18

9:10 *inscribed by the finger of God.* This bold anthropomorphism is an example of synecdoche, which uses a part of something to stand for the whole. God was the author of the "ten words" (see note on Ex 34:28). This metaphor suggests that divine presence and power wrote the ten words. Most likely each tablet contained a full copy of the ten words. *finger of God.* See note on Ex 8:19. In Egyptian mythology the finger of the Egyptian god Seth had been used to damage the "Eye of Horus." Until it was removed, Horus's eye would not heal. The phrase "finger(s) of the god(s)" is also found in Mesopotamian texts. In two Babylonian texts the outstretched finger of the ritualist while sealing an oath is a sign, in that context, of danger or threat from the god.

prayed to the LORD and said, "Sovereign LORD, do not destroy your people, your own inheritance that you redeemed by your great power and brought out of Egypt with a mighty hand.[c] 27 Remember your servants Abraham, Isaac and Jacob. Overlook the stubbornness of this people, their wickedness and their sin. 28 Otherwise, the country from which you brought us will say, 'Because the LORD was not able to take them into the land he had promised them, and because he hated them, he brought them out to put them to death in the wilderness.'[d] 29 But they are your people, your inheritance[e] that you brought out by your great power and your outstretched arm.[f]"

Tablets Like the First Ones

10 At that time the LORD said to me, "Chisel out two stone tablets[g] like the first ones and come up to me on the mountain. Also make a wooden ark.[a] 2 I will write on the tablets the words that were on the first tablets, which you broke. Then you are to put them in the ark."[h]

3 So I made the ark out of acacia wood[i] and chiseled[j] out two stone tablets like the first ones, and I went up on the mountain with the two tablets in my hands. 4 The LORD wrote on these tablets what he had written before, the Ten Commandments he had proclaimed[k] to you on the mountain, out of the fire, on the day of the assembly. And the LORD gave them to me. 5 Then I came back down the mountain[l] and put the tablets in the ark[m] I had made, as the LORD commanded me, and they are there now.[n]

6 (The Israelites traveled from the wells of Bene Jaakan to Moserah.[o] There Aaron died and was buried, and Eleazar his son succeeded him as priest.[p] 7 From there they traveled to Gudgodah and on to Jotbathah, a land with streams of water.[q] 8 At that time the LORD set apart the tribe of Levi[r] to carry the ark of the covenant of the LORD, to stand before the LORD to minister[s] and to pronounce blessings[t] in his name, as they still do today. 9 That is why the Levites have no share or inheritance among their fellow Israelites; the LORD is their inheritance,[u] as the LORD your God told them.)

10 Now I had stayed on the mountain forty days and forty nights, as I did the first time, and the LORD listened to me at this time also. It was not his will to destroy you.[v] 11 "Go," the LORD said to me, "and lead the people on their way, so that they may enter and possess the land I swore to their ancestors to give them."

Fear the LORD

12 And now, Israel, what does the LORD your God ask of you[w] but to fear the LORD your God, to walk in obedience to him, to love him,[x] to serve the LORD your God with all your heart[y] and with all your soul, 13 and to observe the LORD's commands and decrees that I am giving you today for your own good?

14 To the LORD your God belong the heavens, even the highest heavens,[z] the earth and everything in it.[a] 15 Yet the LORD set his affection on your ancestors and loved[b]

[a] *1* That is, a chest

9:26 [c] Ex 32:11 **9:28** [d] Ex 32:12; Nu 14:16 **9:29** [e] Dt 4:20; 1Ki 8:51 [f] Dt 4:34; Ne 1:10 **10:1** [g] Ex 25:10; 34:1-2 **10:2** [h] Ex 25:16, 21; Dt 4:13 **10:3** [i] Ex 25:5, 10; 37:1-9 [j] Ex 34:4 **10:4** [k] Ex 20:1 **10:5** [l] Ex 34:29 [m] Ex 40:20 [n] 1Ki 8:9 **10:6** [o] Nu 33:30-31,38 [p] Nu 20:25-28 **10:7** [q] Nu 33:32-34 **10:8** [r] Nu 3:6 [s] Dt 18:5 [t] Dt 21:5 **10:9** [u] Nu 18:20; Dt 18:1-2; Eze 44:28 **10:10** [v] Ex 33:17; 34:28; Dt 9:18-19,25 **10:12** [w] Mic 6:8 [x] Dt 5:33; 6:13; Mt 22:37 [y] Dt 6:5 **10:14** [z] 1Ki 8:27 [a] Ex 19:5 **10:15** [b] Dt 4:37

9:28 Gods in the ancient Near East were not omnipotent, and could fail to accomplish something they set out to do. In addition, they were not seen to be friendly, predictable, reliable or forthright. An example from Mesopotamia is the god Ea telling the human Adapa that he will die from eating bread that would have made him immortal. Mortuary texts in Egypt are targeted against hostile deities. The Sumerian city laments feature gods who decide that it is simply time for a city to be destroyed. The gods were not characterized by foresight and they did not work according to long-range plans. In all of these areas, Yahweh was distinct in his consistency and his ultimate goodness.

10:3 *ark.* The ark of the covenant law was a wooden chest carried by poles inserted into rings attached to the corners of the chest. Similar construction patterns have been uncovered in Egypt from the tomb of Tutankhamun (1336 – 1327 BC). All of the features of the ark (portable shrine, carrying poles, priestly care for it, winged creatures, gilded wood) were present in Egypt (1479 – 1069 BC). *acacia wood.* A primary wood in Egypt for various kinds of carpentry. It grew in the Sinai area and was fairly common in the thirteenth century BC. It was relatively light, but strong and hard, making it ideal for furniture. The compound wooden bow made of this material was in use then and was bound together by smaller pieces of wood and glue. The strong gates at Lachish were made of acacia wood. Sources of acacia today are only a fraction of what was available in antiquity.

10:6 – 7 Itineraries similar to this one are known from Mesopotamia (e.g., the annals of Tukulti-Ninurta II, 890 – 884 BC). In fact, such itineraries and geography are found throughout antiquity in the ancient Near East: Old Babylonian itineraries of the eighteenth century BC, Mari itineraries and Egyptian itineraries constituting the military directions for New Kingdom pharaohs (sixteenth – fifteenth centuries BC), with some toponymn lists coming from the Late Bronze Age. This itinerary and others in the OT (e.g., Ge 14; Nu 33) were part and parcel of the ancient Near Eastern world.

10:6 *Jaakan.* The location of the Jaakanites is not certain, but the name possibly relates it to the family of Akan (see Ge 36:27). *Moserah.* Its location is still uncertain; it is likely near to or the same as Mount Hor.

10:7 *Gudgodah ... Jotbathah.* Gudgodah is possibly Bir Taba, located on the west side of the Arabah and south of the Dead Sea. Jotbathah was in the same area as, but east of, Gudgodah. Both places were probably watering locations. The locations may have been, respectively, at Ain el-Gattar and Ain el-Weibah, on the east side of the Arabah about 20 miles (32 kilometers) south of the Dead Sea.

them, and he chose you, their descendants, above all the nations — as it is today. 16 Circumcise[c] your hearts, therefore,
and do not be stiff-necked[d] any longer.
17 For the LORD your God is God of gods[e]
and Lord of lords, the great God, mighty
and awesome, who shows no partiality[f]
and accepts no bribes. 18 He defends the
cause of the fatherless and the widow,[g]
and loves the foreigner residing among
you, giving them food and clothing. 19 And
you are to love those who are foreigners, for you yourselves were foreigners
in Egypt.[h] 20 Fear the LORD your God and
serve him.[i] Hold fast[j] to him and take your
oaths in his name.[k] 21 He is the one you
praise;[l] he is your God, who performed for
you those great and awesome wonders[m]
you saw with your own eyes. 22 Your ancestors who went down into Egypt were
seventy in all,[n] and now the LORD your
God has made you as numerous as the
stars in the sky.[o]

Love and Obey the LORD

11 Love[p] the LORD your God and keep
his requirements, his decrees, his
laws and his commands always.[q] 2 Remember today that your children were not the
ones who saw and experienced the discipline of the LORD your God:[r] his majesty,
his mighty hand, his outstretched arm;
3 the signs he performed and the things he
did in the heart of Egypt, both to Pharaoh
king of Egypt and to his whole country;
4 what he did to the Egyptian army, to its
horses and chariots, how he overwhelmed
them with the waters of the Red Sea[a][s] as
they were pursuing you, and how the LORD
brought lasting ruin on them. 5 It was not
your children who saw what he did for
you in the wilderness until you arrived at
this place, 6 and what he did[t] to Dathan
and Abiram, sons of Eliab the Reubenite,
when the earth opened its mouth right
in the middle of all Israel and swallowed
them up with their households, their tents
and every living thing that belonged to
them. 7 But it was your own eyes that saw
all these great things the LORD has done.

8 Observe therefore all the commands I
am giving you today, so that you may have
the strength to go in and take over the land
that you are crossing the Jordan to possess,[u] 9 and so that you may live long[v] in
the land the LORD swore[w] to your ancestors
to give to them and their descendants, a
land flowing with milk and honey.[x]

10:16 [c] Jer 4:4 [d] Dt 9:6 **10:17** [e] Jos 22:22; Da 2:47 [f] Ac 10:34; Ro 2:11; Eph 6:9 **10:18** [g] Ps 68:5 **10:19** [h] Lev 19:34 **10:20** [i] Mt 4:10 [j] Dt 11:22 [k] Ps 63:11 **10:21** [l] Ex 15:2; Jer 17:14 [m] Ps 106:21-22 **10:22** [n] Ge 46:26-27 [o] Ge 15:5; Dt 1:10 **11:1** [p] Dt 10:12 [q] Zec 3:7 **11:2** [r] Dt 5:24; 8:5 **11:4** [s] Ex 14:27 **11:6** [t] Nu 16:1-35 **11:8** [u] Jos 1:7 **11:9** [v] Dt 4:40; Pr 10:27 [w] Dt 9:5 [x] Ex 3:8

[a] 4 Or *the Sea of Reeds*

10:16 *Circumcise your hearts.* The metaphoric concept of the heart was and is central to Biblical anthropology, spirituality and theology (see notes on 6:5,6). The heart was the focus of moral fortitude and character development and was considered a gift of the gods; hence, it was metaphorically referred to as a "god." A circumcised heart responded, panting after the law of the Lord and his covenant. It trusted in the moral, ethical, religious and spiritual guidance of the covenant and the Torah. It communed within its chamber with the "law of the LORD" and his presence "day and night" (cf. Ps 1:2). *Circumcise.* See the article "Circumcision," p. 46. To circumcise one's heart in order to become a part of the Lord's covenant people was the internal equivalent of covenantal commitment to the Lord, observable by God, not a human being. Circumcised Israelites loved God from the inside out, and God sustained their trust in him.

10:17 *God of gods and Lord of lords, the great God, mighty and awesome.* This powerful language recalls the God of the exodus and urges the reader to make the connection (cf. vv. 20 – 21). Titles, especially royal titles, were popular in the ancient Near East. The title "Lord of kings" appears in a Philistine letter to Pharaoh and also is found as a title in Phoenician. The exact title "Lord of lords" is present in Assyrian texts, usually occurring before the late kings of Assyria. The "mighty and awesome" God is an epithet also at Ugarit (*mlk rb*). *accepts no bribes.* In ancient Near Eastern religion, gods could be manipulated because they had needs (see the article "Great Symbiosis," p. 186). By providing food, clothing and shelter for the god, an individual could win favor. Yahweh here makes it clear that he will not distort justice for personal gain.

10:18 *He defends the cause of the fatherless and the widow.* This language is a mainstay in the laws and the prologues/epilogues in the ancient Near East (e.g., the Code of Hammurapi; also those found at Ugarit in the Aqhat Legend). Lipit-Ishtar's prologue and epilogue (1934 – 1924 BC) imply this act of justice. The concern is expressed among the Hittite kings as well, as kings and gods gave special attention and protection to these groups of people. These ancient Near Eastern texts emphasize that, as socially vulnerable classes, widows and orphans must be protected with extra care. Using the terms "widow" and "fatherless" together may have been a way of designating disadvantaged classes in general. Groups other than true widows and orphans easily might have fallen into this category (see note on 15:7).

10:22 *seventy.* The number 70 has a rich use in the Bible and in the ancient Near East, primarily in the Northwest Semitic and Egyptian areas. The multiplication from 70 persons (literal) who migrated to Egypt into an unlimited host (metaphoric) describes Israel's amazing multiplication into an innumerable number. The number 70 also expresses totality. Panammuwa slew 70 of his brothers (all of them) to become king of Sam'al/Zinjirli. The number 70 also indicates potential (cf. Ex 1:1 – 7). Anatu slew an innumerable number of sacrificial animals for the god Baal in the Ugaritic Baal Cycle — 70 at a time. The 70 sons (divine) of Athirat are mentioned in texts at Ugarit. In Egyptian literature the phrase "seventy kings in seventy days" may refer to the 70 "creative forces" in Heliopolitan cosmology. The Lord was Israel's sole creative force, responsible for both creation and procreation.

11:4 *horses and chariots.* Chariots in the ancient Near East for millennia trumped cavalry. Until the Eighteenth or Nineteenth Dynasty (roughly the sixth to twelfth centuries BC), Egypt did not use cavalry except to serve the chariots in battle. In the time of Shalmaneser III (858 – 824 BC) and Tiglath-Pileser III (744 – 727 BC), cavalry began to play a greatly expanded role in warfare.

10 The land you are entering to take over is
not like the land of Egypt, from which you
have come, where you planted your seed
and irrigated it by foot as in a vegetable
garden. 11 But the land you are crossing the
Jordan to take possession of is a land of
mountains and valleys that drinks rain
from heaven.[y] 12 It is a land the LORD your
God cares for; the eyes[z] of the LORD your
God are continually on it from the beginning of the year to its end.
13 So if you faithfully obey[a] the commands I am giving you today — to love[b]
the LORD your God and to serve him with
all your heart and with all your soul —
14 then I will send rain[c] on your land in its
season, both autumn and spring rains,[d] so
that you may gather in your grain, new
wine and olive oil. 15 I will provide grass[e]
in the fields for your cattle, and you will
eat and be satisfied.[f]
16 Be careful, or you will be enticed to
turn away and worship other gods and
bow down to them.[g] 17 Then the LORD's
anger[h] will burn against you, and he will
shut up[i] the heavens so that it will not rain
and the ground will yield no produce, and
you will soon perish[j] from the good land
the LORD is giving you. 18 Fix these words
of mine in your hearts and minds; tie them
as symbols on your hands and bind them
on your foreheads.[k] 19 Teach them to your
children,[l] talking about them when you
sit at home and when you walk along the
road, when you lie down and when you
get up.[m] 20 Write them on the doorframes
of your houses and on your gates,[n] 21 so
that your days and the days of your children may be many[o] in the land the LORD
swore to give your ancestors, as many as
the days that the heavens are above the
earth.[p]
22 If you carefully observe[q] all these commands I am giving you to follow — to love
the LORD your God, to walk in obedience
to him and to hold fast[r] to him — 23 then
the LORD will drive out all these nations
before you, and you will dispossess nations larger and stronger than you.[s] 24 Every place where you set your foot will be
yours:[t] Your territory will extend from the
desert to Lebanon, and from the Euphrates
River to the Mediterranean Sea. 25 No one
will be able to stand against you. The LORD
your God, as he promised you, will put the
terror and fear of you on the whole land,
wherever you go.[u]
26 See, I am setting before you today a
blessing and a curse[v] — 27 the blessing[w]
if you obey the commands of the LORD
your God that I am giving you today; 28 the
curse if you disobey[x] the commands of the
LORD your God and turn from the way that
I command you today by following other
gods, which you have not known. 29 When
the LORD your God has brought you into
the land you are entering to possess, you
are to proclaim on Mount Gerizim the

11:11 [y] Dt 8:7
11:12 [z] 1Ki 9:3
11:13 [a] Dt 6:17 [b] Dt 10:12
11:14 [c] Lev 26:4; Dt 28:12 [d] Joel 2:23; Jas 5:7
11:15 [e] Ps 104:14 [f] Dt 6:11
11:16 [g] Dt 8:19; 29:18; Job 31:9, 27
11:17 [h] Dt 6:15 [i] 1Ki 8:35; 2Ch 6:26 [j] Dt 4:26
11:18 [k] Dt 6:6-8
11:19 [l] Dt 6:7 [m] Dt 4:9-10
11:20 [n] Dt 6:9
11:21 [o] Pr 3:2; 4:10 [p] Ps 72:5
11:22 [q] Dt 6:17 [r] Dt 10:20
11:23 [s] Dt 4:38; 9:1
11:24 [t] Ge 15:18; Ex 23:31; Jos 1:3; 14:9
11:25 [u] Ex 23:27; Dt 7:24
11:26 [v] Dt 30:1, 15, 19
11:27 [w] Dt 28:1-14
11:28 [x] Dt 28:15

11:10 *irrigated it by foot.* In Egypt, agriculture depended on irrigation systems of some kind. By contrast, the land of Canaan soaked up the rain and produced crops over a large area and in many settings. Small channels dug by one's foot watered the small ribbon of irrigated land in Egypt. Land not covered by the annual Nile flood had to be irrigated manually. Watering a plot of land was a constant chore in Egypt and is so depicted in the Egyptian Satire on the Trades. The gardener had to water the vegetables daily, or else they would fail: "In the morning he waters vegetables, the evening he spends with the herbs." In the fertile land of Canaan, rain sent by the Lord watered the land, a condition attested by writings of the Egyptian fugitive Sinuhe.

Some scholars detect a bit of mockery in the phrase "irrigated it by foot" by taking the Hebrew phrase as a euphemistic idiom referring to urination ("waters of the feet"). In this case, the reference is to the purity of the water. In any case, the potential multiple resources for water in Canaan exceeded those in Egypt.

11:13 – 17 *So if you faithfully obey ... then I will send rain ... Be careful, or you will be enticed to turn away ... Then the LORD's anger will burn.* In ancient Near Eastern treaties, the gods rewarded fealty to a treaty or covenant; failure to comply incurred the wrath of the gods who had been entreated to judge the participants of the document according to the oaths they had taken. Rain was absolutely necessary to the land of Canaan. The Lord would send both early and latter rains to prosper Israel's crops, if the Israelites carefully kept the covenant stipulations.

The visitation of pestilence and drought were signs of the displeasure of the god(s), as in the time of a devastating drought in the reign of the Hittite King Mursili in Hatti (c. 1330 – 1295 BC) and in Israel in the days of Elijah (c. 870 BC). In Canaan, Baal could be the source of devastations. The Egyptian god Seth could create drought conditions in Hatti. The anger of Pharaoh Rameses II could keep rain from the Hittites. Threats to shut down rain were among the curses in Hittite treaties.

11:24 *from the desert to Lebanon, and from the Euphrates River to the Mediterranean Sea.* Hittite and Assyrian treaties have descriptive approaches for their territories similar to those here. The Assyrian king Adadnirari boasted that his conquered territory stretched "as far as the Great Sea of the Rising Sun (and) from the banks of the Euphrates." The Euphrates River and Mount Lebanon were favorite ancient Near Eastern territorial markers.

11:26 – 28 Threats of blessings or curses were tied to covenant fealty in a prophetic utterance found at Mari. A theology of the heart was imbedded within its formal ancient Near Eastern covenant/treaty form. Likewise, Israel's faithfulness to her covenant God determined whether she received a curse or a blessing.

11:29 *Mount Gerizim ... Mount Ebal.* These mountains, situated on the main north-south road, and the valley between them form an east-west entrance into Canaan. The curses and blessings of the covenant could be recited antiphonally by the participants, positioned in the narrowest part of the valley, opposite each other (cf. 27:12 – 26).

The lower north slope of Mount Gerizim was excavated in 1968, uncovering a structure that served as a temple in the Middle Bronze Age (c. 1650 – 1540). This is earlier

blessings, and on Mount Ebal the curses.[y] 30As you know, these mountains are
across the Jordan, westward, toward the
setting sun, near the great trees of Moreh,[z] in the territory of those Canaanites
living in the Arabah in the vicinity of Gilgal.[a] 31You are about to cross the Jordan
to enter and take possession[b] of the land
the LORD your God is giving you. When
you have taken it over and are living there,
32be sure that you obey all the decrees and
laws I am setting before you today.

The One Place of Worship

12 These are the decrees and laws you
must be careful to follow in the
land that the LORD, the God of your ancestors, has given you to possess—as long as
you live in the land.[c] 2Destroy completely
all the places on the high mountains, on
the hills and under every spreading tree,[d]
where the nations you are dispossessing
worship their gods. 3Break down their altars, smash[e] their sacred stones and burn
their Asherah poles in the fire; cut down
the idols of their gods and wipe out their
names from those places.

4You must not worship the LORD your
God in their way. 5But you are to seek the
place the LORD your God will choose from
among all your tribes to put his Name
there for his dwelling.[f] To that place you
must go; 6there bring your burnt offerings
and sacrifices, your tithes[g] and special
gifts, what you have vowed to give and
your freewill offerings, and the firstborn
of your herds and flocks. 7There, in the
presence of the LORD your God, you and
your families shall eat and shall rejoice[h] in
everything you have put your hand to, because the LORD your God has blessed you.

8You are not to do as we do here today,
everyone doing as they see fit, 9since you
have not yet reached the resting place and
the inheritance the LORD your God is giving you. 10But you will cross the Jordan
and settle in the land the LORD your God is
giving[i] you as an inheritance, and he will
give you rest from all your enemies around
you so that you will live in safety. 11Then
to the place the LORD your God will choose
as a dwelling for his Name[j]—there you
are to bring everything I command you:
your burnt offerings and sacrifices, your
tithes and special gifts, and all the choice
possessions you have vowed to the LORD.
12And there rejoice[k] before the LORD your
God—you, your sons and daughters, your
male and female servants, and the Levites
from your towns who have no allotment
or inheritance[l] of their own. 13Be careful
not to sacrifice your burnt offerings anywhere you please. 14Offer them only at
the place the LORD will choose[m] in one of
your tribes, and there observe everything
I command you.

15Nevertheless, you may slaughter your
animals in any of your towns and eat as
much of the meat as you want, as if it were
gazelle or deer,[n] according to the blessing
the LORD your God gives you. Both the ceremonially unclean and the clean may eat
it. 16But you must not eat the blood;[o] pour
it out on the ground like water.[p] 17You
must not eat in your own towns the tithe
of your grain and new wine and olive oil,
or the firstborn of your herds and flocks,
or whatever you have vowed to give, or
your freewill offerings or special gifts. 18In-
stead, you are to eat[q] them in the presence
of the LORD your God at the place the LORD
your God will choose[r]—you, your sons
and daughters, your male and female servants, and the Levites from your towns—
and you are to rejoice[s] before the LORD
your God in everything you put your hand

11:29 [y] Dt 27:12-13; Jos 8:33
11:30 [z] Ge 12:6 [a] Jos 4:19
11:31 [b] Dt 9:1; Jos 1:11
12:1 [c] Dt 4:9-10; 1Ki 8:40
12:2 [d] 2Ki 16:4; 17:10
12:3 [e] Nu 33:52; Dt 7:5; Jdg 2:2
12:5 [f] ver 11, 13; 2Ch 7:12, 16
12:6 [g] Dt 14:22-23
12:7 [h] ver 12, 18; Lev 23:40; Dt 14:26
12:10 [i] Dt 11:31
12:11 [j] ver 5; Dt 15:20; 16:2
12:12 [k] ver 7 [l] Dt 10:9; 14:29
12:14 [m] ver 11
12:15 [n] ver 20-23; Dt 14:5; 15:22
12:16 [o] Ge 9:4; Lev 7:26; 17:10-12 [p] Dt 15:23
12:18 [q] Dt 14:23 [r] ver 5 [s] ver 7, 12

than Israel's settlement in the land but indicates that the mountain has a history of serving as sacred space. On Mount Ebal are ruins of a structure dating to the Iron Age (just after the Israelite settlement) that most scholars consider to be an altar. No evidence connects it to the Israelites.

12:2 *places on the high mountains, on the hills and under every spreading tree.* Mountains and hills were recognized as prime spots for worship and ritual in ancient Near Eastern texts. The phrase "hilltop" is linked with sites featuring leafy green trees. Trees and mountains were often believed to be endowed with a sacred aura in the ancient Near East, both in Israel (Ge 2:9; 3:22,24; Pr 3:18) and in other nations. Mount Hermon in Syria was considered a sacred mountain by many nations, and a mountain located near ancient Ugarit was the site of a shrine to Baal. In Hatti, the gods were thought to assemble under a hawthorn tree. A tree or group of trees could represent fertility goddesses. The "tree of life for the sunfolk" is mentioned in the Great Cairo Hymn of Praise to Amun-Re. The goddess Asherah was connected to a sacred tree or pole, a symbol of fertility and a place of worship.

Being in the supposed presence of a deity was an awe-inspiring experience (cf. Ex 3:5; 24:9–11), and the religious objects at these locations threatened Israel's faithfulness to the Lord (see Dt 7:5). Israel was not to worship like the prior inhabitants of the land at the high hills and green trees. Hence, the Israelites were to erase the names of foreign deities at all these locations by destroying all of their objects (v. 3).

12:5 *put his Name there.* The names of gods were attached to the places where they appeared or were connected to a given location, such as a shrine. As a result of this practice, God instructs Israel that he will put his name at those places that he chooses to be recognized and worshiped. The name of a deity in the ancient Near East defined in an essential way the character and nature and function of a deity. Hence, when a god's name was "placed" somewhere (e.g., Baal Peor), the god was there.

12:16 *not eat the blood.* See note on Lev 1:5.

to. 19Be careful not to neglect the Levites[t]
as long as you live in your land.
20When the LORD your God has enlarged
your territory[u] as he promised[v] you, and
you crave meat and say, "I would like some
meat," then you may eat as much of it as
you want. 21If the place where the LORD
your God chooses to put his Name is too
far away from you, you may slaughter animals from the herds and flocks the LORD
has given you, as I have commanded you,
and in your own towns you may eat as
much of them as you want. 22Eat them as
you would gazelle or deer.[w] Both the ceremonially unclean and the clean may eat.
23But be sure you do not eat the blood,[x]

12:19 [t]Dt 14:27 12:20 [u]Dt 19:8 [v]Ge 15:18; Dt 11:24 12:22 [w]ver 15 12:23 [x]ver 16; Ge 9:4; Lev 17:11,14

DEUTERONOMY 12:4

Ancient Near Eastern Worship

We now know a fair amount about the worship of the Canaanites, including their mythology and ritual practices. Without exception they were polytheistic, worshiping royal pantheons, and were much concerned with the care and sustenance of their gods (see the article "Great Symbiosis," p. 186). At Ugarit, on the northern edge of Canaan, there were temples, one for Baal and one for Dagan. The Baal temple is typical of the Middle Bronze Age in Syria and has typical features for that era. Most of the temple furniture has been unearthed as well. The palace chapel was a raised construction to which the many gods would "go up," and it was dedicated to Dagan and Baal. Altars of crafted masonry were found with steps leading up to them, in contrast to Israel's expected practice (see Ex 20:26).

There was a temple at Shechem as well (twelfth century BC). El, the high god in Canaan, was connected with the bull symbol and was considered the creator of the earth and the human race, as well as the progenitor of the gods, while Athirat was the progenitress. But Baal, who came to rival Yahweh in Israel, was the most popular god. He manifested himself in various places, and his name appeared in various locations, thus binding him to that location. His followers believed that he controlled rain, lightning and thunder.

The people at Ugarit worshiped Anat, goddess and consort of Baal. A yearly schedule of sacrifices was scheduled at the various temples, including "holocausts" (whole burnt offerings), peace/well-being offerings and libation offerings. Gods were believed to visit these temples during worship. Often the king had a part in the ceremonies, and a full temple staff functioned in Ugarit, offering sacrifices for various types of sin(s). Confession of sins occurred both at Ugarit and among Hittite kings, and the collective guilt of a people or community could be expressed. A Ugaritic "Day of Atonement" is described, and a day of purification for the king. Most Hebrew offerings are analogous to those in the cult at Ugarit and/or Egypt.

Bronze figurine possibly of Anat, Syria, early second millennium BC. The people at Ugarit worshiped Anat, goddess and consort of Baal.

Wikimedia Commons/Walters Art Museum, CC BY-SA 3.0

continued on next page

In temples at larger cities like Emar, Ebla and Hazor (thirteenth to twelfth centuries BC) seven-year cycles were observed. High priestesses formed part of the temple personnel, and a nine-day ritual from Emar recounts the installation of the high priestess of the storm-god and the removal of a previous high priestess. A seven-day feast was celebrated during this time.

Official religious prostitution is considered by some to have been a part of worship at Ugarit, but the evidence for it is not definitive, and most recent studies conclude that it was not practiced. Divination at Ugarit employed models of livers, as it did in many parts of Canaan. Omens were read when unusual births, deformed births or the unusual behavior of animals took place. This latter practice recalls similar practices in the Babylonian text *Shumma izbu* and many other Mesopotamian divination texts. Prayer for national safety and well-being was a common theme in all royal divination systems.

Farther south in Canaan, the remains of many well-preserved temples have been unearthed. At Lachish, a mud brick altar is located near a thirteenth-century BC temple, which was rebuilt twice by 1230 BC. Divine images were housed in niches in a rear wall, where gifts also could be deposited. Entire assemblages of the remains of offerings and ritual texts have been unearthed. Among the remains are various animal bones and bird bones. Incense was used in rituals. High places, however, are more scarcely attested.

There is no clear archaeological evidence for the practice of child sacrifice in Mesopotamia, Syria or Canaan, but the OT testifies to child sacrifice and high places among the Canaanites, and later classical authors mentioned child sacrifice among the Phoenicians. Divination, sacred prostitution, a cult of the dead, prayer and a kingly role in religion are all witnessed to, in part at least, by various texts and archaeological indicators. The shades of the dead (*rephaim*) were deified and even worshiped at Ugarit. Some scholars now believe that all uses of the term *rephaim* refer to the deified dead, often kings.

While much of this information about foreign ritual and religious practice helps us see the commonly shared aspects of Israel and her world, polytheism, mythology, nature worship, divination, divine kingship, omens, necromancy, ancestor worship and use of images, all stand in sharp contrast to the way Israel was to worship before her God. ◆

Baal Epic, the account of Baal's death and his victory over Mot.

because the blood is the life, and you must
not eat the life with the meat. 24 You must
not eat the blood; pour it out on the ground
like water. 25 Do not eat it, so that it may go
well[y] with you and your children after you,
because you will be doing what is right[z] in
the eyes of the LORD.
26 But take your consecrated things and

12:25 [y] Dt 4:40; Isa 3:10 [z] Ex 15:26; Dt 13:18; 1Ki 11:38
12:26 [a] ver 17; Nu 5:9-10
12:27 [b] Lev 1:5, 9, 13

whatever you have vowed to give,[a] and go
to the place the LORD will choose. 27 Present your burnt offerings[b] on the altar of
the LORD your God, both the meat and the
blood. The blood of your sacrifices must
be poured beside the altar of the LORD
your God, but you may eat the meat. 28 Be
careful to obey all these regulations I am

giving you, so that it may always go well[c]
with you and your children after you, because you will be doing what is good and
right in the eyes of the LORD your God.
29 The LORD your God will cut off[d] before you the nations you are about to invade and dispossess. But when you have
driven them out and settled in their land,
30 and after they have been destroyed before you, be careful not to be ensnared by
inquiring about their gods, saying, "How
do these nations serve their gods? We will
do the same." 31 You must not worship the
LORD your God in their way, because in
worshiping their gods, they do all kinds
of detestable things the LORD hates.[e] They
even burn their sons[f] and daughters in the
fire as sacrifices to their gods.
32 See that you do all I command you; do
not add[g] to it or take away from it.[a]

Worshiping Other Gods

13 [b] If a prophet,[h] or one who foretells
by dreams, appears among you
and announces to you a sign or wonder,
2 and if the sign or wonder spoken of takes
place, and the prophet says, "Let us follow
other gods"[i] (gods you have not known)
"and let us worship them," 3 you must
not listen to the words of that prophet or
dreamer. The LORD your God is testing[j] you
to find out whether you love him with all
your heart and with all your soul. 4 It is
the LORD your God you must follow,[k] and
him you must revere. Keep his commands
and obey him; serve him and hold fast[l] to
him. 5 That prophet or dreamer must be
put to death for inciting rebellion against
the LORD your God, who brought you out
of Egypt and redeemed you from the land
of slavery. That prophet or dreamer tried
to turn you from the way the LORD your
God commanded you to follow. You must
purge the evil[m] from among you.
6 If your very own brother, or your son
or daughter, or the wife you love, or your
closest friend secretly entices[n] you, saying,
"Let us go and worship other gods" (gods
that neither you nor your ancestors have
known, 7 gods of the peoples around you,
whether near or far, from one end of the
land to the other), 8 do not yield[o] to them
or listen to them. Show them no pity. Do
not spare them or shield them. 9 You must
certainly put them to death.[p] Your hand
must be the first in putting them to death,
and then the hands of all the people.
10 Stone them to death, because they tried
to turn you away from the LORD your God,
who brought you out of Egypt, out of the
land of slavery. 11 Then all Israel will hear
and be afraid,[q] and no one among you will
do such an evil thing again.
12 If you hear it said about one of the
towns the LORD your God is giving you to
live in 13 that troublemakers[r] have arisen
among you and have led the people of
their town astray, saying, "Let us go and
worship other gods" (gods you have not
known), 14 then you must inquire, probe
and investigate it thoroughly. And if it is
true and it has been proved that this detestable thing has been done among you,
15 you must certainly put to the sword all
who live in that town. You must destroy it
completely,[c] both its people and its livestock. 16 You are to gather all the plunder
of the town into the middle of the public

12:28 [c] ver 25; Dt 4:40 **12:29** [d] Jos 23:4 **12:31** [e] Dt 9:5 [f] Dt 18:10; Jer 32:35 **12:32** [g] Dt 4:2; Jos 1:7; Rev 22:18-19 **13:1** [h] Mt 24:24; Mk 13:22; 2Th 2:9 **13:2** [i] ver 6, 13 **13:3** [j] Dt 8:2, 16 **13:4** [k] 2Ki 23:3; 2Ch 34:31 [l] Dt 10:20 **13:5** [m] Dt 17:7, 12; 1Co 5:13 **13:6** [n] Dt 17:2-7; 29:18 **13:8** [o] Pr 1:10 **13:9** [p] Dt 17:5, 7 **13:11** [q] Dt 19:20 **13:13** [r] ver 2, 6; 1Jn 2:19

[a] *32* In Hebrew texts this verse (12:32) is numbered 13:1. [b] In Hebrew texts 13:1-18 is numbered 13:2-19. [c] *15* The Hebrew term refers to the irrevocable giving over of things or persons to the LORD, often by totally destroying them.

12:31 *They … burn their sons and daughters in the fire as sacrifices to their gods.* Human sacrifice in the ancient Near East took various forms. In Mesopotamia, it was common to ritually kill the attendants to important people, as well as to place human sacrifices in the foundations of new buildings. In Syria and Canaan, expiatory sacrifices took place in times of crisis, as did propitiatory sacrifices on special occasions. There is good reason to believe that religious child sacrifice was practiced in Mesopotamia, but absolute proof is lacking. Human sacrifice in late texts at Carthage (Punic) is more likely but still not certain.

Alternatively, the evidence for cremation and strong involvement in rituals for the dead has been proven in Syria, Canaan and Mesopotamia, and this may be what is being condemned here.

13:1 – 18 This chapter treats the problem of disloyalty to Yahweh. Dreams (v. 1) were a means of obtaining knowledge/wisdom from the gods across the ancient Near East and were also recognized channels of revelation in Israel. However, no dream could supersede the covenantal laws given by the Lord at Sinai. Immorality and unfaithfulness to divine precepts were condemned by all wise men outside or inside Israel. See the article "Balaam," p. 268, and the article "Prophets and Prophecy," p. 1110.

13:10 *Stone them to death.* Execution by stoning is prescribed in the Hadad Inscription to deal with a possible assassin or murderer, whether male or female. Hittite, Aramaic and Assyrian treaties deal openly and gravely with sedition and rebellion.

Esarhaddon's succession treaty deals with the possibility of disloyalty to himself or his son Ashurbanipal. Disloyalty is treated severely by immediate and summary execution of a disloyal subject or anyone in the royal house when the king's life is endangered by such an act. In this case even the relatives of a rebel were to be executed. This conclusion is further supported by the stipulations in the Zakatu Treaty. Hence, execution of a false prophet who foments disloyalty toward the Lord falls into place in its ancient Near Eastern setting.

13:16 *gather all the plunder of the town into the middle of the public square and completely burn the town.* This constitutes a typical ancient Near Eastern covenantal curse/threat. A city was burned so that it would not be rebuilt from the same materials. Ruin reflects the Hebrew word *tel* (Arabic *tell*), meaning a heap, ruin. This ultimate curse could befall a city — to become a ruin instead of a place

square and completely burn the town and all its plunder as a whole burnt offering to the LORD your God.[s] That town is to remain a ruin[t] forever, never to be rebuilt, 17and none of the condemned things[a] are to be found in your hands. Then the LORD will turn from his fierce anger,[u] will show you mercy, and will have compassion[v] on you. He will increase your numbers,[w] as he promised[x] on oath to your ancestors—18because you obey the LORD your God by keeping all his commands that I am giving you today and doing what is right[y] in his eyes.

Clean and Unclean Food

14:3-20pp — Lev 11:1-23

14 You are the children[z] of the LORD your God. Do not cut yourselves or shave the front of your heads for the dead, 2for you are a people holy to the LORD your God.[a] Out of all the peoples on the face of the earth, the LORD has chosen you to be his treasured possession.[b]

3Do not eat any detestable thing.[c] 4These are the animals you may eat:[d] the ox, the sheep, the goat, 5the deer, the gazelle, the roe deer, the wild goat, the ibex, the antelope and the mountain sheep.[b] 6You may eat any animal that has a divided hoof and that chews the cud. 7However, of those that chew the cud or that have a divided hoof you may not eat the camel, the rabbit or the hyrax. Although they chew the cud, they do not have a divided hoof; they are ceremonially unclean for you. 8The pig is also unclean; although it has a divided hoof, it does not chew the cud. You are not to eat their meat or touch their carcasses.[e]

9Of all the creatures living in the water, you may eat any that has fins and scales. 10But anything that does not have fins and scales you may not eat; for you it is unclean.

11You may eat any clean bird. 12But these you may not eat: the eagle, the vulture, the black vulture, 13the red kite, the black kite, any kind of falcon, 14any kind of raven, 15the horned owl, the screech owl, the gull, any kind of hawk, 16the little owl, the great owl, the white owl, 17the desert owl, the osprey, the cormorant, 18the stork, any kind of heron, the hoopoe and the bat.

19All flying insects are unclean to you; do not eat them. 20But any winged creature that is clean you may eat.

21Do not eat anything you find already dead.[f] You may give it to the foreigner residing in any of your towns, and they may eat it, or you may sell it to any other foreigner. But you are a people holy to the LORD your God.[g]

Do not cook a young goat in its mother's milk.[h]

Tithes

22Be sure to set aside a tenth[i] of all that your fields produce each year. 23Eat the tithe of your grain, new wine and olive oil, and the firstborn of your herds and flocks in the presence of the LORD your God at the place he will choose as a dwelling for his Name,[j] so that you may learn[k] to revere the LORD your God always. 24But if that place is too distant and you have been blessed by the LORD your God and cannot carry your tithe (because the place where the LORD will choose to put his Name is

13:16 [s]Jos 6:24 [t]Jos 8:28; Jer 49:2 **13:17** [u]Nu 25:4 [v]Dt 30:3 [w]Dt 7:13 [x]Ge 22:17; 26:4, 24; 28:14 **13:18** [y]Dt 12:25, 28 **14:1** [z]Lev 19:28; 21:5; Jer 16:6; 41:5; Ro 8:14; 9:8; Gal 3:26 **14:2** [a]Lev 20:26 [b]Dt 7:6; 26:18-19 **14:3** [c]Eze 4:14 **14:4** [d]Lev 11:2-45; Ac 10:14 **14:8** [e]Lev 11:26-27 **14:21** [f]Lev 17:15; 22:8 [g]ver 2 [h]Ex 23:19; 34:26 **14:22** [i]Lev 27:30; Dt 12:6, 17; Ne 10:37 **14:23** [j]Dt 12:5 [k]Dt 4:10

[a] *17* The Hebrew term refers to the irrevocable giving over of things or persons to the LORD, often by totally destroying them. [b] *5* The precise identification of some of the birds and animals in this chapter is uncertain.

of joyful habitation. The ancient city of Ur (c. 2000 BC) was laid waste and became a ruin by an act of the gods toward it. The Sefire Treaty inscription (c. 750 BC) between Bargahdah and Matihdel records curses against Matihdel, king of Arpad, if he breaks the covenant, including: "And may Arpad become a mound [ruin] to [house the desert animal] ... May [this] city not be mentioned."

Through time, these ruins became hills or huge mounds of successive layers of debris from the destruction of cities and villages across the centuries and millennia. In this case the city was to remain so permanently. The threat of a flood could likewise turn a city and its land into an uninhabitable ruin. The treaty of Ushshur-Nerari II with the Hittite king records a threat against the Hittites if they are disloyal: "Then may Assur, father of the gods, who grants kingship, turn your land into a battlefield, your people to devastation, your cities into mounds, and your houses into ruins." In the Baal Myth at Ugarit, "two ruin-mounds" (mountains) seem to set off the land of the dead from the land of the living, thus making a plausible parallel between those mythological constructs and historical cities that lay dead in ruins.

14:1 *Do not cut yourselves or shave the front of your heads for the dead.* See note on Lev 19:28.

14:8 *The pig is ... unclean.* See note on Lev 11:7.

14:21 *Do not eat anything you find already dead.* Letting good meat go to waste would have been unthinkable in a protein-starved area such as Israel. However, Israelites were not permitted to eat it, because it contained blood. Nevertheless, they were allowed to distribute it to resident aliens or sell it to foreigners. *in its mother's milk.* Early Jewish rabbis extrapolated from this law the custom—still current among observant practitioners of traditional Judaism—of not combining in one meal milk or milk byproducts together with any form of meat (represented by the "kid"). The actual meaning of this prohibition remains speculative. One of the more popular notions in the mid-twentieth century was that this command was directed at a particular religious practice of nearby polytheistic societies. It is also possible that the prohibition may involve a nursing animal (which may have mother's milk in its stomach), or the possibility that the milk might contain blood and would thus contaminate the meat.

so far away), 25then exchange your tithe for silver, and take the silver with you and go to the place the LORD your God will choose. 26Use the silver to buy whatever you like: cattle, sheep, wine or other fermented drink, or anything you wish. Then you and your household shall eat there in the presence of the LORD your God and rejoice.[l] 27And do not neglect the Levites[m] living in your towns, for they have no allotment or inheritance of their own.[n]

28At the end of every three years, bring all the tithes of that year's produce and store it in your towns,[o] 29so that the Levites (who have no allotment[p] or inheritance of their own) and the foreigners,[q] the fatherless and the widows who live in your towns may come and eat and be satisfied, and so that the LORD your God may bless[r] you in all the work of your hands.

The Year for Canceling Debts

15:1-11Ref — Lev 25:8-38

15 At the end of every seven years you must cancel debts.[s] 2This is how it is to be done: Every creditor shall cancel any loan they have made to a fellow Israelite. They shall not require payment from anyone among their own people, because the LORD's time for canceling debts has been proclaimed. 3You may require payment from a foreigner,[t] but you must cancel any debt your fellow Israelite owes you. 4However, there need be no poor people among you, for in the land the LORD your God is giving you to possess as your inheritance, he will richly bless[u] you, 5if only you fully obey the LORD your God and are careful to follow[v] all these commands I am giving you today. 6For the LORD your God will bless you as he has promised, and you will lend to many nations but will borrow from none. You will rule over many nations but none will rule over you.[w]

7If anyone is poor among your fellow Israelites in any of the towns of the land the LORD your God is giving you, do not be hardhearted or tightfisted[x] toward them. 8Rather, be openhanded[y] and freely lend them whatever they need. 9Be careful not to harbor this wicked thought: "The seventh year, the year for canceling debts,[z] is near," so that you do not show ill will[a] toward the needy among your fellow Israelites and give them nothing. They may then appeal to the LORD against you, and you will be found guilty of sin.[b] 10Give generously to them and do so without a grudging heart;[c] then because of this the LORD your God will bless[d] you in all your work and in everything you put your hand to. 11There will always be poor people in the land. Therefore I command you to be openhanded toward your fellow Israelites who are poor and needy in your land.[e]

Freeing Servants

15:12-18pp — Ex 21:2-6
15:12-18Ref — Lev 25:38-55

12If any of your people — Hebrew men or women — sell themselves to you and serve you six years, in the seventh year you must let them go free.[f] 13And when you release them, do not send them away empty-handed. 14Supply them liberally from your flock, your threshing floor and your winepress. Give to them as the LORD

14:26 [l] Dt 12:7-8 **14:27** [m] Dt 12:19 [n] Nu 18:20 **14:28** [o] Dt 26:12 **14:29** [p] ver 27 [q] Dt 26:12 [r] Dt 15:10; Mal 3:10 **15:1** [s] Dt 31:10 **15:3** [t] Dt 23:20 **15:4** [u] Dt 28:8 **15:5** [v] Dt 28:1 **15:6** [w] Dt 28:12-13,44 **15:7** [x] 1Jn 3:17 **15:8** [y] Mt 5:42; Lk 6:34 **15:9** [z] ver 1 [a] Mt 20:15 [b] Dt 24:15 **15:10** [c] 2Co 9:5 [d] Dt 14:29; 24:19 **15:11** [e] Mt 26:11; Mk 14:7; Jn 12:8 **15:12** [f] Ex 21:2; Lev 25:39; Jer 34:14

15:1 *every seven years ... cancel debts.* A cycle of seven years also occurs in the Ugaritic calendar, but the similarity likely only reflects literary convention. The Ugaritic cycle was tied to the agricultural year and agricultural prosperity, not to debt release, though debt release regulation was practically ubiquitous in the ancient Near East. Decrees releasing debts were promulgated by kings in many locations: Aleppo, Alalakh, Emar, Babylon and Assyria.

In the Old Babylonian period, e.g. (which had Sumerian antecedents), edicts issued by the kings canceled debts, released some hostages or slaves, and helped the oppressed and impoverished persons in Babylonian society. Land reverted to its original owners. The most outstanding example is the one issued by Ammisaduqa, the tenth king in the Dynasty of Hammurapi (c. 1646–1626 BC). These edicts were issued at fairly regular intervals at the word of a particular king. Some scholars argue that Israelites adapted this policy as the Sabbatical Year (vv. 1–4; Lev 25) for the covenantal community of Yahweh. However, there is more contrast between the relevant texts than comparison with Israel's weekly Sabbath, Sabbatical Year and Year of Jubilee (see next note).

15:7 *If anyone is poor among your fellow Israelites.* The homeless, powerless or disadvantaged in the ancient Near East were ideally defended and supported in various ways by righteous kings (see note on 10:18). In the Sumerian Nanshe Hymn, the goddess Nanshe is lifted up as a goddess who cares for and "knows" the widow, the poor, the orphan (Nanshe is a mother of the orphan), the oppressed debtor and the weak.

Justice and righteousness for these persons was the special task of the king. Concern for the poor, along with the alien and the widow, is emphasized in the prologues and/or epilogues of the collected legal sayings from Mesopotamia (e.g., Hammurapi, Ur-Nammu, Lipit-Ishtar of Isin). Hammurapi cared for the poor, as did the Babylonian kings Uruinimgina and Ur-Nammu in the third millennium BC. Sinuhe, an Egyptian having returned home from a journey through Canaan, exalts the pharaoh, saying, "You deliver the poor from harm." Canaanite documents from Ugarit and Egyptian tomb inscriptions prescribe special care and concern for these persons.

15:12 *Hebrew.* A social, rather than ethnic designation; it refers to one who does not own land (see note on Ge 14:13). The individual in mind here is an Israelite, but one who has become destitute or returned from foreign lands. Non-Israelite slaves had no right of release. *sell themselves to you.* See note on Lev 25:39.

your God has blessed you. 15 Remember
that you were slaves[g] in Egypt and the
LORD your God redeemed you.[h] That is
why I give you this command today.
16 But if your servant says to you, "I
do not want to leave you," because he
loves you and your family and is well off
with you, 17 then take an awl and push it
through his earlobe into the door, and he
will become your servant for life. Do the
same for your female servant.
18 Do not consider it a hardship to set
your servant free, because their service to
you these six years has been worth twice
as much as that of a hired hand. And the
LORD your God will bless you in everything
you do.

The Firstborn Animals

19 Set apart for the LORD your God every firstborn male[i] of your herds and
flocks. Do not put the firstborn of your
cows to work, and do not shear the firstborn of your sheep. 20 Each year you and
your family are to eat them in the presence of the LORD your God at the place
he will choose.[j] 21 If an animal has a defect, is lame or blind, or has any serious
flaw, you must not sacrifice it to the LORD
your God.[k] 22 You are to eat it in your own
towns. Both the ceremonially unclean and
the clean may eat it, as if it were gazelle
or deer.[l] 23 But you must not eat the blood;
pour it out on the ground like water.[m]

The Passover

16:1-8pp — Ex 12:14-20; Lev 23:4-8; Nu 28:16-25

16 Observe the month of Aviv[n] and
celebrate the Passover of the LORD
your God, because in the month of Aviv he
brought you out of Egypt by night. 2 Sacrifice as the Passover to the LORD your God
an animal from your flock or herd at the
place the LORD will choose as a dwelling
for his Name.[o] 3 Do not eat it with bread
made with yeast, but for seven days eat
unleavened bread, the bread of affliction,[p]
because you left Egypt in haste[q] — so that
all the days of your life you may remember the time of your departure from Egypt.[r]
4 Let no yeast be found in your possession
in all your land for seven days. Do not let
any of the meat you sacrifice on the evening of the first day remain until morning.[s]
5 You must not sacrifice the Passover in
any town the LORD your God gives you 6 except in the place he will choose as a dwelling for his Name. There you must sacrifice
the Passover in the evening, when the sun
goes down, on the anniversary[a][t] of your
departure from Egypt. 7 Roast[u] it and eat it
at the place the LORD your God will choose.
Then in the morning return to your tents.
8 For six days eat unleavened bread and on
the seventh day hold an assembly[v] to the
LORD your God and do no work.

The Festival of Weeks

16:9-12pp — Lev 23:15-22; Nu 28:26-31

9 Count off seven weeks[w] from the time
you begin to put the sickle to the standing grain.[x] 10 Then celebrate the Festival of
Weeks to the LORD your God by giving a
freewill offering in proportion to the blessings the LORD your God has given you.
11 And rejoice[y] before the LORD your God
at the place he will choose as a dwelling
for his Name — you, your sons and daughters, your male and female servants, the
Levites[z] in your towns, and the foreigners, the fatherless and the widows living

15:15 [g] Dt 5:15 [h] Dt 16:12 **15:19** [i] Ex 13:2 **15:20** [j] Dt 12:5-7, 17, 18; 14:23 **15:21** [k] Lev 22:19-25 **15:22** [l] Dt 12:15, 22 **15:23** [m] Dt 12:16 **16:1** [n] Ex 12:2; 13:4

16:2 [o] Dt 12:5, 26 **16:3** [p] Ex 12:8, 39; 34:18 [q] Ex 12:11, 15, 19 [r] Ex 13:3, 6-7 **16:4** [s] Ex 12:10; 34:25 **16:6** [t] Ex 12:6; Dt 12:5 **16:7** [u] Ex 12:8; 2Ch 35:13 **16:8** [v] Ex 12:16; 13:6; Lev 23:8 **16:9** [w] Ex 34:22; Lev 23:15 [x] Ex 23:16; Nu 28:26 **16:11** [y] Dt 12:7 [z] Dt 12:12

[a] 6 Or *down, at the time of day*

15:17 *take an awl and push it through his earlobe into the door.* An Akkadian parallel indicates that piercing the ear of a slave in Israel may have indicated a declaration of ownership of the slave in a public and permanent manner. The Akkadian ritual called for a "parallel" activity in which a peg was driven into the mouth of a small statue of the slave. This act symbolized the slave's becoming the property of his new owner.

The Code of Hammurapi (sections 280; 282) mentions the slave who has disavowed his master by declaring, "You are not my master." The master could bring charges and proofs against such a "rebellious" slave to prove that he was his slave. If the master successfully established his claim over the slave, he could cut off the slave's ear, and the person became an *unwilling* slave for the rest of his life.

In Israel, the slave who desired to pledge perpetual love/obedience to his master, because he loved his master (or, more likely, because he wanted to preserve a family he established while in servitude; cf. Ex 21:5 – 6) is highlighted. The master happily "adopts" him forever. The mark on the Israelite's ear was a sign of mutually desired ownership, a slave-master relationship forever.

15:18 This law concerns native Israelites and recognizes their superiority as God's chosen people, contrasting the service received with that of a mere "hired hand." The Code of Hammurapi treats native slaves, male or female, with respect to their native owners, more than for the slaves themselves and their well-being. A slave purchased in a foreign land by someone could be redeemed without cost to their former master(s), if the masters were both natives of the same country. The Biblical text rather says a word on behalf of the native Israelite slave.

16:1 *month of Aviv.* The OT contains certain month names that the Israelites shared with or borrowed from their Canaanite neighbors. Four are used as such: Aviv, the first month; Ziv, the second month; Ethanim, the seventh month; Bul, the eighth month. Aviv and Ziv have been found in Canaanite or Phoenician sources. In later centuries Israel borrowed Babylonian calendar names: Nisan (1), Sivan (3), Elul (6), Kislev (9), Tebet (10), Shebat (11), Adar (12). The Babylonian Nisannu is equivalent to Hebrew Nisan, which was equal to the older Canaanite Aviv, for the first month.

among you. 12 Remember that you were
slaves in Egypt,[a] and follow carefully these
decrees.

The Festival of Tabernacles

16:13-17pp — Lev 23:33-43; Nu 29:12-39

13 Celebrate the Festival of Tabernacles
for seven days after you have gathered the
produce of your threshing floor[b] and your
winepress.[c] 14 Be joyful[d] at your festival—
you, your sons and daughters, your male
and female servants, and the Levites, the
foreigners, the fatherless and the widows
who live in your towns. 15 For seven days
celebrate the festival to the LORD your God
at the place the LORD will choose. For the
LORD your God will bless you in all your
harvest and in all the work of your hands,
and your joy[e] will be complete.
16 Three times a year all your men must
appear before the LORD your God at the
place he will choose: at the Festival of Unleavened Bread, the Festival of Weeks and
the Festival of Tabernacles.[f] No one should
appear before the LORD empty-handed:[g]
17 Each of you must bring a gift in proportion to the way the LORD your God has
blessed you.

Judges

18 Appoint judges[h] and officials for each
of your tribes in every town the LORD your
God is giving you, and they shall judge
the people fairly. 19 Do not pervert justice[i]
or show partiality.[j] Do not accept a bribe,[k]
for a bribe blinds the eyes of the wise and
twists the words of the innocent. 20 Follow
justice and justice alone, so that you may
live and possess the land the LORD your
God is giving you.

Worshiping Other Gods

21 Do not set up any wooden Asherah
pole[l] beside the altar you build to the LORD
your God,[m] 22 and do not erect a sacred
stone,[n] for these the LORD your God hates.

17 Do not sacrifice to the LORD your
God an ox or a sheep that has any
defect[o] or flaw in it, for that would be detestable to him.[p]
2 If a man or woman living among you
in one of the towns the LORD gives you is
found doing evil in the eyes of the LORD
your God in violation of his covenant,[q]
3 and contrary to my command[r] has worshiped other gods, bowing down to them
or to the sun[s] or the moon or the stars
in the sky, 4 and this has been brought to
your attention, then you must investigate
it thoroughly. If it is true and it has been
proved that this detestable thing has been
done in Israel,[t] 5 take the man or woman
who has done this evil deed to your city
gate and stone that person to death.[u] 6 On
the testimony of two or three witnesses a
person is to be put to death, but no one is
to be put to death on the testimony of only
one witness.[v] 7 The hands of the witnesses

16:12 [a] Dt 15:15 **16:13** [b] Lev 23:34 [c] Ex 23:16 **16:14** [d] ver 11 **16:15** [e] Lev 23:39 **16:16** [f] Ex 23:14, 16 [g] Ex 34:20 **16:18** [h] Dt 1:16 **16:19** [i] Ex 23:2, 8 [j] Lev 19:15; Dt 1:17 [k] Ecc 7:7 **16:21** [l] Dt 7:5 [m] Ex 34:13; 2Ki 17:16; 21:3; 2Ch 33:3 **16:22** [n] Lev 26:1 **17:1** [o] Mal 1:8, 13 [p] Dt 15:21 **17:2** [q] Dt 13:6-11 **17:3** [r] Jer 7:22-23 [s] Job 31:26 **17:4** [t] Dt 13:12-14 **17:5** [u] Lev 24:14 **17:6** [v] Nu 35:30; Dt 19:15; Jos 7:25; Mt 18:16; Jn 8:17; 2Co 13:1; 1Ti 5:19; Heb 10:28

16:19 *Do not pervert justice or show partiality.* In Mesopotamia, a major part of the king's mission was to establish justice and to liberate the oppressed—a high calling. Nevertheless, justice was elusive and almost inaccessible to the lower classes. The ideal of the king remained, even when only the upper classes benefited. Social reforms were put into place in Mesopotamia and Egypt to see that justice was rendered, especially with respect to the weak in society. In Mesopotamia, various legal collections and promulgations (Ur-Nammu, 2064–2046 BC; Lipit-Ishtar, 1875–1864 BC; Eshnunna, nineteenth century BC) were set forth to "establish justice" in the lands. Akkadian anthologies of jurisprudence were compiled by Hammurapi and Eshnunna. However, even in societies with three-tiered structures of persons these efforts tended to protect the less powerful and help the poor and others who were less fortunate.

This socio-theological activity was meant to enable the kings' servants to serve the gods properly. The kings could issue special proclamations of mercy as needed. In Egypt the king, or pharaoh, likewise maintained *maat*—order and justice. The vizier, the second-in-command, and his secretary were to see that uprightness was carried out. This theme is carried through into the New Kingdom and beyond (1570–1070 BC). Even during the chaotic intermediate periods the attempt to preserve justice was important. Pharaoh Khety says, "[I did] what people love and gods praise: I gave bread to the hungry, clothes to the naked; I listened to the plea of the widow, I gave a home to the orphan." In Canaan, the righteous legendary character Danel of Ugarit was described as pursuing justice for all.

17:1 *defect or flaw.* Neither the Proto-Sinaitic inscriptions nor sacrificial instructions at Ugarit describe conditions of a sacrificial animal. Certain texts may imply a strong concern for a high quality of sacrificial animals, unblemished, in religious rituals. Gudea, a king of ancient Lagash (c. 2094–2047 BC), while praising his god Ningirsu, was careful to present only a perfect ox and a perfect he-goat. A Mesopotamian text depicts Anu of Uruk offering "fine, fattened, ritually pure sheep that had eaten barley for two years." The purity of animals is praised in an imagined world by an Akkadian diviner. Hittite "Instructions to Priests and Temple Officials" likewise insists on a pure animal for sacrifice.

17:5 *city gate.* Where disputes and legal trials were handled by the elders of a village or city (cf. 21:19). The righteous Danel, a character in Ugaritic epic literature, processed justice and carried out judgment at the city gate. The problems and issues of the town were discussed and justice meted out at the city gate(s), where the elders of that city congregated. Cuneiform documents from Babylonia indicate that these classes of society, as in Israel, dealt with the administration of justice: the elders, the priests, and the king and his officials. See note on Ge 19:1.

17:6 *two or three witnesses.* Certain Middle Assyrian laws possibly required a minimum of two witnesses (sections A 12, 17, 40), but this is not certain. The law has a plural form for witnesses and does not limit them explicitly to two,

must be the first in putting that person to
death, and then the hands of all the people. You must purge the evil[w] from among
you.

Law Courts

8 If cases come before your courts that
are too difficult for you to judge—whether bloodshed, lawsuits or assaults[x]—take
them to the place the LORD your God will
choose.[y] 9 Go to the Levitical priests and
to the judge who is in office at that time.
Inquire of them and they will give you the
verdict.[z] 10 You must act according to the
decisions they give you at the place the
LORD will choose. Be careful to do everything they instruct you to do. 11 Act according to whatever they teach you and the
decisions they give you. Do not turn aside
from what they tell you, to the right or to
the left.[a] 12 Anyone who shows contempt[b]
for the judge or for the priest who stands
ministering there to the LORD your God is
to be put to death. You must purge the evil
from Israel. 13 All the people will hear and
be afraid, and will not be contemptuous
again.[c]

The King

14 When you enter the land the LORD
your God is giving you and have taken
possession of it and settled in it, and you
say, "Let us set a king over us like all the
nations around us,"[d] 15 be sure to appoint
over you a king the LORD your God chooses. He must be from among your fellow
Israelites.[e] Do not place a foreigner over
you, one who is not an Israelite. 16 The

17:7 [w] Dt 13:5,9 **17:8** [x] 2Ch 19:10 [y] Dt 12:5; Hag 2:11 **17:9** [z] Dt 19:17; Eze 44:24 **17:11** [a] Dt 25:1 **17:12** [b] Nu 15:30 **17:13** [c] Dt 13:11; 19:20 **17:14** [d] Dt 11:31; 1Sa 8:5, 19-20 **17:15** [e] Jer 30:21

and this seems to suggest what we have in this Mosaic text.

17:8 *take them to the place the LORD your God will choose.* In the second millennium BC, there were locations where cases were examined and judgments rendered, as well as specific places where judgments were enacted. In Egypt, certain persons were entitled "overseer of the law courts." They served at the "six great houses" and could cite the laws issued by Pharaoh or his close attendant(s). A group called "the thirty" acted as "judges." Judgment was pronounced at the gates or entrances of temples or palaces. The New Kingdom featured great courts where high-ranking members served and lesser courts functioned under them. The vizier oversaw both town and temple courts. Justice also was meted out at temple gates, palaces, porticos and forecourts.

In the Old Babylonian period, a mayor and elders governed a city and served as court functionaries. Wards were established in the city. The king was the highest court and the authority of final appeal. The palace functioned somewhat as a supreme court building. Similar structures and personnel operated in the Middle Babylonian, Middle Assyrian and Nuzi eras. The Hittites, as well as cities such as Emar, Alalakh and Ugarit, and much of Syria and Canaan, had many of these same features.

In Canaanite city-states, kings acted as judges, as did priests. The elders in Israel and at Ugarit pronounced judgments and took oaths. The elders were especially important in Israel, but also at Alalakh, Ugarit and in texts from El-Amarna. At Alalakh the elders were involved in international cases, as well as in local affairs. In an El-Amarna text, a city elder appeals to the pharaoh of Egypt. In Mesopotamia some elders engaged in areas of specialization and rendered decisions. In Israel, as in Mesopotamia, the temple and tabernacle were places where oaths were taken by various persons, including accusers, the accused, elders, priests and others (see note on Ex 18:22).

17:14 *When you ... say, "Let us set a king over us like all the nations around us."* Israel does ask for this king in 1Sa 8:4–5. Samuel sets before the people the political, military and economic reality they are asking for. The real cost of a king like the kings of the nations is enormous. The state machinery of a monarchy demands crops and personal property, to say nothing of "state enslavement" for cheap labor. Mari, Ugarit, Alalakh and later cities and mini-kingdoms should have made Israel aware of the cost of kingship. In times of war, oppression intensified beyond imagination. The model put forth in vv. 15–20 tries to control major abuses beforehand and to set Israel's kingship within a Yahwistic covenantal framework that circumscribes its practice and ideology over against the current realpolitik and its abuses.

Models of kingship abound in the literature of the ancient world. In Egypt, the god-king-priest was central and was to imitate, control, guarantee and communicate the order of the cosmos and society, as well as to regulate religious, moral, political and military issues. In Mesopotamia, Assyrian and Babylonian kings ate the food of the gods and were to provide a paragon of rulership and virtue. Prior to human kings, gods had purportedly ruled, but then they had subsequently lowered kingship down to humans at Ur for finite periods of rulership.

17:15 *a king the LORD ... chooses.* In the ancient Near East the king was invariably chosen by the chief god(s) of a nation, picked to lead the people and honor the god(s) who had chosen him. For a king to be successful, a legitimate chain of approval, including connections with the chief god and the people, was necessary. If no immediate link or legitimacy existed for the new king, it had to be created. The gods put the right king on the throne—which had to be the case. Hattusili III (1275–1245 BC) was chosen by the goddess Shaushga to be the Great King of the Hittites. Sargon, king of Agade (2296–2240 BC), was anointed and given kingship by Enlil and Anu (sky-god). Hammurapi was chosen by the sun-god Shamash and Marduk, Babylon's patron god. Likewise, Assyrian, Neo-Babylonian and Persian kings were chosen by the gods. *Do not place a foreigner over you.* Neither Israel nor Judah ever had a foreign ruler until their respective exiles. Given the way foreign rulers tended to oppress the native populations in the ancient Near East, it was to Israel's advantage, during the monarchy or during the divided kingdom, not to have had one.

Egypt suffered under the foreign rule of the Hyksos (shepherd-kings or possibly "rulers of foreign lands," c. 1649–1540 BC). Their rule was oppressive in certain areas. The ancient historian of Egypt, Manetho, described this period: "A blast of god smote us." The Egyptians finally cast off this foreign element under Pharaoh Ahmose (c. 1552–1527). A foreign ruler would most likely be an enemy of the god of the conquered land, as when the Elamites conquered Babylon, carried the god Enlil to Elam, and installed a ruler who was not of Babylonian descent. Because of Israel's theocracy, it was imperative that her king be of Davidic descent (at least in Judah).

king, moreover, must not acquire great
numbers of horses for himself[f] or make
the people return to Egypt[g] to get more of
them,[h] for the LORD has told you, "You are
not to go back that way again."[i] 17He must
not take many wives,[j] or his heart will be
led astray. He must not accumulate large
amounts of silver and gold.
18When he takes the throne of his kingdom, he is to write[k] for himself on a scroll
a copy of this law, taken from that of the
Levitical priests. 19It is to be with him, and
he is to read it all the days of his life[l] so
that he may learn to revere the LORD his
God and follow carefully all the words of
this law and these decrees 20and not consider himself better than his fellow Israelites and turn from the law[m] to the right or
to the left.[n] Then he and his descendants
will reign a long time over his kingdom
in Israel.

17:16 [f] 1Ki 4:26; 10:26 [g] Isa 31:1; Hos 11:5 [h] 1Ki 10:28; Eze 17:15 [i] Ex 13:17 **17:17** [j] 1Ki 11:3 **17:18** [k] Dt 31:22, 24 **17:19** [l] Jos 1:8 **17:20** [m] 1Ki 15:5 [n] Dt 5:32

18:1 [o] Dt 10:9; 1Co 9:13 **18:3** [p] Lev 7:28-34 **18:4** [q] Ex 22:29; Nu 18:12 **18:5** [r] Ex 28:1 [s] Dt 10:8

Offerings for Priests and Levites

18 The Levitical priests—indeed, the
whole tribe of Levi—are to have no
allotment or inheritance with Israel. They
shall live on the food offerings presented
to the LORD, for that is their inheritance.[o]
2They shall have no inheritance among
their fellow Israelites; the LORD is their inheritance, as he promised them.
3This is the share due the priests from
the people who sacrifice a bull or a sheep:
the shoulder, the internal organs and the
meat from the head.[p] 4You are to give
them the firstfruits of your grain, new
wine and olive oil, and the first wool from
the shearing of your sheep,[q] 5for the LORD
your God has chosen them[r] and their descendants out of all your tribes to stand
and minister[s] in the LORD's name always.
6If a Levite moves from one of your towns
anywhere in Israel where he is living, and

In Mesopotamia, Babylonian kings gave way to the Kassites, a people from the Zagros Mountains area, east of the Tigris River. They held power for about 400 years (c. 1530–1155 BC). Although they were relatively successful rulers, the Babylonians removed them and seized their own destiny. Both the Kassites and the Hyksos became acculturated to some extent in the countries they conquered. But they remained a foreign element, separate from the peoples they had subjugated. They powerfully influenced the culture and religion of those over whom they ruled. While they adopted the gods of the nations they controlled, they also changed and added to their pantheons. Such an action was strictly forbidden in Israel.

Assyrians ruled Babylon several times by placing an Assyrian on the throne, thus creating practically a dual monarchy. This empire greatly influenced the Babylonians, since the position of king included the charge to represent the people and the gods over whom he ruled.

17:17 *not take many wives.* In the present verse the prohibition was political and intended to keep Israel from striking covenants with foreign nations. This injunction forbids marriages for political purposes, for they might bring devastating religious consequences and were a means of filling the king's harem. The history of the ancient Near East is replete with these arrangements between nations and royal dynasties. A few sample illustrations can be offered, but the point could be multiplied many times over. Each foreign wife represented a connection to a foreign god as well as to a pagan political entity. The king's wives, in effect, made up a royal harem that had its own living quarters in or near the royal palace. Amenhotep III of Egypt (1403–1364 BC) offered to marry the daughter of Arzawa in a shrewd political move against the Hittites. He would recognize the gods of King Tarhumdaradu of Arzawa, and that king would reciprocate, thus sealing a religious-political-military coup by a treaty cemented through marriage. Amenhotep also married the daughter of Tushratta, Taduhepa of Mitanni. Similarly, the Great King of Hatti strengthened his relationship with his subjects by giving the subject rulers a female relation of the Great King as wife. A Mitannian princess married Thutmose IV to demonstrate both friendship and agreement between the two kings. Babylon and Assyria sealed their rapprochement by way of the daughter of Ashur-Uballit given to the son of Burnaburiash II. Elam and Babylon, Assyria and smaller states, secured their treaties and friendships with dynastic marriages. *large amounts of silver and gold.* The kings of the ancient Near East prided themselves in the accumulation of wealth. Solomon's cache was actually modest compared to the claimed wealth of other kings in Egypt or the Midas of legendary fame. Solomon's yearly 25 tons (23 metric tons) of gold (666 talents, 1Ki 10:14) was pocket change compared to the wealth of Pharaoh Osorkon I, who presented 383 tons (347 metric tons) of gold as offerings to the gods and temples of Egypt. Persian wealth of over 1,000 tons (900 metric tons) of gold was taken by Alexander the Great out of Susa alone.

17:18 *write for himself on a scroll.* Some kings in the ancient Near East could write, and writing was highly developed in Alalakh, Emar and Ugarit. Much further back, Shulgi (2094–2047 BC), king during the Third Dynasty of Ur, claimed to be a superb writer of tablets and boasted that he had attended "the tablet-house" for training. Kings received praise in ancient Near Eastern texts for their skill in writing.

17:19 *read it all the days of his life.* In the ancient Near East, instructions for future kings or leaders were recorded in various works of wisdom literature. In Egypt, Ptahhotep instructed his son about how to be a successful vizier over Egypt. Pharaoh Amenemhet I (c. 1960 BC), the first pharaoh of the Twelfth Dynasty, left written instructions for his son and successor to read and study. More words of instruction for a successor come from a pharaoh of the Twenty-Second Dynasty. Among other things he enjoins the future king to "advance the great men, so that they may carry out thy laws," and further to "copy thy fathers and thy ancestors." According to ancient Sumerian wisdom, the king who implemented justice in his land and faithfully observed the worship of his gods would enjoy long life.

17:20 *not … turn from the law.* In Mesopotamia, the king was not technically "above the law," but there was no means to bring him to justice; he was accountable only to the gods. This may have also been true in Israel, though the prophets, as spokesmen for the Lord, could hold the king accountable.

comes in all earnestness to the place the
LORD will choose,[t] 7he may minister in the
name of the LORD his God like all his fellow
Levites who serve there in the presence of
the LORD. 8He is to share equally in their
benefits, even though he has received money from the sale of family possessions.[u]

Occult Practices

9When you enter the land the LORD
your God is giving you, do not learn to
imitate[v] the detestable ways of the nations there. 10Let no one be found among
you who sacrifices their son or daughter in the fire, who practices divination[w]
or sorcery, interprets omens, engages in
witchcraft,[x] 11or casts spells, or who is a
medium or spiritist or who consults the
dead. 12Anyone who does these things is
detestable to the LORD; because of these
same detestable practices the LORD your
God will drive out those nations before

18:6 [t] Nu 35:2-3 **18:8** [u] 2Ch 31:4; Ne 12:44,47 **18:9** [v] Dt 12:29-31 **18:10** [w] Dt 12:31 [x] Lev 19:31

18:10 *sorcery.* The OT refers to a variety of practices that can all be placed under the rubric of divination and incantation, including activities such as hexing and necromancy (see also v. 11). It is difficult to determine the precise nature of these activities. Some might be included in what is sometimes referred to as "magic," but that realm of activity cannot easily be distinguished from the realm of "religion" in the ancient world. Activities included identifying future events through dreams, consultation with the dead, and probably the observation and interpretation of physical phenomena (e.g., stars, animal behavior). The activity of a sorceress likely involved the casting of spells or curses (see note on v. 11).

18:11 *casts spells.* The use of curses in general was not forbidden in ancient Israel. Joshua issued a curse on anyone who might try to rebuild the city of Jericho (Jos 6:26). Nu 5:16–28 imposes potential curses on a woman suspected of adultery. Even Yahweh himself is spoken of as bringing curses on the Israelites if they are disobedient (Dt 28:15–68). In ancient Israel, some curses were legitimate; others were not.

This was also the case in other ancient Near Eastern societies. The clearest evidence comes from Mesopotamia, where different terms were used for legitimate and illegitimate practitioners. Some practices that are counted among divination practices were legitimate. As high priest, Aaron carried special paraphernalia (the Urim and Thummim, see the article "Urim and Thummim," p. 162), which were the "means of making decisions for the Israelites" (Ex 28:30) and which, presumably, gave him access to special communications from Yahweh. The casting of lots, another activity whose details are rather obscure, was also practiced. Such activities were condoned, encouraged and even commanded (e.g., Lev 16:8). Moses performed wonders with what mere observers might take for a magical staff (Ex 7–11).

DEUTERONOMY 18:10–11

MAGIC

When people think of magic today, they either think of illusion or some intrinsic power that a person has (this latter generally only in the fantasy media). In the ancient world magic involved tapping into external sources of power or knowledge. Hexes, spells, incantations and exorcisms were all ways to wield power. Necromancy was a way to gain information from the dead. Divination, of which there were many different sorts, was a way to gain knowledge from the gods or about the gods. Magic of this sort was integrated into religion, rather than being something separate or the polar opposite. They did not have the categories of "black" magic and "white" magic as we might think today. Magic could have its destructive uses, but generally was based on the agenda of the practitioner rather than the nature of the powers that were tapped. Power could be wielded by practitioners either by connecting to gods or to spirits. Magic was also prominent in the practice of medicine. Often divination experts would work alongside herbal specialists, as both strategies were used to combat illness.

Israelites were forbidden to use any of the power-wielding forms of magic, though occasionally God would work similar wonders through specific individuals (Moses, Elisha). Most divination was also forbidden to Israel, with the exceptions being binary forms that required no interpretation (such as casting of lots) and inspired forms for which God provided the interpreter (dreams and prophecy). ◆

you.[y] 13You must be blameless before the
LORD your God.

The Prophet

14The nations you will dispossess listen
to those who practice sorcery or divination. But as for you, the LORD your God
has not permitted you to do so. 15The LORD
your God will raise up for you a prophet
like me from among you, from your fellow
Israelites.[z] You must listen to him. 16For
this is what you asked of the LORD your
God at Horeb on the day of the assembly
when you said, "Let us not hear the voice
of the LORD our God nor see this great fire
anymore, or we will die."[a]
17The LORD said to me: "What they say
is good. 18I will raise up for them a prophet like you from among their fellow Israelites, and I will put my words[b] in his
mouth. He will tell them everything I command him.[c] 19I myself will call to account[d]
anyone who does not listen to my words
that the prophet speaks in my name. 20But
a prophet who presumes to speak in my
name anything I have not commanded, or
a prophet who speaks in the name of other
gods,[e] is to be put to death."[f]
21You may say to yourselves, "How can
we know when a message has not been
spoken by the LORD?" 22If what a prophet
proclaims in the name of the LORD does not
take place or come true, that is a message
the LORD has not spoken.[g] That prophet
has spoken presumptuously,[h] so do not be
alarmed.

18:12 [y] Lev 18:24; Dt 9:4
18:15 [z] Jn 1:21; Ac 3:22*; 7:37*
18:16 [a] Ex 20:19; Dt 5:23-27
18:18 [b] Isa 51:16; Jn 17:8 [c] Jn 4:25-26; 8:28; 12:49-50
18:19 [d] Ac 3:23*
18:20 [e] Jer 14:14 [f] Dt 13:1-5
18:22 [g] Jer 28:9 [h] ver 20
19:1 [i] Dt 12:29
19:6 [j] Nu 35:12

Cities of Refuge

19:1-14Ref — Nu 35:6-34; Dt 4:41-43; Jos 20:1-9

19 When the LORD your God has destroyed the nations whose land he
is giving you, and when you have driven
them out and settled in their towns and
houses,[i] 2then set aside for yourselves
three cities in the land the LORD your God
is giving you to possess. 3Determine the
distances involved and divide into three
parts the land the LORD your God is giving you as an inheritance, so that a person
who kills someone may flee for refuge to
one of these cities.
4This is the rule concerning anyone who
kills a person and flees there for safety—
anyone who kills a neighbor unintentionally, without malice aforethought. 5For
instance, a man may go into the forest
with his neighbor to cut wood, and as he
swings his ax to fell a tree, the head may
fly off and hit his neighbor and kill him.
That man may flee to one of these cities
and save his life. 6Otherwise, the avenger
of blood[j] might pursue him in a rage, overtake him if the distance is too great, and
kill him even though he is not deserving
of death, since he did it to his neighbor
without malice aforethought. 7This is why
I command you to set aside for yourselves
three cities.
8If the LORD your God enlarges your territory, as he promised on oath to your ancestors, and gives you the whole land he
promised them, 9because you carefully follow all these laws I command you today—

18:22 If God, who hates deception, was the source of prophecy, then prophecy had to be true and sound (with rare exceptions in particular circumstances, cf. Eze 14:9). In Mari, this principle was recognized; prophecies were "tested" to evaluate their validity by getting another opinion. Royal written records were kept about prophecies in order to check their fulfillment or nonfulfillment. This practice was followed in Nineveh as well. In this way prophecies could be tested over a long period of time if necessary.

False prophecy often confirmed a shrewd political maneuver. In Egypt, Amenemhet I (1990–1960 BC), founder of the Egyptian Twelfth Dynasty, was supported by a *vaticana ex eventu* ("prophecy after the event"), the prophecy of Neferti. This prophecy was given an artificial setting in the time of Snefru, Fourth Dynasty (2600 BC); it predicted Amenemhet I as a redeemer figure for the current era. Similarly, false prophecy is found in "Tales of the Magicians."

19:6 *the avenger of blood.* Because of the kin-based social structure of Israel, the relative designated as the "avenger of blood" (*goel haddam*) of a slain person was authorized to avenge/reclaim the blood of his relative. To control this volatile situation, Israel set up a unique institution in the ancient Near East: cities of refuge. These cities provided protection for the person who had accidentally slain another person.

Cities of refuge were not paralleled in Babylon or Assyria at the familial level on account of various social, political, religious and economic factors. The Sefire Treaty (3.9–14) calls for the assassination of a ruler or any relative to be avenged by a treaty partner. The ruler would avenge a slain fellow ruler, a grandson would avenge a slain grandson of the ruler, and so on. Surprisingly, the "slayer" or guilty party to be slain could be a city as well as an individual.

The Babylonian king Burnaburiash (fourteenth century BC) demanded that the Egyptian pharaoh Amenhotep IV apprehend and slay certain murderers who had killed Babylonians in Egypt on business. Outside of Israel, a "lord of blood" (*bel dame*), referring to both the slayer and the representative from the family of the slain person, seems to have operated among the royal families. In a proclamation the Hittite king Telipinu, in order to ensure proper dynastic succession, declares that the "lord of the blood" would determine whether any guilty person would live or die, except that a person who had slain a king would die without recourse.

In the laws of Mesopotamia, the formal jurisdiction of the state dealt with homicide, and blood feuds and the families of both the slain and the slayer were involved. Thus, cities of refuge were not needed. In this milieu, Biblical and Mesopotamian law (and the rest of the ancient Near East) differed greatly. In Mesopotamia there were no "blood avengers," for state institutions, including the king or other judges, remedied certain homicide cases. Assyria permitted a role for both the family of the slayer and the victim.

to love the LORD your God and to walk
always in obedience to him[k]—then you
are to set aside three more cities. 10Do this
so that innocent blood will not be shed
in your land, which the LORD your God is
giving you as your inheritance, and so that
you will not be guilty of bloodshed.[l]

11But if out of hate someone lies in wait,
assaults and kills a neighbor,[m] and then
flees to one of these cities, 12the killer shall
be sent for by the town elders, be brought
back from the city, and be handed over
to the avenger of blood to die. 13Show no
pity.[n] You must purge from Israel the guilt
of shedding innocent blood,[o] so that it
may go well with you.

14Do not move your neighbor's boundary stone set up by your predecessors in
the inheritance you receive in the land the
LORD your God is giving you to possess.[p]

Witnesses

15One witness is not enough to convict
anyone accused of any crime or offense
they may have committed. A matter must
be established by the testimony of two or
three witnesses.[q]

16If a malicious witness[r] takes the stand
to accuse someone of a crime, 17the two
people involved in the dispute must stand
in the presence of the LORD before the
priests and the judges[s] who are in office
at the time. 18The judges must make a
thorough investigation, and if the witness
proves to be a liar, giving false testimony against a fellow Israelite, 19then do to
the false witness as that witness intended
to do to the other party.[t] You must purge
the evil from among you. 20The rest of the
people will hear of this and be afraid,[u]
and never again will such an evil thing be
done among you. 21Show no pity:[v] life for
life, eye for eye, tooth for tooth, hand for
hand, foot for foot.[w]

Going to War

20 When you go to war against your
enemies and see horses and chariots and an army greater than yours,[x] do
not be afraid[y] of them,[z] because the LORD
your God, who brought you up out of
Egypt, will be with you. 2When you are
about to go into battle, the priest shall
come forward and address the army. 3He
shall say: "Hear, Israel: Today you are going into battle against your enemies. Do
not be fainthearted[a] or afraid; do not panic
or be terrified by them. 4For the LORD your
God is the one who goes with you to fight[b]
for you against your enemies to give you
victory."

5The officers shall say to the army: "Has

19:9 [k] Jos 20:7-8
19:10 [l] Nu 35:33; Dt 21:1-9
19:11 [m] Nu 35:16
19:13 [n] Dt 7:2 [o] 1Ki 2:31
19:14 [p] Dt 27:17; Pr 22:28; Hos 5:10
19:15 [q] Nu 35:30; Dt 17:6; Mt 18:16*; Jn 8:17; 2Co 13:1*; 1Ti 5:19; Heb 10:28
19:16 [r] Ex 23:1; Ps 27:12
19:17 [s] Dt 17:9
19:19 [t] Pr 19:5,9
19:20 [u] Dt 17:13; 21:21
19:21 [v] ver 13 [w] Ex 21:24; Lev 24:20; Mt 5:38*
20:1 [x] Ps 20:7; Isa 31:1 [y] Dt 31:6,8 [z] 2Ch 32:7-8
20:3 [a] Jos 23:10
20:4 [b] Dt 1:30; 3:22; Jos 23:10

19:11 *lies in wait, assaults and kills.* Killing a person with prior intent defined murder, as reflected in the Mesopotamian laws of Ur-Nammu and in some Hittite laws. In the Hittite laws, there is an assumption of intent to kill a person even though it is during a quarrel. There is a clear concern for intent here. In the Old Babylonian period, premeditated killing was punished by death. Regarding Israelite law, in the case of premeditation the guilty person could not find asylum by fleeing to a city of refuge like the person who had committed manslaughter, a crime committed without prior intent (see note on Nu 35:22–28).

19:14 *boundary stone.* Stones often marked boundaries and they were not to be moved under threat of heavy penalties. The movement of a boundary marker was worthy of a curse (27:17). The wisdom saying in chapter 6 of the Egyptian work of Amenemope, who determined the boundaries of the land, forbade carrying off landmarks of arable land or encroachment. Some boundary stones (called *kudurrus*) in the ancient Near East bore inscriptions that appealed to divine sanction and divine protection for the owner's rights. The first such stones are found after the time of Hammurapi (c. 1600 BC). They appear in the eleventh and tenth centuries BC in Babylon. Some features of these stones reflect Israel's covenantal forms/content.

Some Hittite laws of the Old Kingdom (1650–1500 BC) concern boundaries and property rights (e.g., Law 168). They assert that the one who takes even a furrow of another's field will, as a penalty, pay a fine and lose a section of his own field to the owner of the field he has violated. In Law 169 a violator confesses his guilt and presents an offering to the sun-god or storm-god. A Babylonian inscription (c. 893 BC), similar to a *kudurru* stone, engraved on a hard black stone, records a royal grant of land and income to a priest.

19:16 *a malicious witness.* See note on Ex 20:16.

19:21 *eye for eye.* See note on Lev 24:20.

20:1 *When you go to war against your enemies.* In the ancient Near East war at the command of a god was common. Divination priests sought the signs that indicated whether a nation should go to war, using various methods (e.g., divination, omens, oracles, dreams and magic). A frequently sought formulaic answer was "god X delivers the enemy into the hand of king X." The king in the ancient Near East performed as leader of the army and often as priest. Scribes were in the vanguard of ancient Near Eastern armies to render encouragement to the troops, to record battles and to serve as experts on the technicalities of military procedure.

The god was the divine warrior (cf. Ex 15:3), and war was part of the divine plan, especially according to Egyptian thinking. A pharaoh engaged in war by divine commission only. Divine warriors in Mesopotamia and Hatti included the gods Ninurta or Teshub, respectively. Among Hittites and Assyrians war could be a lawsuit with the god serving as judge-warrior. The gods in the ancient Near Eastern worldviews were invoked to participate in warfare and even the battle itself in Egypt and Mesopotamia from the earliest ages (c. 2500 BC). The Hittite king won battles only with the aid of his divine warrior god.

The conquered enemy became the property of the god, the divine warrior. Among the Hittites, as in Israel, they were at times subject to *herem* ("total destruction"). Victory was always attributed to the divine warrior gods, never to the king alone, and the enemies engaged were ultimately the enemies of the gods. Divine wars and victories were then remembered in cult rituals and were recorded in the annals of the state.

20:5–9 Military officers also announced acceptable

anyone built a new house and not yet begun to live in[c] it? Let him go home, or he
may die in battle and someone else may
begin to live in it. 6Has anyone planted
a vineyard and not begun to enjoy it? Let
him go home, or he may die in battle and
someone else enjoy it. 7Has anyone become pledged to a woman and not married her? Let him go home, or he may die
in battle and someone else marry her.[d]"
8Then the officers shall add, "Is anyone
afraid or fainthearted? Let him go home
so that his fellow soldiers will not become
disheartened too."[e] 9When the officers
have finished speaking to the army, they
shall appoint commanders over it.
10When you march up to attack a city,
make its people an offer of peace.[f] 11If they
accept and open their gates, all the people in it shall be subject to forced labor[g]
and shall work for you. 12If they refuse to
make peace and they engage you in battle, lay siege to that city. 13When the LORD
your God delivers it into your hand, put to
the sword all the men in it.[h] 14As for the
women, the children, the livestock[i] and

20:5 [c] Ne 12:27 **20:7** [d] Dt 24:5 **20:8** [e] Jdg 7:3 **20:10** [f] Lk 14:31-32 **20:11** [g] 1Ki 9:21 **20:13** [h] Nu 31:7 **20:14** [i] Jos 8:2; 22:8

---

conditions under which some soldiers could refrain from going to battle. Gilgamesh, the great Sumerian hero, finds 50 men to help him accomplish his journey to the distant land of the living. He allows only single males to accompany him; those who have a house or a mother can go to their house or mother. He requests that only soldiers stout of heart accompany him against Kish.

As many as seven ranks of officers were used in the Hittite army, and the highest level of officers was even allowed to function in place of the king to direct military operations. Officers also kept rituals that bolstered the morale of the Hittite army when needed.

20:14 *take these as plunder.* Warfare was endemic in the ancient Near East. Hittite military procedures illustrate this devastating horror. In general, a conquered city was looted and torched. The leaders may have been spared, but usually they were executed while only the common people were more likely to be spared. Sometimes the Hittites respected the deities of a conquered city to the extent that they were moved to spare the city. Normally various valuables, herds and people were collected and used to augment the wealth and strength of the conquering nations. Some of these persons ended up as slaves, some as new faithful subjects of their conquerors. Others ended up serving on the estates of the deities of the Hittites.

The site of the destroyed city might be sown with

MAJOR SOCIAL CONCERNS IN THE COVENANT

1. **Personhood**
Everyone's person is to be secure (Ex 20:13; Dt 5:17; see also Ex 21:16–21,26–32; Lev 19:14; Dt 24:7; 27:18).
2. **False Accusation**
Everyone is to be secure against slander and false accusation (Ex 20:16; Dt 5:20; Ex 23:1–3,6–8; Lev 19:16; Dt 19:15–21).
3. **Women**
No woman is to be taken advantage of within her subordinate status in society (Ex 21:7–11,20,26–32; 22:16–17; Nu 27:1–11; 36:1–12; Dt 21:10–14; 22:13–30; 24:1–5).
4. **Punishment**
Punishment for wrongdoing shall not be excessive so that the culprit is dehumanized (Dt 25:1–3).
5. **Dignity**
Every Israelite's dignity and right to be God's servant are to be honored and safeguarded (Ex 21:2,5–6; Lev 25; Dt 15:12–18).
6. **Inheritance**
Every Israelite's inheritance in the promised land is to be secure (Lev 25; Nu 27:5–7; 36:1–9; Dt 25:5–10).
7. **Property**
Everyone's property is to be secure (Ex 20:15; Dt 5:19; see also Ex 21:33–36; 22:1–15; 23:4–5; Lev 19:35–36; Dt 22:1–4; 25:13–15).
8. **Fruit of Labor**
Everyone is to receive the fruit of their labors (Lev 19:13; Dt 24:14; 25:4).
9. **Fruit of the Ground**
Everyone is to share the fruit of the ground (Ex 23:10–11; Lev 19:9–10; 23:22; 25:3–55; Dt 14:28–29; 24:19–21).
10. **Rest on Sabbath**
Everyone, down to the humblest servant and the resident foreigner, is to share in the weekly rest of God's Sabbath (Ex 20:8–11; Dt 5:12–15; see also Ex 23:12).
11. **Marriage**
The marriage relationship is to be kept inviolate (Ex 20:14; Dt 5:18; see also Lev 18:6–23; 20:10–21; Dt 22:13–30).
12. **Exploitation**
No one, however disabled, impoverished or powerless, is to be oppressed or exploited (Ex 22:21–27; Lev 19:14,33–34; 25:35–36; Dt 23:19; 24:6,12–15,17; 27:18).
13. **Fair Trial**
Everyone is to have free access to the courts and is to be afforded a fair trial (Ex 23:6–8; Lev 19:15; Dt 1:17; 10:17–18; 16:18–20; 17:8–13; 19:15–21).
14. **Social Order**
Every person's God-given place in the social order is to be honored (Ex 20:12; Dt 5:16; see also Ex 21:15,17; 22:28; Lev 19:3,32; 20:9; Dt 17:8–13; 21:15–21; 27:16).
15. **Law**
No one shall be above the law, not even the king (Dt 17:18–20).
16. **Animals**
Concern for the welfare of other creatures is to be extended to the animal world (Ex 23:5,11; Lev 25:7; Dt 22:4,6–7; 25:4).

everything else in the city, you may take
these as plunder for yourselves. And you
may use the plunder the LORD your God
gives you from your enemies. 15This is
how you are to treat all the cities that are
at a distance from you and do not belong
to the nations nearby.
16However, in the cities of the nations
the LORD your God is giving you as an inheritance, do not leave alive anything that
breathes.[j] 17Completely destroy[a] them—
the Hittites, Amorites, Canaanites, Perizzites, Hivites and Jebusites—as the LORD
your God has commanded you. 18Other-
wise, they will teach you to follow all the
detestable things they do in worshiping
their gods,[k] and you will sin[l] against the
LORD your God.
19When you lay siege to a city for a long
time, fighting against it to capture it, do not
destroy its trees by putting an ax to them,
because you can eat their fruit. Do not cut
them down. Are the trees people, that you
should besiege them?[b] 20However, you may
cut down trees that you know are not fruit
trees and use them to build siege works
until the city at war with you falls.

Atonement for an Unsolved Murder

21 If someone is found slain, lying in
a field in the land the LORD your
God is giving you to possess, and it is not
known who the killer was, 2your elders
and judges shall go out and measure the
distance from the body to the neighboring
towns. 3Then the elders of the town nearest the body shall take a heifer that has
never been worked and has never worn
a yoke 4and lead it down to a valley that
has not been plowed or planted and where
there is a flowing stream. There in the valley they are to break the heifer's neck.
5The Levitical priests shall step forward,
for the LORD your God has chosen them to
minister and to pronounce blessings[m] in
the name of the LORD and to decide all cases of dispute and assault.[n] 6Then all the
elders of the town nearest the body shall
wash their hands[o] over the heifer whose
neck was broken in the valley, 7and they
shall declare: "Our hands did not shed this
blood, nor did our eyes see it done. 8Ac-
cept this atonement for your people Israel,
whom you have redeemed, LORD, and do
not hold your people guilty of the blood of
an innocent person." Then the bloodshed
will be atoned for,[p] 9and you will have
purged[q] from yourselves the guilt of shedding innocent blood, since you have done
what is right in the eyes of the LORD.

20:16 [j] Ex 23:31-33; Nu 21:2-3; Dt 7:2; Jos 11:14
20:18 [k] Ex 34:16; Dt 7:4; 12:30-31 [l] Ex 23:33
21:5 [m] 1Ch 23:13 [n] Dt 17:8-11
21:6 [o] Mt 27:24
21:8 [p] Nu 35:33-34
21:9 [q] Dt 19:13

[a] *17* The Hebrew term refers to the irrevocable giving over of things or persons to the LORD, often by totally destroying them. [b] *19* Or *down to use in the siege, for the fruit trees are for the benefit of people.*

fennel weeds to erase its previous existence. Certain conquered cities could be offered treaties that would be confirmed by oracles. Tribute was imposed on defeated peoples and their cities. This basic scenario played out repeatedly in Egypt, Syria, Canaan and Mesopotamia.

20:19 *do not destroy its trees by putting an ax to them.* The flora in the land of Canaan was vital to the survival of its inhabitants. Over 15 species of trees are mentioned in Scripture. Nearly every part of a date palm tree (34:3) was used in daily life. Pomegranate trees, fig trees, grape vines, sycamore trees, almond trees and pistachio trees were crucial to life.

The Lord did not instruct Israel to follow a scorched-earth policy. Egypt's warrior king, Thutmose III (1490–1436 BC) often pursued just such a policy, cutting down all kinds of trees in his Asiatic campaigns. In the Barkal Stele he records that he cut down all the fruitful groves: "I took away the *very sources of life*, for I cut down their grain and felled all their groves and their pleasant trees." He used the wood to construct siege equipment. It is clear that in the first millennium BC the Assyrians cut down fruit trees. The Assyrian Shalmaneser attacked Hazael of Damascus and in his annals records: "I cut down his orchards."

21:1 *If someone is found slain.* In Old Kingdom Hittite laws, if a dead person was found in a field in the open country, designated persons (village elders, councils, civil officials, priests, local judges, etc.) measured out a radius of three miles (4.8 kilometers) in every direction. The villages that fell within that radius were forced to present payments to the heir of the dead person. If no village lay within that area the heir forfeited his claim. In the case of robbery, the city and governors in whose territory the robbery took place made up the lost property or paid one mina to the relative(s) of a person who was killed. Blood spilled on the ground at Ugarit threatened the fertility of the ground. In the Ugaritic Aqhat Legend, Danel locates the place where his son was murdered and curses the unknown murderer and the cities near the crime. At Nuzi, likewise, the nearest town was held responsible for any unsolved crime.

21:4 *break the heifer's neck.* The purpose of killing the heifer was to atone for the death of the victim beside a "flowing stream" and at an area of land not cultivated. This served to eliminate the bloodguilt created by the crime from the community, while killing a cow reenacted the murder as well. Both Hittite and Mesopotamian texts seem to suggest likewise. These rites "remove pollution from the community or inhabited area to an area uninhabited or separate from the community's concerns."

Hittite rituals disposed of impurity in seas, rivers, enemy lands, mountains and open country (e.g., the Ambazzi ritual and the Tunnavi ritual) (see the article "Azazel," p. 207). A female ritualistic priestess would throw combs used to cull evil from a patient into a river nearby. In Mesopotamia, the Akitu festival and the Shurpu rituals contained rites that removed evil from a person by taking it into open country. A priest decapitated a ram and eventually threw its carcass in the river. The same was done with the ram's head. Before this slaughter the room was wiped with the carcass of the dead ram and incantations of exorcism were carried out.

21:7 *Our hands did not shed this blood.* A similar exculpatory oath is found in Ugarit, concerning a woman whose husband was murdered in the city of Arzigana. The local leaders must declare, "We did not kill the husband of the woman ... in the city. We do not know who killed him." See the article "Divine Verdict," p. 152.

Marrying a Captive Woman

10When you go to war against your enemies and the LORD your God delivers them
into your hands[r] and you take captives,
11if you notice among the captives a beautiful woman and are attracted to her, you
may take her as your wife. 12Bring her into
your home and have her shave her head,[s]
trim her nails 13and put aside the clothes
she was wearing when captured. After she
has lived in your house and mourned her
father and mother for a full month,[t] then
you may go to her and be her husband
and she shall be your wife. 14If you are not
pleased with her, let her go wherever she
wishes. You must not sell her or treat her
as a slave, since you have dishonored her.[u]

The Right of the Firstborn

15If a man has two wives, and he loves
one but not the other, and both bear him
sons but the firstborn is the son of the
wife he does not love,[v] 16when he wills
his property to his sons, he must not give
the rights of the firstborn to the son of the
wife he loves in preference to his actual
firstborn, the son of the wife he does not
love.[w] 17He must acknowledge the son of
his unloved wife as the firstborn by giving
him a double share of all he has. That son
is the first sign of his father's strength.[x]
The right of the firstborn belongs to him.[y]

A Rebellious Son

18If someone has a stubborn and rebellious son who does not obey his father
and mother[z] and will not listen to them
when they discipline him, 19his father and
mother shall take hold of him and bring
him to the elders at the gate of his town.
20They shall say to the elders, "This son
of ours is stubborn and rebellious. He will
not obey us. He is a glutton and a drunkard." 21Then all the men of his town are
to stone him to death. You must purge the
evil[a] from among you. All Israel will hear
of it and be afraid.[b]

Various Laws

22If someone guilty of a capital offense[c]
is put to death and their body is exposed
on a pole, 23you must not leave the body
hanging on the pole overnight.[d] Be sure
to bury it that same day, because anyone who is hung on a pole is under God's
curse.[e] You must not desecrate[f] the land
the LORD your God is giving you as an inheritance.

22 If you see your fellow Israelite's ox
or sheep straying, do not ignore it
but be sure to take it back to its owner.[g] 2If
they do not live near you or if you do not
know who owns it, take it home with you
and keep it until they come looking for it.
Then give it back. 3Do the same if you find

21:10 [r] Jos 21:44 **21:12** [s] Lev 14:9; Nu 6:9 **21:13** [t] Ps 45:10 **21:14** [u] Ge 34:2 **21:15** [v] Ge 29:33 **21:16** [w] 1Ch 26:10 **21:17** [x] Ge 49:3 [y] Ge 25:31

21:18 [z] Pr 1:8; Isa 30:1; Eph 6:1-3 **21:21** [a] Dt 19:19; 1Co 5:13* [b] Dt 13:11 **21:22** [c] Dt 22:26; Mk 14:64; Ac 23:29 **21:23** [d] Jos 8:29; 10:27; Jn 19:31 [e] Gal 3:13* [f] Lev 18:25; Nu 35:34 **22:1** [g] Ex 23:4-5

21:10 – 14 The Mari texts also instruct that clothing and jobs be provided to captive women. The rights given to the former captive are similar to those of Israelite women and demonstrate that there was no reduction of her status if divorce were to occur. Similar concerns are reflected in Assyrian laws, in which married former captives are required to dress like ordinary Assyrian women of that social class.

21:16 *rights of the firstborn.* See the article "Inheritance Rights and Birthrights," p. 62.

21:18 *a stubborn and rebellious son.* In the West Semitic Hadad inscription from near Zinjirli, death by stoning was administered to persons, male or female, who had committed an assassination — an understandable penalty for such a crime. Rebellion against established authority was the major issue, whether against the royal house of King Panammuwa I of Sam'al or the parental line of authority set up by God in Israel. The Code of Hammurapi discusses a son who commits a grave offense against his parents and sets forth the penalty as disinheritance. Penalties elsewhere involved enslavement, mutilation or disinheritance.

The parallel law in Ex 21:15 requires the death penalty for a son who strikes his parents, an act that is probably included in the rebelliousness in mind in this passage. In Israel rebellion against one's parents was equivalent to rebellion against the Lord. In the ancient Near East it was basically a societal issue, but still was a grave offense.

21:23 *you must not leave the body hanging on the pole overnight.* The burial of the dead was important for several reasons in the ancient Near East, and improper burial was a catastrophe as far back as ancient Sumer. Improper burial could lead to baneful consequences involving ghosts, demons and other evils. The Assyrians used the practice of hanging an enemy on a pole in a time of war instead of burying them so that birds would eat the corpse. The dead bodies of the enemy were also mutilated, fed to animals, and finally removed. The threat of not being buried continued into the Persian era and even later.

In Babylonian anthropological thinking the physical body provided the habitation for the dead person's ghost (*etemmu*) to be received by the community of the dead. The body was to be buried, because burial of the body maintained the identity of the deceased. Rites that would feed and renew the memory of them then provided for the dead. Destroying a person's corpse deprived the person of a future identity among the dead. Burning, mutilation or the consumption of a body by animals also destroyed the person's identity and future life. Those whose bodies were not buried had a gruesome chaotic existence to face.

At the city of Emar the dead were referred to as divine beings or "gods." According to certain Sumerian texts the dead should be buried within "the shade of one's house," so that they would enjoy their new lives among the dead in this vicinity. Within this religious and cognitive kind of thinking it is easy to see why in Israel a dead body desecrated the Lord's land, both literally and symbolically.

22:1 – 4 Rather than permitting the Israelites to envy the property of their neighbors, the Lord instructs them to be their brother's helpers and keepers. Israelite houses had a stable area on the ground floor where animals were kept and cared for. A lost animal was to be treated as one's own. The Hittite laws of the Old Kingdom (c. 1650 – 1500 BC) instructed a person who found a stray animal (ox, horse, mule) to take it to the gate of the king

their donkey or cloak or anything else they have lost. Do not ignore it.

4If you see your fellow Israelite's donkey[h] or ox fallen on the road, do not ignore it. Help the owner get it to its feet.

5A woman must not wear men's clothing, nor a man wear women's clothing, for the LORD your God detests anyone who does this.

6If you come across a bird's nest beside the road, either in a tree or on the ground, and the mother is sitting on the young or on the eggs, do not take the mother with the young.[i] 7You may take the young, but be sure to let the mother go, so that it may go well with you and you may have a long life.[j]

8When you build a new house, make a parapet around your roof so that you may not bring the guilt of bloodshed on your house if someone falls from the roof.

9Do not plant two kinds of seed in your vineyard;[k] if you do, not only the crops you plant but also the fruit of the vineyard will be defiled.[a]

10Do not plow with an ox and a donkey yoked together.[l]

11Do not wear clothes of wool and linen woven together.[m]

12Make tassels on the four corners of the cloak you wear.[n]

22:4 [h]Ex 23:5
22:6 [i]Lev 22:28
22:7 [j]Dt 4:40
22:9 [k]Lev 19:19
22:10 [l]2Co 6:14
22:11 [m]Lev 19:19
22:12 [n]Nu 15:37-41; Mt 23:5

Marriage Violations

13If a man takes a wife and, after sleeping with her[o], dislikes her 14and slanders her and gives her a bad name, saying, "I married this woman, but when I approached her, I did not find proof of her virginity," 15then the young woman's father and mother shall bring to the town elders at the gate proof that she was a virgin. 16Her father will say to the elders, "I gave my daughter in marriage to this man, but he dislikes her. 17Now he has slandered her and said, 'I did not find your daughter to be a virgin.' But here is the proof of my daughter's virginity." Then her parents shall display the cloth before the elders of the town, 18and the elders[p] shall take the man and punish him. 19They shall fine him a hundred shekels[b] of silver and give them to the young woman's father, because this man has given an Israelite virgin a bad name. She shall continue to be his wife; he must not divorce her as long as he lives.

20If, however, the charge is true and no proof of the young woman's virginity can be found, 21she shall be brought to the door of her father's house and there the men of her town shall stone her to death.

22:13 [o]Dt 24:1
22:18 [p]Ex 18:21

[a] *9* Or *be forfeited to the sanctuary* [b] *19* That is, about 2 1/2 pounds or about 1.2 kilograms

---

or to the elders of the nearest town. The finder could use the animal until the owner happened to locate it with the finder. The finder would be considered a thief if he were not to then turn the animal over to the owner. The Code of Hammurapi has near parallels, but they are in a different context and the issue is more clearly theft by the finder.

22:5 *A woman must not wear men's clothing.* In Mesopotamian literature the goddess Ishtar is androgynous (both psychologically and physiologically), marginal and ambiguous. She shatters the boundaries of male/female, war/love, divine/human and more. Known also as Inanna-Ishtar, she breaks all gender and socioeconomic distinctions. Some scholars suggest that Israel's reaction to this type of description/perversion was to prohibit its occurrence in Israel. Hittite texts also report the use of gender-related clothes and objects (mirror and distaff for women, weapons for men) in magical rituals used to influence one's sexual status or to alter the gender status of an adversary. Most instances that mention cross-dressing are religious or legal in nature.

Hittite texts illuminate the larger issue of gender confusion as abnormal and depict it as a shaming technique in certain circumstances. In the Ritual and Prayer to Ishtar of Nineveh, males captured by the Hittites have their manhood shamefully insulted and removed by being dressed to look like women. A scarf worn by women was placed on them, and they were forced to do women's work with a distaff and spindle in their hand. This was an act of shaming punished soldiers who broke an oath of allegiance to the king.

22:8 *make a parapet around your roof.* An Israelite is to fulfill his responsibilities toward the safety of others when they are on his property. Law 58 of the Laws of Eshnunna indicates that when a wall collapses and causes the death of a free man, it is a capital offense and must be brought before the highest legal authority in the land, the king. One scholar notes that a specific punishment is not set here in Deuteronomy, but he suggests that "the guilt of bloodshed" may refer to polluting the building or making it unclean, or to actually bringing bloodguilt on the household. The penalty for the latter could be execution. In Hittite Law 6, a general case refers to a fine of a portion of the owner's property.

22:9 – 11 See note on Lev 19:19.

22:12 *tassels.* See note on Nu 15:38.

22:13 – 19 A man could take a wife and subsequently divorce her, but not without being challenged in many instances. He could not slander or impugn her. A Babylonian dossier from the reign of Samsu-iluna (c. 1749 – 1712 BC) touches on a provision in the Code of Hammurapi involving a charge of the Ama-sukkal against his bride of not being a virgin when he married her. His charge was not sustained. Charges against a virgin in the laws of Lipit-Ishtar also failed. It was of great value to a woman, her father and her family for her to be a virgin at marriage. Cases at Mari and Nippur indicate that a betrothed woman who was penetrated before marriage had broken her vow and could be divorced.

22:21 *the men of her town shall stone her to death.* This penalty is not paralleled in the ancient Near East if the sexual activity was understood to have taken place before a betrothal. This legal equality between a married woman and a betrothed woman is mirrored in various laws of the ancient Near East. In the Laws of Eshnunna (Law 26), a man who rapes a betrothed daughter is executed. The woman's death by stoning demonstrated that this was not a "sacrificial" act.

She has done an outrageous thing[q] in Israel by being promiscuous while still in
her father's house. You must purge the evil
from among you.
[22]If a man is found sleeping with another man's wife, both the man who slept
with her and the woman must die.[r] You
must purge the evil from Israel.
[23]If a man happens to meet in a town a
virgin pledged to be married and he sleeps
with her, [24]you shall take both of them to
the gate of that town and stone them to
death — the young woman because she
was in a town and did not scream for help,
and the man because he violated another
man's wife. You must purge the evil from
among you.[s]
[25]But if out in the country a man happens to meet a young woman pledged to
be married and rapes her, only the man
who has done this shall die. [26]Do nothing to the woman; she has committed no
sin deserving death. This case is like that
of someone who attacks and murders a
neighbor, [27]for the man found the young
woman out in the country, and though the
betrothed woman screamed, there was no
one to rescue her.
[28]If a man happens to meet a virgin who
is not pledged to be married and rapes her
and they are discovered,[t] [29]he shall pay her
father fifty shekels[a] of silver. He must marry
the young woman, for he has violated her.
He can never divorce her as long as he lives.
[30]A man is not to marry his father's wife;
he must not dishonor his father's bed.[b][u]

22:21 [q]Ge 34:7; Dt 13:5; 23:17-18; Jdg 20:6; 2Sa 13:12 **22:22** [r]Lev 20:10; Jn 8:5 **22:24** [s]ver 21-22; 1Co 5:13* **22:28** [t]Ex 22:16 **22:30** [u]Lev 18:8; 20:11; Dt 27:20; 1Co 5:1

Exclusion From the Assembly

23 [c] No one who has been emasculated by crushing or cutting may enter the assembly of the LORD.

[a] *29* That is, about 1 1/4 pounds or about 575 grams
[b] *30* In Hebrew texts this verse (22:30) is numbered 23:1.
[c] In Hebrew texts 23:1-25 is numbered 23:2-26.

22:22 *If a man is found sleeping with another man's wife.* The laws in vv. 22 – 29 treat in three scenarios sexual sins that can dissolve a marriage or betrothal covenant or pledge. Adultery was termed the "great sin" in various documents in Egypt and Ugarit and in the ancient Near East in general. The Code of Hammurapi (Law 129) parallels v. 22 and assigns the penalty for both of the persons involved; they were to be bound and drowned. The husband could show mercy to his wife; if so, then the guilty man could be set free also.

Hittite laws and Middle Assyrian laws recognize these same conditions. In Hittite laws the manner of execution is not given. In Egypt, adultery was prominent in legal cases, but there was evidently no officially enforced death penalty. Adulterers were rebuked or possibly beaten, sometimes in public. A betrayed husband was urged to get a new wife. In a famous list of sins confessed by persons before they died, they asserted that they did not commit adultery.

Extramarital activities by the husband were not punishable offenses in ancient Mesopotamia, but an adulterous wife was put to death. Drowning and impalement were vicious punishments, but forgiveness from the husband was possible, and both the offending wife and her paramour could go free. In the case of adultery by the wife, the sins and accusations set forth in the case invariably involved more than adultery: sorcery, deceit and slander were included in the charges. There is little from Ugarit on adultery. In Israel it appears that adultery was considered a religious crime against the Lord. See the article "Penalties for Sexual Offenses in Biblical and Mesopotamian Law," p. 216.

22:23 – 24 The circumstances of rape/adultery helped determine blame and penalty in each case in Israel and in the ancient Near East (see the article "Penalties for Sexual Offenses in Biblical and Mesopotamian Law," p. 216). This text discusses a betrothed virgin (fiancée). Similar conditions for a married woman are noted in Hittite laws, where the woman is culpable if the rape is in a populated area and she does not cry out. The Code of Hammurapi (Law 150) describes a situation in which a man clearly overpowers and holds down a betrothed virgin who is still living in her father's household. The rapist is executed; she is set free and is not considered guilty.

In the Laws of Ur-Nammu, the "violation" of a betrothed "virgin wife" resulted in the criminal's execution. According to Middle Assyrian Law 55 (fifteenth century BC), the father could have the rapist's wife ravished (see note on Ex 21:31) and could even take her to himself as an additional wife. But a father could allow his daughter to marry the one who raped her. The rapist must pay the father a dowry of the price of a virgin, and he could not divorce her. Alternatively, the father could keep the money and marry his daughter to whomever he desired (see note on Ex 22:16). According to the Laws of Eshnunna (c. 1766 BC), in the case of a man who brings a bride's offering to obtain a man's daughter without her parents' consent, then abducts and ravishes her, the one who abducted her is executed.

22:25 – 27 In this case a betrothed woman has clearly been subjected to forced rape. The man, as in other ancient Near Eastern law codes, is to be executed. The Code of Hammurapi prescribed death for the man alone. A woman seized and raped in the mountains of the land of Hatti was likewise allowed to go free, and her attacker was executed.

22:29 *fifty shekels.* The amount of money paid equaled the *mohar* ("bride-price"). In the Sumerian Laws of Ur-Nammu, if a man divorced his wife of first rank, he had to pay a penalty of 60 shekels. Silver was weighed out since coins were not minted. In this case the daughter was not yet pledged in marriage (v. 28), but this law protected her and any possible child from being abandoned without support. In some school-text laws it is recorded that a man who had deflowered a virgin daughter in the city, whose parents were free citizens and who did not know that she was "in the street," could be forced to marry their daughter whom he had raped.

22:30 *A man is not to marry his father's wife.* This prohibition is common among the sexual taboos of the ancient Near East. The Code of Hammurapi prohibits this relationship, as do the Hittite laws. In Babylonian documents the penalty is the death of both persons by burning. Such deviant acts involving a person's mother or daughter, or a father with his own son, were capital crimes. In case a father was already dead, a son cohabiting with his stepmother was disinherited only.

23:1 *emasculated.* In certain cases of adultery or sodomy in the Middle Assyrian era, the guilty parties were turned

2No one born of a forbidden marriage[a] nor any of their descendants may enter the assembly of the LORD, not even in the tenth generation.

3No Ammonite or Moabite or any of their descendants may enter the assembly of the LORD, not even in the tenth generation.[v] 4For they did not come to meet you with bread and water on your way when you came out of Egypt, and they hired Balaam[w] son of Beor from Pethor in Aram Naharaim[b] to pronounce a curse on you. 5However, the LORD your God would not listen to Balaam but turned the curse[x] into a blessing for you, because the LORD your God loves you. 6Do not seek a treaty of friendship with them as long as you live.[y]

7Do not despise an Edomite, for the Edomites are related to you.[z] Do not despise an Egyptian, because you resided as foreigners in their country.[a] 8The third generation of children born to them may enter the assembly of the LORD.

Uncleanness in the Camp

9When you are encamped against your enemies, keep away from everything impure. 10If one of your men is unclean because of a nocturnal emission, he is to go outside the camp and stay there.[b] 11But as evening approaches he is to wash himself, and at sunset he may return to the camp.

12Designate a place outside the camp where you can go to relieve yourself. 13As part of your equipment have something to dig with, and when you relieve yourself, dig a hole and cover up your excrement. 14For the LORD your God moves[c] about in your camp to protect you and to deliver your enemies to you. Your camp must be holy,[d] so that he will not see among you anything indecent and turn away from you.

Miscellaneous Laws

15If a slave has taken refuge with you, do not hand them over to their master.[e] 16Let them live among you wherever they like and in whatever town they choose. Do not oppress[f] them.

17No Israelite man[g] or woman is to become a shrine prostitute.[h] 18You must not bring the earnings of a female prostitute or of a male prostitute[c] into the house of the

23:3 [v] Ne 13:2 **23:4** [w] Nu 22:5-6; 23:7; 2Pe 2:15 **23:5** [x] Pr 26:2 **23:6** [y] Ezr 9:12 **23:7** [z] Ge 25:26; Ob 1:10, 12 [a] Ex 22:21; 23:9; Lev 19:34; Dt 10:19 **23:10** [b] Lev 15:16 **23:14** [c] Lev 26:12 [d] Ex 3:5 **23:15** [e] 1Sa 30:15 **23:16** [f] Ex 22:21 **23:17** [g] Ge 19:25; 2Ki 23:7 [h] Lev 19:29; Dt 22:21

[a] *2* Or *one of illegitimate birth* [b] *4* That is, Northwest Mesopotamia [c] *18* Hebrew *of a dog*

into eunuchs by having their testicles crushed. Hittite texts attest to the presence of eunuchs in the "house of the king," indicating that eunuchs played a major role in the royal structure of the ancient Near East and in Hittite administration, but they did not serve in the military. Anuwanze, a eunuch, served as supervisor over the scribes who wrote/copied a Hittite New Kingdom text concerning the founding of a new temple. In contrast, the presence of eunuchs as elite military troops at Mari is well attested.

In Assyria, eunuchs were disqualified from serving as priests, but they served in lower capacities. They could serve as a treasurer of the temple or (rarely) as a temple administrator. The Chief Eunuch was a high-ranking military leader, and eunuchs held other high military positions. Eunuchs were normally made, not born. At an early age a child was castrated or their testicles were crushed. Captives from war or persons given in tribute were the main source for eunuchs. The mother goddess Ninmah created some from birth, according to ancient Sumerian tradition. In Israel, emasculation disqualified a priest from serving and from offering animals for sacrifice (Lev 21:20–21; 22:24).

23:4 *Balaam.* See the article "Balaam," p. 268.

23:9 *keep away from everything impure.* This prohibition included physical cleanliness that crossed over into religious spheres according to Israel's worldview.

23:12–14 To let human excrement remain uncovered was an "abomination" and "indecent" in the Lord's eyes.

23:13 *something to dig with.* The tool used to cover human excrement is referred to in Hebrew as a *yated*—a dibble (similar to a gardener's pointed tool for planting seeds) or trowel.

23:15–25 This series of miscellaneous laws reveals both contrast and positive comparison between Israel's laws and those of her ancient Near Eastern neighbors. Verses 15–17 show that Israel, in contrast to the rest of the ancient Near East, was to provide refuge for a fugitive slave. Israel's fugitive status in Egypt and in Canaan sensitized her toward such humane issues. Harboring a runaway slave was a capital offense in Babylonia (the Code of Hammurapi, Laws 15–20).

Treaties between Hatti and Egypt and Hatti and Amurru mandate the mutual extradition of slaves. If the policy was not followed, the treaty was considered broken. In treaties from Alalakh, fugitive slaves had to be returned to the land of their owner(s). If the elders of a city or country where slaves were found misrepresented the situation and harbored a fugitive slave, their hands were cut off and a fine of 6,000 shekels exacted.

23:17–18 If religious prostitution did function in Israel, this legislation would have cut off a significant source of income for the temple in Israel; the activity was possibly approved in some ancient Near Eastern cultic activities in Mesopotamia. Some scholars conclude that OT evidence and ancient Near Eastern evidence does not establish the long-held assumption of religious prostitution. Religious prostitution indicates an activity fostered officially by the religious and state authorities in the sanctuary or its vicinity in order to support the sanctuary itself and to carry out effective religious rituals and ceremonies.

Prostitution in general was legally and socially tolerated in the ancient Near East, although it was ridiculed. Its religious function was prohibited in Israel. However, internal textual Biblical arguments do suggest that those referred to in Hebrew as the *qedeshim* in Israel did perform sexual rituals (here; Ge 38; see note on Ge 38:15) The holy persons, male or female (Hebrew *qadesh*, *qedeshah*), while considered holy outside Israel, were not recognized in official Yahwism. Although similar "holy" personnel (*qdshm*) were active in Babylonian religion in some nonofficial way, men scoffed at them as unsuitable to marry. These functionaries were outlawed in Israel, whatever their real roles were.

LORD your God to pay any vow, because the LORD your God detests them both.

19 Do not charge a fellow Israelite interest, whether on money or food or anything else that may earn interest.[i] 20 You may charge a foreigner interest, but not a fellow Israelite, so that the LORD your God may bless[j] you in everything you put your hand to in the land you are entering to possess.

21 If you make a vow to the LORD your God, do not be slow to pay it, for the LORD your God will certainly demand it of you and you will be guilty of sin.[k] 22 But if you refrain from making a vow, you will not be guilty. 23 Whatever your lips utter you must be sure to do, because you made your vow freely to the LORD your God with your own mouth.

24 If you enter your neighbor's vineyard, you may eat all the grapes you want, but do not put any in your basket. 25 If you enter your neighbor's grainfield, you may pick kernels with your hands, but you must not put a sickle to their standing grain.[l]

24

If a man marries a woman who becomes displeasing to him[m] because he finds something indecent about her, and he writes her a certificate of divorce,[n] gives it to her and sends her from his house, 2 and if after she leaves his house she becomes the wife of another man, 3 and her second husband dislikes her and writes her a certificate of divorce, gives it to her and sends her from his house, or if he dies, 4 then her first husband, who divorced her, is not allowed to marry her again after she has been defiled. That would be detestable in the eyes of the LORD. Do not bring sin upon the land the LORD[o] your God is giving you as an inheritance.

5 If a man has recently married, he must not be sent to war or have any other duty laid on him. For one year he is to be free to stay at home and bring happiness to the wife he has married.[p]

6 Do not take a pair of millstones—not even the upper one—as security for a debt, because that would be taking a person's livelihood as security.

23:19 [i] Ex 22:25; Lev 25:35-37
23:20 [j] Dt 15:10; 28:12
23:21 [k] Nu 30:1-2; Ecc 5:4-5; Mt 5:33
23:25 [l] Mt 12:1; Mk 2:23; Lk 6:1
24:1 [m] Dt 22:13 [n] Mt 5:31*; 19:7-9; Mk 10:4-5
24:4 [o] Jer 3:1
24:5 [p] Dt 20:7

23:19–20 Interest was charged regularly and widely in the ancient Near East. The Laws of Eshnunna and the Code of Hammurapi were the first law codes to provide for interest. Rates of interest were sometimes expressed; the rate charged was normally 20 percent for most loans, but 33 1/3 percent for grain crops. However, "excessive" interest was frowned upon. Israel condemned taking interest from a fellow Israelite by virtue of the ideal of covenantal compassion.

Loans at high rates of interest were extended throughout the ancient Near East, and temples were often the most-used creditors. In some cases interest could be forfeited, such as if a catastrophe struck the debtor. Since the purpose of a loan was to help the poor or someone in a crisis situation, it was unjust to exact interest from the debtor. The excessive rates charged reached 25 percent or more a year, with additional demands tacked on. Certain Assyrian Aramaic inscriptions (c. 650 BC) had this provision.

Especially in a time of need or crisis among the people of Israel, interest was not to be placed on fellow Israelites, but Israelites could charge interest to foreigners. In Ugarit, class-conscious free men did not charge each other interest. Persons could stand in pledge and serve as laborers in place of interest. Surety for debt was firmly exacted.

24:1–4 According to the OT, a husband could divorce his wife simply for personal reasons or for economic purposes. The husband could declare, "You are not my wife," in an appropriate legal setting. By contrast, it was difficult for the wife to divorce her husband or leave a marriage. A wife does not appear to have had a right to divorce her husband in Mesopotamia.

All of the grandiose rituals performed during a marriage ceremony were reversed in the divorce proceedings. The husband cut the hem of his wife's clothing, thus separating them and making it possible for them to remarry. The wife could lose her dowry in this process, depending on the reason for the divorce. In the case of a blameless wife, her dowry might be returned. A husband could divorce his wife if she could not bear children or simply because he wanted to end a marriage relationship and start a new one. In serious cases where the wife had committed an egregious offense, she could be stripped naked and forced out of her house. Divorce became more complex once children were born. The husband became liable to stiffer penalties to help curb divorce and to protect the wife and offspring economically.

Hittite law permitted a husband to divorce a wife and sell her for 12 shekels of silver. Because part of the text is missing, what she may have done to merit her husband's action is not clear. In a Late Bronze Age text from Alalakh, a prenuptial agreement states reasons for a divorce: If the wife does not bear children within seven years, a second wife may be taken, and abuse by a husband may be grounds for divorce. The first husband is not permitted to remarry his ex-wife. This may be a restriction placed on a practice that had been taking place in Israel.

What God sees as "detestable" (v. 4; cf. 23:18) in the actions of the husband is that the husband's actions would come perilously close to mirroring adultery, according to many commentators and legal experts. The act of taking a wife back under these circumstances unfairly humiliates the woman who declared her deficiency publicly (Hebrew *huttammaah*, "she has been made to declare herself unclean," NIV "defiled"). A similar concept of what God finds "detestable" is inscribed in coffin texts of Tabneh, priest of Astoreth and king of Sidon. The ritual abominations extended to sexual relations.

24:5 *recently married.* The joy of a new marriage is respected and adulated. The possibility of producing a child and heir in the family was highest during the first year of marriage in the cultural milieu and age spans of the ancient Near East. Note that a military exemption could be suspended in unusual circumstances. This custom was observed at Ugarit, but it was waived in the case of war undertaken on behalf of King Keret in the Ugaritic epic texts.

24:6 *pair of millstones.* Necessary for a household to produce groats, meal or flour for cooking and food preparation, usually operated by women, slaves or servants

7If someone is caught kidnapping a fellow Israelite and treating or selling them
as a slave, the kidnapper must die.[q] You
must purge the evil from among you.
8In cases of defiling skin diseases,[a] be
very careful to do exactly as the Levitical
priests instruct you. You must follow carefully what I have commanded them.[r] 9Re-
member what the LORD your God did to
Miriam along the way after you came out
of Egypt.[s]
10When you make a loan of any kind
to your neighbor, do not go into their
house to get what is offered to you as a
pledge. 11Stay outside and let the neighbor
to whom you are making the loan bring
the pledge out to you. 12If the neighbor is
poor, do not go to sleep with their pledge
in your possession. 13Return their cloak by
sunset[t] so that your neighbor may sleep in
it. Then they will thank you, and it will be
regarded as a righteous act in the sight of
the LORD your God.[u]
14Do not take advantage of a hired worker who is poor and needy, whether that
worker is a fellow Israelite or a foreigner
residing in one of your towns.[v] 15Pay them
their wages each day before sunset, because they are poor[w] and are counting on
it.[x] Otherwise they may cry to the LORD
against you, and you will be guilty of sin.[y]
16Parents are not to be put to death for
their children, nor children put to death
for their parents; each will die for their
own sin.[z]
17Do not deprive the foreigner or the fatherless of justice,[a] or take the cloak of the

24:7 [q] Ex 21:16 **24:8** [r] Lev 13:1-46; 14:2 **24:9** [s] Nu 12:10 **24:13** [t] Ex 22:26 [u] Dt 6:25; Da 4:27 **24:14** [v] Lev 25:35-43; Dt 15:12-18 **24:15** [w] Jer 22:13 [x] Lev 19:13 [y] Dt 15:9; Jas 5:4 **24:16** [z] 2Ki 14:6; 2Ch 25:4; Jer 31:29-30; Eze 18:20 **24:17** [a] Dt 1:17; 10:17-18; 16:19

[a] *8* The Hebrew word for *defiling skin diseases*, traditionally translated "leprosy," was used for various diseases affecting the skin.

(cf. Ex 11:5 ["handmill"]; Isa 47:2). Two stones were used, so that to take one as a pledge or guarantee removed a family's means of sustenance and livelihood. This insensitive seizing of property was an exception to what the creditor could normally do with property of a debtor.

Millstones were used in homes, and the officials of the state in milling houses used large millstones. The millhouse existed as a part of Mesopotamian culture. Two stone slabs were used, one concave lower stone and an upper stone shaped like a loaf. Grain was placed on the lower stone to be ground. The upper stone was moved up and down by hand on the lower stone to grind the grain between them. Sixteen grindstones have been found in place at Ebla.

24:7 *kidnapping.* A form of theft and murder, because removing a person from the community cut off a fellow Israelite from the community of God's people and from the promised covenant land itself. Kidnapping dealt with persons as if they were merchandise. The Code of Hammurapi (Law 14) says that the person who kidnapped a young man must be executed. In the Old Babylonian period, kidnapping slaves and free persons for enslavement was common.

In Hittite laws, kidnapping did not carry a death penalty. Depending on who the abductor was and who was abducted, the abductor was subject to various penalties: The abductor's house could be taken, six persons in place of the abducted person as restitution might be exacted, 12 shekels of silver paid, or the abducted male slave returned with no further penalty. The purpose of kidnapping in Deuteronomy was probably to enslave the victim or to reap a monetary gain. In ancient law codes, even a betrothed woman could be kidnapped and then married to her kidnapper, who then paid to the previously promised groom any expenses he had paid out before the kidnapping (e.g., Hittite Law 28). Outright "eloping" occurred with subsequent marriage (Law 37); however, this act was illegal.

24:8 *defiling skin diseases.* See note on Ex 4:6.

24:13 *Return their cloak.* The confiscation of a worker's garment in texts from Ugarit is reported. The action was hotly contested by the owner of the clothing, a farm worker. A duly registered complaint written in Biblical Hebrew (ninth century BC) on an ostracon records a field hand's vehement charge that his garment had been unjustly seized. Allegedly it was taken because he failed to meet his expected quota of grain. He sought reparation through the military governor, Hoshaiah, attempting to have his garment returned. A similar incident involving the return of a cloak is reported in some Syrian Semitic texts. Keeping these garments humiliated the owner.

24:14 *Do not take advantage of a hired worker.* The Code of Hammurapi records the pay of a hired man who received a daily ration of six barleycorns of silver (0.01 ounces or 0.279 grams) for the first five months of the year and five barleycorns of silver (0.008 ounces or 0.233 grams) for the remaining seven months of the year. In Mesopotamia a shekel was equal to about 0.3 ounces (8.4 grams). One shekel equaled 180 barleycorns (one barleycorn = 1/180 of a shekel). A worker received, therefore, less than 0.93 of a shekel per month for five months (0.01 ounces [0.279 grams] x 28 days) and only 0.75 of a shekel per month for seven months (0.008 ounces [0.233 grams] x 28 days)—totaling nine shekels of silver per year.

Weighing procedures in ancient Mesopotamia allowed for a margin of error of 3 percent or more, and the absolute value of an ancient shekel is not certain (see the article "Weights and Measures," p. 214). Skilled craftsmen were hired at a rate of four to five barleycorns of silver per day, but they probably worked fewer hours. The hired man depended on his daily wage to survive and to care for his family.

24:16 *Parents are not to be put to death for their children.* But see note on Ex 21:31.

24:17 *foreigner ... fatherless ... widow.* This powerful injunction of social justice is widespread and found in documents at Ugarit, in Akkadian texts and in texts from Nuzi. A common social and legal concern for persons in these situations was part of the ancient Near Eastern culture, but nowhere as it was in Israel. Four classes of persons outside the normal safety nets of these ancient societies are highlighted: widow, orphan, foreigner (Hebrew *ger*) and the poor. All four groups were vulnerable and subject to abuse. *foreigner.* Not mentioned along with the other three in the law collections outside Israel. The Moabite Stone records the death of "*grn*" and "*grt*," male and female sojourners, among those whom Mesha, the king of Moab, killed in his war against Israel. Israel had experienced firsthand what it was to be a foreigner in a strange land and culture (v. 18), and thus the foreigner was specifically written into her laws. Showing hospitality to the stranger was far from providing for them in the laws

widow as a pledge. 18Remember that you
were slaves in Egypt and the LORD your
God redeemed you from there. That is why
I command you to do this.
19When you are harvesting in your field
and you overlook a sheaf, do not go back
to get it.[b] Leave it for the foreigner, the fatherless and the widow, so that the LORD
your God may bless[c] you in all the work
of your hands. 20When you beat the olives from your trees, do not go over the
branches a second time.[d] Leave what remains for the foreigner, the fatherless and
the widow. 21When you harvest the grapes
in your vineyard, do not go over the vines
again. Leave what remains for the foreigner, the fatherless and the widow. 22Re-
member that you were slaves in Egypt.
That is why I command you to do this.[e]
25 When people have a dispute, they
are to take it to court and the judges will decide the case,[f] acquitting the
innocent and condemning the guilty.[g] 2If
the guilty person deserves to be beaten,[h]
the judge shall make them lie down and
have them flogged in his presence with the
number of lashes the crime deserves, 3but
the judge must not impose more than forty
lashes.[i] If the guilty party is flogged more
than that, your fellow Israelite will be degraded in your eyes.[j]
4Do not muzzle an ox while it is treading out the grain.[k]
5If brothers are living together and one
of them dies without a son, his widow
must not marry outside the family. Her
husband's brother shall take her and marry her and fulfill the duty of a brother-in-
law to her.[l] 6The first son she bears shall
carry on the name of the dead brother so
that his name will not be blotted out from
Israel.[m]
7However, if a man does not want to
marry his brother's wife, she shall go to
the elders at the town gate and say, "My
husband's brother refuses to carry on his
brother's name in Israel. He will not fulfill the duty of a brother-in-law to me."[n]
8Then the elders of his town shall summon him and talk to him. If he persists in
saying, "I do not want to marry her," 9his
brother's widow shall go up to him in the
presence of the elders, take off one of his
sandals,[o] spit in his face and say, "This
is what is done to the man who will not
build up his brother's family line." 10That
man's line shall be known in Israel as The
Family of the Unsandaled.
11If two men are fighting and the wife of
one of them comes to rescue her husband
from his assailant, and she reaches out
and seizes him by his private parts, 12you
shall cut off her hand. Show her no pity.[p]
13Do not have two differing weights in
your bag—one heavy, one light.[q] 14Do
not have two differing measures in your

24:19 [b]Lev 19:9; 23:22 [c]Pr 19:17
24:20 [d]Lev 19:10
24:22 [e]ver 18
25:1 [f]Dt 19:17 [g]Dt 1:16-17
25:2 [h]Lk 12:47-48
25:3 [i]2Co 11:24 [j]Job 18:3
25:4 [k]Pr 12:10; 1Co 9:9*; 1Ti 5:18*
25:5 [l]Mt 22:24; Mk 12:19; Lk 20:28
25:6 [m]Ge 38:9; Ru 4:5,10
25:7 [n]Ru 4:1-2,5-6
25:9 [o]Ru 4:7-8,11
25:12 [p]Dt 19:13
25:13 [q]Lev 19:35-37; Pr 11:1; Eze 45:10; Mic 6:11

of a nation. These foreigners were residents in various countries but did not enjoy citizenship; hence, they were denied significant legal rights. Israel's God heard their cry. *fatherless ... widow.* See notes on 10:18; 15:7.

25:2–3 *flogged in his presence ... not impose more than forty lashes.* This law seeks to protect a guilty party from being destroyed emotionally and spiritually by excessive humiliation. The Code of Hammurapi (Law 202) limits the number of lashes to 60 for insubordination. Note also the NT, where 39 lashes were prescribed to ensure that the law not be broken (2Co 11:24). The "lashes" were likely administered with something like a rod (cf. Ex 21:20). In the Code of Hammurapi an oxtail whip was used in public to administer punishment. In the Middle Assyrian Laws flogging normally entailed from 30 to 100 lashes. The most often prescribed penalty was 50 lashes, though the total range was from 5 to 100.

Tablet A (57) of the Middle Assyrian Laws instructs the punishment to be done "in the presence of the judges." This provision guaranteed that the penalty was administered and was delivered as prescribed. According to the status of the guilty person and what the offense had been, an appropriate penalty was framed. A harlot who was spotted in the street wearing a veil to disguise herself was flogged 50 times with staves or rods, and hot pitch was poured on her head.

25:4 In Israel work animals were to be treated with compassion (cf. 5:14,21). The ox was an immensely important piece of property and an invaluable work animal throughout the ancient Near East (cf. Ex 21:28–32,35–36). It was the primary work animal in agriculture. Oxen pulled sledges that had been outfitted with studs of flint or basalt embedded into wooden boards. They pulled these across the grain to loosen the grain from the stalks. The lack of muzzle allowed the animal to eat a portion of the grain as its "wage." An Egyptian relief pictures an ox that has stopped to eat grain, and it has no muzzle on its snout.

25:5 *duty of a brother-in-law.* See note on Ge 38:8; see also the article "Levirate Marriage," p. 85.

25:10 *The Family of the Unsandaled.* Sandals of various types were worn in Canaan, Syria and Mesopotamia from the most ancient times. They could be used in a symbolic way at Nuzi, perhaps as token payments. At Nuzi the seller removed his foot from a piece of land he was selling and placed the buyer's foot in its place. Then shoes were transferred. A pair of shoes and garments are presented as a fictitious payment to "accommodate" some unusual transactions. The brother-in-law (here) who refused to honor his dead brother by preserving his seed and inheritance brought shame on himself and his house. Honor, shame and covenant relations were central concerns in the ancient Near East.

25:11–12 The harshness of the penalty in this law is surprising. In the Middle Assyrian Laws, if in a fight between two men, a woman intervenes and crushes a testicle of one of them, one of her fingers is cut off. If the man suffers the damage or loss of the other testicle because of complications, then the woman's eyes were torn out (or, possibly, both nipples were ripped off). In the second case, in both Deuteronomy and the Middle Assyrian Laws, the penalty approaches *lex talionis* (the law of retaliation, where the punishment matches the offense), and the offender suffers punishment according to her deed.

25:13 *differing weights.* In the ancient Near East, the king

house—one large, one small. 15You must
have accurate and honest weights and
measures, so that you may live long[r] in
the land the LORD your God is giving you.
16For the LORD your God detests anyone
who does these things, anyone who deals
dishonestly.[s]
17Remember what the Amalekites[t] did
to you along the way when you came out
of Egypt. 18When you were weary and
worn out, they met you on your journey
and attacked all who were lagging behind;
they had no fear of God.[u] 19When the LORD
your God gives you rest from all the enemies around you in the land he is giving
you to possess as an inheritance, you shall
blot out the name of Amalek[v] from under
heaven. Do not forget!

Firstfruits and Tithes

26 When you have entered the land
the LORD your God is giving you as
an inheritance and have taken possession
of it and settled in it, 2take some of the
firstfruits[w] of all that you produce from the
soil of the land the LORD your God is giving
you and put them in a basket. Then go to
the place the LORD your God will choose as
a dwelling for his Name[x] 3and say to the
priest in office at the time, "I declare today
to the LORD your God that I have come to
the land the LORD swore to our ancestors
to give us." 4The priest shall take the basket from your hands and set it down in
front of the altar of the LORD your God.
5Then you shall declare before the LORD
your God: "My father was a wandering
Aramean,[y] and he went down into Egypt
with a few people[z] and lived there and became a great nation, powerful and numerous. 6But the Egyptians mistreated us and
made us suffer,[a] subjecting us to harsh labor. 7Then we cried out to the LORD, the
God of our ancestors, and the LORD heard
our voice[b] and saw[c] our misery, toil and
oppression. 8So the LORD brought us out
of Egypt with a mighty hand and an outstretched arm, with great terror and with
signs and wonders.[d] 9He brought us to this
place and gave us this land, a land flowing
with milk and honey;[e] 10and now I bring
the firstfruits of the soil that you, LORD,
have given me." Place the basket before
the LORD your God and bow down before
him. 11Then you and the Levites[f] and the
foreigners residing among you shall rejoice[g] in all the good things the LORD your
God has given to you and your household.
12When you have finished setting aside
a tenth[h] of all your produce in the third
year, the year of the tithe,[i] you shall give it
to the Levite, the foreigner, the fatherless
and the widow, so that they may eat in
your towns and be satisfied. 13Then say to
the LORD your God: "I have removed from
my house the sacred portion and have giv-

25:15 [r] Ex 20:12 **25:16** [s] Pr 11:1 **25:17** [t] Ex 17:8 **25:18** [u] Ps 36:1; Ro 3:18 **25:19** [v] 1Sa 15:2-3 **26:2** [w] Ex 22:29; 23:16, 19; Nu 18:13; Pr 3:9 [x] Dt 12:5

26:5 [y] Hos 12:12 [z] Ge 43:1-2; 45:7, 11; 46:27; Dt 10:22 **26:6** [a] Ex 1:11, 14 **26:7** [b] Ex 2:23-25 [c] Ex 3:9 **26:8** [d] Dt 4:34 **26:9** [e] Ex 3:8 **26:11** [f] Dt 12:7 [g] Dt 16:11 **26:12** [h] Lev 27:30 [i] Nu 18:24; Dt 14:28-29; Heb 7:5, 9

was especially responsible to see that the weights used in business or personal transactions were fair and that everyone used the same set of weights. Unfortunately a uniform universal system of weights was not adopted in ancient times, but whatever system was used to begin a transaction had to be used to complete it. A lender could potentially sell using one set of weights, but receive payment using another set. In the Laws of Ur-Nammu (2112–2095 BC), a faltering attempt was made to standardize weights and measures.

In the Egyptian "Instruction of Amenemope," the falsification of weights was prohibited, as well as "leaning" on them. Measuring devices were not to be tampered with, and the god Thoth was believed to have a sacred ape (or baboon) that watched constantly over the system of scales in use. In the document relating the "negative confession of sins," the confessor asserts that he has not "added to ... the balance" or "tampered with ... plummet of the scales." The "Eloquent Peasant" in Egypt mentions the evil practice of "tipping the scales" in one's favor.

In Mesopotamia, a specific provision in a contract could stipulate that a certain standard be employed, such as the mina of Shamash (i.e., the system of balances employed in transactions in the temple of Shamash). A cheating merchant, if caught, could forfeit everything due to him. In a hymn to the god Shamash, it is asserted that Shamash was especially wary of a misuse of honest weights and measures.

25:19 *Amalek.* The Amalekites were nomadic/seminomadic people and were descendants of Esau. Israel was not the only nation that at the command of her God blotted out memories of whole peoples, such as Amalek (Ex 17:14–16), who had, in fact, first tried to destroy Israel at the nation's birth at the exodus. Pharaoh Merneptah (1209 BC) laid down his claim that he had stamped out the seed of Israel—"its seed is not." The irony of the claim is that it is, in fact, presently the only major ancient Near Eastern unequivocal witness to the existence of Israel's "seed" in the land of Canaan at this early date.

26:5 *wandering Aramean.* The Arameans are attested as early as the fourteenth century BC (Amenhotep III, 1380 BC; Merneptah, 1200 BC) on the west bend of the Euphrates River. They then appear in Syria, to the west and south. The Israelites clearly recognized a biological and geographic connection between themselves and the Arameans. Nahor, Bethuel and Laban had remained in Aram as Arameans. Wives of Isaac and Jacob came from this Aramaic branch of the family (see Ge 24:15,29). Hence, this verse seems justified, as an assertion of origin for Israel, as a particular branch of the much larger classification of people known as Arameans (cf. Ge 10:22–23). Some scholars prefer to see "Aramean" as primarily a geographic term rather than an ethnic term.

26:12 *a tenth of all your produce in the third year.* See note on Nu 18:21.

26:13–14 After a positive affirmative of obedience to protocol, a negative confession in v. 14 disavows any sacrifice to the dead. In this instruction it is possible to see a reference to giving a part of one's tithe to Baal, the "Dead One," who, however, was purportedly resurrected again and again in the spring according to the fertility rites recorded in the Ugaritic Baal Cycle. This is also, of course, a reference to the fact that a funerary cult was to be avoided that involved feeding, nourishing and

en it to the Levite, the foreigner, the fatherless and the widow, according to all
you commanded. I have not turned aside
from your commands nor have I forgotten
any of them.[j] 14I have not eaten any of the
sacred portion while I was in mourning,
nor have I removed any of it while I was
unclean,[k] nor have I offered any of it to
the dead. I have obeyed the LORD my God;
I have done everything you commanded
me. 15Look down from heaven,[l] your holy
dwelling place, and bless your people Israel and the land you have given us as you
promised on oath to our ancestors, a land
flowing with milk and honey."

Follow the LORD's Commands

16The LORD your God commands you
this day to follow these decrees and laws;
carefully observe them with all your heart
and with all your soul.[m] 17You have declared this day that the LORD is your God
and that you will walk in obedience to
him, that you will keep his decrees, commands and laws — that you will listen to
him. 18And the LORD has declared this day
that you are his people, his treasured possession[n] as he promised, and that you are
to keep all his commands. 19He has declared that he will set you in praise, fame
and honor high above all the nations[o] he
has made and that you will be a people
holy[p] to the LORD your God, as he promised.

The Altar on Mount Ebal

27 Moses and the elders of Israel commanded the people: "Keep all these
commands that I give you today. 2When
you have crossed the Jordan into the land
the LORD your God is giving you, set up
some large stones and coat them with
plaster.[q] 3Write on them all the words of
this law when you have crossed over to
enter the land the LORD your God is giving
you, a land flowing with milk and honey,[r]
just as the LORD, the God of your ancestors, promised you. 4And when you have
crossed the Jordan, set up these stones on
Mount Ebal,[s] as I command you today,
and coat them with plaster. 5Build there
an altar[t] to the LORD your God, an altar of
stones. Do not use any iron tool[u] on them.
6Build the altar of the LORD your God with
fieldstones and offer burnt offerings on it
to the LORD your God. 7Sacrifice fellowship offerings there, eating them and rejoicing in the presence of the LORD your
God. 8And you shall write very clearly all
the words of this law on these stones you
have set up."

Curses From Mount Ebal

9Then Moses and the Levitical priests
said to all Israel, "Be silent, Israel, and
listen! You have now become the people
of the LORD your God.[v] 10Obey the LORD
your God and follow his commands and
decrees that I give you today."

11On the same day Moses commanded
the people:

12When you have crossed the Jordan,
these tribes shall stand on Mount Gerizim[w] to bless the people: Simeon, Levi,
Judah, Issachar, Joseph and Benjamin.[x]
13And these tribes shall stand on Mount
Ebal to pronounce curses: Reuben, Gad,
Asher, Zebulun, Dan and Naphtali.

26:13 [j] Ps 119:141, 153, 176 **26:14** [k] Lev 7:20; Hos 9:4 **26:15** [l] Isa 63:15; Zec 2:13 **26:16** [m] Dt 4:29 **26:18** [n] Ex 6:7; 19:5; Dt 7:6; 14:2; 28:9 **26:19** [o] Dt 4:7-8; 28:1, 13, 44 [p] Ex 19:6; Dt 7:6; 1Pe 2:9

27:2 [q] Jos 8:31 **27:3** [r] Dt 26:9 **27:4** [s] Dt 11:29 **27:5** [t] Jos 8:31 [u] Ex 20:25 **27:9** [v] Dt 26:18 **27:12** [w] Dt 11:29 [x] Jos 8:35

communicating with the dead of a family. Such tasks were passed on within the family at Nuzi, Emar and perhaps Ugarit. Mari and Ebla seem to have lacked these practices. This negative confession formula was also spoken in Egypt, and the confessor specifically disavowed ever having been guilty of any sins with respect to the temple, gods or other holy things, including foods.

26:17 – 18 *You have declared this day. … And the LORD has declared this day.* Assyrian kings and their vassals exchanged oaths. Various ancient Near Eastern treaties/covenants reflect this clearly. Later Assyrian treaties include the assertions by the vassal that the vassal "does swear" to the terms of the treaty; later vassal treaties include actions by word and ceremony that were to effect the treaty. Earlier Hittite treaties/covenants featured this as well. Extensive ratification rites are included in the Hittite treaty between Kurtiwaza and Suppiluliuma. In the expanded covenant/treaty of Deuteronomy these vv. 16 – 19 connect the material in chs. 26 – 28. Even the gods were thought to exchange oaths in marriage, as when Dumuzi and Inanna were married.

27:2 *set up some large stones and coat them with plaster.* Some Syrian and Canaanite treaty/covenant sections provided engraved blessings and cursings. These stones were whitewashed with an application of lime plaster, and then laws were written on them (cf. Da 5:5). Several such inscriptions are known at Sukkoth and Kuntillet Ajrud. Many other stone inscriptions are well known from the ancient Near East. This method and type of writing and this peculiar preparation reflects Egyptian influence (cf. Jos 24:27). In Egypt black ink was used, especially for decorative flourishes or headings. Red ocher or red oxide was substituted for the carbon. In Egypt, Syria and Canaan, stone was used for permanence and for public display. Plaster was used to improve the writing quality of the stone.

27:5 *altar.* This altar was not intended to be a permanent installation (another reason to use fieldstones) but was set up for the purposes of the celebration ceremonies of this occasion. It is specifically burnt offerings and fellowship offerings that are offered here (v. 7) — no purification or reparation offerings generally associate with purifying a sanctuary (v. 7). *Do not use any iron tool.* The use of unhewn stone distinguishes it from the (carved) stone altars found in sanctuaries, though it is not clear why one sort was used over another.

27:12 – 13 *to bless … to pronounce curses.* These introductory verses and the ceremony reciting key curses (vv. 15 – 26) constitute a ritual that Israel was to carry out when the people entered the land. The list of curses and

14The Levites shall recite to all the people of Israel in a loud voice:

15"Cursed is anyone who makes an idol[y] — a thing detestable to the LORD, the work of skilled hands — and sets it up in secret."

Then all the people shall say, "Amen!"

16"Cursed is anyone who dishonors their father or mother."[z]

Then all the people shall say, "Amen!"

17"Cursed is anyone who moves their neighbor's boundary stone."[a]

Then all the people shall say, "Amen!"

18"Cursed is anyone who leads the blind astray on the road."[b]

Then all the people shall say, "Amen!"

19"Cursed is anyone who withholds justice from the foreigner,[c] the fatherless or the widow."[d]

Then all the people shall say, "Amen!"

20"Cursed is anyone who sleeps with his father's wife, for he dishonors his father's bed."[e]

Then all the people shall say, "Amen!"

21"Cursed is anyone who has sexual relations with any animal."[f]

Then all the people shall say, "Amen!"

22"Cursed is anyone who sleeps with his sister, the daughter of his father or the daughter of his mother."[g]

Then all the people shall say, "Amen!"

23"Cursed is anyone who sleeps with his mother-in-law."[h]

Then all the people shall say, "Amen!"

24"Cursed is anyone who kills[i] their neighbor secretly."

Then all the people shall say, "Amen!"

25"Cursed is anyone who accepts a bribe to kill an innocent person."[j]

Then all the people shall say, "Amen!"

26"Cursed is anyone who does not uphold the words of this law by carrying them out."[k]

Then all the people shall say, "Amen!"

Blessings for Obedience

28 If you fully obey the LORD your God and carefully follow all his com-

27:15 [y]Ex 20:4; 34:17; Lev 19:4; 26:1; Dt 4:16,23; 5:8; Isa 44:9 **27:16** [z]Ex 20:12; 21:17; Lev 19:3; 20:9 **27:17** [a]Dt 19:14; Pr 22:28 **27:18** [b]Lev 19:14 **27:19** [c]Ex 22:21; Dt 24:19 [d]Dt 10:18 **27:20** [e]Lev 18:7; Dt 22:30 **27:21** [f]Lev 18:23 **27:22** [g]Lev 18:9; 20:17 **27:23** [h]Lev 20:14 **27:24** [i]Lev 24:17; Nu 35:31 **27:25** [j]Ex 23:7-8; Dt 10:17; Eze 22:12 **27:26** [k]Jer 11:3; Gal 3:10*

blessings of the renewal of the Sinai covenant is contained in Dt 28. The presence of blessings *and* curses argues strongly for a Late Bronze Age (c. 1550 – 1200 BC) origin for the treaty form of Deuteronomy itself; there are (1) ancient Near Eastern parallels for nearly every curse in Dt 28, and (2) most parallels (about 30 treaties dated before 1200 BC) link up to the second millennium BC much better than to the seventh century BC.

27:18 *leads the blind astray.* The blind were to be treated with care and compassion. Blindness was relatively common in the ancient Near East (cf. 10:18; 24:17 and notes). The Egyptian "Instruction of Amenemope" (c. 1300 BC) prohibits laughing at a blind person or a dwarf, or doing injury to a lame person. Blindness could, however, be visited on a mortal who had offended a god in some way. In the myth of Enki, the god of wisdom, and Ninmah, the mother goddess, various kinds of persons with disabilities are created. Enki gave them appropriate roles. The one born blind was placed before the king in a place of honor as the chief musician. Each person with disabilities is placed appropriately.

27:20 – 23 The accursed sexual behaviors mentioned in these verses are condemned in several ancient law codes. A plethora of punishments was meted out to the persons involved, such as banishment, drowning, monetary restitution, loss of dowry and potential daughter-in-law, burning or disinheritance. Hittite laws considered sexual relations with one's mother, daughter or son to be a capital crime, but the king could spare the offender's life. Having sexual relations with a living brother's wife was a capital crime. Bestiality was permitted with certain animals, especially in the Hittite laws. The penalty for lying carnally with cattle, pigs, dogs or sheep was death, but, strangely, not so with a horse or mule (no punishment, but see note on Lev 22:3 – 9). Nevertheless, the king could spare the guilty person's life.

27:24 *kills their neighbor.* Murder of whatever kind was usually punishable by blood revenge or compensation. In Assyria, both options were available in all the periods for which we have texts. Interestingly, among the Hittites only compensatory penalties were in place, except for the case of a royal murder, which was still able to be settled by compensation or blood revenge. In Babylonia, evidence suggests that the death penalty was an option, at least for wives and their accomplices who were involved in murdering husbands.

27:25 *bribe.* It is unclear whether this refers to the payment of an assassin or a bribe made to a judge or witness in order to condemn an innocent man to death. The one who took a bribe was usually a judge or official of some kind (cf. 16:18 – 20), so it is probable that a judge is in mind here. In the Code of Hammurapi, if a judge who has officially decided a case and rendered a sealed judgment changes his decision, that judge is condemned and ejected from the assembly and his place of judgment permanently. Bribery may have blinded him to act perversely.

A text found in Assurbanipal's library (668 – 663 BC), but which undoubtedly has a much earlier origin, praises the universal sun-god, Shamash. Shamash punished a person who accepted bribes, because he was perverting justice. This text notes that a person who rejects bribes would likewise intercede for the weak, who could be innocent victims.

28:1 – 2 These verses state the conditions under which the following blessings (vv. 3 – 14) will be received, a feature common to other ancient Near Eastern lists of blessings. However, in other similar lists it is typically the king

According to Dt 27 – 31, the Israelites were instructed to remember God's covenant by proclaiming God's blessings from Mt. Gerizim (left ridge) and potential curses from Mt. Ebal (right ridge).

mands[l] I give you today, the LORD your God will set you high above all the nations on earth.[m] 2All these blessings will come on you[n] and accompany you if you obey the LORD your God:

3You will be blessed[o] in the city
and blessed in the country.[p]
4The fruit of your womb will be blessed, and the crops of your land and the young of your livestock — the calves of your herds and the lambs of your flocks.[q]
5Your basket and your kneading trough will be blessed.
6You will be blessed when you come in and blessed when you go out.[r]

7The LORD will grant that the enemies who rise up against you will be defeated before you. They will come at you from one direction but flee from you in seven.[s]
8The LORD will send a blessing on your barns and on everything you put your hand to. The LORD your God will bless you in the land he is giving you.

28:1 [l] Ex 15:26; Lev 26:3; Dt 7:12-26 [m] Dt 26:19 **28:2** [n] Zec 1:6 **28:3** [o] Ps 128:1, 4 [p] Ge 39:5 **28:4** [q] Ge 49:25; Pr 10:22 **28:6** [r] Ps 121:8 **28:7** [s] Lev 26:8, 17

whose honor is primary, not the honor of the particular god involved, as is the case in Israel. The king implores that those who observe his laws and respect his inscriptions may receive the pleasure and blessing of a god or gods; e.g., Lipit-Ishtar, king of the First Dynasty of Isin (1934 – 1924 BC), offers these blessings for the one who respects his laws, promotes his stele, and does not place his name over the king's (pseudepigraphy was strongly condemned centuries before the intertestamental period): "May he be granted life and breath of long days; may he raise his neck to heaven in the Ekur temple; may the god Enlil's brilliant countenance be turned upon him from above."

Hammurapi implores that those who follow his laws may have their reign lengthened and may shepherd their people with justice by the help of Shamash, god of justice. The kings of Egypt and Hatti wished goodwill on those who kept their treaty/covenant. Hundreds are called upon to bless any Egyptian or Hittite who keeps the Hittite treaty.

28:3 – 6 The far-ranging blessings of these verses are covered in a summary way in a treaty hoping for peace, health, happiness and success on persons and their country in Hittite and Egyptian treaties. The higher echelons of society and government receive special emphasis. Suppiluliuma 1 (1370 – 1330 BC) implores that Kurtiwaza may return to its high place among the nations that it had before, and that it may prosper and expand.

However, mixed with the blessings for Israel from her God is a clear recognition and realization that she is his holy people, if they keep his covenantal laws. This overarching theological concept is not paralleled in the blessings of other ancient Near Eastern treaties. To breach or break a covenant or treaty, which was, in fact, an act of unfaithfulness by a covenant partner, brought down terrible curses on an offending party. The Hittite king Mursili II (c. 1330 – 1295 BC) attributed a terrible plague upon his people during his reign to the peoples' failure and the failure of Suppiluliuma I (c. 1370 – 1330) to keep a treaty with the Egyptians even though it had been enacted under a previous king.

ANCIENT NEAR EASTERN TREATIES

		ANATOLIA	EGYPT	SYRO-PALESTINE	MESOPOTAMIA
THIRD MILLENNIUM	1.			EBLA-ABARSAL	
	2.				Eannatum/LAGASH-UMMA
	3.				Ḫita/AWAN- Ňaram-Sin/AKKAD
EARLY AND MIDDLE SECOND MILLENNIUM	4.				Ilum-gamil/URUK-?
	5.			Abba-AN/YAMḪAD- Yarimlim/ALALAKH	
	6.			Niqmepa/ALALAKH- IR.IM/TUNIP	
	7.	Pilliya/KIZZUWADNA —		Idrimi/ALALAKH	
	8.	Arnuwandas (I?)/ḪATTI- Ishmerikka people			
	9.	ḪATTI — Šunaššura/KIZZUWADNA			
	10.	Telepinu/ḪATTI — Ishputaša/KIZZUWADNA			
	11.	Zidanza/ḪATTI — Pilliya/KIZZUWADNA			
	12.	ḪATTI — Paddatissu/KIZZUWADNA			
	13.	ḪATTI		HABIRU	
	14.	ḪATTI — ?			
LATE SECOND MILLENNIUM	15.	Šuppiluliuma I/ḪATTI — Šunaššura/KIZZUWADNA			
	16.	Šuppiluliuma I/ḪATTI		"Mattiwaza"/MITANNI	
	17.	Šuppiluliuma I/ḪATTI		"Mattiwaza"/MITANNI	
	18.	Šuppiluliuma I/ḪATTI		Tette/NUḪASSE	
	19.	Šuppiluliuma I/ḪATTI		Aziru/AMURRU	
	20.	Šuppiluliuma I/ḪATTI Ḫukkanas/ḪAYASA			
	21.	Šuppiluliuma I/ḪATTI		Šarrikušuh/CARCHEMISH	
	22.	Mursil II/ḪATTI		Duppi-Tešub/AMURRU	
	23.	Mursil II/ḪATTI		Niqmepa/UGARIT	
	24.	Mursil II/ḪATTI Targasnallis/ḪAPALLA			
	25.	Mursil II/ḪATTI Kupanta-KAL/MIRA/KUWALIYA			
	26.	Mursil II/ḪATTI Manapa-Datta/SEḪA RIVER LAND			
	27.	Mursil II/ḪATTI		Talmi-Sarruma/ALEPPO	
	28.	Muwatallis/ḪATTI — Alaksandus/ WILUSA			
	29.	Ḫattusil III/ḪATTI		Benteshina/AMURRU	

		ANATOLIA	EGYPT	SYRO-PALESTINE	MESOPOTAMIA
LATE SECOND MILLENNIUM (CONTINUED)	30.	Ḫattusil III/ḪATTI	Ramesses II/EGYPT		
	31.	Ḫattusil III/ḪATTI	Ramesses II/EGYPT		
	32.	Tudḫalia IV/ḪATTI		Šaušgamuwa/AMURRU	
	33.	Tudḫalia IV/ḪATTI Ulmi-Tešub/DATASSA			
	34.	ḪATTI		Labu & Elders/TUNIP	
	35.	Ḫattusil III/ḪATTI — TILIURA			
	36.	Šuppiluliuma II/ḪATTI		Talmi-Tešub/CARCHEMISH	
	37.	(Šuppiluliuma II)/ḪATTI		ALAŠIA (CYPRUS)	
	38.	(Šuppiluliuma II)/ḪATTI — Eḫli-Sarruma/ISUWA			
	39.	Arnuwandas (III?)/ḪATTI-KASKEANS			
	40. – 42.	Parts of three treaties with the Kaskeans			
	43.	ḪATTI — KIZZUWADNA			
	44.	ḪATTI – KURUSTAMA (?)			
	45.	ḪATTI		Mukish	
FIRST MILLENNIUM	46.			Bar-Ga'yah/KTK-Matiel/ARPAD	
	47.			Bar-Ga'yah/KTK-Matiel/ARPAD	
	48.			Bar-Ga'yah/KTK-Matiel/ARPAD	
	49.			Matiel/ARPAD	Aššur-nirari/ASSYRIA
	50.				Marduk-zakir-šumi/BABYLON-Šamši-AdadV/ASSYRIA
	51.				Sennacherib/ASSYRIA-?
	52.				Esarhaddon/ASSYRIA-7 Median Rulers
	53.			Baal/TYRE	Esarhaddon/ASSYRIA
	54.			(Esarhaddon)/ASSYRIA-?	
	55.				Aššurbanipal/ASSYRIA-Samaš-sum-ukin (?) BABYLON
	56.			Abiate/QEDAR	Aššurbanipal/ASSYRIA
	57.				Sin-šar-iskun/ASSYRIA (?)

9The LORD will establish you as his holy
people,[t] as he promised you on oath, if
you keep the commands of the LORD your
God and walk in obedience to him. 10Then
all the peoples on earth will see that you
are called by the name[u] of the LORD, and
they will fear you. 11The LORD will grant
you abundant prosperity—in the fruit of
your womb, the young of your livestock
and the crops of your ground—in the land
he swore to your ancestors to give you.[v]
12The LORD will open the heavens, the
storehouse of his bounty, to send rain[w] on
your land in season and to bless all the
work of your hands. You will lend to many
nations but will borrow from none.[x] 13The
LORD will make you the head, not the tail.
If you pay attention to the commands of
the LORD your God that I give you this day
and carefully follow them, you will always
be at the top, never at the bottom. 14Do
not turn aside from any of the commands
I give you today, to the right or to the left,[y]
following other gods and serving them.

Curses for Disobedience

15However, if you do not obey[z] the LORD
your God and do not carefully follow all
his commands and decrees I am giving
you today, all these curses will come on
you and overtake you:[a]

16You will be cursed in the city and
cursed in the country.
17Your basket and your kneading
trough will be cursed.
18The fruit of your womb will be
cursed, and the crops of your land,
and the calves of your herds and the
lambs of your flocks.
19You will be cursed when you
come in and cursed when you go out.

20The LORD will send on you curses,[b]
confusion and rebuke[c] in everything you
put your hand to, until you are destroyed
and come to sudden ruin[d] because of the
evil you have done in forsaking him.[a]
21The LORD will plague you with diseases
until he has destroyed you from the land
you are entering to possess.[e] 22The LORD
will strike you with wasting disease, with
fever and inflammation, with scorching
heat and drought,[f] with blight and mildew,
which will plague you until you perish.[g]
23The sky over your head will be bronze,
the ground beneath you iron.[h] 24The LORD
will turn the rain of your country into dust
and powder; it will come down from the
skies until you are destroyed.
25The LORD will cause you to be defeated before your enemies. You will come
at them from one direction but flee from
them in seven,[i] and you will become a
thing of horror to all the kingdoms on
earth.[j] 26Your carcasses will be food for
all the birds and the wild animals, and
there will be no one to frighten them
away.[k] 27The LORD will afflict you with the
boils of Egypt[l] and with tumors, festering
sores and the itch, from which you cannot be cured. 28The LORD will afflict you
with madness, blindness and confusion of
mind. 29At midday you will grope[m] about
like a blind person in the dark. You will be
unsuccessful in everything you do; day after day you will be oppressed and robbed,
with no one to rescue you.
30You will be pledged to be married to a
woman, but another will take her and rape
her.[n] You will build a house, but you will
not live in it.[o] You will plant a vineyard,
but you will not even begin to enjoy its
fruit.[p] 31Your ox will be slaughtered before
your eyes, but you will eat none of it. Your
donkey will be forcibly taken from you
and will not be returned. Your sheep will
be given to your enemies, and no one will
rescue them. 32Your sons and daughters
will be given to another nation,[q] and you
will wear out your eyes watching for them
day after day, powerless to lift a hand. 33A
people that you do not know will eat what
your land and labor produce, and you will
have nothing but cruel oppression all your
days.[r] 34The sights you see will drive you
mad. 35The LORD will afflict your knees
and legs with painful boils[s] that cannot
be cured, spreading from the soles of your
feet to the top of your head.
36The LORD will drive you and the king[t]
you set over you to a nation unknown to
you or your ancestors.[u] There you will

28:9 [t]Ex 19:6; Dt 7:6 **28:10** [u]2Ch 7:14 **28:11** [v]Dt 30:9; Pr 10:22 **28:12** [w]Lev 26:4 [x]Dt 15:3,6 **28:14** [y]Dt 5:32 **28:15** [z]Lev 26:14 [a]Jos 23:15; Da 9:11; Mal 2:2 **28:20** [b]Mal 2:2 [c]Isa 51:20; 66:15 [d]Dt 4:26 **28:21** [e]Lev 26:25; Jer 24:10 **28:22** [f]Lev 26:16 [g]Am 4:9 **28:23** [h]Lev 26:19 **28:25** [i]Isa 30:17 [j]Jer 15:4; 24:9; Eze 23:46 **28:26** [k]Jer 7:33; 16:4; 34:20 **28:27** [l]ver 60-61; 1Sa 5:6 **28:29** [m]Job 5:14; Isa 59:10 **28:30** [n]Job 31:10; Jer 8:10 [o]Am 5:11 [p]Jer 12:13 **28:32** [q]ver 41 **28:33** [r]Jer 5:15-17 **28:35** [s]ver 27 **28:36** [t]2Ki 17:4,6; 24:12,14; 25:7,11 [u]Jer 16:13

[a] *20* Hebrew *me*

28:23 *bronze ... iron.* The depiction of a drought featuring a bronze sky and iron ground is matched in a canonical West Semitic inscription that may go back to the seventh century BC: "The earth was bronze, the heavens, of iron, the sod, in a bad/arid state." Esarhaddon's vassal treaty curses mention the soil being turned to iron and the sky to copper.

28:25–29 These verses encompass curses that result in Israel's complete defeat and humiliation at the hands of her enemies, in addition to a terrifying buffeting by plagues from the Lord because Israel has broken the covenant (cf. Ex 15:22–24). Parallels exist in Aramaic and Akkadian with curses listed in the vassal treaties of Esarhaddon, but only partially and not in the same order. This is the situation with most of the curses found in ch. 28. Ugaritic, Aramaic and Akkadian texts speak of blindness as a curse because of murder. The epilogue in the Code of Hammurapi contains relatively close parallels concerning dispersion and exile and defeat by enemies (v. 25); boils, tumors and itch (v. 27), as well as blindness and mental confusion (vv. 28–29).

worship other gods, gods of wood and
stone.[v] 37 You will become a thing of horror, a byword and an object of ridicule
among all the peoples where the LORD will
drive you.[w]
38 You will sow much seed in the field
but you will harvest little,[x] because locusts
will devour[y] it. 39 You will plant vineyards
and cultivate them but you will not drink
the wine or gather the grapes, because
worms will eat them.[z] 40 You will have olive trees throughout your country but you
will not use the oil, because the olives will
drop off.[a] 41 You will have sons and daughters but you will not keep them, because
they will go into captivity.[b] 42 Swarms of
locusts will take over all your trees and the
crops of your land.
43 The foreigners who reside among you
will rise above you higher and higher, but
you will sink lower and lower.[c] 44 They
will lend to you, but you will not lend to
them.[d] They will be the head, but you will
be the tail.[e]
45 All these curses will come on you.
They will pursue you and overtake you
until you are destroyed,[f] because you did
not obey the LORD your God and observe
the commands and decrees he gave you.
46 They will be a sign and a wonder to you
and your descendants forever.[g] 47 Because
you did not serve[h] the LORD your God joyfully and gladly[i] in the time of prosperity,
48 therefore in hunger and thirst, in nakedness and dire poverty, you will serve the
enemies the LORD sends against you. He
will put an iron yoke[j] on your neck until
he has destroyed you.
49 The LORD will bring a nation against
you from far away, from the ends of the
earth,[k] like an eagle[l] swooping down, a
nation whose language you will not understand, 50 a fierce-looking nation without respect for the old[m] or pity for the
young. 51 They will devour the young of
your livestock and the crops of your land
until you are destroyed. They will leave
you no grain, new wine or olive oil, nor
any calves of your herds or lambs of your
flocks until you are ruined.[n] 52 They will
lay siege to all the cities throughout your
land until the high fortified walls in which
you trust fall down. They will besiege all
the cities throughout the land the LORD
your God is giving you.[o]

28:36 [v] Dt 4:28
28:37 [w] Jer 24:9
28:38 [x] Mic 6:15; Hag 1:6,9 [y] Joel 1:4
28:39 [z] Isa 5:10; 17:10-11
28:40 [a] Mic 6:15
28:41 [b] ver 32
28:43 [c] ver 13
28:44 [d] ver 12 [e] ver 13
28:45 [f] ver 15
28:46 [g] Isa 8:18; Eze 14:8
28:47 [h] Dt 32:15 [i] Ne 9:35
28:48 [j] Jer 28:13-14
28:49 [k] Jer 5:15; 6:22 [l] La 4:19; Hos 8:1
28:50 [m] Isa 47:6
28:51 [n] ver 33
28:52 [o] Jer 10:18; Zep 1:14-16, 17
28:53 [p] Lev 26:29; 2Ki 6:28-29; Jer 19:9; La 2:20; 4:10
28:56 [q] ver 54
28:58 [r] Mal 1:14 [s] Ex 6:3
28:60 [t] ver 27
28:61 [u] Dt 4:25-26
28:62 [v] Dt 4:27; 10:22; Ne 9:23
28:63 [w] Jer 32:41 [x] Pr 1:26 [y] Jer 12:14; 45:4
28:64 [z] Lev 26:33; Dt 4:27 [a] Ne 1:8
28:65 [b] Lev 26:16,36

53 Because of the suffering your enemy
will inflict on you during the siege, you
will eat the fruit of the womb, the flesh
of the sons and daughters the LORD your
God has given you.[p] 54 Even the most gentle and sensitive man among you will
have no compassion on his own brother
or the wife he loves or his surviving children, 55 and he will not give to one of them
any of the flesh of his children that he is
eating. It will be all he has left because
of the suffering your enemy will inflict
on you during the siege of all your cities.
56 The most gentle and sensitive[q] woman
among you—so sensitive and gentle that
she would not venture to touch the ground
with the sole of her foot—will begrudge
the husband she loves and her own son or
daughter 57 the afterbirth from her womb
and the children she bears. For in her dire
need she intends to eat them secretly because of the suffering your enemy will inflict on you during the siege of your cities.
58 If you do not carefully follow all the
words of this law, which are written in
this book, and do not revere[r] this glorious and awesome name[s]—the LORD your
God— 59 the LORD will send fearful plagues
on you and your descendants, harsh and
prolonged disasters, and severe and lingering illnesses. 60 He will bring on you all
the diseases of Egypt[t] that you dreaded,
and they will cling to you. 61 The LORD will
also bring on you every kind of sickness
and disaster not recorded in this Book of
the Law, until you are destroyed.[u] 62 You
who were as numerous as the stars in the
sky[v] will be left but few in number, because you did not obey the LORD your God.
63 Just as it pleased[w] the LORD to make you
prosper and increase in number, so it will
please[x] him to ruin and destroy you. You
will be uprooted[y] from the land you are
entering to possess.
64 Then the LORD will scatter[z] you among
all nations,[a] from one end of the earth to
the other. There you will worship other
gods—gods of wood and stone, which
neither you nor your ancestors have
known. 65 Among those nations you will
find no repose, no resting place for the
sole of your foot. There the LORD will give
you an anxious mind, eyes weary with
longing, and a despairing heart.[b] 66 You
will live in constant suspense, filled with

28:53 *eat the fruit of the womb.* Ugaritic texts describe prayers offered on behalf of a city under siege. Sumerian texts record deaths from famine at the time of the destruction of Ur and Sumer. The horrors of siege warfare often resulted in unbelievable acts of human cannibalism. The ancient Atrahasis epic contains a description of cannibalism in a city oppressed with hunger.

These conditions were also set forth in the vassal treaties of Esarhaddon (c. 690 BC):

- Mothers would lock out daughters
- Flesh of children devoured by parents
- Dogs and pigs will devour you
- Spirit will be uncared for
- No libations poured out when you are dead

dread both night and day, never sure of your life. [67]In the morning you will say, "If only it were evening!" and in the evening, "If only it were morning!"—because of the terror that will fill your hearts and the sights that your eyes will see.[c] [68]The LORD will send you back in ships to Egypt on a journey I said you should never make again. There you will offer yourselves for sale to your enemies as male and female slaves, but no one will buy you.

Renewal of the Covenant

29[a] These are the terms of the covenant the LORD commanded Moses to make with the Israelites in Moab, in addition to the covenant he had made with them at Horeb.[d]

[2]Moses summoned all the Israelites and said to them:

Your eyes have seen all that the LORD did in Egypt to Pharaoh, to all his officials and to all his land.[e] [3]With your own eyes you saw those great trials, those signs and great wonders.[f] [4]But to this day the LORD has not given you a mind that understands or eyes that see or ears that hear.[g] [5]Yet the LORD says, "During the forty years that I led you through the wilderness, your clothes did not wear out, nor did the sandals on your feet.[h] [6]You ate no bread and drank no wine or other fermented drink. I did this so that you might know that I am the LORD your God."[i]

[7]When you reached this place, Sihon[j] king of Heshbon and Og king of Bashan came out to fight against us, but we defeated them.[k] [8]We took their land and gave it as an inheritance to the Reubenites, the Gadites and the half-tribe of Manasseh.[l]

[9]Carefully follow[m] the terms of this covenant, so that you may prosper in everything you do.[n] [10]All of you are standing today in the presence of the LORD your God—your leaders and chief men, your elders and officials, and all the other men of Israel, [11]together with your children and your wives, and the foreigners living in your camps who chop your wood and carry your water.[o] [12]You are standing here in order to enter into a covenant with the LORD your God, a covenant the LORD is making with you this day and sealing with an oath, [13]to confirm you this day as his people,[p] that he may be your God[q] as he promised you and as he swore to your fathers, Abraham, Isaac and Jacob. [14]I am making this covenant,[r] with its oath, not only with you [15]who are standing here with us today in the presence of the LORD our God but also with those who are not here today.[s]

[16]You yourselves know how we lived in Egypt and how we passed through the countries on the way here. [17]You saw among them their detestable images and idols of wood and stone, of silver and gold.[t] [18]Make sure there is no man or woman, clan or tribe among you today whose heart turns away from the LORD our God to go and worship the gods of those nations; make sure there is no root among you that produces such bitter poison.[u]

[19]When such a person hears the words of this oath and they invoke a blessing on themselves, thinking, "I will be safe, even though I persist in going my own way," they will bring disaster on the watered land as well as the dry. [20]The LORD will never be willing to forgive them; his wrath and zeal[v] will burn[w] against them. All the curses written in this book will fall on them, and the LORD will blot[x] out their names from under heaven. [21]The LORD will single them out from all the tribes of Israel for disaster, according to all the curses of the covenant written in this Book of the Law.

[a] In Hebrew texts 29:1 is numbered 28:69, and 29:2-29 is numbered 29:1-28.

28:67 [c] ver 34; Job 7:4
29:1 [d] Dt 5:2-3
29:2 [e] Ex 19:4
29:3 [f] Dt 4:34; 7:19
29:4 [g] Isa 6:10; Ac 28:26-27; Ro 11:8*; Eph 4:18
29:5 [h] Dt 8:4
29:6 [i] Dt 8:3
29:7 [j] Dt 2:32; 3:1 [k] Nu 21:21-24, 33-35
29:8 [l] Nu 32:33; Dt 3:12-13
29:9 [m] Dt 4:6; Jos 1:7 [n] 1Ki 2:3
29:11 [o] Jos 9:21, 23, 27
29:13 [p] Dt 28:9 [q] Ge 17:7; Ex 6:7
29:14 [r] Jer 31:31
29:15 [s] Ac 2:39
29:17 [t] Dt 28:36
29:18 [u] Dt 11:16; Heb 12:15
29:20 [v] Eze 23:25 [w] Ps 74:1; 79:5 [x] Ex 32:33; Dt 9:14

28:68 *send you back in ships to Egypt.* One way for this to happen would be for the Assyrians to press their Israelite captives/vassals into service in naval actions from the Phoenician coast. Another option is for them to fall victim to the Egyptian slave trade in Canaan, where slaves were transported by ship. Either way, this curse represents oppression from foreign enemies.

29:4 *mind that understands … ears that hear.* God created human beings with the ability to see and hear (see Ex 4:11–12), but spiritual, moral and intellectual perception is in mind in this verse. All these functions work together in the Egyptian Ennead of gods: "eyes see, the ears' hearing … to the heart [which] causes every conclusion to emerge." Ears and eyes that function properly inform the heart (Hebrew *leb*), which produces knowledge, speech and action that is also morally and ethically discerning. This is expressed in the action of the Egyptian god Ptah, creator of the world. The sight of the eyes, the hearing of the ears and the sense of smell are connected to Ptah's heart, understanding and intelligence.

For Israel to truly "hear" with their whole being, they needed to keep the covenant, but they had not done so. Only faithful obedience to the Lord and his covenant could open the way for God to give them an understanding mind (Hebrew *leb*; cf. 6:4–5).

29:19 *I will be safe, even though I persist in going my own way.* The vassal treaty of Esarhaddon (690–669 BC), with the god Assur as witness, puts forth similar conditions: "If you, as you stand on the soil where this oath (is sworn), swear the oath with *words and lips (only)*, do not swear with your entire heart, do not transmit it to your sons … if you take this curse upon yourselves but do not plan to keep the treaty of Esarhaddon." Duplicity and deceit were not acceptable to Assur or to Esarhaddon—or to the Lord of Israel.

22 Your children who follow you in later generations and foreigners who come
from distant lands will see the calamities
that have fallen on the land and the diseases with which the LORD has afflicted
it.[y] 23 The whole land will be a burning
waste[z] of salt[a] and sulfur—nothing planted, nothing sprouting, no vegetation growing on it. It will be like the destruction of
Sodom and Gomorrah,[b] Admah and Zeboyim, which the LORD overthrew in fierce
anger. 24 All the nations will ask: "Why has
the LORD done this to this land?[c] Why this
fierce, burning anger?"
25 And the answer will be: "It is because
this people abandoned the covenant of
the LORD, the God of their ancestors, the
covenant he made with them when he
brought them out of Egypt. 26 They went
off and worshiped other gods and bowed
down to them, gods they did not know,
gods he had not given them. 27 Therefore
the LORD's anger burned against this land,
so that he brought on it all the curses written in this book.[d] 28 In furious anger and in
great wrath the LORD uprooted[e] them from
their land and thrust them into another
land, as it is now."
29 The secret things belong to the LORD
our God, but the things revealed belong
to us and to our children forever, that we
may follow all the words of this law.

Prosperity After Turning to the LORD

30 When all these blessings and curses[f] I have set before you come on
you and you take them to heart wherever
the LORD your God disperses you among
the nations,[g] 2 and when you and your
children return[h] to the LORD your God and
obey him with all your heart and with all
your soul according to everything I command you today, 3 then the LORD your God
will restore your fortunes[a][i] and have compassion on you and gather[j] you again from
all the nations where he scattered you.[k]
4 Even if you have been banished to the
most distant land under the heavens, from
there the LORD your God will gather you
and bring you back.[l] 5 He will bring[m] you
to the land that belonged to your ancestors, and you will take possession of it.
He will make you more prosperous and
numerous than your ancestors. 6 The LORD
your God will circumcise your hearts and
the hearts of your descendants,[n] so that
you may love him with all your heart and
with all your soul, and live. 7 The LORD
your God will put all these curses on your
enemies who hate and persecute you.[o]
8 You will again obey the LORD and follow
all his commands I am giving you today.
9 Then the LORD your God will make you
most prosperous in all the work of your
hands and in the fruit of your womb, the
young of your livestock and the crops of
your land.[p] The LORD will again delight in
you and make you prosperous, just as he
delighted in your ancestors, 10 if you obey
the LORD your God and keep his commands and decrees that are written in this
Book of the Law and turn to the LORD your
God with all your heart and with all your
soul.[q]

The Offer of Life or Death

11 Now what I am commanding you today is not too difficult for you or beyond
your reach.[r] 12 It is not up in heaven, so
that you have to ask, "Who will ascend
into heaven to get it and proclaim it to us
so we may obey it?"[s] 13 Nor is it beyond the
sea, so that you have to ask, "Who will
cross the sea to get it and proclaim it to us
so we may obey it?" 14 No, the word is very
near you; it is in your mouth and in your
heart so you may obey it.
15 See, I set before you today life and
prosperity, death and destruction.[t] 16 For I

29:22 [y] Jer 19:8 **29:23** [z] Isa 34:9 [a] Jer 17:6 [b] Ge 19:24, 25; Zep 2:9 **29:24** [c] 1Ki 9:8; Jer 22:8-9 **29:27** [d] Da 9:11, 13, 14 **29:28** [e] 1Ki 14:15; 2Ch 7:20; Ps 52:5; Pr 2:22 **30:1** [f] ver 15, 19; Dt 11:26 [g] Lev 26:40-45; Dt 28:64; 29:28; 1Ki 8:47 **30:2** [h] Dt 4:30; Ne 1:9 **30:3** [i] Ps 126:4 [j] Ps 147:2; Jer 32:37; Eze 34:13

[k] Jer 29:14 **30:4** [l] Ne 1:8-9; Isa 43:6 **30:5** [m] Jer 29:14 **30:6** [n] Dt 10:16; Jer 32:39 **30:7** [o] Dt 7:15 **30:9** [p] Dt 28:11; Jer 31:28; 32:41 **30:10** [q] Dt 4:29 **30:11** [r] Isa 45:19, 23 **30:12** [s] Ro 10:6* **30:15** [t] Dt 11:26

[a] 3 Or *will bring you back from captivity*

29:23 *salt and sulfur.* Burning, salting and weeds are mentioned in inscriptions from Sefire, in a treaty context, as curses on those who break the treaty or covenant. Salt and sulfur wither and dry up vegetation. The cities of Jericho and Shechem experienced this kind of devastation.

29:25–28 *this people abandoned the covenant ... Therefore the LORD's anger burned ... the LORD uprooted them.* Ashurbanipal records that all of the kings he set up in his provinces rebelled and broke their covenant and oaths. Therefore, he proceeded to punish them with the curses contained in the treaties. Covenant rebels were given their due—the curses of their respective treaties or covenants. The gods involved were the covenant prosecutors and executioners through the legal and military machinery of the suzerain whom the vassals had betrayed.

In the case of Ashurbanipal (668–633 BC) the treaty language, as in Deuteronomy, anticipates the questions of an astonished rebel vassal who asks, "On account of what have these calamities befallen Arabia?" He himself responds, "Because we did not keep the solemn oaths (sworn by) Assur, because we offended the friendliness of Assurbanipal, the king, beloved of Enlil." The guilty vassals could not claim lack of knowledge, for the terms of the covenant or treaty and the will of the gods and suzerain stood in the publicly accessible document that had been sworn by all the parties involved (cf. v. 29).

30:15 *life ... death.* To live was to receive the blessings; to die was to encounter the divine displeasure through the curses. Thus, two ways are set before Israel—life or death. The "Noah" character of Babylonian legends, Utnapishtim, was encouraged to seek life by following the words of the gods, with the result that prosperity and health would follow. Pharaoh Akhenaten, who alone knew the Aten (sun-disk/god), believed that to follow him was to experience life. The king's heart was to stay focused on his god.

The victory stele of Piye (c. 734 BC), king of Egypt,

command you today to love the LORD your
God, to walk in obedience to him, and to
keep his commands, decrees and laws;
then you will live and increase, and the
LORD your God will bless you in the land
you are entering to possess.
17But if your heart turns away and you
are not obedient, and if you are drawn
away to bow down to other gods and worship them, 18I declare to you this day that
you will certainly be destroyed.[u] You will
not live long in the land you are crossing
the Jordan to enter and possess.
19This day I call the heavens and the
earth as witnesses against you[v] that I have
set before you life and death, blessings
and curses.[w] Now choose life, so that you
and your children may live 20and that you
may love[x] the LORD your God, listen to his
voice, and hold fast to him. For the LORD
is your life,[y] and he will give you many
years in the land he swore to give to your
fathers, Abraham, Isaac and Jacob.

Joshua to Succeed Moses

31 Then Moses went out and spoke
these words to all Israel: 2"I am
now a hundred and twenty years old[z] and
I am no longer able to lead you.[a] The LORD
has said to me, 'You shall not cross the
Jordan.'[b] 3The LORD your God himself will
cross[c] over ahead of you.[d] He will destroy
these nations before you, and you will
take possession of their land. Joshua also
will cross[e] over ahead of you, as the LORD
said. 4And the LORD will do to them what
he did to Sihon and Og, the kings of the
Amorites, whom he destroyed along with
their land. 5The LORD will deliver[f] them
to you, and you must do to them all that
I have commanded you. 6Be strong and
courageous.[g] Do not be afraid or terrified[h]
because of them, for the LORD your God
goes with you;[i] he will never leave you[j]
nor forsake[k] you."
7Then Moses summoned Joshua and
said[l] to him in the presence of all Israel,
"Be strong and courageous, for you must
go with this people into the land that
the LORD swore to their ancestors to give
them, and you must divide it among them
as their inheritance. 8The LORD himself
goes before you and will be with you;[m]
he will never leave you nor forsake you.
Do not be afraid; do not be discouraged."

Public Reading of the Law

9So Moses wrote down this law and
gave it to the Levitical priests, who carried[n] the ark of the covenant of the LORD,
and to all the elders of Israel. 10Then Moses commanded them: "At the end of every seven years, in the year for canceling
debts,[o] during the Festival of Tabernacles,[p] 11when all Israel comes to appear[q]
before the LORD your God at the place he

30:18 [u] Dt 8:19 **30:19** [v] Dt 4:26 [w] ver 1 **30:20** [x] Dt 6:5; 10:20 [y] Ps 27:1; Jn 11:25 **31:2** [z] Dt 34:7 [a] Nu 27:17; 1Ki 3:7 [b] Dt 3:23, 26 **31:3** [c] Nu 27:18 [d] Dt 9:3 [e] Dt 3:28 **31:5** [f] Dt 7:2 **31:6** [g] Jos 10:25; 1Ch 22:13 [h] Dt 7:18 [i] Dt 1:29; 20:4 [j] Jos 1:5 [k] Heb 13:5* **31:7** [l] Dt 1:38; 3:28 **31:8** [m] Ex 13:21; 33:14 **31:9** [n] ver 25; Nu 4:15; Jos 3:3 **31:10** [o] Dt 15:1 [p] Lev 23:34 **31:11** [q] Dt 16:16

reports that as he approached a town, he sent messengers saying, "Look, two ways are before you; choose as you wish. Open, you live; close, you die." Those who follow the word of their lord prolong their life, but shorten it if they rebel. Moral behavior was a key to a good and long life in Egyptian thinking.

Consistently across the ancient Near East, life is found in a god when one has found favor with that god. God is the source of life; he can give it and take it away. Even though different cultures had different ideas of what would gain divine favor, those became the pursuits of religious belief. For many peoples, that meant the faithful performance of rituals. For Israel, it meant faithful adherence to the covenant.

30:19 *I call the heavens and the earth as witnesses.* Calling out witnesses and writing down a list of divine witnesses to a covenant or treaty in the Late Bronze Age Hittite documents was tedious, but necessary in order to activate the covenant. In the treaty between the Hittite king Mursili and Duppi-Teshub, the list of deities and witnesses begins: "Let the thousand gods stand by for this oath! Let them observe and listen!" The list runs for 40 lines and concludes with "mountains, rivers, springs, great sea, heaven and earth, winds, clouds. Let these be witnesses to the treaty and to the oath!" For the king and country, but also for the king's agents who were faithful, a blessing of long life was extended. In addition to life, health, multitudes of years and length of days were rewards for the faithful covenant keeper.

31:2 *I am now a hundred and twenty years old.* Old age was a blessing from the gods in the thinking of the ancient Near East. The kings before the flood in the Sumerian King List were attributed heroic lives of thousands of years. The age of 110 represented a fulfilled life in Egypt. Rameses II lived to be about 90 years old. Moses reached the Biblical ideal of 120 years (see Ge 6:3; cf. Ge 50:26).

Ptahhotep, one of Egypt's ancient viziers and wise men, instructed his son concerning how to live and think in order to enjoy a successful and long life. He himself attained 110 years through the favor of the king and the god Horus. In more recent texts found at Emar the ideal age of 120 years has surfaced and was already known in *Enlil and Namzitara.* The average lifespan in the ancient Near East was, in fact, only about 45 years. Moses, Joshua, Job, and a high priest named Jehoiada were the only persons, besides persons in the patriarchal era, who lived to 100 years or more.

Various phrases used to describe old age, such as "length of days," have been found outside the OT at Kuntillet Ajrud (ninth to eighth century BC). Ancient Near Eastern parallels in West Semitic and Akkadian occur. Nabonidus, a king of the Neo-Babylonian era, had a mother who was made famous for her old age by the god Sin, who extended her life and, more importantly, maintained her full mental capacity and reasoning powers. Nabonidus himself prayed to Sin for a "present life of long days."

31:10 – 11 *At the end of every seven years ... you shall read this law.* Hittite treaties provided for the deposition of treaty/covenant documents (of whatever material: iron, bronze, clay, stone, silver, etc.). It was desirable to have a copy of these documents on file, but also to make future public periodic reading possible. The document was deposited "before the god" and was read in the presence of the king and the "sons of the Hatti country." Curses

will choose, you shall read this law[r] before them in their hearing. 12Assemble the
people — men, women and children, and
the foreigners residing in your towns —
so they can listen and learn[s] to fear the
LORD your God and follow carefully all the
words of this law. 13Their children,[t] who
do not know this law, must hear it and
learn to fear the LORD your God as long as
you live in the land you are crossing the
Jordan to possess."

Israel's Rebellion Predicted

14The LORD said to Moses, "Now the day
of your death[u] is near. Call Joshua and
present yourselves at the tent of meeting,
where I will commission him." So Moses
and Joshua came and presented themselves at the tent of meeting.
15Then the LORD appeared at the tent
in a pillar of cloud, and the cloud stood
over the entrance to the tent.[v] 16And the
LORD said to Moses: "You are going to rest
with your ancestors, and these people will
soon prostitute[w] themselves to the foreign
gods of the land they are entering. They
will forsake[x] me and break the covenant I
made with them. 17And in that day I will
become angry[y] with them and forsake[z]
them; I will hide[a] my face from them, and
they will be destroyed. Many disasters and
calamities will come on them, and in that
day they will ask, 'Have not these disasters come on us because our God is not
with us?'[b] 18And I will certainly hide my
face in that day because of all their wickedness in turning to other gods.
19"Now write down this song and teach
it to the Israelites and have them sing it,
so that it may be a witness for me against
them. 20When I have brought them into
the land flowing with milk and honey, the
land I promised on oath to their ancestors,[c]
and when they eat their fill and thrive, they
will turn to other gods[d] and worship them,
rejecting me and breaking my covenant.[e]
21And when many disasters and calamities come on them,[f] this song will testify
against them, because it will not be forgotten by their descendants. I know what
they are disposed to do,[g] even before I
bring them into the land I promised them
on oath." 22So Moses wrote[h] down this
song that day and taught it to the Israelites.
23The LORD gave this command[i] to Joshua son of Nun: "Be strong and courageous,[j] for you will bring the Israelites into
the land I promised them on oath, and I
myself will be with you."
24After Moses finished writing in a book
the words of this law from beginning to
end, 25he gave this command to the Levites who carried the ark of the covenant
of the LORD: 26"Take this Book of the Law
and place it beside the ark of the covenant
of the LORD your God. There it will remain

31:11 [r] Jos 8:34-35; 2Ki 23:2 **31:12** [s] Dt 4:10 **31:13** [t] Dt 11:2; Ps 78:6-7 **31:14** [u] Nu 27:13; Dt 32:49-50 **31:15** [v] Ex 33:9 **31:16** [w] Jdg 2:12 [x] Jdg 10:6, 13 **31:17** [y] Jdg 2:14, 20 [z] Jdg 6:13; 2Ch 15:2 [a] Dt 32:20; Isa 1:15; 8:17

[b] Nu 14:42 **31:20** [c] Dt 6:10-12 [d] Dt 32:15-17 [e] ver 16 **31:21** [f] ver 17 [g] Hos 5:3 **31:22** [h] ver 19 **31:23** [i] ver 7 [j] Jos 1:6

were declared against anyone who would be so bold as to remove, damage, destroy or deface the treaty or covenant document. Curses were set forth for the person who would change the document.

In a covenant between the Hittites and King Kurtiwaza in Mitanni, the covenantal documents were deposited before the gods or goddesses for periodic reading. An inscribed public monument could serve the same function. A copy was placed before the goddess Arinna in Hatti and one was placed before Teshub in Mitanni mainly done for safekeeping by both parties. But the ancients also considered the words of the text and their reading to aid in keeping the agreement in force.

At Emar in Syria, a *Zukru* festival reflects a number of significant features of the covenant in Deuteronomy. A covenant renewal ceremony was held every seven years, which parallels the seven-year cycle of covenant reading and covenant renewal laid out in these two verses at the Festival of Tabernacles. The ritual calendar of this religious festival began on the first full moon of the year. This *Zukru* festival included all those who functioned as the essential parties in the festival. The king was there, though he was not the key participant. The seventh year was also special in Ugarit.

Seven-year cycles with a preparatory period in the sixth year are also found. In the sixth year preparations were made for the seventh year. The *Zukru* festival was directed to the gods, a total of 70, and involved a treaty or covenant bond between Emar and its god Dagan (grain-god).

31:14 *tent of meeting.* See note on Ex 33:7; see also the article "The Tabernacle," p. 158.

31:16 *rest with your ancestors.* See notes on Ge 23:4; 25:8.

31:19 *Now write down this song ... that it may be a witness.* The flexibility of ancient Near Eastern treaty/covenant forms permitted additional sections to be added. Here the Biblical author places witnesses following the blessings and curses, a feature found in Hittite treaties, especially those between Tudhaliya IV and Kurunta. There the required deposition of the treaty documents is located between stipulations, and other stipulations are added after the curses and blessings as well as a list of sanctions. The Hittites, Syrians and Assyrians adjusted treaties depending on whether they were dealing with individuals, peoples or kingdoms. Terminology, structure and tone could vary with the purpose of the treaty.

31:22 The interplay between writing and literacy is well illustrated here. Ancient Israel was not a modern literate nation, but the Israelites were acquainted with writing (see the article "Literacy," p. 140). Israelites used writing to help disseminate knowledge and wisdom by repeating or teaching it to the people orally, not by having them produce a thousand copies of the Song of Moses or the Book of the Law or the Blessings of Moses.

This oral-literate interplay is reflected here and in v. 30, as the written words of Moses are to be repeated and spoken. Ancient Near Eastern materials — e.g., some letters of Arad, a Deir Alla inscription, the Gezer Calendar, an Izbet Sartah inscription, inscriptions at Kuntillet Ajrud, Lachish ostraca (broken pottery fragments used as writing material), the Mesha Stele, etc. — all reflect the interesting interaction of oral and written words.

31:26 The only objects inside the ark were the tablets; the Book of the Law is placed before the ark along with

as a witness against you.[k] 27For I know
how rebellious and stiff-necked[l] you are.
If you have been rebellious against the
LORD while I am still alive and with you,
how much more will you rebel after I die!
28Assemble before me all the elders of
your tribes and all your officials, so that
I can speak these words in their hearing
and call the heavens and the earth to testify against them.[m] 29For I know that after
my death you are sure to become utterly
corrupt[n] and to turn from the way I have
commanded you. In days to come, disaster[o] will fall on you because you will do
evil in the sight of the LORD and arouse his
anger by what your hands have made."

The Song of Moses

30And Moses recited the words of this
song from beginning to end in the hearing
of the whole assembly of Israel:

32 Listen, you heavens,[p] and I will speak;
hear, you earth, the words of my mouth.
2Let my teaching fall like rain
and my words descend like dew,[q]
like showers[r] on new grass,
like abundant rain on tender plants.
3I will proclaim the name of the LORD.[s]
Oh, praise the greatness[t] of our God!
4He is the Rock,[u] his works are perfect,[v]
and all his ways are just.
A faithful God[w] who does no wrong,
upright and just is he.
5They are corrupt and not his children;
to their shame they are a warped and crooked generation.[x]
6Is this the way you repay[y] the LORD,
you foolish and unwise people?[z]
Is he not your Father,[a] your Creator,[a]
who made you and formed you?[b]
7Remember the days of old;
consider the generations long past.
Ask your father and he will tell you,
your elders, and they will explain to you.[c]
8When the Most High gave the nations their inheritance,
when he divided all mankind,[d]
he set up boundaries for the peoples
according to the number of the sons of Israel.[b]
9For the LORD's portion[e] is his people,
Jacob his allotted inheritance.[f]
10In a desert[g] land he found him,
in a barren and howling waste.
He shielded him and cared for him;
he guarded him as the apple of his eye,[h]
11like an eagle that stirs up its nest
and hovers over its young,[i]
that spreads its wings to catch them
and carries them aloft.

31:26 [k]ver 19 **31:27** [l]Ex 32:9; Dt 9:6,24 **31:28** [m]Dt 4:26; 30:19; 32:1 **31:29** [n]Dt 32:5; Jdg 2:19 [o]Dt 28:15 **32:1** [p]Isa 1:2 **32:2** [q]Isa 55:11 [r]Ps 72:6 **32:3** [s]Ex 33:19 [t]Dt 3:24 **32:4** [u]ver 15, 18,30 [v]2Sa 22:31 [w]Dt 7:9 **32:5** [x]Dt 31:29 **32:6** [y]Ps 116:12 [z]Ps 74:2 [a]Dt 1:31; Isa 63:16 [b]ver 15 **32:7** [c]Ex 13:14 **32:8** [d]Ge 11:8; Ac 17:26 **32:9** [e]Jer 10:16 [f]1Ki 8:51,53 **32:10** [g]Jer 2:6 [h]Ps 17:8; Zec 2:8 **32:11** [i]Ex 19:4

[a] 6 Or *Father, who bought you* [b] 8 Masoretic Text; Dead Sea Scrolls (see also Septuagint) *sons of God*

Aaron's rod and a jar of manna. In Egypt, important documents confirmed by oath, such as international treaties, were deposited beneath the feet of the deity. The ark is the footstool of God, so that is where the book is being placed.
31:30 *Moses recited the words.* See note on v. 22.
32:6 *Is he not your Father . . . ?* The fatherhood of the gods was a common theological feature of the peoples of the ancient Near East and contributed to the idea, e.g., that Enlil (Sumer) "was a friendly, fatherly deity who watches over the safety and well-being of all humans, *particularly* the inhabitants of Sumer." However, the overall concept is somewhat jumbled because of the seemingly contradictory way the material is presented and the strangeness of the worldview being propounded. *your Creator.* Many "father gods"—e.g., in Sumer (e.g., An, Enlil, Utu), Egypt (Atum, Ptah, Re, Geb) and Ugarit (El, Baal)—were involved in the production and creation not only of the cosmos but of other gods as well. As an example, in the Ugaritic myths (c. 1350 BC), Baal, the Bull, is described as the creator of the gods. In Egypt, Amun was the ultimate source and cause of gods and the cosmos. This language is echoed in the designation of even a subordinate ruler such as Azatiwata, "mother and father" of the Danua people. In the Emar *Zukru* festival, Dagan (grain-god; storm-god) is referred to as the "lord of creation."

These examples demonstrate that Israel talked about Yahweh in much the same ways that other peoples in the ancient world talked about their own gods. Even though the God of Israel was very different in nature, many of his attributes could be expressed using similar metaphors to those used throughout the ancient world.

32:8 *according to the number of the sons of Israel.* The NIV follows the Hebrew text here. Many scholars prefer the reading of the Septuagint, the pre-Christian translation of the OT, and some Dead Sea Scrolls, which read "according to the sons of God" (see NIV text note). This text is closely connected to Ge 10, where 70 nations are listed, but Israel is not included among them. It is possible that, according to the Septuagint, God "divided" (Hebrew *prd,* in both Ge 10 and this verse) the nations among 70 subordinate, created, divine beings (see the article "Divine Council," p. 615). This reading is increasingly favored by scholars.

A Ugaritic text refers to the "seventy sons of Athirat," sired by El, which comprised his council of divine beings. Seventy gods are also mentioned at Emar. A divine council of gods was common in the ancient Near East. A Phoenician inscription also refers to the whole "group of the children of the gods." In other Babylonian literature, we generally read of the gods distributing the cosmos among themselves, but not the nations, as here.

This is part of the broader context, but these verses are intended to contrast the fact that the Lord has set Israel *apart unto himself* from among all the nations, and Israel is not numbered with them, for the Israelites are "his people," his "allotted inheritance" (v. 9)".
32:10 *apple of his eye.* This is an English idiom, not a Hebrew one. The Hebrew means "pupil" and refers to a sensitive, protected and significant part of the body.
32:11 *like an eagle . . . spreads its wings . . . and carries them aloft.* The story of Etana, a quasi-historical king of Kish mentioned in the Sumerian King List, rode upon an eagle that cared for him as it carried Etana on his back. Etana is

Cylinder seal shows Etana ascending on an eagle's back, twenty-third century BC. There is a parallel of Etana's story and the Biblical text. Note on Dt 32:11 explains parallel between Etana's story and the biblical text.

12 The LORD alone led him;
no foreign god was with him.[j]
13 He made him ride on the heights[k] of the land
and fed him with the fruit of the fields.
He nourished him with honey from the rock,
and with oil[l] from the flinty crag,
14 with curds and milk from herd and flock
and with fattened lambs and goats,
with choice rams of Bashan
and the finest kernels of wheat.[m]
You drank the foaming blood of the grape.[n]

32:12 [j]ver 39
32:13 [k]Isa 58:14 [l]Job 29:6
32:14 [m]Ps 81:16; 147:14 [n]Ge 49:11
32:15 [o]Dt 31:20 [p]ver 6; Isa 1:4, 28 [q]ver 4
32:16 [r]1Co 10:22 [s]Ps 78:58
32:17 [t]Dt 28:64 [u]Jdg 5:8

15 Jeshurun[a] grew fat[o] and kicked;
filled with food, they became heavy and sleek.
They abandoned[p] the God who made them
and rejected the Rock[q] their Savior.
16 They made him jealous[r] with their foreign gods
and angered[s] him with their detestable idols.
17 They sacrificed to false gods, which are not God—
gods they had not known,[t]
gods that recently appeared,[u]
gods your ancestors did not fear.

[a] 15 *Jeshurun* means *the upright one,* that is, Israel.

pictured ascending on an eagle's back on a cylinder seal of the twenty-third century BC.

The story line in the Etana myth is helpful. It depicts an eagle as the instrument through whom Etana successfully gets a son. The eagle imagery here and in Ex 19:4 is tied to the Lord's rescue of his son Israel on eagles' wings. Etana beseeches the eagle to "change my destiny"; the eagle obliges, but only after giving Etana a magnificent but dangerous ride toward heaven and back down to earth. The eagle drops but retrieves Etana at three miles (4.8 kilometers), two miles (3.2 kilometers), one mile (1.6 kilometers), and three feet (1 meter) above the ground.

The parallel with the Biblical text is not dependent on naturalists observing certain behavior patterns of eagles with their young, but on the story line of the Etana text. It took an eagles' wings for Etana's goal to be met: his acquisition of a son. God brought Israel to the mountain of God, Sinai, and births/nurtures his only son (cf. v. 8).

Some believe that the "eagles' wings" protective imagery originated in Egypt and moved throughout the ancient Near East. The actual bird in the Egyptian iconography is considered to be the griffon vulture. The Hebrew word translated "eagle" can also be translated "vulture."

A misconception refuted by naturalist observations of birds in the wild is that eagles/vultures teach their young to fly by nudging them out of the nests and then catching them when they fail to fly. In fact, however, these birds do not take their first flight until they are three to four months old and nearly full grown.

It is more likely that the picture painted here makes use of political imagery. In Egypt, the goddess Nekhbet is portrayed in the shape of a vulture and is notably maternal in her protection of the pharaoh. She is often seen protecting him with her wings. This vulture deity cared for its young and protected the pharaoh.

32:13 *ride on the heights.* Cities were built on hills, because hills boasted natural defensibility and strategic value. This metaphor refers to victory and security.

32:17 *gods.* The Hebrew word here is the plural *shedim* (singular *shed*). Israel had rebelled by sacrificing to a god(s) *shdym* (cf. Ps 106:37; cf. Akkadian *shedu*). The Hebrew word could be related to either the cognate Akkadian *shedu* or to the Aramaic *shdyn*, found in the Deir Alla Balaam

18 You deserted the Rock, who fathered you;
you forgot[v] the God who gave you birth.

19 The LORD saw this and rejected them[w]
because he was angered by his sons and daughters.[x]
20 "I will hide my face[y] from them," he said,
"and see what their end will be;
for they are a perverse generation,[z]
children who are unfaithful.
21 They made me jealous[a] by what is no god
and angered me with their worthless idols.[b]
I will make them envious by those who are not a people;
I will make them angry by a nation that has no understanding.[c]
22 For a fire will be kindled by my wrath,
one that burns down to the realm of the dead below.[d]
It will devour the earth and its harvests
and set afire the foundations of the mountains.

23 "I will heap calamities[e] on them
and spend my arrows[f] against them.
24 I will send wasting famine against them,
consuming pestilence[g] and deadly plague;[h]
I will send against them the fangs of wild beasts,[i]
the venom of vipers[j] that glide in the dust.
25 In the street the sword will make them childless;
in their homes terror will reign.[k]
The young men and young women will perish,
the infants and those with gray hair.[l]
26 I said I would scatter[m] them
and erase their name from human memory,[n]
27 but I dreaded the taunt of the enemy,
lest the adversary misunderstand
and say, 'Our hand has triumphed;
the LORD has not done all this.' "[o]

28 They are a nation without sense,
there is no discernment in them.
29 If only they were wise and would understand this[p]
and discern what their end will be!
30 How could one man chase a thousand,
or two put ten thousand to flight,[q]
unless their Rock had sold them,
unless the LORD had given them up?[r]
31 For their rock is not like our Rock,
as even our enemies concede.
32 Their vine comes from the vine of Sodom
and from the fields of Gomorrah.
Their grapes are filled with poison,
and their clusters with bitterness.
33 Their wine is the venom of serpents,
the deadly poison of cobras.[s]

34 "Have I not kept this in reserve
and sealed it in my vaults?[t]

32:18 [v] Isa 17:10
32:19 [w] Jer 44:21-23 [x] Ps 106:40
32:20 [y] Dt 31:17,29 [z] ver 5
32:21 [a] 1Co 10:22 [b] 1Ki 16:13,26 [c] Ro 10:19*
32:22 [d] Ps 18:7-8; Jer 15:14; La 4:11
32:23 [e] Dt 29:21 [f] Ps 7:13; Eze 5:16
32:24 [g] Dt 28:22 [h] Ps 91:6 [i] Lev 26:22 [j] Am 5:18-19
32:25 [k] Eze 7:15 [l] 2Ch 36:17; La 2:21
32:26 [m] Dt 4:27 [n] Ps 34:16
32:27 [o] Isa 10:13
32:29 [p] Dt 5:29; Ps 81:13
32:30 [q] Lev 26:8 [r] Ps 44:12
32:33 [s] Ps 58:4
32:34 [t] Jer 2:22; Hos 13:12

inscription. The Akkadian word (*shedu*) describes only minor deities, if deities at all (cf. Ps 106:36–38), and it is connected to spirits of the dead. The *shedu* would not have been the recipients of sacrifices. In contrast, the Aramaic *shdyn* were gods, members of the divine council, who were worshiped in Transjordan and Canaan, and therefore could have been the same gods referred to in the Biblical texts. In the Deir Allah Balaam inscription, these "gods" sit in the divine assembly with other gods and decree a catastrophe on the earth, but then inform Balaam of this by a dream or vision (cf. Nu 22:8–9,12,19). It is therefore possible that they could be involved in Israel's illegitimate cultic practice. No evidence concerning their moral nature or relationship to Israel's God can be determined; Yahweh is occasionally depicted as holding assembly with other divine beings (1Ki 22:20–22; Job 1:6–7) which may be comparable to the *shdyn*. Whether the Bible's term is related to the Akkadian or Aramaic, these *shedim* were forbidden in Israelite religion. In neither case, however, would they have been considered demons.

32:20 *I will hide my face from them.* When God hides his face, he is displeased with his people, and catastrophe strikes them. In a famous Egyptian theological treatise, a deceased person expresses despair that he can no longer see the face of Atum: "It is too much for me, my Lord, not to see your face." When the great god Erra (Nirgal) was enthroned, the other gods "began to look at his face." Telipinu, a weather- or storm-god of sorts at Hatti, turned his face away and left his people because of their insolence toward him. When he left, he took with him all kinds of blessings, especially fertility. People could not conceive, nor could they, if pregnant, give birth. The hills dried up, trees withered, and the grass died. Hunger set in. An incantation finally resulted in the god's return, and subsequent blessings at his return ensued when he was again with his people. The royal house prospered.

The abandonment of a people by its god occurred several times during Babylon's history. In the Tukulti-Ninurta Epic, the gods abandon the Kassite Babylonian king because he had broken his covenant with Assyria. The third-century BC priest-historian Manetho reported that the Hyksos invasion of Egypt (seventeenth century BC) was a result of "God's displeasure upon us." Cyrus the Great (538 BC) proclaimed that Marduk, Babylon's chief god, gave Babylon into his power because the last king, Nabonidus, forsook the worship of Marduk and worshiped other gods.

32:23 *I will heap calamities on them.* Curses are found in various texts in the ancient Near East. At Ugarit, the god Resheph, a storm-god, was a god of war and a god of pestilence. These threats became realities in warfare. The support of a national god was crucial for a king, such as Hadad of northern Syria. In this case, Panammuwa, son of a king named Qarli, claimed support from many gods: Hadad, for whom a statue was erected, but also El, Rashap, Rakib-El and Shamash. Fulfilled curses include vivid

[35]It is mine to avenge; I will repay.[u]
In due time their foot will slip;[v]
their day of disaster is near
and their doom rushes upon them.[w]"

[36]The LORD will vindicate his people
and relent concerning his servants[x]
when he sees their strength is gone
and no one is left, slave or free.[a]
[37]He will say: "Now where are their gods,
the rock they took refuge in,[y]
[38]the gods who ate the fat of their sacrifices
and drank the wine of their drink offerings?
Let them rise up to help you!
Let them give you shelter!

[39]"See now that I myself am he![z]
There is no god besides me.[a]
I put to death and I bring to life,[b]
I have wounded and I will heal,[c]
and no one can deliver out of my hand.[d]
[40]I lift my hand to heaven and solemnly swear:
As surely as I live forever,
[41]when I sharpen my flashing sword[e]
and my hand grasps it in judgment,
I will take vengeance on my adversaries
and repay those who hate me.[f]
[42]I will make my arrows drunk with blood,[g]
while my sword devours flesh:[h]
the blood of the slain and the captives,
the heads of the enemy leaders."

[43]Rejoice,[i] you nations, with his people,[b,c]
for he will avenge the blood of his servants;[j]
he will take vengeance on his enemies
and make atonement for his land and people.[k]

32:35 [u]Ro 12:19*; Heb 10:30* [v]Jer 23:12 [w]Eze 7:8-9 **32:36** [x]Dt 30:1-3; Ps 135:14; Joel 2:14 **32:37** [y]Jdg 10:14; Jer 2:28 **32:39** [z]Isa 41:4 [a]Isa 45:5 [b]1Sa 2:6; Ps 68:20 [c]Hos 6:1 [d]Ps 50:22 **32:41** [e]Isa 34:6; 66:16; Eze 21:9-10 [f]Jer 50:29 **32:42** [g]ver 23 [h]Jer 46:10, 14 **32:43** [i]Ro 15:10* [j]2Ki 9:7 [k]Ps 65:3; 85:1; Rev 19:2

32:44 [l]Nu 13:8, 16 **32:46** [m]Eze 40:4 **32:47** [n]Dt 30:20 **32:49** [o]Nu 27:12 **32:50** [p]Ge 25:8 **32:51** [q]Nu 20:11-13 [r]Nu 27:14 **32:52** [s]Dt 34:1-3 [t]Dt 1:37 **33:1** [u]Jos 14:6 **33:2** [v]Ex 19:18; Ps 68:8 [w]Jdg 5:4 [x]Hab 3:3

[44]Moses came with Joshua[d][l] son of Nun and spoke all the words of this song in the hearing of the people. [45]When Moses finished reciting all these words to all Israel, [46]he said to them, "Take to heart all the words I have solemnly declared to you this day,[m] so that you may command your children to obey carefully all the words of this law. [47]They are not just idle words for you—they are your life.[n] By them you will live long in the land you are crossing the Jordan to possess."

Moses to Die on Mount Nebo

[48]On that same day the LORD told Moses, [49]"Go up into the Abarim[o] Range to Mount Nebo in Moab, across from Jericho, and view Canaan, the land I am giving the Israelites as their own possession. [50]There on the mountain that you have climbed you will die[p] and be gathered to your people, just as your brother Aaron died on Mount Hor and was gathered to his people. [51]This is because both of you broke faith with me in the presence of the Israelites at the waters of Meribah Kadesh in the Desert of Zin[q] and because you did not uphold my holiness among the Israelites.[r] [52]Therefore, you will see the land only from a distance;[s] you will not enter[t] the land I am giving to the people of Israel."

Moses Blesses the Tribes

33:1-29Ref — Ge 49:1-28

33 This is the blessing that Moses the man of God[u] pronounced on the Israelites before his death. [2]He said:

"The LORD came from Sinai[v]
and dawned over them from Seir;[w]
he shone forth from Mount Paran.[x]

[a] 36 Or *and they are without a ruler or leader*
[b] 43 Or *Make his people rejoice, you nations*
[c] 43 Masoretic Text; Dead Sea Scrolls (see also Septuagint) *people, / and let all the angels worship him, /*
[d] 44 Hebrew *Hoshea,* a variant of *Joshua*

descriptions of besieged cities, such as Sumer and Ur. In several ancient treaties, a specific stipulation was followed by a specific curse administered by a particular god.

32:49 *Abarim Range to Mount Nebo.* The Abarim mountain range sits northeast of the Dead Sea. Mount Nebo (c. 1,435 feet or 440 meters) is a part of this range (cf. Nu 27:12; 33:47–48). It is located near the city Nebo (Nu 32:3), and the area forms a northwestern rim of the tableland of Moab. Mount Nebo (cf. Dt 34:1) is closely connected to Mount Pisgah, which is tied to descriptions of southern Gilead. The Spring of Moses on the north and the Wadi Afirt help frame the mountain.

The view from Nebo is panoramic, including the Dead Sea, the Jordan Valley, and the Jordan Desert from Tekoa to Jerusalem. Even the mountains of Samaria are visible from it. In the Mesha Stele of Moab (c. 830 BC), Nebo is considered an Israelite city conquered by the Moabites.

33:1–29 Compare the blessings of Isaac (Ge 27) and the blessings of Jacob (Ge 48–49). Outside of the OT, there are similar final blessings recorded in the second millennium BC, especially in texts at Nuzi. Many features of Yahweh presented in this chapter are paralleled by descriptions of the great storm-god in the ancient Near East, especially under his name Baal. In general, the Canaanite setting of several tribes is depicted just before Moses' death. There are close connections with Canaanite mythology, as evidenced in the literary style, language and vocabulary of the poem. Language reminiscent of the storm-gods of the ancient Near East depicts the Lord's kingship and his theophany (see especially vv. 2–3,13–16,26–29).

33:2 Mount Paran is clearly a Hebrew poetic parallel with Sinai and Seir (Edom area). Sinai is the primary referent, which is near or possibly in the Desert of Paran.

This entire theophany of God's awesome appearance shares features with texts from Ugarit (Baal) and Mesopotamia (e.g., Assur), among others. El "shines forth" in a text

He came with[a] myriads of holy ones[y]
from the south, from his mountain slopes.[b]
3 Surely it is you who love[z] the people;
all the holy ones are in your hand.[a]
At your feet they all bow down,[b]
and from you receive instruction,
4 the law that Moses gave us,[c]
the possession of the assembly of Jacob.[d]
5 He was king over Jeshurun[c]
when the leaders of the people assembled,
along with the tribes of Israel.

6 "Let Reuben live and not die,
nor[d] his people be few."

7 And this he said about Judah:[e]

"Hear, LORD, the cry of Judah;
bring him to his people.
With his own hands he defends his cause.
Oh, be his help against his foes!"

8 About Levi he said:

"Your Thummim and Urim[f] belong
to your faithful servant.
You tested him at Massah;
you contended with him at the waters of Meribah.[g]
9 He said of his father and mother,[h]
'I have no regard for them.'
He did not recognize his brothers
or acknowledge his own children,
but he watched over your word
and guarded your covenant.[i]
10 He teaches your precepts to Jacob
and your law to Israel.[j]
He offers incense before you
and whole burnt offerings on your altar.[k]
11 Bless all his skills, LORD,
and be pleased with the work of his hands.[l]
Strike down those who rise against him,
his foes till they rise no more."

12 About Benjamin he said:

"Let the beloved of the LORD rest
secure in him,[m]
for he shields him all day long,
and the one the LORD loves rests
between his shoulders.[n]"

13 About Joseph[o] he said:

"May the LORD bless his land
with the precious dew from heaven above
and with the deep waters that lie below;[p]
14 with the best the sun brings forth
and the finest the moon can yield;
15 with the choicest gifts of the ancient mountains[q]
and the fruitfulness of the everlasting hills;
16 with the best gifts of the earth and its fullness
and the favor of him who dwelt in the burning bush.[r]
Let all these rest on the head of Joseph,
on the brow of the prince among[e] his brothers.
17 In majesty he is like a firstborn bull;
his horns are the horns of a wild ox.[s]
With them he will gore[t] the nations,
even those at the ends of the earth.
Such are the ten thousands of Ephraim;
such are the thousands of Manasseh."

18 About Zebulun[u] he said:

"Rejoice, Zebulun, in your going out,
and you, Issachar, in your tents.
19 They will summon peoples to the mountain[v]
and there offer the sacrifices of the righteous;[w]
they will feast on the abundance of the seas,[x]
on the treasures hidden in the sand."

20 About Gad[y] he said:

"Blessed is he who enlarges Gad's domain!
Gad lives there like a lion,
tearing at arm or head.

33:2 [y] Da 7:10; Ac 7:53; Rev 5:11 **33:3** [z] Hos 11:1 [a] Dt 14:2 [b] Lk 10:39 **33:4** [c] Jn 1:17 [d] Ps 119:111 **33:7** [e] Ge 49:10 **33:8** [f] Ex 28:30 [g] Ex 17:7 **33:9** [h] Ex 32:26-29 [i] Mal 2:5 **33:10** [j] Lev 10:11; Dt 31:9-13 [k] Ps 51:19 **33:11** [l] 2Sa 24:23 **33:12** [m] Dt 12:10 [n] Ex 28:12 **33:13** [o] Ge 49:25 [p] Ge 27:28 **33:15** [q] Hab 3:6 **33:16** [r] Ex 3:2 **33:17** [s] Nu 23:22 [t] 1Ki 22:11; Ps 44:5 **33:18** [u] Ge 49:13-15 **33:19** [v] Ex 15:17; Isa 2:3 [w] Ps 4:5 [x] Isa 60:5, 11 **33:20** [y] Ge 49:19

[a] 2 Or *from* [b] 2 The meaning of the Hebrew for this phrase is uncertain. [c] 5 *Jeshurun* means *the upright one*, that is, Israel; also in verse 26. [d] 6 Or *but let* [e] 16 Or *of the one separated from*

in Hebrew (Phoenician script) from Kuntillet Ajrud. In Ugaritic texts Baal marches forth. The divine allies of Baal and ancient Near Eastern storm-gods parallel Yahweh's "myriads." A divine assembly to perform the bidding of the chief god is present in Canaanite and similar mythological texts in Assyrian, Assyrian-Babylonian and Hittite texts.
33:8 *Thummim and Urim.* See the article "Urim and Thummim," p. 162.
33:13–17 In essence, Yahweh fulfills the functions performed by the chief fertility god, Baal, in Canaan. The "deep waters" (v. 13) are tied to the "abyss" in both Ugaritic liturgical texts and mythological texts. The bull imagery applied to Joseph in v. 17 has similarities with Ugaritic metaphoric descriptions of gods in which Mot and Baal "gore like wild oxen," and El is called "the bull." A Hittite document describes the strength of the bull that moved a mountain. Even Horus in Egypt is pictured as a young, strong bull.

21 He chose the best land for himself;[z]
the leader's portion was kept for him.
When the heads of the people
assembled,
he carried out the LORD's righteous
will,[a]
and his judgments concerning
Israel."

22 About Dan[b] he said:

"Dan is a lion's cub,
springing out of Bashan."

23 About Naphtali he said:

"Naphtali is abounding with the favor
of the LORD
and is full of his blessing;
he will inherit southward to the lake."

24 About Asher[c] he said:

"Most blessed of sons is Asher;
let him be favored by his brothers,
and let him bathe his feet in oil.[d]
25 The bolts of your gates will be iron and
bronze,
and your strength will equal your
days.[e]
26 "There is no one like the God of
Jeshurun,[f]
who rides across the heavens to help
you[g]
and on the clouds in his majesty.
27 The eternal God is your refuge,[h]
and underneath are the everlasting
arms.
He will drive out your enemies before
you,[i]
saying, 'Destroy them!'[j]

33:21 [z] Nu 32:1-5, 31-32 [a] Jos 4:12; 22:1-3 **33:22** [b] Ge 49:16 **33:24** [c] Ge 49:21 [d] Ge 49:20; Job 29:6 **33:25** [e] Dt 4:40; 32:47 **33:26** [f] Ex 15:11 [g] Ps 104:3 **33:27** [h] Ps 90:1 [i] Jos 24:18 [j] Dt 7:2

28 So Israel will live in safety;[k]
Jacob will dwell[a] secure
in a land of grain and new wine,
where the heavens drop dew.[l]
29 Blessed are you, Israel![m]
Who is like you,[n]
a people saved by the LORD?[o]
He is your shield and helper[p]
and your glorious sword.
Your enemies will cower before you,
and you will tread on their
heights.[q]"

The Death of Moses

34 Then Moses climbed Mount Nebo
from the plains of Moab to the top
of Pisgah, across from Jericho.[r] There the
LORD showed[s] him the whole land — from
Gilead to Dan, 2 all of Naphtali, the territory of Ephraim and Manasseh, all the land
of Judah as far as the Mediterranean Sea,[t]
3 the Negev and the whole region from the
Valley of Jericho, the City of Palms,[u] as
far as Zoar. 4 Then the LORD said to him,
"This is the land I promised on oath[v] to
Abraham, Isaac and Jacob when I said, 'I
will give it[w] to your descendants.' I have
let you see it with your eyes, but you will
not cross[x] over into it."
5 And Moses the servant of the LORD[y] died[z]
there in Moab, as the LORD had said. 6 He
buried him[b] in Moab, in the valley opposite
Beth Peor,[a] but to this day no one knows
where his grave is.[b] 7 Moses was a hundred
and twenty years old[c] when he died, yet his
eyes were not weak[d] nor his strength gone.
8 The Israelites grieved for Moses in the

33:28 [k] Nu 23:9; Jer 23:6 [l] Ge 27:28 **33:29** [m] Ps 144:15 [n] Ps 18:44 [o] 2Sa 7:23 [p] Ps 115:9-11 [q] Dt 32:13 **34:1** [r] Dt 32:49 [s] Dt 32:52 **34:2** [t] Dt 11:24 **34:3** [u] Jdg 1:16; 3:13; 2Ch 28:15 **34:4** [v] Ge 28:13 [w] Ge 12:7 [x] Dt 3:27 **34:5** [y] Nu 12:7 [z] Dt 32:50; Jos 1:1-2 **34:6** [a] Dt 3:29 [b] Jude 1:9 **34:7** [c] Dt 31:2 [d] Ge 27:1

[a] 28 Septuagint; Hebrew *Jacob's spring is* [b] 6 Or *He was buried*

33:26 *who rides across the heavens ... on the clouds.* This language closely resembles language used to depict Baal. He is presented as a warrior-god who prepares to smash his enemies and to take his everlasting kingdom and dominion (cf. Ps 68:4 – 5). However, Baal was also the bringer of rain. A bit less striking, but still helpful, is the depiction in a Sumerian myth of the weather-god Ishkur in "Enki and the Ordering of the World." In this case Ishkur is put in charge of the entire weather system. In the case of Yahweh, Israel's God shows that he is in control of all of this, such that he can destroy Israel's enemies (v. 27).

33:29 *heights.* Exactly what the Hebrew word (*bamotemo*) refers to is still debated. Several high places (Hebrew *bamot*) have recently been uncovered. These were possibly places where local shrines were situated and pagan religious rites were practiced. To Israel's detriment, these places fostered syncretism and enticed Israel to become involved in forbidden worship. Asherahs (Hebrew *matstsebot*, sacred poles or trees) and altars were featured. These high places often had a *lishka*, a room for sacred meals, connected to them.

34:1 – 3 This description of the promised land mentions only key points of focus. The view given here surveys the scene by looking straight ahead (north) and then to the left (west).

34:1 *Dan.* The city and tribe of Dan were located just south of Mount Hermon, about 100 miles (160 kilometers) distant.

34:3 *Zoar.* Probably located at the southern tip of the Dead Sea (cf. Ge 13:10).

34:5 *the servant of the LORD.* This description of Moses has connotations of intimacy and of obedience. The legendary King Keret in the Ugaritic literature is depicted as "the beloved, Lad of El," "the Servant of El" (3x), with the context of each occurrence implying the care and concern of El for his chosen servant.

34:7 *a hundred and twenty years old.* Moses' eyesight and vigor are still not gone at 120 years of age. No wonder! In the ancient Near East "the face of a god radiated light and life to those fortunate enough to gaze upon it." Only kings could, however, claim this blessing. Moses had lived in the presence of God 40 days and nights and then conversed with the Lord without his veil for an indefinite period of time. In some ancient Near Eastern traditions, the radiant faces of the gods (e.g., Enlil, Assur, Ninlil) strengthened the kings they looked upon. The faces of the gods were both radiant and life-giving, a belief recorded in an inscription of Samsu-iluna (c. 1749 – 1712 BC), grandson of Hammurapi.

plains of Moab thirty days, until the time of
weeping and mourning[e] was over.
9Now Joshua son of Nun was filled with
the spirit[a] of wisdom[f] because Moses had
laid his hands on him.[g] So the Israelites
listened to him and did what the LORD had
commanded Moses.
10Since then, no prophet has risen in
Israel like Moses,[h] whom the LORD knew
face to face,[i] 11who did all those signs
and wonders[j] the LORD sent him to do
in Egypt—to Pharaoh and to all his officials[k] and to his whole land. 12For no one
has ever shown the mighty power or performed the awesome deeds that Moses did
in the sight of all Israel.

34:8 [e]Ge 50:3, 10; 2Sa 11:27 **34:9** [f]Ge 41:38; Isa 11:2; Da 6:3 [g]Nu 27:18,23 **34:10** [h]Dt 18:15,18 [i]Ex 33:11; Nu 12:6,8; Dt 5:4 **34:11** [j]Dt 4:34 [k]Dt 7:19

[a] 9 Or *Spirit*

DEUTERONOMY 34

The Death of Moses and the Authorship of Deuteronomy

It is not unusual for an ancient document to be updated in various ways as it is copied by later generations of scribes. Moses' responsibility for at least parts of Deuteronomy was to have them written down. Other parts, such as his sermons, song (Dt 32) and blessing (Dt 33), are said to have been delivered orally and were likely preserved orally for some time before being written down.

Moses well could have had scribal training himself, but more likely would have employed scribes to do the writing. The resulting documents would be stored in an archive and would eventually be used to compile the book that we now call Deuteronomy. Moses is appropriately attributed as the authoritative source for the material in the book, though we do not know when it took its final literary shape. In the ancient world, the oral form was often more important than the written form, though some formal documents (e.g., treaties) were preserved in writing and periodically read. As scribes copied the documents of this archive generation after generation, details could be updated (such as the location of Dan in the north in Dt 34:1, even though Dan did not move north until the period of the judges). ◆

OLD TESTAMENT

NARRATIVE LITERATURE

GOD WORKING THROUGH EVENTS AND OUTCOMES

Introduction to Narrative Literature

Comparative Studies and Historical Literature

Cultural studies from the ancient Near East can provide much information to fill in the background of the second and first millennia BC. Royal Inscriptions are particularly helpful as we try to reconstruct the political events that impacted the lives of the peoples of this period. Some actually refer to Israel or to various kings of Israel. Others give information about kings who interacted with Israel on various levels. Archaeological excavations help to reconstruct the daily life of the people. Biblical genres such as genealogies or conquest accounts can be explored profitably in relation to genres in the ancient Near East. Others try to establish lines of comparison between sections of the OT and ancient Near Eastern literary works such as the Middle Assyrian Epic of Tukulti-Ninurta.

Beyond the reconstruction of the events of ancient history and the study of the genres in which history is recorded, comparative studies can also help us to penetrate how people in the ancient world thought about history and what their values were in recording it ("historiography"). Studies in ancient historiography help us to assess how to read the literature in a way that will honor the ideas, intentions and values of the authors. Some of the conclusions from this sort of study alert us to important differences between the ancient and modern worlds. We learn that while our modern historians often ignore deity altogether, in the ancient world, one of the main values of history writing was to clarify what the gods were doing.

This radical difference can be explained when we understand that ancient historians were not recording events as much as they were interpreting outcomes. The truth of what "really happened" was not assessed by what the eyewitness saw, but by what the final outcome was. As a result they did not promote the role of the eyewitness as our history writing tends to do. Instead, the various subgenres of historiography promoted various people or ideas. Royal inscriptions characteristically promoted the king as they articulated what the gods were doing through his kingship. Biblical historiography often promoted the prophetic role to articulate what Yahweh was doing, particularly with regard to the covenant. This general survey indicates just a few of the ways that comparative and cultural studies will impact and illuminate our study of the historical literature in this volume. ◆

NARRATIVE LITERATURE

JOSHUA

Historical Background

The era of the exodus is normally dated to the Late Bronze Age (c. 1550 – 1200 BC). A more precise date for the events recorded in the book of Joshua depends upon when one chooses to date the exodus (see the article "The Timing of the Exodus," p. 118). Extra-Biblical texts that illuminate the history of the Late Bronze Age in Palestine are few. Prominent among them are the Amarna letters, which comprise communication from the governors and petty kings of city-states in Palestine to Pharaoh that inform him of the political situation they are facing.

KEY CONCEPTS

- God, not their own strength, gives Israel the land. Victory belongs to the Lord.
- The land is distributed to Israel to fulfill covenant promises.

Literary Form

The search for comparisons between the book of Joshua and other ancient Near Eastern literature include annals of military campaigns, suzerain-vassal treaties, itineraries of Egyptian campaigns, Egyptian scribal exercises recounting visits to Canaan, Hittite instructions for the royal bodyguard and for the border fort commanders, Hittite boundary descriptions in treaties, personal names, town lists among the West Semitic archives of Alalakh and Ugarit, cultic calendars from Emar, Old Babylonian laws, rhetorical forms in the Amarna letters from Canaan and other literary sources. However, none of these encompasses the overall form of the book of Joshua. The most productive source for comparison with the book of Joshua is the genre of land grants. These differ from treaties and particularly from suzerain-vassal treaties in that treaties focus on the rights of the suzerain, whereas land grants emphasize the rights of the vassal.

In the West Semitic world, of which Abram and later Israel were a part, there are land grants from Late Bronze Age Ugarit and from Middle Bronze Age Alalakh. One Alalakh grant (see the article "Land Grants," p. 361) describes the gift from one king to another of a city along with its villages and lands. The gift is thus a city-state or kingdom rather than a parcel of land. In fact, this text describes the legal deeding of the kingdom of Alalakh to the king who would begin a dynasty at the site. It is this text that provides the closest parallel to the overall structure to the book of Joshua. Joshua resembles the royal grant of Alalakh (and others) in that the text itself functions as the actual grant from God to the tribes of Israel. ◆

Joshua Installed as Leader

1 After the death of Moses the servant
of the LORD,[a] the LORD said to Joshua[b] son of Nun, Moses' aide: 2"Moses my
servant is dead. Now then, you and all
these people, get ready to cross the Jordan
River[c] into the land I am about to give to
them—to the Israelites. 3I will give you
every place where you set your foot,[d] as
I promised Moses. 4Your territory will extend from the desert to Lebanon, and from
the great river, the Euphrates[e]—all the
Hittite country—to the Mediterranean Sea
in the west.[f] 5No one will be able to stand
against you[g] all the days of your life. As I
was with[h] Moses, so I will be with you;
I will never leave you nor forsake[i] you.
6Be strong and courageous, because you
will lead these people to inherit the land
I swore to their ancestors[j] to give them.
7"Be strong and very courageous. Be
careful to obey all the law my servant Moses gave you; do not turn from it to the
right or to the left,[k] that you may be successful wherever you go.[l] 8Keep this Book
of the Law always on your lips; meditate

1:1 [a] Nu 12:7; Dt 34:5 [b] Ex 24:13; Dt 1:38 **1:2** [c] ver 11 **1:3** [d] Dt 11:24 **1:4** [e] Ge 15:18 [f] Nu 34:2-12 **1:5** [g] Dt 7:24 [h] Jos 3:7; 6:27 [i] Dt 31:6-8 **1:6** [j] Dt 31:23 **1:7** [k] Dt 5:32; 28:14 [l] Jos 11:15

1:1 *After the death of Moses.* In both ancient and modern times, the transition of leadership has been one of the most precarious times in the security of a state. More than any other time, this can become a period of potential revolts and civil wars. Of all such transitional periods, the most dangerous are those in which the transition is not dynastic, but involves the enthronement of a ruler unrelated to his or her predecessor. Among these, David's acquisition of power after the deaths of Saul and Jonathan required that much of the text of 1 Samuel justify his kingship and explain how he was not disloyal to his predecessor. This was not unique to the Bible. From Sargon I in the third millennium BC to Cambyses and Darius in the first millennium BC, many rulers succeeded in place of the expected successor. In Jos 1, a major concern of the author is to describe how Joshua is the legitimate successor of Moses as leader of God's people. Although Joshua is not biologically related to Moses, God has already established Joshua as successor with public demonstrations of his approval. Jos 1:1–9 confirms Joshua as divinely appointed. The remainder of ch. 1 illustrates the manner in which Joshua acted to establish authority, as well as the respect he received from the civil authorities (vv. 10–11) and from the tribes least likely to follow him (vv. 12–18). In common with other ancient Near Eastern rulers who rose to power outside of an established dynasty, Joshua recorded both the divine and human approval that he gained for his leadership. *servant of.* This title is a common form of many personal names found in the ancient West Semitic world of the fifteenth through twelfth centuries BC, and not as frequently earlier or later. At Ugarit, Alalakh, Emar and Ekalte, as well as the towns of Palestine and Syria represented by the Amarna letters, the personal name formation "servant of X," where X represents the name of a god or goddess, is found in many examples. These are often leaders of population centers. The epithet "servant of the LORD" is first applied to Moses at the end of his life (Dt 34:5) and remains reserved for a few major leaders early in Israel's history. Joshua is the second person to receive it, and he does so only at the end of his life (24:29).
1:4 *Your territory.* The territory of the promised land is defined elsewhere in Ge 10:19; Nu 13:17,21–22; 34:3–12. The name of Canaan and the territory it defines in these early Biblical texts is identical to the territory that the Egyptian New Kingdom Empire (c. 1550–1150 BC) referred to as Canaan. Only in this period do both the Bible and Egypt apply the term to this territory, and the extent of the territory for both is the same. This territory is defined in the south by an arc from the southeastern Mediterranean to the southern tip of the Dead Sea. The eastern border traveled north along the rift valley marked by the Dead Sea, the Jordan Valley, the Sea of Kinnereth (Galilee), the Huleh basin, the Beqa' and northeast to the Euphrates. The western border to Canaan was the Mediterranean Sea. The northern border did not reach as far as Ugarit or Alalakh, but lay to the south of these kingdoms. *all the Hittite country.* Although the Hittites of the Late Bronze Age can be identified with the kingdom whose capital was at Hattusas in central Anatolia, these people did not actually refer to themselves as Hittites. Rather, the Hittite land here may be identified with northern Canaan, an area controlled by the Hittite Empire, whose vacillating border saw clashes with Egyptian penetration to the north. If the northern border of Canaan is as defined above, then this cannot be a reference to the Neo-Hittite states of the first millennium BC that extended farther north into Anatolia. Rather, "the Hittite country" is a term that would have been applied by the Egyptians to (the northern part of) the region of Canaan, as it was, e.g., in the Merneptah Stele of 1209 BC. Thus, "the Hittite country" was a part of Canaan that was given to the Israelites.
1:5 *forsake.* The Hebrew verb describes a divine abandonment, which would imply that Joshua and the Israelites would face certain defeat at the hands of their enemies. However, the expression involves more than a casual change of sides. Elsewhere in Joshua it can be used of Israel's abandonment of its God to worship other deities (24:16,20). In military usage, it describes how the warriors abandon Ai (8:17) and how the Transjordanian tribes did not abandon their other tribal brothers in the wars west of the Jordan River. In fact, the Akkadian cognate of this Hebrew term also describes the betrayal by someone who switches sides in a battle. It is often used in the fourteenth-century BC Amarna letters to describe the manner in which Canaanites showed disloyalty to the pharaoh by joining his enemies. God's promise in v. 5 shows his faithfulness toward Joshua and Israel, because it confirms that he will remain on their side and fight for them.
1:8 *Keep this Book of the Law always on your lips.* This expression describes the importance of the covenantal document that the Israelites have received and the need for the leader to know it as well and as completely as possible. *Law.* Lit. "Torah," or "instruction." The formal relationship between various legal documents in the Pentateuch and Joshua—the Decalogue (see Dt 5:6–21 and note), the book of Deuteronomy, Jos 24—has been compared to the ancient Near Eastern treaty structure (see the article "Decrees and Laws," p. 301). In particular, the treaties preserved by the Hittite Empire provide a close correspondence with the structure of these covenants. Of interest here is the value placed upon the writing and reading of the covenant. Dt 31 records how Moses wrote the words of the covenant (Dt 31:24) and the periodic public reading of the text (Dt 31:10–12). In particular, the king must copy the words of the covenant and read them at intervals (Dt 17:18–19). The same requirement appears on some Hittite treaties. There the king is responsible for regularly copying and reading

JOSHUA 1:3–4

LAND GRANTS

The most productive source for comparison with the book of Joshua is the genre of land grants. These differ from treaties and particularly from suzerain-vassal treaties, to which they have been compared (see the article "Decrees and Laws," p. 301; see also note on Dt 6:5). Treaties tend to follow a careful and recognized form; land grants are diverse in their organization and presentation. Treaties use diplomatic language that can be recognized; land grants do not necessarily use such language, but have phrases that occur in other types of literature. Treaties focus on the rights of the suzerain; land grants emphasize the rights of the vassal. The curses reflect these different emphases in the two types of documents.

Of the land grants in the Bible, the most famous is the divine grant of the promised land given to Abram. It first appears in Ge 12:1–3 and is then developed over the next ten chapters. In the West Semitic world, of which Abram and later Israel were a part, there are land grants from Late Bronze Age Ugarit and from Middle Bronze Age Alalakh. Those at Ugarit function as grants of usufruct by the king for his loyal servants. The land remains within the kingdom of Ugarit and under the control of the king. A text from Alalakh, the neighboring state to the north of Ugarit, describes the gift from one king to another of a city along with its villages and lands. The gift is thus a city-state or kingdom rather than a parcel of land. In fact, this text describes the legal deeding of the kingdom of Alalakh to the king who would begin a dynasty at the site. It is this text that provides the closest parallel to the overall structure to the book of Joshua. Unlike the divine grant to Abram, the text of Joshua does not focus on a promise; it only obliquely refers to this promise in its expression to Moses (Jos 1:3). Rather, Joshua resembles the royal grant of Alalakh (and others), in that the text itself functions as the actual grant from God to the tribes of Israel. Unlike the grant to Abram, it is not in any sense unconditional. Instead, both the royal grants and that of Joshua are given on the basis of continuing loyalty or faithfulness to the suzerain. In the case of the book of Joshua, of course, God takes on the role of the suzerain (chs. 7–8; 23–24). The gift of the land, like that of the city of Alalakh, is conditional. Israel keeps the land as long as the nation remains faithful to its suzerain. ◆

This stone tablet is a copy of a deed recording the restoration of certain lands (land grant) by the Babylonian king Nabu-apla-iddina to a priest of the same name, 870 BC.

on it day and night, so that you may be
careful to do everything written in it. Then
you will be prosperous and successful.[m]
9 Have I not commanded you? Be strong
and courageous. Do not be afraid;[n] do not
be discouraged, for the LORD your God will
be with you wherever you go."[o]
10 So Joshua ordered the officers of the
people: 11 "Go through the camp and tell
the people, 'Get your provisions ready.
Three days from now you will cross the
Jordan here to go in and take possession[p]
of the land the LORD your God is giving
you for your own.' "
12 But to the Reubenites, the Gadites
and the half-tribe of Manasseh,[q] Joshua
said, 13 "Remember the command that Moses the servant of the LORD gave you after he said, 'The LORD your God will give
you rest[r] by giving you this land.' 14 Your
wives, your children and your livestock
may stay in the land that Moses gave you
east of the Jordan, but all your fighting
men, ready for battle, must cross over
ahead of your fellow Israelites. You are
to help them 15 until the LORD gives them
rest, as he has done for you, and until
they too have taken possession of the land
the LORD your God is giving them. After
that, you may go back and occupy your
own land, which Moses the servant of the
LORD gave you east of the Jordan toward
the sunrise."[s]
16 Then they answered Joshua, "Whatever you have commanded us we will do,
and wherever you send us we will go.
17 Just as we fully obeyed Moses, so we
will obey you.[t] Only may the LORD your
God be with you as he was with Moses.
18 Whoever rebels against your word and
does not obey it, whatever you may command them, will be put to death. Only be
strong and courageous!"

1:8 [m] Dt 29:9; Ps 1:1-3 **1:9** [n] Ps 27:1 [o] ver 7; Dt 31:7-8; Jer 1:8 **1:11** [p] Joel 3:2 **1:12** [q] Nu 32:20-22 **1:13** [r] Dt 3:18-20 **1:15** [s] Jos 22:1-4 **1:17** [t] ver 5,9

Rahab and the Spies

2 Then Joshua son of Nun secretly sent
two spies[u] from Shittim.[v] "Go, look
over the land," he said, "especially Jericho." So they went and entered the house
of a prostitute named Rahab[w] and stayed
there.
2 The king of Jericho was told, "Look,
some of the Israelites have come here tonight to spy out the land." 3 So the king of
Jericho sent this message to Rahab: "Bring
out the men who came to you and entered
your house, because they have come to
spy out the whole land."
4 But the woman had taken the two men
and hidden them.[x] She said, "Yes, the men
came to me, but I did not know where
they had come from. 5 At dusk, when it
was time to close the city gate, they left. I
don't know which way they went. Go after them quickly. You may catch up with
them." 6 (But she had taken them up to the
roof and hidden them under the stalks of
flax[y] she had laid out on the roof.)[z] 7 So the
men set out in pursuit of the spies on the
road that leads to the fords of the Jordan,
and as soon as the pursuers had gone out,
the gate was shut.
8 Before the spies lay down for the night,
she went up on the roof 9 and said to them,
"I know that the LORD has given you this
land and that a great fear[a] of you has fall-
en on us, so that all who live in this country are melting in fear because of you.
10 We have heard how the LORD dried up[b]
the water of the Red Sea[a] for you when

2:1 [u] Jas 2:25 [v] Nu 25:1; Jos 3:1 [w] Heb 11:31 **2:4** [x] 2Sa 17:19-20 **2:6** [y] Jas 2:25 [z] Ex 1:17, 19; 2Sa 17:19 **2:9** [a] Ge 35:5; Ex 23:27; Dt 2:25 **2:10** [b] Ex 14:21

[a] 10 Or *the Sea of Reeds*

the text. In both cases, the vassal ruler is required periodically to study the treaty/covenant so as to be familiar with its words and to obey it.

1:16–18 Egyptian New Kingdom scholars contend that (as with rulers at other times) when a new pharaoh came to power he required his vassals from Canaan to swear a new loyalty oath to him. The response of the two and a half tribes (v. 12) in these verses represents such an oath. The pharaoh might come to Canaan, perhaps to a center such as Gaza or Gezer, and the Canaanite rulers would arrive and swear an oath to the pharaoh. This would assure the recognition of the pharaoh as the new ruler of the Egyptian Empire. It would guarantee the succession of the new leader and assist in the prevention of any revolt. The oath form of vv. 16–18 could have been used by the other tribes as well. The two and a half tribes are mentioned here because they are the tribes that had the least incentive to cross over the Jordan and fight alongside the other tribes. They had already received their land from Moses east of the Jordan and therefore could occupy it with no need for additional land acquisition or warfare (Dt 3:12–20).

2:1 *Jericho.* Tell es-Sultan is the location of ancient Jericho, a site occupied from as early as the ninth millennium BC. Its location, 10 miles (16 kilometers) north of the Dead Sea in the Jordan Valley, suggests its importance in terms of trade routes along the Jordan Valley and westward to Jerusalem, Bethel and Ophrah. This strategic location, combined with the ideal agricultural climate of the south Jordan Valley, made the region and this site, which boasts its own spring, valuable. *house of a prostitute.* In the second millennium BC, the West Semitic world and that of its Hittite neighbors to the north associated innkeepers, whom Rahab is assumed to be in this story, with prostitutes. In the first millennium BC, this seems to have changed, perhaps due to sociological changes brought about by developments in the brewing of alcohol. The role of the prostitute as innkeeper is attested in the eighteenth-century BC Code of Hammurapi.

2:5 *At dusk, when it was time to close the city gate.* It was not unusual for a walled town to close its gates at night, especially when there was an enemy nearby. City gates were massive structures with several sequential chambers and entrances (see note on Jdg 16:3).

2:9–11 For the reputation Yahweh gained in the light of the exodus, see the article "Yahweh's Victory," p. 137.

you came out of Egypt,[c] and what you did
to Sihon and Og,[d] the two kings of the
Amorites east of the Jordan, whom you
completely destroyed.[a] 11When we heard
of it, our hearts melted in fear and everyone's courage failed because of you,[e] for
the LORD your God is God in heaven above
and on the earth[f] below.
12"Now then, please swear to me by the
LORD that you will show kindness to my
family, because I have shown kindness to
you. Give me a sure sign[g] 13that you will
spare the lives of my father and mother,
my brothers and sisters, and all who belong to them—and that you will save us
from death."
14"Our lives for your lives!" the men assured her. "If you don't tell what we are
doing, we will treat you kindly and faithfully[h] when the LORD gives us the land."
15So she let them down by a rope
through the window,[i] for the house she
lived in was part of the city wall. 16She
said to them, "Go to the hills so the pursuers will not find you. Hide yourselves
there three days[j] until they return, and
then go on your way."[k]
17Now the men had said to her, "This
oath[l] you made us swear will not be binding on us 18unless, when we enter the
land, you have tied this scarlet cord in the
window through which you let us down,
and unless you have brought your father
and mother, your brothers and all your
family[m] into your house. 19If any of them
go outside your house into the street, their
blood will be on their own heads;[n] we will
not be responsible. As for those who are
in the house with you, their blood will be
on our head[o] if a hand is laid on them.
20But if you tell what we are doing, we
will be released from the oath you made
us swear."
21"Agreed," she replied. "Let it be as you
say."
So she sent them away, and they departed. And she tied the scarlet cord in the
window.
22When they left, they went into the hills
and stayed there three days, until the pursuers had searched all along the road and
returned without finding them. 23Then the
two men started back. They went down
out of the hills, forded the river and came
to Joshua son of Nun and told him everything that had happened to them. 24They
said to Joshua, "The LORD has surely giv-
en the whole land into our hands;[p] all the
people are melting in fear because of us."

Crossing the Jordan

3 Early in the morning Joshua and all
the Israelites set out from Shittim[q] and
went to the Jordan, where they camped
before crossing over. 2After three days the

2:10 [c] Nu 23:22 [d] Nu 21:21, 24, 34-35 **2:11** [e] Ex 15:14; Jos 5:1; 7:5; Ps 22:14; Isa 13:7 [f] Dt 4:39 **2:12** [g] ver 18 **2:14** [h] Jdg 1:24; Mt 5:7 **2:15** [i] Ac 9:25 **2:16** [j] Jas 2:25 [k] Heb 11:31 **2:17** [l] Ge 24:8 **2:18** [m] ver 12; Jos 6:23 **2:19** [n] Eze 33:4 [o] Mt 27:25 **2:24** [p] ver 9; Jos 6:2 **3:1** [q] Jos 2:1

[a] *10* The Hebrew term refers to the irrevocable giving over of things or persons to the LORD, often by totally destroying them.

2:11 *the LORD your God is God.* Rahab acknowledges Yahweh as "God in heaven above and on the earth below," which classifies him as a cosmic deity and powerful national patron god. It is not an expression of monotheism, or a conversion to Israelite religion; she has not renounced her gods, and we have no reason to think she has any knowledge of the Mosaic Law. Hittite, Assyrian and Babylonian texts all speak of divine warriors who terrify their enemies.
2:12 *my family.* Lit. "the house of my father," which refers to Rahab's extended family, including the relations described in v. 13. The house of the father forms the basic sociological unit of West Semitic society (including Canaan and Israel) in the Bronze and Iron Ages. Traditionally, this family unit is led by the eldest male. Here, in a unique manner, Rahab negotiates on behalf of her extended family.
2:15 *part of the city wall.* Excavations in the 1930s revealed an important fortified center at ancient Jericho with mud brick walls. However, work two decades later confirmed that these walls dated centuries earlier than any time that the Israelites could have entered Palestine. Although some have challenged this change in dating, most ceramicists who study the evidence from Tell es-Sultan affirm the absence of preserved walls in the Late Bronze Age. In itself this is not surprising; sites such as Lachish and Megiddo have preserved no Late Bronze Age walls, yet it is clear from Egyptian accounts of the site during this period that Megiddo was fortified by a wall. Perhaps the same was the case at Jericho. Perhaps the walls eroded after their destruction in ch. 6 and before Jericho was rebuilt hundreds of years later in the ninth century BC (1Ki 16:34). If these walls were mud brick and more easily subject to erosion, a more likely possibility could be that a small circle of mud brick houses was built so as to form a continuous wall around the site of Jericho. The descent from Rahab's window to the ground outside Jericho could have been as small as a single story (from the second-story window to the ground), or the fort could have been built beside a precipice formed by the tell, and thus the descent could have been much longer.
2:16 *Hide ... three days.* Cf. v. 22. The use of "three days" as a measure of time may indicate a general period of time lasting more than one or two days but not specific beyond that. However, the Late Bronze Age Hittite "Instructions to the Commander of the Border Fortress" specifies this length of time for the pursuit of the enemy, followed by the demand that any officer who does not kill this enemy must be turned over to the king for punishment. This provides a precedent for Rahab's advice to Jericho's enemies and a measure of her personal risk in not surrendering the spies to Jericho's leadership.
2:18,21 *scarlet cord.* The Hebrew word here for "cord" is distinct from the rope used to lower the spies (v. 15). It normally describes a simple "thread," something of low value (Ge 14:23). The Hebrew term for "scarlet" appears elsewhere in the Bible to describe textiles used to decorate the tabernacle (e.g., Ex 25:4), for cleansing rituals (e.g., Lev 14:4), to denote a bright color (e.g., Ge 38:28) and to identify the wealthy or special (e.g., Pr 31:21).
3:1–4 The crossing of the Jordan River, unlike the crossing of the Red (Reed) Sea of the previous generation

officers went throughout the camp,[r] 3giv-
ing orders to the people: "When you see
the ark of the covenant[s] of the LORD your
God, and the Levitical priests[t] carrying it,
you are to move out from your positions
and follow it. 4Then you will know which
way to go, since you have never been this
way before. But keep a distance of about
two thousand cubits[a] between you and
the ark; do not go near it."

5Joshua told the people, "Consecrate
yourselves,[u] for tomorrow the LORD will
do amazing things among you."

6Joshua said to the priests, "Take up the
ark of the covenant and pass on ahead of
the people." So they took it up and went
ahead of them.

7And the LORD said to Joshua, "Today I
will begin to exalt you[v] in the eyes of all Israel, so they may know that I am with you
as I was with Moses.[w] 8Tell the priests[x]
who carry the ark of the covenant: 'When
you reach the edge of the Jordan's waters,
go and stand in the river.' "

9Joshua said to the Israelites, "Come
here and listen to the words of the LORD
your God. 10This is how you will know
that the living God[y] is among you and that
he will certainly drive out before you the
Canaanites, Hittites, Hivites, Perizzites,
Girgashites, Amorites and Jebusites.[z]
11See, the ark of the covenant of the Lord
of all the earth[a] will go into the Jordan
ahead of you. 12Now then, choose twelve
men[b] from the tribes of Israel, one from
each tribe. 13And as soon as the priests
who carry the ark of the LORD—the Lord
of all the earth[c]—set foot in the Jordan,
its waters flowing downstream[d] will be cut
off and stand up in a heap.[e]"

14So when the people broke camp to
cross the Jordan, the priests carrying the
ark of the covenant[f] went ahead[g] of them.
15Now the Jordan is at flood stage[h] all
during harvest. Yet as soon as the priests
who carried the ark reached the Jordan
and their feet touched the water's edge,
16the water from upstream stopped flowing.[i] It piled up in a heap a great distance
away, at a town called Adam in the vicinity of Zarethan,[j] while the water flowing
down[k] to the Sea of the Arabah[l] (that is,
the Dead Sea[m]) was completely cut off. So
the people crossed over opposite Jericho.
17The priests who carried the ark of the
covenant of the LORD stopped in the middle of the Jordan and stood on dry ground,
while all Israel passed by until the whole
nation had completed the crossing on dry
ground.[n]

3:2 [r] Jos 1:11 **3:3** [s] Nu 10:33 [t] Dt 31:9 **3:5** [u] Ex 19:10, 14; Lev 20:7; Jos 7:13; 1Sa 16:5; Joel 2:16 **3:7** [v] Jos 4:14; 1Ch 29:25 [w] Jos 1:5 **3:8** [x] ver 3 **3:10** [y] Dt 5:26; 1Sa 17:26, 36; 2Ki 19:4, 16; Hos 1:10; Mt 16:16; 1Th 1:9 [z] Ex 33:2; Dt 7:1

3:11 [a] ver 13; Job 41:11; Zec 6:5 **3:12** [b] Jos 4:2, 4 **3:13** [c] ver 11 [d] ver 16 [e] Ex 15:8; Ps 78:13 **3:14** [f] Ps 132:8 [g] Ac 7:44-45 **3:15** [h] Jos 4:18; 1Ch 12:15 **3:16** [i] Ps 66:6; 74:15 [j] 1Ki 4:12; 7:46 [k] ver 13 [l] Dt 1:1 [m] Ge 14:3 **3:17** [n] Ex 14:22, 29

[a] *4* That is, about 3,000 feet or about 900 meters

(Ex 14–15), was accomplished in an orderly fashion. Most of this chapter is taken up with the detailed procedure by which Israel was to cross the river. The God of Israel moves in the midst of his people in a procession that leads them into enemy territory. This forms a military procession and resembles the military marches of Egypt and the other powers of the ancient Near East. Although few descriptions remain of the procedure of such marches, there is a detailed description found in the second-millennium BC Hittite "Instruction for the Royal Bodyguard." This tablet describes the responsibilities of the palace guard for the protection of the king. Most of it concerns the movement of the king in a cart from his palace to the place where he gives judgment and the return at the end of the day. Although there are many differences, of special interest is the manner in which the location of the guard is specified. They surround the king and protect him on all sides. This reminds us of the Israelite camp's order of march through the wilderness (Nu 10:14–28). However, the Hittite instructions also require that the guards keep a specific distance from the king when they march. As the guards are required to stay at a certain distance from the cart carrying the king, so the Israelites are commanded to stay 3,000 feet (900 meters) from the ark representing God in its movement across the Jordan River (see v. 4 and NIV text note). The specific directions and the whole ceremony of Jos 3–4 suggest a movement comparable to that of a king surrounded by his army as they march to battle.

3:5 *Consecrate yourselves.* At Mount Sinai, Israel consecrated itself by washing their clothes and abstaining from sex (Ex 19:10–15). In the Kirta epic from Ugarit, the god El instructs the king to prepare for his campaign by washing and rouging himself and by sacrificing animals.

3:10 *Canaanites, Hittites, Hivites, Perizzites, Girgashites, Amorites and Jebusites.* Cf. Ge 15:19–21. *Canaanites.* See note on Dt 1:7; see also the article "The Canaanites," p. 294. *Hittites.* See notes on Ge 23:3; Dt 7:1. *Hivites.* See note on Dt 7:1. *Perizzites.* See note on Dt 7:1. *Girgashites.* See note on Dt 7:1. *Amorites.* See notes on Nu 13:29; Dt 1:7. *Jebusites.* See note on Dt 7:1.

3:15 *flood stage all during harvest.* After the winter rains, the spring harvest of the grains also represents the time when the Jordan River would reach maximum levels, above its average 90–100 feet (27–30 meters) in width and 3–10 feet (1–3 meters) in depth.

3:16 *water from upstream stopped flowing. It piled up … at a town called Adam in the vicinity of Zarethan.* Adam is Tell ed-Damieh, almost 17 miles (27 kilometers) north of Jericho. Zarethan lies east of the Jordan River. Either it is Tell es-Sa'idiyeh, 22 miles (17.7 kilometers) north of Adam, or it is Tell umm H'amid, 2.8 miles (4.5 kilometers) north of Adam. Adam has been a traditional crossing point of the Jordan River. Close to where the Jabbok River joins from the east and the Wadi el-Fara from the west, the site marks the spot where the southerly flow of the Jordan River becomes more difficult to cross. Adam is 16.75 miles (27 kilometers) from the Dead Sea. This means that some 29 percent of the Jordan Valley was affected by this "amazing thing" (see v. 5). The high banks in the region and the tectonic nature of the Jordan Valley have contributed to periodic collapses of earthen mounds into the river, damming it temporarily. This occurred at least three times in recent history: 1267, 1906, 1927. On the last occasion the river was blocked for some 21 hours. No natural explanation is necessary, but neither would something that we call a "natural" explanation diminish God's hand.

JOSHUA 3:14–17

DIVINE WARFARE

It is not proper to call this "holy war," because in the ancient Near East there was no other kind of war. The divine warrior motif depicts the deity fighting and defeating the deities of the enemy. The gods empowered the king and fought before/beside him. Warfare was a divine undertaking, because it was generally understood as a response to unrest. Deities were responsible for bringing rest and maintaining it for their people, so unrest had to be addressed.

In Assyria, the god Nergal is the King of Battle, and Ishtar is viewed also as a war goddess. The Canaanite Baal and the Babylonian Marduk are divine warriors. In situations of impending battle, prayers would be made and omens asked to assure the god's presence. Standards or statues of the deity were usually carried to symbolize their presence. Assyrian kings of the ninth and eighth centuries BC regularly refer to the divine standard that goes before them. The ark of the covenant, as Yahweh's standard, represents the Lord as clearing the way before the Israelites and leading the armies into Canaan. Nearly every army in the ancient Near East included priests and diviners (as seen in the Mari tablets), prophets (cf. 2Ki 3), and portable sacred objects (Assyrian annals of Shalmaneser III [858–824 BC]). In this way, the god(s) could be consulted on the battlefield or invoked to lead the soldiers to victory. In this worldview, human warfare is simply a representation of warfare among the gods. The stronger god would be victorious regardless of the strengths or weaknesses in the human combatants. Therefore, if Yahweh fought on their behalf, the Israelites would be convinced that they would be victorious.

Divine wars were not wars intended to "wipe out the infidel" or to force conversion to the worship of the victorious god. The reasons for war were practical, not ideological. Wars were fought to provide/ensure prosperity for the nation, which, in turn, provided prosperity for the god. Modern nations view prosperity as a result of market forces, and our philosophy of war is consequently shaped in economic terms. In the ancient world, prosperity was seen as a result of divine activity, so the philosophy of war was constructed in religious terms. Warfare served to bring additional wealth into the coffers of the temple. In cultures where the care of the gods was viewed as a primary responsibility, more wealth meant more luxury and grandeur for a god, who would be anticipated to then respond with blessings. The god was the one who commanded war to be undertaken (usually through oracles or divination) and who vouchsafed the victory.

In Israel, the wars of Yahweh were often designed to bring judgment on peoples whose offenses called for their destruction. This is explicitly stated with regard to Sodom and Gomorrah (Ge 18:20–21,26), as well as Nineveh (Jnh 1:2; 3:10), but it is also true of God fighting against Israel when they became unfaithful (from the book of Judges to the destruction of Jerusalem by Nebuchadnezzar). For the inhabitants of Canaan, they are being driven out not as punishment for offenses but so they do not become a snare to Israel. More specifically, offenses were at times committed against the Israelites (such as the Amalekites preying on the stragglers, Ex 17). In these cases, the Israelites became the instrument of God's judgment. In all these instances, the wars conducted by Yahweh were designed for God to uphold his part of the covenant. ◆

4 When the whole nation had finished
crossing the Jordan,[o] the LORD said
to Joshua, 2"Choose twelve men[p] from
among the people, one from each tribe,
3and tell them to take up twelve stones[q]
from the middle of the Jordan, from right
where the priests are standing, and carry
them over with you and put them down at
the place where you stay tonight.[r]"
4So Joshua called together the twelve
men he had appointed from the Israelites,
one from each tribe, 5and said to them,
"Go over before the ark of the LORD your
God into the middle of the Jordan. Each of
you is to take up a stone on his shoulder,
according to the number of the tribes of
the Israelites, 6to serve as a sign among
you. In the future, when your children
ask you, 'What do these stones mean?'[s]
7tell them that the flow of the Jordan was
cut off[t] before the ark of the covenant of
the LORD. When it crossed the Jordan, the
waters of the Jordan were cut off. These
stones are to be a memorial[u] to the people
of Israel forever."
8So the Israelites did as Joshua commanded them. They took twelve stones
from the middle of the Jordan, according
to the number of the tribes of the Israelites, as the LORD had told Joshua;[v] and
they carried them over with them to their
camp, where they put them down. 9Josh-
ua set up the twelve stones[w] that had
been[a] in the middle of the Jordan at the
spot where the priests who carried the ark
of the covenant had stood. And they are
there to this day.
10Now the priests who carried the ark
remained standing in the middle of the
Jordan until everything the LORD had commanded Joshua was done by the people,
just as Moses had directed Joshua. The
people hurried over, 11and as soon as all
of them had crossed, the ark of the LORD
and the priests came to the other side
while the people watched. 12The men of
Reuben, Gad and the half-tribe of Manasseh crossed over, ready for battle, in front
of the Israelites,[x] as Moses had directed
them. 13About forty thousand armed for
battle crossed over before the LORD to the
plains of Jericho for war.
14That day the LORD exalted[y] Joshua in
the sight of all Israel; and they stood in
awe of him all the days of his life, just as
they had stood in awe of Moses.
15Then the LORD said to Joshua, 16"Command the priests carrying the ark of the
covenant law[z] to come up out of the Jordan."
17So Joshua commanded the priests,
"Come up out of the Jordan."
18And the priests came up out of the
river carrying the ark of the covenant of
the LORD. No sooner had they set their feet
on the dry ground than the waters of the
Jordan returned to their place and ran at
flood stage[a] as before.
19On the tenth day of the first month
the people went up from the Jordan and
camped at Gilgal[b] on the eastern border of
Jericho. 20And Joshua set up at Gilgal the
twelve stones[c] they had taken out of the
Jordan. 21He said to the Israelites, "In the
future when your descendants ask their
parents, 'What do these stones mean?'[d]
22tell them, 'Israel crossed the Jordan on
dry ground.'[e] 23For the LORD your God
dried up the Jordan before you until you
had crossed over. The LORD your God did
to the Jordan what he had done to the Red
Sea[b] when he dried it up before us until
we had crossed over.[f] 24He did this so that
all the peoples of the earth might know[g]
that the hand of the LORD is powerful[h] and
so that you might always fear the LORD
your God.[i]"

5 Now when all the Amorite kings west
of the Jordan and all the Canaanite
kings along the coast[j] heard how the LORD
had dried up the Jordan before the Israelites until they[c] had crossed over, their

4:1 [o] Dt 27:2
4:2 [p] Jos 3:12
4:3 [q] ver 20 [r] ver 19
4:6 [s] ver 21; Ex 12:26; 13:14
4:7 [t] Jos 3:13 [u] Ex 12:14
4:8 [v] ver 20
4:9 [w] Ge 28:18; Jos 24:26; 1Sa 7:12
4:12 [x] Nu 32:27
4:14 [y] Jos 3:7
4:16 [z] Ex 25:22
4:18 [a] Jos 3:15
4:19 [b] Jos 5:9
4:20 [c] ver 3,8
4:21 [d] ver 6
4:22 [e] Jos 3:17
4:23 [f] Ex 14:21
4:24 [g] 1Ki 8:42-43; 2Ki 19:19; Ps 106:8; Jer 10:7 [h] Ex 15:16; 1Ch 29:12; Ps 89:13 [i] Ex 14:31
5:1 [j] Nu 13:29

[a] 9 Or *Joshua also set up twelve stones* [b] 23 Or *the Sea of Reeds* [c] 1 Another textual tradition *we*

4:7 *These stones are to be a memorial to the people of Israel forever.* The use of uncarved standing stones for various cultic purposes is well attested in the West Semitic world. Like Jacob at Bethel (Ge 28) and Moses at Mount Sinai (Ex 24), these stones could be erected as a memorial to a vow or for another dedicatory purpose. More often, however, standing stones have been ascribed religious significance either in the sense of some sort of representation of a deity or as a symbol of a sacred spot for veneration. Their association with the worship of other gods is condemned in the Bible (Lev 26:1; Dt 7:5; 16:21–22; 1Ki 14:22–23). In the Negev and Eastern Sinai, some 142 independent sites of standing stones have been found, most with origins dating thousands of years before Israel's appearance. They are generally thought to represent deities and were venerated by libations and other offerings. Here in Joshua, they symbolize the unity of the people rather than gods, but they resemble the other usages insofar as they are associated with a religious center (Gilgal), with a divine act (crossing the Jordan River) and with a memorial for every generation. Since they are taken from the river, they are likely rocks that could be carried by one person.

4:13 *forty thousand armed for battle.* The Hebrew word for "thousand" (*aleph*) can carry the sense of a group of soldiers or a squad of indeterminate number. Especially in military contexts such as this one, the idea of an organized squad is implied. The orderly march, maintaining a distance from the ark and between squads, may be compared with instructions given to the Hittite palace guard (see note on 3:1–4).

4:24 *hand of the LORD is powerful.* See note on Ex 6:1.

5:1 *hearts melted in fear ... no longer had the courage.* The

hearts melted in fear[k] and they no longer had the courage to face the Israelites.

Circumcision and Passover at Gilgal

2At that time the LORD said to Joshua, "Make flint knives[l] and circumcise the Israelites again." 3So Joshua made flint knives and circumcised the Israelites at Gibeath Haaraloth.[a]

4Now this is why he did so: All those who came out of Egypt—all the men of military age—died in the wilderness on the way after leaving Egypt.[m] 5All the people that came out had been circumcised, but all the people born in the wilderness during the journey from Egypt had not.
6The Israelites had moved about in the wilderness forty years[n] until all the men who were of military age when they left Egypt had died, since they had not obeyed the LORD. For the LORD had sworn to them that they would not see the land he had solemnly promised their ancestors to give us,[o] a land flowing with milk and honey.[p]
7So he raised up their sons in their place, and these were the ones Joshua circumcised. They were still uncircumcised because they had not been circumcised on the way. 8And after the whole nation had been circumcised, they remained where they were in camp until they were healed.[q]

9Then the LORD said to Joshua, "Today I have rolled away the reproach of Egypt from you." So the place has been called Gilgal[b] to this day.

10On the evening of the fourteenth day of the month,[r] while camped at Gilgal on the plains of Jericho, the Israelites celebrated the Passover. 11The day after the Passover, that very day, they ate some of the produce of the land:[s] unleavened bread and roasted grain.[t] 12The manna stopped the

5:1 [k]Jos 2:9-11
5:2 [l]Ex 4:25
5:4 [m]Dt 2:14
5:6 [n]Dt 2:7 [o]Nu 14:23, 29-35; Dt 2:14 [p]Ex 3:8
5:8 [q]Ge 34:25
5:10 [r]Ex 12:6
5:11 [s]Nu 15:19 [t]Lev 23:14

[a] 3 *Gibeath Haaraloth* means *the hill of foreskins.*
[b] 9 *Gilgal* sounds like the Hebrew for *roll.*

fear of enemy leaders is a common motif in ancient Near Eastern battle accounts. As in many such accounts, it forms a prelude to victory over the enemy.
5:2–12 Although war accounts are replete with sacrifices given to appease the gods before a battle, there is little in the comparative literature to compare with the circumcision and celebration of the Passover (with no mention of a lamb or any other animal in these verses).
5:2 *flint knives.* Better understood as obsidian, the use of such smooth and sharp stones for cutting is attested long after the introduction of bronze and iron.
5:10 *the Passover.* The Passover celebration culminates the crossing of the Jordan River and the entrance into the promised land. The Passover occurs on the 14th day of the first month at the time of the barley harvest. Therefore, the "wave offering" of the barley sheaf takes place at this time (Lev 23:10–14). It is the presentation of the firstfruits of the barley, a grain that matures around this time and forms the most important staple for the inhabitants of Canaan. The Passover and the Festival of Unleavened Bread constitute both a memory of the exodus and a celebration of gratitude for the firstfruits of barley.
5:11 *unleavened bread.* Required time to make; as a complement the roasted grain could be made more quickly (1Sa 17:17).
5:12 *The manna stopped.* The change in diet, from manna

Cylinder seal impression showing presentation of grain sheaf. The Israelites had an offering of the barley sheaf at Passover (Lev 23:10–14) and then would eat some of the produce the following day (Jos 5:11).

Kim Walton. The Oriental Institute Museum, The University of Chicago.

day after[a] they ate this food from the land; there was no longer any manna for the Israelites, but that year they ate the produce of Canaan.[u]

The Fall of Jericho

[13]Now when Joshua was near Jericho, he looked up and saw a man[v] standing in front of him with a drawn sword[w] in his hand. Joshua went up to him and asked, "Are you for us or for our enemies?"

[14]"Neither," he replied, "but as commander of the army of the LORD I have now come." Then Joshua fell facedown[x] to the ground in reverence, and asked him, "What message does my Lord[b] have for his servant?"

5:12 [u]Ex 16:35
5:13 [v]Ge 18:2; 32:24 [w]Nu 22:23
5:14 [x]Ge 17:3

[a] *12* Or *the day* [b] *14* Or *lord*

to grain, provides one more signal that the period of the wilderness has ended and a new age is dawning.

5:14 *commander of the army of the LORD.* The presence of this supernatural being is another indication that Yahweh is going to be responsible for Israel's military successes. In the ancient Near East, war was usually carried out according to divine instructions, following a divine plan. In the Ugaritic Keret epic, the god El brings Keret instructions for battle in a dream. The Babylonian king Samsu-iluna receives instructions for battle from supernatural messengers from Enlil. In the case of Joshua, later theologians sometimes wondered whether this was God himself or perhaps even a preincarnate Christ, but the role of messengers in the ancient world fully accounts for everything in this passage. The instructions given in Jos 6 are likely presented to Joshua by this commander.

JOSHUA 5:13—6:27

The Fall of Jericho

Given the absence of much, though not all, archaeological evidence for settlement at Jericho in the Late Bronze Age period, the picture of a small settlement surrounded by mud brick walls (see note on Jos 2:15) seems reasonable. Indeed, the term translated "city" (Hebrew *'ir*) in Jos 6:3 can describe a "citadel" (e.g., 2Sa 12:26) or a fort (e.g., 2Sa 5:7,9), perhaps within a city. This seems a more reasonable understanding of Jericho in light of our current knowledge of the site gained through excavations. It may have been primarily a military compound, a small fort, rather than a civilian population center. As such it would have been designed to guard strategic passes east and west, a major ford across the Jordan, and the north-south road on behalf of towns in the hill country, such as Bethel and Jerusalem. This would be an ideal location for an inn or hostel, such as the one Rahab operated with her family. The "king" of Jericho (Jos 6:2) would then have been a military commander under the authority of hill country leaders. From about the same time period the Amarna letters reveal the West Semitic root for "king" (*mlk*), used in Joshua, to apply as well to commissioners and others under a higher authority.

The Amarna letters also provide examples of the size of armies in Canaan in the fourteenth century BC, textual evidence that is closer than any other to the period in which the Bible places the story of Joshua. Here many princes of Canaan request forces from the pharaoh to supplement their own in order to fight their enemies. The numbers requested are never higher than a few hundred and sometimes a low as 20. These are reinforcements, not the whole number of defenders. Nevertheless, it would not make sense to request reinforcements unless they significantly enhanced the strength of the existing force, increasing it by at least a fourth, or more likely something on the order of doubling the force. Jericho, a smaller site than Jerusalem, could have 100 soldiers or fewer guarding it.

If this is so, then why does the book of Joshua make so much of the attack on Jericho? From a comparative perspective, the importance of Jericho is that it is the first victory of a new leader. Whatever the actual size of Jericho, this victory would serve to confirm Joshua as the true leader and successor of Moses in the eyes of

continued on next page

15 The commander of the LORD's army replied, "Take off your sandals, for the place
where you are standing is holy."[y] And
Joshua did so.

6
Now the gates of Jericho[z] were securely barred because of the Israelites. No
one went out and no one came in.
2 Then the LORD said to Joshua, "See, I
have delivered[a] Jericho into your hands,
along with its king and its fighting men.
3 March around the city once with all the
armed men. Do this for six days. 4 Have
seven priests carry trumpets of rams'
horns in front of the ark. On the seventh
day, march around the city seven times,
with the priests blowing the trumpets.[b]

5:15 [y] Ex 3:5; Ac 7:33
6:1 [z] Jos 24:11
6:2 [a] Dt 7:24; Jos 2:9,24; 8:1
6:4 [b] Lev 25:9; Nu 10:8

This person is identified as the commander of God's armies. As such he is worthy of highest respect. He is also serving in the role of God's messenger, which means that he can speak for God. Apparently the message that he has begins in 6:2. At times in the history of the church, people who were eager to find every possible connection to Christ interpreted this figure to be a preincarnate appearance of Christ. Nothing in this context requires anything that radical, nor does the NT suggest such a connection.

6:3 *Do this for six days.* In the Ugaritic Keret epic, the army is instructed by the god El to stay quiet for six days without attacking. On the seventh day, the city would offer tribute for them to leave. A passage like this suggests that the strategy proposed to Joshua may not have sounded as outlandish to him as it does to us, whether or not Joshua was familiar with the tales from Ugarit.

6:4 *trumpets of rams' horns.* The trumpet (*shofar*) is capable of a variety of tones, but cannot play a tune,

Israel (Jos 3:7), and it would further demoralize the Canaanite opponents (Jos 5:1). Furthermore, Jericho did represent a strategic foothold that offered access to several other regions. The lengthy account of initial battles should also be noted. This occurs, e.g., in the campaign of Thutmose III during years 22–42 of his reign (c. 1458–1438 BC), where his initial battle at Megiddo receives the fullest report. So in Joshua the first battles at Jericho and Ai receive more detailed discussion than the later ones. ◆

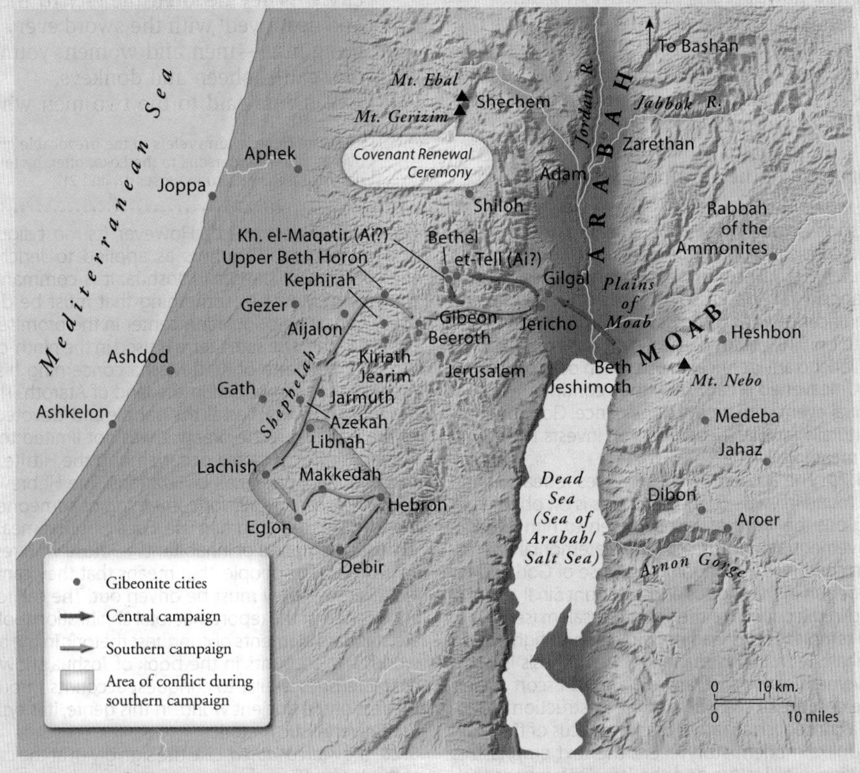

Conquest of Canaan.

5 When you hear them sound a long blast[c]
on the trumpets, have the whole army
give a loud shout;[d] then the wall of the
city will collapse and the army will go up,
everyone straight in."
6 So Joshua son of Nun called the priests
and said to them, "Take up the ark of the
covenant of the LORD and have seven
priests carry trumpets in front of it." 7 And
he ordered the army, "Advance[e]! March
around the city, with an armed guard going ahead of the ark of the LORD."
8 When Joshua had spoken to the people, the seven priests carrying the seven
trumpets before the LORD went forward,
blowing their trumpets, and the ark of
the LORD's covenant followed them. 9 The
armed guard marched ahead of the priests
who blew the trumpets, and the rear
guard[f] followed the ark. All this time the
trumpets were sounding. 10 But Joshua had
commanded the army, "Do not give a war
cry, do not raise your voices, do not say
a word until the day I tell you to shout.
Then shout![g]" 11 So he had the ark of the
LORD carried around the city, circling it
once. Then the army returned to camp and
spent the night there.
12 Joshua got up early the next morning
and the priests took up the ark of the LORD.
13 The seven priests carrying the seven
trumpets went forward, marching before
the ark of the LORD and blowing the trumpets. The armed men went ahead of them
and the rear guard followed the ark of
the LORD, while the trumpets kept sounding. 14 So on the second day they marched
around the city once and returned to the
camp. They did this for six days.
15 On the seventh day, they got up at
daybreak and marched around the city
seven times in the same manner, except
that on that day they circled the city seven
times.[h] 16 The seventh time around, when
the priests sounded the trumpet blast,
Joshua commanded the army, "Shout! For
the LORD has given you the city! 17 The city
and all that is in it are to be devoted[a][i] to
the LORD. Only Rahab the prostitute and
all who are with her in her house shall be
spared, because she hid[j] the spies we sent.
18 But keep away from the devoted things,[k]
so that you will not bring about your own
destruction by taking any of them. Otherwise you will make the camp of Israel liable to destruction[l] and bring trouble[m] on
it. 19 All the silver and gold and the articles
of bronze and iron[n] are sacred to the LORD
and must go into his treasury."
20 When the trumpets sounded,[o] the
army shouted, and at the sound of the
trumpet, when the men gave a loud
shout,[p] the wall collapsed; so everyone
charged straight in, and they took the
city.[q] 21 They devoted the city to the LORD
and destroyed[r] with the sword every living
thing in it—men and women, young and
old, cattle, sheep and donkeys.
22 Joshua said to the two men who had

6:5 [c] Ex 19:13 [d] ver 20; 1Sa 4:5; Ps 42:4; Isa 42:13 **6:7** [e] Ex 14:15 **6:9** [f] ver 13; Isa 52:12 **6:10** [g] ver 20

6:15 [h] 1Ki 18:44 **6:17** [i] Lev 27:28; Dt 20:17 [j] Jos 2:4 **6:18** [k] Jos 7:1 [l] Jos 7:12 [m] Jos 7:25,26 **6:19** [n] ver 24; Nu 31:22 **6:20** [o] Jdg 6:34; Jer 4:21; Am 2:2 [p] ver 5 [q] Heb 11:30 **6:21** [r] Dt 20:16

[a] *17* The Hebrew term refers to the irrevocable giving over of things or persons to the LORD, often by totally destroying them; also in verses 18 and 21.

and as such is used mostly for signaling, using a preset code consisting of combinations of short and long blasts. *seventh day.* The number seven here has a twofold significance. First, the Passover takes on a special and new significance with the crossing of the Jordan River (see note on 5:10). Second, the seven days of marching around Jericho are identical to the seven days of the Festival of Unleavened Bread. They thus continue to invest this annual event with a new significance. God routinely uses culturally familiar ideas but then invests them with deeper meaning.

6:6 – 15,20 The account in these verses repeats all the phrases found in vv. 3 – 5. The emphasis is on obedience, carrying out the word of Joshua given to him by God. The movement around the city is a ceremonial procession that continues the ongoing purpose of God and his people begun in the exodus and at Mount Sinai and culminating in the deposit of the ark in Jerusalem (see 2Sa 6) and the temple. God is leading, moving and fighting on their behalf. Seen in this manner, the emphasis is upon the movement of the ark (Yahweh) and its escort (Israel). Thus the collapse of the wall and the destruction of Jericho are a consequence rather than the focus of the main action. Unlike modern storytellers, the text emphasizes the obedience of Joshua and the Israelite army as they accompany Yahweh in his work.

6:17 *devoted.* This is the same term used by Rahab in 2:10 to describe Israel's treatment of Sihon and Og ("completely destroyed"). However, its most significant and controversial usage is as applied to Jericho and the subsequent battles in Joshua. It is commanded in the Law of Moses as something that must be done to every Canaanite population center in the promised land (Dt 20:16 – 18). The same term is used in the ninth-century BC Moabite Stone of King Mesha concerning his treatment of the men of Gad in the land of Ataroth. The text describes how he killed all the people and "devoted them to the ban." Thus the practice was not limited to Israel. Indeed, similar customs occur among the Hittite, Egyptian and Mesopotamian civilizations. The Hebrew word used here, *herem* calls for something or someone to be made ineligible for human use. For a city, that means that it must be emptied of inhabitants—those who resist are to be killed. For people, that means that they cannot be assimilated—they must be driven out. The call for total annihilation or the report that total annihilation took place are standard elements of conquest rhetoric in the ancient world. The accounts in the book of Joshua show many characteristics similar to conquest accounts throughout the rest of the ancient world. In this genre, it is typical to use universalistic rhetoric.

6:20 *the wall collapsed.* Like the sign given at the crossing of the Jordan River, this sign indicates God's presence with his people and the futility of resistance. Those who heard of the destruction of this site would have understood the significance of Israel's mission and the power of its God.

spied out the land, "Go into the prostitute's house and bring her out and all who
belong to her, in accordance with your
oath to her.[s]" 23So the young men who had
done the spying went in and brought out
Rahab, her father and mother, her brothers
and sisters and all who belonged to her.[t]
They brought out her entire family and put
them in a place outside the camp of Israel.
24Then they burned the whole city and
everything in it, but they put the silver and
gold and the articles of bronze and iron[u]
into the treasury of the LORD's house. 25But
Joshua spared Rahab the prostitute,[v] with
her family and all who belonged to her,
because she hid the men Joshua had sent
as spies to Jericho[w]—and she lives among
the Israelites to this day.
26At that time Joshua pronounced this
solemn oath: "Cursed before the LORD is
the one who undertakes to rebuild this
city, Jericho:

"At the cost of his firstborn son
he will lay its foundations;
at the cost of his youngest
he will set up its gates."[x]

27So the LORD was with Joshua,[y] and his
fame spread[z] throughout the land.

Achan's Sin

7 But the Israelites were unfaithful in
regard to the devoted things[a];[a] Achan
son of Karmi, the son of Zimri,[b] the son of
Zerah,[b] of the tribe of Judah, took some of
them. So the LORD's anger burned against
Israel.
2Now Joshua sent men from Jericho to
Ai, which is near Beth Aven[c] to the east
of Bethel, and told them, "Go up and spy
out the region." So the men went up and
spied out Ai.
3When they returned to Joshua, they
said, "Not all the army will have to go up
against Ai. Send two or three thousand
men to take it and do not weary the whole
army, for only a few people live there." 4So
about three thousand went up; but they
were routed by the men of Ai,[d] 5who killed
about thirty-six of them. They chased the
Israelites from the city gate as far as the
stone quarries and struck them down on
the slopes. At this the hearts of the people
melted in fear[e] and became like water.
6Then Joshua tore his clothes[f] and fell
facedown to the ground before the ark of
the LORD, remaining there till evening. The
elders of Israel did the same, and sprinkled
dust[g] on their heads. 7And Joshua said,
"Alas, Sovereign LORD, why did you ever
bring this people across the Jordan to deliver us into the hands of the Amorites to
destroy us?[h] If only we had been content
to stay on the other side of the Jordan!
8Pardon your servant, Lord. What can I
say, now that Israel has been routed by its
enemies? 9The Canaanites and the other
people of the country will hear about this
and they will surround us and wipe out
our name from the earth.[i] What then will
you do for your own great name?"
10The LORD said to Joshua, "Stand up!
What are you doing down on your face?
11Israel has sinned; they have violated my
covenant,[j] which I commanded them to
keep. They have taken some of the devoted things; they have stolen, they have lied,[k]
they have put them with their own possessions. 12That is why the Israelites cannot stand against their enemies;[l] they turn
their backs and run because they have been
made liable to destruction.[m] I will not be
with you anymore unless you destroy whatever among you is devoted to destruction.
13"Go, consecrate the people. Tell them,
'Consecrate yourselves[n] in preparation
for tomorrow; for this is what the LORD,
the God of Israel, says: There are devoted things among you, Israel. You cannot
stand against your enemies until you remove them.
14" 'In the morning, present yourselves
tribe by tribe. The tribe the LORD chooses[o] shall come forward clan by clan; the
clan the LORD chooses shall come forward

6:22 [s] Jos 2:14; Heb 11:31 **6:23** [t] Jos 2:13 **6:24** [u] ver 19 **6:25** [v] Heb 11:31 [w] Jos 2:6 **6:26** [x] 1Ki 16:34 **6:27** [y] Ge 39:2; Jos 1:5 [z] Jos 9:1 **7:1** [a] Jos 6:18 [b] Jos 22:20 **7:2** [c] Jos 18:12; 1Sa 13:5; 14:23 **7:4** [d] Lev 26:17; Dt 28:25 **7:5** [e] Lev 26:36; Jos 2:9,11; Eze 21:7; Na 2:10 **7:6** [f] Ge 37:29 [g] 1Sa 4:12; 2Sa 13:19; Ne 9:1; Job 2:12; La 2:10; Rev 18:19 **7:7** [h] Ex 5:22 **7:9** [i] Ex 32:12; Dt 9:28 **7:11** [j] Jos 6:17-19 [k] Ac 5:1-2 **7:12** [l] Nu 14:45; Jdg 2:14 [m] Jos 6:18 **7:13** [n] Jos 3:5; 6:18 **7:14** [o] Pr 16:33

[a] *1* The Hebrew term refers to the irrevocable giving over of things or persons to the LORD, often by totally destroying them; also in verses 11, 12, 13 and 15.
[b] *1* See Septuagint and 1 Chron. 2:6; Hebrew *Zabdi*; also in verses 17 and 18.

7:2 *Ai, which is near Beth Aven to the east of Bethel.* There were three main routes that led from Jericho westward into the hill country. The best known was the southerly road to Jerusalem. The northernmost road led to Ophrah. In between there was a road that led to Beitin, with Ai functioning as a fort (like Jericho) to guard the approach.
7:5 *stone quarries.* The Hebrew word *shebarim* describes the steep slopes of the Wadi el-Makkuk, about 3.5 miles (5.6 kilometers) east-southeast from Ai along the road to Jericho.
7:13 *consecrate the people.* The story of Jos 7 is one of an attempt by the Israelites to pursue a military campaign against Ai apart from God, their failure, their confession before God and the subsequent identification and eradication of the sin of Achan. Ancient Near Eastern literature does not often address failed military campaigns, since most of this literature served royal interests of legitimation of the king through the success given him by the gods. The Hittite rituals include one for an army that is defeated by the enemy, but it is very different from the events of Jos 7. The presence of an event like this in Joshua is therefore further confirmation that this is not just standard ancient-world propaganda to serve a political agenda. It also demonstrates the theological point that God is the one bringing victory (as well as defeat).

family by family; and the family the LORD
chooses shall come forward man by man.
15Whoever is caught with the devoted
things shall be destroyed by fire, along
with all that belongs to him.[p] He has violated the covenant[q] of the LORD and has
done an outrageous thing in Israel!' "[r]
16Early the next morning Joshua had
Israel come forward by tribes, and Judah
was chosen. 17The clans of Judah came
forward, and the Zerahites were chosen.[s]
He had the clan of the Zerahites come forward by families, and Zimri was chosen.
18Joshua had his family come forward
man by man, and Achan son of Karmi, the
son of Zimri, the son of Zerah, of the tribe
of Judah, was chosen.
19Then Joshua said to Achan, "My son,
give glory[t] to the LORD, the God of Israel,
and honor him. Tell[u] me what you have
done; do not hide it from me."
20Achan replied, "It is true! I have
sinned against the LORD, the God of Israel.
This is what I have done: 21When I saw in
the plunder a beautiful robe from Babylonia,[a] two hundred shekels[b] of silver and a
bar of gold weighing fifty shekels,[c] I coveted[v] them and took them. They are hidden in the ground inside my tent, with the
silver underneath."
22So Joshua sent messengers, and they
ran to the tent, and there it was, hidden
in his tent, with the silver underneath.
23They took the things from the tent,
brought them to Joshua and all the Israelites and spread them out before the LORD.
24Then Joshua, together with all Israel,
took Achan son of Zerah, the silver, the
robe, the gold bar, his sons and daughters,
his cattle, donkeys and sheep, his tent and
all that he had, to the Valley of Achor.[w]
25Joshua said, "Why have you brought
this trouble[x] on us? The LORD will bring
trouble on you today."
Then all Israel stoned him,[y] and after
they had stoned the rest, they burned
them. 26Over Achan they heaped up a
large pile of rocks, which remains to this
day. Then the LORD turned from his fierce
anger.[z] Therefore that place has been
called the Valley of Achor[d][a] ever since.

Ai Destroyed

8 Then the LORD said to Joshua, "Do not
be afraid;[b] do not be discouraged.[c]
Take the whole army[d] with you, and go
up and attack Ai. For I have delivered[e] into
your hands the king of Ai, his people, his
city and his land. 2You shall do to Ai and
its king as you did to Jericho and its king,
except that you may carry off their plunder and livestock for yourselves.[f] Set an
ambush behind the city."

7:15 [p] 1Sa 14:39 [q] ver 11 [r] Ge 34:7 **7:17** [s] Nu 26:20 **7:19** [t] 1Sa 6:5; Jer 13:16; Jn 9:24* [u] 1Sa 14:43 **7:21** [v] Dt 7:25; Eph 5:5; 1Ti 6:10
7:24 [w] ver 26; Jos 15:7 **7:25** [x] Jos 6:18 [y] Dt 17:5 **7:26** [z] Nu 25:4; Dt 13:17 [a] ver 24; Isa 65:10; Hos 2:15 **8:1** [b] Dt 31:6 [c] Dt 1:21; 7:18; Jos 1:9 [d] Jos 10:7 [e] Jos 6:2 **8:2** [f] ver 27; Dt 20:14

[a] 21 Hebrew *Shinar* [b] 21 That is, about 5 pounds or about 2.3 kilograms [c] 21 That is, about 1 1/4 pounds or about 575 grams [d] 26 *Achor* means *trouble.*

7:21 *beautiful robe from Babylonia ... a bar of gold weighing fifty shekels.* Inventory lists contemporary with early Israel are found in Babylonia and Egypt, as well as the culturally closer city-states of Ugarit and Alalakh. Two hundred shekels of silver would amount to about 6 pounds (2.7 kilograms), while 50 shekels would calculate to about 1.25 pounds (0.56 kilograms). Such an extravagant amount would have taken a common worker a lifetime to earn. The note of a garment followed by its place of origin is found repeatedly on inventories from thirteenth-century BC Ugarit. A letter from Old Babylonian Mari carries a close parallel to the incident described here. Though fragmentary, its message is clear: At the time of a victory, the soldiers were forbidden to take any of the spoil. Anyone doing so would be breaking the *asakku* (taboo) of Addu and Shamash. One man did ignore the prohibition, taking two bronze containers, some silver and gold. The penalty for his action was death.

7:23–25 *spread them out before the LORD ... they burned them.* The items that Achan had taken had been designated as ineligible for human use and had to be destroyed (or, in the case of gold, given to the temple). The expression "spread them out before the LORD" may suggest a formal display of these items before the ark of the covenant as part of the ceremony to appease the divine wrath directed against Israel. In the Old Babylonian period, the theft of temple property was a serious offense. It is among the first of the laws in the Code of Hammurapi. The punishment for theft of property dedicated to a deity (*asakku*) was death by burning. The Israelite approach appears more merciful, with death by stoning preceding the incineration.

7:24 *Achan ... his sons and daughters.* In the ancient Near East, a person found identity within a group. Integration and interdependence were important values. Consequently, individual behavior would not be viewed independently from the group. When one family member sinned, the whole family shared the responsibility. This is true on the national level as well; Achan, as a member of the group of Israel, infects the entire nation with his sin (v. 1). When the law forbids children to be punished for the sin of the parents (Dt 24:16), it refers to the children being subject to punishment in place of the parents. The punishment for violating the ban was to be put under the ban, which entails the elimination of the family line.

8:1 *attack Ai.* With the sin of Achan fully addressed (ch. 7), the narrative now turns to the attack against the leader of Ai, his forces and his stronghold. The particulars of the plan used here are not unusual; however, the comprehensive description of this battle has no parallel in the writings of the ancient Near East. This is not to say that battles were not described; rather, the emphasis on the Israelite forces remains surprising. Most of the detailed contemporary battle accounts emphasized the role of the commander and hardly mentioned that of the soldiers involved. Here there is no doubt that Joshua is the leader, but the soldiers with him receive full credit for their work in the military expedition. Thus the story is not of a sole king or leader, such as the Egyptian accounts of campaigns in which the pharaoh reigns triumphant. Instead, the unity of the army of Israel is emphasized, in contrast to the partial force of Jos 7. In this manner, success is assured, and the victory belongs to the nation and its God rather than to the individual leader.

8:2 *Set an ambush behind the city.* See also v. 4. The use of an ambush in warfare has great antiquity. It occurs in Canaan in the thirteenth century BC as recorded by the

3 So Joshua and the whole army moved
out to attack Ai. He chose thirty thousand
of his best fighting men and sent them out
at night 4 with these orders: "Listen carefully. You are to set an ambush behind the
city. Don't go very far from it. All of you
be on the alert. 5 I and all those with me
will advance on the city, and when the
men come out against us, as they did before, we will flee from them. 6 They will
pursue us until we have lured them away
from the city, for they will say, 'They are
running away from us as they did before.'
So when we flee from them, 7 you are to
rise up from ambush and take the city.
The LORD your God will give it into your
hand.[g] 8 When you have taken the city,
set it on fire.[h] Do what the LORD has commanded.[i] See to it; you have my orders."
9 Then Joshua sent them off, and they
went to the place of ambush[j] and lay in
wait between Bethel and Ai, to the west
of Ai—but Joshua spent that night with
the people.
10 Early the next morning[k] Joshua mustered his army, and he and the leaders of
Israel[l] marched before them to Ai. 11 The
entire force that was with him marched
up and approached the city and arrived in
front of it. They set up camp north of Ai,
with the valley[y] between them and the city.
12 Joshua had taken about five thousand
men and set them in ambush between
Bethel and Ai, to the west of the city. 13 So
the soldiers took up their positions—with
the main camp to the north of the city and
the ambush to the west of it. That night
Joshua went into the valley.
14 When the king of Ai saw this, he and
all the men of the city hurried out early
in the morning to meet Israel in battle at
a certain place overlooking the Arabah.[m]
But he did not know[n] that an ambush
had been set against him behind the city.
15 Joshua and all Israel let themselves be
driven back[o] before them, and they fled
toward the wilderness.[p] 16 All the men of
Ai were called to pursue them, and they
pursued Joshua and were lured away[q]
from the city. 17 Not a man remained in Ai
or Bethel who did not go after Israel. They
left the city open and went in pursuit of
Israel.
18 Then the LORD said to Joshua, "Hold
out toward Ai the javelin[r] that is in your
hand,[s] for into your hand I will deliver the
city." So Joshua held out toward the city
the javelin that was in his hand.[t] 19 As soon
as he did this, the men in the ambush rose
quickly[u] from their position and rushed
forward. They entered the city and captured it and quickly set it on fire.[v]
20 The men of Ai looked back and saw
the smoke of the city rising up into the
sky,[w] but they had no chance to escape
in any direction; the Israelites who had
been fleeing toward the wilderness had
turned back against their pursuers. 21 For
when Joshua and all Israel saw that the
ambush had taken the city and that smoke
was going up from it, they turned around
and attacked the men of Ai. 22 Those in the
ambush also came out of the city against
them, so that they were caught in the middle, with Israelites on both sides. Israel cut
them down, leaving them neither survivors
nor fugitives.[x] 23 But they took the king of
Ai alive[y] and brought him to Joshua.
24 When Israel had finished killing all
the men of Ai in the fields and in the wilderness where they had chased them, and
when every one of them had been put to
the sword, all the Israelites returned to Ai
and killed those who were in it. 25 Twelve
thousand men and women fell that day—
all the people of Ai.[z] 26 For Joshua did not
draw back the hand that held out his javelin until he had destroyed[a][a] all who lived
in Ai.[b] 27 But Israel did carry off for themselves the livestock and plunder of this
city, as the LORD had instructed Joshua.[c]

8:7 [g] Jdg 7:7; 1Sa 23:4 **8:8** [h] Jdg 20:29-38 [i] ver 19 **8:9** [j] 2Ch 13:13 **8:10** [k] Ge 22:3 [l] Jos 7:6 **8:14** [m] Dt 1:1 [n] Jdg 20:34 **8:15** [o] Jdg 20:36 [p] Jos 15:61; 16:1; 18:12 **8:16** [q] Jdg 20:31 **8:18** [r] Job 41:26; Ps 35:3 [s] Ex 4:2; 14:16; 17:9-12 [t] ver 26 **8:19** [u] Jdg 20:33 [v] ver 8 **8:20** [w] Jdg 20:40 **8:22** [x] Dt 7:2; Jos 10:1 **8:23** [y] 1Sa 15:8 **8:25** [z] Dt 20:16-18 **8:26** [a] Nu 21:2 [b] Ex 17:12 **8:27** [c] ver 2

[a] *26* The Hebrew term refers to the irrevocable giving over of things or persons to the LORD, often by totally destroying them.

Egyptians in the Papyrus Anastasi I. It appears again in the strategy of a tenth-century BC Assyrian king; there it resembles the tactic used by Israel in this chapter. Also comparable is the ambush by the Israelites against the Benjamites at Gibeah in Jdg 20. There as well the topography allowed for a hiding place near the target.

8:3 *sent them out at night.* Maneuvers and whole battles might be fought at night. There are examples centuries earlier at Mari of night warfare. Night marches and attacks were used by the fourteenth-century BC Hittite king Mursili II and by the opponents of a military commander from thirteenth-century BC Ugarit.

8:9,12,17 *Bethel.* Located perhaps 1 mile (1.5 kilometers) west of Ai (according to the traditional designations of the sites), Bethel represents the main population center of the immediate area. If Ai is indeed a fort intended to guard Bethel, then it was probably staffed by soldiers from Bethel, so the two armies would have been parts of one and the same military force. For this reason, Joshua takes Bethel into account in his strategy and, as expected, the army of Bethel joins Ai in the apparent rout of the Israelites.

8:18,26 *javelin.* The Hebrew *kidon* was actually a curved sword, either a sickle sword or a scimitar (in the Philistine version of 1Sa 17). In Egyptian it was called the *khopesh.*

8:27 *Israel did carry off for themselves the livestock and plunder of this city.* This verse (cf. v. 2) demonstrates the flexibility of the *herem.* God varied the rules in comparison with what he had commanded at Jericho (6:21). At Ai, the Israelites could and did carry off the plunder for themselves. This would be crucial for the people. The manna had stopped before they attacked Jericho. While

Assyrians impaling prisoners from the palace of Tiglath-Pileser III, c. 730–727 BC. The treatment of Ai's commander (Jos 8:29) is characteristic of the method of execution for enemy leaders.

28So Joshua burned[d] Ai[a][e] and made it a
permanent heap of ruins,[f] a desolate place
to this day.[g] 29He impaled the body of the
king of Ai on a pole and left it there until
evening. At sunset,[h] Joshua ordered them
to take the body from the pole and throw
it down at the entrance of the city gate.
And they raised a large pile of rocks[i] over
it, which remains to this day.

The Covenant Renewed at Mount Ebal

30Then Joshua built on Mount Ebal[j] an
altar[k] to the LORD, the God of Israel, 31as
Moses the servant of the LORD had commanded the Israelites. He built it according to what is written in the Book of the
Law of Moses — an altar of uncut stones,
on which no iron tool[l] had been used. On
it they offered to the LORD burnt offerings and sacrificed fellowship offerings.[m]
32There, in the presence of the Israelites,
Joshua wrote on stones a copy of the law
of Moses.[n] 33All the Israelites, with their
elders, officials and judges, were standing
on both sides of the ark of the covenant
of the LORD, facing the Levitical[o] priests

8:28 [d] Nu 31:10 [e] Jos 7:2; Jer 49:3 [f] Dt 13:16; Jos 10:1 [g] Ge 35:20 **8:29** [h] Dt 21:23; Jn 19:31 [i] 2Sa 18:17 **8:30** [j] Dt 11:29 [k] Ex 20:24 **8:31** [l] Ex 20:25 [m] Dt 27:6-7 **8:32** [n] Dt 27:8 **8:33** [o] Dt 31:12

[a] 28 *Ai* means *the ruin.*

---

in the fertile Jordan Valley, they might enjoy both cultivated and wild barley that was ready for harvest. Now that they were in the less fertile highland and the rather arid region of Ai, they might have found less available food growing naturally. Thus, the livestock and other supplies provided essential support for the continued success of the army.

8:29 *impaled the body of the king of Ai on a pole and left it there until evening.* This treatment of Ai's commander resembles that of the five Amorite kings in 10:26–27. This is not the mode of execution, but the treatment of the corpse after execution used on enemy leaders, especially those whom the victor wishes to use as an example.

8:31 *altar of uncut stones, on which no iron tool had been used.* This is the type of altar commanded to be built in Ex 20:22–26 and specifically for Mount Ebal in Dt 27:5. A parallel occurs in the Iron Age II sanctuary at Tel Arad in southern Judah (tenth–ninth century BC), which contains an Israelite-period altar made of field stones. Otherwise, altars (and other cultic objects) within Canaan were constructed of carefully cut stones.

8:32 *Joshua wrote on stones a copy of the law of Moses.* Here Joshua fulfills the Law of Moses regarding the king who must copy and read the law (Dt 17:18–19). He also fulfills the command to coat the stones with plaster and to write on them the words of the law at Mount Ebal (Dt 27:4,8). Writing on plaster is known in the ninth century BC from sites in the northern Sinai and the Jordan

who carried it. Both the foreigners living
among them and the native-born[p] were
there. Half of the people stood in front of
Mount Gerizim and half of them in front
of Mount Ebal,[q] as Moses the servant of
the LORD had formerly commanded when
he gave instructions to bless the people
of Israel.

34 Afterward, Joshua read all the words
of the law — the blessings and the curses — just as it is written in the Book of the
Law.[r] 35 There was not a word of all that
Moses had commanded that Joshua did
not read to the whole assembly of Israel,
including the women and children, and
the foreigners who lived among them.[s]

8:33 [p] Lev 16:29 [q] Dt 11:29; 27:11-14
8:34 [r] Dt 28:61; 31:11; Jos 1:8
8:35 [s] Ex 12:38; Dt 31:12

Valley. In both cases, this occurs in religious contexts. Writing in alphabetic (proto-) Hebrew script is known in the second millennium BC, and examples have been found in the land of Israel from the thirteenth and twelfth centuries BC onward through every subsequent century in all major areas of the land and reflecting a variety of writers. Basic literacy was common enough, but for official documents scribes would have been used.

JOSHUA 8:30 – 35

ALTAR ON MOUNT EBAL

The Hebrew Bible clearly states that Joshua built an altar of uncut stones on Mount Ebal in accordance with divine instruction to Moses (Dt 27:2 – 8). A site located on the third highest peak near the ridge facing an open area where a large number of people could easily gather has been identified as an open-air altar with two levels of occupation. Evidence suggests that a rather simple pit was built and used for sacrifices in the second half of the thirteenth century BC. This was followed peacefully by a more elaborate structure built of field stones, surrounded by a veranda, and accessed by a ramp, in the first half of the twelfth century BC. The main animals killed there (for sacrifice) were cattle, sheep and a local species of deer; no pigs were slaughtered at the site. Current consensus is that this represents an anomalous Early Iron Age ritual site that has no clear cultural antecedents anywhere in the region, but no evidence connects it directly to the Israelites or the events in Deuteronomy or Joshua. ◆

The Mount Ebal altar shows two levels of occupation: a simple pit from the second half of the thirteenth century BC and the more elaborate structure in the first half of twelfth century BC.

Bill Schlegel/www.BiblePlaces.com

The Gibeonite Deception

9 Now when all the kings west of the Jordan heard about these things — the kings in the hill country, in the western foothills, and along the entire coast of the Mediterranean Sea[t] as far as Lebanon (the kings of the Hittites, Amorites, Canaanites, Perizzites, Hivites and Jebusites)[u] — 2they came together to wage war against Joshua and Israel.

3However, when the people of Gibeon[v] heard what Joshua had done to Jericho and Ai, 4they resorted to a ruse: They went as a delegation whose donkeys were loaded[a] with worn-out sacks and old wineskins, cracked and mended. 5They put worn and patched sandals on their feet and wore old clothes. All the bread of their food supply was dry and moldy. 6Then they went to Joshua in the camp at Gilgal[w] and said to him and the Israelites, "We have come from a distant country; make a treaty with us."

7The Israelites said to the Hivites,[x] "But perhaps you live near us, so how can we make a treaty[y] with you?"

8"We are your servants,[z]" they said to Joshua.

But Joshua asked, "Who are you and where do you come from?"

9They answered: "Your servants have come from a very distant country[a] because of the fame of the LORD your God. For we have heard reports[b] of him: all that he did in Egypt, 10and all that he did to the two kings of the Amorites east of the Jordan — Sihon king of Heshbon, and Og king of Bashan,[c] who reigned in Ashtaroth.[d] 11And our elders and all those living in our country said to us, 'Take provisions for your journey; go and meet them and say to them, "We are your servants; make a treaty with us." ' 12This bread of ours was warm when we packed it at home on the day we left to come to you. But now see how dry and moldy it is. 13And these wineskins that we filled were new, but see how cracked they are. And our clothes and sandals are worn out by the very long journey."

14The Israelites sampled their provisions but did not inquire[e] of the LORD. 15Then Joshua made a treaty of peace[f] with them to let them live, and the leaders of the assembly ratified it by oath.

16Three days after they made the treaty with the Gibeonites, the Israelites heard that they were neighbors, living near them. 17So the Israelites set out and on the third day came to their cities: Gibeon, Kephirah, Beeroth[g] and Kiriath Jearim.[h] 18But the Israelites did not attack them, because the leaders of the assembly had sworn an oath[i] to them by the LORD, the God of Israel.

The whole assembly grumbled[j] against the leaders, 19but all the leaders answered, "We have given them our oath by the LORD, the God of Israel, and we cannot touch them now. 20This is what we will do to them: We will let them live, so that God's wrath will not fall on us for breaking the oath we swore to them." 21They continued, "Let them live,[k] but let them be woodcutters and water carriers[l] in the service of the whole assembly." So the leaders' promise to them was kept.

22Then Joshua summoned the Gibeonites and said, "Why did you deceive us by saying, 'We live a long way[m] from you,' while actually you live near[n] us? 23You are now under a curse:[o] You will never be released from service as woodcutters and water carriers for the house of my God."

24They answered Joshua, "Your servants were clearly told[p] how the LORD your God had commanded his servant Moses to give you the whole land and to wipe out all its inhabitants from before you. So we feared for

9:1 [t] Nu 34:6 [u] Ex 3:17; Jos 3:10 **9:3** [v] ver 17; Jos 10:2; 2Sa 2:12; 2Ch 1:3; Isa 28:21 **9:6** [w] Jos 5:10 **9:7** [x] ver 1; Jos 11:19 [y] Ex 23:32; Dt 7:2 **9:8** [z] Dt 20:11; 2Ki 10:5 **9:9** [a] Dt 20:15 [b] ver 24; Jos 2:9 **9:10** [c] Nu 21:33 [d] Nu 21:24, 35
9:14 [e] Nu 27:21 **9:15** [f] Ex 23:32; Jos 11:19; 2Sa 21:2 **9:17** [g] Jos 18:25 [h] 1Sa 7:1-2 **9:18** [i] Ps 15:4 [j] Ex 15:24 **9:21** [k] ver 15 [l] Dt 29:11 **9:22** [m] ver 6 [n] ver 16 **9:23** [o] Ge 9:25 **9:24** [p] ver 9

[a] 4 Most Hebrew manuscripts; some Hebrew manuscripts, Vulgate and Syriac (see also Septuagint) *They prepared provisions and loaded their donkeys*

9:4 *they resorted to a ruse.* Despite the absence of an exact parallel, the Hittite annals of Mursili II do record examples of willing capitulation of a region that leads to servitude instead of annihilation, of the use of vulnerable "emissaries" instead of the leader to negotiate, and of elders of a town coming and subjugating themselves.

9:6 *Gilgal.* If this is the Gilgal of 4:19 – 20 and 5:9 – 10, then the story would appear to be out of sequence, as the Israelites appear at the end of ch. 8 to be based in the central hill country near Shechem. However, Gilgal may be a description of any oval-shaped site. El-'Unuq, east of Shechem, could qualify.

9:11,16 *treaty.* The suzerain-vassal treaty has many examples preserved from the Hittite archives. It was used by that empire for making official agreements with neighboring states of lesser strength. This would have been the type of treaty made with the Gibeonites. An element of such a treaty is the list of gods of each side who are called upon to uphold the treaty.

9:17 *Kephirah, Beeroth and Kiriath Jearim.* That these cities are mentioned along with Gibeon suggests that there was a league of four cities of Hivites in what would become the heart of the territory of Benjamin. All these towns lay close to one another. The region should not take three days to reach from the area of Mount Ebal (8:30 – 35). Either the Israelites were interrupted on their journey, perhaps by unrecorded battles, or the term "third day" signifies a general period of time rather than a specific number of days.

9:18 *sworn an oath to them by the LORD.* If an oath was not kept, the invoked deity's name was being held as worthless and powerless. In a culture where gods were active and powerful, treating them with contempt had serious consequences, which are demonstrated when this same oath is broken in 2Sa 21.

our lives because of you, and that is why we
did this. 25We are now in your hands.[q] Do to
us whatever seems good and right to you."
26So Joshua saved them from the Israelites, and they did not kill them. 27That day
he made the Gibeonites woodcutters and
water carriers for the assembly, to provide
for the needs of the altar of the LORD at the
place the LORD would choose.[r] And that is
what they are to this day.

The Sun Stands Still

10 Now Adoni-Zedek king of Jerusalem[s] heard that Joshua had taken
Ai[t] and totally destroyed[a][u] it, doing to Ai
and its king as he had done to Jericho and
its king, and that the people of Gibeon had
made a treaty of peace[v] with Israel and had
become their allies. 2He and his people
were very much alarmed at this, because
Gibeon was an important city, like one of
the royal cities; it was larger than Ai, and all
its men were good fighters. 3So Adoni-Zedek king of Jerusalem appealed to Hoham
king of Hebron,[w] Piram king of Jarmuth,
Japhia king of Lachish[x] and Debir king of
Eglon. 4"Come up and help me attack Gibeon," he said, "because it has made peace[y]
with Joshua and the Israelites."
5Then the five kings of the Amorites[z]—
the kings of Jerusalem, Hebron, Jarmuth,
Lachish and Eglon—joined forces. They
moved up with all their troops and took up
positions against Gibeon and attacked it.
6The Gibeonites then sent word to Joshua in the camp at Gilgal: "Do not abandon
your servants. Come up to us quickly and
save us! Help us, because all the Amorite
kings from the hill country have joined
forces against us."
7So Joshua marched up from Gilgal with
his entire army,[a] including all the best
fighting men. 8The LORD said to Joshua,
"Do not be afraid[b] of them; I have given
them into your hand. Not one of them will
be able to withstand you."
9After an all-night march from Gilgal,
Joshua took them by surprise. 10The LORD
threw them into confusion before Israel,[c]
so Joshua and the Israelites defeated them
completely at Gibeon. Israel pursued them
along the road going up to Beth Horon[d]
and cut them down all the way to Azekah[e] and Makkedah. 11As they fled before
Israel on the road down from Beth Horon
to Azekah, the LORD hurled large hailstones[f] down on them, and more of them
died from the hail than were killed by the
swords of the Israelites.

9:25 [q] Ge 16:6
9:27 [r] Dt 12:5
10:1 [s] Jdg 1:7 [t] Jos 8:1 [u] Dt 20:16; Jos 8:22 [v] Jos 9:15
10:3 [w] Ge 13:18 [x] 2Ch 11:9; 25:27; Ne 11:30; Isa 36:2; 37:8; Jer 34:7; Mic 1:13
10:4 [y] Jos 9:15
10:5 [z] Nu 13:29
10:7 [a] Jos 8:1
10:8 [b] Dt 3:2; Jos 1:9
10:10 [c] Dt 7:23 [d] Jos 16:3,5 [e] Jos 15:35
10:11 [f] Ps 18:12; Isa 28:2,17

[a] *1* The Hebrew term refers to the irrevocable giving over of things or persons to the LORD, often by totally destroying them; also in verses 28, 35, 37, 39 and 40.

9:27 *he made the Gibeonites woodcutters and water carriers for the assembly, to provide for the needs of the altar of the LORD.* Assuming that the Gibeonites remained in their cities (as ch. 10 suggests), it seems reasonable to assume that part of the community and at least one sanctuary were located in the region of Gibeon. This may refer to the high place at Gibeon that Solomon later visited (1Ki 3:4–5). An Israelite sanctuary, like those of their neighbors, would require wood to burn the incense and sacrifices, and water to keep the altar and sanctuary clean from the blood and gore of the animal sacrifices. The menial nature of the work gave them permanent lower-class status.

10:1–43 Perhaps more than any other chapter of the book of Joshua, ch. 10 is filled with material that possesses parallels in ancient Near Eastern literature and can be further illuminated by comparisons with aspects of contemporary culture. In its totality, it resembles the annalistic accounts of the ancient Near East. Thus the Ten Year Annals of Mursili II include near their beginning a description of hostilities taken against Mursili and his response in the destruction of two cities. This is followed by the Kashka enemy all gathering together against him for war and his defeat of them. Then, in subsequent years, there is an iterative construction in which the same phrases are used repeatedly to describe the assault and defeat of enemy city after enemy city. This bears a surprising resemblance to the book of Joshua, where the Israelites first defeat two "cities," Jericho and Ai (chs. 6; 8). This is followed by a coalition coming together to oppose them (10:1–5). There follows a description of town after town being attacked and destroyed in an iterative fashion (vv. 28–42). Also of interest are the annals of Thutmose III covering years 22–42 of his reign (c. 1458–1438 BC). Here as well there is the threat of the enemy consolidating diverse forces and coming together at Megiddo to battle the pharaoh. The first battle at Megiddo and its immediate background receive the greatest detail of coverage. This resembles Joshua's initial battle from Gibeon to Makkedah (vv. 9–27). In both cases the far greater detail of the initial battle contrasts with the briefer more repetitious descriptions of the following battles in the campaign, whether the 16 of Thutmose or the five or six of Jos 10. The similarities in style argue that Jos 10 was styled in the manner of royal annals and followed forms known and used in the Late Bronze Age.

10:4 *Come up and help me attack Gibeon … because it has made peace with Joshua and the Israelites.* This is the only Biblical example of a reported message from one Canaanite king to another. Although most likely a summary of what was sent, it preserves rhetorical forms not unlike the Amarna letters from Canaan in the fourteenth century BC. The use of threefold repetition in the verbs ("come up," "help me," "attack") and in the identification of the king's enemy (here: Gibeon, Joshua, the Israelites)—all have their parallels in letters from Canaanite kings of Jerusalem and Shechem. Even the manner in which "peace" becomes a pretext for war has a parallel. Thus the message reflects authentic style of this period.

10:11 *the LORD hurled large hailstones down on them.* Again, there are parallels to such divine intervention in the annals of ancient kings and their battles. Close in type is that of the eighth-century BC Assyrian king Sargon, who writes concerning one campaign: "The rest of the people, who had fled to save their lives, whom he had abandoned that the glorious might of Ashur, my lord, might be magnified, Adad, the violent, the son of Anu, the valiant, uttered his loud cry against them; and with the flood cloud and hailstones, he totally annihilated the remainder."

JOSHUA 10:12 – 13

The Sun Stands Still and the Moon Stops

This event has motivated interpreters to seek a variety of solutions, and it remains among the most widely contested of events in the Bible. The traditional interpretation of this passage is that Joshua's prayer takes place as daylight is waning, and he feels that with just a few extra daylight hours, he can finish off the enemy. Unfortunately, this interpretation has failed to take into account the details given in the text. The passage explicitly notes that the sun is over Gibeon and the moon over the Valley of Aijalon. Since Gibeon is east and Aijalon is west, we must conclude that Joshua prays in the morning. Consequently we begin to wonder why Joshua would even bother to request a longer period of daylight if it is still morning. This critique is also true of a second view, namely, that Joshua is seeking relief from the heat of the sun. A third view, that a solar eclipse is in view, is impossible, because a solar eclipse cannot take place if sun and moon are on opposite horizons.

We can now try to understand the text as an ancient text rather than a modern one. As such, we must begin with the idea that the text operates in the world of omens, not the world of physics and astronomy. Then we must consider the possibility that the correct interpretation of this passage is that Joshua was praying for the Amorites to see a bad omen. The argument for this position is as follows: If the sun is in the east and moon is in the west, we can conclude that not only is it morning, but it is morning at the time of the full moon. On the first official day of the full moon, the orb of the sun is fully visible above the eastern horizon line and the orb of the moon is fully visible above the western horizon line for about four minutes. When we explore ancient celestial omen texts, we find that this is one of the most important times of the month for getting an important omen.

In the ancient Near East, the months were not standardized in length, but varied according to the phases of the moon. This lunar calendar was then periodically adjusted to the solar year so as to retain the relationship of months with the seasons. The beginning of a month was calculated by the first appearance of the new moon. The full moon came in the middle of the month and was identified by the fact that the moon set just minutes after the sun rose. The day of the month on which the full moon occurred served as an indicator of how many days the month would have. When the opposition of sun and moon — the full moon — occurred on the 14th day of the month, that meant that the new crescent would be seen on the 30th day. Such a month was considered the "right" length, and all would be in harmony. It was then considered a full-length month made up of full-length days. Longer or shorter months were believed to contain longer or shorter days. Thus, seeing the full moon on the morning of the 14th day was a good omen.

As a result of these beliefs about omens, the horizon was observed very carefully in the middle section of the month hoping for this opposition of sun and moon to come on the propitious day (the 14th). Opposition on the wrong day was believed to be an omen of all sorts of disaster, including military defeat and overthrow of cities. In this way, the movements of the sun and the moon became monthly omens of good fortune or ill. As is evident from Jos 10:13, on the day of Joshua's battle, he requests that the sun and moon would not give an omen that the Amorites would have hoped for. In the ancient Near East, great significance was attached to these omens, and they

continued on next page

well might have been used to determine whether or not battle should be engaged on a particular day. As noted above, the positions reported in Joshua for the sun and moon suggest that it is near sunrise in the full-moon phase. Since Joshua wants the Amorites to receive a negative omen, we can reason that it must not be the 14th day of the month. If what Joshua prays for takes place, the Amorites would feel that their battle was doomed.

Not only are the focus and the timing right, the language also supports this sort of interpretation. The Mesopotamian celestial omens use verbs like "wait," "stand" and "stop" to record the relative movements and positions of the celestial bodies. When the moon and/or sun do not wait, the moon sinks over the horizon before the sun rises and no opposition occurs. When the moon and sun wait or stand, it indicates that the opposition does occur for the determination of the full-moon day. The omens in the series known as *Enuma Anu Enlil* often speak of changing velocities of the moon in its course to effect or avoid opposition with the sun.

The major objections to this interpretation of the passage as involving an understanding of omens come from Jos 10:13. Most standard translations are relatively close to the NIV: "So the sun stood still, and the moon stopped, till the nation avenged itself on its enemies, as it is written in the Book of Jashar. The sun stopped in the middle of the sky and delayed going down about a full day." Four Hebrew terms deserve some attention:

1. *Till.* This translation gives the impression that the described situation was sustained until victory was achieved. In fact, however, the Hebrew preposition used here can be rendered "before" in precisely the sort of syntactic arrangement used in this verse. A good example is found in Eze 33:22.

2. *Middle.* By "middle," we should not assume that the text refers to midday. At midday, the moon would not be visible in the west; neither would Joshua know he needed extended light at midday. A more likely treatment would be to see it as a reference to its half of the sky (i.e., the eastern half of the sky)

3. *Delayed.* Here the text says that the sun "did not hasten." The same phrasing is found in an omen text concerning Mars: "It will not stand in it [in its midst], it will not become stationary [= wait] and not tarry [= rest]; it went forth hurriedly." Furthermore, some translations say that it did not hasten *to set*. The Hebrew verb is sometimes translated that way, but it is the basic verb "to go, enter" and could feasibly be used for any transition from one section to another.

4. *Full.* This is the most difficult term to assess. A couple of options are worthy of consideration. In Akkadian omen texts, a "full-length" month (30 days) is made up of "full-length" days. When the full moon is on the 14th, it will be a full-length month filled with full-length days. If the month is not going to be 30 days, as here, then they are not full-length days. It may not make sense immediately to us, but it is how the texts are interpreted. Alternatively, rather than translate "full-length" we might consider the possibility of translating the Hebrew adjective *tammim* as "propitious." In this case, the phrase would be translated "the sun did not hasten to its entry as on a propitious day."

Beyond these lexical discussions, some object to this reading, because all of the omen texts are Neo-Assyrian and therefore many centuries later than the time of Joshua. Furthermore, the interest in celestial divination is strongest in the seventh century BC and in the area of Assyria. We have little information concerning the use of omens from the Levant in the mid-second millennium BC. Nevertheless, recent study has shown that even the Neo-Assyrian sources have their roots in the second millennium BC, and the Levant is not totally lacking evidence (cf. Emar).

The lexical issues remain vexing and problematic, but they can be addressed. Even if we acknowledge that we have not yet sorted out the lexical details, the presence of terms such as "stop," "stand" and "wait" gain new possibilities in light of the language of celestial omens, and the fact that the context is one that is just right for an

continued on next page

omen application (i.e., on the brink of battle). Certainly a reading of the text in light of omens is more likely for an ancient text than a reading in light of physics.

It should be noted that the text does not suggest the astronomical phenomena were unique. Instead, Jos 10:14 says plainly that what was unique was the Lord accepting a battle strategy from a man ("the LORD listened to a human being"). A Mesopotamian lamentation (first millennium BC) shows this same type of terminology for divine judgment when it speaks of the heavens rumbling, the earth shaking, the sun lying at the horizon and the moon stopping in the sky, and evil storms sweeping through the land. Joshua's knowledge of the Amorites' dependence on omens may have led him to ask the Lord for one that he knew would deflate their morale — for the opposition to occur on an unpropitious day. ◆

12On the day the LORD gave the Amorites[g] over to Israel, Joshua said to the LORD in the presence of Israel:

"Sun, stand still over Gibeon,
and you, moon, over the Valley of Aijalon.[h]"
13So the sun stood still,[i]
and the moon stopped,
till the nation avenged itself on[a] its enemies,

as it is written in the Book of Jashar.[j]

The sun stopped[k] in the middle of the sky and delayed going down about a full day. 14There has never been a day like it before or since, a day when the LORD listened to a human being. Surely the LORD was fighting[l] for Israel!

15Then Joshua returned with all Israel to the camp at Gilgal.[m]

Five Amorite Kings Killed

16Now the five kings had fled and hidden in the cave at Makkedah. 17When Joshua was told that the five kings had been found hiding in the cave at Makkedah, 18he said, "Roll large rocks up to the mouth of the cave, and post some men there to guard it. 19But don't stop; pursue your enemies! Attack them from the rear and don't let them reach their cities, for the LORD your God has given them into your hand."

20So Joshua and the Israelites defeated them completely,[n] but a few survivors managed to reach their fortified cities. 21The whole army then returned safely to Joshua in the camp at Makkedah, and no one uttered a word against the Israelites.

22Joshua said, "Open the mouth of the cave and bring those five kings out to me." 23So they brought the five kings out of the cave — the kings of Jerusalem, Hebron, Jarmuth, Lachish and Eglon. 24When they had brought these kings to Joshua, he summoned all the men of Israel and said to the army commanders who had come with him, "Come here and put your feet[o] on the necks of these kings." So they came forward and placed their feet[p] on their necks.

25Joshua said to them, "Do not be afraid; do not be discouraged. Be strong and courageous.[q] This is what the LORD will do to all the enemies you are going to fight." 26Then Joshua put the kings to death and exposed their bodies on five poles, and they were left hanging on the poles until evening.

27At sunset[r] Joshua gave the order and they took them down from the poles and threw them into the cave where they had been hiding. At the mouth of the cave they placed large rocks, which are there to this day.

Southern Cities Conquered

28That day Joshua took Makkedah. He put the city and its king to the sword and totally destroyed everyone in it. He left no survivors.[s] And he did to the king of Makkedah as he had done to the king of Jericho.[t]

29Then Joshua and all Israel with him moved on from Makkedah to Libnah and attacked it. 30The LORD also gave that city and its king into Israel's hand. The city and everyone in it Joshua put to the sword. He left no survivors there. And he did to its king as he had done to the king of Jericho.

10:12 [g] Am 2:9 [h] Jdg 1:35; 12:12 **10:13** [i] Hab 3:11 [j] 2Sa 1:18 [k] Isa 38:8 **10:14** [l] ver 42; Ex 14:14; Dt 1:30; Ps 106:43; 136:24 **10:15** [m] ver 43 **10:20** [n] Dt 20:16

10:24 [o] Mal 4:3 [p] Ps 110:1 **10:25** [q] Dt 31:6 **10:27** [r] Dt 21:23; Jos 8:9,29 **10:28** [s] Dt 20:16 [t] Jos 6:21

[a] 13 *Or nation triumphed over*

10:26 *exposed their bodies on five poles.* Compare the fate of the king of Ai (see 8:29 and note).

31Then Joshua and all Israel with him
moved on from Libnah to Lachish; he
took up positions against it and attacked
it. 32The LORD gave Lachish into Israel's
hands, and Joshua took it on the second
day. The city and everyone in it he put
to the sword, just as he had done to Libnah. 33Meanwhile, Horam king of Gezer[u]
had come up to help Lachish, but Joshua
defeated him and his army — until no survivors were left.

34Then Joshua and all Israel with him
moved on from Lachish to Eglon; they
took up positions against it and attacked
it. 35They captured it that same day and
put it to the sword and totally destroyed
everyone in it, just as they had done to
Lachish.

36Then Joshua and all Israel with him
went up from Eglon to Hebron[v] and attacked it. 37They took the city and put it
to the sword, together with its king, its
villages and everyone in it. They left no
survivors. Just as at Eglon, they totally destroyed it and everyone in it.

38Then Joshua and all Israel with him
turned around and attacked Debir.[w]
39They took the city, its king and its villages, and put them to the sword. Everyone
in it they totally destroyed. They left no
survivors. They did to Debir and its king
as they had done to Libnah and its king
and to Hebron.

40So Joshua subdued the whole region,
including the hill country, the Negev,[x]
the western foothills and the mountain
slopes,[y] together with all their kings.[z] He
left no survivors. He totally destroyed all
who breathed, just as the LORD, the God
of Israel, had commanded.[a] 41Joshua subdued them from Kadesh Barnea[b] to Gaza[c]
and from the whole region of Goshen[d] to
Gibeon. 42All these kings and their lands
Joshua conquered in one campaign, because the LORD, the God of Israel, fought[e]
for Israel.

43Then Joshua returned with all Israel to
the camp at Gilgal.[f]

Northern Kings Defeated

11 When Jabin[g] king of Hazor[h] heard
of this, he sent word to Jobab king
of Madon, to the kings of Shimron[i] and
Akshaph, 2and to the northern kings who
were in the mountains, in the Arabah[j]
south of Kinnereth,[k] in the western foothills and in Naphoth Dor[l] on the west; 3to
the Canaanites in the east and west; to the
Amorites, Hittites, Perizzites and Jebusites
in the hill country; and to the Hivites[m]

10:33 [u] Jos 16:3, 10; Jdg 1:29; 1Ki 9:15
10:36 [v] Jos 14:13; 15:13; Jdg 1:10
10:38 [w] Jos 15:15; Jdg 1:11
10:40 [x] Ge 12:9; Jos 12:8 [y] Dt 1:7 [z] Dt 7:24 [a] Dt 20:16-17
10:41 [b] Ge 14:7 [c] Ge 10:19 [d] Jos 11:16; 15:51
10:42 [e] ver 14
10:43 [f] ver 15; Jos 5:9
11:1 [g] Jdg 4:2, 7,23 [h] ver 10; 1Sa 12:9 [i] Jos 19:15
11:2 [j] Jos 12:3 [k] Nu 34:11 [l] Jos 17:11; Jdg 1:27; 1Ki 4:11
11:3 [m] Dt 7:1; Jdg 3:3,5; 1Ki 9:20

10:40 *the hill country, the Negev, the western foothills and the mountain slopes.* This summarizes the whole region south of Gibeon. *hill country.* Includes the region immediately south and dominated by sites such as Jerusalem and Hebron, with Arad and Beersheba at the southern tip. *Negev.* In the Bible refers to the region around the Beersheba Valley at the southern end of the region of Judah. *the western foothills and the mountain slopes.* Seems to describe the same area, that which is located between the coastal plain and the hill country. It is called the Shephelah (Hebrew for "western foothills").
10:41 *Kadesh Barnea.* The place where the previous generation reached the southern border of the promised land, but was unable to enter (Nu 11). *Gaza.* The traditional southwestern corner of the land of Canaan and the first Canaanite city that the Egyptians reached when traveling from their country across the northern Sinai. *region of Goshen.* Mentioned as a southern boundary in Canaan in 11:16 and as an otherwise unattested hill country town of Judah in 15:51. This is not the region of Egypt where the Israelites lived before the exodus; rather, it may refer to a region at the south central or southeastern edge of Canaan (and Judah).
11:1 *Jabin king of Hazor.* From the time of the Middle Bronze Age Mari letters (eighteenth century BC), the leader at Hazor was a Yabni-Addu; the first part of the name sounds like Jabin but is not identical to it, and in fact is derived from a different root. The form, *ib-ni,* also occurs in a Middle Bronze letter from Hazor as part of a personal name. It is possible that this was a dynastic name at Hazor that was preserved in the Bible, both in Jos 11 and in Jdg 4 – 5, but with a different vocalization added later. *Hazor.* The site, including its lower tel, covers some 175 acres (70.8 hectares), the largest city in ancient Israel. It was destroyed by violent conflagration in the thirteenth century BC, which may relate to the events of Jos 11. *Madon.* Occurs elsewhere only in 12:19, and should probably be identified with Merom. The *d* and *r* resemble one another in Biblical Hebrew, so this could be a copyist error. Alternatively, there could be two slightly different names for the same place, perhaps dialectical variants. The battle at the Waters of Merom (vv. 5 – 7) would then have been near a site that itself was close to Hazor, Tel Qarnei Hittin, on the heights west of the Sea of Galilee. *Shimron.* Tel Shimron, 5 miles (8 kilometers) west of Nazareth at the western end of the Jezreel Valley. *Akshaph.* It may be Tell Keisan, 4.5 miles (7.3 kilometers) south of Akko on the plain, or it may be Tel Regev, at the foot of Mount Carmel and at the entrance to the Jokneam Pass to the Jezreel Valley.
11:2 *northern kings who were in the mountains.* Like the summary of the southern coalition region in 10:40, the description here divides the north into four areas. The description begins in the north and proceeds in a clockwise direction. This term includes the towns in the Galilean highlands north of the Jezreel Valley. *in the Arabah south of Kinnereth.* Kinnereth is Tel Kinrot, overlooking the northwest shore of the Sea of Galilee. The Arabah is the whole region of the Sea of Galilee and the northern half of the Jordan Valley. *in the western foothills.* In Hebrew, the Shephelah (see note on 10:40). *Naphoth Dor.* There is no certain translation of "Naphoth." Dor lies on the Mediterranean coast, south of Mount Carmel. This expression could refer to the coastal plain in that region.
11:3 The northern assembly is composed of diverse groups, perhaps reflecting the international cultural and commercial importance of the north, as seen in the later history of the northern kingdom of Israel. *Jebusites.* Encountered around Jerusalem (15:8,63; 18:16). *hill country.* May be the central hill country and may reflect their presence well north of Jerusalem. *Hivites below Hermon*

below Hermon in the region of Mizpah.[n]
[4]They came out with all their troops and
a large number of horses and chariots — a
huge army, as numerous as the sand on
the seashore.[o] [5]All these kings joined forces[p] and made camp together at the Waters
of Merom to fight against Israel.
[6]The LORD said to Joshua, "Do not be
afraid of them, because by this time tomorrow I will hand[q] all of them, slain,
over to Israel. You are to hamstring[r] their
horses and burn their chariots."
[7]So Joshua and his whole army came
against them suddenly at the Waters of
Merom and attacked them, [8]and the LORD
gave them into the hand of Israel. They
defeated them and pursued them all the
way to Greater Sidon, to Misrephoth
Maim,[s] and to the Valley of Mizpah on the
east, until no survivors were left. [9]Joshua
did to them as the LORD had directed: He
hamstrung their horses and burned their
chariots.
[10]At that time Joshua turned back and
captured Hazor and put its king to the
sword. (Hazor had been the head of all
these kingdoms.) [11]Everyone in it they
put to the sword. They totally destroyed[a]
them, not sparing anyone that breathed,[t]
and he burned Hazor itself.
[12]Joshua took all these royal cities and
their kings and put them to the sword. He
totally destroyed them, as Moses the servant of the LORD had commanded.[u] [13]Yet
Israel did not burn any of the cities built
on their mounds — except Hazor, which
Joshua burned. [14]The Israelites carried off

11:3 [n] Ge 31:49; Jos 15:38; 18:26 **11:4** [o] Jdg 7:12; 1Sa 13:5 **11:5** [p] Jdg 5:19 **11:6** [q] Jos 10:8 [r] 2Sa 8:4 **11:8** [s] Jos 13:6 **11:11** [t] Dt 20:16-17 **11:12** [u] Nu 33:50-52; Dt 7:2

[a] *11* The Hebrew term refers to the irrevocable giving over of things or persons to the LORD, often by totally destroying them; also in verses 12, 20 and 21.

in the region of Mizpah. For the Hivites located around Gibeon, see v. 19; 9:7. In Ge 34:2, there are Hivites living in Shechem. Here the description takes the reader farther north. If Hermon is equated with Sirion and Senir in Dt 3:9, then Mizpah could refer to the eastern part of the Litani River, which flows south from the Beqa and turns westward toward Tyre at a point close to the northern end of the Huleh Basin. This would be the region of Dan and the northern limits of the Israelite settlement.

11:5 *Waters of Merom.* Perhaps these are to be located north of Tel Qarnei Hittin at Wadi el-Hamam. This site lay on the ancient road north to Hazor and would provide a staging point for the coalition.

11:6 *hamstring their horses and burn their chariots.* The presence of chariots among the northern coalition suggests a sophistication not found in the south. Here in the north, the leaders had more wealth and power, such that they could afford to field the most advanced weaponry of the era. Horses were not used for transportation (or cavalry) by themselves, but only for pulling chariots. The chariots functioned as mobile fighting platforms, particularly serving to move archers quickly across the battlefield and to aid in their effectiveness. Hamstringing the horses would render them useless for battle. Chariots needed to be light and were often built of wood. Hence they could be burned. Bronze or iron could be used as linchpins for the wheels and perhaps as plating to protect the wood; hence the description of "chariots fitted with iron" (17:16,18; see note on Jdg 1:19).

11:13 *Israel did not burn any of the cities built on their mounds — except Hazor.* Jos 6:24; 8:28 record that Jericho and Ai were also burned, though archaeological

Aerial view of Hazor (Jos 11:1,10).

Z. Radovan/www.BibleLandPictures.com

for themselves all the plunder and livestock of these cities, but all the people
they put to the sword until they completely destroyed them, not sparing anyone
that breathed.[v] 15 As the LORD commanded
his servant Moses, so Moses commanded
Joshua, and Joshua did it; he left nothing
undone of all that the LORD commanded
Moses.[w]
16 So Joshua took this entire land: the hill country, all
the Negev, the whole region
of Goshen, the western foothills,[x] the Arabah and the
mountains of Israel with their
foothills, 17 from Mount Halak, which rises toward Seir,
to Baal Gad in the Valley of
Lebanon[y] below Mount Hermon. He captured all their
kings and put them to death.[z]
18 Joshua waged war against
all these kings for a long time.
19 Except for the Hivites living
in Gibeon,[a] not one city made
a treaty of peace with the Israelites, who took them all in
battle. 20 For it was the LORD
himself who hardened their
hearts[b] to wage war against
Israel, so that he might destroy them totally, extermi-
nating them without mercy,
as the LORD had commanded
Moses.[c]
21 At that time Joshua went
and destroyed the Anakites[d]
from the hill country: from
Hebron, Debir and Anab,
from all the hill country of
Judah, and from all the hill
country of Israel. Joshua totally destroyed them and their
towns. 22 No Anakites were
left in Israelite territory; only
in Gaza, Gath[e] and Ashdod[f]
did any survive.
23 So Joshua took the en-
tire land,[g] just as the LORD
had directed Moses, and he gave it as an
inheritance[h] to Israel according to their
tribal divisions.[i] Then the land had rest
from war.[j]

11:14 [v] Nu 31:11-12 **11:15** [w] Ex 34:11; Jos 1:7 **11:16** [x] Jos 10:41 **11:17** [y] Jos 12:7 [z] Dt 7:24 **11:19** [a] Jos 9:3

11:20 [b] Ex 14:17; Ro 9:18 [c] Dt 7:16; Jdg 14:4 **11:21** [d] Nu 13:22, 33; Dt 9:2 **11:22** [e] 1Sa 17:4; 1Ki 2:39; 1Ch 8:13 [f] 1Sa 5:1; Isa 20:1 **11:23** [g] Jos 21:43-45 [h] Dt 1:38; 12:9-10; 25:19 [i] Nu 26:53 [j] Jos 14:15

THE NORTHERN CAMPAIGN

Late Bronze Age Hazor was burned by Joshua (Jos 11:13). Excavations have revealed three clearly datable destruction layers, one of which may provide the strongest evidence yet for a historically verifiable date for the conquest.

The excavator thought Joshua burned the latest level c. 1230 BC, but others argue that it must actually have been the earliest of the three levels, c. 1400 BC (see note on Jos 11:13).

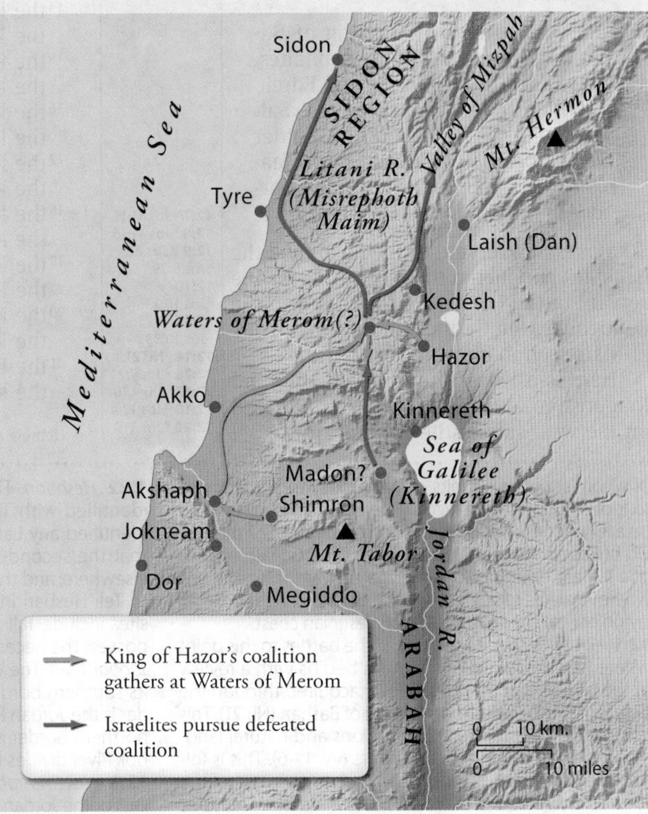

evidence at these two sites is lacking. However, there is no record of other towns of either the southern or northern coalition being burned. This may explain why archaeologists have not found destruction layers, characterized by evidence of burning, at the many other sites listed in chs. 10–11. Hazor does evidence a very clear burn layer, but there is still controversy over whether it can be attributed to Joshua's armies.
11:17 *from Mount Halak, which rises toward Seir, to Baal Gad in the Valley of Lebanon below Mount Hermon.* In 12:7 Mount Halak lies between Israel and Edom. Jebel Halaq is located midway between Kadesh Barnea and the southern end of the Dead Sea. If it marks the southern end of Israel's activity, Baal Gad marks the northern end. If Mount Hermon is the Anti-Lebanon range, then the Valley of Lebanon could be the Beqa or the Valley of Mizpah to its south.
11:21 *the Anakites.* The Bible associates the sons of Anak with the Nephilim (Nu 13:33) and they are in turn connected to the Rephaim (Dt 2:11). These as a whole are best understood as mighty warriors who fell in battle, often slain by Israel. They are not a race but an ethnic group (see notes on Nu 13:22,33). The thirteenth-century BC Egyptian Papyrus Anastasi I notes that among the Canaanites are "some

List of Defeated Kings

12 These are the kings of the land
whom the Israelites had defeated
and whose territory they took over east
of the Jordan, from the Arnon Gorge to
Mount Hermon,[k] including all the eastern
side of the Arabah:

2 Sihon king of the Amorites, who
reigned in Heshbon.
He ruled from Aroer on the rim of
the Arnon Gorge — from the middle
of the gorge — to the Jabbok River,
which is the border of the Ammonites. This included half of Gilead.[l]
3 He also ruled over the eastern Arabah from the Sea of Galilee[a][m] to
the Sea of the Arabah (that is, the
Dead Sea), to Beth Jeshimoth,[n] and
then southward below the slopes of
Pisgah.

4 And the territory of Og king of Bashan,[o] one of the last of the Rephaites,
who reigned in Ashtaroth[p] and Edrei.
5 He ruled over Mount Hermon, Salekah,[q] all of Bashan to the border
of the people of Geshur[r] and Maakah,[s] and half of Gilead to the border of Sihon king of Heshbon.

6 Moses, the servant of the LORD, and the
Israelites conquered them. And Moses the
servant of the LORD gave their land to the
Reubenites, the Gadites and the half-tribe
of Manasseh to be their possession.[t]
7 Here is a list of the kings of the land
that Joshua and the Israelites conquered
on the west side of the Jordan, from Baal
Gad in the Valley of Lebanon[u] to Mount
Halak, which rises toward Seir. Joshua
gave their lands as an inheritance to the
tribes of Israel according to their tribal divisions. 8 The lands included the hill country, the western foothills, the Arabah, the
mountain slopes, the wilderness and the
Negev.[v] These were the lands of the Hittites, Amorites, Canaanites, Perizzites, Hivites and Jebusites. These were the kings:

9 the king of Jericho[w] one
the king of Ai[x] (near Bethel) one
10 the king of Jerusalem[y] one
the king of Hebron one
11 the king of Jarmuth one
the king of Lachish one
12 the king of Eglon one
the king of Gezer[z] one
13 the king of Debir one
the king of Geder one
14 the king of Hormah one
the king of Arad[a] one
15 the king of Libnah one
the king of Adullam one
16 the king of Makkedah one
the king of Bethel[b] one
17 the king of Tappuah one
the king of Hepher[c] one
18 the king of Aphek[d] one
the king of Lasharon one
19 the king of Madon one
the king of Hazor one
20 the king of Shimron Meron one
the king of Akshaph[e] one
21 the king of Taanach one
the king of Megiddo one

12:1 [k] Dt 3:8
12:2 [l] Dt 2:36
12:3 [m] Jos 11:2 [n] Jos 13:20
12:4 [o] Nu 21:21, 33; Dt 3:11 [p] Dt 1:4
12:5 [q] Dt 3:10 [r] 1Sa 27:8 [s] Dt 3:14
12:6 [t] Nu 32:29, 33; Jos 13:8
12:7 [u] Jos 11:17
12:8 [v] Jos 11:16
12:9 [w] Jos 6:2 [x] Jos 8:29
12:10 [y] Jos 10:23
12:12 [z] Jos 10:33
12:14 [a] Nu 21:1
12:16 [b] Jos 7:2
12:17 [c] 1Ki 4:10
12:18 [d] Jos 13:4
12:20 [e] Jos 11:1

[a] 3 Hebrew *Kinnereth*

of whom are of four cubits or five cubits (from) their nose to foot and have fierce faces." Five Egyptian cubits would be a few inches/centimeters short of nine feet (2.7 meters). Og of Bashan (see Nu 21:33 and note) and Goliath of Gath (1Sa 17) are examples of this type of warrior. The towns where Anakites remained — Gaza, Gath and Ashdod — all lay on or near the southwestern Palestinian coast.

12:1 – 24 This chapter reviews all the battles to this point where Israel acquired land. Thus it begins with a review of the land east of the Jordan River acquired through the defeat of Sihon of Heshbon and Og of Bashan (Nu 21). This review lists their territories by regions and natural landmarks such as mountains and rivers (vv. 1 – 6). This is followed by a list of the leaders and their towns west of the Jordan River that Israel defeated. There are three features of note that are also common in ancient Near Eastern war documents: summarizing texts, selectivity in lists and the use of itinerary lists. Summarizing texts, such as vv. 1 – 6, occur in annalistic inscriptions.

12:1 *from the Arnon Gorge to Mount Hermon.* The southernmost and northernmost extent of Sihon's kingdom and of Israel's possessions. *Arnon Gorge.* Lay between Moab to the south and the tribal territories of Reuben and Gad to the north. The Arnon River (Wadi el-Mujib) flows into the Dead Sea at a point across the Dead Sea from the location of En Gedi. *Mount Hermon.* See note on 11:3.

12:2 *Heshbon.* This town in Joshua at times has been identified with Tell Hesban, but excavations have not identified any Late Bronze occupation there. It may be that the second-millennium BC site should be sought elsewhere, and that the name shifted from the other site to Tell Hesban in the Iron Age. Candidates from other sites include Tall Jalul and Tall al-Umayri, both of which possess the necessary occupation levels. *Aroer.* Tell 'Ara'ir. *Jabbok River.* The Wadi ez-Zerqa (see note on 3:16). *Gilead.* Its southern border is the Arnon Gorge; its western border is the Jordan River; its eastern border is the desert; its northern border is perhaps the Yarmuk River, as the Jabbok River divides the area in half.

12:3 *eastern Arabah.* This constitutes the Jordan Valley east of the Jordan River. *Sea of the Arabah.* The Salt Sea, i.e., the Dead Sea. *Beth Jeshimoth.* Possibly Tell 'Azeimeh. *Pisgah.* Whether or not Pisgah is Ras es-Siyagha, the slopes of Pisgah are found at the northwestern edge of the Moabite tableland where it descends into the Jordan Valley.

12:4 *Rephaites.* See note on Dt 2:11.

12:7 *Here is a list of the kings.* The phrase is followed by a list of place-names, most of which have occurred previously in Jos 1 – 11. Jos 12:10 – 16 includes southern sites, many of which are mentioned in ch. 10. Jos 12:17 – 24 includes northern places, many of which are mentioned in ch. 11.

12:21 *Megiddo.* Arabic Tell el-Mutesellim or Hebrew Tel

22 the king of Kedesh[f] one
the king of Jokneam in Carmel[g] one
23 the king of Dor (in Naphoth Dor[h]) one
the king of Goyim in Gilgal one
24 the king of Tirzah one
thirty-one kings in all.[i]

Land Still to Be Taken

13 When Joshua had grown old,[j] the
LORD said to him, "You are now
very old, and there are still very large areas of land to be taken over.

2 "This is the land that remains: all the
regions of the Philistines and Geshurites, 3 from the Shihor River[k] on the
east of Egypt to the territory of Ekron[l]
on the north, all of it counted as Canaanite though held by the five Philistine rulers[m] in Gaza, Ashdod, Ashkelon, Gath and Ekron; the territory
of the Avvites[n] 4 on the south; all the
land of the Canaanites, from Arah of
the Sidonians as far as Aphek[o] and
the border of the Amorites;[p] 5 the area
of Byblos;[q] and all Lebanon[r] to the
east, from Baal Gad below Mount
Hermon to Lebo Hamath.

6 "As for all the inhabitants of the mountain regions from Lebanon to Misrephoth
Maim,[s] that is, all the Sidonians, I myself
will drive them out before the Israelites.
Be sure to allocate this land to Israel for an
inheritance, as I have instructed you,[t] 7 and
divide it as an inheritance[u] among the nine
tribes and half of the tribe of Manasseh."

Division of the Land East of the Jordan

8 The other half of Manasseh,[a] the Reubenites and the Gadites had received the inheritance that Moses had given them east

12:22 [f] Jos 19:37; 20:7; 21:32 [g] 1Sa 15:12 **12:23** [h] Jos 11:2 **12:24** [i] Ps 135:11; Dt 7:24 **13:1** [j] Ge 24:1; Jos 14:10 **13:3** [k] Jer 2:18 [l] Jdg 1:18 [m] Jdg 3:3 [n] Dt 2:23 **13:4** [o] Jos 12:18; 19:30 [p] Am 2:10 **13:5** [q] 1Ki 5:18; Ps 83:7; Eze 27:9 [r] Jos 12:7 **13:6** [s] Jos 11:8 [t] Nu 33:54 **13:7** [u] Jos 11:23; Ps 78:55

[a] 8 Hebrew *With it* (that is, with the other half of Manasseh)

Megiddo. It was assigned to Manasseh, but not captured by the Israelites until the period of the monarchy (1Ki 4:12; 9:15).

12:22 *Jokneam in Carmel.* Arabic Tell Qeimûn or Hebrew Tel Yoqneam. The city was destroyed in the thirteenth century BC following the collapse of Egyptian control, and again at the end of the eleventh century BC, perhaps as part of the Israelite expansion to the north.

12:23 *Dor (in Naphoth Dor).* The Egyptian story of Wen-Amon's adventure (eleventh century BC) indicates that the Philistines settled here. It was assigned to Manasseh, but not conquered until the reign of Solomon (1Ki 4:11). *Goyim in Gilgal.* The Septuagint (the pre-Christian Greek translation of the OT) identifies this as Goyim in Galilee. As with Dor and Jokneam before it, this has the same construction of two place-names, in which the first is a town and the second should be a region. Galilee is a region; Gilgal is usually thought of as a town or cult site. However, both Gilgal and Galilee come from the same root (*gll*). Therefore, these could be variants of the same place-name. It is probably related to Harosheth Haggoyim in or near Galilee (see Jdg 4:13,16). If so, it may come from a region of pharaonic royal estates known from the Amarna letters in this area. An Arabic site possibly preserving the name is Jiljuliyey, a few miles/kilometers north of Aphek.

13:1—19:51 Several Hittite treaties offer boundary lists similar to those found in Joshua. The lists indicate the borders of the land entrusted to the vassal by the suzerain, who offers local control and delineates the boundaries that define the legal relationship. It is the role of the suzerain to define boundaries that demonstrates the suzerain's control over the vassals and their land. Such lists often operate by simply naming cities that are counted in the region rather than drawing imaginary lines that circumscribe the territory.

13:2 *all the regions of the Philistines and Geshurites.* Before the settlement can be completed, there is a list of regions and towns within Canaan that have not been defeated by Israel. The allotments will include these areas, however, so that the picture created is one in which the document that follows remains in use through the period of the monarchy for various legal and royal purposes. Although Geshur has been previously mentioned (12:5), this is the first and only mention of the Philistines in the book of Joshua. Three traditional Philistine cities connected with the Anakites appeared in 11:22, but there was no explicit association with the Philistines.

13:3 *Shihor River.* Either the easternmost branch of the Nile (Pelusiac) or the Wadi el-Arish in northeastern Sinai. The latter would fit better as a border for the known sites of the Philistines. *Ekron.* Modern Tel Miqne. Ekron was the most northeastern of the five cities of the Philistines. Thus, the region between the Shihor River and Ekron would have been the home of the Philistine newcomers. *rulers.* This term (Hebrew *seren*) is unique to the Philistines in the Bible. It is generally regarded as a Philistine term brought from their Aegean and Mycenaean homeland and possibly reflected in the later Greek word for a type of leader, *tyrannos*, from which the English "tyrant" is derived. *Gaza, Ashdod, Ashkelon, Gath and Ekron.* These cities comprise the traditional pentapolis of the Philistines and are here so associated for the first time. Ashkelon and Ekron are mentioned here for the first time in Joshua. *Avvites.* Also called the Avvim, they are the pre-Philistine inhabitants of this region (Dt 2:23).

13:4–5 The description in these verses constitutes the coastal area and the entire northern region of Canaan.

13:4 *Arah of the Sidonians.* Arah is not identified, but the coastal region of the Sidonians includes the region north of the area of the Philistines (which here may include other Sea People settlements such as the Sikil at Dor) to Aphek. *Aphek.* Tell Afqa, near the sources of the Nahr Ibrahim and southeast of Byblos. *Amorites.* Here refers to people of the ancient kingdom of Amurru, which flourished only in the Late Bronze Age. Their territory could have included the Lebanon mountain range and some of the Beqa to the east.

13:5 *Byblos.* Constituted the third major coastal division, after that of the Philistines and the Sidonians. *Baal Gad.* The northern limit of Israel's activity in 11:17, located somewhere north of Galilee in the Beqa. *Lebo Hamath.* The northern limit of Canaan, perhaps as Lebweh. Thus, the entire region north of Galilee remained, as did the coast.

13:6 *Misrephoth Maim.* Located just north of Galilee and would form the northern boundary of Israel's control before the united monarchy.

of the Jordan, as he, the servant of the
LORD, had assigned[v] it to them.

9It extended from Aroer[w] on the rim of
the Arnon Gorge, and from the town
in the middle of the gorge, and included the whole plateau[x] of Medeba
as far as Dibon,[y] 10and all the towns
of Sihon king of the Amorites, who
ruled in Heshbon, out to the border
of the Ammonites.[z] 11It also included Gilead, the territory of the people
of Geshur and Maakah, all of Mount
Hermon and all Bashan as far as Salekah[a]— 12that is, the whole kingdom
of Og in Bashan,[b] who had reigned
in Ashtaroth[c] and Edrei. (He was the
last of the Rephaites.[d]) Moses had
defeated them and taken over their
land. 13But the Israelites did not drive
out the people of Geshur[e] and Maakah,[f] so they continue to live among
the Israelites to this day.

14But to the tribe of Levi he gave no inheritance, since the food offerings presented to the LORD, the God of Israel, are their
inheritance, as he promised them.[g]

15This is what Moses had given to the tribe
of Reuben, according to its clans:

16The territory from Aroer[h] on the
rim of the Arnon Gorge, and from
the town in the middle of the gorge,
and the whole plateau past Medeba[i]
17to Heshbon and all its towns on the
plateau, including Dibon,[j] Bamoth
Baal, Beth Baal Meon,[k] 18Jahaz,[l] Kedemoth, Mephaath,[m] 19Kiriathaim,[n]
Sibmah, Zereth Shahar on the hill in
the valley, 20Beth Peor,[o] the slopes of
Pisgah, and Beth Jeshimoth— 21all
the towns on the plateau and the entire realm of Sihon king of the Amorites, who ruled at Heshbon. Moses
had defeated him and the Midianite
chiefs,[p] Evi, Rekem, Zur, Hur and
Reba[q]—princes allied with Sihon—
who lived in that country. 22In addition to those slain in battle, the
Israelites had put to the sword Balaam son of Beor,[r] who practiced divination. 23The boundary of the Reubenites was the bank of the Jordan.
These towns and their villages were
the inheritance of the Reubenites, according to their clans.

24This is what Moses had given to the tribe
of Gad, according to its clans:

25The territory of Jazer,[s] all the towns
of Gilead and half the Ammonite
country as far as Aroer, near Rabbah;
26and from Heshbon[t] to Ramath Mizpah and Betonim, and from Mahanaim to the territory of Debir;[u] 27and in
the valley, Beth Haram, Beth Nimrah,
Sukkoth[v] and Zaphon with the rest
of the realm of Sihon king of Heshbon (the east side of the Jordan, the
territory up to the end of the Sea of
Galilee[a][w]). 28These towns and their
villages were the inheritance of the
Gadites,[x] according to their clans.

29This is what Moses had given to the
half-tribe of Manasseh, that is, to half the
family of the descendants of Manasseh,
according to its clans:

30The territory extending from Mahanaim[y] and including all of Bashan,
the entire realm of Og king of Bashan—all the settlements of Jair[z] in
Bashan, sixty towns, 31half of Gilead,
and Ashtaroth and Edrei (the royal
cities of Og in Bashan). This was for
the descendants of Makir[a] son of Manasseh—for half of the sons of Makir,
according to their clans.

32This is the inheritance Moses had giv-
en when he was in the plains of Moab
across the Jordan east of Jericho. 33But to
the tribe of Levi, Moses had given no inheritance; the LORD, the God of Israel, is
their inheritance,[b] as he promised them.[c]

13:8 [v] Jos 12:6 **13:9** [w] ver 16; Jdg 11:26 [x] Jer 48:8, 21 [y] Nu 21:30 **13:10** [z] Nu 21:24 **13:11** [a] Jos 12:5 **13:12** [b] Dt 3:11 [c] Jos 12:4 [d] Ge 14:5 **13:13** [e] Jos 12:5 [f] Dt 3:14 **13:14** [g] ver 33; Dt 18:1-2 **13:16** [h] ver 9; Jos 12:2 [i] Nu 21:30 **13:17** [j] Nu 32:3 [k] 1Ch 5:8 **13:18** [l] Nu 21:23 [m] Jer 48:21 **13:19** [n] Nu 32:37 **13:20** [o] Dt 3:29 **13:21** [p] Nu 25:15 [q] Nu 31:8 **13:22** [r] Nu 22:5; 31:8 **13:25** [s] Nu 21:32; Jos 21:39 **13:26** [t] Nu 21:25; Jer 49:3 [u] Jos 10:3 **13:27** [v] Ge 33:17 [w] Nu 34:11 **13:28** [x] Nu 32:33 **13:30** [y] Ge 32:2 [z] Nu 32:41 **13:31** [a] Ge 50:23 **13:33** [b] Nu 18:20 [c] ver 14; Jos 18:7

[a] 27 Hebrew *Kinnereth*

13:9 *Aroer.* See note on 12:2. *Arnon Gorge.* See note on 12:1. *the town in the middle of the gorge.* May be Khirbet el-Medeineh at the junction of Wadi Saliyeh and the Wadi Sarideh. *Dibon.* Although Tell Dhibân may be the Iron Age site of Dibon, there is a lack of evidence for a Late Bronze Age occupation there. Nevertheless, Egyptian scribes of the thirteenth century BC knew of the existence of a Dibon in this area.
13:22 *Balaam.* See Nu 22 and notes; see also the article "Balaam," p. 268.
13:25 *Jazer.* Perhaps Khirbet Jazzir. *Rabbah.* May be at the Amman acropolis.
13:26 *Ramath Mizpah.* Perhaps Khirbet Jel'ad. *Betonim.* Perhaps Khirbet Batneh. *Mahanaim.* Perhaps Khirbet ed-Dhahab el-Garbi on the north side of the Zerqa Valley. *Debir.* As Lo-debar it may be Tell Dober on the southwestern tip of the Golan Heights and north of the Yarmuk Valley.
13:27 *Beth Haram.* May be Tell Iktanu. *Beth Nimrah.* May possibly be Tell el-Bleibil. *Sukkoth.* May be Tell Deir ʿAlla. *Zaphon.* May possibly be Tell el-Qôs.
13:30 *settlements of Jair.* This is the only place-name in the description of Manasseh not mentioned earlier. Jair, a son of Manasseh, occupied a territory east of the Sea of Galilee containing 60 settlements (Nu 32:41; Dt 3:13–14; 1Ki 4:13; but 23 settlements in 1Ch 2:22–23) ruled by 30 sons (Jdg 10:4). They would have been tent encampments, but the nine towns named as part of the land of Geshur may constitute some of what becomes the settlements of Jair.

Division of the Land West of the Jordan

14 Now these are the areas the Israelites received as an inheritance in the land of Canaan, which Eleazar the priest, Joshua son of Nun and the heads of the tribal clans of Israel allotted to them.[d] 2Their inheritances were assigned by lot[e] to the nine and a half tribes, as the LORD had commanded through Moses. 3Moses had granted the two and a half tribes their inheritance east of the Jordan[f] but had not granted the Levites an inheritance among the rest,[g] 4for Joseph's descendants had become two tribes — Manasseh and Ephraim.[h] The Levites received no share of the land but only towns to live in, with pasturelands for their flocks and herds. 5So the Israelites divided the land, just as the LORD had commanded Moses.[i]

Allotment for Caleb

6Now the people of Judah approached Joshua at Gilgal, and Caleb son of Jephunneh[j] the Kenizzite said to him, "You know what the LORD said to Moses the man of God at Kadesh Barnea[k] about you and me. 7I was forty years old when Moses the servant of the LORD sent me from Kadesh Barnea to explore the land.[l] And I brought him back a report according to my convictions,[m] 8but my fellow Israelites who went up with me made the hearts of the people melt in fear.[n] I, however, followed the LORD my God wholeheartedly.[o] 9So on that day Moses swore to me, 'The land on which your feet have walked will be your inheritance and that of your children[p] forever, because you have followed the LORD my God wholeheartedly.'[a]

10"Now then, just as the LORD promised,[q] he has kept me alive for forty-five years since the time he said this to Moses, while Israel moved about in the wilderness. So here I am today, eighty-five years old! 11I am still as strong[r] today as the day Moses sent me out; I'm just as vigorous to go out to battle now as I was then. 12Now give me this hill country that the LORD promised me that day. You yourself heard then that the Anakites[s] were there and their cities were large and fortified,[t] but, the LORD helping me, I will drive them out just as he said."

13Then Joshua blessed[u] Caleb son of Jephunneh and gave him Hebron[v] as his inheritance.[w] 14So Hebron has belonged to Caleb son of Jephunneh the Kenizzite ever since, because he followed the LORD, the God of Israel, wholeheartedly. 15(Hebron used to be called Kiriath Arba[x] after Arba,[y] who was the greatest man among the Anakites.)

Then the land had rest[z] from war.

Allotment for Judah

15:15-19pp — Jdg 1:11-15

15 The allotment for the tribe of Judah, according to its clans, extended down to the territory of Edom,[a] to the Desert of Zin[b] in the extreme south.

2Their southern boundary started from the bay at the southern end of the Dead Sea, 3crossed south of Scorpion Pass,[c] continued on to Zin and went over to the south of Kadesh Barnea. Then it ran past Hezron up to

[a] 9 Deut. 1:36

14:1 [d] Nu 34:17-18 **14:2** [e] Nu 26:55 **14:3** [f] Nu 32:33 [g] Jos 13:14 **14:4** [h] Ge 41:52; 48:5 **14:5** [i] Nu 34:13; 35:2; Jos 21:2 **14:6** [j] Nu 13:6; 14:30 [k] Nu 13:26 **14:7** [l] Nu 13:17 [m] Nu 13:30; 14:6-9 **14:8** [n] Nu 13:31 [o] Nu 14:24 **14:9** [p] Nu 14:24; Dt 1:36 **14:10** [q] Nu 14:30 **14:11** [r] Dt 34:7 **14:12** [s] Nu 13:33 [t] Nu 13:28 **14:13** [u] Jos 22:6,7 [v] Jos 10:36 [w] Jdg 1:20; 1Ch 6:56 **14:15** [x] Ge 23:2 [y] Jos 15:13 [z] Jos 11:23 **15:1** [a] Nu 34:3 [b] Nu 33:36 **15:3** [c] Nu 34:4

14:1 *Eleazar the priest.* The son and successor to Aaron the high priest. He will oversee the allotment of the land (17:4; 19:51), the assignment of the priestly towns (21:1), and the mediation with the Transjordanian tribes (22:13,31 – 32).
14:2 *assigned by lot.* Divination was widely practiced in the ancient Near East. Types of divination include prophecy and necromancy, but also numerous other practices that involved a variety of techniques based on interpreting observations of signs in the sky, unusual births, or other abnormal occurrences in the world around them. However, in Israel, the only approved instruments for the determination of God's will were the Urim and Thummim (see the article "Urim and Thummim," p. 162). These are mentioned as fitting into the breastpiece of the high priest (Ex 28:30; Lev 8:8) and as subject to the use of the priest (Nu 27:21; Dt 33:8; Ezr 2:63; Ne 7:65). They may well have been the lots used in the division of the land. Note their association with Eleazar the priest in v. 1, although Joshua seems to use them in 18:6 – 10. Behind the casting of lots is the principle that the ownership of the land, and therefore the right to give it according to his wishes, belongs to God. As with the land grant of the king of Alalakh (see the article "Land Grants," p. 361), the suzerain has the right to assign the land to whom he will.
14:4 *pasturelands.* In addition to the towns for the Levites, they received pasturelands for their flocks and herds. The Hebrew term (*migrash*) describes districts or regions that were allotted to the Levites, who otherwise did not receive land for farming, etc. It would appear that in the West Semitic world, towns normally had specific areas set aside for use by the townspeople for grazing and perhaps for some gardening.
15:1 – 4 These verses describe the southern boundary of Judah.
15:1 *territory of Edom.* East of the Arabah during the period of the settlement. Unless this represents an otherwise unattested incursion to the west, Judah's land would have "touched" only south of the Dead Sea. *Desert of Zin.* First mentioned in Nu 13:21 and last mentioned in Jos 15:3. It describes the desert area around Kadesh Barnea on the edge of Judah's settlement. *the extreme south.* May be transliterated as Teiman, a desert region in the south whose name is attested in the ninth-century BC inscriptions from Kuntillet 'Ajrud, south of Kadesh Barnea in the northeastern Sinai.
15:2 *the bay … of the Dead Sea.* The southern extension, the Lisan.
15:3 *Scorpion Pass.* Probably Naqb es-Safa. *Zin.* See note on v. 1. *Kadesh Barnea.* See note on 10:41. *Addar.* Ain Qedeis. *Karka.* Ain Qoṣeimeh.

Addar and curved around to Karka.
4 It then passed along to Azmon[d] and
joined the Wadi of Egypt,[e] ending at
the Mediterranean Sea. This is their[a]
southern boundary.
5 The eastern boundary[f] is the Dead
Sea as far as the mouth of the Jordan.
The northern boundary[g] started
from the bay of the sea at the mouth
of the Jordan, 6 went up to Beth Hoglah[h] and continued north of Beth Arabah to the Stone of Bohan[i] son of
Reuben. 7 The boundary then went
up to Debir from the Valley of Achor[j]
and turned north to Gilgal, which
faces the Pass of Adummim south of
the gorge. It continued along to the
waters of En Shemesh and came out
at En Rogel.[k] 8 Then it ran up the Valley of Ben Hinnom along the southern slope of the Jebusite[l] city (that is,
Jerusalem). From there it climbed to
the top of the hill west of the Hinnom
Valley at the northern end of the Valley of Rephaim. 9 From the hilltop the
boundary headed toward the spring
of the waters of Nephtoah,[m] came
out at the towns of Mount Ephron
and went down toward Baalah[n] (that
is, Kiriath Jearim). 10 Then it curved
westward from Baalah to Mount Seir,
ran along the northern slope of Mount
Jearim (that is, Kesalon), continued
down to Beth Shemesh and crossed
to Timnah.[o] 11 It went to the northern
slope of Ekron, turned toward Shik-
keron, passed along to Mount Baalah
and reached Jabneel.[p] The boundary
ended at the sea.
12 The western boundary is the
coastline of the Mediterranean Sea.[q]

These are the boundaries around the
people of Judah by their clans.

13 In accordance with the LORD's command to him, Joshua gave to Caleb son
of Jephunneh a portion in Judah—Kiriath Arba, that is, Hebron. (Arba was the
forefather of Anak.)[r] 14 From Hebron Caleb
drove out the three Anakites[s]—Sheshai,
Ahiman and Talmai,[t] the sons of Anak.[u]
15 From there he marched against the people living in Debir (formerly called Kiriath
Sepher). 16 And Caleb said, "I will give my
daughter Aksah[v] in marriage to the man
who attacks and captures Kiriath Sepher."
17 Othniel[w] son of Kenaz, Caleb's brother,
took it; so Caleb gave his daughter Aksah
to him in marriage.
18 One day when she came to Othni-
el, she urged him[b] to ask her father for a
field. When she got off her donkey, Caleb
asked her, "What can I do for you?"
19 She replied, "Do me a special favor.
Since you have given me land in the Negev, give me also springs of water." So Caleb gave her the upper and lower springs.

20 This is the inheritance of the tribe of
Judah, according to its clans:
21 The southernmost towns of the tribe of
Judah in the Negev toward the boundary
of Edom were:
Kabzeel, Eder,[x] Jagur, 22 Kinah, Di-
monah, Adadah, 23 Kedesh, Hazor,
Ithnan, 24 Ziph,[y] Telem, Bealoth, 25 Hazor Hadattah, Kerioth Hezron (that is,
Hazor), 26 Amam, Shema, Moladah,[z]
27 Hazar Gaddah, Heshmon, Beth Pelet,
28 Hazar Shual, Beersheba,[a] Biziothiah,
29 Baalah,[b] Iyim, Ezem, 30 Eltolad,[c] Kesil, Hormah, 31 Ziklag,[d] Madmannah,
Sansannah, 32 Lebaoth, Shilhim, Ain
and Rimmon[e]—a total of twenty-nine
towns and their villages.

33 In the western foothills:
Eshtaol,[f] Zorah, Ashnah, 34 Zanoah,[g] En Gannim, Tappuah, Enam,
35 Jarmuth,[h] Adullam,[i] Sokoh, Aze-

15:4 [d] Nu 34:5 [e] Ge 15:18 **15:5** [f] Nu 34:10 [g] Jos 18:15-19 **15:6** [h] Jos 18:19,21 [i] Jos 18:17 **15:7** [j] Jos 7:24 [k] 2Sa 17:17; 1Ki 1:9 **15:8** [l] ver 63; Jos 18:16,28; Jdg 1:21; 19:10 **15:9** [m] Jos 18:15 [n] 1Ch 13:6 **15:10** [o] Ge 38:12; Jdg 14:1 **15:11** [p] Jos 19:33 **15:12** [q] Nu 34:6 **15:13** [r] Jos 14:13-15 **15:14** [s] Nu 13:33 [t] Nu 13:22 [u] Jdg 1:10,20 **15:16** [v] Jdg 1:12 **15:17** [w] Jdg 3:9, 11 **15:21** [x] Ge 35:21 **15:24** [y] 1Sa 23:14 **15:26** [z] 1Ch 4:28 **15:28** [a] Ge 21:31 **15:29** [b] ver 9 **15:30** [c] Jos 19:4 **15:31** [d] 1Sa 27:6 **15:32** [e] Jdg 20:45 **15:33** [f] Jdg 13:25; 16:31 **15:34** [g] 1Ch 4:18; Ne 3:13 **15:35** [h] Jos 10:3 [i] 1Sa 22:1

[a] 4 Septuagint; Hebrew *your* [b] 18 Hebrew and some Septuagint manuscripts; other Septuagint manuscripts (see also note at Judges 1:14) *Othniel, he urged her*

15:4 Proceeding farther westward, the border passes Azmon (Ain Muweilih) and reaches the Wadi of Egypt (Wadi el-Arish).

15:5–11 The northern boundary proceeds from the mouth of the Jordan River westward. This boundary list is the most detailed, reflecting the use of this list throughout the period of the monarchy to determine boundary disputes between Judah and its northern tribal neighbors.

15:18 *she urged him to ask her father for a field.* Following the Hebrew text, this understanding suggests that the women in this society retained some right over their dowry, although it became part of their husband's property. Aksah asks her husband to request her dowry from her father, Caleb. However, she then requests additional water sources directly from her father (v. 19).

15:20–63 The town list in these verses forms the longest and most complex for any tribe. Many of the sites are not otherwise known, although some can be identified. The lists are divided according to regions that are identified at the beginning of each section. Each section and subsection concludes with a summary statement of the total number of towns and villages.

15:21–32 These verses list the towns in the southern Negev.

15:33–47 These verses list the towns in the western foothills, or Shephelah. The towns in the western foothills are divided into three districts (vv. 33–36,37–41,42–44). Each district is organized between the east-west valleys from north to south: from the Sorek Valley to the Elah Valley, from the Elah Valley to Nahal Lachish, and from Nahal Lachish to the Negev. A fourth district in this region includes the towns on the coastal plain (vv. 45–47) that were not occupied (13:2–3) until the united monarchy.

kah, 36Shaaraim, Adithaim and Gederah[j] (or Gederothaim)[a]—fourteen
towns and their villages.
37Zenan, Hadashah, Migdal Gad,
38Dilean, Mizpah, Joktheel,[k] 39La-
chish,[l] Bozkath,[m] Eglon, 40Kabbon,
Lahmas, Kitlish, 41Gederoth, Beth Dagon, Naamah and Makkedah[n]—sixteen towns and their villages.
42Libnah, Ether, Ashan,[o] 43Iphtah,
Ashnah, Nezib, 44Keilah, Akzib[p] and
Mareshah[q]—nine towns and their
villages.
45Ekron, with its surrounding settlements and villages; 46west of Ekron, all that were in the vicinity of
Ashdod, together with their villages; 47Ashdod,[r] its surrounding settlements and villages; and Gaza, its
settlements and villages, as far as the
Wadi of Egypt[s] and the coastline of
the Mediterranean Sea.[t]

48In the hill country:
Shamir, Jattir,[u] Sokoh, 49Dannah,
Kiriath Sannah (that is, Debir[v]),
50Anab, Eshtemoh,[w] Anim, 51Goshen,[x]
Holon and Giloh—eleven towns and
their villages.
52Arab, Dumah,[y] Eshan, 53Janim,
Beth Tappuah, Aphekah, 54Humtah,
Kiriath Arba (that is, Hebron) and
Zior—nine towns and their villages.
55Maon, Carmel,[z] Ziph, Juttah,
56Jezreel,[a] Jokdeam, Zanoah, 57Kain,
Gibeah[b] and Timnah—ten towns and
their villages.
58Halhul, Beth Zur,[c] Gedor, 59Ma-
arath, Beth Anoth and Eltekon—six
towns and their villages.[b]
60Kiriath Baal (that is, Kiriath Jearim[d]) and Rabbah[e]—two towns and
their villages.

61In the wilderness:
Beth Arabah, Middin, Sekakah,
62Nibshan, the City of Salt and En
Gedi[f]—six towns and their villages.
63Judah could not[g] dislodge the Jebusites[h], who were living in Jerusalem; to
this day the Jebusites live there with the
people of Judah.

Allotment for Ephraim and Manasseh

16 The allotment for Joseph began at the Jordan, east of the
springs of Jericho, and went up from
there through the desert[i] into the hill
country of Bethel. 2It went on from
Bethel (that is, Luz[j]),[c] crossed over to
the territory of the Arkites in Ataroth,
3descended westward to the territory
of the Japhletites as far as the region
of Lower Beth Horon[k] and on to Gezer,[l] ending at the Mediterranean Sea.
4So Manasseh and Ephraim, the descendants of Joseph, received their inheritance.[m]

5This was the territory of Ephraim, according to its clans:

The boundary of their inheritance
went from Ataroth Addar[n] in the east
to Upper Beth Horon 6and continued
to the Mediterranean Sea. From Mikmethath[o] on the north it curved eastward to Taanath Shiloh, passing by it
to Janoah on the east. 7Then it went
down from Janoah to Ataroth[p] and
Naarah, touched Jericho and came
out at the Jordan. 8From Tappuah the
border went west to the Kanah Ravine[q] and ended at the Mediterranean
Sea. This was the inheritance of the
tribe of the Ephraimites, according
to its clans. 9It also included all the
towns and their villages that were set

15:36 [j] 1Ch 12:4 **15:38** [k] 2Ki 14:7 **15:39** [l] Jos 10:3; 2Ki 14:19 [m] 2Ki 22:1 **15:41** [n] Jos 10:10 **15:42** [o] 1Sa 30:30 **15:44** [p] Jdg 1:31 [q] Mic 1:15 **15:47** [r] Jos 11:22 [s] ver 4 [t] Nu 34:6 **15:48** [u] 1Sa 30:27 **15:49** [v] Jos 10:3 **15:50** [w] Jos 21:14 **15:51** [x] Jos 10:41; 11:16 **15:52** [y] Ge 25:14 **15:55** [z] Jos 12:22 **15:56** [a] Jos 17:16 **15:57** [b] Jos 18:28; Jdg 19:12 **15:58** [c] 1Ch 2:45 **15:60** [d] Jos 18:14 [e] Dt 3:11 **15:62** [f] 1Sa 23:29 **15:63** [g] Jdg 1:21 [h] 2Sa 5:6 **16:1** [i] Jos 8:15; 18:12 **16:2** [j] Jos 18:13 **16:3** [k] 2Ch 8:5 [l] Jos 10:33; 1Ki 9:15 **16:4** [m] Jos 17:14 **16:5** [n] Jos 18:13 **16:6** [o] Jos 17:7 **16:7** [p] 1Ch 7:28 **16:8** [q] Jos 17:9

[a] 36 Or *Gederah and Gederothaim* [b] 59 The Septuagint adds another district of eleven towns, including Tekoa and Ephrathah (Bethlehem). [c] 2 Septuagint; Hebrew *Bethel to Luz*

15:48–60 The hill country includes five districts in the region. The first three are in the south and include Debir and Hebron (vv. 48–51,52–54,55–57). A region to the north appears in vv. 58–59. The Hebrew text of v. 60 preserves only two towns, Kiriath Jearim and Rabbah. However, the Septuagint (the pre-Christian Greek translation of the OT) adds eleven additional towns immediately before these two. This includes Ephrath (Bethlehem), otherwise not found in the Hebrew list of Judah.
15:61–62 The final list of six towns in the desert includes En Gedi and other towns that lay along the western coast of the Dead Sea.
16:1 The southeastern boundary of Ephraim begins at the Jordan River and passes through Jericho (see note on 2:1) and Bethel (see note on 8:9,12,17).
16:2 *Bethel (that is, Luz).* The association of the name of Bethel with Luz occurs three times in Genesis (Ge 28:19; 35:6; 48:3), twice in Joshua (here; 18:13), and twice in Judges (Jdg 1:23,26). The last occurrence in Judges suggests that a survivor of the Israelite destruction of the town there went to the land of the Hittites and built a city called Luz. Among the proposed connections with Luz is the kingdom of Lydia in Iron Age southwestern Anatolia, and a Hebrew version of a known Hittite city such as Lahhuwiyassi. *Arkites.* Unattested outside this reference (Ge 10:17 is a different spelling in the Hebrew and therefore a different group), except in reference to David's diplomat Hushai, who is described as one (2Sa 16:16).
16:3 *Japhletites.* This group is unattested other than perhaps a son of Heber who carries the name Japhlet in 1Ch 7:32–33.
16:6–7 *Mikmethath ... Taanath Shiloh ... Janoah ... Naarah.* These previously unattested sites move from west to east along the northern border of Ephraim and the southern border of Manasseh.

aside for the Ephraimites within the
inheritance of the Manassites.
10They did not dislodge the Canaanites living in Gezer; to this day the Canaanites
live among the people of Ephraim but are
required to do forced labor.[r]
17 This was the allotment for the tribe
of Manasseh as Joseph's firstborn,[s]
that is, for Makir,[t] Manasseh's firstborn.
Makir was the ancestor of the Gileadites,
who had received Gilead and Bashan because the Makirites were great soldiers.
2So this allotment was for the rest of the
people of Manasseh—the clans of Abiezer,[u] Helek, Asriel, Shechem, Hepher and
Shemida. These are the other male descendants of Manasseh son of Joseph by
their clans.
3Now Zelophehad son of Hepher,[v] the
son of Gilead, the son of Makir, the son of
Manasseh, had no sons but only daughters,[w] whose names were Mahlah, Noah,
Hoglah, Milkah and Tirzah. 4They went to
Eleazar the priest, Joshua son of Nun, and
the leaders and said, "The LORD commanded Moses to give us an inheritance among
our relatives." So Joshua gave them an inheritance along with the brothers of their
father, according to the LORD's command.[x]
5Manasseh's share consisted of ten tracts
of land besides Gilead and Bashan east of
the Jordan, 6because the daughters of the
tribe of Manasseh received an inheritance
among the sons. The land of Gilead belonged to the rest of the descendants of
Manasseh.
7The territory of Manasseh extended from Asher to Mikmethath[y] east of
Shechem.[z] The boundary ran southward from there to include the people
living at En Tappuah. 8(Manasseh had
the land of Tappuah, but Tappuah[a] itself, on the boundary of Manasseh,
belonged to the Ephraimites.) 9Then
the boundary continued south to the
Kanah Ravine.[b] There were towns belonging to Ephraim lying among the
towns of Manasseh, but the boundary
of Manasseh was the northern side of
the ravine and ended at the Mediterranean Sea. 10On the south the land
belonged to Ephraim, on the north to
Manasseh. The territory of Manasseh
reached the Mediterranean Sea and
bordered Asher on the north and Issachar[c] on the east.
11Within Issachar and Asher, Manasseh also had Beth Shan,[d] Ibleam
and the people of Dor,[e] Endor,[f] Taanach and Megiddo,[g] together with
their surrounding settlements (the
third in the list is Naphoth[a]).
12Yet the Manassites were not able[h] to occupy these towns, for the Canaanites were
determined to live in that region. 13Howev-
er, when the Israelites grew stronger, they
subjected the Canaanites to forced labor
but did not drive them out completely.[i]
14The people of Joseph said to Joshua,
"Why have you given us only one allotment and one portion for an inheritance?
We are a numerous people, and the LORD
has blessed us abundantly."[j]
15"If you are so numerous," Joshua answered, "and if the hill country of Ephraim
is too small for you, go up into the forest

16:10 [r] Jos 17:13; Jdg 1:28-29; 1Ki 9:16
17:1 [s] Ge 41:51 [t] Ge 50:23
17:2 [u] Nu 26:30; 1Ch 7:18
17:3 [v] Nu 27:1 [w] Nu 26:33
17:4 [x] Nu 27:5-7
17:7 [y] Jos 16:6 [z] Ge 12:6; Jos 21:21
17:8 [a] Jos 16:8
17:9 [b] Jos 16:8
17:10 [c] Ge 30:18
17:11 [d] 1Sa 31:10; 1Ki 4:12; 1Ch 7:29 [e] Jos 11:2 [f] 1Sa 28:7; Ps 83:10 [g] 1Ki 9:15
17:12 [h] Jdg 1:27
17:13 [i] Jos 16:10
17:14 [j] Nu 26:28-37

[a] *11* That is, Naphoth Dor

16:10 *required to do forced labor.* This reference, part of the customary note at the end of a tribal allotment regarding unconquered land, refers to the *mas* or forced labor (corvée) that was extracted from subject towns by a more powerful ruler. It was a form of taxation known in Late Bronze Age and Iron Age Canaan. The term appears in a fourteenth-century BC Amarna letter from the leader of Megiddo who is using a corvée to cultivate the pharaoh's land near Shunem. Solomon also uses this type of labor (1Ki 4:6). Here it may have come as a result of the battles of either Jos 11 or Jdg 4–5.
17:1 *Makir.* The part of the tribe of Manasseh that settled east of the Jordan River and north of Reuben and Gad (13:31).
17:2 *Abiezer, Helek, Asriel, Shechem, Hepher and Shemida.* These are the remaining clans other than Makir. In the Samaria ostraca of the first half of the eighth century BC, these clan names appear as regions and towns neighboring Samaria. In relation to the city of Samaria: Abiezer lies to the south; Helek is immediately southeast; Asriel is farther south than Abiezer; Shechem (Tell Balata) is farther southeast than Helek; Hepher is northeast; Shemida is west.
17:3 *daughters … Mahlah, Noah, Hoglah, Milkah and Tirzah.* For Zelophehad's daughters, see note on Nu 27:1. Zelophehad's daughters were the granddaughters of Hepher, and thus the names of their towns are located northeast and east of Samaria by the beginning of the eighth century BC (see note on v. 2).
17:11 *Beth Shan, Ibleam … Endor.* These are the only towns among those belonging to Manasseh that did not appear earlier in the book of Joshua.
17:12 *Canaanites were determined to live in that region.* These towns are better known, because they are larger and more prominent centers in and around the Jezreel Valley. Many of these names appear in Egyptian sources and in Amarna letters from the Late Bronze Age. The wealth of such towns in terms of agriculture in the fertile valley and, above all, in terms of trade, made them highly desirable prizes that the Canaanites held on to, in some cases until the period of the united monarchy.
17:13 *forced labor.* See note on 16:10.
17:15 *If you are so numerous … and if the hill country of Ephraim is too small for you, go up into the forest and clear land for yourselves there.* The sudden appearance of some 300 villages dating to the first half of the twelfth century BC and situated in the hill country occupied by Manasseh and, to a lesser extent, Ephraim, attests to the presence of Israel and its expansion in the region suggested in this verse. *Perizzites.* See note on Dt 7:1. *Rephaites.* See note on Dt 2:11.

and clear land for yourselves there in the land of the Perizzites and Rephaites.[k]" 16 The people of Joseph replied, "The hill country is not enough for us, and all the Canaanites who live in the plain have chariots fitted with iron,[l] both those in Beth Shan and its settlements and those in the Valley of Jezreel."

17 But Joshua said to the tribes of Joseph — to Ephraim and Manasseh — "You are numerous and very powerful. You will have not only one allotment 18 but the forested hill country as well. Clear it, and its farthest limits will be yours; though the Canaanites have chariots fitted with iron[m] and though they are strong, you can drive them out."

Division of the Rest of the Land

18 The whole assembly of the Israelites gathered at Shiloh[n] and set up the tent of meeting[o] there. The country was brought under their control, 2 but there were still seven Israelite tribes who had not yet received their inheritance.

3 So Joshua said to the Israelites: "How long will you wait before you begin to take possession of the land that the LORD, the God of your ancestors, has given you? 4 Appoint three men from each tribe. I will send them out to make a survey of the land and to write a description of it, according to the inheritance of each.[p] Then they will return to me. 5 You are to divide the land into seven parts. Judah is to remain in its territory on the south[q] and the tribes of Joseph in their territory on the north.[r] 6 After you have written descriptions of the seven parts of the land, bring them here to me and I will cast lots[s] for you in the presence of the LORD our God. 7 The Levites, however, do not get a portion among you, because the priestly service of the LORD is their inheritance.[t] And Gad, Reuben and the half-tribe of Manasseh have already received their inheritance on the east side of the Jordan. Moses the servant of the LORD gave it to them.[u]"

8 As the men started on their way to map out the land, Joshua instructed them, "Go and make a survey of the land and write a description of it. Then return to me, and I will cast lots for you here at Shiloh[v] in the presence of the LORD." 9 So the men left and went through the land. They wrote its description on a scroll, town by town, in seven parts, and returned to Joshua in the camp at Shiloh. 10 Joshua then cast lots[w] for them in Shiloh in the presence[x] of the LORD, and there he distributed the land to the Israelites according to their tribal divisions.[y]

Allotment for Benjamin

11 The first lot came up for the tribe of Benjamin according to its clans. Their allotted territory lay between the tribes of Judah and Joseph:

12 On the north side their boundary began at the Jordan, passed the northern slope of Jericho and headed west into the hill country, coming out at the wilderness[z] of Beth Aven.[a] 13 From there it crossed to the south slope of Luz[b] (that is, Bethel[c]) and went down to Ataroth Addar[d] on the hill south of Lower Beth Horon.

14 From the hill facing Beth Horon[e] on the south the boundary turned south along the western side and came out at Kiriath Baal (that is, Kiriath Jearim), a town of the people of Judah. This was the western side.

15 The southern side began at the outskirts of Kiriath Jearim on the west, and the boundary came out at the spring of the waters of Nephtoah.[f] 16 The boundary went down to the foot of the hill facing the Valley of Ben Hinnom, north of the Valley of Rephaim. It continued down the Hinnom Valley[g] along the southern slope of the Jebusite city and so to En Rogel.[h] 17 It then curved north, went to En Shemesh, continued to Geliloth, which faces the Pass of Adummim, and ran down to the Stone of Bohan[i] son of Reuben. 18 It continued to the northern slope of Beth Arabah[a][j] and on down into the Arabah. 19 It then went to the northern slope of Beth Hoglah and came out at the northern bay of the Dead Sea,[k] at the mouth of the Jordan in the south. This was the southern boundary.

[a] 18 Septuagint; Hebrew *slope facing the Arabah*

17:15 [k] Ge 14:5
17:16 [l] Jdg 1:19; 4:3, 13
17:18 [m] ver 16
18:1 [n] Jos 19:51; 21:2; Jdg 18:31; 21:12, 19; 1Sa 1:3; 4:3; Jer 7:12; 26:6 [o] Ex 27:21
18:4 [p] Mic 2:5
18:5 [q] Jos 15:1 [r] Jos 16:1-4
18:6 [s] Jos 14:2
18:7 [t] Jos 13:33 [u] Jos 13:8
18:8 [v] ver 1
18:10 [w] Nu 34:13 [x] ver 1; Jer 7:12 [y] Nu 33:54; Jos 19:51
18:12 [z] Jos 16:1 [a] Jos 7:2
18:13 [b] Ge 28:19 [c] Jdg 1:23 [d] Jos 16:5
18:14 [e] Jos 10:10
18:15 [f] Jos 15:9
18:16 [g] Jos 15:8; 2Ki 23:10 [h] Jos 15:7
18:17 [i] Jos 15:6
18:18 [j] Jos 15:6
18:19 [k] Ge 14:3

17:16,18 *chariots fitted with iron.* See note on 11:6.
18:1 *Shiloh.* Probably Khirbet Seilûn, where excavations uncovered a Middle Bronze Age shrine and a Late Bronze Age population center. Occupation continued into the Iron Age until it was destroyed in the eleventh century BC, perhaps by Philistines. *tent of meeting.* Mentioned only here and in 19:51 in Joshua.
18:11 – 28 The allotments for Benjamin include the largest number of towns of any of the allotment descriptions and are second only to the allotments of Judah. Whatever the significance of these lists, the number of sites is out of proportion to those of other tribes. Like the towns of Judah and Simeon, this suggests the ongoing use of these documents for administrative purposes right to the end of the monarchy in Judah, when the population of the region was much larger and the towns far more numerous. The boundaries of Benjamin (vv. 12 – 20) match those of their surrounding tribes. The following town lists are divided into the eastern (vv. 21 – 24) and western (vv. 25 – 28) lists.

20The Jordan formed the boundary
on the eastern side.
These were the boundaries that marked
out the inheritance of the clans of Benjamin on all sides.[l]

21The tribe of Benjamin, according to its
clans, had the following towns:
Jericho, Beth Hoglah, Emek Keziz,
22Beth Arabah, Zemaraim, Bethel,[m]
23Avvim, Parah, Ophrah, 24Kephar
Ammoni, Ophni and Geba[n]—twelve
towns and their villages.
25Gibeon,[o] Ramah,[p] Beeroth,[q]
26Mizpah,[r] Kephirah, Mozah, 27Re-
kem, Irpeel, Taralah, 28Zelah,[s] Ha-
leph, the Jebusite city[t] (that is,
Jerusalem[u]), Gibeah[v] and Kiriath—
fourteen towns and their villages.
This was the inheritance of Benjamin for
its clans.

Allotment for Simeon

19:2-10pp — 1Ch 4:28-33

19 The second lot came out for the
tribe of Simeon according to its
clans. Their inheritance lay within the territory of Judah.[w] 2It included:
Beersheba[x] (or Sheba),[a] Moladah,
3Hazar Shual, Balah, Ezem, 4Eltolad,
Bethul, Hormah, 5Ziklag, Beth Markaboth, Hazar Susah, 6Beth Lebaoth
and Sharuhen—thirteen towns and
their villages;
7Ain, Rimmon, Ether and Ashan[y]—
four towns and their villages— 8and
all the villages around these towns as
far as Baalath Beer (Ramah in the Negev).[z]
This was the inheritance of the tribe of the
Simeonites, according to its clans. 9The
inheritance of the Simeonites was taken
from the share of Judah,[a] because Judah's
portion was more than they needed. So
the Simeonites received their inheritance
within the territory of Judah.[b]

Allotment for Zebulun

10The third lot came up for Zebulun[c] according to its clans:
The boundary of their inheritance
went as far as Sarid. 11Going west it
ran to Maralah, touched Dabbesheth,
and extended to the ravine near Jokneam.[d] 12It turned east from Sarid
toward the sunrise to the territory of
Kisloth Tabor and went on to Daberath and up to Japhia. 13Then it continued eastward to Gath Hepher and
Eth Kazin; it came out at Rimmon[e]
and turned toward Neah. 14There the
boundary went around on the north
to Hannathon and ended at the Valley
of Iphtah El. 15Included were Kattath,
Nahalal, Shimron, Idalah and Bethlehem.[f] There were twelve towns and
their villages.
16These towns and their villages were the
inheritance of Zebulun,[g] according to its
clans.[h]

Allotment for Issachar

17The fourth lot came out for Issachar[i]
according to its clans. 18Their territory included:
Jezreel,[j] Kesulloth, Shunem,[k]
19Hapharaim, Shion, Anaharath,
20Rabbith, Kishion, Ebez, 21Remeth,
En Gannim, En Haddah and Beth Paz-
zez. 22The boundary touched Tabor,[l]
Shahazumah and Beth Shemesh,[m]
and ended at the Jordan. There were
sixteen towns and their villages.
23These towns and their villages were the
inheritance of the tribe of Issachar,[n] according to its clans.[o]

Allotment for Asher

24The fifth lot came out for the tribe of
Asher[p] according to its clans. 25Their territory included:
Helkath, Hali, Beten, Akshaph,
26Allammelek, Amad and Mishal.
On the west the boundary touched
Carmel[q] and Shihor Libnath. 27It
then turned east toward Beth Dagon, touched Zebulun[r] and the Valley of Iphtah El, and went north to
Beth Emek and Neiel, passing Kabul[s]

18:20 [l]Jos 21:4, 17; 1Sa 9:1 **18:22** [m]Jos 16:1 **18:24** [n]Isa 10:29 **18:25** [o]Jos 9:3 [p]Jdg 4:5 [q]Jos 9:17 **18:26** [r]Jos 11:3 **18:28** [s]2Sa 21:14 [t]Jos 15:8 [u]Jos 10:1 [v]Jos 15:57 **19:1** [w]ver 9; Ge 49:7 **19:2** [x]Ge 21:14; 1Ki 19:3 **19:7** [y]Jos 15:42 **19:8** [z]Jos 10:40 **19:9** [a]Ge 49:7 [b]Eze 48:24 **19:10** [c]Jos 21:7, 34 **19:11** [d]Jos 12:22 **19:13** [e]Jos 15:32 **19:15** [f]Ge 35:19 **19:16** [g]ver 10; Jos 21:7 [h]Eze 48:26 **19:17** [i]Ge 30:18 **19:18** [j]Jos 15:56 [k]1Sa 28:4; 2Ki 4:8 **19:22** [l]Jdg 4:6, 12; Ps 89:12 [m]Jos 15:10 **19:23** [n]Jos 17:10 [o]Ge 49:15; Eze 48:25 **19:24** [p]Jos 17:7 **19:26** [q]Jos 12:22 **19:27** [r]ver 10 [s]1Ki 9:13

[a] 2 Or *Beersheba, Sheba;* 1 Chron. 4:28 does not have *Sheba.*

19:1–9 The Simeon allotment is, like Benjamin's allotment (18:11–28), divided into eastern (19:2–6) and western (vv. 7–8) lists.

19:10–16 The allotment for Zebulon lies in the western part of lower Galilee, north of the Jezreel Valley and reaching north to include the fertile Beit Netofa Valley. The southern boundary (vv. 10–11) proceeds to the east (vv. 12–13) and then turns north (vv. 14–15).

19:15 *Bethlehem.* Northwest of Nahalal in Zebulun; it should not be confused with the well-known town in Judah. The judge Ibzan was buried here (Jdg 12:9–10), and a modern village nearby is still called Beit-Lahm.

19:17–23 Issachar's inheritance includes only a town list, the southern part of which overlaps with towns belonging to Manasseh. Issachar reaches the Beth Shan Valley in the south and the Valley of Yiptah-el in the north with towns on the edge of cliffs, on the basalt heights, and in the Jezreel Valley.

19:24–31 Asher includes the territories from Carmel to the south along the Akko Plain to the north as far as Tyre and Greater Sidon. Kabul (Khirbet Rosh Zayit) and the eastern region was given to Hiram by Solomon (1Ki 9:11–13).

DIVIDING THE LAND

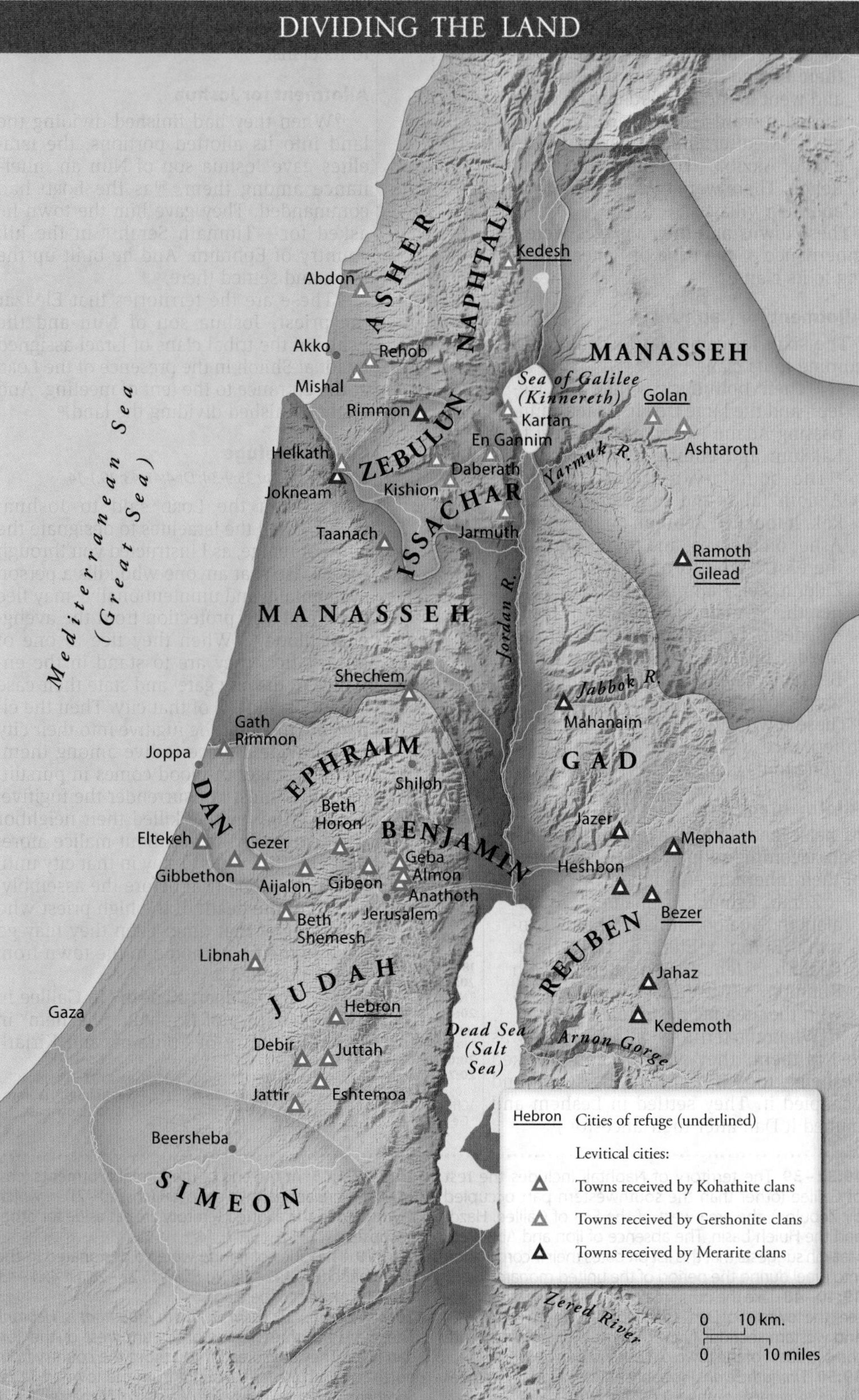
ASHER
NAPHTALI
Kedesh
Abdon
Akko
Rehob
Mishal
MANASSEH
Sea of Galilee
(Kinnereth)
Golan
Rimmon
Kartan
ZEBULUN
En Gannim
Ashtaroth
Helkath
Yarmuk R.
Daberath
Jokneam
Kishion
ISSACHAR
Mediterranean Sea
(Great Sea)
Taanach
Jarmuth
Ramoth
Gilead
MANASSEH
Jordan R.
Shechem
Jabbok R.
Mahanaim
Gath
Rimmon
Joppa
EPHRAIM
GAD
DAN
Shiloh
Beth
Horon
BENJAMIN
Jazer
Eltekeh
Gezer
Mephaath
Geba
Gibbethon
Aijalon
Gibeon
Almon
Heshbon
Anathoth
Jerusalem
Bezer
Beth
Shemesh
REUBEN
Libnah
JUDAH
Jahaz
Gaza
Hebron
Kedemoth
Dead Sea
(Salt
Sea)
Arnon Gorge
Debir
Juttah
Eshtemoa
Jattir
Beersheba
SIMEON
Hebron Cities of refuge (underlined)
Levitical cities:
Towns received by Kohathite clans
Towns received by Gershonite clans
Towns received by Merarite clans
Zered River
0 10 km.
0 10 miles

on the left. 28It went to Abdon,[a] Rehob,[t] Hammon[u] and Kanah, as far
as Greater Sidon.[v] 29The boundary
then turned back toward Ramah[w]
and went to the fortified city of Tyre,[x]
turned toward Hosah and came out
at the Mediterranean Sea in the region of Akzib,[y] 30Ummah, Aphek and
Rehob. There were twenty-two towns
and their villages.
31These towns and their villages were the
inheritance of the tribe of Asher,[z] according to its clans.

Allotment for Naphtali

32The sixth lot came out for Naphtali according to its clans:
33Their boundary went from He-
leph and the large tree in Zaanannim,
passing Adami Nekeb and Jabneel to
Lakkum and ending at the Jordan.
34The boundary ran west through
Aznoth Tabor and came out at Huk-
kok. It touched Zebulun on the south,
Asher on the west and the Jordan[b] on
the east. 35The fortified towns were
Ziddim, Zer, Hammath, Rakkath, Kinnereth,[a] 36Adamah, Ramah,[b] Hazor,[c]
37Kedesh, Edrei,[d] En Hazor, 38Iron,
Migdal El, Horem, Beth Anath and
Beth Shemesh. There were nineteen
towns and their villages.
39These towns and their villages were the
inheritance of the tribe of Naphtali, according to its clans.[e]

Allotment for Dan

40The seventh lot came out for the tribe of
Dan according to its clans. 41The territory
of their inheritance included:
Zorah, Eshtaol, Ir Shemesh, 42Sha-
alabbin, Aijalon,[f] Ithlah, 43Elon, Timnah,[g] Ekron, 44Eltekeh, Gibbethon,
Baalath, 45Jehud, Bene Berak, Gath
Rimmon,[h] 46Me Jarkon and Rakkon,
with the area facing Joppa.[i]
47(When the territory of the Danites was
lost to them,[j] they went up and attacked
Leshem[k], took it, put it to the sword and
occupied it. They settled in Leshem and
named it Dan after their ancestor.)[l]
48These towns and their villages were the
inheritance of the tribe of Dan,[m] according
to its clans.

Allotment for Joshua

49When they had finished dividing the
land into its allotted portions, the Israelites gave Joshua son of Nun an inheritance among them, 50as the LORD had
commanded. They gave him the town he
asked for — Timnath Serah[c][n] in the hill
country of Ephraim. And he built up the
town and settled there.
51These are the territories that Eleazar
the priest, Joshua son of Nun and the
heads of the tribal clans of Israel assigned
by lot at Shiloh in the presence of the LORD
at the entrance to the tent of meeting. And
so they finished dividing the land.[o]

Cities of Refuge

20:1-9Ref — Nu 35:9-34; Dt 4:41-43; 19:1-14

20 Then the LORD said to Joshua:
2"Tell the Israelites to designate the
cities of refuge, as I instructed you through
Moses, 3so that anyone who kills a person
accidentally and unintentionally[p] may flee
there and find protection from the avenger of blood.[q] 4When they flee to one of
these cities, they are to stand in the entrance of the city gate[r] and state their case
before the elders[s] of that city. Then the elders are to admit the fugitive into their city
and provide a place to live among them.
5If the avenger of blood comes in pursuit,
the elders must not surrender the fugitive,
because the fugitive killed their neighbor
unintentionally and without malice aforethought. 6They are to stay in that city until
they have stood trial before the assembly[t]
and until the death of the high priest who
is serving at that time. Then they may go
back to their own home in the town from
which they fled."
7So they set apart Kedesh[u] in Galilee in
the hill country of Naphtali, Shechem[v] in
the hill country of Ephraim, and Kiriath

19:28 [t] Jdg 1:31 [u] 1Ch 6:76 [v] Ge 10:19; Jos 11:8 **19:29** [w] Jos 18:25 [x] 2Sa 5:11; 24:7; Isa 23:1; Jer 25:22; Eze 26:2 [y] Jdg 1:31 **19:31** [z] Ge 30:13; Eze 48:2 **19:35** [a] Jos 11:2 **19:36** [b] Jos 18:25 [c] Jos 11:1 **19:37** [d] Nu 21:33 **19:39** [e] Dt 33:23; Eze 48:3 **19:42** [f] Jdg 1:35 **19:43** [g] Ge 38:12 **19:45** [h] Jos 21:24; 1Ch 6:69 **19:46** [i] 2Ch 2:16; Jnh 1:3 **19:47** [j] Jdg 18:1 [k] Jdg 18:7,14 [l] Jdg 18:27,29 **19:48** [m] Ge 30:6 **19:50** [n] Jos 24:30 **19:51** [o] Jos 14:1; 18:10; Ac 13:19 **20:3** [p] Lev 4:2 [q] Nu 35:12 **20:4** [r] Ru 4:1; Jer 38:7 [s] Jos 7:6 **20:6** [t] Nu 35:12 **20:7** [u] Jos 21:32; 1Ch 6:76 [v] Ge 12:6

a 28 Some Hebrew manuscripts (see also 21:30); most Hebrew manuscripts *Ebron* *b* 34 Septuagint; Hebrew *west, and Judah, the Jordan,* *c* 50 Also known as *Timnath Heres* (see Judges 2:9)

19:32 – 39 The territory of Naphtali includes the rest of Galilee (other than the southwestern part occupied by Zebulon), the area west of the Sea of Galilee, Hazor and the Huleh basin. The absence of Ijon and Abel Beth Maakah suggests that this list predates their incorporation into Israel during the period of the united monarchy.
19:40 – 48 Like the other major town lists in these chapters, the town list of Dan is divided into eastern (vv. 41 – 44) and western sections (vv. 45 – 47). It is coordinated with the conquest of the town of Leshem/Dan in Jdg 18:11.
19:50 *Timnath Serah.* Probably Khirbet Tibnah, 16 miles (25.7 kilometers) southwest of Shechem.
20:1 — 21:45 At the end of the formal allotments (chs. 14 – 19) there appear two chapters (chs. 20 – 21) in which towns within the allotted territory are set aside for other purposes.
20:1 – 9 The cities of refuge were so designated in the Pentateuch (Ex 21:12 – 14; Nu 35:9 – 15,22 – 28; Dt 4:41 – 43; 19:1 – 10) and occur here again.
20:7 *Kedesh ... Shechem ... Kiriath Arba (that is, Hebron).* These are the three towns of asylum west of the Jordan River. They are spread throughout the country from north to south. *Kedesh.* Distinct from the town in 12:22. *Shechem.* Although the name of a clan of Manasseh (17:2),

Arba (that is, Hebron[w]) in the hill country of Judah.[x] 8East of the Jordan (on the
other side from Jericho) they designated
Bezer[y] in the wilderness on the plateau in
the tribe of Reuben, Ramoth in Gilead[z] in
the tribe of Gad, and Golan in Bashan in
the tribe of Manasseh. 9Any of the Israelites or any foreigner residing among them
who killed someone accidentally could
flee to these designated cities and not be
killed by the avenger of blood prior to
standing trial before the assembly.[a]

Towns for the Levites

21:4-39pp — 1Ch 6:54-80

21 Now the family heads of the Levites approached Eleazar the priest,
Joshua son of Nun, and the heads of the
other tribal families of Israel[b] 2at Shiloh[c]
in Canaan and said to them, "The LORD
commanded through Moses that you give
us towns to live in, with pasturelands for
our livestock."[d] 3So, as the LORD had commanded, the Israelites gave the Levites the
following towns and pasturelands out of
their own inheritance:

4The first lot came out for the Kohathites, according to their clans. The Levites
who were descendants of Aaron the priest
were allotted thirteen towns from the tribes
of Judah, Simeon and Benjamin.[e] 5The rest
of Kohath's descendants were allotted ten
towns from the clans of the tribes of Ephraim, Dan and half of Manasseh.[f]

6The descendants of Gershon were allotted thirteen towns from the clans of the
tribes of Issachar,[g] Asher, Naphtali and the
half-tribe of Manasseh in Bashan.

7The descendants of Merari,[h] according
to their clans, received twelve towns from
the tribes of Reuben, Gad and Zebulun.[i]

8So the Israelites allotted to the Levites
these towns and their pasturelands, as the
LORD had commanded through Moses.

9From the tribes of Judah and Simeon
they allotted the following towns by name
10(these towns were assigned to the descendants of Aaron who were from the
Kohathite clans of the Levites, because the
first lot fell to them):

11They gave them Kiriath Arba
(that is, Hebron[j]), with its surrounding pastureland, in the hill country
of Judah. (Arba was the forefather
of Anak.) 12But the fields and villages around the city they had given to
Caleb son of Jephunneh as his possession.

13So to the descendants of Aaron
the priest they gave Hebron (a city
of refuge for one accused of murder),
Libnah,[k] 14Jattir,[l] Eshtemoa,[m] 15Ho-
lon,[n] Debir, 16Ain, Juttah[o] and Beth
Shemesh,[p] together with their pasturelands — nine towns from these
two tribes.

17And from the tribe of Benjamin
they gave them Gibeon, Geba,[q] 18An-
athoth and Almon, together with
their pasturelands — four towns.

19The total number of towns for the
priests, the descendants of Aaron, came to
thirteen, together with their pasturelands.

20The rest of the Kohathite clans of the Levites were allotted towns from the tribe of
Ephraim:

21In the hill country of Ephraim
they were given Shechem[r] (a city
of refuge for one accused of murder) and Gezer, 22Kibzaim and Beth
Horon,[s] together with their pasturelands — four towns.[t]

23Also from the tribe of Dan they
received Eltekeh, Gibbethon, 24Aija-
lon and Gath Rimmon,[u] together with
their pasturelands — four towns.

25From half the tribe of Manasseh they received Taanach and Gath
Rimmon, together with their pasturelands — two towns.

26All these ten towns and their pasturelands were given to the rest of the Kohathite clans.

20:7 [w] Jos 10:36; 21:11 [x] Lk 1:39 **20:8** [y] Jos 21:36; 1Ch 6:78 [z] Jos 12:2 **20:9** [a] Ex 21:13; Nu 35:15 **21:1** [b] Jos 14:1 **21:2** [c] Jos 18:1 [d] Nu 35:2-3 **21:4** [e] ver 19 **21:5** [f] ver 26 **21:6** [g] Ge 30:18 **21:7** [h] Ex 6:16 [i] Jos 19:10 **21:11** [j] Jos 15:13; 1Ch 6:55 **21:13** [k] Jos 15:42; 1Ch 6:57 **21:14** [l] Jos 15:48 [m] Jos 15:50 **21:15** [n] Jos 15:51 **21:16** [o] Jos 15:55 [p] Jos 15:10 **21:17** [q] Jos 18:24 **21:21** [r] Jos 17:7; 20:7 **21:22** [s] Jos 10:10 [t] 1Sa 1:1 **21:24** [u] Jos 19:45

Shechem is a recognized town elsewhere (17:7). *Kiriath Arba (that is, Hebron).* See Ge 23:2; see also note on Nu 13:22. Although Dt 19:1 – 10 suggests an additional three towns west of the Jordan River, they are not allocated. Perhaps this is due to a failure to achieve a complete conquest. These towns would have been fortified and provided a safe refuge from the blood avenger (see notes on Dt 19:6,11). In particular, excavations at Shechem have revealed a remarkably strong wall and gate system built of cyclopean stones and dating from the Middle Bronze Age (early second millennium BC).

20:8 *Bezer ... Ramoth ... Golan.* These are the three towns of asylum east of the Jordan River. They are spread throughout the country from south to north.

21:2 *The LORD commanded through Moses that you give us towns to live in, with pasturelands for our livestock.* The instructions here require that not only the town, but also the surrounding pastures for up to 3,000 feet (900 meters) be given to the Levites (see note on Nu 35:2 – 15). That priests and priestly assistants should receive provision certainly has support throughout the ancient Near East. In particular the Egyptian temples were endowed with lands and settlements to provide food and income for the priests. The famous temple of Amun Re in Thebes owned 56 towns in Egypt during the time of Rameses III, not to mention nine additional estates in Palestine and Nubia. The Levitical town system is a simplification of this. There was no central temple to whom these towns and their lands were given. Further, the Levites lived in the towns and worked the lands themselves. The complex and almost certainly oppressive Egyptian system was alien to the Israelite system.

27 The Levite clans of the Gershonites were
given:
from the half-tribe of Manasseh,
Golan in Bashan[v] (a city of refuge
for one accused of murder[w]) and Be
Eshterah, together with their pasturelands — two towns;
28 from the tribe of Issachar,[x]
Kishion, Daberath, 29 Jarmuth and En
Gannim, together with their pasturelands — four towns;
30 from the tribe of Asher,[y]
Mishal, Abdon, 31 Helkath and Rehob,
together with their pasturelands —
four towns;
32 from the tribe of Naphtali,
Kedesh[z] in Galilee (a city of refuge for
one accused of murder[a]), Hammoth
Dor and Kartan, together with their
pasturelands — three towns.
33 The total number of towns of the Gershonite[b] clans came to thirteen, together
with their pasturelands.

34 The Merarite clans (the rest of the Levites) were given:
from the tribe of Zebulun,[c]
Jokneam, Kartah, 35 Dimnah and Nahalal, together with their pasturelands — four towns;
36 from the tribe of Reuben,
Bezer,[d] Jahaz, 37 Kedemoth and Mephaath, together with their pasturelands — four towns;
38 from the tribe of Gad,
Ramoth[e] in Gilead (a city of refuge for
one accused of murder), Mahanaim,[f]
39 Heshbon and Jazer, together with
their pasturelands — four towns in all.
40 The total number of towns allotted to the
Merarite clans, who were the rest of the
Levites, came to twelve.
41 The towns of the Levites in the territory held by the Israelites were forty-eight
in all, together with their pasturelands.[g]
42 Each of these towns had pasturelands
surrounding it; this was true for all these
towns.

43 So the LORD gave Israel all the land
he had sworn to give their ancestors,[h]
and they took possession[i] of it and settled there.[j] 44 The LORD gave them rest[k] on
every side, just as he had sworn to their
ancestors. Not one of their enemies[l] with-
stood them; the LORD gave all their enemies[m] into their hands.[n] 45 Not one of all
the LORD's good promises[o] to Israel failed;
every one was fulfilled.

Eastern Tribes Return Home

22 Then Joshua summoned the Reubenites, the Gadites and the half-
tribe of Manasseh 2 and said to them, "You
have done all that Moses the servant of
the LORD commanded,[p] and you have
obeyed me in everything I commanded.
3 For a long time now — to this very day —
you have not deserted your fellow Israelites but have carried out the mission the
LORD your God gave you. 4 Now that the
LORD your God has given them rest as he
promised, return to your homes[q] in the
land that Moses the servant of the LORD
gave you on the other side of the Jordan.[r]
5 But be very careful to keep the commandment[s] and the law that Moses the servant
of the LORD gave you: to love the LORD
your God, to walk in obedience to him, to
keep his commands,[t] to hold fast to him
and to serve him with all your heart and
with all your soul.[u]"
6 Then Joshua blessed[v] them and sent
them away, and they went to their homes.
7 (To the half-tribe of Manasseh Moses had
given land in Bashan,[w] and to the other
half of the tribe Joshua gave land on the
west side[x] of the Jordan along with their
fellow Israelites.) When Joshua sent them
home, he blessed them, 8 saying, "Return to
your homes with your great wealth — with
large herds of livestock,[y] with silver, gold,
bronze and iron, and a great quantity of
clothing — and divide[z] the plunder[a] from
your enemies with your fellow Israelites."
9 So the Reubenites, the Gadites and the
half-tribe of Manasseh left the Israelites
at Shiloh in Canaan to return to Gilead,[b]
their own land, which they had acquired
in accordance with the command of the
LORD through Moses.
10 When they came to Geliloth near the
Jordan in the land of Canaan, the Reubenites, the Gadites and the half-tribe of Manasseh built an imposing altar there by the

21:27 [v] Jos 12:5 [w] Nu 35:6 **21:28** [x] Ge 30:18 **21:30** [y] Jos 17:7 **21:32** [z] Jos 12:22 [a] Nu 35:6; Jos 20:7 **21:33** [b] ver 6 **21:34** [c] Jos 19:10; 1Ch 6:77 **21:36** [d] Jos 20:8 **21:38** [e] Dt 4:43 [f] Ge 32:2 **21:41** [g] Nu 35:7 **21:43** [h] Dt 34:4 [i] Dt 11:31 [j] Dt 17:14 **21:44** [k] Ex 33:14; Jos 1:13 [l] Dt 6:19 [m] Ex 23:31 [n] Dt 7:24; 21:10 **21:45** [o] Jos 23:14; Ne 9:8 **22:2** [p] Nu 32:25 **22:4** [q] Nu 32:22; Dt 3:20 [r] Nu 32:18; Jos 1:13-15 **22:5** [s] Isa 43:22 [t] Dt 5:29 [u] Dt 6:6, 17 **22:6** [v] Ex 39:43 **22:7** [w] Nu 32:33; Jos 12:5 [x] Jos 17:2, 5 **22:8** [y] Dt 20:14 [z] Nu 31:27 [a] Ge 49:27; 1Sa 30:16; Isa 9:3 **22:9** [b] Nu 32:26, 29

22:1 – 34 On the one hand, this is a story about the building of an altar and thus might be compared to 8:30 – 35. However, there are no examples of an altar built purely as a memorial. The erection of standing stones of special significance seems to have served that purpose elsewhere (see note on 4:7). This account provides a dramatic visual and verbal means to affirm the ongoing unity of Israel and its boundaries. The Transjordanian tribes affirm their unity with the rest of the nation, and by doing so and extracting a confession from the other tribes, they also seek to guarantee that their own lands and borders will be respected. There will not come some future time when the tribes west of the Jordan see them as non-Israelites who worship other deities and thus attack and seize their land. Both Joshua the commander and Phinehas the priest confirm the loyalty and faithfulness of the Transjordanian tribes (vv. 1 – 8,31). In the context of Joshua, the altar serves as a witness, because there are no other deities than the God of Israel that can be recognized. For this reason the altar is named "A Witness Between Us — that the LORD is God" (v. 34).

Jordan. 11And when the Israelites heard
that they had built the altar on the border of Canaan at Geliloth near the Jordan
on the Israelite side, 12the whole assembly
of Israel gathered at Shiloh[c] to go to war
against them.
13So the Israelites sent Phinehas[d] son
of Eleazar,[e] the priest, to the land of Gilead — to Reuben, Gad and the half-tribe of
Manasseh. 14With him they sent ten of the
chief men, one from each of the tribes of
Israel, each the head of a family division
among the Israelite clans.[f]
15When they went to Gilead — to Reuben, Gad and the half-tribe of Manasseh —
they said to them: 16"The whole assembly
of the LORD says: 'How could you break
faith[g] with the God of Israel like this?
How could you turn away from the LORD
and build yourselves an altar in rebellion[h]
against him now? 17Was not the sin of
Peor[i] enough for us? Up to this very day
we have not cleansed ourselves from that
sin, even though a plague fell on the community of the LORD! 18And are you now
turning away from the LORD?
" 'If you rebel against the LORD today,
tomorrow he will be angry with the whole
community[j] of Israel. 19If the land you
possess is defiled, come over to the LORD's
land, where the LORD's tabernacle stands,
and share the land with us. But do not rebel against the LORD or against us by building an altar for yourselves, other than the
altar of the LORD our God. 20When Achan
son of Zerah was unfaithful in regard to
the devoted things,[a][k] did not wrath[l] come
on the whole community of Israel? He was
not the only one who died for his sin.' "[m]
21Then Reuben, Gad and the half-tribe
of Manasseh replied to the heads of the
clans of Israel: 22"The Mighty One, God,
the LORD! The Mighty One, God,[n] the
LORD![o] He knows![p] And let Israel know! If
this has been in rebellion or disobedience
to the LORD, do not spare us this day. 23If
we have built our own altar to turn away
from the LORD and to offer burnt offerings
and grain offerings,[q] or to sacrifice fellowship offerings on it, may the LORD himself
call us to account.[r]
24"No! We did it for fear that some day
your descendants might say to ours, 'What
do you have to do with the LORD, the God
of Israel? 25The LORD has made the Jordan
a boundary between us and you — you
Reubenites and Gadites! You have no
share in the LORD.' So your descendants
might cause ours to stop fearing the LORD.
26"That is why we said, 'Let us get ready
and build an altar — but not for burnt offerings or sacrifices.' 27On the contrary, it
is to be a witness[s] between us and you
and the generations that follow, that we
will worship the LORD at his sanctuary
with our burnt offerings, sacrifices and
fellowship offerings.[t] Then in the future
your descendants will not be able to say
to ours, 'You have no share in the LORD.'
28"And we said, 'If they ever say this to
us, or to our descendants, we will answer:
Look at the replica of the LORD's altar,
which our ancestors built, not for burnt
offerings and sacrifices, but as a witness
between us and you.'
29"Far be it from us to rebel[u] against the
LORD and turn away from him today by
building an altar for burnt offerings, grain
offerings and sacrifices, other than the altar of the LORD our God that stands before
his tabernacle.[v]"
30When Phinehas the priest and the
leaders of the community — the heads of
the clans of the Israelites — heard what
Reuben, Gad and Manasseh had to say,
they were pleased. 31And Phinehas son of
Eleazar, the priest, said to Reuben, Gad
and Manasseh, "Today we know that the
LORD is with us,[w] because you have not
been unfaithful to the LORD in this matter.
Now you have rescued the Israelites from
the LORD's hand."
32Then Phinehas son of Eleazar, the
priest, and the leaders returned to Canaan
from their meeting with the Reubenites
and Gadites in Gilead and reported to the
Israelites. 33They were glad to hear the report and praised God.[x] And they talked no
more about going to war against them to
devastate the country where the Reubenites and the Gadites lived.
34And the Reubenites and the Gadites
gave the altar this name: A Witness[y] Between Us — that the LORD is God.

Joshua's Farewell to the Leaders

23 After a long time had passed and
the LORD had given Israel rest[z] from
all their enemies around them, Joshua, by

22:12 [c] Jos 18:1 **22:13** [d] Nu 25:7 [e] Nu 3:32; Jos 24:33 **22:14** [f] Nu 1:4 **22:16** [g] Dt 13:14 [h] Dt 12:13-14 **22:17** [i] Nu 25:1-9 **22:18** [j] Lev 10:6; Nu 16:22 **22:20** [k] Jos 7:1 [l] Ps 7:11 [m] Jos 7:5 **22:22** [n] Dt 10:17 [o] Ps 50:1 [p] 1Ki 8:39; Job 10:7; Ps 44:21; Jer 17:10 **22:23** [q] Jer 41:5 [r] Dt 12:11; 18:19; 1Sa 20:16 **22:27** [s] Ge 21:30; Jos 24:27 [t] Dt 12:6 **22:29** [u] Jos 24:16 [v] Dt 12:13-14 **22:31** [w] Lev 26:11-12; 2Ch 15:2 **22:33** [x] 1Ch 29:20; Da 2:19; Lk 2:28 **22:34** [y] Ge 21:30 **23:1** [z] Dt 12:9; Jos 21:44

[a] 20 The Hebrew term refers to the irrevocable giving over of things or persons to the LORD, often by totally destroying them.

22:15 *Gilead.* See note on 12:2.

22:17 *sin of Peor.* This was stopped by Phinehas at Baal Peor in Transjordan (Nu 25:6–18; see notes on Nu 25).

23:1–16 This is the final sermon of Joshua. It will be followed by a covenant renewal (24:1–28). However, even here aspects of ancient Near Eastern treaty appear. The first part, vv. 1–14, reviews Israel's experience in the promised land and the manner in which God enabled the nation to have success against all of its enemies. It concludes with observations about the manner in which God has blessed the people. Thus, v. 10—"One of you routs a thousand, because the LORD your God fights for you"—

then a very old man,[a] 2summoned all Israel — their elders,[b] leaders, judges and officials[c] — and said to them: "I am very old. 3You yourselves have seen everything the LORD your God has done to all these nations for your sake; it was the LORD your God who fought for you.[d] 4Remember how I have allotted[e] as an inheritance for your tribes all the land of the nations that remain — the nations I conquered — between the Jordan and the Mediterranean Sea[f] in the west. 5The LORD your God himself will push them out for your sake. He will drive them out before you, and you will take possession of their land, as the LORD your God promised you.[g]

6"Be very strong; be careful to obey all that is written in the Book of the Law of Moses, without turning aside to the right or to the left.[h] 7Do not associate with these nations that remain among you; do not invoke the names of their gods or swear[i] by them. You must not serve them or bow down[j] to them. 8But you are to hold fast to the LORD[k] your God, as you have until now.

9"The LORD has driven out before you great and powerful nations;[l] to this day no one has been able to withstand you.[m] 10One of you routs a thousand,[n] because the LORD your God fights for you,[o] just as he promised. 11So be very careful to love the LORD[p] your God.

12"But if you turn away and ally yourselves with the survivors of these nations that remain among you and if you intermarry with them[q] and associate with them,[r] 13then you may be sure that the LORD your God will no longer drive out these nations before you. Instead, they will become snares[s] and traps for you, whips on your backs and thorns in your eyes,[t] until you perish from this good land, which the LORD your God has given you.

14"Now I am about to go the way of all the earth.[u] You know with all your heart and soul that not one of all the good promises the LORD your God gave you has failed. Every promise has been fulfilled; not one has failed.[v] 15But just as all the good things the LORD your God has promised you have come to you, so he will bring on you all the evil things he has threatened, until the LORD your God has destroyed you from this good land he has given you.[w] 16If you violate the covenant of the LORD your God, which he commanded you, and go and serve other gods and bow down to them, the LORD's anger will burn against you, and you will quickly perish from the good land he has given you.[x]"

23:1 [a]Jos 13:1 **23:2** [b]Jos 7:6 [c]Jos 24:1 **23:3** [d]Ex 14:14 **23:4** [e]Jos 19:51 [f]Nu 34:6 **23:5** [g]Ex 23:30; Nu 33:53 **23:6** [h]Dt 5:32; Jos 1:7 **23:7** [i]Ex 23:13; Ps 16:4; Jer 5:7 [j]Ex 20:5 **23:8** [k]Dt 10:20 **23:9** [l]Dt 11:23 [m]Dt 7:24 **23:10** [n]Lev 26:8 [o]Ex 14:14; Dt 3:22 **23:11** [p]Jos 22:5 **23:12** [q]Dt 7:3 [r]Ex 34:16; Ps 106:34-35 **23:13** [s]Ex 23:33 [t]Nu 33:55 **23:14** [u]1Ki 2:2 [v]Jos 21:45 **23:15** [w]Lev 26:17; Dt 28:15 **23:16** [x]Dt 4:25-26 **24:1** [y]Jos 23:2

The Covenant Renewed at Shechem

24 Then Joshua assembled all the tribes of Israel at Shechem. He summoned the elders, leaders, judges and officials of Israel,[y] and they presented themselves before God.

2Joshua said to all the people, "This is what the LORD, the God of Israel, says: 'Long ago your ancestors, including Terah

---

sounds similar to the blessings of ancient Near Eastern treaties of the second millennium BC, although the latter are more general. The same is true of vv. 15 – 16, which resemble curses such as may be found in many treaties, with an emphasis upon divine judgment. When we see details like this that correspond with literary forms well-known in the ancient Near East, it reminds us that Israel was part of a larger ancient Near Eastern world and that God was inclined to use their familiarity with that world to communicate effectively to them.

23:2 *all Israel — their elders, leaders, judges and officials.* This is a good example of the use of the term "all Israel" in a context where it is immediately qualified by the leadership that represented the nation. Thus, neither here nor elsewhere in the book does "all Israel" imply every man, woman and child in the nation. This type of rhetorical expression has parallels in the ancient Near Eastern annals.

23:7 The equation of invoking the names of the deities with service and worship of them brings to mind the use of their names in the ancient Near Eastern treaties that occur at this time. Every treaty that has not had its latter section destroyed preserves a listing of divine witnesses.

24:1 *Joshua assembled all the tribes of Israel at Shechem.* The earlier covenant ceremony of 8:30 – 35 was at Mount Ebal, just north of Shechem. Because ch. 24 does not mention Mount Ebal, whereas ch. 8 does not mention Shechem, it is possible that the location of this covenant renewal was not at the same place as that of ch. 8 (which itself is portrayed as a fulfillment of Dt 27:2 – 8). However, no attack or conquest of Shechem is ever mentioned. This has raised the question of how Israel came to occupy this city. It is possible that there was a battle that was simply not recorded. Alternatively, it may be that Israel peacefully occupied the region and did not fight against the inhabitants of Shechem. Although this latter suggestion seems to contradict 11:19, it is possible that some other accommodation was made at Shechem. We cannot be certain. The assembly point at Shechem suggests that, despite the important role Shiloh was taking on, it did not replace Shechem (and Mount Ebal?) as a center for other national meetings, for covenant renewal and for religious acts such as the erection of a sacred memorial stone (v. 26). Furthermore, Shechem was the first place where Abram built an altar when he first came to Canaan (Ge 12:6) and the first place where Jacob came when he returned from Aram, as well as where he built an altar (Ge 33:18 – 20). Further, land nearby is associated with the burial place for Joseph as one of the early patriarchal plots purchased by Jacob (Ge 33:19) where Joseph would be buried (see Jos 24:32). *elders, leaders, judges and officials of Israel.* See note on 23:2.

24:2 *Terah.* The father of Abram and Nahor, the brother of Abram (Ge 11:26). *beyond the Euphrates River.* The area north and east of Canaan across the Euphrates River. The area discussed here lay in the Balikh River region and other rivers that flow into and form the Euphrates

Shechem.

the father of Abraham and Nahor, lived
beyond the Euphrates River and worshiped other gods.[z] 3But I took your father
Abraham from the land beyond the Euphrates and led him throughout Canaan[a]
and gave him many descendants.[b] I gave
him Isaac,[c] 4and to Isaac I gave Jacob and
Esau.[d] I assigned the hill country of Seir[e]
to Esau, but Jacob and his family went
down to Egypt.[f]
5" 'Then I sent Moses and Aaron,[g] and I
afflicted the Egyptians by what I did there,
and I brought you out. 6When I brought
your people out of Egypt, you came to the
sea, and the Egyptians pursued them with
chariots and horsemen[a][h] as far as the Red
Sea.[b] 7But they cried to the LORD for help,
and he put darkness[i] between you and the
Egyptians; he brought the sea over them
and covered them.[j] You saw with your
own eyes what I did to the Egyptians.
Then you lived in the wilderness for a
long time.[k]
8" 'I brought you to the land of the Amorites who lived east of the Jordan. They
fought against you, but I gave them into
your hands. I destroyed them from before you, and you took possession of their
land.[l] 9When Balak son of Zippor,[m] the
king of Moab, prepared to fight against Israel, he sent for Balaam son of Beor to put
a curse on you.[n] 10But I would not listen
to Balaam, so he blessed you[o] again and
again, and I delivered you out of his hand.
11" 'Then you crossed the Jordan[p] and
came to Jericho.[q] The citizens of Jericho
fought against you, as did also the Amorites,
Perizzites, Canaanites, Hittites, Girgashites,

24:2 [z] Ge 11:32 **24:3** [a] Ge 12:1 [b] Ge 15:5 [c] Ge 21:3 **24:4** [d] Ge 25:26 [e] Dt 2:5 [f] Ge 46:5-6 **24:5** [g] Ex 3:10 **24:6** [h] Ex 14:9 **24:7** [i] Ex 14:20 [j] Ex 14:28 [k] Dt 1:46 **24:8** [l] Nu 21:31 **24:9** [m] Nu 22:2 [n] Nu 22:6 **24:10** [o] Nu 23:11; Dt 23:5 **24:11** [p] Jos 3:16-17 [q] Jos 6:1

[a] 6 Or *charioteers* [b] 6 Or *the Sea of Reeds*

River in northern Syria. *worshiped other gods.* The nearby sites of Mari and Alalakh have yielded archives of cuneiform tablets from this period that attest to many deities worshiped by peoples of the region and same linguistic background as the patriarchs. This demonstrates that Abram did not come from a long line of unbroken monotheism.

24:5 *I brought you out.* Here and in many of the following phrases, note the switch to the second person. This report of a covenant renewal follows treaty language, in which a significant part of the historical reminiscence is directed to the actual recipient(s) of the treaty/covenant rather than previous generations. The emphasis is upon what God did for that generation and what they witnessed with their own eyes. While Rahab (2:9–11) mentions the drying up of the Red Sea as part of her confession, no mention of that is made here. More than the miracles, this covenant renewal review emphasizes God's acts of deliverance of his people from their enemies.

24:11 *citizens of Jericho.* As the first enemies in the promised land, these symbolize the rest. The term is used of a group or assembly that makes decisions for the towns of Shechem (Jdg 9:2) and Keilah (1Sa 23:11–12). At Ampi in the Amarna letters, they appear as a council who make decisions along with the governor.

Hivites and Jebusites, but I gave them into
your hands.[r] 12 I sent the hornet[s] ahead of
you, which drove them out before you—
also the two Amorite kings. You did not
do it with your own sword and bow. 13 So I
gave you a land on which you did not toil
and cities you did not build; and you live
in them and eat from vineyards and olive
groves that you did not plant.'[t]
14 "Now fear the LORD and serve him with
all faithfulness.[u] Throw away the gods[v] your
ancestors worshiped beyond the Euphrates
River and in Egypt,[w] and serve the LORD.
15 But if serving the LORD seems undesirable
to you, then choose for yourselves this day
whom you will serve, whether the gods
your ancestors served beyond the Euphrates, or the gods of the Amorites,[x] in whose
land you are living. But as for me and my
household, we will serve the LORD."[y]
16 Then the people answered, "Far be it
from us to forsake the LORD to serve other
gods! 17 It was the LORD our God himself
who brought us and our parents up out of
Egypt, from that land of slavery, and performed those great signs before our eyes.
He protected us on our entire journey and
among all the nations through which we
traveled. 18 And the LORD drove out before
us all the nations, including the Amorites,
who lived in the land. We too will serve
the LORD, because he is our God."
19 Joshua said to the people, "You are
not able to serve the LORD. He is a holy
God;[z] he is a jealous God.[a] He will not
forgive your rebellion[b] and your sins. 20 If
you forsake the LORD[c] and serve foreign
gods, he will turn[d] and bring disaster on
you and make an end of you,[e] after he has
been good to you."
21 But the people said to Joshua, "No!
We will serve the LORD."
22 Then Joshua said, "You are witnesses
against yourselves that you have chosen[f]
to serve the LORD."
"Yes, we are witnesses," they replied.
23 "Now then," said Joshua, "throw
away the foreign gods[g] that are among
you and yield your hearts[h] to the LORD,
the God of Israel."
24 And the people said to Joshua, "We will
serve the LORD our God and obey him."[i]
25 On that day Joshua made a covenant[j]
for the people, and there at Shechem he
reaffirmed for them decrees and laws.[k]
26 And Joshua recorded these things in the
Book of the Law of God.[l] Then he took a
large stone[m] and set it up there under the
oak near the holy place of the LORD.
27 "See!" he said to all the people. "This
stone will be a witness[n] against us. It has
heard all the words the LORD has said to
us. It will be a witness against you if you
are untrue to your God."
28 Then Joshua dismissed the people,
each to their own inheritance.

24:11 [r] Ex 23:23; Dt 7:1 **24:12** [s] Ex 23:28; Dt 7:20; Ps 44:3,6-7 **24:13** [t] Dt 6:10-11 **24:14** [u] Dt 10:12; 18:13; 1Sa 12:24; 2Co 1:12 [v] ver 23 [w] Eze 23:3 **24:15** [x] Jdg 6:10; Ru 1:15 [y] Ru 1:16; 1Ki 18:21 **24:19** [z] Lev 19:2; 20:26 [a] Ex 20:5 [b] Ex 23:21 **24:20** [c] 1Ch 28:9, 20 [d] Ac 7:42 [e] Jos 23:15 **24:22** [f] Ps 119:30,173 **24:23** [g] ver 14 [h] 1Ki 8:58; Ps 119:36; 141:4 **24:24** [i] Ex 19:8; 24:3,7; Dt 5:27 **24:25** [j] Ex 24:8 [k] Ex 15:25 **24:26** [l] Dt 31:24 [m] Ge 28:18 **24:27** [n] Jos 22:27

24:12 *the hornet.* Although some have suggested that the hornet is Egypt, this seems unlikely, because this identification is nowhere made in the Bible. The use of insects in warfare is attested, but not found in the war chronicles of Israel unlike, e.g., the use of (hail)stones that God also sends. The hornet may be a symbol of terror or perhaps the term for hornet should be read as "terror." This would exemplify the terror that is elsewhere attributed to the battles of Israel as in 2:9–11; 5:1; 6:27; Ex 15:14–16.

24:13 *vineyards and olive groves.* These constitute important nutritional sources for Israel. Mentioned some 185 times in the OT, wine was the most commonly consumed beverage. Wine culture in the region was known from the third millennium BC. Water could be contaminated, and other beverages were not available. Olive trees grow well in the climate and soil of the hill country of Israel. They do not compete with the staple diet grains that grow in different soil. Because it can take many years for olive trees to mature and yield fruit, the presence of these groves, as well as vineyards, suggests the replacement of one civilization by the other without the destruction of the natural resources. At seventh-century BC Ekron, the city processed 1,000 tons (900 metric tons) of olive oil annually, most of which was exported. Olive oil was used for food, medicine and lamp fuel, and as a base for cosmetics. It was also used in anointing kings and in ritual contexts.

24:22 *You are witnesses ... Yes, we are witnesses.* The confession of the people is to agree with the covenant stipulations just as the vassal in a suzerain-vassal treaty must accept the treaty stipulations. Of course, in treaties the witnesses are customarily the gods of the parties involved. Therefore, it is of greatest interest that the reference to "witnesses" is followed immediately by a charge from Joshua that the people should throw away their divine images of other gods and goddesses (v. 23). There is the context of the town of Shechem and the manner in which Jacob's family responded to his charge to do away with their divine images by handing them over to Jacob so that he could bury them under the oak at Shechem (Ge 35:2–4). However, in the context of a treaty/covenant and the reference to witnesses, Joshua's exhortation denies to the images any validity to function as witnesses to this covenant. The response of the people here is "We will serve the LORD our God and obey him" (v. 24). This sounds optimistic, but it is an ominous indicator that no mention is made of any Israelite relinquishing their images to Joshua, unlike the earlier 'Israel' who relinquished their images to Jacob.

24:25 *Joshua made a covenant for the people ... he reaffirmed for them decrees and laws.* The text provides no further information, although such a treaty/covenant would likely include the sorts of statements that Joshua charged the people with in vv. 14–24. It may even be larger, along the lines of the Book of the Covenant (Ex 20:22—23:33). On the role of writing and the significance of God's covenant for Joshua, see note on 1:8.

24:26 *a large stone ... under the oak near the holy place of the LORD.* Although the oak or great tree at Shechem had a long history of association with Israel's ancestors and their worship of God (Ge 12:6; 35:4; cf. Jdg 9:6), there is no known preservation of this tree. On the other hand, there is a standing stone that is visible in the cult center of the ancient site. Whatever association it may have with the account here is not known.

Standing stone at Schechem (see note on 24:26).
Kim Walton

Buried in the Promised Land

24:29-31pp — Jdg 2:6-9

[29]After these things, Joshua son of Nun,
the servant of the LORD, died at the age
of a hundred and ten.[o] [30]And they buried
him in the land of his inheritance, at Timnath Serah[a][p] in the hill country of Ephraim, north of Mount Gaash.
[31]Israel served the LORD throughout the
lifetime of Joshua and of the elders[q] who
outlived him and who had experienced everything the LORD had done for Israel.
[32]And Joseph's bones, which the Israelites had brought up from Egypt,[r] were
buried at Shechem in the tract of land[s]
that Jacob bought for a hundred pieces of
silver[b] from the sons of Hamor, the father
of Shechem. This became the inheritance
of Joseph's descendants.
[33]And Eleazar son of Aaron[t] died and
was buried at Gibeah, which had been
allotted to his son Phinehas[u] in the hill
country of Ephraim.

24:29 [o]Jdg 2:8 **24:30** [p]Jos 19:50 **24:31** [q]Jdg 2:7 **24:32** [r]Ge 50:25; Ex 13:19 [s]Ge 33:19; Jn 4:5; Ac 7:16 **24:33** [t]Jos 22:13 [u]Ex 6:25

[a] *30* Also known as *Timnath Heres* (see Judges 2:9)
[b] *32* Hebrew *hundred kesitahs;* a kesitah was a unit of money of unknown weight and value.

24:29 *the age of a hundred and ten.* This age matches that of Joseph, who also appears here (v. 32). In addition, both the age of Joseph and that of Joshua are mentioned twice in the Bible (Ge 50:22,26; Jdg 2:8).
24:30 *Mount Gaash.* This site is otherwise unknown, although the phrase "ravines of Gaash" occurs in the duplicate texts of 2Sa 23:30 and 1Ch 11:32. The Hebrew root behind "Gaash" means "to belch forth" or "to rise and fall," and may suggest that this describes a kind of topographic feature rather than a proper name. Unlike the patriarchs who had to purchase their burial tracts (see Ge 23 and notes), Joshua is buried in a land claimed by conquest (see note on Ge 47:29).

NARRATIVE LITERATURE

JUDGES

Literary Background

Many of the events and customs described or alluded to in the book of Judges, as well as the literary forms incorporated therein, find counterparts in extra-Biblical writings from the second and first millennia BC. The book contains annalistic summaries of conquests, a victory hymn, prayers, prophecies, political speeches, a fable, geographic equations (Bethel = Luz), reports of scouting expeditions and many other types of stories — all of which are attested outside the Bible. However, the literary style represented by the book of Judges is unlike anything found outside the Bible in the ancient Near East.

Whereas archaeologists' spades have unearthed inscriptions that have literary links with virtually every type of writing found in Judges, nowhere do we find a coherent portrayal of history incorporating the forms and contents of these documents like we find in Judges. Whereas other ancient Near Eastern societies managed to preserve literary artifacts that contain snippets of historical and cultural information, these remain isolated and unintegrated; they provide the raw materials necessary for historical composition, but none represents the kind of intentional historiography found in the book of Judges. Whenever the book was compiled, the editor employed a variety of sources, undoubtedly oral and literary, and crafted a document that represents a remarkable literary achievement.

KEY CONCEPTS

- Leadership was lacking in the time of the judges, which worked to the disadvantage of the people.
- Israel worshiped other gods alongside Yahweh and thus failed to keep the covenant.

Historical Background

For the most part, the events described in the book of Judges take place in Canaan, the small strip of land on the eastern Mediterranean sandwiched between Egypt to the south and the territories occupied by the Phoenicians and Arameans in the north.

According to chronologies established by archaeologists, the events described in Judges transpired in the Late Bronze Age (1550 – 1200 BC) and the Early Iron Age (1, 1200 – 1000 BC). Establishing the chronological sequence of the events described in Judges poses special problems. While many of the places named in the book can be firmly identified geographically, not a single character in the book is named in any contemporary ancient Near Eastern literature.

Efforts to gain a contextual ancient Near Eastern perspective on events described in Judges are aided greatly by extra-Biblical textual and material evidence. These are referred to regularly in the notes, but it may be helpful to summarize here their significance for understanding the period of the judges. With respect to literary evidence, the Merneptah Stele, erected in c. 1209/08 BC to commemorate the Egyptian pharaoh's Libyan victories, concludes with a stanza celebrating his conquests in Canaan. This document provides the earliest extra-Biblical attestation of an entity known as "Israel," confirming that by the end of the thirteenth century BC, the nation was a significant force in Canaan.

The so-called Amarna letters, discovered at Tell el-Amarna in Egypt in 1888 – 1889, provide the clearest window into the Canaanite political situation at the beginning of the period of the judges. This cache of more than 300 clay tablets inscribed in Akkadian, the language of trade and diplomacy in the fourteenth century BC, contains the written correspondence between the Egyptian king Amenhotep IV (also called Akhenaten, c. 1352 – 1336 BC) and his vassal kingdoms in Canaan and Syria. These letters describe a political landscape dominated by small city-states often at odds with each other and harassed by a troublesome group of landless people known as Apiru.

The religious situation in Canaan during this period has been illuminated by the discovery of several collections of clay tablets from twelfth-century BC Ugarit on the Mediterranean coast in northern Syria. Discovered in palace and temple libraries, these texts were written in alphabetic and syllabic Akkadian cuneiform, and they have yielded a host of invaluable ritual and mythological texts, clarifying the relationships among the Canaanite deities mentioned in Judges and the nature of Canaanite religion.

Later in the book of Judges the Philistines become major players. Our knowledge of the culture of the Philistines has been greatly enhanced in recent decades by archaeological excavations at Ashdod, Ekron, Ashkelon and Tel Qasile. Archaeological excavations have illuminated many critical elements in the narratives of Judges, including the accounts of the demise of Abimelek (Jdg 9), especially the fortifications of Shechem and the conquest of the northern city of Dan/Laish (Jdg 18) and many others. ◆

Israel Fights the Remaining Canaanites

1:11-15pp — Jos 15:15-19

1 After the death[a] of Joshua, the Israelites
asked the LORD, "Who of us is to go up
first[b] to fight against the Canaanites?[c]"
²The LORD answered, "Judah[d] shall
go up; I have given the land into their
hands.[e]"
³The men of Judah then said to the Simeonites their fellow Israelites, "Come up
with us into the territory allotted to us, to
fight against the Canaanites. We in turn
will go with you into yours." So the Simeonites[f] went with them.
⁴When Judah attacked, the LORD gave the
Canaanites and Perizzites[g] into their hands,
and they struck down ten thousand men at
Bezek.[h] ⁵It was there that they found Adoni-Bezek and fought against him, putting to
rout the Canaanites and Perizzites. ⁶Adoni-
Bezek fled, but they chased him and caught
him, and cut off his thumbs and big toes.
⁷Then Adoni-Bezek said, "Seventy
kings with their thumbs and big toes cut

1:1 [a] Jos 24:29 [b] Nu 27:21 [c] ver 27; Jdg 3:1-6 **1:2** [d] Ge 49:8 [e] ver 4; Jdg 3:28 **1:3** [f] ver 17 **1:4** [g] Ge 13:7; Jos 3:10 [h] 1Sa 11:8

1:1 *asked the LORD.* In OT times, military leaders would generally consult their gods before embarking on military campaigns. To determine the will of the gods they resorted to a variety of oracular means, such as examining the liver of a slaughtered sheep for special markings or observing astrological phenomena. Sometimes the reception of an oracle was preceded by sacrificial rituals. The present text is silent on the method used by the Israelites to determine the will of Yahweh. The fact that in a later analogous situation the Israelites went to Bethel, where the ark of the covenant law of God was located, and where Phinehas, son of Eleazar, the son of Aaron, served as high priest (20:27–28), suggests the divine will on the matter was ascertained by manipulating the Urim and Thummim, as prescribed for Joshua in Nu 27:21 (cf. 1Sa 28:6; see the article "Urim and Thummim," p. 162). *to go up.* The choice of the Hebrew verb reflects the mountainous terrain of much of Palestine and the common Canaanite practice of fortifying settlements on hilltops or mounds. Since campaigns of conquest often involved sieges of fortified towns rather than pitched battles between two armies in the open field, this Hebrew verb became idiomatic for "to attack." *Canaanites.* See the article "The Canaanites," p. 294.

1:2 *I have given the land into their hands.* This *committal formula* reflects the ancient belief that the outcome of battles was always determined by the gods. This statement portrays Yahweh as a divine warrior who marches before his people, defeats the enemy and hands the enemy's territory over to those on whose behalf he was fighting. A seventh-century BC oracle in support of Esarhaddon, king of Assyria, uses similar wording to indicate that Marduk will deliver all the countries into his hands.

1:3 *Judah then said to the Simeonites their fellow Israelites.* In ancient tribal contexts, tribes were often named after their "eponymous" ancestor. Although the original Judah and Simeon were full brothers, the sons of Jacob and his first wife Leah (Ge 29:33,35), political and military allies would also frequently be referred to as brothers. According to Jos 19:1–9, the territorial allotment of Simeon consisted of scattered towns within the grant of Judah. Within a century or two, Simeon ceased to exist as a separate tribe; Simeon is missing in Moses' blessing of the tribes (Dt 33) and in the Song of Deborah (Jdg 5). The reference to Simeon as a tribe therefore evidences the antiquity of the document.

1:4 *Perizzites.* See note on Dt 7:1. *ten thousand men.* This is obviously a rounded figure, perhaps a conventional generic number for "innumerable." Although this figure correlates well with the figures given for the registration of Israel's men of military age in Nu 2 and Nu 26 and with the song composed to celebrate David's victory over Goliath (1Sa 18:7), in the light of archaeological evidence for population levels in Canaan at this time it seems inordinately high. Based on a comparison of these numbers with those found in Assyrian records, some conclude that the numbers should be interpreted not literally but as intentionally and conventionally hyperbolic. A more likely option is to reinterpret the expression *elep*, usually rendered "1,000." Since the consonantal form of this Hebrew word (*'lp*) can also mean "clan," or "head of a clan," the Hebrew word may refer to the leader of a contingent of troops a clan could muster, or it may function as a collective for the troop itself. See the article "Numbers in Numbers," p. 235.

1:6 *they … cut off his thumbs and big toes.* The mutilation of captives was common in the ancient world. Although we have no ancient records of the torturous cutting off of toes and thumbs, this action recalls the brutality of the Assyrians. The purpose of this kind of torture is not merely to incapacitate an enemy or to cause pain, but also to humiliate them (see next note) and prevent them from ever again serving as soldiers.

1:7 *scraps under my table.* By cutting off the fingers and toes of his enemies, Adoni-Bezek had treated them like dogs and reduced them to scavenging scraps under his table. They are displayed as a sign of their conqueror's power. In accounts from Ugarit, the god El treats enemy gods in this manner. *God has paid me back.* As any ancient Near Easterner would have done, the governor of Bezek interprets his fate theologically: Adoni-Bezek's reference to God is ambiguous. In ascribing responsibility for his punishment to deity he uses the generic designation "*elohim*," which could refer either to Yahweh by the generic title or to his own pagan god. Since he was a Canaanite, we would not necessarily expect him to refer to Yahweh, the God of Israel. *Jerusalem.* The earliest extra-Biblical attestation of the place-name derives from the nineteenth- to eighteenth-century BC Execration Texts from Egypt. According to the Amarna letters (clay tablets found in Egypt), in the fourteenth century BC, the city (spelled *Urusalim*) was ruled by Abdi-Hiba, a vassal of the Egyptian pharaoh Amenhotep IV (Akhenaten). The common Biblical name for this place, Jebus (cf. v. 21), is unattested outside the OT. Jerusalem at this time is still considered a foreign city. First, 2Sa 5:6–9 reports that David wrested Jerusalem out of Jebusite hands. Second, according to Jdg 1:21 and Jos 15:8, Jerusalem was occupied by Jebusites (rather than Canaanites and Perizzites). Additionally, according to Jos 18:16,28, the city was located within the territory allotted to Benjamin. The most likely explanation recognizes Jerusalem as a border city, located on the boundary between Judah and Benjamin. The city that was burned in v. 8 probably identifies the Jebusite fortress on the southern hill of the city, between the Kidron and Hinnom Valleys, which David eventually captured and made his capital. Accordingly, the unsuccessful Benjamite effort in v. 21 may have been directed against a citadel on the north end of the city. The fact that David had to reconquer Jerusalem suggests that the Judahite hold on the city was weak and short-lived. It seems that shortly after they had sacked it the Jebusites moved in from the north and took control, which they then held for several centuries.

off have picked up scraps under my table.
Now God has paid me back[i] for what I did
to them." They brought him to Jerusalem,
and he died there.
8The men of Judah attacked Jerusalem[j]
also and took it. They put the city to the
sword and set it on fire.
9After that, Judah went down to fight
against the Canaanites living in the hill
country,[k] the Negev[l] and the western foothills. 10They advanced against the Canaanites living in Hebron[m] (formerly called Kiriath Arba[n]) and defeated Sheshai, Ahiman
and Talmai.[o] 11From there they advanced
against the people living in Debir[p] (formerly called Kiriath Sepher).

1:7 [i] Lev 24:19
1:8 [j] ver 21; Jos 15:63
1:9 [k] Nu 13:17 [l] Nu 21:1
1:10 [m] Ge 13:18 [n] Ge 35:27 [o] Jos 15:14
1:11 [p] Jos 15:15

JUDGES 1

Judges 1 as Annalistic Military Reporting

Although Jdg 1 is dependent upon the narrative account of the conquest of Canaan found in Jos 13 – 19, the literary form adopted here resembles that of Assyrian summary inscriptions of military campaigns. Although these accounts often begin with a chronological note, they arrange events not necessarily chronologically, but according to geography. The descriptions tend to be short, telescoping relatively long periods of time into brief spans of reading time. Summary inscriptions tend to describe a static world in general terms, rather than dynamic scenes of action developing a narrative plot. They are often characterized by iterative schemes, they regularly resort to hyperbole and other forms of rhetorical flourish, and they often refer to the involvement of deity. Jdg 1 does indeed begin with a chronological note, but after that it is impossible to construct a chronology of the conquest from Jdg 1. Except for the anecdotal notes (which represent insertions from other sources interested less in tribal achievements than in personal fates/fortunes), the accounts of individual campaigns are brief, static and without characterization or plot. Accordingly, the present document is intended as a summary of Israel's fortunes after the death of Joshua.

Even so, since Jdg 1 recounts more failures than successes, a summary inscription of military conquests is transformed ironically into an *anti-conquest account*. Unlike most ancient military reports, the aim of this document is not to celebrate the achievements of the generation of Israelites that survived Joshua, but to lament their sorry response to the divine mandate to occupy the land and eliminate the Canaanites. ◆

Clay prism of Tiglath-Pileser I summarizing his military achievements, c. 1114 – 1076 BC.

12 And Caleb said, "I will give my daughter Aksah in marriage to the man who
attacks and captures Kiriath Sepher."
13 Othniel son of Kenaz, Caleb's younger
brother, took it; so Caleb gave his daughter Aksah to him in marriage.
14 One day when she came to Othni-
el, she urged him[a] to ask her father for a
field. When she got off her donkey, Caleb
asked her, "What can I do for you?"
15 She replied, "Do me a special favor.
Since you have given me land in the Negev, give me also springs of water." So Caleb gave her the upper and lower springs.
16 The descendants of Moses' father-in-
law,[q] the Kenite,[r] went up from the City of
Palms[b][s] with the people of Judah to live
among the inhabitants of the Desert of Judah in the Negev near Arad.[t]
17 Then the men of Judah went with the
Simeonites[u] their fellow Israelites and attacked the Canaanites living in Zephath,
and they totally destroyed[c] the city. Therefore it was called Hormah.[d][v] 18 Judah also
took[e] Gaza,[w] Ashkelon and Ekron—each
city with its territory.
19 The LORD was with[x] the men of Judah.
They took possession of the hill country,
but they were unable to drive the people
from the plains, because they had chariots
fitted with iron.[y] 20 As Moses had promised, Hebron[z] was given to Caleb, who
drove from it the three sons of Anak.[a]
21 The Benjamites, however, did not drive
out[b] the Jebusites, who were living in Jerusalem;[c] to this day the Jebusites live
there with the Benjamites.
22 Now the tribes of Joseph attacked
Bethel, and the LORD was with them.
23 When they sent men to spy out Bethel
(formerly called Luz),[d] 24 the spies saw a
man coming out of the city and they said

1:16 [q] Nu 10:29 [r] Ge 15:19; Jdg 4:11 [s] Dt 34:3; Jdg 3:13 [t] Nu 21:1 **1:17** [u] ver 3 [v] Nu 21:3 **1:18** [w] Jos 11:22 **1:19** [x] ver 2 [y] Jos 17:16 **1:20** [z] Jos 14:9; 15:13-14 [a] ver 10; Jos 14:13 **1:21** [b] Jos 15:63 [c] ver 8 **1:23** [d] Ge 28:19

[a] 14 Hebrew; Septuagint and Vulgate *Othniel, he urged her* [b] 16 That is, Jericho [c] 17 The Hebrew term refers to the irrevocable giving over of things or persons to the LORD, often by totally destroying them. [d] 17 *Hormah* means *destruction.* [e] 18 Hebrew; Septuagint *Judah did not take*

1:12 *I will give my daughter Aksah.* Some modern readers find Caleb's treatment of his daughter offensive, as if she is mere property, an object to be awarded by one man to another for a job well done. However, in this world, where clan loyalties are high and the well-being of the extended family takes precedence over personal and individual interests, Aksah could well have felt honored to be given in marriage to a military hero like Othniel. As in the patricentric and patrilocal world around Israel, where fathers regularly gave their daughters in marriage to their husbands, Caleb's actions would have been viewed as perfectly normal. Caleb's offer of a valuable marriage contract, allowing an increase in status to the recipient, is made to entice a hero to step forward.
1:16 *descendants of Moses' father-in-law, the Kenite.* Since Moses' father-in-law is referred to elsewhere as a Midianite priest (Ex 3:1; 18:1), either Moses had more than one wife, or the Israelites were fluid in their identification of the nomadic groups that migrated back and forth in the desert regions south of Judah. Otherwise, "Kenite" may refer to a Midianite clan or subgroup. *City of Palms.* This expression is elsewhere used of Jericho (Jdg 3:13), but could feasibly refer to any oasis that featured date palms. Since all of the activity of this section takes place much farther south than Jericho, it likely refers to a fortified oasis settlement in that region, perhaps Tamar on the western edge of the Arabah south of the Dead Sea.
1:17 *Zephath ... called Hormah.* The location of this site is unknown. *totally destroyed the city.* The treatment of the city appears on the surface to be according to the law of *herem* as reflected not only in Dt 7:1–5, but also according to the ninth-century BC Mesha Stele, in which he describes his sacking of Nebo, an Israelite town, and his destruction of its citizens consigning them to *herem* status for the gods Ashtar and Kemosh (see article, "Divine Warfare," p. 365). The renaming of the site accords with common ancient Near Eastern practice of conquerors renaming conquered territories and with the Danites' renaming of Laish as Dan in Jdg 18:29. The new name, Hormah (*hormh*), which means "destruction," plays on the term *herem*, "devoted [to God] for destruction," the technical expression for Israel's mandate to destroy the Canaanites utterly.
1:19 *chariots fitted with iron.* Judah's failure to dislodge the inhabitants of the lowland regions is attributed to the Canaanites' technological superiority: they possessed iron chariots. Chariots were useless in the highlands of Judah, but in the valleys and the river plains they proved a great advantage. The author's note that these were chariots "fitted with iron" is extremely significant, not only because it expresses the impressive nature of the Canaanites' military hardware, but also because it announces the beginning of the Iron Age in Palestine. Textual and archaeological evidence shows that iron was known in the ancient Near East prior to what is known as the Iron Age (c. 1200–586 BC), but because of the difficulty in refining it (the ore has to be heated to 1530°C [2786°F]), the refined metal was rare and precious. However, the discovery of the process of carburization at the beginning of this period ushered in a new technological age, which the Canaanites exploited to full advantage. How much iron was used in the chariots is an open question. Obviously the chariots were not made entirely of iron, but the metal could have been used on the hubs or rims of wheels or to reinforce other features of the chariot or simply as decoration.
1:24 *Show us how to get into the city.* If Bethel were a walled town like some of the major cities of Canaan in the Middle Bronze Age and Israel's fortified towns of the Iron Age, then the request to be shown the entrance to the city sounds ridiculous, since any passerby could have observed the nature of the walls and the location of the gates. However, the archaeological record suggests that in the Late Bronze Period (1550–1200 BC), the defenses of many towns involved a perimeter of houses constructed close together, a practice that continued into the following Iron Age. Presumably the spies wanted to know the best route of access into Bethel. Their appeal to a local citizen for aid is illuminated by second-millennium BC Mesopotamian correspondence between Zimri-Lim and his officials, who report the use of local people as scouts and guides when their army entered unfamiliar territory.

to him, "Show us how to get into the
city and we will see that you are treated
well.[e]" 25So he showed them, and they put
the city to the sword but spared[f] the man
and his whole family. 26He then went to
the land of the Hittites, where he built a
city and called it Luz, which is its name
to this day.
27But Manasseh did not drive out the
people of Beth Shan or Taanach or Dor or
Ibleam[g] or Megiddo and their surrounding
settlements, for the Canaanites[h] were determined to live in that land. 28When Israel
became strong, they pressed the Canaanites into forced labor but never drove them
out completely. 29Nor did Ephraim drive
out the Canaanites living in Gezer,[i] but the
Canaanites continued to live there among
them.[j] 30Neither did Zebulun drive out the
Canaanites living in Kitron or Nahalol, so
these Canaanites lived among them, but
Zebulun did subject them to forced labor.
31Nor did Asher drive out those living in
Akko or Sidon or Ahlab or Akzib[k] or Hel-
bah or Aphek or Rehob. 32The Asherites
lived among the Canaanite inhabitants of
the land because they did not drive them
out. 33Neither did Naphtali drive out those

1:24 [e] Jos 2:12, 14
1:25 [f] Jos 6:25
1:27 [g] Jos 17:11 [h] ver 1
1:29 [i] 1Ki 9:16 [j] Jos 16:10
1:31 [k] Jdg 10:6

1:25 *spared the man and his whole family.* Contrary to the *herem* law, the house of Joseph not only spared the life of the "traitor" (from the Canaanite point of view) but also allowed him to leave and build his own city and continue his life as a Hittite (v. 26).

1:26 *land of the Hittites.* In these texts, the Hittites are presented as one of the Canaanite ethnic groups (presumably the "descendants of Heth" [see NIV text note on Ge 23:3]). It is doubtful that the territory in question should be identified with the Hittites, whose capital was in Hattusas in Anatolia and who vied with Egypt for hegemony over Canaan in the Late Bronze Age. Rather, the Merneptah Stele of 1209 BC confirms that the "land of the Hittites" refers to a region of Hatti in the northern part of the territory assigned by Yahweh to the Israelites. Technically, Luz/Bethel was conquered, but in reality the city was simply transferred to a new site, and continued to function as a sanctioned symbol of "the Canaanites ... among them" (v. 29).

1:27 *Beth Shan ... Taanach ... Dor ... Ibleam ... Megiddo.* The Manassite failure to fulfill the divine mandate is summarized by listing a series of unconquered cities and their respective dependent territories in a narrow strip of land extending from the Jordan in the east to the Mediterranean in the west. The order in which these towns are named does not follow a normal east-west itinerary. Rather, the narrator moves in a straight line from the eastern extremity (Beth Shan) to the center (Taanach) to the western extremity (Dor) and then from the southernmost (Ibleam) to the northernmost site (Megiddo). The effect is not only to highlight Canaanite control of the fertile Valley of Jezreel, but also to highlight the geographic wedge this created between the northern tribes and Ephraim to the south. *Beth Shan.* An important city at the junction of the Jordan and Jezreel Valleys. *Taanach.* A site five miles (eight kilometers) south-east of Megiddo, with which it is often linked (5:19; Jos 12:21; 17:11; 1Ki 4:12). *Dor.* An important coastal town just south of the Carmel ridge. *Ibleam.* Probably to be identified with Khirbet Belameh, guarding the easternmost pass from the Ephraimite highlands into the Valley of Jezreel. *Megiddo.* A major fortress in the Valley of Jezreel. Its strategic location was recognized by Solomon, who rebuilt the city as a major Israelite military fortress. *surrounding settlements.* The villages surrounding the captured sites are traditionally referred to as "daughters." The expression refers to the satellite villages within the economic and political orbit of the town named. Since most of these were unfortified, in time of war the inhabitants would have sought protection in the "mother" town. Some have estimated that in the Late Bronze Age the radius of the areas of influence of these small-scale city-states may have averaged 12 miles (20 kilometers) — the distance one could travel in a one-day round trip. In the OT the expression usually translated "city" or "town," refers by definition to a settlement fortified with walls and defensive gate structures.

1:28 *forced labor.* Refers to the common ancient Near Eastern practice of conquerors subjecting conquered populations into slavery, though evidence for lifetime servitude is scanty. In Mesopotamia, captives could be ransomed, but until the money was raised they would be put to work. The meaning of the expression is illustrated by the treatment of the Gibeonites in Jos 9:21 and Solomon's treatment of the remnant of the original population in 1Ki 9:20 – 21. This practice is distinguished from the corvée service Solomon imposed on his own people (1Ki 9:22).

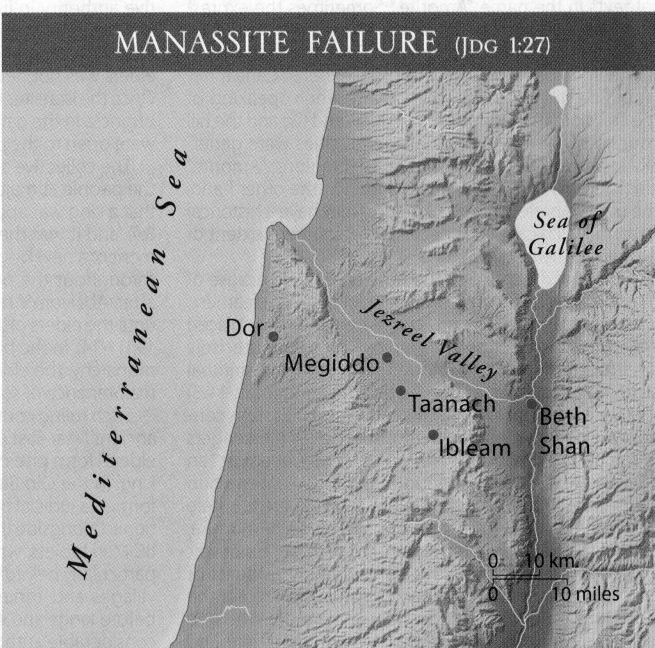

living in Beth Shemesh or Beth Anath[l]; but
the Naphtalites too lived among the Canaanite inhabitants of the land, and those
living in Beth Shemesh and Beth Anath
became forced laborers for them. 34The
Amorites[m] confined the Danites to the hill
country, not allowing them to come down
into the plain. 35And the Amorites were
determined also to hold out in Mount Heres, Aijalon[n] and Shaalbim, but when the
power of the tribes of Joseph increased,
they too were pressed into forced labor.
36The boundary of the Amorites was from
Scorpion Pass[o] to Sela and beyond.

The Angel of the LORD at Bokim

2 The angel of the LORD[p] went up from
Gilgal to Bokim[q] and said, "I brought
you up out of Egypt[r] and led you into the
land I swore to give to your ancestors.[s] I
said, 'I will never break my covenant with
you,[t] 2and you shall not make a covenant
with the people of this land,[u] but you
shall break down their altars.[v]' Yet you
have disobeyed me. Why have you done
this? 3And I have also said, 'I will not drive
them out before you;[w] they will become
traps[x] for you, and their gods will become
snares[y] to you.' "
4When the angel of the LORD had spoken these things to all the Israelites, the
people wept aloud, 5and they called that
place Bokim.[a] There they offered sacrifices
to the LORD.

Disobedience and Defeat

2:6-9pp — Jos 24:29-31

6After Joshua had dismissed the Israelites, they went to take possession of the
land, each to their own inheritance. 7The
people served the LORD throughout the
lifetime of Joshua and of the elders who
outlived him and who had seen all the
great things the LORD had done for Israel.

1:33 [l] Jos 19:38 **1:34** [m] Ex 3:17 **1:35** [n] Jos 19:42 **1:36** [o] Jos 15:3 **2:1** [p] Jdg 6:11 [q] ver 5 [r] Ex 20:2 [s] Ge 17:8 [t] Lev 26:42-44; Dt 7:9 **2:2** [u] Ex 23:32; 34:12; Dt 7:2 [v] Ex 34:13 **2:3** [w] Jos 23:13 [x] Nu 33:55 [y] Dt 7:16; Jdg 3:6; Ps 106:36

[a] 5 *Bokim* means *weepers.*

1:34 *Amorites.* The name is related to Akkadian Amurru, "the west," which could designate a direction, region or people. The heartland of the Amorites (Amurru) as described in Mesopotamian texts was located in northern Syria, between the western Euphrates and the Khabur and Balikh Rivers. When the Amurru/Amorites migrated west and south into the region of Palestine is not clear. It seems, however, that by the seventeenth century BC, the term "Amurru" was increasingly used to designate central and southern Syria, and by the fifteenth century BC, "the Kingdom of Amurru" had come to denote a realm in the mountains of northern Lebanon. In time the expression could be used of the mountainous region farther south as well. These Amurru have left their mark on the Biblical texts in the name "Amorite." Sometimes the expression was used in a limited sense of a specific subgroup of the pre-Israelite populations of Palestine (e.g., Dt 7:1). Sometimes narrators use "Amorite" where "Canaanite" would be inappropriate, particularly when speaking of the Transjordanian kingdoms of Sihon and Og and the hill country of the Cisjordan. "Canaanite" cities were generally located in the valleys and coastal regions; "Amorite" cities tended to be in the highlands. On the other hand, the present preference for "Amorite" may have a historical base, in which case v. 36 declares the southern extent of Amorite settlement.

2:1 *angel of the LORD.* See the note on Ex 3:2. Because of the popular modern misconception of angels as feathery, winged creatures, the term "angel" here may be replaced with either "messenger" or "envoy," for this is precisely what the term means. Although the moral and spiritual scolding of an entire nation by this messenger (vv. 1 – 3) is quite exceptional within the ancient Near Eastern context, the notion of human beings sent out as messengers of the gods is common. In "The Report of Wenamun," an Egyptian text from the period of the judges, Wenamun advises the prince of Byblos in Phoenicia to erect a stele and inscribe on it the following message: "Amun-Re, King of the Gods, sent me Amun-of-the-Road, his envoy, together with Wenamun, his human envoy, in quest of timber for the great noble bark of Amun-Re, King of the Gods." *my covenant.* The covenant spoken of is the one ratified by Yahweh and Israel at Mount Sinai. Here and elsewhere it is always referred to as Yahweh's covenant — never Israel's. This accords with the pattern of suzerainty treaties contracted between Hittite overlords and their vassal kings of the late second millennium BC (see the articles "Treaty Formats and Biblical Covenants," p. 303; "Covenants," p. 143).

2:7 *elders.* The book of Judges has elders governing both tribes on the move (here) and settled communities, villages and towns (8:14,16). Later, the elders of Gilead contract with Jephthah to lead their forces against the Ammonites (11:5 – 11). It is not clear how fixed the body of elders in Israelite communities were, nor how men attained this status. Nevertheless, it is clear that the title "elders" designated senior leadership with collective authority in judicial and administrative matters that affected the whole village or tribe (see note on Ru 4:2). Although age was undoubtedly a factor, the body of elders was not necessarily composed purely of old men. Once the Israelites had settled down, they conducted their business in the gates of the towns, and their deliberations were open to the public (Ru 4:1 – 12; see note on Ge 19:1).

The collective assembly of Israelite elders represented the people at major gatherings. It was at their instigation that a king was appointed over Israel in the first place (1Sa 8:4), and it was their prerogative to endorse the appointment of a new king (1Ch 11:3). Their importance continued throughout the period of the monarchy. David himself after Absalom's rebellion did not return to the throne until the elders of Judah came out to bring him back (2Sa 19:11 – 14). In the postexilic period too in the absence of a monarchy, the elders had a significant role to play in the maintenance of social justice and order.

Such ruling councils of elders are attested widely in the ancient Near East. In the tale of Gilgamesh and Agga, "the elders" form one of the two committees who advise the king. In the Old Babylonian period, the elders of the city formed a judicial body that decided local cases and functioned alongside the royal courts. The eighteenth-century BC Mari tablets, where tribal organization dominated, are particularly helpful in illuminating how elders represented villages and tribes in conversation with outsiders and before kings and demonstrate that the elders exercised considerable authority.

8Joshua son of Nun, the servant of the
LORD, died at the age of a hundred and ten.
9And they buried him in the land of his inheritance, at Timnath Heres[a][z] in the hill
country of Ephraim, north of Mount Gaash.
10After that whole generation had been
gathered to their ancestors, another generation grew up who knew neither the LORD
nor what he had done for Israel.[a] 11Then
the Israelites did evil in the eyes of the
LORD[b] and served the Baals.[c] 12They forsook the LORD, the God of their ancestors,
who had brought them out of Egypt. They
followed and worshiped various gods[d] of
the peoples around them.[e] They aroused
the LORD's anger 13because they forsook
him and served Baal and the Ashtoreths.[f]
14In his anger[g] against Israel the LORD gave
them into the hands[h] of raiders who plundered them. He sold them[i] into the hands
of their enemies all around, whom they
were no longer able to resist.[j] 15Whenever
Israel went out to fight, the hand of the
LORD was against them to defeat them, just
as he had sworn to them. They were in
great distress.
16Then the LORD raised up judges,[b][k]
who saved[l] them out of the hands of these
raiders. 17Yet they would not listen to their
judges but prostituted[m] themselves to other gods and worshiped them. They quickly
turned from the ways of their ancestors,
who had been obedient to the LORD's commands.[n] 18Whenever the LORD raised up
a judge for them, he was with the judge
and saved them out of the hands of their
enemies as long as the judge lived; for the
LORD relented[o] because of their groaning[p]
under those who oppressed and afflicted
them. 19But when the judge died, the people returned to ways even more corrupt[q]
than those of their ancestors, following
other gods and serving and worshiping
them.[r] They refused to give up their evil
practices and stubborn ways.
20Therefore the LORD was very angry[s]
with Israel and said, "Because this nation
has violated the covenant I ordained for
their ancestors and has not listened to me,

2:9 [z] Jos 19:50
2:10 [a] Ex 5:2; 1Sa 2:12; 1Ch 28:9; Gal 4:8
2:11 [b] Jdg 3:12; 4:1; 6:1; 10:6 [c] Jdg 3:7; 8:33
2:12 [d] Ps 106:36 [e] Dt 31:16; Jdg 10:6
2:13 [f] Jdg 10:6
2:14 [g] Dt 31:17 [h] Ps 106:41 [i] Dt 32:30; Jdg 3:8 [j] Dt 28:25
2:16 [k] Ac 13:20 [l] Ps 106:43
2:17 [m] Ex 34:15 [n] ver 7
2:18 [o] Dt 32:36; Jos 1:5 [p] Ps 106:44
2:19 [q] Jdg 3:12 [r] Jdg 4:1; 8:33
2:20 [s] ver 14; Jos 23:16

[a] *9* Also known as *Timnath Serah* (see Joshua 19:50 and 24:30) [b] *16* Or *leaders*; similarly in verses 17-19

2:8 *servant of the LORD.* That the notion of human beings as servants of deities was common in the ancient Near East is reflected in the many theophoric names (names involving a title or name of a deity) that are found in Hebrew (e.g., Obadiah, "one who serves Yahweh"), and also in the Semitic world surrounding ancient Israel. Although "servant" is often interpreted as a designation for a menial role, the fact that a court official in the ancient world was called "servant of the king" demonstrates that in contexts like this it actually bears honorific significance (cf. 2Ki 25:8).
2:10 *gathered to their ancestors.* This expression functions euphemistically for "they died and were buried." The idiom derives from the Israelite custom of burying the deceased in family/ancestral tombs. See the notes on Ge 23:4; 25:8.
2:11 *the Baals.* When applied to a god, the name Baal functions as a title ("divine lord, master") rather than a personal name, and is used as an appellative for many gods in the ancient world, like the Babylonian god Marduk, also known as Bel. Occurring as a divine title more than 70 times in the OT, *baal* usually refers to the storm/weather-god, who in the Canaanite mythological literature goes by the name Hadad, as well as several other titles: "the victor Baal," "Rider of the Clouds," "son of Dagan," "the prince lord of the earth," "Baal of Zaphan." The present plural form, "the Baals," does not refer to a multiplicity of gods, but to numerous manifestations of the one weather-god, on whose blessing the fertility of the land was thought to depend. These manifestations are reflected in the Biblical place-names bearing Baal as an element: Baal Peor (Dt 4:3), Baal Hazor (2Sa 13:23), Baal Gad (Jos 11:17), Baal Hermon (Jdg 3:3), Baal Shalishah (2Ki 4:42), Baal Tamar (Jdg 20:33).
2:13 *the Ashtoreths.* Refers to the deity Astarte, who was worshiped widely as the goddess of love and war. This deity was identified in Ebla as Ashtar and in Mesopotamia as Ishtar. Although in the Ugaritic mythological literature Anath usually functions as Baal's consort, Astarte also appears as his spouse, which agrees with the broader ancient Near Eastern world reflected in the OT. Like "the Baals" (see v. 11 and note), the present plural form refers to the local manifestations of the deity. Together these two gods formed a powerful force in ancient Near Eastern spirituality. Israel's abandonment of Yahweh may be attributable to an inability to conceive of Yahweh as the God of this land where Baal and Astarte ruled with apparent effectiveness. The newcomers had experienced Yahweh's power in Egypt, at Mount Sinai, and in the wilderness, but once they crossed the Jordan, they found it easier to change allegiance to the gods of this land than to transfer to Yahweh the fertility functions of a territorial god.
2:14 – 20 *In his anger against Israel ... the LORD was very angry with Israel.* The notion of divine anger with the people over whom the deity served as patron/matron is common in the ancient Near East. Where these non-Israelite accounts give reasons for the divine fury, the cause tends to be the people's failure to satisfy the god with proper rituals. Here, the cause is the Israelites' failure to be devoted exclusively to Yahweh. While Yahweh's intolerance of the worship of other deities was unique within the ancient Near Eastern context, his expression of anger would have been familiar to many outside Israel. In the ancient world, divine fury was typically expressed by the deity leaving the city and allowing enemy forces to move in and wreak havoc on the place.
2:16 *judges.* Unlike the English expression "judge," which is usually associated with judicial activity, the meaning of the title in the book of Judges is established in 2:16 – 19: each judge functioned as a deliverer/liberator, who rescued the Israelites from outside oppressors. Although the verb "judge" is applied to several individuals in the book, none of these persons is portrayed as exercising judicial function. The expression should therefore be interpreted more broadly to mean govern, administer, exercise leadership — either in internal or external affairs. These "judges" should be perceived like all other Canaanite princes or petty chieftains of the presettlement time.
2:18 *judge.* See note on v. 16.

21 I will no longer drive out[t] before them
any of the nations Joshua left when he
died. 22 I will use them to test[u] Israel and
see whether they will keep the way of the
LORD and walk in it as their ancestors did."
23 The LORD had allowed those nations to
remain; he did not drive them out at once
by giving them into the hands of Joshua.

3 These are the nations the LORD left to
test[v] all those Israelites who had not
experienced any of the wars in Canaan
2 (he did this only to teach warfare to the
descendants of the Israelites who had not
had previous battle experience): 3 the five[w]
rulers of the Philistines, all the Canaanites,
the Sidonians, and the Hivites living in
the Lebanon mountains from Mount Baal
Hermon to Lebo Hamath. 4 They were left
to test[x] the Israelites to see whether they
would obey the LORD's commands, which
he had given their ancestors through Moses.
5 The Israelites lived[y] among the Canaanites, Hittites, Amorites, Perizzites, Hivites
and Jebusites. 6 They took their daughters
in marriage and gave their own daughters
to their sons, and served their gods.[z]

Othniel

7 The Israelites did evil in the eyes of the
LORD; they forgot the LORD[a] their God and
served the Baals and the Asherahs.[b] 8 The
anger of the LORD burned against Israel so
that he sold[c] them into the hands of Cushan-Rishathaim king of Aram Naharaim,[a]

2:21 [t] Jos 23:13 **2:22** [u] Dt 8:2, 16; Jdg 3:1,14 **3:1** [v] Jdg 2:21-22 **3:3** [w] Jos 13:3 **3:4** [x] Dt 8:2; Jdg 2:22 **3:5** [y] Ps 106:35 **3:6** [z] Ex 34:16; Dt 7:3-4 **3:7** [a] Dt 4:9 [b] Ex 34:13; Jdg 2:11,13 **3:8** [c] Jdg 2:14

[a] *8* That is, Northwest Mesopotamia

2:22 *to test Israel.* In most instances in the OT, the test is performed either for quality control (a superior's check on the loyalty of the inferior) or quality enhancement (a superior's effort to improve the loyalty of the inferior). According to v. 20, the nations do not represent the actual test; in accordance with Ex 19:5, the test consists in whether or not the Israelites will listen to Yahweh's voice.

3:3 *Philistines.* The Hebrew *pelishtim* identifies one of several groups of Sea Peoples who swept into Palestine from Anatolia and the Mediterranean in the twelfth and eleventh centuries BC, leaving in their wake a trail of ruins. Biblical tradition, which traces their origins to Crete, accords with the archaeological record, which suggests they came from the Aegean. However, how they arrived in Palestine is the subject of some debate—some arguing they came by sea, others that they came overland via Anatolia and down through Syria. It seems their original goal was to settle in Egypt, but Rameses III was able to defeat them in about 1190 BC. He settled the vanquished forces in the coastal towns of southern Canaan, but in the mid-twelfth century BC, the Philistines succeeded in driving out their Egyptian overlords and forming the Philistine Pentapolis, a federation of five major city-states: Ashdod, Ashkelon, Ekron, Gath, and Gaza. *Canaanites.* See the article "The Canaanites," p. 294. *Sidonians.* They do not figure in the stereotypical lists of Canaanite nations whom the Israelites will displace (e.g., Dt 7:1). Here the term functions generally for all the Phoenicians living along the Mediterranean coast north of the region occupied by the Philistines. *Hivites.* Some have associated them with the Hurrians (Horites) of Ge 36:2,20. Although Jos 9:7; 11:19 link the Gibeonites to the Hivites, our text seems to use the expression generally for the peoples occupying the regions north of the Sea of Galilee, in the Lebanon mountains, west of a line running "from Mount Baal Hermon to Lebo Hamath." *Lebo Hamath.* Some interpret this as "the Pass of Hamath," but it is more likely to be identified with a specific place, modern Lebweh, some 45 miles (72.5 kilometers) north of Damascus. The name appears as Lab'u in the Egyptian texts and Laba'û in Assyrian inscriptions. In later times Lebo Hamath constituted the northern border of Solomon's kingdom (1Ki 8:65), and of Jeroboam II's northern kingdom of Israel (2Ki 14:25).

3:7 *the Baals.* See note on 2:11. *the Asherahs.* Whereas in 2:13 the female counterpart to the Baals is identified as the Ashtoreths, here the text speaks of Asherahs. Since the Asherahs are known from other Biblical contexts to have been made of wood, and their demolition involved chopping them down, the KJV translated the term as "groves"—i.e., sacred trees. However, in the light of the Ugaritic evidence that has surfaced more recently, Asherah (also identified as Athirat) is now known to have been a prominent goddess in Canaanite mythology, the wife of the high god El and the mother of 70 gods. Her titles in the Ugaritic myths include "Lady Athirat of the Sea" and "Creatress of the Gods," which reflects her role as mother of the gods who are referred to elsewhere as "the seventy sons of Athirat." The seductive power of the Canaanite Asherah cult to the Israelites is attested by several Hebrew inscriptions, in the form of blessings, from the eighth century BC that speak of "Yahweh and his Asherah," the latter apparently being viewed as Yahweh's consort by those who wrote these words. Even with this new information, the mention of Asherah alongside Baal in our text (presumably as his consort) is surprising, especially since 2:13 had associated the Baals with the Ashtartes. Either the author confuses the two deities, or he recognizes both as consorts of Baal in this fertility religion.

3:8 *Cushan-Rishathaim king of Aram Naharaim.* The title of this man appears straightforward. Aram, rendered "Syria" in the Septuagint (the pre-Christian Greek translation of the OT), is the name given to the area populated primarily by Arameans, one of the most important ethnic groups in the late second and early first millennia BC. Their territory extended from northeast of the Sea of Galilee to the Taurus Mountains in the north and eastward beyond the Habur tributary of the upper Euphrates River. While his capital is not identified, the addition of Naharaim, "of the two rivers" (cf. English Mesopotamia, "between the rivers"), fixes his home somewhere near or east of the great bend of the Euphrates. During the fourteenth and thirteenth centuries BC, this region was politically subservient to the empire of the Hittites, serving as a buffer to the Assyrians to the east and the Egyptians to the south. Their influence is reflected in the first appearance of Aram as the name of a region in the fourteenth-century BC Egyptian inscription of Amenhotep III.

There is no consensus on who Cushan-Rishathaim might have been, though a variety of identifications have been proposed: a leader of the Kassites, who controlled Babylonia from 1600–1150 BC (see Ge 10:8); a Nubian (= Cush); an Asiatic usurper in Egypt, known in Egyptian sources as Arsu or Irsu; a Midianite chieftain (cf. Nu 12:1; Hab 3:7); a surviving chieftain of southern Judah. Josephus (*Antiquities* 5.180) proposes an identification with Chusarsathus, king of the Assyrians, which might

to whom the Israelites were subject for
eight years. 9But when they cried out[d] to
the LORD, he raised up for them a deliverer, Othniel[e] son of Kenaz, Caleb's younger
brother, who saved them. 10The Spirit of
the LORD came on him,[f] so that he became
Israel's judge[a] and went to war. The LORD
gave Cushan-Rishathaim king of Aram
into the hands of Othniel, who overpowered him. 11So the land had peace for forty
years, until Othniel son of Kenaz died.

Ehud

12Again the Israelites did evil in the eyes
of the LORD,[g] and because they did this
evil the LORD gave Eglon king of Moab[h]

3:9 [d] ver 15; Jdg 6:6,7; 10:10; Ps 106:44 [e] Jdg 1:13 **3:10** [f] Nu 11:25, 29; 24:2; Jdg 6:34; 11:29; 13:25; 14:6, 19; 1Sa 11:6 **3:12** [g] Jdg 2:11, 14 [h] 1Sa 12:9

[a] *10* Or *leader*

suggest Tiglath-Pileser I of Assyria (1114–1076 BC), but this is too late for Othniel. The name is similar to common Hurrian names (such as Kuzzari-rishti) and he is perhaps the leader of a displaced tribe seeking a new homeland. However, it seems best to see in Cushan-Rishathaim of Aram-Naharaim one of the Akhlamu Aramean adventurers who established a base of power in the Aramean heartland, claimed the title of "king," and embarked on a southward campaign of terror that eventually brought him into conflict with the newly arrived Israelites. In the end it is impossible to link Cushan-Rishathaim with any known historical figure.

3:10 *The LORD gave Cushan-Rishathaim ... into the hands of Othniel.* The attribution of Othniel's successes over such a formidable foe as Cushan-Rishathaim to Yahweh would have been understood by all ancient Near Easterners. It was universally acknowledged that rulers governed by the will of the gods and especially that the outcomes of battles depended ultimately on the intervention of the gods. The annals of Tiglath-Pileser I (1114–1076 BC), an Assyrian contemporary of the later deliverers, are laced with references to the involvement of Ashur, the patron divinity of Assyria. Centuries later, a Neo-Assyrian successor to Tiglath-Pileser, Shalmaneser III (854–824 BC) credited Ashur with his victory over a western alliance of kings that included Hadadezer of Damascus and Ahab the Israelite.

3:12 *Eglon king of Moab.* Moab designates the nation state that emerged on the plateau east and northeast of the Dead Sea in the late second millennium BC (see the article "Moab," p. 450). Ge 19:30–38 suggests the Moabites were relatives of the Israelites, having descended from an eponymous ancestor. Whether Eglon was the king of a highly developed sedentary population or the foremost ruler over a group of tribes, each led by an elder or sheikh, is not clear, though his present residence in Jericho shows his preference for the town over tents. Eglon's capital has not yet been discovered, nor has any other Moabite capital from the time of the judges.

THE PATTERN OF CHRONOLOGICAL NOTICES IN JUDGES

TEXT	OPPRESSOR	YEARS	PERIOD OF PEACE	YEARS	JUDGESHIP	YEARS	TOTAL YEARS
3:8	Cushan-Rishathaim	8					8
3:11			After Othniel (Judah)	40			40
3:14	Moab	18					18
3:30			After Ehud (Benjamin)	80			80
4:2	Jabin	20					20
5:31			After Barak (Naphtali)	40			40
6:1	Midianites	7					7
8:28			After/During Gideon (Manasseh)	40			40
9:22					Abimelek	3	3
10:2					Tola (Issachar)	23	23
10:3					Jair (Gilead)	22	22
10:8	Ammonites	18					18
12:7					Jephthah (Gilead)	6	6
12:9					Ibzan (Zebulun or Judah?)	7	7
12:11					Elon (Zebulun)	10	10
12:14					Abdon (Ephraim?)	8	8
13:1	Philistines	40					40
15:20					Samson (Dan)	20	20
16:31							—
Totals		111		200		99	410

power over Israel. 13Getting the Ammonites and Amalekites to join him, Eglon
came and attacked Israel, and they took
possession of the City of Palms.[a][i] 14The
Israelites were subject to Eglon king of
Moab for eighteen years.

15Again the Israelites cried out to the
LORD, and he gave them a deliverer[j] —
Ehud, a left-handed man, the son of Gera
the Benjamite. The Israelites sent him with
tribute to Eglon king of Moab. 16Now Ehud
had made a double-edged sword about a
cubit[b] long, which he strapped to his right
thigh under his clothing. 17He presented
the tribute to Eglon king of Moab, who
was a very fat man.[k] 18After Ehud had
presented the tribute, he sent on their way
those who had carried it. 19But on reaching the stone images near Gilgal he himself went back to Eglon and said, "Your
Majesty, I have a secret message for you."

The king said to his attendants, "Leave
us!" And they all left.

20Ehud then approached him while he
was sitting alone in the upper room of his
palace[c] and said, "I have a message from
God for you." As the king rose from his
seat, 21Ehud reached with his left hand,
drew the sword from his right thigh and
plunged it into the king's belly. 22Even the
handle sank in after the blade, and his
bowels discharged. Ehud did not pull the
sword out, and the fat closed in over it.
23Then Ehud went out to the porch[d]; he
shut the doors of the upper room behind
him and locked them.

24After he had gone, the servants came
and found the doors of the upper room
locked. They said, "He must be relieving
himself[l] in the inner room of the palace."
25They waited to the point of embarrassment,[m] but when he did not open the
doors of the room, they took a key and

3:13 [i] Jdg 1:16
3:15 [j] ver 9; Ps 78:34; 107:13
3:17 [k] ver 12
3:24 [l] 1Sa 24:3
3:25 [m] 2Ki 2:17; 8:11

[a] *13* That is, Jericho [b] *16* That is, about 18 inches or about 45 centimeters [c] *20* The meaning of the Hebrew for this word is uncertain; also in verse 24. [d] *23* The meaning of the Hebrew for this word is uncertain.

3:13 *Ammonites.* See notes on Ge 19:37–38; Dt 2:19. *Amalekites.* See note on Nu 13:29. *City of Palms.* Jericho (Dt 34:3; 2Ch 28:15; see note on Jos 2:1). Eglon seems to have selected Jericho as the base of his rule west of the Jordan, probably because of its desirable location at an oasis in the Jordan Valley, and because of its longstanding history as a strategic Canaanite settlement.

3:15 *Ehud, a left-handed man.* Ehud has traditionally been identified as "left-handed" in English translations, though the Septuagint (the pre-Christian Greek translation of the OT) identifies him as ambidextrous. The Biblical text, however, describes him as bound or limited with regard to the right hand—an unusual way to identify someone who is left-handed. Furthermore, in 20:16, a whole troop of Benjamites are described this way. Based on this evidence, it is preferable to interpret the phrase as describing warriors who have been trained to use either their left or right hand with equal effectiveness, just as highly skilled athletes today. Since he had training to teach him the use of his left hand, we deduce that he is not left-handed. This training allowed him an advantage in approaching Eglon.

3:16 *double-edged sword.* This weapon facilitated a straight stab rather than a hacking stroke, slicing cleanly into the king's flesh. Because the present text uses a term that occurs only here, it is not clear whether this dagger was a full cubit (about 18 inches or 45 centimeters) in length or a fraction thereof. Given the need for concealment, it is likely considerably shorter. Since most men were right-handed, the weapon would have been worn on the left side. Exploiting the benefits of his training, Ehud fastened the dagger under his garment to his right hip, where no one would suspect it.

3:17 *tribute.* In the OT this term is used most often of gift offerings made to God as an expression of gratitude and reverence, but it is also used for a voluntary gift of homage (Ge 32:14,19,21) or political friendship (2Ki 20:12). Here it applies to the tribute required of a vassal by a superior. This was an ancient and widespread practice in the ancient Near East. The present text does not describe the nature of the tribute. The most valued items would have been precious metals, silver and gold, but other items were often included.

3:19 *stone images.* The Hebrew word used here always denotes sculpted pagan images elsewhere in the OT, but this meaning is ill suited to the context. By itself the Hebrew word means simply "carved images [of stone]." Here it seems best to interpret these objects as steles either marking the boundary of the territory claimed by Eglon or as a monument to a battle by which Eglon achieved control over this region. Outside Israel such markers often contained the following features: (1) They were made of stone. (2) They were inscribed with text. (3) They often contained sculpted imagery that complemented the text. (4) The inscription closed with curses on any who would damage or deface the monument. (5) The monument was erected in a public place for public observation. (6) Royal monuments commemorated achievements emblematic of the king's role, such as military victories or building projects. (7) Royal monuments were treasured as trophies by victorious opponents. (8) After the death of the king the monuments served as his memorial. It is easy to imagine these were intended for some such function. *attendants.* This is a technical expression for courtiers of the king, those who have official access to his presence. These could include his ministers, advisors and body guards, charged with securing the safety of the monarch. Ancient Near Eastern kings seem to have employed such guards as a matter of course.

3:20 *upper room.* This Hebrew phrase is generally interpreted something like "cool roof chamber," based on the obvious meaning of the first word ("upper") and a derivation of the second from a root meaning "to be cold." In ancient Israel, and undoubtedly among Israel's neighbors, the houses of the wealthy often included upper stories to which the family would retreat for the sake of comfort. However, it has been rightly noted that not only is "cool" not an architectural term, but to escape the heat in the southern Jordan Valley near the Dead Sea one does not build upward but burrows down into the ground. Alternative interpretation of the Hebrew phrase used here suggests the plausible option that the present phrase means "the room over the beams," i.e., the raised throne room.

unlocked them. There they saw their lord
fallen to the floor, dead.
26 While they waited, Ehud got away. He
passed by the stone images and escaped to
Seirah. 27 When he arrived there, he blew
a trumpet[n] in the hill country of Ephraim, and the Israelites went down with him
from the hills, with him leading them.
28 "Follow me," he ordered, "for the LORD
has given Moab, your enemy, into your
hands.[o]" So they followed him down and
took possession of the fords of the Jordan[p]
that led to Moab; they allowed no one to
cross over. 29 At that time they struck down
about ten thousand Moabites, all vigorous
and strong; not one escaped. 30 That day
Moab was made subject to Israel, and the
land had peace[q] for eighty years.

3:27 [n] Jdg 6:34; 1Sa 13:3 **3:28** [o] Jdg 7:9, 15 [p] Jos 2:7; Jdg 7:24; 12:5 **3:30** [q] ver 11

3:31 [r] Jdg 5:6 [s] Jos 23:10 **4:1** [t] Jdg 2:19 **4:2** [u] Jos 11:1 [v] ver 13, 16; 1Sa 12:9; Ps 83:9 **4:3** [w] Jdg 1:19 [x] Ps 106:42

Shamgar

31 After Ehud came Shamgar son of
Anath,[r] who struck down six hundred[s]
Philistines with an oxgoad. He too saved
Israel.

Deborah

4 Again the Israelites did evil[t] in the eyes
of the LORD, now that Ehud was dead.
2 So the LORD sold them into the hands of
Jabin king of Canaan, who reigned in Hazor.[u] Sisera,[v] the commander of his army,
was based in Harosheth Haggoyim. 3 Because he had nine hundred chariots fitted
with iron[w] and had cruelly oppressed[x] the
Israelites for twenty years, they cried to
the LORD for help.
4 Now Deborah, a prophet, the wife of

3:27 *trumpet.* The ram's horn (*shofar*). See note on Jos 6:4.
3:28 *the fords of the Jordan.* Although the Jordan rift valley averages six miles (9.5 kilometers) wide and is 15 miles (24 kilometers) wide at Jericho, the river itself is modest in size. The Romans were the first to build bridges across the river. Until then, people had to wade across. Except in the rainy season there were many places where this was possible—which is probably why the narrator does not specify where the present fords are.
3:29 *ten thousand.* On the interpretation of seemingly inordinately high numbers in Judges, see note on 1:4.
3:31 *Shamgar son of Anath.* The name of this deliverer is a riddle. Since the Hebrew vocabulary (like that of most Semitic languages) is based on triliteral roots, the presence of four strong consonants (*sh-m-g-r*) suggests he was not an Israelite. The presence of analogous forms of the name in Nuzi texts suggests he may have been a Hurrian mercenary in Canaan. Equally puzzling is his characterization as "son of Anath." In the past, interpreters have assumed this meant that Shamgar was a resident of Beth Anath in Galilee. Now it seems more likely this is intended as a dedicatory expression: Shamgar was devoted to the service of Anath. What this means may be learned from extra-Biblical sources. In Canaanite mythology, Anath was at the same time the consort of Baal and Canaanite goddess of war. But the fame of Anath extended far beyond Palestine. At the beginning of the Nineteenth Dynasty (thirteenth century BC), she was accepted into the Egyptian pantheon, functioning particularly as the goddess of war and personal protectress of the pharaoh. But of special interest is an inscription from the Wadi Hammâmaât dated in the third year of Rameses IV (1166–60 BC), which reads: "*'prw* of the troop of 'An[ath] eight hundred men." Shamgar may have been one of these *'prw* (Apiru, see note on Ge 14:13), among whom were found a variety of ethnic elements, including Hurrians. As a member of an Apiru troop of mercenaries in Pharaoh's army named after the Canaanite goddess of war, and a man of valor, he bore the widely used military cognomen "ben Anath" ("son of Anath"). Since at first the Sea Peoples' base of land operations in Canaan was located in northern Lebanon, and the Song of Deborah (Jdg 5) associates Shamgar with problems in northern Israel, the latter's confrontation with the Philistines probably occurred in the north at the beginning of the twelfth century BC. As an officer under the command of the Egyptian pharaoh, Shamgar ben Anath was not intentionally serving Israelite interests, yet Yahweh still provided deliverance by his hand. It must be recalled that even the Israelite judges were not consciously trying to serve Yahweh, yet God used them nonetheless. *oxgoad.* This Hebrew word occurs only here in the OT, but in post-Biblical Hebrew the word identifies a guiding instrument, a pointer (in the Mishnah see *Sanhedrin* 10:28a). The present instrument, normally used to train and control livestock, was made of hard wood and probably tipped with metal.
4:2 *Jabin king of Canaan, who reigned in Hazor.* The person bearing the name Jabin here is not to be confused with the Jabin who ruled Hazor at least 30 or 40 years earlier, and who headed an alliance of Canaanite forces against Joshua in Jos 11:1–15. In the ancient Near East, royal names were commonly repeated and even took on the form of dynastic names (e.g., Rameses I–XI). The first part of the name has surfaced in a fragment of a royal letter found at Hazor from the eighteenth or seventeenth century BC addressed to Ibni (= Yabin/Jabin). From Egypt, the topographic list of Rameses II at Karnak includes the entry Qishon of Jabin. The present text identifies Jabin as "king of Canaan," suggesting he had recaptured for Hazor the dominant position among Canaanite cities that had not fallen into Israelite control. *Sisera.* Unknown as a Canaanite name. The name seems not to be Semitic, suggesting he may have been a Hittite or Hurrian mercenary like Shamgar in 3:31, or a member of the Sea Peoples. *Harosheth Haggoyim.* While prevailing opinion understands the first element in this name to mean "forested area," the fact that Sisera's forces included 900 chariots, which could be deployed only in coastal and alluvial plains (1:19), renders this interpretation problematic. A more logical solution relates the expression to an Akkadian cognate that means "cultivated land." Accordingly, Harosheth Haggoyim probably means "cultivated field of the Gentiles," an explanation that not only suits the fertile alluvial plain between Taanach and Megiddo, but also accords with the present linkage with chariots, the reference to the Canaanite chariot bases in the river plains in 1:19 and the location of the battle in 5:19.
4:3 *nine hundred chariots fitted with iron.* In view of the claim of Thutmose III in the fifteenth century BC to have captured 924 chariots at Megiddo, including the chariot of the ruler of Megiddo, which was decorated with gold, this reference is feasible. Whether the number is interpreted literally or as epic hyperbole, in the light of 1:19, this superior technology had rendered the Canaanites invincible to Israelite armies marching out in their own strength.
4:4 *a prophet, the wife.* This epithet brings Deborah's

JUDGES 3:23–25

Keys and Locks

"Ehud ... shut the doors of the upper room behind him and locked them [the doors]" (Jdg 3:23). "[The servants] took a key and unlocked them [the doors]" (Jdg 3:25). The logistics of Ehud's actions are difficult: how would Ehud escape the throne room if the door were locked from the inside? The answer lies in the nature of locks and keys in the ancient world. SS 5:4–6 provides a clue in noting that the character thrust his hand through the hole in the door and unlocked the bolt. If the door can be unlocked from the outside, it can also be locked from the outside.

In ancient Israel the doors of palaces, temples, granaries and domestic dwellings were locked with a wooden bolt and a tumbler lock mounted on the inside of the door. A wooden box containing loose pins was attached to the inside of the door above the wooden bolt, oarlock case, into which the pins drop when the bar is moved into the locked position. To unlock the door the key is inserted into a slot in the bolt until the matching teeth of the key push up the movable pins so that the sliding bolt can be drawn. When the key is withdrawn, the bolt can be secured by sliding it horizontally into a position in which the pins drop from the box into the slots of the bolt. To make the tumbler locks more difficult to pick, they were mounted on the inside of the door and reached by passing one's hand and key through a hole in the door.

Keys came in various sizes, from 10 to 20 inches (from 25 to 50 centimeters) long, with some so large they were carried on the shoulders (Isa 22:22). Some resembled large toothbrushes with handles bent near the end. Doors could be locked without the key simply by sliding the bolt in place and waiting for the pins to drop, but they could not be unlocked without the key.

In the present instance, after Ehud stabs Eglon he goes out through the door of the throne room and closes it behind him. Reaching his hand through the keyhole, he slides the bolt back into place. When he hears the pins drop, he turns around and flees

continued on next page

Lappidoth, was leading[a] Israel at that
time. 5She held court under the Palm of
Deborah between Ramah and Bethel[y] in
the hill country of Ephraim, and the Israelites went up to her to have their disputes decided. 6She sent for Barak son of
Abinoam[z] from Kedesh in Naphtali and
said to him, "The LORD, the God of Israel, commands you: 'Go, take with you
ten thousand men of Naphtali and Zebulun and lead them up to Mount Tabor. 7I
will lead Sisera, the commander of Jabin's
army, with his chariots and his troops to
the Kishon River[a] and give him into your
hands.'"

4:5 [y] Ge 35:8
4:6 [z] Heb 11:32
4:7 [a] Ps 83:9

[a] *4* Traditionally *judging*

profession and gender to the reader's attention. A prophet serves as a spokesperson for deity to the people. Not only was the institution of prophecy widespread in the ancient Near East, but Mesopotamian prophecy in particular involved an unusually large proportion of female prophets. In the patricentric world of the OT, few if any standing leadership offices were open to women. By contrast, there seems to have been no hesitation in Israel to engage women as prophets. This may be because in Israel the prophetic office had an ad hoc character. Whereas elsewhere, especially in the Neo-Assyrian courts, prophets tended to function as part of the courts of kings, in Israel they were engaged directly by Yahweh, and in monarchic times especially often worked in opposition to kings.

4:5 *held court.* This reading reflects too legal an interpretation of the Hebrew verb, which means simply "to sit." Deborah functions here as the agent through whom the people expect a divine word regarding their present crisis—a common role of prophets. Seated beneath the palm, the people come to her for a divine judgment on the crisis created by the Canaanites. The divine response is to call Barak to rescue the people.

4:6,10 *ten thousand men.* On this seemingly high number, see note on 1:4.

4:7 *lead Sisera ... to the Kishon River.* The flat plains would normally favor chariots but the overflowing river (5:20–21) would have muddied the battlefield and bogged down the chariots, neutralizing their advantage.

through the pillared portico. However, to enter the king's room his servants will need to retrieve the key to unlock the door — by which time Eglon is long dead. A number of obscure words combined with our inadequate understanding of the architectural design leave many unanswered questions about the logistics of this daring deed and escape. ◆

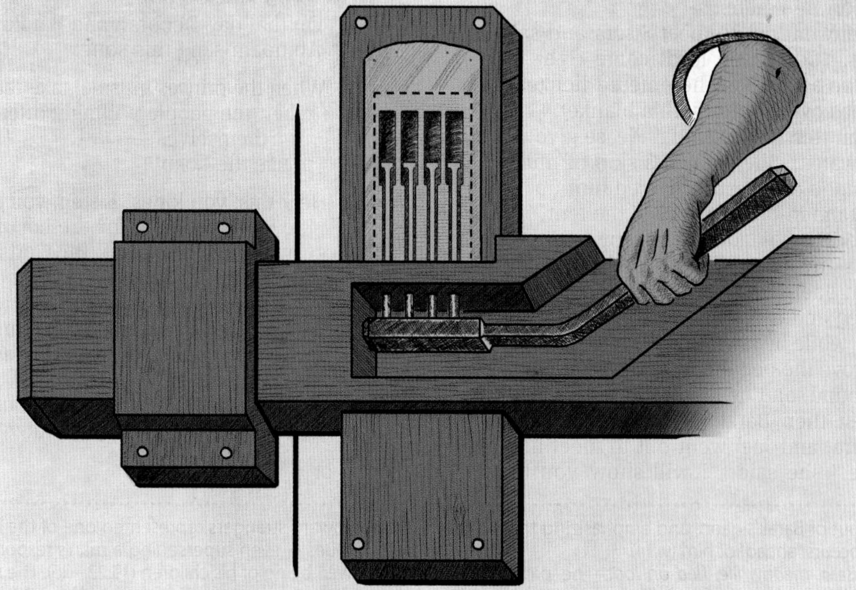

A tumbler (or "Egyptian") lock with slot and key in the bolt. This type of key is mentioned in Jdg 3:25.

8Barak said to her, "If you go with me,
I will go; but if you don't go with me, I
won't go."
9"Certainly I will go with you," said
Deborah. "But because of the course you
are taking, the honor will not be yours, for
the LORD will deliver Sisera into the hands
of a woman." So Deborah went with Barak to Kedesh.[b] 10There Barak summoned[c]
Zebulun and Naphtali, and ten thousand
men went up under his command. Deborah also went up with him.
11Now Heber the Kenite had left the other Kenites,[d] the descendants of Hobab,[e]
Moses' brother-in-law,[a] and pitched his
tent by the great tree in Zaanannim[f] near
Kedesh.
12When they told Sisera that Barak son
of Abinoam had gone up to Mount Tabor,
13Sisera summoned from Harosheth Haggoyim to the Kishon River all his men and
his nine hundred chariots fitted with iron.[g]
14Then Deborah said to Barak, "Go! This
is the day the LORD has given Sisera into
your hands. Has not the LORD gone ahead[h]
of you?" So Barak went down Mount Tabor, with ten thousand men following
him. 15At Barak's advance, the LORD routed[i] Sisera and all his chariots and army by

4:9 [b] ver 21; Jdg 2:14 **4:10** [c] ver 14; Jdg 5:15,18 **4:11** [d] Jdg 1:16 [e] Nu 10:29 [f] Jos 19:33 **4:13** [g] ver 3 **4:14** [h] Dt 9:3; 2Sa 5:24; Ps 68:7 **4:15** [i] Jos 10:10; Ps 83:9-10

[a] *11* Or *father-in-law*

4:15 *routed.* The Hebrew verb, which means "to bring into motion and confusion," recalls several other texts, most notably Yahweh's action against the Egyptians in Ex 14:24, in which natural phenomena are marshaled to effect the rout. The description of Yahweh's involvement is reminiscent of Assyrian accounts that speak of the awe-inspiring terror of Ashur going before the Assyrian king. Whereas the Assyrian accounts, cast in bombastic autobiographical style, are written intentionally to magnify the victorious human king, in this Biblical account the role of Barak is deliberately diminished, not only by retaining Yahweh as the subject of the verb, but also by taking the

the sword, and Sisera got down from his
chariot and fled on foot.
16Barak pursued the chariots and army
as far as Harosheth Haggoyim, and all Sisera's troops fell by the sword; not a man
was left.[j] 17Sisera, meanwhile, fled on foot
to the tent of Jael, the wife of Heber the
Kenite, because there was an alliance between Jabin king of Hazor and the family
of Heber the Kenite.
18Jael went out to meet Sisera and said
to him, "Come, my lord, come right in.
Don't be afraid." So he entered her tent,
and she covered him with a blanket.
19"I'm thirsty," he said. "Please give me
some water." She opened a skin of milk,[k]
gave him a drink, and covered him up.
20"Stand in the doorway of the tent," he
told her. "If someone comes by and asks
you, 'Is anyone in there?' say 'No.'"
21But Jael, Heber's wife, picked up a
tent peg and a hammer and went quietly
to him while he lay fast asleep, exhausted.
She drove the peg through his temple into
the ground, and he died.[l]
22Just then Barak came by in pursuit
of Sisera, and Jael went out to meet him.
"Come," she said, "I will show you the
man you're looking for." So he went in
with her, and there lay Sisera with the tent
peg through his temple—dead.
23On that day God subdued[m] Jabin king
of Canaan before the Israelites. 24And the
hand of the Israelites pressed harder and
harder against Jabin king of Canaan until
they destroyed him.

4:16 [j] Ps 83:9
4:19 [k] Jdg 5:25
4:21 [l] Jdg 5:26
4:23 [m] Ne 9:24; Ps 18:47
5:1 [n] Ex 15:1
5:2 [o] 2Ch 17:16; Ps 110:3 [p] ver 9
5:3 [q] Ps 27:6
5:4 [r] Dt 33:2 [s] Ps 68:8

The Song of Deborah

5 On that day Deborah and Barak son of
Abinoam sang this song:[n]

2"When the princes in Israel take the lead,
when the people willingly offer[o]
themselves—
praise the LORD![p]

3"Hear this, you kings! Listen, you rulers!
I, even I, will sing to[a] the LORD;
I will praise the LORD, the God of
Israel, in song.[q]

4"When you, LORD, went out from Seir,[r]
when you marched from the land of
Edom,
the earth shook, the heavens poured,
the clouds poured down water.[s]

[a] 3 Or *of*

sword out of Barak's hand, and emphasizing that all the action occurs "ahead" of him (v. 14).

4:17 *Sisera, meanwhile, fled on foot.* The picture of a defeated general fleeing for his life from the scene of battle is found in many Assyrian annals. The annals of Ashurnasirpal II recount how Nūr-Adad, the rebel sheikh of the land of Dagara, "to save his life, climbed up a rugged mountain," in the face of his overwhelming defeat by the Assyrians. An even more colorful account involves Ursā, a prince of Urartu, who, terrorized by the might of Adad and defeated by Sargon II (721–705 BC), fled for his life. Recognizing that with Jabin's main forces decimated no protection was to be found in the capital (cf. v. 23), Sisera continued running northward until he came to the tent of Heber the Kenite, a recognized ally of Jabin. *tent of Jael.* In ancient Israel, households often consisted of several branches of an extended family, hence the designation for "family" means "clan." Accordingly, the homes of a family would often be more like a compound, consisting of several houses. Since Heber is a Kenite (see note on 1:16), making the transition from a nomadic to a sedentary lifestyle, it is not surprising to read that his household lives in tents (vv. 11,17–18,20–22), and since his clan represents a significant political force in this context, it is not surprising to read that his compound in Zaanannim (v. 11) consisted of more than one tent. Apparently Jael had her own tent. It is unclear whether Heber had other wives who would have had their own tents, but presumably as the head of this household he would have had his own.

4:18–21 In her actions Jael violates a series of fundamental social norms: (1) In offering hospitality to Sisera she usurps her husband's exclusive right as a male to offer hospitality to a male. (2) In killing Sisera she violates the covenant between Heber and Sisera's superior. (3) In killing Sisera, who had sought hospitality and protection in her house, she violates the fundamental rights of guests. As in the Middle East today, in the ancient Near East hospitality toward strangers represented one of the highest social values—even superseding a man's responsibility for the well-being of his children (19:22–26). The story of Jael in these verses represents one of the most blatant violations of this value in the literature of the ancient world; nonetheless, God used such actions to accomplish his objectives.

5:4 *When you, LORD, went out from Seir, when you marched from the land of Edom.* The song portrays Yahweh as a divine warrior marching forth from Seir/Edom to the aid of his people. In terms reminiscent of his descent on Mount Sinai in Ex 19, the song celebrates the arrival of Yahweh. Scholars have long been intrigued by the association of Yahweh, not only with Sinai (v. 5), but also with Seir/Edom in this text, as well as in several other ancient and/or archaizing poems, such as Dt 33:2, in which Yahweh is described as coming from Sinai/Seir/Mount Paran; Hab 3:3, in which God comes from Teman/Mount Paran. In Ps 78:40 God encounters Israel in the wasteland. This portrayal of Yaweh marching forth from the south (Sinai/Seir/Edom) represents a deliberate polemic against the perspectives cherished by the kings whom the poet has summoned to listen (v. 3)—Canaanites, whose god Baal resided in the north, on Mount Zaphon. Yahweh had triumphed over Baal. *Seir.* Means "hairy." It functions as a personal name in Ge 36:20–21; 1Ch 1:38, identifying the ancestor of an ethnic group associated with the Horites, who lived in the hill country of Seir (Ge 14:6). But elsewhere Seir is always a geographic designation for the mountainous region south of the Dead Sea occupied by the Edomites. Most agree that these mountains are to be located to the east of the Arabah, south of Moab. However, perhaps because of the encroachment of the Seir-based Edomites into the territory adjoining Judah, sometimes the name is applied to the region west of the Arabah. *Edom.* See note on Ge 36:9.

[5]The mountains quaked[t] before the
LORD, the One of Sinai,
before the LORD, the God of Israel.

[6]"In the days of Shamgar son of
Anath,[u]
in the days of Jael,[v] the highways[w]
were abandoned;
travelers took to winding paths.
[7]Villagers in Israel would not fight;
they held back until I, Deborah,
arose,
until I arose, a mother in Israel.
[8]God chose new leaders[x]
when war came to the city gates,
but not a shield or spear was seen
among forty thousand in Israel.
[9]My heart is with Israel's princes,
with the willing volunteers[y] among
the people.
Praise the LORD!

[10]"You who ride on white donkeys,[z]
sitting on your saddle blankets,
and you who walk along the road,
consider [11]the voice of the singers[a] at
the watering places.
They recite the victories[a] of the
LORD,
the victories of his villagers in Israel.

"Then the people of the LORD
went down to the city gates.[b]
[12]'Wake up,[c] wake up, Deborah!
Wake up, wake up, break out in song!
Arise, Barak!
Take captive your captives,[d] son of
Abinoam.'
[13]"The remnant of the nobles came
down;
the people of the LORD came down to
me against the mighty.
[14]Some came from Ephraim, whose roots
were in Amalek;[e]
Benjamin was with the people who
followed you.
From Makir captains came down,
from Zebulun those who bear a
commander's[a] staff.
[15]The princes of Issachar were with
Deborah;[f]

5:5 [t] Ex 19:18; Ps 68:8; 97:5; Isa 64:3 **5:6** [u] Jdg 3:31 [v] Jdg 4:17 [w] Isa 33:8 **5:8** [x] Dt 32:17 **5:9** [y] ver 2 **5:10** [z] Jdg 10:4; 12:14 **5:11** [a] 1Sa 12:7; Mic 6:5 [b] ver 8 **5:12** [c] Ps 57:8 [d] Ps 68:18; Eph 4:8 **5:14** [e] Jdg 3:13 **5:15** [f] Jdg 4:10

[a] *11,14* The meaning of the Hebrew for this word is uncertain.

5:5 *the One of Sinai.* This epithet occurs only here and in the derivative Ps 68:8, and may be considered an archaic title of Yahweh. Yahweh's status is reinforced by the storm imagery, which the Canaanite religion generally associates with Baal as the "rider of the clouds." The poet draws from this well-known imagery to describe Yahweh as riding the clouds to the aid of his people. At the same time, the storm imagery anticipates the cosmic aspects of the victory later in the poem (vv. 19–21).
5:6 *highways were abandoned.* In this lawless period, roads were dangerous, and travelers were subject to attack by bandits. Farmers and merchants traveled by hillside tracks instead. The roads of the ancient Near East were for the most part unpaved (except for a few roads in the Late Assyrian period). Although unpaved, those which were intended for wheeled transport (called "wagon roads" in the Nuzi tablets) had to be staked out, leveled and consistently maintained. However, very few texts describe the construction and maintenance of these roads. Roads for heavy transport were somewhat rare, and were primarily located along the trade routes. Thus, a vassal king complained to the king of Mari that he had to arrive at the Syrian capital by a roundabout route along a major highway. Assyrian kings rarely boasted of their road constructions, as it appeared to be the duty of the local populations.
5:7 *Villagers.* The Hebrew word used here functions as a collective designation for residents of rural unwalled settlements, in contrast to describing "towns," which were by definition fortified with protective walls. Unlike the walled Canaanite towns of the valleys and plains, Israelite villages in the hill country were unfortified and vulnerable to outside harassment (cf. Eze 38:11). Instead, defense was based on their elevated hilltop locations and the arrangement of houses on the village perimeters. This absence of true fortifications undoubtedly is the result of the economic and military superiority of the Canaanites living in the fertile valleys, but it may also be a leftover effect of Merneptah's campaign in Palestine in 1207 BC.
5:8 *gates.* Since the Israelites lived in unwalled villages, this probably refers to the fortified Canaanite towns in the valleys (see previous note). *not a shield or spear.* Israel's lack of military technology is also noted by 1Sa 13:19–22. Either they were forced to turn in their weapons to their Philistine and Canaanite overlords, or they lacked the knowledge to make them.
5:9 *willing volunteers.* Highlights the contrast between the way this army was raised and the typical ancient Near Eastern pattern of conscripted and professional armies, reflected in Samuel's warning to the elders of Israel in 1Sa 8:11–12, where military forces consisted largely of conscripts forced into military duty.
5:10 *white donkeys.* While donkeys were used primarily as pack and draft animals, they were also ridden by the upper classes. The NIV's "white" translates a Hebrew word that occurs only here in the OT, meaning "tawny," i.e., light colored animals, brownish orange to light brown. Because female donkeys of this color would have been rare, as symbols of status the rich preferred them over the generic gray animals. Among the Canaanites the economically powerful advertised their social standing further by dressing the donkeys with luxurious "saddle blankets." In a time of trouble for Israel, Canaanite merchants rode up and down the public roads in confidence, on their equivalents to luxury limousines.
5:11,13 *people of the LORD.* Occurs only here in Judges, highlighting the notion that it is as the people of their divine patron that the Israelites have volunteered for military service. Many of the patron deities around Israel were perceived either as local manifestations or functional territorial deities. Accordingly the Baals were viewed as manifestations of the storm-god, and Marduk was viewed primarily as the god of the city Babylon. These divine patrons related to specific people secondarily as a consequence of their being in his territory. In Israel's case, Yahweh's relationship was primarily with his covenant people and secondarily with the land.

FIVE CITIES OF THE PHILISTINES

Gaza, Ashkelon, Ashdod, Ekron and Gath comprise a list of familiar Biblical names. Each of these cities was a commercial emporium with important connections both north (as far as Mesopotamia) and south (as far as Egypt) by way of the coastal highway that served as one of the major highways of the ancient world. Also the ships of Phoenicia, Cyprus, Crete and the Aegean called at Philistia's seaports. Among these seaports was a place today called Tel Qasile on the Yarkon River (the "Kanah Ravine" of Jos 16:8; 17:9) just north of modern Tel Aviv. A Philistine temple has been found at Tel Qasile.

The Philistine plain itself was an arid, loam-covered lowland between the Mediterranean Sea and the foothills of the Judahite plateau on the east. To the south lay a stretch of undulating sand dunes adjacent to the sea. No area in Biblical history was more frequently contested than the western foothills, lying on the border between Judah and Philistia. Originally a part of Judah's tribal allotment, the coastal area was never totally wrested away from the Philistines. Beth Shemesh, Timnah, Azekah and Ziklag were among the towns coveted by both Israelites and Philistines, and they figure in the stories of Samson, Goliath and David. The area to the north of Philistia, the plain of Sharon, was also contested at various periods. During Saul's reign the Philistines even held Beth Shan and the Valley of Jezreel. Later, from about the time of Baasha on, a long border war was conducted by the Israelites at Gibbethon.

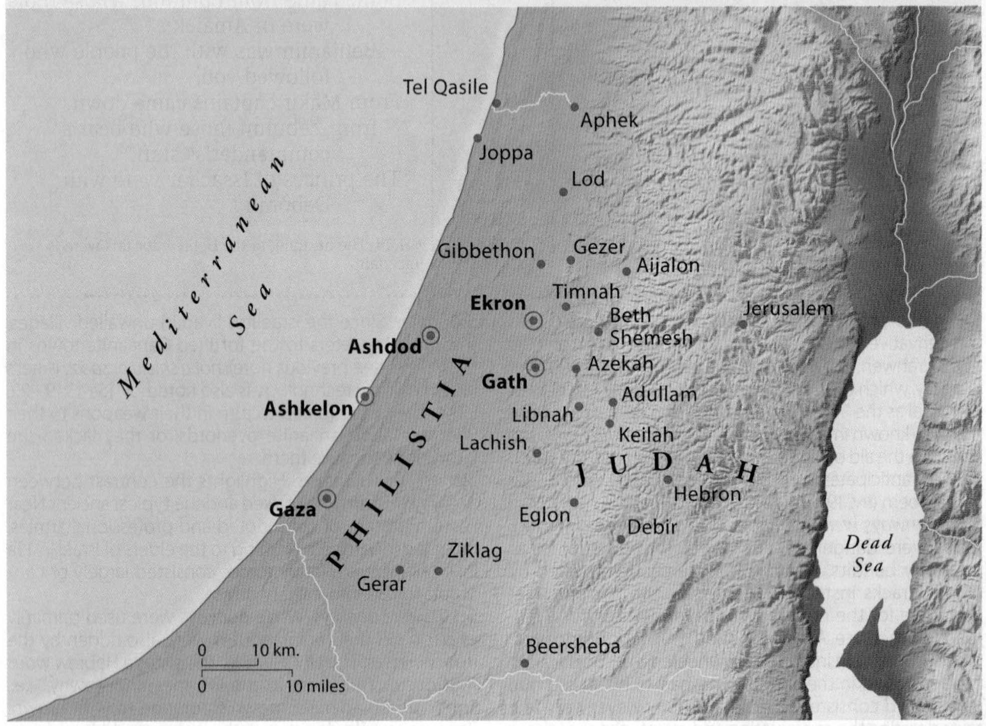

yes, Issachar was with Barak,
sent under his command into the valley.
In the districts of Reuben
there was much searching of heart.
16 Why did you stay among the sheep pens[a]
to hear the whistling for the flocks?[g]
In the districts of Reuben
there was much searching of heart.
17 Gilead stayed beyond the Jordan.
And Dan, why did he linger by the ships?
Asher remained on the coast[h]
and stayed in his coves.

5:16 [g] Nu 32:1
5:17 [h] Jos 19:29

[a] 16 Or *the campfires*; or *the saddlebags*

5:16 *whistling.* Occurs elsewhere only in Jer 18:16, where it speaks of derisive hissing ("object of ... scorn"). In Da 3:5,10,15 an Aramaic word from the same root refers to a "pipe" used in Nebuchadnezzar's orchestra. The instrument in question here was probably a flute of some type made of a reed, or the bone of a bird or goat.
5:17 *why did he linger by the ships?* According to the song the Danites were too busy in the shipping industry—presumably as clients of the Phoenicians or perhaps the Sea Peoples. The association of Dan with the northern tribe of Asher suggests that the battle with the Canaanites occurred later than the events described in chs. 17–18, and that the Danites had already arrived in the Huleh valley north of the Sea of Galilee. When they took over the territory around Laish they also gained control of the east-west trade from Banias along the Litani River to

18 The people of Zebulun risked their
very lives;
so did Naphtali on the terraced
fields.[i]
19 "Kings came[j], they fought,
the kings of Canaan fought.
At Taanach, by the waters of Megiddo,[k]
they took no plunder of silver.[l]
20 From the heavens[m] the stars fought,
from their courses they fought
against Sisera.
21 The river Kishon[n] swept them away,
the age-old river, the river Kishon.
March on, my soul; be strong!
22 Then thundered the horses' hooves—
galloping, galloping go his mighty
steeds.
23 'Curse Meroz,' said the angel of the
LORD.
'Curse its people bitterly,
because they did not come to help the
LORD,
to help the LORD against the mighty.'

24 "Most blessed of women be Jael,[o]
the wife of Heber the Kenite,
most blessed of tent-dwelling
women.
25 He asked for water, and she gave him
milk;[p]
in a bowl fit for nobles she brought
him curdled milk.
26 Her hand reached for the tent peg,
her right hand for the workman's
hammer.
She struck Sisera, she crushed his
head,
she shattered and pierced his temple.[q]
27 At her feet he sank,
he fell; there he lay.
At her feet he sank, he fell;
where he sank, there he fell—dead.

28 "Through the window peered Sisera's
mother;
behind the lattice she cried out,[r]
'Why is his chariot so long in coming?
Why is the clatter of his chariots
delayed?'
29 The wisest of her ladies answer her;
indeed, she keeps saying to herself,
30 'Are they not finding and dividing the
spoils:[s]
a woman or two for each man,
colorful garments as plunder for Sisera,
colorful garments embroidered,
highly embroidered garments for my
neck—
all this as plunder?'

31 "So may all your enemies perish, LORD!
But may all who love you be like the
sun[t]
when it rises in its strength."
Then the land had peace[u] forty years.

Gideon

6 The Israelites did evil in the eyes of
the LORD,[v] and for seven years he gave
them into the hands of the Midianites.[w]
2 Because the power of Midian was so oppressive,[x] the Israelites prepared shelters
for themselves in mountain clefts, caves
and strongholds.[y] 3 Whenever the Israelites
planted their crops, the Midianites, Amalekites[z] and other eastern peoples invaded

5:18 [i] Jdg 4:6, 10 **5:19** [j] Jos 11:5; Jdg 4:13 [k] Jdg 1:27 [l] ver 30 **5:20** [m] Jos 10:11 **5:21** [n] Jdg 4:7 **5:24** [o] Jdg 4:17 **5:25** [p] Jdg 4:19 **5:26** [q] Jdg 4:21

5:28 [r] Pr 7:6 **5:30** [s] Ex 15:9; 1Sa 30:24 **5:31** [t] 2Sa 23:4; Ps 19:4; 89:36 [u] Jdg 3:11 **6:1** [v] Jdg 2:11 [w] Nu 25:15-18; 31:1-3 **6:2** [x] 1Sa 13:6; Isa 8:21 [y] Heb 11:38 **6:3** [z] Jdg 3:13

Tyre. Those who gained control of the trade route inevitably came into contact with Phoenician merchants, and some may even have taken positions on board their ships.
5:20 *from their courses.* While most interpret this to mean that the stars functioned like an army, each in its place, it is preferable to see here the heavenly bodies leaving their normal orbits to fight against Israel's enemy. In this imagery, Deborah draws on a common ancient Near Eastern mythological motif, according to which the gods intervene on their devotees' behalf by engaging the heavenly hosts (see next note).
5:21 *The river Kishon swept them away.* The sudden flooding of the Kishon, and the crippling of Sisera's chariotry echo what had happened to Pharaoh's armies at the Red (Reed) Sea (Ex 15:4). This association of the stars fighting from heaven (v. 20) and the flooding of the Kishon seems odd to the modern reader, but both may be understood as evidences of the arrival of Yahweh (cf. vv. 4–5), who usurps the signs of theophanic advent that Canaanites had associated with Baal. Indeed in some Ugaritic texts the stars are declared to be the source of rain.
5:23 *Meroz.* Mentioned only here in the OT. Though it cannot be located, it must have been within a triangle whose apexes are marked by Mount Tabor on the east, where Barak assembled his troops (4:6,12,14), the Kishon River in the west, and Megiddo or Taanach in the south, perhaps near Sarid. A closer identification is not possible. *angel of the LORD.* See note on 2:1.
5:30 *dividing the spoils.* Although ancient Near Easterners justified warfare as having been commanded by the gods or as having served the king's/nation's honor, there was always plunder to be gained—both by the people and the conquering gods. The items Deborah lists represent the highest prizes of war: women and luxury garments. *colorful garments ... highly embroidered garments.* In addition to the colorful dyes used, the luxury clothes were also decorated with fine needlework, embroidered with geometric patterns and images. Such garments were considered luxuries worn by priests (Ex 28:15–20) and royalty (Ps 45:14; Eze 16:10). Eze 27:7,16 single out Egypt and Edom as producers of embroidered goods. The needles used in embroidery would have been made of bronze or bone or ivory.
6:1 *Midianites.* Known by name only from Biblical texts, which portray them as a seminomadic Bedouin people of the Sinai peninsula and western Arabia who relied on the camel for transportation (cf. v. 5). The archaeological site of Qurayya has yielded evidence of walls and a citadel, and distinctive pottery, known as "Qurayya ware," or "Midianite ware." This pottery has been dated to the thirteenth and twelfth centuries BC, which fits the context of Jdg 6–8.
6:3 *Amalekites.* See note on Nu 13:29. *eastern peoples.* Lit.

the country. 4 They camped on the land
and ruined the crops[a] all the way to Gaza
and did not spare a living thing for Israel, neither sheep nor cattle nor donkeys.
5 They came up with their livestock and
their tents like swarms of locusts.[b] It was
impossible to count them or their camels;[c]
they invaded the land to ravage it. 6 Midian so impoverished the Israelites that they
cried out[d] to the LORD for help.

7 When the Israelites cried out to the
LORD because of Midian, 8 he sent them a
prophet, who said, "This is what the LORD,
the God of Israel, says: I brought you up
out of Egypt,[e] out of the land of slavery.
9 I rescued you from the hand of the Egyptians. And I delivered you from the hand
of all your oppressors; I drove them out
before you and gave you their land.[f] 10 I
said to you, 'I am the LORD your God; do
not worship[g] the gods of the Amorites,[h]
in whose land you live.' But you have not
listened to me."

11 The angel of the LORD[i] came and sat
down under the oak in Ophrah that belonged to Joash the Abiezrite,[j] where his
son Gideon[k] was threshing wheat in a
winepress to keep it from the Midianites.
12 When the angel of the LORD appeared to
Gideon, he said, "The LORD is with you,[l]
mighty warrior."

13 "Pardon me, my lord," Gideon replied,
"but if the LORD is with us, why has all
this happened to us? Where are all his
wonders that our ancestors told[m] us about
when they said, 'Did not the LORD bring
us up out of Egypt?' But now the LORD has
abandoned[n] us and given us into the hand
of Midian."

14 The LORD turned to him and said, "Go
in the strength you have[o] and save Israel
out of Midian's hand. Am I not sending
you?"

15 "Pardon me, my lord," Gideon replied,
"but how can I save Israel? My clan is the
weakest in Manasseh, and I am the least
in my family.[p]"

16 The LORD answered, "I will be with
you[q], and you will strike down all the
Midianites, leaving none alive."

17 Gideon replied, "If now I have found
favor in your eyes, give me a sign[r] that it
is really you talking to me. 18 Please do not
go away until I come back and bring my
offering and set it before you."

And the LORD said, "I will wait until you
return."

19 Gideon went inside, prepared a young
goat, and from an ephah[a] of flour he made
bread without yeast. Putting the meat in a

6:4 [a] Lev 26:16; Dt 28:30,51 **6:5** [b] Jdg 7:12 [c] Jdg 8:10 **6:6** [d] Jdg 3:9 **6:8** [e] Jdg 2:1 **6:9** [f] Ps 44:2 **6:10** [g] 2Ki 17:35 [h] Jer 10:2 **6:11** [i] Ge 16:7 [j] Jos 17:2 [k] Heb 11:32 **6:12** [l] Jos 1:5; Jdg 13:3; Lk 1:11,28

6:13 [m] Ps 44:1 [n] 2Ch 15:2 **6:14** [o] Heb 11:34 **6:15** [p] Ex 3:11; 1Sa 9:21 **6:16** [q] Ex 3:12; Jos 1:5 **6:17** [r] ver 36-37; Ge 24:14; Isa 38:7-8

[a] *19* That is, probably about 36 pounds or about 16 kilograms

"sons of the east," a vague label used by westerners to denote the nomadic groups that migrated about the Arabian desert, often raiding the settled communities of the Transjordan and, as opportunity provided, of Cisjordan.

6:5 *locusts.* This undoubtedly refers to *schistocerca gregaria*, a species of desert locust that is normally a solitary insect, but in certain conditions, such as overcrowding, undergoes morphological and behavioral changes, resulting in migratory swarms capable of devastating regions on an international scale. The swarm of locusts that invaded Somaliland in AD 1957 is estimated to have numbered 16 trillion and to have weighed 50,000 tons (45,350 metric tons). Since each insect eats its own weight in green food every day, the devastation a swarm of locusts can cause is almost unimaginable. *camels.* Partially domesticated as early as the third millennium BC; by the middle of the second millennium BC they were quite widely used as pack animals in southern Arabia. In the present context the Midianites appear not as caravanners, but as camel-riding warriors, a practice not yet documented archaeologically, who may have been driven by the need to supplement the (inadequate) foodstuffs being produced in their own territory. In any case, the camels served as pack animals to carry the loot collected in the Midianites' forays into Israelite and Canaanite territory.

6:11 *angel of the LORD.* See note on 2:1. *threshing wheat.* See note on Ru 3:2. Gideon resorts to beating the grain under an oak in a sheltered vat used for pressing grapes. *winepress.* Generally involved two excavated depressions in the rock, one above the other. The grapes would be gathered and trampled in the upper, while a conduit would drain the juices to the lower. The present location might have been satisfactory for beating out the grain, but separating the grain from the chaff in these instances would have been more difficult. Either Gideon would have had to wait for a very windy day, or the grain and chaff mixture would have to be carried quickly to an exposed area, tossed in the air, and the grain quickly whisked away.

6:12 *mighty warrior.* See note on Ru 2:1.

6:13 *if the LORD is with us, why has all this happened to us?* The theological world of ancient Near Easterners was complex, and people often recognized divinities to be operative at four levels: cosmic, national/state, clan, and ancestral (deceased ancestors elevated to semi-divine status). While Yahweh had demonstrated his cosmic sovereignty through the wonders he had performed in Egypt (Dt 4:32–40), and his role as Israel's national God by rescuing them from Egypt and entering into relationship with them at Sinai (cf. Jdg 6:8–10), during the period of the judges the Israelites apparently had difficulty conceiving of him as a personal and family deity. Consequently, they turned to local manifestations of the gods of the Canaanites to take care of them at this level. These are the gods on whom one depended for the fertility of livestock, of the soil and of their own wives.

6:15 *weakest in Manasseh ... least in my family.* Gideon is claiming lack of status and authority. He cannot call out soldiers from his own clan or family, much less other tribes. Command is the prerogative of status, and he has none.

6:16 *I will.* Typical of ancient Near Eastern official messenger style, speaking on behalf of Yahweh, the divine envoy uses the first person (see note on Ex 3:2).

6:18 *offering.* The Hebrew word means "gift" and is not necessarily indicative of a sacrifice. The kid is prepared and presented as meat, not brought live and slaughtered, which suggests the context of a meal.

6:19 *ephah of flour.* About 36 pounds (16 kilograms), which points either to a single huge loaf or up to a dozen

basket and its broth in a pot, he brought
them out and offered them to him under
the oak.[s]
20The angel of God said to him, "Take
the meat and the unleavened bread, place
them on this rock,[t] and pour out the
broth." And Gideon did so. 21Then the angel of the LORD touched the meat and the
unleavened bread[u] with the tip of the staff
that was in his hand. Fire flared from the
rock, consuming the meat and the bread.
And the angel of the LORD disappeared.
22When Gideon realized[v] that it was the
angel of the LORD, he exclaimed, "Alas,
Sovereign LORD! I have seen the angel of
the LORD face to face!"[w]
23But the LORD said to him, "Peace! Do
not be afraid.[x] You are not going to die."
24So Gideon built an altar to the LORD
there and called[y] it The LORD Is Peace. To
this day it stands in Ophrah[z] of the Abiezrites.
25That same night the LORD said to him,
"Take the second bull from your father's
herd, the one seven years old.[a] Tear down
your father's altar to Baal and cut down
the Asherah pole[b][a] beside it. 26Then build a
proper kind of[c] altar to the LORD your God
on the top of this height. Using the wood
of the Asherah pole that you cut down, offer the second[d] bull as a burnt offering."
27So Gideon took ten of his servants and
did as the LORD told him. But because he
was afraid of his family and the townspeople, he did it at night rather than in
the daytime.
28In the morning when the people of the
town got up, there was Baal's altar,[b] demolished, with the Asherah pole beside it
cut down and the second bull sacrificed
on the newly built altar!
29They asked each other, "Who did
this?"
When they carefully investigated, they
were told, "Gideon son of Joash did it."
30The people of the town demanded of
Joash, "Bring out your son. He must die,
because he has broken down Baal's altar
and cut down the Asherah pole beside it."
31But Joash replied to the hostile crowd
around him, "Are you going to plead Baal's cause? Are you trying to save him?
Whoever fights for him shall be put to
death by morning! If Baal really is a god,
he can defend himself when someone
breaks down his altar." 32So because Gideon broke down Baal's altar, they gave him
the name Jerub-Baal[e][c] that day, saying,
"Let Baal contend with him."
33Now all the Midianites, Amalekites
and other eastern peoples[d] joined forces
and crossed over the Jordan and camped
in the Valley of Jezreel.[e] 34Then the Spirit
of the LORD came on[f] Gideon, and he blew
a trumpet,[g] summoning the Abiezrites to
follow him. 35He sent messengers throughout Manasseh, calling them to arms, and
also into Asher, Zebulun and Naphtali,[h] so
that they too went up to meet them.
36Gideon said to God, "If you will save[i]
Israel by my hand as you have promised—
37look, I will place a wool fleece on the
threshing floor.[j] If there is dew only on
the fleece and all the ground is dry, then
I will know[k] that you will save Israel by
my hand, as you said." 38And that is what
happened. Gideon rose early the next day;

6:19 [s]Ge 18:7-8 **6:20** [t]Jdg 13:19 **6:21** [u]Lev 9:24 **6:22** [v]Jdg 13:16, 21 [w]Ge 32:30; Ex 33:20; Jdg 13:22 **6:23** [x]Da 10:19 **6:24** [y]Ge 22:14 [z]Jdg 8:32 **6:25** [a]Ex 34:13; Dt 7:5 **6:28** [b]1Ki 16:32 **6:32** [c]Jdg 7:1; 8:29, 35; 1Sa 12:11 **6:33** [d]ver 3 [e]Jos 17:16 **6:34** [f]Jdg 3:10; 1Ch 12:18; 2Ch 24:20 [g]Jdg 3:27 **6:35** [h]Jdg 4:6 **6:36** [i]ver 14 **6:37** [j]Ex 4:3-7 [k]Ge 24:14

[a] 25 Or *Take a full-grown, mature bull from your father's herd* [b] 25 That is, a wooden symbol of the goddess Asherah; also in verses 26, 28 and 30 [c] 26 Or *build with layers of stone an* [d] 26 Or *full-grown*; also in verse 28 [e] 32 *Jerub-Baal* probably means *let Baal contend.*

flat cakes—an extremely generous meal in these hard times.

6:20–21 It is the angel who instructs Gideon to place the food on the rock (v. 20), where it is consumed (v. 21), transforming the meal into a sacrifice.

6:31 *If Baal really is a god, he can defend himself.* Ancient Near Easterners perceived deities to be present in the images that represented them. By an elaborate process, an object made with human hands was transformed into a representative of the god, indwelled by his spirit/breath. Once an object had been transformed into a god, it should have been able to defend itself. The NIV's insertion of "really" may suggest to some that Gideon's actions have tested Baal's divinity, and that Joash's rhetorical question anticipates a negative answer: "No, Baal is not a god." However, it seems quite unlikely that the sponsor of the Baal installation at Ophrah would have conceded this so quickly. When a desecration takes place, it is the role of the deity to defend itself (Lev 10:1–3; 1Sa 6:19; 2Sa 6:7). Joash is declaring that anyone who takes retribution into their own hands will be considered guilty of bloodshed and subject to clan retribution.

6:34 *the Spirit of the LORD came on Gideon.* According to the normal use of this form of this Hebrew verb ("to clothe"), the Hebrew reads "the Spirit of the LORD put on Gideon," suggesting that the Spirit "wears" Gideon, i.e., the Spirit is inside him, rather than Gideon "wearing" the Spirit, as an external force. This raises the question whether the Spirit functions as an internal or external force. A statement in an Akkadian wisdom text raises the same issue: "The demon has clothed himself in my body as with a garment; sleep covers me like a net." The verb reflected in the NIV and most English translations assumes the present idiom represents a stronger version of the divine empowerment formula than "the Spirit of the LORD came on" in 3:10; 11:29, and a more colorful version than "The Spirit of the Lord came powerfully upon" in 14:6,19; 15:14. This interpretation finds some support in Job 29:14, but especially in extra-Biblical texts, which often use clothing imagery to describe a person as covered or overwhelmed by divine or demonic forces. One Akkadian text reads, "He [the *asakku*-demon] enveloped the miserable man like a garment."

The Spirit of the Lord usually appears in Judges to facilitate the calling of an army. Since Israel has no central authority, only Yahweh has the ability to call out the tribes, and his authority is recognized in anyone who does so.

JUDGES 6:36–40

Gideon's Fleece: Testing the Deity

Gideon's demands have much in common with divination. First, as in many extra-Biblical contexts, a military crisis precipitated the present ritual performances. Second, even more so than in the reading of omens, like the liver of a sheep (called "extispicy"), Gideon's demand that Yahweh treat his fleece differently than the environment around it operated on simple binary principles — it could only yield a yes or no answer. Third, in keeping with a common purpose of Mesopotamian divination, Gideon's aim was to reassure himself of divine support for the venture against the Midianites. Fourth, like many ancient diviners, Gideon apparently was not confident in the verdict of a single sign; he needed reinforcement through a second performance of the test. Indeed, the results of his first test could be explained as what would normally happen. Irregular events or observations were needed to gain omens. So, when soft and absorbent material is left overnight on the hard ground or the rocky surface of a threshing floor, in the morning it will feel wetter than the ground around it. This is normal. Gideon therefore demands reiteration through a reversal of the phenomena: wet fleece, dry ground, followed by dry fleece, wet ground. His request that Yahweh do something that would be regarded as abnormal is analogous to diviners seeking reinforcement through signs of a different genre and involving a different realm. Celestial omens would be sought out to try to confirm terrestrial omens or extispicy (examination of the entrails of sacrificed animals). It is likely that Gideon only requested the normal occurrence the first night to give Yahweh the benefit of the doubt. The angel had already told him that he would be the deliverer. Gideon is simply giving an opportunity to change the instructions.

continued on next page

he squeezed the fleece and wrung out the
dew — a bowlful of water.
39Then Gideon said to God, "Do not be
angry with me. Let me make just one more
request.[l] Allow me one more test with the
fleece, but this time make the fleece dry
and let the ground be covered with dew."
40That night God did so. Only the fleece
was dry; all the ground was covered with
dew.

Gideon Defeats the Midianites

7 Early in the morning, Jerub-Baal[m] (that
is, Gideon) and all his men camped at
the spring of Harod. The camp of Midian
was north of them in the valley near the
hill of Moreh.[n] 2The LORD said to Gideon,
"You have too many men. I cannot deliver
Midian into their hands, or Israel would
boast against me, 'My own strength[o] has
saved me.' 3Now announce to the army,
'Anyone who trembles with fear may turn
back and leave Mount Gilead.[p]' " So twenty-two thousand men left, while ten thousand remained.
4But the LORD said to Gideon, "There are
still too many[q] men. Take them down to
the water, and I will thin them out for you
there. If I say, 'This one shall go with you,'
he shall go; but if I say, 'This one shall not
go with you,' he shall not go."
5So Gideon took the men down to the
water. There the LORD told him, "Separate
those who lap the water with their tongues
as a dog laps from those who kneel down
to drink." 6Three hundred of them drank

6:39 [l] Ge 18:32 **7:1** [m] Jdg 6:32 [n] Ge 12:6 **7:2** [o] Dt 8:17; 2Co 4:7 **7:3** [p] Dt 20:8 **7:4** [q] 1Sa 14:6

7:3 *Mount Gilead.* The traditional reading reflected in the NIV creates impossible problems, because the only Gilead known in the OT is the mountainous region east of the Jordan. It seems best to associate the place with the modern name of the spring, Ain Galud. *twenty-two thousand men left, while ten thousand remained.* On the seemingly inordinately high numbers, see note on 1:4.

As in the case of divination by extispicy following a prophetic or celestial omen, the form of divination here is provoked rather than passive divination. Whereas most forms of divination involve the observance of phenomena over which the observer has no control, Gideon prescribes for Yahweh both the method and the meaning of the results. In this respect, the present case differs significantly from the Urim and the Thummim, which were inaccessible to Gideon. In the Urim and Thummim, Yahweh both provided the instruments and prescribed the method whereby the high priest could establish Yahweh's will in such contexts (see Nu 27:21; see also the article "Urim and Thummim," p. 162). Finally, unlike prevailing custom, according to which kings or generals would engage professional diviners to determine the will of the gods, Gideon takes matters into his own hands. The fact that Gideon, an ordinary citizen from a minor clan of Israel, even thinks about demanding signs suggests that common people may have had their own ad hoc divinatory practices by which they sought to determine the will of the gods in their own domestic affairs. However, since Yahweh is calling on him to deliver the nation from the Midianites, the stakes are much higher here. ◆

Clay tablet representing sheep liver, used for divination.

from cupped hands, lapping like dogs. All
the rest got down on their knees to drink.
7The LORD said to Gideon, "With the
three hundred men that lapped I will save
you and give the Midianites into your
hands. Let all the others go home."[r] 8So
Gideon sent the rest of the Israelites home
but kept the three hundred, who took over
the provisions and trumpets of the others.
Now the camp of Midian lay below him
in the valley. 9During that night the LORD
said to Gideon, "Get up, go down against
the camp, because I am going to give it
into your hands.[s] 10If you are afraid to attack, go down to the camp with your servant Purah 11and listen to what they are
saying. Afterward, you will be encouraged
to attack the camp." So he and Purah his
servant went down to the outposts of the
camp. 12The Midianites, the Amalekites[t]
and all the other eastern peoples had settled in the valley, thick as locusts.[u] Their
camels[v] could no more be counted than
the sand on the seashore.[w]
13Gideon arrived just as a man was telling a friend his dream. "I had a dream,"

7:7 [r] 1Sa 14:6
7:9 [s] Jos 2:24; 10:8; 11:6
7:12 [t] Jdg 8:10 [u] Jdg 6:5 [v] Jer 49:29 [w] Jos 11:4

7:13 *I had a dream.* In the OT, most dreams involve non-Israelites (e.g., Ge 20:3,6; 31:24; 40–41; Da 2:1–3). Portentous dreams were a common feature of ancient Near Eastern life. These dreams tended to be of one of two types. *Message dreams* often involved theophanies through which a clear and simple message was communicated. They required no outside interpreter. The accounts available to us usually involve monarchs and serve one or more of four purposes: (1) to assure the recipient of the deity's presence and care; (2) to issue a warning or offer counsel; (3) to foretell events in the future; and (4) to command the recipient to particular action.

The present account involves a *symbolic dream,* which apparently occurred less frequently than message dreams. Symbolic dreams involved little if any dialogue; instead, in the dream, the recipient witnessed a symbolic event that typically required interpretation by an outsider after the person awoke. The present text is exceptional

GIDEON'S BATTLES

The story of Gideon begins with a graphic portrayal of one of the most striking facts of life in the Fertile Crescent: the periodic migration of nomadic peoples into the settled areas of Canaan. Each spring the tents of the Bedouin herdsmen appeared overnight almost as if by magic, scattered on the hills and fields of the farming districts. Conflict between these two ways of life (herdsmen and farmers) was inevitable.

1 In the Biblical period, the vast numbers and warlike practice of the herdsmen reduced the village people to near vassalage. God's answer was twofold: (1) religious reform, starting with Gideon's own family; and (2) military action, based on a coalition of northern Israelite tribes. The location of Gideon's hometown, "Ophrah of the Abiezrites" (6:24), is not known with certainty, but it probably was ancient Aper (modern Afula) in the Valley of Jezreel.

2 The battle at the spring of Harod is justly celebrated for its strategic brilliance. Denied the use of the only local water source, the Midianites camped in the valley and fell victim to the small band of Israelites that attacked them from the heights of the hill of Moreh.

3 The main battle took place north of the hill near the village of En-dor at the foot of Mount Tabor. Fleeing by way of the Jordan valley, the Midianites were trapped when the Ephraimites seized the fords of the Jordan from below Beth Shan to Beth Barah near Adam.

he was saying. "A round loaf of barley
bread came tumbling into the Midianite
camp. It struck the tent with such force
that the tent overturned and collapsed."
14His friend responded, "This can be
nothing other than the sword of Gideon
son of Joash, the Israelite. God has given
the Midianites and the whole camp into
his hands."
15When Gideon heard the dream and its
interpretation, he bowed down and worshiped.[x] He returned to the camp of Israel
and called out, "Get up! The LORD has giv-
en the Midianite camp into your hands."
16Dividing the three hundred men[y] into
three companies,[z] he placed trumpets and
empty jars in the hands of all of them,
with torches inside.
17"Watch me," he told them. "Follow
my lead. When I get to the edge of the
camp, do exactly as I do. 18When I and
all who are with me blow our trumpets,[a]
then from all around the camp blow yours
and shout, 'For the LORD and for Gideon.'"
19Gideon and the hundred men with
him reached the edge of the camp at the
beginning of the middle watch, just after
they had changed the guard. They blew
their trumpets and broke the jars that
were in their hands. 20The three companies blew the trumpets and smashed the
jars. Grasping the torches in their left
hands and holding in their right hands the
trumpets they were to blow, they shouted,
"A sword[b] for the LORD and for Gideon!"
21While each man held his position around
the camp, all the Midianites ran, crying
out as they fled.[c]
22When the three hundred trumpets
sounded,[d] the LORD caused the men

7:15 [x] 1Sa 15:31 **7:16** [y] Ge 14:15 [z] 2Sa 18:2
7:18 [a] Jdg 3:27 **7:20** [b] ver 14 **7:21** [c] 2Ki 7:7 **7:22** [d] Jos 6:20

in that, although for the dreamer and the interpreter the dream communicated a disastrous message, for Gideon, who overheard the telling and the interpretation, it offered a welcome word of assurance.

7:16 *trumpets ... empty jars ... torches.* By ancient Near Eastern standards (as by our own), the weapons with which Gideon attacked the Midianites were ridiculous. *trumpets.* Refers to a *shofar,* the ram's horn (see note on Jos 6:4). *jars.* Identifies a small- to medium-sized storage jar. *torches.* Probably sticks with rags soaked in oil and wrapped around their ends, or, since it was harvest time, reeds or stalks of grain tightly bound and attached to short sticks. So long as the lit torches were covered by the jars, they would smolder, but once the jars were removed they would fan into flame. While the sound of smashing pottery undoubtedly awakened the Midianites, they probably were intended to misinterpret the sight of 300 torches lighting up the night sky: they likely deduced that with so many men available to sound signals and hold torches to light the perimeter, there must be many more attacking the camp.

throughout the camp to turn on each other[e] with their swords. The army fled to
Beth Shittah toward Zererah as far as the
border of Abel Meholah[f] near Tabbath.
23Israelites from Naphtali, Asher and all
Manasseh were called out,[g] and they pursued the Midianites. 24Gideon sent messengers throughout the hill country of
Ephraim, saying, "Come down against the
Midianites and seize the waters of the Jordan[h] ahead of them as far as Beth Barah."
So all the men of Ephraim were called
out and they seized the waters of the Jordan as far as Beth Barah. 25They also captured two of the Midianite leaders, Oreb
and Zeeb[i]. They killed Oreb at the rock of
Oreb,[j] and Zeeb at the winepress of Zeeb.
They pursued the Midianites and brought
the heads of Oreb and Zeeb to Gideon,
who was by the Jordan.[k]

Zebah and Zalmunna

8 Now the Ephraimites asked Gideon,
"Why have you treated us like this?
Why didn't you call us when you went to
fight Midian?"[l] And they challenged him
vigorously.[m]
2But he answered them, "What have I
accomplished compared to you? Aren't the
gleanings of Ephraim's grapes better than
the full grape harvest of Abiezer? 3God
gave Oreb and Zeeb,[n] the Midianite leaders, into your hands. What was I able to
do compared to you?" At this, their resentment against him subsided.
4Gideon and his three hundred men, exhausted yet keeping up the pursuit, came
to the Jordan[o] and crossed it. 5He said to
the men of Sukkoth,[p] "Give my troops
some bread; they are worn out, and I am
still pursuing Zebah and Zalmunna,[q] the
kings of Midian."
6But the officials of Sukkoth said, "Do
you already have the hands of Zebah
and Zalmunna in your possession? Why
should we give bread[r] to your troops?"[s]
7Then Gideon replied, "Just for that,
when the LORD has given Zebah and Zalmunna[t] into my hand, I will tear your
flesh with desert thorns and briers."
8From there he went up to Peniel[a][u] and
made the same request of them, but they
answered as the men of Sukkoth had.
9So he said to the men of Peniel, "When
I return in triumph, I will tear down this
tower."[v]
10Now Zebah and Zalmunna were in
Karkor with a force of about fifteen thousand men, all that were left of the armies
of the eastern peoples; a hundred and
twenty thousand swordsmen had fallen.[w]
11Gideon went up by the route of the nomads east of Nobah[x] and Jogbehah[y] and
attacked the unsuspecting army. 12Zebah
and Zalmunna, the two kings of Midian,
fled, but he pursued them and captured
them, routing their entire army.
13Gideon son of Joash then returned
from the battle by the Pass of Heres. 14He
caught a young man of Sukkoth and questioned him, and the young man wrote
down for him the names of the seventy-
seven officials of Sukkoth, the elders of
the town. 15Then Gideon came and said to
the men of Sukkoth, "Here are Zebah and
Zalmunna, about whom you taunted me
by saying, 'Do you already have the hands
of Zebah and Zalmunna in your possession? Why should we give bread to your
exhausted men?[z]' " 16He took the elders of
the town and taught the men of Sukkoth
a lesson[a] by punishing them with desert
thorns and briers. 17He also pulled down
the tower of Peniel and killed the men of
the town.[b]
18Then he asked Zebah and Zalmunna,
"What kind of men did you kill at Tabor?[c]"
"Men like you," they answered, "each
one with the bearing of a prince."
19Gideon replied, "Those were my
brothers, the sons of my own mother. As
surely as the LORD lives, if you had spared

7:22 [e] 1Sa 14:20; 2Ch 20:23 [f] 1Ki 4:12; 19:16 **7:23** [g] Jdg 6:35 **7:24** [h] Jdg 3:28 **7:25** [i] Jdg 8:3; Ps 83:11 [j] Isa 10:26 [k] Jdg 8:4 **8:1** [l] Jdg 12:1 [m] 2Sa 19:41 **8:3** [n] Jdg 7:25; Pr 15:1 **8:4** [o] Jdg 7:25 **8:5** [p] Ge 33:17 [q] Ps 83:11 **8:6** [r] 1Sa 25:11 [s] ver 15 **8:7** [t] Jdg 7:15 **8:8** [u] Ge 32:30; 1Ki 12:25 **8:9** [v] ver 17 **8:10** [w] Jdg 6:5; 7:12; Isa 9:4 **8:11** [x] Nu 32:42 [y] Nu 32:35 **8:15** [z] ver 6 **8:16** [a] ver 7 **8:17** [b] ver 9 **8:18** [c] Jos 19:22; Jdg 4:6

[a] 8 Hebrew *Penuel,* a variant of *Peniel;* also in verses 9 and 17

8:5 *Sukkoth.* This place-name (meaning "Booths") should not be confused with the first stopping place of the Israelites when they came out of Egypt (Ex 12:37; Nu 33:5). This place is generally identified with Tell Deir 'Allah in the Transjordan. *kings of Midian.* Whereas in 7:25 Oreb and Zeeb had been identified as "leaders," these men are identified as "kings." Since the Midianites are commonly thought to have been a seminomadic migratory desert tribe we might have expected the narrator to identify them either as "chiefs" or "princes"/"rulers." However, the archaeological evidence of Qurayya in the Sinai points to a more sedentary community than we have previously imagined (see note on 6:1). Furthermore, the boundaries between the office of chief or chieftain and king were often blurred, the critical factor apparently being the number and levels of bureaucratic officials who were involved in the administration of the society, i.e., how far removed the ruler was from the common people.
8:6 *Do you already have the hands of Zebah and Zalmunna in your possession?* Lit. "Are the palms of Zebah and Zalmunna now in your hand?" which alludes to the ancient Near Eastern military practice of cutting off the hands of captives, taking these back to the base, and using them to tally the number of casualties in battle.
8:9 *tower.* Although no evidence of fortifications in Peniel has been found, this reference suggests that Sukkoth was a fortified town, a notion reinforced by the designation of her leaders as "officials" (military commanders) in v. 6.
8:10 *fifteen thousand men ... a hundred and twenty thousand swordsmen.* On these seemingly inordinately high numbers, see note on 1:4. *eastern peoples.* See note on 6:3.

their lives, I would not kill you." 20 Turning to Jether, his oldest son, he said, "Kill
them!" But Jether did not draw his sword,
because he was only a boy and was afraid.
21 Zebah and Zalmunna said, "Come,
do it yourself. 'As is the man, so is his
strength.'" So Gideon stepped forward and
killed them, and took the ornaments[d] off
their camels' necks.

Gideon's Ephod

22 The Israelites said to Gideon, "Rule
over us—you, your son and your grandson—because you have saved us from the
hand of Midian."
23 But Gideon told them, "I will not rule
over you, nor will my son rule over you.
The LORD will rule[e] over you." 24 And he
said, "I do have one request, that each of
you give me an earring from your share
of the plunder." (It was the custom of the
Ishmaelites[f] to wear gold earrings.)
25 They answered, "We'll be glad to give
them." So they spread out a garment, and
each of them threw a ring from his plunder onto it. 26 The weight of the gold rings
he asked for came to seventeen hundred
shekels,[a] not counting the ornaments,
the pendants and the purple garments
worn by the kings of Midian or the chains
that were on their camels' necks. 27 Gideon made the gold into an ephod,[g] which
he placed in Ophrah, his town. All Israel
prostituted themselves by worshiping it
there, and it became a snare[h] to Gideon
and his family.

Gideon's Death

28 Thus Midian was subdued before the
Israelites and did not raise its head again.
During Gideon's lifetime, the land had
peace[i] forty years.
29 Jerub-Baal[j] son of Joash went back
home to live. 30 He had seventy sons[k] of his
own, for he had many wives. 31 His concubine, who lived in Shechem, also bore him

8:21 [d] ver 26; Ps 83:11 **8:23** [e] Ex 16:8; 1Sa 8:7; 10:19; 12:12 **8:24** [f] Ge 25:13

8:27 [g] Jdg 17:5; 18:14 [h] Dt 7:16; Ps 106:39 **8:28** [i] Jdg 5:31 **8:29** [j] Jdg 7:1 **8:30** [k] Jdg 9:2, 5, 18, 24

[a] *26* That is, about 43 pounds or about 20 kilograms

8:21 *took the ornaments off their camels' necks.* An image of a conqueror claiming the customary trophies of victory—the crescent ornaments, worn on the necks of "royal" camels.
8:23 *I will not rule over you.* Although Gideon appears to reject the Israelites' invitation to rule over them and found a hereditary dynasty, by ancient Near Eastern standards all his actions hereafter are typical of kings: (1) he claims the lion's share of the plunder from battle for himself (vv. 24–26); (2) he claims the purple garments of the Midianite kings (v. 26); (3) he establishes a national cult center complete with divine image (v. 27); (4) he is identified by patronymic ("Jerub-Baal son of Joash," v. 29) and lives in his house; (5) he establishes a large harem and fathers 70 sons (vv. 30–31); (6) he names his son Abimelek, which means "my father is king" (v. 31).
8:24 *earring.* In the ancient Near East both men and women wore earrings. The earrings involved in the accounts of Jacob's family gods (Ge 35:1–7), the golden calf (Ex 32:1–6) and the present story are not simply arbitrary items of jewelry. Rather, the earrings symbolize the relationship between the deity and the worshiper at several levels: (1) Since deities are often portrayed with holes in their ears or as wearing earrings, they represent precious gifts from devotee to deity. (2) Analogous to piercing the ear of a slave who chose not to leave his master (Ex 21:5–6; Dt 15:16–17), the pierced ear symbolized the worshiper's devotion to the deity. (3) Attached to the organ of listening, the earrings reminded the devotee to be ever attentive to the voice of the deity. Like Aaron in Ex 32, Gideon melted down the gold and used this "sacred" metal to create a new religious symbol (v. 27). *Ishmaelites.* In the ancient Near East, ethnic designations were not always used with precision. According to Ge 25:12, strictly speaking Ishmael was the (elder) son of Abraham by Hagar. However, the present identification of Midianites as Ishmaelites (cf. also Ge 37:27–28,36) suggests that either the latter could also be used of desert people (Bedouins?) in general, or the Midianite alliance extended beyond the Amalekites and the "eastern peoples" mentioned earlier (v. 10). In the latter case Zebah and Zalmunna may actually have belonged to the Ishmaelite branch of this alliance.
8:26 *seventeen hundred shekels.* Calculated at 2/5 ounce (11.5 grams) per shekel, 1,700 shekels of gold amounts to 43 pounds (about 20 kilograms).
8:27 *ephod.* The nature of this object is not clear. Elsewhere in the OT it denotes the priest's special breastpiece (Ex 28:15–30). In Jdg 17:5; 18:14–20; the same word refers to the priestly vestments of Micah. However, because this object was erected in Gideon's city and became an object of pagan worship, this meaning seems unlikely here. The solution to the present problem may be suggested by the Akkadian cognate (*epattu*), which in several old Assyrian texts apparently refers to the costly garments that were worn by high officials and/or were draped over images of the gods. In the present context, the part stands for the whole, i.e., the word "ephod" represents not only the garment that clothed a sacred image, but also the image over which the garment was draped and which became the object of worship for the Israelites.
8:30 *seventy.* This number of his sons sounds like an idealized number, perhaps the number of a complete royal household. This use of the number occurs not only in the OT (Jdg 1:7; 12:14; Ge 46:27; Ex 24:1; 2Ki 10:1–7) but also in extra-Biblical texts. In the eighth-century BC Aramaic inscription from Samal (Zinjirli), Bar-rakib reports that his father Panammuwa had assassinated his own father and 70 of his own brothers.
8:31 *concubine.* The etymology of this Hebrew word is obscure, but the word always identifies female persons. In most contexts in the OT, the concubine was considered a legal but second-ranked wife, subordinate to a full-status wife (e.g., Ge 16:2–3; 29:24,29), and was more easily divorced (Ge 21:10–14). It seems that in most instances concubines began as servants or slaves, and were legally elevated to their status with the consent of the husband's full-status wife or wives, without bringing with them a dowry, either to provide offspring for the husband or simply to serve him as a contracted sexual partner. Gideon's marriage to this woman reinforces the impression that he is behaving like a typical Near Eastern king on two counts: (1) she represents an addition to an already large harem, and (2) she is a Canaanite. By marrying a Shechemite, Gideon seems either to have been establishing a claim to

a son, whom he named Abimelek.[l] 32Gid-
eon son of Joash died at a good old age[m]
and was buried in the tomb of his father
Joash in Ophrah of the Abiezrites.
33No sooner had Gideon died than the
Israelites again prostituted themselves to
the Baals.[n] They set up Baal-Berith[o] as
their god[p] 34and did not remember[q] the
LORD their God, who had rescued them
from the hands of all their enemies on every side. 35They also failed to show any
loyalty to the family of Jerub-Baal (that is,
Gideon) in spite of all the good things he
had done for them.[r]

Abimelek

9 Abimelek[s] son of Jerub-Baal went to
his mother's brothers in Shechem and
said to them and to all his mother's clan,
2"Ask all the citizens of Shechem, 'Which
is better for you: to have all seventy of Jerub-Baal's sons rule over you, or just one
man?' Remember, I am your flesh and
blood.[t]"
3When the brothers repeated all this
to the citizens of Shechem, they were inclined to follow Abimelek, for they said,
"He is related to us." 4They gave him seventy shekels[a] of silver from the temple of
Baal-Berith,[u] and Abimelek used it to hire
reckless scoundrels,[v] who became his followers. 5He went to his father's home in
Ophrah and on one stone murdered his
seventy brothers,[w] the sons of Jerub-Baal.
But Jotham, the youngest son of Jerub-
Baal, escaped by hiding.[x] 6Then all the
citizens of Shechem and Beth Millo gathered beside the great tree at the pillar in
Shechem to crown Abimelek king.
7When Jotham was told about this, he
climbed up on the top of Mount Gerizim[y]
and shouted to them, "Listen to me, citizens of Shechem, so that God may listen
to you. 8One day the trees went out to
anoint a king for themselves. They said to
the olive tree, 'Be our king.'
9"But the olive tree answered, 'Should
I give up my oil, by which both gods and
humans are honored, to hold sway over
the trees?'
10"Next, the trees said to the fig tree,
'Come and be our king.'
11"But the fig tree replied, 'Should I give
up my fruit, so good and sweet, to hold
sway over the trees?'
12"Then the trees said to the vine, 'Come
and be our king.'
13"But the vine answered, 'Should I give
up my wine,[z] which cheers both gods and
humans, to hold sway over the trees?'
14"Finally all the trees said to the thornbush, 'Come and be our king.'
15"The thornbush said to the trees, 'If
you really want to anoint me king over
you, come and take refuge in my shade;[a]
but if not, then let fire come out[b] of the
thornbush and consume the cedars of Lebanon!'[c]
16"Have you acted honorably and in
good faith by making Abimelek king?
Have you been fair to Jerub-Baal and his
family? Have you treated him as he deserves? 17Remember that my father fought

8:31 [l] Jdg 9:1 **8:32** [m] Ge 25:8 **8:33** [n] Jdg 2:11, 13, 19 [o] Jdg 9:4 [p] Jdg 9:27, 46 **8:34** [q] Jdg 3:7; Dt 4:9; Ps 78:11, 42 **8:35** [r] Jdg 9:16 **9:1** [s] Jdg 8:31 **9:2** [t] Ge 29:14; Jdg 8:30 **9:4** [u] Jdg 8:33 [v] Jdg 11:3; 2Ch 13:7 **9:5** [w] ver 2; Jdg 8:30 [x] 2Ki 11:2 **9:7** [y] Dt 11:29; 27:12; Jn 4:20 **9:13** [z] Ecc 2:3 **9:15** [a] Isa 30:2 [b] ver 20 [c] Isa 2:13

[a] 4 That is, about 1 3/4 pounds or about 800 grams

this town or to have entered into a marriage alliance with the rulers of the town.

8:33 *Baal-Berith.* This name, which occurs only here and in 9:4, is lit. "Lord/Baal of the Covenant." In view of the prominence of Baal in the book and especially in the Judges narratives, one's immediate response is to equate this Baal with the Canaanite storm and warrior deity. However, the issue is complicated by the reference to the Shechemite "temple of El-Berith" in 9:46. It is possible that Baal-Berith and El-Berith represent two separate deities, both of whom were worshiped in Shechem, but it is more likely that Baal and El were interchangeable designations for the same god. Many understand El to have been the patron deity of Canaanite Shechem. This theory may be supported by the second part of the phrase ("covenant"). In the expression some see an allusion to a political treaty between Shechem and some other Canaanite state, perhaps even Israel, in which El\Baal-Berith was invoked as the divine guardian and guarantor. However, it is preferable to see in El/Baal-Berith an allusion to a treaty between Shechem and El that knit the deity and the population of the city in a special relationship, analogous to (but certainly different in many ways from) Yahweh's covenant with Israel.

9:1 *Abimelek son of Jerub-Baal.* If Abimelek's mother were from the ruling clan, his violent actions to regain control of the city (v. 5) are somewhat understandable. On the other hand, since Abimelek also represents the new Israelite population, some may have considered him one of the Apiru, a designation found in the Amarna letters for troublesome segments of society accused of disloyalty, taking over cities, looting and robbery. Unlike the surrounding narratives of the deliverer governors, this account is not concerned with an external threat, but a problem of internal politics.

9:5 *on one stone.* This phrase suggests ritual execution, maybe even implying a sacrificial altar, but there are no known instances of human sacrifice of rival claimants to the throne in the ancient Near East.

9:7 *Mount Gerizim.* Identified with modern Jebel et-Tor on the south side of the Nablus valley, which overlooked the city of Shechem from the south. Jotham issued his speech from an acoustically advantageous location on the mountain.

9:9 *oil.* See notes on 1Sa 2:10; 10:1.

9:14 *thornbush.* The Hebrew word used here denotes a species of buckthorn, usually equated with *lycium europaeum*. However, the present context also requires something larger—it gives a significant amount of shade and when it burns provides fuel for a great conflagration (vv. 15,20). If the reference to shade is not sarcastic, it is preferable to equate this with Christ Thorn (Latin *Ziziphus spina-Christi*), a stately evergreen that grows to a height of 30 feet (9 meters), and whose branches are armed with spines.

JUDGES 9:8 – 15

Fables in the Ancient World

Judges 9:8 – 15 contains one of the finest examples of fables from the ancient world. By definition, a fable typically involves a short narrative in poetry or prose that teaches a moral lesson and involves creatures, plants and/or inanimate objects speaking or behaving like human characters. The best-known examples of ancient fables are found in the Greek collection associated with Aesop, but the ancient Semitic world has also produced several examples. The text bearing the closest resemblance to Jotham's fable is an ancient Babylonian text called "The Dispute Between the Tamarisk and the Date Palm," in which these two trees debate who is greater. ◆

for you and risked his life to rescue you from the hand of Midian. 18 But today you have revolted against my father's family. You have murdered his seventy sons[d] on a single stone and have made Abimelek, the son of his female slave, king over the citizens of Shechem because he is related to you. 19 So have you acted honorably and in good faith toward Jerub-Baal and his family today? If you have, may Abimelek be your joy, and may you be his, too! 20 But if you have not, let fire come out[e] from Abimelek and consume you, the citizens of Shechem and Beth Millo, and let fire come out from you, the citizens of Shechem and Beth Millo, and consume Abimelek!"

21 Then Jotham fled, escaping to Beer, and he lived there because he was afraid of his brother Abimelek.

22 After Abimelek had governed Israel three years, 23 God stirred up animosity[f] between Abimelek and the citizens of Shechem so that they acted treacherously against Abimelek. 24 God did this in order that the crime against Jerub-Baal's seventy sons, the shedding[g] of their blood, might be avenged[h] on their brother Abimelek and on the citizens of Shechem, who had helped him[i] murder his brothers. 25 In opposition to him these citizens of Shechem set men on the hilltops to ambush and rob everyone who passed by, and this was reported to Abimelek.

26 Now Gaal son of Ebed moved with his clan into Shechem, and its citizens put their confidence in him. 27 After they had gone out into the fields and gathered the grapes and trodden[j] them, they held a festival in the temple of their god.[k] While they were eating and drinking, they cursed Abimelek. 28 Then Gaal son of Ebed said, "Who[l] is Abimelek, and why should we Shechemites be subject to him? Isn't he Jerub-Baal's son, and isn't Zebul his deputy? Serve the family of Hamor,[m] Shechem's father! Why should we serve Abimelek? 29 If only this people were under my command![n] Then I would get rid of him. I would say to Abimelek, 'Call out your whole army!' "[a]

9:18 [d] ver 5-6; Jdg 8:30
9:20 [e] ver 15
9:23 [f] 1Sa 16:14, 23; 18:10; 1Ki 22:22; Isa 19:14; 33:1
9:24 [g] Nu 35:33; 1Ki 2:32
[h] ver 56-57
[i] Dt 27:25
9:27 [j] Am 9:13
[k] Jdg 8:33
9:28 [l] 1Sa 25:10; 1Ki 12:16
[m] Ge 34:2,6
9:29 [n] 2Sa 15:4

[a] 29 Septuagint; Hebrew *him." Then he said to Abimelek, "Call out your whole army!"*

9:23 *stirred up animosity.* The NIV's translation carries a strong sense of God's activity here. Other translations such as the KJV render this as God sending an "evil spirit" in this situation. To understand the meaning of this phrase, two considerations must be borne in mind. First, the Hebrew word, translated "evil" (KJV), can refer either to moral malignancy or experiential misfortune, analogous to English "ill," as in "ill will" (NKJV), "ill repute," "ill feelings toward someone." In this and other similar contexts, the word is not to be interpreted in a moral sense, but in the profane sense of "bad, unfavorable" as opposed to "good, favorable." The activity attributed to God's actions (or the "spirit") here comes close to the role attributed to demons in ancient Near Eastern thought. In general, what we refer to as demons were perceived as agents of the gods, whose role was to execute divinely decreed blessings and punishments for sin, the latter usually by inflicting their victims with illnesses. Although in later Jewish magical texts this phrase came to be understood as "demon," in our passages the identity remains vague, but its role is clearly subservient to Yahweh.

30 When Zebul the governor of the city
heard what Gaal son of Ebed said, he was
very angry. 31 Under cover he sent messengers to Abimelek, saying, "Gaal son
of Ebed and his clan have come to Shechem and are stirring up the city against
you. 32 Now then, during the night you and
your men should come and lie in wait[o]
in the fields. 33 In the morning at sunrise,
advance against the city. When Gaal and
his men come out against you, seize the
opportunity to attack them.[p]"
34 So Abimelek and all his troops set out
by night and took up concealed positions
near Shechem in four companies. 35 Now
Gaal son of Ebed had gone out and was
standing at the entrance of the city gate
just as Abimelek and his troops came out
from their hiding place.[q]
36 When Gaal saw them, he said to Zebul, "Look, people are coming down from
the tops of the mountains!"
Zebul replied, "You mistake the shadows of the mountains for men."
37 But Gaal spoke up again: "Look, people are coming down from the central
hill,[a] and a company is coming from the
direction of the diviners' tree."
38 Then Zebul said to him, "Where is
your big talk now, you who said, 'Who
is Abimelek that we should be subject to
him?' Aren't these the men you ridiculed?[r]
Go out and fight them!"
39 So Gaal led out[b] the citizens of Shechem and fought Abimelek. 40 Abimelek
chased him all the way to the entrance
of the gate, and many were killed as they
fled. 41 Then Abimelek stayed in Arumah,
and Zebul drove Gaal and his clan out of
Shechem.
42 The next day the people of Shechem
went out to the fields, and this was reported to Abimelek. 43 So he took his men, divided them into three companies[s] and set
an ambush in the fields. When he saw the
people coming out of the city, he rose to
attack them. 44 Abimelek and the companies with him rushed forward to a position
at the entrance of the city gate. Then two
companies attacked those in the fields and
struck them down. 45 All that day Abimelek pressed his attack against the city until
he had captured it and killed its people.
Then he destroyed the city[t] and scattered
salt[u] over it.
46 On hearing this, the citizens in the
tower of Shechem went into the stronghold of the temple[v] of El-Berith. 47 When
Abimelek heard that they had assembled
there, 48 he and all his men went up Mount
Zalmon.[w] He took an ax and cut off some
branches, which he lifted to his shoulders.
He ordered the men with him, "Quick! Do
what you have seen me do!" 49 So all the
men cut branches and followed Abimelek.
They piled them against the stronghold
and set it on fire with the people still inside. So all the people in the tower of Shechem, about a thousand men and women,
also died.
50 Next Abimelek went to Thebez[x] and
besieged it and captured it. 51 Inside the
city, however, was a strong tower, to which
all the men and women—all the people
of the city—had fled. They had locked
themselves in and climbed up on the tower roof. 52 Abimelek went to the tower and
attacked it. But as he approached the entrance to the tower to set it on fire, 53 a
woman dropped an upper millstone on his
head and cracked his skull.[y]
54 Hurriedly he called to his armor-bearer, "Draw your sword and kill me,[z] so that
they can't say, 'A woman killed him.'" So
his servant ran him through, and he died.
55 When the Israelites saw that Abimelek
was dead, they went home.
56 Thus God repaid the wickedness that
Abimelek had done to his father by murdering his seventy brothers. 57 God also
made the people of Shechem pay for all
their wickedness.[a] The curse of Jotham
son of Jerub-Baal came on them.

Tola

10 After the time of Abimelek, a man
of Issachar[b] named Tola son of
Puah,[c] the son of Dodo, rose to save[d] Israel. He lived in Shamir, in the hill country

9:32 [o] Jos 8:2
9:33 [p] 1Sa 10:7
9:35 [q] Ps 32:7; Jer 49:10
9:38 [r] ver 28-29
9:43 [s] Jdg 7:16
9:45 [t] ver 20; 2Ki 3:25 [u] Dt 29:23
9:46 [v] Jdg 8:33
9:48 [w] Ps 68:14
9:50 [x] 2Sa 11:21
9:53 [y] 2Sa 11:21
9:54 [z] 1Sa 31:4; 2Sa 1:9
9:57 [a] ver 20
10:1 [b] Ge 30:18 [c] Ge 46:13 [d] Jdg 2:16; 6:14

[a] *37* The Hebrew for this phrase means *the navel of the earth.* [b] *39* Or *Gaal went out in the sight of*

9:45 *destroyed the city and scattered salt over it.* The significance of Abimelek's action in salting the conquered site is not clear. Some have suggested that since salt renders a land infertile, by spreading salt on a city a conqueror may have sought to guarantee that it would never rise again. It seems best to interpret Abimelek's scattering salt over Shechem as a nonverbal gesture, equivalent to the curse that Yahweh had pronounced upon Jericho through the mouth of Joshua (Jos 6:26).

9:46 *stronghold of the temple of El-Berith.* Excavations at Shechem may have yielded the foundations of what was probably the temple fortress referred to here. This two-story structure was huge by Canaanite standards, measuring 70 feet (21 meters) wide and 86 feet (26 meters) long, easily large enough for 1,000 people to huddle inside. It is evident from the ruins that the temple was destroyed by a massive fire.

9:53 *upper millstone.* It is doubtful this refers to the large upper stone of a rotary quern at the mill, which came into general use in the Iron Age. Rather, we should imagine the smaller round muller used to grind grain spread out on a larger slightly concaved bottom stone. It would have been basalt and weighed four or five pounds (about two kilograms).

of Ephraim. 2He led[a] Israel twenty-three years; then he died, and was buried in Shamir.

Jair

3He was followed by Jair of Gilead, who led Israel twenty-two years. 4He had thirty sons, who rode thirty donkeys. They controlled thirty towns in Gilead, which to this day are called Havvoth Jair.[b][e] 5When Jair died, he was buried in Kamon.

Jephthah

6Again the Israelites did evil in the eyes of the LORD.[f] They served the Baals and the Ashtoreths,[g] and the gods of Aram, the gods of Sidon, the gods of Moab, the gods of the Ammonites and the gods of the Philistines.[h] And because the Israelites forsook the LORD[i] and no longer served him, 7he became angry[j] with them. He sold them[k] into the hands of the Philistines and the Ammonites, 8who that year shattered and crushed them. For eighteen years they oppressed all the Israelites on the east side of the Jordan in Gilead, the land of the Amorites. 9The Ammonites also crossed the Jordan to fight against Judah, Benjamin and Ephraim; Israel was in great distress. 10Then the Israelites cried out to the LORD, "We have sinned against you, forsaking our God and serving the Baals."[l]

11The LORD replied, "When the Egyptians,[m] the Amorites, the Ammonites,[n] the Philistines,[o] 12the Sidonians, the Amalekites and the Maonites[c] oppressed you[p] and you cried to me for help, did I not save you from their hands? 13But you have forsaken me and served other gods, so I will no longer save you. 14Go and cry out to the gods you have chosen. Let them save you when you are in trouble![q]"

15But the Israelites said to the LORD, "We have sinned. Do with us whatever you think best,[r] but please rescue us now." 16Then they got rid of the foreign gods among them and served the LORD.[s] And he could bear Israel's misery[t] no longer.[u]

17When the Ammonites were called to arms and camped in Gilead, the Israelites assembled and camped at Mizpah.[v] 18The leaders of the people of Gilead said to each other, "Whoever will take the lead in attacking the Ammonites will be head[w] over all who live in Gilead."

11 Jephthah[x] the Gileadite was a mighty warrior.[y] His father was Gilead; his mother was a prostitute. 2Gilead's wife also bore him sons, and when they were grown up, they drove Jephthah away. "You are not going to get any inheritance in our family," they said, "because you are the son of another woman." 3So Jephthah fled from his brothers and settled in the land of Tob,[z] where a gang of

10:4 [e] Nu 32:41 **10:6** [f] Jdg 2:11 [g] Jdg 2:13 [h] Jdg 2:12 [i] Dt 32:15 **10:7** [j] Dt 31:17 [k] Dt 32:30; Jdg 2:14; 1Sa 12:9 **10:10** [l] 1Sa 12:10 **10:11** [m] Ex 14:30 [n] Nu 21:21; Jdg 3:13 [o] Jdg 3:31 **10:12** [p] Ps 106:42 **10:14** [q] Dt 32:37 **10:15** [r] 1Sa 3:18; 2Sa 15:26 **10:16** [s] Jos 24:23; Jer 18:8 [t] Isa 63:9 [u] Dt 32:36; Ps 106:44-45 **10:17** [v] Ge 31:49; Jdg 11:29 **10:18** [w] Jdg 11:8,9 **11:1** [x] Heb 11:32 [y] Jdg 6:12 **11:3** [z] 2Sa 10:6,8

[a] 2 Traditionally *judged*; also in verse 3 [b] 4 Or *called the settlements of Jair* [c] 12 Hebrew; some Septuagint manuscripts *Midianites*

10:4 *thirty sons.* Suggests a multiplicity of wives, which may suggest that Jair functioned as a major chieftain or a minor monarch. Interpreted sociopolitically, the territory governed by Jair seems to have consisted of a confederacy of 30 cities. *thirty donkeys.* The significance of the donkeys is not clear, though the narrator's choice of terms seems to highlight their function as riding rather than pack animals. The prestige associated with owning asses is reflected not only in the Song of Deborah (5:10), but in extra-Biblical writings as well. To describe each son as riding on his own donkey is like saying each son was given his own Porsche.

10:10 *We have sinned against you, forsaking our God and serving the Baals.* This confession of sin arises out of the distress caused by the Israelites' defeat at the hands of the Ammonites (v. 9). The conviction expressed here, that this distress represented divine punishment for sin, would have been at home among most ancient Near Eastern peoples. However, the cause of the anger is distinctively Israelite. Whereas orthodox Yahwism demanded exclusive devotion to Yahweh (see Dt 6:4–5), elsewhere divinities did not take great offense at their devotees worshiping other gods. Indeed, in one of his plague prayers, Mursilis II pleads with the storm-god and defends his case, expressly declaring his attention to all the gods: "When I celebrated the festivals, I busied myself for all the gods. I did not pick out any single temple." Pagan deities were particularly infuriated through improper attention to ritual practice (since they depended upon their worshipers to meet their needs through sacrifice and other rituals) or violation of some taboo.

10:17 *Mizpah.* This Mizpah, located in Gilead, is not to be confused with the Benjamite town of the same name in chs. 19–21. The location is unknown.

10:18 *Whoever will take the lead … will be head.* Elders and tribal leaders were willing to submit to the authority of a military leader in times of crisis. This same political structure is seen among the Babylonian gods, where Marduk assumes leadership of the pantheon to counter the threat posed by the younger gods. This type of arrangement between elders and military leaders is what eventually led to the development of monarchy in the ancient Near East.

11:1 *prostitute.* In the ancient world, women would often resort to prostitution if they had no other means of economic support, especially if they were widows or orphans. However, Jephthah also illustrates the plight of the children of prostitutes in the ancient Near East. Without legal attachment to the head of a household, they were generally denied inheritance of property and social standing within the community, and were often forced into a life of prostitution simply to survive.

11:2 *drove Jephthah away.* The reason for Jephthah's expulsion is not family shame; in a culture with polygamy and sanctioned religious prostitution, "illegitimate" children would have been common. The dispute is over inheritance: one less share means more for everyone else.

11:3 *Tob.* Its location is uncertain, though the present context suggests a sparsely populated district north of the Jabbok. *scoundrels.* The Hebrew term ("empty men") intentionally reflects the narrator's negative evaluation

scoundrels[a] gathered around him and followed him.
4Some time later, when the Ammonites[b]
were fighting against Israel, 5the elders of
Gilead went to get Jephthah from the land
of Tob. 6"Come," they said, "be our commander, so we can fight the Ammonites."
7Jephthah said to them, "Didn't you
hate me and drive me from my father's
house?[c] Why do you come to me now,
when you're in trouble?"
8The elders of Gilead said to him, "Nevertheless, we are turning to you now;
come with us to fight the Ammonites, and
you will be head[d] over all of us who live
in Gilead."
9Jephthah answered, "Suppose you take
me back to fight the Ammonites and the
LORD gives them to me—will I really be
your head?"
10The elders of Gilead replied, "The
LORD is our witness;[e] we will certainly do
as you say." 11So Jephthah went with the
elders of Gilead, and the people made him
head and commander over them. And he
repeated all his words before the LORD in
Mizpah.[f]
12Then Jephthah sent messengers to the
Ammonite king with the question: "What
do you have against me that you have attacked my country?"
13The king of the Ammonites answered
Jephthah's messengers, "When Israel
came up out of Egypt, they took away my
land from the Arnon to the Jabbok,[g] all
the way to the Jordan. Now give it back
peaceably."
14Jephthah sent back messengers to the
Ammonite king, 15saying:

"This is what Jephthah says: Israel
did not take the land of Moab[h] or
the land of the Ammonites.[i] 16But
when they came up out of Egypt,
Israel went through the wilderness
to the Red Sea[a][j] and on to Kadesh.[k]
17Then Israel sent messengers[l] to
the king of Edom, saying, 'Give us
permission to go through your country,'[m] but the king of Edom would
not listen. They sent also to the king
of Moab, and he refused.[n] So Israel
stayed at Kadesh.
18"Next they traveled through
the wilderness, skirted the lands of
Edom[o] and Moab, passed along the
eastern side[p] of the country of Moab,
and camped on the other side of the
Arnon.[q] They did not enter the territory of Moab, for the Arnon was its
border.
19"Then Israel sent messengers
to Sihon king of the Amorites, who
ruled in Heshbon, and said to him,
'Let us pass through your country to
our own place.'[r] 20Sihon, however, did
not trust Israel[b] to pass through his
territory. He mustered all his troops
and encamped at Jahaz and fought
with Israel.[s]
21"Then the LORD, the God of Israel, gave Sihon and his whole army
into Israel's hands, and they defeated
them. Israel took over all the land of
the Amorites who lived in that country, 22capturing all of it from the Arnon to the Jabbok and from the desert to the Jordan.[t]
23"Now since the LORD, the God of
Israel, has driven the Amorites out
before his people Israel, what right
have you to take it over? 24Will you
not take what your god Chemosh[u]

11:3 [a] Jdg 9:4
11:4 [b] Jdg 10:9
11:7 [c] Ge 26:27
11:8 [d] Jdg 10:18
11:10 [e] Ge 31:50; Jer 42:5
11:11 [f] Jos 11:3; Jdg 10:17; 20:1; 1Sa 10:17
11:13 [g] Ge 32:22; Nu 21:24
11:15 [h] Dt 2:9 [i] Dt 2:19
11:16 [j] Nu 14:25; Dt 1:40 [k] Nu 20:1
11:17 [l] Nu 20:14 [m] Nu 20:18, 21 [n] Jos 24:9
11:18 [o] Nu 21:4 [p] Dt 2:8 [q] Nu 21:13
11:19 [r] Nu 21:21-22; Dt 2:26-27
11:20 [s] Nu 21:23; Dt 2:32
11:22 [t] Dt 2:36
11:24 [u] Nu 21:29; Jos 3:10; 1Ki 11:7

[a] 16 Or *the Sea of Reeds* [b] 20 Or *however, would not make an agreement for Israel*

of these men. This characterization invites comparison with the Apiru mentioned frequently in the Amarna letters. The Apiru represented a loosely defined, generally inferior social class on the edges of settled society, with no ethnic or linguistic relation to each other, usually serving as mercenaries, outlaws or slaves (see note on Ge 14:13).

11:11 *he repeated all his words before the LORD in Mizpah.* In solemnizing the agreement between Jephthah and the leaders of Gilead at the sanctuary in the presence of the deity, the parties to this contract follow regular ancient Near Eastern custom. Deities were invoked as witnesses to agreements and as guarantors of the fidelity of the parties.

11:12 *Jephthah sent messengers to the Ammonite king.* Jephthah acts remarkably kinglike—dispatching envoys, negotiating directly with the king of Bene Ammon, dealing with the conflicting issues as if they were personal between him and the Ammonite king and claiming the land as his own. *Ammonite king.* The identity of this king is unknown. This may have been the predecessor to Nahash (c. 1030–1000 BC), the first Ammonite king identifiable by name, who appears in 1Sa 11:1–12; 12:12; 2Sa 10:2. Based on the Biblical and extra-Biblical evidence, 11 Ammonite kings can now be identified.

11:14–27 As to style and form, Jephthah's speech (delivered by the envoys) is formal and conventional, incorporating many features of the ancient Near Eastern lawsuit genre that would be a typical way of pressing international claims.

11:24 *Will you not take what your god Chemosh gives you.* The ninth-century BC Mesha Stele illuminates this comment on two counts. First, Mesha's perspective on the role of deities in determining who rules over specific territories is much like that of Jephthah, who claims in v. 21 that Yahweh, the God of Israel, gave Sihon into Israel's hands. In lines 14–15, Mesha's scribe writes (on his behalf): "Kemosh said to me: 'Go take Nebo from Israel!' And I went in the night, and I fought against it from the break of dawn until noon." Second, in his question Jephthah refers to the deity involved in the present territorial debate as Chemosh. The deity Chemosh is well

gives you? Likewise, whatever the
LORD our God has given us, we will
possess. 25Are you any better than
Balak son of Zippor,[v] king of Moab?
Did he ever quarrel with Israel or
fight with them?[w] 26For three hundred years Israel occupied[x] Heshbon,
Aroer, the surrounding settlements
and all the towns along the Arnon.
Why didn't you retake them during
that time? 27I have not wronged you,
but you are doing me wrong by waging war against me. Let the LORD, the
Judge,[y] decide[z] the dispute this day
between the Israelites and the Ammonites."

28The king of Ammon, however, paid no
attention to the message Jephthah sent
him.
29Then the Spirit[a] of the LORD came on
Jephthah. He crossed Gilead and Manasseh, passed through Mizpah of Gilead,
and from there he advanced against the
Ammonites. 30And Jephthah made a vow[b]
to the LORD: "If you give the Ammonites
into my hands, 31whatever comes out of
the door of my house to meet me when
I return in triumph from the Ammonites
will be the LORD's, and I will sacrifice it as
a burnt offering."
32Then Jephthah went over to fight the
Ammonites, and the LORD gave them into
his hands. 33He devastated twenty towns
from Aroer to the vicinity of Minnith,[c] as
far as Abel Keramim. Thus Israel subdued
Ammon.
34When Jephthah returned to his
home in Mizpah, who should come out
to meet him but his daughter, dancing to
the sound of timbrels![d] She was an only
child. Except for her he had neither son
nor daughter. 35When he saw her, he tore
his clothes and cried, "Oh no, my daughter! You have brought me down and I am
devastated. I have made a vow to the LORD
that I cannot break.[e]"
36"My father," she replied, "you have
given your word to the LORD. Do to me just
as you promised,[f] now that the LORD has
avenged you of your enemies,[g] the Ammonites. 37But grant me this one request,"
she said. "Give me two months to roam
the hills and weep with my friends, because I will never marry."
38"You may go," he said. And he let her
go for two months. She and her friends
went into the hills and wept because
she would never marry. 39After the two
months, she returned to her father, and he
did to her as he had vowed. And she was
a virgin.
From this comes the Israelite tradition
40that each year the young women of Israel go out for four days to commemorate
the daughter of Jephthah the Gileadite.

11:25 [v] Nu 22:2 [w] Jos 24:9 **11:26** [x] Nu 21:25 **11:27** [y] Ge 18:25 [z] Ge 16:5; 31:53; 1Sa 24:12, 15 **11:29** [a] Nu 11:25; Jdg 3:10; 6:34; 14:6, 19; 15:14; 1Sa 11:6; 16:13; Isa 11:2 **11:30** [b] Ge 28:20 **11:33** [c] Eze 27:17 **11:34** [d] Ex 15:20; Jer 31:4 **11:35** [e] Nu 30:2; Ecc 5:2, 4, 5 **11:36** [f] Lk 1:38 [g] 2Sa 18:19

attested in extra-Biblical texts, not only in the Mesha Stele referred to above, but also in documents as early as the third-millennium BC tablets from Ebla, in northern Syria in twelfth-century BC texts from Ugarit and in the first-millennium BC Neo-Assyrian texts. The problem with Jephthah's comment is that, as a national deity, Chemosh is known to us not as the god of the Ammonites, but as the patron deity of Moab. This is confirmed not only by the Mesha Stele, but also by a series of personal names that scholars generally recognize to be Moabite. The patron deity of the Ammonites is Milkom. Nevertheless the relations between the two may have resulted in their worship of one another's deities.

11:26 *three hundred years.* If this number is understood chronologically rather than rhetorically, it would indicate that Israel possessed the land as early as 1400 BC.

11:30 *Jephthah made a vow to the LORD.* Analogues to Jephthah's vow are found in both Biblical and extra-Biblical texts. People uttered such vows when they were anxious about issues like a safe return from a journey, a need for a military victory or when they were desperate to have children. Jephthah's vow was an expression of piety adding force to a prayer by making a contract with God.

11:31 *whatever comes out of the door of my house.* Although we might find it strange for Jephthah to speak of a sheep or calf coming out of his house, the word "house" refers to a complex domestic structure known as the four-room house, which included rooms for the animals. However, since livestock do not usually greet a person returning from a journey, Jephthah's promise expresses a readiness to sacrifice a member of his own family. By not naming a specific individual, he in effect leaves the choice up to Yahweh.

11:34 *timbrels.* This Hebrew word refers to a variety of handheld percussion instruments often associated with dancing. Where musicians are identified in the Bible they are usually female. Unlike modern tambourines, the instruments did not have metal jingles on the sides, but consisted of a circular wood frame about ten inches (25 centimeters) in diameter, over which was stretched a piece of goatskin leather. *She was an only child.* This emphatic statement heightens the crisis that the appearance of Jephthah's daughter creates for him, for he realizes that if he does with her as he had vowed, he not only sacrifices his daughter, but he also sacrifices himself. In the ancient world people were thought to live on through their children—daughters and sons alike. Accordingly, the worst fate one could experience was to have his "descendants" cut off and his "name" destroyed from his father's household (cf. 1Sa 24:21).

11:39 *he did to her as he had vowed.* The statement should be interpreted in the light of the Canaanized Israelite society and culture to which Jephthah belonged. In 10:10, the narrator testifies to the fact that at this time the Israelites worshiped Milkom, the Ammonite god, and Chemosh, the god of the Moabites, whose leaders are known to have sacrificed children on occasion (2Ki 3:27). For these people, vows to sacrifice children were not rash or impulsive, but deadly serious expressions of devotion. Though Yahweh would have found such an act to be abhorrent, he often allows his people to suffer the consequences of their bad choices.

JUDGES 11:30–40

WOMEN SERVING IN THE TABERNACLE

Some interpreters suggest that Jephthah's vow involved dedicating his daughter to cultic service, rather than offering her as a literal sacrifice. This option could be supported by appeal to the presence of women involved at the tabernacle in the Bible (Ex 38:8; 1Sa 2:22) and in temple service in the ancient Near East, though there is no reason to think that these were lifelong dedications with vows of celibacy. The attractiveness of this solution to some is that it would also give an explanation of why she is mourning her virginity rather than her imminent death (Jdg 11:37–39). The problem with this option is that the language of the text ("burnt offering," Jdg 11:31) cannot easily support it, and the logical arguments based on theological assumptions are mitigated by the fact that this is the period of the judges, when "everyone did as they saw fit" (Jdg 17:6; 21:25). ◆

Jephthah and Ephraim

12 The Ephraimite forces were called
out, and they crossed over to Zaphon. They said to Jephthah, "Why did
you go to fight the Ammonites without
calling us to go with you?[h] We're going to
burn down your house over your head."
2Jephthah answered, "I and my people
were engaged in a great struggle with the
Ammonites, and although I called, you
didn't save me out of their hands. 3When I
saw that you wouldn't help, I took my life
in my hands[i] and crossed over to fight the
Ammonites, and the LORD gave me the victory over them. Now why have you come
up today to fight me?"
4Jephthah then called together the men
of Gilead and fought against Ephraim. The
Gileadites struck them down because the
Ephraimites had said, "You Gileadites are
renegades from Ephraim and Manasseh."
5The Gileadites captured the fords of the
Jordan[j] leading to Ephraim, and whenever
a survivor of Ephraim said, "Let me cross
over," the men of Gilead asked him, "Are
you an Ephraimite?" If he replied, "No,"
6they said, "All right, say 'Shibboleth.'" If
he said, "Sibboleth," because he could not
pronounce the word correctly, they seized
him and killed him at the fords of the Jordan. Forty-two thousand Ephraimites were
killed at that time.
7Jephthah led[a] Israel six years. Then
Jephthah the Gileadite died and was buried in a town in Gilead.

Ibzan, Elon and Abdon

8After him, Ibzan of Bethlehem led Israel. 9He had thirty sons and thirty daughters. He gave his daughters away in marriage to those outside his clan, and for his
sons he brought in thirty young women
as wives from outside his clan. Ibzan led
Israel seven years. 10Then Ibzan died and
was buried in Bethlehem.

12:1 [h] Jdg 8:1 **12:3** [i] 1Sa 19:5; 28:21; Job 13:14 **12:5** [j] Jos 22:11; Jdg 3:28

[a] 7 Traditionally *judged*; also in verses 8-14

12:5 *fords of the Jordan.* See note on 3:28.
12:6 *Shibboleth … Sibboleth.* The Gileadites' plan to identify Ephraimites involves a dialectical contrast between a "sh" sound and an "s" sound. This is a case of differentiation in the pronunciation of the same sibilant in different regions. To the Gileadites, the Ephraimite pronunciation of the two sounded exactly alike. Accordingly, whenever the Gileadites demanded that an Ephraimite say, "Shibboleth" (pronounced "thibboleth" by the Gileadites), he would have betrayed his origin by saying, "Sibboleth." *killed him at the fords of the Jordan.* This event reflects and reinforces the significance of the Jordan River as a geographic and psychological barrier between eastern and western Israelites. *Forty-two thousand Ephraimites were killed.* On the seemingly inordinately high numbers, see note on 1:4.
12:9 *marriage to those outside his clan … wives from outside his clan.* Ibzan's sending his daughters away reflects the patrilocal pattern of marriage. These marriages probably cemented clan alliances and extended the scope of his political influence. At the same time, Ibzan's initiative in all of these marriages arose out of a concern to build a community with sound foundations, perhaps even a dynasty.

11 After him, Elon the Zebulunite led Israel ten years. 12 Then Elon died and was buried in Aijalon in the land of Zebulun.

13 After him, Abdon son of Hillel, from Pirathon, led Israel. 14 He had forty sons and thirty grandsons,[k] who rode on seventy donkeys.[l] He led Israel eight years. 15 Then Abdon son of Hillel died and was buried at Pirathon in Ephraim, in the hill country of the Amalekites.[m]

The Birth of Samson

13 Again the Israelites did evil in the eyes of the LORD, so the LORD delivered them into the hands of the Philistines[n] for forty years.

2 A certain man of Zorah,[o] named Manoah, from the clan of the Danites, had a wife who was childless, unable to give birth. 3 The angel of the LORD[p] appeared to her[q] and said, "You are barren and childless, but you are going to become pregnant and give birth to a son.[r] 4 Now see to it that you drink no wine or other fermented drink and that you do not eat anything unclean.[s] 5 You will become pregnant and have a son whose head is never to be touched by a razor[t] because the boy is to be a Nazirite,[u] dedicated to God from the womb. He will take the lead[v] in delivering Israel from the hands of the Philistines."

6 Then the woman went to her husband and told him, "A man of God[w] came to me. He looked like an angel of God,[x] very awesome. I didn't ask him where he came from, and he didn't tell me his name. 7 But he said to me, 'You will become pregnant and have a son. Now then, drink no wine or other fermented drink and do not eat anything unclean, because the boy will be a Nazirite of God from the womb until the day of his death.' "

8 Then Manoah prayed to the LORD: "Pardon your servant, Lord. I beg you to let the man of God you sent to us come again to teach us how to bring up the boy who is to be born."

9 God heard Manoah, and the angel of God came again to the woman while she was out in the field; but her husband Manoah was not with her. 10 The woman hurried to tell her husband, "He's here! The man who appeared to me the other day!"

11 Manoah got up and followed his wife. When he came to the man, he said, "Are you the man who talked to my wife?"

"I am," he said.

12 So Manoah asked him, "When your words are fulfilled, what is to be the rule that governs the boy's life and work?"

13 The angel of the LORD answered, "Your wife must do all that I have told her. 14 She must not eat anything that comes from the grapevine, nor drink any wine or other fermented drink[y] nor eat anything unclean.[z] She must do everything I have commanded her."

15 Manoah said to the angel of the LORD, "We would like you to stay until we prepare a young goat[a] for you."

16 The angel of the LORD replied, "Even though you detain me, I will not eat any of your food. But if you prepare a burnt offering,[b] offer it to the LORD." (Manoah did not realize that it was the angel of the LORD.)

17 Then Manoah inquired of the angel of the LORD, "What is your name,[c] so that we may honor you when your word comes true?"

18 He replied, "Why do you ask my name?[d] It is beyond understanding.[a]" 19 Then Manoah took a young goat, together with the grain offering, and sacrificed it on a rock[e] to the LORD. And the LORD did an amazing thing while Manoah and his wife watched: 20 As the flame[f] blazed up from the altar toward heaven, the angel of the LORD ascended in the flame. Seeing this, Manoah and his wife fell with their

[a] 18 Or *is wonderful*

12:14 [k] Jdg 10:4 [l] Jdg 5:10
12:15 [m] Jdg 5:14
13:1 [n] Jdg 2:11; 1Sa 12:9
13:2 [o] Jos 15:33; 19:41
13:3 [p] ver 6, 8; Jdg 6:12 [q] ver 10 [r] Lk 1:13
13:4 [s] ver 14; Nu 6:2-4; Lk 1:15
13:5 [t] Nu 6:5; 1Sa 1:11 [u] Nu 6:2, 13 [v] 1Sa 7:13
13:6 [w] ver 8; 1Sa 2:27; 9:6 [x] ver 17-18; Mt 28:3
13:14 [y] Nu 6:4 [z] ver 4
13:15 [a] ver 3; Jdg 6:19
13:16 [b] Jdg 6:20
13:17 [c] Ge 32:29
13:18 [d] Isa 9:6
13:19 [e] Jdg 6:20
13:20 [f] Lev 9:24

12:14 *forty sons . . . thirty grandsons . . . seventy donkeys.* See note on 10:4.
13:1 *Philistines.* See note on 3:3.
13:3 *angel of the LORD.* See note on 2:1. *you are going to . . . give birth to a son.* Given the androcentric social structures of ancient Israel, the announcement to Manoah's wife that the child would be a son would have been especially welcome. A son would not only carry on the family name, but also provide leadership in the home and in the community. In the world outside Israel, a son was also the key to a person's well-being here and now, as well as in the afterlife.
13:4 *drink no wine or other fermented drink.* See the article "Nazirites," p. 242. *do not eat anything unclean.* The Israelite regulations concerning clean and unclean food are found in Lev 11; Dt 14.
13:5 *Nazirite.* See the article "Nazirites," p. 242.
13:15 *We would like you to stay until we prepare a young goat for you.* Like Gideon's response in 6:18, Manoah's invitation to the envoy to stay for a meal represents typical ancient Near Eastern hospitality. *young goat.* As in 6:18 (see note there).
13:18 *It is beyond understanding.* Instead of acceding to Manoah's request and giving his name, the divine envoy describes it: his name is extraordinary. *understanding.* The Hebrew word reflects the awe-inspiring numinosity of divinity, here perceived by Manoah to be fatal to a human observer (v. 22). The extraordinary nature of this being may be compared to Mesopotamia where the *melammu*, a divine brilliance, distinguishes the gods. While the *melammu* would strike terror in the hearts of those who saw it, it was not deemed to be fatal. At the same time, no abnormal appearance characterizes this messenger because his appearance gave nothing away.

faces to the ground.[g] 21 When the angel of
the LORD did not show himself again to
Manoah and his wife, Manoah realized[h]
that it was the angel of the LORD.
22 "We are doomed[i] to die!" he said to
his wife. "We have seen[j] God!"
23 But his wife answered, "If the LORD
had meant to kill us, he would not have
accepted a burnt offering and grain offering from our hands, nor shown us all
these things or now told us this."[k]
24 The woman gave birth to a boy and
named him Samson.[l] He grew[m] and the
LORD blessed him,[n] 25 and the Spirit of the
LORD began to stir[o] him while he was in
Mahaneh Dan,[p] between Zorah and Eshtaol.

Samson's Marriage

14 Samson went down to Timnah[q] and
saw there a young Philistine woman. 2 When he returned, he said to his father and mother, "I have seen a Philistine
woman in Timnah; now get her for me as
my wife."[r]
3 His father and mother replied, "Isn't
there an acceptable woman among your
relatives or among all our people?[s] Must
you go to the uncircumcised[t] Philistines
to get a wife?[u]"
But Samson said to his father, "Get her
for me. She's the right one for me." 4 (His
parents did not know that this was from
the LORD, who was seeking an occasion to
confront the Philistines;[v] for at that time
they were ruling over Israel.)[w]
5 Samson went down to Timnah together
with his father and mother. As they approached the vineyards of Timnah, suddenly a young lion came roaring toward
him. 6 The Spirit of the LORD came powerfully upon him[x] so that he tore the lion
apart with his bare hands as he might have
torn a young goat. But he told neither his
father nor his mother what he had done.
7 Then he went down and talked with the
woman, and he liked her.
8 Some time later, when he went back to
marry her, he turned aside to look at the
lion's carcass, and in it he saw a swarm of
bees and some honey. 9 He scooped out the
honey with his hands and ate as he went
along. When he rejoined his parents, he
gave them some, and they too ate it. But

13:20 [g] 1Ch 21:16; Eze 1:28; Mt 17:6 **13:21** [h] ver 16; Jdg 6:22 **13:22** [i] Dt 5:26 [j] Ge 32:30; Jdg 6:22 **13:23** [k] Ps 25:14 **13:24** [l] Heb 11:32 [m] 1Sa 3:19 [n] Lk 1:80 **13:25** [o] Jdg 3:10 [p] Jdg 18:12 **14:1** [q] Ge 38:12 **14:2** [r] Ge 21:21; 34:4 **14:3** [s] Ge 24:4 [t] Dt 7:3 [u] Ex 34:16 **14:4** [v] Jos 11:20 [w] Jdg 13:1 **14:6** [x] Jdg 3:10; 13:25

13:24 *The woman ... named him Samson.* In ancient Israel, either parent could name a child, though the OT reports mothers naming their children more often than fathers. *Samson.* The name consists of the Hebrew word for sun with the diminutive ending, hence, "little sun." It is tempting to give the name a positive spin as a celebration of the ray of light, which the birth of this boy represented in the dark days of the judges. Some have suggested it was given in anticipation of his "sunlike" strength. A more common view links the name with the worship of the sun, which provides the background for the Samson narratives. The fact that Samson's name incorporates the same element as Beth Shemesh (1:33, lit. "house of Shemesh"), the name of an important town just a few miles/kilometers from Zorah and Eshtaol down the Sorek Valley, once the focal point of sun worship, offers strong support for this interpretation. Consequently, this may be understood as yet another example of the Canaanization of the Israelites in this period. Theophoric names involving Shemesh/Shamash were common in the ancient Near East, and exemplified in the OT by Shimshai in Ezr 4:8.

14:2 *get her for me as my wife.* Though parentally arranged marriages are nowhere mandated in the OT, this tended to be the practice, a fact reflected in expressions like "give your daughters to their sons" (e.g., Dt 7:3). In contrast to modern Western marriages, where marriage tends to be an individual matter and driven by personal desire for companionship and romance, arranged marriages in the ancient world often represented alliances intended to ensure the continuation of the families through progeny.

14:3 *acceptable woman among your relatives or among all our people.* In Israel, marriages were generally endogamous—i.e., within the clan or tribe—though there were no laws against marrying someone from another tribe. For an Israelite to marry a Philistine poses a special problem, a commitment to peaceful coexistence and mutual acceptance between the clans (cf. Ge 34:14–17). This is precisely what Dt 7:1–8 forbids on spiritual and theological grounds: Israel is Yahweh's holy people. Since the Philistines are not listed in Dt 7:1, technically one might argue that they are excluded from the prohibition. However, to Samson's parents, his proposition to marry a Philistine appears simply a cultural and ethnic issue—they say nothing of Yahweh's prohibition on intermarriage with non-Israelites, Samson's call to special Nazirite status within Israel or Yahweh's agenda for him to deliver Israel from Philistine oppression. *uncircumcised Philistines.* An intentionally pejorative slur, used in the Bible only of the Philistines (cf. 15:18; 1Sa 14:6; 17:26,36; 31:4 [1Ch 10:4]; 2Sa 1:20). Although the origins of circumcision are unknown, the practice was widespread in the ancient world, being attested not only in Israel, but also among Egyptians, Ammonites, Moabites, Edomites, and perhaps Midianites (Ex 4:24–26), but not among the eastern Semites of Mesopotamia (see the article "Circumcision," p. 46). It is unknown whether ancient Canaanites practiced circumcision, though the account of Jacob's sons and the Shechemites in Ge 34 suggests they did not.

14:5 *lion.* Although lions are found in Israel only in captivity today, in ancient times Asiatic lions were common throughout the Fertile Crescent. Indeed, in ancient Assyria the lion symbolized chaos and the untamed world in all its forms. Through their successes as lion hunters, Neo-Assyrian kings demonstrated their authority over evil forces, both cosmic and human, and proved that they deserved the title "Master of the Beasts." In Jdg 14–15, Samson proves himself "Master of the Beasts," first by overpowering a lion effortlessly, and later by capturing and manipulating 300 foxes (15:4–5).

14:8 *lion's carcass, and in it ... a swarm of bees and some honey.* Bees do not normally inhabit cadavers; flies and maggots do. Apparently this carcass dehydrated quickly, eliminating putrefaction, and in no time at all provided a hospitable environment for bees not only to live but also to produce their honey.

he did not tell them that he had taken the
honey from the lion's carcass.
10 Now his father went down to see the
woman. And there Samson held a feast, as
was customary for young men. 11 When the
people saw him, they chose thirty men to
be his companions.
12 "Let me tell you a riddle,[y]" Samson
said to them. "If you can give me the answer within the seven days of the feast,[z]
I will give you thirty linen garments and
thirty sets of clothes.[a] 13 If you can't tell me
the answer, you must give me thirty linen
garments and thirty sets of clothes."
"Tell us your riddle," they said. "Let's
hear it."
14 He replied,

"Out of the eater, something to eat;
out of the strong, something sweet."

For three days they could not give the answer.
15 On the fourth[a] day, they said to Samson's wife, "Coax[b] your husband into explaining the riddle for us, or we will burn
you and your father's household to death.[c]
Did you invite us here to steal our property?"
16 Then Samson's wife threw herself on
him, sobbing, "You hate me! You don't
really love me.[d] You've given my people a
riddle, but you haven't told me the answer."
"I haven't even explained it to my father
or mother," he replied, "so why should I
explain it to you?" 17 She cried the whole
seven days[e] of the feast. So on the seventh
day he finally told her, because she continued to press him. She in turn explained
the riddle to her people.
18 Before sunset on the seventh day the
men of the town said to him,

"What is sweeter than honey?
What is stronger than a lion?"[f]

Samson said to them,

"If you had not plowed with my heifer,
you would not have solved my
riddle."

19 Then the Spirit of the LORD came powerfully upon him.[g] He went down to Ashkelon, struck down thirty of their men,
stripped them of everything and gave their
clothes to those who had explained the
riddle. Burning with anger,[h] he returned
to his father's home. 20 And Samson's wife
was given to one of his companions[i] who
had attended him at the feast.

14:12 [y] 1Ki 10:1; Eze 17:2 [z] Ge 29:27 [a] Ge 45:22; 2Ki 5:5 **14:15** [b] Jdg 16:5; Ecc 7:26 [c] Jdg 15:6 **14:16** [d] Jdg 16:15 **14:17** [e] Est 1:5 **14:18** [f] ver 14 **14:19** [g] Nu 11:25; Jdg 3:10; 6:34; 11:29; 13:25; 15:14; 1Sa 11:6; 16:13; 1Ki 18:46; 2Ch 24:20; Isa 11:2 [h] 1Sa 11:6 **14:20** [i] Jdg 15:2,6; Jn 3:29

[a] 15 Some Septuagint manuscripts and Syriac; Hebrew *seventh*

14:10 *Samson held a feast, as was customary.* The word for "feast" in this context refers to a seven-day feast at the home of the bride's parents, climaxing in the consummation of the marriage. The picture of drunken revelry at a Philistine event is quite realistic. The seriousness of the issue for Samson is heightened, inasmuch as his Nazirite status specifically prohibits him from consuming products derived from grapes. We know of no civil or sacred ceremonies for marriage in the ancient world. People were officially married when their families came to agreement, the dowry and bride-price were exchanged, and the match was officially celebrated. The marriage then was consummated, and the two became man and wife.

14:11 *thirty men to be his companions.* Their role is uncertain. Traditionally, the response of the Philistines has been interpreted as arising out of a concern to maintain Philistine custom. Apparently grooms did not host such feasts without attendants. On the surface, the Philistines' action appears to be a gesture of goodwill—they are providing companions for him. However, since Samson is a stranger in this town, and "friendship" implies a measure of intimacy, it is doubtful the narrator looks upon these men as Samson's friends. Either the expression is used ironically, or these 30 men are "friends" of the Philistine guests.

14:13 *thirty linen garments and thirty sets of clothes.* The first expression is cognate to an Akkadian term that refers to an item of clothing. Traditionally the former has been understood as a luxurious cape, and the latter as festal clothing, in contrast to everyday garments.

14:15 *wife.* The Hebrew word denotes both "woman" and "wife." If the Philistines followed the custom reflected in Ge 29:23,27, the marriage would not have been consummated until the seventh day of the feast, but in this cultural context the status of a betrothed woman was not sharply distinguished from that of a wife (but see NIV text note).

14:18 *If you had not plowed with my heifer.* The Philistines' answer to Samson's riddle is a riddle in itself, indicating the means by which they solved it. *my heifer.* Samson's reference to his new bride is as disparaging in the Hebrew as it is in the English.

14:19 *stripped … of.* The expression occurs elsewhere only in 2Sa 2:21, where it denotes the equipment stripped from a slain man, particularly the belt from which weapons and tools were hung. Carrying these items 20 miles (32 kilometers) back to Timnah in a mocking gesture, Samson presents them to the Philistine guards as their promised change of clothes. *returned to his father's home.* Within the context of ancient Near Eastern marriage customs, the fact that Samson went home after the wedding was probably not unusual. In a cultural context where marriages were patrilocal, his new father-in-law could have interpreted his action as a return home to get the house in order. These periods of separation often lasted several months. Meanwhile, the wife continued to live at home, and the husband would visit her at more or less regular intervals, bringing gifts and enjoying a night of love. According to 15:1, Samson seems to think he can return to his wife at any time.

14:20 *Samson's wife was given to one of his companions.* It is probably not surprising that the author later gives us only the father-in-law's interpretation of Samson's departure (15:2). Not a word is said about the feelings of Samson's wife. Did she have any say in whether or not her father would give her to another man? Did she love Samson? Did she want him back? In the ancient world, most women in this situation would probably have longed for their husbands to return.

Samson's Vengeance on the Philistines

15 Later on, at the time of wheat harvest, Samson took a young goat[j] and went to visit his wife. He said, "I'm going to my wife's room." But her father would not let him go in.

2"I was so sure you hated her," he said, "that I gave her to your companion.[k] Isn't her younger sister more attractive? Take her instead."

3Samson said to them, "This time I have a right to get even with the Philistines; I will really harm them." 4So he went out and caught three hundred foxes and tied them tail to tail in pairs. He then fastened a torch to every pair of tails, 5lit the torches and let the foxes loose in the standing grain of the Philistines. He burned up the shocks and standing grain, together with the vineyards and olive groves.

6When the Philistines asked, "Who did this?" they were told, "Samson, the Timnite's son-in-law, because his wife was given to his companion."

So the Philistines went up and burned her and her father to death.[l] 7Samson said to them, "Since you've acted like this, I swear that I won't stop until I get my revenge on you." 8He attacked them viciously and slaughtered many of them. Then he went down and stayed in a cave in the rock of Etam.

9The Philistines went up and camped in Judah, spreading out near Lehi.[m] 10The people of Judah asked, "Why have you come to fight us?"

"We have come to take Samson prisoner," they answered, "to do to him as he did to us."

11Then three thousand men from Judah went down to the cave in the rock of Etam and said to Samson, "Don't you realize that the Philistines are rulers over us?[n] What have you done to us?"

15:1 [j]Ge 38:17 **15:2** [k]Jdg 14:20 **15:6** [l]Jdg 14:15 **15:9** [m]ver 14, 17, 19 **15:11** [n]Jdg 13:1; 14:4; Ps 106:40-42

He answered, "I merely did to them what they did to me."

12They said to him, "We've come to tie you up and hand you over to the Philistines."

Samson said, "Swear to me that you won't kill me yourselves."

13"Agreed," they answered. "We will only tie you up and hand you over to them. We will not kill you." So they bound him with two new ropes and led him up from the rock. 14As he approached Lehi, the Philistines came toward him shouting. The Spirit of the LORD came powerfully upon him.[o] The ropes on his arms became like charred flax, and the bindings dropped from his hands. 15Finding a fresh jawbone of a donkey, he grabbed it and struck down a thousand men.[p]

16Then Samson said,

"With a donkey's jawbone
 I have made donkeys of them.[a]
With a donkey's jawbone
 I have killed a thousand men."

17When he finished speaking, he threw away the jawbone; and the place was called Ramath Lehi.[b]

18Because he was very thirsty, he cried out to the LORD,[q] "You have given your servant this great victory. Must I now die of thirst and fall into the hands of the uncircumcised?" 19Then God opened up the hollow place in Lehi, and water came out of it. When Samson drank, his strength returned and he revived.[r] So the spring was called En Hakkore,[c] and it is still there in Lehi.

20Samson led[d] Israel for twenty years[s] in the days of the Philistines.

15:14 [o]Jdg 3:10; 14:19; 1Sa 11:6 **15:15** [p]Lev 26:8; Jos 23:10; Jdg 3:31 **15:18** [q]Jdg 16:28 **15:19** [r]Ge 45:27; Isa 40:29 **15:20** [s]Jdg 13:1; 16:31; Heb 11:32

[a] *16* Or *made a heap or two*; the Hebrew for *donkey* sounds like the Hebrew for *heap*. [b] *17 Ramath Lehi* means *jawbone hill*. [c] *19 En Hakkore* means *caller's spring*. [d] *20* Traditionally *judged*

15:2 *I was so sure you hated her.* At the climax of the wedding festivities, Samson had left his wife in anger (14:19), and her family assumed logically that he had repudiated the marriage and rejected his wife (14:20). The bride's father's assessment of the situation is expressed emphatically with the infinitive absolute and finite verb and may be interpreted as "you have surely divorced her," with no intention of returning to claim her.

15:4 – 5 *went out ... caught ... tied ... fastened ... lit ... let ... loose ... burned up.* The rapid succession of verbs in the description creates the impression that Samson's actions took no effort at all.

15:4 *foxes.* The Hebrew word used here applied to both foxes and jackals. Since the latter were more common in Canaan, and since foxes are solitary animals, Samson was probably dealing with jackals, which live in packs. Jackals are certainly intended in Eze 13:4; La 5:18; Ps 63:10, where the same Hebrew word is used.

15:5 *burned up.* This specific sort of strategy is undocumented anywhere else in the ancient world, though burning the crops of the enemy is common enough.

15:13 *new ropes.* The reference in v. 14 to "charred flax" (lit. "flax that had been burned with fire") suggests that the "new ropes" were made of flax fibers. Flax fibers are among the strongest and longest natural fibers in use by human beings, and they gain in strength when they are wet. In the present instance, the "new ropes" were undoubtedly ropes made of fresh fibers harvested from that year's crop.

15:15 *fresh jawbone of a donkey.* Reminiscent of Shamgar's victory over the Philistines using an oxgoad (3:31), Samson used a fresh jawbone to slaughter "a thousand men." The image is intended to be comical. Being only about nine inches (23 centimeters) long, a donkey's jawbone is an unlikely weapon. *a thousand.* Used as a way to indicate a band, so it is difficult to know how many Samson fought.

Samson and Delilah

16 One day Samson went to Gaza,
where he saw a prostitute. He went
in to spend the night with her. 2The people
of Gaza were told, "Samson is here!" So
they surrounded the place and lay in wait
for him all night at the city gate.[t] They
made no move during the night, saying,
"At dawn we'll kill him."

3But Samson lay there only until the
middle of the night. Then he got up and
took hold of the doors of the city gate, together with the two posts, and tore them
loose, bar and all. He lifted them to his
shoulders and carried them to the top of
the hill that faces Hebron.[u]

4Some time later, he fell in love[v] with a
woman in the Valley of Sorek whose name
was Delilah. 5The rulers of the Philistines[w]
went to her and said, "See if you can lure[x]
him into showing you the secret of his
great strength and how we can overpower him so we may tie him up and subdue
him. Each one of us will give you eleven
hundred shekels[a] of silver."[y]

6So Delilah said to Samson, "Tell me the
secret of your great strength and how you
can be tied up and subdued."

7Samson answered her, "If anyone ties
me with seven fresh bowstrings that have
not been dried, I'll become as weak as any
other man."

8Then the rulers of the Philistines
brought her seven fresh bowstrings that
had not been dried, and she tied him with
them. 9With men hidden in the room,[z] she
called to him, "Samson, the Philistines are
upon you!" But he snapped the bowstrings
as easily as a piece of string snaps when
it comes close to a flame. So the secret of
his strength was not discovered.

10Then Delilah said to Samson, "You
have made a fool of me;[a] you lied to me.
Come now, tell me how you can be tied."

11He said, "If anyone ties me securely with new ropes[b] that have never been
used, I'll become as weak as any other
man."

12So Delilah took new ropes and tied
him with them. Then, with men hidden
in the room, she called to him, "Samson, the Philistines are upon you!" But he
snapped the ropes off his arms as if they
were threads.

13Delilah then said to Samson, "All this
time you have been making a fool of me
and lying to me. Tell me how you can be
tied."

He replied, "If you weave the sev-
en braids of my head into the fabric on
the loom and tighten it with the pin, I'll
become as weak as any other man." So
while he was sleeping, Delilah took the
seven braids of his head, wove them into
the fabric 14and[b] tightened it with the pin.

Again she called to him, "Samson, the
Philistines are upon you!"[c] He awoke from
his sleep and pulled up the pin and the
loom, with the fabric.

15Then she said to him, "How can you
say, 'I love you,'[d] when you won't confide
in me? This is the third time[e] you have
made a fool of me and haven't told me
the secret of your great strength.[f]" 16With
such nagging she prodded him day after
day until he was sick to death of it.

17So he told her everything.[g] "No razor
has ever been used on my head," he said,
"because I have been a Nazirite[h] dedi-

16:2 [t] 1Sa 23:26; Ps 118:10-12; Ac 9:24 **16:3** [u] Jos 10:36 **16:4** [v] Ge 24:67 **16:5** [w] Jos 13:3 [x] Ex 10:7; Jdg 14:15 [y] ver 18 **16:9** [z] ver 12

16:10 [a] ver 13 **16:11** [b] Jdg 15:13 **16:14** [c] ver 9,20 **16:15** [d] Jdg 14:16 [e] Nu 24:10 [f] ver 5 **16:17** [g] Mic 7:5 [h] Nu 6:2,5; Jdg 13:5

[a] *5* That is, about 28 pounds or about 13 kilograms
[b] *13,14* Some Septuagint manuscripts; Hebrew *replied, "I can if you weave the seven braids of my head into the fabric on the loom."* 14*So she*

16:3 *doors of the city gate.* The gates of major fortifications had to be wide enough for chariots to drive through. The gates themselves consisted of double doors made of wood; to prevent easy entry by an enemy, they had to be made of thick boards. They were barred on the side by means of a heavy horizontal beam slid through slots in the doorposts. The doors were braced by wooden posts, the outside of which pivoted in stone sockets. The gates of Gaza that Samson pulled out of their sockets and hoisted onto his shoulders must have weighed at least 400 or 500 pounds (about 200 kilograms). *carried them to the top of the hill that faces Hebron.* As the crow flies, the distance from Gaza to Hebron is 40 miles (65 kilometers). But if Samson followed the route along the Wadi Guvrin, as is most likely, the distance would have been even greater. It is not clear how far Samson carried the gates. *carried ... to.* Since elsewhere the idiom simply means "in the direction of," it seems most likely that Samson headed off in the direction of Hebron, and when he reached the top of the hill—probably overlooking Gaza—he deposited the gates.

16:5 *The rulers of the Philistines.* There were five (see note on 3:3). *eleven hundred shekels of silver.* About 28 pounds (13 kilograms) of silver. In the OT, the shekel was the primary unit of weight, used especially to measure commodities in business transactions. The reward the Philistine rulers offer Delilah for betraying her husband is exorbitant: 5,500 shekels of silver—1,100 shekels per governor. Calculated according to the standard of ancient wages, if the average wage of a day laborer was ten shekels a year (cf. 17:10), this amount is equivalent to 550 years' wages.

16:7 *bowstrings.* The meaning of this noun is uncertain, but the Hebrew word is used elsewhere of bowstrings (Job 30:11; Ps 11:2) and a tent peg (4:21), made from the tendons of a sheep or a cow. Normally these would have been laid out to dry, but in specifying that these were to be "fresh" and "not ... dried," Samson again trivializes his Nazirite vow. He assumes the Philistines will understand these unprocessed sinews to have magical powers, to counter the assumed magical source of his strength.

16:17 *If my head were shaved, my strength would leave me.* A number of well-known tales from the Aegean region (where the Philistines had come from) feature a hero with hair that made him invincible and who was defeated when it was cut. The Philistines may well have retained

cated to God from my mother's womb. If
my head were shaved, my strength would
leave me, and I would become as weak as
any other man."

18 When Delilah saw that he had told
her everything, she sent word to the rulers of the Philistines[i], "Come back once
more; he has told me everything." So the
rulers of the Philistines returned with the
silver in their hands. 19 After putting him to
sleep on her lap, she called for someone to
shave off the seven braids of his hair, and
so began to subdue him.[a] And his strength
left him.[j]

20 Then she called, "Samson, the Philistines are upon you!"

He awoke from his sleep and thought,
"I'll go out as before and shake myself
free." But he did not know that the LORD
had left him.[k]

21 Then the Philistines[l] seized him,
gouged out his eyes[m] and took him down
to Gaza. Binding him with bronze shackles, they set him to grinding grain[n] in the
prison. 22 But the hair on his head began to
grow again after it had been shaved.

The Death of Samson

23 Now the rulers of the Philistines assembled to offer a great sacrifice to Dagon[o] their god and to celebrate, saying,
"Our god has delivered Samson, our enemy, into our hands."

24 When the people saw him, they
praised their god,[p] saying,

"Our god has delivered our enemy
into our hands,[q]
the one who laid waste our land
and multiplied our slain."

25 While they were in high spirits,[r] they
shouted, "Bring out Samson to entertain
us." So they called Samson out of the prison, and he performed for them.

When they stood him among the pillars,
26 Samson said to the servant who held his
hand, "Put me where I can feel the pillars that support the temple, so that I may
lean against them." 27 Now the temple was
crowded with men and women; all the rulers of the Philistines were there, and on the
roof[s] were about three thousand men and
women watching Samson perform. 28 Then
Samson prayed to the LORD,[t] "Sovereign
LORD, remember me. Please, God, strength-
en me just once more, and let me with one
blow get revenge[u] on the Philistines for my
two eyes." 29 Then Samson reached toward
the two central pillars on which the temple stood. Bracing himself against them, his
right hand on the one and his left hand on
the other, 30 Samson said, "Let me die with
the Philistines!" Then he pushed with all

16:18 [i] Jos 13:3; 1Sa 5:8 **16:19** [j] Pr 7:26-27 **16:20** [k] Nu 14:42; Jos 7:12; 1Sa 16:14; 18:12; 28:15 **16:21** [l] Jer 47:1 [m] Nu 16:14 [n] Job 31:10; Isa 47:2 **16:23** [o] 1Sa 5:2; 1Ch 10:10

16:24 [p] Da 5:4 [q] 1Sa 31:9; 1Ch 10:9 **16:25** [r] Jdg 9:27; Ru 3:7; Est 1:10 **16:27** [s] Dt 22:8; Jos 2:8 **16:28** [t] Jdg 15:18 [u] Jer 15:15

[a] *19* Hebrew; some Septuagint manuscripts *and he began to weaken*

these traditions, and, if so, would recognize this kind of thinking. Even though Samson has violated his Nazirite vow many times by now, it is the cutting of the hair that brings an end to the vow.

16:21 *gouged out his eyes.* A common ancient Near Eastern custom. In Mesopotamia, defeated enemies were often blinded by having their eyes gouged and then humiliated by being forced to perform the most menial of tasks, customarily assigned to slaves and women. Hittite sources report that captors blinded particularly dangerous captives to prevent them from taking up arms or trying to flee.

16:23 *a great sacrifice to Dagon their god.* One may assume from the presentation of "a great sacrifice" that the festivities described in vv. 23 – 24 took place in the temple of Dagon, the patron deity of the Philistines. Although the Philistines were non-Semitic peoples, having originated in the Aegean, they appear to have adapted quickly to prevailing religious ideologies in Canaan. See the article "Dagon," p. 468. *Our god has delivered Samson, our enemy, into our hands.* This is a Hebrew version of the divine committal formula, variations of which occur in many extra-Biblical texts. The direct quotation here, which may have been chanted by the governors, captures the theme of the celebration, and in so doing reflects several important features of common ancient Near Eastern theology. First, even though Dagon has been out of the picture in the preceding episodes, the narrator presents the captivity of Samson, not as the result of human decision and machinations, but as a divine accomplishment. Second, although Dagon may have been primarily associated with grain and harvest (still open to much debate), this chant portrays him in a military role, giving the enemy into the Philistines' hands.

16:26 *pillars that support the temple.* While no Philistine temple to Dagon has been discovered in Gaza, excavations further north at Tel Qasile have revealed a Philistine building that illuminates this text. The temple was a complex structure 40 feet (12 meters) long and 25 feet (7.5 meters) wide. Two cedar pillars slightly less than 10 feet (16 meters) apart set on round stone bases supported the roof and upper story of this large temple. In the temple in this account, the pillars must have been closer together than that.

16:27 *roof.* Here the Hebrew word that usually means "roof" may refer to a balcony or terrace surrounding the central courtyard where Samson was standing. Ancient public buildings, including temples, often included central courtyards, surrounded by rooms and balconies on the second floor. It seems that all the rulers and undoubtedly the temple functionaries, were on the ground floor, where Samson was entertaining them, while 3,000 spectators looked on from above. *three thousand.* The number seems inordinately high, but it should be interpreted along the lines of other high figures in the book (see note on 1:4).

16:29 *central pillars.* May either be solid pieces of cedar spanning the entire height, or thick disks of stone piled atop one another. In either case, it was the weight of the roof that held them in place.

16:30 *pushed.* The Hebrew verb describing Samson's act that caused the collapse is unclear, but would have involved either pushing or twisting the central pillars off their stone bases.

his might, and down came the temple on
the rulers and all the people in it. Thus he
killed many more when he died than while
he lived.
31 Then his brothers and his father's
whole family went down to get him. They
brought him back and buried him between Zorah and Eshtaol in the tomb of
Manoah[v] his father. He had led[aw] Israel
twenty years.[x]

Micah's Idols

17 Now a man named Micah[y] from the
hill country of Ephraim 2 said to his
mother, "The eleven hundred shekels[b] of
silver that were taken from you and about
which I heard you utter a curse — I have
that silver with me; I took it."
Then his mother said, "The LORD bless
you,[z] my son!"
3 When he returned the eleven hundred
shekels of silver to his mother, she said, "I
solemnly consecrate my silver to the LORD
for my son to make an image overlaid with
silver.[a] I will give it back to you."
4 So after he returned the silver to his
mother, she took two hundred shekels[c] of
silver and gave them to a silversmith, who
used them to make the idol.[b] And it was
put in Micah's house.
5 Now this man Micah had a shrine,[c] and
he made an ephod[d] and some household
gods[e] and installed[f] one of his sons as his
priest.[g] 6 In those days Israel had no king;[h]
everyone did as they saw fit.[i]
7 A young Levite from Bethlehem in Judah,[j] who had been living within the clan
of Judah, 8 left that town in search of some
other place to stay. On his way[d] he came
to Micah's house in the hill country of
Ephraim.
9 Micah asked him, "Where are you
from?"
"I'm a Levite from Bethlehem in Judah," he said, "and I'm looking for a place
to stay."

16:31 [v] Jdg 13:2 [w] Ru 1:1; 1Sa 4:18 [x] Jdg 15:20 **17:1** [y] Jdg 18:2, 13 **17:2** [z] Ru 2:20; 1Sa 15:13; 2Sa 2:5 **17:3** [a] Ex 20:4, 23; 34:17; Lev 19:4 **17:4** [b] Ex 32:4; Isa 17:8 **17:5** [c] Isa 44:13; Eze 8:10 [d] Jdg 8:27 [e] Ge 31:19; Jdg 18:14 [f] Nu 16:10 [g] Ex 29:9; Jdg 18:24 **17:6** [h] Jdg 18:1; 19:1; 21:25 [i] Dt 12:8 **17:7** [j] Jdg 19:1; Ru 1:1-2; Mic 5:2; Mt 2:1

[a] *31* Traditionally *judged* [b] *2* That is, about 28 pounds or about 13 kilograms [c] *4* That is, about 5 pounds or about 2.3 kilograms [d] *8* Or *To carry on his profession*

16:31 *in the tomb of Manoah his father.* See note on Ge 25:8.

17:2 *curse.* This Hebrew verb for "cursing" is relatively rare, and serves as an abbreviated version of the curse formula, which more often involves a different verb plus the noun. In general, the text indicates a conditional curse, in this case the invocation of some horrendous fate on someone who commits a crime. *The LORD bless you, my son!* By exchanging the curse for a blessing, Micah's mother seeks to prevent the disaster threatened by the previous curse. Her blessing is cast in typical form, "May my son be blessed by Yahweh," which bears a close resemblance to the syncretistic blessings on two Hebrew inscriptions from southern Judah:

Kuntillet 'Ajrud pithos: "May you be blessed by Yahweh of Samaria and by his Asherah."

Khirbet el-Qom: "May Uriyahu be blessed by Yahweh."

Utterances like this characteristically express the speaker's grateful response to a good deed done for him or her by the third party on whose behalf the blessing is invoked. The fact that Micah's mother commends Micah to Yahweh, rather than Baal or some other Canaanite deity, suggests she is devoted to the covenant God of Israel — though this devotion is not firm, as the sequel demonstrates.

17:3 *I solemnly consecrate my silver to the LORD.* In the ancient world, the manufacture of images of gods was a complex process that began with the consecration of the materials out of which the images were to be made. A bull calf statuette found at Ashkelon, apparently associated with the worship of El or Baal, is 4.1 inches (10 centimeters) high and 4.3 inches (11 centimeters) long, and weighs just under a pound (0.45 kilograms). Its body was made of solid cast bronze, and still retained some of the thick overleaf of pure silver that once covered the entire body. While the icon from Ashkelon consisted mostly of bronze, which is much cheaper than silver, divine images were often carved out of wood and then plated with precious metals. Five pounds (2.25 kilograms) of silver (the weight of the 200 shekels offered here) could plate an image much more impressive than this calf. *an image overlaid with silver.* Lit. "a sculpture and something poured," which reflects the process of idol manufacture, i.e., "a carved image overlaid with molten metal."

17:5 *shrine.* Lit. "house of god," which reflects the primary function of temples in the ancient world — a residence for deity. Being a family shrine or chapel, the present structure must have been modest in size, perhaps consisting of a small building in which the image was housed. This shrine was intended to serve the needs of the family by providing a means of securing divine assistance in conception and childbirth, fertility of flocks and fields, and protection from natural calamities and enemies. *ephod.* See note on 8:27. *household gods.* In Ge 31:19, the Hebrew word rendered "household gods" (*teraphim*) seems to refer to miniature images of ancestors (see the article "Household Gods," p. 72). But the form and function of these "*teraphim*" in the ancient Near East remains unclear. The most likely explanation refers to "a spirit which can on some occasions be regarded as protective and on others as malevolent." Zec 10:2 links idols with diviners who prophesy through visions and dreams, suggesting these objects may have had a divinatory function. The fact that in 1Sa 19:11 – 17 Michal made use of one that was mistaken for a sick man suggests these images were anthropomorphic, lending support to the view that they were figurines representing deceased ancestors. *installed one of his sons as his priest.* In most instances, the Hebrew idiom for "installation" (lit. "to fill the hands") is used of the consecration of priests. The Hebrew word suggests it involved the placement of some symbol of authority into the hands of the person being installed. This action posed a direct challenge to the officially authorized Aaronic priesthood.

17:6 *In those days Israel had no king.* During the settlement period, Israel had a decentralized government, and each tribe was governed by its own chieftains, leaving local communities much freedom to govern their own lives. This also meant that there was likely no centralized control over religious matters, leaving Micah and his household with complete independence in shaping the cult in their own household.

10 Then Micah said to him, "Live with
me and be my father and priest,[k] and I'll
give you ten shekels[a] of silver a year, your
clothes and your food." 11 So the Levite
agreed to live with him, and the young
man became like one of his sons to him.
12 Then Micah installed[l] the Levite, and the
young man became his priest and lived in
his house. 13 And Micah said, "Now I know
that the LORD will be good to me, since this
Levite has become my priest."

The Danites Settle in Laish

18 In those days Israel had no king.[m]
And in those days the tribe of the
Danites was seeking a place of their own
where they might settle, because they had
not yet come into an inheritance among
the tribes of Israel.[n] 2 So the Danites[o] sent
five of their leading men from Zorah and
Eshtaol to spy out the land and explore
it. These men represented all the Danites.
They told them, "Go, explore the land."[p]
So they entered the hill country of
Ephraim and came to the house of Micah,[q] where they spent the night. 3 When
they were near Micah's house, they recognized the voice of the young Levite; so
they turned in there and asked him, "Who
brought you here? What are you doing in
this place? Why are you here?"
4 He told them what Micah had done for
him, and said, "He has hired me and I am
his priest.[r]"
5 Then they said to him, "Please inquire
of God[s] to learn whether our journey will
be successful."
6 The priest answered them, "Go in
peace[t]. Your journey has the LORD's approval."
7 So the five men left and came to Laish,[u]
where they saw that the people were living in safety, like the Sidonians, at peace
and secure. And since their land lacked
nothing, they were prosperous.[b] Also, they
lived a long way from the Sidonians[v] and
had no relationship with anyone else.[c]
8 When they returned to Zorah and Eshtaol, their fellow Danites asked them,
"How did you find things?"
9 They answered, "Come on, let's attack them! We have seen the land, and
it is very good. Aren't you going to do
something? Don't hesitate to go there and

17:10 [k] Jdg 18:19 **17:12** [l] Nu 16:10 **18:1** [m] Jdg 17:6; 19:1 [n] Jos 19:47 **18:2** [o] Jdg 13:25 [p] Jos 2:1 [q] Jdg 17:1 **18:4** [r] Jdg 17:12 **18:5** [s] 1Ki 22:5 **18:6** [t] 1Ki 22:6 **18:7** [u] Jos 19:47 [v] ver 28

[a] *10* That is, about 4 ounces or about 115 grams
[b] *7* The meaning of the Hebrew for this clause is uncertain.
[c] *7* Hebrew; some Septuagint manuscripts *with the Arameans*

17:10 *ten shekels of silver a year.* This was the typical annual salary for laborers. The Pentateuch never stipulates the salary for priests or Levites, who would theoretically be provided for by sacrifices. *silver.* The offering of precious metals constitutes a bribe.

18:1 *the tribe of the Danites.* According to Jos 19:40 – 48, the original Danite territorial allotment was located west of the Benjamite land, between the territories of Ephraim and Judah. The present events must have happened soon after the death of Joshua and prior to the events described in Jdg 13 – 16. First, the Levitical priest is identified in 18:30 as "Jonathan son of Gershom, the son of Moses," which would suggest placing these events within two generations of the conquest (though at times generations can be skipped). Second, the Philistines claimed a large part of the territory allotted to the Danites. However, there is no hint of Philistine involvement here — unless, of course, their presence was the reason the Danites could not occupy the land assigned to them. *inheritance.* Although most English versions translate the word used here with inheritance terminology, this is a feudal expression, referring primarily to land given by a superior to his vassals as a reward for past service (usually military service) and in anticipation of future service. This designation is appropriate for the territory originally given to Israel by Yahweh and distributed by Joshua by lot among the tribes, but it does not suit territory seized by force, particularly when it is at another Israelite tribe's expense.

18:5 *inquire of God.* Before embarking on an adventure like this, which had military implications, leaders would consult their deities to determine their disposition toward the mission. To the Danites the Levitical priest was the equivalent of an Assyrian *baru* priest or a prophet at Mari. Sometimes such an intermediary would attempt to curry the favor of the deity through sacrifices. The present context gives no indication how — or even if — the Levitical priest sought his oracle from Yahweh. Presumably he used the household gods or ephod mentioned in 17:5.

18:6 *Go in peace.* This is stereotypical, involving the word meaning "peace, well-being." *Your journey has the LORD's approval.* Most translations (including the NIV) interpret this positively, but in fact it is quite ambiguous. The Hebrew reads lit. "Before Yahweh is your course on which you are going." This could mean that it has the approval of Yahweh's watchful eye, but it could also mean the opposite, i.e., the conduct of the scouts and the Danites as a tribe is under critical scrutiny by Yahweh. Such ambiguity was characteristic of many ancient prophecies. In this instance, the Danite scouts should have come back and asked the Levite what he meant by the oracle.

18:7 *like the Sidonians.* A paraphrastic idiom suggesting that Laish was located within the sphere of Sidon, a major Phoenician coastal city. This accords with what we know of Sidon's status at the end of the second millennium BC. Although Sidon existed in the shadow of Tyre from the time of Solomon, prior to this, she had been the premiere Phoenician city. In the OT, the non-Semitic "Sidonians" stands for "Phoenicians." *a long way from the Sidonians.* The Sidonians, separated from Laish by the Lebanon mountains and preoccupied with their maritime interests, apparently had neither time for nor interest in exerting political control in the interior. *no relationship with anyone else.* Nestled in the shadow of Mount Hermon, between the Lebanon and Anti-Lebanon mountain ranges, the people of Laish lived in isolation from the Arameans to the east and north and in independence from Sidon to the west. Recent archaeological excavations of Dan may have unearthed one more reason for the Laishite smugness: their massive defensive ramparts. Like most Canaanite cities of the time, Laish was not defended by stone walls, but by huge ramparts consisting of alternating layers of soil from the surrounding region and debris from previous settlements.

take it over.[w] 10When you get there, you
will find an unsuspecting people and a
spacious land that God has put into your
hands, a land that lacks nothing[x] whatever.[y]"
11Then six hundred men[z] of the Danites,[a] armed for battle, set out from Zorah
and Eshtaol. 12On their way they set up
camp near Kiriath Jearim in Judah. This
is why the place west of Kiriath Jearim is
called Mahaneh Dan[a][b] to this day. 13From
there they went on to the hill country of
Ephraim and came to Micah's house.
14Then the five men who had spied out
the land of Laish said to their fellow Danites, "Do you know that one of these houses has an ephod, some household gods
and an image overlaid with silver?[c] Now
you know what to do." 15So they turned in
there and went to the house of the young
Levite at Micah's place and greeted him.
16The six hundred Danites,[d] armed for battle, stood at the entrance of the gate. 17The
five men who had spied out the land went
inside and took the idol, the ephod and
the household gods[e] while the priest and
the six hundred armed men stood at the
entrance of the gate.
18When the five men went into Micah's
house and took[f] the idol, the ephod and
the household gods, the priest said to
them, "What are you doing?"
19They answered him, "Be quiet![g] Don't
say a word. Come with us, and be our father and priest.[h] Isn't it better that you
serve a tribe and clan in Israel as priest
rather than just one man's household?"
20The priest was very pleased. He took the
ephod, the household gods and the idol
and went along with the people. 21Putting
their little children, their livestock and
their possessions in front of them, they
turned away and left.
22When they had gone some distance
from Micah's house, the men who lived
near Micah were called together and overtook the Danites. 23As they shouted after
them, the Danites turned and said to Micah, "What's the matter with you that you
called out your men to fight?"
24He replied, "You took the gods I made,
and my priest, and went away. What else
do I have? How can you ask, 'What's the
matter with you?' "
25The Danites answered, "Don't argue
with us, or some of the men may get angry
and attack you, and you and your family
will lose your lives." 26So the Danites went
their way, and Micah, seeing that they
were too strong for him,[i] turned around
and went back home.
27Then they took what Micah had
made, and his priest, and went on to Laish, against a people at peace and secure.[j]
They attacked them with the sword and
burned down their city.[k] 28There was no
one to rescue them because they lived a
long way from Sidon[l] and had no relationship with anyone else. The city was in a
valley near Beth Rehob.[m]
The Danites rebuilt the city and settled
there. 29They named it Dan[n] after their
ancestor Dan, who was born to Israel—
though the city used to be called Laish.[o]
30There the Danites set up for themselves
the idol, and Jonathan son of Gershom,[p]
the son of Moses,[b] and his sons were
priests for the tribe of Dan until the time
of the captivity of the land. 31They continued to use the idol Micah had made, all
the time the house of God[q] was in Shiloh.[r]

A Levite and His Concubine

19 In those days Israel had no king.
Now a Levite who lived in a remote
area in the hill country of Ephraim[s] took
a concubine from Bethlehem in Judah.[t]

18:9 [w] Nu 13:30; 1Ki 22:3 **18:10** [x] ver 7, 27; Dt 8:9 [y] 1Ch 4:40 **18:11** [z] ver 16, 17 [a] Jdg 13:2 **18:12** [b] Jdg 13:25 **18:14** [c] Ge 31:19; Jdg 17:5 **18:16** [d] ver 11 **18:17** [e] Ge 31:19; Mic 5:13 **18:18** [f] Isa 46:2; Jer 43:11; Hos 10:5 **18:19** [g] Job 21:5; 29:9; 40:4; Mic 7:16 [h] Jdg 17:10 **18:26** [i] Ps 18:17; 35:10 **18:27** [j] ver 7, 10 [k] Ge 49:17; Jos 19:47 **18:28** [l] ver 7 [m] Nu 13:21; 2Sa 10:6 **18:29** [n] Ge 14:14 [o] Jos 19:47; 1Ki 15:20 **18:30** [p] Ex 2:22; Jdg 17:3,5 **18:31** [q] Jdg 19:18 [r] Jos 18:1; Jer 7:14 **19:1** [s] Jdg 18:1 [t] Ru 1:1

[a] 12 *Mahaneh Dan* means *Dan's camp.* [b] 30 Many Hebrew manuscripts, some Septuagint manuscripts and Vulgate; many other Hebrew manuscripts and some other Septuagint manuscripts *Manasseh*

18:14 *an ephod, some household gods and an image overlaid with silver.* Cf. v. 17; see notes on 8:27; 17:3,5.
18:17 When the Danites seized the idol and the articles associated with this cult center, they were following normal ancient customs. In the conquest of cities, the invaders would as a matter of course aim for the temple, seize the images and take them out of the city, thereby asserting their dominance over the place and demonstrating the deity's inability to defend his worshipers against attack. Furthermore, temples were storehouses for valuable objects and metals, as well as for grain.
18:27 *attacked them with the sword and burned down their city.* Technically, the slaughter of the population and the torching of the city looks like the application of the "ban" mandated by Yahweh (Dt 7:1 – 5). However, this was common practice in ancient Near Eastern warfare. Total destruction of a city is not always an expression of the "ban" and the theology associated with it. Archaeological excavations at Laish indicate the city was destroyed by a massive conflagration in the mid-eleventh century BC, leaving a layer of ash and rubble two to four feet (0.6 to 1.2 meters) thick in some places. Whether those remains point to the events described here is uncertain.
18:28 *The Danites rebuilt the city.* Accords with the archaeological evidence, which suggests that despite the total destruction of the city people continued to occupy it. The walls of the previous occupation continued in use and the material culture continued without appreciable change.
18:31 *the house of God was in Shiloh.* For some time prior to the establishment of the monarchy Shiloh functioned as the religious center for the nation (21:19; 1Sa 1:3), being home to the tabernacle, which housed the ark of the covenant law. Excavations at Shiloh have identified a couple of possible places on the site where the installation may have been (see note on 1Sa 1:3).
19:1 *concubine.* See note on 8:31.

2 But she was unfaithful to him. She left him and went back to her parents' home in Bethlehem, Judah. After she had been there four months, 3 her husband went to her to persuade her to return. He had with him his servant and two donkeys. She took him into her parents' home, and when her father saw him, he gladly welcomed him. 4 His father-in-law, the woman's father, prevailed on him to stay; so he remained with him three days, eating and drinking,[u] and sleeping there.

5 On the fourth day they got up early and he prepared to leave, but the woman's father said to his son-in-law, "Refresh yourself[v] with something to eat; then you can go." 6 So the two of them sat down to eat and drink together. Afterward the woman's father said, "Please stay tonight and enjoy yourself.[w]" 7 And when the man got up to go, his father-in-law persuaded him, so he stayed there that night. 8 On the morning of the fifth day, when he rose to go, the woman's father said, "Refresh yourself. Wait till afternoon!" So the two of them ate together.

9 Then when the man, with his concubine and his servant, got up to leave, his father-in-law, the woman's father, said, "Now look, it's almost evening. Spend the night here; the day is nearly over. Stay and enjoy yourself. Early tomorrow morning you can get up and be on your way home." 10 But, unwilling to stay another night, the man left and went toward Jebus[x] (that is, Jerusalem), with his two saddled donkeys and his concubine.

11 When they were near Jebus and the day was almost gone, the servant said to his master, "Come, let's stop at this city of the Jebusites[y] and spend the night."

12 His master replied, "No. We won't go into any city whose people are not Israelites. We will go on to Gibeah." 13 He added, "Come, let's try to reach Gibeah or Ramah[z] and spend the night in one of those places." 14 So they went on, and the sun set as they neared Gibeah in Benjamin.[a] 15 There they stopped to spend the night. They went and sat in the city square,[b] but no one took them in for the night.

16 That evening[c] an old man from the hill country of Ephraim,[d] who was living in Gibeah (the inhabitants of the place were Benjamites), came in from his work in the fields. 17 When he looked and saw the traveler in the city square, the old man asked, "Where are you going? Where did you come from?"[e]

18 He answered, "We are on our way from Bethlehem in Judah to a remote area in the hill country of Ephraim where I live. I have been to Bethlehem in Judah and now I am going to the house of the LORD.[a][f] No one has taken me in for the night. 19 We have both straw and fodder[g] for our donkeys and bread and wine[h] for ourselves your servants—me, the woman and the young man with us. We don't need anything."

20 "You are welcome at my house," the old man said. "Let me supply whatever you need. Only don't spend the night in the square." 21 So he took him into his house and fed his donkeys. After they had washed their feet, they had something to eat and drink.[i]

22 While they were enjoying themselves,[j] some of the wicked men[k] of the city surrounded the house. Pounding on the door,

19:4 [u] Ex 32:6 **19:5** [v] ver 8; Ge 18:5 **19:6** [w] ver 9, 22; Jdg 16:25 **19:10** [x] Ge 10:16; Jos 15:8; 1Ch 11:4-5 **19:11** [y] Jos 3:10 **19:13** [z] Jos 18:25 **19:14** [a] 1Sa 10:26; Isa 10:29 **19:15** [b] Ge 19:2 **19:16** [c] Ps 104:23 [d] ver 1 **19:17** [e] Ge 29:4 **19:18** [f] Jdg 18:31 **19:19** [g] Ge 24:25 [h] Ge 14:18 **19:21** [i] Ge 24:32-33; Lk 7:44 **19:22** [j] Jdg 16:25 [k] Dt 13:13

[a] *18* Hebrew, Vulgate, Syriac and Targum; Septuagint *going home*

19:4 *he remained with him three days, eating and drinking, and sleeping there.* This account is all about hospitality, an extremely important ancient Near Eastern value. The fact that the man feasted with his father-in-law for three days indicates that whatever the cause of the tension between the man and his concubine, unlike Samson's case, the relationship between husband and father-in-law appears not to have been strained. On the contrary, the latter is portrayed as a model of hospitality, exceeding even the Near Eastern standards honored by Abraham in Ge 18.

19:12 *Gibeah.* It is not clear whether Gibeah of Benjamin should be identified with modern Tell El-Fûl, a northern part of the ridge that includes the Mount of Olives and Mount Scopus north of Jerusalem, or Jaba', some 5.6 miles (9 kilometers) north of Jerusalem. In either case, having left too late in the afternoon to reach home in one day, this party of travelers is forced to seek a place to spend the night. In order to avoid contact with the Jebusites, they would probably have taken the road around the west of Jerusalem, and then through Anathoth and on to Gibeah.

19:15 *city square.* Its presence in Gibeah assumes some town planning, if not a defensive wall and a gate entrance. The town square was typically located just inside the city gates. The square provided space for events that involved the whole community: a marketplace for merchants, a rallying place for political leaders, a gathering place for religious festivities. On a normal day, all the residents would pass through the square and through the gate in the morning on the way to work out in the fields, and would return through the gate and square in the evening. In times of crisis the gates would be closed to traffic at night in order that all should be safe. The present travelers assumed that, as the residents returned and passed by them, surely someone would invite them to their home for the night. The square is the last place a visitor would choose to spend the night; the Levite's predicament demonstrates the general inhospitability of the town.

19:21 *After they had washed their feet, they had something to eat and drink.* These are all important elements of ancient hospitality (cf. Ge 18:4; 19:2). Like their neighbors, ancient Israelites either went barefoot or wore leather sandals. In either case, to wash a guest's feet was a welcoming convention of hospitality, intended not only to remove the dust, but also to refresh the visitor after a hot and dusty trip. The meal served two purposes: to nourish the guests and to express solidarity with them.

19:22 *Bring out the man ... so we can have sex with him.* Information on homosexuality in the ancient world

they shouted to the old man who owned
the house, "Bring out the man who came
to your house so we can have sex with
him.[l]"
23The owner of the house went outside[m]
and said to them, "No, my friends, don't
be so vile. Since this man is my guest,
don't do this outrageous thing.[n] 24Look,
here is my virgin daughter,[o] and his concubine. I will bring them out to you now,
and you can use them and do to them
whatever you wish. But as for this man,
don't do such an outrageous thing."
25But the men would not listen to him.
So the man took his concubine and sent
her outside to them, and they raped her
and abused her[p] throughout the night, and
at dawn they let her go. 26At daybreak the
woman went back to the house where her
master was staying, fell down at the door
and lay there until daylight.
27When her master got up in the morning and opened the door of the house
and stepped out to continue on his way,
there lay his concubine, fallen in the doorway of the house, with her hands on the
threshold. 28He said to her, "Get up; let's
go." But there was no answer. Then the
man put her on his donkey and set out
for home.
29When he reached home, he took a
knife[q] and cut up his concubine, limb by
limb, into twelve parts and sent them into
all the areas of Israel.[r] 30Everyone who
saw it was saying to one another, "Such
a thing has never been seen or done, not
since the day the Israelites came up out of
Egypt.[s] Just imagine! We must do something! So speak up![t]"

The Israelites Punish the Benjamites

20 Then all Israel[u] from Dan to Beersheba[v] and from the land of Gilead
came together as one[w] and assembled[x] before the LORD in Mizpah. 2The leaders of
all the people of the tribes of Israel took
their places in the assembly of God's people, four hundred thousand men[y] armed
with swords. 3(The Benjamites heard that
the Israelites had gone up to Mizpah.)
Then the Israelites said, "Tell us how this
awful thing happened."
4So the Levite, the husband of the murdered woman, said, "I and my concubine
came to Gibeah[z] in Benjamin to spend the
night.[a] 5During the night the men of Gib-

19:22 [l] Ge 19:4-5; Jdg 20:5; Ro 1:26-27 **19:23** [m] Ge 19:6 [n] Ge 34:7; Lev 19:29; Dt 22:21; Jdg 20:6; 2Sa 13:12; Ro 1:27 **19:24** [o] Ge 19:8; Dt 21:14 **19:25** [p] 1Sa 31:4 **19:29** [q] Ge 22:6 [r] Jdg 20:6; 1Sa 11:7 **19:30** [s] Hos 9:9 [t] Jdg 20:7; Pr 13:10 **20:1** [u] Jdg 21:5 [v] 1Sa 3:20; 2Sa 3:10; 1Ki 4:25 [w] 1Sa 11:7 [x] 1Sa 7:5 **20:2** [y] Jdg 8:10 **20:4** [z] Jos 15:57 [a] Jdg 19:15

outside the OT is sketchy. In Mesopotamia, the disposition toward male homosexuals ranged from toleration to contempt to outright prohibition. It seems that in the broader ancient Near East the religious community was most tolerant toward homosexuality; this is especially true with respect to those involved in the worship of Ishtar. Apparently, people viewed homosexuality with contempt because such acts did not serve the purpose of having children, and thus contributed nothing to the community. Hittite laws categorize illegal sexual couplings along with bestiality, intercourse with one's mother, daughter or son, with one's stepmother while one's father is living, with one's sister-in-law while one's brother is living or with a free woman and her mother or her sister. In demanding to have sexual intercourse with the Levite, the residents of Gibeah, these "wicked men" violate three fundamental social/moral laws: the law of hospitality, the proscription on intercourse outside of marriage, and proscription on homosexual intercourse, clearly laid out in the laws in the Pentateuch (Lev 18:22; 20:13).

19:24 *here is … his concubine.* The Levite's concubine is a legal extension of him and should be protected by the same standards of hospitality. In offering her, the Ephraimite is abandoning his role as host. The situation here is comparable to that in Ge 19: in both accounts the host is saved by his guests (where the opposite should be true), but the resolution created by Lot's guests is far more desirable (Ge 19:19).

19:29 *took a knife and cut up his concubine, limb by limb, into twelve parts and sent them into all the areas of Israel.* No parallels to this course of action are found in the ancient Near East. The closest Biblical analogue to this horrific scene is found in 1Sa 11:7, where Saul cuts up his team of oxen and sends the pieces throughout the land of Israel as a symbolic act to coerce people to enlist in his army. There the messengers who delivered the pieces to their intended destination expressly declared the significance of the action: "This is what will be done to the oxen of anyone who does not follow Saul and Samuel." The effect is to strike divine terror on all the people, causing them to turn out in full force. Our text offers no such interpretation, expressing only the shocking effect of the Levite's action on the population of Israel.

20:1 *from Dan to Beersheba.* This is the first occurrence of this merismic geographic definition of the territory of Israel, spanning a distance of about 160 miles (257 kilometers). This stereotypical phrase reflects the narrator's own perspective of the nation of Israel as an ideal state consisting of all 12 tribes and occupying all the land promised to the ancestors.

20:2 *assembly of God's people.* The expression "God's people" usually points to the nation of Israel as a community of people united in their religious allegiance to Yahweh, but here indicates the perception of Israel as a vassal community covenantally committed to Yahweh. The proceedings that follow include the presentation of evidence by a witness (the Levite, vv. 4–6), the call for a verdict (v. 7), the announcement of the sentence (vv. 8–10), the preparations for the execution of the sentence (v. 11) and the effort to arrive at a negotiation resolution with the community to which the offenders belonged (vv. 12–13). These represent essential elements of an ancient legal process. *four hundred thousand men armed with swords.* The Hebrew specifies these troops as "foot men," in contrast to cavalry or charioteers, like Sisera's forces in 4:3,15. The Israelites' economy and organizational structures had not developed enough to produce a more sophisticated military force. Like many other numbers in the book, 400,000 seems inordinately high (see note on 1:4). Whether the key word is interpreted as "thousand" or the contingents mustered by individual clans (in comparison with the numbers in Nu 1; 26), since they had entered the land, the population of Israel had fallen by one-third since they left Egypt.

eah came after me and surrounded the
house, intending to kill me.[b] They raped
my concubine, and she died.[c] 6I took my
concubine, cut her into pieces and sent
one piece to each region of Israel's inheritance,[d] because they committed this lewd
and outrageous act[e] in Israel. 7Now, all
you Israelites, speak up and tell me what
you have decided to do.[f]"
8All the men rose up together as one,
saying, "None of us will go home. No, not
one of us will return to his house. 9But
now this is what we'll do to Gibeah: We'll
go up against it in the order decided by
casting lots.[g] 10We'll take ten men out of
every hundred from all the tribes of Israel, and a hundred from a thousand, and
a thousand from ten thousand, to get
provisions for the army. Then, when the
army arrives at Gibeah[a] in Benjamin, it
can give them what they deserve for this
outrageous act done in Israel." 11So all the
Israelites got together and united as one
against the city.[h]
12The tribes of Israel sent messengers
throughout the tribe of Benjamin, saying,
"What about this awful crime that was
committed among you? 13Now turn those
wicked men[i] of Gibeah over to us so that
we may put them to death and purge the
evil from Israel.[j]"
But the Benjamites would not listen to
their fellow Israelites. 14From their towns
they came together at Gibeah to fight
against the Israelites. 15At once the Benjamites mobilized twenty-six thousand
swordsmen from their towns, in addition
to seven hundred able young men from
those living in Gibeah. 16Among all these
soldiers there were seven hundred select
troops who were left-handed,[k] each of
whom could sling a stone at a hair and
not miss.

20:5 [b]Jdg 19:22 [c]Jdg 19:25-26 **20:6** [d]Jdg 19:29 [e]Jos 7:15; Jdg 19:23 **20:7** [f]Jdg 19:30 **20:9** [g]Lev 16:8 **20:11** [h]ver 1 **20:13** [i]Dt 13:13; Jdg 19:22 [j]Dt 17:12 **20:16** [k]Jdg 3:15; 1Ch 12:2

20:18 [l]ver 26-27; Nu 27:21 [m]ver 23,28 **20:21** [n]ver 25 **20:23** [o]Jos 7:6 [p]ver 18 **20:25** [q]ver 21 **20:26** [r]ver 23 [s]Jdg 21:4 **20:27** [t]Jos 18:1 **20:28** [u]Jos 24:33

17Israel, apart from Benjamin, mustered
four hundred thousand swordsmen, all of
them fit for battle.
18The Israelites went up to Bethel[b] and
inquired of God.[l] They said, "Who of us
is to go up first to fight[m] against the Benjamites?"
The LORD replied, "Judah shall go first."
19The next morning the Israelites got up
and pitched camp near Gibeah. 20The Israelites went out to fight the Benjamites and
took up battle positions against them at
Gibeah. 21The Benjamites came out of Gibeah and cut down twenty-two thousand
Israelites[n] on the battlefield that day. 22But
the Israelites encouraged one another and
again took up their positions where they
had stationed themselves the first day.
23The Israelites went up and wept before
the LORD until evening,[o] and they inquired
of the LORD. They said, "Shall we go up
again to fight[p] against the Benjamites, our
fellow Israelites?"
The LORD answered, "Go up against
them."
24Then the Israelites drew near to Benjamin the second day. 25This time, when
the Benjamites came out from Gibeah
to oppose them, they cut down another
eighteen thousand Israelites,[q] all of them
armed with swords.
26Then all the Israelites, the whole
army, went up to Bethel, and there they
sat weeping before the LORD.[r] They fasted that day until evening and presented
burnt offerings and fellowship offerings
to the LORD.[s] 27And the Israelites inquired
of the LORD. (In those days the ark of the
covenant of God[t] was there, 28with Phinehas son of Eleazar,[u] the son of Aaron,

[a] *10* One Hebrew manuscript; most Hebrew manuscripts *Geba,* a variant of *Gibeah* [b] *18* Or *to the house of God;* also in verse 26

20:9 *decided by casting lots.* Whereas in 1:1–2 the narrator intimates that the tribes had inquired of Yahweh directly to see who was to lead the attack against the Canaanites, here there is no reference to Yahweh, only the method by which his reply will be determined: the lot. The use of the lot is required in the absence of a leader, who would normally have chosen his troops. This kind of divination, which assumed that the gods determined the way the lots fell (Pr 16:33), was widespread in the ancient Near East, though the forms it took varied greatly. Active forms included lots, rhabdomancy (throwing arrows or sticks in the air and observing the pattern when they landed), and hydromancy (observing the color patterns of oil poured on water). While Dt 18:9–13 forbade most forms of divination for the Israelites, in the Urim and Thummim, which were to be manipulated by the priest, they possessed a divinely sanctioned form of divination (Nu 27:21; see the article "Urim and Thummim," p. 162). This will probably be the case in vv. 27–28, where Phinehas, the grandson of Aaron, will be involved, but here there is no mention of the priest or these sacred lots.

20:10 Although all the numbers in this verse seem inflated, the present proportion of one tenth of the force being assigned supply duty finds a close parallel in a report from Mari that notes that in a force of 12,000 troops 1,000 were appointed to transport food.

20:15 *twenty-six thousand swordsmen.* On the large number, see notes on v. 2; 1:4. The decline in Benjamin's military force since the exodus (cf. Nu 1:37 [35,400 men]; 26:41 [45,600 men]) is proportional to the drop in Israel as a whole.

20:16 *left-handed.* See note on 3:15. *could sling a stone at a hair and not miss.* See note on 1Sa 17:40.

20:21 *twenty-two thousand Israelites.* On the seemingly high number, see note on 1:4.

20:27 *ark of the covenant of God.* This is the only reference to the ark of the covenant law in Judges. It seems the Israelites had brought the ark to Bethel from Shiloh, presumably to function as a palladium, a symbol of God's presence and "good luck charm" in the battle against the Benjamites. A likely analogue is found in 1Sa 4, where the ark is brought up to secure victory for the Israelites after

ministering before it.)[v] They asked, "Shall we go up again to fight against the Benjamites, our fellow Israelites, or not?"

The LORD responded, "Go, for tomorrow I will give them into your hands.[w]"

29 Then Israel set an ambush[x] around Gibeah. 30 They went up against the Benjamites on the third day and took up positions against Gibeah as they had done before. 31 The Benjamites came out to meet them and were drawn away[y] from the city. They began to inflict casualties on the Israelites as before, so that about thirty men fell in the open field and on the roads—the one leading to Bethel and the other to Gibeah. 32 While the Benjamites were saying, "We are defeating them as before,"[z] the Israelites were saying, "Let's retreat and draw them away from the city to the roads."

33 All the men of Israel moved from their places and took up positions at Baal Tamar, and the Israelite ambush charged out of its place[a] on the west[a] of Gibeah.[b] 34 Then ten thousand of Israel's able young men made a frontal attack on Gibeah. The fighting was so heavy that the Benjamites did not realize[b] how near disaster was.[c] 35 The LORD defeated Benjamin[d] before Israel, and on that day the Israelites struck down 25,100 Benjamites, all armed with swords. 36 Then the Benjamites saw that they were beaten.

Now the men of Israel had given way[e] before Benjamin, because they relied on the ambush they had set near Gibeah. 37 Those who had been in ambush made a sudden dash into Gibeah, spread out and put the whole city to the sword.[f] 38 The Israelites had arranged with the ambush that they should send up a great cloud of smoke[g] from the city, 39 and then the Israelites would counterattack.

The Benjamites had begun to inflict casualties on the Israelites (about thirty), and they said, "We are defeating them as in the first battle."[h] 40 But when the column of smoke began to rise from the city, the Benjamites turned and saw the whole city going up in smoke.[i] 41 Then the Israelites counterattacked, and the Benjamites were terrified, because they realized that disaster had come on them. 42 So they fled before the Israelites in the direction of the wilderness, but they could not escape the battle. And the Israelites who came out of the towns cut them down there. 43 They surrounded the Benjamites, chased them and easily[c] overran them in the vicinity of Gibeah on the east. 44 Eighteen thousand Benjamites fell, all of them valiant fighters.[j] 45 As they turned and fled toward the wilderness to the rock of Rimmon,[k] the Israelites cut down five thousand men along the roads. They kept pressing after the Benjamites as far as Gidom and struck down two thousand more.

46 On that day twenty-five thousand Benjamite swordsmen fell, all of them valiant fighters. 47 But six hundred of them turned and fled into the wilderness to the rock of Rimmon, where they stayed four months. 48 The men of Israel went back to Benjamin and put all the towns to the sword, including the animals and everything else they found. All the towns they came across they set on fire.[l]

Wives for the Benjamites

21 The men of Israel had taken an oath[m] at Mizpah:[n] "Not one of us will give[o] his daughter in marriage to a Benjamite."

2 The people went to Bethel,[d] where they sat before God until evening, raising their voices and weeping bitterly. 3 "LORD, God of Israel," they cried, "why has this happened to Israel? Why should one tribe be missing from Israel today?"

4 Early the next day the people built an altar and presented burnt offerings and fellowship offerings.[p]

5 Then the Israelites asked, "Who from

20:28 [v] Dt 18:5 [w] Jdg 7:9 **20:29** [x] Jos 8:2,4 **20:31** [y] Jos 8:16 **20:32** [z] ver 39 **20:33** [a] Jos 8:19 **20:34** [b] Jos 8:14 [c] Isa 47:11 **20:35** [d] 1Sa 9:21 **20:36** [e] Jos 8:15 **20:37** [f] Jos 8:19 **20:38** [g] Jos 8:20 **20:39** [h] ver 32 **20:40** [i] Jos 8:20 **20:44** [j] Ps 76:5 **20:45** [k] Jos 15:32; Jdg 21:13 **20:48** [l] Jdg 21:23 **21:1** [m] Jos 9:18 [n] Jdg 20:1 [o] ver 7,18 **21:4** [p] Jdg 20:26; 2Sa 24:25

[a] 33 Some Septuagint manuscripts and Vulgate; the meaning of the Hebrew for this word is uncertain. [b] 33 Hebrew *Geba,* a variant of *Gibeah* [c] 43 The meaning of the Hebrew for this word is uncertain. [d] 2 Or *to the house of God*

a disastrous defeat at the hands of the Philistines. If this comparison is sound, the Israelites treated the ark like their neighbors treated the images of their deities—as a physical and magical symbol of Yahweh's protective presence as they engaged the enemy in battle.

20:48 *All the towns they came across they set on fire.* This extreme policy toward conquered peoples has some similarities to the *herem*-style action that designates cities, including their plunder and animals, ineligible for human use and their people as not to be assimilated lest they corrupt the Israelite population. The action is not always punitive, but here it is. On this policy in ancient warfare and in Israel, see article "Divine Warfare," p. 365.

21:1 *an oath.* This is the first reference to an oath in the book. In the ancient world, oaths and curses were thought to derive their potency through people's appeals to the gods to guarantee by divine sanction that promises made in agreements would be fulfilled. Accordingly, although breaking an agreement could pose a legal problem to be resolved by the courts, through their own agents the gods meted out punishment for perjury. An oath typically spelled out the consequences that would be experienced by the person who swore it in the form of self-imprecation. The deities appealed to in oaths were those of one's own city or country. Since the Israelites had "assembled before the LORD in Mizpah" (20:1) and "before the LORD" (21:5), we may assume that Yahweh was invoked as the guarantor of the present agreement. This is confirmed

all the tribes of Israel[q] has failed to assemble before the LORD?" For they had taken
a solemn oath that anyone who failed to
assemble before the LORD at Mizpah was
to be put to death.
6Now the Israelites grieved for the tribe
of Benjamin, their fellow Israelites. "Today one tribe is cut off from Israel," they
said. 7"How can we provide wives for
those who are left, since we have taken
an oath[r] by the LORD not to give them any
of our daughters in marriage?" 8Then they
asked, "Which one of the tribes of Israel
failed to assemble before the LORD at Mizpah?" They discovered that no one from
Jabesh Gilead[s] had come to the camp for
the assembly. 9For when they counted the
people, they found that none of the people
of Jabesh Gilead were there.
10So the assembly sent twelve thousand fighting men with instructions to
go to Jabesh Gilead and put to the sword
those living there, including the women
and children. 11"This is what you are to
do," they said. "Kill every male and every woman who is not a virgin.[t]" 12They
found among the people living in Jabesh
Gilead four hundred young women who
had never slept with a man, and they took
them to the camp at Shiloh[u] in Canaan.
13Then the whole assembly sent an offer
of peace[v] to the Benjamites at the rock of
Rimmon.[w] 14So the Benjamites returned at
that time and were given the women of
Jabesh Gilead who had been spared. But
there were not enough for all of them.
15The people grieved for Benjamin,[x]
because the LORD had made a gap in the

21:5 [q] Jdg 5:23; 20:1
21:7 [r] ver 1
21:8 [s] 1Sa 11:1; 31:11
21:11 [t] Nu 31:17-18
21:12 [u] Jos 18:1
21:13 [v] Dt 20:10 [w] Jdg 20:47
21:15 [x] ver 6

tribes of Israel. 16And the elders of the assembly said, "With the women of Benjamin destroyed, how shall we provide wives
for the men who are left? 17The Benjamite
survivors must have heirs," they said, "so
that a tribe of Israel will not be wiped out.
18We can't give them our daughters as
wives, since we Israelites have taken this
oath: 'Cursed be anyone who gives[y] a wife
to a Benjamite.' 19But look, there is the annual festival of the LORD in Shiloh,[z] which
lies north of Bethel, east of the road that
goes from Bethel to Shechem, and south
of Lebonah."
20So they instructed the Benjamites, saying, "Go and hide in the vineyards 21and
watch. When the young women of Shiloh come out to join in the dancing,[a] rush
from the vineyards and each of you seize
one of them to be your wife. Then return
to the land of Benjamin. 22When their fathers or brothers complain to us, we will
say to them, 'Do us the favor of helping
them, because we did not get wives for
them during the war. You will not be guilty
of breaking your oath because you did not
give[b] your daughters to them.'"
23So that is what the Benjamites did.
While the young women were dancing,
each man caught one and carried her off
to be his wife. Then they returned to their
inheritance and rebuilt the towns and settled in them.[c]
24At that time the Israelites left that
place and went home to their tribes and
clans, each to his own inheritance.
25In those days Israel had no king; everyone did as they saw fit.[d]

21:18 [y] ver 1
21:19 [z] Jos 18:1; Jdg 18:31; 1Sa 1:3
21:21 [a] Ex 15:20; Jdg 11:34
21:22 [b] ver 1, 18
21:23 [c] Jdg 20:48
21:25 [d] Dt 12:8; Jdg 17:6; 18:1; 19:1

later in v. 7. The commitment to which they bound themselves is stated in the next clause of v. 1.

21:10 *twelve thousand fighting men.* On the seemingly high number, see note on 1:4.

21:19 *annual festival.* The Hebrew term used here is a generic term for any periodic pilgrimage festival, but which specific festival is in mind is not clear. According to Dt 16:1 – 17, all Israelite males were required to appear before Yahweh in the place that he would approve and establish as his authorized cult site three times a year: (1) the Passover and Festival of Unleavened Bread, (2) the Festival of Weeks (also known as the Festival of Harvest) and (3) the Festival of Tabernacles (also known as the Festival of Ingathering). Only adult males were obligated to attend these festivals (Ex 23:17; Dt 16:16), though women and children were also welcome (Dt 16:11,14).

21:21 *young women of Shiloh.* This expression suggests a special professional class of female dancers associated with the religious institution of Shiloh. The inspiration for such religious personnel and such activity may well have come from Canaanite religious customs, which often involved women. In the Late Bronze Age at Emar, in Syria, the great festivals were headed by the high priestess and involved several additional classes of priestesses. While the regulations concerning worship in Israel freely admitted women and children to participate in the festivals (Dt 12:12; 31:10 – 12), and the narratives occasionally highlight the role of women in celebrative dance (Ex 15:20), the ritual of Yahweh at the tabernacle and later the temple never involved women in priestly roles. This annual festival may have simply involved cultic dance in joyful celebration of Yahweh, especially if this "annual festival" (v. 19) is one of the three festivals obligatory for all males (see note on v. 19). The instructions to the Benjamites to "hide in the vineyards" (v. 20) may suggest a festival of thanksgiving for the grape harvest, which would be characterized by revelry, music and dance. *Shiloh.* See note on 1Sa 1:3.

NARRATIVE LITERATURE

RUTH

Author

Nothing is known of the author of the book, though the book of Ruth stands in contrast to the book of Judges: Judges details the faithlessness of Israel and its leadership, while Ruth offers a vignette of faithfulness among common folks — even a Moabite woman.

KEY CONCEPTS

- Faithfulness generates faithfulness.
- David's ancestry was populated by faithful people.

Historical Setting

The opening statement of Ruth (1:1) embeds the events of the book in the chaotic era reflected in the book of Judges, when there was no central authority and "everyone did as they saw fit" (Jdg 21:25). Depending upon when the exodus occurred, the span can be either c. 1400 – 1050 BC or c. 1220 – 1050 BC. Not only was Israel embroiled in chaos, but most of the ancient world was as well. Egypt, the Hittite Empire and Mesopotamia were in general decline; Greece was undergoing political upheaval, and the Sea Peoples (which included the Philistines) were wreaking havoc in the Mediterranean basin. The reasons for these disruptions are difficult to determine, but environmental stresses of some kind, in conjunction with a flurry of earthquakes, may have contributed to the situation. The deterioration of the major superpowers allowed a number of smaller peoples and states to germinate in the Levant. Among them are the Moabites, Phoenicians, Syrians, Ammonites, Philistines and, of course, the Israelites. ◆

Naomi Loses Her Husband and Sons

1 In the days when the judges ruled,[a][a]
there was a famine in the land.[b] So a
man from Bethlehem in Judah, together
with his wife and two sons, went to live
for a while in the country of Moab.[c] 2The
man's name was Elimelek, his wife's
name was Naomi, and the names of his
two sons were Mahlon and Kilion. They
were Ephrathites from Bethlehem,[d] Judah.
And they went to Moab and lived there.
3Now Elimelek, Naomi's husband, died,
and she was left with her two sons. 4They
married Moabite women, one named Orpah and the other Ruth.[e] After they had
lived there about ten years, 5both Mahlon
and Kilion also died, and Naomi was left
without her two sons and her husband.

Naomi and Ruth Return to Bethlehem

6When Naomi heard in Moab that the
LORD had come to the aid of his people[f]
by providing food[g] for them, she and her
daughters-in-law prepared to return home
from there. 7With her two daughters-in-
law she left the place where she had been

1:1 [a] Jdg 2:16-18 [b] Ge 12:10; Ps 105:16 [c] Jdg 3:30 **1:2** [d] Ge 35:19 **1:4** [e] Mt 1:5 **1:6** [f] Ex 4:31; Jer 29:10; Zep 2:7 [g] Ps 132:15; Mt 6:11

[a] 1 Traditionally *judged*

1:1 *In the days when the judges ruled.* The events of the book take place in the chaotic era reflected in the book of Judges, when Israel lacked central authority, and "everyone did as they saw fit" (Jdg 21:25). Depending upon when the exodus occurred, the span of the period of the judges might be either c. 1400 – 1050 BC or c. 1220 – 1050 BC. Not only was Israel embroiled in chaos at this time, but most of the ancient world was as well. The Egyptians, Hittites and Mesopotamians were in general decline; Greece was undergoing political upheaval; and the Sea Peoples (which included the Philistines) were wreaking havoc in the Mediterranean basin. The reasons for these disruptions are difficult to determine, but environmental stresses of some kind in conjunction with a flurry of earthquakes may have contributed to the demise. The deterioration of the major superpowers allowed a number of smaller peoples and states to germinate in the Levant. Among them are the Moabites, Phoenicians, Syrians, Ammonites, Philistines and, of course, the Israelites. *famine.* Famines were not uncommon in the Levant. Sometimes they could be local as prophesied by Amos (see Am 4:7 – 8), but the phrase normally implies a wide-spread famine. Several factors could precipitate a famine in addition to lack of rainfall. An adequate amount of rain, but at the wrong time, could destroy the crops. Additionally, plant disease (e.g., Dt 28:21; 1Ki 8:37; Am 4:9; Hab 2:17), insect infestation (e.g., Am 4:9 – 10; Joel 1) and warfare (e.g., 2Ki 6:24 – 25; Isa 1:7) could effectively serve as famines. The Bible notes a number of famines, some of which precipitated departures from Canaan — Abraham went to Egypt (Ge 12:10); Isaac sojourned in Gerar (Ge 26:1); and Jacob and his family descended to Egypt (Ge 43 – 50). Overall, the pattern of famine and plenty in the Levant is unpredictable. *Bethlehem.* The name means "house of bread." Ironically, the house of plenty has failed Elimelek, forcing his exodus to Moab. Bethlehem is about five miles (eight kilometers) south of Jerusalem on the main north-south road that passes along the ridge of the central mountains. The area is generally productive with wheat, barley, almonds and grapes, which may have factored into the significance of the town's name. It would become the birthplace of David. *live for a while.* The Hebrew word here is often rendered "sojourn" and is a technical social term applied to a class of people who are neither native nor simply foreigners living in the land. They had no blood ties to the residents and only had legal rights as the dominant peoples permitted, which were often whimsically granted and withdrawn. The people of Sodom refer to Lot in this way and use it as a slur (see "foreigner" in Ge 19:9).

1:2 *names.* With the exception of the wordplay that Naomi injects regarding her own name (v. 20), the names of the major personalities — Elimelek, Naomi, Mahlon, Kilion, Ruth and Orpah — have neither meanings nor etymologies that play literary roles in the narrative. The equivalents of Elimelek, Naomi and Kilion are preserved in Ugarit, Amorite and/or Akkadian (demonstrating that they are authentic period names), while Mahlon, Ruth and Orpah have not been identified. *Ephrathites.* The matriarch, Rachel, had died on the way to Ephrath (Ge 35:16 – 19), which was an earlier name of Bethlehem (familiar to us from Mic 5:2, a well-known passage read around Christmas). The use of Ephrathite may reflect an old aristocratic family of Ephrath/Bethlehem from which Elimelek descended.

1:3 *Elimelek … died.* The hazards of widowhood in antiquity were great. In most rural areas, women would have had little opportunity to pursue independent careers, and therefore overwhelmingly depended upon their husbands for sustenance. Women certainly had significant roles in the household, but these usually did not extend to commercial enterprises, contrary to the idealized description of the noble woman of Pr 31. Upon her husband's death, the widow normally relied upon her sons for support; if she had none, she might have to sell herself into slavery, resort to prostitution or die. It is in part to prevent this harshness for which the guardian-redeemer legislation exists (Lev 25:39 – 55). The Mosaic Law was concerned for the widows and the poor (Dt 10:17 – 18; cf. Ps 68:5; 146:9; Jer 49:11), and issued instructions for their preservation (e.g., Ex 22:22 – 24; Dt 14:28 – 29; 24:17 – 20; 26:12 – 13; 27:19). Many of these concerns with widows, the poor and orphans are mirrored in surrounding cultures from whom laws and customs have been preserved; among them are laws from the Code of Hammurapi, instructions relative to widows and orphans in Egypt and justice for the widow and orphan in the gate at Ugarit.

In view of the events that followed — particularly the deaths of Naomi's two sons — we may infer that she is stripped of all male protection. Her plight, then, would often be connected to that of the orphan and foreigner (e.g., Mal 3:5) and the poor (e.g., Isa 10:2). The lapse of ten years (v. 4) implies that Naomi is past childbearing age, or at least near the end of such, so that her prospect of finding a husband would be significantly reduced. Her decision to return to Bethlehem was the most reasonable option; there she might at least find sustenance by gleaning if no extended family members were to care for her.

If the marriages in the narrative followed typical ancient Near Eastern tradition, Naomi probably had married in her mid-teens and had likely borne her two sons by age 20. The sons would have married a little earlier than age 20 to young women similarly in their mid-teens. By the time she decides to return to Judah, Naomi is likely in her mid-40s and Ruth and Orpah are likely in their mid- to late 20s.

living and set out on the road that would
take them back to the land of Judah.
8Then Naomi said to her two daughters-in-law, "Go back, each of you, to your
mother's home. May the LORD show you
kindness,[h] as you have shown kindness to
your dead husbands[i] and to me. 9May the
LORD grant that each of you will find rest[j]
in the home of another husband."
Then she kissed them goodbye and they
wept aloud 10and said to her, "We will go
back with you to your people."

1:8 [h] Ru 2:20; 2Ti 1:16 [i] ver 5 **1:9** [j] Ru 3:1

1:8 *mother's home.* The OT implies that the mother's house has to do with preparation for marriage (Ge 24:28, SS 3:4; 8:2). This corresponds to Egypt and Mesopotamia, where the mother was the protector of the daughter and the advisor and supervisor in matters of love, sex and marriage. The suggestion to return to their mother does not primarily encourage seeking legal protection (Ruth's father is still alive, cf. 2:11), but rather presents the option to have a new family.

RUTH 1:1

MOAB

Moab, as a geographic or political entity, is attested as early as the reign of Ramses II (thirteenth century BC), who refers to Moab on a pylon at Luxor. Moab consists of three main regions. The northernmost section spans the plains of Moab to the northeast of the Dead Sea. The middle section extends from the plains of Moab southward to the Arnon and is generally a fairly level tableland at 2,000 – 2,400 feet (610 – 730 meters) elevation. The third and southernmost section is higher, with elevations over 4,000 feet (1,220 meters) and extending from the Arnon to the Zered at the southern end of the Dead Sea.

The relationship between Moab and early Israel is difficult to clarify. The Bible notes that Reuben and Gad lived in some of the area later attributed to Moab (see Nu 32; Jos 13:15 – 28). Mesha, king of Moab (late ninth century BC), states that the people of Gad had lived in the area "forever." Since the core of Moab seems to have been to the south, the northern regions may have been much more fluid and multicultural in nature.

The text gives no indication of where Elimelek settles in Moab. To reach the borders, however, would have taken several days, since the maximum rate of travel on foot would be about 20 miles (32 kilometers) a day. The distance involved in the move made the decision a serious one, inhibiting easy access to the homeland. If he took the family to northern Moab, he would have traveled northward to Jerusalem and descended to Jericho where he would have crossed the Jordan into Moab. Alternatively, he might have traveled southward to Hebron, descended eastward to the Dead Sea, crossed the sea to the Lisan (i.e., the peninsula that extends into the Dead Sea) and climbed into the interior of Moab. This would have been the shortest route to Moab. ◆

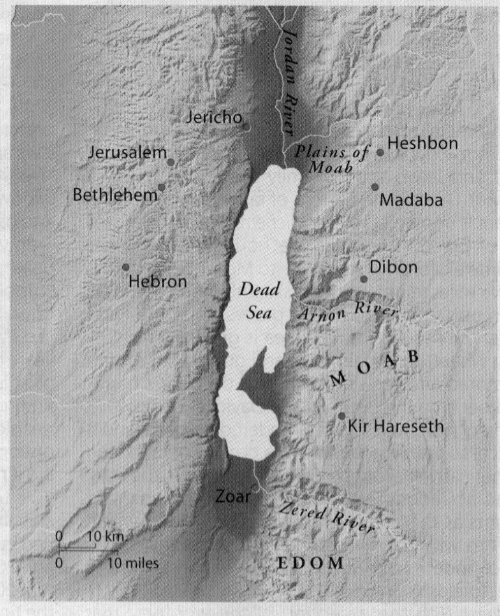

11But Naomi said, "Return home, my
daughters. Why would you come with
me? Am I going to have any more sons,
who could become your husbands?[k] 12Re-
turn home, my daughters; I am too old to
have another husband. Even if I thought
there was still hope for me — even if I had
a husband tonight and then gave birth to
sons — 13would you wait until they grew
up? Would you remain unmarried for
them? No, my daughters. It is more bitter
for me than for you, because the LORD's
hand has turned against me![l]"
14At this they wept aloud again. Then
Orpah kissed her mother-in-law[m] goodbye, but Ruth clung to her.[n]
15"Look," said Naomi, "your sister-in-
law is going back to her people and her
gods.[o] Go back with her."
16But Ruth replied, "Don't urge me to
leave you[p] or to turn back from you. Where
you go I will go, and where you stay I will
stay. Your people will be my people and
your God my God.[q] 17Where you die I will
die, and there I will be buried. May the
LORD deal with me, be it ever so severely,[r] if
even death separates you and me." 18When
Naomi realized that Ruth was determined
to go with her, she stopped urging her.[s]
19So the two women went on until they
came to Bethlehem. When they arrived in
Bethlehem, the whole town was stirred[t]
because of them, and the women exclaimed, "Can this be Naomi?"

1:11 [k] Ge 38:11; Dt 25:5
1:13 [l] Jdg 2:15; Job 4:5; 19:21; Ps 32:4
1:14 [m] Ru 2:11 [n] Pr 17:17; 18:24
1:15 [o] Jos 24:14; Jdg 11:24
1:16 [p] 2Ki 2:2 [q] Ru 2:11, 12
1:17 [r] 1Sa 3:17; 25:22; 2Sa 19:13; 2Ki 6:31
1:18 [s] Ac 21:14
1:19 [t] Mt 21:10

1:11 *sons … become your husbands.* The Bible provides specific legislation for family preservation, often called levirate marriage (Dt 25:5 – 10; see the article "Levirate Marriage," p. 85) — if a man married a woman and he died before there were offspring, his brother would marry the widow and raise up children in the name of the deceased. Since Naomi does not mention the prospect of marrying her husband's brother, technically, her proposed scenario would not be levirate marriage, since the husband she might hypothetically secure would not, in a patrilineal society, produce brothers to her deceased sons. Instead she emphasizes how futile was any prospect of securing husbands for her widowed daughters-in-law, in contrast to the implied resources of their "mother's home" (v. 8; see note there).

1:15 *her people and her gods.* While "people" and "gods" may refer to her personal allegiances, they also may extend to her tribe's social and religious associations. Ancient societies often had a hierarchical slate of deities who resided in their area — sometimes connected with geography or geographic features. This is indicated when the Aramean king's officials described Israel's gods as "gods of the hills" and not of "the plains" (1Ki 20:23). A god's domain, however, might expand geographically through conquest as indicated in Ashurnasirpal's bombast of himself and the sponsorship of a host of Assyrian deities. These national gods apparently were often considered beyond the reach of the common person, who alternatively appealed to an array of lesser deities and spirits who were more easily accessible and task specific — hence the proliferation of the personal family worship that may have been at odds with the national religious expression.

1:16 *your God my God.* The national god of Moab was Chemosh. Mesha, a later Moabite king, commented that Chemosh had been angry with the land and permitted Omri to subdue the country. Chemosh was an ancient god in the Levant for whom we have evidence as early as the late third millennium BC at Ebla. We have no evidence of his perceived character at the period, although he may have been a god of war similar to the Mesopotamian god, Nergal. Ruth's statement suggests that she will adopt the worship of Naomi's people in Bethlehem. This is an expression of her loyalty to Naomi, and it would be the general practice of someone joining a new family and community in a new area. Though the high God of the region is Yahweh, the syncretism of the judges period would likely have featured gods at various family and clan levels. Ruth would not be able to continue worshiping her gods (Chemosh or any others), for there would not have been sacred places dedicated to them. Ruth's decision is born of loyalty to Naomi, not necessarily of any theological convictions about Yahweh as the one true God. However, it is enough of a foothold for Yahweh to reveal himself.

1:17 *there I will be buried.* Ruth's commitment to leave her family for a land where she apparently has never been, potentially totally isolated from her own kin, commands admiration and respect. While she has probably become familiar with some Hebrew customs and beliefs, to saturate herself in the different culture has dimensions that one can only appreciate by experience. Some suggest that her loyalty surpasses that of Abraham, since he was called by divine direction (Ge 12:1 – 5) and Ruth was not. To most Westerners, there is usually little emotional trauma in being buried away from the family plot. Such a casual approach to death was unknown to the people of ancient Canaan. The Bible often refers to death as being gathered to one's people (e.g., Ge 25:8,17; 35:29; 49:33; Nu 20:24,26; Dt 32:50), and Jacob and Joseph gave specific instructions that their remains be conveyed to the family homeland (Ge 49:29 – 32; 50:24 – 26). These requests are apparently not unique to the Israelites. Archaeology has uncovered a number of cemeteries, many of which yield evidence that the deceased had passed away elsewhere and their bones had been interred in the cemetery sometime after death and decomposition had occurred. Our text gives no indication that Naomi had brought her husband's and sons' remains back to the family plot in Bethlehem, but if she did not, she likely was returning with them on this journey.

A proper burial was a matter of great concern for people in the ancient world. Goals were to keep the deceased connected to the community of living relatives and descendants as well as to help them transition into the community of the ancestors who had already died. The maintenance of the dead was a common practice as implied in the often elaborate tombs designed to accommodate the extended family. Continued care for the dead was a common practice in the ancient world and was believed to affect the afterlife of the deceased.

1:19 *stirred.* The Hebrew word elsewhere denotes considerable excitement and commotion (cf. 1Sa 4:5; 1Ki 1:45). Ancient towns were little more than small villages. Demographic studies indicate that the typical village had a population of only a few hundred. Additionally, the population of the town may have diminished because of the famine — either by death or by its inhabitants emigrating, as Elimelek and his family had done.

20"Don't call me Naomi,[a]" she told
them. "Call me Mara,[b] because the Almighty[c][u] has made my life very bitter.[v] 21I
went away full, but the LORD has brought
me back empty.[w] Why call me Naomi?
The LORD has afflicted[d] me; the Almighty
has brought misfortune upon me."

22So Naomi returned from Moab accompanied by Ruth the Moabite, her daughter-
in-law, arriving in Bethlehem as the barley
harvest[x] was beginning.[y]

Ruth Meets Boaz in the Grain Field

2 Now Naomi had a relative[z] on her
husband's side, a man of standing
from the clan of Elimelek,[a] whose name
was Boaz.[b]

2And Ruth the Moabite said to Naomi,
"Let me go to the fields and pick up the
leftover grain[c] behind anyone in whose
eyes I find favor."

Naomi said to her, "Go ahead, my
daughter." 3So she went out, entered a
field and began to glean behind the harvesters. As it turned out, she was working in a field belonging to Boaz, who was
from the clan of Elimelek.

4Just then Boaz arrived from Bethlehem
and greeted the harvesters, "The LORD be
with you![d]"

"The LORD bless you![e]" they answered.

1:20 [u] Ex 6:3 [v] ver 13; Job 6:4 **1:21** [w] Job 1:21 **1:22** [x] Ex 9:31; Ru 2:23 [y] 2Sa 21:9 **2:1** [z] Ru 3:2, 12 [a] Ru 1:2 [b] Ru 4:21

2:2 [c] ver 7; Lev 19:9; 23:22; Dt 24:19 **2:4** [d] Jdg 6:12; Lk 1:28; 2Th 3:16 [e] Ps 129:7-8

[a] *20 Naomi* means *pleasant.* [b] *20 Mara* means *bitter.* [c] *20* Hebrew *Shaddai*; also in verse 21 [d] *21* Or *has testified against*

1:22 *barley harvest.* Barley and wheat were usually sown at the same time, but barley matured a month before wheat and was harvested from mid- to late April. Barley was not the preferred grain of consumption—it yielded a course, hearty bread. Since barley matures first, though, it is suitable as the firstfruits offering (Lev 23:10). The arrival of the barley was a time of rejoicing, and it heralded the prospect of security as the remaining crops would come in.
2:1 *man of standing.* The Hebrew phrase used here is often rendered "mighty man of valor" (cf. "best fighting men" in Jos 10:7; "valiant soldier" in 2Ki 5:1), but sometimes it simply refers to a person of ability (1Ki 11:28) or of wealth (2Ki 15:20). The connection with wealth suggests that the "man of standing/valor" was wealthy enough to leave his place of livelihood, having his own weapons of war to serve as necessary when there was not a standing army. Even though there is no evidence of military conflict or turmoil in the book of Ruth, Boaz's description as a man of standing may be significant, since the events are placed within the context of the chaos and anarchy of the period of the judges (Ru 1:1), when there was occasional need to call people for military duty (cf. Jdg 3:28–29; 4:10; 7:1,23). *clan of Elimelek.* The clan was a social grouping in size between that of the tribe (e.g., Judah) and that of the extended family. The clan definition was based on descent from a common ancestor and from within this context the function of the guardian/redeemer (cf. Lev 25) of the narrative will unfold. The clan would normally be responsible for maintaining the social and economic survival of the relatives and in times of crisis would even contribute personnel to the defense of the emerging tribal nation.
2:2 *pick up the leftover grain.* Commonly called gleaning. Mosaic Law decreed that landowners were not to harvest the full extent of their fields, but were to leave produce in the hard-to-reach areas. The remaining harvest was for the poor and foreigners who might be in the land (Lev 19:9–10; Dt 24:19–22). Ruth expects to gather the cut remnants that the reapers have accidentally dropped. Obadiah (Ob 5) and Jeremiah (Jer 49:9) allude to the expectations of gleaning in their indictments of Edom. *in whose eyes I find favor.* Even though Mosaic Law prescribed the landowner to permit gleaning, part of the challenge of the period of the judges was that the people did not generally follow God's law. Ruth's statement implies not only an awareness of etiquette to request permission, but also the potential danger to herself, particularly as a foreigner. Later prophets reveal that the Israelites did not always follow God's direction relative to the poor and oppressed (Isa 1:17; Am 5:10–15; 8:4–6; Mic 3:1–3), and almost certainly this abuse would often manifest itself in the refusal to allow them to glean. Corroboration of this is the Egyptian instruction from the Ramesside period: Do not "pounce on a widow when you find her in the fields. And then fail to be patient with her reply." It is not clear if this instruction reflects a widespread custom or law in Egypt, or if it simply represents Amenemope's perception of civility and humanitarianism.
2:3 *behind the harvesters.* Whether the harvesters were from Boaz's household cannot be ascertained. The Bible notes that natives and foreigners might hire themselves out for work (Dt 24:14) either on a daily basis (Lev 19:13; Dt 24:15; cf. Mt 20:1–16) or annually (Lev 25:53). The Laws of Eshnunna specified a shekel of silver for a month's wages, plus a grain provision. The Code of Hammurapi decrees a per diem wage—for the first half of the year, it was to be six barleycorn of silver per day and for the second half, five barleycorn of silver per day. We do not know the pay scale for the time of Ruth in Judah. Harvesting crops apparently was not a favored occupation (cf. Job 7:1–2; 14:6), and the person's welfare would inevitably be at the mercy of the overseer (Jer 22:13; Mal 3:5). *a field belonging to Boaz.* People typically lived in small towns or villages, which provided safety as well as a sense of community, especially since the people were usually tribally related. The population of the town seldom exceeded a few hundred. The fields were away from the town and it was necessary for the people to leave the security of the town to work in the fields. The fields were marked off in family plots, often with small piles of stones serving as boundary markers. It would be somewhat easy for an unscrupulous person to move these stones over a little at a time to increase his land holdings at the expense of a neighbor. Reflecting this reality, the Bible has injunctions against illicitly moving boundary markers (Dt 19:14; 27:17; Pr 22:28; 23:10; cf. Job 24:2; Hos 5:10). A similar prohibition against land theft with instructions for compensation appears in Hittite laws. The production of these small piles of stones, and sometimes low walls, were also a convenient means by which to remove the stones from the cultivable fields.
2:4 *"The LORD be with you!" "The LORD bless you!"* The exchange of greetings imploring the Lord is not unusual. It may denote an element of devotion, but it may also simply have been a customary greeting. In this text, the reader is certainly supposed to read significance in it even if it is conventional. In Ps 129, the psalmist uses agricultural imagery to describe the interaction with his enemies; the final verse (Ps 129:8) implies that a blessing including the divine name was common. One greeting in the Hebrew Bible was simply "shalom," meaning "peace" (cf. Jdg 6:23; 1Sa 25:6; 2Sa 18:28).

Gleaning scene from the Tomb of Menna. Two small girls quarrel with each other and pull at each other's hair. A basket lies on the ground between them, so it would appear that they were also gathering ears of wheat before they started their argument. Ruth meets Boaz as she gleans in his field (Ru 2:7 – 8).

Manna Nader, Gabana Studios Cairo

5Boaz asked the overseer of his harvesters, "Who does that young woman belong to?"
6The overseer replied, "She is the Moabite[f] who came back from Moab with Naomi. 7She said, 'Please let me glean and
gather among the sheaves behind the harvesters.' She came into the field and has
remained here from morning till now, except for a short rest in the shelter."
8So Boaz said to Ruth, "My daughter,
listen to me. Don't go and glean in another field and don't go away from here. Stay
here with the women who work for me.
9Watch the field where the men are harvesting, and follow along after the wom-
en. I have told the men not to lay a hand
on you. And whenever you are thirsty, go
and get a drink from the water jars the
men have filled."
10At this, she bowed down with her face
to the ground.[g] She asked him, "Why have

2:6 [f] Ru 1:22
2:10 [g] 1Sa 25:23

2:5 *the overseer.* The Hebrew word used here is sometimes translated "young man," but the term encompasses much more. Ugaritic and Egyptian sources use a cognate word to refer to people of military rank. Similarly, people in the Bible who are so designated are often servants or retainers of some kind (Nu 22:22; Jdg 7:10 – 11; 19:3; 2Ki 4:12) or military personnel (Ge 14:24; 1Sa 25:5; 2Sa 2:14; 1Ki 20:14). It can also apply to someone who manages an estate, such as Ziba, who had custody of Saul's estate (2Sa 9:9; 19:18). As far as age is concerned, the age of demarcation appears to vary depending on the function of the person involved — for military service, it was age 20 (Ex 30:14; Nu 1:3,18); for Levitical service outside the tent of meeting, it was age 25 (Nu 8:24); for service in the tent of meeting, it was age 30 (Nu 4).
2:7 *from morning till now.* The Hebrew text is difficult to decipher. The NIV has opted for a rendering that describes the agricultural custom of rising early to work in the fields. Farmers typically rise at or before dawn to take advantage of the cooler morning temperatures. In pre-industrial societies, and especially in a hot climate like that of Israel, it would be normal to take an afternoon break during the heat of the day and resume the field work in the later afternoon. This is part of the context for David's late afternoon walk on his roof after his rest (2Sa 11:2). *short rest in the shelter.* Again the Hebrew is difficult. The NIV has opted to render the verse to reflect Ruth's industriousness. She has not stopped working "except for a short rest in the shelter." Work in the hot sun can quickly drain one's energy. The shelter was a kind of brush arbor set up as a break shade for the workers. Because of Israel's low humidity, retreat into the shade yields a dramatic differential in temperature, since the dry air rapidly evaporates the perspiration and accentuates the cooling effects.
2:9 *follow ... after the women.* It appears there was a division of labor, the men doing the cutting (v. 15) and the women doing the binding (vv. 8 – 9), although this separation is not necessarily absolute. *men not to lay a hand on you.* Ruth's presence on the scene as a stranger and especially as a foreigner would naturally draw attention and almost invite abuse by some in society. *lay a hand on.* The Hebrew word carries several nuances including to strike (see Ge 32:25,32; Jos 8:15 ["be driven back"]; Job 1:19), to inflict injury (see Ge 26:11,29) and to have sexual relations (see Ge 20:6; Pr 6:29). Unless Boaz suspected his employees to be of the basest sort, it is unlikely that sexual relations (i.e., rape) would be the point of his prohibition; more likely it was that they were not to strike or abuse her or inflict upon her verbal abuse (cf. the Egyptian "Instruction of Amenemope" in the note on v. 2). *water jars.* The young men were to permit her to drink from the jars they had filled. Without a readily available water supply in the field, it was necessary to prepare for the day's activities. While not necessarily exclusively so, drawing water was commonly a woman's job (Ge 24:11,13; 1Sa 9:11). Ugaritic materials reflect the activity as predominantly a woman's task. The Israelites sometimes coerced foreigners into the job (Dt 29:10 – 11; Jos 9:21 – 27).
2:10 *bowed down with her face to the ground.* While we

I found such favor in your eyes that you
notice me[h]—a foreigner?[i]"
11 Boaz replied, "I've been told all about
what you have done for your mother-in-
law[j] since the death of your husband—
how you left your father and mother and
your homeland and came to live with a
people you did not know before.[k] 12 May
the LORD repay you for what you have
done. May you be richly rewarded by the
LORD,[l] the God of Israel, under whose
wings[m] you have come to take refuge.[n]"
13 "May I continue to find favor in your
eyes, my lord," she said. "You have put
me at ease by speaking kindly to your servant—though I do not have the standing
of one of your servants."
14 At mealtime Boaz said to her, "Come
over here. Have some bread and dip it in
the wine vinegar."
When she sat down with the harvesters,
he offered her some roasted grain. She ate
all she wanted and had some left over.[o]
15 As she got up to glean, Boaz gave orders
to his men, "Let her gather among the
sheaves and don't reprimand her. 16 Even
pull out some stalks for her from the bundles and leave them for her to pick up, and
don't rebuke her."
17 So Ruth gleaned in the field until evening. Then she threshed the barley she
had gathered, and it amounted to about
an ephah.[a] 18 She carried it back to town,
and her mother-in-law saw how much she
had gathered. Ruth also brought out and
gave her what she had left over[p] after she
had eaten enough.
19 Her mother-in-law asked her, "Where
did you glean today? Where did you work?
Blessed be the man who took notice of
you![q]"
Then Ruth told her mother-in-law about
the one at whose place she had been
working. "The name of the man I worked
with today is Boaz," she said.
20 "The LORD bless him!" Naomi said to
her daughter-in-law. "He has not stopped
showing his kindness[r] to the living and
the dead." She added, "That man is our
close relative; he is one of our guardian-
redeemers.[b][s]"
21 Then Ruth the Moabite said, "He even
said to me, 'Stay with my workers until
they finish harvesting all my grain.' "
22 Naomi said to Ruth her daughter-in-
law, "It will be good for you, my daughter,
to go with the women who work for him,
because in someone else's field you might
be harmed."
23 So Ruth stayed close to the women of

2:10 [h] Ps 41:1 [i] Dt 15:3 **2:11** [j] Ru 1:14 [k] Ru 1:16-17 **2:12** [l] 1Sa 24:19 [m] Ps 17:8; 36:7; 57:1; 61:4; 63:7; 91:4 [n] Ru 1:16 **2:14** [o] ver 18

2:18 [p] ver 14 **2:19** [q] ver 10; Ps 41:1 **2:20** [r] Ru 3:10; 2Sa 2:5; Pr 17:17 [s] Ru 3:9,12; 4:1,14

[a] *17* That is, probably about 30 pounds or about 13 kilograms [b] *20* The Hebrew word for *guardian-redeemer* is a legal term for one who has the obligation to redeem a relative in serious difficulty (see Lev. 25:25-55).

cannot be absolutely sure of the posture involved, the Black Obelisk depicts Jehu of Israel bowing before Shalmaneser III with his face on the ground.

2:12 *under whose wings.* In this case, Boaz likely simply alludes to the protective covering of the Lord's care. The Lord elsewhere is portrayed as providing such protection (Ps 36:7; 57:1; 61:4; 91:4). Occasional artistic depictions of deities spreading their wings over their subjects can be seen in a Syrian goddess spreading her wings over two children who nurse at her breasts. An Egyptian statue depicts Horus as a falcon hovering behind the king, Khafre, and another shows the wings of Isis protectively surrounding Osiris. Boaz's imagery might draw from the wing-protected ark of the covenant law with its cherubim (Ex 25:17–22).

2:14 *At mealtime.* The day's meals normally began with a light breakfast and a light noon meal such as reflected in this narrative. The evening meal was the main meal of the day and usually consisted of basically a one-pot stew mainly of vegetables; the stew was sopped with bread. *wine vinegar.* May have been a type of vinegar-based sauce. An inscription preserved from Arad lists this commodity (Hebrew *homets*) as being requisitioned along with wine; however, earlier Ugaritic materials seem to list it as a synonym of wine. Linguistically, the item, alternatively, could render a commonly used chick pea sauce, hummus, prevalent through the Mediterranean world into which bread is dipped. The roasted grain was a common addition to the meal (1Sa 17:17; 25:18; 2Sa 17:28).

2:17 *threshed the barley.* To thresh this personal harvest for herself and Naomi, Ruth beat the grain with a stick to separate the grains from the chaff (cf. Gideon in Jdg 6:11). It would be necessary for her then to winnow it as well (see note on 3:2). Her take for the day was impressive—an ephah (about two-thirds of a bushel, or 23 liters) is an exceptional quantity and implies that the workers complied with Boaz's request (vv. 15–16). This was the same amount that Jesse instructs David to deliver to his three brothers serving in Saul's army (1Sa 17:13–17).

2:20 *the living and the dead.* Some cultures worked to maintain the dead by giving food offerings and sacrifices on their behalf; there is no indication that Naomi has this in mind—she more likely alludes to God's preservation of the memory of the dead (i.e., Elimelek, Mahlon and Kilion) by taking care of their widows (i.e., Naomi and Ruth). She recognizes that Boaz is a potential source of hope as their guardian-redeemer (Hebrew *goel*). *guardian-redeemers.* This role was multifaceted and served to stabilize a disrupted family circumstance. Mosaic Law prescribed that the guardian-redeemer reacquire property lost by family members who had fallen on hard times (Lev 25:25–30; cf. Jer 32:6–15). He also was to redeem relatives who, because of poverty, had sold themselves into slavery (Lev 25:47–55). In addition, he was to avenge relatives who had died at the hands of others (Nu 35:12,19–27; Dt 19:6,12; Jos 20:2–3,5,9), be the recipient of payments owed to deceased relatives (Nu 5:8) and generally serve to alleviate wrongs that relatives might not be able to alleviate for themselves (Job 19:25; Ps 119:154; Pr 23:11; Jer 50:34; La 3:58). The legislation says nothing explicitly regarding taking the wife of the deceased as part of the redemption procedure, although it appears that the Israelites sometimes understood a connection between the two.

2:23 *barley and wheat harvests.* The time involved would normally be two to two and one-half months, taking the wheat harvest into June. If the narrative is chronological,

14So she lay at his feet until morning, but
got up before anyone could be recognized;
and he said, "No one must know that a
woman came to the threshing floor."[g]
15He also said, "Bring me the shawl you
are wearing and hold it out." When she
did so, he poured into it six measures of
barley and placed the bundle on her. Then
he[a] went back to town.
16When Ruth came to her mother-in-
law, Naomi asked, "How did it go, my
daughter?"
Then she told her everything Boaz
had done for her 17and added, "He gave
me these six measures of barley, saying,
'Don't go back to your mother-in-law
empty-handed.'"
18Then Naomi said, "Wait, my daughter,
until you find out what happens. For the
man will not rest until the matter is settled
today."[h]

Boaz Marries Ruth

4 Meanwhile Boaz went up to the town
gate and sat down there just as the
guardian-redeemer[b] he had mentioned[i]
came along. Boaz said, "Come over here,
my friend, and sit down." So he went over
and sat down.
2Boaz took ten of the elders[j] of the town
and said, "Sit here," and they did so.
3Then he said to the guardian-redeemer,
"Naomi, who has come back from Moab,
is selling the piece of land that belonged to
our relative Elimelek. 4I thought I should
bring the matter to your attention and
suggest that you buy it in the presence of
these seated here and in the presence of
the elders of my people. If you will redeem
it, do so. But if you[c] will not, tell me, so I
will know. For no one has the right to do it
except you,[k] and I am next in line."
"I will redeem it," he said.
5Then Boaz said, "On the day you buy
the land from Naomi, you also acquire
Ruth the Moabite, the[d] dead man's widow, in order to maintain the name of the
dead with his property."[l]
6At this, the guardian-redeemer said,
"Then I cannot redeem[m] it because I might
endanger my own estate. You redeem it
yourself. I cannot do it."
7(Now in earlier times in Israel, for the
redemption and transfer of property to become final, one party took off his sandal

3:14 [g] Ro 14:16; 2Co 8:21 **3:18** [h] Ps 37:3-5 **4:1** [i] Ru 3:12 **4:2** [j] 1Ki 21:8; Pr 31:23
4:4 [k] Lev 25:25; Jer 32:7-8 **4:5** [l] Ge 38:8; Dt 25:5-6; Ru 3:13; Mt 22:24 **4:6** [m] Lev 25:25; Ru 3:13

[a] *15* Most Hebrew manuscripts; many Hebrew manuscripts, Vulgate and Syriac *she* [b] *1* The Hebrew word for *guardian-redeemer* is a legal term for one who has the obligation to redeem a relative in serious difficulty (see Lev. 25:25-55); also in verses 3, 6, 8 and 14. [c] *4* Many Hebrew manuscripts, Septuagint, Vulgate and Syriac; most Hebrew manuscripts *he* [d] *5* Vulgate and Syriac; Hebrew (see also Septuagint) *Naomi and from Ruth the Moabite, you acquire the*

3:14 *No one must know.* See previous note. Obscurity is important for propriety, but it is also important that rumors of immorality do not interfere with the day's legal proceedings
3:17 *six measures.* The "measure" is not identified, but it would not have been the ephah since six ephahs would equal approximately 200 pounds (90 kilograms). The seah is more likely; six seahs would equal 60–90 pounds (27–41 kilograms). An alternative would be an omer, which was approximately one-tenth of an ephah, in which case the amount would be a little over half the quantity she had gleaned in her first outing (see 2:17 and note).
4:1 *the town gate.* See note on Ge 19:1. *guardian-redeemer.* See note on 2:20.
4:2 *elders.* References to elders who oversee the people of antiquity appear in the Gilgamesh Epic and in Hittite law. The Bible indicates that Moab and Midian had elders serving a similar function (Nu 22:4,7) as did the Gibeonites (Jos 9:11). Over time, the term came to apply not only to those of a certain age, but to those who administrated the affairs of the community. They were assumed to be people who had experienced sufficient vicissitudes of life to be able to tap into those experiences to guide the community (1Ki 12:6–11; Job 12:20; Jer 26:17–19). Additionally, they sometimes represented the people before God (Lev 4:13–15), and would oversee murder trials and questions of asylum (Dt 19:11–12; 21:1–9; Jos 20:1–6) and disputes regarding virginity (Dt 22:15–19). They also sometimes served as social witnesses to issues of the guardian-redeemer and levirate marriages (Ru 4:9–11; Dt 25:5–10). The Bible notes that there were elders over tribal and clan affairs (e.g., Jdg 11:5), as well as over national affairs (Dt 31:28). In addition, cities had their own appointments (Dt 19:11–12). How many elders a town should have is not indicated in the Bible. Gideon was informed that Sukkoth had 77 elders and officials (Jdg 8:14). This statement in Ruth (i.e., "ten of the elders") indicates that there were more than ten for Bethlehem.
4:5 *the dead man's widow.* See the article "Levirate Marriage," p. 85.
4:6 *I might endanger my own estate.* The man fails to elaborate how serving as the guardian-redeemer with Ruth as part of the deal would endanger his estate. Since the purpose of the levirate marriage was to perpetuate the name of the deceased, the inheritance would be through another's line than the guardian-redeemer himself. An investment to redeem the land for Naomi, who was apparently past childbearing age (1:11–13), would likely keep the property in his own line, and would be an attractive business proposal, but the prospect of marrying Ruth, who came with the property and the implied responsibilities, would indicate that not only would the investment to redeem the property be forfeited to any offspring that might be born, but there would be the added burden of supporting Ruth and Naomi, as well as any additional offspring that might come from the union.
4:7–8 *took off his sandal ... removed his sandal.* The text implies that the guardian-redeemer relinquished his sandal to Boaz. The image perhaps derives from property rights and the right of the person who owns a piece of land to be the one who walks on it. God had revealed to Abraham that wherever he might walk in Canaan, the land would belong to him (Ge 13:17). This foot-placement motif is reflected in the Nuzi materials in which "to make a transfer of real estate more valid, a man would 'lift up his foot from his property,' and 'placed the foot of the other man on it.'" With similar imagery, God declares possession of Edom with the metaphor of casting his sandal over the land (Ps 60:8; 108:9).
4:7 *earlier times.* Indicates that some time has passed

Boaz to glean until the barley and wheat
harvests[t] were finished. And she lived
with her mother-in-law.

Ruth and Boaz at the Threshing Floor

3 One day Ruth's mother-in-law Naomi said to her, "My daughter, I must
find a home[a][u] for you, where you will be
well provided for. 2 Now Boaz, with whose
women you have worked, is a relative[v] of
ours. Tonight he will be winnowing barley on the threshing floor. 3 Wash, put on
perfume,[w] and get dressed in your best
clothes. Then go down to the threshing
floor, but don't let him know you are there
until he has finished eating and drinking.
4 When he lies down, note the place where
he is lying. Then go and uncover his feet
and lie down. He will tell you what to do."
5 "I will do whatever you say,"[x] Ruth answered. 6 So she went down to the threshing floor and did everything her mother-
in-law told her to do.
7 When Boaz had finished eating and
drinking and was in good spirits,[y] he went
over to lie down at the far end of the grain
pile. Ruth approached quietly, uncovered
his feet and lay down. 8 In the middle of
the night something startled the man; he
turned — and there was a woman lying at
his feet!
9 "Who are you?" he asked.
"I am your servant Ruth," she said.
"Spread the corner of your garment[z] over
me, since you are a guardian-redeemer[b][a]
of our family."
10 "The LORD bless you, my daughter," he
replied. "This kindness is greater than that
which you showed earlier: You have not
run after the younger men, whether rich
or poor. 11 And now, my daughter, don't be
afraid. I will do for you all you ask. All
the people of my town know that you are
a woman of noble character.[b] 12 Although
it is true that I am a guardian-redeemer of
our family,[c] there is another who is more
closely related than[d] I. 13 Stay here for the
night, and in the morning if he wants to
do his duty as your guardian-redeemer,[e]
good; let him redeem you. But if he is not
willing, as surely as the LORD lives[f] I will
do it. Lie here until morning."

2:23 [t] Dt 16:9
3:1 [u] Ru 1:9
3:2 [v] Dt 25:5-10; Ru 2:1
3:3 [w] 2Sa 14:2
3:5 [x] Eph 6:1; Col 3:20
3:7 [y] Jdg 19:6, 9,22; 2Sa 13:28; 1Ki 21:7; Est 1:10
3:9 [z] Eze 16:8 [a] ver 12; Ru 2:20
3:11 [b] Pr 12:4; 31:10
3:12 [c] ver 9 [d] Ru 4:1
3:13 [e] Dt 25:5; Ru 4:5; Mt 22:24 [f] Jdg 8:19; Jer 4:2

[a] 1 Hebrew *find rest* (see 1:9) [b] 9 The Hebrew word for *guardian-redeemer* is a legal term for one who has the obligation to redeem a relative in serious difficulty (see Lev. 25:25-55); also in verses 12 and 13.

the winnowing of barley does not commence until ch. 3; it appears the barley winnowing was put on hold until the wheat harvest had come in. If this is the case, it implies a significant harvest in view of the recently terminated famine.

3:2 *winnowing barley.* Winnowing was often done as a community activity. Winnowing takes place after the threshing (see below), and it is a very labor-intensive process to separate the grains from the plant stalks. The process was conducted typically outside of the town where the person, using a pitchfork, would throw the mixture into the air. The breezes blew away the unwanted, lighter components (cf. Hos 13:3), allowing the heavier grains to fall to the ground. The process would be repeated until the grains were relatively free from the plant stalks. The breezes usually came up in mid-afternoon and died out about sunset; it is possible that Naomi's reference to Boaz winnowing at night accommodates the festivities that normally followed a successful harvest and winnowing. Transport of the grain to the threshing and winnowing floor was either in animal-drawn carts (cf. Am 2:13) or in baskets. *threshing floor.* A large flat area, usually bared bedrock, slick from the polishing effect of the intensive activity, with the straw acting as a polishing agent. It was situated to take advantage of the prevailing winds, which were critical for the process. Sometimes it was near the city gate (1Ki 22:10; Jer 15:7); Ugaritic literature also cites the placement of a threshing floor near the gate. Threshing could be done several ways. Ruth had beaten out her fairly small volume with a stick (see note at 2:17). A larger volume, however, required more intensive and efficient threshing. Sometimes animals walked over the grain and their hooves beat the grain to separate the grain from the stalk (cf. a metaphoric allusion in Mic 4:13). Mosaic legislation demanded that the animals be allowed to eat of the harvest (Dt 25:4). A more efficient tool was to use a threshing sledge, which would be pulled by an animal or two (cf. the metaphor in Isa 41:15). The sledge consisted of two to three wide boards with upturned ends to slide easily over the grain; the underside of the boards would have holes drilled or slots cut into them into which teeth of flint or iron were driven. The teeth would separate the components of the grain. Isaiah also alludes to the wheels of carts along with the animals hooves being used to thresh (Isa 28:28).

3:4 *uncover his feet.* The instruction is seen by some as a double entendre. Sometimes the Hebrew word translated "feet" is a euphemism for the genital region (see Isa 7:20; Eze 16:25; and perhaps Ex 4:25; Jdg 3:24; 1Sa 24:3), but most of the time "feet" simply means feet. Complicating the interpretation, however, is the use of "uncover" (*glh*) which sometimes referred to sexual relations (Lev 18 [14 times]; Lev 20 [6 times]; Dt 22:30; 27:20; Eze 16:35 – 39). Nevertheless, Naomi instructs Ruth to uncover "the place of his feet," and given the noble character reflected of both Boaz and Ruth, there is no reason to infer that anything more than uncovering the feet occurs. The meaning of this apparently significant action is unknown to us.

3:7 *far end of the grain pile.* Boaz probably remained at the threshing floor to protect against thieves.

3:9 *Who are you?* As to what startled Boaz awake is not revealed, but it likely was the subconscious realization that someone was nearby. *Spread the corner of your garment over me.* Ruth's request is an idiom for marriage. The phrase is the same as applies to marriage when God later described his marriage to Israel (Eze 16:8). The imagery brings to mind Boaz's own blessing of coming under the Lord's wing for protection (2:12). Ruth explains that the invitation is important because he is her "guardian-redeemer" (see note on 2:20). *corner of your garment.* Applies to either a wing or the edge of a garment.

3:13 *Stay … the night.* The Hebrew word does not have sexual connotations.

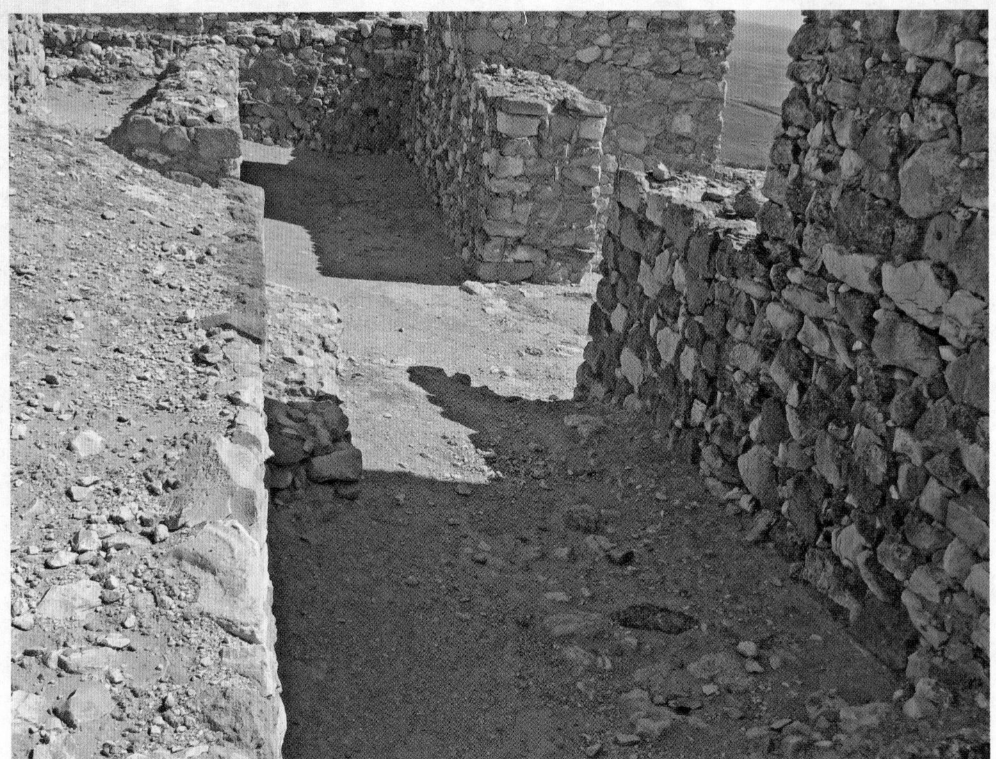

Gate chamber at Arad showing bench (middle left) where people would sit to conduct business. At the town gate Boaz announced to the elders that he bought Naomi's property and took Ruth as his wife (Ru 4).

Kim Walton

and gave it to the other. This was the method of legalizing transactions in Israel.)[n]
8So the guardian-redeemer said to Boaz,
"Buy it yourself." And he removed his
sandal.
9Then Boaz announced to the elders
and all the people, "Today you are witnesses that I have bought from Naomi all
the property of Elimelek, Kilion and Mahlon. 10I have also acquired Ruth the Moabite, Mahlon's widow, as my wife, in order
to maintain the name of the dead with his
property, so that his name will not disappear from among his family or from his
hometown.[o] Today you are witnesses!"
11Then the elders and all the people at
the gate said, "We are witnesses.[p] May the
LORD make the woman who is coming into
your home like Rachel and Leah,[q] who together built up the family of Israel. May
you have standing in Ephrathah[r] and be
famous in Bethlehem. 12Through the offspring the LORD gives you by this young
woman, may your family be like that of
Perez,[s] whom Tamar bore to Judah."

4:7 [n] Dt 25:7-9 **4:10** [o] Dt 25:6 **4:11** [p] Dt 25:9 [q] Ps 127:3; 128:3 [r] Ge 35:16 **4:12** [s] ver 18; Ge 38:29 **4:13** [t] Ge 29:31; 33:5; Ru 3:11 **4:14** [u] Lk 1:58 **4:15** [v] Ru 1:16-17; 2:11-12; 1Sa 1:8

Naomi Gains a Son

13So Boaz took Ruth and she became
his wife. When he made love to her, the
LORD enabled her to conceive,[t] and she
gave birth to a son. 14The women[u] said
to Naomi: "Praise be to the LORD, who
this day has not left you without a guardian-redeemer. May he become famous
throughout Israel! 15He will renew your
life and sustain you in your old age. For
your daughter-in-law, who loves you and
who is better to you than seven sons,[v] has
given him birth."
16Then Naomi took the child in her

from the events of the narrative and when it was recorded, although the Hebrew term sometimes refers to a single generation's separation (cf. Job 42:11).

4:10 *maintain the name of the dead.* Similar explanation appears in the levirate marriage legislation (Dt 25:6). "Name," however, does not serve just as nomenclature; it also refers to being remembered and honored, a kind of eternal life in having offspring to connect with the deceased. Its broader use has to do with inheritance and "the reality and significance of a man's deeds and life." If a man had no sons, the name might be preserved through daughters, as implied in the request of Zelophehad's daughters and their petition to Moses (Nu 27:1 – 11); however, they were required to marry only within their own tribe (Nu 36).

arms and cared for him. [17]The women living there said, "Naomi has a son!" And
they named him Obed. He was the father
of Jesse,[w] the father of David.

The Genealogy of David

4:18-22pp — 1Ch 2:5-15; Mt 1:3-6; Lk 3:31-33

[18]This, then, is the family line of Perez[x]:

Perez was the father of Hezron,
[19]Hezron the father of Ram,
Ram the father of Amminadab,[y]
[20]Amminadab the father of Nahshon,
Nahshon the father of Salmon,[a]
[21]Salmon the father of Boaz,[z]
Boaz the father of Obed,
[22]Obed the father of Jesse,
and Jesse the father of David.

4:17 [w] ver 22; 1Sa 16:1, 18; 1Ch 2:12, 13 **4:18** [x] Mt 1:3-6 **4:19** [y] Ex 6:23 **4:21** [z] Ru 2:1

[a] *20* A few Hebrew manuscripts, some Septuagint manuscripts and Vulgate (see also verse 21 and Septuagint of 1 Chron. 2:11); most Hebrew manuscripts *Salma*

4:17 *Naomi has a son!* It is possible that this refers to a legal adoption, but it more likely recognizes that Naomi is the legal mother of the child (Boaz substituting for Elimelek) and that she will play a significant role in his upbringing.

4:18–22 Genealogies in the ancient world served to communicate connectedness and identity. Sometimes a genealogy may associate a person to someone well-known in their past. Here, the genealogy indicates how the famous king David descended from these very unusual roots. The point is not that he descended from a Moabite woman, but that he descended from a line in which there was faithfulness, in contrast to the tenor of the judges period.

Literary Setting

Determining precisely what genre(s) one is reading is not always an easy task, especially when one is reading texts from a distant time and place. In seeking to discover what the books of Samuel should be "read as," we must bear in mind the broader ancient Near Eastern literary culture in which the texts were first written.

Underneath the broad genre categories of story (narrative) and poem, the books of Samuel seem to incorporate a number of more specific literary forms or subgenres: e.g., birth narratives, call narratives, dream theophanies, prophetic judgment speeches, battle reports, accession accounts, court intrigues, regnal formulas/summaries — just to name a few. In one way or another, these subgenres are attested not only in the Bible but also in the ancient Near East more generally.

David is without doubt the central character in the books of Samuel. And, though the Biblical writers show no reticence to expose his serious failings, David is defended from start to finish as rightly occupying the throne of Israel. Royal apologies are well known from the ancient Near East, and though no exemplar of the genre comes close to the books of Samuel in terms of length, depth, complexity or tone, there are some shared traits. Ancient Near Eastern royal apologies, like the books of Samuel, offer a defense of the right of a certain individual to occupy the throne. This individual is typically not the hereditary heir to the throne and has often come to the throne by a path that some, then as now, would regard as suspicious. The charge of usurpation is often a catalyst for the writing of a royal apology. Some ancient Near Eastern royal apologies may, of course, amount to little more than deceptive political propaganda. But the mere fact that circumstances may be such that an individual, such as David, requires defense, in no way proves that the individual is unworthy of defense.

Difficulty in putting a date on texts that refuse to date themselves is self-evident, and the books of Samuel have been assigned dates across a wide spectrum — from quite early (close to the events they describe) to quite late (in the exilic period). A possible scenario would see the book as containing early sources that have been edited to one degree or another in order to incorporate them into a larger corpus. ◆

NARRATIVE LITERATURE

1 SAMUEL

Introduction to 1 – 2 Samuel.

Historical Setting

The events described in the books of Samuel took place in the eleventh and early tenth centuries BC. This time period (falling mostly within what archaeologists call Iron Age I, c. 1200 – 1000 BC) was one in which the superpowers of the preceding Bronze Ages were having little impact in Syro-Palestine. The Anatolian kingdom of the Hittites had been essentially destroyed by the Sea Peoples and other land-based movements. The Egyptians exercised limited control along the coast of Canaan until the mid-twelfth century BC and then withdrew. The Assyrians were occupied with troubles closer to home, not least was their rivalry with Babylonia to their south. The Assyrian king Tiglath-Pileser I did push as far west as the northern Mediterranean coast near the end of the twelfth century BC, defeating some Aramean territories along the way, but he did not move south into Syro-Palestine itself. Babylonia too in the period in question, was incapable of giving much, if any, attention to Syro-Palestine, finding plenty to keep it busy protecting its interests against neighboring Assyria and Elam. Thus, as the books of Samuel open, the land in which they are set was experiencing what has been described as an eclipse of the great powers. Conditions were ripe for the emergence of smaller territorial powers such as the kingdom ascribed to David in the text of Samuel (see the article "David's 'Empire,'" p. 528).

The transition to monarchy was a departure in the political and religious life of tribal Israel. But it was not a surprising or unanticipated development. The concept of kingship was well known and widely observable in the ancient Near East from at least early in the third millennium BC. Understanding ancient Near Eastern patterns of royal accession and vassal kingship, the interplay of religion and politics, the interaction of prophets with kings, and so forth will help us in grasping the social and religious dynamics reflected in the pages of Samuel.

KEY CONCEPTS

- Samuel is established as a recognized and verified man of God.
- God established a kingship covenant with David and his descendants.
- The key to successful kingship is the recognition that Yahweh is the true king, therefore a king's reign must reflect Yahweh's values (represented in the law and the covenant).
- It is important to honor the presence of God (ark, temple).

The Birth of Samuel

1 There was a certain man from Ramathaim, a Zuphite[a] from the hill country[a] of Ephraim, whose name was Elkanah[b] son of Jeroham, the son of Elihu, the
son of Tohu, the son of Zuph, an Ephraimite. 2He had two wives;[c] one was called
Hannah and the other Peninnah. Peninnah
had children, but Hannah had none.
3Year after year[d] this man went up from
his town to worship[e] and sacrifice to the
LORD Almighty at Shiloh,[f] where Hophni
and Phinehas, the two sons of Eli, were
priests of the LORD. 4Whenever the day
came for Elkanah to sacrifice,[g] he would
give portions of the meat to his wife Peninnah and to all her sons and daughters.
5But to Hannah he gave a double portion
because he loved her, and the LORD had
closed her womb.[h] 6Because the LORD had
closed Hannah's womb, her rival kept provoking her in order to irritate her.[i] 7This
went on year after year. Whenever Hannah
went up to the house of the LORD, her rival
provoked her till she wept and would not
eat. 8Her husband Elkanah would say to
her, "Hannah, why are you weeping? Why
don't you eat? Why are you downhearted?
Don't I mean more to you than ten sons?[j]"
9Once when they had finished eating
and drinking in Shiloh, Hannah stood up.
Now Eli the priest was sitting on his chair

1:1 [a] Jos 17:17-18 [b] 1Ch 6:27, 34
1:2 [c] Dt 21:15-17; Lk 2:36
1:3 [d] ver 21; Ex 23:14; 34:23; Lk 2:41 [e] Dt 12:5-7 [f] Jos 18:1
1:4 [g] Dt 12:17-18
1:5 [h] Ge 16:1; 30:2
1:6 [i] Job 24:21
1:8 [j] Ru 4:15

[a] *1* See Septuagint and 1 Chron. 6:26-27,33-35; or *from Ramathaim Zuphim.*

1:2 *He had two wives.* On polygyny (having more than one wife), see note on Ge 16:2. Most cases of polygyny among commoners occurred prior to the time of the monarchy. The practice was not especially common among the Israelites and generally occurred when the first wife married was barren, when marriage was required to provide offspring for a deceased brother, or for the political reasons of building alliances. *Peninnah had children, but Hannah had none.* Hannah found herself not only in the difficult position of having a rival wife, but in the pitiable position of having no children (see note on Ge 11:30). Given the order in which she and Peninnah are named, Hannah was probably Elkanah's first wife, and it may have been her barrenness that prompted Elkanah to take a second wife. In the broader ancient Near East, fertility was a major concern for women and even for men, the more so as fertility was regarded as under the control of God (v. 5) or the gods, and lack of fertility could be understood as a curse.
1:3 *Year after year this man went up from his town to worship and sacrifice.* Religious life in the ancient Near East, as in the Bible, was marked by feasts and festivals. The Pentateuch makes reference to three annual pilgrim festivals: the Festival of Unleavened Bread, the Festival of Weeks and the Festival of Tabernacles (Dt 16:16; cf. Ex 23:14–17; 34:18–23; Dt 16:1–15). An "annual festival of the LORD in Shiloh" is mentioned in Jdg 21:19, and it may have been this festival to which Elkanah and his family went, or they may have gone to Shiloh simply in observance of a family ceremony (the existence of family ceremonies is suggested by David's excuse in 1Sa 20:6). *LORD Almighty.* This divine appellation, referring to Yahweh as the commander of armies (heavenly hosts) occurs here for the first time in the OT. *Shiloh.* Biblical Shiloh is identified with modern Khirbet Seilun, which lies midway between Shechem to the north and Bethel and Jerusalem to the south. First mentioned in Jos 18:1, Shiloh was the place where Joshua designated the tribal allotments after the initial conquest (Jos 19:51). Shiloh became the site of an annual festival during the period of the judges (Jdg 21:19), and at least by the end of the judges period Shiloh had become the home of the priestly family of Eli and of the ark of the covenant (1Sa 4:3; 14:3). Ps 78:60 and especially Jer 7:12 suggest that Shiloh may have served as Israel's first "central sanctuary," and Jer 7:14; 26:6,9 imply that the city was destroyed or at least abandoned after Israel's defeat by the Philistines in 1Sa 4. *Hophni and Phinehas, the two sons of Eli, were priests of the LORD.* That Eli is simply mentioned without further introduction suggests that he must have been well-known to the original audience(s) of this story. He appears to have been both judge (cf. 4:18) and high priest as the period of the judges was drawing to a close—though he is never explicitly called high priest. Combining the evidence of several Biblical passages (e.g., 14:3; 22:9,11,20; 1Ch 24:3), we may conclude that Eli descended from Aaron's fourth son, Ithamar, rather than from his third son, Eleazar, whose line had occupied the high priestly office at the beginning of the period of the judges (see, e.g., Jos 22:31–32; Jdg 20:28). How the transfer of responsibility from the house of Eleazar to the house of Ithamar took place remains obscure, as the question is not addressed in Scripture.
1:4 *give portions of the meat.* While some sacrifices were completely consumed by fire (e.g., whole burnt offerings; see Lev 1 and notes), others such as the fellowship offerings (see Lev 3 and notes; 7:11–34) stipulated portions to be eaten by those participating in the sacrifice (see note on Lev 3:1).
1:5 *to Hannah he gave a double portion.* Dt 21:17 speaks of a "double share" being given to the firstborn son, even if he is the son of an unloved wife. Many commentators assume a similar meaning here, i.e., a "double portion" given to the beloved but barren wife. The Hebrew expression in the present context is, however, different from the expression in Dt 21:17, and its sense is much debated. Whatever the nature of this portion, it could not compensate for other factors such as the social stigma associated with barrenness, the need for offspring to assure the social security of aging parents, etc.
1:9 *the LORD's house.* Mention of "the LORD's house" at this stage in Israel's history may seem anachronistic, inasmuch as Solomon's temple in Jerusalem would not be built until more than 70 years later, and, in any case, 2Sa 7:6 indicates clearly that the Lord's house prior to King David's time was a tent. This is confirmed by Ps 78:60, which speaks unmistakably of the Lord's "tent" at Shiloh. The best approach is to understand the "house" here and also in 3:3 as referring to the tabernacle. Given the fact that the tabernacle is designated in several different ways in Samuel—e.g., "the house of the LORD" (v. 7; 3:15) and "the tent of meeting" (2:22)—and the fact that other portions of Scripture exhibit a similar variety of expression (e.g., Ps 27:4–5), one should not make too much of the fact that the tabernacle is called the Lord's "house." That said, the mention of the "doorpost" here and the "doors" in 3:15 does seem to suggest a more permanent structure than has typically been associated with the tabernacle, and, indeed, there may have a been a more substantial "house" at Shiloh that held

by the doorpost of the LORD's house.[k] 10In
her deep anguish[l] Hannah prayed to the
LORD, weeping bitterly. 11And she made a
vow, saying, "LORD Almighty, if you will
only look on your servant's misery and remember[m] me, and not forget your servant
but give her a son, then I will give him to
the LORD for all the days of his life, and no
razor[n] will ever be used on his head."
12As she kept on praying to the LORD,
Eli observed her mouth. 13Hannah was
praying in her heart, and her lips were
moving but her voice was not heard. Eli
thought she was drunk 14and said to her,
"How long are you going to stay drunk?
Put away your wine."
15"Not so, my lord," Hannah replied,
"I am a woman who is deeply troubled.
I have not been drinking wine or beer;
I was pouring[o] out my soul to the LORD.
16Do not take your servant for a wicked
woman; I have been praying here out of
my great anguish and grief."
17Eli answered, "Go in peace,[p] and may
the God of Israel grant you what you have
asked of him.[q]"
18She said, "May your servant find favor
in your eyes.[r]" Then she went her way and
ate something, and her face was no longer
downcast.[s]
19Early the next morning they arose
and worshiped before the LORD and then
went back to their home at Ramah. Elkanah made love to his wife Hannah, and the
LORD remembered[t] her. 20So in the course
of time Hannah became pregnant and gave
birth to a son. She named[u] him Samuel,[a]
saying, "Because I asked the LORD for him."

Hannah Dedicates Samuel

21When her husband Elkanah went up
with all his family to offer the annual[v] sacrifice to the LORD and to fulfill his vow,[w]
22Hannah did not go. She said to her husband, "After the boy is weaned, I will take
him and present[x] him before the LORD, and
he will live there always."[b]
23"Do what seems best to you," her husband Elkanah told her. "Stay here until
you have weaned him; only may the LORD
make good[y] his[c] word." So the woman
stayed at home and nursed her son until
she had weaned him.
24After he was weaned, she took the boy
with her, young as he was, along with a
three-year-old bull,[d][z] an ephah[e] of flour
and a skin of wine, and brought him to
the house of the LORD at Shiloh. 25When
the bull had been sacrificed, they brought
the boy to Eli, 26and she said to him, "Pardon me, my lord. As surely as you live, I
am the woman who stood here beside you
praying to the LORD. 27I prayed[a] for this
child, and the LORD has granted me what
I asked of him. 28So now I give him to the
LORD. For his whole life[b] he will be given
over to the LORD." And he worshiped the
LORD there.

Hannah's Prayer

2 Then Hannah prayed and said:[c]

"My heart rejoices[d] in the LORD;
  in the LORD my horn[f][e] is lifted high.
My mouth boasts over my enemies,
  for I delight in your deliverance.

2"There is no one holy[f] like the LORD;
  there is no one besides you;
  there is no Rock[g] like our God.

1:9 [k]1Sa 3:3 **1:10** [l]Job 7:11 **1:11** [m]Ge 8:1; 28:20; 29:32 [n]Nu 6:1-21; Jdg 13:5 **1:15** [o]Ps 42:4; 62:8; La 2:19 **1:17** [p]Jdg 18:6; 1Sa 25:35; 2Ki 5:19; Mk 5:34 [q]Ps 20:3-5 **1:18** [r]Ru 2:13 [s]Ecc 9:7; Ro 15:13 **1:19** [t]Ge 4:1; 30:22 **1:20** [u]Ge 41:51-52; Ex 2:10, 22; Mt 1:21 **1:21** [v]ver 3 [w]Dt 12:11

1:22 [x]ver 11, 28; Lk 2:22 **1:23** [y]ver 17; Nu 30:7 **1:24** [z]Nu 15:8-10; Dt 12:5; Jos 18:1 **1:27** [a]ver 11-13; Ps 66:19-20 **1:28** [b]ver 11, 22; Ge 24:26, 52 **2:1** [c]Lk 1:46-55 [d]Ps 9:14; 13:5 [e]Ps 89:17, 24; 92:10; Isa 12:2-3 **2:2** [f]Ex 15:11; Lev 19:2 [g]Dt 32:30-31; 2Sa 22:2, 32

[a] *20 Samuel* sounds like the Hebrew for *heard by God.* [b] *22* Masoretic Text; Dead Sea Scrolls *always. I have dedicated him as a Nazirite—all the days of his life."* [c] *23* Masoretic Text; Dead Sea Scrolls, Septuagint and Syriac *your* [d] *24* Dead Sea Scrolls, Septuagint and Syriac; Masoretic Text *with three bulls* [e] *24* That is, probably about 36 pounds or about 16 kilograms [f] *1 Horn* here symbolizes strength; also in verse 10.

the tabernacle inside it, though no archaeological evidence of such a structure has been uncovered at Shiloh.
1:11 *made a vow.* The making of vows was a common practice in the OT world and in the ancient Near East generally, including among Mesopotamians, Hittites, Phoenicians, Egyptians and the people of Ugarit. Often the vow was made to God (or a god) and involved an agreement by the one making the vow to do a particular thing (offer a sacrifice, erect a stele, etc.), on the condition that the deity would fulfill a request. (see note on Jdg 11:30). *no razor will ever be used on his head.* Recalls the second prohibition of the so-called Nazirite vow (Nu 6:1–21). While a Nazirite vow was commonly made for a limited period of time (the end of which would be marked by the shaving of the head and the return of the individual to "normal" status), Hannah consecrated her son for "all the days of his life." In this respect, Hannah's vow is reminiscent of the Nazirite charge included in the annunciation of Samson's birth (Jdg 13:3–7). No similar vows are known from the rest of the ancient world.
1:13 *Hannah was praying in her heart.* While spontaneous prayer is quite common in the Bible, silent prayer is mentioned explicitly only here. An interesting parallel is found in the Egyptian "Instruction of Any," which encourages the worshiper to pray words hidden in their hearts.
1:22 *After the boy is weaned.* In antiquity, a child might be nursed for three years or more. Because the return of ovulation after giving birth can be delayed by breast-feeding, an extended period of nursing may have served as a kind of natural contraceptive.
2:1 *horn.* Refers, of course, at a literal level to the antlers or horns that served as weapons for various animals; the OT uses "horn" to describe the natural headgear of rams and wild oxen, and even for the tusks of elephants. It is not surprising, therefore, that horns regularly appear in depictions of Mesopotamian deities and kings. As a general metaphor, one's horn represents one's strength, pride and security. See the article "Moses' Horns," p. 172.
2:2 *there is no Rock like our God.* The term "rock" (or "mountain") occurs in theophoric personal names (names that make a statement of some sort about God) in both the ancient Near East and the OT. As a title (and not a mere

3 "Do not keep talking so proudly
or let your mouth speak such
arrogance,[h]
for the LORD is a God who knows,
and by him deeds[i] are weighed.[j]
4 "The bows of the warriors are
broken,[k]
but those who stumbled are armed
with strength.
5 Those who were full hire themselves
out for food,
but those who were hungry are
hungry no more.
She who was barren[l] has borne seven
children,
but she who has had many sons
pines away.

6 "The LORD brings death and makes
alive;[m]
he brings down to the grave and
raises up.[n]
7 The LORD sends poverty and
wealth;[o]
he humbles and he exalts.[p]
8 He raises[q] the poor from the dust
and lifts the needy from the ash heap;
he seats them with princes
and has them inherit a throne of
honor.[r]

"For the foundations[s] of the earth are
the LORD's;
on them he has set the world.
9 He will guard the feet[t] of his faithful
servants,
but the wicked will be silenced in
the place of darkness.[u]

"It is not by strength[v] that one prevails;
10 those who oppose the LORD will be
broken.[w]
The Most High will thunder[x] from
heaven;
the LORD will judge[y] the ends of the
earth.

"He will give strength[z] to his king
and exalt the horn[a] of his anointed."

11 Then Elkanah went home to Ramah, but the boy ministered[b] before the LORD under Eli the priest.

2:3 [h] Pr 8:13 [i] 1Sa 16:7; 1Ki 8:39 [j] Pr 16:2; 24:11-12 **2:4** [k] Ps 37:15 **2:5** [l] Ps 113:9; Jer 15:9 **2:6** [m] Dt 32:39 [n] Isa 26:19 **2:7** [o] Dt 8:18 [p] Job 5:11; Ps 75:7 **2:8** [q] Ps 113:7-8 [r] Job 36:7 [s] Job 38:4 **2:9** [t] Ps 91:12 [u] Mt 8:12 [v] Ps 33:16-17 **2:10** [w] Ps 2:9 [x] Ps 18:13 [y] Ps 96:13 [z] Ps 21:1 [a] Ps 89:24 **2:11** [b] ver 18; 1Sa 3:1

metaphor) for the God of the Bible, the term is concentrated in poetic passages such as the song of Moses in Dt 32, the song of David in 2Sa 22, the Psalms and Isaiah. Modern readers, familiar with the use of explosives and heavy machinery to move or even pulverize rocks, must use their imaginations to grasp the sense of "impervious solidity" that a large rock would have evoked in the minds of ancient people. In the Bible, "Rock" is suggestive of God's strength and sovereignty and of the security, stability and salvation of those who trust in him.

2:6 *The LORD brings death and makes alive; he brings down to the grave and raises up.* Cf. vv. 3 – 8. The conviction that the fate of human beings is in the hands of God (or the gods) runs deep in ancient Near Eastern cultures. In the Akkadian creation epic known as the *Enuma Elish*, we read the following lines: "Thou, Marduk, art the most honored of the great gods, Thy decree is unrivaled, thy word is Anu [i.e., it has the authority of the sky-god Anu]. From this day unchangeable shall be thy pronouncement. To raise or bring low — these shall be (in) thy hand." And from the Egyptian "Instruction of Amenemope" the following: "He [the deity] tears down and builds up every day, he makes a thousand poor as he wishes, and makes a thousand people overseers, when he is in his hour of life." See also note on Dt 32:6.

2:10 *thunder from heaven.* Few displays of nature evoked such a sense of power and danger among ancient people as a severe thunderstorm. Not surprisingly, the ancients often perceived booming thunder as evidence of the powerful presence and judgment of the deity. In the Akkadian flood stories, it is the weather-god Adad that rumbles and thunders in the clouds. In Hittite mythology, Telipinu, also a weather-god, comes raging with lightning and thunder. In Ugaritic texts, the Canaanite god Baal makes "his voice ring out in the clouds, by flashing his lightning to the earth"; he opens "a rift" in the clouds and makes "his holy voice" resound. Since the Israelites lived in the same culture as these other nations, they were used to using similar conventions and imagery to describe their God, even though he had revealed himself as unique from the gods of the nations. *He will give strength to his king.* That Hannah should refer to the Lord's "king" may seem surprising, inasmuch as kingship had in her day not yet been introduced in Israel. Kingship was certainly well known among Israel's neighbors, and it was widely practiced in Egypt and Mesopotamia from at least the third millennium BC. Israel itself had flirted with the idea of kingship already in the days of Abimelek (Jdg 9). Jotham's fabled response to Abimelek's bid for power explicitly mentions anointing a king (Jdg 9:8). Prior to the book of Judges, numerous references in the Pentateuch make clear that God intended for Israel one day to have a king (e.g., Ge 17:6; 49:10; Nu 24:7,17 – 19; Dt 17:14 – 20; 28:36). We also find that the word translated "king" here can designate the governor or chieftain of a settlement or city-state (note "the king of Jericho" in Jos 2:2). *his anointed.* Anointing with oil was widely practiced in ancient Israel and in the ancient Near East. Egyptian officials were anointed to high office, though it is unclear whether the Egyptian king himself, the pharaoh, was also anointed. From the Amarna letters, it appears that local kings in Palestine were anointed as an expression of vassalage to their Egyptian suzerain. Among the Hittites also, it was common for the suzerain to bind his vassals to him by formal rites undergirded by religious sanctions. Among these rites was the anointing of the vassal ruler. Hittite kings themselves were also anointed with the "holy oil of kingship," and their titles sometimes referred to their anointed status, e.g., "Tabarna, the Anointed, the Great King." Similar practices are represented in the OT. While both religious objects and religious personnel were anointed (Ex 30:22 – 33), it was the king who ultimately held the title "the LORD's anointed" (e.g., 1Sa 16:6) or, in shortened form, "his anointed" (e.g., 12:5) This title expressed the king's vassal status as the Lord's earthly representative and his consecration to and authorization for divine service (on vassal kingship, see notes on 8:7; 10:1; 12:3; 24:6). The king's status as the "anointed" implied his divine enabling and his inviolability.

Eli's Wicked Sons

12 Eli's sons were scoundrels; they had
no regard[c] for the LORD. 13 Now it was the
practice of the priests that, whenever any
of the people offered a sacrifice, the priest's
servant would come with a three-pronged
fork in his hand while the meat[d] was being boiled 14 and would plunge the fork
into the pan or kettle or caldron or pot.
Whatever the fork brought up the priest
would take for himself. This is how they
treated all the Israelites who came to Shiloh. 15 But even before the fat was burned,
the priest's servant would come and say to
the person who was sacrificing, "Give the
priest some meat to roast; he won't accept
boiled meat from you, but only raw."

16 If the person said to him, "Let the fat
be burned first, and then take whatever
you want," the servant would answer,
"No, hand it over now; if you don't, I'll
take it by force."

17 This sin of the young men was very
great in the LORD's sight, for they[a] were
treating the LORD's offering with contempt.[e]

18 But Samuel was ministering[f] before
the LORD—a boy wearing a linen ephod.[g]
19 Each year his mother made him a little
robe and took it to him when she went
up with her husband to offer the annual[h]
sacrifice. 20 Eli would bless Elkanah and
his wife, saying, "May the LORD give you
children by this woman to take the place
of the one she prayed[i] for and gave to[b] the
LORD." Then they would go home. 21 And
the LORD was gracious to Hannah;[j] she
gave birth to three sons and two daughters. Meanwhile, the boy Samuel grew[k] up
in the presence of the LORD.

22 Now Eli, who was very old, heard
about everything his sons were doing
to all Israel and how they slept with the
women[l] who served at the entrance to
the tent of meeting. 23 So he said to them,
"Why do you do such things? I hear from
all the people about these wicked deeds
of yours. 24 No, my sons; the report I hear
spreading among the LORD's people is not
good. 25 If one person sins against another,
God[c] may mediate for the offender; but if
anyone sins against the LORD, who will[m]
intercede[n] for them?" His sons, however,
did not listen to their father's rebuke, for
it was the LORD's will to put them to death.

26 And the boy Samuel continued to
grow[o] in stature and in favor with the
LORD and with people.

Prophecy Against the House of Eli

27 Now a man of God[p] came to Eli and
said to him, "This is what the LORD says:
'Did I not clearly reveal myself to your an-

2:12 [c] Jer 2:8; 9:6
2:13 [d] Lev 7:29-34
2:17 [e] Mal 2:7-9
2:18 [f] ver 11; 1Sa 3:1 [g] ver 28
2:19 [h] 1Sa 1:3
2:20 [i] 1Sa 1:11, 27-28; Lk 2:34
2:21 [j] Ge 21:1 [k] ver 26; Jdg 13:24; 1Sa 3:19; Lk 2:40
2:22 [l] Ex 38:8
2:25 [m] Nu 15:30; Jos 11:20 [n] Dt 1:17; 1Sa 3:14; Heb 10:26
2:26 [o] ver 21; Lk 2:52
2:27 [p] Ex 4:14-16; 1Ki 13:1

[a] *17* Dead Sea Scrolls and Septuagint; Masoretic Text *people* [b] *20* Dead Sea Scrolls; Masoretic Text *and asked from* [c] *25* Or *the judges*

2:13 *three-pronged fork.* This and other implements such as tongs were used in religious practice for various purposes—e.g., adjusting sacrificial animals on the altar. Here Eli's wicked sons are simply plunging the fork into the pot of sacrificial meat, contrary to procedures prescribed in the Pentateuch, which stated that only certain portions of the sacrificial animal were to be eaten by the priests (Lev 10:14–15).

2:15 *even before the fat was burned.* See note on Lev 3:4. The priest's duty was to burn the fat on the altar as a pleasing aroma to the Lord (Lev 3:16; 7:31). Both fat and blood were barred from human consumption (Lev 3:17; cf. Lev 7:33; Eze 39:19; 44:7,15), and anyone who offended in this matter was to be "cut off from their people" (Lev 7:25). Against this background, the abuses of the sons of Eli, described in 1Sa 2:12 as "scoundrels," were very grave indeed (v. 17). Ritual rules about sacrificial portions and priestly prebends varied from culture to culture and from ritual to ritual. Violation of such rules by the priests who were supposed to safeguard proper practice was always dangerous.

2:18 *ephod.* The term seems to refer to three distinct but related items in the Bible: (1) the simple linen garment worn by priests (as in the present context); (2) the very elaborate high priestly ephod described especially in Ex 28; 39, upon which was attached a breastplate containing the Urim and Thummim (oracular devices of some sort; see 1Sa 14:3,18–19); and (3) some other object, perhaps an idol or, more likely, a sacred garment that clothed an idol. (see note on Lev 3:11). What all three types of ephod have in common is their character as a sacred vestment of some sort. Outside the Bible, Old Assyrian texts from Cappadocia attest the possibly cognate term *epattu,* which designates a "rich and costly garment." The notice that the boy Samuel was wearing a linen ephod indicates that he had entered the priestly service as an apprentice.

2:19 *robe.* Probably an outer garment of some sort to be worn over the linen priestly ephod (see note on v. 18). In both the Bible and the ancient Near East generally, robes or special garments often carried symbolic significance or marked the wearer as holding a particular office or status (see note on 18:3–4).

2:22 *women who served at the entrance to the tent of meeting.* The "tent of meeting," first mentioned in Ex 27:21, is used frequently in the OT to refer to the pre-Solomonic portable sanctuary where the Lord would appear to his people and their leaders, initially and especially to Moses. In its use here, the designation may be virtually synonymous with the tabernacle. Commentators sometimes have assumed that the women referred to here were engaged in religious prostitution and have likened their activities to those of fertility cults believed to have existed in Canaan. Recent studies have questioned the linkage between prostitution and fertility, however, and have expressed doubt that such prostitution was at all prevalent in the ancient Near East (see note on Ge 38:15). Finally, unlike many of its neighbors, ancient Israel seems not to have included women in the priesthood. On the linguistic level, this is indicated by the absence of a word for "priestess," in contradistinction to references to priestesses among the Assyrians, Phoenicians and others.

2:27 *man of God.* Often used in the OT as a synonym for "prophet" (cf. 9:8–11). The phenomenon of prophecy is widely attested in the ancient Near East, from Meso-

cestor's family when they were in Egypt
under Pharaoh? 28I chose[q] your ancestor out of all the tribes of Israel to be my
priest, to go up to my altar, to burn incense, and to wear an ephod[r] in my presence. I also gave your ancestor's family
all the food offerings presented by the
Israelites. 29Why do you[a] scorn my sacrifice and offering[s] that I prescribed for my
dwelling?[t] Why do you honor your sons
more than me by fattening yourselves on
the choice parts of every offering made by
my people Israel?'
30"Therefore the LORD, the God of Israel,
declares: 'I promised that members of your
family would minister before me forever.[u]'
But now the LORD declares: 'Far be it from
me! Those who honor me I will honor,[v]
but those who despise[w] me will be disdained. 31The time is coming when I will
cut short your strength and the strength
of your priestly house, so that no one in it
will reach old age,[x] 32and you will see distress in my dwelling. Although good will
be done to Israel, no one in your family
line will ever reach old age.[y] 33Every one
of you that I do not cut off from serving at
my altar I will spare only to destroy your
sight and sap your strength, and all your
descendants will die in the prime of life.
34" 'And what happens to your two
sons, Hophni and Phinehas, will be a sign
to you — they will both die[z] on the same
day.[a] 35I will raise up for myself a faithful priest,[b] who will do according to what
is in my heart and mind. I will firmly establish his priestly house, and they will
minister before my anointed[c] one always.
36Then everyone left in your family line
will come and bow down before him for
a piece of silver and a loaf of bread and
plead, "Appoint me to some priestly office
so I can have food to eat.[d]" ' "

2:28 [q] Ex 28:1 [r] Lev 8:7-8 **2:29** [s] ver 12-17 [t] Dt 12:5; Mt 10:37 **2:30** [u] Ex 29:9 [v] Ps 50:23; 91:15 [w] Mal 2:9 **2:31** [x] 1Sa 4:11-18; 22:16-20 **2:32** [y] 1Ki 2:26-27; Zec 8:4 **2:34** [z] 1Sa 4:11 [a] 1Ki 13:3 **2:35** [b] 1Sa 12:3; 1Ki 2:35 [c] 1Sa 16:13; 2Sa 7:11,27; 1Ki 11:38

The LORD Calls Samuel

3 The boy Samuel ministered[e] before the
LORD under Eli. In those days the word
of the LORD was rare;[f] there were not many
visions.[g]
2One night Eli, whose eyes[h] were becoming so weak that he could barely see,
was lying down in his usual place. 3The
lamp[i] of God had not yet gone out, and
Samuel was lying down in the house of
the LORD, where the ark of God was. 4Then
the LORD called Samuel.
Samuel answered, "Here I am.[j]" 5And
he ran to Eli and said, "Here I am; you
called me."
But Eli said, "I did not call; go back and
lie down." So he went and lay down.
6Again the LORD called, "Samuel!" And
Samuel got up and went to Eli and said,
"Here I am; you called me."
"My son," Eli said, "I did not call; go
back and lie down."
7Now Samuel did not yet know the
LORD: The word of the LORD had not yet
been revealed[k] to him.
8A third time the LORD called, "Samuel!"
And Samuel got up and went to Eli and
said, "Here I am; you called me."
Then Eli realized that the LORD was calling the boy. 9So Eli told Samuel, "Go and
lie down, and if he calls you, say, 'Speak,
LORD, for your servant is listening.' " So
Samuel went and lay down in his place.
10The LORD came and stood there, calling as at the other times, "Samuel! Samuel!"

2:36 [d] 1Ki 2:27 **3:1** [e] 1Sa 2:11 [f] Ps 74:9 [g] Am 8:11 **3:2** [h] 1Sa 4:15 **3:3** [i] Lev 24:1-4 **3:4** [j] Isa 6:8 **3:7** [k] Ac 19:12

a 29 The Hebrew is plural.

potamia (Uruk, Mari, Assyria, etc.) to Anatolia (where the Hittites also referred to prophets as "men of God") to Syria and Palestine (Ebla, Emar, Ugarit, Phoenicia, Aram, Ammon) to Egypt. Although definitions of "prophecy" range from "foretelling the future" to "decrying injustice," the key element in Biblical (and some ancient Near Eastern) prophecy is that it constitutes inspired speech at the initiative of a divine power. The key distinction between Biblical and other ancient Near Eastern prophecy is the identity of the divine power at whose behest the prophet speaks.

2:28 *ephod.* See note on v. 18. The present context, which speaks of Eli's ancestral family approaching the altar and burning incense, suggests that the high priestly ephod is in view.

3:1 *not many visions.* Judging from the extant evidence, ancient Near Eastern cultures were deeply theological in outlook. It is not surprising, therefore, that "visionaries," or prophets, who (ostensibly) brought messages from the gods to the people, were a regular feature in most ancient societies. Should any god refuse to communicate through the prophets, it would be a sign of divine displeasure.

3:3 *lying down in the house of the LORD, where the ark of God was.* This statement has led some to speculate that Samuel may have been engaging in a well-attested ancient Near Eastern practice called "incubation," which involves spending a night in the temple precinct in the hope of receiving a divine vision or oracular dream. The practice is attested among the Egyptians, with manuals of dream interpretation being used as early as the New Kingdom period, among the Hittites of Anatolia and in Canaan during the Biblical period. However, there is no hint in the text that Samuel intended to incubate a revelatory dream — quite the contrary, as he repeatedly assumed that the voice he heard was Eli's. Rather, Samuel's experience would best be called an (unanticipated) auditory dream theophany. No accidental incubation dreams are known from the ancient Near East. The closest to it is found in an Egyptian story in which the prince who was to become Thutmose IV receives a dream while sleeping between the paws of the sphinx (not a temple, but arguably sacred space). Extra-Biblical examples of auditory dream theophanies, or auditory message dreams as they are sometimes called, come from Egypt, Ugarit, Hatti and Babylonia. *house of the LORD.* See note on 1:9. *ark of God.* See note on Ex 25:16.

Then Samuel said, "Speak, for your servant is listening."

11 And the LORD said to Samuel: "See, I am about to do something in Israel that will make the ears of everyone who hears about it tingle.[l] 12 At that time I will carry out against Eli everything[m] I spoke against his family—from beginning to end. 13 For I told him that I would judge his family forever because of the sin he knew about; his sons blasphemed God,[a] and he failed to restrain[n] them. 14 Therefore I swore to the house of Eli, 'The guilt of Eli's house will never be atoned[o] for by sacrifice or offering.' "

15 Samuel lay down until morning and then opened the doors of the house of the LORD. He was afraid to tell Eli the vision, 16 but Eli called him and said, "Samuel, my son."

Samuel answered, "Here I am."

17 "What was it he said to you?" Eli asked. "Do not hide it from me. May God deal with you, be it ever so severely,[p] if you hide from me anything he told you." 18 So Samuel told him everything, hiding nothing from him. Then Eli said, "He is the LORD; let him do what is good in his eyes."[q]

19 The LORD was with[r] Samuel as he grew[s] up, and he let none[t] of Samuel's words fall to the ground. 20 And all Israel from Dan to Beersheba[u] recognized that Samuel was attested as a prophet of the LORD. 21 The LORD continued to appear at Shiloh, and there he revealed[v] himself to Samuel through his word.

4 And Samuel's word came to all Israel.

The Philistines Capture the Ark

Now the Israelites went out to fight against the Philistines. The Israelites camped at Ebenezer,[w] and the Philistines at Aphek.[x] 2 The Philistines deployed their forces to meet Israel, and as the battle spread, Israel was defeated by the Philistines, who killed about four thousand of them on the battlefield. 3 When the soldiers returned to camp, the elders of Israel asked, "Why[y] did the LORD bring defeat on us today before the Philistines? Let us bring the ark[z] of the LORD's covenant from Shiloh, so that he may go with us and save us from the hand of our enemies."

4 So the people sent men to Shiloh, and they brought back the ark of the covenant of the LORD Almighty, who is enthroned between the cherubim.[a] And Eli's two sons, Hophni and Phinehas, were there with the ark of the covenant of God.

5 When the ark of the LORD's covenant came into the camp, all Israel raised such a great shout[b] that the ground shook. 6 Hearing the uproar, the Philistines asked, "What's all this shouting in the Hebrew camp?"

When they learned that the ark of the LORD had come into the camp, 7 the Philistines were afraid.[c] "A god has[b] come into the camp," they said. "Oh no! Nothing like this has happened before. 8 We're doomed! Who will deliver us from the hand of these mighty gods? They are the gods who struck the Egyptians with all kinds of plagues in the wilderness. 9 Be strong, Philistines! Be men, or you will be subject to the Hebrews, as they[d] have been to you. Be men, and fight!"

10 So the Philistines fought, and the Israelites were defeated[e] and every man fled to his tent. The slaughter was very great; Israel lost thirty thousand foot soldiers. 11 The ark of God was captured, and Eli's two sons, Hophni and Phinehas, died.[f]

Death of Eli

12 That same day a Benjamite ran from the battle line and went to Shiloh with his clothes torn and dust[g] on his head. 13 When he arrived, there was Eli[h] sitting on his chair by the side of the road, watching, because his heart feared for the ark of God. When the man entered the town and told what had happened, the whole town sent up a cry.

14 Eli heard the outcry and asked, "What is the meaning of this uproar?"

The man hurried over to Eli, 15 who was ninety-eight years old and whose eyes[i] had failed so that he could not see. 16 He told

3:11 [l] 2Ki 21:12; Jer 19:3 **3:12** [m] 1Sa 2:27-36 **3:13** [n] 1Sa 2:12, 17, 22, 29-31 **3:14** [o] Lev 15:30-31; 1Sa 2:25; Isa 22:14 **3:17** [p] Ru 1:17; 2Sa 3:35 **3:18** [q] Job 2:10; Isa 39:8 **3:19** [r] Ge 21:22; 39:2 [s] 1Sa 2:21 [t] 1Sa 9:6 **3:20** [u] Jdg 20:1 **3:21** [v] ver 10 **4:1** [w] 1Sa 7:12 [x] Jos 12:18; 1Sa 29:1 **4:3** [y] Jos 7:7 [z] Nu 10:35; Jos 6:7 **4:4** [a] Ex 25:22; 2Sa 6:2 **4:5** [b] Jos 6:5, 10 **4:7** [c] Ex 15:14 **4:9** [d] Jdg 13:1; 1Co 16:13 **4:10** [e] ver 2; Dt 28:25; 2Sa 18:17; 2Ki 14:12 **4:11** [f] 1Sa 2:34; Ps 78:61, 64 **4:12** [g] Jos 7:6; 2Sa 1:2; 15:32; Ne 9:1; Job 2:12 **4:13** [h] ver 18; 1Sa 1:9 **4:15** [i] 1Sa 3:2

[a] *13* An ancient Hebrew scribal tradition (see also Septuagint); Masoretic Text *sons made themselves contemptible* [b] *7* Or *"Gods have* (see Septuagint)

4:1 *Philistines.* See notes on Ge 21:32; Jdg 3:3.

4:4 *cherubim.* See note on Ex 25:18.

4:6 *Hebrew.* The first occurrence of this designation in the books of Samuel. It is perhaps not surprising that this label is found on the lips of a non-Israelite people. Throughout the books of Samuel, as well as elsewhere in the Hebrew Bible, the designation "Hebrew(s)" is often used by foreigners or in the presence of foreigners. A possible explanation for this phenomenon has to do with the much debated link between the "Hebrews" and the so-called Habiru/Apiru known from many documents throughout the ancient Near East, particularly in the second millennium BC (see note on Ge 14:13).

4:10 *thirty thousand foot soldiers.* See the article "Numbers in Numbers," p. 235. See also note on Jos 4:13.

4:12 *his clothes torn and dust on his head.* The Benjamite messenger's appearance leaves no doubt that he brings bad news. Grief and distress are often indicated in the Bible (both OT and NT) by actions such as fasting, wailing, breast-beating, tearing of one's garments, putting on sackcloth or throwing dust (dirt or ashes) on one's head.

Eli, "I have just come from the battle line;
I fled from it this very day."
Eli asked, "What happened, my son?"
17 The man who brought the news replied, "Israel fled before the Philistines,
and the army has suffered heavy losses.
Also your two sons, Hophni and Phinehas, are dead, and the ark of God has been
captured."
18 When he mentioned the ark of God,
Eli fell backward off his chair by the side
of the gate. His neck was broken and he
died, for he was an old man, and he was
heavy. He had led[a][j] Israel forty years.
19 His daughter-in-law, the wife of Phinehas, was pregnant and near the time of
delivery. When she heard the news that
the ark of God had been captured and that
her father-in-law and her husband were
dead, she went into labor and gave birth,
but was overcome by her labor pains. 20 As
she was dying, the women attending her
said, "Don't despair; you have given birth
to a son." But she did not respond or pay
any attention.
21 She named the boy Ichabod,[b][k] saying,
"The Glory[l] has departed from Israel" —
because of the capture of the ark of God
and the deaths of her father-in-law and
her husband. 22 She said, "The Glory has
departed from Israel, for the ark of God
has been captured."

4:18 [j] ver 13
4:21 [k] Ge 35:18 [l] Ps 26:8; Jer 2:11

The Ark in Ashdod and Ekron

5 After the Philistines had captured the
ark of God, they took it from Ebenezer[m] to Ashdod.[n] 2 Then they carried the
ark into Dagon's temple and set it beside
Dagon.[o] 3 When the people of Ashdod rose
early the next day, there was Dagon, fall-
en[p] on his face on the ground before the
ark of the LORD! They took Dagon and put
him back in his place. 4 But the following
morning when they rose, there was Dagon,
fallen on his face on the ground before the
ark of the LORD! His head and hands had
been broken[q] off and were lying on the
threshold; only his body remained. 5 That
is why to this day neither the priests of
Dagon nor any others who enter Dagon's
temple at Ashdod step on the threshold.[r]
6 The LORD's hand[s] was heavy on the
people of Ashdod and its vicinity; he
brought devastation[t] on them and afflicted them with tumors.[c][u] 7 When the people
of Ashdod saw what was happening, they

5:1 [m] 1Sa 4:1; 7:12 [n] Jos 13:3
5:2 [o] Jdg 16:23
5:3 [p] Isa 19:1; 46:7
5:4 [q] Eze 6:6; Mic 1:7
5:5 [r] Zep 1:9
5:6 [s] ver 7; Ex 9:3; Ps 32:4; Ac 13:11 [t] ver 11; Ps 78:66 [u] Dt 28:27; 1Sa 6:5

[a] 18 Traditionally *judged* [b] 21 *Ichabod* means *no glory.* [c] 6 Hebrew; Septuagint and Vulgate *tumors. And rats appeared in their land, and there was death and destruction throughout the city*

5:1 *Ashdod.* In the OT period it was one of the cities of the Philistine pentapolis (see note on Jdg 3:3). The city, along with "its surrounding settlements and villages" (Jos 15:47), was assigned to the tribe of Judah, but from the arrival of the Sea Peoples in the late thirteenth and early twelfth century BC until the time of King David (tenth century BC), the city seems to have been in Philistine hands. The city appears to have been a major seaport.
5:2 *they carried the ark into Dagon's temple and set it beside Dagon.* Ancient Near Eastern peoples were convinced that their fates were ultimately in the hands of the gods. In keeping with this (poly)theistic mindset, battles were viewed as contests not just between the human opponents but, more importantly, between the deities of the respective sides. A defeat, therefore, was a humiliation not only for the human participants but also for the gods of the losing side. As part of the victor's despoiling the vanquished, the gods of the losing side were typically carried off and deposited in the temple of the winning god(s) as adjunct deities and/or as a sign of the inferiority and subordination of the captured gods. References to this practice are ubiquitous in ancient Near Eastern battle reports. Although not an idol, the ark of God was treated as such by the Philistines.
5:3–4 *there was Dagon ... His head and hands had been broken off.* Decapitation of defeated foes was common practice in the ancient Near East and, indeed, in the books of Samuel (17:51; 31:9; 2Sa 4:7; 16:9). The Assyrian king Tiglath-Pileser I (1114–1076 BC), e.g., boasts of his defeat of 20,000 men-at-arms and five kings of the land of Kadmuhu: "Like a storm demon I piled up the corpses of their warriors on the battlefield (and) made their blood flow into the hollows and plains of the mountains. I cut off their heads (and) stacked them like grain piles around their cities." Severing hands (and sometimes other body parts, see note on 1Sa 18:25) was a convenient way of tabulating and demonstrating enemy casualties. Dagon's loss of head and hands, therefore, was a sign of unmistakable defeat by the supposedly captive Israelite God, Yahweh, as symbolized by the ark. A variety of occurrences that happened to statues, whether of gods or kings, were often interpreted as omens in the ancient Near East.
5:5 *step on the threshold.* Peoples of the ancient Near East had a sense of sacred precincts and even of especially sacred spaces within the sacred precincts. In Israel, e.g., one may think of the Most Holy Place within the temple. In the book of Ezekiel, thresholds appear to be of some special significance (Eze 9:3; 10:4,18; 46:2; 47:1). The avoidance of stepping on the threshold of a sacred precinct was known, if not approved, in Israel (Zep 1:9). Philistine avoidance of thresholds may have begun with the humiliation of Dagon described in the present episode, or it may have been a preexisting practice that the Biblical narrator, for purposes of irony and ridicule, links to the fall and destruction of Dagon at the threshold.
5:6 *afflicted them with tumors.* Debate over the nature of the Philistine affliction has revolved around two main possibilities: bubonic plague (characterized by tumors, or swellings of the lymph nodes) and bacillary dysentery. Both afflictions could be caused by pathogen-bearing rodents, a particular bane for coastal cities such as Ashdod, where infected rodents could arrive by ship. See the NIV text note on this verse for the long reading of this verse in the Septuagint (the pre-Christian Greek translation of the OT), which mentions rats appearing in the land and bringing death and destruction. That the Philistines suspected their woes to be the result of infestation may be inferred also from the Hebrew text of the next chapter, which mentions rodents several times (6:4,11,18).

1 SAMUEL 5:2

DAGON

The worship of Dagon (spelled "Dagan" in ancient Near Eastern literature outside the Bible) is widely attested in Mesopotamia from as early as the third millennium BC. In Canaan, the existence of Dagon worship already in the second half of the second millennium BC is evidenced by a proper name in the Amarna letters that includes the theophoric element "Dagon."

In Philistia — judging from Biblical evidence — Dagon was apparently the head of the pantheon of gods. Jdg 16:23 speaks of the rulers of the Philistines assembling

Artist's recreation of Dagon fallen before the ark.

Jonathan Walton

continued on next page

to offer a "great sacrifice to Dagon their god" after their capture and humiliation of Samson, and 1Ch 10:10 mentions that after King Saul's death, the Philistines placed his armor in the temple of their gods and "hung up his head in the temple of Dagon."

The vexing question of what kind of deity Dagon must have been has elicited several etymological theories. The first, favored by Jerome, some Jewish tradition, and promoted by Wellhausen in the nineteenth century AD, is that Dagon was a fish-god, the chief evidence being the similarity of the deity's name to the Hebrew word for fish (*dag*). This etymology of Dagon has not gained general acceptance.

A second theory links the name to the Hebrew word for grain (*dagan*), but again there are problems, namely, that the etymology is uniquely West Semitic and would not account for the presence of the name in Mesopotamia. There is some evidence, however, that Dagon/Dagan may have been regarded in Mesopotamian religion as inventor of the plow and that his consort may have been the goddess Shala, an agricultural deity whose symbol was a barley stalk. This lends some support to the "grain" etymology.

A third theory links the name Dagon to an Arabic root (*dajana*) for "gloomy, cloudy," which makes Dagon a storm-god, a notion that finds some support in the positioning of Dagon as the father of Baal, also a storm-god. None of these three major theories has gained a general consensus, and while Dagon/Dagan is frequently attested in Mesopotamian literature, these attestations do little to clarify the deity's specific character and role. In a *Zukru* festival tablet from Emar, e.g., Dagan is variously referred to as "Lord of the Brickwork," "Lord of the Firstborn," "Lord of Creation," "Lord of the Camp," "Lord of Habitations," "Lord of the Valley," "Lord of Shade and Protection," "Lord of the Fortress," "Lord of the Quiver" and "Lord of" several villages.

Given the evidence at hand, many specific questions regarding Dagon must remain open. What can be said is that Dagon was widely worshiped in Mesopotamia over a vast stretch of time (even as late as the second-century BC Maccabean period; in the Apocrypha see 1 Maccabees 10:83–85), and that his ascendancy to the head of the Philistine pantheon possibly took place after the Sea Peoples' arrival in Canaan. ◆

said, "The ark of the god of Israel must
not stay here with us, because his hand is
heavy on us and on Dagon our god." 8So
they called together all the rulers of the
Philistines and asked them, "What shall
we do with the ark of the god of Israel?"

They answered, "Have the ark of the
god of Israel moved to Gath.[v]" So they
moved the ark of the God of Israel.

9But after they had moved it, the LORD's
hand was against that city, throwing it into
a great panic.[w] He afflicted the people of
the city, both young and old, with an outbreak of tumors.[a] 10So they sent the ark of
God to Ekron.

As the ark of God was entering Ekron,
the people of Ekron cried out, "They have
brought the ark of the god of Israel around
to us to kill us and our people." 11So they
called together all the rulers[x] of the Philistines and said, "Send the ark of the god of
Israel away; let it go back to its own place,
or it[b] will kill us and our people." For
death had filled the city with panic; God's
hand was very heavy on it. 12Those who
did not die were afflicted with tumors, and
the outcry of the city went up to heaven.

The Ark Returned to Israel

6 When the ark of the LORD had been in
Philistine territory seven months, 2the
Philistines called for the priests and the diviners[y] and said, "What shall we do with
the ark of the LORD? Tell us how we should
send it back to its place."

3They answered, "If you return the ark
of the god of Israel, do not send it back

5:8 [v] ver 11 **5:9** [w] ver 6, 11; Dt 2:15; 1Sa 7:13; Ps 78:66 **5:11** [x] ver 6, 8-9

6:2 [y] Ge 41:8; Ex 7:11; Isa 2:6

[a] 9 Or *with tumors in the groin* (see Septuagint)
[b] 11 Or *he*

5:8 *Gath.* Some 12 miles (19 kilometers) east-southeast of Ashdod, the city to which the Philistines first brought the ark in the aftermath of the battle of Ebenezer (4:1—5:1).

6:2 *Tell us how we should sent it back to its place.* In the ancient world, an outbreak of plague was often considered the work of an angry deity, perhaps the god of an enemy people. In one Hittite text, an enemy god is assumed to be responsible for an outbreak of plague, and in response a chosen animal is decorated and driven back into enemy territory in the hope of pacifying the angry god and ending the plague. This procedure loosely parallels the Philistines' actions in ch. 6. A second Hittite

to him without a gift;[z] by all means send
a guilt offering[a] to him. Then you will be
healed, and you will know why his hand[b]
has not been lifted from you."
4The Philistines asked, "What guilt offering should we send to him?"
They replied, "Five gold tumors and
five gold rats, according to the number[c]
of the Philistine rulers, because the same
plague has struck both you and your rulers. 5Make models of the tumors[d] and of
the rats that are destroying the country,
and give glory[e] to Israel's god. Perhaps
he will lift his hand from you and your
gods and your land. 6Why do you harden[f]
your hearts as the Egyptians and Pharaoh
did? When Israel's god dealt harshly with
them, did they[g] not send the Israelites out
so they could go on their way?
7"Now then, get a new cart[h] ready, with
two cows that have calved and have never
been yoked.[i] Hitch the cows to the cart,
but take their calves away and pen them
up. 8Take the ark of the LORD and put it on
the cart, and in a chest beside it put the
gold objects you are sending back to him
as a guilt offering. Send it on its way, 9but
keep watching it. If it goes up to its own
territory, toward Beth Shemesh,[j] then the
LORD has brought this great disaster on us.
But if it does not, then we will know that
it was not his hand that struck us but that
it happened to us by chance."
10So they did this. They
took two such cows and
hitched them to the cart and
penned up their calves. 11They
placed the ark of the LORD on
the cart and along with it the
chest containing the gold rats
and the models of the tumors.
12Then the cows went straight
up toward Beth Shemesh,
keeping on the road and lowing all the way; they did not
turn to the right or to the left.
The rulers of the Philistines
followed them as far as the
border of Beth Shemesh.
13Now the people of Beth
Shemesh were harvesting
their wheat in the valley, and
when they looked up and saw
the ark, they rejoiced at the
sight. 14The cart came to the
field of Joshua of Beth She-

6:3 [z]Ex 23:15; Dt 16:16 [a]Lev 5:15 [b]ver 9
6:4 [c]ver 17-18; Jos 13:3; Jdg 3:3
6:5 [d]1Sa 5:6-11 [e]Jos 7:19; Isa 42:12; Jn 9:24; Rev 14:7
6:6 [f]Ex 7:13; 8:15; 9:34; 14:17
[g]Ex 12:31,33
6:7 [h]2Sa 6:3 [i]Nu 19:2
6:9 [j]ver 3; Jos 15:10; 21:16

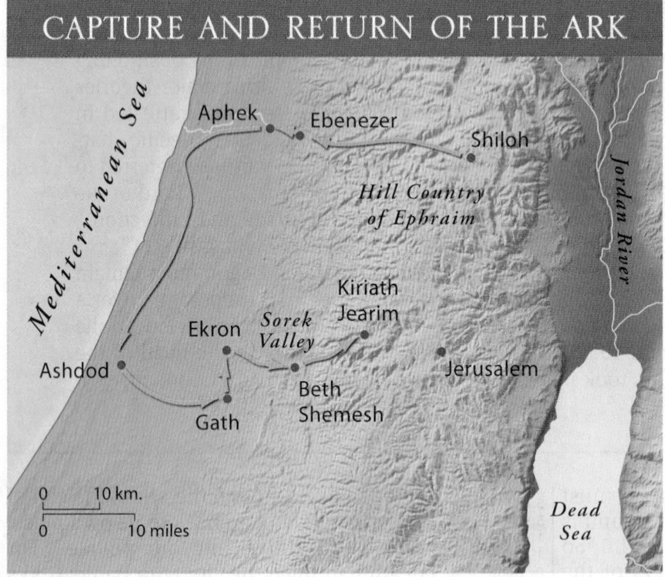

ritual text offers further parallels, except that it involves human beings (enemy captives) as scapegoats. The last lines describe a kind of apotropaic (turning away) ritual that vaguely resembles the scapegoat ritual in Lev 16:7–10,21–22 and is even closer (though certainly not identical) to the procedure enacted by the Philistines here in 1Sa 6—both the Philistines and the Hittites express some uncertainty regarding whether their plague was caused by an offended deity (cf. v. 9); both return something or someone representative of the plague or its agents back to enemy territory accompanied by "all the lords" (cf. "the rulers of the Philistines" in v. 12); and both are concerned that the apotropaic objects or persons be of value sufficient to pacify the offended deity. The Philistine account is distinctive in its references to sending a "guilt offering" (v. 3) and to giving "glory to Israel's god" (v. 5).

6:4 *Five gold tumors and five gold rats.* It seems likely, especially given their stated intent to "give glory to Israel's god" (v. 5), that the use of gold is a sign of honor and submission. Further, the golden objects (tumors/mice) probably served an apotropaic function (see previous note). Like the Israelite scapegoat of Lev 16 that was to "carry on itself all their sins to a remote place" (Lev 16:22; see note on Lev 16:10), the golden tumors/mice were meant to bear away the plague afflicting the Philistines. A similar procedure involving a mouse is attested in the Hittite Ambazzi ritual, wherein the practitioner declares: "I have taken away from you evil and I have put it on the mouse. Let this mouse take it to the high mountains, the deep valleys and the distant ways!" (Ambazzi ii 37–40).

6:7–9 In keeping with the ritual character of the proceedings, the Philistines prepared a new cart (thus ritually clean), to which they attached cows that had recently calved. The point of the exercise, as explicitly stated in v. 9, was to determine whether their distress was wrought by the Israelites' God or whether it had come upon them for some other unknown reason. As v. 7 explains, the cows chosen to pull the cart had never been yoked before and had recently given birth to calves. If, contrary to nature, they should forsake their calves and, accepting the yoke, pull the cart toward Israelite territory, this abnormal behavior would be a sure sign that Israel's God, Yahweh, was the cause of their recent distress. For partial analogues to the ritual procedure, see note on v. 2. The aims of the Philistine procedure were to ascertain the cause of their affliction, to pacify the offended deity if necessary, and to bear the plague away by sympathetic magic.

mesh, and there it stopped beside a large rock. The people chopped up the wood of the cart and sacrificed the cows as a burnt offering[k] to the LORD. 15The Levites[l] took down the ark of the LORD, together with the chest containing the gold objects, and placed them on the large rock. On that day the people of Beth Shemesh offered burnt offerings and made sacrifices to the LORD. 16The five rulers of the Philistines saw all this and then returned that same day to Ekron.

17These are the gold tumors the Philistines sent as a guilt offering to the LORD — one each[m] for Ashdod, Gaza, Ashkelon, Gath and Ekron. 18And the number of the gold rats was according to the number of Philistine towns belonging to the five rulers — the fortified towns with their country villages. The large rock on which the Levites set the ark of the LORD is a witness to this day in the field of Joshua of Beth Shemesh.

19But God struck down[n] some of the inhabitants of Beth Shemesh, putting seventy[a] of them to death because they looked[o] into the ark of the LORD. The people mourned because of the heavy blow the LORD had dealt them. 20And the people of Beth Shemesh asked, "Who can stand[p] in the presence of the LORD, this holy[q] God? To whom will the ark go up from here?"

21Then they sent messengers to the people of Kiriath Jearim,[r] saying, "The Philistines have returned the ark of the LORD. Come down and take it up to your town."

7 1So the men of Kiriath Jearim came and took up the ark of the LORD. They brought it to Abinadab's[s] house on the hill and consecrated Eleazar his son to guard the ark of the LORD. 2The ark remained at Kiriath Jearim a long time — twenty years in all.

Samuel Subdues the Philistines at Mizpah

Then all the people of Israel turned back to the LORD. 3So Samuel said to all the Israelites, "If you are returning[t] to the LORD with all your hearts, then rid[u] yourselves of the foreign gods and the Ashtoreths[v] and commit[w] yourselves to the LORD and serve him only,[x] and he will deliver you out of the hand of the Philistines." 4So the Israelites put away their Baals and Ashtoreths, and served the LORD only.

5Then Samuel said, "Assemble all Israel at Mizpah,[y] and I will intercede with the LORD for you." 6When they had assembled at Mizpah, they drew water and poured[z] it out before the LORD. On that day they fasted and there they confessed, "We have sinned against the LORD." Now Samuel was serving as leader[b][a] of Israel at Mizpah.

7When the Philistines heard that Israel had assembled at Mizpah, the rulers of the

6:14 [k]2Sa 24:22; 1Ki 19:21 **6:15** [l]Jos 3:3 **6:17** [m]ver 4 **6:19** [n]2Sa 6:7 [o]Ex 19:21; Nu 4:5,15,20 **6:20** [p]2Sa 6:9; Mal 3:2; Rev 6:17 [q]Lev 11:45 **6:21** [r]Jos 9:17; 15:9,60; 1Ch 13:5-6

7:1 [s]2Sa 6:3 **7:3** [t]Dt 30:10; Isa 55:7; Hos 6:1 [u]Ge 35:2; Jos 24:14 [v]Jdg 2:12-13; 1Sa 31:10 [w]Joel 2:12 [x]Dt 6:13; Mt 4:10; Lk 4:8 **7:5** [y]Jdg 20:1 **7:6** [z]Ps 62:8; La 2:19 [a]Jdg 10:10; Ne 9:1; Ps 106:6

[a] *19* A few Hebrew manuscripts; most Hebrew manuscripts and Septuagint *50,070* [b] *6* Traditionally *judge*; also in verse 15

6:19 *struck down ... because they looked into the ark.* The text gives no indication of the mode of death inflicted here. The number given of those who died (70) may simply be a convention indicating a large number (some manuscripts indicate 50,070; see the article "Numbers in Numbers," p. 235). Nu 4:4,15,20 forbids even priests from looking at the ark, but this passage indicates that the victims engaged in more than incidental glances. Treating a holy object as a common curiosity violates the sanctity of the ark and would have been recognized as an act of desecration.
7:4 *Baals and Ashtoreths.* See notes on Jdg 2:11,13.
7:6 *they drew water and poured it out before the LORD.* Although this apparently ritual act of pouring out water before the Lord (called a "libation") is without specific parallel elsewhere in the OT, its association with fasting and confession in the present context suggests that at least in this instance it is meant to imply repentance and a desire to do serious business with God. Water (as well as beer and wine) libations are attested throughout the ancient Near East. Water libations in Mesopotamia and in Syria-Canaan appear to have been offered as drink for the gods, just as animal sacrifices represented food for the gods. For ancient Israel, however, such practices appear to have been emptied of their literal significance even while being retained as ritual features with symbolic significance. *fasted.* Fasting is not commonly found in the ancient Near East, except in the context of mourning (see note on 2Sa 12:16). In the OT, it can be seen as part of a purification process, usually in connection with making a request before God. *leader.* The Hebrew word here is the same word elsewhere rendered "judge" (e.g., Jdg 2:16; 3:10). Samuel is depicted as combining several roles, namely, prophet, priest and judge. The transitional period in which Samuel served, along with the dint of his own personality and divine calling, may well account for his combining of roles that would, at a later period in Israel's development, have been kept quite separate.
7:7 *the Philistines heard that Israel had assembled.* That word of an Israelite assembly in progress should raise concern among the Philistines is understandable, given the fact that in the ancient Near East impending battles were typically preceded by religious assemblies designed to entreat the deity for a favorable oracle. Babylonian and Assyrian historical texts ranging in time from Hammurapi (eighteenth century BC) to the siege of Jerusalem by Sennacherib a thousand years later make frequent reference to trust-inspiring oracles from the deity/deities prior to battle. Mediation of the oracle through prophets or priests is not explicitly mentioned in these passages, though the king sometimes assumes the title of high priest. An inscription from the reign of Ashurnasirpal II (884–858 BC), however, distinguishes "king" and "diviner" among the conquered forces of Karduniash, and it is particularly noteworthy that the diviner is also described as a "commanding officer," suggesting a combined religious and military role. In the OT it was customary to "consecrate" war and to speak of warriors as "consecrated." An attempt to consult Yahweh, through priest or prophet or otherwise, generally preceded battle and was sometimes accompanied by sacrifice and/or prayer (see the article "Divine Warfare," p. 365).

Tomb painting of a libation offering, Thebes, Egypt, fourteenth century BC.

Kim Walton. The Israel Museum, Jerusalem.

Philistines came up to attack them. When
the Israelites heard of it, they were afraid[b]
because of the Philistines. 8They said to
Samuel, "Do not stop crying[c] out to the
LORD our God for us, that he may rescue
us from the hand of the Philistines." 9Then
Samuel[d] took a suckling lamb and sacrificed it as a whole burnt offering to the
LORD. He cried out to the LORD on Israel's
behalf, and the LORD answered him.[e]
10While Samuel was sacrificing the
burnt offering, the Philistines drew near
to engage Israel in battle. But that day the
LORD thundered[f] with loud thunder against
the Philistines and threw them into such
a panic[g] that they were routed before the
Israelites. 11The men of Israel rushed out
of Mizpah and pursued the Philistines,
slaughtering them along the way to a
point below Beth Kar.
12Then Samuel took a stone[h] and set it
up between Mizpah and Shen. He named

7:7 [b] 1Sa 17:11 **7:8** [c] 1Sa 12:19, 23; Isa 37:4; Jer 15:1 **7:9** [d] Ps 99:6 [e] Jer 15:1 **7:10** [f] 1Sa 2:10; 2Sa 22:14-15 [g] Jos 10:10 **7:12** [h] Ge 35:14; Jos 4:9

In the light of all this, it is perfectly understandable that the Philistines would have been concerned that the assembly of Israelites at Mizpah at a time unconnected to a regular festival might signal a precursor to war.

7:8 – 9 *"Do not stop crying out to the LORD our God for us . . ." Then Samuel took a suckling lamb and sacrificed it as a whole burnt offering.* Samuel's sacrifice accompanied his crying out to Yahweh in a time of military distress. This combination of prayer and sacrifice in a context of military crisis is found also in a Ugaritic prayer-song to the god El.

7:10 *the LORD thundered . . . against the Philistines.* See note on 2:10.

7:12 *took a stone and set it up . . . named it Ebenezer.* The use of (often inscribed) boundary stones was widespread

it Ebenezer,[a] saying, "Thus far the LORD
has helped us."
13So the Philistines were subdued[i] and
they stopped invading Israel's territory.
Throughout Samuel's lifetime, the hand
of the LORD was against the Philistines.
14The towns from Ekron to Gath that the
Philistines had captured from Israel were
restored to Israel, and Israel delivered the
neighboring territory from the hands of
the Philistines. And there was peace between Israel and the Amorites.
15Samuel[j] continued as Israel's leader all
the days of his life. 16From year to year he
went on a circuit from Bethel to Gilgal to
Mizpah, judging Israel in all those places. 17But he always went back to Ramah,[k]
where his home was, and there he also
held court for Israel. And he built an altar[l]
there to the LORD.

Israel Asks for a King

8 When Samuel grew old, he appointed[m] his sons as Israel's leaders.[b] 2The
name of his firstborn was Joel and the
name of his second was Abijah, and they
served at Beersheba.[n] 3But his sons did
not follow his ways. They turned aside
after dishonest gain and accepted bribes[o]
and perverted justice.
4So all the elders of Israel gathered together and came to Samuel at Ramah.[p]
5They said to him, "You are old, and your
sons do not follow your ways; now appoint a king[q] to lead[c] us, such as all the
other nations have."
6But when they said, "Give us a king
to lead us," this displeased[r] Samuel; so
he prayed to the LORD. 7And the LORD told
him: "Listen to all that the people are saying to you; it is not you they have rejected,
but they have rejected me as their king.[s]
8As they have done from the day I brought
them up out of Egypt until this day, forsaking me and serving other gods, so they
are doing to you. 9Now listen to them; but
warn them solemnly and let them know[t]
what the king who will reign over them
will claim as his rights."
10Samuel told all the words of the LORD
to the people who were asking him for
a king. 11He said, "This is what the king

7:13 [i] Jdg 13:1, 5; 1Sa 13:5 **7:15** [j] ver 6; 1Sa 12:11 **7:17** [k] 1Sa 1:19; 8:4 [l] Jdg 21:4 **8:1** [m] Dt 16:18-19 **8:2** [n] Ge 22:19; 1Ki 19:3; Am 5:4-5

8:3 [o] Ex 23:8; Dt 16:19; Ps 15:5 **8:4** [p] 1Sa 7:17 **8:5** [q] Dt 17:14-20 **8:6** [r] 1Sa 15:11 **8:7** [s] Ex 16:8; 1Sa 10:19 **8:9** [t] ver 11-18; 1Sa 10:25

[a] *12* Ebenezer means *stone of help.* [b] *1* Traditionally *judges* [c] *5* Traditionally *judge*; also in verses 6 and 20

throughout the ancient Near East. The stones were sometimes named and were believed to be under divine protection. Curses against those who might move them were sometimes included in the inscription.

7:14 *Amorites.* In the books of Samuel, the Amorites are mentioned only here and in 2Sa 21:2 (the Gibeonites being survivors from a former Amorite population). Along with the Canaanites, the Amorites are frequently mentioned as among the early inhabitants of the land of promise prior to the arrival of Israel. See note on Jdg 1:34.

7:17 *he built an altar there to the LORD.* With Shiloh having suffered destruction at the hands of the Philistines in the aftermath of the Israelite loss in ch. 4, sacrifices could no longer be offered there (on Shiloh, see note on 1:3). Whether Samuel's altar at Ramah was intended for sacrifice or merely as a memorial is not specified by the text, but the former seems more likely. While the proliferation of local altars was discouraged after the establishment of Jerusalem as Israel's central sanctuary, there was no absolute prohibition at earlier periods, only a command not to sacrifice in the Canaanite way (Dt 12).

8:3 *accepted bribes and perverted justice.* It is not only in the Bible that accepting bribes and perverting justice is considered a serious offense. In a well-attested Hittite text containing instructions from "His Majesty Arnuwanda the great king" to his officials in border towns, the king insists that "border governors" (perhaps analogous to the role held by Samuel's sons) are to judge each case appropriately and make things right or else refer it to the king himself. The recipient is specifically warned against perverting justice by taking a bribe and consequently swinging a case in the favor of one party or another. Samuel's sons are therefore guilty of actions that would be considered criminal in other nations as well as Israel.

8:7 *they have rejected me as their king.* Not just in Israel, but in the ancient Near East generally, kingship was intertwined with religion. While in Egypt the king himself was worshiped as divine, in Mesopotamia kingship was regarded as one of the basic institutions of human life devised by the gods for mankind. The concept of divine sponsorship of kingship was foundational in the cognitive environment of the ancient Near East. In Israel, the emphasis fell on God himself as the Great King, with the human king to serve not as a demigod, but as vice-regent (vassal) to the Great King. The "law of the king" in Dt 17:14–20 makes it clear that the king in Israel was to be subservient to the divine law and was "not [to] consider himself better than his fellow Israelites" (Dt 17:20). The people have not concluded that they don't want God leading them anymore: No one in the ancient Near East would want that, and that is not a king like the nations have. Rather they want a king who would successfully bring the deity into play so that they could carry out their national agendas instead of waiting on the action of the deity alone (as when he appointed judges over them). They wanted God's power, but not his control.

8:11–17 Whatever advantages the elders imagined a king like those of the nations would bring, Samuel—speaking for Yahweh—was intent on making plain the disadvantages that kingship, particularly if self-serving in character, would bring. Perhaps Samuel's warning progresses from the less obviously abusive royal practices (v. 11) to the more obviously abusive ones (v. 17). In any case, it is understandable that a centralized monarchical government would require courtiers and servants of the court, agricultural workers for the king's fields, artisans to craft the king's weapons (v. 12), domestic workers to prepare meals for the court and to keep the palace (v. 13), and a standing army to protect it all (vv. 11–12). To make all this happen, there would be royal taxation and expropriation of "the best" of the fields, flocks and servants of the people (vv. 14–17). The end result, Samuel warned, would be that "you yourselves will become his slaves" (v. 17). These were the realities of kingship at the end of the second millennium BC.

8:11 *He will take your sons.* Sons were particularly important in the ancient Near East—for reasons relating to

who will reign over you will claim as his
rights: He will take[u] your sons and make
them serve with his chariots and horses,
and they will run in front of his chariots.[v]
12Some he will assign to be commanders[w]
of thousands and commanders of fifties,
and others to plow his ground and reap
his harvest, and still others to make weapons of war and equipment for his chariots. 13He will take your daughters to be
perfumers and cooks and bakers. 14He will
take the best of your[x] fields and vineyards[y]
and olive groves and give them to his attendants. 15He will take a tenth of your
grain and of your vintage and give it to
his officials and attendants. 16Your male
and female servants and the best of your
cattle[a] and donkeys he will take for his
own use. 17He will take a tenth of your
flocks, and you yourselves will become his
slaves. 18When that day comes, you will
cry out for relief from the king you have
chosen, but the LORD will not answer[z] you
in that day."
19But the people refused[a] to listen to
Samuel. "No!" they said. "We want a king
over us. 20Then we will be like all the other nations,[b] with a king to lead us and to
go out before us and fight our battles."
21When Samuel heard all that the people
said, he repeated[c] it before the LORD. 22The
LORD answered, "Listen[d] to them and give
them a king."
Then Samuel said to the Israelites, "Everyone go back to your own town."

8:11 [u] 1Sa 10:25; 14:52 [v] Dt 17:16; 2Sa 15:1
8:12 [w] 1Sa 22:7
8:14 [x] Eze 46:18 [y] 1Ki 21:7, 15
8:18 [z] Pr 1:28; Isa 1:15; Mic 3:4
8:19 [a] Isa 66:4; Jer 44:16
8:20 [b] ver 5
8:21 [c] Jdg 11:11
8:22 [d] ver 7

9:1 [e] 1Sa 14:51; 1Ch 8:33; 9:39
9:2 [f] 1Sa 10:24 [g] 1Sa 10:23
9:4 [h] Jos 24:33 [i] 2Ki 4:42
9:5 [j] 1Sa 1:1 [k] 1Sa 10:2
9:6 [l] Dt 33:1; 1Ki 13:1 [m] 1Sa 3:19
9:7 [n] 1Ki 14:3; 2Ki 5:5, 15; 8:8

Samuel Anoints Saul

9 There was a Benjamite, a man of standing, whose name was Kish[e] son of Abiel, the son of Zeror, the son of Bekorath,
the son of Aphiah of Benjamin. 2Kish had
a son named Saul, as handsome a young
man as could be found[f] anywhere in Israel,
and he was a head taller[g] than anyone else.
3Now the donkeys belonging to Saul's
father Kish were lost, and Kish said to his
son Saul, "Take one of the servants with
you and go and look for the donkeys."
4So he passed through the hill[h] country
of Ephraim and through the area around
Shalisha,[i] but they did not find them.
They went on into the district of Shaalim,
but the donkeys were not there. Then he
passed through the territory of Benjamin,
but they did not find them.
5When they reached the district of
Zuph,[j] Saul said to the servant who was
with him, "Come, let's go back, or my father will stop thinking about the donkeys
and start worrying[k] about us."
6But the servant replied, "Look, in this
town there is a man of God;[l] he is highly
respected, and everything[m] he says comes
true. Let's go there now. Perhaps he will
tell us what way to take."
7Saul said to his servant, "If we go,
what can we give the man? The food in
our sacks is gone. We have no gift[n] to take
to the man of God. What do we have?"
8The servant answered him again.

[a] 16 Septuagint; Hebrew *young men*

---

the security and continuity of the family line—but, as Samuel warned, the king "will take your sons" to serve the king. *make them serve with his chariots and horses, and they will run in front of his chariots.* The practice Samuel describes finds a loose analogy in a Hittite text prescribing the protocol to be followed by the royal guard whenever the king travels. Samuel's warning that they would be required to run in front of the king's chariot may not have sounded particularly negative to Israel's elders. Indeed, a couple of eighth-century BC Aramaic inscriptions seem to suggest that "running at the wheel" of one's lord was an honor, though the fact remains that the absence of sons would prove a hardship, e.g., at harvest time.

9:1 *a Benjamite, a man of standing ... Kish.* As a small tribe wedged between the much more powerful tribes of Judah to the south and Ephraim to the north, and as the home of the yet to be conquered city of Jerusalem, Benjamin, which had nearly been annihilated in the judges period, was an ideal choice as home of Israel's first centralized regime, as it would have been less likely to provoke jealousy among the other tribes.

9:2 *Saul, as handsome a young man as could be found.* In the ancient Near East, a high priority was placed on the commanding appearance and heroic qualities of leaders (e.g., Gilgamesh). By ancient Near Eastern standards, therefore, Saul showed great potential.

9:7 *what can we give the man?* In the ancient Near East, prophets, prophetesses, diviners and the like were sought out for consultation on all manner of issues ranging from health and fertility to religious observance, political fortune, military enterprises, lost items, and more. Recipients of services naturally expected to pay and generally did so without need of reminder. Remuneration for solicited prophetic services is well attested in the Mari corpus, where payment is occasionally even explicitly demanded. Unsolicited prophetic revelations, which would describe most Biblical prophecies, were often delivered without expectation of payment. In fact, the Biblical writing prophets express disapproval of those who prophesy for money: Amos denies being such a prophet (Am 7:12–15), and Micah explicitly condemns prophets who divine for money (Mic 3:5,11; cf. Jer 6:13). The attitude of preliterary Yahwistic prophecy is less clear, however, making it difficult to decide whether Saul's concern to pay the "man of God" was normal or, as Josephus suggests (*Antiquities* 6.48), yet another hint of religious ignorance.

9:8 *quarter of a shekel of silver.* Silver was a common form of currency in Canaan, as well as in Assyria and Babylonia. In Hebrew, the word for "silver" eventually came to mean "money" as well. A quarter shekel would have weighed about one-tenth ounce (three grams) and would likely have represented several days' wage for any ordinary worker. It seems likely, then, that the quarter shekel available to Saul would have been a more or less appropriate payment for a solicited inquiry.

"Look," he said, "I have a quarter of a shekel[a] of silver. I will give it to the man of God so that he will tell us what way to take." 9(Formerly in Israel, if someone went to inquire of God, they would say, "Come, let us go to the seer," because the prophet of today used to be called a seer.)[o]

10"Good," Saul said to his servant. "Come, let's go." So they set out for the town where the man of God was.

11As they were going up the hill to the town, they met some young women coming out to draw[p] water, and they asked them, "Is the seer here?"

12"He is," they answered. "He's ahead of you. Hurry now; he has just come to our town today, for the people have a sacrifice[q] at the high place.[r] 13As soon as you enter the town, you will find him before he goes up to the high place to eat. The people will not begin eating until he comes, because he must bless the sacrifice; afterward, those who are invited will eat. Go up now; you should find him about this time."

14They went up to the town, and as they were entering it, there was Samuel, coming toward them on his way up to the high place.

15Now the day before Saul came, the LORD had revealed this to Samuel: 16"About this time tomorrow I will send you a man from the land of Benjamin. Anoint[s] him ruler over my people Israel; he will deliver[t] them from the hand of the Philistines. I have looked on my people, for their cry has reached me."

17When Samuel caught sight of Saul, the LORD said to him, "This[u] is the man I spoke to you about; he will govern my people."

18Saul approached Samuel in the gateway and asked, "Would you please tell me where the seer's house is?"

19"I am the seer," Samuel replied. "Go up ahead of me to the high place, for today you are to eat with me, and in the morning I will send you on your way and will tell you all that is in your heart. 20As for the donkeys[v] you lost three days ago, do not worry about them; they have been found. And to whom is all the desire[w] of Israel turned, if not to you and your whole family line?"

21Saul answered, "But am I not a Benjamite, from the smallest tribe[x] of Israel, and is not my clan the least of all the clans of the tribe of Benjamin?[y] Why do you say such a thing to me?"

22Then Samuel brought Saul and his servant into the hall and seated them at the head of those who were invited—about thirty in number. 23Samuel said to the cook, "Bring the piece of meat I gave you, the one I told you to lay aside."

24So the cook took up the thigh[z] with what was on it and set it in front of Saul. Samuel said, "Here is what has been kept for you. Eat, because it was set aside for you for this occasion from the time I said, 'I have invited guests.'" And Saul dined with Samuel that day.

25After they came down from the high place to the town, Samuel talked with Saul on the roof[a] of his house. 26They rose about daybreak, and Samuel called to Saul on the roof, "Get ready, and I will send you on your way." When Saul got ready, he and Samuel went outside together. 27As they were going down to the edge of the town,

9:9 [o] 2Sa 24:11; 2Ki 17:13; 1Ch 9:22; 26:28; 29:29; Isa 30:10; Am 7:12 **9:11** [p] Ge 24:11, 13 **9:12** [q] Nu 28:11-15; 1Sa 7:17 [r] Ge 31:54; 1Sa 10:5; 1Ki 3:2 **9:16** [s] 1Sa 10:1 [t] Ex 3:7-9 **9:17** [u] 1Sa 16:12
9:20 [v] ver 3 [w] 1Sa 8:5; 12:13 **9:21** [x] 1Sa 15:17 [y] Jdg 20:35,46 **9:24** [z] Lev 7:32-34; Nu 18:18 **9:25** [a] Dt 22:8; Ac 10:9

[a] *8* That is, about 1/10 ounce or about 3 grams

9:9 *prophet … seer.* Prophets and seers perform similar functions, but their roles in society are structured differently (not dissimilar from the difference between a "king" and a "judge.") The emphasis in this passage is on terminology, however, not sociology. "Seer" emphasizes the source of the message (received in visions); "prophet" emphasizes the proclamation of the message to its target audience. See the article "Prophets and Prophecy," p. 1110.
9:11 *they met some young women coming out to draw water.* At least until underground water systems were developed (e.g., see notes on 2Sa 2:13; 5:8), village dwellers had to make periodic trips to draw water from the nearest source, often near the base of the hills on which most towns were situated. Wells or springs, located on the outskirts of towns, were often the places where newcomers to town first met townspeople, often women, who typically bore the responsibility of porting water.
9:12 *high place.* "High places" (Hebrew *bamot*; singular, *bamah*) are mentioned over a hundred times in the OT. The word is used in the OT in a mundane sense to mean "hill," "height," "ridge," and in a religious sense to mean a sacred "high place," either a worship site on a natural elevation or a raised platform. Often sites of Canaanite worship, "high places" are viewed in the OT as endangering the purity of Israelite worship (see, e.g., Nu 33:52; Dt 12:2–3; Jer 2:20). Nevertheless, in the period between the destruction of the sanctuary at Shiloh and the building of the temple in Jerusalem, worship of Yahweh at "high places" was sometimes conducted without explicit censure, as in the present passage. After the division of the kingdom, worship at "high places" constituted a severe problem both in the north (1Ki 12:31–32; 13:32–34) and in the south (1Ki 14:22–24). Removal of the "high places" became a major goal of reform movements under southern kings such as Hezekiah (e.g., 2Ki 18:4) and Josiah (e.g., 2Ki 23:5). With Shiloh destroyed and the ark in exile, this might be serving as the central sanctuary.
9:15 *the LORD had revealed this.* On the various modes of divine revelation, see notes on 28:3,7; see also the article "Consulting a 'Spirit,'" p. 508.
9:24 *Eat, because it was set aside for you for this occasion.* Having instructed the cook to set aside a special cut of meat (v. 23), namely, the shank (NIV "thigh"), Samuel has it placed before Saul. Special portions of meat were often reserved for important personages, as in the case of an officiating priest, who was to receive the right shank of the sacrificial animal (Lev 7:32–34). That a special portion had been set aside for Saul in advance of his arrival suggests both the momentousness of the occasion and its providential direction.

Samuel said to Saul, "Tell the servant to
go on ahead of us"—and the servant did
so—"but you stay here for a while, so that
I may give you a message from God."

10 Then Samuel took a flask[b] of olive
oil and poured it on Saul's head
and kissed him, saying, "Has not the LORD
anointed[c] you ruler over his inheritance?[a][d]
2 When you leave me today, you will meet
two men near Rachel's tomb,[e] at Zelzah
on the border of Benjamin. They will say
to you, 'The donkeys[f] you set out to look
for have been found. And now your father
has stopped thinking about them and is
worried[g] about you. He is asking, "What
shall I do about my son?"'

3 "Then you will go on from there until
you reach the great tree of Tabor. Three
men going up to worship God at Bethel[h]
will meet you there. One will be carrying
three young goats, another three loaves of
bread, and another a skin of wine. 4 They
will greet you and offer you two loaves of
bread, which you will accept from them.

5 "After that you will go to Gibeah of God,
where there is a Philistine outpost.[i] As you
approach the town, you will meet a procession of prophets coming down from the
high place[j] with lyres, timbrels, pipes and
harps[k] being played before them, and they
will be prophesying.[l] 6 The Spirit[m] of the
LORD will come powerfully upon you, and
you will prophesy with them; and you will
be changed into a different person. 7 Once
these signs are fulfilled, do whatever[n] your
hand finds to do, for God is with[o] you.

8 "Go down ahead of me to Gilgal.[p] I will
surely come down to you to sacrifice burnt
offerings and fellowship offerings, but you
must wait seven days until I come to you
and tell you what you are to do."

Saul Made King

9 As Saul turned to leave Samuel, God
changed[q] Saul's heart, and all these signs
were fulfilled that day. 10 When he and his
servant arrived at Gibeah, a procession of
prophets met him; the Spirit of God came
powerfully upon him, and he joined in their
prophesying.[r] 11 When all those who had
formerly known him saw him prophesying
with the prophets, they asked each other,
"What is this[s] that has happened to the son
of Kish? Is Saul also among the prophets?"[t]

12 A man who lived there answered,
"And who is their father?" So it became a

10:1 [b] 1Sa 16:13; 2Ki 9:1,3,6 [c] Ps 2:12 [d] Dt 32:9; Ps 78:62,71 **10:2** [e] Ge 35:20 [f] 1Sa 9:4 [g] 1Sa 9:5 **10:3** [h] Ge 28:22; 35:7-8 **10:5** [i] 1Sa 13:3 [j] 1Sa 9:12 [k] 2Ki 3:15 [l] 1Sa 19:20; 1Co 14:1 **10:6** [m] ver 10; Nu 11:25; 1Sa 19:23-24 **10:7** [n] Ecc 9:10 [o] Jos 1:5; Jdg 6:12; Heb 13:5 **10:8** [p] 1Sa 11:14-15 **10:9** [q] ver 6 **10:10** [r] ver 5-6; 1Sa 19:20 **10:11** [s] Mt 13:54; Jn 7:15 [t] 1Sa 19:24

[a] *1* Hebrew; Septuagint and Vulgate *over his people Israel? You will reign over the LORD's people and save them from the power of their enemies round about. And this will be a sign to you that the LORD has anointed you ruler over his inheritance:*

10:1 *flask.* Connotes a small jug or vial. Special oils and cosmetics, because of their preciousness, were often held in tiny containers in antiquity, as today. *poured [oil] on Saul's head.* Anointing is known from Hittite enthronement texts; Egyptian and Mesopotamian kings were not anointed, though the pharaohs anointed their vassals and officials. It is possible that anointing represents a contract between the ruler and the people, hence the anointing of David by the people in 2Sa 2:4. Texts from Nuzi show individuals anointing each other when entering a business agreement, and anointing with oil occurred in Egyptian wedding ceremonies. *ruler.* In this context means something like "king-elect" or "one who is designated as leader of the people." *inheritance.* The Lord's "inheritance" comprised both the land and the people of Israel (Dt 32:9). In acceding to the people's demand for a king, Yahweh did not relinquish his rights as Great King over his inheritance to the human monarch. Rather, the human king was to be Yahweh's vice-regent and was to subordinate himself within an authority structure that Yahweh himself would stipulate (v. 25). Prior to the monarchy, judges had been raised up by Yahweh on an ad hoc basis and had both received and carried out Yahweh's instructions. With the inauguration of kingship, however, the tasks of receiving and carrying out Yahweh's instructions were initially divided between prophet (Samuel) and king (Saul). The former would be Yahweh's mouthpiece to the king, and the king was to carry out Yahweh's instructions as received through the prophet. This authority structure is evidenced in the first charge Saul receives in vv. 7–8, and grasping its significance is essential to understanding the nature of the eventual breach between Saul and Samuel/Yahweh.

10:5 *a procession of prophets ... prophesying.* Though prophets and prophecy were not unknown in Israel's premonarchical period—e.g., Abraham, Moses, Miriam and many others were described as prophets—it was with the inception of monarchy that the prophetic office and the prophetic guild came into their own. Prophecy was a skill in which one could train, and groups of these trainees, described as "sons of the prophets," began to appear, often under the leadership of a prominent individual. 1Sa 19:20 will find Samuel himself presiding over such a group of prophets. It was one such band that Saul encounters at Gibeah, and they are playing musical instruments and prophesying (a word that implies a trancelike state). The use of instruments was intended to induce a trancelike state ("ecstasy") in which one might become receptive to prophetic oracles. The Mari tablets describe an entire class of ecstatic prophets who served as temple personnel.

10:6 *The Spirit of the LORD will come powerfully upon you, and you will prophesy with them; and you will be changed into a different person.* Bestowal of the divine Spirit often connoted God's empowering of an individual for the accomplishment of a particular task, usually involving calling out the tribes to war, something only Yahweh has the authority to do. Conversely, the Spirit of God might thwart someone intent on a particular action (e.g., 19:23). Verse 10 of the present episode describes the "Spirit of God" coming "powerfully" upon Saul, a verbatim repetition of what was often said of Samson in the book of Judges (Jdg 14:6,19; 15:14). Such visitations of the Spirit appear to have been temporary and designed to empower (or prevent) a particular action. In Akkadian texts the presence of a deity with a king was indicated by the king receiving the *melammu*—a glow that regularly accompanied deity.

10:9 *God changed Saul's heart, and all these signs were fulfilled.* See note on v. 6.

10:10 *the Spirit of God came powerfully upon him.* See note on v. 6.

saying: "Is Saul also among the prophets?" 13After Saul stopped prophesying, he went to the high place.

14Now Saul's uncle[u] asked him and his servant, "Where have you been?"

"Looking for the donkeys," he said. "But when we saw they were not to be found, we went to Samuel."

15Saul's uncle said, "Tell me what Samuel said to you."

16Saul replied, "He assured us that the donkeys[v] had been found." But he did not tell his uncle what Samuel had said about the kingship.

17Samuel summoned the people of Israel to the LORD at Mizpah[w] 18and said to them, "This is what the LORD, the God of Israel, says: 'I brought Israel up out of Egypt, and I delivered you from the power of Egypt and all the kingdoms that oppressed[x] you.' 19But you have now rejected your God, who saves you out of all your disasters and calamities. And you have said, 'No, appoint a king[y] over us.' So now present[z] yourselves before the LORD by your tribes and clans."

20When Samuel had all Israel come forward by tribes, the tribe of Benjamin was taken by lot. 21Then he brought forward the tribe of Benjamin, clan by clan, and Matri's clan was taken. Finally Saul son of Kish was taken. But when they looked for him, he was not to be found. 22So they inquired[a] further of the LORD, "Has the man come here yet?"

And the LORD said, "Yes, he has hidden himself among the supplies."

23They ran and brought him out, and as he stood among the people he was a head taller[b] than any of the others. 24Samuel said to all the people, "Do you see the man the LORD has chosen?[c] There is no one like him among all the people."

Then the people shouted, "Long live[d] the king!"

25Samuel explained to the people the rights and duties[e] of kingship. He wrote them down on a scroll and deposited it before the LORD. Then Samuel dismissed the people to go to their own homes.

26Saul also went to his home in Gibeah,[f] accompanied by valiant men whose hearts God had touched. 27But some scoundrels[g] said, "How can this fellow save us?" They despised him and brought him no gifts.[h] But Saul kept silent.

Saul Rescues the City of Jabesh

11 Nahash[a][i] the Ammonite went up and besieged Jabesh Gilead.[j] And all the men of Jabesh said to him, "Make a treaty[k] with us, and we will be subject to you."

[a] 1 Masoretic Text; Dead Sea Scrolls *gifts. Now Nahash king of the Ammonites oppressed the Gadites and Reubenites severely. He gouged out all their right eyes and struck terror and dread in Israel. Not a man remained among the Israelites beyond the Jordan whose right eye was not gouged out by Nahash king of the Ammonites, except that seven thousand men fled from the Ammonites and entered Jabesh Gilead. About a month later,* [i]*Nahash*

10:14 [u] 1Sa 14:50 **10:16** [v] 1Sa 9:20 **10:17** [w] Jdg 20:1; 1Sa 7:5 **10:18** [x] Jdg 6:8-9 **10:19** [y] 1Sa 8:5-7; 12:12 [z] Jos 7:14; 24:1 **10:22** [a] 1Sa 23:2,4, 9-11

10:23 [b] 1Sa 9:2 **10:24** [c] Dt 17:15; 2Sa 21:6 [d] 1Ki 1:25,34,39 **10:25** [e] Dt 17:14-20; 1Sa 8:11-18 **10:26** [f] 1Sa 11:4 **10:27** [g] Dt 13:13 [h] 1Ki 10:25; 2Ch 17:5 **11:1** [i] 1Sa 12:12 [j] Jdg 21:8 [k] 1Ki 20:34; Eze 17:13

10:25 *Samuel explained to the people the rights and duties of kingship. He wrote them down on a scroll and deposited it before the LORD.* The notice of this verse raises three interesting questions: What were these "rights and duties of kingship"? What was the state of writing and literacy in Samuel's day? And what did it mean to deposit something before the Lord? None of these questions can be answered with certainty, but studied conjectures can be offered. The "rights and duties of kingship" would likely have stipulated the responsibilities of the people to the king, the king to the people, and, most significantly, the king to Yahweh (perhaps along lines similar to the law of the king in Dt 17:14–20). Assyrian kings would sometimes make formal agreements (*adu*-agreements) with their servants "in front of the great gods." Something similar may be implied in the verse here, but the text offers little detail.

The question of popular literacy in ancient Israel is widely debated, but Samuel's upbringing as a priest in the house of Eli would likely have afforded educational opportunities beyond the ordinary. Evidence suggests that a basic level of literacy was common, but most people would rarely have occasion to read or write. A formal document like the one mentioned here would be executed by someone with scribal training.

The statement that the document was deposited "before the LORD" suggests that it was deposited in the sanctuary. In the ancient Near East as well—e.g., among the Hittites—covenant documents were frequently deposited in sanctuaries. Other Biblical references to documents deposited before the Lord include Dt 31:26; Jos 24:26.The rationale is not given, but presumably this was intended to keep the information visible to the deity.

10:27 *some scoundrels said, "How can this fellow save us?"* While culpable for refusing to accept the one whom Yahweh had chosen, the "scoundrels" ("insurrectionists") nevertheless asked a valid question, especially when viewed against the typical process by which leaders in the ancient Near East often came to power. As several studies have shown, the accession process in the ancient Near East typically comprised three stages: (1) divine designation of the new leader, (2) some kind of demonstration by the new leader that would gain public attention and rally support, (3) public confirmation of the new leader. If all had gone according to plan, Saul's anointing and first charge (vv. 1–8) would have served as his designation (stage 1); an attack on the Philistine outpost in Gibeah of God would have served as the demonstration (stage 2); and a public confirmation of Saul as Israel's first king would have followed (stage 3). Saul's failure to execute stage 2 meant that he did not come to public attention. To rectify this situation, Samuel convened the assembly at Mizpah, where Saul was selected by lot (vv. 17–24). This meant, however, that Saul had still done nothing to distinguish himself or gain public confidence; in fact, he had been dragged from hiding among the supplies (vv. 22–23). Eventually (ch. 11), Saul's victory over the Ammonites would silence the dissenters, but it would leave his first charge—intended to test his fitness as a vassal-king to Yahweh—yet unfulfilled. Only in ch. 13 would the first charge come back into play, and there Saul would fail.

11:1 *Nahash.* See note on Jdg 11:12. *Ammonite.* See notes on Ge 19:37–38; Dt 2:19.

2But Nahash the Ammonite replied, "I
will make a treaty with you only on the
condition that I gouge[l] out the right eye of
every one of you and so bring disgrace[m]
on all Israel."
3The elders of Jabesh said to him, "Give
us seven days so we can send messengers
throughout Israel; if no one comes to rescue us, we will surrender to you."
4When the messengers came to Gibeah[n]
of Saul and reported these terms to the
people, they all wept[o] aloud. 5Just then
Saul was returning from the fields, behind
his oxen, and he asked, "What is wrong
with everyone? Why are they weeping?"
Then they repeated to him what the men
of Jabesh had said.
6When Saul heard their words, the
Spirit[p] of God came powerfully upon
him, and he burned with anger. 7He took
a pair of oxen, cut them into pieces, and
sent the pieces by messengers throughout Israel,[q] proclaiming, "This is what
will be done to the oxen of anyone[r] who
does not follow Saul and Samuel." Then
the terror of the LORD fell on the people, and they came out together as one.
8When Saul mustered[s] them at Bezek,[t]
the men of Israel numbered three hundred thousand and those of Judah thirty
thousand.
9They told the messengers who had
come, "Say to the men of Jabesh Gilead,
'By the time the sun is hot tomorrow, you
will be rescued.'" When the messengers
went and reported this to the men of Jabesh, they were elated. 10They said to the
Ammonites, "Tomorrow we will surrender[u] to you, and you can do to us whatever you like."
11The next day Saul separated his men
into three divisions;[v] during the last watch
of the night they broke into the camp of
the Ammonites and slaughtered them until the heat of the day. Those who survived
were scattered, so that no two of them
were left together.

Saul Confirmed as King

12The people then said to Samuel,
"Who[w] was it that asked, 'Shall Saul reign
over us?' Turn these men over to us so that
we may put them to death."
13But Saul said, "No one will be put to
death today,[x] for this day the LORD has rescued[y] Israel."
14Then Samuel said to the people,
"Come, let us go to Gilgal[z] and there renew the kingship.[a]" 15So all the people
went to Gilgal[b] and made Saul king in the
presence of the LORD. There they sacrificed
fellowship offerings before the LORD, and
Saul and all the Israelites held a great celebration.

Samuel's Farewell Speech

12 Samuel said to all Israel, "I have
listened[c] to everything you said to
me and have set a king[d] over you. 2Now
you have a king as your leader.[e] As for

11:2 [l] Nu 16:14 [m] 1Sa 17:26 **11:4** [n] 1Sa 10:5, 26; 15:34 [o] Jdg 2:4; 1Sa 30:4 **11:6** [p] Jdg 3:10; 6:34; 13:25; 14:6; 1Sa 10:10; 16:13 **11:7** [q] Jdg 19:29 [r] Jdg 21:5 **11:8** [s] Jdg 20:2 [t] Jdg 1:4 **11:10** [u] ver 3 **11:11** [v] Jdg 7:16 **11:12** [w] 1Sa 10:27; Lk 19:27 **11:13** [x] 2Sa 19:22 [y] Ex 14:13; 1Sa 19:5 **11:14** [z] 1Sa 10:8 [a] 1Sa 10:25 **11:15** [b] 1Sa 10:8, 17 **12:1** [c] 1Sa 8:7 [d] 1Sa 10:24; 11:15 **12:2** [e] 1Sa 8:5

11:2 *gouge out the right eye.* In the ancient Near East, losing a battle sometimes resulted in physical mutilation of one sort or another, and punitive action by regimes against those considered rebels often included mutilation such as the removal of eyes, ears or hands. In the present context, submission to mutilation is presented as a precondition for avoiding battle. Such a precondition is so far unattested in other ancient Near Eastern literature. The purposes of blinding the vanquished varied, as the Bible itself indicates: Samson was blinded by the Philistines to humiliate and incapacitate him (Jdg 16:21); King Zedekiah of Judah was blinded by the king of Babylon in order that his last visual memory might be the slaughter of his own sons (2Ki 25:7; cf. Jer 39:6–7). In the case before us, the Ammonite king's intention was certainly to humiliate the Jabesh Gileadites, but also, it seems likely, to render the fighting men ineffectual in battle. As Josephus (who was a successful general before he became a historian) explains, "Since the left eye was covered by the buckler" (i.e., the shield), blinding the right would render the warriors "utterly unserviceable" (*Antiquities* 6.68–72). Right-handed warriors (the majority) would be able to see very little in battle, unless they were willing to lower their shields or literally stick their necks out. In any case, with only one eye, they would lack depth perception and thus be at a severe disadvantage in hand-to-hand combat. Sparing the left eye would leave them capable of agricultural work and menial tasks, but little else.

11:4 *When the messengers came to Gibeah of Saul.* The Hebrew text of this verse could as well be rendered, "So the messengers came to Gibeah of Saul." It seems likely that the messengers were in fact sent directly to Gibeah and not "throughout Israel" (the elders' request in v. 3 involving an element of deception). Not only would this have been a logical action after the assembly in Mizpah in which Saul was selected as Israel's king-elect, but pragmatic considerations make a more general dispersal of messengers unlikely. The rate of march for armies in the ancient Near East was about 15–20 miles (25–30 kilometers) a day. Messengers on an urgent mission could probably double that rate. The distance from Jabesh Gilead to Gibeah would have been 50–60 miles (80–100 kilometers), depending on the route taken. This would place the messengers in Gibeah late on the second day. Their subsequent dispersal "throughout Israel" (v. 7) would have taken another two or three days, leaving two or three days of the permitted seven days for the general muster at Bezek (vv. 7–8).

11:7 *He took a pair of oxen, cut them into pieces, and sent the pieces by messengers throughout Israel.* The intent is to evoke a strong reaction, reinforced by the threat that those who do not respond may suffer similar treatment. The ancient Near East was accustomed to gruesome actions intended to prompt a certain response. A tablet from Mari (ARM 2.48), e.g., records a request for permission to sever the head of a prisoner and parade it throughout the territory so as to shock reticent warriors into assembling for battle.

me, I am old and gray, and my sons are here with you. I have been your leader from my youth until this day. [3]Here I stand. Testify against me in the presence of the LORD and his anointed.[f] Whose ox have I taken? Whose donkey[g] have I taken? Whom have I cheated? Whom have I oppressed? From whose hand have I accepted a bribe[h] to make me shut my eyes? If I have done[i] any of these things, I will make it right."

[4]"You have not cheated or oppressed us," they replied. "You have not taken anything from anyone's hand."

[5]Samuel said to them, "The LORD is witness against you, and also his anointed is witness this day, that you have not found anything[j] in my hand.[k]"

"He is witness," they said.

[6]Then Samuel said to the people, "It is the LORD who appointed Moses and Aaron and brought[l] your ancestors up out of Egypt. [7]Now then, stand here, because I am going to confront[m] you with evidence before the LORD as to all the righteous acts performed by the LORD for you and your ancestors.

[8]"After Jacob entered Egypt, they cried[n] to the LORD for help, and the LORD sent[o] Moses and Aaron, who brought your ancestors out of Egypt and settled them in this place.

[9]"But they forgot[p] the LORD their God; so he sold them into the hand of Sisera,[q] the commander of the army of Hazor, and into the hands of the Philistines[r] and the king of Moab,[s] who fought against them. [10]They cried out to the LORD and said, 'We have sinned; we have forsaken[t] the LORD and served the Baals and the Ashtoreths.[u] But now deliver us from the hands of our enemies, and we will serve you.' [11]Then the LORD sent Jerub-Baal,[a][v] Barak,[b][w] Jephthah[x] and Samuel,[c] and he delivered you from the hands of your enemies all around you, so that you lived in safety.

[12]"But when you saw that Nahash[y] king[z] of the Ammonites was moving against you, you said to me, 'No, we want a king to rule[a] over us' — even though the LORD your God was your king. [13]Now here is the king[b] you have chosen, the one you asked[c] for; see, the LORD has set a king over you. [14]If you fear[d] the LORD and serve and obey him and do not rebel against his commands, and if both you and the king who reigns over you follow the LORD your God — good! [15]But if you do not obey the LORD, and if you rebel against[e] his commands, his hand will be against you, as it was against your ancestors.

[16]"Now then, stand still and see[f] this great thing the LORD is about to do before your eyes! [17]Is it not wheat harvest[g] now? I will call[h] on the LORD to send thunder and rain.[i] And you will realize what an evil[j] thing you did in the eyes of the LORD when you asked for a king."

[18]Then Samuel called on the LORD, and that same day the LORD sent thunder and rain. So all the people stood in awe[k] of the LORD and of Samuel.

[19]The people all said to Samuel, "Pray[l] to the LORD your God for your servants so that we will not die, for we have added to all our other sins the evil of asking for a king."

[20]"Do not be afraid," Samuel replied. "You have done all this evil; yet do not turn away from the LORD, but serve the LORD with all your heart. [21]Do not turn away after useless[m] idols.[n] They can do you no good, nor can they rescue you, because they are useless. [22]For the sake[o] of his great name[p] the LORD will not reject[q] his people, because the LORD was pleased to make[r] you his own. [23]As for me, far be it from me that I should sin against the LORD by failing to pray[s] for you. And I will teach[t] you the way that is good and right. [24]But be sure to fear[u] the LORD and serve him faithfully with all your heart; consider[v] what great[w] things he has done for you. [25]Yet if you persist[x] in doing evil, both you and your king will perish."[y]

[a] *11* Also called *Gideon* [b] *11* Some Septuagint manuscripts and Syriac; Hebrew *Bedan* [c] *11* Hebrew; some Septuagint manuscripts and Syriac *Samson*

12:3 [f] 1Sa 10:1; 24:6; 2Sa 1:14 [g] Nu 16:15 [h] Dt 16:19 [i] Ac 20:33
12:5 [j] Ac 23:9; 24:20 [k] Ex 22:4
12:6 [l] Ex 6:26; Mic 6:4
12:7 [m] Isa 1:18; Mic 6:1-5
12:8 [n] Ex 2:23 [o] Ex 3:10; 4:16
12:9 [p] Jdg 3:7 [q] Jdg 4:2 [r] Jdg 10:7; 13:1 [s] Jdg 3:12
12:10 [t] Jdg 10:10, 15 [u] Jdg 2:13
12:11 [v] Jdg 6:14, 32 [w] Jdg 4:6 [x] Jdg 11:1
12:12 [y] 1Sa 11:1 [z] 1Sa 8:5 [a] Jdg 8:23; 1Sa 8:6, 19
12:13 [b] 1Sa 8:5; Hos 13:11 [c] 1Sa 10:24
12:14 [d] Jos 24:14
12:15 [e] ver 9; Jos 24:20; Isa 1:20
12:16 [f] Ex 14:13
12:17 [g] 1Sa 7:9-10 [h] Jas 5:18 [i] Pr 26:1 [j] 1Sa 8:6-7
12:18 [k] Ex 14:31
12:19 [l] ver 23; Ex 9:28; Jas 5:18; 1Jn 5:16
12:21 [m] Isa 41:24, 29; Jer 16:19; Hab 2:18 [n] Dt 11:16
12:22 [o] Ps 106:8 [p] Jos 7:9 [q] 1Ki 6:13 [r] Dt 7:7; 1Pe 2:9
12:23 [s] Ro 1:9-10; Col 1:9; 2Ti 1:3 [t] 1Ki 8:36; Ps 34:11; Pr 4:11
12:24 [u] Ecc 12:13 [v] Isa 5:12 [w] Dt 10:21
12:25 [x] 1Sa 31:1-5 [y] Jos 24:20

12:3 *Testify against me in the presence of the LORD and his anointed.* It was widely understood in the ancient Near East that those in positions of power were responsible to execute justice and to protect the vulnerable in society (see notes on 8:3; 2Sa 7:1; 15:4; 21:17; cf. 2Sa 5:12; 12:1–4). When rulers were deposed, it was not uncommon for those who replaced them to trump up charges of injustice against them and seek to eliminate them. Thus, Samuel was intent on clearing his name, before redefining his leadership role. While the context is markedly different, the "negative penance" section of the Egyptian "Book of the Dead" employs phrases in some respects similar to Samuel's protestations: e.g., "I have committed no injustice against men. I have not mistreated the cattle (of God) ... I have not done violence to a poor man ... I have neither increased nor diminished the bushel." Similar protests are attested in the archival records of Hittite court cases.

12:17 *Is it not wheat harvest now?* Wheat harvest took place early in Israel's dry season (in May–June). In this period of almost complete drought, Yahweh's sending of "thunder and rain" at Samuel's request would serve both as a sign of divine approval for Samuel and as a mild punishment for Israel's sin, as rain is never welcome at harvest time. Specifically, rain at harvest time can cause what is called preharvest sprouting: Water is absorbed into the head of the grain, stimulating hormone production leading to germination. The end effect is a lower-quality yield.

Samuel Rebukes Saul

13 Saul was thirty[a] years old when he
became king, and he reigned over
Israel forty-[b] two years.
2 Saul chose three thousand men from
Israel; two thousand were with him at
Mikmash and in the hill country of Bethel, and a thousand were with Jonathan at
Gibeah[z] in Benjamin. The rest of the men
he sent back to their homes.
3 Jonathan attacked the Philistine outpost[a] at Geba, and the Philistines heard
about it. Then Saul had the trumpet blown
throughout the land and said, "Let the Hebrews hear!" 4 So all Israel heard the news:
"Saul has attacked the Philistine outpost,
and now Israel has become obnoxious[b] to
the Philistines." And the people were summoned to join Saul at Gilgal.
5 The Philistines assembled to fight Israel, with three thousand[c] chariots, six
thousand charioteers, and soldiers as numerous as the sand[c] on the seashore. They
went up and camped at Mikmash, east of
Beth Aven. 6 When the Israelites saw that
their situation was critical and that their
army was hard pressed, they hid in caves
and thickets, among the rocks, and in
pits and cisterns.[d] 7 Some Hebrews even
crossed the Jordan to the land of Gad[e]
and Gilead.
Saul remained at Gilgal, and all the
troops with him were quaking with fear.
8 He waited seven[f] days, the time set by
Samuel; but Samuel did not come to Gilgal, and Saul's men began to scatter. 9 So
he said, "Bring me the burnt offering and
the fellowship offerings." And Saul offered[g] up the burnt offering. 10 Just as he
finished making the offering, Samuel[h] arrived, and Saul went out to greet him.
11 "What have you done?" asked Samuel.
Saul replied, "When I saw that the men
were scattering, and that you did not
come at the set time, and that the Philistines were assembling at Mikmash,[i] 12 I

13:2 [z] 1Sa 10:26
13:3 [a] 1Sa 10:5
13:4 [b] Ge 34:30
13:5 [c] Jos 11:4
13:6 [d] Jdg 6:2
13:7 [e] Nu 32:33
13:8 [f] 1Sa 10:8
13:9 [g] 2Sa 24:25; 1Ki 3:4
13:10 [h] 1Sa 15:13
13:11 [i] ver 2,5, 16,23

[a] *1* A few late manuscripts of the Septuagint; Hebrew does not have *thirty.* [b] *1* Probable reading of the original Hebrew text (see Acts 13:21); Masoretic Text does not have *forty-.* [c] *5* Some Septuagint manuscripts and Syriac; Hebrew *thirty thousand*

13:1 *Saul was thirty years old when he became king, and he reigned over Israel forty-two years.* As the NIV text notes indicate, the numerals "thirty" and "forty" do not actually appear in the Hebrew text, which reads literally, "Saul was a year old when he became king, and he reigned over Israel two years." This appears to be a (defective?) regnal formula. In the historiography of the OT, regnal formulae stating the age of the king at accession and the length of his reign typically mark the official beginning of a king's reign (cf., e.g., 2Sa 2:10; 5:4; 1Ki 14:21). Clearly, Saul could not have been literally a year old when he began to reign. Perhaps the number is to be understood differently—e.g., perhaps it had been a year since Saul's anointing, and perhaps the two-year reign referred to the time elapsed between Saul's inauguration and his definitive rejection by God in 1Sa 15:23,28. If the regnal formula is to be read literally, however, then we must assume that one or two numerals are missing from the text. Examples of omitted numerals do occur in the ancient Near East: e.g., in two economic texts from Ur, in a list of personal names from the Old Babylonian period, in the Sumerian King List, in the Babylonian Chronicles, and more. At present the question of Saul's age at accession must remain open, but a rough estimate would make him at least 40, assuming that the events of ch. 13, in which Saul's son Jonathan is already in charge of troops, took place early in his reign.

In one place, Josephus accords Saul a reign of 20 years (*Antiquities* 10.143). In another place, the text of Josephus states that Saul reigned 18 years during Samuel's lifetime and "two and twenty" thereafter. But the "twenty" is text-critically and logically dubious; if Saul reigned 22 years after Samuel's death, and David became king at age 30, upon Saul's death, then at the time of Samuel's death David would have been only 8 years old, having already killed Goliath, served as a commander in Saul's army, incurred Saul's jealousy, escaped to the Philistines, gathered a troop of 600 men while on the run in the wilderness and so on. Full discussion is not possible here, but a reign of about 20 or 22 years for Saul seems to work best.

13:2 *three thousand.* This is probably a number of retainers, not the actual size of the mustered army, which would have been larger. Three "thousand" might also refer to three "units" or companies (see the article "Numbers in Numbers," p. 235). Standing armies usually consisted of trained soldiers and/or mercenaries, and would be deployed in border posts, garrisons or the royal guard.

13:3 *trumpet.* Hebrew *shofar,* which designates a "sounding horn" crafted (usually) from the horn of a ram (see note on Jos 6:4).

13:5 *three thousand chariots.* It is possible that this number represents the accepted and familiar practice of hyperbole in military reports. If not, see note on Jdg 4:3. Further information to consider is that the Hebrew text refers to 30,000 chariots, while the Septuagint (the pre-Christian Greek translation of the OT) and Syriac attest the number 3,000. Even the lower figure seems high by ancient Near Eastern standards, though not impossible: e.g., Sisera had 900 (Jdg 4:3); David killed 700 Aramean charioteers (2Sa 10:18); Solomon had 1,400 chariots (1Ki 10:26); Tukulti-Ninurta II had "2,702 horses in teams [and chariots], more than ever before." If the NIV is correct in reading also "six thousand charioteers," then this would further confirm that the Philistines had 3,000 (and not 30,000) chariots. The word translated "charioteer" can also be rendered "horseman/cavalryman" and "(chariot) horse." In view of the fairly late introduction of cavalry in Canaan and the pictorial evidence of traveling bands of Philistines comprising three main elements: chariots, infantry, and noncombatants, but no cavalry, the decision of many modern translations to read "cavalry" or "horsemen" seems misguided. Moreover, if the Philistines, like the Hittites, employed three-man chariot crews, then the number 6,000 would best refer to the chariot horses, not the charioteers (which would have numbered about 9,000). That said, some variation of the chariot team is certainly possible. Assyrian chariot crews could consist of two, three or even four men. There is also possible evidence of two-man chariots among the Mycenaeans, to whom the Philistines are thought to be related.

thought, 'Now the Philistines will come
down against me at Gilgal, and I have not
sought the LORD's favor.[j]' So I felt compelled to offer the burnt offering."
13"You have done a foolish thing,[k]"
Samuel said. "You have not kept[l] the
command the LORD your God gave you; if
you had, he would have established your
kingdom over Israel for all time. 14But now
your kingdom[m] will not endure; the LORD
has sought out a man after his own heart[n]
and appointed[o] him ruler of his people,
because you have not kept the LORD's
command."
15Then Samuel left Gilgal[a] and went up
to Gibeah[p] in Benjamin, and Saul counted
the men who were with him. They numbered about six hundred.

Israel Without Weapons

16Saul and his son Jonathan and the
men with them were staying in Gibeah[b]
in Benjamin, while the Philistines camped
at Mikmash. 17Raiding[q] parties went out
from the Philistine camp in three detachments. One turned toward Ophrah[r] in the
vicinity of Shual, 18another toward Beth
Horon,[s] and the third toward the border-
land overlooking the Valley of Zeboyim[t]
facing the wilderness.
19Not a blacksmith[u] could be found in
the whole land of Israel, because the Philistines had said, "Otherwise the Hebrews
will make swords or spears!" 20So all Israel went down to the Philistines to have
their plow points, mattocks, axes and sick-
les[c] sharpened. 21The price was two-thirds
of a shekel[d] for sharpening plow points
and mattocks, and a third of a shekel[e] for
sharpening forks and axes and for repoint-
ing goads.
22So on the day of the battle not a soldier with Saul and Jonathan[v] had a sword
or spear[w] in his hand; only Saul and his
son Jonathan had them.

Jonathan Attacks the Philistines

23Now a detachment of Philistines had
14 gone out to the pass[x] at Mikmash.
1One day Jonathan son of Saul said
to his young armor-bearer, "Come, let's go
over to the Philistine outpost on the other
side." But he did not tell his father.
2Saul was staying on the outskirts of
Gibeah[y] under a pomegranate tree in Migron.[z] With him were about six hundred
men, 3among whom was Ahijah, who was
wearing an ephod. He was a son of Ichabod's[a] brother Ahitub[b] son of Phinehas,

13:12 [j] Jer 26:19 **13:13** [k] 2Ch 16:9 [l] 1Sa 15:23,24 **13:14** [m] 1Sa 15:28 [n] Ac 7:46; 13:22 [o] 2Sa 6:21 **13:15** [p] 1Sa 14:2 **13:17** [q] 1Sa 14:15 [r] Jos 18:23 **13:18** [s] Jos 18:13-14 [t] Ne 11:34 **13:19** [u] 2Ki 24:14; Jer 24:1 **13:22** [v] 1Ch 9:39 [w] Jdg 5:8 **13:23** [x] 1Sa 14:4 **14:2** [y] 1Sa 13:15 [z] Isa 10:28 **14:3** [a] 1Sa 4:21 [b] 1Sa 22:11,20

[a] *15* Hebrew; Septuagint *Gilgal and went his way; the rest of the people went after Saul to meet the army, and they went out of Gilgal* [b] *16* Two Hebrew manuscripts; most Hebrew manuscripts *Geba,* a variant of *Gibeah* [c] *20* Septuagint; Hebrew *plow points*
[d] *21* That is, about 1/4 ounce or about 8 grams
[e] *21* That is, about 1/8 ounce or about 4 grams

13:14 *after his own heart.* Probably means "of his own choosing." The phrase does not necessarily reflect the piety of David, but demonstrates God's exercise of will in the rejection of Saul. In the Babylonian "Chronicle Concerning the Early Years of Nebuchadnezzar II," Nebuchadnezzar captures Judah and puts a king of his own choice ("according to his own heart") on the throne. This descriptive phrase is also used commonly in royal inscriptions dating more than a thousand years earlier to indicate that the king met the god's criteria. Saul, in contrast, had met only the people's criteria.

13:19 *Not a blacksmith could be found in the whole land of Israel.* Whether the Philistines led their neighbors in ironworking technology or simply were militarily powerful enough in this period to deny Israel access to blacksmiths remains an open question. Iron objects are not unknown prior to the so-called Iron Age, but at earlier periods iron was generally not preferred to bronze (an alloy of copper and tin), because bronze was in fact stronger than simple wrought iron. Only when iron was "carburized" (had carbon added to it) and "quenched" (doused in cold water) did it become steel. Because of its higher melting temperature (1528°C [2782°F], as opposed to 1200°C [2192°F] for copper), iron could not be melted and cast; ancient furnaces could achieve at best 1300–1400°C (2372–2552°F). The only solution was "forging"—repeatedly heating and then hammering the spongy hot iron to remove slag and compact the metallic iron. In most parts of the ancient Near East, iron ore was in fact more common and available than copper or tin, but the technological challenges of smelting iron meant that its use for weapons and tools did not become widespread until shortages of (often imported) copper and tin created a necessity that could not be ignored. There are even earlier references to metallic iron (cf. Og's bed decorated with iron [Dt 3:11]), which treat it as a luxury item, obtained most often from meteors (the Egyptian word for iron means "metal of heaven"). The point, in any case, is that the Philistines prevented the Israelites from arming themselves properly. Since bronze weapons (i.e., weapons produced without iron technology) would still have been useful to the Israelites, this verse probably means the Philistines prohibited metalworking of any sort.

13:21 *two-thirds of a shekel . . . a third of a shekel.* If the average monthly wage was one shekel, then these charges were exorbitant.

14:1 *armor-bearer.* He not only is a porter of equipment, but also serves a function similar to a squire or apprentice while fighting alongside the king.

14:2 *Saul was staying on the outskirts of Gibeah under a pomegranate tree in Migron.* The word "tree" is not present in the Hebrew text; "pomegranate" may refer to a certain large cave in the south wall of the wadi. The cave's pitted interior gives it the resemblance of an open pomegranate and may have earned it the name "Rimmon" (Hebrew for "pomegranate"). Jdg 20:45 speaks of "the rock of Rimmon" to which 600 Benjamites fled, and so it is conceivable that the 600 men with Saul could have been stationed "under the Pomegranate." Saul's location in a cave would also explain his need for lookouts to inform him of activities in the Philistine camp (v. 16).

14:3 *ephod.* See note on 2:18. In the present context, the ephod that Ahijah is "wearing" (or "carrying"—the Hebrew verb can mean either) was probably the high

the son of Eli,[c] the LORD's priest in Shiloh.
No one was aware that Jonathan had left.
4 On each side of the pass[d] that Jonathan
intended to cross to reach the Philistine
outpost was a cliff; one was called Bozez
and the other Seneh. 5 One cliff stood to
the north toward Mikmash, the other to
the south toward Geba.
6 Jonathan said to his young armor-bearer, "Come, let's go over to the outpost of
those uncircumcised[e] men. Perhaps the
LORD will act in our behalf. Nothing[f] can
hinder the LORD from saving, whether by
many[g] or by few.[h]"
7 "Do all that you have in mind," his armor-bearer said. "Go ahead; I am with you
heart and soul."
8 Jonathan said, "Come on, then; we will
cross over toward them and let them see
us. 9 If they say to us, 'Wait there until we
come to you,' we will stay where we are
and not go up to them. 10 But if they say,
'Come up to us,' we will climb up, because
that will be our sign[i] that the LORD has giv-
en them into our hands."
11 So both of them showed themselves
to the Philistine outpost. "Look!" said the
Philistines. "The Hebrews are crawling out
of the holes they were hiding[j] in." 12 The
men of the outpost shouted to Jonathan
and his armor-bearer, "Come up to us and
we'll teach you a lesson.[k]"
So Jonathan said to his armor-bearer,
"Climb up after me; the LORD has given
them into the hand[l] of Israel."
13 Jonathan climbed up, using his hands
and feet, with his armor-bearer right behind him. The Philistines fell before Jonathan, and his armor-bearer followed
and killed behind him. 14 In that first attack Jonathan and his armor-bearer killed
some twenty men in an area of about half
an acre.

Israel Routs the Philistines

15 Then panic[m] struck the whole army—
those in the camp and field, and those in
the outposts and raiding[n] parties—and
the ground shook. It was a panic sent by
God.[a]
16 Saul's lookouts[o] at Gibeah in Benjamin saw the army melting away in all directions. 17 Then Saul said to the men who
were with him, "Muster the forces and see
who has left us." When they did, it was
Jonathan and his armor-bearer who were
not there.
18 Saul said to Ahijah, "Bring[p] the ark
of God." (At that time it was with the Israelites.)[b] 19 While Saul was talking to the
priest, the tumult in the Philistine camp
increased more and more. So Saul said to
the priest,[q] "Withdraw your hand."

14:3 [c] 1Sa 2:28 **14:4** [d] 1Sa 13:23 **14:6** [e] 1Sa 17:26, 36; Jer 9:26 [f] Heb 11:34 [g] Jdg 7:4 [h] 1Sa 17:46-47 **14:10** [i] Ge 24:14; Jdg 6:36-37 **14:11** [j] 1Sa 13:6 **14:12** [k] 1Sa 17:43-44 [l] 2Sa 5:24 **14:15** [m] Ge 35:5; 2Ki 7:5-7 [n] 1Sa 13:17 **14:16** [o] 2Sa 18:24 **14:18** [p] 1Sa 30:7 **14:19** [q] Nu 27:21

[a] *15 Or a terrible panic* [b] *18* Hebrew; Septuagint *"Bring the ephod." (At that time he wore the ephod before the Israelites.)*

priestly ephod containing the Urim and Thummim, devices used in divine inquiry (see notes on vv. 18–19; Ex 28:15; see also the article "Urim and Thummim," p. 162). The presence of these oracular instruments among Saul's entourage might encourage hope that Saul would seek and receive divine guidance, as David did on several occasions, using the ephod (1Sa 23:9–12; 30:7–8). *Ichabod's brother Ahitub son of Phinehas, the son of Eli.* The bearer of the ephod, Ahijah, is provided with a genealogy that not only identifies him as a member of the rejected priestly house of Eli, but makes a rather unusual step sideways to mention an uncle, Ichabod, whose name means something like "no glory" (see NIV text note on 4:21). Commentators have struggled to explain this genealogy, but its purpose is probably to recall, if only indirectly, that Saul's glory too is much diminished after the events of ch. 13.

14:6 *uncircumcised men.* See note on Jdg 14:3. *Nothing can hinder the LORD from saving, whether by many or by few.* Though distinctive in its monotheism, Israel's belief that the Divine Warrior ultimately decided the outcome of battles was not without analogy among neighboring peoples. The ancient Near Eastern pantheons included gods or goddesses of war—Baal and Anat in Canaan, Nergal and Ishtar in Assyria, Marduk in Babylon and so forth. Battles were regarded as ultimately decided by the gods, the stronger god defeating the weaker. Thus, an inferior human force led by a superior deity could defeat a superior human force led by a lesser deity. In the present instance, Jonathan's faith in the power of Yahweh emboldens him to go over, accompanied only by his armor-bearer, to confront an entire Philistine troop.

14:15 *the ground shook. It was a panic sent by God.* In keeping with their belief that in warfare the gods actually did battle (see notes on v. 6; Jdg 1:2; 3:10; see also the article "Combat by Champions," p. 491), peoples of the ancient Near East associated this divine activity with dramatic manifestations in nature, the shaking of the earth, the splitting of the heavens, thunder and storm and so forth (cf. 2Sa 22:8–10). In the present passage, Yahweh manifests himself by causing the ground to shake and by throwing the Philistines into confusion so that their swords are turned upon each other (v. 20).

14:18–19 *Bring the ark ... Withdraw your hand.* Having learned that Jonathan and his armor-bearer had left the camp, Saul orders Ahijah to "bring the ark of God." Mention of the "ark" is surprising at this point in the narrative for the following reasons: (1) in v. 3 Ahijah is in possession of an "ephod," not the ark; (2) judging from 7:1 and 2Sa 6, the ark appears to have remained at the town of Kiriath Jearim throughout the reign of Saul (1Ch 13:3 confirms that the ark was not sought during Saul's reign); (3) Saul's order that Ahijah "bring" the object seems appropriate in reference to an ephod (cf. 23:9; 30:7) but not in reference to the ark; (4) Saul's command in v. 19 to "withdraw your hand" makes little sense if the ark is in view, but excellent sense if Ahijah is in the process of grasping the Urim and Thummim, or the container holding them, in the breastpiece of the priestly ephod. Based on Akkadian evidence, it is possible that oracular inquiry using the Urim and Thummim was a form of psephomancy, "divination by means of white and black stones" (see the article "Urim and Thummim," p. 162). Considerations such as these have led a majority of commentators to follow the Septuagint (the pre-Christian Greek translation

[20]Then Saul and all his men assembled and went to the battle. They found
the Philistines in total confusion, striking[r]
each other with their swords. [21]Those Hebrews who had previously been with the
Philistines and had gone up with them to
their camp went[s] over to the Israelites who
were with Saul and Jonathan. [22]When all
the Israelites who had hidden[t] in the hill
country of Ephraim heard that the Philistines were on the run, they joined the
battle in hot pursuit. [23]So on that day the
LORD saved[u] Israel, and the battle moved
on beyond Beth Aven.[v]

Jonathan Eats Honey

[24]Now the Israelites were in distress that
day, because Saul had bound the people
under an oath,[w] saying, "Cursed be anyone who eats food before evening comes,
before I have avenged myself on my enemies!" So none of the troops tasted food.
[25]The entire army entered the woods,
and there was honey on the ground.
[26]When they went into the woods, they
saw the honey oozing out; yet no one
put his hand to his mouth, because they
feared the oath. [27]But Jonathan had not
heard that his father had bound the people
with the oath, so he reached out the end of
the staff that was in his hand and dipped it
into the honeycomb.[x] He raised his hand
to his mouth, and his eyes brightened.[a]
[28]Then one of the soldiers told him, "Your
father bound the army under a strict oath,
saying, 'Cursed be anyone who eats food
today!' That is why the men are faint."
[29]Jonathan said, "My father has made
trouble[y] for the country. See how my eyes
brightened when I tasted a little of this
honey. [30]How much better it would have
been if the men had eaten today some of
the plunder they took from their enemies.
Would not the slaughter of the Philistines
have been even greater?"
[31]That day, after the Israelites had
struck down the Philistines from Mikmash to Aijalon,[z] they were exhausted.
[32]They pounced on the plunder[a] and, taking sheep, cattle and calves, they butchered them on the ground and ate them,
together with the blood.[b] [33]Then someone
said to Saul, "Look, the men are sinning
against the LORD by eating meat that has
blood in it."
"You have broken faith," he said. "Roll
a large stone over here at once." [34]Then
he said, "Go out among the men and tell
them, 'Each of you bring me your cattle
and sheep, and slaughter them here and
eat them. Do not sin against the LORD by
eating meat with blood still in it.'"
So everyone brought his ox that night
and slaughtered it there. [35]Then Saul built
an altar[c] to the LORD; it was the first time
he had done this.
[36]Saul said, "Let us go down and pursue the Philistines by night and plunder
them till dawn, and let us not leave one
of them alive."
"Do whatever seems best to you," they
replied.
But the priest said, "Let us inquire of
God here."
[37]So Saul asked God, "Shall I go down
and pursue the Philistines? Will you give
them into Israel's hand?" But God did not
answer[d] him that day.

14:20 [r] Jdg 7:22; 2Ch 20:23 **14:21** [s] 1Sa 29:4 **14:22** [t] 1Sa 13:6 **14:23** [u] Ex 14:30; Ps 44:6-7 [v] 1Sa 13:5 **14:24** [w] Jos 6:26 **14:27** [x] ver 43; 1Sa 30:12 **14:29** [y] Jos 7:25; 1Ki 18:18 **14:31** [z] Jos 10:12 **14:32** [a] 1Sa 15:19 [b] Ge 9:4; Lev 3:17; 7:26; 17:10-14; 19:26; Dt 12:16,23-24 **14:35** [c] 1Sa 7:17 **14:37** [d] 1Sa 10:22; 28:6,15

[a] 27 Or *his strength was renewed*; similarly in verse 29

of the OT) (cf. also Josephus, *Antiquities* 6.115) in reading "ephod" instead of "ark" in the present context—the two words are orthographically fairly similar in Hebrew. It seems likely, then, that Saul initiated an oracular inquiry involving the ephod but almost immediately aborted the process when it became apparent that the battle was heating up. Having failed to wait for Samuel in ch. 13, Saul now finds it difficult even to wait the few minutes necessary to inquire of Yahweh regarding the battle in progress, and this trend of increasing indifference to gaining divine direction adds to the unfavorable portrayal of Saul. On the customary practice in the Bible and the ancient Near East of seeking divine guidance before entering battle, see note on 7:7.

14:21 *Hebrews who had previously been with the Philistines ... went over to the Israelites.* This statement seems to distinguish "Hebrews" from Israelites. The "Hebrews" here may refer to the Habiru/Apiru, landless, troublesome mercenaries who may have shifted allegiances opportunistically (see note on 4:6).

14:24 *Cursed be anyone who eats food.* In the ancient Near East, fasting is often associated with mourning, but is unattested in battle contexts such as this.

14:33 *sinning against the LORD by eating meat that has blood in it.* Not just in the OT but throughout Egypt, Mesopotamia and the Levant, blood was regarded with awe as the medium that carried and contained life. As such, it gave rise to seemingly conflicting attitudes. Contact with it was regulated by taboos, yet ways to use its power were developed in ritual. In the OT, control over the lifeblood was understood to belong to God, the giver of life, and prohibitions against eating blood were pervasive (e.g., Ge 9:4; Lev 3:17; 7:26–27; 17:10,12; 19:26; Dt 15:23; Eze 33:25).

14:35 *Saul built an altar.* When an animal was laid on an altar, in the process of sacrifice the blood drained out as regulations required. By building an altar, Saul is facilitating proper sacrifice. Consequently we can see that though he has some ritual knowledge and sensitivities, he still lacks an overall sense of doing what is necessary to please God (obedience).

14:37 *God did not answer him that day.* Though Urim and Thummim represent some sort of system like lots (see the article "Urim and Thummim," p. 162), and therefore tend to address binary questions (yes/no), it is likely that the same answer had to be drawn several times in a row to confirm that the answer came from God. If this is so, it would explain how an answer could fail to result from the inquiry process.

38 Saul therefore said, "Come here, all you who are leaders of the army, and let us find out what sin has been committed[e] today. 39 As surely as the LORD who rescues Israel lives,[f] even if the guilt lies with my son Jonathan, he must die." But not one of them said a word.

40 Saul then said to all the Israelites, "You stand over there; I and Jonathan my son will stand over here."

"Do what seems best to you," they replied.

41 Then Saul prayed to the LORD, the God of Israel, "Why have you not answered your servant today? If the fault is in me or my son Jonathan, respond with Urim, but if the men of Israel are at fault,[a] respond with Thummim." Jonathan and Saul were taken by lot, and the men were cleared. 42 Saul said, "Cast the lot between me and Jonathan my son." And Jonathan was taken.

43 Then Saul said to Jonathan, "Tell me what you have done."[g]

So Jonathan told him, "I tasted a little honey[h] with the end of my staff. And now I must die!"

44 Saul said, "May God deal with me, be it ever so severely,[i] if you do not die, Jonathan.[j]"

45 But the men said to Saul, "Should Jonathan die — he who has brought about this great deliverance in Israel? Never! As surely as the LORD lives, not a hair[k] of his head will fall to the ground, for he did this today with God's help." So the men rescued[l] Jonathan, and he was not put to death.

46 Then Saul stopped pursuing the Philistines, and they withdrew to their own land.

47 After Saul had assumed rule over Israel, he fought against their enemies on every side: Moab, the Ammonites,[m] Edom, the kings[b] of Zobah,[n] and the Philistines. Wherever he turned, he inflicted punishment on them.[c] 48 He fought valiantly and defeated the Amalekites,[o] delivering Israel from the hands of those who had plundered them.

Saul's Family

49 Saul's sons were Jonathan, Ishvi and Malki-Shua.[p] The name of his older daughter was Merab, and that of the younger was Michal.[q] 50 His wife's name was Ahinoam daughter of Ahimaaz. The name of the commander of Saul's army was Abner son of Ner, and Ner was Saul's uncle. 51 Saul's father Kish[r] and Abner's father Ner were sons of Abiel.

52 All the days of Saul there was bitter war with the Philistines, and whenever Saul saw a mighty or brave man, he took[s] him into his service.

The LORD Rejects Saul as King

15 Samuel said to Saul, "I am the one the LORD sent to anoint[t] you king over his people Israel; so listen now to the message from the LORD. 2 This is what the LORD Almighty says: 'I will punish the Amalekites[u] for what they did to Israel when they waylaid them as they came up from Egypt. 3 Now go, attack the Amalekites and totally[v] destroy[d] all that belongs to them. Do not spare them; put to death men and women, children and infants, cattle and sheep, camels and donkeys.' "

4 So Saul summoned the men and mustered them at Telaim — two hundred thousand foot soldiers and ten thousand from Judah. 5 Saul went to the city of Amalek and set an ambush in the ravine. 6 Then he said to the Kenites,[w] "Go away, leave the Amalekites so that I do not destroy you along with them; for you showed kindness to all the Israelites when they came up out of Egypt." So the Kenites moved away from the Amalekites.

7 Then Saul attacked the Amalekites[x] all the way from Havilah to Shur,[y] near the eastern border of Egypt. 8 He took Agag king of the Amalekites alive,[z] and all his people he totally destroyed with the sword. 9 But Saul and the army spared[a] Agag and the best of the sheep and cattle, the fat calves[e] and lambs — everything that was good. These they were unwilling to destroy completely, but everything that was despised and weak they totally destroyed.

14:38 [e] Jos 7:11; 1Sa 10:19 **14:39** [f] 2Sa 12:5 **14:43** [g] Jos 7:19 [h] ver 27 **14:44** [i] Ru 1:17 [j] ver 39 **14:45** [k] 1Ki 1:52; Lk 21:18; Ac 27:34 [l] 2Sa 14:11 **14:47** [m] 1Sa 11:1-13 [n] ver 52; 2Sa 10:6 **14:48** [o] 1Sa 15:2,7 **14:49** [p] 1Sa 31:2; 1Ch 8:33 [q] 1Sa 18:17-20 **14:51** [r] 1Sa 9:1 **14:52** [s] 1Sa 8:11 **15:1** [t] 1Sa 9:16 **15:2** [u] Ex 17:8-14; Nu 24:20; Dt 25:17-19 **15:3** [v] Nu 24:20; Dt 20:16-18; Jos 6:17; 1Sa 22:19 **15:6** [w] Ex 18:10, 19; Nu 10:29-32; 24:22; Jdg 1:16; 4:1 **15:7** [x] 1Sa 14:48 [y] Ge 16:7; 25:17-18; Ex 15:22 **15:8** [z] 1Sa 30:1 **15:9** [a] ver 3, 15

a 41 Septuagint; Hebrew does not have *"Why . . . at fault.* *b* 47 Masoretic Text; Dead Sea Scrolls and Septuagint *king* *c* 47 Hebrew; Septuagint *he was victorious* *d* 3 The Hebrew term refers to the irrevocable giving over of things or persons to the LORD, often by totally destroying them; also in verses 8, 9, 15, 18, 20 and 21. *e* 9 Or *the grown bulls*; the meaning of the Hebrew for this phrase is uncertain.

15:2 *Amalekites.* See note on Nu 13:29. Ex 17:14 singles out the Amalekites as enemies of Israel. The severity of the treatment of the Amalekites commanded by Yahweh here in vv. 2 – 3 must be seen in the light of this status and ongoing opposition to Israel (see, e.g., Jdg 3:13; 6:3 – 5,33; 7:12; 10:12).
15:3 *totally destroy.* See note on Dt 2:34.
15:4 *two hundred thousand foot soldiers.* See the article "Numbers in Numbers," p. 235.

15:6 *Kenites.* See note on Jdg 1:16. Not only in the present context of Saul's battle against the Amalekites but elsewhere in the Bible (e.g., Nu 24:20 – 21) Kenites and Amalekites are mentioned together. But whereas the Amalekites were consistently hostile toward Israel, the Kenites were consistently friendly, and so Saul was careful to send the Kenites away from danger before attacking the Amalekites.

10 Then the word of the LORD came to
Samuel: 11 "I regret[b] that I have made Saul
king, because he has turned[c] away from
me and has not carried out my instructions."[d] Samuel was angry,[e] and he cried
out to the LORD all that night.
12 Early in the morning Samuel got up
and went to meet Saul, but he was told,
"Saul has gone to Carmel.[f] There he has
set up a monument in his own honor and
has turned and gone on down to Gilgal."
13 When Samuel reached him, Saul said,
"The LORD bless you! I have carried out
the LORD's instructions."
14 But Samuel said, "What then is this
bleating of sheep in my ears? What is this
lowing of cattle that I hear?"
15 Saul answered, "The soldiers brought
them from the Amalekites; they spared
the best of the sheep and cattle to sacrifice to the LORD your God, but we totally
destroyed the rest."
16 "Enough!" Samuel said to Saul. "Let
me tell you what the LORD said to me last
night."
"Tell me," Saul replied.
17 Samuel said, "Although you were once
small[g] in your own eyes, did you not become the head of the tribes of Israel? The
LORD anointed you king over Israel. 18 And
he sent you on a mission, saying, 'Go and
completely destroy those wicked people,
the Amalekites; wage war against them
until you have wiped them out.' 19 Why
did you not obey the LORD? Why did you
pounce on the plunder[h] and do evil in the
eyes of the LORD?"
20 "But I did obey[i] the LORD," Saul said.
"I went on the mission the LORD assigned
me. I completely destroyed the Amalekites
and brought back Agag their king. 21 The
soldiers took sheep and cattle from the
plunder, the best of what was devoted to
God, in order to sacrifice them to the LORD
your God at Gilgal."
22 But Samuel replied:

"Does the LORD delight in burnt
offerings and sacrifices
as much as in obeying the LORD?
To obey is better than sacrifice,[j]
and to heed is better than the fat of
rams.
23 For rebellion is like the sin of
divination,[k]
and arrogance like the evil of
idolatry.
Because you have rejected[l] the word of
the LORD,
he has rejected you as king."

24 Then Saul said to Samuel, "I have
sinned.[m] I violated the LORD's command
and your instructions. I was afraid[n] of the
men and so I gave in to them. 25 Now I beg
you, forgive[o] my sin and come back with
me, so that I may worship the LORD."
26 But Samuel said to him, "I will not
go back with you. You have rejected[p] the
word of the LORD, and the LORD has rejected you as king over Israel!"
27 As Samuel turned to leave, Saul caught
hold of the hem of his robe, and it tore.[q]
28 Samuel said to him, "The LORD has torn[r]
the kingdom of Israel from you today and
has given it to one of your neighbors—
to one better than you. 29 He who is the

15:11 [b] Ge 6:6; 2Sa 24:16 [c] Jos 22:16 [d] 1Sa 13:13; 1Ki 9:6-7 [e] ver 35 **15:12** [f] Jos 15:55 **15:17** [g] 1Sa 9:21 **15:19** [h] 1Sa 14:32 **15:20** [i] ver 13 **15:22** [j] Ps 40:6-8; 51:16; Isa 1:11-15; Jer 7:22; Hos 6:6; Mic 6:6-8; Mt 12:7; Mk 12:33; Heb 10:6-9 **15:23** [k] Dt 18:10 [l] 1Sa 13:13 **15:24** [m] 2Sa 12:13 [n] Pr 29:25; Isa 51:12-13 **15:25** [o] Ex 10:17 **15:26** [p] 1Sa 13:14 **15:27** [q] 1Ki 11:11,31 **15:28** [r] 1Sa 28:17; 1Ki 11:31

15:12 *Carmel.* See note on 25:2; cf. 23:24. *he has set up a monument in his own honor.* It was common practice in the ancient Near East for victorious kings to set up monuments, or victory steles, with inscriptions celebrating their glorious achievements and crediting their success to their god(s). The ninth-century BC Assyrian king Ashurnasirpal II, e.g., makes repeated reference to erecting steles or statues in praise of his mighty power. In the aftermath of one victory, apparently not content with a single monument to himself, he erected a "colossal royal statue of [him]self" in the palace of his vanquished foe and also deposited steles in praise of his own might in the enemy's gate. Saul's monument may have been such a victory stele. Absalom will later honor himself similarly with a monument (2Sa 18:18).

15:23 *rebellion.* The same Hebrew word used of Israel's contentiousness in the wilderness; it refers to "pressing one's case." *divination.* Acquiring information about the desires of deity by indirect means. Here, Saul's "case" is that he (thinks he) knows what will please Yahweh (sacrifices from the plunder), so his assertion of that knowledge in his own defense (his "case" or "rebellion") is like divination. *idolatry.* The word in the original Hebrew text is "teraphim," see the article "Household Gods," p. 72.

15:27 *Saul caught hold of the hem of his robe, and it tore.* The precise significance, or intent, of Saul's seizing the hem of Samuel's robe is uncertain. In addition to several texts in Akkadian, at least one reference to this action can be found in Old Aramaic, as well as one other in the OT, namely, Zec 8:23: "This is what the LORD Almighty says: 'In those days ten people from all languages and nations will take firm hold of one Jew by the hem of his robe and say, "Let us go with you, because we have heard that God is with you."'" In the light of these texts, Saul's grasping of Samuel's hem might be read positively, as indicating supplication or submission. However, this positive construal of Saul's action assumes more regarding Saul's motives than the context will support. A further instance of grasping the hem is found in the Ugaritic myth of Baal and Mot, in which Anat seizes the hem of Mot's garment in order to constrain him. Anat's action, in context, is suggestive of supplication but hardly of penitence or submission; when she next "seizes" Mot, Anat "hacks him up, pulverizes him, and scatters his remains for the birds to eat." Taking this evidence together, we may conclude that grasping the hem can mean various things in various contexts. In the present context, Saul's grasping and (inadvertently?) tearing the hem of Samuel's robe is best understood as a last desperate attempt to rescue a situation that has gone badly wrong and to wrest from the prophet a word of comfort or concession. As it happened, however, the torn robe became simply a symbol of the kingdom now "torn" from Saul (v. 28).

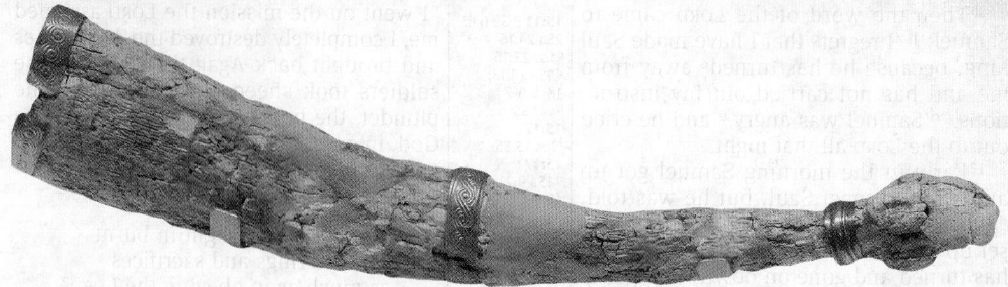

Ivory and gold anointing horn found at Megiddo, c. fourteenth century BC. Samuel anointed David with a horn filled with oil (1Sa 16:1).

Kim Walton. The Israel Museum, Jerusalem.

Glory of Israel does not lie[s] or change[t] his
mind; for he is not a human being, that he
should change his mind."
30 Saul replied, "I have sinned. But
please honor[u] me before the elders of my
people and before Israel; come back with
me, so that I may worship the LORD your
God." 31 So Samuel went back with Saul,
and Saul worshiped the LORD.
32 Then Samuel said, "Bring me Agag
king of the Amalekites."
Agag came to him in chains.[a] And he
thought, "Surely the bitterness of death is
past."
33 But Samuel said,

"As your sword has made women
childless,
so will your mother be childless
among women."[v]

And Samuel put Agag to death before the
LORD at Gilgal.
34 Then Samuel left for Ramah,[w] but
Saul went up to his home in Gibeah[x] of
Saul. 35 Until the day Samuel[y] died, he did
not go to see Saul again, though Samuel
mourned[z] for him. And the LORD regretted
that he had made Saul king over Israel.

Samuel Anoints David

16 The LORD said to Samuel, "How
long will you mourn[a] for Saul, since
I have rejected[b] him as king over Israel? Fill
your horn with oil[c] and be on your way; I
am sending you to Jesse[d] of Bethlehem. I
have chosen[e] one of his sons to be king."
2 But Samuel said, "How can I go? If Saul
hears about it, he will kill me."
The LORD said, "Take a heifer with you
and say, 'I have come to sacrifice to the
LORD.' 3 Invite Jesse to the sacrifice, and
I will show[f] you what to do. You are to
anoint[g] for me the one I indicate."
4 Samuel did what the LORD said. When
he arrived at Bethlehem,[h] the elders of the
town trembled when they met him. They
asked, "Do you come in peace?[i]"
5 Samuel replied, "Yes, in peace; I have
come to sacrifice to the LORD. Consecrate[j]
yourselves and come to the sacrifice with
me." Then he consecrated Jesse and his
sons and invited them to the sacrifice.
6 When they arrived, Samuel saw Eliab[k]
and thought, "Surely the LORD's anointed
stands here before the LORD."
7 But the LORD said to Samuel, "Do not
consider his appearance or his height, for I
have rejected him. The LORD does not look
at the things people look at. People look
at the outward appearance,[l] but the LORD
looks at the heart."[m]
8 Then Jesse called Abinadab[n] and had
him pass in front of Samuel. But Samuel
said, "The LORD has not chosen this one
either." 9 Jesse then had Shammah pass
by, but Samuel said, "Nor has the LORD
chosen this one." 10 Jesse had seven of his
sons pass before Samuel, but Samuel said
to him, "The LORD has not chosen these."

15:29 [s] 1Ch 29:11; Titus 1:2 [t] Nu 23:19; Eze 24:14 **15:30** [u] Isa 29:13; Jn 5:44; 12:43 **15:33** [v] Ge 9:6; Jdg 1:7 **15:34** [w] 1Sa 7:17 [x] 1Sa 11:4 **15:35** [y] 1Sa 19:24 [z] 1Sa 16:1 **16:1** [a] 1Sa 15:35 [b] 1Sa 15:23 [c] 2Ki 9:1 [d] Ru 4:17; 1Sa 9:16 [e] Ps 78:70; Ac 13:22 **16:3** [f] Ex 4:15 [g] Dt 17:15; 1Sa 9:16 **16:4** [h] Ge 48:7; Lk 2:4 [i] 1Ki 2:13; 2Ki 9:17 **16:5** [j] Ex 19:10, 22 **16:6** [k] 1Sa 17:13 **16:7** [l] Ps 147:10 [m] 1Ki 8:39; 1Ch 28:9; Isa 55:8 **16:8** [n] 1Sa 17:13

[a] *32* The meaning of the Hebrew for this phrase is uncertain.

15:29 *the Glory of Israel does not lie or change his mind.* The ninth-century BC Assyrian king Ashurnasirpal II begins one of the longest extant Assyrian royal inscriptions with line after line of praise to the god Ninurta, whom he describes as, among other things, "the splendid god who never changes (his mind)." In the context of the trial of Saul, the sense seems to be similar: No amount of cajoling or manipulation will succeed in mitigating the sentence that has been pronounced against Saul, for it has been issued by Yahweh, whose judgment is supreme.

16:1 *Fill your horn with oil.* See 10:1.

16:7 *the LORD looks at the heart.* In the ancient Near East, the heart was viewed as far more than the seat of blind passions. Some Babylonian texts speak of the deity Shamash seeing into or searching the heart of an individual. The Hebrew concept of the heart as the center of intellectual, ethical, moral and religious consciousness was similar.

16:10 – 11 *Jesse had seven of his sons pass before Samuel ... "There is still the youngest."* Ascendancy of a younger brother over his elder brothers is a common motif in the Bible and in the ancient Near East generally. One

[11]So he asked Jesse, "Are these all[o] the
sons you have?"
"There is still the youngest," Jesse answered. "He is tending the sheep."
Samuel said, "Send for him; we will not sit down until he arrives."
[12]So he[p] sent for him and had him
brought in. He was glowing with health and had a fine appearance and handsome[q] features.
Then the LORD said, "Rise and anoint him; this is the one."
[13]So Samuel took the horn of oil and
anointed him in the presence of his brothers, and from that day on the Spirit of the LORD[r] came powerfully upon David.[s] Samuel then went to Ramah.

16:11 [o] 1Sa 17:12 **16:12** [p] 1Sa 9:17 [q] Ge 39:6; 1Sa 17:42 **16:13** [r] Nu 27:18; Jdg 11:29 [s] 1Sa 10:1,6, 9-10; 11:6 **16:14** [t] Jdg 16:20 [u] Jdg 9:23; 1Sa 18:10 **16:16** [v] ver 23; 1Sa 18:10; 19:9; 2Ki 3:15

David in Saul's Service

[14]Now the Spirit of the LORD had departed[t] from Saul, and an evil[a] spirit[u] from the LORD tormented him.
[15]Saul's attendants said to him, "See,
an evil spirit from God is tormenting you.
[16]Let our lord command his servants here
to search for someone who can play the lyre.[v] He will play when the evil spirit from God comes on you, and you will feel better."

[a] 14 Or *and a harmful*; similarly in verses 15, 16 and 23

particularly interesting parallel is offered by a mid-third-millennium BC Sumerian epic in which the eighth son, one Lugalbanda, joins seven older brothers and performs heroically in their attempt to conquer a city.

16:12 *anoint him.* See note on 2:10.

16:14 *the Spirit of the LORD had departed from Saul, and an evil spirit from the LORD tormented him.* See note on Jdg 9:23. In the ancient Near East, unworthy kings could provoke similar displeasure and disciplinary actions from their deities. For instance, near the end of the Code of Hammurapi a curse is invoked upon anyone who should disobey the law such that divine favor would be withdrawn from the offender, as it was withdrawn from Saul. The Akkadian notion of "a spirit or demon representing the individual's vital force," which could become alienated from the individual or driven away by evil, may offer some degree of conceptual parallel, as also to a lesser degree the Akkadian phrase referring to a good or evil spirit.

DAVID'S FAMILY TREE

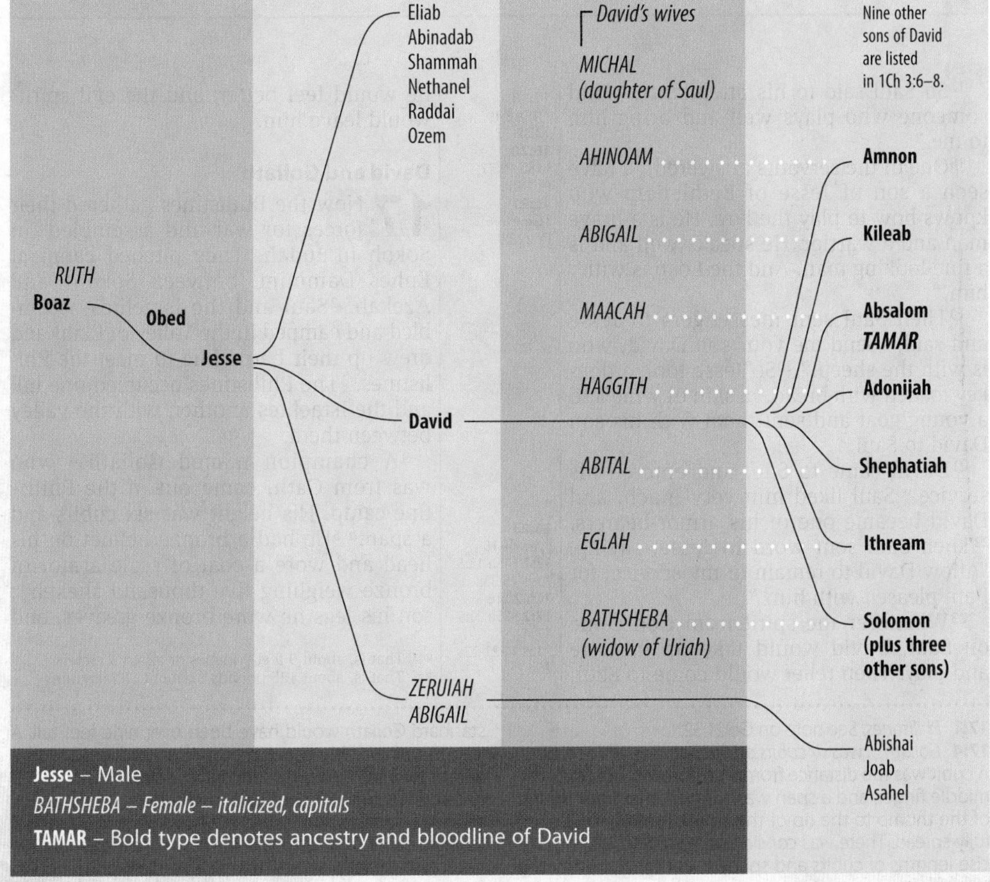

1 SAMUEL 16:16,18

LYRE

The precise identification of some Hebrew musical terms is uncertain, since the Biblical contexts do not always bring clarity. There were several types of lyres in antiquity. The type of lyre that David played (the *kinnor*) was presumably the "Eastern," or "thin," lyre, which was strung with 4 to 8 strings and was played with a plectrum. The "thick" lyre (the *nebel*) had 10 to 13 strings and was played with the fingers. To date, no evidence of thick lyres has been discovered in Palestine. Lyres were constructed using a rectangular sound box, two asymmetrical arms, and an oblique yoke, with strings stretched between the sound box and the yoke. ◆

Harpist on jug, eleventh century BC, Megiddo. David would play his lyre for Saul to bring him relief (1Sa 16:23).

Kim Walton. The Israel Museum, Jerusalem.

[17]So Saul said to his attendants, "Find
someone who plays well and bring him
to me."
[18]One of the servants answered, "I have
seen a son of Jesse of Bethlehem who
knows how to play the lyre. He is a brave
man and a warrior. He speaks well and is
a fine-looking man. And the LORD is with[w]
him."
[19]Then Saul sent messengers to Jesse
and said, "Send me your son David, who
is with the sheep." [20]So Jesse took a donkey loaded with bread,[x] a skin of wine and
a young goat and sent them with his son
David to Saul.
[21]David came to Saul and entered his
service.[y] Saul liked him very much, and
David became one of his armor-bearers.
[22]Then Saul sent word to Jesse, saying,
"Allow David to remain in my service, for
I am pleased with him."
[23]Whenever the spirit from God came
on Saul, David would take up his lyre
and play. Then relief would come to Saul;
he would feel better, and the evil spirit[z]
would leave him.

16:18 [w] 1Sa 3:19; 17:32-37 **16:20** [x] 1Sa 10:27; Pr 18:16 **16:21** [y] Ge 41:46; Pr 22:29 **16:23** [z] ver 14-16 **17:1** [a] 1Sa 13:5 [b] Jos 15:35; 2Ch 28:18 **17:2** [c] 1Sa 21:9 **17:4** [d] Jos 11:21-22; 2Sa 21:19

David and Goliath

17 Now the Philistines gathered their
forces for war and assembled[a] at
Sokoh in Judah. They pitched camp at
Ephes Dammim, between Sokoh[b] and
Azekah. [2]Saul and the Israelites assembled and camped in the Valley of Elah[c] and
drew up their battle line to meet the Philistines. [3]The Philistines occupied one hill
and the Israelites another, with the valley
between them.
[4]A champion named Goliath,[d] who
was from Gath, came out of the Philistine camp. His height was six cubits and
a span.[a] [5]He had a bronze helmet on his
head and wore a coat of scale armor of
bronze weighing five thousand shekels[b];
[6]on his legs he wore bronze greaves, and

[a] 4 That is, about 9 feet 9 inches or about 3 meters
[b] 5 That is, about 125 pounds or about 58 kilograms

17:1 *Philistines.* See note on Ge 21:32.

17:4 *Goliath . . . was six cubits and a span.* See NIV text note. A cubit was the distance from the elbow to the tip of the middle finger, and a span was the distance from the tip of the thumb to the tip of the smallest finger of a hand fully spread. There was considerable variation in the precise lengths of cubits and spans in antiquity, but by any standard Goliath would have been over nine feet tall. A number of credible Greek manuscripts reduce Goliath's height by a third to four cubits and a span, making him about six feet nine inches (205 centimeters) — still tall by ancient standards, to be sure, but not a giant (a claim that the Biblical text never makes in any case). It should be noted, however, that examples of giantism on the order

a bronze javelin[e] was slung on his back.
7His spear shaft was like a weaver's rod,[f]
and its iron point weighed six hundred
shekels.[a] His shield bearer[g] went ahead
of him.

8Goliath stood and shouted to the ranks
of Israel, "Why do you come out and line
up for battle? Am I not a Philistine, and
are you not the servants of Saul? Choose[h]
a man and have him come down to me.
9If he is able to fight and kill me, we will
become your subjects; but if I overcome
him and kill him, you will become our
subjects and serve us." 10Then the Philistine said, "This day I defy[i] the armies of
Israel! Give me a man and let us fight each
other." 11On hearing the Philistine's words,
Saul and all the Israelites were dismayed
and terrified.

12Now David was the son of an Ephrathite named Jesse,[j] who was from Bethlehem[k] in Judah. Jesse had eight[l] sons, and
in Saul's time he was very old. 13Jesse's
three oldest sons had followed Saul to the
war: The firstborn was Eliab;[m] the second,
Abinadab; and the third, Shammah.[n] 14Da-
vid was the youngest. The three oldest
followed Saul, 15but David went back and
forth from Saul to tend his father's sheep[o]
at Bethlehem.

16For forty days the Philistine came forward every morning and evening and took
his stand.

17Now Jesse said to his son David,
"Take this ephah[b] of roasted grain[p] and
these ten loaves of bread for your brothers and hurry to their camp. 18Take along
these ten cheeses to the commander of
their unit. See how your brothers[q] are and
bring back some assurance[c] from them.
19They are with Saul and all the men of
Israel in the Valley of Elah, fighting against
the Philistines."

20Early in the morning David left the
flock in the care of a shepherd, loaded
up and set out, as Jesse had directed. He
reached the camp as the army was going
out to its battle positions, shouting the
war cry. 21Israel and the Philistines were
drawing up their lines facing each other.
22David left his things with the keeper of
supplies, ran to the battle lines and asked
his brothers how they were. 23As he was
talking with them, Goliath, the Philistine
champion from Gath, stepped out from
his lines and shouted his usual[r] defiance,
and David heard it. 24Whenever the Israelites saw the man, they all fled from him
in great fear.

25Now the Israelites had been saying,
"Do you see how this man keeps coming
out? He comes out to defy Israel. The king
will give great wealth to the man who kills
him. He will also give him his daughter[s] in
marriage and will exempt his family from
taxes in Israel."

26David asked the men standing near
him, "What will be done for the man
who kills this Philistine and removes this

17:6 [e] ver 45 **17:7** [f] 2Sa 21:19 [g] ver 41 **17:8** [h] 1Sa 8:17 **17:10** [i] ver 26, 45; 2Sa 21:21 **17:12** [j] Ru 4:17; 1Ch 2:13-15 [k] Ge 35:19 [l] 1Sa 16:11 **17:13** [m] 1Sa 16:6 [n] 1Sa 16:9 **17:15** [o] 1Sa 16:19 **17:17** [p] 1Sa 25:18 **17:18** [q] Ge 37:14 **17:23** [r] ver 8-10 **17:25** [s] Jos 15:16; 1Sa 18:17

[a] *7* That is, about 15 pounds or about 6.9 kilograms [b] *17* That is, probably about 36 pounds or about 16 kilograms [c] *18* Or *some token*; or *some pledge of spoils*

of what the Hebrew text claims for Goliath are attested in numerous sources both ancient and modern. Within the Bible itself, both giant individuals (e.g., King Og of Bashan, Dt 3:11) and entire races of giants are described (e.g., the Anakites [see notes on Nu 13:22; Dt 2:10] and Rephaites [see note on Dt 2:11], the latter being the race of which Og was a remnant). A noteworthy extra-Biblical reference is found in the thirteenth-century BC Egyptian Papyrus Anastasi I, which "describes bedouin in Canaan, 'some of whom are of four cubits or five cubits (from) their nose to foot and have fierce faces.'" Joshua, during the conquest period, was largely successful in wiping out the Anakites, but there were some survivors in the Philistine cities of Gaza, Gath and Ashdod (Jos 11:21–22). Goliath may well have been one of these survivors.

17:18 *bring back some assurance from them.* The English translation of this instruction from Jesse to David suggests that David was to bring back assurance that his brothers were faring well. This is one possible understanding of the Hebrew ("some pledge" or "some token," see NIV text note). There may also be a sense that David was to bring back some indication that he had fulfilled his mission and delivered the goods. In view of the responsibility of local populations to supply troops in their area, a further possibility is that David was to bring back a token as proof that Jesse had met his obligations to supply the army.

17:22 *David left his things with the keeper of supplies.* If the grain and loaves brought by David (v. 17) were for the resupply of the troops, his depositing them with the "keeper of supplies" marked the fulfillment of that part of the errand. If, on the other hand, his task was to deliver the grain and loaves directly to his brothers (and the cheeses to the commanding officer, v. 18), then he was simply placing them in safekeeping so long as attention was directed toward the battle lines.

17:25 *exempt his family from taxes in Israel.* Taxes are not explicitly mentioned in the Hebrew text; rather, the term "exempt" is simply "free," most often used to distinguish those who are not slaves. Attempts have been made on the basis of similar sounding terms in Akkadian and Ugaritic to liken these "free" people to particular social classes in ancient Near Eastern societies (craftsmen, farmers, serfs, etc. who fell midway between slaves and landowners), but there is no evidence of this usage or this class in Israel. Certainty of what precisely the promised freedom would have been is elusive, but it may well have involved exemption from further obligations to the king (including the obligation to pay taxes), or perhaps it even involved the right of the hero's family to live as pensioners of the royal house.

17:26 *uncircumcised Philistine.* See note on Jdg 14:3. David's words reflect a theologically based confidence similar to that of Jonathan when in ch. 14 he too went up against the Philistines despite apparently unfavorable odds.

The Valley of Elah where David fought Goliath.
Kim Walton

disgrace[t] from Israel? Who is this uncircumcised[u] Philistine that he should defy[v]
the armies of the living[w] God?"
27They repeated to him what they had
been saying and told him, "This is what
will be done for the man who kills him."
28When Eliab, David's oldest brother, heard him speaking with the men, he
burned with anger[x] at him and asked,
"Why have you come down here? And
with whom did you leave those few sheep
in the wilderness? I know how conceited
you are and how wicked your heart is; you
came down only to watch the battle."
29"Now what have I done?" said David.
"Can't I even speak?" 30He then turned
away to someone else and brought up the
same matter, and the men answered him as
before. 31What David said was overheard
and reported to Saul, and Saul sent for him.
32David said to Saul, "Let no one lose
heart[y] on account of this Philistine; your
servant will go and fight him."
33Saul replied,[z] "You are not able to go
out against this Philistine and fight him;
you are only a young man, and he has
been a warrior from his youth."

17:26 [t] 1Sa 11:2 [u] 1Sa 14:6 [v] ver 10 [w] Dt 5:26
17:28 [x] Ge 37:4, 8, 11; Pr 18:19; Mt 10:36
17:32 [y] Dt 20:3; 1Sa 16:18
17:33 [z] Nu 13:31
17:34 [a] Jer 49:19; Am 3:12
17:37 [b] 2Co 1:10 [c] 2Ti 4:17 [d] 1Sa 20:13; 1Ch 22:11, 16

34But David said to Saul, "Your servant has been keeping his father's sheep.
When a lion[a] or a bear came and carried
off a sheep from the flock, 35I went after
it, struck it and rescued the sheep from its
mouth. When it turned on me, I seized it
by its hair, struck it and killed it. 36Your
servant has killed both the lion and the
bear; this uncircumcised Philistine will be
like one of them, because he has defied
the armies of the living God. 37The LORD
who rescued[b] me from the paw of the
lion[c] and the paw of the bear will rescue
me from the hand of this Philistine."
Saul said to David, "Go, and the LORD
be with[d] you."
38Then Saul dressed David in his own
tunic. He put a coat of armor on him and
a bronze helmet on his head. 39David fastened on his sword over the tunic and
tried walking around, because he was not
used to them.
"I cannot go in these," he said to Saul,
"because I am not used to them." So he
took them off. 40Then he took his staff in
his hand, chose five smooth stones from
the stream, put them in the pouch of his

17:37 *the lion.* Probably of the Asiatic variety (*Panthera leo persica*), which closely resembles the African lion, but is now virtually extinct—there are less than 300 still in the wild in the Gir Forest of northwestern India and 200 or so in zoos worldwide. The last sure evidence of a lion in Palestine was one killed in the thirteenth century AD. See note on Jdg 14:5. *the bear.* A brown bear, probably of the subspecies *Ursus arctos syriacus*, a somewhat smaller and paler relative of the well-known grizzly bear (*Ursus arctos horribilis*). These paler-than-normal brown bears can still be found in parts of the Middle East, but they disappeared from the area around Israel in the first half of the twentieth century AD. Preferring fruits and wild forage, bears would likely have menaced livestock mostly in winter months when such vegetarian fare was scarce. Despite their seemingly gentler eating habits, bears may have been even more feared than lions because of their greater strength and more erratic behavior. Tangible evidence of lions and bears—in the form of their remains—has been unearthed by archaeologists excavating Iron Age levels in Palestine (the period of the settlement and monarchy).

17:40 *sling.* In Israel, slings were used mainly by shepherds to ward off marauding animals, but they were used in Egypt and Assyria as weapons of war. These slings consisted of a patch of leather or cloth, with leather straps or rope cords tied to opposite ends. Holding the ends of the cords firmly in his hand, the warrior would swing the loaded sling around above his head and then, when it had reached maximum speed, release one of the cords. The sling stones could reach speeds of 100–150 miles per hour (160–240 kilometers per hour). The stones used by the Assyrians at Lachish in the eighth century BC were two and a half to three inches (six to seven and a half centimeters) in diameter and weighed about nine ounces (250 grams). Slings were affordable but effective weapons that were used, e.g., by shepherds to drive off predators.

1 SAMUEL 17

Combat by Champions

The contest joined between the "champion" Goliath and David is perhaps the best known example from antiquity of a military conflict decided by "single combat," namely, a fight between representatives of the warring factions intended to get an initial indication of how the general battle would go. The logic behind such contests was grounded in the belief that battles were ultimately decided by God or the gods, and that the champion representing the more powerful deity would triumph. The premise that the people of the loser would serve the people of the winner did not suggest that the general battle would not be fought; it just gave an assessment of the expected outcome. A superior champion would serve as a ready instrument for the god, but the gods were not constrained to the relative skills and strength of the combatants. In a match as lopsided as this, a victory by David would serve as incontrovertible evidence of the superiority of Yahweh.

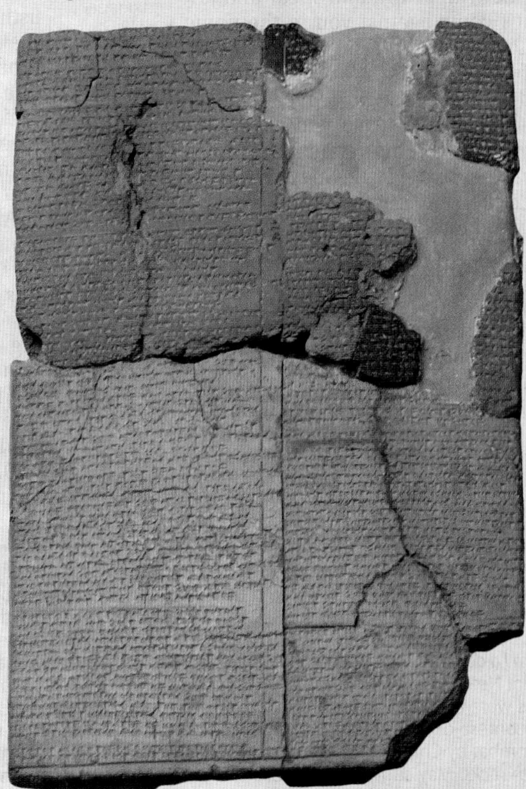

Hittite Apology of Hattushili, c. 1267 – 1237 BC. The story of Hattushili personally defeating his enemy is a strong parallel to the story of David and Goliath.

Kim Walton. The Istanbul Archaeological Museums, Turkey.

Other examples of similar situations from ancient sources are well-known, such as those in Homer's *Iliad* (Paris versus Menelaus, Hector versus Ajax) and the Egyptian *Story of Sinuhe*, in which Sinuhe defeats a Syrian challenger. Sinuhe uses an arrow in place of David's sling, but, like David, he then uses his opponent's own sword to complete the victory. While certain similarities with the story of David's triumph over Goliath are striking, it is important to distinguish between duels settling personal grievances and representative combat. A good example of the latter is found in an account by Hattushili III, who defeated the champion of the enemy with the result that the rest of the army fled. We can therefore see that David's confrontation with Goliath illustrates a practice that was familiar in the ancient world. By any account, it should have been Saul, who had been chosen to lead the armies, who represented the Israelites in battle. ◆

shepherd's bag and, with his sling in his
hand, approached the Philistine.
41 Meanwhile, the Philistine, with his
shield bearer in front of him, kept coming
closer to David. 42 He looked David over
and saw that he was little more than a
boy, glowing with health and handsome,[e]
and he despised[f] him. 43 He said to David,
"Am I a dog,[g] that you come at me with
sticks?" And the Philistine cursed David
by his gods. 44 "Come here," he said, "and
I'll give your flesh to the birds and the
wild animals![h]"
45 David said to the Philistine, "You come
against me with sword and spear and javelin, but I come against you in the name[i]
of the LORD Almighty, the God of the armies of Israel, whom you have defied.[j]
46 This day the LORD will deliver you into
my hands, and I'll strike you down and
cut off your head. This very day I will give
the carcasses[k] of the Philistine army to the
birds and the wild animals, and the whole
world[l] will know that there is a God in Israel.[m] 47 All those gathered here will know
that it is not by sword[n] or spear that the
LORD saves;[o] for the battle[p] is the LORD's,
and he will give all of you into our hands."
48 As the Philistine moved closer to attack him, David ran quickly toward the
battle line to meet him. 49 Reaching into
his bag and taking out a stone, he slung it
and struck the Philistine on the forehead.
The stone sank into his forehead, and he
fell facedown on the ground.
50 So David triumphed over the Philistine
with a sling[q] and a stone; without a sword
in his hand he struck down the Philistine
and killed him.
51 David ran and stood over him. He took
hold of the Philistine's sword and drew it
from the sheath. After he killed him, he
cut[r] off his head with the sword.[s]
When the Philistines saw that their hero
was dead, they turned and ran. 52 Then the
men of Israel and Judah surged forward
with a shout and pursued the Philistines
to the entrance of Gath[a] and to the gates of
Ekron.[t] Their dead were strewn along the
Shaaraim[u] road to Gath and Ekron. 53 When
the Israelites returned from chasing the Philistines, they plundered their camp.
54 David took the Philistine's head and
brought it to Jerusalem; he put the Philistine's weapons in his own tent.
55 As Saul watched David[v] going out to
meet the Philistine, he said to Abner, commander of the army, "Abner, whose son is
that young man?"
Abner replied, "As surely as you live,
Your Majesty, I don't know."
56 The king said, "Find out whose son
this young man is."
57 As soon as David returned from killing the Philistine, Abner took him and
brought him before Saul, with David still
holding the Philistine's head.
58 "Whose son are you, young man?"
Saul asked him.
David said, "I am the son of your servant Jesse[w] of Bethlehem."

17:42 [e] 1Sa 16:12 [f] Ps 123:3-4; Pr 16:18 **17:43** [g] 1Sa 24:14; 2Sa 3:8; 9:8; 2Ki 8:13 **17:44** [h] 1Ki 20:10-11 **17:45** [i] 2Sa 22:33, 35; 2Ch 32:8; Ps 124:8; Heb 11:32-34 [j] ver 10 **17:46** [k] Dt 28:26 [l] Jos 4:24; 1Ki 8:43; Isa 52:10 [m] 1Ki 18:36; 2Ki 19:19; Isa 37:20 **17:47** [n] Hos 1:7; Zec 4:6 [o] 1Sa 14:6; 2Ch 14:11 [p] 2Ch 20:15; Ps 44:6-7 **17:50** [q] 2Sa 23:21 **17:51** [r] Heb 11:34 [s] 1Sa 21:9 **17:52** [t] Jos 15:11 [u] Jos 15:36 **17:55** [v] 1Sa 16:21 **17:58** [w] ver 12

[a] *52* Some Septuagint manuscripts; Hebrew *of a valley*

David's background as a shepherd would have afforded him opportunity to develop considerable skill in the use of a sling.

17:43 *Am I a dog . . . ?* Dogs were not highly esteemed in the ancient Near East (see note on 24:14). Goliath's taunting words were typical in prebattle situations, especially when a contest of champions was involved (see the article "Combat by Champions," p. 491; cf. 2Sa 2:14). *come at me with sticks.* May suggest that Goliath did not see David's sling, which he would certainly have known to be a dangerous weapon in skilled hands (see note on v. 40). Among the ailments that often attend giantism is poor eyesight, often a kind of tunnel vision. The shepherd's simple sling hanging limp in his hand may have appeared to Goliath as no more than a stick, though we know from v. 40 that David had both a staff and a sling in his hands.

17:49 *struck the Philistine on the forehead.* Not enough specifics are known about the type of helmet Goliath wore to determine what size area was vulnerable to David's sling stone. We cannot even judge by typical Philistine headgear, because we don't know whether Goliath's armor was typical. A sling can be wielded with great accuracy and Goliath's choice of armor and weapons kept him stationary, making him an easier target. It is difficult to decide between these two interpretations, but the result in either case was that Goliath was toppled and quickly dispatched by David, using Goliath's own sword (v. 51). The text does not clarify whether the sling stone or the sword actually ended Goliath's life. The language would allow that the stone stunned Goliath and that he was then killed by decapitation, but it is also possible that he was already dead and David cut his head off to use for the typical display.

17:51 *he cut off his head.* Decapitation of enemy dead was a common practice in the ancient Near East and a recurrent motif in 1 Samuel (see notes on 5:3–4; 31:4,9; cf. note on 2Sa 4:12). Sometimes, as here, the enemy's own weapon was used to do the deed. Having bested his opponent with an arrow in his neck, the Egyptian hero Sinuhe boasts: "He cried out and fell on his nose. I felled him with his (own) battle-axe and raised my cry of victory over his back, while every Asiatic roared." Cf. also Benaiah's killing of a "huge Egyptian" with the Egyptian's own sword (2Sa 23:21).

17:55 *whose son . . . ?* See also v. 58. As a musician for Saul (16:14–23; 18:10; 19:9), David may have been one of many adjutants who served Saul and to whom he paid little attention. Though he would have known David's name and family at one point, that information may not have been retained. Here it is important for him to know from which family David has come, because benefits have been offered to that family (v. 25). Furthermore, Samuel has already announced to Saul that a replacement has been chosen (15:26–28), so Saul would suddenly be very interested in this potential challenger whose deed would make him immediately popular.

Saul's Growing Fear of David

18 After David had finished talking with Saul, Jonathan became one in spirit with David, and he loved[x] him as himself.[y] 2From that day Saul kept David with him and did not let him return home to his family. 3And Jonathan made a covenant[z] with David because he loved him as himself. 4Jonathan took off the robe[a] he was wearing and gave it to David, along with his tunic, and even his sword, his bow and his belt.

5Whatever mission Saul sent him on, David was so successful that Saul gave him a high rank in the army. This pleased all the troops, and Saul's officers as well.

6When the men were returning home after David had killed the Philistine, the women came out from all the towns of Israel to meet King Saul with singing and dancing,[b] with joyful songs and with timbrels[c] and lyres. 7As they danced, they sang:[d]

"Saul has slain his thousands,
and David his tens[e] of thousands."

8Saul was very angry; this refrain displeased him greatly. "They have credited David with tens of thousands," he thought, "but me with only thousands. What more can he get but the kingdom?[f]" 9And from that time on Saul kept a close eye on David.

10The next day an evil[a] spirit[g] from God came forcefully on Saul. He was prophesying in his house, while David was playing the lyre, as he usually[h] did. Saul had a spear in his hand 11and he hurled it, saying to himself,[i] "I'll pin David to the wall." But David eluded[j] him twice.

12Saul was afraid[k] of David, because the LORD[l] was with[m] David but had departed from Saul. 13So he sent David away from him and gave him command over a thousand men, and David led[n] the troops in their campaigns.[o] 14In everything he did he had great success,[p] because the LORD was with[q] him. 15When Saul saw how successful he was, he was afraid of him. 16But all Israel and Judah loved David, because he led them in their campaigns.[r]

17Saul said to David, "Here is my older daughter[s] Merab. I will give her to you in marriage; only serve me bravely and fight the battles[t] of the LORD." For Saul said to himself,[u] "I will not raise a hand against him. Let the Philistines do that!"

18But David said to Saul, "Who am I,[v] and what is my family or my clan in Israel, that I should become the king's son-in-law?[w]" 19So[b] when the time came for Merab,[x] Saul's daughter, to be given to David, she was given in marriage to Adriel of Meholah.[y]

20Now Saul's daughter Michal[z] was in love with David, and when they told Saul about it, he was pleased. 21"I will give her to him," he thought, "so that she may be a snare[a] to him and so that the hand of the Philistines may be against him." So Saul said to David, "Now you have a second opportunity to become my son-in-law."

22Then Saul ordered his attendants: "Speak to David privately and say, 'Look, the king likes you, and his attendants all love you; now become his son-in-law.'"

23They repeated these words to David. But David said, "Do you think it is a small matter to become the king's son-in-law? I'm only a poor man and little known."

24When Saul's servants told him what

18:1 [x] 2Sa 1:26 [y] Ge 44:30 **18:3** [z] 1Sa 20:8, 16, 17, 42 **18:4** [a] Ge 41:42 **18:6** [b] Ex 15:20 [c] Jdg 11:34; Ps 68:25 **18:7** [d] Ex 15:21 [e] 1Sa 21:11; 29:5 **18:8** [f] 1Sa 15:8 **18:10** [g] 1Sa 16:14 [h] 1Sa 19:7 **18:11** [i] 1Sa 20:7, 33 [j] 1Sa 19:10 **18:12** [k] ver 15, 29 [l] 1Sa 16:13 [m] 1Sa 28:15 **18:13** [n] ver 16; Nu 27:17 [o] 2Sa 5:2 **18:14** [p] Ge 39:3 [q] Ge 39:2, 23; Jos 6:27; 1Sa 16:18 **18:16** [r] ver 5 **18:17** [s] 1Sa 17:25 [t] Nu 21:14; 1Sa 25:28 [u] ver 25 **18:18** [v] 1Sa 9:21; 2Sa 7:18 [w] ver 23 **18:19** [x] 2Sa 21:8 [y] Jdg 7:22 **18:20** [z] ver 28 **18:21** [a] ver 17, 26

[a] 10 Or *a harmful* [b] 19 Or *However,*

18:3–4 *Jonathan made a covenant with David … Jonathan took off the robe he was wearing and gave it to David.* In the light of Jonathan's later references to David's ascendancy (20:14–15; 23:17), the act here seems to symbolize a transference of the right to the throne to David. Jonathan's action may perhaps be likened to symbolic acts performed by the prophets, but it almost certainly also had legal significance. Texts from Ugarit and Emar, e.g., illustrate the symbolic significance of mantles (robes) in matters relating to inheritance or even royal succession. Two texts describe how "a son who refuses to obey his father is forced to leave the house and deposit his mantle on the stool or the door-bolt." The implication is that the son no longer holds legal status as a member of the family. Another addresses a situation in which a prince must choose whether to stay with his father, Ammistamru, king of Ugarit, or follow his divorced mother. Should he choose to follow his mother, he must leave his mantle on the throne and depart, with the implication that he has relinquished his legal status as prince. These and other extra-Biblical examples do not fully match Jonathan's action, as they mention only the relinquishment of the mantle, not its transference to another, but the general point seems clear. A special robe or mantle could serve as a symbol of a person's identity and status, so that to transfer it to another signified a transfer of status. In this instance (as in the later instances mentioned above), Jonathan acknowledges David's right to the throne.

18:6 *singing and dancing … timbrels and lyres.* Judging from both the (Biblical) textual evidence and artifactual evidence unearthed by archaeologists, we may fairly conclude that dancing, often accompanied by music, was a common feature in religious and secular celebrations in tenth-century BC Israel, as well as in other periods. Indeed, dancing seems to have been an integral part of ritual ceremonies among Israel's neighbors as well, in Philistia, Phoenicia, etc. Representations of dancers and musicians are found throughout the ancient Near East. The Biblical writers employ a dozen different verbal roots to designate dancing but do not describe the dances in any detail. For more on dancing in ancient Israel, see note on 2Sa 6:14.

18:16 *all Israel and Judah loved David.* On "love" as political loyalty and service, see notes on 2Sa 1:26; 19:6.

David had said, 25 Saul replied, "Say to David, 'The king wants no other price[b] for
the bride than a hundred Philistine foreskins, to take revenge on his enemies.'"
Saul's plan[c] was to have David fall by the
hands of the Philistines.
26 When the attendants told David these
things, he was pleased to become the
king's son-in-law. So before the allotted
time elapsed, 27 David took his men with
him and went out and killed two hundred
Philistines and brought back their foreskins. They counted out the full number
to the king so that David might become
the king's son-in-law. Then Saul gave him
his daughter Michal[d] in marriage.
28 When Saul realized that the LORD was
with David and that his daughter Michal
loved David, 29 Saul became still more
afraid of him, and he remained his enemy
the rest of his days.
30 The Philistine commanders continued
to go out to battle, and as often as they
did, David met with more success[e] than
the rest of Saul's officers, and his name
became well known.

Saul Tries to Kill David

19 Saul told his son Jonathan[f] and all
the attendants to kill[g] David. But
Jonathan had taken a great liking to David
2 and warned him, "My father Saul is looking for a chance to kill you. Be on your
guard tomorrow morning; go into hiding
and stay there. 3 I will go out and stand
with my father in the field where you are.
I'll speak[h] to him about you and will tell
you what I find out."
4 Jonathan spoke[i] well of David to Saul
his father and said to him, "Let not the
king do wrong[j] to his servant David; he
has not wronged you, and what he has
done has benefited you greatly. 5 He took
his life in his hands when he killed the
Philistine. The LORD won a great victory[k] for all Israel, and you saw it and were
glad. Why then would you do wrong to an
innocent[l] man like David by killing him
for no reason?"

6 Saul listened to Jonathan and took this
oath: "As surely as the LORD lives, David
will not be put to death."
7 So Jonathan called David and told him
the whole conversation. He brought him to
Saul, and David was with Saul as before.[m]
8 Once more war broke out, and David
went out and fought the Philistines. He
struck them with such force that they fled
before him.
9 But an evil[a] spirit[n] from the LORD came
on Saul as he was sitting in his house with
his spear in his hand. While David was
playing the lyre, 10 Saul tried to pin him to
the wall with his spear, but David eluded[o]
him as Saul drove the spear into the wall.
That night David made good his escape.
11 Saul sent men to David's house to
watch[p] it and to kill him in the morning.
But Michal, David's wife, warned him, "If
you don't run for your life tonight, tomorrow you'll be killed." 12 So Michal let David down through a window,[q] and he fled
and escaped. 13 Then Michal took an idol
and laid it on the bed, covering it with a
garment and putting some goats' hair at
the head.
14 When Saul sent the men to capture
David, Michal said,[r] "He is ill."
15 Then Saul sent the men back to see
David and told them, "Bring him up to me
in his bed so that I may kill him." 16 But
when the men entered, there was the idol
in the bed, and at the head was some
goats' hair.
17 Saul said to Michal, "Why did you
deceive me like this and send my enemy
away so that he escaped?"
Michal told him, "He said to me, 'Let
me get away. Why should I kill you?'"
18 When David had fled and made his
escape, he went to Samuel at Ramah[s] and
told him all that Saul had done to him.
Then he and Samuel went to Naioth and
stayed there. 19 Word came to Saul: "David is in Naioth at Ramah"; 20 so he sent
men to capture him. But when they saw a

[a] 9 Or *But a harmful*

18:25 [b] Ge 34:12; Ex 22:17; 1Sa 14:24 [c] ver 17
18:27 [d] ver 13; 2Sa 3:14
18:30 [e] ver 5; 2Sa 11:1
19:1 [f] 1Sa 18:1 [g] 1Sa 18:9
19:3 [h] 1Sa 20:12
19:4 [i] 1Sa 20:32; Pr 31:8, 9; Jer 18:20 [j] Ge 42:22; Pr 17:13
19:5 [k] 1Sa 11:13; 17:49-50; 1Ch 11:14 [l] Dt 19:10-13; 1Sa 20:32; Mt 27:4
19:7 [m] 1Sa 16:21; 18:2, 13
19:9 [n] 1Sa 16:14; 18:10-11
19:10 [o] 1Sa 18:11
19:11 [p] Ps 59 Title
19:12 [q] Jos 2:15; Ac 9:25
19:14 [r] Jos 2:4
19:18 [s] 1Sa 7:17

18:25 *price for the bride.* Kings in the ancient world made alliances by marriage. Such alliances could be with international allies, wealthy countrymen, politically powerful families or with families of those that had significant benefits to offer the monarch (e.g., wisdom of an advisor or prowess of a military champion). Payment of a bride-price was common enough in the OT world, as it is still in some cultures today. It was the prerogative of the bride's father to set the price, and Saul set it dangerously high at 100 Philistine foreskins. Body parts (heads, hands, etc.) often served as trophies of war, and Saul's unusual choice was designed to assure that David actually killed Philistines—others among Israel's neighbors would likely have been circumcised (see note on Jdg 14:3). Merneptah's Great Libyan War Inscription from Karnak repeatedly mentions that the "phalli with foreskins" were being collected from slain enemies. David met Saul's challenge twice over, presenting 200 foreskins (1Sa 18:27). This success was viewed by Saul as evidence that Yahweh was with David (v. 28), and his fear of him grew into full-blown enmity (v. 29).

19:13 *Michal took an idol and laid it on the bed.* See the article "Household Gods," p. 72. While Rachel was able to conceal *teraphim* from Laban's household in the camel's saddle upon which she was sitting (Ge 31:34–35), Michal's *teraphim* was apparently large enough to simulate a reclining David.

19:20 *a group of prophets prophesying.* See note on 3:1

group of prophets[t] prophesying, with Samuel standing there as their leader, the Spirit of God came on[u] Saul's men, and they also prophesied.[v] 21Saul was told about it, and he sent more men, and they prophesied too. Saul sent men a third time, and they also prophesied. 22Finally, he himself left for Ramah and went to the great cistern at Seku. And he asked, "Where are Samuel and David?"

"Over in Naioth at Ramah," they said.

23So Saul went to Naioth at Ramah. But the Spirit of God came even on him, and he walked along prophesying[w] until he came to Naioth. 24He stripped[x] off his garments, and he too prophesied in Samuel's presence. He lay naked all that day and all that night. This is why people say, "Is Saul also among the prophets?"[y]

David and Jonathan

20 Then David fled from Naioth at Ramah and went to Jonathan and asked, "What have I done? What is my crime? How have I wronged[z] your father, that he is trying to kill me?"

2"Never!" Jonathan replied. "You are not going to die! Look, my father doesn't do anything, great or small, without letting me know. Why would he hide this from me? It isn't so!"

3But David took an oath[a] and said, "Your father knows very well that I have found favor in your eyes, and he has said to himself, 'Jonathan must not know this or he will be grieved.' Yet as surely as the LORD lives and as you live, there is only a step between me and death."

4Jonathan said to David, "Whatever you want me to do, I'll do for you."

5So David said, "Look, tomorrow is the New Moon feast,[b] and I am supposed to dine with the king; but let me go and hide[c] in the field until the evening of the day after tomorrow. 6If your father misses me at all, tell him, 'David earnestly asked my permission to hurry to Bethlehem,[d] his hometown, because an annual[e] sacrifice is being made there for his whole clan.' 7If he says, 'Very well,' then your servant is safe. But if he loses his temper,[f] you can be sure that he is determined to harm me. 8As for you, show kindness to your servant, for you have brought him into a covenant[g] with you before the LORD. If I am guilty, then kill[h] me yourself! Why hand me over to your father?"

9"Never!" Jonathan said. "If I had the least inkling that my father was determined to harm you, wouldn't I tell you?"

10David asked, "Who will tell me if your father answers you harshly?"

11"Come," Jonathan said, "let's go out into the field." So they went there together.

12Then Jonathan said to David, "I swear by the LORD, the God of Israel, that I will surely sound out my father by this time the day after tomorrow! If he is favorably disposed toward you, will I not send you word and let you know? 13But if my father intends to harm you, may the LORD deal with Jonathan, be it ever so severely,[i] if I do not let you know and send you away in peace. May the LORD be with[j] you as he has been with my father. 14But show me unfailing kindness like the LORD's kindness as long as I live, so that I may not be killed, 15and do not ever cut off your kindness from my family[k]—not even when the LORD has cut off every one of David's enemies from the face of the earth."

16So Jonathan made a covenant[l] with the house of David, saying, "May the LORD call David's enemies to account." 17And Jonathan had David reaffirm his oath[m] out of love for him, because he loved him as he loved himself.

18Then Jonathan said to David, "Tomorrow is the New Moon feast. You will be missed, because your seat will be empty.[n] 19The day after tomorrow, toward evening, go to the place where you hid[o] when this trouble began, and wait by the stone Ezel. 20I will shoot three arrows to the side of it, as though I were shooting at a target. 21Then I will send a boy and say, 'Go, find the arrows.' If I say to him, 'Look, the arrows are on this side of you; bring them here,' then come, because, as surely as the LORD lives, you are safe; there is no danger. 22But if I say to the boy, 'Look, the

19:20 [t] ver 11, 14; Jn 7:32, 45 [u] Nu 11:25 [v] 1Sa 10:5; Joel 2:28 **19:23** [w] 1Sa 10:13 **19:24** [x] 2Sa 6:20; Isa 20:2; Mic 1:8 [y] 1Sa 10:11 **20:1** [z] 1Sa 24:9 **20:3** [a] Dt 6:13 **20:5** [b] Nu 10:10; 28:11 [c] 1Sa 19:2 **20:6** [d] 1Sa 17:58 [e] Dt 12:5 **20:7** [f] 1Sa 25:17

20:8 [g] 1Sa 18:3; 23:18 [h] 2Sa 14:32 **20:13** [i] Ru 1:17; 1Sa 3:17 [j] Jos 1:5; 1Sa 17:37; 18:12; 1Ch 22:11, 16 **20:15** [k] 2Sa 9:7 **20:16** [l] 1Sa 25:22 **20:17** [m] 1Sa 18:3 **20:18** [n] ver 5, 25 **20:19** [o] 1Sa 19:2

19:24 *He stripped off his garments.* Both in the Bible and the ancient Near East more broadly, special garments often served to mark a person's identity, status or rank (see note on 18:3–4). Saul's (involuntary) divestment of his royal robes in the present context serves as yet another reminder that, in Yahweh's eyes, he is no longer rightful king (cf. 15:28).

20:5 *tomorrow is the New Moon feast.* The Mesopotamian calendar included various festivals, or special days. Many were celebrated on certain days of the month, the seventh day, the fifteenth or the beginning of the month (the new moon). In Israel too the New Moon feast was a time of rejoicing. Marked by special sacrifices (Nu 28:11–15), the sounding of trumpets (Nu 10:10; cf. Ps 81:3), etc., the feast was often mentioned in conjunction with the most regular of special days, the Sabbath (2Ki 4:23), and it may have been subject to similar regulations (Am 8:5). Judging from the prominence of the king in ancient Near Eastern festival celebrations and from Biblical passages such as Eze 45:17, David's absence from Saul's table may have had political repercussions. Observance of the New Moon feast continued into the postexilic period (Ne 10:33), and it is mentioned once in the NT (Col 2:16).

arrows are beyond[p] you,' then you must
go, because the LORD has sent you away.
23 And about the matter you and I discussed — remember, the LORD is witness[q]
between you and me forever."
24 So David hid in the field, and when
the New Moon feast came, the king sat
down to eat. 25 He sat in his customary
place by the wall, opposite Jonathan,[a] and
Abner sat next to Saul, but David's place
was empty.[r] 26 Saul said nothing that day,
for he thought, "Something must have
happened to David to make him ceremonially unclean — surely he is unclean.[s]"
27 But the next day, the second day of the
month, David's place was empty again.
Then Saul said to his son Jonathan, "Why
hasn't the son of Jesse come to the meal,
either yesterday or today?"
28 Jonathan answered, "David earnestly
asked me for permission[t] to go to Bethlehem. 29 He said, 'Let me go, because
our family is observing a sacrifice in the
town and my brother has ordered me to be
there. If I have found favor in your eyes,
let me get away to see my brothers.' That
is why he has not come to the king's table."
30 Saul's anger flared up at Jonathan and
he said to him, "You son of a perverse and
rebellious woman! Don't I know that you
have sided with the son of Jesse to your
own shame and to the shame of the mother who bore you? 31 As long as the son of
Jesse lives on this earth, neither you nor
your kingdom will be established. Now
send someone to bring him to me, for he
must die!"
32 "Why[u] should he be put to death?
What[v] has he done?" Jonathan asked his
father. 33 But Saul hurled his spear at him
to kill him. Then Jonathan knew that his
father intended[w] to kill David.
34 Jonathan got up from the table in
fierce anger; on that second day of the
feast he did not eat, because he was
grieved at his father's shameful treatment
of David.

20:22 [p] ver 37 **20:23** [q] ver 14-15; Ge 31:50 **20:25** [r] ver 18 **20:26** [s] Lev 7:20-21; 15:5; 1Sa 16:5 **20:28** [t] ver 6

20:32 [u] 1Sa 19:4; Mt 27:23 [v] Ge 31:36; Lk 23:22 **20:33** [w] ver 7; 1Sa 18:11, 17

[a] 25 Septuagint; Hebrew *wall. Jonathan arose*

20:26 *ceremonially unclean.* The issue is not so much one of physical purity as of ritual purity, though the boundary between these two was vague, if present at all, in the ancient Near East (see note on Lev 21:1; see also the article "Consecration," p. 165.)

DAVID THE FUGITIVE

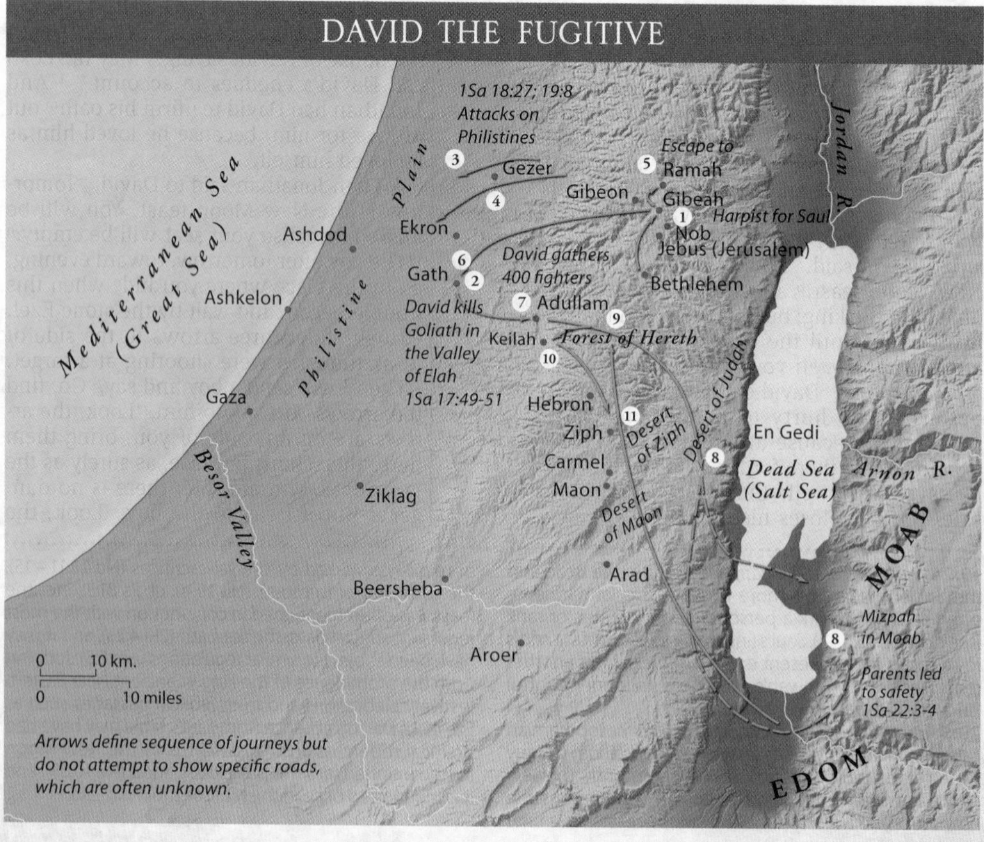

35 In the morning Jonathan went out to
the field for his meeting with David. He
had a small boy with him, 36 and he said to
the boy, "Run and find the arrows I shoot."
As the boy ran, he shot an arrow beyond
him. 37 When the boy came to the place
where Jonathan's arrow had fallen, Jonathan called out after him, "Isn't the arrow
beyond[x] you?" 38 Then he shouted, "Hurry!
Go quickly! Don't stop!" The boy picked
up the arrow and returned to his master.
39 (The boy knew nothing about all this;
only Jonathan and David knew.) 40 Then
Jonathan gave his weapons to the boy and
said, "Go, carry them back to town."
41 After the boy had gone, David got
up from the south side of the stone and
bowed down before Jonathan three times,
with his face to the ground. Then they
kissed each other and wept together — but
David wept the most.
42 Jonathan said to David, "Go in peace,[y]
for we have sworn friendship[z] with each
other in the name of the LORD, saying,
'The LORD is witness between you and me,
and between your descendants and my descendants forever.' " Then David left, and
Jonathan went back to the town.[a]

David at Nob

21 [b] David went to Nob,[a] to Ahimelek
the priest. Ahimelek trembled[b]
when he met him, and asked, "Why are
you alone? Why is no one with you?"
2 David answered Ahimelek the priest,
"The king sent me on a mission and said
to me, 'No one is to know anything about
the mission I am sending you on.' As for
my men, I have told them to meet me at
a certain place. 3 Now then, what do you
have on hand? Give me five loaves of
bread, or whatever you can find."
4 But the priest answered David, "I don't
have any ordinary bread[c] on hand; however, there is some consecrated[d] bread
here — provided the men have kept[e] themselves from women."
5 David replied, "Indeed women have
been kept from us, as usual whenever[c] I
set out. The men's bodies are holy[f] even
on missions that are not holy. How much
more so today!" 6 So the priest gave him
the consecrated bread,[g] since there was no
bread there except the bread of the Presence that had been removed from before
the LORD and replaced by hot bread on the
day it was taken away.
7 Now one of Saul's servants was there
that day, detained before the LORD; he was
Doeg[h] the Edomite,[i] Saul's chief shepherd.
8 David asked Ahimelek, "Don't you
have a spear or a sword here? I haven't
brought my sword or any other weapon,
because the king's mission was urgent."
9 The priest replied, "The sword[j] of Goliath the Philistine, whom you killed in
the Valley of Elah,[k] is here; it is wrapped
in a cloth behind the ephod. If you want
it, take it; there is no sword here but that
one."
David said, "There is none like it; give
it to me."

David at Gath

10 That day David fled from Saul and
went[l] to Achish king of Gath. 11 But the
servants of Achish said to him, "Isn't this
David, the king of the land? Isn't he the
one they sing about in their dances:

" 'Saul has slain his thousands,
and David his tens of thousands'?"[m]

12 David took these words to heart and
was very much afraid of Achish king of
Gath. 13 So he pretended to be insane[n] in

20:37 [x] ver 22 **20:42** [y] ver 22; 1Sa 1:17 [z] 2Sa 1:26; Pr 18:24 **21:1** [a] 1Sa 14:3; 22:9, 19; Ne 11:32; Isa 10:32 [b] 1Sa 16:4 **21:4** [c] Lev 24:8-9 [d] Ex 25:30; Mt 12:4 [e] Ex 19:15 **21:5** [f] 1Th 4:4 **21:6** [g] Lev 24:8-9; Mt 12:3-4; Mk 2:25-28; Lk 6:1-5 **21:7** [h] 1Sa 22:9, 22 [i] 1Sa 14:47; Ps 52 Title **21:9** [j] 1Sa 17:51 [k] 1Sa 17:2 **21:10** [l] 1Sa 27:2 **21:11** [m] 1Sa 18:7; 29:5; Ps 56 Title **21:13** [n] Ps 34 Title

[a] *42* In Hebrew texts this sentence (20:42b) is numbered 21:1. [b] In Hebrew texts 21:1-15 is numbered 21:2-16. [c] *5* Or *from us in the past few days since*

20:41 *they kissed each other.* See note on 2Sa 20:9. Here, Jonathan and David, in the face of the dire situation they face, kiss one another as an expression of their friendship and the covenant existing between them. The Gilgamesh Epic speaks of a similar exchange between the hero Gilgamesh, apparently about to embark on a dangerous venture, and Enkidu, who has failed to dissuade him: "They kissed each other and formed a friendship." No evidence would suggest that this is any more than the greeting of friends. The gods kiss one another in greeting in the Babylonian creation epic (*Enuma Elish* III.132).
21:4 *there is some consecrated bread here — provided the men have kept themselves from women.* Consecration, or purification, of soldiers prior to battle was a common practice in the ancient Near East, as in the OT (see note on Jos 3:5). Ritual purity would be all the more required before handling "consecrated bread," usually reserved for the priests. Uncleanness could be brought about in various ways (see note on 20:26). Sexual intercourse could lead to a state of ritual uncleanness (see Lev 15:18 and note on Lev 15:16), and abstention was often ordered for a period prior to an auspicious occasion (Ex 19:15). Fear of contaminating the camp may have played some part in Uriah's refusal to visit his wife Bathsheba (2Sa 11:11 – 12).
21:7 *Doeg the Edomite.* Doeg is probably a mercenary employed by Saul, probably as a messenger or spy. *chief shepherd.* A common administrative title.
21:9 *ephod.* All three senses of the term "ephod" (see note on 2:18) have in common that they designate a sacred garment of some sort. In the ancient Near East, ornate vestments not only were worn by high officials but also sometimes adorned the statues of deities. In the present context, with the ark unavailable (6:21 — 7:2a), the ephod at Nob may have been the holiest relic of the sanctuary, lending plausibility to the notion that captured trophies such as Goliath's sword would have been placed near it, as the ark had earlier been placed in the temple of Dagon (5:2).
21:13 *pretended to be insane.* Presumably, David went to

their presence; and while he was in their
hands he acted like a madman, making
marks on the doors of the gate and letting
saliva run down his beard.
14Achish said to his servants, "Look at
the man! He is insane! Why bring him to
me? 15Am I so short of madmen that you
have to bring this fellow here to carry on
like this in front of me? Must this man
come into my house?"

David at Adullam and Mizpah

22 David left Gath and escaped to the
cave[o] of Adullam. When his brothers and his father's household heard about
it, they went down to him there. 2All those
who were in distress or in debt or discontented gathered[p] around him, and he became their commander. About four hundred men were with him.
3From there David went to Mizpah in
Moab and said to the king of Moab, "Would
you let my father and mother come and
stay with you until I learn what God will
do for me?" 4So he left them with the king
of Moab, and they stayed with him as long
as David was in the stronghold.
5But the prophet Gad[q] said to David,
"Do not stay in the stronghold. Go into
the land of Judah." So David left and went
to the forest of Hereth.

Saul Kills the Priests of Nob

6Now Saul heard that David and his
men had been discovered. And Saul was
seated,[r] spear in hand, under the tamarisk[s]
tree on the hill at Gibeah, with all his officials standing at his side. 7He said to them,
"Listen, men of Benjamin! Will the son of
Jesse give all of you fields and vineyards?
Will he make all of you commanders[t] of
thousands and commanders of hundreds?
8Is that why you have all conspired against
me? No one tells me when my son makes
a covenant[u] with the son of Jesse. None
of you is concerned[v] about me or tells me
that my son has incited my servant to lie
in wait for me, as he does today."
9But Doeg[w] the Edomite, who was
standing with Saul's officials, said, "I saw
the son of Jesse come to Ahimelek son of
Ahitub at Nob.[x] 10Ahimelek inquired[y] of
the LORD for him; he also gave him provisions[z] and the sword of Goliath the Philistine."
11Then the king sent for the priest Ahimelek son of Ahitub and all the men of his
family, who were the priests at Nob, and
they all came to the king. 12Saul said, "Listen now, son of Ahitub."
"Yes, my lord," he answered.
13Saul said to him, "Why have you conspired[a] against me, you and the son of
Jesse, giving him bread and a sword and
inquiring of God for him, so that he has rebelled against me and lies in wait for me,
as he does today?"
14Ahimelek answered the king, "Who[b]
of all your servants is as loyal as David,
the king's son-in-law, captain of your
bodyguard and highly respected in your
household? 15Was that day the first time I
inquired of God for him? Of course not! Let
not the king accuse your servant or any of
his father's family, for your servant knows
nothing at all about this whole affair."
16But the king said, "You will surely die,
Ahimelek, you and your whole family."
17Then the king ordered the guards at
his side: "Turn and kill the priests of the
LORD, because they too have sided with
David. They knew he was fleeing, yet they
did not tell me."
But the king's officials were unwilling[c]

22:1 [o] 2Sa 23:13; Ps 57 Title; 142 Title **22:2** [p] 1Sa 23:13; 25:13; 2Sa 15:20 **22:5** [q] 2Sa 24:11; 1Ch 21:9; 29:29; 2Ch 29:25 **22:6** [r] Jdg 4:5 [s] Ge 21:33 **22:7** [t] 1Sa 8:14 **22:8** [u] 1Sa 18:3; 20:16 [v] 1Sa 23:21 **22:9** [w] 1Sa 21:7; Ps 52 Title [x] 1Sa 21:1 **22:10** [y] Nu 27:21; 1Sa 10:22 [z] 1Sa 21:6 **22:13** [a] ver 8 **22:14** [b] 1Sa 19:4 **22:17** [c] Ex 1:17

Gath to offer his services as a mercenary. Theoretically the Philistines would have welcomed a military hero with motive to help depose their enemy, Saul. Instead, they remember David's celebrated status as a killer of Philistines and distrust him. David's feigned madness serves two purposes. First, the only reason they think he is the famous David is that he said he was; if he is insane, what he says has no significance. Second, madness is a divine affliction, similar to the ecstatic state experienced by the prophets. Because the prophet is possessed by a god, he must be allowed to live, but he is also not kept around. David is counting on both of these: being left alive and being turned out of (allowed to leave) the city.

22:2 *those who were in distress or in debt or discontented gathered around him.* Shifting alliances were characteristic of the ancient Near East, as is illustrated, e.g., by the behaviors of the marginalized Habiru/Apiru in the second millennium BC (see note on 4:6). The judge Jephthah, during his own period of marginalization, was joined by a gang of "scoundrels" (see Jdg 11:3 and note; NRSV, "outlaws"; JPS, "men of low character"). To David was drawn a motley band of marginal people who were suffering in various ways, they had suffered some great loss, were economically deprived, homeless, etc., and as a result they were eager for change. David's attraction to these disfranchised people was far more than a partisan attraction similar to southerners against northerners.

22:3 *David went to Mizpah in Moab.* David's reception by the Moabite king may be related to David's Moabite ancestry through Ruth (Ru 4:13–17). The Bible offers several examples of individuals seeking refuge in foreign territories (e.g., Jacob, Joseph, Moses, Absalom). An interesting ancient Near Eastern example is the tale of King Idrimi of Aleppo, who was forced to flee his native land, find refuge among his mother's kin, and eventually take up with the Habiru/Apiru in northern Canaan for seven years, before returning to become king of Alalakh in northwestern Syria.

22:7 *give all of you fields and vineyards.* The practice of both rewarding and encouraging loyalty to the king by royal grants of land, houses, vineyards, wells, etc. was widespread in the ancient Near East. Royal rewards and incentives are evidenced, e.g., in Babylonian, Assyrian, Hittite and Ugaritic documents.

to raise a hand to strike the priests of the
LORD.
18The king then ordered Doeg, "You
turn and strike down the priests." So
Doeg the Edomite turned and struck them
down. That day he killed eighty-five men
who wore the linen ephod.[d] 19He also put
to the sword[e] Nob, the town of the priests,
with its men and women, its children and
infants, and its cattle, donkeys and sheep.
20But one son of Ahimelek son of Ahitub, named Abiathar,[f] escaped and fled
to join David.[g] 21He told David that Saul
had killed the priests of the LORD. 22Then
David said to Abiathar, "That day, when
Doeg[h] the Edomite was there, I knew he
would be sure to tell Saul. I am responsible for the death of your whole family.
23Stay with me; don't be afraid. The man
who wants to kill you[i] is trying to kill me
too. You will be safe with me."

David Saves Keilah

23 When David was told, "Look, the
Philistines are fighting against Keilah[j] and are looting the threshing floors,"
2he inquired[k] of the LORD, saying, "Shall I
go and attack these Philistines?"
The LORD answered him, "Go, attack the
Philistines and save Keilah."
3But David's men said to him, "Here
in Judah we are afraid. How much more,
then, if we go to Keilah against the Philistine forces!"
4Once again David inquired of the LORD,
and the LORD answered him, "Go down to
Keilah, for I am going to give the Philistines into your hand.[l]" 5So David and his
men went to Keilah, fought the Philistines
and carried off their livestock. He inflicted
heavy losses on the Philistines and saved
the people of Keilah. 6(Now Abiathar[m] son
of Ahimelek had brought the ephod down
with him when he fled to David at Keilah.)

Saul Pursues David

7Saul was told that David had gone to
Keilah, and he said, "God has delivered
him into my hands, for David has imprisoned himself by entering a town with
gates and bars." 8And Saul called up all
his forces for battle, to go down to Keilah
to besiege David and his men.
9When David learned that Saul was
plotting against him, he said to Abiathar[n]
the priest, "Bring the ephod." 10David
said, "LORD, God of Israel, your servant
has heard definitely that Saul plans to
come to Keilah and destroy the town on
account of me. 11Will the citizens of Keilah surrender me to him? Will Saul come
down, as your servant has heard? LORD,
God of Israel, tell your servant."
And the LORD said, "He will."
12Again David asked, "Will the citizens
of Keilah surrender[o] me and my men to
Saul?"
And the LORD said, "They will."
13So David and his men,[p] about six hundred in number, left Keilah and kept moving from place to place. When Saul was
told that David had escaped from Keilah,
he did not go there.
14David stayed in the wilderness strongholds and in the hills of the Desert of
Ziph.[q] Day after day Saul searched[r] for
him, but God did not[s] give David into his
hands.
15While David was at Horesh in the
Desert of Ziph, he learned that[a] Saul had
come out to take his life. 16And Saul's son
Jonathan went to David at Horesh and
helped him find strength[t] in God. 17"Don't
be afraid," he said. "My father Saul will
not lay a hand on you. You will be king[u]
over Israel, and I will be second to you.
Even my father Saul knows this." 18The
two of them made a covenant[v] before the
LORD. Then Jonathan went home, but David remained at Horesh.
19The Ziphites[w] went up to Saul at Gibeah and said, "Is not David hiding among
us[x] in the strongholds at Horesh, on the
hill of Hakilah,[y] south of Jeshimon? 20Now,
Your Majesty, come down whenever it

22:18 [d] 1Sa 2:18,31 **22:19** [e] 1Sa 15:3 **22:20** [f] 1Sa 23:6, 9; 30:7; 1Ki 2:22,26,27 [g] 1Sa 2:32 **22:22** [h] 1Sa 21:7 **22:23** [i] 1Ki 2:26 **23:1** [j] Jos 15:44 **23:2** [k] ver 4, 12; 1Sa 30:8; 2Sa 5:19,23 **23:4** [l] Jos 8:7; Jdg 7:7 **23:6** [m] 1Sa 22:20

23:9 [n] ver 6; 1Sa 22:20; 30:7 **23:12** [o] ver 20 **23:13** [p] 1Sa 22:2; 25:13 **23:14** [q] Jos 15:24, 55 [r] Ps 54:3-4 [s] Ps 32:7 **23:16** [t] 1Sa 30:6 **23:17** [u] 1Sa 20:31; 24:20 **23:18** [v] 1Sa 18:3; 20:16,42; 2Sa 9:1; 21:7 **23:19** [w] 1Sa 26:1 [x] Ps 54 Title [y] 1Sa 26:3

[a] 15 Or *he was afraid because*

22:19 *put to the sword Nob, the town of the priests.* The massacre of the inhabitants of the priestly town of Nob strikes the modern reader as an illegal outrage. A recent study considering the present episode in the light of Hittite literature, however, maintains that priests in Israel were obliged by oaths of loyalty to the royal authority, just as were Hittite priests. The penalty for disloyalty could be extreme. In the Hittite "Instructions to Priests and Temple Officials," e.g., offenses against human superiors or a god were punished quite severely, potentially including the "total annihilation of the 'sinner' and his house." On the basis of such comparisons, one might argue that Saul's annihilation of the inhabitants of Nob was neither illegal nor outrageous. From a literary standpoint, though, Saul is no longer the rightful king from the perspective of 1 Samuel, having been rejected by Yahweh in 15:28, and so he has no right either to expect loyalty or to punish those who lack it. We should also note that Saul's own officers refuse to obey, which indicates that they are not being asked to do something expected.

23:1 *looting the threshing floors.* In the agricultural societies of the ancient Near East, grain was a highly valued commodity. Grain that reached the threshing floor was at the end of a lengthy process of labor-intensive cultivation and harvesting, and the looting of the threshing floors was thus a particularly effective means of weakening an adversary. The story of the judge Gideon offers a parallel example of agricultural looting and destruction (Jdg 6:3–6).

23:9 *Bring the ephod.* See note on 2:18.

pleases you to do so, and we will be responsible for giving[z] him into your hands."
[21]Saul replied, "The LORD bless you for
your concern[a] for me. [22]Go and get more
information. Find out where David usually goes and who has seen him there.
They tell me he is very crafty. [23]Find out
about all the hiding places he uses and
come back to me with definite information. Then I will go with you; if he is in
the area, I will track him down among all
the clans of Judah."
[24]So they set out and went to Ziph ahead
of Saul. Now David and his men were in
the Desert of Maon,[b] in the Arabah south
of Jeshimon. [25]Saul and his men began the
search, and when David was told about
it, he went down to the rock and stayed
in the Desert of Maon. When Saul heard
this, he went into the Desert of Maon in
pursuit of David.
[26]Saul[c] was going along one side of the
mountain, and David and his men were on
the other side, hurrying to get away from
Saul. As Saul and his forces were closing in on David and his men to capture
them, [27]a messenger came to Saul, saying,
"Come quickly! The Philistines are raiding
the land." [28]Then Saul broke off his pursuit of David and went to meet the Philistines. That is why they call this place
Sela Hammahlekoth.[a] [29]And David went
up from there and lived in the strongholds
of En Gedi.[bd]

David Spares Saul's Life

24[c] After Saul returned from pursuing
the Philistines, he was told, "Da-
vid is in the Desert of En Gedi.[e]" [2]So Saul
took three thousand able young men from
all Israel and set out to look[f] for David and
his men near the Crags of the Wild Goats.
[3]He came to the sheep pens along the
way; a cave[g] was there, and Saul went
in to relieve[h] himself. David and his men
were far back in the cave. [4]The men said,
"This is the day the LORD spoke[i] of when
he said[d] to you, 'I will give your enemy
into your hands for you to deal with as
you wish.'"[j] Then David crept up unnoticed and cut off a corner of Saul's robe.
[5]Afterward, David was conscience-
stricken[k] for having cut off a corner of his
robe. [6]He said to his men, "The LORD forbid that I should do such a thing to my
master, the LORD's anointed,[l] or lay my
hand on him; for he is the anointed of the
LORD." [7]With these words David sharply
rebuked his men and did not allow them
to attack Saul. And Saul left the cave and
went his way.
[8]Then David went out of the cave and
called out to Saul, "My lord the king!"
When Saul looked behind him, David
bowed down and prostrated himself with
his face to the ground.[m] [9]He said to Saul,
"Why do you listen when men say, 'David is bent on harming you'? [10]This day
you have seen with your own eyes how
the LORD delivered you into my hands
in the cave. Some urged me to kill you,
but I spared you; I said, 'I will not lay my
hand on my lord, because he is the LORD's
anointed.' [11]See, my father, look at this
piece of your robe in my hand! I cut off
the corner of your robe but did not kill
you. See that there is nothing in my hand
to indicate that I am guilty[n] of wrongdoing or rebellion. I have not wronged you,
but you are hunting[o] me down to take my
life. [12]May the LORD judge[p] between you
and me. And may the LORD avenge[q] the
wrongs you have done to me, but my hand
will not touch you. [13]As the old saying
goes, 'From evildoers come evil deeds,'[r]
so my hand will not touch you.
[14]"Against whom has the king of Israel come out? Who are you pursuing?
A dead dog?[s] A flea?[t] [15]May the LORD be

23:20 [z] ver 12 **23:21** [a] 1Sa 22:8 **23:24** [b] Jos 15:55; 1Sa 25:2 **23:26** [c] Ps 17:9 **23:29** [d] 2Ch 20:2 **24:1** [e] 1Sa 23:28-29 **24:2** [f] 1Sa 26:2 **24:3** [g] Ps 57 Title; 142 Title [h] Jdg 3:24

24:4 [i] 1Sa 25:28-30 [j] 1Sa 23:17; 26:8 **24:5** [k] 2Sa 24:10 **24:6** [l] 1Sa 26:11 **24:8** [m] 1Sa 25:23-24 **24:11** [n] Ps 7:3 [o] 1Sa 23:14, 23; 26:20 **24:12** [p] Ge 16:5; 31:53; Job 5:8 [q] Jdg 11:27; 1Sa 26:10 **24:13** [r] Mt 7:20 **24:14** [s] 1Sa 17:43; 2Sa 9:8 [t] 1Sa 26:20

[a] *28 Sela Hammahlekoth* means *rock of parting.* [b] *29* In Hebrew texts this verse (23:29) is numbered 24:1. [c] In Hebrew texts 24:1-22 is numbered 24:2-23. [d] *4* Or *"Today the LORD is saying*

24:3 *a cave was there.* While caves certainly abound in the area, attempts to identify the specific cave in question out of the innumerable possibilities have not succeeded. *relieve himself.* Lit. "cover his feet." Its occurrence also in Jdg 3:24 confirms its use as a euphemism. That Saul entered alone into the very cave where David and his men were hiding is an unmistakably providential irony.
24:4–5 *David … cut off a corner of Saul's robe … was conscience-stricken.* For the significance of robes and hems and their removal, see note on 15:27. In the present episode, David displays the severed hem of Saul's robe as evidence that he had been close enough to Saul to kill him, but had refrained to do so, despite the encouragement of his men (vv. 10–11). However, the fact that no sooner had David "cut off the corner of Saul's robe" than his conscience began to strike him (v. 5) suggests that David's motive may not have been first or foremost to demonstrate his innocence to Saul but, rather, to divest Saul symbolically of his rule (see notes on 2:19; 18:3–4).
24:6 *The LORD forbid that I should do such a thing to … the LORD's anointed, or lay my hand on him.* Political assassination sets a very bad precedent for a future ruler. The claim to divine right to the throne is only valuable as long as the mystique of that claim is upheld and respected.
24:8 *bowed down and prostrated himself with his face to the ground.* A very common way in the ancient Near East of showing submission, deference and sometimes fear.
24:14 *dead dog.* As the dog was not considered "man's best friend" in the ancient Near East but was regarded with some disdain or at least as entirely insignificant, "dog" was a favorite term both in insults and in expressions of self-abasement. To be a "dead dog" was worse still (on this usage, see also 2Sa 9:8; 16:9, the only other occurrences in the Bible). David's self-deprecation before Saul was

our judge[u] and decide between us. May
he consider my cause and uphold[v] it; may
he vindicate[w] me by delivering[x] me from
your hand."
16When David finished saying this, Saul
asked, "Is that your voice,[y] David my
son?" And he wept aloud. 17"You are more
righteous than I,"[z] he said. "You have
treated me well,[a] but I have treated you
badly. 18You have just now told me about
the good you did to me; the LORD delivered[b] me into your hands, but you did not
kill me. 19When a man finds his enemy,
does he let him get away unharmed? May
the LORD reward you well for the way you
treated me today. 20I know that you will
surely be king[c] and that the kingdom[d] of
Israel will be established in your hands.
21Now swear[e] to me by the LORD that you
will not kill off my descendants or wipe
out my name from my father's family.[f]"
22So David gave his oath to Saul. Then
Saul returned home, but David and his
men went up to the stronghold.[g]

David, Nabal and Abigail

25 Now Samuel died,[h] and all Israel
assembled and mourned[i] for him;
and they buried him at his home in Ramah.[j] Then David moved down into the
Desert of Paran.[a]
2A certain man in Maon,[k] who had property there at Carmel, was very wealthy. He
had a thousand goats and three thousand
sheep, which he was shearing in Carmel.
3His name was Nabal and his wife's name
was Abigail.[l] She was an intelligent and
beautiful woman, but her husband was
surly and mean in his dealings — he was
a Calebite.[m]
4While David was in the wilderness, he
heard that Nabal was shearing sheep. 5So
he sent ten young men and said to them,
"Go up to Nabal at Carmel and greet him
in my name. 6Say to him: 'Long life to
you! Good health[n] to you and your household! And good health to all that is yours![o]
7" 'Now I hear that it is sheep-shearing
time. When your shepherds were with us,
we did not mistreat[p] them, and the whole
time they were at Carmel nothing of theirs
was missing. 8Ask your own servants and
they will tell you. Therefore be favorable
toward my men, since we come at a festive time. Please give your servants and
your son David whatever[q] you can find for
them.' "
9When David's men arrived, they gave
Nabal this message in David's name. Then
they waited.
10Nabal answered David's servants,
"Who[r] is this David? Who is this son of
Jesse? Many servants are breaking away
from their masters these days. 11Why
should I take my bread[s] and water, and
the meat I have slaughtered for my shearers, and give it to men coming from who
knows where?"
12David's men turned around and went
back. When they arrived, they reported every word. 13David said to his men, "Each
of you strap on your sword!" So they did,
and David strapped his on as well. About
four hundred men went[t] up with David,
while two hundred stayed with the supplies.[u]
14One of the servants told Abigail, Nabal's wife, "David sent messengers from
the wilderness to give our master his greetings,[v] but he hurled insults at them. 15Yet
these men were very good to us. They did

a *1* Hebrew and some Septuagint manuscripts; other Septuagint manuscripts *Maon*

24:15 [u] ver 12 [v] Ps 35:1, 23; Mic 7:9 [w] Ps 43:1 [x] Ps 119:134, 154 **24:16** [y] 1Sa 26:17 **24:17** [z] Ge 38:26; 1Sa 26:21 [a] Mt 5:44 **24:18** [b] 1Sa 26:23 **24:20** [c] 1Sa 23:17 [d] 1Sa 13:14 **24:21** [e] Ge 21:23; 2Sa 21:1-9 [f] 1Sa 20:14-15 **24:22** [g] 1Sa 23:29 **25:1** [h] 1Sa 28:3 [i] Nu 20:29; Dt 34:8 [j] Ge 21:21; 2Ch 33:20 **25:2** [k] Jos 15:55; 1Sa 23:24 **25:3** [l] Pr 31:10 [m] Jos 15:13 **25:6** [n] Ps 122:7; Lk 10:5 [o] 1Ch 12:18 **25:7** [p] ver 15 **25:8** [q] Ne 8:10 **25:10** [r] Jdg 9:28 **25:11** [s] Jdg 8:6 **25:13** [t] 1Sa 23:13 [u] 1Sa 30:24 **25:14** [v] 1Sa 13:10

meant to assure Saul that his pursuit of him was neither necessary nor worthy. Reference to oneself as a "dog" was a stereotypical way in the ancient Near East of showing deference to one in a superior position, as is evidenced, e.g., in the Lachish and Amarna letters. *flea.* If to be a (dead) dog was to be insignificant, then to be a "single flea" (so the Hebrew reads) was to be almost nothing at all. This usage of "single" to connote something like "mere" is paralleled in several Amarna letters that refer to a "single dog" — e.g., "Who am I, a mere dog, that I should not go?"
25:2 *Carmel.* Not to be confused with Mount Carmel, a mountain range along the coast to the northwest of Samaria, the town of Carmel with which Nabal was identified lay just about a mile (1.5 kilometers) north of Maon and some eight miles (almost 13 kilometers) southeast of Hebron. In the Biblical period, Carmel was both politically and economically important. Its political importance derived from its strategic position as part of the defense system of the Judean wilderness, and its economic importance was based on its suitability to animal breeding. In the aftermath of his battle against the Amalekites, Saul had raised a monument to himself at the town of Carmel (see note on 15:12). In so doing, he had laid claim to sovereignty over the area. This fact, perhaps along with some sense of indebtedness to Saul for expelling the Amalekites, may have contributed to Nabal's utter disregard for David (vv. 10 – 11).
25:3 *Calebite.* Since the time of the Israelite conquest and settlement of the Negev, Hebron was associated with the hero Caleb (Jos 14:13 – 15; Jdg 1:20). Quite possibly — in view of the genealogical information in 1Ch 2:18 – 55, which links the settlement of Bethlehem with the descendants of Caleb (see especially 1Ch 2:19,50 – 51,54) — Nabal the Calebite was a kinsman of David, making David's request of him all the more reasonable.
25:4 *shearing sheep.* Shearing time (in the spring) would have been a time of abundance and gladness and, one would hope, generosity. If, as early second-millennium BC texts from the Babylonian city of Larsa indicate, one sheep would produce over two pounds (1 kilogram) of wool at shearing time, then Nabal's 3,000 sheep (v. 2) would have produced over three tons (2.7 metric tons) of wool. Further evidence of Nabal's wealth is the quantity of the goods that Abigail brings to David in v. 18.

not mistreat[w] us, and the whole time we
were out in the fields near them nothing
was missing.[x] 16 Night and day they were
a wall[y] around us the whole time we were
herding our sheep near them. 17 Now think
it over and see what you can do, because
disaster is hanging over our master and
his whole household. He is such a wicked[z]
man that no one can talk to him."

18 Abigail acted quickly. She took two
hundred loaves of bread, two skins of
wine, five dressed sheep, five seahs[a] of
roasted grain, a hundred cakes of raisins[a]
and two hundred cakes of pressed figs,
and loaded them on donkeys.[b] 19 Then she
told her servants, "Go on ahead;[c] I'll follow you." But she did not tell her husband
Nabal.

20 As she came riding her donkey into a
mountain ravine, there were David and his
men descending toward her, and she met
them. 21 David had just said, "It's been useless—all my watching over this fellow's
property in the wilderness so that nothing
of his was missing. He has paid[d] me back
evil for good. 22 May God deal with David,[b]
be it ever so severely,[e] if by morning I leave
alive one male[f] of all who belong to him!"

23 When Abigail saw David, she quickly
got off her donkey and bowed down before David with her face to the ground.[g]
24 She fell at his feet and said: "Pardon
your servant, my lord, and let me speak
to you; hear what your servant has to
say. 25 Please pay no attention, my lord, to
that wicked man Nabal. He is just like his
name—his name means Fool,[h] and folly
goes with him. And as for me, your servant, I did not see the men my lord sent.
26 And now, my lord, as surely as the LORD
your God lives and as you live, since the
LORD has kept you from bloodshed[i] and
from avenging[j] yourself with your own
hands, may your enemies and all who are
intent on harming my lord be like Nabal.[k]
27 And let this gift,[l] which your servant has
brought to my lord, be given to the men
who follow you.

28 "Please forgive[m] your servant's presumption. The LORD your God will certainly make a lasting[n] dynasty for my lord, because you fight the LORD's battles,[o] and no
wrongdoing[p] will be found in you as long
as you live. 29 Even though someone is pursuing you to take your life, the life of my
lord will be bound securely in the bundle
of the living by the LORD your God, but the

[a] *18* That is, probably about 60 pounds or about 27 kilograms [b] *22* Some Septuagint manuscripts; Hebrew *with David's enemies*

25:15 [w] ver 7 [x] ver 21
25:16 [y] Ex 14:22; Job 1:10
25:17 [z] 1Sa 20:7
25:18 [a] 1Ch 12:40 [b] 2Sa 16:1
25:19 [c] Ge 32:20
25:21 [d] Ps 109:5
25:22 [e] 1Sa 3:17; 20:13 [f] 1Ki 14:10; 21:21; 2Ki 9:8
25:23 [g] 1Sa 20:41
25:25 [h] Pr 14:16
25:26 [i] ver 33 [j] Heb 10:30 [k] 2Sa 18:32
25:27 [l] Ge 33:11; 1Sa 30:26
25:28 [m] ver 24 [n] 2Sa 7:11,26 [o] 1Sa 18:17 [p] 1Sa 24:11

25:16 *Night and day they were a wall around us.* With these words, one of Nabal's servants explicitly confirmed to Abigail that David's claim to have safeguarded Nabal's flocks (vv. 7,15) was true. For this service, Nabal's servants had as much reason to be grateful to David as Nabal himself. In the ancient Near East, sheep owners often contracted with shepherds to tend their flocks (who in turn might contract out the actual care of the sheep to shepherd-boys). At certain times of the year, it may have been possible for the flocks to graze near the home of their owner, returning each evening, but in the dry summer months shepherds would often have to travel considerable distances to find suitable pasturage for the flocks and be gone for long stretches of time. As a reward for fulfilling their duties, the shepherds could expect a certain amount of wool per adult sheep, as well as milk while in the field, meat at slaughter time, etc. For their part, shepherds assumed liability for the welfare of the sheep and were responsible to return the right total at shearing time (calculated on the basis of normal rates of birth and natural attrition, and with agreed upon means of proving loss by disease or animal attack). Should the shepherds come up short, they would themselves have to make up the lack.
25:18 These further gifts were in keeping with a time of festival and were suggestive of hospitality, not simply of repayment. In ancient societies, gift-giving, as distinct from the simple exchange of goods (which would constitute commerce), played an important and complex role. Chiefly, of course, Abigail's immediate concern was to make amends for her foolish husband's actions and to appease the affronted David. David was affronted not simply by Nabal's unwillingness to compensate for services rendered (even if they were technically unsolicited), but also by the dishonor/shame that Nabal's refusal to recognize him as more than a runaway slave heaped upon David.
25:22 *May God deal . . . ever so severely.* Saul said this earlier too (14:44), and also got talked out of it. It is a standard oath formula, and would therefore be assumed to be binding. It was nevertheless recognized that changing conditions could be reason to negate an oath. The only one to enforce such an oath was the deity, and presumably the change in the situation here would suggest that Yahweh would not be displeased by David's failure to follow through.
25:25 *his name means Fool.* The name Nabal, sounds like a Hebrew adjective meaning "churlish, foolish," and his portrayal throughout ch. 25 confirms the appropriateness of the name. It seems hardly likely, however, that Nabal's parents would have saddled him with a name of such negative connotation, nor is it likely that the name arose as a nickname by those who knew Nabal—nicknames do not typically focus on character deficiencies. Rather, it was probably the case that the meaning(s) associated with the name Nabal in the minds of his parents were favorable. In the OT it is common for the author to draw links between a name and similar sounding words (e.g., Isaac, see Ge 17:19 and NIV text note; 18:10–15; 21:3–6). On various linguistic grounds, four suggestions are offered: (1) fire/flame/arrow; (2) one sent; (3) noble/noble-minded/generous; (4) skilled/clever.
25:29 *your life . . . will be bound securely in the bundle of the living . . . the lives of your enemies he will hurl away as from the pocket of a sling.* Two main theories of explanation have been proposed. One is that the "bundle of the living" is a document that has been bound, or tied up—thus, "Document of the Living." The concept of a heavenly ledger is present in the ancient Near East from earliest times. In Mesopotamia, destinies were determined by the gods, and their decisions were inscribed on "tablets of destiny." Thus, prayers often include petitions such as the follow-

lives of your enemies he will hurl[q] away
as from the pocket of a sling. 30When the
LORD has fulfilled for my lord every good
thing he promised concerning him and
has appointed him ruler[r] over Israel, 31my
lord will not have on his conscience the
staggering burden of needless bloodshed
or of having avenged himself. And when
the LORD your God has brought my lord
success, remember[s] your servant."
32David said to Abigail, "Praise[t] be
to the LORD, the God of Israel, who has
sent you today to meet me. 33May you
be blessed for your good judgment and
for keeping me from bloodshed[u] this day
and from avenging myself with my own
hands. 34Otherwise, as surely as the LORD,
the God of Israel, lives, who has kept me
from harming you, if you had not come
quickly to meet me, not one male belonging to Nabal would have been left alive by
daybreak."
35Then David accepted from her hand
what she had brought him and said, "Go
home in peace. I have heard your words
and granted[v] your request."
36When Abigail went to Nabal, he was
in the house holding a banquet like that
of a king. He was in high[w] spirits and very
drunk.[x] So she told[y] him nothing at all until daybreak. 37Then in the morning, when
Nabal was sober, his wife told him all
these things, and his heart failed him and
he became like a stone. 38About ten days
later, the LORD struck[z] Nabal and he died.
39When David heard that Nabal was
dead, he said, "Praise be to the LORD, who
has upheld my cause against Nabal for
treating me with contempt. He has kept
his servant from doing wrong and has
brought Nabal's wrongdoing down on his
own head."
Then David sent word to Abigail, asking her to become his wife. 40His servants
went to Carmel and said to Abigail, "David has sent us to you to take you to become his wife."
41She bowed down with her face to the
ground and said, "I am your servant and
am ready to serve you and wash the feet
of my lord's servants." 42Abigail[a] quickly
got on a donkey and, attended by her five
female servants, went with David's messengers and became his wife. 43David had
also married Ahinoam[b] of Jezreel, and
they both were his wives.[c] 44But Saul had
given his daughter Michal, David's wife,
to Paltiel[a][d] son of Laish, who was from
Gallim.[e]

25:29 [q] Jer 10:18 **25:30** [r] 1Sa 13:14 **25:31** [s] Ge 40:14 **25:32** [t] Ge 24:27; Ex 18:10; Lk 1:68 **25:33** [u] ver 26 **25:35** [v] Ge 19:21; 1Sa 20:42; 2Ki 5:19 **25:36** [w] 2Sa 13:23 [x] Pr 20:1; Isa 5:11, 22; Hos 4:11 [y] ver 19 **25:38** [z] 1Sa 26:10; 2Sa 6:7 **25:42** [a] Ge 24:61-67 **25:43** [b] Jos 15:56 [c] 1Sa 27:3; 30:5 **25:44** [d] 2Sa 3:15 [e] Isa 10:30 **26:1** [f] 1Sa 23:19 [g] Ps 54 Title **26:2** [h] 1Sa 13:2; 24:2 **26:5** [i] 1Sa 14:50; 17:55 **26:6** [j] Jdg 7:10-11; 1Ch 2:16

David Again Spares Saul's Life

26 The Ziphites[f] went to Saul at Gibeah and said, "Is not David hiding[g]
on the hill of Hakilah, which faces Jeshimon?"
2So Saul went down to the Desert of
Ziph, with his three thousand select Israelite troops, to search[h] there for David.
3Saul made his camp beside the road on
the hill of Hakilah facing Jeshimon, but
David stayed in the wilderness. When he
saw that Saul had followed him there, 4he
sent out scouts and learned that Saul had
definitely arrived.
5Then David set out and went to the
place where Saul had camped. He saw
where Saul and Abner[i] son of Ner, the
commander of the army, had lain down.
Saul was lying inside the camp, with the
army encamped around him.
6David then asked Ahimelek the Hittite and Abishai son of Zeruiah,[j] Joab's

[a] 44 Hebrew *Palti*, a variant of *Paltiel*

ing by Nebuchadrezzar: "On your [Nabu's] unchangeable tablet, which establishes the boundaries of heaven and earth, proclaim length of days for me, inscribe long life." A second theory is that shepherds would have kept a tally of their sheep by carrying a bag of small stones, each of which represented one of the sheep. When a sheep was bought or sold, a stone was added or removed.

25:39b *David sent word to Abigail, asking her to become his wife.* While modern, Western readers might read these lines as a tale of romance, in the ancient Near East marriage and politics were often intertwined. Whatever may have been David's personal feelings for Abigail — "an intelligent and beautiful woman" (v. 3) — he undoubtedly benefited politically from this and other marriages. David's earlier marriage to Saul's daughter Michal (18:27) brought him into the royal family, his marriages to Ahinoam of Jezreel (see v. 43 and note) and to Abigail (here) would have strengthened his ties to the southern region around Hebron. For polygamy in antiquity, see note on Ge 16:2.

25:43 *David had also married Ahinoam of Jezreel.* While first mentioned here, David's marriage to Ahinoam of Jezreel had apparently preceded his marriage to Abigail, bringing the sum of David's wives, including Saul's daughter Michal, to three so far. *Ahinoam.* She has piqued the curiosity of scholars. Combining the fact that the OT mentions only one other Ahinoam — the wife of Saul listed in 14:50 — with Nathan's statement to David in 2Sa 12:8 that the Lord had given David's "master's wives into [his] arms," one scholar has suggested that David's Ahinoam may have once been Saul's wife, though this seems unlikely. More likely, Nathan's comment refers in a formulaic fashion to David's inheritance of all that had belonged to Saul, once David became king over both Judah and Israel (2Sa 5:1 – 5). *Jezreel.* Almost certainly not the Jezreel Valley but, rather, a town in the hill country of Judah somewhere in the vicinity of Maon, Carmel, Ziph, etc. (Jos 15:55 – 56). The precise location of this town is uncertain.

25:44 *Saul had given his daughter Michal, David's wife, to Paltiel.* Saul's giving of Michal to Paltiel must have been in part at least politically motivated, effectively distancing David from the royal family — a situation that David will be quick to rectify at the earliest opportunity (see note on 2Sa 3:13).

brother, "Who will go down into the camp
with me to Saul?"
"I'll go with you," said Abishai.
7So David and Abishai went to the army
by night, and there was Saul, lying asleep
inside the camp with his spear stuck in
the ground near his head. Abner and the
soldiers were lying around him.
8Abishai said to David, "Today God has
delivered your enemy into your hands.
Now let me pin him to the ground with
one thrust of the spear; I won't strike him
twice."
9But David said to Abishai, "Don't destroy him! Who can lay a hand on the
LORD's anointed[k] and be guiltless?[l] 10As
surely as the LORD lives," he said, "the
LORD himself will strike[m] him, or his time[n]
will come and he will die,[o] or he will go
into battle and perish. 11But the LORD forbid that I should lay a hand on the LORD's
anointed. Now get the spear and water jug
that are near his head, and let's go."
12So David took the spear and water jug
near Saul's head, and they left. No one
saw or knew about it, nor did anyone
wake up. They were all sleeping, because
the LORD had put them into a deep sleep.[p]
13Then David crossed over to the other side and stood on top of the hill some
distance away; there was a wide space between them. 14He called out to the army
and to Abner son of Ner, "Aren't you going
to answer me, Abner?"

26:9 [k] 2Sa 1:14 [l] 1Sa 24:5
26:10 [m] 1Sa 25:38; Ro 12:19 [n] Ge 47:29; Dt 31:14; Ps 37:13 [o] 1Sa 31:6; 2Sa 1:1
26:12 [p] Ge 2:21; 15:12

26:11 *get the spear and water jug that are near his head, and let's go.* Again Saul is found with his spear at his side or, in this instance, "stuck in the ground near his head" (v. 7) while he sleeps. The regular association of Saul with his spear (18:10; 19:9; 22:6; 2Sa 1:6) may suggest that it served as a kind of royal emblem, but, be that as it may, it also recalls his earlier acts of violence against others and foreshadows his final act of violence against himself (31:4). The loss of spear and water jug in the desert (1Sa 26:2) could be life-threatening, and David used the items effectively to demonstrate that even though Saul had again fallen into his hands, he had refused to lay a hand on him (v. 23). That David did not intend to harm Saul, even indirectly, is evidenced by his return of the spear in v. 22.

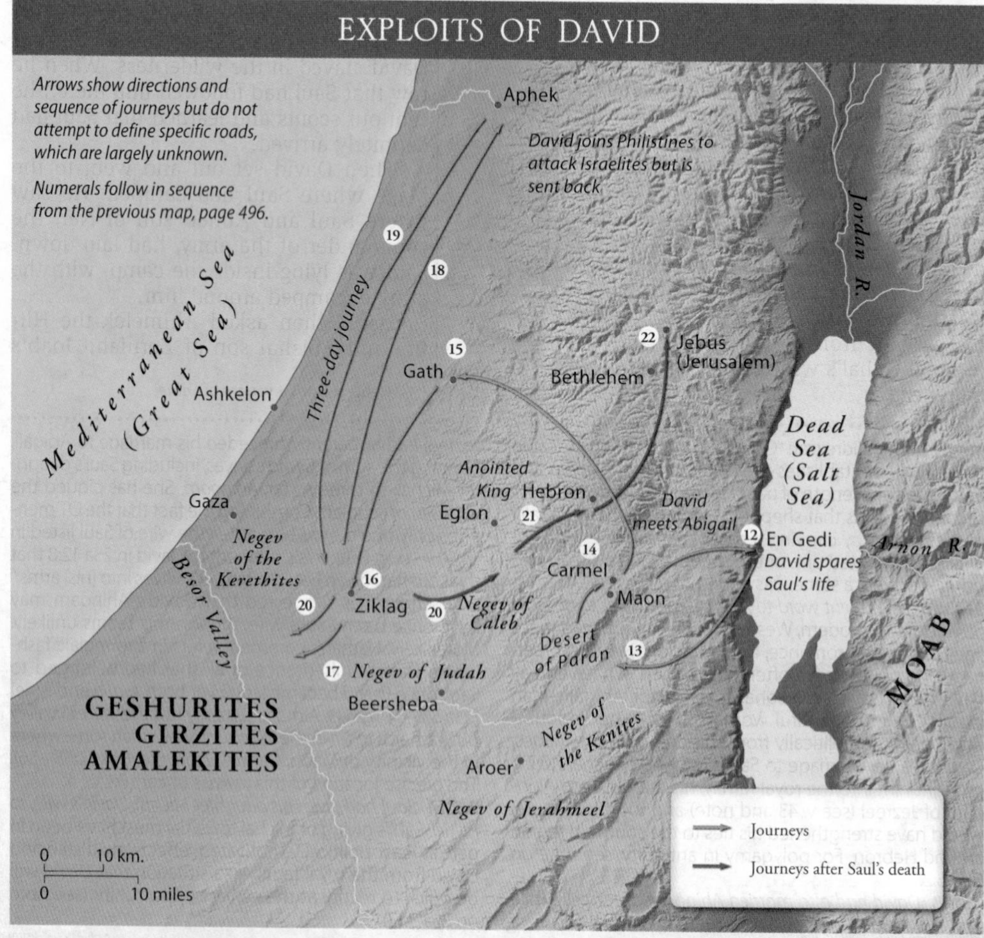

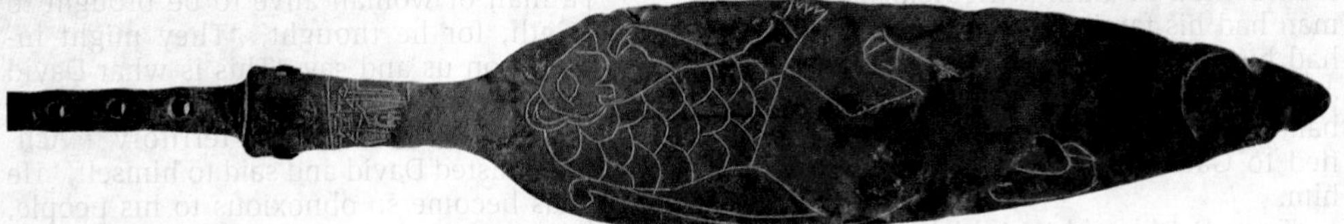

Copper spearhead inscribed with "Lugal, king of Kish," c. 2600 BC. In the OT, Saul is often described as having his spear by his side (1Sa 26:11).

Wikimedia Commons

Abner replied, "Who are you who calls
to the king?"
15 David said, "You're a man, aren't you?
And who is like you in Israel? Why didn't
you guard your lord the king? Someone
came to destroy your lord the king. 16 What
you have done is not good. As surely as
the LORD lives, you and your men must
die, because you did not guard your master, the LORD's anointed. Look around you.
Where are the king's spear and water jug
that were near his head?"
17 Saul recognized David's voice and
said, "Is that your voice,[q] David my son?"
David replied, "Yes it is, my lord the
king." 18 And he added, "Why is my lord
pursuing his servant? What have I done,
and what wrong[r] am I guilty of? 19 Now
let my lord the king listen to his servant's
words. If the LORD has incited you against
me, then may he accept an offering.[s] If,
however, people have done it, may they be
cursed before the LORD! They have driven
me today from my share in the LORD's inheritance[t] and have said, 'Go, serve other
gods.' 20 Now do not let my blood fall to the
ground far from the presence of the LORD.
The king of Israel has come out to look for
a flea[u] — as one hunts a partridge in the
mountains."
21 Then Saul said, "I have sinned.[v] Come
back, David my son. Because you considered my life precious[w] today, I will not try
to harm you again. Surely I have acted like
a fool and have been terribly wrong."
22 "Here is the king's spear," David answered. "Let one of your young men come
over and get it. 23 The LORD rewards[x] everyone for their righteousness[y] and faithfulness. The LORD delivered you into my
hands today, but I would not lay a hand
on the LORD's anointed. 24 As surely as I
valued your life today, so may the LORD
value my life and deliver[z] me from all
trouble."
25 Then Saul said to David, "May you be
blessed, David my son; you will do great
things and surely triumph."
So David went on his way, and Saul returned home.

26:17 [q] 1Sa 24:16 **26:18** [r] 1Sa 24:9, 11-14 **26:19** [s] 2Sa 16:11 [t] 2Sa 14:16 **26:20** [u] 1Sa 24:14 **26:21** [v] Ex 9:27; 1Sa 15:24 [w] 1Sa 24:17 **26:23** [x] Ps 62:12 [y] Ps 7:8; 18:20, 24 **26:24** [z] Ps 54:7 **27:2** [a] 1Sa 25:13 [b] 1Sa 21:10 [c] 1Ki 2:39

David Among the Philistines

27 But David thought to himself, "One
of these days I will be destroyed by
the hand of Saul. The best thing I can do
is to escape to the land of the Philistines.
Then Saul will give up searching for me
anywhere in Israel, and I will slip out of
his hand."
2 So David and the six hundred men[a]
with him left and went[b] over to Achish[c]
son of Maok king of Gath. 3 David and his

26:19 *Go, serve other gods.* While peoples of the ancient Near East often associated their deities with particular territories and even particular holy places, Yahweh, according to mainstream OT thinking, was not so limited. In their recent history, Israel had seen Yahweh lay his heavy hand on the Philistines and the Ammonites (chs. 6; 11), to say nothing of David's encounter with the Philistine Goliath (ch. 17). The sense of David's complaint that he was being forced to serve other gods and was being driven from the presence of Yahweh should not be understood in any absolute sense but in the purely practical sense that, as a fugitive, he was being driven from the familiar places where Yahweh was worshiped.

26:20 *a flea ... a partridge in the mountains.* David's self-description may have suggested not only humility but the difficulty of Saul's accomplishing his goal, "to look for a flea." Further, David began his exchange with Saul when he "called out" to Abner from atop a distant hill (vv. 13 – 14), but now David likens himself to "a partridge in the mountains." The word for "partridge" in Hebrew is literally "caller"; just as a hunter might pursue a single partridge ("caller") in the mountains with little hope of success, so Saul is in futile pursuit of David, himself a caller in the mountains (cf. v. 14).

27:2 *David ... went over to Achish son of Maok king of Gath.* As a fugitive seeking refuge in foreign territory, and perhaps employment as a mercenary, David was following a widely attested practice in the ancient Near East. The landless or disfranchised — e.g., the Habiru/Apiru (see note on 4:6), with whom David and his men have been compared — sometimes hired themselves out as fighters in exchange for favors such as land. In addition to the desire to better their own circumstances, mercenaries were also sometimes motivated by grievances toward their former ruler. At the famous Battle of Marathon, e.g., the Persian army benefited from the defection of Greek tyrants who, having been expelled from their positions, joined the ultimately unsuccessful Persians in fighting against the Greeks.

David's departure to the Philistines (though not a full

men settled in Gath with Achish. Each
man had his family with him, and David
had his two wives:[d] Ahinoam of Jezreel
and Abigail of Carmel, the widow of Nabal. 4When Saul was told that David had
fled to Gath, he no longer searched for
him.
5Then David said to Achish, "If I have
found favor in your eyes, let a place be
assigned to me in one of the country
towns, that I may live there. Why should
your servant live in the royal city with
you?"
6So on that day Achish gave him Ziklag,[e] and it has belonged to the kings of
Judah ever since. 7David lived[f] in Philistine territory a year and four months.
8Now David and his men went up and
raided the Geshurites,[g] the Girzites and
the Amalekites.[h] (From ancient times
these peoples had lived in the land extending to Shur[i] and Egypt.) 9Whenever
David attacked an area, he did not leave a
man or woman alive,[j] but took sheep and
cattle, donkeys and camels, and clothes.
Then he returned to Achish.
10When Achish asked, "Where did
you go raiding today?" David would say,
"Against the Negev of Judah" or "Against
the Negev of Jerahmeel[k]" or "Against the
Negev of Kenites.[l]" 11He did not leave
a man or woman alive to be brought to
Gath, for he thought, "They might inform on us and say, 'This is what David
did.' " And such was his practice as long
as he lived in Philistine territory. 12Ach-
ish trusted David and said to himself, "He
has become so obnoxious to his people,
the Israelites, that he will be my servant
for life."

28 In those days the Philistines gathered[m] their forces to fight against
Israel. Achish said to David, "You must
understand that you and your men will
accompany me in the army."
2David said, "Then you will see for
yourself what your servant can do."
Achish replied, "Very well, I will make
you my bodyguard for life."

Saul and the Medium at Endor

3Now Samuel was dead,[n] and all Israel had mourned for him and buried him
in his own town of Ramah.[o] Saul had expelled the mediums and spiritists[p] from
the land.
4The Philistines assembled and came
and set up camp at Shunem,[q] while Saul
gathered all Israel and set up camp at Gilboa.[r] 5When Saul saw the Philistine army,
he was afraid; terror filled his heart. 6He
inquired[s] of the LORD, but the LORD did not

27:3 [d] 1Sa 25:43; 30:3 **27:6** [e] Jos 15:31; 19:5; Ne 11:28 **27:7** [f] 1Sa 29:3 **27:8** [g] Jos 13:2, 13 [h] Ex 17:8; 1Sa 15:7-8 [i] Ex 15:22 **27:9** [j] 1Sa 15:3 **27:10** [k] 1Sa 30:29; 1Ch 2:9, 25 [l] Jdg 1:16
28:1 [m] 1Sa 29:1 **28:3** [n] 1Sa 25:1 [o] 1Sa 7:17 [p] Ex 22:18; Lev 19:31; 20:27; Dt 18:10-11; 1Sa 15:23 **28:4** [q] Jos 19:18; 2Ki 4:8 [r] 1Sa 31:1, 3 **28:6** [s] 1Sa 14:37; 1Ch 10:13-14; Pr 1:28

defection, as subsequent events demonstrated), was largely prompted by his grievous treatment at the hands of Saul. Later, after David became king, he too employed mercenaries, the Kerethites and Pelethites (i.e., Cretans and Philistines), who served as his personal bodyguard (2Sa 8:18; cf. 2Sa 23:22–23). Although David's sojourn among the Philistines has rightly been characterized as one of the most disreputable in David's career, from a pragmatic standpoint it did accomplish several things: It placed him out of Saul's reach; it allowed him to learn Philistine ways, including their technologies and military practices; it put him in a position surreptitiously to destroy some of Israel's longtime foes, while benefiting from their wealth and using some of it to curry favor with leaders in Judah, who would one day be his subjects. See note on 1Ki 1:38.

27:7 *David lived in Philistine territory a year and four months.* During this period Saul died, and following it David became king in Hebron at the age of 30 (2Sa 5:4). Thus, David would have been about 28 when he fled to Philistine territory.

28:2 *I will make you my bodyguard for life.* Shows how supremely successful was David's deception of Achish. *bodyguard.* This Hebrew word is not the same as that used elsewhere in Samuel (cf. 22:14; 2Sa 23:23) or anywhere else in the Bible. The phrase literally reads "keeper/guard of my head" and may have carried a sense similar to the colloquial expression in English "you've got my back." The irony of this choice of words by Achish of Gath—given the fact that David has already collected the head of Goliath, another citizen of Gath—is only heightened by the complaint of the Philistine commanders in 29:4 that David might turn in battle and "regain his master's favor ... by taking the heads of our own men"!

28:3 *Saul had expelled the mediums and spiritists.* Cultures throughout the ancient Near East evidenced a desire to make contact with the spirit world, and a complex array of rites and practitioners arose in an effort to satisfy this desire. For Israel, however, participation in the kinds of rites practiced by its polytheistic neighbors in Canaan was condemned in the strongest possible terms and strictly forbidden, both in the book of Deuteronomy (Dt 18:9–13; see notes on Dt 18:10,11; see also the article "Magic," p. 326) and in the priestly legislation of Leviticus (Lev 19:31; 20:27). The basis of this proscription of occult practices may in part have had to do with the distinction between magic and religion, i.e., between the occult magical arts, on the one hand, which seek to harness knowledge and power for selfish ends, and religious observance, on the other, which seeks to bring the worshiper into communion with the deity. But the distinction between magic and religion is not always easy to maintain, and the OT itself reports without censure certain acts that might be considered magic (a staff becoming a snake, the casting of lots, causing an axhead to float, etc.). The more fundamental reason for banning occult practices in Israel was that they involved engaging false gods or demonic powers rather than the one true God, Yahweh. In any case, Saul's expulsion of mediums and spiritists was fully in accord with Mosaic Law. However, other motivations more related to eliminating an unsavory group of people from society may have been behind Saul's action. About all that can be said at present is that purging the land of occult specialists could have been motivated by a variety of reasons, but whatever Saul's initial motivation, he lost no time in seeking out a medium when the accepted methods of divine inquiry failed him, and he showed that a medium could easily be found despite his purge.

answer him by dreams[t] or Urim[u] or prophets. 7Saul then said to his attendants,
"Find me a woman who is a medium,[v] so
I may go and inquire of her."
"There is one in Endor,[w]" they said.
8So Saul disguised[x] himself, putting on
other clothes, and at night he and two
men went to the woman. "Consult[y] a spirit for me," he said, "and bring up for me
the one I name."
9But the woman said to him, "Surely
you know what Saul has done. He has cut
off[z] the mediums and spiritists from the
land. Why have you set a trap for my life
to bring about my death?"

28:6 [t] Nu 12:6 [u] Ex 28:30; Nu 27:21 **28:7** [v] Ac 16:16 [w] Jos 17:11 **28:8** [x] 2Ch 18:29; 35:22 [y] Dt 18:10-11; 1Ch 10:13; Isa 8:19 **28:9** [z] ver 3

10Saul swore to her by the LORD, "As
surely as the LORD lives, you will not be
punished for this."
11Then the woman asked, "Whom shall
I bring up for you?"
"Bring up Samuel," he said.
12When the woman saw Samuel, she
cried out at the top of her voice and said
to Saul, "Why have you deceived me? You
are Saul!"
13The king said to her, "Don't be afraid.
What do you see?"
The woman said, "I see a ghostly figure[a]
coming up out of the earth."

[a] 13 Or *see spirits*; or *see gods*

28:7 *medium.* The term is most often paired with "spiritist" in Biblical references (e.g., vv. 3,9), and the chief function of such practitioners was evidently to communicate with the spirit world, particularly with the dead. In the present instance, the Hebrew word for "medium" is lit. "ghostwife" or perhaps "ghostmistress." The "ghost" was understood as the spirit of the dead, and the function of the medium was to call up the spirit through necromancy, in order that it might speak. Necromancy was practiced throughout the ancient Near East. In Mesopotamia, the necromancer would rub salve on his or her face in an effort to contact or perhaps embody the spirit of the dead, or would employ skulls or figurines as temporary houses for the spirit that was being summoned. Although evidence of specifics is sparse, similar practices apparently took place in Hittite Anatolia, where a distinguishing feature was the prominent role played by old women. Necromancy is first attested in Egypt in the first half of the first millennium BC, but there is evidence, such as the "Letters to the Dead," that necromancy may have been practiced much earlier. Egyptian necromancy sometimes employed cadavers or scrying (gazing) cups. From Ugarit, the "Protocol of a Necromancy" (KTU 1:124) offers direct evidence of the practice, and there is other, more indirect evidence as well. The only direct evidence of necromancy being practiced in Israel is the present encounter between Saul and the medium at Endor, and in this context the practice is evaluated negatively.

28:13 *a ghostly figure coming up out of the earth.* Background information cannot resolve the many questions swirling around this event. Texts do not offer explanations of the phenomenon that was experienced in this necromancy, or how it may have differed from the norm. We do not know why the woman was startled and how she deduced that Saul was before her. From a literary

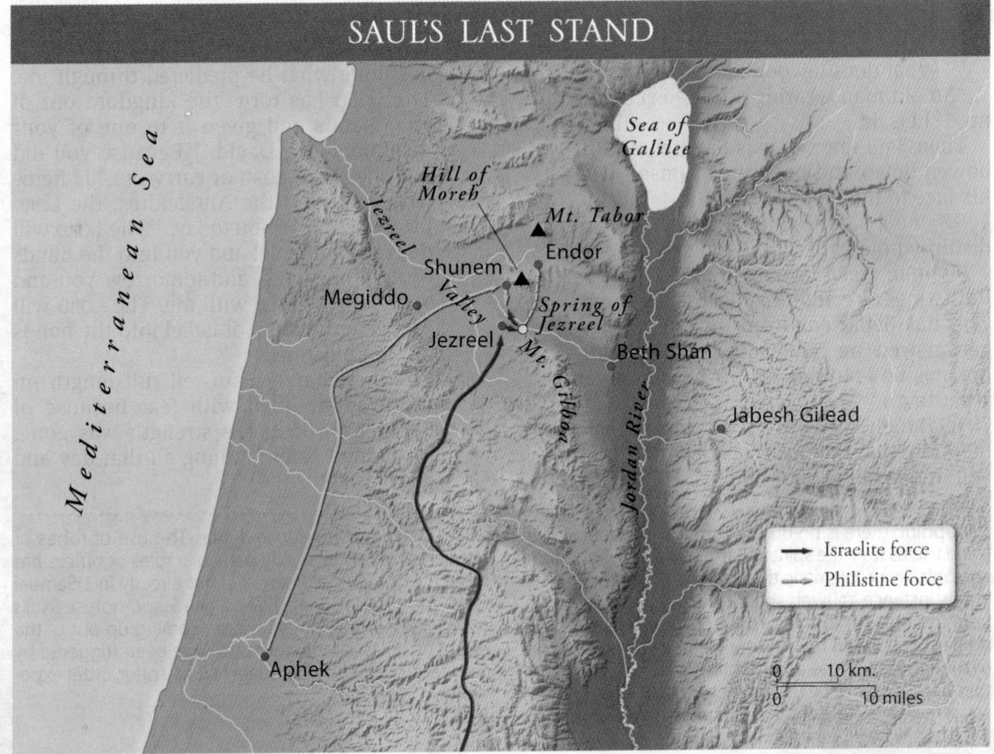

1 SAMUEL 28:8–25

CONSULTING A "SPIRIT"

The word Saul uses for "spirit" in 1Sa 28:8 refers to the "ghost" or "spirit" of one who has died (see notes on 1Sa 28:3,7). The etymological origin of this term is much debated, but one attractive proposal in the light of the present context (note, e.g., the "ghostly figure coming up out of the earth" in 1Sa 28:13) is that the word derives from a non-Semitic loanword meaning "sacrificial pit" on the basis of the occurrence of a cognate word in Hittite religious texts. Scholars have identified additional cognates in Sumerian, Akkadian, Hurrian and Ugaritic. The Hebrew term, like its Hittite cognate, should then be understood as designating a pit dug in the ground, which served as a means of access between infernal spirits of gods or deceased persons and the upper world. Among the Hittites rituals were carried out which involved the opening up of such pits in places selected by oracle, the lowering of offerings into the pits and the luring up of spirits out of the pits to eat the sacrifices and drink the blood libations and show their favor and superior knowledge to the sacrificers.

Among the offerings lowered into the pits were foodstuffs, often including a black sacrificial animal (a hog or a dog), and silver objects such as a model of a human ear (symbolizing the practitioner's desire to hear from the underworld) and a ladder or staircase (to encourage the spirit to ascend). Sumerian and Akkadian versions of the Gilgamesh Epic also attest the use of pits or holes in the ground as portals through which the dead could ascend from the underworld; Gilgamesh used such a pit to summon his departed companion Enkidu. ◆

14"What does he look like?" he asked.
"An old man wearing a robe[a] is coming
up," she said.
Then Saul knew it was Samuel, and he
bowed down and prostrated himself with
his face to the ground.
15Samuel said to Saul, "Why have you
disturbed me by bringing me up?"
"I am in great distress," Saul said. "The
Philistines are fighting against me, and
God has departed[b] from me. He no longer answers me, either by prophets or by
dreams. So I have called on you to tell me
what to do."
16Samuel said, "Why do you consult
me, now that the LORD has departed from
you and become your enemy? 17The LORD
has done what he predicted through me.
The LORD has torn[c] the kingdom out of
your hands and given it to one of your
neighbors—to David. 18Because you did
not obey[d] the LORD or carry out his fierce
wrath[e] against the Amalekites, the LORD
has done this to you today. 19The LORD will
deliver both Israel and you into the hands
of the Philistines, and tomorrow you and
your sons[f] will be with me. The LORD will
also give the army of Israel into the hands
of the Philistines."
20Immediately Saul fell full length on
the ground, filled with fear because of
Samuel's words. His strength was gone,
for he had eaten nothing all that day and
all that night.

28:14 [a] 1Sa 15:27; 24:8 **28:15** [b] ver 6; 1Sa 18:12
28:17 [c] 1Sa 15:28 **28:18** [d] 1Sa 15:20 [e] 1Ki 20:42 **28:19** [f] 1Sa 31:2

standpoint, there is no question that we should understand this as truly the spirit of Samuel, however phenomenologically problematic that conclusion might be. That in this instance Yahweh should deign to return Samuel from the grave—to the surprise of the woman and the dismay of Saul—in no way represents a validation either of the efficacy or the acceptability of necromancy. Furthermore, it cannot be used to deduce revealed theology concerning the state of the dead or the nature of the soul since it may be an exceptional situation.

28:14 *An old man wearing a robe.* The use of robes or special garments to signify particular roles or offices has been encountered numerous times already in 1 Samuel (see 2:19; 15:27; 18:3–4; 19:24; 24:4–5 and notes). Saul's recognition of the "ghostly figure coming up out of the earth" (v. 13) as Samuel seems to have been triggered by Samuel's robe (with which Saul had had prior, bitter experience [15:27–28]).

21 When the woman came to Saul and
saw that he was greatly shaken, she said,
"Look, your servant has obeyed you. I
took my life[g] in my hands and did what
you told me to do. 22 Now please listen to
your servant and let me give you some
food so you may eat and have the strength
to go on your way."
23 He refused[h] and said, "I will not eat."
But his men joined the woman in urging him, and he listened to them. He got
up from the ground and sat on the couch.
24 The woman had a fattened calf at the
house, which she butchered at once. She
took some flour, kneaded it and baked
bread without yeast. 25 Then she set it before Saul and his men, and they ate. That
same night they got up and left.

Achish Sends David Back to Ziklag

29 The Philistines gathered[i] all their
forces at Aphek,[j] and Israel camped
by the spring in Jezreel.[k] 2 As the Philistine
rulers marched with their units of hundreds and thousands, David and his men
were marching at the rear[l] with Achish.
3 The commanders of the Philistines asked,
"What about these Hebrews?"
Achish replied, "Is this not David, who
was an officer of Saul king of Israel? He
has already been with me for over a year,[m]
and from the day he left Saul until now, I
have found no fault in him."
4 But the Philistine commanders were
angry with Achish and said, "Send[n] the
man back, that he may return to the place
you assigned him. He must not go with
us into battle, or he will turn[o] against us
during the fighting. How better could he
regain his master's favor than by taking
the heads of our own men? 5 Isn't this the
David they sang about in their dances:

" 'Saul has slain his thousands,
and David his tens of thousands'?"[p]

6 So Achish called David and said to
him, "As surely as the LORD lives, you have
been reliable, and I would be pleased to
have you serve with me in the army. From
the day[q] you came to me until today, I
have found no fault in you, but the rulers[r]
don't approve of you. 7 Now turn back and
go in peace; do nothing to displease the
Philistine rulers."
8 "But what have I done?" asked David. "What have you found against your
servant from the day I came to you until
now? Why can't I go and fight against the
enemies of my lord the king?"
9 Achish answered, "I know that you
have been as pleasing in my eyes as an
angel[s] of God; nevertheless, the Philistine
commanders[t] have said, 'He must not go
up with us into battle.' 10 Now get up early, along with your master's servants who
have come with you, and leave[u] in the
morning as soon as it is light."
11 So David and his men got up early in
the morning to go back to the land of the
Philistines, and the Philistines went up to
Jezreel.

David Destroys the Amalekites

30 David and his men reached Ziklag[v]
on the third day. Now the Amalekites[w] had raided the Negev and Ziklag.
They had attacked Ziklag and burned it,
2 and had taken captive the women and
everyone else in it, both young and old.
They killed none of them, but carried
them off as they went on their way.
3 When David and his men reached Ziklag, they found it destroyed by fire and
their wives and sons and daughters taken
captive. 4 So David and his men wept aloud
until they had no strength left to weep.
5 David's two wives[x] had been captured —
Ahinoam of Jezreel and Abigail, the widow of Nabal of Carmel. 6 David was greatly
distressed because the men were talking of
stoning[y] him; each one was bitter in spirit because of his sons and daughters. But
David found strength[z] in the LORD his God.
7 Then David said to Abiathar[a] the
priest, the son of Ahimelek, "Bring me
the ephod.[b]" Abiathar brought it to him,
8 and David inquired[c] of the LORD, "Shall I
pursue this raiding party? Will I overtake
them?"
"Pursue them," he answered. "You will
certainly overtake them and succeed[d] in
the rescue."
9 David and the six hundred men[e] with
him came to the Besor Valley, where some
stayed behind. 10 Two hundred of them
were too exhausted[f] to cross the valley,
but David and the other four hundred continued the pursuit.
11 They found an Egyptian in a field and
brought him to David. They gave him water to drink and food to eat — 12 part of a
cake of pressed figs and two cakes of raisins. He ate and was revived,[g] for he had
not eaten any food or drunk any water for
three days and three nights.
13 David asked him, "Who do you belong
to? Where do you come from?"
He said, "I am an Egyptian, the slave of
an Amalekite. My master abandoned me
when I became ill three days ago. 14 We

28:21 [g] Jdg 12:3; 1Sa 19:5; Job 13:14 **28:23** [h] 2Ki 5:13 **29:1** [i] 1Sa 28:1 [j] Jos 12:18; 1Sa 4:1 [k] 2Ki 9:30 **29:2** [l] 1Sa 28:2 **29:3** [m] 1Sa 27:7; Da 6:5 **29:4** [n] 1Ch 12:19 [o] 1Sa 14:21 **29:5** [p] 1Sa 18:7; 21:11 **29:6** [q] 1Sa 27:8-12 [r] ver 3
29:9 [s] 2Sa 14:17, 20; 19:27 [t] ver 4 **29:10** [u] 1Ch 12:19 **30:1** [v] 1Sa 29:4, 11 [w] 1Sa 15:7; 27:8 **30:5** [x] 1Sa 25:43; 2Sa 2:2 **30:6** [y] Ex 17:4; Jn 8:59 [z] Ps 27:14; 56:3-4, 11; Ro 4:20 **30:7** [a] 1Sa 22:20 [b] 1Sa 23:9 **30:8** [c] 1Sa 23:2 [d] ver 18 **30:9** [e] 1Sa 27:2 **30:10** [f] ver 9, 21 **30:12** [g] Jdg 15:19

29:3 *Hebrews.* See note on 4:6.
30:7 *Abiathar the priest.* See 22:20. *Bring me the ephod.* See note on 2:18. Cf. Saul's instructions to Ahijah in 14:18 – 19 (see note there).

raided the Negev of the Kerethites,[h] some
territory belonging to Judah and the Negev of Caleb.[i] And we burned[j] Ziklag."
15David asked him, "Can you lead me
down to this raiding party?"
He answered, "Swear to me before God
that you will not kill me or hand me over
to my master, and I will take you down
to them."
16He led David down, and there they
were, scattered over the countryside, eating, drinking and reveling[k] because of the
great amount of plunder[l] they had taken
from the land of the Philistines and from
Judah. 17David fought[m] them from dusk
until the evening of the next day, and none
of them got away, except four hundred
young men who rode off on camels and
fled.[n] 18David recovered[o] everything the
Amalekites had taken, including his two
wives. 19Nothing was missing: young or
old, boy or girl, plunder or anything else
they had taken. David brought everything
back. 20He took all the flocks and herds,
and his men drove them ahead of the other
livestock, saying, "This is David's plunder."
21Then David came to the two hundred
men who had been too exhausted[p] to follow him and who were left behind at the
Besor Valley. They came out to meet David and the men with him. As David and
his men approached, he asked them how
they were. 22But all the evil men and troublemakers among David's followers said,
"Because they did not go out with us, we
will not share with them the plunder we
recovered. However, each man may take
his wife and children and go."
23David replied, "No, my brothers, you
must not do that with what the LORD has
given us. He has protected us and delivered into our hands the raiding party that
came against us. 24Who will listen to what
you say? The share of the man who stayed
with the supplies is to be the same as that
of him who went down to the battle. All
will share alike.[q]" 25David made this a
statute and ordinance for Israel from that
day to this.
26When David reached Ziklag, he sent
some of the plunder to the elders of Judah,
who were his friends, saying, "Here is a
gift for you from the plunder of the LORD's
enemies."
27David sent it to those who were in
Bethel,[r] Ramoth[s] Negev and Jattir;[t] 28to
those in Aroer,[u] Siphmoth, Eshtemoa[v]
29and Rakal; to those in the towns of the
Jerahmeelites[w] and the Kenites;[x] 30to those
in Hormah,[y] Bor Ashan,[z] Athak 31and Hebron;[a] and to those in all the other places
where he and his men had roamed.

30:14 [h] 2Sa 8:18; 1Ki 1:38,44; Eze 25:16; Zep 2:5 [i] ver 16; Jos 14:13; 15:13 [j] ver 1
30:16 [k] Lk 12:19 [l] ver 14
30:17 [m] 1Sa 11:11 [n] 1Sa 15:3
30:18 [o] Ge 14:16
30:21 [p] ver 10
30:24 [q] Nu 31:27; Jos 22:8
30:27 [r] Jos 7:2 [s] Jos 19:8 [t] Jos 15:48
30:28 [u] Jos 13:16 [v] Jos 15:50
30:29 [w] 1Sa 27:10 [x] Jdg 1:16; 1Sa 15:6
30:30 [y] Nu 14:45; Jdg 1:17 [z] Jos 15:42
30:31 [a] Jos 14:13; 2Sa 2:1,4

Saul Takes His Life

31:1-13pp — 2Sa 1:4-12; 1Ch 10:1-12

31 Now the Philistines fought against
Israel; the Israelites fled before
them, and many fell dead on Mount Gil-

30:17 *rode off on camels.* The possession of camels by the Amalekites was encountered already in 15:3. Of the six living species of camels, only two appear to have inhabited the world of the ancient Near East, the one-humped dromedary (*Camelus dromedarius*) and the two-humped bactrian (*Camelus bactrianus*). The Hebrew term for camel used in the Bible is generic, like its English equivalent, and does not clearly specify which species of camel is in view (though the one-humped, or Arabian, camel would be most likely in this range). Biblical references to domesticated camels in the patriarchal period continue to be challenged as anachronistic by some scholars, but other scholars point out that Pentateuchal references to riding camels are quite limited, and there is some evidence for the domestication of camels as early as 3000 BC. This evidence converges nicely with the Biblical texts, in which cameleering is associated mainly with peoples such as the Amalekites and Midianites (Jdg 6:5; 7:12; 8:21,26) who lived in the arid regions to the south and east of Judah. Because of their stamina — namely, their ability to go several days without drinking — and their speed, camels made effective mounts for travel and for battle.

30:24 *All will share alike.* While the taking of plunder in battle is subjected to ethical questioning nowadays, in antiquity it was regarded as a legitimate aspect of warfare. In the thought world of the ancient Near East, both victory in battle and the spoils of battle were regarded as gifts of the gods. Furthermore, soldiers who were not mercenaries were often not paid directly for their services but were allowed loot by way of compensation. With some exceptions, however, plundering the vanquished foe in the ancient Near East was regarded as a legitimate aspect of warfare, not in itself a legitimate ground for initiating a conflict. The quantity of spoils captured, whether measured in human captives, livestock or material goods, served as a measure of the magnitude of the victory and bolstered the prestige of the triumphant army, especially its leader, and was often celebrated in inscriptions and reliefs. In most circumstances, the spoils of war were collected and then carefully distributed in the aftermath of the battle, according to guidelines established either before or after the battle. As a general rule, significant (not merely symbolic) quantities of spoils went to the temple and the temple service. Any allies involved in the conflict or in certain covenantal relationships also received a share — one may think in this regard of David's sending "some of the plunder to the elders of Judah" (v. 26), among whom he had found refuge for a time during his fugitive period. The king or leader, of course, received a significant share, and the soldiers along with auxiliary personnel also received distributions. Among such auxiliary personnel in the present episode might be counted the 200 soldiers who remained behind at the Besor Valley (vv. 9 – 10; cf. the 200 who "stayed with the supplies" as David and 400 others went up against Nabal in 25:13). Thus, David's insistence that those who stayed behind were not to be denied a share was in keeping with wider practices in the ancient Near East and in the Bible (e.g., Nu 31; Jos 22).

31:1 *Mount Gilboa.* The Gilboa range runs north to border the Jezreel Valley on the southeast side. The military

boa.[b] 2 The Philistines were in hot pursuit
of Saul and his sons, and they killed his
sons Jonathan, Abinadab and Malki-Shua.
3 The fighting grew fierce around Saul,
and when the archers overtook him, they
wounded[c] him critically.
4 Saul said to his armor-bearer, "Draw
your sword and run me through,[d] or these
uncircumcised[e] fellows will come and run
me through and abuse me."
But his armor-bearer was terrified and
would not do it; so Saul took his own
sword and fell on it. 5 When the armor-
bearer saw that Saul was dead, he too fell
on his sword and died with him. 6 So Saul
and his three sons and his armor-bearer
and all his men died together that same
day.
7 When the Israelites along the valley
and those across the Jordan saw that the
Israelite army had fled and that Saul and
his sons had died, they abandoned their
towns and fled. And the Philistines came
and occupied them.
8 The next day, when the Philistines
came to strip the dead, they found Saul
and his three sons fallen on Mount Gilboa.
9 They cut off his head and stripped off his
armor, and they sent messengers throughout the land of the Philistines to proclaim
the news[f] in the temple of their idols and
among their people.[g] 10 They put his armor
in the temple of the Ashtoreths[h] and fastened his body to the wall of Beth Shan.[i]
11 When the people of Jabesh Gilead[j] heard what the Philistines had done
to Saul, 12 all their valiant men marched
through the night to Beth Shan. They took
down the bodies of Saul and his sons from
the wall of Beth Shan and went to Jabesh,
where they burned[k] them. 13 Then they
took their bones[l] and buried them under a
tamarisk[m] tree at Jabesh, and they fasted[n]
seven days.[o]

31:1 [b] 1Sa 28:4; 1Ch 10:1-12 **31:3** [c] 2Sa 1:6 **31:4** [d] Jdg 9:54; 2Sa 1:6,10 [e] 1Sa 14:6 **31:9** [f] 2Sa 1:20 [g] Jdg 16:24 **31:10** [h] Jdg 2:12-13; 1Sa 7:3 [i] Jos 17:11; 2Sa 21:12 **31:11** [j] 1Sa 11:1 **31:12** [k] 2Sa 2:4-7; 2Ch 16:14; Am 6:10 **31:13** [l] 2Sa 21:12-14 [m] 1Sa 22:6 [n] 2Sa 1:12 [o] Ge 50:10

superiority that chariots afforded the Philistines in the relatively flat battleground of the Jezreel Valley led to a rapid Philistine victory and put the Israelites to flight. Many Israelites were slain on Mount Gilboa, perhaps as they sought to gain the advantage of high ground or rougher terrain, where chariots would be less effective, or simply because they were overmatched and had been routed. In antiquity, chariots often served as mobile firing platforms for chariots, and that may have been the case here. The position of the Philistines at Aphek (29:1), which was near Shunem, might have threatened to cut Saul off from the northern Israelite territory, which might explain why he was forced to fight them in a place where they held such a tactical advantage.

31:4 *armor-bearer.* See note on 14:1. *Draw your sword and run me through.* In view of the kind of treatment ancient Near Eastern prisoners of war in general, and defeated kings in particular, could expect, Saul's fear of being abused by the Philistines was well founded. From Assyrian inscriptions around the time of David and later, we gain an impression of unremitting cruelty to prisoners of war. One particularly gruesome relief from the reign of Sargon II shows the vanquished king of Hamath literally being flayed alive in public. Although Saul managed to end his life before falling into the hands of the Philistines, their treatment of his corpse (vv. 8 – 10) confirms the cruelty that Saul had feared. Saul's attempt to have his armor-bearer run him through finds its closest analogy in the death scene of the less than admirable Abimelek in Jdg 9:54. Outside the Bible, Assyrian texts also attest a king asking his armor-bearer to finish him off. For suicide in the ancient Near East, see note on 2Sa 17:23. *uncircumcised fellows.* See note on Jdg 14:3.

31:9 *They cut off his head.* In the ancient Near East, a king's head was a prized trophy. See note on 5:3 – 4.

31:10 *put his armor in the temple of the Ashtoreths.* Cf. the placement of Goliath's sword behind the ephod in the sanctuary at Nob (21:9). Cf. also the general practice of deporting enemy gods/idols and depositing them in one's own sanctuary (see note on 5:2). *Ashtoreths.* See note on Jdg 2:13.

31:12 *took down the bodies ... burned them.* Cremation was not a common burial practice in most parts of the ancient Near East, though it is attested especially among the Hurrian-influenced Hittites of Anatolia. There is some sparse evidence of cremation burials in Judah from as early as the second half of the eleventh century BC, though some of what little evidence there is may have resulted from accidental causes, such as tomb fires. In the OT, burning in the fire or burning with fire is associated mostly with purification (Lev 13:57), with the punishment of capital offenders (Lev 20:14; 21:9), or both (Jos 7:25). Cremation as a burial custom per se is unknown in the OT, unless the present episode in which the mutilated bodies of Saul and his sons are burned provides an exception.

NARRATIVE LITERATURE

2 SAMUEL

David Hears of Saul's Death

1:4-12pp — 1Sa 31:1-13; 1Ch 10:1-12

1 After the death[a] of Saul, David returned from striking down[b] the Amalekites and stayed in Ziklag two days. 2On
the third day a man[c] arrived from Saul's
camp with his clothes torn and dust on his
head.[d] When he came to David, he fell to
the ground to pay him honor.
3"Where have you come from?" David
asked him.
He answered, "I have escaped from the
Israelite camp."
4"What happened?" David asked.
"Tell me."
"The men fled from the battle," he replied. "Many of them fell and died. And
Saul and his son Jonathan are dead."
5Then David said to the young man who
brought him the report, "How do you know
that Saul and his son Jonathan are dead?"
6"I happened to be on Mount Gilboa,[e]"
the young man said, "and there was Saul,
leaning on his spear, with the chariots
and their drivers in hot pursuit. 7When he
turned around and saw me, he called out
to me, and I said, 'What can I do?'
8"He asked me, 'Who are you?'
" 'An Amalekite,[f]' I answered.
9"Then he said to me, 'Stand here by me
and kill me! I'm in the throes of death, but
I'm still alive.'
10"So I stood beside him and killed him,
because I knew that after he had fallen he
could not survive. And I took the crown[g]
that was on his head and the band on his
arm and have brought them here to my
lord."
11Then David and all the men with him
took hold of their clothes and tore[h] them.
12They mourned and wept and fasted till
evening for Saul and his son Jonathan,
and for the army of the LORD and for the
nation of Israel, because they had fallen
by the sword.
13David said to the young man who
brought him the report, "Where are you
from?"
"I am the son of a foreigner, an Amalekite,[i]" he answered.
14David asked him, "Why weren't you
afraid to lift your hand to destroy the
LORD's anointed?[j]"
15Then David called one of his men and
said, "Go, strike him down!"[k] So he struck

1:1 [a] 1Sa 31:6 [b] 1Sa 30:17
1:2 [c] 2Sa 4:10 [d] 1Sa 4:12
1:6 [e] 1Sa 28:4; 31:2-4
1:8 [f] 1Sa 15:2; 30:13, 17
1:10 [g] Jdg 9:54; 2Ki 11:12
1:11 [h] Ge 37:29; 2Sa 3:31; 13:31
1:13 [i] ver 8
1:14 [j] 1Sa 24:6; 26:9
1:15 [k] 2Sa 4:12

1:1 *Amalekites.* See note on 1Sa 15:2.

1:2 *with his clothes torn and dust on his head.* Signs of distress and mourning (see note on 1Sa 4:12).

1:6 *chariots.* See note on 1Sa 13:5. While chariots are not mentioned in the account of Saul's death in 1Sa 31 (where Saul's injuries are inflicted by archers, see 1Sa 31:3), there is no necessary discrepancy here, as chariots often served as mobile firing platforms for archers. *drivers.* Lit. "horse-masters" or "master horsemen," a phrase that occurs only here in the Hebrew Bible. In light of the late introduction of cavalry to Syria and Palestine, they are probably to be thought of as "charioteers."

1:10 *the crown … on his head and the band on his arm.* From the evidence of reliefs, it is apparent that crowns of many shapes and sizes were worn by gods, kings and other important individuals throughout the ancient Near East from earliest times. The specific character of the Saul's crown and armband is unknown, but given the fact that Saul was able to wear them into battle, it is fair to assume that they were of lightweight construction. Further support for this assumption comes from the fact that the Hebrew word here rendered "crown," more properly connotes something like a "diadem" (i.e., a circular, ornamental headdress, sometimes bearing precious stones). Diadems could be added to the turbans frequently worn by ancient Near Eastern kings, priests and others. Israel's high priest wore not only a fine linen turban, but a diadem as well, from the front of which hung a gold plate engraved with the words "HOLY TO THE LORD" (Ex 28:36). Saul's crown may have been a similar diadem with royal insignia attached. The nature of Saul's armband is also uncertain, there being only one other mention of such

him down, and he died.[l] 16For David had
said to him, "Your blood be on your own
head.[m] Your own mouth testified against
you when you said, 'I killed the LORD's
anointed.' "

David's Lament for Saul and Jonathan

17David took up this lament[n] concerning Saul and his son Jonathan, 18and he
ordered that the people of Judah be taught
this lament of the bow (it is written in the
Book of Jashar):[o]

19"A gazelle[a] lies slain on your heights, Israel.
How the mighty have fallen![p]

20"Tell it not in Gath,[q]
proclaim it not in the streets of Ashkelon,
lest the daughters of the Philistines[r] be glad,
lest the daughters of the uncircumcised rejoice.[s]

21"Mountains of Gilboa,[t]
may you have neither dew nor rain,
may no showers fall on your terraced fields.[b][u]
For there the shield of the mighty was despised,
the shield of Saul—no longer rubbed with oil.[v]

22"From the blood[w] of the slain,
from the flesh of the mighty,
the bow[x] of Jonathan did not turn back,
the sword of Saul did not return unsatisfied.

23Saul and Jonathan—
in life they were loved and admired,
and in death they were not parted.
They were swifter than eagles,[y]
they were stronger than lions.[z]

24"Daughters of Israel,
weep for Saul,
who clothed you in scarlet and finery,
who adorned your garments with ornaments of gold.

25"How the mighty have fallen in battle!
Jonathan lies slain on your heights.
26I grieve for you, Jonathan my brother;[a]
you were very dear to me.
Your love for me was wonderful,[b]
more wonderful than that of women.

27"How the mighty have fallen!
The weapons of war have perished!"[c]

1:15 [l] 2Sa 4:10 **1:16** [m] Lev 20:9; 2Sa 3:28-29; 1Ki 2:32; Mt 27:24-25; Ac 18:6 **1:17** [n] 2Ch 35:25 **1:18** [o] Jos 10:13; 1Sa 31:3 **1:19** [p] ver 27 **1:20** [q] Mic 1:10 [r] 1Sa 31:8 [s] Ex 15:20; 1Sa 18:6 **1:21** [t] ver 6; 1Sa 31:1 [u] Eze 31:15 [v] Isa 21:5 **1:22** [w] Isa 34:3, 7 [x] Dt 32:42; 1Sa 18:4 **1:23** [y] Dt 28:49; Jer 4:13 [z] Jdg 14:18 **1:26** [a] 1Sa 20:42 [b] 1Sa 18:1 **1:27** [c] ver 19, 25; 1Sa 2:4

[a] 19 *Gazelle* here symbolizes a human dignitary.
[b] 21 Or / *nor fields that yield grain for offerings*

an "armlet" in the Bible (Nu 31:50), but it too must have served to symbolize Saul's royal status.

1:17–27 Among the various lamentations and elegies known from the ancient Near East, the best known is Gilgamesh's lament for his dead friend Enkidu. David's lament over Saul and Jonathan exhibits a number of general similarities—e.g., a broad public is addressed (v. 18); martial imagery is prevalent and deeds of valor are celebrated (vv. 21–22); physical prowess is highlighted (v. 23); deep affection and grief are expressed (v. 26); and there is a recurring refrain (vv. 19,25,27). Parallels like this do not suggest that David has borrowed an ancient Near Eastern lament; they just situate David in the literary world of the time, using genres and motifs that were familiar in those days.

1:18 *lament of the bow.* The sense of this title has puzzled commentators and sparked several explanations. The word "lament" is not explicitly stated in the Hebrew text, and the Septuagint (the pre-Christian Greek translation of the OT) omits the word "bow." The sense then would be that David is ordering that the lament he is about to take up should be taught to the children of Israel. If the word "bow" is retained, however, it may refer to Jonathan (whose bow is mentioned in v. 22) and serve as a title for the lament. Referring to Jonathan or Saul by the weapon(s) they wielded appears to be attested in the closing line of the lament, where "weapons of war" (v. 27) probably stands for Saul and Jonathan. The later designation of Elijah and Elisha as "the chariots and horsemen of Israel" (2Ki 13:14) offers an analogue. *Book of Jashar.* Appears to have been a book of early Israelite poetry, now lost. In addition to the present passage, it is mentioned in Jos 10:12–13 in the account of Joshua's exceptional day in defense of the Gibeonites. The name is generally assumed to derive from the Hebrew word meaning "upright, just, righteous," and the like, suggesting that the Book of Jashar may have celebrated the exploits of heroic individuals in Israel or of the Israelites as a whole, as the Lord's "upright" people. Alternatively, the name may reflect the Hebrew word for "song," yielding simply the "Book of Song."

1:20 *uncircumcised.* See note on Jdg 14:3.

1:21 *shield of Saul—no longer rubbed with oil.* Ancient Near Eastern shields came in a variety of shapes and sizes. One of the most prevalent constructions involved a wooden shield covered with leather. Fifteenth-century BC wall paintings from the tomb of the Egyptian Rekhmire illustrate the various steps in the construction of such shields. To preserve and condition leather shields, oil was periodically rubbed into them (cf. Isa 21:5). An Old Babylonian text from Tell Asmar records "one sila of oil to rub the shield(s)."

1:26 *Jonathan my brother . . . Your love for me was . . . more wonderful than that of women.* Some modern readers, unaware or neglectful of the Biblical and ancient Near Eastern background to such expressions of love, have tried to read a homosexual nuance into David's words. However, "love language" was often used to express loyalty in legal contexts, where the legal (and not sexual) connotations of words such as "dear" and "beloved" is evident. The same is true of the Hebrew word for "love" in many contexts. Commentators have perhaps been led astray by David's extolling of Jonathan's love as "more wonderful than that of women," but David's intent may simply have been to underscore the remarkably selfless character of Jonathan's loyalty to David and willingness to defer to him with regard to the kingship (1Sa 18:3–4).

David Anointed King Over Judah

2 In the course of time, David inquired[d]
of the LORD. "Shall I go up to one of
the towns of Judah?" he asked.
The LORD said, "Go up."
David asked, "Where shall I go?"
"To Hebron,"[e] the LORD answered.
2So David went up there with his two
wives,[f] Ahinoam of Jezreel and Abigail,[g]
the widow of Nabal of Carmel. 3David also
took the men who were with him,[h] each
with his family, and they settled in Hebron
and its towns. 4Then the men of Judah
came to Hebron,[i] and there they anointed[j]
David king over the tribe of Judah.
When David was told that it was the
men from Jabesh Gilead[k] who had buried
Saul, 5he sent messengers to them to say
to them, "The LORD bless[l] you for showing this kindness to Saul your master by
burying him. 6May the LORD now show
you kindness and faithfulness,[m] and I too
will show you the same favor because you
have done this. 7Now then, be strong and
brave, for Saul your master is dead, and
the people of Judah have anointed me
king over them."

2:1 [d] 1Sa 23:2, 11-12 [e] Ge 13:18; 1Sa 30:31 **2:2** [f] 1Sa 25:43; 30:5 [g] 1Sa 25:42 **2:3** [h] 1Sa 27:2; 30:9 **2:4** [i] 1Sa 30:31 [j] 1Sa 2:35; 2Sa 5:3-5 [k] 1Sa 31:11-13 **2:5** [l] 1Sa 23:21 **2:6** [m] Ex 34:6; 1Ti 1:16

War Between the Houses of David and Saul

3:2-5pp — 1Ch 3:1-4

8Meanwhile, Abner[n] son of Ner, the
commander of Saul's army, had taken Ish-
Bosheth son of Saul and brought him over
to Mahanaim.[o] 9He made him king over
Gilead,[p] Ashuri[q] and Jezreel, and also
over Ephraim, Benjamin and all Israel.[r]
10Ish-Bosheth son of Saul was forty
years old when he became king over Israel, and he reigned two years. The tribe of
Judah, however, remained loyal to David.
11The length of time David was king in Hebron over Judah was seven years and six
months.[s]
12Abner son of Ner, together with the
men of Ish-Bosheth son of Saul, left Mahanaim and went to Gibeon.[t] 13Joab[u] son
of Zeruiah and David's men went out
and met them at the pool of Gibeon. One
group sat down on one side of the pool
and one group on the other side.
14Then Abner said to Joab, "Let's have
some of the young men get up and fight
hand to hand in front of us."
"All right, let them do it," Joab said.

2:8 [n] 1Sa 14:50 [o] Ge 32:2 **2:9** [p] Nu 32:26 [q] Jdg 1:32 [r] 1Ch 12:29 **2:11** [s] 2Sa 5:5 **2:12** [t] Jos 18:25 **2:13** [u] 2Sa 8:16; 1Ch 2:16; 11:6

2:2 *Ahinoam of Jezreel and Abigail ... of Carmel.* See notes on 1Sa 25:39b; 25:43.

2:4a *anointed David king.* See note on 1Sa 2:10. Several factors converge to make the anointing of David as king by the major southern tribe of Judah understandable: (1) the recent successes of the Philistines in the battle of Gilboa may have limited the ability of more northerly tribes to participate, even had they wanted to; (2) the death of most of Saul's house would have created uncertainty regarding the succession, even for those unaware of or unwilling to accept the fact that Saul's house had been rejected; (3) government by city-kings was well-known in Canaan and a previous attempt to establish a king had been initiated by a tribe (Jdg 9).

2:4b – 7 Jabesh-Gilead represented a strong constituency of Saul since he rescued them (1Sa 11). David is arguing that since Saul and his family are dead, there is no further loyalty owed to them; they have "repaid" Saul by giving him proper burial, and David will see to their defense in the same way Saul had. By gaining favor from these staunch supporters of Saul, David hopes to sway others to follow him as well.

2:8 *Abner ... had taken Ish-Bosheth son of Saul ... to Mahanaim.* In the aftermath of Israel's defeat by the Philistines at the battle of Gilboa, Abner had little choice but to seek to establish a rump kingdom in Transjordan. The former heart of the kingdom of Saul west of the Jordan would have been too vulnerable to repeated Philistine attack.

2:9 *He made him king over ... all Israel.* Both the specific sites over which Ish-Bosheth is to have been made king, as well as the summary of his domain as "all Israel," probably represent merely the territories to which Ish-Bosheth laid claim, irrespective of whether he actually exercised control over them. The scenario of a military strongman (in this instance Abner) propping up a weak heir to the throne is not without precedent in the ancient Near East.

2:13 *Joab son of Zeruiah.* Joab, who served as commander of David's forces (see 8:16), is here mentioned for the first time in the Bible. He was a nephew of David, being one of three sons of David's sister Zeruiah (1Ch 2:13 – 16). *pool of Gibeon.* A pool excavated at Gibeon was created by carving a cylinder some 39 feet (12 meters) in diameter and 35 feet (10.5 meters) deep into limestone bedrock, removing some 3,000 tons (2,720 metric tons) of limestone in the process. A 5-foot-wide (1.5-meter-wide) staircase spirals down the side of the cylinder, providing access to the flat floor of the large cylinder. The stairs do not end here, however, but continue in a narrower shaft some 45 feet (13.7 meters) farther down, until they reach the water table. The purpose of this two-part construction is somewhat mysterious, but it has been suggested that the large cylinder may have been a first phase, intended to serve as a cistern. (Given the dry summer season, larger settlements in Canaan found it necessary to find ways to capture and preserve water.) The narrower shaft may have been dug when it was determined that the spring feeding the other water system at Gibeon lay somewhere below the large cylinder.

2:14 The Hebrew terminology employed in this verse has led some interpreters to assume that the event involved some kind of sport or exhibition that became overly serious and turned out badly. The Hebrew word rendered "young men" can mean "youths," and the Hebrew word rendered "fight" often means "play" or "sport"; thus, Abner's suggestion would be that youths from the opposing sides arise and make sport (perhaps engage in mock fighting) for the entertainment of the others. More likely, however, what we have here is an example of representative combat by a team of select warriors to decide the fates of the opposing armies. The concept of representative combat has been encountered already in the contest between David and Goliath, where David gained a decisive victory, killing Goliath and putting the Philistine army to flight (see the article "Combat by Champions," p. 491). The term "young men" then refers here, as in other military contexts, to professional soldiers. The line between

15So they stood up and were counted
off — twelve men for Benjamin and Ish-
Bosheth son of Saul, and twelve for David.
16Then each man grabbed his opponent by
the head and thrust his dagger into his opponent's side, and they fell down together.
So that place in Gibeon was called Helkath
Hazzurim.[a]
17The battle that day was very fierce,
and Abner and the Israelites were defeated[v] by David's men.
18The three sons of Zeruiah[w] were there:
Joab,[x] Abishai[y] and Asahel.[z] Now Asahel
was as fleet-footed as a wild gazelle.[a] 19He
chased Abner, turning neither to the right
nor to the left as he pursued him. 20Ab-
ner looked behind him and asked, "Is that
you, Asahel?"

"It is," he answered.

21Then Abner said to him, "Turn aside to
the right or to the left; take on one of the
young men and strip him of his weapons."
But Asahel would not stop chasing him.
22Again Abner warned Asahel, "Stop
chasing me! Why should I strike you
down? How could I look your brother Joab
in the face?"[b]
23But Asahel refused to give up the pursuit; so Abner thrust the butt of his spear
into Asahel's stomach,[c] and the spear
came out through his back. He fell there
and died on the spot. And every man
stopped when he came to the place where
Asahel had fallen and died.[d]
24But Joab and Abishai pursued Abner,
and as the sun was setting, they came to
the hill of Ammah, near Giah on the way
to the wasteland of Gibeon. 25Then the
men of Benjamin rallied behind Abner.
They formed themselves into a group and
took their stand on top of a hill.
26Abner called out to Joab, "Must the
sword devour[e] forever? Don't you realize
that this will end in bitterness? How long
before you order your men to stop pursuing their fellow Israelites?"
27Joab answered, "As surely as God
lives, if you had not spoken, the men
would have continued pursuing them until morning."
28So Joab[f] blew the trumpet,[g] and all the
troops came to a halt; they no longer pursued Israel, nor did they fight anymore.
29All that night Abner and his men
marched through the Arabah. They
crossed the Jordan, continued through the
morning hours[b] and came to Mahanaim.[h]
30Then Joab stopped pursuing Abner
and assembled the whole army. Besides
Asahel, nineteen of David's men were
found missing. 31But David's men had
killed three hundred and sixty Benjamites
who were with Abner. 32They took Asahel and buried him in his father's tomb[i]
at Bethlehem. Then Joab and his men
marched all night and arrived at Hebron
by daybreak.

3 The war between the house of Saul
and the house of David lasted a long
time.[j] David grew stronger and stronger,[k]
while the house of Saul grew weaker and
weaker.[l]
2Sons were born to David in Hebron:

His firstborn was Amnon the son of
Ahinoam[m] of Jezreel;

2:17 [v] 2Sa 3:1 **2:18** [w] 2Sa 3:39 [x] 2Sa 3:30 [y] 1Sa 26:6 [z] 1Ch 2:16 [a] 1Ch 12:8 **2:22** [b] 2Sa 3:27 **2:23** [c] 2Sa 3:27; 4:6 [d] 2Sa 20:12 **2:26** [e] Dt 32:42; Jer 46:10, 14 **2:28** [f] 2Sa 18:16 [g] Jdg 3:27 **2:29** [h] ver 8 **2:32** [i] Ge 49:29 **3:1** [j] 1Ki 14:30 [k] 2Sa 5:10 [l] 2Sa 2:17 **3:2** [m] 1Sa 25:43; 1Ch 3:1-3

[a] 16 *Helkath Hazzurim* means *field of daggers* or *field of hostilities.* [b] 29 See Septuagint; the meaning of the Hebrew for this phrase is uncertain.

the two understandings of the contest, mock fighting or contest of champions, should perhaps not be too sharply drawn — one need only think of medieval jousting to understand that the line between sport and battle may have been thin. The purpose of "single combat," or "representative combat," whether by individuals or, as here, by a group of elite soldiers, was to decide victory without the necessity of wider bloodshed. The outcome here was decidedly inconclusive. However, "each man grabbed his opponent by the head and thrust his dagger into his opponent's side, and they fell down together" (v. 16), with the result that "the battle that day was very fierce" (v. 17).

2:21 *strip him of his weapons.* The rank or status of a soldier was indicated by the quality of his weapons, which would become the property of the victor if he was defeated in combat. Asahel wants to claim the enemy commander's gear.

2:23 *Abner thrust the butt of his spear into Asahel's stomach.* Unless the text should read "with a backward thrust," then Abner's ability to kill a man with the butt of his spear reflects both his own physical prowess and the fact that the butt end of spears would have typically been fitted with a metal casing useful for prodding and for sticking the spear into the ground (without damaging the spearhead itself); recall 1Sa 26:7, where Saul's spear was "stuck in the ground near his head." Archaeological excavations have uncovered numerous such end casings, and they can be seen also in wall paintings.

2:28 *trumpet.* Used as a signaling device (see note on Jos 6:4).

2:32 *buried him in his father's tomb at Bethlehem.* In Israel's monarchal period, it was common practice for important families to bury succeeding generations of their dead in rock-cut or cave tombs or tomb complexes — thus perhaps explaining the expression "rest with your ancestors" (7:12) or "gathered to his people" (Ge 25:8; see note there). The bones of earlier burials would be either collected in a "charnel pit" or simply pushed to the periphery of the tomb, while the most recently deceased would be placed on a bench shelf, often surrounded by personal items (see note on Ge 23:4).

3:2 – 5 The numeric growth of David's family attests to the growing strength of his house, in contrast to the house of Saul (v. 1). Four additional wives (or concubines) aid in the process of David's siring six sons, and in 5:13 – 16, after David's arrival in Jerusalem, further wives/concubines will be added, and at least eleven more children will be born to David (cf. 1Ch 3:1 – 9). It was common practice among powerful kings in the ancient Near East to multiply wives and children. Kings established their political strength

3 his second, Kileab the son of Abigail[n] the widow of Nabal of Carmel;
the third, Absalom[o] the son of Maakah daughter of Talmai king of Geshur;[p]
4 the fourth, Adonijah[q] the son of
Haggith;
the fifth, Shephatiah the son of Abi-
tal;
5 and the sixth, Ithream the son of
David's wife Eglah.
These were born to David in Hebron.

Abner Goes Over to David

6 During the war between the house of
Saul and the house of David, Abner had
been strengthening his own position in the
house of Saul. 7 Now Saul had had a concubine[r] named Rizpah[s] daughter of Aiah.
And Ish-Bosheth said to Abner, "Why did
you sleep with my father's concubine?"
8 Abner was very angry because of what
Ish-Bosheth said. So he answered, "Am I a
dog's head[t]—on Judah's side? This very
day I am loyal to the house of your father
Saul and to his family and friends. I haven't
handed you over to David. Yet now you accuse me of an offense involving this woman! 9 May God deal with Abner, be it ever so
severely, if I do not do for David what the
LORD promised[u] him on oath 10 and transfer
the kingdom from the house of Saul and
establish David's throne over Israel and
Judah from Dan to Beersheba."[v] 11 Ish-Bosheth did not dare to say another word to
Abner, because he was afraid of him.
12 Then Abner sent messengers on his
behalf to say to David, "Whose land is it?
Make an agreement with me, and I will
help you bring all Israel over to you."
13 "Good," said David. "I will make an
agreement with you. But I demand one
thing of you: Do not come into my presence unless you bring Michal daughter of
Saul when you come to see me."[w] 14 Then
David sent messengers to Ish-Bosheth son
of Saul, demanding, "Give me my wife Mi-

3:3 [n] 1Sa 25:42 [o] 2Sa 13:1, 28 [p] 1Sa 27:8; 2Sa 13:37; 14:32; 15:8 **3:4** [q] 1Ki 1:5, 11 **3:7** [r] 2Sa 16:21-22 [s] 2Sa 21:8-11
3:8 [t] 1Sa 24:14; 2Sa 9:8; 16:9 **3:9** [u] 1Sa 15:28; 1Ki 19:2 **3:10** [v] Jdg 20:1; 1Sa 3:20 **3:13** [w] Ge 43:5; 1Sa 18:20

through the network that was established through marriage alliances. The Biblical narrator withholds judgment for the time being on David's "royal" behavior, though the instruction in Dt 17:14–20 to future kings of Israel is that they "must not take many wives" (Dt 17:17).

3:7 *Why did you sleep with my father's concubine?* In the ancient Near East, a household might at times include a primary wife and one or more subordinate wives or concubines, the latter being defined as women by whom a man might father children, but who brought no dowry into the relationship and thus did not enjoy the status of full wife. While monogamy may have been the (flexible) norm among common folk in the ancient Near East (see note on 1Sa 1:2), polygamy was common among the powerful, especially kings (for David's growing harem, see notes on 1Sa 25:39b,43). A king's wives and concubines were a reflection of his power and position, often involving political alliances through marriage, and so for an outsider to sleep with one of these women was, among other things, a direct assault on the husband's status and position. In the Bible, to sleep with a royal wife or concubine was tantamount to usurping the throne (see note on 2Sa 16:21), and even to ask to marry a concubine of a deceased king was considered treason (1Ki 2:22). In the present episode, the narrator does not state explicitly whether Abner had or had not slept with Saul's concubine Rizpah, but it does state that "Abner had been strengthening his own position in the house of Saul" (v. 6), perhaps aggravating Ish-Bosheth's suspicions. Abner's incensed response in v. 8 to Ish-Bosheth's charge—unless he was simply feigning indignation—suggests that he was innocent of the specific charge.

3:8 *dog's head.* This expression is found nowhere else in Biblical or ancient Near Eastern literature, and so its significance can only be surmised. Dogs were not highly regarded in the ancient Near East, and to be a "dog" was at best to be insignificant, to be a "dead dog" was to be less significant still (see note on 1Sa 24:14), and to be a "dog's head" was to be perhaps worst of all (particularly if "head" is being used euphemistically for the opposing end of the dog). In the OT specifically, dogs were considered unclean (Lev 11:26–28), aggressive scavengers (2Ki 9:35–36), and disgusting (Pr 26:11), so Abner's choice of image aptly captures his sense of outrage at Ish-Bosheth's accusation.

3:13 *bring Michal daughter of Saul when you come.* Several ancient Near Eastern law codes stipulate what was to be done when a husband was either voluntarily or involuntarily absent from his wife for a long period. The Mesopotamian Laws of Eshnunna, e.g., state that if a man is taken prisoner by an invading force and carried away to a foreign country, he shall receive his wife back upon his return, even if she has been taken by another man, but if a man "repudiates his city and his master and then flees," he shall have no right to reclaim his wife upon his return. The Code of Hammurapi addresses the issue similarly, adding that a woman incurs no blame by entering the house of another man, but only if "there are not sufficient provisions in [her absent husband's] house." If the husband has voluntarily deserted his city and his wife and she "enters another's house," then upon his return "because he repudiated his city and fled, the wife of the deserter will not return to her husband." Middle Assyrian laws run along similar lines, but qualify the code in further respects. To name but one example, even if a woman was voluntarily deserted by her husband and was left without "oil or wool or clothing or provisions or anything else," she was still required to "remain [the exclusive object of rights] for her husband for five years" before considering other options. In the light of ancient Near Eastern legal tradition, David was within his rights to demand the return of his wife Michal—his absence from her was involuntary, necessitated by Saul's attempts to kill him—and Saul should probably be faulted for giving her to another man (1Sa 25:44). Saul's treatment of Michal was almost certainly motivated more by political considerations than by concern for her best interests, and the same can probably be said of David's motivation in demanding her back. She is a pawn in a power play. Michal was David's tie to the former royal house of Benjamin, and her return to his own house would have served his own royal ambitions. Further, the text's poignant picture of Paltiel "weeping behind her all the way" (v. 16) seems intended to contrast Paltiel's affection with David's political maneuvering.

chal,[x] whom I betrothed to myself for the
price of a hundred Philistine foreskins.”
15So Ish-Bosheth gave orders and had
her taken away from her husband[y] Paltiel[z] son of Laish. 16Her husband, however,
went with her, weeping behind her all the
way to Bahurim.[a] Then Abner said to him,
“Go back home!” So he went back.
17Abner conferred with the elders[b] of Israel and said, “For some time you have
wanted to make David your king. 18Now
do it! For the LORD promised David, ‘By
my servant David I will rescue my people
Israel from the hand of the Philistines[c] and
from the hand of all their enemies.[d]’ ”
19Abner also spoke to the Benjamites in
person. Then he went to Hebron to tell David everything that Israel and the whole
tribe of Benjamin[e] wanted to do. 20When
Abner, who had twenty men with him,
came to David at Hebron, David prepared
a feast for him and his men. 21Then Abner
said to David, “Let me go at once and assemble all Israel for my lord the king, so
that they may make a covenant[f] with you,
and that you may rule over all that your
heart desires.”[g] So David sent Abner away,
and he went in peace.

Joab Murders Abner

22Just then David’s men and Joab returned from a raid and brought with them
a great deal of plunder. But Abner was no
longer with David in Hebron, because David had sent him away, and he had gone
in peace. 23When Joab and all the soldiers
with him arrived, he was told that Abner
son of Ner had come to the king and that
the king had sent him away and that he
had gone in peace.
24So Joab went to the king and said,
“What have you done? Look, Abner came
to you. Why did you let him go? Now he
is gone! 25You know Abner son of Ner;
he came to deceive you and observe your
movements and find out everything you
are doing.”
26Joab then left David and sent messengers after Abner, and they brought him
back from the cistern at Sirah. But David
did not know it. 27Now when Abner[h] returned to Hebron, Joab took him aside
into an inner chamber, as if to speak with
him privately. And there, to avenge the
blood of his brother Asahel, Joab stabbed
him in the stomach, and he died.[i]
28Later, when David heard about this, he
said, “I and my kingdom are forever innocent[j] before the LORD concerning the blood
of Abner son of Ner. 29May his blood[k] fall
on the head of Joab and on his whole family![l] May Joab’s family never be without
someone who has a running sore[m] or leprosy[a] or who leans on a crutch or who falls
by the sword or who lacks food.”
30(Joab and his brother Abishai murdered Abner because he had killed their
brother Asahel in the battle at Gibeon.)
31Then David said to Joab and all the
people with him, “Tear your clothes and
put on sackcloth[n] and walk in mourning[o]
in front of Abner.” King David himself
walked behind the bier. 32They buried Abner in Hebron, and the king wept[p] aloud
at Abner’s tomb. All the people wept also.
33The king sang this lament[q] for Abner:

“Should Abner have died as the
lawless die?
34 Your hands were not bound,
your feet were not fettered.
You fell as one falls before the
wicked.”

3:14 [x] 1Sa 18:27 **3:15** [y] Dt 24:1-4 [z] 1Sa 25:44 **3:16** [a] 2Sa 16:5; 19:16 **3:17** [b] Jdg 11:11 **3:18** [c] 1Sa 9:16 [d] 1Sa 15:28; 2Sa 8:6 **3:19** [e] 1Sa 10:20-21; 1Ch 12:2, 16, 29 **3:21** [f] ver 10, 12 [g] 1Ki 11:37

3:27 [h] 2Sa 2:8 [i] 2Sa 2:22; 20:9-10; 1Ki 2:5 **3:28** [j] ver 37; Dt 21:9 **3:29** [k] Lev 20:9 [l] 1Ki 2:31-33 [m] Lev 15:2 **3:31** [n] 2Sa 1:2, 11; Ps 30:11; Isa 20:2 [o] Ge 37:34 **3:32** [p] Nu 14:1; Pr 24:17 **3:33** [q] 2Sa 1:17

[a] *29* The Hebrew for *leprosy* was used for various diseases affecting the skin.

3:27 *Joab took him aside into an inner chamber.* City gateways in ancient Israel were not simple openings, but complex affairs often involving several chambers, where elders would sit and business was transacted. Joab’s action would not have aroused Abner’s suspicion but, as the text indicates, would only have suggested that Joab wished to have a private word with him. Given the prominence of the city of Hebron in David’s day, it likely would have had a sizable gate complex in which Joab could catch Abner unawares.

3:29 David would have gained much benefit from an alliance with Abner, so he is truly distressed by Joab’s unsanctioned act of violence. In distancing himself from Joab’s egregious murder of Abner, David curses Joab using formulaic language familiar from elsewhere in the ancient Near East. First, he calls down upon Joab’s family the worst of chronic and socially ostracizing diseases. Appended to the Code of Hammurapi, e.g., is a curse threatening any potential offender with divine action that would “inflict upon him in his body a grievous malady, an evil disease, a serious wound that never heals, whose nature no physician knows, which he cannot allay with bandages, which like a deadly bite cannot be rooted out.” David concludes his curse by invoking death (“falls by the sword”) and poverty (“lacks food”) on Joab’s family. Less certain in its interpretation is the middle element in which David expresses his desire that the family of Joab never be without someone “who leans on a crutch.” While the NIV rendering is traditional, it seems less likely than two other possibilities. One is that David is condemning Joab’s male descendants to be effeminate and unworthy of warfare. This reading is based on the fact that the Hebrew word rendered “crutch” by the NIV is more likely, in view of Semitic cognates and its rendering in Pr 31:19, to mean “spindle” or “distaff,” a weaving tool associated in the ancient Near East with female activities. The Hittite Soldier’s Oath offers an example of the curse of effeminacy on disloyal soldiers. Their oaths would “change” those who were disloyal into women by having them dress as women, break their weapons, and be given women’s accessories. Alternatively, taking the key word to mean “work-duty” or “tax in the form of conscripted labor,”

And all the people wept over him again.
35 Then they all came and urged David
to eat something while it was still day;
but David took an oath, saying, "May God
deal with me, be it ever so severely,[r] if I
taste bread[s] or anything else before the
sun sets!"
36 All the people took note and were
pleased; indeed, everything the king did
pleased them. 37 So on that day all the people there and all Israel knew that the king
had no part[t] in the murder of Abner son
of Ner.
38 Then the king said to his men, "Do
you not realize that a commander and a
great man has fallen[u] in Israel this day?
39 And today, though I am the anointed
king, I am weak, and these sons of Zeruiah[v] are too strong for me.[w] May the LORD
repay[x] the evildoer according to his evil
deeds!"

Ish-Bosheth Murdered

4 When Ish-Bosheth son of Saul heard
that Abner[y] had died in Hebron, he lost
courage, and all Israel became alarmed.
2 Now Saul's son had two men who were
leaders of raiding bands. One was named
Baanah and the other Rekab; they were
sons of Rimmon the Beerothite from the
tribe of Benjamin—Beeroth[z] is considered
part of Benjamin, 3 because the people of
Beeroth fled to Gittaim[a] and have resided
there as foreigners to this day.
4 (Jonathan[b] son of Saul had a son who
was lame in both feet. He was five years
old when the news[c] about Saul and Jonathan came from Jezreel. His nurse picked
him up and fled, but as she hurried to
leave, he fell and became disabled.[d] His
name was Mephibosheth.)[e]
5 Now Rekab and Baanah, the sons of
Rimmon the Beerothite, set out for the
house of Ish-Bosheth,[f] and they arrived
there in the heat of the day while he was
taking his noonday rest. 6 They went into
the inner part of the house as if to get
some wheat, and they stabbed[g] him in the
stomach. Then Rekab and his brother Baanah slipped away.
7 They had gone into the house while he
was lying on the bed in his bedroom. After
they stabbed and killed him, they cut off
his head. Taking it with them, they traveled all night by way of the Arabah. 8 They
brought the head of Ish-Bosheth to David
at Hebron and said to the king, "Here is
the head of Ish-Bosheth son of Saul,[h] your
enemy, who tried to kill you. This day the
LORD has avenged my lord the king against
Saul and his offspring."
9 David answered Rekab and his brother Baanah, the sons of Rimmon the Beerothite, "As surely as the LORD lives, who
has delivered[i] me out of every trouble,
10 when someone told me, 'Saul is dead,'
and thought he was bringing good news,
I seized him and put him to death in
Ziklag.[j] That was the reward I gave him
for his news! 11 How much more—when
wicked men have killed an innocent man
in his own house and on his own bed—
should I not now demand his blood[k] from
your hand and rid the earth of you!"
12 So David gave an order to his men,
and they killed them.[l] They cut off their
hands and feet and hung the bodies by the
pool in Hebron. But they took the head of
Ish-Bosheth and buried it in Abner's tomb
at Hebron.

David Becomes King Over Israel

5:1-3pp — 1Ch 11:1-3

5 All the tribes of Israel[m] came to David
at Hebron and said, "We are your own
flesh and blood.[n] 2 In the past, while Saul
was king over us, you were the one who
led Israel on their military campaigns.[o]
And the LORD said to you, 'You will shepherd[p] my people Israel, and you will become their ruler.[q]' "
3 When all the elders of Israel had come
to King David at Hebron, the king made
a covenant[r] with them at Hebron before
the LORD, and they anointed[s] David king
over Israel.
4 David was thirty years old[t] when he
became king, and he reigned[u] forty[v] years.
5 In Hebron he reigned over Judah seven
years and six months,[w] and in Jerusalem
he reigned over all Israel and Judah thirty-three years.

3:35 [r] Ru 1:17; 1Sa 3:17 [s] 1Sa 31:13; 2Sa 1:12; 12:17; Jer 16:7 **3:37** [t] ver 28 **3:38** [u] 2Sa 1:19 **3:39** [v] 2Sa 2:18 [w] 2Sa 19:5-7 [x] 1Ki 2:5-6, 33-34; Ps 41:10; 101:8 **4:1** [y] 2Sa 3:27; Ezr 4:4 **4:2** [z] Jos 9:17; 18:25 **4:3** [a] Ne 11:33 **4:4** [b] 1Sa 18:1 [c] 1Sa 31:1-4 [d] Lev 21:18 [e] 2Sa 9:3,6; 1Ch 8:34; 9:40 **4:5** [f] 2Sa 2:8 **4:6** [g] 2Sa 2:23

4:8 [h] 1Sa 24:4; 25:29 **4:9** [i] Ge 48:16; 1Ki 1:29 **4:10** [j] 2Sa 1:2-16 **4:11** [k] Ge 9:5; Ps 9:12 **4:12** [l] 2Sa 1:15 **5:1** [m] 2Sa 19:43 [n] 1Ch 11:1 **5:2** [o] 1Sa 18:5, 13,16 [p] 1Sa 16:1; 2Sa 7:7 [q] 1Sa 25:30 **5:3** [r] 2Sa 3:21 [s] 2Sa 2:4 **5:4** [t] Lk 3:23 [u] 1Ki 2:11; 1Ch 3:4 [v] 1Ch 26:31; 29:27 **5:5** [w] 2Sa 2:11; 1Ch 3:4

David's curse may have been that Joab's family would never be without someone working on a "chain gang," i.e., forced labor (see note on Jos 16:10).

4:4 *a son who was lame in both feet.* That Jonathan's son, Mephibosheth—called Merib-Baal in 1Ch 8:34; 9:40 (on intentional name distortions, see note on 1Sa 25:25)—is described as lame in both feet may suggest that he had received a spinal cord injury. It is possible, however, that he received (compound) fractures that either were not or could not be set properly. Medicine designed to treat illness and injury was practiced in the ancient Near East from early times, and although splinting was practiced, compound fractures were generally hopeless.

4:12 *They cut off their hands and feet and hung the bodies by the pool.* See note on 1Sa 31:4; cf. 1Sa 5:3–4. Though mutilation of this sort was not uncommon in the ancient Near East, there may be a special significance here, namely, removal of the offending members—hands that committed the murder and feet that brought the news.

5:3 *elders of Israel.* See note on Jdg 2:7.

DAVID'S CONQUESTS

Once he had become king over all Israel (2Sa 5:1–5), David

(1) conquered the Jebusite fortress of Zion/Jerusalem and made it his royal city (5:6–10);

(2) received the recognition of and assurance of friendship from Hiram of Tyre, king of the Phoenicians (5:11–12);

(3) decisively defeated the Philistines so that their hold on Israelite territory was broken and their threat to Israel eliminated (5:17–25; 8:1);

(4) defeated the Moabites and imposed his authority over them (8:2);

(5) crushed the Aramean kingdoms of Hadadezer (king of Zobah), Damascus and Maakah and put them under tribute (8:3–8; 10:6–19). Talmai, the Aramean king of Geshur, apparently had made peace with David while he was still reigning in Hebron and sealed the alliance by giving his daughter Maakah in marriage to David (3:3);

(6) subdued Edom and incorporated it into his empire (8:13–14);

(7) defeated the Ammonites and brought them into subjection (12:26–31);

(8) subjugated the remaining Canaanite cities that had previously maintained their independence from Israel, such as Beth Shan, Megiddo, Taanach and Dor.

Since David had earlier crushed the Amalekites (1Sa 30:17–18), his wars thus completed the conquest begun by Joshua and secured all the borders of Israel. His empire (united Israel plus the subjugated kingdoms) reached from Ezion Geber on the eastern arm of the Red Sea to the Euphrates River.

David Conquers Jerusalem

5:6-10pp — 1Ch 11:4-9
5:11-16pp — 1Ch 3:5-9; 14:1-7

[6]The king and his men marched to Jerusalem[x] to attack the Jebusites,[y] who lived
there. The Jebusites said to David, "You
will not get in here; even the blind and
the lame can ward you off." They thought,
"David cannot get in here." [7]Nevertheless,
David captured the fortress of Zion —
which is the City of David.[z]
[8]On that day David had said, "Anyone
who conquers the Jebusites will have to
use the water shaft to reach those 'lame
and blind' who are David's enemies.[a]"
That is why they say, "The 'blind and
lame' will not enter the palace."
[9]David then took up residence in the
fortress and called it the City of David.
He built up the area around it, from the
terraces[b][a] inward. [10]And he became more
and more powerful,[b] because the LORD
God Almighty was with him.
[11]Now Hiram[c] king of Tyre sent envoys
to David, along with cedar logs and carpenters and stonemasons, and they built a
palace for David. [12]Then David knew that

5:6 [x] Jdg 1:8 [y] Jos 15:8 **5:7** [z] 2Sa 6:12, 16; 1Ki 2:10 **5:9** [a] ver 7; 1Ki 9:15, 24 **5:10** [b] 2Sa 3:1 **5:11** [c] 1Ki 5:1, 18; 1Ch 14:1

[a] 8 Or *are hated by David* [b] 9 Or *the Millo*

5:6 *Jerusalem.* David's interest in Jerusalem (where he would eventually establish his royal capital) likely stemmed from its strategic location and relatively independent status. Occupied already in the third millennium BC (and even earlier), Jerusalem in the time of David lay within the territorial allotment of the small tribe of Benjamin, close to the northern border of Judah, but it had never come under full Israelite control. The city had been conquered by Judah in the period of the judges (Jdg 1:8), but neither Judah nor Benjamin had been successful in permanently occupying the city or in driving out its Jebusite inhabitants (Jos 15:63; Jdg 1:21). Thus, David may have viewed Jerusalem as an ideal candidate for a national capital — centrally located between the northern and southern tribes within one of the smaller tribes that would be unlikely to evoke jealousy from the others, and not yet conquered. *Jebusites.* See note on Dt 7:1. *even the blind and the lame can ward you off.* An exchange of taunts or insults prior to battle was common practice in the ancient Near East. The meaning of the Jebusites' taunt has elicited considerable discussion and numerous suggestions, but no interpretation has achieved a consensus. Perhaps it was suggestive of over-confidence — i.e., "even our handicapped can keep you at bay" — or simply of a determination to fight to the last man (even be he blind or lame). Or perhaps it involved some kind of hex, or harked back to a prior treaty between David and the Jebusites in which the blind or lame were invoked in the ratification ceremony. Perhaps the precise meaning of the taunt is beyond recovery (apart from the basic Biblical explanation that by it the Jebusites meant "David cannot get in here").
5:7 *fortress of Zion.* The etymology of the name "Zion," which occurs here for the first time in the Bible, has not been firmly established, but suggestions include "castle," "bare place," "bare hill," etc. The fortress of Zion probably referred originally to a stronghold atop the recently discovered stepped stone structure on the northeast side of the city overlooking the Kidron Valley. The name eventually was extended to designate Jerusalem itself (e.g., 2Ki 19:21; Isa 2:3) or even the entire nation of Israel (e.g., Ps 149:2; Isa 46:13).
5:8 *water shaft.* Since Charles Warren's discovery in 1867 of an approximately 50-foot (15-meter) vertical shaft not too far from the Gihon spring but within the walls of the ancient City of David, many scholars have assumed that David's instructions to "use the water shaft to reach those 'lame and blind' who are David's enemies" must relate to what came to be called "Warren's Shaft." This view was never universally accepted, however, and has recently been rejected by many scholars. In the end, it is difficult to retrace with any confidence Joab's daring entry into the Jebusite city. Certainly, the general notion that he entered through some kind of water shaft or water tunnel system, even if not the specific structure discovered by Warren, seems reasonable enough.
5:9 *called it the City of David.* The practice of renaming a captured (or purchased) city and making it one's capital and principal residence is attested elsewhere in the ancient Near East. Such cities, which were often considered part of the ruler's personal estate, not only enjoyed the most ambitious building projects but also, as far as the administrative personnel were concerned (typically relatives of the king), enjoyed such privileges as exemption for taxation, military duty or corvée labor. These latter privileges stemmed not least from the fact that from Mesopotamia to Egypt such cities were typically "temple cities," which were to be governed by the god alone and therefore free of obligations toward the government.
5:11 *Hiram king of Tyre.* Tyre was a major Phoenician seaport city situated on an island off the Mediterranean coast some 30 miles (48 kilometers) north of Mount Carmel and 25 miles (40 kilometers) south of Sidon. Only about 100 miles (160 kilometers) north of Jerusalem, Tyre's commercial and cultural influence was felt throughout the ancient world and throughout the duration of Israel's history. In the time of David, Tyre, under king Hiram I, experienced its first golden age. Hiram's generosity to David is a testimony to the impressiveness of David's own accomplishments, but it was likely also motivated by self-interest: Hiram may well have wanted to make sure that David did not deny him access to inland trade routes and necessary agricultural produce (cf. the goods supplied to Sidon and Tyre in Ezr 3:7). Hiram I is not mentioned in ancient Near Eastern texts outside the Bible, but the much later Assyrian king Tiglath-Pileser III (745 – 727 BC) includes a different Hiram of Tyre in a list of those from whom he received tribute. Yet another Hiram is attested in the early tenth-century BC sarcophagus inscription of Ahiram, king of Byblos. *cedar logs.* The cedars of Lebanon (*Cedrus libani*), which could grow to heights of 130 feet (40 meters) and live as long as 3,000 years, were much admired in the ancient Near East, and their timbers were much coveted for the construction of temples and palaces. The beauty, aroma and durability of the wood was unsurpassed, and the kings of Mesopotamia and Egypt were importing cedar timbers from the Lebanese region as early as the fourth millennium BC. About a century before David's reign, the Assyrian king Tiglath-Pileser I (1115 – 1076 BC) includes the following in a report of an expedition to Lebanon and the Mediterranean: "I went to Lebanon (Lab-na-a-ni). I cut (there) timber cedars for the temple of Anu and Adad, the great gods, my lords, and carried (them to Ashur)."

the LORD had established him as king over
Israel and had exalted his kingdom for the
sake of his people Israel.
13After he left Hebron, David took more
concubines and wives[d] in Jerusalem, and
more sons and daughters were born to
him. 14These are the names of the children born to him there:[e] Shammua, Shobab, Nathan, Solomon, 15Ibhar, Elishua,
Nepheg, Japhia, 16Elishama, Eliada and
Eliphelet.

David Defeats the Philistines

5:17-25pp — 1Ch 14:8-17

17When the Philistines heard that David
had been anointed king over Israel, they
went up in full force to search for him, but
David heard about it and went down to
the stronghold.[f] 18Now the Philistines had
come and spread out in the Valley of Rephaim;[g] 19so David inquired[h] of the LORD,
"Shall I go and attack the Philistines? Will
you deliver them into my hands?"
The LORD answered him, "Go, for I will
surely deliver the Philistines into your
hands."
20So David went to Baal Perazim, and
there he defeated them. He said, "As waters break out, the LORD has broken out
against my enemies before me." So that
place was called Baal Perazim.[a][i] 21The Philistines abandoned their idols there, and
David and his men carried them off.[j]
22Once more the Philistines came up
and spread out in the Valley of Rephaim;
23so David inquired of the LORD, and he answered, "Do not go straight up, but circle
around behind them and attack them in
front of the poplar trees. 24As soon as you
hear the sound[k] of marching in the tops
of the poplar trees, move quickly, because
that will mean the LORD has gone out in
front[l] of you to strike the Philistine army."
25So David did as the LORD commanded
him, and he struck down the Philistines all
the way from Gibeon[b][m] to Gezer.[n]

The Ark Brought to Jerusalem

6:1-11pp — 1Ch 13:1-14
6:12-19pp — 1Ch 15:25 – 16:3

6 David again brought together all the
able young men of Israel — thirty thousand. 2He and all his men went to Baalah[c][o]

5:13 [d] Dt 17:17; 1Ch 3:9 **5:14** [e] 1Ch 3:5 **5:17** [f] 2Sa 23:14; 1Ch 11:16 **5:18** [g] Jos 15:8; 17:15; 18:16 **5:19** [h] 1Sa 23:2; 2Sa 2:1 **5:20** [i] Isa 28:21 **5:21** [j] Dt 7:5; 1Ch 14:12; Isa 46:2 **5:24** [k] 2Ki 7:6 [l] Jdg 4:14 **5:25** [m] Isa 28:21 [n] 1Ch 14:16 **6:2** [o] Jos 15:9

[a] 20 *Baal Perazim* means *the lord who breaks out.*
[b] 25 Septuagint (see also 1 Chron. 14:16); Hebrew *Geba*
[c] 2 That is, Kiriath Jearim (see 1 Chron. 13:6)

5:13 *David took more concubines and wives.* See notes on 1Sa 25:39b,43.
5:17 *the Philistines . . . went up in full force.* David's rule over Judah from Hebron had not been contested by the Philistines, but the extension of his domain to include the northern tribes posed a threat to Philistine interests that they could not ignore. *stronghold.* Its identity is debated. In the present context, one naturally thinks of the "fortress of Zion" captured by David in v. 7 and occupied by him in v. 9. (The Hebrew for "fortress" is the same as that for "stronghold.) However, some regard the expression "went down" as inappropriate in reference to Jerusalem and suggest that David returned to a stronghold of prior acquaintance, perhaps at Adullam.
5:18 *Valley of Rephaim.* Generally identified with the Wadi el-Ward, the Valley of Rephaim would have run essentially east-west about a mile (1.5 kilometers) south of the present-day Old City of Jerusalem. The deployment of Philistines in this valley made good strategic sense, as it would have hindered Judahite reinforcements from joining David in Jerusalem.
5:21 *Philistines abandoned their idols.* On ancient Near Eastern conceptions of the involvement of the god(s) in warfare and on the common practice of carrying off defeated deities, see note on 1Sa 5:2. While the captured gods of defeated foes were often placed in the temples of the more powerful, victorious deities, the Biblical text here gives no indication that David followed this practice. The parallel account in Chronicles completes the picture: "The Philistines had abandoned their gods there, and David gave orders to burn them in the fire" (1Ch 14:12; cf. the instructions of Dt 7:5,25). While less common than subordinating (or simply adding) captured gods to the existing pantheon, the practice of denigrating the power of and even destroying captured gods is known in the ancient Near East. Ashurbanipal, e.g., exemplifies the former practice with the following remark regarding the gods of the Elamites: "I counted their gods and goddesses as powerless ghosts." In another place, he attests the latter practice as well, again in reference to the Elamite gods: "I smashed their gods and thereby soothed the heart of the lord of lords."
5:23 – 24 Though there are uncertainties of interpretation in these verses — e.g., are we to read "poplar trees" or, perhaps, a place-name? — two typical aspects of Israelite warfare are evident: clever strategies capitalizing on deception and surprise and divine assistance through the orchestration of natural or supernatural events (cf. 2Ki 7:6, where Yahweh "caused the Arameans to hear the sound of chariots and horses and a great army"). Here it is not clear whether only David and his army could hear the sound or whether the Philistines also heard it and thought they were being attacked by a much larger force.
5:24 *the LORD has gone out in front of you.* The concept of the Divine Warrior was not unique to Israel (see note on 1Sa 14:6). A major tenet of Divine Warrior theology was that God or the gods went before the troops to enable victory by demoralizing, confusing or terrifying the enemy. At times the deity would "thunder" against the enemy (1Sa 2:10; see note there), cause the earth to shake (see 1Sa 14:15 and note) or in other ways befuddle, trick and dispirit the enemy.
6:1 – 23 Various studies have compared the present episode to ancient Near Eastern accounts of ceremonies accompanying the return of a deity to its temple. While aspects of these studies are illuminating, the more pertinent analogues to David's bringing the ark up to Jerusalem are ancient Near Eastern accounts of the introduction of a national god to a new royal city. Examples include inscriptions of the Assyrian kings Sargon II (721 – 705 BC), Sennacherib (704 – 681 BC), and Esarhaddon (680 – 669 BC), each of which recounts the arrival or restoration of a deity in a (new) royal city. Most lavish of all is the account of Ashurbanipal II's inauguration of the palace in Calah:

in Judah to bring up from there the ark[p]
of God, which is called by the Name,[a][q]
the name of the LORD Almighty, who is
enthroned[r] between the cherubim[s] on the
ark. 3They set the ark of God on a new cart[t]
and brought it from the house of Abinadab,
which was on the hill. Uzzah and Ahio,
sons of Abinadab, were guiding the new
cart 4with the ark of God on it,[b] and Ahio
was walking in front of it. 5David and all
Israel were celebrating with all their might
before the LORD, with castanets,[c] harps,
lyres, timbrels, sistrums and cymbals.[u]
6When they came to the threshing
floor of Nakon, Uzzah reached out and
took hold of[v] the ark of God, because the
oxen stumbled. 7The LORD's anger burned
against Uzzah because of his irreverent
act;[w] therefore God struck him down,[x] and
he died there beside the ark of God.
8Then David was angry because the
LORD's wrath[y] had broken out against Uzzah, and to this day that place is called
Perez Uzzah.[d][z]
9David was afraid of the LORD that day
and said, "How[a] can the ark of the LORD
ever come to me?" 10He was not willing
to take the ark of the LORD to be with him
in the City of David. Instead, he took it to
the house of Obed-Edom[b] the Gittite. 11The
ark of the LORD remained in the house of
Obed-Edom the Gittite for three months,
and the LORD blessed him and his entire
household.[c]
12Now King David[d] was told, "The LORD
has blessed the household of Obed-Edom
and everything he has, because of the ark
of God." So David went to bring up the
ark of God from the house of Obed-Edom
to the City of David with rejoicing. 13When
those who were carrying the ark of the
LORD had taken six steps, he sacrificed[e] a
bull and a fattened calf. 14Wearing a lin-
en ephod,[f] David was dancing[g] before the

6:2 p 1Sa 4:4; 7:1 q Lev 24:16; Isa 63:14 r Ps 99:1 s Ex 25:22; 1Ch 13:5-6 **6:3** t Nu 7:4-9; 1Sa 6:7 **6:5** u 1Sa 18:6-7; Ezr 3:10; Ps 150:5 **6:6** v Nu 4:15, 19-20; 1Ch 13:9 **6:7** w 1Ch 15:13-15 x Ex 19:22; 1Sa 6:19 **6:8** y Ps 7:11 z Ge 38:29 **6:9** a Ps 119:120 **6:10** b 1Ch 13:13; 26:4-5 **6:11** c Ge 30:27; 39:5 **6:12** d 1Ki 8:1; 1Ch 15:25 **6:13** e 1Ki 8:5, 62 **6:14** f Ex 19:6; 1Sa 2:18 g Ex 15:20

a 2 Hebrew; Septuagint and Vulgate do not have *the Name.* *b* 3,4 Dead Sea Scrolls and some Septuagint manuscripts; Masoretic Text *cart* *4and they brought it with the ark of God from the house of Abinadab, which was on the hill* *c* 5 Masoretic Text; Dead Sea Scrolls and Septuagint (see also 1 Chron. 13:8) *songs* *d* 8 *Perez Uzzah* means *outbreak against Uzzah.*

First, "he invited into it Ashur, the great lord and the gods of his entire country," to whom he, secondly, offered sacrifices of extraordinary quantity and variety, and then, thirdly, "treated for ten days with food and drink 47,074 persons, men and women," along with other guests, bringing the total to 69,574. David's actions here in ch. 6 follow a similar pattern: Yahweh, as represented by the ark of God, is brought into the new royal city of David, sacrifices are offered, and the people are treated to a banquet.

6:2 *Baalah in Judah.* Another name for Kiriath Jearim (cf. 1Sa 6:21). If the site has been correctly identified, then the journey from Baalah to Jerusalem would have been seven to eight miles (about 12 kilometers). *the ark of God.* See note on Ex 25:16. *cherubim.* See note on Ex 25:18.

6:3 *new cart.* While the choice of a "new" cart was doubtless motivated by a desire for ritual purity, it was nevertheless an inappropriate choice. Recalling Philistine precedent set in 1Sa 6:7, this mode of transporting the ark entirely neglected the divine directive that the ark, equipped with rings and poles (Ex 25:12–14; 37:5), was to be carried, not carted (e.g., Nu 4:15,19; 7:9; Dt 10:8; Jos 3:8).

6:5 The musical instruments mentioned in this verse are for the most part well-known both in the Bible and in the ancient Near East generally (see 1Sa 10:5; 18:6; see the articles "Lyre," p. 488; "Music and Musicians," p. 524). *sistrums.* Mentioned only here in the Bible, a sistrum was a metallic instrument known particularly among the ancient Egyptians. Several wires were attached to a metal hoop in such a way that shaking the instrument would produce a jingling sound. The etymology of the Hebrew word suggests that the key aspect of the instrument was that it was a "shaker" of some sort. This has led to the alternative suggestion that the instrument may have been a "(pottery) rattle." Dozens of pottery rattles, averaging about four inches (ten centimeters) in height, have been discovered in ancient Palestine. Used from as early as the second millennium BC until they were generally replaced by metal bells in the ninth century BC, these rattles consisted of enclosed hollow pottery vessels containing one or more small pellets.

6:13 *six steps.* The nature of the ritual procedure described in this verse has been described in two distinct ways. The first, reflected in the NIV translation, is that after those carrying the ark had taken their first six steps without incident, a sacrifice was performed in thanksgiving for the apparent divine approval of David's second attempt to transport the ark to Jerusalem. The second, likelier interpretation is that a sacrifice was offered each time the bearers of the ark had taken six steps. While the number of sacrificial animals would have been considerable (though not compared with Solomon's ceremony to install the ark in the temple, 1Ki 8:5,63) and the ritual procession rather slow moving, Assyrian sources offer a possible analogue to such a procession. When restoring the image of Marduk to Babylon, the Assyrian king Ashurbanipal offered a sacrifice every two miles (three kilometers) over a distance of 250 miles (400 kilometers). David would have made the same number of sacrifices as Ashurbanipal within a half mile (0.8 kilometers).

6:14 *ephod.* See note on 1Sa 2:18; David apparently laid aside his royal insignia and clothed himself in a priestly garment (or perhaps the attire of a dancer) in order to participate in the procession. *dancing.* Scrutiny of the Hebrew words used to describe David's dancing suggest that it was an exuberant, energetic leaping and whirling about. While ancient Near Eastern literature provides no other examples of kings dancing in such processions, instances of the queen joining in a ritual dance, followed by other dignitaries, are known from Hittite sources. Depictions of dancers in a broad range of ancient Near Eastern pictorial sources give some sense of what this dancing may have been like. Dancing was done either in groups or singly, and was often quite acrobatic. Dancing took place in a variety of settings and for a variety of reasons, as it has in most cultures up to the present time. It could be a spontaneous expression of joy and playfulness; on occasion it could verge into eroticism; and it was often a component of cultic ceremonies. Dancing was not always evaluated positively; an Akkadian letter from the first half of the second millennium BC criticizes a woman who had "greatly aggravated the matter." The letter explains: "In addition to dancing about every day, she has slighted us by consis-

LORD with all his might, 15while he and all
Israel were bringing up the ark of the LORD
with shouts and the sound of trumpets.[h]
16As the ark of the LORD was entering
the City of David,[i] Michal daughter of
Saul watched from a window. And when
she saw King David leaping and dancing
before the LORD, she despised him in her
heart.
17They brought the ark of the LORD and
set it in its place inside the tent that David
had pitched for it,[j] and David sacrificed
burnt offerings[k] and fellowship offerings
before the LORD. 18After he had finished
sacrificing[l] the burnt offerings and fellowship offerings, he blessed the people in
the name of the LORD Almighty. 19Then he
gave a loaf of bread, a cake of dates and
a cake of raisins[m] to each person in the
whole crowd of Israelites, both men and
women.[n] And all the people went to their
homes.
20When David returned home to bless
his household, Michal daughter of Saul
came out to meet him and said, "How the
king of Israel has distinguished himself today, going around half-naked[o] in full view
of the slave girls of his servants as any
vulgar fellow would!"
21David said to Michal, "It was before
the LORD, who chose me rather than your
father or anyone from his house when
he appointed[p] me ruler over the LORD's
people Israel—I will celebrate before the
LORD. 22I will become even more undignified than this, and I will be humiliated in
my own eyes. But by these slave girls you
spoke of, I will be held in honor."
23And Michal daughter of Saul had no
children to the day of her death.

God's Promise to David

7:1-17pp — 1Ch 17:1-15

7 After the king was settled in his palace[q] and the LORD had given him rest
from all his enemies around him, 2he said
to Nathan the prophet, "Here I am, living
in a house[r] of cedar, while the ark of God
remains in a tent."[s]
3Nathan replied to the king, "Whatever
you have in mind, go ahead and do it, for
the LORD is with you."
4But that night the word of the LORD
came to Nathan, saying:
5"Go and tell my servant David,
'This is what the LORD says: Are you[t]
the one to build me a house to dwell
in?[u] 6I have not dwelt in a house from
the day I brought the Israelites up out
of Egypt to this day. I have been moving from place to place with a tent[v]
as my dwelling.[w] 7Wherever I have
moved with all the Israelites,[x] did I
ever say to any of their rulers whom I
commanded to shepherd[y] my people

6:15 [h] Ps 47:5; 98:6
6:16 [i] 2Sa 5:7
6:17 [j] 1Ch 15:1; 2Ch 1:4 [k] Lev 1:1-17; 1Ki 8:62-64
6:18 [l] 1Ki 8:22
6:19 [m] Hos 3:1 [n] Ne 8:10
6:20 [o] ver 14, 16
6:21 [p] 1Sa 13:14; 15:28
7:1 [q] 1Ch 17:1
7:2 [r] 2Sa 5:11 [s] Ex 26:1; Ac 7:45-46
7:5 [t] 1Ki 8:19; 1Ch 22:8 [u] 1Ki 5:3-5
7:6 [v] Ex 40:18, 34 [w] 1Ki 8:16
7:7 [x] Dt 23:14 [y] 2Sa 5:2

tently behaving thoughtlessly." Mostly, though, dancing was deemed a reflex of joy and well-being. David's whirling dance apparently combined personal exuberance with cultic performance.

6:15 *trumpets.* See note on Jos 6:4.

6:20 *How the king of Israel has distinguished himself today.* David's humbling of himself before Yahweh finds at least general analogy in Mesopotamian ritual texts. A ritual text from the reign of late thirteenth- or early twelfth-century BC Assyrian king Tukulti-Ninurta I, e.g., describes the king's divestment of royal insignia and humble appearance as supplicant before the god Assur. Following his humiliation, the king is "reinvested with the symbols of office, is crowned, and is extolled with praises and wishes for a long reign."

7:1 *rest.* Pertains to God's provision of stability and security for the kingdom or community. In the ancient Near East, kings built temples to provide rest for the god (a place where the god would be cared for). God had promised to provide rest for his people Israel in Dt 12:10, and here has provided it for his chosen king. When rest is achieved, the king can rule as he maintains order and justice for his people. These same desires for both God and king are common in the ancient world.

7:2 *Nathan the prophet.* Mentioned here for the first time. He will play a significant role also in ch. 12 and in 1Ki 1. That David should approach a prophet to seek (oracular) approval for his intent to build a temple is in keeping with general ancient Near Eastern practice. From the late third millennium BC, we have the example of Gudea of Lagash who set out to build a temple for his god, but not without first receiving divine approval. Examples of kings seeking divine sanction for temple building could easily be multiplied, and there are also instances of divine sanction being withheld. We only learn of these latter instances from later kings reporting on the failures of their predecessors, and the reasons are not given. See the article "Prophets and Prophecy," p. 1110. *a house of cedar.* The mention of cedar is suggestive of the refinement and luxury of David's palace (on cedar, see note on 5:11). David evidently viewed his palace as in some sense symbolic of his now established rule (cf. 5:11–12) and thought it only appropriate that God's rulership be similarly symbolized by a permanent dwelling for the ark. In wishing to build a temple for the God who had given him victory, David was not unlike other ancient Near Eastern monarchs, who liked to crown their achievements with temples to their patron deities. David's focus on the ark links ch. 7 with ch. 6, which recounts David's bringing of the ark to Jerusalem.

7:5–16 Texts from Mari offer instructive parallels to this dynastic oracle. These include divine installation of the king (cf. v. 8), father-son imagery (cf. v. 14), reference to a sanctuary as a "house" (cf. vv. 6,7,13), "house" as a palace/dynasty (cf. v. 11b,16), mention of throne (cf. vv. 13,16), land/kingdom (cf. vv. 12,13,16) and extent of rule (cf. v. 16). Besides these common features, the dynastic oracles from Mari and the Bible differ markedly in some respects; chiefly, the Mari oracles are "obligatory," i.e., conditional, placing the king under obligation, while the Davidic oracle is promissory, and thus unconditional (for David had already met the conditions). Furthermore, while Yahweh rejects David's desire to build him a temple, the deity of the Mari oracles (Adad) is adamant that the king, Zimri-Lim, should build him a temple.

2 SAMUEL 6:5

Music and Musicians

The Scriptures and the ancient Near Eastern evidence attest to a wide variety of musical instruments. Evidence is both textual and iconographic, the latter being most important in trying to understand precisely what instruments are being referred to in the texts. A number of different categories of instrument are attested, divided according to sound: idiophones, membranophones, chordophones and aerophones. Several different instruments are mentioned in Chronicles. Five occur in 1Ch 13:8.

The *kinnor* is a lyre, mentioned 42 times in the OT in a wide variety of situations, both secular and sacred. It is frequently associated with the *nebel*, a similar instrument in type and function. The *nebel* also seems to be a lyre, but it differs in the number of strings (it has more than the *kinnor*) and in the method of performance (strings were plucked with the fingers rather than with a plectrum, Josephus, *Antiquities* 7.306). See the article "Lyre," p. 488.

The *mesiltayim* are cymbals. This identification is reinforced by the fact that the form of the Hebrew word is dual (designating a pair of something [e.g., cymbals] by the form of the word itself). 1Ch 15:19 and Josephus (*Antiquities* 7.306) indicate that they are made of bronze.

The *hasosera* is a trumpet and is the only instrument for which we have a fairly detailed description of its material and construction. It is made of beaten or hammered silver (Nu 10:2). Josephus says it is nearly a cubit (18 inches or 45 centimeters) in length, with a narrow body and a broad bell-shaped end (*Antiquities* 3.291). Two different types of sound are produced: a powerful, sustained sound and a shorter blast. Each combination of sounds signifies something different. It is primarily a priestly instrument (Nu 10:8, 2Ch 5:12).

These four instruments are associated with the Levitical divisions of musicians. Josephus (*Antiquities* 8.94) says that the two-stringed instruments were invented

Coins depicting a three-stringed lyre and trumpets and a paleo-Hebrew inscription, AD 134–135.

continued on next page

Clay figurines of women playing drums/tambourines, Achzib, eighth–seventh century BC.
Kim Walton. The Israel Museum, Jerusalem.

for the singing of hymns. The lyres and the cymbals are played together at specific religious ceremonies, such as the transfer of the ark or the dedication of the temple (e.g., 1Ch 15:28; 2Ch 5:12 – 13). They are also apparently used on an ongoing basis to accompany both the sacrifices and the liturgy associated with the ark (1Ch 16:39 – 42; 2Ch 29:25 – 28).

The *tup* is a hand drum and is almost exclusively a woman's instrument. A large number of terracotta figurines of women playing this instrument have been recovered. There are no indications in the Scriptures regarding its size or shape, but modern interpretations agree that it is a small frame drum, resembling what we refer to as a tambourine or a timbrel, though without the metal jingles attached to it. It is held in the hand (Ex 15:20). It is never mentioned in connection with temple music, but it does appear in the context of religious hymns, dances and processions.

Finally, of the instruments specifically mentioned in Chronicles (e.g., 1Ch 15:28), the *shofar* is the most frequently mentioned instrument in the OT. It is identified as a naturally occurring horn, that of either a goat or a ram. It could be of two different shapes — straight or curved — and used on different occasions. A mouthpiece is inserted in order to play it. It is primarily a solo instrument and has a wide variety of functions, both religious and secular. ◆

Israel, "Why have you not built me a
house of cedar?[z]" '
8"Now then, tell my servant David, 'This is what the LORD Almighty
says: I took you from the pasture,
from tending the flock,[a] and appointed you ruler[b] over my people Israel.[c]
9I have been with you wherever you
have gone,[d] and I have cut off all your
enemies from before you.[e] Now I will
make your name great, like the names
of the greatest men on earth. 10And I
will provide a place for my people Israel and will plant[f] them so that they
can have a home of their own and no
longer be disturbed. Wicked[g] people
will not oppress them anymore,[h] as
they did at the beginning 11and have
done ever since the time I appointed leaders[a][i] over my people Israel. I
will also give you rest from all your
enemies.[j]
" 'The LORD declares to you that the
LORD himself will establish[k] a house[l]
for you: 12When your days are over
and you rest[m] with your ancestors, I
will raise up your offspring to succeed
you, your own flesh and blood,[n] and
I will establish his kingdom. 13He is
the one who will build a house for my
Name,[o] and I will establish the throne
of his kingdom forever.[p] 14I will be
his father, and he will be my son.[q]
When he does wrong, I will punish
him with a rod[r] wielded by men, with
floggings inflicted by human hands.
15But my love will never be taken
away from him, as I took it away from

7:7 [z] Lev 26:11-12 **7:8** [a] 1Sa 16:11 [b] 2Sa 6:21 [c] Ps 78:70-72; 2Co 6:18* **7:9** [d] 2Sa 5:10 [e] Ps 18:37-42 **7:10** [f] Ex 15:17; Isa 5:1-7 [g] Ps 89:22-23 [h] Isa 60:18 **7:11** [i] Jdg 2:16; 1Sa 12:9-11 [j] ver 1 [k] 1Sa 25:28 [l] ver 27 **7:12** [m] 1Ki 2:1 [n] Ps 132:11-12 **7:13** [o] 1Ki 5:5; 8:19,29 **7:13** [p] Isa 9:7 **7:14** [q] Ps 89:26; Heb 1:5* [r] Ps 89:30-33

7:15 [s] 1Sa 15:23,28 **7:16** [t] Ps 89:36-37 [u] ver 13 **7:18** [v] Ex 3:11; 1Sa 18:18 **7:19** [w] Isa 55:8-9 **7:20** [x] Jn 21:17 [y] 1Sa 16:7 **7:22** [z] Ps 48:1; 86:10; Jer 10:6 [a] Dt 3:24 [b] Ex 15:11 [c] Ex 10:2; Ps 44:1 **7:23** [d] Dt 4:32-38 [e] Dt 10:21

Saul,[s] whom I removed from before
you. 16Your house and your kingdom
will endure forever before me[b]; your
throne[t] will be established forever.[u]' "

17Nathan reported to David all the
words of this entire revelation.

David's Prayer

7:18-29pp — 1Ch 17:16-27

18Then King David went in and sat before the LORD, and he said:

"Who am I,[v] Sovereign LORD, and
what is my family, that you have
brought me this far? 19And as if this
were not enough in your sight, Sovereign LORD, you have also spoken
about the future of the house of your
servant—and this decree,[w] Sovereign
LORD, is for a mere human![c]
20"What more can David say to
you? For you know[x] your servant,[y]
Sovereign LORD. 21For the sake of your
word and according to your will, you
have done this great thing and made
it known to your servant.
22"How great[z] you are,[a] Sovereign
LORD! There is no one like you, and
there is no God[b] but you, as we have
heard with our own ears.[c] 23And who
is like your people Israel[d]—the one
nation on earth that God went out to
redeem as a people for himself, and
to make a name for himself, and to
perform great and awesome wonders[e]

[a] 11 Traditionally *judges* [b] 16 Some Hebrew manuscripts and Septuagint; most Hebrew manuscripts *you* [c] 19 Or *for the human race*

7:14 *I will be his father, and he will be my son.* The father-son relationship between God and king is seen at various times in the ancient Near East and in different places. At times this is linked with the idea of divine kingship, such as in Egypt and the Ur III Dynasty in Mesopotamia. In Egypt the king was seen as the son of Re, the sun-god. The Ur III kings were the sons of the goddess Ninsun and the deified Lugalbanda, and some of them were deified even during their lifetime. At other times kings are more reticent to claim the kinship of the gods.

It is noticeable in Assyria that the claims of kings become more grandiose the greater the size of the kingdom, although they still stop short of claims to divine kinship. Closer to home, in Ugaritic literature, the Kirta epic describes Kirta, king of Bêtu-Hubur, as the son of the god El, the chief god of the Canaanite pantheon. Aramean kings even included such claims among their throne names: Ben-Hadad, e.g., means "son of Hadad." There is no concept of divine kinship here. These sorts of examples show us that royal ideology in Israel followed the established patterns of kingship in the ancient world. Yahweh used much of the same rhetoric that would have been familiar to people of this time.

7:15 *my love will never be taken away from him.* On "love" language used in ancient Near Eastern contexts to express covenant loyalty or the like, see notes on 1:26; 19:6. Covenantal use of love language is well illustrated in a later Biblical passage describing the relationship of Hiram, king of Tyre, to David: "When Hiram king of Tyre heard that Solomon had been anointed king to succeed his father David, he sent his envoys to Solomon, because he had always been on friendly terms with [lit. "had been one loving (or a lover of)] David" (1Ki 5:1). A noteworthy conceptual parallel to the present passage, though involving a covenant agreement between two human rulers, is found in the Hittite Bronze Tablet introduced in the note on Lev 19:18. The "Great King" Tudhaliya IV promises the vassal Kurunta that the treaty between them will remain in force and will apply even to Kurunta's descendants. Even should a son or grandson of Kurunta commit treason, the covenant will remain inalienable: "I ... will not throw out your son." The offender, if proven guilty, will be punished, to be sure: "they shall do to him whatever the king of the land of Hatti decides. But they may not take from him his 'house' [i.e., dynasty] and land ..." Similar with respect to succession is a section of a treaty between the Hittite king Hattusili III and Ulmi-Teshshup. In general, the gods of the ancient Near East did not seek "love" (either emotional or legal) from their worshipers, nor did they make covenant relations with them.

7:22 *no God but you.* See the article "Monotheism, Monolatry and Henotheism," p. 308.

by driving out nations and their gods
from before your people, whom you
redeemed[f] from Egypt?[a] 24You have
established your people Israel as your
very own[g] forever, and you, LORD,
have become their God.[h]
25"And now, LORD God, keep forever the promise you have made concerning your servant and his house.
Do as you promised, 26so that your
name will be great forever. Then
people will say, 'The LORD Almighty
is God over Israel!' And the house
of your servant David will be established in your sight.
27"LORD Almighty, God of Israel,
you have revealed this to your servant, saying, 'I will build a house
for you.' So your servant has found
courage to pray this prayer to you.
28Sovereign LORD, you are God! Your
covenant is trustworthy,[i] and you
have promised these good things to
your servant. 29Now be pleased to
bless the house of your servant, that
it may continue forever in your sight;
for you, Sovereign LORD, have spoken,
and with your blessing[j] the house of
your servant will be blessed forever."

7:23 [f] Dt 9:26; 15:15 **7:24** [g] Dt 26:18 [h] Ex 6:6-7; Ps 48:14 **7:28** [i] Ex 34:6; Jn 17:17 **7:29** [j] Nu 6:23-27 **8:2** [k] Ge 19:37; Nu 24:17 **8:3** [l] 2Sa 10:16, 19 [m] 1Sa 14:47

David's Victories

8:1-14pp — 1Ch 18:1-13

8 In the course of time, David defeated
the Philistines and subdued them, and
he took Metheg Ammah from the control
of the Philistines.
2David also defeated the Moabites.[k] He
made them lie down on the ground and
measured them off with a length of cord.
Every two lengths of them were put to
death, and the third length was allowed
to live. So the Moabites became subject to
David and brought him tribute.
3Moreover, David defeated Hadadezer[l] son of Rehob, king of Zobah,[m] when
he went to restore his monument at[b] the
Euphrates River. 4David captured a thousand of his chariots, seven thousand

[a] 23 See Septuagint and 1 Chron. 17:21; Hebrew *wonders for your land and before your people, whom you redeemed from Egypt, from the nations and their gods.* [b] 3 Or *his control along*

8:1 *he took Metheg Ammah from the control of the Philistines.* Whether Metheg Ammah is to be understood as a proper place-name or as two simple common nouns is unclear. If the former, the site is attested only here (but cf. "hill of Ammah" in 2:24), and its location remains unknown. If, following the second option, one takes the combination as two common nouns, various readings are possible. One might read the words as "the reins of the forearm," an idiomatic usage suggesting control or supremacy, in this instance over the Philistines. Or, with slight emendation, one might read "the common lands," yielding the sense that David took control of the outlying (nonurban) lands from the Philistines. The parallel phrase in 1Ch 18:1 reads "Gath and its surrounding villages [or daughters]." Gath was viewed by early rabbinical scholars as the foremost of Philistine cities, so that supremacy over Gath constituted effective supremacy over the Philistines.

8:2 *Every two lengths of them were put to death.* Unparalleled in Biblical and extra-Biblical literature, David's method of casting lots to reduce the soldiers of Moab by two-thirds strikes modern readers as cruel and arbitrary, especially in view of the fact that David had earlier trusted the Moabites (1Sa 22:3). A case could be made, however, that, in an ancient Near Eastern context, in which combatants were often either all sold into slavery or all executed, the sparing of one third of the enemy soldiers to return to their homes was not without mercy. Furthermore, even when defeated combatants were retained as slaves, they were often mutilated (e.g., blinded) to keep them under control (see note on 1Sa 11:2); long-term imprisonment of large numbers of prisoners was not an option, though brief internment was sometimes practiced where repatriation or political negotiations were anticipated. *the Moabites became subject to David and brought him tribute.* In the ancient Near East, subjugated territories were typically expected to send tribute in the form of various kinds of payment (e.g., precious metals and other goods, agricultural produce, livestock, even labor forces). In addition to the symbolic and, indeed, economic value of the conqueror's receiving tribute, this system had the effect of depressing the economy of the conquered land and helping to assure its continued submission, much in the same way that deportation (or, as in the present instance, execution) depleted the workforce and defense forces of the conquered land. From as early as Sumerian times in the first half of the third millennium BC, references to tribute can be found in the extant literature. Assyrian sources contain numerous references to Israel having to pay tribute. The most famous instance—that of Jehu bringing tribute and bowing before Shalmaneser III (858–824 BC)—is depicted on the well-known Black Obelisk. Other explicit references to Assyria exacting tribute from Israel can be found in the records of Adadnirari III (810–782 BC), Tiglath-Pileser III (745–727 BC), Sargon II (722–705 BC), Sennacherib (705–681 BC), Esarhaddon (681–669 BC) and Ashurbanipal (668–627 BC).

8:3 *he went to restore his monument at the Euphrates River.* Ambiguity regarding the antecedent of "he" has given rise to debate as to whether it was David or Hadadezer who went to "restore his monument" (or possibly "restore his control" [see NIV text note]). On the one hand, it can be argued that, because David would have passed through the territory of Hadadezer en route to the Euphrates River (probably in the vicinity of Emar) and would otherwise not likely have encountered Hadadezer so far north, it may have been David who went to "restore his monument." On the other hand, however, if it was Hadadezer who had to restore order in his northern territories, David may have seized the opportunity of Hadadezer's preoccupation with the north to attack him from the south.

8:4 *hamstrung all but a hundred of the chariot horses.* See note on Jos 11:6. According to the "law of the king" in Dt 17:16, Israel's kings "must not acquire great numbers of horses." Prior to Joshua's encounter with the Hazor coalition of northern Canaanite kings, Yahweh had instructed Joshua to "hamstring their horses and burn their chariots," which he did (Jos 11:6,9). David's action is thus largely in keeping with these precedents, though his retention of "a hundred" of the chariot horses may suggest an early stage in a growing reliance on military might (see note on 24:1).

2 SAMUEL 8

DAVID'S "EMPIRE"

To call the kingdom ruled by David (and later Solomon) an "empire" can be misleading, if one's points of comparison are the massive empires of the ancient Egyptians, Assyrians, Persians or Romans. Terminology defies consensus definitions, and disagreement is entrenched in questions pertaining to duration, size or the complexity of social and political structures. David certainly has a kingdom, and one that has a number of territories under a variety of regimented relationships.

The summary of David's victories in 2Sa 8 says that David "subdued" (or "humbled") the Philistines (2Sa 8:1), fought and "defeated" the Moabites (2Sa 8:2), the Zobahites (2Sa 8:3 – 4) and the Arameans (2Sa 8:5 – 8), and that he received congratulatory greetings from Tou king of Hamath, who sent gifts by the agency of his son Joram (2Sa 8:9 – 10). In 2Sa 8:11 – 12 the Edomites, Ammonites and Amalekites are added to the list of peoples "subdued" by David. The reference to the Edomites anticipates 2Sa 8:13 – 14. The reference to the Ammonites may anticipate 2Sa 10, and the reference to the Amalekites recalls 2Sa 1:1, etc.

The summary in 2Sa 8 of David's kingdom suggests the following distinctions. While the Philistines were "subdued" (or "humbled"), there is no mention of their becoming servants of David or of their sending tribute. By contrast, Moab and Aram are explicitly reduced to tributary status, as are also, apparently, Edom and Ammon. Hamath welcomes David's defeat of Aram and allies itself to David without the necessity of conquest. Taken together, these data present a multitiered Davidic kingdom comprising heartland (Judah and Israel, but not Philistia), conquered territories (Edom, Moab, Ammon and Aram), and subject-allies (Hamath). Over these constituent parts of his empire, David gained political control by various means and exercised dominion in different ways. The general concept of a multitiered kingdom is appropriate to David's time and place in the southern Levant. Three other similar kingdoms in the Late Bronze Age Levant have been inferred from Biblical and extra-Biblical evidence (especially Hittite hieroglyphic and Mesopotamian cuneiform texts): they are those of Hadadezer of Aram, of Carchemish and of Tabal. ◆

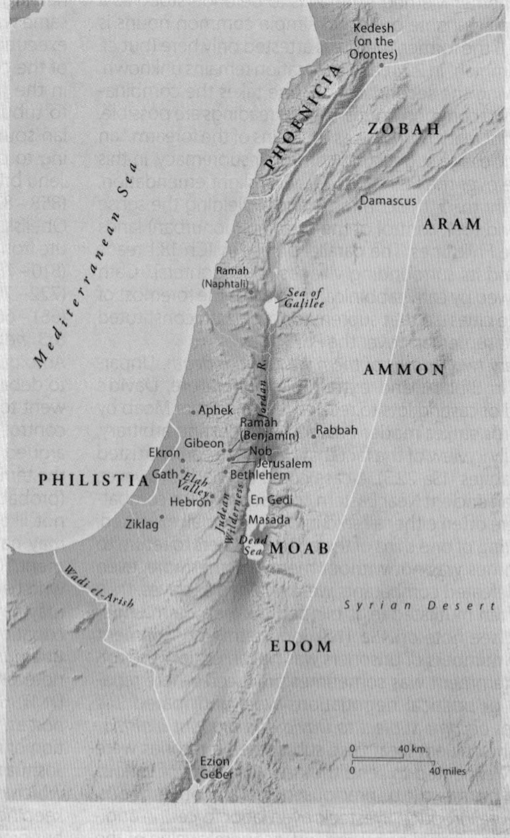

charioteers[a] and twenty thousand foot soldiers. He hamstrung[n] all but a hundred of
the chariot horses.
5 When the Arameans of Damascus[o]
came to help Hadadezer king of Zobah,
David struck down twenty-two thousand
of them. 6 He put garrisons in the Aramean
kingdom of Damascus, and the Arameans
became subject to him and brought tribute. The LORD gave David victory wherever
he went.[p]
7 David took the gold shields[q] that belonged to the officers of Hadadezer and
brought them to Jerusalem. 8 From Tebah[b]
and Berothai,[r] towns that belonged to
Hadadezer, King David took a great quantity of bronze.
9 When Tou[c] king of Hamath[s] heard
that David had defeated the entire army
of Hadadezer, 10 he sent his son Joram[d] to
King David to greet him and congratulate
him on his victory in battle over Hadadezer, who had been at war with Tou. Joram
brought with him articles of silver, of gold
and of bronze.
11 King David dedicated[t] these articles to
the LORD, as he had done with the silver
and gold from all the nations he had subdued: 12 Edom[e] and Moab,[u] the Ammonites[v] and the Philistines,[w] and Amalek.[x]
He also dedicated the plunder taken from
Hadadezer son of Rehob, king of Zobah.
13 And David became famous[y] after he
returned from striking down eighteen
thousand Edomites[f] in the Valley of Salt.[z]
14 He put garrisons throughout Edom,
and all the Edomites[a] became subject
to David.[b] The LORD gave David victory
wherever he went.[c]

8:4 [n] Jos 11:9 **8:5** [o] 1Ki 11:24 **8:6** [p] ver 14; 2Sa 3:18; 7:9 **8:7** [q] 1Ki 10:16 **8:8** [r] Eze 47:16 **8:9** [s] 1Ki 8:65; 2Ch 8:4 **8:11** [t] 1Ki 7:51; 1Ch 26:26 **8:12** [u] ver 2 [v] 2Sa 10:14 [w] 2Sa 5:25 [x] 1Sa 27:8 **8:13** [y] 2Sa 7:9 [z] 2Ki 14:7; 1Ch 18:12 **8:14** [a] Nu 24:17-18 [b] Ge 27:29, 37-40 [c] ver 6 **8:16** [d] 2Sa 19:13; 1Ch 11:6 [e] 2Sa 20:24; 1Ki 4:3 **8:17** [f] 2Sa 15:24, 29; 1Ch 16:39; 24:3

David's Officials

8:15-18pp — 1Ch 18:14-17

15 David reigned over all Israel, doing
what was just and right for all his people.
16 Joab[d] son of Zeruiah was over the army;
Jehoshaphat[e] son of Ahilud was recorder; 17 Zadok[f] son of Ahitub and Ahimelek
son of Abiathar were priests; Seraiah was

[a] *4* Septuagint (see also Dead Sea Scrolls and 1 Chron. 18:4); Masoretic Text *captured seventeen hundred of his charioteers* [b] *8* See some Septuagint manuscripts (see also 1 Chron. 18:8); Hebrew *Betah.* [c] *9* Hebrew *Toi*, a variant of *Tou*; also in verse 10 [d] *10* A variant of *Hadoram* [e] *12* Some Hebrew manuscripts, Septuagint and Syriac (see also 1 Chron. 18:11); most Hebrew manuscripts *Aram* [f] *13* A few Hebrew manuscripts, Septuagint and Syriac (see also 1 Chron. 18:12); most Hebrew manuscripts *Aram* (that is, Arameans)

8:7 *gold shields.* Should probably read "bow (and arrow) cases," a judgment based on Aramaic technical terminology and supportive Semitic cognates.

8:10 *sent his son Joram.* That the king of Hamath's son should bear the name Joram ("Yahweh is exalted") seems surprising, and indeed his original name may have been Hadoram ("[the god] Haddu/Hadad is exalted"), as in 1Ch 18:10. Perhaps the name Joram was adopted or imposed in keeping with Israel's growing dominance under David. The adoption of a second name in royal circles is a practice well attested throughout the Near East.

8:11 *dedicated these articles to the LORD.* In keeping with the common ancient Near Eastern belief that the gods gave victory (see the article "Divine Warfare," p. 365), it was appropriate and expected that a valuable portion of the spoils of victory would be dedicated to the deity. While no battle was fought against Hamath to gain the gifts brought by Tou's son Joram — "articles of silver, of gold and of bronze" (v. 10) — it was David's victory over Hadadezer that prompted Tou king of Hamath to subordinate himself voluntarily to David (see the article "David's 'Empire,'" p. 528). While in some instances that which was dedicated to God was killed or destroyed, precious metals would typically be placed in the sacred precinct, under the administration of the priests and for the maintenance of the sanctuary (cf. 1Ch 26:26 – 28). The gift signals the commencement of diplomatic relations between the two states. There is no indication that Tou is accepting a vassal-suzerain relationship with David. Rather, as one powerful king to another he is employing the age-old diplomatic protocol of exchanging commodities such as precious metals (1Ch 18:10). *all the nations he had subdued.* See the article "David's 'Empire,'" p. 528.

8:13 *David became famous.* Lit. "David made a name," which may recall Yahweh's promise to David in 7:9 that he would "make [David's] name great, like the names of the greatest men on earth." Alternatively, "name" may connote a victory monument of some sort. The effect, in either case, may have been much the same. The Old Assyrian king Shamshi-Adad I (1813 – 1781 BC), e.g., boasts: "I established my great name and my steles in the land of Lebanon on the shore of the Great Sea." Making a name is accomplished by anything that provides for perpetuating the memory of someone, whether great accomplishments, successful kingship, or something as basic as having a family (family members are most likely to remember someone after they die).

8:16 – 17 *over the army ... recorder ... priests ... secretary.* See the similar, if fuller, listing at 20:23 – 26. Each of these titles designates a high-ranking official in David's government. Among Israel's ancient Near Eastern neighbors, similar "cabinets" of high-ranking officials are attested. The Neo-Assyrian cabinet, e.g., included the following: treasurer, palace herald, chief cupbearer, chief eunuch, chief judge, grand vizier, and commander-in-chief. *over the army.* The fact that in the list of David's officers the chief military commander, Joab, is named first, is typical of ancient Near Eastern governments, in which the military leader ranked second only to the king himself. *recorder.* An office mentioned here for the first time in the OT. The title has led some to assume that this official's primary responsibilities must have included keeping the state records, but the Hebrew word might better (if inelegantly) be rendered "remembrancer," or "herald." The "recorder," like the Egyptian "herald," probably had two chief functions: (1) the task of handling the communications between the king and the country, and (2) the care of the ceremonial tasks at the royal audiences. Thus, Jehoshaphat as "recorder" might be compared to both a modern press secretary and a chief of protocol. Jehoshaphat continued his service in this capacity during the administration of Solomon (1Ki 4:3). *priests.* David's court also included two priests: Zadok, mentioned here for the first time in the OT, and Abiathar (1Sa 22:20). While Zadok and Abiathar both

secretary;[g] 18Benaiah[h] son of Jehoiada was
over the Kerethites[i] and Pelethites; and
David's sons were priests.[a]

David and Mephibosheth

9 David asked, "Is there anyone still left
of the house of Saul to whom I can
show kindness for Jonathan's sake?"[j]
2Now there was a servant of Saul's
household named Ziba.[k] They summoned
him to appear before David, and the king
said to him, "Are you Ziba?"
"At your service," he replied.
3The king asked, "Is there no one still
alive from the house of Saul to whom I
can show God's kindness?"
Ziba answered the king, "There is still
a son of Jonathan;[l] he is lame[m] in both
feet."
4"Where is he?" the king asked.
Ziba answered, "He is at the house of
Makir[n] son of Ammiel in Lo Debar."
5So King David had him brought from
Lo Debar, from the house of Makir son of
Ammiel.
6When Mephibosheth son of Jonathan,
the son of Saul, came to David, he bowed
down to pay him honor.[o]
David said, "Mephibosheth!"
"At your service," he replied.
7"Don't be afraid," David said to him,
"for I will surely show you kindness for
the sake of your father Jonathan. I will
restore to you all the land that belonged
to your grandfather Saul, and you will always eat at my table."[p]
8Mephibosheth bowed down and said,
"What is your servant, that you should notice a dead dog[q] like me?"
9Then the king summoned Ziba, Saul's
steward, and said to him, "I have given
your master's grandson everything that
belonged to Saul and his family. 10You and
your sons and your servants are to farm
the land for him and bring in the crops, so
that your master's grandson[r] may be provided for. And Mephibosheth, grandson of
your master, will always eat at my table."
(Now Ziba had fifteen sons and twenty
servants.)
11Then Ziba said to the king, "Your servant will do whatever my lord the king
commands his servant to do." So Mephibosheth ate at David's[b] table like one of the
king's sons.[s]
12Mephibosheth had a young son
named Mika, and all the members of Ziba's household were servants of Mephibosheth.[t] 13And Mephibosheth lived in Jerusalem, because he always ate at the king's
table; he was lame in both feet.

8:17 [g] 1Ki 4:3; 2Ki 12:10
8:18 [h] 2Sa 20:23; 1Ki 1:8,38; 1Ch 18:17 [i] 1Sa 30:14
9:1 [j] 1Sa 20:14-17,42
9:2 [k] 2Sa 16:1-4; 19:17,26,29
9:3 [l] 1Sa 20:14 [m] 2Sa 4:4
9:4 [n] 2Sa 17:27-29
9:6 [o] 2Sa 16:4; 19:24-30
9:7 [p] ver 1, 3; 2Sa 12:8; 19:28; 1Ki 2:7; 2Ki 25:29
9:8 [q] 2Sa 16:9
9:10 [r] ver 7, 11, 13; 2Sa 19:28
9:11 [s] Job 36:7; Ps 113:8
9:12 [t] 1Ch 8:34

[a] *18* Or *were chief officials* (see Septuagint and Targum; see also 1 Chron. 18:17) [b] *11* Septuagint; Hebrew *my*

functioned as priests during David's reign, the latter was removed from office by Solomon (1Ki 1:7–8), thus fulfilling the judgment pronounced on the house of Eli in 1Sa 2:31. *secretary.* Would have been among the highest-ranking civil servants (cf. 2Ki 12:10; 25:19). His duties likely including presiding over the secretariat, where official documents were written and where the state records were kept. The name of David's "secretary," Seraiah, is spelled in several different ways elsewhere in the OT (2Sa 20:25; 1Ch 18:16; possibly 1Ki 4:3), which may suggest a non-Israelite origin—perhaps Egypt, where the scribal and administrative traditions were well established.

8:18 *Benaiah.* A man of outstanding military credentials (23:20–22). *Kerethites and Pelethites.* Professional troops who served apparently as David's personal army (see note on 1Sa 27:2). Using foreign mercenaries for a personal army such as this provided trained military personnel who would not be inclined to take sides politically or to get involved in court intrigue. See note on 1Ki 1:38. *David's sons were priests.* Given the multiplicity of priestly roles attested both in the Bible and in the ancient Near East (where royal and familial priests were not uncommon), the notion that David's sons served a (royal) priestly role is less problematic than is sometimes supposed. It is true that in Israel the care of the temple was given into the hands of those from the tribe of Levi. Some of these were priests serving in the temple precinct, while other Levites served across the towns of Israel. Given the possibility of multiple distinct priestly roles, it is not clear that David's sons are assigned a status that should have been reserved for Levites. No other Biblical examples feature priests from any other tribe, but having some from the royal family would not be surprising.

9:1–13 Given the harsh treatment often meted out to former or potential rivals, David's actions were gracious. An extreme example is the cruel treatment that the much later Assyrian king Ashurbanipal (669–633 BC) gave to those who "had plotted against me"... "I fed their corpses, cut into small pieces, to dogs, pigs, vultures, the birds of the sky and (also) to the fish of the ocean." The Bible itself describes instances of rather rough executions of justice (e.g., Jdg 1:6–7) and even the massacre of rival royal families (e.g., 1Ki 15:29). In view of such practices, David's sparing of Mephibosheth was indeed gracious. On the other hand, bringing Mephibosheth into the royal court and to the king's table may also have served David's own interests, as it would have placed Mephibosheth under immediate surveillance. From his own experience, he must have recognized the potential dangers of allowing a rival into the royal court (note Ziba's actions in 16:1–4). Granted, Mephibosheth's crippled condition would have made him an unlikely candidate for the throne, but he did have a young son named Mika (v. 12).

9:3 *lame in both feet.* See note on 4:4.

9:7 *eat at my table.* In the ancient Near East, political prisoners were not kept in cells, but in the palace, where they could be closely observed. Ration lists from Babylon and Assyria show clothing, food and oil allotted to "guests" of the king. In Persia, political detainees were kept in the king's presence. Within the court, Mephibosheth may be free, but he is still essentially a prisoner. Still, for Jonathan's sake he is kept alive and cared for. It would be reckless to just give him his freedom. That had been the general nature of Jonathan's request from David.

9:8 *dead dog.* See notes on 3:8; 1Sa 17:43; 24:14.

David Defeats the Ammonites

10:1-19pp — 1Ch 19:1-19

10 In the course of time, the king of
the Ammonites died, and his son
Hanun succeeded him as king. 2David
thought, "I will show kindness to Hanun
son of Nahash,[u] just as his father showed
kindness to me." So David sent a delegation to express his sympathy to Hanun
concerning his father.

When David's men came to the land
of the Ammonites, 3the Ammonite commanders said to Hanun their lord, "Do
you think David is honoring your father
by sending envoys to you to express sympathy? Hasn't David sent them to you only
to explore the city and spy it out and overthrow it?" 4So Hanun seized David's envoys, shaved off half of each man's beard,[v]
cut off their garments at the buttocks,[w]
and sent them away.

5When David was told about this, he
sent messengers to meet the men, for
they were greatly humiliated. The king
said, "Stay at Jericho till your beards have
grown, and then come back."

6When the Ammonites realized that
they had become obnoxious[x] to David,
they hired twenty thousand Aramean[y] foot
soldiers from Beth Rehob[z] and Zobah, as
well as the king of Maakah[a] with a thousand men, and also twelve thousand men
from Tob.

7On hearing this, David sent Joab out
with the entire army of fighting men. 8The
Ammonites came out and drew up in battle formation at the entrance of their city
gate, while the Arameans of Zobah and
Rehob and the men of Tob and Maakah
were by themselves in the open country.

9Joab saw that there were battle lines
in front of him and behind him; so he selected some of the best troops in Israel
and deployed them against the Arameans. 10He put the rest of the men under
the command of Abishai his brother and
deployed them against the Ammonites.
11Joab said, "If the Arameans are too
strong for me, then you are to come to
my rescue; but if the Ammonites are too
strong for you, then I will come to rescue you. 12Be strong,[b] and let us fight
bravely for our people and the cities of
our God. The LORD will do what is good
in his sight."[c]

13Then Joab and the troops with him
advanced to fight the Arameans, and they
fled before him. 14When the Ammonites
realized that the Arameans were fleeing,
they fled before Abishai and went inside
the city. So Joab returned from fighting the
Ammonites and came to Jerusalem.

15After the Arameans saw that they had
been routed by Israel, they regrouped.
16Hadadezer had Arameans brought from
beyond the Euphrates River; they went to
Helam, with Shobak the commander of
Hadadezer's army leading them.

17When David was told of this, he gathered all Israel, crossed the Jordan and
went to Helam. The Arameans formed
their battle lines to meet David and fought

10:2 [u] 1Sa 11:1
10:4 [v] Lev 19:27; Isa 15:2; Jer 48:37 [w] Isa 20:4
10:6 [x] Ge 34:30 [y] 2Sa 8:5 [z] Jdg 18:28 [a] Dt 3:14
10:12 [b] Dt 31:6; 1Co 16:13; Eph 6:10 [c] Jdg 10:15; 1Sa 3:18; Ne 4:14

10:2 *show kindness.* Suggests that a treaty or covenant relationship had existed between David and Hanun's father, Nahash, even though it had been the latter's aggression toward Israel that had in part contributed to Saul's rise to power (1Sa 11:1 – 11; 12:12). David's fugitive period, when he was on the run from Saul, would have been a logical time for him to enter into some kind of agreement with Nahash, and it probably would have been something akin to a "parity treaty" (between more or less equal partners), as distinguished from a "suzerain-vassal treaty" (between a greater and a lesser power). Both kinds of treaties are well attested in the ancient Near East. In a parity treaty between the Hittite king Hattushili III and the Egyptian pharaoh Rameses II, the two kings agree to mutual nonaggression, mutual defense, extradition of fugitives, and even assistance in cases of contested royal accession. It was designed to "establish good peace (and) good brotherhood be[tween us] forever." That Hanun should dishonor David's emissaries (v. 4) was, in essence, to renounce the treaty of peace that had existed between his father and David and was wittingly or unwittingly to invite retaliation by David.

10:4 *envoys.* In the ancient world, heads of state generally did not travel to other countries on diplomatic missions. Messengers were used who, like ambassadors, were understood as fully representing the person and authority of the king. They spoke as the king and they were to be treated as if they were the king. *shaved off half of each man's beard, cut off their garments at the buttocks.* The records from the ancient Near East reveal no direct parallels to the treatment given to David's representatives, so it is difficult to unpack the specific symbolism. But Hanun's treatment of the envoys clearly constituted a calculated, direct affront to David and, not surprisingly, started a war between the two states. David's beard was in effect shaved half off, and his garments were cut off at the buttocks.

10:9 *battle lines in front of him and behind him.* How Joab found himself caught between the Aramean and the Ammonite forces is a matter of conjecture. Perhaps he made a tactical mistake by marching directly to Rabbah (the probable Ammonite city of v. 8; modern Amman) via Jericho or Heshbon, rather than crossing the Jordan at Adam and intercepting the Aramean forces in the region of Helam (a considerable distance north of Rabbah), as David apparently did in v. 17. Whether Joab arrived in his initial predicament by strategic error or simply because it could not be avoided, his decision to divide his troops and fight on two fronts was, though risky, ultimately successful, at least to the point of a draw. No enemy casualties are mentioned in the text however, only the enemy's flight, with the Ammonites escaping to the safety of their city, after which Joab returned to Jerusalem. It remained for David, in a second encounter, to soundly defeat the Arameans (vv. 15 – 19).

against him. 18But they fled before Israel,
and David killed seven hundred of their
charioteers and forty thousand of their
foot soldiers.[a] He also struck down Shobak the commander of their army, and he
died there. 19When all the kings who were
vassals of Hadadezer saw that they had
been routed by Israel, they made peace
with the Israelites and became subject[d] to
them.

So the Arameans[e] were afraid to help
the Ammonites anymore.

David and Bathsheba

11 In the spring,[f] at the time when
kings go off to war, David sent
Joab[g] out with the king's men and the
whole Israelite army.[h] They destroyed the
Ammonites and besieged Rabbah.[i] But David remained in Jerusalem.

2One evening David got up from his
bed and walked around on the roof[j] of the
palace. From the roof he saw[k] a woman
bathing. The woman was very beautiful,
3and David sent someone to find out about
her. The man said, "She is Bathsheba,[l] the
daughter of Eliam[m] and the wife of Uriah[n]
the Hittite." 4Then David sent messengers
to get her.[o] She came to him, and he slept[p]
with her. (Now she was purifying herself
from her monthly uncleanness.)[q] Then
she went back home. 5The woman conceived and sent word to David, saying, "I
am pregnant."

6So David sent this word to Joab: "Send
me Uriah[r] the Hittite." And Joab sent him
to David. 7When Uriah came to him, David
asked him how Joab was, how the soldiers
were and how the war was going. 8Then
David said to Uriah, "Go down to your
house and wash your feet."[s] So Uriah left
the palace, and a gift from the king was

10:19 [d] 2Sa 8:6 [e] 1Ki 11:25; 2Ki 5:1 **11:1** [f] 1Ki 20:22, 26 [g] 2Sa 2:18 [h] 1Ch 20:1 [i] 2Sa 12:26-28 **11:2** [j] Dt 22:8; Jos 2:8 [k] Mt 5:28 **11:3** [l] 1Ch 3:5 [m] 2Sa 23:34 [n] 2Sa 23:39 **11:4** [o] Lev 20:10; Ps 51 Title; Jas 1:14-15 [p] Dt 22:22 [q] Lev 15:25-30; 18:19 **11:6** [r] 1Ch 11:41 **11:8** [s] Ge 18:4; 43:24; Lk 7:44

[a] *18* Some Septuagint manuscripts (see also 1 Chron. 19:18); Hebrew *horsemen*

11:1 *In the spring, at the time when kings go off to war.* As straightforward as this notice seems in the English translation, it is not without complications in the Hebrew text, which reads lit. "at the return of the year, at the time of the messengers' going forth." This has led to the suggestion that the campaign described in ch. 11 was launched on the one-year anniversary of David's first sending of a delegation to Hanun, the new king of the Ammonites (10:2). The first delegation had been treated shamefully by Hanun (see note on 10:4), and the timing of the present delegation would leave no doubt of its retaliatory purpose. The more traditional reading (reflected in the NIV) is not without defense however; e.g., the Hebrew words "king" and "messenger" sound and are spelled much alike (differing only by one "silent" consonant), making confusion in transmission a possibility. Further, the Hebrew verb meaning "go forth" is often used for "going forth (to battle/war)." In any case, the spring of the year would have been a typical time for military campaigning in the ancient Near East; the winter rains would have stopped and the labor-intensive harvest time would not yet have arrived, thus leaving able-bodied men available for military exploits. Assyrian and Babylonian annals, which often mention the month in which a military campaign was launched, typically name the first month of the year (Nisanu) or the second (Aiaru), the new year beginning in the springtime. Other events occurring in various months are, of course, mentioned, but the beginnings of military operations are typically linked to the spring months. *David remained in Jerusalem.* The reason why David elected to remain behind when the army went out is not given. Although it was customary for kings to accompany armies, they did not always do so. Affairs of state, physical condition, or domestic issues might hinder him from going. In a parallel situation when Nebuchadnezzar laid siege to Jerusalem in 589 BC, he was not there in person for the duration of the siege. Nor was he there when the city itself fell in 586; he was at Riblah in Lebanon. The capture of Jerusalem was overseen by Nebuzaradan (Nabû-zemr-iddina), the "commander of the imperial guard" (2Ki 25:10). Similarly, when Babylon fell to Cyrus in 539 BC, Cyrus remained at Sippar until he could enter Babylon in a well-orchestrated victory parade. Perhaps because it was a siege situation, David may have felt he did not have to involve himself personally until the very end. See note on 12:28.

11:2 *he saw a woman bathing.* As v. 4 indicates, Bathsheba's bathing was likely the purification rite prescribed in Lev 15:19–24 that was to follow menstruation. It is generally assumed that Bathsheba was in full view of the king and therefore some wonder about her intention or discretion. However, such an assumption is unwarranted. Even if Bathsheba was being appropriately discrete and the king's actual view was limited, he knows what is taking place—he saw that she was bathing—and his imagination would be able to do the rest. *a woman.* Though most translations make it sound as if David did not know the identity of the woman, the city of Jerusalem was very small (10 acres or 4 hectares) at this point and most of the people living in it were likely part of the administration. Since Bathsheba's husband and father have long been part of David's group of select warriors, it is highly unlikely that David does not know her. It is also unimaginable that he does not know whose house he is looking at. Consequently, we should understand "David sent someone to find out about her" (v. 3) as a requisition (not just to discover who she was).

11:3 *find out about her.* See previous note. *Eliam.* Given the typically economic style of Biblical narratives, the explicit naming of Bathsheba's father invites explanation. If he is the same Eliam as is mentioned in 23:34 ("Eliam son of Ahithophel"), then the fact that Ahithophel was Bathsheba's grandfather may help to explain Ahithophel's later betrayal of David in favor of Absalom's conspiracy (15:12; 16:15). Absalom was aggrieved over David's failure to execute justice (15:4,6), and Ahithophel would certainly have nursed a similar grievance. *Uriah the Hittite.* He is listed as the last of David's "mighty warriors" (23:8,39). *Hittite.* As with other people groups living amongst the Israelites, the Hittites may have served as mercenaries for David, or as part of his personal troops, as did the Kerethites and Pelethites (see notes on 8:18; 1Sa 27:2).

11:4 *she was purifying herself from her monthly uncleanness.* This notice indicates that Bathsheba has just finished menstruating, eliminating any possibility that Bathsheba could have been pregnant by her husband, thus complicating David's attempt to cover up his misdeed.

11:8 *Go down to your house and wash your feet.* Whether or not "wash your feet" was a euphemism for sexual intercourse, Uriah certainly understood what David was implying (v. 11). If sexual abstinence was a requirement for

Clay figurine of a woman bathing found at Achzib, eighth–sixth century BC, a few centuries after David saw Bathsheba bathing.
Kim Walton. The Israel Museum, Jerusalem.

sent after him. [9]But Uriah slept at the entrance to the palace with all his master's
servants and did not go down to his house.
[10]David was told, "Uriah did not go
home." So he asked Uriah, "Haven't you
just come from a military campaign? Why
didn't you go home?"
[11]Uriah said to David, "The ark[t] and Israel and Judah are staying in tents,[a] and
my commander Joab and my lord's men
are camped in the open country. How
could I go to my house to eat and drink
and make love to my wife? As surely as
you live, I will not do such a thing!"
[12]Then David said to him, "Stay here
one more day, and tomorrow I will send
you back." So Uriah remained in Jerusalem that day and the next. [13]At David's
invitation, he ate and drank with him, and
David made him drunk. But in the evening
Uriah went out to sleep on his mat among
his master's servants; he did not go home.
[14]In the morning David wrote a letter[u]
to Joab and sent it with Uriah. [15]In it he
wrote, "Put Uriah out in front where the
fighting is fiercest. Then withdraw from
him so he will be struck down[v] and die.[w]"

11:11 [t]2Sa 7:2 **11:14** [u]1Ki 21:8 **11:15** [v]2Sa 12:9 [w]2Sa 12:12

[16]So while Joab had the city under siege,
he put Uriah at a place where he knew the
strongest defenders were. [17]When the men
of the city came out and fought against
Joab, some of the men in David's army
fell; moreover, Uriah the Hittite died.
[18]Joab sent David a full account of the
battle. [19]He instructed the messenger:
"When you have finished giving the king
this account of the battle, [20]the king's anger may flare up, and he may ask you,
'Why did you get so close to the city to
fight? Didn't you know they would shoot
arrows from the wall? [21]Who killed Abimelek[x] son of Jerub-Besheth[b]? Didn't a woman drop an upper millstone on him from
the wall,[y] so that he died in Thebez? Why
did you get so close to the wall?' If he asks
you this, then say to him, 'Moreover, your
servant Uriah the Hittite is dead.' "
[22]The messenger set out, and when he
arrived he told David everything Joab had
sent him to say. [23]The messenger said to
David, "The men overpowered us and
came out against us in the open, but we
drove them back to the entrance of the
city gate. [24]Then the archers shot arrows
at your servants from the wall, and some
of the king's men died. Moreover, your
servant Uriah the Hittite is dead."
[25]David told the messenger, "Say this to
Joab: 'Don't let this upset you; the sword
devours one as well as another. Press the
attack against the city and destroy it.' Say
this to encourage Joab."
[26]When Uriah's wife heard that her husband was dead, she mourned for him. [27]Af-
ter the time of mourning was over, David
had her brought to his house, and she became his wife and bore him a son. But the
thing David had done displeased[z] the LORD.

Nathan Rebukes David

11:1; 12:29-31pp — 1Ch 20:1-3

12 The LORD sent Nathan[a] to David.[b]
When he came to him,[c] he said,
"There were two men in a certain town,

11:21 [x]Jdg 8:31 [y]Jdg 9:50-54 **11:27** [z]2Sa 12:9; Ps 51:4-5 **12:1** [a]2Sa 7:2; 1Ki 20:35-41 [b]Ps 51 Title [c]2Sa 14:4

[a] 11 Or *staying at Sukkoth* [b] 21 Also known as *Jerub-Baal* (that is, Gideon)

soldiers on active duty, as may be inferred from 1Sa 21:5 (cf. Dt 23:10), David may have been seeking to entrap Uriah in a ritual infraction and thereby find legal grounds for eliminating him. In any case, David's hope was that Uriah would sleep with Bathsheba and thus cloud the paternity issue. Uriah's refusal to indulge himself while the armies of Israel were in the field must have been a stinging rebuke to David, whether Uriah intended it to be so or not (we are left in the dark about what Uriah did or did not know of David's affair).

11:26 *she mourned for him.* The Biblical text offers no indication of Bathsheba's feelings for Uriah, except to observe that she mourned for him.

11:27 *time of mourning.* Probably seven days, which seems to have been the customary period (Ge 50:10; 1Sa 31:13). National leaders were sometimes mourned for longer periods; Aaron and Moses were each mourned for 30 days (Nu 20:29; Dt 34:8) and the Egyptians mourned for Jacob a full 70 days (Ge 50:3). A chronicle from the reign of the Neo-Babylonian king Nabonidus (556–539 BC) states that when the wife of the king died, she was mourned "from the 27th day of Arahshamnu till the 3rd day of Nisanu"—over four months.

12:1–4 While Nathan's parable did not speak of adultery and murder per se, Nathan's rich man did resemble David in two specific respects: first, he ignored the many sheep

one rich and the other poor. 2The rich man had a very large number of sheep and cattle, 3but the poor man had nothing except one little ewe lamb he had bought. He raised it, and it grew up with him and his children. It shared his food, drank from his cup and even slept in his arms. It was like a daughter to him.

4"Now a traveler came to the rich man, but the rich man refrained from taking one of his own sheep or cattle to prepare a meal for the traveler who had come to him. Instead, he took the ewe lamb that belonged to the poor man and prepared it for the one who had come to him."

5David[d] burned with anger against the man and said to Nathan, "As surely as the LORD lives, the man who did this must die! 6He must pay for that lamb four times over,[e] because he did such a thing and had no pity."

7Then Nathan said to David, "You are the man! This is what the LORD, the God of Israel, says: 'I anointed[f] you[g] king over Israel, and I delivered you from the hand of Saul. 8I gave your master's house to you,[h] and your master's wives into your arms. I gave you all Israel and Judah. And if all this had been too little, I would have given you even more. 9Why did you despise[i] the word of the LORD by doing what is evil in his eyes? You struck down[j] Uriah the Hittite with the sword and took his wife to be your own. You killed him with the sword of the Ammonites. 10Now, therefore, the sword[k] will never depart from your house, because you despised me and took the wife of Uriah the Hittite to be your own.'

11"This is what the LORD says: 'Out of your own household I am going to bring calamity on you.[l] Before your very eyes I will take your wives and give them to one who is close to you, and he will sleep with your wives in broad daylight. 12You did it in secret,[m] but I will do this thing in broad daylight[n] before all Israel.'"

13Then David said to Nathan, "I have sinned[o] against the LORD."

Nathan replied, "The LORD has taken away[p] your sin.[q] You are not going to die.[r] 14But because by doing this you have shown utter contempt for[a] the LORD,[s] the son born to you will die."

15After Nathan had gone home, the LORD struck[t] the child that Uriah's wife had borne to David, and he became ill. 16David pleaded with God for the child. He fasted and spent the nights lying[u] in sackcloth[b] on the ground. 17The elders of his household stood beside him to get him up from the ground, but he refused, and he would not eat any food with them.[v]

18On the seventh day the child died. David's attendants were afraid to tell him that the child was dead, for they thought, "While the child was still living, he wouldn't listen to us when we spoke to him. How can we now tell him the child is dead? He may do something desperate."

19David noticed that his attendants were whispering among themselves, and he realized the child was dead. "Is the child dead?" he asked.

"Yes," they replied, "he is dead."

20Then David got up from the ground. After he had washed,[w] put on lotions and changed his clothes,[x] he went into the house of the LORD and worshiped. Then he went to his own house, and at his request they served him food, and he ate.

21His attendants asked him, "Why are you acting this way? While the child was alive, you fasted and wept,[y] but now that the child is dead, you get up and eat!"

22He answered, "While the child was

a *14* An ancient Hebrew scribal tradition; Masoretic Text *for the enemies of* *b* *16* Dead Sea Scrolls and Septuagint; Masoretic Text does not have *in sackcloth*.

12:5 [d] 1Ki 20:40 **12:6** [e] Ex 22:1; Lk 19:8 **12:7** [f] 1Sa 16:13 [g] 1Ki 20:42 **12:8** [h] 2Sa 9:7 **12:9** [i] Nu 15:31; 1Sa 15:19 [j] 2Sa 11:15 **12:10** [k] 2Sa 13:28; 18:14-15; 1Ki 2:25 **12:11** [l] Dt 28:30; 2Sa 16:21-22 **12:12** [m] 2Sa 11:4-15 [n] 2Sa 16:22 **12:13** [o] Ge 13:13; Nu 22:34; 1Sa 15:24; 2Sa 24:10 [p] Ps 32:1-5; 51:1,9; 103:12; Zec 3:4,9 [q] Pr 28:13; Mic 7:18-19 [r] Lev 20:10; 24:17 **12:14** [s] Isa 52:5; Ro 2:24 **12:15** [t] 1Sa 25:38 **12:16** [u] 2Sa 13:31; Ps 5:7 **12:17** [v] 2Sa 3:35 **12:20** [w] Mt 6:17 [x] Job 1:20 **12:21** [y] Jdg 20:26

that he had and took the one precious lamb of the poor man (a lamb that was like a "daughter" to him (v. 3); the Hebrew word *bat* ["daughter"] is the first syllable of the name Bathsheba); second, he followed his first offense with an act of audacious hypocrisy (i.e., his apparent show of hospitality in v. 4). Fundamentally, the rich man's crime involved an abuse of power, just as did David's.

12:6 *pay for that lamb four times over.* While David's emotional response was that the offender should die (v. 5), he restrained himself to remain within the law. Fourfold restitution for sheep theft is mandated in Ex 22:1. The Code of Hammurapi required thirtyfold restitution for theft of livestock from the temple or the state and tenfold restitution for theft from a private citizen; should the offender be unable to make restitution, he was to die.

12:8 *I gave … your master's wives into your arms.* In the ancient Near East, the royal harem of the former monarch would become the responsibility of the new king, if only in order to honor diplomatic relationships often established through royal marriages. After all, the harem was not considered family, but state property supporting state alliances.

12:11 *he will sleep with your wives in broad daylight.* See note on 16:21.

12:16 *He fasted and spent the nights lying in sackcloth on the ground.* David is engaged in mourning rituals even though the child has not yet died (though David may well consider him virtually dead due to either the prophecy or the child's tenuous condition or both). Mourning rituals are generally designed to associate the mourner with the dead. David hopes that Yahweh may yet show compassion and spare the child, but there is nothing in his behavior that suggests he is trying to appease God or leverage the situation. When the Ninevites used similar ritual tactics, they were demonstrating their repentance in the only ways they knew (cf. Jnh 3). There is no evidence in this description that David's actions are penitential in nature, though Ps 51 shows that David was indeed repentant.

still alive, I fasted and wept. I thought,
'Who knows?[z] The LORD may be gracious
to me and let the child live.'[a] 23But now
that he is dead, why should I go on fasting? Can I bring him back again? I will go
to him,[b] but he will not return to me."[c]
24Then David comforted his wife Bathsheba,[d] and he went to her and made love
to her. She gave birth to a son, and they
named him Solomon.[e] The LORD loved
him; 25and because the LORD loved him,
he sent word through Nathan the prophet
to name him Jedidiah.[a][f]
26Meanwhile Joab fought against Rabbah[g] of the Ammonites and captured the
royal citadel. 27Joab then sent messengers
to David, saying, "I have fought against
Rabbah and taken its water supply. 28Now
muster the rest of the troops and besiege
the city and capture it. Otherwise I will take
the city, and it will be named after me."
29So David mustered the entire army
and went to Rabbah, and attacked and
captured it. 30David took the crown[h] from
their king's[b] head, and it was placed on
his own head. It weighed a talent[c] of gold,
and it was set with precious stones. David took a great quantity of plunder from
the city 31and brought out the people who
were there, consigning them to labor with
saws and with iron picks and axes, and
he made them work at brickmaking.[d] David did this to all the Ammonite[i] towns.
Then he and his entire army returned to
Jerusalem.

Amnon and Tamar

13 In the course of time, Amnon[j] son of
David fell in love with Tamar,[k] the
beautiful sister of Absalom[l] son of David.
2Amnon became so obsessed with his
sister Tamar that he made himself ill. She
was a virgin, and it seemed impossible for
him to do anything to her.
3Now Amnon had an adviser named
Jonadab son of Shimeah,[m] David's brother. Jonadab was a very shrewd man. 4He
asked Amnon, "Why do you, the king's
son, look so haggard morning after morning? Won't you tell me?"
Amnon said to him, "I'm in love with
Tamar, my brother Absalom's sister."
5"Go to bed and pretend to be ill," Jonadab said. "When your father comes to see
you, say to him, 'I would like my sister
Tamar to come and give me something to
eat. Let her prepare the food in my sight
so I may watch her and then eat it from
her hand.'"
6So Amnon lay down and pretended to
be ill. When the king came to see him, Amnon said to him, "I would like my sister Tamar to come and make some special bread
in my sight, so I may eat from her hand."
7David sent word to Tamar at the palace: "Go to the house of your brother Amnon and prepare some food for him." 8So
Tamar went to the house of her brother
Amnon, who was lying down. She took
some dough, kneaded it, made the bread
in his sight and baked it. 9Then she took
the pan and served him the bread, but he
refused to eat.
"Send everyone out of here,"[n] Amnon
said. So everyone left him. 10Then Amnon said to Tamar, "Bring the food here

12:22 [z] Jnh 3:9 [a] Isa 38:1-5
12:23 [b] Ge 37:35 [c] 1Sa 31:13; 2Sa 13:39; Job 7:10; 10:21
12:24 [d] 1Ki 1:11 [e] 1Ki 1:10; 1Ch 22:9; 28:5; Mt 1:6
12:25 [f] Ne 13:26
12:26 [g] Dt 3:11; 1Ch 20:1-3
12:30 [h] 1Ch 20:2; Est 8:15; Ps 21:3; 132:18
12:31 [i] 1Sa 14:47
13:1 [j] 2Sa 3:2 [k] 2Sa 14:27; 1Ch 3:9 [l] 2Sa 3:3
13:3 [m] 1Sa 16:9
13:9 [n] Ge 45:1

[a] *25 Jedidiah* means *loved by the LORD.* [b] *30* Or *from Milkom's* (that is, Molek's) [c] *30* That is, about 75 pounds or about 34 kilograms [d] *31* The meaning of the Hebrew for this clause is uncertain.

12:24–25 *named him Solomon ... Jedidiah.* In the ancient Near East, naming meant more than assigning a label for purposes of identification. Rather, a name was to capture something of the essence of an individual. Thus, names were not usually decided in advance of birth, but were usually triggered by something that happened or was said in connection with the birth (cf. the naming of Samuel [1Sa 1:20] and of Ichabod [1Sa 4:21]). The name Solomon sounds something like the Hebrew word for "peace" (1Ch 22:9) and also like the Hebrew word "replacement" (i.e., for the first child of Bathsheba, which died). The name Jedidiah sounds like "beloved of Yah(weh)" and must have signaled hope for the future of the Davidic house, a hope in keeping with the remarkable promises made in 7:14–15.

12:26–27 *royal citadel ... water supply.* Joab's notice that both the royal citadel and the water supply have been taken is sufficient to indicate that Rabbah cannot withstand Israelite pressure much longer. In the ancient Near East, particularly in the semiarid regions east and west of the Jordan, cities could not hold out under siege once their water supply was cut off. Conversely, elaborate water works were often constructed to secure access to springs and other water supplies.

12:28 Ancient Near Eastern kings did not always accompany their armies on campaigns and did not often lead from the front when they did, but it would still be customary for the king to lead the march into the conquered city. The king's absence from this final phase might indicate to his subjects or detractors that he is unworthy of his position. David himself has experienced how his own victories drew loyalty away from Saul and ultimately led to his ascension. Joab is reminding David what will happen if David does not return to the field and another is given credit as the conqueror.

12:30 *the crown.* This crown was quite different from Saul's lightweight crown, or diadem, that was handed over to David in 1:10. Not only is this crown described with a different Hebrew word, but its weight of almost 75 pounds (34 kilograms) would have made it difficult to wear for any length of time, much less to wear into battle. *from their king's.* The NIV retains the traditional reading, but it is far more likely (as per the NIV text note) that the crown sat atop a statue representing the Ammonites' god Milkom. Ammonite statues showing individuals (gods or kings) wearing large crowns have survived to the present day.

into my bedroom so I may eat from your
hand." And Tamar took the bread she had
prepared and brought it to her brother
Amnon in his bedroom. 11But when she
took it to him to eat, he grabbed[o] her and
said, "Come to bed with me, my sister."[p]
12"No, my brother!" she said to him.
"Don't force me! Such a thing should not
be done in Israel![q] Don't do this wicked
thing.[r] 13What about me?[s] Where could I
get rid of my disgrace? And what about
you? You would be like one of the wicked
fools in Israel. Please speak to the king;
he will not keep me from being married to
you." 14But he refused to listen to her, and
since he was stronger than she, he raped
her.[t]
15Then Amnon hated her with intense
hatred. In fact, he hated her more than he
had loved her. Amnon said to her, "Get up
and get out!"
16"No!" she said to him. "Sending me
away would be a greater wrong than what
you have already done to me."
But he refused to listen to her. 17He
called his personal servant and said, "Get
this woman out of my sight and bolt the
door after her." 18So his servant put her
out and bolted the door after her. She was
wearing an ornate[a] robe,[u] for this was the
kind of garment the virgin daughters of the
king wore. 19Tamar put ashes[v] on her head
and tore the ornate robe she was wearing.
She put her hands on her head and went
away, weeping aloud as she went.
20Her brother Absalom said to her, "Has
that Amnon, your brother, been with you?
Be quiet for now, my sister; he is your
brother. Don't take this thing to heart."
And Tamar lived in her brother Absalom's
house, a desolate woman.
21When King David heard all this, he
was furious.[w] 22And Absalom never said
a word to Amnon, either good or bad;[x] he
hated[y] Amnon because he had disgraced
his sister Tamar.

Absalom Kills Amnon

23Two years later, when Absalom's
sheepshearers[z] were at Baal Hazor near
the border of Ephraim, he invited all the
king's sons to come there. 24Absalom went
to the king and said, "Your servant has
had shearers come. Will the king and his
attendants please join me?"
25"No, my son," the king replied. "All
of us should not go; we would only be a
burden to you." Although Absalom urged
him, he still refused to go but gave him
his blessing.
26Then Absalom said, "If not, please let
my brother Amnon come with us."
The king asked him, "Why should he go
with you?" 27But Absalom urged him, so
he sent with him Amnon and the rest of
the king's sons.
28Absalom[a] ordered his men, "Listen!
When Amnon is in high[b] spirits from
drinking wine and I say to you, 'Strike
Amnon down,' then kill him. Don't be
afraid. Haven't I given you this order? Be
strong and brave.[c]" 29So Absalom's men
did to Amnon what Absalom had ordered.
Then all the king's sons got up, mounted
their mules and fled.
30While they were on their way, the report came to David: "Absalom has struck
down all the king's sons; not one of
them is left." 31The king stood up, tore[d]
his clothes and lay down on the ground;
and all his attendants stood by with their
clothes torn.
32But Jonadab son of Shimeah, David's
brother, said, "My lord should not think
that they killed all the princes; only Amnon is dead. This has been Absalom's express intention ever since the day Amnon
raped his sister Tamar. 33My lord the king
should not be concerned about the report
that all the king's sons are dead. Only Amnon is dead."
34Meanwhile, Absalom had fled.
Now the man standing watch looked up
and saw many people on the road west of
him, coming down the side of the hill. The
watchman went and told the king, "I see
men in the direction of Horonaim, on the
side of the hill."[b]
35Jonadab said to the king, "See, the
king's sons have come; it has happened
just as your servant said."

13:11 [o] Ge 39:12 [p] Ge 38:16 **13:12** [q] Lev 20:17; Jdg 20:6 [r] Ge 34:7; Jdg 19:23 **13:13** [s] Ge 20:12; Lev 18:9; Dt 22:21, 23-24 **13:14** [t] Ge 34:2; Dt 22:25; Eze 22:11 **13:18** [u] Ge 37:23; Jdg 5:30 **13:19** [v] Jos 7:6; 1Sa 4:12; 2Sa 1:2; Est 4:1; Da 9:3 **13:21** [w] Ge 34:7 **13:22** [x] Ge 31:24 [y] Lev 19:17-18; 1Jn 2:9-11 **13:23** [z] 1Sa 25:7 **13:28** [a] 2Sa 3:3 [b] Jdg 19:6, 9, 22; Ru 3:7; 1Sa 25:36 [c] 2Sa 12:10 **13:31** [d] Nu 14:6; 2Sa 1:11; 12:16

[a] *18* The meaning of the Hebrew for this word is uncertain; also in verse 19. [b] *34* Septuagint; Hebrew does not have this sentence.

13:12 *Don't force me!* Incestuous relationships are clearly prohibited in Lev 18; 21, and were also considered taboo in many ancient Near Eastern cultures.

13:19 *put ashes on her head.* Putting dust or ashes on the head was a gesture of mourning and distress throughout the ancient Near East (see note on 1Sa 4:12). *tore the ornate robe she was wearing.* Tamar's ornate robe marked her as a virgin daughter of the king (v. 18). Her tearing of the robe not only demonstrated her anguish, it also dramatically underscored her changed status.

13:23 *Absalom's sheepshearers were at Baal Hazor.* Shearing time would have been an occasion of celebration, abundance and generosity (see note on 1Sa 25:4). Thus, an invitation to join the shearing party would normally have been most welcome. The 14-mile (22-kilometer) distance between Jerusalem and Absalom's sheepshearers was short enough to make an invitation to David and his sons plausible, but long enough to mask Absalom's true intent.

36As he finished speaking, the king's
sons came in, wailing loudly. The king, too,
and all his attendants wept very bitterly.
37Absalom fled and went to Talmai[e] son
of Ammihud, the king of Geshur. But King
David mourned many days for his son.
38After Absalom fled and went to Geshur, he stayed there three years. 39And
King David longed to go to Absalom,[f] for
he was consoled[g] concerning Amnon's
death.

Absalom Returns to Jerusalem

14 Joab[h] son of Zeruiah knew that the
king's heart longed for Absalom.
2So Joab sent someone to Tekoa[i] and had
a wise woman[j] brought from there. He
said to her, "Pretend you are in mourning. Dress in mourning clothes, and don't
use any cosmetic lotions.[k] Act like a woman who has spent many days grieving for
the dead. 3Then go to the king and speak
these words to him." And Joab[l] put the
words in her mouth.
4When the woman from Tekoa went[a]
to the king, she fell with her face to the
ground to pay him honor, and she said,
"Help me, Your Majesty!"
5The king asked her, "What is troubling
you?"
She said, "I am a widow; my husband is
dead. 6I your servant had two sons. They
got into a fight with each other in the field,
and no one was there to separate them.
One struck the other and killed him. 7Now
the whole clan has risen up against your
servant; they say, 'Hand over the one who
struck his brother down, so that we may
put him to death[m] for the life of his brother whom he killed; then we will get rid of
the heir[n] as well.' They would put out the
only burning coal I have left,[o] leaving my
husband neither name nor descendant on
the face of the earth."
8The king said to the woman, "Go
home,[p] and I will issue an order in your
behalf."
9But the woman from Tekoa said to him,
"Let my lord the king pardon[q] me and my
family,[r] and let the king and his throne be
without guilt.[s]"
10The king replied, "If anyone says anything to you, bring them to me, and they
will not bother you again."
11She said, "Then let the king invoke the
LORD his God to prevent the avenger[t] of
blood from adding to the destruction, so
that my son will not be destroyed."
"As surely as the LORD lives," he said,
"not one hair[u] of your son's head will fall
to the ground.[v]"
12Then the woman said, "Let your servant speak a word to my lord the king."
"Speak," he replied.
13The woman said, "Why then have you
devised a thing like this against the people of God? When the king says this, does
he not convict himself,[w] for the king has
not brought back his banished son?[x] 14Like
water[y] spilled on the ground, which cannot be recovered, so we must die.[z] But that
is not what God desires; rather, he devises
ways so that a banished person[a] does not
remain banished from him.

[a] 4 Many Hebrew manuscripts, Septuagint, Vulgate and Syriac; most Hebrew manuscripts *spoke*

13:37 [e] ver 34; 2Sa 3:3; 14:23, 32
13:39 [f] 2Sa 14:13 [g] 2Sa 12:19-23
14:1 [h] 2Sa 2:18
14:2 [i] 2Ch 11:6; Ne 3:5; Jer 6:1; Am 1:1 [j] 2Sa 20:16 [k] Ru 3:3; 2Sa 12:20; Isa 1:6
14:3 [l] ver 19
14:7 [m] Nu 35:19 [n] Mt 21:38 [o] Dt 19:10-13
14:8 [p] 1Sa 25:35
14:9 [q] 1Sa 25:24 [r] Mt 27:25 [s] 1Sa 25:28; 1Ki 2:33
14:11 [t] Nu 35:12, 21 [u] Mt 10:30 [v] 1Sa 14:45
14:13 [w] 2Sa 12:7; 1Ki 20:40 [x] 2Sa 13:38-39
14:14 [y] Job 14:11; Ps 58:7; Isa 19:5 [z] Job 10:8; 17:13; 30:23; Ps 22:15; Heb 9:27 [a] Nu 35:15, 25-28; Job 34:15

13:37 *Talmai son of Ammihud, the king of Geshur.* Talmai was, according to 3:3, Absalom's maternal grandfather. The Geshur in view here lay in Transjordan, in the southern part of the Golan Heights. Absalom's flight took him more than 50 miles (80 kilometers) farther north and across the Jordan River, where he remained in exile for three years.

14:2 *wise woman.* While the designation has not yet been discovered outside the Bible, women in the ancient Near East did sometimes fulfill priestly, prophetic, or other religious or civic functions. The OT also cites women as fulfilling prophetic (though not priestly) and other roles. In the books of Samuel, "wise woman" is specifically used of two women — the one here and another at 20:16, where a "wise woman" intervenes decisively to save the city of Abel Beth Maakah. Abigail should probably be included as well, though she is not explicitly called a wise woman (in 1Sa 25:3,33 she is said to be "intelligent" and to have "good judgment"). The wisdom in view seems to connote skill in speech capable of persuading someone to follow a certain course of action (cf. the "wisdom" of Jonadab in 13:3, where the NIV translates the same Hebrew word for "wise" as "shrewd"). That such wisdom was highly prized in the ancient Near East is illustrated, e.g., in the so-called Protests of the Eloquent Peasant, in which the wronged peasant is retained at court simply to regale the courtiers with his eloquent and persuasive speeches.

14:3 *Joab put the words in her mouth.* By prompting the wise woman of Tekoa to raise issues of blood revenge (v. 11) and the survival of her family line on its ancestral property, Joab covertly forces David to render a verdict on the very issues he is facing, namely, his duty to avenge the blood of Amnon and his desire that Absalom not be cut off. The dynamic of the present episode recalls an earlier occasion in which David was drawn by a fictional story into indicting himself (12:1 – 10). An analogue to the present scenario of disguise, deception and self-indictment is found in the Egyptian myth of Horus and Seth, in which Isis, the mother of Horus, disguises herself as a maiden and tricks Seth into pronouncing a verdict against himself and in favor of Horus.

14:7 *get rid of the heir … put out the only burning coal I have left.* The paralleling of "heir" and "burning coal" is in keeping with the virtually universal use of the hearth-fire to symbolize family life. Not only in the Bible does light/lamp symbolize life and hope (e.g., 21:17; Job 18:5 – 6) but in the ancient Near East it does as well. Mesopotamian texts speak of family misfortune metaphorically as the oven or hearth-fire being extinguished. In Sumerian, the word used for "heir" may connote "one who keeps the oil (lamp) burning."

15“And now I have come to say this to
my lord the king because the people have
made me afraid. Your servant thought, ‘I
will speak to the king; perhaps he will
grant his servant’s request. 16Perhaps the
king will agree to deliver his servant from
the hand of the man who is trying to cut
off both me and my son from God’s inheritance.’[b]
17“And now your servant says, ‘May the
word of my lord the king secure my inheritance, for my lord the king is like an angel[c]
of God in discerning[d] good and evil. May
the LORD your God be with you.’ ”
18Then the king said to the woman,
“Don’t keep from me the answer to what I
am going to ask you.”
“Let my lord the king speak,” the woman said.
19The king asked, “Isn’t the hand of
Joab[e] with you in all this?”
The woman answered, “As surely as
you live, my lord the king, no one can turn
to the right or to the left from anything my
lord the king says. Yes, it was your servant
Joab who instructed me to do this and
who put all these words into the mouth
of your servant. 20Your servant Joab did
this to change the present situation. My
lord has wisdom[f] like that of an angel of
God—he knows everything that happens
in the land.[g]”
21The king said to Joab, “Very well, I
will do it. Go, bring back the young man
Absalom.”
22Joab fell with his face to the ground to
pay him honor, and he blessed the king.[h]
Joab said, “Today your servant knows that
he has found favor in your eyes, my lord
the king, because the king has granted his
servant’s request.”
23Then Joab went to Geshur and brought
Absalom back to Jerusalem. 24But the king
said, “He must go to his own house; he
must not see my face.” So Absalom went
to his own house and did not see the face
of the king.
25In all Israel there was not a man so
highly praised for his handsome appearance as Absalom. From the top of his head
to the sole of his foot there was no blemish
in him. 26Whenever he cut the hair of his
head[i]—he used to cut his hair once a year
because it became too heavy for him—he
would weigh it, and its weight was two
hundred shekels[a] by the royal standard.
27Three sons[j] and a daughter were born
to Absalom. His daughter’s name was Tamar,[k] and she became a beautiful woman.

28Absalom lived two years in Jerusalem
without seeing the king’s face. 29Then Absalom sent for Joab in order to send him to
the king, but Joab refused to come to him.
So he sent a second time, but he refused
to come. 30Then he said to his servants,
“Look, Joab’s field is next to mine, and he
has barley[l] there. Go and set it on fire.” So
Absalom’s servants set the field on fire.
31Then Joab did go to Absalom’s house,
and he said to him, “Why have your servants set my field on fire?[m]”
32Absalom said to Joab, “Look, I sent
word to you and said, ‘Come here so I can
send you to the king to ask, “Why have I
come from Geshur?[n] It would be better for
me if I were still there!” ’ Now then, I want
to see the king’s face, and if I am guilty of
anything, let him put me to death.”[o]
33So Joab went to the king and told him
this. Then the king summoned Absalom,
and he came in and bowed down with his
face to the ground before the king. And
the king kissed[p] Absalom.

Absalom’s Conspiracy

15 In the course of time,[q] Absalom
provided himself with a chari-
ot[r] and horses and with fifty men to run
ahead of him. 2He would get up early and
stand by the side of the road leading to
the city gate.[s] Whenever anyone came
with a complaint to be placed before the
king for a decision, Absalom would call
out to him, “What town are you from?”
He would answer, “Your servant is from
one of the tribes of Israel.” 3Then Absalom
would say to him, “Look, your claims are
valid and proper, but there is no representative of the king to hear you.”[t] 4And Absalom would add, “If only I were appointed judge in the land![u] Then everyone who
has a complaint or case could come to me
and I would see that they receive justice.”
5Also, whenever anyone approached
him to bow down before him, Absalom
would reach out his hand, take hold of
him and kiss him. 6Absalom behaved
in this way toward all the Israelites who
came to the king asking for justice, and so
he stole the hearts[v] of the people of Israel.
7At the end of four[b] years, Absalom said
to the king, “Let me go to Hebron and fulfill a vow I made to the LORD. 8While your
servant was living at Geshur[w] in Aram, I
made this vow:[x] ‘If the LORD takes me back

14:16 [b] Ex 34:9; 1Sa 26:19 **14:17** [c] ver 20; 1Sa 29:9; 2Sa 19:27 [d] 1Ki 3:9; Da 2:21 **14:19** [e] ver 3 **14:20** [f] 1Ki 3:12, 28; Isa 28:6 [g] ver 17; 2Sa 18:13; 19:27 **14:22** [h] Ge 47:7 **14:26** [i] 2Sa 18:9; Eze 44:20 **14:27** [j] 2Sa 18:18 [k] 2Sa 13:1 **14:30** [l] Ex 9:31 **14:31** [m] Jdg 15:5 **14:32** [n] 2Sa 3:3 [o] 1Sa 20:8 **14:33** [p] Ge 33:4; Lk 15:20 **15:1** [q] 2Sa 12:11 [r] 1Sa 8:11; 1Ki 1:5 **15:2** [s] Ge 23:10; 2Sa 19:8 **15:3** [t] Pr 12:2 **15:4** [u] Jdg 9:29 **15:6** [v] Ro 16:18 **15:8** [w] 2Sa 3:3; 13:37-38 [x] Ge 28:20

[a] 26 That is, about 5 pounds or about 2.3 kilograms
[b] 7 Some Septuagint manuscripts, Syriac and Josephus; Hebrew *forty*

15:4 *If only I were appointed judge.* Absalom did not directly challenge his father’s right to be king, but by questioning the administration of justice under David he effectively planted the seeds of discontent. First and foremost among the responsibilities of the ancient Near Eastern king was the administration of justice.

offered sacrifices until all the people had
finished leaving the city.
[25]Then the king said to Zadok, "Take the
ark of God back into the city. If I find favor
in the LORD's eyes, he will bring me back
and let me see it and his dwelling place[q]
again. [26]But if he says, 'I am not pleased
with you,' then I am ready; let him do to
me whatever seems good to him.[r]"
[27]The king also said to Zadok the priest,
"Do you understand?[s] Go back to the city
with my blessing. Take your son Ahimaaz
with you, and also Abiathar's son Jonathan.[t] You and Abiathar return with your
two sons. [28]I will wait at the fords[u] in the
wilderness until word comes from you
to inform me." [29]So Zadok and Abiathar
took the ark of God back to Jerusalem and
stayed there.
[30]But David continued up the Mount of
Olives, weeping[v] as he went; his head[w]
was covered and he was barefoot. All
the people with him covered their heads
too and were weeping as they went up.
[31]Now David had been told, "Ahithophel[x]
is among the conspirators with Absalom."
So David prayed, "LORD, turn Ahithophel's
counsel into foolishness."
[32]When David arrived at the summit,
where people used to worship God, Hushai the Arkite[y] was there to meet him, his
robe torn and dust[z] on his head. [33]David
said to him, "If you go with me, you will
be a burden[a] to me. [34]But if you return to
the city and say to Absalom, 'Your Majesty, I will be your servant; I was your father's servant in the past, but now I will
be your servant,'[b] then you can help me by
frustrating Ahithophel's advice. [35]Won't
the priests Zadok and Abiathar be there
with you? Tell them anything you hear in
the king's palace.[c] [36]Their two sons, Ahimaaz son of Zadok and Jonathan[d] son of
Abiathar, are there with them. Send them
to me with anything you hear."

[37]So Hushai,[e] David's confidant, arrived
at Jerusalem as Absalom[f] was entering the
city.

David and Ziba

16 When David had gone a short distance beyond the summit, there
was Ziba,[g] the steward of Mephibosheth,
waiting to meet him. He had a string of
donkeys saddled and loaded with two
hundred loaves of bread, a hundred cakes
of raisins, a hundred cakes of figs and a
skin of wine.[h]
[2]The king asked Ziba, "Why have you
brought these?"
Ziba answered, "The donkeys are for
the king's household to ride on, the bread
and fruit are for the men to eat, and the
wine is to refresh[i] those who become exhausted in the wilderness."
[3]The king then asked, "Where is your
master's grandson?"[j]
Ziba said to him, "He is staying in Jerusalem, because he thinks, 'Today the Israelites will restore to me my grandfather's
kingdom.'"
[4]Then the king said to Ziba, "All that
belonged to Mephibosheth is now yours."
"I humbly bow," Ziba said. "May I find
favor in your eyes, my lord the king."

Shimei Curses David

[5]As King David approached Bahurim,[k]
a man from the same clan as Saul's family came out from there. His name was
Shimei[l] son of Gera, and he cursed[m] as
he came out. [6]He pelted David and all the
king's officials with stones, though all the
troops and the special guard were on David's right and left. [7]As he cursed, Shimei
said, "Get out, get out, you murderer, you
scoundrel! [8]The LORD has repaid you for
all the blood you shed in the household of
Saul, in whose place you have reigned.[n]
The LORD has given the kingdom into the

15:25 [q]Ex 15:13; Ps 43:3; Jer 25:30
15:26 [r]1Sa 3:18; 2Sa 22:20; 1Ki 10:9
15:27 [s]1Sa 9:9 [t]2Sa 17:17
15:28 [u]2Sa 17:16
15:30 [v]2Sa 19:4; Ps 126:6 [w]Est 6:12; Isa 20:2-4
15:31 [x]ver 12; 2Sa 16:23; 17:14,23
15:32 [y]Jos 16:2 [z]2Sa 1:2
15:33 [a]2Sa 19:35
15:34 [b]2Sa 16:19
15:35 [c]2Sa 17:15-16
15:36 [d]ver 27; 2Sa 17:17
15:37 [e]2Sa 16:16-17; 1Ch 27:33 [f]2Sa 16:15
16:1 [g]2Sa 9:1-13 [h]1Sa 25:18
16:2 [i]2Sa 17:27-29
16:3 [j]2Sa 9:9-10; 19:26-27
16:5 [k]2Sa 3:16 [l]2Sa 19:16-23; 1Ki 2:8-9,36,44 [m]Ex 22:28
16:8 [n]2Sa 21:9

15:25 *Take the ark of God back into the city.* Although the ark is a powerful talisman, David recognizes that if he is out of favor with Yahweh, it will do him no good to bring it along. Sending the ark back to Jerusalem also provides cover for his spies Zadok and Abiathar.

15:28 *I will wait at the fords in the wilderness.* As 17:16 indicates, the fords in question would have been at the Jordan River, almost 20 miles (32 kilometers) east of Jerusalem. David and his followers would undoubtedly be exhausted after covering that distance, and overnighting on the west side of the Jordan would serve the symbolic purpose of not abandoning the land entirely.

15:30 *his head was covered and he was barefoot.* Both were signs of sorrow and distress (cf. Est 6:12; Isa 20:2 – 4; Jer 14:3 – 4; Mic 1:8).

15:32 *the summit, where people used to worship God.* The identity and location of this place of worship has not been determined. One suggestion is the priestly town of Nob, which lay within a couple of miles/kilometers of Jerusalem and whose priests were massacred by Saul (see 1Sa 22:19 and note), thus perhaps the present notice that "people used to worship" there.

16:5 *As King David approached Bahurim ... Shimei son of Gera ... cursed.* Shimei, as a kinsman of Saul, may have held David responsible for the deaths of Abner and Ish-Bosheth, and he may have resented David's permitting the execution of seven of Saul's descendants by the Gibeonites (see 21:1 – 14). Furthermore, as a resident of Bahurim, Shimei may have witnessed David's treatment of Michal, Saul's daughter, as it had been at Bahurim that Paltiel, Michal's second husband, was ordered to cease following after his wife as she was being forcibly returned to David (3:16). The underlying grievance, of course, was that the kingdom once held by Saul, the Benjamite, had been forfeited to David.

to Jerusalem, I will worship
the LORD in Hebron.[a]' "
9The king said to him, "Go
in peace." So he went to Hebron.
10Then Absalom sent secret messengers throughout the tribes of Israel to say, "As soon as you hear the sound of the trumpets,[y] then say, 'Absalom is king in Hebron.' "
11Two hundred men from Jerusalem had accompanied Absalom. They had been invited as guests and went quite innocently, knowing nothing about the matter.
12While Absalom was offering sacrifices, he also sent for Ahithophel[z] the Gilonite, David's counselor,[a] to come from Giloh,[b] his hometown. And so the conspiracy gained strength, and Absalom's following kept on increasing.[c]

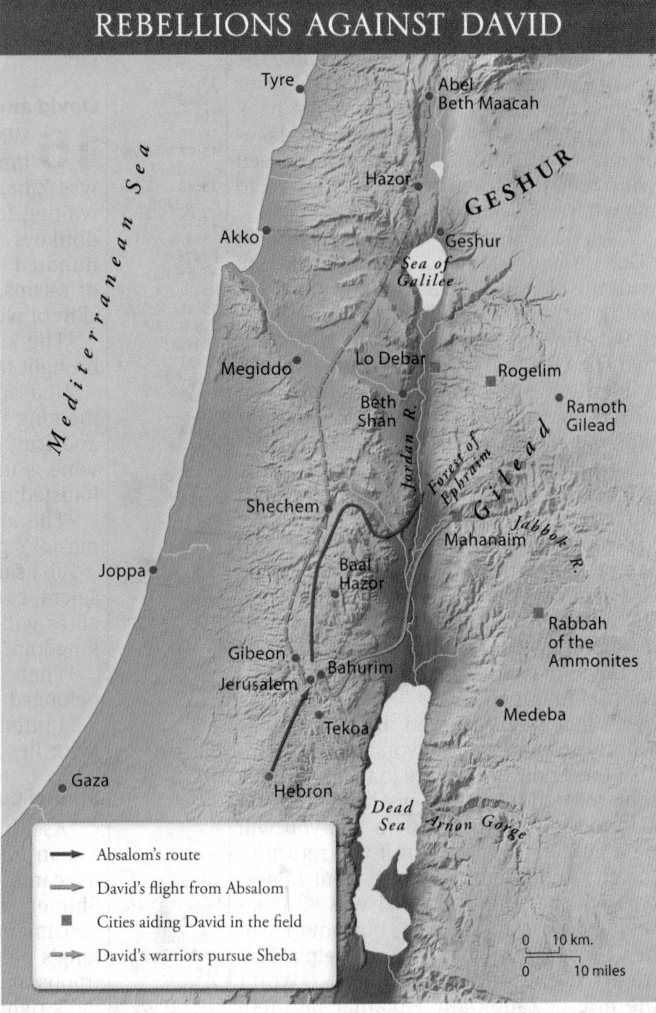

David Flees

13A messenger came and told David, "The hearts of the people of Israel are with Absalom."
14Then David said to all his officials who were with him in Jerusalem, "Come! We must flee,[d] or none of us will escape from Absalom.[e] We must leave immediately, or he will move quickly to overtake us and bring ruin on us and put the city to the sword."
15The king's officials answered him, "Your servants are ready to do whatever our lord the king chooses."
16The king set out, with his entire household following him; but he left ten concubines[f] to take care of the palace.
17So the king set out, with all the people following him, and they halted at the edge of the city.
18All his men marched past him, along with all the Kerethites[g] and Pelethites; and all the six hundred Gittites who had accompanied him from Gath marched before the king.
19The king said to Ittai[h] the Gittite, "Why should you come along with us? Go back and stay with King Absalom. You are a foreigner,[i] an exile from your homeland.
20You came only yesterday. And today shall I make you wander[j] about with us, when I do not know where I am going? Go back, and take your people with you. May the LORD show you kindness and faithfulness."[b][k]
21But Ittai replied to the king, "As surely
as the LORD lives, and as my lord the king lives, wherever my lord the king may be, whether it means life or death, there will your servant be."[l]
22David said to Ittai, "Go ahead, march on." So Ittai the Gittite marched on with all his men and the families that were with him.
23The whole countryside wept aloud as all the people passed by. The king also crossed the Kidron Valley,[m] and all the people moved on toward the wilderness.
24Zadok[n] was there, too, and all the Levites who were with him were carrying the ark[o] of the covenant of God. They set down the ark of God, and Abiathar[p]

15:10 [y] 1Ki 1:34, 39; 2Ki 9:13 **15:12** [z] ver 31, 34; 2Sa 16:15, 23; 1Ch 27:33 [a] Job 19:14; Ps 41:9; 55:13; Jer 9:4 [b] Jos 15:51 [c] Ps 3:1 **15:14** [d] 2Sa 12:11; 1Ki 2:26; Ps 3 Title; 132:1 [e] 2Sa 19:9 **15:16** [f] 2Sa 16:21-22; 20:3 **15:18** [g] 1Sa 30:14; 2Sa 8:18; 20:7, 23; 1Ki 1:38, 44; 1Ch 18:17 **15:19** [h] 2Sa 18:2 [i] Ge 31:15 **15:20** [j] 1Sa 23:13 [k] 2Sa 2:6

[a] *8* Some Septuagint manuscripts; Hebrew does not have *in Hebron.* [b] *20* Septuagint; Hebrew *May kindness and faithfulness be with you*

15:21 [l] Ru 1:16-17; Pr 17:17 **15:23** [m] 2Ch 29:16 **15:24** [n] 2Sa 8:17 [o] Nu 4:15 [p] 1Sa 22:20

hands of your son Absalom. You have
come to ruin because you are a murderer!"
9Then Abishai[o] son of Zeruiah said to
the king, "Why should this dead dog curse
my lord the king? Let me go over and cut
off his head."[p]
10But the king said, "What does this
have to do with you, you sons of Zeruiah?[q] If he is cursing because the LORD said
to him, 'Curse David,' who can ask, 'Why
do you do this?' "[r]
11David then said to Abishai and all
his officials, "My son,[s] my own flesh and
blood, is trying to kill me. How much
more, then, this Benjamite! Leave him
alone; let him curse, for the LORD has told
him to.[t] 12It may be that the LORD will look
upon my misery[u] and restore to me his
covenant blessing[v] instead of his curse today.[w]"
13So David and his men continued along
the road while Shimei was going along the
hillside opposite him, cursing as he went
and throwing stones at him and shower-
ing him with dirt. 14The king and all the
people with him arrived at their destination exhausted.[x] And there he refreshed
himself.

The Advice of Ahithophel and Hushai

15Meanwhile, Absalom[y] and all the men
of Israel came to Jerusalem, and Ahithophel[z] was with him. 16Then Hushai[a] the
Arkite, David's confidant, went to Absalom and said to him, "Long live the king!
Long live the king!"
17Absalom said to Hushai, "So this is
the love you show your friend? If he's your
friend, why didn't you go with him?"[b]
18Hushai said to Absalom, "No, the one
chosen by the LORD, by these people, and
by all the men of Israel—his I will be, and
I will remain with him. 19Furthermore,
whom should I serve? Should I not serve
the son? Just as I served your father, so I
will serve you."[c]
20Absalom said to Ahithophel, "Give us
your advice. What should we do?"
21Ahithophel answered, "Sleep with
your father's concubines whom he left
to take care of the palace. Then all Israel will hear that you have made yourself
obnoxious to your father, and the hands
of everyone with you will be more resolute." 22So they pitched a tent for Absalom
on the roof, and he slept with his father's
concubines in the sight of all Israel.[d]
23Now in those days the advice[e] Ahithophel gave was like that of one who inquires of God. That was how both David[f]
and Absalom regarded all of Ahithophel's
advice.

17 Ahithophel said to Absalom, "I
would[a] choose twelve thousand
men and set out tonight in pursuit of David. 2I would attack him while he is weary
and weak.[g] I would strike him with terror,
and then all the people with him will flee.
I would strike down only the king[h] 3and
bring all the people back to you. The death
of the man you seek will mean the return
of all; all the people will be unharmed."
4This plan seemed good to Absalom and
to all the elders of Israel.
5But Absalom said, "Summon also Hushai[i] the Arkite, so we can hear what he
has to say as well." 6When Hushai came
to him, Absalom said, "Ahithophel has
given this advice. Should we do what he
says? If not, give us your opinion."
7Hushai replied to Absalom, "The advice Ahithophel has given is not good this
time. 8You know your father and his men;
they are fighters, and as fierce as a wild
bear robbed of her cubs.[j] Besides, your
father is an experienced fighter;[k] he will
not spend the night with the troops. 9Even
now, he is hidden in a cave or some other place.[l] If he should attack your troops
first,[b] whoever hears about it will say,
'There has been a slaughter among the
troops who follow Absalom.' 10Then even
the bravest soldier, whose heart is like the
heart of a lion,[m] will melt[n] with fear, for
all Israel knows that your father is a fighter and that those with him are brave.[o]

16:9 [o] 2Sa 9:8 [p] Ex 22:28; Lk 9:54
16:10 [q] 2Sa 19:22 [r] Ro 9:20
16:11 [s] 2Sa 12:11 [t] Ge 45:5
16:12 [u] Ps 4:1; 25:18 [v] Dt 23:5; Ro 8:28 [w] Ps 109:28
16:14 [x] 2Sa 17:2
16:15 [y] 2Sa 15:37 [z] 2Sa 15:12
16:16 [a] 2Sa 15:37
16:17 [b] 2Sa 19:25
16:19 [c] 2Sa 15:34
16:22 [d] 2Sa 12:11-12; 15:16
16:23 [e] 2Sa 17:14,23 [f] 2Sa 15:12
17:2 [g] 2Sa 16:14 [h] 1Ki 22:31; Zec 13:7
17:5 [i] 2Sa 15:32
17:8 [j] Hos 13:8 [k] 1Sa 16:18
17:9 [l] Jer 41:9
17:10 [m] 1Ch 12:8 [n] Jos 2:9,11; Eze 21:15 [o] 2Sa 23:8; 1Ch 11:11

[a] 1 Or *Let me* [b] 9 Or *When some of the men fall at the first attack*

16:16 *Hushai the Arkite, David's confidant.* The Hebrew word rendered "confidant" here is not the normal Hebrew word for "confidant" or "friend," though it looks much like it, and it may actually represent a borrowing from the Egyptian honorific "acquaintance of the king." In other words, "Confidant / Friend of David" may have been an official court title held by Hushai in David's government, a sort of "privy counselor." In this light, Absalom's questions to Hushai in v. 17, twice using the normal Hebrew word for "friend" or "confidant," must be seen as involving an ironic wordplay, something like: "Is this how you show friendship to the one you serve as Friend?"
16:21 *Sleep with your father's concubines.* In the ancient Near East a king's wives and concubines were regarded as indicative of his power and position (see note on 3:7). Their acquisition often involved diplomacy or conquest. For an outsider to sleep with a member of the royal harem, therefore, was a direct affront to the monarch and tantamount to usurpation. The Assyrian king Sennacherib boasts of divesting King Hezekiah of his "daughters, concubines," and much more besides; he did much the same to Marduk-Baladan of Babylon, entering his palace, taking charge of "the property and goods (laid up) therein," including "his wife, his harem," etc. Ahithophel knew whereof he spoke, when he counseled Absalom that lying with his father's concubines would make him "obnoxious" to his father.

11"So I advise you: Let all Israel, from Dan to Beersheba[p]—as numerous as the sand[q] on the seashore—be gathered to you, with you yourself leading them into battle. 12Then we will attack him wherever he may be found, and we will fall on him as dew settles on the ground. Neither he nor any of his men will be left alive. 13If he withdraws into a city, then all Israel will bring ropes to that city, and we will drag it down to the valley[r] until not so much as a pebble is left."

14Absalom and all the men of Israel said, "The advice[s] of Hushai the Arkite is better than that of Ahithophel."[t] For the LORD had determined to frustrate[u] the good advice of Ahithophel in order to bring disaster[v] on Absalom.[w]

15Hushai told Zadok and Abiathar, the priests, "Ahithophel has advised Absalom and the elders of Israel to do such and such, but I have advised them to do so and so. 16Now send a message at once and tell David, 'Do not spend the night at the fords in the wilderness;[x] cross over without fail, or the king and all the people with him will be swallowed up.[y]'"

17Jonathan[z] and Ahimaaz were staying at En Rogel.[a] A female servant was to go and inform them, and they were to go and tell King David, for they could not risk being seen entering the city. 18But a young man saw them and told Absalom. So the two of them left at once and went to the house of a man in Bahurim.[b] He had a well in his courtyard, and they climbed down into it. 19His wife took a covering and spread it out over the opening of the well and scattered grain over it. No one knew anything about it.[c]

20When Absalom's men came to the woman[d] at the house, they asked, "Where are Ahimaaz and Jonathan?"

The woman answered them, "They crossed over the brook."[a] The men searched but found no one, so they returned to Jerusalem.

21After they had gone, the two climbed out of the well and went to inform King David. They said to him, "Set out and cross the river at once; Ahithophel has advised such and such against you." 22So David and all the people with him set out and crossed the Jordan. By daybreak, no one was left who had not crossed the Jordan.

23When Ahithophel saw that his advice[e] had not been followed, he saddled his donkey and set out for his house in his hometown. He put his house in order[f] and then hanged himself. So he died and was buried in his father's tomb.

Absalom's Death

24David went to Mahanaim,[g] and Absalom crossed the Jordan with all the men of Israel. 25Absalom had appointed Amasa[h] over the army in place of Joab. Amasa was the son of Jether,[b][i] an Ishmaelite[c] who had married Abigail,[d] the daughter of Nahash and sister of Zeruiah the mother of Joab. 26The Israelites and Absalom camped in the land of Gilead.

27When David came to Mahanaim, Shobi son of Nahash[j] from Rabbah[k] of the Ammonites, and Makir[l] son of Ammiel from Lo Debar, and Barzillai[m] the Gileadite[n] from Rogelim 28brought bedding and bowls and articles of pottery. They also brought wheat and barley, flour and roasted grain, beans and lentils,[e] 29honey and

17:11 [p]Jdg 20:1 [q]Ge 12:2; 22:17; Jos 11:4 **17:13** [r]Mic 1:6 **17:14** [s]2Sa 16:23 [t]2Sa 15:12 [u]2Sa 15:34; Ne 4:15 [v]Ps 9:16 [w]2Ch 10:8 **17:16** [x]2Sa 15:28 [y]2Sa 15:35 **17:17** [z]2Sa 15:27, 36 [a]Jos 15:7; 18:16 **17:18** [b]2Sa 3:16; 16:5 **17:19** [c]Jos 2:6 **17:20** [d]Ex 1:19; Jos 2:3-5; 1Sa 19:12-17 **17:23** [e]2Sa 15:12; 16:23 [f]2Ki 20:1; Mt 27:5 **17:24** [g]Ge 32:2; 2Sa 2:8 **17:25** [h]2Sa 19:13; 20:4,9-12; 1Ki 2:5,32; 1Ch 12:18 [i]1Ch 2:13-17 **17:27** [j]1Sa 11:1 [k]Dt 3:11; 2Sa 10:1-2; 12:26,29 [l]2Sa 9:4 [m]2Sa 19:31-39; 1Ki 2:7 [n]2Sa 19:31; Ezr 2:61

[a] 20 Or *"They passed by the sheep pen toward the water."* [b] 25 Hebrew *Ithra*, a variant of *Jether* [c] 25 Some Septuagint manuscripts (see also 1 Chron. 2:17); Hebrew and other Septuagint manuscripts *Israelite* [d] 25 Hebrew *Abigal*, a variant of *Abigail* [e] 28 Most Septuagint manuscripts and Syriac; Hebrew *lentils, and roasted grain*

17:13 *all Israel will bring ropes to that city, and we will drag it down to the valley.* See the article "Siege Warfare," p. 1157.
17:18 *went to the house of a man in Bahurim.* Bahurim was the site of Shimei's cursing (see note on 16:5). That Jonathan and Ahimaaz are able to find an ally there indicates that David was not without supporters even in this Saulide village.
17:19 *took a covering and spread it out over the opening of the well.* Because of the semiarid climate of the land of Palestine, wells were both numerous and important. Wells were constructed by digging a vertical shaft down to the water table. The top opening of wells was typically 5 to 6.5 feet (1.5 to 2 meters) in diameter, and the depth varied depending on the water table, some being quite deep—one of several wells discovered at Lachish was about 140 feet (42.5 meters) deep. To prevent collapse, the shafts of wells were often lined with field stones, and to prevent contamination of the water or danger to unwary people or animals, the opening was covered in some way (e.g., with a stone slab). Flat covers could be disguised so as to prevent discovery of the well, as appears to have been done here.
17:23 *He ... hanged himself.* Wise enough to recognize that Absalom's failure to follow his advice would lead to a victory and a return to power for David, Ahithophel must have understood that his life was forfeit because of his treason. In taking his own life, Ahithophel may have felt that he was only hastening the inevitable on his own terms (after having "put his house in order"). The Hebrew Bible does not contain any explicit evaluation of suicide, but of the six reported incidents, Abimelek and Saul are hardly to be read as heroic in their actions (see note on 1Sa 31:4), Saul's armor-bearer is a lesser character who was simply demonstrating loyalty to his deceased master (1Sa 31:4), Samson gave his life not so much as an act of suicide but in order to rain down a crushing defeat on the Philistines (Jdg 16:28–31), and the erstwhile Israelite king Zimri (like Ahithophel) understood that his failed power play left him with little hope of survival in any case (1Ki 16:18). In ancient Mesopotamian thought, suicide was a means of retrieving honor, but in ancient Egypt, it was generally frowned on, although allowed as an option for officials facing capital crimes.

curds, sheep, and cheese from cows' milk
for David and his people to eat.[o] For they
said, "The people have become exhausted and hungry and thirsty in the wilderness.[p]"

18 David mustered the men who were
with him and appointed over them
commanders of thousands and commanders of hundreds. 2David sent out his
troops,[q] a third under the command of
Joab, a third under Joab's brother Abishai[r]
son of Zeruiah, and a third under Ittai[s] the
Gittite. The king told the troops, "I myself
will surely march out with you."

3But the men said, "You must not go
out; if we are forced to flee, they won't
care about us. Even if half of us die, they
won't care; but you are worth ten[t] thousand of us.[a] It would be better now for you
to give us support from the city."[u]

4The king answered, "I will do whatever
seems best to you."

So the king stood beside the gate while
all his men marched out in units of hundreds and of thousands. 5The king commanded Joab, Abishai and Ittai, "Be gentle with the young man Absalom for my
sake." And all the troops heard the king
giving orders concerning Absalom to each
of the commanders.

6David's army marched out of the city
to fight Israel, and the battle took place
in the forest[v] of Ephraim. 7There Israel's
troops were routed by David's men, and
the casualties that day were great — twenty thousand men. 8The battle spread out
over the whole countryside, and the forest
swallowed up more men that day than the
sword.

9Now Absalom happened to meet David's men. He was riding his mule, and as
the mule went under the thick branches
of a large oak, Absalom's hair[w] got caught
in the tree. He was left hanging in midair, while the mule he was riding kept on
going.

10When one of the men saw what had
happened, he told Joab, "I just saw Absalom hanging in an oak tree."

11Joab said to the man who had told him
this, "What! You saw him? Why didn't you
strike[x] him to the ground right there? Then
I would have had to give you ten shekels[b]
of silver and a warrior's belt.[y]"

12But the man replied, "Even if a thousand shekels[c] were weighed out into my
hands, I would not lay a hand on the king's
son. In our hearing the king commanded
you and Abishai and Ittai, 'Protect the
young man Absalom for my sake.[d]' 13And
if I had put my life in jeopardy[e] — and
nothing is hidden from the king[z] — you
would have kept your distance from me."

14Joab[a] said, "I'm not going to wait like
this for you." So he took three javelins in
his hand and plunged them into Absalom's heart while Absalom was still alive
in the oak tree. 15And ten of Joab's armor-
bearers surrounded Absalom, struck him
and killed him.[b]

16Then Joab[c] sounded the trumpet, and
the troops stopped pursuing Israel, for
Joab halted them. 17They took Absalom,
threw him into a big pit in the forest and
piled up[d] a large heap of rocks[e] over him.
Meanwhile, all the Israelites fled to their
homes.

18During his lifetime Absalom had taken

17:29 [o] 1Ch 12:40 [p] 2Sa 16:2; Ro 12:13 **18:2** [q] Jdg 7:16; 1Sa 11:11 [r] 1Sa 26:6 [s] 2Sa 15:19 **18:3** [t] 1Sa 18:7 [u] 2Sa 21:17 **18:6** [v] Jos 17:18 **18:9** [w] 2Sa 14:26 **18:11** [x] 2Sa 3:39 [y] 1Sa 18:4 **18:13** [z] 2Sa 14:19-20 **18:14** [a] 2Sa 2:18; 14:30 **18:15** [b] 2Sa 12:10 **18:16** [c] 2Sa 2:28; 20:22 **18:17** [d] Jos 7:26 [e] Jos 8:29

[a] *3* Two Hebrew manuscripts, some Septuagint manuscripts and Vulgate; most Hebrew manuscripts *care; for now there are ten thousand like us* [b] *11* That is, about 4 ounces or about 115 grams [c] *12* That is, about 25 pounds or about 12 kilograms [d] *12* A few Hebrew manuscripts, Septuagint, Vulgate and Syriac; most Hebrew manuscripts may be translated *Absalom, whoever you may be.* [e] *13* Or *Otherwise, if I had acted treacherously toward him*

18:8 *the forest swallowed up more men that day than the sword.* Forests are recognized as places of danger *par excellence* in ancient Near Eastern texts, as is evident when Gilgamesh and Enkidu go hunting for Huwawa in the Gilgamesh Epic. Whether through temptation to desertion (which would have been facilitated by the thick cover) or through the advantages that savvy fighters can exploit in terrain where troop movements are impeded, the forest contributed to the success of David's cause. Outnumbered but well-trained troops often fair best in difficult terrain.

18:9 *Absalom's hair got caught in the tree.* Absalom's vanity regarding his hair (14:25 – 26) tempts the reader to see a fine irony in his hair getting caught in a tree. It is possible that Absalom was suddenly caught up and suspended in midair when the disturbance of his passage released branches previously pinned in a flexed position by other branches. Whatever the case, this points toward an allusion that to be hung on a tree signified, according to Dt 21:23, God's curse, though Dt 21:23 had a different action in mind.

18:11 *ten shekels of silver.* About four ounces (113 grams); it represents approximately one year's wages. *belt.* The Hebrew word used here never designates a piece of military gear, but may indicate a ceremonial belt or sash worn on special occasions.

18:14 – 15 The standard translations of these two verses have raised questions; e.g., if three javelins were driven into Absalom's heart (v. 14), how could it possibly be necessary that Joab's men subsequently strike and kill him (v. 15)? A better understanding of the Hebrew text might be that Joab took three stout sticks in his hands and hit Absalom in the chest in order to dislodge him from the tree, after which Joab's men swarmed and killed him. The result would be that no one person, least of all Joab, could be held directly responsible for Absalom's death.

18:16 *trumpet.* Used as a signaling device (see note on Jos 6:4).

18:17 *piled up a large heap of rocks over him.* This was a form of burial often reserved for criminals or defeated enemies (e.g., Jos 7:26; 8:29).

a pillar and erected it in the King's Valley[f] as a monument[g] to himself, for he
thought, "I have no son[h] to carry on the
memory of my name." He named the pillar after himself, and it is called Absalom's
Monument to this day.

David Mourns

19 Now Ahimaaz[i] son of Zadok said, "Let
me run and take the news to the king that
the LORD has vindicated him by delivering
him from the hand of his enemies.[j]"
20 "You are not the one to take the news
today," Joab told him. "You may take the
news another time, but you must not do
so today, because the king's son is dead."
21 Then Joab said to a Cushite, "Go, tell
the king what you have seen." The Cushite bowed down before Joab and ran off.
22 Ahimaaz son of Zadok again said to
Joab, "Come what may, please let me run
behind the Cushite."
But Joab replied, "My son, why do you
want to go? You don't have any news that
will bring you a reward."
23 He said, "Come what may, I want to
run."
So Joab said, "Run!" Then Ahimaaz ran
by way of the plain[a] and outran the Cushite.
24 While David was sitting between the
inner and outer gates, the watchman[k]
went up to the roof of the gateway by the
wall. As he looked out, he saw a man running alone. 25 The watchman called out to
the king and reported it.
The king said, "If he is alone, he must
have good news." And the runner came
closer and closer.
26 Then the watchman saw another runner, and he called down to the gatekeeper,
"Look, another man running alone!"
The king said, "He must be bringing
good news,[l] too."
27 The watchman said, "It seems to me
that the first one runs like[m] Ahimaaz son
of Zadok."
"He's a good man," the king said. "He
comes with good news."
28 Then Ahimaaz called out to the king,
"All is well!" He bowed down before the
king with his face to the ground and said,
"Praise be to the LORD your God! He has
delivered up those who lifted their hands
against my lord the king."
29 The king asked, "Is the young man
Absalom safe?"
Ahimaaz answered, "I saw great confusion just as Joab was about to send the
king's servant and me, your servant, but I
don't know what it was."
30 The king said, "Stand aside and wait
here." So he stepped aside and stood there.
31 Then the Cushite arrived and said,
"My lord the king, hear the good news!
The LORD has vindicated you today by delivering you from the hand of all who rose
up against you."
32 The king asked the Cushite, "Is the
young man Absalom safe?"
The Cushite replied, "May the enemies
of my lord the king and all who rise up to
harm you be like that young man."[n]
33 The king was shaken. He went up to
the room over the gateway and wept. As

18:18 [f] Ge 14:17 [g] Ge 50:5; Nu 32:42; 1Sa 15:12 [h] 2Sa 14:27 **18:19** [i] 2Sa 15:36 [j] ver 31; Jdg 11:36 **18:24** [k] 1Sa 14:16; 2Sa 19:8; 2Ki 9:17; Jer 51:12

18:26 [l] 1Ki 1:42; Isa 52:7; 61:1 **18:27** [m] 2Ki 9:20 **18:32** [n] Jdg 5:31; 1Sa 25:26

[a] *23* That is, the plain of the Jordan

18:23 *Ahimaaz ... outran the Cushite.* Messengers were among the chief means of communication in the ancient Near East, including in battle situations (see notes on 10:4; 1Sa 11:4). In all likelihood, as texts from Mari indicate, messengers would have been of various sorts and served for delivering various kinds of messages. Mari, e.g., attests regular messengers, letter carriers, fast couriers, express messengers, mounted messengers, etc. Of particular interest are the messengers whose task, it seems, was to deliver the good news of a military victory. In the present context, v. 27 suggests a correlation between the messenger chosen and the content of the message—whether good, bad or mixed. Thus, Joab's disinclination to send Ahimaaz may have been prompted not simply by concern for Ahimaaz's safety, given David's likely reaction to the news, but also by a desire not to appear as himself taking too much pleasure in Absalom's demise (v. 22). In the end, Joab allows Ahimaaz to run, but only after releasing an earlier messenger. Ahimaaz, however, took a faster route by way of the plain—as distinct from a perhaps shorter but more treacherous route through the forest—and arrived first.

18:24 *sitting between the inner and outer gates.* Because city gates served a dual function in the ancient Near East—military and civic—their design reflected a compromise between these two competing aims. For civic and commercial purposes, the gate needed to be open and accessible, but for military purposes, the gate needed to be narrow, difficult to navigate by chariots or large numbers of troops, and defensible. Several different types of gates are attested, some flanked by guard towers, some in which the towers became virtual small forts into which city leaders could retreat in times of danger from without or within the city, many with several chambers or rooms as part of the gate complex, and many with both inner and outer gates. Often a sharp turn was required when moving from the outer to the inner gates, the purpose again being to prevent easy passage of attacking chariots or troops. Important city gates in the time of David would have involved some combination of the above features—multiple chambers (four being perhaps the most common number in Canaan before the time of Solomon), guard towers, inner and outer gates, etc. All of these features, along with a generally stepped approach to the gate (which would hinder chariots), made gateways more defensible while leaving them wide enough to accommodate commercial traffic and civic activity. Excavations at the ancient site of Tell Dan have uncovered structures that illustrate the outer and inner gates, with a (presumably canopied) seat/throne for the city ruler between them. It may have been on such a throne that "David was sitting between the inner and outer gates."

he went, he said: "O my son Absalom! My
son, my son Absalom! If only I had died[o]
instead of you—O Absalom, my son, my
son!"[a][p]

19 [b] Joab was told, "The king is weeping and mourning for Absalom."
2 And for the whole army the victory that
day was turned into mourning, because
on that day the troops heard it said, "The
king is grieving for his son." 3 The men
stole into the city that day as men steal in
who are ashamed when they flee from battle. 4 The king covered his face and cried
aloud, "O my son Absalom! O Absalom,
my son, my son!"

5 Then Joab went into the house to the
king and said, "Today you have humiliated all your men, who have just saved
your life and the lives of your sons and
daughters and the lives of your wives and
concubines. 6 You love those who hate you
and hate those who love you. You have
made it clear today that the commanders and their men mean nothing to you. I
see that you would be pleased if Absalom
were alive today and all of us were dead.
7 Now go out and encourage your men. I
swear by the LORD that if you don't go out,
not a man will be left with you by nightfall. This will be worse for you than all
the calamities that have come on you from
your youth till now."[q]

8 So the king got up and took his seat
in the gateway. When the men were told,
"The king is sitting in the gateway,[r]" they
all came before him.

Meanwhile, the Israelites had fled to
their homes.

David Returns to Jerusalem

9 Throughout the tribes of Israel, all the
people were arguing among themselves,
saying, "The king delivered us from the
hand of our enemies; he is the one who
rescued us from the hand of the Philistines.[s] But now he has fled the country
to escape from Absalom;[t] 10 and Absalom,
whom we anointed to rule over us, has
died in battle. So why do you say nothing
about bringing the king back?"

11 King David sent this message to Zadok[u] and Abiathar, the priests: "Ask the
elders of Judah, 'Why should you be the
last to bring the king back to his palace,
since what is being said throughout Israel
has reached the king at his quarters? 12 You
are my relatives, my own flesh and blood.
So why should you be the last to bring
back the king?' 13 And say to Amasa,[v] 'Are
you not my own flesh and blood?[w] May
God deal with me, be it ever so severely,[x]
if you are not the commander of my army
for life in place of Joab.[y]' "

14 He won over the hearts of the men of
Judah so that they were all of one mind.
They sent word to the king, "Return, you
and all your men." 15 Then the king returned and went as far as the Jordan.

Now the men of Judah had come to Gilgal[z] to go out and meet the king and bring
him across the Jordan. 16 Shimei[a] son of
Gera, the Benjamite from Bahurim, hurried down with the men of Judah to meet
King David. 17 With him were a thousand
Benjamites, along with Ziba,[b] the steward of Saul's household,[c] and his fifteen
sons and twenty servants. They rushed to
the Jordan, where the king was. 18 They
crossed at the ford to take the king's
household over and to do whatever he
wished.

When Shimei son of Gera crossed the
Jordan, he fell prostrate before the king
19 and said to him, "May my lord not hold
me guilty. Do not remember how your servant did wrong on the day my lord the
king left Jerusalem.[d] May the king put it
out of his mind. 20 For I your servant know
that I have sinned, but today I have come
here as the first from the tribes of Joseph
to come down and meet my lord the king."

21 Then Abishai[e] son of Zeruiah said,
"Shouldn't Shimei be put to death for this?
He cursed[f] the LORD's anointed."[g]

22 David replied, "What does this have to
do with you, you sons of Zeruiah?[h] What
right do you have to interfere? Should anyone be put to death in Israel today?[i] Don't

18:33 [o] Ex 32:32 [p] Ge 43:14; 2Sa 19:4; Ro 9:3 **19:7** [q] Pr 14:28 **19:8** [r] 2Sa 15:2 **19:9** [s] 2Sa 8:1-14 [t] 2Sa 15:14

19:11 [u] 2Sa 15:24 **19:13** [v] 2Sa 17:25 [w] Ge 29:14 [x] Ru 1:17; 1Ki 19:2; 8:16 [y] 2Sa 2:13 **19:15** [z] Jos 5:9; 1Sa 11:15 **19:16** [a] 2Sa 16:5-13; 1Ki 2:8 **19:17** [b] 2Sa 9:2; 16:1-2 [c] Ge 43:16 **19:19** [d] 1Sa 22:15; 2Sa 16:6-8 **19:21** [e] 1Sa 26:6 [f] Ex 22:28 [g] 1Sa 12:3; 26:9; 2Sa 16:7-8 **19:22** [h] 2Sa 2:18; 16:10 [i] 1Sa 11:13

[a] *33* In Hebrew texts this verse (18:33) is numbered 19:1. [b] In Hebrew texts 19:1-43 is numbered 19:2-44.

19:6 *You love those who hate you and hate those who love you.* "Love" language is used in the ancient Near East and in the Bible to connote political loyalty (see notes on 1:26; 7:15). This is clear, e.g., from the Amarna letters. In one, Akizzi (mayor of Qatna) writes: "My lord, just as I love the king, my lord, so too the king of . . .; all of these kings are my lord's servants." An even closer parallel to Joab's words is found in the following complaint by 'Abdi-Heba of Jerusalem: "Why do you love the 'Apiru but hate the mayors?"

19:8 *the king got up and took his seat in the gateway.* This action visibly signaled David's resumption of his kingly duties, as gateways were frequently the place where official duties were performed. The Ugaritic Aqhat Legend, e.g., describes the ruler Danel taking a seat at the city gate, in the company of the leaders, and judging cases of widows and orphans. The nature of David's duties in the present circumstances would have included the encouragement of his victorious troops (v. 7) and perhaps the beginning of the process of reconciliation with those who had sided with Absalom (vv. 9–14).

19:22 *Should anyone be put to death in Israel today?* In the ancient Near East, victors could and sometimes did inflict terrible punishments upon the vanquished (see note on 9:1–13), but in many instances, especially when the political situation remained delicate, they showed

I know that today I am king over Israel?"
23So the king said to Shimei, "You shall
not die." And the king promised him on
oath.[j]
24Mephibosheth,[k] Saul's grandson, also
went down to meet the king. He had not
taken care of his feet or trimmed his mustache or washed his clothes from the day
the king left until the day he returned
safely. 25When he came from Jerusalem to
meet the king, the king asked him, "Why
didn't you go with me,[l] Mephibosheth?"
26He said, "My lord the king, since I
your servant am lame,[m] I said, 'I will
have my donkey saddled and will ride on
it, so I can go with the king.' But Ziba[n]
my servant betrayed me. 27And he has
slandered your servant to my lord the
king. My lord the king is like an angel[o]
of God; so do whatever you wish. 28All
my grandfather's descendants deserved
nothing but death[p] from my lord the
king, but you gave your servant a place
among those who eat at your table.[q] So
what right do I have to make any more
appeals to the king?"
29The king said to him, "Why say more?
I order you and Ziba to divide the land."
30Mephibosheth said to the king, "Let
him take everything, now that my lord the
king has returned home safely."
31Barzillai[r] the Gileadite also came
down from Rogelim to cross the Jordan
with the king and to send him on his way
from there. 32Now Barzillai was very old,
eighty years of age. He had provided for
the king during his stay in Mahanaim, for
he was a very wealthy[s] man. 33The king
said to Barzillai, "Cross over with me and
stay with me in Jerusalem, and I will provide for you."
34But Barzillai answered the king, "How
many more years will I live, that I should
go up to Jerusalem with the king? 35I am
now eighty[t] years old. Can I tell the difference between what is enjoyable and what
is not? Can your servant taste what he eats
and drinks? Can I still hear the voices of
male and female singers?[u] Why should
your servant be an added[v] burden to my
lord the king? 36Your servant will cross
over the Jordan with the king for a short
distance, but why should the king reward
me in this way? 37Let your servant return,
that I may die in my own town near the
tomb of my father[w] and mother. But here
is your servant Kimham.[x] Let him cross
over with my lord the king. Do for him
whatever you wish."
38The king said, "Kimham shall cross
over with me, and I will do for him whatever you wish. And anything you desire
from me I will do for you."
39So all the people crossed the Jordan,
and then the king crossed over. The king
kissed Barzillai and bid him farewell,[y] and
Barzillai returned to his home.
40When the king crossed over to Gilgal,
Kimham crossed with him. All the troops
of Judah and half the troops of Israel had
taken the king over.
41Soon all the men of Israel were coming
to the king and saying to him, "Why did
our brothers, the men of Judah, steal the
king away and bring him and his household across the Jordan, together with all
his men?"[z]
42All the men of Judah answered the
men of Israel, "We did this because the
king is closely related to us. Why are you
angry about it? Have we eaten any of the
king's provisions? Have we taken anything
for ourselves?"
43Then the men of Israel[a] answered the
men of Judah, "We have ten shares in the
king; so we have a greater claim on David than you have. Why then do you treat
us with contempt? Weren't we the first to
speak of bringing back our king?"
But the men of Judah pressed their
claims even more forcefully than the men
of Israel.

19:23 [j] 1Ki 2:8, 42 **19:24** [k] 2Sa 4:4; 9:6-10 **19:25** [l] 2Sa 16:17 **19:26** [m] Lev 21:18 [n] 2Sa 9:2 **19:27** [o] 1Sa 29:9; 2Sa 14:17, 20 **19:28** [p] 2Sa 16:8; 21:6-9 [q] 2Sa 9:7, 13 **19:31** [r] 2Sa 17:27-29; 1Ki 2:7 **19:32** [s] 1Sa 25:2; 2Sa 17:27 **19:35** [t] Ps 90:10 [u] 2Ch 35:25; Ezr 2:65; Ecc 2:8; 12:1; Isa 5:11-12 [v] 2Sa 15:33 **19:37** [w] Ge 49:29; 1Ki 2:7 [x] ver 40; Jer 41:17 **19:39** [y] Ge 31:55; 47:7 **19:41** [z] Jdg 8:1; 12:1 **19:43** [a] 2Sa 5:1

clemency toward those who had sought to harm them. The Hittite kings Telipinu (seventeenth century BC) and Hattushili III (thirteenth century BC), e.g., left behind records of such clemency: "They did me harm, yet I will not do them harm"; "Why should they die? Let them rather hide their faces." Preference for imprisonment of rivals, rather than execution, appears to have been motivated by the political need to win over as many of the former supporters of the rival as possible. Even where the accession was not challenged, a new king might, at the time of his accession and periodically thereafter, choose to proclaim a general amnesty, particularly relating to debts owed.

19:29 *I order you and Ziba to divide the land.* A Hittite text recounts a case in which an individual guilty of unprovoked attacks on Hattushili is required by the crown to relinquish half of his estate for damages. Having earlier awarded all of Mephibosheth's property to his servant Ziba, David here adjusts this to a fifty-fifty split. This compromise arrangement suggests that David either is uncertain of the veracity of Mephibosheth's version of events or is simply unwilling to call Ziba to account, lest he jeopardize support from that quarter.

19:42 *Have we eaten any of the king's provisions?* In the ancient Near East, those who were afforded the privilege of eating at the king's table were expected to respond with loyalty to their royal benefactor. In Mari, e.g., many tablets recording daily provisions for the king's table have been recovered. The Judahites' protest to the northern tribes is that their loyalty to David has not been bought by privileges extended and enjoyed, but by kinship: "We did this because the king is closely related to us."

Sheba Rebels Against David

20 Now a troublemaker named Sheba son of Bikri, a Benjamite, happened to be there. He sounded the trumpet and shouted,

"We have no share[b] in David,[c]
no part in Jesse's son![d]
Every man to his tent, Israel!"

2So all the men of Israel deserted David to follow Sheba son of Bikri. But the men of Judah stayed by their king all the way from the Jordan to Jerusalem.

3When David returned to his palace in Jerusalem, he took the ten concubines[e] he had left to take care of the palace and put them in a house under guard. He provided for them but had no sexual relations with them. They were kept in confinement till the day of their death, living as widows.

4Then the king said to Amasa,[f] "Summon the men of Judah to come to me within three days, and be here yourself." 5But when Amasa went to summon Judah, he took longer than the time the king had set for him.

6David said to Abishai,[g] "Now Sheba son of Bikri will do us more harm than Absalom did. Take your master's men and pursue him, or he will find fortified cities and escape from us."[a] 7So Joab's men and the Kerethites[h] and Pelethites and all the mighty warriors went out under the command of Abishai. They marched out from Jerusalem to pursue Sheba son of Bikri.

8While they were at the great rock in Gibeon,[i] Amasa came to meet them. Joab[j] was wearing his military tunic, and strapped over it at his waist was a belt with a dagger in its sheath. As he stepped forward, it dropped out of its sheath.

9Joab said to Amasa, "How are you, my brother?" Then Joab took Amasa by the beard with his right hand to kiss him. 10Amasa was not on his guard against the dagger[k] in Joab's[l] hand, and Joab plunged it into his belly, and his intestines spilled out on the ground. Without being stabbed again, Amasa died. Then Joab and his brother Abishai pursued Sheba son of Bikri.

11One of Joab's men stood beside Amasa and said, "Whoever favors Joab, and whoever is for David, let him follow Joab!" 12Amasa lay wallowing in his blood in the middle of the road, and the man saw that all the troops came to a halt[m] there. When he realized that everyone who came up to Amasa stopped, he dragged him from the road into a field and threw a garment over him. 13After Amasa had been removed from the road, everyone went on with Joab to pursue Sheba son of Bikri.

14Sheba passed through all the tribes of Israel to Abel Beth Maakah and through the entire region of the Bikrites,[b][n] who gathered together and followed him. 15All the troops with Joab came and besieged Sheba in Abel Beth Maakah.[o] They built a siege ramp[p] up to the city, and it stood against the outer fortifications. While they were battering the wall to bring it down, 16a wise woman[q] called from the city, "Listen! Listen! Tell Joab to come here so I can speak to him." 17He went toward her, and she asked, "Are you Joab?"

"I am," he answered.

She said, "Listen to what your servant has to say."

"I'm listening," he said.

18She continued, "Long ago they used to say, 'Get your answer at Abel,' and that settled it. 19We are the peaceful[r] and faithful in

20:1 [b]Ge 31:14 [c]Ge 29:14; 1Ki 12:16 [d]1Sa 22:7-8; 2Ch 10:16 **20:3** [e]2Sa 15:16; 16:21-22 **20:4** [f]2Sa 17:25; 19:13 **20:6** [g]2Sa 21:17 **20:7** [h]1Sa 30:14; 2Sa 8:18; 15:18; 1Ki 1:38 **20:8** [i]Jos 9:3 [j]2Sa 2:18 **20:10** [k]Jdg 3:21; 2Sa 2:23; 3:27 [l]1Ki 2:5 **20:12** [m]2Sa 2:23 **20:14** [n]Nu 21:16 **20:15** [o]1Ki 15:20; 2Ki 15:29 [p]2Ki 19:32; Isa 37:33; Jer 6:6; 32:24 **20:16** [q]2Sa 14:2 **20:19** [r]Dt 2:26

[a] 6 Or *and do us serious injury* [b] 14 See Septuagint and Vulgate; Hebrew *Berites*.

20:1 *Sheba son of Bikri.* If "Bikri" is linked to "Bekorath" of the genealogy of Saul (1Sa 9:1), then Sheba may have been not only a Benjamite but a relative of Saul, and this may have contributed to his apparent eagerness to precipitate a general withdrawal of support from David.
20:3 *he took the ten concubines ... provided for them.* The reference is to the concubines left in Jerusalem in 15:16 to care for the palace during David's flight from Absalom; they were violated by Absalom in 16:22 (on the offense, see note on 16:21). Unable or unwilling to reinstate the concubines in his harem, David provides for them as if they were widows in his household. In ancient Near Eastern legal codes, provisions were often made for the care of unmarried kinswomen or widows. The Code of Hammurapi states that a wife who becomes unfit to perform her wifely duty may be replaced, but her husband "shall continue to support her as long as she lives."
20:8 *dropped out of its sheath.* The normal understanding is that Joab was able to tip the dagger out of the sheath so he could pick it up and be holding it nonthreateningly as he approached Amasa.
20:9 *Joab took Amasa by the beard with his right hand to kiss him.* In the ancient Near East, a kiss might connote many things: obeisance, reconciliation, friendship, affection, etc. In the books of Samuel, Saul's anointing is accompanied by a kiss of honor by Samuel (1Sa 10:1; cf. 2Sa 19:39); Jonathan and David kissed one another in affection and sorrow (see note on 1Sa 20:41); and David used a kiss to effect a (partial?) reconciliation with Absalom (2Sa 14:33), only to have Absalom subsequently steal the people's affection and loyalty with a kiss (15:5–6). Here, Joab's kiss feigns honor or reconciliation, but facilitates treachery. The purpose of the unusually detailed description of his grasping the beard with his right hand is to enable to the reader to visualize how Amasa could have been caught off guard.
20:15 *siege ramp ... they were battering the wall.* See the article "Siege Warfare," p. 1157.
20:16 *wise woman.* See note on 14:2.
20:19 *a city that is a mother in Israel.* Lit "a city and a mother in Israel." This curious expression suggests several possible interpretations: (1) The "wise woman" (v. 16) is

Israel. You are trying to destroy a city that
is a mother in Israel. Why do you want to
swallow up the LORD's inheritance?"[s]
20 "Far be it from me!" Joab replied, "Far
be it from me to swallow up or destroy!
21 That is not the case. A man named Sheba son of Bikri, from the hill country of
Ephraim, has lifted up his hand against
the king, against David. Hand over this
one man, and I'll withdraw from the city."
The woman said to Joab, "His head[t] will
be thrown to you from the wall."
22 Then the woman went to all the people with her wise advice,[u] and they cut off
the head of Sheba son of Bikri and threw
it to Joab. So he sounded the trumpet, and
his men dispersed from the city, each returning to his home. And Joab went back
to the king in Jerusalem.

David's Officials

23 Joab[v] was over Israel's entire army;
Benaiah son of Jehoiada was over the
Kerethites and Pelethites; 24 Adoniram[a][w]
was in charge of forced labor; Jehoshaphat[x] son of Ahilud was recorder; 25 Sheva
was secretary; Zadok[y] and Abiathar were
priests; 26 and Ira the Jairite[b] was David's
priest.

The Gibeonites Avenged

21 During the reign of David, there
was a famine[z] for three successive years; so David sought[a] the face of
the LORD. The LORD said, "It is on account
of Saul and his blood-stained house; it is
because he put the Gibeonites to death."
2 The king summoned the Gibeonites[b]
and spoke to them. (Now the Gibeonites
were not a part of Israel but were survivors of the Amorites; the Israelites had
sworn to spare them, but Saul in his zeal
for Israel and Judah had tried to annihilate them.) 3 David asked the Gibeonites,
"What shall I do for you? How shall I
make atonement so that you will bless the
LORD's inheritance?"[c]
4 The Gibeonites answered him, "We
have no right to demand silver or gold

20:19 [s] 1Sa 26:19; 2Sa 21:3 **20:21** [t] 2Sa 4:8 **20:22** [u] Ecc 9:13 **20:23** [v] 2Sa 2:28; 8:16-18; 24:2 **20:24** [w] 1Ki 4:6; 5:14; 12:18; 2Ch 10:18 [x] 2Sa 8:16; 1Ki 4:3 **20:25** [y] 1Sa 2:35; 2Sa 8:17 **21:1** [z] Ge 12:10; Dt 32:24 [a] Ex 32:11 **21:2** [b] Jos 9:15 **21:3** [c] 1Sa 26:19; 2Sa 20:19

[a] *24* Some Septuagint manuscripts (see also 1 Kings 4:6 and 5:14); Hebrew *Adoram* [b] *26* Hebrew; some Septuagint manuscripts and Syriac (see also 23:38) *Ithrite*

referring not only to her city but also to herself, a mother in Israel (cf. Deborah's self-description as "a mother in Israel" in Jdg 5:7). (2) Taking the phrase as a hendiadys (a single concept expressed with two coordinated terms) and reading it in the light of the general Hebrew perception of cities and regions as, figuratively speaking, the mothers of their inhabitants, it means "a mother city," i.e., a major city (cf. the Hebrew phrase "a city and its daughters" [i.e., towns or villages]). (3) Perhaps the most likely interpretation is to relate the Hebrew term "mother" to cognates from Old Babylonian (Mari), Ugaritic, Phoenician, etc. that mean something like "mother unit" or "clan." The wise women's charge in the present passage, then, would be "You are trying to destroy a city and family (or, rather, clan) in Israel."

20:23 – 26 Despite David's attempt to diminish Joab's power (19:13), Joab has managed to murder (20:8) his way back to the position of commander over "Israel's entire army" (v. 23). Thus, Joab again heads the list of David's chief officials, as he did in the somewhat shorter register of officers in 8:16 – 18 (see the notes there for descriptions of the various offices). Additions to the present list include Adoniram who was in charge of "forced labor," Zadok and Abiathar the priests, and Ira the Jairite as "David's priest" (perhaps replacing his sons; see note on 8:18). The narrative placement of David's list of court officials at the end of ch. 20 is logical: First, just as the section recounting the full establishment of David's kingdom ended with a summary of his officers (8:16 – 18), so the section recounting his reestablishment of control after the rebellions of Absalom and Sheba ends with such a summary; second, the official summary draws the narrative to a fitting close before the epilogue (chs. 21 – 24) that follows.

20:24 *forced labor.* Probably comprised of war captives and non-Israelite Canaanite survivors (cf. Jos 16:10; Jdg 1:28), suggestive of David's growing power and desire to develop the infrastructure of the kingdom: roads, fortresses, civic administrative buildings, etc. The title of officer "over the forced labor" is used in the Bible only in the administrations of David, Solomon and Rehoboam, but outside the Bible it is attested also in a seventh-century BC Hebrew seal.

21:1 *During the reign of David, there was a famine for three successive years.* In the ancient Near East generally, the king was regarded as representing the people, and his behavior could bring blessing or curse on all those under his rule. The three-year famine is placed very generally "during the reign of David," and it seems almost certain that it occurred earlier rather than later in his reign. Shimei's outraged reference to "all the blood you shed in the household of Saul" (16:8) may allude to the actions David takes in the present chapter to end the famine. Famines were common occurrences in Canaan and the ancient Near East more broadly, and were typically viewed as manifestations of divine displeasure. As has often been noted, the plague prayers of the fourteenth-century BC Hittite king Mursili II offer a number of comparisons to the present episode. In both episodes, the cause of divine displeasure lies not with the current king but with a predecessor: "It is on account of Saul and his blood-stained house" (here) / "the offense ... was committed in the days of my father." In both, the specific offense had to do with a breach of covenant: Saul putting Gibeonites to death in breach of the covenant Israel made with them in Jos 9, and Mursili II's predecessor having broken an "oath of the gods" sworn with respect to the Egyptians. And in both, the treaty violation led to national catastrophe. The ancient Near East is replete with other instances of sacral desecration bringing national catastrophe and requiring sacral remedy.

21:2 *Saul in his zeal for Israel and Judah had tried to annihilate them.* Political pragmatism, not religious zeal, appears to have motivated Saul's decimation of the Gibeonites. The Gibeonites' strategic position within the centrally located tribe of Benjamin also posed a serious danger to the political unity of north and south, especially were the Gibeonites to form an alliance with the Philistines to their west.

from Saul or his family, nor do we have
the right to put anyone in Israel to death."[d]
"What do you want me to do for you?"
David asked.
5 They answered the king, "As for the
man who destroyed us and plotted against
us so that we have been decimated and
have no place anywhere in Israel, 6 let sev-
en of his male descendants be given to
us to be killed and their bodies exposed[e]
before the LORD at Gibeah of Saul—the
LORD's chosen[f] one."
So the king said, "I will give them to
you."
7 The king spared Mephibosheth[g] son of
Jonathan, the son of Saul, because of the
oath[h] before the LORD between David and
Jonathan son of Saul. 8 But the king took
Armoni and Mephibosheth, the two sons
of Aiah's daughter Rizpah,[i] whom she
had borne to Saul, together with the five
sons of Saul's daughter Merab,[a] whom
she had borne to Adriel son of Barzillai
the Meholathite.[j] 9 He handed them over
to the Gibeonites, who killed them and
exposed their bodies on a hill before the
LORD. All seven of them fell together; they
were put to death[k] during the first days of
the harvest, just as the barley harvest was
beginning.[l]
10 Rizpah daughter of Aiah took sackcloth and spread it out for herself on a
rock. From the beginning of the harvest
till the rain poured down from the heavens on the bodies, she did not let the birds
touch them by day or the wild animals
by night.[m] 11 When David was told what
Aiah's daughter Rizpah, Saul's concubine,
had done, 12 he went and took the bones
of Saul[n] and his son Jonathan from the
citizens of Jabesh Gilead. (They had stolen their bodies from the public square
at Beth Shan,[o] where the Philistines had
hung[p] them after they struck Saul down
on Gilboa.) 13 David brought the bones of
Saul and his son Jonathan from there, and
the bones of those who had been killed
and exposed were gathered up.
14 They buried the bones of Saul and
his son Jonathan in the tomb of Saul's father Kish, at Zela[q] in Benjamin, and did
everything the king commanded. After
that,[r] God answered prayer[s] in behalf of
the land.

21:4 [d] Nu 35:33-34 **21:6** [e] Nu 25:4 [f] 1Sa 10:24 **21:7** [g] 2Sa 4:4 [h] 1Sa 18:3; 20:8, 15; 2Sa 9:7 **21:8** [i] 2Sa 3:7 [j] 1Sa 18:19 **21:9** [k] 2Sa 16:8 [l] Ru 1:22 **21:10** [m] ver 8; Dt 21:23; 1Sa 17:44 **21:12** [n] 1Sa 31:11-13 [o] Jos 17:11 [p] 1Sa 31:10 **21:14** [q] Jos 18:28 [r] Jos 7:26 [s] 2Sa 24:25 **21:15** [t] 2Sa 5:25 **21:17** [u] 2Sa 20:6 [v] 1Ki 11:36 [w] 2Sa 18:3

Wars Against the Philistines

21:15-22pp — 1Ch 20:4-8

15 Once again there was a battle between the Philistines[t] and Israel. David
went down with his men to fight against
the Philistines, and he became exhausted. 16 And Ishbi-Benob, one of the descendants of Rapha, whose bronze spearhead
weighed three hundred shekels[b] and who
was armed with a new sword, said he
would kill David. 17 But Abishai[u] son of
Zeruiah came to David's rescue; he struck
the Philistine down and killed him. Then
David's men swore to him, saying, "Never
again will you go out with us to battle, so
that the lamp[v] of Israel will not be extinguished.[w]"
18 In the course of time, there was another battle with the Philistines, at Gob. At

a 8 Two Hebrew manuscripts, some Septuagint manuscripts and Syriac (see also 1 Samuel 18:19); most Hebrew and Septuagint manuscripts *Michal* *b* 16 That is, about 7 1/2 pounds or about 3.5 kilograms

21:6 *seven of his male descendants.* The number seven signifies completeness, suggesting full restitution—not, e.g., the number of Gibeonites slain by Saul, which would likely have been much higher. *their bodies exposed.* Some uncertainty surrounds the correct understanding of the term rendered "exposed," but regardless, the bodies of the seven executed sons of Saul were in fact exposed to the elements (vv. 9–10). The withholding of proper burial and the exposure of the bodies of the slain is a practice attested elsewhere in the ancient Near East in contexts of treaty violations (see next note).

21:10 *she did not let the birds touch them.* As in the ancient Near East generally, in Israel also it was considered a disgrace when the bodies of the slain were allowed to become carrion for birds and beasts, with no one to frighten them away (e.g., Dt 28:26; 1Sa 17:44,46). Threatened exposure of corpses to the elements was a frequent feature of curse formulations, as the following excerpt from a vassal treaty of Esarhaddon illustrates: "May Ninurta, leader of the gods, fell you with his fierce arrow, and fill the plain with your corpses, give your flesh to eagles and vultures to feed upon." It was precisely to drive away the birds that Rizpah set a vigil by the bodies of her sons "from the beginning of the harvest till the rain poured down." The harvest in question was the barley harvest (v. 9), which began in April. Thus, the "rain" should presumably be understood as an unseasonal downpour that ended the famine, rather than the beginning of "winter rains," which would not commence until late October.

21:16 *descendants of Rapha.* This epithet has occasioned considerable discussion. While certainty is unobtainable at present, Rapha is probably best understood not as the name of a deity in Gath, as some have suggested, but as a collective noun to be associated with the Rephaites—pre-Israelite inhabitants of the land of Canaan (Ge 14:5; 15:20; Dt 2:20; Jos 17:15). The Rephaites were noted for their gigantic proportions (see note on 1Sa 17:4). Among the Rephaites were sometimes counted such peoples as the Emites, Zamzummites and Anakites (Dt 2:10–11,20–21), all peoples distinguished for their strength and stature. According to Jos 11:21–22, the Anakites were driven from the hill country of Israel and Judah by Joshua but were able to survive in the cities of Gaza, Gath and Ashdod—thus in the general area in view in the present context.

21:17 *lamp.* On its metaphoric use, see note on 14:7. Kings in the ancient Near East were often associated with light, in the sense of that which brings hope, justice and well-being. A Babylonian idiom speaks of a family with no descendants as a brazier that has gone out.

that time Sibbekai[x] the Hushathite killed
Saph, one of the descendants of Rapha.
[19]In another battle with the Philistines
at Gob, Elhanan son of Jair[a] the Bethlehemite killed the brother of[b] Goliath the
Gittite, who had a spear with a shaft like
a weaver's rod.[y]
[20]In still another battle, which took
place at Gath, there was a huge man with
six fingers on each hand and six toes on
each foot — twenty-four in all. He also was
descended from Rapha. [21]When he taunted Israel, Jonathan son of Shimeah,[z] David's brother, killed him.
[22]These four were descendants of Rapha
in Gath, and they fell at the hands of David and his men.

David's Song of Praise

22:1-51pp — Ps 18:1-50

22 David sang[a] to the LORD the words
of this song when the LORD delivered him from the hand of all his enemies
and from the hand of Saul. [2]He said:

"The LORD is my rock,[b] my fortress[c]
and my deliverer;[d]
[3] my God is my rock, in whom I take
refuge,[e]
my shield[c][f] and the horn[d][g] of my
salvation.
He is my stronghold,[h] my refuge and
my savior —
from violent people you save me.
[4]"I called to the LORD, who is worthy[i] of
praise,
and have been saved from my
enemies.
[5]The waves[j] of death swirled about me;
the torrents of destruction
overwhelmed me.
[6]The cords of the grave[k] coiled around me;
the snares of death confronted me.
[7]"In my distress[l] I called[m] to the LORD;
I called out to my God.
From his temple he heard my voice;
my cry came to his ears.
[8]The earth[n] trembled and quaked,[o]
the foundations[p] of the heavens[e]
shook;
they trembled because he was
angry.
[9]Smoke rose from his nostrils;
consuming fire[q] came from his
mouth,
burning coals blazed out of it.
[10]He parted the heavens and came
down;
dark clouds[r] were under his feet.
[11]He mounted the cherubim and flew;
he soared[f] on the wings of the
wind.[s]
[12]He made darkness his canopy around
him —
the dark[g] rain clouds of the sky.
[13]Out of the brightness of his presence
bolts of lightning[t] blazed forth.
[14]The LORD thundered[u] from heaven;
the voice of the Most High
resounded.
[15]He shot his arrows[v] and scattered the
enemy,
with great bolts of lightning he
routed them.
[16]The valleys of the sea were exposed
and the foundations of the earth laid
bare
at the rebuke[w] of the LORD,
at the blast of breath from his
nostrils.

21:18 [x] 1Ch 11:29; 20:4; 27:11 **21:19** [y] 1Sa 17:7 **21:21** [z] 1Sa 16:9 **22:1** [a] Ex 15:1; Jdg 5:1; Ps 18:2-50 **22:2** [b] Dt 32:4; Ps 71:3 [c] Ps 31:3; 91:2 [d] Ps 144:2 **22:3** [e] Dt 32:37; Jer 16:19 [f] Ge 15:1 [g] Lk 1:69 [h] Ps 9:9 **22:4** [i] Ps 48:1; 96:4 **22:5** [j] Ps 69:14-15; 93:4; Jnh 2:3 **22:6** [k] Ps 116:3
22:7 [l] Ps 120:1 [m] Ps 34:6, 15; 116:4 **22:8** [n] Jdg 5:4; Ps 97:4 [o] Ps 77:18 [p] Job 26:11 **22:9** [q] Ps 97:3; Heb 12:29 **22:10** [r] 1Ki 8:12; Na 1:3 **22:11** [s] Ps 104:3 **22:13** [t] ver 9 **22:14** [u] 1Sa 2:10 **22:15** [v] Dt 32:23 **22:16** [w] Na 1:4

[a] *19* See 1 Chron. 20:5; Hebrew *Jaare-Oregim.* [b] *19* See 1 Chron. 20:5; Hebrew does not have *the brother of.* [c] *3* Or *sovereign* [d] *3* *Horn* here symbolizes strength. [e] *8* Hebrew; Vulgate and Syriac (see also Psalm 18:7) *mountains* [f] *11* Many Hebrew manuscripts (see also Psalm 18:10); most Hebrew manuscripts *appeared* [g] *12* Septuagint (see also Psalm 18:11); Hebrew *massed*

21:20 *six fingers ... six toes.* Polydactylism (extra digits on hands or feet) was, like other physical abnormalities, a subject of considerable interest in antiquity. In Mesopotamia, priests and diviners would be consulted regarding the significance of physical abnormalities. A seventh-century BC Assyrian text runs through various possible cases of polydactylism and interprets them: "If a woman gives birth, and [the child] has six fingers on the right hand — poverty will seize the house of the man. If ... on the left hand — [the mother] is endowed with prosperity; [the man's] adversary will die." The list continues, describing all the possible configurations, and concludes: "If a woman gives birth, and [the child] has six fingers [and toes] on each of its right and left hands and right and left feet — the land will live undisturbed." The prevalence of this genetic abnormality, particularly common in inbred societies, is masked in the modern Western world by cosmetic surgical intervention at birth.

22:3 *rock ... horn.* Both are metaphors for refuge and strength. *rock.* See note on 1Sa 2:2. *horn.* See note on 1Sa 2:1.

22:5 *waves of death ... torrents of destruction.* In the ancient Near Eastern mindset, the power of water was such that only God or the gods could control it. Uncontrolled, it brought death and destruction. In the present context, David's being overwhelmed by "waves" and "torrents" led to a cry for help (v. 7), which God, who alone was capable of rescue, answered with an awesome display of power (vv. 8 – 20).

22:7 *distress.* In Hebrew, the concept of distress is expressed in terms of being in a narrow or tightly confined space, and it was from just such a "tight spot" that Yahweh brought David into "a spacious place" (v. 20).

22:8 – 10 *The earth trembled and quaked ... He parted the heavens and came down.* A Ugaritic passage describing a triumphant campaign by Baal, the storm-god, employs similar imagery: he "opened a rift in the clouds. Baal sounded his holy voice, Baal repeated it from his lips; he uttered his holy voice and the earth quaked."

17 "He reached down from on high[x] and
took hold of me;
he drew[y] me out of deep waters.
18 He rescued me from my powerful
enemy,
from my foes, who were too strong
for me.
19 They confronted me in the day of my
disaster,
but the LORD was my support.[z]
20 He brought me out into a spacious[a]
place;
he rescued[b] me because he
delighted[c] in me.[d]

21 "The LORD has dealt with me according
to my righteousness;[e]
according to the cleanness of my
hands[f] he has rewarded me.
22 For I have kept[g] the ways of the LORD;
I am not guilty of turning from my
God.
23 All his laws are before me;[h]
I have not turned[i] away from his
decrees.
24 I have been blameless[j] before him
and have kept myself from sin.
25 The LORD has rewarded me according
to my righteousness,[k]
according to my cleanness[*a*] in his
sight.

26 "To the faithful you show yourself
faithful,
to the blameless you show yourself
blameless,
27 to the pure[l] you show yourself pure,
but to the devious you show yourself
shrewd.[m]
28 You save the humble,[n]
but your eyes are on the haughty to
bring them low.[o]
29 You, LORD, are my lamp;[p]
the LORD turns my darkness into
light.
30 With your help I can advance against a
troop[*b*];
with my God I can scale a wall.

31 "As for God, his way is perfect:[q]
The LORD's word is flawless;[r]
he shields all who take refuge in
him.
32 For who is God besides the LORD?
And who is the Rock[s] except our
God?
33 It is God who arms me with strength[*c*]
and keeps my way secure.
34 He makes my feet like the feet of a
deer;[t]
he causes me to stand on the
heights.[u]
35 He trains my hands[v] for battle;
my arms can bend a bow of bronze.
36 You make your saving help my
shield;[w]
your help has made[*d*] me great.
37 You provide a broad path[x] for my feet,
so that my ankles do not give way.

38 "I pursued my enemies and crushed
them;
I did not turn back till they were
destroyed.
39 I crushed[y] them completely, and they
could not rise;
they fell beneath my feet.
40 You armed me with strength for battle;
you humbled my adversaries before
me.[z]
41 You made my enemies turn their
backs[a] in flight,
and I destroyed my foes.
42 They cried for help,[b] but there was no
one to save them—[c]
to the LORD, but he did not answer.
43 I beat them as fine as the dust of the
earth;
I pounded and trampled[d] them like
mud[e] in the streets.

44 "You have delivered[f] me from the
attacks of the peoples;
you have preserved[g] me as the head
of nations.
People[h] I did not know now serve me,
45 foreigners cower[i] before me;
as soon as they hear of me, they
obey me.
46 They all lose heart;
they come trembling[*e*j] from their
strongholds.

47 "The LORD lives! Praise be to my Rock!
Exalted be my God, the Rock, my
Savior![k]
48 He is the God who avenges me,[l]
who puts the nations under me,
49 who sets me free from my
enemies.[m]
You exalted me above my foes;
from a violent man you rescued me.
50 Therefore I will praise you, LORD,
among the nations;
I will sing the praises of your name.[n]

51 "He gives his king great victories;[o]
he shows unfailing kindness to his
anointed,[p]
to David[q] and his descendants
forever."[r]

22:17 [x] Ps 144:7 [y] Ex 2:10 **22:19** [z] Ps 23:4 **22:20** [a] Ps 31:8 [b] Ps 118:5 [c] Ps 22:8 [d] 2Sa 15:26 **22:21** [e] 1Sa 26:23 [f] Ps 24:4 **22:22** [g] Ge 18:19; Ps 128:1; Pr 8:32 **22:23** [h] Dt 6:4-9; Ps 119:30-32 [i] Ps 119:102 **22:24** [j] Ge 6:9; Eph 1:4 **22:25** [k] ver 21 **22:27** [l] Mt 5:8 [m] Lev 26:23-24 **22:28** [n] Ex 3:8; Ps 72:12-13 [o] Isa 2:12, 17; 5:15 **22:29** [p] Ps 27:1 **22:31** [q] Dt 32:4; Mt 5:48 [r] Ps 12:6; 119:140; Pr 30:5-6 **22:32** [s] 1Sa 2:2 **22:34** [t] Hab 3:19 [u] Dt 32:13 **22:35** [v] Ps 144:1 **22:36** [w] Eph 6:16 **22:37** [x] Pr 4:11 **22:39** [y] Mal 4:3 **22:40** [z] Ps 44:5 **22:41** [a] Ex 23:27 **22:42** [b] Isa 1:15 [c] Ps 50:22 **22:43** [d] Mic 7:10 [e] Isa 10:6; Mic 7:10 **22:44** [f] 2Sa 3:1 [g] Dt 28:13 [h] 2Sa 8:1-14; Isa 55:3-5 **22:45** [i] Ps 66:3; 81:15 **22:46** [j] Mic 7:17 **22:47** [k] Ps 89:26 **22:48** [l] Ps 94:1; 144:2; 1Sa 25:39 **22:49** [m] Ps 140:1,4 **22:50** [n] Ro 15:9* **22:51** [o] Ps 144:9-10 [p] Ps 89:20 [q] 2Sa 7:13 [r] Ps 89:24, 29

[a] 25 Hebrew; Septuagint and Vulgate (see also Psalm 18:24) *to the cleanness of my hands* [b] 30 Or *can run through a barricade* [c] 33 Dead Sea Scrolls, some Septuagint manuscripts, Vulgate and Syriac (see also Psalm 18:32); Masoretic Text *who is my strong refuge* [d] 36 Dead Sea Scrolls; Masoretic Text *shield; / you stoop down to make* [e] 46 Some Septuagint manuscripts and Vulgate (see also Psalm 18:45); Masoretic Text *they arm themselves*

David's Last Words

23 These are the last words of David:

"The inspired utterance of David son
of Jesse,
the utterance of the man exalted[s] by
the Most High,
the man anointed[t] by the God of Jacob,
the hero of Israel's songs:

2 "The Spirit[u] of the LORD spoke through
me;
his word was on my tongue.
3 The God of Israel spoke,
the Rock[v] of Israel said to me:
'When one rules over people in
righteousness,[w]
when he rules in the fear of God,[x]
4 he is like the light of morning at sunrise[y]
on a cloudless morning,
like the brightness after rain
that brings grass from the earth.'

5 "If my house were not right with God,
surely he would not have made with
me an everlasting covenant,[z]
arranged and secured in every part;
surely he would not bring to fruition
my salvation
and grant me my every desire.
6 But evil men are all to be cast aside
like thorns,[a]
which are not gathered with the hand.
7 Whoever touches thorns
uses a tool of iron or the shaft of a
spear;
they are burned up where they lie."

David's Mighty Warriors

23:8-39pp — 1Ch 11:10-41

8 These are the names of David's mighty
warriors:
Josheb-Basshebeth,[a] a Tahkemonite,[b]
was chief of the Three; he raised his spear
against eight hundred men, whom he
killed[c] in one encounter.
9 Next to him was Eleazar son of Dodai[b]
the Ahohite.[c] As one of the three mighty
warriors, he was with David when they
taunted the Philistines gathered at Pas
Dammim[d] for battle. Then the Israelites
retreated, 10 but Eleazar stood his ground
and struck down the Philistines till his
hand grew tired and froze to the sword.
The LORD brought about a great victory
that day. The troops returned to Eleazar,
but only to strip the dead.
11 Next to him was Shammah son of Agee
the Hararite. When the Philistines banded together at a place where there was a
field full of lentils, Israel's troops fled from
them. 12 But Shammah took his stand in
the middle of the field. He defended it and
struck the Philistines down, and the LORD
brought about a great victory.
13 During harvest time, three of the thirty chief warriors came down to David at
the cave of Adullam,[d] while a band of
Philistines was encamped in the Valley
of Rephaim.[e] 14 At that time David was in
the stronghold,[f] and the Philistine garrison was at Bethlehem.[g] 15 David longed
for water and said, "Oh, that someone
would get me a drink of water from the
well near the gate of Bethlehem!" 16 So the
three mighty warriors broke through the
Philistine lines, drew water from the well
near the gate of Bethlehem and carried it
back to David. But he refused to drink it;
instead, he poured[h] it out before the LORD.
17 "Far be it from me, LORD, to do this!"
he said. "Is it not the blood[i] of men who
went at the risk of their lives?" And David
would not drink it.
Such were the exploits of the three
mighty warriors.
18 Abishai[j] the brother of Joab son of
Zeruiah was chief of the Three.[e] He raised
his spear against three hundred men,
whom he killed, and so he became as famous as the Three. 19 Was he not held in
greater honor than the Three? He became
their commander, even though he was not
included among them.
20 Benaiah[k] son of Jehoiada, a valiant

23:1 [s] 2Sa 7:8-9; Ps 78:70-71; 89:27 [t] 1Sa 16:12-13; Ps 89:20
23:2 [u] Mt 22:43; 2Pe 1:21
23:3 [v] Dt 32:4; 2Sa 22:2, 32 [w] Ps 72:2 [x] 2Ch 19:7,9; Isa 11:1-5
23:4 [y] Jdg 5:31; Ps 89:36
23:5 [z] Ps 89:29; Isa 55:3
23:6 [a] Mt 13:40-41
23:9 [b] 1Ch 27:4 [c] 1Ch 8:4
23:13 [d] 1Sa 22:1 [e] 2Sa 5:18
23:14 [f] 1Sa 22:4-5 [g] Ru 1:19
23:16 [h] Ge 35:14
23:17 [i] Lev 17:10-12
23:18 [j] 2Sa 10:10,14; 1Ch 11:20
23:20 [k] 2Sa 8:18; 20:23

[a] 8 Hebrew; some Septuagint manuscripts suggest *Ish-Bosheth,* that is, *Esh-Baal* (see also 1 Chron. 11:11 *Jashobeam*). [b] 8 Probably a variant of *Hakmonite* (see 1 Chron. 11:11) [c] 8 Some Septuagint manuscripts (see also 1 Chron. 11:11); Hebrew and other Septuagint manuscripts *Three; it was Adino the Eznite who killed eight hundred men* [d] 9 See 1 Chron. 11:13; Hebrew *gathered there.* [e] 18 Most Hebrew manuscripts (see also 1 Chron. 11:20); two Hebrew manuscripts and Syriac *Thirty*

23:4 *light of morning at sunrise … brightness after rain that brings grass from the earth.* In the ancient Near East, kings were often described as lamps, lights or even the sun, giving light to the land. The fourteenth-century BC Hittite king Suppiluliuma, e.g., introduces himself in a treaty document this way: "I, the Sun Suppiluliuma, the great king, the king of the Hatti land, the valiant, the favorite of the Storm-god, went to war." In an early second millennium BC Egyptian hymn to the god Amon-Re, the "goodly ruler" is described as "The lord of rays, who makes brilliance, To whom the gods give thanksgiving, Who extends his arms to him whom he loves, (But) his enemy is consumed by a flame."

23:20 *killed a lion.* The lion hunt is a regular motif in royal reliefs, the ferocity of the "king of beasts" serving to prove the mettle of the one able to conquer him. In a legend extolling his hunting prowess, the fifteenth-century BC pharaoh Thutmose III is credited with killing "seven lions by shooting in the completion of a moment." In the present account, the added detail that it was "on a snowy day," with the slippery footing that this suggests, further dramatizes Benaiah's valorous feat. The "pit" presumably would have been designed to trap the lion.

Assyrian King Ashurbanipal killing a lion, c. 645 BC. Heroes and kings were often portrayed fighting lions (2Sa 23:20).

fighter from Kabzeel,[l] performed great exploits. He struck down Moab's two mightiest warriors. He also went down into a pit
on a snowy day and killed a lion. 21 And he
struck down a huge Egyptian. Although
the Egyptian had a spear in his hand, Benaiah went against him with a club. He
snatched the spear from the Egyptian's
hand and killed him with his own spear.
22 Such were the exploits of Benaiah son
of Jehoiada; he too was as famous as the
three mighty warriors. 23 He was held in
greater honor than any of the Thirty, but
he was not included among the Three.
And David put him in charge of his bodyguard.

24 Among the Thirty were:
Asahel[m] the brother of Joab,
Elhanan son of Dodo from Bethlehem,
25 Shammah the Harodite,[n]
Elika the Harodite,
26 Helez[o] the Paltite,
Ira son of Ikkesh from Tekoa,
27 Abiezer from Anathoth,[p]
Sibbekai[a] the Hushathite,
28 Zalmon the Ahohite,
Maharai[q] the Netophathite,[r]
29 Heled[b] son of Baanah the Netophathite,
Ithai son of Ribai from Gibeah[s] in Benjamin,
30 Benaiah the Pirathonite,[t]
Hiddai[c] from the ravines of Gaash,[u]
31 Abi-Albon the Arbathite,
Azmaveth the Barhumite,[v]
32 Eliahba the Shaalbonite,
the sons of Jashen,
Jonathan 33 son of[d] Shammah the Hararite,
Ahiam son of Sharar[e] the Hararite,
34 Eliphelet son of Ahasbai the Maakathite,
Eliam[w] son of Ahithophel[x] the Gilonite,
35 Hezro the Carmelite,[y]
Paarai the Arbite,
36 Igal son of Nathan from Zobah,[z]
the son of Hagri,[f]
37 Zelek the Ammonite,
Naharai the Beerothite, the armor-bearer of Joab son of Zeruiah,

23:20 [l] Jos 15:21 **23:24** [m] 2Sa 2:18 **23:25** [n] Jdg 7:1; 1Ch 11:27 **23:26** [o] 1Ch 27:10 **23:27** [p] Jos 21:18 **23:28** [q] 1Ch 27:13 [r] 2Ki 25:23; Ne 7:26 **23:29** [s] Jos 15:57 **23:30** [t] Jdg 12:13 [u] Jos 24:30 **23:31** [v] 2Sa 3:16 **23:34** [w] 2Sa 11:3 [x] 2Sa 15:12 **23:35** [y] Jos 12:22 **23:36** [z] 1Sa 14:47

[a] *27* Some Septuagint manuscripts (see also 21:18; 1 Chron. 11:29); Hebrew *Mebunnai* [b] *29* Some Hebrew manuscripts and Vulgate (see also 1 Chron. 11:30); most Hebrew manuscripts *Heleb* [c] *30* Hebrew; some Septuagint manuscripts (see also 1 Chron. 11:32) *Hurai* [d] *33* Some Septuagint manuscripts (see also 1 Chron. 11:34); Hebrew does not have *son of.* [e] *33* Hebrew; some Septuagint manuscripts (see also 1 Chron. 11:35) *Sakar* [f] *36* Some Septuagint manuscripts (see also 1 Chron. 11:38); Hebrew *Haggadi*

38Ira the Ithrite,[a]
Gareb the Ithrite
39and Uriah[b] the Hittite.
There were thirty-seven in all.

David Enrolls the Fighting Men

24:1-17pp — 1Ch 21:1-17

24 Again[c] the anger of the LORD
burned against Israel, and he incited David against them, saying, "Go and
take a census of[d] Israel and Judah."
2So the king said to Joab[e] and the army
commanders[a] with him, "Go throughout
the tribes of Israel from Dan to Beersheba[f]
and enroll the fighting men, so that I may
know how many there are."
3But Joab replied to the king, "May the
LORD your God multiply the troops a hundred times over,[g] and may the eyes of my
lord the king see it. But why does my lord
the king want to do such a thing?"
4The king's word, however, overruled
Joab and the army commanders; so they
left the presence of the king to enroll the
fighting men of Israel.
5After crossing the Jordan, they camped
near Aroer,[h] south of the town in the
gorge, and then went through Gad and
on to Jazer.[i] 6They went to Gilead and the
region of Tahtim Hodshi, and on to Dan
Jaan and around toward Sidon.[j] 7Then
they went toward the fortress of Tyre[k] and
all the towns of the Hivites and Canaanites. Finally, they went on to Beersheba[l] in
the Negev[m] of Judah.
8After they had gone through the entire
land, they came back to Jerusalem at the
end of nine months and twenty days.
9Joab reported the number of the fighting men to the king: In Israel there were
eight hundred thousand able-bodied men
who could handle a sword, and in Judah
five hundred thousand.[n]
10David was conscience-stricken[o] after
he had counted the fighting men, and he
said to the LORD, "I have sinned[p] greatly in
what I have done. Now, LORD, I beg you,
take away the guilt of your servant. I have
done a very foolish thing.[q]"
11Before David got up the next morning,
the word of the LORD had come to Gad[r]
the prophet, David's seer:[s] 12"Go and tell
David, 'This is what the LORD says: I am
giving you three options. Choose one of
them for me to carry out against you.'"
13So Gad went to David and said to him,
"Shall there come on you three[b] years of
famine[t] in your land? Or three months of
fleeing from your enemies while they pursue you? Or three days of plague[u] in your
land? Now then, think it over and decide
how I should answer the one who sent me."
14David said to Gad, "I am in deep distress. Let us fall into the hands of the
LORD, for his mercy[v] is great; but do not
let me fall into human hands."
15So the LORD sent a plague on Israel
from that morning until the end of the
time designated, and seventy thousand of
the people from Dan to Beersheba died.[w]
16When the angel stretched out his hand to
destroy Jerusalem, the LORD relented[x] concerning the disaster and said to the angel
who was afflicting the people, "Enough!
Withdraw your hand." The angel of the
LORD[y] was then at the threshing floor of
Araunah the Jebusite.
17When David saw the angel who was
striking down the people, he said to the
LORD, "I have sinned; I, the shepherd,[c]
have done wrong. These are but sheep.[z]
What have they done? Let your hand fall
on me and my family."[a]

David Builds an Altar

24:18-25pp — 1Ch 21:18-26

18On that day Gad went to David and
said to him, "Go up and build an altar to
the LORD on the threshing floor of Arau-

23:38 [a] 2Sa 20:26; 1Ch 2:53 **23:39** [b] 2Sa 11:3 **24:1** [c] Jos 9:15 [d] 1Ch 27:23 **24:2** [e] 2Sa 20:23 [f] Jdg 20:1; 2Sa 3:10 **24:3** [g] Dt 1:11 **24:5** [h] Dt 2:36; Jos 13:9 [i] Nu 21:32 **24:6** [j] Ge 10:19; Jos 19:28; Jdg 1:31 **24:7** [k] Jos 19:29 [l] Ge 21:22-33 [m] Dt 1:7; Jos 11:3 **24:9** [n] Nu 1:44-46; 1Ch 21:5 **24:10** [o] 1Sa 24:5 [p] 2Sa 12:13 [q] Nu 12:11; 1Sa 13:13 **24:11** [r] 1Sa 22:5 [s] 1Sa 9:9; 1Ch 29:29 **24:13** [t] Dt 28:38-42, 48; Eze 14:21 [u] Lev 26:25 **24:14** [v] Ne 9:28; Ps 51:1; 103:8, 13; 130:4 **24:15** [w] 1Ch 27:24 **24:16** [x] Ge 6:6; 1Sa 15:11 [y] Ex 12:23; Ac 12:23 **24:17** [z] Ps 74:1 [a] Jnh 1:12

[a] 2 Septuagint (see also verse 4 and 1 Chron. 21:2); Hebrew *Joab the army commander* [b] 13 Septuagint (see also 1 Chron. 21:12); Hebrew *seven* [c] 17 Dead Sea Scrolls and Septuagint; Masoretic Text does not have *the shepherd*.

24:1 *take a census.* Census-taking was a regular practice in the ancient Near East. Evidence exists from as early as the third millennium BC in Mesopotamia and on into the first millennium BC. Unlike modern censuses designed to study long-term trends and demographics, ancient censuses were directed to specific, contemporary needs, such as assessing taxes, allocating land, determining the strength of the national militia, etc. In the OT, taking a census does not seem to have been regarded as wrong per se (cf. Nu 1:1 – 2; 4:1 – 2; 26:1 – 4), although Ex 30:11 – 12 does raise the possibility of plague accompanying it. Here, God's anger for undisclosed offenses is what prompts David to take the census. One way to assuage the anger of deity is to buy favor with gifts to the sanctuary, which could be collected as taxes, hence the census. Yahweh does not wish to be appeased in this way, so the judgment is both punishment for the original offense, and for theological impropriety.

24:8 *nine months and twenty days.* Given that the distances involved in the itinerary described could have been covered in a matter of weeks, the vast majority of the time must have been spent taking the census itself.

24:9 *eight hundred thousand.* On large numbers and population estimates, see the article "Numbers in Numbers," p. 235.

24:16 *the angel who was afflicting the people.* This is the same terminology used of the destroyer angel in Ex 12. The Mesopotamian epic "Erra and Ishum" depicts the plague-god Nergal embarking on a campaign of destruction until he is pacified by his subordinate Ishum.

24:18 *the threshing floor of Araunah the Jebusite.* In the agrarian societies of the ancient Near East, large flat out-

nah the Jebusite." [19]So David went up, as the LORD had commanded through Gad. [20]When Araunah looked and saw the king and his officials coming toward him, he went out and bowed down before the king with his face to the ground.

[21]Araunah said, "Why has my lord the king come to his servant?"

"To buy your threshing floor," David answered, "so I can build an altar to the LORD, that the plague on the people may be stopped."[b]

[22]Araunah said to David, "Let my lord the king take whatever he wishes and offer it up. Here are oxen[c] for the burnt offering, and here are threshing sledges and ox yokes for the wood. [23]Your Majesty, Araunah[a] gives[d] all this to the king." Araunah also said to him, "May the LORD your God accept you."

[24]But the king replied to Araunah, "No, I insist on paying you for it. I will not sacrifice to the LORD my God burnt offerings that cost me nothing."[e]

So David bought the threshing floor and the oxen and paid fifty shekels[b] of silver for them. [25]David built an altar[f] to the LORD there and sacrificed burnt offerings and fellowship offerings. Then the LORD answered his prayer[g] in behalf of the land, and the plague on Israel was stopped.

24:21 [b]Nu 16:44-50 **24:22** [c]1Sa 6:14; 1Ki 19:21 **24:23** [d]Eze 20:40-41 **24:24** [e]Mal 1:13-14 **24:25** [f]1Sa 7:17 [g]2Sa 21:14

[a] *23* Some Hebrew manuscripts and Septuagint; most Hebrew manuscripts *King Araunah* [b] *24* That is, about 1 1/4 pounds or about 575 grams

croppings of bedrock, frequently elevated to catch the breeze needed for winnowing, were often used as threshing floors (see note on Ru 3:2). Their prominence and spaciousness lent to their use also as public gathering places. The harvest activity conducted at threshing floors would often have been accompanied by religious celebration, with the result that they were sometimes vested with religious significance. In this light, it is plausible that the threshing floor of Araunah may have had some religious associations prior to its purchase by David. It would be at this very site that the temple of Yahweh would one day be built (2Ch 3:1). At this time in history, the city did not yet extend this far north.

NARRATIVE LITERATURE

1 KINGS

Introduction to 1 – 2 Kings.

Historical Setting

The historical setting of 1 Kings can be understood either as the time of the book's composition or, alternatively, as the same era as the final events described in the book. Its composition, along with 2 Kings, is likely to be sometime late in the Judahite monarchy (the late 600s BC), when the northern kingdom had gone into exile and a similar devastation of the Davidic dynasty seemed unavoidable. The actual events recounted in Kings are known to have transpired between 1000 and 562 BC. This can be known from the good number of extra-Biblical texts and archaeological finds that corroborate the Biblical record.

KEY CONCEPTS

- The two books of Kings, like the book of Judges, document covenant failure.
- The exiles are shown that the cause of the judgment was apostasy and idolatry.
- The kings were frequently warned by the prophets.
- Recurrent themes are the sins of Jeroboam (the golden calves) and the promises to David (covenant).

The era of David and Solomon is commonly known as the united monarchy. This period (1000 – 931 BC) was a time in which Israel became the dominant nation in the ancient Near East (1Ki 1 – 11). David's successful military campaigns extended his control over neighboring and distant lands, while Solomon's administration capitalized upon Israel's strength to bring vast wealth and cultural resources into the kingdom. Israel became a mini-empire that conformed to the conventional Near Eastern model, complete with alliances, cosmopolitan influences and fortified administrative centers with palaces and military garrisons.

After the division of the monarchy, two less powerful Israelite kingdoms (the northern kingdom of Israel and the southern kingdom of Judah) fought each other and their neighbors for supremacy in the region. Both suffered crushing defeats when Pharaoh Shishak of Egypt made a lightning raid through the region. After decades of infighting, the two kingdoms entered a period of detente and cooperation. Alliances were forged with neighbors (most important, the Arameans and Phoenicians). By the mid-ninth century BC, Ahab of Israel was identified as the most powerful member of a united coalition that fought Assyria in 853 BC against the Assyrian king Shalmaneser III, whose annals recorded Ahab's significant role.

The ebb and flow of Israel's and Judah's fortunes continues in the book of 2 Kings, which spans the period from 850 to 586 BC. Following Ahab's reign, struggles with the Assyrians and Arameans continued for several decades until Jeroboam II of Israel and Uzziah of Judah restored peace and prosperity. The heyday ended in 732 BC when the age of nationalism came to a tumultuous end and imperial powers returned, this time in the form of a new and powerful Assyrian military invasion. A series of attacks beginning with those of Tiglath-Pileser III and ending with those of Sargon II led to the annihilation of the capital city (Samaria) and the captivity of Israel (2Ki 15–17). Judah and its capital (Jerusalem) survived for another century — only to meet the same fate at the hands of the Babylonian Empire in 586 BC.

Cultural and Religious Setting

During the era of David and Solomon, the needs of the state began to encroach on the concerns of the tribe. This is reflected in the increased size and number of cities and also in a new level of interaction with surrounding cultures. Distinctive architectural forms, such as palaces, fortified cities with distinctive gateways, and ornate masonry found their way from Phoenicia to the largest cities in Judah and Israel. Administrative and military activity increased significantly, as did the level of prosperity.

Literary Setting

The compiler of the books of Kings, like the scribes of most ancient Near Eastern kingdoms, had available to him the copious records of key events in the life of the court and the history of the state such as royal archives. Royal archives from Egypt, Babylon, Assyria, Mari, Emar and other kingdoms contained annals of military events, king lists and chronicles, as well as a variety of royal inscriptions. The Babylonian Chronicle and the Assyrian Eponym List are good examples of the detailed records kept in state archives in the second and first millennia BC. Frequent allusions to documents of this sort are found in Kings, so there can be no doubt that the court in Jerusalem contained an archive similar to those of surrounding nations. The annals referred to in Kings would seem to have much in common with those of other ancient kingdoms, but the great historical work into which they are crafted has few, if any, parallels in the ancient Near East. ◆

Adonijah Sets Himself Up as King

1 When King David was very old, he
could not keep warm even when they
put covers over him. 2So his attendants
said to him, "Let us look for a young virgin to serve the king and take care of him.
She can lie beside him so that our lord the
king may keep warm."
3Then they searched throughout Israel
for a beautiful young woman and found
Abishag, a Shunammite,[a] and brought her
to the king. 4The woman was very beautiful; she took care of the king and waited
on him, but the king had no sexual relations with her.
5Now Adonijah,[b] whose mother was
Haggith, put himself forward and said, "I
will be king." So he got chariots[c] and horses[a] ready, with fifty men to run ahead of
him. 6(His father had never rebuked[d] him
by asking, "Why do you behave as you
do?" He was also very handsome and was
born next after Absalom.)
7Adonijah conferred with Joab[e] son of
Zeruiah and with Abiathar[f] the priest, and
they gave him their support. 8But Zadok[g]
the priest, Benaiah[h] son of Jehoiada, Nathan[i] the prophet, Shimei[j] and Rei and David's special guard[k] did not join Adonijah.
9Adonijah then sacrificed sheep, cattle
and fattened calves at the Stone of Zoheleth near En Rogel.[l] He invited all his
brothers, the king's sons, and all the royal
officials of Judah, 10but he did not invite
Nathan the prophet or Benaiah or the special guard or his brother Solomon.[m]
11Then Nathan asked Bathsheba,[n] Solomon's mother, "Have you not heard that
Adonijah,[o] the son of Haggith, has become
king, and our lord David knows nothing
about it? 12Now then, let me advise[p] you
how you can save your own life and the
life of your son Solomon. 13Go in to King
David and say to him, 'My lord the king,
did you not swear[q] to me your servant:
"Surely Solomon your son shall be king
after me, and he will sit on my throne"?
Why then has Adonijah become king?'
14While you are still there talking to the
king, I will come in and add my word to
what you have said."
15So Bathsheba went to see the aged
king in his room, where Abishag[r] the Shunammite was attending him. 16Bathsheba
bowed down, prostrating herself before
the king.
"What is it you want?" the king asked.
17She said to him, "My lord, you yourself
swore[s] to me your servant by the LORD your
God: 'Solomon your son shall be king after me, and he will sit on my throne.' 18But
now Adonijah has become king, and you,
my lord the king, do not know about it.
19He has sacrificed[t] great numbers of cattle,
fattened calves, and sheep, and has invit-

1:3 [a] Jos 19:18 **1:5** [b] 2Sa 3:4 [c] 2Sa 15:1 **1:6** [d] 2Sa 3:3-4 **1:7** [e] 1Ki 2:22, 28; 1Ch 11:6 [f] 1Sa 22:20; 2Sa 20:25 **1:8** [g] 2Sa 20:25 [h] 2Sa 8:18 [i] 2Sa 12:1 [j] 1Ki 4:18 [k] 2Sa 23:8 **1:9** [l] 2Sa 17:17 **1:10** [m] 2Sa 12:24 **1:11** [n] 2Sa 12:24 [o] 2Sa 3:4 **1:12** [p] Pr 15:22 **1:13** [q] ver 30; 1Ch 22:9-13 **1:15** [r] ver 1 **1:17** [s] ver 13,30 **1:19** [t] ver 9

[a] 5 Or *charioteers*

1:1 *King David was very old.* A comparison of dates given in 2 Samuel and 1 Kings indicates that David is well over 70 years old as he lies on his deathbed, much older than the average lifespan in the first millennium BC as suggested by the analysis of anthropological remains, though royal inscriptions often indicate that royalty tended to live longer.

1:3 *Abishag, a Shunammite.* Biblical and ancient Near Eastern sources give special attention to the status of women in the royal court. The size and makeup of the king's harem was a measure of his power and prestige. In this case, the beautiful Abishag slept next to the king, but was never added to his harem. Yet, as a consequence of this intimate association with the king, any interest in marrying her would be interpreted as a challenge to the throne (cf. 2:13–25). It is noteworthy that Abishag was from Shunem in Galilee, not far from Nazareth. Her selection may have been a way to maintain strong ties between the Judahite monarch and the rival northern tribes.

1:5 *I will be king.* Because Adonijah was the next in line after Absalom's death, his statement was in keeping with the customs of Israel and its neighbors. Legal documents dating to the second millennium BC from places such as Mari, Nuzi and Assyria stipulate that the oldest surviving son always received the privileged position. Likewise, the Israelites were expected to give the firstborn son a double portion of property and to establish him as the head of the household (see the article "Inheritance Rights and Birthrights," p. 62). This practice, which was the norm for households and royal courts alike, served to preserve family resources and regulate generational transitions. Rank and status were assigned by societal norms rather than the father's love for a particular wife or son. Many Biblical characters did not adhere to this tradition, but examination of the passage's ancient context clearly shows that Adonijah and some of the king's advisors anticipated that David would. *he got chariots and horses ready, with fifty men to run ahead of him.* See note on 2Sa 18:23.

1:7–8 *gave him their support ... did not join.* Two factions emerged in the court because of David's failure to follow cultural norms and announce a successor when he became incapacitated. The failure of David's special guard to join Adonijah's followers was a clear indicator that David had yet to act. Adonijah's entrance with chariots and a royal guard (v. 5) not only increased the tension between the king and traditional institutions, but perhaps represented a premature appeal to power by force that violated religious and cultural protocols (though it is possible that an heir to the throne would normally enjoy such perquisites). David's inaction therefore emboldened both parties and created a national crisis with rifts in the military, the priesthood and the prophets.

1:9 *Adonijah then sacrificed sheep, cattle and fattened calves at the Stone of Zoheleth near En Rogel.* The religious pretext for the sacrifice is unclear, though it likely was intended to initiate a feast that would seal an alliance between those gathered. Adonijah achieved political relations with the Israelite aristocracy by inviting them to his gathering (v. 25). Conversely, he did not invite his own brother Solomon or the opposing prophet, priest and commander (Nathan, Zadok and Benaiah, v. 10).

ed all the king's sons, Abiathar the priest
and Joab the commander of the army, but
he has not invited Solomon your servant.
20My lord the king, the eyes of all Israel are
on you, to learn from you who will sit on
the throne of my lord the king after him.
21Otherwise, as soon as my lord the king
is laid to rest[u] with his ancestors, I and my
son Solomon will be treated as criminals."
22While she was still speaking with the
king, Nathan the prophet arrived. 23And
the king was told, "Nathan the prophet
is here." So he went before the king and
bowed with his face to the ground.
24Nathan said, "Have you, my lord the
king, declared that Adonijah shall be king
after you, and that he will sit on your
throne? 25Today he has gone down and
sacrificed great numbers of cattle, fattened
calves, and sheep. He has invited all the
king's sons, the commanders of the army
and Abiathar the priest. Right now they
are eating and drinking with him and saying, 'Long live King Adonijah!' 26But me
your servant, and Zadok the priest, and
Benaiah son of Jehoiada, and your servant
Solomon he did not invite.[v] 27Is this something my lord the king has done without
letting his servants know who should sit
on the throne of my lord the king after
him?"

David Makes Solomon King

1:28-53pp — 1Ch 29:21-25

28Then King David said, "Call in Bathsheba." So she came into the king's presence and stood before him.
29The king then took an oath: "As surely
as the LORD lives, who has delivered me
out of every trouble,[w] 30I will surely carry
out this very day what I swore[x] to you by
the LORD, the God of Israel: Solomon your
son shall be king after me, and he will sit
on my throne in my place."
31Then Bathsheba bowed down with her
face to the ground, prostrating herself before the king, and said, "May my lord King
David live forever!"
32King David said, "Call in Zadok the
priest, Nathan the prophet and Benaiah
son of Jehoiada." When they came before
the king, 33he said to them: "Take your
lord's servants with you and have Solomon my son mount my own mule[y] and
take him down to Gihon.[z] 34There have
Zadok the priest and Nathan the prophet anoint[a] him king over Israel. Blow the
trumpet[b] and shout, 'Long live King Solomon!' 35Then you are to go up with him,
and he is to come and sit on my throne
and reign in my place. I have appointed
him ruler over Israel and Judah."
36Benaiah son of Jehoiada answered the
king, "Amen! May the LORD, the God of
my lord the king, so declare it. 37As the
LORD was with my lord the king, so may
he be with[c] Solomon to make his throne
even greater[d] than the throne of my lord
King David!"
38So Zadok[e] the priest, Nathan the
prophet, Benaiah son of Jehoiada, the Kerethites[f] and the Pelethites went down and
had Solomon mount King David's mule,
and they escorted him to Gihon.[g] 39Zadok
the priest took the horn of oil[h] from the
sacred tent and anointed Solomon. Then
they sounded the trumpet and all the people shouted,[i] "Long live King Solomon!"
40And all the people went up after him,
playing pipes and rejoicing greatly, so that
the ground shook with the sound.
41Adonijah and all the guests who were
with him heard it as they were finishing
their feast. On hearing the sound of the

1:21 [u] Dt 31:16; 1Ki 2:10 **1:26** [v] ver 8, 10 **1:29** [w] 2Sa 4:9 **1:30** [x] ver 13, 17
1:33 [y] 2Sa 20:6-7 [z] 2Ch 32:30; 33:14 **1:34** [a] 1Sa 10:1; 16:3, 12; 1Ki 19:16; 2Ki 9:3, 13 [b] ver 25; 2Sa 5:3; 15:10 **1:37** [c] Jos 1:5, 17; 1Sa 20:13 [d] ver 47 **1:38** [e] ver 8 [f] 2Sa 8:18 [g] ver 33 **1:39** [h] Ex 30:23-32; Ps 89:20 [i] ver 34; 1Sa 10:24

1:21 *I and my son Solomon will be treated as criminals.* Coup attempts were common in the ancient Near East. They inevitably led to bloodshed. A good example is the ascension of Esarhaddon, an Assyrian king in 680 BC. Rival siblings killed his father and disputed his claim to the throne. Upon his victory he meted out collective punishment by killing the rebels, their aides and their male descendants. In light of the ancient Near Eastern background, Bathsheba's concern is an understatement.
1:33 *have Solomon my son mount my own mule and take him down to Gihon.* David's quick action rendered Adonijah's feast an act of rebellion in practice and not just theory. He handed to Solomon several overt symbols of kingship, including his personal means of transportation as well as the go-ahead for anointing him in a public declaration at one of the royal city's main landmarks. Mules were the preferred means of transportation among royalty, a fact corroborated by second-millennium BC letters from the kingdom of Mari.
1:34 *anoint him king over Israel.* See notes on 1Sa 2:10; 10:1. Typically it was the prophet's role to anoint a king. The unusual participation of the priest may have been a response to the support that Adonijah received from the rival priest, Abiathar. Priestly participation may also represent the completion of David's work to establish Jerusalem (now also known as Zion with its preexisting Jebusite traditions) as the religious and political capital of Yahweh's people (2Sa 7). Note how the priest personally brought the horn of oil specifically from the tent (v. 39), Yahweh's original residence in the holy city.
1:38 *the Kerethites and the Pelethites.* These two groups are mentioned together so often in the Bible that it is reasonable to suggest a common ethnic and geographic origin. They are described as David's royal guard. By hiring foreigners for this service he ensured that his personal security was not dependent on Israelites who could become involved with persons or causes opposed to the king. Like many other attributes of David and Solomon's kingdom, this practice is well attested in the Near East from the days of Abraham to the days of Jesus. The Code of Hammurapi and other Mesopotamian texts refer to reliable, well-paid mercenaries. See notes on 1Sa 27:2; 2Sa 8:18.
1:40 *playing pipes and rejoicing greatly.* See note on 1Sa 18:6.
1:41 *What's the meaning of all the noise in the city?* Adonijah's

trumpet, Joab asked, "What's the meaning
of all the noise in the city?"
42 Even as he was speaking, Jonathan[j]
son of Abiathar the priest arrived. Adonijah said, "Come in. A worthy man like you
must be bringing good news."[k]
43 "Not at all!" Jonathan answered. "Our
lord King David has made Solomon king.
44 The king has sent with him Zadok the
priest, Nathan the prophet, Benaiah son
of Jehoiada, the Kerethites and the Pelethites, and they have put him on the king's
mule, 45 and Zadok the priest and Nathan
the prophet have anointed him king at Gihon. From there they have gone up cheering, and the city resounds[l] with it. That's
the noise you hear. 46 Moreover, Solomon
has taken his seat on the royal throne.
47 Also, the royal officials have come to
congratulate our lord King David, saying,
'May your God make Solomon's name
more famous than yours and his throne
greater[m] than yours!' And the king bowed
in worship on his bed 48 and said, 'Praise
be to the LORD, the God of Israel, who has
allowed my eyes to see a successor[n] on my
throne today.'"
49 At this, all Adonijah's guests rose in
alarm and dispersed. 50 But Adonijah, in
fear of Solomon, went and took hold of
the horns[o] of the altar. 51 Then Solomon
was told, "Adonijah is afraid of King Solomon and is clinging to the horns of the
altar. He says, 'Let King Solomon swear to
me today that he will not put his servant
to death with the sword.'"
52 Solomon replied, "If he shows himself
to be worthy, not a hair[p] of his head will
fall to the ground; but if evil is found in
him, he will die." 53 Then King Solomon
sent men, and they brought him down
from the altar. And Adonijah came and
bowed down to King Solomon, and Solomon said, "Go to your home."

David's Charge to Solomon

2:10-12pp — 1Ch 29:26-28

2 When the time drew near for David
to die,[q] he gave a charge to Solomon
his son.
2 "I am about to go the way of all the
earth,"[r] he said. "So be strong,[s] act like
a man, 3 and observe[t] what the LORD your
God requires: Walk in obedience to him,
and keep his decrees and commands, his
laws and regulations, as written in the
Law of Moses. Do this so that you may
prosper[u] in all you do and wherever you
go 4 and that the LORD may keep his promise[v] to me: 'If your descendants watch
how they live, and if they walk faithfully[w]
before me with all their heart and soul,
you will never fail to have a successor on
the throne of Israel.'
5 "Now you yourself know what Joab[x]
son of Zeruiah did to me — what he did
to the two commanders of Israel's armies,
Abner[y] son of Ner and Amasa[z] son of Jether. He killed them, shedding their blood
in peacetime as if in battle, and with that
blood he stained the belt around his waist
and the sandals on his feet. 6 Deal with
him according to your wisdom,[a] but do
not let his gray head go down to the grave
in peace.
7 "But show kindness to the sons of Barzillai[b] of Gilead and let them be among
those who eat at your table.[c] They stood
by me when I fled from your brother Absalom.

1:42 [j] 2Sa 15:27, 36 [k] 2Sa 18:26 **1:45** [l] ver 40 **1:47** [m] ver 37; Ge 47:31 **1:48** [n] 2Sa 7:12; 1Ki 3:6 **1:50** [o] 1Ki 2:28 **1:52** [p] 1Sa 14:45; 2Sa 14:11

2:1 [q] Ge 47:29; Dt 31:14 **2:2** [r] Jos 23:14 [s] Dt 31:7,23; Jos 1:6 **2:3** [t] Dt 17:14-20; Jos 1:7 [u] 1Ch 22:13 **2:4** [v] 2Sa 7:13, 25; 1Ki 8:25 [w] 2Ki 20:3; Ps 132:12 **2:5** [x] 2Sa 2:18; 18:5, 12, 14 [y] 2Sa 3:27 [z] 2Sa 20:10 **2:6** [a] ver 9 **2:7** [b] 2Sa 17:27; 19:31-39 [c] 2Sa 9:7

entire company at En Rogel heard the commotion and the trumpet from the Gihon spring, because they were less than a mile (0.5 kilometers) away, around a turn in the Kidron Valley. The swiftness of events and the messengers was due to the close proximity of the two groups, despite their inability to see one another.

1:50 *took hold of the horns of the altar.* Though horned altars are ubiquitous in the ancient world, the purpose of the horns protruding from the altar is not known. Adonijah went to this location because, according to Biblical tradition, it was a place of asylum for those who inadvertently committed murder (Ex 21:13 – 14). Although he had not killed anyone, Adonijah expected to be executed for his actions and apparently thought the horns of the altar would be the best place from which to beg for his life and vow allegiance. This form of seeking asylum is so far unattested in the rest of the ancient Near East.

1:52 The expectation was that Adonijah would be killed for his insurrection. As David had done after Absalom's revolt (2Sa 15 – 16), Solomon chooses to spare the usurper. The uncustomary nature of this action is reminiscent of an edict issued by King Telipinu of the Hittite Empire in 1500 BC. In response to decades of brutal fighting over the throne, Telipinu implemented a prohibition on the killing of political rivals and usurpers, regardless of social standing.

2:2 – 9 A remarkably similar set of concerns is found in a treatise on kingship delivered by an aging Egyptian pharaoh during the late third millennium BC. Besides a summary of King Merikare's reign, this text "lays down all the laws of kingship." It advises the successor on methods of ethically suppressing rebellion, maintaining good relations with the aristocracy and commoners alike and dealing justly in all situations. Comparative compositions such as this one can increase our appreciation for the pressing issues that David and Solomon faced during their reigns and the judicious manner in which they responded.

2:5 *with that blood he stained the belt ... and the sandals.* Joab twice murdered his political rivals against David's intentions. The stability of the kingdom requires that he be punished as a criminal. *belt ... sandals.* Do not refer to military gear and may be intended to emphasize that these killings took place in circumstances other than combat.

2:7 *let them ... eat at your table.* In the ancient Near East, eating together was a symbol of friendship and cooperation that carried with it the obligation to protect one other and provide hospitality. In addition to these cultural

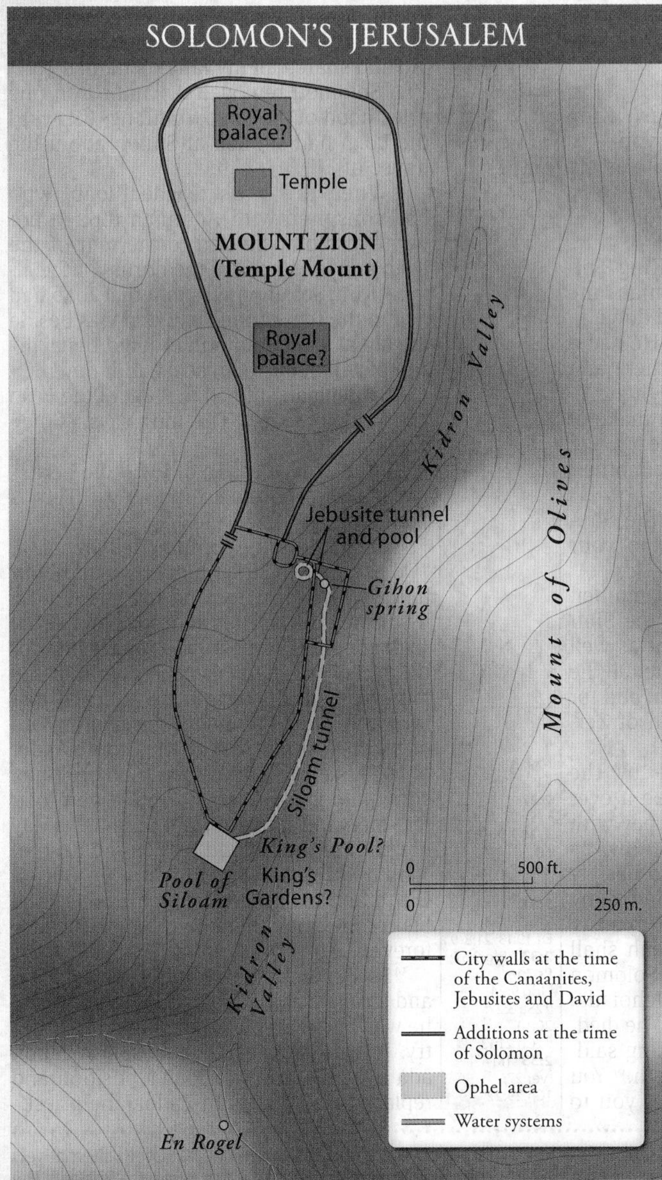

c. 950 BC

Solomon extended the city northward from the original site and there built his magnificent temple.

His royal residence was nearby, but its exact location is unknown.

8"And remember, you have
with you Shimei[d] son of Gera,
the Benjamite from Bahurim,
who called down bitter curses
on me the day I went to Mahanaim. When he came down
to meet me at the Jordan, I
swore[e] to him by the LORD: 'I
will not put you to death by
the sword.' 9But now, do not
consider him innocent. You
are a man of wisdom;[f] you
will know what to do to him.
Bring his gray head down to
the grave in blood."
10Then David rested with
his ancestors and was buried[g] in the City of David.[h]
11He had reigned[i] forty years
over Israel — seven years in
Hebron and thirty-three in Jerusalem. 12So Solomon sat on
the throne[j] of his father David, and his rule was firmly
established.[k]

Solomon's Throne Established

13Now Adonijah, the son of
Haggith, went to Bathsheba,
Solomon's mother. Bathsheba asked him, "Do you come
peacefully?"[l]
He answered, "Yes, peace-
fully." 14Then he added, "I
have something to say to you."
"You may say it," she replied.
15"As you know," he said,
"the kingdom was mine. All
Israel looked to me as their
king. But things changed, and
the kingdom has gone to my

2:8 [d] 2Sa 16:5-13 [e] 2Sa 19:18-23
2:9 [f] ver 6 **2:10** [g] Ac 2:29; 13:36 [h] 2Sa 5:7
2:11 [i] 2Sa 5:4,5 **2:12** [j] 1Ch 29:23 [k] 2Ch 1:1
2:13 [l] 1Sa 16:4

expectations, those who sat at the king's table were considered special friends to be provided for, protected and housed near the king's palace. A lively depiction of the king's banquet table is preserved on a wall relief from Ashurbanipal's palace in Nineveh.

2:10 *rested with his ancestors.* Conceptually indicates that a person has joined the ancestors in the netherworld. It is more tangibly expressed in the common burial practices that interred each individual in a family tomb wherein they literally rested with their ancestors (see notes on Ge 23:4; 25:8). We have no reason to assume that David's ancestors were buried in Jerusalem ("the City of David"), so here the expression reflects the focus on joining his deceased ancestors. The royal tombs of David and his progeny were the only burials to be located within the confines of Jerusalem. *buried.* Kings from Macedonia to Egypt built lavish tombs, but Israelite burials were more modest, rock-cut chambers whose features emulated the foyers, doorways and cornices of contemporary palaces. The tomb was known as late as the first century AD (cf. Ac 2:29), but the modern-day "David's tomb" is a much later construction on a nearby hill erroneously ascribed to David by Crusader pilgrims.

brother; for it has come to him from the
LORD. 16Now I have one request to make
of you. Do not refuse me."
"You may make it," she said.
17So he continued, "Please ask King
Solomon—he will not refuse you—to
give me Abishag[m] the Shunammite as my
wife."
18"Very well," Bathsheba replied, "I will
speak to the king for you."
19When Bathsheba went to King Solomon to speak to him for Adonijah, the
king stood up to meet her, bowed down to
her and sat down on his throne. He had a
throne brought for the king's mother,[n] and
she sat down at his right hand.[o]
20"I have one small request to make of
you," she said. "Do not refuse me."
The king replied, "Make it, my mother;
I will not refuse you."
21So she said, "Let Abishag[p] the Shunammite be given in marriage to your
brother Adonijah."
22King Solomon answered his mother,
"Why do you request Abishag[q] the Shunammite for Adonijah? You might as well
request the kingdom for him—after all, he
is my older brother[r]—yes, for him and for
Abiathar the priest and Joab son of Zeruiah!"
23Then King Solomon swore by the
LORD: "May God deal with me, be it ever
so severely,[s] if Adonijah does not pay with
his life for this request! 24And now, as
surely as the LORD lives—he who has established me securely on the throne of my
father David and has founded a dynasty
for me as he promised[t]—Adonijah shall
be put to death today!" 25So King Solomon
gave orders to Benaiah[u] son of Jehoiada,
and he struck down Adonijah and he died.
26To Abiathar[v] the priest the king said,
"Go back to your fields in Anathoth.[w] You
deserve to die, but I will not put you to
death now, because you carried the ark[x]
of the Sovereign LORD before my father David and shared all my father's hardships."[y]
27So Solomon removed Abiathar from the
priesthood of the LORD, fulfilling[z] the word
the LORD had spoken at Shiloh about the
house of Eli.
28When the news reached Joab, who
had conspired with Adonijah though not
with Absalom, he fled to the tent of the
LORD and took hold of the horns[a] of the altar. 29King Solomon was told that Joab had
fled to the tent of the LORD and was beside
the altar. Then Solomon ordered Benaiah[b]
son of Jehoiada, "Go, strike him down!"
30So Benaiah entered the tent of the LORD
and said to Joab, "The king says, 'Come
out!'[c]"
But he answered, "No, I will die here."
Benaiah reported to the king, "This is
how Joab answered me."
31Then the king commanded Benaiah,
"Do as he says. Strike him down and bury
him, and so clear me and my whole family of the guilt of the innocent blood[d] that
Joab shed. 32The LORD will repay[e] him for
the blood he shed,[f] because without my
father David knowing it he attacked two
men and killed them with the sword. Both
of them—Abner son of Ner, commander
of Israel's army, and Amasa[g] son of Jether,
commander of Judah's army—were better[h] men and more upright than he. 33May
the guilt of their blood rest on the head of
Joab and his descendants forever. But on
David and his descendants, his house and
his throne, may there be the LORD's peace
forever."
34So Benaiah son of Jehoiada went up
and struck down Joab and killed him, and
he was buried at his home out in the country. 35The king put Benaiah[i] son of Jehoiada over the army in Joab's position and
replaced Abiathar with Zadok[j] the priest.

2:17 [m] 1Ki 1:3 **2:19** [n] 1Ki 15:13 [o] Ps 45:9 **2:21** [p] 1Ki 1:3 **2:22** [q] 2Sa 12:8; 1Ki 1:3 [r] 1Ch 3:2 **2:23** [s] Ru 1:17 **2:24** [t] 2Sa 7:11; 1Ch 22:10 **2:25** [u] 2Sa 8:18 **2:26** [v] 1Sa 22:20 [w] Jos 21:18
[x] 2Sa 15:24 [y] 1Sa 23:6 **2:27** [z] 1Sa 2:27-36 **2:28** [a] 1Ki 1:7, 50 **2:29** [b] ver 25 **2:30** [c] Ex 21:14 **2:31** [d] Nu 35:33; Dt 19:13; 21:8-9 **2:32** [e] Jdg 9:57; Ps 7:16 [f] Jdg 9:24 [g] 2Sa 3:27; 20:10 [h] 2Ch 21:13 **2:35** [i] 1Ki 4:4 [j] ver 27; 1Ch 29:22

2:17 *give me Abishag the Shunammite as my wife.* Adonijah's request to marry Abishag and Solomon's harsh response must be understood against the backdrop of Abishag's ambiguous status (1:3–4) and the revolt of Absalom in 2Sa 16:21–22. In the ancient world, control of the harem accompanied accession to the throne. A public appearance with the king's concubines was a political statement of control. Records from Ugarit, e.g., indicate a similar process in Canaanite culture. Although Abishag had never been an official concubine of David, her close association with him meant that her marriage to Solomon's political rival might be interpreted by the populace as an acquisition of power and a challenge to the new king. In light of the fight over succession, Solomon had no other choice but to interpret Adonijah's request as a rebellious act (v. 22), and thus Solomon eliminated him (v. 25).

2:19 *a throne ... for the king's mother.* There are three different kinds of queens in the ancient world. The first includes primary wives of the king (e.g., Esther), who were sometimes treated as ornaments, but could alternatively be delegated power (as is later the case with Jezebel). The second is the wife or mother of the king who assumes his place when he dies, such as Athaliah of Judah or Hatshepsut of Egypt. The third is the "queen mother," whose royal husband has died but who continues to hold influence over his successor, such as Maakah of Judah, Sammuramat of Assyria and, in this context, Bathsheba. The amount of power and influence would have depended upon the personality of the individual. The queen mother is named for nearly every king in Judah, but not for those of Israel, suggesting that the queen mother was an especially important figure in the southern kingdom.

2:34 *Joab ... was buried at his home.* Despite the guilt assigned to him (see 2:5 and note), Joab was given a proper burial in his family tomb at the edge of the wilderness near Bethlehem. There he would rest secure with his ancestors on the family plot. The shame and eternal curse of an improper burial would be too severe for even Joab's crimes.

36Then the king sent for Shimei[k] and
said to him, "Build yourself a house in
Jerusalem and live there, but do not go
anywhere else. 37The day you leave and
cross the Kidron Valley,[l] you can be sure
you will die; your blood will be on your
own head."[m]
38Shimei answered the king, "What you
say is good. Your servant will do as my
lord the king has said." And Shimei stayed
in Jerusalem for a long time.
39But three years later, two of Shimei's
slaves ran off to Achish[n] son of Maakah,
king of Gath, and Shimei was told, "Your
slaves are in Gath." 40At this, he saddled
his donkey and went to Achish at Gath in
search of his slaves. So Shimei went away
and brought the slaves back from Gath.
41When Solomon was told that Shimei had gone from Jerusalem to Gath and
had returned, 42the king summoned Shimei and said to him, "Did I not make you
swear by the LORD and warn you, 'On the
day you leave to go anywhere else, you
can be sure you will die'? At that time you
said to me, 'What you say is good. I will
obey.' 43Why then did you not keep your
oath to the LORD and obey the command
I gave you?"
44The king also said to Shimei, "You
know in your heart all the wrong[o] you did
to my father David. Now the LORD will repay you for your wrongdoing. 45But King
Solomon will be blessed, and David's
throne will remain secure[p] before the LORD
forever."
46Then the king gave the order to Benaiah son of Jehoiada, and he went out and
struck Shimei down and he died.
The kingdom was now established[q] in
Solomon's hands.

Solomon Asks for Wisdom

3:4-15pp — 2Ch 1:2-13

3 Solomon made an alliance with Pharaoh king of Egypt and married[r] his
daughter.[s] He brought her to the City of David[t] until he finished building his palace[u]
and the temple of the LORD, and the wall
around Jerusalem. 2The people, however,
were still sacrificing at the high places,[v] because a temple had not yet been built for
the Name of the LORD. 3Solomon showed
his love[w] for the LORD by walking according
to the instructions[x] given him by his father
David, except that he offered sacrifices and
burned incense on the high places.
4The king went to Gibeon[y] to offer sacrifices, for that was the most important high
place, and Solomon offered a thousand
burnt offerings on that altar. 5At Gibeon
the LORD appeared[z] to Solomon during the
night in a dream,[a] and God said, "Ask for
whatever you want me to give you."

2:36 [k] ver 8; 2Sa 16:5 **2:37** [l] 2Sa 15:23 [m] Lev 20:9; Jos 2:19; 2Sa 1:16 **2:39** [n] 1Sa 27:2 **2:44** [o] 1Sa 25:39; 2Sa 16:5-13; Eze 17:19 **2:45** [p] 2Sa 7:13; Pr 25:5 **2:46** [q] ver 12; 2Ch 1:1 **3:1** [r] 1Ki 7:8 [s] 1Ki 9:24 [t] 2Sa 5:7 [u] 1Ki 7:1; 9:15, 19 **3:2** [v] Lev 17:3-5; Dt 12:2, 4-5; 1Ki 22:43 **3:3** [w] Dt 6:5; Ps 31:23; 1Co 8:3 [x] 1Ki 2:3; 9:4; 11:4, 6, 38 **3:4** [y] 1Ch 16:39 **3:5** [z] 1Ki 9:2 [a] Nu 12:6; Mt 1:20

2:39 *two of Shimei's slaves ran off to Achish.* Some Near Eastern states in Solomon's day had treaties that forbade the harboring of runaway slaves or political fugitives. For example: "If a fugitive flees from Hatti [and goes to the land of Mittanni, the Mittanians shall seize and] return him." Shimei probably expected the cooperation of Achish when his slaves were discovered there. Philistia lay to the west of Judah and was connected to the highlands by way of several ridge routes. During this period, unlike the prior decades, the border was quiet and Shimei likely could pass into the Philistine pentapolis unhindered.
3:1 *Solomon made an alliance with Pharaoh king of Egypt and married his daughter.* In antiquity, treaties and alliances between monarchs were often consummated through an exchange of daughters as wives. Israel's new dominance in the region led to a series of alliances and hence a large number of wives for Solomon (11:1). The marriage to Pharaoh's daughter was significant because the powerful Egyptians had seldom been in a weak enough position to derive benefit from giving their women to other monarchs. In keeping with this prestigious acquisition, Solomon built his bride a palace (7:8). The dowry included the site of Gezer (9:16), located near Joppa at an important crossroads between the road into Jerusalem and the international coastal route traversing the coast of Israel from Egypt to Syria and then inland to Mesopotamia. Archaeological excavations at Gezer have unearthed a large Israelite city wall, gate, and other structures that Solomon built at this time (9:15,17). During this period of waning Egyptian influence, the Twenty-First Dynasty ruled Egypt from Tanis in the delta. When the dates of Solomon (970 – 930 BC) are correlated with Egyptian chronology, Siamun emerges as the pharaoh who forged this alliance with Solomon. Effectively, in a rare anomaly of history, the Israelites under Solomon displaced the mighty pharaoh's hegemony of the southern Levant and its all-important trade routes. Indeed, only a few decades later the Egyptians attempted to disrupt Israelite supremacy in the region through the campaign of Pharaoh Shishak in 927 BC.
3:2 *high places.* Throughout their history, the people of Israel navigated the fine line between adapting local customs and preserving their distinctive religious and ethnic identity rooted in Yahweh. The comparison between Israelite worship atop the *bamah* (Hebrew for "high place," vv. 2 – 4) and that of Ugaritic, Canaanite and Akkadian cultures illustrates this tension. When the Israelites entered the promised land, non-Israelite high places were to be destroyed (Nu 33:52; Dt 7:5), whereas Israelite ones would be tolerated until such time that the temple was completed. It seems that problems did not arise from the *bamah* itself, which was merely an enclosed, stepped platform for worship and sacrifice, but rather from the temptation to adopt local pagan belief and practice.
3:4 *offered a thousand burnt offerings.* Such a large number of offerings must represent a momentous event in Israel's history (cf. 8:63). Although this number sounds excessive, comparable numbers occur in other ancient Near Eastern texts, and in this case the Hebrew verb for "offered" can mean ongoing sacrifice over time. Some scholars compare this passage to Dt 1:11, in which the number "a thousand" appears to convey the idea of "a great many."
3:5 *At Gibeon the LORD appeared to Solomon.* The high place at Gibeon is a site of legitimate worship (see note on 2Ch 1:3). *dream.* Dream narratives are common in ancient

6 Solomon answered, "You have shown
great kindness to your servant, my father
David, because he was faithful[b] to you
and righteous and upright in heart. You
have continued this great kindness to him
and have given him a son[c] to sit on his
throne this very day.
7 "Now, LORD my God, you have made
your servant king in place of my father
David. But I am only a little child[d] and
do not know how to carry out my duties.
8 Your servant is here among the people
you have chosen,[e] a great people, too numerous to count or number.[f] 9 So give your
servant a discerning[g] heart to govern your
people and to distinguish[h] between right
and wrong. For who is able[i] to govern this
great people of yours?"
10 The LORD was pleased that Solomon
had asked for this. 11 So God said to him,
"Since you have asked[j] for this and not for
long life or wealth for yourself, nor have
asked for the death of your enemies but
for discernment in administering justice,
12 I will do what you have asked.[k] I will
give you a wise[l] and discerning heart, so
that there will never have been anyone
like you, nor will there ever be. 13 Moreover, I will give you what you have not[m]
asked for—both wealth and honor[n]—so
that in your lifetime you will have no
equal[o] among kings. 14 And if you walk[p]
in obedience to me and keep my decrees
and commands as David your father did,
I will give you a long life."[q] 15 Then Solomon awoke[r]—and he realized it had been
a dream.
He returned to Jerusalem, stood before
the ark of the LORD's covenant and sacrificed burnt offerings[s] and fellowship of-

3:6 [b] 1Ki 2:4; 9:4 [c] 1Ki 1:48 **3:7** [d] Nu 27:17; 1Ch 29:1 **3:8** [e] Dt 7:6 [f] Ge 15:5 **3:9** [g] 2Sa 14:17; Jas 1:5 [h] Pr 2:3-9; Heb 5:14 [i] Ps 72:1-2 **3:11** [j] Jas 4:3 **3:12** [k] 1Jn 5:14-15 [l] 1Ki 4:29, 30, 31; 5:12; 10:23; Ecc 1:16 **3:13** [m] Mt 6:33; Eph 3:20 [n] 1Ki 4:21-24; Pr 3:1-2, 16 [o] 1Ki 10:23 **3:14** [p] ver 6; Pr 3:1-2, 16 [q] Ps 61:6; 91:16 **3:15** [r] Ge 41:7 [s] 1Ki 8:65 [t] Mk 6:21 [u] Est 1:3, 9; Da 5:1 **3:26** [v] Ge 43:30; Isa 49:15; Jer 31:20; Hos 11:8

ferings.[t] Then he gave a feast[u] for all his
court.

A Wise Ruling

16 Now two prostitutes came to the king
and stood before him. 17 One of them said,
"Pardon me, my lord. This woman and I
live in the same house, and I had a baby
while she was there with me. 18 The third
day after my child was born, this woman
also had a baby. We were alone; there was
no one in the house but the two of us.
19 "During the night this woman's son
died because she lay on him. 20 So she got
up in the middle of the night and took
my son from my side while I your servant
was asleep. She put him by her breast and
put her dead son by my breast. 21 The next
morning, I got up to nurse my son—and
he was dead! But when I looked at him
closely in the morning light, I saw that it
wasn't the son I had borne."
22 The other woman said, "No! The living one is my son; the dead one is yours."
But the first one insisted, "No! The dead
one is yours; the living one is mine." And
so they argued before the king.
23 The king said, "This one says, 'My son
is alive and your son is dead,' while that
one says, 'No! Your son is dead and mine
is alive.'"
24 Then the king said, "Bring me a
sword." So they brought a sword for the
king. 25 He then gave an order: "Cut the
living child in two and give half to one and
half to the other."
26 The woman whose son was alive was
deeply moved[v] out of love for her son and
said to the king, "Please, my lord, give her
the living baby! Don't kill him!"

Near Eastern literature, especially among kings facing new challenges. Thus, King Gudea of Mesopotamia (third millennium BC) received instruction to build a temple to Ningirsu and place the statues of the deity inside, the Egyptian pharaoh Netjer-er-khet was warned of impending famine, Amenhotep II received battle plans from the god Amon, and King Kirta of Ugarit gained instruction for conquest and personal restoration from the deity. See the article "Dreams and Temple Building in the Ancient Near East," p. 718.

3:7 *you have made your servant king.* Like David before him, Solomon was "sponsored" by Yahweh. One text among many that portrays divine backing for a king is the monumental inscription from Tell Dan in which an Aramean king boasts of his god, Hadad, making him king and "going forth before" him. The kings of Israel spoke of their divinely sponsored acts with the same conventions used by monarchs in surrounding lands. *little child.* Solomon is an adult at this time, but he compares himself to a child, because he feels that he lacks the maturity that comes from experience, which would help him be an effective ruler.

3:12 *a wise and discerning heart.* Solomon's appeal for wisdom and the LORD's promise of wealth and long life could be taken from the pages of any Near Eastern king. Note, e.g., the prayer for the Assyrian king Tukulti-Ninurta I, a century before Solomon: "May Assur give you authority, obedience, concord, justice, and peace!" See note on 2Ch 1:10. At the same time, Solomon's request is commendable because it would not have been unusual for a king to request wealth and military success from the god, as Zimri-Lim of Mari is recorded to have done many centuries earlier. In the royal ideology of the ancient world, the highest expectation of a king was that he be wise and just, and Solomon's request reflects this lofty aspiration.

3:16 *prostitutes.* Brothels and prostitutes were a part of everyday life in the Biblical and ancient Near Eastern world. Solomon's judicious handling of the two prostitutes indicates that even persons of the lowest stature could gain an audience with the king. The Mesopotamian Lipit-Ishtar Code of the early second millennium BC ensures that child-bearing prostitutes be guaranteed provision, but not the status of wife. The Code of Hammurapi considers prostitutes to be unmarriageable, but possessing limited rights. The stories of Rahab (Jos 2) and Tamar (Ge 38) convey the relative freedom that prostitutes had in ancient Israel.

But the other said, "Neither I nor you
shall have him. Cut him in two!"
27 Then the king gave his ruling: "Give
the living baby to the first woman. Do not
kill him; she is his mother."
28 When all Israel heard the verdict the
king had given, they held the king in awe,
because they saw that he had wisdom[w]
from God to administer justice.

Solomon's Officials and Governors

4 So King Solomon ruled over all Israel.
2 And these were his chief officials:

Azariah[x] son of Zadok—the priest;
3 Elihoreph and Ahijah, sons of Shisha—secretaries;
Jehoshaphat[y] son of Ahilud—recorder;
4 Benaiah[z] son of Jehoiada—commander in chief;
Zadok[a] and Abiathar—priests;
5 Azariah son of Nathan—in charge of the district governors;
Zabud son of Nathan—a priest and adviser to the king;
6 Ahishar—palace administrator;
Adoniram son of Abda—in charge of forced labor.

7 Solomon had twelve district governors
over all Israel, who supplied provisions for
the king and the royal household. Each
one had to provide supplies for one month
in the year. 8 These are their names:

Ben-Hur—in the hill country[b] of Ephraim;
9 Ben-Deker—in Makaz, Shaalbim,[c] Beth Shemesh[d] and Elon Bethhanan;
10 Ben-Hesed—in Arubboth (Sokoh[e] and all the land of Hepher[f] were his);
11 Ben-Abinadab—in Naphoth Dor[g] (he was married to Taphath daughter of Solomon);
12 Baana son of Ahilud—in Taanach and Megiddo, and in all of Beth Shan[h] next to Zarethan[i] below Jezreel, from Beth Shan to Abel Meholah[j] across to Jokmeam;[k]
13 Ben-Geber—in Ramoth Gilead (the settlements of Jair[l] son of Manasseh in Gilead were his, as well as the region of Argob in Bashan and its sixty large walled cities[m] with bronze gate bars);
14 Ahinadab son of Iddo—in Mahanaim;[n]
15 Ahimaaz[o]—in Naphtali (he had married Basemath daughter of Solomon);
16 Baana son of Hushai[p]—in Asher and in Aloth;
17 Jehoshaphat son of Paruah—in Issachar;
18 Shimei[q] son of Ela—in Benjamin;
19 Geber son of Uri—in Gilead (the country of Sihon king of the Amorites

3:28 [w] ver 9, 11-12; Col 2:3 **4:2** [x] 1Ch 6:10 **4:3** [y] 2Sa 8:16 **4:4** [z] 1Ki 2:35 [a] 1Ki 2:27 **4:8** [b] Jos 24:33 **4:9** [c] Jdg 1:35 [d] Jos 21:16 **4:10** [e] Jos 15:35 [f] Jos 12:17 **4:11** [g] Jos 11:2 **4:12** [h] Jos 17:11; Jdg 5:19 [i] Jos 3:16 [j] 1Ki 19:16 [k] 1Ch 6:68 **4:13** [l] Nu 32:41 [m] Dt 3:4 **4:14** [n] Jos 13:26 **4:15** [o] 2Sa 15:27 **4:16** [p] 2Sa 15:32 **4:18** [q] 1Ki 1:8

3:28 *wisdom from God to administer justice.* One of the most important ways that wisdom is demonstrated is in a keen understanding of human nature. This is exactly what Solomon demonstrates here. The ideal king is also a fair and consistent judge, as Solomon is shown to be in this passage. He is in good company, as kings of the entire Near East are depicted in similar ways in law codes and monument inscriptions. A representative example is Hammurapi of Babylon, "whose deeds are pleasing to the goddess Ishtar ... who proclaims the truth, who guides the population properly, who restores its benevolent protective spirit to the city of Assur." As the Bible attributes Solomon's discernment to Yahweh, so this Babylonian law code credits its patron deity with wisdom and sound judgment. The Assyrian king Sargon credited the gods Ea and Belet-ili with making him the wisest ruler in the world, and Ashurbanipal takes pride in his great learning and wisdom, as well as technical knowledge and ability to debate the learned, courtesy of Adad and Shamash. See note on 2Ch 1:10.

4:1 – 6 Under Solomon, the kingdom of Israel became a small-scale empire that required new organization. The changes can be seen through the proliferation of titles and the increased number of royal officials from the time of David's reign through the latter part of Solomon's reign. The empires of the Near East required large bureaucracies, and it is no surprise that at the height of Israel's fortune Solomon required the same. The names of many officials can be found on clay seals and stone inscriptions dated to the centuries following Solomon. Although they are later, they demonstrate the commonality of the titles of many officials, such as scribe and royal steward, who are said to be those "who are over the household."

4:7 – 19 Samuel's original concerns were proven to be justified as the tribal league strained under the increasing power of a centralized bureaucracy (1Sa 8:10 – 22). The traditional institutions of Israel throughout the land now had to compete with a large, well-staffed palace-temple establishment in Jerusalem. The purpose of Solomon's 12 new administrative districts appears to have been to increase the tax base, reduce tribal autonomy (particularly in the restless north) and incorporate territories secured by David. While many of the districts roughly matched the original tribal allotments, the core northern tribes of Manasseh and Ephraim were carved up into smaller districts. The borders of these new units are described by means of topographic features, tribal borders, and strategic cities, though not all of them are clearly delineated in the text.

A number of the districts incorporated adjacent non-Israelite regions, some dominated by large Canaanite cities. Solomon named each of the 12 districts after its chief officer; they took turns financing the kingdom for a month at a time. Judah was exempt, a fact that would exacerbate tribal tensions in the future. Administrative districting in the ancient Near East can be traced back to the districts ("nomes") of Egypt and the city-states of Mesopotamia in the third millennium BC. Solomon's administrative reforms were a natural outgrowth of his kingdom's great size.

and the country of Og[r] king of Bashan). He was the only governor
over the district.

Solomon's Daily Provisions

20The people of Judah and Israel were
as numerous as the sand[s] on the seashore; they ate, they drank and they were
happy. 21And Solomon ruled[t] over all the
kingdoms from the Euphrates River[u] to
the land of the Philistines, as far as the
border of Egypt.[v] These countries brought
tribute[w] and were Solomon's subjects all
his life.
22Solomon's daily provisions were thirty
cors[a] of the finest flour and sixty cors[b] of
meal, 23ten head of stall-fed cattle, twenty
of pasture-fed cattle and a hundred sheep
and goats, as well as deer, gazelles, roe-
bucks and choice fowl. 24For he ruled over
all the kingdoms west of the Euphrates
River, from Tiphsah[x] to Gaza, and had
peace[y] on all sides. 25During Solomon's
lifetime Judah and Israel, from Dan to Beersheba,[z] lived in safety,[a] everyone under
their own vine and under their own fig
tree.[b]
26Solomon had four[c] thousand stalls for
chariot horses,[c] and twelve thousand horses.[d]
27The district governors,[d] each in his
month, supplied provisions for King Solomon and all who came to the king's table.
They saw to it that nothing was lacking.
28They also brought to the proper place
their quotas of barley and straw for the
chariot horses and the other horses.

Solomon's Wisdom

29God gave Solomon wisdom[e] and very
great insight, and a breadth of understanding as measureless as the sand on the seashore. 30Solomon's wisdom was greater
than the wisdom of all the people of the

4:19 [r] Dt 3:8-10 **4:20** [s] Ge 22:17; 32:12; 1Ki 3:8 **4:21** [t] 2Ch 9:26; Ps 72:11 [u] Jos 1:4; Ps 72:8 [v] Ge 15:18 [w] Ps 68:29 **4:24** [x] Ps 72:11 [y] 1Ch 22:9 **4:25** [z] Jdg 20:1 [a] Jer 23:6 [b] Mic 4:4; Zec 3:10 **4:26** [c] 1Ki 10:26; 2Ch 1:14 **4:27** [d] ver 7 **4:29** [e] 1Ki 3:12

[a] 22 That is, probably about 5 1/2 tons or about 5 metric tons [b] 22 That is, probably about 11 tons or about 10 metric tons [c] 26 Some Septuagint manuscripts (see also 2 Chron. 9:25); Hebrew *forty* [d] 26 Or *charioteers*

4:21 *from the Euphrates River to the land of the Philistines, as far as the border of Egypt.* David left Solomon with a kingdom that stretched from the northwestern bend of the Euphrates to the border of Egypt (Wadi el-Arish), including the southern coast that was so frequently the domain of Egypt. Ironically, the frontiers of the kingdom began to destabilize during Solomon's prosperous reign. Revolts in Edom and Aram created uncertainty on the northern and eastern borders, as a trade deficit resulted in the transfer of the Asher plain to Phoenicia. Meanwhile, Egypt could always be counted on to foment rebellion among Solomon's neighbors. Beyond the core territories of Israel, Solomon's sphere of influence nevertheless persisted until the close of his reign through conquered territories, vassals and regional allies across northern Syria, Transjordan and the entire eastern Mediterranean.

4:22–23,27–28 The new administrative system no doubt increased the efficiency of taxation. Bureaucratic records were a necessity, but they also conveyed the size and complexity of the kingdom. The kings of Ugarit, Mari and Assyria maintained careful records of taxes received, produce gathered, and plunder conquered, which testified to the wealth and largesse of their domains. A good illustration is the roster of village payments at Ugarit that listed the units of flour and barley contributed to the throne. The list of provisions in these verses seems staggering until one considers that the king's family, the royal guard, and a host of officials and their families required daily deliveries. The amounts are on par with a monarch comparable to the Egyptian pharaoh, and may even be listed in accordance with Egyptian record-keeping practice, as the units of measure are Egyptian rather than Hebrew (cor = homer).

4:25 *Dan to Beersheba.* A common expression referring to the entirety of the heartland's length and breadth (cf. Jdg 20:1; 1Sa 3:20). *everyone under their own vine and under their own fig tree.* This is the classic Biblical statement on the security and peace that comes with following Yahweh. *vine … fig tree.* Implies long-term care through cultivation, nourishment through harvesting, and the rooted security of the family dwelling within a larger family compound. Deuteronomy and most of the Prophets (e.g., Mic 4:4; Zec 3:10) uphold this image as an ideal that Yahweh grants to those who align their hearts to him. The converse is also true, as the blessings and curses of these same books show.

4:26 *four thousand stalls for chariot horses, and twelve thousand horses.* The description of Solomon's vast force informs us that the transformation of Israel's army from a local militia to a well-equipped professional fighting force was complete. Some argue that the large numbers of stalls, chariots and horses are a case of literary hyperbole. That may indeed be the case, since comparable large numbers appear in the annals of other monarchs. However, archaeological remains of chariot cities such as Megiddo and the consistently large numbers of chariots recorded in ancient Near Eastern and Biblical battles support the possibility that these numbers are indeed accurate.

4:29–34 Alongside chariots, bureaucracy and administrative districts, wisdom can be seen as a common denominator to the cultures and empires of the ancient Near East. Regardless of geographic location and cultural heritage, ancient wisdom texts contain similar yet profound truths about morality, ethics, relationships, society and nature.

The timeless nature of wisdom is seen in the shared concerns of wisdom traditions throughout the ancient Near East. From far in the East came practical wisdom traditions recognized by the author of Job (Job 1:3). From Egypt's wisdom tradition, which exerted strong influence on Israel at all times, came the Ptahhotep father-son teachings, the pithy sayings of the "Wisdom of Amenemope" a hundred years before Solomon (cf. Pr 22:17—24:22), and the reflections of the Eloquent Peasant. Akkadian wisdom included large numbers of proverbs, theodicies, school texts and the Job-like *Words of Ahiqar.*

Verses 32–34 describe Solomon's knowledge of the natural world, plants, and animals. Because the wise were known to comprehend the underlying order of life, they often appealed to "nature wisdom," the classification of living things, and the natural world to illustrate their points. Given the vast corpus of ancient Near Eastern wisdom and its extensive overlap with Biblical wisdom in both style and content, the Biblical statement that

East,[f] and greater than all the wisdom of
Egypt.[g] 31He was wiser[h] than anyone else,
including Ethan the Ezrahite — wiser than
Heman, Kalkol and Darda, the sons of Mahol. And his fame spread to all the surrounding nations. 32He spoke three thousand proverbs[i] and his songs[j] numbered a
thousand and five. 33He spoke about plant
life, from the cedar of Lebanon to the hyssop that grows out of walls. He also spoke
about animals and birds, reptiles and fish.
34From all nations people came to listen to
Solomon's wisdom, sent by all the kings[k]
of the world, who had heard of his wisdom.[a]

Preparations for Building the Temple

5:1-16pp — 2Ch 2:1-18

5 [b] When Hiram[l] king of Tyre heard that
Solomon had been anointed king to
succeed his father David, he sent his envoys to Solomon, because he had always
been on friendly terms with David. 2Sol-
omon sent back this message to Hiram:

3"You know that because of the
wars[m] waged against my father David from all sides, he could not build
a temple for the Name of the LORD his
God until the LORD put his enemies
under his feet. 4But now the LORD my
God has given me rest[n] on every side,
and there is no adversary or disaster.
5I intend, therefore, to build a temple[o]
for the Name of the LORD my God, as
the LORD told my father David, when
he said, 'Your son whom I will put on
the throne in your place will build the
temple for my Name.'[p]
6"So give orders that cedars of Lebanon be cut for me. My men will work
with yours, and I will pay you for your
men whatever wages you set. You
know that we have no one so skilled
in felling timber as the Sidonians."

7When Hiram heard Solomon's message, he was greatly pleased and said,

4:30 [f] Ge 25:6 [g] Ac 7:22 **4:31** [h] 1Ki 3:12; 1Ch 2:6; 6:33; 15:19; Ps 89 Title **4:32** [i] Pr 1:1; Ecc 12:9 [j] SS 1:1 **4:34** [k] 1Ki 10:1; 2Ch 9:23 **5:1** [l] ver 10, 18; 2Sa 5:11; 1Ch 14:1 **5:3** [m] 1Ch 22:8; 28:3 **5:4** [n] 1Ki 4:24; 1Ch 22:9 **5:5** [o] 1Ch 17:12 [p] 2Sa 7:13; 1Ch 22:10

[a] *34* In Hebrew texts 4:21-34 is numbered 5:1-14. [b] In Hebrew texts 5:1-18 is numbered 5:15-32.

"Solomon's wisdom was greater than the wisdom of all the people of the East" is profound indeed (v. 30).

4:31 *Ethan ... Heman, Kalkol and Darda, the sons of Mahol.* These individuals were known for their intellectual prowess, which Solomon was said to surpass. Little is known about them, although 1Ch 2:6 lists them as descendants of Tamar and Judah. The first two are described in the psalm titles of Ps 88–89 as "Ezrahites," a possible reference to service in Levitical circles. Here, the author of 1 Kings is emphasizing that even these men, skilled in music, wisdom and perhaps dance (if the Hebrew word *mahol* ["dancer"] is properly understood), were no match for the prodigious Solomon.

4:33 *plant life.* This does not concern the kind of matters modern botanists would be interested in, but involves medicinal, industrial, dietary and magical functions of plants ("herb lore"). Botanical wisdom can also relate to agricultural pursuits concerning seeds and the entire planting, growing and harvesting process. The context's emphasis on trees may indicate the use of tree-based parables and fables in his wisdom teaching, such as the one related in Jdg 9:8–15 by Jotham or the Sumerian parable of the Tamarisk and the Palm. *animals.* Probably refers to telling stories about animals like those found in Aesop's fables (see the article "Fables in the Ancient World," p. 428). The Egyptian "Instruction of Amenemope" and the Mesopotamian *Words of Ahiqar* are both filled with parables and sayings about animals and plants.

5:1 *Hiram king of Tyre.* The Phoenicians were seafaring Canaanites whose fleet served as conduit for trade between the inland regions of the eastern Mediterranean and the west, as well as between the Egyptians and the north Syrian coast. They established numerous cities in the western Mediterranean during the first millennium BC. Their primary natural resource was wood from the mountain ranges adjoining their territory, but they were almost entirely dependent on trade. Thus, Hiram naturally sought good relations with the ascendant Israelite nation.

Hiram's reign from the city-state of Tyre, just south of Sidon, is thought to have lasted from 980–950 BC. This contemporary of Solomon is not attested in extra-Biblical sources, though several Phoenician kings with the same name are attested in later periods. During much of this time, Solomon provided food in exchange for timber and laborers, since lack of farmland was the Phoenicians' greatest liability. For more details on Hiram's ties to Israel, see note on 9:11.

5:3 *because of the wars waged against my father David from all sides, he could not build a temple.* The account of Solomon's temple construction fits precisely into a recognizable literary device known as a "building account." This genre, attested for over two millennia in Mesopotamia and the Levant, includes the rationale for the project, the consent of the deity, preparations for construction, building description, dedication of the building, prayer of blessing and recitation of blessings and curses (see note on 2Ch 2:1). David did not succeed in the first stage of building a temple, and in this he was not alone among the monarchs of the ancient world. Naram-Sin, Zimri-Lim, Nabonidus — all powerful leaders of ancient Mesopotamia — for one reason or another failed to secure their deity's approval to build a temple at one point in their reign. David's unsuitability for temple building should not be understood as unheard of in ancient Near Eastern culture. *put his enemies under his feet.* This expression, which refers to the defeat and humiliation of an enemy, may also be noted in texts and in art ranging from the third-millennium BC monument of Naram-Sin (king of Akkad in Mesopotamia) to the Narmer Palette (memorializing Narmer's unification of Egypt, third millennium BC) and the portrayal of Rameses II's battle with the Hittites at Qadesh (1285 BC). In his letter to Solomon, Hiram uses an expression that occurs in the Bible and can be heard to this day in the Middle East.

5:6 *cedars of Lebanon.* Cedars grew only in select areas of the Lebanon mountain range. As tall, massive trees with strong, durable wood, there was a high demand for them, particularly for the construction of ships and crossbeams in large public buildings. A symbol of luxury in architecture, they were used for lining the walls of palaces and temples. This precious building material, together with the many cultural connections of the region, ensured Phoenicia's wealth and influence.

1 KINGS 5

NEW KINGS AND TEMPLES

Mesopotamian kings are known to have started their reigns with the planning and implementation of new building projects or the repair of famous temples. The sequence of events prior to and following the Biblical building account fits precisely the pattern of Mesopotamian building accounts from the third through first millennia BC. A similar pattern is found in the Baal Cycle, a text from Ugarit, a second-millennium BC city on the shores of northern Syria. Baal's house is rebuilt when it is recognized that unlike other gods, he lacks a dwelling.

Solomon commenced building in the fourth year of his reign. The Jewish historian Josephus quotes Phoenician sources that date Solomon's temple 143 years prior to the founding of Carthage. When these two dates are used, the most likely date for Solomon's fourth year is 967 BC.

As with many ancient Near Eastern building accounts, the date of the temple's founding is related to other significant dates in the nation's history. In Solomon's case, the Hebrew Bible places the temple construction 480 years after the Israelites left Egypt. This would place the exodus at 1447 BC. Many scholars consider the 480 years to be a schematic number representing 12 generations, which allows for a later date of the exodus (1280 BC). This late date for the exodus places the entry into Canaan at a time when the Egyptian Empire was in retreat, and it resolves the anachronism of Rameses, a thirteenth-century BC city that the Israelites are said to have built, but could not have if the early date is followed (Ex 1:11; 12:37).

The Biblical description of the temple fits comfortably into the ever-growing typology of Syrian temples. Its features as described in 1 Kings indicate that it is of Syrian or Phoenician influence and that it dates to the late second or early first millennium BC. ◆

Building and restoring temples were important undertakings for kings in the ancient world. Here Gudea has the plans for a temple on his lap, 2120 BC.

Kim Walton. The Louvre.

"Praise be to the LORD today, for he has
given David a wise son to rule over this
great nation."
8So Hiram sent word to Solomon:

"I have received the message you
sent me and will do all you want
in providing the cedar and juniper
logs. 9My men will haul them down
from Lebanon to the Mediterranean
Sea[q], and I will float them as rafts by
sea to the place you specify. There I
will separate them and you can take
them away. And you are to grant my
wish by providing food[r] for my royal
household."

10In this way Hiram kept Solomon supplied with all the cedar and juniper logs he
wanted, 11and Solomon gave Hiram twenty thousand cors[a] of wheat as food for his
household, in addition to twenty thousand
baths[b,c] of pressed olive oil. Solomon continued to do this for Hiram year after year.
12The LORD gave Solomon wisdom,[s] just as
he had promised him. There were peaceful relations between Hiram and Solomon,
and the two of them made a treaty.[t]
13King Solomon conscripted laborers[u]
from all Israel—thirty thousand men.
14He sent them off to Lebanon in shifts of
ten thousand a month, so that they spent
one month in Lebanon and two months
at home. Adoniram[v] was in charge of the
forced labor. 15Solomon had seventy thousand carriers and eighty thousand stonecutters in the hills, 16as well as thirty-three
hundred[d] foremen[w] who supervised the
project and directed the workers. 17At the
king's command they removed from the
quarry[x] large blocks of high-grade stone[y]
to provide a foundation of dressed stone
for the temple. 18The craftsmen of Solomon and Hiram and workers from Byblos[z]
cut and prepared the timber and stone for
the building of the temple.

5:9 [q] Ezr 3:7 [r] Eze 27:17; Ac 12:20 5:12 [s] 1Ki 3:12 [t] Am 1:9 5:13 [u] 1Ki 9:15 5:14 [v] 1Ki 4:6; 2Ch 10:18 5:16 [w] 1Ki 9:23 5:17 [x] 1Ki 6:7 [y] 1Ch 22:2 5:18 [z] Jos 13:5

Solomon Builds the Temple

6:1-29pp — 2Ch 3:1-14

6 In the four hundred and eightieth[e]
year after the Israelites came out of
Egypt, in the fourth year of Solomon's
reign over Israel, in the month of Ziv, the

[a] *11* That is, probably about 3,600 tons or about 3,250 metric tons [b] *11* Septuagint (see also 2 Chron. 2:10); Hebrew *twenty cors* [c] *11* That is, about 120,000 gallons or about 440,000 liters [d] *16* Hebrew; some Septuagint manuscripts (see also 2 Chron. 2:2,18) *thirty-six hundred* [e] *1* Hebrew; Septuagint *four hundred and fortieth*

5:13 *Solomon conscripted laborers from all Israel.* Solomon's building projects required additional labor, which he extracted from the Canaanites, who apparently were now subdued and hence subject to the governance of the Israelites. Although such conscription was not uncommon in the ancient world, in this case it sowed the seeds of the schism between north and south (see 9:15; 12:1–33). Conscript labor is evident in the Levant as early as the Alalakh texts and the Amarna texts of the mid-second millennium BC. Conscription was designed to meet the needs of state projects, including irrigation, construction of public and administrative buildings, digging canals, construction of garrisons or fortifications and many other projects that were done away from one's home. It was often imposed by a conqueror on a subjugated people. Such an act expressed bondage.

It is unclear whether Solomon raised a corvée labor force from the Israelite population, and, if so, whether it differed from the labor imposed on foreigners. On the one hand, texts such as 2Ch 2:17–18; 8:9 indicate that Solomon did not impose slavery on Israelites; on the other hand, texts such as this verse imply that Israelites were also conscripted for royal work projects. The difference may simply lie in the distinction between the slavery-style labor placed on the foreign population and the required national service expected of Israelites.

It is possible that the drama of Rehoboam's confrontation with the elders of the northern kingdom (ch. 12) must be understood in light of the distinction between Jeroboam as an officer of the corvée and Adoniram as the overseer of the forced labor gangs. This difference in terminology likely implies different categories of state workers. Thus, Rehoboam was backing up his verbal rhetoric by sending the overseer of harsher work to the north. One proposal is that Israelites performed national service on a rotating basis (service for one out of every three months), whereas foreigners were conscripted on a more permanent basis.

Certainly, the conscription of citizens for national interests such as warfare and infrastructure projects was not uncommon in the ancient Near East. Note that Egypt used a three-month corvée program based on the cycle of the inundation of the Nile River. Similarly, special taxes might be imposed on the citizenry to help underwrite the cost of the raw materials associated with such projects. In the cylinders of Gudea the text notes that the "whole country" participated in his temple project through physical labor and financial contributions. The raising of a corvée from the citizenry carried a negative nuance that could be exploited by political rivals (as with Jeroboam). Thus, the Persian ruler Cyrus refers to the Babylonian king Nabonidus in the Cyrus Cylinder as "an incompetent person" who imposed corvée on his citizens "unrelentingly, ruining them all." See the article "Temples and Sacred Space," p. 724.

5:18 *workers from Byblos.* Stonemasons from Byblos were added to the work force at this time. Because the Phoenicians were a central trading partner for neighboring nations, they absorbed artistic and cultural influences from adjacent regions and from Mesopotamia and Egypt, the two great civilizations of the ancient world. Many artifacts uncovered in Israel and Syria bear the characteristic features of Phoenicia's eclectic art and brilliant artisans. From dagger handles to public buildings, the influence is unmistakable. Solomon's building projects no doubt bore the trademark features of Phoenician art, including the tripartite temple, the palace with a throne room and columned porch and the embossed style of masonry that persisted until the end of the Israelite kingdoms.

Despite his extensive borrowing of Phoenician resources and know-how, Solomon did not succumb to the attendant paganism of his neighbor until the latter

second month, he began to build the temple of the LORD.[a]
2The temple[b] that King Solomon built
for the LORD was sixty cubits long, twenty wide and thirty high.[a] 3The portico at
the front of the main hall of the temple
extended the width of the temple, that is
twenty cubits,[b] and projected ten cubits[c]
from the front of the temple. 4He made
narrow windows[c] high up in the temple
walls. 5Against the walls of the main hall
and inner sanctuary he built a structure
around the building, in which there were
side rooms.[d] 6The lowest floor was five
cubits[d] wide, the middle floor six cubits[e]
and the third floor seven.[f] He made offset
ledges around the outside of the temple
so that nothing would be inserted into the
temple walls.
7In building the temple, only blocks
dressed[e] at the quarry were used, and no
hammer, chisel or any other iron tool[f] was
heard at the temple site while it was being built.
8The entrance to the lowest[g] floor was
on the south side of the temple; a stairway led up to the middle level and from
there to the third. 9So he built the temple
and completed it, roofing it with beams
and cedar[g] planks. 10And he built the side
rooms all along the temple. The height of
each was five cubits, and they were attached to the temple by beams of cedar.
11The word of the LORD came to Solomon: 12"As for this temple you are building, if you follow my decrees, observe my
laws and keep all my commands and obey
them, I will fulfill through you the promise[h] I gave to David your father. 13And I
will live among the Israelites and will not
abandon[i] my people Israel."
14So Solomon built the temple and completed[j] it. 15He lined its interior walls with
cedar boards, paneling them from the
floor of the temple to the ceiling,[k] and covered the floor of the temple with planks
of juniper. 16He partitioned off twenty cubits at the rear of the temple with cedar
boards from floor to ceiling to form within
the temple an inner sanctuary, the Most
Holy Place.[l] 17The main hall in front of
this room was forty cubits[h] long. 18The inside of the temple was cedar,[m] carved with
gourds and open flowers. Everything was
cedar; no stone was to be seen.
19He prepared the inner sanctuary[n]
within the temple to set the ark of the
covenant[o] of the LORD there. 20The inner
sanctuary[p] was twenty cubits long, twenty wide and twenty high. He overlaid the

6:1 [a] Ac 7:47 **6:2** [b] Eze 41:1 **6:4** [c] Eze 40:16; 41:16 **6:5** [d] ver 16, 19-21; Eze 41:5-6 **6:7** [e] Ex 20:25 [f] Dt 27:5 **6:9** [g] ver 14, 38 **6:12** [h] 2Sa 7:12-16; 1Ki 2:4; 9:5 **6:13** [i] Ex 25:8; Lev 26:11; Dt 31:6; Heb 13:5 **6:14** [j] ver 9, 38 **6:15** [k] 1Ki 7:7 **6:16** [l] Ex 26:33; Lev 16:2; 1Ki 8:6 **6:18** [m] 1Ki 7:24; Ps 74:6 **6:19** [n] 1Ki 8:6 [o] 1Sa 3:3 **6:20** [p] Eze 41:3-4

[a] *2* That is, about 90 feet long, 30 feet wide and 45 feet high or about 27 meters long, 9 meters wide and 14 meters high [b] *3* That is, about 30 feet or about 9 meters; also in verses 16 and 20 [c] *3* That is, about 15 feet or about 4.5 meters; also in verses 23-26 [d] *6* That is, about 7 1/2 feet or about 2.3 meters; also in verses 10 and 24 [e] *6* That is, about 9 feet or about 2.7 meters [f] *6* That is, about 11 feet or about 3.2 meters [g] *8* Septuagint; Hebrew *middle* [h] *17* That is, about 60 feet or about 18 meters

part of his reign. Up until that point, his selective borrowing from Phoenicia was a stark contrast to Ahab's later wholesale embrace of Phoenician customs, religion and ethics.

6:2 *temple.* The Hebrew word is *bayit* ("house"), a ubiquitous term that has a wide semantic range in many Semitic languages. *sixty cubits long, twenty wide and thirty high.* See note on 2Ch 3:3.

6:3 *portico.* Best described as a porch. Perched atop a broad staircase, it served as a type of transitional passageway linking the courtyard to the temple's main room. Identical temple porches are known from Syria and Phoenicia. In Syrian and Mesopotamian temples, the porch was the access point to the interior of the temple, a mysterious and holy place where the deity was believed to reside.

6:7 *blocks dressed at the quarry.* The stones for the temple were prepared at some distance from the construction site. Gudea's account of building a temple demanded silence at the construction site; the taboo against dressed stone for sacred altars might also be in view here. However, it may be for practical rather than religious reasons, as seen in Assyrian reliefs depicting completed stones and statues being removed from a quarry. Sennacherib of Assyria, for his part, built a temple to Ashur complete with limestone foundations from nearby mountains.

6:8 *stairway.* The entrance on the southern side room parallels the design of the 'Ain Dara temple in Syria. This indicates that the temple was oriented east-west. Most temples of the "long room" type (long sides with shorter ends) are found in northern Israel or in Syria and are oriented in the same direction. The means of ascent was not a ladder, as some translations suggest, but rather a substantial return staircase fashioned from wood or stone. Examples are known from the palace at Alalakh and the temple of 'Ain Dara, both in Syria.

6:15 *cedar boards.* Expensive wood such as cedar is found in burnt houses at various Iron Age cities in Israel. Because cedar had to be imported from Lebanon, it was reserved for special buildings or structures requiring long beams (see note on 5:6). Texts and reliefs from Egypt and Mesopotamia indicate that nations throughout the eastern Mediterranean imported cedars from Lebanon for use in architecture and, in the case of Egypt, for building fleets. The second-millennium BC Egyptian *Report of Wenamun*, e.g., describes the importation of large planks for boat construction in Egypt. Comparable traces of cedar paneling have been uncovered in several palaces and temples in northern Syria. In some structures the holes for attaching the paneling are all that remain.

6:19 *inner sanctuary.* This was the Most Holy Place, the holiest place in the temple, where the ark was located. It was accessible only by ascent through increasing spheres of holiness from the outer courtyard, the porch and the main hall. In addition to being centrally located, the Most Holy Place was elevated. North Syrian temples at Tayinat, Munbaqa, 'Ain Dara and Ebla have elevated areas in the back third of their main temple rooms. This would explain the smaller size of the inner shrine in comparison to the dimensions of the temple. The symmetry of its cube shape is attested in Mesopotamian and Anatolian temples.

TEMPLE FURNISHINGS

Glimpses of the rich ornamentation of Solomon's temple can be gained through recent discoveries that illumine the text of 1Ki 6–7.

1 ARK OF THE COVENANT
Cherubim with wings flanking a royal throne are attested in Egyptian, Israelite and Phoenician art (e.g., at Megiddo).

2 MOVABLE BRONZE BASIN
An extremely close parallel to the wheeled portable basins used in the courtyard of the temple has come from archaeological excavations on Cyprus. This representation combines elements from the Biblical text with the archaeological evidence.

3 INCENSE ALTAR
A stone incense altar having four horns on the corners was found at Megiddo. It provides a clear idea of the shape of the gold incense altar in the temple.

4 TABLE FOR THE BREAD OF THE PRESENCE
The table for the bread of the Presence was made of gold.

5 LAMPSTAND
Ten lampstands were in the temple, five on each side of the sanctuary (1Ki 7:49), to which were added ten tables (2Ch 4:8). Ritual sevenfold lamps have been found at several places in Israel, including Hazor and Dothan. The stand itself is modeled on bronze ones from the excavations at Megiddo.

inside with pure gold, and he also overlaid
the altar of cedar. 21Solomon covered the
inside of the temple with pure gold, and
he extended gold chains across the front
of the inner sanctuary, which was overlaid with gold. 22So he overlaid the whole
interior with gold. He also overlaid with
gold the altar that belonged to the inner
sanctuary.
23For the inner sanctuary he made a pair
of cherubim[q] out of olive wood, each ten
cubits high. 24One wing of the first cherub
was five cubits long, and the other wing
five cubits—ten cubits from wing tip to
wing tip. 25The second cherub also measured ten cubits, for the two cherubim were
identical in size and shape. 26The height of
each cherub was ten cubits. 27He placed
the cherubim[r] inside the innermost room
of the temple, with their wings spread out.
The wing of one cherub touched one wall,
while the wing of the other touched the

6:23 [q] Ex 37:1-9
6:27 [r] Ex 25:20; 37:9; 1Ki 8:7; 2Ch 5:8

6:22 *overlaid the whole interior with gold.* Although the dimensions of the temple are widely accepted, many scholars approach its lavish decoration with considerable skepticism. There is, however, a large body of comparative evidence that proves the temple's wealth to be entirely plausible. The third-millennium BC kings of Lagash in Mesopotamia covered their temples with gold and silver, while Esarhaddon, an Assyrian monarch of the seventh century BC, is documented as coating the walls of Ashur's shrine with gold. Egyptian documents recount that monuments and pillars in the second millennium BC Karnak temple were plated with gold and electrum. The vast gold of King Tutankhamun's famous tomb, with its myriad utensils and miniature shrines, further strengthens the claims of this Biblical verse.

6:23–28 Winged sphinxes or cherub figures, fearsome composite or hybrid creatures, from religious and royal iconography in Egypt, Mesopotamia and the Levant correspond nicely to the creatures described in the temple's Most Holy Place (see note on 8:7). A wall relief at Mari depicts such creatures flanking a fertile tree of life as a divine being summons the king. Several of the north Syrian temples yielded stone cherubim that are reminiscent of the ones described in this passage. They crouch at the entrance of the temples in order, it would seem, to reinforce the fearful power of the deity and to demarcate the perimeter of his presence. The cherubim and the ark in the innermost part of the temple most likely represented the footstool of Yahweh (see notes on Ex 25:16,18).

1 KINGS 6

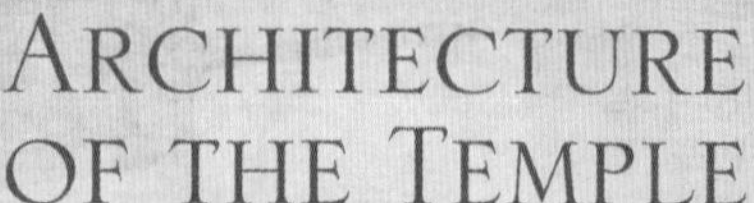

Architecture of the Temple

The Hebrew expression translated "narrow windows high up in the temple walls" (1Ki 6:4), i.e., windows near the roofline designed to let in light, reads lit. "framed, blocked windows" or "recessed, latticed windows." An examination of cognate languages suggests windows that are blocked, perhaps by a screen or some other ornamentation. Further clarity comes through a comparison with the windows of the well-preserved temple at 'Ain Dara in Syria, which is the closest parallel to Solomon's temple in size and features. Images of windows with screens and frames were carved into its basalt rock walls. The Hebrew expression could therefore mean ornamental faux windows instead of clerestory windows.

Against the walls of the main hall and inner sanctuary Solomon built a structure around the building, in which there were "side rooms" (1Ki 6:5). The Hebrew terms translated "side rooms" indicate "ribs" or "sides," which here are best understood as a multistoried structure that surrounded the building on three sides. This conclusion is based on parallel architecture in Egypt, Syria and Anatolia. The three stories of the side rooms increase in width from lowest to highest (1Ki 6:6). At first glance this seems to defy common sense because one would expect that wider rooms on the upper floors would be difficult to support. This problem was solved by using stair-like recesses on the outer face of the temple's main wall. The design may reflect the architect's desire to avoid inserting beams into the walls of the main shrine. Cedar beams attached the side rooms to the temple's main structure (1Ki 6:10). While the side rooms may have been used for priestly storage space, it is possible that ritual processions passed through the corridors on the first floor. This interpretation is supported by the odd presence of fine relief on the interior of the 'Ain Dara temple side rooms and by the description of the processions through the temple itself at the city of Emar in northern Syria.

The vast majority of temples in Syria, Phoenicia and Mesopotamia contain an elevated area at the back of the main room that was originally blocked off by wood paneling. In some cases the rear partition was constructed of stone or mud brick, as at Tell Tayinat in Syria. The partition was comparable to the ambulatory or chancel screen in some churches. It separated from view the most sacred space in the temple.

Visual reminders of creation and Eden could be found throughout this meeting point between heaven, earth and the world below. Carvings on the entry pillars, doors and walls depicted palm trees, sacred floral designs and cherubim (1Ki 6:29). These were all motifs from the garden, whose story had always factored into the theology of Israel.

The plan of the temple reflected spheres of increasing holiness, each with its protocol for worship. Behind them all was housed the ark of the covenant and the cherub throne of God, from which judgment was proclaimed (cf. Ps 76:8–9).

The design and features of Solomon's temple project have a number of points of connection and shared vocabulary with several Late Bronze and Iron Age temples throughout Syria and Canaan from the third to the first millennium BC. The most distinguishing point of connection between these temples is that of the threefold (tripartite) structure within a rectangular footprint that included a courtyard (portico;

continued on next page

porch; forecourt), a central temple chamber (main hall; forecourt; Holy Place) and an inner sanctuary (Most Holy Place).

Since temples were fashioned to some degree according to celestial archetypes and featured paradisiacal motifs of creation beauty, the common threefold structure may reflect prevailing cosmological thought. For example, the tripartite temple at the northern Syrian city of Ebla (c. twenty-fourth century BC) was of a similar size and proportion as Solomon's temple and, like Solomon's temple, was connected to the royal palace complex. In addition, the tenth-century BC temple discovered at Tell Tayinat in the Orontes Basin was also tripartite in layout and featured two columns at the entrance with lion images at the base (cf. Jakin and Boaz, 2Ch 3:17) and was also located adjacent to the royal palace.

Similarly, the tenth-century BC northwest-Syrian temple at the Aramaic capital of 'Ain Dara also featured a tripartite footprint, side storage rooms and carved basalt orthostats with lions and cherubs/sphinxes. Other temples that have similarity with Solomon's temple include ninth-century BC temples at Alalakh and Arad, an eighth-century BC temple from Hamath and acropolis temples from Zinjirli and Tell Halaf.

In addition to a similar floor plan, there are other points of architectural connection between Solomon's temple and other ancient Near Eastern temples. For example, dressed masonry with interlaced wooden beams was a common feature of Middle and Late Bronze Age monumental construction technique, as seen in the Syrian palace structures at Alalakh and Ugarit as well as the Canaanite buildings at Hazor. Moreover, fine examples of ashlar masonry (finely hewn blocks of building stone) at Israelite administrative centers from the tenth and ninth centuries BC such as Jerusalem, Gezer, Hazor and Megiddo nicely fit the Biblical description of Phoenician assistance in craftsmanship. See the article "Temples and Sacred Space," p. 724. ◆

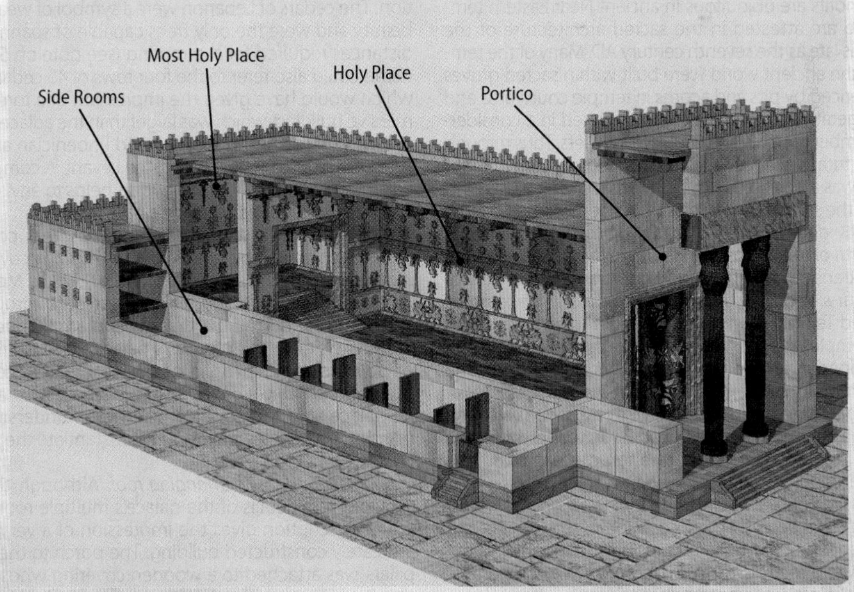

Solomon's temple.

other wall, and their wings touched each other in the middle of the room. 28He overlaid the cherubim with gold.

29On the walls all around the temple, in both the inner and outer rooms, he carved cherubim,[s] palm trees and open flowers. 30He also covered the floors of both the inner and outer rooms of the temple with gold.

31For the entrance to the inner sanctuary he made doors out of olive wood that were one fifth of the width of the sanctuary. 32And on the two olive-wood doors he carved cherubim, palm trees and open flowers, and overlaid the cherubim and palm trees with hammered gold. 33In the same way, for the entrance to the main hall he made doorframes out of olive wood that were one fourth of the width of the hall. 34He also made two doors out of juniper wood, each having two leaves that turned in sockets. 35He carved cherubim, palm trees and open flowers on them and overlaid them with gold hammered evenly over the carvings.

36And he built the inner courtyard of three courses[t] of dressed stone and one course of trimmed cedar beams.

37The foundation of the temple of the LORD was laid in the fourth year, in the month of Ziv. 38In the eleventh year in the month of Bul, the eighth month, the temple was finished in all its details according to its specifications.[u] He had spent seven years building it.

Solomon Builds His Palace

7 It took Solomon thirteen years, however, to complete the construction of his palace.[v] 2He built the Palace[w] of the Forest of Lebanon[x] a hundred cubits long, fifty wide and thirty high,[a] with four rows of cedar columns supporting trimmed cedar beams. 3It was roofed with cedar above the beams that rested on the columns—forty-five beams, fifteen to a row. 4Its windows were placed high in sets of three, facing each other. 5All the doorways had rectangular frames; they were in the front part in sets of three, facing each other.[b]

6He made a colonnade fifty cubits long and thirty wide.[c] In front of it was a portico, and in front of that were pillars and an overhanging roof.

6:29 [s] ver 32,35
6:36 [t] 1Ki 7:12; Ezr 6:4
6:38 [u] Heb 8:5
7:1 [v] 1Ki 9:10; 2Ch 8:1
7:2 [w] 2Sa 7:2 [x] 1Ki 10:17; 2Ch 9:16

[a] 2 That is, about 150 feet long, 75 feet wide and 45 feet high or about 45 meters long, 23 meters wide and 14 meters high [b] 5 The meaning of the Hebrew for this verse is uncertain. [c] 6 That is, about 75 feet long and 45 feet wide or about 23 meters long and 14 meters wide

6:29 *carved cherubim, palm trees and open flowers.* The ornate carvings of flowers, vines, rosettes and the palm tree or tree of life combine to evoke images of paradise. These motifs are ubiquitous in ancient Near Eastern temples and are attested in the sacred architecture of the region as late as the seventh century AD. Many of the temples in the ancient world were built within sacred groves as evidenced by pits and acorns in temple courtyards and lush vegetation in temple scenes depicted in a considerable number of Egyptian and Assyrian reliefs. Thus through architectural decor as well as adjoining gardens, vibrant fertility was associated with sacred space, which was considered the source of that fertility, as Eden had first been.

6:31 – 33 *doors ... one fifth of the width ... doorframes ... one fourth of the width.* The Hebrew words used here are usually translated as "five-sided doorframes/door jambs" and "four-sided doorframes/door jambs." The temples at Ur and Tell Tayinat allow for a better interpretation. In those temples the main door frame is "rabbeted," possessing stepped indents on three sides. Most commonly the frames have four indented steps, but in some cases, as at the Ningal temple at Ur, they have five. This was also the case with Solomon's temple. In addition to their indented frames, the doors in Solomon's temple exhibited the same garden-like motifs as the walls.

6:36 *three courses of dressed stone and one course of trimmed cedar beams.* The description of the inner courtyard suggests that the sacred precinct, or temenos, of the temple was already large in Solomon's day. A comparable inner courtyard was unearthed in the lower city of Hazor. The walls were made with a layer of cedar planking interspersed between every three layers (courses) of stone, perhaps to compensate for irregularities in stone size and provide greater stability to the wall. Walls of this kind are attested at Ugarit, throughout Anatolia, at the palace of Knossos in Crete and at other Mycenaean sites.

7:2 *Palace of the Forest of Lebanon.* The origin of the building's name is not known, though it likely reflects the Phoenician inspiration of its design and cedar construction. The cedars of Lebanon were a symbol of wealth and beauty and were the only trees capable of spanning the distances required for the roofing (see note on 5:6). The name could also refer to the four rows of 45 cedar pillars, which would have given the impression of a forest. This massive building, which was larger than the adjacent temple, was typical of north Syrian and Phoenician architecture known from excavation in the Levant. A comparable pillared building at Kition on Cyprus helps to envision the size and grandeur or Solomon's palace.

The architectural components of the complex described in the Bible are similar to those discovered at Zinjirli in modern Turkey and Palace 1723 at Megiddo. These so-called *bit-hilani* palaces, attested throughout the Near East during the first millennium BC, are architecturally similar to Solomon's palace. Because remains of Solomon's main buildings have been uncovered, these extra-Biblical buildings (and especially the Israelite palace at Megiddo) provide a better understanding of Solomon's achievements and substantiate the Biblical record.

7:6 *pillars and an overhanging roof.* Although the text provides few details of the palace's multiple rooms, the entire description gives the impression of a very costly, intricately constructed building. The porch to the hall of pillars was attached to a wooden covering whose function is unclear. An identical covering protruded from the temple in precisely the same location of the building relative to the entrance (Eze 41:26). Because the courtyard of the palace, like the courtyard of the temple, was the venue for public gatherings, it is likely that this feature was a protective cornice or awning in front of the porch.

7He built the throne hall, the Hall of Justice, where he was to judge,[y] and he covered
it with cedar from floor to ceiling.[a][z] 8And
the palace in which he was to live, set farther back, was similar in design. Solomon
also made a palace like this hall for Pharaoh's daughter, whom he had married.[a]
9All these structures, from the outside to
the great courtyard and from foundation to
eaves, were made of blocks of high-grade
stone cut to size and smoothed on their
inner and outer faces. 10The foundations
were laid with large stones of good quality, some measuring ten cubits[b] and some
eight.[c] 11Above were high-grade stones,
cut to size, and cedar beams. 12The great
courtyard was surrounded by a wall of
three courses[b] of dressed stone and one
course of trimmed cedar beams, as was
the inner courtyard of the temple of the
LORD with its portico.

The Temple's Furnishings

7:23-26pp — 2Ch 4:2-5
7:38-51pp — 2Ch 4:6,10 – 5:1

13King Solomon sent to Tyre and
brought Huram,[d][c] 14whose mother was
a widow from the tribe of Naphtali and
whose father was from Tyre and a skilled
craftsman in bronze. Huram was filled
with wisdom,[d] with understanding and
with knowledge to do all kinds of bronze
work. He came to King Solomon and did
all[e] the work assigned to him.
15He cast two bronze pillars,[f] each eighteen cubits high and twelve cubits in circumference.[e] 16He also made two capitals[g]
of cast bronze to set on the tops of the
pillars; each capital was five cubits[f] high.
17A network of interwoven chains adorned
the capitals on top of the pillars, seven for
each capital. 18He made pomegranates in
two rows[g] encircling each network to decorate the capitals on top of the pillars.[h]
He did the same for each capital. 19The
capitals on top of the pillars in the portico were in the shape of lilies, four cubits[i] high. 20On the capitals of both pillars,
above the bowl-shaped part next to the
network, were the two hundred pomegranates[h] in rows all around. 21He erected
the pillars at the portico of the temple. The
pillar to the south he named Jakin[j] and the
one to the north Boaz.[k][i] 22The capitals on
top were in the shape of lilies. And so the
work on the pillars was completed.
23He made the Sea[j] of cast metal, circular in shape, measuring ten cubits from
rim to rim and five cubits high. It took a
line of thirty cubits[l] to measure around it.

7:7 [y] Ps 122:5; Pr 20:8 [z] 1Ki 6:15 **7:8** [a] 1Ki 3:1; 2Ch 8:11 **7:12** [b] 1Ki 6:36 **7:13** [c] 2Ch 2:13 **7:14** [d] Ex 31:2-5; 35:31; 36:1; 2Ch 2:14 [e] 2Ch 4:11,16 **7:15** [f] 2Ki 25:17; 2Ch 3:15; 4:12; Jer 52:17,21 **7:16** [g] 2Ki 25:17 **7:20** [h] 2Ch 3:16; 4:13; Jer 52:23 **7:21** [i] 1Ki 6:3; 2Ch 3:17 **7:23** [j] 2Ki 25:13; 1Ch 18:8; Jer 52:17

[a] *7* Vulgate and Syriac; Hebrew *floor* [b] *10* That is, about 15 feet or about 4.5 meters; also in verse 23 [c] *10* That is, about 12 feet or about 3.6 meters [d] *13* Hebrew *Hiram,* a variant of *Huram;* also in verses 40 and 45 [e] *15* That is, about 27 feet high and 18 feet in circumference or about 8.1 meters high and 5.4 meters in circumference [f] *16* That is, about 7 1/2 feet or about 2.3 meters; also in verse 23 [g] *18* Two Hebrew manuscripts and Septuagint; most Hebrew manuscripts *made the pillars, and there were two rows* [h] *18* Many Hebrew manuscripts and Syriac; most Hebrew manuscripts *pomegranates* [i] *19* That is, about 6 feet or about 1.8 meters; also in verse 38 [j] *21* *Jakin* probably means *he establishes.* [k] *21* *Boaz* probably means *in him is strength.* [l] *23* That is, about 45 feet or about 14 meters

7:14 *Huram was filled with wisdom, with understanding and with knowledge to do all kinds of bronze work.* Ancient Israelite art, judging from the artifacts discovered to date, did not stand out as being particularly sophisticated or noteworthy. Monarchs of the period routinely acquired craftsmen or artisans from other lands by means of conquest or treaty. Ancient records point to a well-developed system of trade from mines and merchants to production centers and artisan households that in turn exported their products to the court or the wealthier classes.

Guilds of artisans and families of craftsmen persisted in state and entrepreneurial ventures from the fourth millennium BC to the time of Solomon and beyond. One of the best-documented production centers is the thirteenth-century BC city of Ugarit, where merchants and artisans from distant lands produced crafts of hybrid Egyptian, Mesopotamian, Greek and Canaanite styles. In hiring one such merchant (v. 13), Solomon followed the conventions of the cosmopolitan eastern Mediterranean culture in which he lived.

7:15 – 22 The porch of most ancient Near Eastern temples resembled a gateway into the mysterious domain of the deity. The pillars resembled ceremonial gates. Based on architectural parallels it is safe to conclude that the pillars of Solomon's temple were load bearing and had an architectural function. In order to visualize the capitals one must rely almost entirely on ancient models and reliefs.

The pillars were 18 cubits (about 27 feet or 8.1 meters) high (cf. 2Ch 3:15 and note) and hollow, each made of cast bronze (v. 15). Each pillar was surmounted by a bowl-shaped capital. The capitals were elaborately decorated, with nets of checker work (wreaths of chain work) and two rows of pomegranates (vv. 17 – 18). These have been interpreted variously as columns with dedicatory inscriptions, representations of the doorways into the divine abode, and flowering trees representing the virile attributes of the divinity and the fertility of his creation. The pomegranate is a ubiquitous symbol of agricultural produce and fertility in ancient Near Eastern art. The fact that such pillars were a common feature of a number of ancient Near Eastern temples has prompted much speculation by scholars looking to unearth some kind of significant religious or cosmological symbolism (such as stylized trees of life) expressed by the pillars and their names (Jakin and Boaz, v. 21). All told, however, there is no indication in the text of any symbolism meant by the pillars, although they may have played a role in Israelite covenantal ceremonies. The "names" of the pillars might be the first words of the inscriptions carved on them.

7:23 – 26 The imagery of the Sea of cast metal (commonly referred to as the "bronze Sea") is compelling in light of ancient Near Eastern symbols. The bronze Sea has parallels with Assyrian reliefs and temple fixtures including those from the time frame of Sargon II (eighth century BC). The Sea is also reminiscent of temple scenes from

24 Below the rim, gourds encircled it — ten
to a cubit. The gourds were cast in two
rows in one piece with the Sea.
25 The Sea stood on twelve bulls,[k] three
facing north, three facing west, three facing south and three facing east. The Sea
rested on top of them, and their hind-
quarters were toward the center. 26 It was
a handbreadth[a] in thickness, and its rim
was like the rim of a cup, like a lily blossom. It held two thousand baths.[b]
27 He also made ten movable stands[l] of
bronze; each was four cubits long, four
wide and three high.[c] 28 This is how the
stands were made: They had side panels
attached to uprights. 29 On the panels between the uprights were lions, bulls and
cherubim — and on the uprights as well.
Above and below the lions and bulls were
wreaths of hammered work. 30 Each stand[m]
had four bronze wheels with bronze axles, and each had a basin resting on four
supports, cast with wreaths on each side.
31 On the inside of the stand there was an
opening that had a circular frame one cubit[d] deep. This opening was round, and
with its basework it measured a cubit and
a half.[e] Around its opening there was engraving. The panels of the stands were
square, not round. 32 The four wheels were
under the panels, and the axles of the
wheels were attached to the stand. The
diameter of each wheel was a cubit and a
half. 33 The wheels were made like chariot
wheels; the axles, rims, spokes and hubs
were all of cast metal.
34 Each stand had four handles, one on
each corner, projecting from the stand.
35 At the top of the stand there was a circular band half a cubit[f] deep. The supports
and panels were attached to the top of
the stand. 36 He engraved cherubim, lions
and palm trees on the surfaces of the supports and on the panels, in every available space, with wreaths all around. 37 This
is the way he made the ten stands. They
were all cast in the same molds and were
identical in size and shape.
38 He then made ten bronze basins,[n]
each holding forty baths[g] and measuring
four cubits across, one basin to go on each
of the ten stands. 39 He placed five of the
stands on the south side of the temple and
five on the north. He placed the Sea on
the south side, at the southeast corner of
the temple. 40 He also made the pots[h] and
shovels and sprinkling bowls.
So Huram finished all the work he had
undertaken for King Solomon in the temple of the LORD:

41 the two pillars;
the two bowl-shaped capitals on top
of the pillars;
the two sets of network decorating
the two bowl-shaped capitals on
top of the pillars;
42 the four hundred pomegranates for
the two sets of network (two rows
of pomegranates for each network
decorating the bowl-shaped capitals[o] on top of the pillars);
43 the ten stands with their ten basins;
44 the Sea and the twelve bulls under it;
45 the pots, shovels and sprinkling
bowls.[p]

7:25 [k] 2Ch 4:4-5; Jer 52:20 **7:27** [l] ver 38; 2Ch 4:14 **7:30** [m] 2Ki 16:17 **7:38** [n] Ex 30:18; 2Ch 4:6 **7:42** [o] ver 20 **7:45** [p] Ex 27:3

[a] *26* That is, about 3 inches or about 7.5 centimeters [b] *26* That is, about 12,000 gallons or about 44,000 liters; the Septuagint does not have this sentence. [c] *27* That is, about 6 feet long and wide and about 4 1/2 feet high or about 1.8 meters long and wide and 1.4 meters high [d] *31* That is, about 18 inches or about 45 centimeters [e] *31* That is, about 2 1/4 feet or about 68 centimeters; also in verse 32 [f] *35* That is, about 9 inches or about 23 centimeters [g] *38* That is, about 240 gallons or about 880 liters [h] *40* Many Hebrew manuscripts, Septuagint, Syriac and Vulgate (see also verse 45 and 2 Chron. 4:11); many other Hebrew manuscripts *basins*

Luxor showing Amenhotep III appearing before the gods along with what appears to be water tanks.

In addition, the bronze Sea is replete with bull imagery, including 300 bull images inscribed below the rim of the container and 12 larger bulls on which the container rested. The use of bulls together with the Sea is intriguing given the connection between bovines and the Sea in several ancient Near Eastern literary texts. In such accounts, disorder (chaos) is portrayed via the aquatic realm (the primordial deep as well as sea creatures such as Leviathan), imagery likewise utilized in OT mythopoetic accounts (cf. Job 26:12 – 13; Ps 74:13 – 15; Isa 27:1; 51:9). Such accounts often intersect with the motif of the divine warrior facilitating order within the created realm. In some cases, the establishment of order culminates in the construction of a divine temple or palace. In short, the bronze Sea may have functioned as a symbolic representation of Yahweh sitting "enthroned over the flood" (Ps 29:10), signifying his mastery over the ancient Near Eastern symbol of chaos and disorder, the sea. Cf. 2Ch 4:2 – 4.

7:25 *stood on twelve bulls.* The bulls that supported the basin were no doubt intended to convey Yahweh's power, strength and fertility, since "bull" is a well-known epithet for the male deities of the ancient Near East. Moreover, large bulls were routinely depicted on religious seals, stands and architecture, intended to evoke awe and reverence from the beholder. In many depictions the deity is pictured atop the animal, as if riding it.

7:26 *two thousand baths.* A bath is commonly understood to be six gallons (22 liters), based on the Mesopotamian parallels and the measurements of the bronze Sea itself. The capacity of the Sea of cast metal was therefore approximately 12,000 gallons (44,000 liters), a large reservoir indeed.

7:27 – 37 The movable stands aided in the transport of water to different areas of the temple courtyard. The Biblical author describes the stands in painstaking detail but they are still difficult to envision. Fortunately, archaeologists in Cyprus have uncovered an almost precise parallel, complete with four-wheeled design, cherubim and floral/faunal ornamentation.

Wheeled bronze stand, Cyprus, 1225 – 1100 BC. This design has similarities to Solomon's movable stands of bronze (1Ki 7:27 – 37).

Kim Walton. The British Museum.

All these objects that Huram made for
King Solomon for the temple of the LORD
were of burnished bronze. 46The king had
them cast in clay molds in the plain[q] of the
Jordan between Sukkoth[r] and Zarethan.[s]
47Solomon left all these things unweighed,[t]
because there were so many; the weight of
the bronze was not determined.
48Solomon also made all the furnishings
that were in the LORD's temple:

the golden altar;
the golden table[u] on which was the
bread of the Presence;[v]
49the lampstands[w] of pure gold (five
on the right and five on the left, in
front of the inner sanctuary);
the gold floral work and lamps and
tongs;
50the pure gold basins, wick trimmers,
sprinkling bowls, dishes and censers;[x]
and the gold sockets for the doors of
the innermost room, the Most Holy
Place, and also for the doors of the
main hall of the temple.

51When all the work King Solomon had
done for the temple of the LORD was finished, he brought in the things his father
David had dedicated[y] — the silver and gold
and the furnishings — and he placed them
in the treasuries of the LORD's temple.

The Ark Brought to the Temple

8:1-21pp — 2Ch 5:2 – 6:11

8 Then King Solomon summoned into
his presence at Jerusalem the elders
of Israel, all the heads of the tribes and the
chiefs[z] of the Israelite families, to bring up
the ark[a] of the LORD's covenant from Zion,
the City of David.[b] 2All the Israelites came
together to King Solomon at the time of
the festival[c] in the month of Ethanim, the
seventh month.[d]
3When all the elders of Israel had arrived, the priests[e] took up the ark, 4and
they brought up the ark of the LORD and
the tent of meeting[f] and all the sacred furnishings in it. The priests and Levites carried them up, 5and King Solomon and the
entire assembly of Israel that had gathered
about him were before the ark, sacrificing[g]
so many sheep and cattle that they could
not be recorded or counted.
6The priests then brought the ark of
the LORD's covenant[h] to its place in the
inner sanctuary of the temple, the Most
Holy Place, and put it beneath the wings
of the cherubim.[i] 7The cherubim spread
their wings over the place of the ark and
overshadowed the ark and its carrying
poles. 8These poles were so long that their
ends could be seen from the Holy Place in
front of the inner sanctuary, but not from
outside the Holy Place; and they are still
there today.[j] 9There was nothing in the ark
except the two stone tablets[k] that Moses
had placed in it at Horeb, where the LORD
made a covenant with the Israelites after
they came out of Egypt.
10When the priests withdrew from the

7:46 [q] 2Ch 4:17 [r] Ge 33:17; Jos 13:27 [s] Jos 3:16
7:47 [t] 1Ch 22:3
7:48 [u] Ex 37:10 [v] Ex 25:30
7:49 [w] Ex 25:31-38
7:50 [x] 2Ki 25:13
7:51 [y] 2Sa 8:11
8:1 [z] Nu 7:2 [a] 2Sa 6:17 [b] 2Sa 5:7
8:2 [c] 2Ch 7:8 [d] Lev 23:34
8:3 [e] Nu 7:9; Jos 3:3
8:4 [f] 1Ki 3:4; 2Ch 1:3
8:5 [g] 2Sa 6:13
8:6 [h] 2Sa 6:17 [i] 1Ki 6:19,27
8:8 [j] Ex 25:13-15
8:9 [k] Ex 24:7-8; 25:21; 40:20; Dt 10:2-5; Heb 9:4

7:51 *treasuries of the LORD's temple.* Second-millennium BC temple treasuries are known from Karnak in Egypt and Hattusas, the capital of the Hittites. However the design of these temples and the style of construction were very different from the sacred architecture of the Levant. With the discovery of the multistoried, ornate hallways that enclose the 'Ain Dara temple, a new understanding of the treasuries in Solomon's temple is possible. The multistoried treasury enclosed the temple on three sides.

We cannot rule out the possibility that the lowest floor of the side structures at 'Ain Dara and Jerusalem were used for some religious ritual. The itineraries of processions and sacred rites at Emar show an expansive vocabulary of priestly processions through the temple corridors. The rituals required a significant number of provisions that were transported from nearby storage facilities. It may be that similar activity took place between the walls of the side chambers of the Solomonic temple.

8:7 *cherubim spread their wings over the place of the ark.* The cherubim figure prominently in ancient Near Eastern iconography as the guardians of the deity (see note on Ex 25:18).

Holy Place, the cloud[l] filled the temple of
the LORD. 11And the priests could not perform their service because of the cloud,
for the glory of the LORD filled his temple.
12Then Solomon said, "The LORD has
said that he would dwell in a dark cloud;[m]
13I have indeed built a magnificent temple
for you, a place for you to dwell[n] forever."
14While the whole assembly of Isra-
el was standing there, the king turned
around and blessed[o] them. 15Then he
said:

"Praise be to the LORD,[p] the God of
Israel, who with his own hand has
fulfilled what he promised with his
own mouth to my father David. For
he said, 16'Since the day I brought my
people Israel out of Egypt, I have not
chosen a city in any tribe of Israel to
have a temple built so that my Name[q]
might be there, but I have chosen[r] David[s] to rule my people Israel.'
17"My father David had it in his
heart to build a temple[t] for the Name
of the LORD, the God of Israel. 18But
the LORD said to my father David, 'You
did well to have it in your heart to
build a temple for my Name. 19Never-
theless, you[u] are not the one to build
the temple, but your son, your own
flesh and blood—he is the one who
will build the temple for my Name.'[v]
20"The LORD has kept the promise
he made: I have succeeded David my
father and now I sit on the throne
of Israel, just as the LORD promised,
and I have built[w] the temple for the
Name of the LORD, the God of Israel. 21I have provided a place there for
the ark, in which is the covenant of
the LORD that he made with our ancestors when he brought them out of
Egypt."

8:10 [l] Ex 40:34-35; 2Ch 7:1-2 **8:12** [m] Ps 18:11; 97:2 **8:13** [n] Ex 15:17; 2Sa 7:13; Ps 132:13 **8:14** [o] 2Sa 6:18 **8:15** [p] 2Sa 7:12-13; 1Ch 29:10, 20; Ne 9:5; Lk 1:68 **8:16** [q] Dt 12:5 [r] 1Sa 16:1 [s] 2Sa 7:4-6, 8 **8:17** [t] 2Sa 7:2; 1Ch 17:1 **8:19** [u] 2Sa 7:5 [v] 2Sa 7:13; 1Ki 5:3, 5 **8:20** [w] 1Ch 28:6

8:22 [x] Ex 9:29; Ezr 9:5 **8:23** [y] 1Sa 2:2; 2Sa 7:22 [z] Dt 7:9, 12; Ne 1:5; 9:32; Da 9:4 **8:25** [a] 1Ki 2:4 **8:26** [b] 2Sa 7:25 **8:27** [c] Ac 7:48 [d] 2Ch 2:6; Ps 139:7-16; Isa 66:1; Jer 23:24 **8:29** [e] 2Ch 7:15; Ne 1:6 [f] Da 6:10 [g] Dt 12:11

Solomon's Prayer of Dedication

8:22-53pp — 2Ch 6:12-40

22Then Solomon stood before the altar
of the LORD in front of the whole assembly of Israel, spread out his hands[x] toward
heaven 23and said:

"LORD, the God of Israel, there is
no God like[y] you in heaven above or
on earth below—you who keep your
covenant of love[z] with your servants
who continue wholeheartedly in your
way. 24You have kept your promise to
your servant David my father; with
your mouth you have promised and
with your hand you have fulfilled it—
as it is today.
25"Now LORD, the God of Israel,
keep for your servant David my father the promises[a] you made to him
when you said, 'You shall never fail
to have a successor to sit before me
on the throne of Israel, if only your
descendants are careful in all they do
to walk before me faithfully as you
have done.' 26And now, God of Israel, let your word that you promised[b]
your servant David my father come
true.
27"But will God really dwell[c] on
earth? The heavens, even the highest
heaven, cannot contain[d] you. How
much less this temple I have built!
28Yet give attention to your servant's
prayer and his plea for mercy, LORD
my God. Hear the cry and the prayer
that your servant is praying in your
presence this day. 29May your eyes be
open[e] toward[f] this temple night and
day, this place of which you said,
'My Name[g] shall be there,' so that
you will hear the prayer your servant prays toward this place. 30Hear
the supplication of your servant and

8:11 *the glory of the LORD filled his temple.* The gods of other ancient Near Eastern cultures (most notably, Baal of the Canaanites) are described in language and imagery similar to the Biblical description of Yahweh's glory and his entry into the temple. The expression and pattern of theophany seems to be replicated in a range of cultures, regardless of the deity in question. This indicates that the presence of Yahweh in his temple was expressed to Israel in terms that were familiar not only to them, but to anyone in the ancient Near East. Thus, the function of the temple, the architecture of the temple, and the ideology of the temple were all elements that the Israelites held in common with their neighbors. All of this similarity does nothing to minimize the unique nature of Israel's God.

8:12 *The LORD has said that he would dwell in a dark cloud.* The largely windowless architecture of most ancient Near Eastern and Aegean temples ensured that the deity would be worshiped in a dark place shrouded in smoke from fire, lamps and incense. The darkness and cloud reinforced the mysterious, supernatural quality of the divine being residing in the temple.

8:13 *I have indeed built a magnificent temple for you, a place for you to dwell forever.* The Sumerian king Gudea made a similar appeal for deity to come and dwell in the temple that had been built on his dedication of a temple to the deity Ningirsu in the third millennium BC. *magnificent temple.* The vocabulary of these Hebrew words is well-known from the descriptions of deities and their heavenly abodes as recorded in the religious texts from Ugarit and Mesopotamia. The semantic range of the Semitic root used encompasses "princely," "heavenly" and "exalted," all of which are appropriate adjectives for Solomon's temple at the highest elevation in his capital city.

8:30 *Hear from heaven, your dwelling place.* The Israelite temple, like its contemporaries in Canaan and Syria, was understood to be a meeting point between heaven, earth and the world below. It was a replica of the heavenly abode that lay above the sky and heavens, and it served

of your people Israel when they pray
toward this place. Hear from heaven,
your dwelling place, and when you
hear, forgive.[h]
31 "When anyone wrongs their
neighbor and is required to take an
oath and they come and swear the
oath[i] before your altar in this temple, 32 then hear from heaven and act.
Judge between your servants, condemning the guilty by bringing down
on their heads what they have done,
and vindicating the innocent by treating them in accordance with their innocence.[j]
33 "When your people Israel have
been defeated[k] by an enemy because
they have sinned[l] against you, and
when they turn back to you and give
praise to your name, praying and
making supplication to you in this
temple, 34 then hear from heaven and
forgive the sin of your people Israel
and bring them back to the land you
gave to their ancestors.
35 "When the heavens are shut up
and there is no rain[m] because your
people have sinned against you, and
when they pray toward this place and
give praise to your name and turn
from their sin because you have afflicted them, 36 then hear from heaven
and forgive the sin of your servants,
your people Israel. Teach[n] them the
right way[o] to live, and send rain on
the land you gave your people for an
inheritance.
37 "When famine[p] or plague comes
to the land, or blight[q] or mildew, locusts or grasshoppers, or when an enemy besieges them in any of their cities, whatever disaster or disease may
come, 38 and when a prayer or plea is
made by anyone among your people
Israel — being aware of the afflictions
of their own hearts, and spreading
out their hands toward this temple —
39 then hear from heaven, your dwelling place. Forgive and act; deal with
everyone according to all they do,
since you know[r] their hearts (for you
alone know every human heart), 40 so
that they will fear[s] you all the time
they live in the land you gave our ancestors.
41 "As for the foreigner who does
not belong to your people Israel but
has come from a distant land because
of your name — 42 for they will hear
of your great name and your mighty
hand[t] and your outstretched arm —
when they come and pray toward
this temple, 43 then hear from heaven,
your dwelling place. Do whatever the
foreigner asks of you, so that all the
peoples of the earth may know[u] your
name and fear[v] you, as do your own
people Israel, and may know that this
house I have built bears your Name.
44 "When your people go to war
against their enemies, wherever you
send them, and when they pray to the
LORD toward the city you have chosen and the temple I have built for
your Name, 45 then hear from heaven
their prayer and their plea, and uphold their cause.
46 "When they sin against you — for
there is no one who does not sin[w] —
and you become angry with them and
give them over to their enemies, who
take them captive[x] to their own lands,
far away or near; 47 and if they have
a change of heart in the land where
they are held captive, and repent and
plead[y] with you in the land of their
captors and say, 'We have sinned,
we have done wrong, we have acted
wickedly';[z] 48 and if they turn back to
you with all their heart[a] and soul in
the land of their enemies who took
them captive, and pray[b] to you toward the land you gave their ancestors, toward the city you have chosen and the temple[c] I have built for
your Name; 49 then from heaven, your
dwelling place, hear their prayer and
their plea, and uphold their cause.
50 And forgive your people, who have
sinned against you; forgive all the offenses they have committed against
you, and cause their captors to show
them mercy;[d] 51 for they are your people and your inheritance,[e] whom you
brought out of Egypt, out of that iron-
smelting furnace.[f]
52 "May your eyes be open to your
servant's plea and to the plea of your
people Israel, and may you listen to
them whenever they cry out to you.
53 For you singled them out from all
the nations of the world to be your
own inheritance,[g] just as you declared through your servant Moses
when you, Sovereign LORD, brought
our ancestors out of Egypt."

8:30 [h] Ps 85:2
8:31 [i] Ex 22:11
8:32 [j] Dt 25:1
8:33 [k] Lev 26:17; Dt 28:25 [l] Lev 26:39
8:35 [m] Lev 26:19; Dt 28:24
8:36 [n] 1Sa 12:23; Ps 25:4; 94:12 [o] Ps 5:8; 27:11; Jer 6:16
8:37 [p] Lev 26:26 [q] Dt 28:22
8:39 [r] 1Sa 16:7; 1Ch 28:9; Ps 11:4; Jer 17:10; Jn 2:24; Ac 1:24
8:40 [s] Ps 130:4
8:42 [t] Dt 3:24
8:43 [u] 1Sa 17:46; 2Ki 19:19 [v] Ps 102:15
8:46 [w] Pr 20:9; Ecc 7:20; Ro 3:9; 1Jn 1:8-10 [x] Lev 26:33-39; Dt 28:64
8:47 [y] Lev 26:40; Ne 1:6 [z] Ps 106:6; Da 9:5
8:48 [a] Dt 4:29; Jer 29:12-14 [b] Da 6:10 [c] Jnh 2:4
8:50 [d] 2Ch 30:9; Ps 106:46
8:51 [e] Dt 4:20; 9:29; Ne 1:10 [f] Jer 11:4
8:53 [g] Ex 19:5; Dt 9:26-29

as an access point to that permanent, inaccessible dwelling of God.
8:31 – 32 *When … they come and swear the oath before your altar … Judge.* Legal texts and treaty formulas in Egypt and Mesopotamia reflect the same appeal to divine witness for personal accountability on matters of property, robbery and the like. See note on Ex 22:11.

54When Solomon had finished all these
prayers and supplications to the LORD, he
rose from before the altar of the LORD,
where he had been kneeling with his
hands spread out toward heaven. 55He
stood and blessed[h] the whole assembly of
Israel in a loud voice, saying:

56"Praise be to the LORD, who
has given rest[i] to his people Israel
just as he promised. Not one word
has failed of all the good promises[j]
he gave through his servant Moses.
57May the LORD our God be with us
as he was with our ancestors; may
he never leave us nor forsake[k] us.
58May he turn our hearts[l] to him, to
walk in obedience to him and keep
the commands, decrees and laws he
gave our ancestors. 59And may these
words of mine, which I have prayed
before the LORD, be near to the LORD
our God day and night, that he may
uphold the cause of his servant and
the cause of his people Israel according to each day's need, 60so that all
the peoples[m] of the earth may know
that the LORD is God and that there is
no other.[n] 61And may your hearts be
fully committed[o] to the LORD our God,
to live by his decrees and obey his
commands, as at this time."

The Dedication of the Temple

8:62-66pp — 2Ch 7:1-10

62Then the king and all Israel with him
offered sacrifices before the LORD. 63Solo-
mon offered a sacrifice of fellowship offerings to the LORD: twenty-two thousand
cattle and a hundred and twenty thousand
sheep and goats. So the king and all the
Israelites dedicated the temple of the LORD.
64On that same day the king consecrated
the middle part of the courtyard in front
of the temple of the LORD, and there he
offered burnt offerings, grain offerings
and the fat of the fellowship offerings, because the bronze altar[p] that stood before
the LORD was too small to hold the burnt
offerings, the grain offerings and the fat of
the fellowship offerings.
65So Solomon observed the festival[q]
at that time, and all Israel with him — a
vast assembly, people from Lebo Hamath[r]
to the Wadi of Egypt.[s] They celebrated it
before the LORD our God for seven days
and seven days more, fourteen days in all.
66On the following day he sent the people away. They blessed the king and then
went home, joyful and glad in heart for all
the good things the LORD had done for his
servant David and his people Israel.

The LORD Appears to Solomon

9:1-9pp — 2Ch 7:11-22

9 When Solomon had finished[t] building
the temple of the LORD and the royal
palace, and had achieved all he had desired to do, 2the LORD appeared[u] to him a
second time, as he had appeared to him at
Gibeon. 3The LORD said to him:

"I have heard[v] the prayer and plea
you have made before me; I have consecrated this temple, which you have
built, by putting my Name there forever. My eyes[w] and my heart will always be there.

4"As for you, if you walk before
me faithfully with integrity of heart[x]
and uprightness, as David[y] your father did, and do all I command and
observe my decrees and laws, 5I will
establish[z] your royal throne over Israel forever, as I promised David your
father when I said, 'You shall never
fail[a] to have a successor on the throne
of Israel.'

6"But if you[a] or your descendants
turn away[b] from me and do not observe the commands and decrees I
have given you[a] and go off to serve
other gods and worship them, 7then I
will cut off Israel from the land[c] I have
given them and will reject this temple
I have consecrated for my Name.[d] Israel will then become a byword[e] and
an object of ridicule[f] among all peoples. 8This temple will become a heap
of rubble. All[b] who pass by will be
appalled and will scoff and say, 'Why

8:55 [h] ver 14; 2Sa 6:18 **8:56** [i] Dt 12:10 [j] Jos 21:45; 23:15 **8:57** [k] Dt 31:6; Jos 1:5; Heb 13:5 **8:58** [l] Ps 119:36 **8:60** [m] Jos 4:24; 1Sa 17:46 [n] Dt 4:35; 1Ki 18:39; Jer 10:10-12 **8:61** [o] 1Ki 11:4; 15:3, 14; 2Ki 20:3 **8:64** [p] 2Ch 4:1 **8:65** [q] ver 2; Lev 23:34 [r] Nu 34:8; Jos 13:5; Jdg 3:3; 2Ki 14:25 [s] Ge 15:18 **9:1** [t] 1Ki 7:1; 2Ch 8:6 **9:2** [u] 1Ki 3:5 **9:3** [v] 2Ki 20:5; Ps 10:17 [w] Dt 11:12; 1Ki 8:29 **9:4** [x] Ge 17:1 [y] 1Ki 15:5 **9:5** [z] 1Ch 22:10 [a] 2Sa 7:15; 1Ki 2:4 **9:6** [b] 2Sa 7:14 **9:7** [c] 2Ki 17:23; 25:21 [d] Jer 7:14 [e] Ps 44:14 [f] Dt 28:37

[a] 6 The Hebrew is plural. [b] 8 See some Septuagint manuscripts, Old Latin, Syriac, Arabic and Targum; Hebrew *And though this temple is now imposing, all*

8:63 *fellowship offerings to the LORD: twenty-two thousand cattle and a hundred and twenty thousand sheep and goats.* The parameters of the fellowship offering are not clear, but the amount of meat generated could certainly have fed a large percentage of the people gathered for the temple dedication ceremony. Sacrifices numbering thousands of animals were not uncommon in the temple and palace dedications of Egyptian pharaohs and Assyrian monarchs.

9:3 – 4 *My eyes and my heart will always be there ... if you ... do all I command and observe my decrees and laws.* The Lord's commitment to the temple and his mindfulness of its location are dependent on Solomon and his people living up to their responsibilities. This relationship is consistent with the pattern of ancient Near Eastern temple accounts. The patron deity of the city typically expressed its dedication to the local temple as long as the king, priesthood and people maintained the building and its rituals. The Sumerian king Gudea received a commitment from his patron deity that resonates with Solomon's experience. In Israel the responsibilities of the people extend beyond maintenance and ritual performance to the keeping of the Torah.

has the LORD done such a thing to this
land and to this temple?’[g] 9People will
answer, ‘Because they have forsaken
the LORD their God, who brought their
ancestors out of Egypt, and have embraced other gods, worshiping and
serving them — that is why the LORD
brought all this disaster on them.’ ”

Solomon’s Other Activities

9:10-28pp — 2Ch 8:1-18

10At the end of twenty years, during
which Solomon built these two buildings — the temple of the LORD and the royal palace — 11King Solomon gave twenty
towns in Galilee to Hiram king of Tyre, because Hiram had supplied him with all the
cedar and juniper and gold[h] he wanted.
12But when Hiram went from Tyre to see
the towns that Solomon had given him, he
was not pleased with them. 13“What kind
of towns are these you have given me, my
brother?” he asked. And he called them
the Land of Kabul,[a][i] a name they have to
this day. 14Now Hiram had sent to the king
120 talents[b] of gold.
15Here is the account of the forced labor King Solomon conscripted[j] to build
the LORD’s temple, his own palace, the terraces,[c][k] the wall of Jerusalem, and Hazor,[l]
Megiddo and Gezer.[m] 16(Pharaoh king of
Egypt had attacked and captured Gezer. He
had set it on fire. He killed its Canaanite
inhabitants and then gave it as a wedding
gift to his daughter, Solomon’s wife. 17And
Solomon rebuilt Gezer.) He built up Lower
Beth Horon,[n] 18Baalath,[o] and Tadmor[d] in
the desert, within his land, 19as well as all
his store cities[p] and the towns for his chariots[q] and for his horses[e] — whatever he
desired to build in Jerusalem, in Lebanon
and throughout all the territory he ruled.
20There were still people left from the
Amorites, Hittites, Perizzites, Hivites and
Jebusites (these peoples were not Israelites). 21Solomon conscripted the descendants[r] of all these peoples remaining in
the land — whom the Israelites could not
exterminate[f][s] — to serve as slave labor,[t]
as it is to this day. 22But Solomon did not
make slaves[u] of any of the Israelites; they
were his fighting men, his government officials, his officers, his captains, and the
commanders of his chariots and charioteers. 23They were also the chief officials[v]
in charge of Solomon’s projects — 550 officials supervising those who did the work.
24After Pharaoh’s daughter[w] had come
up from the City of David to the palace
Solomon had built for her, he constructed
the terraces.[x]
25Three[y] times a year Solomon sacrificed
burnt offerings and fellowship offerings on
the altar he had built for the LORD, burning
incense before the LORD along with them,
and so fulfilled the temple obligations.

9:8 [g] Dt 29:24; Jer 22:8-9 **9:11** [h] 2Ch 8:2 **9:13** [i] Jos 19:27 **9:15** [j] Jos 16:10; 1Ki 5:13 [k] ver 24; 2Sa 5:9 [l] Jos 19:36 [m] Jos 17:11 **9:17** [n] Jos 16:3; 2Ch 8:5 **9:18** [o] Jos 19:44 **9:19** [p] ver 1 [q] 1Ki 4:26 **9:21** [r] Ge 9:25-26 [s] Jos 15:63; 17:12; Jdg 1:21, 27, 29 [t] Ezr 2:55, 58 **9:22** [u] Lev 25:39 **9:23** [v] 1Ki 5:16 **9:24** [w] 1Ki 3:1; 7:8 [x] 2Sa 5:9; 1Ki 11:27; 2Ch 32:5 **9:25** [y] Ex 23:14; 2Ch 8:12-13, 16

[a] 13 *Kabul* sounds like the Hebrew for *good-for-nothing.*
[b] 14 That is, about 4 1/2 tons or about 4 metric tons
[c] 15 Or *the Millo*; also in verse 24
[d] 18 The Hebrew may also be read *Tamar.*
[e] 19 Or *charioteers*
[f] 21 The Hebrew term refers to the irrevocable giving over of things or persons to the LORD, often by totally destroying them.

9:11 *Solomon gave twenty towns in Galilee to Hiram king of Tyre.* Land and cities were a common form of exchange between kingdoms of the ancient Near East, particularly when they were in need of friendly border adjustments. The cause for the exchange is unclear, but it likely reflects Tyre’s increasing strength and the final settling of accounts after its contribution to Solomon’s building campaign. Hiram desired a hinterland for his coastal kingdom, whereas Solomon sought to secure inland trade routes.
9:13 *brother.* Ancient Near Eastern treaties and letters indicate that this term expresses agreement or understanding between two equal parties, both kings (cf. 20:3 and note).
9:14 *120 talents of gold.* The weight of one talent is calculated by multiplying the number of shekels per talent (3,000) by the weight of a shekel (0.4 ounces or 11.5 grams) as determined by weights and measures found in the archaeological record; therefore, one talent is about 75 pounds or 34 kilograms. Thus Hiram delivers about 4.5 tons (4 metric tons) of gold to Solomon as part of the ongoing trade negotiations between the two kingdoms.
9:15 *forced labor.* Solomon’s projects relied on forced labor or corvée service demanded of the foreigners (and especially Canaanites) in his kingdom. A census determined the capacity of this labor force (v. 21). Textual records from larger ancient Near Eastern kingdoms often include abbreviated accounts of taxation, conscription and building projects that characterize a rise in status and regional influence. Solomon’s royal building program and its administration reflect programs that can be traced as far back as the early civilizations of Mesopotamia.
9:19 *store cities and the towns for his chariots and for his horses.* There is abundant evidence for administrative centers and chariot cities in the Levant and adjacent regions. During the Egyptian rule of Canaan in the fifteenth to twelfth centuries BC, garrisons were established in Megiddo, Beth Shan and other cities. They are mentioned in Egyptian annals and appear in the archaeological record as “governor’s residences.” Megiddo is the best example of an administrative center for storage and chariots dating to Solomon’s era, though substantial finds from this period have been discovered at other sites as well.
9:20 *Amorites.* See note on Nu 13:29. *Hittites.* See notes on Ge 23:3; Dt 7:1. *Perizzites, Hivites and Jebusites.* See note on Dt 7:1.
9:22–23 *fighting men ... government officials ... officers ... captains ... commanders of his chariots and charioteers ... chief officials in charge of Solomon’s projects.* The robust terminology for court officials is to be expected in ancient kingdoms that became regional hegemonies. Although Solomon’s bureaucracy is most often compared to the court of the pharaoh in nearby Egypt, the range of officials is attested in the third through first millennium BC in Syria and Mesopotamia as well.

26 King Solomon also built ships[z] at Ezion Geber,[a] which is near Elath in Edom,
on the shore of the Red Sea.[a] 27 And Hiram sent his men—sailors[b] who knew the
sea—to serve in the fleet with Solomon's
men. 28 They sailed to Ophir[c] and brought
back 420 talents[b] of gold, which they delivered to King Solomon.

The Queen of Sheba Visits Solomon

10:1-13pp — 2Ch 9:1-12

10 When the queen of Sheba[d] heard
about the fame of Solomon and his
relationship to the LORD, she came to test
Solomon with hard questions.[e] 2 Arriving
at Jerusalem with a very great caravan—
with camels carrying spices, large quantities of gold, and precious stones—she
came to Solomon and talked with him
about all that she had on her mind. 3 Solomon answered all her questions; nothing
was too hard for the king to explain to her.
4 When the queen of Sheba saw all the wisdom of Solomon and the palace he had
built, 5 the food on his table,[f] the seating of
his officials, the attending servants in their
robes, his cupbearers, and the burnt offerings he made at[c] the temple of the LORD,
she was overwhelmed.

6 She said to the king, "The report I
heard in my own country about your
achievements and your wisdom is true.
7 But I did not believe these things until I
came and saw with my own eyes. Indeed,
not even half was told me; in wisdom and
wealth[g] you have far exceeded the report I
heard. 8 How happy your people must be!
How happy your officials, who continually
stand before you and hear[h] your wisdom!
9 Praise[i] be to the LORD your God, who has
delighted in you and placed you on the
throne of Israel. Because of the LORD's
eternal love for Israel, he has made you
king to maintain justice[j] and righteousness."

10 And she gave the king 120 talents[d] of
gold,[k] large quantities of spices, and precious stones. Never again were so many
spices brought in as those the queen of
Sheba gave to King Solomon.

11 (Hiram's ships brought gold from
Ophir;[l] and from there they brought great
cargoes of almugwood[e] and precious
stones. 12 The king used the almugwood

9:26 [z] 1Ki 22:48 [a] Nu 33:35; Dt 2:8 **9:27** [b] 1Ki 10:11; Eze 27:8 **9:28** [c] 1Ch 29:4 **10:1** [d] Ge 10:7, 28; Mt 12:42; Lk 11:31 [e] Jdg 14:12 **10:5** [f] 1Ch 26:16 **10:7** [g] 1Ch 29:25 **10:8** [h] Pr 8:34 **10:9** [i] 1Ki 5:7 [j] 2Sa 8:15; Ps 33:5; 72:2 **10:10** [k] ver 2 **10:11** [l] Ge 10:29; 1Ki 9:27-28

[a] *26* Or *the Sea of Reeds* [b] *28* That is, about 16 tons or about 14 metric tons [c] *5* Or *the ascent by which he went up to* [d] *10* That is, about 4 1/2 tons or about 4 metric tons [e] *11* Probably a variant of *algumwood;* also in verse 12

9:26 *ships.* The most successful Israelite and Judahite kings are credited with maritime operations, though this was the exception for the Israelites, not the rule. Israel, and later Judah, offered a vital link between the ports of the Mediterranean and the sources of exotic goods in Arabia and east Africa. See note on 2Ch 8:18. *Ezion Geber.* The most likely site is modern Jezirat Faraun, a small island in the Gulf of Aqaba/Eilat.

9:28 *Ophir.* Most often thought to be east Africa, perhaps along the Somali coast. The items attributed to Ophir in the Biblical text are also known to originate from Arabia and Yemen, which lie opposite. Other proposals range from India to coastal Africa (including Punt and Nubia; "Nub" means gold). Gold sourced from Ophir is noted in various ancient Near Eastern documents and receipts, including a notation on an eighth-century BC ostracon discovered at Tel Qasile (Tel Aviv). See 2Ch 8:18.

10:1 *queen of Sheba.* It is not clear whether the queen herself is a ruler or she has been dispatched by her husband on a diplomatic venture. Later Assyrian contacts with Arabia often dealt with powerful queens. *Sheba.* Its location is likely to be in the vicinity of Yemen on the western edge of Arabia. Several first-millennium BC kingdoms are known to have existed in that region, as recorded in eighth-century BC Assyrian texts, and there can be little doubt that there were tribal kingdoms in the region during the days of Solomon. The journey is 1,400 miles (2,250 kilometers) long and would have taken several months.

10:2 *camels.* Domesticated camels appeared in the Levant at least by the late second millennium BC, although they were utilized much earlier in the Arabian peninsula. They were incorporated into the Assyrian army in the eighth century BC as evidenced in palace reliefs, but the archaeological record for earlier periods is scarce. *spices, large quantities of gold, and precious stones.* Trade in spice, gold and precious stones is well documented from the third millennium BC through the Arab conquest in the seventh century AD. These products, derived from Arabia and east Africa, are depicted in the Egyptian reliefs at the Hatshepsut temple in Upper Egypt along with wild animals, birds and other goods known only from Africa and Arabia.

10:5 *the food on his table, the seating of his officials, the attending servants in their robes, his cupbearers.* An analogous visual commentary on this description of Solomon's wealth is found in the banquet scenes depicted in Assyrian reliefs of the eighth and seventh centuries BC as well as in a Phoenician bronze bowl found in Cyprus. An earlier example of festivities before the king, replete with varieties of animals, food and gifts, is found in the Royal Standard of Ur, a third-millennium BC ornate box from ancient Sumer. The variety of officials in attendance and the extent of his temple offerings are reflective of a large kingdom or even an empire. The diplomatic nature of the visit is further highlighted by Solomon's overwhelming hospitality, as banquets and meals were an integral part of any personal or public relationship.

10:9 *to maintain justice and righteousness.* As the agent of the deity, the ancient Near Eastern monarch was expected to maintain order, prosperity and justice in his kingdom and to expand his domain whenever possible. In Egypt, the king regulated *maat* (truth and justice), and in Mesopotamia the monarch implemented throughout his land the just decrees of his patron god. David and Solomon performed the same function on behalf of Yahweh, as recorded in this verse and many of the psalms.

10:11 *almugwood.* Unlike the almugwood imported from Lebanon (cf. 2Ch 9:10–11), the almugwood of this verse was imported from the land of Ophir. This large timber was mostly likely a sandalwood or "Grecian juniper" that originated in Ceylon or India. Biblical and ancient Near Eastern sources indicate that it was used in the construction of large buildings and musical instruments.

to make supports[a] for the temple of the
LORD and for the royal palace, and to
make harps and lyres for the musicians.
So much almugwood has never been imported or seen since that day.)
13King Solomon gave the queen of Sheba all she desired and asked for, besides
what he had given her out of his royal
bounty. Then she left and returned with
her retinue to her own country.

Solomon's Splendor

10:14-29pp — 2Ch 1:14-17; 9:13-28

14The weight of the gold[m] that Solomon
received yearly was 666 talents,[b] 15not including the revenues from merchants and
traders and from all the Arabian kings and
the governors of the territories.
16King Solomon made two hundred large
shields[n] of hammered gold; six hundred
shekels[c] of gold went into each shield. 17He
also made three hundred small shields of
hammered gold, with three minas[d] of gold
in each shield. The king put them in the
Palace of the Forest of Lebanon.[o]
18Then the king made a great throne
covered with ivory and overlaid with fine
gold. 19The throne had six steps, and its
back had a rounded top. On both sides of
the seat were armrests, with a lion standing beside each of them. 20Twelve lions
stood on the six steps, one at either end
of each step. Nothing like it had ever been
made for any other kingdom. 21All King
Solomon's goblets were gold, and all the
household articles in the Palace of the Forest of Lebanon were pure gold. Nothing
was made of silver, because silver was
considered of little value in Solomon's
days. 22The king had a fleet of trading
ships[e][p] at sea along with the ships of Hiram. Once every three years it returned,
carrying gold, silver and ivory, and apes
and baboons.

10:14 [m] 1Ki 9:28
10:16 [n] 1Ki 14:26-28
10:17 [o] 1Ki 7:2
10:22 [p] 1Ki 9:26

[a] *12* The meaning of the Hebrew for this word is uncertain. [b] *14* That is, about 25 tons or about 23 metric tons [c] *16* That is, about 15 pounds or about 6.9 kilograms; also in verse 29 [d] *17* That is, about 3 3/4 pounds or about 1.7 kilograms; or perhaps reference is to double minas, that is, about 7 1/2 pounds or about 3.5 kilograms. [e] *22* Hebrew *of ships of Tarshish*

10:12 *lyres.* See the articles "Lyre," p. 488; "Music and Musicians," p. 524.

10:14 *666 talents.* Although this number (about 25 tons or 23 metric tons) seems exaggerated, the quantities recorded in the Bible are consistent with the revenues recorded in the empires of the ancient Near East. This amount of gold no doubt reflects Solomon's control of most trade routes on the eastern Mediterranean seaboard.

10:16 *shields of hammered gold.* Ancient shields came in a wide variety of shapes and sizes and from a range of raw materials. The Hebrew words in this verse most likely depict a small, round shield. Egyptian models and frescoes show the military and ceremonial use of shields in the second millennium BC, while the Assyrian reliefs of Sargon and Ashurbanipal are the closest to Solomon chronologically. In light of their great worth and the ineffectiveness of gold for a shield, most likely the gold shields of Solomon were made for ceremonial purposes alone; such opulent ceremonial weapons were not intended for battle, but instead provided tangible proof of a kingdom's wealth and prestige. References to gold shields and weapons are found in the gift lists of several Amarna letters and a gold-plated shield is noted in a Hittite votive text. Numerous gold ceremonial weapons have been uncovered in archaeological digs, particularly in the tomb of the Egyptian pharaoh Tutankhamen. Also, in detailing his eighth-century BC looting of Urartu, Sargon includes his seizing of ceremonial weapons, including one gold dagger weighing 27 pounds (12.25 kilograms) and six gold shields from the temple at Musasir weighing more than 100 pounds (45 kilograms) each. Similarly, the Chronicler notes that David took the gold shields carried by the officers of Hadadezer back to Jerusalem (1Ch 18:7). Shortly after Solomon's death, the Egyptian pharaoh Shishak seizes the gold shields made by Solomon following his raid on the southern kingdom (2Ch 12:9).

10:18 – 20 Solomon's regnal throne was a magnificent work of art that featured stylistics seen in other ancient Near Eastern thrones, particularly in the use of lion imagery (i.e., 12 lions on each side of six steps, and a lion next to each armrest). The throne of the Egyptian pharaoh Tutankhamun (King Tut), e.g., was a finely crafted wooden chair plated with gold and adorned with a colorful variety of precious stones and featured armrests with animal heads and animal claws at its base and the rays of the Aten as hands. The Phoenician king Ahiram is portrayed on his sarcophagus on a throne flanked by winged lions. Other images of regnal thrones with points of similarity to Solomon's throne include the throne of the Aramean king Bar Rakab, and an ivory plaque from Megiddo dating to the same period depicts a delegation with prisoners before a throne that resembles a winged sphinx. As these examples suggest, animal images were a common ancient Near Eastern royal motif as these noble beasts project strength, dominance and fortitude. Solomon's throne was also inlaid with ivory, a material prized in the ancient world for its smoothness. The use of ivory in art and architecture was an area of Phoenician expertise. Moreover, gold-covered ivory was used in the Assyrian royal palace at Nimrud (Calah). In both literary and artistic depictions the king, human or divine, sits on a throne that is elevated above his subjects. These images and the Biblical description of Solomon's six-stepped throne with sphinx-like armrests are reminiscent of the Yahweh's throne described in ch. 6.

10:22 *trading ships.* A more common translation of this verse reads "ships of Tarshish" (see NIV text note). When Biblical references are considered, Tarshish may refer either to a kind of boat or to a distant port — perhaps a city in Spain, in Cilicia (Tarsus), or in North Africa, an idea supported by a seventh-century BC Assyrian inscription that places "Tarsisi" west of Greece. It is safe to assume that Tarshish was a remote destination because the boats in this verse are recorded as returning only every three years. Because the items transported in these boats were of African origin, Tarshish may have been a trade outlet for the African interior, or it may be that in this instance the phrase "ships of Tarshish" refers generally to large cargo ships with sails. The luxury items it transported were the

[23]King Solomon was greater in riches[q]
and wisdom[r] than all the other kings of
the earth. [24]The whole world sought audience with Solomon to hear the wisdom[s]
God had put in his heart. [25]Year after year,
everyone who came brought a gift — articles of silver and gold, robes, weapons
and spices, and horses and mules.
[26]Solomon accumulated chariots and
horses;[t] he had fourteen hundred chariots
and twelve thousand horses,[a] which he
kept in the chariot cities and also with him
in Jerusalem. [27]The king made silver as
common[u] in Jerusalem as stones, and cedar as plentiful as sycamore-fig trees in the
foothills. [28]Solomon's horses were imported from Egypt and from Kue[b] — the royal
merchants purchased them from Kue at
the current price. [29]They imported a chariot from Egypt for six hundred shekels of
silver, and a horse for a hundred and fifty.[c]
They also exported them to all the kings of
the Hittites[v] and of the Arameans.

Solomon's Wives

11 King Solomon, however, loved
many foreign women[w] besides
Pharaoh's daughter — Moabites, Ammonites, Edomites, Sidonians and Hittites.
[2]They were from nations about which the
LORD had told the Israelites, "You must not
intermarry[x] with them, because they will
surely turn your hearts after their gods."
Nevertheless, Solomon held fast to them
in love. [3]He had seven hundred wives of
royal birth and three hundred concubines,
and his wives led him astray. [4]As Solomon
grew old, his wives turned his heart after
other gods, and his heart was not fully devoted[y] to the LORD his God, as the heart of
David his father had been. [5]He followed
Ashtoreth[z] the goddess of the Sidonians,
and Molek[a] the detestable god of the Ammonites. [6]So Solomon did evil in the eyes

10:23 [q] 1Ki 3:13 [r] 1Ki 4:30 **10:24** [s] 1Ki 3:9, 12, 28 **10:26** [t] Dt 17:16; 1Ki 4:26; 9:19; 2Ch 1:14; 9:25 **10:27** [u] Dt 17:17 **10:29** [v] 2Ki 7:6-7 **11:1** [w] Dt 17:17; Ne 13:26 **11:2** [x] Ex 34:16; Dt 7:3-4 **11:4** [y] 1Ki 8:61; 9:4 **11:5** [z] ver 33; Jdg 2:13; 2Ki 23:13 [a] ver 7

[a] *26* Or *charioteers* [b] *28* Probably *Cilicia* [c] *29* That is, about 3 3/4 pounds or about 1.7 kilograms

expected accoutrements of an imperial court even if they strained the linguistic and artistic abilities of Solomon's scribes and artisans (cf. v. 12). See note on 2Ch 8:18.

10:26 *chariots.* Corroborative evidence for Solomon's 1,400 chariots is found in the Qarqar inscription of 853 BC, which credits Ahab, the ninth-century BC king of northern Israel, with possessing 2,000 chariots. See 4:26 and note.

10:27 *silver as common in Jerusalem as stones.* Jerusalem was not a large city in Solomon's day, but it was wealthy. Some scholars argue that there is a dearth of archaeological material dating to David and Solomon, so that this Biblical account of the city's wealth is based on an idealized image of the city. However, this verse claims that Jerusalem was immensely wealthy, not that it encompassed vast territory. When the city is brought down to "Biblical size," one can envision a wealthy regional capital whose acreage was smaller than most of the royal cities such as Megiddo and Hazor. Pharaoh Shishak's plundering of the city after Solomon's death (described in both the Bible and in Egyptian records) is further evidence that the Jerusalem had huge wealth in the days of Solomon.

10:28–29 *imported from Egypt and from Kue ... exported them to all the kings of the Hittites and of the Arameans.* Solomon's dominance of the Levant trade routes brought him into contact with Egypt in the south and Kue in the north, the Neo-Hittite kingdom on the coastal plain below the Amanus and Taurus Mountains in what is today south-central Turkey. Through conquest or alliance (it is unclear which), Solomon controlled both Syria and the entrance to Egypt. From this position of strength he was able to broker horses from the region of Cilicia and chariots from Egypt, not to mention the spice trade from Arabia and lucrative products from Mesopotamia that reached the Mediterranean through Tadmor, Syria, Galilee and Phoenicia. See the article "All the King's Horses," p. 720.

11:1 *loved many foreign women.* In Bible times, marriages were arranged primarily for the economic and political benefit of family, clan and tribe. The number and geographic distribution of Solomon's wives is a reflection of this principle, but on the level of international relations. Solomon sealed his alliances and treaties with surrounding nations through marriage, in most cases in order to secure the continued cooperation of his vassals. Despite its prohibition in Dt 17:17, this practice was an expected part of diplomacy in the ancient Near Eastern world. As he gained power, Solomon had to participate in such diplomacy, just like the monarchs of Syria, Mesopotamia and Egypt. Ancient archives from the second millennium BC indicate that such marriage arrangements were commonplace throughout the ancient Near East. King Zimri-Lim of Mari, e.g., married a princess of Aleppo, a neighboring kingdom, and Rameses II married a Hittite princess in order to cement his peaceful relations with his past enemy. Solomon's marriage to Pharaoh's daughter is indicative of Israel's regional dominance in the tenth century BC, because the Egyptians rarely gave their daughters in marriage and only to imperial powers.

11:3 *seven hundred wives of royal birth and three hundred concubines.* In addition to being a status symbol, the royal harem maintained close ties to Solomon's constituents through marriage into families of varying clans, tribes and social classes, including wives of higher status who were counted among the royalty. Counting royal women by the hundreds was not unusual during the Iron Age. Assyrian wine lists from Nimrud indicate that as many as 300 women of various ranks lived at that palace. Extensive harems produced a large pool of heirs to ensure the enduring strength of the dynasty. In the OT world, royal marriage was not about establishing families, but about establishing alliances. A large harem is indicative not of lust on the part of the king, but of his power in international relations.

11:5 *Ashtoreth.* A goddess of fertility and the famous consort of the Canaanite god Baal. Known in Mesopotamia and Syria as Ishtar and Athirat, this goddess is best known as Astarte, the primary deity of Phoenician coastal cities. She appears in numerous texts and is depicted in painted pottery, metal plaques, and ivory from Judah, Israel and their neighbors. In the Bible, she is also referred to as "Queen of Heaven" and is presented with bread and cakes (Jer 7:18), as was the practice in ancient Phoenicia, Syria and Mesopotamia. *Molek.* Alternately named Milkom, Malik and Milku, this god was known in second-millennium BC Syria, but is figured most prominently as an Ammonite deity mentioned in Ammonite inscriptions. Identified as Canaanite Baal, this deity is associated with

of the LORD; he did not follow the LORD
completely, as David his father had done.
[7]On a hill east[b] of Jerusalem, Solomon
built a high place for Chemosh[c] the detestable god of Moab, and for Molek[d] the
detestable god of the Ammonites. [8]He did
the same for all his foreign wives, who
burned incense and offered sacrifices to
their gods.
[9]The LORD became angry with Solomon
because his heart had turned away from
the LORD, the God of Israel, who had appeared[e] to him twice. [10]Although he had
forbidden Solomon to follow other gods,[f]
Solomon did not keep the LORD's command.[g] [11]So the LORD said to Solomon,
"Since this is your attitude and you have
not kept my covenant and my decrees,
which I commanded you, I will most certainly tear[h] the kingdom away from you
and give it to one of your subordinates.
[12]Nevertheless, for the sake of David your
father, I will not do it during your lifetime.
I will tear it out of the hand of your son.
[13]Yet I will not tear the whole kingdom
from him, but will give him one tribe[i] for
the sake[j] of David my servant and for the
sake of Jerusalem, which I have chosen."[k]

Solomon's Adversaries

[14]Then the LORD raised up against Solomon an adversary, Hadad the Edomite, from the royal line of Edom. [15]Earli-
er when David was fighting with Edom,
Joab the commander of the army, who
had gone up to bury the dead, had struck
down all the men in Edom.[l] [16]Joab and all
the Israelites stayed there for six months,
until they had destroyed all the men in
Edom. [17]But Hadad, still only a boy, fled
to Egypt with some Edomite officials who
had served his father. [18]They set out from
Midian and went to Paran.[m] Then taking
people from Paran with them, they went
to Egypt, to Pharaoh king of Egypt, who
gave Hadad a house and land and provided him with food.
[19]Pharaoh was so pleased with Hadad
that he gave him a sister of his own wife,
Queen Tahpenes, in marriage. [20]The sister
of Tahpenes bore him a son named Genubath, whom Tahpenes brought up in the
royal palace. There Genubath lived with
Pharaoh's own children.
[21]While he was in Egypt, Hadad heard
that David rested with his ancestors and
that Joab the commander of the army was
also dead. Then Hadad said to Pharaoh,
"Let me go, that I may return to my own
country."
[22]"What have you lacked here that you
want to go back to your own country?"
Pharaoh asked.
"Nothing," Hadad replied, "but do let
me go!"
[23]And God raised up against Solomon
another adversary,[n] Rezon son of Eliada,
who had fled from his master, Hadadezer[o]

11:7 [b] 2Ki 23:13 [c] Nu 21:29; Jdg 11:24 [d] Lev 20:2-5; Ac 7:43 **11:9** [e] ver 2-3; 1Ki 3:5; 9:2 **11:10** [f] 1Ki 9:6 [g] 1Ki 6:12 **11:11** [h] ver 31; 1Ki 12:15-16; 2Ki 17:21 **11:13** [i] 1Ki 12:20 [j] 2Sa 7:15 [k] Dt 12:11 **11:15** [l] Dt 20:13; 2Sa 8:14; 1Ch 18:12 **11:18** [m] Nu 10:12 **11:23** [n] ver 14 [o] 2Sa 8:3

---

child sacrifice in Punic inscriptions from Carthage and in the Biblical record (2Ki 23:10; Lev 18:21; 20:2–5; Jer 32:35; see notes on 2Ki 16:3; Lev 20:2; Jer 7:31). The prophetic condemnation of child sacrifice to Molek may refer to this deity or to pagan practices named after him.

11:7 *high place.* High places (Hebrew *bamot*) proliferated throughout ancient Israel even as the prophets and Biblical writers routinely condemned them (see note on 3:2). The typical high place included a pile of stones or a staircase on a high hill. Such sites were alternate locations for improper worship of Yahweh or the veneration of pagan deities, often through sacrifice and the erection of a commemorative standing stone (Hebrew *matstsebah*) (cf. 14:23). *Chemosh.* This national god of the Moabites is described in the Mesha Stone, a ninth-century BC monumental inscription celebrating Chemosh's victory over Israel after a period of defeat and punishment. The language and nationalist expressions are reminiscent of the Bible's characterization of Yahweh, though this deity is known from other sources to have been venerated in Syria and Mesopotamia as well. The intense rivalry and animosity between Israel and its eastern neighbor is reflected in this verse and in the taunts of the Mesha Stone.

11:14–17 Long the archenemies of Judah, the Edomites are now able to exploit Solomon's internal weaknesses by operating under the patronage of Egypt. Like Solomon's internal rival, Jeroboam, Hadad will bide his time in Egypt until Israelite tribal unity becomes fragile enough for his return. Surveys and excavations in recent years have shown that Edom was a powerful tribal kingdom with settled towns as early as the second millennium BC.

11:15 *bury the dead.* The dead required proper burial, usually in the family tomb, in order ensure well-being in the afterlife. Defilement of the dead was the worst possible dishonor, a social reality that explains Joab's return to Edom as well as the horrific fate of enemy dead that is showcased in the Bible and ancient Near Eastern texts.

11:18 *Pharaoh ... gave Hadad a house and land and provided him with food.* Egypt had a long tradition of harboring foreigners during times of famine or strife in the Levant, but in this instance Egypt's motive was to cultivate allies for a return to military and economic exploitation of its northern neighbors. They would be housed, tied to their patron by marriage, and then sent back to cause as much trouble as they could, draining enemy resources and perhaps opening opportunity for conquest. The Middle Kingdom *Story of Sinuhe* brings to life Egypt's rich hospitality and manipulation of political rivals through cultivating rebels from adjacent lands. Although Hadad resided in Egypt for some time and married into the royal family of the Twenty-First Dynasty, it is not known whether his patron was Pharaoh Shishak of the Biblical record or a prior king such as Siamun (see 3:1 and note). If his patron is the same Siamun who has a treaty with Solomon, releasing Hadad to cause havoc puts the pharaoh in a very awkward position, which might explain why he encourages Hadad to stay (vv. 19–22).

11:23 *Rezon son of Eliada, who had fled from his master, Hadadezer king of Zobah.* The Aramean kingdom of

THE DIVIDED KINGDOM

930–586 BC

The division of Solomon's kingdom had geographical and political causes, with roots reaching back to earlier tribal rivalries. Israel was closer to Phoenician cities and major trade routes than Judah, whose heartland was a plateau-like ridge higher than the district around Samaria.

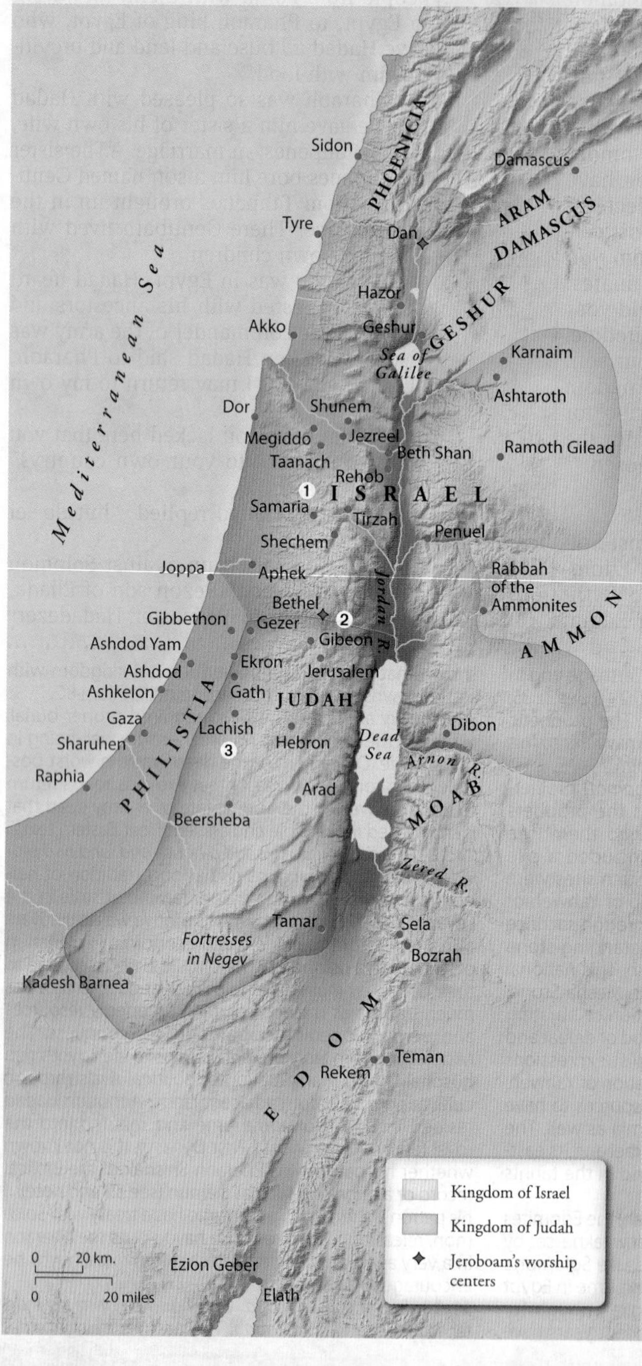

The Aramean wars were fierce and destructive contests between the kingdom of Damascus and Israel during the greater part of the ninth century. These so-called Aramean-Ephraimitic wars ended with the conquests of Jeroboam II and an era of great prosperity for Israel.

The campaigns of Tiglath-Pileser III of Assyria were enormously destructive, following a celebrated pattern of siege warfare. By 732 BC the northern kingdom was tributary to the Assyrians.

1 The final capture and destruction of Samaria took place in 722/721 BC after a long siege. The surviving inhabitants were exiled to distant places in the Assyrian Empire, and new settlers were brought to Samaria.

2 The Benjamite frontier was an issue that brought Judah and Israel into conflict early in their history. After a struggle between Asa and Baasha, the border was finally fixed south of Bethel in the territory of Benjamin.

The role of Mesha, king of Moab, was first that of a vassal and then a rebel, as both the Bible and the Mesha stele make clear.

Periods of expansion and contraction characterized the two kingdoms during the period 930–722 BC. Judah was to some extent protected by its geography, but Israel was forced to develop an efficient standing army with substantial chariotry to defend against frequent attacks. Assyrian records mention that Ahab of Israel provided 2,000 chariots—by far the largest contingent in the anti-Assyrian alliance—in the battle of Qarqar in 853 BC.

3 Judah's prosperity was intermittent and depended in large part on control of the trade routes to Egypt and the Red Sea. Border fortresses in the Judahite desert guarded the approaches from Edom. The "front door" of Judah was through Lachish and from there up to Hebron and Jerusalem. The capital was besieged many times, most forcefully by the Assyrians in 701 BC and by the Babylonians in 597 and 586, leading to the destruction of Jerusalem by Nebuchadnezzar and marking the end of the monarchy.

An impressive devotion to the Davidic dynastic line characterized the southern kingdom and helped to maintain stability, in contrast to the more mercurial northern kingdom.

king of Zobah. 24When David destroyed
Zobah's army, Rezon gathered a band of
men around him and became their leader; they went to Damascus,[p] where they
settled and took control. 25Rezon was Israel's adversary as long as Solomon lived,
adding to the trouble caused by Hadad.
So Rezon ruled in Aram[q] and was hostile
toward Israel.

Jeroboam Rebels Against Solomon

26Also, Jeroboam son of Nebat rebelled[r]
against the king. He was one of Solomon's
officials, an Ephraimite from Zeredah, and
his mother was a widow named Zeruah.

27Here is the account of how he rebelled
against the king: Solomon had built the
terraces[a][s] and had filled in the gap in the
wall of the city of David his father. 28Now
Jeroboam was a man of standing,[t] and
when Solomon saw how well[u] the young
man did his work, he put him in charge
of the whole labor force of the tribes of
Joseph.

29About that time Jeroboam was going
out of Jerusalem, and Ahijah[v] the prophet
of Shiloh met him on the way, wearing a
new cloak. The two of them were alone
out in the country, 30and Ahijah took hold
of the new cloak he was wearing and tore[w]
it into twelve pieces. 31Then he said to Jeroboam, "Take ten pieces for yourself, for
this is what the LORD, the God of Israel,
says: 'See, I am going to tear[x] the kingdom out of Solomon's hand and give you
ten tribes. 32But for the sake of my servant
David and the city of Jerusalem, which I
have chosen out of all the tribes of Israel, he will have one tribe. 33I will do this
because they have[b] forsaken me and worshiped[y] Ashtoreth the goddess of the Sidonians, Chemosh the god of the Moabites,
and Molek the god of the Ammonites, and
have not walked in obedience to me, nor
done what is right in my eyes, nor kept
my decrees[z] and laws as David, Solomon's
father, did.

34" 'But I will not take the whole kingdom out of Solomon's hand; I have made
him ruler all the days of his life for the
sake of David my servant, whom I chose
and who obeyed my commands and decrees. 35I will take the kingdom from his
son's hands and give you ten tribes. 36I
will give one tribe[a] to his son so that David my servant may always have a lamp[b]
before me in Jerusalem, the city where
I chose to put my Name. 37However, as
for you, I will take you, and you will rule
over all that your heart desires;[c] you will
be king over Israel. 38If you do whatever
I command you and walk in obedience to
me and do what is right in my eyes by
obeying my decrees[d] and commands, as
David my servant did, I will be with you.
I will build you a dynasty[e] as enduring as
the one I built for David and will give Israel to you. 39I will humble David's descendants because of this, but not forever.' "

40Solomon tried to kill Jeroboam, but
Jeroboam fled to Egypt, to Shishak[f] the
king, and stayed there until Solomon's
death.

Solomon's Death

11:41-43pp — 2Ch 9:29-31

41As for the other events of Solomon's
reign — all he did and the wisdom he displayed — are they not written in the book
of the annals of Solomon? 42Solomon
reigned in Jerusalem over all Israel forty
years. 43Then he rested with his ancestors
and was buried in the city of David his
father. And Rehoboam[g] his son succeeded
him as king.

Israel Rebels Against Rehoboam

12:1-24pp — 2Ch 10:1 – 11:4

12 Rehoboam went to Shechem, for
all Israel had gone there to make
him king. 2When Jeroboam son of Nebat

11:24 p 2Sa 8:5; 10:8, 18 **11:25** q 2Sa 10:19 **11:26** r 2Sa 20:21; 1Ki 12:2; 2Ch 13:6 **11:27** s 1Ki 9:24 **11:28** t Ru 2:1 u Pr 22:29 **11:29** v 1Ki 12:15; 14:2; 2Ch 9:29 **11:30** w 1Sa 15:27 **11:31** x ver 11 **11:33** y ver 5-7 z 1Ki 3:3 **11:36** a ver 13; 1Ki 12:17 b 1Ki 15:4; 2Ki 8:19 **11:37** c 2Sa 3:21 **11:38** d Dt 17:19 e Jos 1:5; 2Sa 7:11, 27 **11:40** f 2Ch 12:2 **11:43** g 1Ki 14:21; Mt 1:7

[a] 27 Or *the Millo* [b] 33 Hebrew; Septuagint, Vulgate and Syriac *because he has*

Zobah lay in the Beqaa Valley northwest of Damascus. It had a history of fomenting rebellion against David (cf. 2Sa 8:3 – 8). After David defeated its king, Hadadezer, a commander named Rezon formed his own military force and overtook Damascus. Late in Solomon's reign, Rezon became a powerful northern rival, gaining supremacy over Aram and northern Mesopotamia. These developments are known primarily from the Biblical text, although Hadadezer's name persists into the eighth century BC on an Aramaic seal.

11:30 *Ahijah took hold of the new cloak he was wearing and tore it into twelve pieces.* Unlike the prophets from Mesopotamia and Syria, who primarily sanctioned the actions of the king and mediated the intentions of the gods, Israelite prophets often played a strategic role in dynastic change. The tearing of garments usually accompanied mourning and impending doom (cf. Samuel's confrontation with Saul, 1Sa 15:27 – 31). Ahijah's tearing of the garment (a new one, no less) was a tangible means of asserting that his words would come to pass. A further indication of Ahijah's investment in Jeroboam may be seen indirectly from Mesopotamian legal documents that describe one's garment as a legal extension of the person and their ability to bring about change. Symbolic gestures become an important means by which the prophets convey their message (see note on Eze 6:11).

11:40 *Shishak.* See note on 14:25.

11:43 *he rested with his ancestors and was buried in the city of David his father.* See note on 2:10.

12:1 *Rehoboam went to Shechem, for all Israel had gone there to make him king.* Shechem was a logical place for such a national gathering (see note on Jos 20:7). Like prior

1 KINGS 12

The Geographic Setting of Kings

Throughout the course of ancient Near Eastern history the land of the Bible served as a bridge between Mesopotamia in the north and Egypt in the south. The book of 1 Kings documents the first time that a local kingdom was able to exert its power beyond the traditional confines of the land up to the borders of Egypt and Mesopotamia. David and Solomon created a political hegemony that included the entire Levant (Phoenicia, Aram, Israel, Philistia, Ammon, Moab, Edom) and perhaps even Egypt. The height of Israel's fortune therefore represents an anomaly in the history of the ancient Near East.

After Solomon, the southern tribe of Judah was largely confined to the central hill country and was bordered by desert regions to the south and the east. The northern tribes were spread across diverse fertile regions, such as Galilee and Samaria, that were open to foreign invasion and cultural influence. Given the geographic settings of the northern and southern tribes, it is not at all surprising that Israel split into northern and southern kingdoms soon after Solomon's death. It was a return to the natural state of affairs. Judah maintained the stable, more insular Davidic dynasty, whereas Israel, Judah's more prosperous neighbor to the north, suffered dynastic intrigue, pagan religion and premature exile. See map, p. 586. ◆

heard this (he was still in Egypt, where
he had fled[h] from King Solomon), he returned from[a] Egypt. 3So they sent for Jeroboam, and he and the whole assembly of
Israel went to Rehoboam and said to him:
4"Your father put a heavy yoke[i] on us, but
now lighten the harsh labor and the heavy
yoke he put on us, and we will serve you."
5Rehoboam answered, "Go away for
three days and then come back to me." So
the people went away.
6Then King Rehoboam consulted the
elders[j] who had served his father Solomon during his lifetime. "How would you
advise me to answer these people?" he
asked.
7They replied, "If today you will be a
servant to these people and serve them
and give them a favorable answer,[k] they
will always be your servants."
8But Rehoboam rejected the advice the
elders gave him and consulted the young
men who had grown up with him and
were serving him. 9He asked them, "What

12:2 [h] 1Ki 11:40 **12:4** [i] 1Sa 8:11-18; 1Ki 4:20-28 **12:6** [j] 1Ki 4:2 **12:7** [k] Pr 15:1

[a] 2 Or *he remained in*

Israelite kings, Rehoboam had to be ratified by the tribal leaders (cf. 1:18–21). Rehoboam was at a disadvantage by meeting in Shechem and not in Jerusalem because the strong traditions associated with Shechem most likely reminded the northern tribes of their supremacy until the days of David. Solomon lacked David's charisma and record of conquest, and his policies exacerbated traditional tribal rivalries (4:7–20). *all Israel.* Here likely refers to the northern tribes without Judah and Benjamin of the south.

12:4 *yoke.* Refers to the corvée labor noted in 9:15 (see notes on 5:13; 9:15). The Akkadian expression for yoke implies "rule" or "service." The delicate balance between royal demands and the tolerance of the populace was not an uncommon issue faced by ancient kings. The Hittite king Tudhaliya, e.g., describes an adjustment to his burdensome forced labor and taxation in a treaty document of the second millennium BC.

12:8 *Rehoboam rejected the advice the elders gave him.* Like their counterparts in the Near East, the elders of Israel seem to have been both an amorphous group in daily life settings and a recognized social stratum within the court. Kingly councils, including one in the famous Gilgamesh Epic, can be traced as far back as Sumerian texts from more than a thousand years before David and Solomon. The elders in Rehoboam's day seem to have had a much longer frame of reference than did the young courtiers who opposed them. The advice and preferences of such stratified groups could vary widely because of the varied interests of such groups. In the setting of this passage and the parallel account in 2Ch 10, the "young men" may have consisted of the royal princes aligned with Rehoboam.

is your advice? How should we answer
these people who say to me, 'Lighten the
yoke your father put on us'?"
10The young men who had grown up
with him replied, "These people have said
to you, 'Your father put a heavy yoke on
us, but make our yoke lighter.' Now tell
them, 'My little finger is thicker than my
father's waist. 11My father laid on you a
heavy yoke; I will make it even heavier.
My father scourged you with whips; I will
scourge you with scorpions.' "
12Three days later Jeroboam and all
the people returned to Rehoboam, as the
king had said, "Come back to me in three
days." 13The king answered the people
harshly. Rejecting the advice given him
by the elders, 14he followed the advice
of the young men and said, "My father
made your yoke heavy; I will make it even
heavier. My father scourged[l] you with
whips; I will scourge you with scorpions."
15So the king did not listen to the people,
for this turn of events was from the LORD,[m]
to fulfill the word the LORD had spoken to
Jeroboam son of Nebat through Ahijah[n]
the Shilonite.
16When all Israel saw that the king refused to listen to them, they answered the
king:

"What share do we have in David,
what part in Jesse's son?
To your tents, Israel![o]
Look after your own house, David!"

So the Israelites went home. 17But as for
the Israelites who were living in the towns
of Judah,[p] Rehoboam still ruled over them.

12:14 [l] Ex 1:14; 5:5-9, 16-18
12:15 [m] ver 24; Dt 2:30; Jdg 14:4; 2Ch 22:7; 25:20 [n] 1Ki 11:29
12:16 [o] 2Sa 20:1
12:17 [p] 1Ki 11:13, 36
12:18 [q] 2Sa 20:24; 1Ki 4:6; 5:14
12:19 [r] 2Ki 17:21
12:20 [s] 1Ki 11:13, 32
12:21 [t] 2Ch 11:1
12:22 [u] 2Ch 12:5-7
12:25 [v] Jdg 9:45 [w] Jdg 8:8, 17

18King Rehoboam sent out Adoniram,[a][q]
who was in charge of forced labor, but all
Israel stoned him to death. King Rehoboam, however, managed to get into his
chariot and escape to Jerusalem. 19So Israel has been in rebellion against the house
of David[r] to this day.
20When all the Israelites heard that Jeroboam had returned, they sent and called
him to the assembly and made him king
over all Israel. Only the tribe of Judah remained loyal to the house of David.[s]
21When Rehoboam arrived in Jerusalem, he mustered all Judah and the tribe
of Benjamin — a hundred and eighty thousand able young men — to go to war[t]
against Israel and to regain the kingdom
for Rehoboam son of Solomon.
22But this word of God came to Shemaiah[u] the man of God: 23"Say to Rehoboam
son of Solomon king of Judah, to all Judah and Benjamin, and to the rest of the
people, 24'This is what the LORD says: Do
not go up to fight against your brothers,
the Israelites. Go home, every one of you,
for this is my doing.' " So they obeyed the
word of the LORD and went home again, as
the LORD had ordered.

Golden Calves at Bethel and Dan

25Then Jeroboam fortified Shechem[v]
in the hill country of Ephraim and lived
there. From there he went out and built
up Peniel.[b][w]
26Jeroboam thought to himself, "The

[a] 18 Some Septuagint manuscripts and Syriac (see also 4:6 and 5:14); Hebrew *Adoram* [b] 25 Hebrew *Penuel,* a variant of *Peniel*

A similar situation is found in the Sumerian story "Gilgamesh and Akka." This narrative describes a time of tension between the ancient Mesopotamian cities of Kish (ruled by Akka) and Uruk (ruled by Gilgamesh) over the workload demanded by Akka in the digging of wells. Although Uruk was under the control of Kish, Gilgamesh sought to rebel, a notion supported by his youthful advisors but not supported by the city's assembly of elders. In the end, like Rehoboam, Gilgamesh rejected the counsel of the elders for that of his "youthful" advisors, who, incidentally, nominated Gilgamesh to be their king.

12:11 *scorpions.* This may be metaphoric, or it may refer to a kind of whip embedded with fragments of metal or glass, though these are unattested prior to Roman times. An Akkadian list does mention a copper "scorpion" along with copper fetters for slaves, and some have suggested this refers to the tip of a scourge.

12:16 *What share do we have in David, what part in Jesse's son? To your tents, Israel!* The scene is almost a repeat of prior revolts in Israel (cf. 2Sa 20:1). The division of the monarchy is commonly referred to as the "schism," but in reality the division into northern and southern kingdoms was a return to the natural state of affairs based on geographic realities and long-held tribal associations. The tensions of the tribal league described in Judges will now manifest themselves in military conflict between neighboring polities. *Look after your own house, David!* The people of the north may be referring to the relative inferiority of Judah's resources in comparison to the large, well-watered north.

12:21 *a hundred and eighty thousand.* See the article "Numbers in Numbers," p. 235.

12:24 *This is what the LORD says: Do not go up to fight against your brothers.* Israel is not alone in the practice of consulting prophets regarding potential military action, though prophets from the ancient world generally encourage the king to pursue his agenda for battle. The prophetic caution against military invasion such as is found in this passage, while far less common in non-Israelite prophetic traditions, is attested in a small number of texts, including a stern warning to King Zimri-Lim of the second-millennium BC kingdom of Mari not to proceed into battle. Overall, prophets in Israel were much more likely than their ancient Near Eastern counterparts to resist the king's desires or to criticize him.

12:25 *Jeroboam fortified Shechem ... and built up Peniel.* Traces of Jeroboam's building activities at Shechem have been unearthed, though they are unimpressive when compared to the massive walls, gates and public buildings of the second-millennium Middle Bronze Age city. Jeroboam's royal initiatives at other strategic centers are attested in a beautiful seal that bears his name. Found at Megiddo in the Jezreel Valley, it bears the name of

kingdom will now likely revert to the
house of David. 27 If these people go up to
offer sacrifices at the temple of the LORD
in Jerusalem,[x] they will again give their
allegiance to their lord, Rehoboam king
of Judah. They will kill me and return to
King Rehoboam."
28 After seeking advice, the king made
two golden calves.[y] He said to the people,
"It is too much for you to go up to Jerusalem. Here are your gods, Israel, who
brought you up out of Egypt."[z] 29 One he
set up in Bethel,[a] and the other in Dan.[b]
30 And this thing became a sin;[c] the people came to worship the one at Bethel and
went as far as Dan to worship the other.[a]
31 Jeroboam built shrines[d] on high places and appointed priests[e] from all sorts of
people, even though they were not Levites.
32 He instituted a festival on the fifteenth
day of the eighth[f] month, like the festival
held in Judah, and offered sacrifices on

12:27 [x]Dt 12:5-6 **12:28** [y]Ex 32:4; 2Ki 10:29; 17:16 [z]Ex 32:8 **12:29** [a]Ge 28:19 [b]Jdg 18:27-31 **12:30** [c]1Ki 13:34; 2Ki 17:21 **12:31** [d]1Ki 13:32 [e]Nu 3:10; 1Ki 13:33; 2Ki 17:32; 2Ch 11:14-15; 13:9 **12:32** [f]Lev 23:33-34; Nu 29:12

[a] *30* Probable reading of the original Hebrew text; Masoretic Text *people went to the one as far as Dan*

"Shema, servant of Jeroboam." Recent analysis of the seal's original context in the gate of Megiddo indicates that it may well have belonged to this tenth-century BC king. *Peniel.* Identified with Tell edh-Dhahab, it lay near the mouth of the Jabbok canyon in Transjordan, not far from the broad Jordan Valley. Its selection as an alternate capital city most likely reflects Jeroboam's need for a place of retreat should his fledgling kingdom suffer invasion. His attention to the site may also be explained by his desire to forge close ties with the Israelite tribes of Gad and Reuben in the mountains of Gilead. It was in any case a sufficiently important city to be included in Shishak's list of destroyed towns in his campaign shortly after Solomon's death.

12:28 *golden calves.* Ancient Near Eastern religious tradition reinforced the power and virility of key deities through association with the bull and calf (see note on 7:23 – 26). In the Canaanite tradition, e.g., both the patron god El and the warrior-god of fertility, Baal, were often referred to as "bull" or "calf." The image is used repeatedly in the Ugaritic myths as well. It is important to note that these creatures represented not the gods themselves but only their attributes. Whether they were cast in metal or incorporated into architecture or incense stands, the bovines were the pedestal or footstool on which the deity was thought to stand.

This iconography and the principles that underlie it are closely related to the ornate thrones of earthly kings. In seeking to replace traditional worship of Yahweh in Jerusalem, Jeroboam initiated a syncretistic pattern that culminated in national Baal worship under the reign of Ahab and Jezebel. Bronze or composite bull or calf figurines have been found in several archaeological excavations (e.g., Mount Gilboa, Hazor and Ashkelon; also a ceramic one at Shiloh), but these are only three to seven inches (seven to eighteen centimeters) long.

Variations of bovine (including calves, bulls and cows) were commonly portrayed in connection with divinity in Mesopotamia, Persia, Egypt, Canaan and Anatolia. The specific association of bovine with the divine realm varied and included the animal as god/goddess, the animal as a bearer (or pedestal) of a god (recall the 12 large bulls on which the "bronze Sea" rested in 7:25), and the animal as an emblematic symbol whose potency, strength and fertility (fecundity) represented attributes of the divine realm.

In Egypt, the Apis bull was understood as a manifestation of the creator god Ptah while the Egyptian goddess of love (Hathor) was typically depicted as cow and the Egyptian god Monto was known as the mighty bull. Also, in Coffin Text 261 the Egyptian god Heka addresses the "bulls of heaven" in his claim to supremacy among the pantheon. Similarly, the Sumerian god Nanna (later associated with the Babylonian moon-god Sin) is described in a praise hymn as a "ferocious bull whose horn is thick" and, like the Canaanite Baal, is described as the "Bull of Heaven." In Canaan and Syria, the god Baal (Hadad) was depicted with bronze, silver and golden calf idols, and his divine sister (Anat) is depicted as a cow in conjunction with her liaison with Baal, who mounts her "like a bull." Lastly, golden calves as a religious symbol are reflected in the discovery of golden calves in the tomb of the priestess of Nanna at Ur.

Given the range of bovine imagery in the ancient Near East, Jeroboam's calves (like those of Aaron in Ex 32) may not be intended as deity (in violation of the first commandment). Rather, they may reflect growing syncretism with neighboring religious systems (likely Egyptian or Canaanite influence) or may reflect the human tendency to make an image of Israel's God in line with a common means of representing deity in the ancient Near East (in violation of the second commandment). See the article "The Golden Calf," p. 167.

12:29 *Bethel ... Dan.* Jeroboam chose these locations based on preexisting traditions and geopolitical considerations. The setting of Dan in the north held great promise as a pagan shrine because of its abundant water and vegetation, as well as its position at the foot of majestic Mount Hermon, which towers nearly 10,000 feet (3,000 meters) above the plain. These abundant images of fertility and provision figured prominently in Israelite and ancient Near Eastern ritual and iconography and were considered to be the physical manifestations of the deity's power and virility. The altars, calves and religious practices drew on the existing syncretism of the northern tribes that reached its zenith in the days of Ahab (ninth century BC) and Jeroboam II (eighth century BC). Dan also lay on the northern perimeter of Jeroboam's kingdom on the main route connecting Israel to Aram, Damascus and the interior of Mesopotamia.

To the south, Bethel's appeal was its location on the border of Judah and the rich spiritual and ethnic heritage of the site from the days of Abraham to the period of the monarchy. Because it lay on the route to Jerusalem, Bethel was perfectly situated to entice Israelites away from the traditional and legitimate religious center in Jerusalem. It was also a convenient rallying place on the plateau between Israel and Judah. Just as David had united the tribes around a new shrine in Jerusalem, so Jeroboam combined diplomacy and religion to draw his people to Dan and Bethel.

12:31 *appointed priests from all sorts of people ... not Levites.* Jeroboam is worried that the Levitical priesthood will not be supportive of him, so he appoints new priests with securer loyalties. The priesthood had significant power in the ancient Near East. Akhenaten of Egypt and Nabonidus of Babylon both tried to reform their state religions, and both dynasties lost their power as the slighted priesthood took revenge.

The high place at Dan, built by Jeroboam (1Ki 12:31).
Kim Walton

the altar. This he did in Bethel, sacrificing
to the calves he had made. And at Bethel
he also installed priests at the high places
he had made. 33On the fifteenth day of the
eighth month, a month of his own choosing, he offered sacrifices on the altar he
had built at Bethel.[g] So he instituted the
festival for the Israelites and went up to
the altar to make offerings.

The Man of God From Judah

13 By the word of the LORD a man of
God[h] came from Judah to Bethel,[i]
as Jeroboam was standing by the altar
to make an offering. 2By the word of the
LORD he cried out against the altar: "Altar,
altar! This is what the LORD says: 'A son
named Josiah[j] will be born to the house of
David. On you he will sacrifice the priests
of the high places who make offerings
here, and human bones will be burned
on you.' " 3That same day the man of God
gave a sign:[k] "This is the sign the LORD has
declared: The altar will be split apart and
the ashes on it will be poured out."
4When King Jeroboam heard what the
man of God cried out against the altar at
Bethel, he stretched out his hand from the
altar and said, "Seize him!" But the hand
he stretched out toward the man shriveled
up, so that he could not pull it back. 5Also,
the altar was split apart and its ashes
poured out according to the sign given by
the man of God by the word of the LORD.

12:33 [g] Nu 15:39; 1Ki 13:1; Am 7:13
13:1 [h] 2Ki 23:17 [i] 1Ki 12:32-33
13:2 [j] 2Ki 23:15-16,20
13:3 [k] Jdg 6:17; Isa 7:14; Jn 2:11; 1Co 1:22

12:33 *he instituted the festival for the Israelites.* It is unclear whether Jeroboam's new festival coincided with the Festival of Tabernacles or the New Year Festival practiced in Jerusalem. Scheduling it simultaneously to a pilgrimage festival such as the New Year Festival would be a logical choice, as it would approximate and displace the Jerusalem experience.

13:2 *he cried out against the altar.* It is not unusual for a prophet in the ancient Near East to declare a shrine illegitimate. *human bones will be burned on you.* Although there is debate as to whether the Israelites ever practiced human sacrifice, it did occur in the Canaanite and Phoenician cultures. The so-called Tophet at Carthage is a prime example. An Egyptian relief of an assault on a Canaanite town may include a depiction of human sacrifice. The defenders hold incense stands, raise their hands, and cast individuals out of a fortified tower.

13:3 *This is the sign the LORD has declared: The altar will be split apart and the ashes on it will be poured out.* The test of a prophet's veracity was whether or not the prediction came true, or more dramatically, the production of a miraculous sign, in this case the destruction of both the altar and (the ashes of) the gift that had been offered on it. Altars were normally made of limestone; impurities or improper preparation could cause them to crack when exposed to heat.

6Then the king said to the man of God,
"Intercede[l] with the LORD your God and
pray for me that my hand may be restored." So the man of God interceded
with the LORD, and the king's hand was
restored and became as it was before.
7The king said to the man of God,
"Come home with me for a meal, and I
will give you a gift."[m]
8But the man of God answered the king,
"Even if you were to give me half your
possessions,[n] I would not go with you, nor
would I eat bread[o] or drink water here.
9For I was commanded by the word of the
LORD: 'You must not eat bread or drink water or return by the way you came.' " 10So
he took another road and did not return by
the way he had come to Bethel.
11Now there was a certain old prophet living in Bethel, whose sons came and
told him all that the man of God had done
there that day. They also told their father
what he had said to the king. 12Their father asked them, "Which way did he go?"
And his sons showed him which road the
man of God from Judah had taken. 13So
he said to his sons, "Saddle the donkey
for me." And when they had saddled the
donkey for him, he mounted it 14and rode
after the man of God. He found him sitting
under an oak tree and asked, "Are you the
man of God who came from Judah?"
"I am," he replied.
15So the prophet said to him, "Come
home with me and eat."
16The man of God said, "I cannot turn
back and go with you, nor can I eat bread[p]
or drink water with you in this place. 17I
have been told by the word of the LORD:
'You must not eat bread or drink water
there or return by the way you came.' "
18The old prophet answered, "I too am
a prophet, as you are. And an angel said
to me by the word of the LORD: 'Bring him
back with you to your house so that he
may eat bread and drink water.' " (But he
was lying[q] to him.) 19So the man of God
returned with him and ate and drank in
his house.
20While they were sitting at the table,
the word of the LORD came to the old
prophet who had brought him back. 21He
cried out to the man of God who had come

13:6 [l] Ex 8:8; 9:28; 10:17; Lk 6:27-28; Ac 8:24; Jas 5:16
13:7 [m] 1Sa 9:7; 2Ki 5:15
13:8 [n] Nu 22:18; 24:13 [o] ver 16
13:16 [p] ver 8
13:18 [q] Dt 13:3

13:21 [r] ver 26
13:24 [s] 1Ki 20:36
13:30 [t] Jer 22:18
13:31 [u] 2Ki 23:18
13:32 [v] ver 2; Lev 26:30 [w] 1Ki 16:24,28 [x] 2Ki 23:16
13:33 [y] 1Ki 12:31; 2Ch 11:15; 13:9

from Judah, "This is what the LORD says:
'You have defied[r] the word of the LORD and
have not kept the command the LORD your
God gave you. 22You came back and ate
bread and drank water in the place where
he told you not to eat or drink. Therefore
your body will not be buried in the tomb
of your ancestors.' "
23When the man of God had finished
eating and drinking, the prophet who had
brought him back saddled his donkey for
him. 24As he went on his way, a lion[s] met
him on the road and killed him, and his
body was left lying on the road, with both
the donkey and the lion standing beside
it. 25Some people who passed by saw the
body lying there, with the lion standing
beside the body, and they went and reported it in the city where the old prophet
lived.
26When the prophet who had brought
him back from his journey heard of it, he
said, "It is the man of God who defied the
word of the LORD. The LORD has given him
over to the lion, which has mauled him
and killed him, as the word of the LORD
had warned him."
27The prophet said to his sons, "Saddle the donkey for me," and they did so.
28Then he went out and found the body
lying on the road, with the donkey and the
lion standing beside it. The lion had neither eaten the body nor mauled the donkey. 29So the prophet picked up the body
of the man of God, laid it on the donkey,
and brought it back to his own city to
mourn for him and bury him. 30Then he
laid the body in his own tomb, and they
mourned over him and said, "Alas, my
brother!"[t]
31After burying him, he said to his sons,
"When I die, bury me in the grave where
the man of God is buried; lay my bones[u]
beside his bones. 32For the message he declared by the word of the LORD against the
altar in Bethel and against all the shrines
on the high places[v] in the towns of Samaria[w] will certainly come true."[x]
33Even after this, Jeroboam did not
change his evil ways, but once more appointed priests for the high places from
all sorts[y] of people. Anyone who wanted to become a priest he consecrated for

13:7 *Come home with me for a meal, and I will give you a gift.* Middle Eastern hospitality was as central in Biblical times as it is today. The sharing of a meal signified a bond of friendship that was not easily broken. The host typically shared his finest produce, as can be seen in Mesopotamian banquet scenes from Ur and Assyria. Gifts were often exchanged at such gatherings. Given this cultural setting, the prophet's rejection of hospitality is jarring and signifies overt hostility (v. 8; cf. 2:7).

13:13 *donkey.* The most common pack animal in antiquity. Horses were reserved for military use and for pulling large carts or chariots.

13:26 *given him over to the lion.* In the many treaties from the ancient Near East, one of the curses found is, "May Bethel and Anath-Bethel deliver you to a man-eating lion." This was a punishment for breaking an oath. In this passage, the prophet's encounter with a lion is interpreted as God's punishment for oath breaking.

the high places. 34This was the sin[z] of the
house of Jeroboam that led to its downfall and to its destruction[a] from the face
of the earth.

Ahijah's Prophecy Against Jeroboam

14 At that time Abijah son of Jeroboam became ill, 2and Jeroboam said
to his wife, "Go, disguise yourself, so you
won't be recognized as the wife of Jeroboam. Then go to Shiloh. Ahijah[b] the prophet is there — the one who told me I would
be king over this people. 3Take ten loaves
of bread[c] with you, some cakes and a jar
of honey, and go to him. He will tell you
what will happen to the boy." 4So Jeroboam's wife did what he said and went to
Ahijah's house in Shiloh.
Now Ahijah could not see; his sight was
gone because of his age. 5But the LORD had
told Ahijah, "Jeroboam's wife is coming
to ask you about her son, for he is ill, and
you are to give her such and such an answer. When she arrives, she will pretend
to be someone else."
6So when Ahijah heard the sound of
her footsteps at the door, he said, "Come
in, wife of Jeroboam. Why this pretense?
I have been sent to you with bad news.
7Go, tell Jeroboam that this is what the
LORD, the God of Israel, says: 'I raised you
up from among the people and appointed
you ruler[d] over my people Israel. 8I tore[e]
the kingdom away from the house of David and gave it to you, but you have not
been like my servant David, who kept my
commands and followed me with all his
heart, doing only what was right[f] in my
eyes. 9You have done more evil than all
who lived before you. You have made for
yourself other gods, idols[g] made of metal; you have aroused my anger and turned
your back on me.[h]
10" 'Because of this, I am going to bring
disaster on the house of Jeroboam. I will
cut off from Jeroboam every last male in
Israel — slave or free.[a][i] I will burn up the
house of Jeroboam as one burns dung, until it is all gone.[j] 11Dogs[k] will eat those belonging to Jeroboam who die in the city,
and the birds will feed on those who die in
the country. The LORD has spoken!'
12"As for you, go back home. When you
set foot in your city, the boy will die. 13All
Israel will mourn for him and bury him.
He is the only one belonging to Jeroboam
who will be buried, because he is the only
one in the house of Jeroboam in whom
the LORD, the God of Israel, has found anything good.[l]
14"The LORD will raise up for himself a
king over Israel who will cut off the family
of Jeroboam. Even now this is beginning
to happen.[b] 15And the LORD will strike Israel, so that it will be like a reed swaying in
the water. He will uproot[m] Israel from this
good land that he gave to their ancestors
and scatter them beyond the Euphrates
River, because they aroused[n] the LORD's
anger by making Asherah[o] poles.[c] 16And
he will give Israel up because of the sins[p]
Jeroboam has committed and has caused
Israel to commit."
17Then Jeroboam's wife got up and
left and went to Tirzah.[q] As soon as she
stepped over the threshold of the house,
the boy died. 18They buried him, and all
Israel mourned for him, as the LORD had
said through his servant the prophet Ahijah.
19The other events of Jeroboam's reign,
his wars and how he ruled, are written in

13:34 [z] 1Ki 12:30 [a] 1Ki 14:10
14:2 [b] 1Sa 28:8; 2Sa 14:2; 1Ki 11:29
14:3 [c] 1Sa 9:7
14:7 [d] 2Sa 12:7-8; 1Ki 16:2
14:8 [e] 1Ki 11:31, 33, 38 [f] 1Ki 15:5
14:9 [g] Ex 34:17; 1Ki 12:28; 2Ch 11:15 [h] Ne 9:26; Ps 50:17; Eze 23:35
14:10 [i] Dt 32:36; 1Ki 21:21; 2Ki 9:8-9; 14:26 [j] 1Ki 15:29
14:11 [k] 1Ki 16:4; 21:24
14:13 [l] 2Ch 12:12; 19:3
14:15 [m] Dt 29:28; 2Ki 15:29; 17:6; Ps 52:5 [n] Jos 23:15-16 [o] Ex 34:13; Dt 12:3
14:16 [p] 1Ki 12:30; 13:34; 15:30, 34; 16:2
14:17 [q] ver 12; 1Ki 15:33; 16:6-9

[a] 10 Or *Israel — every ruler or leader* [b] 14 The meaning of the Hebrew for this sentence is uncertain. [c] 15 That is, wooden symbols of the goddess Asherah; here and elsewhere in 1 Kings

14:3 *Take ten loaves of bread with you, some cakes and a jar of honey.* It was common practice to present votive gifts when visiting a prophet or person of authority, particularly if a favor was to be requested. *honey.* It is unclear whether the honey in this instance was wild or cultivated, as there is no mention of hive cultivation activity in the Bible. Nevertheless, the Egyptians were producing honey centuries before, and beehives have been excavated from this time period at Tel Rehov indicating that Israelites were also doing so.

14:9 – 10 *you have aroused my anger … Because of this, I am going to bring disaster.* In this verse and throughout the historical record of Israel, Yahweh rewards and punishes his subjects individually and corporately. The Bible is not unique in explaining the demise of kings and empires as divine retribution for religious disobedience. One of the best ancient Near Eastern parallels to this Biblical retribution theme is found in the Curse of Agade. In this account, a successful Mesopotamian king named Naram-Sin desecrates a temple of the god Enlil, who is credited with the eventual demise of his kingdom. As a result, the impulsive king loses the very kingdom he strove so hard to build.

14:11 *Dogs will eat … birds will feed on.* In the ancient world, desecration of the deceased put in jeopardy the well-being and repose of that person in the underworld. If a body was not buried, the spirit could not pass into the netherworld and would roam the earth causing problems to the living. The body gave the dead person identity in the netherworld. In Babylonian thinking, burial gave the spirit a place to reside once the body transitioned to the netherworld through decomposition. With no identity in the world of the dead, the individual would find no rest, receive no care and have no hope. No punishment could be greater than to be consumed by roaming dogs and fowl. Some rulers enforced their treaties by threatening disloyal subjects with just such a fate. The Assyrian king Esarhaddon employed this threat in one of his treaties. The prophets of 1 Kings raised the prospect of this treatment repeatedly, but even such horrific images did not produce moral correction.

14:19 *the book of the annals of the kings of Israel.* The author of 1,2 Kings makes frequent reference to the "book of the annals" (e.g., v. 29; 15:7,23,31; 2Ki 15:6,11,15,21,26,31,36). This

the book of the annals of the kings of Israel. 20He reigned for twenty-two years and
then rested with his ancestors. And Nadab
his son succeeded him as king.

Rehoboam King of Judah

14:21,25-31pp — 2Ch 12:9-16

21Rehoboam son of Solomon was king
in Judah. He was forty-one years old when
he became king, and he reigned seventeen years in Jerusalem, the city the LORD
had chosen out of all the tribes of Israel in
which to put his Name. His mother's name
was Naamah; she was an Ammonite.[r]
22Judah[s] did evil in the eyes of the LORD.
By the sins they committed they stirred
up his jealous anger[t] more than those
who were before them had done. 23They
also set up for themselves high places, sacred stones[u] and Asherah poles on every
high hill and under every spreading tree.[v]
24There were even male shrine prostitutes[w]
in the land; the people engaged in all the
detestable practices of the nations the LORD
had driven out before the Israelites.
25In the fifth year of King Rehoboam,
Shishak king of Egypt attacked[x] Jerusalem. 26He carried off the treasures of the
temple[y] of the LORD and the treasures of
the royal palace. He took everything, including all the gold shields[z] Solomon had
made. 27So King Rehoboam made bronze
shields to replace them and assigned these
to the commanders of the guard on duty at

14:21 [r]ver 31; 1Ki 11:1; 2Ch 12:13
14:22 [s]2Ch 12:1 [t]Dt 32:21; Ps 78:58; 1Co 10:22
14:23 [u]Dt 16:22; 2Ki 17:9-10; Eze 16:24-25 [v]Dt 12:2; Isa 57:5
14:24 [w]Dt 23:17; 1Ki 15:12; 2Ki 23:7
14:25 [x]1Ki 11:40; 2Ch 12:2
14:26 [y]1Ki 15:15,18 [z]1Ki 10:17

---

was likely part of a robust court record of the type discovered in ancient Mesopotamia, Anatolia and Egypt. Vast archives from these empires and regional kingdoms such as Ebla and Mari provide a glimpse of the size and range of topics that likely characterized the lost court records of ancient Israel. These archives include letters from and to the king, court documents and records of military campaigns. A fine illustration is the court archival material from the capital of the Hittite Empire, dating to the middle of the second millennium BC. It describes a range of activities that took place in the court.

14:23 *high places, sacred stones and Asherah poles.* Because the Biblical (and especially prophetic) condemnation of pagan cultic practices was so extensive, one can conclude that these practices were ubiquitous during much of the period recorded in 1 Kings. The archaeological record largely corroborates these condemnations. *high places.* See notes on 3:2; 11:7. *sacred stones.* In the ancient world, cult symbols such as standing stones are abundantly observable. These standing stones could at times be deified (i.e., considered to contain the essence of a deity), probably the function of the two found in the vicinity of the Iron Age temple unearthed at Israelite Arad. Others were believed to represent ancestral spirits; still others simply stood as memorials of treaties or special events (notice the 12 set up by Moses in Ex 24:4 – 8). *Asherah poles.* The people venerated Asherah, consort of the main Canaanite deity El, by setting up poles of wood or stone. This practice, similar to the setting up of standing stones (Hebrew *matstsebot*), is well documented both in the Bible and in archaeological discoveries.

14:24 *male shrine prostitutes.* See note on Dt 23:17 – 18.

14:25 *fifth year of King Rehoboam.* Most likely 926 BC. Rehoboam began his reign following the death of Solomon (c. 931 BC), with the division of the kingdom occurring shortly thereafter. The Chronicler, in his parallel account of Rehoboam's reign (2Ch 10 – 12), notes that there was a three-year period in which Rehoboam was loyal to Yahweh (c. 930 – 927 BC) followed by apostasy, providing a context (theological and historical) for the time leading up to Shishak's invasion (2Ch 11:17 — 12:1). *Shishak king of Egypt.* The last pharaoh of the Twenty-First Dynasty (Psusennes II, c. 965 – 931 BC) did not have a male son and thus promoted a Libyan military commander named Sheshonq I (Biblical Shishak; variously spelled as Sheshonq, Sheshonk, Shosheng and Shusheq by Egyptologists) to a position of virtual heir to the throne. When Psusennes II died, Sheshonq became the pharaoh, founding the Twenty-Second Dynasty. He facilitated the reunification of Upper (Southern) and Lower (Northern) Egypt through deft political decisions, strategic priestly appointments and key marriage arrangements. This internal unity in turn strengthened Egypt's ability to expand trading activities and international influence, particularly in Phoenicia and Canaan. *attacked Jerusalem.* The summary of Shishak's invasion in the parallel account in 2Ch 12 provides additional details of Shishak's campaign over those disclosed in 1Ki 14, such as the extent of Shishak's invasion, the number of chariots involved in the battle (1,200), the number of cavalry/horsemen (60,000) and the multiethnic composition of his military coalition (Libyans, Sukkites and Cushites [Nubians or Ethiopians]). The details of Shishak's invasion are celebrated on the southwest wall of the Karnak temple in Thebes — a topographic inventory of more than 150 hieroglyphic place-names recorded as part of his expansion of the temple via the Bubastite Gate. Of this number, approximately 30 names have been effaced and other names are proposed reconstructions. The upper register of Shishak's list contains a number of towns in what was primarily the territory of the northern kingdom of Israel, including cities along the coastal highway (such as Soko and Yaham), places in the Jezreel Valley (such as Taanach and Megiddo), towns in the Beth Shan (Shean) Valley (including Beth Shan and Rehob) and places in the Transjordan region (such as Adam and Penuel). These victories undoubtedly restored Egyptian domination over important trade routes through these areas. In the upper register of his temple inscription Shishak also records the defeat of several towns in the territory of the southern kingdom of Judah, including Gibeon (in the central hill country) and Aijalon (one of Rehoboam's fortified cities in the Shephelah). Moreover, the lower register of Shishak's list focuses on towns in the southern region of Judah (the Biblical Negev), perhaps aimed at reasserting Egyptian control over trade routes to Arabia. The absence of Jerusalem in Shishak's lists is noteworthy, although any notations summarizing the plundering of Jerusalem may have been among the destroyed sections of the inscription.

14:26 *He took everything.* Shishak's goal was not only to reassert Egyptian supremacy in the southern Levant. He had his sights set on Solomon's famed treasury. An appreciation for the geographic environs of Jerusalem can help to explain how Shishak could extract such riches from Solomon without destroying Jerusalem. A broad highland plateau lies north of the city in the center of Benjamin's tribal territory. Convenient routes connect this plateau to Gezer and the coast in the west, to Jericho

the entrance to the royal palace. 28When-
ever the king went to the LORD's temple,
the guards bore the shields, and afterward
they returned them to the guardroom.
29As for the other events of Rehoboam's
reign, and all he did, are they not written in the book of the annals of the kings
of Judah? 30There was continual warfare[a]
between Rehoboam and Jeroboam. 31And
Rehoboam rested with his ancestors and
was buried with them in the City of David.
His mother's name was Naamah; she was
an Ammonite.[b] And Abijah[a] his son succeeded him as king.

Abijah King of Judah

15:1-2,6-8pp — 2Ch 13:1-2,22 – 14:1

15 In the eighteenth year of the reign
of Jeroboam son of Nebat, Abijah[b]
became king of Judah, 2and he reigned in
Jerusalem three years. His mother's name
was Maakah[c] daughter of Abishalom.[c]
3He committed all the sins his father
had done before him; his heart was not
fully devoted[d] to the LORD his God, as the
heart of David his forefather had been.
4Nevertheless, for David's sake the LORD
his God gave him a lamp[e] in Jerusalem
by raising up a son to succeed him and
by making Jerusalem strong. 5For David
had done what was right in the eyes of the
LORD and had not failed to keep[f] any of the
LORD's commands all the days of his life —
except in the case of Uriah[g] the Hittite.
6There was war[h] between Abijah[d] and
Jeroboam throughout Abijah's lifetime.
7As for the other events of Abijah's reign,
and all he did, are they not written in the
book of the annals of the kings of Judah?
There was war between Abijah and Jeroboam. 8And Abijah rested with his ancestors and was buried in the City of David.
And Asa his son succeeded him as king.

Asa King of Judah

15:9-22pp — 2Ch 14:2-3; 15:16 – 16:6
15:23-24pp — 2Ch 16:11 – 17:1

9In the twentieth year of Jeroboam king
of Israel, Asa became king of Judah, 10and
he reigned in Jerusalem forty-one years.
His grandmother's name was Maakah[i]
daughter of Abishalom.
11Asa did what was right in the eyes of
the LORD, as his father David had done.
12He expelled the male shrine prostitutes[j]
from the land and got rid of all the idols
his ancestors had made. 13He even deposed his grandmother Maakah from her
position as queen mother, because she had
made a repulsive image for the worship of
Asherah. Asa cut it down[k] and burned it
in the Kidron Valley. 14Although he did not
remove the high places, Asa's heart was
fully committed[l] to the LORD all his life.
15He brought into the temple of the LORD
the silver and gold and the articles that he
and his father had dedicated.[m]
16There was war[n] between Asa and Baasha king of Israel throughout their reigns.
17Baasha king of Israel went up against Judah and fortified Ramah[o] to prevent anyone from leaving or entering the territory
of Asa king of Judah.
18Asa then took all the silver and gold

14:30 [a] 1Ki 12:21; 15:6 **14:31** [b] ver 21; 2Ch 12:16 **15:2** [c] 2Ch 11:20; 13:2 **15:3** [d] 1Ki 11:4; Ps 119:80 **15:4** [e] 2Sa 21:17; 1Ki 11:36; 2Ch 21:7 **15:5** [f] 1Ki 9:4; 14:8 [g] 2Sa 11:2-27; 12:9 **15:6** [h] 1Ki 14:30 **15:10** [i] ver 2 **15:12** [j] 1Ki 14:24; 22:46 **15:13** [k] Ex 32:20 **15:14** [l] ver 3; 1Ki 8:61; 22:43 **15:15** [m] 1Ki 7:51 **15:16** [n] ver 32 **15:17** [o] Jos 18:25; 1Ki 12:27

[a] *31* Some Hebrew manuscripts and Septuagint (see also 2 Chron. 12:16); most Hebrew manuscripts *Abijam*
[b] *1* Some Hebrew manuscripts and Septuagint (see also 2 Chron. 12:16); most Hebrew manuscripts *Abijam*; also in verses 7 and 8
[c] *2* A variant of *Absalom*; also in verse 10
[d] *6* Some Hebrew manuscripts and Syriac *Abijam* (that is, Abijah); most Hebrew manuscripts *Rehoboam*

in the east, and to Jerusalem in the south and Shechem in the north. Though Jerusalem served as an admirable capital city for a number of strategic reasons (water supply, surrounding topography, and access to north-south trade routes), it did not connect directly to any convenient routes from the coast or Transjordan. It therefore relied largely on the Benjamin region for access to the outside world.

In a move taken by many invaders before and after his day, Shishak effectively held Jerusalem hostage by seizing the cities of the plateau in Benjamin. It is unclear whether the pharaoh was unable to take Jerusalem or whether tribute was sufficient not to advance further. Rehoboam paid handsomely to avoid a siege and to restore his access to the outside world. This is reminiscent of the words used to describe Sennacherib's attack on Judah in 701 BC, even before he laid siege to Jerusalem. Hezekiah in his capital city was "like a bird in a cage."

15:13 *queen mother.* Like Bathsheba before her (cf. 2:19), Maakah exercised extensive power as queen mother. Hittite records offer a useful parallel to the considerable activism of the Judahite queen mother in affairs of state. Although Maakah venerated Asherah and was condemned for this, her influence does not account adequately for the chronological and geographic scope of Asherah-related artifacts excavated to date in the region of ancient Judah.

15:17 *Ramah.* Jerusalem's fate was so tied to the strategic Benjamin plateau that the capture of Ramah by an enemy effectively cut off Judah altogether. The city's name is preserved in er-Ram, the name of the modern town, under which the ancient site presumably lies. It is noteworthy that even the capture of a town several miles/kilometers north of strategic Gibeon in the northern part of the plateau could block all traffic in and out of Judah.

15:18 *Ben-Hadad.* This Aramean king was one of several who bore the name Ben-Hadad. As a result, there is some confusion in determining the sequence of conflicts between the Israelites and the Arameans as recorded in 1 Kings. The other names in this verse are unattested. It is most likely that this is Ben-Hadad I, who ruled roughly during the first part of the ninth century BC. He is not mentioned in any extra-Biblical sources. After Asa bribed Ben-Hadad, the latter exploited the situation and conquered the cities of both trunk routes, the vicinity of Hazor, and the hilly region of Naphtali to the west, thereby expanding the western reaches and maritime trade routes of his Damascus-based kingdom.

that was left in the treasuries of the LORD's
temple[p] and of his own palace. He entrusted it to his officials and sent[q] them
to Ben-Hadad[r] son of Tabrimmon, the son
of Hezion, the king of Aram, who was ruling in Damascus. 19“Let there be a treaty
between me and you,” he said, “as there
was between my father and your father.
See, I am sending you a gift of silver and
gold. Now break your treaty with Baasha king of Israel so he will withdraw
from me.”
20Ben-Hadad agreed with King Asa and
sent the commanders of his forces against
the towns of Israel. He conquered[s] Ijon,
Dan, Abel Beth Maakah and all Kinnereth
in addition to Naphtali. 21When Baasha
heard this, he stopped building Ramah
and withdrew to Tirzah. 22Then King Asa
issued an order to all Judah — no one was
exempt — and they carried away from Ramah the stones and timber Baasha had
been using there. With them King Asa
built up Geba[t] in Benjamin, and also
Mizpah.
23As for all the other events of Asa's
reign, all his achievements, all he did and
the cities he built, are they not written in
the book of the annals of the kings of Judah? In his old age, however, his feet became diseased. 24Then Asa rested with his
ancestors and was buried with them in the
city of his father David. And Jehoshaphat[u]
his son succeeded him as king.

Nadab King of Israel

25Nadab son of Jeroboam became king
of Israel in the second year of Asa king
of Judah, and he reigned over Israel two
years. 26He did evil in the eyes of the LORD,
following the ways of his father[v] and committing the same sin his father had caused
Israel to commit.
27Baasha son of Ahijah from the tribe
of Issachar plotted against him, and he
struck him down[w] at Gibbethon,[x] a Philis-

15:18 [p] ver 15; 1Ki 14:26 [q] 2Ki 12:18 [r] 1Ki 11:23-24
15:20 [s] Jdg 18:29; 2Sa 20:14; 2Ki 15:29
15:22 [t] Jos 18:24; 21:17
15:24 [u] Mt 1:8
15:26 [v] 1Ki 12:30; 14:16
15:27 [w] 1Ki 14:14 [x] Jos 19:44; 21:23

15:22 *Geba.* Modern Jeba; it lay six miles (almost 10 kilometers) northeast of Jerusalem and dominated the main road to Jericho. *Mizpah.* Modern Tell en-Nasbeh; it was directly between Bethel to the north and the widening of the Benjamin plateau to the south. There are expansive remains and evidence of massive fortification and administrative architecture exposed in modern excavations. In some places the walls are 13 – 19 feet (4 – 6 meters) thick. These features bear witness to the strategic position of the town and Asa's determination to define the border once and for all. Two of the gates were preserved to a height of several feet/meters and sections of the city wall towered nearly 50 feet (15 meters) above ground level.

1 KINGS 15

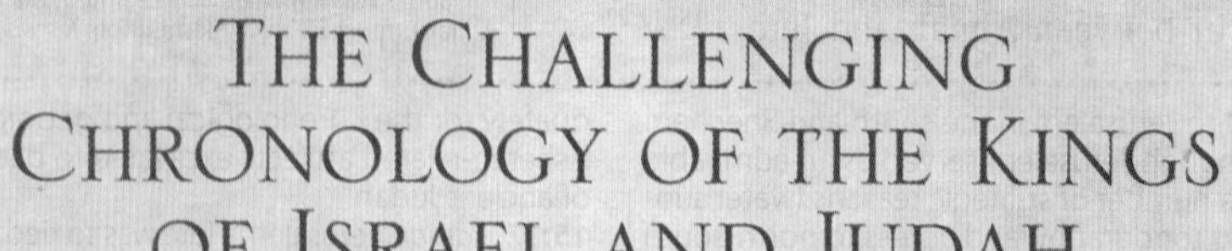

THE CHALLENGING CHRONOLOGY OF THE KINGS OF ISRAEL AND JUDAH

The historical account of 1 – 2 Kings includes a dizzying number of Israelite kings and international events that together generate a chronology of Israel's ancient monarchies. There are a good number of seeming discrepancies in this chronology that must be addressed by any reader of these books. The first step is to frame the events of the book within the known history of the ancient Near East. While there is basic harmony between the Biblical account and the records of ancient Near Eastern kingdoms, the regnal years of Israelite and Judahite kings do not always seem to match up. There are many explanations for this, such as the different calendars used by the Judahite and Israelite scribes, the tendency of kings to form coregencies with their successors, and slight discrepancies between the Hebrew and Greek versions of the OT. With each new discovery of written records from the ancient Near East comes an additional anchor for reconstructing the chronology of the Israelite kingdoms. See chart, p. 620. ◆

tine town, while Nadab and all Israel were
besieging it. 28Baasha killed Nadab in the
third year of Asa king of Judah and succeeded him as king.
29As soon as he began to reign, he killed
Jeroboam's whole family.[y] He did not
leave Jeroboam anyone that breathed, but
destroyed them all, according to the word
of the LORD given through his servant Ahijah the Shilonite. 30This happened because
of the sins[z] Jeroboam had committed and
had caused Israel to commit, and because
he aroused the anger of the LORD, the God
of Israel.
31As for the other events of Nadab's
reign, and all he did, are they not written in the book of the annals of the kings
of Israel? 32There was war[a] between Asa
and Baasha king of Israel throughout their
reigns.

Baasha King of Israel

33In the third year of Asa king of Judah,
Baasha son of Ahijah became king of all
Israel in Tirzah, and he reigned twenty-
four years. 34He did evil[b] in the eyes of the
LORD, following the ways of Jeroboam and
committing the same sin Jeroboam had
caused Israel to commit.
16 Then the word of the LORD came to
Jehu[c] son of Hanani[d] concerning
Baasha: 2"I lifted you up from the dust[e]
and appointed you ruler[f] over my people
Israel, but you followed the ways of Jeroboam and caused[g] my people Israel to sin
and to arouse my anger by their sins. 3So
I am about to wipe out Baasha and his
house,[h] and I will make your house like
that of Jeroboam son of Nebat. 4Dogs[i] will
eat those belonging to Baasha who die in
the city, and birds will feed on those who
die in the country."
5As for the other events of Baasha's
reign, what he did and his achievements,
are they not written in the book of the annals[j] of the kings of Israel? 6Baasha rested with his ancestors and was buried in
Tirzah.[k] And Elah his son succeeded him
as king.
7Moreover, the word of the LORD came[l]
through the prophet Jehu[m] son of Hanani
to Baasha and his house, because of all
the evil he had done in the eyes of the
LORD, arousing his anger by the things he
did, becoming like the house of Jeroboam—and also because he destroyed it.

Elah King of Israel

8In the twenty-sixth year of Asa king of
Judah, Elah son of Baasha became king of
Israel, and he reigned in Tirzah two years.
9Zimri, one of his officials, who had
command of half his chariots, plotted
against him. Elah was in Tirzah at the
time, getting drunk[n] in the home of Arza,
the palace administrator[o] at Tirzah. 10Zim-
ri came in, struck him down and killed
him in the twenty-seventh year of Asa
king of Judah. Then he succeeded him as
king.
11As soon as he began to reign and was
seated on the throne, he killed off Baasha's whole family.[p] He did not spare a
single male, whether relative or friend.
12So Zimri destroyed the whole family of
Baasha, in accordance with the word of
the LORD spoken against Baasha through
the prophet Jehu— 13because of all the
sins Baasha and his son Elah had committed and had caused Israel to commit, so
that they aroused the anger of the LORD,
the God of Israel, by their worthless idols.[q]
14As for the other events of Elah's reign,
and all he did, are they not written in the
book of the annals of the kings of Israel?

Zimri King of Israel

15In the twenty-seventh year of Asa king
of Judah, Zimri reigned in Tirzah seven
days. The army was encamped near Gibbethon,[r] a Philistine town. 16When the Israelites in the camp heard that Zimri had
plotted against the king and murdered
him, they proclaimed Omri, the commander of the army, king over Israel that
very day there in the camp. 17Then Omri
and all the Israelites with him withdrew
from Gibbethon and laid siege to Tirzah.
18When Zimri saw that the city was taken,
he went into the citadel of the royal palace and set the palace on fire around him.
So he died, 19because of the sins he had

15:29 [y] 1Ki 14:10,14 **15:30** [z] 1Ki 14:9,16 **15:32** [a] ver 16 **15:34** [b] ver 26; 1Ki 12:28-29; 13:33; 14:16 **16:1** [c] ver 7; 2Ch 19:2; 20:34 [d] 2Ch 16:7 **16:2** [e] 1Sa 2:8 [f] 1Ki 14:7-9 [g] 1Ki 15:34 **16:3** [h] ver 11; 1Ki 14:10; 15:29; 21:22 **16:4** [i] 1Ki 14:11 **16:5** [j] 1Ki 14:19; 15:31 **16:6** [k] 1Ki 14:17; 15:33 **16:7** [l] 1Ki 15:27, 29 [m] ver 1

16:9 [n] 2Ki 9:30-33 [o] 1Ki 18:3 **16:11** [p] ver 3 **16:13** [q] Dt 32:21; 1Sa 12:21; Isa 41:29 **16:15** [r] Jos 19:44; 1Ki 15:27

15:29 *killed Jeroboam's whole family.* Beyond the practical purpose of eliminating every member of the outgoing rival dynasty, the literary traditions of Israel and its neighbors also interpreted such barbaric acts. They were considered a reckoning for offenses committed against the ruling deity.
16:4 *Dogs will eat ... birds will feed.* See note on 14:11.
16:6 *rested with his ancestors.* See note on 2:10.
16:14 *the book of the annals of the kings of Israel.* See note on 14:19.
16:15–16 *The army ... proclaimed Omri ... king over Israel.* It was not normally the job of the army to declare a king, but military support is essential for a successful reign. Military coups might be more common than records indicate, because kings usually like to portray themselves as ascending legitimately, and the violent overthrow of a ruler does not set a healthy precedent.
16:18 *set the palace on fire.* Zimri's apparent suicide is surprisingly similar to the death of Shamash-shum-ukin, the Assyrian king who died in a burning building in Babylon during the desperate last days of the Assyrian Empire. In both cases the victim suffered the indignity of murder and mutilation.

Relief of Sennacherib's camp at the siege of Lachish shows the oval-walled defensive towers and a road that passes through the middle that is flanked by pavilions and tents. This gives an idea of what the camp (1Ki 16:16) may have looked like.

Kim Walton. The British Museum.

committed, doing evil in the eyes of the
LORD and following the ways of Jeroboam
and committing the same sin Jeroboam
had caused Israel to commit.
20 As for the other events of Zimri's
reign, and the rebellion he carried out, are
they not written in the book of the annals
of the kings of Israel?

Omri King of Israel

21 Then the people of Israel were split
into two factions; half supported Tibni son
of Ginath for king, and the other half supported Omri. 22 But Omri's followers proved
stronger than those of Tibni son of Ginath.
So Tibni died and Omri became king.
23 In the thirty-first year of Asa king of
Judah, Omri became king of Israel, and
he reigned twelve years, six of them in Tirzah.[s] 24 He bought the hill of Samaria from
Shemer for two talents[a] of silver and built
a city on the hill, calling it Samaria,[t] after
Shemer, the name of the former owner of
the hill.

16:23 [s] 1Ki 15:21 **16:24** [t] 1Ki 13:32; Jn 4:4

[a] *24* That is, about 150 pounds or about 68 kilograms

16:23 *Omri became king.* Omri made several decisions that put Israel on a new trajectory and prepared the way for his son Ahab. Ahab's prominence in the eastern Mediterranean during the ninth century BC is noteworthy. Omri's policy changes included a new alliance with Phoenicia (sealed through his son's marriage to Jezebel), a powerful new capital city (Samaria) and aggressive military expansion such as the attack on Moab recorded by its king, Mesha: "Omri was the king of Israel, and he oppressed Moab for many days."

Biblical and ancient Near Eastern texts suggest that Omri and Ahab were powerful kings, and the archaeological record of wealth and construction supports this description. Like Solomon of the tenth century BC, these ninth-century BC kings exploited the relative absence of great international powers. One indicator of Omri's success is the frequency with which Assyrian annals refer to him, most notably in the campaign records of Shalmaneser III and the Black Obelisk that shows "Jehu, son of Omri" bowing before the Assyrian monarch. In this case "son of" likely indicates the dynastic line rather than direct sonship.

16:24 *Samaria.* In contrast to the defensive positions of Tirzah and Penuel, Samaria was in a forward position that afforded direct access to the coastal plain to the west, the strategic Jezreel Valley to the north and the Israelite highlands to the southeast. Unhindered access to the Dothan and Jezreel Valleys encouraged both Israelite expansion and foreign invasion. Despite the vulnerability of its position, the large natural hill made Samaria significantly more defensible than Shechem, the traditional center of the northern Ephraimite highlands. *Shemer.* His estate was a small village with excellent wine and olive yields and

25 But Omri did evil[u] in the eyes of the
LORD and sinned more than all those before him. 26 He followed completely the
ways of Jeroboam son of Nebat, committing the same sin Jeroboam had caused[v]
Israel to commit, so that they aroused the
anger of the LORD, the God of Israel, by
their worthless idols.[w]
27 As for the other events of Omri's reign,
what he did and the things he achieved,
are they not written in the book of the annals of the kings of Israel? 28 Omri rested
with his ancestors and was buried in Samaria. And Ahab his son succeeded him
as king.

Ahab Becomes King of Israel

29 In the thirty-eighth year of Asa king of
Judah, Ahab son of Omri became king of
Israel, and he reigned in Samaria over Israel twenty-two years. 30 Ahab son of Omri
did more[x] evil in the eyes of the LORD than
any of those before him. 31 He not only
considered it trivial to commit the sins of
Jeroboam son of Nebat, but he also married[y] Jezebel daughter[z] of Ethbaal king of
the Sidonians, and began to serve Baal[a]
and worship him. 32 He set up an altar for
Baal in the temple[b] of Baal that he built
in Samaria. 33 Ahab also made an Asherah
pole[c] and did more[d] to arouse the anger of
the LORD, the God of Israel, than did all the
kings of Israel before him.
34 In Ahab's time, Hiel of Bethel rebuilt
Jericho. He laid its foundations at the cost
of his firstborn son Abiram, and he set up
its gates at the cost of his youngest son
Segub, in accordance with the word of the
LORD spoken by Joshua son of Nun.[e]

Elijah Announces a Great Drought

17 Now Elijah[f] the Tishbite, from Tishbe[a] in Gilead,[g] said to Ahab, "As
the LORD, the God of Israel, lives, whom I
serve, there will be neither dew nor rain[h]
in the next few years except at my word."

16:25 [u] Dt 4:25; Mic 6:16 **16:26** [v] ver 19 [w] Dt 32:21 **16:30** [x] ver 25; 1Ki 14:9 **16:31** [y] Dt 7:3; 1Ki 11:2 [z] Jdg 18:7; 2Ki 9:34 [a] 2Ki 10:18; 17:16 **16:32** [b] 2Ki 10:21, 27; 11:18 **16:33** [c] 2Ki 13:6 [d] ver 29, 30; 1Ki 14:9; 21:25 **16:34** [e] Jos 6:26 **17:1** [f] Mal 4:5; Jas 5:17 [g] Jdg 12:4 [h] Dt 10:8; 1Ki 18:1; 2Ki 3:14; Lk 4:25

[a] *1* Or *Tishbite, of the settlers*

a commanding view in all directions. American excavations uncovered scattered dwellings and olive presses on the acropolis. Above this small original settlement lay the large courtyards, terraces and the impressive palace of Ahab's great ninth-century BC city.

16:26 *worthless idols.* The idols and plaques represented various deities or in some cases a human worshiper. Figurines could also accompany rituals that sought to ensure good fortune in day-to-day activities. Israelite idols and votives had much in common with those of Canaan/Syria and Egypt in terms of iconography, motifs and cultic use, because these clay and metal images signified and invoked the presence of a deity.

16:29 *Ahab.* Just as Solomon had been able to capitalize on David's strategic successes, so Ahab consolidated a mighty kingdom built on Omri's foresight. Comparison might be made with Tukulti-Ninurta I, who built the Assyrian Empire against great odds, overcame internal strife and paved the way for Assyrian campaigns abroad. Through synchronism with Judahite king lists and ancient Near Eastern sources, it is possible to date Ahab's rule to 873 – 852 BC and to reconstruct many details of his reign. Ahab's military might is recorded in the annals of his enemy, the Assyrian king Shalmaneser III. The "2,000 chariots and 10,000 troops of Ahab the Israelite" comprise the second largest contingent of the coalition against the Assyrian attack. Ahab's military and civic structures are well represented at excavated sites such as Megiddo, Hazor, Tell Dan, Samaria, Dothan and Jezreel. They include storage facilities, palaces with characteristic Phoenician masonry, large solid city walls and pillared buildings associated with chariotry.

16:31 *married Jezebel daughter of Ethbaal king of the Sidonians.* This reestablishment of Phoenician-Israelite ties secured inland markets for the Phoenicians and Mediterranean trade for Israel. It effectively cut Aram-Damascus out of the trade routes passing from Arabia and the Red Sea up the King's Highway of Transjordan and on to the Mediterranean Sea. This alliance is one of the major causes for the century of warfare between Aram-Damascus and Israel in the ninth and eighth centuries BC. For the significance of marriage in ancient political alliances, see note on 3:1. Ahab tightened the cultural ties between Israel and Phoenicia to the point of embracing Canaanite/Phoenician religion. *Jezebel.* Excavators at Samaria uncovered a beautiful seal of Jezebel that may be associated with Ahab's queen. It depicts stylized Egyptian griffins and her name in Phoenician script. Jezebel would have used a seal like this to secure royal edicts and correspondence (cf. 21:8). *Ethbaal.* He reigned 887 – 856 BC and controlled most of the Phoenician coastland, including the port of Sidon, and he dominated western Cyprus as well. He, like many local kings, faced the Assyrian invasions of the mid- and late- ninth century BC.

16:32 *temple of Baal that he built in Samaria.* Only small fragments of this structure were exposed during the excavations at Samaria. Long, tripartite Baal temples are known from Ugarit, Byblos and other sites in the Levant. Each had a stepped, pillared entrance and a long hall with an elevated holy of holies in the back, upon which sat an image of the deity. It is likely that a high percentage of early first-millennium BC temples in Syria were dedicated to local expressions of Baal. Each had its own designation, such as Baal Hamon, Baal Hadad and so on. *Baal.* In Jezebel's home country, the major deity was (Baal)-Melqart. Aside from a few brief references in inscriptions, little is known about him aside from his identity as a warrior-god. Nevertheless, it is unlikely that Ahab and Jezebel were seeking to import Melqart into Israel. The religious center being established in Samaria probably focused on a local manifestation of Baal, which perhaps would have been designated "Baal of Samaria." See the article "Baal," p. 600.

16:34 *He laid its foundations ... and he set up its gates.* In the literature of the ancient Near East, including the Bible, one measure of a ruler's greatness is the extent of his or her building activity. King Mesha of Moab, e.g., boasted of building the citadel, gates, towers and reservoir of his capital city, Karcho. His good fortune was expressed in the tangible projects he undertook or in the ability of his enemies to destroy those symbols of his power, such as towers, fortifications and public buildings (see note on 9:15).

17:1 *neither dew nor rain.* Periodic droughts are recorded in antiquity and occur today as well. The catastrophic

1 KINGS 16:32

With his embrace of Baal and Canaanite religion, Ahab completed the strategic program initiated by his father, Omri. The alliance with Phoenicia brought not only commercial and military ties, but also state-sponsored religious syncretism. Yet, because the prophets and Biblical authors were so consistently critical of Israel's pagan practices, it must be assumed that to some degree Ahab simply made official what had for many years been unofficial popular religious practice.

Baal and the large pantheon of Canaanite gods are not only attacked in the Biblical text but are also well represented in archaeological and textual records of the ancient Mediterranean world. Finds include statues, reliefs, high places and a plethora of inscriptions and texts from the Levant and the Aegean. Baal, the god of fertility and storms, is depicted as a strident warrior bearing a lightning bolt. His annual death and revival is recorded in the Baal Cycle, a religious text from the ancient port city of Ugarit. After delivering the winter rains and the spring vegetation, Baal was vanquished for the summer by Mot, the deity of death, only to be resurrected in the following year. Baal's life cycle coincided with the physical seasons and may also have reflected the ebb and flow of political power and cosmic equilibrium. Baal fought with other gods as well, such as Yamm, the chaotic deity of the sea, and usually had the support of his sister/consort Anat, a fierce goddess of war and sensuality.

In accepting Baal, Ahab was simply bringing his kingdom closer to the mainstream of ancient Near Eastern thought and practice. In fact, most cities and kingdoms in the region had their local versions of Baal. In some cases, the deity had a different name or epithet based on local conditions but his qualities and the mode of his worship was for the most part the same. In many Syrian cities, e.g., he was named Hadad. Under Ahab, Israel became yet another Baal-worshiping nation-state.

Perhaps Ahab and Jezebel exceeded all others simply by the degree or extent of their apostasy, but it may also be that the distinction was in what they attempted.

continued on next page

Elijah Fed by Ravens

²Then the word of the LORD came to Elijah: ³"Leave here, turn eastward and hide
in the Kerith Ravine, east of the Jordan.
⁴You will drink from the brook, and I have
directed the ravens[i] to supply you with
food there."
⁵So he did what the LORD had told him.
He went to the Kerith Ravine, east of the
Jordan, and stayed there. ⁶The ravens
brought him bread and meat in the morning[j] and bread and meat in the evening,
and he drank from the brook.

Elijah and the Widow at Zarephath

⁷Some time later the brook dried up because there had been no rain in the land.
⁸Then the word of the LORD came to him:
⁹"Go at once to Zarephath[k] in the region
of Sidon and stay there. I have directed
a widow[l] there to supply you with food."
¹⁰So he went to Zarephath. When he came

17:4 [i] Ge 8:7
17:6 [j] Ex 16:8
17:9 [k] Ob 1:20 [l] Lk 4:26

nature of this drought is seen in the absence of dew, which is vital to vineyards and trees during the dry summer months. Elijah, through confronting Ahab in this manner, began the process of neutering Baal, the Canaanite god of storms and fertility. In the myths of Ugarit, Baal is described as the one who waters and provides bread and who defeats the forces of death and famine. The confrontation on Mount Carmel (18:16–40) was the culmination of this showdown. By stopping the rain and dew, the prophet effectively rendered impotent both Baal and his priesthood.

17:4 *ravens.* Known to roost in the wadis and other desolate areas, storing excess food in rocky crags. Elijah might be observing these caches and stealing them. Regardless of whether Elijah is active or passive, God is the one acting to provide for his needs.

17:10 *widow.* See notes on Ge 38:11; Dt 10:18; 15:7. *bring me a little water.* Elijah's request would have been mod-

In ancient polytheism deities existed in hierarchical structures, both politically and cosmically. Some gods were manifest in cosmic elements (sun, moon, storm, waters), and some had political clout among the council of the gods. Ruling deities were connected to large empires and national entities, while cities had their patron deities. Lower echelon deities typically served in connection with clans and families and at times ancestors were seen as divinized in some sense and capable of bringing protection and succor.

Through much of the judges period and revived in the more recent monarchy, the worship of Baal and Asherah most likely arose to serve the people's concerns about fertility. Yahweh would have still been viewed as their national god, but the mentality in the ancient world was to posit a variety of deities in a variety of functions rather than to have a single, all-purpose deity. In this past history, then, Yahweh would not have been replaced by Baal and Asherah, but they simply would have been brought in alongside him. One possible variation with the movement led by Ahab and Jezebel is that rather than simply bringing Baal in as a second-level fertility deity in conjunction with Yahweh as national deity, they were attempting to replace Yahweh as national deity with the Baal of Samaria. Standing against this attempted transition, Elijah becomes the champion of Yahweh's kingship. ◆

Baal, the god of fertility and storms, is depicted as a strident warrior bearing a lightning bolt, Ras Shamra-Ugarit, c. 1499 – 1299 BC.
Wikimedia Commons

to the town gate, a widow was there gathering sticks. He called to her and asked,
"Would you bring me a little water in a
jar so I may have a drink?"[m] 11As she was
going to get it, he called, "And bring me,
please, a piece of bread."
12"As surely as the LORD your God lives,"
she replied, "I don't have any bread — only
a handful of flour in a jar and a little olive
oil[n] in a jug. I am gathering a few sticks
to take home and make a meal for myself
and my son, that we may eat it — and die."
13Elijah said to her, "Don't be afraid.
Go home and do as you have said. But
first make a small loaf of bread for me
from what you have and bring it to me,
and then make something for yourself and
your son. 14For this is what the LORD, the
God of Israel, says: 'The jar of flour will
not be used up and the jug of oil will not
run dry until the day the LORD sends rain
on the land.' "
15She went away and did as Elijah had
told her. So there was food every day for
Elijah and for the woman and her family.
16For the jar of flour was not used up and
the jug of oil did not run dry, in keeping
with the word of the LORD spoken by Elijah.

17:10 [m] Ge 24:17; Jn 4:7 **17:12** [n] ver 1; 2Ki 4:2

est in terms of normal hospitality. At this time, however, it exposes the strain caused by drought and famine.

17:12 *the LORD your God.* Elijah is recognizable as an Israelite, and the Sidonian woman is greeting him in the name of his own god, as per common protocol. This statement does not indicate any belief of the woman in Yahweh.

17:16 *the jar of flour was not used up and the jug of oil did not run dry.* The importance of this is to show Yahweh's superiority to Baal. Not only could Yahweh provide food for his own prophet, he now sent that prophet up into Baal's home territory, where there was a drought, to provide for Baal's people.

17 Some time later the son of the woman who owned the house became ill. He grew worse and worse, and finally stopped breathing. 18 She said to Elijah, "What do you have against me, man of God? Did you come to remind me of my sin[o] and kill my son?"

19 "Give me your son," Elijah replied. He took him from her arms, carried him to the upper room where he was staying, and laid him on his bed. 20 Then he cried out to the LORD, "LORD my God, have you brought tragedy even on this widow I am staying with, by causing her son to die?" 21 Then he stretched[p] himself out on the boy three times and cried out to the LORD, "LORD my God, let this boy's life return to him!"

22 The LORD heard Elijah's cry, and the boy's life returned to him, and he lived. 23 Elijah picked up the child and carried him down from the room into the house. He gave him to his mother and said, "Look, your son is alive!"

24 Then the woman said to Elijah, "Now I know[q] that you are a man of God and that the word of the LORD from your mouth is the truth."[r]

17:18 [o] 2Ki 3:13; Lk 5:8 **17:21** [p] 2Ki 4:34; Ac 20:10 **17:24** [q] Jn 3:2; 16:30 [r] Ps 119:43; Jn 17:17 **18:1** [s] 1Ki 17:1; Lk 4:25; Jas 5:17 [t] Dt 28:12

Elijah and Obadiah

18 After a long time, in the third[s] year, the word of the LORD came to Elijah: "Go and present yourself to Ahab, and I will send rain[t] on the land." 2 So Elijah went to present himself to Ahab.

Now the famine was severe in Samaria, 3 and Ahab had summoned Obadiah, his palace administrator.[u] (Obadiah was a devout believer[v] in the LORD. 4 While Jezebel[w] was killing off the LORD's prophets, Obadiah had taken a hundred prophets and hidden[x] them in two caves, fifty in each, and had supplied them with food and water.) 5 Ahab had said to Obadiah, "Go through the land to all the springs and valleys. Maybe we can find some grass to keep the horses and mules alive so we will not have to kill any of our animals." 6 So they divided the land they were to cover, Ahab going in one direction and Obadiah in another.

7 As Obadiah was walking along, Elijah met him. Obadiah recognized[y] him, bowed down to the ground, and said, "Is it really you, my lord Elijah?"

8 "Yes," he replied. "Go tell your master, 'Elijah is here.' "

9 "What have I done wrong," asked Obadiah, "that you are handing your servant over to Ahab to be put to death? 10 As surely as the LORD your God lives, there is not a nation or kingdom where my master has not sent someone to look[z] for you. And whenever a nation or kingdom claimed you were not there, he made them swear they could not find you. 11 But now you tell me to go to my master and say, 'Elijah is here.' 12 I don't know where the Spirit[a] of the LORD may carry you when I leave you. If I go and tell Ahab and he doesn't

18:3 [u] 1Ki 16:9 [v] Ne 7:2 **18:4** [w] 2Ki 9:7 [x] ver 13; Isa 16:3 **18:7** [y] 2Ki 1:8 **18:10** [z] 1Ki 17:3 **18:12** [a] 2Ki 2:16; Eze 3:14; Ac 8:39

17:18 *kill my son.* As an inhabitant of Phoenician Zarephath, this woman thinks about God the way that Phoenicians did. Gods could become angry over small slights and strike severely. As a prophet, Elijah lives in the aura of the divine, and therefore those around him are more subject to divine scrutiny. The woman fears that although her connections to the prophet have thus far brought benefits, she is now experiencing the downside.
17:21 This verse and 2Ki 4:34–35 are among the most blatant examples of magical procedures used by Israel's prophets. Incantation literature from Assyria indicates the belief that demons exercise power over an individual by touching part to part. It is an expression of possession. Here Elijah is imitating that procedure to reverse the effects as vitality and life force are transferred. Nonetheless, here, as the prayer indicates, the power of Yahweh is at work. In the ancient world, sharp lines were not drawn between magic and religion. Both are related to interacting with the world of the divine. Incantations in the ancient world also represented attempts to tap the power of deity through words of power, but in Israel, unlike her neighbors, God could not be bound or obligated by such words or by accompanying rituals. As is often seen to be the case throughout the OT, Yahweh regularly uses ideas and practices that are familiar to the Israelites in their culture to accomplish his work.
18:3 *palace administrator.* Lit. "who was over the household." This expression is found in the imprints of royal seals discovered in the Holy Land and also in an inscription above an elegant rock-cut tomb in Jerusalem dating to the days of Isaiah: "This is the tomb of Shebna who is over the household." Obadiah was probably the executive officer of Ahab's court.
18:4 *Jezebel was killing off the LORD's prophets.* To the modern reader this may look like religious persecution, but it must be understood in its context. The polytheism of the ancient world was an open system—there was always room for more gods, and if a god was deemed to be active and powerful in the region, it was logical to acknowledge that deity. This was not an issue of theological ideology; it was a matter of practical necessity. People worshiped gods by caring for their needs, such as providing food for them. As a result, the deity would not become angry and the attention he received brought benefits to the people. No question arose in ancient Near Eastern theology of whether a certain god was a "true god" or not, though there were discussions of some gods being stronger than others. The relative strength of gods was a political matter as one country, empowered by its gods, sought to impose its will on another country, despite the will of its patron deities. We must therefore seek a motive for the slaughter of Yahweh's prophets in politics rather than in theology. Prophets in the ancient world often served in the hire of the king and, more than anything else, served as mouthpiece for the gods to support the legitimacy and programs of the king. The prophets of Yahweh, therefore, would not likely offer support for the legitimacy of Ahab and Jezebel's rule, and this made them enemies of the state.

find you, he will kill me. Yet I your servant
have worshiped the LORD since my youth.
13 Haven't you heard, my lord, what I did
while Jezebel was killing the prophets of
the LORD? I hid a hundred of the LORD's
prophets in two caves, fifty in each, and
supplied them with food and water. 14 And
now you tell me to go to my master and
say, 'Elijah is here.' He will kill me!"
15 Elijah said, "As the LORD Almighty
lives, whom I serve, I will surely present[b]
myself to Ahab today."

Elijah on Mount Carmel

16 So Obadiah went to meet Ahab and
told him, and Ahab went to meet Elijah.
17 When he saw Elijah, he said to him, "Is
that you, you troubler[c] of Israel?"
18 "I have not made trouble for Israel,"
Elijah replied. "But you[d] and your father's
family have. You have abandoned[e] the
LORD's commands and have followed the
Baals. 19 Now summon the people from
all over Israel to meet me on Mount Carmel.[f] And bring the four hundred and fifty prophets of Baal and the four hundred
prophets of Asherah, who eat at Jezebel's
table."
20 So Ahab sent word throughout all Israel and assembled the prophets on Mount
Carmel. 21 Elijah went before the people
and said, "How long will you waver[g] between two opinions? If the LORD is God,
follow him; but if Baal is God, follow him."
But the people said nothing.
22 Then Elijah said to them, "I am the
only one of the LORD's prophets left,[h] but
Baal has four hundred and fifty prophets.[i]
23 Get two bulls for us. Let Baal's prophets
choose one for themselves, and let them
cut it into pieces and put it on the wood
but not set fire to it. I will prepare the other bull and put it on the wood but not set
fire to it. 24 Then you call on the name of
your god, and I will call on the name of
the LORD. The god who answers by fire[j]—
he is God."
Then all the people said, "What you say
is good."
25 Elijah said to the prophets of Baal,
"Choose one of the bulls and prepare it
first, since there are so many of you. Call
on the name of your god, but do not light
the fire." 26 So they took the bull given
them and prepared it.
Then they called on the name of Baal
from morning till noon. "Baal, answer
us!" they shouted. But there was no response;[k] no one answered. And they
danced around the altar they had made.

18:15 [b] 1Ki 17:1 **18:17** [c] Jos 7:25; 1Ki 21:20; Ac 16:20 **18:18** [d] 1Ki 16:31,33; 21:25 [e] 2Ch 15:2 **18:19** [f] Jos 19:26 **18:21** [g] Jos 24:15; 2Ki 17:41; Mt 6:24 **18:22** [h] 1Ki 19:10 [i] ver 19 **18:24** [j] ver 38; 1Ch 21:26 **18:26** [k] Ps 115:4-5; Jer 10:5; 1Co 8:4; 12:2

18:19 *Mount Carmel.* It rises over 500 meters (1,600 ft) above the Mediterranean Sea and defines both the western edge of the Jezreel Valley and the coastline of the sea. Known in Egyptian texts as "the antelope's nose," it has been a key landmark for seafarers and land-based travelers since the third millennium BC. It is one of the country's most lush and evergreen regions, and in the winter one can see from its summit the snow-capped Lebanon and Anti-Lebanon ranges. These qualities and the mountain's position between Phoenicia and Israel, the sea and the land, made it the perfect location for the religious and cultural showdown that was about to transpire. *prophets of Baal and ... prophets of Asherah, who eat at Jezebel's table.* Baal was the storm-god of Canaanite mythology, whereas Asherah was the consort of the patriarchal deity El (see the article "Baal," p. 600). In Ahab's day, Asherah was recast as Yahweh's consort, a syncretistic approach that opened the door for Baal worship as well. A series of ninth-century BC inscriptions from a fortified way station at Kuntillet 'Ajrud in the Negev wilderness sheds light on this issue. They include statements such as "Yahweh of Samaria and his Asherah." Painted images of dancing figures and a deity sitting on a throne are strong indicators that some Israelites worshiped Asherah as a consort of El. In the myths of Ugarit, Baal was said to receive the help of Asherah when he requested from El that he be permitted to build a house. Ahab and Jezebel had chosen prophets of Baal and Asherah to be their official advisors. Just as these prophets were identified as those "who eat at Jezebel's table," prophets in the ancient world often enjoyed the patronage of the king. Prophets of the Levant at places such as Emar, Ugarit and Damascus acted as intermediaries, more often than not handing down favorable words of encouragement to the king. A study of the prophetic texts available from the ancient world has shown that these sponsored prophets rarely had anything negative to say about the king or his policies. Only a couple of examples are extant in which these prophets proclaim any indictment or judgment on the king. They more often provide instruction to the king (often regarding cultic actions to be taken) and almost always give support and encouragement to the king in his undertakings. In contrast we find Elijah offering no support at all of the king's policies. Instead, he has stinging indictments and horrific judgments that he pronounces on the royal house. Such an adversarial role is unattested in the ancient Near East, though that does not mean such a role did not exist. It must be remembered that most of the literature we have from the ancient world was preserved by the palace and temple. These sources would be less likely to preserve the antagonistic words of any who stood against the throne.

18:23 *two bulls.* As was common in the ancient Near East, the animals were slaughtered and prepared prior to being placed on the altar. In effect the altar was a table on which the deity consumed the animal. Texts from Ugarit describe the ritual of sacrifice as an attempt to appease the Canaanite pantheon. The prophets of Baal in this chapter were doing the same thing. Other forms of appeasement included clapping hands, wearing special garments and handing over gifts to the priests.

18:26 *danced around the altar.* The frenzied dance most likely included music and chanting. Depictions of ritual dancers using instruments such as tambourines, flutes and lyres are found on seals, pottery paintings and frescoes in Late Bronze Age and Iron Age Phoenicia and Palestine. The variety of poses, configurations and artistic media of the artwork indicate that this was a common practice. The dancing, music and chanting no doubt were intended to get the attention of the deity.

27At noon Elijah began to taunt them.
"Shout louder!" he said. "Surely he is a
god! Perhaps he is deep in thought, or
busy, or traveling. Maybe he is sleeping
and must be awakened."[l] 28So they shouted louder and slashed[m] themselves with
swords and spears, as was their custom,
until their blood flowed. 29Midday passed,
and they continued their frantic prophesying until the time for the evening sacrifice.[n] But there was no response, no one
answered, no one paid attention.[o]
30Then Elijah said to all the people,
"Come here to me." They came to him,
and he repaired the altar[p] of the LORD,
which had been torn down. 31Elijah took
twelve stones, one for each of the tribes
descended from Jacob, to whom the word
of the LORD had come, saying, "Your name
shall be Israel."[q] 32With the stones he built
an altar in the name[r] of the LORD, and he
dug a trench around it large enough to
hold two seahs[a] of seed. 33He arranged[s]
the wood, cut the bull into pieces and laid
it on the wood. Then he said to them, "Fill
four large jars with water and pour it on
the offering and on the wood."
34"Do it again," he said, and they did
it again.
"Do it a third time," he ordered, and
they did it the third time. 35The water ran
down around the altar and even filled the
trench.
36At the time of sacrifice, the prophet Elijah stepped forward and prayed: "LORD, the
God of Abraham,[t] Isaac and Israel, let it be
known[u] today that you are God in Israel
and that I am your servant and have done
all these things at your command.[v] 37An-
swer me, LORD, answer me, so these people
will know that you, LORD, are God, and that
you are turning their hearts back again."
38Then the fire[w] of the LORD fell and
burned up the sacrifice, the wood, the
stones and the soil, and also licked up the
water in the trench.

18:27 [l] Hab 2:19 **18:28** [m] Lev 19:28; Dt 14:1 **18:29** [n] Ex 29:41 [o] ver 26 **18:30** [p] 1Ki 19:10 **18:31** [q] Ge 32:28; 35:10; 2Ki 17:34 **18:32** [r] Col 3:17 **18:33** [s] Ge 22:9; Lev 1:6-8 **18:36** [t] Ex 3:6; Mt 22:32 [u] 1Ki 8:43; 2Ki 19:19 [v] Nu 16:28 **18:38** [w] Lev 9:24; Jdg 6:21; 1Ch 21:26; 2Ch 7:1; Job 1:16

[a] 32 That is, probably about 24 pounds or about 11 kilograms

18:27 *Perhaps he is deep in thought, or busy, or traveling. Maybe he is sleeping and must be awakened.* The gods of Canaan, Mesopotamia and Greece were understood to possess many human characteristics, including vices and some bodily functions. Elijah was therefore taunting the prophets with their own possible explanations for Baal's indifference. A passage in the Baal Cycle from Ugarit describes the challenge of finding Baal when he is not in his house, and another text describes his death, an integral part of the annual cycle. The humanlike attributes of Sumerian gods are also seen in the Myth of Enki and Ninmah. A passage from that story provides a most instructive context for Elijah's mockery: "Enki lay on his bed and would not rise from his sleep ... 'you are sleeping and slumbering ... arise!'"
18:28 *slashed themselves with swords and spears, as was their custom, until their blood flowed.* Self-flagellation represents a more desperate attempt to invoke Baal's presence, and it is a behavior that is well attested in the Canaanite, Hittite and Mesopotamian cultures. The shedding of blood draws the attention of the gods. The prayers of the Hittite king Mursili II, e.g., sought to "make restitution by spilling blood." In the myths of Ugarit, El mourns the death of Baal by cutting himself with razors and "plowing his chest like a garden." In another text the mourners of Kirta "rend their skin" in sorrow as they sacrifice to the gods. *slashed.* This Hebrew word is translated "passed over" in Ex 12:27, and might therefore mean "stood guard" (see the article "Passover," p. 129).
18:30 *repaired the altar of the LORD.* It was common practice in the ancient Near East to destroy or desecrate the altars and divine statues of rival peoples. The burned and overturned temples of Hazor's lower city are a good example. In a violent Late Bronze Age conflagration, statues of the gods were beheaded and violated, and the temple courtyards were ransacked. Given the cultural background and archaeological parallels, Jezebel's religious persecution is the most likely explanation for the ruined altar of Yahweh (see note on 19:10).
18:32 *two seahs of seed.* A seah (7 quarts or 7.5 liters) is a dry measure typically used for cereals and grains, and its use in this verse is unclear. If this is the volume of the trench, it is a small trench. The reference may be to the size of a container used to hold that amount, as a reference to indicate the trench's depth.
18:33 *large jars.* These containers are no doubt smaller versions of the large storage jars that are ubiquitous in the Levant from the seventeenth through the fourth centuries BC. The *nebel* or "Canaanite jar" and "Israelite jar" held over eight gallons (32 liters) of wine or water, whereas the smaller *kad* of this verse held half of that volume. The typology of Israelite pottery shows that the volume of water is almost 50 gallons. *water.* The source for filling these jars is not known, though several springs at the foot of Mount Carmel's eastern slopes are known to this day. Since the text does not specify "fresh" water, the Mediterranean is also a possible source. It is possible that one of Elijah's purposes in pouring out the water at the altar was to make a libation offering to Yahweh (cf. 1Sa 7:6). Such offerings to the gods are well-known in ancient Near Eastern religions, as, e.g., upon the wall relief at Mari, where liquid offerings are poured out before the gods.
18:38 *fire of the LORD fell.* Fire is the clearest possible indicator of the divine presence, an impressive theophany. The irony of Yahweh's victory is all the more potent when one considers the Canaanite religious tradition that Baal controlled lightning and rain. In one passage from Ugarit, Baal states, "I understand lightning, which not even the heavens know."

The lightning, however, is more than just an impressive show of power. The sacrifices were ostensibly offered along with petitions for rain, typically sent by storm-gods. The fire indicated that God was listening to and answering Elijah's prayer, so that when the rain came in the following verses, it was clear that it was sent by Yahweh rather than by Baal. The lightning was also one of the weapons of the divine warrior; thus, here we see the warfare going on between Baal and Yahweh in the last couple of chapters brought to a climax.

It is natural, then, that this should result in the slaughter of the prophets of Baal and Asherah, for the worship of Yahweh did not tolerate prophets of other gods among the Israelites. As a result of this contest, the petition of Elijah is heard (the sacrifice is consumed), Yahweh sends rain (the drought ends), and the warfare with Baal is con-

39 When all the people saw this, they
fell prostrate and cried, "The LORD—he is
God! The LORD—he is God!"[x]
40 Then Elijah commanded them, "Seize
the prophets of Baal. Don't let anyone get
away!" They seized them, and Elijah had
them brought down to the Kishon Valley[y]
and slaughtered[z] there.
41 And Elijah said to Ahab, "Go, eat and
drink, for there is the sound of a heavy
rain." 42 So Ahab went off to eat and drink,
but Elijah climbed to the top of Carmel,
bent down to the ground and put his face
between his knees.[a]
43 "Go and look toward the sea," he told
his servant. And he went up and looked.
"There is nothing there," he said.
Seven times Elijah said, "Go back."
44 The seventh time the servant reported,
"A cloud[b] as small as a man's hand is rising from the sea."
So Elijah said, "Go and tell Ahab, 'Hitch
up your chariot and go down before the
rain stops you.'"
45 Meanwhile, the sky grew black with
clouds, the wind rose, a heavy rain started
falling and Ahab rode off to Jezreel. 46 The
power[c] of the LORD came on Elijah and,
tucking his cloak into his belt,[d] he ran
ahead of Ahab all the way to Jezreel.

18:39 [x] ver 24
18:40 [y] Jdg 4:7 [z] Dt 13:5; 18:20; 2Ki 10:24-25
18:42 [a] ver 19-20; Jas 5:18
18:44 [b] Lk 12:54
18:46 [c] 2Ki 3:15 [d] 2Ki 4:29; 9:1

Elijah Flees to Horeb

19 Now Ahab told Jezebel everything
Elijah had done and how he had
killed[e] all the prophets with the sword. 2 So
Jezebel sent a messenger to Elijah to say,
"May the gods deal with me, be it ever so
severely,[f] if by this time tomorrow I do not
make your life like that of one of them."
3 Elijah was afraid[a] and ran[g] for his life.
When he came to Beersheba in Judah, he
left his servant there, 4 while he himself
went a day's journey into the wilderness.
He came to a broom bush, sat down under
it and prayed that he might die. "I have
had enough, LORD," he said. "Take my
life;[h] I am no better than my ancestors."
5 Then he lay down under the bush and
fell asleep.[i]
All at once an angel touched him and
said, "Get up and eat." 6 He looked around,
and there by his head was some bread
baked over hot coals, and a jar of water.
He ate and drank and then lay down again.
7 The angel of the LORD came back a second time and touched him and said, "Get
up and eat, for the journey is too much for
you." 8 So he got up and ate and drank.
Strengthened by that food, he traveled

19:1 [e] 1Ki 18:40
19:2 [f] 1Ki 20:10; 2Ki 6:31; Ru 1:17
19:3 [g] Ge 31:21
19:4 [h] Nu 11:15; Jer 20:18; Jnh 4:8
19:5 [i] Ge 28:11

[a] 3 Or *Elijah saw*

cluded (prophets are slain), with Yahweh having demonstrated himself superior to Baal in Baal's own terms.

18:40 *Kishon Valley.* Runs along the eastern edge of Mount Carmel. It drains the entire western half of the Jezreel Valley as far east as Mount Tabor and the outskirts of Tell Jezreel, the winter palace of the Israelite kings. The entire region drains through a narrow break in the ridge connecting Mount Carmel and the ridge on which lie Nazareth and the ancient city of Sepphoris. In antiquity the river swelled during the winter months and flooded the entire region between Megiddo and Nazareth, making passage nearly impossible. This is the reason the prophet urged Ahab to return to Jezreel without delay (v. 44).

18:45 *the sky grew black with clouds, the wind rose, a heavy rain started falling.* Rainfall in the Holy Land typically occurs only when storms push their way across the Mediterranean Sea, usually accompanied by strong winds and dramatic clouds. There is no better location at which to experience these storms than the summit of Mount Carmel. The Canaanites attributed the power of such storms to Baal, as in this passage from the Baal Cycle from Ugarit: "Baal (can) send his rain in due season … shout aloud in the clouds … shoot (his) lightning-bolts to the earth." Such descriptions of Baal highlight the fact that it was Yahweh who in the end possessed these qualities and broke the three-year drought (see note on v. 38). *Ahab rode off to Jezreel.* Ahab most likely followed the high road along the periphery of the valley next to the Carmel range.

18:46 *Elijah … ran ahead of Ahab all the way to Jezreel.* Elijah's specific action is unclear in the text. It seems that he either accompanied the king as an attendant or raced Ahab to Jezreel by taking a more direct route that the heavy chariot could not attempt. In light of ancient Near Eastern parallels and Biblical contexts, the former explanation is more compelling. By running ahead of the king's chariot, the prophet may have been symbolically representing Yahweh, the king's new patron deity. Hittite kings were known to describe their chariots as vehicles led by the gods. Rameses II of thirteenth-century BC Egypt noted the advance of the god Montu running before his chariot as he advanced into battle. It is equally likely, however, that Elijah's position ahead of the chariot was one of respect and allegiance. This precise intent is conveyed in the eighth-century BC Bar Rakub inscription, in which a Syrian vassal shows his devotion to Tiglath-Pileser III by "running at his wheel" as an outrunner.

19:2 *May the gods deal with me, be it ever so severely.* This is a common ancient Near Eastern oath formula, indicating that a horrible fate awaits one who breaks a covenant or acts in treachery against another. In effect, Jezebel is making a treaty with herself.

19:3 *Beersheba.* One of the regional centers of the Biblical Negev, which served as a major gateway into Judah via Hebron. By mentioning Elijah's arrival at Beersheba the Biblical author most likely intended to note that the prophet was far beyond the borders of Ahab's kingdom and about to enter the dangerous and foreboding wilderness that lay beyond the southern kingdom of Judah.

19:4 *broom bush. Retama raetum* can grow to a height of 10 feet (3 meters). It produces small white flowers in spring. To this day broom bushes in the arid Negev and northern Sinai offer much-needed shade. Because vegetation is so sparse in the great wilderness, this particular bush may have been the only shade available to Elijah for several miles/kilometers.

19:8 *traveled forty days and forty nights until he reached Horeb.* The long journey places Elijah deep in the Sinai peninsula or on the border of Arabia. *Horeb.* The location of Horeb/Mount Sinai is uncertain (see the article "Mount Sinai," p. 144).

forty[j] days and forty nights until he reached
Horeb,[k] the mountain of God. 9There he
went into a cave[l] and spent the night.

The LORD Appears to Elijah

And the word of the LORD came to him:
"What are you doing here, Elijah?"
10He replied, "I have been very zealous[m] for the LORD God Almighty. The Israelites have rejected your covenant, torn
down your altars, and put your prophets
to death with the sword. I am the only
one left,[n] and now they are trying to kill
me too."
11The LORD said, "Go out and stand on
the mountain[o] in the presence of the LORD,
for the LORD is about to pass by."
Then a great and powerful wind[p] tore
the mountains apart and shattered the
rocks before the LORD, but the LORD was
not in the wind. After the wind there was
an earthquake, but the LORD was not in the
earthquake. 12After the earthquake came
a fire, but the LORD was not in the fire.
And after the fire came a gentle whisper.[q]
13When Elijah heard it, he pulled his cloak
over his face[r] and went out and stood at
the mouth of the cave.
Then a voice said to him, "What are you
doing here, Elijah?"
14He replied, "I have been very zealous
for the LORD God Almighty. The Israelites
have rejected your covenant, torn down
your altars, and put your prophets to death
with the sword. I am the only one left,[s] and
now they are trying to kill me too."
15The LORD said to him, "Go back the
way you came, and go to the Desert of
Damascus. When you get there, anoint
Hazael[t] king over Aram. 16Also, anoint[u]
Jehu son of Nimshi king over Israel, and
anoint Elisha[v] son of Shaphat from Abel
Meholah to succeed you as prophet.

19:8 [j] Ex 24:18; 34:28; Dt 9:9-11, 18; Mt 4:2 [k] Ex 3:1
19:9 [l] Ex 33:22
19:10 [m] Nu 25:13 [n] 1Ki 18:4, 22; Ro 11:3*
19:11 [o] Ex 24:12 [p] Eze 1:4; 37:7
19:12 [q] Job 4:16; Zec 4:6
19:13 [r] ver 9; Ex 3:6
19:14 [s] ver 10
19:15 [t] 2Ki 8:7-15
19:16 [u] 2Ki 9:1-3, 6 [v] ver 21; 2Ki 2:9, 15

Ivory representation of Hazael (see note on 19:15).
Kim Walton

19:10 *torn down your altars, and put your prophets to death with the sword.* Such desecration and religious purging have good parallels in the reforms of Akhenaten in fourteenth-century BC Egypt and the efforts made at restoring traditional Egyptian religion after his death.
19:11 *the LORD is about to pass by.* The wind, earthquake and fire (vv. 11b – 12) are recognizable elements of theophany in the ancient world. The presence of the god either in anger or in battle can wreak havoc, as it threatens human life. Some of these same features are evident in Yahweh's theophany on Mount Sinai (Ex 19:16 – 19). Yahweh also approaches Job in the whirlwind (Job 38:1). Sumerian, Hittite, Akkadian and Ugaritic texts all attest to the power of the divine warrior.
19:12 *gentle whisper.* This is unusual and is without parallel in the ancient world (see previous note). In a theophany, the voice of the god usually thunders, but in all the destructive emanations there had been no message from Yahweh. The "gentle whisper" does not indicate the demeanor or the volume of Yahweh's communication. Rather, it identifies that Yahweh speaks in the reverberating silence that follows tumultuous disasters. Here this indicates that Yahweh has not just been about judging Ahab and Jezebel as divine warrior, he has also been transitioning to a new era in which new leadership will take control (vv. 15 – 16).
19:15 *anoint Hazael king over Aram.* Israel was not the only nation that anointed kings. This method of installing kings was also practiced in ancient Egypt and possibly in Canaan as well. Hazael was the most powerful king Aram would ever know. He ruled during the last four decades of the ninth century BC. For most of his reign he campaigned tirelessly against the kingdom of Israel that had been weakened by an unstable dynasty after the house of Omri was obliterated through Ahab's demise in 852 BC. Hazael's destructive attacks on sites such as Rehov in Galilee and Gath and Zeitah in Philistia are seen in excavated destruction layers that are dated securely by radiocarbon dating. After fighting off Shalmaneser III of Assyria, Hazael successfully cut off Israel and Judah on three sides and

LIVES OF ELIJAH AND ELISHA

The life-and-death struggle with Baalism, acute in Elijah's day, intensified under Elisha and culminated in bloody purges of the priests of Baal. Ahab's line was overthrown, and reforms were promulgated by Jehu.

Elijah's rugged figure became a model of the ideal prophet in Israel. Jesus fulfilled 40 days and nights of desert fasting, as Elijah had done; many believed he was a reincarnated Elijah (see 1Ki 19:8; Mt 4:2 and note; 16:14).

Elisha also became a model for the prophets. Jesus' miracle of feeding the 5,000 was similar to Elisha's feeding 100 men with 20 barley loaves.

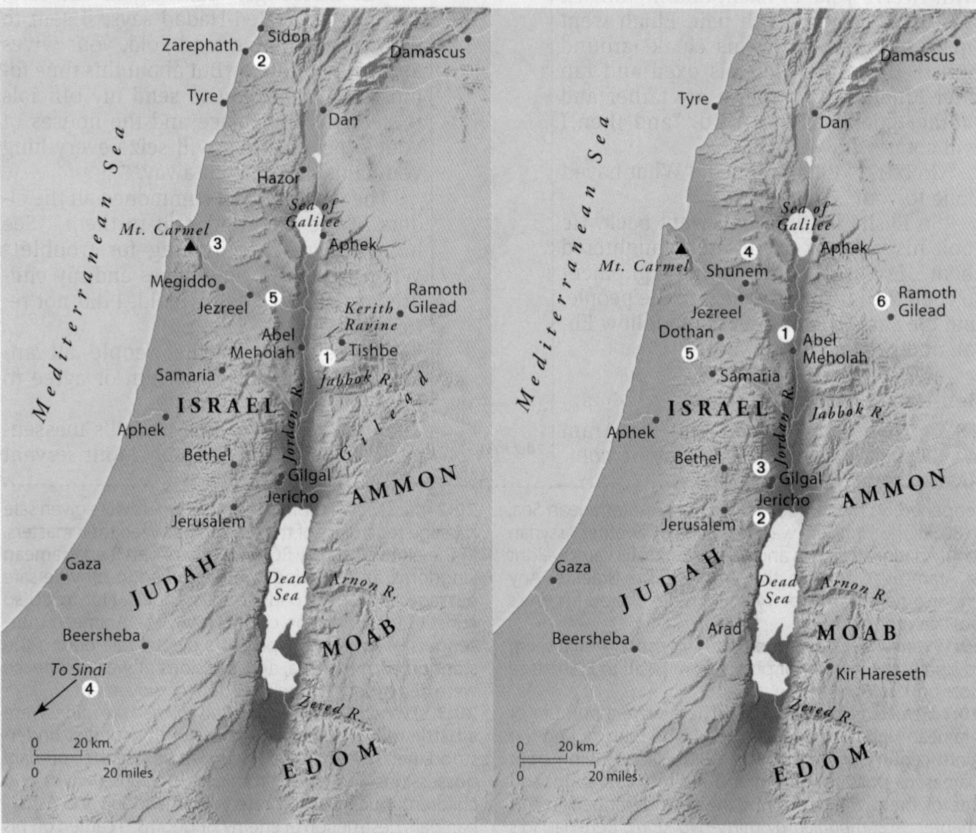

ELIJAH

Elijah of Tishbe was instrumental in Israel's reaction to Baalism. Jezebel of Tyre was symbolic of the nation's corruption.

1 Fed by ravens

2 Miracle of the widow's jar of oil

3 After the triumph on Mount Carmel, Elijah ordered the people to slaughter the prophets of Baal.

4 Elijah was so discouraged that he wanted to die. Fleeing to Sinai, he was told to anoint a new generation of political and religious leaders.

5 At Naboth's vineyard in Jezreel, God's servant confronted Jezebel's puppet, the king.

ELISHA

Elisha, like Elijah, performed miracles and was called "the chariots and horsemen of Israel" (2Ki 13:14).

1 Born west of the Jordan, the prophet frequented shrines at Mount Carmel and Gilgal. Dothan, a flourishing town in this period, was probably his residence.

2 Spring healed

3 Jeered by youths

4 Elisha journeyed from Mount Carmel to Shunem to raise a child from the dead, as Elijah had done at Zarephath.

5 Vision of chariots of fire

6 Elisha and his servant anointed Hazael and Jehu, completing Elijah's commission at Horeb.

17 Jehu will put to death any who escape the sword of Hazael,[w] and Elisha will put to death any who escape the sword of Jehu. 18 Yet I reserve[x] seven thousand in Israel — all whose knees have not bowed down to Baal and whose mouths have not kissed[y] him."

The Call of Elisha

19 So Elijah went from there and found Elisha son of Shaphat. He was plowing with twelve yoke of oxen, and he himself was driving the twelfth pair. Elijah went up to him and threw his cloak[z] around him. 20 Elisha then left his oxen and ran after Elijah. "Let me kiss my father and mother goodbye,"[a] he said, "and then I will come with you."

"Go back," Elijah replied. "What have I done to you?"

21 So Elisha left him and went back. He took his yoke of oxen[b] and slaughtered them. He burned the plowing equipment to cook the meat and gave it to the people, and they ate. Then he set out to follow Elijah and became his servant.[c]

Ben-Hadad Attacks Samaria

20 Now Ben-Hadad[d] king of Aram mustered his entire army. Accompanied by thirty-two kings with their horses and chariots, he went up and besieged Samaria and attacked it. 2 He sent messengers into the city to Ahab king of Israel, saying, "This is what Ben-Hadad says: 3 'Your silver and gold are mine, and the best of your wives and children are mine.' "

4 The king of Israel answered, "Just as you say, my lord the king. I and all I have are yours."

5 The messengers came again and said, "This is what Ben-Hadad says: 'I sent to demand your silver and gold, your wives and your children. 6 But about this time tomorrow I am going to send my officials to search your palace and the houses of your officials. They will seize everything you value and carry it away.' "

7 The king of Israel summoned all the elders of the land and said to them, "See how this man is looking for trouble![e] When he sent for my wives and my children, my silver and my gold, I did not refuse him."

8 The elders and the people all answered, "Don't listen to him or agree to his demands."

9 So he replied to Ben-Hadad's messengers, "Tell my lord the king, 'Your servant

19:17 [w] 2Ki 8:12,29; 9:14; 13:3,7,22
19:18 [x] Ro 11:4* [y] Hos 13:2
19:19 [z] 2Ki 2:8, 14
19:20 [a] Mt 8:21-22; Lk 9:61
19:21 [b] 2Sa 24:22 [c] ver 16
20:1 [d] 1Ki 15:18; 22:31; 2Ki 6:24
20:7 [e] 2Ki 5:7

reopened his own trade links to the Mediterranean Sea. In 805 BC his kingdom was destroyed by another Assyrian king, Adadnirari III. This anointing would still carry weight in Aram even though the prophet was Israelite. Any endorsement from a deity could be exploited for one's political ambitions.

19:19 *threw his cloak around him.* This action would seem to signify the transfer of power from Elijah to Elisha (see note on 1Sa 18:3 – 4).

20:1 *Ben-Hadad king of Aram.* There were a number of Aramean kings named Ben-Hadad who ruled during the ninth century BC. There was a Ben-Hadad ruling from Damascus prior to, during and after Ahab's reign, and one of them was no doubt the king described in this chapter. *Accompanied by thirty-two kings.* Ben-Hadad's ability to recruit so many other kings and chieftains was a rare achievement in the ancient Near East and is a testimony to Aram's ascendancy in the mid-ninth century BC. *besieged Samaria and attacked it.* Ahab's battles with Aram reflect an ongoing trade war between Aram and Israel that originated with the alliance between Israel and Phoenicia. This new arrangement, sealed by the marriage of Jezebel and Ahab, severely curtailed Aram's access to the lucrative trade of Mediterranean ports. Ben-Hadad's purpose was to isolate Israel and not necessarily destroy its capital city of Samaria. Because of the geographic distribution of messages, scouts and troop movement, the battle description in ch. 20 apparently does not involve a protracted localized siege of Samaria. Instead, ch. 20 must be read against the backdrop of the ongoing trade wars, the geography of the Israelite highlands, and the translation of the Hebrew word translated "in their tents" in v. 12 (see note there). These contextual data help to explain Ahab's victory and the subsequent hesitation of Ben-Hadad to engage Israel in the hills (v. 23).

20:2 *messengers.* Diplomatic messengers were given safe passage regardless of the tension between their masters. In the eighth-century BC Sefire treaty between Aramean kingdoms, all local kings were required to provide safe passage and open roads to messengers. Not to do so constituted a violation of the treaty. The Aramean messengers of Ben-Hadad played a pivotal role during the standoff with Samaria, and decisions of war and peace were dependent on their freedom of movement.

20:3 *silver and gold ... wives and children are mine.* Were a battle to be fought, both sides of the conflict understood that the vanquished party would lose their primary possessions and most prominent persons ("wives and children"). Such was the case in Esarhaddon's and Ashurbanipal's destruction of enemy kingdoms: "I carried off his wife, his children, the personnel of his palace, gold, silver ... many valuables" (cf. v. 3). The Egyptian victors did the same. Amenhotep II boasts of seizing wives, children, animals and "all of their property without end." Reliefs from Tiglath-Pileser III show captives and animals leaving Babylon, providing a chilling visual commentary to such texts.

20:4 *all I have are yours.* Because he was outnumbered, Ahab's compliance is nothing less than a surrender. His words resemble that of a vassal responding to a lord in the deferential language of covenant treaties from the ancient Near Eastern world.

20:6 *I am going to send my officials to search your palace and the houses of your officials.* While the actions described in the preceding three verses resonate with coercive ancient Near Eastern surrenders, the thoroughness of the threatened search was a declaration of war. This escalation and the ability of Ahab's advisors and commanders to crisscross the region help to explain Ahab's abrupt change of tone.

20:8 *The elders and the people all answered, "Don't listen to*

will do all you demanded the first time,
but this demand I cannot meet.' " They left
and took the answer back to Ben-Hadad.
10Then Ben-Hadad sent another message to Ahab: "May the gods deal with
me, be it ever so severely, if enough dust[f]
remains in Samaria to give each of my
men a handful."
11The king of Israel answered, "Tell him:
'One who puts on his armor should not
boast[g] like one who takes it off.' "
12Ben-Hadad heard this message while
he and the kings were drinking[h] in their
tents,[a] and he ordered his men: "Prepare
to attack." So they prepared to attack the
city.

Ahab Defeats Ben-Hadad

13Meanwhile a prophet came to Ahab
king of Israel and announced, "This is what
the LORD says: 'Do you see this vast army?
I will give it into your hand today, and then
you will know[i] that I am the LORD.' "
14"But who will do this?" asked Ahab.
The prophet replied, "This is what the
LORD says: 'The junior officers under the
provincial commanders will do it.' "
"And who will start[j] the battle?" he
asked.
The prophet answered, "You will."
15So Ahab summoned the 232 junior
officers under the provincial commanders. Then he assembled the rest of the
Israelites, 7,000 in all. 16They set out at
noon while Ben-Hadad and the 32 kings
allied with him were in their tents getting
drunk.[k] 17The junior officers under the
provincial commanders went out first.
Now Ben-Hadad had dispatched scouts,
who reported, "Men are advancing from
Samaria."
18He said, "If they have come out for
peace, take them alive; if they have come
out for war, take them alive."
19The junior officers under the provincial commanders marched out of the city
with the army behind them 20and each one
struck down his opponent. At that, the Arameans fled, with the Israelites in pursuit.
But Ben-Hadad king of Aram escaped on
horseback with some of his horsemen.
21The king of Israel advanced and overpowered the horses and chariots and inflicted heavy losses on the Arameans.
22Afterward, the prophet[l] came to the
king of Israel and said, "Strengthen your
position and see what must be done, because next spring[m] the king of Aram will
attack you again."
23Meanwhile, the officials of the king
of Aram advised him, "Their gods are
gods[n] of the hills. That is why they were
too strong for us. But if we fight them
on the plains, surely we will be stronger
than they. 24Do this: Remove all the kings
from their commands and replace them
with other officers. 25You must also raise
an army like the one you lost—horse for
horse and chariot for chariot—so we can
fight Israel on the plains. Then surely we
will be stronger than they." He agreed
with them and acted accordingly.
26The next spring[o] Ben-Hadad mustered
the Arameans and went up to Aphek[p] to
fight against Israel. 27When the Israelites
were also mustered and given provisions,
they marched out to meet them. The

20:10 [f] 2Sa 22:43; 1Ki 19:2 **20:11** [g] Pr 27:1; Jer 9:23 **20:12** [h] ver 16; 1Ki 16:9 **20:13** [i] ver 28; Ex 6:7 **20:14** [j] Jdg 1:1 **20:16** [k] ver 12; 1Ki 16:9
20:22 [l] ver 13 [m] ver 26; 2Sa 11:1 **20:23** [n] 1Ki 14:23; Ro 1:21-23 **20:26** [o] ver 22 [p] 2Ki 13:17

[a] 12 Or *in Sukkoth*; also in verse 16

him or agree to his demands." This verse runs against common practice in the ancient world. Public outcry was seldom an option in the theocracies and monarchies of the ancient world. *the people.* In this verse they are most likely the elders and clan leaders of the northern kingdom, who represent the views of the people. The semantic range of the Hebrew word is broad enough to comprise military commanders and advisors, which may be the intent here (cf. 12:8).

20:11 *One who puts on his armor should not boast like one who takes it off.* The language of royal correspondence and diplomacy often invoked pithy sayings and proverbs. A good parallel to Ahab's caustic reply is found in a letter from a local king to the pharaoh of Egypt: "When ants are struck ... they bite the hands that strike them." These idioms expressing the concept of "don't act like you've won before the battle starts" continue the evidence throughout this chapter that the cultural behavior of the Israelites is very much like that with which we are familiar from the ancient world.

20:12 *in their tents.* The Hebrew (*bassukkot*) can also be translated "in Sukkoth" (see NIV text note), presumably a staging area in Transjordan. The movements of messengers and troops in the verses that follow would not be possible were Samaria under a tight siege. For this reason and because both Zimri (16:9) and David (2Sa 11) previously had launched campaigns from the nearby region of Sukkoth, a city in the Jordan Valley, the alternative translation "in Sukkoth" is probably intended. This interpretation also helps to explain the relatively free movement of Ahab's army in vv. 17–20.

20:15 *junior officers under the provincial commanders.* Relatively few details are known about the organization of the Israelite army. *junior officers.* The Hebrew word (*naar*) can denote a soldier or "young officer" as in the texts of Ugarit and Late Bronze Age Egypt, but the cognate terms do not guarantee this translation. *provincial commanders.* The meaning of this term is unclear. *7,000 in all.* This would be a sizeable force, but this may also designate seven clan divisions, which would likely be considerably smaller (see the article "Numbers in Numbers," p. 235).

20:23 *Their gods are gods of the hills.* People in the ancient world often recognized divinities as being confined to regions (see note on Jdg 6:13). *if we fight them on the plains ... we will be stronger.* Chariotry and archers were better suited to the traditional battlegrounds of the open plain than to the narrow defiles of the central range. Moreover, Ben-Hadad had no desire to repeat the disaster recorded in the preceding verses.

Israelites camped op-
posite them like two
small flocks of goats,
while the Arameans
covered the country-
side.[q]
28The man of God
came up and told the
king of Israel, "This
is what the LORD
says: 'Because the
Arameans think the
LORD is a god of the
hills and not a god[r]
of the valleys, I will
deliver this vast army
into your hands, and
you will know[s] that I
am the LORD.' "
29For seven days
they camped oppo-
site each other, and
on the seventh day
the battle was joined.
The Israelites inflict-
ed a hundred thou-
sand casualties on
the Aramean foot
soldiers in one day.
30The rest of them
escaped to the city of Aphek,[t] where the
wall collapsed on twenty-seven thousand
of them. And Ben-Hadad fled to the city
and hid[u] in an inner room.
31His officials said to him, "Look, we
have heard that the kings of Israel are merciful. Let us go to the king of Israel with
sackcloth[v] around our waists and ropes
around our heads. Perhaps he will spare
your life."
32Wearing sackcloth around their waists
and ropes around their heads, they went
to the king of Israel and said, "Your servant Ben-Hadad says: 'Please let me live.' "
The king answered, "Is he still alive? He
is my brother."
33The men took this as a good sign and
were quick to pick up his word. "Yes, your
brother Ben-Hadad!" they said.
"Go and get him," the king said. When
Ben-Hadad came out, Ahab had him come
up into his chariot.
34"I will return the cities[w] my father
took from your father," Ben-Hadad offered.

Sappers, or siege soldiers who tunneled under defensive walls, undermining the foundations of a wall. Sappers could have caused the wall at Aphek to collapse (1Ki 20:30).

The British Museum. © James C. Martin.

20:27 [q] Jdg 6:6; 1Sa 13:6
20:28 [r] ver 23 [s] ver 13
20:30 [t] ver 26 [u] 1Ki 22:25; 2Ch 18:24
20:31 [v] Ge 37:34
20:34 [w] 1Ki 15:20

20:29 *a hundred thousand casualties . . . in one day.* See the article "Numbers in Numbers," p. 235.
20:30 *wall collapsed.* The massive walls of ancient Israelite cities required large foundations, which could be undermined by sapper work, as depicted in many Assyrian reliefs (see the article "Siege Warfare," p. 1157). *inner room.* The expression may or may not be a technical term for a specific room. It is unclear where this "inner room" was located, but it was most likely a fortified space within the citadel of the city. A Hittite historiographic document describes an associate of the king going into the "inner chamber" and sitting before him on the right. The context implies a throne room or some portion of the king's secure quarters.
20:32 *Wearing sackcloth.* A clear sign of submission that has parallels in both textual and artistic expressions in other ancient Near Eastern cultures. In a similar act of surrender King Shurpria of Urartu faced his Assyrian opponent and "took off his royal garment and wrapped his body in sackcloth befitting a (penitent) sinner." *ropes around their heads.* Most likely a sign of their submission and willingness to be bound. Pharaoh Shishak's Karnak relief shows local kings on their knees before the king, with ropes around their necks. By placing ropes on their heads, the Arameans appear to have been acquiescing to Ahab in advance of being captured. *He is my brother.* This common diplomatic usage of the term "brother" indicates that Ahab still acknowledged the equal power and position of Ben-Hadad, whom he had just defeated. Compare the diplomatic parity reflected in the friendly dialogue between the kings of Tyre and Ugarit in the thirteenth century BC: "To the king of Ugarit, my brother, say . . ." The expression is often found in the preamble or conclusion of treaties between kings, as is the case here. By inviting Ben Hadad into his chariot (v. 33) rather than making him walk in submission by the wheel, Ahab was acknowledging publicly the agreement between the two kings. Rather than making Ben-Hadad into a vassal, he was extracting from him key territorial and economic concessions in return for his freedom.
20:34 *market areas in Damascus.* The treaty made in this verse is a further indicator that trade and economic gain were the motivation of this battle and the Aramean-Israelite wars generally. A good precedent of such tax-

"You may set up your own market areas in
Damascus,[x] as my father did in Samaria."
Ahab said, "On the basis of a treaty[y]
I will set you free." So he made a treaty
with him, and let him go.

A Prophet Condemns Ahab

35 By the word of the LORD one of the
company of the prophets said to his companion, "Strike me with your weapon,"
but he refused.[z]
36 So the prophet said, "Because you
have not obeyed the LORD, as soon as you
leave me a lion[a] will kill you." And after
the man went away, a lion found him and
killed him.
37 The prophet found another man and
said, "Strike me, please." So the man
struck him and wounded him. 38 Then the
prophet went and stood by the road waiting for the king. He disguised himself with
his headband down over his eyes. 39 As the
king passed by, the prophet called out to
him, "Your servant went into the thick of
the battle, and someone came to me with
a captive and said, 'Guard this man. If he
is missing, it will be your life for his life,[b]
or you must pay a talent[a] of silver.' 40 While
your servant was busy here and there, the
man disappeared."
"That is your sentence," the king of Israel said. "You have pronounced it yourself."
41 Then the prophet quickly removed the
headband from his eyes, and the king of
Israel recognized him as one of the prophets. 42 He said to the king, "This is what
the LORD says: 'You have set free a man I
had determined should die.[b][c] Therefore it
is your life for his life,[d] your people for his
people.'" 43 Sullen and angry,[e] the king of
Israel went to his palace in Samaria.

Naboth's Vineyard

21 Some time later there was an incident involving a vineyard belonging to Naboth[f] the Jezreelite. The vineyard was in Jezreel,[g] close to the palace of
Ahab king of Samaria. 2 Ahab said to Naboth, "Let me have your vineyard to use
for a vegetable garden, since it is close to
my palace. In exchange I will give you a
better vineyard or, if you prefer, I will pay
you whatever it is worth."
3 But Naboth replied, "The LORD forbid
that I should give you the inheritance[h] of
my ancestors."
4 So Ahab went home, sullen and angry[i]
because Naboth the Jezreelite had said,
"I will not give you the inheritance of my
ancestors." He lay on his bed sulking and
refused to eat.
5 His wife Jezebel came in and asked
him, "Why are you so sullen? Why won't
you eat?"
6 He answered her, "Because I said to
Naboth the Jezreelite, 'Sell me your vineyard; or if you prefer, I will give you another vineyard in its place.' But he said, 'I
will not give you my vineyard.'"
7 Jezebel his wife said, "Is this how you
act as king over Israel? Get up and eat!
Cheer up. I'll get you the vineyard[j] of Naboth the Jezreelite."
8 So she wrote letters in Ahab's name,
placed his seal[k] on them, and sent them

20:34 [x] Jer 49:23-27 [y] Ex 23:32 **20:35** [z] 1Ki 13:21; 2Ki 2:3-7 **20:36** [a] 1Ki 13:24 **20:39** [b] 2Ki 10:24 **20:42** [c] Jer 48:10 [d] ver 39; Jos 2:14; 1Ki 22:31-37

20:43 [e] 1Ki 21:4 **21:1** [f] 2Ki 9:21 [g] 1Ki 18:45-46 **21:3** [h] Lev 25:23; Nu 36:7; Eze 46:18 **21:4** [i] 1Ki 20:43 **21:7** [j] 1Sa 8:14 **21:8** [k] Ge 38:18; Est 3:12; 8:8, 10

[a] *39* That is, about 75 pounds or about 34 kilograms
[b] *42* The Hebrew term refers to the irrevocable giving over of things or persons to the LORD, often by totally destroying them.

free trading centers is the Assyrian colonies in Anatolia that brought copper ore into Mesopotamia. These *karums* or land-based ports thrived in the second millennium BC.

20:39 *a talent of silver.* A talent is 75 pounds (34 kilograms); therefore, this is an impossibly large sum for an ordinary person, and it virtually assured that it would be a life for a life if the man went missing. This was the price of two or more slaves in Mesopotamia and Egypt. Such a large sum of money, though exorbitant, is in keeping with the penalties recorded in other ancient Near Eastern cultures.

21:2 *vineyard to use for a vegetable garden.* Assyrian palace reliefs depict royal gardens adjacent to the king's residence much like the sacred gardens that surrounded temples and holy sites. The city plan of most ancient cities included a royal complex with palace, gardens and administrative buildings. The temple and its courtyard lay adjacent to the royal complex and its palace as at Zinjirli, Tell Tayinat and Jerusalem. Such distinct districts can be identified not only by a contrast in architecture but also in the concentration of expensive or imported finds that they produce in archaeological excavations. *vegetable.* This Hebrew word occurs only two other times in the OT and in those contexts refers to small agriculture for food. Its basic root refers to greenery, but other terms could have been used here if Ahab intended a park of trees and flowers. A vegetable garden is not unlikely, since the palace kitchens would have needed a place to grow the food for the king's table.

21:3 *the inheritance of my ancestors.* Naboth can make this claim on the covenant basis of land inheritance. Each Israelite family viewed the land as their little piece of the covenant. At the same time, temporary land grants could be made, so it is likely that Naboth is maintaining his covenant right of possession as an expression of antagonism toward Ahab and Jezebel.

21:4–6 This passage demonstrates differences in the social structure of Israelite and Phoenician monarchies. In Phoenicia, though still accountable to the gods, the king was above the law, and the land was considered to be the ultimate property of the crown, given out through grants. In Israel, the king is bound by the same covenant laws as the people, and the land is ultimately Yahweh's to distribute.

21:8 *wrote letters in Ahab's name, placed his seal on them.* Most documents and decrees were written in ink on leather or papyrus. Official communication was secured

to the elders and nobles who lived in Naboth's city with him. 9In those letters she
wrote:

"Proclaim a day of fasting and seat
Naboth in a prominent place among
the people. 10But seat two scoundrels[l]
opposite him and have them bring
charges that he has cursed[m] both God
and the king. Then take him out and
stone him to death."

11So the elders and nobles who lived
in Naboth's city did as Jezebel directed
in the letters she had written to them.
12They proclaimed a fast[n] and seated Naboth in a prominent place among the people. 13Then two scoundrels came and sat
opposite him and brought charges against
Naboth before the people, saying, "Naboth has cursed both God and the king."
So they took him outside the city and
stoned him to death.[o] 14Then they sent
word to Jezebel: "Naboth has been stoned
to death."

15As soon as Jezebel heard that Naboth
had been stoned to death, she said to
Ahab, "Get up and take possession of the
vineyard[p] of Naboth the Jezreelite that he
refused to sell you. He is no longer alive,
but dead." 16When Ahab heard that Naboth was dead, he got up and went down
to take possession of Naboth's vineyard.

17Then the word of the LORD came to Elijah the Tishbite: 18"Go down to meet Ahab
king of Israel, who rules in Samaria. He is
now in Naboth's vineyard, where he has
gone to take possession of it. 19Say to him,
'This is what the LORD says: Have you not
murdered a man and seized his property?'
Then say to him, 'This is what the LORD
says: In the place where dogs licked up
Naboth's blood,[q] dogs[r] will lick up your
blood—yes, yours!'"

20Ahab said to Elijah, "So you have
found me, my enemy!"[s]

"I have found you," he answered, "because you have sold[t] yourself to do evil in
the eyes of the LORD. 21He says, 'I am going
to bring disaster on you. I will wipe out
your descendants and cut off from Ahab
every last male[u] in Israel—slave or free.[a]
22I will make your house[v] like that of Jeroboam son of Nebat and that of Baasha
son of Ahijah, because you have aroused
my anger and have caused Israel to sin.'[w]

23"And also concerning Jezebel the LORD
says: 'Dogs[x] will devour Jezebel by the
wall of[b] Jezreel.'

24"Dogs[y] will eat those belonging to
Ahab who die in the city, and the birds
will feed on those who die in the country."

25(There was never[z] anyone like Ahab,
who sold himself to do evil in the eyes of
the LORD, urged on by Jezebel his wife.
26He behaved in the vilest manner by going after idols, like the Amorites[a] the LORD
drove out before Israel.)

27When Ahab heard these words, he
tore his clothes, put on sackcloth[b] and
fasted. He lay in sackcloth and went
around meekly.

28Then the word of the LORD came to
Elijah the Tishbite: 29"Have you noticed
how Ahab has humbled himself before
me? Because he has humbled himself, I
will not bring this disaster in his day, but
I will bring it on his house in the days of
his son."[c]

21:10 [l] Ac 6:11 [m] Ex 22:28; Lev 24:15-16 **21:12** [n] Isa 58:4 **21:13** [o] 2Ki 9:26 **21:15** [p] 1Sa 8:14 **21:19** [q] 2Ki 9:26; Ps 9:12; Isa 14:20 [r] 1Ki 22:38 **21:20** [s] 1Ki 18:17 [t] ver 25; 2Ki 17:17; Ro 7:14 **21:21** [u] 1Ki 14:10; 2Ki 9:8 **21:22** [v] 1Ki 15:29; 16:3 [w] 1Ki 12:30 **21:23** [x] 2Ki 9:10, 34-36 **21:24** [y] 1Ki 14:11; 16:4 **21:25** [z] ver 20; 1Ki 16:33 **21:26** [a] Ge 15:16; Lev 18:25-30; 2Ki 21:11 **21:27** [b] Ge 37:34; 2Sa 3:31; 2Ki 6:30 **21:29** [c] 2Ki 9:26

[a] *21* Or *Israel—every ruler or leader* [b] *23* Most Hebrew manuscripts; a few Hebrew manuscripts, Vulgate and Syriac (see also 2 Kings 9:26) *the plot of ground at*

by string, held together by a clay seal impressed with the official's seal. Personalized stone seals or stamps were commonly used in the ancient Near East in order to indicate the ownership of pottery vessels or to authenticate letters. In the latter case the seal impression was made on a wet clay "bulla," which was then affixed to the string tied around the document in order to seal it. It is usually possible still to see traces of the string and of the papyrus fibers on the reverse side of Hebrew bullae, which does confirm that sheets of papyrus were in widespread use in Israel and Judah in the eighth to the sixth centuries BC—the time period from which most of the seal impressions come. Hundreds of such stone seals or the impressions they made on pottery or bullae have been discovered all over Syria and Palestine. They are often inscribed with artwork and usually display the name of the seal's owner and some further information about the owner (e.g., father's and grandfather's name; title). In about a dozen examples of specifically Hebrew seal inscriptions, the inscription derives from an Israelite woman rather than a man, suggesting that at least some women in that culture were authorized to sign contracts and other documents.

21:9 *Proclaim a day of fasting.* The king can declare a fast as part of some sort of critical petition (cf. Jnh 3:7–9) in order to relieve a calamity such as a drought. The assumption would have been that someone's offense had brought disaster on them all. Once Naboth is identified as the responsible party, his death is supposed to rectify whatever offense caused the problem by appeasing God. *seat Naboth in a prominent place.* Naboth's prominent position indicates high status, which means he could potentially be responsible for whatever affects the entire community.

21:10 *seat two scoundrels opposite him.* Placed near Naboth so that they can claim to have overheard Naboth curse God and the king (see next note).

21:13 *cursed both God and the king.* Refers to placing blame for the situation, which demonstrates disloyalty and is judged as treasonous.

21:16 *take possession.* Technically, Ahab had the right to the property if Naboth had been deemed a law breaker. A similar royal takeover of property is recorded in a text from Alalakh in the late second millennium BC, and also from fourteenth-century BC Ugarit.

21:24 *Dogs will eat ... birds will feed.* See note on 14:11.

Micaiah Prophesies Against Ahab

22:1-28pp — 2Ch 18:1-27

22 For three years there was no war
between Aram and Israel. [2]But in
the third year Jehoshaphat king of Judah
went down to see the king of Israel. [3]The
king of Israel had said to his officials,
"Don't you know that Ramoth Gilead[d] belongs to us and yet we are doing nothing
to retake it from the king of Aram?"
[4]So he asked Jehoshaphat, "Will you go
with me to fight[e] against Ramoth Gilead?"
Jehoshaphat replied to the king of Israel, "I am as you are, my people as your
people, my horses as your horses." [5]But
Jehoshaphat also said to the king of Israel,
"First seek the counsel[f] of the LORD."
[6]So the king of Israel brought together
the prophets — about four hundred men —
and asked them, "Shall I go to war against
Ramoth Gilead, or shall I refrain?"
"Go,"[g] they answered, "for the Lord will
give it into the king's hand."
[7]But Jehoshaphat asked, "Is there no
longer a prophet[h] of the LORD here whom
we can inquire of?"
[8]The king of Israel answered Jehoshaphat, "There is still one prophet through
whom we can inquire of the LORD, but I
hate[i] him because he never prophesies
anything good[j] about me, but always bad.
He is Micaiah son of Imlah."
"The king should not say such a thing,"
Jehoshaphat replied.
[9]So the king of Israel called one of his
officials and said, "Bring Micaiah son of
Imlah at once."
[10]Dressed in their royal robes, the king
of Israel and Jehoshaphat king of Judah
were sitting on their thrones at the threshing floor[k] by the entrance of the gate of
Samaria, with all the prophets prophesying before them. [11]Now Zedekiah son of
Kenaanah had made iron horns[l] and he
declared, "This is what the LORD says:
'With these you will gore the Arameans
until they are destroyed.' "
[12]All the other prophets were prophesying the same thing. "Attack Ramoth Gilead and be victorious," they said, "for the
LORD will give it into the king's hand."
[13]The messenger who had gone to summon Micaiah said to him, "Look, the other
prophets without exception are predicting
success for the king. Let your word agree
with theirs, and speak favorably."
[14]But Micaiah said, "As surely as the
LORD lives, I can tell him only what the
LORD tells me."[m]
[15]When he arrived, the king asked him,
"Micaiah, shall we go to war against Ramoth Gilead, or not?"
"Attack and be victorious," he answered,
"for the LORD will give it into the king's
hand."
[16]The king said to him, "How many times
must I make you swear to tell me nothing
but the truth in the name of the LORD?"
[17]Then Micaiah answered, "I saw all Israel scattered on the hills like sheep without a shepherd,[n] and the LORD said, 'These
people have no master. Let each one go
home in peace.' "
[18]The king of Israel said to Jehoshaphat,
"Didn't I tell you that he never prophesies
anything good about me, but only bad?"
[19]Micaiah continued, "Therefore hear
the word of the LORD: I saw the LORD sitting
on his throne[o] with all the multitudes[p] of
heaven standing around him on his right
and on his left. [20]And the LORD said, 'Who
will entice Ahab into attacking Ramoth
Gilead and going to his death there?'

22:3 [d]Dt 4:43; Jos 21:38 **22:4** [e]2Ki 3:7 **22:5** [f]Ex 33:7; 2Ki 3:11 **22:6** [g]1Ki 18:19 **22:7** [h]2Ki 3:11 **22:8** [i]Am 5:10 [j]Isa 5:20 **22:10** [k]ver 6
22:11 [l]Dt 33:17; Zec 1:18-21 **22:14** [m]Nu 22:18; 24:13; 1Ki 18:10, 15 **22:17** [n]ver 34-36; Nu 27:17; Mt 9:36 **22:19** [o]Isa 6:1; Eze 1:26; Da 7:9 [p]Job 1:6; 2:1; Ps 103:20-21; Mt 18:10; Heb 1:7, 14

22:5 *First seek the counsel of the LORD.* Texts as early as the early third millennium BC record royal consultation with professional seers before battle. Many of the prophetic terms and procedures described in the Mari archive have close parallels in the Bible. The Mari archive includes numerous examples of prophetic warnings or approvals of the king's military and political plans. A ninth-century BC inscription of King Zakkur of Hamath describes the assurances he received from Baal Shamayim, his patron deity, during a siege. His seers and diviners said, "Don't be afraid! Since I have made you king I will stand beside you!" The rhetoric and vocabulary of these prophets is similar to prophetic utterances in the Biblical books of Kings and Chronicles. Ahab and Jehoshaphat were no doubt hoping for such assurance.

22:11 *made iron horns.* This symbolic action evokes images of power and domination. Bulls and their horns are used as metaphors for the king's power in Egyptian and Mesopotamian texts and iconography. The same image shows the power of the gods. In the Ugaritic myths the patron deity El is described as a strong bull calf, "the bull, the gracious one," and in one Mesopotamian text the goddess Ninlil gores her enemies "with her strong horns."

22:12 *Attack Ramoth Gilead … for the LORD will give it into the king's hand.* The unanimous answer of the prophets did not match the dire situation that Ahab and Jehoshaphat faced. The prophets of Mari likewise inclined to offer their king Zimri-Lim an overly positive assessment of the situation. Ahab's admonition to Micaiah (v. 16) indicates that he, like Zimri-Lim a millennium before, had his doubts about prophetic consensus.

22:17 *like sheep without a shepherd.* The concept of shepherd-king is as ubiquitous in the ancient Near Eastern world as it is in the Bible. The monarchs of Assyria, e.g., were described as unrivaled princes who shepherded their people. A well-known Babylonian proverb further exemplifies the nexus between king and shepherd: "A people without a king (is like) a sheep without a shepherd."

22:19 *the LORD sitting on his throne with all the multitudes of heaven standing around him.* These images fit comfortably within the religious traditions of Egypt, Syria and Mesopotamia, where the gods are seen as sitting in their heavenly council before the throne of El.

"One suggested this, and another that.
21 Finally, a spirit came forward, stood before the LORD and said, 'I will entice him.'
22 " 'By what means?' the LORD asked.
" 'I will go out and be a deceiving[q] spirit
in the mouths of all his prophets,' he said.
" 'You will succeed in enticing him,' said
the LORD. 'Go and do it.'
23 "So now the LORD has put a deceiving
spirit in the mouths of all these prophets[r]
of yours. The LORD has decreed disaster
for you."
24 Then Zedekiah[s] son of Kenaanah
went up and slapped[t] Micaiah in the face.
"Which way did the spirit from[a] the LORD
go when he went from me to speak to
you?" he asked.
25 Micaiah replied, "You will find out on
the day you go to hide[u] in an inner room."
26 The king of Israel then ordered, "Take
Micaiah and send him back to Amon the
ruler of the city and to Joash the king's son
27 and say, 'This is what the king says: Put
this fellow in prison[v] and give him nothing
but bread and water until I return safely.' "
28 Micaiah declared, "If you ever return
safely, the LORD has not spoken[w] through
me." Then he added, "Mark my words, all
you people!"

Ahab Killed at Ramoth Gilead

22:29-36pp — 2Ch 18:28-34

29 So the king of Israel and Jehoshaphat
king of Judah went up to Ramoth Gilead.
30 The king of Israel said to Jehoshaphat, "I
will enter the battle in disguise,[x] but you
wear your royal robes." So the king of Israel disguised himself and went into battle.
31 Now the king of Aram had ordered
his thirty-two chariot commanders, "Do
not fight with anyone, small or great, except the king[y] of Israel." 32 When the chariot commanders saw Jehoshaphat, they
thought, "Surely this is the king of Israel."
So they turned to attack him, but when
Jehoshaphat cried out, 33 the chariot commanders saw that he was not the king of
Israel and stopped pursuing him.
34 But someone drew his bow[z] at random
and hit the king of Israel between the sections of his armor. The king told his chariot driver, "Wheel around and get me out
of the fighting. I've been wounded." 35 All
day long the battle raged, and the king
was propped up in his chariot facing the
Arameans. The blood from his wound ran
onto the floor of the chariot, and that evening he died. 36 As the sun was setting, a
cry spread through the army: "Every man
to his town. Every man to his land!"[a]
37 So the king died and was brought
to Samaria, and they buried him there.
38 They washed the chariot at a pool in Samaria (where the prostitutes bathed),[b] and
the dogs[b] licked up his blood, as the word
of the LORD had declared.
39 As for the other events of Ahab's
reign, including all he did, the palace he
built and adorned with ivory,[c] and the cities he fortified, are they not written in the
book of the annals of the kings of Israel? 40 Ahab rested with his ancestors. And
Ahaziah his son succeeded him as king.

Jehoshaphat King of Judah

22:41-50pp — 2Ch 20:31 – 21:1

41 Jehoshaphat son of Asa became king
of Judah in the fourth year of Ahab king of
Israel. 42 Jehoshaphat was thirty-five years
old when he became king, and he reigned

22:22 [q] Jdg 9:23; 1Sa 16:14; 18:10; 19:9; Eze 14:9; 2Th 2:11 **22:23** [r] Eze 14:9 **22:24** [s] ver 11 [t] Ac 23:2 **22:25** [u] 1Ki 20:30 **22:27** [v] 2Ch 16:10 **22:28** [w] Dt 18:22 **22:30** [x] 2Ch 35:32 **22:31** [y] 2Sa 17:2 **22:34** [z] 2Ch 35:23 **22:36** [a] 2Ki 14:12 **22:38** [b] 1Ki 21:19 **22:39** [c] 2Ch 9:17; Am 3:15

[a] 24 Or *Spirit of* [b] 38 Or *Samaria and cleaned the weapons*

22:21 *a spirit came forward.* There are ancient precedents for deities and spirits offering guidance to the king in this manner. In the Ugaritic Keret epic, it is El, the patriarch of the gods, who blesses the human and sends a message to him.

22:24 *slapped Micaiah in the face.* The inappropriateness of this action is attested in the Code of Hammurapi itself. Although it dates to the prior millennium and is a product of Babylonian culture, this legal collection has much in common with the Biblical laws. Hammurapi's collection lists a series of fines for striking a commoner or one above or below one's own social status. The penalty for striking a fellow commoner was ten shekels of silver (about a year's pay), plus the cost of a medical treatment.

22:27 *Put this fellow in prison.* In the Mari letters prisoners describe the king's practice of confining them for some time before deciding their fate, and this may be the case in this verse as well.

22:31 *chariot commanders.* Chariotry would accompany infantry in the initial charge, but would then break away from the melee in order to pursue other objectives, such as containing the perimeter or hunting down a specific target, as here.

22:34 *between the sections of his armor.* An identical scene replete with detailed relief of pierced armor is recorded on a panel of Thutmose III's chariot dating to the sixteenth century BC. Interconnected scales of armor have been excavated at various Late Bronze and Iron Age sites. These can be reconstructed into sleeveless vests of interconnected plates.

22:39 *adorned with ivory.* Ivory was a prized symbol of wealth. It was typically used for the manufacture of combs, cosmetic boxes, small tools and handles, as well as inlay in furniture. Excavators at Samaria found hundreds of ivory pieces in a large burned building that may be the palace described here. The intricate images of architecture, lions and bulls, cherubs, lotus flowers, mythical scenes and women were common in the Levant, Cyprus, and particularly in Phoenicia. These finds are a concrete manifestation of the syncretistic and excessive practices of Ahab described in 1 Kings. A house with ivory-paneled walls would have represented opulence and indulgence taken to unprecedented levels. Further evidence of great wealth among the kingdom's aristocracy was uncovered at Shechem, where a large house with wealthy contents is a good parallel to Ahab's ivory house.

1 KINGS 22:19 – 23

Divine Council

In the ancient world, most cultures believed in many gods, and they imagined that the business of the gods was done in council (as typically happened in human governance). This council was made up of prominent members of the pantheon and presided over by the chief god (at various times and places, gods such as Enlil, Marduk, Asshur or El). Unlike Israel's understanding of Yahweh, the gods of these pantheons had no overarching plan. It rather seems that decisions were made ad hoc. This means of corporate operation was a reflection of the idea prominent in the ancient world that one's identity was found in their community. Just as individual people found their most significant identity in their clan, so the gods also experienced community and acted in corporate solidarity.

The idea that the gods operated in community, however, posed serious problems for the theology of Israel, in which only one being had divine authority. This theology did not eradicate the divine council from Israelite thinking; instead the council was transformed. Rather than being comprised of various gods, the council featured the "sons of God" over whom Yahweh presided and whose activities he delegated (Job 1:6, see NIV text note there on "angels"). These council members were not gods who had autonomous divine authority on a par with Yahweh's, but they were spirit beings given a role in Yahweh's governance of the world. Intimations of the divine council in the Bible include the plurals in Ge 1:26; 3:22; 11:7; Dt 32:8 (see NIV text note rendering "sons of God," likely the correct reading); Job 1:6; 2:1 (see NIV text notes on Job 1:6; 2:1, which both read "sons of God," likely the correct reading); Isa 6:8 — but the passage in 1Ki 22 is the clearest attestation. It was logical to portray divine operations this way because just as a king had the prerogative of having a court of minions to do his bidding, Yahweh also functioned as a king and would be considered to have such prerogatives. ◆

Limestone boundary stone recording a gift of land; the symbols above the writing represent gods doing business "in council," c. 1125 – 1100 BC.

Kim Walton. The British Museum.

The temple at Arad.
Kim Walton

in Jerusalem twenty-five years. His mother's name was Azubah daughter of Shilhi. 43In everything he followed the ways
of his father Asa[d] and did not stray from
them; he did what was right in the eyes of
the LORD. The high places,[e] however, were
not removed, and the people continued to
offer sacrifices and burn incense there.[a]
44Jehoshaphat was also at peace with the
king of Israel.
45As for the other events of Jehoshaphat's reign, the things he achieved and
his military exploits, are they not written
in the book of the annals of the kings of
Judah? 46He rid the land of the rest of the
male shrine prostitutes[f] who remained
there even after the reign of his father Asa.
47There was then no king[g] in Edom; a provincial governor ruled.
48Now Jehoshaphat built a fleet of trading ships[b][h] to go to Ophir for gold, but
they never set sail—they were wrecked at
Ezion Geber. 49At that time Ahaziah son of
Ahab said to Jehoshaphat, "Let my men
sail with yours," but Jehoshaphat refused.
50Then Jehoshaphat rested with his ancestors and was buried with them in the
city of David his father. And Jehoram his
son succeeded him as king.

Ahaziah King of Israel

51Ahaziah son of Ahab became king of
Israel in Samaria in the seventeenth year of
Jehoshaphat king of Judah, and he reigned
over Israel two years. 52He did evil[i] in the
eyes of the LORD, because he followed the
ways of his father and mother and of Jeroboam son of Nebat, who caused Israel to
sin. 53He served and worshiped Baal[j] and
aroused the anger of the LORD, the God of
Israel, just as his father[k] had done.

22:43 [d] 2Ch 17:3 [e] 1Ki 3:2; 15:14; 2Ki 12:3
22:46 [f] Dt 23:17; 1Ki 14:24; 15:12
22:47 [g] 2Sa 8:14; 2Ki 3:9; 8:20
22:48 [h] 1Ki 9:26; 10:22
22:52 [i] 1Ki 15:26; 21:25
22:53 [j] Jdg 2:11 [k] 1Ki 16:30-32

[a] *43* In Hebrew texts this sentence (22:43b) is numbered 22:44, and 22:44-53 is numbered 22:45-54.
[b] *48* Hebrew *of ships of Tarshish*

22:43 *high places.* See notes on 3:2; 11:7.
22:48 *ships … wrecked at Ezion Geber.* Dozens of ancient Mediterranean shipwrecks have been identified off the coasts of Turkey and Israel. A series of Iron Age wreckages have been excavated under the eastern Mediterranean using the new technologies of underwater archaeology. The sunken ships held hundreds of large storage jars, utensils for the crew, and large stone anchors. *Ophir.* See note on 9:28.

NARRATIVE
LITERATURE

2 KINGS

The LORD's Judgment on Ahaziah

1 After Ahab's death, Moab[a] rebelled
against Israel. 2Now Ahaziah had fall-
en through the lattice of his upper room
in Samaria and injured himself. So he sent
messengers,[b] saying to them, "Go and
consult Baal-Zebub,[c] the god of Ekron,[d] to
see if I will recover[e] from this injury."
3But the angel[f] of the LORD said to Elijah[g] the Tishbite, "Go up and meet the
messengers of the king of Samaria and
ask them, 'Is it because there is no God
in Israel[h] that you are going off to consult
Baal-Zebub, the god of Ekron?' 4Therefore
this is what the LORD says: 'You will not
leave[i] the bed you are lying on. You will
certainly die!' " So Elijah went.
5When the messengers returned to the
king, he asked them, "Why have you
come back?"
6"A man came to meet us," they replied.
"And he said to us, 'Go back to the king
who sent you and tell him, "This is what
the LORD says: Is it because there is no God
in Israel that you are sending messengers
to consult Baal-Zebub, the god of Ekron?
Therefore you will not leave the bed you
are lying on. You will certainly die!" ' "
7The king asked them, "What kind of
man was it who came to meet you and
told you this?"
8They replied, "He had a garment of
hair[a][j] and had a leather belt around his
waist."
The king said, "That was Elijah the
Tishbite."
9Then he sent[k] to Elijah a captain[l] with
his company of fifty men. The captain
went up to Elijah, who was sitting on the
top of a hill, and said to him, "Man of
God, the king says, 'Come down!' "
10Elijah answered the captain, "If I am
a man of God, may fire come down from
heaven and consume you and your fifty
men!" Then fire[m] fell from heaven and
consumed the captain and his men.
11At this the king sent to Elijah another captain with his fifty men. The captain
said to him, "Man of God, this is what the
king says, 'Come down at once!' "
12"If I am a man of God," Elijah replied,
"may fire come down from heaven and
consume you and your fifty men!" Then
the fire of God fell from heaven and consumed him and his fifty men.
13So the king sent a third captain with
his fifty men. This third captain went up
and fell on his knees before Elijah. "Man
of God," he begged, "please have respect
for my life[n] and the lives of these fifty
men, your servants! 14See, fire has fallen
from heaven and consumed the first two
captains and all their men. But now have
respect for my life!"
15The angel[o] of the LORD said to Elijah,
"Go down with him; do not be afraid[p] of
him." So Elijah got up and went down
with him to the king.
16He told the king, "This is what the
LORD says: Is it because there is no God in
Israel for you to consult that you have sent
messengers[q] to consult Baal-Zebub, the
god of Ekron? Because you have done this,
you will never leave[r] the bed you are lying
on. You will certainly die!" 17So he died,[s]

1:1 [a] Ge 19:37; 2Sa 8:2; 2Ki 3:5
1:2 [b] ver 16 [c] Mk 3:22 [d] 1Sa 6:2; Isa 2:6; 14:29; Mt 10:25 [e] Jdg 18:5; 2Ki 8:7-10
1:3 [f] ver 15; Ge 16:7 [g] 1Ki 17:1 [h] 1Sa 28:8
1:4 [i] ver 6, 16; Ps 41:8
1:8 [j] 1Ki 18:7; Zec 13:4; Mt 3:4; Mk 1:6
1:9 [k] 2Ki 6:14 [l] Ex 18:25; Isa 3:3
1:10 [m] 1Ki 18:38; Lk 9:54; Rev 11:5; 13:13
1:13 [n] 1Sa 26:21; Ps 72:14
1:15 [o] ver 3 [p] Isa 51:12; 57:11; Jer 1:17; Eze 2:6
1:16 [q] ver 2 [r] ver 4
1:17 [s] 2Ki 8:15; Jer 20:6; 28:17

[a] 8 Or *He was a hairy man*

1:2 *Samaria.* See note on 1Ki 16:24.
1:10 *may fire come down from heaven.* The idea of gods raining down fire to destroy enemies is well known in the ancient world. Here the power of Elijah's God is signaled as a sign that Elijah is Yahweh's prophet. (For another instance of messengers of a king who come to find a prophet and find themselves incapacitated, see 1Sa 19:18–24. For signs given of a king's doom, see Jeroboam in 1Ki 13:1–6.)

2 KINGS 1:2

Lord of the Flies

The god mentioned in 2Ki 1:2 is the Canaanite storm and fertility deity Baal-Hadad, in one of his many localized manifestations. Here he is Baal-Zebub, which would most naturally be taken to mean "Baal/lord of the flies." If this is correct, it is possibly a deliberate Israelite corruption of "Baal-Zebul" ("Baal the prince") intended to express the Biblical authors' scorn of or hostility toward this "deity." Alternatively, Baal-Zebub, rather than being a corruption, is a title indicating mastery over flies, the spreaders of pestilence, and thus over the curing of disease. An Ugaritic deity named El Dhubub may signify something similar.

Ahaziah himself does not scorn this deity, however, but regards him as a source of information and power. In this our authors depict the king as only one of those many Israelites who, in the monarchic period, prefers Baal to Yahweh — or at least does not wish to give Yahweh exclusive allegiance. It is not made clear in the Biblical text why Ahaziah must send messengers on a 60-mile (almost 100-kilometer) trip for such a consultation, although the implication appears to be that a localized manifestation of Baal can only be consulted in his locale. On Baal, see the article "Baal," p. 600. ◆

according to the word of the LORD that Elijah had spoken.

Because Ahaziah had no son, Joram[a][t]
succeeded him as king in the second year
of Jehoram son of Jehoshaphat king of Judah.
18 As for all the other events of Ahaziah's reign, and what he did, are they not written in the book of the annals of the kings of Israel?

Elijah Taken Up to Heaven

2 When the LORD was about to take[u] Elijah up to heaven in a whirlwind,[v] Elijah and Elisha[w] were on their way from
Gilgal.[x]
2 Elijah said to Elisha, "Stay here;[y] the LORD has sent me to Bethel."

But Elisha said, "As surely as the LORD lives and as you live, I will not leave you."[z] So they went down to Bethel.

3 The company[a] of the prophets at Bethel came out to Elisha and asked, "Do you know that the LORD is going to take your master from you today?"

1:17 [t] 2Ki 3:1; 8:16 **2:1** [u] Ge 5:24; Heb 11:5 [v] ver 11; 1Ki 19:11; Isa 5:28; 66:15; Jer 4:13; Na 1:3 [w] 1Ki 19:16,21 [x] Dt 11:30; 2Ki 4:38 **2:2** [y] ver 6 [z] Ru 1:16; 1Sa 1:26; 2Ki 4:30 **2:3** [a] 1Sa 10:5; 2Ki 4:1,38

2:4 [b] Jos 3:16; 6:26 **2:5** [c] ver 3 **2:6** [d] ver 2 [e] Jos 3:15 [f] Ru 1:16 **2:8** [g] 1Ki 19:19 [h] ver 14

"Yes, I know," Elisha replied, "so be quiet."

4 Then Elijah said to him, "Stay here, Elisha; the LORD has sent me to Jericho.[b]"

And he replied, "As surely as the LORD lives and as you live, I will not leave you." So they went to Jericho.

5 The company[c] of the prophets at Jericho went up to Elisha and asked him, "Do you know that the LORD is going to take your master from you today?"

"Yes, I know," he replied, "so be quiet."

6 Then Elijah said to him, "Stay here;[d] the LORD has sent me to the Jordan."[e]

And he replied, "As surely as the LORD lives and as you live, I will not leave you."[f] So the two of them walked on.

7 Fifty men from the company of the prophets went and stood at a distance, facing the place where Elijah and Elisha
had stopped at the Jordan.
8 Elijah took his cloak,[g] rolled it up and struck[h] the water

[a] 17 Hebrew *Jehoram*, a variant of *Joram*

1:18 *book of the annals of the kings of Israel.* See note on 1Ki 14:19.

2:1 *take … up to heaven.* Extra-Biblical texts underline the unusual nature in the ancient Near Eastern context of any idea that mortals can enter and remain in heaven, the best known of which is the Akkadian myth of Adapa, the son of Ea, who visits heaven and almost obtains eternal life but is compelled in the end to return to earth. Another tale of a journey from earth to heaven is told of Etana, one of the fabled rulers of the Sumerian dynasty of Kish, who is compelled to visit heaven (with the help of an eagle) in order to obtain the plant of birth and overcome his childlessness.

Here it is unclear whether Elijah is taken to heaven, referring to the dwelling place of God, or to the heaven, referring to the sky. The other prophets assume the latter since they go looking for where he might have come down. The same Hebrew verb is used with regard to Enoch in Ge 5:24, but there the destination is unspecified.

Elijah's ascent.

Jonathan Walton

with it. The water divided[i] to the right and
to the left, and the two of them crossed
over on dry[j] ground.
9When they had crossed, Elijah said to
Elisha, "Tell me, what can I do for you before I am taken from you?"
"Let me inherit a double[k] portion of
your spirit,"[l] Elisha replied.
10"You have asked a difficult thing," Elijah said, "yet if you see me when I am tak-
en from you, it will be yours — otherwise,
it will not."
11As they were walking along and talking together, suddenly a chariot
of fire[m] and horses of fire appeared and separated the two
of them, and Elijah went up to
heaven[n] in a whirlwind.[o] 12Eli-
sha saw this and cried out, "My
father! My father! The chariots[p]
and horsemen of Israel!" And
Elisha saw him no more. Then
he took hold of his garment and
tore[q] it in two.
13Elisha then picked up Elijah's cloak that had fallen from
him and went back and stood
on the bank of the Jordan. 14He
took the cloak[r] that had fallen
from Elijah and struck[s] the water with it. "Where now is the
LORD, the God of Elijah?" he
asked. When he struck the water, it divided to the right and
to the left, and he crossed over.
15The company[t] of the prophets from Jericho, who were
watching, said, "The spirit[u]
of Elijah is resting on Elisha."
And they went to meet him and
bowed to the ground before
him. 16"Look," they said, "we
your servants have fifty able
men. Let them go and look for
your master. Perhaps the Spirit[v] of the LORD has picked him
up[w] and set him down on some
mountain or in some valley."
"No," Elisha replied, "do not
send them."
17But they persisted until he was too
embarrassed[x] to refuse. So he said, "Send
them." And they sent fifty men, who
searched for three days but did not find
him. 18When they returned to Elisha, who
was staying in Jericho, he said to them,
"Didn't I tell you not to go?"

Healing of the Water

19The people of the city said to Elisha,
"Look, our lord, this town is well situated,

2:8 [i]Ex 14:21 [j]Ex 14:22,29 **2:9** [k]Dt 21:17 [l]Nu 11:17 **2:11** [m]2Ki 6:17; Ps 68:17; 104:3, 4; Isa 66:15; Hab 3:8; Zec 6:1 [n]Ge 5:24 [o]ver 1 **2:12** [p]2Ki 6:17; 13:14 [q]Ge 37:29 **2:14** [r]1Ki 19:19 [s]ver 8 **2:15** [t]ver 7; 1Sa 10:5 [u]Nu 11:17 **2:16** [v]1Ki 18:12 [w]Ac 8:39 **2:17** [x]2Ki 8:11

2:9 *a double portion of your spirit.* This is the language of inheritance. Elisha requests of Elijah what an eldest son would expect of a father in Israel (cf. v. 12): a double portion (cf. Dt 21:15 – 17). In this case, however, the inheritance is not land — Elisha has already left normal life and normal rules of inheritance behind (cf. 1Ki 19:19 – 21). Elisha is asking to receive the status of the principal successor of Elijah.
2:11 *chariot of fire.* Commonly associated with divine manifestation. Some deities, like the sun-god Shamash and the storm-god Hadad, are assigned charioteers or depicted in chariots. It is possible that Yahweh is here appearing as a familiar manifestation of a storm-god.
2:12 *took hold of his garment and tore it in two.* Elisha tears his clothing in the customary gesture of sorrow (cf. Ge 37:34; 2Sa 13:31; Isa 37:1), but perhaps also to indicate the end of an old life and the beginning of a new one as Elijah's successor, symbolized by the picking up of Elijah's cloak (v. 13) — "new" clothing (see next note).
2:13 *cloak.* The "mantle" has passed, quite literally, from Elijah to Elisha; and the cloak that was used in 1Ki 19:19 – 21 to symbolize Elisha's prophetic call has now become Elisha's permanent possession. New clothing was also symbolic of new life elsewhere in the ancient Near East. In the Akkadian myth of Adapa and the South Wind (see note on v. 1), Adapa is offered in heaven both the food of life and a new garment, which he declines.

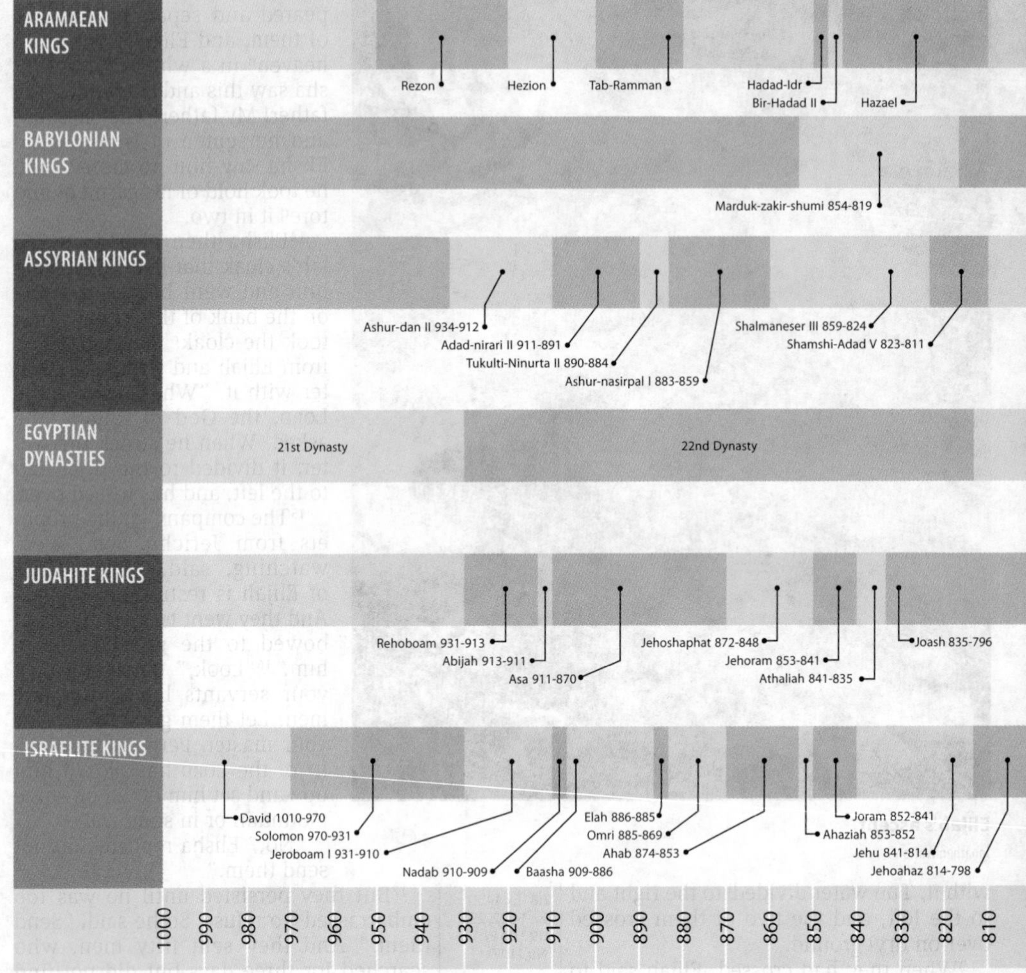

as you can see, but the water is bad and
the land is unproductive."
20"Bring me a new bowl," he said, "and
put salt in it." So they brought it to him.
21Then he went out to the spring and
threw[y] the salt into it, saying, "This is
what the LORD says: 'I have healed this
water. Never again will it cause death or
make the land unproductive.'" 22And the
water has remained pure[z] to this day, according to the word Elisha had spoken.

Elisha Is Jeered

23From there Elisha went up to Bethel.
As he was walking along the road, some
boys came out of the town and jeered[a] at
him. "Get out of here, baldy!" they said.
"Get out of here, baldy!" 24He turned
around, looked at them and called down a
curse[b] on them in the name[c] of the LORD.
Then two bears came out of the woods
and mauled forty-two of the boys. 25And
he went on to Mount Carmel[d] and from
there returned to Samaria.

Moab Revolts

3 Joram[a][e] son of Ahab became king of
Israel in Samaria in the eighteenth
year of Jehoshaphat king of Judah, and he
reigned twelve years. 2He did evil[f] in the
eyes of the LORD, but not as his father[g]
and mother had done. He got rid of the

2:21 [y] Ex 15:25; 2Ki 4:41; 6:6 **2:22** [z] Ex 15:25 **2:23** [a] Ex 22:28; 2Ch 36:16; Job 19:18; Ps 31:18 **2:24** [b] Ge 4:11; Ne 13:25-27 [c] Dt 18:19 **2:25** [d] 1Ki 18:20; 2Ki 4:25 **3:1** [e] 2Ki 1:17 **3:2** [f] 1Ki 15:26 [g] 1Ki 16:30-32

[a] *1* Hebrew *Jehoram,* a variant of *Joram;* also in verse 6

2:24 *boys.* The age of the mockers is uncertain. The Hebrew can refer to prepubescent children, but can also refer to "the younger generation"; the same Hebrew word describes Rehoboam's peers in 1Ki 12:8 ("young men"), and they are over 40. This is probably a group of young teens. **3:2** *sacred stone of Baal.* See note on 1Ki 14:23.

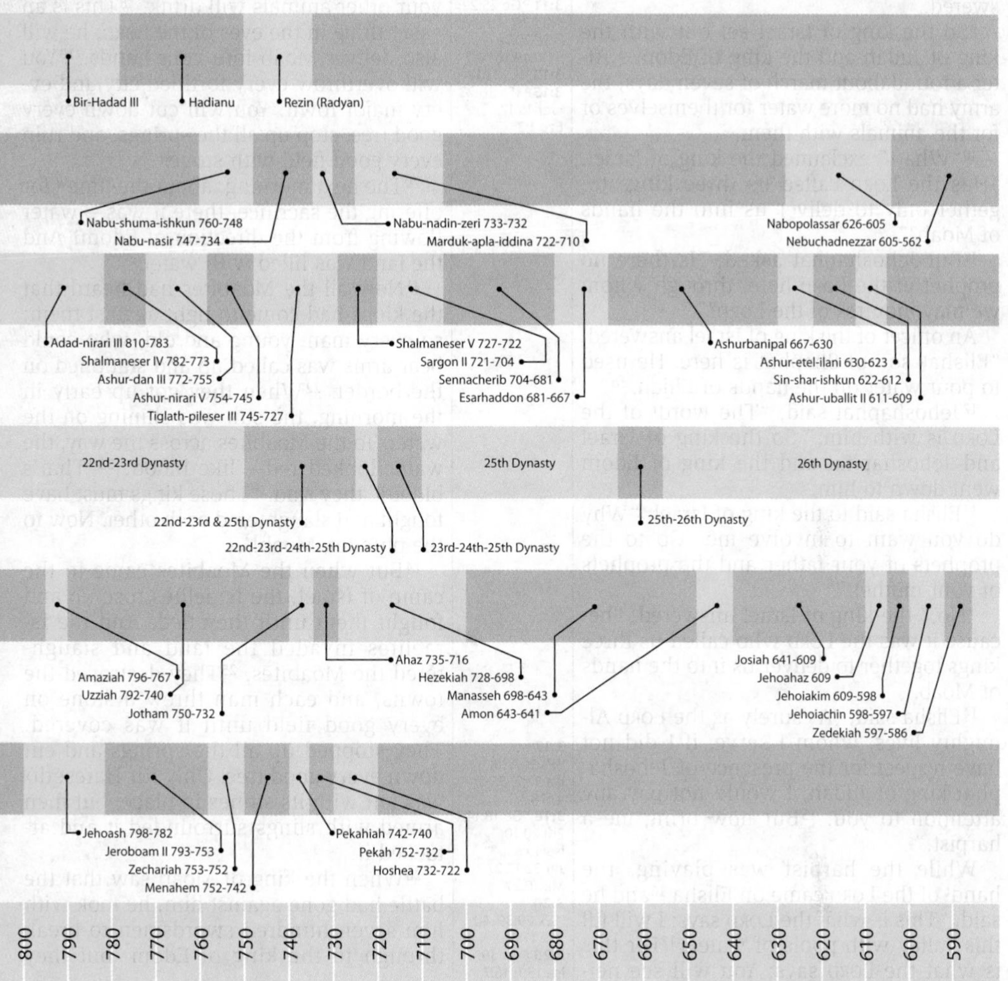

sacred stone[h] of Baal that his father had
made. [3]Nevertheless he clung to the sins[i]
of Jeroboam son of Nebat, which he had
caused Israel to commit; he did not turn
away from them.

[4]Now Mesha king of Moab[j] raised
sheep, and he had to pay the king of Israel a tribute of a hundred thousand lambs[k]
and the wool of a hundred thousand
rams. [5]But after Ahab died, the king of
Moab rebelled[l] against the king of Israel.

[6]So at that time King Joram set out from
Samaria and mobilized all Israel. [7]He also
sent this message to Jehoshaphat king of
Judah: "The king of Moab has rebelled
against me. Will you go with me to fight[m]
against Moab?"

"I will go with you," he replied. "I am
as you are, my people as your people, my
horses as your horses."

[8]"By what route shall we attack?" he
asked.

3:2 [h] Ex 23:24; 2Ki 10:18, 26-28 **3:3** [i] 1Ki 12:28-32; 14:9, 16 **3:4** [j] Ge 19:37; 2Ki 1:1 [k] Ezr 7:17; Isa 16:1 **3:5** [l] 2Ki 1:1 **3:7** [m] 1Ki 22:4

3:4 *Mesha.* A ninth-century BC Moabite king, the successor of his father, Chemosh-yatti, according to the Moabite Stone. He began his reign under the dominion of the Israelite house of Omri. *pay … tribute.* As was true of most subservient peoples in the ancient Near East, Mesha had to pay his overlord "tribute" (i.e., taxes). In Mesopotamia and Assyria this could involve the handing over of a percentage of agricultural products or of flocks and herds, or indeed people (forced labor). The present verse describes the taxation in this more local case as involving sheep and wool, which is understandable given the importance of sheep in the economy of ancient Palestine. After Ahab's death, however, Mesha took advantage of the new situation and rebelled, inciting Ahab's son Joram to launch the campaign described in this chapter. *a hundred thousand lambs.* This is an immense tribute, but nowhere near the 800,000 sheep Sennacherib claimed to have taken from Babylon, so we can see that the amounts are not beyond what is attested in other ancient Near Eastern records.

3:8 *Desert of Edom.* The idea was to attack Moab from

"Through the Desert of Edom," he answered.
9So the king of Israel set out with the
king of Judah and the king of Edom.[n] After a roundabout march of seven days, the
army had no more water for themselves or
for the animals with them.
10"What!" exclaimed the king of Israel.
"Has the LORD called us three kings together only to deliver us into the hands
of Moab?"
11But Jehoshaphat asked, "Is there no
prophet of the LORD here, through whom
we may inquire[o] of the LORD?"
An officer of the king of Israel answered,
"Elisha[p] son of Shaphat is here. He used
to pour water on the hands of Elijah.[a][q]"
12Jehoshaphat said, "The word[r] of the
LORD is with him." So the king of Israel
and Jehoshaphat and the king of Edom
went down to him.
13Elisha said to the king of Israel, "Why
do you want to involve me? Go to the
prophets of your father and the prophets
of your mother."
"No," the king of Israel answered, "because it was the LORD who called us three
kings together to deliver us into the hands
of Moab."
14Elisha said, "As surely as the LORD Almighty lives, whom I serve, if I did not
have respect for the presence of Jehoshaphat king of Judah, I would not pay any
attention to you. 15But now bring me a
harpist."[s]
While the harpist was playing, the
hand[t] of the LORD came on Elisha 16and he
said, "This is what the LORD says: I will fill
this valley with pools of water. 17For this
is what the LORD says: You will see neither wind nor rain, yet this valley will be
filled with water,[u] and you, your cattle and
your other animals will drink. 18This is an
easy[v] thing in the eyes of the LORD; he will
also deliver Moab into your hands. 19You
will overthrow every fortified city and every major town. You will cut down every
good tree, stop up all the springs, and ruin
every good field with stones."
20The next morning, about the time[w] for
offering the sacrifice, there it was — water
flowing from the direction of Edom! And
the land was filled with water.[x]
21Now all the Moabites had heard that
the kings had come to fight against them;
so every man, young and old, who could
bear arms was called up and stationed on
the border. 22When they got up early in
the morning, the sun was shining on the
water. To the Moabites across the way, the
water looked red — like blood. 23"That's
blood!" they said. "Those kings must have
fought and slaughtered each other. Now to
the plunder, Moab!"
24But when the Moabites came to the
camp of Israel, the Israelites rose up and
fought them until they fled. And the Israelites invaded the land and slaughtered the Moabites. 25They destroyed the
towns, and each man threw a stone on
every good field until it was covered.
They stopped up all the springs and cut
down every good tree. Only Kir Hareseth[y]
was left with its stones in place, but men
armed with slings surrounded it and attacked it.
26When the king of Moab saw that the
battle had gone against him, he took with
him seven hundred swordsmen to break
through to the king of Edom, but they

3:9 [n] 1Ki 22:47
3:11 [o] Ge 25:22; 1Ki 22:7 [p] Ge 20:7 [q] 1Ki 19:16
3:12 [r] Nu 11:17
3:15 [s] 1Sa 16:23 [t] Jer 15:17; Eze 1:3
3:17 [u] Ps 107:35; Isa 32:2; 35:6; 41:18
3:18 [v] Ge 18:14; 2Ki 20:10; Isa 49:6; Jer 32:17, 27; Mk 10:27
3:20 [w] Ex 29:39-40 [x] Ex 17:6
3:25 [y] ver 19; Isa 15:1; 16:7; Jer 48:31, 36

[a] *11* That is, he was Elijah's personal servant.

---

the south rather than from the north, which was possible because Edom was under Judahite rule and Edom's "king" was Jehoshaphat's deputy rather than an independent monarch (1Ki 22:47).

3:11 *Elisha ... used to pour water on the hands of Elijah.* This classifies Elisha as an attendant of the famous prophet. Despite the insignificance of the task, Elisha's association with Elijah is enough to provide hope for divine aid.

3:13 *the prophets of your father and the prophets of your mother.* Refers to the prophets of Baal who serve Ahab and Jezebel (see note on 1Ki 18:19). Either Joram consulted Yahweh specifically to begin this campaign or, more likely, the oracle was taken by Jehoshaphat. In either case, it is Yahweh who has led them there, and now Yahweh must be dealt with. The divine direction is now perceived by Joram as intending to destroy them.

3:15 *bring me a harpist.* The implication is that music plays its part in Elisha's attainment of the prophetic "state" in which he utters his prophecy. This connection between music and prophecy is also hinted at in 1Sa 10:5 – 11, and suggests that, on this occasion at least, Elisha was engaged in "ecstatic" prophetic behavior of a kind similar to that evidenced at Mari. Another example of ecstatic prophecy is recorded in an eleventh-century BC Egyptian text. It describes the visit of the traveler Wenamun to the Phoenician city of Byblos and the following event that took place during a temple ritual: "Now while he [the prince of Byblos] was making offering to his gods, the god seized one of his youths and made him possessed. And he [the young man] said to him [the prince]: "Bring up the god! Bring the messenger who is carrying him [i.e., Wenamun]. Amun is the one who sent him out."

3:20 *water flowing from the direction of Edom.* The campaign is probably close to the Wadi Zered, which drains runoff from high elevations and so can suddenly fill with water even if no rain falls in the area. Prophetic knowledge of flooding due to rain elsewhere is also demonstrated by Deborah in Jdg 4:14 – 16 (see note on Jdg 4:7).

3:22 *the water looked red — like blood.* It is easy to see how water in a sandstone region under a red sky would appear like blood, but it is not so easy to see why they didn't notice the lack of corpses. More likely they thought they saw a deserted camp. A Mesopotamian omen dictates that if a river carries blood, internal strife will cause an army to do battle with itself. The Moabites probably see the water as such an omen.

failed. [27]Then he took his firstborn[z] son, who was to succeed him as king, and offered him as a sacrifice on the city wall. The fury against Israel was great; they withdrew and returned to their own land.

The Widow's Olive Oil

4 The wife of a man from the company[a] of the prophets cried out to Elisha, "Your servant my husband is dead, and you know that he revered the LORD. But now his creditor[b] is coming to take my two boys as his slaves."

[2]Elisha replied to her, "How can I help you? Tell me, what do you have in your house?"

"Your servant has nothing there at all," she said, "except a small jar of olive oil."[c]

[3]Elisha said, "Go around and ask all your neighbors for empty jars. Don't ask for just a few. [4]Then go inside and shut the door behind you and your sons. Pour oil into all the jars, and as each is filled, put it to one side."

[5]She left him and shut the door behind her and her sons. They brought the jars to her and she kept pouring. [6]When all the jars were full, she said to her son, "Bring me another one."

But he replied, "There is not a jar left." Then the oil stopped flowing.

[7]She went and told the man of God,[d] and he said, "Go, sell the oil and pay your debts. You and your sons can live on what is left."

The Shunammite's Son Restored to Life

[8]One day Elisha went to Shunem.[e] And a well-to-do woman was there, who urged him to stay for a meal. So whenever he came by, he stopped there to eat. [9]She said to her husband, "I know that this man who often comes our way is a holy man of God. [10]Let's make a small room on the roof and put in it a bed and a table, a chair and a lamp for him. Then he can stay[f] there whenever he comes to us."

[11]One day when Elisha came, he went up to his room and lay down there. [12]He said to his servant Gehazi, "Call the Shunammite."[g] So he called her, and she stood before him. [13]Elisha said to him, "Tell her, 'You have gone to all this trouble for us. Now what can be done for you? Can we speak on your behalf to the king or the commander of the army?' "

She replied, "I have a home among my own people."

[14]"What can be done for her?" Elisha asked.

Gehazi said, "She has no son, and her husband is old."

[15]Then Elisha said, "Call her." So he called her, and she stood in the doorway. [16]"About this time[h] next year," Elisha said, "you will hold a son in your arms."

"No, my lord!" she objected. "Please, man of God, don't mislead your servant!"

[17]But the woman became pregnant, and the next year about that same time she gave birth to a son, just as Elisha had told her.

[18]The child grew, and one day he went out to his father, who was with the reapers.[i] [19]He said to his father, "My head! My head!"

His father told a servant, "Carry him to his mother." [20]After the servant had lifted him up and carried him to his mother, the boy sat on her lap until noon, and then he died. [21]She went up and laid him on the bed[j] of the man of God, then shut the door and went out.

[22]She called her husband and said, "Please send me one of the servants and a donkey so I can go to the man of God quickly and return."

[23]"Why go to him today?" he asked. "It's not the New Moon[k] or the Sabbath."

"That's all right," she said.

[24]She saddled the donkey and said to her servant, "Lead on; don't slow down for me unless I tell you." [25]So she set out and came to the man of God at Mount Carmel.[l]

When he saw her in the distance, the man of God said to his servant Gehazi, "Look! There's the Shunammite! [26]Run to meet her and ask her, 'Are you all right? Is your husband all right? Is your child all right?' "

3:27 [z] Dt 12:31; 2Ki 16:3; 21:6; 2Ch 28:3; Ps 106:38; Jer 19:4-5; Am 2:1; Mic 6:7 **4:1** [a] 1Sa 10:5; 2Ki 2:3 [b] Ex 22:26; Lev 25:39-43; Ne 5:3-5; Job 22:6; 24:9 **4:2** [c] 1Ki 17:12 **4:7** [d] 1Ki 12:22 **4:8** [e] Jos 19:18 **4:10** [f] Mt 10:41; Ro 12:13

4:12 [g] 2Ki 8:1 **4:16** [h] Ge 18:10 **4:18** [i] Ru 2:3 **4:21** [j] ver 32 **4:23** [k] Nu 10:10; 1Ch 23:31; Ps 81:3 **4:25** [l] 1Ki 18:20; 2Ki 2:25

3:27 *he took his firstborn son ... and offered him as a sacrifice.* See notes on 16:3; 1Ki 11:5; Lev 20:2; Jer 7:31. Here the mechanism of sacrifice is not explicitly described. We are only told that the child was the king's firstborn son—the sacrifice of something exceedingly precious in an exceedingly critical situation. Jephthah's vow is similar to this, though his sacrifice of his daughter comes after the fact (Jdg 11:30–40).

4:1 *his creditor is coming to take my two boys as his slaves.* Indebtedness was a problem commonly found throughout the ancient Near East and could lead to the loss of property, home, fields and ultimately the freedom of the debtor or a family member of the debtor, who then became a "debt-slave" to the person looking for payment. See notes on Ex 13:15; 21:4,8.

4:23 *It's not the New Moon or the Sabbath.* The implication is that it was the custom in Israel to consult prophets only on particular rest days and that to do anything else was unusual. Am 8:5 associates New Moons (marking the beginning of each month) with Sabbaths in terms of cessation of work when it attacks avaricious people for their anxiety that "the New Moon be over that we may sell grain, and the Sabbath be ended that we may market wheat" (cf. also 1Sa 20:5–34; Hos 2:11). The practice of celebrating on the first of the month had ancient roots; the New Moon was already one of the principal lunar festivals of Old Babylonian times.

"Everything is all right," she said.
27When she reached the man of God at
the mountain, she took hold of his feet.
Gehazi came over to push her away, but
the man of God said, "Leave her alone!
She is in bitter distress,[m] but the LORD has
hidden it from me and has not told me
why."
28"Did I ask you for a son, my lord?"
she said. "Didn't I tell you, 'Don't raise
my hopes'?"
29Elisha said to Gehazi, "Tuck your
cloak into your belt,[n] take my staff[o] in
your hand and run. Don't greet anyone
you meet, and if anyone greets you, do not
answer. Lay my staff on the boy's face."
30But the child's mother said, "As surely
as the LORD lives and as you live, I will not
leave you." So he got up and followed her.
31Gehazi went on ahead and laid the
staff on the boy's face, but there was no
sound or response. So Gehazi went back
to meet Elisha and told him, "The boy has
not awakened."
32When Elisha reached the house, there
was the boy lying dead on his couch.[p]
33He went in, shut the door on the two of
them and prayed[q] to the LORD. 34Then he
got on the bed and lay on the boy, mouth
to mouth, eyes to eyes, hands to hands. As
he stretched[r] himself out on him, the boy's
body grew warm. 35Elisha turned away
and walked back and forth in the room
and then got on the bed and stretched out
on him once more. The boy sneezed seven
times[s] and opened his eyes.[t]
36Elisha summoned Gehazi and said,
"Call the Shunammite." And he did. When
she came, he said, "Take your son."[u] 37She
came in, fell at his feet and bowed to the
ground. Then she took her son and went
out.

Death in the Pot

38Elisha returned to Gilgal[v] and there
was a famine[w] in that region. While the
company of the prophets was meeting
with him, he said to his servant, "Put on
the large pot and cook some stew for these
prophets."
39One of them went out into the fields
to gather herbs and found a wild vine and
picked as many of its gourds as his garment could hold. When he returned, he
cut them up into the pot of stew, though
no one knew what they were. 40The stew
was poured out for the men, but as they
began to eat it, they cried out, "Man of
God, there is death in the pot!" And they
could not eat it.
41Elisha said, "Get some flour." He put it
into the pot and said, "Serve it to the people to eat." And there was nothing harmful in the pot.[x]

Feeding of a Hundred

42A man came from Baal Shalishah,[y]
bringing the man of God twenty loaves[z]
of barley bread[a] baked from the first ripe
grain, along with some heads of new
grain. "Give it to the people to eat," Elisha said.
43"How can I set this before a hundred
men?" his servant asked.
But Elisha answered, "Give it to the
people to eat.[b] For this is what the LORD
says: 'They will eat and have some left
over.[c]' " 44Then he set it before them, and
they ate and had some left over, according
to the word of the LORD.

Naaman Healed of Leprosy

5 Now Naaman was commander of the
army of the king of Aram.[d] He was a
great man in the sight of his master and
highly regarded, because through him the
LORD had given victory to Aram. He was a
valiant soldier, but he had leprosy.[a][e]
2Now bands of raiders[f] from Aram had
gone out and had taken captive a young

4:27 [m] 1Sa 1:15 **4:29** [n] 1Ki 18:46; 2Ki 2:8, 14; 9:1 [o] Ex 4:2; 7:19; 14:16 **4:32** [p] ver 21 **4:33** [q] 1Ki 17:20; Mt 6:6 **4:34** [r] 1Ki 17:21; Ac 20:10 **4:35** [s] Jos 6:15 [t] 2Ki 8:5 **4:36** [u] Heb 11:35 **4:38** [v] 2Ki 2:1 [w] Lev 26:26; 2Ki 8:1

4:41 [x] Ex 15:25; 2Ki 2:21 **4:42** [y] 1Sa 9:4 [z] Mt 14:17; 15:36 [a] 1Sa 9:7 **4:43** [b] Lk 9:13 [c] Mt 14:20; Jn 6:12 **5:1** [d] Ge 10:22; 2Sa 10:19 [e] Ex 4:6; Nu 12:10; Lk 4:27 **5:2** [f] 2Ki 6:23; 13:20; 24:2

[a] *1* The Hebrew for *leprosy* was used for various diseases affecting the skin; also in verses 3, 6, 7, 11 and 27.

4:29 *staff.* This is a different Hebrew word than that used for Moses' rod; it connotes a crutch or cane. It appears that Elisha and Gehazi thought the staff would be enough to revive the boy. In Akkadian incantation texts, a staff is a component used in the exorcism of disease-causing spirits. Because the boy's head was hurt, the staff is laid on the boy's face.
4:34–35 See note on 1Ki 17:21.
4:40 *death in the pot!* The poisonous ingredient is generally considered to be "apples of Sodom" (colocynths, a yellow gourd), which can be fatal.
4:41 *Get some flour.* Flour is often mentioned as having magical power, though it is not normally used in this manner. Sometimes a doughy paste is made into a figurine, other times it is sprinkled around in a circle. Elisha's procedure has some similarity to magic, but lacks the exact procedure or any of the ritual elements.
5:1 *leprosy.* It is clear from Lev 13–14 that the Hebrew word here in fact refers to a wide range of patchy disfigurements of skin or material (see note on Lev 13:2), which may or may not have included what is now commonly called leprosy (Hansen's disease). "Skin disease" may be a better way to categorize this (see NIV text note). Such an ailment signified to the Hebrew reader ritual uncleanness or defilement (cf. Lev 13–14) and the judgment of God (cf. 2Ki 15:5; Nu 12:1–15; 2Sa 3:28–29). Naaman is one who is in every sense "outside the camp" (Lev 13:46; see note there)—a foreigner, as well as a leper. An interesting analogy is found in an Old Babylonian omen text which says that "if the skin of a man exhibits white *pusu*-areas or is dotted with *nuqdu* dots, such a man has been rejected by his god and is to be rejected by mankind." A Neo-Assyrian text similarly maintains that "if a man has the surface of his flesh covered with black and white spots, the disease is the *mamitu* (curse/tabu)."

girl from Israel, and she served Naaman's
wife. [3]She said to her mistress, "If only
my master would see the prophet[g] who
is in Samaria! He would cure him of his
leprosy."
[4]Naaman went to his master and told
him what the girl from Israel had said.
[5]"By all means, go," the king of Aram replied. "I will send a letter to the king of
Israel." So Naaman left, taking with him
ten talents[a] of silver, six thousand shekels[b]
of gold and ten sets of clothing.[h] [6]The letter that he took to the king of Israel read:
"With this letter I am sending my servant
Naaman to you so that you may cure him
of his leprosy."
[7]As soon as the king of Israel read the
letter,[i] he tore his robes and said, "Am I
God?[j] Can I kill and bring back to life?[k]
Why does this fellow send someone to me
to be cured of his leprosy? See how he is
trying to pick a quarrel[l] with me!"
[8]When Elisha the man of God heard that
the king of Israel had torn his robes, he
sent him this message: "Why have you
torn your robes? Have the man come to
me and he will know that there is a prophet[m] in Israel." [9]So Naaman went with his
horses and chariots and stopped at the
door of Elisha's house. [10]Elisha sent a messenger to say to him, "Go, wash[n] yourself
seven times[o] in the Jordan, and your flesh
will be restored and you will be cleansed."
[11]But Naaman went away angry and
said, "I thought that he would surely
come out to me and stand and call on the
name of the LORD his God, wave his hand[p]
over the spot and cure me of my leprosy.
[12]Are not Abana and Pharpar, the rivers
of Damascus, better than all the waters[q]
of Israel? Couldn't I wash in them and be
cleansed?" So he turned and went off in
a rage.[r]
[13]Naaman's servants went to him and
said, "My father,[s] if the prophet had
told you to do some great thing, would
you not have done it? How much more,
then, when he tells you, 'Wash and be
cleansed'!" [14]So he went down and dipped
himself in the Jordan seven times,[t] as the
man of God had told him, and his flesh
was restored[u] and became clean like that
of a young boy.[v]
[15]Then Naaman and all his attendants
went back to the man of God[w]. He stood
before him and said, "Now I know[x] that
there is no God in all the world except in
Israel. So please accept a gift[y] from your
servant."
[16]The prophet answered, "As surely as
the LORD lives, whom I serve, I will not accept a thing." And even though Naaman
urged him, he refused.[z]
[17]"If you will not," said Naaman,
"please let me, your servant, be given as
much earth[a] as a pair of mules can carry, for your servant will never again make
burnt offerings and sacrifices to any other
god but the LORD. [18]But may the LORD forgive your servant for this one thing: When

5:3 [g]Ge 20:7 **5:5** [h]ver 22; Ge 24:53; Jdg 14:12; 1Sa 9:7 **5:7** [i]2Ki 19:14 [j]Ge 30:2 [k]Dt 32:39; 1Sa 2:6 [l]1Ki 20:7 **5:8** [m]1Ki 22:7 **5:10** [n]Jn 9:7 [o]Ge 33:3; Lev 14:7 **5:11** [p]Ex 7:19 **5:12** [q]Isa 8:6 [r]Pr 14:17, 29; 19:11; 29:11 **5:13** [s]2Ki 6:21; 13:14 **5:14** [t]Ge 33:3; Lev 14:7; Jos 6:15 [u]Ex 4:7 [v]Job 33:25; Lk 4:27 **5:15** [w]Jos 2:11 [x]Jos 4:24; 1Sa 17:46; Da 2:47 [y]1Sa 9:7; 25:27 **5:16** [z]ver 20, 26; Ge 14:23; Da 5:17 **5:17** [a]Ex 20:24

[a] 5 That is, about 750 pounds or about 340 kilograms
[b] 5 That is, about 150 pounds or about 69 kilograms

5:5 *ten talents of silver.* The "talent" was an ancient measure of weight. Its origin probably lies in the load that a man could carry, but it is estimated to have represented around 75 pounds (34 kilograms). It was widely regarded in the ancient Near East as equivalent to 3,000 shekels (see Ex 38:25 – 26 and NIV text notes there). The larger amount of silver in Naaman's gift when compared to the gold reflects the much greater value of the latter metal. *six thousand shekels of gold.* The value of the gift is more clearly understood when it is realized that 6,000 shekels of gold represented the combined annual wages of 600 common laborers. Converted to today's buying power, it equals about 750 million dollars.

5:7 *he tore his robes.* As well as indicating sorrow (cf. Ge 37:34; 2Sa 13:31; Isa 37:1), the tearing of clothes could signify consternation (cf. the actions of King Josiah in 2Ki 22:11 – 13, when faced with the prospect of the covenant curses taking effect as a result of the breach of Torah). The king of Israel's distress here arises from the king of Aram's delegation to him of a task that only divinity can accomplish.

5:10 *wash yourself seven times in the Jordan.* A Mesopotamian ritual involves submerging seven times facing downstream and seven times facing upstream, allowing the river to carry impurities into the underworld. Gifts for the god Ea were also released into the stream. Elisha's procedure is cosmetically similar, yet also distinct from familiar magical rituals.

5:11 *wave his hand over the spot and cure me of my leprosy.* Akkadian inscriptions from this period depict a magical specialist with raised hand offering an invocation and prayer for the removal of disease and evil. A magical ritual would have required the supervision of such a specialist to conduct or oversee the proper rituals. Elisha is careful to remove himself from this role, leading Naaman to think that any source of water would serve the cleansing purpose. He expects the presence of the practitioner to be the key to the success of the ritual.

5:17 *as much earth as a pair of mules can carry.* The transportation of the earth is connected here with the making of burnt offerings and sacrifices to Yahweh, which implies that the earth is to be used in the construction of an altar. The OT does itself mention "earth" or "ground" (Hebrew *adamah*) as one of the materials used in the construction of altars (Ex 20:24 – 25). Most likely we are to envisage a mud brick altar constructed from clods of clay, taken from the Lord's own land.

5:18 *Rimmon.* In the OT, the storm-god Hadad is almost always called by the name "Baal" (which is, strictly speaking, a title; see the article "Baal," p. 600). Zec 12:11, however, mentions a postexilic cult of Hadad Rimmon associated with the central portion of the Jezreel Valley near the city of Megiddo, and this deity is referred to here in shortened form. The epithet's Akkadian form is *ramman*, from the verb *rmm*, "to roar"; the full name Hadad Ramman thus means "Hadad the thunderer." It is under this name of

my master enters the temple of Rimmon to bow down and he is leaning[b] on my arm and I have to bow there also — when I bow down in the temple of Rimmon, may the LORD forgive your servant for this."

19 "Go in peace,"[c] Elisha said.

After Naaman had traveled some distance, 20 Gehazi, the servant of Elisha the man of God, said to himself, "My master was too easy on Naaman, this Aramean, by not accepting from him what he brought. As surely as the LORD[d] lives, I will run after him and get something from him."

21 So Gehazi hurried after Naaman. When Naaman saw him running toward him, he got down from the chariot to meet him. "Is everything all right?" he asked.

22 "Everything is all right," Gehazi answered. "My master sent me to say, 'Two young men from the company of the prophets have just come to me from the hill country of Ephraim. Please give them a talent[a] of silver and two sets of clothing.' "[e]

23 "By all means, take two talents," said Naaman. He urged Gehazi to accept them, and then tied up the two talents of silver in two bags, with two sets of clothing. He gave them to two of his servants, and they carried them ahead of Gehazi. 24 When Gehazi came to the hill, he took the things from the servants and put them away in the house. He sent the men away and they left.

25 When he went in and stood before his master, Elisha asked him, "Where have you been, Gehazi?"

"Your servant didn't go anywhere," Gehazi answered.

26 But Elisha said to him, "Was not my spirit with you when the man got down from his chariot to meet you? Is this the time[f] to take money or to accept clothes — or olive groves and vineyards, or flocks and herds, or male and female slaves?[g] 27 Naaman's leprosy[h] will cling to you and to your descendants forever." Then Gehazi[i] went from Elisha's presence and his skin was leprous — it had become as white as snow.[j]

5:18 [b] 2Ki 7:2 **5:19** [c] 1Sa 1:17; Ac 15:33 **5:20** [d] Ex 20:7 **5:22** [e] ver 5; Ge 45:22 **5:26** [f] ver 16 [g] Jer 45:5 **5:27** [h] Nu 12:10; 2Ki 15:5 [i] Col 3:5 [j] Ex 4:6 **6:1** [k] 1Sa 10:5; 2Ki 4:38 **6:6** [l] Ex 15:25; 2Ki 2:21

An Axhead Floats

6 The company[k] of the prophets said to Elisha, "Look, the place where we meet with you is too small for us. 2 Let us go to the Jordan, where each of us can get a pole; and let us build a place there for us to meet."

And he said, "Go."

3 Then one of them said, "Won't you please come with your servants?"

"I will," Elisha replied. 4 And he went with them.

They went to the Jordan and began to cut down trees. 5 As one of them was cutting down a tree, the iron axhead fell into the water. "Oh no, my lord!" he cried out. "It was borrowed!"

6 The man of God asked, "Where did it fall?" When he showed him the place, Elisha cut a stick and threw[l] it there, and made the iron float. 7 "Lift it out," he said. Then the man reached out his hand and took it.

Elisha Traps Blinded Arameans

8 Now the king of Aram was at war with Israel. After conferring with his officers, he said, "I will set up my camp in such and such a place."

[a] *22* That is, about 75 pounds or about 34 kilograms

Hadad Ramman/Rimmon that Hadad was worshiped in the kingdom of Damascus in the period of the divided monarchy in Israel, with both parts of the name appearing in royal names or titles of the period — e.g., Tabrimmon ("Rimmon is good," 1Ki 15:18) and Barhadad ("son of Hadad").

5:22 *a talent of silver.* Gehazi's request is modest compared to what Naaman was prepared to offer, but it is still the equivalent of 300 years' wages, which Naaman doubles (v. 23).

5:26 *olive groves and vineyards, or flocks and herds, or male and female slaves.* This is describing the life of luxury Gehazi will be able to purchase with this ill-gotten loot.

5:27 *Naaman's leprosy will cling to you.* The punishment inflicted threatens neither his life nor health, but condemns him as a social outcast. *white as snow.* Refers to flakiness, not color; "white" has been added by translators.

6:5 *iron axhead.* Iron technology was becoming more widely available at this time, but implements of iron were still expensive and valuable.

6:6 *cut a stick ... made the iron float.* Ancient magic included a category called transference, where properties or characteristics of one object were passed to another. In this case, the buoyancy of the wood is passed to the axhead. While the text is unclear whether Elisha was actually practicing magic or not, his actions would have appeared that way to an ancient observer.

6:8 *the king of Aram was at war with Israel.* Aram had already become a thorn in Israel's side during the reigns of Baasha, Omri and Ahab (1Ki 15:16 – 22; 20:1 – 43; 22:1 – 36), although the two states sometimes became allies when a greater threat confronted them. The Assyrian Monolith Inscription mentions Ahab fighting alongside the king of Damascus against the Assyrians at Qarqar in southern Syria in 853 BC. It was shortly afterward, however, when the Assyrian threat had waned, that conflict between Israel and Damascus was renewed and Ahab lost his life fighting to recover Ramoth Gilead (1Ki 22:1 – 36). Thereafter, there is no evidence of any Israelite presence at known battles between Shalmaneser and the Syro-Palestinian alliance. This external evidence, combined with the internal evidence of the Biblical text, suggests a general breakdown of relations between Israel and Damascus in the aftermath of Ahab's death, which sometimes exhibited itself in the form of an uneasy truce between them (cf. 5:1 – 8, noting especially the Israelite king's reaction in 5:7)

2 KINGS 6:1–7

PRACTICE OF MAGIC

Magic is typically forbidden to Israel for a number of reasons: (1) Magic is human encroachment into the divine realm. (2) Magic is used to manipulate deity. (3) Magic involves relying on a power other than Yahweh. If that is the reason, a sanctioned prophet would be able to bypass all three; his office already enters the divine realm, and the power comes from Yahweh, even though the prophet appears to have some autonomy in using it. The prophets are called to wield divine authority at some level. ◆

[9]The man of God sent word to the king[m]
of Israel: "Beware of passing that place,
because the Arameans are going down
there." [10]So the king of Israel checked on
the place indicated by the man of God.
Time and again Elisha warned[n] the king,
so that he was on his guard in such places.
[11]This enraged the king of Aram. He
summoned his officers and demanded of
them, "Tell me! Which of us is on the side
of the king of Israel?"
[12]"None of us, my lord the king[o]," said
one of his officers, "but Elisha, the prophet
who is in Israel, tells the king of Israel the
very words you speak in your bedroom."
[13]"Go, find out where he is," the king
ordered, "so I can send men and capture
him." The report came back: "He is in Dothan."[p] [14]Then he sent[q] horses and chariots and a strong force there. They went by
night and surrounded the city.
[15]When the servant of the man of God
got up and went out early the next morning, an army with horses and chariots had
surrounded the city. "Oh no, my lord!
What shall we do?" the servant asked.
[16]"Don't be afraid,"[r] the prophet answered. "Those who are with us are more[s]
than those who are with them."
[17]And Elisha prayed, "Open his eyes,
LORD, so that he may see." Then the LORD
opened the servant's eyes, and he looked
and saw the hills full of horses and chariots[t] of fire all around Elisha.
[18]As the enemy came down toward him,
Elisha prayed to the LORD, "Strike this

6:9 [m] ver 12 **6:10** [n] Jer 11:18 **6:12** [o] ver 9

6:13 [p] Ge 37:17 **6:14** [q] 2Ki 1:9 **6:16** [r] Ge 15:1 [s] 2Ch 32:7; Ps 55:18; Ro 8:31; 1Jn 4:4 **6:17** [t] 2Ki 2:11, 12; Ps 68:17; Zec 6:1-7

---

and sometimes in the outbreak of full hostilities, as here in 6:8—7:20. It may have been during this war that Ramoth Gilead was recovered by Israel, since we are later told that Joram was wounded at a defensive battle at this city (8:28; 9:14–15). Our knowledge of interactions between Israel and Damascus in this period or in any other is, however, limited in view of the number and nature of the sources available to us, and specifically by the limited number of native Aramean records.

6:9 *Beware of passing that place.* Prophetic messages were often sought and/or offered in the ancient Near East in relation to military campaigns. In the case of Zimri-Lim of Mari, the information we have does not portray the king actively consulting prophets or personally encountering them, but only receiving their words through intermediaries. Prophetic messages were subjected to testing by other, more common means of divine communication (e.g., divination procedures such as extispicy). For divination regarding military tactics, see note on 1Sa 14:18–19. For differences between prophecy and divination, see the article "Balaam," p. 268.

At least during the reigns of the Assyrian kings Esarhaddon and Ashurbanipal, prophecy was highly esteemed and considered on a par with astrology and extispicy in terms of sources of information from deity. These kings received prophecies, as did Zimri-Lim, during their military campaigns, and prophets were included among the Assyrian forces as they marched. The Assyrian royal inscriptions mention kings receiving oracles during battles; and one Neo-Assyrian source lists "Quqi the prophet" in a lodging list alongside three high-ranking military officers: Nergal-mukin-ahi, chariot owner; Nabu-sarru-usur, cohort commander; and Wazaru, bodyguard of the queen mother.

6:17 *hills full of horses and chariots of fire all around Elisha.* The text does not speak of the mountains surrounding Dothan, but of the mount where Elisha stands. It refers then not to an army in the hills, but to Elisha's heavenly bodyguard. They are not there to attack the Aramean army, but to protect Elisha from harm. This differs from the examples in the ancient Near East, in which the king is protected by the deity himself in that it is Yahweh's army acting on his behalf.

6:18 *blindness.* It is often assumed that this refers to a total loss of physical sight. Yet the Arameans would not doubt their location just because they could no longer physically see it; and the "seeing" of the closely preceding vv. 15–17, which lies in contrastive parallel with this "not seeing," is certainly not physical. It seems much more likely that the text refers to a dazed mental condition, in

army with blindness."[u] So he struck them
with blindness, as Elisha had asked.
19 Elisha told them, "This is not the road
and this is not the city. Follow me, and I
will lead you to the man you are looking
for." And he led them to Samaria.
20 After they entered the city, Elisha said,
"LORD, open the eyes of these men so they
can see." Then the LORD opened their eyes
and they looked, and there they were, inside Samaria.
21 When the king of Israel saw them, he
asked Elisha, "Shall I kill them, my father?[v] Shall I kill them?"
22 "Do not kill them," he answered.
"Would you kill those you have captured[w]
with your own sword or bow? Set food and
water before them so that they may eat and
drink and then go back to their master."
23 So he prepared a great feast for them, and
after they had finished eating and drinking, he sent them away, and they returned
to their master. So the bands[x] from Aram
stopped raiding Israel's territory.

Famine in Besieged Samaria

24 Some time later, Ben-Hadad[y] king
of Aram mobilized his entire army and
marched up and laid siege[z] to Samaria.
25 There was a great famine[a] in the city;
the siege lasted so long that a donkey's
head sold for eighty shekels[a] of silver, and
a quarter of a cab[b] of seed pods[c][b] for five
shekels.[d]
26 As the king of Israel was passing by on
the wall, a woman cried to him, "Help me,
my lord the king!"
27 The king replied, "If the LORD does not
help you, where can I get help for you?
From the threshing floor? From the winepress?" 28 Then he asked her, "What's the
matter?"
She answered, "This woman said to me,
'Give up your son so we may eat him today, and tomorrow we'll eat my son.' 29 So
we cooked my son and ate[c] him. The next
day I said to her, 'Give up your son so we
may eat him,' but she had hidden him."
30 When the king heard the woman's
words, he tore[d] his robes. As he went
along the wall, the people looked, and
they saw that, under his robes, he had
sackcloth[e] on his body. 31 He said, "May
God deal with me, be it ever so severely, if
the head of Elisha son of Shaphat remains
on his shoulders today!"
32 Now Elisha was sitting in his house,
and the elders[f] were sitting with him.
The king sent a messenger ahead, but
before he arrived, Elisha said to the elders, "Don't you see how this murderer[g]
is sending someone to cut off my head?[h]
Look, when the messenger comes, shut
the door and hold it shut against him. Is
not the sound of his master's footsteps behind him?" 33 While he was still talking to
them, the messenger came down to him.
The king said, "This disaster is from the
LORD. Why should I wait[i] for the LORD any
longer?"
7 Elisha replied, "Hear the word of the
LORD. This is what the LORD says:
About this time tomorrow, a seah[e] of the

6:18 [u] Ge 19:11; Ac 13:11
6:21 [v] 2Ki 5:13
6:22 [w] Dt 20:11; 2Ch 28:8-15; Ro 12:20
6:23 [x] 2Ki 5:2
6:24 [y] 1Ki 15:18; 20:1; 2Ki 8:7 [z] Dt 28:52
6:25 [a] Lev 26:26; Ru 1:1 [b] Isa 36:12
6:29 [c] Lev 26:29; Dt 28:53-55
6:30 [d] 2Ki 18:37; Isa 22:15 [e] Ge 37:34; 1Ki 21:27
6:32 [f] Eze 8:1; 14:1; 20:1 [g] 1Ki 18:4 [h] ver 31
6:33 [i] Lev 24:11; Job 2:9; 14:14; Isa 40:31

[a] *25* That is, about 2 pounds or about 920 grams
[b] *25* That is, probably about 1/4 pound or about 100 grams [c] *25* Or *of doves' dung* [d] *25* That is, about 2 ounces or about 58 grams [e] *1* That is, probably about 12 pounds or about 5.5 kilograms of flour; also in verses 16 and 18

which the Arameans are open to suggestion and manipulation, but are still able to follow the prophet to Samaria. They believe Elisha when he tells them that they are in the wrong place (v. 19), and they do not realize that he has tricked them until the daze has passed (v. 20). An analogy to the idea of a god "blinding" enemy troops is found in the Tukulti-Ninurta Epic, where Shamash, the sun-god, "blinded the eyesight of the army of Sumer and Akkad."

6:25 *a donkey's head sold for eighty shekels of silver.* It is not likely that the inhabitants of any city would have moved quickly to slaughter and eat animals valuable to them in respect of their livelihoods. The Assyrian reliefs depicting Sennacherib's conquest of Judahite Lachish in 701 BC underline this by showing animals (some of them looking more emaciated than the captured people) emerging from the city after the siege. That they are thus emaciated, but at least alive, indicates that their owners chose to eat their animals' food before eating their animals. The people of Samaria, by contrast, were reduced not only to slaughtering and eating animals valuable to them, but also to consuming body parts that would not normally be consumed—and purchasing them for exorbitant prices. The cost of a live horse in 1Ki 10:29 is only 150 shekels of silver. *seed pods.* Lit. "dove's dung," which is sometimes interpreted as the popular name for something other than it at first appears (e.g., NIV's "seed pods" and NEB's "locust beans"). Yet we know that ancient city sieges often led to extremes among the besieged populations, including the eating of dung, and the people of Samaria were certainly in dire straits. A "quarter of a cab" is equivalent to about a quarter pound (100 grams). During the siege, then, a quarter pound of dove's dung cost five shekels (what the average worker could make in six months).

6:28 *Give up your son so we may eat him today.* Describing his two-year siege of Babylon that ended in 648 BC, the Assyrian king Ashurbanipal says that "famine seized them; for in their hunger they ate the flesh of their sons and daughters." Later he tells of a siege of King Uate of Arabia and his army in the mountain stronghold of Hukkuruna, where "famine broke out among them and they ate the flesh of their children against their hunger." The Bible itself knows of other instances of this gruesome reality of cannibalism arising from long siege (e.g., La 2:20; 4:10; Eze 5:10).

6:31 *May God deal with me, be it ever so severely, if the head of Elisha son of Shaphat remains on his shoulders today!* Even though the prophets spoke on behalf of the deity, the people often held them responsible for the results as if they had the power to stop judgment or to enact deliverance. The office of prophet was therefore a dangerous one that could exact a high personal price.

finest flour will sell for a shekel[a] and two seahs[b] of barley for a shekel[j] at the gate of Samaria."

2The officer on whose arm the king was leaning[k] said to the man of God, "Look, even if the LORD should open the floodgates[l] of the heavens, could this happen?"

"You will see it with your own eyes," answered Elisha, "but you will not eat[m] any of it!"

The Siege Lifted

3Now there were four men with leprosy[c][n] at the entrance of the city gate. They said to each other, "Why stay here until we die? 4If we say, 'We'll go into the city'—the famine is there, and we will die. And if we stay here, we will die. So let's go over to the camp of the Arameans and surrender. If they spare us, we live; if they kill us, then we die."

5At dusk they got up and went to the camp of the Arameans. When they reached the edge of the camp, no one was there, 6for the Lord had caused the Arameans to hear the sound[o] of chariots and horses and a great army, so that they said to one another, "Look, the king of Israel has hired[p] the Hittite[q] and Egyptian kings to attack us!" 7So they got up and fled[r] in the dusk and abandoned their tents and their horses and donkeys. They left the camp as it was and ran for their lives.

8The men who had leprosy[s] reached the edge of the camp, entered one of the tents and ate and drank. Then they took silver, gold and clothes, and went off and hid them. They returned and entered another tent and took some things from it and hid them also.

9Then they said to each other, "What we're doing is not right. This is a day of good news and we are keeping it to ourselves. If we wait until daylight, punishment will overtake us. Let's go at once and report this to the royal palace."

10So they went and called out to the city gatekeepers and told them, "We went into the Aramean camp and no one was there—not a sound of anyone—only tethered horses and donkeys, and the tents left just as they were." 11The gatekeepers shouted the news, and it was reported within the palace.

12The king got up in the night and said to his officers, "I will tell you what the Arameans have done to us. They know we are starving; so they have left the camp to hide[t] in the countryside, thinking, 'They will surely come out, and then we will take them alive and get into the city.'"

13One of his officers answered, "Have some men take five of the horses that are left in the city. Their plight will be like that of all the Israelites left here—yes, they will only be like all these Israelites who are doomed. So let us send them to find out what happened."

14So they selected two chariots with their horses, and the king sent them after the Aramean army. He commanded the drivers, "Go and find out what has happened." 15They followed them as far as the Jordan, and they found the whole road strewn with the clothing and equipment the Arameans had thrown away in their headlong flight. So the messengers returned and reported to the king. 16Then the people went out and plundered[u] the camp of the Arameans. So a seah of the finest flour sold for a shekel, and two seahs of barley sold for a shekel,[v] as the LORD had said.

17Now the king had put the officer on whose arm he leaned in charge of the gate, and the people trampled him in the gateway, and he died,[w] just as the man of God had foretold when the king came down to his house. 18It happened as the man of God had said to the king: "About this time tomorrow, a seah of the finest flour will sell for a shekel and two seahs of barley for a shekel at the gate of Samaria."

19The officer had said to the man of God, "Look, even if the LORD should open the floodgates[x] of the heavens, could this happen?" The man of God had replied, "You

7:1 [j] ver 16
7:2 [k] 2Ki 5:18 [l] ver 19; Ge 7:11; Ps 78:23; Mal 3:10 [m] ver 17
7:3 [n] Lev 13:45-46; Nu 5:1-4
7:6 [o] Ex 14:24; 2Sa 5:24; Eze 1:24 [p] 2Sa 10:6; Jer 46:21 [q] Nu 13:29
7:7 [r] Jdg 7:21; Ps 48:4-6; Pr 28:1; Isa 30:17
7:8 [s] Isa 33:23; 35:6
7:12 [t] Jos 8:4; 2Ki 6:25-29
7:16 [u] Isa 33:4, 23 [v] ver 1
7:17 [w] ver 2; 2Ki 6:32
7:19 [x] ver 2

[a] *1* That is, about 2/5 ounce or about 12 grams; also in verses 16 and 18 [b] *1* That is, probably about 20 pounds or about 9 kilograms of barley; also in verses 16 and 18 [c] *3* The Hebrew for *leprosy* was used for various diseases affecting the skin; also in verse 8.

7:2 *officer.* Refers to the member of the chariot crew whose job it was to hold the shield and protect archer and driver. Eventually the term evolved to designate the king's armor bearer (see note on 1Sa 14:1) or administrative assistant. *floodgates of the heavens.* See note on Ge 7:11. This expression is usually used of sending rain, but the officer is using it more broadly to describe God's provision, since the shortage here is food, not water.
7:6 *hired the Hittite and Egyptian kings.* The Aramean army was deceived into thinking that a mercenary army, drawn from Egypt to the south and the Hittites to the north, had been summoned to Samaria to lift the siege. The "hiring" of armies was not unusual in the ancient Near East, as the Kulamuwa Inscription (c. 830–832 BC) from Sam'al illustrates: "My father's house was in the midst of mighty kings. Everybody stretched forth his hand to eat it. But I was in the hands of the kings like a fire that eats the beard, like a fire that eats the hand. The king of the Danunians tried to overpower me; but I hired against him the king of Assyria."
7:15 The Samarians suspect the common tactic of setting an ambush after pretending to give up and go home. A well-known application of this ruse was used by the Greeks against Troy. The Moabites were tricked the same way by Israel in ch. 3.

will see it with your own eyes, but you
will not eat any of it!" 20And that is exactly what happened to him, for the people
trampled him in the gateway, and he died.

The Shunammite's Land Restored

8 Now Elisha had said to the woman[y]
whose son he had restored to life, "Go
away with your family and stay for a while
wherever you can, because the LORD has
decreed a famine[z] in the land that will last
seven years."[a] 2The woman proceeded to
do as the man of God said. She and her
family went away and stayed in the land
of the Philistines seven years.

3At the end of the seven years she came
back from the land of the Philistines and
went to appeal to the king for her house
and land. 4The king was talking to Gehazi, the servant of the man of God, and had
said, "Tell me about all the great things
Elisha has done." 5Just as Gehazi was telling the king how Elisha had restored[b] the
dead to life, the woman whose son Elisha
had brought back to life came to appeal to
the king for her house and land.

Gehazi said, "This is the woman, my
lord the king, and this is her son whom
Elisha restored to life." 6The king asked
the woman about it, and she told him.

Then he assigned an official to her case
and said to him, "Give back everything
that belonged to her, including all the income from her land from the day she left
the country until now."

Hazael Murders Ben-Hadad

7Elisha went to Damascus,[c] and Ben-Hadad[d] king of Aram was ill. When the king
was told, "The man of God has come all the
way up here," 8he said to Hazael,[e] "Take a
gift[f] with you and go to meet the man of
God. Consult[g] the LORD through him; ask
him, 'Will I recover from this illness?' "

9Hazael went to meet Elisha, taking
with him as a gift forty camel-loads of all
the finest wares of Damascus. He went in
and stood before him, and said, "Your son
Ben-Hadad king of Aram has sent me to
ask, 'Will I recover from this illness?' "

10Elisha answered, "Go and say to him,
'You will certainly recover.'[h] Nevertheless,[a] the LORD has revealed to me that he
will in fact die." 11He stared at him with a
fixed gaze until Hazael was embarrassed.[i]
Then the man of God began to weep.[j]

12"Why is my lord weeping?" asked
Hazael.

"Because I know the harm[k] you will do
to the Israelites," he answered. "You will
set fire to their fortified places, kill their
young men with the sword, dash[l] their little children[m] to the ground, and rip open[n]
their pregnant women."

13Hazael said, "How could your servant,
a mere dog,[o] accomplish such a feat?"

"The LORD has shown me that you will
become king[p] of Aram," answered Elisha.

14Then Hazael left Elisha and returned
to his master. When Ben-Hadad asked,
"What did Elisha say to you?" Hazael replied, "He told me that you would certainly recover." 15But the next day he took a
thick cloth, soaked it in water and spread
it over the king's face, so that he died.[q]
Then Hazael succeeded him as king.

8:1 [y] 2Ki 4:8-37 [z] Lev 26:26; Dt 28:22; Ru 1:1 [a] Ge 12:10; Ps 105:16; Hag 1:11 **8:5** [b] 2Ki 4:35 **8:7** [c] 2Sa 8:5; 1Ki 11:24 [d] 2Ki 6:24 **8:8** [e] 1Ki 19:15 [f] Ge 32:20; 1Sa 9:7; 2Ki 1:2 [g] Jdg 18:5 **8:10** [h] Isa 38:1 **8:11** [i] Jdg 3:25 [j] Lk 19:41 **8:12** [k] 1Ki 19:17; 2Ki 10:32; 12:17; 13:3, 7 [l] Ps 137:9; Isa 13:16; Hos 13:16; Na 3:10; Lk 19:44 [m] Ge 34:29 [n] 2Ki 15:16; Am 1:13 **8:13** [o] 1Sa 17:43; 2Sa 3:8 [p] 1Ki 19:15 **8:15** [q] 2Ki 1:17

[a] 10 The Hebrew may also be read *Go and say, 'You will certainly not recover,' for.*

8:3 *she ... went to appeal to the king for her house and land.* In the woman's absence, her house and land had been taken by others—possibly by the king himself, displaying the same land-grabbing tendencies as his parents (cf. 1Ki 21). The king was now the recipient of her appeal, as the person with primary responsibility under God for the establishment and maintenance of order and justice throughout the kingdom.

8:6 *Give back ... all the income from her land.* Normally, a person would not receive income from land reclaimed after a period of absence. The income would instead go to the caretakers and workers who had kept it up during that period.

8:7–15 Hazael's seizure of the throne of Aram from Ben-Hadad II, known to the Assyrians as Adad-idri, is recorded not only in these verses but also in a fragmentary Assyrian text on a basalt statue of Shalmaneser III, which refers to Hazael as the "son of nobody," perhaps reflecting his lowly, nonroyal origins. This dismissive notation is interestingly matched by Hazael's own self-deprecating speech in v. 13, where he refers to himself as "a mere dog"—a conventional humility matched in one of the Lachish ostraca of the later seventh century BC, in which a subordinate addresses a superior thus: "I am nothing but a dog; why should you think of me?"

Hazael came to power at some point between Shalmaneser's campaign in the west in his 14th year (845 BC), when we know that Adad-idri was still on the throne, and the campaign of Shalmaneser's 18th year (841 BC), which records Hazael now as king. He reigned for around 40 years as one of Israel's most bitter enemies.

8:8 *Take a gift with you and go to meet the man of God.* Ben-Hadad II consulted Israel's God about his future in much the same way that King Ahaziah of Israel earlier consulted Baal-Zebub of Ekron in ch. 1. It appears to have been customary when consulting prophets for this and other purposes to offer some payment—in this case an extravagant gift of 40 camel-loads of wares (v. 9). The gift is meant to buy the favor of the deity in exchange for a favorable oracle, which would in turn carry the deity's power with it.

8:12 *set fire to their fortified places, kill their young men ... dash their little children to the ground, and rip open their pregnant women.* These tactics are all standard procedure for a conqueror hoping to prevent future rebellion. Destruction of the cities prevents their use as defensive or staging points, and the execution of men, women and unborn children decimates any current or future army. Tiglath-Pileser I is said to have ripped open pregnant women, and Assyrian conquest accounts mention the burning of young boys and girls.

Jehoram King of Judah

8:16-24pp — 2Ch 21:5-10,20

16 In the fifth year of Joram[r] son of Ahab
king of Israel, when Jehoshaphat was king
of Judah, Jehoram[s] son of Jehoshaphat began his reign as king of Judah. 17 He was
thirty-two years old when he became king,
and he reigned in Jerusalem eight years.
18 He followed the ways of the kings of Israel, as the house of Ahab had done, for
he married a daughter[t] of Ahab. He did
evil in the eyes of the LORD. 19 Nevertheless, for the sake of his servant David, the
LORD was not willing to destroy[u] Judah.
He had promised to maintain a lamp[v] for
David and his descendants forever.

20 In the time of Jehoram, Edom rebelled
against Judah and set up its own king.[w]
21 So Jehoram[a] went to Zair with all his
chariots. The Edomites surrounded him
and his chariot commanders, but he rose
up and broke through by night; his army,
however, fled back home. 22 To this day
Edom has been in rebellion[x] against Judah. Libnah[y] revolted at the same time.

23 As for the other events of Jehoram's
reign, and all he did, are they not written
in the book of the annals of the kings of
Judah? 24 Jehoram rested with his ancestors and was buried with them in the City
of David. And Ahaziah his son succeeded
him as king.

Ahaziah King of Judah

8:25-29pp — 2Ch 22:1-6

25 In the twelfth[z] year of Joram son of
Ahab king of Israel, Ahaziah son of Jehoram king of Judah began to reign. 26 Ahaziah was twenty-two years old when he
became king, and he reigned in Jerusalem
one year. His mother's name was Athaliah,[a] a granddaughter of Omri[b] king of Israel. 27 He followed the ways of the house of
Ahab[c] and did evil[d] in the eyes of the LORD,
as the house of Ahab had done, for he was
related by marriage to Ahab's family.

28 Ahaziah went with Joram son of Ahab
to war against Hazael king of Aram at Ramoth Gilead.[e] The Arameans wounded Joram; 29 so King Joram returned to Jezreel[f]
to recover from the wounds the Arameans
had inflicted on him at Ramoth[b] in his battle with Hazael[g] king of Aram.

Then Ahaziah son of Jehoram king of Judah went down to Jezreel to see Joram son
of Ahab, because he had been wounded.

Jehu Anointed King of Israel

9 The prophet Elisha summoned a man
from the company[h] of the prophets
and said to him, "Tuck your cloak into
your belt,[i] take this flask of olive oil[j] with
you and go to Ramoth Gilead.[k] 2 When you
get there, look for Jehu son of Jehoshaphat, the son of Nimshi. Go to him, get
him away from his companions and take
him into an inner room. 3 Then take the
flask and pour the oil[l] on his head and declare, 'This is what the LORD says: I anoint
you king over Israel.' Then open the door
and run; don't delay!"

4 So the young prophet went to Ramoth
Gilead. 5 When he arrived, he found the
army officers sitting together. "I have a
message for you, commander," he said.

"For which of us?" asked Jehu.

"For you, commander," he replied.

8:16 [r] 2Ki 1:17; 3:1 [s] 2Ch 21:1-4 **8:18** [t] ver 26; 2Ki 11:1 **8:19** [u] Ge 6:13 [v] 2Sa 21:17; 7:13; 1Ki 11:36; Rev 21:23 **8:20** [w] 1Ki 22:47 **8:22** [x] Ge 27:40 [y] Nu 33:20; Jos 21:13; 2Ki 19:8 **8:25** [z] 2Ki 9:29 **8:26** [a] ver 18 [b] 1Ki 16:23 **8:27** [c] 1Ki 16:30 [d] 1Ki 15:26 **8:28** [e] Dt 4:43; 1Ki 22:3,29 **8:29** [f] 2Ki 9:15 [g] 1Ki 19:15,17 **9:1** [h] 1Sa 10:5 [i] 2Ki 4:29 [j] 1Sa 10:1 [k] 2Ki 8:28 **9:3** [l] 1Ki 19:16

[a] *21* Hebrew *Joram,* a variant of *Jehoram;* also in verses 23 and 24 [b] *29* Hebrew *Ramah,* a variant of *Ramoth*

8:16 *Jehoram son of Jehoshaphat.* Jehoshaphat is the king of Judah credited in 1,2 Kings with making peace with the king of Israel in the aftermath of the struggles that arose out of the division of the kingdoms under Jeroboam and Rehoboam (1Ki 22:44), and from his reign forward the fortunes of the Omrides and Davidides were closely interconnected. The two royal houses fought together (vv. 28 – 29; ch. 3) and were linked by intermarriage, in that Jehoshaphat's son Jehoram married Ahab's daughter Athaliah (vv. 18,26). Over time they came to share a similar religious policy, such that both King Jehoram and his successor, Ahaziah, are portrayed in Kings as idolaters under the influence of the house of Ahab (vv. 18,27).

8:19 *a lamp for David.* See notes on 2Sa 14:7; 21:17; 23:4.

8:22 *Libnah.* Likely a Judahite city to the southwest of Jerusalem (Jos 15:1,42), near the Philistine border, although its identification is disputed. This verse makes clear that even Jehoram's rule in Judah itself was not entirely secure. 2Ch 21:2 – 4 adds to our knowledge of Jehoram's reign by telling us that he had previously executed all his brothers, as well as certain others who (we can assume) were perceived as offering some threat to his position, and 2Ch 21:16 – 17 informs us of attacks from the very Philistines and Arabs who had given tribute to Jehoram's father. The picture is clearly that of a weak king.

8:26 *Omri king of Israel.* Omri was the first king of the northern kingdom of Israel to successfully establish a dynasty following the period of relative instability that ensued after the division of Israel into two kingdoms (1Ki 12 – 16). Of Omri himself we know very little, whether from Biblical or other sources, apart from the manner of his accession to the throne, his purchase of the hill of Samaria, the building of the new northern capital there (1Ki 16:23 – 28) and his domination of Moab. Yet the northern kingdom became so identified with this Omride dynasty in the eyes of the outside world that even after the Omride period it was referred to in Assyrian records as "the land of Omri." This suggests that Omri was perhaps a more substantial international figure than can be deduced simply from 1 Kings. See note on 1Ki 16:23; see also the article "Omri and Jehu in History," p. 632.

9:2 *Jehu son of Jehoshaphat, the son of Nimshi.* Although King Joram of Israel himself had retired wounded to Jezreel (8:28 – 29), his army was still at Ramoth Gilead; Jehu, elsewhere simply called "Jehu son of Nimshi" (e.g., v. 20; 1Ki 19:16), was one of its commanders, now destined to be Israel's next king. He appears as such in Assyrian records.

1 KINGS 16:21 – 28; 2 KINGS 9:1 — 10:36

OMRI AND JEHU IN HISTORY

There are numerous references to the "land of Omri" (Bit-Humria = Israel) in Assyrian texts. Examples include an inscription from the palace of Sargon II (722 – 705 BC) in ancient Dur Sharrukin ("fortress of Sargon," modern Khorsabad) that summarizes the king's campaigns, and one found on a pavement slab for the gates at Dur Sharrukin:

The Mesha Inscription, or Moabite Stone, was discovered in 1868 near the ruins of ancient Dibon in Transjordan, which lay a short distance north of the Arnon River. Its content as well as its style indicates that it is a mid-ninth century BC text, whose purpose is to describe the blessing of Moab's chief deity, Chemosh, in his deliverance of Moab from the control of its neighbor Israel. It is of interest to readers of the

Jehu King of Israel giving tribute to King Shalmaneser III of Assyria, on the Black Obelisk of Shalmaneser III from Nimrud, c. 827 BC.

continued on next page

6 Jehu got up and went into the house.
Then the prophet poured the oil[m] on Jehu's
head and declared, "This is what the LORD,
the God of Israel, says: 'I anoint you king
over the LORD's people Israel. 7 You are to
destroy the house of Ahab your master, and
I will avenge[n] the blood of my servants[o] the
prophets and the blood of all the LORD's servants
shed by Jezebel.[p] 8 The whole house[q]
of Ahab will perish. I will cut off from Ahab
every last male[r] in Israel — slave or free.[a]
9 I will make the house of Ahab like the
house of Jeroboam[s] son of Nebat and like
the house of Baasha[t] son of Ahijah. 10 As for
Jezebel, dogs[u] will devour her on the plot
of ground at Jezreel, and no one will bury
her.' " Then he opened the door and ran.
11 When Jehu went out to his fellow officers,
one of them asked him, "Is every-

9:6 [m] 1Ki 19:16; 2Ch 22:7
9:7 [n] Ge 4:24; Rev 6:10 [o] Dt 32:43 [p] 1Ki 18:4; 21:15
9:8 [q] 2Ki 10:17 [r] Dt 32:36; 1Sa 25:22; 1Ki 21:21; 2Ki 14:26
9:9 [s] 1Ki 14:10; 15:29; 16:3, 11 [t] 1Ki 16:3
9:10 [u] ver 35-36; 1Ki 21:23

[a] 8 Or *Israel — every ruler or leader*

9:10 *no one will bury her.* It was considered a terrible thing in Israel not to be afforded a proper burial (see Dt 28:25 – 26; Jer 16:4, which capture the horror well). A similar view of burial is reflected in a curse that concludes the inscription on a ninth-century BC boundary stone found at Sippar in Mesopotamia. The curse inflicts the violator with having no children, a hard life and no proper burial.

Certainly in Mesopotamia the importance of the

Bible chiefly because it appears to refer, from a Moabite point of view, to the revolt of King Mesha against Israel that is mentioned in 2Ki 1:1; 3:4 – 5. It refers to Omri by name and recounts some of the interactions between Israel and Moab.

As for Jehu, we are told and shown in pictorial form that Shalmaneser collected tribute from "Jehu the Israelite" as well as from Tyre and Sidon. The detail of the campaign is given in various of Shalmaneser's inscriptions, including one engraved on a statue of the king found at Calah and dating from 839 to 838 BC (the Kurba'il Statue, dedicated to the god Adad of the city of Kurba'il).

The Black Obelisk of Shalmaneser III is a four-sided biographical monument of black limestone discovered at ancient Calah (modern Nimrud) and dating from 828 to 827 BC. It stands some seven feet (two meters) tall and is inscribed with both text and relief sculptures depicting battles and other events from Shalmaneser's reign. Among the reliefs is one that shows Jehu kneeling before the Assyrian emperor in the course of his western campaign of 841 BC — the only contemporary portrait in existence of an Israelite king. The relief is accompanied by the following caption: "The tribute of Jehu, son of Omri: I received from him silver, gold, a golden bowl, a golden vase with pointed bottom, golden tumblers, golden buckets, tin, a staff for a king, and javelins." ◆

The basalt Mesha Inscription (c. 840 BC) references the "land of Omri." It also bears the earliest certain extra-Biblical reference to the Israelite God Yahweh.

thing all right? Why did this maniac[v] come to you?"

"You know the man and the sort of things he says," Jehu replied.

12"That's not true!" they said. "Tell us."

Jehu said, "Here is what he told me: 'This is what the LORD says: I anoint you king over Israel.' "

13They quickly took their cloaks and spread[w] them under him on the bare steps. Then they blew the trumpet[x] and shouted, "Jehu is king!"

9:11 [v] Jer 29:26; Jn 10:20; Ac 26:24
9:13 [w] Mt 21:8; Lk 19:36 [x] 2Sa 15:10; 1Ki 1:34,39

Jehu Kills Joram and Ahaziah

9:21-29pp — 2Ch 22:7-9

14So Jehu son of Jehoshaphat, the son of Nimshi, conspired against Joram. (Now Joram and all Israel had been defending

burial of the body was connected with a belief that, without burial, the *etemmu* (ghost) of the deceased would not find its natural place among the community of the dead and would therefore have no rest. In addition, the lack of a burial prevented the ongoing care of the dead at the burial site in the form of mortuary rites — it dissolved community between the living and the dead. One way to ensure that a dead individual did indeed lose his or her individual and social identity was, as this verse implies, to feed the body to animals (see note on 1Ki 14:11). In such a case, some Mesopotamian texts suggest, the dead person was consigned to

Ramoth Gilead[y] against Hazael king of Aram, 15but King Joram[a] had returned to Jezreel to recover[z] from the wounds the Arameans had inflicted on him in the battle with Hazael king of Aram.) Jehu said, "If you desire to make me king, don't let anyone slip out of the city to go and tell the news in Jezreel." 16Then he got into his chariot and rode to Jezreel, because Joram was resting there and Ahaziah[a] king of Judah had gone down to see him.

17When the lookout[b] standing on the tower in Jezreel saw Jehu's troops approaching, he called out, "I see some troops coming."

"Get a horseman," Joram ordered. "Send him to meet them and ask, 'Do you come in peace?[c]'"

18The horseman rode off to meet Jehu and said, "This is what the king says: 'Do you come in peace?'"

"What do you have to do with peace?" Jehu replied. "Fall in behind me."

The lookout reported, "The messenger has reached them, but he isn't coming back."

19So the king sent out a second horseman. When he came to them he said, "This is what the king says: 'Do you come in peace?'"

Jehu replied, "What do you have to do with peace? Fall in behind me."

20The lookout reported, "He has reached them, but he isn't coming back either. The driving is like[d] that of Jehu son of Nimshi—he drives like a maniac."

21"Hitch up my chariot," Joram ordered. And when it was hitched up, Joram king of Israel and Ahaziah king of Judah rode out, each in his own chariot, to meet Jehu. They met him at the plot of ground that had belonged to Naboth[e] the Jezreelite. 22When Joram saw Jehu he asked, "Have you come in peace, Jehu?"

"How can there be peace," Jehu replied, "as long as all the idolatry and witchcraft of your mother Jezebel[f] abound?"

23Joram turned about and fled, calling out to Ahaziah, "Treachery,[g] Ahaziah!"

24Then Jehu drew his bow[h] and shot Joram between the shoulders. The arrow pierced his heart and he slumped down in his chariot. 25Jehu said to Bidkar, his chariot officer, "Pick him up and throw him on the field that belonged to Naboth the Jezreelite. Remember how you and I were riding together in chariots behind Ahab his father when the LORD spoke this prophecy[i] against him: 26'Yesterday I saw the blood of Naboth[j] and the blood of his sons, declares the LORD, and I will surely make you pay for it on this plot of ground, declares the LORD.'[b] Now then, pick him up and throw him on that plot, in accordance with the word of the LORD."[k]

27When Ahaziah king of Judah saw what had happened, he fled up the road to Beth Haggan.[c] Jehu chased him, shouting, "Kill him too!" They wounded him in his chariot on the way up to Gur near Ibleam,[l] but he escaped to Megiddo[m] and died there. 28His servants took him by chariot[n] to Jerusalem and buried him with his ancestors in his tomb in the City of David. 29(In the eleventh[o] year of Joram son of Ahab, Ahaziah had become king of Judah.)

Jezebel Killed

30Then Jehu went to Jezreel. When Jezebel heard about it, she put on eye makeup,[p] arranged her hair and looked out of a window. 31As Jehu entered the gate, she asked, "Have you come in peace, you Zimri,[q] you murderer of your master?"[d]

32He looked up at the window and called out, "Who is on my side? Who?"

[a] *15* Hebrew *Jehoram,* a variant of *Joram;* also in verses 17 and 21-24 [b] *26* See 1 Kings 21:19. [c] *27* Or *fled by way of the garden house* [d] *31* Or *"Was there peace for Zimri, who murdered his master?"*

9:14 [y] Dt 4:43; 2Ki 8:28
9:15 [z] 2Ki 8:29
9:16 [a] 2Ch 22:7
9:17 [b] Isa 21:6 [c] 1Sa 16:4
9:20 [d] 2Sa 18:27
9:21 [e] ver 26; 1Ki 21:1-7, 15-19
9:22 [f] 1Ki 16:30-33; 18:19; 2Ch 21:13; Rev 2:20
9:23 [g] 2Ki 11:14
9:24 [h] 1Ki 22:34
9:25 [i] 1Ki 21:19-22, 24-29
9:26 [j] 1Ki 21:19 [k] 1Ki 21:29
9:27 [l] Jdg 1:27 [m] 2Ki 23:29
9:28 [n] 2Ki 14:20; 23:30
9:29 [o] 2Ki 8:25
9:30 [p] Jer 4:30; Eze 23:40
9:31 [q] 1Ki 16:9-10

---

a formless and chaotic reality and perhaps even to the world of demons.

9:22 A similar accusation is made by Hittite king Mursili II to depose his late father's Babylonian wife on the grounds that she practiced sorcery.

9:30 *she put on eye makeup, arranged her hair and looked out of a window.* The significance of these actions is not entirely clear. It could mean nothing more than that Jezebel meets her end proudly, dressed up as a queen should be. It is intriguing nonetheless that her posture echoes the "woman in the window" motif found on carved ivory plaques from various ancient Near Eastern sites, which may represent the goddess Astarte, one of the consorts of Baal. In this case, Jezebel is represented as the very incarnation of the religion she brought into Israel from Sidon. Alternatively, Jezebel's reference to Zimri (v. 31) may be a not-so-subtle warning about the failure of Israel's last military coup. By making herself alluring, she may be encouraging him to take over the harem and thus establish his legitimacy through her.

9:32 *eunuchs.* It was common practice in the ancient world for the king to have a harem (cf. 1Ki 11:3) and for the harem to be provided with guards. These guards were typically eunuchs (castrated men), so that the king could be sure that the males who were in close proximity to his women were not capable of sexual relationships with them.

Eunuchs also performed an important role in the official hierarchy of the ancient Near East more generally. In Neo-Assyrian sources, e.g., they are attested at the royal court, in the army, in the bureaucracy, and in the provincial administration. They functioned, among many roles, as the king's personal attendants, cooks, palace guards, scribes and envoys to foreign rulers. They belonged to an official guild or corps, headed by the *rab ša reši,* who was one of the king's closest advisors. It was a great honor to belong to this corps, and it was also a path to material advancement.

2 KINGS 8:25 – 29; 9:14 – 29

THE TELL DAN STELE

The joint campaign conducted by Joram of Israel and Ahaziah of Judah against Aram provides the background against which our Biblical sources describe the death of both kings. It is probably to these same events that the fragmentary ninth-century BC Tell Dan inscription also alludes. Tell Dan was located in the northern region of Israel at the foot of Mount Hermon, and the discoveries were made in 1993 and 1994. The inscription appears to commemorate a victory by an Aramean king over kings of Israel and Judah and to claim responsibility for their deaths, naming them as Ahaziah of Judah and Jehoram of Israel.

If this is so, the Aramean king is presumably Hazael, and he is likely engaging in the oversimplification and hyperbole that is typical of victory steles; for although the deaths of Ahaziah of Judah and Jehoram of Israel certainly followed their conflict with Hazael, the Biblical testimony suggests that the events surrounding them were more complex than the stele implies. Perhaps Hazael regarded Jehu as a vassal and felt justified in claiming Jehu's feats as his own. We may further deduce that the stele was set up in Dan during a period of Damascus/Aramean control of the city and was later reused as building material by Israelite builders (the main fragment of the stele formed part of a pavement when it was found). ◆

House of David Inscription from Tell Dan, 870 – 750 BC.

Kim Walton. The Israel Museum, Jerusalem.

Two or three eunuchs looked down at
him. 33"Throw her down!" Jehu said. So
they threw her down, and some of her
blood spattered the wall and the horses as
they trampled her underfoot.[r]
34Jehu went in and ate and drank.
"Take care of that cursed woman," he
said, "and bury her, for she was a king's
daughter."[s] 35But when they went out to
bury her, they found nothing except her
skull, her feet and her hands. 36They went
back and told Jehu, who said, "This is the

9:33 [r] Ps 7:5
9:34 [s] 1Ki 16:31; 21:25

Perhaps in order that their loyalty should be assured, Assyrian eunuchs received significant grants of arable land and laborers from the king and various tax exemptions. Although this has been a matter of dispute among Assyriologists, it now seems more than likely that the beardless figures found in various Neo-Assyrian reliefs are intended as representations of eunuchs — a contention supported by the numerous seals of Neo-Assyrian officials (the majority of all the Neo-Assyrian seals) that likewise depict beardless worshipers.

9:36 *dogs will devour Jezebel's flesh.* Jezebel's gruesome end is paralleled in the Egyptian *Tale of Two Brothers,* in

word of the LORD that he spoke through
his servant Elijah the Tishbite: On the plot
of ground at Jezreel dogs[t] will devour Jezebel's flesh.[a][u] 37Jezebel's body will be like
dung[v] on the ground in the plot at Jezreel,
so that no one will be able to say, 'This
is Jezebel.' "

Ahab's Family Killed

10 Now there were in Samaria[w] seventy sons[x] of the house of Ahab.
So Jehu wrote letters and sent them to
Samaria: to the officials of Jezreel,[b][y] to
the elders and to the guardians[z] of Ahab's
children. He said, 2"You have your master's sons with you and you have chariots and horses, a fortified city and weapons. Now as soon as this letter reaches
you, 3choose the best and most worthy
of your master's sons and set him on his
father's throne. Then fight for your master's house."

4But they were terrified and said, "If two
kings could not resist him, how can we?"

5So the palace administrator, the city
governor, the elders and the guardians
sent this message to Jehu: "We are your
servants[a] and we will do anything you say.
We will not appoint anyone as king; you
do whatever you think best."

6Then Jehu wrote them a second letter,
saying, "If you are on my side and will
obey me, take the heads of your master's
sons and come to me in Jezreel by this
time tomorrow."

Now the royal princes, seventy of them,
were with the leading men of the city,
who were rearing them. 7When the letter
arrived, these men took the princes and
slaughtered all seventy[b] of them. They put
their heads[c] in baskets and sent them to
Jehu in Jezreel. 8When the messenger arrived, he told Jehu, "They have brought
the heads of the princes."

Then Jehu ordered, "Put them in two
piles at the entrance of the city gate until
morning."

9The next morning Jehu went out.
He stood before all the people and said,
"You are innocent. It was I who conspired
against my master and killed him, but
who killed all these? 10Know, then, that
not a word the LORD has spoken against
the house of Ahab will fail. The LORD has
done what he announced[d] through his
servant Elijah."[e] 11So Jehu[f] killed everyone in Jezreel who remained of the house
of Ahab, as well as all his chief men, his
close friends and his priests, leaving him
no survivor.[g]

12Jehu then set out and went toward Samaria. At Beth Eked of the Shepherds, 13he
met some relatives of Ahaziah king of Judah and asked, "Who are you?"

They said, "We are relatives of Ahaziah,[h] and we have come down to greet
the families of the king and of the queen
mother.[i]"

9:36 [t] Ps 68:23; Jer 15:3 [u] 1Ki 21:23 **9:37** [v] Ps 83:10; Isa 5:25; Jer 8:2; 9:22; 16:4; 25:33; Zep 1:17 **10:1** [w] 1Ki 13:32 [x] Jdg 8:30 [y] 1Ki 21:1 [z] ver 5 **10:5** [a] Jos 9:8; 1Ki 20:4,32 **10:7** [b] 1Ki 21:21 [c] 2Sa 4:8 **10:10** [d] 2Ki 9:7-10 [e] 1Ki 21:29 **10:11** [f] Hos 1:4 [g] ver 14; Job 18:19 **10:13** [h] 2Ki 8:24, 29; 2Ch 22:8 [i] 1Ki 2:19

[a] *36* See 1 Kings 21:23. [b] *1* Hebrew; some Septuagint manuscripts and Vulgate *of the city*

which the elder brother kills his own wife for her treachery, casts her to the dogs, and then sits mourning for his young brother, who had fled because of his older brother's false accusation. For the significance of animals eating the flesh, see note on 9:10.

10:5 *palace administrator.* The Hebrew is "who was over the house"—an important position at the royal court, which is also mentioned in 15:5; 18:18,37; 19:2. The power of the palace administrator, at least in Judah, is indicated in Isa 22:22; next to the king, he had complete power over Judah, somewhat akin to the power of vizier in Egypt. Both the title and sometimes the names of its holders are found in extra-Biblical inscriptions.

One of these is the inscription over a tomb from the monarchic period found on the slopes of the village of Siloam to the east of Jerusalem, which reads: "This is [the tomb of x]yahu, palace administrator. There is neither silver nor gold here, only [his bones] and the bones of his maidservant with him. Cursed be the man who would open this [tomb]!"

10:7 *took the princes and slaughtered all seventy of them.* This kind of drastic action against a royal household was not uncommon in the ancient world, as present incumbents of thrones tried to ensure their own future. The Aramaic Panammuwa Inscription, found at Zinjirli on a statue erected by Panammuwa of Sam'al's son Bar-Rakib around 733–727 BC, records that Panammuwa himself was the survivor of a palace coup in which a brother killed his father Barsur, along with 70 brothers of his father. This text, along with Jdg 9:5, where Abimelech kills 70 of his brothers prior to being crowned king, may suggest that the number 70 in such contexts is a matter of literary convention rather than strict accounting.

10:8 *two piles at the entrance of the city gate.* The piling of the severed heads of victims at the city gate evokes both the Baal Cycle myth from Ugarit (see note on 9:30), in which Anat in victory kicks her enemies' heads around like soccer balls, and also the literal case of the Assyrian king Ashurnasirpal II, who records in an inscription decorating the walls and floor of the Ninurta temple in Calah a campaign that included the siege of the city of Dammusa. Ashurnasirpal claims that he cut off the heads of 600 enemy troops and "took the live soldiers and the heads to the city of Amedu, his royal city, and built a pile of heads before his gate. I hung the live soldiers on stakes around about his city." Visual evidence for the practice of collecting the heads of the enemy slain is available from the much later time of Sennacherib in the form of a wall relief portraying plunder taken from a town in southern Babylonia.

10:11 *close friends.* This designation does not refer to personal acquaintances, but rather to those who enjoyed the patronage of the court. They are royal wards, and probably not Israelites. Ahab's family, administration and priesthood are also killed.

10:12 *relatives of Ahaziah.* Ahaziah is Joram's nephew, so his relatives are at least distantly related to Ahab, which is enough to warrant their deaths.

14“Take them alive!” he ordered. So they took them alive and slaughtered them by the well of Beth Eked — forty-two of them. He left no survivor.

15After he left there, he came upon Jehonadab[j] son of Rekab,[k] who was on his way to meet him. Jehu greeted him and said, “Are you in accord with me, as I am with you?”

“I am,” Jehonadab answered.

“If so,” said Jehu, “give me your hand.”[l] So he did, and Jehu helped him up into the chariot. 16Jehu said, “Come with me and see my zeal[m] for the LORD.” Then he had him ride along in his chariot.

17When Jehu came to Samaria, he killed all who were left there of Ahab’s family;[n] he destroyed them, according to the word of the LORD spoken to Elijah.

Servants of Baal Killed

18Then Jehu brought all the people together and said to them, “Ahab served[o] Baal a little; Jehu will serve him much. 19Now summon[p] all the prophets of Baal, all his servants and all his priests. See that no one is missing, because I am going to hold a great sacrifice for Baal. Anyone who fails to come will no longer live.” But Jehu was acting deceptively in order to destroy the servants of Baal.

20Jehu said, “Call an assembly[q] in honor of Baal.” So they proclaimed it. 21Then he sent word throughout Israel, and all the servants of Baal came; not one stayed away. They crowded into the temple of Baal until it was full from one end to the other. 22And Jehu said to the keeper of the wardrobe, “Bring robes for all the servants of Baal.” So he brought out robes for them.

23Then Jehu and Jehonadab son of Rekab went into the temple of Baal. Jehu said to the servants of Baal, “Look around and see that no one who serves the LORD is here with you — only servants of Baal.” 24So they went in to make sacrifices and burnt offerings. Now Jehu had posted eighty men outside with this warning: “If one of you lets any of the men I am placing in your hands escape, it will be your life for his life.”[r]

25As soon as Jehu had finished making the burnt offering, he ordered the guards and officers: “Go in and kill[s] them; let no one escape.”[t] So they cut them down with the sword. The guards and officers threw the bodies out and then entered the inner shrine of the temple of Baal. 26They brought the sacred stone[u] out of the temple of Baal and burned it. 27They demolished the sacred stone of Baal and tore down the temple[v] of Baal, and people have used it for a latrine to this day.

28So Jehu[w] destroyed Baal worship in Israel. 29However, he did not turn away from the sins[x] of Jeroboam son of Nebat, which he had caused Israel to commit — the worship of the golden calves[y] at Bethel[z] and Dan.

30The LORD said to Jehu, “Because you have done well in accomplishing what is right in my eyes and have done to the house of Ahab all I had in mind to do, your descendants will sit on the throne of Israel to the fourth generation.”[a] 31Yet Jehu was not careful[b] to keep the law of the LORD, the God of Israel, with all his heart. He did not turn away from the sins[c] of Jeroboam, which he had caused Israel to commit.

32In those days the LORD began to reduce[d] the size of Israel. Hazael[e] overpowered the Israelites throughout their territory 33east of the Jordan in all the land of Gilead (the region of Gad, Reuben and Manasseh), from Aroer[f] by the Arnon Gorge through Gilead to Bashan.

34As for the other events of Jehu’s reign, all he did, and all his achievements, are they not written in the book of the annals[g] of the kings of Israel?

10:15 [j] Jer 35:6, 14-19 [k] 1Ch 2:55; Jer 35:2 [l] Ezr 10:19; Eze 17:18 **10:16** [m] Nu 25:13; 1Ki 19:10 **10:17** [n] 2Ki 9:8 **10:18** [o] Jdg 2:11; 1Ki 16:31-32 **10:19** [p] 1Ki 18:19; 22:6 **10:20** [q] Ex 32:5; Joel 1:14

10:24 [r] 1Ki 20:39 **10:25** [s] Ex 22:20; 2Ki 11:18 [t] 1Ki 18:40 **10:26** [u] 1Ki 14:23 **10:27** [v] 1Ki 16:32 **10:28** [w] 1Ki 19:17 **10:29** [x] 1Ki 12:30 [y] 1Ki 12:28-29 [z] 1Ki 12:32 **10:30** [a] ver 35; 2Ki 15:12 **10:31** [b] Pr 4:23 [c] 1Ki 12:30 **10:32** [d] 2Ki 13:25 [e] 1Ki 19:17; 2Ki 8:12 **10:33** [f] Nu 32:34; Dt 2:36; Jdg 11:26; Isa 17:2 **10:34** [g] 1Ki 15:31

10:19 *great sacrifice.* It was common rhetoric for a new king to proclaim himself a more pious devotee of the national cult. This would usually include promises to repair or expand the sanctuary and was intended to gain the support of the priesthood and the populace, and also hopefully bring the favor of the deity on his reign. The celebration is probably an enthronement ceremony, in which Jehu will be crowned a vassal in the service of Baal. Absence from such an event could easily be considered treason.

10:20 *Call an assembly in honor of.* The Hebrew word translated “assembly” is comparatively rare; the entire phrase is unparalleled in Hebrew. However, a Ugaritic text about gaining protection for the royal ancestors of King Ammurapi of Ugarit suggests that the phrase represents genuine Canaanite religious terminology, referring to the convening of a solemn meeting.

10:22 *robes.* These are cultic robes used in the worship of Baal. It is possible that the use of these robes is partly to prevent weapons from being worn, making the job easier.

10:27 *latrine.* Temples were usually built on the site of earlier temples, because the ground had already been considered holy. By turning the site into a latrine (or possibly garbage dump), Jehu ensures that it will never be used as a temple again, making the revival of the cult in Samaria difficult.

10:29 *golden calves at Bethel and Dan.* Jeroboam installed these images of a young bull made from gold in the northernmost and southernmost ends of his new kingdom after leading Israel in revolt against the house of David (1Ki 12:25 – 30). The religion that ensued is not regarded by the authors of Kings as explicitly Baal worship (note the contrast between this verse and v. 28; cf. 1Ki 16:31 – 33), although it is regarded as idolatrous.

35 Jehu rested with his ancestors and
was buried in Samaria. And Jehoahaz his
son succeeded him as king. 36 The time
that Jehu reigned over Israel in Samaria
was twenty-eight years.

Athaliah and Joash

11:1-21pp — 2Ch 22:10 – 23:21

11 When Athaliah[h] the mother of Ahaziah saw that her son was dead,
she proceeded to destroy the whole royal
family. 2 But Jehosheba, the daughter of
King Jehoram[a] and sister of Ahaziah, took
Joash[i] son of Ahaziah and stole him away
from among the royal princes, who were
about to be murdered. She put him and
his nurse in a bedroom to hide him from
Athaliah; so he was not killed.[j] 3 He remained hidden with his nurse at the temple of the LORD for six years while Athaliah ruled the land.

4 In the seventh year Jehoiada sent for
the commanders of units of a hundred,
the Carites[k] and the guards and had them
brought to him at the temple of the LORD.
He made a covenant with them and put
them under oath at the temple of the
LORD. Then he showed them the king's
son. 5 He commanded them, saying, "This
is what you are to do: You who are in the
three companies that are going on duty
on the Sabbath[l] — a third of you guarding the royal palace,[m] 6 a third at the Sur
Gate, and a third at the gate behind the
guard, who take turns guarding the temple — 7 and you who are in the other two
companies that normally go off Sabbath
duty are all to guard the temple for the
king. 8 Station yourselves around the king,
each of you with weapon in hand. Anyone who approaches your ranks[b] is to be
put to death. Stay close to the king wherever he goes."

9 The commanders of units of a hundred
did just as Jehoiada the priest ordered.
Each one took his men — those who were
going on duty on the Sabbath and those
who were going off duty — and came to
Jehoiada the priest. 10 Then he gave the
commanders the spears and shields[n] that
had belonged to King David and that were
in the temple of the LORD. 11 The guards,
each with weapon in hand, stationed
themselves around the king — near the altar and the temple, from the south side to
the north side of the temple.

12 Jehoiada brought out the king's son
and put the crown on him; he presented
him with a copy of the covenant[o] and proclaimed him king. They anointed[p] him,
and the people clapped their hands[q] and
shouted, "Long live the king!"[r]

13 When Athaliah heard the noise made
by the guards and the people, she went to
the people at the temple of the LORD. 14 She
looked and there was the king, standing
by the pillar,[s] as the custom was. The officers and the trumpeters were beside the
king, and all the people of the land were
rejoicing and blowing trumpets.[t] Then
Athaliah tore[u] her robes and called out,
"Treason! Treason!"[v]

15 Jehoiada the priest ordered the commanders of units of a hundred, who were
in charge of the troops: "Bring her out
between the ranks[c] and put to the sword
anyone who follows her." For the priest
had said, "She must not be put to death
in the temple[w] of the LORD." 16 So they
seized her as she reached the place where
the horses enter[x] the palace grounds, and
there she was put to death.[y]

17 Jehoiada then made a covenant[z] between the LORD and the king and people
that they would be the LORD's people.
He also made a covenant between the
king and the people.[a] 18 All the people of
the land went to the temple[b] of Baal and
tore it down. They smashed[c] the altars
and idols to pieces and killed Mattan the
priest[d] of Baal in front of the altars.

Then Jehoiada the priest posted guards
at the temple of the LORD. 19 He took with
him the commanders of hundreds, the
Carites,[e] the guards and all the people of
the land, and together they brought the
king down from the temple of the LORD
and went into the palace, entering by way
of the gate of the guards. The king then
took his place on the royal throne. 20 All
the people of the land rejoiced,[f] and the
city was calm, because Athaliah had been
slain with the sword at the palace.

21 Joash[d] was seven years old when he
began to reign.[e]

11:1 [h] 2Ki 8:18 **11:2** [i] ver 21; 2Ki 12:1 [j] Jdg 9:5 **11:4** [k] ver 19 **11:5** [l] 1Ch 9:25 [m] 1Ki 14:27 **11:10** [n] 2Sa 8:7; 1Ch 18:7 **11:12** [o] Ex 25:16; 2Ki 23:3 [p] 1Sa 9:16; 1Ki 1:39 [q] Ps 47:1; 98:8; Isa 55:12 [r] 1Sa 10:24 **11:14** [s] 1Ki 7:15; 2Ki 23:3; 2Ch 34:31 [t] 1Ki 1:39 [u] Ge 37:29 [v] 2Ki 9:23 **11:15** [w] 1Ki 2:30 **11:16** [x] Ne 3:28; Jer 31:40 [y] Ge 4:14 **11:17** [z] Ex 24:8; 2Sa 5:3; 2Ch 15:12; 23:3; 29:10; 34:31; Ezr 10:3 [a] 2Ki 23:3; Jer 34:8 **11:18** [b] 1Ki 16:32 [c] Dt 12:3 [d] 1Ki 18:40; 2Ki 10:25; 23:20 **11:19** [e] ver 4 **11:20** [f] Pr 11:10; 28:12; 29:2

[a] 2 Hebrew *Joram,* a variant of *Jehoram* [b] 8 Or *approaches the precincts* [c] 15 Or *out from the precincts* [d] 21 Hebrew *Jehoash,* a variant of *Joash* [e] 21 In Hebrew texts this verse (11:21) is numbered 12:1.

11:4 *Carites.* They also appear in the consonantal Hebrew text of 2Sa 20:23 as part of the elite royal bodyguard alongside the Pelethites. They may well be essentially the same body as the Kerethites, with whom the Pelethites normally appear in the OT (2Sa 8:18; 15:18; 20:7,23; 1Ki 1:38,44). The Pelethites were perhaps Philistines, and the Kerethites Cretans — mercenaries who served as David's bodyguard in the period after his service to Achish king of Gath (1Sa 27; 29); the Carites were the later royal bodyguard of Davidic kings.

11:14 *the pillar.* This probably refers to one of the two pillars (Jakin and Boaz) that were found at the temple entrance (see 1Ki 7:15 – 22,41 – 42), flanking the temple forecourt, just as the monumental gateways of major ancient Near Eastern cities marked the entrance to their own sacred enclosures.

Joash Repairs the Temple

12:1-21pp — 2Ch 24:1-14; 24:23-27

12[a] In the seventh year of Jehu, Joash[b][g] became king, and he reigned in Jerusalem forty years. His mother's name was Zibiah; she was from Beersheba. 2 Joash did what was right in the eyes of the LORD all the years Jehoiada the priest instructed him. 3 The high places,[h] however, were not removed; the people continued to offer sacrifices and burn incense there.

4 Joash said to the priests, "Collect[i] all the money that is brought as sacred offerings[j] to the temple of the LORD — the money collected in the census,[k] the money received from personal vows and the money brought voluntarily[l] to the temple. 5 Let every priest receive the money from one of the treasurers, then use it to repair whatever damage is found in the temple."

6 But by the twenty-third year of King Joash the priests still had not repaired the temple. 7 Therefore King Joash summoned Jehoiada the priest and the other priests and asked them, "Why aren't you repairing the damage done to the temple? Take no more money from your treasurers, but hand it over for repairing the temple." 8 The priests agreed that they would not collect any more money from the people and that they would not repair the temple themselves.

9 Jehoiada the priest took a chest and bored a hole in its lid. He placed it beside the altar, on the right side as one enters the temple of the LORD. The priests who guarded the entrance[m] put into the chest all the money[n] that was brought to the temple of the LORD. 10 Whenever they saw that there was a large amount of money in the chest, the royal secretary[o] and the high priest came, counted the money that had been brought into the temple of the LORD and put it into bags. 11 When the amount had been determined, they gave the money to the men appointed to supervise the work on the temple. With it they paid those who worked on the temple of the LORD — the carpenters and builders, 12 the masons and stonecutters.[p] They purchased timber and blocks of dressed stone for the repair of the temple of the LORD, and met all the other expenses of restoring the temple.

13 The money brought into the temple was not spent for making silver basins, wick trimmers, sprinkling bowls, trumpets or any other articles of gold[q] or silver for the temple of the LORD; 14 it was paid to the

12:1 [g] 2Ki 11:2 **12:3** [h] 1Ki 3:3; 2Ki 14:4; 15:35; 18:4 **12:4** [i] 2Ki 22:4 [j] Ex 35:5 [k] Ex 30:12 [l] Ex 35:29; 1Ch 29:3-9

12:9 [m] Jer 35:4 [n] 2Ch 24:8; Mk 12:41; Lk 21:1 **12:10** [o] 2Sa 8:17 **12:12** [p] 2Ki 22:5-6 **12:13** [q] 1Ki 7:48-51; 2Ch 24:14

[a] In Hebrew texts 12:1-21 is numbered 12:2-22.
[b] 1 Hebrew *Jehoash,* a variant of *Joash;* also in verses 2, 4, 6, 7 and 18

12:3 *high places.* See notes on 1Ki 3:2; 11:7.
12:4 *money that is brought as sacred offerings.* The text appears to differentiate two sorts of income that represent regular temple income — payments made in relation to the periodic census of male Israelites (Ex 30:11 – 16), and payments connected with personal vows (monetary equivalents for things dedicated to God, Lev 27:1 – 25). A third sort of income derives from a special fund-raising campaign similar to that initiated by Moses, at God's command (Ex 35).
12:5 *treasurers.* The Hebrew word (*makkar*) occurs in the OT only here and in v. 7, and it is of uncertain meaning. Older translations (e.g., KJV) derived it from the root *nkr,* "regard, recognize," and translated it as "acquaintances." The NIV's "treasurers" connects the word with Ugaritic *mkr,* a functionary referred to on lists of temple personnel whose precise occupation is unfortunately uncertain. In addition, Akkadian has the cognate *makkuru,* which means "valuables, treasures, property, assets, estate" and can be used specifically to refer to temple or palace property or estates; we also know of the *tamkaru* — Assyrian traders and credit merchants. Perhaps the *makkarim* were merchants associated with the sacrificial cult of the temple who also invested temple money. The temple was, after all, not only a political and religious center in Israel but also an economic center — a secure stronghold in which were stored the national assets and revenues of the state (e.g., tribute from vassals, plunder from conquered peoples, and profits from the sacrificial system). *repair ... the temple.* The Jerusalem temple, like other temple buildings in the ancient Near East, was not merely a worship site. It was the dwelling place on earth for the deity (in this case, the God of Israel) and as such the preeminently important symbol of the presence of a god with the king and the nation. Similarly to the palace of a god, it had to be a fine dwelling place, built and furnished with the finest and most expensive of materials and cared for with the greatest of care. To neglect a temple in the ancient world was to neglect its deity and to risk his or her disapproval and the possible undermining of a king's legitimate authority to rule. This is why a king like Esarhaddon of Assyria had servants such as his minister Mar-Ištar traveling around his realm and sending him reports about the state of temples and their cults and the political and religious issues arising from them. Conversely, a deity's approval of the ruling king was often communicated in the ancient Near East through the construction of a temple or, if a major shift in political power was taking place, through the renewal or renovation of an existing temple. This construction or renovation of a temple, it was believed, would bring peace and prosperity to all the inhabitants of the kingdom. It is against this background that Joash's actions are to be understood, as the Davidic dynasty sought to reestablish itself in the aftermath of Athaliah's coup.
12:7 *treasurers.* See note on v. 5.
12:9 – 16 The measures described in this and the following verses and designed to ensure shared responsibility between the crown and the priesthood for the distribution of funds in respect of the temple restoration are interestingly paralleled in a letter from the crown official Mar-Ištar to King Esarhaddon of Assyria concerning necessary repair work to the temples of Uruk and Der. This may suggest that Jehoiada did not himself invent the procedures described in these verses, but simply adapted practices already used in the temples of neighboring lands.

workers, who used it to repair the temple.
15They did not require an accounting from
those to whom they gave the money to
pay the workers, because they acted with
complete honesty.[r] 16The money from the
guilt offerings[s] and sin offerings[a][t] was not
brought into the temple of the LORD; it belonged[u] to the priests.
17About this time Hazael[v] king of Aram
went up and attacked Gath and captured
it. Then he turned to attack Jerusalem.
18But Joash king of Judah took all the sacred objects dedicated by his predecessors—Jehoshaphat, Jehoram and Ahaziah, the kings of Judah—and the gifts he
himself had dedicated and all the gold
found in the treasuries of the temple of
the LORD and of the royal palace, and he
sent[w] them to Hazael king of Aram, who
then withdrew[x] from Jerusalem.
19As for the other events of the reign of
Joash, and all he did, are they not written
in the book of the annals of the kings of
Judah? 20His officials[y] conspired against
him and assassinated[z] him at Beth Millo,[a]
on the road down to Silla. 21The officials
who murdered him were Jozabad son of
Shimeath and Jehozabad son of Shomer.
He died and was buried with his ancestors
in the City of David. And Amaziah his son
succeeded him as king.

Jehoahaz King of Israel

13 In the twenty-third year of Joash
son of Ahaziah king of Judah, Jehoahaz son of Jehu became king of Israel in Samaria, and he reigned seventeen
years. 2He did evil[b] in the eyes of the LORD
by following the sins of Jeroboam son of
Nebat, which he had caused Israel to commit, and he did not turn away from them.
3So the LORD's anger[c] burned against Israel, and for a long time he kept them under
the power[d] of Hazael king of Aram and
Ben-Hadad[e] his son.
4Then Jehoahaz sought[f] the LORD's favor, and the LORD listened to him, for he
saw[g] how severely the king of Aram was
oppressing[h] Israel. 5The LORD provided a
deliverer[i] for Israel, and they escaped from
the power of Aram. So the Israelites lived
in their own homes as they had before.
6But they did not turn away from the sins[j]
of the house of Jeroboam, which he had
caused Israel to commit; they continued in
them. Also, the Asherah pole[b][k] remained
standing in Samaria.
7Nothing had been left[l] of the army of
Jehoahaz except fifty horsemen, ten chariots and ten thousand foot soldiers, for
the king of Aram had destroyed the rest
and made them like the dust[m] at threshing time.
8As for the other events of the reign of
Jehoahaz, all he did and his achievements,
are they not written in the book of the annals of the kings of Israel? 9Jehoahaz rested with his ancestors and was buried in
Samaria. And Jehoash[c] his son succeeded
him as king.

Jehoash King of Israel

10In the thirty-seventh year of Joash
king of Judah, Jehoash son of Jehoahaz
became king of Israel in Samaria, and he
reigned sixteen years. 11He did evil in the
eyes of the LORD and did not turn away
from any of the sins of Jeroboam son of

12:15 [r] 2Ki 22:7; 1Co 4:2 **12:16** [s] Lev 5:14-19; Nu 18:9 [t] Lev 4:1-35 [u] Lev 7:7 **12:17** [v] 2Ki 8:12 **12:18** [w] 1Ki 15:18; 2Ch 21:16-17 [x] 1Ki 15:21 **12:20** [y] 2Ki 14:5 [z] 2Ch 24:25 [a] Jdg 9:6 **13:2** [b] 1Ki 12:26-33

13:3 [c] Dt 31:17; Jdg 2:14 [d] 1Ki 8:12; 12:17; 19:17 [e] ver 24 **13:4** [f] Dt 4:29; Ps 78:34 [g] Ex 3:7; Dt 26:7 [h] 2Ki 14:26 **13:5** [i] ver 25; 2Ki 14:25,27 **13:6** [j] 1Ki 12:30 [k] 1Ki 16:33 **13:7** [l] 2Ki 10:32-33 [m] 2Sa 22:43

[a] 16 Or *purification offerings* [b] 6 That is, a wooden symbol of the goddess Asherah; here and elsewhere in 2 Kings [c] 9 Hebrew *Joash*, a variant of *Jehoash*; also in verses 12-14 and 25

12:17 *Hazael ... attacked Gath ... Jerusalem.* Hazael king of Aram already controlled the entire Israelite Transjordan (10:32–33). Now he brings the Arameans right into the heart of Israelite territory to the west of the Jordan and threatens Jerusalem. The capture of the Philistine city of Gath in fact presupposes that Hazael could move at will through Israelite territory to the north. The campaign is best explained in terms of an attempt by Damascus to gain control over the western part of the incense trade that in later times came from south Arabia via the Wadi Arabah to southern Philistia. It is best dated during the reign of Jehu's son Jehoahaz (c. 815–799), who, according to 13:1–7,22–23, fared even worse than his father at the hands of Aram and thus provided no bulwark of defense (conscious or unconscious) for Judah.

12:19 *the book of the annals of the kings of Judah.* These were in all likelihood analogous to the royal annals of Assyria—personal memorials of individual Judahite kings that provide accounts of royal achievements, especially military campaigns. See note on 1Ki 14:19.

13:5 *The LORD provided a deliverer for Israel.* The identity of this "savior" who rescues Israel from their extremity in the face of Damascene assaults is not made explicit in the text. However, it seems likely that we are hearing a veiled reference to the resurgence of Assyrian interest in Syria and Palestine that results in a measure of relief for Israel as Assyria begins to occupy the attention of Damascus again in the north. The first explicit evidence of this interest can be found in the Saba'a Stele of Adadnirari III, which speaks of a campaign in the west in 806 BC during which the Assyrians besiege Damascus and exact tribute.

This appears to have been one of several campaigns west of the Euphrates during the first half of Adadnirari's reign, although several of these military expeditions were probably organized by provincial governors rather than by the king himself. The paucity of the records for Adadnirari's reign makes it difficult to be certain about their exact number and date.

13:6 *Asherah pole.* See notes on 1Ki 14:23; Dt 7:5.

13:7 *like the dust at threshing time.* This simile is drawn from agricultural practice. In separating the grain from the remainder of the crop, the crop was threshed and then winnowed (see note on Ru 3:2). The threshed material was thrown into the air to allow the breeze to blow away the chaff, or "dust." Jehoahaz's armed forces have been scattered just like chaff on the breeze.

Nebat, which he had caused Israel to commit; he continued in them.
12As for the other events of the reign of
Jehoash, all he did and his achievements,
including his war against Amaziah[n] king of
Judah, are they not written in the book of
the annals[o] of the kings of Israel? 13Jehoash
rested with his ancestors, and Jeroboam[p]
succeeded him on the throne. Jehoash was
buried in Samaria with the kings of Israel.
14Now Elisha had been suffering from
the illness from which he died. Jehoash
king of Israel went down to see him and
wept over him. "My father! My father!"
he cried. "The chariots[q] and horsemen of
Israel!"
15Elisha said, "Get a bow and some arrows,"[r] and he did so. 16"Take the bow in
your hands," he said to the king of Israel. When he had taken it, Elisha put his
hands on the king's hands.
17"Open the east window," he said, and
he opened it. "Shoot!"[s] Elisha said, and
he shot. "The LORD's arrow of victory, the
arrow of victory over Aram!" Elisha declared. "You will completely destroy the
Arameans at Aphek."[t]
18Then he said, "Take the arrows,"
and the king took them. Elisha told him,
"Strike the ground." He struck it three
times and stopped. 19The man of God was
angry with him and said, "You should
have struck the ground five or six times;
then you would have defeated Aram and
completely destroyed it. But now you will
defeat it only three times."[u]
20Elisha died and was buried.
Now Moabite raiders[v] used to enter the
country every spring. 21Once while some
Israelites were burying a man, suddenly
they saw a band of raiders; so they threw
the man's body into Elisha's tomb. When
the body touched Elisha's bones, the man
came to life[w] and stood up on his feet.

13:12 [n] 2Ki 14:15 [o] 1Ki 15:31 **13:13** [p] 2Ki 14:23; Hos 1:1 **13:14** [q] 2Ki 2:12 **13:15** [r] 1Sa 20:20 **13:17** [s] Jos 8:18 [t] 1Ki 20:26 **13:19** [u] ver 25 **13:20** [v] 2Ki 3:7; 24:2 **13:21** [w] Mt 27:52

13:22 [x] 1Ki 19:17; 2Ki 8:12 **13:23** [y] Ge 13:16-17; Ex 2:24 [z] Dt 29:20 [a] Ex 33:15; 2Ki 14:27; 17:18; 24:3,20 **13:24** [b] ver 3 **13:25** [c] ver 18, 19 [d] 2Ki 10:32 **14:4** [e] 2Ki 12:3; 16:4 **14:5** [f] 2Ki 21:24 [g] 2Ki 12:20 **14:6** [h] Dt 28:61

22Hazael king of Aram oppressed[x] Israel throughout the reign of Jehoahaz. 23But
the LORD was gracious to them and had
compassion and showed concern for them
because of his covenant[y] with Abraham,
Isaac and Jacob. To this day he has been
unwilling to destroy[z] them or banish them
from his presence.[a]
24Hazael king of Aram died, and Ben-
Hadad[b] his son succeeded him as king.
25Then Jehoash son of Jehoahaz recaptured from Ben-Hadad son of Hazael the
towns he had taken in battle from his father Jehoahaz. Three times[c] Jehoash defeated him, and so he recovered[d] the Israelite towns.

Amaziah King of Judah

14:1-7pp — 2Ch 25:1-4,11-12
14:8-22pp — 2Ch 25:17–26:2

14 In the second year of Jehoash[a] son
of Jehoahaz king of Israel, Amaziah son of Joash king of Judah began to
reign. 2He was twenty-five years old when
he became king, and he reigned in Jerusalem twenty-nine years. His mother's
name was Jehoaddan; she was from Jerusalem. 3He did what was right in the eyes
of the LORD, but not as his father David
had done. In everything he followed the
example of his father Joash. 4The high
places,[e] however, were not removed; the
people continued to offer sacrifices and
burn incense there.
5After the kingdom was firmly in his
grasp, he executed[f] the officials[g] who had
murdered his father the king. 6Yet he did
not put the children of the assassins to
death, in accordance with what is written
in the Book of the Law[h] of Moses where
the LORD commanded: "Parents are not
to be put to death for their children, nor

[a] *1* Hebrew *Joash,* a variant of *Jehoash;* also in verses 13, 23 and 27

13:15–19 Perhaps in the background of this part of the story lie ancient beliefs about omens and their importance as conveyors of divine messages. These beliefs gave rise to the widely practiced art of divination. The diviner would attempt to read significance out of unusual natural phenomena or out of divinatory rituals. One form of divination, known as belomancy, involved arrows that could be used in various ways. For example, a number of different instructions might be attached to a set of arrows, which were then fired. The instruction on the arrow that flew the farthest, or was found first, would be obeyed. Alternatively, the instructions on the first arrow drawn from a quiver would be taken, or the arrows could be thrown to the ground and the practitioner would travel in the direction they pointed as they settled.
13:21 *threw the man's body into Elisha's tomb.* Tombs in ancient Israel were often dug out of soft rock or located in caves. They did not present to people in a hurry the difficulties of access that more modern, Western forms of burial do. Cave tombs are in fact much more frequently attested in the southern Levant of the tenth to the eighth centuries BC than during any previous or subsequent periods.
13:25 *Three times Jehoash defeated him.* It was during the reign of Hazael's successor Ben-Hadad III that Israel began to recover territory, as Ben-Hadad was preoccupied by the Assyrian threat to his north. At the same time, it is evident that Israel itself did not entirely escape Assyrian attention. Both the Calah and the Tell er-Rimah inscriptions of Adad-nirari claim that tribute passed from Israel to Assyria in this period, and the Rimah inscription explicitly mentions Jehoash of Israel as a tribute-payer. Yet the Assyrian threat and the infighting among the various Syrian kingdoms nevertheless allowed for a limited Israelite recovery vis-à-vis Damascus. Jehoash's successes were later spectacularly exceeded by his son Jeroboam II, once the Assyrian threat had entirely (if temporarily) receded.
14:4 *high places.* See notes on 1Ki 3:2; 11:7.

children put to death for their parents;
each will die for their own sin."[a][i]
7He was the one who defeated ten thousand Edomites in the Valley of Salt[j] and
captured Sela[k] in battle, calling it Joktheel,
the name it has to this day.
8Then Amaziah sent messengers to Jehoash son of Jehoahaz, the son of Jehu,
king of Israel, with the challenge: "Come,
let us face each other in battle."
9But Jehoash king of Israel replied to
Amaziah king of Judah: "A thistle[l] in Lebanon sent a message to a cedar in Lebanon, 'Give your daughter to my son in
marriage.' Then a wild beast in Lebanon
came along and trampled the thistle underfoot. 10You have indeed defeated Edom
and now you are arrogant.[m] Glory in your
victory, but stay at home! Why ask for
trouble and cause your own downfall and
that of Judah also?"
11Amaziah, however, would not listen,
so Jehoash king of Israel attacked. He and
Amaziah king of Judah faced each other
at Beth Shemesh[n] in Judah. 12Judah was
routed by Israel, and every man fled to his
home.[o] 13Jehoash king of Israel captured
Amaziah king of Judah, the son of Joash,
the son of Ahaziah, at Beth Shemesh.
Then Jehoash went to Jerusalem and
broke down the wall[p] of Jerusalem from
the Ephraim Gate[q] to the Corner Gate[r]—a
section about four hundred cubits long.[b]
14He took all the gold and silver and all the
articles found in the temple of the LORD
and in the treasuries of the royal palace.

14:6 [i] Nu 26:11; Job 21:20; Jer 31:30; 44:3; Eze 18:4, 20 **14:7** [j] 2Sa 8:13; 2Ch 25:11 [k] Jdg 1:36 **14:9** [l] Jdg 9:8-15 **14:10** [m] Dt 8:14; 2Ch 26:16; 32:25 **14:11** [n] Jos 15:10 **14:12** [o] 2Sa 18:17 **14:13** [p] 1Ki 3:1; 2Ch 33:14; 36:19; Jer 39:2 [q] Ne 8:16; 12:39 [r] 2Ch 25:23; Jer 31:38; Zec 14:10 **14:15** [s] 2Ki 13:12 **14:19** [t] 2Ki 12:20 [u] Jos 10:3; 2Ki 18:14, 17 **14:20** [v] 2Ki 9:28 **14:21** [w] 2Ki 15:1; 2Ch 26:23 **14:22** [x] 1Ki 9:26; 2Ki 16:6 **14:23** [y] 2Ki 13:13

He also took hostages and returned to Samaria.
15As for the other events of the reign
of Jehoash, what he did and his achievements, including his war[s] against Amaziah
king of Judah, are they not written in the
book of the annals of the kings of Israel?
16Jehoash rested with his ancestors and
was buried in Samaria with the kings of
Israel. And Jeroboam his son succeeded
him as king.
17Amaziah son of Joash king of Judah
lived for fifteen years after the death of Jehoash son of Jehoahaz king of Israel. 18As
for the other events of Amaziah's reign,
are they not written in the book of the annals of the kings of Judah?
19They conspired[t] against him in Jerusalem, and he fled to Lachish,[u] but they sent
men after him to Lachish and killed him
there. 20He was brought back by horse[v]
and was buried in Jerusalem with his ancestors, in the City of David.
21Then all the people of Judah took Azariah,[c][w] who was sixteen years old, and
made him king in place of his father Amaziah. 22He was the one who rebuilt Elath[x]
and restored it to Judah after Amaziah
rested with his ancestors.

Jeroboam II King of Israel

23In the fifteenth year of Amaziah son
of Joash king of Judah, Jeroboam[y] son
of Jehoash king of Israel became king in

[a] *6* Deut. 24:16 [b] *13* That is, about 600 feet or about 180 meters [c] *21* Also called *Uzziah*

14:7 *defeated ten thousand Edomites.* Edom had revolted against Judahite rule during the reign of Jehoram (8:20–22). Amaziah, established on the throne of Judah in the wake of his father Joash's assassination (12:19–21), is not noted as reestablishing Judahite control over Edom, but he did win an important battle that had implications for Judah's ability to trade (cf. v. 22). *Valley of Salt.* Best identified with Wadi el-Milh, east of Beersheba (cf. 2Sa 8:13). *Sela.* Meaning "rock," it has commonly been identified with the famous rock-city Petra, halfway between the Dead Sea and the Gulf of Aqaba, although archaeological evidence does not suggest settlement there earlier than the seventh century BC. It may more plausibly be identified with Khirbet Sil', a couple of miles/kilometers north of Buseira (Biblical Bozrah), which was a fortified city from the ninth to the seventh centuries BC.

14:13 *Ephraim Gate ... Corner Gate.* The assault on Jerusalem that followed the battle of Beth Shemesh resulted in the destruction of about 600 feet (183 meters) of city wall on the northern side of the city between these two gates. *Ephraim Gate.* As its name suggests, it was the main gate in the center of the northern wall and exited to the road that led to the mountains of Ephraim via the central Benjamin plateau. *Corner Gate.* Its location is uncertain (as indeed the precise location of the city walls more generally in this period is uncertain), but it is assumed to have been at the northwestern corner of the city.

14:19 *Lachish.* Identified with Tell ed-Duweir, now called Tel Lachish, situated near the Wadi Ghafr—a main route from the coastal plain to the Hebron hills. Archaeological excavations there have revealed (level IV) a large fortified city in this period, which we may assume was constructed during the reign of Rehoboam (2Ch 11:5–12,23). Among the finds were an impressive city-gate complex in the southwestern wall (the city's only gate), and a palace-fort in the center of the city attached to a storehouse and a stable. It was to this city, then—the most important fortified city in Judah after Jerusalem—that Amaziah fled when Jerusalem was lost.

14:22 *Elath.* Elath was a port town on the northern coast of the Gulf of Aqaba (the Red Sea), closely associated with Ezion Geber and the trade of the Solomonic era with the wider world (1Ki 9:26). It stood at the southern end of the great King's Highway, which ran all the way north through the Transjordan to Damascus and facilitated trade connections especially with southern Arabia (see note on Nu 20:17). Presumably Elath was lost to Judah when Edom revolted during Jehoram's reign (2Ki 8:20–22), just as both Israelite and Judahite control of the highway was challenged as a result of both that revolt and also the earlier Moabite uprising (1:1; 3:4–5) and the constant pressure from Damascus. It was only in the aftermath of Amaziah's victory over the Edomites (v. 7) and with the decline of Damascus that Azariah, Amaziah's son, was able once again to reassert control of Elath.

Samaria, and he reigned forty-one years. 24He did evil in the eyes of the LORD and did not turn away from any of the sins of Jeroboam son of Nebat, which he had caused Israel to commit.[z] 25He was the one who restored the boundaries of Israel from Lebo Hamath[a] to the Dead Sea,[ab] in accordance with the word of the LORD, the God of Israel, spoken through his servant Jonah[c] son of Amittai, the prophet from Gath Hepher.

26The LORD had seen how bitterly everyone in Israel, whether slave or free,[d] was suffering;[be] there was no one to help them.[f] 27And since the LORD had not said he would blot out[g] the name of Israel from under heaven, he saved[h] them by the hand of Jeroboam son of Jehoash.

28As for the other events of Jeroboam's reign, all he did, and his military achievements, including how he recovered for Israel both Damascus[i] and Hamath,[j] which had belonged to Judah, are they not written in the book of the annals[k] of the kings of Israel? 29Jeroboam rested with his ancestors, the kings of Israel. And Zechariah his son succeeded him as king.

Azariah King of Judah

15:1-7pp — 2Ch 26:3-4,21-23

15 In the twenty-seventh year of Jeroboam king of Israel, Azariah[cl] son of Amaziah king of Judah began to reign. 2He was sixteen years old when he became king, and he reigned in Jerusalem fifty-two years. His mother's name was Jekoliah; she was from Jerusalem. 3He did what was right in the eyes of the LORD, just as his father Amaziah had done. 4The high places, however, were not removed; the people continued to offer sacrifices and burn incense there.

5The LORD afflicted[m] the king with leprosy[d] until the day he died, and he lived in a separate house.[en] Jotham[o] the king's son had charge of the palace[p] and governed the people of the land.

6As for the other events of Azariah's reign, and all he did, are they not written in the book of the annals of the kings of Judah? 7Azariah rested[q] with his ancestors and was buried near them in the City of David. And Jotham[r] his son succeeded him as king.

Zechariah King of Israel

8In the thirty-eighth year of Azariah king of Judah, Zechariah son of Jeroboam became king of Israel in Samaria, and he reigned six months. 9He did evil[s] in the eyes of the LORD, as his predecessors had done. He did not turn away from the sins of Jeroboam son of Nebat, which he had caused Israel to commit.

10Shallum son of Jabesh conspired

14:24 [z] 1Ki 15:30
14:25 [a] Nu 13:21; 1Ki 8:65 [b] Dt 3:17 [c] Jnh 1:1; Mt 12:39
14:26 [d] Dt 32:36 [e] 2Ki 13:4 [f] Ps 18:41; 22:11; 72:12; 107:12; Isa 63:5; La 1:7
14:27 [g] 2Ki 13:23 [h] Jdg 6:14
14:28 [i] 2Sa 8:5; 1Ki 11:24 [j] 2Ch 8:3 [k] 1Ki 15:31
15:1 [l] ver 32; 2Ki 14:21
15:5 [m] Ge 12:17 [n] Lev 13:46 [o] 2Ch 27:1 [p] Ge 41:40
15:7 [q] Isa 6:1; 14:28 [r] ver 5
15:9 [s] 1Ki 15:26

[a] 25 Hebrew *the Sea of the Arabah* [b] 26 Or *Israel was suffering. They were without a ruler or leader, and* [c] 1 Also called *Uzziah*; also in verses 6, 7, 8, 17, 23 and 27 [d] 5 The Hebrew for *leprosy* was used for various diseases affecting the skin. [e] 5 Or *in a house where he was relieved of responsibilities*

14:25 *restored the boundaries of Israel.* In the aftermath of Assyria's assault on Syria, which had evidently seriously weakened the kingdoms of that region, and in a period of relative Assyrian quiescence in Syria and Palestine, Jeroboam II was able to further the Israelite recovery begun by his father. Assyria did not apparently trouble Syria or Palestine much in the period between Adadnirari III (811 – 783 BC) and Tiglath-Pileser III (745 – 727 BC). Assyria's kings — Shalmaneser IV (783 – 773 BC), Ashur-Dan III (773 – 755 BC) and Ashurnirari V (755 – 745 BC) — were beset by other troubles and only infrequently ventured out on military campaigns in the west. *Lebo Hamath.* Hamath was situated in central Syria at the place where the main road from the north crossed the Orontes River, about 133 miles (214 kilometers) north of Damascus (v. 28), and Lebo Hamath ("entrance to Hamath") was presumably a closely associated city or geographic feature. As we can see from 1Ki 8:65, Jeroboam II restored the territory of northern Israel to its previous greatest extent under Solomon. He not only recovered all the territory in Transjordan captured by Hazael in 2Ki 10:32 – 33, but in fact now claimed dominion over Aram and the Syrian kingdoms beyond Damascus, to the ideal boundaries of the promised land described elsewhere as including territory "from the Euphrates River to the land of the Philistines, as far as the border of Egypt" and "from Tiphsah to Gaza" (1Ki 4:21,24; cf. 2Ki 15:16). Whatever Lebo Hamath is, therefore, it cannot be (as many have suggested) a city to the south of Hamath itself (e.g., modern Lebweh in the Lebanon Valley). It must be looked for to the north. *Gath Hepher.* Jos 19:13 suggests that it was a town on the eastern border of the territory of Zebulun, and traditionally it has been identified with Khirbet el-Zurra'a near the modern settlement of Mashhad, a couple of miles/kilometers east of Sepphoris, which, in fact, contains a tomb opportunistically attributed to Jonah.

15:4 *high places.* See notes on 1Ki 3:2; 11:7.

15:5 *leprosy.* See note on 5:1. *in a separate house.* Lit. "in the house of freedom," the meaning of which is unclear. The second NIV text note on this verse is probably on the right track in taking the phrase as a metaphor for Azariah's being relieved of (set free from) responsibility in government. More than that, however, the suggestion is perhaps that the king, being seriously incapacitated, was regarded as effectively dead. The Hebrew word *hopshi* ("free") appears in connection with the world of the dead in Job 3:19; Ps 88:5 ("set apart"), and there is one reference in the Ugaritic Baal Cycle to the netherworld as the *bt hptt*, "the place of seclusion."

15:8 – 16 With Jeroboam II's death around 748 BC (14:29) and the assassination very shortly thereafter of his son Zechariah (vv. 8 – 12), the northern kingdom, after its brief period of recovery, was on its way to destruction (722 BC). The assassin Shallum held on to power for a mere month before losing both crown and life to Menahem (vv. 13 – 15), whose power base was apparently in the old Israelite capital of Tirzah (vv. 14,16; cf. 1Ki 16:23 – 24; see next note).

2 KINGS 15:1 – 7

Azariah King of Judah

Azariah (also known in the Biblical texts as Uzziah, e.g., 2Ki 15:13,30,32,34) consolidated the Judahite recovery initiated by his father, Amaziah (2Ki 14:21 – 22), and at some point during his long reign may indeed have risen to a position of preeminence among the Syro-Palestinian kingdoms. The evidence is implicit and disputed, however. It comes from two textual fragments that some scholars view as forming parts of one text from the reign of Tiglath-Pileser III (745 – 727 BC), but that others claim derive from different Assyrian kings (Tiglath-Pileser III and the later Sargon II or Sennacherib). The composite text has been interpreted as suggesting that Azariah stood at the head of an anti-Assyrian alliance during the early years of renewed Assyrian activity in the west in 743 – 738 BC — the period in which our Biblical sources suggest that his son Jotham was exercising effective governmental power in Judah as a result of his father's illness (2Ki 15:5).

The first fragment identifies a person apparently called "Azriau" of "Ia-u-da-a-a" as a payer of tribute to Assyria. The second fragment comes from the annals of Tiglath-Pileser III (745 – 727 BC) and describes an unnamed group of kings who had taken 19 districts and cities of the coast belonging to Hamath and had given them to one "Azriau." The identification of "Azriau" with Azariah of Judah is disputed. However, even if it were shown to be indisputably the case that the first fragment belongs to the records of a king later than Tiglath-Pileser III, the fact remains that the second fragment contains a name Az-ri-a-a-u that is written in an Israelite, not an Aramean, form and that we know of no king of this name in this period other than Azariah of Judah. These points taken together favor identifying Az-ri-a-a-u with Azariah, at least in the case of the second fragment. ◆

against Zechariah. He attacked him in
front of the people,[a] assassinated[t] him
and succeeded him as king. 11 The other
events of Zechariah's reign are written
in the book of the annals[u] of the kings of
Israel. 12 So the word of the LORD spoken
to Jehu was fulfilled:[v] "Your descendants
will sit on the throne of Israel to the fourth
generation."[b]

Shallum King of Israel

13 Shallum son of Jabesh became king
in the thirty-ninth year of Uzziah king of
Judah, and he reigned in Samaria[w] one
month. 14 Then Menahem son of Gadi
went from Tirzah[x] up to Samaria. He attacked Shallum son of Jabesh in Samaria,
assassinated[y] him and succeeded him as
king.

15 The other events of Shallum's reign,
and the conspiracy he led, are written in
the book of the annals[z] of the kings of Israel.

16 At that time Menahem, starting out
from Tirzah, attacked Tiphsah[a] and everyone in the city and its vicinity, because
they refused to open[b] their gates. He
sacked Tiphsah and ripped open all the
pregnant women.

15:10 [t] 2Ki 12:20 **15:11** [u] 1Ki 15:31 **15:12** [v] 2Ki 10:30 **15:13** [w] ver 1,8 **15:14** [x] 1Ki 14:17 [y] 2Ki 12:20 **15:15** [z] 1Ki 15:31 **15:16** [a] 1Ki 4:24 [b] 2Ki 8:12; Hos 13:16

[a] *10* Hebrew; some Septuagint manuscripts *in Ibleam*
[b] *12* 2 Kings 10:30

15:16 *Tirzah.* Probably Tell el-Far'ah, six miles (almost 10 kilometers) northeast of Nablus. *Tiphsah.* An important city on the Euphrates River located about 75 miles (120 kilometers) south of Carchemish on the main trade route connecting Mesopotamia with Syria. Menahem made one last attempt to retain for Israel Solomon-like influence in the north by engaging in a campaign that took him as far north as Tiphsah (cf. 1Ki 4:24). Such a campaign would likely have taken place early in his reign, either before the Assyrian campaigns of 743 – 740 BC began, or during these years as part of the anti-Assyrian struggle in the region. It is in this same struggle that Azariah and Jotham of Judah each may have been involved in a leading role (see the article "Azariah King of Judah," p. 644. *ripped open all the pregnant women.* See note on 8:12.

Menahem King of Israel

17In the thirty-ninth year of Azariah
king of Judah, Menahem son of Gadi became king of Israel, and he reigned in Samaria ten years. 18He did evil in the eyes
of the LORD. During his entire reign he did
not turn away from the sins of Jeroboam
son of Nebat, which he had caused Israel
to commit.
19Then Pul[a,c] king of Assyria invaded the
land, and Menahem gave him a thousand
talents[b] of silver to gain his support and
strengthen his own hold on the kingdom.
20Menahem exacted this money from Israel. Every wealthy person had to contribute fifty shekels[c] of silver to be given to
the king of Assyria. So the king of Assyria
withdrew[d] and stayed in the land no longer.
21As for the other events of Menahem's
reign, and all he did, are they not written
in the book of the annals of the kings of
Israel? 22Menahem rested with his ancestors. And Pekahiah his son succeeded him
as king.

Pekahiah King of Israel

23In the fiftieth year of Azariah king of
Judah, Pekahiah son of Menahem became
king of Israel in Samaria, and he reigned
two years. 24Pekahiah did evil in the eyes
of the LORD. He did not turn away from
the sins of Jeroboam son of Nebat, which
he had caused Israel to commit. 25One of
his chief officers, Pekah[e] son of Remaliah,
conspired against him. Taking fifty men
of Gilead with him, he assassinated[f] Pekahiah, along with Argob and Arieh, in the
citadel of the royal palace at Samaria. So
Pekah killed Pekahiah and succeeded him
as king.
26The other events of Pekahiah's reign,
and all he did, are written in the book of
the annals of the kings of Israel.

Pekah King of Israel

27In the fifty-second year of Azariah
king of Judah, Pekah[g] son of Remaliah[h]
became king of Israel in Samaria, and he
reigned twenty years. 28He did evil in the
eyes of the LORD. He did not turn away
from the sins of Jeroboam son of Nebat,
which he had caused Israel to commit.
29In the time of Pekah king of Israel, Tiglath-Pileser[i] king of Assyria came and took

15:19 [c] 1Ch 5:6, 26 **15:20** [d] 2Ki 12:18 **15:25** [e] 2Ch 28:6; Isa 7:1 [f] 2Ki 12:20 **15:27** [g] 2Ch 28:6; Isa 7:1 [h] Isa 7:4 **15:29** [i] 2Ki 16:7; 17:6; 1Ch 5:26; 2Ch 28:20; Jer 50:17

[a] *19* Also called *Tiglath-Pileser* [b] *19* That is, about 38 tons or about 34 metric tons [c] *20* That is, about 1 1/4 pounds or about 575 grams

15:19 *Pul.* The Hebrew version of the Akkadian "Pulu"—a short name for Tiglath-Pileser, not found in any of the inscriptions contemporary with him but known from the Babylonian king lists. During the reigns of Menahem in Israel and Azariah and his son Jotham in Judah, the relative lull in Assyrian military activity in Syria and Palestine came to a decisive end with the appearance of the armies of Tiglath-Pileser III. Tiglath-Pileser's first campaigns represent the beginning of a process through which, within a short period, northern Israel and most of the Syro-Hittite states to its north were incorporated into the Assyrian Empire. His goal was apparently to establish an Assyrian trading center on the border with Egypt, and he required control of the intervening regions to accomplish this and to ensure safe passage for trade between Philistia and Assyria. *Menahem gave him a thousand talents of silver.* The payment of tribute bought Assyrian support for Menahem's rule, which had been seized by force and would not have been regarded as legitimate by many. Menahem is mentioned in two texts dating from the reign of Tiglath-Pileser III as a king paying tribute to Assyria. The first text comes from Tiglath-Pileser's royal annals from Calah, compiled during the final years of his reign but now in a fragmentary and difficult state, and relates to 738 BC: "I received tribute from ... Rezin of Damascus, Menahem of Samaria, Hiram of Tyre." The second text is found on the only known stele of Tiglath-Pileser III, set up in western Iran on the border of one of the states defeated during the 737 BC campaign. It may look back on the year 738 BC, or possibly an earlier year: "Rezin, the Damascene, Menahem, the Samarian, Tuba'il, the Tyrian ... I imposed on them tribute of silver, gold, tin, iron."
15:27 *Pekah ... reigned twenty years.* It seems clear that if Menahem was king of Israel in 738 BC and Pekah was succeeded by Hoshea around 732 BC, Pekah could not have reigned for 20 years over Israel. Indeed, if we were simply to add together the regnal years for Hoshea (17:1), Pekahiah (v. 23) and Pekah, and work backward from the fall of Samaria at the juncture of the reigns of the Assyrian kings Shalmaneser V and Sargon II in 722 BC, we would arrive at a starting date for Pekah's reign of around 753 BC—well before the accession of Tiglath-Pileser III in 745 BC. The best solution is to assume that before succeeding Pekahiah in Samaria, Pekah had already ruled as governor over at least part of the Israelite territory mentioned in v. 29. Verse 25 appears to locate his power base in Gilead. Pekah then counted his regnal years from the earlier period (during which he was not really a king) as a way of claiming legitimacy, perhaps as the "true" successor to Jeroboam II.
15:29 *In the time of Pekah king of Israel, Tiglath-Pileser ... came.* In 733–732 BC, Tiglath-Pileser met with concerted opposition in Syria and Palestine, led by Rezin (Rakhianu in cuneiform sources) of Damascus and supported by Pekah of Israel and others. The kingdom of Judah, an ally of Assyria at this point (v. 37; 16:5–9), itself came under attack from this coalition. The Assyrian response was to launch campaigns against Damascus and its allies in both 733 and 732 BC. Damascus was eventually captured in 732 BC, and in the course of the campaigns Israel also suffered major losses, relinquishing territory on both sides of the Jordan River as far south as Megiddo and Ramoth Gilead, respectively. *deported the people to Assyria.* The first recorded example of the deportation of people groups by the Assyrians comes from the reign of Tukulti-Ninurta I (c. 1243–1207 BC), whose defeat of the Hittites was followed by the transportation of a large group of that conquered people from Syria to labor camps in Assyria. By this means Assyrian kings could not only increase their labor force for building projects or the development of uncultivated land in order to increase the food supply, but also reduce the possibility of further opposition among the subjugated peoples. Tiglath-Pileser III made deportation

ASSYRIAN CAMPAIGNS AGAINST ISRAEL AND JUDAH

The Assyrian invasions of the eighth century BC were the most traumatic political events in the entire history of Israel.

The brutal Assyrian style of warfare relied on massive armies, superbly equipped with the world's first great siege machines manipulated by an efficient corps of engineers.

Psychological terror, however, was Assyria's most effective weapon. It was ruthlessly applied, with corpses impaled on stakes, severed heads stacked in heaps and captives skinned alive.

The shock of bloody military sieges on both Israel and Judah was profound. The prophets did not fail to speak out against their horror, while at the same time pleading with the people to see God's hand in history, to recognize spiritual causes in the present punishment.

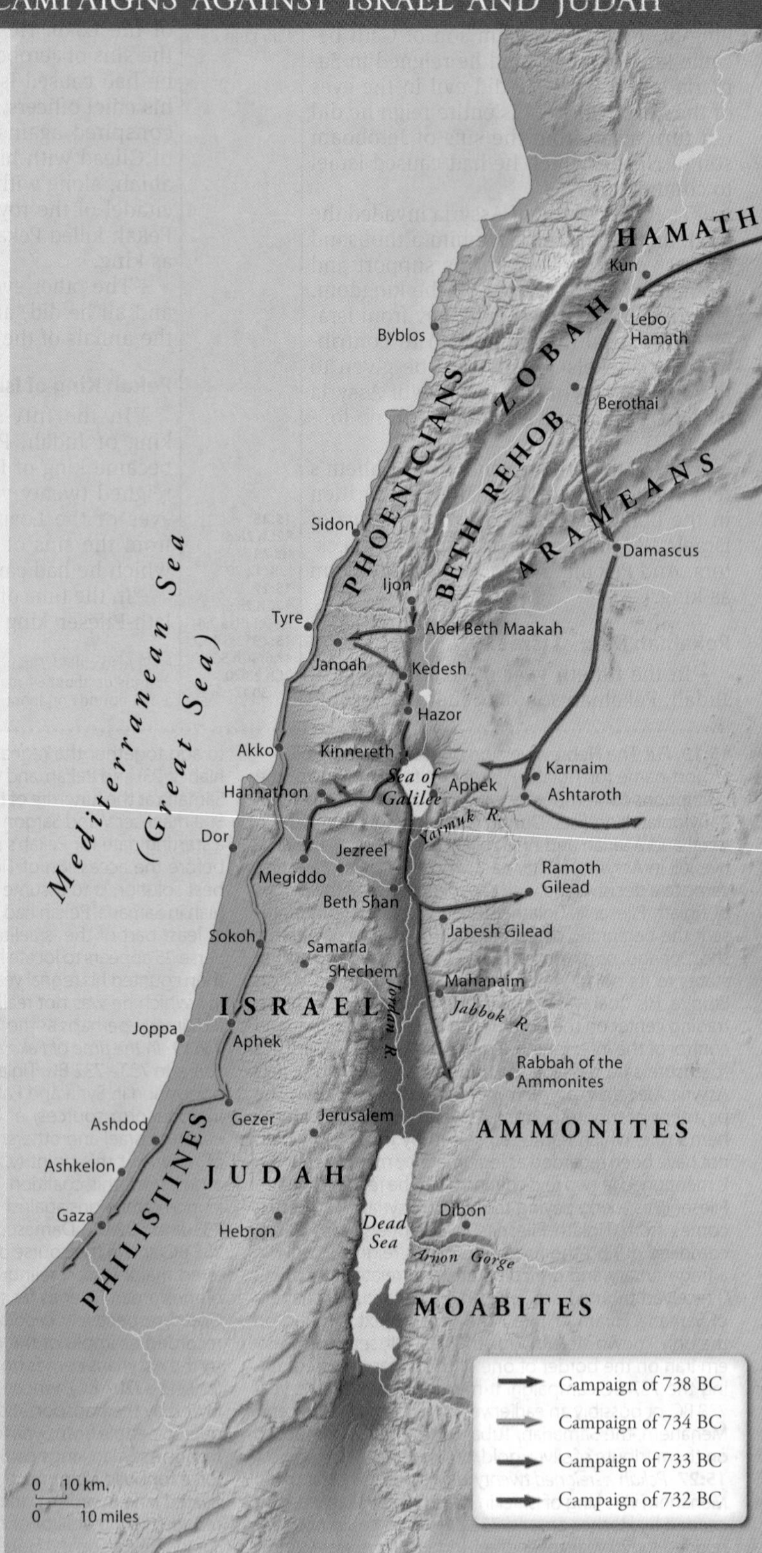

1. CAMPAIGNS OF TIGLATH-PILESER III (738–732 BC)

King Tiglath-Pileser of Assyria (745–727 BC) proved to be a vigorous campaigner, first exacting tribute from Menahem and then annexing Hamath, Philistia, Galilee, Gilead and Damascus (738–732 BC) during the reign of Pekah.

The ferocious onslaught against the northern tribes left only central Israel and the capital city of Samaria intact. By this time Israel was a tiny nation wracked by pro- and anti-Assyrian factions, multiple assassinations, hypocrisy, arrogance and fear.

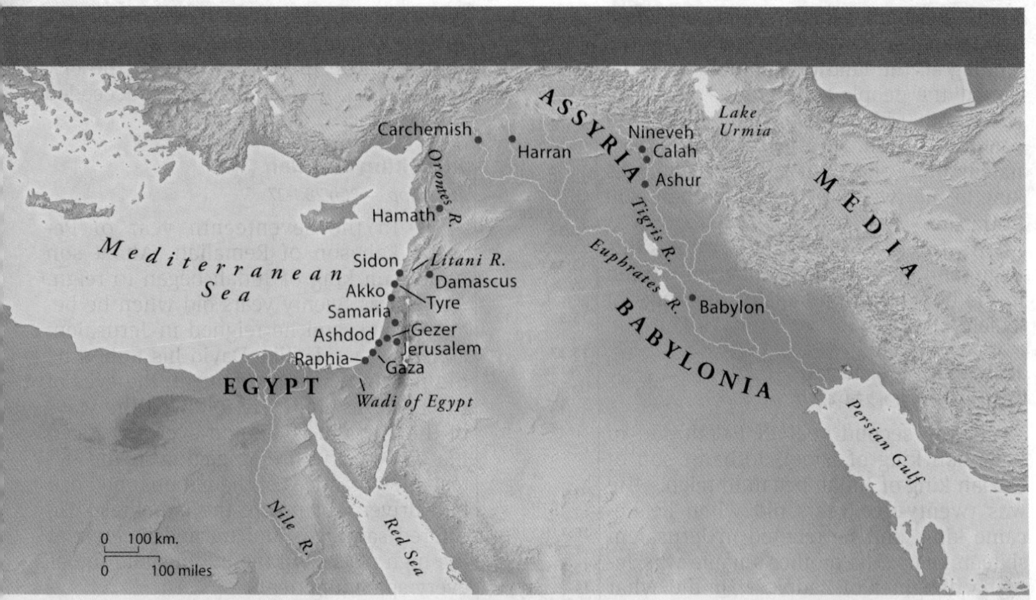

2. CAMPAIGN OF SHALMANESER V (725–722 BC)

The last king of Israel, Hoshea, conspired with Egypt and withheld the annual tribute to the Assyrians.

A protracted three-year siege conducted by Shalmaneser and concluded by Sargon II saw the end of the Israelite kingdom in 722–721 BC.

At that time, according to Assyrian annals, "I [Sargon] besieged and conquered Samaria, led away as plunder 27,290 inhabitants . . . I installed over [those remaining] an officer of mine and imposed upon them the tribute of the former king."

3. SENNACHERIB'S CAMPAIGN AGAINST JUDAH (701 BC)

In the 14th year of Hezekiah, the Assyrians finally attacked Judah. The Prism of Sennacherib calls Hezekiah "overbearing and proud," indicating that he was part of Philistia's and Egypt's effort to rebel against Assyria.

A battle in the plain of Eltekeh was won by Assyria; the Egyptian and Cushite charioteers fled. Lachish was besieged and taken. Sennacherib's annals note: "As for Hezekiah the Jew, he did not submit to my yoke. I laid siege to 46 of his strong cities, walled forts and the countless small villages in their vicinity, and conquered them by means of well-tamped earth ramps and battering-rams brought near to the walls combined with the attack by foot-soldiers, using mines, breaches and sapper work. I drove out 200,150 people, young and old, male and female, horses, mules, donkeys, camels, large and small cattle beyond counting, and considered them plunder. Himself I made a prisoner in Jerusalem, his royal residence, like a bird in a cage."

Nowhere, however, does the boastful Assyrian king record the disaster mentioned in 2Ki 19:35-36; 2Ch 32:21; Isa 37:36-37.

Ijon,[j] Abel Beth Maakah, Janoah, Kedesh
and Hazor. He took Gilead and Galilee, including all the land of Naphtali,[k] and deported[l] the people to Assyria. 30 Then Hoshea[m] son of Elah conspired against Pekah
son of Remaliah. He attacked and assassinated[n] him, and then succeeded him as
king in the twentieth year of Jotham son
of Uzziah.
31 As for the other events of Pekah's
reign, and all he did, are they not written
in the book of the annals of the kings of
Israel?

Jotham King of Judah

15:33-38pp — 2Ch 27:1-4,7-9

32 In the second year of Pekah son of
Remaliah king of Israel, Jotham[o] son of
Uzziah king of Judah began to reign. 33 He
was twenty-five years old when he became king, and he reigned in Jerusalem
sixteen years. His mother's name was Jerusha daughter of Zadok. 34 He did what
was right[p] in the eyes of the LORD, just as
his father Uzziah had done. 35 The high
places,[q] however, were not removed; the
people continued to offer sacrifices and
burn incense there. Jotham rebuilt the Upper Gate[r] of the temple of the LORD.
36 As for the other events of Jotham's
reign, and what he did, are they not written in the book of the annals of the kings
of Judah? 37 (In those days the LORD began
to send Rezin[s] king of Aram and Pekah
son of Remaliah against Judah.) 38 Jotham
rested with his ancestors and was buried
with them in the City of David, the city
of his father. And Ahaz his son succeeded
him as king.

Ahaz King of Judah

16:1-20pp — 2Ch 28:1-27

16 In the seventeenth year of Pekah son of Remaliah, Ahaz[t] son
of Jotham king of Judah began to reign.
2 Ahaz was twenty years old when he became king, and he reigned in Jerusalem
sixteen years. Unlike David his father, he
did not do what was right[u] in the eyes of
the LORD his God. 3 He followed the ways
of the kings of Israel and even sacrificed
his son[v] in the fire, engaging in the detestable[w] practices of the nations the LORD
had driven out before the Israelites. 4 He
offered sacrifices and burned incense at
the high places, on the hilltops and under
every spreading tree.[x]
5 Then Rezin[y] king of Aram and Pekah
son of Remaliah king of Israel marched up
to fight against Jerusalem and besieged
Ahaz, but they could not overpower him.
6 At that time, Rezin[z] king of Aram recovered Elath[a] for Aram by driving out the
people of Judah. Edomites then moved
into Elath and have lived there to this day.
7 Ahaz sent messengers to say to Tiglath-Pileser[b] king of Assyria, "I am your
servant and vassal. Come up and save[c] me

15:29 [j] 1Ki 15:20 [k] 2Ki 16:9; 17:24; 2Ch 16:4; Isa 9:1 [l] 2Ki 24:14-16; 1Ch 5:22; Isa 14:6, 17; 36:17; 45:13 **15:30** [m] 2Ki 17:1 [n] 2Ki 12:20 **15:32** [o] 1Ch 5:17 **15:34** [p] ver 3; 1Ki 14:8; 2Ch 26:4-5 **15:35** [q] 2Ki 12:3 [r] 2Ch 23:20 **15:37** [s] 2Ki 16:5; Isa 7:1 **16:1** [t] Isa 1:1; 14:28 **16:2** [u] 1Ki 14:8 **16:3** [v] Lev 18:21; 2Ki 21:6 [w] Lev 18:3; Dt 9:4; 12:31 **16:4** [x] Dt 12:2; Eze 6:13 **16:5** [y] 2Ki 15:37; Isa 7:1,4 **16:6** [z] Isa 9:12 [a] 2Ki 14:22; 2Ch 26:2 **16:7** [b] 2Ki 15:29 [c] Isa 2:6; Jer 2:18; Eze 16:28; Hos 10:6

---

of this kind a major feature of his imperial policy, and it was imitated often by subsequent rulers. It is estimated that 250,000–500,000 people were deported during the reigns of Assyrian kings. With only occasional exceptions, they were deported to environments similar to those from which they originated—some to cities, others to underpopulated rural areas, and still others to regions of the empire depopulated by an earlier deportation after a rebellion. One major consequence was that Assyrian cities in particular became cosmopolitan and multilingual.

15:30 *Hoshea ... succeeded him.* Although much of northern Israel had been absorbed into the Assyrian Empire by 732 BC, a smaller state confined to the hill country of Ephraim survived for another ten years as Assyria's vassal. The new king, Hoshea, was on the throne of that kingdom when Samaria eventually fell in 722 BC. It seems that the Assyrians were content to allow some territories a relative degree of autonomy in relation to the empire, refusing the trouble of absorbing a state (or in this case, all of a state) where they did not think it necessary for their ends. It was no doubt useful to them to have a "buffer zone" of semi-independent peoples between the borders of their empire and the borders of Egypt. A summary inscription of Tiglath-Pileser III, inscribed on a pavement slab, also records this transition of power and describes the deportations and payment of tribute associated with it.

15:35 *high places.* See notes on 1Ki 3:2; 11:7. *Upper Gate of the temple.* The "gate behind the guard" (11:6) that was located in a wall separating the temple and palace complexes. It is intriguing that Jotham should give attention to the boundary marker between temple and palace when it is precisely the transgression of that boundary for which 2Ch 26:16–21 blames his father.

16:3 *sacrificed his son in the fire.* Child sacrifice was a prominent feature of at least some of the polytheistic Canaanite religions practiced in ancient times in Syria and Palestine (see notes on 3:27; 1Ki 11:5; Lev 20:2; Jer 7:31). In the aftermath of Jotham's relatively orthodox reign comes a renewed period of officially sanctioned idolatry in Judah, as King Ahaz "followed the ways of the kings of Israel" and the high places became centers, not of the worship of Yahweh, but of the worship of Baal Hadad.

16:4 *high places.* See notes on 1Ki 3:2; 11:7.

16:6 *Elath.* Elath had only recently been won back for Judah by Azariah (see note on 14:22). It is here implied, however, that Rezin was able to reestablish Aramean control over the entirety of the King's Highway in Transjordan, from Damascus to Elath (see note on Nu 20:17). He then apparently gave it to the Edomites, who appear to have taken part as allies in the assault on Judah along with the Philistines (2Ch 28:17–18).

16:7–9 Besieged in Jerusalem, King Ahaz's response was to call on Tiglath-Pileser for help, sending at the same time a large gift to encourage compliance (possibly the same tribute referred to in an Assyrian text from Tiglath-Pileser's time). The help is represented in 2 Kings as the Assyrian campaigns in Syria and Palestine of 733–732 BC that resulted in the capture of Damascus and the death of Rezin, as well as the annexation of large parts of northern Israel and the death of Pekah (15:29–30).

out of the hand of the king of Aram and of
the king of Israel, who are attacking me."
8And Ahaz took the silver and gold found
in the temple of the LORD and in the treasuries of the royal palace and sent it as a
gift[d] to the king of Assyria. 9The king of
Assyria complied by attacking Damascus[e]
and capturing it. He deported its inhabitants to Kir[f] and put Rezin to death.
10Then King Ahaz went to Damascus to
meet Tiglath-Pileser king of Assyria. He
saw an altar in Damascus and sent to Uriah[g] the priest a sketch of the altar, with
detailed plans for its construction. 11So
Uriah the priest built an altar in accordance with all the plans that King Ahaz
had sent from Damascus and finished it
before King Ahaz returned. 12When the
king came back from Damascus and saw
the altar, he approached it and presented

16:8 [d] 2Ki 12:18 **16:9** [e] 2Ki 15:29 [f] Isa 22:6; Am 1:5; 9:7 **16:10** [g] Isa 8:2

16:10–16 For the Biblical authors, the direct intervention of Assyria into Judahite affairs in 734–732 BC was fateful for Judah in terms of its religious, not just its political, consequences. A king open to foreign influence in his religious policy from the beginning (cf. vv. 2–4), Ahaz is presented here as traveling to Damascus to pay homage to the Assyrian king and being so impressed by an altar there that he reorganizes worship in Jerusalem around its facsimile. The origin of the altar—Assyrian or Aramean—is not stated, but it was most likely the latter. The assumption that it was an Assyrian altar has led some to suggest that implicit in this story is the imposition of Assyrian religion on Judah as a vassal state. There is, however, no compelling reason to think that Tiglath-Pileser imposed Assyrian religious architecture on a vassal state, and nothing in Ahaz's actions upon returning to Jerusalem implies specifically Assyrian religious practice as such. 2Ch 28:23 explicitly says that in fact it was "the gods of Damascus" that Ahaz introduced into Jerusalem—a particular variant of the Baal worship that had so recently plagued northern Israel (see note on 2Ki 5:18). If some of the things that Ahaz did were "in deference to the king of Assyria" (16:18), these are less likely to

2 KINGS 16:5–20

ISRAEL AND DAMASCUS VERSUS JUDAH

The pressure on Judah from Rezin king of Aram/Damascus and Pekah king of Israel has already been mentioned in 2Ki 15:37 with respect to Jotham's reign, and in 2Ki 16 it is mentioned with respect to Ahaz's reign. In all probability this father and son shared some years of coregency around the time of the crisis (cf. 2Ki 15:30, which has 732/731 BC as Jotham's 20th year, whereas 2Ki 15:33 tells us that he reigned for only 16 years), just as the reigns of Azariah and Jotham had previously overlapped.

This crisis is usually referred to as the Syro-Ephraimite War. It began around 734 BC in the context of the opposition to Tiglath-Pileser III led by Rezin of Damascus and supported by Pekah of Israel and others (see note on 15:29), which led in turn to the Assyrian campaigns of 733–732 BC against Damascus and its allies. The motive for the attack on Judah is never explicitly given in the Biblical sources. However, even if Judah was involved in anti-Assyrian resistance early in Tiglath-Pileser's reign (as the "Azriau of Judah" text may imply [see the article "Azariah of Judah," p. 644]), the evidence suggests that Judah had been in a tributary relationship with Assyria since that time and would have had no desire to fight against the empire. It was no doubt this pro-Assyrian stance on the part of Judah under Jotham and Ahaz that prompted the Syro-Ephraimite assault.

A list of tributary kings of Syria and Canaan, found on the only complete building inscription of Tiglath-Pileser III, from Calah and dating from around 729 BC, mentions King Ahaz (here given his fuller name of Jehoahaz) as a vassal paying tribute in the context of the Assyrian campaigns of this period, without explicating the circumstances. It is unclear whether it alludes to the same payment of tribute that is mentioned in 2Ki 16:8 or to an earlier instance. ◆

offerings[a][h] on it. 13He offered up his burnt
offering[i] and grain offering, poured out
his drink offering, and splashed the blood
of his fellowship offerings[j] against the altar. 14As for the bronze altar[k] that stood
before the LORD, he brought it from the
front of the temple — from between the
new altar and the temple of the LORD —
and put it on the north side of the new
altar.
15King Ahaz then gave these orders to
Uriah the priest: "On the large new altar,
offer the morning[l] burnt offering and the
evening grain offering, the king's burnt of-

16:12 [h]2Ch 26:16 **16:13** [i]Lev 6:8-13 [j]Lev 7:11-21 **16:14** [k]2Ch 4:1 **16:15** [l]Ex 29:38-41

[a] 12 Or *and went up*

have been impositions than voluntary attempts to please the Assyrian king, in part by incorporating into Judahite religion further elements of the worship of Hadad. Nevertheless, the altar could simply represent artistic innovation rather than religious syncretism.

16:15 *seeking guidance.* The new and impressively large Hadad altar displaced the bronze altar that had been used for sacrifice since the days of Solomon (v. 14; 1Ki 8:22 – 23,62 – 64; 9:25), the latter now being reserved for Ahaz's practice of "seeking" oracles. This no doubt refers to the use of the bronze altar for divination (the interpretation of omens). It is probably specifically a reference to extispicy — the examination of the entrails of sacrificial animals in order to divine the will and intentions of the gods, most importantly focusing on the inspection of the liver (hepatoscopy; Lev 13:36; 27:33 use the same verb for ritual examination; see the article "Extispicy," p. 650). Although the OT describes legitimate ways of seeking divine guidance that are not dissimilar to some forms of divination elsewhere in the ancient world (e.g., the use of the Urim and Thummim, see the article "Urim and Thummim," p. 162), there is no question that the authors of Kings intend the reader to disapprove of Ahaz's reassignment of the bronze altar for this divinatory practice. Whereas Ahaz's own word for the practice is the innocuous "seeking," 2Ki 17:17 appears to be looking back at Ahaz above all others when it speaks of those Israelites who "sacrificed their sons and daughters in the fire ... practiced divination and sought omens," recalling the explicit prohibition of Dt 18:10 that "no one be found among you who sacrifices his son or daughter in the fire, who practices divination ... interprets omens" (see notes on Dt 18:10 – 11).

2 KINGS 16:15

Extispicy

Ahab's use of the altar for "seeking guidance" suggests the practice of extispicy that is well-known in the ancient world. Extispicy is attested in the ancient Near East from early in the second millennium BC and played an important role not only at royal courts, but also in the everyday lives of ordinary people. It is attested not just in Mesopotamia, but also in Syria and Canaan, where clay models of livers used by the apprentice diviner to learn his craft have been found (e.g., at Megiddo and Hazor). Such models typically have inscriptions on them indicating interesting features observed on the organ that has been modeled or informing the handler of the circumstances in which the consultation took place, as in this example from Ugarit: "This liver model is for Agaptarri when he was to buy the boy of the Alashian [Cyprus]."

Extispicy focused on abnormalities in animal entrails, and its practice led to the accumulation of extispicy reports, which detailed past findings in the hope of guiding future enquiries. The different parts of the entrails, especially the liver, had their own names and significances, both individually and when added up to give the final conclusion.

We possess particularly good information about divination, and specifically extispicy, from the city of Mari, where eighteenth century BC letters share this common theme. Here too we find documents that list previous phenomena as a guide to the diviner in the present.

Hadad himself was one of the cosponsors of Mesopotamian divination, along with Shamash, the sun-god. It was from these deities (through oil and liver divination) that Enmedurranki, the ancient king of Sippar, was believed to have first received the secrets of heaven and earth, so that he could later pass them on to wise men in the cities of Sippar, Nippur and Babylon. ◆

fering and his grain offering, and the burnt offering of all the people of the land, and their grain offering and their drink offering. Splash against this altar the blood of all the burnt offerings and sacrifices. But I will use the bronze altar for seeking guidance."[m] 16And Uriah the priest did just as King Ahaz had ordered.

17King Ahaz cut off the side panels and removed the basins from the movable stands. He removed the Sea from the bronze bulls that supported it and set it on a stone base.[n] 18He took away the Sabbath canopy[a] that had been built at the temple and removed the royal entryway outside the temple of the LORD, in deference to the king of Assyria.[o]

19As for the other events of the reign of Ahaz, and what he did, are they not written in the book of the annals of the kings of Judah? 20Ahaz rested with his ancestors and was buried with them in the City of David. And Hezekiah his son succeeded him as king.

Hoshea Last King of Israel

17:3-7pp — 2Ki 18:9-12

17 In the twelfth year of Ahaz king of Judah, Hoshea[p] son of Elah became king of Israel in Samaria, and he reigned nine years. 2He did evil in the eyes of the LORD, but not like the kings of Israel who preceded him.

3Shalmaneser[q] king of Assyria came up to attack Hoshea, who had been Shalmaneser's vassal and had paid him tribute. 4But the king of Assyria discovered that Hoshea was a traitor, for he had sent envoys to So[b] king of Egypt, and he no longer paid tribute to the king of Assyria, as he had done year by year. Therefore Shalmaneser seized him and put him in prison. 5The king of Assyria invaded the entire land, marched against Samaria and laid siege[r] to it for three years. 6In the ninth year of Hoshea, the king of Assyria captured Samaria[s] and deported[t] the Israelites to Assyria. He settled them in Halah, in Gozan[u] on the Habor River and in the towns of the Medes.

Israel Exiled Because of Sin

7All this took place because the Israelites had sinned[v] against the LORD their God, who had brought them up out of Egypt[w] from under the power of Pharaoh king of Egypt. They worshiped other gods 8and followed the practices of the nations[x] the LORD had driven out before them, as well as the practices that the kings of Israel had introduced. 9The Israelites secretly did things against the LORD their God that were not right. From watchtower to fortified city[y] they built themselves high places in all their towns. 10They set up sacred stones and Asherah poles[z] on every high hill and under every spreading tree.[a] 11At every high place they burned incense, as the nations whom the LORD had driven out before them had done. They did wicked things that aroused the LORD's anger. 12They worshiped idols,[b] though the LORD had said, "You shall not do this."[c] 13The LORD warned Israel and Judah through all his prophets and seers:[c] "Turn from your evil ways.[d] Observe my commands and decrees, in accordance with the entire Law that I commanded your ancestors to obey and that I delivered to you through my servants the prophets."

14But they would not listen and were as stiff-necked[e] as their ancestors, who did not trust in the LORD their God. 15They rejected his decrees and the covenant[f] he had made with their ancestors and the statutes he had warned them to keep. They followed worthless idols[g] and themselves became worthless. They imitated the nations[h] around them although the LORD had ordered them, "Do not do as they do."

16They forsook all the commands of the LORD their God and made for themselves two idols cast in the shape of calves,[i] and

16:15 [m] 1Sa 9:9
16:17 [n] 1Ki 7:27
16:18 [o] Eze 16:28
17:1 [p] 2Ki 15:30
17:3 [q] 2Ki 18:9-12; Hos 10:14
17:5 [r] Hos 13:16
17:6 [s] Hos 13:16 [t] Dt 28:36,64; 2Ki 18:10-11
[u] 1Ch 5:26
17:7 [v] Jos 23:16; Jdg 6:10 [w] Ex 14:15-31
17:8 [x] Lev 18:3; Dt 18:9; 2Ki 16:3
17:9 [y] 2Ki 18:8
17:10 [z] Ex 34:13; Mic 5:14 [a] 1Ki 14:23
17:12 [b] Ex 20:4
17:13 [c] 1Sa 9:9 [d] Jer 18:11; 25:5; 35:15
17:14 [e] Ex 32:9; Dt 31:27; Ac 7:51
17:15 [f] Dt 29:25 [g] Dt 32:21; Ro 1:21-23 [h] Dt 12:30-31
17:16 [i] 1Ki 12:28

[a] 18 Or *the dais of his throne* (see Septuagint) [b] 4 *So* is probably an abbreviation for *Osorkon.* [c] 12 Exodus 20:4,5

17:4 *So king of Egypt.* As well as failing to render tribute to Assyria, Hoshea had also entered a conspiracy with Egypt. The Egyptian ruler of the time is apparently named in this verse, although it is not certain that "So" is intended as a personal name rather than a place-name (perhaps "Sais"). The pharaoh in question may have been Osorkon IV (see NIV text note), the last pharaoh of the Dynasty 22 (730–715 BC, with "So" being an abbreviation of Osorkon) or Tefnakht, founder of the overlapping and rising Dynasty 24 (727–720 BC), which was based in Sais.
17:6 *He settled them in Halah, in Gozan on the Habor River and in the towns of the Medes.* Deportation became a standard tactic of Assyrian kings after Tiglath-Pileser III (see note on 15:29), which was in part designed to reduce the chance of future trouble from a conquered city or state by dispelling any strong sense of community and leadership. *Halah.* Possibly a town and district northeast of Nineveh. *Gozan.* Tell Halaf on the modern Turkish-Syrian border. *Habor River.* A tributary of the Euphrates River now named al-Khabur. *Medes.* A people of central western Iran who would shortly ally themselves with the Babylonians to overthrow the Assyrian Empire in 612 BC.
17:9 *high places.* See notes on 1Ki 3:2; 11:7.
17:10 *sacred stones and Asherah poles.* See notes on 1Ki 14:23; Dt 7:5.
17:16 *calves.* See notes on 10:29; 1Ki 12:28–29. *Baal.* See the article "Baal," p. 600. *starry hosts.* The worship of the starry hosts, along with sorcery (v. 17), has not been introduced to us thus far in the narrative. Both will appear in the account of Manasseh's reign (21:3–6; see note on 21:3; see also the article "Manasseh of Judah and Ashurbanipal," p. 665).

2 KINGS 17:3–6

SHALMANESER

Hoshea reigned only a few years in Israel before a failure to render tribute to Assyria brought down on him the wrath of Tiglath-Pileser's successor, Shalmaneser V (727–722 BC), who imprisoned Hoshea and laid siege to Samaria. It is Shalmaneser who is identified in Biblical tradition as the eventual conqueror of Samaria around 722 BC after a three-year siege (2Ki 17:5–6; 18:9–10). Extra-Biblical tradition possibly speaks with two voices on the subject, however. The Babylonian Chronicle does indeed identify Shalmaneser V as Samaria's besieger and conqueror, but Shalmaneser's successor, Sargon II (722–705 BC), also takes this honor for himself in his inscriptions.

It is possible that Sargon absorbed Shalmaneser's conquest of Samaria into his own record in order to claim more success for himself than he actually achieved and perhaps also to give himself legitimacy (as a usurper of the Assyrian throne) by connecting himself with the previous reign. It was certainly Sargon and not Shalmaneser who brought the final end to Israelite independence, however, following up the successes of his predecessor in Syria and Canaan, consolidating them, and transforming Israel into the Assyrian province of Samerina. This ongoing campaign included Sargon's own brief siege and speedy reconquest of Samaria in 720 BC.

The Babylonian Chronicle is an important source for ancient Near Eastern history in the Assyrian period from 745 BC on; it is a year-by-year account of political events as they affected the region of Babylonia; it also provides useful cross-references for the claims of Assyrian texts. The Chronicle touches on the events surrounding the fall of the city of Samaria in 722 BC.

Sargon II's own inscriptions, however—in addition to celebrating a later victory in 720 BC over a coalition of forces that included the army of Samaria—appear to claim the conquest of Samaria in 722 BC for himself in a summary inscription from the wall slabs of some of the rooms in Sargon's palace in Dur Sharrukin (modern Khorsabad) as well as on a text from a pavement slab for the gates at Dur Sharrukin. ◆

an Asherah[j] pole. They bowed down to
all the starry hosts,[k] and they worshiped
Baal.[l] 17 They sacrificed[m] their sons and
daughters in the fire. They practiced divination and sought omens[n] and sold[o]
themselves to do evil in the eyes of the
LORD, arousing his anger.
18 So the LORD was very angry with Israel and removed them from his presence.
Only the tribe of Judah was left, 19 and
even Judah did not keep the commands
of the LORD their God. They followed the
practices Israel had introduced.[p] 20 Therefore the LORD rejected all the people of Israel; he afflicted them and gave them into
the hands of plunderers,[q] until he thrust
them from his presence.
21 When he tore[r] Israel away from the
house of David, they made Jeroboam son
of Nebat their king.[s] Jeroboam enticed
Israel away from following the LORD and
caused them to commit a great sin. 22 The
Israelites persisted in all the sins of Jeroboam and did not turn away from them
23 until the LORD removed them from his
presence, as he had warned through all his

17:16 [j] 1Ki 14:15, 23 [k] 2Ki 21:3 [l] 1Ki 16:31
17:17 [m] Dt 18:10-12; 2Ki 16:3 [n] Lev 19:26 [o] 1Ki 21:20
17:19 [p] 1Ki 14:22-23; 2Ki 16:3
17:20 [q] 2Ki 15:29
17:21 [r] 1Ki 11:11 [s] 1Ki 12:20

17:17 *sacrificed their sons and daughters in the fire.* See notes on 3:27; 16:3; 1Ki 11:5; Lev 20:2; Jer 7:31). *divination.* See notes on Ge 30:27; Dt 18:10–11; see also the article "Balaam," p. 268. *sought omens.* Prohibited by Dt 18:10 and probably itself is to be understood as divination (see note on 2Ki 16:15), as implied by the NIV translation in Dt 18:10: "Let no one be found among you who sacrifices their son or daughter in the fire, who practices divination or sorcery, interprets omens." (Note further that this same Hebrew term is translated "divination" in Ge 30:27; 44:5,15). No doubt a distinction is intended in Dt 18:10 (see note there) between two different kinds of divination, but we cannot be sure what the distinction is.

EXILE OF THE NORTHERN KINGDOM

The mass deportation policy of the Assyrians was a companion piece to the brutal and calculated terror initiated by Ashurnasirpal and followed by all his successors. It was intended to forestall revolts but, like all Draconian measures, it merely spread misery and engendered hatred. In the end, it hastened the disintegration of the Assyrian Empire.

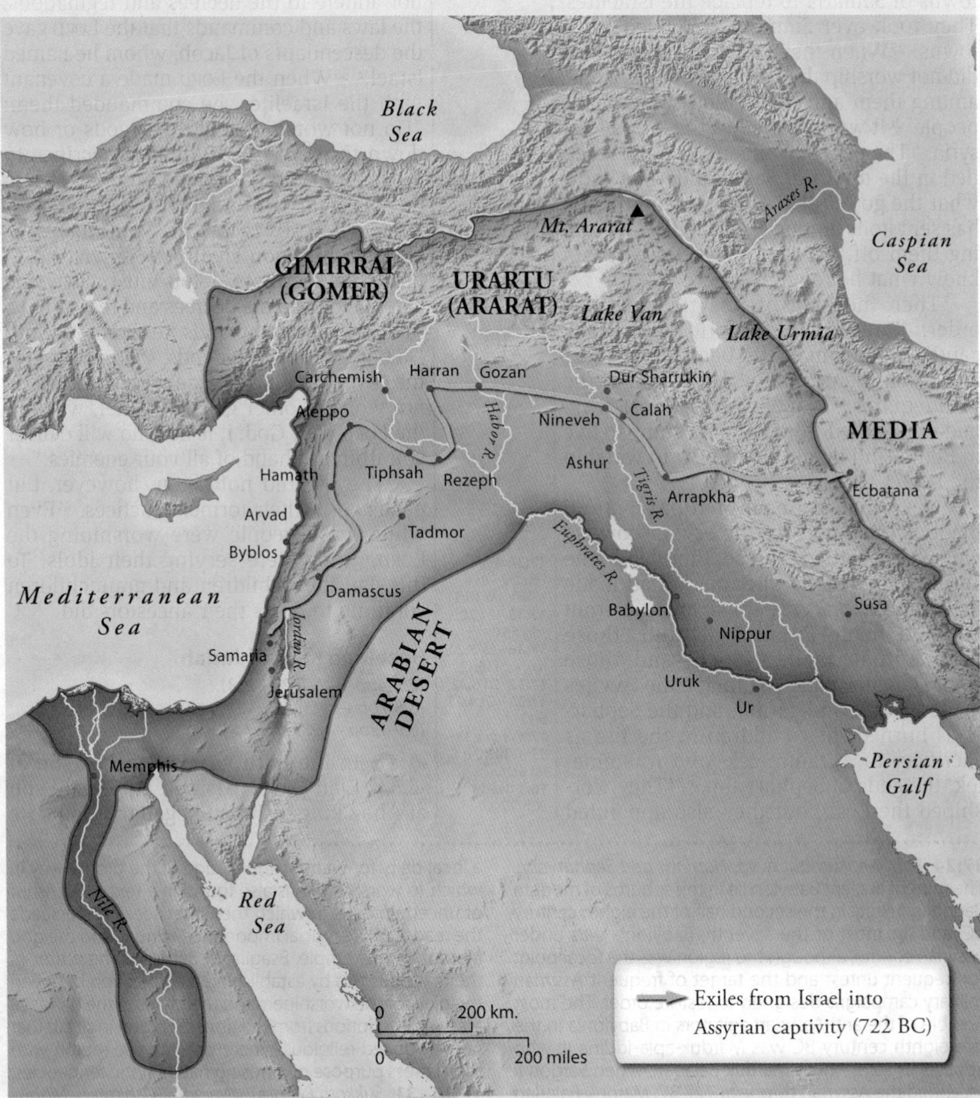

There is some evidence that Israel experienced its first deportations under Tiglath-Pileser III (745–727 BC), a cruelty repeated by Sargon II (721–705 BC) at the time of the fall of Samaria. The latter king's inscriptions boast of carrying away 27,290 inhabitants of the city "as plunder." According to 2Ki 17:6, they were sent to Assyria, to Halah, to Gozan on the Habor River, and apparently to the eastern frontiers of the empire (to the towns of the Medes, most probably somewhere in the vicinity of Ecbatana, the modern Hamadan).

The sequel is provided by the inscriptions of Sargon: "The Arabs who live far away in the desert, who know neither overseers nor officials, and who had not yet brought their tribute to any king, I deported ... and settled them in Samaria."

Much mythology has developed around the theme of the so-called ten lost tribes of Israel. A close examination of Assyrian records reveals that the deportations approximated only a limited percentage of the population, usually consisting of noble families. Agricultural workers, no doubt the majority, were deliberately left to care for the crops (compare the Babylonian practice, 2Ki 24:14; 25:12).

servants the prophets. So the people of Israel were taken from their homeland into exile in Assyria, and they are still there.

Samaria Resettled

24The king of Assyria[t] brought people from Babylon, Kuthah, Avva, Hamath and Sepharvaim[u] and settled them in the towns of Samaria to replace the Israelites. They took over Samaria and lived in its towns. 25When they first lived there, they did not worship the LORD; so he sent lions[v] among them and they killed some of the people. 26It was reported to the king of Assyria: "The people you deported and resettled in the towns of Samaria do not know what the god of that country requires. He has sent lions among them, which are killing them off, because the people do not know what he requires."

27Then the king of Assyria gave this order: "Have one of the priests you took captive from Samaria go back to live there and teach the people what the god of the land requires." 28So one of the priests who had been exiled from Samaria came to live in Bethel and taught them how to worship the LORD.

29Nevertheless, each national group made its own gods in the several towns[w] where they settled, and set them up in the shrines[x] the people of Samaria had made at the high places.[y] 30The people from Babylon made Sukkoth Benoth, those from Kuthah made Nergal, and those from Hamath made Ashima; 31the Avvites made Nibhaz and Tartak, and the Sepharvites burned their children in the fire as sacrifices to Adrammelek[z] and Anammelek, the gods of Sepharvaim.[a] 32They worshiped the LORD, but they also appointed all sorts[b] of their own people to officiate for them as priests in the shrines at the high places. 33They worshiped the LORD, but they also served their own gods in accordance with the customs of the nations from which they had been brought.

34To this day they persist in their former practices. They neither worship the LORD nor adhere to the decrees and regulations, the laws and commands that the LORD gave the descendants of Jacob, whom he named Israel.[c] 35When the LORD made a covenant with the Israelites, he commanded them: "Do not worship[d] any other gods or bow down to them, serve them or sacrifice to them. 36But the LORD, who brought you up out of Egypt with mighty power and outstretched arm,[e] is the one you must worship. To him you shall bow down and to him offer sacrifices. 37You must always be careful[f] to keep the decrees and regulations, the laws and commands he wrote for you. Do not worship other gods. 38Do not forget[g] the covenant I have made with you, and do not worship other gods. 39Rather, worship the LORD your God; it is he who will deliver you from the hand of all your enemies."

40They would not listen, however, but persisted in their former practices. 41Even while these people were worshiping the LORD,[h] they were serving their idols. To this day their children and grandchildren continue to do as their ancestors did.

Hezekiah King of Judah

18:2-4pp — 2Ch 29:1-2; 31:1
18:5-7pp — 2Ch 31:20-21
18:9-12pp — 2Ki 17:3-7

18 In the third year of Hoshea son of Elah king of Israel, Hezekiah[i] son of Ahaz king of Judah began to reign. 2He

17:24 [t] Ezr 4:2, 10 [u] 2Ki 18:34
17:25 [v] Ge 37:20
17:29 [w] Jer 2:28 [x] 1Ki 12:31 [y] Mic 4:5
17:31 [z] 2Ki 19:37 [a] ver 24
17:32 [b] 1Ki 12:31
17:34 [c] Ge 32:28; 35:10; 1Ki 18:31
17:35 [d] Ex 20:5; Jdg 6:10
17:36 [e] Ex 3:20; 6:6; Ps 136:12
17:37 [f] Dt 5:32
17:38 [g] Dt 4:23; 6:12
17:41 [h] ver 32-33; 1Ki 18:21; Mt 6:24
18:1 [i] Isa 1:1; 2Ch 28:27

17:24 *Babylon, Kuthah, Avva, Hamath and Sepharvaim.* The ruins of ancient Babylon lie in the suburbs of modern Baghdad in Iraq. In the second half of the eighth century BC, and for most of the seventh, Babylonia was under Assyrian control, although the region was the focal point for frequent unrest and the target of frequent Assyrian military campaigns designed to restore order. The most notable of the anti-Assyrian agitators in Babylonia in the late eighth century BC was Marduk-apla-iddina II, who appears in 20:12–19 as Marduk-Baladan. When Sargon II ascended the Assyrian throne in 722 BC, Marduk-Baladan had himself crowned king at Babylon. It is the ongoing attempts to depose Marduk-Baladan that provide a possible context for deportations to the cities of Samaria from Babylon and Kuthah (commonly identified with Tell Ibrahim, 20 miles [32 kilometers] northeast of Babylon).

17:25 *lions.* Wild beasts were one of the ways deities could express displeasure, along with famine and disease. Devastation by wild animals was linked to treaty violations, and Assyrian negative omens from the period commonly refer to lions and wolves.

17:26 *The people ... do not know what the god of that country requires.* The idea that people could run afoul of a local deity for want of knowledge of the proper way in which to worship him is also found in a text from Ashur of uncertain date, in which the writer seeks to persuade the reader of the crucial importance of honoring the god Marduk in his temple, Esagila, in Babylon. The writer of the text does this by establishing a connection between the piety of the worshipers and their fates at the hands of Marduk. Inscriptions from the time of Sargon indicate that he introduced religious syncretism into the region with the express purpose of diffusing nationalistic tendencies.

17:30–31 *Sukkoth Benoth ... Nergal ... Ashima ... Nibhaz and Tartak ... Adrammelek and Anammelek.* The only deities in this list who are clearly known from other sources are the West Semitic god Ashima and the Mesopotamian god Nergal, who was an underworld god associated with famine, drought, plague and death and whose cult was centered in the city of Kuthah. The combination Sukkoth Benoth alludes at least to the goddess Banitu and possibly also to Sakkut (Ninurta). Nibhaz and Tartak may be Elamite deities, while Adrammelek and Anammelek may be Phoenician and Emarite gods, respectively.

18:1 *Hezekiah ... began to reign.* With the fall of Samaria and the incorporation of much of Syria and Palestine into

was twenty-five years old when he became king, and he reigned in Jerusalem
twenty-nine years.[j] His mother's name
was Abijah[a] daughter of Zechariah. 3He
did what was right in the eyes of the LORD,
just as his father David[k] had done. 4He removed[l] the high places, smashed the sacred stones[m] and cut down the Asherah
poles. He broke into pieces the bronze
snake[n] Moses had made, for up to that
time the Israelites had been burning incense to it. (It was called Nehushtan.[b])
5Hezekiah trusted[o] in the LORD, the
God of Israel. There was no one like him
among all the kings of Judah, either before him or after him. 6He held fast[p] to
the LORD and did not stop following him;
he kept the commands the LORD had giv-
en Moses. 7And the LORD was with him;
he was successful[q] in whatever he undertook. He rebelled[r] against the king of Assyria and did not serve him. 8From watchtower to fortified city,[s] he defeated the
Philistines, as far as Gaza and its territory.
9In King Hezekiah's fourth year,[t] which
was the seventh year of Hoshea son of
Elah king of Israel, Shalmaneser king of
Assyria marched against Samaria and laid
siege to it. 10At the end of three years the
Assyrians took it. So Samaria was captured in Hezekiah's sixth year, which was
the ninth year of Hoshea king of Israel.

18:2 [j] Isa 38:5 **18:3** [k] Isa 38:5 **18:4** [l] 2Ch 31:1 [m] Ex 23:24 [n] Nu 21:9 **18:5** [o] 2Ki 19:10; 23:25 **18:6** [p] Dt 10:20; Jos 23:8 **18:7** [q] Ge 39:3; 1Sa 18:14 [r] 2Ki 16:7 **18:8** [s] 2Ki 17:9; Isa 14:29 **18:9** [t] Isa 1:1

[a] 2 Hebrew *Abi*, a variant of *Abijah* [b] 4 *Nehushtan* sounds like the Hebrew for both *bronze* and *snake*.

the Assyrian Empire, only Judah was left as a relatively independent remnant of what had been Israel. Although Ahaz's son Hezekiah attained regal status just a few years before the end of the northern kingdom (727 BC), he was not yet sole ruler of the kingdom; his 14th year in v. 13 is in fact correlated with Sennacherib of Assyria's invasion of Judah in 701 BC, implying a sole accession date of 714 BC and a period of coregency with Ahaz from 727–714 BC. **18:4** *high places.* See notes on 1Ki 3:2; 11:7. Even the most righteous of Judahite kings thus far had always failed to remove the "high places" (man-made structures, sometimes located on mountain tops or on raised platforms, within which or upon which cultic acts were performed), and the possibility always existed, therefore, that they would become focal points for the kind of slide from true worship of Yahweh into apostasy that occurred during the reign of Ahaz (cf. 16:4). Hezekiah now appears as the one who addresses this issue, although it is not clear from the evidently generalized and perhaps hyperbolic language of the text what this closure of the high places might have looked like "on the ground" in terms of its severity and geographic extent. *sacred stones ... Asherah poles.* See notes on 1Ki 14:23; Dt 7:5.

2 KINGS 18:4

NEHUSHTAN

The bronze snake that Moses had made in the desert (Nu 21:4–9) had perhaps been deposited in the temple in Jerusalem, like other religious items from the Mosaic age (cf. 1Ki 8:1–9). Nehushtan is not presented in the OT tradition as having originally been made for worship (see note on Nu 21:8); nor is it likely that the authors of Kings meant that it was, in fact, worshiped continually even in the monarchic period, but it eventually became in practice a focal point for idolatry, perhaps because of the association of snakes with the goddess Asherah. Snakes fashioned from copper alloy or bronze and used as cultic images have been found throughout the ancient Near East, and in general the snake was a popular religious symbol that adorned many artifacts (see notes on Ex 7:10). A particularly striking copper alloy serpent with gold foil overlay was found at Timna, about 19 miles (30 kilometers) north of Eilat/Elath. Snakes often appear in this religious iconography in the hands of a god or goddess; among these is the goddess Asherah, who is sometimes called Qdš in the Ugaritic texts and is attested by this name in Egypt, where she appears on reliefs and amulets and is characteristically represented holding snakes in one hand and sometimes both hands. An eighth-century BC bronze bowl found at ancient Calah in Assyria, which perhaps came there as tribute to Tiglath-Pileser III from Hezekiah's father (Ahaz), has engraved on its rim a winged snake mounted on a standard of just the kind envisaged by our Biblical texts. ◆

11 The king[u] of Assyria deported Israel to
Assyria and settled them in Halah, in Gozan on the Habor River and in towns of
the Medes. 12 This happened because they
had not obeyed the LORD their God, but
had violated his covenant[v]—all that Moses the servant of the LORD commanded.[w]
They neither listened to the commands[x]
nor carried them out.
13 In the fourteenth year of King Hezekiah's reign, Sennacherib king of Assyria attacked all the fortified cities of Judah[y] and
captured them. 14 So Hezekiah king of Judah sent this message to the king of Assyria
at Lachish: "I have done wrong.[z] Withdraw
from me, and I will pay whatever you demand of me." The king of Assyria exacted
from Hezekiah king of Judah three hundred
talents[a] of silver and thirty talents[b] of gold.
15 So Hezekiah gave[a] him all the silver that
was found in the temple of the LORD and in
the treasuries of the royal palace.
16 At this time Hezekiah king of Judah
stripped off the gold with which he had
covered the doors and doorposts of the
temple of the LORD, and gave it to the king
of Assyria.

18:11 [u] Isa 37:12
18:12 [v] 2Ki 17:15 [w] Da 9:6, 10 [x] 1Ki 9:6
18:13 [y] 2Ch 32:1; Isa 1:7; Mic 1:9
18:14 [z] Isa 24:5
18:15 [a] 1Ki 15:18; 2Ki 16:8
18:17 [b] Isa 20:1 [c] 2Ki 20:20; 2Ch 32:4, 30; Isa 7:3
18:18 [d] 2Ki 19:2; Isa 22:20 [e] Isa 22:15

Sennacherib Threatens Jerusalem

18:13,17-37pp — Isa 36:1-22
18:17-35pp — 2Ch 32:9-19

17 The king of Assyria sent his supreme
commander,[b] his chief officer and his field
commander with a large army, from Lachish to King Hezekiah at Jerusalem. They
came up to Jerusalem and stopped at the
aqueduct of the Upper Pool,[c] on the road
to the Washerman's Field. 18 They called
for the king; and Eliakim[d] son of Hilkiah
the palace administrator, Shebna[e] the secretary, and Joah son of Asaph the recorder
went out to them.
19 The field commander said to them,
"Tell Hezekiah:

"'This is what the great king, the
king of Assyria, says: On what are
you basing this confidence of yours?
20 You say you have the counsel and
the might for war—but you speak
only empty words. On whom are you
depending, that you rebel against
me? 21 Look, I know you are depend-

[a] *14* That is, about 11 tons or about 10 metric tons
[b] *14* That is, about 1 ton or about 1 metric ton

18:13 *Sennacherib ... attacked all the fortified cities of Judah and captured them.* After Sargon II's death in 705 BC, the new Assyrian king Sennacherib (705–681 BC) was involved in a campaign in southern Mesopotamia (703–702 BC) against the erstwhile king of Babylon Marduk-apla-iddina II (Biblical Marduk-Baladan), who was leading a revolt there in renewed pursuit of his own royal claims. It was only after dealing with this closer threat that Sennacherib was able to turn his attention to Syria and Palestine (in 701 BC). The rebellion there quickly collapsed, according to Assyrian records, and Hezekiah found himself without effective allies and without fortresses.
18:14–16 Sennacherib's records report that Hezekiah paid about 30 talents (1 ton or 0.9 metric tons) of gold and 800 talents of silver (3 tons or 2.7 metric tons). Assyrian texts are more detailed, specifying a wide variety of persons and objects.
18:14 *Lachish.* One of the most important cities in Judah, it guarded a main route from the coastal plain to the Hebron hills (see note on 14:19), and it received particular attention from Sennacherib during this campaign. The main Assyrian attack was carried out in the southwest corner of the city—the only part of the city not protected by a deep valley—where a siege ramp of boulders was erected to allow the approach of the Assyrian forces. The city was eventually captured and burned to the ground.

When King Sennacherib later in his reign constructed his royal palace at Nineveh, he commissioned a set of stone reliefs to commemorate his famous conquest of the city of Lachish. They depict the besieged city itself (portrayed in the center of the series), the attack on it, Assyrian soldiers carrying plunder away from the city, the deported inhabitants leaving it, Sennacherib sitting on his throne facing the city and, finally, the Assyrian camp. The detail is extraordinary and gives us a vivid impression of these events.

Inscribed in a rectangular block to the left of the figure of the king are the following words: "Sennacherib, king of the world, king of Assyria, sat upon a *nimedu*-throne and passed in review the plunder from Lachish." The choice of the assault on Lachish for this impressive artistic representation is interesting in that it serves to underline (without meaning to do so) that Sennacherib did not capture Jerusalem.
18:17 *sent his supreme commander, his chief officer and his field commander.* While still besieging Lachish and having apparently decided after all not to accept Hezekiah's attempt to persuade him to withdraw (vv. 14–15), Sennacherib sent an army to Jerusalem to pressure Hezekiah into a full surrender. We have an analogy to the practice of besieging a major city while continuing operations elsewhere in the surrounding region in Tiglath-Pileser III's campaigns in Syria in 743–740 BC. *supreme commander.* The *turtanu* (Hebrew *tartan*), one of two persons in the Assyrian army with this title who often led campaigns on behalf of the emperor. *chief officer.* The *rab-saris* (lit. "chief eunuch"), who was often dispatched on campaigns at the head of Assyrian forces; the title does not necessarily indicate that he himself was physically a eunuch. *field commander.* The *rab-shakeh* (lit. "chief cupbearer") did not normally take part in military campaigns, but he would have accompanied the emperor as a personal attendant. His presence in this delegation is no doubt to be explained in terms of his linguistic abilities, as he spoke the local language. He may well himself have been of Aramean or Israelite origin, for although his first speech in vv. 19–35 reveals many parallels with the Neo-Assyrian annals, he clearly not only knew the local language, but also displayed good knowledge of Judahite customs.
18:18 *palace administrator ... secretary ... recorder.* Three of the most important of the Judahite officials went out to parley with the three Assyrian officials. *palace administrator.* See note on 10:5. *secretary.* In charge of royal correspondence and, as such, was a royal counselor. *recorder.* Also a royal counselor, somewhat akin to a modern secretary of state but absorbing also the role of the king's official spokesman.
18:21 *Egypt.* The Assyrian push to the Mediterranean

2 KINGS 18:17 — 19:37

HEZEKIAH AND ASSYRIA

Since at least 733–732 BC, and probably since near the end of Azariah's reign, Judah was in tributary relationship with Assyria and had avoided the fate meted out to other states in the region — absorption into the Assyrian provincial system and the deportation of significant segments of their populations (especially the leading members of communities). Hezekiah, however, was not his father (Ahaz), and eventually he rebelled against his Assyrian overlord.

Hezekiah might have begun on this path as early as 720 BC, when one of Sargon II's inscriptions describes Sargon as "the subduer of the country Judah which lies far away," apparently in connection with a campaign undertaken to crush a revolt that had broken out in Syria and Canaan under the leadership of Hamath. If the so-called Azekah Inscription belongs to Sargon II rather than his successor Sennacherib, Hezekiah may also have been involved immediately after his sole accession to the throne (714 BC) in a revolt against Assyria spearheaded by the Philistine city of Ashdod that led to the absorption of Ashdod into the Assyrian provincial system in 712 BC. However, the first event described in Assyrian records that can be securely related to the statement in 2Ki 18:7 that Hezekiah "rebelled against the king of Assyria" is the widespread revolt that broke out in Syria-Palestine, as in other parts of the empire, after Sargon's unexpected death on the battlefield in 705 BC.

Assyrian records from Sargon II's reign tell us of an effort by the Philistine city of Ashdod to woo "neighboring kings" away from Assyria, and of an Assyrian assault on Ashdod and other Philistine cities. The only clear evidence that any attempt to win Judah over was successful, however, is the so-called Azekah Inscription, whose relevance to these events is disputed. If the Assyrian king in question is Sargon, then this inscription probably relates to his campaign against Ashdod and Judah. If Judah was involved, we must assume that Hezekiah came to some arrangement with Assyria before judgment descended, for there is no evidence that Judah suffered any Assyrian penalties after the revolt was over; only Azekah (Tell Zakariya) is said to have been destroyed. The text may in fact relate, however, to the later invasion of Canaan by Sennacherib in 701 BC, or its two parts may not belong together at all. Sennacherib's own account of the campaign of 701 BC is found in its earliest form on the Rassam Cylinder, which dates from immediately after the events (700 BC). ◆

ing on Egypt,[f] that splintered reed
of a staff,[g] which pierces the hand
of anyone who leans on it! Such is
Pharaoh king of Egypt to all who depend on him. 22But if you say to me,
"We are depending on the LORD our
God" — isn't he the one whose high
places and altars Hezekiah removed,
saying to Judah and Jerusalem, "You
must worship before this altar in Jerusalem"?
23" 'Come now, make a bargain
with my master, the king of Assyria:
I will give you two thousand horses — if you can put riders on them!
24How can you repulse one officer[h]

18:21 [f] Isa 20:5; Eze 29:6 [g] Isa 30:5, 7
18:24 [h] Isa 10:8

in pursuit of sea trade, begun with the campaigns of Tiglath-Pileser III, inevitably brought Assyria into conflict with Egypt. Throughout the later eighth and early seventh centuries BC, the kingdoms in Syria and Palestine often looked to Egypt for help in resisting the Assyrians. Hoshea of northern Israel had sought military support against the Assyrians from "So King of Egypt" just prior to the fall of Samaria (17:4), and in 712 BC it was to Egypt that the rebel ruler of the city of Ashdod fled when all was lost: "When Yamani heard about the advance of my [Sargon II's] expedition ... he fled into the territory of Egypt ... and his hiding-place could not be detected." In 701 BC, Hezekiah also looks to Egypt for help.

of the least of my master's officials,
even though you are depending on
Egypt for chariots and horsemen[a]?
25Furthermore, have I come to attack
and destroy this place without word
from the LORD?[i] The LORD himself told
me to march against this country and
destroy it.' "

26Then Eliakim son of Hilkiah, and
Shebna and Joah said to the field commander,
"Please speak to your servants
in Aramaic,[j] since we understand it. Don't
speak to us in Hebrew in the hearing of
the people on the wall."
27But the commander replied, "Was it
only to your master and you that my master
sent me to say these things, and not to
the people sitting on the wall—who, like
you, will have to eat their own excrement
and drink their own urine?"
28Then the commander stood and called
out in Hebrew, "Hear the word of the great
king, the king of Assyria! 29This is what
the king says: Do not let Hezekiah deceive[k]
you. He cannot deliver you from my hand.
30Do not let Hezekiah persuade you to trust
in the LORD when he says, 'The LORD will
surely deliver us; this city will not be given
into the hand of the king of Assyria.'
31"Do not listen to Hezekiah. This is
what the king of Assyria says: Make peace
with me and come out to me. Then each
of you will eat fruit from your own vine
and fig tree[l] and drink water from your
own cistern,[m] 32until I come and take you
to a land like your own—a land of grain
and new wine, a land of bread and vineyards,
a land of olive trees and honey.
Choose life[n] and not death!
"Do not listen to Hezekiah, for he is
misleading you when he says, 'The LORD
will deliver us.' 33Has the god[o] of any nation
ever delivered his land from the hand
of the king of Assyria? 34Where are the
gods of Hamath[p] and Arpad?[q] Where are
the gods of Sepharvaim, Hena and Ivvah?
Have they rescued Samaria from my hand?
35Who of all the gods of these countries
has been able to save his land from me?
How then can the LORD deliver Jerusalem
from my hand?"[r]

18:25 [i] 2Ki 19:6, 22 **18:26** [j] Ezr 4:7 **18:29** [k] 2Ki 19:10 **18:31** [l] Nu 13:23; 1Ki 4:25 [m] Jer 14:3; La 4:4 **18:32** [n] Dt 8:7-9; 30:19 **18:33** [o] 2Ki 19:12; Isa 10:10-11 **18:34** [p] 2Ki 17:24; 19:13 [q] Isa 10:9 **18:35** [r] Ps 2:1-2

36But the people remained silent and
said nothing in reply, because the king
had commanded, "Do not answer him."
37Then Eliakim son of Hilkiah the palace
administrator, Shebna the secretary,
and Joah son of Asaph the recorder went
to Hezekiah, with their clothes torn,[s] and
told him what the field commander had
said.

Jerusalem's Deliverance Foretold

19:1-13pp — Isa 37:1-13

19 When King Hezekiah heard this, he
tore[t] his clothes and put on sackcloth
and went into the temple of the LORD.
2He sent Eliakim the palace administrator,
Shebna the secretary and the leading
priests, all wearing sackcloth, to the prophet
Isaiah[u] son of Amoz. 3They told him,
"This is what Hezekiah says: This day is
a day of distress and rebuke and disgrace,
as when children come to the moment of
birth and there is no strength to deliver
them. 4It may be that the LORD your God
will hear all the words of the field commander,
whom his master, the king of Assyria,
has sent to ridicule[v] the living God,
and that he will rebuke[w] him for the words
the LORD your God has heard. Therefore
pray for the remnant that still survives."
5When King Hezekiah's officials came
to Isaiah, 6Isaiah said to them, "Tell your
master, 'This is what the LORD says: Do
not be afraid of what you have heard—
those words with which the underlings
of the king of Assyria have blasphemed[x]
me. 7Listen! When he hears a certain report,
I will make him want to return to his
own country, and there I will have him cut
down with the sword.[y]' "
8When the field commander heard that
the king of Assyria had left Lachish,[z] he
withdrew and found the king fighting
against Libnah.
9Now Sennacherib received a report
that Tirhakah, the king of Cush,[b] was
marching out to fight against him. So he
again sent messengers to Hezekiah with
this word: 10"Say to Hezekiah king of Judah:
Do not let the god you depend[a] on

18:37 [s] 2Ki 6:30 **19:1** [t] Ge 37:34; 1Ki 21:27; 2Ch 32:20-22 **19:2** [u] Isa 1:1 **19:4** [v] 2Ki 18:35 [w] 2Sa 16:12 **19:6** [x] 2Ki 18:25 **19:7** [y] ver 37 **19:8** [z] 2Ki 18:14 **19:10** [a] 2Ki 18:5

[a] 24 Or *charioteers* [b] 9 That is, the upper Nile region

18:26 *Please speak ... in Aramaic.* Aramaic was the language of the Assyrian Empire west of the Euphrates and would have been understood by the educated royal officials, but not by the ordinary people on the city wall. The Assyrians are trying to appeal to the people over the heads of their rulers, however, and so their choice of Hebrew is understandable. They want the people to be fully aware of the hopelessness of their situation and the consequences of a long siege (they will "eat their own excrement and drink their own urine," v. 27). Perhaps the people will even turn on their leaders.

19:9 *Tirhakah, the king of Cush.* At some point during Sennacherib's 701 BC campaign, as the Biblical and Assyrian records agree, an Egyptian army marched into Palestine to aid the rebels. The Egyptian forces were led by Taharqa (Hebrew "Tirhakah"), who would not become pharaoh for another 11 years (690–664 BC), but is referred to here under his later title. He was in fact a Cushite and the third king of the Twenty-Fifth Dynasty in Egypt, founded by Shabako (716–702 BC), who was then followed by Shebitku (702–690 BC). These kings were descendants of the Nubian/Cushite rulers who had pushed north toward

deceive[b] you when he says, 'Jerusalem
will not be given into the hands of the
king of Assyria.' 11Surely you have heard
what the kings of Assyria have done to all
the countries, destroying them completely.
And will you be delivered? 12Did the gods
of the nations that were destroyed by my
predecessors deliver[c] them—the gods of
Gozan,[d] Harran,[e] Rezeph and the people
of Eden who were in Tel Assar? 13Where is
the king of Hamath or the king of Arpad?
Where are the kings of Lair, Sepharvaim,
Hena and Ivvah?"[f]

Hezekiah's Prayer

19:14-19pp — Isa 37:14-20

14Hezekiah received the letter from the
messengers and read it. Then he went up
to the temple of the LORD and spread it out
before the LORD. 15And Hezekiah prayed
to the LORD: "LORD, the God of Israel, enthroned between the cherubim,[g] you alone
are God over all the kingdoms of the earth.
You have made heaven and earth. 16Give
ear,[h] LORD, and hear;[i] open your eyes,[j]
LORD, and see; listen to the words Sennacherib has sent to ridicule the living God.

17"It is true, LORD, that the Assyrian
kings have laid waste these nations and
their lands. 18They have thrown their gods
into the fire and destroyed them, for they
were not gods[k] but only wood and stone,
fashioned by human hands.[l] 19Now, LORD
our God, deliver us from his hand, so that
all the kingdoms[m] of the earth may know[n]
that you alone, LORD, are God."

Isaiah Prophesies Sennacherib's Fall

19:20-37pp — Isa 37:21-38
19:35-37pp — 2Ch 32:20-21

20Then Isaiah son of Amoz sent a message to Hezekiah: "This is what the LORD,
the God of Israel, says: I have heard[o] your
prayer concerning Sennacherib king of Assyria. 21This is the word that the LORD has
spoken against him:

"'Virgin Daughter[p] Zion
despises you and mocks[q] you.
Daughter Jerusalem
tosses her head[r] as you flee.
22Who is it you have ridiculed and
blasphemed?
Against whom have you raised your
voice
and lifted your eyes in pride?
Against the Holy One[s] of Israel!
23By your messengers
you have ridiculed the Lord.
And you have said,[t]
"With my many chariots[u]
I have ascended the heights of the
mountains,
the utmost heights of Lebanon.
I have cut down its tallest cedars,
the choicest of its junipers.
I have reached its remotest parts,
the finest of its forests.
24I have dug wells in foreign lands
and drunk the water there.
With the soles of my feet
I have dried up all the streams of
Egypt."

25"'Have you not heard?[v]
Long ago I ordained it.
In days of old I planned[w] it;
now I have brought it to pass,
that you have turned fortified cities
into piles of stone.[x]
26Their people, drained of power,
are dismayed[y] and put to shame.
They are like plants in the field,
like tender green shoots,[z]
like grass sprouting on the roof,
scorched[a] before it grows up.

27"'But I know[b] where you are
and when you come and go
and how you rage against me.

19:10 [b] 2Ki 18:29 **19:12** [c] 2Ki 18:33 [d] 2Ki 17:6 [e] Ge 11:31 **19:13** [f] 2Ki 18:34 **19:15** [g] Ex 25:22 **19:16** [h] Ps 31:2 [i] 1Ki 8:29 [j] ver 4; 2Ch 6:40 **19:18** [k] Isa 44:9-11; Jer 10:3-10 [l] Ps 115:4; Ac 17:29 **19:19** [m] 1Ki 8:43 [n] Ps 83:18 **19:20** [o] 2Ki 20:5 **19:21** [p] Jer 14:17; La 2:13 [q] Ps 22:7-8 [r] Job 16:4; Ps 109:25 **19:22** [s] Ps 71:22; Isa 5:24 **19:23** [t] Isa 10:18 [u] Ps 20:7 **19:25** [v] Isa 40:21,28 [w] Isa 10:5; 45:7 [x] Mic 1:6 **19:26** [y] Ps 6:10 [z] Isa 4:2 [a] Ps 129:6 **19:27** [b] Ps 139:1-4

Egypt (and had eventually annexed Egypt to Cush) in the same period that the Assyrians were pushing south toward the same destination. Tirhakah's entire life was marked by conflict with the Assyrians, from his leadership as a young man of the Egyptian forces helping Hezekiah through the period of his own rule, which ended in defeat at the hands of Esarhaddon and Ashurbanipal. The battle in 701 BC took place at Eltekeh, probably Khirbet el-Mukennah, about 12 miles (19 kilometers) east of the Mediterranean on the eastern border of the coastal plain. Sennacherib claims to have defeated the Egyptian force at Eltekeh, and we have no reason to disbelieve him. It may be that it was after this Assyrian victory that Hezekiah, in an attempt to buy more time, released Padi of Ekron, whom Sennacherib claims to have "made" come from Jerusalem and to have reestablished on his throne (see the article "Hezekiah and Assyria," p. 657).

19:15 *enthroned between the cherubim.* The OT envisions the God of Israel as dwelling in a special way (though not an exclusive way, cf. 1Ki 8:27–30) in the Jerusalem temple, and as being invisibly enthroned in the Most Holy Place on two enormous cherubim, overlaid with gold, which functioned as a covering for the ark of the covenant (1Ki 8:6–7; see note on Ex 25:16). The cherubim served as guardians to both royal and divine thrones in the ancient world (see note on Ex 25:18). Yahweh, however, was not visibly depicted on this throne.

19:23–24 *I have ascended the heights of the mountains ... I have dried up all the streams of Egypt.* Sennacherib never literally conquered Egypt, nor did he ever literally ascend the heights of the mountains with his chariots and cut down Lebanon's tallest trees, although he may have taken some cedar back to Assyria with him as his predecessor, Ashurnasirpal II, claims to have done. The point of the text is that Sennacherib thinks of himself as a god. These words reflect the exaggerated view that Sennacherib and other Assyrian kings often had of their own persons and their accomplishments.

28 Because you rage against me
and because your insolence has
reached my ears,
I will put my hook[c] in your nose
and my bit[d] in your mouth,
and I will make you return[e]
by the way you came.'

29 "This will be the sign[f] for you, Hezekiah:

"This year you will eat what grows by
itself,[g]
and the second year what springs
from that.
But in the third year sow and reap,
plant vineyards[h] and eat their fruit.
30 Once more a remnant of the kingdom
of Judah
will take root[i] below and bear fruit
above.
31 For out of Jerusalem will come a
remnant,
and out of Mount Zion a band of
survivors.

"The zeal[j] of the LORD Almighty will accomplish this.

32 "Therefore this is what the LORD says concerning the king of Assyria:

" 'He will not enter this city
or shoot an arrow here.
He will not come before it with shield
or build a siege ramp against it.
33 By the way that he came he will return;[k]
he will not enter this city,
declares the LORD.
34 I will defend[l] this city and save it,
for my sake and for the sake of
David[m] my servant.' "

35 That night the angel of the LORD[n] went out and put to death a hundred and eighty-five thousand in the Assyrian camp. When the people got up the next morning—there were all the dead bodies![o]
36 So Sennacherib king of Assyria broke camp and withdrew. He returned to Nineveh[p] and stayed there.
37 One day, while he was worshiping in the temple of his god Nisrok, his sons Adrammelek and Sharezer killed him with the sword,[q] and they escaped to the land of Ararat.[r] And Esarhaddon[s] his son succeeded him as king.

19:28 [c]Eze 19:9; 29:4 [d]Isa 30:28 [e]ver 33
19:29 [f]2Ki 20:8-9; Lk 2:12 [g]Lev 25:5 [h]Ps 107:37
19:30 [i]2Ch 32:22-23
19:31 [j]Isa 9:7
19:33 [k]ver 28
19:34 [l]2Ki 20:6 [m]1Ki 11:12-13
19:35 [n]Ex 12:23 [o]Job 24:24
19:36 [p]Ge 10:11; Jnh 1:2
19:37 [q]ver 7 [r]Ge 8:4 [s]Ezr 4:2

Hezekiah's Illness

20:1-11pp — 2Ch 32:24-26; Isa 38:1-8

20 In those days Hezekiah became ill and was at the point of death. The prophet Isaiah son of Amoz went to him and said, "This is what the LORD says: Put your house in order, because you are going to die; you will not recover."

19:28 *put my hook in your nose and my bit in your mouth.* This metaphor may reflect actual Assyrian practice. After his second campaign against Egypt in 671 BC, King Esarhaddon erected several victory steles, the most famous of which depicts Esarhaddon as leading two prisoners, apparently Baal I of Tyre and Taharqa/Tirhakah of Egypt, by ropes tied to a ring that pierced their lips. Ashurbanipal, his successor, further records an act of humiliation against Uate, king of Arabia, in which he "pierced his cheeks with the sharp-edged spear … put the ring to his jaw, placed a dog collar around his neck and made him guard the bar of the east gate of Nineveh."
19:29 *what grows by itself … what springs from that.* The sign that Judah will recover from the Assyrian assault is to be found in the way that the survivors will be provided for in the short term. Initially the people will only be able to survive because of the crops that spring up from what is already in the ground; but in the third year it will be possible to resume normal agricultural practice. The initial fragility of both human and economic conditions should not be a reason for despair.
19:32 *He will not … build a siege ramp against it.* According to Isaiah's message here to Hezekiah, Sennacherib will return home before the army encamped outside the city of Jerusalem can take military action against it—before an arrow is fired, a shield raised or a siege ramp is built against its walls. See the article "Siege Warfare," p. 1157.
19:35 *the angel of the LORD … put to death.* One of Ashurbanipal's inscriptions claims that the plague-god Erra wiped out an Arabian king and his army in response to a treaty violation.
19:36 *Sennacherib king of Assyria … returned to Nineveh and stayed there.* Nowhere in his own account of his campaign does Sennacherib claim to have taken Jerusalem, nor even to have received tribute from Hezekiah in the immediate aftermath of the siege. He tells us only that after his return to Nineveh (the occasion of which he does not describe), Hezekiah sent tribute. His silence on the way in which the siege ended when compared to what he says in this same account about other kings in the region requires some explanation. Our Biblical sources give us some hints in the direction of this when they tell of a mysterious reversal suffered by the Assyrians while Jerusalem lay at their mercy (v. 35).

A considerable time after these events, in the middle of the fifth century BC, the Greek historian Herodotus heard an Egyptian story about Sennacherib's campaign that also ascribed the Assyrian withdrawal from Palestine to a miracle. The presence of mice in his story has suggested to some the possibility of plague afflicting the Assyrian army.
19:37 *his god Nisrok.* The identity of this deity is unknown, though it may be a variant form of the name Marduk, Nusku or Ninurta. *Esarhaddon.* Ruled Assyria 681–669 BC. Unlike his father, Sennacherib, who took a harsh stance in relation to Babylonian unrest led by Marduk-Baladan and others (see notes on 17:24; 20:12) and ultimately destroyed Babylon itself in 689 BC, Esarhaddon pursued a conciliatory policy, which gave him peace in the south and enabled him to give his full attention to the west. As far as we can tell, Judah was in tributary relationship with him throughout his reign and was even compelled at some point to receive deportees from other parts of the Assyrian Empire (Ezr 4:2).
20:1–19 These verses are a "flashback" to the period around 713/712 BC (see note on v. 12).

2 KINGS 19:37

The Death of Sennacherib

The Babylonian Chronicle reports the death of Sennacherib as taking place in 681 BC, during an insurrection led by his son, but not Esarhaddon, the son who ascended to the throne in the aftermath. Esarhaddon describes the events surrounding his accession to the throne at greater length. He identifies himself as the youngest son of Sennacherib, yet chosen as successor by his father. He claims that he drove the assassins out of the country. A letter to Esarhaddon, found in the royal archives of the Sargonid Dynasty at Nineveh, identifies one of the assassins as Arad-Mullissu — probably the Adrammelek of the Biblical text (2Ki 19:37). ◆

2Hezekiah turned his face to the wall
and prayed to the LORD, 3"Remember,[t]
LORD, how I have walked before you faithfully[u] and with wholehearted devotion
and have done what is good in your eyes."
And Hezekiah wept bitterly.
4Before Isaiah had left the middle court,
the word of the LORD came to him: 5"Go
back and tell Hezekiah, the ruler of my
people, 'This is what the LORD, the God
of your father David, says: I have heard[v]
your prayer and seen your tears;[w] I will
heal you. On the third day from now you
will go up to the temple of the LORD. 6I will
add fifteen years to your life. And I will
deliver you and this city from the hand of
the king of Assyria. I will defend[x] this city
for my sake and for the sake of my servant
David.' "
7Then Isaiah said, "Prepare a poultice
of figs." They did so and applied it to the
boil,[y] and he recovered.

20:3 [t] Ne 13:22 [u] 2Ki 18:3-6 **20:5** [v] 1Sa 9:16; 1Ki 9:3; 2Ki 19:20 [w] Ps 39:12; 56:8 **20:6** [x] 2Ki 19:34 **20:7** [y] Isa 38:21

8Hezekiah had asked Isaiah, "What will
be the sign that the LORD will heal me and
that I will go up to the temple of the LORD
on the third day from now?"
9Isaiah answered, "This is the LORD's
sign[z] to you that the LORD will do what
he has promised: Shall the shadow go
forward ten steps, or shall it go back ten
steps?"
10"It is a simple matter for the shadow
to go forward ten steps," said Hezekiah.
"Rather, have it go back ten steps."
11Then the prophet Isaiah called on the
LORD, and the LORD made the shadow go
back[a] the ten steps it had gone down on
the stairway of Ahaz.

20:9 [z] Dt 13:2; Jer 44:29 **20:11** [a] Jos 10:13

Envoys From Babylon

20:12-19pp — Isa 39:1-8
20:20-21pp — 2Ch 32:32-33

12At that time Marduk-Baladan son of
Baladan king of Babylon sent Hezekiah

20:3 *Remember ... I have walked before you faithfully and with wholehearted devotion.* Kings in the ancient world would be likely to offer prayers to deity when their health or kingdom were threatened, as Hezekiah does here. A prayer of Ashurbanipal is preserved in which he asks for healing on the basis of faithfulness to Ishtar. He speaks of his humility, reverence, his tears and anxiety, the many rituals he has carried out and himself as beloved of the deity.
20:7 *poultice of figs.* Figs had long been cultivated in Palestine, and as well as being eaten fresh, they could be dried and made into cakes or fermented and made into wine. However, it is specifically their medicinal use that is in view here: A fig poultice is applied to what may have been an abscess. The belief that figs had medicinal qualities is also attested later in Rome and earlier at Ugarit. Sweet substances such as figs and dates were used to combat infection in the ancient world, and they do have antibacterial properties.
20:9 *Shall the shadow go forward ten steps, or shall it go back ten steps?* It has often been assumed that this refers to a device designed to tell time, but if so this is the only mention of such a device in the OT. Scholars refer in this context to ancient sundials in general (dating back to fifteenth-century BC Babylonia and Egypt) and in particular to the model of a house excavated in Egypt that contained two flights of stairs used for telling time. This is, however, to read a considerable amount into the Biblical text. It may be a device used in the worship of astral deities, or it may simply be a flight of steps on which shadows can be observed.
20:12 *Marduk-Baladan son of Baladan king of Babylon.* When Sargon II ascended the Assyrian throne in 722 BC,

letters and a gift, because he had heard
of Hezekiah's illness. 13 Hezekiah received
the envoys and showed them all that was
in his storehouses — the silver, the gold,
the spices and the fine olive oil — his armory and everything found among his
treasures. There was nothing in his palace
or in all his kingdom that Hezekiah did
not show them.
14 Then Isaiah the prophet went to King
Hezekiah and asked, "What did those men
say, and where did they come from?"
"From a distant land," Hezekiah replied. "They came from Babylon."
15 The prophet asked, "What did they
see in your palace?"
"They saw everything in my palace,"
Hezekiah said. "There is nothing among
my treasures that I did not show them."
16 Then Isaiah said to Hezekiah, "Hear
the word of the LORD: 17 The time will surely come when everything in your palace,
and all that your predecessors have stored
up until this day, will be carried off to Babylon.[b] Nothing will be left, says the LORD.
18 And some of your descendants,[c] your
own flesh and blood who will be born to
you, will be taken away, and they will become eunuchs in the palace of the king of
Babylon."
19 "The word of the LORD you have spoken is good," Hezekiah replied. For he
thought, "Will there not be peace and security in my lifetime?"
20 As for the other events of Hezekiah's
reign, all his achievements and how he
made the pool[d] and the tunnel by which
he brought water into the city, are they not
written in the book of the annals of the
kings of Judah? 21 Hezekiah rested with his
ancestors. And Manasseh his son succeeded him as king.

Manasseh King of Judah

21:1-10pp — 2Ch 33:1-10
21:17-18pp — 2Ch 33:18-20

21 Manasseh was twelve years old
when he became king, and he
reigned in Jerusalem fifty-five years. His
mother's name was Hephzibah.[e] 2 He did
evil[f] in the eyes of the LORD, following
the detestable practices[g] of the nations
the LORD had driven out before the Israelites. 3 He rebuilt the high places[h] his father
Hezekiah had destroyed; he also erected altars to Baal[i] and made an Asherah
pole, as Ahab king of Israel had done. He
bowed down to all the starry hosts[j] and
worshiped them. 4 He built altars[k] in the
temple of the LORD, of which the LORD had
said, "In Jerusalem I will put my Name."[l]
5 In the two courts[m] of the temple of the
LORD, he built altars to all the starry hosts.
6 He sacrificed his own son[n] in the fire,
practiced divination, sought omens, and
consulted mediums and spiritists.[o] He did
much evil in the eyes of the LORD, arousing his anger.
7 He took the carved Asherah pole[p] he
had made and put it in the temple, of

20:17 [b] 2Ki 24:13; 25:13; 2Ch 36:10; Jer 27:22; 52:17-23
20:18 [c] 2Ki 24:15; 2Ch 33:11; Da 1:3
20:20 [d] Ne 3:16
21:1 [e] Isa 62:4
21:2 [f] Jer 15:4 [g] 2Ki 16:3
21:3 [h] 2Ki 18:4 [i] Jdg 6:28; 1Ki 16:32 [j] Dt 17:3; 2Ki 17:16
21:4 [k] Jer 32:34 [l] 2Sa 7:13; 1Ki 8:29
21:5 [m] 1Ki 7:12; 2Ki 23:12
21:6 [n] Lev 18:21; Dt 18:10; 2Ki 16:3; 17:17 [o] Lev 19:31
21:7 [p] Dt 16:21; 2Ki 23:4

Marduk-Baladan (Marduk-apla-iddina II) had himself crowned king in Babylon, and there ensued a period of ongoing if intermittent conflict in Mesopotamia that lasted until Esarhaddon's reign (see notes on 17:24; 19:37). The visit of Marduk-Baladan's envoys to Jerusalem is best set during the period in which he was still enjoying his first spell of kingship in Babylon (722 – 710 BC), before Sargon II reconquered Babylonia after 710 BC and drove Marduk-Baladan into exile.

2Ki 20:1 – 19 as a whole, in fact, represents a "flashback" to the period around 713/712 BC, 15 years before Hezekiah's death (cf. v. 6). The visit suggests that the anti-Assyrian resistance that arose after Sargon's death in different parts of the empire was coordinated rather than coincidental and had its roots in long-term prior contacts between the different groups involved. Hezekiah may have been involved at this time in a revolt against Assyria spearheaded by the Philistine city of Ashdod (see the article "Hezekiah and Assyria," p. 657).

21:3 *starry hosts.* In the ancient Near East generally, the stars and the planets were identified with specific gods and goddesses and worshiped as such, and their movements were carefully studied for astrological reasons. The sun was worshiped in Mesopotamia as Shamash, the moon as Sin and the planet Venus as Ishtar (the goddess of love and sexuality). At Ugarit in Syria the sun was worshiped as the goddess Shapash, the moon as Yarikh and Venus as Astarte.

Israel encountered astral worship of this kind as soon as it entered Canaan (Israel "served Baal and the Ashtoreths" [Jdg 2:13]). Ashtoreth is the Biblical name for Astarte, and the plural refers to various local manifestations of the goddess (see note on Jdg 2:13). The cult was revived during the monarchic period by Solomon (1Ki 11:5,33) and may well have been promoted, along with other aspects of astral worship (2Ki 23:11), under Manasseh, in part to display his loyalty to the Assyrian king.

Certainly we find no lack in the archaeological record in Palestine of religious art that reflects this indigenous worship of heavenly powers. A bulla from Jerusalem dating from the seventh century BC displays the crescent moon standard of the god Sin, while a seventh-century BC scaraboid from Shechem shows the moon-god in anthropomorphic form, enthroned on a low stool and with his arms raised in blessing.

21:6 All the terms in this verse appear in Dt 18:10 – 11 (see notes there). *sacrificed his own son in the fire.* See notes on 3:27; 16:3; 1Ki 11:5; Lev 20:2; Jer 7:31). *divination.* See notes on Ge 30:27; Dt 18:10; see also the article "Balaam," p. 268. *sought omens.* See notes on 16:15; 17:17; see also the article "Extispicy," p. 650. *mediums and spiritists.* Practiced not divination in general but necromancy specifically (divination by inquiring of the dead). The best narrative example of necromancy in the Bible is found in 1Sa 28:8 – 25, where the spirit of the prophet Samuel is apparently summoned from the world of the dead (see note on 1Sa 28:7; see also the article "Consulting a 'Spirit,'" p. 508). Necromancy was a popular form of divination in the ancient Near East.

2 KINGS 20:20

Hezekiah's Tunnel

Settled existence in Syria-Palestine required adequate water supplies, or at least water supplies that could be made adequate by human interference with nature. Towns were often built, therefore, beside rivers and springs, so that the course of the rivers could be altered and the flow of springs could be improved. Wells were dug in order to access underground water, and rainwater from the wet months was collected in cisterns or reservoirs for later use. Particular attention had to be given to ensuring that towns possessed water sources that would enable them to withstand siege.

In the case of Jerusalem, the Gihon spring in the Kidron Valley was the crucial resource, and a complex water system was created early in order to secure and access its water. An impressive tower was constructed in the Middle Bronze Age (eighteenth to seventeenth centuries BC) to protect the spring, and a large, quarter-mile-long (0.4-kilometer-long) conduit (often known as the Siloam Tunnel) channeled the water from there to the reservoir at Birket el-Hamra (perhaps the Lower [Old] Pool of Isa 22:9 – 11) at the southern end of the City of David, gathering as it went run-off water from above and irrigating adjacent fields. Although well protected by large boulders wedged in the channel, this water supply lay outside the city's walls and was vulnerable in time of siege.

However, the Middle Bronze Age water system also contained a subsidiary tunnel that led from the Siloam conduit, near to its beginning point by the Gihon spring, into a large rock-cut pool, from which Jerusalem residents could draw water from above by way of a further tunnel that began inside the city walls. This water supply would have been especially useful in time of siege. Later, in preparation for the Assyrian attack, King Hezekiah had a tunnel cut that diverted water from the Gihon spring directly underground to the Pool of Siloam (Birket es-Silwan) at the southern end of the Tyropoeon Valley — which by this time lay within the city walls. This not only secured his own water supply, but also deprived the Assyrians of one (see 2Ch 32:4,30). At this point the old water system was apparently abandoned.

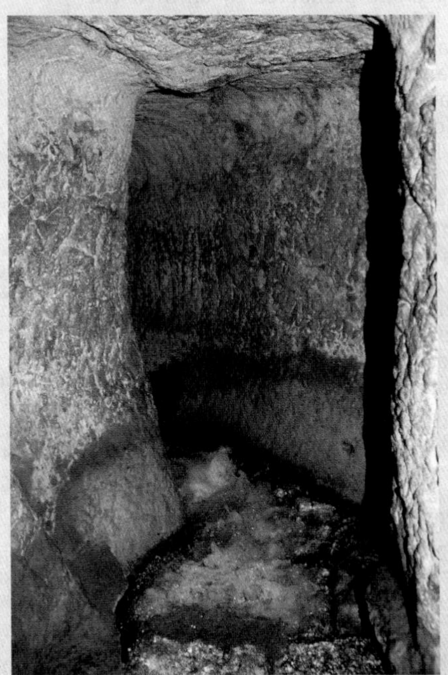

Hezekiah's tunnel.

An inscription cut into the tunnel wall (known as the Siloam Tunnel Inscription) commemorates King Hezekiah's accomplishment in building a tunnel that brought water from the Gihon spring directly underground to the Pool of Siloam. The feat was considered remarkable partly because the tunnel was cut by two teams working toward each other from opposite directions and yet meeting accurately in the middle. ◆

which the LORD had said to David and to
his son Solomon, "In this temple and in
Jerusalem, which I have chosen out of all
the tribes of Israel, I will put my Name[q]
forever. 8I will not again[r] make the feet of
the Israelites wander from the land I gave
their ancestors, if only they will be careful
to do everything I commanded them and
will keep the whole Law that my servant
Moses[s] gave them." 9But the people did
not listen. Manasseh led them astray, so
that they did more evil[t] than the nations[u]
the LORD had destroyed before the Israelites.

10The LORD said through his servants the
prophets: 11"Manasseh king of Judah has
committed these detestable sins. He has
done more evil[v] than the Amorites[w] who
preceded him and has led Judah into sin
with his idols. 12Therefore this is what the
LORD, the God of Israel, says: I am going
to bring such disaster[x] on Jerusalem and
Judah that the ears of everyone who hears
of it will tingle.[y] 13I will stretch out over
Jerusalem the measuring line used against
Samaria and the plumb line[z] used against
the house of Ahab. I will wipe[a] out Jerusalem as one wipes a dish, wiping it and
turning it upside down. 14I will forsake[b]
the remnant[c] of my inheritance and give
them into the hands of enemies. They will
be looted and plundered by all their enemies; 15they have done evil[d] in my eyes
and have aroused[e] my anger from the day
their ancestors came out of Egypt until
this day."

16Moreover, Manasseh also shed so
much innocent blood[f] that he filled Jerusalem from end to end—besides the sin
that he had caused Judah to commit, so
that they did evil in the eyes of the LORD.

17As for the other events of Manasseh's
reign, and all he did, including the sin he
committed, are they not written in the
book of the annals of the kings of Judah?
18Manasseh rested with his ancestors and
was buried in his palace garden,[g] the garden of Uzza. And Amon his son succeeded
him as king.

Amon King of Judah

21:19-24pp — 2Ch 33:21-25

19Amon was twenty-two years old when
he became king, and he reigned in Jerusalem two years. His mother's name was
Meshullemeth daughter of Haruz; she was
from Jotbah. 20He did evil[h] in the eyes
of the LORD, as his father Manasseh had
done. 21He followed completely the ways
of his father, worshiping the idols his father had worshiped, and bowing down to
them. 22He forsook the LORD, the God of
his ancestors, and did not walk[i] in obedience to him.

23Amon's officials conspired against
him and assassinated[j] the king in his palace. 24Then the people of the land killed[k]
all who had plotted against King Amon,
and they made Josiah his son king in his
place.

25As for the other events of Amon's
reign, and what he did, are they not written in the book of the annals of the kings
of Judah? 26He was buried in his tomb in
the garden[l] of Uzza. And Josiah his son
succeeded him as king.

The Book of the Law Found

22:1-20pp — 2Ch 34:1-2,8-28

22 Josiah was eight years old when
he became king, and he reigned
in Jerusalem thirty-one years. His mother's name was Jedidah daughter of Adaiah; she was from Bozkath.[m] 2He did what
was right[n] in the eyes of the LORD and followed completely the ways of his father
David, not turning aside to the right[o] or
to the left.

3In the eighteenth year of his reign, King
Josiah sent the secretary, Shaphan[p] son of
Azaliah, the son of Meshullam, to the temple of the LORD. He said: 4"Go up to Hilkiah the high priest and have him get ready
the money that has been brought into the
temple of the LORD, which the doorkeepers have collected[q] from the people. 5Have
them entrust it to the men appointed to
supervise the work on the temple. And
have these men pay the workers who repair[r] the temple of the LORD— 6the carpenters, the builders and the masons. Also
have them purchase timber and dressed
stone to repair the temple.[s] 7But they need
not account for the money entrusted to
them, because they are honest in their
dealings."[t]

8Hilkiah the high priest said to Shaphan
the secretary, "I have found the Book of
the Law[u] in the temple of the LORD." He
gave it to Shaphan, who read it. 9Then

21:7 [q] 2Sa 7:13; 1Ki 8:29; 9:3; 2Ki 23:27; Jer 32:34
21:8 [r] 2Sa 7:10 [s] 2Ki 18:12
21:9 [t] Pr 29:12 [u] Dt 9:4
21:11 [v] 2Ki 24:3-4 [w] Ge 15:16; 1Ki 21:26
21:12 [x] 2Ki 23:26; 24:3; Jer 15:4 [y] 1Sa 3:11; Jer 19:3
21:13 [z] Isa 34:11; La 2:8; Am 7:7-9 [a] 2Ki 23:27
21:14 [b] Ps 78:58-60 [c] 2Ki 19:4; Mic 2:12
21:15 [d] Ex 32:22 [e] Jer 25:7
21:16 [f] 2Ki 24:4
21:18 [g] ver 26
21:20 [h] ver 2-6
21:22 [i] 1Ki 11:33
21:23 [j] 2Ki 12:20; 2Ch 33:24-25
21:24 [k] 2Ki 14:5
21:26 [l] ver 18
22:1 [m] Jos 15:39
22:2 [n] Dt 17:19 [o] Dt 5:32
22:3 [p] 2Ch 34:20; Jer 39:14
22:4 [q] 2Ki 12:4-5
22:5 [r] 2Ki 12:5, 11-14
22:6 [s] 2Ki 12:11-12
22:7 [t] 2Ki 12:15
22:8 [u] Dt 31:24

21:18 *his palace garden, the garden of Uzza.* This burial site is of uncertain location, but the implication may be that it lay outside the "City of David" (i.e., the original settled area on the southern hill), which is noted as the resting place of preceding kings (e.g., Ahaz in 16:20). It is tempting, in view of Manasseh's worship of astral deities (v. 3), to associate Uzza with the Arabian goddess al-'Uzza, who was identified with Venus, and to speculate that the garden of Uzza was an enclosure dedicated to her on the temple mount. An equally plausible suggestion is that this enclosure was at the southern end of the Kidron Valley, just outside the city walls, where we know that there was a "king's garden" (25:4; Ne 3:15).

22:8 *found the Book of the Law.* We are not told the range of content that was included in the document that was

2 KINGS 21:1 – 18

MANASSEH OF JUDAH AND ASHURBANIPAL

The records of Esarhaddon's son and successor Ashurbanipal (669 – c. 630 BC) indicate that Manasseh remained a loyal vassal of Assyria at least throughout the early part of Ashurbanipal's reign. Manasseh's Judahite forces fought on the Assyrian side in 667 BC during the king's first campaign there, when Ashurbanipal recaptured Memphis and laid the foundation for his capture of Thebes a few years later in 664 BC.

However, Esarhaddon had divided his kingdom between two of his sons rather than bequeathing it to one, and Ashurbanipal therefore ruled directly only over Assyria, with Shamash-shum-ukin in charge of Babylonia. Open war between the two was the eventual result (652 – 648 BC), with Ashurbanipal the victor. While he was campaigning in Babylonia, there was widespread disaffection in Syria-Palestine. Although 2 Kings gives no hint of these events, it is likely that they are alluded to in 2Ch 33:11 – 13, which perhaps implies that Manasseh was suspected of being involved in disloyal activities and was summoned to Babylon to answer charges either during the siege or after the fall of Babylon (648 BC). He was subsequently restored and appears to have enjoyed a degree of freedom under Assyrian overlordship in the subsequent period, perhaps because Ashurbanipal wished to have Judah as a strong buffer state between Syria and Canaan, and Egypt.

Egypt had itself withheld tribute a few years before Shamash-shum-ukin's rebellion, and afterward Egypt never came under the Assyrian domination that it had earlier experienced during the reigns of both Esarhaddon and Ashurbanipal. After the rebellion, with Ashurbanipal occupied with troubles elsewhere in his empire, Pharaoh Psammetichus I gradually extended Egypt's influence once again into Syria-Palestine and became more of a presence there. ◆

Shaphan the secretary went to the king
and reported to him: "Your officials have
paid out the money that was in the temple
of the LORD and have entrusted it to the
workers and supervisors at the temple."
10Then Shaphan the secretary informed
the king, "Hilkiah the priest has given me
a book." And Shaphan read from it in the
presence of the king.[v]
11When the king heard the words of the
Book of the Law, he tore his robes. 12He
gave these orders to Hilkiah the priest,
Ahikam[w] son of Shaphan, Akbor son
of Micaiah, Shaphan the secretary and

22:10 [v] Jer 36:21 **22:12** [w] 2Ki 25:22; Jer 26:24

discovered. It is clearly a covenant document of some sort. Given that the foundation and structure of ancient Near Eastern buildings were often used as a repository for dedicatory inscriptions and the storage of royal annals, Hilkiah's "discovery" of the Book of the Law is not as peculiar as it may at first appear. Such foundation tablets would often include instructions of religious and architectural significance for those who might be involved in future temple restoration. For example, in the palace of Sin-kasid at Uruk, a large number of clay tablets were intentionally built into the foundation of the temple in regular intervals of approximately 16.5 inches (42 centimeters).

In the context of Josiah's religious reforms and temple restoration (23:8 – 13), there may have even been an intentional search for such guiding documents given the supreme importance of properly handling sacred space. Discovered texts were commonly reburied in conjunction with a temple refurbishing project, as reflected by the Assyrian king Tukulti-Ninurta I, who redeposited foundation tablets from the time of Adadnirari I into the wall of the Aššurimtu temple at Assur.

The discovery of ancient foundation documents at a holy place such as a temple could also impact contemporary religious thought, since these texts carried an implicit level of authority. Pharaoh Shabako claimed to have found a forgotten theological text describing the creation of the world by Ptah, now called the Memphite Theology, which he had inscribed on stone. A similar process is seen by the reforms enacted by Josiah following the discovery of the Book of the Law.

2 KINGS 22:10

Books and Literacy

The Hebrew word translated "book" in 2Ki 22:10 refers generally to a document, which could have been composed of various materials (clay tablet, parchment, papyrus, wax tablet). Bound books had not yet been invented, and written material tended to be used for official documents stored in archives. Temples had archives as well as foundation deposits, and this document could have been found in such locations. While basic literacy was widespread, and kings would likely have had a higher level of literacy, it was still conventional for documents to be read before the king by a scribe rather than the king reading them himself. Though many parts of Deuteronomy are traced back to Moses, we do not know when the entire book we know as Deuteronomy was compiled. It may be that such material was still only transmitted in numerous individual documents found in archives and in the oral traditions that preserved them. ◆

Assyrian foundation tablets from the Temple of Mamu, 875–865 BC. Bound books had not yet been invented, and written material tended to be used for official documents stored in archives.

Asaiah the king's attendant: [13]"Go and inquire of the LORD for me and for the people
and for all Judah about what is written
in this book that has been found. Great is
the LORD's anger[x] that burns against us because those who have gone before us have
not obeyed the words of this book; they
have not acted in accordance with all that
is written there concerning us."
[14]Hilkiah the priest, Ahikam, Akbor,
Shaphan and Asaiah went to speak to
the prophet Huldah, who was the wife of

22:13 [x] Dt 29:24-28; 31:17

22:14 *the prophet Huldah ... wife of Shallum ... keeper of the wardrobe.* It is not clear whether Shallum was in charge of the king's wardrobe or the wardrobe of the priests in the temple (cf. 10:22). It is consequently unclear whether Huldah was the wife of a court official or perhaps one of the temple personnel. Female prophets are well-known in the

Shallum son of Tikvah, the son of Harhas,
keeper of the wardrobe. She lived in Jerusalem, in the New Quarter.
15She said to them, "This is what the
LORD, the God of Israel, says: Tell the man
who sent you to me, 16'This is what the
LORD says: I am going to bring disaster[y]
on this place and its people, according to
everything written in the book[z] the king
of Judah has read. 17Because they have
forsaken[a] me and burned incense to other gods and aroused my anger by all the
idols their hands have made,[a] my anger
will burn against this place and will not be
quenched.' 18Tell the king of Judah, who
sent you to inquire[b] of the LORD, 'This is
what the LORD, the God of Israel, says concerning the words you heard: 19Because
your heart was responsive and you humbled[c] yourself before the LORD when you
heard what I have spoken against this
place and its people—that they would become a curse[b][d] and be laid waste[e]—and
because you tore your robes and wept in
my presence, I also have heard you, declares the LORD. 20Therefore I will gather
you to your ancestors, and you will be buried in peace.[f] Your eyes will not see all the
disaster I am going to bring on this place.'"
So they took her answer back to the
king.

Josiah Renews the Covenant

23:1-3pp — 2Ch 34:29-32
23:4-20Ref — 2Ch 34:3-7,33
23:21-23pp — 2Ch 35:1,18-19
23:28-30pp — 2Ch 35:20–36:1

23 Then the king called together all
the elders of Judah and Jerusalem.
2He went up to the temple of the LORD with
the people of Judah, the inhabitants of Jerusalem, the priests and the prophets—all
the people from the least to the greatest.
He read[g] in their hearing all the words of
the Book of the Covenant, which had been
found in the temple of the LORD. 3The king
stood by the pillar and renewed the covenant[h] in the presence of the LORD—to
follow[i] the LORD and keep his commands,
statutes and decrees with all his heart and
all his soul, thus confirming the words of
the covenant written in this book. Then
all the people pledged themselves to the
covenant.
4The king ordered Hilkiah the high
priest, the priests next in rank and the
doorkeepers[j] to remove[k] from the temple of the LORD all the articles made for
Baal and Asherah and all the starry hosts.
He burned them outside Jerusalem in the
fields of the Kidron Valley and took the
ashes to Bethel. 5He did away with the
idolatrous priests appointed by the kings
of Judah to burn incense on the high places of the towns of Judah and on those
around Jerusalem—those who burned incense to Baal, to the sun and moon, to the
constellations and to all the starry hosts.[l]
6He took the Asherah pole from the temple
of the LORD to the Kidron Valley outside
Jerusalem and burned it there. He ground
it to powder and scattered the dust over
the graves of the common people.[m] 7He
also tore down the quarters of the male
shrine prostitutes[n] that were in the temple
of the LORD, the quarters where women
did weaving for Asherah.
8Josiah brought all the priests from the
towns of Judah and desecrated the high

22:16 [y] Dt 31:29; Jos 23:15 [z] Dt 29:27; Da 9:11
22:17 [a] Dt 29:25-27
22:18 [b] 2Ch 34:26; Jer 21:2
22:19 [c] Ex 10:3; 1Ki 21:29; Ps 51:17; Isa 57:15; Mic 6:8 [d] Jer 26:6 [e] Lev 26:31
22:20 [f] Isa 57:1
23:2 [g] Dt 31:11; 2Ki 22:8
23:3 [h] 2Ki 11:14, 17 [i] Dt 13:4
23:4 [j] 2Ki 25:18 [k] 2Ki 21:7
23:5 [l] 2Ki 21:3; Jer 8:2
23:6 [m] Jer 26:23
23:7 [n] 1Ki 14:24; 15:12; Eze 16:16

[a] *17* Or *by everything they have done* [b] *19* That is, their names would be used in cursing (see Jer. 29:22); or, others would see that they are cursed.

ancient Near East, sometimes addressing kings (as here) on important matters such as their personal security.

23:3 *the pillar.* See note on 11:14.

23:4 *Kidron Valley.* Lay to the east of the Old City of David, separating it from the Mount of Olives. It ran from north to south to join first the Tyropoeon Valley at the southern end of the city and then, farther on, the Hinnom Valley. The stream that ran through the valley, then, progressed southeast and emptied into the Dead Sea. Associated with idolatry since the time of Solomon (1Ki 11:7), the Kidron Valley became during Josiah's reformation a convenient place to destroy cult objects, thus not only removing them from Jerusalem but also desecrating the valley itself as a religious site. *Bethel.* Jeroboam I had focused his new cult on Bethel and Dan (1Ki 12–13; see note on 1Ki 12:29), and this cult lived on in the activities of the new settlers in the land of Israel (cf. 2Ki 17:24–41). Most scholars identify Bethel with Tell Beitin. Josiah is here envisaged as seeking to reform worship both in Judah and in territory that had belonged to the northern kingdom of Israel (cf. 2Ch 34:3–7), which he now implicitly claims back as his own. It is certainly clear from a consideration of the political circumstances of the period that the opportunity existed from early in Josiah's reign for increasing activity to the north of his capital. Ashurbanipal died around 630 BC, plunging the Assyrian Empire into an extended period of civil war and general strife, out of which the city of Babylon eventually emerged as the new imperial power in the east. Palestine was far from the center of events throughout the period, and after 630 BC Assyria was little interested in or capable of exercising effective control there. The major power in Syria and Palestine was increasingly Egypt, but there is no reason to think that in the midst of the many larger matters that concerned them, the Egyptians would have cared much about Josiah's interest in the territory to his north that did not directly affect their interests. The evidence suggests, in fact, that Egyptian interest in Palestine in this period was limited to commerce and trade, and it did not extend to possession of territory as such—albeit they expected to be able to move troops through Palestine when they wished to do so (see note on v. 29).

23:7 *male shrine prostitutes.* See note on Dt 23:17–18. *weaving for Asherah.* This probably refers to the manufacture of ritual garments for worship of the goddess Asherah (cf. 10:22).

places, from Geba[o] to Beersheba, where the
priests had burned incense. He broke down
the gateway at the entrance of the Gate
of Joshua, the city governor, which was
on the left of the city gate. 9 Although the
priests of the high places did not serve[p] at
the altar of the LORD in Jerusalem, they ate
unleavened bread with their fellow priests.
10 He desecrated Topheth,[q] which was
in the Valley of Ben Hinnom,[r] so no one
could use it to sacrifice their son[s] or
daughter in the fire to Molek. 11 He removed from the entrance to the temple of
the LORD the horses that the kings of Judah had dedicated to the sun. They were
in the court[a] near the room of an official
named Nathan-Melek. Josiah then burned
the chariots dedicated to the sun.[t]
12 He pulled down the altars the kings
of Judah had erected on the roof[u] near
the upper room of Ahaz, and the altars
Manasseh had built in the two courts[v] of
the temple of the LORD. He removed them
from there, smashed them to pieces and
threw the rubble into the Kidron Valley.
13 The king also desecrated the high places
that were east of Jerusalem on the south
of the Hill of Corruption—the ones Solomon[w] king of Israel had built for Ashtoreth the vile goddess of the Sidonians,
for Chemosh the vile god of Moab, and
for Molek the detestable god of the people
of Ammon. 14 Josiah smashed[x] the sacred
stones and cut down the Asherah poles
and covered the sites with human bones.
15 Even the altar[y] at Bethel, the high
place made by Jeroboam[z] son of Nebat,
who had caused Israel to sin—even that
altar and high place he demolished. He
burned the high place and ground it to
powder, and burned the Asherah pole
also. 16 Then Josiah[a] looked around, and
when he saw the tombs that were there
on the hillside, he had the bones removed
from them and burned on the altar to defile it, in accordance with the word of the
LORD proclaimed by the man of God who
foretold these things.
17 The king asked, "What is that tomb-
stone I see?"
The people of the city said, "It marks
the tomb of the man of God who came
from Judah and pronounced against the
altar of Bethel the very things you have
done to it."
18 "Leave it alone," he said. "Don't
let anyone disturb his bones[b]." So they
spared his bones and those of the prophet
who had come from Samaria.
19 Just as he had done at Bethel, Josiah
removed all the shrines at the high places that the kings of Israel had built in the
towns of Samaria and that had aroused
the LORD's anger. 20 Josiah slaughtered[c] all
the priests of those high places on the altars and burned human bones[d] on them.
Then he went back to Jerusalem.
21 The king gave this order to all the people: "Celebrate the Passover[e] to the LORD
your God, as it is written in this Book of
the Covenant." 22 Neither in the days of
the judges who led Israel nor in the days
of the kings of Israel and the kings of Judah had any such Passover been observed.
23 But in the eighteenth year of King Josiah,
this Passover was celebrated to the LORD
in Jerusalem.
24 Furthermore, Josiah got rid of the
mediums and spiritists,[f] the household
gods,[g] the idols and all the other detestable things seen in Judah and Jerusalem.
This he did to fulfill the requirements of
the law written in the book that Hilkiah

23:8 [o] 1Ki 15:22 **23:9** [p] Eze 44:10-14 **23:10** [q] Isa 30:33; Jer 7:31, 32; 19:6 [r] Jos 15:8 [s] Lev 18:21; Dt 18:10 **23:11** [t] Dt 4:19 **23:12** [u] Jer 19:13; Zep 1:5 [v] 2Ki 21:5 **23:13** [w] 1Ki 11:7 **23:14** [x] Ex 23:24; Dt 7:5, 25 **23:15** [y] 1Ki 13:1-3 [z] 1Ki 12:33 **23:16** [a] 1Ki 13:2 **23:18** [b] 1Ki 13:31 **23:20** [c] Ex 22:20; 2Ki 10:25; 11:18 [d] 1Ki 13:2 **23:21** [e] Ex 12:11; Nu 9:2; Dt 16:1-8 **23:24** [f] Lev 19:31; Dt 18:11; 2Ki 21:6 [g] Ge 31:19

[a] *11* The meaning of the Hebrew for this word is uncertain.

23:10 *Topheth ... the Valley of Ben Hinnom ... Molek.* The Hinnom Valley ran along the western and southern sides of ancient Jerusalem until it met the Kidron Valley, running from north to south. Like the Kidron Valley, it was associated with idolatry—in particular with the worship of Molek (see note on 1Ki 11:5). Topheth was apparently the cultic site where this worship was practiced, lying at the juncture of the Kidron and Hinnom Valleys near En Rogel.
23:11 *horses ... dedicated to the sun.* On the worship of the starry host, including the sun, see note on 21:3. The practice of dedicating horses to the sun appears to have been distinctively Assyrian (by way of the Hurrian peoples of Mitanni in northern Mesopotamia and Syria in the second half of the second millennium BC), but is also known in Ugarit. The sun-god was thought to ride across the sky in a chariot drawn by horses. These horses may be dedicated to a foreign solar deity, or perhaps to a syncretistic version of Yahweh as a sun-god.
23:12 *altars ... on the roof.* A text from Ugarit that describes the ritual for the annual celebration of the grape harvest at the temple of Baal in that city also mentions a king sacrificing at an altar on a roof (on this occasion, the roof of the Baal temple), in the context of the worship of Shapash, the female sun-god at Ugarit. The roof is a natural location for worshiping the starry host.
23:13 *Hill of Corruption.* Because it hosted the idolatrous altars here mentioned, the Mount of Olives is named the "Hill of Corruption." The mountain was the central summit on a ridge of three running to the east of Jerusalem and the Kidron Valley. *Ashtoreth.* See note on 1Ki 11:5. *Chemosh.* The chief god of the Moabites, although he was already known in ancient Ebla in Syria (Tell Mardikh) as Kamish and is probably to be identified with the Mesopotamian deity Nergal, an underworld god associated with famine, drought, plague and death. *Molek.* See note on 1Ki 11:5.
23:14 *human bones.* It is possible that these were added to the refuse so that no one would disturb it, because of the taboo of coming into contact with dead bodies.
23:19 *high places.* See notes on 1Ki 3:2; 11:7.
23:24 *mediums and spiritists.* See note on 2Ki 21:6. *household gods.* See the article "Household Gods," p. 72.

the priest had discovered in the temple of
the LORD. 25 Neither before nor after Josiah
was there a king like him who turned[h] to
the LORD as he did — with all his heart and
with all his soul and with all his strength,
in accordance with all the Law of Moses.
26 Nevertheless, the LORD did not turn
away from the heat of his fierce anger,
which burned against Judah because of all
that Manasseh[i] had done to arouse his anger. 27 So the LORD said, "I will remove[j] Judah also from my presence[k] as I removed
Israel, and I will reject Jerusalem, the city
I chose, and this temple, about which I
said, 'My Name shall be there.'[a]"
28 As for the other events of Josiah's
reign, and all he did, are they not written
in the book of the annals of the kings of
Judah?
29 While Josiah was king, Pharaoh Necho[l] king of Egypt went up to the Euphrates River to help the king of Assyria. King
Josiah marched out to meet him in battle, but Necho faced him and killed him
at Megiddo.[m] 30 Josiah's servants brought
his body in a chariot[n] from Megiddo to Jerusalem and buried him in his own tomb.
And the people of the land took Jehoahaz
son of Josiah and anointed him and made
him king in place of his father.

Jehoahaz King of Judah

23:31-34pp — 2Ch 36:2-4

31 Jehoahaz[o] was twenty-three years old
when he became king, and he reigned
in Jerusalem three months. His mother's
name was Hamutal[p] daughter of Jeremiah; she was from Libnah. 32 He did evil in
the eyes of the LORD, just as his predecessors had done. 33 Pharaoh Necho put him
in chains at Riblah[q] in the land of Hamath[r]
so that he might not reign in Jerusalem,
and he imposed on Judah a levy of a hundred talents[b] of silver and a talent[c] of gold.
34 Pharaoh Necho made Eliakim[s] son of Josiah king in place of his father Josiah and
changed Eliakim's name to Jehoiakim.
But he took Jehoahaz and carried him off
to Egypt, and there he died.[t] 35 Jehoiakim
paid Pharaoh Necho the silver and gold he
demanded. In order to do so, he taxed the
land and exacted the silver and gold from
the people of the land according to their
assessments.[u]

Jehoiakim King of Judah

23:36 – 24:6pp — 2Ch 36:5-8

36 Jehoiakim[v] was twenty-five years old
when he became king, and he reigned
in Jerusalem eleven years. His mother's
name was Zebidah daughter of Pedaiah;
she was from Rumah. 37 And he did evil in
the eyes of the LORD, just as his predecessors had done.

24 During Jehoiakim's reign, Nebuchadnezzar[w] king of Babylon invaded the land, and Jehoiakim became his

23:25 [h] 2Ki 18:5 **23:26** [i] 2Ki 21:12; Jer 15:4 **23:27** [j] 2Ki 21:13 [k] 2Ki 18:11 **23:29** [l] Jer 46:2 [m] Zec 12:11 **23:30** [n] 2Ki 9:28 **23:31** [o] 1Ch 3:15; Jer 22:11 [p] 2Ki 24:18 **23:33** [q] 2Ki 25:6 [r] 1Ki 8:65 **23:34** [s] 1Ch 3:15; 2Ch 36:5-8 [t] Jer 22:12; Eze 19:3-4 **23:35** [u] ver 33 **23:36** [v] Jer 26:1 **24:1** [w] Jer 25:1, 9; Da 1:1

[a] *27* 1 Kings 8:29 [b] *33* That is, about 3 3/4 tons or about 3.4 metric tons [c] *33* That is, about 75 pounds or about 34 kilograms

23:29 *Pharaoh Necho king of Egypt went … to help the king of Assyria.* After the death of Ashurbanipal of Assyria around 630 BC, Egypt gradually emerged as the major power in Syria-Palestine and indeed as the ally of Assyria in its struggle with Babylon, sending troops northward at least from 616 BC on to join with the Assyrians in battle. The campaign mentioned here took place in 609 BC, as Pharaoh Necho II marched north for what was apparently the last joint Assyrian-Egyptian engagement with the Babylonians (and their allies, the Medes). After this we no longer hear of the last Assyrian ruler, Ashur-Uballit II, who had set himself up as king in Harran after the fall of Nineveh in 612 BC and was now trying to retake Harran (with Necho's help) from the Babylonians, who had captured it the previous year.

To accomplish the movement of troops to the north, the Egyptians needed effective control of the Coastal Highway, the international highway that ran from Egypt along the western coast of Palestine and then northeast via Megiddo and Damascus. The city of Megiddo controlled this highway as it entered the Jezreel Valley. Josiah's decision to confront the Egyptian army there implies that he had captured Megiddo from either the Egyptians or the Assyrians prior to the battle.

The motives for Josiah's intervention are not clear; perhaps he is attempting early in the reign of the new pharaoh (who had succeeded his father, Psammetichus, in 610 BC) to establish his independence from an increasingly powerful Egypt, hoping to benefit from being seen as taking the Babylonians' side. If so, the attempt ends in disaster. Josiah is killed, and any limited independence that Judah may have had during the period of Assyrian decline in Syria-Palestine is now lost.

23:33 *Riblah.* Located in a wide plain about seven miles (11 kilometers) south of Kadesh on the eastern bank of the Orontes River. It was an ideal place for Necho and his army to encamp on their journey back from the unsuccessful siege of Harran in 609 BC. Shortly after Josiah's death, the new king of Judah, Jehoahaz (also known as Shallum, 1Ch 3:15; Jer 22:11), was summoned to Necho's headquarters at Riblah, removed from power, and subsequently imprisoned in Egypt.

24:1 *Jehoiakim.* Jehoahaz's brother Eliakim replaced him on the throne, ruling as an Egyptian vassal under the name of Jehoiakim. It was during his reign that King Nebuchadnezzar of Babylon (605 – 562 BC) invaded Palestine in pursuit of complete victory over Egypt. Early in 605 BC, he defeated the Egyptian army at Carchemish on the Euphrates River, following up this victory with a march the following year that reached as far as Ashkelon in Philistia. An Aramaic letter, written to Pharaoh Necho of Egypt by Adon king of Ekron just prior to the Babylonian assault on that city, pleads for Egyptian help, but to no avail. Nebuchadnezzar was never able to defeat Egypt finally. An attack on Egypt itself was repulsed by Necho in 601 BC with heavy losses on the Babylonian side. Egyptian influence over Syria-Palestine was nevertheless removed, as v. 7 indicates: "The king of Egypt did

NEBUCHADNEZZAR'S CAMPAIGNS AGAINST JUDAH

605–586 BC

Events in Judah moved swiftly following the death of Josiah. Pharaoh Necho pressed his advantage by deporting Jehoahaz, the new ruler, and appointing a second son of Josiah, Jehoiakim, as king.

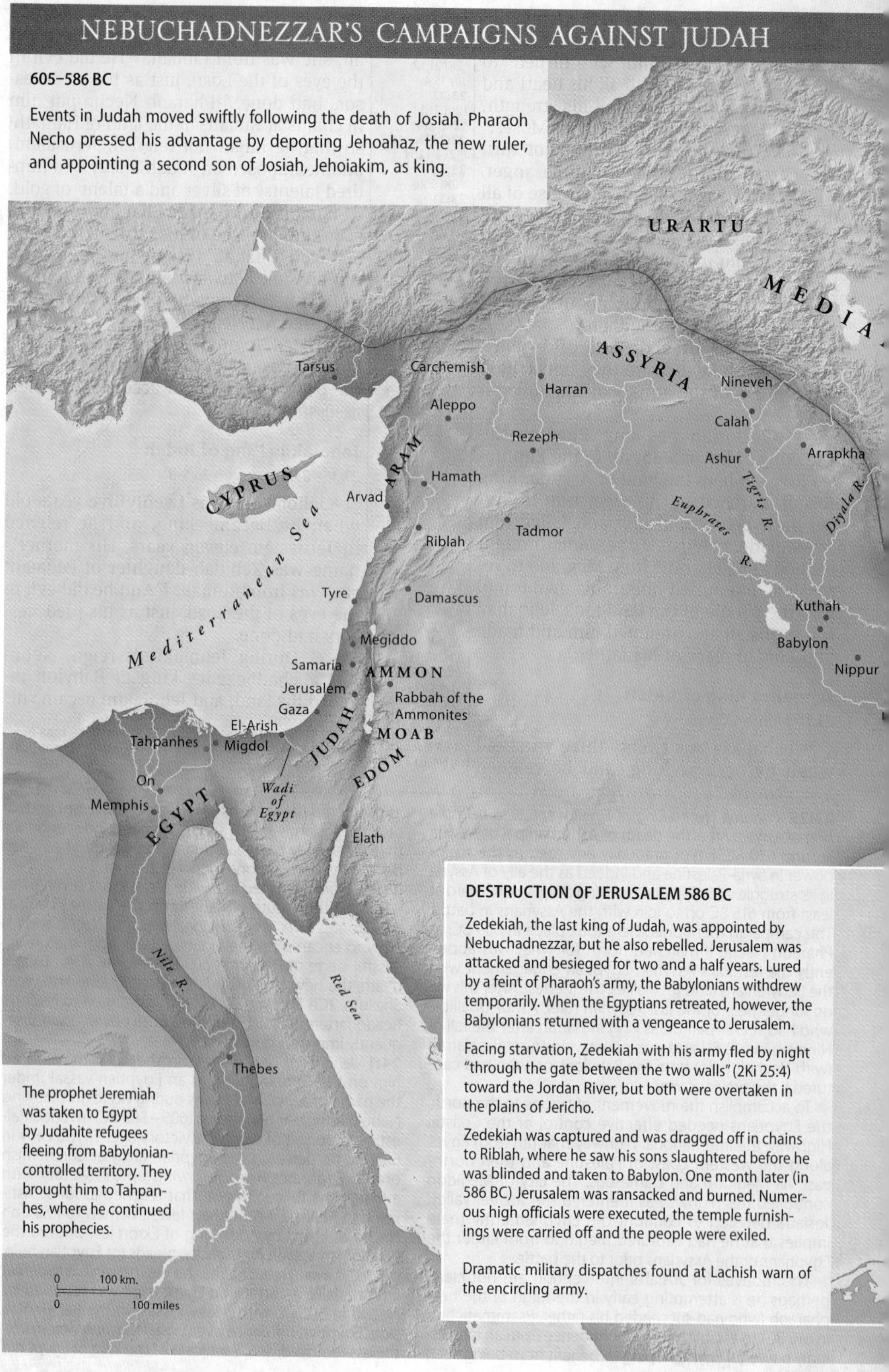

URARTU
MEDIA
ASSYRIA
Tarsus
Carchemish
Harran
Nineveh
Aleppo
Calah
Rezeph
Ashur
Arrapkha
ARAM
Hamath
CYPRUS
Arvad
Tigris R.
Euphrates R.
Diyala R.
Tadmor
Riblah
Mediterranean Sea
Tyre
Damascus
Kuthah
Babylon
Nippur
Megiddo
Samaria
AMMON
Jerusalem
Rabbah of the Ammonites
Gaza
El-Arish
JUDAH
MOAB
Tahpanhes
Migdol
EDOM
On
Wadi of Egypt
Memphis
EGYPT
Elath
Nile R.
Red Sea
Thebes

The prophet Jeremiah was taken to Egypt by Judahite refugees fleeing from Babylonian-controlled territory. They brought him to Tahpanhes, where he continued his prophecies.

0 100 km.
0 100 miles

DESTRUCTION OF JERUSALEM 586 BC

Zedekiah, the last king of Judah, was appointed by Nebuchadnezzar, but he also rebelled. Jerusalem was attacked and besieged for two and a half years. Lured by a feint of Pharaoh's army, the Babylonians withdrew temporarily. When the Egyptians retreated, however, the Babylonians returned with a vengeance to Jerusalem.

Facing starvation, Zedekiah with his army fled by night "through the gate between the two walls" (2Ki 25:4) toward the Jordan River, but both were overtaken in the plains of Jericho.

Zedekiah was captured and was dragged off in chains to Riblah, where he saw his sons slaughtered before he was blinded and taken to Babylon. One month later (in 586 BC) Jerusalem was ransacked and burned. Numerous high officials were executed, the temple furnishings were carried off and the people were exiled.

Dramatic military dispatches found at Lachish warn of the encircling army.

e Chaldeans (Kaldu), as the Neo-Babylonians were called, had important nnections at Ur and Harran, centers of worship of the moon-god Sin. ey also developed the trade routes across North Arabia, where Tema was rticularly important, becoming the residence of Nabonidus during the last ys of the kingdom.

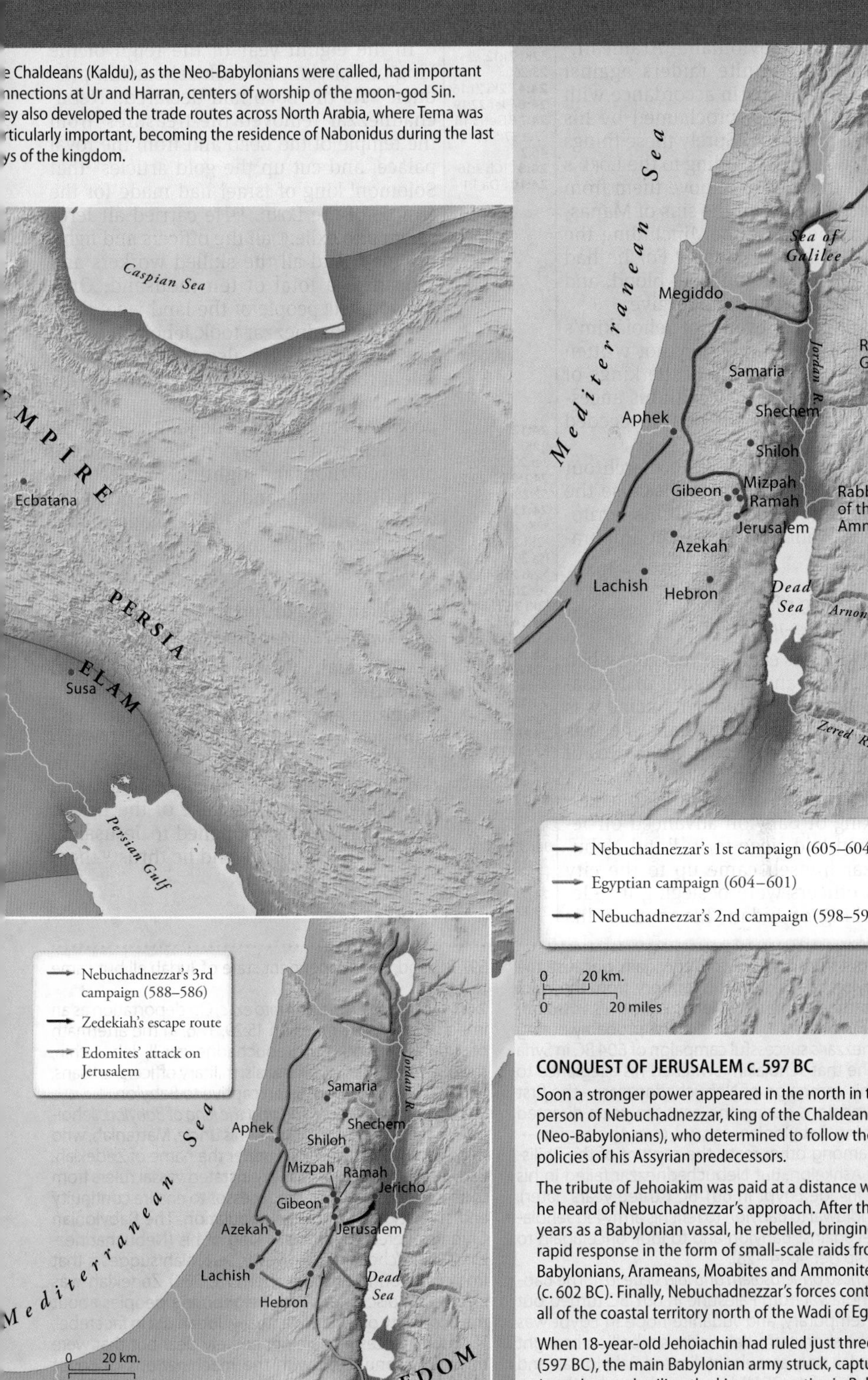

CONQUEST OF JERUSALEM c. 597 BC

Soon a stronger power appeared in the north in the person of Nebuchadnezzar, king of the Chaldeans (Neo-Babylonians), who determined to follow the fierce policies of his Assyrian predecessors.

The tribute of Jehoiakim was paid at a distance when he heard of Nebuchadnezzar's approach. After three years as a Babylonian vassal, he rebelled, bringing a rapid response in the form of small-scale raids from Babylonians, Arameans, Moabites and Ammonites (c. 602 BC). Finally, Nebuchadnezzar's forces controlled all of the coastal territory north of the Wadi of Egypt.

When 18-year-old Jehoiachin had ruled just three months (597 BC), the main Babylonian army struck, capturing Jerusalem and exiling the king as a captive in Babylon. Ten thousand persons were deported.

vassal for three years. But then he turned
against Nebuchadnezzar and rebelled.
2The LORD sent Babylonian,[a] Aramean,[x]
Moabite and Ammonite raiders against
him to destroy[y] Judah, in accordance with
the word of the LORD proclaimed by his
servants the prophets. 3Surely these things
happened to Judah according to the LORD's
command,[z] in order to remove them from
his presence because of the sins of Manasseh[a] and all he had done, 4including the
shedding of innocent blood.[b] For he had
filled Jerusalem with innocent blood, and
the LORD was not willing to forgive.
5As for the other events of Jehoiakim's
reign, and all he did, are they not written
in the book of the annals of the kings of
Judah? 6Jehoiakim rested[c] with his ancestors. And Jehoiachin his son succeeded
him as king.
7The king of Egypt[d] did not march out
from his own country again, because the
king of Babylon[e] had taken all his territory, from the Wadi of Egypt to the Euphrates River.

Jehoiachin King of Judah

24:8-17pp — 2Ch 36:9-10

8Jehoiachin[f] was eighteen years old when
he became king, and he reigned in Jerusalem three months. His mother's name was
Nehushta daughter of Elnathan; she was
from Jerusalem. 9He did evil in the eyes of
the LORD, just as his father had done.
10At that time the officers of Nebuchadnezzar[g] king of Babylon advanced on Jerusalem and laid siege to it, 11and Nebuchadnezzar himself came up to the city
while his officers were besieging it. 12Je-
hoiachin king of Judah, his mother, his
attendants, his nobles and his officials all
surrendered[h] to him.
In the eighth year of the reign of the
king of Babylon, he took Jehoiachin prisoner. 13As the LORD had declared,[i] Nebuchadnezzar removed the treasures[j] from
the temple of the LORD and from the royal
palace, and cut up the gold articles[k] that
Solomon[l] king of Israel had made for the
temple of the LORD. 14He carried all Jerusalem into exile:[m] all the officers and fighting men, and all the skilled workers and
artisans — a total of ten thousand. Only
the poorest[n] people of the land were left.
15Nebuchadnezzar took Jehoiachin captive to Babylon. He also took from Jerusalem to Babylon the king's mother,[o] his
wives, his officials and the prominent
people[p] of the land. 16The king of Babylon
also deported to Babylon the entire force
of seven thousand fighting men, strong
and fit for war, and a thousand skilled
workers and artisans.[q] 17He made Mattaniah, Jehoiachin's uncle, king in his place
and changed his name to Zedekiah.[r]

Zedekiah King of Judah

24:18-20pp — 2Ch 36:11-16; Jer 52:1-3

18Zedekiah[s] was twenty-one years old
when he became king, and he reigned
in Jerusalem eleven years. His mother's
name was Hamutal[t] daughter of Jeremiah; she was from Libnah. 19He did evil in
the eyes of the LORD, just as Jehoiakim
had done. 20It was because of the LORD's
anger that all this happened to Jerusalem
and Judah, and in the end he thrust[u] them
from his presence.

[a] 2 Or *Chaldean*

24:2 [x] Jer 35:11 [y] Jer 25:9
24:3 [z] 2Ki 18:25 [a] 2Ki 21:12; 23:26
24:4 [b] 2Ki 21:16
24:6 [c] Jer 22:19
24:7 [d] Ge 15:18 [e] Jer 37:5-7; 46:2
24:8 [f] 1Ch 3:16
24:10 [g] Da 1:1
24:12 [h] 2Ki 25:27; Jer 22:24-30; 24:1; 25:1; 29:2; 52:28
24:13 [i] 2Ki 20:17 [j] 2Ki 25:15; Isa 39:6 [k] 2Ki 25:14; Jer 20:5 [l] 1Ki 7:51
24:14 [m] Jer 24:1; 52:28 [n] 2Ki 25:12; Jer 40:7; 52:16
24:15 [o] Jer 22:24-28 [p] Est 2:6; Eze 17:12-14
24:16 [q] Jer 52:28
24:17 [r] 1Ch 3:15; 2Ch 36:11; Jer 37:1
24:18 [s] Jer 52:1 [t] 2Ki 23:31
24:20 [u] Dt 4:26; 29:27

---

not march out from his own country again, because the king of Babylon had taken all his territory, from the Wadi of Egypt to the Euphrates River." *became his vassal for three years. But then he ... rebelled.* It was probably during Nebuchadnezzar's successful campaign of 604 BC in Syria and Palestine that Jehoiakim switched his allegiance to Babylon. This campaign of Nebuchadnezzar — the first of eight campaigns during the next ten years directed at establishing Babylonian control over the region — produced, among other feats, the capture of the Philistine city of Ashkelon. But Nebuchadnezzar failed in his attempt to invade Egypt in 601 BC ("three years" later), and his withdrawal to Babylon to refit his army led Jehoiakim to rebel against Babylon and to look once again to Egypt for help (Jer 46:14 – 28).

24:10 *advanced on Jerusalem and laid siege to it.* The Babylonian withdrawal from Palestine in 601 BC turned out to be only temporary, and Judahite hope in Egypt was illusory. In the short term, Jehoiakim's rebellion brought down on Judah only assaults by limited Babylonian and allied forces (v. 2, cf. Jer 35:11). However, the end of the year 598 BC saw the main Babylonian army before the gates of Jerusalem and no Egyptian forces on hand to help. The city surrendered to the Babylonians on Mar. 15 or Mar. 16, 597 BC, and the independent state of Judah all but came to its end.

24:14 *carried all Jerusalem into exile.* On deportation as an imperial tactic, see notes on 15:29; 17:6. In the aftermath of Judah's surrender to Nebuchadnezzar II, Jehoiachin, the queen mother, royal officials, military officers, artisans, and 7,000 soldiers were taken captive to Babylon.

24:20 *Zedekiah rebelled against the king of Babylon.* Jehoiachin's replacement as king was his uncle, Mattaniah, who ruled as a Babylonian vassal under the name of Zedekiah. Babylonian conquerors usually instated vassal rulers from the same house as their predecessor to ensure continuity and stability with the local population. The Babylonian Chronicle refers to him as "a king of his [Nebuchadnezzar's] liking/choosing." However, Jeremiah suggests that from early on in his reign (Jer 27:1; 28:1) Zedekiah was involved in discussions with neighboring peoples about the possibility of revolt. Eventually, Judah did in fact rebel, in circumstances that are not entirely clear but that were no doubt connected with the machinations of Egypt under Necho's successor, Psammetichus II (595 – 589 BC).

Zedekiah stopped paying tribute, and a new siege of Jerusalem followed. This siege was temporarily lifted when the new pharaoh Apries (589 – 570 BC) sent an army

The Fall of Jerusalem

25:1-12pp — Jer 39:1-10
25:1-21pp — 2Ch 36:17-20; Jer 52:4-27
25:22-26pp — Jer 40:7-9; 41:1-3,16-18

Now Zedekiah rebelled against the king of Babylon.

25 So in the ninth year of Zedekiah's reign, on the tenth day of the tenth month, Nebuchadnezzar[v] king of Babylon marched against Jerusalem with his whole army. He encamped outside the city and built siege works[w] all around it. [2]The city was kept under siege until the eleventh year of King Zedekiah.

[3]By the ninth day of the fourth[a] month the famine[x] in the city had become so severe that there was no food for the people to eat. [4]Then the city wall was broken through,[y] and the whole army fled at night through the gate between the two walls near the king's garden, though the Babylonians[b] were surrounding[z] the city. They fled toward the Arabah,[c] [5]but the Babylonian[d] army pursued the king and overtook him in the plains of Jericho. All his soldiers were separated from him and scattered,[a] [6]and he was captured.[b]

He was taken to the king of Babylon at Riblah,[c] where sentence was pronounced on him. [7]They killed the sons of Zedekiah before his eyes. Then they put out his eyes, bound him with bronze shackles and took him to Babylon.[d]

[8]On the seventh day of the fifth month, in the nineteenth year of Nebuchadnezzar king of Babylon, Nebuzaradan commander of the imperial guard, an official of the king of Babylon, came to Jerusalem. [9]He set fire[e] to the temple of the LORD, the royal palace and all the houses of Jerusalem. Every important building he burned down.[f] [10]The whole Babylonian army under the commander of the imperial guard broke down the walls[g] around Jerusalem.

25:1 [v]Jer 34:1-7 [w]Eze 24:2 **25:3** [x]Jer 14:18; La 4:9 **25:4** [y]Eze 33:21 [z]Jer 4:17 **25:5** [a]Eze 12:14 **25:6** [b]Jer 34:21-22 [c]2Ki 23:33 **25:7** [d]Jer 21:7; 32:4-5; Eze 12:11 **25:9** [e]Isa 60:7 [f]Ps 74:3-8; Jer 2:15; Am 2:5; Mic 3:12 **25:10** [g]Ne 1:3 **25:11** [h]2Ki 24:14 [i]2Ki 24:1 **25:12** [j]2Ki 24:14 **25:14** [k]Ex 27:3; 1Ki 7:47-50 **25:17** [l]1Ki 7:15-22 **25:18** [m]1Ch 6:14; Ezr 7:1; Ne 11:11 [n]Jer 21:1; 29:25

[11]Nebuzaradan the commander of the guard carried into exile[h] the people who remained in the city, along with the rest of the populace and those who had deserted to the king of Babylon.[i] [12]But the commander left behind some of the poorest people[j] of the land to work the vineyards and fields.

[13]The Babylonians broke up the bronze pillars, the movable stands and the bronze Sea that were at the temple of the LORD and they carried the bronze to Babylon. [14]They also took away the pots, shovels, wick trimmers, dishes and all the bronze articles[k] used in the temple service. [15]The commander of the imperial guard took away the censers and sprinkling bowls — all that were made of pure gold or silver.

[16]The bronze from the two pillars, the Sea and the movable stands, which Solomon had made for the temple of the LORD, was more than could be weighed. [17]Each pillar[l] was eighteen cubits[e] high. The bronze capital on top of one pillar was three cubits[f] high and was decorated with a network and pomegranates of bronze all around. The other pillar, with its network, was similar.

[18]The commander of the guard took as prisoners Seraiah[m] the chief priest, Zephaniah[n] the priest next in rank and the three doorkeepers. [19]Of those still in the city, he took the officer in charge of the fighting men, and five royal advisers. He also took the secretary who was chief officer in charge of conscripting the people of the land and sixty of the conscripts who

[a] *3* Probable reading of the original Hebrew text (see Jer. 52:6); Masoretic Text does not have *fourth.*
[b] *4* Or *Chaldeans*; also in verses 13, 25 and 26
[c] *4* Or *the Jordan Valley*
[d] *5* Or *Chaldean*; also in verses 10 and 24
[e] *17* That is, about 27 feet or about 8.1 meters
[f] *17* That is, about 4 1/2 feet or about 1.4 meters

---

into Palestine (Jer 37:1 – 10), but it was resumed when the Egyptian army withdrew. The city eventually fell in 586 BC, after nearly two years of siege and with all supplies of food exhausted.

25:4 *through the gate between the two walls.* As the city wall of Jerusalem was being breached (probably on the northern side), Zedekiah managed to escape by night with his troops through an exit in the southeastern wall that is probably to be identified with the Fountain Gate of Ne 3:15. The mention of "two walls" likely alludes to the old wall of the City of David and the new wall built in the eighth century BC in order to enclose the western hill and the Pool of Siloam. *fled toward the Arabah.* Zedekiah's plan was to flee to the Arabah (the great rift valley of Palestine that runs from the Sea of Galilee to the Red Sea and forms the barrier between Israel and Transjordan), apparently by way of the Wadi Kelt in the vicinity of Jericho to Jerusalem's northeast. The Babylonians overtook him near Jericho, however, on the road from Jerusalem to Jericho (v. 5).

25:8 *Nebuzaradan commander of the imperial guard.* He may also be named as a high official of Nebuchadnezzar's court on a prism found in Babylon and now located in Istanbul: "I ordered the following court officials in exercise of their duties to take up position in my official suite: as *mašennu*-officials, Nabuzeriddinam."

25:9 – 11 *set fire to the temple … the royal palace and all the houses … broke down the walls around Jerusalem … carried into exile the people.* The systematic destruction of the city, including prominent buildings such as the temple, the palace and the city defenses, was overseen by Nebuzaradan, a Babylonian officer who also organized the deportations (and indeed the executions, vv. 18 – 21). Jer 52:28 – 30 counts the number of the exiles taken to Babylon from Jerusalem at this time as totaling 832 people in all. It was a sizable deportation of people important for the independent rule and prosperity of Judah, and it was designed to have a detrimental effect on the ability of the Judahites in the future to organize for rebellion.

EXILE OF THE SOUTHERN KINGDOM

Knowledge about the destiny of the captives from Israel and Judah is sparse in the period following the capture of Samaria and the later destruction of Jerusalem.

Assyrians and Babylonians treated their subject peoples essentially the same: overwhelming military force used in a manner inspiring psychological terror, along with mass deportations and heavy tribute.

Three deportations are mentioned in Jer 52:28–30, the largest one consisting of 3,023 Jews who were taken to Babylon along with King Jehoiachin in 597 BC.

After the destruction of Jerusalem by Nebuzaradan, the commander of the Babylonian army, hundreds of exiles were taken to Riblah in the land of Hamath, where, in addition to Zedekiah's sons, at least 61 were executed.

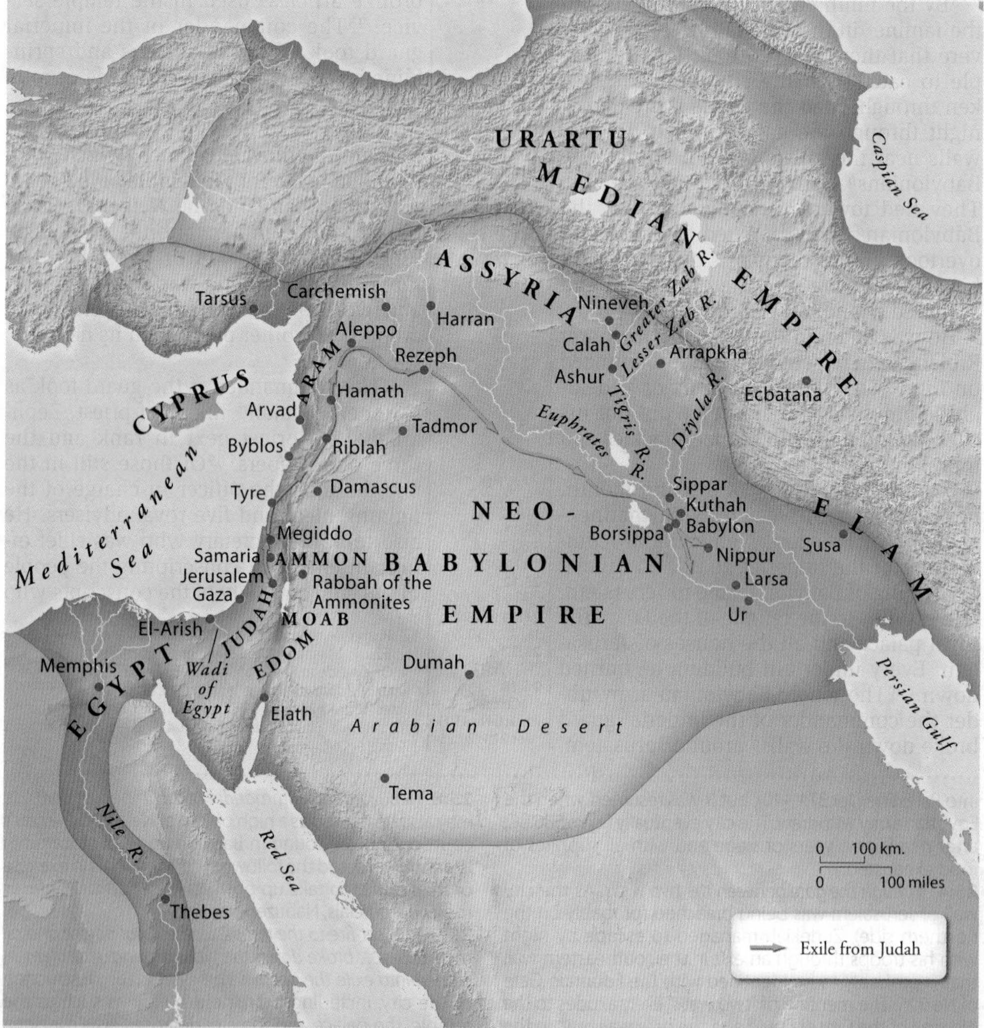

Clay tablets from the fifth century BC called the Murashu archives have been found at Nippur. They document the commercial transactions with Jewish families who remained in Mesopotamia following Ezra's return to Jerusalem.

Eze 1:1–3 and 3:15 indicate that other captives were placed at Tel Aviv and at the Kebar River, both probably in the locale of Nippur, as were other villages mentioned in Ezr 2:59; 8:15,17; Ne 7:61.

Jehoiachin and his family were kept in Babylon, where clay ration receipts bearing his name and the names of his sons have been found.

Cuneiform text listing rations for Jehoiachin and his sons.

Kim Walton, Vorderasiatisches Museum.

were found in the city. [20]Nebuzaradan the
commander took them all and brought
them to the king of Babylon at Riblah.
[21]There at Riblah, in the land of Hamath,
the king had them executed.

So Judah went into captivity, away from
her land.[o]

[22]Nebuchadnezzar king of Babylon appointed Gedaliah[p] son of Ahikam, the
son of Shaphan, to be over the people he
had left behind in Judah. [23]When all the
army officers and their men heard that
the king of Babylon had appointed Gedaliah as governor, they came to Gedaliah
at Mizpah—Ishmael son of Nethaniah, Johanan son of Kareah, Seraiah son of Tanhumeth the Netophathite, Jaazaniah the son of
the Maakathite, and their men.
[24]Gedaliah took an oath to reassure them and their men. "Do
not be afraid of the Babylonian officials," he said. "Settle
down in the land and serve the
king of Babylon, and it will go
well with you."

[25]In the seventh month, however,
Ishmael son of Nethaniah, the son of
Elishama, who was of royal blood, came
with ten men and assassinated Gedaliah
and also the men of Judah and the Babylonians who were with him at Mizpah.
[26]At this, all the people from the least to
the greatest, together with the army officers, fled to Egypt[q] for fear of the Babylonians.

25:21 [o]Ge 12:7; Dt 28:64; Jos 23:13; 2Ki 23:27
25:22 [p]Jer 39:14; 40:5,7
25:26 [q]Isa 30:2; Jer 43:7
25:27 [r]2Ki 24:12; Jer 52:31-34
25:28 [s]Ezr 5:5; Ne 2:1; Da 2:48
25:29 [t]2Sa 9:7
25:30 [u]Est 2:9; Jer 28:4

Jehoiachin Released

25:27-30pp — Jer 52:31-34

[27]In the thirty-seventh year of the exile
of Jehoiachin king of Judah, in the year
Awel-Marduk became king of Babylon, he
released Jehoiachin[r] king of Judah from
prison. He did this on the twenty-seventh
day of the twelfth month. [28]He spoke kindly to him and gave him a seat of honor[s]
higher than those of the other kings who
were with him in Babylon. [29]So Jehoiachin
put aside his prison clothes and for the
rest of his life ate regularly at the king's
table.[t] [30]Day by day the king gave Jehoiachin a regular allowance as long as he
lived.[u]

25:23 *Mizpah.* The site that Gedaliah chose for his new administrative center was Mizpah (located at Tell en-Nasbeh, about eight miles [almost 13 kilometers] from Jerusalem on Judah's northern border)—a significant fortress that appears to have escaped destruction in the course of the Babylonian campaign. Jer 41:4–6 may imply that it became not only Judah's new capital, but also its new worship center, for these verses describe a pilgrimage in order to offer grain and frankincense at the "house of the LORD"—perhaps in Mizpah itself. *Jaazaniah.* Among the archaeological discoveries at Mizpah is an onyx seal dating from the sixth century BC and inscribed "belonging to Jaazaniah, servant of the king." This may be the person named in this verse.

25:27 *Awel-Marduk.* Nebuchadnezzar's son and successor, ruling 562–560 BC. He is known for virtually nothing other than his release of the Judahite king Jehoiachin from prison.

25:29–30 *Jehoiachin … ate regularly at the king's table … a regular allowance as long as he lived.* Jehoahaz was exiled to Egypt and died there (23:34), while the fate of Zedekiah in Babylon is never made clear (v. 7). But news of Jehoiachin at the end of the books of Kings seems designed to foster hope that the destruction of Jerusalem and the exile of its people does not mean that there is no future for the Davidic line. One of the most interesting extra-Biblical texts that touch on the deportation of Judahites to Babylon is in fact an administrative document that lists rations for Jehoiachin and his sons, apparently in captivity in Babylon.

NARRATIVE LITERATURE

1 CHRONICLES

Introduction to 1 – 2 Chronicles.

Historical Setting

The closing verses of the book, which record the advent of Cyrus the Great of Persia and his proclamation, demonstrate that the book is compiled sometime after 539 BC. Other indications in the book, particularly the list of postexilic descendants of David (1Ch 3:17 – 24), may point to a still later date, possibly in the second half of the fourth century BC, toward the end of the Persian period.

When Cyrus the Great conquered Babylon in 539 BC and established Persian rule in the ancient Near East, he set in motion a series of events that concerned the Jews. His proclamation, which gave permission for the rebuilding of the temple in Jerusalem, gave rise to a series of returns from exile by deportees and descendants of deportees. Although Cyrus is looked upon by the Jews as a benefactor, it should be noted that his "beneficence" was not directed solely toward the Jews but formed only part of a wider foreign policy.

It should be borne in mind when discussing the historical setting of Chronicles that during the Persian period (and later) there was a significant Jewish community outside the land of Israel: in Babylonia, Elam, Persia, Egypt and even into Asia Minor. The indication is that Jews traveled to other places from Babylonia in the course of trade or as mercenaries in the Babylonian, then Persian, army. Once there, Jews held a variety of occupations and social states in the lands in which they settled, and some (e.g., Nehemiah) even rose to high positions within the Persian administration. It is clear from the book of Nehemiah and from the archive of letters dating to the fifth century BC from Elephantine in Upper Egypt that contact was maintained with the community in Israel itself. It also seems clear that, at least on the part of some Jews, there was intermarriage with non-Jews and some religious syncretism, as witnessed by the invocation of foreign deities and a readiness to call their children by names that had a foreign deity as a component. From early in the exile, there appears to have been a fair degree of freedom of movement,

KEY CONCEPTS

- These books seek to help readers understand the basis for continuity, transformation and theological stability.
- These books highlight retribution theology and the role of the priests and Levites.
- These books also lead the post-exilic community to refocus from monarchy to theocracy.
- Recurrent themes are reform and repentance as a means to God's blessing.

and this increased in the postexilic period. There was also the freedom for Jews to engage in commerce, even to become comparatively wealthy in their adopted country. Jews lived side-by-side with people of all nationalities, interacted with them on a daily basis, and even entered into business partnerships with them. It may be stated, therefore, that at least some Jews did not pursue a rigorous policy of separation.

The Jews were part of the Persian Empire, under the direct authority of the king, albeit filtered through different levels of administration, and were constantly monitored both by their superiors and by their peers. Even though they did have some freedom, their autonomy and their liberty were limited. These constraints would have effectively and quickly curbed any hope of a swift restoration of the Davidic monarchy.

Literary Setting

Chronicles shares similarities with a number of different text genres that are represented in ancient Near Eastern literature. It is immediately apparent to the reader of Chronicles that its compiler is heavily dependent on lists of all kinds: genealogical records, census records, administrative lists, etc. Lists per se are well attested in the ancient Near East. From Mesopotamia in particular a large number of lists on many different topics have been recovered. It seems that there was a desire, at least in Mesopotamia, to order and to categorize everything, including the pantheon. The incorporation of lists of different kinds into literary texts also has parallels within ancient Near Eastern literature as a whole and within the Hebrew Bible itself. At times genealogical records may be included in Near Eastern royal inscriptions, but they very rarely go beyond the third generation. ◆

Historical Records From Adam to Abraham

To Noah's Sons

1 Adam,[a] Seth, Enosh, [2]Kenan,[b] Mahalalel,[c] Jared,[d] [3]Enoch,[e] Methuselah,[f]
Lamech,[g] Noah.[h]

4 The sons of Noah:[a][i]
Shem, Ham and Japheth.[j]

The Japhethites

1:5-7pp — Ge 10:2-5

5 The sons[b] of Japheth:
Gomer, Magog, Madai, Javan, Tubal, Meshek and Tiras.
6 The sons of Gomer:
Ashkenaz, Riphath[c] and Togarmah.
7 The sons of Javan:
Elishah, Tarshish, the Kittites and the Rodanites.

The Hamites

1:8-16pp — Ge 10:6-20

8 The sons of Ham:
Cush, Egypt, Put and Canaan.
9 The sons of Cush:
Seba, Havilah, Sabta, Raamah and Sabteka.
The sons of Raamah:
Sheba and Dedan.
10 Cush was the father[d] of
Nimrod, who became a mighty warrior on earth.
11 Egypt was the father of
the Ludites, Anamites, Lehabites,
Naphtuhites, [12]Pathrusites, Kaslu-
hites (from whom the Philistines came) and Caphtorites.
13 Canaan was the father of
Sidon his firstborn,[e] and of the Hittites, [14]Jebusites, Amorites, Girgashites, [15]Hivites, Arkites, Sinites,
[16]Arvadites, Zemarites and Hamathites.

The Semites

1:17-23pp — Ge 10:21-31; 11:10-27

17 The sons of Shem:
Elam, Ashur, Arphaxad, Lud and Aram.
The sons of Aram:[f]
Uz, Hul, Gether and Meshek.
18 Arphaxad was the father of Shelah,
and Shelah the father of Eber.
19 Two sons were born to Eber:
One was named Peleg,[g] because in his time the earth was divided; his brother was named Joktan.
20 Joktan was the father of
Almodad, Sheleph, Hazarmaveth,
Jerah, [21]Hadoram, Uzal, Diklah,
[22]Obal,[h] Abimael, Sheba, [23]Ophir,
Havilah and Jobab. All these were sons of Joktan.

24 Shem,[k] Arphaxad,[i] Shelah,
25 Eber, Peleg, Reu,
26 Serug, Nahor, Terah
27 and Abram (that is, Abraham).

The Family of Abraham

28 The sons of Abraham:
Isaac and Ishmael.

Descendants of Hagar

1:29-31pp — Ge 25:12-16

29 These were their descendants:
Nebaioth the firstborn of Ishmael,
Kedar, Adbeel, Mibsam, [30]Mishma,
Dumah, Massa, Hadad, Tema, [31]Je-
tur, Naphish and Kedemah. These were the sons of Ishmael.

Descendants of Keturah

1:32-33pp — Ge 25:1-4

32 The sons born to Keturah, Abraham's concubine:[l]
Zimran, Jokshan, Medan, Midian, Ishbak and Shuah.
The sons of Jokshan:
Sheba and Dedan.[m]
33 The sons of Midian:
Ephah, Epher, Hanok, Abida and Eldaah.
All these were descendants of Keturah.

Descendants of Sarah

1:35-37pp — Ge 36:10-14

34 Abraham[n] was the father of Isaac.[o]
The sons of Isaac:
Esau and Israel.[p]

Esau's Sons

35 The sons of Esau:[q]
Eliphaz, Reuel,[r] Jeush, Jalam and Korah.

1:1 [a] Ge 5:1-32; Lk 3:36-38 **1:2** [b] Ge 5:9 [c] Ge 5:12 [d] Ge 5:15 **1:3** [e] Ge 5:18; Jude 1:14 [f] Ge 5:21 [g] Ge 5:25 [h] Ge 5:29 **1:4** [i] Ge 6:10; 10:1 [j] Ge 5:32
1:24 [k] Ge 10:21-25; Lk 3:34-36 **1:32** [l] Ge 22:24 [m] Ge 10:7 **1:34** [n] Lk 3:34 [o] Ge 21:2-3; Mt 1:2; Ac 7:8 [p] Ge 17:5; 25:25-26 **1:35** [q] Ge 36:19 [r] Ge 36:4

[a] *4* Septuagint; Hebrew does not have this line. [b] *5* *Sons* may mean *descendants* or *successors* or *nations*; also in verses 6-9, 17 and 23. [c] *6* Many Hebrew manuscripts and Vulgate (see also Septuagint and Gen. 10:3); most Hebrew manuscripts *Diphath* [d] *10* *Father* may mean *ancestor* or *predecessor* or *founder*; also in verses 11, 13, 18 and 20. [e] *13* Or *of the Sidonians, the foremost* [f] *17* One Hebrew manuscript and some Septuagint manuscripts (see also Gen. 10:23); most Hebrew manuscripts do not have this line. [g] *19* *Peleg* means *division.* [h] *22* Some Hebrew manuscripts and Syriac (see also Gen. 10:28); most Hebrew manuscripts *Ebal* [i] *24* Hebrew; some Septuagint manuscripts *Arphaxad, Cainan* (see also note at Gen. 11:10)

1:28–54 The descendants of Ishmael and Keturah equate with Arab tribes who lived in the Syro-Arabian desert. Various of these descendants and their settlements are mentioned in inscriptions of the Assyrian king Ashurbanipal. The last king of the Chaldean dynasty, Nabonidus, led an extensive campaign against Tema and other Arabian states in the mid-sixth century BC.

36 The sons of Eliphaz:
Teman, Omar, Zepho,[a] Gatam and Kenaz;
by Timna: Amalek.[b][s]
37 The sons of Reuel:[t]
Nahath, Zerah, Shammah and Mizzah.

The Assyrian King List, seventh century BC. Several features of the genealogy in 1Ch 1 are striking when compared with this. There is no introduction; the scribe has drawn lines across the tablet, dividing it into four sections, two of which are lists of names without kinship terms, alternating with two lists in which relations are specified; both segmented and linear genealogies are used. This suggests the Chronicler was following a known literary pattern.

The People of Seir in Edom

1:38-42pp — Ge 36:20-28

38 The sons of Seir:
Lotan, Shobal, Zibeon, Anah, Dishon, Ezer and Dishan.
39 The sons of Lotan:
Hori and Homam. Timna was Lotan's sister.
40 The sons of Shobal:
Alvan,[c] Manahath, Ebal, Shepho and Onam.
The sons of Zibeon:
Aiah and Anah.[u]
41 The son of Anah:
Dishon.
The sons of Dishon:
Hemdan,[d] Eshban, Ithran and Keran.
42 The sons of Ezer:
Bilhan, Zaavan and Akan.[e]
The sons of Dishan[f]:
Uz and Aran.

The Rulers of Edom

1:43-54pp — Ge 36:31-43

43 These were the kings who reigned in Edom before any Israelite king reigned:
Bela son of Beor, whose city was named Dinhabah.
44 When Bela died, Jobab son of Zerah from Bozrah succeeded him as king.
45 When Jobab died, Husham from the land of the Temanites[v] succeeded him as king.
46 When Husham died, Hadad son of Bedad, who defeated Midian in the country of Moab, succeeded him as king. His city was named Avith.
47 When Hadad died, Samlah from Masrekah succeeded him as king.
48 When Samlah died, Shaul from Rehoboth on the river[g] succeeded him as king.
49 When Shaul died, Baal-Hanan son of Akbor succeeded him as king.
50 When Baal-Hanan died, Hadad succeeded him as king. His city was named Pau,[h] and his wife's name was Mehetabel daughter of Matred, the daughter of Me-Zahab. 51 Hadad also died.

The chiefs of Edom were:
Timna, Alvah, Jetheth, 52 Oholibamah, Elah, Pinon, 53 Kenaz, Teman, Mibzar, 54 Magdiel and Iram. These were the chiefs of Edom.

1:36 [s] Ex 17:14
1:37 [t] Ge 36:17
1:40 [u] Ge 36:2
1:45 [v] Ge 36:11

Israel's Sons

2:1-2pp — Ge 35:23-26

2 These were the sons of Israel:
Reuben, Simeon, Levi, Judah, Issachar, Zebulun, 2 Dan, Joseph, Benjamin, Naphtali, Gad and Asher.

[a] *36* Many Hebrew manuscripts, some Septuagint manuscripts and Syriac (see also Gen. 36:11); most Hebrew manuscripts *Zephi* [b] *36* Some Septuagint manuscripts (see also Gen. 36:12); Hebrew *Gatam, Kenaz, Timna and Amalek* [c] *40* Many Hebrew manuscripts and some Septuagint manuscripts (see also Gen. 36:23); most Hebrew manuscripts *Alian* [d] *41* Many Hebrew manuscripts and some Septuagint manuscripts (see also Gen. 36:26); most Hebrew manuscripts *Hamran* [e] *42* Many Hebrew and Septuagint manuscripts (see also Gen. 36:27); most Hebrew manuscripts *Zaavan, Jaakan* [f] *42* See Gen. 36:28; Hebrew *Dishon,* a variant of *Dishan* [g] *48* Possibly the Euphrates [h] *50* Many Hebrew manuscripts, some Septuagint manuscripts, Vulgate and Syriac (see also Gen. 36:39); most Hebrew manuscripts *Pai*

1:36 *Amalek.* See notes on Nu 13:29; Dt 25:19.

1 CHRONICLES 1–8

The Significance of Genealogies for a Postexilic Audience

On genealogies in the ancient world, see the article "Genealogies," p. 16. The intended readers of Chronicles are those who have returned from the Babylonian exile in the sixth and fifth centuries BC and who have reestablished themselves in the land of Palestine. A clear genealogy was crucial to provide them with claims to territory within the restored community. According to Lev 25:23, the land belonged to the Lord, and the people were his tenants. This land had been allocated to the different families of Israelites and remained in their possession (cf. 1Ki 21:3). Any claim to that land, therefore, had to be accompanied by proof of belonging to the correct family.

Moreover, certain offices within Israel, particularly those relating to temple worship, had been allocated to specific families. Those wishing to exercise such functions had to be able to show their pedigree (cf. Ezr 2:61–63). Admittedly, most of the genealogies in 1Ch 2–8 stop far short of the exile. However, a preoccupation with lineage in the author's own time may have sparked an interest in the genealogies of certain key figures in the narrative. While prerogatives of land rights and office entitlements explains tracing lineage back as far as Abraham, it is intriguing that the Chronicler goes all the way back to Adam (1Ch 1:1). This suggests an even broader purpose beyond tribe, clan and individual identity to Israelite identity.

The Israelites had returned to the land in the sixth and fifth centuries BC. The books of Chronicles were compiled several decades later, perhaps about 400 BC. By this time, any momentum associated with the return had dissipated, and hopes of a restored Davidic empire had waned. This group of people needed a new vision of who they were. The genealogies provide this information. They are the people of God whose lineage traces back through all the worthies of the past, not just to Abraham, but to Adam. They are part of the community that finds its identity in the kingdom of God—a spiritual kingdom, not just a political one.

Corporate identity was important in the ancient world and these genealogies rooted the corporate identity of Israel not just in the present (where their hopes and dreams about restoration stood unfulfilled), but linked it with generations and ancestors of the past who had experienced God's good work and who together with them made up the kingdom of God. ◆

Judah

2:5-15pp — Ru 4:18-22; Mt 1:3-6

To Hezron's Sons

3 The sons of Judah:[w]
Er, Onan and Shelah.[x] These three
were born to him by a Canaanite
woman, the daughter of Shua.[y] Er,
Judah's firstborn, was wicked in the
LORD's sight; so the LORD put him to
death.[z] 4 Judah's daughter-in-law[a]
Tamar[b] bore Perez[c] and Zerah to Judah. He had five sons in all.

5 The sons of Perez:[d]
Hezron[e] and Hamul.

6 The sons of Zerah:
Zimri, Ethan, Heman, Kalkol and Darda[a]—five in all.

2:3 [w] Ge 29:35; 38:2-10 [x] Ge 38:5 [y] Ge 38:2 [z] Nu 26:19 **2:4** [a] Ge 11:31 [b] Ge 38:11-30 [c] Ge 38:29 **2:5** [d] Ge 46:12 [e] Nu 26:21

[a] *6* Many Hebrew manuscripts, some Septuagint manuscripts and Syriac (see also 1 Kings 4:31); most Hebrew manuscripts *Dara*

2:3 *Canaanite woman.* See note on Dt 1:7 ("the land of the Canannites").

7 The son of Karmi:
Achar,[a f] who brought trouble on Israel by violating the ban on taking
devoted things.[b g]
8 The son of Ethan:
Azariah.
9 The sons born to Hezron[h] were:
Jerahmeel, Ram and Caleb.[c]

From Ram Son of Hezron

10 Ram[i] was the father of
Amminadab[j], and Amminadab the
father of Nahshon,[k] the leader of
the people of Judah. 11 Nahshon
was the father of Salmon,[d] Salmon
the father of Boaz, 12 Boaz[l] the father of Obed and Obed the father
of Jesse.[m]
13 Jesse[n] was the father of
Eliab[o] his firstborn; the second
son was Abinadab, the third Shimea, 14 the fourth Nethanel, the fifth
Raddai, 15 the sixth Ozem and the
seventh David. 16 Their sisters were
Zeruiah[p] and Abigail. Zeruiah's[q]
three sons were Abishai, Joab[r] and
Asahel. 17 Abigail was the mother of
Amasa,[s] whose father was Jether
the Ishmaelite.

Caleb Son of Hezron

18 Caleb son of Hezron had children by
his wife Azubah (and by Jerioth).
These were her sons: Jesher, Shobab and Ardon. 19 When Azubah
died, Caleb[t] married Ephrath, who
bore him Hur. 20 Hur was the father
of Uri, and Uri the father of Bezalel.[u]
21 Later, Hezron, when he was sixty
years old, married the daughter
of Makir the father of Gilead.[v] He
made love to her, and she bore him
Segub. 22 Segub was the father of
Jair, who controlled twenty-three
towns in Gilead. 23 (But Geshur and
Aram captured Havvoth Jair,[e w] as
well as Kenath[x] with its surrounding settlements — sixty towns.) All
these were descendants of Makir
the father of Gilead.
24 After Hezron died in Caleb Ephrathah, Abijah the wife of Hezron
bore him Ashhur[y] the father[f] of Tekoa.

2:7 [f] Jos 7:1 [g] Jos 6:18 **2:9** [h] Nu 26:21 **2:10** [i] Lk 3:32-33 [j] Ex 6:23 [k] Nu 1:7 **2:12** [l] Ru 2:1 [m] Ru 4:17 **2:13** [n] Ru 4:17 [o] 1Sa 16:6 **2:16** [p] 1Sa 26:6 [q] 2Sa 2:18 [r] 2Sa 2:13 **2:17** [s] 2Sa 17:25 **2:19** [t] ver 42, 50 **2:20** [u] Ex 31:2 **2:21** [v] Nu 27:1 **2:23** [w] Nu 32:41; Dt 3:14; Jos 13:30 [x] Nu 32:42 **2:24** [y] 1Ch 4:5 **2:36** [z] 1Ch 11:41

Jerahmeel Son of Hezron

25 The sons of Jerahmeel the firstborn of
Hezron:
Ram his firstborn, Bunah, Oren,
Ozem and[g] Ahijah. 26 Jerahmeel had
another wife, whose name was Ata-
rah; she was the mother of Onam.
27 The sons of Ram the firstborn of Jerahmeel:
Maaz, Jamin and Eker.
28 The sons of Onam:
Shammai and Jada.
The sons of Shammai:
Nadab and Abishur.
29 Abishur's wife was named Abihail,
who bore him Ahban and Molid.
30 The sons of Nadab:
Seled and Appaim. Seled died without children.
31 The son of Appaim:
Ishi, who was the father of Sheshan.
Sheshan was the father of Ahlai.
32 The sons of Jada, Shammai's brother:
Jether and Jonathan. Jether died
without children.
33 The sons of Jonathan:
Peleth and Zaza.
These were the descendants of Jerahmeel.
34 Sheshan had no sons — only daughters.
He had an Egyptian servant named
Jarha. 35 Sheshan gave his daughter
in marriage to his servant Jarha,
and she bore him Attai.
36 Attai was the father of Nathan,
Nathan the father of Zabad,[z]
37 Zabad the father of Ephlal,
Ephlal the father of Obed,
38 Obed the father of Jehu,
Jehu the father of Azariah,
39 Azariah the father of Helez,
Helez the father of Eleasah,
40 Eleasah the father of Sismai,
Sismai the father of Shallum,
41 Shallum the father of Jekamiah,
and Jekamiah the father of Elishama.

[a] 7 *Achar* means *trouble*; *Achar* is called *Achan* in Joshua. [b] 7 The Hebrew term refers to the irrevocable giving over of things or persons to the LORD, often by totally destroying them. [c] 9 Hebrew *Kelubai*, a variant of *Caleb* [d] 11 Septuagint (see also Ruth 4:21); Hebrew *Salma* [e] 23 Or *captured the settlements of Jair* [f] 24 *Father* may mean *civic leader* or *military leader*; also in verses 42, 45, 49-52 and possibly elsewhere. [g] 25 Or *Oren and Ozem, by*

2:7 *ban.* See notes on Jos 6:17; 7:24.
2:23 *Havvoth Jair, as well as Kenath.* These settlements in Transjordan were taken by the Manassites from the Amorites before the conquest (Nu 32:39 – 42). Geshur and Aram are states from farther north toward Mount Hermon. David married the daughter of the king of Geshur, and the settlements of Jair are mentioned within the list of Solomon's governors (1Ki 4:13). These settlements were captured after this time, therefore, probably in the ninth century BC, when Aram was becoming strong. The affiliation of these settlements with Judah is found only here.

The Clans of Caleb

[42]The sons of Caleb[a] the brother of Jerahmeel:
Mesha his firstborn, who was the father of Ziph, and his son Mareshah,[a]
who was the father of Hebron.
[43]The sons of Hebron:
Korah, Tappuah, Rekem and Shema. [44]Shema was the father of
Raham, and Raham the father of
Jorkeam. Rekem was the father of
Shammai. [45]The son of Shammai
was Maon[b], and Maon was the father of Beth Zur.[c]
[46]Caleb's concubine Ephah was the
mother of Haran, Moza and Gazez.
Haran was the father of Gazez.
[47]The sons of Jahdai:
Regem, Jotham, Geshan, Pelet,
Ephah and Shaaph.
[48]Caleb's concubine Maakah was the
mother of Sheber and Tirhanah.
[49]She also gave birth to Shaaph the
father of Madmannah[d] and to Sheva the father of Makbenah and Gib-
ea. Caleb's daughter was Aksah.[e]
[50]These were the descendants of
Caleb.

The sons of Hur[f] the firstborn of Ephrathah:
Shobal the father of Kiriath Jearim,[g]
[51]Salma the father of Bethlehem, and
Hareph the father of Beth Gader.
[52]The descendants of Shobal the father
of Kiriath Jearim were:
Haroeh, half the Manahathites,
[53]and the clans of Kiriath Jearim: the
Ithrites,[h] Puthites, Shumathites and
Mishraites. From these descended
the Zorathites and Eshtaolites.
[54]The descendants of Salma:
Bethlehem, the Netophathites,[i] Atroth Beth Joab, half the Manahathites, the Zorites, [55]and the clans of
scribes[b] who lived at Jabez: the Ti-
rathites, Shimeathites and Sucath-
ites. These are the Kenites[j] who
came from Hammath,[k] the father
of the Rekabites.[c][l]

2:42 [a] ver 19
2:45 [b] Jos 15:55 [c] Jos 15:58
2:49 [d] Jos 15:31 [e] Jos 15:16
2:50 [f] 1Ch 4:4 [g] ver 19
2:53 [h] 2Sa 23:38
2:54 [i] Ezr 2:22; Ne 7:26; 12:28
2:55 [j] Ge 15:19; Jdg 1:16; Jdg 4:11 [k] Jos 19:35 [l] 2Ki 10:15, 23; Jer 35:2-19
3:1 [m] 1Ch 14:3; 28:5 [n] Jos 15:56 [o] 1Sa 25:42
3:2 [p] 1Ki 2:22
3:4 [q] 2Sa 5:4; 1Ch 29:27 [r] 2Sa 2:11; 5:5
3:5 [s] 2Sa 11:3; 12:24
3:9 [t] 2Sa 13:1 [u] 1Ch 14:4

The Sons of David

3:1-4pp — 2Sa 3:2-5
3:5-8pp — 2Sa 5:14-16; 1Ch 14:4-7

3 These were the sons of David[m] born to
him in Hebron:
The firstborn was Amnon the son
of Ahinoam of Jezreel;[n]
the second, Daniel the son of Abigail[o] of Carmel;
[2]the third, Absalom the son of Maakah daughter of Talmai king of Geshur;
the fourth, Adonijah[p] the son of
Haggith;
[3]the fifth, Shephatiah the son of Abi-
tal;
and the sixth, Ithream, by his wife
Eglah.
[4]These six were born to David in
Hebron,[q] where he reigned seven
years and six months.[r]
David reigned in Jerusalem thirty-three
years, [5]and these were the children born
to him there:
Shammua,[d] Shobab, Nathan and
Solomon. These four were by
Bathsheba[e][s] daughter of Ammiel.
[6]There were also Ibhar, Elishua,[f]
Eliphelet, [7]Nogah, Nepheg, Japhia,
[8]Elishama, Eliada and Eliphelet —
nine in all. [9]All these were the sons
of David, besides his sons by his
concubines. And Tamar[t] was their
sister.[u]

[a] *42* The meaning of the Hebrew for this phrase is uncertain. [b] *55* Or *of the Sopherites* [c] *55* Or *father of Beth Rekab* [d] *5* Hebrew *Shimea,* a variant of *Shammua* [e] *5* One Hebrew manuscript and Vulgate (see also Septuagint and 2 Samuel 11:3); most Hebrew manuscripts *Bathshua* [f] *6* Two Hebrew manuscripts (see also 2 Samuel 5:15 and 1 Chron. 14:5); most Hebrew manuscripts *Elishama*

2:42–55 Caleb was given a special land grant near Hebron. Since the genealogies are being used for land claims (see the article "The Significance of Genealogies for a Postexilic Audience," p. 680) it is important that his claim is recognized.
2:55 *clans of scribes.* See the article "Books and Literacy," p. 666.
3:1 *Hebron.* The city held particular significance for the Israelites. Abraham had camped close by, and he and the other patriarchs were buried there. Caleb, Judah's hero of the conquest, was given Hebron and its environs as his inheritance, and the city itself was one of the Levitical cities of refuge (Jos 20:7). Later, when Absalom rebelled against David, his father, he made Hebron his capital. It was also an important commercial center, sitting astride the important trade routes that ran north to Jerusalem and south to Beersheba and Arad.
3:2 *Maakah daughter of Talmai king of Geshur.* Diplomatic marriages were common in the ancient Near East to form alliances between states. During David's reign in Hebron, Saul's son Ish-Bosheth had set up a rival kingdom. Centered in Mahanaim in Transjordan, his kingdom included Gilead. An alliance of David with the king of Geshur to the north of Gilead made sound strategic sense, since the war could potentially then be fought on two fronts. If, however, the marriage took place after Ish-Bosheth's two-year reign was over, it would have aided the consolidation of the kingdom and the pacification of one of Israel's close neighbors. *Geshur.* The land of Geshur can be fixed with a high degree of confidence in the Golan between Mount Hermon on the north, Bashan on the east, and Gilead on the south. The Amarna letters mention a "Land of Garu" (EA 256), a large tract of territory covering the most fertile part of the Golan Heights, identical with Biblical Geshur. The difference between the names can be explained by the scribal omission of a cuneiform sign on the part of the Amarna scribe.

The Kings of Judah

10 Solomon's son was Rehoboam,[v]
Abijah his son,
Asa his son,
Jehoshaphat[w] his son,
11 Jehoram[a][x] his son,
Ahaziah[y] his son,
Joash[z] his son,
12 Amaziah[a] his son,
Azariah his son,
Jotham[b] his son,
13 Ahaz[c] his son,
Hezekiah[d] his son,
Manasseh[e] his son,
14 Amon[f] his son,
Josiah[g] his son.
15 The sons of Josiah:
Johanan the firstborn,
Jehoiakim[h] the second son,
Zedekiah[i] the third,
Shallum[j] the fourth.
16 The successors of Jehoiakim:
Jehoiachin[b][k] his son,
and Zedekiah.[l]

The Royal Line After the Exile

17 The descendants of Jehoiachin the captive:
Shealtiel[m] his son, 18 Malkiram, Pedaiah, Shenazzar,[n] Jekamiah, Hoshama and Nedabiah.[o]
19 The sons of Pedaiah:
Zerubbabel[p] and Shimei.
The sons of Zerubbabel:
Meshullam and Hananiah.
Shelomith was their sister.
20 There were also five others:
Hashubah, Ohel, Berekiah, Hasadiah and Jushab-Hesed.
21 The descendants of Hananiah:
Pelatiah and Jeshaiah, and the sons of Rephaiah, of Arnan, of Obadiah and of Shekaniah.
22 The descendants of Shekaniah:
Shemaiah and his sons:
Hattush,[q] Igal, Bariah, Neariah and Shaphat — six in all.

3:10 [v] 1Ki 11:43; 14:21-31; 2Ch 12:16 [w] 2Ch 17:1-21:3 **3:11** [x] 2Ki 8:16-24; 2Ch 21:1 [y] 2Ch 22:1-10 [z] 2Ki 11:1-12:21 **3:12** [a] 2Ki 14:1-22; 2Ch 25:1-28 [b] Isa 1:1; Hos 1:1; Mic 1:1 **3:13** [c] 2Ki 16:1-20; 2Ch 28:1; Isa 7:1 [d] 2Ki 18:1-20:21; 2Ch 29:1; Jer 26:19 [e] 2Ch 33:1 **3:14** [f] 2Ki 21:19-26; 2Ch 33:21; Zep 1:1 [g] 2Ch 34:1; Jer 1:2; 3:6; 25:3 **3:15** [h] 2Ki 23:34 [i] Jer 37:1 [j] 2Ki 23:31 **3:16** [k] 2Ki 24:6, 8; Mt 1:11 [l] 2Ki 24:18 **3:17** [m] Ezr 3:2 **3:18** [n] Ezr 1:8; 5:14 [o] Jer 22:30 **3:19** [p] Ezr 2:2; 3:2; 5:2; Ne 7:7; 12:1; Hag 1:1; 2:2; Zec 4:6 **3:22** [q] Ezr 8:2-3

23 The sons of Neariah:
Elioenai, Hizkiah and Azrikam — three in all.
24 The sons of Elioenai:
Hodaviah, Eliashib, Pelaiah, Akkub, Johanan, Delaiah and Anani — seven in all.

Other Clans of Judah

4 The descendants of Judah:[r]
Perez, Hezron,[s] Karmi, Hur and Shobal.
2 Reaiah son of Shobal was the father of Jahath, and Jahath the father of Ahumai and Lahad. These were the clans of the Zorathites.
3 These were the sons[c] of Etam:
Jezreel, Ishma and Idbash. Their sister was named Hazzelelponi.
4 Penuel was the father of Gedor, and Ezer the father of Hushah.
These were the descendants of Hur,[t] the firstborn of Ephrathah and father[d] of Bethlehem.[u]
5 Ashhur[v] the father of Tekoa had two wives, Helah and Naarah.
6 Naarah bore him Ahuzzam, Hepher, Temeni and Haahashtari. These were the descendants of Naarah.
7 The sons of Helah:
Zereth, Zohar, Ethnan, 8 and Koz, who was the father of Anub and Hazzobebah and of the clans of Aharhel son of Harum.

9 Jabez was more honorable than his
brothers. His mother had named him Jabez,[e] saying, "I gave birth to him in pain."
10 Jabez cried out to the God of Israel, "Oh,
that you would bless me and enlarge my
territory! Let your hand be with me, and

4:1 [r] Ge 29:35; 46:12; 1Ch 2:3 [s] Nu 26:21 **4:4** [t] 1Ch 2:50 [u] Ru 1:19 **4:5** [v] 1Ch 2:24

[a] *11* Hebrew *Joram*, a variant of *Jehoram*
[b] *16* Hebrew *Jeconiah*, a variant of *Jehoiachin*; also in verse 17
[c] *3* Some Septuagint manuscripts (see also Vulgate); Hebrew *father*
[d] *4* *Father* may mean *civic leader* or *military leader*; also in verses 12, 14, 17, 18 and possibly elsewhere.
[e] *9* *Jabez* sounds like the Hebrew for *pain*.

3:17–24 The presence of Jehoiachin and five of his sons (seven are mentioned here) in Babylon was established beyond doubt by the discovery of four ration lists, one of which dates from the 13th year of Nebuchadnezzar (i.e., the 6th year of Jehoiachin's captivity; see note on 2Ki 25:29–30). If Jehoiachin was only 18 when he became king, his sons must have been very young at this point. The importance of David's line continues into the postexilic period. Given the covenant God made with David, the preservation of his line was essential. Of the names given in this list, only two are mentioned elsewhere: Zerubbabel (v. 19) was one of the initial returnees, while Hattush (v. 22) returned with Ezra (Ezr 8:2). Given Ezra's efforts to ensure that all classes of officiators were present with him so that the temple could function effectively, it is possible that a "son of David" was included so that, should an opportunity arise, the monarchy could be restored. The seven generations listed here show the preservation of the Davidic line down to the end of the fifth or the beginning of the fourth century BC. Given that Hattush himself returned from Babylon, it is probable that the majority of the individuals listed here resided in Babylon.

4:9 *Jabez.* In the ancient world, almost anything that could happen (including things that were highly improbable if not impossible) was considered to be portentous. Consequently, action was often taken to avert a threatening evil. Sometimes this could be quite elaborate, involving a specialist magician. Jabez's name, a close variant of the word for "pain," held evil foreboding because of that obtuse relationship. The means of averting this was not some elaborate magical ritual, but prayer to the God of Israel (v. 10).

4:10 *enlarge my territory!* The connection between divine

keep me from harm so that I will be free from pain." And God granted his request.

11 Kelub, Shuhah's brother, was the father of Mehir, who was the father of Eshton. 12Eshton was the father of Beth Rapha, Paseah and Tehinnah the father of Ir Nahash.[a] These were the men of Rekah.

13 The sons of Kenaz:
Othniel[w] and Seraiah.
The sons of Othniel:
Hathath and Meonothai.[b] 14Meonothai was the father of Ophrah.
Seraiah was the father of Joab,
the father of Ge Harashim.[c] It was called this because its people were skilled workers.
15 The sons of Caleb son of Jephunneh:
Iru, Elah and Naam.
The son of Elah:
Kenaz.
16 The sons of Jehallelel:
Ziph, Ziphah, Tiria and Asarel.
17 The sons of Ezrah:
Jether, Mered, Epher and Jalon.
One of Mered's wives gave birth
to Miriam,[x] Shammai and Ishbah
the father of Eshtemoa. 18(His wife
from the tribe of Judah gave birth
to Jered the father of Gedor, Heber
the father of Soko, and Jekuthiel
the father of Zanoah.[y]) These were
the children of Pharaoh's daughter
Bithiah, whom Mered had married.
19 The sons of Hodiah's wife, the sister of Naham:
the father of Keilah[z] the Garmite,
and Eshtemoa the Maakathite.[a]
20 The sons of Shimon:
Amnon, Rinnah, Ben-Hanan and Tilon.
The descendants of Ishi:
Zoheth and Ben-Zoheth.
21 The sons of Shelah[b] son of Judah:
Er the father of Lekah, Laadah the
father of Mareshah and the clans of
the linen workers at Beth Ashbea,
22Jokim, the men of Kozeba, and
Joash and Saraph, who ruled in
Moab and Jashubi Lehem. (These
records are from ancient times.)
23They were the potters who lived
at Netaim and Gederah; they stayed
there and worked for the king.

4:13 [w] Jos 15:17
4:17 [x] Ex 15:20
4:18 [y] Jos 15:34
4:19 [z] Jos 15:44
[a] Dt 3:14
4:21 [b] Ge 38:5

Simeon

4:28-33pp — Jos 19:2-10

24 The descendants of Simeon:[c]
Nemuel, Jamin, Jarib,[d] Zerah and Shaul;
25 Shallum was Shaul's son, Mibsam his son and Mishma his son.
26 The descendants of Mishma:
Hammuel his son, Zakkur his son and Shimei his son.

27Shimei had sixteen sons and six
daughters, but his brothers did not have
many children; so their entire clan did
not become as numerous as the people of
Judah. 28They lived in Beersheba,[e] Moladah,[f] Hazar Shual, 29Bilhah, Ezem,[g] To-
lad, 30Bethuel, Hormah,[h] Ziklag, 31Beth
Markaboth, Hazar Susim, Beth Biri and
Shaaraim.[i] These were their towns until
the reign of David. 32Their surrounding
villages were Etam, Ain,[j] Rimmon, Token
and Ashan[k]—five towns— 33and all the
villages around these towns as far as Ba-
lath.[d] These were their settlements. And
they kept a genealogical record.

34Meshobab, Jamlech, Joshah son of
Amaziah, 35Joel, Jehu son of Joshi-
biah, the son of Seraiah, the son of
Asiel, 36also Elioenai, Jaakobah, Jesh-
ohaiah, Asaiah, Adiel, Jesimiel, Benaiah, 37and Ziza son of Shiphi, the son
of Allon, the son of Jedaiah, the son
of Shimri, the son of Shemaiah.

38The men listed above by name were
leaders of their clans. Their families increased greatly, 39and they went to the
outskirts of Gedor[l] to the east of the valley in search of pasture for their flocks.

4:24 [c] Ge 29:33
[d] Nu 26:12
4:28 [e] Ge 21:14
[f] Jos 15:26
4:29 [g] Jos 15:29
4:30 [h] Nu 14:45
4:31 [i] Jos 15:36
4:32 [j] Nu 34:11
[k] Jos 15:42
4:39 [l] Jos 15:58

[a] 12 Or *of the city of Nahash* [b] 13 Some Septuagint manuscripts and Vulgate; Hebrew does not have *and Meonothai.* [c] 14 *Ge Harashim* means *valley of skilled workers.* [d] 33 Some Septuagint manuscripts (see also Joshua 19:8); Hebrew *Baal*

---

support or blessing and the enlargement of territory is also to be found in Assyrian royal inscriptions, although there it is in the context of conquest. Here there are no such connotations.

4:21 *clans of the linen workers.* The Alalakh texts from the fifteenth century BC list various "houses" of craftsmen, including coppersmiths, leather workers, jewelers and joiners. Given the nature of the industry, textile production generally required a sizable workforce on a permanent basis, though it could be done on a small scale at home. Textual sources for textile production exist from the mid-third millennium BC at Ebla onward.

4:23 *potters.* The construction of pottery was a basic necessity for every family. When the size of the royal household and associated government departments are considered, most likely royal potteries were needed. Producing pottery involves two requirements: a good supply of clay and a plentiful supply of water. For fired pottery, fuel for the kilns is also needed. Presumably, therefore, the towns mentioned here had all these. In addition it may be surmised that both the potters and the materials mentioned here were of the best quality.

4:39 *pasture for their flocks.* The increase in population among the Simeonites led to the need for economic migration and the search for fresh pastureland. The place they found was one of "rich, good pasture" (v. 40). Armed

40 They found rich, good pasture, and the
land was spacious, peaceful and quiet.[m]
Some Hamites had lived there formerly.
41 The men whose names were listed
came in the days of Hezekiah king of Judah. They attacked the Hamites in their
dwellings and also the Meunites[n] who were
there and completely destroyed[a] them, as
is evident to this day. Then they settled in
their place, because there was pasture for
their flocks. 42 And five hundred of these
Simeonites, led by Pelatiah, Neariah, Rephaiah and Uzziel, the sons of Ishi, invaded the hill country of Seir.[o] 43 They killed the
remaining Amalekites[p] who had escaped,
and they have lived there to this day.

Reuben

5 The sons of Reuben[q] the firstborn of
Israel (he was the firstborn, but when
he defiled his father's marriage bed,[r] his
rights as firstborn were given to the sons
of Joseph[s] son of Israel;[t] so he could not
be listed in the genealogical record in accordance with his birthright,[u] 2 and though
Judah[v] was the strongest of his brothers
and a ruler[w] came from him, the rights of
the firstborn[x] belonged to Joseph) — 3 the
sons of Reuben[y] the firstborn of Israel:
Hanok, Pallu,[z] Hezron and Karmi.
4 The descendants of Joel:
Shemaiah his son, Gog his son,
Shimei his son, 5 Micah his son,
Reaiah his son, Baal his son,
6 and Beerah his son, whom Tiglath-
Pileser[b][a] king of Assyria took into
exile. Beerah was a leader of the
Reubenites.
7 Their relatives by clans,[b] listed according to their genealogical records:
Jeiel the chief, Zechariah, 8 and
Bela son of Azaz, the son of Shema, the son of Joel. They settled in
the area from Aroer[c] to Nebo and
Baal Meon. 9 To the east they occupied the land up to the edge of the
desert that extends to the Euphrates River, because their livestock
had increased in Gilead.[d]
10 During Saul's reign they waged
war against the Hagrites[e], who were
defeated at their hands; they occupied the dwellings of the Hagrites
throughout the entire region east of
Gilead.

Gad

11 The Gadites[f] lived next to them in Bashan, as far as Salekah:[g]
12 Joel was the chief, Shapham the
second, then Janai and Shaphat, in
Bashan.
13 Their relatives, by families, were:
Michael, Meshullam, Sheba, Jorai,
Jakan, Zia and Eber — seven in all.
14 These were the sons of Abihail son
of Huri, the son of Jaroah, the son
of Gilead, the son of Michael, the
son of Jeshishai, the son of Jahdo,
the son of Buz.
15 Ahi son of Abdiel, the son of Guni,
was head of their family.
16 The Gadites lived in Gilead, in Bashan and its outlying villages, and
on all the pasturelands of Sharon as
far as they extended.
17 All these were entered in the genealogical records during the reigns of Jotham[h]
king of Judah and Jeroboam[i] king of Israel.
18 The Reubenites, the Gadites and the
half-tribe of Manasseh had 44,760 men
ready for military service[j] — able-bodied
men who could handle shield and sword,

4:40 [m] Jdg 18:7-10 **4:41** [n] 2Ch 20:1; 26:7 **4:42** [o] Ge 14:6 **4:43** [p] 1Sa 15:8; 30:17; 2Sa 8:12; Est 3:1; 9:16 **5:1** [q] Ge 29:32 [r] Ge 35:22; 49:4 [s] Ge 48:16,22; 49:26 [t] Ge 48:5 [u] 1Ch 26:10 **5:2** [v] Ge 49:10, 12 [w] 1Sa 9:16; 12:12; 2Sa 6:21; 1Ch 11:2; 2Ch 7:18; Ps 60:7; Mic 5:2; Mt 2:6 [x] Ge 25:31 **5:3** [y] Ge 29:32; 46:9; Ex 6:14; Nu 26:5-11 [z] Nu 26:5 **5:6** [a] ver 26; 2Ki 15:19; 16:10; 2Ch 28:20 **5:7** [b] ver 17 **5:8** [c] Nu 32:34 **5:9** [d] Nu 32:26; Jos 22:9 **5:10** [e] ver 18-21 **5:11** [f] Jos 13:24-28 [g] Dt 3:10; Jos 13:11 **5:17** [h] 2Ki 15:32 [i] 2Ki 14:16,28 **5:18** [j] Nu 1:3

[a] *41* The Hebrew term refers to the irrevocable giving over of things or persons to the LORD, often by totally destroying them. [b] *6* Hebrew *Tilgath-Pilneser,* a variant of *Tiglath-Pileser;* also in verse 26

expansion to solve economic difficulties is a common feature in the ancient world. It was used, e.g., to justify the expansionist policies of the Assyrians. This passage implies that the Simeonites were essentially herdsmen. Their new pastureland cannot be located with any precision.

4:41 *Meunites.* A number of opinions have been expressed on their identity. From the general description given here, it seems likely that they are to be found to the south of Palestine. It is possible, therefore, that they are the Mu'unaya mentioned in the inscriptions of Tiglath-Pileser III, and who seem to be located in northern Sinai. See note on 2Ch 20:1 – 30.

5:1 *rights as firstborn.* See the article "Inheritance Rights and Birthrights," p. 62.

5:6 *Tiglath-Pileser king of Assyria.* See note on v. 26.

5:10 *Hagrites.* Little is known of these people other than that they inhabited the region east of Gilead. They are mentioned in Ps 83 among those allied against Israel. Some have linked them with a tribe of Arameans called the Hagaranu mentioned in the inscriptions of Tiglath-Pileser III.

5:11 – 16 The bulk of the Gadite territory seems to have been in Gilead, a plateau some 2,000 feet (600 meters) above sea level. This land had rich grazing lands and plenty of moisture — the primary reasons that the three Transjordanian tribes opted to remain there in the first place (cf. Nu 32:1 – 5,33 – 44).

5:16 *Sharon.* Mentioned also in the Mesha Stele, this name has not been precisely identified. This "Sharon" should not be confused with the "Sharon" mentioned elsewhere in Scripture (SS 2:1) — the coastal plain between Joppa and Mount Carmel.

5:17 *genealogical records during the reigns of Jotham ... Jeroboam.* This is likely an unknown census in the days of Jotham. There is no indication from 1 – 2 Kings that Jotham and Jeroboam II were contemporaries, but chronological studies of the period have shown them to be at least partly synchronous.

King of Assyria Tiglath-Pileser III, who "took the Reubenites, the Gadites and the half-tribe of Manasseh into exile" (1Ch 5:26).
Wikimedia Commons

who could use a bow, and who were
trained for battle. 19 They waged war against
the Hagrites, Jetur,[k] Naphish and Nodab.
20 They were helped[l] in fighting them, and
God delivered the Hagrites and all their allies into their hands, because they cried[m]
out to him during the battle. He answered
their prayers, because they trusted[n] in him.
21 They seized the livestock of the Hagrites — fifty thousand camels, two hundred
fifty thousand sheep and two thousand
donkeys. They also took one hundred thousand people captive, 22 and many others fell
slain, because the battle[o] was God's. And
they occupied the land until the exile.[p]

The Half-Tribe of Manasseh

23 The people of the half-tribe of Manasseh were numerous; they settled in the
land from Bashan to Baal Hermon, that is,
to Senir (Mount Hermon).[q]
24 These were the heads of their fam-

5:19 [k] ver 10; Ge 25:15; 1Ch 1:31
5:20 [l] Ps 37:40 [m] 1Ki 8:44; 2Ch 13:14; 14:11; Ps 20:7-9; 22:5 [n] Ps 26:1; Da 6:23
5:22 [o] 2Ch 32:8 [p] 2Ki 15:29; 17:6
5:23 [q] Dt 3:8,9; SS 4:8
5:25 [r] Dt 32:15-18; 2Ki 17:7; 1Ch 9:1; 2Ch 26:16 [s] Ex 34:15
5:26 [t] 2Ki 15:19 [u] 2Ki 15:29 [v] 2Ki 17:6; 18:11
6:1 [w] Ge 46:11; Ex 6:16; Nu 26:57; 1Ch 23:6

ilies: Epher, Ishi, Eliel, Azriel, Jeremiah,
Hodaviah and Jahdiel. They were brave
warriors, famous men, and heads of their
families. 25 But they were unfaithful[r] to
the God of their ancestors and prostituted[s] themselves to the gods of the peoples
of the land, whom God had destroyed before them. 26 So the God of Israel stirred
up the spirit of Pul[t] king of Assyria (that
is, Tiglath-Pileser[u] king of Assyria), who
took the Reubenites, the Gadites and the
half-tribe of Manasseh into exile. He took
them to Halah,[v] Habor, Hara and the river
of Gozan, where they are to this day.

Levi

6[a] The sons of Levi:[w]
Gershon, Kohath and Merari.
2 The sons of Kohath:
Amram, Izhar, Hebron and Uzziel.

[a] In Hebrew texts 6:1-15 is numbered 5:27-41, and 6:16-81 is numbered 6:1-66.

5:19 *waged war against the Hagrites, Jetur, Naphish and Nodab.* The allies of the Hagrites (see note on v. 10) are all Arabian tribes. Alliances between small states to form larger fighting forces were common throughout the ancient Near East, through all periods. The offensive this time seems to be on the part of the Transjordanian tribes against the Arabs. *Jetur, Naphish.* Both are known from the list of Ishmael's descendants (Ge 25:15). *Jetur.* By Roman times they were known as the Itureans (cf. Lk 3:1), located in an area northeast of Palestine. It cannot be necessarily concluded, however, that this is where they were to be found at this time. *Naphish.* Mentioned in a seventh-century BC letter to the Assyrian king Ashurbanipal. *Nodab.* Not known from elsewhere, unless it is to be identified with Adbeel, another of Ishmael's sons (Ge 25:13).

5:21 *seized the livestock ... people.* The numbers given here for livestock and captives are colossal, but the nature of the spoil is consistent with the enemy fought, and it is not inconceivable to contemplate such numbers of livestock (see 2Ki 3:4 and note).

5:26 *Pul.* See note on 2Ki 15:19. *took ... into exile.* Tiglath-Pileser III (744 – 727 BC) invaded upper and lower Galilee in 733 BC and the years following, and reduced the northern kingdom of Israel to Samaria and its surroundings. From

3 The children of Amram:
Aaron, Moses and Miriam.
The sons of Aaron:
Nadab, Abihu,[x] Eleazar and Ithamar.
4 Eleazar was the father of Phinehas,
Phinehas the father of Abishua,
5 Abishua the father of Bukki,
Bukki the father of Uzzi,
6 Uzzi the father of Zerahiah,
Zerahiah the father of Meraioth,
7 Meraioth the father of Amariah,
Amariah the father of Ahitub,
8 Ahitub the father of Zadok,[y]
Zadok the father of Ahimaaz,
9 Ahimaaz the father of Azariah,
Azariah the father of Johanan,
10 Johanan the father of Azariah[z] (it
was he who served as priest in the
temple Solomon built in Jerusalem),
11 Azariah the father of Amariah,
Amariah the father of Ahitub,
12 Ahitub the father of Zadok,
Zadok the father of Shallum,
13 Shallum the father of Hilkiah,[a]
Hilkiah the father of Azariah,
14 Azariah the father of Seraiah,[b]
and Seraiah the father of Jozadak.[a]
15 Jozadak[c] was deported when the
LORD sent Judah and Jerusalem into
exile by the hand of Nebuchadnezzar.

16 The sons of Levi:[d]
Gershon,[b] Kohath and Merari.[e]
17 These are the names of the sons of
Gershon:
Libni and Shimei.
18 The sons of Kohath:
Amram, Izhar, Hebron and Uzziel.
19 The sons of Merari:[f]
Mahli and Mushi.
These are the clans of the Levites list-
ed according to their fathers:
20 Of Gershon:
Libni his son, Jahath his son,
Zimmah his son, 21 Joah his son,
Iddo his son, Zerah his son
and Jeatherai his son.

6:3 [x] Lev 10:1
6:8 [y] 2Sa 8:17; 15:27; Ezr 7:2
6:10 [z] 1Ki 4:2; 6:1; 2Ch 3:1; 26:17-18
6:13 [a] 2Ki 22:1-20; 2Ch 34:9; 35:8
6:14 [b] 2Ki 25:18; Ezr 2:2; Ne 11:11
6:15 [c] 2Ki 25:18; Ne 12:1; Hag 1:1, 14; 2:2, 4; Zec 6:11
6:16 [d] Ge 29:34; Ex 6:16; Nu 3:17-20 [e] Nu 26:57
6:19 [f] Ge 46:11; 1Ch 23:21; 24:26
6:22 [g] Ex 6:24
6:24 [h] 1Ch 15:5
6:27 [i] 1Sa 1:1 [j] 1Sa 1:20
6:28 [k] ver 33; 1Sa 8:2
6:31 [l] 1Ch 25:1; 2Ch 29:25-26; Ne 12:45 [m] 1Ch 9:33; 15:19; Ezr 3:10; Ps 68:25
6:33 [n] 1Ki 4:31; 1Ch 15:17; 25:1 [o] ver 28
6:34 [p] 1Sa 1:1

22 The descendants of Kohath:
Amminadab his son, Korah[g] his
son,
Assir his son, 23 Elkanah his son,
Ebiasaph his son, Assir his son,
24 Tahath his son, Uriel[h] his son,
Uzziah his son and Shaul his son.
25 The descendants of Elkanah:
Amasai, Ahimoth,
26 Elkanah his son,[c] Zophai his son,
Nahath his son, 27 Eliab his son,
Jeroham his son, Elkanah[i] his son
and Samuel[j] his son.[d]
28 The sons of Samuel:
Joel[e][k] the firstborn
and Abijah the second son.
29 The descendants of Merari:
Mahli, Libni his son,
Shimei his son, Uzzah his son,
30 Shimea his son, Haggiah his son
and Asaiah his son.

The Temple Musicians

6:54-80pp — Jos 21:4-39

31 These are the men[l] David put in charge
of the music[m] in the house of the LORD after the ark came to rest there. 32 They ministered with music before the tabernacle,
the tent of meeting, until Solomon built
the temple of the LORD in Jerusalem. They
performed their duties according to the
regulations laid down for them.
33 Here are the men who served, together with their sons:
From the Kohathites:
Heman,[n] the musician,
the son of Joel,[o] the son of Samuel,
34 the son of Elkanah,[p] the son of Jeroham,

[a] *14* Hebrew *Jehozadak*, a variant of *Jozadak*; also in verse 15 [b] *16* Hebrew *Gershom*, a variant of *Gershon*; also in verses 17, 20, 43, 62 and 71 [c] *26* Some Hebrew manuscripts, Septuagint and Syriac; most Hebrew manuscripts *Ahimoth* *26and Elkanah. The sons of Elkanah:* [d] *27* Some Septuagint manuscripts (see also 1 Samuel 1:19,20 and 1 Chron. 6:33,34); Hebrew does not have *and Samuel his son.* [e] *28* Some Septuagint manuscripts and Syriac (see also 1 Samuel 8:2 and 1 Chron. 6:33); Hebrew does not have *Joel.*

the northern kingdom he deported 13,520 people (see notes on 2Ki 15:29; 17:6).

6:3 *sons of Aaron.* There were two families from the line of Aaron from whom high priests came. (1) The house of Eli (descended from Ithamar) was disqualified from office by the activities of Eli's two sons, Hophni and Phinehas (1Sa 2:27 – 36; 1Ki 2:27). (2) The Zadokites (descended from Eliezer) are given here. The importance of the preservation of the priestly line for the continued functioning of the temple in the postexilic period need hardly be stated (see notes on Ezr 2:40,59).

6:31 – 32 *the house of the LORD … the tabernacle … the temple.* These three distinct structures seem to be referred to in the NIV of these verses: (1) The "house of the LORD" refers to the tent David erected in Jerusalem to house the ark, once it was brought there (15:1 — 16:6). (2) The "tabernacle" was the tent constructed in the time of Moses; it was located at this period in Gibeon (16:39). (3) The "temple" was built by Solomon and superseded the other two.

6:31 *music in the house of the LORD.* See the article "Music and Musicians," p. 524.

6:32 *according to the regulations.* There are no stipulations given for music in relation to the tabernacle. Nor are there any indications regarding the function of music in organized worship in the books of Samuel or Kings. The divisions of the singers and their duties are given in 1Ch 25. Akkadian and Sumerian texts tell us much about musical instruments and styles used in a variety of situations, including rituals. Some texts even provide the basis for understanding musical notation and theory. No texts, however, offer stipulations or regulations comparable to what is found here.

the son of Eliel, the son of Toah,
35 the son of Zuph, the son of Elkanah,
the son of Mahath, the son of Amasai,
36 the son of Elkanah, the son of Joel,
the son of Azariah, the son of Zephaniah,
37 the son of Tahath, the son of Assir,
the son of Ebiasaph, the son of Korah,[q]
38 the son of Izhar,[r] the son of Kohath,
the son of Levi, the son of Israel;
39 and Heman's associate Asaph,[s] who served at his right hand:
Asaph son of Berekiah, the son of Shimea,[t]
40 the son of Michael, the son of Baaseiah,[a]
the son of Malkijah, 41 the son of Ethni,
the son of Zerah, the son of Adaiah,
42 the son of Ethan, the son of Zimmah,
the son of Shimei, 43 the son of Jahath,
the son of Gershon, the son of Levi;
44 and from their associates, the Merarites, at his left hand:
Ethan son of Kishi, the son of Abdi,
the son of Malluk, 45 the son of Hashabiah,
the son of Amaziah, the son of Hilkiah,
46 the son of Amzi, the son of Bani,
the son of Shemer, 47 the son of Mahli,
the son of Mushi, the son of Merari,
the son of Levi.

48 Their fellow Levites[u] were assigned to all the other duties of the tabernacle, the house of God. 49 But Aaron and his descendants were the ones who presented offerings on the altar[v] of burnt offering and on the altar of incense[w] in connection with all that was done in the Most Holy Place, making atonement for Israel, in accordance with all that Moses the servant of God had commanded.

50 These were the descendants of Aaron:
Eleazar his son, Phinehas his son,
Abishua his son, 51 Bukki his son,
Uzzi his son, Zerahiah his son,
52 Meraioth his son, Amariah his son,
Ahitub his son, 53 Zadok[x] his son
and Ahimaaz his son.

54 These were the locations of their settlements[y] allotted as their territory (they were assigned to the descendants of Aaron who were from the Kohathite clan, because the first lot was for them):
55 They were given Hebron in Judah with its surrounding pasturelands.
56 But the fields and villages around the city were given to Caleb son of Jephunneh.[z]
57 So the descendants of Aaron were given Hebron (a city of refuge), and Libnah,[b][a] Jattir,[b] Eshtemoa, 58 Hilen, Debir,[c] 59 Ashan,[d] Juttah[c] and Beth Shemesh, together with their pasturelands. 60 And from the tribe of Benjamin they were given Gibeon,[d] Geba, Alemeth and Anathoth,[e] together with their pasturelands.
The total number of towns distributed among the Kohathite clans came to thirteen.
61 The rest of Kohath's descendants were allotted ten towns from the clans of half the tribe of Manasseh.
62 The descendants of Gershon, clan by clan, were allotted thirteen towns from the tribes of Issachar, Asher and Naphtali, and from the part of the tribe of Manasseh that is in Bashan.
63 The descendants of Merari, clan by clan, were allotted twelve towns from the tribes of Reuben, Gad and Zebulun.
64 So the Israelites gave the Levites these towns[f] and their pasturelands. 65 From the tribes of Judah, Simeon and Benjamin they allotted the previously named towns.
66 Some of the Kohathite clans were given as their territory towns from the tribe of Ephraim.
67 In the hill country of Ephraim they were given Shechem (a city of refuge), and Gezer,[e][g] 68 Jokmeam,[h] Beth Horon,[i] 69 Aijalon[j] and Gath Rimmon,[k] together with their pasturelands.
70 And from half the tribe of Manasseh the Israelites gave Aner and Bileam, together with their pasturelands, to the rest of the Kohathite clans.

71 The Gershonites[l] received the following:
From the clan of the half-tribe of Manasseh

6:37 [q] Ex 6:24 **6:38** [r] Ex 6:21 **6:39** [s] 1Ch 25:1, 9; 2Ch 29:13; Ne 11:17 [t] 1Ch 15:17 **6:48** [u] 1Ch 23:32 **6:49** [v] Ex 27:1-8 [w] Ex 30:1-7, 10; 2Ch 26:18 **6:53** [x] 2Sa 8:17 **6:54** [y] Nu 31:10 **6:56** [z] Jos 14:13; 15:13 **6:57** [a] Nu 33:20 [b] Jos 15:48 **6:58** [c] Jos 10:3 **6:59** [d] Jos 15:42 **6:60** [e] Jer 1:1 **6:64** [f] Nu 35:1-8; Jos 21:3, 41-42 **6:67** [g] Jos 10:33 **6:68** [h] 1Ki 4:12 [i] Jos 10:10 **6:69** [j] Jos 10:12 [k] Jos 19:45 **6:71** [l] 1Ch 23:7

[a] *40* Most Hebrew manuscripts; some Hebrew manuscripts, one Septuagint manuscript and Syriac *Maaseiah* [b] *57* See Joshua 21:13; Hebrew *given the cities of refuge: Hebron, Libnah.* [c] *59* Syriac (see also Septuagint and Joshua 21:16); Hebrew does not have *Juttah.* [d] *60* See Joshua 21:17; Hebrew does not have *Gibeon.* [e] *67* See Joshua 21:21; Hebrew *given the cities of refuge: Shechem, Gezer.*

6:54–81 The Levites were not allotted specific territories as their inheritance (Jos 13:14). Rather, they were given cities among the inheritance of the other Israelite tribes. The holdings of the priests, the descendants of Aaron, are all within the territories of Judah and Benjamin. The towns allotted to the rest of the Levite families were in what later became the northern kingdom of Israel on both sides of the Jordan.

they received Golan in Bashan[m]
and also Ashtaroth, together with
their pasturelands;
72 from the tribe of Issachar
they received Kedesh, Daberath,[n]
73 Ramoth and Anem, together with
their pasturelands;
74 from the tribe of Asher
they received Mashal, Abdon,[o]
75 Hukok[p] and Rehob,[q] together
with their pasturelands;
76 and from the tribe of Naphtali
they received Kedesh in Galilee,
Hammon[r] and Kiriathaim,[s] together with their pasturelands.

77 The Merarites (the rest of the Levites)
received the following:
From the tribe of Zebulun
they received Jokneam, Kartah,[a]
Rimmono and Tabor, together with
their pasturelands;
78 from the tribe of Reuben across the
Jordan east of Jericho
they received Bezer[t] in the wilderness, Jahzah, 79 Kedemoth[u] and
Mephaath, together with their pasturelands;
80 and from the tribe of Gad
they received Ramoth in Gilead,[v]
Mahanaim,[w] 81 Heshbon and Jazer,[x]
together with their pasturelands.[y]

Issachar

7 The sons of Issachar:[z]
Tola, Puah,[a] Jashub and Shimron—four in all.
2 The sons of Tola:
Uzzi, Rephaiah, Jeriel, Jahmai, Ib-
sam and Samuel—heads of their
families. During the reign of David, the descendants of Tola listed
as fighting men in their genealogy
numbered 22,600.
3 The son of Uzzi:
Izrahiah.
The sons of Izrahiah:
Michael, Obadiah, Joel and Ishiah.
All five of them were chiefs. 4 According to their family genealogy,
they had 36,000 men ready for battle, for they had many wives and
children.
5 The relatives who were fighting men
belonging to all the clans of Issachar, as listed in their genealogy,
were 87,000 in all.

Benjamin

6 Three sons of Benjamin:[b]
Bela, Beker and Jediael.
7 The sons of Bela:
Ezbon, Uzzi, Uzziel, Jerimoth and
Iri, heads of families—five in all.
Their genealogical record listed
22,034 fighting men.
8 The sons of Beker:
Zemirah, Joash, Eliezer, Elioenai,
Omri, Jeremoth, Abijah, Anathoth
and Alemeth. All these were the
sons of Beker. 9 Their genealogical
record listed the heads of families
and 20,200 fighting men.
10 The son of Jediael:
Bilhan.
The sons of Bilhan:
Jeush, Benjamin, Ehud, Kenaanah, Zethan, Tarshish and Ahisha-
har. 11 All these sons of Jediael were
heads of families. There were 17,200
fighting men ready to go out to war.
12 The Shuppites and Huppites were
the descendants of Ir, and the Hu-
shites[b] the descendants of Aher.

Naphtali

13 The sons of Naphtali:[c]
Jahziel, Guni, Jezer and Shillem[c]—
the descendants of Bilhah.

Manasseh

14 The descendants of Manasseh:[d]
Asriel was his descendant through
his Aramean concubine. She gave
birth to Makir the father of Gilead.[e]
15 Makir took a wife from among the
Huppites and Shuppites. His sister's
name was Maakah.
Another descendant was named
Zelophehad,[f] who had only daughters.
16 Makir's wife Maakah gave birth
to a son and named him Peresh. His
brother was named Sheresh, and his
sons were Ulam and Rakem.
17 The son of Ulam:
Bedan.
These were the sons of Gilead[g] son of
Makir, the son of Manasseh. 18 His
sister Hammoleketh gave birth to
Ishhod, Abiezer[h] and Mahlah.
19 The sons of Shemida were:
Ahian, Shechem, Likhi and Aniam.

Ephraim

20 The descendants of Ephraim:[i]
Shuthelah, Bered his son,
Tahath his son, Eleadah his son,
Tahath his son, 21 Zabad his son
and Shuthelah his son.

6:71 [m] Jos 20:8 **6:72** [n] Jos 19:12 **6:74** [o] Jos 19:28 **6:75** [p] Jos 19:34 [q] Nu 13:21 **6:76** [r] Jos 19:28 [s] Nu 32:37 **6:78** [t] Jos 20:8 **6:79** [u] Dt 2:26 **6:80** [v] Jos 20:8 [w] Ge 32:2 **6:81** [x] Nu 21:32 [y] 2Ch 11:14 **7:1** [z] Ge 30:18; Nu 26:23 [a] Ge 46:13 **7:6** [b] Ge 46:21; Nu 26:38; 1Ch 8:1-40

7:13 [c] Ge 30:8; 46:24 **7:14** [d] Ge 41:51; Jos 17:1; 1Ch 5:23 [e] Nu 26:30 **7:15** [f] Nu 26:33; 36:1-12 **7:17** [g] Nu 26:30; 1Sa 12:11 **7:18** [h] Jos 17:2 **7:20** [i] Ge 41:52; Nu 1:33; 26:35

[a] *77* See Septuagint and Joshua 21:34; Hebrew does not have *Jokneam, Kartah.* [b] *12* Or *Ir. The sons of Dan: Hushim,* (see Gen. 46:23); Hebrew does not have *The sons of Dan.* [c] *13* Some Hebrew and Septuagint manuscripts (see also Gen. 46:24 and Num. 26:49); most Hebrew manuscripts *Shallum*

Ezer and Elead were killed by the
native-born men of Gath, when they
went down to seize their livestock.
22Their father Ephraim mourned for
them many days, and his relatives
came to comfort him. 23Then he
made love to his wife again, and she
became pregnant and gave birth to a
son. He named him Beriah,[a] because
there had been misfortune in his family. 24His daughter was Sheerah, who
built Lower and Upper Beth Horon[j] as
well as Uzzen Sheerah.
25 Rephah was his son, Resheph his son,[b]
Telah his son, Tahan his son,
26 Ladan his son, Ammihud his son,
Elishama his son, 27Nun his son
and Joshua his son.
28Their lands and settlements included
Bethel and its surrounding villages, Naa-
ran to the east, Gezer[k] and its villages to
the west, and Shechem and its villages all
the way to Ayyah and its villages. 29Along
the borders of Manasseh were Beth Shan,[l]
Taanach, Megiddo and Dor,[m] together
with their villages. The descendants of Joseph son of Israel lived in these towns.

Asher

30 The sons of Asher:[n]
Imnah, Ishvah, Ishvi and Beriah.
Their sister was Serah.
31 The sons of Beriah:
Heber and Malkiel, who was the father of Birzaith.
32 Heber was the father of Japhlet, Shomer and Hotham and of their sister
Shua.
33 The sons of Japhlet:
Pasak, Bimhal and Ashvath.
These were Japhlet's sons.
34 The sons of Shomer:
Ahi, Rohgah,[c] Hubbah and Aram.
35 The sons of his brother Helem:
Zophah, Imna, Shelesh and Amal.
36 The sons of Zophah:
Suah, Harnepher, Shual, Beri, Im-
rah, 37Bezer, Hod, Shamma, Shil-
shah, Ithran[d] and Beera.
38 The sons of Jether:
Jephunneh, Pispah and Ara.
39 The sons of Ulla:
Arah, Hanniel and Rizia.
40All these were descendants of Asher—
heads of families, choice men, brave warriors and outstanding leaders. The number
of men ready for battle, as listed in their
genealogy, was 26,000.

7:24 [j] Jos 10:10; 16:3,5 **7:28** [k] Jos 10:33; 16:7 **7:29** [l] Jos 17:11 [m] Jos 11:2 **7:30** [n] Ge 46:17; Nu 1:40; 26:44

The Genealogy of Saul the Benjamite

8:28-38pp — 1Ch 9:34-44

8 Benjamin[o] was the father of Bela his
firstborn,
Ashbel the second son, Aharah the
third,
2 Nohah the fourth and Rapha the
fifth.
3 The sons of Bela were:
Addar,[p] Gera, Abihud,[e] 4Abishua,
Naaman, Ahoah,[q] 5Gera, Shephu-
phan and Huram.
6 These were the descendants of Ehud,[r]
who were heads of families of
those living in Geba and were deported to Manahath:
7 Naaman, Ahijah, and Gera, who
deported them and who was the
father of Uzza and Ahihud.
8 Sons were born to Shaharaim in
Moab after he had divorced his
wives Hushim and Baara. 9By his
wife Hodesh he had Jobab, Zib-
ia, Mesha, Malkam, 10Jeuz, Sakia
and Mirmah. These were his sons,
heads of families. 11By Hushim he
had Abitub and Elpaal.
12 The sons of Elpaal:
Eber, Misham, Shemed (who built
Ono[s] and Lod with its surrounding
villages), 13and Beriah and Shema, who were heads of families of
those living in Aijalon[t] and who
drove out the inhabitants of Gath.[u]
14 Ahio, Shashak, Jeremoth, 15Zebadiah,
Arad, Eder, 16Michael, Ishpah and
Joha were the sons of Beriah.
17 Zebadiah, Meshullam, Hizki, Heber,
18Ishmerai, Izliah and Jobab were
the sons of Elpaal.
19 Jakim, Zikri, Zabdi, 20Elienai, Zillethai, Eliel, 21Adaiah, Beraiah and
Shimrath were the sons of Shimei.
22 Ishpan, Eber, Eliel, 23Abdon, Zikri,
Hanan, 24Hananiah, Elam, Antho-
thijah, 25Iphdeiah and Penuel were
the sons of Shashak.
26 Shamsherai, Shehariah, Athaliah,
27Jaareshiah, Elijah and Zikri were
the sons of Jeroham.
28All these were heads of families, chiefs
as listed in their genealogy, and they lived
in Jerusalem.

8:1 [o] Ge 46:21; 1Ch 7:6 **8:3** [p] Ge 46:21 **8:4** [q] 2Sa 23:9 **8:6** [r] Jdg 3:12-30; 1Ch 2:52 **8:12** [s] Ezr 2:33; Ne 6:2; 7:37; 11:35 **8:13** [t] Jos 10:12 [u] Jos 11:22

[a] 23 *Beriah* sounds like the Hebrew for *misfortune.* [b] 25 Some Septuagint manuscripts; Hebrew does not have *his son.* [c] 34 Or *of his brother Shomer: Rohgah* [d] 37 Possibly a variant of *Jether* [e] 3 Or *Gera the father of Ehud*

8:12 *Ono and Lod.* The mention of building these cities represents an expansion on the part of Benjamin toward the west. Ono, Lod and Aijalon all lay within the territory allotted to Dan (Jos 19:40–46). The Danites had difficulty taking possession of their territory. Some, as a result, migrated to the far north of the country. It appears that the Benjamites, at least in some regions, achieved what the Danites could not.

29 Jeiel[a] the father[b] of Gibeon lived in
Gibeon.[v]
His wife's name was Maakah,
30 and his firstborn son was Abdon,
followed by Zur, Kish, Baal, Ner,[c]
Nadab, 31 Gedor, Ahio, Zeker 32 and
Mikloth, who was the father of
Shimeah. They too lived near their
relatives in Jerusalem.
33 Ner[w] was the father of Kish,[x] Kish the
father of Saul[y], and Saul the father
of Jonathan, Malki-Shua, Abinadab
and Esh-Baal.[dz]
34 The son of Jonathan:[a]
Merib-Baal,[eb] who was the father
of Micah.
35 The sons of Micah:
Pithon, Melek, Tarea and Ahaz.
36 Ahaz was the father of Jehoaddah, Jehoaddah was the father of
Alemeth, Azmaveth and Zimri,
and Zimri was the father of Moza.
37 Moza was the father of Binea; Ra-
phah was his son, Eleasah his son
and Azel his son.
38 Azel had six sons, and these were
their names:
Azrikam, Bokeru, Ishmael, Sheariah, Obadiah and Hanan. All these
were the sons of Azel.
39 The sons of his brother Eshek:
Ulam his firstborn, Jeush the second son and Eliphelet the third.
40 The sons of Ulam were brave
warriors who could handle the
bow. They had many sons and
grandsons — 150 in all.
All these were the descendants of
Benjamin.[c]

9 All Israel was listed in the genealogies
recorded in the book of the kings of Israel and Judah. They were taken captive to
Babylon because of their unfaithfulness.[d]

The People in Jerusalem

9:1-17pp — Ne 11:3-19

2 Now the first to resettle on their own
property in their own towns[e] were some
Israelites, priests, Levites and temple servants.[f]

3 Those from Judah, from Benjamin, and
from Ephraim and Manasseh who lived in
Jerusalem were:
4 Uthai son of Ammihud, the son of
Omri, the son of Imri, the son of
Bani, a descendant of Perez son of
Judah.[g]
5 Of the Shelanites[f]:
Asaiah the firstborn and his sons.
6 Of the Zerahites:
Jeuel.
The people from Judah numbered
690.
7 Of the Benjamites:
Sallu son of Meshullam, the son of
Hodaviah, the son of Hassenuah;
8 Ibneiah son of Jeroham; Elah son
of Uzzi, the son of Mikri; and Meshullam son of Shephatiah, the son
of Reuel, the son of Ibnijah.
9 The people from Benjamin, as listed in their genealogy, numbered
956. All these men were heads of
their families.
10 Of the priests:
Jedaiah; Jehoiarib; Jakin;
11 Azariah son of Hilkiah, the son of
Meshullam, the son of Zadok, the
son of Meraioth, the son of Ahitub,
the official in charge of the house
of God;
12 Adaiah son of Jeroham, the son of
Pashhur,[h] the son of Malkijah; and
Maasai son of Adiel, the son of Jah-
zerah, the son of Meshullam, the
son of Meshillemith, the son of Immer.
13 The priests, who were heads of
families, numbered 1,760. They
were able men, responsible for
ministering in the house of God.
14 Of the Levites:
Shemaiah son of Hasshub, the son
of Azrikam, the son of Hashabiah,
a Merarite; 15 Bakbakkar, Heresh,

8:29 [v] Jos 9:3
8:33 [w] 1Sa 28:19 [x] 1Sa 9:1 [y] 1Sa 14:49 [z] 2Sa 2:8
8:34 [a] 2Sa 9:12 [b] 2Sa 4:4
8:40 [c] Nu 26:38
9:1 [d] 1Ch 5:25
9:2 [e] Jos 9:27; Ezr 2:70 [f] Ezr 2:43, 58; 8:20; Ne 7:60
9:4 [g] Ge 38:29; 46:12
9:12 [h] Ezr 2:38; 10:22; Ne 10:3; Jer 21:1; 38:1

[a] 29 Some Septuagint manuscripts (see also 9:35); Hebrew does not have *Jeiel.* [b] 29 *Father* may mean *civic leader* or *military leader.* [c] 30 Some Septuagint manuscripts (see also 9:36); Hebrew does not have *Ner.* [d] 33 Also known as *Ish-Bosheth* [e] 34 Also known as *Mephibosheth* [f] 5 See Num. 26:20; Hebrew *Shilonites.*

9:1 *genealogies.* There are various reasons both why genealogical records were kept by the king and why they were periodically updated. First, possession of land in Israel was based on "inheritance"; i.e., it was tied to families (cf. 1Ki 21:1 – 3; see note on 1Ki 21:3). Thus, the keeping of accurate, up-to-date records was essential in the settlement of disputes over land ownership. Second, conscription to service — whether duties in the temple (23:1 — 26:32), corvée labor (27:25 – 31) or military service (27:1 – 24) — was all done on the basis of census figures. In texts from Mari censuses also were conducted for military conscription and land allocation. A lot of the lists from Alalakh and Ugarit mentioning names of persons with their land and property appear to be census lists. Such censuses were typically arranged according to genealogical principles.

9:3 *Who lived in Jerusalem.* The list that follows addresses the resettlement of Jerusalem by those whose families had not been residents before the exile. The general pattern was for families to return to their ancestral holdings (v. 2; cf. Ezr 2:70). However, the population of Jerusalem had been decimated by Nebuchadnezzar, both by the deportations in 597 BC and earlier and at its destruction in 586. See notes on Ne 7:73; 11:1.

Galal and Mattaniah[i] son of Mika,
the son of Zikri, the son of Asaph;
16 Obadiah son of Shemaiah, the
son of Galal, the son of Jeduthun;
and Berekiah son of Asa, the son of
Elkanah, who lived in the villages
of the Netophathites.[j]
17 The gatekeepers:[k]
Shallum, Akkub, Talmon, Ahiman
and their fellow Levites, Shallum
their chief 18 being stationed at the
King's Gate[l] on the east, up to the
present time. These were the gatekeepers belonging to the camp
of the Levites. 19 Shallum[m] son of
Kore, the son of Ebiasaph, the son
of Korah, and his fellow gatekeepers from his family (the Korahites)
were responsible for guarding the
thresholds of the tent just as their
ancestors had been responsible for
guarding the entrance to the dwelling of the LORD. 20 In earlier times
Phinehas[n] son of Eleazar was the
official in charge of the gatekeepers, and the LORD was with him.
21 Zechariah[o] son of Meshelemiah
was the gatekeeper at the entrance
to the tent of meeting.
22 Altogether, those chosen to be gatekeepers[p] at the thresholds numbered 212.
They were registered by genealogy in their
villages. The gatekeepers had been assigned to their positions of trust by David
and Samuel the seer.[q] 23 They and their descendants were in charge of guarding the
gates of the house of the LORD — the house
called the tent of meeting. 24 The gatekeepers were on the four sides: east, west,
north and south. 25 Their fellow Levites
in their villages had to come from time
to time and share their duties for seven-
day[r] periods. 26 But the four principal gatekeepers, who were Levites, were entrusted
with the responsibility for the rooms and
treasuries[s] in the house of God. 27 They
would spend the night stationed around
the house of God,[t] because they had to
guard it; and they had charge of the key[u]
for opening it each morning.
28 Some of them were in charge of the
articles used in the temple service; they
counted them when they were brought in
and when they were taken out. 29 Others
were assigned to take care of the furnishings and all the other articles of the sanctuary,[v] as well as the special flour and
wine, and the olive oil, incense and spices. 30 But some[w] of the priests took care
of mixing the spices. 31 A Levite named
Mattithiah, the firstborn son of Shallum
the Korahite, was entrusted with the responsibility for baking the offering bread.
32 Some of the Kohathites, their fellow
Levites, were in charge of preparing for
every Sabbath the bread set out on the
table.[x]
33 Those who were musicians,[y] heads of
Levite families, stayed in the rooms of the
temple and were exempt from other duties because they were responsible for the
work day and night.[z]
34 All these were heads of Levite families, chiefs as listed in their genealogy, and
they lived in Jerusalem.

The Genealogy of Saul

9:34-44pp — 1Ch 8:28-38

35 Jeiel[a] the father[a] of Gibeon lived in
Gibeon.
His wife's name was Maakah,
36 and his firstborn son was Abdon,
followed by Zur, Kish, Baal, Ner,
Nadab, 37 Gedor, Ahio, Zechariah

9:15 [i] 2Ch 20:14; Ne 11:22 **9:16** [j] Ne 12:28 **9:17** [k] ver 22; 1Ch 26:1; 2Ch 8:14; 31:14; Ezr 2:42; Ne 7:45 **9:18** [l] 1Ch 26:14; Eze 43:1; 46:1 **9:19** [m] Jer 35:4 **9:20** [n] Nu 25:7-13 **9:21** [o] 1Ch 26:2, 14 **9:22** [p] ver 17; 1Ch 26:1-2; 2Ch 31:15, 18 [q] 1Sa 9:9 **9:25** [r] 2Ki 11:5; 2Ch 23:8 **9:26** [s] 1Ch 26:22 **9:27** [t] Nu 3:38; 1Ch 23:30-32 [u] Isa 22:22 **9:29** [v] Nu 3:28; 1Ch 23:29 **9:30** [w] Ex 30:23-25 **9:32** [x] Lev 24:5-8; 1Ch 23:29; 2Ch 13:11 **9:33** [y] 1Ch 6:31; 25:1-31 [z] Ps 134:1 **9:35** [a] 1Ch 8:29

[a] 35 *Father* may mean *civic leader* or *military leader.*

9:17 *gatekeepers.* In the ancient world temples were not open to the general public. Certain areas were accessible, but the more sacred areas were only open to certain individuals, sometimes only at specified times. In Akkadian the term *erib biti* ("temple enterer") denotes a person who held that status. Thus, the task of gatekeepers became more important. They had to control access to the temple precinct and prevent the defilement of sacred areas by those who were unconsecrated. The consequences of such an intrusion were potentially dire, both for the individual concerned and for the whole priesthood (Nu 18:1 – 7). Their job also entailed guarding the temple treasuries, which were at times substantial, from misappropriation by those who did not fear divine retribution. This meant a round-the-clock vigil in shifts.

The most important role the priests had was to maintain the purity of sacred space. Otherwise the deity would be offended and might abandon the place, leaving the people without his blessing and protection. Purity was maintained by making sure that (1) only those who entered were qualified to do so (in either status or purity), (2) rituals that were needed were performed, and performed properly, and (3) the people were instructed with pertinent information concerning their roles in maintaining sacred space. Since the temple was viewed as the center of the cosmos and the base of operations for the deity, the priests, and to a lesser degree, the people, played a role in the smooth operation of the cosmos as they meticulously carried out their duties. They facilitated and enabled the god to do his job.

9:28 – 32 All kinds of duties and skills were demanded of the Levitical families. Accounting for the various sacred vessels and utensils, many of them made of gold, and constant provision of ingredients for offerings involved inventory procedures and detailed records. The mixing of oil or spices to special recipes (Ex 30:22 – 38) or the baking of the offering bread also fell to certain Levites, as did the maintenance of the furnishings. Only in Israel were such activities restricted to one particular extended family (Nu 4). Elsewhere, various unrelated individuals served in the tasks associated with the service of the temples.

and Mikloth. 38Mikloth was the father of Shimeam. They too lived near their relatives in Jerusalem.
39Ner[b] was the father of Kish,[c] Kish the father of Saul, and Saul the father of Jonathan,[d] Malki-Shua, Abinadab and Esh-Baal.[a][e]
40The son of Jonathan:
Merib-Baal,[b][f] who was the father of Micah.
41The sons of Micah:
Pithon, Melek, Tahrea and Ahaz.[c]
42Ahaz was the father of Jadah, Jadah[d] was the father of Alemeth, Azmaveth and Zimri, and Zimri was the father of Moza. 43Moza was the father of Binea; Rephaiah was his son, Eleasah his son and Azel his son.
44Azel had six sons, and these were their names:
Azrikam, Bokeru, Ishmael, Sheariah, Obadiah and Hanan. These were the sons of Azel.

Saul Takes His Life

10:1-12pp — 1Sa 31:1-13; 2Sa 1:4-12

10 Now the Philistines fought against Israel; the Israelites fled before them, and many fell dead on Mount Gilboa. 2The Philistines were in hot pursuit of Saul and his sons, and they killed his sons Jonathan, Abinadab and Malki-Shua.
3The fighting grew fierce around Saul, and when the archers overtook him, they wounded him.
4Saul said to his armor-bearer, "Draw your sword and run me through, or these uncircumcised fellows will come and abuse me."

But his armor-bearer was terrified and would not do it; so Saul took his own sword and fell on it. 5When the armor-bearer saw that Saul was dead, he too fell on his sword and died. 6So Saul and his three sons died, and all his house died together.

7When all the Israelites in the valley saw that the army had fled and that Saul and his sons had died, they abandoned their towns and fled. And the Philistines came and occupied them.

8The next day, when the Philistines came to strip the dead, they found Saul and his sons fallen on Mount Gilboa.
9They stripped him and took his head and his armor, and sent messengers throughout the land of the Philistines to proclaim the news among their idols and their people. 10They put his armor in the temple of their gods and hung up his head in the temple of Dagon.[g]

11When all the inhabitants of Jabesh Gilead[h] heard what the Philistines had done to Saul, 12all their valiant men went and took the bodies of Saul and his sons and brought them to Jabesh. Then they buried their bones under the great tree in Jabesh, and they fasted seven days.

13Saul died[i] because he was unfaithful[j] to the LORD; he did not keep[k] the word of the LORD and even consulted a medium[l] for guidance, 14and did not inquire of the LORD. So the LORD put him to death and turned[m] the kingdom[n] over to David son of Jesse.

David Becomes King Over Israel

11:1-3pp — 2Sa 5:1-3

11 All Israel[o] came together to David at Hebron[p] and said, "We are your own flesh and blood. 2In the past, even while Saul was king, you were the one who led Israel on their military campaigns.[q] And the LORD your God said to

9:39 [b] 1Ch 8:33 [c] 1Sa 9:1 [d] 1Sa 13:22 [e] 2Sa 2:8 **9:40** [f] 2Sa 4:4
10:10 [g] Jdg 16:23 **10:11** [h] Jdg 21:8 **10:13** [i] 2Sa 1:1 [j] 1Sa 15:23; 1Ch 5:25 [k] 1Sa 13:13 [l] Lev 19:31; 20:6; Dt 18:9-14; 1Sa 28:7 **10:14** [m] 1Ch 12:23 [n] 1Sa 13:14; 15:28 **11:1** [o] 1Ch 9:1 [p] Ge 13:18; 23:19 **11:2** [q] 1Sa 18:5, 16

[a] *39* Also known as *Ish-Bosheth* [b] *40* Also known as *Mephibosheth* [c] *41* Vulgate and Syriac (see also Septuagint and 8:35); Hebrew does not have *and Ahaz.* [d] *42* Some Hebrew manuscripts and Septuagint (see also 8:36); most Hebrew manuscripts *Jarah, Jarah*

10:4 *armor-bearer.* See note on 1Sa 14:1.
10:9 *They ... took his head.* See note on 1Sa 17:51.
10:10 *put his armor in the temple.* See note on 1Sa 5:2. *temple of their gods.* Identified in 1Sa 31:10 as the "temple of the Ashtoreths" (i.e., of Astarte) in Beth Shan (see notes on Jdg 2:13; 1Sa 31:10). It is likely, given the close proximity of the expressions, that the "temple of Dagon" was also there. Three Iron Age Canaanite temples have been discovered at the site.
10:13 *Saul died.* In the ancient world the defeat of kings and of kingdoms was linked with divine displeasure. Put simply, losers were seen as bad and obviously deserving of their fate—for if they were not bad, the gods would have brought them victory. The Cyrus Cylinder, e.g., describes the Babylonian king Nabonidus as impious and irreverent; conversely, Cyrus is portrayed as a conquering hero. Similarly, oppression by a foreign power was viewed as the result of divine anger. At the same time, we should remember that the Cyrus Cylinder and other such documents are pieces of political propaganda written by a conqueror in his own interests. Such assessments may need to be treated with a generous helping of salt. It could be argued that this negative assessment of Saul was written by a supporter of David, Saul's successor, and should therefore be treated in the same way. However, the general frankness of the Biblical writers about the misdemeanors of the kings of Israel and Judah, even about those who were not defeated and shamed, leads to the conclusion that this is an accurate and impartial assessment of Saul's behavior in relation to Yahweh.
11:2 *shepherd my people.* The concept of the king as a "shepherd" is common in ancient Near Eastern literature. Examples include the Code of Hammurapi and the Cyrus Cylinder. See note on 1Ki 22:17.

Beth Shan, the place where the Philistines put Saul's armor in the temple of their gods (1Ch 10:10).

you, 'You will shepherd[r] my people Israel,
and you will become their ruler.[s]' "
3When all the elders of Israel had come
to King David at Hebron, he made a covenant with them at Hebron before the
LORD, and they anointed[t] David king over
Israel, as the LORD had promised through
Samuel.

David Conquers Jerusalem

11:4-9pp — 2Sa 5:6-10

4David and all the Israelites marched to
Jerusalem (that is, Jebus). The Jebusites[u]
who lived there 5said to David, "You will
not get in here." Nevertheless, David captured the fortress of Zion — which is the
City of David.
6David had said, "Whoever leads the
attack on the Jebusites will become commander-in-chief." Joab[v] son of Zeruiah
went up first, and so he received the command.
7David then took up residence in the
fortress, and so it was called the City of
David. 8He built up the city around it,
from the terraces[a][w] to the surrounding
wall, while Joab restored the rest of the
city. 9And David became more and more
powerful,[x] because the LORD Almighty was
with him.

David's Mighty Warriors

11:10-41pp — 2Sa 23:8-39

10These were the chiefs of David's
mighty warriors — they, together with all
Israel,[y] gave his kingship strong support
to extend it over the whole land, as the
LORD had promised[z] — 11this is the list of
David's mighty warriors:[a]
Jashobeam,[b] a Hakmonite, was chief of
the officers[c]; he raised his spear against
three hundred men, whom he killed in
one encounter.
12Next to him was Eleazar son of Dodai
the Ahohite, one of the three mighty warriors. 13He was with David at Pas Dammim when the Philistines gathered there

11:2 [r] Ps 78:71; Mt 2:6 [s] 1Ch 5:2
11:3 [t] 1Sa 16:1-13
11:4 [u] Ge 10:16; 15:18-21; Jos 3:10; 15:8; Jdg 1:21; 19:10
11:6 [v] 2Sa 2:13; 8:16
11:8 [w] 2Sa 5:9; 2Ch 32:5
11:9 [x] 2Sa 3:1; Est 9:4
11:10 [y] ver 1 [z] ver 3; 1Ch 12:23
11:11 [a] 2Sa 17:10

[a] 8 Or *the Millo* [b] 11 Possibly a variant of *Jashob-Baal*
[c] 11 Or *Thirty*; some Septuagint manuscripts *Three* (see also 2 Samuel 23:8)

11:3 *elders.* In the ancient Near East, with the exception of Egypt, elders had an important role to play. See note on Jdg 2:7. *covenant.* The elders of Israel and David formally declare his kingship. This likely includes drawing up a written document, which affirms the tribes' loyalty to David and lays out the terms by which he should rule. By this means, the accountability of the king is established. In Babylon, part of the New Year celebrations revolved around the accountability of the king and an annual declaration that he had ruled appropriately. *anointed.* See notes on 1Sa 2:10; 10:1.

11:4 *Jerusalem.* See notes on Jdg 1:7; 2Sa 5:6. *Jebusites.* See note on Dt 7:1.

11:7 *City of David.* See note on 2Sa 5:9.

for battle. At a place where there was a
field full of barley, the troops fled from the
Philistines. 14 But they took their stand in
the middle of the field. They defended it
and struck the Philistines down, and the
LORD brought about a great victory.[b]
15 Three of the thirty chiefs came down
to David to the rock at the cave of Adullam, while a band of Philistines was encamped in the Valley[c] of Rephaim. 16 At
that time David was in the stronghold,[d]
and the Philistine garrison was at Bethlehem. 17 David longed for water and said,
"Oh, that someone would get me a drink
of water from the well near the gate of
Bethlehem!" 18 So the Three broke through
the Philistine lines, drew water from the
well near the gate of Bethlehem and carried it back to David. But he refused to
drink it; instead, he poured[e] it out to the
LORD. 19 "God forbid that I should do this!"
he said. "Should I drink the blood of these
men who went at the risk of their lives?"
Because they risked their lives to bring it
back, David would not drink it.
Such were the exploits of the three
mighty warriors.
20 Abishai[f] the brother of Joab was chief
of the Three. He raised his spear against
three hundred men, whom he killed, and
so he became as famous as the Three. 21 He
was doubly honored above the Three and
became their commander, even though he
was not included among them.
22 Benaiah son of Jehoiada, a valiant
fighter from Kabzeel,[g] performed great exploits. He struck down Moab's two mightiest warriors. He also went down into a pit
on a snowy day and killed a lion.[h] 23 And
he struck down an Egyptian who was five
cubits[a] tall. Although the Egyptian had a
spear like a weaver's rod[i] in his hand, Benaiah went against him with a club. He
snatched the spear from the Egyptian's
hand and killed him with his own spear.
24 Such were the exploits of Benaiah son
of Jehoiada; he too was as famous as the
three mighty warriors. 25 He was held in
greater honor than any of the Thirty, but
he was not included among the Three.
And David put him in charge of his bodyguard.
26 The mighty warriors were:
Asahel[j] the brother of Joab,
Elhanan son of Dodo from Bethlehem,
27 Shammoth[k] the Harorite,
Helez the Pelonite,
28 Ira son of Ikkesh from Tekoa,
Abiezer[l] from Anathoth,
29 Sibbekai[m] the Hushathite,
Ilai the Ahohite,
30 Maharai the Netophathite,
Heled son of Baanah the Netophathite,
31 Ithai son of Ribai from Gibeah in
Benjamin,
Benaiah[n] the Pirathonite,[o]
32 Hurai from the ravines of Gaash,
Abiel the Arbathite,
33 Azmaveth the Baharumite,
Eliahba the Shaalbonite,
34 the sons of Hashem the Gizonite,
Jonathan son of Shagee the Hararite,
35 Ahiam son of Sakar the Hararite,
Eliphal son of Ur,
36 Hepher the Mekerathite,
Ahijah the Pelonite,
37 Hezro the Carmelite,
Naarai son of Ezbai,
38 Joel the brother of Nathan,
Mibhar son of Hagri,
39 Zelek the Ammonite,
Naharai the Berothite, the armor-
bearer of Joab son of Zeruiah,
40 Ira the Ithrite,
Gareb the Ithrite,
41 Uriah[p] the Hittite,
Zabad[q] son of Ahlai,
42 Adina son of Shiza the Reubenite,
who was chief of the Reubenites,
and the thirty with him,
43 Hanan son of Maakah,
Joshaphat the Mithnite,
44 Uzzia the Ashterathite,[r]
Shama and Jeiel the sons of Hotham the Aroerite,
45 Jediael son of Shimri,
his brother Joha the Tizite,
46 Eliel the Mahavite,
Jeribai and Joshaviah the sons of
Elnaam,
Ithmah the Moabite,
47 Eliel, Obed and Jaasiel the Mezoba-
ite.

Warriors Join David

12 These were the men who came to
David at Ziklag,[s] while he was banished from the presence of Saul son of Kish
(they were among the warriors who helped
him in battle; 2 they were armed with bows
and were able to shoot arrows or to sling
stones right-handed or left-handed;[t] they

11:14 [b] Ex 14:30; 1Sa 11:13
11:15 [c] 1Ch 14:9; Isa 17:5
11:16 [d] 2Sa 5:17
11:18 [e] Dt 12:16
11:20 [f] 1Sa 26:6
11:22 [g] Jos 15:21 [h] 1Sa 17:36
11:23 [i] 1Sa 17:7
11:26 [j] 2Sa 2:18
11:27 [k] 1Ch 27:8
11:28 [l] 1Ch 27:12
11:29 [m] 2Sa 21:18
11:31 [n] 1Ch 27:14 [o] Jdg 12:13
11:41 [p] 2Sa 11:6 [q] 1Ch 2:36
11:44 [r] Dt 1:4
12:1 [s] Jos 15:31; 1Sa 27:2-6
12:2 [t] Jdg 3:15; 20:16

[a] *23* That is, about 7 feet 6 inches or about 2.3 meters

11:22 *killed a lion.* See note on 2Sa 23:20.
12:2 *sling stones.* See note on 1Sa 17:40. *right-handed or left-handed.* See note on Jdg 3:15.

were relatives of Saul[u] from the tribe of
Benjamin):

3Ahiezer their chief and Joash the
sons of Shemaah the Gibeathite; Je-
ziel and Pelet the sons of Azmaveth;
Berakah, Jehu the Anathothite, 4and
Ishmaiah the Gibeonite, a mighty
warrior among the Thirty, who was
a leader of the Thirty; Jeremiah, Jahaziel, Johanan, Jozabad the Gederathite,[a][v] 5Eluzai, Jerimoth, Bealiah,
Shemariah and Shephatiah the Haru-
phite; 6Elkanah, Ishiah, Azarel, Joe-
zer and Jashobeam the Korahites;
7and Joelah and Zebadiah the sons of
Jeroham from Gedor.[w]

8Some Gadites[x] defected to David at his
stronghold in the wilderness. They were
brave warriors, ready for battle and able
to handle the shield and spear. Their faces
were the faces of lions,[y] and they were as
swift as gazelles[z] in the mountains.

9Ezer was the chief,
Obadiah the second in command, Eliab the third,
10Mishmannah the fourth, Jeremiah the
fifth,
11Attai the sixth, Eliel the seventh,
12Johanan the eighth, Elzabad the
ninth,
13Jeremiah the tenth and Makbannai
the eleventh.

14These Gadites were army commanders; the least was a match for a hundred,[a]
and the greatest for a thousand.[b] 15It was
they who crossed the Jordan in the first
month when it was overflowing all its
banks,[c] and they put to flight everyone living in the valleys, to the east and to the
west.
16Other Benjamites[d] and some men from
Judah also came to David in his stronghold.
17David went out to meet them and said to
them, "If you have come to me in peace
to help me, I am ready for you to join me.
But if you have come to betray me to my
enemies when my hands are free from violence, may the God of our ancestors see it
and judge you."
18Then the Spirit[e] came on Amasai,[f]
chief of the Thirty, and he said:

"We are yours, David!
We are with you, son of Jesse!
Success,[g] success to you,
and success to those who help you,
for your God will help you."

So David received them and made them
leaders of his raiding bands.
19Some of the tribe of Manasseh defected to David when he went with the Philistines to fight against Saul. (He and his
men did not help the Philistines because,
after consultation, their rulers sent him
away. They said, "It will cost us our heads
if he deserts to his master Saul.")[h] 20When
David went to Ziklag,[i] these were the men
of Manasseh who defected to him: Adnah,
Jozabad, Jediael, Michael, Jozabad, Elihu
and Zillethai, leaders of units of a thousand in Manasseh. 21They helped David
against raiding bands, for all of them were
brave warriors, and they were commanders in his army. 22Day after day men came
to help David, until he had a great army,
like the army of God.[b]

Others Join David at Hebron

23These are the numbers of the men
armed for battle who came to David at
Hebron[j] to turn[k] Saul's kingdom over to
him, as the LORD had said:[l]

12:2 [u] 2Sa 3:19 **12:4** [v] Jos 15:36 **12:7** [w] Jos 15:58 **12:8** [x] Ge 30:11 [y] 2Sa 17:10 [z] 2Sa 2:18 **12:14** [a] Lev 26:8 [b] Dt 32:30 **12:15** [c] Jos 3:15 **12:16** [d] 2Sa 3:19 **12:18** [e] Jdg 3:10; 6:34; 1Ch 28:12; 2Ch 15:1; 20:14; 24:20 [f] 2Sa 17:25 [g] 1Sa 25:5-6 **12:19** [h] 1Sa 29:2-11 **12:20** [i] 1Sa 27:6 **12:23** [j] 2Sa 2:3-4 [k] 1Ch 10:14 [l] 1Sa 16:1; 1Ch 11:10

[a] *4* In Hebrew texts the second half of this verse (*Jeremiah . . . Gederathite*) is numbered 12:5, and 12:5-40 is numbered 12:6-41. [b] *22* Or *a great and mighty army*

12:15 *the first month.* Began in March. At this time the spring temperatures were melting the snow in the mountains, and the water from the various tributaries swelled the river, causing it to burst its banks in the flood plain around Jericho (cf. Jos 3:15), where the river was usually fordable. Crossing the Jordan at this time was more dangerous, but doing so afforded an element of surprise to any attack. Frequently in Neo-Assyrian inscriptions, the kings relate that they crossed the Euphrates when it was in flood, apparently by the use of pontoons. Shalmaneser III of Assyria records several times that he crossed the Euphrates in flood. He did so on "rafts (made of inflated) goatskins." In his 11th regnal year he states that he crossed the Euphrates in flood "for the ninth time."

12:21 *his army.* Forces were conscripted from the whole population of serviceable age, most of whom were farmers. As a result, military campaigning was conducted in spring, after the winter rains and before the harvest had to be gathered in, when every available hand was needed in the fields. Even after the introduction of a standing army this pattern continued, since the majority of the troops had to be mustered. The advantage of having a standing army was that it was always in training and its troops were expected to be more effective than those more experienced in handling a plowshare. The disadvantage was that it needed feeding and paying—an expensive business. In Israel, the growth of the standing army began with the establishment of the monarchy—Saul began to take into his service any mighty or brave man that he saw (1Sa 14:52). Assyrian and Babylonian annals often include the note that a military campaign began either in Nisan or Iyyar, i.e., the first or second month of the year (March–May).

12:23–40 This list illustrates two aspects of the situation. First, the listing according to tribal affiliation shows that Israel is still very much a tribal society, despite having a permanent leader in the person of the king. Any ruler over all Israel must have the backing of all the tribes. Second, it is clear that any would-be ruler must also have the support of the armed forces.

24 from Judah, carrying shield and
spear — 6,800 armed for battle;
25 from Simeon, warriors ready for battle — 7,100;
26 from Levi — 4,600, 27 including Jehoiada, leader of the family of Aaron,
with 3,700 men, 28 and Zadok,[m] a
brave young warrior, with 22 officers from his family;
29 from Benjamin,[n] Saul's tribe — 3,000,
most[o] of whom had remained loyal
to Saul's house until then;
30 from Ephraim, brave warriors, famous in their own clans — 20,800;
31 from half the tribe of Manasseh, designated by name to come and make
David king — 18,000;
32 from Issachar, men who understood
the times and knew what Israel
should do[p] — 200 chiefs, with all
their relatives under their command;
33 from Zebulun, experienced soldiers
prepared for battle with every type
of weapon, to help David with undivided loyalty — 50,000;
34 from Naphtali — 1,000 officers, together with 37,000 men carrying
shields and spears;
35 from Dan, ready for battle — 28,600;
36 from Asher, experienced soldiers prepared for battle — 40,000;
37 and from east of the Jordan, from
Reuben, Gad and the half-tribe of
Manasseh, armed with every type
of weapon — 120,000.

38 All these were fighting men who volunteered to serve in the ranks. They came
to Hebron fully determined to make David
king over all Israel.[q] All the rest of the Israelites were also of one mind to make David king. 39 The men spent three days there
with David, eating and drinking,[r] for their
families had supplied provisions for them.
40 Also, their neighbors from as far away
as Issachar, Zebulun and Naphtali came
bringing food on donkeys, camels, mules
and oxen. There were plentiful supplies[s] of
flour, fig cakes, raisin[t] cakes, wine, olive
oil, cattle and sheep, for there was joy[u]
in Israel.

Bringing Back the Ark

13:1-14pp — 2Sa 6:1-11

13 David conferred with each of his
officers, the commanders of thousands and commanders of hundreds. 2 He
then said to the whole assembly of Israel,
"If it seems good to you and if it is the will
of the LORD our God, let us send word far
and wide to the rest of our people throughout the territories of Israel, and also to the
priests and Levites who are with them in
their towns and pasturelands, to come and
join us. 3 Let us bring the ark of our God
back to us,[v] for we did not inquire[w] of[a]
it[b] during the reign of Saul." 4 The whole
assembly agreed to do this, because it
seemed right to all the people.

5 So David assembled all Israel,[x] from
the Shihor River[y] in Egypt to Lebo Hamath,[z] to bring the ark of God from Kiriath
Jearim.[a] 6 David and all Israel went to Baalah[b] of Judah (Kiriath Jearim) to bring up
from there the ark of God the LORD, who
is enthroned between the cherubim[c] — the
ark that is called by the Name.

7 They moved the ark of God from Abinadab's[d] house on a new cart, with Uzzah
and Ahio guiding it. 8 David and all the Israelites were celebrating with all their might
before God, with songs and with harps,
lyres, timbrels, cymbals and trumpets.[e]

9 When they came to the threshing floor
of Kidon, Uzzah reached out his hand to
steady the ark, because the oxen stumbled. 10 The LORD's anger[f] burned against
Uzzah, and he struck him down[g] because
he had put his hand on the ark. So he died
there before God.

11 Then David was angry because the
LORD's wrath had broken out against Uz-
zah, and to this day that place is called
Perez Uzzah.[c]

12 David was afraid of God that day and
asked, "How can I ever bring the ark of
God to me?" 13 He did not take the ark to
be with him in the City of David. Instead,
he took it to the house of Obed-Edom[i] the
Gittite. 14 The ark of God remained with
the family of Obed-Edom in his house for
three months, and the LORD blessed his
household[j] and everything he had.

David's House and Family

14:1-7pp — 2Sa 5:11-16; 1Ch 3:5-8

14 Now Hiram king of Tyre sent messengers to David, along with cedar
logs,[k] stonemasons and carpenters to build
a palace for him. 2 And David knew that
the LORD had established him as king over

[a] 3 Or *we neglected* [b] 3 Or *him* [c] 11 *Perez Uzzah* means *outbreak against Uzzah.*

12:28 [m] 2Sa 8:17; 1Ch 6:8; 15:11; 16:39; 27:17
12:29 [n] 2Sa 3:19 [o] 2Sa 2:8-9
12:32 [p] Est 1:13
12:38 [q] 2Sa 5:1-3; 1Ch 9:1
12:39 [r] 2Sa 3:20; Isa 25:6-8
12:40 [s] 2Sa 16:1; 17:29 [t] 1Sa 25:18 [u] 1Ch 29:22
13:3 [v] 1Sa 7:1-2 [w] 2Ch 1:5
13:5 [x] 1Ch 11:1; 15:3 [y] Jos 13:3 [z] Nu 13:21 [a] 1Sa 6:21; 7:2
13:6 [b] Jos 15:9; 2Sa 6:2 [c] Ex 25:22; 2Ki 19:15
13:7 [d] Nu 4:15; 1Sa 7:1
13:8 [e] 2Sa 6:5; 1Ch 15:16, 19, 24; 2Ch 5:12; Ps 92:3
13:10 [f] 1Ch 15:13, 15 [g] Lev 10:2
13:11 [h] 1Ch 15:13; Ps 7:11
13:13 [i] 1Ch 15:18, 24; 16:38; 26:4-5, 15
13:14 [j] 2Sa 6:11; 1Ch 26:4-5
14:1 [k] 2Ch 2:3; Ezr 3:7

13:3 *ark of our God.* See note on Ex 25:16.
13:6 *enthroned between the cherubim.* See note on 2Ki 19:15.
13:7 *new cart.* See note on 2Sa 6:3.
13:8 *with songs and with harps ... trumpets.* See the article "Music and Musicians," p. 524.
14:1 *Hiram.* See notes on 2Sa 5:11; 1Ki 5:1. *cedar logs.* See notes on 2Sa 5:11; 1Ki 5:6; 6:15. *stonemasons and carpenters.* The use of foreign artisans in constructing monumental architecture is also documented in relation to the temple (2Ch 2:7), although Solomon also had his own skilled craftsmen. Perhaps in the time of David the Israelites had little experience constructing the large buildings that go with a

Israel and that his kingdom had been highly exalted[l] for the sake of his people Israel.
3In Jerusalem David took more wives
and became the father of more sons[m]
and daughters. 4These are the names of
the children born to him there:[n] Shammua, Shobab, Nathan, Solomon, 5Ibhar,
Elishua, Elpelet, 6Nogah, Nepheg, Japhia,
7Elishama, Beeliada[a] and Eliphelet.

David Defeats the Philistines

14:8-17pp — 2Sa 5:17-25

8When the Philistines heard that David
had been anointed king over all Israel,[o]
they went up in full force to search for
him, but David heard about it and went
out to meet them. 9Now the Philistines
had come and raided the Valley[p] of Rephaim; 10so David inquired of God: "Shall I
go and attack the Philistines? Will you deliver them into my hands?"

The LORD answered him, "Go, I will deliver them into your hands."

11So David and his men went up to Baal
Perazim,[q] and there he defeated them. He
said, "As waters break out, God has broken out against my enemies by my hand."
So that place was called Baal Perazim.[b]
12The Philistines had abandoned their
gods there, and David gave orders to burn[r]
them in the fire.[s]

13Once more the Philistines raided the
valley;[t] 14so David inquired of God again,
and God answered him, "Do not go directly
after them, but circle around them and attack them in front of the poplar trees. 15As
soon as you hear the sound of marching in
the tops of the poplar trees, move out to
battle, because that will mean God has gone
out in front of you to strike the Philistine
army." 16So David did as God commanded
him, and they struck down the Philistine
army, all the way from Gibeon[u] to Gezer.[v]

17So David's fame[w] spread throughout
every land, and the LORD made all the nations fear[x] him.

The Ark Brought to Jerusalem

15:25 – 16:3pp — 2Sa 6:12-19

15 After David had constructed buildings for himself in the City of David, he prepared[y] a place for the ark of
God and pitched[z] a tent for it. 2Then David
said, "No one but the Levites[a] may carry[b]
the ark of God, because the LORD chose
them to carry the ark of the LORD and to
minister[c] before him forever."

3David assembled all Israel[d] in Jerusalem to bring up the ark of the LORD to the
place he had prepared for it. 4He called
together the descendants of Aaron and the
Levites:

5From the descendants of Kohath,
Uriel the leader and 120 relatives;
6from the descendants of Merari,
Asaiah the leader and 220 relatives;
7from the descendants of Gershon,[c]
Joel the leader and 130 relatives;
8from the descendants of Elizaphan,[e]
Shemaiah the leader and 200 relatives;
9from the descendants of Hebron,[f]
Eliel the leader and 80 relatives;
10from the descendants of Uzziel,
Amminadab the leader and 112 relatives.

11Then David summoned Zadok[g] and
Abiathar[h] the priests, and Uriel, Asaiah,
Joel, Shemaiah, Eliel and Amminadab
the Levites. 12He said to them, "You are
the heads of the Levitical families; you
and your fellow Levites are to consecrate[i] yourselves and bring up the ark of
the LORD, the God of Israel, to the place I
have prepared for it. 13It was because you,
the Levites,[j] did not bring it up the first
time that the LORD our God broke out in
anger against us.[k] We did not inquire of
him about how to do it in the prescribed
way." 14So the priests and Levites consecrated themselves in order to bring up the
ark of the LORD, the God of Israel. 15And
the Levites carried the ark of God with the
poles on their shoulders, as Moses had
commanded[l] in accordance with the word
of the LORD.

16David told the leaders of the Levites to
appoint their fellow Levites as musicians[m]
to make a joyful sound with musical instruments: lyres, harps and cymbals.[n]

17So the Levites appointed Heman[o] son

14:2 [l] Nu 24:7; Dt 26:19
14:3 [m] 1Ch 3:1
14:4 [n] 1Ch 3:9
14:8 [o] 1Ch 11:1
14:9 [p] ver 13; Jos 15:8; 1Ch 11:15
14:11 [q] Isa 28:21
14:12 [r] Ex 32:20 [s] Jos 7:15
14:13 [t] ver 9
14:16 [u] Jos 9:3 [v] Jos 10:33
14:17 [w] Jos 6:27; 2Ch 26:8 [x] Ex 15:14-16; Dt 2:25
15:1 [y] Ps 132:1-18
[z] 1Ch 16:1; 17:1
15:2 [a] Nu 4:15; Dt 10:8; 2Ch 5:5 [b] Dt 31:9 [c] 1Ch 23:13
15:3 [d] 1Ki 8:1; 1Ch 13:5
15:8 [e] Ex 6:22
15:9 [f] Ex 6:18
15:11 [g] 1Ch 12:28 [h] 1Sa 22:20
15:12 [i] Ex 19:14-15; Lev 11:44; 2Ch 35:6
15:13 [j] 1Ki 8:4 [k] 2Sa 6:3; 1Ch 13:7-10
15:15 [l] Ex 25:14; Nu 4:5, 15
15:16 [m] Ps 68:25 [n] 1Ch 13:8; 25:1; Ne 12:27, 36
15:17 [o] 1Ch 6:33

[a] 7 A variant of *Eliada*
[b] 11 *Baal Perazim* means *the lord who breaks out.*
[c] 7 Hebrew *Gershom,* a variant of *Gershon*

centralized administration and a monarchy. Egyptian tomb reliefs depict various craftsmen at work, including stoneworkers and woodworkers and display the different tools employed. Some of the tools used for carpentry include the drill, saw, mallet and chisel, adze and polishing stone.

14:3 *David took more wives.* See notes on 1Sa 25:39b,43; 2Sa 3:2–5,7.

14:10 *David inquired of God.* See the article "Urim and Thummim," p. 162.

14:12 *abandoned their gods.* See note on 2Sa 5:21.

14:15 *hear ... marching in the tops of the poplar trees.* See note on 2Sa 5:23–24. *God has gone out.* See the article "Divine Warfare," p. 365.

14:17 *the LORD made all the nations fear him.* In Assyrian inscriptions there is the frequent assertion that Assur (their god) caused various nations to fear Assyria. There the usual consequence is that they bring tribute and bow to the Assyrian yoke. Here, in contrast, there is no direct reference to any action on the part of the surrounding nations other than a fear of David.

of Joel; from his relatives, Asaph[p] son
of Berekiah; and from their relatives the
Merarites,[q] Ethan son of Kushaiah; 18and
with them their relatives next in rank:
Zechariah,[a] Jaaziel, Shemiramoth, Jehiel,
Unni, Eliab, Benaiah, Maaseiah, Mattithiah, Eliphelehu, Mikneiah, Obed-Edom[r]
and Jeiel,[b] the gatekeepers.
19The musicians Heman,[s] Asaph and
Ethan were to sound the bronze cymbals; 20Zechariah, Jaaziel,[c] Shemiramoth,
Jehiel, Unni, Eliab, Maaseiah and Benaiah were to play the lyres according to
alamoth,[d] 21and Mattithiah, Eliphelehu,
Mikneiah, Obed-Edom, Jeiel and Azaziah
were to play the harps, directing according
to *sheminith*.[d] 22Kenaniah the head Levite
was in charge of the singing; that was his
responsibility because he was skillful at it.
23Berekiah and Elkanah were to be
doorkeepers for the ark. 24Shebaniah,
Joshaphat, Nethanel, Amasai, Zechariah, Benaiah and Eliezer the priests were
to blow trumpets[t] before the ark of God.
Obed-Edom and Jehiah were also to be
doorkeepers for the ark.
25So David and the elders of Israel and
the commanders of units of a thousand
went to bring up the ark[u] of the covenant
of the LORD from the house of Obed-Edom,
with rejoicing. 26Because God had helped
the Levites who were carrying the ark of
the covenant of the LORD, seven bulls and
seven rams[v] were sacrificed. 27Now David
was clothed in a robe of fine linen, as were
all the Levites who were carrying the ark,
and as were the musicians, and Kenaniah,

15:17 [p] 1Ch 6:39 [q] 1Ch 6:44
15:18 [r] 1Ch 26:4-5
15:19 [s] 1Ch 25:6
15:24 [t] ver 28; 1Ch 16:6; 2Ch 7:6
15:25 [u] 1Ch 13:13; 2Ch 1:4
15:26 [v] Nu 23:1-4, 29

[a] 18 Three Hebrew manuscripts and most Septuagint manuscripts (see also verse 20 and 16:5); most Hebrew manuscripts *Zechariah son and* or *Zechariah, Ben and*
[b] 18 Hebrew; Septuagint (see also verse 21) *Jeiel and Azaziah*
[c] 20 See verse 18; Hebrew *Aziel*, a variant of *Jaaziel*.
[d] 20,21 Probably a musical term

15:21 *sheminith*. This musical term means "eighth." It may be an instrument with eight strings or an instrument an octave removed from the basic tone.
15:26 *seven bulls and seven rams*. Seven was a universally sacred number throughout the ancient Near East. It symbolized completeness or perfection. Frequently, rituals were to be performed seven times in order to be effective.
15:27 *robe of fine linen*. See note on 1Sa 2:19. *linen ephod*. See note on 1Sa 2:18.

THE CITY OF THE JEBUSITES/DAVID'S JERUSALEM

Substantial historical evidence, both Biblical and extra-Biblical, places the temple of Solomon on the holy spot where King David built an altar to the Lord. David had purchased the land from Araunah the Jebusite, who was using the exposed bedrock as a threshing floor (2Sa 24:18–25). Tradition claims a much older sanctity for the site, associating it with the altar of Abraham on Mount Moriah (Ge 22:1–19; see 2Ch 3:1). The writer of Genesis equates Moriah with "the mountain of the LORD" (Ge 22:14).

c. 1000 BC

Less than 11 acres in size, Jebus, a Canaanite city, could well defend itself against attack, with walls atop steep canyons and shafts reaching an underground water source. David captured the stronghold c. 1000 BC and made it his capital.

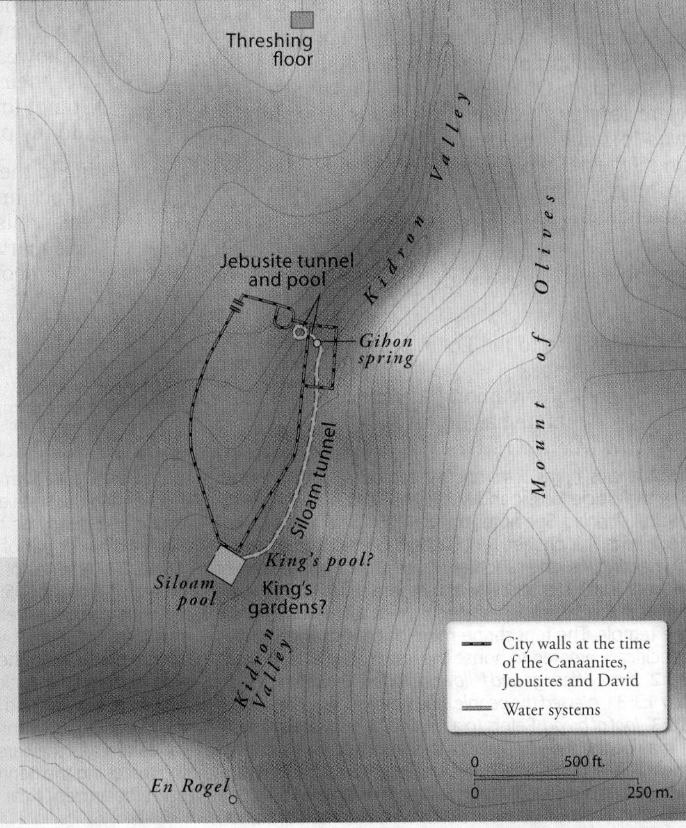

who was in charge of the singing of the
choirs. David also wore a linen ephod.
28So all Israel brought up the ark of the
covenant of the LORD with shouts, with the
sounding of rams' horns[w] and trumpets,
and of cymbals, and the playing of lyres
and harps.
29As the ark of the covenant of the LORD
was entering the City of David, Michal
daughter of Saul watched from a window.
And when she saw King David dancing and
celebrating, she despised him in her heart.

Ministering Before the Ark

16:8-22pp — Ps 105:1-15
16:23-33pp — Ps 96:1-13
16:34-36pp — Ps 106:1,47-48

16 They brought the ark of God and
set it inside the tent that David had
pitched[x] for it, and they presented burnt
offerings and fellowship offerings before
God. 2After David had finished sacrificing
the burnt offerings and fellowship offerings, he blessed[y] the people in the name of
the LORD. 3Then he gave a loaf of bread, a
cake of dates and a cake of raisins to each
Israelite man and woman.
4He appointed some of the Levites to
minister[z] before the ark of the LORD, to extol,[a] thank, and praise the LORD, the God
of Israel: 5Asaph was the chief, and next
to him in rank were Zechariah, then Jaaziel,[b] Shemiramoth, Jehiel, Mattithiah, Eliab, Benaiah, Obed-Edom and Jeiel. They
were to play the lyres and harps, Asaph
was to sound the cymbals, 6and Benaiah
and Jahaziel the priests were to blow the
trumpets regularly before the ark of the
covenant of God.
7That day David first appointed Asaph
and his associates to give praise[a] to the
LORD in this manner:

8Give praise[b] to the LORD, proclaim his
name;
make known among the nations[c]
what he has done.

15:28 [w] 1Ch 13:8
16:1 [x] 1Ch 15:1
16:2 [y] Ex 39:43
16:4 [z] 1Ch 15:2
16:7 [a] 2Sa 23:1
16:8 [b] ver 34; Ps 136:1 [c] 2Ki 19:19
16:9 [d] Ex 15:1
16:11 [e] 1Ch 28:9; 2Ch 7:14; Ps 24:6; 119:2, 58
16:12 [f] Ps 77:11 [g] Ps 78:43
16:14 [h] Isa 26:9
16:16 [i] Ge 12:7; 15:18; 17:2; 22:16-18; 26:3; 28:13; 35:11
16:17 [j] Ge 35:9-12
16:18 [k] Ge 13:14-17
16:19 [l] Ge 34:30; Dt 7:7
16:21 [m] Ge 12:17; 20:3; Ex 7:15-18
16:22 [n] Ge 20:7

9Sing to him, sing praise[d] to him;
tell of all his wonderful acts.
10Glory in his holy name;
let the hearts of those who seek the
LORD rejoice.
11Look to the LORD and his strength;
seek[e] his face always.

12Remember[f] the wonders he has done,
his miracles,[g] and the judgments he
pronounced,
13you his servants, the descendants of
Israel,
his chosen ones, the children of
Jacob.
14He is the LORD our God;
his judgments[h] are in all the earth.

15He remembers[c] his covenant forever,
the promise he made, for a thousand
generations,
16the covenant[i] he made with Abraham,
the oath he swore to Isaac.
17He confirmed it to Jacob[j] as a decree,
to Israel as an everlasting covenant:
18"To you I will give the land of
Canaan[k]
as the portion you will inherit."

19When they were but few in number,[l]
few indeed, and strangers in it,
20they[d] wandered from nation to nation,
from one kingdom to another.
21He allowed no one to oppress them;
for their sake he rebuked kings:[m]
22"Do not touch my anointed ones;
do my prophets[n] no harm."

23Sing to the LORD, all the earth;
proclaim his salvation day after day.
24Declare his glory among the nations,
his marvelous deeds among all
peoples.

[a] *4* Or *petition*; or *invoke* [b] *5* See 15:18,20; Hebrew *Jeiel*, possibly another name for *Jaaziel*. [c] *15* Some Septuagint manuscripts (see also Psalm 105:8); Hebrew *Remember* [d] *18-20* One Hebrew manuscript, Septuagint and Vulgate (see also Psalm 105:12); most Hebrew manuscripts *inherit, / 19though you are but few in number, / few indeed, and strangers in it." / 20They*

15:28 *rams' horns ... trumpets ... cymbals ... lyres ... harps.* See the article "Music and Musicians," p. 524.
15:29 *dancing.* See notes on 1Sa 18:6; 2Sa 6:14.
16:1 *tent.* This pitched tent is distinguished from the tent of meeting (i.e., the sanctuary constructed in the time of Moses). That latter tent was at this time still in Gibeon (see note on 2Ch 1:3) and remained there until the building of the temple. The tent shrine mentioned in this verse was specifically erected to house the ark.
16:2 *burnt offerings and fellowship offerings.* See notes on Lev 1:3; 3:1. *blessed the people.* See note on Nu 6:24–26.
16:3 *loaf of bread.* Refers to a round-shaped loaf of bread. It may be that two or three of these constituted a normal meal (1Sa 10:3, unless Saul is being given a double portion), while prison fare and charity provision was only one (1Sa 2:36; Jer 37:21). *cake of dates.* A traditional translation but of uncertain etymology and meaning. It only occurs here and in the parallel passage in 2Sa 6:19. *cake of raisins.* Could apparently be made with any dried fruit and was likely a block or ball of compressed dried fruit.
16:8 – 36 A series of partial quotations from three different psalms: Ps 105; 96; 106. The contextualization of different psalms is well-known in Scripture, both through insertion into narrative texts and from historical comments made in the headings to various psalms. This has no parallel in the ancient Near East. In Mesopotamia, the historical background to a hymn might be inferred from its content, but hymns of praise are not inserted into narrative texts as they are here. Admittedly, however, nothing matching the genre and scope of Chronicles is known from the ancient Near East.

25 For great is the LORD and most worthy
of praise;[o]
he is to be feared[p] above all gods.[q]
26 For all the gods of the nations are
idols,
but the LORD made the heavens.[r]
27 Splendor and majesty are before him;
strength and joy are in his dwelling
place.
28 Ascribe to the LORD, all you families of
nations,
ascribe to the LORD glory and
strength.[s]
29 Ascribe to the LORD the glory due his
name;
bring an offering and come before
him.
Worship the LORD in the splendor of
his[a] holiness.[t]
30 Tremble[u] before him, all the earth!
The world is firmly established; it
cannot be moved.
31 Let the heavens rejoice, let the earth be
glad;[v]
let them say among the nations,
"The LORD reigns![w]"
32 Let the sea resound, and all that is in it;[x]
let the fields be jubilant, and
everything in them!
33 Let the trees[y] of the forest sing,
let them sing for joy before the LORD,
for he comes to judge[z] the earth.
34 Give thanks[a] to the LORD, for he is good;[b]
his love endures forever.[c]
35 Cry out, "Save us, God our Savior;[d]
gather us and deliver us from the
nations,
that we may give thanks to your holy
name,
and glory in your praise."
36 Praise be to the LORD, the God of
Israel,[e]
from everlasting to everlasting.

Then all the people said "Amen" and
"Praise the LORD."

37 David left Asaph and his associates
before the ark of the covenant of the LORD
to minister there regularly, according to
each day's requirements.[f] 38 He also left
Obed-Edom[g] and his sixty-eight associates to minister with them. Obed-Edom
son of Jeduthun, and also Hosah,[h] were
gatekeepers.
39 David left Zadok[i] the priest and his
fellow priests before the tabernacle of the
LORD at the high place in Gibeon[j] 40 to present burnt offerings to the LORD on the
altar of burnt offering regularly, morning and evening, in accordance with everything written in the Law[k] of the LORD,
which he had given Israel. 41 With them
were Heman[l] and Jeduthun and the rest
of those chosen and designated by name
to give thanks to the LORD, "for his love
endures forever." 42 Heman and Jeduthun
were responsible for the sounding of the
trumpets and cymbals and for the playing
of the other instruments for sacred song.[m]
The sons of Jeduthun were stationed at
the gate.
43 Then all the people left, each for their
own home, and David returned home to
bless his family.

God's Promise to David

17:1-15pp — 2Sa 7:1-17

17 After David was settled in his palace, he said to Nathan the proph-
et, "Here I am, living in a house of cedar,
while the ark of the covenant of the LORD
is under a tent.[n]"
2 Nathan replied to David, "Whatever you
have in mind,[o] do it, for God is with you."
3 But that night the word of God came to
Nathan, saying:
4 "Go and tell my servant David,
'This is what the LORD says: You[p]
are not the one to build me a house
to dwell in. 5 I have not dwelt in a
house from the day I brought Israel

16:25 [o] Ps 48:1 [p] Ps 76:7; 89:7 [q] Dt 32:39 **16:26** [r] Lev 19:4; Ps 102:25 **16:28** [s] Ps 29:1-2 **16:29** [t] Ps 29:1-2 **16:30** [u] Ps 114:7 **16:31** [v] Isa 44:23; 49:13 [w] Ps 93:1 **16:32** [x] Ps 98:7 **16:33** [y] Isa 55:12 [z] Ps 96:10; 98:9 **16:34** [a] ver 8 [b] Na 1:7 [c] 2Ch 5:13; 7:3; Ezr 3:11; Ps 136:1-26; Jer 33:11 **16:35** [d] Mic 7:7 **16:36** [e] Dt 27:15; 1Ki 8:15; Ps 72:18-19
16:37 [f] 2Ch 8:14 **16:38** [g] 1Ch 13:13 [h] 1Ch 26:10 **16:39** [i] 2Sa 8:17; 1Ch 15:11 [j] 1Ki 3:4; 2Ch 1:3 **16:40** [k] Ex 29:38; Nu 28:1-8 **16:41** [l] 1Ch 6:33; 25:1-6; 2Ch 5:13 **16:42** [m] 2Ch 7:6 **17:1** [n] 1Ch 15:1 **17:2** [o] 2Ch 6:7 **17:4** [p] 1Ch 28:3

[a] 29 Or *LORD with the splendor of*

16:26 *all the gods of the nations are idols.* See note on Ps 97:5 ("Lord of all the earth").
16:39 *the high place in Gibeon.* See note on 2Ch 1:3.
17:1 *under a tent.* Important activities of ancient Near Eastern monarchs in peacetime included constructing monumental architecture, strengthening fortifications, and especially building temples. From earliest times in Mesopotamia and elsewhere, rulers founded, rebuilt or repaired shrines to their deities and left behind building inscriptions to document it.

Such activity was a gesture of gratitude to the deity for help granted, but there was also another side to it. The proper maintenance of temples was essential for the well-being of the land as a whole and was therefore the duty of the ruler. A temple where the god or goddess could reside and in which he or she could be properly looked after ensured that the deity would both remain among and be well disposed toward the people. Building inscriptions mostly contain prayers for the blessing and longevity of the ruler himself in a reciprocation of benefit.

In addition, the construction of monumental architecture was a kind of immortality for the monarch — the buildings remained long after he himself had gone. Consequently, Mesopotamian building inscriptions are very egocentric. They are written in the first person and glorify the monarch as much as, if not more than, the deity. David's intention to build a temple in Jerusalem, therefore, may have been to express (or ensure) the permanence of the relationship between the Lord and Israel, and it may also have had the effect of uniting the political and religious centers of the kingdom in one place.

up out of Egypt to this day. I have
moved from one tent site to another,
from one dwelling place to another.
6Wherever I have moved with all the
Israelites, did I ever say to any of their
leaders[a] whom I commanded to shepherd my people, "Why have you not
built me a house of cedar?" '
7"Now then, tell my servant David, 'This is what the LORD Almighty
says: I took you from the pasture,
from tending the flock, and appointed you ruler[q] over my people Israel.
8I have been with you wherever you
have gone, and I have cut off all your
enemies from before you. Now I will
make your name like the names of
the greatest men on earth. 9And I will
provide a place for my people Israel
and will plant them so that they can
have a home of their own and no longer be disturbed. Wicked people will
not oppress them anymore, as they
did at the beginning 10and have done
ever since the time I appointed leaders[r] over my people Israel. I will also
subdue all your enemies.
" 'I declare to you that the LORD
will build a house for you: 11When
your days are over and you go to be
with your ancestors, I will raise up
your offspring to succeed you, one
of your own sons, and I will establish his kingdom. 12He is the one
who will build[s] a house for me, and
I will establish his throne forever.[t] 13I
will be his father,[u] and he will be my
son.[v] I will never take my love away
from him, as I took it away from
your predecessor. 14I will set him
over my house and my kingdom forever; his throne[w] will be established
forever.[x]' "
15Nathan reported to David all the
words of this entire revelation.

David's Prayer

17:16-27pp — 2Sa 7:18-29

16Then King David went in and sat before the LORD, and he said:
"Who am I, LORD God, and what
is my family, that you have brought
me this far? 17And as if this were not
enough in your sight, my God, you
have spoken about the future of the
house of your servant. You, LORD
God, have looked on me as though I
were the most exalted of men.
18"What more can David say to you
for honoring your servant? For you
know your servant, 19LORD. For the
sake[y] of your servant and according
to your will, you have done this great
thing and made known all these great
promises.[z]
20"There is no one like you, LORD,
and there is no God but you,[a] as we
have heard with our own ears. 21And
who is like your people Israel—the
one nation on earth whose God went
out to redeem[b] a people for himself,
and to make a name for yourself, and
to perform great and awesome wonders by driving out nations from before your people, whom you redeemed
from Egypt? 22You made your people
Israel your very own forever,[c] and you,
LORD, have become their God.
23"And now, LORD, let the promise[d] you have made concerning your
servant and his house be established
forever. Do as you promised, 24so that
it will be established and that your
name will be great forever. Then people will say, 'The LORD Almighty, the
God over Israel, is Israel's God!' And
the house of your servant David will
be established before you.
25"You, my God, have revealed to
your servant that you will build a
house for him. So your servant has
found courage to pray to you. 26You,
LORD, are God! You have promised
these good things to your servant.
27Now you have been pleased to bless
the house of your servant, that it may
continue forever in your sight;[e] for
you, LORD, have blessed it, and it will
be blessed forever."

17:7 [q] 2Sa 6:21
17:10 [r] Jdg 2:16
17:12 [s] 1Ki 5:5 [t] 2Ch 7:18
17:13 [u] 2Co 6:18 [v] Lk 1:32; Heb 1:5*
17:14 [w] 1Ki 2:12; 1Ch 28:5 [x] Ps 132:11; Jer 33:17
17:19 [y] 2Sa 7:16-17; 2Ki 20:6; Isa 9:7; 37:35; 55:3 [z] 2Sa 7:25
17:20 [a] Ex 8:10; 9:14; 15:11; Isa 44:6; 46:9
17:21 [b] Ex 6:6
17:22 [c] Ex 19:5-6
17:23 [d] 1Ki 8:25
17:27 [e] Ps 16:11; 21:6

[a] 6 Traditionally *judges*; also in verse 10

17:6 *shepherd my people.* See note on 11:2.
17:7 *I took you.* The claim to divine sponsorship is common in Mesopotamian and Hittite royal inscriptions. Ashurnasirpal II of Assyria, e.g., speaks of being "called by name" by Ashur and given sovereignty. The coronation hymn of Ashurbanipal also delineates the king's relationship to various deities.
17:12 *He ... will build a house for me.* The "autobiography" of Adad-Guppi, the mother of Nabonidus, relates a dream of hers in which she was told that her son would restore the temple of the moon-god Sin in Harran. That, however, was a work of rebuilding, not a fresh construction. In addition, Adad-Guppi was not a ruler, nor did her dream predate the accession of Nabonidus to the throne.
17:13 *I will be his father, and he will be my son.* See note on 2Sa 7:14.
17:20 *no God but you.* In the ancient world, the existence of a god was understood in terms of their effective activity as a god. A being who was inactive, ineffectual, incompetent or lacking power or authority was not a god. This statement in Chronicles identifies Yahweh as the only being justifiably classified as a god. See the article "Monotheism, Monolatry and Henotheism," p. 308.

David's Victories

18:1-13pp — 2Sa 8:1-14

18 In the course of time, David defeated the Philistines and subdued them, and he took Gath and its surrounding villages from the control of the Philistines.

2David also defeated the Moabites,[f] and they became subject to him and brought him tribute.

3Moreover, David defeated Hadadezer king of Zobah,[g] in the vicinity of Hamath, when he went to set up his monument at[a] the Euphrates River.[h] 4David captured a thousand of his chariots, seven thousand charioteers and twenty thousand foot soldiers. He hamstrung[i] all but a hundred of the chariot horses.

5When the Arameans of Damascus[j] came to help Hadadezer king of Zobah, David struck down twenty-two thousand of them. 6He put garrisons in the Aramean kingdom of Damascus, and the Arameans became subject to him and brought him tribute. The LORD gave David victory wherever he went.

7David took the gold shields carried by the officers of Hadadezer and brought them to Jerusalem. 8From Tebah[b] and Kun, towns that belonged to Hadadezer, David took a great quantity of bronze, which Solomon used to make the bronze Sea,[k] the pillars and various bronze articles.

9When Tou king of Hamath heard that David had defeated the entire army of Hadadezer king of Zobah, 10he sent his son Hadoram to King David to greet him and congratulate him on his victory in battle over Hadadezer, who had been at war with Tou. Hadoram brought all kinds of articles of gold, of silver and of bronze.

11King David dedicated these articles to the LORD, as he had done with the silver and gold he had taken from all these nations: Edom[l] and Moab, the Ammonites and the Philistines, and Amalek.[m]

12Abishai son of Zeruiah struck down eighteen thousand Edomites[n] in the Valley of Salt. 13He put garrisons in Edom, and all the Edomites became subject to David. The LORD gave David victory wherever he went.

David's Officials

18:14-17pp — 2Sa 8:15-18

14David reigned[o] over all Israel,[p] doing what was just and right for all his people. 15Joab[q] son of Zeruiah was over the army; Jehoshaphat son of Ahilud was recorder; 16Zadok[r] son of Ahitub and Ahimelek[c][s] son of Abiathar were priests; Shavsha was secretary; 17Benaiah son of Jehoiada was over the Kerethites and Pelethites;[t] and David's sons were chief officials at the king's side.

David Defeats the Ammonites

19:1-19pp — 2Sa 10:1-19

19 In the course of time, Nahash king of the Ammonites[u] died, and his son succeeded him as king. 2David thought, "I will show kindness to Hanun son of Nahash, because his father showed kindness to me." So David sent a delegation to express his sympathy to Hanun concerning his father.

When David's envoys came to Hanun in the land of the Ammonites to express sympathy to him, 3the Ammonite commanders said to Hanun, "Do you think David is honoring your father by sending envoys to you to express sympathy? Haven't his envoys come to you only to explore and spy out[v] the country and overthrow it?" 4So Hanun seized David's envoys, shaved them, cut off their garments at the buttocks, and sent them away.

5When someone came and told David about the men, he sent messengers to meet them, for they were greatly humiliated. The king said, "Stay at Jericho till your beards have grown, and then come back."

6When the Ammonites realized that they had become obnoxious[w] to David,

18:2 [f] Nu 21:29 **18:3** [g] 1Ch 19:6 [h] Ge 2:14 **18:4** [i] Ge 49:6 **18:5** [j] 2Ki 16:9; 1Ch 19:6 **18:8** [k] 1Ki 7:23; 2Ch 4:12, 15-16 **18:11** [l] Nu 24:18 [m] Nu 24:20 **18:12** [n] 1Ki 11:15

18:14 [o] 1Ch 29:26 [p] 1Ch 11:1 **18:15** [q] 2Sa 5:6-8; 1Ch 11:6 **18:16** [r] 2Sa 8:17; 1Ch 6:8 [s] 1Ch 24:6 **18:17** [t] 1Sa 30:14; 2Sa 8:18; 15:18 **19:1** [u] Ge 19:38; Jdg 10:17-11:33; 2Ch 20:1-2; Zep 2:8-11 **19:3** [v] Nu 21:32 **19:6** [w] Ge 34:30

[a] *3* Or *to restore his control over* [b] *8* Hebrew *Tibhath,* a variant of *Tebah* [c] *16* Some Hebrew manuscripts, Vulgate and Syriac (see also 2 Samuel 8:17); most Hebrew manuscripts *Abimelek*

18:4 *chariots ... hamstrung ... the chariot horses.* See notes on Dt 11:4; Jos 11:6; Jdg 1:19; 4:7.

18:7 *gold shields.* See note on 2Sa 8:7.

18:15 – 16 *over the army ... recorder ... priests ... secretary.* See note on 2Sa 8:16 – 17.

18:17 *Kerethites and Pelethites.* See notes on 1Sa 27:2; 2Sa 8:18; 1Ki 1:38; 2Ki 11:4. *chief officials at the king's side.* Placing family members in key administrative positions made good sense. It created an efficient and stable administration, and was designed to effect a smooth transfer of power after the king's death. This would have been particularly valuable to maintain stability in areas toward the fringes of the realm. This ancient practice is attested, e.g., within the Ur III Empire in Mesopotamia. The sons (and daughters) of the Ur III kings were given governorships (or were married to governors) in different parts of the empire with the intention of binding it all together. Such a ploy was successful for some time, although, inevitably, it could not bind disparate groups together indefinitely. A similar practice is attested among the Hittites.

19:2 *show kindness.* See note on 2Sa 10:2.

19:4 See note on 2Sa 10:4.

19:6 *a thousand talents of silver.* This sum is considerable, amounting to about 38 tons (34 metric tons) of silver. This is the same amount that was sent by Menahem of Israel to Tiglath-Pileser III of Assyria (2Ki 15:19) and considerably outstrips other sums of money recorded in Scripture as being sent as tribute to the kings of Egypt or Assyria. It was common for states to band together against a common enemy, for small states to enlist the help of more

Hanun and the Ammonites sent a thousand talents[a] of silver to hire chariots and charioteers from Aram Naharaim,[b] Aram Maakah and Zobah.[x] 7They hired thirty-two thousand chariots and charioteers, as well as the king of Maakah with his troops, who came and camped near Medeba,[y] while the Ammonites were mustered from their towns and moved out for battle.
8On hearing this, David sent Joab out with the entire army of fighting men. 9The Ammonites came out and drew up in battle formation at the entrance to their city, while the kings who had come were by themselves in the open country.
10Joab saw that there were battle lines in front of him and behind him; so he selected some of the best troops in Israel and deployed them against the Arameans. 11He put the rest of the men under the command of Abishai[z] his brother, and they were deployed against the Ammonites. 12Joab said, "If the Arameans are too strong for me, then you are to rescue me; but if the Ammonites are too strong for you, then I will rescue you. 13Be strong, and let us fight bravely for our people and the cities of our God. The LORD will do what is good in his sight."
14Then Joab and the troops with him advanced to fight the Arameans, and they fled before him. 15When the Ammonites realized that the Arameans were fleeing, they too fled before his brother Abishai and went inside the city. So Joab went back to Jerusalem.
16After the Arameans saw that they had been routed by Israel, they sent messengers and had Arameans brought from beyond the Euphrates River, with Shophak the commander of Hadadezer's army leading them.
17When David was told of this, he gathered all Israel[a] and crossed the Jordan; he advanced against them and formed his battle lines opposite them. David formed his lines to meet the Arameans in battle, and they fought against him. 18But they fled before Israel, and David killed seven thousand of their charioteers and forty thousand of their foot soldiers. He also killed Shophak the commander of their army.
19When the vassals of Hadadezer saw that they had been routed by Israel, they made peace with David and became subject to him.

So the Arameans were not willing to help the Ammonites anymore.

19:6 [x] 1Ch 18:3, 5,9 **19:7** [y] Nu 21:30; Jos 13:9,16 **19:11** [z] 1Sa 26:6 **19:17** [a] 1Ch 9:1

The Capture of Rabbah

20:1-3pp — 2Sa 11:1; 12:29-31

20 In the spring, at the time when kings go off to war, Joab led out the armed forces. He laid waste the land of the Ammonites and went to Rabbah[b] and besieged it, but David remained in Jerusalem. Joab attacked Rabbah and left it in ruins.[c] 2David took the crown from the head of their king[c]—its weight was found to be a talent[d] of gold, and it was set with precious stones—and it was placed on David's head. He took a great quantity of plunder from the city 3and brought out the people who were there, consigning them to labor with saws and with iron picks and axes.[d] David did this to all the Ammonite towns. Then David and his entire army returned to Jerusalem.

War With the Philistines

20:4-8pp — 2Sa 21:15-22

4In the course of time, war broke out with the Philistines, at Gezer.[e] At that time Sibbekai the Hushathite killed Sippai, one of the descendants of the Rephaites,[f] and the Philistines were subjugated.
5In another battle with the Philistines,

20:1 [b] Dt 3:11; 2Sa 12:26 [c] Am 1:13-15 **20:3** [d] Dt 29:11 **20:4** [e] Jos 10:33 [f] Ge 14:5

[a] 6 That is, about 38 tons or about 34 metric tons
[b] 6 That is, Northwest Mesopotamia
[c] 2 Or *of Milkom,* that is, Molek
[d] 2 That is, about 75 pounds or about 34 kilograms

---

powerful ones, and for a superior to demand help from a vassal relationship. Given the size of the sum of money involved, it is likely that Hanun has weighed up the situation and is approaching Hadadezer the king of Zobah in order to become his vassal. Hadadezer in turn sees this as a good opportunity to deal with his southern rival and to gain control of the important trade route that led east of the Jordan through Ammonite territory en route to Damascus.

19:19 *the vassals of Hadadezer ... became subject to him.* Once David gained the victory over Hadadezer and his army, his erstwhile vassals seized the opportunity to transfer allegiance to David. States in the ancient Near East were conscious of the way in which the political wind was blowing, and loyalty was often ephemeral (despite the curses built into treaties and loyalty oaths). Such states were all too ready to look to another, more powerful, ruler should one arise. It seems that the vassals who became subject to David may even have included the Arameans from the Euphrates region (18:3). The result was that the Ammonites were left to fend for themselves without any ally.

20:1 *In the spring, at the time when kings go off to war ... David remained in Jerusalem.* See note on 2Sa 11:1.

20:2 *took the crown from the head of their king.* See note on 2Sa 12:30.

20:3 *consigning them to labor.* Captured nations were a valuable source of forced labor. They were used to repair the damage induced by the war and to execute building projects in the conquered territory. The use of foreign conscripts for projects involving heavy labor was also attractive because it saved levying (and trying the patience of) the local people. See note on Jos 16:10.

Elhanan son of Jair killed Lahmi the brother of Goliath the Gittite, who had a spear
with a shaft like a weaver's rod.[g]
6 In still another battle, which took place
at Gath, there was a huge man with six
fingers on each hand and six toes on each
foot—twenty-four in all. He also was descended from Rapha. 7 When he taunted
Israel, Jonathan son of Shimea, David's
brother, killed him.
8 These were descendants of Rapha in
Gath, and they fell at the hands of David
and his men.

David Counts the Fighting Men

21:1-26pp — 2Sa 24:1-25

21 Satan[h] rose up against Israel and
incited David to take a census[i] of
Israel. 2 So David said to Joab and the commanders of the troops, "Go and count[j] the
Israelites from Beersheba to Dan. Then report back to me so that I may know how
many there are."
3 But Joab replied, "May the LORD multiply his troops a hundred times over.[k] My
lord the king, are they not all my lord's
subjects? Why does my lord want to do
this? Why should he bring guilt on Israel?"
4 The king's word, however, overruled
Joab; so Joab left and went throughout
Israel and then came back to Jerusalem.
5 Joab reported the number of the fighting
men to David: In all Israel[l] there were one
million one hundred thousand men who
could handle a sword, including four hundred and seventy thousand in Judah.
6 But Joab did not include Levi and
Benjamin in the numbering, because the
king's command was repulsive to him.
7 This command was also evil in the sight
of God; so he punished Israel.
8 Then David said to God, "I have sinned
greatly by doing this. Now, I beg you, take
away the guilt of your servant. I have done
a very foolish thing."
9 The LORD said to Gad,[m] David's seer,[n]
10 "Go and tell David, 'This is what the
LORD says: I am giving you three options.
Choose one of them for me to carry out
against you.'"
11 So Gad went to David and said to him,
"This is what the LORD says: 'Take your
choice: 12 three years of famine,[o] three
months of being swept away[a] before your
enemies, with their swords overtaking
you, or three days of the sword[p] of the
LORD[q]—days of plague in the land, with
the angel of the LORD ravaging every part
of Israel.' Now then, decide how I should
answer the one who sent me."
13 David said to Gad, "I am in deep distress. Let me fall into the hands of the
LORD, for his mercy[r] is very great; but do
not let me fall into human hands."
14 So the LORD sent a plague on Israel,
and seventy thousand men of Israel fell
dead.[s] 15 And God sent an angel[t] to destroy
Jerusalem.[u] But as the angel was doing so,
the LORD saw it and relented[v] concerning
the disaster and said to the angel who was
destroying[w] the people, "Enough! Withdraw your hand." The angel of the LORD
was then standing at the threshing floor
of Araunah[b] the Jebusite.
16 David looked up and saw the angel
of the LORD standing between heaven and
earth, with a drawn sword in his hand extended over Jerusalem. Then David and
the elders, clothed in sackcloth, fell facedown.[x]
17 David said to God, "Was it not I who
ordered the fighting men to be counted?
I, the shepherd,[c] have sinned and done
wrong. These are but sheep.[y] What have
they done? LORD my God, let your hand
fall on me and my family,[z] but do not let
this plague remain on your people."

David Builds an Altar

18 Then the angel of the LORD ordered
Gad to tell David to go up and build an
altar to the LORD on the threshing floor[a]
of Araunah the Jebusite. 19 So David went
up in obedience to the word that Gad had
spoken in the name of the LORD.
20 While Araunah was threshing wheat,[b]
he turned and saw the angel; his four
sons who were with him hid themselves.
21 Then David approached, and when
Araunah looked and saw him, he left the

20:5 [g] 1Sa 17:7
21:1 [h] 2Ch 18:21; Ps 109:6 [i] 2Ch 14:8; 25:5
21:2 [j] 1Ch 27:23-24
21:3 [k] Dt 1:11
21:5 [l] 1Ch 9:1
21:9 [m] 1Sa 22:5 [n] 1Sa 9:9
21:12 [o] Dt 32:24 [p] Eze 30:25 [q] Ge 19:13
21:13 [r] Ps 6:4; 86:15; 130:4,7
21:14 [s] 1Ch 27:24
21:15 [t] Ge 32:1 [u] Ps 125:2 [v] Ge 6:6; Ex 32:14 [w] Ge 19:13
21:16 [x] Nu 14:5; Jos 7:6
21:17 [y] 2Sa 7:8; Ps 74:1 [z] Jnh 1:12
21:18 [a] 2Ch 3:1
21:20 [b] Jdg 6:11

[a] *12* Hebrew; Septuagint and Vulgate (see also 2 Samuel 24:13) *of fleeing* [b] *15* Hebrew *Ornan,* a variant of *Araunah;* also in verses 18-28 [c] *17* Probable reading of the original Hebrew text (see 2 Samuel 24:17 and note); Masoretic Text does not have *the shepherd.*

20:6 *six fingers ... six toes ... twenty-four in all.* See note on 2Sa 21:20.
20:8 *descendants of Rapha.* See note on 2Sa 21:16.
21:1 *Satan.* See the article "Satan," p. 820. Here, the responsibility for inciting David to take a census is leveled at an adversary described by the Hebrew word "satan." The nature of this foe cannot be automatically identified in the OT as the devil, designated Satan in the NT. Other cultures of the ancient Near East, while recognizing the existence of demons in general, do not have a figure heading up the forces of evil comparable to what we find by the NT period. In the parallel account in 2Sa 24, the word "satan" is not used; rather, the instigator of David's action is designated by a pronoun referring back to "the anger of the LORD." This is not a contradiction between the two books, only the identification of an extra level of causation. *census.* See note on 2Sa 24:1.
21:14 *the LORD sent a plague.* See note on 2Sa 24:16.
21:18 *threshing floor of Araunah.* See note on 2Sa 24:18.

threshing floor and bowed down before
David with his face to the ground.
22David said to him, "Let me have the
site of your threshing floor so I can build
an altar to the LORD, that the plague on the
people may be stopped. Sell it to me at the
full price."
23Araunah said to David, "Take it! Let
my lord the king do whatever pleases him.
Look, I will give the oxen for the burnt
offerings, the threshing sledges for the
wood, and the wheat for the grain offering. I will give all this."
24But King David replied to Araunah,
"No, I insist on paying the full price. I
will not take for the LORD what is yours,
or sacrifice a burnt offering that costs me
nothing."
25So David paid Araunah six hundred
shekels[a] of gold for the site. 26David built
an altar to the LORD there and sacrificed
burnt offerings and fellowship offerings.
He called on the LORD, and the LORD answered him with fire[c] from heaven on the
altar of burnt offering.
27Then the LORD spoke to the angel, and
he put his sword back into its sheath. 28At
that time, when David saw that the LORD
had answered him on the threshing floor
of Araunah the Jebusite, he offered sacrifices there. 29The tabernacle of the LORD,
which Moses had made in the wilderness,
and the altar of burnt offering were at that
time on the high place at Gibeon.[d] 30But
David could not go before it to inquire of
God, because he was afraid of the sword
of the angel of the LORD.

22 Then David said, "The house of the
LORD God[e] is to be here, and also
the altar of burnt offering for Israel."

Preparations for the Temple

2So David gave orders to assemble the
foreigners[f] residing in Israel, and from
among them he appointed stonecutters[g]
to prepare dressed stone for building
the house of God. 3He provided a large
amount of iron to make nails for the doors
of the gateways and for the fittings, and
more bronze than could be weighed.[h] 4He
also provided more cedar logs[i] than could
be counted, for the Sidonians and Tyrians
had brought large numbers of them to David.
5David said, "My son Solomon is young[j]
and inexperienced, and the house to be
built for the LORD should be of great magnificence and fame and splendor in the
sight of all the nations. Therefore I will
make preparations for it." So David made
extensive preparations before his death.
6Then he called for his son Solomon
and charged him to build[k] a house for the
LORD, the God of Israel. 7David said to Solomon: "My son, I had it in my heart[l] to
build[m] a house for the Name[n] of the LORD
my God. 8But this word of the LORD came
to me: 'You have shed much blood and
have fought many wars.[o] You are not to
build a house for my Name,[p] because you
have shed much blood on the earth in my
sight. 9But you will have a son who will
be a man of peace[q] and rest, and I will
give him rest from all his enemies on every side. His name will be Solomon,[b][r] and
I will grant Israel peace and quiet[s] during
his reign. 10He is the one who will build a
house for my Name.[t] He will be my son,[u]
and I will be his father. And I will establish the throne of his kingdom over Israel
forever.'[v]
11"Now, my son, the LORD be with[w] you,
and may you have success and build the
house of the LORD your God, as he said
you would. 12May the LORD give you discretion and understanding[x] when he puts
you in command over Israel, so that you
may keep the law of the LORD your God.
13Then you will have success if you are
careful to observe the decrees and laws[y]
that the LORD gave Moses for Israel. Be
strong and courageous.[z] Do not be afraid
or discouraged.
14"I have taken great pains to provide
for the temple of the LORD a hundred thou-

21:26 [c] Lev 9:24; Jdg 6:21
21:29 [d] 1Ki 3:4; 1Ch 16:39
22:1 [e] Ge 28:17; 1Ch 21:18-29; 2Ch 3:1
22:2 [f] 1Ki 9:21; Isa 56:6 [g] 1Ki 5:17-18
22:3 [h] ver 14; 1Ki 7:47; 1Ch 29:2-5
22:4 [i] 1Ki 5:6
22:5 [j] 1Ki 3:7; 1Ch 29:1
22:6 [k] Ac 7:47
22:7 [l] 1Ch 17:2 [m] 2Sa 7:2; 1Ki 8:17 [n] Dt 12:5, 11
22:8 [o] 1Ki 5:3 [p] 1Ch 28:3
22:9 [q] 1Ki 5:4 [r] 2Sa 12:24 [s] 1Ki 4:20
22:10 [t] 1Ch 17:12 [u] 2Sa 7:13 [v] 2Sa 7:14; 2Ch 6:15
22:11 [w] ver 16
22:12 [x] 1Ki 3:9-12; 2Ch 1:10
22:13 [y] 1Ch 28:7 [z] Dt 31:6; Jos 1:6-9; 1Ch 28:20

[a] *25* That is, about 15 pounds or about 6.9 kilograms
[b] *9* *Solomon* sounds like and may be derived from the Hebrew for *peace.*

21:29 *the high place at Gibeon.* See note on 2Ch 1:3.

22:2 *stonecutters.* There was an abundance of stone available in ancient Israel of various types, from Galilee basalt to coastal sandstone. Harder limestone was available in the hill country, and granite could be quarried in the southern Arabah near Eilat. Excavations at various quarry sites have shed light on the methods used for quarrying. Blocks of stone were outlined by digging narrow channels on the four sides using iron picks. They were then pried loose or split along the grain of the rock by driving wooden wedges into cracks and then soaking them with water. As the wood expanded, it split the rock. Stones were then dressed either at the quarry or at the building site. In the case of the temple, stones were dressed off site, so that the noise of chisels would not be heard. At this period, the way in which the stone was prepared is known as Ashlar masonry. The margin around the edges only was dressed smooth using an iron chisel. The center of the block was left with rough surface (see 1Ki 7:9).

22:3 *iron to make nails.* Iron was in general use in Palestine by about 1200 BC. The Philistines were workers of iron and were careful to keep the secrets from the Israelites during the time of Saul. David remedied this lack, and iron became freely available. It appears that the iron here is for decorative use, possibly to attach plates or bands to the doors and gates.

22:4 *cedar logs.* See notes on 2Sa 5:11; 1Ki 5:6; 6:15.

22:14 *a hundred thousand talents of gold.* A talent

sand talents[a] of gold, a million talents[b]
of silver, quantities of bronze and iron
too great to be weighed, and wood and
stone. And you may add to them.[a] 15 You
have many workers: stonecutters, masons
and carpenters, as well as those skilled
in every kind of work 16 in gold and silver, bronze and iron — craftsmen[b] beyond
number. Now begin the work, and the
LORD be with you."
17 Then David ordered[c] all the leaders of
Israel to help his son Solomon. 18 He said
to them, "Is not the LORD your God with
you? And has he not granted you rest[d] on
every side?[e] For he has given the inhabitants of the land into my hands, and the
land is subject to the LORD and to his people. 19 Now devote your heart and soul to
seeking the LORD your God.[f] Begin to build
the sanctuary of the LORD God, so that you
may bring the ark of the covenant of the
LORD and the sacred articles belonging to
God into the temple that will be built for
the Name of the LORD."

The Levites

23 When David was old and full of
years, he made his son Solomon[g]
king over Israel.[h]
2 He also gathered together all the leaders of Israel, as well as the priests and
Levites. 3 The Levites thirty years old or
more[i] were counted, and the total number
of men was thirty-eight thousand.[j] 4 David
said, "Of these, twenty-four thousand are
to be in charge[k] of the work of the temple of the LORD and six thousand are to
be officials and judges.[l] 5 Four thousand
are to be gatekeepers and four thousand
are to praise the LORD with the musical instruments[m] I have provided for that purpose."[n]
6 David separated[o] the Levites into divisions corresponding to the sons of Levi:
Gershon, Kohath and Merari.

Gershonites

7 Belonging to the Gershonites:
Ladan and Shimei.
8 The sons of Ladan:
Jehiel the first, Zetham and Joel —
three in all.
9 The sons of Shimei:
Shelomoth, Haziel and Haran —
three in all.
These were the heads of the families of Ladan.
10 And the sons of Shimei:
Jahath, Ziza,[c] Jeush and Beriah.
These were the sons of Shimei —
four in all.
11 Jahath was the first and Ziza the
second, but Jeush and Beriah did
not have many sons; so they were
counted as one family with one assignment.

Kohathites

12 The sons of Kohath:[p]
Amram, Izhar, Hebron and Uzziel — four in all.
13 The sons of Amram:[q]
Aaron and Moses.
Aaron was set apart,[r] he and his descendants forever, to consecrate the
most holy things, to offer sacrifices
before the LORD, to minister before
him and to pronounce blessings[s] in
his name forever. 14 The sons of Moses the man[t] of God were counted
as part of the tribe of Levi.
15 The sons of Moses:
Gershom and Eliezer.[u]
16 The descendants of Gershom:[v]
Shubael was the first.
17 The descendants of Eliezer:
Rehabiah was the first.
Eliezer had no other sons, but the
sons of Rehabiah were very numerous.
18 The sons of Izhar:
Shelomith was the first.
19 The sons of Hebron:[w]
Jeriah the first, Amariah the second, Jahaziel the third and Jekameam the fourth.
20 The sons of Uzziel:
Micah the first and Ishiah the second.

22:14 [a] ver 3; 1Ch 29:2-5, 19 **22:16** [b] ver 11; 2Ch 2:7 **22:17** [c] 1Ch 28:1-6 **22:18** [d] ver 9; 1Ch 23:25 [e] 2Sa 7:1 **22:19** [f] ver 7; 1Ki 8:6; 1Ch 28:9; 2Ch 5:7; 7:14 **23:1** [g] 1Ki 1:33-39; 1Ch 28:5 [h] 1Ki 1:30; 1Ch 29:28 **23:3** [i] ver 24; Nu 8:24 [j] Nu 4:3-49 **23:4** [k] Ezr 3:8 [l] 1Ch 26:29; 2Ch 19:8 **23:5** [m] 1Ch 15:16 [n] Ne 12:45 **23:6** [o] 2Ch 8:14; 29:25

23:12 [p] Ex 6:18 **23:13** [q] Ex 6:20; 28:1 [r] Ex 30:7-10; Dt 21:5 [s] Nu 6:23 **23:14** [t] Dt 33:1 **23:15** [u] Ex 18:4 **23:16** [v] 1Ch 26:24-28 **23:19** [w] 1Ch 24:23

[a] *14* That is, about 3,750 tons or about 3,400 metric tons
[b] *14* That is, about 37,500 tons or about 34,000 metric tons
[c] *10* One Hebrew manuscript, Septuagint and Vulgate (see also verse 11); most Hebrew manuscripts *Zina*

weighed about 75 pounds (34 kilograms). Thus, the total weight here was about 3,750 tons (3,400 metric tons). In today's currency, the monetary value of such a hoard would be tens of billions of dollars. It is an immense amount of gold, though it is possible that any ancient reader would have understood these amounts to be rhetorical rather than actual. The tabernacle, by comparison, was much more modest. The total amount of gold used in its construction weighed just over one ton (about 1 metric ton, see NIV text note on Ex 38:24). Outside Chronicles, the largest amount of gold mentioned is 666 talents (nearly 25 tons [23 metric tons]), the base rate of gold that Solomon received per year (1Ki 10:14). In Assyrian and Babylonian royal inscriptions, a figure is rarely placed on how much gold is collected, but it must have been considerable. *a million talents of silver.* Once again, this is a colossal figure, representing about 37,500 tons (34,000 metric tons), worth nearly ten billion dollars on today's market. The figure far exceeds any other Biblical or extra-Biblical references, and again, may be rhetorical in nature (= "countless").

Merarites

21 The sons of Merari:[x]
Mahli and Mushi.
The sons of Mahli:
Eleazar and Kish.
22 Eleazar died without having sons:
he had only daughters. Their cousins, the sons of Kish, married them.
23 The sons of Mushi:
Mahli, Eder and Jerimoth — three
in all.

24 These were the descendants of Levi
by their families — the heads of families
as they were registered under their names
and counted individually, that is, the
workers twenty years old or more[y] who
served in the temple of the LORD. 25 For David had said, "Since the LORD, the God of
Israel, has granted rest[z] to his people and
has come to dwell in Jerusalem forever,
26 the Levites no longer need to carry the
tabernacle or any of the articles used in its
service."[a] 27 According to the last instructions of David, the Levites were counted
from those twenty years old or more.
28 The duty of the Levites was to help
Aaron's descendants in the service of the
temple of the LORD: to be in charge of the
courtyards, the side rooms, the purification[b] of all sacred things and the performance of other duties at the house of God.
29 They were in charge of the bread set out
on the table,[c] the special flour for the grain
offerings,[d] the thin loaves made without
yeast, the baking and the mixing, and
all measurements of quantity and size.[e]
30 They were also to stand every morning
to thank and praise the LORD. They were
to do the same in the evening[f] 31 and whenever burnt offerings were presented to the
LORD on the Sabbaths, at the New Moon[g]
feasts and at the appointed festivals.[h]
They were to serve before the LORD regularly in the proper number and in the way
prescribed for them.
32 And so the Levites[i] carried out their
responsibilities for the tent of meeting,[j] for
the Holy Place and, under their relatives
the descendants of Aaron, for the service
of the temple of the LORD.[k]

The Divisions of Priests

24 These were the divisions[l] of the descendants of Aaron:[m]
The sons of Aaron were Nadab, Abihu, Eleazar and Ithamar.[n] 2 But Nadab and
Abihu died before their father did,[o] and
they had no sons; so Eleazar and Ithamar served as the priests. 3 With the help
of Zadok[p] a descendant of Eleazar and
Ahimelek a descendant of Ithamar, David separated them into divisions for their
appointed order of ministering. 4 A larger
number of leaders were found among Eleazar's descendants than among Ithamar's,
and they were divided accordingly: sixteen
heads of families from Eleazar's descendants and eight heads of families from Ithamar's descendants. 5 They divided them
impartially by casting lots,[q] for there were
officials of the sanctuary and officials of
God among the descendants of both Eleazar and Ithamar.
6 The scribe Shemaiah son of Nethanel,
a Levite, recorded their names in the presence of the king and of the officials: Zadok
the priest, Ahimelek[r] son of Abiathar and
the heads of families of the priests and of
the Levites — one family being taken from
Eleazar and then one from Ithamar.

7 The first lot fell to Jehoiarib,
the second to Jedaiah,[s]
8 the third to Harim,[t]
the fourth to Seorim,
9 the fifth to Malkijah,
the sixth to Mijamin,
10 the seventh to Hakkoz,
the eighth to Abijah,[u]
11 the ninth to Jeshua,
the tenth to Shekaniah,
12 the eleventh to Eliashib,
the twelfth to Jakim,
13 the thirteenth to Huppah,
the fourteenth to Jeshebeab,
14 the fifteenth to Bilgah,
the sixteenth to Immer,[v]
15 the seventeenth to Hezir,[w]
the eighteenth to Happizzez,
16 the nineteenth to Pethahiah,
the twentieth to Jehezkel,
17 the twenty-first to Jakin,
the twenty-second to Gamul,
18 the twenty-third to Delaiah
and the twenty-fourth to Maaziah.

19 This was their appointed order of ministering when they entered the temple of
the LORD, according to the regulations prescribed for them by their ancestor Aaron,
as the LORD, the God of Israel, had commanded him.

The Rest of the Levites

20 As for the rest of the descendants of
Levi:[x]

23:21 [x] 1Ch 24:26 **23:24** [y] Nu 4:3; 10:17,21 **23:25** [z] 1Ch 22:9 **23:26** [a] Nu 4:5, 15; 7:9; Dt 10:8 **23:28** [b] 2Ch 29:15; Ne 13:9; Mal 3:3 **23:29** [c] Ex 25:30 [d] Lev 2:4-7; 6:20-23 [e] Lev 19:35-36; 1Ch 9:29,32 **23:30** [f] 1Ch 9:33; Ps 134:1 **23:31** [g] 2Ki 4:23 [h] Lev 23:4; Nu 28:9-29:39; Isa 1:13-14; Col 2:16 **23:32** [i] Nu 1:53; 1Ch 6:48 [j] Nu 3:6-8,38 [k] 2Ch 23:18; 31:2; Eze 44:14 **24:1** [l] 1Ch 23:6; 28:13; 2Ch 5:11; 8:14; 23:8; 31:2; 35:4,5; Ezr 6:18 [m] Nu 3:2-4 [n] Ex 6:23 **24:2** [o] Lev 10:1-2; Nu 3:4

24:3 [p] 2Sa 8:17 **24:5** [q] ver 31; 1Ch 25:8 **24:6** [r] 1Ch 18:16 **24:7** [s] Ezr 2:36; Ne 12:6 **24:8** [t] Ezr 2:39; Ne 10:5 **24:10** [u] Ne 12:4, 17; Lk 1:5 **24:14** [v] Jer 20:1 **24:15** [w] Ne 10:20 **24:20** [x] 1Ch 23:6

23:27 *twenty years old or more.* No reason is given for the change in age from v. 3. Nu 4 gives the period of Levitical service as being between 30 and 50. Perhaps it was changed in order to bring it into line with the age given for the commencement of military service (Nu 1:20). **23:28** *duty of the Levites.* See note on 9:28 – 32 **24:6** *scribe.* See note on Jer 36:4; see also the article "Books and Literacy," p. 666.

from the sons of Amram: Shubael;
from the sons of Shubael: Jehdeiah.
21 As for Rehabiah,[y] from his sons:
Ishiah was the first.
22 From the Izharites: Shelomoth;
from the sons of Shelomoth: Jahath.
23 The sons of Hebron:[z] Jeriah the first,[a]
Amariah the second, Jahaziel the third and Jekameam the fourth.
24 The son of Uzziel: Micah;
from the sons of Micah: Shamir.
25 The brother of Micah: Ishiah;
from the sons of Ishiah: Zechariah.
26 The sons of Merari:[a] Mahli and Mushi.
The son of Jaaziah: Beno.
27 The sons of Merari:
from Jaaziah: Beno, Shoham, Zakkur and Ibri.
28 From Mahli: Eleazar, who had no sons.
29 From Kish: the son of Kish:
Jerahmeel.
30 And the sons of Mushi: Mahli, Eder and Jerimoth.

These were the Levites, according to
their families. 31 They also cast lots,[b] just
as their relatives the descendants of Aaron
did, in the presence of King David and of
Zadok, Ahimelek, and the heads of families of the priests and of the Levites. The
families of the oldest brother were treated
the same as those of the youngest.

The Musicians

25 David, together with the commanders of the army, set apart some of
the sons of Asaph,[c] Heman[d] and Jeduthun[e] for the ministry of prophesying,[f] accompanied by harps, lyres and cymbals.[g]
Here is the list of the men[h] who performed this service:[i]

2 From the sons of Asaph:
Zakkur, Joseph, Nethaniah and Asarelah. The sons of Asaph were under the supervision of Asaph, who prophesied under the king's supervision.

24:21 [y] 1Ch 23:17 **24:23** [z] 1Ch 23:19 **24:26** [a] 1Ch 6:19; 23:21 **24:31** [b] ver 5 **25:1** [c] 1Ch 6:39 [d] 1Ch 6:33 [e] 1Ch 16:41, 42; Ne 11:17 [f] 1Sa 10:5; 2Ki 3:15 [g] 1Ch 15:16 [h] 1Ch 6:31 [i] 2Ch 5:12; 8:14; 34:12; 35:15; Ezr 3:10

25:3 [j] 1Ch 16:41-42 [k] Ge 4:21; Ps 33:2 **25:6** [l] 1Ch 15:16

Anatolian trumpeters, eighth–sixth centuries BC. Music was a significant part of life in the ancient Near East. The Bible mentions several instruments, five of which are listed in 1Ch 15:28 (several more are mentioned in Ps 150:3–5; Da 3:5).

Caryn Reeder. The British Museum, London.

3 As for Jeduthun, from his sons:[j]
Gedaliah, Zeri, Jeshaiah, Shimei,[b] Hashabiah and Mattithiah, six in all, under the supervision of their father Jeduthun, who prophesied, using the harp[k] in thanking and praising the LORD.
4 As for Heman, from his sons:
Bukkiah, Mattaniah, Uzziel, Shubael and Jerimoth; Hananiah, Hanani, Eliathah, Giddalti and Romamti-Ezer; Joshbekashah, Mallothi, Hothir and Mahazioth. 5 (All these were sons of Heman the king's seer. They were given him through the promises of God to exalt him. God gave Heman fourteen sons and three daughters.)

6 All these men were under the supervision of their father[l] for the music of the

[a] 23 Two Hebrew manuscripts and some Septuagint manuscripts (see also 23:19); most Hebrew manuscripts *The sons of Jeriah:* [b] 3 One Hebrew manuscript and some Septuagint manuscripts (see also verse 17); most Hebrew manuscripts do not have *Shimei.*

25:1 *prophesying, accompanied by harps, lyres and cymbals.* In the ancient Near East, prophecy was sometimes connected with an ecstatic or a trance-like state induced by various means. At Mari there was a whole class of temple personnel known as "ecstatics," who provided prophetic messages (see note on 2Ki 3:15). Here, the whole activity of the singers is described as "prophecy." It may be that prophesying here refers primarily to the three principal heads of the families of singers—Asaph, Heman and Jeduthun—who were responsible for composing the temple psalmody and thus had some claim to divine inspiration. Indeed, this facet of their work may have continued throughout the generations as new psalms were added to the liturgy. In their singing, these Levites were proclaiming the praises of God and thereby instructing the people about God—much like the Divine Liturgy of Saint John Chrysostom, used in the traditional Orthodox service, does today. *harps, lyres and cymbals.* See the articles "Lyre," p. 488; "Music and Musicians," p. 524.
25:2–5 The listing of the sons of Asaph at the head probably indicates they were the most important. In 16:37–42, Asaph and his associates remained with the ark in Jerusalem, while the other two divisions were dispatched to Gibeon to the tent of meeting. Numerically the sons of Asaph were in the minority and the sons of Heman in the majority. After the exile, however, only the descendants of Asaph are mentioned as returning in the first wave (Ezr 2:41), and only one of the descendants of Jeduthun (Ne 11:17). The descendants of Heman seem to have vanished.

temple of the LORD, with cymbals, lyres and
harps, for the ministry at the house of God.
Asaph, Jeduthun and Heman[m] were under the supervision of the king.[n] 7 Along
with their relatives — all of them trained
and skilled in music for the LORD — they
numbered 288. 8 Young and old alike,
teacher as well as student, cast lots[o] for
their duties.

9 The first lot, which was for
Asaph,[p] fell to Joseph,
his sons and relatives[a] 12[b]
the second to Gedaliah,
him and his relatives
and sons 12
10 the third to Zakkur,
his sons and relatives 12
11 the fourth to Izri,[c]
his sons and relatives 12
12 the fifth to Nethaniah,
his sons and relatives 12
13 the sixth to Bukkiah,
his sons and relatives 12
14 the seventh to Jesarelah,[d]
his sons and relatives 12
15 the eighth to Jeshaiah,
his sons and relatives 12
16 the ninth to Mattaniah,
his sons and relatives 12
17 the tenth to Shimei,
his sons and relatives 12
18 the eleventh to Azarel,[e]
his sons and relatives 12
19 the twelfth to Hashabiah,
his sons and relatives 12
20 the thirteenth to Shubael,
his sons and relatives 12
21 the fourteenth to Mattithiah,
his sons and relatives 12
22 the fifteenth to Jerimoth,
his sons and relatives 12
23 the sixteenth to Hananiah,
his sons and relatives 12
24 the seventeenth to
Joshbekashah,
his sons and relatives 12
25 the eighteenth to Hanani,
his sons and relatives 12
26 the nineteenth to Mallothi,
his sons and relatives 12
27 the twentieth to Eliathah,
his sons and relatives 12
28 the twenty-first to Hothir,
his sons and relatives 12
29 the twenty-second to Giddalti,
his sons and relatives 12
30 the twenty-third to Mahazioth,
his sons and relatives 12
31 the twenty-fourth to Romamti-
Ezer,
his sons and relatives 12.[q]

25:6 [m] 1Ch 15:19 [n] 2Ch 23:18; 29:25 **25:8** [o] 1Ch 26:13 **25:9** [p] 1Ch 6:39 **25:31** [q] 1Ch 9:33

The Gatekeepers

26 The divisions of the gatekeepers:[r]

From the Korahites: Meshelemiah son
of Kore, one of the sons of Asaph.
2 Meshelemiah had sons:
Zechariah[s] the firstborn,
Jediael the second,
Zebadiah the third,
Jathniel the fourth,
3 Elam the fifth,
Jehohanan the sixth
and Eliehoenai the seventh.
4 Obed-Edom also had sons:
Shemaiah the firstborn,
Jehozabad the second,
Joah the third,
Sakar the fourth,
Nethanel the fifth,
5 Ammiel the sixth,
Issachar the seventh
and Peullethai the eighth.
(For God had blessed Obed-Edom.[t])

6 Obed-Edom's son Shemaiah also had
sons, who were leaders in their
father's family because they were
very capable men. 7 The sons of
Shemaiah: Othni, Rephael, Obed
and Elzabad; his relatives Elihu and
Semakiah were also able men. 8 All
these were descendants of Obed-
Edom; they and their sons and
their relatives were capable men
with the strength to do the work —
descendants of Obed-Edom, 62 in
all.
9 Meshelemiah had sons and relatives,
who were able men — 18 in all.

10 Hosah the Merarite had sons: Shimri
the first (although he was not the
firstborn, his father had appointed
him the first),[u] 11 Hilkiah the second, Tabaliah the third and Zechariah the fourth. The sons and relatives of Hosah were 13 in all.

12 These divisions of the gatekeepers,
through their leaders, had duties for ministering[v] in the temple of the LORD, just
as their relatives had. 13 Lots[w] were cast
for each gate, according to their families,
young and old alike.

14 The lot for the East Gate[x] fell to Shelemiah.[f] Then lots were cast for his son
Zechariah,[y] a wise counselor, and the lot
for the North Gate fell to him. 15 The lot for

26:1 [r] 1Ch 9:17 **26:2** [s] 1Ch 9:21 **26:5** [t] 2Sa 6:10; 1Ch 13:13; 16:38 **26:10** [u] Dt 21:16; 1Ch 5:1 **26:12** [v] 1Ch 9:22 **26:13** [w] 1Ch 24:5,31; 25:8 **26:14** [x] 1Ch 9:18 [y] 1Ch 9:21

[a] 9 See Septuagint; Hebrew does not have *his sons and relatives.* [b] 9 See the total in verse 7; Hebrew does not have *twelve.* [c] 11 A variant of *Zeri* [d] 14 A variant of *Asarelah* [e] 18 A variant of *Uzziel* [f] 14 A variant of *Meshelemiah*

26:12 *gatekeepers.* See note on 9:17.

Treasury at Delphi, 490 BC. The Levites were in charge of the "treasuries of the house of God" (1Ch 26:20).

the South Gate fell to Obed-Edom,[z] and
the lot for the storehouse fell to his sons.
16The lots for the West Gate and the Shal-
leketh Gate on the upper road fell to Shup-
pim and Hosah.
Guard was alongside of guard: 17There
were six Levites a day on the east, four a
day on the north, four a day on the south
and two at a time at the storehouse. 18As
for the court[a] to the west, there were four
at the road and two at the court[a] itself.
19These were the divisions of the gatekeepers who were descendants of Korah
and Merari.[a]

The Treasurers and Other Officials

20Their fellow Levites[b] were[b] in charge
of the treasuries of the house of God and
the treasuries for the dedicated things.[c]
21The descendants of Ladan, who were
Gershonites through Ladan and who were
heads of families belonging to Ladan the
Gershonite,[d] were Jehieli, 22the sons of Jehieli, Zetham and his brother Joel. They
were in charge of the treasuries[e] of the
temple of the LORD.

23From the Amramites, the Izharites, the
Hebronites and the Uzzielites:[f]
24Shubael,[g] a descendant of Gershom son of Moses, was the official in charge of the treasuries.
25His relatives through Eliezer: Rehabiah his son, Jeshaiah his son, Joram his son, Zikri his son and Shelomith[h] his son.
26Shelomith and his relatives were in charge of all the treasuries for the things dedicated[i] by King David, by the heads of families who were the commanders of thousands and commanders of hundreds, and by the other army commanders.
27Some of the plunder taken in battle they dedicated for the repair of the temple of the LORD.
28And everything dedicated by Samuel the seer[j] and by Saul son of Kish, Abner son of Ner and Joab son of Zeruiah, and all the

26:15 [z] 1Ch 13:13; 2Ch 25:24 **26:19** [a] 2Ch 35:15; Ne 7:1; Eze 44:11 **26:20** [b] 2Ch 24:5 [c] 1Ch 28:12 **26:21** [d] 1Ch 23:7; 29:8 **26:22** [e] 1Ch 9:26 **26:23** [f] Nu 3:27 **26:24** [g] 1Ch 23:16 **26:25** [h] 1Ch 23:18 **26:26** [i] 2Sa 8:11 **26:28** [j] 1Sa 9:9

[a] *18* The meaning of the Hebrew for this word is uncertain. [b] *20* Septuagint; Hebrew *As for the Levites, Ahijah was*

26:15,17 *storehouse.* This Hebrew term is only found elsewhere in Ne 12:25, where the term is translated "storerooms at the gates." The Akkadian cognate also refers to outbuildings in a compound and is associated with the gates. This fits well with the general duties of Obed-Edom and his sons.

26:18 *court.* This Hebrew term (*parbar*) is thought to be a Persian loanword. It is an obscure architectural term that may refer to an open colonnade with pillars. Its location is west of the sanctuary to the rear.

26:20 *treasuries of the house of God.* See note on 9:17.

other dedicated things were in the
care of Shelomith and his relatives.
29 From the Izharites: Kenaniah and his
sons were assigned duties away
from the temple, as officials and
judges[k] over Israel.
30 From the Hebronites: Hashabiah[l]
and his relatives — seventeen hundred able men — were responsible
in Israel west of the Jordan for all
the work of the LORD and for the
king's service. 31 As for the Hebronites,[m] Jeriah was their chief according to the genealogical records of
their families. In the fortieth[n] year
of David's reign a search was made
in the records, and capable men
among the Hebronites were found
at Jazer in Gilead. 32 Jeriah had
twenty-seven hundred relatives,
who were able men and heads of
families, and King David put them
in charge of the Reubenites, the
Gadites and the half-tribe of Manasseh for every matter pertaining
to God and for the affairs of the
king.

Army Divisions

27 This is the list of the Israelites —
heads of families, commanders of
thousands and commanders of hundreds,
and their officers, who served the king in
all that concerned the army divisions that
were on duty month by month throughout
the year. Each division consisted of 24,000
men.

2 In charge of the first division, for the
first month, was Jashobeam[o] son of
Zabdiel. There were 24,000 men in
his division. 3 He was a descendant of
Perez and chief of all the army officers for the first month.
4 In charge of the division for the second
month was Dodai[p] the Ahohite; Mikloth was the leader of his division.
There were 24,000 men in his division.
5 The third army commander, for the
third month, was Benaiah[q] son of Jehoiada the priest. He was chief and
there were 24,000 men in his division. 6 This was the Benaiah who was
a mighty warrior among the Thirty
and was over the Thirty. His son Am-

26:29 [k] Dt 17:8-13; 1Ch 23:4; Ne 11:16
26:30 [l] 1Ch 27:17
26:31 [m] 1Ch 23:19 [n] 2Sa 5:4
27:2 [o] 2Sa 23:8; 1Ch 11:11
27:4 [p] 2Sa 23:9
27:5 [q] 2Sa 23:20
27:7 [r] 2Sa 2:18; 1Ch 11:26
27:8 [s] 1Ch 11:27
27:9 [t] 2Sa 23:26; 1Ch 11:28
27:10 [u] 2Sa 23:26; 1Ch 11:27
27:11 [v] 2Sa 21:18
27:12 [w] 2Sa 23:27; 1Ch 11:28
27:13 [x] 2Sa 23:28; 1Ch 11:30
27:14 [y] 1Ch 11:31
27:15 [z] 2Sa 23:29 [a] Jos 15:17
27:17 [b] 1Ch 26:30 [c] 2Sa 8:17; 1Ch 12:28

mizabad was in charge of his division.
7 The fourth, for the fourth month, was
Asahel[r] the brother of Joab; his son
Zebadiah was his successor. There
were 24,000 men in his division.
8 The fifth, for the fifth month, was the
commander Shamhuth[s] the Izrahite.
There were 24,000 men in his division.
9 The sixth, for the sixth month, was Ira[t]
the son of Ikkesh the Tekoite. There
were 24,000 men in his division.
10 The seventh, for the seventh month,
was Helez[u] the Pelonite, an Ephraimite. There were 24,000 men in his division.
11 The eighth, for the eighth month, was
Sibbekai[v] the Hushathite, a Zerahite.
There were 24,000 men in his division.
12 The ninth, for the ninth month, was
Abiezer[w] the Anathothite, a Benjamite. There were 24,000 men in his
division.
13 The tenth, for the tenth month, was Maharai[x] the Netophathite, a Zerahite.
There were 24,000 men in his division.
14 The eleventh, for the eleventh month,
was Benaiah[y] the Pirathonite, an
Ephraimite. There were 24,000 men
in his division.
15 The twelfth, for the twelfth month, was
Heldai[z] the Netophathite, from the
family of Othniel.[a] There were 24,000
men in his division.

Leaders of the Tribes

16 The leaders of the tribes of Israel:
over the Reubenites: Eliezer son of
Zikri;
over the Simeonites: Shephatiah son
of Maakah;
17 over Levi: Hashabiah[b] son of Kemuel;
over Aaron: Zadok;[c]
18 over Judah: Elihu, a brother of David;
over Issachar: Omri son of Michael;
19 over Zebulun: Ishmaiah son of Obadiah;
over Naphtali: Jerimoth son of Azriel;
20 over the Ephraimites: Hoshea son of
Azaziah;
over half the tribe of Manasseh: Joel
son of Pedaiah;

27:1 – 22 Two separate lists are given here (vv. 2 – 15, 16 – 22). The first list concerns the organization of troops according to a militia system, which probably distributed the various tribes among the divisions so that it had the least possible effect on agricultural productivity. Each division was placed under the command of one of David's "mighty warriors" and had to serve one month in the year to provide a rotating standing army. This was in addition to the professional army and the mercenaries. The second list has to do with the more traditional tribal units, which could be called upon when needed, since it was the duty of every Israelite to serve the king in the army.

21 over the half-tribe of Manasseh in Gilead: Iddo son of Zechariah;
over Benjamin: Jaasiel son of Abner;
22 over Dan: Azarel son of Jeroham.
These were the leaders of the tribes of
Israel.

23 David did not take the number of the
men twenty years old or less,[d] because the
LORD had promised to make Israel as numerous as the stars[e] in the sky. 24 Joab son
of Zeruiah began to count the men but did
not finish. God's wrath came on Israel on
account of this numbering,[f] and the number was not entered in the book[a] of the
annals of King David.

The King's Overseers

25 Azmaveth son of Adiel was in charge
of the royal storehouses.
Jonathan son of Uzziah was in charge
of the storehouses in the outlying districts,
in the towns, the villages and the watchtowers.
26 Ezri son of Kelub was in charge of the
workers who farmed the land.
27 Shimei the Ramathite was in charge of
the vineyards.
Zabdi the Shiphmite was in charge of
the produce of the vineyards for the wine
vats.
28 Baal-Hanan the Gederite was in charge
of the olive and sycamore-fig[g] trees in the
western foothills.
Joash was in charge of the supplies of
olive oil.
29 Shitrai the Sharonite was in charge of
the herds grazing in Sharon.
Shaphat son of Adlai was in charge of
the herds in the valleys.
30 Obil the Ishmaelite was in charge of
the camels.
Jehdeiah the Meronothite was in charge
of the donkeys.
31 Jaziz the Hagrite[h] was in charge of the
flocks.
All these were the officials in charge of
King David's property.

32 Jonathan, David's uncle, was a counselor, a man of insight and a scribe. Jehiel son of Hakmoni took care of the king's
sons.
33 Ahithophel[i] was the king's counselor.
Hushai[j] the Arkite was the king's confidant. 34 Ahithophel was succeeded by Jehoiada son of Benaiah and by Abiathar.[k]
Joab[l] was the commander of the royal
army.

David's Plans for the Temple

28 David summoned all the officials[m]
of Israel to assemble at Jerusalem:
the officers over the tribes, the commanders of the divisions in the service of the
king, the commanders of thousands and
commanders of hundreds, and the officials
in charge of all the property and livestock
belonging to the king and his sons, together with the palace officials, the warriors
and all the brave fighting men.
2 King David rose to his feet and said:
"Listen to me, my fellow Israelites, my
people. I had it in my heart[n] to build a
house as a place of rest for the ark of the
covenant of the LORD, for the footstool[o] of
our God, and I made plans to build it. 3 But
God said to me,[p] 'You are not to build a
house for my Name,[q] because you are a
warrior and have shed blood.'[r]
4 "Yet the LORD, the God of Israel, chose
me[s] from my whole family[t] to be king over
Israel forever. He chose Judah[u] as leader,
and from the tribe of Judah he chose my
family, and from my father's sons he was
pleased to make me king over all Israel.
5 Of all my sons—and the LORD has given
me many[v]—he has chosen my son Solomon[w] to sit on the throne of the kingdom
of the LORD over Israel. 6 He said to me: 'Solomon your son is the one who will build
my house and my courts, for I have chosen
him to be my son,[x] and I will be his father.
7 I will establish his kingdom forever if he is
unswerving in carrying out my commands
and laws,[y] as is being done at this time.'
8 "So now I charge you in the sight of
all Israel and of the assembly of the LORD,
and in the hearing of our God: Be careful
to follow all the commands[z] of the LORD
your God, that you may possess this good
land and pass it on as an inheritance to
your descendants forever.[a]
9 "And you, my son Solomon, acknowledge the God of your father, and serve him
with wholehearted devotion[b] and with a

[a] 24 Septuagint; Hebrew *number*

27:23 [d] 1Ch 21:2-5 [e] Ge 15:5 **27:24** [f] 2Sa 24:15; 1Ch 21:7 **27:28** [g] 1Ki 10:27; 2Ch 1:15 **27:31** [h] 1Ch 5:10 **27:33** [i] 2Sa 15:12 [j] 2Sa 15:37 **27:34** [k] 1Ki 1:7 [l] 1Ch 11:6 **28:1** [m] 1Ch 11:10; 27:1-31 **28:2** [n] 1Ch 17:2 [o] Ps 99:5; 132:7 **28:3** [p] 2Sa 7:5 [q] 1Ch 22:8 [r] 1Ki 5:3; 1Ch 17:4 **28:4** [s] 1Ch 17:23, 27; 2Ch 6:6 [t] 1Sa 16:1-13 [u] Ge 49:10; 1Ch 5:2 **28:5** [v] 1Ch 3:1 [w] 1Ch 22:9; 23:1 **28:6** [x] 2Sa 7:13; 1Ch 22:9-10 **28:7** [y] 1Ch 22:13 **28:8** [z] Dt 6:1 [a] Dt 4:1 **28:9** [b] 1Ch 29:19

27:24 *God's wrath came on Israel.* See note on 2Sa 24:16.
27:31 *King David's property.* Property that had no heirs reverted to the crown, so the overseers in vv. 25–31 had oversight of these estates. Those who had somehow become debtors also worked for the king. The crown also owned flocks and herds that grazed throughout the land.
28:1 *all the officials of Israel.* The categories listed here give a summary of Israelite royal administration. Those listed relate to the political and military administration of the kingdom rather than the religious—the priests and Levites are not mentioned as being present. Lower levels of administration existed, of course, as they did throughout the Near East and had since earliest times. But the concern here is with the state. Two issues are dealt with: the succession of the monarchy and the construction of the temple. Both require the cooperation of the officers of the realm.
28:2 *footstool.* See note on Ex 25:16.

willing mind, for the LORD searches every heart[c] and understands every desire and every thought. If you seek him,[d] he will be found by you; but if you forsake[e] him, he will reject[f] you forever. [10]Consider now, for the LORD has chosen you to build a house as the sanctuary. Be strong and do the work."

[11]Then David gave his son Solomon the plans[g] for the portico of the temple, its buildings, its storerooms, its upper parts, its inner rooms and the place of atonement. [12]He gave him the plans of all that the Spirit[h] had put in his mind for the courts of the temple of the LORD and all the surrounding rooms, for the treasuries of the temple of God and for the treasuries for the dedicated things.[i] [13]He gave him instructions for the divisions[j] of the priests and Levites, and for all the work of serving in the temple of the LORD, as well as for all the articles to be used in its service. [14]He designated the weight of gold for all the gold articles to be used in various kinds of service, and the weight of silver for all the silver articles to be used in various kinds of service: [15]the weight of gold for the gold lampstands[k] and their lamps, with the weight for each lampstand and its lamps; and the weight of silver for each silver lampstand and its lamps, according to the use of each lampstand; [16]the weight of gold for each table[l] for consecrated bread; the weight of silver for the silver tables; [17]the weight of pure gold for the forks, sprinkling bowls[m] and pitchers; the weight of gold for each gold dish; the weight of silver for each silver dish; [18]and the weight of the refined gold for the altar of incense.[n] He also gave him the plan for the chariot,[o] that is, the cherubim of gold that spread their wings and overshadow[p] the ark of the covenant of the LORD.

[19]"All this," David said, "I have in writing as a result of the LORD's hand on me, and he enabled me to understand all the details[q] of the plan.[r]"

[20]David also said to Solomon his son, "Be strong and courageous,[s] and do the work. Do not be afraid or discouraged, for the LORD God, my God, is with you. He will not fail you or forsake[t] you until all the work for the service of the temple of the LORD is finished.[u] [21]The divisions of the priests and Levites are ready for all the work on the temple of God, and every willing person skilled[v] in any craft will help you in all the work. The officials and all the people will obey your every command."

Gifts for Building the Temple

29 Then King David said to the whole assembly: "My son Solomon, the one whom God has chosen, is young and inexperienced.[w] The task is great, because this palatial structure is not for man but for the LORD God. [2]With all my resources I have provided for the temple of my God—gold[x] for the gold work, silver for the silver, bronze for the bronze, iron for the iron and wood for the wood, as well as onyx for the settings, turquoise,[a][y] stones of various colors, and all kinds of fine stone and marble—all of these in large quantities.[z] [3]Besides, in my devotion to the temple of my

28:9 [c] 1Sa 16:7; Ps 7:9 [d] Ps 40:16; Jer 29:13 [e] Jos 24:20; 2Ch 15:2 [f] Ps 44:23 **28:11** [g] Ex 25:9 **28:12** [h] 1Ch 12:18 [i] 1Ch 26:20 **28:13** [j] 1Ch 24:1 **28:15** [k] Ex 25:31 **28:16** [l] Ex 25:23 **28:17** [m] Ex 27:3 **28:18** [n] Ex 30:1-10 [o] Ex 25:18-22 [p] Ex 25:20 **28:19** [q] 1Ki 6:38 [r] Ex 25:9 **28:20** [s] Dt 31:6; 1Ch 22:13; 2Ch 19:11; Hag 2:4 [t] Dt 4:31; Jos 24:20 [u] 1Ki 6:14; 2Ch 7:11 **28:21** [v] Ex 35:25-36:5 **29:1** [w] 1Ki 3:7; 1Ch 22:5; 2Ch 13:7 **29:2** [x] ver 7, 14, 16; Ezr 1:4; 6:5; Hag 2:8 [y] Isa 54:11 [z] 1Ch 22:2-5

[a] *2* The meaning of the Hebrew for this word is uncertain.

28:11 *plans.* The plans and instructions that David gives to Solomon are detailed. It would be essential that the plans were followed exactly. Moses received instructions and plans for the construction of the tabernacle on Mount Sinai (Ex 25:40). Similarly, Ezekiel was given detailed plans pertaining to the restored temple (Eze 40–48). Gudea, the third-millennium BC king of Lagash, received a vision in which he caught a glimpse of the temple that he was to build. In contrast to the Scriptures, he had great difficulty obtaining detailed plans for the structure.

Since the temple was the dwelling place for Yahweh, it was considered important that he be consulted for every detail of the plans. This includes not only the architectural plans, but even those related to the furniture, the functionaries, the location, the orientation, the trappings, etc. The temple was to become the hub of the cosmos from which the business of the cosmos would be run. It was the center of order in the cosmos, and, as such, should be ordered in meticulous detail.

28:18 *chariot, that is, the cherubim of gold.* The connection between the cherubim and a chariot motif occurs only here. The association of the cherubim with "wheels" is well-known from Ezekiel (cf. Eze 1; 10), but nowhere there is the concept of a chariot explicitly mentioned. The construction of chariots for deities is attested in Mesopotamia, particularly in the Isin-Larsa period in the early second millennium BC. Those, however, were literal chariots designed to transport the image of the deity, notably on festal occasions. In this verse, it is likely that this was a chariot fashioned for Yahweh much like the ark was fashioned as a footstool for the throne of Yahweh. In both cases, Yahweh himself remains invisible. *cherubim.* See notes on Ge 3:24; Ex 25:18.

29:2 *onyx.* The precise identification of this stone is uncertain. It has been suggested that the carnelian is a more likely candidate. Both onyx and carnelian are composed of silicon dioxide. Carnelian is a red stone, onyx is banded. *turquoise.* This Hebrew term is obscure. Elsewhere, it is known as a black paste used as an eye cosmetic (e.g., 2Ki 9:30). Its link with stones of various colors may suggest it was "antimony" or a dark-colored mortar. If so, then the "stones of various colors" may refer to the use of mosaics made from colored pebbles and laid out in geometric designs. *marble.* True marble is not found in Palestine, but must be imported from Greece or Italy, and is not evidenced in the region until the Persian period. Another possibility for the meaning of the Hebrew word is alabaster, but real alabaster is soft and scratches easily. The term here probably refers to noncrystalline limestone capable of being smoothed and polished. White or yellow stone of this character is abundant in Palestine.

God I now give my personal treasures of
gold and silver for the temple of my God,
over and above everything I have provided[a] for this holy temple: 4three thousand
talents[a] of gold (gold of Ophir)[b] and seven
thousand talents[b] of refined silver,[c] for the
overlaying of the walls of the buildings, 5for
the gold work and the silver work, and for
all the work to be done by the craftsmen.
Now, who is willing to consecrate themselves to the LORD today?"

6Then the leaders of families, the officers of the tribes of Israel, the commanders of thousands and commanders of hundreds, and the officials[d] in charge of the
king's work gave willingly.[e] 7They[f] gave
toward the work on the temple of God five
thousand talents[c] and ten thousand darics[d] of gold, ten thousand talents[e] of silver,
eighteen thousand talents[f] of bronze and
a hundred thousand talents[g] of iron. 8Any-
one who had precious stones[g] gave them
to the treasury of the temple of the LORD in
the custody of Jehiel the Gershonite.[h] 9The
people rejoiced at the willing response of
their leaders, for they had given freely and
wholeheartedly[i] to the LORD. David the
king also rejoiced greatly.

David's Prayer

10David praised the LORD in the presence
of the whole assembly, saying,

"Praise be to you, LORD,
the God of our father Israel,
from everlasting to everlasting.
11 Yours, LORD, is the greatness and the
power[j]
and the glory and the majesty and
the splendor,
for everything in heaven and earth is
yours.[k]
Yours, LORD, is the kingdom;
you are exalted as head over all.[l]
12 Wealth and honor[m] come from you;
you are the ruler[n] of all things.
In your hands are strength and power
to exalt and give strength to all.
13 Now, our God, we give you thanks,
and praise your glorious name.

14"But who am I, and who are my people, that we should be able to give as generously as this? Everything comes from
you, and we have given you only what
comes from your hand. 15We are foreigners and strangers[o] in your sight, as were
all our ancestors. Our days on earth are
like a shadow,[p] without hope. 16LORD our
God, all this abundance that we have provided for building you a temple for your
Holy Name comes from your hand, and
all of it belongs to you. 17I know, my God,
that you test the heart[q] and are pleased
with integrity. All these things I have giv-
en willingly and with honest intent. And
now I have seen with joy how willingly
your people who are here have given to
you.[r] 18LORD, the God of our fathers Abraham, Isaac and Israel, keep these desires
and thoughts in the hearts of your people forever, and keep their hearts loyal
to you. 19And give my son Solomon the
wholehearted devotion[s] to keep your commands, statutes and decrees[t] and to do everything to build the palatial structure for
which I have provided."[u]

20Then David said to the whole assembly, "Praise the LORD your God." So they
all praised the LORD, the God of their fathers; they bowed down, prostrating themselves before the LORD and the king.

Solomon Acknowledged as King

29:21-25pp — 1Ki 1:28-53

21The next day they made sacrifices to
the LORD and presented burnt offerings to
him:[v] a thousand bulls, a thousand rams
and a thousand male lambs, together with
their drink offerings, and other sacrifices
in abundance for all Israel. 22They ate and
drank with great joy[w] in the presence of
the LORD that day.

Then they acknowledged Solomon son
of David as king a second time, anointing
him before the LORD to be ruler and Zadok[x] to be priest. 23So Solomon sat on the
throne[y] of the LORD as king in place of his

29:3 [a] 2Ch 24:10; 31:3; 35:8 **29:4** [b] Ge 10:29 [c] 1Ch 22:14 **29:6** [d] 1Ch 27:1; 28:1 [e] ver 9; Ex 25:1-8; 35:20-29; 36:2; 2Ch 24:10; Ezr 7:15 **29:7** [f] Ex 25:2; Ne 7:70-71 **29:8** [g] Ex 35:27 [h] 1Ch 26:21 **29:9** [i] 1Ki 8:61; 2Co 9:7 **29:11** [j] Ps 24:8; 59:17; 62:11 [k] Ps 89:11 [l] Rev 5:12-13 **29:12** [m] 2Ch 1:12 [n] 2Ch 20:6; Ro 11:36 **29:15** [o] Ps 39:12; Heb 11:13 [p] Job 14:2 **29:17** [q] Ps 139:23; Pr 15:11; 17:3; Jer 11:20; 17:10 [r] 1Ch 28:9; Ps 15:1-5 **29:19** [s] 1Ch 28:9 [t] Ps 72:1 [u] 1Ch 22:14 **29:21** [v] 1Ki 8:62 **29:22** [w] 1Ch 23:1 [x] 1Ki 1:33-39 **29:23** [y] 1Ki 2:12

[a] 4 That is, about 110 tons or about 100 metric tons
[b] 4 That is, about 260 tons or about 235 metric tons
[c] 7 That is, about 190 tons or about 170 metric tons
[d] 7 That is, about 185 pounds or about 84 kilograms
[e] 7 That is, about 380 tons or about 340 metric tons
[f] 7 That is, about 675 tons or about 610 metric tons
[g] 7 That is, about 3,800 tons or about 3,400 metric tons

29:3 *I now give my personal treasures of gold and silver.* See notes on 22:14.
29:4 *gold of Ophir.* Became synonymous with gold of high quality. Outside the Bible it is mentioned on an eighth-century BC ostracon discovered at Tel Qasile, a Philistine settlement on the outskirts of Tel Aviv. *Ophir.* Its exact location is uncertain (see note on 1Ki 9:28). Gold from there was shipped to Ezion Geber.
29:7 *darics.* The mention of darics here is an example of the Chronicler converting an amount into contemporary currency. Although historians credit the Lydians in western Turkey with inventing coinage, coins were not in common use until the Persian period when Darius the Great, presumably having borrowed the idea from the Lydians, introduced them. The term *daric* probably derived its name from Darius. It bore the image of an archer and weighed about one-tenth of a gram. The daric was about 95 percent gold and 3 percent copper in order to give it some hardness. "Ten thousand darics," therefore, weighed about 185 pounds (84 kilograms) and was worth just over one million dollars in today's currency.

father David. He prospered and all Israel
obeyed him. 24All the officers and warriors,
as well as all of King David's sons, pledged
their submission to King Solomon.
25The LORD highly exalted Solomon in
the sight of all Israel and bestowed on him
royal splendor[z] such as no king over Israel
ever had before.[a]

The Death of David

29:26-28pp — 1Ki 2:10-12

26David son of Jesse was king[b] over all
Israel. 27He ruled over Israel forty years —
seven in Hebron and thirty-three in Jerusalem.[c]
28He died[d] at a good old age, having enjoyed long life, wealth and honor.
His son Solomon succeeded him as king.[e]
29As for the events of King David's
reign, from beginning to end, they are
written in the records of Samuel the seer,[f]
the records of Nathan[g] the prophet and
the records of Gad[h] the seer, 30together
with the details of his reign and power,
and the circumstances that surrounded
him and Israel and the kingdoms of all
the other lands.

29:25 [z] 2Ch 1:1, 12 [a] 1Ki 3:13; Ecc 2:9 **29:26** [b] 1Ch 18:14 **29:27** [c] 2Sa 5:4-5; 1Ki 2:11; 1Ch 3:4 **29:28** [d] Ge 15:15; Ac 13:36 [e] 1Ch 23:1 **29:29** [f] 1Sa 9:9 [g] 2Sa 7:2 [h] 1Sa 22:5

29:29 *records of Samuel … records of Nathan … records of Gad.* Most of the records listed have not survived, though they probably include the canonical documents of Samuel and Kings. The sources mentioned are attributed to three famous prophets from the time of David, but we do not know what kind of documents they would have been and no other records of a court prophet have ever been found. The works of prophets would likely not have been compiled into literary works such as we have in our Bibles until sometime after their lives, but certainly individual documents recording prophecies would not have been uncommon. They would have been kept in archives where scribes, though not the general public, could access them.

NARRATIVE LITERATURE

2 CHRONICLES

Solomon Asks for Wisdom

1:2-13pp — 1Ki 3:4-15
1:14-17pp — 1Ki 10:26-29; 2Ch 9:25-28

1 Solomon son of David established[a]
himself firmly over his kingdom, for
the LORD his God was with[b] him and made
him exceedingly great.[c]
2 Then Solomon spoke to all Israel[d]—to
the commanders of thousands and commanders of hundreds, to the judges and
to all the leaders in Israel, the heads of
families— 3 and Solomon and the whole
assembly went to the high place at Gibeon, for God's tent of meeting[e] was there,
which Moses[f] the LORD's servant had
made in the wilderness. 4 Now David had
brought up the ark[g] of God from Kiriath
Jearim to the place he had prepared for
it, because he had pitched a tent[h] for it in
Jerusalem. 5 But the bronze altar[i] that Bezalel[j] son of Uri, the son of Hur, had made
was in Gibeon in front of the tabernacle
of the LORD; so Solomon and the assembly inquired[k] of him there. 6 Solomon went
up to the bronze altar before the LORD in
the tent of meeting and offered a thousand
burnt offerings on it.
7 That night God appeared[l] to Solomon
and said to him, "Ask for whatever you
want me to give you."
8 Solomon answered God, "You have
shown great kindness to David my father
and have made me[m] king in his place.
9 Now, LORD God, let your promise[n] to my
father David be confirmed, for you have
made me king over a people who are as numerous as the dust of the earth.[o] 10 Give me

1:1 [a] 1Ki 2:12, 26; 2Ch 12:1 [b] Ge 21:22; 39:2; Nu 14:43 [c] 1Ch 29:25 **1:2** [d] 1Ch 9:1; 28:1 **1:3** [e] Ex 36:8 [f] Ex 40:18 **1:4** [g] 2Sa 6:2; 1Ch 15:25 [h] 2Sa 6:17; 1Ch 15:1 **1:5** [i] Ex 38:2 [j] Ex 31:2 [k] 1Ch 13:3 **1:7** [l] 2Ch 7:12 **1:8** [m] 1Ch 23:1; 28:5 **1:9** [n] 2Sa 7:25; 1Ki 8:25 [o] Ge 12:2

1:1 *the LORD his God was with him.* The notions of divine election, divine presence and divine enablement concerning kings are seen in a number of ancient Near Eastern texts. For example, the Egyptian pharaoh Thutmose IV (fifteenth century BC) is assured by his god Harmakhis-Khepri-Re-Atum that "I am with thee; I am thy guide." Similarly, the Hittite king Muwattalli (c. fifteenth century BC) refers to himself as the "Beloved of the Storm-god." In addition, the twenty-second-century BC Sumerian king Gudea notes that the god Ningirsu set him "firm upon his throne." Likewise, the Neo-Babylonian king Nabopolassar (seventh century BC) notes that he was called by Shazu (= Marduk) to be lord over the country and to be successful in everything he did. Similarly, Nabopolassar's son Nebuchadnezzar is noted as being "permanently selected by Marduk." All of this underscores the importance that the favor of the deity be understood as resting upon the ruler. They demonstrate that culturally, God interacted with Israel in terms that were familiar to them. These are the sorts of promises that gods typically made to kings in the ancient world.

1:3 *the high place at Gibeon.* High places are religious sites typically associated with hills or mountains—the added elevation providing a sense of closeness to the supernatural realm. High places were used in conjunction with the worship of a number of gods and had a variety of forms (roofs, open air, platforms, stairs, podiums, etc.), sizes (recall that the high place in the district of Zuph accommodated Samuel, Saul and 30 or so other guests, 1Sa 9:22) and functions. Prior to the construction of the temple, high places in Israel were simply generic places where worship or cultic activity took place, reflecting a non-centralized worship context. Following the completion of the temple, however, high places became associated with idolatry and syncretism. Consequently, the removal or nonremoval of high places became a litmus test for the religious fidelity of a given king. With this in mind, much is done within the context of Chronicles to show that the high place at Gibeon was a legitimate place of worship. Earlier the Chronicler noted that David appointed Zadok the priest to serve "before the tabernacle ... at the high place in Gibeon" and to present burnt offerings on the bronze altar "in accordance with everything written in the Law of the LORD" (1Ch 16:39–40). We learn in the present context (2Ch 1:5) that, along with the tabernacle made by Moses, the bronze altar crafted by Bezalel, was also at Gibeon. The tabernacle underscores continuity with the Mosaic tradition, while the bronze altar connects the site with the Aaronic priesthood. All these details together stress that Gibeon was a legitimate sacred place.

1:7 *That night God appeared to Solomon.* See note on 1Ki 3:5.

1:10 *wisdom and knowledge.* Solomon's request for wisdom and knowledge connects with the ancient Near

2 CHRONICLES 1:7 – 12

Dreams and Temple Building in the Ancient Near East

In the context of ancient Near Eastern texts, revelatory dreams frequently intersected with temple building and refurbishing, given the importance of securing divine approval for such plans. The proposal for the construction of a temple might be prompted by the deity (as with Nabonidus and the rebuilding of the temple of Sin) or initiated by the ruler (as with Esarhaddon and the restoration of the temple of Shamash).

In some cases, the revelatory dream precedes the building effort, whereas in other cases the dream follows the completion of the task. Occasionally, revelatory dreams frame the temple building project (as with Solomon, cf. 2Ch 7:12 – 22). The goddess Ishtar, e.g., appears to the Assyrian king Ashurbanipal (seventh century BC) via a dream and converses with the king following his efforts to bring order to the temple of Ishtar. Similarly, the auditory message-dream of the Neo-Babylonian king Nabonidus (sixth century BC) commemorates his rebuilding of three temples, especially the temple of the moon-god Sin in Harran.

The account of Solomon's temple building is often compared with the account of the Sumerian king Gudea of Lagash (c. 2100 BC, around the onset of the Third Dynasty of Ur). This account is a building dedication hymn that celebrates Gudea's intent to build the Eninnu temple for the god Ningirsu (and his consort Baba), a desire that was birthed, confirmed and designed in a series of dreams. Reminiscent of Solomon, Gudea is described as "a man of wide wisdom" at the outset of his temple building project and "wise and knowledgeable" at its completion (cf. 2Ch 1:10 – 12; 9:22 – 23) and is described as establishing righteous judgment over his subjects. Additional noteworthy parallels between the temple building accounts of Gudea and Solomon are as follows:

- affirmation of the divine choice of the ruler
- the deity's intentions to bless the ruler (e.g., long life, established reign, peace, wealth, descendants)
- divine call and approval of temple building project
- importance of building the temple in exact accordance with the deity's plan
- commitment of the ruler to the project
- raising of materials and workers for the project

continued on next page

wisdom and knowledge, that I may lead[p]
this people, for who is able to govern this
great people of yours?"
11God said to Solomon, "Since this is
your heart's desire and you have not asked
for wealth,[q] possessions or honor, nor for
the death of your enemies, and since you
have not asked for a long life but for wis-

1:10 [p] Nu 27:17; 2Sa 5:2; Pr 8:15-16
1:11 [q] Dt 17:17

Eastern motif of "the king as sage." Ancient Near Eastern kings were commonly portrayed as wise sages who received their wisdom as an act of favor by their respective deities. Such descriptions frequently include an assessment that the king's wisdom surpasses that of all others (cf. 2Ch 9:22). Hammurapi, e.g., refers to the "breadth of vision" given to him by the god Ea and declares, "My words are precious, my wisdom is unrivaled." Likewise, in the eighth-century BC Phoenician Karatepe Stele, Azatiwata (Azitawadda) boasts that "every king made me father to himself because of my wisdom and my goodness." In the ancient Near East, wisdom was not as much abstract as it was functional. Thus, from the perspective of the king, wisdom had functionality in important areas such as practical knowledge, decision making and temple building. In the realm of knowledge, wisdom was characterized by mastery of areas such as botany, zoology, music, law, diplomacy, flora, fauna, literature and other elements of the cultured life (cf. 1Ki 4:32 – 33). With respect to decision making, note that Solomon's request for wisdom is connected to his ability to judge ("govern") God's people and facilitate an ordered society. In like manner, ancient Near Eastern kings

• request by the ruler for the deity to inhabit the temple
• seven-day temple dedication ceremony including public assembly, prayers and sacrifice

With these noted, it is important not to overstate the parallels. Thus, unlike Solomon's dream at Gibeon, Gudea's initial dream required the services of a dream interpreter, and Gudea's second and third revelatory dreams needed to be incubated by spending days and nights in a temple, by establishing peace among his subjects and by offerings. Moreover, the Gudea Cylinders present the temple construction process as laden with step-by-step ritual, with Gudea needing to nearly pry specifics from Ningirsu. It should also be noted that the Gudea Cylinders lack the overarching literary context (and related theology) found within Solomon's temple building texts (i.e., 2Ch 1 – 8; 1Ki 5 – 9). Lastly, it should be noted that in the case of Solomon, the plans for the temple were given to him not by God in his dream but rather by his father David, who noted that the temple plans were put in his mind by the Spirit of God (see 1Ch 28:11 – 12) and "in writing as a result of the LORD's hand on me" (1Ch 28:19). ◆

The Cylinder of Nabonidus commemorates the reconstruction of three temples, c. 555 – 540 BC.

dom and knowledge to govern my people over whom I have made you king, 12therefore wisdom and knowledge will be given you. And I will also give you wealth, possessions and honor,[r] such as no king who was before you ever had and none after you will have.[s]"

13Then Solomon went to Jerusalem from

1:12 [r] 1Ch 29:12 [s] 1Ch 29:25; 2Ch 9:22; Ne 13:26

are commonly portrayed as champions of justice and protectors of the disenfranchised. The Babylonian king Hammurapi (eighteenth century BC), e.g., noted that the gods Anu and Bel called him to cause justice, enlightenment and welfare to prevail in the land. With respect to royal building, particularly of temples, divinely gifted wisdom is stressed in a number of ancient Near Eastern texts. In the temple building account of Gudea (twenty-seventh century BC), the notion of royal wisdom is interwoven through the text (see the article "Dreams and Temple Building in the Ancient Near East," p. 718). Likewise, the prologue to the legal code of the Babylonian king Hammurapi (eighteenth century BC) refers to his wisdom in the context of rebuilding the religious shrines of several deities. Similarly, the Babylonian king Nebuchadnezzar (sixth century BC) is described as a "wise expert who is attentive to the ways of the gods" in conjunction with his refurbishing work on the shrines of Marduk and Nabu. Later, the Babylonian king Nabonidus records in the Sippar Cylinder that during an auspicious day he was instilled with wisdom by the gods Shamash and Adad in conjunction with his work on the temple of the moon god Sin. In the case of Solomon, the

the high place at Gibeon, from before the
tent of meeting. And he reigned over Israel.
14Solomon accumulated chariots[t] and
horses; he had fourteen hundred chariots
and twelve thousand horses,[a] which he
kept in the chariot cities and also with him
in Jerusalem. 15The king made silver and
gold[u] as common in Jerusalem as stones,

1:14 [t] 1Sa 8:11; 1Ki 4:26; 9:19
1:15 [u] 1Ki 9:28; Isa 60:5

[a] 14 Or *charioteers*

stress on his divinely gifted wisdom connects him with Bezalel, who is similarly noted as being given wisdom and knowledge by God for the task of constructing the tabernacle in the wilderness (cf. Ex. 31:1–5; 35:30–35; 36:1). *this great people of yours.* The notion of the ownership of people, kingdom and throne is sometimes blurred between the ruler and the deity. As such, the king may be portrayed as a divine vice-regent or divine son (perhaps elected or adopted as such; cf. 1Ch 28:6). Thutmose III, e.g., notes the following concerning his god Amon: "He is my father and I am his son," and Amon commanded that "I should be upon his throne." Similarly, Thutmose IV is told by his god in a revelatory dream that "thou art my son ... I am thy father" and "I shall give thee my kingdom." In the case of the Israelite monarchy, numerous Biblical texts make it clear that the people led by the king are God's people (here), the kingdom is God's kingdom (13:8; 1Ch 17:14) and the king sits on God's throne (2Ch 9:8).

1:14 *accumulated chariots and horses.* See note on 1Ki 4:26.

1:15 *cedar.* See notes on 2Sa 5:11; 1Ki 5:6; 6:15.

2 CHRONICLES 1:16–17

ALL THE KING'S HORSES

The notion that Solomon imported horses from Egypt is commonly dismissed. Yet, there is evidence that northeast Africa (Egypt, Cush and Nubia) was known for its horses both before and after the time of Solomon. A number of texts indicate that certain Egyptian horses (especially Nubian horses) were a large and prized breed of horses in contrast to the smaller horses common in the northern regions.

Moreover, the Sudan was known as a horse-breeding region, with the Dangola Reach (Cush) being known for the finest horses. Texts from the thirteenth century BC mention scores of horses in the east delta region of Egypt. Rameses II (thirteenth century BC) is noted to have built large stable facilities in the Nile delta region. In light of the quality of his horses, Rameses II was asked to send horses to the Hittite king in Anatolia. Following Solomon's time frame, Sargon II of Assyria (eighth century BC) speaks of 12 large Egyptian horses unlike any found in Assyria given to him by the Egyptian pharaoh Osorkon IV. Lastly, it should not be missed that the prohibition against an Israelite king getting horses from Egypt (Dt 17:14–20) would imply that a king would wish to do so!

Kue can be equated with Cilicia in southeast Anatolia in the lowlands of modern southeastern Turkey, an area known for ample pasturage for equine breeding.

With respect to the price of a horse noted 2Ch 1:17 (150 shekels), a text from Nuzi (fifteenth–fourteenth centuries BC) reflects the immense value of a horse vis-à-vis other animals. In this text, a single horse was deemed equal in value to the sum of the following ten animals: one ox, three goats, and six sheep. In addition, a text from Mari (eighteenth century BC) indicates that a horse cost 300 shekels, and later texts from Ugarit (thirteenth century BC) indicate a price point of 200 shekels, illustrating that the 150 shekels paid by Solomon's royal merchants in the tenth century BC fits the declining price curve for horses. By the sixth century BC, another text indicates that the price for a quality horse had gone up, with 230 shekels noted as the price for a top-quality horse. Other early texts indicate much lower prices for horses (particularly young colts and unbroken horses), implying a wide range of prices corresponding to size, age, color, pedigree, function, training, etc. (as is the case today).

2Ch 1:17 indicates that Solomon functions as a broker/middle man between Aramean and Neo-Hittite states in the north and Egypt in the south, reflecting the growing regional prominence of ancient Israel. From this perspective, Solomon's "royal merchants" (2Ch 1:16) are engaging in trade in much the same way as the rulers of

continued on next page

and cedar as plentiful as sycamore-fig trees
in the foothills. 16Solomon's horses were
imported from Egypt and from Kue[a]—the
royal merchants purchased them from Kue
at the current price. 17They imported a
chariot[v] from Egypt for six hundred shekels[b] of silver, and a horse for a hundred and
fifty.[c] They also exported them to all the
kings of the Hittites and of the Arameans.

1:17 [v] SS 1:9

[a] *16* Probably Cilicia [b] *17* That is, about 15 pounds or about 6.9 kilograms [c] *17* That is, about 3 3/4 pounds or about 1.7 kilograms

1:17 *imported a chariot from Egypt.* While the data for prices of chariots are limited, it seems clear that the price point of 600 shekels of silver (about 15 pounds or 6.9 kilograms) for a chariot is quite steep. This price point suggests that these are no ordinary chariots, but rather richly appointed chariots that would be utilized by royalty in processions and state ceremonies. Such chariots, commonly adorned with gold and precious stones such as lapis lazuli (a greatly prized deep blue gemstone), were viewed as surrogate thrones and status symbols for ancient Near Eastern monarchs. Thus, in the Gilgamesh Epic, the goddess Ishtar tries to woo Gilgamesh by offering him an abundant life that includes a chariot adorned with gold and lapis lazuli.

The most famous Egyptian gold chariot is that of King Tut in the Egyptian museum (c. 1330s BC). Another mention of gold chariots from Egypt is found in an Amarna letter sent from Egypt to Babylon in which the Egyptian

Carchemish bartered trade between Anatolia and Mesopotamia (including the trade of horses). With respect to brokering the export of chariots from Egypt, Solomon is leveraging his kingdom's position as a land bridge between the kingdoms of the south (Egypt, Nubia, Kush) and those of the north (Aram/Syria, Mesopotamia, Anatolia).

The brokering of horses from Kue to Neo-Hittite and Aramean states, however, requires more explanation. While the notion of Solomon's "royal merchants" importing horses from Kue (treated above) is not problematic, the detail that Solomon was able to broker the sale of horses originating in Kue to "all the kings of the Hittites and of the Arameans" (2Ch 1:17) implies that Solomon exerted significant control over these northern territories. Interestingly, the Bible stresses that this is exactly what had begun during David's rule (recall David's subjugation of northern Aram and Damascus, 2Sa 8:3 – 11). As a result, Solomon was able to build and fortify storage cities in Hamath in northern Aram/Syria (an ideal place for his "royal merchants" to rear and keep horses because of the ample amount of pasturage in the region) as well as Tadmor, an oasis city on the main trade route between Mesopotamia and Canaan (2Ch 8:3 – 4). These locations gave Solomon control over important trade routes for commerce with Aramean and Neo-Hittite states. ◆

Horses and riders, Achzib, eight–sixth centuries BC.

Kim Walton. The Israel Museum, Jerusalem.

Preparations for Building the Temple

2:1-18pp — 1Ki 5:1-16

2[a] Solomon gave orders to build a temple[w] for the Name of the LORD and
a royal palace for himself.[x] 2 He conscripted 70,000 men as carriers and 80,000 as
stonecutters in the hills and 3,600 as foremen over them.[y]
3 Solomon sent this message to Hiram[b][z]
king of Tyre:

"Send me cedar logs[a] as you did
for my father David when you sent
him cedar to build a palace to live in.
4 Now I am about to build a temple[b]
for the Name of the LORD my God and
to dedicate it to him for burning fragrant incense[c] before him, for setting
out the consecrated bread[d] regularly,
and for making burnt offerings[e] every morning and evening and on the
Sabbaths,[f] at the New Moons and at
the appointed festivals of the LORD
our God. This is a lasting ordinance
for Israel.
5 "The temple I am going to build
will be great,[g] because our God is
greater than all other gods.[h] 6 But who
is able to build a temple for him, since
the heavens, even the highest heavens,
cannot contain him?[i] Who then am I[j]
to build a temple for him, except as
a place to burn sacrifices before him?
7 "Send me, therefore, a man skilled
to work in gold and silver, bronze
and iron, and in purple, crimson and
blue yarn, and experienced in the art
of engraving, to work in Judah and
Jerusalem with my skilled workers,[k]
whom my father David provided.
8 "Send me also cedar, juniper and
algum[c] logs from Lebanon, for I know

2:1 [w] Dt 12:5 [x] Ecc 2:4 **2:2** [y] ver 18; 2Ch 10:4 **2:3** [z] 2Sa 5:11 [a] 1Ch 14:1 **2:4** [b] ver 1; Dt 12:5 [c] Ex 30:7 [d] Ex 25:30 [e] Ex 29:42; 2Ch 13:11 [f] Nu 28:9-10 **2:5** [g] 1Ch 22:5; Ps 135:5 [h] 1Ch 16:25 **2:6** [i] 1Ki 8:27; 2Ch 6:18; Jer 23:24 [j] Ex 3:11 **2:7** [k] ver 13-14; Ex 35:31; 1Ch 22:16

a In Hebrew texts 2:1 is numbered 1:18, and 2:2-18 is numbered 2:1-17. *b* 3 Hebrew *Huram,* a variant of *Hiram;* also in verses 11 and 12 *c* 8 Probably a variant of *almug*

---

pharaoh notes that he has sent the Babylonian king two chariots overlaid with gold. Similarly, Papyrus Anastasi IV describes the chariots of the pharaoh as being made of ornate wood and adorned with gold and ivory. The combination of Nubian acacia wood (noted for its quality and hardness) and the use of ivory may have added to the value of Egyptian chariots.

Egypt also acquired gold chariots in battle, as reflected in Thutmose III's claim that he acquired "magnificent chariots of gold and silver" in plunder from Megiddo (fifteenth century BC). Egyptian pharaohs also received gold chariots as gifts. In a diplomatic letter sent from the king of Assyria to the king of Egypt, the Assyrian king (Ashur-Uballit) notes that he sent the Egyptian pharaoh "a beautiful royal chariot," along with two white horses. Similarly, Tushratta king of Mitanni sent a chariot covered with 320 shekels of gold as a wedding gift to Pharaoh Nimmureya.

2:1 *Solomon gave orders to build a temple.* Unlike the account of Solomon's building activities in 1 Kings (e.g., 1Ki 7:1 – 12), the Chronicler only mentions Solomon's palace in passing (2Ch 8:1). Instead, the central narrative focus of chs. 2 – 9 is the construction of the Jerusalem temple (chs. 2 – 7). The construction of a new temple or refurbishing of an important religious shrine was an important task for a new king, and preparations for the project would begin soon after the monarch's enthronement. In order to tangibly illustrate the king's devotion and to acknowledge the role of the deity in his reign, emphasis was placed on showing that no expense was spared in the procurement of materials for the temple.

Similarly, temple construction accounts stressed the skill and workmanship of the craftsmen employed to build the temple. For example, the Old Babylonian king Shamshi-Adad notes that his temple project for the god Enlil was "methodically made by the skilled work of the building trade." In addition, in the Sippar Cylinder the Babylonian king Nabonidus notes that he rebuilt the temple for the moon-god Sin from "its foundation to its parapet." All in all, each royal temple builder wanted to show that the goal of his building campaign was to build, in the words of the Sumerian king Gudea, the "foremost temple of all the lands."

The construction of Solomon's temple began in his 4th year as king (c. 967 BC) and was completed in the 11th year of his reign (c. 960 BC). The fact that Solomon did not begin the temple construction until his 4th year reflects the significant amount of preparation and planning that still needed to take place beyond that accomplished by David. See the article "New Kings and Temples," p. 568.

2:2 *conscripted … carriers and … stonecutters.* See notes on 1Ch 20:3; Jos 16:10; 1Ki 5:13; 9:15.

2:3 *Solomon sent this message to Hiram.* The exchange of letters between Hiram and Solomon reflects standard practice for official ancient Near Eastern correspondence. Such diplomatic correspondence typically contained expressions of warmth, divine blessings, and even "love" (referring to a relationship loyal to agreed-upon terms). Depending on the history between the two parties, such blessings might include a short review of the relations between the nations and previous rulers. This is seen in an Amarna letter wherein the king of Mitanni notes that the ancestors of the Egyptian pharaoh have "always showed love to my ancestors." Typically, such letters are geared toward a request from one party to the other, as in the request of the Babylonian king for the Egyptian pharaoh to "send me much gold" for his temple project, noting in return, "whatever you want from my country, write me so that it may be taken to you." Beyond precious metals and gifts, skilled workmen (e.g., Huram) were another desired "gift." It is noteworthy that Solomon (like David, cf. 1Ch 22:1 – 5) readily seeks Phoenician assistance in the building of Yahweh's temple. The Phoenicians were noted for both supplying crucial building materials as well as the technical expertise to construct buildings and fashion raw materials into artistic objects. See note on 1Ki 5:18. *cedar logs.* See notes on 2Sa 5:11; 1Ki 5:6; 6:15.

2:5 *greater than all other gods.* This rhetoric would be expected of any nation. Claims to divine superiority are usually founded in military supremacy or acts of power, and are strongest when coming from the mouths of the former worshipers of the now-deemed-inferior deities (cf. Rahab [Jos 2:11]; Naaman [2Ki 5:15]). See the article "Monotheism, Monolatry and Henotheism," p. 308.

2:8 *cedar.* See notes on 2Sa 5:11; 1Ki 5:6; 6:15. *algum.* Probably a variant of almugwood.

that your servants are skilled in cutting timber there. My servants will work with yours [9]to provide me with plenty of lumber, because the temple I build must be large and magnificent. [10]I will give your servants, the woodsmen who cut the timber, twenty thousand cors[a] of ground wheat, twenty thousand cors[b] of barley, twenty thousand baths[c] of wine and twenty thousand baths of olive oil.[l]"

[11]Hiram king of Tyre replied by letter to Solomon:

"Because the LORD loves[m] his people, he has made you their king."

[12]And Hiram added:

"Praise be to the LORD, the God of Israel, who made heaven and earth![n] He has given King David a wise son, endowed with intelligence and discernment, who will build a temple for the LORD and a palace for himself.

[13]"I am sending you Huram-Abi,[o] a man of great skill, [14]whose mother was from Dan[p] and whose father was from Tyre. He is trained[q] to work in gold and silver, bronze and iron, stone and wood, and with purple and blue[r] and crimson yarn and fine linen. He is experienced in all kinds of engraving and can execute any design given to him. He will work with your skilled workers and with those of my lord, David your father.

[15]"Now let my lord send his servants the wheat and barley and the olive oil[s] and wine he promised, [16]and we will cut all the logs from Lebanon that you need and will float them as rafts by sea down to Joppa.[t] You can then take them up to Jerusalem."

[17]Solomon took a census of all the foreigners[u] residing in Israel, after the census[v] his father David had taken; and they were found to be 153,600. [18]He assigned[w] 70,000 of them to be carriers and 80,000 to be stonecutters in the hills, with 3,600 foremen over them to keep the people working.

Solomon Builds the Temple

3:1-14pp — 1Ki 6:1-29

3 Then Solomon began to build[x] the temple of the LORD[y] in Jerusalem on Mount Moriah, where the LORD had appeared to his father David. It was on the threshing

2:10 [l]Ezr 3:7 **2:11** [m]1Ki 10:9; 2Ch 9:8 **2:12** [n]Ne 9:6; Ps 8:3; 33:6; 102:25 **2:13** [o]1Ki 7:13 **2:14** [p]Ex 31:6 [q]Ex 35:31 [r]Ex 35:35 **2:15** [s]ver 10; Ezr 3:7 **2:16** [t]Jos 19:46; Jnh 1:3 **2:17** [u]1Ch 22:2 [v]2Sa 24:2 **2:18** [w]ver 2; 1Ch 22:2; 2Ch 8:8 **3:1** [x]Ac 7:47 [y]Ge 28:17

[a] *10* That is, probably about 3,600 tons or about 3,200 metric tons of wheat [b] *10* That is, probably about 3,000 tons or about 2,700 metric tons of barley [c] *10* That is, about 120,000 gallons or about 440,000 liters

2:10 *I will give your servants.* Solomon's payment of agricultural products and derivatives to Hiram's workers is formidable and would provide a combination of rations for the Phoenician guest workers and payment for their services. *cors.* The "cor" is a unit of dry measure equivalent to approximately six bushels (220 liters), making the trade amounts in wheat and barley amount to 120,000 bushels (26.4 million liters) each, i.e., 3,600 tons (3,200 metric tons) of wheat and 3,000 tons (2,700 metric tons) of barley. Twenty thousand cors of grain would have required about 260 acres (slightly more than 100 hectares) of crop from each of Solomon's 12 districts. *wheat ... barley ... wine ... olive oil.* These agricultural products were part of Israel's natural resources (especially the northern tribal regions and portions of the Transjordan). Note that such trade with Tyre/Phoenicia is also implied in the prophecy against Tyre in Ezekiel (Eze 27:17). *baths.* The "bath" is a unit of liquid measure equivalent to approximately six gallons (22 liters), making Solomon's shipments of wine and olive oil equal to about 120,000 gallons (440,000 liters) each. Agricultural products from Israel were perhaps transported and stored in cylindrical storage jars (called "sausage jars") discovered at the Phoenician city of Tyre having features consistent with pottery vessels manufactured in Israel.

The trade interaction noted here between Solomon and Hiram provides an excellent insight into Iron Age trading and barter practices. As reflected here, the natural resources of one region were traded for the natural resources of another at a rate that would be a combination of supply and demand as well as the relative strength and relationship of the trading parties. In this transaction, Solomon's setting of the price of the trade implies that he is the stronger party in the transaction.

The amounts here describe the "budget" for the project, but each individual worker would have been paid a daily wage. These amounts would have provided rations for 6,000–8,000 workers over three years.

2:12 *wise.* See note on 1:10.

2:14 *purple and blue and crimson yarn and fine linen.* See note on Ex 25:4.

2:16 *float them as rafts by sea down to Joppa.* The transporting of wood by means of floating of logs was a practical logistical option for city-states and nations that had access to a seaport. Such transportation of wood over sea is seen in Assyrian reliefs showing logs being towed by Phoenician ships. In addition, the account of Gudea's temple building project provides a poetic description of the watery journey experienced by the cedar and cypress logs, noting that the logs moved "like majestic snakes floating on water." Solomon's ability to transport this wood from the seaport inland to Jerusalem implies his control over the coastal area in the environs of Joppa as well as the Shephelah (low hills) heading eastward to Jerusalem. The journey from Tyre to the port city of Joppa is approximately 100 miles (160 kilometers) and the trip inland to Jerusalem is another 30 miles (50 kilometers) or so.

3:1 *Mount Moriah.* The location of Mount Moriah is connected with the place where Yahweh appeared to David (1Ch 21) and is described as the place Yahweh chose for the location of the temple (2Ch 7:12). Also, though the historical-geographical connection is tenuous, the name Moriah connects with God's provision of a substitutionary sacrifice for Abraham, after which the area is called the "mountain of the LORD" (Ge 22:14). This care reflects the importance in the ancient Near East that a religious shrine/temple be located on a divinely chosen or divinely confirmed place. Such concern is also reflected in the Gudea account, wherein Gudea receives signs in

2 CHRONICLES 2–3

TEMPLES AND SACRED SPACE

Temples and palaces were understood as tangible and spatial extensions of divine order and governance over the created realm and as such were centerpieces of ancient Near Eastern cultures. The importance of a temple relates directly to the notion of sacred space — a place wherein the human realm could intersect with the divine realm, a sort of *axis mundi* that linked heaven and earth and acted as a conduit for divine presence and blessing. In addition, the temple functioned as an earthly expression of divine order that was understood to extend into the social, political and religious structures of an ancient society.

The meeting place between the divine realm and the human realm was often associated with elevated structures in the ancient Near East: mountain tops in Syria and Canaan, ziggurats in Mesopotamia (stepped structures — stairways from heaven — from which the deity would descend to earth, cf. Ge 28) and primordial hillocks (mounds) in Egypt. The notion of temple in ancient Near Eastern cultures was also associated with the localization of deity in a spatial (as well as temporal) setting, which necessitated a wide range of procedures, incantations, etc. in order to attain (or maintain) the deity's favor. Since ancient Near Eastern temples were understood to be sacred space (holy ground), the layout, features and requisite rituals of these temples were laden with symbolism connected to the attributes and provisions of the deity.

In ancient Israel, the mediation of divine presence was the driving force behind the great importance attached to the proper procedures of approaching the holy space, usage of sanctified items, and human holiness. In addition to engaging the presence of God, the temple also functioned as a place of human community through feasts and festivals. The careful attention to the design of the temple structure and the legal stipulations pertaining to entering the temple reflects the importance of properly

continued on next page

floor of Araunah[a][z] the Jebusite, the place
provided by David. [2]He began building on
the second day of the second month in the
fourth year of his reign.[a]

[3]The foundation Solomon laid for building the temple of God was sixty cubits long and twenty cubits wide[b][b] (using the cubit of the old standard). [4]The portico at the front of the temple was twenty cubits[c] long across the width of the building and twenty[d] cubits high.

3:1 [z] 2Sa 24:18; 1Ch 21:18
3:2 [a] Ezr 5:11
3:3 [b] Eze 41:2

[a] *1* Hebrew *Ornan*, a variant of *Araunah* [b] *3* That is, about 90 feet long and 30 feet wide or about 27 meters long and 9 meters wide [c] *4* That is, about 30 feet or about 9 meters; also in verses 8, 11 and 13 [d] *4* Some Septuagint and Syriac manuscripts; Hebrew *and a hundred and twenty*

dreams designating the divinely chosen location for Ningirsu's temple. Such a divinely chosen place comes to be understood as holy ground, a notion that contributes to the notion of sacred space (see the article "Temples and Sacred Space," p. 724).

3:3 *the cubit of the old standard.* The system of linear measurement used in ancient Israel was also employed in Egypt and Mesopotamia and was the result of standardizing commonly used measurements based on the length of fingers, hands (four fingers; length of the palm), and forearms (as horses are still measured in "hands" today). (See note on Ex 25:10.) The Chronicler's statement here reveals the fact that the standard of the cubit would have more than one option in the mind of his audience. While it is difficult to state unequivocally which cubit length the Chronicler had in view, the position here is that the older standard cubit was somewhat longer (about 21 inches) than the more recent standard (about 18 inches).

Using the longer cubit, Solomon's temple would have been just over 100 feet long and 32 feet wide (just over 30 meters long and 10 meters wide), not counting the portico/porch in the front of the temple (v. 4), which measured 20 by 20 cubits (35 by 35 feet or 10.5 meters by 10.5 meters). Alternatively, if the shorter cubit was in view by the Chronicler, the temple would have measured 90 feet long and 30 feet wide. By way of comparison, an NBA basketball court is 94 feet long and 50 feet wide (28.6 meters long and 15.2 meters wide), making the length of the temple quite comparable and its width narrower by 20 feet.

navigating sacred space. Such procedures and protocols functioned to establish and maintain proper boundaries between the sacred and the human realm.

The importance of maintaining boundaries for sacred space is also reflected in the use of veils, curtains and boards to separate the innermost area of the temple (cf. 2Ch 3:14). The function of these items was to provide a spatial barrier marker between the localized presence of God and humans. Moreover, such barriers served as a reminder of the necessity of approaching — and worshiping — God on his terms. Although lacking the sustained concern for divine holiness and human sinfulness, cultic documents from the ancient Near East oftentimes provided the extremely detailed procedures and rituals necessary for priests and others entering a temple complex. An Egyptian text for Theban priests, e.g., details dozens of spells to be said when lighting the fire, approaching the holy place, putting incense in a bowl, etc. — all associated with daily morning rituals at the Karnak temple during the New Kingdom. ◆

Ziggurat of Ur. The meeting place between the divine realm and the human realm was often associated with elevated structures in the ancient Near East.

Wikimedia Commons

He overlaid the inside with pure gold.
5He paneled the main hall with juniper
and covered it with fine gold and decorated it with palm tree[c] and chain designs.
6He adorned the temple with precious
stones. And the gold he used was gold of
Parvaim. 7He overlaid the ceiling beams,
doorframes, walls and doors of the temple with gold, and he carved cherubim[d]
on the walls.
8He built the Most Holy Place,[e] its
length corresponding to the width of the
temple — twenty cubits long and twenty
cubits wide. He overlaid the inside with

3:5 [c] Eze 40:16
3:7 [d] Ge 3:24; 1Ki 6:29-35; Eze 41:18
3:8 [e] Ex 26:33

3:4b *overlaid the inside with pure gold.* See note on 1Ki 6:22.
3:5 *palm tree.* A common symbol of fertility, life and agricultural bounty in the ancient Near East, given the ubiquitous date fruit. As such, palm trees are found in palace and temple wall paintings (such as the prominent palms trees in the courtyard at the Mari palace) and on inscribed reliefs, and are referenced in texts. *chain designs.* Also found on the pillar capitals (1Ki 7:17); it may signify some aspect of God's character (such as his eternality) or may simply be a common architectural motif. These chains were at the top of the pillars and were adorned with pomegranates (see note on 1Ki 7:15 – 22).
3:6 *gold of Parvaim.* The text mentions several grades of gold that increase in purity as one draws closer to the Most Holy Place. *Parvaim.* Its meaning is uncertain, but most likely refers to a location, perhaps in Arabia.
3:8 – 9 *six hundred talents of fine gold ... gold nails.* Temple building texts customarily list the various precious metals used to construct everything from gold sun disks to bronze fastening pegs. The covering of the interior of a temple in gold is attested in several ancient Near Eastern temple projects. Nebuchadnezzar II, e.g., notes that he used "shiny gold" instead of plaster in his refurbishing work on Marduk's temple. Similarly, the Assyrian king Esarhaddon notes that he covered walls and doors with gold "as if with plaster" in his restoration of Ashur's shrine. Also, the last Babylonian king, Nabonidus, covered the walls of the temple of the moon-god Sin with gold and silver, while the Egyptian pharaoh Amenhotep III (fourteenth century BC) plated parts of the temple to Amun at Thebes with gold and silver.

In this text the 600 talents used inside the Most Holy

six hundred talents[a] of fine gold. 9The
gold nails[f] weighed fifty shekels.[b] He also
overlaid the upper parts with gold.
10For the Most Holy Place he made a
pair[g] of sculptured cherubim and overlaid
them with gold. 11The total wingspan of
the cherubim was twenty cubits. One wing
of the first cherub was five cubits[c] long
and touched the temple wall, while its
other wing, also five cubits long, touched
the wing of the other cherub. 12Similarly
one wing of the second cherub was five
cubits long and touched the other temple
wall, and its other wing, also five cubits
long, touched the wing of the first cherub.
13The wings of these cherubim[h] extended
twenty cubits. They stood on their feet,
facing the main hall.[d]
14He made the curtain[i] of blue, purple
and crimson yarn and fine linen, with
cherubim[j] worked into it.
15For the front of the temple he made
two pillars,[k] which together were thirty-five cubits[e] long, each with a capital[l]
five cubits high. 16He made interwoven
chains[f][m] and put them on top of the pillars. He also made a hundred pomegranates[n] and attached them to the chains.
17He erected the pillars in the front of the
temple, one to the south and one to the
north. The one to the south he named Jakin[g] and the one to the north Boaz.[h]

3:9 [f] Ex 26:32
3:10 [g] Ex 25:18
3:13 [h] Ex 25:18
3:14 [i] Ex 26:31, 33; Heb 9:3 [j] Ge 3:24
3:15 [k] 1Ki 7:15; Rev 3:12 [l] 1Ki 7:22
3:16 [m] 1Ki 7:17 [n] 1Ki 7:20

The Temple's Furnishings

4:2-6,10 – 5:1pp — 1Ki 7:23-26,38-51

4 He made a bronze altar[o] twenty cubits
long, twenty cubits wide and ten cubits
high.[i] 2He made the Sea[p] of cast metal, circular in shape, measuring ten cubits from
rim to rim and five cubits[j] high. It took a
line of thirty cubits[k] to measure around it.
3Below the rim, figures of bulls encircled
it — ten to a cubit.[l] The bulls were cast in
two rows in one piece with the Sea.
4The Sea stood on twelve bulls, three
facing north, three facing west, three facing south and three facing east.[q] The Sea
rested on top of them, and their hind-
quarters were toward the center. 5It was
a handbreadth[m] in thickness, and its rim
was like the rim of a cup, like a lily blossom. It held three thousand baths.[n]
6He then made ten basins[r] for washing

[a] 8 That is, about 23 tons or about 21 metric tons [b] 9 That is, about 1 1/4 pounds or about 575 grams [c] 11 That is, about 7 1/2 feet or about 2.3 meters; also in verse 15 [d] 13 Or *facing inward* [e] 15 That is, about 53 feet or about 16 meters [f] 16 Or possibly *made chains in the inner sanctuary*; the meaning of the Hebrew for this phrase is uncertain. [g] 17 *Jakin* probably means *he establishes.* [h] 17 *Boaz* probably means *in him is strength.* [i] 1 That is, about 30 feet long and wide and 15 feet high or about 9 meters long and wide and 4.5 meters high [j] 2 That is, about 7 1/2 feet or about 2.3 meters [k] 2 That is, about 45 feet or about 14 meters [l] 3 That is, about 18 inches or about 45 centimeters [m] 5 That is, about 3 inches or about 7.5 centimeters [n] 5 That is, about 18,000 gallons or about 66,000 liters

4:1 [o] Ex 20:24; 27:1-2; 40:6; 1Ki 8:64; 2Ki 16:14
4:2 [p] Rev 4:6; 15:2
4:4 [q] Nu 2:3-25; Eze 48:30-34; Rev 21:13
4:6 [r] Ex 30:18

Place would be equivalent to about 23 tons (21 metric tons) of gold, while the weight of the gold "nails" or pegs (50 shekels) amounts to about 1.25 pounds (575 grams) each. While the amount of gold indicated here is significant, it is not without points of comparison to other ancient Near Eastern texts summarizing royal temple donations. The Egyptian pharaoh Thutmose III (fifteenth century BC) presented over 200 talents of gold (about 7.5 tons or 6.8 metric tons) to the Amun temple, the details of which (along with other gifts of silver and precious stones) have been inscribed on the walls of the Karnak temple in Thebes (Luxor), Egypt.

Similarly, the twelfth-century BC pharaoh Rameses III lists a wide range of gifts of gold, silver and other precious items to the temples at Thebes (including Medinet Habu, Karnak and Luxor), Heliopolis, Memphis and others. In the Theban section of his Prayer to Amun, Rameses III notes that he "filled its treasury with the products of the lands of Egypt: gold, silver [and] every costly stone by the hundred-thousand." Later, the tenth-century BC pharaoh Osorkon I enumerates gifts he provided for the various gods and goddesses of Egypt, totaling 375 tons (340 metric tons) of gold and silver (over 10,000 talents of gold and silver). Osorkon's father was Shishak, who had invaded Israel and had been paid massive amounts of gold and silver that had belonged to Solomon. Therefore, the gift Osorkon made to the gods may well have been inherited from his father, who either received it in tribute or plundered it from Solomon's successor. Finally, in Mesopotamia, the Assyrian king Sargon II (727 – 705 BC) claims to have donated 154 talents of gold (5.75 tons or 5.25 metric tons) to his gods. Thus, within this broader historical context, the 600 talents of gold recorded in Solomon's temple project should not be dismissed by a modern reader as unrealistic.

3:10 – 13 See note on 1Ki 6:23 – 28.

3:15 *two pillars, which together were thirty-five cubits.* The two pillars covered with polished bronze stationed in the front of Solomon's temple are noted as "together" totaling 35 cubits (about 53 feet or 16 meters) in height (17.5 cubits each, i.e., 26.5 feet or 8 meters). Each impressive pillar had a five-cubit (7.5-foot or 2.25-meter) capital, an ornate top that would have mostly overlapped the top portion of each pillar, creating a stylized arboreal image. The notation in the account in 1Ki 7:15 (cf. 2Ki 25:17; Jer 52:21) specifies a length of 18 cubits per pillar (36 total) versus the 35 cubits noted here (and in the Septuagint, the pre-Christian Greek translation of the OT, of Jer 52:21). The difference between the 18-cubit measurement and the 17.5-cubit measurement can be understood as related to the part of the capital extending beyond the top of the pillar (0.5 cubits per pillar). See note on 1Ki 7:15 – 22.

3:16 *interwoven chains.* See note on v. 5. *pomegranates.* See note on 1Ki 7:15 – 22.

4:2 *the Sea of cast metal.* See note on 1Ki 7:23 – 26.

4:5 *a handbreadth.* The measurement of the width of the palm (four fingers) and thus about three inches (7.5 centimeters). *three thousand baths.* The capacity (volume) of the bronze Sea is noted at 3,000 baths, which is approximately 18,000 gallons (66,000 liters), an amount comparable to a large above-ground swimming pool.

4:6 *basins.* The ten basins were mounted on wheels and adorned with various images including cherubim (see 1Ki 7:27 – 39 and note on 7:27 – 37). These basins are reminiscent of wheeled basins featuring composite creatures found in Phoenicia as well as on the island of Cyprus

DAVID AND SOLOMON'S EMPIRE

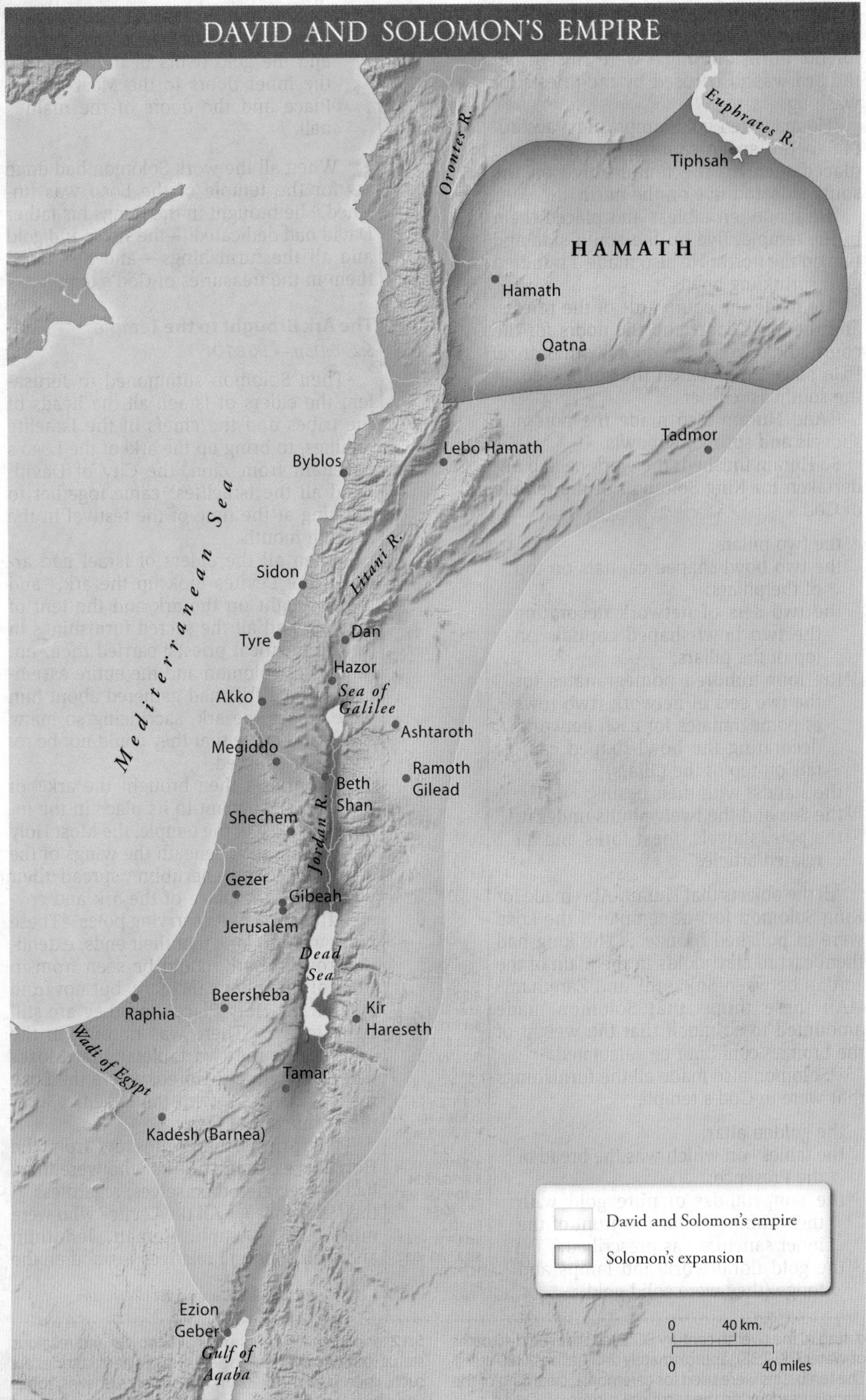
Euphrates R.
Orontes R.
Tiphsah
HAMATH
Hamath
Qatna
Tadmor
Lebo Hamath
Byblos
Mediterranean Sea
Litani R.
Sidon
Tyre
Dan
Hazor
Sea of Galilee
Akko
Ashtaroth
Megiddo
Ramoth Gilead
Beth Shan
Shechem
Jordan R.
Gezer
Gibeah
Jerusalem
Dead Sea
Raphia
Beersheba
Kir Hareseth
Wadi of Egypt
Tamar
Kadesh (Barnea)
David and Solomon's empire
Solomon's expansion
Ezion Geber
Gulf of Aqaba
0
40 km.
0
40 miles

and placed five on the south side and five
on the north. In them the things to be used
for the burnt offerings[s] were rinsed, but
the Sea was to be used by the priests for
washing.
7 He made ten gold lampstands[t] according to the specifications[u] for them and
placed them in the temple, five on the
south side and five on the north.
8 He made ten tables[v] and placed them
in the temple, five on the south side and
five on the north. He also made a hundred
gold sprinkling bowls.[w]
9 He made the courtyard[x] of the priests,
and the large court and the doors for the
court, and overlaid the doors with bronze.
10 He placed the Sea on the south side, at
the southeast corner.
11 And Huram also made the pots and
shovels and sprinkling bowls.
So Huram finished[y] the work he had undertaken for King Solomon in the temple
of God:

12 the two pillars;
the two bowl-shaped capitals on top
of the pillars;
the two sets of network decorating
the two bowl-shaped capitals on
top of the pillars;
13 the four hundred pomegranates for
the two sets of network (two rows
of pomegranates for each network,
decorating the bowl-shaped capitals on top of the pillars);
14 the stands[z] with their basins;
15 the Sea and the twelve bulls under it;
16 the pots, shovels, meat forks and all
related articles.

All the objects that Huram-Abi[a] made for
King Solomon for the temple of the LORD
were of polished bronze. 17 The king had
them cast in clay molds in the plain of the
Jordan between Sukkoth[b] and Zarethan.[a]
18 All these things that Solomon made
amounted to so much that the weight of
the bronze[c] could not be calculated.
19 Solomon also made all the furnishings
that were in God's temple:

the golden altar;
the tables[d] on which was the bread of
the Presence;
20 the lampstands[e] of pure gold with
their lamps, to burn in front of the
inner sanctuary as prescribed;
21 the gold floral work and lamps and
tongs (they were solid gold);
22 the pure gold wick trimmers, sprinkling bowls, dishes[f] and censers;[g]
and the gold doors of the temple:
the inner doors to the Most Holy
Place and the doors of the main
hall.

5 When all the work Solomon had done
for the temple of the LORD was finished,[h] he brought in the things his father
David had dedicated[i] — the silver and gold
and all the furnishings — and he placed
them in the treasuries of God's temple.

The Ark Brought to the Temple

5:2 – 6:11pp — 1Ki 8:1-21

2 Then Solomon summoned to Jerusalem the elders of Israel, all the heads of
the tribes and the chiefs of the Israelite
families, to bring up the ark[j] of the LORD's
covenant from Zion, the City of David.
3 And all the Israelites[k] came together to
the king at the time of the festival in the
seventh month.
4 When all the elders of Israel had arrived, the Levites took up the ark, 5 and
they brought up the ark and the tent of
meeting and all the sacred furnishings in
it. The Levitical priests[l] carried them up;
6 and King Solomon and the entire assembly of Israel that had gathered about him
were before the ark, sacrificing so many
sheep and cattle that they could not be recorded or counted.
7 The priests then brought the ark[m] of
the LORD's covenant to its place in the inner sanctuary of the temple, the Most Holy
Place, and put it beneath the wings of the
cherubim. 8 The cherubim[n] spread their
wings over the place of the ark and covered the ark and its carrying poles. 9 These
poles were so long that their ends, extending from the ark, could be seen from in
front of the inner sanctuary, but not from
outside the Holy Place; and they are still
there today. 10 There was nothing in the
ark except[o] the two tablets[p] that Moses
had placed in it at Horeb, where the LORD
made a covenant with the Israelites after
they came out of Egypt.
11 The priests then withdrew from the
Holy Place. All the priests who were there
had consecrated themselves, regardless of
their divisions.[q] 12 All the Levites who were
musicians[r] — Asaph, Heman, Jeduthun
and their sons and relatives — stood on the

4:6 [s] Ne 13:5,9; Eze 40:38
4:7 [t] Ex 25:31 [u] Ex 25:40
4:8 [v] Ex 25:23 [w] Nu 4:14
4:9 [x] 1Ki 6:36; 2Ki 21:5; 2Ch 33:5
4:11 [y] 1Ki 7:14
4:14 [z] 1Ki 7:27-30
4:16 [a] 1Ki 7:13
4:17 [b] Ge 33:17
4:18 [c] 1Ki 7:23
4:19 [d] Ex 25:23, 30
4:20 [e] Ex 25:31
4:22 [f] Nu 7:14 [g] Lev 10:1
5:1 [h] 1Ki 6:14 [i] 2Sa 8:11
5:2 [j] Nu 3:31; 2Sa 6:12; 1Ch 15:25
5:3 [k] 1Ch 9:1; 2Ch 7:8-10
5:5 [l] Nu 3:31; 1Ch 15:2
5:7 [m] Rev 11:19
5:8 [n] Ge 3:24
5:10 [o] Heb 9:4 [p] Ex 16:34; Dt 10:2
5:11 [q] 1Ch 24:1
5:12 [r] 1Ki 10:12; 1Ch 25:1; Ps 68:25

[a] *17* Hebrew *Zeredatha,* a variant of *Zarethan*

dating to the twelfth century BC. Each basin held 40 baths of water (1Ki 7:38), approximately 240 gallons (880 liters). The ten basins were used for ceremonial cleansing of the utensils used within the sacrificial system.

5:12 *fine linen.* A symbol of wealth, power and religious status (purity) in several ancient Near Eastern cultures. As such, linen gifts in the form of garments, shawls, robes and shoes are found in several gift lists in the Amarna

east side of the altar, dressed in fine linen
and playing cymbals, harps and lyres.
They were accompanied by 120 priests
sounding trumpets.[s] 13 The trumpeters and
musicians joined in unison to give praise
and thanks to the LORD. Accompanied by
trumpets, cymbals and other instruments,
the singers raised their voices in praise to
the LORD and sang:

"He is good;
his love endures forever."[t]

Then the temple of the LORD was filled
with the cloud, 14 and the priests could
not perform[u] their service because of the
cloud,[v] for the glory[w] of the LORD filled the
temple of God.

6 Then Solomon said, "The LORD has
said that he would dwell in a dark
cloud;[x] 2 I have built a magnificent temple
for you, a place for you to dwell forever.[y]"
3 While the whole assembly of Israel was
standing there, the king turned around
and blessed them. 4 Then he said:

"Praise be to the LORD, the God of
Israel, who with his hands has fulfilled what he promised with his
mouth to my father David. For he
said, 5 'Since the day I brought my
people out of Egypt, I have not chosen a city in any tribe of Israel to have
a temple built so that my Name might
be there, nor have I chosen anyone to
be ruler over my people Israel. 6 But
now I have chosen Jerusalem[z] for my
Name[a] to be there, and I have chosen
David[b] to rule my people Israel.'

7 "My father David had it in his
heart[c] to build a temple for the
Name of the LORD, the God of Israel.
8 But the LORD said to my father David, 'You did well to have it in your
heart to build a temple for my Name.
9 Nevertheless, you are not the one to
build the temple, but your son, your
own flesh and blood—he is the one
who will build the temple for my
Name.'

10 "The LORD has kept the promise
he made. I have succeeded David my
father and now I sit on the throne of
Israel, just as the LORD promised, and
I have built the temple for the Name
of the LORD, the God of Israel. 11 There
I have placed the ark, in which is the
covenant[d] of the LORD that he made
with the people of Israel."

5:12 [s] 1Ch 13:8; 15:24 **5:13** [t] 1Ch 16:34, 41; 2Ch 7:3; 20:21; Ezr 3:11; Ps 100:5; 136:1; Jer 33:11 **5:14** [u] Ex 40:35; Rev 15:8 [v] Ex 19:16 [w] Ex 29:43; 2Ch 7:2 **6:1** [x] Ex 19:9; 1Ki 8:12-50 **6:2** [y] Ezr 6:12; 7:15; Ps 135:21 **6:6** [z] Dt 12:5; Isa 14:1 [a] Ex 20:24; 2Ch 12:13 [b] 1Ch 28:4 **6:7** [c] 1Sa 10:7; 1Ch 17:2; 28:2; Ac 7:46 **6:11** [d] Dt 10:2; 2Ch 5:10; Ps 25:10; 50:5

6:13 [e] Ne 8:4 [f] Ps 95:6 **6:14** [g] Ex 8:10; 15:11 [h] Dt 7:9 **6:15** [i] 1Ch 22:10 **6:16** [j] 2Sa 7:13, 15; 1Ki 2:4; 2Ch 7:18; 23:3 [k] Ps 132:12 **6:18** [l] Rev 21:3 [m] 2Ch 2:6; Ps 11:4; Isa 40:22; 66:1; Ac 7:49 **6:20** [n] Ex 3:16; Ps 34:15 [o] Dt 12:11 [p] 2Ch 7:14; 30:20 **6:21** [q] Ps 51:1; Isa 33:24; 40:2; 43:25; 44:22; 55:7; Mic 7:18

Solomon's Prayer of Dedication

6:12-40pp — 1Ki 8:22-53
6:41-42pp — Ps 132:8-10

12 Then Solomon stood before the altar
of the LORD in front of the whole assembly
of Israel and spread out his hands. 13 Now
he had made a bronze platform,[e] five cubits long, five cubits wide and three cubits
high,[a] and had placed it in the center of
the outer court. He stood on the platform
and then knelt down[f] before the whole assembly of Israel and spread out his hands
toward heaven. 14 He said:

"LORD, the God of Israel, there is
no God like you[g] in heaven or on
earth—you who keep your covenant
of love[h] with your servants who continue wholeheartedly in your way.
15 You have kept your promise to your
servant David my father; with your
mouth you have promised[i] and with
your hand you have fulfilled it—as
it is today.

16 "Now, LORD, the God of Israel,
keep for your servant David my father the promises you made to him
when you said, 'You shall never fail[j]
to have a successor to sit before me
on the throne of Israel, if only your
descendants are careful in all they do
to walk before me according to my
law,[k] as you have done.' 17 And now,
LORD, the God of Israel, let your word
that you promised your servant David
come true.

18 "But will God really dwell[l] on
earth with humans? The heavens,[m]
even the highest heavens, cannot
contain you. How much less this temple I have built! 19 Yet, LORD my God,
give attention to your servant's prayer
and his plea for mercy. Hear the cry
and the prayer that your servant is
praying in your presence. 20 May your
eyes[n] be open toward this temple day
and night, this place of which you
said you would put your Name[o] there.
May you hear[p] the prayer your servant prays toward this place. 21 Hear
the supplications of your servant and
of your people Israel when they pray
toward this place. Hear from heaven,
your dwelling place; and when you
hear, forgive.[q]

[a] *13* That is, about 7 1/2 feet long and wide and 4 1/2 feet high or about 2.3 meters long and wide and 1.4 meters high

letters, such as the gifts exchanged between the queens of Egypt and Hatti. Similarly, the eleventh-century BC (Egyptian New Kingdom) report of Wenamun's trip from Egypt to Phoenicia speaks of an array of linen products produced in Egypt that Wenamun was able to trade for timber, suggesting the value of linen at this time. See note on Ex 39:27. *cymbals, harps and lyres.* See the articles "Lyre," p. 488; "Music and Musicians," p. 524.

22 “When anyone wrongs their neighbor and is required to take an oath[r] and they come and swear the oath before your altar in this temple, 23 then hear from heaven and act. Judge between your servants, condemning[s] the guilty and bringing down on their heads what they have done, and vindicating the innocent by treating them in accordance with their innocence.

24 “When your people Israel have been defeated[t] by an enemy because they have sinned against you and when they turn back and give praise to your name, praying and making supplication before you in this temple, 25 then hear from heaven and forgive the sin of your people Israel and bring them back to the land you gave to them and their ancestors.

26 “When the heavens are shut up and there is no rain[u] because your people have sinned against you, and when they pray toward this place and give praise to your name and turn from their sin because you have afflicted them, 27 then hear from heaven and forgive[v] the sin of your servants, your people Israel. Teach them the right way to live, and send rain on the land you gave your people for an inheritance.

28 “When famine[w] or plague comes to the land, or blight or mildew, locusts or grasshoppers, or when enemies besiege them in any of their cities, whatever disaster or disease may come, 29 and when a prayer or plea is made by anyone among your people Israel—being aware of their afflictions and pains, and spreading out their hands toward this temple—30 then hear from heaven, your dwelling place. Forgive,[x] and deal with everyone according to all they do, since you know their hearts (for you alone know the human heart),[y] 31 so that they will fear you[z] and walk in obedience to you all the time they live in the land you gave our ancestors.

32 “As for the foreigner who does not belong to your people Israel but has come[a] from a distant land because of your great name and your mighty hand[b] and your outstretched arm—when they come and pray toward this temple, 33 then hear from heaven, your dwelling place. Do whatever the foreigner[c] asks of you, so that all the peoples of the earth may know your name and fear you, as do your own people Israel, and may know that this house I have built bears your Name.

34 “When your people go to war against their enemies,[d] wherever you send them, and when they pray[e] to you toward this city you have chosen and the temple I have built for your Name, 35 then hear from heaven their prayer and their plea, and uphold their cause.

36 “When they sin against you—for there is no one who does not sin[f]—and you become angry with them and give them over to the enemy, who takes them captive[g] to a land far away or near; 37 and if they have a change of heart[h] in the land where they are held captive, and repent and plead with you in the land of their captivity and say, ‘We have sinned, we have done wrong and acted wickedly’; 38 and if they turn back to you with all their heart and soul in the land of their captivity where they were taken, and pray toward the land you gave their ancestors, toward the city you have chosen and toward the temple I have built for your Name; 39 then from heaven, your dwelling place, hear their prayer and their pleas, and uphold their cause. And forgive your people, who have sinned against you.

40 “Now, my God, may your eyes be open and your ears attentive[i] to the prayers offered in this place.

41 “Now arise,[j] LORD God, and come
to your resting place,[k]
you and the ark of your might.
May your priests,[l] LORD God, be
clothed with salvation,
may your faithful people rejoice
in your goodness.[m]
42 LORD God, do not reject your
anointed one.
Remember the great love[n]
promised to David your
servant.”

The Dedication of the Temple

7:1-10pp — 1Ki 8:62-66

7 When Solomon finished praying, fire[o] came down from heaven and consumed the burnt offering and the sacrifices, and the glory of the LORD filled[p] the temple.[q] 2 The priests could not enter[r] the temple of the LORD because the glory[s] of the LORD filled it. 3 When all the Israelites saw the fire coming down and the

6:22 [r] Ex 22:11 **6:23** [s] Isa 3:11; 65:6; Mt 16:27 **6:24** [t] Lev 26:17 **6:26** [u] Lev 26:19; Dt 11:17; 28:24; 2Sa 1:21; 1Ki 17:1 **6:27** [v] ver 30, 39; 2Ch 7:14 **6:28** [w] 2Ch 20:9 **6:30** [x] ver 27 [y] 1Sa 16:7; 1Ch 28:9; Ps 7:9; 44:21; Pr 16:2; 17:3 **6:31** [z] Ps 103:11, 13; Pr 8:13 **6:32** [a] 2Ch 9:6; Jn 12:20; Ac 8:27 [b] Ex 3:19, 20 **6:33** [c] 2Ch 7:14

6:34 [d] Dt 28:7 [e] 1Ch 5:20 **6:36** [f] Job 15:14; Ps 143:2; Ecc 7:20; Jer 17:9; Jas 3:1; 1Jn 1:8-10 [g] Lev 26:44 **6:37** [h] 2Ch 7:14; 33:12, 19, 23; Jer 29:13 **6:40** [i] 2Ch 7:15; Ne 1:6, 11; Ps 17:1, 6 **6:41** [j] Isa 33:10 [k] 1Ch 28:2 [l] Ps 132:16 [m] Ps 116:12 **6:42** [n] Ps 89:24, 28; Isa 55:3 **7:1** [o] Lev 9:24; 1Ki 18:38 [p] Ex 16:10 [q] Ps 26:8 **7:2** [r] 1Ki 8:11 [s] Ex 29:43; 40:35; 2Ch 5:14

7:1 *fire came down from heaven.* See note on 1Ki 18:38.

glory of the LORD above the temple, they
knelt on the pavement with their faces to
the ground, and they worshiped and gave
thanks to the LORD, saying,

“He is good;
his love endures forever.”[t]

4 Then the king and all the people offered
sacrifices before the LORD. 5 And King Solomon offered a sacrifice of twenty-two
thousand head of cattle and a hundred
and twenty thousand sheep and goats. So
the king and all the people dedicated the
temple of God. 6 The priests took their positions, as did the Levites[u] with the LORD’s
musical instruments,[v] which King David
had made for praising the LORD and which
were used when he gave thanks, saying,
“His love endures forever.” Opposite the
Levites, the priests blew their trumpets,
and all the Israelites were standing.
7 Solomon consecrated the middle part
of the courtyard in front of the temple of
the LORD, and there he offered burnt offerings and the fat of the fellowship offerings, because the bronze altar he had
made could not hold the burnt offerings,
the grain offerings and the fat portions.
8 So Solomon observed the festival[w] at
that time for seven days, and all Israel
with him — a vast assembly, people from
Lebo Hamath to the Wadi of Egypt.[x] 9 On
the eighth day they held an assembly, for
they had celebrated the dedication of the
altar for seven days and the festival[y] for
seven days more. 10 On the twenty-third
day of the seventh month he sent the people to their homes, joyful and glad in heart
for the good things the LORD had done for
David and Solomon and for his people Israel.

The LORD Appears to Solomon

7:11-22pp — 1Ki 9:1-9

11 When Solomon had finished the temple of the LORD and the royal palace, and
had succeeded in carrying out all he had
in mind to do in the temple of the LORD
and in his own palace, 12 the LORD appeared to him at night and said:

“I have heard your prayer and have
chosen this place for myself[z] as a
temple for sacrifices.
13 “When I shut up the heavens so
that there is no rain,[a] or command
locusts to devour the land or send a
plague among my people, 14 if my people, who are called by my name, will
humble[b] themselves and pray and
seek my face[c] and turn[d] from their
wicked ways, then I will hear from
heaven, and I will forgive[e] their sin
and will heal[f] their land. 15 Now my
eyes will be open and my ears attentive to the prayers offered in this
place.[g] 16 I have chosen[h] and consecrated this temple so that my Name
may be there forever. My eyes and my
heart will always be there.
17 “As for you, if you walk before
me faithfully[i] as David your father
did, and do all I command, and observe my decrees and laws, 18 I will
establish your royal throne, as I covenanted with David your father when
I said, ‘You shall never fail to have a
successor[j] to rule over Israel.’[k]
19 “But if you[a] turn away[l] and forsake[m] the decrees and commands I
have given you[a] and go off to serve
other gods and worship them, 20 then
I will uproot[n] Israel from my land,[o]
which I have given them, and will
reject this temple I have consecrated
for my Name. I will make it a byword
and an object of ridicule[p] among all
peoples. 21 This temple will become a
heap of rubble. All[b] who pass by will
be appalled and say,[q] ‘Why has the
LORD done such a thing to this land
and to this temple?’ 22 People will
answer, ‘Because they have forsak-
en the LORD, the God of their ancestors, who brought them out of Egypt,
and have embraced other gods, worshiping and serving them — that is
why he brought all this disaster on
them.’ ”

7:3 [t] 1Ch 16:34; 2Ch 5:13; 20:21 **7:6** [u] 1Ch 15:16 [v] 2Ch 5:12 **7:8** [w] 2Ch 30:26 [x] Ge 15:18 **7:9** [y] Lev 23:36 **7:12** [z] Dt 12:5 **7:13** [a] 2Ch 6:26-28; Am 4:7 **7:14** [b] Lev 26:41; 2Ch 6:37; Jas 4:10 [c] 1Ch 16:11 [d] Isa 55:7; Zec 1:4 [e] 2Ch 6:27 [f] 2Ch 30:20; Isa 30:26; 57:18 **7:15** [g] 2Ch 6:40 **7:16** [h] ver 12; 2Ch 6:6 **7:17** [i] 1Ki 9:4 **7:18** [j] 2Ch 6:16 [k] 2Sa 7:13; 2Ch 13:5 **7:19** [l] Dt 28:15 [m] Lev 26:14,33 **7:20** [n] Dt 29:28 [o] 1Ki 14:15 [p] Dt 28:37 **7:21** [q] Dt 29:24 **8:5** [r] 1Ch 7:24; 2Ch 14:7

Solomon’s Other Activities

8:1-18pp — 1Ki 9:10-28

8 At the end of twenty years, during
which Solomon built the temple of
the LORD and his own palace, 2 Solomon
rebuilt the villages that Hiram[c] had given
him, and settled Israelites in them. 3 Solomon then went to Hamath Zobah and captured it. 4 He also built up Tadmor in the
desert and all the store cities he had built
in Hamath. 5 He rebuilt Upper Beth Horon[r]
and Lower Beth Horon as fortified cities,

[a] *19* The Hebrew is plural. [b] *21* See some Septuagint manuscripts, Old Latin, Syriac, Arabic and Targum; Hebrew *And though this temple is now so imposing, all* [c] *2* Hebrew *Huram,* a variant of *Hiram;* also in verse 18

8:2 *Solomon rebuilt the villages that Hiram had given him.* The relationship between this verse and 1Ki 9:10–14 (where Solomon is described as giving Hiram 20 cities in the region of Galilee) is uncertain. One possibility is that the land was given to Hiram as collateral during the massive flow of Phoenician supplies and workmanship into Israel (1Ki 9:10–14), with the return of this land taking place following the settling of debts (see notes on 2:3,10).

with walls and with gates and bars, 6as well as Baalath and all his store cities, and all the cities for his chariots and for his horses[a]—whatever he desired to build in Jerusalem, in Lebanon and throughout all the territory he ruled.

7There were still people left from the Hittites, Amorites, Perizzites, Hivites and Jebusites[s] (these people were not Israelites). 8Solomon conscripted[t] the descendants of all these people remaining in the land—whom the Israelites had not destroyed—to serve as slave labor, as it is to this day. 9But Solomon did not make slaves of the Israelites for his work; they were his fighting men, commanders of his captains, and commanders of his chariots and charioteers. 10They were also King Solomon's chief officials—two hundred and fifty officials supervising the men.

11Solomon brought Pharaoh's daughter[u] up from the City of David to the palace he had built for her, for he said, "My wife must not live in the palace of David king of Israel, because the places the ark of the LORD has entered are holy."

12On the altar[v] of the LORD that he had built in front of the portico, Solomon sacrificed burnt offerings to the LORD, 13according to the daily requirement[w] for offerings commanded by Moses for the Sabbaths,[x] the New Moons and the three[y] annual festivals—the Festival of Unleavened Bread, the Festival of Weeks[z] and the Festival of Tabernacles. 14In keeping with the ordinance of his father David, he appointed the divisions[a] of the priests for their duties, and the Levites[b] to lead the praise and to assist the priests according to each day's requirement. He also appointed the gatekeepers[c] by divisions for the various gates, because this was what David the man of God[d] had ordered.[e] 15They did not deviate from the king's commands to the priests or to the Levites in any matter, including that of the treasuries.

16All Solomon's work was carried out, from the day the foundation of the temple of the LORD was laid until its completion. So the temple of the LORD was finished.

17Then Solomon went to Ezion Geber and Elath on the coast of Edom. 18And Hiram sent him ships commanded by his own men, sailors who knew the sea. These, with Solomon's men, sailed to Ophir and brought back four hundred and fifty talents[b] of gold,[f] which they delivered to King Solomon.

The Queen of Sheba Visits Solomon

9:1-12pp — 1Ki 10:1-13

9 When the queen of Sheba[g] heard of Solomon's fame, she came to Jerusalem to test him with hard questions. Arriving with a very great caravan—with camels carrying spices, large quantities of gold, and precious stones—she came to Solomon and talked with him about all she had on her mind. 2Solomon answered all her questions; nothing was too hard for him to explain to her. 3When the queen of Sheba saw the wisdom of Solomon,[h] as well as the palace he had built, 4the food on his table, the seating of his officials, the attending servants in their robes, the cupbearers in their robes and the burnt offer-

[a] 6 Or *charioteers*   [b] 18 That is, about 17 tons or about 15 metric tons

8:7 [s] Ge 10:16 **8:8** [t] 1Ki 4:6; 9:21 **8:11** [u] 1Ki 3:1; 7:8 **8:12** [v] 1Ki 8:64; 2Ch 4:1; 15:8 **8:13** [w] Ex 29:38; Nu 28:3 [x] Nu 28:9 [y] Ex 23:14; Dt 16:16 [z] Ex 23:16 **8:14** [a] 1Ch 24:1 [b] 1Ch 25:1 [c] 1Ch 9:17; 26:1 [d] Ne 12:24, 36 [e] 1Ch 23:6; Ne 12:45 **8:18** [f] 2Ch 9:9 **9:1** [g] Ge 10:7; Eze 23:42; Mt 12:42; Lk 11:31 **9:3** [h] 1Ki 5:12

8:6 *store cities, and all the cities for his chariots and for his horses.* See note on 1Ki 9:19.

8:11 *brought Pharaoh's daughter … to the palace he had built for her.* See note on 1Ki 3:1.

8:18 *ships … sailors.* Solomon's arrangements with Phoenicia extended into maritime trade, with the Phoenicians supplying both ships and experienced sailors. The Phoenicians were noted sailors in the ancient world and built on the accomplishments of earlier merchants such as those of the northern Syrian port city of Ugarit. The Egyptian language even came to include the term "Byblos Ship" to denote high quality vessels from Phoenicia. A painting in the tomb of Qenamon/Kenamon at Thebes (c. 1400 BC) depicts what might be Phoenician ships unloading cargo at an Egyptian port. In addition, an eighth/seventh-century BC Hebrew seal shows a clear image of a sailing ship, perhaps of the Phoenician type utilized by Solomon; this reflects a functioning maritime economy in ancient Israel. Such trading vessels typically ranged from 40 to 80 feet (12 to 24 meters) in length and were powered by sails (single mast) and oars. Commercial shipping was attested in the ancient Near East from at least as early as the third millennium BC, including the shipping routes from along the Mediterranean coast between Egypt and ports in Phoenicia (e.g., Byblos, Tyre, Sidon), Syria (e.g., Ugarit) and beyond, as well as routes from Egypt to Africa (e.g., Punt) and Arabia. The description of these ships as "ships that could go to Tarshish" (see NIV text note on 9:21) together with their three-year trading journey (9:21) implies that these ships could manage the high seas and undertake long-distance sea travel, although most travel was within sight of land (see note on 1Ki 10:22). Note that a three-year sea journey is also the length of time recorded for a trip circumnavigating Africa during the reign of pharaoh Necho II (seventh century BC) as recorded in Herodotus 4.42. In addition to the exchange of normal trade items such as regional agricultural products, metals and timber, such maritime journeys also featured the acquisition of exotic cargo (note the "apes and baboons," 2Ch 9:21), reflecting the penchant of ancient Near Eastern monarchs for unusual items. Rulers often boasted about their collections of exotic animals (such as two-humped camels, "river oxen," antelopes, elephants, baboons and peacocks) and even dancing pygmies. These exotic items were depicted in scenes inscribed on the walls of the temples (such as Deir el-Bahri in Egypt) and woven into literature (such as the Story of the Shipwrecked Sailor). *Ophir.* See note 1Ki 9:28.

9:1 *queen of Sheba.* See note on 1Ki 10:1.

9:3 *wisdom.* See note on 1:10.

9:4 *food on his table.* See note on 1Ki 10:5.

ings he made at[a] the temple of the LORD,
she was overwhelmed.
5She said to the king, "The report I
heard in my own country about your
achievements and your wisdom is true.
6But I did not believe what they said until
I came[i] and saw with my own eyes. Indeed, not even half the greatness of your
wisdom was told me; you have far exceeded the report I heard. 7How happy your
people must be! How happy your officials, who continually stand before you
and hear your wisdom! 8Praise be to the
LORD your God, who has delighted in you
and placed you on his throne[j] as king to
rule for the LORD your God. Because of the
love of your God for Israel and his desire
to uphold them forever, he has made you
king[k] over them, to maintain justice and
righteousness."
9Then she gave the king 120 talents[b] of
gold,[l] large quantities of spices, and precious stones. There had never been such
spices as those the queen of Sheba gave to
King Solomon.
10(The servants of Hiram and the servants of Solomon brought gold from
Ophir;[m] they also brought algumwood[c]
and precious stones. 11The king used the
algumwood to make steps for the temple
of the LORD and for the royal palace, and
to make harps and lyres for the musicians.
Nothing like them had ever been seen in
Judah.)
12King Solomon gave the queen of Sheba all she desired and asked for; he gave
her more than she had brought to him.
Then she left and returned with her retinue to her own country.

Solomon's Splendor

9:13-28pp — 1Ki 10:14-29; 2Ch 1:14-17

13The weight of the gold that Solomon
received yearly was 666 talents,[d] 14not including the revenues brought in by merchants and traders. Also all the kings of
Arabia[n] and the governors of the territories brought gold and silver to Solomon.
15King Solomon made two hundred
large shields of hammered gold; six hundred shekels[e] of hammered gold went into
each shield. 16He also made three hundred
small shields[o] of hammered gold, with
three hundred shekels[f] of gold in each
shield. The king put them in the Palace of
the Forest of Lebanon.[p]
17Then the king made a great throne
covered with ivory[q] and overlaid with
pure gold. 18The throne had six steps,
and a footstool of gold was attached to it.
On both sides of the seat were armrests,
with a lion standing beside each of them.
19Twelve lions stood on the six steps, one
at either end of each step. Nothing like it
had ever been made for any other kingdom. 20All King Solomon's goblets were
gold, and all the household articles in the
Palace of the Forest of Lebanon were pure
gold. Nothing was made of silver, because
silver was considered of little value in Solomon's day. 21The king had a fleet of trading ships[g] manned by Hiram's[h] servants.
Once every three years it returned, carrying gold, silver and ivory, and apes and
baboons.
22King Solomon was greater in riches and wisdom than all the other kings
of the earth.[r] 23All the kings[s] of the earth
sought audience with Solomon to hear the
wisdom God had put in his heart. 24Year
after year, everyone who came brought
a gift[t] — articles of silver and gold, and
robes, weapons and spices, and horses
and mules.
25Solomon had four thousand stalls for
horses and chariots,[u] and twelve thousand
horses,[i] which he kept in the chariot cities and also with him in Jerusalem. 26He
ruled[v] over all the kings from the Euphrates River[w] to the land of the Philistines,
as far as the border of Egypt.[x] 27The king
made silver as common in Jerusalem as

9:6 [i] 2Ch 6:32
9:8 [j] 1Ki 2:12; 1Ch 17:14; 28:5; 29:23; 2Ch 13:8 [k] 2Ch 2:11
9:9 [l] 2Ch 8:18
9:10 [m] 2Ch 8:18
9:14 [n] 2Ch 17:11; Isa 21:13; Jer 25:24; Eze 27:21; 30:5
9:16 [o] 2Ch 12:9 [p] 1Ki 7:2
9:17 [q] 1Ki 22:39
9:22 [r] 1Ki 3:13; 2Ch 1:12
9:23 [s] 1Ki 4:34
9:24 [t] 2Ch 32:23; Ps 45:12; 68:29; 72:10; Isa 18:7
9:25 [u] 1Sa 8:11; 1Ki 4:26
9:26 [v] 1Ki 4:21 [w] Ps 72:8-9 [x] Ge 15:18-21

[a] 4 Or *and the ascent by which he went up to*
[b] 9 That is, about 4 1/2 tons or about 4 metric tons
[c] 10 Probably a variant of *almugwood*
[d] 13 That is, about 25 tons or about 23 metric tons
[e] 15 That is, about 15 pounds or about 6.9 kilograms
[f] 16 That is, about 7 1/2 pounds or about 3.5 kilograms
[g] 21 Hebrew *of ships that could go to Tarshish*
[h] 21 Hebrew *Huram*, a variant of *Hiram*
[i] 25 Or *charioteers*

9:9 *120 talents of gold.* A talent was about 75 pounds, meaning Sheba's gift was about 4.5 tons (4 metric tons) of gold. It is possible that this large gift was part of a broader commercial trading agreement negotiated between Solomon and the queen of Sheba (see note on 1Ki 10:1).
9:10 *gold from Ophir.* See note on 1Ki 9:28.
9:13 *gold ... received yearly was 666 talents.* See note on 1Ki 10:14.
9:15 *shields of hammered gold.* See note on 1Ki 10:16.
9:16 *Palace of the Forest of Lebanon.* This palace is given further description in 1Ki 7 (see notes on 1Ki 7:2,6) and probably derives its name from its dozens of cedar pillars inside (which would have a tree-like appearance) along with the cedar paneling on the walls and cedar beams on the ceiling. This palace may have functioned as an alternate residence for the king, as well as a more convenient place to meet trading partners and dignitaries from the north.
9:17 – 19 See note on 1Ki 10:18 – 20.
9:21 *trading ships.* See notes on 8:18; 1Ki 10:22.
9:22,23 *wisdom.* See note on 1:10.
9:25 *four thousand stalls for horses and chariots.* See note on 1Ki 4:26.
9:27 *silver as common in Jerusalem as stones.* See note on 1Ki 10:27. *cedar.* See notes on 2Sa 5:11; 1Ki 5:6; 6:15.

stones, and cedar as plentiful as sycamore-fig trees in the foothills. 28 Solomon's horses were imported from Egypt and from all other countries.

Solomon's Death

9:29-31pp — 1Ki 11:41-43

29 As for the other events of Solomon's reign, from beginning to end, are they not written in the records of Nathan[y] the prophet, in the prophecy of Ahijah[z] the Shilonite and in the visions of Iddo the seer concerning Jeroboam[a] son of Nebat? 30 Solomon reigned in Jerusalem over all Israel forty years. 31 Then he rested with his ancestors and was buried in the city of David[b] his father. And Rehoboam his son succeeded him as king.

Israel Rebels Against Rehoboam

10:1 – 11:4pp — 1Ki 12:1-24

10 Rehoboam went to Shechem, for all Israel had gone there to make him king. 2 When Jeroboam[c] son of Nebat heard this (he was in Egypt, where he had fled[d] from King Solomon), he returned from Egypt. 3 So they sent for Jeroboam, and he and all Israel[e] went to Rehoboam and said to him: 4 "Your father put a heavy yoke on us,[f] but now lighten the harsh labor and the heavy yoke he put on us, and we will serve you."

5 Rehoboam answered, "Come back to me in three days." So the people went away.

6 Then King Rehoboam consulted the elders[g] who had served his father Solomon during his lifetime. "How would you advise me to answer these people?" he asked.

7 They replied, "If you will be kind to these people and please them and give them a favorable answer,[h] they will always be your servants."

8 But Rehoboam rejected[i] the advice the elders[j] gave him and consulted the young men who had grown up with him and were serving him. 9 He asked them, "What is your advice? How should we answer these people who say to me, 'Lighten the yoke your father put on us'?"

10 The young men who had grown up with him replied, "The people have said to you, 'Your father put a heavy yoke on us, but make our yoke lighter.' Now tell them, 'My little finger is thicker than my father's waist. 11 My father laid on you a heavy yoke; I will make it even heavier. My father scourged you with whips; I will scourge you with scorpions.' "

12 Three days later Jeroboam and all the people returned to Rehoboam, as the king had said, "Come back to me in three days." 13 The king answered them harshly. Rejecting the advice of the elders, 14 he followed the advice of the young men and said, "My father made your yoke heavy; I will make it even heavier. My father scourged you with whips; I will scourge you with scorpions." 15 So the king did not listen to the people, for this turn of events was from God,[k] to fulfill the word the LORD had spoken to Jeroboam son of Nebat through Ahijah the Shilonite.[l]

16 When all Israel[m] saw that the king refused to listen to them, they answered the king:

"What share do we have in David,[n]
  what part in Jesse's son?
To your tents, Israel!
  Look after your own house, David!"

So all the Israelites went home. 17 But as for the Israelites who were living in the towns of Judah, Rehoboam still ruled over them.

18 King Rehoboam sent out Adoniram,[a][o] who was in charge of forced labor, but the Israelites stoned him to death. King Rehoboam, however, managed to get into his chariot and escape to Jerusalem. 19 So Israel has been in rebellion against the house of David to this day.

11 When Rehoboam arrived in Jerusalem,[p] he mustered Judah and Benjamin — a hundred and eighty thousand able young men — to go to war against Israel and to regain the kingdom for Rehoboam.

2 But this word of the LORD came to Shemaiah[q] the man of God: 3 "Say to Rehoboam son of Solomon king of Judah and to all Israel in Judah and Benjamin, 4 'This is what the LORD says: Do not go up to fight against your fellow Israelites.[r] Go home, every one of you, for this is my doing.' " So they obeyed the words of the LORD and turned back from marching against Jeroboam.

Rehoboam Fortifies Judah

5 Rehoboam lived in Jerusalem and built up towns for defense in Judah: 6 Bethlehem, Etam, Tekoa, 7 Beth Zur, Soko, Adul-

9:29 [y] 2Sa 7:2; 1Ch 29:29 [z] 1Ki 11:29 [a] 2Ch 10:2 **9:31** [b] 1Ki 2:10 **10:2** [c] 2Ch 9:29 [d] 1Ki 11:40 **10:3** [e] 1Ch 9:1 **10:4** [f] 2Ch 2:2 **10:6** [g] Job 8:8-9; 12:12; 15:10; 32:7 **10:7** [h] Pr 15:1 **10:8** [i] 2Sa 17:14 [j] Pr 13:20 **10:15** [k] 2Ch 11:4; 25:16-20 [l] 1Ki 11:29 **10:16** [m] 1Ch 9:1 [n] ver 19; 2Sa 20:1 **10:18** [o] 1Ki 5:14 **11:1** [p] 1Ki 12:21 **11:2** [q] 2Ch 12:5-7,15 **11:4** [r] 2Ch 28:8-11

[a] 18 Hebrew *Hadoram,* a variant of *Adoniram*

9:28 *horses were imported from Egypt.* See note on 1Ki 10:28–29; see also the article "All the King's Horses," p. 720.
10:4 *harsh labor.* See note on 1Ki 12:4.
10:11 *scorpions.* See note on 1Ki 12:11.
10:16 *What share do we have in David … Look after your own house, David!* See note on 1Ki 12:16.
11:1 *a hundred and eighty thousand.* See the article "Numbers in Numbers," p. 235.
11:5 – 12 Rehoboam's fortified cities address the strategic threats to Judah following the division of the kingdom, including the erstwhile foes to the east (Moab, Ammon, Edom), the perennial enemy to the west (Philistines), and

lam, 8Gath, Mareshah, Ziph, 9Adoraim, Lachish, Azekah, 10Zorah, Aijalon and Hebron. These were fortified cities in Judah and Benjamin. 11He strengthened their defenses and put commanders in them, with supplies of food, olive oil and wine. 12He put shields and spears in all the cities, and made them very strong. So Judah and Benjamin were his.

13The priests and Levites from all their districts throughout Israel sided with him. 14The Levites[s] even abandoned their pasturelands and property[t] and came to Judah and Jerusalem, because Jeroboam and his sons had rejected them as priests of the LORD 15when he appointed[u] his own priests[v] for the high places and for the goat[w] and calf[x] idols he had made. 16Those from every tribe of Israel[y] who set their hearts on seeking the LORD, the God of Israel, followed the Levites to Jerusalem to offer sacrifices to the LORD, the God of their ancestors. 17They strengthened[z] the kingdom of Judah and supported Rehoboam son of Solomon three years, following the ways of David and Solomon during this time.

Rehoboam's Family

18Rehoboam married Mahalath, who was the daughter of David's son Jerimoth and of Abihail, the daughter of Jesse's son Eliab. 19She bore him sons: Jeush, Shemariah and Zaham. 20Then he married Maakah[a] daughter of Absalom, who bore him Abijah,[b] Attai, Ziza and Shelomith. 21Rehoboam loved Maakah daughter of Absalom more than any of his other wives and concubines. In all, he had eighteen wives[c] and sixty concubines, twenty-eight sons and sixty daughters.

22Rehoboam appointed Abijah[d] son of Maakah as crown prince among his brothers, in order to make him king. 23He acted wisely, dispersing some of his sons throughout the districts of Judah and Benjamin, and to all the fortified cities. He gave them abundant provisions and took many wives for them.

Shishak Attacks Jerusalem

12:9-16pp — 1Ki 14:21,25-31

12 After Rehoboam's position as king was established[e] and he had become strong,[f] he and all Israel[a] with him abandoned the law of the LORD. 2Because they had been unfaithful[g] to the LORD, Shishak[h] king of Egypt attacked Jerusalem in the fifth year of King Rehoboam. 3With twelve hundred chariots and sixty thousand horsemen and the innumerable troops of Libyans, Sukkites and Cushites[b][i] that came with him from Egypt, 4he captured the fortified cities[j] of Judah and came as far as Jerusalem.

5Then the prophet Shemaiah[k] came to Rehoboam and to the leaders of Judah who had assembled in Jerusalem for fear of Shishak, and he said to them, "This is what the LORD says, 'You have abandoned me; therefore, I now abandon[l] you to Shishak.' "

6The leaders of Israel and the king humbled themselves and said, "The LORD is just."[m]

7When the LORD saw that they humbled themselves, this word of the LORD came to Shemaiah: "Since they have humbled themselves, I will not destroy them but will soon give them deliverance.[n] My wrath will not be poured out on Jerusalem through Shishak. 8They will, however, become subject[o] to him, so that they may learn the difference between serving me and serving the kings of other lands."

9When Shishak king of Egypt attacked Jerusalem, he carried off the treasures of the temple of the LORD and the treasures of the royal palace. He took everything, including the gold shields[p] Solomon had made. 10So King Rehoboam made bronze shields to replace them and assigned these to the commanders of the guard on duty at the entrance to the royal palace. 11Whenever the king went to the LORD's temple, the guards went with him, bearing the shields, and afterward they returned them to the guardroom.

12Because Rehoboam humbled himself, the LORD's anger turned from him, and he was not totally destroyed. Indeed, there was some good[q] in Judah.

13King Rehoboam established himself firmly in Jerusalem and continued as king. He was forty-one years old when he became king, and he reigned seventeen years in Jerusalem, the city the LORD had chosen out of all the tribes of Israel in which

11:14 [s] Nu 35:2-5 [t] 2Ch 13:9
11:15 [u] 1Ki 13:33 [v] 1Ki 12:31 [w] Lev 17:7 [x] 1Ki 12:28; 2Ch 13:8
11:16 [y] 2Ch 15:9
11:17 [z] 2Ch 12:1
11:20 [a] 1Ki 15:2 [b] 2Ch 13:2
11:21 [c] Dt 17:17
11:22 [d] Dt 21:15-17
12:1 [e] ver 13 [f] 2Ch 11:17
12:2 [g] 1Ki 14:22-24 [h] 1Ki 11:40
12:3 [i] 2Ch 16:8; Na 3:9
12:4 [j] 2Ch 11:10
12:5 [k] 2Ch 11:2 [l] Dt 28:15; 2Ch 15:2
12:6 [m] Ex 9:27; Da 9:14
12:7 [n] 1Ki 21:29; Ps 78:38
12:8 [o] Dt 28:48
12:9 [p] 2Ch 9:16
12:12 [q] 1Ki 14:13; 2Ch 19:3

[a] *1* That is, Judah, as frequently in 2 Chronicles
[b] *3* That is, people from the upper Nile region

the threat of Egypt to the south. All told, the focal point is the defense of access points to Jerusalem.

11:15 *goat ... idols.* Their significance is uncertain, but they may be a representation of satyr-like demons understood to traverse deserted wastelands. Alternatively, gold and silver statues of goats from Ur may imply a possible connection with the tree of life and/or Asherah, as these statues portray the goats standing upright with their forelegs fastened to a tree. *calf idols.* See note on 1Ki 12:28.

12:2 *Shishak king of Egypt attacked.* See note on 1Ki 14:25.

12:3 *Libyans, Sukkites and Cushites.* See note on 1Ki 14:25.

12:13 *His mother's name was Naamah ... an Ammonite.* See note on 1Ki 2:19.

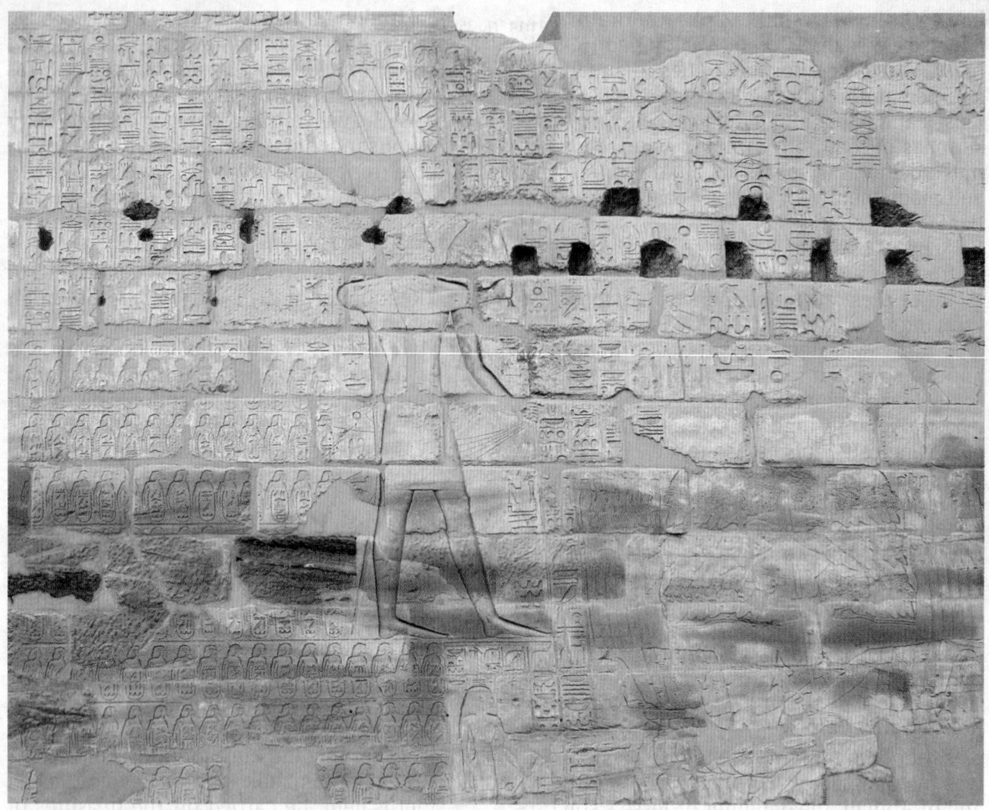

Cartouches (oblong hieroglyphs of conquered towns) along the wall of the Karnak temple describe Shishak's military campaign in Canaan. Shishak's attack on Jerusalem is recorded in 2Ch 12:2 – 4.

to put his Name.[r] His mother's name was
Naamah; she was an Ammonite. 14He did
evil because he had not set his heart on
seeking the LORD.
15As for the events of Rehoboam's
reign, from beginning to end, are they
not written in the records of Shemaiah[s]
the prophet and of Iddo the seer that deal
with genealogies? There was continual
warfare between Rehoboam and Jeroboam. 16Rehoboam rested with his ancestors and was buried in the City of David.
And Abijah[t] his son succeeded him as
king.

12:13 [r]Dt 12:5; 2Ch 6:6
12:15 [s]2Ch 9:29; 11:2
12:16 [t]2Ch 11:20

Abijah King of Judah

13:1-2,22 – 14:1pp — 1Ki 15:1-2,6-8

13 In the eighteenth year of the reign
of Jeroboam, Abijah became king
of Judah, 2and he reigned in Jerusalem
three years. His mother's name was Maakah,[a] a daughter[b] of Uriel of Gibeah.
There was war between Abijah[u] and
Jeroboam.[v] 3Abijah went into battle with
an army of four hundred thousand able

13:2 [u]2Ch 11:20 [v]1Ki 15:6

[a] 2 Most Septuagint manuscripts and Syriac (see also 11:20 and 1 Kings 15:2); Hebrew *Micaiah*
[b] 2 Or *granddaughter*

12:15 *continual warfare between Rehoboam and Jeroboam.* On top of the losses inflicted by Pharaoh Shishak, the northern kingdom and southern kingdom engaged in prolonged strife and conflict. Much of the warfare between Rehoboam and Jeroboam consisted of a back-and-forth battle for Benjamin (particularly the central Benjamin plateau), the strategic tribal area just to the north of Jerusalem.
13:2 *war between Abijah and Jeroboam.* The conflict that began between Jeroboam and Rehoboam (12:15) continued into the reign of Abijah, successor to Rehoboam in Judah. Even though Jeroboam's army is described as being double that of Abijah's, the battle highlighted in ch. 13 implies that Abijah is on the offensive. His rhetoric suggests that it is his intention to reunite the north and south, by conquest if necessary. Abijah's victory over Jeroboam gives Judah control of the two major north-south highways connecting the southern kingdom and northern kingdom and control over the coveted Benjamin plateau, as well as a portion of the Ephraimite hill country. The remark in v. 20 that "Jeroboam did not regain power" may be related to Aramean pressure on the northern kingdom as facilitated by a treaty Abijah apparently made with Ben-Hadad of Aram (Syria).
13:3 For the size of these armies, see the article "Numbers in Numbers," p. 235.

fighting men, and Jeroboam drew up a
battle line against him with eight hundred
thousand able troops.
4Abijah stood on Mount Zemaraim,[w]
in the hill country of Ephraim, and said,
"Jeroboam and all Israel,[x] listen to me!
5Don't you know that the LORD, the God
of Israel, has given the kingship of Israel
to David and his descendants forever[y] by
a covenant of salt?[z] 6Yet Jeroboam son of
Nebat, an official of Solomon son of David, rebelled[a] against his master. 7Some
worthless scoundrels[b] gathered around
him and opposed Rehoboam son of Solomon when he was young and indecisive
and not strong enough to resist them.
8"And now you plan to resist the kingdom of the LORD, which is in the hands
of David's descendants. You are indeed a
vast army and have with you the golden
calves[c] that Jeroboam made to be your
gods. 9But didn't you drive out the priests
of the LORD,[d] the sons of Aaron, and the
Levites, and make priests of your own as
the peoples of other lands do? Whoever
comes to consecrate himself with a young
bull[e] and seven rams may become a priest
of what are not gods.[f]
10"As for us, the LORD is our God, and
we have not forsaken him. The priests
who serve the LORD are sons of Aaron, and
the Levites assist them. 11Every morning
and evening[g] they present burnt offerings
and fragrant incense to the LORD. They set
out the bread on the ceremonially clean
table[h] and light the lamps on the gold
lampstand every evening. We are observing the requirements of the LORD our God.
But you have forsaken him. 12God is with
us; he is our leader. His priests with their
trumpets will sound the battle cry against
you.[i] People of Israel, do not fight against
the LORD,[j] the God of your ancestors, for
you will not succeed."
13Now Jeroboam had sent troops around
to the rear, so that while he was in front
of Judah the ambush[k] was behind them.
14Judah turned and saw that they were being attacked at both front and rear. Then
they cried out[l] to the LORD. The priests
blew their trumpets 15and the men of Judah raised the battle cry. At the sound of
their battle cry, God routed Jeroboam and
all Israel[m] before Abijah and Judah. 16The
Israelites fled before Judah, and God delivered[n] them into their hands. 17Abijah and
his troops inflicted heavy losses on them,
so that there were five hundred thousand
casualties among Israel's able men. 18The
Israelites were subdued on that occasion,
and the people of Judah were victorious
because they relied[o] on the LORD, the God
of their ancestors.
19Abijah pursued Jeroboam and took
from him the towns of Bethel, Jeshanah
and Ephron, with their surrounding villages. 20Jeroboam did not regain power
during the time of Abijah. And the LORD
struck him down and he died.
21But Abijah grew in strength. He married fourteen wives and had twenty-two
sons and sixteen daughters.
22The other events of Abijah's reign,
what he did and what he said, are written
in the annotations of the prophet Iddo.

14 [a] And Abijah rested with his ancestors and was buried in the City of
David. Asa his son succeeded him as king,
and in his days the country was at peace
for ten years.

Asa King of Judah

14:2-3pp — 1Ki 15:11-12

2Asa did what was good and right in the
eyes of the LORD his God. 3He removed the
foreign altars and the high places, smashed
the sacred stones and cut down the Asherah poles.[b][p] 4He commanded Judah to seek
the LORD, the God of their ancestors, and to
obey his laws and commands. 5He removed
the high places and incense altars[q] in every town in Judah, and the kingdom was at
peace under him. 6He built up the fortified
cities of Judah, since the land was at peace.
No one was at war with him during those
years, for the LORD gave him rest.[r]
7"Let us build up these towns," he said
to Judah, "and put walls around them,
with towers, gates and bars. The land is
still ours, because we have sought the
LORD our God; we sought him and he has
given us rest on every side." So they built
and prospered.
8Asa had an army of three hundred
thousand men from Judah, equipped with
large shields and with spears, and two
hundred and eighty thousand from Benjamin, armed with small shields and with
bows. All these were brave fighting men.

13:4 [w] Jos 18:22 [x] 1Ch 11:1 **13:5** [y] 2Sa 7:13 [z] Lev 2:13; Nu 18:19 **13:6** [a] 1Ki 11:26 **13:7** [b] Jdg 9:4 **13:8** [c] 1Ki 12:28; 2Ch 11:15 **13:9** [d] 2Ch 11:14-15 [e] Ex 29:35-36 [f] Jer 2:11 **13:11** [g] Ex 29:39; 2Ch 2:4 [h] Lev 24:5-9 **13:12** [i] Nu 10:8-9 [j] Ac 5:39 **13:13** [k] Jos 8:9 **13:14** [l] 2Ch 14:11 **13:15** [m] 2Ch 14:12 **13:16** [n] 2Ch 16:8 **13:18** [o] 1Ch 5:20; 2Ch 14:11; Ps 22:5 **14:3** [p] Ex 34:13; Dt 7:5; 1Ki 15:12-14 **14:5** [q] 2Ch 34:4,7 **14:6** [r] 1Ch 22:9; 2Ch 15:15

[a] In Hebrew texts 14:1 is numbered 13:23, and 14:2-15 is numbered 14:1-14. [b] *3* That is, wooden symbols of the goddess Asherah; here and elsewhere in 2 Chronicles

13:5 *covenant of salt.* See note on Lev 2:13.
13:8 *have with you the golden calves.* It was common practice to carry images representing the gods into battle. See the article "Divine Warfare," p. 365.
14:3 *high places.* See notes on 1:3; 1Ki 3:2; 11:7. *sacred stones . . . Asherah poles.* See notes on Dt 7:5; 1Ki 14:23.
14:5 *high places.* See notes on 1:3; 1Ki 3:2; 11:7.
14:6 *fortified cities of Judah.* Likely the same cities fortified by Solomon and Rehoboam but destroyed by Shishak (see notes on 11:5 – 12; 1Ki 14:25).
14:8 *three hundred thousand.* See the article "Numbers in Numbers," p. 235.

9 Zerah the Cushite[s] marched out against
them with an army of thousands upon
thousands and three hundred chariots,
and came as far as Mareshah.[t] 10 Asa went
out to meet him, and they took up battle
positions in the Valley of Zephathah near
Mareshah.
11 Then Asa called[u] to the LORD his God
and said, "LORD, there is no one like you
to help the powerless against the mighty.
Help us, LORD our God, for we rely[v] on
you, and in your name[w] we have come
against this vast army. LORD, you are our
God; do not let mere mortals prevail[x]
against you."
12 The LORD struck down[y] the Cushites
before Asa and Judah. The Cushites fled,
13 and Asa and his army pursued them
as far as Gerar.[z] Such a great number of
Cushites fell that they could not recover;
they were crushed before the LORD and
his forces. The men of Judah carried off a
large amount of plunder. 14 They destroyed
all the villages around Gerar, for the terror[a] of the LORD had fallen on them. They
looted all these villages, since there was
much plunder there. 15 They also attacked
the camps of the herders and carried off
droves of sheep and goats and camels.
Then they returned to Jerusalem.

Asa's Reform

15:16-19pp — 1Ki 15:13-16

15 The Spirit of God came on[b] Azariah
son of Oded. 2 He went out to meet
Asa and said to him, "Listen to me, Asa
and all Judah and Benjamin. The LORD is
with you[c] when you are with him.[d] If you
seek[e] him, he will be found by you, but if
you forsake him, he will forsake you.[f] 3 For
a long time Israel was without the true
God, without a priest to teach[g] and without the law.[h] 4 But in their distress they
turned to the LORD, the God of Israel, and
sought him,[i] and he was found by them.
5 In those days it was not safe to travel
about,[j] for all the inhabitants of the lands
were in great turmoil. 6 One nation was
being crushed by another and one city
by another,[k] because God was troubling
them with every kind of distress. 7 But as
for you, be strong[l] and do not give up, for
your work will be rewarded."[m]
8 When Asa heard these words and the
prophecy of Azariah son of[a] Oded the
prophet, he took courage. He removed the
detestable idols from the whole land of Judah and Benjamin and from the towns he
had captured[n] in the hills of Ephraim. He
repaired the altar[o] of the LORD that was in
front of the portico of the LORD's temple.
9 Then he assembled all Judah and
Benjamin and the people from Ephraim, Manasseh and Simeon who had settled among them, for large numbers[p] had
come over to him from Israel when they
saw that the LORD his God was with him.
10 They assembled at Jerusalem in the
third month of the fifteenth year of Asa's
reign. 11 At that time they sacrificed to the
LORD seven hundred head of cattle and
seven thousand sheep and goats from the
plunder[q] they had brought back. 12 They
entered into a covenant[r] to seek the LORD,[s]
the God of their ancestors, with all their
heart and soul. 13 All who would not seek
the LORD, the God of Israel, were to be put
to death,[t] whether small or great, man or
woman. 14 They took an oath to the LORD
with loud acclamation, with shouting and
with trumpets and horns. 15 All Judah rejoiced about the oath because they had
sworn it wholeheartedly. They sought
God[u] eagerly, and he was found by them.
So the LORD gave them rest[v] on every side.
16 King Asa also deposed his grandmother Maakah from her position as queen
mother, because she had made a repulsive
image for the worship of Asherah.[w] Asa
cut it down, broke it up and burned it in
the Kidron Valley. 17 Although he did not
remove the high places from Israel, Asa's
heart was fully committed to the LORD all
his life. 18 He brought into the temple of
God the silver and gold and the articles
that he and his father had dedicated.
19 There was no more war until the thir-
ty-fifth year of Asa's reign.

Asa's Last Years

16:1-6pp — 1Ki 15:17-22
16:11 – 17:1pp — 1Ki 15:23-24

16 In the thirty-sixth year of Asa's
reign Baasha[x] king of Israel went
up against Judah and fortified Ramah to
prevent anyone from leaving or entering
the territory of Asa king of Judah.
2 Asa then took the silver and gold out of

14:9 [s] 2Ch 12:3; 16:8 [t] 2Ch 11:8 **14:11** [u] 2Ch 13:14 [v] 2Ch 13:18 [w] 1Sa 17:45 [x] 1Sa 14:6; Ps 9:19 **14:12** [y] 2Ch 13:15 **14:13** [z] Ge 10:19 **14:14** [a] Ge 35:5; 2Ch 17:10 **15:1** [b] Nu 11:25, 26; 24:2; 2Ch 20:14; 24:20 **15:2** [c] ver 4, 15; 2Ch 20:17 [d] Jas 4:8 [e] Jer 29:13 [f] 1Ch 28:9; 2Ch 24:20 **15:3** [g] Lev 10:11 [h] 2Ch 17:9; La 2:9 **15:4** [i] Dt 4:29 **15:5** [j] Jdg 5:6 **15:6** [k] Mt 24:7 **15:7** [l] Jos 1:7, 9 [m] Ps 58:11 **15:8** [n] 2Ch 13:19 [o] 2Ch 8:12 **15:9** [p] 2Ch 11:16-17 **15:11** [q] 2Ch 14:13 **15:12** [r] 2Ki 11:17; 2Ch 23:16; 34:31 [s] 1Ch 16:11 **15:13** [t] Ex 22:20; Dt 13:9-16 **15:15** [u] Dt 4:29 [v] 1Ch 22:9; 2Ch 14:7 **15:16** [w] Ex 34:13; 2Ch 14:2-5 **16:1** [x] Jer 41:9

[a] 8 Vulgate and Syriac (see also Septuagint and verse 1); Hebrew does not have *Azariah son of*.

14:9 *Zerah the Cushite.* Although Egypt is not named within the account of vv. 9 – 15, the close connection between the region of Cush/Nubia and Egypt, as well as the inclusion of Libyans along with Cushites in 16:8, may imply that Zerah was a field general on behalf of an Egyptian pharaoh (presumably Osorkon I). Alternatively, Zerah may have been the chief of an Arab coalition (from the Sinai region), given the pairing of Cushites with Midianites in OT texts and the references to camels and herdsmen in v. 15.

15:16 *queen mother.* See note on 1Ki 2:19. *Asherah.* Refers to an Asherah pole (see notes on Dt 7:5; 1Ki 14:23).

16:1 *Ramah.* See note on 1Ki 15:17.

16:2 *Ben-Hadad.* See note on 1Ki 15:18.

the treasuries of the LORD's temple and of
his own palace and sent it to Ben-Hadad
king of Aram, who was ruling in Damascus. 3"Let there be a treaty[y] between me
and you," he said, "as there was between
my father and your father. See, I am sending you silver and gold. Now break your
treaty with Baasha king of Israel so he will
withdraw from me."
4Ben-Hadad agreed with King Asa and
sent the commanders of his forces against
the towns of Israel. They conquered Ijon,
Dan, Abel Maim[a] and all the store cities
of Naphtali. 5When Baasha heard this, he
stopped building Ramah and abandoned
his work. 6Then King Asa brought all the
men of Judah, and they carried away from
Ramah the stones and timber Baasha had
been using. With them he built up Geba
and Mizpah.
7At that time Hanani[z] the seer came to
Asa king of Judah and said to him: "Because you relied on the king of Aram and
not on the LORD your God, the army of
the king of Aram has escaped from your
hand. 8Were not the Cushites[b][a] and Libyans a mighty army with great numbers
of chariots and horsemen[c]? Yet when you
relied on the LORD, he delivered[b] them
into your hand. 9For the eyes[c] of the LORD
range throughout the earth to strengthen
those whose hearts are fully committed to
him. You have done a foolish[d] thing, and
from now on you will be at war."
10Asa was angry with the seer because
of this; he was so enraged that he put him
in prison. At the same time Asa brutally
oppressed some of the people.
11The events of Asa's reign, from beginning to end, are written in the book of the
kings of Judah and Israel. 12In the thirty-ninth year of his reign Asa was afflicted with a disease in his feet. Though his
disease was severe, even in his illness he
did not seek help from the LORD,[e] but only
from the physicians. 13Then in the forty-
first year of his reign Asa died and rested
with his ancestors. 14They buried him in
the tomb that he had cut out for himself in
the City of David. They laid him on a bier
covered with spices and various blended
perfumes,[f] and they made a huge fire[g] in
his honor.

16:3 [y] 2Ch 20:35 **16:7** [z] 1Ki 16:1 **16:8** [a] 2Ch 12:3; 14:9 [b] 2Ch 13:16 **16:9** [c] Pr 15:3; Jer 16:17; Zec 4:10 [d] 1Sa 13:13 **16:12** [e] Jer 17:5-6 **16:14** [f] Ge 50:2; Jn 19:39-40 [g] 2Ch 21:19; Jer 34:5

Jehoshaphat King of Judah

17 Jehoshaphat his son succeeded him
as king and strengthened himself
against Israel. 2He stationed troops in all
the fortified cities of Judah and put garrisons in Judah and in the towns of Ephraim
that his father Asa had captured.[h]
3The LORD was with Jehoshaphat because he followed the ways of his father
David[i] before him. He did not consult the
Baals 4but sought[j] the God of his father and
followed his commands rather than the
practices of Israel. 5The LORD established
the kingdom under his control; and all Judah brought gifts[k] to Jehoshaphat, so that
he had great wealth and honor.[l] 6His heart
was devoted[m] to the ways of the LORD; furthermore, he removed the high places[n] and
the Asherah poles[o] from Judah.[p]
7In the third year of his reign he sent
his officials Ben-Hail, Obadiah, Zechariah, Nethanel and Micaiah to teach[q] in the
towns of Judah. 8With them were certain
Levites[r] — Shemaiah, Nethaniah, Zebadiah, Asahel, Shemiramoth, Jehonathan,
Adonijah, Tobijah and Tob-Adonijah —
and the priests Elishama and Jehoram.
9They taught throughout Judah, taking
with them the Book of the Law[s] of the
LORD; they went around to all the towns of
Judah and taught the people.
10The fear[t] of the LORD fell on all the
kingdoms of the lands surrounding Judah, so that they did not go to war against
Jehoshaphat. 11Some Philistines brought
Jehoshaphat gifts and silver as tribute,
and the Arabs[u] brought him flocks:[v] seven
thousand seven hundred rams and seven
thousand seven hundred goats.
12Jehoshaphat became more and more
powerful; he built forts and store cities
in Judah 13and had large supplies in the

17:2 [h] 2Ch 15:8 **17:3** [i] 1Ki 22:43 **17:4** [j] 1Ki 12:28; 2Ch 22:9 **17:5** [k] 1Sa 10:27 [l] 2Ch 18:1 **17:6** [m] 1Ki 8:61; 2Ch 15:17 [n] 1Ki 15:14; 2Ch 19:3; 20:33 [o] Ex 34:13 [p] 2Ch 21:12 **17:7** [q] Lev 10:11; Dt 6:4-9; 2Ch 15:3; 35:3 **17:8** [r] 2Ch 19:8; Ne 8:7-8 **17:9** [s] Dt 6:4-9; 28:61 **17:10** [t] Ge 35:5; Dt 2:25; 2Ch 14:14 **17:11** [u] 2Ch 9:14; 26:8 [v] 2Ch 21:16

[a] 4 Also known as *Abel Beth Maakah* [b] 8 That is, people from the upper Nile region [c] 8 Or *charioteers*

16:12 *disease in his feet.* Asa's affliction has been attributed to gout (uncommon in Biblical times) or gangrene. *physicians.* Specialists in magical and/or herbal remedies; they operated under the aegis of various gods and in their power.
16:14 *made a huge fire in his honor.* A funerary pyre was a statement of respect and honor for the deceased and was typically only available for those of high position. Such fires were honorary acts rather than a means of cremation. Attendees would then have made a pile of stones over the place to commemorate the dead king. Similar rites of burning are evident in the Neo-Assyrian substitute king rituals in which the performance of the burning (Akkadian *šuruptu*) took place after the burial.
17:3 *The LORD was with Jehoshaphat.* See note on 1:1.
17:6 *high places.* See notes on 1:3; 1Ki 3:2; 11:7. *Asherah poles.* See notes on Dt 7:5; 1Ki 14:23.
17:11 *gifts and silver as tribute … flocks.* This tribute, together with statements of military fortifications (vv. 13,19), makes it clear that the southern kingdom now controls the caravan routes across the Arabah and Negev and on to the Coastal Highway (see note on 2Ki 23:29), providing a lucrative source of tax and tribute income for Jehoshaphat's administration. This economic and political stability will in turn allow for further military strengthening, building projects and governmental expansion (vv. 12 – 19). *Arabs.* Likely seminomadic tribes in the desert regions to the south of the Judahite Negev and portions of the Sinaitic and (perhaps) Arabian peninsulas.

towns of Judah. He also kept experienced
fighting men in Jerusalem. 14Their enroll-
ment[w] by families was as follows:

From Judah, commanders of units
of 1,000:
Adnah the commander, with
300,000 fighting men;
15next, Jehohanan the commander,
with 280,000;
16next, Amasiah son of Zikri, who
volunteered[x] himself for the service of the LORD, with 200,000.
17From Benjamin:[y]
Eliada, a valiant soldier, with
200,000 men armed with bows
and shields;
18next, Jehozabad, with 180,000 men
armed for battle.

19These were the men who served the
king, besides those he stationed in the fortified cities[z] throughout Judah.[a]

Micaiah Prophesies Against Ahab

18:1-27pp — 1Ki 22:1-28

18 Now Jehoshaphat had great wealth
and honor,[b] and he allied[c] himself
with Ahab[d] by marriage. 2Some years later he went down to see Ahab in Samaria.
Ahab slaughtered many sheep and cattle for
him and the people with him and urged him
to attack Ramoth Gilead. 3Ahab king of Israel asked Jehoshaphat king of Judah, "Will
you go with me against Ramoth Gilead?"

Jehoshaphat replied, "I am as you are,
and my people as your people; we will
join you in the war." 4But Jehoshaphat
also said to the king of Israel, "First seek
the counsel of the LORD."

5So the king of Israel brought together
the prophets — four hundred men — and
asked them, "Shall we go to war against
Ramoth Gilead, or shall I not?"

"Go," they answered, "for God will give
it into the king's hand."

6But Jehoshaphat asked, "Is there no
longer a prophet of the LORD here whom
we can inquire of?"

7The king of Israel answered Jehoshaphat, "There is still one prophet through
whom we can inquire of the LORD, but
I hate him because he never prophesies
anything good about me, but always bad.
He is Micaiah son of Imlah."

"The king should not say such a thing,"
Jehoshaphat replied.

8So the king of Israel called one of his
officials and said, "Bring Micaiah son of
Imlah at once."

9Dressed in their royal robes, the king
of Israel and Jehoshaphat king of Judah
were sitting on their thrones at the threshing floor by the entrance of the gate of Samaria, with all the prophets prophesying
before them. 10Now Zedekiah son of Kenaanah had made iron horns, and he declared, "This is what the LORD says: 'With
these you will gore the Arameans until
they are destroyed.' "

11All the other prophets were prophesying the same thing. "Attack Ramoth Gilead[e] and be victorious," they said, "for the
LORD will give it into the king's hand."

12The messenger who had gone to summon Micaiah said to him, "Look, the other
prophets without exception are predicting
success for the king. Let your word agree
with theirs, and speak favorably."

13But Micaiah said, "As surely as the
LORD lives, I can tell him only what my
God says."[f]

14When he arrived, the king asked him,
"Micaiah, shall we go to war against Ramoth Gilead, or shall I not?"

"Attack and be victorious," he answered,
"for they will be given into your hand."

15The king said to him, "How many times
must I make you swear to tell me nothing
but the truth in the name of the LORD?"

16Then Micaiah answered, "I saw all Israel[g] scattered on the hills like sheep without a shepherd,[h] and the LORD said, 'These
people have no master. Let each one go
home in peace.' "

17The king of Israel said to Jehoshaphat,
"Didn't I tell you that he never prophesies
anything good about me, but only bad?"

18Micaiah continued, "Therefore hear
the word of the LORD: I saw the LORD sitting on his throne[i] with all the multitudes
of heaven standing on his right and on his
left. 19And the LORD said, 'Who will entice
Ahab king of Israel into attacking Ramoth
Gilead and going to his death there?'

"One suggested this, and another that.
20Finally, a spirit came forward, stood before the LORD and said, 'I will entice him.'

" 'By what means?' the LORD asked.

21" 'I will go and be a deceiving spirit[j]
in the mouths of all his prophets,' he said.

" 'You will succeed in enticing him,' said
the LORD. 'Go and do it.'

17:14 [w] 2Sa 24:2 **17:16** [x] Jdg 5:9; 1Ch 29:9 **17:17** [y] Nu 1:36 **17:19** [z] 2Ch 11:10 [a] 2Ch 25:5 **18:1** [b] 2Ch 17:5 [c] 2Ch 19:1-3; 22:3 [d] 2Ch 21:6
18:11 [e] 2Ch 22:5 **18:13** [f] Nu 22:18, 20, 35 **18:16** [g] 1Ch 9:1 [h] Nu 27:17; Eze 34:5-8 **18:18** [i] Da 7:9 **18:21** [j] 1Ch 21:1; Job 1:6; Zec 3:1; Jn 8:44

17:14 – 18 For these large numbers of fighting men, see the article "Numbers in Numbers," p. 235.
18:1 *Jehoshaphat ... allied himself with Ahab by marriage.* Despite the initial posture of uncertainty (or hostility) toward the northern kingdom (17:1 – 2), Jehoshaphat ultimately attained peace with Ahab, a diplomatic act culminating in a political marriage between Jehoshaphat's son Jehoram and Ahab's daughter Athaliah (21:5 – 6). See notes on 1Sa 18:25; 25:39b.
18:18 *multitudes of heaven.* See the article "Divine Council," p. 615.

22“So now the LORD has put a deceiving
spirit in the mouths of these prophets of
yours.[k] The LORD has decreed disaster for
you.”
23Then Zedekiah son of Kenaanah
went up and slapped[l] Micaiah in the face.
“Which way did the spirit from[a] the LORD
go when he went from me to speak to
you?” he asked.
24Micaiah replied, “You will find out on
the day you go to hide in an inner room.”
25The king of Israel then ordered, “Take
Micaiah and send him back to Amon the
ruler of the city and to Joash the king’s son,
26and say, ‘This is what the king says: Put
this fellow in prison[m] and give him nothing
but bread and water until I return safely.’ ”
27Micaiah declared, “If you ever return
safely, the LORD has not spoken through
me.” Then he added, “Mark my words, all
you people!”

Ahab Killed at Ramoth Gilead

18:28-34pp — 1Ki 22:29-36

28So the king of Israel and Jehoshaphat
king of Judah went up to Ramoth Gilead. 29The king of Israel said to Jehoshaphat, “I will enter the battle in disguise,
but you wear your royal robes.” So the
king of Israel disguised[n] himself and went
into battle.
30Now the king of Aram had ordered his
chariot commanders, “Do not fight with
anyone, small or great, except the king
of Israel.” 31When the chariot commanders saw Jehoshaphat, they thought, “This
is the king of Israel.” So they turned to
attack him, but Jehoshaphat cried out,[o]
and the LORD helped him. God drew them
away from him, 32for when the chariot
commanders saw that he was not the king
of Israel, they stopped pursuing him.
33But someone drew his bow at random and hit the king of Israel between the
breastplate and the scale armor. The king
told the chariot driver, “Wheel around
and get me out of the fighting. I’ve been
wounded.” 34All day long the battle raged,
and the king of Israel propped himself up
in his chariot facing the Arameans until
evening. Then at sunset he died.[p]

19 When Jehoshaphat king of Judah
returned safely to his palace in Jerusalem, 2Jehu[q] the seer, the son of Hanani,
went out to meet him and said to the king,
“Should you help the wicked[r] and love[b]
those who hate the LORD?[s] Because of this,
the wrath[t] of the LORD is on you. 3There is,
however, some good[u] in you, for you have
rid the land of the Asherah poles[v] and have
set your heart on seeking God.[w]”

Jehoshaphat Appoints Judges

4Jehoshaphat lived in Jerusalem, and he
went out again among the people from Beersheba to the hill country of Ephraim and
turned them back to the LORD, the God of
their ancestors. 5He appointed judges[x] in the
land, in each of the fortified cities of Judah.
6He told them, “Consider carefully what you
do,[y] because you are not judging for mere
mortals[z] but for the LORD, who is with you
whenever you give a verdict. 7Now let the
fear of the LORD be on you. Judge carefully,
for with the LORD our God there is no injustice[a] or partiality[b] or bribery.”
8In Jerusalem also, Jehoshaphat appointed some of the Levites, priests and
heads of Israelite families to administer[c]
the law of the LORD and to settle disputes.
And they lived in Jerusalem. 9He gave
them these orders: “You must serve faithfully and wholeheartedly in the fear of
the LORD. 10In every case that comes before you from your people who live in the
cities — whether bloodshed or other concerns of the law, commands, decrees or
regulations — you are to warn them not to
sin against the LORD;[d] otherwise his wrath
will come on you and your people. Do
this, and you will not sin.
11“Amariah the chief priest will be over
you in any matter concerning the LORD,
and Zebadiah son of Ishmael, the leader
of the tribe of Judah, will be over you in
any matter concerning the king, and the
Levites will serve as officials before you.
Act with courage,[e] and may the LORD be
with those who do well.”

Jehoshaphat Defeats Moab and Ammon

20 After this, the Moabites and Ammonites with some of the Meunites[c][f]
came to wage war against Jehoshaphat.
2Some people came and told Jehoshaphat, “A vast army is coming against you

[a] 23 Or *Spirit of* [b] 2 Or *and make alliances with*
[c] 1 Some Septuagint manuscripts; Hebrew *Ammonites*

18:22 [k] Job 12:16; Isa 19:14; Eze 14:9 **18:23** [l] Jer 20:2; Mk 14:65; Ac 23:2 **18:26** [m] 2Ch 16:10; Heb 11:36 **18:29** [n] 1Sa 28:8 **18:31** [o] 2Ch 13:14 **18:34** [p] 2Ch 22:5 **19:2** [q] 1Ki 16:1 [r] 2Ch 16:2-9 [s] Ps 139:21-22 [t] 2Ch 24:18; 32:25; Ps 7:11 **19:3** [u] 1Ki 14:13; 2Ch 12:12 [v] 2Ch 17:6 [w] 2Ch 18:1; 20:35; 25:7; Ezr 7:10 **19:5** [x] Ge 47:6; Ex 18:26 **19:6** [y] Lev 19:15 [z] Dt 1:17; 16:18-20; 17:8-13 **19:7** [a] Ge 18:25; Dt 32:4 [b] Dt 10:17; Job 34:19; Ro 2:11; Col 3:25 **19:8** [c] 2Ch 17:8-9 **19:10** [d] Dt 17:8-13 **19:11** [e] 1Ch 28:20 **20:1** [f] 1Ch 4:41

19:3 *Asherah poles.* See notes on Dt 7:5; 1Ki 14:23.

19:5 – 11 Jehoshaphat’s appointment of judges in the fortified cities of Judah (v. 5) and his exhortation to these judges (vv. 6 – 7) suggests a reform of the judiciary. Likewise, his appointment of select Levites, priests and family leaders within Jerusalem to handle appeals (vv. 8 – 11) suggests a centralization of the judicial system within the southern kingdom. Such reforms were common in conjunction with a new administration, as seen in the similar reforms enacted by the fourteenth-century BC Egyptian pharaoh Horemheb. Legal disputes sometimes involved oracular judgments, or the seeking of divine verdicts by religious professionals (see the article “Divine Verdict,” p. 152), which is why the Levites and priests are involved.

20:1 – 30 Sensing weakness following the defeat of Jehoshaphat and Ahab at Ramoth Gilead, an eastern

from Edom,[a] from the other side of the
Dead Sea. It is already in Hazezon Tamar[g]"
(that is, En Gedi). 3 Alarmed, Jehoshaphat
resolved to inquire of the LORD, and he
proclaimed a fast[h] for all Judah. 4 The people of Judah came together to seek help
from the LORD; indeed, they came from every town in Judah to seek him.
5 Then Jehoshaphat stood up in the assembly of Judah and Jerusalem at the
temple of the LORD in the front of the new
courtyard 6 and said:

"LORD, the God of our ancestors,[i]
are you not the God who is in heav-
en?[j] You rule over all the kingdoms[k]
of the nations. Power and might are
in your hand, and no one can withstand you. 7 Our God, did you not
drive out the inhabitants of this land
before your people Israel and give it
forever to the descendants of Abraham your friend?[l] 8 They have lived in
it and have built in it a sanctuary[m]
for your Name, saying, 9 'If calamity
comes upon us, whether the sword
of judgment, or plague or famine,[n]
we will stand in your presence before
this temple that bears your Name and
will cry out to you in our distress, and
you will hear us and save us.'
10 "But now here are men from Ammon, Moab and Mount Seir, whose
territory you would not allow Israel to
invade when they came from Egypt;[o]
so they turned away from them and
did not destroy them. 11 See how they
are repaying us by coming to drive
us out of the possession[p] you gave
us as an inheritance. 12 Our God, will
you not judge them?[q] For we have no
power to face this vast army that is
attacking us. We do not know what to
do, but our eyes are on you.[r]"

13 All the men of Judah, with their wives
and children and little ones, stood there
before the LORD.
14 Then the Spirit[s] of the LORD came on
Jahaziel son of Zechariah, the son of Benaiah, the son of Jeiel, the son of Mattaniah, a Levite and descendant of Asaph, as
he stood in the assembly.

20:2 [g] Ge 14:7
20:3 [h] 1Sa 7:6; 2Ch 19:3; Ezr 8:21; Jer 36:9; Jnh 3:5,7
20:6 [i] Mt 6:9 [j] Dt 4:39 [k] 1Ch 29:11-12
20:7 [l] Isa 41:8; Jas 2:23
20:8 [m] 2Ch 6:20
20:9 [n] 2Ch 6:28
20:10 [o] Nu 20:14-21; Dt 2:4-6,9, 18-19
20:11 [p] Ps 83:1-12
20:12 [q] Jdg 11:27 [r] Ps 25:15; 121:1-2
20:14 [s] 2Ch 15:1
20:15 [t] 2Ch 32:7 [u] Ex 14:13-14; 1Sa 17:47
20:17 [v] Ex 14:13; 2Ch 15:2
20:18 [w] Ex 4:31
20:20 [x] Isa 7:9 [y] Ge 39:3; Pr 16:3
20:21 [z] 1Ch 16:29; Ps 29:2 [a] 2Ch 5:13; Ps 136:1
20:22 [b] Jdg 7:22; 2Ch 13:13
20:23 [c] Ge 19:38 [d] 2Ch 21:8 [e] Jdg 7:22; 1Sa 14:20; Eze 38:21

15 He said: "Listen, King Jehoshaphat
and all who live in Judah and Jerusalem!
This is what the LORD says to you: 'Do not
be afraid or discouraged[t] because of this
vast army. For the battle[u] is not yours, but
God's. 16 Tomorrow march down against
them. They will be climbing up by the Pass
of Ziz, and you will find them at the end
of the gorge in the Desert of Jeruel. 17 You
will not have to fight this battle. Take up
your positions; stand firm and see[v] the
deliverance the LORD will give you, Judah
and Jerusalem. Do not be afraid; do not
be discouraged. Go out to face them tomorrow, and the LORD will be with you.' "
18 Jehoshaphat bowed down[w] with his
face to the ground, and all the people of
Judah and Jerusalem fell down in worship
before the LORD. 19 Then some Levites from
the Kohathites and Korahites stood up and
praised the LORD, the God of Israel, with a
very loud voice.
20 Early in the morning they left for the
Desert of Tekoa. As they set out, Jehoshaphat stood and said, "Listen to me, Judah
and people of Jerusalem! Have faith[x] in
the LORD your God and you will be upheld;
have faith in his prophets and you will be
successful.[y]" 21 After consulting the people,
Jehoshaphat appointed men to sing to the
LORD and to praise him for the splendor of
his[b] holiness[z] as they went out at the head
of the army, saying:

"Give thanks to the LORD,
for his love endures forever."[a]

22 As they began to sing and praise, the
LORD set ambushes[b] against the men of
Ammon and Moab and Mount Seir who
were invading Judah, and they were defeated. 23 The Ammonites[c] and Moabites
rose up against the men from Mount Seir[d]
to destroy and annihilate them. After they
finished slaughtering the men from Seir,
they helped to destroy one another.[e]
24 When the men of Judah came to the
place that overlooks the desert and looked
toward the vast army, they saw only dead

[a] *2* One Hebrew manuscript; most Hebrew manuscripts, Septuagint and Vulgate *Aram* [b] *21* Or *him with the splendor of*

coalition joins forces against Jehoshaphat. This account (not found in 2 Kings) has two areas of uncertainty as to the makeup of this coalition. (1) The Hebrew text has "Ammonites" where the NIV has posited "Meunites" (v. 1). This NIV reading is attested in the Septuagint, the pre-Christian Greek translation of the OT, and alleviates what would seem to be an unlikely expression (i.e., "Moabites and Ammonites with some of the Ammonites"). Moreover, since the "men from ... Mount Seir" function later in the passage (see vv. 10,22) as synonyms for the third part of the coalition (Meunites), the proposal has merit. The Meunites were an Arabian tribe who lived in the southern region of the Transjordan and parts of the Sinai; they paid tribute to Judah during the reign of Uzziah (26:7–8) and are mentioned in Assyrian annals as paying tribute to Tiglath-Pileser III (eighth century BC). (2) The Hebrew text notes that the coalition is attacking "from Aram" (v. 2), which the NIV has rendered "from Edom." If Aram is the intended nation, the passage would indicate that these eastern nations were being supported (if not incited) by Damascus, perhaps as a means of reprisal against Jehoshaphat in his help of Ahab's assault on Ramoth Gilead.

bodies lying on the ground; no one had escaped. 25 So Jehoshaphat and his men went
to carry off their plunder, and they found
among them a great amount of equipment
and clothing[a] and also articles of value —
more than they could take away. There
was so much plunder that it took three
days to collect it. 26 On the fourth day they
assembled in the Valley of Berakah, where
they praised the LORD. This is why it is
called the Valley of Berakah[b] to this day.
27 Then, led by Jehoshaphat, all the men
of Judah and Jerusalem returned joyfully to Jerusalem, for the LORD had given
them cause to rejoice over their enemies.
28 They entered Jerusalem and went to the
temple of the LORD with harps and lyres
and trumpets.
29 The fear[f] of God came on all the surrounding kingdoms when they heard how
the LORD had fought[g] against the enemies
of Israel. 30 And the kingdom of Jehoshaphat was at peace, for his God had given
him rest[h] on every side.

The End of Jehoshaphat's Reign

20:31 – 21:1pp — 1Ki 22:41-50

31 So Jehoshaphat reigned over Judah.
He was thirty-five years old when he became king of Judah, and he reigned in Jerusalem twenty-five years. His mother's
name was Azubah daughter of Shilhi. 32 He
followed the ways of his father Asa and
did not stray from them; he did what was
right in the eyes of the LORD. 33 The high
places,[i] however, were not removed, and
the people still had not set their hearts on
the God of their ancestors.
34 The other events of Jehoshaphat's
reign, from beginning to end, are written in the annals of Jehu[j] son of Hanani, which are recorded in the book of the
kings of Israel.
35 Later, Jehoshaphat king of Judah
made an alliance[k] with Ahaziah king of
Israel, whose ways were wicked.[l] 36 He
agreed with him to construct a fleet of
trading ships.[c] After these were built at
Ezion Geber, 37 Eliezer son of Dodavahu
of Mareshah prophesied against Jehoshaphat, saying, "Because you have made an
alliance with Ahaziah, the LORD will destroy what you have made." The ships[m]
were wrecked and were not able to set sail
to trade.[d]

21 Then Jehoshaphat rested with his
ancestors and was buried with
them in the City of David. And Jehoram[n]
his son succeeded him as king. 2 Jehoram's
brothers, the sons of Jehoshaphat, were
Azariah, Jehiel, Zechariah, Azariahu, Michael and Shephatiah. All these were sons
of Jehoshaphat king of Israel.[e] 3 Their father had given them many gifts[o] of silver
and gold and articles of value, as well as
fortified cities[p] in Judah, but he had given
the kingdom to Jehoram because he was
his firstborn son.

Jehoram King of Judah

21:5-10,20pp — 2Ki 8:16-24

4 When Jehoram established[q] himself
firmly over his father's kingdom, he put
all his brothers[r] to the sword along with
some of the officials of Israel. 5 Jehoram
was thirty-two years old when he became
king, and he reigned in Jerusalem eight
years. 6 He followed the ways of the kings
of Israel,[s] as the house of Ahab had done,
for he married a daughter of Ahab.[t] He
did evil in the eyes of the LORD. 7 Nevertheless, because of the covenant the LORD
had made with David,[u] the LORD was not
willing to destroy the house of David.[v] He
had promised to maintain a lamp[w] for him
and his descendants forever.
8 In the time of Jehoram, Edom[x] rebelled
against Judah and set up its own king. 9 So
Jehoram went there with his officers and
all his chariots. The Edomites surrounded him and his chariot commanders, but
he rose up and broke through by night.
10 To this day Edom has been in rebellion
against Judah.
Libnah[y] revolted at the same time, because Jehoram had forsaken the LORD, the
God of his ancestors. 11 He had also built
high places on the hills of Judah and had
caused the people of Jerusalem to prostitute themselves and had led Judah astray.
12 Jehoram received a letter from Elijah[z]
the prophet, which said:

> "This is what the LORD, the God of
> your father[a] David, says: 'You have
> not followed the ways of your father
> Jehoshaphat or of Asa[b] king of Judah.
> 13 But you have followed the ways of
> the kings of Israel, and you have led
> Judah and the people of Jerusalem
> to prostitute themselves, just as the
> house of Ahab did.[c] You have also

20:29 [f] Ge 35:5; Dt 2:25; 2Ch 14:14; 17:10 [g] Ex 14:14 **20:30** [h] 1Ch 22:9; 2Ch 14:6-7; 15:15 **20:33** [i] 2Ch 17:6; 19:3 **20:34** [j] 1Ki 16:1 **20:35** [k] 2Ch 16:3 [l] 2Ch 19:1-3 **20:37** [m] 1Ki 9:26; 2Ch 9:21 **21:1** [n] 1Ch 3:11

21:3 [o] 2Ch 11:23 [p] 2Ch 11:10 **21:4** [q] 1Ki 2:12 [r] Jdg 9:5 **21:6** [s] 1Ki 12:28-30 [t] 2Ch 18:1; 22:3 **21:7** [u] 2Sa 7:13 [v] 2Sa 7:15; 2Ch 23:3 [w] 2Sa 21:17; 1Ki 11:36 **21:8** [x] 2Ch 20:22-23 **21:10** [y] Nu 33:20 **21:12** [z] 2Ki 1:16-17 [a] 2Ch 17:3-6 [b] 2Ch 14:2 **21:13** [c] ver 6, 11; 1Ki 16:29-33

[a] 25 Some Hebrew manuscripts and Vulgate; most Hebrew manuscripts *corpses* [b] 26 *Berakah* means *praise.* [c] 36 Hebrew *of ships that could go to Tarshish* [d] 37 Hebrew *sail for Tarshish* [e] 2 That is, Judah, as frequently in 2 Chronicles

20:28 *harps and lyres and trumpets.* See the articles "Lyre," p. 488; "Music and Musicians," p. 524.
20:34 *annals.* See note on 1Ki 14:19.
20:36 *trading ships.* See notes on 8:18; 1Ki 10:22.
21:4 *Jehoram ... put all his brothers to the sword.* See note on 2Ki 10:7.
21:7 *lamp.* See note on 2Ki 8:19.
21:10 *Libnah.* See note on 2Ki 8:22.

murdered your own brothers, members of your own family, men who were better[d] than you. 14So now the LORD is about to strike your people, your sons, your wives and everything that is yours, with a heavy blow. 15You yourself will be very ill with a lingering disease[e] of the bowels, until the disease causes your bowels to come out.' "

16The LORD aroused against Jehoram the hostility of the Philistines and of the Arabs[f] who lived near the Cushites. 17They attacked Judah, invaded it and carried off all the goods found in the king's palace, together with his sons and wives. Not a son was left to him except Ahaziah,[a] the youngest.[g]

18After all this, the LORD afflicted Jehoram with an incurable disease of the bowels. 19In the course of time, at the end of the second year, his bowels came out because of the disease, and he died in great pain. His people made no funeral fire in his honor,[h] as they had for his predecessors.

20Jehoram was thirty-two years old when he became king, and he reigned in Jerusalem eight years. He passed away, to no one's regret, and was buried[i] in the City of David, but not in the tombs of the kings.

Ahaziah King of Judah

22:1-6pp — 2Ki 8:25-29
22:7-9pp — 2Ki 9:21-29

22 The people[j] of Jerusalem[k] made Ahaziah, Jehoram's youngest son, king in his place, since the raiders,[l] who came with the Arabs into the camp, had killed all the older sons. So Ahaziah son of Jehoram king of Judah began to reign.

2Ahaziah was twenty-two[b] years old when he became king, and he reigned in Jerusalem one year. His mother's name was Athaliah, a granddaughter of Omri.

3He too followed[m] the ways of the house of Ahab,[n] for his mother encouraged him to act wickedly. 4He did evil in the eyes of the LORD, as the house of Ahab had done, for after his father's death they became his advisers, to his undoing. 5He also followed their counsel when he went with Joram[c] son of Ahab king of Israel to wage war against Hazael king of Aram at Ramoth Gilead.[o] The Arameans wounded Joram; 6so he returned to Jezreel to recover from the wounds they had inflicted on him at Ramoth[d] in his battle with Hazael[p] king of Aram.

Then Ahaziah[e] son of Jehoram king of Judah went down to Jezreel to see Joram son of Ahab because he had been wounded.

7Through Ahaziah's[q] visit to Joram, God brought about Ahaziah's downfall. When Ahaziah arrived, he went out with Joram to meet Jehu son of Nimshi, whom the LORD had anointed to destroy the house of Ahab. 8While Jehu was executing judgment on the house of Ahab,[r] he found the officials of Judah and the sons of Ahaziah's relatives, who had been attending Ahaziah, and he killed them. 9He then went in search of Ahaziah, and his men captured him while he was hiding[s] in Samaria. He was brought to Jehu and put to death. They buried him, for they said, "He was a son of Jehoshaphat, who sought[t] the LORD with all his heart." So there was no one in the house of Ahaziah powerful enough to retain the kingdom.

Athaliah and Joash

22:10–23:21pp — 2Ki 11:1-21

10When Athaliah the mother of Ahaziah saw that her son was dead, she proceeded to destroy the whole royal family of the house of Judah. 11But Jehosheba,[f] the daughter of King Jehoram, took Joash son of Ahaziah and stole him away from among the royal princes who were about to be murdered and put him and his nurse in a bedroom. Because Jehosheba,[f] the daughter of King Jehoram and wife of the priest Jehoiada, was Ahaziah's sister, she hid the child from Athaliah so she could not kill him. 12He remained hidden with

21:13 [d] ver 4; 1Ki 2:32
21:15 [e] ver 18-19; Nu 12:10
21:16 [f] 2Ch 17:10-11; 22:1; 26:7
21:17 [g] 2Ki 12:18; 2Ch 22:1; 25:23; Joel 3:5
21:19 [h] 2Ch 16:14
21:20 [i] 2Ch 24:25; 28:27; 33:20; Jer 22:18, 28
22:1 [j] 2Ch 33:25; 36:1 [k] 2Ch 23:20-21; 26:1 [l] 2Ch 21:16-17
22:3 [m] 2Ch 18:1 [n] 2Ch 21:6
22:5 [o] 2Ch 18:11, 34
22:6 [p] 1Ki 19:15; 2Ki 8:13-15; 9:15
22:7 [q] 2Ki 9:16; 2Ch 10:15
22:8 [r] 2Ki 10:13
22:9 [s] Jdg 9:5 [t] 2Ch 17:4

[a] *17* Hebrew *Jehoahaz,* a variant of *Ahaziah*
[b] *2* Some Septuagint manuscripts and Syriac (see also 2 Kings 8:26); Hebrew *forty-two*
[c] *5* Hebrew *Jehoram,* a variant of *Joram;* also in verses 6 and 7
[d] *6* Hebrew *Ramah,* a variant of *Ramoth*
[e] *6* Some Hebrew manuscripts, Septuagint, Vulgate and Syriac (see also 2 Kings 8:29); most Hebrew manuscripts *Azariah*
[f] *11* Hebrew *Jehoshabeath,* a variant of *Jehosheba*

21:16–17 *the Philistines and ... the Arabs ... attacked Judah.* In addition to the rebellion of Edom and Libnah (vv. 8–10), Jehoram also faced attacks on Judah (including Jerusalem) from regional foes to the south and west. These Arabs were located in the desert regions to the south of the Judahite Negev into portions of the Sinai peninsula. The Cushites noted here as adjacent to the Arabs might relate to the battle of Zerah, which would place them in the vicinity of Gerar, in the southern region of the Negev (14:9–13). The Arab raiders are credited with killing all of Jehoram's sons except Ahaziah (22:1). In addition to the difficulties of fighting battles on multiple fronts, the loss of Judah's hegemony over these areas entailed the loss of tribute payments and caravan (trade) revenue.

21:20 *not in the tombs of the kings.* As with the withholding of a fire in the honor of Jehoram following his death (v. 19; see note on 16:14), Jehoram was also denied the honor of being buried in the royal cemetery. See note on 1Ki 2:10.

22:1 *The people of Jerusalem.* See note on 23:20. *the Arabs.* See note on 21:16–17.

them at the temple of God for six years while Athaliah ruled the land.

23 In the seventh year Jehoiada showed his strength. He made a covenant with the commanders of units of a hundred: Azariah son of Jeroham, Ishmael son of Jehohanan, Azariah son of Obed, Maaseiah son of Adaiah, and Elishaphat son of Zikri. 2 They went throughout Judah and gathered the Levites[u] and the heads of Israelite families from all the towns. When they came to Jerusalem, 3 the whole assembly made a covenant[v] with the king at the temple of God.

Jehoiada said to them, "The king's son shall reign, as the LORD promised concerning the descendants of David.[w] 4 Now this is what you are to do: A third of you priests and Levites who are going on duty on the Sabbath are to keep watch at the doors, 5 a third of you at the royal palace and a third at the Foundation Gate, and all the others are to be in the courtyards of the temple of the LORD. 6 No one is to enter the temple of the LORD except the priests and Levites on duty; they may enter because they are consecrated, but all the others are to observe[x] the LORD's command not to enter.[a] 7 The Levites are to station themselves around the king, each with weapon in hand. Anyone who enters the temple is to be put to death. Stay close to the king wherever he goes."

8 The Levites and all the men of Judah did just as Jehoiada the priest ordered.[y] Each one took his men—those who were going on duty on the Sabbath and those who were going off duty—for Jehoiada the priest had not released any of the divisions.[z] 9 Then he gave the commanders of units of a hundred the spears and the large and small shields that had belonged to King David and that were in the temple of God. 10 He stationed all the men, each with his weapon in his hand, around the king—near the altar and the temple, from the south side to the north side of the temple.

11 Jehoiada and his sons brought out the king's son and put the crown on him; they presented him with a copy[a] of the covenant and proclaimed him king. They anointed him and shouted, "Long live the king!"

12 When Athaliah heard the noise of the people running and cheering the king, she went to them at the temple of the LORD. 13 She looked, and there was the king,[b] standing by his pillar[c] at the entrance. The officers and the trumpeters were beside the king, and all the people of the land were rejoicing and blowing trumpets, and musicians with their instruments were leading the praises. Then Athaliah tore her robes and shouted, "Treason! Treason!"

14 Jehoiada the priest sent out the commanders of units of a hundred, who were in charge of the troops, and said to them: "Bring her out between the ranks[b] and put to the sword anyone who follows her." For the priest had said, "Do not put her to death at the temple of the LORD." 15 So they seized her as she reached the entrance of the Horse Gate[d] on the palace grounds, and there they put her to death.

16 Jehoiada then made a covenant[e] that he, the people and the king[c] would be the LORD's people. 17 All the people went to the temple of Baal and tore it down. They smashed the altars and idols and killed[f] Mattan the priest of Baal in front of the altars.

18 Then Jehoiada placed the oversight of the temple of the LORD in the hands of the Levitical priests,[g] to whom David had made assignments in the temple,[h] to present the burnt offerings of the LORD as written in the Law of Moses, with rejoicing and singing, as David had ordered. 19 He also stationed gatekeepers[i] at the gates of the LORD's temple so that no one who was in any way unclean might enter.

20 He took with him the commanders of hundreds, the nobles, the rulers of the people and all the people of the land and

23:2 [u] Nu 35:2-5 **23:3** [v] 2Ki 11:17 [w] 2Sa 7:12; 1Ki 2:4; 2Ch 6:16; 7:18; 21:7 **23:6** [x] 1Ch 23:28-29; Zec 3:7 **23:8** [y] 2Ki 11:9 [z] 1Ch 24:1

23:11 [a] Ex 25:16; Dt 17:18; 1Sa 10:24 **23:13** [b] 1Ki 1:41 [c] 1Ki 7:15 **23:15** [d] Ne 3:28; Jer 31:40 **23:16** [e] 2Ch 29:10; 34:31; Ne 9:38 **23:17** [f] Dt 13:6-9 **23:18** [g] 1Ch 23:28-32; 2Ch 5:5 [h] 1Ch 23:6; 25:6 **23:19** [i] 1Ch 9:22

[a] 6 Or *are to stand guard where the LORD has assigned them* [b] 14 Or *out from the precincts* [c] 16 Or *covenant between the LORD and the people and the king that they* (see 2 Kings 11:17)

23:1–11 This episode in the history of Judah illustrates the power behind the priesthood. The power of the priest extending into the political realm is similar to the degree of power and privilege afforded priests in other ancient Near Eastern societies. Priests have land holdings and assets, and the emotional support of the people. Jehoiada is also Joram's son-in-law and so is connected by marriage to the royal line.

23:19 *gatekeepers.* See note on 1Ch 9:17.

23:20 *people of the land.* The sociopolitical group designated the "people of the land" factors into several significant regnal change narratives, including those of Joash (here; vv. 13,21), Josiah (33:25), and Jehoahaz (36:1). This group is also referenced several times in Jeremiah (Jer 1:18; 34:19; 44:21) in a way that implies these individuals were regular citizens, perhaps clan leadership rather than royal officials. Nevertheless, the ability of this group to impact regnal changes shows that the "people of the land" functioned as power brokers regardless of their official status within the kingdom.

While it is difficult to completely deduce the political and/or religious objectives of the "people of the land," the pivotal nature of the contexts in which they appear and influence the political (regnal) process is noteworthy. The "people of the land" facilitate the coronation of Jehoahaz (36:1) following the death of Josiah at Megiddo (35:20–24). In putting Jehoahaz onto the throne, the "people of the land" pass over the oldest son of Josiah (Eliakim), implying

brought the king down from the temple
of the LORD. They went into the palace
through the Upper Gate[j] and seated the
king on the royal throne. 21 All the people of the land rejoiced, and the city was
calm, because Athaliah had been slain
with the sword.[k]

Joash Repairs the Temple

24:1-14pp — 2Ki 12:1-16
24:23-27pp — 2Ki 12:17-21

24 Joash was seven years old when
he became king, and he reigned in
Jerusalem forty years. His mother's name
was Zibiah; she was from Beersheba. 2 Joash did what was right in the eyes of the
LORD[l] all the years of Jehoiada the priest.
3 Jehoiada chose two wives for him, and he
had sons and daughters.

4 Some time later Joash decided to restore the temple of the LORD. 5 He called
together the priests and Levites and said
to them, "Go to the towns of Judah and
collect the money[m] due annually from all
Israel,[n] to repair the temple of your God.
Do it now." But the Levites[o] did not act
at once.

6 Therefore the king summoned Jehoiada the chief priest and said to him, "Why
haven't you required the Levites to bring
in from Judah and Jerusalem the tax imposed by Moses the servant of the LORD
and by the assembly of Israel for the tent
of the covenant law?"[p]

7 Now the sons of that wicked woman
Athaliah had broken into the temple of
God and had used even its sacred objects
for the Baals.

8 At the king's command, a chest was
made and placed outside, at the gate of the
temple of the LORD. 9 A proclamation was
then issued in Judah and Jerusalem that
they should bring to the LORD the tax that
Moses the servant of God had required of
Israel in the wilderness. 10 All the officials
and all the people brought their contributions gladly,[q] dropping them into the chest
until it was full. 11 Whenever the chest was
brought in by the Levites to the king's officials and they saw that there was a large
amount of money, the royal secretary and
the officer of the chief priest would come
and empty the chest and carry it back to
its place. They did this regularly and collected a great amount of money. 12 The
king and Jehoiada gave it to those who
carried out the work required for the temple of the LORD. They hired[r] masons and
carpenters to restore the LORD's temple,
and also workers in iron and bronze to repair the temple.

13 The men in charge of the work were
diligent, and the repairs progressed under them. They rebuilt the temple of God
according to its original design and reinforced it. 14 When they had finished, they
brought the rest of the money to the king
and Jehoiada, and with it were made articles for the LORD's temple: articles for the
service and for the burnt offerings, and
also dishes and other objects of gold and
silver. As long as Jehoiada lived, burnt offerings were presented continually in the
temple of the LORD.

15 Now Jehoiada was old and full of
years, and he died at the age of a hundred and thirty. 16 He was buried with the
kings in the City of David, because of the
good he had done in Israel for God and
his temple.

The Wickedness of Joash

17 After the death of Jehoiada, the officials of Judah came and paid homage to
the king, and he listened to them. 18 They
abandoned[s] the temple of the LORD, the
God of their ancestors, and worshiped
Asherah poles and idols.[t] Because of
their guilt, God's anger[u] came on Judah
and Jerusalem. 19 Although the LORD sent

23:20 [j] 2Ki 15:35
23:21 [k] 2Ch 22:1
24:2 [l] 2Ch 25:2; 26:5
24:5 [m] Ex 30:16; Ne 10:32-33; Mt 17:24 [n] 1Ch 11:1 [o] 1Ch 26:20
24:6 [p] Ex 30:12-16; Nu 1:50
24:10 [q] Ex 25:2; 1Ch 29:3, 6, 9
24:12 [r] 2Ch 34:11
24:18 [s] ver 4; Jos 24:20; 2Ch 7:19 [t] Ex 34:13; 1Ki 14:23; 2Ch 33:3; Jer 17:2 [u] Jos 22:20; 2Ch 19:2

---

that they see Jehoahaz as a better fit for their agenda, which may have been pro-Babylonian and anti-Egyptian (as Josiah's actions at Megiddo reflect).

This possibility is bolstered by the fact that Pharaoh Necho II deposes Jehoahaz after three months and replaces him with Eliakim (Jehoiakim). Similarly, note the role of the "people of the land" in the political dynamics surrounding the assassination of Amon (33:24 – 25). All told, the usage of this expression at pivotal moments in Judah's history provides some insight into the social dynamics of ancient Judah, including contrasting views of foreign policy and perhaps even tensions between urban and rural citizenry.

24:1 *Joash.* Began his reign as a seven-year-old child, no doubt under the close guidance of Jehoiada the priest. Joash's long reign (c. 835 – 796 BC) overlaps with those of Jehu and Jehoahaz in the northern kingdom and reflects a time of Aramean resurgence under Hazael and Ben-Hadad and continued strength in Assyria, particular under the rule of Shalmaneser III and Adadnirari III.

24:4 – 14 As with the construction of a new temple, the refurbishing of an existing religious shrine was an important task for a new ruler, as reflected in Joash's efforts as well as those of Hezekiah (29:3 – 36) and Josiah (34:8 – 13). See notes on 2:1; 2Ki 12:5.

24:15 *old and full of years.* Death at an old age was considered to be a divine blessing on a life well lived. Death at an old age is the summary remark in the tomb inscription of the Egyptian leader Ahmose, who is credited with expelling the Hyksos from Egypt. Likewise, in the OT, the attaining of old age is seen as a blessing of God (e.g., Ps 91:16) as well as a by-product of wisdom (Pr 3:16). Idealized numbers for time of death include 110 in Egyptian thought and 120 in Mesopotamian thought.

24:18 *Asherah poles.* See notes on Dt 7:5; 1Ki 14:23.

prophets to the people to bring them back
to him, and though they testified against
them, they would not listen.[v]
20Then the Spirit[w] of God came on Zechariah[x] son of Jehoiada the priest. He stood
before the people and said, "This is what
God says: 'Why do you disobey the LORD's
commands? You will not prosper.[y] Because
you have forsaken the LORD, he has forsak-
en[z] you.'"
21But they plotted against him, and
by order of the king they stoned[a] him to
death[b] in the courtyard of the LORD's temple.[c] 22King Joash did not remember the
kindness Zechariah's father Jehoiada had
shown him but killed his son, who said as
he lay dying, "May the LORD see this and
call you to account."[d]
23At the turn of the year,[a] the army of
Aram marched against Joash; it invaded
Judah and Jerusalem and killed all the
leaders of the people.[e] They sent all the
plunder to their king in Damascus. 24Al-
though the Aramean army had come with
only a few men,[f] the LORD delivered into
their hands a much larger army.[g] Because
Judah had forsaken the LORD, the God of
their ancestors, judgment was executed on
Joash. 25When the Arameans withdrew,
they left Joash severely wounded. His officials conspired against him for murdering
the son of Jehoiada the priest, and they
killed him in his bed. So he died and was
buried[h] in the City of David, but not in the
tombs of the kings.
26Those who conspired against him
were Zabad,[b] son of Shimeath an Ammonite woman, and Jehozabad, son of Shim-
rith[c][i] a Moabite woman.[j] 27The account
of his sons, the many prophecies about
him, and the record of the restoration of
the temple of God are written in the annotations on the book of the kings. And
Amaziah his son succeeded him as king.

Amaziah King of Judah

25:1-4pp — 2Ki 14:1-6
25:11-12pp — 2Ki 14:7
25:17-28pp — 2Ki 14:8-20

25 Amaziah was twenty-five years
old when he became king, and he
reigned in Jerusalem twenty-nine years.
His mother's name was Jehoaddan; she
was from Jerusalem. 2He did what was
right in the eyes of the LORD, but not
wholeheartedly.[k] 3After the kingdom was
firmly in his control, he executed the officials who had murdered his father the
king. 4Yet he did not put their children to
death, but acted in accordance with what
is written in the Law, in the Book of Moses,[l] where the LORD commanded: "Parents shall not be put to death for their children, nor children be put to death for their
parents; each will die for their own sin."[d][m]
5Amaziah called the people of Judah
together and assigned them according to
their families to commanders of thousands
and commanders of hundreds for all Judah and Benjamin. He then mustered[n]
those twenty years old[o] or more and found
that there were three hundred thousand
men fit for military service,[p] able to handle the spear and shield. 6He also hired a
hundred thousand fighting men from Israel for a hundred talents[e] of silver.
7But a man of God came to him and
said, "Your Majesty, these troops from
Israel[q] must not march with you, for the
LORD is not with Israel — not with any of
the people of Ephraim. 8Even if you go
and fight courageously in battle, God will
overthrow you before the enemy, for God
has the power to help or to overthrow."[r]
9Amaziah asked the man of God, "But
what about the hundred talents I paid for
these Israelite troops?"
The man of God replied, "The LORD can
give you much more than that."[s]
10So Amaziah dismissed the troops who
had come to him from Ephraim and sent
them home. They were furious with Judah
and left for home in a great rage.[t]
11Amaziah then marshaled his strength
and led his army to the Valley of Salt,
where he killed ten thousand men of Seir.
12The army of Judah also captured ten
thousand men alive, took them to the top
of a cliff and threw them down so that all
were dashed to pieces.[u]
13Meanwhile the troops that Amaziah
had sent back and had not allowed to take
part in the war raided towns belonging to

24:19 [v] Nu 11:29; Jer 7:25; Zec 1:4 **24:20** [w] Jdg 3:10; 1Ch 12:18; 2Ch 20:14 [x] Mt 23:35; Lk 11:51 [y] Nu 14:41 [z] Dt 31:17; 2Ch 15:2 **24:21** [a] Jos 7:25; Ac 7:58-59 [b] Ne 9:26; Jer 26:21 [c] Jer 20:2; Mt 23:35 **24:22** [d] Ge 9:5 **24:23** [e] 2Ki 12:17-18 **24:24** [f] 2Ch 14:9; 16:8; 20:2, 12 [g] Lev 26:23-25; Dt 28:25 **24:25** [h] 2Ch 21:20 **24:26** [i] 2Ki 12:21 [j] Ru 1:4

25:2 [k] ver 14; 1Ki 8:61; 2Ch 24:2 **25:4** [l] Dt 28:61 [m] Nu 26:11; Dt 24:16 **25:5** [n] 2Sa 24:2 [o] Ex 30:14 [p] Nu 1:3; 1Ch 21:1; 2Ch 17:14-19 **25:7** [q] 2Ch 16:2-9; 19:1-3 **25:8** [r] 2Ch 14:11; 20:6 **25:9** [s] Dt 8:18; Pr 10:22 **25:10** [t] ver 13 **25:12** [u] Ps 141:6; Ob 1:3

[a] 23 Probably in the spring [b] 26 A variant of *Jozabad* [c] 26 A variant of *Shomer* [d] 4 Deut. 24:16 [e] 6 That is, about 3 3/4 tons or about 3.4 metric tons; also in verse 9

24:23 – 27 See note on 2Ki 12:17.
25:5 *three hundred thousand men.* See the article "Numbers in Numbers," p. 235.
25:12 *threw them down … dashed to pieces.* Throwing enemy prisoners off a cliff is not known outside this passage. It was likely employed for convenience given the geographic location.
25:13 *raided towns belonging to Judah.* Following a prophetic challenge, Amaziah decides against using the mercenary troops from Israel, which prompts them to plunder Judahite cities from "Samaria to Beth Horon." Given that the northern kingdom capital Samaria was not a Judahite town and that it was over 50 miles (80 kilometers) away, Samaria here may be the name of a Judahite town or may reflect a textual transmission issue. The statement may also simply reflect the direction of the attack on Judahite towns.

Judah from Samaria to Beth Horon. They
killed three thousand people and carried
off great quantities of plunder.
14When Amaziah returned from slaughtering the Edomites, he brought back the
gods of the people of Seir. He set them up
as his own gods,[v] bowed down to them
and burned sacrifices to them. 15The anger of the LORD burned against Amaziah,
and he sent a prophet to him, who said,
"Why do you consult this people's gods,
which could not save[w] their own people
from your hand?"
16While he was still speaking, the king
said to him, "Have we appointed you an
adviser to the king? Stop! Why be struck
down?"
So the prophet stopped but said, "I
know that God has determined to destroy
you, because you have done this and have
not listened to my counsel."
17After Amaziah king of Judah consulted his advisers, he sent this challenge
to Jehoash[a] son of Jehoahaz, the son of
Jehu, king of Israel: "Come, let us face
each other in battle."
18But Jehoash king of Israel replied to
Amaziah king of Judah: "A thistle[x] in Lebanon sent a message to a cedar in Lebanon, 'Give your daughter to my son in
marriage.' Then a wild beast in Lebanon
came along and trampled the thistle underfoot. 19You say to yourself that you
have defeated Edom, and now you are arrogant and proud. But stay at home! Why
ask for trouble and cause your own downfall and that of Judah also?"
20Amaziah, however, would not listen,
for God so worked that he might deliver
them into the hands of Jehoash, because
they sought the gods of Edom.[y] 21So Jehoash king of Israel attacked. He and Amaziah king of Judah faced each other at Beth
Shemesh in Judah. 22Judah was routed by
Israel, and every man fled to his home.
23Jehoash king of Israel captured Amaziah
king of Judah, the son of Joash, the son of
Ahaziah,[b] at Beth Shemesh. Then Jehoash
brought him to Jerusalem and broke down
the wall of Jerusalem from the Ephraim
Gate[z] to the Corner Gate[a]—a section
about four hundred cubits[c] long. 24He took
all the gold and silver and all the articles
found in the temple of God that had been
in the care of Obed-Edom,[b] together with
the palace treasures and the hostages, and
returned to Samaria.
25Amaziah son of Joash king of Judah
lived for fifteen years after the death of
Jehoash son of Jehoahaz king of Israel.
26As for the other events of Amaziah's
reign, from beginning to end, are they not
written in the book of the kings of Judah
and Israel? 27From the time that Amaziah
turned away from following the LORD, they
conspired against him in Jerusalem and he
fled to Lachish[c], but they sent men after
him to Lachish and killed him there. 28He
was brought back by horse and was buried
with his ancestors in the City of Judah.[d]

Uzziah King of Judah

26:1-4pp — 2Ki 14:21-22; 15:1-3
26:21-23pp — 2Ki 15:5-7

26 Then all the people of Judah[d] took
Uzziah,[e] who was sixteen years
old, and made him king in place of his
father Amaziah. 2He was the one who rebuilt Elath and restored it to Judah after
Amaziah rested with his ancestors.
3Uzziah was sixteen years old when he
became king, and he reigned in Jerusalem
fifty-two years. His mother's name was
Jekoliah; she was from Jerusalem. 4He did
what was right in the eyes of the LORD,
just as his father Amaziah had done. 5He
sought God during the days of Zechariah,
who instructed him in the fear[f] of God.[e]
As long as he sought the LORD, God gave
him success.[f]
6He went to war against the Philistines[g]
and broke down the walls of Gath, Jabneh
and Ashdod.[h] He then rebuilt towns near
Ashdod and elsewhere among the Philistines. 7God helped him against the Philistines and against the Arabs[i] who lived in
Gur Baal and against the Meunites.[j] 8The
Ammonites[k] brought tribute to Uzziah,
and his fame spread as far as the border
of Egypt, because he had become very
powerful.

25:14 [v] Ex 20:3; 2Ch 28:23; Isa 44:15
25:15 [w] Ps 96:5; Isa 36:20
25:18 [x] Jdg 9:8-15
25:20 [y] 1Ki 12:15; 2Ch 10:15; 22:7
25:23 [z] 2Ki 14:13; Ne 8:16; 12:39 [a] 2Ch 26:9; Jer 31:38
25:24 [b] 1Ch 26:15
25:27 [c] Jos 10:3
26:1 [d] 2Ch 22:1
26:5 [e] 2Ch 15:2; 24:2; Da 1:17 [f] 2Ch 27:6
26:6 [g] Isa 2:6; 11:14; 14:29; Jer 25:20 [h] Am 1:8; 3:9
26:7 [i] 2Ch 21:16 [j] 2Ch 20:1
26:8 [k] Ge 19:38; 2Ch 17:11

[a] *17* Hebrew *Joash,* a variant of *Jehoash*; also in verses 18, 21, 23 and 25 [b] *23* Hebrew *Jehoahaz,* a variant of *Ahaziah* [c] *23* That is, about 600 feet or about 180 meters [d] *28* Most Hebrew manuscripts, Septuagint, Vulgate and Syriac (see also 2 Kings 14:20) *David* [e] *1* Also called *Azariah* [f] *5* Many Hebrew manuscripts, Septuagint and Syriac; other Hebrew manuscripts *vision*

25:14 *gods of the people of Seir.* The national god of Seir (i.e., Edom) is Qos. Though sometimes the gods of the enemy were smashed or subjugated, it is not unusual to offer worship to the gods of defeated enemies if there is some sense that those gods fought on your side. Their favor could be considered as important as that of native gods.
25:24 *hostages.* The taking of hostages was a common way to ensure continued power over a conquered area, as reflected in the tactics of the Assyrian king Sennacherib, who took the relatives of Marduk-Baladan and those who were assisting him to discourage his ongoing acts of rebellion.
25:27 *Lachish.* See note on 2Ki 14:19.
26:1 *the people of Judah.* See note on 23:20.
26:2 *rebuilt Elath and restored it to Judah.* See note on 2Ki 14:22.

[9]Uzziah built towers in Jerusalem at the Corner Gate,[l] at the Valley Gate[m] and at the angle of the wall, and he fortified them. [10]He also built towers in the wilderness and dug many cisterns, because he had much livestock in the foothills and in the plain. He had people working his fields and vineyards in the hills and in the fertile lands, for he loved the soil.

[11]Uzziah had a well-trained army, ready to go out by divisions according to their numbers as mustered by Jeiel the secretary and Maaseiah the officer under the direction of Hananiah, one of the royal officials. [12]The total number of family leaders over the fighting men was 2,600. [13]Under their command was an army of 307,500 men trained for war, a powerful force to support the king against his enemies. [14]Uzziah provided shields, spears, helmets, coats of armor, bows and slingstones for the entire army.[n] [15]In Jerusalem he made devices invented for use on the towers and on the corner defenses so that soldiers could shoot arrows and hurl large stones from the walls. His fame spread far and wide, for he was greatly helped until he became powerful.

[16]But after Uzziah became powerful, his pride[o] led to his downfall.[p] He was unfaithful[q] to the LORD his God, and entered the temple of the LORD to burn incense[r] on the altar of incense. [17]Azariah[s] the priest with eighty other courageous priests of the LORD followed him in. [18]They confronted King Uzziah and said, "It is not right for you, Uzziah, to burn incense to the LORD. That is for the priests,[t] the descendants[u] of Aaron,[v] who have been consecrated to burn incense.[w] Leave the sanctuary, for you have been unfaithful; and you will not be honored by the LORD God."

[19]Uzziah, who had a censer in his hand ready to burn incense, became angry. While he was raging at the priests in their presence before the incense altar in the LORD's temple, leprosy[a][x] broke out on his forehead. [20]When Azariah the chief priest and all the other priests looked at him, they saw that he had leprosy on his forehead, so they hurried him out. Indeed, he himself was eager to leave, because the LORD had afflicted him.

[21]King Uzziah had leprosy until the day he died. He lived in a separate house[b][y]—leprous, and banned from the temple of the LORD. Jotham his son had charge of the palace and governed the people of the land.

[22]The other events of Uzziah's reign, from beginning to end, are recorded by the prophet Isaiah[z] son of Amoz. [23]Uzziah[a] rested with his ancestors and was buried near them in a cemetery that belonged to the kings, for people said, "He had leprosy." And Jotham his son succeeded him as king.[b]

Jotham King of Judah

27:1-4,7-9pp — 2Ki 15:33-38

27 Jotham[c] was twenty-five years old when he became king, and he reigned in Jerusalem sixteen years. His mother's name was Jerusha daughter of Zadok. [2]He did what was right in the eyes of the LORD, just as his father Uzziah had done, but unlike him he did not enter the temple of the LORD. The people, however, continued their corrupt practices. [3]Jotham rebuilt the Upper Gate of the temple of the LORD and did extensive work on the wall at the hill of Ophel.[d] [4]He built towns in the hill country of Judah and forts and towers in the wooded areas.

[5]Jotham waged war against the king of the Ammonites[e] and conquered them.

[a] *19* The Hebrew for *leprosy* was used for various diseases affecting the skin; also in verses 20, 21 and 23.
[b] *21* Or *in a house where he was relieved of responsibilities*

26:9 [l] 2Ki 14:13; 2Ch 25:23 [m] Ne 2:13; 3:13
26:14 [n] Jer 46:4
26:16 [o] 2Ki 14:10 [p] Dt 32:15; 2Ch 25:19 [q] 1Ch 5:25 [r] 2Ki 16:12
26:17 [s] 1Ki 4:2; 1Ch 6:10
26:18 [t] Nu 16:39 [u] Nu 18:1-7 [v] Ex 30:7 [w] 1Ch 6:49
26:19 [x] Nu 12:10; 2Ki 5:25-27
26:21 [y] Ex 4:6; Lev 13:46; 14:8; Nu 5:2; 19:12
26:22 [z] 2Ki 15:1; Isa 1:1; 6:1
26:23 [a] Isa 1:1; 6:1 [b] 2Ki 14:21; 15:7; Am 1:1
27:1 [c] 2Ki 15:5, 32; 1Ch 3:12
27:3 [d] 2Ch 33:14; Ne 3:26
27:5 [e] Ge 19:38

26:13 *307,500 men.* See the article "Numbers in Numbers," p. 235.

26:14 *shields, spears, helmets, coats of armor, bows and slingstones.* Assyrian reliefs indicate a wide variety of shields, spears, bows and battle armament, including coats of armor used for chariot warfare. Uzziah's impressive efforts for his army are an indirect statement on the economic and political stability of Judah at this time.

26:15 *devices invented for use on the towers and on the corner defenses so that soldiers could shoot arrows and hurl large stones from the walls.* The specifics of these military machines are not clear. Their design and the remark that Uzziah's fame spread far and wide as a result of this equipment implies that these were impressive devices (at least within a Judahite context). While catapult-like devices are not known in the ancient world until several hundred years later, the view that these "devices" were essentially shields to protect soldiers as they shot arrows or threw stones ignores the engineering and design emphasis of the passage. In any case, these devices created a military advantage for a city under siege.

26:19 *leprosy.* See notes on Ex 4:6; Lev 13:2. Yahdun-Lim of Mari calls down a curse of leprosy on whoever desecrates the temple he is dedicating, so the association of the disease with cultic impropriety seems to be a known theme.

27:5 *Jotham waged war against the king of the Ammonites.* Jotham continued the domination of Ammon attained by his father, Uzziah. Since the northern kingdom retained the Transjordan tribes (Gad, Reuben and part of Manasseh) and exercised hegemony over Transjordan nations such as Moab, Uzziah and Jotham's expansion of southern kingdom–interests to Ammon are impressive and likely relate to the warmed relations between Israel and Judah during this time. *the Ammonites paid him.* The amount of silver tribute received by Jotham noted here is staggering. A talent weighed about 75 pounds, so that Ammon's tribute was about 3.75 tons (3.4 metric tons) of silver.

That year the Ammonites paid him a hundred talents[a] of silver, ten thousand cors[b]
of wheat and ten thousand cors[c] of barley. The Ammonites brought him the same
amount also in the second and third years.
6Jotham grew powerful[f] because he
walked steadfastly before the LORD his
God.
7The other events in Jotham's reign, including all his wars and the other things
he did, are written in the book of the kings
of Israel and Judah. 8He was twenty-five
years old when he became king, and he
reigned in Jerusalem sixteen years. 9Jo-
tham rested with his ancestors and was
buried in the City of David. And Ahaz his
son succeeded him as king.

Ahaz King of Judah

28:1-27pp — 2Ki 16:1-20

28 Ahaz[g] was twenty years old when
he became king, and he reigned in
Jerusalem sixteen years. Unlike David his
father, he did not do what was right in the
eyes of the LORD. 2He followed the ways of
the kings of Israel and also made idols[h] for
worshiping the Baals. 3He burned sacrifices in the Valley of Ben Hinnom[i] and sacrificed his children[j] in the fire, engaging in
the detestable[k] practices of the nations the
LORD had driven out before the Israelites.
4He offered sacrifices and burned incense
at the high places, on the hilltops and under every spreading tree.
5Therefore the LORD his God delivered him into the hands of the king of
Aram.[l] The Arameans defeated him and
took many of his people as prisoners and
brought them to Damascus.
He was also given into the hands of
the king of Israel, who inflicted heavy casualties on him. 6In one day Pekah[m] son
of Remaliah killed a hundred and twenty thousand soldiers in Judah[n] — because
Judah had forsaken the LORD, the God of
their ancestors. 7Zikri, an Ephraimite warrior, killed Maaseiah the king's son, Azrikam the officer in charge of the palace,
and Elkanah, second to the king. 8The
men of Israel took captive from their fellow Israelites who were from Judah[o] two
hundred thousand wives, sons and daughters. They also took a great deal of plunder, which they carried back to Samaria.[p]
9But a prophet of the LORD named Oded
was there, and he went out to meet the
army when it returned to Samaria. He said
to them, "Because the LORD, the God of
your ancestors, was angry[q] with Judah, he
gave them into your hand. But you have
slaughtered them in a rage that reaches to
heaven.[r] 10And now you intend to make
the men and women of Judah and Jerusalem your slaves.[s] But aren't you also guilty
of sins against the LORD your God? 11Now
listen to me! Send back your fellow Israelites you have taken as prisoners, for the
LORD's fierce anger rests on you.[t]"
12Then some of the leaders in Ephraim — Azariah son of Jehohanan, Berekiah son of Meshillemoth, Jehizkiah son of
Shallum, and Amasa son of Hadlai — confronted those who were arriving from the
war. 13"You must not bring those prisoners
here," they said, "or we will be guilty before the LORD. Do you intend to add to our
sin and guilt? For our guilt is already great,
and his fierce anger rests on Israel."
14So the soldiers gave up the prisoners
and plunder in the presence of the officials
and all the assembly. 15The men designated by name took the prisoners, and from
the plunder they clothed all who were
naked. They provided them with clothes
and sandals, food and drink,[u] and healing balm. All those who were weak they
put on donkeys. So they took them back to
their fellow Israelites at Jericho, the City of
Palms,[v] and returned to Samaria.
16At that time King Ahaz sent to the
kings[d] of Assyria[w] for help. 17The Edomites[x] had again come and attacked Judah
and carried away prisoners,[y] 18while the
Philistines[z] had raided towns in the foothills and in the Negev of Judah. They
captured and occupied Beth Shemesh, Aijalon[a] and Gederoth, as well as Soko, Timnah and Gimzo, with their surrounding
villages. 19The LORD had humbled Judah
because of Ahaz king of Israel,[e] for he had
promoted wickedness in Judah and had
been most unfaithful[b] to the LORD. 20Tig-
lath-Pileser[f][c] king of Assyria came to him,
but he gave him trouble instead of help.[d]
21Ahaz took some of the things from the
temple of the LORD and from the royal palace and from the officials and presented
them to the king of Assyria, but that did
not help him.

27:6 [f] 2Ch 26:5
28:1 [g] 1Ch 3:13; Isa 1:1
28:2 [h] Ex 34:17; 2Ch 22:3
28:3 [i] Jos 15:8; 2Ki 23:10 [j] Lev 18:21; 2Ki 3:27; 2Ch 33:6; Eze 20:26 [k] Dt 18:9; 2Ch 33:2
28:5 [l] Isa 7:1
28:6 [m] 2Ki 15:25,27 [n] ver 8; Isa 9:21; 11:13
28:8 [o] Dt 28:25-41; 2Ch 11:4 [p] 2Ch 29:9
28:9 [q] 2Ch 25:15; Isa 10:6; 47:6; Zec 1:15 [r] Ezr 9:6; Rev 18:5
28:10 [s] Lev 25:39-46
28:11 [t] 2Ch 11:4; Jas 2:13
28:15 [u] 2Ki 6:22; Pr 25:21-22 [v] Dt 34:3; Jdg 1:16
28:16 [w] 2Ki 16:7
28:17 [x] Ps 137:7; Isa 34:5 [y] 2Ch 29:9
28:18 [z] Eze 16:27,57 [a] Jos 10:12
28:19 [b] 2Ch 21:2
28:20 [c] 2Ki 15:29; 1Ch 5:6 [d] 2Ki 16:7

[a] *5* That is, about 3 3/4 tons or about 3.4 metric tons
[b] *5* That is, probably about 1,800 tons or about 1,600 metric tons of wheat [c] *5* That is, probably about 1,500 tons or about 1,350 metric tons of barley
[d] *16* Most Hebrew manuscripts; one Hebrew manuscript, Septuagint and Vulgate (see also 2 Kings 16:7) *king*
[e] *19* That is, Judah, as frequently in 2 Chronicles
[f] *20* Hebrew *Tilgath-Pilneser*, a variant of *Tiglath-Pileser*

28:3 *sacrificed his children in the fire.* See notes on Lev 20:2; 1Ki 11:5; 2Ki 3:27; 16:3; Jer 7:31.
28:6 *a hundred and twenty thousand soldiers.* See the article "Numbers in Numbers," p. 235.
28:16 – 21 See the article "Israel and Damascus Versus Judah," p. 649.

22In his time of trouble King Ahaz became even more unfaithful[e] to the LORD.
23He offered sacrifices to the gods[f] of Damascus, who had defeated him; for he
thought, "Since the gods of the kings of
Aram have helped them, I will sacrifice
to them so they will help me."[g] But they
were his downfall and the downfall of all
Israel.
24Ahaz gathered together the furnishings from the temple of God[h] and cut them
in pieces. He shut the doors[i] of the LORD's
temple and set up altars[j] at every street
corner in Jerusalem. 25In every town in Judah he built high places to burn sacrifices
to other gods and aroused the anger of the
LORD, the God of his ancestors.
26The other events of his reign and all
his ways, from beginning to end, are written in the book of the kings of Judah and
Israel. 27Ahaz rested[k] with his ancestors
and was buried[l] in the city of Jerusalem,
but he was not placed in the tombs of the
kings of Israel. And Hezekiah his son succeeded him as king.

Hezekiah Purifies the Temple

29:1-2pp — 2Ki 18:2-3

29 Hezekiah[m] was twenty-five years
old when he became king, and he
reigned in Jerusalem twenty-nine years.
His mother's name was Abijah daughter
of Zechariah. 2He did what was right in
the eyes of the LORD, just as his father David[n] had done.
3In the first month of the first year of his
reign, he opened the doors of the temple of
the LORD and repaired[o] them. 4He brought
in the priests and the Levites, assembled
them in the square on the east side 5and
said: "Listen to me, Levites! Consecrate[p]
yourselves now and consecrate the temple of the LORD, the God of your ancestors.
Remove all defilement from the sanctuary.
6Our parents[q] were unfaithful;[r] they did
evil in the eyes of the LORD our God and
forsook him. They turned their faces away
from the LORD's dwelling place and turned
their backs on him. 7They also shut the
doors of the portico and put out the lamps.
They did not burn incense or present any
burnt offerings at the sanctuary to the God
of Israel. 8Therefore, the anger of the LORD
has fallen on Judah and Jerusalem; he has
made them an object of dread and horror[s]
and scorn,[t] as you can see with your own
eyes. 9This is why our fathers have fall-
en by the sword and why our sons and
daughters and our wives are in captivity.[u] 10Now I intend to make a covenant[v]
with the LORD, the God of Israel, so that
his fierce anger will turn away from us.
11My sons, do not be negligent now, for
the LORD has chosen you to stand before
him and serve him,[w] to minister[x] before
him and to burn incense."
12Then these Levites[y] set to work:
from the Kohathites,
Mahath son of Amasai and Joel son
of Azariah;
from the Merarites,
Kish son of Abdi and Azariah son
of Jehallelel;
from the Gershonites,
Joah son of Zimmah and Eden[z] son
of Joah;
13from the descendants of Elizaphan,
Shimri and Jeiel;
from the descendants of Asaph,[a]
Zechariah and Mattaniah;
14from the descendants of Heman,
Jehiel and Shimei;
from the descendants of Jeduthun,
Shemaiah and Uzziel.
15When they had assembled their fellow
Levites and consecrated themselves, they
went in to purify[b] the temple of the LORD,
as the king had ordered, following the
word of the LORD. 16The priests went into
the sanctuary of the LORD to purify it. They
brought out to the courtyard of the LORD's
temple everything unclean that they found
in the temple of the LORD. The Levites took
it and carried it out to the Kidron Valley.[c]
17They began the consecration on the first
day of the first month, and by the eighth
day of the month they reached the portico of the LORD. For eight more days they
consecrated the temple of the LORD itself,
finishing on the sixteenth day of the first
month.
18Then they went in to King Hezekiah
and reported: "We have purified the entire temple of the LORD, the altar of burnt
offering with all its utensils, and the table for setting out the consecrated bread,
with all its articles. 19We have prepared
and consecrated all the articles[d] that King
Ahaz removed in his unfaithfulness while
he was king. They are now in front of the
LORD's altar."
20Early the next morning King Hezekiah gathered the city officials together and
went up to the temple of the LORD. 21They
brought seven bulls, seven rams, seven
male lambs and seven male goats as a sin

28:22 [e] Jer 5:3
28:23 [f] 2Ch 25:14 [g] Jer 44:17-18
28:24 [h] 2Ki 16:18 [i] 2Ch 29:7 [j] 2Ch 30:14
28:27 [k] Isa 14:28-32 [l] 2Ch 21:20; 24:25
29:1 [m] 1Ch 3:13
29:2 [n] 2Ch 28:1; 34:2
29:3 [o] 2Ch 28:24
29:5 [p] 2Ch 35:6
29:6 [q] Ps 106:6-47; Jer 2:27 [r] 1Ch 5:25; Eze 8:16
29:8 [s] Dt 28:25; 2Ch 24:18 [t] Jer 18:16; 19:8; 25:9, 18
29:9 [u] 2Ch 28:5-8, 17
29:10 [v] 2Ch 15:12; 23:16
29:11 [w] Nu 3:6; 8:6, 14 [x] 1Ch 15:2
29:12 [y] Nu 3:17-20 [z] 2Ch 31:15
29:13 [a] 1Ch 6:39
29:15 [b] ver 5; 1Ch 23:28; 2Ch 30:12
29:16 [c] 2Sa 15:23
29:19 [d] 2Ch 28:24

28:24 *set up altars at every street corner.* Babylonian texts refer to small, open-air shrines located on street corners. The city of Babylon was said to contain 180 of them dedicated to Ishtar.

28:27 *not placed in the tombs of the kings of Israel.* See note on 21:20.

offering[a][e] for the kingdom, for the sanctuary and for Judah. The king commanded
the priests, the descendants of Aaron, to
offer these on the altar of the LORD. 22So
they slaughtered the bulls, and the priests
took the blood and splashed it against the
altar; next they slaughtered the rams and
splashed their blood against the altar; then
they slaughtered the lambs and splashed
their blood[f] against the altar. 23The goats
for the sin offering were brought before
the king and the assembly, and they laid
their hands[g] on them. 24The priests then
slaughtered the goats and presented their
blood on the altar for a sin offering to
atone[h] for all Israel, because the king had
ordered the burnt offering and the sin offering for all Israel.

25He stationed the Levites in the temple
of the LORD with cymbals, harps and lyres
in the way prescribed by David[i] and Gad[j]
the king's seer and Nathan the prophet;
this was commanded by the LORD through
his prophets. 26So the Levites stood ready
with David's instruments,[k] and the priests
with their trumpets.[l]

27Hezekiah gave the order to sacrifice
the burnt offering on the altar. As the offering began, singing to the LORD began
also, accompanied by trumpets and the instruments[m] of David king of Israel. 28The
whole assembly bowed in worship, while
the musicians played and the trumpets
sounded. All this continued until the sacrifice of the burnt offering was completed.

29When the offerings were finished, the
king and everyone present with him knelt
down and worshiped.[n] 30King Hezekiah
and his officials ordered the Levites to
praise the LORD with the words of David
and of Asaph the seer. So they sang praises with gladness and bowed down and
worshiped.

31Then Hezekiah said, "You have now
dedicated yourselves to the LORD. Come
and bring sacrifices[o] and thank offerings
to the temple of the LORD." So the assembly brought sacrifices and thank offerings, and all whose hearts were willing[p]
brought burnt offerings.

32The number of burnt offerings the
assembly brought was seventy bulls, a
hundred rams and two hundred male
lambs—all of them for burnt offerings to
the LORD. 33The animals consecrated as
sacrifices amounted to six hundred bulls
and three thousand sheep and goats. 34The
priests, however, were too few to skin all
the burnt offerings;[q] so their relatives the
Levites helped them until the task was finished and until other priests had been consecrated,[r] for the Levites had been more
conscientious in consecrating themselves
than the priests had been. 35There were
burnt offerings in abundance, together
with the fat[s] of the fellowship offerings[t]
and the drink offerings[u] that accompanied
the burnt offerings.

So the service of the temple of the LORD
was reestablished. 36Hezekiah and all the
people rejoiced at what God had brought
about for his people, because it was done
so quickly.

Hezekiah Celebrates the Passover

30 Hezekiah sent word to all Israel
and Judah and also wrote letters
to Ephraim and Manasseh,[v] inviting them
to come to the temple of the LORD in Jerusalem and celebrate the Passover[w] to the
LORD, the God of Israel. 2The king and his
officials and the whole assembly in Jerusalem decided to celebrate[x] the Passover in
the second month. 3They had not been able
to celebrate it at the regular time because
not enough priests had consecrated[y] themselves and the people had not assembled in
Jerusalem. 4The plan seemed right both to
the king and to the whole assembly. 5They
decided to send a proclamation throughout
Israel, from Beersheba to Dan,[z] calling the
people to come to Jerusalem and celebrate
the Passover to the LORD, the God of Israel.
It had not been celebrated in large numbers
according to what was written.

6At the king's command, couriers went
throughout Israel and Judah with letters
from the king and from his officials, which
read:

"People of Israel, return to the LORD,
the God of Abraham, Isaac and Israel, that he may return to you who are
left, who have escaped from the hand
of the kings of Assyria. 7Do not be like
your parents[a] and your fellow Israelites, who were unfaithful to the LORD,
the God of their ancestors, so that he
made them an object of horror,[b] as
you see. 8Do not be stiff-necked,[c] as
your ancestors were; submit to the
LORD. Come to his sanctuary, which
he has consecrated forever. Serve the
LORD your God, so that his fierce anger[d] will turn away from you. 9If you
return[e] to the LORD, then your fellow
Israelites and your children will be
shown compassion[f] by their captors
and will return to this land, for the
LORD your God is gracious and compassionate.[g] He will not turn his face
from you if you return to him."

10The couriers went from town to town
in Ephraim and Manasseh, as far as Zeb-

29:21 [e] Lev 4:13-14 **29:22** [f] Lev 4:18 **29:23** [g] Lev 4:15 **29:24** [h] Ex 29:36; Lev 4:26 **29:25** [i] 1Ch 25:6; 2Ch 8:14 [j] 1Sa 22:5; 2Sa 24:11 **29:26** [k] 1Ch 15:16 [l] 1Ch 15:24; 23:5; 2Ch 5:12 **29:27** [m] 2Ch 23:18 **29:29** [n] 2Ch 20:18 **29:31** [o] Heb 13:15-16 [p] Ex 25:2; 35:22 **29:34** [q] 2Ch 35:11 [r] 2Ch 30:3, 15

29:35 [s] Ex 29:13; Lev 3:16 [t] Lev 7:11-21 [u] Nu 15:5-10 **30:1** [v] Ge 41:52 [w] Ex 12:11; Nu 28:16 **30:2** [x] Nu 9:10 **30:3** [y] 2Ch 29:34 **30:5** [z] Jdg 20:1 **30:7** [a] Ps 78:8, 57; 106:6; Eze 20:18 [b] 2Ch 29:8 **30:8** [c] Ex 32:9 [d] Nu 25:4; 2Ch 29:10 **30:9** [e] Dt 30:2-5; Isa 1:16; 55:7 [f] 1Ki 8:50; Ps 106:46 [g] Ex 34:6-7; Dt 4:31; Mic 7:18

[a] 21 Or *purification offering*; also in verses 23 and 24

ulun, but people scorned and ridiculed[h] them. 11Nevertheless, some from Asher, Manasseh and Zebulun humbled themselves and went to Jerusalem.[i] 12Also in Judah the hand of God was on the people to give them unity[j] of mind to carry out what the king and his officials had ordered, following the word of the LORD.

13A very large crowd of people assembled in Jerusalem to celebrate the Festival of Unleavened Bread[k] in the second month. 14They removed the altars[l] in Jerusalem and cleared away the incense altars and threw them into the Kidron Valley.[m]

15They slaughtered the Passover lamb on the fourteenth day of the second month. The priests and the Levites were ashamed and consecrated[n] themselves and brought burnt offerings to the temple of the LORD. 16Then they took up their regular positions[o] as prescribed in the Law of Moses the man of God. The priests splashed against the altar the blood handed to them by the Levites. 17Since many in the crowd had not consecrated themselves, the Levites had to kill[p] the Passover lambs for all those who were not ceremonially clean and could not consecrate their lambs[a] to the LORD. 18Although most of the many people who came from Ephraim, Manasseh, Issachar and Zebulun had not purified themselves,[q] yet they ate the Passover, contrary to what was written. But Hezekiah prayed for them, saying, "May the LORD, who is good, pardon everyone 19who sets their heart on seeking God—the LORD, the God of their ancestors—even if they are not clean according to the rules of the sanctuary." 20And the LORD heard[r] Hezekiah and healed[s] the people.[t]

21The Israelites who were present in Jerusalem celebrated the Festival of Unleavened Bread[u] for seven days with great rejoicing, while the Levites and priests praised the LORD every day with resounding instruments dedicated to the LORD.[b]

22Hezekiah spoke encouragingly to all the Levites, who showed good understanding of the service of the LORD. For the seven days they ate their assigned portion and offered fellowship offerings and praised[c] the LORD, the God of their ancestors.

23The whole assembly then agreed to celebrate[v] the festival seven more days; so for another seven days they celebrated joyfully. 24Hezekiah king of Judah provided[w] a thousand bulls and seven thousand sheep and goats for the assembly, and the officials provided them with a thousand bulls and ten thousand sheep and goats. A great number of priests consecrated themselves. 25The entire assembly of Judah rejoiced, along with the priests and Levites and all who had assembled from Israel[x], including the foreigners who had come from Israel and also those who resided in Judah. 26There was great joy in Jerusalem, for since the days of Solomon[y] son of David king of Israel there had been nothing like this in Jerusalem. 27The priests and the Levites stood to bless[z] the people, and God heard them, for their prayer reached heaven, his holy dwelling place.

31 When all this had ended, the Israelites who were there went out to the towns of Judah, smashed the sacred stones and cut down[a] the Asherah poles. They destroyed the high places and the altars throughout Judah and Benjamin and in Ephraim and Manasseh. After they had destroyed all of them, the Israelites returned to their own towns and to their own property.

Contributions for Worship

31:20-21pp — 2Ki 18:5-7

2Hezekiah[b] assigned the priests and Levites to divisions[c]—each of them according to their duties as priests or Levites—to offer burnt offerings and fellowship offerings, to minister,[d] to give thanks and to sing praises[e] at the gates of the LORD's dwelling.[f] 3The king contributed[g] from his own possessions for the morning and evening burnt offerings and for the burnt offerings on the Sabbaths, at the New Moons and at the appointed festivals as written in the Law of the LORD.[h] 4He ordered the people living in Jerusalem to give the portion[i] due the priests and Levites so they could devote themselves to the Law of the LORD. 5As soon as the order went out, the Israelites generously gave the firstfruits[j] of their grain, new wine,[k] olive oil and honey and all that the fields produced. They brought a great amount, a tithe of everything. 6The people of Israel and Judah who lived in the towns of Judah also brought a tithe[l] of their herds and flocks and a tithe of the holy things dedicated to the LORD their God, and they piled them in heaps.[m] 7They began doing this in the third month and finished in the seventh month.[n] 8When Hezekiah and his officials

30:10 [h] 2Ch 36:16 **30:11** [i] ver 25 **30:12** [j] Jer 32:39; Eze 11:19; Php 2:13 **30:13** [k] Nu 28:16 **30:14** [l] 2Ch 28:24 [m] 2Sa 15:23 **30:15** [n] 2Ch 29:34 **30:16** [o] 2Ch 35:10 **30:17** [p] 2Ch 29:34 **30:18** [q] Ex 12:43-49; Nu 9:6-10 **30:20** [r] 2Ch 6:20 [s] 2Ch 7:14; Mal 4:2 [t] Jas 5:16 **30:21** [u] Ex 12:15, 17; 13:6 **30:23** [v] 1Ki 8:65; 2Ch 7:9 **30:24** [w] 1Ki 8:5; 2Ch 29:34; 35:7; Ezr 6:17; 8:35

30:25 [x] ver 11 **30:26** [y] 2Ch 7:8 **30:27** [z] Ex 39:43; Nu 6:23; Dt 26:15; 2Ch 23:18; Ps 68:5 **31:1** [a] 2Ki 18:4; 2Ch 32:12; Isa 36:7 **31:2** [b] 2Ch 29:9 [c] 1Ch 24:1 [d] 1Ch 15:2 [e] Ps 7:17; 9:2; 47:6; 71:22 [f] 1Ch 23:28-32 **31:3** [g] 1Ch 29:3; 2Ch 35:7; Eze 45:17 [h] Nu 28:1-29:40 **31:4** [i] Nu 18:8; Dt 18:8; Ne 13:10; Mal 2:7 **31:5** [j] Nu 18:12, 24; Ne 13:12; Eze 44:30 [k] Dt 12:17 **31:6** [l] Lev 27:30; Ne 13:10-12 [m] Dt 14:28; Ru 3:7 **31:7** [n] Ex 23:16

[a] *17* Or *consecrate themselves* [b] *21* Or *priests sang to the LORD every day, accompanied by the LORD's instruments of praise* [c] *22* Or *and confessed their sins to*

31:1 *sacred stones ... Asherah poles.* See notes on Dt 7:5; 1Ki 14:23. *high places.* See notes on 1:3; 1Ki 3:2; 11:7.

came and saw the heaps, they praised the LORD and blessed[o] his people Israel.

9 Hezekiah asked the priests and Levites about the heaps; 10 and Azariah the chief priest, from the family of Zadok,[p] answered, "Since the people began to bring their contributions to the temple of the LORD, we have had enough to eat and plenty to spare, because the LORD has blessed his people, and this great amount is left over."[q]

11 Hezekiah gave orders to prepare storerooms in the temple of the LORD, and this was done. 12 Then they faithfully brought in the contributions, tithes and dedicated gifts. Konaniah,[r] a Levite, was the overseer in charge of these things, and his brother Shimei was next in rank. 13 Jehiel, Azaziah, Nahath, Asahel, Jerimoth, Jozabad,[s] Eliel, Ismakiah, Mahath and Benaiah were assistants of Konaniah and Shimei his brother. All these served by appointment of King Hezekiah and Azariah the official in charge of the temple of God.

14 Kore son of Imnah the Levite, keeper of the East Gate, was in charge of the freewill offerings given to God, distributing the contributions made to the LORD and also the consecrated gifts. 15 Eden,[t] Miniamin, Jeshua, Shemaiah, Amariah and Shekaniah assisted him faithfully in the towns[u] of the priests, distributing to their fellow priests according to their divisions, old and young alike.

16 In addition, they distributed to the males three years old or more whose names were in the genealogical records[v]— all who would enter the temple of the LORD to perform the daily duties of their various tasks, according to their responsibilities and their divisions. 17 And they distributed to the priests enrolled by their families in the genealogical records and likewise to the Levites twenty years old or more, according to their responsibilities and their divisions. 18 They included all the little ones, the wives, and the sons and daughters of the whole community listed in these genealogical records. For they were faithful in consecrating themselves.

19 As for the priests, the descendants of Aaron, who lived on the farmlands around their towns or in any other towns,[w] men were designated by name to distribute portions to every male among them and to all who were recorded in the genealogies of the Levites.

20 This is what Hezekiah did throughout Judah, doing what was good and right and faithful[x] before the LORD his God. 21 In everything that he undertook in the service of God's temple and in obedience to the law and the commands, he sought his God and worked wholeheartedly. And so he prospered.[y]

Sennacherib Threatens Jerusalem

32:9-19pp — 2Ki 18:17-35; Isa 36:2-20
32:20-21pp — 2Ki 19:35-37; Isa 37:36-38

32 After all that Hezekiah had so faithfully done, Sennacherib[z] king of Assyria came and invaded Judah. He laid siege to the fortified cities, thinking to conquer them for himself. 2 When Hezekiah saw that Sennacherib had come and that he intended to wage war against Jerusalem,[a] 3 he consulted with his officials and military staff about blocking off the water from the springs outside the city, and they helped him. 4 They gathered a large group of people who blocked all the springs[b] and the stream that flowed through the land. "Why should the kings[a] of Assyria come and find plenty of water?" they said. 5 Then he worked hard repairing all the broken sections of the wall[c] and building towers on it. He built another wall outside that one and reinforced the terraces[b][d] of the City of David. He also made large numbers of weapons[e] and shields.

6 He appointed military officers over the people and assembled them before him in the square at the city gate and encouraged them with these words: 7 "Be strong and courageous.[f] Do not be afraid or discouraged[g] because of the king of Assyria and the vast army with him, for there is a greater power with us than with him.[h] 8 With him is only the arm of flesh,[i] but with us[j] is the LORD our God to help us and to fight our battles."[k] And the people gained confidence from what Hezekiah the king of Judah said.

9 Later, when Sennacherib king of Assyria and all his forces were laying siege to Lachish,[l] he sent his officers to Jerusalem with this message for Hezekiah king of Judah and for all the people of Judah who were there:

10 "This is what Sennacherib king of Assyria says: On what are you basing

[a] 4 Hebrew; Septuagint and Syriac *king* [b] 5 Or *the Millo*

31:8 [o] Ps 144:13-15 **31:10** [p] 2Sa 8:17 [q] Ex 36:5; Eze 44:30; Mal 3:10-12 **31:12** [r] 2Ch 35:9 **31:13** [s] 2Ch 35:9 **31:15** [t] 2Ch 29:12 [u] Jos 21:9-19 **31:16** [v] 1Ch 23:3; Ezr 3:4 **31:19** [w] ver 12-15; Lev 25:34; Nu 35:2-5 **31:20** [x] 2Ki 20:3; 22:2 **31:21** [y] Dt 29:9 **32:1** [z] 2Ki 18:13-19; Isa 36:1; 37:9, 17, 37 **32:2** [a] Isa 22:7; Jer 1:15 **32:4** [b] 2Ki 18:17; 20:20; Isa 22:9, 11; Na 3:14 **32:5** [c] 2Ch 25:23; Isa 22:10 [d] 1Ki 9:24; 1Ch 11:8 [e] Isa 22:8 **32:7** [f] Dt 31:6; 1Ch 22:13 [g] 2Ch 20:15 [h] Nu 14:9; 2Ki 6:16 **32:8** [i] Job 40:9; Isa 52:10; Jer 17:5; 32:21 [j] Dt 3:22; 1Sa 17:45; 2Ch 13:12 [k] 1Ch 5:22; 2Ch 20:17; Ps 20:7; Isa 28:6 **32:9** [l] Jos 10:3, 31

31:11 *storerooms in the temple.* See the article "Architecture of the Temple," p. 572. Hezekiah's efforts are either a revamping of existing storage in Solomon's temple or an expansion of storage capacity in light of the renewed focus on temple worship.

32:1 *Sennacherib king of Assyria … invaded Judah.* See note on 2Ki 18:13; see also the article "Hezekiah and Assyria," p. 657.

32:9 *Lachish.* See notes on 2Ki 14:19; 18:14. *officers.* See note on 2Ki 18:17.

Sennacherib watching over the exile of Lachish. These scenes were found in Sennacherib's palace in Nineveh (seventh century BC).

your confidence,[m] that you remain in
Jerusalem under siege? 11 When Hezekiah says, 'The LORD our God will
save us from the hand of the king of
Assyria,' he is misleading[n] you, to let
you die of hunger and thirst. 12 Did
not Hezekiah himself remove this
god's high places and altars, saying
to Judah and Jerusalem, 'You must
worship before one altar[o] and burn
sacrifices on it'?

13 "Do you not know what I and my
predecessors have done to all the peoples of the other lands? Were the gods
of those nations ever able to deliver
their land from my hand?[p] 14 Who
of all the gods of these nations that
my predecessors destroyed has been
able to save his people from me? How
then can your god deliver you from
my hand? 15 Now do not let Hezekiah deceive[q] you and mislead you like
this. Do not believe him, for no god of
any nation or kingdom has been able
to deliver[r] his people from my hand
or the hand of my predecessors.[s] How
much less will your god deliver you
from my hand!"

16 Sennacherib's officers spoke further
against the LORD God and against his servant Hezekiah. 17 The king also wrote letters[t] ridiculing[u] the LORD, the God of Israel, and saying this against him: "Just as
the gods[v] of the peoples of the other lands
did not rescue their people from my hand,
so the god of Hezekiah will not rescue his
people from my hand." 18 Then they called
out in Hebrew to the people of Jerusalem
who were on the wall, to terrify them and
make them afraid in order to capture the
city. 19 They spoke about the God of Jerusalem as they did about the gods of the
other peoples of the world — the work of
human hands.[w]

20 King Hezekiah and the prophet Isaiah
son of Amoz cried out in prayer to heaven
about this. 21 And the LORD sent an angel,[x]
who annihilated all the fighting men and
the commanders and officers in the camp
of the Assyrian king. So he withdrew to
his own land in disgrace. And when he
went into the temple of his god, some of
his sons, his own flesh and blood, cut him
down with the sword.[y]

22 So the LORD saved Hezekiah and the
people of Jerusalem from the hand of

32:10 [m] Eze 29:16 **32:11** [n] Isa 37:10 **32:12** [o] 2Ch 31:1 **32:13** [p] ver 15 **32:15** [q] Isa 37:10 [r] Da 3:15 [s] Ex 5:2 **32:17** [t] Isa 37:14 [u] Ps 74:22; Isa 37:4, 17 [v] 2Ki 19:12 **32:19** [w] 2Ki 19:18; Ps 115:4-8; Isa 2:8; 17:8 **32:21** [x] Ge 19:13 [y] 2Ki 19:7

32:21 *some of his sons ... cut him down with the sword.* See the article "The Death of Sennacherib," p. 661. In order to close out the account, the death notice of Sennacherib is given, although his actual death does not come for another 20 years.

Sennacherib king of Assyria and from the hand of all others. He took care of them[a] on every side. 23 Many brought offerings to Jerusalem for the LORD and valuable gifts[z] for Hezekiah king of Judah. From then on he was highly regarded by all the nations.

Hezekiah's Pride, Success and Death

32:24-33pp — 2Ki 20:1-21; Isa 37:21-38; 38:1-8

24 In those days Hezekiah became ill and was at the point of death. He prayed to the LORD, who answered him and gave him a miraculous sign. 25 But Hezekiah's heart was proud[a] and he did not respond to the kindness shown him; therefore the LORD's wrath[b] was on him and on Judah and Jerusalem. 26 Then Hezekiah repented[c] of the pride of his heart, as did the people of Jerusalem; therefore the LORD's wrath did not come on them during the days of Hezekiah.[d]

27 Hezekiah had very great wealth and honor,[e] and he made treasuries for his silver and gold and for his precious stones, spices, shields and all kinds of valuables. 28 He also made buildings to store the harvest of grain, new wine and olive oil; and he made stalls for various kinds of cattle, and pens for the flocks. 29 He built villages and acquired great numbers of flocks and herds, for God had given him very great riches.[f]

30 It was Hezekiah who blocked[g] the upper outlet of the Gihon[h] spring and channeled the water down to the west side of the City of David. He succeeded in everything he undertook. 31 But when envoys were sent by the rulers of Babylon[i] to ask him about the miraculous sign[j] that had occurred in the land, God left him to test[k] him and to know everything that was in his heart.

32 The other events of Hezekiah's reign and his acts of devotion are written in the vision of the prophet Isaiah son of Amoz in the book of the kings of Judah and Israel. 33 Hezekiah rested with his ancestors and was buried on the hill where the tombs of David's descendants are. All Judah and the people of Jerusalem honored him when he died. And Manasseh his son succeeded him as king.

Manasseh King of Judah

33:1-10pp — 2Ki 21:1-10
33:18-20pp — 2Ki 21:17-18

33 Manasseh[l] was twelve years old when he became king, and he reigned in Jerusalem fifty-five years. 2 He did evil in the eyes of the LORD,[m] following the detestable[n] practices of the nations the LORD had driven out before the Israelites. 3 He rebuilt the high places his father Hezekiah had demolished; he also erected altars to the Baals and made Asherah poles.[o] He bowed down[p] to all the starry hosts and worshiped them. 4 He built altars in the temple of the LORD, of which the LORD had said, "My Name[q] will remain in Jerusalem forever." 5 In both courts of the temple of the LORD,[r] he built altars to all the starry hosts. 6 He sacrificed his children[s] in the fire in the Valley of Ben Hinnom, practiced divination and witchcraft, sought omens, and consulted mediums[t] and spiritists.[u] He did much evil in the eyes of the LORD, arousing his anger.

7 He took the image he had made and put it in God's temple,[v] of which God had said to David and to his son Solomon, "In this temple and in Jerusalem, which I have chosen out of all the tribes of Israel, I will put my Name forever. 8 I will not again make the feet of the Israelites leave the land[w] I assigned to your ancestors, if only they will be careful to do everything I commanded them concerning all the laws, decrees and regulations given through Moses." 9 But Manasseh led Judah and the people of Jerusalem astray, so that they did more evil than the nations the LORD had destroyed before the Israelites.[x]

10 The LORD spoke to Manasseh and his people, but they paid no attention. 11 So the LORD brought against them the army commanders of the king of Assyria, who took Manasseh prisoner,[y] put a hook in his nose, bound him with bronze shackles[z] and took him to Babylon. 12 In his distress he sought the favor of the LORD his God and humbled[a] himself greatly before the God of his ancestors. 13 And when he prayed to him, the LORD was moved by his entreaty and listened to his plea; so he brought him back to Jerusalem and to his kingdom. Then Manasseh knew that the LORD is God.

14 Afterward he rebuilt the outer wall of the City of David, west of the Gihon[b] spring in the valley, as far as the entrance of the Fish Gate[c] and encircling the hill of Ophel;[d] he also made it much higher. He stationed military commanders in all the fortified cities in Judah.

32:23 [z] 2Ch 9:24; 17:5; Isa 45:14; Zec 14:16-17
32:25 [a] 2Ki 14:10; 2Ch 26:16 [b] 2Ch 19:2; 24:18
32:26 [c] Jer 26:18-19 [d] 2Ch 34:27,28; Isa 39:8
32:27 [e] 1Ch 29:12
32:29 [f] 1Ch 29:12
32:30 [g] 2Ki 18:17 [h] 1Ki 1:33
32:31 [i] Isa 39:1 [j] ver 24; Isa 38:7 [k] Ge 22:1; Dt 8:16
33:1 [l] 1Ch 3:13
33:2 [m] Jer 15:4 [n] Dt 18:9; 2Ch 28:3
33:3 [o] Dt 16:21-22 [p] Dt 17:3; 2Ch 31:1
33:4 [q] 2Ch 7:16
33:5 [r] 2Ch 4:9
33:6 [s] Lev 18:21; Dt 18:10; 2Ch 28:3 [t] Lev 19:31 [u] 1Sa 28:13
33:7 [v] 2Ch 7:16
33:8 [w] 2Sa 7:10
33:9 [x] Jer 15:4
33:11 [y] Dt 28:36 [z] Ps 149:8
33:12 [a] 2Ch 6:37; 32:26; 1Pe 5:6
33:14 [b] 1Ki 1:33 [c] Ne 3:3; 12:39; Zep 1:10 [d] 2Ch 27:3; Ne 3:26

[a] 22 Hebrew; Septuagint and Vulgate *He gave them rest*

32:31 *envoys were sent by the rulers of Babylon.* See note on 2Ki 20:12.
33:3 *high places.* See notes on 1:3; 1Ki 3:2; 11:7. *Asherah poles.* See notes on Dt 7:5; 1Ki 14:23. *starry hosts.* See note on 2Ki 21:3.
33:6 *sacrificed his children in the fire.* See notes on Lev 20:2; 1Ki 11:5; 2Ki 3:27; 16:3; Jer 7:31.
33:11 *the king of Assyria . . . took Manasseh prisoner.* See the article "Manasseh of Judah and Ashurbanipal," p. 665.

15He got rid of the foreign gods and removed[e] the image from the temple of the
LORD, as well as all the altars he had built
on the temple hill and in Jerusalem; and
he threw them out of the city. 16Then he
restored the altar of the LORD and sacrificed fellowship offerings and thank offerings[f] on it, and told Judah to serve
the LORD, the God of Israel. 17The people,
however, continued to sacrifice at the high
places, but only to the LORD their God.

18The other events of Manasseh's reign,
including his prayer to his God and the
words the seers spoke to him in the name
of the LORD, the God of Israel, are written
in the annals of the kings of Israel.[a] 19His
prayer and how God was moved by his entreaty, as well as all his sins and unfaithfulness, and the sites where he built high
places and set up Asherah poles and idols
before he humbled[g] himself — all these are
written in the records of the seers.[b][h] 20Ma-
nasseh rested with his ancestors and was
buried[i] in his palace. And Amon his son
succeeded him as king.

Amon King of Judah

33:21-25pp — 2Ki 21:19-24

21Amon[j] was twenty-two years old when
he became king, and he reigned in Jerusalem two years. 22He did evil in the eyes
of the LORD, as his father Manasseh had
done. Amon worshiped and offered sacrifices to all the idols Manasseh had made.
23But unlike his father Manasseh, he did
not humble[k] himself before the LORD;
Amon increased his guilt.

24Amon's officials conspired against
him and assassinated him in his palace.
25Then the people[l] of the land killed all
who had plotted against King Amon, and
they made Josiah his son king in his place.

Josiah's Reforms

34:1-2pp — 2Ki 22:1-2
34:3-7Ref — 2Ki 23:4-20
34:8-13pp — 2Ki 22:3-7

34 Josiah[m] was eight years old when
he became king,[n] and he reigned in
Jerusalem thirty-one years. 2He did what
was right in the eyes of the LORD and followed the ways of his father David,[o] not
turning aside to the right or to the left.

3In the eighth year of his reign, while
he was still young, he began to seek the
God[p] of his father David. In his twelfth
year he began to purge Judah and Jerusalem of high places, Asherah poles and
idols. 4Under his direction the altars of the
Baals were torn down; he cut to pieces
the incense altars that were above them,
and smashed the Asherah poles[q] and
the idols. These he broke to pieces and
scattered over the graves of those who
had sacrificed to them.[r] 5He burned[s] the
bones of the priests on their altars, and so
he purged Judah and Jerusalem. 6In the
towns of Manasseh, Ephraim and Simeon, as far as Naphtali, and in the ruins
around them, 7he tore down the altars and
the Asherah poles and crushed the idols to
powder[t] and cut to pieces all the incense
altars throughout Israel. Then he went
back to Jerusalem.

8In the eighteenth year of Josiah's reign,
to purify the land and the temple, he sent
Shaphan son of Azaliah and Maaseiah the
ruler of the city, with Joah son of Joahaz,
the recorder, to repair the temple of the
LORD his God.

9They went to Hilkiah[u] the high priest
and gave him the money that had been
brought into the temple of God, which
the Levites who were the gatekeepers had
collected from the people of Manasseh,
Ephraim and the entire remnant of Israel and from all the people of Judah and
Benjamin and the inhabitants of Jerusalem. 10Then they entrusted it to the men
appointed to supervise the work on the
LORD's temple. These men paid the workers who repaired and restored the temple.
11They also gave money[v] to the carpenters
and builders to purchase dressed stone,
and timber for joists and beams for the
buildings that the kings of Judah had allowed to fall into ruin.[w]

12The workers labored faithfully.[x] Over
them to direct them were Jahath and Obadiah, Levites descended from Merari, and
Zechariah and Meshullam, descended
from Kohath. The Levites — all who were
skilled in playing musical instruments —[y]
13had charge of the laborers[z] and supervised all the workers from job to job. Some
of the Levites were secretaries, scribes and
gatekeepers.

The Book of the Law Found

34:14-28pp — 2Ki 22:8-20
34:29-32pp — 2Ki 23:1-3

14While they were bringing out the
money that had been taken into the temple of the LORD, Hilkiah the priest found
the Book of the Law of the LORD that had

33:15 [e] ver 3-7; 2Ki 23:12
33:16 [f] Lev 7:11-18
33:19 [g] 2Ch 6:37 [h] 2Ki 21:17
33:20 [i] 2Ki 21:18; 2Ch 21:20
33:21 [j] 1Ch 3:14
33:23 [k] ver 12; Ex 10:3; 2Ch 7:14; Ps 18:27; 147:6; Pr 3:34
33:25 [l] 2Ch 22:1
34:1 [m] 1Ch 3:14 [n] Zep 1:1
34:2 [o] 2Ch 29:2
34:3 [p] 1Ki 13:2; 1Ch 16:11; 2Ch 15:2; 33:17,22
34:4 [q] Ex 34:13 [r] Ex 32:20; Lev 26:30; 2Ki 23:11; Mic 1:5
34:5 [s] 1Ki 13:2
34:7 [t] Ex 32:20; 2Ch 31:1
34:9 [u] 1Ch 6:13; 2Ch 35:8
34:11 [v] 2Ch 24:12 [w] 2Ch 33:4-7
34:12 [x] 2Ki 12:15 [y] 1Ch 25:1
34:13 [z] 1Ch 23:4

[a] *18* That is, Judah, as frequently in 2 Chronicles
[b] *19* One Hebrew manuscript and Septuagint; most Hebrew manuscripts *of Hozai*

33:19 *high places.* See notes on 1:3; 1Ki 3:2; 11:7. *Asherah poles.* See notes on Dt 7:5; 1Ki 14:23.
33:25 *people of the land.* See note on 23:20.
34:8 *repair the temple of the LORD.* See note on 24:4–14.
34:14 *found the Book of the Law.* See note on 2Ki 22:8.

been given through Moses. 15Hilkiah said
to Shaphan the secretary, "I have found
the Book of the Law[a] in the temple of the
LORD." He gave it to Shaphan.
16Then Shaphan took the book to the
king and reported to him: "Your officials
are doing everything that has been committed to them. 17They have paid out the
money that was in the temple of the LORD
and have entrusted it to the supervisors
and workers." 18Then Shaphan the secretary informed the king, "Hilkiah the priest
has given me a book." And Shaphan read
from it in the presence of the king.
19When the king heard the words of the
Law,[b] he tore[c] his robes. 20He gave these
orders to Hilkiah, Ahikam son of Shaphan[d], Abdon son of Micah,[a] Shaphan
the secretary and Asaiah the king's attendant: 21"Go and inquire of the LORD for me
and for the remnant in Israel and Judah
about what is written in this book that
has been found. Great is the LORD's anger
that is poured out[e] on us because those
who have gone before us have not kept
the word of the LORD; they have not acted
in accordance with all that is written in
this book."
22Hilkiah and those the king had sent
with him[b] went to speak to the prophet[f]
Huldah, who was the wife of Shallum son
of Tokhath,[c] the son of Hasrah,[d] keeper of
the wardrobe. She lived in Jerusalem, in
the New Quarter.
23She said to them, "This is what the
LORD, the God of Israel, says: Tell the man
who sent you to me, 24'This is what the
LORD says: I am going to bring disaster[g] on
this place and its people[h]—all the curses[i]
written in the book that has been read in
the presence of the king of Judah. 25Be-
cause they have forsaken me[j] and burned
incense to other gods and aroused my anger by all that their hands have made,[e] my
anger will be poured out on this place and
will not be quenched.' 26Tell the king of Judah, who sent you to inquire of the LORD,
'This is what the LORD, the God of Israel, says concerning the words you heard:
27Because your heart was responsive[k] and
you humbled[l] yourself before God when
you heard what he spoke against this
place and its people, and because you
humbled yourself before me and tore your
robes and wept in my presence, I have
heard you, declares the LORD. 28Now I will
gather you to your ancestors,[m] and you
will be buried in peace. Your eyes will not
see all the disaster I am going to bring on
this place and on those who live here.'"[n]

So they took her answer back to the
king.
29Then the king called together all the
elders of Judah and Jerusalem. 30He went
up to the temple of the LORD[o] with the
people of Judah, the inhabitants of Jerusalem, the priests and the Levites—all
the people from the least to the greatest.
He read in their hearing all the words of
the Book of the Covenant, which had been
found in the temple of the LORD. 31The
king stood by his pillar[p] and renewed the
covenant[q] in the presence of the LORD—to
follow[r] the LORD and keep his commands,
statutes and decrees with all his heart and
all his soul, and to obey the words of the
covenant written in this book.
32Then he had everyone in Jerusalem
and Benjamin pledge themselves to it; the
people of Jerusalem did this in accordance
with the covenant of God, the God of their
ancestors.
33Josiah removed all the detestable[s]
idols from all the territory belonging to the
Israelites, and he had all who were present
in Israel serve the LORD their God. As long
as he lived, they did not fail to follow the
LORD, the God of their ancestors.

Josiah Celebrates the Passover

35:1,18-19pp — 2Ki 23:21-23

35 Josiah celebrated the Passover[t]
to the LORD in Jerusalem, and the
Passover lamb was slaughtered on the
fourteenth day of the first month. 2He appointed the priests to their duties and encouraged them in the service of the LORD's
temple. 3He said to the Levites, who instructed[u] all Israel and who had been consecrated to the LORD: "Put the sacred ark
in the temple that Solomon son of David
king of Israel built. It is not to be carried
about on your shoulders. Now serve the
LORD your God and his people Israel. 4Pre-
pare yourselves by families in your divisions,[v] according to the instructions written by David king of Israel and by his son
Solomon.
5"Stand in the holy place with a group
of Levites for each subdivision of the families of your fellow Israelites, the lay people. 6Slaughter the Passover lambs, consecrate yourselves[w] and prepare the lambs
for your fellow Israelites, doing what the
LORD commanded through Moses."

[a] 20 Also called *Akbor son of Micaiah* [b] 22 One Hebrew manuscript, Vulgate and Syriac; most Hebrew manuscripts do not have *had sent with him.* [c] 22 Also called *Tikvah* [d] 22 Also called *Harhas* [e] 25 Or *by everything they have done*

34:15 [a] 2Ki 22:8; Ezr 7:6; Ne 8:1 **34:19** [b] Dt 28:3-68 [c] Jos 7:6; Isa 36:22; 37:1 **34:20** [d] 2Ki 22:3 **34:21** [e] 2Ch 29:8; La 2:4; 4:11; Eze 36:18 **34:22** [f] Ex 15:20; Ne 6:14 **34:24** [g] Pr 16:4; Isa 3:9; Jer 40:2; 42:10; 44:2,11 [h] 2Ch 36:14-20 [i] Dt 28:15-68 **34:25** [j] 2Ch 33:3-6; Jer 22:9 **34:27** [k] 2Ch 12:7; 32:26 [l] Ex 10:3; 2Ch 6:37 **34:28** [m] 2Ch 35:20-25 [n] 2Ch 32:26

34:30 [o] 2Ki 23:2; Ne 8:1-3 **34:31** [p] 1Ki 7:15; 2Ki 11:14 [q] 2Ki 11:17; 2Ch 23:16; 29:10 [r] Dt 13:4 **34:33** [s] ver 3-7; Dt 18:9 **35:1** [t] Ex 12:1-30; Nu 9:3; 28:16 **35:3** [u] Dt 33:10; 1Ch 23:26; 2Ch 5:7; 17:7 **35:4** [v] ver 10; 1Ch 9:10-13; 24:1; 2Ch 8:14; Ezr 6:18 **35:6** [w] Lev 11:44; 2Ch 29:5,15

34:22 *the prophet Huldah ... wife of Shallum ... keeper of the wardrobe.* See note on 2Ki 22:14.

7Josiah provided for all the lay people who were there a total of thirty thousand lambs and goats for the Passover offerings,[x] and also three thousand cattle—all from the king's own possessions.[y]

8His officials also contributed[z] voluntarily to the people and the priests and Levites. Hilkiah,[a] Zechariah and Jehiel, the officials in charge of God's temple, gave the priests twenty-six hundred Passover offerings and three hundred cattle. 9Also Konaniah[b] along with Shemaiah and Nethanel, his brothers, and Hashabiah, Jeiel and Jozabad,[c] the leaders of the Levites, provided five thousand Passover offerings and five hundred head of cattle for the Levites.

10The service was arranged and the priests stood in their places with the Levites in their divisions[d] as the king had ordered.[e] 11The Passover lambs were slaughtered,[f] and the priests splashed against the altar the blood handed to them, while the Levites skinned the animals. 12They set aside the burnt offerings to give them to the subdivisions of the families of the people to offer to the LORD, as it is written in the Book of Moses. They did the same with the cattle. 13They roasted the Passover animals over the fire as prescribed,[g] and boiled the holy offerings in pots, caldrons and pans and served them quickly to all the people. 14After this, they made preparations for themselves and for the priests, because the priests, the descendants of Aaron, were sacrificing the burnt offerings and the fat portions[h] until nightfall. So the Levites made preparations for themselves and for the Aaronic priests.

15The musicians,[i] the descendants of Asaph, were in the places prescribed by David, Asaph, Heman and Jeduthun the king's seer. The gatekeepers at each gate did not need to leave their posts, because their fellow Levites made the preparations for them.

16So at that time the entire service of the LORD was carried out for the celebration of the Passover and the offering of burnt offerings on the altar of the LORD, as King Josiah had ordered. 17The Israelites who were present celebrated the Passover at that time and observed the Festival of Unleavened Bread for seven days. 18The Passover had not been observed like this in Israel since the days of the prophet Samuel; and none of the kings of Israel had ever celebrated such a Passover as did Josiah, with the priests, the Levites and all Judah and Israel who were there with the people of Jerusalem. 19This Passover was celebrated in the eighteenth year of Josiah's reign.

The Death of Josiah

35:20–36:1pp — 2Ki 23:28-30

20After all this, when Josiah had set the temple in order, Necho king of Egypt went up to fight at Carchemish[j] on the Euphrates,[k] and Josiah marched out to meet him in battle. 21But Necho sent messengers to him, saying, "What quarrel is there, king of Judah, between you and me? It is not you I am attacking at this time, but the house with which I am at war. God has told[l] me to hurry; so stop opposing God, who is with me, or he will destroy you."

22Josiah, however, would not turn away from him, but disguised[m] himself to engage him in battle. He would not listen to what Necho had said at God's command but went to fight him on the plain of Megiddo.

23Archers[n] shot King Josiah, and he told his officers, "Take me away; I am badly wounded." 24So they took him out of his chariot, put him in his other chariot and brought him to Jerusalem, where he died. He was buried in the tombs of his ancestors, and all Judah and Jerusalem mourned for him.

25Jeremiah composed laments for Josiah, and to this day all the male and female singers commemorate Josiah in the laments.[o] These became a tradition in Israel and are written in the Laments.

26The other events of Josiah's reign and his acts of devotion in accordance with what is written in the Law of the LORD—27all the events, from beginning to end, are written in the book of the kings of Israel and Judah.

36 1And the people of the land took Jehoahaz son of Josiah and made him king in Jerusalem in place of his father.

Jehoahaz King of Judah

36:2-4pp — 2Ki 23:31-34

2Jehoahaz[a] was twenty-three years old when he became king, and he reigned in Jerusalem three months. 3The king of Egypt dethroned him in Jerusalem and imposed on Judah a levy of a hundred talents[b] of silver and a talent[c] of gold. 4The king of Egypt made Eliakim, a brother of

35:7 [x] 2Ch 30:24 [y] 2Ch 31:3 **35:8** [z] 1Ch 29:3; 2Ch 29:31-36 [a] 1Ch 6:13 **35:9** [b] 2Ch 31:12 [c] 2Ch 31:13 **35:10** [d] ver 4; Ezr 6:18 [e] 2Ch 30:16 **35:11** [f] 2Ch 29:22, 34; 30:17 **35:13** [g] Ex 12:2-11; Lev 6:25; 1Sa 2:13-15 **35:14** [h] Ex 29:13 **35:15** [i] 1Ch 25:1; 26:12-19; 2Ch 29:30; Ne 12:46; Ps 68:25

35:20 [j] Isa 10:9; Jer 46:2 [k] Ge 2:14 **35:21** [l] 1Ki 13:18; 2Ki 18:25 **35:22** [m] Jdg 5:19; 1Sa 28:8; 2Ch 18:29 **35:23** [n] 1Ki 22:34 **35:25** [o] Jer 22:10, 15-16

[a] *2* Hebrew *Joahaz,* a variant of *Jehoahaz;* also in verse 4 [b] *3* That is, about 3 3/4 tons or about 3.4 metric tons [c] *3* That is, about 75 pounds or about 34 kilograms

35:20 *Necho king of Egypt.* See note on 2Ki 23:29.
36:1 *people of the land.* See note on 23:20.
36:4 *changed Eliakim's name to Jehoiakim.* See note on Ge 2:20.

Jehoahaz, king over Judah and Jerusalem
and changed Eliakim's name to Jehoiakim.
But Necho[p] took Eliakim's brother Jehoahaz and carried him off to Egypt.

Jehoiakim King of Judah

36:5-8pp — 2Ki 23:36 – 24:6

5 Jehoiakim[q] was twenty-five years old
when he became king, and he reigned in
Jerusalem eleven years. He did evil in the
eyes of the LORD his God. 6 Nebuchadnezzar[r] king of Babylon attacked him and
bound him with bronze shackles to take
him to Babylon.[s] 7 Nebuchadnezzar also
took to Babylon articles from the temple
of the LORD and put them in his temple[a]
there.[t]
8 The other events of Jehoiakim's reign,
the detestable things he did and all that
was found against him, are written in the
book of the kings of Israel and Judah. And
Jehoiachin his son succeeded him as king.

Jehoiachin King of Judah

36:9-10pp — 2Ki 24:8-17

9 Jehoiachin[u] was eighteen[b] years old
when he became king, and he reigned
in Jerusalem three months and ten days.
He did evil in the eyes of the LORD. 10 In
the spring, King Nebuchadnezzar sent for
him and brought him to Babylon,[v] together with articles of value from the temple
of the LORD, and he made Jehoiachin's
uncle,[c] Zedekiah, king over Judah and Jerusalem.

Zedekiah King of Judah

36:11-16pp — 2Ki 24:18-20; Jer 52:1-3

11 Zedekiah[w] was twenty-one years old
when he became king, and he reigned
in Jerusalem eleven years. 12 He did evil
in the eyes of the LORD[x] his God and did
not humble[y] himself before Jeremiah the
prophet, who spoke the word of the LORD.
13 He also rebelled against King Nebuchadnezzar, who had made him take an oath[z]
in God's name. He became stiff-necked[a]
and hardened his heart and would not
turn to the LORD, the God of Israel. 14 Furthermore, all the leaders of the priests and
the people became more and more unfaithful,[b] following all the detestable practices of the nations and defiling the temple
of the LORD, which he had consecrated in
Jerusalem.

The Fall of Jerusalem

36:17-20pp — 2Ki 25:1-21; Jer 52:4-27
36:22-23pp — Ezr 1:1-3

15 The LORD, the God of their ancestors,
sent word to them through his messengers[c] again and again,[d] because he had
pity on his people and on his dwelling
place. 16 But they mocked God's messengers, despised his words and scoffed[e] at
his prophets until the wrath[f] of the LORD
was aroused against his people and there
was no remedy.[g] 17 He brought up against
them the king of the Babylonians,[d] who
killed their young men with the sword in
the sanctuary, and did not spare young
men[h] or young women, the elderly or the
infirm. God gave them all into the hands of
Nebuchadnezzar.[i] 18 He carried to Babylon
all the articles[j] from the temple of God,
both large and small, and the treasures of
the LORD's temple and the treasures of the
king and his officials. 19 They set fire[k] to
God's temple[l] and broke down the wall[m]
of Jerusalem; they burned all the palaces
and destroyed[n] everything of value there.[o]
20 He carried into exile[p] to Babylon the
remnant, who escaped from the sword,
and they became servants[q] to him and
his successors until the kingdom of Persia
came to power. 21 The land enjoyed its sabbath rests;[r] all the time of its desolation it
rested,[s] until the seventy years[t] were completed in fulfillment of the word of the
LORD spoken by Jeremiah.
22 In the first year of Cyrus[u] king of Per-

36:4 [p] Jer 22:10-12 **36:5** [q] Jer 22:18; 26:1; 35:1 **36:6** [r] Jer 25:9; 27:6; Eze 29:18 [s] 2Ch 33:11; Eze 19:9; Da 1:1 **36:7** [t] 2Ki 24:13; Ezr 1:7; Da 1:2 **36:9** [u] Jer 22:24-28; 52:31 **36:10** [v] ver 18; 2Ki 20:17; Ezr 1:7; Jer 22:25; 24:1; 29:1; 37:1; Eze 17:12 **36:11** [w] 2Ki 24:17; Jer 27:1; 28:1 **36:12** [x] Jer 37:1-39:18 [y] Dt 8:3; 2Ch 7:14; 33:23; Jer 21:3-7 **36:13** [z] Eze 17:13 [a] 2Ki 17:14; 2Ch 30:8 **36:14** [b] 1Ch 5:25 **36:15** [c] Isa 5:4; 44:26; Jer 7:25; Hag 1:13; Zec 1:4; Mal 2:7; 3:1 [d] Jer 7:13, 25; 25:3-4; 35:14, 15; 44:4-6 **36:16** [e] 2Ki 2:23; Pr 1:25; Jer 5:13 [f] Ezr 5:12; Pr 1:30-31 [g] 2Ch 30:10; Pr 29:1; Zec 1:2 **36:17** [h] Jer 6:11 [i] Ezr 5:12; Jer 32:28 **36:18** [j] ver 7, 10 **36:19** [k] Jer 11:16; 17:27; 21:10, 14; 22:7; 32:29; 39:8; La 4:11; Eze 20:47; Am 2:5; Zec 11:1 [l] 1Ki 9:8-9 [m] 2Ki 14:13 [n] La 2:6 [o] Ps 79:1-3 **36:20** [p] Lev 26:44; 2Ki 24:14; Ezr 2:1; Ne 7:6 [q] Jer 27:7

[a] 7 Or *palace* [b] 9 One Hebrew manuscript, some Septuagint manuscripts and Syriac (see also 2 Kings 24:8); most Hebrew manuscripts *eight* [c] 10 Hebrew *brother,* that is, relative (see 2 Kings 24:17) [d] 17 Or *Chaldeans*

36:21 [r] Lev 25:4; 26:34 [s] 1Ch 22:9 [t] Jer 1:1; 25:11; 27:22; 29:10; 40:1; Da 9:2; Zec 1:12; 7:5 **36:22** [u] Isa 44:28; 45:1, 13; Jer 25:12; 29:10; Da 1:21; 6:28; 10:1

36:6 *Nebuchadnezzar king of Babylon attacked.* See note on 2Ki 24:10.
36:10 *brought him to Babylon.* See note on 2Ki 24:14.
36:13 *also rebelled against King Nebuchadnezzar.* See note on 2Ki 24:20.
36:21 *seventy years.* The beginning point and ending point of Jeremiah's prophecy of 70 years of exile (Jer 25:8 – 14) is not exactly specified within the Biblical material. One option is to see the destruction of the temple in 586/585 BC as inaugurating this period, which then comes to a close with the dedication of the rebuilt temple in 516/515 BC. Another option is understanding the decree of Cyrus (539 BC; see v. 22; Ezr 1:1 – 4) as signaling the end of the 70 years, which implies a beginning point at the death of Josiah, at which point the southern kingdom lost its independence and became a pawn to the geopolitical interests of Egypt and Babylonia.
36:22 – 23 The death of Nebuchadnezzar II in 562 BC set in motion the beginning of the end of the Babylonian Empire. His son Awel-Marduk was assassinated after two years and the next two Babylonian kings (Neriglissar [probably "Nergal-Sharezer, Jer 39:3] and Labashi-Marduk) reigned for a combined five years or so before Nabonidus assumed the throne. Nabonidus ruled Babylon 556 – 539 BC, but his interest in the moon-god Sin (rather than Marduk) caused numerous issues, and within

sia, in order to fulfill the word of the LORD spoken by Jeremiah, the LORD moved the heart of Cyrus king of Persia to make a proclamation throughout his realm and also to put it in writing:

23 "This is what Cyrus king of Persia says:

" 'The LORD, the God of heaven, has given me all the kingdoms of the earth and he has appointed[v] me to build a temple for him at Jerusalem in Judah. Any of his people among you may go up, and may the LORD their God be with them.' "

36:23
[v] Jdg 4:10

a few years Nabonidus departed for the Arabian oasis city of Tema (some 500 miles [800 kilometers] from Babylon) and appointed his son Belshazzar to rule in his stead.

Meanwhile, Persia continued to gain strength and encroach on Babylonian territory, so that by 546 BC Persia was controlling much of the southern region of Babylonia and closing in on Babylon. In 539 BC, Cyrus the Persian (559 – 530 BC) took Babylon with hardly a fight and presented himself as a loyal worshiper of Marduk and the liberator of the Babylonian people. The Persian Empire ruled the ancient Near East 539 – 333 BC.

By conquering the Babylonian Empire, Cyrus inherited various nations exiled to Babylon and overturned the foreign policy of the Babylonians by allowing peoples previously deported to return to their homeland if they so desired. Thus, within the first year of his rule Cyrus issued proclamations to this effect, as reflected in the Cyrus Cylinder (Clay Barrel; see illustration in "Ancient Texts Relating to the Old Testament," p. xxviii). Cyrus also sought to placate the gods of these people groups by encouraging traditional worship of local deities, as reflected in his respect of Marduk and his reverential words toward Yahweh (v. 23). One way to do this was by returning religious articles seized by the Babylonians and by funding rebuilding efforts of temples and shrines (Ezr 1:2 – 8; 6:1 – 12).

NARRATIVE LITERATURE

EZRA

Introduction to Ezra and Nehemiah.

Historical Setting

The Persian Empire, established by the Achaemenids, extended from India to Cush (Est 1:1) and lasted from 550 BC until Alexander's conquests (323 BC). Cyrus was the founder of the Persian Empire and the greatest Achaemenid king. He reigned over the Persians from 559 to 530 BC. He established Persian dominance over the Medes in 550 BC, conquered Lydia and Ionia in 547 – 46 BC, and captured Babylon in 539 BC. It was Cyrus who permitted the Jews who wished to do so to return to their homeland (Ezr 1:1 – 4).

The Jewish territory of Yehud (Judah) belonged to the Persian satrapy called Abarnahara (meaning "beyond [or across] the river"). The governor of Abarnahara who came to investigate the conflict between the Jews and their neighbors was Tattenai, a figure who appears in cuneiform sources as *Tattanu*, and he is known to have held this position between 520 and 502 BC.

The refortification of Jerusalem by Nehemiah may have been part of the imperial Persian strategy against the dangers of Athenian imperialism, which included the coastal Palestinian city of Dor in its Delian League. Extra-Biblical examples of local leaders who cooperated (some would say collaborated) with Persian authorities may be cited, most notably an Egyptian priest named Udjahorresnet, who served both Cambyses and Darius I. Since Darius I authorized the codification of Egyptian laws, some scholars have argued that Artaxerxes I may have had a similar motive in sending Ezra back to establish the Torah. It is quite significant that as the cupbearer to Artaxerxes I, Nehemiah was a highly trusted official who was sent forth as the Persian governor of Judah. ◆

KEY CONCEPTS

- God had declared through the prophets, especially Jeremiah, that after he judged his people and gave them over to the Babylonians, he would bring them back 70 years later.
- Prayer is an important expression of trust.
- The law takes its proper place as the foundation of society.
- Even pagan kings are under God's control.

Cyrus Helps the Exiles to Return

1:1-3pp — 2Ch 36:22-23

1 In the first year of Cyrus king of Persia,
in order to fulfill the word of the LORD
spoken by Jeremiah,[a] the LORD moved the
heart[b] of Cyrus king of Persia to make a
proclamation throughout his realm and
also to put it in writing:

2"This is what Cyrus king of Persia
says:
" 'The LORD, the God of heaven,
has given me all the kingdoms of the
earth and he has appointed[c] me to
build[d] a temple for him at Jerusalem
in Judah. 3Any of his people among
you may go up to Jerusalem in Judah
and build the temple of the LORD, the
God of Israel, the God who is in Jerusalem, and may their God be with
them. 4And in any locality where survivors[e] may now be living, the people
are to provide them with silver and
gold, with goods and livestock, and
with freewill offerings[f] for the temple
of God in Jerusalem.' "[g]

5Then the family heads of Judah and
Benjamin,[h] and the priests and Levites —
everyone whose heart God had moved[i] —
prepared to go up and build the house[j] of
the LORD in Jerusalem. 6All their neighbors
assisted them with articles of silver and
gold, with goods and livestock, and with
valuable gifts, in addition to all the freewill offerings.
7Moreover, King Cyrus brought out the
articles belonging to the temple of the
LORD, which Nebuchadnezzar had carried

1:1 [a] Jer 25:11-12; 29:10-14 [b] 2Ch 36:22,23 **1:2** [c] Isa 44:28; 45:13 [d] Ezr 5:13 **1:4** [e] Isa 10:20-22 [f] Nu 15:3; Ps 50:14; 54:6; 116:17 [g] Ezr 4:3; 5:13; 6:3,14 **1:5** [h] Ezr 4:1; Ne 11:4 [i] ver 1; Ex 35:20-22; 2Ch 36:22; Hag 1:14; Php 2:13 [j] Ps 127:1

1:1 *first year of Cyrus king of Persia.* When Cyrus the Great conquered Babylon in 539 BC and established Persian rule in the ancient world, he set in motion a series of events important for the Jews. His proclamation recorded in vv. 2 – 4 and 2Ch 36:23 gave permission for the rebuilding of the temple in Jerusalem, which resulted in a series of returns from exile by deportees and the descendants of deportees. Although the Jews regarded Cyrus as a benefactor, as well they might, it should be noted that his "beneficence" was not directed solely toward the Jews, but formed part of a wider foreign policy. The Cyrus Cylinder, in which Cyrus decrees that some exiled populations can return, mentions a number of deities and peoples whom he restored to their own places. The thinking behind this, no doubt, was to foster goodwill among the subjects of his kingdom. This was especially desirable in the case of the province of Yehud, since it lay on the fringe of the empire and acted as a buffer between an Egypt that had not yet been subjugated and the rest of the realm. Through the decree of Cyrus (see note on 2Ch 36:22 – 23), those exiled to Babylonia were given the opportunity to return home and rebuild what was left of Judah (Ezr 2:1 – 35; Ne 7:5 – 73). *the word of the LORD spoken by Jeremiah.* Jeremiah's prediction (Jer 25:1 – 12; 29:10; cf. 51:11) of a 70-year Babylonian captivity. The first deportations began in 605 BC, in the third year of Jehoiakim (Da 1:1). The 70th year would be 536 BC.
1:2 *God of heaven.* This title ascribed to Yahweh does not necessarily reflect Cyrus's personal beliefs. In the Cyrus Cylinder, he attributes his conquest of Babylon to the city's patron, Marduk. Marduk, Yahweh and any other gods would have been seen by Cyrus as members of the forces of light under the head of Ahura Mazda, the god of the Persian Zoroastrian religion. Similar deference is made to other gods in decrees pertaining to the restoration of their shrines.
1:7 *articles belonging to the temple of the LORD.* Conquerors customarily carried off the statues of the gods of conquered cities (see note on 1Sa 5:2). The Cyrus Cylinder records Cyrus returning sacred objects throughout his

RETURN FROM EXILE

Restoration of the Jewish exiles began under Cyrus (559–530 BC), who allowed them to return to Judah with the captured temple treasures. The temple was consecrated in 516 BC by official permission of Darius I (522–486 BC).

Ezra won the approval of Artaxerxes I (465–424 BC) to return with additional exiles and to promote obedience to the law; Nehemiah, to rebuild the walls of Jerusalem.

Babylon and vicinity long retained a large and prosperous Jewish community, as clay tablets from the Murashu archives at Nippur testify.

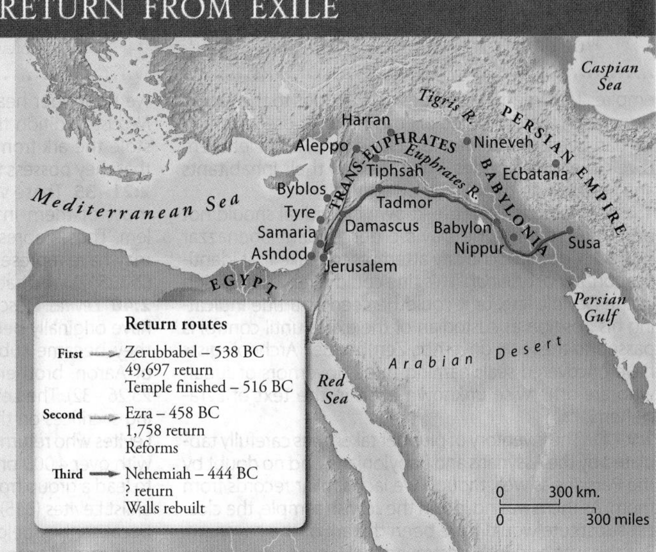

away from Jerusalem and had placed in
the temple of his god.[a][k] 8 Cyrus king of Persia had them brought by Mithredath the
treasurer, who counted them out to Sheshbazzar[l] the prince of Judah.
9 This was the inventory:

gold dishes	30
silver dishes	1,000
silver pans[b]	29
10 gold bowls	30
matching silver bowls	410
other articles	1,000

11 In all, there were 5,400 articles of
gold and of silver. Sheshbazzar brought
all these along with the exiles when they
came up from Babylon to Jerusalem.

The List of the Exiles Who Returned

2:1-70pp — Ne 7:6-73

2 Now these are the people of the province who came up from the captivity of the exiles,[m] whom Nebuchadnezzar
king of Babylon[n] had taken captive to
Babylon (they returned to Jerusalem and
Judah, each to their own town,[o] 2 in company with Zerubbabel,[p] Joshua,[q] Nehemiah, Seraiah,[r] Reelaiah, Mordecai, Bilshan,
Mispar, Bigvai, Rehum and Baanah):

The list of the men of the people of
Israel:

3 the descendants of Parosh[s]	2,172
4 of Shephatiah	372
5 of Arah	775
6 of Pahath-Moab (through the line of Jeshua and Joab)	2,812
7 of Elam	1,254
8 of Zattu	945
9 of Zakkai	760
10 of Bani	642
11 of Bebai	623
12 of Azgad	1,222
13 of Adonikam[t]	666
14 of Bigvai	2,056
15 of Adin	454
16 of Ater (through Hezekiah)	98
17 of Bezai	323
18 of Jorah	112
19 of Hashum	223
20 of Gibbar	95
21 the men of Bethlehem[u]	123
22 of Netophah	56
23 of Anathoth	128
24 of Azmaveth	42
25 of Kiriath Jearim,[c] Kephirah and Beeroth	743
26 of Ramah[v] and Geba	621
27 of Mikmash	122
28 of Bethel and Ai[w]	223
29 of Nebo	52
30 of Magbish	156
31 of the other Elam	1,254
32 of Harim	320
33 of Lod, Hadid and Ono	725
34 of Jericho[x]	345
35 of Senaah	3,630

36 The priests:

the descendants of Jedaiah[y] (through the family of Jeshua)	973
37 of Immer[z]	1,052
38 of Pashhur[a]	1,247
39 of Harim[b]	1,017

40 The Levites:[c]

the descendants of Jeshua[d] and Kadmiel (of the line of Hodaviah)	74

1:7 [k] 2Ki 24:13; 2Ch 36:7, 10; Ezr 5:14; 6:5 1:8 [l] Ezr 5:14 2:1 [m] 2Ch 36:20; Ne 7:6 [n] 2Ki 24:16; 25:12 [o] Ne 7:73 2:2 [p] 1Ch 3:19 [q] Ezr 3:2 [r] Ne 10:2 2:3 [s] Ezr 8:3 2:13 [t] Ezr 8:13 2:21 [u] Mic 5:2 2:26 [v] Jos 18:25 2:28 [w] Ge 12:8 2:34 [x] 1Ki 16:34; 2Ch 28:15 2:36 [y] 1Ch 24:7 2:37 [z] 1Ch 24:14 2:38 [a] 1Ch 9:12 2:39 [b] 1Ch 24:8 2:40 [c] Ge 29:34; Nu 3:9; Dt 18:6-7; 1Ch 16:4; Ezr 7:7; 8:15; Ne 12:24 [d] Ezr 3:9

[a] *7* Or *gods* [b] *9* The meaning of the Hebrew for this word is uncertain. [c] *25* See Septuagint (see also Neh. 7:29); Hebrew *Kiriath Arim.*

empire: "I returned the (images of) the gods to the sacred centers [on the other side of] the Tigris whose sanctuaries had been abandoned for a long time, and I let them dwell in eternal abodes. I gathered all their inhabitants and returned (to them) their dwellings."

1:8 *Sheshbazzar.* This little-known individual should not be confused with the Davidic descendant Shenazzar (1Ch 3:18), despite scholarly attempts to make that identification. *prince of Judah.* This title could refer to a position in the Davidic line, or it could be seen as a title indicating his position as custodian of the exiles until control is passed to the local governor, Zerubbabel. Archeologists have uncovered seals naming three governors of Judah who are otherwise unknown even in the text of Ezra-Nehemiah.

1:9–11 The inventory of plunder taken was carefully tabulated by the Assyrians and Babylonians, and no doubt by the Persians as well, though we lack similar records from them. As there was no idol in the Jewish temple, the closest substitute would have been the ark of the covenant. But this was evidently destroyed by Nebuchadnezzar, as we no longer hear of it. Based on the legendary *Kebra Negast* tradition that the queen of Sheba's son Menelik stole the ark from Solomon, Ethiopian Christians claim that they possess the ark in their cathedral in Aksum.

2:21–35 These verses list a series of villages and towns, most of them in Benjamite territory north of Jerusalem. Those represented by villages rather than families may have represented "the poorest people of the land" (2Ki 25:12), who had no land or property in their own name.

2:40 *Levites.* Descendants of Levi (cf. Ge 29:34). They may have originally been regarded as priests (Dt 18:6–8), but they became subordinate to the priestly descendants of Aaron, brother of Moses (Nu 3:9–10; 1Ch 16:4–42; 23:26–32). The Levites were then prohibited from offering sacrifices on the altar (Nu 16:40; 18:7). The number of Levites who returned (74) is remarkably small as compared with over 4,000 priests (vv. 36–39). When Ezra was ready to lead a group from Babylon in 458 BC, he had to stop to enlist Levites (8:15). Either few Levites had been deported because they belonged to the poorer class, or they may have turned to secular occupations during their exile.

CHRONOLOGY: EZRA–NEHEMIAH

Dates below are given according to a Nisan-to-Nisan Jewish calendar (see chart, p. 130).
Roman numerals represent months; Arabic numerals represent days.

540 BC
530
520
510
500
490
480
470
460
450
440
430

YEAR	MONTH	DAY	EVENT	REFERENCE
539 BC	Oct.	12	Capture of Babylon	Da 5:30
538 537	Mar. to Mar.	24 11	Cyrus's first year	Ezr 1:1–4
537(?)			Return under Sheshbazzar	Ezr 1:11
537	VII		Building of altar	Ezr 3:1
536	II		Work on temple begun	Ezr 3:8
536–530			Opposition during Cyrus's reign	Ezr 4:1–5
530–520			Work on temple ceased	Ezr 4:24
520	VI = Sept.	24 21	Work on temple renewed under Darius	Ezr 5:2; Hag 1:14
516	XII = Mar.	3 12	Temple completed	Ezr 6:15
458	I = Apr.	1 8	Ezra departs from Babylon	Ezr 7:6–9
	V = Aug.	1 4	Ezra arrives in Jerusalem	Ezr 7:8–9
	IX = Dec.	20 19	People assemble	Ezr 10:9
	X = Dec.	1 29	Committee begins investigation	Ezr 10:16
457	I = Mar.	1 27	Committee ends investigation	Ezr 10:17
445 444	Apr. to Apr.	13 2	20th year of Artaxerxes I	Ne 1:1
444	I = Mar.–Apr.		Nehemiah approaches the king	Ne 2:1
	Aug.(?)		Nehemiah arrives in Jerusalem	Ne 2:11
	VI = Oct.	25 2	Completion of wall	Ne 6:15
	VII = Oct. to Nov.	8 5	Public assembly	Ne 7:73—8:1
	VII = Oct.	15-22 22-28	Festival of Tabernacles	Ne 8:14
	VII = Oct.	24 30	Day of Fasting	Ne 9:1
433 432	Apr. to Apr.	1 19	32nd year of Artaxerxes; Nehemiah's recall and return	Ne 5:14; 13:6

[41]The musicians:[e]

the descendants of Asaph 128

[42]The gatekeepers[f] of the temple:

the descendants of
Shallum, Ater, Talmon,
Akkub, Hatita and Shobai 139

[43]The temple servants:[g]

the descendants of
Ziha, Hasupha, Tabbaoth,
[44]Keros, Siaha, Padon,
[45]Lebanah, Hagabah, Akkub,
[46]Hagab, Shalmai, Hanan,
[47]Giddel, Gahar, Reaiah,
[48]Rezin, Nekoda, Gazzam,
[49]Uzza, Paseah, Besai,
[50]Asnah, Meunim, Nephusim,
[51]Bakbuk, Hakupha, Harhur,
[52]Bazluth, Mehida, Harsha,
[53]Barkos, Sisera, Temah,
[54]Neziah and Hatipha

[55]The descendants of the servants of Solomon:

the descendants of
Sotai, Hassophereth, Peruda,
[56]Jaala, Darkon, Giddel,
[57]Shephatiah, Hattil,
Pokereth-Hazzebaim and Ami

[58]The temple servants[h] and the descendants of the servants of Solomon 392

[59]The following came up from the
towns of Tel Melah, Tel Harsha, Ke-
rub, Addon and Immer, but they
could not show that their families
were descended[i] from Israel:

[60]The descendants of
Delaiah, Tobiah and Nekoda 652

[61]And from among the priests:

The descendants of
Hobaiah, Hakkoz and Barzillai
(a man who had married
a daughter of Barzillai the
Gileadite[j] and was called by that
name).
[62]These searched for their family
records, but they could not find them
and so were excluded from the priesthood[k] as unclean. [63]The governor ordered them not to eat any of the most
sacred food[l] until there was a priest
ministering with the Urim and Thummim.[m]

[64]The whole company numbered
42,360, [65]besides their 7,337 male
and female slaves; and they also had
200 male and female singers.[n] [66]They
had 736 horses,[o] 245 mules, [67]435
camels and 6,720 donkeys.

[68]When they arrived at the house of the
LORD in Jerusalem, some of the heads of
the families[p] gave freewill offerings toward the rebuilding of the house of God
on its site. [69]According to their ability they
gave to the treasury for this work 61,000
darics[a] of gold, 5,000 minas[b] of silver and
100 priestly garments.
[70]The priests, the Levites, the musicians,
the gatekeepers and the temple servants
settled in their own towns, along with
some of the other people, and the rest of
the Israelites settled in their towns.[q]

Rebuilding the Altar

3 When the seventh month came and
the Israelites had settled in their
towns,[r] the people assembled[s] together
as one in Jerusalem. [2]Then Joshua[t] son
of Jozadak[u] and his fellow priests and Zerubbabel son of Shealtiel[v] and his associates began to build the altar of the God
of Israel to sacrifice burnt offerings on it,
in accordance with what is written in the
Law of Moses[w] the man of God. [3]Despite

a 69 That is, about 1,100 pounds or about 500 kilograms
b 69 That is, about 3 tons or about 2.8 metric tons

2:41 [e] 1Ch 15:16 **2:42** [f] 1Sa 3:15; 1Ch 9:17 **2:43** [g] 1Ch 9:2; Ne 11:21 **2:58** [h] 1Ki 9:21; 1Ch 9:2 **2:59** [i] Nu 1:18 **2:61** [j] 2Sa 17:27 **2:62** [k] Nu 3:10; 16:39-40 **2:63** [l] Lev 2:3, 10 [m] Ex 28:30; Nu 27:21 **2:65** [n] 2Sa 19:35 **2:66** [o] Isa 66:20 **2:68** [p] Ex 25:2 **2:70** [q] ver 1; 1Ch 9:2; Ne 11:3-4 **3:1** [r] Ne 7:73; 8:1 [s] Lev 23:24 **3:2** [t] Ezr 2:2; Ne 12:1, 8; Hag 2:2 [u] Hag 1:1; Zec 6:11 [v] 1Ch 3:17 [w] Ex 20:24; Dt 12:5-6

2:43 *temple servants.* A long list of names (35 in vv. 43–54; 32 in Ne 7:46–56) follows the heading "temple servants." The Hebrew word used here occurs only in 1Ch 9:2 and in Ezra-Nehemiah. They occupied a special quarter in Jerusalem (Ne 3:26,31; 11:21) and enjoyed exemption from taxes (Ezr 7:24). They participated in rebuilding the wall (Ne 3:26) and signed Nehemiah's covenant (Ne 10:29).
2:59 *they could not show.* Of the exiles who returned, members of three lay families and three priestly families were unable at this time to prove their descent. Some may have derived from proselytes; others may have temporarily lost access to their genealogical records. Genealogies, which occur prominently in Chronicles and Ezra-Nehemiah, were important for many reasons, but especially for priests and Levites. See the article "The Significance of Genealogies for a Postexilic Audience," p. 680.
2:61 *Barzillai.* The case of a man taking his name from his father-in-law is unique in the OT, but it is attested in Mesopotamia as a so-called *erebu* marriage; it is also attested in many other cultures (such as the Japanese), where a family has daughters but no sons.
2:63 *Urim and Thummim.* See the article "Urim and Thummim," p. 162.
2:69 *darics.* The daric was a gold Persian coin, named after Darius I, who began minting it. The coin was famed for its purity, which was guaranteed by the king. It bore the image of an archer and weighed about one-tenth of a gram.
3:2 *Joshua … and Zerubbabel.* Scholars have seen a tension between this statement and that of 5:16, which states that Sheshbazzar laid the foundations for the temple. Moreover, Haggai, who dates his prophetic activity in Hag 1:1 to the "second year of King Darius" (520 BC), mentions Zerubbabel (Hag 1:1) but not Sheshbazzar. It is possible

their fear[x] of the peoples around them,
they built the altar on its foundation and
sacrificed burnt offerings on it to the LORD,
both the morning and evening sacrifices.[y]
4Then in accordance with what is written,
they celebrated the Festival of Tabernacles[z] with the required number of burnt
offerings prescribed for each day. 5After
that, they presented the regular burnt offerings, the New Moon[a] sacrifices and the
sacrifices for all the appointed sacred festivals of the LORD,[b] as well as those brought
as freewill offerings to the LORD. 6On the
first day of the seventh month they began
to offer burnt offerings to the LORD, though
the foundation of the LORD's temple had
not yet been laid.

3:3 [x]Ezr 4:4; Da 9:25 [y]Ex 29:39; Nu 28:1-8 **3:4** [z]Ex 23:16; Nu 29:12-38; Ne 8:14-18; Zec 14:16-19 **3:5** [a]Nu 28:3, 11, 14; Col 2:16 [b]Lev 23:1-44; Nu 29:39 **3:7** [c]1Ch 14:1 [d]Isa 35:2 [e]Ezr 1:2-4; 6:3 **3:8** [f]Zec 4:9 [g]1Ch 23:24 **3:9** [h]Ezr 2:40

Rebuilding the Temple

7Then they gave money to the masons
and carpenters, and gave food and drink
and olive oil to the people of Sidon and
Tyre, so that they would bring cedar logs[c]
by sea from Lebanon[d] to Joppa, as authorized by Cyrus[e] king of Persia.
8In the second month of the second year
after their arrival at the house of God in
Jerusalem, Zerubbabel[f] son of Shealtiel,
Joshua son of Jozadak and the rest of the
people (the priests and the Levites and all
who had returned from the captivity to Jerusalem) began the work. They appointed
Levites twenty[g] years old and older to supervise the building of the house of the
LORD. 9Joshua[h] and his sons and brothers

that a foundation laid by Sheshbazzar had deteriorated over 20 years and had to be done again.

3:4 *Festival of Tabernacles.* See the article "Festivals," p. 220.

3:7 *cedar logs ... from Lebanon.* As with Solomon's temple (1Ch 22:2–4; 2Ch 2:7–15), the Phoenicians cooperated by sending timbers and workmen (1Ki 5:7–12). See notes on 2Sa 5:11; 1Ki 5:6; 6:15.

ZERUBBABEL'S TEMPLE

Construction of the second temple was started in 536 BC on the Solomonic foundations leveled a half-century earlier by the Babylonians. People who remembered the earlier temple wept at the comparison (Ezr 3:12). Not until 516 BC, the sixth year of the Persian emperor Darius I (522–486 BC), was the temple finally completed at the urging of Haggai and Zechariah (Ezr 6:13–15).

Archaeological evidence confirms that the Persian period in the Holy Land was a comparatively impoverished one in terms of material culture. Later Aramaic documents from Elephantine in Upper Egypt illustrate the official process of gaining permission to construct a Jewish place of worship and the opposition engendered by such a project.

Of the temple and its construction, little is known. Consequently, all art reconstructions of it are tentative. Among the few contemporary buildings, the Persian palace at Lachish and the Tobiad monument at Iraq al-Amir may be compared in terms of technique.

Unlike the more famous structures razed in 586 BC and AD 70, the temple begun by Zerubbabel suffered no major hostile destruction, but was gradually repaired and reconstructed over a long period of time. Eventually it was replaced entirely by Herod's magnificent edifice.

and Kadmiel and his sons (descendants of Hodaviah[a]) and the sons of Henadad and their sons and brothers — all Levites — joined together in supervising those working on the house of God.

10 When the builders laid[i] the foundation of the temple of the LORD, the priests in their vestments and with trumpets,[j] and the Levites (the sons of Asaph) with cymbals, took their places to praise[k] the LORD, as prescribed by David[l] king of Israel.[m] 11 With praise and thanksgiving they sang to the LORD:

"He is good;
his love toward Israel endures
forever."[n]

And all the people gave a great shout[o] of praise to the LORD, because the foundation of the house of the LORD was laid. 12 But many of the older priests and Levites and family heads, who had seen the former temple,[p] wept aloud when they saw the foundation of this temple being laid, while many others shouted for joy. 13 No one could distinguish the sound of the shouts of joy[q] from the sound of weeping, because the people made so much noise. And the sound was heard far away.

Opposition to the Rebuilding

4 When the enemies of Judah and Benjamin heard that the exiles were building a temple for the LORD, the God of Israel, 2 they came to Zerubbabel and to the heads of the families and said, "Let us help you build because, like you, we seek your God and have been sacrificing to him since the time of Esarhaddon[r] king of Assyria, who brought us here."[s]

3 But Zerubbabel, Joshua and the rest of the heads of the families of Israel answered, "You have no part with us in building a temple to our God. We alone will build it for the LORD, the God of Israel, as King Cyrus, the king of Persia, commanded us."[t]

3:10 [i] Ezr 5:16 [j] Nu 10:2; 1Ch 16:6 [k] 1Ch 25:1 [l] 1Ch 6:31 [m] Zec 6:12
3:11 [n] 1Ch 16:34, 41; 2Ch 7:3; Ps 107:1; 118:1 [o] Ne 12:24
3:12 [p] Hag 2:3, 9
3:13 [q] Job 8:21; Ps 27:6; Isa 16:9
4:2 [r] 2Ki 17:24; 19:37 [s] 2Ki 17:41
4:3 [t] Ezr 1:1-4; Ne 2:20
4:4 [u] Ezr 3:3
4:6 [v] Est 1:1; Da 9:1 [w] Est 3:13; 9:5
4:7 [x] Ezr 7:1; Ne 2:1 [y] 2Ki 18:26; Isa 36:11; Da 2:4
4:9 [z] Ezr 5:6; 6:6, 13
4:10 [a] ver 17; Ne 4:2

4 Then the peoples around them set out to discourage the people of Judah and make them afraid to go on building.[b][u] 5 They bribed officials to work against them and frustrate their plans during the entire reign of Cyrus king of Persia and down to the reign of Darius king of Persia.

Later Opposition Under Xerxes and Artaxerxes

6 At the beginning of the reign of Xerxes,[c][v] they lodged an accusation against the people of Judah and Jerusalem.[w]

7 And in the days of Artaxerxes[x] king of Persia, Bishlam, Mithredath, Tabeel and the rest of his associates wrote a letter to Artaxerxes. The letter was written in Aramaic script and in the Aramaic[y] language.[d,e]

8 Rehum the commanding officer and Shimshai the secretary wrote a letter against Jerusalem to Artaxerxes the king as follows:

9 Rehum the commanding officer and Shimshai the secretary, together with the rest of their associates[z] — the judges, officials and administrators over the people from Persia, Uruk and Babylon, the Elamites of Susa, 10 and the other people whom the great and honorable Ashurbanipal deported and settled in the city of Samaria and elsewhere in Trans-Euphrates.[a]

11 (This is a copy of the letter they sent him.)

To King Artaxerxes,

From your servants in Trans-Euphrates:

12 The king should know that the people who came up to us from you

[a] 9 Hebrew *Yehudah*, a variant of *Hodaviah* [b] 4 Or *and troubled them as they built* [c] 6 Hebrew *Ahasuerus* [d] 7 Or *written in Aramaic and translated* [e] 7 The text of 4:8 – 6:18 is in Aramaic.

4:2 *we seek your God.* The people who proffered their help were evidently from the area of Samaria, though they are not explicitly described as such. After the fall of Samaria in 722 BC, the Assyrian kings kept importing inhabitants from Mesopotamia and Syria who "worshiped the LORD, but ... also served their own gods" (2Ki 17:33). The newcomers' influence doubtless diluted further the faith of the northerners, who had already apostatized from the sole worship of the Lord in the tenth century BC. Even after the destruction of the temple, worshipers from Shiloh and Shechem in the north came to offer cereals and incense at the site of the ruined temple (Jer 41:5). Moreover, the northerners did not abandon faith in Yahweh, as we see from the Yahwistic names given to Sanballat's sons (Delaiah and Shelemiah) in the Elephantine papyri. Nevertheless, they retained Yahweh not as the sole God, but as one god among many gods. Sanballat's name honors the moon-god Sin. Though Ezra-Nehemiah does not explicitly mention the syncretistic character of the northerners, evidence suggests that the inhabitants of Samaria were syncretists. *Esarhaddon king of Assyria.* See note on 2Ki 19:37.

4:6 *Xerxes.* See Introduction to Esther: Historical Setting.

4:7 *Artaxerxes.* Artaxerxes I (465 – 424 BC), the Persian king during whose reign both Ezra and Nehemiah led the Jewish exiles. Little is known of him from sources outside the Hebrew Bible. Herodotus makes passing reference to his disastrous economic policies. Several revolts were unsuccessful at unseating him, but they did occupy his attention.

4:10 *Ashurbanipal.* See the article "Manasseh of Judah and Ashurbanipal," p. 665.

4:11 *Trans-Euphrates.* Lit. "across the River." This place-name first appears in the reign of Sargon II. Those living west of the Euphrates River, who looked east across the

have gone to Jerusalem and are rebuilding that rebellious and wicked
city. They are restoring the walls and
repairing the foundations.[b]
13 Furthermore, the king should
know that if this city is built and
its walls are restored, no more taxes, tribute or duty[c] will be paid, and
eventually the royal revenues will suffer.[a] 14 Now since we are under obligation to the palace and it is not proper
for us to see the king dishonored, we
are sending this message to inform
the king, 15 so that a search may be
made in the archives[d] of your predecessors. In these records you will
find that this city is a rebellious city,
troublesome to kings and provinces, a
place with a long history of sedition.
That is why this city was destroyed.[e]
16 We inform the king that if this city
is built and its walls are restored, you
will be left with nothing in Trans-Euphrates.

17 The king sent this reply:

To Rehum the commanding officer,
Shimshai the secretary and the rest of
their associates living in Samaria and
elsewhere in Trans-Euphrates:[f]

Greetings.

18 The letter you sent us has been
read and translated in my presence.
19 I issued an order and a search was
made, and it was found that this city
has a long history of revolt[g] against
kings and has been a place of rebellion and sedition. 20 Jerusalem has
had powerful kings ruling over the
whole of Trans-Euphrates,[h] and taxes,
tribute and duty were paid to them.
21 Now issue an order to these men to
stop work, so that this city will not
be rebuilt until I so order. 22 Be careful not to neglect this matter. Why let
this threat grow, to the detriment of
the royal interests?[i]

23 As soon as the copy of the letter of
King Artaxerxes was read to Rehum and
Shimshai the secretary and their associates,[j] they went immediately to the Jews
in Jerusalem and compelled them by force
to stop.

24 Thus the work on the house of God
in Jerusalem came to a standstill until the
second year of the reign of Darius[k] king
of Persia.

Tattenai's Letter to Darius

5 Now Haggai[l] the prophet and Zechariah[m] the prophet, a descendant of
Iddo, prophesied[n] to the Jews in Judah
and Jerusalem in the name of the God of
Israel, who was over them. 2 Then Zerubbabel[o] son of Shealtiel and Joshua[p] son of
Jozadak set to work[q] to rebuild the house

4:12 [b] Ezr 5:3,9 **4:13** [c] Ezr 7:24; Ne 5:4 **4:15** [d] Ezr 5:17; 6:1 [e] Est 3:8 **4:17** [f] ver 10 **4:19** [g] 2Ki 18:7 **4:20** [h] Ge 15:18-21; Ex 23:31; Jos 1:4; 1Ki 4:21; 1Ch 18:3; Ps 72:8-11 **4:22** [i] Da 6:2 **4:23** [j] ver 9 **4:24** [k] Ne 2:1-8; Da 9:25; Hag 1:1,15; Zec 1:1 **5:1** [l] Ezr 6:14; Hag 1:1,3,12; 2:1,10,20 [m] Zec 1:1; 7:1 [n] Hag 1:14-2:9; Zec 4:9-10; 8:9 **5:2** [o] 1Ch 3:19; Hag 1:14; 2:21; Zec 4:6-10 [p] Ezr 2:2; 3:2 [q] ver 8; Hag 2:2-5

[a] *13* The meaning of the Aramaic for this clause is uncertain.

Euphrates, defined the land "across the River" as Mesopotamia (Jos 24:2–3,14–15; 2Sa 10:16). Mesopotamians, who looked west across the Euphrates, saw this region as including Syria, Phoenicia and Israel—the area today referred to by historians of the ancient world as the Levant (cf. 1Ki 4:24).

4:13 *taxes.* Translates a Hebrew (and Aramaic) term borrowed from Akkadian that refers to a fixed annual tax paid by the provinces to the king. The word appears in the Elephantine texts as the rent due from the royal domains in Egypt to the Persians. Estimates suggest that 20–35 million dollars' worth of taxes were collected annually by the Persian king. The Fifth Satrapy, which included the Jewish province of Yehud, had to pay the smallest amount of the western satrapies. The Persians took much of the gold and silver coins and melted them down to be stored as bullion. Very little of the taxes returned to benefit the provinces. *tribute.* The rent tax in Babylonia. Some scholars interpret this word as an impost or duty charged on merchandise (RSV "custom") or as a poll tax. *duty.* Derives from Akkadian and was a land tax.

4:23 *compelled them by force to stop.* After provincial authorities had intervened, the Persian king ordered a halt to the Jewish attempt to rebuild the walls of Jerusalem. Most scholars date the episode of vv. 7–23 to just before 445 BC. The forcible destruction of these recently rebuilt walls rather than the destruction by Nebuchadnezzar is the basis of the report made to Nehemiah (Ne 1).

4:24 *Darius king of Persia.* During his first two years, Darius fought numerous battles against nine rebels. Only after the stabilization of the Persian Empire could efforts to rebuild the temple be permitted. Darius consolidated the administration of the vast empire, setting up satraps, introducing coinage and establishing the famous royal road from Susa to Sardis and a system of mounted couriers.

5:1 *Haggai ... and Zechariah ... prophesied.* Very little progress had been made in the years since the foundation of the temple was first laid. But beginning on Aug. 29, 520 BC (Hag 1:1), and continuing till Dec. 18 (Hag 2:1–9,20–23), the prophet Haggai delivered a series of messages to stir the people to begin work on the temple. Two months after Haggai's first speech, Zechariah joined him (Zec 1:1). Hag 1:6 describes the deplorable situation: housing shortages, disappointing harvests, lack of clothing and jobs, and inadequate funds—perhaps as a result of inflation. Money went into "a purse with holes in it." The people were concerned more about their own houses than about the Lord's house. See the article "Prophets and Prophecy," p. 1110.

5:2 *Zerubbabel.* A Babylonian name referring to his birth in exile, probably before 570 BC. Here (see also Ezr 3:2; Ne 12:1; Hag 1:1) he is described as the "son of Shealtiel." *Shealtiel.* Son of Jehoiachin, second-to-last king of Judah (1Ch 3:17). Though he was replaced by Zedekiah, Jehoiachin was regarded as the last legitimate king of Judah. Zerubbabel was the last of the Davidic line to be entrusted with political authority by the occupying powers.

of God in Jerusalem. And the prophets of
God were with them, supporting them.
3At that time Tattenai,[r] governor of
Trans-Euphrates, and Shethar-Bozenai[s]
and their associates went to them and
asked, "Who authorized you to rebuild
this temple and to finish it?"[t] 4They[a] also
asked, "What are the names of those who
are constructing this building?" 5But the
eye of their God[u] was watching over the
elders of the Jews, and they were not
stopped until a report could go to Darius
and his written reply be received.
6This is a copy of the letter that Tattenai,
governor of Trans-Euphrates, and Shethar-
Bozenai and their associates, the officials
of Trans-Euphrates, sent to King Darius.
7The report they sent him read as follows:

To King Darius:

Cordial greetings.

8The king should know that we
went to the district of Judah, to the
temple of the great God. The people
are building it with large stones and
placing the timbers in the walls. The
work[v] is being carried on with diligence and is making rapid progress
under their direction.
9We questioned the elders and
asked them, "Who authorized you to
rebuild this temple and to finish it?"[w]
10We also asked them their names, so
that we could write down the names
of their leaders for your information.
11This is the answer they gave us:

"We are the servants of the God of
heaven and earth, and we are rebuilding the temple[x] that was built many
years ago, one that a great king of Israel built and finished. 12But because
our ancestors angered[y] the God of
heaven, he gave them into the hands
of Nebuchadnezzar the Chaldean,
king of Babylon, who destroyed this
temple and deported the people to
Babylon.[z]
13"However, in the first year of Cyrus king of Babylon, King Cyrus issued a decree[a] to rebuild this house
of God. 14He even removed from the
temple[b] of Babylon the gold and silver
articles of the house of God, which
Nebuchadnezzar had taken from the
temple in Jerusalem and brought to
the temple[b] in Babylon.[b] Then King
Cyrus gave them to a man named
Sheshbazzar,[c] whom he had appointed governor, 15and he told him, 'Take
these articles and go and deposit them
in the temple in Jerusalem. And rebuild the house of God on its site.'
16"So this Sheshbazzar came and
laid the foundations of the house of
God[d] in Jerusalem. From that day to
the present it has been under construction but is not yet finished."

17Now if it pleases the king, let a
search be made in the royal archives[e]
of Babylon to see if King Cyrus did in
fact issue a decree to rebuild this house
of God in Jerusalem. Then let the king
send us his decision in this matter.

The Decree of Darius

6 King Darius then issued an order, and
they searched in the archives[f] stored
in the treasury at Babylon. 2A scroll was
found in the citadel of Ecbatana in the
province of Media, and this was written
on it:

Memorandum:

3In the first year of King Cyrus, the
king issued a decree concerning the
temple of God in Jerusalem:

Let the temple be rebuilt as a
place to present sacrifices, and let its

5:3 [r] Ezr 6:6 [s] Ezr 6:6 [t] ver 9; Ezr 1:3; 4:12 **5:5** [u] 2Ki 25:28; Ezr 7:6,9, 28; 8:18,22, 31; Ne 2:8, 18; Ps 33:18; Isa 66:14 **5:8** [v] ver 2 **5:9** [w] Ezr 4:12 **5:11** [x] 1Ki 6:1; 2Ch 3:1-2 **5:12** [y] 2Ch 36:16 [z] Dt 21:10; 28:36; 2Ki 24:1; 25:8,9,11; Jer 1:3 **5:13** [a] Ezr 1:1 **5:14** [b] Ezr 1:7; 6:5; Da 5:2 [c] 1Ch 3:18 **5:16** [d] Ezr 3:10; 6:15 **5:17** [e] Ezr 4:15; 6:1,2 **6:1** [f] Ezr 4:15; 5:17

[a] *4* See Septuagint; Aramaic *We.* [b] *14* Or *palace*

5:3 *Tattenai, governor of Trans-Euphrates.* Attestation of this governor (see also v. 6; 6:6,13) has been provided by a cuneiform document that can be dated to June 5, 502 BC, which cites Tattannu as the governor who was subordinate to the satrap over the region of Ebir-nari. From the Mesopotamian point of view, the region "across the River" was the area west of the Euphrates River, including Syria and Palestine (see note on 4:11). Tattenai was a subordinate of the governor of the combined satrapy of Across-the-River and Babylonia.
5:7 *The report they sent … King Darius.* That such inquiries were sent directly to the king has been vividly confirmed by the Elamite texts from Persepolis, where in 1933 – 1934 several thousand tablets and fragments were found in the fortification wall. Some 2,000 fortification tablets, dated from the 13th to the 28th year of Darius (509 – 494 BC), deal with the transfer and payment of food products. In 1936 – 1938, over 100 additional Elamite texts were discovered in the treasury area of Persepolis, dating from the 30th year of Darius to the 7th year of Artaxerxes I (492 – 458 BC). In addition to payment in kind, they include supplementary payment in silver coins, an innovation introduced around 493 BC.
6:2 *Ecbatana.* The capital of Media. Its ancient name is still preserved in the name of the modern Hamadan in northwestern Iran. This is the sole OT reference to the site, though there are numerous references in the Apocryphal books. *Memorandum.* A similar "memorandum" in the Aramaic papyri deals with Persian permission to rebuild the Jewish temple at Elephantine, which Egyptians had destroyed. It includes a response from the Persian governor to a petition from the Jewish garrison serving the Persians on the island of Elephantine near Aswan in Upper Egypt.

foundations be laid.[g] It is to be sixty cubits[a] high and sixty cubits wide,
4with three courses[h] of large stones
and one of timbers. The costs are to
be paid by the royal treasury.[i] 5Also,
the gold[j] and silver articles of the
house of God, which Nebuchadnezzar took from the temple in Jerusalem
and brought to Babylon, are to be returned to their places in the temple in
Jerusalem; they are to be deposited in
the house of God.[k]

6Now then, Tattenai,[l] governor of
Trans-Euphrates, and Shethar-Bozenai[m] and you other officials of that
province, stay away from there. 7Do
not interfere with the work on this
temple of God. Let the governor of
the Jews and the Jewish elders rebuild this house of God on its site.

8Moreover, I hereby decree what
you are to do for these elders of the
Jews in the construction of this house
of God:

Their expenses are to be fully paid
out of the royal treasury,[n] from the
revenues[o] of Trans-Euphrates, so that
the work will not stop. 9Whatever is
needed — young bulls, rams, male
lambs for burnt offerings[p] to the God
of heaven, and wheat, salt, wine and
olive oil, as requested by the priests
in Jerusalem — must be given them
daily without fail, 10so that they may
offer sacrifices pleasing to the God of
heaven and pray for the well-being of
the king and his sons.[q]

11Furthermore, I decree that if anyone defies this edict, a beam is to
be pulled from their house and they
are to be impaled[r] on it. And for this
crime their house is to be made a
pile of rubble.[s] 12May God, who has
caused his Name to dwell there,[t]
overthrow any king or people who
lifts a hand to change this decree or
to destroy this temple in Jerusalem.

I Darius[u] have decreed it. Let it be
carried out with diligence.

Completion and Dedication of the Temple

13Then, because of the decree King Darius had sent, Tattenai, governor of Trans-
Euphrates, and Shethar-Bozenai and their
associates[v] carried it out with diligence.
14So the elders of the Jews continued to
build and prosper under the preaching[w] of
Haggai the prophet and Zechariah, a descendant of Iddo. They finished building
the temple according to the command of
the God of Israel and the decrees of Cyrus,[x] Darius[y] and Artaxerxes,[z] kings of Persia. 15The temple was completed on the
third day of the month Adar, in the sixth
year of the reign of King Darius.[a]

16Then the people of Israel — the priests,
the Levites and the rest of the exiles — celebrated the dedication[b] of the house of
God with joy. 17For the dedication of this
house of God they offered[c] a hundred
bulls, two hundred rams, four hundred
male lambs and, as a sin offering[b] for all
Israel, twelve male goats, one for each of
the tribes of Israel. 18And they installed the
priests in their divisions[d] and the Levites

6:3 [g] Ezr 3:10; Hag 2:3 **6:4** [h] 1Ki 6:36 [i] ver 8; Ezr 7:20 **6:5** [j] 1Ch 29:2 [k] Ezr 1:7; 5:14 **6:6** [l] Ezr 5:3 [m] Ezr 5:3 **6:8** [n] ver 4 [o] 1Sa 9:20 **6:9** [p] Lev 1:3, 10 **6:10** [q] Ezr 7:23; 1Ti 2:1-2

6:11 [r] Dt 21:22-23; Est 2:23; 5:14; 9:14 [s] Ezr 7:26; Da 2:5; 3:29 **6:12** [t] Ex 20:24; Dt 12:5; 1Ki 9:3; 2Ch 6:2 [u] ver 14 **6:13** [v] Ezr 4:9 **6:14** [w] Ezr 5:1 [x] Ezr 1:1-4 [y] ver 12 [z] Ezr 7:1; Ne 2:1 **6:15** [a] Zec 1:1; 4:9 **6:16** [b] 1Ki 8:63; 2Ch 7:5 **6:17** [c] 2Sa 6:13; 2Ch 29:21; 30:24; Ezr 8:35 **6:18** [d] 1Ch 23:6; 2Ch 35:4; Lk 1:5

[a] *3* That is, about 90 feet or about 27 meters [b] *17* Or *purification offering*

6:4 *three courses of large stones and one of timbers.* See note on 1Ki 6:36.

6:7 *on its site.* When Babylonian kings such as Nebuchadnezzar and Nabonidus rebuilt temples, they searched carefully to discover the exact outlines of the former buildings. An inscription of Nabonidus reads: "I discovered its [i.e., the Ebabbara in Sippar] ancient foundation, which Sargon, a former king, had made. I laid its brick foundations solidly on the foundation that Sargon had made, neither protruding nor receding an inch." See note on 2Ki 12:5 ("repair ... the temple").

6:8 *Their expenses are to be fully paid out of the royal treasury.* As the accounts in Haggai and Zechariah do not speak of support from the Persian treasury, some have questioned the promises made here. Extra-Biblical evidence, however, makes it clear that Persian kings consistently helped restore sanctuaries in their empire. Cyrus repaired the Eanna temple at Uruk and the Enunmah structure at Ur. Cambyses gave funds for the temple at Sais in Egypt, according to the important inscription of Udjahorresnet. The temple of Amon at Hibis in the Khargah Oasis was rebuilt from top to bottom by order of Darius.

6:10 *so that they may offer sacrifices ... and pray.* Darius commanded that the Jews be allowed to "pray for the well-being of the king and his sons." In the Cyrus Cylinder the king asks, "May all the gods whom I have resettled in their sacred cities ask daily Bel and Nebo for a long life for me." The Jews of Elephantine wrote to Bagoas, the Persian governor of Judah, that if he helped them get their temple rebuilt, "the meal-offering, incense and burnt offering will be offered in your name, and we shall pray for you at all times, we, and our wives and our children." Herodotus reported that among the Persians anyone who offered a sacrifice had to pray for the king.

6:11 *impaled.* See note on Est 2:23.

6:15 *third day of the month Adar.* The temple was finished on Mar. 12, 515 BC, a little over 70 years after its destruction. As the renewed work on the temple had begun in September, 520 BC (see Hag 1:4 – 15), sustained effort had continued for over four years. According to Hag 2:3, the older members, who could remember the splendor of Solomon's temple, were disappointed when they saw the smaller size of Zerubbabel's temple. Nonetheless, the second temple, though not as grand as the first, lasted much longer.

6:18 *priests in their divisions.* As there were more priests than necessary for services in the Jerusalem temple, they were divided into rotations. There are 21 rotations mentioned in Ne 10:3 – 9; 24 in 1Ch 24:1 – 19. Since the priests

in their groups[e] for the service of God at Jerusalem, according to what is written in the Book of Moses.[f]

The Passover

19 On the fourteenth day of the first month, the exiles celebrated the Passover.[g] 20 The priests and Levites had purified themselves and were all ceremonially clean. The Levites slaughtered[h] the Passover lamb for all the exiles, for their relatives the priests and for themselves. 21 So the Israelites who had returned from the exile ate it, together with all who had separated themselves[i] from the unclean practices[j] of their Gentile neighbors in order to seek the LORD,[k] the God of Israel. 22 For seven days they celebrated with joy the Festival of Unleavened Bread,[l] because the LORD had filled them with joy by changing the attitude[m] of the king of Assyria so that he assisted them in the work on the house of God, the God of Israel.

Ezra Comes to Jerusalem

7 After these things, during the reign of Artaxerxes[n] king of Persia, Ezra son of Seraiah, the son of Azariah, the son of Hilkiah,[o] 2 the son of Shallum, the son of Zadok,[p] the son of Ahitub,[q] 3 the son of Amariah, the son of Azariah, the son of Meraioth, 4 the son of Zerahiah, the son of Uzzi, the son of Bukki, 5 the son of Abishua, the son of Phinehas, the son of Eleazar, the son of Aaron the chief priest— 6 this Ezra[r] came up from Babylon. He was a teacher well versed in the Law of Moses, which the LORD, the God of Israel, had given. The king had granted him everything he asked, for the hand of the LORD his God was on him.[s] 7 Some of the Israelites, including priests, Levites, musicians, gatekeepers and temple servants, also came up to Jerusalem in the seventh year of King Artaxerxes.[t]

8 Ezra arrived in Jerusalem in the fifth month of the seventh year of the king. 9 He had begun his journey from Babylon on the first day of the first month, and he arrived in Jerusalem on the first day of the fifth month, for the gracious hand of his God was on him.[u] 10 For Ezra had devoted himself to the study and observance of the Law of the LORD, and to teaching[v] its decrees and laws in Israel.

King Artaxerxes' Letter to Ezra

11 This is a copy of the letter King Artaxerxes had given to Ezra the priest, a teacher of the Law, a man learned in matters concerning the commands and decrees of the LORD for Israel:

12 Artaxerxes, king of kings,[w]

To Ezra the priest, teacher of the Law of the God of heaven:

Greetings.

13 Now I decree that any of the Israelites in my kingdom, including priests and Levites, who volunteer to go to Jerusalem with you, may go. 14 You are sent by the king and his seven advisers[x] to inquire about Judah and Jerusalem with regard to the Law of your God, which is in your hand. 15 Moreover, you are to take with you the silver and gold that the king and his advisers have freely given[y] to the God of Israel, whose dwelling[z] is in Jerusalem, 16 together with all the silver and gold[a] you may obtain from the province of Babylon, as well as the freewill offerings of the people and priests for the temple of their God in Jerusalem.[b] 17 With this money be sure to buy bulls, rams and male lambs,[c] together with their grain offerings and drink offerings,[d] and sacrifice[e] them on the altar of the temple of your God in Jerusalem.

18 You and your fellow Israelites may then do whatever seems best with the rest of the silver and gold, in accordance with the will of your God. 19 Deliver[f] to the God of Jerusalem all the articles entrusted to you for worship in the temple of your God. 20 And anything else needed for the temple of your God that you are responsible to supply, you may provide from the royal treasury.[g]

6:18 [e] 1Ch 24:1 [f] Nu 3:6-9; 8:9-11; 18:1-32 **6:19** [g] Ex 12:11; Nu 28:16 **6:20** [h] 2Ch 30:15, 17; 35:11 **6:21** [i] Ezr 9:1; Ne 9:2 [j] Dt 18:9; Ezr 9:11; Eze 36:25 [k] 1Ch 22:19; Ps 14:2 **6:22** [l] Ex 12:17 [m] Ezr 1:1 **7:1** [n] Ezr 4:7; 6:14; Ne 2:1 [o] 2Ki 22:4 **7:2** [p] 1Ki 1:8; 1Ch 6:8 [q] Ne 11:11 **7:6** [r] Ne 12:36 [s] Ezr 5:5; Isa 41:20 **7:7** [t] Ezr 8:1 **7:9** [u] ver 6 **7:10** [v] ver 25; Dt 33:10; Ne 8:1-8 **7:12** [w] Eze 26:7; Da 2:37 **7:14** [x] Est 1:14 **7:15** [y] 1Ch 29:6 [z] 1Ch 29:6, 9; 2Ch 6:2 **7:16** [a] Ezr 8:25 [b] Zec 6:10 **7:17** [c] 2Ki 3:4 [d] Nu 15:5-12 [e] Dt 12:5-11 **7:19** [f] Ezr 5:14; Jer 27:22 **7:20** [g] Ezr 6:4

---

served a week at a time, they normally served at Jerusalem twice a year.

6:20 *ceremonially clean.* See notes on Lev 21:1; 22:3–9.

6:21 *all who had separated themselves.* The returning exiles were not uncompromising separatists; they were willing to accept those who separated themselves from the syncretism of the foreigners introduced into the area by the Assyrians. Gentiles, such as Rahab and Ruth, who were willing to join themselves to Israel (Ex 12:44–48), had been accepted as members of the elect community (Jos 6:25; Ru 1:16; 4:13). The same openness is expressed in Ne 10:28–29. The repeated reference to "Israel" (12 times in Ezr 1–6) was designed to include more than just the Jews, namely, the returning exiles of those who had been deported from Judah.

7:1 *Ezra.* The name is a shortened form of Azariah, meaning "Yahweh has helped." He was from a priestly lineage; his ancestors are listed back 16 generations to Aaron. One can compare the list of 1Ch 6:3–15, where 23 high priests are listed from Aaron to the exile.

7:6 *teacher.* The Hebrew word is the common word for "scribe." See the articles "Literacy," p. 140; "Books and Literacy," p. 666.

7:12–26 The style of the Aramaic document recording the commission given to Ezra by Artaxerxes I bears every indication of an official document.

21 Now I, King Artaxerxes, decree
that all the treasurers of Trans-Euphrates are to provide with diligence whatever Ezra the priest, the teacher of the
Law of the God of heaven, may ask of
you— 22 up to a hundred talents[a] of silver, a hundred cors[b] of wheat, a hundred baths[c] of wine, a hundred baths[c]
of olive oil, and salt without limit.
23 Whatever the God of heaven has prescribed, let it be done with diligence
for the temple of the God of heaven.
Why should his wrath fall on the realm
of the king and of his sons?[h] 24 You are
also to know that you have no authority to impose taxes, tribute or duty[i] on
any of the priests, Levites, musicians,
gatekeepers, temple servants or other
workers at this house of God.[j]
25 And you, Ezra, in accordance
with the wisdom of your God, which
you possess, appoint[k] magistrates and
judges to administer justice to all the
people of Trans-Euphrates—all who
know the laws of your God. And you
are to teach[l] any who do not know
them. 26 Whoever does not obey the
law of your God and the law of the
king must surely be punished by
death, banishment, confiscation of
property, or imprisonment.[d][m]

27 Praise be to the LORD, the God of our
ancestors, who has put it into the king's
heart[n] to bring honor[o] to the house of the
LORD in Jerusalem in this way 28 and who
has extended his good favor[p] to me before
the king and his advisers and all the king's
powerful officials. Because the hand of the
LORD my God was on me,[q] I took courage
and gathered leaders from Israel to go up
with me.

7:23 [h] Ezr 6:10 **7:24** [i] Ezr 4:13 [j] Ezr 8:36 **7:25** [k] Ex 18:21, 26; Dt 16:18 [l] ver 10; Lev 10:11 **7:26** [m] Ezr 6:11 **7:27** [n] Ezr 1:1; 6:22 [o] 1Ch 29:12 **7:28** [p] 2Ki 25:28 [q] Ezr 5:5; 9:9 **8:1** [r] Ezr 7:7

List of the Family Heads Returning With Ezra

8 These are the family heads and those
registered with them who came up
with me from Babylon during the reign of
King Artaxerxes:[r]

2 of the descendants of Phinehas, Gershom;
of the descendants of Ithamar, Daniel;
of the descendants of David, Hattush
3 of the descendants of Shekaniah;[s]

of the descendants of Parosh,[t] Zechariah, and with him were registered
150 men;
4 of the descendants of Pahath-Moab,[u]
Eliehoenai son of Zerahiah, and
with him 200 men;
5 of the descendants of Zattu,[e] Shekaniah son of Jahaziel, and with him
300 men;
6 of the descendants of Adin,[v] Ebed son
of Jonathan, and with him 50 men;
7 of the descendants of Elam, Jeshaiah
son of Athaliah, and with him 70
men;
8 of the descendants of Shephatiah,
Zebadiah son of Michael, and with
him 80 men;
9 of the descendants of Joab, Obadiah son of Jehiel, and with him 218
men;
10 of the descendants of Bani,[f] Shelomith son of Josiphiah, and with
him 160 men;
11 of the descendants of Bebai, Zechariah son of Bebai, and with him 28
men;
12 of the descendants of Azgad, Johanan
son of Hakkatan, and with him 110
men;
13 of the descendants of Adonikam,[w] the
last ones, whose names were Eliphelet, Jeuel and Shemaiah, and with
them 60 men;
14 of the descendants of Bigvai, Uthai
and Zakkur, and with them 70
men.

8:3 [s] 1Ch 3:22 [t] Ezr 2:3 **8:4** [u] Ezr 2:6 **8:6** [v] Ezr 2:15; Ne 7:20; 10:16 **8:13** [w] Ezr 2:13

[a] *22* That is, about 3 3/4 tons or about 3.4 metric tons [b] *22* That is, probably about 18 tons or about 16 metric tons [c] *22* That is, about 600 gallons or about 2,200 liters [d] *26* The text of 7:12-26 is in Aramaic. [e] *5* Some Septuagint manuscripts (also 1 Esdras 8:32); Hebrew does not have *Zattu.* [f] *10* Some Septuagint manuscripts (also 1 Esdras 8:36); Hebrew does not have *Bani.*

7:22 *a hundred talents of silver.* A talent weighed about 75 pounds (34 kilograms), so 100 talents was an enormous sum—about 3.75 tons (3.4 metric tons) of silver. *a hundred cors of wheat.* A "cor" was a donkey load, about six bushels (220 liters). The 100 cors of wheat was 600 bushels (22,000 liters), equal to 18 tons (16 metric tons). The grain would be used in meal offerings. *a hundred baths of wine.* A "bath" was a liquid measure of about 6 gallons (22 liters). The 100 baths of wine was about 600 gallons (2,200 liters) of wine. *a hundred baths of olive oil.* About 600 gallons (2,200 liters) of olive oil. *salt without limit.* Lit. "salt without prescribing (how much)."

7:24 Priests and other temple personnel were often given exemptions from enforced labor or taxes. An important letter of Darius to Gadates, the Persian governor in Ionia (modern western Turkey), rebuked him for disregarding his orders concerning the collection of "tribute" from cultic personnel of Apollo at Aulai.

7:26 *punished by death, banishment, confiscation of property, or imprisonment.* The extensive powers given to Ezra are striking and extend to secular realms. Some suggest the implementation of these provisions may have involved Ezra in much traveling, which would explain the silence about Ezra's activities between 458 and 445 BC. Though some have questioned the wide authority given to Ezra, extra-Biblical parallels show that it was Persian policy to encourage both moral and religious authority that would enhance public order. An outstanding parallel to the king's commissioning of Ezra is found in a similar commission of Darius I to Udjahorresnet, an Egyptian

The Return to Jerusalem

[15]I assembled them at the canal that flows toward Ahava,[x] and we camped there three days. When I checked among the people and the priests, I found no Levites[y] there. [16]So I summoned Eliezer, Ariel, Shemaiah, Elnathan, Jarib, Elnathan, Nathan, Zechariah and Meshullam, who were leaders, and Joiarib and Elnathan, who were men of learning, [17]and I ordered them to go to Iddo, the leader in Kasiphia. I told them what to say to Iddo and his fellow Levites, the temple servants[z] in Kasiphia, so that they might bring attendants to us for the house of our God. [18]Because the gracious hand of our God was on us,[a] they brought us Sherebiah, a capable man, from the descendants of Mahli son of Levi, the son of Israel, and Sherebiah's sons and brothers, 18 in all; [19]and Hashabiah, together with Jeshaiah from the descendants of Merari, and his brothers and nephews, 20 in all. [20]They also brought 220 of the temple servants[b]—a body that David and the officials had established to assist the Levites. All were registered by name.

[21]There, by the Ahava Canal,[c] I proclaimed a fast, so that we might humble ourselves before our God and ask him for a safe journey[d] for us and our children, with all our possessions. [22]I was ashamed to ask the king for soldiers[e] and horsemen to protect us from enemies on the road, because we had told the king, "The gracious hand of our God is on everyone[f] who looks to him, but his great anger is against all who forsake him.[g]" [23]So we fasted[h] and petitioned our God about this, and he answered our prayer.

[24]Then I set apart twelve of the leading priests, namely, Sherebiah,[i] Hashabiah and ten of their brothers, [25]and I weighed out[j] to them the offering of silver and gold and the articles that the king, his advisers, his officials and all Israel present there had donated for the house of our God. [26]I weighed out to them 650 talents[a] of silver, silver articles weighing 100 talents,[b] 100 talents[b] of gold, [27]20 bowls of gold valued at 1,000 darics,[c] and two fine articles of polished bronze, as precious as gold.

[28]I said to them, "You as well as these articles are consecrated to the LORD.[k] The silver and gold are a freewill offering to the LORD, the God of your ancestors. [29]Guard them carefully until you weigh them out in the chambers of the house of the LORD in Jerusalem before the leading priests and the Levites and the family heads of Israel." [30]Then the priests and Levites received the silver and gold and sacred articles that had been weighed out to be taken to the house of our God in Jerusalem.

[31]On the twelfth day of the first month we set out from the Ahava Canal[l] to go to Jerusalem. The hand of our God was on us, and he protected us from enemies and bandits along the way. [32]So we arrived in Jerusalem, where we rested three days.[m]

[33]On the fourth day, in the house of our God, we weighed out the silver and gold and the sacred articles into the hands of Meremoth[n] son of Uriah, the priest. Eleazar son of Phinehas was with him, and so were the Levites Jozabad son of Jeshua and Noadiah son of Binnui.[o] [34]Everything was accounted for by number and weight, and the entire weight was recorded at that time.

[35]Then the exiles who had returned from captivity sacrificed burnt offerings to the God of Israel: twelve bulls for all Israel, ninety-six rams, seventy-seven male lambs and, as a sin offering,[d] twelve male goats.[p] All this was a burnt offering to the LORD. [36]They also delivered the king's orders[q] to the royal satraps and to the governors of Trans-Euphrates, who then gave assistance to the people and to the house of God.[r]

Ezra's Prayer About Intermarriage

9 After these things had been done, the leaders came to me and said, "The people of Israel, including the priests and

8:15 [x] ver 21,31 [y] Ezr 2:40; 7:7 **8:17** [z] Ezr 2:43 **8:18** [a] Ezr 5:5 **8:20** [b] 1Ch 9:2; Ezr 2:43 **8:21** [c] ver 15; 2Ch 20:3 [d] Ps 5:8; 107:7 **8:22** [e] Ne 2:9; Ezr 7:6,9, 28 [f] Ezr 5:5 [g] Dt 31:17; 2Ch 15:2 **8:23** [h] 2Ch 20:3; 33:13 **8:24** [i] ver 18 **8:25** [j] ver 33; Ezr 7:15,16
8:28 [k] Lev 21:6; 22:2-3 **8:31** [l] ver 15 **8:32** [m] Ge 40:13; Ne 2:11 **8:33** [n] Ne 3:4, 21 [o] Ne 3:24 **8:35** [p] 2Ch 29:21; Ezr 6:17 **8:36** [q] Ezr 7:21-24 [r] Est 9:3

[a] *26* That is, about 24 tons or about 22 metric tons
[b] *26* That is, about 3 3/4 tons or about 3.4 metric tons
[c] *27* That is, about 19 pounds or about 8.4 kilograms
[d] *35* Or *purification offering*

priest, scholar and military leader, who had also served under Cambyses.

8:17 *Kasiphia.* May be related to the word for "silver" (Aramaic *kaspam*) and may have been named after a guild of silversmiths. The NIV has left untranslated the word *hammaqom* ("the place"), which occurs twice after "Kasiphia" in this verse. As this word is sometimes used for the temple (Dt 12:5; 1Ki 8:29), some have wondered if the Babylonian exiles had a sanctuary, similar to that attested for the Jewish community in Elephantine, Egypt.

8:28 *consecrated to the LORD.* Both people and objects could be considered sacred, consecrated to God. Ezra carefully weighed out the treasures and entrusted them to others (vv. 29–30). He instilled a sense of the holiness of the mission and the gravity of each individual's responsibility. Each was responsible to guard his deposit. The data were carefully recorded and rechecked at the journey's end (v. 34).

9:1 *neighboring peoples.* The "peoples of the lands" included the pagan newcomers brought into Samaria by the Assyrians, as well as Edomites and others who had encroached on former Judahite territories. The eight groups listed designate the original inhabitants of Canaan before the Hebrew conquest (cf. Ex 3:8,17; 13:5; 23:23,28; Dt 7:1; 20:17; Jos 3:10; 9:1; 12:8; Jdg 3:5; 1Ki 9:20). Only the Ammonites, Moabites and Egyptians were still extant in the postexilic period (cf. 2Ch 8:7; Ne 9:8). *Canaanites.* See note on Dt 1:7; see also the article "The Canaanites," p. 294.

EZRA 9

Mixed Marriages

Marriage with foreigners as such was not prohibited in the Torah. Joseph was given an Egyptian wife, Asenath (Ge 41:45). Moses married both Zipporah, a Midianite (Ex 2:16–21), and a Cushite woman (Nu 12:1). Ruth, a Moabite (Ru 1:4), had an honored place in Jesus' genealogy (Mt 1:5). There was, however, always the danger that marriage with non-Israelite women could lead to apostasy, as in the case of the numerous foreign wives of Solomon (1Ki 11:1–3). Malachi, who prophesied in the early fifth century BC, prior to Ezra's mission, indicates in Mal 2:10–16 that some Jews had broken off marriages to their wives to marry women who worshiped "a foreign god" (Mal 2:11).

The situation for the returning exiles was probably aggravated by demographic and economic factors. A large proportion of the newcomers returning from exile were males, who perhaps would have had difficulty finding Jewish wives. Though the actions of Ezra and later of Nehemiah may strike some readers as harsh, the measures taken were more than racial or cultural; they were felt necessary to preserve the spiritual heritage of Israel. Both from the principle and from exceptions to the rule, warnings against intermarriage were clearly concerned not so much about racial intermarriage as about spiritual adulteration. ◆

the Levites, have not kept themselves separate[s] from the neighboring peoples with
their detestable practices, like those of
the Canaanites, Hittites, Perizzites, Jebusites, Ammonites,[t] Moabites, Egyptians
and Amorites.[u] 2They have taken some of
their daughters[v] as wives for themselves
and their sons, and have mingled the holy
race[w] with the peoples around them. And
the leaders and officials have led the way
in this unfaithfulness."[x]
3When I heard this, I tore my tunic and
cloak, pulled hair from my head and beard
and sat down appalled. 4Then everyone
who trembled[y] at the words of the God of
Israel gathered around me because of this
unfaithfulness of the exiles. And I sat there
appalled until the evening sacrifice.
5Then, at the evening sacrifice,[z] I rose
from my self-abasement, with my tunic
and cloak torn, and fell on my knees with
my hands spread out to the LORD my God
6and prayed:

"I am too ashamed and disgraced,
my God, to lift up my face to you,
because our sins are higher than our
heads and our guilt has reached to the
heavens.[a] 7From the days of our ancestors[b] until now, our guilt has been
great. Because of our sins, we and our
kings and our priests have been subjected to the sword[c] and captivity,[d] to
pillage and humiliation[e] at the hand
of foreign kings, as it is today.
8"But now, for a brief moment, the
LORD our God has been gracious[f] in
leaving us a remnant[g] and giving us
a firm place[a][h] in his sanctuary, and
so our God gives light to our eyes[i]
and a little relief in our bondage.
9Though we are slaves,[j] our God has
not forsaken us in our bondage. He
has shown us kindness[k] in the sight
of the kings of Persia: He has granted
us new life to rebuild the house of our
God and repair its ruins,[l] and he has
given us a wall of protection in Judah
and Jerusalem.
10"But now, our God, what can we
say after this? For we have forsaken
the commands[m] 11you gave through

9:1 [s] Ezr 6:21; Ne 9:2 [t] Ge 19:38 [u] Ex 13:5 **9:2** [v] Ex 34:16 [w] Ex 22:31 [x] Ezr 10:2 **9:4** [y] Ezr 10:3 **9:5** [z] Ex 29:41 **9:6** [a] 2Ch 28:9; Job 42:6; Ps 38:4; Rev 18:5 **9:7** [b] 2Ch 29:6 [c] Eze 21:1-32 [d] Dt 28:64 [e] Dt 28:37 **9:8** [f] Ps 25:16; Isa 33:2 [g] Ge 45:7 [h] Ecc 12:11; Isa 22:23 [i] Ps 13:3 **9:9** [j] Ex 1:14; Ne 9:36 [k] Ezr 7:28 [l] Ps 69:35; Isa 43:1; Jer 32:44 **9:10** [m] Dt 11:8; Isa 1:19-20

[a] 8 Or *a foothold*

Hittites. See notes on Ge 23:3; Dt 7:1. *Perizzites.* See note on Dt 7:1. *Jebusites.* See notes on Nu 13:29; Dt 7:1. *Ammonites.* See notes on Ge 19:37–38; Dt 2:19. *Moabites.* See notes on Ge 19:37–38; Dt 2:9; see also the article "Moab," p. 450. *Amorites.* See note on Nu 13:29.

your servants the prophets when you
said: 'The land you are entering to
possess is a land polluted[n] by the corruption of its peoples. By their detestable practices[o] they have filled it with
their impurity from one end to the
other. 12Therefore, do not give your
daughters in marriage to their sons or
take their daughters for your sons. Do
not seek a treaty of friendship with
them[p] at any time, that you may be
strong and eat the good things of the
land and leave it to your children as
an everlasting inheritance.'
13"What has happened to us is a
result of our evil deeds and our great
guilt, and yet, our God, you have
punished us less than our sins deserved[q] and have given us a remnant
like this. 14Shall we then break your
commands again and intermarry[r]
with the peoples who commit such
detestable practices? Would you not
be angry enough with us to destroy
us,[s] leaving us no remnant[t] or survivor? 15LORD, the God of Israel, you
are righteous![u] We are left this day as
a remnant. Here we are before you
in our guilt, though because of it not
one of us can stand[v] in your presence.[w]"

The People's Confession of Sin

10 While Ezra was praying and confessing,[x] weeping and throwing
himself down before the house of God,
a large crowd of Israelites — men, wom-
en and children — gathered around him.
They too wept bitterly. 2Then Shekaniah
son of Jehiel, one of the descendants of
Elam, said to Ezra, "We have been unfaithful[y] to our God by marrying foreign
women from the peoples around us. But
in spite of this, there is still hope for Israel.[z] 3Now let us make a covenant[a] before
our God to send away[b] all these women
and their children, in accordance with the
counsel of my lord and of those who fear
the commands of our God. Let it be done
according to the Law. 4Rise up; this matter
is in your hands. We will support you, so
take courage and do it."
5So Ezra rose up and put the leading
priests and Levites and all Israel under
oath[c] to do what had been suggested. And
they took the oath. 6Then Ezra withdrew
from before the house of God and went
to the room of Jehohanan son of Eliashib.
While he was there, he ate no food and
drank no water,[d] because he continued to
mourn over the unfaithfulness of the exiles.
7A proclamation was then issued
throughout Judah and Jerusalem for all
the exiles to assemble in Jerusalem. 8Any-
one who failed to appear within three
days would forfeit all his property, in accordance with the decision of the officials
and elders, and would himself be expelled
from the assembly of the exiles.

9Within the three days, all the men of
Judah and Benjamin[e] had gathered in Jerusalem. And on the twentieth day of the
ninth month, all the people were sitting in
the square before the house of God, greatly distressed by the occasion and because
of the rain. 10Then Ezra the priest stood
up and said to them, "You have been unfaithful; you have married foreign wom-
en, adding to Israel's guilt. 11Now honor[a]
the LORD, the God of your ancestors, and
do his will. Separate yourselves from the
peoples around you and from your foreign
wives."[f]
12The whole assembly responded with a
loud voice:[g] "You are right! We must do as
you say. 13But there are many people here
and it is the rainy season; so we cannot
stand outside. Besides, this matter cannot
be taken care of in a day or two, because
we have sinned greatly in this thing. 14Let
our officials act for the whole assembly.
Then let everyone in our towns who has
married a foreign woman come at a set
time, along with the elders and judges[h] of
each town, until the fierce anger[i] of our
God in this matter is turned away from
us." 15Only Jonathan son of Asahel and
Jahzeiah son of Tikvah, supported by Meshullam and Shabbethai[j] the Levite, opposed this.
16So the exiles did as was proposed.
Ezra the priest selected men who were
family heads, one from each family divi-

9:11 [n] Lev 18:25-28 [o] Dt 9:4
9:12 [p] Ex 34:15; Dt 7:3; 23:6
9:13 [q] Job 11:6; Ps 103:10
9:14 [r] Ne 13:27 [s] Dt 9:8 [t] Dt 9:14
9:15 [u] Ge 18:25; Ps 51:4; Jer 12:1; Da 9:7 [v] Ne 9:33; Ps 130:3; Mal 3:2 [w] 1Ki 8:47
10:1 [x] 2Ch 20:9; Da 9:20
10:2 [y] Ezr 9:2; Ne 13:27 [z] Dt 30:8-10
10:3 [a] 2Ch 34:31 [b] Ex 34:16; Dt 7:2-3; Ezr 9:4
10:5 [c] Ne 5:12; 13:25
10:6 [d] Ex 34:28; Dt 9:18
10:9 [e] Ezr 1:5
10:11 [f] ver 3; Dt 24:1; Ne 9:2; Mal 2:10-16
10:12 [g] Jos 6:5
10:14 [h] Dt 16:18 [i] Nu 25:4; 2Ch 29:10; 30:8
10:15 [j] Ne 11:16

[a] 11 Or *Now make confession to*

10:8 *within three days.* As the territory of Judah had been much reduced, all could travel to Jerusalem "within three days." The borders were Bethel in the north, Beersheba in the south, Jericho in the east and Ono in the west — about 35 miles (56 kilometers) north to south and 25 miles (40 kilometers) east to west. *would forfeit.* From Hebrew *hrm,* it means to ban from profane use and to devote either to destruction (e.g., Ex 22:20; Dt 13:13 – 17) or for use in the temple (e.g., 1 Esdras 9:4; cf. Lev 27:28 – 29; Jos 6:18 – 19; 7:1 – 26). This verse, which is the earliest attestation of excommunication, is probably a modification of the more ancient capital punishment: to be "cut off" from Israel (see notes on Lev 7:20; Nu 15:30).

10:9 *ninth month.* Kislev (November–December); it is in the middle of the rainy season, which begins with light showers in October and lasts to mid-April. *rain.* The Hebrew (using a plural of intensity) indicates heavy torrential rains.

10:14 *elders.* See note on Jdg 2:7.

sion, and all of them designated by name. On the first day of the tenth month they sat down to investigate the cases, [17]and by the first day of the first month they finished dealing with all the men who had married foreign women.

Those Guilty of Intermarriage

[18]Among the descendants of the priests, the following had married foreign women:[k]

From the descendants of Joshua[l] son of Jozadak, and his brothers: Maaseiah, Eliezer, Jarib and Gedaliah. [19](They all gave their hands[m] in pledge to put away their wives, and for their guilt they each presented a ram from the flock as a guilt offering.)[n]

[20]From the descendants of Immer:[o]
Hanani and Zebadiah.

[21]From the descendants of Harim:[p]
Maaseiah, Elijah, Shemaiah, Jehiel and Uzziah.

[22]From the descendants of Pashhur:[q]
Elioenai, Maaseiah, Ishmael, Nethanel, Jozabad and Elasah.

[23]Among the Levites:[r]
Jozabad, Shimei, Kelaiah (that is, Kelita), Pethahiah, Judah and Eliezer.

[24]From the musicians:
Eliashib.[s]
From the gatekeepers:
Shallum, Telem and Uri.

[25]And among the other Israelites:
From the descendants of Parosh:[t]
Ramiah, Izziah, Malkijah, Mijamin, Eleazar, Malkijah and Benaiah.

[26]From the descendants of Elam:[u]
Mattaniah, Zechariah, Jehiel, Abdi, Jeremoth and Elijah.

[27]From the descendants of Zattu:
Elioenai, Eliashib, Mattaniah, Jeremoth, Zabad and Aziza.

[28]From the descendants of Bebai:
Jehohanan, Hananiah, Zabbai and Athlai.

[29]From the descendants of Bani:
Meshullam, Malluk, Adaiah, Jashub, Sheal and Jeremoth.

[30]From the descendants of Pahath-Moab:
Adna, Kelal, Benaiah, Maaseiah, Mattaniah, Bezalel, Binnui and Manasseh.

[31]From the descendants of Harim:
Eliezer, Ishijah, Malkijah, Shemaiah, Shimeon, [32]Benjamin, Malluk and Shemariah.

[33]From the descendants of Hashum:
Mattenai, Mattattah, Zabad, Eliphelet, Jeremai, Manasseh and Shimei.

[34]From the descendants of Bani:
Maadai, Amram, Uel, [35]Benaiah, Bedeiah, Keluhi, [36]Vaniah, Meremoth, Eliashib, [37]Mattaniah, Mattenai and Jaasu.

[38]From the descendants of Binnui:[a]
Shimei, [39]Shelemiah, Nathan, Adaiah, [40]Maknadebai, Shashai, Sharai, [41]Azarel, Shelemiah, Shemariah, [42]Shallum, Amariah and Joseph.

[43]From the descendants of Nebo:
Jeiel, Mattithiah, Zabad, Zebina, Jaddai, Joel and Benaiah.

[44]All these had married foreign women, and some of them had children by these wives.[b]

10:18 [k]Jdg 3:6 [l]Ezr 2:2
10:19 [m]2Ki 10:15 [n]Lev 5:15; 6:6
10:20 [o]1Ch 24:14
10:21 [p]1Ch 24:8
10:22 [q]1Ch 9:12
10:23 [r]Ne 8:7; 9:4
10:24 [s]Ne 3:1; 12:10; 13:7,28
10:25 [t]Ezr 2:3
10:26 [u]ver 2

[a] *37,38* See Septuagint (also 1 Esdras 9:34); Hebrew *Jaasu* [38]*and Bani and Binnui,* [b] *44* Or *and they sent them away with their children*

NARRATIVE LITERATURE

NEHEMIAH

Nehemiah's Prayer

1 The words of Nehemiah son of Hakaliah:

In the month of Kislev[a] in the twentieth
year, while I was in the citadel of Susa,
2 Hanani,[b] one of my brothers, came from
Judah with some other men, and I questioned them about the Jewish remnant[c]
that had survived the exile, and also about
Jerusalem.

3 They said to me, "Those who survived
the exile and are back in the province are
in great trouble and disgrace. The wall of
Jerusalem is broken down, and its gates
have been burned with fire.[d]"

4 When I heard these things, I sat down
and wept.[e] For some days I mourned and
fasted[f] and prayed before the God of heav-
en. 5 Then I said:

"LORD, the God of heaven, the great
and awesome God,[g] who keeps his
covenant of love[h] with those who
love him and keep his commandments, 6 let your ear be attentive and
your eyes open to hear[i] the prayer[j]
your servant is praying before you
day and night for your servants, the
people of Israel. I confess the sins we
Israelites, including myself and my father's family, have committed against
you. 7 We have acted very wickedly[k]
toward you. We have not obeyed the
commands, decrees and laws you
gave your servant Moses.

8 "Remember[l] the instruction you
gave your servant Moses, saying, 'If
you are unfaithful, I will scatter[m] you
among the nations, 9 but if you return
to me and obey my commands, then
even if your exiled people are at the
farthest horizon, I will gather[n] them
from there and bring them to the
place I have chosen as a dwelling for
my Name.'[o]

10 "They are your servants and
your people, whom you redeemed by
your great strength and your mighty
hand.[p] 11 Lord, let your ear be attentive[q] to the prayer of this your servant
and to the prayer of your servants
who delight in revering your name.
Give your servant success today by
granting him favor in the presence of
this man."

I was cupbearer[r] to the king.

1:1 [a] Ne 10:1; Zec 7:1 **1:2** [b] Ne 7:2 [c] Jer 52:28 **1:3** [d] 2Ki 25:10; Ne 2:3, 13, 17 **1:4** [e] Ps 137:1 [f] Ezr 9:4 **1:5** [g] Dt 7:21; Ne 4:14 [h] Ex 20:6; Da 9:4 **1:6** [i] 1Ki 8:29 [j] Da 9:17 **1:7** [k] Dt 28:14-15; Ps 106:6 **1:8** [l] 2Ki 20:3 [m] Lev 26:33 **1:9** [n] Dt 30:4 [o] 1Ki 8:48; Jer 29:14 **1:10** [p] Ex 32:11; Dt 9:29 **1:11** [q] ver 6 [r] Ge 40:1

1:1 *Nehemiah.* Cupbearer (see note on v. 11) to Artaxerxes I of Persia, who reigned from 465–424 BC. In 460 a revolt broke out in Egypt that took five years to put down. A satrap north of Mesopotamia named Megabyzus also rebelled in 488 BC. Because of the turbulence of the times, the Persians may have been willing to ally themselves with minority groups such as the Jews, which may explain the high position held by Nehemiah.
1:3 *The wall of Jerusalem is broken down.* The wall of Jerusalem that had been destroyed by Nebuchadnezzar, despite abortive attempts to rebuild them, remained in ruins for almost a century and a half. Such a lamentable situation obviously made Jerusalem vulnerable to numerous enemies. Yet, from a mixture of apathy and fear, the Jews failed to rectify this glaring deficiency. The narrative is describing a recent failed attempt to rebuild the wall (see note on Ezr 4:23), not the original destruction of the city and its wall over a century prior.
1:4 *God of heaven.* See note on Ezr 1:2. The title of Ahura Mazda, the god of Zoroastrianism, the religion of Persia. Nehemiah, however, does not mind attributing this title to Yahweh. (See the article "Zoroastrianism," p. 1433.
1:11 *cupbearer.* An important official with ready access to the king. Since he also came in contact with the harem, he was often a eunuch, but there is no evidence that this was the case with Nehemiah. The cupbearer was the chief financial officer and bearer of the signet ring (see notes on Est 3:10,11) and in later sources is said to be the wine taster, whose job it was to sample royal beverages to test for poison.

Ashurnasirpal court scene depicts a eunuch offering the king the royal cup, Nimrud, 865–860 BC. Nehemiah was also cupbearer to the king (Ne 1:11).

Artaxerxes Sends Nehemiah to Jerusalem

2 In the month of Nisan in the twentieth year of King Artaxerxes,[s] when
wine was brought for him, I took the wine
and gave it to the king. I had not been
sad in his presence before, [2]so the king
asked me, "Why does your face look so
sad when you are not ill? This
can be nothing but sadness of
heart."
I was very much afraid,
[3]but I said to the king, "May
the king live forever![t] Why
should my face not look sad
when the city[u] where my ancestors are buried lies in ruins, and its gates have been
destroyed by fire?[v]"
[4]The king said to me,
"What is it you want?"
Then I prayed to the God of
heaven, [5]and I answered the
king, "If it pleases the king
and if your servant has found
favor in his sight, let him send
me to the city in Judah where
my ancestors are buried so
that I can rebuild it."
[6]Then the king[w], with the
queen sitting beside him, asked
me, "How long will your journey take, and when will you
get back?" It pleased the king
to send me; so I set a time.
[7]I also said to him, "If it
pleases the king, may I have
letters to the governors of
Trans-Euphrates,[x] so that they
will provide me safe-conduct
until I arrive in Judah? [8]And
may I have a letter to Asaph,
keeper of the royal park, so he
will give me timber to make beams for the
gates of the citadel[y] by the temple and for
the city wall and for the residence I will
occupy?" And because the gracious hand
of my God was on me,[z] the king granted
my requests. [9]So I went to the governors

2:1 [s] Ezr 7:1
2:3 [t] 1Ki 1:31; Da 2:4; 5:10; 6:6, 21 [u] Ps 137:6 [v] Ne 1:3
2:6 [w] Ne 5:14; 13:6
2:7 [x] Ezr 8:36
2:8 [y] Ne 7:2 [z] ver 18; Ezr 5:5; 7:6

2:1 *Artaxerxes.* See note on Ezr 4:7. *sad in his presence.* Given the self-indulgence of the Persian monarchs, it seems in character that they would prohibit their subjects from imposing grief on them. Herodotus writes of people with complaints gathering outside the king's gate and wailing without bringing their trouble within the palace. In one instance, the wife of a condemned noble stood outside the palace gate, weeping until Darius relented and agreed to spare her husband. In this situation Nehemiah expresses fear when the Persian king notes that Nehemiah has come before him with a sad look on his face (see v. 2 and note).
2:2 *I was very much afraid.* Possibly, Nehemiah expected to be punished for bringing his sorrow before the king (cf. Est 4:2) In Persian reliefs, courtiers cover their faces in the king's presence, possibly as a sign of deference. The facial expressions would be somewhat masked; however, it would be expected that the joy of working in the king's service would be shown on every face.
2:5 *where my ancestors are buried.* Family ties were extremely important in the ancient Near East. One of the primary family responsibilities was to care for the remains or tombs of one's ancestors. Artaxerxes would have been sympathetic to this appeal of Nehemiah to rebuild the city where his ancestors were buried lest it become a ruin and a wasteland. See notes on Ge 23:4; 25:8.
2:7 *letters ... provide me safe-conduct.* Due to the unrest of the times, Nehemiah might have been worried about encountering hostility. He may have also expected political opposition due to the nature of his undertaking. The primary function of such letters is to instruct regional officials to supply provisions from the royal stores, as demonstrated by a fifth-century BC Aramaic document. *governors.* Can refer to either the major provincial rulers, called satraps, or to lesser regional governors.
2:8 *park.* The Hebrew (*pardes*) is a loanword from Persian that originally meant "beyond the wall," hence an enclosure, a pleasant retreat, or a park. See note on Est 1:5. *the citadel.* May refer to the fortress north of the temple. The majority of the construction of these structures would have been mud brick and stone. Cedar timber would have been used primarily for paneling,

of Trans-Euphrates and gave them the king's letters. The king had also sent army officers and cavalry[a] with me.

[10]When Sanballat[b] the Horonite and Tobiah[c] the Ammonite official heard about this, they were very much disturbed that someone had come to promote the welfare of the Israelites.[d]

2:9 [a] Ezr 8:22 **2:10** [b] ver 19; Ne 4:1,7 [c] Ne 4:3; 13:4-7 [d] Est 10:3 **2:11** [e] Ge 40:13

Nehemiah Inspects Jerusalem's Walls

[11]I went to Jerusalem, and after staying there three days[e] [12]I set out during the night with a few others. I had not told anyone what my God had put in my heart to do for Jerusalem. There were no mounts with me except the one I was riding on.

[13]By night I went out through the Valley Gate[f] toward the Jackal[a] Well and the Dung Gate,[g] examining the walls[h] of Jerusalem, which had been broken down, and its gates, which had been destroyed

2:13 [f] 2Ch 26:9 [g] Ne 3:13 [h] Ne 1:3

[a] *13* Or *Serpent* or *Fig*

though the lintel and side-posts of gates would also use beams of wood.

2:10 *Sanballat.* Sanballat was the chief political opponent of Nehemiah. Although not called governor, he had that position over Samaria (4:1 – 2). An important Elephantine papyrus, a letter to Bagoas (the governor of Judah), refers to "Delaiah and Shelemiah, the sons of Sanballat the governor of Samaria." It is interesting that Sanballat's sons both bear Yahwistic names. Bagoas and Delaiah authorized the Jews to petition the satrap Arsames about rebuilding their temple at Elephantine. *Tobiah.* He may have been a Judaizing Ammonite, but more probably he was a Yahwist Jew as indicated by his name and that of his son, Jehohanan (6:18). Some scholars speculate that Tobiah descended from an aristocratic family that owned estates in Gilead and was influential in Transjordan and in Jerusalem even as early as the eighth century BC. *official.* The Hebrew (*ebed*) is lit. "slave" or "servant." The RSV believes this term was meant derisively: "Tobias, the Ammonite, the slave." But *ebed* is often used of high officials both in Biblical and in extra-Biblical texts. He may have been governor of Ammon, as his grandson (also named Tobiah) was.

2:13 *Jackal Well.* The Hebrew (*en hattannin*) is "spring of the dragon," using the same Hebrew word as Ge 1:21, referring to the chaos creatures of the water (see note on Ge 1:21). The NIV and RSV emend the word to read *tannim* ("jackals"). It is possible that this may be the major spring of Jerusalem, the Gihon, and that the name "Tannin" is derived from the serpentine course of the waters of the spring to the Pool of Siloam.

JERUSALEM OF THE RETURNING EXILES

AFTER 458 BC

A smaller city was rebuilt, with new walls higher on the eastern hill. Temple worship was restored in a rebuilt temple on the former site. Rebuilding on the western hill did not occur until later.

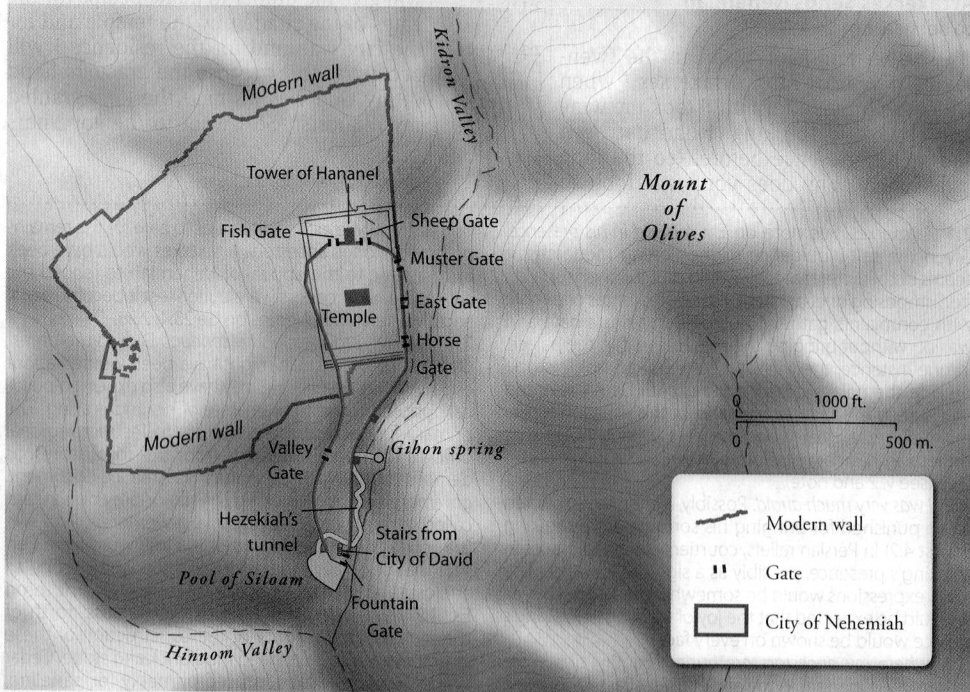

by fire. 14Then I moved on toward the
Fountain Gate[i] and the King's Pool,[j] but
there was not enough room for my mount
to get through; 15so I went up the valley by
night, examining the wall. Finally, I turned
back and reentered through the Valley
Gate. 16The officials did not know where I
had gone or what I was doing, because as
yet I had said nothing to the Jews or the
priests or nobles or officials or any others
who would be doing the work.

17Then I said to them, "You see the
trouble we are in: Jerusalem lies in ruins, and its gates have been burned with
fire.[k] Come, let us rebuild the wall[l] of Jerusalem, and we will no longer be in disgrace.[m]" 18I also told them about the gracious hand of my God on me[n] and what
the king had said to me.

They replied, "Let us start rebuilding."
So they began this good work.

19But when Sanballat the Horonite, Tobiah the Ammonite official and Geshem[o]
the Arab heard about it, they mocked
and ridiculed us.[p] "What is this you are
doing?" they asked. "Are you rebelling
against the king?"

20I answered them by saying, "The God
of heaven will give us success. We his servants will start rebuilding, but as for you,
you have no share[q] in Jerusalem or any
claim or historic right to it."

Builders of the Wall

3 Eliashib[r] the high priest and his fellow priests went to work and rebuilt[s]
the Sheep Gate.[t] They dedicated it and set
its doors in place, building as far as the
Tower of the Hundred, which they dedicated, and as far as the Tower of Hananel.[u]
2The men of Jericho[v] built the adjoining
section, and Zakkur son of Imri built next
to them.

3The Fish Gate[w] was rebuilt by the sons
of Hassenaah. They laid its beams and put
its doors and bolts and bars in place. 4Mer-
emoth son of Uriah, the son of Hakkoz,
repaired the next section. Next to him Meshullam son of Berekiah, the son of Meshezabel, made repairs, and next to him
Zadok son of Baana also made repairs.
5The next section was repaired by the men
of Tekoa,[x] but their nobles would not put

2:14 [i] Ne 3:15 [j] 2Ki 18:17 **2:17** [k] Ne 1:3 [l] Ps 102:16; Isa 30:13; 58:12 [m] Eze 5:14 **2:18** [n] 2Sa 2:7 **2:19** [o] Ne 6:1, 2, 6 [p] Ps 44:13-16 **2:20** [q] Ezr 4:3 **3:1** [r] Ezr 10:24 [s] Isa 58:12 [t] ver 32; Ne 12:39 [u] Ne 12:39; Jer 31:38; Zec 14:10 **3:2** [v] Ne 7:36 **3:3** [w] 2Ch 33:14; Ne 12:39 **3:5** [x] 2Sa 14:2

2:14 *Fountain Gate.* Possibly in the southeast wall facing toward En Rogel. According to 2Ki 20:20 (cf. 2Ch 32:30), Hezekiah diverted the overflow from his Siloam tunnel to irrigate the royal gardens (2Ki 25:4; see the article "Hezekiah's Tunnel," p. 663) located at the junction of the Kidron and Tyropoeon Valleys.

2:19 *Geshem the Arab.* In addition to Sanballat and Tobiah, a new opponent is named, this one an Arab. Biblical and extra-Biblical documents indicate that Arabs became dominant in the Transjordanian area from the Assyrian to the Persian periods. A Lihyanite inscription from Dedan in northwest Arabia reads: "Jašm son of Šahr and 'Abd, governor of Dedan." This Jašm is identified with the Biblical Geshem. In 1947, several silver vessels, some with Aramaic inscriptions dating to the late fifth century BC, were discovered near the Suez Canal. One inscription bore the name "Qaynu the son of Gashmu, the king of Qedar." Geshem was thus in charge of a powerful north Arabian confederacy of tribes that controlled vast areas from northeast Egypt to northern Arabia to southern Palestine.

It is noteworthy that the Edomites, who occupied the territory southeast of Judah, are not mentioned as a foe, though they are denounced particularly by the prophet Obadiah for taking advantage of the Babylonian occupation of Judah. Epigraphic evidence indicates the integration of Edom into the Persian ruled territory of greater Arabia.

3:1–32 This chapter describes how Nehemiah effectively organized work crews to repair sections of the city wall, beginning at the Sheep Gate in the north and proceeding in a counterclockwise direction for the 1.5-mile (2.4-kilometer) circuit of the wall. Some cities, such as Bethlehem, are not represented; some segments of society, such as "the nobles" of Tekoa, refused to participate (v. 5), but others repaired double sections (v. 27). Archaeological evidence indicates that Nehemiah must have abandoned areas on the steep eastern slope of Ophel. Only one crew was needed to repair the southern half of the western wall (from the Valley Gate to the Dung Gate). On the other hand, the eastern section required twice as many work crews as the western section.

3:1 *Eliashib the high priest.* He was the son of Joiakim and father of Joiada (12:10). His "house" is mentioned in 3:20–21. It was fitting that the high priest should set the example. Among the Sumerians, the king himself would carry bricks (or at least the ceremonial first brick) for the building of the temple, a practice attested as late as the Assyrian king Ashurbanipal. *Sheep Gate.* The only gate that was "dedicated" by the priests. No doubt, it was used to bring in sheep for sacrifices in the temple. It was located in the northern section of the wall. Jn 5:2 locates a Sheep Gate near the Bethesda Pool, whose ruins have been excavated on the grounds of Saint Anne's Church near the current Saint Stephen's Gate in the northeastern part of the Ottoman walls. This may have replaced the earlier Benjamin Gate (Jer 37:13; 38:7) that led to Anathoth in Benjamin (Zec 14:10). *Tower of the Hundred.* Mentioned only here and in 12:39. What the "hundred" refers to is unclear—its height (100 cubits), or 100 steps, or a military unit (cf. Dt 1:15). *Tower of Hananel.* Also mentioned in Jer 31:38 and Zec 14:10 as the northernmost part of the city. Some scholars believe that the "Tower of the Hundred" may be a popular name for this tower, but other scholars believe that these were two separate towers, with the Tower of Hananel to the west of the Tower of the Hundred. The towers were associated with "the citadel by the temple" (2:8) in protecting the vulnerable northwestern approaches to the city.

3:3 *Fish Gate.* Known in the days of the first temple as one of Jerusalem's main entrances. It may be the same as the Gate of Ephraim (8:16; 12:39), which led out to the main road north from Jerusalem and then descended to the coastal plain through Beth Horon. It was called the Fish Gate, because merchants brought fish either from Tyre or from the Sea of Galilee through it to the fish market.

3:5 *Tekoa.* A small town five miles (eight kilometers) south of Bethlehem, famed as the home of the prophet

NEHEMIAH 2:10

THE MURASHU TEXTS AND THE ELEPHANTINE PAPYRI

Two collections of valuable documents illuminate the lives of Jews living in the Diaspora (the dispersion) during the Persian era: the Murashu cuneiform texts from Mesopotamia and the Elephantine papyri from Egypt.

Murashu and his sons were wealthy bankers and brokers who loaned almost everything at a price. About 700 of the cuneiform texts from their archives, which span the period from 454 to 404 BC, have now been published. In documents like these, theophoric names with various forms of the name Yahweh (Yah, Yeho, Yahu, Ia, Iama) may be recognized as Jewish. Among 2,500 individuals mentioned in the texts, about 70 (approximately 3 percent) are likely Jews. Jews were found in 28 of 200 settlements in the region around Nippur in southern Mesopotamia.

Aramaic papyri from a Jewish military garrison serving the Persians, on the island of Elephantine near Aswan, shed valuable light on a Jewish community in Egypt from 495 to 398 BC. About 40 of the 95 Jewish names from Elephantine contain some form of the name Yahweh. The letters reveal that Egyptians had destroyed the Jewish temple in their area. The papyri reveal the incidence of mixed marriages, which led to syncretistic practices. One papyrus names the sons of Sanballat, thus confirming that Nehemiah's opponent was indeed the governor of Samaria. ◆

One document of the Elephantine papyri. This letter is a request for the rebuilding of a Jewish temple at Elephantine, which had been destroyed by Egyptian pagans. The letter is dated year 17 of king Darius (II), which corresponds to 407 BC.

Wikimedia Commons

their shoulders to the work under their supervisors.[a]

6The Jeshanah[b] Gate[y] was repaired by
Joiada son of Paseah and Meshullam son
of Besodeiah. They laid its beams and put
its doors with their bolts and bars in place.
7Next to them, repairs were made by men
from Gibeon[z] and Mizpah — Melatiah of
Gibeon and Jadon of Meronoth — places under the authority of the governor of
Trans-Euphrates. 8Uzziel son of Harhaiah,
one of the goldsmiths, repaired the next
section; and Hananiah, one of the perfume-makers, made repairs next to that.
They restored Jerusalem as far as the
Broad Wall.[a] 9Rephaiah son of Hur, ruler of a half-district of Jerusalem, repaired
the next section. 10Adjoining this, Jedaiah
son of Harumaph made repairs opposite
his house, and Hattush son of Hashabneiah made repairs next to him. 11Malkijah
son of Harim and Hasshub son of Pahath-
Moab repaired another section and the
Tower of the Ovens.[b] 12Shallum son of
Hallohesh, ruler of a half-district of Jerusalem, repaired the next section with the
help of his daughters.

13The Valley Gate[c] was repaired by Hanun and the residents of Zanoah.[d] They
rebuilt it and put its doors with their bolts
and bars in place. They also repaired a
thousand cubits[c] of the wall as far as the
Dung Gate.[e]

14The Dung Gate was repaired by Malkijah son of Rekab, ruler of the district of
Beth Hakkerem.[f] He rebuilt it and put its
doors with their bolts and bars in place.

15The Fountain Gate was repaired by
Shallun son of Kol-Hozeh, ruler of the
district of Mizpah. He rebuilt it, roofing it
over and putting its doors and bolts and
bars in place. He also repaired the wall of
the Pool of Siloam,[d][g] by the King's Garden, as far as the steps going down from
the City of David. 16Beyond him, Nehemiah son of Azbuk, ruler of a half-district
of Beth Zur,[h] made repairs up to a point
opposite the tombs[e][i] of David, as far as the
artificial pool and the House of the Heroes.

3:6 [y] Ne 12:39
3:7 [z] Jos 9:3; Ne 2:7
3:8 [a] Ne 12:38
3:11 [b] Ne 12:38
3:13 [c] 2Ch 26:9 [d] Jos 15:34 [e] Ne 2:13
3:14 [f] Jer 6:1
3:15 [g] Isa 8:6; Jn 9:7
3:16 [h] Jos 15:58 [i] Ac 2:29

[a] 5 Or *their Lord* or *the governor*   [b] 6 Or *Old*
[c] 13 That is, about 1,500 feet or about 450 meters
[d] 15 Hebrew *Shelah,* a variant of *Shiloah,* that is, Siloam
[e] 16 Hebrew; Septuagint, some Vulgate manuscripts and Syriac *tomb*

Amos (Am 1:1). Some have suggested that its southern location near the territory of Geshem may have meant that the nobles were influenced to cooperate with him. *their nobles.* These aristocrats disdained manual labor. *would not put their shoulders to the work.* The Hebrew word for "shoulders" specifically refers to the back of the neck. This expression is drawn from the imagery of oxen that refuse to yield to the yoke.

3:7 *under the authority.* Lit. "to the chair" or "throne." Fragments of a lion's paw and a bronze cylinder that belonged to the foot of a Persian throne similar to those depicted at Persepolis were found in Samaria. The phrase can be interpreted in different ways: (1) as the satrap's residence in Jerusalem; (2) as the satrap's residence at Damascus or Aleppo; or (3) with the "chair" as a symbol for the jurisdiction of the governor over the places from which the builders came, such as Mizpah (NIV interpretation).

3:8 *one of … one of.* Reflects the Hebrew word *ben* ("son of," i.e., a member of a guild). *goldsmiths … perfume-makers.* The industrial district of the goldsmiths and perfumers may have been located outside the wall. Craft guilds were often made up of families that had perfected their own secrets and techniques that would be passed down from generation to generation. *perfume-makers.* Translates *raqqahim*, which occurs only here, with the feminine form in 1Sa 8:13. As demonstrated by other derived forms of the same root and cognates in other Semitic languages, it pertains to mixing ointments and spices. *They restored.* Comes from the Hebrew word *azab*, which means "to abandon" (the Septuagint, the pre-Christian Greek translation of the OT, uses *kataleipo*, "to leave"). Some scholars, whose view the NIV has followed, believe that the word here must be a homonym that means "to restore" or "to fortify," citing words in cognate languages. Nevertheless, it could also mean that Nehemiah abandoned areas as far as the Broad Wall. *Broad Wall.* Often understood as a thick wall, but it can be interpreted to mean a long, extensive wall. In 1970 – 1971 a wall about 7.5 yards (7 meters) thick was discovered in the Jewish Quarter of the walled city that was cleared for some 44 yards (40 meters). This wall, dating to the early seventh century BC, was probably built by Hezekiah (2Ch 32:5). It is postulated that the great expansion to and beyond the Broad Wall that caused a three- to fourfold expansion of the city was occasioned by the influx of refugees from the fall of Samaria in 722 BC.

3:11 *Tower of the Ovens.* This is preferable to the alternative translation: "tower of the furnaces" (e.g., KJV). This tower is mentioned only here and was located on the western wall, perhaps in the same location as the one Uzziah built at the Corner Gate. The ovens may have been those situated in the bakers' street. Another possibility is that they overlooked the potters' quarter.

3:12 *Hallohesh.* The Hebrew (*hallohesh*) is not a proper name but a participle that means "whisperer," in the sense of a snake charmer or an enchanter. *with the help of his daughters.* A unique reference to women working at the wall, which may refer to either his biological daughters or associates who practice divination. When the Athenians attempted to rebuild their walls after the Persians had destroyed them, it was decreed that "the whole population of the city, men, women and children, should take part in the wall-building." Less likely is the attempt to translate the word "daughters" as "dependent" villages (cf. 11:25 – 31).

3:14 *Beth Hakkerem.* Meaning "house of the vineyard," it is mentioned in Jer 6:1 as a fire signal point.

3:15 *Kol-Hozeh.* Lit. "everyone a seer"; it may indicate that the family practiced divination. Divination (i.e., the art of foretelling the future) was widely practiced in the ancient world, in Mesopotamia, Egypt, Canaan, Greece and Rome. There are also references to such practices in Israel (see note on Isa 2:6; see also the articles "Magic," p. 326; "Practice of Magic," p. 627).

3:16 *tombs of David.* Several references (1Ki 2:10; 2Ch 21:20; 32:33; Ac 2:29) confirm that David was buried in the city area (Ne 2:5), though the site of the royal tombs has not yet been discovered. See note on 1Ki 2:10.

17 Next to him, the repairs were made
by the Levites under Rehum son of Bani.
Beside him, Hashabiah, ruler of half the
district of Keilah,[j] carried out repairs for
his district. 18 Next to him, the repairs were
made by their fellow Levites under Binnui[a]
son of Henadad, ruler of the other half-district of Keilah. 19 Next to him, Ezer son of
Jeshua, ruler of Mizpah, repaired another
section, from a point facing the ascent to
the armory as far as the angle of the wall.
20 Next to him, Baruch son of Zabbai zeal-
ously repaired another section, from the
angle to the entrance of the house of Eliashib the high priest. 21 Next to him, Meremoth[k] son of Uriah, the son of Hakkoz, repaired another section, from the entrance
of Eliashib's house to the end of it.
22 The repairs next to him were made by
the priests from the surrounding region.
23 Beyond them, Benjamin and Hasshub
made repairs in front of their house; and
next to them, Azariah son of Maaseiah, the
son of Ananiah, made repairs beside his
house. 24 Next to him, Binnui[l] son of Henadad repaired another section, from Azariah's house to the angle and the corner,
25 and Palal son of Uzai worked opposite
the angle and the tower projecting from the
upper palace near the court of the guard.[m]
Next to him, Pedaiah son of Parosh[n] 26 and
the temple servants[o] living on the hill of
Ophel[p] made repairs up to a point opposite
the Water Gate[q] toward the east and the
projecting tower. 27 Next to them, the men
of Tekoa[r] repaired another section, from the
great projecting tower[s] to the wall of Ophel.

28 Above the Horse Gate,[t] the priests
made repairs, each in front of his own
house. 29 Next to them, Zadok son of Immer made repairs opposite his house.
Next to him, Shemaiah son of Shekaniah,
the guard at the East Gate, made repairs.
30 Next to him, Hananiah son of Shelemiah, and Hanun, the sixth son of Zalaph,
repaired another section. Next to them,
Meshullam son of Berekiah made repairs
opposite his living quarters. 31 Next to him,
Malkijah, one of the goldsmiths, made repairs as far as the house of the temple
servants and the merchants, opposite the
Inspection Gate, and as far as the room
above the corner; 32 and between the room
above the corner and the Sheep Gate[u] the
goldsmiths and merchants made repairs.

3:17 [j] Jos 15:44 **3:21** [k] Ezr 8:33 **3:24** [l] Ezr 8:33 **3:25** [m] Jer 32:2; 37:21; 39:14 [n] Ezr 2:3 **3:26** [o] Ne 7:46; 11:21 [p] 2Ch 33:14 [q] Ne 8:1, 3, 16; 12:37 **3:27** [r] ver 5 [s] Ps 48:12 **3:28** [t] 2Ki 11:16; 2Ch 23:15; Jer 31:40 **3:32** [u] ver 1; Jn 5:2

Opposition to the Rebuilding

4 [b] When Sanballat[v] heard that we were
rebuilding the wall, he became angry
and was greatly incensed. He ridiculed the
Jews, 2 and in the presence of his associates[w] and the army of Samaria, he said,
"What are those feeble Jews doing? Will
they restore their wall? Will they offer sacrifices? Will they finish in a day? Can they
bring the stones back to life from those
heaps of rubble[x]—burned as they are?"
3 Tobiah[y] the Ammonite, who was at his
side, said, "What they are building—even
a fox climbing up on it would break down
their wall of stones!"[z]

4 Hear us, our God, for we are despised.[a]
Turn their insults back on their own
heads. Give them over as plunder in a land
of captivity. 5 Do not cover up their guilt[b]
or blot out their sins from your sight,[c] for
they have thrown insults in the face of[c]
the builders.

6 So we rebuilt the wall till all of it
reached half its height, for the people
worked with all their heart.
7 But when Sanballat, Tobiah,[d] the
Arabs, the Ammonites and the people of
Ashdod heard that the repairs to Jerusalem's walls had gone ahead and that the
gaps were being closed, they were very
angry. 8 They all plotted together[e] to come
and fight against Jerusalem and stir up
trouble against it. 9 But we prayed to our
God and posted a guard day and night to
meet this threat.
10 Meanwhile, the people in Judah said,
"The strength of the laborers[f] is giving out,
and there is so much rubble that we cannot rebuild the wall."
11 Also our enemies said, "Before they
know it or see us, we will be right there
among them and will kill them and put an
end to the work."
12 Then the Jews who lived near them
came and told us ten times over, "Wherever you turn, they will attack us."
13 Therefore I stationed some of the people behind the lowest points of the wall at
the exposed places, posting them by fam-

4:1 [v] Ne 2:10 **4:2** [w] Ezr 4:9-10 [x] Ps 79:1; Jer 26:18 **4:3** [y] Ne 2:10 [z] Job 13:12; 15:3 **4:4** [a] Ps 44:13; 79:12; 123:3-4; Jer 33:24 **4:5** [b] Isa 2:9; La 1:22 [c] 2Ki 14:27; Ps 51:1; 69:27-28; 109:14; Jer 18:23 **4:7** [d] Ne 2:10 **4:8** [e] Ps 2:2; 83:1-18 **4:10** [f] 1Ch 23:4

[a] *18* Two Hebrew manuscripts and Syriac (see also Septuagint and verse 24); most Hebrew manuscripts *Bavvai* [b] In Hebrew texts 4:1-6 is numbered 3:33-38, and 4:7-23 is numbered 4:1-17. [c] *5* Or *have aroused your anger before*

4:2 *army of Samaria.* The governor of Samaria had an army to aid the Persian king, but it is not certain if the troops mentioned are a garrison regiment or a local militia.
4:7 *Ashdod.* Along with Ashkelon, Gaza, Ekron and Gath, it was one of the five major Philistine cities (see note on Jdg 3:3) as early as the Late Bronze Age (1550–1200 BC). Ashdod was overrun by the Assyrians in 711 BC and was later conquered by the Babylonians. With the Persian conquest, alternate patches of the Palestinian coast were parceled out to the Phoenician cities of Tyre and Sidon, which provided ships for the Persian navy. During this period Ashdod was the most important city so used. As it was inland, it had a separate harbor at the coastal site of Ashdod-Yam.

ilies, with their swords, spears and bows.
14 After I looked things over, I stood up
and said to the nobles, the officials and
the rest of the people, "Don't be afraid[g] of
them. Remember[h] the Lord, who is great
and awesome,[i] and fight[j] for your families,
your sons and your daughters, your wives
and your homes."
15 When our enemies heard that we were
aware of their plot and that God had frustrated it,[k] we all returned to the wall, each
to our own work.
16 From that day on, half of my men
did the work, while the other half were
equipped with spears, shields, bows and
armor. The officers posted themselves behind all the people of Judah 17 who were
building the wall. Those who carried materials did their work with one hand and
held a weapon[l] in the other, 18 and each of
the builders wore his sword at his side as
he worked. But the man who sounded the
trumpet[m] stayed with me.
19 Then I said to the nobles, the officials
and the rest of the people, "The work
is extensive and spread out, and we are
widely separated from each other along
the wall. 20 Wherever you hear the sound
of the trumpet,[n] join us there. Our God
will fight[o] for us!"
21 So we continued the work with half
the men holding spears, from the first light
of dawn till the stars came out. 22 At that
time I also said to the people, "Have every
man and his helper stay inside Jerusalem
at night, so they can serve us as guards
by night and as workers by day." 23 Neither I nor my brothers nor my men nor
the guards with me took off our clothes;
each had his weapon, even when he went
for water.[a]

Nehemiah Helps the Poor

5 Now the men and their wives raised a
great outcry against their fellow Jews.
2 Some were saying, "We and our sons and
daughters are numerous; in order for us
to eat and stay alive, we must get grain."
3 Others were saying, "We are mort-
gaging our fields,[p] our vineyards and our
homes to get grain during the famine."[q]
4 Still others were saying, "We have had
to borrow money to pay the king's tax[r] on
our fields and vineyards. 5 Although we are
of the same flesh and blood[s] as our fellow Jews and though our children are as
good as theirs, yet we have to subject our
sons and daughters to slavery.[t] Some of
our daughters have already been enslaved,
but we are powerless, because our fields
and our vineyards belong to others."[u]
6 When I heard their outcry and these
charges, I was very angry. 7 I pondered
them in my mind and then accused the
nobles and officials. I told them, "You are
charging your own people interest!"[v] So
I called together a large meeting to deal

4:14 [g] Ge 28:15; Nu 14:9; Dt 1:29 [h] Ne 1:8 [i] Ne 1:5 [j] 2Sa 10:12 **4:15** [k] 2Sa 17:14; Job 5:12 **4:17** [l] Ps 149:6 **4:18** [m] Nu 10:2 **4:20** [n] Eze 33:3 [o] Ex 14:14; Dt 1:30; 20:4; Jos 10:14

5:3 [p] Ps 109:11 [q] Ge 47:23 **5:4** [r] Ezr 4:13 **5:5** [s] Ge 29:14 [t] Lev 25:39-43, 47; 2Ki 4:1; Isa 50:1 [u] Dt 15:7-11; 2Ki 4:1 **5:7** [v] Ex 22:25-27; Lev 25:35-37; Dt 23:19-20; 24:10-13

[a] 23 The meaning of the Hebrew for this clause is uncertain.

4:18 *trumpet.* See note on Jos 6:4.

5:1 – 19 The economic crisis faced by Nehemiah is described in ch. 5, in the middle of his major effort to rebuild the wall of Jerusalem. Since this building project lasted only 52 days (6:15), some scholars have considered it unlikely that Nehemiah would have called a great assembly (5:7) in the midst of such a project. They suggest that the assembly was called only after the rebuilding of the wall, taking v. 14 as retrospective. Nevertheless, the economic pressure created by the rebuilding program may have brought to light problems long simmering that had to be solved before work could proceed. Among the classes affected by the economic crisis were the landless, who were short of food (v. 2), the landowners compelled to mortgage their properties (v. 3), those forced to borrow money at exorbitant rates because of oppressive taxation (v. 4), and those forced to sell their children into slavery (v. 5).

5:1 *raised a great outcry.* The gravity of the situation is underscored in that the wives joined in the protest as the people ran short of funds and supplies to feed their families. This may have been exacerbated by people being required to work the wall instead of their fields during critical harvest time. Also significant, their complaints were not lodged against the foreign authorities, but against their own fellow countrymen, who were exploiting their poorer brethren at a time when both were needed to defend the country.

5:4 *king's tax.* See note on Ezr 4:13.

5:5 *our daughters have already been enslaved.* In times of economic distress, families would borrow funds using members of the family as collateral. If a man could not repay the loan and its interest, his daughters, his sons, his wife or even the man himself could be sold into bondage. A Hebrew who fell into debt would serve his creditor as a hired servant (see note on Lev 25:39). He was to be released in the seventh year, unless he chose to stay voluntarily. The Code of Hammurapi limited such bond service to three years. The ironic tragedy of the situation for the exiles was that at least in Mesopotamia their families were together; now, because of dire economic necessities, their children were being sold into slavery.

5:7 *You are charging your own people interest!* The Hebrew word *mashsha,* which occurs only here, in v. 10 and in 10:31, does not technically mean the exaction of interest, often at exorbitant rates. Rather, it means to impose a burden or claim for repayment of debt because a loan has been made for a pledge. Compare the related word *mashshaah* ("secured loan based on security"; Dt 24:10; Pr 22:26). Nehemiah is therefore lamenting the abuse of a system of loans secured by pledges. A letter on a Hebrew ostracon from Mesdad Hashavyahu on the coast (seventh century BC) bears the poignant plea of a poor farmer whose garment had been taken by the governor's officer and had not been returned (in contravention of Ex 22:26 – 27). The OT passages prohibiting the giving of loans at interest were intended not to prohibit commercial loans but rather to prohibit charging interest to the impoverished so as to make a profit from the helplessness of one's neighbors (see notes on Lev 25:36; Dt 23:19 – 20).

with them 8and said: "As far as possible,
we have bought[w] back our fellow Jews
who were sold to the Gentiles. Now you
are selling your own people, only for them
to be sold back to us!" They kept quiet,
because they could find nothing to say.[x]
9So I continued, "What you are doing
is not right. Shouldn't you walk in the
fear of our God to avoid the reproach[y] of
our Gentile enemies? 10I and my brothers
and my men are also lending the people
money and grain. But let us stop charging interest![z] 11Give back to them immediately their fields, vineyards, olive groves
and houses, and also the interest[a] you are
charging them—one percent of the money, grain, new wine and olive oil."
12"We will give it back," they said. "And
we will not demand anything more from
them. We will do as you say."
Then I summoned the priests and made
the nobles and officials take an oath[b] to do
what they had promised. 13I also shook[c]
out the folds of my robe and said, "In this
way may God shake out of their house and
possessions anyone who does not keep
this promise. So may such a person be
shaken out and emptied!"
At this the whole assembly said,
"Amen,"[d] and praised the LORD. And the
people did as they had promised.
14Moreover, from the twentieth year of
King Artaxerxes,[e] when I was appointed
to be their governor[f] in the land of Judah, until his thirty-second year—twelve
years—neither I nor my brothers ate the
food allotted to the governor. 15But the
earlier governors—those preceding me—
placed a heavy burden on the people and
took forty shekels[a] of silver from them in
addition to food and wine. Their assistants
also lorded it over the people. But out of
reverence for God[g] I did not act like that.
16Instead,[h] I devoted myself to the work
on this wall. All my men were assembled
there for the work; we[b] did not acquire
any land.
17Furthermore, a hundred and fifty Jews
and officials ate at my table, as well as
those who came to us from the surrounding nations. 18Each day one ox, six choice
sheep and some poultry[i] were prepared
for me, and every ten days an abundant
supply of wine of all kinds. In spite of all
this, I never demanded the food allotted to
the governor, because the demands were
heavy on these people.
19Remember[j] me with favor, my God, for
all I have done for these people.

Further Opposition to the Rebuilding

6 When word came to Sanballat, Tobiah,[k] Geshem[l] the Arab and the rest of
our enemies that I had rebuilt the wall and
not a gap was left in it—though up to that
time I had not set the doors in the gates—
2Sanballat and Geshem sent me this message: "Come, let us meet together in one
of the villages[c] on the plain of Ono.[m]"

5:8 [w] Lev 25:47 [x] Jer 34:8 **5:9** [y] Isa 52:5 **5:10** [z] Ex 22:25 **5:11** [a] Isa 58:6 **5:12** [b] Ezr 10:5 **5:13** [c] Mt 10:14; Ac 18:6 [d] Dt 27:15-26 **5:14** [e] Ne 2:6; 13:6 [f] Ge 42:6; Ezr 6:7; Jer 40:7; Hag 1:1 **5:15** [g] Ge 20:11 **5:16** [h] 2Th 3:7-10 **5:18** [i] 1Ki 4:23 **5:19** [j] Ge 8:1; 2Ki 20:3; Ne 1:8; 13:14, 22,31 **6:1** [k] Ne 2:10 [l] Ne 2:19 **6:2** [m] 1Ch 8:12

[a] *15* That is, about 1 pound or about 460 grams
[b] *16* Most Hebrew manuscripts; some Hebrew manuscripts, Septuagint, Vulgate and Syriac *I*
[c] *2* Or *in Kephirim*

5:8 *you are selling your own people.* Though it was possible to use a poor fellow Israelite as a bondservant, he was not to be sold as a slave (Lev 25:39–42). The sale of fellow Israelites as slaves to Gentiles was a particularly callous offense and was always forbidden (Ex 21:8). Joseph's brothers nonetheless sold him to the foreign traders (Ge 37:12–36). We know from Joel 3:6 that Jews were being sold to Greeks (c. 520 BC).
5:10 *lending the people money and grain.* The granting of loans is not condemned, nor is the making of profit (cf. Sirach 42:1–5a). Nonetheless, in view of the urgency of the situation, Nehemiah urges the creditors to relinquish their rights to repayment with interest. Solon, the great Athenian reformer (594 BC), adopted a similar policy.
5:11 *one percent.* Lit. the "hundred" (pieces of silver). But in the context it must mean one percent of interest (i.e., per month).
5:15 *earlier governors.* "Governors" is the plural of Hebrew *pehah* (also the same in Aramaic), which is used of Sheshbazzar, Zerubbabel and various Persian officials. It was once believed that Judah did not have governors before Nehemiah, and that this refers to governors of Samaria. New archaeological evidence, however, confirms that the reference is to previous governors of Judah. A collection of bullae (seal impressions) yields the names of some of the governors prior to Nehemiah.
5:18 *some poultry.* Poultry were domesticated in the Indus River Valley by 2000 BC and were brought to Egypt by the reign of Thutmose III (fifteenth century BC). Poultry were known in Mesopotamia and Greece by the eighth century BC. The earliest evidence in Palestine is the seal of Jaazaniah (c. 600 BC), which depicts a fighting cock. *food allotted to the governor.* As governor, Nehemiah is expected to entertain both domestic and foreign dignitaries, as well as pay the salaries of the 150 officials (v. 17). The cost of this is supposed to be offset by the "food allotted to the governor" (taxes levied, cf. v. 14), which Nehemiah has refrained from collecting, meaning that these "business expenses" are coming out of his own pocket.
5:19 *Remember me with favor.* Some have suggested that Nehemiah's memoirs were inscribed as a memorial set up in the temple. A parallel to Nehemiah's prayer is found in Nebuchadnezzar II's prayer to his god: "O Marduk, my lord, do remember my deeds favorably as good [deeds], may (these) my good deeds be always before your mind." An even more striking parallel is found on the stele of a chief physician named Udjahorresnet in which he identifies himself as a good man who provided relief and protection for his people. He therefore calls on his god to remember his altruism, treat him well and make his name endure, as Nehemiah also does.
6:2 *Ono.* Located 27 miles (43.5 kilometers) northwest of Jerusalem and 7 miles (11 kilometers) southeast of Joppa, near Lod (Lydda). It was in the westernmost area settled by the returning Jews (7:37; 11:35; Ezr 2:33). There is disagreement among scholars as to whether Ono was part of Judah.

But they were scheming to harm me;
3so I sent messengers to them with this reply: "I am carrying on a great project and
cannot go down. Why should the work
stop while I leave it and go down to you?"
4Four times they sent me the same message, and each time I gave them the same
answer.
5Then, the fifth time, Sanballat[n] sent his
aide to me with the same message, and in
his hand was an unsealed letter 6in which
was written:

"It is reported among the nations —
and Geshem[a o] says it is true — that
you and the Jews are plotting to revolt, and therefore you are building the wall. Moreover, according to
these reports you are about to become
their king 7and have even appointed
prophets to make this proclamation
about you in Jerusalem: 'There is a
king in Judah!' Now this report will
get back to the king; so come, let us
meet together."

8I sent him this reply: "Nothing like
what you are saying is happening; you are
just making it up out of your head."
9They were all trying to frighten us,
thinking, "Their hands will get too weak
for the work, and it will not be completed."
But I prayed, "Now strengthen my
hands."
10One day I went to the house of Shemaiah son of Delaiah, the son of Mehetabel,
who was shut in at his home. He said, "Let
us meet in the house of God, inside the
temple[p], and let us close the temple doors,
because men are coming to kill you — by
night they are coming to kill you."
11But I said, "Should a man like me run
away? Or should someone like me go into
the temple to save his life? I will not go!"
12I realized that God had not sent him,
but that he had prophesied against me[q]
because Tobiah and Sanballat[r] had hired
him. 13He had been hired to intimidate me
so that I would commit a sin by doing this,
and then they would give me a bad name
to discredit me.[s]
14Remember[t] Tobiah and Sanballat,[u] my
God, because of what they have done; remember also the prophet[v] Noadiah and
how she and the rest of the prophets[w]
have been trying to intimidate me. 15So the
wall was completed on the twenty-fifth of
Elul, in fifty-two days.

Opposition to the Completed Wall

16When all our enemies heard about
this, all the surrounding nations were
afraid and lost their self-confidence, because they realized that this work had
been done with the help of our God.
17Also, in those days the nobles of Judah were sending many letters to Tobiah,
and replies from Tobiah kept coming to
them. 18For many in Judah were under
oath to him, since he was son-in-law to
Shekaniah son of Arah, and his son Jehohanan had married the daughter of Meshullam son of Berekiah. 19Moreover, they
kept reporting to me his good deeds and
then telling him what I said. And Tobiah
sent letters to intimidate me.

7 After the wall had been rebuilt and I
had set the doors in place, the gatekeepers,[x] the musicians[y] and the Levites[z]
were appointed. 2I put in charge of Jerusalem my brother Hanani,[a] along with
Hananiah[b] the commander of the citadel,[c] because he was a man of integrity
and feared[d] God more than most people
do. 3I said to them, "The gates of Jerusalem are not to be opened until the sun
is hot. While the gatekeepers are still on
duty, have them shut the doors and bar
them. Also appoint residents of Jerusalem
as guards, some at their posts and some
near their own houses."

The List of the Exiles Who Returned

7:6-73pp — Ezr 2:1-70

4Now the city was large and spacious,
but there were few people in it,[e] and the

6:5 [n] Ne 2:10
6:6 [o] Ne 2:19
6:10 [p] Nu 18:7
6:12 [q] Eze 13:22-23 [r] Ne 2:10
6:13 [s] Jer 20:10
6:14 [t] Ne 1:8 [u] Ne 2:10 [v] Ex 15:20; Eze 13:17-23; Ac 21:9; Rev 2:20 [w] Ne 13:29; Jer 23:9-40; Zec 13:2-3
7:1 [x] 1Ch 9:27; 26:12-19; Ne 6:1, 15 [y] Ps 68:25 [z] Ne 8:9
7:2 [a] Ne 1:2 [b] Ne 10:23 [c] Ne 2:8 [d] 1Ki 18:3
7:4 [e] Ne 11:1

[a] 6 Hebrew *Gashmu,* a variant of *Geshem*

6:5 *unsealed letter.* Letters during this period were ordinarily written on a papyrus or leather sheet, rolled up, tied with a string and sealed with a clay bulla (seal impression) to guarantee its authenticity (see note on 1Ki 21:8). Sanballat obviously intended that the contents should be made known to the public at large.
6:7 *prophets to make this proclamation.* See note on 1Ki 11:30.
6:9 *hands will get too weak.* This idiom uses the Hebrew verb *rapah* ("to become slack"). The Hebrew idiom "to cause the hands to drop" means to demoralize (cf. Ezr 4:4). Jeremiah was accused of "weakening the hands of the soldiers" (Jer 38:4; NIV "discouraging the soldiers"). The Lachish Ostracon VI speaks of people in Jerusalem "who weaken the hands of the land and make the city slack so that it fails."
7:2 *commander of the citadel.* See note on 4:2.
7:3 *gates . . . are not to be opened until the sun is hot.* Normally the gates of a city were opened at dawn. According to one view, in this ruling the opening was to be delayed until the sun was high in the heavens, perhaps due to a shortage of gatekeepers to staff the entrance for a full day. Others believe that the gates were to be closed during the heat of the day while people took a siesta. One famous historical episode, which occurred in 410 BC, that may illustrate the need for a special guard at this time was the attack by Alaric on a gate in Rome while the guards were dozing.
7:4 *large and spacious.* The Hebrew phrase uses the idiom

houses had not yet been rebuilt. 5So my
God put it into my heart to assemble the
nobles, the officials and the common people for registration by families. I found the
genealogical record of those who had been
the first to return. This is what I found
written there:

6These are the people of the province who came up from the captivity
of the exiles[f] whom Nebuchadnezzar king of Babylon had taken captive (they returned to Jerusalem and
Judah, each to his own town, 7in
company with Zerubbabel,[g] Joshua,
Nehemiah, Azariah, Raamiah, Naha-
mani, Mordecai, Bilshan, Mispereth,
Bigvai, Nehum and Baanah):

The list of the men of Israel:

8the descendants of Parosh 2,172
9of Shephatiah 372
10of Arah 652
11of Pahath-Moab (through
the line of Jeshua and
Joab) 2,818
12of Elam 1,254
13of Zattu 845
14of Zakkai 760
15of Binnui 648
16of Bebai 628
17of Azgad 2,322
18of Adonikam 667
19of Bigvai 2,067
20of Adin[h] 655
21of Ater (through Hezekiah) 98
22of Hashum 328
23of Bezai 324
24of Hariph 112
25of Gibeon 95
26the men of Bethlehem and
Netophah[i] 188
27of Anathoth[j] 128
28of Beth Azmaveth 42
29of Kiriath Jearim, Kephirah[k]
and Beeroth[l] 743
30of Ramah and Geba 621
31of Mikmash 122
32of Bethel and Ai[m] 123
33of the other Nebo 52
34of the other Elam 1,254
35of Harim 320
36of Jericho[n] 345
37of Lod, Hadid and Ono[o] 721
38of Senaah 3,930

39The priests:

the descendants of Jedaiah
(through the family
of Jeshua) 973
40of Immer 1,052
41of Pashhur 1,247
42of Harim 1,017

43The Levites:

the descendants of Jeshua
(through Kadmiel through
the line of Hodaviah) 74

44The musicians:[p]

the descendants of Asaph 148

45The gatekeepers:[q]

the descendants of
Shallum, Ater, Talmon,
Akkub, Hatita and Shobai 138

46The temple servants:[r]

the descendants of
Ziha, Hasupha, Tabbaoth,
47Keros, Sia, Padon,
48Lebana, Hagaba, Shalmai,
49Hanan, Giddel, Gahar,
50Reaiah, Rezin, Nekoda,
51Gazzam, Uzza, Paseah,
52Besai, Meunim, Nephusim,
53Bakbuk, Hakupha, Harhur,
54Bazluth, Mehida, Harsha,
55Barkos, Sisera, Temah,
56Neziah and Hatipha

57The descendants of the servants of
Solomon:

the descendants of
Sotai, Sophereth, Perida,
58Jaala, Darkon, Giddel,
59Shephatiah, Hattil,
Pokereth-Hazzebaim and Amon
60The temple servants and the
descendants of the servants
of Solomon[s] 392

61The following came up from the
towns of Tel Melah, Tel Harsha, Ke-
rub, Addon and Immer, but they
could not show that their families
were descended from Israel:

62the descendants of
Delaiah, Tobiah and Nekoda 642

63And from among the priests:

the descendants of
Hobaiah, Hakkoz and Barzillai

7:6 [f] 2Ch 36:20; Ezr 2:1-70; Ne 1:2
7:7 [g] 1Ch 3:19; Ezr 2:2
7:20 [h] Ezr 8:6
7:26 [i] 2Sa 23:28; 1Ch 2:54
7:27 [j] Jos 21:18
7:29 [k] Jos 18:26 [l] Jos 18:25
7:32 [m] Ge 12:8
7:36 [n] Ne 3:2
7:37 [o] 1Ch 8:12
7:44 [p] Ne 11:23
7:45 [q] 1Ch 9:17
7:46 [r] Ne 3:26
7:60 [s] 1Ch 9:2

"wide of two hands and large." This expression means extending to the right and left. As the actual circuit of the wall of the city was smaller than in preexilic times, the expressions must be relative to the number of people who could still be housed once the damaged homes were rebuilt.

7:5 *I found the genealogical record.* See note on Ezr 2:59; see also the article "The Significance of Genealogies for a Postexilic Audience," p. 680.

(a man who had married
a daughter of Barzillai the
Gileadite and was called by that
name).
64 These searched for their family records, but they could not find
them and so were excluded from the
priesthood as unclean. 65 The governor, therefore, ordered them not to
eat any of the most sacred food until
there should be a priest ministering
with the Urim and Thummim.[t]

66 The whole company numbered
42,360, 67 besides their 7,337 male
and female slaves; and they also had
245 male and female singers. 68 There
were 736 horses, 245 mules,[a] 69 435
camels and 6,720 donkeys.

70 Some of the heads of the families
contributed to the work. The governor gave to the treasury 1,000 darics[b]
of gold, 50 bowls and 530 garments
for priests. 71 Some of the heads of the
families[u] gave to the treasury for the
work 20,000 darics[c] of gold and 2,200
minas[d] of silver. 72 The total given by
the rest of the people was 20,000 darics of gold, 2,000 minas[e] of silver and
67 garments for priests.[v]
73 The priests, the Levites, the gatekeepers, the musicians and the temple servants,[w] along with certain of
the people and the rest of the Israelites, settled in their own towns.[x]

Ezra Reads the Law

When the seventh month came and the
8 Israelites had settled in their towns,[y] 1 all
the people came together as one in the
square before the Water Gate.[z] They told
Ezra the teacher of the Law to bring out
the Book of the Law of Moses,[a] which the
LORD had commanded for Israel.
2 So on the first day of the seventh
month[b] Ezra the priest brought the Law[c]
before the assembly, which was made up
of men and women and all who were able
to understand. 3 He read it aloud from daybreak till noon as he faced the square before the Water Gate[d] in the presence of the
men, women and others who could understand. And all the people listened attentively to the Book of the Law.
4 Ezra the teacher of the Law stood on a
high wooden platform[e] built for the occasion. Beside him on his right stood Mattithiah, Shema, Anaiah, Uriah, Hilkiah and
Maaseiah; and on his left were Pedaiah,
Mishael, Malkijah, Hashum, Hashbadda-
nah, Zechariah and Meshullam.
5 Ezra opened the book. All the people
could see him because he was standing[f]
above them; and as he opened it, the people all stood up. 6 Ezra praised the LORD,
the great God; and all the people lifted their hands[g] and responded, "Amen!
Amen!" Then they bowed down and worshiped the LORD with their faces to the
ground.
7 The Levites[h]—Jeshua, Bani, Sherebiah, Jamin, Akkub, Shabbethai, Hodiah,
Maaseiah, Kelita, Azariah, Jozabad, Hanan and Pelaiah—instructed[i] the people
in the Law while the people were standing there. 8 They read from the Book of the

7:65 [t] Ex 28:30; Ne 8:9 **7:71** [u] 1Ch 29:7 **7:72** [v] Ex 25:2 **7:73** [w] Ne 1:10; Ps 34:22; 103:21; 113:1; 135:1 [x] Ezr 3:1; Ne 11:1 [y] Ezr 3:1 **8:1** [z] Ne 3:26 [a] Dt 28:61; 2Ch 34:15; Ezr 7:6 **8:2** [b] Lev 23:23-25; Nu 29:1-6 [c] Dt 31:11 **8:3** [d] Ne 3:26 **8:4** [e] 2Ch 6:13 **8:5** [f] Jdg 3:20 **8:6** [g] Ex 4:31; Ezr 9:5; 1Ti 2:8 **8:7** [h] Ezr 10:23 [i] Lev 10:11; 2Ch 17:7

[a] *68* Some Hebrew manuscripts (see also Ezra 2:66); most Hebrew manuscripts do not have this verse.
[b] *70* That is, about 19 pounds or about 8.4 kilograms
[c] *71* That is, about 375 pounds or about 170 kilograms; also in verse 72
[d] *71* That is, about 1 1/3 tons or about 1.2 metric tons
[e] *72* That is, about 1 1/4 tons or about 1.1 metric tons

7:70 *1,000 darics of gold.* About 19 pounds (8.4 kilograms) of gold.

7:72 *20,000 darics of gold.* About 375 pounds (170 kilograms) of gold. *2,000 minas of silver.* About 1.25 tons (1.1 metric tons) of silver.

7:73 *settled in their own towns.* Many returning exiles may not have been from Jerusalem. These naturally returned to their own hometowns, leaving Jerusalem underpopulated.

8:1 *teacher of the Law.* The Hebrew uses the word usually translated "scribe." The NIV decision to render it "teacher of the Law" reflects the idea that at this period the scribes were taking on a more extensive role (similar to the role played by those called the scribes in the Gospels). Some interpreters see in this development the beginning of what might be referred to as Rabbinic Judaism. Rabbis are recognized as those who instruct the people in the law and lead the synagogues that begin developing around this time as houses of prayer and study distinct from the temple. They gave official interpretations of the text of the law and advised people about how to live in accordance with the law.

8:2 *Book of the Law of Moses.* There are at least four views about what this book represented: (1) a collection of legal documents, (2) the collection of priestly writings, (3) the laws from what we know as the book of Deuteronomy or (4) the Pentateuch as a whole (Genesis–Deuteronomy). Ezra could certainly have brought back with him the Torah, i.e., the Pentateuch, which is the view now favored by most scholars. What we recognize as the books of the Torah, and the Torah itself, would likely have been compiled over time from individual documents (scrolls, tablets, etc.) that had been archived and repeatedly taught and recopied since the time of Moses.

8:3 *read it aloud.* See the articles "Literacy," p. 140; "Books and Literacy," p. 666. Most people in the ancient world, though having basic literacy, did not themselves read documents. They would have had little access to documents and would not need to gain information this way. It was general practice that even those who could read would have documents read aloud to them. Documents were written either to be stored in archives or to be read aloud to others.

8:5 *opened the book.* See the article "Books and Literacy," p. 666.

8:7–8 *instructed the people ... making it clear and giving the meaning.* See note on v. 1.

Law of God, making it clear[a] and giving
the meaning so that the people understood
what was being read.
9Then Nehemiah the governor, Ezra the
priest and teacher of the Law, and the Levites[j] who were instructing the people said
to them all, "This day is holy to the LORD
your God. Do not mourn or weep."[k] For
all the people had been weeping as they
listened to the words of the Law.
10Nehemiah said, "Go and enjoy choice
food and sweet drinks, and send some to
those who have nothing[l] prepared. This
day is holy to our Lord. Do not grieve, for
the joy[m] of the LORD is your strength."
11The Levites calmed all the people, saying, "Be still, for this is a holy day. Do not
grieve."
12Then all the people went away to eat
and drink, to send portions of food and
to celebrate with great joy,[n] because they
now understood the words that had been
made known to them.
13On the second day of the month, the
heads of all the families, along with the
priests and the Levites, gathered around
Ezra the teacher to give attention to the
words of the Law. 14They found written in
the Law, which the LORD had commanded
through Moses, that the Israelites were to
live in temporary shelters during the festival of the seventh month 15and that they
should proclaim this word and spread it
throughout their towns and in Jerusalem:
"Go out into the hill country and bring
back branches from olive and wild olive
trees, and from myrtles, palms and shade
trees, to make temporary shelters"—as it
is written.[b]
16So the people went out and brought
back branches and built themselves temporary shelters on their own roofs, in their
courtyards, in the courts of the house of
God and in the square by the Water Gate
and the one by the Gate of Ephraim.[o]
17The whole company that had returned
from exile built temporary shelters and
lived in them. From the days of Joshua
son of Nun until that day, the Israelites
had not celebrated[p] it like this. And their
joy was very great.
18Day after day, from the first day to the
last, Ezra read[q] from the Book of the Law
of God. They celebrated the festival for
seven days, and on the eighth day, in accordance with the regulation,[r] there was
an assembly.

The Israelites Confess Their Sins

9 On the twenty-fourth day of the same
month, the Israelites gathered together, fasting and wearing sackcloth and putting dust on their heads.[s] 2Those of Israelite descent had separated themselves from
all foreigners.[t] They stood in their places
and confessed their sins and the sins of
their ancestors.[u] 3They stood where they
were and read from the Book of the Law
of the LORD their God for a quarter of the
day, and spent another quarter in confession and in worshiping the LORD their God.
4Standing on the stairs of the Levites[v] were
Jeshua, Bani, Kadmiel, Shebaniah, Bunni,
Sherebiah, Bani and Kenani. They cried
out with loud voices to the LORD their God.
5And the Levites—Jeshua, Kadmiel, Bani,
Hashabneiah, Sherebiah, Hodiah, Shebaniah and Pethahiah—said: "Stand up and
praise the LORD your God,[w] who is from
everlasting to everlasting.[c]"

"Blessed be your glorious name,
and may it be exalted above all blessing and praise. 6You alone are the
LORD.[x] You made the heavens,[y] even
the highest heavens, and all their starry host, the earth[z] and all that is on it,
the seas[a] and all that is in them.[b] You
give life to everything, and the multitudes of heaven worship you.
7"You are the LORD God, who chose
Abram and brought him out of Ur of
the Chaldeans[c] and named him Abraham.[d] 8You found his heart faithful to

8:9 [j]Ne 7:1,65, 70 [k]Dt 12:7,12; 16:14-15 **8:10** [l]1Sa 25:8; Lk 14:12-14 [m]Lev 23:40; Dt 12:18; 16:11, 14-15 **8:12** [n]Est 9:22 **8:16** [o]2Ki 14:13; Ne 12:39 **8:17** [p]2Ch 7:8; 8:13; 30:21 **8:18** [q]Dt 31:11 [r]Lev 23:36,40; Nu 29:35 **9:1** [s]Jos 7:6; 1Sa 4:12 **9:2** [t]Ne 13:3, 30 [u]Ezr 10:11; Ps 106:6 **9:4** [v]Ezr 10:23 **9:5** [w]Ps 78:4 **9:6** [x]Dt 6:4 [y]2Ki 19:15 [z]Ge 1:1; Isa 37:16 [a]Ps 95:5 [b]Dt 10:14 **9:7** [c]Ge 11:31 [d]Ge 17:5

[a] 8 Or *God, translating it* [b] 15 See Lev. 23:37-40. [c] 5 Or *God for ever and ever*

8:15 *branches from olive and wild olive trees ... myrtles, palms and shade trees.* With the exception of palm trees and other leafy trees, the trees mentioned here are not the same as those prescribed in Lev 23:40. Lev 23:40 includes the willow, which is omitted here. *olive ... trees.* Widespread in Mediterranean countries. According to Dt 8:8, it was growing in Canaan before the conquest. It takes an olive tree 30 years to mature, so its cultivation requires peaceful conditions. *wild olive trees.* Rendered "oil trees" (*Olea europaea oleaster*) by the NKJV and "oleaster" by the NABRE. However, this is questionable, since, according to 1Ki 6:23,31–32, the wood of this tree was used as timber, whereas the wood of the wild olive tree had little value for use in the temple's furniture. Also, the oleaster contains very little "oil." The phrase may have meant a resinous tree like the fir. The KJV renders the phrase as "pine." *myrtles.* Evergreen bushes with a pleasing odor. *palms.* Date palms; such trees were common around Jericho.

9:6 *You alone are the LORD.* See the article "Monotheism, Monolatry and Henotheism," p. 308. The reference here is to the personal name of the God of Israel, Yahweh. Since no other god claims the name Yahweh, this should be rendered to convey that Yahweh stands alone—in a class by himself. The description that follows in the prayer (vv. 6–37) enumerates the unique acts of Yahweh that distinguish him from other gods. Though the prayer begins with acts of creation that other peoples would attribute to other gods, most of the list deals with the acts Yahweh performed on behalf of his covenant people Israel. *starry host.* See note on 2Ki 21:3.

you, and you made a covenant with
him to give to his descendants the
land of the Canaanites, Hittites, Amorites, Perizzites, Jebusites and Girgashites.[e] You have kept your promise[f]
because you are righteous.[g]
9“You saw the suffering of our ancestors in Egypt;[h] you heard their cry
at the Red Sea.[a][i] 10You sent signs[j] and
wonders against Pharaoh, against all
his officials and all the people of his
land, for you knew how arrogantly the Egyptians treated them. You
made a name[k] for yourself, which remains to this day. 11You divided the
sea before them,[l] so that they passed
through it on dry ground, but you
hurled their pursuers into the depths,
like a stone into mighty waters.[m] 12By
day you led[n] them with a pillar of
cloud,[o] and by night with a pillar of
fire to give them light on the way they
were to take.
13“You came down on Mount Si-
nai;[p] you spoke[q] to them from heav-
en. You gave them regulations and
laws that are just[r] and right, and decrees and commands that are good.[s]
14You made known to them your holy
Sabbath[t] and gave them commands,
decrees and laws through your servant Moses. 15In their hunger you
gave them bread from heaven[u] and
in their thirst you brought them water from the rock;[v] you told them to
go in and take possession of the land
you had sworn with uplifted hand to
give them.[w]
16“But they, our ancestors, became arrogant and stiff-necked, and
they did not obey your commands.[x]
17They refused to listen and failed
to remember[y] the miracles you performed among them. They became
stiff-necked and in their rebellion appointed a leader in order to return to
their slavery.[z] But you are a forgiving God, gracious and compassionate, slow to anger[a] and abounding
in love.[b] Therefore you did not desert them,[c] 18even when they cast for
themselves an image of a calf[d] and
said, ‘This is your god, who brought
you up out of Egypt,’ or when they
committed awful blasphemies.
19“Because of your great compassion you did not abandon them in the
wilderness. By day the pillar of cloud
did not fail to guide them on their
path, nor the pillar of fire by night to
shine on the way they were to take.
20You gave your good Spirit[e] to instruct them. You did not withhold
your manna[f] from their mouths, and
you gave them water[g] for their thirst.
21For forty years you sustained them
in the wilderness; they lacked nothing,[h] their clothes did not wear out
nor did their feet become swollen.[i]
22“You gave them kingdoms and
nations, allotting to them even the
remotest frontiers. They took over
the country of Sihon[b][j] king of Heshbon and the country of Og king of
Bashan.[k] 23You made their children
as numerous as the stars in the sky,
and you brought them into the land
that you told their parents to enter
and possess. 24Their children went in
and took possession of the land.[l] You
subdued before them the Canaanites,
who lived in the land; you gave the
Canaanites into their hands, along
with their kings and the peoples of
the land, to deal with them as they
pleased. 25They captured fortified cities and fertile land; they took possession of houses filled with all kinds of
good things, wells already dug, vineyards, olive groves and fruit trees in
abundance. They ate to the full and
were well-nourished;[m] they reveled in
your great goodness.[n]
26“But they were disobedient and
rebelled against you; they turned their
backs on your law.[o] They killed your
prophets,[p] who had warned them in
order to turn them back to you; they
committed awful blasphemies.[q] 27So
you delivered them into the hands of
their enemies,[r] who oppressed them.
But when they were oppressed they
cried out to you. From heaven you
heard them, and in your great compassion[s] you gave them deliverers,
who rescued them from the hand of
their enemies.
28“But as soon as they were at rest,
they again did what was evil in your
sight. Then you abandoned them to
the hand of their enemies so that they
ruled over them. And when they cried
out to you again, you heard from

[a] 9 Or *the Sea of Reeds* [b] 22 One Hebrew manuscript and Septuagint; most Hebrew manuscripts *Sihon, that is, the country of the*

9:8 [e]Ge 15:18-21 [f]Jos 21:45 [g]Ge 15:6; Ezr 9:15 **9:9** [h]Ex 3:7 [i]Ex 14:10-30 **9:10** [j]Ex 10:1 [k]Jer 32:20; Da 9:15 **9:11** [l]Ex 14:21; Ps 78:13 [m]Ex 15:4-5,10; Heb 11:29 **9:12** [n]Ex 15:13 [o]Ex 13:21 **9:13** [p]Ex 19:11 [q]Ex 19:19 [r]Ps 119:137 [s]Ex 20:1 **9:14** [t]Ge 2:3; Ex 20:8-11 **9:15** [u]Ex 16:4; Jn 6:31 [v]Ex 17:6; Nu 20:7-13 [w]Dt 1:8,21 **9:16** [x]Dt 1:26-33; 31:29 **9:17** [y]Ps 78:42 [z]Nu 14:1-4 [a]Ex 34:6 [b]Nu 14:17-19 [c]Ps 78:11 **9:18** [d]Ex 32:4

9:20 [e]Nu 11:17; Isa 63:11,14 [f]Ex 16:15 [g]Ex 17:6 **9:21** [h]Dt 2:7 [i]Dt 8:4 **9:22** [j]Nu 21:21 [k]Nu 21:33 **9:24** [l]Jos 11:23 **9:25** [m]Dt 6:10-12 [n]Nu 13:27; Dt 32:12-15 **9:26** [o]1Ki 14:9 [p]Mt 21:35-36 [q]Jdg 2:12-13 **9:27** [r]Jdg 2:14 [s]Ps 106:45

9:18 *image of a calf.* See note on 1Ki 12:28; see also the article “The Golden Calf,” p. 167.
9:22 *Sihon king of Heshbon.* See note on Dt 2:24.
9:25 *wells already dug.* The lack of rainfall during much of the year made it necessary for almost every house to have its own well or cistern to store water from the rainy seasons. See note on Ge 37:20.

heaven, and in your compassion you
delivered them[t] time after time.
29“You warned them in order to
turn them back to your law, but they
became arrogant[u] and disobeyed your
commands. They sinned against your
ordinances, of which you said, ‘The
person who obeys them will live by
them.’[v] Stubbornly they turned their
backs on you, became stiff-necked
and refused to listen.[w] 30For many
years you were patient with them. By
your Spirit you warned them through
your prophets.[x] Yet they paid no attention, so you gave them into the
hands of the neighboring peoples.
31But in your great mercy you did
not put an end[y] to them or abandon
them, for you are a gracious and merciful God.
32“Now therefore, our God, the
great God, mighty[z] and awesome,
who keeps his covenant of love,[a] do
not let all this hardship seem trifling
in your eyes — the hardship that has
come on us, on our kings and leaders,
on our priests and prophets, on our
ancestors and all your people, from
the days of the kings of Assyria until today. 33In all that has happened
to us, you have remained righteous;[b]
you have acted faithfully, while we
acted wickedly.[c] 34Our kings,[d] our
leaders, our priests and our ancestors[e] did not follow your law; they did
not pay attention to your commands
or the statutes you warned them to
keep. 35Even while they were in their
kingdom, enjoying your great goodness[f] to them in the spacious and
fertile land you gave them, they did
not serve you[g] or turn from their evil
ways.
36“But see, we are slaves[h] today,
slaves in the land you gave our ancestors so they could eat its fruit and
the other good things it produces.
37Because of our sins, its abundant
harvest goes to the kings you have
placed over us. They rule over our
bodies and our cattle as they please.
We are in great distress.[i]

The Agreement of the People

38“In view of all this, we are making
a binding agreement,[j] putting it in writing,[k] and our leaders, our Levites and our
priests are affixing their seals to it.”[a]

10 [b] Those who sealed it were:

Nehemiah the governor, the son of Hakaliah.

Zedekiah, 2Seraiah,[l] Azariah, Jeremiah,
3Pashhur,[m] Amariah, Malkijah,
4Hattush, Shebaniah, Malluk,
5Harim,[n] Meremoth, Obadiah,
6Daniel, Ginnethon, Baruch,
7Meshullam, Abijah, Mijamin,
8Maaziah, Bilgai and Shemaiah.
These were the priests.

9The Levites:[o]

Jeshua son of Azaniah, Binnui of the sons of Henadad, Kadmiel,
10and their associates: Shebaniah,
Hodiah, Kelita, Pelaiah, Hanan,
11Mika, Rehob, Hashabiah,
12Zakkur, Sherebiah, Shebaniah,
13Hodiah, Bani and Beninu.

14The leaders of the people:

Parosh, Pahath-Moab, Elam, Zattu, Bani,
15Bunni, Azgad, Bebai,
16Adonijah, Bigvai, Adin,[p]
17Ater, Hezekiah, Azzur,
18Hodiah, Hashum, Bezai,

9:28 [t]Ps 106:43 **9:29** [u]Ps 5:5; Isa 2:11; Jer 43:2 [v]Dt 30:16 [w]Zec 7:11-12 **9:30** [x]2Ki 17:13-18; 2Ch 36:16 **9:31** [y]Isa 48:9; Jer 4:27 **9:32** [z]Ps 24:8 [a]Dt 7:9 **9:33** [b]Ge 18:25 [c]Jer 44:3; Da 9:7-8, 14 **9:34** [d]2Ki 23:11 [e]Jer 44:17 **9:35** [f]Isa 63:7 [g]Dt 28:45-48 **9:36** [h]Dt 28:48; Ezr 9:9 **9:37** [i]Dt 28:33; La 5:5 **9:38** [j]2Ch 23:16 [k]Isa 44:5 **10:2** [l]Ezr 2:2 **10:3** [m]1Ch 9:12 **10:5** [n]1Ch 24:8 **10:9** [o]Ne 12:1 **10:16** [p]Ezr 8:6

[a] *38* In Hebrew texts this verse (9:38) is numbered 10:1.
[b] In Hebrew texts 10:1-39 is numbered 10:2-40.

9:32 *kings of Assyria.* One of these was Shalmaneser III (858 – 824 BC), who reported that he defeated Ahab at the battle of Qarqar in 853 BC, an important battle, but one that is not mentioned in the OT (see the article “Omri and Jehu in History,” p. 632). The first Assyrian king to expand his empire to the Mediterranean was the great Tiglath-Pileser III, also known as Pul. He attacked Phoenicia in 736 BC, Philistia in 734 and Damascus in 732 (see note on 2Ki 15:29; see also the article “Israel and Damascus Versus Judah,” p. 649). Early in his reign (752 – 742 BC), Menahem of Israel paid tribute to him (see note on 2Ki 15:19). During his campaigns against Damascus, he also ravaged Gilead and Galilee and destroyed Hazor and Megiddo. Shalmaneser V (727 – 722 BC) laid siege to Samaria (see the article “Shalmaneser,” p. 652) — a task completed by Sargon II (721 – 705 BC) (see the article “Hezekiah and Assyria,” p. 657). Sennacherib (704 – 681 BC) failed to take Jerusalem in 701 BC, but captured Lachish (see notes on 2Ki 18:13,14; 19:9,36). Esarhaddon (681 – 669 BC) conquered Lower Egypt and extracted tribute from Manasseh of Judah (see note on 2Ki 19:37). Ashurbanipal (669 – 633 BC) also invaded Egypt and proceeded as far south as Thebes. He was probably the king who freed Manasseh from exile and restored him as a puppet king (see the article “Manasseh of Judah and Ashurbanipal,” p. 665).

9:37 *bodies.* The Hebrew term is used 13 times in the OT and characterizes the human being in weakness, oppression or trouble. It is also used of a “corpse” (e.g., see 1Sa 31:10 [“body”]) or of a “carcass” (e.g., Jdg 14:9). The Persian rulers drafted their subjects into military service. Possibly some Jews accompanied Xerxes on his invasion of Greece.

10:1 – 27 This is a legal list, bearing the official seals and containing a roster of 84 names arranged according to the following categories: 2 leaders, 21 priests, 17 Levites and 44 laymen.

19 Hariph, Anathoth, Nebai,
20 Magpiash, Meshullam, Hezir,[q]
21 Meshezabel, Zadok, Jaddua,
22 Pelatiah, Hanan, Anaiah,
23 Hoshea, Hananiah,[r] Hasshub,
24 Hallohesh, Pilha, Shobek,
25 Rehum, Hashabnah, Maaseiah,
26 Ahiah, Hanan, Anan,
27 Malluk, Harim and Baanah.

28 "The rest of the people — priests,
Levites, gatekeepers, musicians, temple servants[s] and all who separated
themselves from the neighboring peoples[t] for the sake of the Law of God,
together with their wives and all their
sons and daughters who are able to
understand — 29 all these now join
their fellow Israelites the nobles, and
bind themselves with a curse and an
oath[u] to follow the Law of God giv-
en through Moses the servant of God
and to obey carefully all the commands, regulations and decrees of the
LORD our Lord.
30 "We promise not to give our
daughters in marriage to the peoples
around us or take their daughters for
our sons.[v]
31 "When the neighboring peoples
bring merchandise or grain to sell on
the Sabbath,[w] we will not buy from
them on the Sabbath or on any holy
day. Every seventh year we will forgo
working the land[x] and will cancel all
debts.[y]
32 "We assume the responsibility for
carrying out the commands to give a
third of a shekel[a] each year for the
service of the house of our God: 33 for
the bread set out on the table;[z] for the
regular grain offerings and burnt offerings; for the offerings on the Sabbaths, at the New Moon[a] feasts and
at the appointed festivals; for the holy
offerings; for sin offerings[b] to make
atonement for Israel; and for all the
duties of the house of our God.[b]
34 "We — the priests, the Levites
and the people — have cast lots[c] to
determine when each of our families
is to bring to the house of our God
at set times each year a contribution
of wood[d] to burn on the altar of the
LORD our God, as it is written in the
Law.
35 "We also assume responsibility
for bringing to the house of the LORD
each year the firstfruits[e] of our crops
and of every fruit tree.[f]
36 "As it is also written in the Law,
we will bring the firstborn[g] of our
sons and of our cattle, of our herds
and of our flocks to the house of our
God, to the priests ministering there.[h]
37 "Moreover, we will bring to the
storerooms of the house of our God,
to the priests, the first of our ground
meal, of our grain offerings, of the
fruit of all our trees and of our new
wine and olive oil.[i] And we will bring
a tithe[j] of our crops to the Levites,[k] for
it is the Levites who collect the tithes
in all the towns where we work.[l] 38 A
priest descended from Aaron is to accompany the Levites when they receive the tithes, and the Levites are to
bring a tenth of the tithes[m] up to the
house of our God, to the storerooms
of the treasury. 39 The people of Israel, including the Levites, are to bring
their contributions of grain, new wine
and olive oil to the storerooms, where
the articles for the sanctuary and for

10:20 [q] 1Ch 24:15 **10:23** [r] Ne 7:2 **10:28** [s] Ps 135:1 [t] 2Ch 6:26; Ne 9:2 **10:29** [u] Nu 5:21; Ps 119:106 **10:30** [v] Ex 34:16; Dt 7:3; Ne 13:23 **10:31** [w] Ne 13:16, 18; Jer 17:27; Eze 23:38; Am 8:5 [x] Ex 23:11; Lev 25:1-7 [y] Dt 15:1 **10:33** [z] Lev 24:6

[a] Nu 10:10; Ps 81:3; Isa 1:14 [b] 2Ch 24:5 **10:34** [c] Lev 16:8 [d] Ne 13:31 **10:35** [e] Ex 22:29; 23:19; Nu 18:12 [f] Dt 26:1-11 **10:36** [g] Ex 13:2; Nu 18:14-16 [h] Ne 13:31 **10:37** [i] Lev 23:17; Nu 18:12 [j] Lev 27:30; Nu 18:21 [k] Dt 14:22-29 [l] Eze 44:30 **10:38** [m] Nu 18:26

[a] 32 That is, about 1/8 ounce or about 4 grams
[b] 33 Or *purification offerings*

10:30 See the article "Mixed Marriages," p. 775.
10:31 *we will not buy ... on the Sabbath.* Though the Sabbath passages in the Torah (e.g., Ex 20:8 – 11; Dt 5:12 – 15) do not explicitly prohibit trading on the Sabbath, this is clearly understood in Jer 17:19 – 27; Am 8:5. The provisions of Ne 10:31 – 34 may have been a code drawn up by Nehemiah to correct the abuses listed in ch. 13 (e.g., 13:15 – 22). Most of the topics addressed in ch. 10 correspond with those found in ch. 13: mixed marriages (compare 10:30 with 13:23 – 30), Sabbath observance (compare 10:31 with 13:15 – 22), wood offering (compare 10:34 with 13:31), firstfruits (compare 10:35 – 36 with 13:31), Levitical tithes (compare 10:37 – 38 with 13:10 – 14) and neglect of the temple (compare 10:39 with 13:11). *Every seventh year we will forgo working the land.* See note on Lev 25:2.
10:32 *a third of a shekel.* Ex 30:13 – 14 states that "a half shekel ... is an offering to the LORD" to be given by each man "twenty years old or more" as a symbolic ransom. Persian subsidies for the temple (Ezr 6:9 – 10; 7:21 – 24) had probably lapsed by this time.
10:33 *for the bread set out on the table.* See note on Ex 25:30.
10:34 *contribution of wood.* Though there is no specific reference to a wood offering in the Pentateuch, the perpetual burning of fires would have required a continual "contribution of wood."
10:35 *firstfruits.* See note on Nu 18:12.
10:37 *tithe of our crops.* Lit. "tithe of our land." The law decreed that a tenth of the plant crops was holy to the Lord (Lev 27:30; Nu 18:23 – 32). There is no reference here to a tithe of cattle (as in Lev 27:32 – 33; cf. 2Ch 31:6). Earlier in the fifth century BC, the prophet Malachi accused the Israelites of robbing God by withholding tithes and offerings (Mal 3:8). Tithes were originally meant for the support of the Levites (Ne 13:10 – 12; Nu 18:21 – 32). A tithe of their tithe was to go to the priests. But we know from Josephus that later on the priests collected the tithes for themselves. Because the tithe was originally expressed in terms of agricultural produce, the burden of the tithe fell disproportionately on farmers.

the ministering priests, the gatekeepers and the musicians are also kept.
"We will not neglect the house of
our God."[n]

The New Residents of Jerusalem

11:3-19pp — 1Ch 9:1-17

11 Now the leaders of the people settled in Jerusalem. The rest of the
people cast lots to bring one out of every ten of them to live in Jerusalem,[o] the
holy city,[p] while the remaining nine were
to stay in their own towns.[q] 2The people
commended all who volunteered to live in
Jerusalem.

3These are the provincial leaders who
settled in Jerusalem (now some Israelites,
priests, Levites, temple servants and descendants of Solomon's servants lived in
the towns of Judah, each on their own
property in the various towns,[r] 4while other people from both Judah and Benjamin[s]
lived in Jerusalem):[t]

From the descendants of Judah:

Athaiah son of Uzziah, the son of
Zechariah, the son of Amariah, the
son of Shephatiah, the son of Mahalalel, a descendant of Perez; 5and Maaseiah son of Baruch, the son of Kol-
Hozeh, the son of Hazaiah, the son
of Adaiah, the son of Joiarib, the son
of Zechariah, a descendant of Shelah. 6The descendants of Perez who
lived in Jerusalem totaled 468 men of
standing.

7From the descendants of Benjamin:

Sallu son of Meshullam, the son of
Joed, the son of Pedaiah, the son of
Kolaiah, the son of Maaseiah, the son
of Ithiel, the son of Jeshaiah, 8and his
followers, Gabbai and Sallai — 928
men. 9Joel son of Zikri was their chief
officer, and Judah son of Hassenuah
was over the New Quarter of the city.

10From the priests:

Jedaiah; the son of Joiarib; Jakin; 11Se-
raiah[u] son of Hilkiah, the son of Meshullam, the son of Zadok, the son of
Meraioth, the son of Ahitub,[v] the official in charge of the house of God,
12and their associates, who carried on
work for the temple — 822 men; Adaiah son of Jeroham, the son of Pelaliah,
the son of Amzi, the son of Zechariah,
the son of Pashhur, the son of Malkijah, 13and his associates, who were
heads of families — 242 men; Amash-
sai son of Azarel, the son of Ahzai, the
son of Meshillemoth, the son of Immer, 14and his[a] associates, who were
men of standing — 128. Their chief officer was Zabdiel son of Haggedolim.

15From the Levites:

Shemaiah son of Hasshub, the son
of Azrikam, the son of Hashabiah,
the son of Bunni; 16Shabbethai[w] and
Jozabad,[x] two of the heads of the Levites, who had charge of the outside
work of the house of God; 17Matta-
niah[y] son of Mika, the son of Zabdi,
the son of Asaph,[z] the director who
led in thanksgiving and prayer; Bakbukiah, second among his associates;
and Abda son of Shammua, the son
of Galal, the son of Jeduthun.[a] 18The
Levites in the holy city[b] totaled 284.

19The gatekeepers:

Akkub, Talmon and their associates,
who kept watch at the gates — 172
men.

20The rest of the Israelites, with the
priests and Levites, were in all the towns
of Judah, each on their ancestral property.
21The temple servants[c] lived on the hill
of Ophel, and Ziha and Gishpa were in
charge of them.

10:39 [n] Dt 12:6; Ne 13:11,12 **11:1** [o] Ne 7:4 [p] ver 18; Isa 48:2; 52:1; 64:10; Zec 14:20-21 [q] Ne 7:73 **11:3** [r] 1Ch 9:2-3; Ezr 2:1 **11:4** [s] Ezr 1:5 [t] Ezr 2:70 **11:11** [u] 2Ki 25:18; Ezr 2:2 [v] Ezr 7:2 **11:16** [w] Ezr 10:15 [x] Ezr 8:33 **11:17** [y] 1Ch 9:15; Ne 12:8 [z] 2Ch 5:12 [a] 1Ch 25:1 **11:18** [b] Rev 21:2 **11:21** [c] Ezr 2:43; Ne 3:26

[a] *14* Most Septuagint manuscripts; Hebrew *their*

11:1 *one out of every ten.* The need for the repopulation of Jerusalem is expressed in 7:4. The practice of redistributing populations was also used to establish Greek and Hellenistic cities. Known as *synoikismos*, the practice involved the forcible transfer from rural settlements to urban centers. The city of Tiberias on the western shore of the Sea of Galilee was populated by such a process by Herod Antipas in AD 18. Archaeological surveys indicate a drop of over 75 percent of the number of occupied sites as a result of the Babylonian conquest of Judah. That they "cast lots" indicates that people do not wish to live in Jerusalem. Since the city is still in a state of disrepair and a focal point of enemy aggression, it is neither a safe nor an attractive place to live. People would also be unwilling to abandon their farms or jeopardize their landholdings.
11:9 *New Quarter.* Translates Hebrew *mishneh*, which some English versions transliterate simply as "Mishneh." Like the "market district" (*maktesh*) in Zep 1:11 (probably the Tyropoeon Valley area), the Mishneh was a new suburb to the west of the temple area.
11:10 *the priests.* To be qualified as a priest, one had to establish his descent through genealogical records, which would trace his ancestry all the way back to Aaron, Moses' brother and the first priest. Hence, priestly genealogies play an important role in the books of Ezra, Nehemiah and Chronicles (see the article "The Significance of Genealogies for a Postexilic Audience," p. 680).
11:20 *ancestral property.* Designates the inalienable hereditary possession including land, buildings and movable goods acquired either by conquest or inheritance. In the OT it describes the land of Canaan as the possession of both Yahweh and Israel, including the individual holdings of tribes and families. It also designated Israel as Yahweh's special possession (see note on Dt 7:6).

22The chief officer of the Levites in Jerusalem was Uzzi son of Bani, the son of
Hashabiah, the son of Mattaniah,[d] the son
of Mika. Uzzi was one of Asaph's descendants, who were the musicians responsible for the service of the house of God.
23The musicians[e] were under the king's orders, which regulated their daily activity.
24Pethahiah son of Meshezabel, one of
the descendants of Zerah[f] son of Judah,
was the king's agent in all affairs relating
to the people.
25As for the villages with their fields,
some of the people of Judah lived in Kiriath Arba[g] and its surrounding settlements,
in Dibon[h] and its settlements, in Jekabzeel
and its villages, 26in Jeshua, in Moladah,
in Beth Pelet,[i] 27in Hazar Shual, in Beersheba[j] and its settlements, 28in Ziklag,[k] in
Mekonah and its settlements, 29in En Rimmon, in Zorah,[l] in Jarmuth,[m] 30Zanoah,
Adullam[n] and their villages, in Lachish[o]
and its fields, and in Azekah[p] and its settlements. So they were living all the way
from Beersheba[q] to the Valley of Hinnom.
31The descendants of the Benjamites
from Geba[r] lived in Mikmash,[s] Aija, Bethel
and its settlements, 32in Anathoth,[t] Nob[u]
and Ananiah, 33in Hazor,[v] Ramah and Gittaim,[w] 34in Hadid, Zeboim[x] and Neballat,
35in Lod and Ono,[y] and in Ge Harashim.
36Some of the divisions of the Levites of
Judah settled in Benjamin.

Priests and Levites

12 These were the priests[z] and Levites
who returned with Zerubbabel[a] son
of Shealtiel and with Joshua:[b]
Seraiah,[c] Jeremiah, Ezra,
2Amariah, Malluk, Hattush,
3Shekaniah, Rehum, Meremoth,
4Iddo,[d] Ginnethon,[a] Abijah,[e]
5Mijamin,[b] Moadiah, Bilgah,
6Shemaiah, Joiarib, Jedaiah,[f]
7Sallu, Amok, Hilkiah and Jedaiah.
These were the leaders of the priests and
their associates in the days of Joshua.
8The Levites were Jeshua, Binnui, Kadmiel, Sherebiah, Judah, and also Mattaniah,[g] who, together with his associates,
was in charge of the songs of thanksgiving. 9Bakbukiah and Unni, their associates, stood opposite them in the services.
10Joshua was the father of Joiakim, Joiakim the father of Eliashib,[h] Eliashib the
father of Joiada, 11Joiada the father of Jonathan, and Jonathan the father of Jaddua.
12In the days of Joiakim, these were the
heads of the priestly families:
of Seraiah's family, Meraiah;
of Jeremiah's, Hananiah;
13of Ezra's, Meshullam;
of Amariah's, Jehohanan;
14of Malluk's, Jonathan;
of Shekaniah's,[c] Joseph;
15of Harim's, Adna;
of Meremoth's,[d] Helkai;
16of Iddo's,[i] Zechariah;
of Ginnethon's, Meshullam;
17of Abijah's, Zikri;
of Miniamin's and of Moadiah's, Pil-
tai;
18of Bilgah's, Shammua;
of Shemaiah's, Jehonathan;
19of Joiarib's, Mattenai;
of Jedaiah's, Uzzi;
20of Sallu's, Kallai;
of Amok's, Eber;
21of Hilkiah's, Hashabiah;
of Jedaiah's, Nethanel.
22The family heads of the Levites in
the days of Eliashib, Joiada, Johanan and

11:22 [d] 1Ch 9:15 **11:23** [e] Ne 7:44 **11:24** [f] Ge 38:30 **11:25** [g] Ge 35:27; Jos 14:15 [h] Nu 21:30 **11:26** [i] Jos 15:27 **11:27** [j] Ge 21:14 **11:28** [k] 1Sa 27:6 **11:29** [l] Jos 15:33 [m] Jos 10:3 **11:30** [n] Jos 15:35 [o] Jos 10:3 [p] Jos 10:10 [q] Jos 15:28 **11:31** [r] Jos 21:17; Isa 10:29 [s] 1Sa 13:2 **11:32** [t] Jos 21:18; Isa 10:30 [u] 1Sa 21:1 **11:33** [v] Jos 11:1 [w] 2Sa 4:3 **11:34** [x] 1Sa 13:18 **11:35** [y] 1Ch 8:12 **12:1** [z] Ne 10:1-8 [a] 1Ch 3:19 [b] Ezr 2:2 [c] Ezr 2:2 **12:4** [d] Zec 1:1 [e] Lk 1:5 **12:6** [f] 1Ch 24:7 **12:8** [g] Ne 11:17 **12:10** [h] Ezr 10:24 **12:16** [i] ver 4

[a] *4* Many Hebrew manuscripts and Vulgate (see also verse 16); most Hebrew manuscripts *Ginnethoi*
[b] *5* A variant of *Miniamin*
[c] *14* Very many Hebrew manuscripts, some Septuagint manuscripts and Syriac (see also verse 3); most Hebrew manuscripts *Shebaniah's*
[d] *15* Some Septuagint manuscripts (see also verse 3); Hebrew *Meraioth's*

11:24 *Pethahiah … was the king's agent in all affairs relating to the people.* Scholars are unsure of the rank of this individual. He may have been a governor who succeeded Nehemiah, or perhaps he was a representative of the interests of the people to the provincial governors or satraps. He may have alternatively represented the Jews at the imperial court in Persia.
11:25–35 There are 17 locations in Judah and 15 in the adjoining territory to the north of Benjamin in these verses. The former locations correspond to earlier lists of Judahite cities. All these names also appear in Jos 15 (except Dibon, Jeshua and Mekonah). The settlements to the south were in areas that were outside the boundary of the province of Yehud, under the influence if not control of the Edomites or Arabs. The list, however, is not comprehensive insofar as several cities listed in Ezr 2:20–34 and Ne 3 are lacking. The limits of the Judahite settlement after the return from Babylon have been confirmed by archaeological evidence; none of the YHD-YHWD (the official designation of the Persian province of Judea) coins have been found outside the area demarcated by these verses.
11:25 *Kiriath Arba.* The archaic name of Hebron (Jos 20:7), an important city 20 miles (32 kilometers) south of Jerusalem (see note on Nu 13:22).
11:30 *Lachish.* See notes on 2Ki 14:19; 18:14.
11:35 *Ge Harashim.* Also known as The Valley of the Craftsmen, this may be the Wadi esh-Shellal, the broad valley between Lod and Ono. The oak trees of the nearby Sharon plain would have been useful to artisans working in either wood or iron.
12:22 *Darius the Persian.* Though some have favored either Nothus (Darius II, 423–404 BC) or Codomannus (Darius III, 335–331 BC, the king whose empire Alexander the Great conquered), the writer probably intended to designate Darius I as "the Persian" in opposition to the enigmatic "Darius the Mede" of Daniel (see note on Da 5:31).

Jaddua, as well as those of the priests,
were recorded in the reign of Darius the
Persian. 23The family heads among the descendants of Levi up to the time of Johanan son of Eliashib were recorded in the
book of the annals. 24And the leaders of
the Levites[j] were Hashabiah, Sherebiah,
Jeshua son of Kadmiel, and their associates, who stood opposite them to give
praise and thanksgiving, one section responding to the other, as prescribed by David the man of God.
25Mattaniah, Bakbukiah, Obadiah, Meshullam, Talmon and Akkub were gatekeepers who guarded the storerooms at
the gates. 26They served in the days of Joiakim son of Joshua, the son of Jozadak,
and in the days of Nehemiah the governor
and of Ezra the priest, the teacher of the
Law.

Dedication of the Wall of Jerusalem

27At the dedication[k] of the wall of Jerusalem, the Levites were sought out from
where they lived and were brought to Jerusalem to celebrate joyfully the dedication with songs of thanksgiving and with
the music of cymbals,[l] harps and lyres.[m]
28The musicians also were brought together from the region around Jerusalem —
from the villages of the Netophathites,[n]
29from Beth Gilgal, and from the area of
Geba and Azmaveth, for the musicians
had built villages for themselves around
Jerusalem. 30When the priests and Levites
had purified themselves ceremonially,
they purified the people,[o] the gates and
the wall.
31I had the leaders of Judah go up on
top of[a] the wall. I also assigned two large
choirs to give thanks. One was to proceed
on top of[b] the wall to the right, toward
the Dung Gate.[p] 32Hoshaiah and half the
leaders of Judah followed them, 33along
with Azariah, Ezra, Meshullam, 34Judah,
Benjamin,[q] Shemaiah, Jeremiah, 35as well
as some priests with trumpets,[r] and also
Zechariah son of Jonathan, the son of
Shemaiah, the son of Mattaniah, the son
of Micaiah, the son of Zakkur, the son of
Asaph, 36and his associates — Shemaiah,
Azarel, Milalai, Gilalai, Maai, Nethanel,
Judah and Hanani — with musical instruments[s] prescribed by David the man of
God.[t] Ezra[u] the teacher of the Law led the
procession. 37At the Fountain Gate[v] they
continued directly up the steps of the City
of David on the ascent to the wall and
passed above the site of David's palace to
the Water Gate[w] on the east.
38The second choir proceeded in the opposite direction. I followed them on top
of[c] the wall, together with half the people — past the Tower of the Ovens[x] to the
Broad Wall,[y] 39over the Gate of Ephraim,[z]
the Jeshanah[d] Gate,[a] the Fish Gate,[b] the
Tower of Hananel[c] and the Tower of the
Hundred,[d] as far as the Sheep Gate.[e] At
the Gate of the Guard they stopped.
40The two choirs that gave thanks then
took their places in the house of God; so
did I, together with half the officials, 41as
well as the priests — Eliakim, Maaseiah,
Miniamin, Micaiah, Elioenai, Zechariah
and Hananiah with their trumpets — 42and
also Maaseiah, Shemaiah, Eleazar, Uzzi,
Jehohanan, Malkijah, Elam and Ezer. The
choirs sang under the direction of Jezra-
hiah. 43And on that day they offered great
sacrifices, rejoicing because God had giv-
en them great joy. The women and children also rejoiced. The sound of rejoicing
in Jerusalem could be heard far away.
44At that time men were appointed to
be in charge of the storerooms[f] for the
contributions, firstfruits and tithes.[g] From
the fields around the towns they were to
bring into the storerooms the portions required by the Law for the priests and the
Levites, for Judah was pleased with the
ministering priests and Levites.[h] 45They
performed the service of their God and
the service of purification, as did also the
musicians and gatekeepers, according to
the commands of David[i] and his son Solomon.[j] 46For long ago, in the days of David
and Asaph,[k] there had been directors for
the musicians and for the songs of praise[l]
and thanksgiving to God. 47So in the days
of Zerubbabel and of Nehemiah, all Israel
contributed the daily portions for the musicians and the gatekeepers. They also set
aside the portion for the other Levites, and
the Levites set aside the portion for the descendants of Aaron.[m]

Nehemiah's Final Reforms

13 On that day the Book of Moses was
read aloud in the hearing of the
people and there it was found written that

12:24 [j] Ezr 2:40 **12:27** [k] Dt 20:5 [l] 2Sa 6:5 [m] 1Ch 15:16, 28; 25:6; Ps 92:3 **12:28** [n] 1Ch 2:54; 9:16 **12:30** [o] Ex 19:10; Job 1:5 **12:31** [p] Ne 2:13 **12:34** [q] Ezr 1:5 **12:35** [r] Ezr 3:10 **12:36** [s] 1Ch 15:16 [t] 2Ch 8:14 [u] Ezr 7:6 **12:37** [v] Ne 2:14; 3:15 [w] Ne 3:26 **12:38** [x] Ne 3:11 [y] Ne 3:8 **12:39** [z] 2Ki 14:13; Ne 8:16 [a] Ne 3:6 [b] 2Ch 33:14; Ne 3:3 [c] Ne 3:1 [d] Ne 3:1 [e] Ne 3:1 **12:44** [f] Ne 13:4, 13 [g] Lev 27:30 [h] Dt 18:8 **12:45** [i] 1Ch 25:1; 2Ch 8:14 [j] 1Ch 6:31; 23:5 **12:46** [k] 2Ch 35:15 [l] 2Ch 29:27; Ps 137:4 **12:47** [m] Nu 18:21; Dt 18:8

[a] 31 Or *go alongside* [b] 31 Or *proceed alongside* [c] 38 Or *them alongside* [d] 39 Or *Old*

12:27 *cymbals, harps and lyres.* See the article "Music and Musicians," p. 524.
12:30 *purified ... the wall.* This idea is unprecedented in the Bible, since purification usually involves consecrating objects or locations used in rituals, though houses with mildew need to be purified (Lev 14:48–53; see note on Lev 14:34). If the former sense is meant, the purification could be the act of consecrating Jerusalem as a "holy city"; if the latter, it may be to remove the corruption of the devastation (corpse contamination, etc.) or the impurity of the idolatry that had been performed there.
13:1 *Book of Moses was read ... no Ammonite or Moabite*

no Ammonite or Moabite should ever be
admitted into the assembly of God,[n] 2be-
cause they had not met the Israelites with
food and water but had hired Balaam[o] to
call a curse down on them.[p] (Our God,
however, turned the curse into a blessing.)[q] 3When the people heard this law,
they excluded from Israel all who were of
foreign descent.[r]

4Before this, Eliashib the priest had been
put in charge of the storerooms[s] of the
house of our God. He was closely associated with Tobiah,[t] 5and he had provided him
with a large room formerly used to store
the grain offerings and incense and temple
articles, and also the tithes[u] of grain, new
wine and olive oil prescribed for the Levites, musicians and gatekeepers, as well
as the contributions for the priests.

6But while all this was going on, I was
not in Jerusalem, for in the thirty-second
year of Artaxerxes[v] king of Babylon I had
returned to the king. Some time later I
asked his permission 7and came back to
Jerusalem. Here I learned about the evil
thing Eliashib[w] had done in providing Tobiah a room in the courts of the house of
God. 8I was greatly displeased and threw
all Tobiah's household goods out of the
room.[x] 9I gave orders to purify the rooms,[y]
and then I put back into them the equipment of the house of God, with the grain
offerings and the incense.

10I also learned that the portions assigned to the Levites had not been giv-
en to them,[z] and that all the Levites and
musicians responsible for the service had
gone back to their own fields. 11So I rebuked the officials and asked them, "Why
is the house of God neglected?"[a] Then I
called them together and stationed them
at their posts.

12All Judah brought the tithes[b] of grain,
new wine and olive oil into the storerooms.[c] 13I put Shelemiah the priest, Zadok the scribe, and a Levite named Pedaiah in charge of the storerooms and made
Hanan son of Zakkur, the son of Mattaniah, their assistant, because they were
considered trustworthy. They were made
responsible for distributing the supplies to
their fellow Levites.[d]

14Remember[e] me for this, my God, and
do not blot out what I have so faithfully done for the house of my God and its
services.

15In those days I saw people in Judah
treading winepresses on the Sabbath and
bringing in grain and loading it on donkeys, together with wine, grapes, figs and
all other kinds of loads. And they were
bringing all this into Jerusalem on the
Sabbath.[f] Therefore I warned them against
selling food on that day. 16People from Tyre
who lived in Jerusalem were bringing in
fish and all kinds of merchandise and selling them in Jerusalem on the Sabbath[g] to
the people of Judah. 17I rebuked the nobles of Judah and said to them, "What is
this wicked thing you are doing—desecrating the Sabbath day? 18Didn't your ancestors do the same things, so that our God
brought all this calamity on us and on this
city? Now you are stirring up more wrath
against Israel by desecrating the Sabbath."[h]

19When evening shadows fell on the
gates of Jerusalem before the Sabbath,[i]
I ordered the doors to be shut and not
opened until the Sabbath was over. I stationed some of my own men at the gates
so that no load could be brought in on
the Sabbath day. 20Once or twice the merchants and sellers of all kinds of goods
spent the night outside Jerusalem. 21But
I warned them and said, "Why do you
spend the night by the wall? If you do this
again, I will arrest you." From that time
on they no longer came on the Sabbath.
22Then I commanded the Levites to purify
themselves and go and guard the gates in
order to keep the Sabbath day holy.

Remember[j] me for this also, my God,
and show mercy to me according to your
great love.

13:1 [n]ver 23; Dt 23:3 **13:2** [o]Nu 22:3-11 [p]Nu 23:7; Dt 23:3 [q]Nu 23:11; Dt 23:4-5 **13:3** [r]ver 23; Ne 9:2 **13:4** [s]Ne 12:44 [t]Ne 2:10 **13:5** [u]Lev 27:30; Nu 18:21 **13:6** [v]Ne 2:6; 5:14 **13:7** [w]Ezr 10:24 **13:8** [x]Mt 21:12-13; Jn 2:13-16 **13:9** [y]1Ch 23:28; 2Ch 29:5 **13:10** [z]Dt 12:19 **13:11** [a]Ne 10:37-39; Hag 1:1-9 **13:12** [b]2Ch 31:6 [c]1Ki 7:51; Ne 10:37-39; Mal 3:10 **13:13** [d]Ne 12:44; Ac 6:1-5 **13:14** [e]Ge 8:1 **13:15** [f]Ex 20:8-11; 34:21; Dt 5:12-15; Ne 10:31 **13:16** [g]Ne 10:31 **13:18** [h]Ne 10:31; Jer 17:21-23 **13:19** [i]Lev 23:32 **13:22** [j]Ge 8:1; Ne 12:30

should ever be admitted into the assembly of God. See Dt 23:3–6.

13:2 *Balaam.* See the article "Balaam," p. 268.

13:6 *I was not in Jerusalem.* The Elephantine papyri provide us with an interesting parallel to Nehemiah's absence. Arsames, the satrap of Egypt, left his post in the 14th year of Darius II (410/409 BC) and was still absent at the Persian court in the 17th year (407/406 BC)—i.e., for three years. As in Nehemiah's case, internal conflict and a breakdown of order took place during the governor's absence.

13:8 *I was greatly displeased.* Nehemiah's expulsion of Tobiah is paralleled somewhat earlier in Egypt by Udjahorresnet's expulsion of squatters from the temple of Neith at Sais. Since wealth, power and prestige were all connected to the temples of the ancient world, it was not uncommon for unsavory and undesirable individuals to infiltrate and exploit the temple for their own gain. Reformers would naturally want to expel such people.

13:16 *Tyre.* In modern times it is located only about 12 miles (19 kilometers) north of the border between Israel and Lebanon. Tyre was renowned for its far-flung maritime trade (see notes on 1Ki 5:1; 2Ch 8:18.

13:19 *When evening shadows fell on the gates ... before the Sabbath.* The gates began to cast long "evening shadows" even before sunset, when the Sabbath began. The Israelites, like the Babylonians, counted their days from sunset to sunset (the Egyptians reckoned their days from dawn to dawn). The precise moment the Sabbath began was heralded by the blowing of a trumpet by a priest.

23Moreover, in those days I saw men
of Judah who had married[k] women from
Ashdod, Ammon and Moab.[l] 24Half of their
children spoke the language of Ashdod
or the language of one of the other peoples, and did not know how to speak the
language of Judah. 25I rebuked them and
called curses down on them. I beat some of
the men and pulled out their hair. I made
them take an oath[m] in God's name and
said: "You are not to give your daughters in
marriage to their sons, nor are you to take
their daughters in marriage for your sons
or for yourselves. 26Was it not because of
marriages like these that Solomon king of
Israel sinned? Among the many nations
there was no king like him.[n] He was loved
by his God,[o] and God made him king over
all Israel, but even he was led into sin by
foreign women.[p] 27Must we hear now that
you too are doing all this terrible wickedness and are being unfaithful to our God
by marrying[q] foreign women?"
28One of the sons of Joiada son of Eliashib[r] the high priest was son-in-law to
Sanballat[s] the Horonite. And I drove him
away from me.

29Remember[t] them, my God, because
they defiled the priestly office and the covenant of the priesthood and of the Levites.

30So I purified the priests and the Levites of everything foreign,[u] and assigned
them duties, each to his own task. 31I also
made provision for contributions of wood[v]
at designated times, and for the firstfruits.

Remember[w] me with favor, my God.

13:23 [k] Ezr 9:1-2; Mal 2:11 [l] ver 1; Ne 10:30 **13:25** [m] Ezr 10:5 **13:26** [n] 1Ki 3:13; 2Ch 1:12 [o] 2Sa 12:25 [p] 1Ki 11:3 **13:27** [q] Ezr 9:14; 10:2 **13:28** [r] Ezr 10:24 [s] Ne 2:10 **13:29** [t] Ne 6:14 **13:30** [u] Ne 10:30 **13:31** [v] Ne 10:34 [w] ver 14,22; Ge 8:1

13:24 *language of Ashdod.* The excavations at Ashdod have uncovered an ostracon from Nehemiah's age in Aramaic script that reads *krm zbdyh* ("[from the] vineyard of Zebadiah"). Unfortunately, the inscription is too brief to shed any light on the Ashdodite language. Possibly the dialect was Phoenician. In the Persian period the Philistine-Palestinian coastal area was divided into several jurisdictions. Ashkelon was under the Tyrians; Ashdod was the center of the Persian province.

13:25 *pulled out their hair.* Contrast Ezra's action (Ezr 9:3), who pulled out his own hair, with Nehemiah's here. Plucking the hair from another's beard was designed to show anger, express an insult and mark someone as worthy of scorn (cf. 2Sa 10:4; Isa 50:6). The *semirasus* ("half-shaven") marked the lowest type of slave or prisoner in Rome. Nehemiah's action was designed to prevent future intermarriages ("you are not to give"), whereas Ezra dissolved the existing unions (Ezr 10:1 – 5).

13:26 *Solomon king of Israel sinned.* See 1Ki 11:1 – 6 and notes.

13:28 *One of the sons of Joiada son of Eliashib the high priest was son-in-law to Sanballat.* The Hebrew is ambiguous since the phrase "high priest" can refer to either Joiada or Eliashib. In the latter case, Eliashib was still alive. More likely, however, "high priest" designates Joiada (cf. 12:10). The offending son would then have been a brother of the man who succeeded Joiada as high priest, Johanan II (12:22 – 23), who was married to a daughter of Sanballat. According to Lev 21:14, the high priest was not to marry a foreigner. The expulsion of Joiada's son may have followed this special ban or the general interdict against intermarriage. Such a union was especially rankling to Nehemiah in the light of Sanballat's enmity.

NARRATIVE LITERATURE

ESTHER

Historical Setting

The book of Esther is set during the era when the Persians ruled over Judah, in the reign of King Xerxes (Hebrew "Ahasuerus"). The Jews became subjects of the Persian Empire when Cyrus the Great, king of Media and Persia, conquered Babylon in 539 BC. (Babylon had taken over Judah in 605 BC, and many Jews were deported to Babylon as captives from 605 to 586 BC.) Even though Cyrus had issued a decree allowing the Jewish captives to return to their homeland, many had chosen to remain in Babylon. After living there for almost half a century, they had become well settled and prosperous. The thought of returning to the ruined and isolated land of Judah had little appeal to them. Some of these Jews made their way even farther east, to the new seat of power in the Eastern world: Susa, the capital of Persia. There they again found that ambitious and capable individuals could attain positions of affluence and influence, as the case of Nehemiah, cupbearer for King Artaxerxes I, demonstrates. Esther's story is set in this community of Persian Jews — far from their homeland, yet true to their heritage.

KEY CONCEPTS

- Chance and circumstance are fully within God's providence.
- Reversal and irony are evidence of God's hand in a book in which he is never mentioned by name.

King Xerxes I (486–465 BC) is well known from the work of the Greek author Herodotus, who wrote *The Histories*, which includes a history of the Persian Wars, around 445 BC. Since the Greeks and the Persians were bitter enemies, Herodotus's account must be read with a critical eye. But even so, with the aid of the 20 or so inscriptions attributed to Xerxes and with information from other classical authors, we can put together a decent profile of his early reign. Xerxes was the son of King Darius I and Queen Atossa, daughter of Cyrus the Great. He was the fourth legitimate monarch of the so-called Achaemenid Dynasty, which ruled Persia from Cyrus until the coming of Alexander the Great in 335 BC.

When Xerxes took the throne, he was confronted with insurrection: Egypt had begun to revolt during the days of Darius, and the province of Babylon revolted soon after Xerxes' enthronement. Both revolts were put down efficiently. Xerxes dealt with Babylon harshly, destroying local temples and carrying away a large statue of the Babylonian principal deity Marduk. It is apparent that Xerxes was not as pious, at least toward foreign deities, as his grandfather Cyrus the Great had been.

Xerxes is most famous for his attempt to invade Greece, chronicled by Herodotus. In

481 BC, Xerxes' forces marched inland and took the city of Athens, but they did not hold it for long. In 479 BC, the Greeks rallied and expelled the Persians from their land. Xerxes never attempted another invasion of Greece. Instead, he seems to have devoted the latter years of his reign to expanding Persepolis, a royal residence and Persian religious center.

The events recorded in Esther span the first half of Xerxes' career. Est 1, in which Vashti is deposed as queen, is dated to the third year of Xerxes' reign (1:3), which would have been before he left on his Greek campaign. The next dated event in the book is Esther's installation as queen (Est 2:16); it is dated to the tenth month of the seventh year of Xerxes' reign, which would have been a few months after his return from Greece. (The preparations of the candidates for queen, which took a full year [Est 2:12], would have begun while Xerxes was away in Greece.)

Our sources record little about events in Xerxes' realm after his return to Persia. As a result, we cannot verify the story of Esther on the basis of external evidence. Indeed, some details of the story are difficult to reconcile with what we do know about Persian history. But scholars who support the historicity of the text argue that none of these difficulties is insurmountable.

Literary Context

One of the preliminary steps in interpreting a Biblical text is identifying its literary genre. Esther (like many Biblical books) has proven something of a challenge in this regard. While the text reads like a historical account (similar to the books of Kings and Chronicles), appearances can be deceptive. Modern novelists can embellish their stories with historical details and local color, not for the purpose of deception but for vividness and realism. Ancient authors often did the same.

The most pertinent examples of this device are found in the genre labeled "court tale," the literary category with which Esther is most often associated. As the name implies, these stories are set in the royal court. The drama occurs when a hero uses skill or luck to foil enemy plots. In the process, the hero receives wealth, power and/or glory. (The Biblical stories of Joseph and Daniel are also examples of court tales.) The Tale of Ahiqar, about an Assyrian courtier who uses his wits to overcome a treacherous nephew's machinations, was well known and loved by both Jews and other Near Eastern peoples. Court tales are frequently based on historical figures, and perhaps even on actual events. We have clear evidence that Ahiqar, though his tale (as it has come down to us) is probably largely fictional, actually existed. The stories told about him incorporate many figures from Assyrian history as well as authentic details of court life.

Besides the court tales, Esther is often compared to the Apocryphal book of Judith, which features a female heroine who uses her "sex appeal" to rescue the Jews from destruction. While not a court tale per se, Judith seems to be representative of a literary style that became popular in the mid to late Second Temple period: the "novel." These novels often feature intrigue, clever heroes and prominent female characters. Another aspect of Esther that researchers have increasingly emphasized is its "comical" nature. Recent studies have demonstrated that humor is an underappreciated aspect of ancient Near Eastern literature. Self-important officials (like the villainous Haman in Esther) are frequently the targets of such lampoons. In the Babylonian story of Gimil-Ninurta, a mayor receives his comeuppance at the hands of a pauper.

Finally, when discussing Esther's literary context, we cannot fail to take note of its conspicuously "secular" character. Not only is Esther the only Biblical book that contains no reference to God; it also contains no prayers, sacrifices or any other religious observances.

To say that this absence is unusual would be an understatement: almost all ancient Near Eastern literature is permeated with religious language. The lack of religious references in the book of Esther is highly remarkable — and almost certainly intentional. Perhaps there is some deliberate irony intended, for God seems to lurk everywhere in the background of this book, in the unlikely coincidences and remarkable deliverances that make the story so entertaining. ◆

Queen Vashti Deposed

1 This is what happened during the time
of Xerxes,[a][a] the Xerxes who ruled over
127 provinces[b] stretching from India to
Cush[b]:[c] 2At that time King Xerxes reigned
from his royal throne in the citadel of
Susa,[d] 3and in the third year of his reign
he gave a banquet[e] for all his nobles and
officials. The military leaders of Persia and
Media, the princes, and the nobles of the
provinces were present.
4For a full 180 days he displayed the
vast wealth of his kingdom and the splendor and glory of his majesty. 5When these
days were over, the king gave a banquet,
lasting seven days,[f] in the enclosed garden[g] of the king's palace, for all the people from the least to the greatest who
were in the citadel of Susa. 6The garden
had hangings of white and blue linen, fastened with cords of white linen and purple
material to silver rings on marble pillars.
There were couches[h] of gold and silver on
a mosaic pavement of porphyry, marble,
mother-of-pearl and other costly stones.
7Wine was served in goblets of gold, each
one different from the other, and the royal
wine was abundant, in keeping with the
king's liberality.[i] 8By the king's command
each guest was allowed to drink with no
restrictions, for the king instructed all the

1:1 [a] Ezr 4:6; Da 9:1 [b] Est 9:30; Da 3:2; 6:1 [c] Est 8:9 **1:2** [d] Ezr 4:9; Ne 1:1; Est 2:8 **1:3** [e] 1Ki 3:15; Est 2:18 **1:5** [f] Jdg 14:17 [g] 2Ki 21:18; Est 7:7-8 **1:6** [h] Est 7:8; Eze 23:41; Am 3:12; 6:4 **1:7** [i] Est 2:18; Da 5:2

THE ACHAEMENID DYNASTY

Cyrus (the Great)	550 – 529 BC
Cambyses I	529 – 522 BC
PseudoSmerdis (illegitimate)	522 BC
Darius I (the Great)	522 – 486 BC
Xerxes I	486 – 465 BC
Artaxerxes I	465 – 425 BC
Xerxes II	425 – 424 BC
Darius II	424 – 405 BC
Artaxerxes II	405 – 359 BC
Artaxerxes III	359 – 338 BC
Arses	338 – 336 BC
Darius III	336 – 330 BC

[a] *1* Hebrew *Ahasuerus*; here and throughout Esther
[b] *1* That is, the upper Nile region

1:1 *India to Cush.* The description of the region encompassed is consistent with descriptions of Xerxes' realm found on the foundation inscription of his palace in Persepolis. *India.* The northwestern region of the Indus River Valley, which had been conquered by Darius. It corresponds to modern western Pakistan. *Cush.* The region south of Egypt. Originally, Cush was an Egyptian name for the area between the second and third cataracts of the Nile River. By Xerxes' time, the term had come to mean southern Egypt, Sudan and northern Ethiopia.
1:3 *banquet for all his nobles and officials.* Eastern kings often threw lavish banquets for members of the nobility. The Greek author Ctesias reported that 15,000 nobles regularly dined at the tables of Persian kings. The Assyrian king Ashurnasirpal I bragged to have entertained 69,574 guests at a ten-day feast on the dedication of his palace at Calah.
1:4 *a full 180 days.* Many scholars understand the text to describe a six-month banquet attended by princes and nobles, during which the king's majesty was on display. Such a long banquet certainly seems excessive, but it is not unprecedented in Jewish literature. The Apocryphal book of Judith tells of an Assyrian king who threw a four-month feast (Judith 1:1).

Alternatively, the Hebrew text does not necessarily mean that the feast lasted six months. Rather, it may imply consecutive acts: first, the feast for the nobles; then, a six-month demonstration of Persian wealth; and finally, a seven-day feast for the people of Susa. The six-month display of wealth might have been more like a tour of his kingdom. King Hezekiah of Judah apparently gave envoys from Babylon such a tour of his kingdom, demonstrating its wealth and glory (2Ki 20:12 – 19) — probably to draw them into an alliance. Some scholars have suggested that Xerxes' demonstration was designed to reassure his nobles and garner support for the coming invasion of Greece.
1:5 *enclosed garden.* In the hot, dry climates of the Near East, gardens often provided some welcome relief. Ancient cuneiform texts describe lavish public gardens constructed in Mesopotamia. Such gardens were often furnished with exotic plants and animals, for the amusement of their visitors (see note on Ge 2:8). The Persians, however, developed monumental gardens to an art form. They served as vacation spots and hunting preserves, as well as displays of royal wealth. Classical writers report that the Persian gardens contained examples of every species of plant or animal in the world. The garden of Cyrus the Great in Pasargadae was one of the most elaborate ever excavated, with stone channels, basins and colonnaded pavilions. The garden was situated so that Cyrus and his guests could see it from his audience hall. The garden of Susa, which has not survived, was probably similar. Such gardens were called by the Persians *paridaida*, "beyond the wall" (i.e., an enclosed area). It is from this word that the Greeks derived their word *paradeisos*, which gives us the English word *paradise*.
1:6 *couches of gold and silver.* These were apparently not gold plated but solid gold. Herodotus reports that the men of Greece plundered such couches from the Persian camp after the Persians were forced to withdraw from Athens. These couches were cushioned with "rich covertures" to make them more comfortable. To the Greeks, such extravagance seemed to epitomize Persian excesses.
1:7 *royal wine.* In Achaemenid Persia, grape wine was primarily a drink for the wealthy. The masses had to be contented with "strong drink," which included beer and date wines. Wine had to be imported from various regions, with inferior brands coming from Babylon. Better wines came from Syria and western Asia. The abundance of wine mentioned here is not meant to convey a sense of debauchery but of wealth and opulence.
1:8 *allowed to drink with no restrictions.* According to Josephus, it was the custom of the Persians to force the guests to drink nonstop, with the servants bringing wine continually to the table. Alternatively, it has been alleged that protocol required guests to drink whenever the king

wine stewards to serve each man what he
wished.
9Queen Vashti also gave a banquet[j] for
the women in the royal palace of King
Xerxes.
10On the seventh day, when King Xerxes
was in high spirits[k] from wine,[l] he commanded the seven eunuchs who served
him — Mehuman, Biztha, Harbona,[m] Big-
tha, Abagtha, Zethar and Karkas — 11to
bring[n] before him Queen Vashti, wearing
her royal crown, in order to display her
beauty[o] to the people and nobles, for she
was lovely to look at. 12But when the attendants delivered the king's command,
Queen Vashti refused to come. Then the

1:9 [j] 1Ki 3:15 **1:10** [k] Jdg 16:25; Ru 3:7 [l] Ge 14:18; Est 3:15; 5:6; 7:2; Pr 31:4-7; Da 5:1-4 [m] Est 7:9 **1:11** [n] SS 2:4 [o] Ps 45:11; Eze 16:14

drank. Xerxes suspended this custom at this banquet, allowing guests to do as they pleased. His laxity in this matter might foreshadow the trouble he would have with a wife who felt his commands could be ignored.

1:9 *Vashti.* The name is unattested in any ancient sources, but appears to be Persian. It has been suggested that the name may derive from words meaning "the best" or "the beloved." It might possibly then have been a title for the queen rather than a proper name. According to Herodotus (7.61), Xerxes' queen (at least in the earlier years of his reign) was a woman named Amestris, daughter of one Otanes, a commander in Xerxes' army. Amestris was reputed to be a powerful, merciless shrew. She was reported to be the mother of Artaxerxes I, Xerxes' successor. *also gave a banquet.* The ancient Persians had no custom requiring that men and women dine separately. Indeed, wives usually accompanied their husbands to dinner banquets. All the same, there is no reason to doubt that segregated dinner affairs could occur. The Persepolis Fortification Tablets, ancient documents excavated from Persepolis, demonstrate that royal wives often acted independently of their husbands. Artystone, one of the wives of Darius I, owned two large estates and had her own servants. One tablet reports that the queen had 512 gallons (1,940 liters) of wine delivered to her house for some occasion, suggesting that she may have been hosting a banquet similar to that given by Vashti.

1:10 *in high spirits from wine.* Lit. "when the heart of the king was good with wine." In Biblical anthropology, the heart is not so much the seat of the emotions as of reason and will. The text implies that wine had impaired the king's judgment. But the Persians would not have regarded Xerxes' inebriation as a problem. Both Herodotus (1.133) and Strabo (15.3.20) report that the Persians typically decided important matters when they were drunk. Herodotus adds that their decisions would be confirmed when they had sobered up. Decisions made when sober were reportedly considered suspect and had to be reconsidered after the parties were fully inebriated. Whether this truly represents Persian custom or is yet another example of how the Greek authors enjoyed ridiculing the Persians is difficult to discern. *eunuchs.* See note on 2Ki 9:32.

1:11 *bring … Queen Vashti … in order to display her beauty.* Jewish tradition holds that Vashti had been ordered to appear naked before the king, but the tradition has no historical support. Some Greek sources imply that the Persian queen was normally sequestered away and eschewed any public appearance; but scholars have demonstrated that this notion is mainly mythical. Royal women in Persia enjoyed high social status and were schooled in a variety

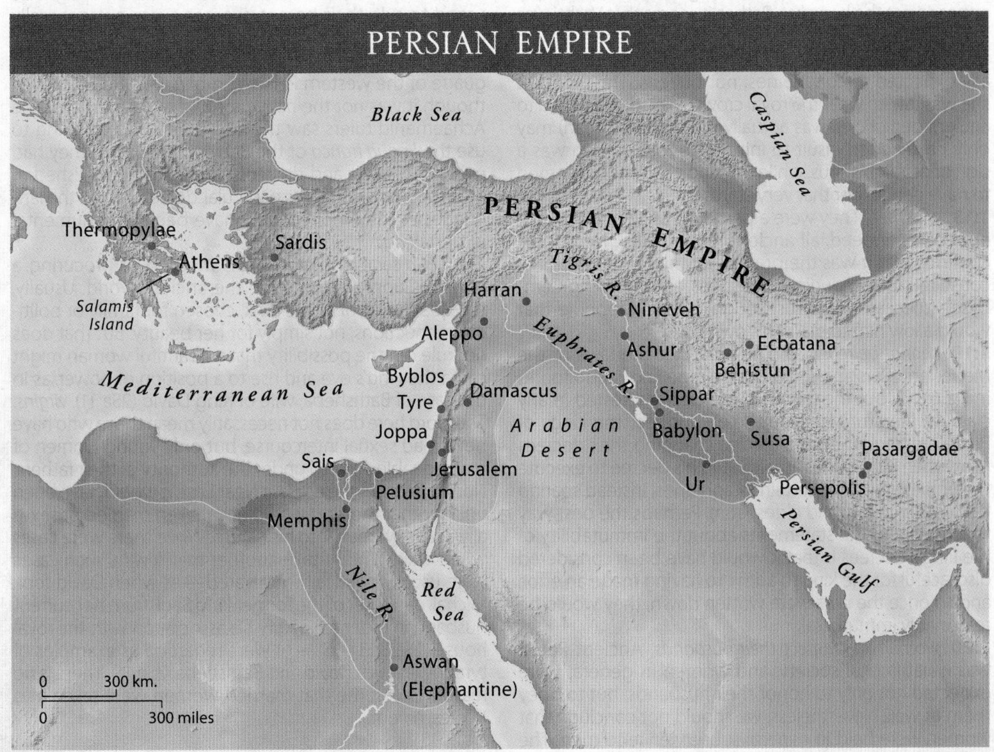

king became furious and burned with
anger.[p]
13Since it was customary for the king
to consult experts in matters of law and
justice, he spoke with the wise men who
understood the times[q] 14and were closest
to the king — Karshena, Shethar, Admatha,
Tarshish, Meres, Marsena and Memukan,
the seven nobles[r] of Persia and Media who
had special access to the king and were
highest in the kingdom.
15"According to law, what must be done
to Queen Vashti?" he asked. "She has not
obeyed the command of King Xerxes that
the eunuchs have taken to her."
16Then Memukan replied in the presence of the king and the nobles, "Queen
Vashti has done wrong, not only against
the king but also against all the nobles and
the peoples of all the provinces of King
Xerxes. 17For the queen's conduct will become known to all the women, and so
they will despise their husbands and say,
'King Xerxes commanded Queen Vashti
to be brought before him, but she would
not come.' 18This very day the Persian and
Median women of the nobility who have
heard about the queen's conduct will respond to all the king's nobles in the same
way. There will be no end of disrespect
and discord.[s]
19"Therefore, if it pleases the king,[t] let
him issue a royal decree and let it be written in the laws of Persia and Media, which
cannot be repealed,[u] that Vashti is never
again to enter the presence of King Xerxes. Also let the king give her royal position to someone else who is better than
she. 20Then when the king's edict is proclaimed throughout all his vast realm, all
the women will respect their husbands,
from the least to the greatest."
21The king and his nobles were pleased
with this advice, so the king did as Memukan proposed. 22He sent dispatches to all
parts of the kingdom, to each province in
its own script and to each people in their
own language,[v] proclaiming that every
man should be ruler over his own household, using his native tongue.

Esther Made Queen

2 Later when King Xerxes' fury had subsided,[w] he remembered Vashti and
what she had done and what he had decreed about her. 2Then the king's personal attendants proposed, "Let a search be
made for beautiful young virgins for the

1:12 [p] Ge 39:19; Est 2:21; 7:7; Pr 19:12 **1:13** [q] 1Ch 12:32; Jer 10:7; Da 2:12 **1:14** [r] 2Ki 25:19; Ezr 7:14

1:18 [s] Pr 19:13; 27:15 **1:19** [t] Ecc 8:4 [u] Est 8:8; Da 6:8,12 **1:22** [v] Ne 13:24; Est 8:9; Eph 5:22-24; 1Ti 2:12 **2:1** [w] Est 1:19-20; 7:10

of skills, including horsemanship and archery. They were known to appear in public, travel with their husbands and host feasts. There was nothing shameful in simply appearing at the banquet. Rather, it seems that Vashti was being commanded to act in a fashion that she believed beneath her station. Public displays of beauty were usually expected of concubines, not queens. The fact that she was told to wear the royal crown (which, according to ancient depictions, was actually more like a turban) may only have added insult to injury: the royal crown was a sign of her high status, while the king's summons seemed to have denied her that very status.

1:13 *wise men.* They were a part of all ancient Near Eastern courts (indeed, all ancient monarchies). Herodotus confirms that it was the practice of the Persian kings to consult judges on judicial questions, as when King Cambyses (successor of Cyrus) sought a legal loophole that would allow him to marry his own sister.

1:19 *cannot be repealed.* The idea that the laws of the Medes and Persians could not be repealed is also found in Da 6:8,12, but the notion is not clearly attested in any classical literature outside the OT. Indeed, the kings of Persia are frequently depicted as changing their decrees (e.g., when King Darius ameliorated his decree to execute the entire family of a certain Intaphernes, instead sparing his brother-in-law and eldest son). Perhaps the best way to understand the statements about the immutability of the king's decrees is that it would have been considered disgraceful for the king to admit to having made an error, and so once the laws were written down, they would be reasonably immutable.

1:20 *women will respect their husbands.* Ancient Persia was a patriarchal society, and women in general were expected not only to honor their husbands, but to obey them as well. Nevertheless, we should not conclude that women were held in general subservience to men. The Persepolis Fortification Tablets reveal that women often worked as managers or directors of various businesses and sometimes supervised men. So while men might be urged to rule their homes, women were not generally oppressed.

1:22 *to each people in their own language.* The official language of the western Persian Empire was Aramaic, even though it was not the native tongue of the Persians. The Achaemenid rulers saw the advantage of continuing to use the *lingua franca* of the Babylonian Empire they had overtaken. Laws and decrees were usually published in Aramaic. Translating this particular decree into all the languages of the empire would have been a monumental undertaking.

2:2 *Let a search be made.* This method of procuring a queen is unprecedented in the ancient world. Usually, the queen was of noble rank, chosen for family or political connections, not simply for her beauty. But that does not rule out the possibility that a beautiful woman might catch the king's eye and rise to a position of power, as in the case of Bathsheba, wife of King David (2Sa 11). *virgins.* The word here does not necessarily mean those who have never had sexual intercourse, but only young women of marriageable age still under the authority of their fathers. Nonetheless, in the ancient Near East, it would have been unlikely that the king would have taken married or sexually active women into his harem. While there were cases when a king might take another man's wife, such cases were usually politically motivated — as when David took Michal, daughter of the former king Saul, from her current husband in order to solidify his association with the royal house (2Sa 3:13 – 15) — or were regarded as examples of tyranny (as with David and Bathsheba, 2Sa 11). There is no reason to assume that married women were taken into Xerxes' harem.

king. 3Let the king appoint commissioners in every province of his realm to bring
all these beautiful young women into the
harem at the citadel of Susa. Let them be
placed under the care of Hegai, the king's
eunuch, who is in charge of the wom-
en; and let beauty treatments be given to
them. 4Then let the young woman who
pleases the king be queen instead of Vashti." This advice appealed to the king, and
he followed it.

5Now there was in the citadel of Susa a
Jew of the tribe of Benjamin, named Mordecai son of Jair, the son of Shimei, the
son of Kish,[x] 6who had been carried into
exile from Jerusalem by Nebuchadnezzar king of Babylon, among those taken
captive with Jehoiachin[a][y] king of Judah.[z]
7Mordecai had a cousin named Hadassah,
whom he had brought up because she
had neither father nor mother. This young
woman, who was also known as Esther,[a]
had a lovely figure[b] and was beautiful.
Mordecai had taken her as his own daughter when her father and mother died.

8When the king's order and edict had
been proclaimed, many young women
were brought to the citadel of Susa[c] and
put under the care of Hegai. Esther also
was taken to the king's palace and entrusted to Hegai, who had charge of the harem.
9She pleased him and won his favor.[d] Immediately he provided her with her beauty
treatments and special food.[e] He assigned
to her seven female attendants selected
from the king's palace and moved her and
her attendants into the best place in the
harem.

10Esther had not revealed her nationality
and family background, because Mordecai
had forbidden her to do so.[f] 11Every day he
walked back and forth near the courtyard
of the harem to find out how Esther was
and what was happening to her.

12Before a young woman's turn came to
go in to King Xerxes, she had to complete
twelve months of beauty treatments prescribed for the women, six months with
oil of myrrh and six with perfumes[g] and
cosmetics. 13And this is how she would
go to the king: Anything she wanted was
given her to take with her from the harem
to the king's palace. 14In the evening she
would go there and in the morning return
to another part of the harem to the care of

2:5 [x] 1Sa 9:1; Est 3:2 **2:6** [y] 2Ki 24:6, 15; 2Ch 36:10, 20 [z] Da 1:1-5; 5:13 **2:7** [a] Ge 41:45 [b] Ge 39:6 **2:8** [c] ver 3, 15; Ne 1:1; Est 1:2; Da 8:2 **2:9** [d] Ge 39:21 [e] ver 3, 12; Ge 37:3; 1Sa 9:22-24; 2Ki 25:30; Eze 16:9-13; Da 1:5 **2:10** [f] ver 20 **2:12** [g] Pr 27:9; SS 1:3; Isa 3:24

[a] 6 Hebrew *Jeconiah,* a variant of *Jehoiachin*

2:3 *in every province of his realm.* The text clearly indicates that the candidates for queen were to be taken from all the different ethnic groups in Xerxes' kingdom. While it would not have been unusual for the king's harem to include women of various nationalities, it may have been exceptional for the queen to be a non-Persian. But there were documented exceptions to the tradition, including Artaxerxes I and Darius II, both of whom had Babylonian queens. *harem.* Lit. "house of women," a special quarters reserved for the king's wives and concubines.
2:5 *tribe of Benjamin ... the son of Shimei, the son of Kish.* The reference to a Benjamite named Kish is reminiscent of Saul, the first king of Israel. Saul was also of Benjamin, and his father was named Kish (1Sa 9:1). The name Shimei too is associated with the house of Saul (2Sa 16:5). Mordecai's forebears named here are probably not the same people mentioned in the books of Samuel (but it is not impossible, since the word "son" in Hebrew can simply mean "descendant"). The allusion to Saul, however, is probably deliberate given Mordecai's antagonism to Haman, who is identified as an Agagite — the known opponent of Saul (see note on 3:1).
2:7 *Hadassah.* Like Mordecai, Esther had a Babylonian name, but her Hebrew name is also recorded. The Hebrew name Hadassah evidently means "myrtle." This name is not attested anywhere else in the OT or in any known ancient records or literature. The Babylonian name "Esther" derives from Ishtar, the name of one of the most widely honored pagan goddesses. Since Ishtar was the goddess of love, the name seems especially fitting for the woman who was destined to win the heart of the Persian king.
2:8 *taken to the king's palace.* Although only one woman would be chosen to replace Vashti, the other women would not be able to return to their homes. Rather, they all would become wives of the king, even if only of "concubine" status (see note on 1Ki 11:3). They remained in the harem even after one was selected to be queen. So Esther did not commit fornication when she finally slept with the king, as some commentators have suggested. Rather, she was fulfilling her conjugal duties as one of the king's wives.
2:9 *special food.* Lit. "her portion of food." The Hebrew word translated "portion" generally means something reserved for those in special positions and offices, such as kings or Levites (2Ch 31:3; Ne 12:44). The text does not necessarily imply that Esther's food was different from that of the other concubines, but apparently the chief eunuch attended to her food personally. Unlike Daniel and his companions (Da 1), Esther seems to have had no qualms about accepting food from the royal household. Indeed, the fact that she had not revealed her nationality (v. 10) implies that she ate the same food as the rest of the women in the harem, since demanding a kosher diet would have betrayed her nationality.
2:11 *he walked ... near the courtyard of the harem.* The Greek author Plutarch, among others, reports that the Persian nobles were jealous of their harems, and any man who approached them would be killed. But Herodotus writes of eunuchs admitting men to the harems, and one nobleman spoke regularly with his daughter, who was one of the royal wives. It was probably not difficult for Mordecai to see his cousin and even speak to her, so long as he had the permission of the chief eunuch.
2:13 According to Greek sources, the royal concubines were expected to entertain the king in various ways throughout the night, ready to provide sexual companionship when requested. We can assume that the women were given items that would help them with their diversions, including musical instruments (harps and flutes), musicians to accompany their singing, and perhaps other tools of entertainment.
2:14 *concubines.* See note on 1Ki 11:3.

Shaashgaz, the king's eunuch who was in
charge of the concubines.[h] She would not
return to the king unless he was pleased
with her and summoned her by name.[i]
15 When the turn came for Esther (the
young woman Mordecai had adopted, the
daughter of his uncle Abihail[j]) to go to the
king,[k] she asked for nothing other than
what Hegai, the king's eunuch who was in
charge of the harem, suggested. And Esther
won the favor[l] of everyone who saw her.
16 She was taken to King Xerxes in the royal
residence in the tenth month, the month
of Tebeth, in the seventh year of his reign.
17 Now the king was attracted to Esther
more than to any of the other women, and
she won his favor and approval more than
any of the other virgins. So he set a royal
crown on her head and made her queen[m]
instead of Vashti. 18 And the king gave a
great banquet,[n] Esther's banquet, for all
his nobles and officials.[o] He proclaimed a
holiday throughout the provinces and distributed gifts with royal liberality.[p]

Mordecai Uncovers a Conspiracy

19 When the virgins were assembled a
second time, Mordecai was sitting at the
king's gate.[q] 20 But Esther had kept secret
her family background and nationality just
as Mordecai had told her to do, for she
continued to follow Mordecai's instructions as she had done when he was bringing her up.[r]
21 During the time Mordecai was sitting
at the king's gate, Bigthana[a] and Teresh,
two of the king's officers[s] who guarded the
doorway, became angry[t] and conspired to
assassinate King Xerxes. 22 But Mordecai
found out about the plot and told Queen
Esther, who in turn reported it to the king,
giving credit to Mordecai. 23 And when the
report was investigated and found to be
true, the two officials were impaled[u] on
poles. All this was recorded in the book
of the annals[v] in the presence of the king.

Haman's Plot to Destroy the Jews

3 After these events, King Xerxes honored Haman son of Hammedatha, the
Agagite,[w] elevating him and giving him a
seat of honor higher than that of all the
other nobles. 2 All the royal officials at the
king's gate knelt down and paid honor to
Haman, for the king had commanded this
concerning him. But Mordecai would not
kneel down or pay him honor.

2:14 [h] 1Ki 11:3; SS 6:8; Da 5:2 [i] Est 4:11
2:15 [j] Est 9:29 [k] Ps 45:14 [l] Ge 18:3; 30:27; Est 5:8
2:17 [m] Est 1:11; Eze 16:9-13
2:18 [n] 1Ki 3:15; Est 1:3 [o] Ge 40:20 [p] Est 1:7
2:19 [q] ver 21; Est 3:2; 4:2; 5:13
2:20 [r] ver 10
2:21 [s] Ge 40:2; Est 6:2 [t] Est 1:12; 3:5; 5:9; 7:7
2:23 [u] Ge 40:19; Ps 7:14-16; Pr 26:27 [v] Est 6:1; 10:2
3:1 [w] ver 10; Ex 17:8-16; Nu 24:7; Dt 25:17-19; 1Sa 14:48; Est 5:11

[a] 21 Hebrew *Bigthan,* a variant of *Bigthana*

2:15 *eunuch ... in charge of the harem.* We know much about the administration of ancient harems from records found primarily in Assyria. These documents demonstrate that harem life was well regulated and under the watchful eye of trusted eunuchs. There were frequent conflicts among the women, as they would sometimes scheme and plot for favors for themselves and any children they had borne. The eunuchs were charged to ensure that such conflicts did not erupt in violence.
2:18 *He proclaimed a holiday.* Lit. "He caused a rest to take place." The phrase is ambiguous and has been interpreted as a release from work, from military service or from taxation.
2:21 *officers.* Lit. "eunuchs" (see note on 2Ki 9:32). The story is reminiscent of an incident in which a eunuch assassinated Artaxerxes III in order to replace him with Artaxerxes' son Arses.
2:23 *impaled on poles.* The Hebrew word translated "poles" literally means "tree" or "wooden object." The text refers to the common practice of impaling victims on wooden stakes. The Code of Hammurapi and Assyrian law codes sometimes prescribe impaling as an actual method of execution, and the Assyrian king Ashurnasirpal II bragged of how he impaled rebellious vassals. But more often, malefactors were executed by other methods, and their dead bodies were impaled for a public display. Also, it has been demonstrated that the Persians practiced crucifixion, and the punishment spoken of here might refer to that practice: impaling people alive on wooden posts and allowing them to die of exposure. *book of the annals ... of the king.* All ancient Near Eastern monarchs kept records of events that occurred during their reigns (see note on 1Ki 14:19).
3:1 *Haman ... Hammedatha.* These names are Persian. *Agagite.* Rendered as a Gentile noun, i.e., an indication of ethnic origin. Ancient interpreters universally understood the text to mean that Haman was a member of the race of Agag, or the Amalekites (see notes on Nu 13:29; Dt 25:19). During the reign of King Saul, God ordered Saul to utterly destroy the Amalekites and to take no plunder from them (see 1Sa 15:2,3 and notes). But Saul saved some of the loot and took the Amalekite king, Agag, as a captive (1Sa 15:7 – 9). The prophet Samuel killed Agag, but not before informing Saul that his disobedience would cost him his throne (1Sa 15:26 – 33). Since Mordecai is associated with the house of Saul (see note on Est 2:5), the clash between Mordecai and Haman is set up as a "rematch" of the Saul-Agag affair. *seat of honor higher than ... all the other nobles.* The exact nature of Haman's position is not explicit in the text. Modern writers frequently call him Xerxes' "vizier" or "prime minister," but it is uncertain that the Achaemenid court had such a position. Another possibility is that he held the position of *hazarpatish,* or "Commander of the Thousand" (called the "chiliarch" by the Greeks). This officer was the head of the king's personal bodyguard, and no one could enter the king's presence without his permission. The Greeks believed the chiliarch was the second great power of the kingdom, but they probably formed a mistaken impression based on the officer's easy access to the throne. Persian sources do not seem to attribute a great deal of authority to the position.
3:2 *knelt down.* According to Herodotus, the Persians were very conscious of social class, observing strict protocols. They would greet equals with a kiss, but would always bow and make obeisance before those of higher standing. Such prostrations were foreign to the Greeks but common throughout the Near East. Ancient Near Eastern peoples often knelt before one another as a sign of respect. Israelites generally had no qualms with such demonstrations (e.g., Ge 33:3; 42:6; 1Sa 20:41; 24:8). Given that prostration was such a common sign of respect, Mordecai's refusal to kneel down or pay Haman honor (v. 3) is a mystery. The rabbis invented a story that Haman car-

3 Then the royal officials at the king's
gate asked Mordecai, "Why do you disobey the king's command?"[x] 4 Day after
day they spoke to him but he refused to
comply.[y] Therefore they told Haman about
it to see whether Mordecai's behavior
would be tolerated, for he had told them
he was a Jew.
5 When Haman saw that Mordecai
would not kneel down or pay him hon-
or, he was enraged.[z] 6 Yet having learned
who Mordecai's people were, he scorned
the idea of killing only Mordecai. Instead
Haman looked for a way[a] to destroy[b] all
Mordecai's people, the Jews,[c] throughout
the whole kingdom of Xerxes.
7 In the twelfth year of King Xerxes, in
the first month, the month of Nisan, the
pur[d] (that is, the lot[e]) was cast in the presence of Haman to select a day and month.
And the lot fell on[a] the twelfth month, the
month of Adar.[f]
8 Then Haman said to King Xerxes,
"There is a certain people dispersed
among the peoples in all the provinces of
your kingdom who keep themselves separate. Their customs[g] are different from
those of all other people, and they do
not obey[h] the king's laws; it is not in the
king's best interest to tolerate them.[i] 9 If it
pleases the king, let a decree be issued to
destroy them, and I will give ten thousand
talents[b] of silver to the king's administrators for the royal treasury."[j]
10 So the king took his signet ring[k] from
his finger and gave it to Haman son of
Hammedatha, the Agagite, the enemy of
the Jews. 11 "Keep the money," the king
said to Haman, "and do with the people
as you please."
12 Then on the thirteenth day of the first
month the royal secretaries were summoned. They wrote out in the script of
each province and in the language[l] of each
people all Haman's orders to the king's satraps, the governors of the various provinces and the nobles of the various peoples. These were written in the name of
King Xerxes himself and sealed[m] with his
own ring. 13 Dispatches were sent by couriers to all the king's provinces with the

Gold signet ring, fifth–fourth century BC, similar to what the king would have used in Est 3:10.

Kim Walton. The British Museum.

3:3 [x] Est 5:9; Da 3:12 **3:4** [y] Ge 39:10 **3:5** [z] Est 2:21; 5:9 **3:6** [a] Pr 16:25 [b] Ps 74:8; 83:4 [c] Est 9:24 **3:7** [d] Est 9:24, 26 [e] Lev 16:8; 1Sa 10:21 [f] ver 13; Ezr 6:15; Est 9:19 **3:8** [g] Ac 16:20-21 [h] Jer 29:7; Da 6:13 [i] Ezr 4:15 **3:9** [j] Est 7:4 **3:10** [k] Ge 41:42; Est 7:6; 8:2

3:12 [l] Ne 13:24 [m] Ge 38:18; 1Ki 21:8; Est 8:8-10

[a] 7 Septuagint; Hebrew does not have *And the lot fell on.*
[b] 9 That is, about 375 tons or about 340 metric tons

ried an idol with him, and it was before this image that Mordecai refused to bow. But this story was moralistic rather than historical, with no textual support. A more likely explanation may be found in Mordecai's assertion that he will not bow to Haman because he (Mordecai) is a Jew (v. 4). It is probably ethnic antagonism between Jews and Amalekites that lies behind Mordecai's refusal to pay Haman the required homage (see note on v. 1).

3:7 *pur.* The Babylonian word for a lot, a form of divination (see the article "Urim and Thummim," p. 162). The form of the lot and how it was used are uncertain. One possibility is that the lot was cast onto a surface that was divided into sections marked with the names of the months and days. The day on which the lot fell would be considered the god's choice. Another possibility is that lots with months and days printed on them would be placed inside a pouch. The pouch would be shaken until one of the lots popped out, thus indicating that a god had chosen that particular date.

3:8 *customs ... laws.* Both words translate the same Hebrew word (*dat*). The Persians regularly allowed subject peoples to follow their own laws and customs, so long as these did not interfere with the peace of the empire. The Jews did, indeed, have unique customs, such as keeping the Sabbath and eating kosher foods, but these presented no danger to Xerxes. More troublesome was the charge that the Jews would not obey the king—i.e., they were rebellious (cf. Ezr 4:14–15). Xerxes had dealt with the revolt in Egypt in the first year of his reign (485 BC), and he ferociously suppressed revolts in Babylon in 484 and 482 BC. In the course of this action, Xerxes showed none of the mollifying tendencies for which Cyrus had been famous. He had no compunctions about using ruthless tactics to secure the compliance of his subjects.

3:9 *ten thousand talents of silver.* The size of the bribe that Haman offered was fantastic. According to the standard established by King Darius, it equaled about 375 tons (340 metric tons) of silver. Based on the figures given in Herodotus, Haman's bribe has been estimated to equal about two-thirds of Persia's annual revenue.

3:10 *signet ring.* Or seal ring. Served as a signature in the ancient world (see note on 1Ki 21:8).

3:11 *Keep the money.* The Hebrew reads lit. "The money is given to you." Many translators follow the Septuagint, the pre-Christian Greek translation of the OT, in understanding that Xerxes told Haman that the king would fund the Jews' destruction himself rather than accept Haman's offer of silver. But since Mordecai states later that Haman's promised funds would go into the royal treasury (4:7), the Hebrew reading seems preferable. The expression probably means that Haman had sufficient funds to do as he had said. It is uncertain where these funds would have come from. If they were his personal funds, they represented a vast fortune. Another possibility is that Haman's position gave him authority over certain public monies, and Xerxes granted him permission to use those funds for the task at hand. Or, perhaps Haman was anticipating a great deal of spoil from the destruction of the Jews, and he intended to use those funds to pay off his mercenaries.

3:13 *the order to ... annihilate all the Jews.* We should

order to destroy, kill and annihilate all the
Jews[n] — young and old, women and children — on a single day, the thirteenth day
of the twelfth month, the month of Adar,[o]
and to plunder[p] their goods. 14A copy of
the text of the edict was to be issued as
law in every province and made known
to the people of every nationality so they
would be ready for that day.[q]
15The couriers went out, spurred on by
the king's command, and the edict was issued in the citadel of Susa.[r] The king and
Haman sat down to drink,[s] but the city of
Susa was bewildered.[t]

Mordecai Persuades Esther to Help

4 When Mordecai learned of all that
had been done, he tore his clothes,[u]
put on sackcloth and ashes,[v] and went out
into the city, wailing[w] loudly and bitterly. 2But he went only as far as the king's
gate,[x] because no one clothed in sackcloth
was allowed to enter it. 3In every province
to which the edict and order of the king
came, there was great mourning among
the Jews, with fasting, weeping and wailing. Many lay in sackcloth and ashes.
4When Esther's eunuchs and female
attendants came and told her about Mordecai, she was in great distress. She sent
clothes for him to put on instead of his
sackcloth, but he would not accept them.
5Then Esther summoned Hathak, one of
the king's eunuchs assigned to attend her,
and ordered him to find out what was
troubling Mordecai and why.
6So Hathak went out to Mordecai in
the open square of the city in front of the
king's gate. 7Mordecai told him everything
that had happened to him, including the
exact amount of money Haman had promised to pay into the royal treasury for the
destruction of the Jews.[y] 8He also gave
him a copy of the text of the edict for their
annihilation, which had been published in
Susa, to show to Esther and explain it to
her, and he told him to instruct her to go
into the king's presence to beg for mercy
and plead with him for her people.
9Hathak went back and reported to Esther what Mordecai had said. 10Then she
instructed him to say to Mordecai, 11"All
the king's officials and the people of the
royal provinces know that for any man or
woman who approaches the king in the
inner court without being summoned[z] the
king has but one law:[a] that they be put
to death unless the king extends the gold
scepter[b] to them and spares their lives.
But thirty days have passed since I was
called to go to the king."
12When Esther's words were reported
to Mordecai, 13he sent back this answer:
"Do not think that because you are in the
king's house you alone of all the Jews will
escape. 14For if you remain silent[c] at this
time, relief[d] and deliverance[e] for the Jews
will arise from another place, but you and
your father's family will perish. And who
knows but that you have come to your
royal position for such a time as this?"[f]
15Then Esther sent this reply to Mordecai: 16"Go, gather together all the Jews
who are in Susa, and fast[g] for me. Do not
eat or drink for three days, night or day.
I and my attendants will fast as you do.

3:13 [n] 1Sa 15:3; Ezr 4:6; Est 8:10-14 [o] ver 7 [p] Est 8:11; 9:10 **3:14** [q] Est 8:8; 9:1 **3:15** [r] Est 8:14 [s] Est 1:10 [t] Est 8:15 **4:1** [u] Nu 14:6 [v] 2Sa 13:19; Eze 27:30-31; Jnh 3:5-6 [w] Ex 11:6; Ps 30:11 **4:2** [x] Est 2:19

4:7 [y] Est 3:9; 7:4 **4:11** [z] Est 2:14 [a] Da 2:9 [b] Est 5:1,2; 8:4 **4:14** [c] Ecc 3:7; Isa 62:1; Am 5:13 [d] Est 9:16, 22 [e] Ge 45:7; Dt 28:29 [f] Ge 50:20 **4:16** [g] 2Ch 20:3; Est 9:31

not think that members of the general public are being offered a license to kill Jews. The verse implies military action and is probably being sent to provincial garrisons.
4:1 *tore his clothes, put on sackcloth.* See notes on 1Sa 4:12; Job 1:20; see also the article "Mourning," p. 828.
4:2 *the king's gate.* See note on Ne 2:1.
4:8 *to show to Esther and explain it to her.* Perhaps the edict was written in Persian and had to be translated into Aramaic for Esther's benefit. Another possibility is that Esther was illiterate and could not read the edict for herself (see the articles "Literacy," p. 140; "Books and Literacy," p. 666). Greek sources tell us that the royal women of Persia were trained in horsemanship, martial arts and other skills, but they make no mention of literary training.
4:11 *any man or woman who approaches the king ... without being summoned ... put to death.* Additional evidence for such a policy is scant. Herodotus makes the point that access to the king was limited, with only the seven noble families of Persia allowed free passage into his presence. Other ancient authors write that no one could enter the king's presence without the permission of the chiliarch, who would demand to know their business. There is clear evidence that few people could march into the king's chamber uninvited. Even so, the text gives us no clues as to why Esther did not simply request an audience with the king, especially since Haman's edict would not be carried out for another 11 months. One possible explanation is that if Haman were, indeed, Xerxes' chiliarch (see note on 3:1), Esther would have had to make an appeal to Haman in order to be admitted into the throne room. Revealing her plans to Haman would have put her in a difficult position, to say the least. *unless the king extends the gold scepter.* The custom of the king extending his scepter in this manner is unattested outside the book of Esther. Many Persian reliefs, however, depict the king holding a scepter, a thin staff about the length of his body with a knob on one end. It seems to have had some function when he was holding court, since the scepter is prominent in scenes of royal audiences. *thirty days have passed since I was called to go to the king.* The queen's contact with the king was physically limited by the fact that she had her own private chamber in the palace and did not regularly dine with the king. Furthermore, since the king had his choice of many concubines, the queen shared his bed infrequently. Nonetheless, the statement that the queen had not been in the king's company for 30 days seems somewhat unusual. It may imply that Esther had fallen out of the king's favor, which could explain her reluctance to appear before him unannounced.
4:16 *fast.* Fasting often accompanied prayer, to demonstrate the deep concern of those making petitions to the Lord (cf. 1Sa 7:6; 2Sa 12:16–22; Ezr 8:21,23; Jnh 3:3–8).

When this is done, I will go
to the king, even though it is
against the law. And if I perish,
I perish."[h]
17So Mordecai went away
and carried out all of Esther's
instructions.

Esther's Request to the King

5 On the third day Esther
put on her royal robes[i] and
stood in the inner court of the
palace, in front of the king's[j]
hall. The king was sitting on
his royal throne in the hall,
facing the entrance. 2When he
saw Queen Esther standing in
the court, he was pleased with
her and held out to her the gold
scepter that was in his hand. So
Esther approached and touched
the tip of the scepter.[k]
3Then the king asked, "What
is it, Queen Esther? What is
your request? Even up to half
the kingdom,[l] it will be given
you."
4"If it pleases the king," replied Esther, "let the king, together with Haman, come today
to a banquet I have prepared for
him."
5"Bring Haman at once," the
king said, "so that we may do
what Esther asks."
So the king and Haman went
to the banquet Esther had prepared. 6As they were drinking
wine,[m] the king again asked Esther, "Now
what is your petition? It will be given you.
And what is your request? Even up to half
the kingdom,[n] it will be granted."[o]
7Esther replied, "My petition and my request is this: 8If the king regards me with
favor[p] and if it pleases the king to grant
my petition and fulfill my request, let the
king and Haman come tomorrow to the
banquet[q] I will prepare for them. Then I
will answer the king's question."

Haman's Rage Against Mordecai

9Haman went out that day happy and in
high spirits. But when he saw Mordecai at
the king's gate and observed that he neither rose nor showed fear in his presence,
he was filled with rage[r] against Mordecai.[s]
10Nevertheless, Haman restrained himself
and went home.
Calling together his friends and Zeresh,[t]
his wife, 11Haman boasted[u] to them about
his vast wealth, his many sons,[v] and all
the ways the king had honored him and
how he had elevated him above the other nobles and officials. 12"And that's not
all," Haman added. "I'm the only person[w]
Queen Esther invited to accompany the
king to the banquet she gave. And she has
invited me along with the king tomorrow.
13But all this gives me no satisfaction as
long as I see that Jew Mordecai sitting at
the king's gate.[x]"

Darius I "the Great" (550 BC – 486 BC), sitting on his throne, Persia, Achaemenid period.

4:16 [h] Ge 43:14
5:1 [i] Est 4:16; Eze 16:13
[j] Est 6:4; Pr 21:1
5:2 [k] Est 4:11; 8:4; Pr 21:1
5:3 [l] Est 7:2; Da 5:16; Mk 6:23
5:6 [m] Est 1:10
[n] Mk 6:23
[o] Est 7:2; 9:12
5:8 [p] Est 2:15; 7:3; 8:5
[q] 1Ki 3:15; Est 6:14
5:9 [r] Est 2:21; Pr 14:17
[s] Est 3:3,5
5:10 [t] Est 6:13
5:11 [u] Pr 13:16
[v] Est 9:7-10, 13
5:12 [w] Job 22:29; Pr 16:18; 29:23 **5:13** [x] Est 2:19

In Esther's case, the fast she calls is designed to implore God's favor on her behalf, even though prayer is never actually mentioned.

5:3 *up to half the kingdom.* This statement should not be taken literally. Its repetition in v. 6 and 7:2, as well as its appearance in Mk 6:23, suggests that this phrase was an idiomatic means of expressing royal favor.

5:4 *come today to a banquet.* Esther's delay in presenting the petition for her people's lives should not be interpreted as a sign of cowardice. Rather, Esther was following typical Near Eastern protocol for presenting a request. She begins by asking for a small favor but eventually she works her way, one concession at a time, to the real issue at hand.

14 His wife Zeresh and all his friends said to him, "Have a pole set up, reaching to a height of fifty cubits,[a][y] and ask the king in the morning to have Mordecai impaled[z] on it. Then go with the king to the banquet and enjoy yourself." This suggestion delighted Haman, and he had the pole set up.

Mordecai Honored

6 That night the king could not sleep;[a] so he ordered the book of the chronicles,[b] the record of his reign, to be brought in and read to him. 2 It was found recorded there that Mordecai had exposed Bigthana and Teresh, two of the king's officers who guarded the doorway, who had conspired to assassinate King Xerxes.

3 "What honor and recognition has Mordecai received for this?" the king asked.

"Nothing has been done for him,"[c] his attendants answered.

4 The king said, "Who is in the court?" Now Haman had just entered the outer court of the palace to speak to the king about impaling Mordecai on the pole he had set up for him.

5 His attendants answered, "Haman is standing in the court."

"Bring him in," the king ordered.

6 When Haman entered, the king asked him, "What should be done for the man the king delights to honor?"

Now Haman thought to himself, "Who is there that the king would rather honor than me?" 7 So he answered the king, "For the man the king delights to honor, 8 have them bring a royal robe[d] the king has worn and a horse[e] the king has ridden, one with a royal crest placed on its head. 9 Then let the robe and horse be entrusted to one of the king's most noble princes. Let them robe the man the king delights to honor, and lead him on the horse through the city streets, proclaiming before him, 'This is what is done for the man the king delights to honor![f]' "

10 "Go at once," the king commanded Haman. "Get the robe and the horse and do just as you have suggested for Mordecai the Jew, who sits at the king's gate. Do not neglect anything you have recommended."

11 So Haman got[g] the robe and the horse. He robed Mordecai, and led him on horseback through the city streets, proclaiming before him, "This is what is done for the man the king delights to honor!"

12 Afterward Mordecai returned to the king's gate. But Haman rushed home, with his head covered[h] in grief, 13 and told Zeresh[i] his wife and all his friends everything that had happened to him.

His advisers and his wife Zeresh said to him, "Since Mordecai, before whom your downfall[j] has started, is of Jewish origin, you cannot stand against him—you will surely come to ruin!" 14 While they were still talking with him, the king's eunuchs arrived and hurried Haman away to the banquet[k] Esther had prepared.

Haman Impaled

7 So the king and Haman went to Queen Esther's banquet,[l] 2 and as they were drinking wine[m] on the second day, the king again asked, "Queen Esther, what is your petition? It will be given you. What is your request? Even up to half the kingdom,[n] it will be granted.[o]"

3 Then Queen Esther answered, "If I have found favor[p] with you, Your Majesty, and if it pleases you, grant me my life—this is my petition. And spare my people—this is my request. 4 For I and my people have been sold to be destroyed, killed and annihilated.[q] If we had merely been sold as male and female slaves, I would have kept quiet, because no such distress would justify disturbing the king.[b]"

5 King Xerxes asked Queen Esther, "Who is he? Where is he—the man who has dared to do such a thing?"

6 Esther said, "An adversary and enemy! This vile Haman!"

Then Haman was terrified before the king and queen. 7 The king got up in a rage,[r] left his wine and went out into the palace garden.[s] But Haman, realizing that the king had already decided his fate,[t] stayed behind to beg Queen Esther for his life.

8 Just as the king returned from the pal-

5:14 [y] Est 7:9 [z] Ezr 6:11; Est 6:4 **6:1** [a] Da 2:1; 6:18 [b] Est 2:23; 10:2 **6:3** [c] Ecc 9:13-16 **6:8** [d] Ge 41:42; Isa 52:1 [e] 1Ki 1:33 **6:9** [f] Ge 41:43

6:11 [g] Ge 41:42 **6:12** [h] 2Sa 15:30; Jer 14:3,4; Mic 3:7 **6:13** [i] Est 5:10 [j] Ps 57:6; Pr 26:27; 28:18 **6:14** [k] 1Ki 3:15; Est 5:8 **7:1** [l] Ge 40:20-22; Mt 22:1-14 **7:2** [m] Est 1:10 [n] Est 5:3 [o] Est 9:12 **7:3** [p] Est 2:15 **7:4** [q] Est 3:9 **7:7** [r] Ge 34:7; Est 1:12; Pr 19:12; 20:1-2 [s] 2Ki 21:18 [t] Est 6:13

[a] 14 That is, about 75 feet or about 23 meters

[b] 4 Or *quiet, but the compensation our adversary offers cannot be compared with the loss the king would suffer*

5:14 *pole.* Refers to a pike for impaling victims (see note on 2:23). But in the reliefs from ancient Assyria, such pikes are usually not much larger than the people impaled on them. It is possible that Haman's 75-foot-tall "pole" includes the hill or platform on which the pike stands.
6:1 *the book of the chronicles.* See note on 2:23 ("book of the annals"). *read.* The form of the Hebrew verb implies continuous, extensive reading rather than a short recitation. Evidently, Xerxes listened to the royal chronicles all through the night, until Haman arrived to present his request (v. 4; cf. 5:14, which says that Haman planned to go "in the morning" to see Xerxes).
7:4 *sold as … slaves.* See note on Lev 25:39.
7:8 *falling on the couch.* The Persian nobles dined reclining on couches rather than sitting. Each guest would have their own couch, which would be decorated in ways befitting their rank. It is unclear if Haman threw himself on the queen or if he merely fell. In either case, he had commit-

ace garden to the banquet hall, Haman
was falling on the couch[u] where Esther
was reclining.[v]
The king exclaimed, "Will he even molest the queen while she is with me in the
house?"[w]
As soon as the word left the king's
mouth, they covered Haman's face.[x] 9Then
Harbona,[y] one of the eunuchs attending
the king, said, "A pole reaching to a height
of fifty cubits[a][z] stands by Haman's house.
He had it set up for Mordecai, who spoke
up to help the king."
The king said, "Impale him on it!"[a] 10So
they impaled Haman[b] on the pole[c] he had
set up for Mordecai.[d] Then the king's fury
subsided.[e]

The King's Edict in Behalf of the Jews

8 That same day King Xerxes gave Queen
Esther the estate of Haman,[f] the enemy of the Jews. And Mordecai came into
the presence of the king, for Esther had
told how he was related to her. 2The king
took off his signet ring,[g] which he had reclaimed from Haman, and presented it to
Mordecai. And Esther appointed him over
Haman's estate.[h]
3Esther again pleaded with the king,
falling at his feet and weeping. She begged
him to put an end to the evil plan of Haman the Agagite, which he had devised
against the Jews. 4Then the king extended
the gold scepter[i] to Esther and she arose
and stood before him.
5"If it pleases the king," she said, "and
if he regards me with favor and thinks it
the right thing to do, and if he is pleased
with me, let an order be written overruling
the dispatches that Haman son of Hammedatha, the Agagite, devised and wrote to
destroy the Jews in all the king's provinces. 6For how can I bear to see disaster fall
on my people? How can I bear to see the
destruction of my family?"[j]
7King Xerxes replied to Queen Esther
and to Mordecai the Jew, "Because Haman
attacked the Jews, I have given his estate
to Esther, and they have impaled him on
the pole he set up. 8Now write another decree[k] in the king's name in behalf of the
Jews as seems best to you, and seal it with
the king's signet ring[l]—for no document
written in the king's name and sealed with
his ring can be revoked."[m]
9At once the royal secretaries were
summoned—on the twenty-third day
of the third month, the month of Sivan.
They wrote out all Mordecai's orders to
the Jews, and to the satraps, governors
and nobles of the 127 provinces stretching from India to Cush.[b][n] These orders
were written in the script of each province and the language of each people and
also to the Jews in their own script and
language.[o] 10Mordecai wrote in the name
of King Xerxes, sealed the dispatches with
the king's signet ring, and sent them by
mounted couriers, who rode fast horses
especially bred for the king.
11The king's edict granted the Jews in
every city the right to assemble and protect themselves; to destroy, kill and annihilate the armed men of any nationality
or province who might attack them and
their women and children,[c] and to plunder[p] the property of their enemies. 12The
day appointed for the Jews to do this in
all the provinces of King Xerxes was the
thirteenth day of the twelfth month, the
month of Adar.[q] 13A copy of the text of
the edict was to be issued as law in every province and made known to the people of every nationality so that the Jews
would be ready on that day[r] to avenge
themselves on their enemies.
14The couriers, riding the royal horses,
went out, spurred on by the king's command, and the edict was issued in the citadel of Susa.

The Triumph of the Jews

15When Mordecai[s] left the king's presence, he was wearing royal garments of
blue and white, a large crown of gold and

7:8 [u] Est 1:6 [v] Ge 39:14 [w] Ge 34:7 [x] Est 6:12 **7:9** [y] Est 1:10 [z] Est 5:14 [a] Ps 7:14-16; 9:16; Pr 11:5-6; 26:27; Mt 7:2 **7:10** [b] Pr 10:28 [c] Est 9:25 [d] Da 6:24 [e] Est 2:1 **8:1** [f] Est 2:7; 7:6; Pr 22:22-23 **8:2** [g] Ge 41:42; Est 3:10 [h] Pr 13:22; Da 2:48 **8:4** [i] Est 4:11; 5:2 **8:6** [j] Est 7:4; 9:1 **8:8** [k] Est 3:12-14 [l] Ge 41:42 [m] Est 1:19; Da 6:15 **8:9** [n] Est 1:1 [o] Est 1:22 **8:11** [p] Est 9:10, 15, 16 **8:12** [q] Est 3:13; 9:1 **8:13** [r] Est 3:14 **8:15** [s] Est 9:4

[a] *9* That is, about 75 feet or about 23 meters [b] *9* That is, the upper Nile region [c] *11* Or *province, together with their women and children, who might attack them;*

ted an egregious error: According to some authors, touching the king's wife was penalized with death. In Assyrian law, no man was allowed to draw within more than seven paces of a member of the king's harem. *covered Haman's face.* In ancient Greece and Rome, it was customary to cover the head of someone condemned to death. However, there is no evidence for this practice among the Persians. It has also been argued that this phrase is a figure of speech simply meaning "to faint," but this suggestion is based on a questionable reading of an Arabic expression. Thus, the meaning of this gesture remains uncertain. In an Assyrian elegy, covering the face is treatment of the dead, so this may indicate that Haman has died and it is his corpse that is impaled (v. 10).

8:11 *right to assemble.* Since the king's first decree could not be revoked (see 1:19 and note), this decree was designed to ameliorate its effects. We can assume that the Jews would have defended themselves against those who tried to kill them. But this decree specifically gave the Jews the right to "assemble." The Hebrew term used here often means to muster an army. Thus, the Jews are authorized to begin gathering and arming soldiers to defend themselves against Haman's mercenaries. Without such a decree, mustering an army would have been viewed as an act of rebellion. This decree was sent everywhere (v. 9), which would presumably discourage anyone from attacking the Jews, knowing that the Jews would be prepared to defend themselves.

a purple robe of fine linen.[t] And the city of
Susa held a joyous celebration.[u] 16For the
Jews it was a time of happiness and joy,[v]
gladness and honor.[w] 17In every province
and in every city to which the edict of the
king came, there was joy[x] and gladness
among the Jews, with feasting and celebrating. And many people of other nationalities became Jews because fear[y] of the
Jews had seized them.[z]

9 On the thirteenth day of the twelfth
month, the month of Adar,[a] the edict
commanded by the king was to be carried
out. On this day the enemies of the Jews
had hoped to overpower them, but now
the tables were turned and the Jews got
the upper hand[b] over those who hated
them.[c] 2The Jews assembled in their cities[d] in all the provinces of King Xerxes to
attack those determined to destroy them.
No one could stand against them,[e] because the people of all the other nationalities were afraid of them. 3And all the
nobles of the provinces, the satraps, the
governors and the king's administrators
helped the Jews,[f] because fear of Mordecai had seized them. 4Mordecai was prominent[g] in the palace; his reputation spread
throughout the provinces, and he became
more and more powerful.[h]
5The Jews struck down all their enemies with the sword, killing and destroying them,[i] and they did what they pleased
to those who hated them. 6In the citadel
of Susa, the Jews killed and destroyed five
hundred men. 7They also killed Parshan-
datha, Dalphon, Aspatha, 8Poratha, Ada-
lia, Aridatha, 9Parmashta, Arisai, Aridai
and Vaizatha, 10the ten sons[j] of Haman
son of Hammedatha, the enemy of the
Jews. But they did not lay their hands on
the plunder.[k]
11The number of those killed in the citadel of Susa was reported to the king that
same day. 12The king said to Queen Esther,
"The Jews have killed and destroyed five
hundred men and the ten sons of Haman
in the citadel of Susa. What have they
done in the rest of the king's provinces?
Now what is your petition? It will be giv-
en you. What is your request? It will also
be granted."[l]
13"If it pleases the king," Esther answered, "give the Jews in Susa permission
to carry out this day's edict tomorrow
also, and let Haman's ten sons[m] be impaled[n] on poles."
14So the king commanded that this be
done. An edict was issued in Susa, and
they impaled[o] the ten sons of Haman.
15The Jews in Susa came together on the
fourteenth day of the month of Adar, and
they put to death in Susa three hundred
men, but they did not lay their hands on
the plunder.[p]
16Meanwhile, the remainder of the Jews
who were in the king's provinces also assembled to protect themselves and get relief[q] from their enemies.[r] They killed seventy-five thousand of them[s] but did not
lay their hands on the plunder. 17This happened on the thirteenth day of the month
of Adar, and on the fourteenth they rested
and made it a day of feasting[t] and joy.
18The Jews in Susa, however, had assembled on the thirteenth and fourteenth,
and then on the fifteenth they rested and
made it a day of feasting and joy.
19That is why rural Jews—those living
in villages—observe the fourteenth of the
month of Adar[u] as a day of joy and feasting, a day for giving presents to each other.[v]

Purim Established

20Mordecai recorded these events, and
he sent letters to all the Jews throughout

8:15 [t]Ge 41:42 [u]Est 3:15 **8:16** [v]Ps 97:10-12 [w]Ps 112:4 **8:17** [x]Est 9:19, 27; Ps 35:27; Pr 11:10 [y]Ex 15:14, 16; Dt 11:25 [z]Est 9:3 **9:1** [a]Est 8:12 [b]Jer 29:4-7 [c]Est 3:12-14; Pr 22:22-23 **9:2** [d]ver 15-18 [e]Est 8:11, 17; Ps 71:13, 24 **9:3** [f]Ezr 8:36 **9:4** [g]Ex 11:3 [h]2Sa 3:1; 1Ch 11:9 **9:5** [i]Ezr 4:6 **9:10** [j]Est 5:11 [k]Ge 14:23; 1Sa 14:32; Est 3:13; 8:11

9:12 [l]Est 5:6; 7:2 **9:13** [m]Est 5:11 [n]Dt 21:22-23 **9:14** [o]Ezr 6:11 **9:15** [p]Ge 14:23; Est 8:11 **9:16** [q]Est 4:14 [r]Dt 25:19 [s]1Ch 4:43 **9:17** [t]1Ki 3:15 **9:19** [u]Est 3:7 [v]ver 22; Dt 16:11, 14; Ne 8:10, 12; Est 2:9; Rev 11:10

8:17 *became Jews.* The Hebrew verb occurs nowhere else in the OT, but there is little question about its translation. Its significance, however, is more problematic. What was the "fear of the Jews" that had seized them? Does the text mean only that many Gentiles sided with the Jews in order to avoid destruction? This interpretation seems unlikely. The lives of the Gentiles were not endangered; the Jews were authorized to kill only those who attacked them. Or is the idea here that the Gentiles were so impressed by the rise of Esther and Mordecai that they converted to Judaism? There is little evidence that Jews were actively seeking proselytes in this era. While they accepted those who wished to adhere to their faith, there is no evidence that the Jewish people were preaching or engaging in activities designed to convert Gentiles. Stories of Gentiles converting to Judaism (Rahab, etc.) were meant to demonstrate the superiority of Judaism to Jewish readers rather than to encourage Gentiles to adopt Judaism.

9:2 *those determined to destroy them.* The Jews did not carry out a general annihilation of everyone who disliked them. Rather, their hostility was reserved for those who attacked them. The total number of the dead—75,000 (v. 16)—is extremely large. By comparison, the number of Persian males in the empire's army was reported to be 120,000 (native Persians were reported to comprise the bulk of the army). The entire population of the Persian Empire in this era has been estimated by modern scholars at 50 million people.

9:10 *did not lay their hands on the plunder.* Xerxes' edict granted the Jews the right to plunder the spoil of their enemies (8:11), completely reversing Haman's decree. The Jews' refusal to touch the plunder might be designed to demonstrate that the slaughter was not motivated by greed. But it seems more likely that their restraint reflects the fact that the conflict is presented as a showdown between Israel and Amalek (see note on 3:1). Since God had forbidden the Israelites from taking plunder from the Amalekites (1Sa 15:3), they took no spoil from their enemies in this battle either.

the provinces of King Xerxes, near and far,
21 to have them celebrate annually the fourteenth and fifteenth days of the month of
Adar 22 as the time when the Jews got relief[w] from their enemies, and as the month
when their sorrow was turned into joy and
their mourning into a day of celebration.[x]
He wrote them to observe the days as days
of feasting and joy and giving presents of
food[y] to one another and gifts to the poor.
23 So the Jews agreed to continue the
celebration they had begun, doing what
Mordecai had written to them. 24 For Haman son of Hammedatha, the Agagite,[z]
the enemy of all the Jews, had plotted
against the Jews to destroy them and had
cast the *pur*[a] (that is, the lot[b]) for their
ruin and destruction. 25 But when the plot
came to the king's attention,[a] he issued
written orders that the evil scheme Haman had devised against the Jews should
come back onto his own head,[c] and that
he and his sons should be impaled[d] on
poles.[e] 26 (Therefore these days were
called Purim, from the word *pur*.[f]) Because of everything written in this letter
and because of what they had seen and
what had happened to them, 27 the Jews
took it on themselves to establish the custom that they and their descendants and
all who join them should without fail observe these two days every year, in the
way prescribed and at the time appointed. 28 These days should be remembered
and observed in every generation by every
family, and in every province and in every
city. And these days of Purim should never fail to be celebrated by the Jews — nor
should the memory of these days die out
among their descendants.
29 So Queen Esther, daughter of Abihail,[g]
along with Mordecai the Jew, wrote with
full authority to confirm this second letter
concerning Purim. 30 And Mordecai sent
letters to all the Jews in the 127 provinces[h] of Xerxes' kingdom — words of goodwill and assurance — 31 to establish these
days of Purim at their designated times, as
Mordecai the Jew and Queen Esther had
decreed for them, and as they had established for themselves and their descendants in regard to their times of fasting[i]
and lamentation.[j] 32 Esther's decree confirmed these regulations about Purim, and
it was written down in the records.

The Greatness of Mordecai

10 King Xerxes imposed tribute
throughout the empire, to its distant shores.[k] 2 And all his acts of power
and might, together with a full account
of the greatness of Mordecai,[l] whom the
king had promoted,[m] are they not written
in the book of the annals[n] of the kings of
Media and Persia? 3 Mordecai the Jew was
second[o] in rank[p] to King Xerxes,[q] preeminent among the Jews, and held in high
esteem by his many fellow Jews, because
he worked for the good of his people and
spoke up for the welfare of all the Jews.[r]

9:22 [w] Est 4:14 [x] Ne 8:12; Ps 30:11-12 [y] 2Ki 25:30 **9:24** [z] Ex 17:8-16 [a] Est 3:7 [b] Lev 16:8 **9:25** [c] Ps 7:16 [d] Dt 21:22-23 [e] Est 7:10 **9:26** [f] ver 20; Est 3:7 **9:29** [g] Est 2:15 **9:30** [h] Est 1:1 **9:31** [i] Est 4:16 [j] Est 4:1-3 **10:1** [k] Ps 72:10; 97:1; Isa 24:15 **10:2** [l] Est 8:15; 9:4 [m] Ge 41:44 [n] Est 2:23 **10:3** [o] Da 5:7 [p] Ge 41:43 [q] Ge 41:40 [r] Ne 2:10; Jer 29:4-7; Da 6:3

[a] 25 Or *when Esther came before the king*

9:22 *days of feasting and joy and giving presents.* Just as the book of Esther seems very "secular," without religious content, so too the celebration of the Jews' victory was designed as a secular celebration. There were no prayers, sacrifices or other religious observances prescribed for the day. In Jewish tradition, the central feature of the celebration (called Purim) is the reading of the scroll of Esther in the synagogue. Through the years, this reading has become a riotous affair, accompanied by noisemakers, costumes and heavy drinking. Indeed, the rabbis commanded Jewish revelers to drink until they could no longer distinguish between "Blessed be Mordecai" and "Cursed be Haman."
9:23 *agreed to continue the celebration.* This festival — the festival of Purim (v. 26) — is the first festival adopted by the Jews that was not commanded by the Mosaic Law. The book of Esther does not demand that its readers observe Purim; rather, it describes how the Jews "establish a custom" (v. 28) to be followed throughout their generations. Another Jewish festival was later established in the same manner, when the Jews added the celebration of Hanukkah, commemorating the Hasmoneans' victory over Antiochus Epiphanes in 164 BC.
9:26 *Purim.* Scholars have questioned whether the title "Purim" could actually be derived from the *"pur"* that Haman cast. First, there is the fact that the festival is called "lots" rather than "lot," since only one lot was cast (3:7; in Hebrew, unlike English, a singular "lot" is cast). The second problem is that the lot plays a minor (and wholly negative) part in the story of the Jews' deliverance. One theory holds that Purim was originally a Babylonian religious festival, and that Mordecai and Esther are Hebraized personifications of the Babylonian gods Marduk and Ishtar. More recently, scholars have contended that Purim was derived from a Babylonian or Persian New Year festival. At such festivals, it was commonly believed that the gods cast "lots" to determine the fates of humanity for the coming year. But there is no evidence of a pagan festival called "Purim," so such reconstructions are wholly hypothetical.

OLD TESTAMENT

WISDOM AND HYMNIC LITERATURE

GOD'S WISDOM AND KINGSHIP

Introduction to Wisdom and Hymnic Literature

In 1Ki 4:30 we are informed that Solomon's wisdom was greater than "all the people of the East." This indicates that there was an international wisdom tradition and that the Israelites were aware of it. Such a tradition is confirmed by the texts that have been unearthed throughout the Near East. There are over a dozen texts from Egypt that are classified as "Instruction" texts. Several literary works from Mesopotamia tackle the problem of the innocent sufferer, as does the book of Job. Collections of proverbs from as early as Sumerian times can be fruitfully compared with the Biblical book of Proverbs.

Hymnic literature is also attested internationally. Comparative literature, mostly from Egypt and Mesopotamia, helps us to understand the genres, literary forms and subject matter of the Biblical psalms. Hymns of praise are most common, but the Biblical psalms of lament find some parallel in the incantation literature as well. There are a few examples in which a case can be made for Biblical psalms being adapted from pieces known from the ancient Near East. Other comparisons suggest that compositions known in the ancient Near East were adapted from Israel's psalms. Comparative study of the book of Psalms will throw into sharp relief some of the key differences that can be identified in Israelite religious thought and practice by locating the Biblical psalms along the continuum of ancient Near Eastern literature. ◆

WISDOM AND HYMNIC LITERATURE

JOB

Date

The date of the story remains a problem, and opinions on this range from the time of the patriarchs in the second millennium BC to the Persian period in the fourth century BC; the seventh to the fifth centuries BC has also been proposed. Job is mentioned as an ancient hero (with Noah and Daniel) in Eze 14:14,20. Noah is the flood hero from the time before Abraham (Ge 6 – 10), and Daniel (Danel) is known from the Late Bronze Age (1350 – 1190 BC) Ugaritic story of Aqhat, which indicates that the story might go back to the international lore of the Bronze Age or second millennium BC, although it could have been written down later and edited in (say) the sixth to fifth centuries BC. The point is that the time period of the events need not be considered the time period of the composition.

KEY CONCEPTS

- The fallen world does not operate by justice.
- There is such a thing as disinterested righteousness, and it is the ideal to be pursued.
- Believing that God is wise, we can trust him to be just.
- In situations of suffering, it is better to focus on the future (what *purpose* God has) rather than the past (what the *cause* of suffering is).

Theme

Central to the book of Job is the question of human suffering — especially why people who are seemingly innocent suffer, which in turn raises the question about the righteousness of a loving God. Job deals with the question of *retribution*, the popular theology according to which the righteous prosper but the wicked suffer, as well as the justice of the deity (so-called *theodicy*). Job's suffering but also his perseverance (e.g., see Jas 5:11) have become proverbial in everyday speech. The problems addressed by the book of Job are truly part of universal human experience and therefore of world literature.

Wisdom accounts of pious and presumed innocent sufferers have surfaced across the ancient Near East (see the article "Innocent Suffering in Ancient Near Eastern Texts," p. 821). These demonstrate that the concern was as universal in the ancient world as it remains today. Analysis of these pieces will reveal some literary similarities and expose some comparable questions and concerns. The book of Job, nevertheless, offers a different and much more sophisticated answer, and rather than seeking to explain Job's suffering, it offers insight into how to think about God. ◆

Prologue

1 In the land of Uz[a] there lived a man
whose name was Job.[b] This man was
blameless[c] and upright; he feared God[d]
and shunned evil. 2He had seven sons and
three daughters,[e] 3and he owned seven
thousand sheep, three thousand camels,
five hundred yoke of oxen and five hundred donkeys, and had a large number of
servants. He was the greatest man[f] among
all the people of the East.

4His sons used to hold feasts in their
homes on their birthdays, and they would
invite their three sisters to eat and drink
with them. 5When a period of feasting had
run its course, Job would make arrangements for them to be purified. Early in the
morning he would sacrifice a burnt offering[g] for each of them, thinking, "Perhaps
my children have sinned[h] and cursed God[i]
in their hearts." This was Job's regular
custom.

1:1 [a] Jer 25:20 [b] Eze 14:14, 20; Jas 5:11 [c] Ge 6:9; 17:1 [d] Ge 22:12; Ex 18:21 **1:2** [e] Job 42:13 **1:3** [f] Job 29:25 **1:5** [g] Ge 8:20; Job 42:8 [h] Job 8:4 [i] 1Ki 21:10, 13

1:1 *the land of Uz.* Job's homeland has yet to be positively identified. Uz is a region, not a city, and "the East" (v. 3) is associated with the Syrian Desert stretching from Mesopotamia to Arabia. In Biblical genealogies, Uz is sometimes connected with Aram (e.g., Ge 10:23; 22:21; 1Ch 1:17) and at other times with Edom (e.g., Ge 36:21,28; 1Ch 1:42; La 4:21 and probably Jer 25:20). Edom has been preferred over Aram, based on Edom's reputation for wisdom and Eliphaz the Temanite's origin from the area of Edom (see 2:11 and note). In an appendix to the book of Job, the Septuagint, the pre-Christian Greek translation of the OT, locates Uz between Idumea and Arabia, causing the earliest analysis to situate it in the south. Regardless of its location, this detail is significant, because it indicates that Job is not an Israelite. His non-Israelite status explains the absence of many key theological elements in the book, including law, covenant, temple and reference to Yahweh. Intriguingly, however, the book frequently evidences an Israelite theological perspective (see the article "How the Book of Job Differs From Ancient Near Eastern Thinking," p. 824, point 5), thus suggesting that the story of the non-Israelite Job has actually been given its literary shape by an Israelite author for an Israelite audience (see the article "Ways in Which Job Thinks Like an Israelite," p. 826).

1:2 *seven sons and three daughters.* Part of the wealth, prosperity and happiness of the blameless and upright Job. The number seven often occurs in Ancient Near Eastern literature; it indicates the ideal family (cf. 1Sa 2:5; Ru 4:15) and is therefore retained in Job 42:13. The gods Baal and Mot have seven assistants ("lads") and Baal has three daughters (Pidray, Tallay and Arsay). The epic of king Keret from Ugarit, which has been compared to the book of Job, deals with his calamities and states that he lost everything when a "seventh" son fell by the sword.

1:5 *burnt offering.* Job's repeated rituals do not suggest that he considers his children to be closet apostates, hurling drunken insults heavenward. Instead, he considers that anytime such revelry occurs, the possibility exists that unguarded statements could be made at which God would take offense despite the innocent intentions of the

JOB 1:1

Chronological Context of the Character Job

Scholars have traditionally placed the events of this book in the patriarchal period, citing the absence of any reference to covenant or law. Two facts join to support the conclusion that the book is set before the time of Moses: Job's service as the family priest and the lack of reference to sanctuary. Against such an inference, we need only note that Job is not an Israelite (he is from the land of Uz). We would therefore not expect any reference to covenant or law, priest or temple.

We could explore some of the potential historical references in the book, such as to the Sabeans (Job 1:15) and Chaldeans (Job 1:17), but such studies do not yield consistent results. Many have also focused on the specialized language of the book, such as the arcane term *qesitah* ("piece of silver," Job 42:11), a unit of money found elsewhere only in early literature (e.g., Ge 33:19; Jos 24:32). But these give little to go on. Scholars do not contest that the book contains arcane features, but there is not sufficient information to date either the setting of the story or the composition of the book with any confidence. Even if we could provide such dates, it would make no difference in the interpretation of the book. ◆

6One day the angels[a][j] came to present
themselves before the LORD, and Satan[b]
also came with them.[k] 7The LORD said to
Satan, "Where have you come from?"
Satan answered the LORD, "From roaming throughout the earth, going back and
forth on it."[l]
8Then the LORD said to Satan, "Have you
considered my servant Job?[m] There is no
one on earth like him; he is blameless and
upright, a man who fears God and shuns
evil."[n]
9"Does Job fear God for nothing?"[o] Satan replied. 10"Have you not put a hedge
around him and his household and everything he has?[p] You have blessed the work
of his hands, so that his flocks and herds
are spread throughout the land.[q] 11But
now stretch out your hand and strike everything he has,[r] and he will surely curse
you to your face."[s]

1:6 [j] Job 38:7 [k] Job 2:1
1:7 [l] 1Pe 5:8
1:8 [m] Jos 1:7; Job 42:7-8 [n] ver 1
1:9 [o] 1Ti 6:5
1:10 [p] Ps 34:7 [q] ver 3; Job 29:6; 31:25; Ps 128:1-2
1:11 [r] Job 19:21 [s] Job 2:5

12The LORD said to Satan, "Very well,
then, everything he has is in your power,
but on the man himself do not lay a finger."
Then Satan went out from the presence
of the LORD.
13One day when Job's sons and daughters were feasting and drinking wine at
the oldest brother's house, 14a messenger
came to Job and said, "The oxen were
plowing and the donkeys were grazing
nearby, 15and the Sabeans[t] attacked and
made off with them. They put the servants
to the sword, and I am the only one who
has escaped to tell you!"
16While he was still speaking, another messenger came and said, "The fire of
God fell from the heavens[u] and burned up
the sheep and the servants,[v] and I am the
only one who has escaped to tell you!"

1:15 [t] Ge 10:7; Job 6:19
1:16 [u] Ge 19:24 [v] Lev 10:2; Nu 11:1-3

[a] 6 Hebrew *the sons of God* [b] 6 Hebrew *satan* means *adversary.*

speaker. In the ancient world outside of Israel, the gods were considered to be unrealistic and almost childish in taking offense. A Neo-Assyrian prayer, e.g., expresses an individual's confusion over all that is going wrong in his life. He begins listing all the unintentional ways that he might have offended some deity or other: Did he accidentally step on sacred space of some known or unknown god? Did he eat some food forbidden by a known or unknown god?

It is worth exploring whether Job was thinking of God in these terms. In the ancient world, religious duty was more concerned with ritual than with ethics. In this view, one could not really know what would please the gods, so they were given gifts to keep them happy. This appeasement mentality carried with it the idea that deity was inclined toward irrational behavior. The gods had needs, and one tried to keep the gods content by meeting those needs (ritually). Ethical behavior was not neglected, but it was not among the primary religious responsibilities. This question is important here, because the chosen example clouds the issue of whether or not Job's behavior demonstrates an appeasement mentality toward an overly sensitive deity. In this way of thinking, God might suddenly become upset if someone were to commit a ritual offense in ignorance. Gods were often suspected of taking offense where none was intended. When Job begins to suffer, we see that he does consider that his troubles might be due to an overly attentive deity (7:17 – 21).

We can see, then, that the description of Job leaves no doubt that he is righteous. However, the chosen example does not clarify his motives for being righteous, and it leaves unresolved the question of Job's picture of God. Once we see the issue in this light, we can see how this verse leads directly to the challenge posed by the adversary, which was precisely on that point. If Job is engaged in the appeasement mentality of the Great Symbiosis (see the articles "Great Symbiosis," p. 186, and "How the Book of Job Differs From Ancient Near Eastern Thinking," p. 824), then it would be legitimate to ask, "Does Job fear God for nothing?" (v. 9). If sacrilege can be inadvertent and if ritual is a shot in the dark to try to appease any such inadvertent word at which that deity make have taken offense, the deity has no integrity, and no motivation remains for righteousness, except to reap benefits from a patronized god. It is Job's fastidious ritual conduct that gives the opportunity for the question to be raised by the adversary.

1:6 *angels.* Lit. "sons of God" (also in 2:1; 38:7; see NIV text notes), as in Ge 6:2,4; Dt 32:8; Ps 29:1, 89:7. *came to present themselves before the LORD.* Sets a scene in heaven in the "divine council," a concept well known in ancient Near Eastern literature (see the article "Divine Council," p. 615).
1:8 *blameless.* As is the case of the high priest Joshua in Zec 3:1 – 2, Job the blameless stands accused. The issue of the suffering of the innocent is also dealt with in other ancient Near Eastern texts. This blamelessness is not absolute, but relative to human standards. Neither the OT nor the literature of the ancient Near East have concepts of original sin that are equivalent to the Christian doctrine. In the ancient Near East, the gods had built evil into human civilization from the beginning. In Israel, it was understood that humans possessed an innate inclination to sin.
1:9 *Does Job fear God for nothing?* The question has roots in the ancient Near East. In what we have called the "Great Symbiosis," (see the articles "Great Symbiosis," p. 186, and "How the Book of Job Differs From Ancient Near Eastern Thinking," p. 824), people find protection and prosperity when they are loyal to the god and meet his needs. The question here is whether or not Job is acting just like everyone else in the ancient Near East — being fastidiously righteous because he is convinced that this is what will bring the favor of a deity. This is based in another common idea in the ancient world called the Retribution Principle: the premise that the righteous will prosper and the wicked will suffer (see the article "Retribution Principle," p. 823).
1:15 *Sabeans.* Not the tribes from southern Arabia (Sheba), but rather those from Tema in northern Arabia (cf. 6:19), although the southern Sabeans might have had commercial colonies in the north. Sabeans are mentioned by the Assyrian kings as having given them gifts. *put ... to the sword.* Killed. The animals were taken away as plunder.
1:16 *fire of God.* Might refer to lightning or thunder. *burned up.* The Hebrew means "ate," as in Nu 26:10, where the fire "devoured" (the same Hebrew verb as is used in Job) 250 rebellious men. Fire could be used by the deity as a form of judgment, as in the Hebrew Bible (e.g., Ge 19:24; 2Ki 1:10,12,14; Ps 21:9; Am 1:4,7,10,12,14; 2:2,5; especially Am 7:4 [also with the verb "eat"]) and other ancient Near Eastern texts. The god Ashur "ignited against the foes the

JOB 1:6

SATAN

The Hebrew word *satan* has traditionally been rendered as the proper name "Satan." This decision leads casual readers to associate this being ("accuser," "adversary"—the meaning of the Hebrew word) with the devil, named as Satan in the NT (e.g., Rev 12:9). However, every time this word occurs in Job, it is preceded by the definite article (*hassatan*). This is strong evidence that *satan* is not a personal name, because Hebrew does not put a definite article in front of personal names. There is therefore also little reason to equate this character with the devil, since it can be used to describe other individuals by function; it is applied to human beings in 1Sa 29:4 ("he [David] will turn against"); 1Ki 5:4 ("adversary" [generic human]); 11:14 ("adversary" [Hadad]); 11:23,25 ("adversary" [Rezon]); Ps 109:6 ("accuser" [generic human]), and even to the angel of the Lord in Nu 22:22 ("oppose"). We should therefore understand the word to indicate the office or function of the individual so designated. The character need not be intrinsically evil. Though interpreters commonly portray this so-called adversary as one who seeks out human failings, God's policies are the true focus of the challenge. Job's character is only the test case. The challenge therefore does not necessarily imply some flaw in God or in Job.

Some infer that this so-called adversary relishes the opportunity to strike at Job, but the text does not attribute to him (or to God) any personal emotional response to Job's tragedy. God carries more responsibility for striking Job than the adversary does (Job 1:12; 2:3), and both lack any sympathetic response. It is arbitrary, therefore, to assume that the adversary enjoys Job's suffering, while God sadly endures it. Nothing intrinsically evil emerges from the profile of the adversary in the book of Job. What he does has negative consequences for Job, a righteous man, but the text is clear that God is at least equally responsible; thus, the actions cannot be implicitly evil. There is no tempting, corrupting, depraving or possessing involved; in fact, there is little if any overlap with the character Satan from the NT. The adversary in Job should therefore not be equated with the devil of later literature. ◆

17While he was still speaking, another messenger came and said, "The Chaldeans[w] formed three raiding parties and
swept down on your camels and made off
with them. They put the servants to the
sword, and I am the only one who has escaped to tell you!"
18While he was still speaking, yet another
messenger came and said, "Your sons and
daughters were feasting and drinking wine at
the oldest brother's house, 19when suddenly
a mighty wind[x] swept in from the desert and
struck the four corners of the house. It collapsed on them and they are dead, and I am
the only one who has escaped to tell you!"
20At this, Job got up and tore his robe[y]
and shaved his head. Then he fell to the
ground in worship[z] 21and said:

1:17 [w] Ge 11:28, 31
1:19 [x] Jer 4:11; 13:24
1:20 [y] Ge 37:29 [z] 1Pe 5:6

deterring fire ... Enlil set the flame in the midst of the foe" and the goddess Ishtar, who is called "Flaming-Fire-of-Battle," describes herself by saying, "I am the burning fire showered upon the land of the foe."

1:17 *Chaldeans.* Not the same peoples as those in the later seventh-century BC imperialistic Neo-Babylonian dynasty who subsequently destroyed Jerusalem in 586 BC. Here it refers to the earlier unsettled tribes who (together with, but still a separate group from Aramean groups) infiltrated Mesopotamia at the beginning of the first millennium BC and are mentioned in Assyrian sources in the tenth century BC as living in southern Mesopotamia. In contrast to the urbanized societies, they lived in tribal groups and were raiders of cities and caravans.

1:19 *wind ... from the desert.* This is not only the scorching eastern desert wind (*sirocco* or *khamsin*, cf. 15:2), but a sudden mighty wind that brought total destruction. As described in Job, it struck the four sides of the house at once.

1:20 *tore his robe ... shaved his head ... fell to the ground.* Gestures of extreme grief and mourning, comparable to the gesture undertaken by the friends in 2:12–13 (see the article "Mourning," p. 828). Tearing the clothes and shaving

"Naked I came from my mother's
womb,
and naked I will depart.[a]a
The LORD gave and the LORD has taken
away;b
may the name of the LORD be
praised."c
22In all this, Job did not sin by charging
God with wrongdoing.d

1:21 a Ecc 5:15; 1Ti 6:7 b 1Sa 2:7 c Job 2:10; Eph 5:20; 1Th 5:18 **1:22** d Job 2:10
2:1 e Job 1:6

2 On another day the angels[b] came to
present themselves before the LORD,
and Satan also came with theme to present
himself before him. 2And the LORD said to
Satan, "Where have you come from?"
Satan answered the LORD, "From roaming throughout the earth, going back and
forth on it."

[a] 21 Or *will return there* [b] 1 Hebrew *the sons of God*

the head to indicate grief are known from the Bible (e.g., 2Sa 1:1–2; Am 8:10) and were prevalent in the ancient Near East. The Mesopotamian king Marduk-Baladan I, e.g., "threw himself to the ground, he rent his [garment], he shaved, and he uttered a lament."
2:1 *Satan also came ... to present himself.* See note on 1:6.

JOB 1:8–22

INNOCENT SUFFERING IN ANCIENT NEAR EASTERN TEXTS

Texts dealing with a seemingly innocent person who suffers were widespread in the ancient world, especially in the ancient Near East. The Egyptian text "The Dialogue of a Man with His Soul" describes someone who asks in his misery whether it would not be better to commit suicide. In other texts (the Ipuwer Papyrus and the Teaching for King Merikare) the "discourse of theodicy" receives attention and the question is asked: "Is he [God] incapable of getting influenced against evil and injustice?"

The Sumerian "A Man and His God," which goes back to the beginning of the second millennium BC, is a long, personal, lamenting monologue, in which a pious sufferer has a feeling of guilt and asks for forgiveness, and the god turns his suffering into joy.

The category closest to the book of Job is that of Akkadian dialogues, such as the Babylonian *Ludlul bel nemeqi* ("I will praise the lord of wisdom") or "The Babylonian Theodicy." The *Ludlul*, from the sixteenth through twelfth centuries BC, describes a pious but not necessarily innocent person who suffers from an illness, which is described in great detail. He is rejected by his peers, and even his brother has become his enemy. Ignored by the gods, he summarizes his dilemma: "What seems good to one's self could be an offence to a god, / What in one's own heart seems abominable could be good to one's god."

"The Babylonian Theodicy" (c. 1000 BC) comes closest to the book of Job. It is in the form of a dialogue, and the sufferer, like Job, is in a dispute with his friends, although he has only one unnamed friend. There is not such harshness in the dispute as found in the book of Job. At the end, the sufferer expresses this wish: "May the god who has cast me off grant help, / May the goddess who has [forsaken me] take pity."

The Mesopotamian examples agree that no one is righteous, that suffering is part and parcel of the human condition and that it is not certain what is right or wrong in the eyes of the gods. Humans cannot fathom the divine mind (Job 11:7–9). This idea was already seen in the quotation from the *Ludlul* above. In "The Babylonian Theodicy": "Divine purpose is as remote as innermost heaven, / It is too difficult to understand." And in "The Dialogue of Pessimism": "Who is tall enough to ascend to the heavens? Who is broad enough to encompass the earth?"

continued on next page

In the polytheistic religions of the ancient Near East, innocent suffering could be attributed to another deity or to demons. There were protective deities to whom one could turn when the main deities could no longer be relied upon. For Job, the situation is more complicated: If there is only one God, what do you do if he has become your enemy? ◆

MESOPOTAMIAN LITERATURE COMPARED WITH JOB

LITERATURE	STATUS	CONDITION	RESOLUTION	OUTCOME	PHILOSOPHY	THEOLOGY
A Man and His God (Sumerian)	Ignorant of offense	Illness; social outcast	Sins confessed	Restored to health	No sinless child born	Results in hymn of praise
Dialogue between a Man and His God (Akkadian)	Ignorant of offense	Illness	Text broken	Restored to health	None offered	Divine favor assured
Sufferer's Salvation[33] (Akkadian, from Ugarit)	No comment	Illness; death imminent; omens obscure	No indication	Restored to health	God brought his suffering then brought his healing	Results in hymn of praise to Marduk
Ludlul bel nemeqi (Akkadian)	Conscientious piety; ignorant of offense	Social outcast; omens obscure; illness; protective spirits chased away; demon oppression	Dream appearance	Purification bringing appeasement; offenses borne away; demons expelled; restored to health	Gods are inscrutable	Results in hymn of praise to Marduk
Babylonian Theodicy (Akkadian)	Claims piety	Family gone; poverty	none	none	Purposes of gods remote; Retribution Principle (RP) unreliable	Gods make people with evil inclinations and prone to suffering
Job (Hebrew)	Claims righteousness and conscientious piety	Family taken; social outcast; illness; wealth taken	Yahweh offers new perspective based on wisdom	Restoration at all levels	Retribution Principle (RP) unreliable; divine wisdom is foundation	God's justice is granted given his wisdom

[3]Then the LORD said to Satan, "Have you
considered my servant Job? There is no
one on earth like him; he is blameless and
upright, a man who fears God and shuns
evil.[f] And he still maintains his integrity,[g]
though you incited me against him to ruin
him without any reason."[h]
[4]"Skin for skin!" Satan replied. "A man
will give all he has for his own life. [5]But
now stretch out your hand and strike his
flesh and bones,[i] and he will surely curse
you to your face."[j]
[6]The LORD said to Satan, "Very well,
then, he is in your hands; but you must
spare his life."[k]
[7]So Satan went out from the presence
of the LORD and afflicted Job with painful sores from the soles of his feet to the

2:3 [f]Job 1:1, 8 [g]Job 27:6 [h]Job 9:17
2:5 [i]Job 19:20 [j]Job 1:11
2:6 [k]Job 1:12

2:7 *sores.* Job suffered from a skin disease, but it is not certain what kind. Leprosy has been proposed because of the resemblance with the description of skin diseases in Lev 13, but the Hebrew word describing the condition in Leviticus is different than the one used in Job. The word used in Job is related to one used in the Ugaritic texts of the god Baal, who grew hot or feverish, and it is also used in the Aramaic prayer of Nabonidus from Qumran,

JOB 1:9 – 10

Retribution Principle

The Retribution Principle (RP) is the conviction that the righteous will prosper and the wicked will suffer, in proportion to both their respective righteousness and wickedness. In Israelite theology, the principle is integral to the belief in God's justice. Since God is just, Israelites believed it was incumbent on him to uphold the RP. Having a worldview in which God is absolutely just and compelled to maintain the RP, the Israelites developed the inevitable converse corollary, which affirmed that those who prospered must be righteous (i.e., favored by God) and those who suffered must be wicked (i.e., experiencing the judgment of God).

The literature of the ancient Near East continually demonstrates that people believed that the administration of justice in the human world was a concern and responsibility of the gods. The questions that swirl around the RP, however, lose their philosophical urgency in the ancient world, because injustice is often blamed on demons and humans, rather than on the gods. In Mesopotamian thinking, evil was built into the fabric of the cosmos by means of the so-called cosmic laws, but even those were not established by the gods. Since evil existed outside of the jurisdiction of the gods, divine administration of justice did not necessarily eliminate suffering. Some misfortune came about simply because of how the world was. In both Egyptian and Mesopotamian thinking, the gods were not considered responsible for evil in the world, and therefore the presence or experience of evil did not have to be resolved in reference to the justice of the gods (this in contrast to Israelite thinking, in which nothing existed totally outside the jurisdiction of God's sovereignty — i.e., the rest of the gods were contingent; Yahweh was not). In the Sumerian "Lament Over the Destruction of Ur," the city is destroyed not as an act of justice or injustice, but because it was time for kingship to be passed on. Likewise with regard to individuals, suffering could sometimes be seen as just one's fate for the present. It is also clear that personal misfortune could result from offending the gods, even if the offense were committed innocently. In such cases, the gods were not unjust — they simply were not very forthcoming about communicating their expectations.

A sense and expectation of RP at a basic level remains evident in the ancient Near East, though the gods are relieved of responsibility because of the way their function in the cosmos is perceived. Even in the areas in which the gods could be held responsible, they, like human judges, may be doing their best to administer justice, but doing so imperfectly.

In this sense, though people of Mesopotamia might have believed that the gods did indeed punish those who earned their wrath, this conviction could not offer an explanation for all suffering. The notion that those who suffer must be wicked could not work, because in the ancient Near Eastern worldview, much of the suffering that people experienced was not orchestrated by the gods. Suffering could be the result of the god's inattention, of simple circumstance or of the nature of the world. Even if the gods abandoned a person because of some offense, they were not responsible for the ensuing evil — they simply did nothing to prevent it, having withdrawn their favor and protection. ◆

JOB 1

How the Book of Job Differs From Ancient Near Eastern Thinking

1. The nature of the suffering is different. In the ancient Near Eastern exemplars, the major difficulty is health related. Because of retribution-principle thinking, sudden serious illness was generally assumed to result from the gods' disfavor. Such illness inevitably led to social rejection, for if a god were angry with the sick individual, one would not want to be associated with that person. If a demon were causing the problem, it would likewise be best to keep one's distance. As the literature indicates, then, serious illness made one a social outcast. In contrast, Job loses his wealth and his family before he loses his health. The Mesopotamian pieces touch on poverty and lost family, but these are not presented as major issues.

2. The nature of the offenses considered in Job are never ritual. In the ancient Near East, ritual offense was the most common sort of misdeed that could be committed; though there were ritual expectations for the people, these were devised by society, not revealed by deity. Deity valued order in society, but moral responsibility was not understood as part of the people's responsibility toward the gods. Instead, humans were to care for the gods (through ritual) and would incur the anger of the gods by failing to provide for them. One cannot then easily speak of "righteousness" in the ancient world, only of piety (which here refers to conscientiousness in ritual activity). There was no orthodoxy (right belief) — only orthopraxy (proper performance). In the Mesopotamian pieces, deity is eventually appeased, whether by prayers, laments or rituals. This appeasement of the deity is necessary in these scenarios because the deity is presumed to be angry or inexplicably moody. In Job, there is no appeasement of Yahweh, given that Yahweh is not angry; furthermore, Job specifically rejects the path of appeasement urged by his friends (Job 27:2 – 6). This refusal is important to the book of Job, for Job's pursuit of appeasement would demonstrate that the adversary was right. Appeasement focuses on regaining benefits and tacitly denies the place of righteousness. The adversary had made that precise claim — that supposedly righteous people weren't really righteous, but only behaved righteously to gain benefits (Job 1:9 – 11). The Mesopotamians pursued appeasement because they considered themselves to be in a symbiotic relationship with the gods. The gods had created people to serve their needs; in response to such service, the gods protected the faithful people and provided for them (e.g., fertile fields). This perspective, called the Great Symbiosis, was the foundation of religious thinking in the ancient world (see the article "Great Symbiosis," p. 186). This symbiosis was benefit based: the gods reaped benefits from the labor of humans, and humans reaped benefits from the favor of the gods. This expectation was not based on the belief that the god was just, only that he or she was sensible. The gods needed what humans provided, and they in return were capable in most circumstances of providing protection. The system did not work this way because the gods were just, but because they were needy. The gods in the ancient world did not care about defending their character; they were only concerned to preserve their prerogatives and their executive perquisites. When a god did not receive the cultic rites to which he was entitled, his status was threatened, and his wrath and/or abandonment was predictable. Appeasement was a vital part of this system, and

continued on next page

if Job had pursued appeasement, he would have shown himself to be a part of this system of thought.

3. In the ancient Near Eastern exemplars, the sufferers stand ready to acknowledge their offenses if they could only be shown what they were. They claim ignorance, while Job claims innocence. This stance would have been difficult to maintain in the ancient Near East, for the gods were the ones who decided where sacred spaces were and what rituals needed to be performed. People who lived in Mesopotamia never believed that their information on these issues was comprehensive. Job, in contrast, is confident in his innocence. He is clearly using different standards to make his claims. Job never acknowledges any offense (unlike his Mesopotamian counterparts), and God does not offer forgiveness in the process of restoration.

4. We can identify a number of Mesopotamian pieces that belong to the declarative praise genre, a genre that likewise appears frequently in the Biblical psalms. This genre is characterized by a lament, a petition, a favorable response by God and an ending of praise. This is far different from the book of Job, which includes no concluding praise of Yahweh. The Mesopotamian pieces seem designed to feature praise, while Job omits it entirely.

5. While the themes of justice (God's) and righteousness (Job's) are central to the book of Job, neither is present in the ancient Near Eastern exemplars. Granted, in the ancient world, the gods were interested in justice being maintained in the human realm; Shamash, e.g., was the god of justice, and kings were accountable to him to maintain justice in society. However, the gods desired an equitable society only because a stable and prosperous community most effectively provided for their needs. The gods themselves were neither just nor unjust: they simply did what they wished. They were neither consistent nor predictable, neither moral nor immoral. Notice that the Mesopotamian pieces do not try to defend the justice of God (in the end, neither does the book of Job), nor do they question whether deity is just. The primary concern is the preservation of the parameters and rules of the Great Symbiosis, not of justice. These pieces are all about the relationship between piety and prosperity. The contrasts in Job show it to be a work thoroughly immersed in the Israelite theological system.

6. Just as the gods were not necessarily just in the ancient world, they were likewise not necessarily responsible for evil or suffering. These elements were understood as built into the fabric of the cosmos, but not by the gods or any other beings. Furthermore, demons or humans could be responsible for suffering or evil without necessarily involving the gods. In Israelite thinking, God could not so easily be removed from the equation, though certainly humans could do evil.

7. The piety/prosperity matrix of the Great Symbiosis serves as the foundation of the adversary's accusation against Job. If Job's response indicates that he is bound to this matrix, the adversary has won his case. In other words, if Job is not different from all of the sufferers in the Mesopotamian literature, the adversary has made his point. In this sense, while all of the Mesopotamian pieces end by affirming the traditional dogmas, in Job those very same traditional dogmas are voiced by the friends and persistently rejected by Job.

8. Job focuses on his own righteousness, not on the piety/prosperity matrix. While his Mesopotamian counterparts are not declared innocent at any point throughout the literature, Job is declared so from beginning to end. Unlike his Mesopotamian counterparts, Job never considers the option that he deserves what he is experiencing.

9. In the ancient Near East, when one offended deity by some sort of ritual neglect or misstep, the deity might react by simply turning his back, leaving one vulnerable to demon attack. In this way the deity was not the one actively bringing harm. These demons were not seen as doing the will of the deity—they were simply acting in character by attacking a vulnerable subject. The adversary in Job, however, is not an independent agent opportunistically fulfilling its nature. Whatever he does, he does through the power of God; all the events of the book are understood as God's

continued on next page

actions. Demons in their ancient Near Eastern role are absent from OT theology, including Job.

10. Finally, it is evident that the philosophical and theological answers provided by the book of Job are quite different from those offered in the ancient Near Eastern exemplars. Job rejects the easy answers of Mesopotamia (divine inscrutability, inherent sinfulness of humanity, gods who make humanity crooked). For Job, these premises are acceptable to a degree, but they are not the answers that the book offers. The Mesopotamian literature concludes that pious people do sometimes suffer, but this suffering has nothing to do with divine injustice—it only means that one can never be fully comprehensive in one's ritual performance, and therefore inadvertent offense is always possible. One can only increase one's piety and call out to the gods for mercy with the hope that perhaps they will answer. Is there pious suffering? Yes. But the suffering is no one's fault, just a possibility inherent in the very nature of the gods and the humans who blindly attempt to serve them in the Great Symbiosis. The texts from Mesopotamia consistently fail to affirm or defend the justice of deity. Instead they affirm pervasive and often ignorant offense by humans and the general inscrutability or, more likely, the capriciousness of the gods. In *Ludlul bel Nemeqi* ("I will praise the lord of wisdom") the sufferer expresses the wish that he could know what pleased the gods because it is not intuitive. He concludes that mortals have no understanding of the ways of the gods. The answer offered by the book of Job is quite different. Here the answer is that yes, sometimes righteous people suffer, but this fact should not be the basis for deducing that God is unjust. Rather, it is a flawed philosophy that concludes that one's suffering or prosperity are directly related to one's behavior. The Great Symbiosis is not at the heart of human experience, but neither is the Retribution Principle. Instead, God's wisdom is at the heart of how the world operates and the resulting human experience. In one sense this does suggest that God is inscrutable, but it is not on account of capriciousness. Yahweh's inscrutability is a result of his infinite wisdom in contrast to our human limitations. ◆

JOB 1

Ways in Which Job Thinks Like an Israelite

1. No symbiosis (God does not have needs, Job 22:3)
2. An interest in the justice of God
3. An interest in righteousness as an abstract concept
4. A sense of personal righteousness that goes beyond what the ancient world would have provided
5. No ritual offenses considered or ritual remedies suggested or pursued
6. No appeasement pursued
7. Worship of celestial deities considered an offense (Job 31:26–28), as it would not have been in the ancient Near East
8. Shape of the Retribution Principle different since God could not be absolved of his role in bringing suffering ◆

crown of his head.[l] [8]Then Job took a piece of broken pottery and scraped himself with it as he sat among the ashes.[m]

[9]His wife said to him, "Are you still maintaining your integrity? Curse God and die!"

[10]He replied, "You are talking like a foolish[a] woman. Shall we accept good from God, and not trouble?"[n]

In all this, Job did not sin in what he said.[o]

[11]When Job's three friends, Eliphaz the Temanite,[p] Bildad the Shuhite[q] and Zophar the Naamathite, heard about all the troubles that had come upon him, they set out from their homes and met together by agreement to go and sympathize with him and comfort him.[r] [12]When they saw him from a distance, they could hardly recognize him; they began to weep aloud, and they tore their robes and sprinkled dust on their heads.[s] [13]Then they sat on the ground with him for seven days and seven nights.[t] No one said a word to him, because they saw how great his suffering was.

Job Speaks

3 After this, Job opened his mouth and cursed the day of his birth. [2]He said:

[3]"May the day of my birth perish,
and the night that said, 'A boy is conceived!'[u]
[4]That day—may it turn to darkness;
may God above not care about it;
may no light shine on it.
[5]May gloom and utter darkness[v] claim it once more;
may a cloud settle over it;
may blackness overwhelm it.
[6]That night—may thick darkness[w] seize it;
may it not be included among the days of the year
nor be entered in any of the months.
[7]May that night be barren;
may no shout of joy be heard in it.
[8]May those who curse days[b] curse that day,
those who are ready to rouse Leviathan.[x]
[9]May its morning stars become dark;
may it wait for daylight in vain
and not see the first rays of dawn,[y]
[10]for it did not shut the doors of the womb on me
to hide trouble from my eyes.

[11]"Why did I not perish at birth,
and die as I came from the womb?[z]
[12]Why were there knees to receive me[a]
and breasts that I might be nursed?

2:7 [l] Dt 28:35; Job 7:5 **2:8** [m] Job 42:6; Jer 6:26; Eze 27:30; Mt 11:21 **2:10** [n] Job 1:21 [o] Job 1:22; Ps 39:1; Jas 1:12; 5:11 **2:11** [p] Ge 36:11; Jer 49:7 [q] Ge 25:2 [r] Job 42:11; Ro 12:15 **2:12** [s] Jos 7:6; Ne 9:1; La 2:10; Eze 27:30 **2:13** [t] Ge 50:10; Eze 3:15 **3:3** [u] Job 10:18-19; Jer 20:14-18 **3:5** [v] Job 10:21, 22; Ps 23:4; Jer 2:6; 13:16 **3:6** [w] Job 23:17 **3:8** [x] Job 41:1, 8, 10, 25 **3:9** [y] Job 41:18 **3:11** [z] Job 10:18 **3:12** [a] Ge 30:3; Isa 66:12

[a] *10* The Hebrew word rendered *foolish* denotes moral deficiency. [b] *8* Or *curse the sea*

where it is said that the king was stricken with an inflammation. As is typical of descriptions of medical conditions and symptoms in the ancient world, these do not offer enough information for confident diagnosis.

2:8 *broken pottery ... ashes.* In Akkadian, the term "place/mound of potsherds" could designate the world of the dead. It might be that Job counted himself already as one dead, as do his friends when they sprinkle dust on their heads (v. 12), thereby identifying themselves with the dead (cf. 17:16). Alternatively, the "ashes" could refer to the town dump outside the city limits where dung was periodically burned. *scraped himself.* This action might have been intended to scratch his itching wounds, but perhaps it is rather a gesture of mourning or, at the least, a form of self-mutilation to express his grief.

2:11 *Eliphaz the Temanite, Bildad the Shuhite and Zophar the Naamathite.* Job's friends come from places or regions that are impossible to identify with certainty, but they are presumably situated in the region of Edom.

3:1 *cursed the day of his birth.* In 2:9, Job's wife advises him, "Curse God and die!" Instead, Job curses the day of his birth. In 2:9, the ambiguous Hebrew word *brk* (also "bless") is used, but here the Hebrew word *qll* instead of the stronger *'rr* is used for "curse." Job's wish that he had never been born is repeated in 10:18 and the prophet Jeremiah does the same: "Cursed [*'rr*] be the day I was born! May the day my mother bore me not be blessed [*brk*]!" (Jer 20:14). In the eighth-century BC Assyrian *Myth of Erra and Ishum* a city governor says to his mother that it would have been better if he had never been born or if he had died with her. A lament in the first person occurs in a letter prayer addressed to the Mesopotamian god Enki. Job's lament, therefore, follows a typical path found in the ancient Near East.

3:4 *darkness.* In contrast to "let there be light" as the first act of God's creation (Ge 1:3), Job wishes for darkness (cf. Am 8:9–10), implying that creation should be returned to nonorder, because his life has reverted to nonorder. This is emphasized by the use of words like "night" (v. 3); "no light" (v. 4); "gloom," "darkness" and "blackness" (v. 5); and "thick darkness" (v. 6).

3:8 *curse days ... rouse Leviathan.* In the ancient Near East, Leviathan was seen as the primeval sea monster of chaos (see the article "Leviathan," p. 874) defeated at creation. It represented the raging, destructive flood waters (22:16), and when it was aroused as part of a curse, it implied that chaos would prevail. Calling forth the forces of chaos might be reflected in later Jewish-Aramaic incantations. In the ancient Near East, those who curse days and rouse chaos creatures are typically demons, but Job's reference here is oblique rather than specific.

3:11 *came from the womb.* In 1:21 Job referred to his "mother's womb," which, in that case, probably referred to the earth as a mother, as in Ps 139:13,15, where "mother's womb" is parallel to "depths of the earth." Here, Job wishes that he had died at birth or after he was born, and that he had been hidden in the ground like a stillborn child (v. 16). The same idea occurs in 10:18; Jer 20:17–18.

3:12 *knees to receive me and breasts that I might be nursed.* The knees might refer to Job's father, on whose knees he sat when he was born, as is known from the ancient Near East. In the Hittite myth of Ullikummi, the god Kumarbi dandles the monster on his knee and gives it a name. In Ge 50:23, the grandchildren were placed at birth on

JOB 2:12–13

MOURNING

In the OT, mourning is described in various texts. In Ge 37:34–35 Jacob tears his clothes, puts on sackcloth and weeps; in Ge 50:3 Joseph's friends mourn with him for seven days; in 2Sa 1:2 David tears his clothes and puts dust on his head; in 2Sa 13:19 Tamar puts ashes on her head, tears her mantle, and then puts her hand on her head and weeps aloud; in Ps 35:13–14 sackcloth and fasting characterize the mourner; in Isa 47:1 mourners sit in the dust (cf. Eze 26:16); in La 1:1; 2:10 mourners sit on the ground, sprinkle dust on their heads and wear sackcloth; in Am 8:10 sackcloth and shaved heads describe mourning; and in Jnh 3:6 the Ninevites don sackcloth and sit in the dust. Mourning is known from Egyptian sources, where there are many depictions of wailing women throwing dust on their heads. Philistine clay figurines depict women with their hands on their heads as a gesture of wailing. When the Ugaritic god El hears of the death of Baal, he leaves his throne and sits on the footstool, and from the footstool he sits on the ground. He pours dust of mourning on his head, puts on a loincloth and scratches his skin with a stone. In Ugaritic legend, wailers mourn seven years over the dead hero Aqhat. Gilgamesh mourned seven days over his dead friend Enkidu, as did Nabonidus after the death of his mother. In the Sumerian myth *Inanna's Descent to the Underworld*, deities sit in the dust dressed in sackcloth and scratch their eyes and mouths. These practices show that the Israelites had practices at most levels of culture that were virtually identical to the people around them rather than being a culturally isolated and unique people. Yahweh's revelation to them in general did not change their culture; it changed their theology—particularly regarding how they thought about God. ◆

Grieving widow puts dust on her head as a sign of mourning, 1350–1300 BC.

Wikimedia Commons

[13]For now I would be lying down[b] in
peace;
I would be asleep and at rest[c]
[14]with kings and rulers of the earth,[d]
who built for themselves places
now lying in ruins,[e]
[15]with princes[f] who had gold,
who filled their houses with silver.[g]
[16]Or why was I not hidden away in
the ground like a stillborn
child,[h]
like an infant who never saw the
light of day?
[17]There the wicked cease from turmoil,
and there the weary are at rest.[i]
[18]Captives also enjoy their ease;
they no longer hear the slave
driver's shout.[j]
[19]The small and the great are there,
and the slaves are freed from their
owners.

[20]"Why is light given to those in
misery,
and life to the bitter of soul,[k]
[21]to those who long for death that
does not come,[l]
who search for it more than for
hidden treasure,[m]
[22]who are filled with gladness
and rejoice when they reach the
grave?
[23]Why is life given to a man
whose way is hidden,
whom God has hedged in?[n]
[24]For sighing has become my daily
food;[o]
my groans pour out like water.[p]
[25]What I feared has come upon me;
what I dreaded[q] has happened
to me.
[26]I have no peace, no quietness;
I have no rest,[r] but only turmoil."

3:13 [b]Job 17:13 [c]Job 7:8-10,21; 10:22; 14:10-12; 19:27; 21:13,23 **3:14** [d]Job 12:17 [e]Job 15:28 **3:15** [f]Job 12:21 [g]Job 27:17 **3:16** [h]Ps 58:8; Ecc 6:3 **3:17** [i]Job 17:16 **3:18** [j]Job 39:7 **3:20** [k]1Sa 1:10; Jer 20:18; Eze 27:30-31 **3:21** [l]Rev 9:6 [m]Pr 2:4 **3:23** [n]Job 19:6, 8, 12; Ps 88:8; La 3:7 **3:24** [o]Job 6:7; 33:20 [p]Ps 42:3,4 **3:25** [q]Job 30:15 **3:26** [r]Job 7:4, 14

4:2 [s]Job 32:20 **4:3** [t]Isa 35:3; Heb 12:12 **4:4** [u]Isa 35:3; Heb 12:12 **4:5** [v]Job 19:21 [w]Job 6:14 **4:6** [x]Pr 3:26 [y]Job 1:1 **4:7** [z]Job 36:7 [a]Job 8:20; Ps 37:25 **4:8** [b]Job 15:35 [c]Pr 22:8; Hos 10:13; Gal 6:7-8 **4:9** [d]Job 15:30; Isa 30:33; 2Th 2:8 [e]Job 40:13 **4:10** [f]Job 5:15; Ps 58:6 **4:11** [g]Job 27:14; Ps 34:10 **4:12** [h]Job 26:14 [i]Job 33:14 **4:13** [j]Job 33:15

Eliphaz

4 Then Eliphaz the Temanite replied:

[2]"If someone ventures a word with you,
will you be impatient?
But who can keep from speaking?[s]
[3]Think how you have instructed many,
how you have strengthened feeble
hands.[t]
[4]Your words have supported those who
stumbled;
you have strengthened faltering
knees.[u]
[5]But now trouble comes to you, and
you are discouraged;
it strikes[v] you, and you are
dismayed.[w]
[6]Should not your piety be your
confidence[x]
and your blameless[y] ways your
hope?

[7]"Consider now: Who, being innocent,
has ever perished?[z]
Where were the upright ever
destroyed?[a]
[8]As I have observed, those who plow
evil[b]
and those who sow trouble reap it.[c]
[9]At the breath of God[d] they perish;
at the blast of his anger they are no
more.[e]
[10]The lions may roar and growl,
yet the teeth of the great lions are
broken.[f]
[11]The lion perishes for lack of prey,[g]
and the cubs of the lioness are
scattered.

[12]"A word was secretly brought to me,
my ears caught a whisper[h] of it.[i]
[13]Amid disquieting dreams in the night,
when deep sleep falls on people,[j]

Joseph's knees, and in Isa 66:12, Jerusalem is said to be like a woman with a child on her knees, nursing it. The most famous ancient Near Eastern comparison is that of the Egyptian goddess Isis nursing the young god Horus on her lap, which was applied in representations of the young pharaoh, but also with mortals. An Egyptian stele depicts a father with his child on his knees.

3:13 *lying down in peace; I would be asleep.* Job would have had peace if he had died, but now he has no rest (cf. v. 26). An inscription in the tomb of the Assyrian king Sennacherib reads, "Palace of sleep, tomb of repose."

3:17 *the weary are at rest.* In the Egyptian "Book of the Dead," the deceased are called "the weary," and the heart is weary when death is near, as stated in the Egyptian *Story of Sinuhe.*

3:18–19 In the underworld, social relations are seen as inverted, because in death all are equal. This idea is also reflected in ancient Near Eastern texts such as the Egyptian Ipuwer Papyrus: "Indeed the land turns around like a potter's wheel. Princes are hungry and perish, Servants are served ... The serf becomes lord of serfs."

4:9 *breath of God.* Usually this phrase refers to God's activity (cf. Ge 2:7), but here it refers to a destructive wind from the desert (cf. Isa 40:7; Hos 13:15). The parallel word used in the second line of the verse (NIV "blast"), is the same as that which blew down the house over Job's children in 1:19. One of the most common portrayals of gods in the ancient world is as storm-gods, a portrayal also ascribed to God in Israel (see note on 37:2–5; see also the article "Baal," p. 600 and note on 1Ki 18:38).

4:11 *The lion perishes.* Eliphaz describes the fate of the wicked: "those who plow evil and those who sow trouble reap it" (v. 8). One of his examples is the lion who perishes. "The Babylonian Theodicy" has: "For the atrocity that lion committed, the pit yawns for him." In the ancient Near East, lions were a symbol of self-assertion, as is known from Akkadian texts, but in the imagery here they are destroyed.

4:13 *dreams in the night.* Terrifying dreams also occur in 7:14; 33:15–16. In the Babylonian text *Ludlul bel nemeqi* ("I will praise the lord of wisdom"), the righteous sufferer also has terrifying dreams. Epiphanies or divine revelations

14 fear and trembling seized me
and made all my bones shake.[k]
15 A spirit glided past my face,
and the hair on my body stood on end.
16 It stopped,
but I could not tell what it was.
A form stood before my eyes,
and I heard a hushed voice:
17 'Can a mortal be more righteous than God?[l]
Can even a strong man be more pure than his Maker?[m]
18 If God places no trust in his servants,
if he charges his angels with error,[n]
19 how much more those who live in houses of clay,[o]
whose foundations[p] are in the dust,[q]
who are crushed more readily than a moth!
20 Between dawn and dusk they are broken to pieces;
unnoticed, they perish forever.[r]
21 Are not the cords of their tent pulled up,[s]
so that they die without wisdom?'[t]

5 "Call if you will, but who will answer you?
To which of the holy ones[u] will you turn?
2 Resentment kills a fool,
and envy slays the simple.[v]
3 I myself have seen a fool taking root,[w]
but suddenly his house was cursed.[x]
4 His children are far from safety,[y]
crushed in court[z] without a defender.
5 The hungry consume his harvest,[a]
taking it even from among thorns,
and the thirsty pant after his wealth.
6 For hardship does not spring from the soil,
nor does trouble sprout from the ground.
7 Yet man is born to trouble[b]
as surely as sparks fly upward.
8 "But if I were you, I would appeal to God;
I would lay my cause before him.[c]
9 He performs wonders that cannot be fathomed,[d]
miracles that cannot be counted.
10 He provides rain for the earth;
he sends water on the countryside.[e]
11 The lowly he sets on high,[f]
and those who mourn are lifted to safety.
12 He thwarts the plans[g] of the crafty,
so that their hands achieve no success.
13 He catches the wise in their craftiness,[h]
and the schemes of the wily are swept away.
14 Darkness[i] comes upon them in the daytime;
at noon they grope as in the night.[j]
15 He saves the needy[k] from the sword in their mouth;
he saves them from the clutches of the powerful.[l]
16 So the poor have hope,
and injustice shuts its mouth.[m]
17 "Blessed is the one whom God corrects;[n]
so do not despise the discipline[o] of the Almighty.[a][p]
18 For he wounds, but he also binds up;[q]
he injures, but his hands also heal.[r]
19 From six calamities he will rescue you;
in seven no harm will touch you.[s]
20 In famine[t] he will deliver you from death,
and in battle from the stroke of the sword.[u]
21 You will be protected from the lash of the tongue,[v]
and need not fear[w] when destruction comes.

4:14 [k] Jer 23:9; Hab 3:16 **4:17** [l] Job 9:2 [m] Job 35:10 **4:18** [n] Job 15:15 **4:19** [o] Job 10:9 [p] Job 22:16 [q] Ge 2:7 **4:20** [r] Job 14:2, 20; 20:7; Ps 90:5-6 **4:21** [s] Job 8:22 [t] Job 18:21; 36:12 **5:1** [u] Job 15:15 **5:2** [v] Pr 12:16 **5:3** [w] Ps 37:35; Jer 12:2 [x] Job 24:18 **5:4** [y] Job 4:11 [z] Am 5:12 **5:5** [a] Job 18:8-10 **5:7** [b] Job 14:1 **5:8** [c] Ps 35:23; 50:15 **5:9** [d] Job 42:3; Ps 40:5 **5:10** [e] Job 36:28 **5:11** [f] Ps 113:7-8 **5:12** [g] Ne 4:15; Ps 33:10 **5:13** [h] 1Co 3:19* **5:14** [i] Job 12:25 [j] Dt 28:29 **5:15** [k] Ps 35:10 [l] Job 4:10 **5:16** [m] Ps 107:42 **5:17** [n] Jas 1:12 [o] Ps 94:12; Pr 3:11 [p] Heb 12:5-11 **5:18** [q] Isa 30:26 [r] 1Sa 2:6 **5:19** [s] Ps 34:19; 91:10 **5:20** [t] Ps 33:19 [u] Ps 144:10 **5:21** [v] Ps 31:20 [w] Ps 91:5

[a] 17 Hebrew *Shaddai*; here and throughout Job

in dreams are well known from the OT and the ancient Near East; they formed part of divination (see note on 1Sa 3:1). There are dream visions in the Mari letters, and a dream omen might come from Ugarit. An inscription from Deir 'Alla reads, "The gods came to him at night, and he beheld a vision." Akkadian texts refer to a similar "hair-raising" experience when someone in a night vision sees various deities in the underworld in hybrid form. Gilgamesh is wakened in the night with a feeling of terror after having a terrible dream. His friend Enkidu dreamed of his death.

4:18 *angels.* Hebrew "messengers" of God, as in Ge 18; Zec 1–2. *error.* Need not refer to some great cosmic event; God commonly holds his messengers accountable and corrects them. Ps 82 refers to just such an occasion. In Job 33:23, the messengers act as mediators. The sufferer of the Babylonian text *Ludlul bel nemeqi* ("I will praise the lord of wisdom") complains that his benevolent angel has been cut off, his protecting spirit frightened off.

5:1 *holy ones.* The Hebrew word *qedoshim* or "saints" occurs 13 times in the OT referring to God, heavenly beings and people, but in this case it refers to heavenly beings (cf. Dt 33:3; Ps 89:5,7; Da 8:13; Zec 14:5), who are part of the heavenly council (Job 1–2). Like the messenger "angels" of 4:18 and 33:23, they function as mediators between God and humans. Some commentators have taken this as the rejection of the Mesopotamian concept of the "personal god," but Eliphaz is merely emphasizing the difference between God and the other heavenly beings, as in 15:15, where God is said to place no trust in them.

5:4 *court.* Lit. "city gate," where legal cases were tried, contracts were concluded, public meetings were held, business deals were made, social interaction occurred and even religion was practiced, as in 29:7; 31:21 (cf. also Dt 25:7; Ru 4:1–12; Pr 22:22; Isa 29:21; Am 5:10). See note on 29:7.

[22] You will laugh at destruction and famine,
and need not fear the wild animals.[x]
[23] For you will have a covenant with the stones[y] of the field,
and the wild animals will be at peace with you.[z]
[24] You will know that your tent is secure;
you will take stock of your property and find nothing missing.[a]
[25] You will know that your children will be many,[b]
and your descendants like the grass of the earth.[c]
[26] You will come to the grave in full vigor,[d]
like sheaves gathered in season.

[27] "We have examined this, and it is true.
So hear it and apply it to yourself."

Job

6

Then Job replied:

[2] "If only my anguish could be weighed
and all my misery be placed on the scales![e]
[3] It would surely outweigh the sand[f] of the seas —
no wonder my words have been impetuous.[g]
[4] The arrows[h] of the Almighty are in me,[i]
my spirit drinks[j] in their poison;
God's terrors[k] are marshaled against me.[l]
[5] Does a wild donkey bray when it has grass,
or an ox bellow when it has fodder?
[6] Is tasteless food eaten without salt,
or is there flavor in the sap of the mallow[a]?
[7] I refuse to touch it;
such food makes me ill.[m]

[8] "Oh, that I might have my request,
that God would grant what I hope for,[n]
[9] that God would be willing to crush me,
to let loose his hand and cut off my life![o]
[10] Then I would still have this consolation —
my joy in unrelenting pain —
that I had not denied the words[p] of the Holy One.[q]

[11] "What strength do I have, that I should still hope?
What prospects, that I should be patient?[r]
[12] Do I have the strength of stone?
Is my flesh bronze?
[13] Do I have any power to help myself,[s]
now that success has been driven from me?

[14] "Anyone who withholds kindness from a friend
forsakes the fear of the Almighty.
[15] But my brothers are as undependable as intermittent streams,[t]
as the streams that overflow
[16] when darkened by thawing ice
and swollen with melting snow,
[17] but that stop flowing in the dry season,
and in the heat[u] vanish from their channels.
[18] Caravans turn aside from their routes;
they go off into the wasteland and perish.
[19] The caravans of Tema[v] look for water,
the traveling merchants of Sheba look in hope.
[20] They are distressed, because they had been confident;
they arrive there, only to be disappointed.[w]
[21] Now you too have proved to be of no help;
you see something dreadful and are afraid.[x]
[22] Have I ever said, 'Give something on my behalf,
pay a ransom for me from your wealth,
[23] deliver me from the hand of the enemy,
rescue me from the clutches of the ruthless'?

[24] "Teach me, and I will be quiet;[y]
show me where I have been wrong.
[25] How painful are honest words![z]
But what do your arguments prove?
[26] Do you mean to correct what I say,
and treat my desperate words as wind?[a]
[27] You would even cast lots[b] for the fatherless
and barter away your friend.

[28] "But now be so kind as to look at me.
Would I lie to your face?[c]
[29] Relent, do not be unjust;
reconsider, for my integrity is at stake.[b][d]
[30] Is there any wickedness on my lips?[e]
Can my mouth not discern[f] malice?

5:22 [x] Ps 91:13; Eze 34:25 **5:23** [y] Ps 91:12 [z] Isa 11:6-9 **5:24** [a] Job 8:6 **5:25** [b] Ps 112:2 [c] Ps 72:16; Isa 44:3-4 **5:26** [d] Ge 15:15 **6:2** [e] Job 31:6 **6:3** [f] Pr 27:3 [g] Job 23:2 **6:4** [h] Ps 38:2 [i] Job 16:12, 13 [j] Job 21:20 [k] Job 30:15 [l] Ps 88:15-18 **6:7** [m] Job 3:24 **6:8** [n] Job 14:13 **6:9** [o] Nu 11:15; 1Ki 19:4 **6:10** [p] Job 22:22; 23:12 [q] Lev 19:2; Isa 57:15 **6:11** [r] Job 21:4 **6:13** [s] Job 26:2 **6:15** [t] Ps 38:11; Jer 15:18 **6:17** [u] Job 24:19 **6:19** [v] Ge 25:15; Isa 21:14 **6:20** [w] Jer 14:3 **6:21** [x] Ps 38:11 **6:24** [y] Ps 39:1 **6:25** [z] Ecc 12:11 **6:26** [a] Job 8:2; 15:3 **6:27** [b] Joel 3:3; Na 3:10; 2Pe 2:3 **6:28** [c] Job 27:4; 33:1, 3; 36:3, 4 **6:29** [d] Job 23:7, 10; 34:5, 36; 42:6 **6:30** [e] Job 27:4 [f] Job 12:11

[a] *6* The meaning of the Hebrew for this phrase is uncertain. [b] *29* Or *my righteousness still stands*

6:15 *undependable as intermittent streams.* As treacherous as the wadis of Canaan: they are dry in summer when water is needed (v. 17), but they can become torrents when it rains. Sudden flooding of watercourses is known, especially in the dry Negev, where the sand and rocks are not so porous, and there is no vegetation to stem the waters from the sudden downpours.

6:19 *Tema.* An important oasis in northern Arabia (Jer 25:23) along the spice route from the south ("Sheba").

7 "Do not mortals have hard service[g] on earth?[h]
Are not their days like those of hired laborers?[i]
2 Like a slave longing for the evening shadows,
or a hired laborer waiting to be paid,[j]
3 so I have been allotted months of futility,
and nights of misery have been assigned to me.[k]
4 When I lie down I think, 'How long before I get up?'[l]
The night drags on, and I toss and turn until dawn.
5 My body is clothed with worms[m] and scabs,
my skin is broken and festering.

6 "My days are swifter than a weaver's shuttle,[n]
and they come to an end without hope.[o]
7 Remember, O God, that my life is but a breath;[p]
my eyes will never see happiness again.[q]
8 The eye that now sees me will see me no longer;
you will look for me, but I will be no more.[r]
9 As a cloud vanishes and is gone,
so one who goes down to the grave[s] does not return.[t]
10 He will never come to his house again;
his place[u] will know him no more.[v]

11 "Therefore I will not keep silent;[w]
I will speak out in the anguish of my spirit,
I will complain in the bitterness of my soul.[x]
12 Am I the sea, or the monster of the deep,[y]
that you put me under guard?
13 When I think my bed will comfort me
and my couch will ease my complaint,[z]
14 even then you frighten me with dreams
and terrify[a] me with visions,
15 so that I prefer strangling and death,[b]
rather than this body of mine.
16 I despise my life;[c] I would not live forever.
Let me alone; my days have no meaning.

17 "What is mankind that you make so much of them,
that you give them so much attention,[d]
18 that you examine them every morning
and test them every moment?[e]
19 Will you never look away from me,
or let me alone even for an instant?[f]
20 If I have sinned, what have I done to you,[g]
you who see everything we do?
Why have you made me your target?[h]
Have I become a burden to you?[a]
21 Why do you not pardon my offenses
and forgive my sins?[i]
For I will soon lie down in the dust;[j]
you will search for me, but I will be no more."

Bildad

8 Then Bildad the Shuhite replied:

2 "How long will you say such things?
Your words are a blustering wind.[k]

7:1 [g] Job 14:14; Isa 40:2 [h] Job 5:7 [i] Job 14:6 **7:2** [j] Lev 19:13 **7:3** [k] Job 16:7; Ps 6:6 **7:4** [l] Dt 28:67 **7:5** [m] Job 17:14; Isa 14:11 **7:6** [n] Job 9:25 [o] Job 13:15; 17:11, 15 **7:7** [p] Ps 78:39; Jas 4:14 [q] Job 9:25 **7:8** [r] Job 20:7, 9, 21 **7:9** [s] Job 11:8 [t] 2Sa 12:23; Job 30:15 **7:10** [u] Job 27:21, 23 [v] Job 8:18 **7:11** [w] Ps 40:9 [x] 1Sa 1:10 **7:12** [y] Eze 32:2-3 **7:13** [z] Job 9:27 **7:14** [a] Job 9:34 **7:15** [b] 1Ki 19:4 **7:16** [c] Job 9:21; 10:1 **7:17** [d] Ps 8:4; 144:3; Heb 2:6 **7:18** [e] Job 14:3 **7:19** [f] Job 9:18 **7:20** [g] Job 35:6 [h] Job 16:12 **7:21** [i] Job 10:14 [j] Job 10:9; Ps 104:29 **8:2** [k] Job 6:26

[a] 20 A few manuscripts of the Masoretic Text, an ancient Hebrew scribal tradition and Septuagint; most manuscripts of the Masoretic Text *I have become a burden to myself.*

7:1 *hard service.* Lit. "army" or "warfare" (also in 14:14; Isa 40:2) can refer to military service, but here it refers to any kind of labor. According to Mesopotamian thought, as reflected by the Atrahasis epic, humans were made to serve the gods and do their work. Israelite kings conscripted people for forced labor (e.g., 1Sa 8:11 – 17; 14:52; 1Ki 5:13 – 14; 9:15 – 22; see notes on Jos 16:10; 1Ki 5:13; 1Ch 20:3). *hired laborers.* A person or object hired for a wage (an animal, Ex 22:14; mercenaries, Jer 46:21).
7:6 *weaver's shuttle.* The device that carries the thread from one side of the loom to the other. This technique goes quite rapidly, but a weaver's shuttle can run out of thread, and here Job considers himself to be without thread or hope. *hope.* The Hebrew word (*tiqwah*) can be translated as "hope" (here) or "thread" (or cord, Jos 2:18), which continues the metaphor from the world of weaving. The same metaphor occurs in Isa 38:12: "Like a weaver I have rolled up my life, and he has cut me off from the loom."
7:12 *the sea ... the monster of the deep.* The sea (Hebrew *yam*) is portrayed as a cosmic power (cf. Ps 93:3 – 4) that has to be kept at bay, as in Job 38:8 – 11. In a Ugaritic text, the god Yamm (the sea-god) is conquered by Baal, and the monster in the sea is defeated by Anat: "I have bound the dragon's jaws, have destroyed it, have smitten the twisting serpent, the closed-coiled one with seven heads." Elsewhere in Ugaritic texts the sea monster has a double tail. It was a symbol of chaos subdued by God (like Leviathan and Rahab; see note on 9:13; see also the article "Identification of Behemoth and Leviathan," p. 871). Here, however, the motif is used to describe the sufferer's protest against God's relentless surveillance.
7:14 *dreams.* See note on 4:13.
7:20 *you who see everything we do.* Usually the divine watcher serves a protective function, but here the emphasis is reversed to portray God as a scrutinizer rather than an observer. The closest ancient Near Eastern parallel is the occasional reference to the seven antediluvian sages (Akkadian *apkallu*) as watchers. Later literature assigned the role of watchers to angels (e.g., Da 4:13,17,23), and eventually to fallen angels (the Apocryphal book of Enoch), though that idea was unknown at this time.

JOB 7:21

DEATH AND SHEOL

The concept of death is central to the book of Job (Job 7:21; 10:21 – 22; 14:10 – 14; 21:21; 30:23; 38:17). In some cases, clay and dust are used to indicate the mortality of humans (e.g., Job 7:21; 13:12; 20:11; 21:26; cf. Ps 22:15,29; Isa 26:19; Da 12:2). The term *Sheol* is used in parallel with death (see note on Job 17:13) in the OT to indicate the grave or the underworld. In Isa 5:14, Sheol ("Death") has a mouth and swallows humanity.

The word *Sheol* is unique to the Hebrew Bible, but the concept of the grave or underworld is well known in the ancient Near East. In Mesopotamian mythology, the underworld is a very inhospitable place from which no one returns; there is no light there, and the inhabitants eat clay or mud and drink unclean water. In the Mesopotamian myths *Descent of Ishtar* and *Nergal and Ereshkigal*, the underworld is described as a place from which those who enter cannot leave, where they see no light, but dwell in darkness. In Enkidu's vision of the netherworld in the Gilgamesh Epic, it is a "House of Dust." The concept of death in Egypt is not so gloomy, and the positive attitude of the ancient Egyptians toward it is common knowledge. They developed a whole program to deal with death and even a complex geography of the underworld. Nevertheless, the underworld is a world reversed, and it holds dangers and darkness.

Death is personified in Hos 13:14: "Where, O death, are your plagues? Where, O grave [Hebrew *sheol*], is your destruction." Hab 2:5 describes Sheol as "greedy" and death as "never satisfied." According to Ps 49:14, humans are like sheep shepherded by death, but according to Isa 25:8, the Lord will swallow up death forever. ◆

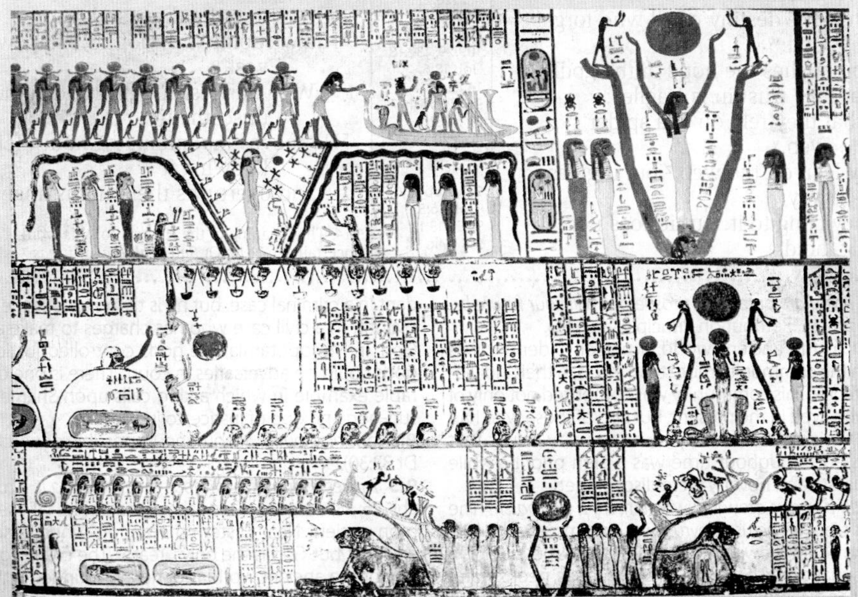

A detail of the painting of the Book of Caverns in the tomb of Ramses VI. The artist depicts the journey of the sun disk through the underworld above the decapitated enemies.

[3]Does God pervert justice?[l]
Does the Almighty pervert what is right?[m]
[4]When your children sinned against him,
he gave them over to the penalty of their sin.[n]
[5]But if you will seek God earnestly
and plead[o] with the Almighty,
[6]if you are pure and upright,
even now he will rouse himself on your behalf[p]
and restore you to your prosperous state.[q]
[7]Your beginnings will seem humble,
so prosperous[r] will your future be.

[8]"Ask the former generations[s]
and find out what their ancestors learned,
[9]for we were born only yesterday and know nothing,[t]
and our days on earth are but a shadow.[u]
[10]Will they not instruct you and tell you?
Will they not bring forth words from their understanding?
[11]Can papyrus grow tall where there is no marsh?
Can reeds thrive without water?
[12]While still growing and uncut,
they wither more quickly than grass.[v]
[13]Such is the destiny of all who forget God;[w]
so perishes the hope of the godless.[x]
[14]What they trust in is fragile[a];
what they rely on is a spider's web.[y]
[15]They lean on the web,[z] but it gives way;
they cling to it, but it does not hold.[a]
[16]They are like a well-watered plant in the sunshine,
spreading its shoots[b] over the garden;[c]
[17]it entwines its roots around a pile of rocks
and looks for a place among the stones.
[18]But when it is torn from its spot,
that place disowns it and says,
'I never saw you.'[d]
[19]Surely its life withers[e] away,
and[b] from the soil other plants grow.[f]
[20]"Surely God does not reject one who is blameless[g]
or strengthen the hands of evildoers.[h]
[21]He will yet fill your mouth with laughter[i]
and your lips with shouts of joy.[j]
[22]Your enemies will be clothed in shame,[k]
and the tents of the wicked will be no more."[l]

Job 9

Then Job replied:

[2]"Indeed, I know that this is true.
But how can mere mortals prove their innocence before God?[m]
[3]Though they wished to dispute with him,
they could not answer him one time out of a thousand.[n]
[4]His wisdom[o] is profound, his power is vast.[p]
Who has resisted him and come out unscathed?[q]
[5]He moves mountains without their knowing it
and overturns them in his anger.[r]

8:3 [l] Dt 32:4; 2Ch 19:7; Ro 3:5 [m] Ge 18:25 **8:4** [n] Job 1:19 **8:5** [o] Job 11:13 **8:6** [p] Ps 7:6 [q] Job 5:24 **8:7** [r] Job 42:12 **8:8** [s] Dt 4:32; 32:7; Job 15:18 **8:9** [t] Ge 47:9 [u] 1Ch 29:15; Job 7:6 **8:12** [v] Ps 129:6; Jer 17:6 **8:13** [w] Ps 9:17 [x] Job 11:20; 13:16; 15:34; Pr 10:28 **8:14** [y] Isa 59:5 **8:15** [z] Job 27:18 [a] Ps 49:11 **8:16** [b] Ps 80:11 [c] Ps 37:35; Jer 11:16 **8:18** [d] Job 7:8; Ps 37:36 **8:19** [e] Job 20:5 [f] Ecc 1:4 **8:20** [g] Job 1:1 [h] Job 21:30 **8:21** [i] Job 5:22 [j] Ps 126:2; 132:16 **8:22** [k] Ps 35:26; 109:29; 132:18 [l] Job 18:6, 14, 21 **9:2** [m] Job 4:17; Ps 143:2; Ro 3:20 **9:3** [n] Job 10:2; 40:2 **9:4** [o] Job 11:6 [p] Job 36:5 [q] 2Ch 13:12 **9:5** [r] Mic 1:4

[a] *14* The meaning of the Hebrew for this word is uncertain. [b] *19* Or *Surely all the joy it has / is that*

8:6–7 *if you are pure … so prosperous will your future be.* See the article "Retribution Principle," p. 823.

8:8–10 In the ancient world, a person's identity was found in the community more than it was in their individual existence. This community was comprised not only of those who lived in the present, but also of those who had lived in the past. Conformity to community values that had existed throughout time was a high priority, while individualism and novelty were discouraged.

8:11 *Can papyrus grow tall where there is no marsh?* The papyrus plant (*Cyperus papyrus*) was common to the Nile delta and could grow as high as 19.5 feet (6 meters); it is a typical aquatic marsh plant, which, like reeds, needs water to grow and can wither like grass (v. 12). It also grew in Canaan, especially in the (now drained) marshes of Huleh. Papyrus was used to make baskets and skiffs, and was used as material on which to write.

9:2 *prove their innocence.* Legal motifs and terms abound in the book of Job, and the book has even been described as a theological lawsuit. Job considers himself a defendant in a criminal case, but he is trying to take the role of plaintiff in a civil case who has charges to make against God. In Mesopotamia, the gods controlled justice, and gods could be adversaries in court. There is one comparable example in which a king calls upon Shamash, the sun-god and god of justice, to judge him.

9:3 *one time out of a thousand.* Impossible odds (cf. 33:23; Dt 32:30).

9:5 *moves mountains without their knowing it.* Ch. 9 (like chs. 26; 38) describes God as the Creator. The OT uses common ancient Near Eastern metaphors when describing creation, but God is the only Creator. The cosmic geography of the ancient world is generally founded on observation and experience, so what does the author have in mind as he describes moving or overturning mountains? Close analysis reveals that the translation should likely go a different direction. The verb the NIV translates "moves" (Hiphil, *ʿtq*) only occurs a few times in the OT; in Genesis it refers to the movement of the patriarchs from place to place (Ge 12:8; 26:22). Therefore, we would translate Job 9:5

[6] He shakes the earth[s] from its place
and makes its pillars tremble.[t]
[7] He speaks to the sun and it does not
shine;
he seals off the light of the stars.[u]
[8] He alone stretches out the heavens[v]
and treads on the waves of the
sea.[w]
[9] He is the Maker of the Bear[a] and
Orion,
the Pleiades and the constellations
of the south.[x]
[10] He performs wonders[y] that cannot
be fathomed,
miracles that cannot be counted.[z]
[11] When he passes me, I cannot see
him;
when he goes by, I cannot perceive
him.[a]
[12] If he snatches away, who can stop
him?[b]
Who can say to him, 'What are you
doing?'[c]
[13] God does not restrain his anger;
even the cohorts of Rahab[d] cowered
at his feet.

9:6 [s] Isa 2:21; Hag 2:6; Heb 12:26 [t] Job 26:11 **9:7** [u] Isa 13:10; Eze 32:8 **9:8** [v] Ge 1:6; Ps 104:2-3 [w] Job 38:16; Ps 77:19 **9:9** [x] Ge 1:16; Job 38:31; Am 5:8 **9:10** [y] Ps 71:15 [z] Job 5:9 **9:11** [a] Job 23:8-9; 35:14 **9:12** [b] Job 11:10 [c] Isa 45:9; Ro 9:20 **9:13** [d] Job 26:12; Ps 89:10; Isa 30:7; 51:9 **9:15** [e] Job 10:15 [f] Job 8:5 **9:17** [g] Job 16:12 [h] Job 30:22 [i] Job 16:14 [j] Job 2:3 **9:18** [k] Job 7:19; 27:2

[14] "How then can I dispute with him?
How can I find words to argue with
him?
[15] Though I were innocent, I could not
answer him;[e]
I could only plead[f] with my Judge
for mercy.
[16] Even if I summoned him and he
responded,
I do not believe he would give me a
hearing.
[17] He would crush me[g] with a storm[h]
and multiply[i] my wounds for no
reason.[j]
[18] He would not let me catch my breath
but would overwhelm me with misery.[k]
[19] If it is a matter of strength, he is
mighty!
And if it is a matter of justice, who
can challenge him[b]?
[20] Even if I were innocent, my mouth
would condemn me;
if I were blameless, it would
pronounce me guilty.

[a] 9 Or *of Leo* [b] 19 See Septuagint; Hebrew *me.*

as "God traverses the mountains." The Akkadian cognate *etequ* means to pass through difficult territory. This would parallel his treading on the seas in v. 8. The next problem is to identify the subject of the verb "to know" ("He traverses mountains and they do not know"). It is not impossible that the mountains here are being personified, but another option is that the subject is those who resisted him in the previous verse (v. 4). These resisters do not emerge unscathed, for God traverses the difficult passes of the mountains without his enemies' knowledge, and thus overthrows them (the resisters, not the mountains).

9:7 *He speaks to the sun.* God orders the cosmos day by day, not just once for all. God's command causes the sun to rise or not rise. This view is to be differentiated from Egyptian mythology in which the sun and the sun-god are indistinguishable. In that view, deity does not call forth the sun—he rises as the sun and chaos causes the sun to darken. *seals off the light of the stars.* Verbs of shutting, when used with this preposition ("off"), mean to lock something in. The seal would be affixed to a closed door to make sure that what is inside is not disturbed. The ancients believed that the stars were engraved on the underside of the solid, rotating firmament and that they moved along paths (in Akkadian literature, the paths of Anu, Enlil and Ea). To seal the stars would not be to inscribe them, but to establish their paths so that they could not change. Such would be an act of creation, bringing order to the cosmos. Alternatively, and perhaps preferably, we might understand the phrase as parallel to the first part of the verse—hence, order is disrupted. Sealing the stars would then refer to shutting them out so they could not enter the paths to shine in the heavens. In Isa 40:26, God "brings out" and "calls forth" the stars (cf. Isa 45:12, where he "marshaled" them); he does not do so here, but he keeps them shut behind sealed doors.

9:9 *the Bear and Orion, the Pleiades.* To interpret this verse, we need a better understanding of constellations in the ancient world. Celestial omens from the ancient world are well known; several sets of tablets give detailed information about the stars and constellations. There are many constellations, but three of the most prominent (judging by their place in the lists and the omens connected to them) are Pleiades (Akkadian *zappu*; Hebrew *kimah*), Orion (Akkadian *šitadallu*; Hebrew *kesil*), and Taurus (Akkadian *alû*, "Bull of Heaven"). We can identify these and the many other constellations in Akkadian and Sumerian texts because of the technical information they include about the times of their rising and setting and their positions in the sky at various times during the year.

In contrast, we have much less information to determine the names of the Hebrew constellations; the OT refers to constellations in only three contexts (here; 38:31–32; Am 5:8). Scholars offer guesses concerning the identity of these constellations from commentary to commentary, based on comparative Semitic etymology or the renderings of the earliest translations (e.g., Greek).

Constellations are often the subject of omens (for good or ill) in Akkadian literature. For example: "If Leo is dark: lions and wolves will rage and cut off traffic with the Westland." Since God is the one who makes the constellations, he is the one who uses them to portend ominous events that are understood as acts of judgment, as in this context.

9:13 *the cohorts of Rahab cowered at his feet.* Rahab is not known from the ancient Near East or in the cognate languages, but like the Tannin and Leviathan (3:8; 41:1), is a sea monster representing chaos. Rahab also occurs in the cosmogony (origin of the cosmos) in 26:12, where it is cut to pieces. In Isa 51:9–10 and Ps 89:10–11, God cuts Rahab to pieces, pierces the "monster" (Hebrew *tannin*) and crushes it. It is used parallel with the drying up of the sea and the waters of the deep (Hebrew *tehom*), over which God rules. Rahab is used for Egypt in Ps 87:4 and Isa 30:7 in the sense of a political enemy.

Chaos creatures in the ancient world were believed to belong to the nonordered world. Nevertheless, the gods could and did control them if they were inclined to do so. They could be domesticated, and they could be used to accomplish tasks for deity, yet they could also be neglected or rebellious.

JOB 9:5 – 10

Cosmic Geography

The ancient Israelites shared many common cosmological (dealing with the structure of the cosmos) and cosmogonic (dealing with the origin of the cosmos) beliefs with the ancient Near Eastern world, although for them there was only one Creator. According to the Hebrew Bible, the cosmos consists of heaven, earth, underworld and sea. In both Egyptian and Mesopotamian thought, the world was understood as a disk resting on the primeval waters. Most people saw their own place as in the center, with the other countries on the periphery. Above was the sky, studded with stars, which were thought to be engraved in the solid sky.

Job 9:6 indicates that the earth rests on pillars, as does Ps 75:3 (cf. foundations/footings in 1Sa 2:8; 2Sa 22:16; Job 38:4,6; Ps 18:15; 82:5 [also shaken]; 104:5). In Job 26:11, the pillars of the *heavens* quake. God shakes the heavens, earth, dry land and sea (Hag 2:6). On a Babylonian *kudurru* (boundary stone), which might depict the world, a large pillar is depicted that undergirds the cosmos. Throughout the Bible and the ancient Near East, what is most important is the role of the gods in the operation of the cosmos. This is generally expressed in relation to the way they viewed the world around them (cosmic geography). In Job, God controls the sun and makes the stars (Job 9:6 – 9). God stretches out the heavens (Job 26:7; cf. Ps 104:2; Isa 40:22) and treads on the waves of the sea (Job 9:8). In the Babylonian creation epic, the god Marduk creates and destroys the constellation to indicate his power. After defeating Tiamat, he splits her in two; half of her he sets up and makes into a cover — heaven, which he stretches out over the cosmos. He then establishes the constellation of the stars.

In Job 9:8, "treads" means to defeat or subjugate, as in Dt 33:29. The image of the ocean as chaos was already seen in Job 3:8 (there called Leviathan) and in Job 7:12 (there it is put under guard), while in Job 38:8 – 11 it is shut up behind doors; its limits are set with doors and bars and halted from going any farther. In Ugaritic myths, the god Baal defeats Yamm, the sea. On a stele from Baal's temple at Ugarit the wavy lines on which the god Baal is standing have been interpreted as the waves of the sea and as the mountains.

All of this demonstrates that the Israelites' thoughts about the world around them were quite similar to those of all their neighbors, though they differed concerning which divine entity/entities were in control. ◆

"Unfinished" Kudurru. Kassite period, attributed to the reign of Melishipak (1186 – 1172 BC) depicts a large pillar that undergirds the cosmos.

Kim Walton. The Louvre.

21 "Although I am blameless,[l]
I have no concern for myself;
I despise my own life.[m]
22 It is all the same; that is why I say,
'He destroys both the blameless and
the wicked.'[n]
23 When a scourge[o] brings sudden death,
he mocks the despair of the
innocent.[p]
24 When a land falls into the hands of the
wicked,[q]
he blindfolds its judges.[r]
If it is not he, then who is it?

25 "My days are swifter than a runner;[s]
they fly away without a glimpse of
joy.
26 They skim past like boats of papyrus,[t]
like eagles swooping down on their
prey.[u]
27 If I say, 'I will forget my complaint,[v]
I will change my expression, and
smile,'
28 I still dread[w] all my sufferings,
for I know you will not hold me
innocent.[x]
29 Since I am already found guilty,
why should I struggle in vain?[y]
30 Even if I washed myself with soap
and my hands[z] with cleansing
powder,[a]
31 you would plunge me into a slime pit
so that even my clothes would
detest me.

32 "He is not a mere mortal like me that
I might answer him,[b]
that we might confront each other in
court.[c]
33 If only there were someone to mediate
between us,[d]
someone to bring us together,
34 someone to remove God's rod
from me,[e]
so that his terror would frighten
me no more.
35 Then I would speak up without fear
of him,
but as it now stands with me,
I cannot.[f]

10 "I loathe my very life;[g]
therefore I will give free rein to
my complaint
and speak out in the bitterness of
my soul.[h]
2 I say to God: Do not declare me
guilty,
but tell me what charges[i] you have
against me.
3 Does it please you to oppress me,[j]
to spurn the work of your hands,[k]
while you smile on the plans of
the wicked?[l]
4 Do you have eyes of flesh?
Do you see as a mortal sees?[m]
5 Are your days like those of a mortal
or your years like those of a strong
man,[n]
6 that you must search out my
faults
and probe after my sin[o] —
7 though you know that I am not
guilty
and that no one can rescue me
from your hand?

8 "Your hands shaped[p] me and made
me.
Will you now turn and destroy me?
9 Remember that you molded me like
clay.[q]
Will you now turn me to dust
again?[r]

9:21 [l] Job 1:1 [m] Job 7:16 **9:22** [n] Job 10:8; Ecc 9:2, 3; Eze 21:3 **9:23** [o] Heb 11:36 [p] Job 24:1, 12 **9:24** [q] Job 10:3; 16:11 [r] Job 12:6 **9:25** [s] Job 7:6 **9:26** [t] Isa 18:2 [u] Hab 1:8 **9:27** [v] Job 7:11 **9:28** [w] Job 3:25; Ps 119:120 [x] Job 7:21 **9:29** [y] Ps 37:33 **9:30** [z] Job 31:7 [a] Jer 2:22 **9:32** [b] Ro 9:20 [c] Ps 143:2; Ecc 6:10 **9:33** [d] 1Sa 2:25 **9:34** [e] Job 13:21; Ps 39:10 **9:35** [f] Job 13:21 **10:1** [g] 1Ki 19:4 [h] Job 7:11 **10:2** [i] Job 9:29 **10:3** [j] Job 9:22 [k] Job 14:15; Ps 138:8; Isa 64:8 [l] Job 21:16; 22:18 **10:4** [m] 1Sa 16:7 **10:5** [n] Ps 90:2, 4; 2Pe 3:8 **10:6** [o] Job 14:16 **10:8** [p] Ps 119:73 **10:9** [q] Isa 64:8 [r] Ge 2:7

9:22 *He destroys both the blameless and the wicked.* This irony also occurs in the Mesopotamian Erra epic: "Like one who plunders a country, I [the god] do not distinguish just from unjust, I fell (them both)."
9:26 *boats of papyrus.* In ancient Egypt, boats made of papyrus (cf. 8:11) were a common sight, and they are often depicted on Egyptian paintings; small models were placed in tombs.
9:30 *soap ... cleansing powder.* Job tries to establish his innocence by referring to the strongest of cleansing agents, soapwort, made of the roots of the plant leontopetalon, and the alkaline solution lye. In ancient times, people did not wash with soap as we do, but applied oil to the skin, which was then scraped off. Washing of hands was a ritual of purification (Dt 21:6), but it could be done in vain (Ps 73:13). This will not cleanse Job, as is described in Jer 2:22.
9:33 *someone to mediate between us.* In the ancient Near East, people sometimes would ask for their personal gods to mediate on their behalf in the divine council. At other times, gods are seen as judges who mediate a person's situations. Arbitration was also carried out in human courts in a variety of ways. One means of mediation was carried out by someone in the family acting on a person's behalf.
10:8 – 9 *shaped me and made me ... molded me like clay.* God is the Creator not only of the universe (ch. 9), but also of humans and even an individual like Job (here). The idea that humans were made from clay also occurs in 33:6. There, a different Hebrew verb is used, which indicates pinching off clay. Job 4:19 refers to "houses of clay" in the literal sense rather than metaphorically to the creation of humans from clay. In Ge 2:7, man (*adam*) was formed from the dust of the ground, and the metaphor of the potter is used in Isa 29:16; 45:9; 64:8; Jer 18:6 (also Ro 9:20 – 21). This was a generally accepted idea in the ancient near East. In Egypt, it was believed that the god Khnum created on a potter's wheel. In the Wisdom of Ani: "Man is clay and straw, the god is his builder." In the Gilgamesh Epic, Enkidu is made by the goddess Aruru from clay, and in "The Babylonian Theodicy" the god Ea created by pinching off clay. In Ugaritic literature, El creates a healer in the same way. According to the Atrahasis epic, a human was created by mixing clay with the flesh and blood of a god. For this reason, God can turn Job to "dust" (v. 9), which indicates death, as described in, e.g., Ge 3:19; Ps 90:3.

10 Did you not pour me out like milk
and curdle me like cheese,
11 clothe me with skin and flesh
and knit me together[s] with bones
and sinews?
12 You gave me life[t] and showed me
kindness,
and in your providence watched
over my spirit.

13 "But this is what you concealed in
your heart,
and I know that this was in your
mind:[u]
14 If I sinned, you would be watching me
and would not let my offense go
unpunished.[v]
15 If I am guilty — woe to me![w]
Even if I am innocent, I cannot lift
my head,[x]
for I am full of shame
and drowned in[a] my affliction.
16 If I hold my head high, you stalk me
like a lion[y]
and again display your awesome
power against me.[z]
17 You bring new witnesses against me[a]
and increase your anger toward me;[b]
your forces come against me wave
upon wave.

18 "Why then did you bring me out of the
womb?[c]
I wish I had died before any eye
saw me.
19 If only I had never come into being,
or had been carried straight from the
womb to the grave!
20 Are not my few days[d] almost over?[e]
Turn away from me[f] so I can have a
moment's joy
21 before I go to the place of no return,[g]
to the land of gloom and utter
darkness,[h]
22 to the land of deepest night,
of utter darkness and disorder,
where even the light is like
darkness."

Zophar

11 Then Zophar the Naamathite replied:

2 "Are all these words to go
unanswered?[i]
Is this talker to be vindicated?
3 Will your idle talk reduce others to
silence?
Will no one rebuke you when you
mock?[j]
4 You say to God, 'My beliefs are
flawless[k]
and I am pure[l] in your sight.'
5 Oh, how I wish that God would speak,
that he would open his lips against
you
6 and disclose to you the secrets of
wisdom,[m]
for true wisdom has two sides.
Know this: God has even forgotten
some of your sin.[n]

7 "Can you fathom[o] the mysteries of
God?
Can you probe the limits of the
Almighty?
8 They are higher than the heavens[p]
above — what can you do?
They are deeper than the depths
below — what can you know?
9 Their measure is longer than the
earth
and wider than the sea.

10 "If he comes along and confines you in
prison
and convenes a court, who can
oppose him?[q]
11 Surely he recognizes deceivers;
and when he sees evil, does he not
take note?[r]
12 But the witless can no more become
wise
than a wild donkey's colt can be
born human.[b]

13 "Yet if you devote your heart[s] to him
and stretch out your hands to him,[t]
14 if you put away the sin that is in your
hand
and allow no evil[u] to dwell in your
tent,[v]
15 then, free of fault, you will lift up your
face;[w]
you will stand firm and without fear.
16 You will surely forget your trouble,[x]
recalling it only as waters gone by.[y]
17 Life will be brighter than noonday,[z]
and darkness will become like
morning.

10:11 [s] Ps 139:13, 15 **10:12** [t] Job 33:4 **10:13** [u] Job 23:13 **10:14** [v] Job 7:21 **10:15** [w] Job 9:13; Isa 3:11 [x] Job 9:15 **10:16** [y] Isa 38:13; La 3:10 [z] Job 5:9 **10:17** [a] Job 16:8 [b] Ru 1:21 **10:18** [c] Job 3:11 **10:20** [d] Job 14:1 [e] Job 7:19 [f] Job 7:16 **10:21** [g] 2Sa 12:23; Job 3:13; 16:22 [h] Ps 23:4; 88:12 **11:2** [i] Job 8:2 **11:3** [j] Job 17:2; 21:3 **11:4** [k] Job 6:10 [l] Job 10:7 **11:6** [m] Job 9:4 [n] Ezr 9:13; Job 15:5 **11:7** [o] Ecc 3:11; Ro 11:33 **11:8** [p] Job 22:12 **11:10** [q] Job 9:12; Rev 3:7 **11:11** [r] Job 34:21-25; Ps 10:14 **11:13** [s] 1Sa 7:3; Ps 78:8 [t] Ps 88:9 **11:14** [u] Ps 101:4 [v] Job 22:23 **11:15** [w] Job 22:26; 1Jn 3:21 **11:16** [x] Isa 65:16 [y] Job 22:11 **11:17** [z] Job 22:28; Ps 37:6; Isa 58:8, 10

[a] 15 Or *and aware of* [b] 12 Or *wild donkey can be born tame*

10:10 *curdle me like cheese.* Another image (see previous note) is here used for the creation of Job. He was formed in his mother's womb like cheese from milk in a churn. Such churns are known from archaeology and depicted on Egyptian tomb paintings.
10:18 – 19 See note on 3:11.
11:13 *stretch out your hands to him.* The stretching out of the arms or hands, raising the hands with the palms outward at face level, is a gesture of prayer typical in the OT (e.g., Ezr 9:5; Ps 28:2; 143:6). It is known from Mesopotamian sources and is depicted in Egyptian art. This gesture is illustrated on a carved ivory casket from Hazor in Canaan dating from the time of the Israelite kings. The gesture also occurs in Ugaritic literature, where the king lifts his hands to heaven while offering a sacrifice.

Egyptian priest Renpetmaa with hands raised in worship before Re-Horakhty, c. 900 BC. The stretching out of the arms or hands, raising the hands with the palms outward at face level, is a gesture of prayer typical in the Old Testament (Job 11:13; Ps 28:2).

Wikimedia Commons

[18] You will be secure, because there is
hope;
you will look about you and take
your rest[a] in safety.[b]
[19] You will lie down, with no one to make
you afraid,[c]
and many will court your favor.[d]
[20] But the eyes of the wicked will fail,[e]
and escape will elude them;[f]
their hope will become a dying gasp."[g]

Job

12 Then Job replied:

[2] "Doubtless you are the only people
who matter,
and wisdom will die with you![h]
[3] But I have a mind as well as you;
I am not inferior to you.
Who does not know all these things?[i]
[4] "I have become a laughingstock[j] to my
friends,
though I called on God and he
answered[k] —
a mere laughingstock, though
righteous and blameless![l]
[5] Those who are at ease have contempt
for misfortune
as the fate of those whose feet are
slipping.
[6] The tents of marauders are
undisturbed,[m]
and those who provoke God are
secure[n] —
those God has in his hand.[a]
[7] "But ask the animals, and they will
teach you,
or the birds in the sky, and they will
tell you;
[8] or speak to the earth, and it will teach
you,
or let the fish in the sea inform you.
[9] Which of all these does not know
that the hand of the LORD has done
this?[o]
[10] In his hand is the life of every creature
and the breath of all mankind.[p]
[11] Does not the ear test words
as the tongue tastes food?[q]
[12] Is not wisdom found among the aged?[r]
Does not long life bring
understanding?[s]
[13] "To God belong wisdom[t] and power;[u]
counsel and understanding are his.[v]
[14] What he tears down[w] cannot be
rebuilt;[x]
those he imprisons cannot be
released.
[15] If he holds back the waters,[y] there is
drought;[z]
if he lets them loose, they devastate
the land.[a]
[16] To him belong strength and insight;
both deceived and deceiver are his.[b]
[17] He leads rulers away stripped[c]
and makes fools of judges.[d]
[18] He takes off the shackles[e] put on by
kings
and ties a loincloth[b] around their
waist.

[a] 6 Or *those whose god is in their own hand*
[b] 18 Or *shackles of kings / and ties a belt*

11:18 [a] Ps 3:5 [b] Lev 26:6; Pr 3:24 **11:19** [c] Lev 26:6 [d] Isa 45:14 **11:20** [e] Dt 28:65; Job 17:5 [f] Job 27:22; 34:22 [g] Job 8:13 **12:2** [h] Job 17:10
12:3 [i] Job 13:2 **12:4** [j] Job 21:3 [k] Ps 91:15 [l] Job 6:29 **12:6** [m] Job 22:18 [n] Job 9:24; 21:9 **12:9** [o] Isa 41:20 **12:10** [p] Job 27:3; 33:4; Ac 17:28 **12:11** [q] Job 34:3 **12:12** [r] Job 15:10 [s] Job 32:7,9 **12:13** [t] Job 11:6 [u] Job 9:4 [v] Job 32:8; 38:36 **12:14** [w] Job 19:10 [x] Job 37:7; Isa 25:2 **12:15** [y] 1Ki 8:35 [z] 1Ki 17:1 [a] Ge 7:11 **12:16** [b] Job 13:7,9 **12:17** [c] Job 19:9 [d] Job 3:14 **12:18** [e] Ps 116:16

12:17,19 *stripped.* The Hebrew word is sometimes translated "barefoot." Ancient Near Eastern art shows prisoners of war being led away naked and barefoot (cf. Isa 20:2 – 4; Mic 1:8). To go barefoot is often a sign of reverence (Ex 3:5) and penitence (2Sa 15:30), but here it represents shame, because stripping someone of clothes indicated a loss of honor (Job 19:9; cf. 22:6; 29:14; 40:10).

12:18 *shackles.* The meaning of the verse is not clear, but it might refer to bound captives. Bound captives are shown frequently in ancient Near Eastern art. Feet can also be fastened in shackles (13:27; cf. 33:11; 36:8).

[19]He leads priests away stripped
and overthrows officials long
established.[f]
[20]He silences the lips of trusted advisers
and takes away the discernment of
elders.[g]
[21]He pours contempt on nobles
and disarms the mighty.
[22]He reveals the deep things of darkness[h]
and brings utter darkness[i] into the
light.[j]
[23]He makes nations great, and destroys
them;[k]
he enlarges nations,[l] and disperses
them.
[24]He deprives the leaders of the earth of
their reason;
he makes them wander in a trackless
waste.[m]
[25]They grope in darkness with no light;[n]
he makes them stagger like
drunkards.[o]

13 "My eyes have seen all this,
my ears have heard and
understood it.
[2]What you know, I also know;
I am not inferior to you.[p]
[3]But I desire to speak to the Almighty
and to argue my case with God.[q]
[4]You, however, smear me with lies;[r]
you are worthless physicians, all of
you!
[5]If only you would be altogether silent!
For you, that would be wisdom.[s]
[6]Hear now my argument;
listen to the pleas of my lips.
[7]Will you speak wickedly on God's
behalf?
Will you speak deceitfully for him?[t]
[8]Will you show him partiality?[u]
Will you argue the case for God?
[9]Would it turn out well if he examined
you?
Could you deceive him as you might
deceive a mortal?[v]
[10]He would surely call you to account
if you secretly showed partiality.
[11]Would not his splendor[w] terrify you?
Would not the dread of him fall on
you?

12:19 [f]Job 24:12, 22; 34:20, 28; 35:9 **12:20** [g]Job 32:9 **12:22** [h]1Co 4:5 [i]Job 3:5 [j]Da 2:22 **12:23** [k]Jer 25:9 [l]Ps 107:38; Isa 9:3; 26:15 **12:24** [m]Ps 107:40 **12:25** [n]Job 5:14 [o]Ps 107:27; Isa 24:20 **13:2** [p]Job 12:3 **13:3** [q]Job 23:3-4 **13:4** [r]Ps 119:69; Jer 23:32 **13:5** [s]Pr 17:28 **13:7** [t]Job 36:4 **13:8** [u]Lev 19:15 **13:9** [v]Job 12:16; Gal 6:7 **13:11** [w]Job 31:23

[12]Your maxims are proverbs of ashes;
your defenses are defenses of clay.
[13]"Keep silent and let me speak;
then let come to me what may.
[14]Why do I put myself in jeopardy
and take my life in my hands?
[15]Though he slay me, yet will I hope[x] in
him;[y]
I will surely[a] defend my ways to his
face.[z]
[16]Indeed, this will turn out for my
deliverance,[a]
for no godless person would dare
come before him!
[17]Listen carefully to what I say;[b]
let my words ring in your ears.
[18]Now that I have prepared my case,[c]
I know I will be vindicated.
[19]Can anyone bring charges against me?[d]
If so, I will be silent and die.[e]
[20]"Only grant me these two things, God,
and then I will not hide from you:
[21]Withdraw your hand[f] far from me,
and stop frightening me with your
terrors.
[22]Then summon me and I will answer,[g]
or let me speak, and you reply
to me.[h]
[23]How many wrongs and sins have
I committed?[i]
Show me my offense and my sin.
[24]Why do you hide your face[j]
and consider me your enemy?[k]
[25]Will you torment a windblown leaf?[l]
Will you chase after dry chaff?[m]
[26]For you write down bitter things
against me
and make me reap the sins of my
youth.[n]
[27]You fasten my feet in shackles;[o]
you keep close watch on all my
paths
by putting marks on the soles of my
feet.
[28]"So man wastes away like something
rotten,
like a garment eaten by moths.[p]

[a] 15 Or *He will surely slay me; I have no hope — / yet I will*

13:15 [x]Job 7:6 [y]Ps 23:4; Pr 14:32 [z]Job 27:5 **13:16** [a]Isa 12:1 **13:17** [b]Job 21:2 **13:18** [c]Job 23:4 **13:19** [d]Job 40:4; Isa 50:8 [e]Job 10:8 **13:21** [f]Ps 39:10 **13:22** [g]Job 14:15 [h]Job 9:16 **13:23** [i]1Sa 26:18 **13:24** [j]Dt 32:20; Ps 13:1; Isa 8:17 [k]Job 19:11; La 2:5 **13:25** [l]Lev 26:36 [m]Job 21:18; Isa 42:3 **13:26** [n]Ps 25:7 **13:27** [o]Job 33:11 **13:28** [p]Isa 50:9; Jas 5:2

13:4 *physicians.* In the ancient world they were experts in the use of herbs and other sorts of treatments, but others were specialists in the magical or supernatural causes of disease. Their remedies could involve something as serious as exorcism, but other times involved incantations and rituals. Since Job's friends are trying to help him identify the causes or solutions to his circumstances, they are playing the role of such physicians.
13:12 *proverbs of ashes.* Ashes could be mixed with water to make a solution for writing, but it was not durable and could easily be erased, similar to modern chalk. *defenses of clay.* Clay might also refer to an unfired clay tablet that could be easily erased. Alternatively, the reference to clay might refer to building material for a city's defensive walls.
13:24 *hide your face.* The hiding of the face of God refers to God's wrath (34:29; Ps 27:9), because he has seemingly become Job's enemy. Job wants God to summon him and show him his sins (vv. 22–23). In Mesopotamia, seeing the face can refer to a deity, but it is also used in a legal context. To see someone's face means to enjoy their favor.
13:27 *shackles.* See note on 12:18. The terminology used in this verse can refer to putting limits or boundaries on the extremities. The shackles function to restrict the movement of the feet.

14 "Mortals, born of woman,
are of few days and full of
trouble.[q]
2 They spring up like flowers[r] and wither
away;[s]
like fleeting shadows,[t] they do not
endure.
3 Do you fix your eye on them?[u]
Will you bring them[a] before you for
judgment?[v]
4 Who can bring what is pure[w] from the
impure?[x]
No one![y]
5 A person's days are determined;
you have decreed the number of his
months[z]
and have set limits he cannot
exceed.
6 So look away from him and let him
alone,[a]
till he has put in his time like a hired
laborer.[b]

7 "At least there is hope for a tree:
If it is cut down, it will sprout
again,
and its new shoots will not fail.
8 Its roots may grow old in the ground
and its stump die in the soil,
9 yet at the scent of water it will bud
and put forth shoots like a plant.
10 But a man dies and is laid low;
he breathes his last and is no more.[c]
11 As the water of a lake dries up
or a riverbed becomes parched and
dry,[d]
12 so he lies down and does not rise;
till the heavens are no more,[e] people
will not awake
or be roused from their sleep.[f]

13 "If only you would hide me in the
grave
and conceal me till your anger has
passed![g]
If only you would set me a time
and then remember me!
14 If someone dies, will they live again?
All the days of my hard service
I will wait for my renewal[b] to come.
15 You will call and I will answer you;[h]
you will long for the creature your
hands have made.
16 Surely then you will count my steps[i]
but not keep track of my sin.[j]
17 My offenses will be sealed up in a
bag;[k]
you will cover over my sin.[l]

18 "But as a mountain erodes and
crumbles
and as a rock is moved from its
place,
19 as water wears away stones
and torrents wash away the soil,
so you destroy a person's hope.[m]
20 You overpower them once for all, and
they are gone;
you change their countenance and
send them away.
21 If their children are honored, they do
not know it;
if their offspring are brought low,
they do not see it.[n]
22 They feel but the pain of their own
bodies
and mourn only for themselves."

Eliphaz

15 Then Eliphaz the Temanite replied:

2 "Would a wise person answer with
empty notions
or fill their belly with the hot east
wind?[o]
3 Would they argue with useless words,
with speeches that have no value?
4 But you even undermine piety
and hinder devotion to God.
5 Your sin prompts your mouth;
you adopt the tongue of the crafty.[p]
6 Your own mouth condemns you, not
mine;
your own lips testify against you.[q]

7 "Are you the first man ever born?[r]
Were you brought forth before the
hills?[s]

14:1 [q] Job 5:7; Ecc 2:23 **14:2** [r] Jas 1:10 [s] Ps 90:5-6 [t] Job 8:9 **14:3** [u] Ps 8:4; 144:3 [v] Ps 143:2 **14:4** [w] Ps 51:10 [x] Eph 2:1-3 [y] Jn 3:6; Ro 5:12 **14:5** [z] Job 21:21 **14:6** [a] Job 7:19 [b] Job 7:1,2; Ps 39:13 **14:10** [c] Job 13:19 **14:11** [d] Isa 19:5 **14:12** [e] Rev 20:11; 21:1 [f] Ac 3:21 **14:13** [g] Isa 26:20 **14:15** [h] Job 13:22 **14:16** [i] Ps 139:1-3; Pr 5:21; Jer 32:19 [j] Job 10:6 **14:17** [k] Dt 32:34 [l] Hos 13:12 **14:19** [m] Job 7:6 **14:21** [n] Ecc 9:5; Isa 63:16 **15:2** [o] Job 6:26 **15:5** [p] Job 5:13 **15:6** [q] Lk 19:22 **15:7** [r] Job 38:21 [s] Ps 90:2; Pr 8:25

[a] 3 Septuagint, Vulgate and Syriac; Hebrew *me*
[b] 14 Or *release*

14:5 *A person's days are determined.* In v. 2, the image of the fleeting shadow is used (cf. 8:9). In Ps 39:4, a mortal's days are shown to be limited. The Gilgamesh Epic and the Aqhat Legend from Ugarit make it clear that death is the fate of humankind and only the deities possess eternal life. Destinies are decreed by the gods and one's fate is sealed in the divine realm. These are typical perceptions in the ancient world.

14:14 *If someone dies, will they live again?* Like everyone in the ancient world, Job believes that life continues after death, but such a belief offers little hope if life in the netherworld is dreary drudgery. Trees can resprout (vv. 7–9), but humans have no such prospects (vv. 10,12); they are more like the riverbed that simply dries up (v. 11). Job wishes that it were otherwise, that he could take refuge in the grave and then be brought back to life (v. 13), but he realizes that such an option does not exist.

15:7 *the first man ever born.* Associated with wisdom in the ancient Near East. According to Mesopotamian tradition, the first sage was Oannes (as preserved by the Jewish historian Josephus), who taught humans civilization, writing, crafts and science. Later came the many *apkallu*, the antediluvian sages who were perfect in wisdom. Adapa was the first of these semidivine sages with supernatural wisdom who served the kings who ruled before the flood. Thus the statement reflects ancient Near Eastern thinking rather than Biblical tradition. Adam was not portrayed as someone of great wisdom until much later.

8 Do you listen in on God's council?[t]
Do you have a monopoly on
wisdom?
9 What do you know that we do not
know?
What insights do you have that we
do not have?[u]
10 The gray-haired and the aged[v] are on
our side,
men even older than your father.
11 Are God's consolations[w] not enough
for you,
words[x] spoken gently to you?[y]
12 Why has your heart[z] carried you away,
and why do your eyes flash,
13 so that you vent your rage against God
and pour out such words from your
mouth?
14 "What are mortals, that they could be
pure,
or those born of woman,[a] that they
could be righteous?[b]
15 If God places no trust in his holy ones,
if even the heavens are not pure in
his eyes,[c]
16 how much less mortals, who are vile
and corrupt,[d]
who drink up evil like water![e]
17 "Listen to me and I will explain to
you;
let me tell you what I have seen,
18 what the wise have declared,
hiding nothing received from their
ancestors[f]
19 (to whom alone the land was given
when no foreigners moved among
them):
20 All his days the wicked man suffers
torment,
the ruthless man through all the
years stored up for him.[g]
21 Terrifying sounds fill his ears;[h]
when all seems well, marauders
attack him.[i]
22 He despairs of escaping the realm of
darkness;
he is marked for the sword.[j]
23 He wanders about[k] for food like a
vulture;
he knows the day of darkness is at
hand.[l]
24 Distress and anguish fill him with
terror;
troubles overwhelm him, like a king
poised to attack,
25 because he shakes his fist at God
and vaunts himself against the
Almighty,[m]
26 defiantly charging against him
with a thick, strong shield.
27 "Though his face is covered with fat
and his waist bulges with flesh,[n]
28 he will inhabit ruined towns
and houses where no one lives,[o]
houses crumbling to rubble.[p]
29 He will no longer be rich and his
wealth will not endure,[q]
nor will his possessions spread over
the land.
30 He will not escape the darkness;[r]
a flame[s] will wither his shoots,
and the breath of God's mouth[t] will
carry him away.
31 Let him not deceive himself by trusting
what is worthless,[u]
for he will get nothing in return.
32 Before his time[v] he will wither,[w]
and his branches will not flourish.[x]
33 He will be like a vine stripped of its
unripe grapes,[y]
like an olive tree shedding its
blossoms.
34 For the company of the godless will be
barren,
and fire will consume the tents of
those who love bribes.[z]
35 They conceive trouble and give birth
to evil;[a]
their womb fashions deceit."

Job
16 Then Job replied:

2 "I have heard many things like these;
you are miserable comforters, all of
you![b]
3 Will your long-winded speeches never
end?
What ails you that you keep on
arguing?[c]
4 I also could speak like you,
if you were in my place;

15:8 [t] Ro 11:34; 1Co 2:11 **15:9** [u] Job 13:2 **15:10** [v] Job 32:6-7 **15:11** [w] 2Co 1:3-4 [x] Zec 1:13 [y] Job 36:16 **15:12** [z] Job 11:13 **15:14** [a] Job 14:4; 25:4 [b] Pr 20:9; Ecc 7:20 **15:15** [c] Job 4:18; 25:5 **15:16** [d] Ps 14:1 [e] Job 34:7; Pr 19:28 **15:18** [f] Job 8:8 **15:20** [g] Job 24:1; 27:13-23 **15:21** [h] Job 18:11; 20:25 [i] Job 27:20; 1Th 5:3 **15:22** [j] Job 19:29; 27:14 **15:23** [k] Ps 59:15; 109:10 [l] Job 18:12 **15:25** [m] Job 36:9 **15:27** [n] Ps 17:10 **15:28** [o] Isa 5:9 [p] Job 3:14 **15:29** [q] Job 27:16-17 **15:30** [r] Job 5:14 [s] Job 22:20 [t] Job 4:9 **15:31** [u] Isa 59:4 **15:32** [v] Ecc 7:17 [w] Job 22:16; Ps 55:23 [x] Job 18:16 **15:33** [y] Hab 3:17 **15:34** [z] Job 8:22 **15:35** [a] Ps 7:14; Isa 59:4; Hos 10:13 **16:2** [b] Job 13:4 **16:3** [c] Job 6:26

15:15 *holy ones.* Refers not to fallen angels but to heavenly beings who are held accountable for the tasks to which they were assigned. See notes on 4:18; 5:1.
15:16 *mortals ... are vile and corrupt.* God does not trust humans, because they are corrupt. In "The Babylonian Theodicy," it is said that the creator deities "gave twisted words to the human race, they endowed them in perpetuity with lies and falsehood." In some of the more radical speeches in Job, God is portrayed in similar ways. By the end of the book these are recognized as flawed views about God.
15:23 *wanders about.* Connected with depression and reflects examples from Mesopotamia. The hero Gilgamesh, e.g., grieves over his dead friend Enkidu and wanders around: "like a lioness deprived of her cubs he paced to and fro, this way and that."
15:27 *fat.* Obesity was a sign of prosperity and therefore of God's blessing, since only the prosperous had the resources to overeat and the leisure to become fat.
15:33 *a vine ... an olive tree.* Symbols of abundance and fertility in the Hebrew Bible; those stripped of unripe grapes and blossoms will not bear any fruit. In the same way, the plans of the wicked will come to naught.

I could make fine speeches against you
and shake my head[d] at you.
5 But my mouth would encourage you;
comfort from my lips would bring you relief.

6 "Yet if I speak, my pain is not relieved;
and if I refrain, it does not go away.
7 Surely, God, you have worn me out;[e]
you have devastated my entire household.
8 You have shriveled me up — and it has become a witness;
my gauntness[f] rises up and testifies against me.[g]
9 God assails me and tears[h] me in his anger
and gnashes his teeth at me;[i]
my opponent fastens on me his piercing eyes.[j]
10 People open their mouths[k] to jeer at me;
they strike my cheek[l] in scorn
and unite together against me.[m]
11 God has turned me over to the ungodly
and thrown me into the clutches of the wicked.[n]
12 All was well with me, but he shattered me;
he seized me by the neck and crushed me.[o]
He has made me his target;[p]
13 his archers surround me.
Without pity, he pierces[q] my kidneys
and spills my gall on the ground.
14 Again and again[r] he bursts upon me;
he rushes at me like a warrior.[s]
15 "I have sewed sackcloth[t] over my skin
and buried my brow in the dust.
16 My face is red with weeping,
dark shadows ring my eyes;
17 yet my hands have been free of violence[u]
and my prayer is pure.

16:4 [d] Ps 22:7; 109:25; La 2:15; Zep 2:15; Mt 27:39 **16:7** [e] Job 7:3 **16:8** [f] Job 19:20 [g] Job 10:17 **16:9** [h] Hos 6:1 [i] Ps 35:16; La 2:16; Ac 7:54 [j] Job 13:24 **16:10** [k] Ps 22:13 [l] Isa 50:6; La 3:30; Mic 5:1; Ac 23:2 [m] Ps 35:15 **16:11** [n] Job 1:15, 17 **16:12** [o] Job 9:17 [p] La 3:12 **16:13** [q] Job 20:24 **16:14** [r] Job 9:17 [s] Joel 2:7 **16:15** [t] Ge 37:34 **16:17** [u] Isa 59:6; Jnh 3:8

16:12 – 14 These verses use the metaphor of God as a warrior attacking Job (cf. 19:8 – 12; 30:12 – 14). In the ancient Near East, the warrior-god Resheph is depicted with a bow, as would befit a divine warrior. An even more vivid illustration might be the scene of target practice on a cylinder seal from Beth Shan, where pharaoh Rameses II is shooting arrows at an ox-hide-shaped target with captives fastened to it.

16:15 *sackcloth.* Expresses mourning (see the article "Mourning," p. 828). *brow.* "Horn" in Hebrew, a symbol of power in the OT (cf. 1Ki 22:11) and the ancient Near East. Asiatic deities and deified rulers wear horned headdresses as symbol of their power. The horn has been debased by being buried in the dust, in the same way that horns could be cut off to render them powerless (e.g., Zec 1:21).

A vivid scene of target practice on a cylinder seal from Beth Shan, where Pharaoh Ramses II is shooting arrows at an ingot with captives fastened to it, c. 1279 – 1212 BC. Job uses the metaphor of God as warrior attacking him (Job 16:12 – 13).

Cylinder Seal with name of Rameses II, 1279 – 1212 BC, from Beth Shean/Rockefeller Archaeological Museum, Jerusalem/The Israel Antiquities Authority Collection/ Bridgeman Images

18 "Earth, do not cover my blood;[v]
may my cry never be laid to rest![w]
19 Even now my witness[x] is in heaven;
my advocate is on high.
20 My intercessor is my friend[a]
as my eyes pour out[y] tears to God;
21 on behalf of a man he pleads[z] with God
as one pleads for a friend.
22 "Only a few years will pass
before I take the path of no return.[a]

17 1 My spirit is broken,
my days are cut short,
the grave awaits me.[b]
2 Surely mockers[c] surround me;
my eyes must dwell on their hostility.

3 "Give me, O God, the pledge you demand.[d]
Who else will put up security[e] for me?[f]
4 You have closed their minds to understanding;
therefore you will not let them triumph.
5 If anyone denounces their friends for reward,
the eyes of their children will fail.[g]

6 "God has made me a byword[h] to everyone,
a man in whose face people spit.
7 My eyes have grown dim with grief;[i]
my whole frame is but a shadow.
8 The upright are appalled at this;
the innocent are aroused[j] against the ungodly.
9 Nevertheless, the righteous[k] will hold to their ways,
and those with clean hands[l] will grow stronger.

10 "But come on, all of you, try again!
I will not find a wise man among you.[m]
11 My days have passed, my plans are shattered.
Yet the desires of my heart[n]
12 turn night into day;
in the face of the darkness light is near.
13 If the only home I hope for is the grave,[o]
if I spread out my bed in the realm of darkness,
14 if I say to corruption,[p] 'You are my father,'
and to the worm,[q] 'My mother' or 'My sister,'
15 where then is my hope—[r]
who can see any hope for me?
16 Will it go down to the gates of death?[s]
Will we descend together into the dust?"

Bildad

18 Then Bildad the Shuhite replied:

2 "When will you end these speeches?
Be sensible, and then we can talk.
3 Why are we regarded as cattle
and considered stupid in your sight?[t]
4 You who tear yourself[u] to pieces in your anger,
is the earth to be abandoned for your sake?
Or must the rocks be moved from their place?

5 "The lamp of a wicked man is snuffed out;[v]
the flame of his fire stops burning.
6 The light in his tent becomes dark;
the lamp beside him goes out.

16:18 [v] Isa 26:21 [w] Ps 66:18-19 **16:19** [x] Ge 31:50; Ro 1:9; 1Th 2:5 **16:20** [y] La 2:19 **16:21** [z] Ps 9:4 **16:22** [a] Ecc 12:5 **17:1** [b] Ps 88:3-4 **17:2** [c] 1Sa 1:6-7 **17:3** [d] Ps 119:122 [e] Pr 6:1 [f] Isa 38:14 **17:5** [g] Job 11:20 **17:6** [h] Job 30:9 **17:7** [i] Job 16:8 **17:8** [j] Job 22:19 **17:9** [k] Pr 4:18 [l] Job 22:30 **17:10** [m] Job 12:2 **17:11** [n] Job 7:6 **17:13** [o] Job 3:13 **17:14** [p] Job 13:28; 30:28,30; Ps 16:10 [q] Job 21:26 **17:15** [r] Job 7:6 **17:16** [s] Job 3:17-19; Jnh 2:6 **18:3** [t] Ps 73:22 **18:4** [u] Job 13:14 **18:5** [v] Job 21:17; Pr 13:9; 20:20; 24:20

[a] 20 Or *My friends treat me with scorn*

16:22 *the path of no return.* See the article "The Old Testament Concept of Resurrection," p. 1160.
17:3 *the pledge you demand.* Legal language (see the article "Negative Confessions and the Oath of Innocence," p. 861). A pledge was a piece of personal property given as a guarantee for later payment (cf. 24:9), as known from ancient Near Eastern law, and as done by Judah in Ge 38, when he gave his seal and staff as a pledge. The pledge can also be a person, as in Ge 43:9; 44:32 (Judah for Benjamin). Here, Job appears to be identifying his own life as a pledge to ascertain his innocence.
17:13 *If the only home I hope for is the grave.* The grave (Hebrew *sheol* [see the article "Death and Sheol," p. 833]) is described as a home (lit. "house," as with death in 30:23). The tomb was the home or house of the dead, but bones were also kept in ossuaries in the form of houses, and one such ossuary found is inscribed with the word "Sheol." *my bed in … darkness.* In Ps 139:8, a bed is made in Sheol (NIV "depths"). Because tombs were dark, lamps were placed in them to provide light; tombs at Ugarit have niches for oil lamps. Sheol is a place of darkness. In Mesopotamian myths, the underworld is described as a place of darkness, deprived of light. In the ancient world, the tomb/grave is considered the entryway to the netherworld, so the same language refers to both tomb and netherworld at the same time.
17:16 *go down to the gates of death … descend … into the dust.* In 21:13 Job also wishes to "go down" to the grave (Sheol). The same idea is found in Ugaritic literature, when the deities El and Anat declare that because Baal is dead, they will also descend into the earth. Dust is often linked with death or Sheol (see the article "Death and Sheol," p. 833). In Mesopotamian myths, the underworld has seven gates through which the goddess Ishtar and the god Nergal must pass; it is a place to where one "goes down," and the inhabitants eat dust. This might be because when people entered tombs, they were found to be full of dust. The Egyptian underworld also had gates, and the Egyptian tomb had a "false door" through which the spirit could enter.

[7] The vigor of his step is weakened;[w]
his own schemes[x] throw him
down.[y]
[8] His feet thrust him into a net;[z]
he wanders into its mesh.
[9] A trap seizes him by the heel;
a snare holds him fast.
[10] A noose is hidden for him on the
ground;
a trap lies in his path.
[11] Terrors startle him on every side[a]
and dog[b] his every step.
[12] Calamity is hungry[c] for him;
disaster is ready for him when he
falls.
[13] It eats away parts of his skin;
death's firstborn devours his
limbs.[d]
[14] He is torn from the security of his
tent[e]
and marched off to the king of
terrors.
[15] Fire resides[a] in his tent;
burning sulfur[f] is scattered over his
dwelling.
[16] His roots dry up below[g]
and his branches wither above.[h]
[17] The memory of him perishes from the
earth;
he has no name in the land.[i]
[18] He is driven from light into the realm
of darkness[j]
and is banished from the world.
[19] He has no offspring[k] or descendants[l]
among his people,
no survivor where once he lived.[m]
[20] People of the west are appalled at his
fate;[n]
those of the east are seized with
horror.
[21] Surely such is the dwelling[o] of an evil
man;
such is the place of one who does
not know God."[p]

Job 19

Then Job replied:

[2] "How long will you torment me
and crush me with words?
[3] Ten times now you have reproached me;
shamelessly you attack me.
[4] If it is true that I have gone astray,
my error[q] remains my concern
alone.
[5] If indeed you would exalt yourselves
above me[r]
and use my humiliation against me,
[6] then know that God has wronged me[s]
and drawn his net[t] around me.

[7] "Though I cry, 'Violence!' I get no
response;[u]
though I call for help, there is no
justice.[v]

18:7 [w] Pr 4:12 [x] Job 5:13 [y] Job 15:6 **18:8** [z] Job 22:10; Ps 9:15; 35:7 **18:11** [a] Job 15:21; Jer 6:25; 20:3 [b] Job 20:8 **18:12** [c] Isa 8:21 **18:13** [d] Zec 14:12 **18:14** [e] Job 8:22 **18:15** [f] Ps 11:6 **18:16** [g] Isa 5:24; Hos 9:1-16; Am 2:9 [h] Job 15:30; Mal 4:1 **18:17** [i] Ps 34:16; Pr 2:22; 10:7 **18:18** [j] Job 5:14 **18:19** [k] Jer 22:30 [l] Isa 14:22 [m] Job 27:14-15 **18:20** [n] Ps 37:13; Jer 50:27,31 **18:21** [o] Job 21:28 [p] Jer 9:3; 1Th 4:5 **19:4** [q] Job 6:24 **19:5** [r] Ps 35:26; 38:16; 55:12 **19:6** [s] Job 27:2 [t] Job 18:8 **19:7** [u] Job 30:20 [v] Job 9:24; Hab 1:2-4

[a] 15 Or *Nothing he had remains*

18:8–10 *net ... mesh ... trap ... snare ... noose ... trap.* In these verses the NIV translates six Hebrew terms for various hunting devices. These traps were used by ordinary people, especially to catch birds (Ps 91:3; Am 3:5). On the net, cf. 19:6 and note. The mesh consisted of branches lightly woven together and placed over a hole, into which the victim would fall. Besides the hunting metaphor, magical spells and hexes were also identified as snares to trap people in their power. It would not be unusual for someone to hire a specialist to put a spell (lay a "snare") for an enemy.

18:13 *death's firstborn.* There has been much discussion on this designation, which only occurs in the OT in the book of Job. Three ancient Near Eastern candidates have been proposed for this demon: (1) the Ugaritic personified Death (Mot), (2) the Syro-Canaanite god of war and pestilence Resheph and (3) Namtar, the Mesopotamian messenger and vizier of the underworld goddess Ereshkigal. None of these three bears the title "firstborn," although Resheph has sons. Namtar is the "offspring" of the underworld-goddess Ereshkigal, but not explicitly called her "firstborn." The intention may be to link the figure with that of Ugaritic Mot, the demon of death, who in Job is personified as having a firstborn son, disease, who is eating away Job's skin. In Ugaritic mythology, Mot is a devourer who swallows the god Baal and humans. It is also possible, however, that the reference is a literary personification that does not have any particular mythological figure or demon in mind.

18:14 *king of terrors.* This designation is unique to Job. The same idea might be reflected in 20:25; 24:17; 27:20; 30:15. For the terrifying character of the Ugaritic Mot, see previous note. In Mesopotamia, the god of the underworld and pestilence Nergal (West Semitic Resheph) is called "king of the land of terror," and his abode "the terrible house." The underworld is described as "filled with terror." See the article "Death and Sheol," p. 833.

18:15 *sulfur.* Brimstone, which burns to produce acid gas and was found in the regions of volcanic activity and the Dead Sea. It was used for fire, fumigation and for medicinal purposes, as is known from Akkadian texts and in rituals of purification to counteract witchcraft. In Ge 19:24 and Rev 14:10 it refers to divine judgment, but is not used with that connotation in most ancient Near Eastern literature.

18:16–17 *roots dry up ... no offspring.* The state of the wicked is described. This destruction occurs in the curses of tomb inscriptions; e.g., whoever desecrates the coffin of Eshmunazar, "let him have no root below or fruit above."

18:20 *People of the west ... those of the east.* People from both directions, i.e., all humankind. The Ugaritic goddess Anat kills people on the seashore (west) and to the east, i.e., all humankind.

19:6 *net.* Cf. Eze 17:20. This is related to the hunt and the idea of the "divine net." The Stele of the Vultures, commissioned by the Sumerian king Eannatum of Lagash, shows enemies caught in a net. The figure holding the net might be Eannatum or the god Ningirsu. Eannatum claims in his inscriptions: "Over the people of Umma I Eannatum threw the net of the god Enlil." The Babylonian god Marduk catches Tiamat and the other monsters with a net, and the god of pestilence Erra also has a net. In a hymn of praise to Hammurapi of Babylon, the king is described as a net over the enemy, evil and offenders.

8 He has blocked my way so I cannot
pass;[w]
he has shrouded my paths in
darkness.[x]
9 He has stripped[y] me of my honor
and removed the crown from my
head.[z]
10 He tears me down[a] on every side till
I am gone;
he uproots my hope[b] like a tree.[c]
11 His anger[d] burns against me;
he counts me among his enemies.[e]
12 His troops advance in force;[f]
they build a siege ramp[g] against me
and encamp around my tent.

13 "He has alienated my family[h] from me;
my acquaintances are completely
estranged from me.[i]
14 My relatives have gone away;
my closest friends have forgotten
me.
15 My guests and my female servants
count me a foreigner;
they look on me as on a stranger.
16 I summon my servant, but he does not
answer,
though I beg him with my own
mouth.
17 My breath is offensive to my wife;
I am loathsome to my own family.
18 Even the little boys[j] scorn me;
when I appear, they ridicule me.
19 All my intimate friends[k] detest me;[l]
those I love have turned against me.
20 I am nothing but skin and bones;[m]
I have escaped only by the skin of
my teeth.[a]

19:8 [w] Job 3:23; La 3:7 [x] Job 30:26 **19:9** [y] Job 12:17 [z] Ps 89:39, 44; La 5:16 **19:10** [a] Job 12:14 [b] Job 7:6 [c] Job 24:20 **19:11** [d] Job 16:9 [e] Job 13:24 **19:12** [f] Job 16:13 [g] Job 30:12 **19:13** [h] Ps 69:8 [i] Job 16:7; Ps 88:8 **19:18** [j] 2Ki 2:23 **19:19** [k] Ps 55:12-13 [l] Ps 38:11 **19:20** [m] Job 33:21; Ps 102:5

21 "Have pity on me, my friends, have
pity,
for the hand of God has struck me.
22 Why do you pursue[n] me as God
does?
Will you never get enough of my
flesh?[o]

23 "Oh, that my words were recorded,
that they were written on a scroll,[p]
24 that they were inscribed with an iron
tool on[b] lead,
or engraved in rock forever!
25 I know that my redeemer[c][q] lives,[r]
and that in the end he will stand
on the earth.[d]
26 And after my skin has been
destroyed,
yet[e] in[f] my flesh I will see God;[s]
27 I myself will see him
with my own eyes—I, and not
another.
How my heart yearns[t] within me!

28 "If you say, 'How we will hound him,
since the root of the trouble lies in
him,[g]'
29 you should fear the sword yourselves;
for wrath will bring punishment by
the sword,[u]
and then you will know that there
is judgment.[h]"[v]

19:22 [n] Job 13:25; 16:11 [o] Ps 69:26 **19:23** [p] Isa 30:8 **19:25** [q] Ps 78:35; Pr 23:11; Isa 43:14; Jer 50:34 [r] Job 16:19 **19:26** [s] Ps 17:15; Mt 5:8; 1Co 13:12; 1Jn 3:2 **19:27** [t] Ps 73:26 **19:29** [u] Job 15:22 [v] Job 22:4; Ps 1:5; 9:7

[a] 20 Or *only by my gums* [b] 24 Or *and* [c] 25 Or *vindicator* [d] 25 Or *on my grave* [e] 26 Or *And after I awake, / though this body has been destroyed, / then* [f] 26 Or *destroyed, / apart from* [g] 28 Many Hebrew manuscripts, Septuagint and Vulgate; most Hebrew manuscripts *me* [h] 29 Or *sword, / that you may come to know the Almighty*

19:12 *siege ramp.* Cf. the war imagery in 16:12–14. Here, Job is attacked by troops advancing in force, who build a siege ramp (cf. 30:12) and encamp around his tent. In the ancient Near East in wartime, the defenders protected themselves behind massive city walls while the city was encircled and attacked by siege troops with siege machines. See the article "Siege Warfare," p. 1157. *my tent.* The reference to a "tent" instead of a city is grim humor.
19:17 *My breath is offensive to my wife.* In the Egyptian Dialogue of a Man with His Soul, the image of the unpleasant smell is used. In the Wisdom of Ani, a name is said to stink. The dead also suffer from bad breath.
19:20 *only by the skin of my teeth.* This is either ironic, given that teeth do not have skin, or, more likely, a reference to the gums (see NIV text note), indicating that the teeth have fallen out. There is no indication that it is used here like the English cliché meaning "barely."
19:23–24 *recorded … on a scroll … engraved in rock.* Job wishes that his words were recorded on a scroll, inscribed with iron and (NIV "on") lead, engraved in rock forever. Scrolls could be of papyrus or leather (vellum). Iron styli or chisels were used to make engravings in stone. The reference to lead may refer to letters filled in or inlaid with lead. Ancient Near Eastern rulers inscribed their deeds in stone on cliffs. Often something was written in this way for the gods to read, rather than for people to read. In the ancient Near East and OT world, memory and remembrance was important, especially after death. For this reason, the Ugaritic hero Danel wants a son who will set up a monument for his clan so that they will be remembered. Letters were even written to the dead in Egypt and Mesopotamia asking for their help. Someone who passed a commemorative funerary stele in Egypt had to say a prayer or bring an offering.
19:25 *I know that my redeemer lives.* This phrase has been made famous by Handel's "I Know That My Redeemer Liveth," from his oratorio *Messiah*, which reflects the popular Christian Messianic interpretation. There are two interpretations—that the Hebrew *goel* (NIV "guardian-redeemer") refers to a vindicator or defender (see NIV text note) of Job's action *against* God, who is his adversary, or that *God* is his Redeemer. Since the word appears in a context in which there is a dispute between God and Job, most consider it unlikely that it refers to God as the redeemer. It might be a personal independent deity, or it might be compared with the mediator/advocate in 9:33; 16:19–21 or the angel/messenger in 33:23–24. Job asks for deliverance not *by* God but *from* God, and the "redeemer" is Job's defense attorney. It is still disputed whether Job here refers to resurrection, but most modern interpreters consider it unlikely (see the article "The Old Testament Concept of the Resurrection," p. 1160).

In ancient Israelite law, the "guardian-redeemer" (Hebrew *goel*) was someone who protected the inter-

Zophar

20 Then Zophar the Naamathite replied:

2 "My troubled thoughts prompt me to answer
because I am greatly disturbed.
3 I hear a rebuke[w] that dishonors me,
and my understanding inspires me to reply.

4 "Surely you know how it has been from of old,
ever since mankind[a] was placed on the earth,
5 that the mirth of the wicked is brief,
the joy of the godless lasts but a moment.[x]
6 Though the pride of the godless person reaches to the heavens
and his head touches the clouds,[y]
7 he will perish forever,[z] like his own dung;
those who have seen him will say, 'Where is he?'[a]
8 Like a dream[b] he flies away,[c] no more to be found,
banished[d] like a vision of the night.[e]
9 The eye that saw him will not see him again;
his place will look on him no more.[f]
10 His children[g] must make amends to the poor;
his own hands must give back his wealth.[h]
11 The youthful vigor[i] that fills his bones
will lie with him in the dust.[j]

12 "Though evil is sweet in his mouth
and he hides it under his tongue,
13 though he cannot bear to let it go
and lets it linger in his mouth,[k]
14 yet his food will turn sour in his stomach;
it will become the venom of serpents within him.
15 He will spit out the riches he swallowed;
God will make his stomach vomit them up.
16 He will suck the poison[l] of serpents;
the fangs of an adder will kill him.[m]
17 He will not enjoy the streams,
the rivers flowing with honey[n] and cream.[o]
18 What he toiled for he must give back uneaten;
he will not enjoy the profit from his trading.
19 For he has oppressed the poor and left them destitute;[p]
he has seized houses he did not build.

20 "Surely he will have no respite from his craving;[q]
he cannot save himself by his treasure.
21 Nothing is left for him to devour;
his prosperity will not endure.[r]
22 In the midst of his plenty, distress will overtake him;
the full force of misery will come upon him.
23 When he has filled his belly,
God will vent his burning anger against him
and rain down his blows on him.[s]
24 Though he flees[t] from an iron weapon,
a bronze-tipped arrow pierces him.
25 He pulls it out of his back,
the gleaming point out of his liver.
Terrors[u] will come over him;[v]
26 total darkness[w] lies in wait for his treasures.
A fire unfanned will consume him[x]
and devour what is left in his tent.
27 The heavens will expose his guilt;
the earth will rise up against him.[y]

20:3 [w] Job 19:3 **20:5** [x] Job 8:12; Ps 37:35-36; 73:19 **20:6** [y] Isa 14:13-14; Ob 1:3-4 **20:7** [z] Job 4:20 [a] Job 7:10; 8:18 **20:8** [b] Ps 73:20 [c] Job 27:21-23 [d] Job 18:18 [e] Ps 90:5 **20:9** [f] Job 7:8 **20:10** [g] Job 5:4 [h] Job 27:16-17 **20:11** [i] Job 13:26 [j] Job 21:26 **20:13** [k] Nu 11:18-20 **20:16** [l] Dt 32:32 [m] Dt 32:24 **20:17** [n] Dt 32:13 [o] Job 29:6 **20:19** [p] Job 24:4, 14; 35:9 **20:20** [q] Ecc 5:12-14 **20:21** [r] Job 15:29 **20:23** [s] Ps 78:30-31 **20:24** [t] Isa 24:18; Am 5:19 **20:25** [u] Job 18:11 [v] Job 16:13 **20:26** [w] Job 18:18 [x] Ps 21:9 **20:27** [y] Dt 31:28

[a] 4 Or *Adam*

ests of his kin by buying property or paying debt and ensuring that the name of a deceased person lived on (Lev 25:25,47 – 49; Dt 25:5 – 10; Ru 4:3 – 6; see note on Ru 2:20). It was usually a near relative (brother, uncle, cousin) or a kinsman. Yahweh can be a redeemer of Israel from Egypt (e.g., Ex 6:6) and the exile (e.g., Isa 44:22 – 23), but also of the needy, widows and orphans (Ps 103:4; 107:2). This is a very different sort of redemption than what Jesus provides, because in this type of redemption, the individual's rightful standing or possession is restored. This redemption views the subject as innocent, whereas the redemption Christ provides assumes their guilt.

20:14,16 *serpents.* In v. 16 it is the serpent's poison, the fangs of an adder, that will kill him. The "serpent" (Hebrew *peten*) in vv. 14,16 is a large snake, and the "adder" in v. 16 is the carpet viper. In ancient texts, "venom" (also called "gall") was understood not only as tasting bitter, but as a poisonous and deadly substance.

20:15 *spit out the riches … vomit them up.* This idea is comparable to the Egyptian "Wisdom of Amenemope," where goods taken from the poor are "a block in the throat, It makes the gullet vomit."

20:24 *iron weapon.* Might be a sword, a weapon used in close combat. *bronze-tipped arrow.* Lit. "bow." If Job is able to flee from the sword, the long-range arrow will get him. Bows of metal or with metal covering were not used; arrows were made of wood or reed with metal tips or points.

20:26 *fire … will consume him.* On divine fire that "eats" things, see note on 1:16.

20:27 *expose … rise up.* In ancient Near Eastern treaties, heaven and earth (in addition to deities) are called as witness (cf. Dt 32:1; Isa 1:2; see note on Dt 4:26).

[28]A flood will carry off his house,[z]
rushing waters[a] on the day of God's
wrath.[a]
[29]Such is the fate God allots the wicked,
the heritage appointed for them by
God."[b]

Job 21

21 Then Job replied:

[2]"Listen carefully to my words;
let this be the consolation you give
me.
[3]Bear with me while I speak,
and after I have spoken, mock on.[c]

[4]"Is my complaint directed to a human
being?
Why should I not be impatient?[d]
[5]Look at me and be appalled;
clap your hand over your mouth.[e]
[6]When I think about this, I am terrified;
trembling seizes my body.
[7]Why do the wicked live on,
growing old and increasing in power?[f]
[8]They see their children established
around them,
their offspring before their eyes.[g]
[9]Their homes are safe and free from
fear;[h]
the rod of God is not on them.
[10]Their bulls never fail to breed;
their cows calve and do not
miscarry.[i]
[11]They send forth their children as a
flock;
their little ones dance about.
[12]They sing to the music of timbrel and
lyre;
they make merry to the sound of the
pipe.[j]
[13]They spend their years in prosperity[k]
and go down to the grave in peace.[b]
[14]Yet they say to God, 'Leave us alone![l]
We have no desire to know your
ways.[m]
[15]Who is the Almighty, that we should
serve him?
What would we gain by praying to
him?'[n]
[16]But their prosperity is not in their own
hands,
so I stand aloof from the plans of the
wicked.

[17]"Yet how often is the lamp of the
wicked snuffed out?[o]
How often does calamity come upon
them,
the fate God allots in his anger?
[18]How often are they like straw before
the wind,
like chaff[p] swept away by a gale?
[19]It is said, 'God stores up the
punishment of the wicked for
their children.'[q]
Let him repay the wicked, so that
they themselves will experience
it!
[20]Let their own eyes see their
destruction;
let them drink[r] the cup of the wrath
of the Almighty.[s]
[21]For what do they care about the
families they leave behind
when their allotted months[t] come to
an end?

[22]"Can anyone teach knowledge to
God,[u]
since he judges even the highest?[v]
[23]One person dies in full vigor,
completely secure and at ease,
[24]well nourished in body,[c]
bones rich with marrow.[w]
[25]Another dies in bitterness of soul,
never having enjoyed anything good.
[26]Side by side they lie in the dust,
and worms cover them both.[x]

[27]"I know full well what you are
thinking,
the schemes by which you would
wrong me.
[28]You say, 'Where now is the house of
the great,[y]
the tents where the wicked lived?'[z]
[29]Have you never questioned those who
travel?
Have you paid no regard to their
accounts—
[30]that the wicked are spared from the
day of calamity,[a]
that they are delivered from[d] the day
of wrath?[b]

20:28 [z]Dt 28:31 [a]Job 21:17, 20, 30 **20:29** [b]Job 27:13 **21:3** [c]Job 16:10 **21:4** [d]Job 6:11 **21:5** [e]Jdg 18:19; Job 29:9; 40:4 **21:7** [f]Job 12:6; Ps 73:3; Jer 12:1; Hab 1:13 **21:8** [g]Ps 17:14 **21:9** [h]Ps 73:5 **21:10** [i]Ex 23:26 **21:12** [j]Ps 81:2 **21:13** [k]Job 36:11 **21:14** [l]Job 22:17 [m]Pr 1:29 **21:15** [n]Ex 5:2; Job 34:9; Mal 3:14 **21:17** [o]Job 18:5 **21:18** [p]Job 13:25; Ps 1:4 **21:19** [q]Ex 20:5; Jer 31:29; Eze 18:2 **21:20** [r]Ps 75:8; Isa 51:17 [s]Jer 25:15; Rev 14:10 **21:21** [t]Job 14:5 **21:22** [u]Job 35:11; 36:22; Isa 40:13-14; Ro 11:34 [v]Ps 82:1 **21:24** [w]Pr 3:8 **21:26** [x]Job 24:20; Ecc 9:2-3; Isa 14:11 **21:28** [y]Job 1:3; 12:21; 31:37 [z]Job 8:22 **21:30** [a]Pr 16:4 [b]Job 20:22, 28; 2Pe 2:9

[a] 28 Or *The possessions in his house will be carried off, / washed away* [b] 13 Or *in an instant* [c] 24 The meaning of the Hebrew for this word is uncertain. [d] 30 Or *wicked are reserved for the day of calamity, / that they are brought forth to*

21:5 *clap your hand over your mouth.* As in 29:9 and 40:4, it can be a gesture of awe and astonishment (cf. Pr 30:32) or of silence (cf. Jdg 18:19; Mic 7:16). It might be depicted on a seal showing the hero Etana, who went to heaven on the back of an eagle; the seal shows one astonished onlooker holding his hand to his mouth.
21:10 *never fail to breed ... do not miscarry.* The prosperity of the wicked is described in terms of fertile bulls and cows. In contrast, in the curses of the ancient Near Eastern Sefire Treaty, "7 rams will cover an ewe, but she will not conceive."
21:12 *timbrel.* A small hand drum. *lyre.* Had a wooden frame with strings, as shown on the Ur Standard and a Megiddo ivory. *pipe.* Made of reed or metal. See the article "Music and Musicians," p. 524.
21:13 *go down to the grave.* See note on 17:16; see also the article "Death and Sheol," p. 833.

Anubis, god of mummification, resting upon a chest of gilded wood from the tomb of Tutankhamen. Because of riches buried with the dead, tombs were concealed and also guarded (Job 21:32).

31 Who denounces their conduct to their
face?
Who repays them for what they
have done?
32 They are carried to the grave,
and watch is kept over their
tombs.
33 The soil in the valley is sweet to
them;[c]
everyone follows after them,
and a countless throng goes[a] before
them.[d]
34 "So how can you console me[e] with
your nonsense?
Nothing is left of your answers but
falsehood!"

Eliphaz

22

Then Eliphaz the Temanite replied:

2 "Can a man be of benefit to God?[f]
Can even a wise person benefit him?
3 What pleasure would it give the
Almighty if you were righteous?
What would he gain if your ways
were blameless?

4 "Is it for your piety that he rebukes
you
and brings charges against you?[g]
5 Is not your wickedness great?
Are not your sins[h] endless?
6 You demanded security[i] from your
relatives for no reason;
you stripped people of their clothing,
leaving them naked.
7 You gave no water to the weary
and you withheld food from the
hungry,[j]
8 though you were a powerful man,
owning land—
an honored man,[k] living on it.
9 And you sent widows away empty-
handed[l]
and broke the strength of the
fatherless.
10 That is why snares are all around
you,
why sudden peril terrifies you,
11 why it is so dark[m] you cannot see,
and why a flood of water covers
you.[n]

12 "Is not God in the heights of heaven?[o]
And see how lofty are the highest
stars!
13 Yet you say, 'What does God know?[p]
Does he judge through such
darkness?[q]
14 Thick clouds[r] veil him, so he does not
see us
as he goes about in the vaulted
heavens.'
15 Will you keep to the old path
that the wicked have trod?
16 They were carried off before their
time,[s]
their foundations washed away by a
flood.[t]
17 They said to God, 'Leave us alone!
What can the Almighty do to us?'[u]

[a] 33 *Or them, / as a countless throng went*

21:33 [c] Job 3:22; 17:16; 24:24 [d] Job 3:19 **21:34** [e] Job 16:2 **22:2** [f] Lk 17:10 **22:4** [g] Job 14:3; 19:29; Ps 143:2 **22:5** [h] Job 11:6; 15:5 **22:6** [i] Ex 22:26; Dt 24:6, 17; Eze 18:12, 16 **22:7** [j] Job 31:17, 21, 31 **22:8** [k] Isa 3:3; 9:15 **22:9** [l] Job 24:3, 21 **22:11** [m] Job 5:14 [n] Ps 69:1-2; 124:4-5; La 3:54 **22:12** [o] Job 11:8 **22:13** [p] Ps 10:11; Isa 29:15 [q] Eze 8:12 **22:14** [r] Job 26:9 **22:16** [s] Job 15:32 [t] Job 14:19; Mt 7:26-27 **22:17** [u] Job 21:15

21:32 *watch is kept over their tombs.* Because of riches buried with the dead, tombs were concealed but also guarded, as is known from ancient Egypt. Tombs were sealed, such as the door of the tomb of Tutankhamun. In Egypt, the guardian of the dead was the jackal-god Anubis, assistant of Osiris the lord of death. One seal impression depicts Anubis, the jackal-god and protector of the dead, with nine bound prisoners.
22:6 *demanded security.* In the OT, a creditor could demand security in the form of clothing, but was supposed to give back a cloak at night (Ex 22:26–27; Dt 24:12–13,17; cf. Am 2:8). A Hebrew letter on an ostracon from Yavneh-Yam might refer to the same custom; someone complains that his garment was taken and he wants it back. Legal collections from the ancient Near East show an interest in protecting debtors from those who would take advantage of them.
22:8 *powerful man.* Lit. "man of arm" (see note on 40:9).
22:14 *vaulted heavens.* In the ancient Near East, heaven was sometimes seen as a dome, but sometimes also disk-shaped. According to Egyptian cosmology, the sky was the goddess Nut, who formed an arch above. See the articles "Cosmic Geography," p. 836, and "The 'Vault' and 'Water Above,'" p. 6.

[18] Yet it was he who filled their houses
with good things,[v]
so I stand aloof from the plans of the
wicked.[w]
[19] The righteous see their ruin and
rejoice;[x]
the innocent mock[y] them, saying,
[20] 'Surely our foes are destroyed,
and fire[z] devours their wealth.'

[21] "Submit to God and be at peace with
him;
in this way prosperity will come to
you.[a]
[22] Accept instruction from his mouth
and lay up his words in your heart.
[23] If you return[b] to the Almighty, you will
be restored:[c]
If you remove wickedness far from
your tent[d]
[24] and assign your nuggets to the dust,
your gold of Ophir to the rocks in
the ravines,[e]
[25] then the Almighty will be your gold,
the choicest silver for you.[f]
[26] Surely then you will find delight in the
Almighty[g]
and will lift up your face to God.
[27] You will pray to him,[h] and he will
hear you,
and you will fulfill your vows.
[28] What you decide on will be done,
and light will shine on your ways.
[29] When people are brought low and you
say, 'Lift them up!'
then he will save the downcast.[i]
[30] He will deliver even one who is not
innocent,
who will be delivered through the
cleanness of your hands."[j]

Job

23 Then Job replied:

[2] "Even today my complaint[k] is
bitter;[l]
his hand*[a]* is heavy in spite of*[b]* my
groaning.
[3] If only I knew where to find him;
if only I could go to his dwelling!
[4] I would state my case[m] before him
and fill my mouth with arguments.
[5] I would find out what he would
answer me,
and consider what he would say
to me.
[6] Would he vigorously oppose me?[n]
No, he would not press charges
against me.
[7] There the upright can establish their
innocence before him,[o]
and there I would be delivered
forever from my judge.

[8] "But if I go to the east, he is not there;
if I go to the west, I do not find him.
[9] When he is at work in the north, I do
not see him;
when he turns to the south, I catch
no glimpse of him.[p]
[10] But he knows the way that I take;
when he has tested me,[q] I will come
forth as gold.[r]
[11] My feet have closely followed his steps;[s]
I have kept to his way without
turning aside.[t]
[12] I have not departed from the
commands of his lips;[u]
I have treasured the words of his
mouth more than my daily
bread.[v]

[13] "But he stands alone, and who can
oppose him?
He does whatever he pleases.[w]
[14] He carries out his decree against me,
and many such plans he still has in
store.[x]
[15] That is why I am terrified before him;
when I think of all this, I fear him.
[16] God has made my heart faint;[y]
the Almighty[z] has terrified me.
[17] Yet I am not silenced by the darkness,[a]
by the thick darkness that covers my
face.

24 "Why does the Almighty not set
times for judgment?[b]
Why must those who know him look
in vain for such days?[c]
[2] There are those who move boundary
stones;[d]
they pasture flocks they have stolen.

22:18 [v] Job 12:6 [w] Job 21:16 **22:19** [x] Ps 58:10; 107:42 [y] Ps 52:6 **22:20** [z] Job 15:30 **22:21** [a] Ps 34:8-10 **22:23** [b] Job 8:5; Isa 31:6; Zec 1:3 [c] Isa 19:22; Ac 20:32 [d] Job 11:14 **22:24** [e] Job 31:25 **22:25** [f] Isa 33:6 **22:26** [g] Job 27:10; Isa 58:14 **22:27** [h] Job 33:26; 34:28; Isa 58:9 **22:29** [i] Mt 23:12; 1Pe 5:5 **22:30** [j] Job 42:7-8 **23:2** [k] Job 7:11 [l] Job 6:3 **23:4** [m] Job 13:18 **23:6** [n] Job 9:4 **23:7** [o] Job 13:3 **23:9** [p] Job 9:11 **23:10** [q] Ps 66:10; 139:1-3 [r] 1Pe 1:7 **23:11** [s] Ps 17:5 [t] Ps 44:18 **23:12** [u] Job 6:10 [v] Jn 4:32,34 **23:13** [w] Ps 115:3 **23:14** [x] 1Th 3:3 **23:16** [y] Dt 20:3; Ps 22:14; Jer 51:46 [z] Job 27:2 **23:17** [a] Job 19:8 **24:1** [b] Jer 46:10 [c] Ac 1:7 **24:2** [d] Dt 19:14; 27:17; Pr 23:10

[a] 2 Septuagint and Syriac; Hebrew / *the hand on me*
[b] 2 Or *heavy on me in*

22:24 *gold of Ophir.* An eighth-century BC ostracon found at Tel Qasile mentions "gold from Ophir," but the location of Ophir is still unknown (East Africa, Arabia or possibly India). It might have been reached via the harbor of Ezion Geber at Elath in the Red Sea. See notes on 1Ch 29:4; 1Ki 9:28.

23:10 *tested ... come forth as gold.* Gold is used as a symbol of testing because of the process of purification it must go through. Job will be tested by God as the faithful are in Ps 26:2; 66:10. That there are grades of purity is evident from the Amarna letters (Nos. 7, 10), in which the Babylonian king writes that the gold that was brought to him was not pure enough. In that text the gold is not metaphoric, as it is here in Job, but it demonstrates the need for diligence in the purification process.

24:2 *boundary stones.* The "boundary stone" or "boundary marker" (as with the Babylonian *kudurru*) was not so much a marker of property as a legal document that contained an inscription describing the owner of the property and curses on those transgressing this legal right. On an Egyptian painting, an official bows down to a small standing stone, puts his hand to his mouth to take

[3] They drive away the orphan's donkey
and take the widow's ox in pledge.[e]
[4] They thrust the needy from the path
and force all the poor[f] of the land
into hiding.[g]
[5] Like wild donkeys in the desert,
the poor go about their labor[h] of
foraging food;
the wasteland provides food for their
children.
[6] They gather fodder in the fields
and glean in the vineyards of the
wicked.
[7] Lacking clothes, they spend the night
naked;
they have nothing to cover
themselves in the cold.[i]
[8] They are drenched by mountain rains
and hug[j] the rocks for lack of shelter.
[9] The fatherless[k] child is snatched from
the breast;
the infant of the poor is seized for a
debt.
[10] Lacking clothes, they go about naked;
they carry the sheaves, but still go
hungry.
[11] They crush olives among the terraces[a];
they tread the winepresses, yet suffer
thirst.
[12] The groans of the dying rise from the
city,
and the souls of the wounded cry
out for help.[l]
But God charges no one with
wrongdoing.[m]

[13] "There are those who rebel against the
light,[n]
who do not know its ways
or stay in its paths.[o]
[14] When daylight is gone, the murderer
rises up,
kills the poor and needy,
and in the night steals forth like a
thief.[p]
[15] The eye of the adulterer watches for
dusk;[q]
he thinks, 'No eye will see me,'[r]
and he keeps his face concealed.

24:3 [e] Dt 24:6, 10, 12, 17; Job 22:6 **24:4** [f] Job 29:12; 30:25; Ps 41:1 [g] Pr 28:28 **24:5** [h] Ps 104:23 **24:7** [i] Ex 22:27; Job 22:6 **24:8** [j] La 4:5 **24:9** [k] Dt 24:17 **24:12** [l] Eze 26:15 [m] Job 9:23 **24:13** [n] Jn 3:19-20 [o] Isa 5:20 **24:14** [p] Ps 10:9 **24:15** [q] Pr 7:8-9 [r] Ps 10:11

24:16 [s] Ex 22:2; Mt 6:19 [t] Jn 3:20 **24:18** [u] Job 9:26 [v] Job 22:16 **24:19** [w] Job 6:17 [x] Job 21:13 **24:20** [y] Job 18:17; Pr 10:7 [z] Ps 31:12; Da 4:14 **24:21** [a] Job 22:9 **24:22** [b] Dt 28:66 **24:23** [c] Job 12:6 [d] Job 11:11 **24:24** [e] Job 14:21; Ps 37:10 [f] Isa 17:5 **24:25** [g] Job 6:28; 27:4 **25:2** [h] Job 9:4; Rev 1:6

[16] In the dark, thieves break into houses,[s]
but by day they shut themselves in;
they want nothing to do with the
light.[t]
[17] For all of them, midnight is their
morning;
they make friends with the terrors of
darkness.

[18] "Yet they are foam[u] on the surface of
the water;[v]
their portion of the land is cursed,
so that no one goes to the vineyards.
[19] As heat and drought snatch away the
melted snow,[w]
so the grave[x] snatches away those
who have sinned.
[20] The womb forgets them,
the worm feasts on them;
the wicked are no longer remembered[y]
but are broken like a tree.[z]
[21] They prey on the barren and childless
woman,
and to the widow they show no
kindness.[a]
[22] But God drags away the mighty by his
power;
though they become established,
they have no assurance of life.[b]
[23] He may let them rest in a feeling of
security,[c]
but his eyes are on their ways.[d]
[24] For a little while they are exalted, and
then they are gone;[e]
they are brought low and gathered
up like all others;
they are cut off like heads of grain.[f]

[25] "If this is not so, who can prove me
false
and reduce my words to nothing?"[g]

Bildad

25 Then Bildad the Shuhite replied:

[2] "Dominion and awe belong to God;[h]
he establishes order in the heights of
heaven.

[a] *11* The meaning of the Hebrew for this word is uncertain.

an oath and swears: "As surely as the great god endures in the heaven, this boundary stone is properly erected." The "Wisdom of Amenemope" advises its readers not to move the markers on the borders of the fields. Moving a boundary stone is regarded as an offense in Dt 19:14; 27:17; Pr 22:28; 23:10.

24:9 *the infant of the poor is seized.* In Mesopotamia children could be offered as collateral, or simply seized from those who could not pay, though the latter was unlawful. In an archive of several generations of divination priests in the ancient town of Emar, several documents concerned the sale of infant children into the family and featured footprints of the children imprinted in clay.

24:11 *crush olives.* Olives were crushed in special presses, such as the one found at Ekron. A huge stone crushing-wheel was rolled over the olives placed on a basin. Stone weights (averaging 650 pounds [300 kilograms]) were attached to a beam, and the oil was squeezed out and ran into a vat. *tread the winepresses.* Wine was made by treading the grapes with the feet in stone troughs in earlier times, as is known from Egyptian paintings. The juice was then collected in a smaller vat before it was stored in wine jars.

25:2 *order.* The Hebrew word is rare and of uncertain meaning, though the NIV choice of "order" is logical given the context. Order was one of the most important issues in the ancient world, so much so that creation narratives were often more concerned with recounting the origins of order than the origins of matter. Order is established through the application of wisdom, and it demonstrates the authority of the one who has established it.

3 Can his forces be numbered?
On whom does his light not rise?[i]
4 How then can a mortal be righteous
before God?
How can one born of woman be
pure?[j]
5 If even the moon[k] is not bright
and the stars are not pure in his
eyes,[l]
6 how much less a mortal, who is but a
maggot —
a human being,[m] who is only a
worm!"[n]

Job 26

Then Job replied:

2 "How you have helped the powerless![o]
How you have saved the arm that is
feeble![p]
3 What advice you have offered to one
without wisdom!
And what great insight you have
displayed!
4 Who has helped you utter these words?
And whose spirit spoke from your
mouth?
5 "The dead are in deep anguish,[q]
those beneath the waters and all that
live in them.
6 The realm of the dead[r] is naked before
God;
Destruction[a] lies uncovered.[s]
7 He spreads out the northern skies[t] over
empty space;
he suspends the earth over nothing.
8 He wraps up the waters[u] in his
clouds,[v]
yet the clouds do not burst under
their weight.
9 He covers the face of the full moon,
spreading his clouds[w] over it.
10 He marks out the horizon on the face
of the waters[x]
for a boundary between light and
darkness.[y]
11 The pillars of the heavens quake,
aghast at his rebuke.

25:3 [i] Jas 1:17 **25:4** [j] Job 4:17; 14:4 **25:5** [k] Job 31:26 [l] Job 15:15 **25:6** [m] Job 7:17 [n] Ps 22:6 **26:2** [o] Job 6:12 [p] Ps 71:9 **26:5** [q] Ps 88:10 **26:6** [r] Ps 139:8 [s] Job 41:11; Pr 15:11; Heb 4:13 **26:7** [t] Job 9:8 **26:8** [u] Pr 30:4 [v] Job 37:11 **26:9** [w] Job 22:14; Ps 97:2 **26:10** [x] Pr 8:27,29 [y] Job 38:8-11

[a] 6 Hebrew *Abaddon*

Babylonian world map (c. 600 BC), the earliest known map of the world. This map shows outer boundaries similar to God marking out the horizon in Job 26:10.

26:5 *The dead.* The Hebrew is "Rephaim," which refers to the inhabitants of the underworld (e.g., Ps 88:10; Isa 14:9; 26:14,19). The Rephaim live beneath the waters of the underworld (water was sometimes associated with the underworld). These were among the blessed and beatified dead and the deified ancestors and rulers in Ugarit, and in the tomb inscriptions of the Phoenician kings Tabnit and Eshmunazar. In other parts of the Hebrew Bible, they are "giants" (e.g., Ge 14:5; 15:20; Dt 2:11,20).
26:6 *Destruction.* See note on Pr 15:11.
26:7 *spreads out the northern skies.* Another cosmogony (as in 9:5 – 10; see the article "Cosmic Geography," p. 836) is described in vv. 7 – 14. In 9:8, Ps 104:2 and Isa 40:22, the Creator "stretches out the heavens" like a tent. *northern.* Hebrew *tsaphon,* which designates "north." Zaphon is also the cosmic mountain *par excellence* (Ps 48:2); it is located north of Israel, in Syria. Here it is synonymous with heaven (cf. Job 37:22; Isa 14:13), where the deity resides. It was originally the deified holy cosmic mountain of Ugaritic mythology (identified with the Jebel al-Aqra, north of Ugarit) where the deities of the North-West Semitic pantheon, and especially the god Baal, were believed to assemble. The concept goes back to the Hittite-Hurrian mountain-god Hazzi and lives on in the Aramaic Amherst Papyrus from the first millennium BC. Philo of Byblos calls the mountain Kassion, as do other Greek texts. The cult of Zeus Kasios lived on until the time of Julian Apostata in AD 363.
26:10 *marks out the horizon.* In 38:5, a "measuring line" is mentioned. This designates the outer limits of the cosmos, beyond which no mortal can go. A "world map" with boundaries is drawn on a seventh-century BC clay tablet with Babylon in the center. In ancient Near Eastern thought, depressions at the western and eastern horizons had cosmic gates through which the sun entered the sky during daytime and again passed through into the underworld at nighttime.
26:11 *pillars of the heavens.* See the article "Cosmic Geography," p. 836. According to Egyptian thought, the god Shu held up the sky, which was identified as his daughter the goddess Nut. The pillars of heaven could also refer to the Mesopotamian idea of a chain of large mountains at the edges of the world supporting the heavens or celestial vault (see the article "The 'Vault' and 'Water Above,'" p. 6).

12 By his power he churned up the sea;[z]
by his wisdom[a] he cut Rahab to pieces.
13 By his breath the skies became fair;
his hand pierced the gliding serpent.[b]
14 And these are but the outer fringe of his works;
how faint the whisper we hear of him!
Who then can understand the thunder of his power?"[c]

Job's Final Word to His Friends

27 And Job continued his discourse:[d]
2 "As surely as God lives, who has denied me justice,[e]
the Almighty, who has made my life bitter,[f]
3 as long as I have life within me,
the breath of God[g] in my nostrils,
4 my lips will not say anything wicked,
and my tongue will not utter lies.[h]
5 I will never admit you are in the right;
till I die, I will not deny my integrity.[i]
6 I will maintain my innocence and never let go of it;
my conscience will not reproach me as long as I live.[j]

7 "May my enemy be like the wicked,
my adversary like the unjust!
8 For what hope have the godless[k] when they are cut off,
when God takes away their life?[l]
9 Does God listen to their cry
when distress comes upon them?[m]
10 Will they find delight in the Almighty?[n]
Will they call on God at all times?

11 "I will teach you about the power of God;
the ways of the Almighty I will not conceal.
12 You have all seen this yourselves.
Why then this meaningless talk?

13 "Here is the fate God allots to the wicked,
the heritage a ruthless man receives from the Almighty:[o]
14 However many his children, their fate is the sword;[p]
his offspring will never have enough to eat.[q]

26:12 [z] Ex 14:21; Isa 51:15; Jer 31:35 [a] Job 12:13 **26:13** [b] Isa 27:1 **26:14** [c] Job 36:29 **27:1** [d] Job 29:1 **27:2** [e] Job 34:5 [f] Job 9:18 **27:3** [g] Job 32:8; 33:4 **27:4** [h] Job 6:28 **27:5** [i] Job 2:9; 13:15 **27:6** [j] Job 2:3 **27:8** [k] Job 8:13 [l] Job 11:20; Lk 12:20 **27:9** [m] Job 35:12; Pr 1:28; Isa 1:15; Jer 14:12; Mic 3:4 **27:10** [n] Job 22:26 **27:13** [o] Job 15:20; 20:29 **27:14** [p] Dt 28:41; Job 15:22; Hos 9:13 [q] Job 20:10

27:15 [r] Ps 78:64 **27:16** [s] Zec 9:3 **27:17** [t] Pr 28:8; Ecc 2:26 **27:18** [u] Job 8:14 [v] Isa 1:8 **27:19** [w] Job 7:8 **27:20** [x] Job 15:21 [y] Job 20:8 **27:21** [z] Job 7:10; 21:18 **27:22** [a] Jer 13:14; Eze 5:11; 24:14 [b] Job 11:20 **27:23** [c] Job 18:18 **28:2** [d] Dt 8:9 **28:3** [e] Ecc 1:13 **28:5** [f] Ps 104:14

15 The plague will bury those who survive him,
and their widows will not weep for them.[r]
16 Though he heaps up silver like dust
and clothes like piles of clay,[s]
17 what he lays up the righteous will wear,[t]
and the innocent will divide his silver.
18 The house he builds is like a moth's cocoon,[u]
like a hut[v] made by a watchman.
19 He lies down wealthy, but will do so no more;[w]
when he opens his eyes, all is gone.
20 Terrors overtake him like a flood;[x]
a tempest snatches him away in the night.[y]
21 The east wind carries him off, and he is gone;
it sweeps him out of his place.[z]
22 It hurls itself against him without mercy[a]
as he flees headlong from its power.[b]
23 It claps its hands in derision
and hisses him out of his place."[c]

Interlude: Where Wisdom Is Found

28 There is a mine for silver
and a place where gold is refined.
2 Iron is taken from the earth,
and copper is smelted from ore.[d]
3 Mortals put an end to the darkness;[e]
they search out the farthest recesses
for ore in the blackest darkness.
4 Far from human dwellings they cut a shaft,
in places untouched by human feet;
far from other people they dangle and sway.
5 The earth, from which food comes,[f]
is transformed below as by fire;
6 lapis lazuli comes from its rocks,
and its dust contains nuggets of gold.
7 No bird of prey knows that hidden path,
no falcon's eye has seen it.
8 Proud beasts do not set foot on it,
and no lion prowls there.
9 People assault the flinty rock with their hands
and lay bare the roots of the mountains.
10 They tunnel through the rock;
their eyes see all its treasures.

26:12–13 *churned up the sea ... cut Rahab to pieces ... pierced the gliding serpent.* See note on 9:13.
27:23 *claps its hands in derision.* The clapping of hands can indicate joy (e.g., Ps 47:1), but clapping in derision is a gesture of scoffing (cf. La 2:15–16) also known from Mesopotamia. See 34:37 for clapping the hands scornfully in contempt of God.

JOB 28

Metals and Mining

Seven metals are known from the ancient Near East: three precious metals—gold, silver and electrum (a naturally occurring alloy of gold and silver), and four base metals—copper, tin, lead and iron. Bronze was an alloy made from copper and tin. Various sources are available to study ancient Near Eastern metallurgy—textual references, excavated objects and metallurgical analysis. The countries of origin of these metals are still a matter of dispute among scholars, but the ancient Near East was the homeland of metallurgy. Gold was mined in southern Arabia and especially in Cush (Nubia) in the Sudan. Silver came from Anatolia and Iran, and copper from Cyprus and Iran. Iron came from Anatolia, Cyprus and Canaan, and tin from Afghanistan. Mining is known from excavations at the copper and turquoise mines of Serabit el-Qadêm in Sinai. A map of an Egyptian gold-mining district in the Wadi Hammamat can be found on a thirteenth-century BC papyrus, and the smelting of metals is depicted in Egyptian paintings.

Various jewels and gemstones are mentioned in Job 28 and Biblical texts such as Ex 28:17–21; 39:10–14 (stones in the breastplate of the high priest); Eze 28:13 (ornaments of the king of Tyre); and Rev 21:19–21 (stones of the New Jerusalem). The Gilgamesh Epic describes the trees of the gods with carnelian fruit, lapis lazuli foliage, coral, agate and hematite. These stones and jewels are sometimes difficult to identify, and they originated from various parts of the ancient world. Sapphire is identified with the deep blue stone lapis lazuli, which came from the province of Badakhshan in Afghanistan. Many stones were found in Egypt and nearby regions. ◆

Egyptian painting from the chapel of Rekhmire. The ancient Near East was the homeland of metallurgy. Here men are accomplishing two tasks, maintaining hearth heat and melting the metal. To stoke the fire, a bellows system has been developed: a leather bag is attached to a white bracket. The worker standing on the bags can change his weight from one foot to the other while he pulls on their strings; pressurized air is delivered directly into the furnace by reed pipes. Adjacent to the furnace is a pile of charcoal and a large vase (perhaps containing water to cool the tools). The crucible containing the metal is placed in, and removed from, the furnace by means of branches of wood.

11 They search[a] the sources of the rivers
and bring hidden things to light.

12 But where can wisdom be found?[g]
Where does understanding dwell?
13 No mortal comprehends its worth;[h]
it cannot be found in the land of
the living.
14 The deep says, "It is not in me";
the sea says, "It is not with me."
15 It cannot be bought with the finest
gold,
nor can its price be weighed out in
silver.[i]
16 It cannot be bought with the gold of
Ophir,
with precious onyx or lapis lazuli.
17 Neither gold nor crystal can compare
with it,
nor can it be had for jewels of
gold.[j]
18 Coral and jasper are not worthy of
mention;
the price of wisdom is beyond
rubies.[k]
19 The topaz of Cush cannot compare
with it;
it cannot be bought with pure gold.[l]

20 Where then does wisdom come from?
Where does understanding dwell?[m]
21 It is hidden from the eyes of every
living thing,
concealed even from the birds in the
sky.
22 Destruction[b][n] and Death say,
"Only a rumor of it has reached our
ears."
23 God understands the way to it
and he alone knows where it
dwells,[o]
24 for he views the ends of the earth[p]
and sees everything under the
heavens.[q]
25 When he established the force of the
wind
and measured out the waters,[r]
26 when he made a decree for the rain
and a path for the thunderstorm,[s]
27 then he looked at wisdom and
appraised it;
he confirmed it and tested it.
28 And he said to the human race,
"The fear of the Lord — that is
wisdom,
and to shun evil is understanding."[t]

Job's Final Defense

29 Job continued his discourse:[u]

2 "How I long for the months gone by,
for the days when God watched over
me,[v]
3 when his lamp shone on my head
and by his light I walked through
darkness![w]
4 Oh, for the days when I was in my
prime,
when God's intimate friendship
blessed my house,[x]
5 when the Almighty was still with me
and my children were around me,
6 when my path was drenched with
cream[y]
and the rock[z] poured out for me
streams of olive oil.[a]

7 "When I went to the gate[b] of the city
and took my seat in the public
square,

28:12 [g] Ecc 7:24 **28:13** [h] Pr 3:15; Mt 13:44-46 **28:15** [i] Pr 3:13-14; 8:10-11; 16:16 **28:17** [j] Pr 16:16 **28:18** [k] Pr 3:15 **28:19** [l] Pr 8:19 **28:20** [m] ver 23, 28 **28:22** [n] Job 26:6 **28:23** [o] Pr 8:22-31 **28:24** [p] Ps 33:13-14 [q] Pr 15:3 **28:25** [r] Job 12:15; Ps 135:7 **28:26** [s] Job 37:3,8,11; 38:25,27 **28:28** [t] Dt 4:6; Ps 111:10; Pr 1:7; 9:10 **29:1** [u] Job 13:12; 27:1 **29:2** [v] Jer 31:28 **29:3** [w] Job 11:17 **29:4** [x] Ps 25:14; Pr 3:32 **29:6** [y] Job 20:17 [z] Ps 81:16 [a] Dt 32:13 **29:7** [b] Job 31:21

[a] 11 Septuagint, Aquila and Vulgate; Hebrew *They dam up* [b] 22 Hebrew *Abaddon*

28:11 *sources of the rivers.* The metallurgist searches this far-off, mysterious and hidden place situated between the two oceans. According to Ugaritic myth, the abode of the chief god El was "at the source of the rivers."
28:12 *wisdom.* See the article "What Is Wisdom?" p. 1040.
28:14 *The deep … the sea.* The hidden wisdom cannot even be found in the primeval oceans, described as the deep or the abyss (Hebrew *tehom*; cf. 38:16,30). In Mesopotamian thought, the Apsu — the deified subterranean water — was the original abode of the antediluvian sages, the *apkallu* (see note on 15:7), and the realm of the crafty god, the god of wisdom Ea or Enki.
28:17 *crystal.* The Hebrew word, which occurs only here in the OT, is taken to refer to glass, which was known as an article of luxury. Glassware in the form of vessels was manufactured by the Phoenicians, and the Egyptians used it for inlays in jewelry.
28:22 *Destruction and Death say.* Here the forces of Destruction (Hebrew *Abaddon*) and Death (*Mawet*) are personified. *Destruction.* See note on Pr 15:11. *Death.* See note on Job 18:13; see also the article "Death and Sheol," p. 833.
28:28 *The fear of the Lord — that is wisdom.* The Lord is the only one who knows where to find wisdom, which is objectified in v. 27. As in the book of Proverbs (Pr 1:7; 9:10), real wisdom is the "fear of the Lord." In the ancient Near East, the Mesopotamian god Ea/Enki was the god of immense wisdom, Marduk had the title "Lord of Wisdom" and the sun-god Shamash granted wisdom. Wisdom in the Hebrew Bible is used to denote the skills of the artisan (e.g., Ex 36:8), intelligence (e.g., 2Sa 14:2), and practical skills in life or an ethical lifestyle (Pr 1 – 2; 5; 11; 14). *wisdom.* The word is feminine in Hebrew, and wisdom is even personified as a woman (Pr 1; 3; 9). Wisdom is sometimes linked with creation (Pr 8:22 – 31).
29:6 *drenched with cream … streams of olive oil.* In Ugaritic texts, the god El has a dream and a vision that when the god Baal becomes alive again, the heavens will rain down oil, the wadis will run with honey — describing abundance and fertility. In other parts of the Hebrew Bible, the promised land is said to be "flowing with milk and honey" (Ex 3:17; Jos 5:6), referring to its fertility and abundance in produce, more precisely dairy farming and agriculture.
29:7 *gate of the city.* See note on 5:4. The gate of the city was not just the entry between the walls, it was the center of commerce and public jurisprudence. Elders met in this public sector to hear and discuss legal cases. News was exchanged there, and business deals concluded. What

8 the young men saw me and stepped
aside
and the old men rose to their feet;
9 the chief men refrained from speaking
and covered their mouths with their
hands;[c]
10 the voices of the nobles were hushed,
and their tongues stuck to the roof of
their mouths.[d]
11 Whoever heard me spoke well of me,
and those who saw me commended
me,
12 because I rescued the poor[e] who cried
for help,
and the fatherless[f] who had none to
assist them.[g]
13 The one who was dying blessed me;[h]
I made the widow's[i] heart sing.
14 I put on righteousness[j] as my clothing;
justice was my robe and my turban.
15 I was eyes[k] to the blind
and feet to the lame.
16 I was a father to the needy;[l]
I took up the case of the stranger.
17 I broke the fangs of the wicked
and snatched the victims from their
teeth.[m]

29:9 [c] Job 21:5
29:10 [d] Ps 137:6
29:12 [e] Job 24:4 [f] Job 31:17, 21 [g] Ps 72:12; Pr 21:13
29:13 [h] Job 31:20 [i] Job 22:9
29:14 [j] Job 27:6; Ps 132:9; Isa 59:17; 61:10; Eph 6:14
29:15 [k] Nu 10:31
29:16 [l] Job 24:4; Pr 29:7
29:17 [m] Ps 3:7
29:18 [n] Ps 30:6
29:19 [o] Job 18:16; Jer 17:8
29:20 [p] Ps 18:34 [q] Ge 49:24
29:22 [r] Dt 32:2

18 "I thought, 'I will die in my own
house,
my days as numerous as the grains
of sand.[n]
19 My roots will reach to the water,[o]
and the dew will lie all night on
my branches.
20 My glory will not fade;
the bow[p] will be ever new in my
hand.'[q]
21 "People listened to me expectantly,
waiting in silence for my counsel.
22 After I had spoken, they spoke no
more;
my words fell gently on their
ears.[r]
23 They waited for me as for
showers
and drank in my words as the
spring rain.
24 When I smiled at them, they scarcely
believed it;
the light of my face was precious
to them.[a]

[a] *24* The meaning of the Hebrew for this clause is uncertain.

---

we call "networking" today took place in the city gate, and here reputations were made or lost. Gates of the Iron Age had a number of chambers along the gateway, with benches lining them where business could be conducted, conversation could take place and cases could be heard. Prominent people in the city were often visible in the gate area, and there their public persona was on display. Both honor and shame found a myriad of ways to be recognized in this arena.

29:9 *covered their mouths with their hands.* See notes on 21:5; 40:4. Here the phrase is used to mean "refrained from speaking," referring to the respect Job enjoyed in earlier times when he was still a local chief. However, now he is shamed. When he used to go to the city gate and sit in the public square, young men stepped aside and old men rose (v. 8). The chiefs and nobles did not speak in his presence (vv. 9 – 10). In the ancient Near East, people of importance sat, while standing and kneeling was a gesture for greeting persons of high status. Such is prescribed in Lev 19:32, and Solomon greeted his mother in this way (1Ki 2:19). In Ugaritic literature, Baal stands in attendance to El; in contrast, the arrogant messengers of the Ugaritic god Yamm do not pay respect to the chief deity by prostrating themselves.

29:14 *clothing ... robe ... turban.* Justice and righteousness can be portrayed as garments (cf. Ps 132:9; Isa 61:10). In Job 30:18, Job wears a collared tunic. *turban.* A head covering formed by a wrapped piece of cloth, kept in place by a headband.

29:16 *I was a father to the needy.* In 22:9, Job was charged with neglecting the needy. He longs for the days when he was still respected, and is described as the ideal patriarch (see vv. 12 – 16) — administering social justice by looking after the needy, the poor, the fatherless, the widow, the lame, the blind and the stranger. This is repeated in 31:13 – 18. Throughout the ancient Near East, the hallmark of the righteous individual or the just king was that they cared for the needy and vulnerable.

29:20 *bow.* Bows had many symbolic and metaphoric associations in the ancient world that are not necessarily transparent to modern readers. The bow is a symbol of glory (Hebrew *kabod*) and power. In 30:11, the unstrung (therefore unusable) bow is part of Job's affliction. The bow (cf. 20:24) is often depicted in scenes of military assault in ancient Near Eastern art as a common offensive weapon. The Ugaritic Aqhat received a bow from the craftsman-god Kothar, but it was coveted by the warrior-goddess Anat, and Aqhat was murdered for it and the bow destroyed. When a bow was broken (Jer 49:35; Hos 1:5), it implied pending destruction. One treaty reads: "May Astarte break your bow in battle." The traditional iconography of the pharaoh of Egypt shows him trampling on nine bows (the traditional enemies of Egypt), and the defeated enemy snaps his bow. An Assyrian relief shows a defeated Elamite cutting his bow as a gesture of defeat and loss of power.

29:23 *waited ... as for showers.* Job's words were awaited like showers and spring rain. In the Ugaritic Keret epic, the farmers wait for the rains of the god Baal and express their joy over the coming rain. This sort of comment makes sense in the meteorological context of the Levant. The success of the agricultural season was dependent on the rains that fell during the winter (the rainy season). The "early rains" and "latter rains" marked the beginning and end of the rainy season that prepared the ground for planting. Whether urban dwellers or farmers, people were heavily dependent on the growth of local crops. A rainy season that began late, ended early or contained less than normal rainfall signaled an underproductive harvest season that could lead to want or even disastrous drought and famine. This background gives poignancy to the metaphor employed here.

29:24 *the light of my face.* This facial expression of joy is known from Ugaritic and Akkadian sources. When the Ugaritic hero Danel hears that a son will be born to him, "his face lit up with joy, His countenance glowed. Signs of worry disappeared from his forehead as he laughed." After eating and drinking, Enkidu in the Gilgamesh Epic

25 I chose the way for them and sat as
their chief;
I dwelt as a king[s] among his
troops;
I was like one who comforts
mourners.[t]

30

"But now they mock me,[u]
men younger than I,
whose fathers I would have disdained
to put with my sheep dogs.
2 Of what use was the strength of their
hands to me,
since their vigor had gone from
them?
3 Haggard from want and hunger,
they roamed[a] the parched land
in desolate wastelands at night.
4 In the brush they gathered salt herbs,
and their food[b] was the root of the
broom bush.
5 They were banished from human
society,
shouted at as if they were thieves.
6 They were forced to live in the dry
stream beds,
among the rocks and in holes in the
ground.
7 They brayed among the bushes
and huddled in the undergrowth.
8 A base and nameless brood,
they were driven out of the land.

9 "And now those young men mock me[v]
in song;[w]
I have become a byword[x] among
them.
10 They detest me and keep their
distance;
they do not hesitate to spit in my
face.[y]
11 Now that God has unstrung my bow
and afflicted me,[z]
they throw off restraint[a] in my
presence.
12 On my right the tribe[c] attacks;
they lay snares for my feet,[b]
they build their siege ramps against
me.[c]
13 They break up my road;[d]
they succeed in destroying me.
'No one can help him,' they say.
14 They advance as through a gaping
breach;
amid the ruins they come rolling in.
15 Terrors overwhelm me;[e]
my dignity is driven away as by the
wind,
my safety vanishes like a cloud.[f]

16 "And now my life ebbs away;[g]
days of suffering grip me.
17 Night pierces my bones;
my gnawing pains never rest.
18 In his great power God becomes like
clothing to me[d];
he binds me like the neck of my
garment.
19 He throws me into the mud,[h]
and I am reduced to dust and ashes.

20 "I cry out to you, God, but you do not
answer;[i]
I stand up, but you merely look at me.
21 You turn on me ruthlessly;[j]
with the might of your hand[k] you
attack me.[l]
22 You snatch me up and drive me before
the wind;[m]
you toss me about in the storm.[n]
23 I know you will bring me down to
death,[o]
to the place appointed for all the
living.[p]
24 "Surely no one lays a hand on a
broken man
when he cries for help in his distress.[q]

29:25 [s] Job 1:3; 31:37 [t] Job 4:4 **30:1** [u] Job 12:4 **30:9** [v] Ps 69:11 [w] Job 12:4; La 3:14, 63 [x] Job 17:6 **30:10** [y] Nu 12:14; Dt 25:9; Isa 50:6; Mt 26:67 **30:11** [z] Ru 1:21 [a] Ps 32:9 **30:12** [b] Ps 140:4-5 [c] Job 19:12 **30:13** [d] Isa 3:12 **30:15** [e] Job 31:23; Ps 55:4-5 [f] Job 3:25; Hos 13:3 **30:16** [g] Job 3:24; Ps 22:14; 42:4 **30:19** [h] Ps 69:2, 14 **30:20** [i] Job 19:7 **30:21** [j] Job 19:6, 22 [k] Job 16:9, 14 [l] Job 10:3 **30:22** [m] Job 27:21 [n] Job 9:17 **30:23** [o] Job 9:22; 10:8 [p] Job 3:19 **30:24** [q] Job 19:7

[a] 3 Or *gnawed* [b] 4 Or *fuel* [c] 12 The meaning of the Hebrew for this word is uncertain. [d] 18 Hebrew; Septuagint *power he grasps my clothing*

became merry, and his face lit up. In contrast, the innocent sufferer in the Babylonian *Ludlul bel nemeqi* ("I will praise the lord of wisdom") complains, "When my ill-wisher heard, his face lit up / When the tidings reached her, my ill-wisher, her mood became radiant."

30:1 *sheep dogs.* Dogs (*Canis familiaris*) are the oldest domesticated animals and were highly valued. In Mesopotamia, the healing-god Gula is sometimes portrayed in dog form. In Egypt, dogs were mummified and formed part of the animal cult. A large dog burial place was found at Ashkelon, possibly linked with a healing cult, though interpretation remains elusive. Dogs were regarded as pets in ancient Egypt and are depicted in Egyptian paintings with collars and sitting under their masters' chairs. One beloved pet was buried in a wooden coffin. On Egyptian paintings they are also used in war, and on Assyrian reliefs they are shown being used for hunting. Shepherd dogs are shown on the cylinder seal depicting Etana (*Illus.* to 21:5). However, in contrast, "man's best friend" is not highly regarded in the OT (1Sa 17:43; Isa 56:10–11; cf. Rev 22:15)! Dogs were not pampered household pets as today; they were dangerous scavengers that ate corpses and the refuse of ancient cities and towns. In the Amarna letters, the vassal calls himself the "dog" of the pharaoh, as does the servant in the Lachish letters.

30:4 *salt herbs.* Refers to saltwort (*Artiplex halimus*), an edible but sour plant. According to the Talmud, the plant was for the poor and starving. *food.* Or "fuel" (see NIV text note). *root of the broom bush.* These roots make good charcoal (Ps 120:4), but are not edible. *broom bush.* The prophet Elijah sat under one (see 1Ki 19:4 and note).

30:22 *drive me before the wind.* Cf. 27:21. For God as a storm-god, see notes on 4:9; 37:2–5; see also the article "Baal," p. 600.

30:23 *bring me down to death, to the place appointed for all the living.* Death (Hebrew *Mawet*) is a house (Hebrew *bet*, NIV "place"), as with Sheol in 17:13. See note on 18:13; see also the article "Death and Sheol," p. 833.

25 Have I not wept for those in trouble?
Has not my soul grieved for the
poor?[r]
26 Yet when I hoped for good, evil came;
when I looked for light, then came
darkness.[s]
27 The churning inside me never stops;[t]
days of suffering confront me.
28 I go about blackened,[u] but not by the
sun;
I stand up in the assembly and cry
for help.[v]
29 I have become a brother of jackals,[w]
a companion of owls.[x]
30 My skin grows black and peels;[y]
my body burns with fever.[z]
31 My lyre is tuned to mourning,[a]
and my pipe to the sound of wailing.

31 "I made a covenant with my eyes
not to look lustfully at a young
woman.[b]
2 For what is our lot from God above,
our heritage from the Almighty on
high?[c]
3 Is it not ruin[d] for the wicked,
disaster for those who do wrong?[e]
4 Does he not see my ways[f]
and count my every step?[g]

5 "If I have walked with falsehood
or my foot has hurried after
deceit[h] —
6 let God weigh me in honest scales[i]
and he will know that I am
blameless —
7 if my steps have turned from the path,[j]
if my heart has been led by my eyes,
or if my hands[k] have been defiled,
8 then may others eat what I have sown,[l]
and may my crops be uprooted.[m]

9 "If my heart has been enticed[n] by a
woman,
or if I have lurked at my neighbor's
door,
10 then may my wife grind another man's
grain,
and may other men sleep with her.[o]
11 For that would have been wicked,
a sin to be judged.[p]
12 It is a fire[q] that burns to Destruction[a];[r]
it would have uprooted my harvest.[s]

13 "If I have denied justice to any of my
servants,
whether male or female,
when they had a grievance against
me,[t]
14 what will I do when God confronts
me?
What will I answer when called to
account?

30:25 [r] Job 24:4; Ps 35:13-14; Ro 12:15 **30:26** [s] Job 3:25-26; 19:8; Jer 8:15 **30:27** [t] La 2:11 **30:28** [u] Ps 38:6; 42:9; 43:2 [v] Job 19:7 **30:29** [w] Ps 44:19 [x] Ps 102:6; Mic 1:8 **30:30** [y] La 4:8 [z] Ps 102:3 **30:31** [a] Isa 24:8 **31:1** [b] Mt 5:28 **31:2** [c] Job 20:29 **31:3** [d] Job 21:30 [e] Job 34:22 **31:4** [f] 2Ch 16:9 [g] Pr 5:21 **31:5** [h] Mic 2:11 **31:6** [i] Job 6:2; 27:5-6 **31:7** [j] Job 23:11 [k] Job 9:30 **31:8** [l] Lev 26:16; Job 20:18 [m] Mic 6:15 **31:9** [n] Job 24:15 **31:10** [o] Dt 28:30; Jer 8:10 **31:11** [p] Ge 38:24; Lev 20:10; Dt 22:22-24 **31:12** [q] Job 15:30 [r] Job 26:6 [s] Job 20:28 **31:13** [t] Dt 24:14-15

[a] *12* Hebrew *Abaddon*

30:28 *blackened.* This is a difficult verse and has been understood as referring to Job's skin, which turned black because of disease (v. 30; 2:7). In the diagnostic medical texts and omen texts from Mesopotamia, black skin lesions (evidence of necrosis) are observed and remedies suggested. Since this is a different Hebrew word than that used in v. 30 ("black"), it could refer to ashes that blacken the skin.
30:29 *jackals ... owls.* In ancient Egypt, the god connected with the dead, the protector of the necropolis and the god of embalming the dead was Anubis. He was represented in the form of a jackal or canine. The reason for the link with these animals might be that canines or jackals often roamed between tombs, even scavenging on the corpses. In Job, the metaphor of the jackal is used because of the wailing sounds they make. Wailing and howling are linked with the jackal and the owl (cf. Mic 1:8, where God wails and howls like a jackal, and moans like an owl). When cities are cursed in treaties they are said to become mounds for foxes and owls, i.e., desolate places. *owls.* The Hebrew word can sometimes be translated "ostriches," but owls are nocturnal and feared for their eerie screeches, so "owls" makes better sense in this context.
30:30 *skin grows black.* See note on v. 28.
30:31 *lyre ... pipe.* See the articles "Lyre," p. 488; "Music and Musicians," p. 524. *mourning.* See note on 2:8; see also the article "Mourning," p. 828.
31:6 *let God weigh me in honest scales.* Scales and weights in various shapes (lions, ducks or cattle) are known from ancient Near Eastern art. These were used to weigh metals such as gold and products for trading. According to Egyptian belief, the heart of the deceased was weighed on a scale to determine whether it was pure (as with metals). Just balances or honest scales were important in the ancient Near East, and are described in the Bible in Lev 19:36; Pr 16:11; Eze 45:10; cf. Am 8:5 ("boosting the price and cheating with dishonest scales"); Mic 6:11 ("dishonest scales, with a bag of false weights"). The problem of false scales is dealt with in Mesopotamian texts such as the hymn to Nanshe. Ancient Near Eastern kings determined the standard of weights to prevent corruption and cheating through the use of false weights. The weights were standardized by the Sumerian king Ur-Nammu. In the Egyptian "Wisdom of Amenemope," the student is advised not to alter the weights. God hates false scales (Pr 11:1), and in a hymn to the god Shamash, merchants who switch weights lose capital.
31:10 *may my wife grind another man's grain.* In OT times, grain was ground by women using a stone millstone, many examples of which were found in Canaan. The millstone consisted of a saddle quern and a hand-operated grinding stone, and was one of the most important implements in the ordinary ancient Israelite home. The law prohibited anyone from taking it as collateral (Dt 24:6), and it was also a symbol of destruction (Jer 25:10). Millstones could be used as weapons (Jdg 9:53; 2Sa 11:21). In 41:24, it is used to describe the strength of the chest of the Leviathan. *sleep with her.* Lit. "bow down to her." In the ancient Near Eastern treaty curses, the same idea occurs in the treaty of the Assyrian king Esarhaddon. In Egypt, young men are warned: "Do not fornicate with a married woman. He who fornicates with a married woman on her bed, his wife will be copulated with on the ground."
31:12 *Destruction.* See note on Pr 15:11.

[15]Did not he who made me in the womb
make them?
Did not the same one form us both
within our mothers?[u]

[16]"If I have denied the desires of the
poor[v]
or let the eyes of the widow[w] grow
weary,
[17]if I have kept my bread to myself,
not sharing it with the fatherless[x]—
[18]but from my youth I reared them as a
father would,
and from my birth I guided the
widow—
[19]if I have seen anyone perishing for lack
of clothing,[y]
or the needy[z] without garments,
[20]and their hearts did not bless me
for warming them with the fleece
from my sheep,
[21]if I have raised my hand against the
fatherless,[a]
knowing that I had influence in
court,
[22]then let my arm fall from the
shoulder,
let it be broken off at the joint.[b]
[23]For I dreaded destruction from God,
and for fear of his splendor[c]
I could not do such things.

[24]"If I have put my trust in gold[d]
or said to pure gold, 'You are my
security,'[e]
[25]if I have rejoiced over my great
wealth,[f]
the fortune my hands had
gained,
[26]if I have regarded the sun[g] in its
radiance
or the moon moving in splendor,

31:15 [u]Job 10:3 **31:16** [v]Job 5:16; 20:19 [w]Job 22:9 **31:17** [x]Job 22:7; 29:12 **31:19** [y]Job 22:6 [z]Job 24:4 **31:21** [a]Job 22:9 **31:22** [b]Job 38:15 **31:23** [c]Job 13:11 **31:24** [d]Job 22:25 [e]Mt 6:24; Mk 10:24 **31:25** [f]Ps 62:10 **31:26** [g]Eze 8:16

31:26 *regarded the sun ... or the moon.* Job refers to the worship of the sun and moon, which was common in the ancient Near East (Mesopotamian deities like Utu/Shamash and Nanna/Sin; Egyptian deities Ra, Aten and Thoth; and Ugaritic deities Shapshu/Shapash and Yarikh), but forbidden by Dt 4:19. In Ps 84:11, the Lord God is described as "a sun." The importance of the sun and moon is indicated by the Ugaritic texts *CAT* 1.24 and 161. Solar

JOB 31:1

Job's Covenant and Arranged Marriages

Job's eyes are being treated as vassals brought under a suzerain's control. Since Job 31:1 as translated seems an obvious statement about sexual ethics, we must consider the textual details carefully. The Hebrew verb (*bin*) describing the forbidden activity (here translated "look lustfully") generally describes close or careful examination of an object. In only one other occurrence (Ps 37:10) is the Hebrew verb *bin* followed by this Hebrew preposition (translated "at" in Job 31:1 and "for" in Ps 37:10), and in Ps 37:10 it refers to seeking out (but not finding) the wicked. No occurrences of this Hebrew verb carry sexual nuance.

This interpretation does not satisfactorily explain why the prohibition to Job's eyes is limited to a particular class of woman (NIV "young woman"). If sexual ethics are truly at stake, it would be more natural for his covenant to extend to any woman. Furthermore, if a girl remains under her father's protection, as does a *betulah* ("young woman") by definition, she is a viable candidate for marriage—and society at this time was comfortably polygamous.

The Hebrew of the second part of the verse begins with a common interrogative particle: "what" (Hebrew *mah*). Although Job's usage of this particle is consistent, most translations choose not to render it in this particular verse (e.g., NIV "not to look"). Typically in Job, this particle introduces a rhetorical question ("what?"), which seems likely here as well. Ps 37:10 employs the same Hebrew verb (*bin*) as this verse to direct the reader to "look" all around for the location of the wicked; within its context, this

continued on next page

directive suggests that if one inquires diligently after the status of the wicked, the search will yield nothing. If we apply this observation to Job's statement, the sense is as follows: "Since I have made a covenant with regard to my eyes, what interest would I have in inquiring after a *betulah* (i.e., investigating her availability)?"

Inquiring after a *betulah* is not the same as inquiring after a prostitute. If the text truly was speaking against lust, the verb *hmd* ("covet") would be a more likely word choice. For another likely wording, see Job 31:9. *Betulah* generally does indicate a virgin, but virginity is more circumstantial than truly representative of the word's core meaning. More to the point, a *betulah* is a marriageable girl still within the household of her father and under his protection. One would inquire after a *betulah* in order to arrange a marriage. Such an inquiry could potentially be motivated by lust (cf. Jdg 14:2), but that is only one of several alternatives and may not be automatically inferred. In point of fact, *any* arranged marriage begins with inquiring after a *betulah*.

In light of this discussion, Job's covenant regarding his eyes cannot be interpreted as a commitment to asceticism, because he already has a wife (as noted not only in Job 2, but also in Job 31:10). The logical alternative is that the statement concerns the acquisition of a harem. A large harem was an indicator of power and status in the ancient world. Job eschews amassing multiple wives and concubines, and characterizes this decision as a covenant regarding his eyes in order to underscore the point that he is not even "on the prowl." This avowal mirrors his statement in Job 31:24 – 25 that he is not absorbed in the pursuit of wealth. Job has undertaken neither a vow of poverty nor a vow of chastity, but rather he avoids the obsessive pursuit of prestige. This interpretation takes account of each word choice the author has made, and therefore presents the most likely interpretation. Accordingly, the verse has nothing to do with sexual ethics, as important as they may be. Instead, it accords with Job's many pronouncements that he has not attempted to consolidate or abuse his power — tempting actions for a person in his position (cf. Samuel's lecture in 1Sa 8:11 – 17 regarding the tactics of a king building a power base). ◆

27 so that my heart was secretly
enticed
and my hand offered them a kiss
of homage,
28 then these also would be sins to be
judged,[h]
for I would have been unfaithful to
God on high.

29 "If I have rejoiced at my enemy's
misfortune[i]
or gloated over the trouble that
came to him[j] —
30 I have not allowed my mouth to
sin
by invoking a curse against their
life —
31 if those of my household have never
said,
'Who has not been filled with Job's
meat?'[k] —
32 but no stranger had to spend the night
in the street,
for my door was always open to the
traveler[l] —

31:28 [h]Dt 17:2-7 **31:29** [i]Ob 1:12 [j]Pr 17:5; 24:17-18
31:31 [k]Job 22:7 **31:32** [l]Ge 19:2-3; Ro 12:13

and lunar worship in ancient Israel is evident from texts such as 2Ki 23:5,11; Eze 8:16; Jer 8:2. The righteous Judahite king Josiah did away with the sun and moon worshipers (2Ki 23:5). Canaanite iconography indicates the importance of astral symbolism in the Assyrian period. However, the book of Job in this verse rejects any cult of the sun or moon as an acceptable form of worship.

31:27 *my hand offered them a kiss of homage.* Kissing can be a form of worship; in Hos 13:2, calf idols are kissed, and in 1Ki 19:18, Baal is kissed by his followers. The gesture of putting the hand to the mouth and "throwing" a kiss to the deity was known in Mesopotamia, as is shown on a statuette of a worshiper from Larsa. This figure has his hand before his mouth without touching it, the thumb and index finger are extended and the three other fingers curled. Cf. notes on 21:5; 29:9.

31:32 *no stranger had to spend the night in the street.* The stranger (Hebrew *ger*) was a foreigner who did not own land and had no home, as in 19:15, but should not be mistreated (cf. Lev 19:33 – 34) or left in the street, as described in Ge 19, because the Israelites themselves and their ancestors used to be strangers in Egypt (Ex 22:21) and in Canaan (Ge 15:13). In contemporary terms, "stranger" describes one who would be designated as landless and disenfranchised.

[33] if I have concealed[m] my sin as
people do,[a]
by hiding[n] my guilt in my heart
[34] because I so feared the crowd[o]
and so dreaded the contempt of the
clans
that I kept silent and would not go
outside—
[35] ("Oh, that I had someone to hear me![p]
I sign now my defense—let the
Almighty answer me;
let my accuser[q] put his indictment
in writing.
[36] Surely I would wear it on my
shoulder,
I would put it on like a
crown.
[37] I would give him an account of
my every step;
I would present it to him as to
a ruler.[r])—

31:33 [m] Pr 28:13 [n] Ge 3:8 **31:34** [o] Ex 23:2 **31:35** [p] Job 19:7; 30:28 [q] Job 27:7; 35:14 **31:37** [r] Job 1:3; 29:25

[a] 33 Or *as Adam did*

31:36 *wear it on my shoulder ... like a crown.* Prominently displayed and worn proudly. An item on the hand, neck or forehead was a constant reminder to the wearer (Ex 13:16; Dt 6:8; 11:18; Pr 6:21).

JOB 31

Negative Confessions and the Oath of Innocence

Job 31 contains what has been called "Job's declaration of innocence." Job lists a catalog of crimes: lust (v. 1); falsehood (v. 5); adultery (v. 9); injustice to servants (v. 13); indifference to the poor, the widow, the fatherless and the naked (vv. 16–20); injustice to the fatherless (v. 21); trust in wealth (vv. 24–25); worship of sun and moon (vv. 26–27); rejoicing over the enemy's misfortune (vv. 29–30); inhospitality (v. 32); hypocrisy (v. 34). Such an oath presumes that if Job swears falsely, God will be obligated to punish him for both the crime and false oath.

According to ancient Egyptian belief, the deceased appeared before a tribunal of divine judges consisting of the underworld-god Osiris and 42 judges. The heart of the deceased was weighed on a scale against the feather of Maat, which represented justice, to determine whether the heart was pure. The weighing was done by the jackal-headed Anubis, the assistant of Osiris, and the result recorded by the scribal god Thoth (represented as an Ibis-headed figure or a baboon) and reported to the enthroned Osiris. In order for the heart not to speak against the deceased, a spell was recited.

The deceased was interrogated by the divine tribunal, and on this occasion "spell" 125 from the Egyptian "Book of the Dead"—called the "declaration of innocence" (or "negative confession")—was recited, which included, e.g., that the person had not committed evil against another person (whether poor or slave) and had not blasphemed.

During the Babylonian Akitu festival the king also uttered a confession contending that he had not sinned, particularly that he had not humiliated citizens.

A "declaration of innocence" also occurs in Akkadian legal texts, and in the seventh-century BC Israelite legal ostracon from Yavneh-Yam, the plaintiff claims to be without guilt. Finally, in a Hittite prayer of the mid-second millennium BC, there is an intriguing declaration of innocence by the king, Kantuzzili. He claims that he has not sworn falsely, eaten forbidden food or stolen ox or sheep, and that he was not selfish (phrased in terms of sharing his food and water). This example has an additional similarity, because Kantuzzili is using his declaration to try to bring an end to a plague. Like Job, he insists that his record be tested to show that he is innocent. ◆

38 “if my land cries out against me[s]
and all its furrows are wet with
tears,
39 if I have devoured its yield without
payment[t]
or broken the spirit of its tenants,[u]
40 then let briers[v] come up instead of
wheat
and stinkweed instead of barley.”

The words of Job are ended.

Elihu

32 So these three men stopped answering Job, because he was righteous in his own eyes.[w] 2 But Elihu son of
Barakel the Buzite,[x] of the family of Ram,
became very angry with Job for justifying
himself rather than God.[y] 3 He was also angry with the three friends, because they
had found no way to refute Job, and yet
had condemned him.[a] 4 Now Elihu had
waited before speaking to Job because
they were older than he. 5 But when he
saw that the three men had nothing more
to say, his anger was aroused.
6 So Elihu son of Barakel the Buzite said:

“I am young in years,
and you are old;[z]
that is why I was fearful,
not daring to tell you what
I know.
7 I thought, ‘Age should speak;
advanced years should teach
wisdom.’
8 But it is the spirit[b] in a person,
the breath of the Almighty,[a] that
gives them understanding.[b]
9 It is not only the old[c] who are wise,[c]
not only the aged who understand
what is right.

10 “Therefore I say: Listen to me;
I too will tell you what I know.
11 I waited while you spoke,
I listened to your reasoning;
while you were searching for
words,
12 I gave you my full attention.
But not one of you has proved Job
wrong;
none of you has answered his
arguments.
13 Do not say, ‘We have found wisdom;[d]
let God, not a man, refute him.’
14 But Job has not marshaled his words
against me,
and I will not answer him with your
arguments.

15 “They are dismayed and have no more
to say;
words have failed them.
16 Must I wait, now that they are silent,
now that they stand there with no
reply?
17 I too will have my say;
I too will tell what I know.
18 For I am full of words,
and the spirit within me compels
me;
19 inside I am like bottled-up wine,
like new wineskins ready to burst.
20 I must speak and find relief;
I must open my lips and reply.
21 I will show no partiality,[e]
nor will I flatter anyone;
22 for if I were skilled in flattery,
my Maker would soon take me
away.

33 “But now, Job, listen to my words;
pay attention to everything I say.[f]
2 I am about to open my mouth;
my words are on the tip of my tongue.
3 My words come from an upright heart;
my lips sincerely speak what I
know.[g]
4 The Spirit of God has made me;[h]
the breath of the Almighty[i] gives me
life.
5 Answer me[j] then, if you can;
stand up[k] and argue your case
before me.

31:38 [s] Ge 4:10
31:39 [t] 1Ki 21:19 [u] Lev 19:13; Jas 5:4
31:40 [v] Ge 3:18
32:1 [w] Job 10:7; 33:9
32:2 [x] Ge 22:21 [y] Job 27:5; 30:21
32:6 [z] Job 15:10
32:8 [a] Job 27:3; 33:4 [b] Pr 2:6
32:9 [c] 1Co 1:26
32:13 [d] Jer 9:23
32:21 [e] Lev 19:15; Job 13:10; Mt 22:16
33:1 [f] Job 13:6
33:3 [g] Job 6:28; 27:4; 36:4
33:4 [h] Ge 2:7; Job 10:3 [i] Job 27:3
33:5 [j] ver 32 [k] Job 13:18

[a] 3 Masoretic Text; an ancient Hebrew scribal tradition *Job, and so had condemned God* [b] 8 Or *Spirit*; also in verse 18 [c] 9 Or *many*; or *great*

31:38 *if my land cries out against me.* Here, “land” possibly refers metonymically to those who work the land on his behalf. In Dt 24:14–15, it is commanded: “Do not take advantage of a hired worker who is poor and needy ... Pay them their wages ... Otherwise they may cry to the LORD against you, and you will be guilty of sin.” Jas 5:4 warns that the wages that one has failed to pay are crying out, and that the cries “have reached the ears of the Lord Almighty.” However, Job denies in v. 39 that he has failed to pay the laborers their wages.

32:2 *Elihu.* Means “he is my God”; it was a common name in the Bible, especially in the time of David. *Barakel the Buzite, of the family of Ram.* The name of Elihu’s father and even his clan (Hebrew *mishpahah*, NIV “family”) are mentioned. Buz was the nephew of Abraham (Ge 22:20–21) and Ram might be related to the Arameans. Jer 25:23–24; 49:32 mentions Buz in connection with Dedan, located in Arabia.

32:19 *new wineskins.* Wine was usually kept in bottles of clay (Jer 19:1), some even with stoppers, as known from Egypt. Wineskins (Jer 13:12) were made of animal skins, and several examples from ancient times have survived. Elihu himself is so “full of words” (v. 18) that if he does not get the chance to speak, he will burst (cf. Jer 20:9). The image is that of bottled-up wine—new wine forms gases as it ferments, which could make the skins burst if the gases could not escape. In the NT parable of the new wine in old wineskins (Mt 9:17), old skins become dried up and are not usable any longer, because the expanding gases of the fermenting new wine will tear them.

6 I am the same as you in God's sight;
I too am a piece of clay.[l]
7 No fear of me should alarm you,
nor should my hand be heavy on
you.[m]

8 "But you have said in my hearing—
I heard the very words—
9 'I am pure,[n] I have done no wrong;[o]
I am clean and free from sin.
10 Yet God has found fault with me;
he considers me his enemy.[p]
11 He fastens my feet in shackles;[q]
he keeps close watch on all my
paths.'[r]

12 "But I tell you, in this you are not
right,
for God is greater than any mortal.[s]
13 Why do you complain to him[t]
that he responds to no one's
words[a]?
14 For God does speak[u]—now one way,
now another—
though no one perceives it.
15 In a dream,[v] in a vision of the night,
when deep sleep falls on people
as they slumber in their beds,
16 he may speak[w] in their ears
and terrify them with warnings,
17 to turn them from wrongdoing
and keep them from pride,
18 to preserve them from the pit,[x]
their lives from perishing by the
sword.[b][y]

19 "Or someone may be chastened on a
bed of pain
with constant distress in their
bones,[z]
20 so that their body finds food[a] repulsive
and their soul loathes the choicest
meal.[b]

33:6 [l] Job 4:19
33:7 [m] Job 9:34; 13:21; 2Co 2:4
33:9 [n] Job 10:7 [o] Job 13:23; 16:17
33:10 [p] Job 13:24
33:11 [q] Job 13:27 [r] Job 14:16
33:12 [s] Ecc 7:20
33:13 [t] Job 40:2; Isa 45:9
33:14 [u] Ps 62:11
33:15 [v] Job 4:13
33:16 [w] Job 36:10, 15
33:18 [x] ver 22, 24, 28, 30 [y] Job 15:22
33:19 [z] Job 30:17
33:20 [a] Ps 107:18 [b] Job 3:24; 6:6
33:21 [c] Job 16:8; 19:20
33:22 [d] Ps 88:3
33:23 [e] Mic 6:8
33:24 [f] Isa 38:17
33:25 [g] 2Ki 5:14
33:26 [h] Job 34:28 [i] Job 22:26 [j] Ps 50:15; 51:12
33:27 [k] 2Sa 12:13 [l] Lk 15:21 [m] Ro 6:21
33:28 [n] Job 22:28
33:29 [o] 1Co 12:6; Eph 1:11; Php 2:13
33:30 [p] Ps 56:13

21 Their flesh wastes away to nothing,
and their bones, once hidden, now
stick out.[c]
22 They draw near to the pit,
and their life to the messengers of
death.[c][d]
23 Yet if there is an angel at their side,
a messenger, one out of a thousand,
sent to tell them how to be upright,[e]
24 and he is gracious to that person and
says to God,
'Spare them from going down to the
pit;[f]
I have found a ransom for them—
25 let their flesh be renewed like a
child's;
let them be restored as in the days
of their youth'[g]—
26 then that person can pray to God and
find favor with him,[h]
they will see God's face and shout
for joy;[i]
he will restore them to full well-
being.[j]
27 And they will go to others and say,
'I have sinned,[k] I have perverted
what is right,[l]
but I did not get what I deserved.[m]
28 God has delivered me from going down
to the pit,
and I shall live to enjoy the light of
life.'[n]

29 "God does all these things to a
person[o]—
twice, even three times—
30 to turn them back from the pit,
that the light of life[p] may shine on
them.

[a] 13 Or *that he does not answer for any of his actions*
[b] 18 Or *from crossing the river*
[c] 22 Or *to the place of the dead*

33:6 *a piece of clay.* See note on 10:8–9.
33:11 *feet in shackles.* See note on 12:18.
33:15 *dream.* See note on 4:13.
33:18 *the pit.* Also vv. 22,30; the grave (see note on 17:13). The Mesopotamian underworld was reached by way of a staircase, but the pit might also refer to the hole dug in the ground to make a grave. *from perishing by the sword.* Cf. 36:12; might be translated "crossing the River" (see NIV text note), which could refer to the so-called river of death—i.e., preserve him from death. In the ancient world, it was believed that the border of the underworld was marked by a river, and that the dead had to cross this "river of death" by boat and had to pay a ferryman. This is the River Styx of classical mythology and the deified Hubur in Mesopotamia. In the Gilgamesh Epic, the "Waters of Death" are crossed with the help of the ferryman Urshanabi, and "The Babylonian Theodicy" mentions the river of the dead. Bitumen boats found in royal tombs at Ur might be related to this belief. Models of boats found in tombs and full-scale boats buried next to the pyramids reflect Egyptian beliefs on the subject. The deceased were believed to travel to Abydos and use boats in the underworld. The Ugaritic word (related to the Hebrew *shalah* in Job) is used for the deified river. Such a deity occurs in Phoenician personal names, and one name might even be linked with the Egyptian underworld-god Osiris.
33:23 *an angel ... a messenger, one out of a thousand.* Da 7:10 reads "Thousands upon thousands attended him; ten thousand times ten thousand stood before him." In the past, this has been interpreted as referring to a guardian angel (cf. Ps 91:11) or an interceding saint, while others have taken it as the Mesopotamian idea of the personal god who acted on behalf of the mortal in the divine assembly. The angel (cf. 1:6; 4:18; see note on 1:6; see also the article "Divine Council," p. 615) is here merely an advocate or defense attorney who acts on his behalf and pleads his case as a mediator.
33:25 *renewed ... restored as in the days of their youth.* Restored youth and physical regeneration have always been the wish of humankind. In the Gilgamesh Epic, the hero receives a magical plant called "Old Man Grown Young," the plant of regeneration, but it is stolen from him by a snake.

31 "Pay attention, Job, and listen to me;
be silent, and I will speak.
32 If you have anything to say, answer me;
speak up, for I want to vindicate you.
33 But if not, then listen to me;
be silent, and I will teach you wisdom.[q]"

34

Then Elihu said:

2 "Hear my words, you wise men;
listen to me, you men of learning.
3 For the ear tests words
as the tongue tastes food.[r]
4 Let us discern for ourselves what is right;
let us learn together what is good.[s]

5 "Job says, 'I am innocent,[t]
but God denies me justice.[u]
6 Although I am right,
I am considered a liar;
although I am guiltless,
his arrow inflicts an incurable wound.'[v]
7 Is there anyone like Job,
who drinks scorn like water?[w]
8 He keeps company with evildoers;
he associates with the wicked.[x]
9 For he says, 'There is no profit
in trying to please God.'[y]

10 "So listen to me, you men of understanding.
Far be it from God to do evil,[z]
from the Almighty to do wrong.[a]
11 He repays everyone for what they have done;[b]
he brings on them what their conduct deserves.[c]
12 It is unthinkable that God would do wrong,
that the Almighty would pervert justice.[d]
13 Who appointed him over the earth?
Who put him in charge of the whole world?[e]
14 If it were his intention
and he withdrew his spirit[a] and breath,[f]
15 all humanity would perish together
and mankind would return to the dust.[g]

16 "If you have understanding, hear this;
listen to what I say.
17 Can someone who hates justice govern?[h]
Will you condemn the just and mighty One?[i]
18 Is he not the One who says to kings,
'You are worthless,'
and to nobles, 'You are wicked,'[j]
19 who shows no partiality[k] to princes
and does not favor the rich over the poor,[l]
for they are all the work of his hands?[m]
20 They die in an instant, in the middle of the night;[n]
the people are shaken and they pass away;
the mighty are removed without human hand.[o]

21 "His eyes are on the ways of mortals;
he sees their every step.[p]
22 There is no deep shadow,[q] no utter darkness,[r]
where evildoers can hide.
23 God has no need to examine people further,
that they should come before him for judgment.[s]
24 Without inquiry he shatters the mighty[t]
and sets up others in their place.[u]
25 Because he takes note of their deeds,
he overthrows them in the night and they are crushed.
26 He punishes them for their wickedness
where everyone can see them,
27 because they turned from following him[v]
and had no regard for any of his ways.[w]
28 They caused the cry of the poor to come before him,
so that he heard the cry of the needy.[x]
29 But if he remains silent, who can condemn him?
If he hides his face, who can see him?
Yet he is over individual and nation alike,
30 to keep the godless from ruling,
from laying snares for the people.[y]

31 "Suppose someone says to God,
'I am guilty but will offend no more.
32 Teach me what I cannot see;[z]
if I have done wrong, I will not do so again.'[a]
33 Should God then reward you on your terms,
when you refuse to repent?[b]
You must decide, not I;
so tell me what you know.

34 "Men of understanding declare,
wise men who hear me say to me,
35 'Job speaks without knowledge;
his words lack insight.'

33:33 [q] Ps 34:11
34:3 [r] Job 12:11
34:4 [s] 1Th 5:21
34:5 [t] Job 33:9 [u] Job 27:2
34:6 [v] Job 6:4
34:7 [w] Job 15:16
34:8 [x] Job 22:15; Ps 50:18
34:9 [y] Job 21:15; 35:3
34:10 [z] Ge 18:25 [a] Dt 32:4; Job 8:3; Ro 9:14
34:11 [b] Ps 62:12; Mt 16:27; Ro 2:6; 2Co 5:10 [c] Jer 32:19; Eze 33:20
34:12 [d] Job 8:3
34:13 [e] Job 38:4,6
34:14 [f] Ps 104:29
34:15 [g] Ge 3:19; Job 9:22
34:17 [h] 2Sa 23:3-4 [i] Job 40:8
34:18 [j] Ex 22:28
34:19 [k] Dt 10:17; Ac 10:34 [l] Lev 19:15 [m] Job 10:3
34:20 [n] Ex 12:29 [o] Job 12:19
34:21 [p] Job 31:4; Pr 15:3
34:22 [q] Am 9:2-3 [r] Ps 139:12
34:23 [s] Job 11:11
34:24 [t] Job 12:19 [u] Da 2:21
34:27 [v] Ps 28:5; Isa 5:12 [w] 1Sa 15:11
34:28 [x] Ex 22:23; Job 35:9; Jas 5:4
34:30 [y] Pr 29:2-12
34:32 [z] Job 35:11; Ps 25:4 [a] Job 33:27
34:33 [b] Job 41:11
34:35 [c] Job 35:16; 38:2

[a] 14 Or *Spirit*

36 Oh, that Job might be tested to the utmost
for answering like a wicked man![d]
37 To his sin he adds rebellion;
scornfully he claps his hands[e]
among us
and multiplies his words against God."[f]

35 Then Elihu said:

2 "Do you think this is just?
You say, 'I am in the right, not God.'
3 Yet you ask him, 'What profit is it to me,[a]
and what do I gain by not sinning?'[g]

4 "I would like to reply to you
and to your friends with you.
5 Look up at the heavens[h] and see;
gaze at the clouds so high above you.[i]
6 If you sin, how does that affect him?
If your sins are many, what does that do to him?[j]
7 If you are righteous, what do you give to him,[k]
or what does he receive[l] from your hand?[m]
8 Your wickedness only affects humans like yourself,
and your righteousness only other people.

9 "People cry out[n] under a load of oppression;
they plead for relief from the arm of the powerful.[o]
10 But no one says, 'Where is God my Maker,[p]
who gives songs in the night,[q]
11 who teaches[r] us more than he teaches[b] the beasts of the earth
and makes us wiser than[c] the birds in the sky?'
12 He does not answer[s] when people cry out
because of the arrogance of the wicked.
13 Indeed, God does not listen to their empty plea;
the Almighty pays no attention to it.[t]
14 How much less, then, will he listen
when you say that you do not see him,[u]
that your case[v] is before him
and you must wait for him,
15 and further, that his anger never punishes
and he does not take the least notice of wickedness.[d]
16 So Job opens his mouth with empty talk;
without knowledge he multiplies words."[w]

36 Elihu continued:

2 "Bear with me a little longer and I will show you
that there is more to be said in God's behalf.
3 I get my knowledge from afar;
I will ascribe justice to my Maker.[x]
4 Be assured that my words are not false;[y]
one who has perfect knowledge[z] is with you.

5 "God is mighty, but despises no one;[a]
he is mighty, and firm in his purpose.[b]
6 He does not keep the wicked alive[c]
but gives the afflicted their rights.[d]
7 He does not take his eyes off the righteous;[e]
he enthrones them with kings[f]
and exalts them forever.
8 But if people are bound in chains,[g]
held fast by cords of affliction,
9 he tells them what they have done—
that they have sinned arrogantly.[h]
10 He makes them listen[i] to correction
and commands them to repent of their evil.[j]
11 If they obey and serve him,[k]
they will spend the rest of their days in prosperity
and their years in contentment.
12 But if they do not listen,
they will perish by the sword[e][l]
and die without knowledge.[m]

13 "The godless in heart[n] harbor resentment;
even when he fetters them, they do not cry for help.
14 They die in their youth,
among male prostitutes of the shrines.[o]
15 But those who suffer he delivers in their suffering;
he speaks to them in their affliction.

34:36 [d] Job 22:15 **34:37** [e] Job 27:23 [f] Job 23:2 **35:3** [g] Job 9:29-31; 34:9 **35:5** [h] Ge 15:5 [i] Job 22:12 **35:6** [j] Pr 8:36 **35:7** [k] Ro 11:35 [l] Pr 9:12 [m] Job 22:2-3; Lk 17:10 **35:9** [n] Ex 2:23 [o] Job 12:19 **35:10** [p] Job 27:10; Isa 51:13 [q] Ps 42:8; 149:5; Ac 16:25 **35:11** [r] Ps 94:12 **35:12** [s] Pr 1:28 **35:13** [t] Job 27:9; Pr 15:29; Isa 1:15; Jer 11:11 **35:14** [u] Job 9:11 [v] Ps 37:6 **35:16** [w] Job 34:35, 37 **36:3** [x] Job 8:3; 37:23 **36:4** [y] Job 33:3 [z] Job 37:5, 16, 23 **36:5** [a] Ps 22:24 [b] Job 12:13 **36:6** [c] Job 8:22 [d] Job 5:15 **36:7** [e] Ps 33:18 [f] Ps 113:8 **36:8** [g] Ps 107:10, 14 **36:9** [h] Job 15:25 **36:10** [i] Job 33:16 [j] 2Ki 17:13 **36:11** [k] Isa 1:19 **36:12** [l] Job 15:22 [m] Job 4:21 **36:13** [n] Ro 2:5 **36:14** [o] Dt 23:17

[a] 3 Or *you* [b] 10,11 Or *night,* / [11] *who teaches us by* [c] 11 Or *us wise by* [d] 15 Symmachus, Theodotion and Vulgate; the meaning of the Hebrew for this word is uncertain. [e] 12 Or *will cross the river*

35:10 *gives songs in the night.* Because the night was a time of danger and was feared by ancient people (cf. 4:13; 33:15; Ps 77:6; 91:5), such songs served the purpose of calming down the distressed. In 38:7, the morning stars sing. Some commentators read, "gives strength in the night."

16 “He is wooing[p] you from the jaws of
distress
to a spacious place free from
restriction,
to the comfort of your table[q] laden
with choice food.
17 But now you are laden with the
judgment due the wicked;
judgment and justice have taken
hold of you.[r]
18 Be careful that no one entices you by
riches;
do not let a large bribe turn you aside.[s]
19 Would your wealth or even all your
mighty efforts
sustain you so you would not be in
distress?
20 Do not long for the night,[t]
to drag people away from their
homes.[a]
21 Beware of turning to evil,[u]
which you seem to prefer to
affliction.[v]

22 “God is exalted in his power.
Who is a teacher like him?[w]
23 Who has prescribed his ways for him,[x]
or said to him, ‘You have done
wrong’?[y]
24 Remember to extol his work,[z]
which people have praised in song.[a]
25 All humanity has seen it;
mortals gaze on it from afar.
26 How great is God — beyond our
understanding![b]
The number of his years is past
finding out.[c]

27 “He draws up the drops of water,
which distill as rain to the streams[b];[d]
28 the clouds pour down their moisture
and abundant showers fall on
mankind.[e]
29 Who can understand how he spreads
out the clouds,
how he thunders from his pavilion?[f]
30 See how he scatters his lightning about
him,
bathing the depths of the sea.
31 This is the way he governs[c] the
nations[g]
and provides food in abundance.[h]
32 He fills his hands with lightning
and commands it to strike its
mark.[i]
33 His thunder announces the coming
storm;
even the cattle make known its
approach.[d]

37

“At this my heart pounds
and leaps from its place.
2 Listen! Listen to the roar of his voice,
to the rumbling that comes from his
mouth.[j]
3 He unleashes his lightning beneath the
whole heaven
and sends it to the ends of the earth.
4 After that comes the sound of his roar;
he thunders with his majestic voice.
When his voice resounds,
he holds nothing back.
5 God’s voice thunders in marvelous
ways;
he does great things beyond our
understanding.[k]

36:16 [p]Hos 2:14 [q]Ps 23:5 **36:17** [r]Job 22:11 **36:18** [s]Job 34:33 **36:20** [t]Job 34:20,25 **36:21** [u]Ps 66:18 [v]Heb 11:25 **36:22** [w]Isa 40:13; 1Co 2:16 **36:23** [x]Job 34:13 [y]Job 8:3 **36:24** [z]Ps 92:5; 138:5 [a]Ps 59:16; Rev 15:3 **36:26** [b]1Co 13:12 [c]Job 10:5; Ps 90:2; 102:24; Heb 1:12 **36:27** [d]Job 38:28; Ps 147:8 **36:28** [e]Job 5:10 **36:29** [f]Job 26:14; 37:16 **36:31** [g]Job 37:13 [h]Ps 136:25; Ac 14:17 **36:32** [i]Job 37:12,15 **37:2** [j]Ps 29:3-9 **37:5** [k]Job 5:9

[a] *20* The meaning of the Hebrew for verses 18-20 is uncertain. [b] *27* Or *distill from the mist as rain* [c] *31* Or *nourishes* [d] *33* Or *announces his coming — / the One zealous against evil*

36:27 *draws up the drops of water.* It would be easy for a modern reader to think of the water cycle of evaporation, condensation and precipitation when reading this verse, but that is not how it would have been read in the ancient world. The processes of drawing out and refining that are indicated by the Hebrew verbs of this verse would have been understood in the ways in which God brings moisture from the waters above and the waters below — these are the cosmic waters that were believed to surround the earth. Elihu’s statements reflect ancient poetical thinking and do not have to be scientifically accounted for or explained.

36:32 *fills his hands with lightning.* This is an example of an ancient explanation (rather than a modern scientific one) of a natural phenomenon. As in Hab 3, God appears as the bringer of lightning and thunder (cf. Job 36:29; 37:3 – 5,11,15). In Hab 3:4, “rays flashed from his hand.” Thunder-gods are shown in the art of the ancient Near East brandishing thunderbolts and lightning in a menacing way, as a gesture of absolute power. The god Baal carries lightning when he goes to the realm of the underworld-god Mot. In another text, Baal is described as holding lightning while enthroned.

37:2 – 5 The Lord is described as a thunder-god in 36:29 — 38:1; cf. 40:9. In 38:1 (cf. 40:6), he answers Job out of the “storm” (or perhaps the “windstorm,” as in the vision of Eze 1). Ancient Near Eastern texts often refer to thunder as the manifestation of the power of deities in times of war, as in 1Sa 7:10. In Ps 18:13 the voice of God is compared to thunder. In Ugarit, the voice of Baal is synonymous to thunder, and he makes the earth shake. Thunder-gods appeared in various manifestations and forms, and also under different names in the ancient Near East. In Mesopotamia, it was Ishkur and Adad/Hadad, although Marduk also uses thunder and wind to defeat Tiamat. The Syro-Canaanite thunder-god was called Baal (Ugarit and Phoenicia) or Hadad (especially among the Arameans). In the Ugaritic myths, Baal is a thunderer, and he carries the title “rider of the clouds.” The Egyptian god Seth was also a god of thunder. He was identified with Baal, and the name “Baal” in hieroglyphs was written with the Seth animal determinative. The Egyptian word for “thunder” is also written with the Seth animal determinative. It is therefore clear that even though the God of Israel is being revealed as distinct from the gods of the ancient Near East in many important ways, at the same time, ideas about deity in the ancient world are adopted and applied to explain Yahweh’s character. Our knowledge of the ancient Near East can help us understand these metaphors and images.

6 He says to the snow,[l] 'Fall on the
earth,'
and to the rain shower, 'Be a mighty
downpour.'[m]
7 So that everyone he has made may
know his work,
he stops all people from their labor.[a n]
8 The animals take cover;
they remain in their dens.[o]
9 The tempest comes out from its
chamber,
the cold from the driving winds.
10 The breath of God produces ice,
and the broad waters become
frozen.[p]
11 He loads the clouds with moisture;
he scatters his lightning through
them.[q]
12 At his direction they swirl around
over the face of the whole earth
to do whatever he commands them.[r]
13 He brings the clouds to punish people,[s]
or to water his earth and show his
love.[t]

14 "Listen to this, Job;
stop and consider God's wonders.
15 Do you know how God controls the
clouds
and makes his lightning flash?
16 Do you know how the clouds hang
poised,
those wonders of him who has
perfect knowledge?[u]
17 You who swelter in your clothes
when the land lies hushed under the
south wind,
18 can you join him in spreading out the
skies,[v]
hard as a mirror of cast bronze?

19 "Tell us what we should say to him;
we cannot draw up our case because
of our darkness.
20 Should he be told that I want to
speak?
Would anyone ask to be swallowed
up?
21 Now no one can look at the sun,
bright as it is in the skies
after the wind has swept them
clean.
22 Out of the north he comes in golden
splendor;
God comes in awesome majesty.
23 The Almighty is beyond our reach and
exalted in power;[w]
in his justice[x] and great
righteousness, he does not
oppress.[y]
24 Therefore, people revere him,[z]
for does he not have regard for all
the wise[a] in heart?[b]"

The LORD Speaks

38 Then the LORD spoke to Job out of
the storm.[b] He said:

2 "Who is this that obscures my plans
with words without knowledge?[c]
3 Brace yourself like a man;
I will question you,
and you shall answer me.[d]

4 "Where were you when I laid the
earth's foundation?[e]
Tell me, if you understand.
5 Who marked off its dimensions?[f]
Surely you know!
Who stretched a measuring line
across it?
6 On what were its footings set,
or who laid its cornerstone[g] —
7 while the morning stars sang together
and all the angels[c] shouted for joy?

37:6 [l] Job 38:22 [m] Job 36:27 **37:7** [n] Job 12:14 **37:8** [o] Job 38:40; Ps 104:22 **37:10** [p] Job 38:29-30; Ps 147:17 **37:11** [q] Job 36:27,29 **37:12** [r] Ps 148:8 **37:13** [s] 1Sa 12:17 [t] Ex 9:18; 1Ki 18:45; Job 38:27 **37:16** [u] Job 36:4 **37:18** [v] Job 9:8; Ps 104:2; Isa 44:24

37:23 [w] Job 9:4; 36:4; 1Ti 6:16 [x] Job 8:3 [y] Isa 63:9; Eze 18:23,32 **37:24** [z] Mt 10:28 [a] Mt 11:25 **38:1** [b] Job 40:6 **38:2** [c] Job 35:16; 42:3; 1Ti 1:7 **38:3** [d] Job 40:7 **38:4** [e] Ps 104:5; Pr 8:29 **38:5** [f] Pr 8:29; Isa 40:12 **38:6** [g] Job 26:7

[a] 7 Or *work, / he fills all people with fear by his power*
[b] 24 Or *for he does not have regard for any who think they are wise.*
[c] 7 Hebrew *the sons of God*

37:18 *the skies, hard as a mirror of cast bronze.* It was thought in the ancient Near East that the sky was a solid dome or a flat roof (see the article "The 'Vault' and 'Water Above,'" p. 6). The idea of the sky as a metal dome appears in Persian cosmogonic texts. *mirror.* In the ancient Near East, mirrors were not made of glass, but were mostly beaten and polished bronze. Many such mirrors with a bronze reflecting surface are known, especially from Egypt.

38:1–41 Whereas the emphasis in ch. 9 was on Job as part of creation (see the article "Cosmic Geography," p. 836), ch. 38 emphasizes God as Creator and the fact that Job was not present ("Where were you ...?" v. 4) at the creation of the world. In the Mesopotamian poem to Erra, rhetorical questions are also used by the creator-god Marduk, as is the case with God in Job.

38:4–6 *earth's foundation ... cornerstone.* Creation is described like the construction of a building, and here the foundation and cornerstone are laid. The link between creation and building terminology is reflected by the prototypical ancient Near Eastern temple, which was seen as a reflection of the cosmos. The Egyptian temple, e.g., had pillars in the form of plants and a roof decorated with stars representing heaven. The shrine represented the primeval hill of creation, and there was a sacred lake within the precinct called the "divine pool." Though the building blocks are being put in place, the interest is in how Yahweh has set up the ordered cosmos to operate at his command.

38:7 *morning stars sang together ... angels shouted.* The stars and "angels" (or "sons of God" [see NIV text note]) that sing together at creation are parallel to one another and considered the same supernatural beings (see 1:6 and note). In a Ugaritic text, the "sons of El/the gods" occur in parallel with "assembly of the stars." In the rest of the ancient world, the stars were divinized, meaning that there was no distinction between the star as an object and the star as a god. In fact, in the ancient world, people did not know that the stars were material objects. In Israel, the stars were not divinized, but they were personified when equated with the heavenly hosts — the sons of God. Here, Israel is still working within the ancient mindset, but the text does not reflect polytheistic thinking.

[8] "Who shut up the sea behind doors[h]
when it burst forth from the womb,[i]
[9] when I made the clouds its garment
and wrapped it in thick darkness,
[10] when I fixed limits for it[j]
and set its doors and bars in place,[k]
[11] when I said, 'This far you may come
and no farther;
here is where your proud waves halt'?[l]

[12] "Have you ever given orders to the morning,
or shown the dawn its place,
[13] that it might take the earth by the edges
and shake the wicked[m] out of it?
[14] The earth takes shape like clay under a seal;
its features stand out like those of a garment.
[15] The wicked are denied their light,[n]
and their upraised arm is broken.[o]

[16] "Have you journeyed to the springs of the sea
or walked in the recesses of the deep?[p]
[17] Have the gates of death[q] been shown to you?
Have you seen the gates of the deepest darkness?

38:8 [h] Jer 5:22 [i] Ge 1:9-10 **38:10** [j] Ps 33:7; 104:9 [k] Job 26:10 **38:11** [l] Ps 89:9 **38:13** [m] Ps 104:35 **38:15** [n] Job 18:5 [o] Ps 10:15 **38:16** [p] Ps 77:19 **38:17** [q] Ps 9:13

38:8 *shut up the sea.* The battle with and control of the sea as symbol of chaos (see notes on 7:12; Ge 1:2; see also the article "Cosmic Geography," p. 836) is observable in the principle cosmogony in the ancient Near East (*Enuma Elish* IV: 139–40). Hints about such a battle can be found in Ps 74:12–23. In most Biblical contexts, God is seen as setting boundaries for the sea and restricting its movements. He is clearly in control.
38:12 *dawn.* Hebrew *shahar*; it is personified, as in Ps 57:8; 108:2, where it is woken up. In Ugaritic literature, Shahar is a god, the child of El, and acts with other gods, such as the sun-goddess; in Job 41:18, it refers to the eyes of the Leviathan. The metaphor in this verse reflects the mindset of the ancient Near East in personifying the dawn, but it does not go as far as to deify the dawn, as other ancient people might have done. From contexts like this, we can see that personification/deification pertains not only to objects in the cosmos, but to functions as well.
38:14 *The earth takes shape like clay under a seal.* In the same way the image on the clay stands out when pressed by a seal, the earth takes shape in the growing light and the landscape becomes clearer.
38:15 *wicked are denied their light ... upraised arm is broken.* The symbolism of light (the sun) versus darkness was common in the ancient Near East, especially when intended to highlight a deity's power. The sun is not mentioned precisely in this sense in Job 38, but it is used as a symbol of righteousness (cf. Mal 4:2). Darkness is a time of danger, but when light appears or the sun rises, then dangerous animals such as lions are dispersed (Ps 104:20–22) with the result that the threat of harm in the darkness is alleviated. In the hymn of the pharaoh Akhenaten to the sun-disk Aten, the rising of the sun introduces life. Darkness is compared to death, and night is portrayed as a time when robbers, lions and serpents harm people. When the Aten shines, darkness is dispelled, and life may flourish. Ancient Near Eastern iconography shows the destruction of evil by the sun: when the sun rises, dangerous forces are dispersed, and their arms are broken.
38:17 *gates of death.* Death (*Mawet*, see note on 18:13; see also the article "Death and Sheol," p. 833) in this verse has gates, as does Sheol (see note on 17:16) and *tsalmawet*—another Hebrew word for death (cf. 24:17 "midnight";

JOB 38

DIVINE DISCOURSE

The divine speech in Job 38 has been compared with the Egyptian name lists or catalogs of things (Onomastica). These lists start with heaven and the stars, deal with meteorological phenomena like rain and thunder, the earth and water, persons and their occupations, towns and buildings, land and products, and end with parts of animals. This tradition is also known from Mesopotamia, where there are lists of trees, domestic and wild animals, birds and fish, and food and drink; but the order in Job is closer to that found in Egypt. Such lists were viewed as displays of wisdom in the ancient world. Sometimes they were lists without elaboration that simply showed a wide knowledge of objects in a similar category. More important, a list such as this one showed insight into how things work—their habits and routines. The presence of such a list, therefore, indicates that Yahweh is showcasing his wisdom. ◆

18 Have you comprehended the vast
expanses of the earth?[r]
Tell me, if you know all this.

19 "What is the way to the abode of light?
And where does darkness reside?
20 Can you take them to their places?
Do you know the paths[s] to their
dwellings?
21 Surely you know, for you were already
born![t]
You have lived so many years!

22 "Have you entered the storehouses of
the snow[u]
or seen the storehouses of the hail,
23 which I reserve for times of trouble,[v]
for days of war and battle?[w]
24 What is the way to the place where the
lightning is dispersed,
or the place where the east winds
are scattered over the earth?
25 Who cuts a channel for the torrents of
rain,
and a path for the thunderstorm,[x]
26 to water[y] a land where no one lives,
an uninhabited desert,
27 to satisfy a desolate wasteland
and make it sprout with grass?[z]
28 Does the rain have a father?[a]
Who fathers the drops of dew?
29 From whose womb comes the ice?
Who gives birth to the frost from the
heavens[b]
30 when the waters become hard as
stone,
when the surface of the deep is
frozen?[c]

31 "Can you bind the chains[a] of the
Pleiades?
Can you loosen Orion's belt?[d]
32 Can you bring forth the constellations
in their seasons[b]
or lead out the Bear[c] with its cubs?
33 Do you know the laws[e] of the heavens?
Can you set up God's[d] dominion
over the earth?

34 "Can you raise your voice to the
clouds
and cover yourself with a flood of
water?[f]
35 Do you send the lightning bolts on
their way?[g]
Do they report to you, 'Here we
are'?
36 Who gives the ibis wisdom[e][h]
or gives the rooster understanding?[f][i]
37 Who has the wisdom to count the
clouds?
Who can tip over the water jars
of the heavens
38 when the dust becomes hard
and the clods of earth stick
together?

39 "Do you hunt the prey for the lioness
and satisfy the hunger of the lions[j]
40 when they crouch in their dens[k]
or lie in wait in a thicket?
41 Who provides food for the raven[l]
when its young cry out to God
and wander about for lack of
food?[m]

39 "Do you know when the mountain
goats[n] give birth?
Do you watch when the doe bears
her fawn?
2 Do you count the months till they
bear?
Do you know the time they give
birth?
3 They crouch down and bring forth
their young;
their labor pains are ended.
4 Their young thrive and grow strong in
the wilds;
they leave and do not return.

5 "Who let the wild donkey[o] go free?
Who untied its ropes?

38:18 [r] Job 28:24 **38:20** [s] Job 26:10 **38:21** [t] Job 15:7 **38:22** [u] Job 37:6 **38:23** [v] Isa 30:30; Eze 13:11 [w] Ex 9:18; Jos 10:11; Rev 16:21 **38:25** [x] Job 28:26 **38:26** [y] Job 36:27 **38:27** [z] Ps 104:14; 107:35 **38:28** [a] Ps 147:8; Jer 14:22 **38:29** [b] Ps 147:16-17 **38:30** [c] Job 37:10 **38:31** [d] Job 9:9; Am 5:8 **38:33** [e] Ps 148:6; Jer 31:36 **38:34** [f] Job 22:11; 36:27-28 **38:35** [g] Job 36:32; 37:3 **38:36** [h] Job 9:4 [i] Job 32:8; Ps 51:6; Ecc 2:26 **38:39** [j] Ps 104:21 **38:40** [k] Job 37:8 **38:41** [l] Lk 12:24 [m] Ps 147:9; Mt 6:26 **39:1** [n] Dt 14:5 **39:5** [o] Job 6:5; 11:12; 24:5

[a] 31 Septuagint; Hebrew *beauty* [b] 32 Or *the morning star in its season* [c] 32 Or *out Leo* [d] 33 Or *their* [e] 36 That is, wisdom about the flooding of the Nile [f] 36 That is, understanding of when to crow; the meaning of the Hebrew for this verse is uncertain.

"darkness"). Mesopotamian descriptions of the underworld tell about the seven gates and a divine gatekeeper.
38:22 *storehouses of the snow ... of the hail.* This expression derives from the cosmic geography of the ancient world. In their view, precipitation was kept in storehouses and taken from the storehouses and put into the clouds, which in turn dropped the water on the earth. These storehouses were believed to be at the horizons. See the article "Cosmic Geography," p. 836.
38:28 *Does the rain have a father? Who fathers the drops of dew?* According to Ugaritic mythology, Baal, the storm-god, had three daughters. The third one's name was Tallay, meaning "dew," or (better) "dewy." One theory in the ancient world was that the dew came from the stars. Such information indicates that this question addresses a known issue in the ancient world, but, of course, in the context of Yahweh's speech, the rhetorical question is meant to indicate things that were not known.
38:38 *clods of earth.* Regions like Syria and Canaan, where there were no large rivers as there were in Egypt and Mesopotamia, were dependent on rain. Without rain, the earth would become dry and the clods of earth would literally stick together.
39:1–30 The thrust of the argument in ch. 39: Does Job know how animals hunt and give birth, or from where their strength and movement come? Only God as Lord-of-animals (a familiar art motif in the ancient world) can control them (cf. Jdg 14:5–6; 15:4–5). But as Lord-of-animals, he does not destroy the animals, but takes care of them—even the lion is fed (Job 38:39).
39:5 *the wild donkey.* The onager; it can be differentiated from the horse because of the much shorter tail of the donkey, the shorter standing mane and the typically

[6]I gave it the wasteland[p] as its home,
the salt flats as its habitat.[q]
[7]It laughs at the commotion in the town;
it does not hear a driver's shout.[r]
[8]It ranges the hills for its pasture
and searches for any green thing.

[9]"Will the wild ox[s] consent to serve you?
Will it stay by your manger at night?
[10]Can you hold it to the furrow with a harness?
Will it till the valleys behind you?
[11]Will you rely on it for its great strength?
Will you leave your heavy work to it?
[12]Can you trust it to haul in your grain
and bring it to your threshing floor?

[13]"The wings of the ostrich flap joyfully,
though they cannot compare
with the wings and feathers of the stork.
[14]She lays her eggs on the ground
and lets them warm in the sand,
[15]unmindful that a foot may crush them,
that some wild animal may trample them.
[16]She treats her young harshly,[t] as if they were not hers;
she cares not that her labor was in vain,
[17]for God did not endow her with wisdom
or give her a share of good sense.[u]
[18]Yet when she spreads her feathers to run,
she laughs at horse and rider.

[19]"Do you give the horse its strength
or clothe its neck with a flowing mane?
[20]Do you make it leap like a locust,[v]
striking terror with its proud snorting?[w]
[21]It paws fiercely, rejoicing in its strength,
and charges into the fray.[x]
[22]It laughs at fear, afraid of nothing;
it does not shy away from the sword.
[23]The quiver rattles against its side,
along with the flashing spear and lance.
[24]In frenzied excitement it eats up the ground;
it cannot stand still when the trumpet sounds.[y]
[25]At the blast of the trumpet[z] it snorts, 'Aha!'
It catches the scent of battle from afar,
the shout of commanders and the battle cry.[a]

[26]"Does the hawk take flight by your wisdom
and spread its wings toward the south?
[27]Does the eagle soar at your command
and build its nest on high?[b]
[28]It dwells on a cliff and stays there at night;
a rocky crag is its stronghold.
[29]From there it looks for food;[c]
its eyes detect it from afar.
[30]Its young ones feast on blood,
and where the slain are, there it is."[d]

40

The LORD said to Job:[e]

[2]"Will the one who contends with the Almighty correct him?
Let him who accuses God answer him!"

39:6 [p] Job 24:5; Ps 107:34; Jer 2:24 [q] Hos 8:9 **39:7** [r] Job 3:18 **39:9** [s] Nu 23:22; Dt 33:17 **39:16** [t] La 4:3 **39:17** [u] Job 35:11 **39:20** [v] Joel 2:4-5 [w] Jer 8:16 **39:21** [x] Jer 8:6 **39:24** [y] Jer 4:5, 19; Eze 7:14; Am 3:6 **39:25** [z] Jos 6:5 [a] Am 1:14; 2:2 **39:27** [b] Jer 49:16; Ob 1:4 **39:29** [c] Job 9:26 **39:30** [d] Mt 24:28; Lk 17:37 **40:1** [e] Job 10:2; 13:3; 23:4; 31:35; 33:13

larger ears. Here the donkey is not the dumb and lazy animal of the popular Western image, but a symbol of the wild, as it cannot be tamed (v. 7; cf. Ge 16:12; Isa 32:14; Jer 2:24; 14:6). Assyrian reliefs depict the hunting of such wild donkeys. People who break treaties are cursed to roam the desert like the wild ass, the desert symbolizing the periphery of civilization. This sequence of animals in ch. 39 includes those that were considered mysterious in the ancient world and had admirable qualities.

39:9 *the wild ox.* This animal is very strong and difficult to tame (cf. Dt 33:17; Ps 92:10). In the Ugaritic texts, the goddess Astarte hunts a bull, as did the Assyrian kings. Ox hunting is also depicted on Assyrian reliefs, and a beautiful golden dish from Ugarit shows a king in his chariot hunting wild bulls.

39:16 *treats her young harshly.* Ancient people thought that the ostrich, out of cruelty (cf. La 4:3: "heartless like ostriches"), left its young after laying the eggs.

39:18 *laughs at horse and rider.* The ostrich can outrun a horse, as observed by Xenophon. Ostriches are depicted in Egyptian paintings, and the ostrich feather was the symbol of the goddess Maat. They are objects of curiosity as demonstrated in art that shows Tutankhamun hunting ostriches and an Assyrian hero pursuing an ostrich.

39:19 *the horse.* Described as a war animal that is used for carrying a quiver, spear and lance (v. 23), and that is familiar with the scent and cry of battle (v. 25). Horses were used to pull chariots, but riding came later. Assyrian reliefs show soldiers on horseback, but cavalry was applied on a large scale only by Alexander the Great, the Scythians and the Parthians. In v. 20, the horse leaps like a locust, and in Joel 2:4 locusts are compared to running horses.

39:26–27 *the hawk ... the eagle.* The last two animals described are birds of prey and large meat eaters. They have mighty wings (v. 26) extending 6.5 feet (2 meters) in length. The young birds drink blood and, like vultures, they eat corpses on the battlefield (v. 30; cf. Mt 24:28).

[3]Then Job answered the LORD:

[4]"I am unworthy[f]—how can I reply to
you?
I put my hand over my mouth.[g]
[5]I spoke once, but I have no
answer[h]—
twice, but I will say no more."[i]

[6]Then the LORD spoke to Job out of the
storm:[j]

[7]"Brace yourself like a man;
I will question you,
and you shall answer me.[k]

[8]"Would you discredit my justice?[l]
Would you condemn me to justify
yourself?
[9]Do you have an arm like God's,[m]
and can your voice thunder like
his?[n]

40:4 [f]Job 42:6 [g]Job 29:9 **40:5** [h]Job 9:3 [i]Job 9:15 **40:6** [j]Job 38:1 **40:7** [k]Job 38:3; 42:4 **40:8** [l]Job 27:2; Ro 3:3 **40:9** [m]2Ch 32:8 [n]Job 37:5; Ps 29:3-4

40:4 *I put my hand over my mouth.* On a relief of the Persian king Darius I, a Median stands with his hand raised to his mouth as a gesture of respect in the presence of someone greater than him. This same gesture is seen much earlier on the stele of Hammurapi as he stands before the god Shamash. Though it is a well-known gesture, its meaning is still subject to various interpretations (see notes on 21:5; 29:9).

40:9 *an arm like God's.* The arm (like the hand) can indicate power and strength, as in the Hebrew of 22:8 (see note there). In Ex 6:6, God saves Israel with an "outstretched arm." In a letter from Ugarit, the hands of the

JOB 40–41

IDENTIFICATION OF BEHEMOTH AND LEVIATHAN

In the dialogues, Job wonders why God is treating him like a chaos creature (Job 7:12); in the discourses, Job suggests that God is acting like a chaos creature (Job 30:20–23). Here in God's second set of speeches, Yahweh picks up both of Job's charges and alters Job's fundamental assumption by implying that chaos creatures are in fact part of God's ordered world.

Most of the ancient world believed that chaos creatures were outside of the established order and often viewed them as a threat to that order. In contrast, the Hebrew Bible consistently expresses God's control of chaos creatures and merges them into the ordered cosmos. For example, they are created (which entails being drawn into the ordered cosmos) in Ge 1:21, and they are passive rather than threatening in Ps 104:26.

The passages about Behemoth and Leviathan appropriately follow Yahweh's challenge to Job to bring low all the proud (Job 40:11), for Leviathan is identified as the king over all who are proud (Job 41:34). Leviathan should be labeled an "anti-cosmos creature" rather than a "chaos creature." These creatures exist on the fringes of the ordered world. Although creation entailed bringing order to the cosmos, the cosmos was not seen as a totally ordered system. The fact that there is a Garden of Eden, where a high level of order exists, but also space outside the garden, where order has yet to be established, evidences the distinction. Liminal creatures (such as coyote, owl and ostrich) are near the boundaries of the ordered world. Nonzoological creatures such as Behemoth, Leviathan, Rahab and Tannin are not viewed as unbridled threats, but neither are they drawn totally into the ordered sphere. Nahash, the serpent of Ge 3, is another example of an anti-cosmos creature. Anti-cosmos creatures are creations of God, but are the "thorns" and "thistles" of the animal world.

Significant problems exist for the suggestions that Behemoth and Leviathan are either zoological specimens or now-extinct creatures that once roamed the earth. In the former category, while Behemoth's location among the lotus plants in the reeds of the marsh (Job 40:21–24) might bring to mind the mighty hippopotamus, the description of the tail (Job 40:17) makes such identification impossible. Likewise, those who

continued on next page

suggest some huge now-extinct plant-eating dinosaur would have trouble explaining how it is concealed among the lotus plants. In the same way, although Leviathan may have some characteristics of a Nile crocodile, its fire breathing (Job 41:18–21) and multiple heads (Ps 74:14) refute that identification. Perhaps those in antiquity would have viewed the hippopotamus and crocodile as reminiscent of Behemoth and Leviathan, and perhaps even as their spawn in some sense, but Behemoth and Leviathan are the archetypes and personify abstractions that hippopotamus and crocodile do to a much lesser degree.

Alternatively, it is not uncommon to see Behemoth and Leviathan identified as throwbacks from ancient mythology. Behemoth would perhaps be represented in figurines and reliefs of a human-headed bison, and Leviathan, also referred to in Ugaritic texts (as Litan), would be the seven-headed dragon that appears on seals and engravings in Mesopotamia.

A third direction taken by interpreters posits Behemoth and Leviathan as figures known from West Semitic mythology, primarily available in the Ugaritic texts. Some scholars associate them with Mot and Yamm, while others prefer to identify Behemoth with El's calf, Atik (Arš), and Leviathan with the Ugaritic mythological sea dragon, Litan. ◆

Human-headed bison, Mesopotamia, 2150–2100 BC. It is common to see Behemoth identified as a throwback from ancient mythology, such as a human-headed bison.

Photo courtesy of Mary Harrsch © 2014

10 Then adorn yourself with glory and splendor,
and clothe yourself in honor and majesty.[o]
11 Unleash the fury of your wrath,[p]
look at all who are proud and bring them low,[q]
12 look at all who are proud and humble them,[r]
crush[s] the wicked where they stand.
13 Bury them all in the dust together;
shroud their faces in the grave.
14 Then I myself will admit to you
that your own right hand can save you.[t]

15 "Look at Behemoth,
which I made along with you
and which feeds on grass like an ox.

40:10 [o] Ps 93:1; 104:1
40:11 [p] Isa 42:25; Na 1:6 [q] Isa 2:11, 12, 17; Da 4:37
40:12 [r] 1Sa 2:7 [s] Isa 13:11; 63:2-3,6
40:14 [t] Ps 20:6; 60:5; 108:6

gods are strong like death, and at Mari, a god's hand destroys cattle and men. The visual representation of deities brandishing weapons in a menacing way also reflects the power of the arm.

40:10 *clothe yourself.* God challenges Job to dress himself in glory, which is ironic, given it refers to something only God can do. God is "clothed with splendor and majesty" (Ps 104:1; cf. Job 37:22). The Mesopotamian deities had power or glamour, called *melammu*; divine statues in the ancient Near East were clothed, and deities are represented as covered in light or stars. Marduk "wore" the auras of seven gods, and the monsters of Tiamat were "clad" with glories.

16 What strength it has in its loins,
what power in the muscles of its belly!
17 Its tail sways like a cedar;
the sinews of its thighs are close-knit.
18 Its bones are tubes of bronze,
its limbs like rods of iron.
19 It ranks first among the works of God,[u]
yet its Maker can approach it with his sword.
20 The hills bring it their produce,[v]
and all the wild animals play[w] nearby.
21 Under the lotus plants it lies,
hidden among the reeds in the marsh.
22 The lotuses conceal it in their shadow;
the poplars by the stream[x] surround it.
23 A raging river does not alarm it;
it is secure, though the Jordan should surge against its mouth.
24 Can anyone capture it by the eyes,
or trap it and pierce its nose?[y]

41 [a] "Can you pull in Leviathan[z] with a fishhook
or tie down its tongue with a rope?
2 Can you put a cord through its nose
or pierce its jaw with a hook?[a]
3 Will it keep begging you for mercy?
Will it speak to you with gentle words?
4 Will it make an agreement with you
for you to take it as your slave for life?[b]
5 Can you make a pet of it like a bird
or put it on a leash for the young women in your house?
6 Will traders barter for it?
Will they divide it up among the merchants?
7 Can you fill its hide with harpoons
or its head with fishing spears?
8 If you lay a hand on it,
you will remember the struggle and never do it again!
9 Any hope of subduing it is false;
the mere sight of it is overpowering.
10 No one is fierce enough to rouse it.[c]
Who then is able to stand against me?[d]
11 Who has a claim against me that I must pay?[e]
Everything under heaven belongs to me.[f]
12 "I will not fail to speak of Leviathan's limbs,
its strength and its graceful form.
13 Who can strip off its outer coat?
Who can penetrate its double coat of armor[b]?
14 Who dares open the doors of its mouth,
ringed about with fearsome teeth?
15 Its back has[c] rows of shields
tightly sealed together;
16 each is so close to the next
that no air can pass between.
17 They are joined fast to one another;
they cling together and cannot be parted.
18 Its snorting throws out flashes of light;
its eyes are like the rays of dawn.[g]
19 Flames stream from its mouth;
sparks of fire shoot out.
20 Smoke pours from its nostrils
as from a boiling pot over burning reeds.
21 Its breath[h] sets coals ablaze,
and flames dart from its mouth.[i]
22 Strength resides in its neck;
dismay goes before it.
23 The folds of its flesh are tightly joined;
they are firm and immovable.
24 Its chest is hard as rock,
hard as a lower millstone.
25 When it rises up, the mighty are terrified;
they retreat before its thrashing.
26 The sword that reaches it has no effect,
nor does the spear or the dart or the javelin.
27 Iron it treats like straw
and bronze like rotten wood.
28 Arrows do not make it flee;
slingstones are like chaff to it.
29 A club seems to it but a piece of straw;
it laughs at the rattling of the lance.
30 Its undersides are jagged potsherds,
leaving a trail in the mud like a threshing sledge.[j]

40:19 [u] Job 41:33 **40:20** [v] Ps 104:14 [w] Ps 104:26 **40:22** [x] Isa 44:4 **40:24** [y] Job 41:2,7,26 **41:1** [z] Job 3:8; Ps 104:26; Isa 27:1 **41:2** [a] Isa 37:29 **41:4** [b] Ex 21:6 **41:10** [c] Job 3:8 [d] Jer 50:44 **41:11** [e] Ro 11:35 [f] Ex 19:5; Dt 10:14; Ps 24:1; 50:12; 1Co 10:26 **41:18** [g] Job 3:9 **41:21** [h] Isa 40:7 [i] Ps 18:8 **41:30** [j] Isa 41:15

[a] In Hebrew texts 41:1-8 is numbered 40:25-32, and 41:9-34 is numbered 41:1-26. [b] *13* Septuagint; Hebrew *double bridle* [c] *15* Or *Its pride is its*

41:9 *sight of it is overpowering.* The Leviathan is so powerful that his very appearance makes one lie low (TEV) or fall to the ground (GNT). The idea of such fear is known from ancient Near Eastern mythology. In the Babylonian creation epic, the gods are powerless against the might of Tiamat. In Ugarit, when the messengers of the sea-god Yamm appear, the gods lower their heads onto their knees. In v. 25, when the Leviathan rises, the "mighty" (Hebrew "gods") are afraid of him and retreat. In the Gilgamesh Epic the deities are afraid when the flood comes. **41:30** *jagged potsherds.* Like the one used by Job in 2:8. *threshing sledge.* Made of parallel boards with sharp stones. The scales on the belly of the Leviathan leave marks like a threshing sledge when it is dragged over the grain.

JOB 41 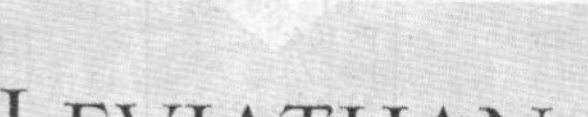

LEVIATHAN

Leviathan is found in Ugaritic texts that contain detailed descriptions of a chaos beast, representing the seas or watery anarchy in the form of a many-headed, twisting sea serpent, who is defeated by Baal. There is a close affinity between the description of Leviathan in Isa 27:1 as a "coiling serpent" and the Ugaritic Baal Cycle, which speaks of how the storm-god "smote Litan the twisting serpent." In both cases, there is a sense of the God of order and fertility vanquishing a chaos monster. Several other passages in the OT mention Leviathan, but most of them, like Ps 74:14, speak in terms of God's creative act that establishes control over watery chaos (personified by the sea serpent). In Isa 27:1, however, that struggle between order and chaos occurs at the end of time. It may be that Satan, portrayed as a seven-headed dragon in Rev 12:3–9, also echoes the Leviathan, "the tyrant with seven heads." Biblically, Leviathan would therefore most easily fit into the category of a "supernatural" creature (like cherubim) as opposed to a natural or purely mythological creature. As such, it may appear in extra-Biblical mythology, as well as being symbolized by something like a crocodile (as in Eze 29:3, though Leviathan is not specifically referenced in that context). The point in Job is that if Job cannot domesticate and control Leviathan, he certainly should not expect to control God.

Some interpret Leviathan as connected to what is called a *chaoskampf* motif—a battle of God against chaos to bring order to the world at its creation. A more substantiable motif for cosmogony is that of the "Lord of the Cosmos." The Hebrew Bible is consistently interested in divine kingship, an interest it holds in common with the rest of the ancient world. Cosmogony is one context in which divine kingship can be demonstrated, but it is only one of many. Yahweh's kingship is expressed over the operations of the cosmos, whether they pertain to precipitation or politics. He is

continued on next page

31 It makes the depths churn like a
boiling caldron
and stirs up the sea like a pot of
ointment.
32 It leaves a glistening wake behind it;
one would think the deep had white
hair.
33 Nothing on earth is its equal[k]—
a creature without fear.
34 It looks down on all that are haughty;
it is king over all that are proud.[l]"

Job

42 Then Job replied to the LORD:

2 "I know that you can do all things;[m]
no purpose of yours can be thwarted.[n]
3 You asked, 'Who is this that obscures
my plans without knowledge?'[o]
Surely I spoke of things I did not
understand,
things too wonderful for me to
know.[p]
4 "You said, 'Listen now, and I will
speak;
I will question you,
and you shall answer me.'[q]
5 My ears had heard of you[r]
but now my eyes have seen you.[s]
6 Therefore I despise myself[t]
and repent in dust and ashes."[u]

Epilogue

7 After the LORD had said these things to Job, he said to Eliphaz the Temanite, "I am angry with you and your two friends,[v] because you have not spoken the truth about me, as my servant Job has. 8 So now take

41:33 [k] Job 40:19 **41:34** [l] Job 28:8 **42:2** [m] Ge 18:14; Mt 19:26 [n] 2Ch 20:6 **42:3** [o] Job 38:2 [p] Ps 40:5; 131:1; 139:6 **42:4** [q] Job 38:3; 40:7 **42:5** [r] Job 26:14; Ro 10:17 [s] Jdg 13:22; Isa 6:5; Eph 1:17-18 **42:6** [t] Job 40:4 [u] Ezr 9:6 **42:7** [v] Job 32:3

42:6 *repent in dust and ashes.* Typical to ancient Israel, the idea of the link between honor and shame is at play here. Job honors God and acknowledges his shame by repenting in dust and ashes, a practice linked with mourning in 2:8,12 (see the article "Mourning," p. 828).

superior to other gods (though he does not bother to fight them and is not said to rule over them — these would give them too high a standing), and he rules nations and empires. Theomachy (God in battle) is typically a motif in contexts in which Yahweh is harnessing those powers that would rebel against his rule. The passages in the Prophets and the Psalms nowhere indicate that the *formation* of the cosmos comes as a result of defeat of other powers, only that Yahweh's *rule* of the cosmos is accomplished as he defeats rebels or harnesses powers. ◆

Seven-headed monster plaque, Mesopotamian, 2450 BC. Leviathan (Job 41:1) is a cosmic monster often thought to have multiple heads.

Z. Radovan/www.BibleLandPictures.com

seven bulls and seven rams[w] and go to my
servant Job and sacrifice a burnt offering[x]
for yourselves. My servant Job will pray
for you, and I will accept his prayer[y] and
not deal with you according to your folly.[z]
You have not spoken the truth about me,
as my servant Job has." 9 So Eliphaz the
Temanite, Bildad the Shuhite and Zophar
the Naamathite did what the LORD told
them; and the LORD accepted Job's prayer.
10 After Job had prayed for his friends,
the LORD restored his fortunes[a] and gave
him twice as much as he had before.[b] 11 All
his brothers and sisters and everyone who
had known him before[c] came and ate with
him in his house. They comforted and
consoled him over all the trouble the LORD
had brought on him, and each one gave
him a piece of silver[a] and a gold ring.
12 The LORD blessed the latter part of
Job's life more than the former part. He
had fourteen thousand sheep, six thousand camels, a thousand yoke of oxen and
a thousand donkeys. 13 And he also had
seven sons and three daughters. 14 The
first daughter he named Jemimah, the second Keziah and the third Keren-Happuch.
15 Nowhere in all the land were there found

42:8 [w] Nu 23:1, 29 [x] Job 1:5 [y] Ge 20:17; Jas 5:15-16; 1Jn 5:16 [z] Job 22:30 **42:10** [a] Dt 30:3; Ps 14:7 [b] Job 1:3; Ps 85:1-3; 126:5-6 **42:11** [c] Job 19:13

[a] *11* Hebrew *him a kesitah*; a kesitah was a unit of money of unknown weight and value.

42:10 *the LORD restored his fortunes.* The Ugaritic king Keret lost seven sons, and he is promised seven, even eight, as with Job, who lost seven sons and three daughters, but whose calamity now will be overturned.
42:11 *piece of silver.* Hebrew *qesitah*. This is not a coin, but a piece of silver used in business transactions. The relatives and friends give Job money in the way that was customary in ancient times before the days of coins and notes. *gold ring.* These are depicted in Egyptian art and worn as jewelry.
42:15 *inheritance.* It was not common for daughters to inherit in the Semitic world and, according to Nu 27, a daughter only inherited when there was no son, whereas Job has sons. The inheritance by daughters does, however, occur in some cases, but it is rather additional inheritance to the normal dowry.

women as beautiful as Job's daughters,
and their father granted them an inheritance along with their brothers.
16 After this, Job lived a hundred and
forty years; he saw his children and
their children to the fourth generation.
17 And so Job died, an old man and full
of years.[d]

42:17 [d]Ge 15:15; 25:8

42:16 *a hundred and forty years.* Might be a doubling of the perfect number of 70 years. Joseph reached an age of 110, the ideal age in Egyptian texts. *fourth generation.* Joseph saw his grandchildren to the third generation (Ge 50:23), Job to the fourth!

42:17 *an old man and full of years.* Used also of Abraham (Ge 25:8), Isaac (Ge 35:29) and David (1Ch 23:1).

WISDOM AND HYMNIC LITERATURE

PSALMS

Ancient Hymnody

Texts containing praise and prayer to gods and goddesses are nearly as old as writing itself. In the late third millennium BC, a high priestess of the Akkadian Empire compiled a cycle of hymns to deities and all the major temples of ancient Mesopotamia. These hymns were placed in related groupings, and a scribal note indicates that at least one later hymn (No. 9) was inserted into the original collection. Although this type of collection is somewhat exceptional, there is evidence that forerunners once existed.

Egypt produced short anthologies of songs organized for a deity or on a specific theme. From Mesopotamia and Egypt, individual texts representing a diverse range of types have been found, counterpart to various kinds of Biblical psalms: hymns to deities and their temples, laments and prayers for kings and other individuals, imprecations against enemies, as well as magical incantations for which there is no Biblical parallel. There are many similarities in formal structure, imagery and thought between these texts from the ancient Near East and the hymns and prayers of the OT.

KEY CONCEPTS

- Many psalms are an expression of emotion, and God responds to us in our emotional highs and lows.
- Psalms is a book with purpose.
- Psalms 1 – 2 embody the message of the book.

At the same time, the book of Psalms is unique as an anthology of songs. Composed and organized in stages over the course of Israel's history, it preserves a sample of inspired music that was used by individuals and the community for worship in God's temple. No other collection from the ancient Near East offers the variety in types of songs or exhibits the degree of internal organization that is increasingly recognized in Psalms. More important, the Psalter's theological content consistently extols Yahweh, the God of Israel, to the exclusion of all other deities, calling for the worship of Yahweh alone even among Israel's neighbors. This is a crucial point to keep in mind when considering the many common elements shared among the songs of worship across the ancient Near East.

Poetry and Genre

The hallmark of rhetoric in ancient Near Eastern literature is repetition; in poetry, this takes the form of what scholars call "parallelism." Frequently, the first line of a verse is echoed in some way by the second line. The second line might repeat the substance of the first line with slightly different emphasis, or perhaps the second line amplifies the first line in some fashion, such as drawing a logical conclusion, illustrating or intensifying the thought. At times the point of the first line is reinforced by a contrast in the second line. Occasionally, more than two lines are parallel. Each of these features, frequently observed in Biblical psalms, is represented in songs from Egypt, Mesopotamia and Ugarit. Unlike English poetry, which often depends on rhyme for its effect, these ancient cultures attained impact on listeners and readers with creative repetition.

Psalms come in several standard subgenres, each with standard formal elements. Praise psalms can be either individual or corporate. Over a third of the psalms in the Psalter are praise psalms. Corporate psalms typically begin with an imperative call to praise (e.g., "Shout for joy to the LORD" [Ps 100:1]) and describe all the good things the Lord has done. Individual praise often begins with a proclamation of intent to praise (e.g., "I will praise you, LORD" [Ps 138:1]) and declare what God has done in a particular situation in the psalmist's life. Mesopotamian and Egyptian hymns generally focus on descriptive praise, often moving from praise to petition. Examples of the proclamation format can be seen in the Mesopotamian wisdom composition, *Ludlul bel nemeqi*. The title is the first line of the piece, which is translated "I will praise the lord of wisdom." As in the individual praise psalms, this Mesopotamian worshiper of Marduk reports about a problem that he had and reports how his god brought him deliverance.

Lament psalms may be personal statements of despair (e.g., Ps 22:1 – 21, dirges following the death of an important person (cf. David's elegy for Saul in 2Sa 1:17 – 27) or communal cries in times of crisis (e.g., Ps 137). The most famous lament form from ancient Mesopotamia is the "Lament Over the Destruction of Ur," which commemorates the capture of the city in 2004 BC by the Elamite king Kindattu. For more information on this latter category, see the article "Neo-Sumerian Laments," p. 1322. In the book of Psalms, more than a third of the psalms are laments, mostly by an individual. The most common complaints concern sickness and oppression by enemies. The lament literature of Mesopotamia is comprised of a number of different subgenres described by various technical terms. Some of these subgenres overlap with Biblical categories, but most of the Mesopotamian pieces are associated with incantations (magical rites being performed to try to rid the person of the problem). Nevertheless, the petitions that accompany lament in the Bible are very similar to those found in prayers from the ancient Near East. They include requests for guidance, protection, favor, attention from the deity, deliverance from crisis, intervention, reconciliation, healing and long life.

Prayers to deities preserved from the ancient Near East share many of the same themes as Biblical prayers. Individuals sensed guilt and divine abandonment (see notes on Ps 6:1,3; 13:1; 32:4; 51:1,5); they felt physical suffering (see notes on Ps 22:14,17; 38:2 – 3), emotional pain and shame (see notes on Ps 6:6; 25:2) and loss of friendship (see note on Ps 31:11); and they faced death (see note on Ps 16:10). At times their afflictions involved legal entanglements accompanied by slander and curses (see notes on Ps 17:2; 41:5 – 6; 62:4). They responded with cries for a divine hearing (see note on Ps 55:17) and justice (see the article "Imprecations and Incantations," p. 937). In ancient Mesopotamia, letters written to gods and deposited in the temple also served to bring requests before the deity. The use of rather generic names in these letters, as well as their transmission through the curriculum of scribal schools, suggests that anyone could relate his or her experience with those recorded in these prayers. In later tradition, similar prayers were cited orally by a priest rather than deposited in the temple.

Much of the language of these prayers and letters, including the Biblical psalms, was general and metaphoric, allowing these texts to serve as examples for others to use in their specific circumstances. While the details of hardship might have differed, the emotional experiences and theological thoughts could be shared by anyone. As in Biblical psalms, the Mesopotamian prayers include protests of innocence, praise to the deity and vows to offer thanks for deliverance. Often specific attributes of the deity are named that correspond to the affliction and desired deliverance of the worshiper. Such elements function within the lament as motivation for the deity to respond to the worshiper's plight. ◆

BOOK I

Psalms 1–41

Psalm 1

[1] Blessed is the one
who does not walk[a] in step with the wicked
or stand in the way that sinners take
or sit[b] in the company of mockers,
[2] but whose delight[c] is in the law of the LORD,[d]
and who meditates[e] on his law day and night.
[3] That person is like a tree[f] planted by streams of water,[g]
which yields its fruit[h] in season
and whose leaf does not wither—
whatever they do prospers.[i]

[4] Not so the wicked!
They are like chaff[j]
that the wind blows away.
[5] Therefore the wicked will not stand[k] in the judgment,[l]
nor sinners in the assembly of the righteous.

[6] For the LORD watches over[m] the way of the righteous,
but the way of the wicked leads to destruction.[n]

Psalm 2

[1] Why do the nations conspire[a]
and the peoples plot[o] in vain?
[2] The kings[p] of the earth rise up
and the rulers band together
against the LORD and against his anointed,[q] saying,
[3] "Let us break their chains
and throw off their shackles."[r]

[4] The One enthroned in heaven laughs;[s]
the Lord scoffs at them.
[5] He rebukes them in his anger
and terrifies them in his wrath,[t] saying,
[6] "I have installed my king
on Zion, my holy mountain."

[7] I will proclaim the LORD's decree:

He said to me, "You are my son;
today I have become your father.[u]

1:1 [a] Pr 4:14 [b] Ps 26:4; Jer 15:17 **1:2** [c] Ps 119:16, 35 [d] Ps 119:1 [e] Jos 1:8 **1:3** [f] Ps 128:3 [g] Jer 17:8 [h] Eze 47:12 [i] Ge 39:3 **1:4** [j] Job 21:18; Isa 17:13 **1:5** [k] Ps 5:5 [l] Ps 9:7-8, 16 **1:6** [m] Ps 37:18; 2Ti 2:19 [n] Ps 9:6 **2:1** [o] Ps 21:11 **2:2** [p] Ps 48:4 [q] Ps 74:18, 23; Jn 1:41; Ac 4:25-26* **2:3** [r] Jer 5:5 **2:4** [s] Ps 37:13; 59:8; Pr 1:26 **2:5** [t] Ps 21:9; 78:49-50 **2:7** [u] Ac 13:33*; Heb 1:5*

[a] *1* Hebrew; Septuagint *rage*

1:3 *a tree planted by streams.* In lands without abundant rainfall, vegetation flourished only where there were natural streams or man-made canals. Along the Nile River in Egypt and the two rivers of Mesopotamia, the fertile soils produced abundantly. Trees in particular were planted closest to the bank, where their roots could reach the supply of water. Paintings from Egypt depict thriving palms beside the river.

1:5 *assembly of the righteous.* The "assembly" is a formal judicial body, just as the assembly of the sons of El was in the Ugaritic texts. This phrase is similar to an idea in 82:1, where God functions in relation to a judicial council as cases are decided. In the heavenly realm, there was a divine council that served this function (see the article "Divine Council," p. 615), but human courts also operated by means of an assembly (Jos 20:9).

1:6 *the way of the righteous … the way of the wicked.* Ancient Near Eastern wisdom maintained that in life there are two destinies for people: Those who live according to the will of the gods experience a long and fruitful life, but those who live as though there is no god come to an early end. Ps 1 shares in the general truth of this wisdom tradition. See the article "Retribution Principle," p. 823.

Ps 2 Changes in kingship created political instability. When a change in kingship occurred in a powerful nation, the rulers of lesser nations under its control might take the opportunity to rebel against their new overlord. Frequently, they formed an alliance to rebel together. The Assyrian king Sennacherib, e.g., faced rebellions after his accession to the throne, including an alliance involving Hezekiah, king of Judah, and Marduk-Baladan of Babylonia. In another case, Esarhaddon forced vassal kings to swear allegiance to his son, Ashurbanipal, and promise not to rebel when Ashurbanipal succeeded him.

Ps 2 celebrates the coronation of a new king in Israel. It warns all the kings of the earth, who ideally are subordinate to Yahweh's king in Israel, not to rebel against him. If such action is folly when plotted against a king such as Sennacherib, how much more foolish is rebellion against the king of David's line who represents the God of all the earth? The poetic style of asking rhetorical questions (v. 1) and citing the words of vassal kings who are wavering on the brink of rebellion (v. 3) is an important theme in Assyrian prophetic oracles that support the Assyrian king's rule over his vassals.

2:2 *his anointed.* See note on 1Sa 2:10.

2:7 *the LORD's decree.* From earliest times in Mesopotamia, it was believed that the gods determined where and upon whom kingship would be placed. King Hammurapi of Babylon (c. 1750 BC) claimed that his kingship came from the council of the gods, and in one inscription he states that the god Shamash granted to him kingship and decreed his supremacy. Egyptian kings likewise received divine proclamation of their status, and some scholars have suggested that the "decree" in Ps 2 refers to a divine proclamation of privileges and duties similar to Egyptian coronations (see note on Ps 110). Perhaps closer in comparison is the covenant relationship set up between Assyrian kings and their gods. One of the Hebrew terms used for a royal covenant (*edut* in Ps 132:12; 2Ki 11:12; note another word for covenant, *berit*, in 2Ki 11:17) is related to the Assyrian word for the covenant between the Assyrian king and the gods (*adu*; see also Ps 132:11). Since the Hebrew word for "decree" in v. 7 is also associated with this covenant term in 81:4–5 (cf. 105:8–10), the idea of a royal covenant is probably in the background to Ps 2. In terms of both theme and structure, Ps 2 is similar to one Assyrian prophetic oracle in particular that affirms the sonship and world dominion of the king. *You are my son.* A parent-child relationship between the gods and the king was common imagery in the ancient world. Such imagery supported the authority of the king and portrayed his role as mediator between the divine realm and the world in which he was to maintain order (for

PSALM 1

PSALM TITLES

Some of the earliest examples of sacred music, from Sumer (third millennium BC), are recorded with notations for musical accompaniment. Some songs contain instructions concerning the ritual actions that accompany the performance. Similarly, the text of a song with musical notation from the site of Ugarit (c. 1300 BC) contains a colophon (scribal conclusion) naming the type of song and the scribe's name. It is no surprise, then, that titles would accompany Biblical psalms. Unfortunately, many of the terms in the psalm titles are no longer clearly understood.

The custom of attaching a title to songs in Israel is illustrated in 2Sa 22:1; Isa 38:9; Hab 3:1,19. This last example is particularly interesting in that it includes an introductory title as well as a conclusion. In the Psalter, all information was eventually placed at the beginning. Regardless of our ability to discern the meaning of the technical terms in the titles, they complemented the indications of authorship for grouping the psalms together in the final form of the Psalter. ◆

in modern transcription

Oldest known music notation, Babylonian, 2000 to 1700 BC.

The Schøyen Collection, Oslo and London, MS 5105, www.schoyencollection.com

"messianic" expectations in the ancient Near East, see note on Ps 72). In Egypt and for a few kings in early Mesopotamia, this relationship was portrayed in terms of a semidivine king. The Egyptian king manifested divinity in his human form in the embodiment of a deified office, and the physical conception of the king might be associated with the seed of a god. In a coronation inscription of Horemheb, the god Amun-Re identifies the king as his son, his heir, and even one who came from his body. Although the king in Mesopotamia was figuratively portrayed as being born, nurtured and nursed by goddesses, the metaphor of relationship was understood in terms of election and decree to kingship. The Assyrian king Esarhaddon is told that the goddess Ishtar is both his father and his mother. In similar fashion, Ashurbanipal declares that he was raised by his goddess, who gave him kingship and ordained eternal life for him. But Assyrian kings were never described with divine titles or worshiped as in Egypt. Kings in David's genealogical line also held their kingship by divine adoption, celebrated on the coronation day in Ps 2. The adoption metaphor in Israel was rooted in the special covenant relationship between Yahweh and the Davidic kings, which used terminology similar to that found in other ancient Near Eastern treaties (cf. 89:3–4,26–27; 2Sa 7:14). The great king was designated as "father," and the vassal king was his "son." In this way of thinking, the Davidic king was the "son" of the great King, Yahweh, who was the "father" (see note on 45:6). All of this, and much other evidence that will be seen throughout the notes, demonstrates that the Israelites thought about kingship in many of the same ways that their neighbors did, and that they used the same rhetoric when talking about kingship. This places Israel firmly within the conceptual world of the ancient Near East. Even though Yahweh is revealing himself as distinct from the other gods, that revelation is configured in terms familiar to anyone in the ancient Near East.

[8]Ask me,
and I will make the nations your inheritance,
the ends of the earth[v] your possession.
[9]You will break them with a rod of iron[a];[w]
you will dash them to pieces[x] like pottery.[y]"

[10]Therefore, you kings, be wise;
be warned, you rulers of the earth.
[11]Serve the LORD with fear
and celebrate his rule[z] with trembling.[a]
[12]Kiss his son,[b] or he will be angry
and your way will lead to your destruction,
for his wrath[c] can flare up in a moment.
Blessed are all who take refuge[d] in him.

2:8 [v]Ps 22:27 **2:9** [w]Rev 12:5 [x]Ps 89:23 [y]Rev 2:27* **2:11** [z]Heb 12:28 [a]Ps 119:119-120 **2:12** [b]Jn 5:23 [c]Rev 6:16 [d]Ps 34:8; Ro 9:33

3:Title [e]2Sa 15:14 **3:2** [f]Ps 71:11 **3:3** [g]Ge 15:1; Ps 28:7 [h]Ps 27:6 **3:4** [i]Ps 2:6 **3:5** [j]Lev 26:6; Pr 3:24

Psalm 3[b]

A psalm of David. When he fled from his son Absalom.[e]

[1]LORD, how many are my foes!
How many rise up against me!
[2]Many are saying of me,
"God will not deliver him."[f][c]

[3]But you, LORD, are a shield[g] around me,
my glory, the One who lifts my head high.[h]
[4]I call out to the LORD,
and he answers me from his holy mountain.[i]

[5]I lie down and sleep;[j]
I wake again, because the LORD sustains me.

[a] 9 Or *will rule them with an iron scepter* (see Septuagint and Syriac) [b] In Hebrew texts 3:1-8 is numbered 3:2-9. [c] 2 The Hebrew has *Selah* (a word of uncertain meaning) here and at the end of verses 4 and 8.

2:9 *break them with a rod of iron.* See NIV text note. Defeating enemies with a scepter, originally a club-like weapon of war, was a common image for ancient Near Eastern kings. *dash them to pieces like pottery.* Egyptian kings attempted to extend control over foreign kings beyond their normal sphere of military control by inscribing their names with curses on pottery jars and then smashing the jars as an invocation of curse. This exact ritual is unknown in Israel, but the breaking of earthen pottery as a symbol of destroying enemies was understood across the ancient Near East. That said, the metaphor is sufficiently facile and transparent.
3:3 *shield.* There is evidence for two basic types of shields used in the ancient Near East. (1) A large, body-length shield protected the entire body, but mobility was sacrificed. It was most suitable for infantry equipped with spears, approaching a fortress or units assigned to protect archers. (2) A round or torso-length shield was more common for infantry engaged in hand to hand combat with swords or spears. The materials were wicker or wood, and leather sometimes served as a cover. Because helmets and body armor were more difficult and expensive to make, the shield was the typical means of defense in combat, so it lends itself to common use as a metaphor of personal protection. Assyrian prophetic oracles (c. 680 BC) would use the image of a shield, along with other military metaphors, to assure the king of the deity's promise of protection. *lifts my head.* See note on 110:7.
3:4 *holy mountain.* See note on 48:1 – 2.

Assyrian panel depicts archers with shields. See note on Ps 3:3.

6 I will not fear[k] though tens of
thousands
assail me on every side.

7 Arise,[l] LORD!
Deliver me,[m] my God!
Strike[n] all my enemies on the jaw;
break the teeth[o] of the wicked.

8 From the LORD comes deliverance.[p]
May your blessing be on your
people.

Psalm 4[a]

For the director of music. With stringed instruments. A psalm of David.

1 Answer me when I call to you,
my righteous God.
Give me relief from my distress;
have mercy[q] on me and hear my
prayer.[r]

2 How long will you people turn my
glory into shame?
How long will you love delusions
and seek false gods[b]?[c][s]
3 Know that the LORD has set apart his
faithful servant[t] for himself;
the LORD hears[u] when I call to
him.

4 Tremble and[d] do not sin;[v]
when you are on your beds,[w]
search your hearts and be silent.
5 Offer the sacrifices of the righteous
and trust in the LORD.[x]

6 Many, LORD, are asking, "Who will
bring us prosperity?"
Let the light of your face shine on
us.[y]
7 Fill my heart[z] with joy[a]
when their grain and new wine
abound.

8 In peace I will lie down and sleep,[b]
for you alone, LORD,
make me dwell in safety.[c]

3:6 [k] Ps 27:3
3:7 [l] Ps 7:6
[m] Ps 6:4
[n] Job 16:10
[o] Ps 58:6
3:8 [p] Isa 43:3, 11
4:1 [q] Ps 25:16
[r] Ps 17:6
4:2 [s] Ps 31:6
4:3 [t] Ps 31:23
[u] Ps 6:8
4:4 [v] Eph 4:26*
[w] Ps 77:6
4:5 [x] Dt 33:19; Ps 37:3
4:6 [y] Nu 6:25
4:7 [z] Ac 14:17
[a] Isa 9:3
4:8 [b] Ps 3:5
[c] Lev 25:18

5:2 [d] Ps 3:4
[e] Ps 84:3
5:3 [f] Ps 88:13
5:4 [g] Ps 11:5; 92:15
5:5 [h] Ps 73:3
[i] Ps 1:5 [j] Ps 11:5
5:6 [k] Ps 55:23; Rev 21:8
5:7 [l] Ps 138:2
5:8 [m] Ps 31:1
[n] Ps 27:11
5:9 [o] Lk 11:44
[p] Ro 3:13*
5:10 [q] Ps 9:16
[r] Ps 107:11

Psalm 5[e]

For the director of music. For pipes. A psalm of David.

1 Listen to my words, LORD,
consider my lament.
2 Hear my cry for help,[d]
my King and my God,[e]
for to you I pray.

3 In the morning,[f] LORD, you hear my
voice;
in the morning I lay my requests
before you
and wait expectantly.
4 For you are not a God who is pleased
with wickedness;
with you, evil people[g] are not
welcome.
5 The arrogant[h] cannot stand[i]
in your presence.
You hate[j] all who do wrong;
6 you destroy those who tell lies.[k]
The bloodthirsty and deceitful
you, LORD, detest.
7 But I, by your great love,
can come into your house;
in reverence I bow down[l]
toward your holy temple.

8 Lead me, LORD, in your righteousness[m]
because of my enemies—
make your way straight[n] before me.
9 Not a word from their mouth can be
trusted;
their heart is filled with malice.
Their throat is an open grave;[o]
with their tongues they tell lies.[p]
10 Declare them guilty, O God!
Let their intrigues be their downfall.
Banish them for their many sins,[q]
for they have rebelled[r] against
you.

[a] In Hebrew texts 4:1-8 is numbered 4:2-9. [b] *2* Or *seek lies* [c] *2* The Hebrew has *Selah* (a word of uncertain meaning) here and at the end of verse 4. [d] *4* Or *In your anger* (see Septuagint) [e] In Hebrew texts 5:1-12 is numbered 5:2-13.

4:2 *people.* The same Hebrew word is translated "highborn" in 62:9 (see note there).

4:6 *light of your face.* This is probably a metaphor of the sun, the radiance of which was associated with light and warmth (see notes on 80:3,7,19; 84:11). There are several parallels to this imagery in ancient Near Eastern texts. In a letter from Ugarit, a man assures his mother of the king's favor upon him asserting that the face of the king shone on him

5:7 *house . . . temple.* The temple was viewed as God's residence, a visible manifestation of his presence on earth (see note on 48:1–2; see also the article "Hymn to Holy Cities," p. 927). Consequently, it was reasonable for an ancient Israelite to look, either physically or figuratively, "toward" Jerusalem and its temple in order to seek the Lord. The underlying premise was that the temple was God's base of operations; therefore, help would come from it.

5:9 *open grave.* Embalming was not practiced in Israel as it was in Egypt, so signs of bodily decay commenced within days of death, and burial was immediate, even for criminals (Dt 21:23). Natural or rock-cut caves were used as tombs (Ge 23:20; 2Ch 16:14). If circumstances dictated, earthen graves were also used, which was probably the custom for the common people (Ge 35:8,20; 1Sa 31:13; 2Ki 23:6). Sometimes the body was left permanently at rest. In other instances, after decomposition of the body, the bones were moved to a central repository in the tomb, and the bench upon which the body was originally laid could be reused. Except for the temporary offset from burial spices, the odor of decomposition was potent, and an open grave is a graphic image of the "rot" issuing forth from the mouth (vocal cords and tongue) of the wicked.

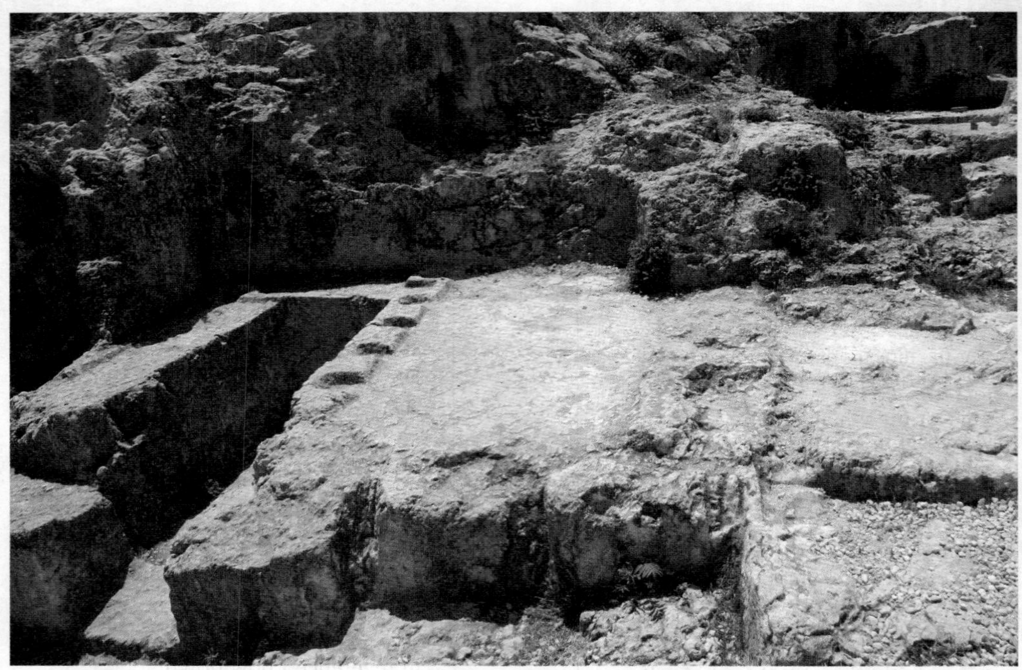

Ketef Hinnom tombs dated to the seventh to sixth century BC. The roof of the tomb has been quarried away, but the slabs where multiple bodies were laid can be seen. It was a common practice in Israel to use natural or rock-cut caves as tombs (see note on Ps 5:9).
Kim Walton

11 But let all who take refuge in you be glad;
let them ever sing for joy.[s]
Spread your protection over them,
that those who love your name[t]
may rejoice in you.[u]

12 Surely, LORD, you bless the righteous;
you surround them[v] with your favor as with a shield.

Psalm 6[a]

For the director of music. With stringed instruments. According to *sheminith.*[b] A psalm of David.

1 LORD, do not rebuke me in your anger[w]
or discipline me in your wrath.

2 Have mercy on me, LORD, for I am faint;
heal me,[x] LORD, for my bones are in agony.[y]
3 My soul is in deep anguish.[z]
How long,[a] LORD, how long?

4 Turn, LORD, and deliver me;
save me because of your unfailing love.[b]
5 Among the dead no one proclaims your name.
Who praises you from the grave?[c]

6 I am worn out[d] from my groaning.

All night long I flood my bed with weeping
and drench my couch with tears.[e]

5:11 [s]Ps 2:12 [t]Ps 69:36 [u]Isa 65:13 5:12 [v]Ps 32:7 6:1 [w]Ps 38:1 6:2 [x]Hos 6:1 [y]Ps 22:14; 31:10 6:3 [z]Jn 12:27 [a]Ps 90:13 6:4 [b]Ps 17:13 6:5 [c]Ps 30:9; 88:10-12; Ecc 9:10; Isa 38:18 6:6 [d]Ps 69:3 [e]Ps 42:3

[a] In Hebrew texts 6:1-10 is numbered 6:2-11. [b] Title: Probably a musical term

6:1 *discipline me in your wrath.* When the worshiper senses that perhaps something is amiss in his or her relationship with God, the possibility of divine discipline enters the mind. A similar question plagued worshipers in Mesopotamia, illustrated in a prayer to the god Nabu, who is recognized as disciplining the worshiper who requests his favor.
6:3 *how long?* This is the natural outcry of one who is suffering, and it finds expression in Mesopotamian laments as well. A Sumerian worshiper whose body is racked with illness complains to his god: "How long will you not care for me, will you not look after me?" In a prayer to the god Nabu, another Mesopotamian worshiper who is ill cries: "How long, a whole year, must I keep on waiting." These are good examples of how the rhetoric of the psalmists is similar to that of Babylonian or Canaanite psalmists. This does not mean that one tradition is borrowing language from another; it is merely indicative that common literary traditions prevailed across the ancient world.
6:5 *Who praises you from the grave?* See note on 88:10.
6:6 *flood my bed with weeping.* The poetical metaphor of crying on one's bed is also found in Ugaritic literature: "His tears are poured forth like shekels upon the

7 My eyes grow weak[f] with sorrow;
they fail because of all my foes.

8 Away from me,[g] all you who do evil,[h]
for the LORD has heard my weeping.
9 The LORD has heard my cry for mercy;[i]
the LORD accepts my prayer.
10 All my enemies will be overwhelmed
with shame and anguish;
they will turn back and suddenly be
put to shame.[j]

Psalm 7[a]

A *shiggaion*[b] of David, which he sang to the LORD concerning Cush, a Benjamite.

1 LORD my God, I take refuge in you;
save and deliver me from all who
pursue me,[k]
2 or they will tear me apart like a lion[l]
and rip me to pieces with no one to
rescue[m] me.

3 LORD my God, if I have done this
and there is guilt on my hands[n]—
4 if I have repaid my ally with evil
or without cause have robbed my
foe—
5 then let my enemy pursue and
overtake me;
let him trample my life to the
ground
and make me sleep in the dust.[c]

6 Arise,[o] LORD, in your anger;
rise up against the rage of my
enemies.[p]
Awake,[q] my God; decree justice.
7 Let the assembled peoples gather
around you,
while you sit enthroned over them
on high.

6:7 [f] Ps 31:9 **6:8** [g] Ps 119:115 [h] Mt 7:23; Lk 13:27 **6:9** [i] Ps 116:1 **6:10** [j] Ps 71:24; 73:19 **7:1** [k] Ps 31:15 **7:2** [l] Isa 38:13 [m] Ps 50:22 **7:3** [n] 1Sa 24:11; Isa 59:3 **7:6** [o] Ps 94:2 [p] Ps 138:7 [q] Ps 44:23

7:8 [r] Ps 18:20; 96:13 **7:9** [s] Ps 37:23 [t] Jer 11:20 [u] 1Ch 28:9; Ps 26:2; Rev 2:23 **7:10** [v] Ps 125:4 **7:11** [w] Ps 50:6 **7:12** [x] Dt 32:41 **7:14** [y] Job 15:35; Isa 59:4; Jas 1:15 **7:15** [z] Job 4:8 **7:17** [a] Ps 71:15-16 [b] Ps 9:2

8 Let the LORD judge the peoples.
Vindicate me, LORD, according to my
righteousness,[r]
according to my integrity, O Most
High.
9 Bring to an end the violence of the
wicked
and make the righteous secure—[s]
you, the righteous God[t]
who probes minds and hearts.[u]
10 My shield[d] is God Most High,
who saves the upright in heart.[v]
11 God is a righteous judge,[w]
a God who displays his wrath
every day.
12 If he does not relent,
he[e] will sharpen his sword;[x]
he will bend and string his bow.
13 He has prepared his deadly weapons;
he makes ready his flaming
arrows.

14 Whoever is pregnant with evil
conceives trouble and gives birth[y] to
disillusionment.
15 Whoever digs a hole and scoops
it out
falls into the pit they have made.[z]
16 The trouble they cause recoils on
them;
their violence comes down on their
own heads.

17 I will give thanks to the LORD because
of his righteousness;[a]
I will sing the praises[b] of the name
of the LORD Most High.

[a] In Hebrew texts 7:1-17 is numbered 7:2-18. [b] Title: Probably a literary or musical term [c] 5 The Hebrew has *Selah* (a word of uncertain meaning) here. [d] 10 Or *sovereign* [e] 12 Or *If anyone does not repent, / God*

ground, like pieces-of-five upon the bed." *bed.* Beds in ancient Israel were most likely like those represented iconographically in the Near East. They were in essence reclining couches and high beds. The poor probably slept on flat mats on the floor, while the average person used a cot.

7:3 *if I have done this.* In some psalms, the psalmist is aware that sin has resulted in divine discipline (e.g., 6:1; 32:4–5; 51:3); however, frequently this is not the case, and the psalmist, like Job, protests his or her innocence. Declaration of innocence by one who is suffering is also a feature of Mesopotamian thought. While some texts preserving lament seem to presume guilt on the part of the worshiper, even if unknown, others complain that the worshiper is innocent.

7:9 *probes minds and hearts.* See note on 19:7.

7:13 *flaming arrows.* The OT never uses the Hebrew word for arrows to describe the flaming arrows used by human armies (see Pr 26:18 where it is "firebrands" in Hebrew). In Akkadian, there are a few references to the use of flaming arrows that kings rain down on the enemy. These arrows were presumably dipped in a type of oil or pitch and set on fire before shooting them. When Yahweh is said to shoot arrows, they are usually considered to be bolts of lightning (see 77:17–18 and its parallel passage in 2Sa 22:15). Lightning would fit well with the concept of flaming arrows in that it is sometimes just called fire. In the divine warrior motif, the deity is fighting the battles and defeating the deities of the enemy (see the article "Divine Warfare," p. 365). In Assyria, Nergal is the King of Battle, and Ishtar is viewed also as a war-goddess. The latter is viewed as raining down flames in war. The Canaanite Baal and the Babylonian Marduk are divine warriors. Thunder and lightning were considered to regularly accompany the presence of a deity in the ancient Near East, often in a battle setting. From the Sumerian Exaltation of Inanna to the Hittite myths about the storm-god to the Akkadian and Ugaritic mythologies, the gods are viewed as thundering in judgment against their enemies. Baal is depicted as grasping a handful of thunderbolts. Thundering terminology is picked up in royal rhetoric as Hittite or Assyrian kings portray themselves as the instruments of the gods, thundering against those who have violated treaties or stood in the way of empire expansion.

Psalm 8[a]

For the director of music. According to *gittith.*[b] A psalm of David.

[1] LORD, our Lord,
how majestic is your name in all the earth!
You have set your glory
in the heavens.[c]
[2] Through the praise of children and infants
you have established a stronghold[d]
against your enemies,
to silence the foe[e] and the avenger.
[3] When I consider your heavens,[f]
the work of your fingers,
the moon and the stars,[g]
which you have set in place,
[4] what is mankind that you are mindful of them,
human beings that you care for them?[c][h]
[5] You have made them[d] a little lower than the angels[e]
and crowned them[d] with glory and honor.[i]
[6] You made them rulers[j] over the works of your hands;
you put everything under their[f] feet:[k]
[7] all flocks and herds,
and the animals of the wild,
[8] the birds in the sky,
and the fish in the sea,
all that swim the paths of the seas.
[9] LORD, our Lord,
how majestic is your name in all the earth![l]

Psalm 9[g,h]

For the director of music. To the tune of "The Death of the Son." A psalm of David.

[1] I will give thanks to you, LORD, with all my heart;[m]
I will tell of all your wonderful deeds.[n]

8:1 [c] Ps 57:5; 113:4; 148:13
8:2 [d] Mt 21:16* [e] Ps 44:16; 1Co 1:27
8:3 [f] Ps 89:11 [g] Ps 136:9
8:4 [h] Job 7:17; Ps 144:3; Heb 2:6
8:5 [i] Ps 21:5; 103:4
8:6 [j] Ge 1:28 [k] 1Co 15:25, 27*; Eph 1:22; Heb 2:6-8*
8:9 [l] ver 1
9:1 [m] Ps 86:12 [n] Ps 26:7

[a] In Hebrew texts 8:1-9 is numbered 8:2-10. [b] Title: Probably a musical term [c] 4 Or *what is a human being that you are mindful of him, / a son of man that you care for him?* [d] 5 Or *him* [e] 5 Or *than God* [f] 6 Or *made him ruler . . . ; / . . . his* [g] Psalms 9 and 10 may originally have been a single acrostic poem in which alternating lines began with the successive letters of the Hebrew alphabet. In the Septuagint they constitute one psalm. [h] In Hebrew texts 9:1-20 is numbered 9:2-21.

8:1 *your glory in the heavens.* In Egyptian cosmology, the sky-goddess Nut was pictured arching over the earth, bearing the stars and heavenly lights on her body (see the illustration in the article "The 'Vault' and 'Water Above,'" p. 6). Mesopotamian religion also viewed the heavenly objects as deities (see notes on 19:1–2; 104:2). In one Egyptian text, the god Amun, the "Hidden One," is conceived in some way as "farther above than heaven"; however, this refers to the mystery that shrouds his nature in comparison to the other Egyptian gods, and even Amun was born out of the waters of chaos. In contrast, the psalmist declares that Yahweh's glory transcends the majestic heavens, even as they are merely his workmanship (see v. 3).
8:3 *stars ... set in place.* In Akkadian literature, the various levels of heaven are made of various types of stone. The lower heavens were considered to be made of jasper, upon which Marduk, the chief god of Babylon, was reported to have drawn (etched) the constellations. The verb "set in place" is used when pictures or reliefs are being made. In *Enuma Elish,* Marduk draws the boundary lines for the year in the heavens. This refers to his setting the courses of the stars. The second half of v. 3 indicates that this psalm also has the heavenly bodies in mind. God elsewhere inscribes with his finger (Ex 31:18; Dt 9:10), but fingers can also be used parallel to hands with regard to handiwork (Isa 2:8).
8:4 *what is mankind ...?* The dignity of human beings is stressed in this passage in a way unparalleled in the ancient Near East. According to Mesopotamian sources, men and women were created to relieve the workload on the lesser gods who were forced to cultivate land in order to feed the gods (see note on 103:14). When the growing human population became too noisy, the gods thought to extinguish human existence through the great flood. As a result of the flood, food offerings to the gods were no longer forthcoming. Only then did the gods find that humans were nonexpendable after all. Although humanity survived the flood, the gods decreed certain afflictions to keep the population from ever growing out of control again. According to Ps 8, far from being expendable slaves to the gods, human beings are the special objects of the Creator's care in the vast universe.
8:5 *angels.* This Hebrew word (*elohim*) can also be translated "God." Here it may refer to the entire class of those who inhabit the heavenly realm, also called the council of "divine beings," which would include both God and those creatures commonly called "angels" (see notes on 29:1; 82:1; 91:11; 103:20; see also the article "Divine Council," p. 615). Mesopotamian myth relegated humanity to a servile status beneath the divine beings (see previous note). Ps 8 places human dignity nearly equal to the council of the heavenly realm.
8:6 *you put everything under their feet.* God created humankind as guardians of creation. The concept of guardianship is illustrated by an inscription of a certain Azatiwata, who in about 700 BC was appointed by a greater king to rule over a district of what is modern Turkey. Azatiwata claims that he brought all things under his guardianship in peaceful and prosperous order: "I placed them under my feet."
8:7–8 The categories of the animal kingdom over which humanity is charged finds a partial parallel in the Egyptian Great Hymn to Aten, who made "All peoples, herds and flocks; / All upon the earth that walk on legs, / All on high that fly on wings."
9:1 *I will give thanks.* The first Hebrew letter of this psalm is the first letter of the Hebrew alphabet, beginning an "acrostic" (see the article "Acrostic Psalms," p. 993).

[2]I will be glad and rejoice[o] in you;
I will sing the praises of your name,[p]
O Most High.

[3]My enemies turn back;
they stumble and perish before you.
[4]For you have upheld my right and my cause,[q]
sitting enthroned as the righteous judge.[r]
[5]You have rebuked the nations and destroyed the wicked;
you have blotted out their name[s] for ever and ever.
[6]Endless ruin has overtaken my enemies,
you have uprooted their cities;
even the memory of them[t] has perished.

[7]The LORD reigns forever;
he has established his throne[u] for judgment.
[8]He rules the world in righteousness[v]
and judges the peoples with equity.
[9]The LORD is a refuge for the oppressed,
a stronghold in times of trouble.[w]
[10]Those who know your name[x] trust in you,
for you, LORD, have never forsaken[y]
those who seek you.

[11]Sing the praises of the LORD, enthroned in Zion;[z]
proclaim among the nations[a] what he has done.[b]
[12]For he who avenges blood[c] remembers;
he does not ignore the cries of the afflicted.

[13]LORD, see how my enemies[d] persecute me!
Have mercy and lift me up from the gates of death,
[14]that I may declare your praises[e]
in the gates of Daughter Zion,
and there rejoice in your salvation.[f]
[15]The nations have fallen into the pit they have dug;[g]
their feet are caught in the net they have hidden.[h]

9:2 [o]Ps 5:11 [p]Ps 92:1; 83:18 9:4 [q]Ps 140:12 [r]1Pe 2:23 9:5 [s]Pr 10:7 9:6 [t]Ps 34:16 9:7 [u]Ps 89:14 9:8 [v]Ps 96:13 9:9 [w]Ps 32:7 9:10 [x]Ps 91:14 [y]Ps 37:28 9:11 [z]Ps 76:2 [a]Ps 107:22 [b]Ps 105:1 9:12 [c]Ge 9:5 9:13 [d]Ps 38:19 9:14 [e]Ps 106:2 [f]Ps 13:5; 51:12 9:15 [g]Ps 7:15-16 [h]Ps 35:8; 57:6

[16]The LORD is known by his acts of justice;
the wicked are ensnared by the work of their hands.[a]
[17]The wicked go down to the realm of the dead,[i]
all the nations that forget God.[j]
[18]But God will never forget the needy;
the hope[k] of the afflicted[l] will never perish.

[19]Arise, LORD, do not let mortals triumph;
let the nations be judged in your presence.
[20]Strike them with terror, LORD;
let the nations know they are only mortal.[m]

Psalm 10[b]

[1]Why, LORD, do you stand far off?[n]
Why do you hide yourself[o] in times of trouble?

[2]In his arrogance the wicked man hunts down the weak,
who are caught in the schemes he devises.
[3]He boasts[p] about the cravings of his heart;
he blesses the greedy and reviles the LORD.
[4]In his pride the wicked man does not seek him;
in all his thoughts there is no room for God.[q]
[5]His ways are always prosperous;
your laws are rejected by[c] him;
he sneers at all his enemies.
[6]He says to himself, "Nothing will ever shake me."
He swears, "No one will ever do me harm."[r]

9:17 [i]Ps 49:14 [j]Job 8:13; Ps 50:22 9:18 [k]Ps 71:5; Pr 23:18 [l]Ps 12:5 9:20 [m]Ps 62:9; Isa 31:3 10:1 [n]Ps 22:1, 11 [o]Ps 13:1 10:3 [p]Ps 94:4 10:4 [q]Ps 14:1; 36:1 10:6 [r]Rev 18:7

[a] 16 The Hebrew has *Higgaion* and *Selah* (words of uncertain meaning) here; *Selah* occurs also at the end of verse 20. [b] Psalms 9 and 10 may originally have been a single acrostic poem in which alternating lines began with the successive letters of the Hebrew alphabet. In the Septuagint they constitute one psalm. [c] 5 See Septuagint; Hebrew / *they are haughty, and your laws are far from*

9:7 *reigns forever.* For this phrase as well as its parallel in v. 11 ("enthroned in Zion"), see notes on 97:5; 99:1.
9:12 *he who avenges blood.* See note on Nu 35:12.
9:13 *gates of death.* See the articles ""Death and Sheol," p. 833; "Death and the Underworld," p. 907.
9:20 *Strike them with terror.* The dread of a deity as a divine warrior was often believed to precede a powerful, successful army into battle. Egyptian and Assyrian texts and reliefs portray the god as a winged disk terrifying the enemy before the arrival of their own armies. Egyptian texts attribute this terror to Amun-Re in the inscriptions of Thutmose III; Hittite, Assyrian and Babylonian texts all have their divine warriors who strike terror into the hearts of the enemy. The concept of deity having an awesome, unapproachable appearance was not limited to Israelite theology, for in Mesopotamia the gods displayed their power through their *melammu*, their divine brilliance. The splendor or "glory" of God overwhelms the enemy. In the face of such divine magnificence, both the gods and the forces of other nations are utterly defeated and forced to submit to the supreme deity.
10:1 *Why ...?* This word begins with the Hebrew letter *lamed*, which continues the acrostic alphabet from Ps 9, uniting the two psalms thematically (see the article "Acrostic Psalms," p. 993). *hide yourself.* See note on 13:1.

7 His mouth is full[s] of lies and threats;[t]
trouble and evil are under his
tongue.[u]
8 He lies in wait near the villages;
from ambush he murders the
innocent.[v]
His eyes watch in secret for his
victims;
9 like a lion in cover he lies in wait.
He lies in wait to catch the helpless;[w]
he catches the helpless and drags
them off in his net.
10 His victims are crushed, they collapse;
they fall under his strength.
11 He says to himself, "God will never
notice;[x]
he covers his face and never sees."

12 Arise, LORD! Lift up your hand,[y]
O God.
Do not forget the helpless.[z]
13 Why does the wicked man revile
God?
Why does he say to himself,
"He won't call me to account"?
14 But you, God, see the trouble[a] of the
afflicted;
you consider their grief and take it
in hand.
The victims commit themselves to
you;[b]
you are the helper[c] of the fatherless.
15 Break the arm of the wicked man;[d]
call the evildoer to account for his
wickedness
that would not otherwise be found
out.

16 The LORD is King for ever and ever;[e]
the nations[f] will perish from his
land.
17 You, LORD, hear the desire of the
afflicted;[g]
you encourage them, and you listen
to their cry,
18 defending the fatherless[h] and the
oppressed,[i]
so that mere earthly mortals
will never again strike terror.

Psalm 11

For the director of music.
Of David.

1 In the LORD I take refuge.[j]
How then can you say to me:
"Flee like a bird to your mountain.
2 For look, the wicked bend their bows;
they set their arrows[k] against the
strings
to shoot from the shadows
at the upright in heart.[l]
3 When the foundations[m] are being
destroyed,
what can the righteous do?"

4 The LORD is in his holy temple;[n]
the LORD is on his heavenly
throne.[o]
He observes everyone on earth;[p]
his eyes examine[q] them.
5 The LORD examines the righteous,[r]
but the wicked, those who love
violence,
he hates with a passion.[s]
6 On the wicked he will rain
fiery coals and burning sulfur;[t]
a scorching wind[u] will be their lot.

7 For the LORD is righteous,[v]
he loves justice;[w]
the upright will see his face.[x]

10:7 [s]Ro 3:14* [t]Ps 73:8 [u]Ps 140:3 **10:8** [v]Ps 94:6 **10:9** [w]Ps 17:12; 59:3; 140:5 **10:11** [x]Job 22:13 **10:12** [y]Ps 17:7; Mic 5:9 [z]Ps 9:12 **10:14** [a]Ps 22:11 [b]Ps 37:5 [c]Ps 68:5 **10:15** [d]Ps 37:17 **10:16** [e]Ps 29:10 [f]Dt 8:20

10:17 [g]1Ch 29:18; Ps 34:15 **10:18** [h]Ps 82:3 [i]Ps 9:9 **11:1** [j]Ps 56:11 **11:2** [k]Ps 7:13 [l]Ps 64:3-4 **11:3** [m]Ps 82:5 **11:4** [n]Ps 18:6 [o]Ps 103:19 [p]Ps 33:13 [q]Ps 34:15-16 **11:5** [r]Ge 22:1; Jas 1:12 [s]Ps 5:5 **11:6** [t]Eze 38:22 [u]Jer 4:11-12 **11:7** [v]Ps 7:9, 11; 45:7 [w]Ps 33:5 [x]Ps 17:15

10:8 *villages.* Most Israelites lived in unwalled villages clustered close to larger walled cities ("surrounding villages" is lit. the "daughter" of the city; cf. 1Ch 7:28). A walled city served as a place of refuge during times of war, provided a central market for villagers to buy and sell goods and produce, and offered important social services such as judicial resources. While traveling to and from cities and fields, people were exposed to danger from robbers lurking among rocks or trees, especially in the more rugged hill country and at night when returning from the fields.

10:16 *King for ever.* See notes on 97:5; 99:1.

11:2 *bend their bows.* Lit. "step on the bow." In order to string a bow, a warrior or hunter would step on the midsection in order to draw the ends of the bow close enough to place the string. A psalmist might mention weapons in contexts alluding to a physical threat to life (cf. 60:4; 76:3); however, weapons might also be used as metaphors for a serious threat to one's legal, economic or social well-being (37:14; 64:3).

11:3 *foundations.* This particular Hebrew word appears only here in the sense of social order, but the concept is found elsewhere in the OT (see note on 82:5). In ancient Egypt, the concept of *maat* (see note on 85:10) referred to the moral and social order of the universe, which was closely linked to the stable and effective rule of the king. Sumerians (third millennium BC) believed that political and social order was established by the gods, who issued decrees concerning civilization to establish controls called "mes." Control of the mes was a matter of divine management. In the city laments (see the article "City Laments," p. 951), the collapse of society meant that this decree for order had been overturned.

11:6 *fiery coals and burning sulfur.* In Akkadian texts, sulfur burned on coals is described as a fumigating agent. The gods Ea and Enlil send down sulfur as a purifier that counteracts witchcraft. In those texts, unlike here, it is not found as part of the divine warrior's arsenal for the judging of enemies. The terms here are reminiscent, though not identical, to those used in the account of the destruction of Sodom and Gomorrah (Ge 19:24; see Eze 38:22).

11:7 *see his face.* Seeing the face of a judge or a god was a metaphor in Mesopotamia and was equivalent to being on their "good side," because it refers to gaining access to their presence. It usually refers to a supplicant or plaintiff gaining an audience with a judge. If a judge or a god turned his face toward you, you were looked upon with favor.

Psalm 12[a]

For the director of music.
According to *sheminith*.[b]
A psalm of David.

[1] Help, LORD, for no one is
faithful anymore;[y]
those who are loyal have
vanished from the
human race.
[2] Everyone lies to their neighbor;
they flatter with their lips
but harbor deception in their
hearts.[z]
[3] May the LORD silence all
flattering lips
and every boastful tongue —[a]
[4] those who say,
"By our tongues we will
prevail;
our own lips will defend
us — who is lord
over us?"
[5] "Because the poor are
plundered and the needy
groan,
I will now arise," says the
LORD.
"I will protect them[b] from
those who malign
them."
[6] And the words of the LORD are
flawless,[c]
like silver purified in a
crucible,
like gold[c] refined seven
times.
[7] You, LORD, will keep the needy safe
and will protect us forever from the
wicked,[d]
[8] who freely strut[e] about
when what is vile is honored by the
human race.

Bird hunter from Palace of Sargon II at Khorsabad, c. 725 BC. "Flee like a bird to your mountain. For look, the wicked bend their bows" (Ps 11:1–2).

Kim Walton. The Louvre.

Psalm 13[d]

For the director of music.
A psalm of David.

[1] How long, LORD? Will you forget me
forever?
How long will you hide your face[f]
from me?
[2] How long must I wrestle with my
thoughts[g]
and day after day have sorrow in my
heart?
How long will my enemy triumph
over me?[h]

12:1 [y] Isa 57:1 **12:2** [z] Ps 10:7; 41:6; 55:21; Ro 16:18 **12:3** [a] Da 7:8; Rev 13:5 **12:5** [b] Ps 10:18; 34:6 **12:6** [c] 2Sa 22:31; Ps 18:30; Pr 30:5 **12:7** [d] Ps 37:28 **12:8** [e] Ps 55:10-11 **13:1** [f] Job 13:24; Ps 44:24 **13:2** [g] Ps 42:4 [h] Ps 42:9

[a] In Hebrew texts 12:1-8 is numbered 12:2-9. [b] Title: Probably a musical term [c] *6* Probable reading of the original Hebrew text; Masoretic Text *earth* [d] In Hebrew texts 13:1-6 is numbered 13:2-6.

12:6 *crucible.* This Hebrew term is found only here in the Bible. Because of the mention of silver, the context implies that what is described may be a clay crucible used for smelting purposes (see note on Pr 17:3). Crucibles appear in Egyptian wall paintings, and clay exemplars have been found by archaeologists. *refined seven times.* Silver often went through the refining process several times to remove all the dross. The imagery here is that if one was purified seven times (the number of completion in Hebrew), he was then completely purified.
13:1 *How long . . . ?* See note on 6:3. *hide your face.* Opposite of showing one's face (cf. 11:7; see note there), hiding one's face is a way of showing displeasure or indifference by turning away the face. This is probably a common metaphor from human experience, and is therefore unsurprisingly found also in other literature of the ancient world. In the Mesopotamian "Poem of the Righteous Sufferer," the worshiper cries, "I called to my god, he did not show his face." Perhaps more heartrending is the Assyrian elegy in memory of a woman who died in child birth: "I prayed to Belet-ili . . . she veiled her face."

[3]Look on me and answer,[i] LORD my
God.
Give light to my eyes,[j] or I will
sleep in death,[k]
[4]and my enemy will say, "I have
overcome him,[l]"
and my foes will rejoice when
I fall.

[5]But I trust in your unfailing love;[m]
my heart rejoices in your
salvation.[n]
[6]I will sing[o] the LORD's praise,
for he has been good to me.

Psalm 14

14:1-7pp — Ps 53:1-6

For the director of music. Of David.

[1]The fool[a] says in his heart,
"There is no God."[p]
They are corrupt, their deeds are
vile;
there is no one who does good.

[2]The LORD looks down from heaven[q]
on all mankind
to see if there are any who
understand,[r]
any who seek God.
[3]All have turned away, all have become
corrupt;[s]
there is no one who does good,[t]
not even one.[u]

[4]Do all these evildoers know nothing?[v]

They devour my people[w] as though
eating bread;
they never call on the LORD.[x]
[5]But there they are, overwhelmed with
dread,
for God is present in the company
of the righteous.
[6]You evildoers frustrate the plans of
the poor,
but the LORD is their refuge.[y]

[7]Oh, that salvation for Israel would
come out of Zion!
When the LORD restores[z] his people,
let Jacob rejoice and Israel be glad!

Psalm 15

A psalm of David.

[1]LORD, who may dwell in your sacred
tent?[a]
Who may live on your holy
mountain?[b]

[2]The one whose walk is blameless,
who does what is righteous,
who speaks the truth[c] from their
heart;
[3]whose tongue utters no slander,[d]
who does no wrong to a neighbor,
and casts no slur on others;
[4]who despises a vile person
but honors[e] those who fear the LORD;
who keeps an oath[f] even when it hurts,
and does not change their mind;
[5]who lends money to the poor without
interest;[g]
who does not accept a bribe[h] against
the innocent.

Whoever does these things
will never be shaken.[i]

Psalm 16

A *miktam*[b] of David.

[1]Keep me safe,[j] my God,
for in you I take refuge.[k]

[2]I say to the LORD, "You are my Lord;
apart from you I have no good
thing."[l]
[3]I say of the holy people who are in the
land,[m]
"They are the noble ones in whom is
all my delight."

13:3 [i]Ps 5:1 [j]Ezr 9:8 [k]Jer 51:39 **13:4** [l]Ps 25:2 **13:5** [m]Ps 52:8 [n]Ps 9:14 **13:6** [o]Ps 116:7 **14:1** [p]Ps 10:4 **14:2** [q]Ps 33:13 [r]Ps 92:6 **14:3** [s]Ps 58:3 [t]Ps 143:2 [u]Ro 3:10-12* **14:4** [v]Ps 82:5 [w]Ps 27:2 [x]Ps 79:6; Isa 64:7 **14:6** [y]Ps 9:9; 40:17 **14:7** [z]Ps 53:6 **15:1** [a]Ps 27:5-6 [b]Ps 24:3-5 **15:2** [c]Ps 24:4; Zec 8:3, 16; Eph 4:25 **15:3** [d]Ex 23:1 **15:4** [e]Ac 28:10 [f]Jdg 11:35 **15:5** [g]Ex 22:25 [h]Ex 23:8; Dt 16:19 [i]2Pe 1:10 **16:1** [j]Ps 17:8 [k]Ps 7:1 **16:2** [l]Ps 73:25 **16:3** [m]Ps 101:6

[a] *1* The Hebrew words rendered *fool* in Psalms denote one who is morally deficient. [b] Title: Probably a literary or musical term

14:3 *All have turned away.* This universal observation did not escape the sensitive heart in Mesopotamia. In an Old Babylonian (c. 1800 BC) prayer for forgiveness, the penitent asks whether any humans are not guilty of sin. This refers to a universal experience of offending God at some point or another. In the larger ancient world, the gods had not revealed themselves, and religious obligation took a ritual form. It was easy to believe that ritual offenses occurred all the time. For Israelites, though ritual offenses could occur, God had revealed his law, and they were more intimately familiar with the sorts of behavior that could offend God. Though they had developed no doctrine of being party to the sin of Adam and Eve, they understood that no one could keep the law perfectly.
14:7 *Zion.* The name for the mount on which God's temple was built in Jerusalem; it represents the center of God's rule (see note on 48:1 – 2).

15:1 *who may dwell in your sacred tent?* Because the space surrounding God's temple was sacred, it required that anyone entering be ceremonially clean and sanctified by the offering of appropriate sacrifices (Lev 1 – 7; 12 – 15). This concerned ritual purity, but in the spirit of worship, those approaching God's presence in the temple were also expected to have exercised obedience to God's instructions for living. The sacredness of temples in the ancient Near East was "guarded" by architectural features such as statues of cherubim (see note on 2Ki 19:15), sphinxes or protective lions. An inscription on a guardian lion at a temple in Assyria identifies the statue as being capable of driving away evil and bringing good. Priests also had the duty to screen would-be worshipers, and perhaps the question and answer format in Ps 15 preserves an entrance liturgy. *sacred tent … holy mountain.* See note on 48:1 – 2.

[4]Those who run after other gods[n] will
suffer[o] more and more.
I will not pour out libations of blood
to such gods
or take up their names[p] on my lips.
[5]LORD, you alone are my portion[q] and
my cup;[r]
you make my lot secure.
[6]The boundary lines have fallen for me
in pleasant places;
surely I have a delightful
inheritance.[s]
[7]I will praise the LORD, who counsels
me;[t]
even at night[u] my heart instructs me.
[8]I keep my eyes always on the LORD.
With him at my right hand,[v] I will
not be shaken.

[9]Therefore my heart is glad[w] and my
tongue rejoices;
my body also will rest secure,[x]
[10]because you will not abandon me to
the realm of the dead,
nor will you let your faithful[a] one
see decay.[y]
[11]You make known to me the path of
life;[z]
you will fill me with joy in your
presence,[a]
with eternal pleasures[b] at your right
hand.

Psalm 17

A prayer of David.

[1]Hear me, LORD, my plea is just;
listen to my cry.[c]
Hear my prayer—
it does not rise from deceitful lips.[d]
[2]Let my vindication come from you;
may your eyes see what is right.
[3]Though you probe my heart,
though you examine me at night and
test me,[e]
you will find that I have planned no
evil;[f]
my mouth has not transgressed.[g]
[4]Though people tried to bribe me,
I have kept myself from the ways of
the violent
through what your lips have
commanded.
[5]My steps have held to your paths;[h]
my feet have not stumbled.[i]

[6]I call on you, my God, for you will
answer me;[j]
turn your ear to me[k] and hear my
prayer.[l]
[7]Show me the wonders of your great
love,[m]
you who save by your right hand[n]
those who take refuge in you from
their foes.
[8]Keep me as the apple of your eye;[o]
hide me in the shadow of your wings
[9]from the wicked who are out to
destroy me,
from my mortal enemies who
surround me.[p]

[10]They close up their callous hearts,[q]
and their mouths speak with
arrogance.[r]
[11]They have tracked me down, they now
surround me,[s]
with eyes alert, to throw me to the
ground.

16:4 [n]Ps 106:37-38 [o]Ps 32:10 [p]Ex 23:13 **16:5** [q]Ps 73:26 [r]Ps 23:5 **16:6** [s]Ps 78:55; Jer 3:19 **16:7** [t]Ps 73:24 [u]Ps 77:6 **16:8** [v]Ps 73:23 **16:9** [w]Ps 4:7; 30:11 [x]Ps 4:8 **16:10** [y]Ac 13:35* **16:11** [z]Mt 7:14 [a]Ac 2:25-28* [b]Ps 36:7-8 **17:1** [c]Ps 61:1 [d]Isa 29:13

17:3 [e]Ps 26:2; 66:10 [f]Job 23:10; Jer 50:20 [g]Ps 39:1 **17:5** [h]Ps 44:18; 119:133 [i]Ps 18:36 **17:6** [j]Ps 86:7 [k]Ps 116:2 [l]Ps 88:2 **17:7** [m]Ps 31:21 [n]Ps 20:6 **17:8** [o]Dt 32:10 **17:9** [p]Ps 31:20; 109:3 **17:10** [q]Ps 73:7 [r]1Sa 2:3 **17:11** [s]Ps 37:14; 88:17

[a] 10 Or *holy*

16:4 *libations of blood.* Other usage in the OT indicates that a libation is a drink offering of wine (Ex 29:40; Lev 23:13; Nu 15:5–10) or beer (perhaps brandy, Nu 28:7). There are no parallels to libations of blood in ancient Near Eastern texts, so the practice to which this refers is unknown at present.
16:6 *boundary lines.* As sovereign Lord of the land, Yahweh allocated Israel's boundaries (Nu 33:50–54) as well as those of the other nations (Dt 32:8). Property delimitation was an important issue in the ancient Near East and closely tied with inheritance rights. OT law regarded the movement of boundary markers as a serious offense (see Dt 19:14 and note; 27:17; Job 24:2; Pr 22:28; 23:10), as did legal custom in Egypt and Mesopotamia. Elaborately decorated and inscribed boundary markers were used in some periods in Mesopotamia. The psalmist celebrates God's goodness to him in terms of desirable land allocation.
16:8 *at my right hand.* A fully armed warrior would hold his weapon in his right hand and his shield in his left. The person to the right of a king would have the privilege of defending him. For a king to put someone there would be an affirmation of trust, and therefore an honor. In contrast, when the Lord takes up his position at someone's right hand, as here, he is in a position to offer defense with his shield (109:31).
16:10 *will not abandon me to the realm of the dead.* In this context, it refers to not allowing someone to be put to death at the hand of malicious enemies. The psalmist will not be consigned to Sheol; he will not see decay because his life will be spared (30:2–3). An early Sumerian text recounts the tale of an individual who is facing capital punishment for the crimes of which he is accused. Instead, however, he finds himself snatched from the jaws of destruction and praises the underworld-goddess Nungal for his deliverance.
17:2 *my vindication.* Legal difficulties were a common experience for people in the ancient Near East, and the defendant naturally sought divine help against his accusers. In the personal library of a family living in Babylon (c. 1500–1200 BC), texts were found describing the theft or misappropriation of farming equipment, which illustrates the type of problems people faced. In the same archive was a prayer, possibly related to litigation, that the god Nabu might judge his case fairly and give a favorable outcome.
17:8 *shadow of your wings.* See note on 36:7.

[12] They are like a lion[t] hungry for prey,
like a fierce lion crouching in cover.
[13] Rise up, LORD, confront them, bring them down;[u]
with your sword rescue me from the wicked.
[14] By your hand save me from such people, LORD,
from those of this world[v] whose reward is in this life.
May what you have stored up for the wicked fill their bellies;
may their children gorge themselves on it,
and may there be leftovers[w] for their little ones.
[15] As for me, I will be vindicated and will see your face;
when I awake, I will be satisfied with seeing your likeness.[x]

Psalm 18[a]

18:Title–50pp — 2Sa 22:1-51

For the director of music. Of David the servant of the LORD. He sang to the LORD the words of this song when the LORD delivered him from the hand of all his enemies and from the hand of Saul. He said:

[1] I love you, LORD, my strength.
[2] The LORD is my rock,[y] my fortress and my deliverer;
my God is my rock, in whom I take refuge,
my shield[b][z] and the horn[c] of my salvation,[a] my stronghold.
[3] I called to the LORD, who is worthy of praise,[b]
and I have been saved from my enemies.
[4] The cords of death[c] entangled me;
the torrents[d] of destruction overwhelmed me.
[5] The cords of the grave coiled around me;
the snares of death[e] confronted me.
[6] In my distress I called to the LORD;
I cried to my God for help.
From his temple he heard my voice;[f]
my cry came before him, into his ears.
[7] The earth trembled and quaked,[g]
and the foundations of the mountains shook;
they trembled because he was angry.[h]
[8] Smoke rose from his nostrils;
consuming fire[i] came from his mouth,
burning coals blazed out of it.
[9] He parted the heavens and came down;[j]
dark clouds were under his feet.

17:12 [t] Ps 7:2; 10:9 **17:13** [u] Ps 7:12; 22:20; 73:18 **17:14** [v] Lk 16:8 [w] Ps 73:3-7 **17:15** [x] Nu 12:8; Ps 4:6-7; 16:11; 1Jn 3:2 **18:2** [y] Ps 19:14 [z] Ps 59:11 [a] Ps 75:10 **18:3** [b] Ps 48:1 **18:4** [c] Ps 116:3 [d] Ps 124:4 **18:5** [e] Ps 116:3 **18:6** [f] Ps 34:15 **18:7** [g] Jdg 5:4 [h] Ps 68:7-8 **18:8** [i] Ps 50:3 **18:9** [j] Ps 144:5

[a] In Hebrew texts 18:1-50 is numbered 18:2-51.
[b] 2 Or *sovereign* [c] 2 *Horn* here symbolizes strength.

17:12 *lion.* See note on 22:13.

18:2 *rock.* In the wilderness regions of southern Judah where David hid from his enemies, the rocky cliffs and caves afforded great protection. One hiding place, named "Sela" in 1Sa 23:28, uses the same word for "rock" as in this verse (Hebrew *sela*). Such places offer a natural fortification (cf. Isa 2:21), which is reinforced by the word "fortress." *fortress.* A very common image for God as a place of safety (31:2; 78:35; 89:26; Dt 32:4; Isa 44:8); it is translated "Crags" in 1Sa 24:2, where David hides from Saul. It is a most appropriate metaphor, then, to refer to God as a place where David takes "refuge." *shield.* See note on 3:3. *horn.* Animal horns were associated with bulls, so they symbolized strength, often with connotations of military victory (e.g., 92:9–11; Dt 33:17). The Assyrian king Ashurbanipal (c. 650 BC) reports how the goddess Ninlil defeated his enemies with her "strong horns." Mesopotamian gods and goddesses were depicted in art with multiple horns, signifying their prowess.

18:4 *cords of death.* Noose snares were commonly used by hunters in the ancient Near East. In this metaphor, death or Sheol is the hunter (see the articles "Death and Sheol," p. 833; "Death and the Underworld," p. 907). Snares and cords are also used to describe magical hexes and curses used to take someone's life.

18:7–15 These verses describe the saving intervention of Yahweh in terms of a great thunderstorm. It alludes to the experience of the nation at Mount Sinai (Ex 19:16–19), and such language was common in ancient Near Eastern accounts of a deity's appearance in battle (see below notes on vv. 7–15).

18:7 *The earth trembled and quaked.* The earth quakes before a divine warrior (cf. 68:7–8; Jdg 5:4–5), as in a Sumerian hymn from the Old Babylonian period (c. 1800 BC) celebrating the coming to power of the storm-god Ishkur, depicted as a fierce lion. He causes the earth to rumble with the roaring of a storm. The same idea can be found in an Egyptian hymn to Amun—when he goes to war the mountains tremble and the earth quakes. Similar to this verse, the connection between an earthquake and the deity's anger is explicit. Even Assyrian kings adopted this warrior image for themselves. Tiglath-Pileser I (c. 1100 BC) boasted that his fierce weapons had caused the four corners of the earth to quake.

18:8 Lightning from a thunderstorm, thought of as fire from heaven, was commonly regarded as an important weapon of divine warriors. One hymn from Egypt (c. 300 BC) describes the god Mar snorting smoke. Assyrian king Esarhaddon is aided by the god Assur, who hurled down fire and hailstones. Ishtar is described as a shining torch who blazes fire against the enemy. Despite these similar texts, the idea of fire coming from a god's mouth is unparalleled in the ancient world.

18:9 *dark clouds.* This term has been found in the Ugaritic Baal Cycle, in which the god Baal is described as the "rider of the clouds" and his "voice" is the sound and fury of thunder and lightning.

[10]He mounted the cherubim[k] and
flew;
he soared on the wings of the
wind.[l]
[11]He made darkness his covering,[m] his
canopy around him—
the dark rain clouds of the sky.
[12]Out of the brightness of his presence[n]
clouds advanced,
with hailstones and bolts of
lightning.[o]
[13]The LORD thundered[p] from heaven;
the voice of the Most High
resounded.[a]
[14]He shot his arrows and scattered the
enemy,
with great bolts of lightning he
routed them.[q]
[15]The valleys of the sea were exposed
and the foundations of the earth laid
bare
at your rebuke,[r] LORD,
at the blast of breath from your
nostrils.
[16]He reached down from on high and
took hold of me;
he drew me out of deep waters.[s]
[17]He rescued me from my powerful
enemy,
from my foes, who were too strong
for me.[t]

18:10 [k]Ps 80:1 [l]Ps 104:3 **18:11** [m]Dt 4:11; Ps 97:2 **18:12** [n]Ps 104:2 [o]Ps 97:3 **18:13** [p]Ps 29:3; 104:7 **18:14** [q]Ps 144:6 **18:15** [r]Ps 76:6; 106:9 **18:16** [s]Ps 144:7 **18:17** [t]Ps 35:10

18:18 [u]Ps 59:16 **18:19** [v]Ps 31:8 [w]Ps 118:5 **18:20** [x]Ps 24:4 **18:21** [y]2Ch 34:33 [z]Ps 119:102 **18:22** [a]Ps 119:30 **18:24** [b]1Sa 26:23 **18:25** [c]1Ki 8:32; Ps 62:12; Mt 5:7

[18]They confronted me in the day of my
disaster,
but the LORD was my support.[u]
[19]He brought me out into a spacious
place;[v]
he rescued me because he delighted
in me.[w]
[20]The LORD has dealt with me according
to my righteousness;
according to the cleanness of my
hands[x] he has rewarded me.
[21]For I have kept the ways of the
LORD;[y]
I am not guilty of turning[z] from
my God.
[22]All his laws are before me;[a]
I have not turned away from his
decrees.
[23]I have been blameless before him
and have kept myself from sin.
[24]The LORD has rewarded me according
to my righteousness,[b]
according to the cleanness of my
hands in his sight.
[25]To the faithful[c] you show yourself
faithful,
to the blameless you show yourself
blameless,

[a] *13* Some Hebrew manuscripts and Septuagint (see also 2 Samuel 22:14); most Hebrew manuscripts *resounded, / amid hailstones and bolts of lightning*

18:10 *mounted.* Refers to riding a chariot. Even as kings rode into battle on chariots (2Ki 9:21), divine warriors were portrayed as chariot riders. Assyrian art portrays the god Assur riding into battle on behalf of the king. The god Baal is described in the Ugaritic Baal Cycle as one who rides the clouds mounted on a chariot (see notes on 68:4; 97:2). This image dates as far back as the Old Akkadian period (c. 2400 BC), from which a cylinder seal depicts the storm-god riding a chariot drawn by a winged lion. Since "cherubim" were guardian spirits with wings, over whom God was enthroned on the ark of the covenant (80:1; Ex 25:18–20; see note on 2Ki 19:15), they naturally are worked into the imagery of God's flying war-chariot (cf. Eze 1).
18:12 *hailstones ... lightning.* In the Assyrian text cited in the note on v. 8, "hailstones" and "lightning" are associated with a deity's appearance in a great thunderstorm. The Canaanite storm-god Baal/Hadad is commonly depicted holding a lightning bolt in his hand (see note on 29:7). Hail is Yahweh's weapon in Ex 9:18,24; Jos 10:11 (see the note on Ps 18:8), and it appears in poetic imagery of his acts of judgment against his enemies (Job 38:22–23; Isa 30:30). In this way and many others, Yahweh is often portrayed in terms and metaphors familiar to the rest of the ancient Near East even as the point is being made concerning how different he is from those gods. Despite the superiority of Yahweh to other gods, there is a common cultural way of describing the activity and nature of a god.
18:14 *arrows.* Lightning bolts were thought of as arrows of the divine warrior. When the Babylonian god Marduk prepared to attack the enemy goddess Tiamat, he mounted his arrows, described as "thunderbolts," on the string. A hymn of Ashurbanipal (c. 650 BC) speaks of the god Marduk defeating the forces of chaos with bow and arrows, swords, and other weapons of war. Another text describes arrows from Marduk's quiver as torches lit from a brazier that rain down on mountains to kill even the strong. An Assyrian carving shows the god Assur riding the sky with wings and shooting an arrow with a flaming head. However, in both texts and art, deities might be depicted shooting more conventional arrows as well. These descriptions depict the power of the deity with the might of the storm.
18:15 *valleys of the sea ... foundations of the earth.* The lowest portions of the sea and the roots of the mountains (see note on 104:5) were thought to be the limits of the earth before descending into the underworld, i.e., death (Dt 32:22; Jnh 2:3–6; see the article "Death and the Underworld," p. 907). In light of the report of deliverance in v. 16, this verse can be understood to mean that David was on the brink of death, from which Yahweh reached down and rescued him.
18:16 *deep waters.* When the Babylonian god Marduk brings restoration he is praised for taking hold of the individual and drawing him out of the waters of the Hubur River. This is the river that flows at the gates of the netherworld, and being drawn from its waters represents being saved from death at the last moment. This imagery continues into Greek mythology with the famous River Styx and even finds its way into Christian literature as indicated by the river of death that flows in front of the golden city in John Bunyan's *Pilgrim's Progress.* Alternatively, the psalmist could simply be referring to the cosmic waters.
18:21 *I have kept the ways of the LORD.* The blameless character of a king before his god was a common theme in royal inscriptions and prayers. In Ramses II's victory hymn, he states that he had not transgressed Amun's command.

26 to the pure you show yourself pure,
but to the devious you show yourself shrewd.[d]
27 You save the humble
but bring low those whose eyes are haughty.[e]
28 You, LORD, keep my lamp burning;
my God turns my darkness into light.[f]
29 With your help[g] I can advance against a troop[a];
with my God I can scale a wall.

30 As for God, his way is perfect:[h]
The LORD's word is flawless;[i]
he shields all who take refuge[j] in him.
31 For who is God besides the LORD?[k]
And who is the Rock[l] except our God?
32 It is God who arms me with strength[m]
and keeps my way secure.
33 He makes my feet like the feet of a deer;[n]
he causes me to stand on the heights.[o]
34 He trains my hands for battle;[p]
my arms can bend a bow of bronze.
35 You make your saving help my shield,
and your right hand sustains[q] me;
your help has made me great.
36 You provide a broad path for my feet,
so that my ankles do not give way.

18:26 [d] Pr 3:34 **18:27** [e] Pr 6:17 **18:28** [f] Job 18:6; 29:3 **18:29** [g] Heb 11:34 **18:30** [h] Dt 32:4; Rev 15:3 [i] Ps 12:6 [j] Ps 17:7 **18:31** [k] Dt 32:39; 86:8; Isa 45:5, 6, 14, 18, 21 [l] Dt 32:31; 1Sa 2:2 **18:32** [m] Isa 45:5 **18:33** [n] Hab 3:19 [o] Dt 32:13 **18:34** [p] Ps 144:1 **18:35** [q] Ps 119:116

18:37 [r] Ps 37:20; 44:5 **18:38** [s] Ps 36:12 [t] Ps 47:3 **18:40** [u] Ps 21:12 [v] Ps 94:23 **18:41** [w] Ps 50:22 [x] Job 27:9; Pr 1:28 **18:43** [y] 2Sa 8:1-14 [z] Isa 52:15; 55:5 **18:44** [a] Ps 66:3 **18:45** [b] Mic 7:17

37 I pursued my enemies[r] and overtook them;
I did not turn back till they were destroyed.
38 I crushed them so that they could not rise;[s]
they fell beneath my feet.[t]
39 You armed me with strength for battle;
you humbled my adversaries before me.
40 You made my enemies turn their backs[u] in flight,
and I destroyed[v] my foes.
41 They cried for help, but there was no one to save them[w]—
to the LORD, but he did not answer.[x]
42 I beat them as fine as windblown dust;
I trampled them[b] like mud in the streets.
43 You have delivered me from the attacks of the people;
you have made me the head of nations.[y]
People I did not know[z] now serve me,
44 foreigners[a] cower before me;
as soon as they hear of me, they obey me.
45 They all lose heart;
they come trembling from their strongholds.[b]

[a] 29 Or *can run through a barricade* [b] 42 Many Hebrew manuscripts, Septuagint, Syriac and Targum (see also 2 Samuel 22:43); Masoretic Text *I poured them out*

18:28 *keep my lamp burning.* See note on 2Sa 14:7.
18:30 *The LORD's word is flawless.* In praising the god Assur for the reliability of his word to bring defeat to his enemies, Ashurbanipal expresses that his god's pronouncement is unchangeable. Of the goddesses who brought him military success he writes that their utterances are valid forever. Similarly, David praises Yahweh's word, which assures his protection. Probably, David is referring to oracles urging him on to victory (e.g., 1Sa 30:8; 2Sa 5:19; see note on Ps 21).
18:32 *God … arms me with strength.* In royal inscriptions, it was proper for a king to attribute his prowess and victory in battle to his god. Esarhaddon reports that he was victorious in battle by the help of his gods. His father, Sennacherib, introduced the annals of his military campaigns by noting that the god Assur "made powerful my weapons" and "all humankind he has brought in submission at my feet." In a text closer to Ps 18 because of its hymnic form, the Assyrian king Ashurbanipal praises his goddess Ishtar by indicating that it was not his strength or the might of his weapons that brought victory, but it was the power of the goddess. Later in this same hymn, similar to v. 39, Ashurbanipal reports that the goddess made the kings "bow down at my feet." Egyptian art shows deities standing behind the pharaoh guiding his hands at the bow. We can therefore see that Israelites praised their God with the same kinds of terms, images and metaphors used by their neighbors for their gods, even though they were learning about the ways in which their God was far more powerful than the other gods.
18:34 *bow of bronze.* If this expression reflects an actual weapon, it may indicate either a wooden bow decorated with bronze or bronze-tipped arrows. On the other hand, it may simply be a poetic way of denoting the strength of the warrior's bow. The bow was a symbol of royal strength in both Assyria and Egypt, as well as one of the weapons of the gods.
18:38 *I crushed them.* The language of battle used in Ps 18 might appear harsh, but it was the common style in royal reports in the ancient world and mild in comparison to many. The imagery in the psalm is not as graphic as many descriptions that can be found in Assyrian records: "I laid low their men-at-arms in the mountains like sheep. Like lambs I cut off their heads (and) made their blood flow into the hollows and plains of the mountains." While this boast of Tiglath-Pileser I (c. 1100 BC) is a narrative report, not a hymnic piece like Ps 18, it illustrates the vividness customary in an ancient and violent culture. The Hittite king, Halparuntiya II (c. 850 BC) similarly claims to have cut off the feet of the men and made eunuchs of the children. Such graphic imagery rarely appears in the psalms, but generally speaking, when it does, it is poetic for the judgment of God, not the celebrated victories of a Judahite king (see notes on 58:10; 137:9).
18:45 A common notion expressed in victory reports is the submission of enemies, whose hearts fail them and who then surrender in fear before the king. Assyrian king Sargon II (c. 720 BC) claims that when he attacked Egypt, the hearts of his enemies palpitated at the sound of his name. Egyptian scribes report of Rameses II (c. 1275 BC) that chiefs and rebels submitted to him out of fear and with trembling.

[46]The LORD lives! Praise be to my Rock!
Exalted be God my Savior![c]
[47]He is the God who avenges me,
who subdues nations[d] under me,
48 who saves[e] me from my enemies.
You exalted me above my foes;
from a violent man you rescued me.
[49]Therefore I will praise you, LORD,
among the nations;
I will sing[f] the praises of your name.[g]

[50]He gives his king great victories;
he shows unfailing love to his anointed,
to David[h] and to his descendants
forever.[i]

Psalm 19[a]

For the director of music. A psalm of David.

[1]The heavens[j] declare[k] the glory of God;
the skies proclaim the work of his
hands.
[2]Day after day they pour forth speech;
night after night they reveal
knowledge.[l]
[3]They have no speech, they use no
words;
no sound is heard from them.
[4]Yet their voice[b] goes out into all the
earth,
their words to the ends of the
world.[m]
In the heavens God has pitched a tent[n]
for the sun.
5 It is like a bridegroom coming out
of his chamber,
like a champion rejoicing to run
his course.
[6]It rises at one end of the heavens
and makes its circuit to the other;[o]
nothing is deprived of its
warmth.

[7]The law of the LORD is perfect,
refreshing the soul.[p]
The statutes of the LORD are
trustworthy,[q]
making wise the simple.[r]
[8]The precepts of the LORD are right,[s]
giving joy to the heart.
The commands of the LORD are
radiant,
giving light to the eyes.
[9]The fear of the LORD is pure,
enduring forever.
The decrees of the LORD are firm,
and all of them are righteous.[t]
[10]They are more precious than gold,[u]
than much pure gold;
they are sweeter than honey,
than honey from the honeycomb.

18:46 [c]Ps 51:14 **18:47** [d]Ps 47:3 **18:48** [e]Ps 59:1 **18:49** [f]Ps 108:1 [g]Ro 15:9* **18:50** [h]Ps 144:10 [i]Ps 89:4 **19:1** [j]Isa 40:22 [k]Ps 50:6; Ro 1:19 **19:2** [l]Ps 74:16 **19:4** [m]Ro 10:18* [n]Ps 104:2 **19:6** [o]Ps 113:3; Ecc 1:5 **19:7** [p]Ps 23:3 [q]Ps 93:5; 111:7 [r]Ps 119:98-100 **19:8** [s]Ps 12:6; 119:128 **19:9** [t]Ps 119:138, 142 **19:10** [u]Pr 8:10

[a] In Hebrew texts 19:1-14 is numbered 19:2-15.
[b] *4* Septuagint, Jerome and Syriac; Hebrew *measuring line*

18:50 *his anointed.* See note on 1Sa 2:10.
19:1 – 2 *The heavens declare ... Day after day ... night after night.* In the Egyptian Papyrus Insinger (a composition from the intertestamental period), it is observed that the hidden work of a god is made known on earth day by day. For the next 20 lines the papyrus describes many aspects of nature that have been created by the god and presumably are involved in this revelation (AEL 3:210). These works of creation included light and darkness; day, month and year; summer and winter; constellations; the birth process; sleep; and the succession of generations. For Mesopotamian and Egyptian thought, the astral bodies were functional manifestations of the deities, and were therefore regarded as appropriate objects to worship. But in the view of the psalmist, the heavenly bodies are not extensions of deities to be worshiped; rather, they should invoke in humanity a sense of wonder at the glory of the God who made them as gifts for human benefit (see notes on 8:1,3).
19:5 *bridegroom ... chamber.* The chamber of a bridegroom was the specially prepared room in which the marriage was consummated. The use in Joel 2:16 suggests this in its parallelism. It has this meaning in early rabbinic Judaism, but after the destruction of the temple in AD 70 it takes on a reference to the pavilion in which the formal wedding ceremony was conducted.
19:6 *rises at one end of the heavens and makes its circuit.* In many ancient Near Eastern cultures, it was assumed that the sun ran a daily course through the heavens. Mesopotamian texts refer to the gates of the heavens where the sun enters and exits. In these texts, all of the heavenly bodies follow paths or courses, which are represented as bands across the sky.
19:7 *The law of the LORD is perfect.* In both Egyptian and Mesopotamian thought, law and justice were closely related to the sun-god, whose penetrating rays illumined every human activity. In the Babylonian Hymn to Shamash, the sun-god even discerns the covetous heart and weighs the fairness of each business transaction. With this divine character in view, King Hammurapi illustrated his famous law code with an engraving of himself standing before Shamash, the sun-god, who sanctions his kingship and law (see note on Ps 72). Egyptian kings, who embodied the sun-god, Ra (or Re), boasted the following epithet: "The Son of Re who lives by Maat (justice)." This background provides an important bridge between the first and second halves of Ps 19. For the psalmist, it is not a deified sun who presides over law and justice; rather, it is Yahweh, whose commands are perfect and who perceives "hidden faults" (v. 12) and every "meditation of [the] heart" (v. 14).
19:10 *pure gold.* This imagery is known from other ancient Near Eastern cultures. A number of inscriptions on doors at a Ptolemaic-period Egyptian temple at Edfu read: "Everyone who enters by this door, beware of entering in impurity, for God loves purity more than millions of possessions, more than hundreds of thousands of fine gold." The Hebrew word translated "pure gold" is somewhat obscure (it is a single word, not a noun with an adjective describing pure or refined). It could refer to a particular grade or to a particular variety, e.g., rose gold or white gold. *honey.* Represents a natural resource, in most occurrences the syrup of the date rather than bees' honey. Since sugar was not available, honey was the most commonly used sweetener. There is evidence of bee domestication at Tel Rehov in Israel, and the Hittites and Canaanites also used honey from domesticated bees

[11] By them your servant is warned;
in keeping them there is great reward.
[12] But who can discern their own errors?
Forgive my hidden faults.[v]
[13] Keep your servant also from willful sins;
may they not rule over me.
Then I will be blameless,
innocent of great transgression.

[14] May these words of my mouth and this meditation of my heart
be pleasing[w] in your sight,
LORD, my Rock[x] and my Redeemer.[y]

Psalm 20[a]

For the director of music. A psalm of David.

[1] May the LORD answer you when you are in distress;
may the name of the God of Jacob[z] protect you.[a]
[2] May he send you help from the sanctuary[b]
and grant you support from Zion.
[3] May he remember[c] all your sacrifices
and accept your burnt offerings.[b][d]
[4] May he give you the desire of your heart[e]
and make all your plans succeed.

[5] May we shout for joy over your victory
and lift up our banners[f] in the name of our God.

May the LORD grant all your requests.[g]

[6] Now this I know:
The LORD gives victory to his anointed.[h]
He answers him from his heavenly sanctuary
with the victorious power of his right hand.
[7] Some trust in chariots and some in horses,[i]
but we trust in the name of the LORD our God.[j]
[8] They are brought to their knees and fall,
but we rise up[k] and stand firm.[l]
[9] LORD, give victory to the king!
Answer us[m] when we call!

Psalm 21[c]

For the director of music. A psalm of David.

[1] The king rejoices in your strength, LORD.
How great is his joy in the victories you give![n]

19:12 [v]Ps 51:2; 90:8; 139:6 **19:14** [w]Ps 104:34 [x]Ps 18:2 [y]Isa 47:4 **20:1** [z]Ps 46:7, 11 [a]Ps 91:14 **20:2** [b]Ps 3:4 **20:3** [c]Ac 10:4 [d]Ps 51:19 **20:4** [e]Ps 21:2; 145:16, 19
20:5 [f]Ps 9:14; 60:4 [g]1Sa 1:17 **20:6** [h]Ps 28:8; 41:11; Isa 58:9 **20:7** [i]Ps 33:17; Isa 31:1 [j]2Ch 32:8 **20:8** [k]Mic 7:8 [l]Ps 37:23 **20:9** [m]Ps 3:7; 17:6 **21:1** [n]Ps 59:16-17

[a] In Hebrew texts 20:1-9 is numbered 20:2-10. [b] *3* The Hebrew has *Selah* (a word of uncertain meaning) here. [c] In Hebrew texts 21:1-13 is numbered 21:2-14.

in their sacrifices. In the Bible, honey occurs in lists with other agricultural products (e.g., 2Ch 31:5). It is possible that the first reference to honey in this verse is date honey, but the second reference is clearly referring to bee honey since the "honeycomb" is mentioned.
19:12 *who can discern their own errors?* The belief in the ancient world was that the gods had many more regulations, requirements and restrictions than were known to people. In a "Prayer to Every God," an Assyrian worshiper goes through an elaborate listing of possible offenses ("the forbidden thing I have eaten, I do not know; the prohibited place on which I have set foot, I do not know") asking that his unwitting sins be pardoned, claiming the offense was committed in ignorance. Additionally the penitential prayers from Mesopotamia known as *shigu* prayers contain frequent reference to being absolved of unknown sins. Egyptians were also concerned with unknown sins, as reflected in a late demotic wisdom piece (Papyrus Insinger), in which the author begs forgiveness for unwitting sin.
Ps 20 Prayers for the king (vv. 6,9) were customary in the ancient world, especially in the face of impending battle, which is the case in v. 5. For example, a prophet's oracle regarding the safety of the Assyrian king Ashurbanipal (650 BC) ends with a prayer that the king be preserved alive in the context of a rebellion against him.
20:2 *support from Zion.* The temple was not only the place of God's residence, it was the center of order in the cosmos and the hub of divine operations (see note on 48:1 – 2; see also the article "Hymns to Holy Cities," p. 927). Therefore, in time of war, God would come forth into the battle to restore order (see notes on 48:7,9). The temple of Yahweh (the "sanctuary") was built on Mount Zion in Jerusalem, which was viewed as the fortress (see notes on 48:3,12 – 13) from which God emerged to do battle against the enemies of his people (see note on 48:9).
20:3 *accept your burnt offerings.* Perhaps as part of the prayer ritual before battle, the king would have offerings and sacrifices presented to the Lord. Egyptian iconography frequently portrays the pharaoh approaching the deity with offerings. In one case the accompanying text provides a fitting parallel to the prayer of Ps 20 as the king offers sacrifices and libations to the god whom he hopes will grant him life. Burnt offerings were a typical sacrifice in Ugaritic ritual as well, but the Ugaritic practice may not have necessitated burning the whole animal as in the case of the OT burnt offering.
20:5 *banners.* The Hebrew word refers to flags held up as rallying points in a military formation or battle, as illustrated in the organization of the tribes marching through the wilderness (note the military implications from Nu 10:35). In the Egyptian army the divisions were named for various gods (e.g., the division of Amun, the division of Seth), and the standards would identify the division by means of some representation of the god. Holding high the banners was evidently a sign of victory.
20:7 *trust in chariots ... horses.* Chariots and horses were prestigious weapons in ancient Near Eastern warfare, and kings often measured military capacity in these terms (cf. Jdg 4:3; 1Ki 4:26; 9:17 – 19). For this reason, the multiplication of them was regarded in the OT as an act of misplaced trust (Dt 17:16). It was Yahweh, not military technology and numbers, who was to be the confidence of Israel in battle, which is the confession of this verse.
Ps 21 This psalm has been compared with a type of prophetic speech that was widespread in the ancient Near East called an "oracle of victory." In the face of impending battle, a spokesperson for the king's god or goddess would offer encouragement to the king. In Syria, a monu-

PSALM 20

PSALM 20 AND PAPYRUS AMHERST 63

Very few pieces of literature from the ancient world show sufficient similarity to a Biblical text to support the claim that they are both representative of the same literary work; the amount of overlap is simply not sufficient to sustain such a claim. The primary exception to that is Papyrus Amherst 63, which contains a version of Ps 20 that is directed to the Egyptian god Horus (also called Baal Shamayn), rather than to Yahweh. Close verbal parallels line by line in the very same sequence show that these are two versions of the same psalm.

Papyrus Amherst 63 is perhaps dated to as early as the fourth century BC, though a strong claim can be made for the second century BC, and it is written in the Aramaic language using a Demotic (Egyptian) script. The papyrus contains a number of cultic texts. Two of them are hymns addressed to Yahweh that are not known from the Hebrew Bible. Hymns to other gods are included as well. Scholars disagree whether Ps 20 is the original composition, with Papyrus Amherst representing a paganized corruption of the Biblical psalm (the majority opinion), or whether Papyrus Amherst represents an original version that the Biblical authors adopted and adapted for praise of Yahweh. An alternative view is that both stem from an earlier non-Israelite version. The importance of this test case is that here we have an incontestable example of the same literary piece having variations that exist both in the Bible and the ancient world, though here the papyrus is a product of the Hellenistic period rather than the ancient world per se. ◆

2 You have granted him his heart's desire[o]
and have not withheld the request of his lips.[a]
3 You came to greet him with rich blessings
and placed a crown of pure gold[p] on his head.
4 He asked you for life, and you gave it to him—
length of days, for ever and ever.[q]
5 Through the victories[r] you gave, his glory is great;
you have bestowed on him splendor and majesty.
6 Surely you have granted him unending blessings
and made him glad with the joy[s] of your presence.[t]
7 For the king trusts in the LORD;
through the unfailing love of the Most High
he will not be shaken.

8 Your hand will lay hold[u] on all your enemies;
your right hand will seize your foes.

21:2 [o]Ps 37:4 **21:3** [p]2Sa 12:30 **21:4** [q]Ps 61:5-6; 91:16; 133:3 **21:5** [r]Ps 18:50 **21:6** [s]Ps 43:4 [t]1Ch 17:27 **21:8** [u]Isa 10:10

[a] 2 The Hebrew has *Selah* (a word of uncertain meaning) here.

ment of Zakkur, the king of Hamath (c. 800 BC), describes how an oracle strengthened him in the face of a terrifying attack against his city. Other examples are common especially in prophetic speech of Assyrian prophets (cf. Ps 110; see note on Ps 110). In Ps 21, the words of an "oracle of victory" might be preserved in vv. 8–12. Perhaps a prophetic psalm, like Ps 21, would have been the source of confidence reflected in a prayer such as in 20:6.

21:8 *lay hold on … seize.* The Hebrew verb used in both instances actually describes attacking the enemy with a weapon, not apprehending him. Most soldiers were right-handed, so one would not seize the foe with the right hand—for that was where the weapon would be held. The right hand, then, was used for offense, and it would "find" its mark. The Hymn to Shamash says that the god's weapon will make straight for the wicked man and that there will be none to save him. In Egyptian reliefs and paintings (also at Ugarit) the king often strikes a pose with his weapon upraised in his right hand, while his left hand lays hold of the enemy. This verse is only describing part of that picture because the lines are parallel, not contrasting. Both lines describe what the right hand does.

9 When you appear for battle,
you will burn them up as in a
blazing furnace.
The LORD will swallow them up in his
wrath,
and his fire will consume them.[v]
10 You will destroy their descendants
from the earth,
their posterity from mankind.[w]
11 Though they plot evil[x] against you
and devise wicked schemes,[y] they
cannot succeed.
12 You will make them turn their backs[z]
when you aim at them with drawn
bow.

13 Be exalted in your strength, LORD;
we will sing and praise your might.

Psalm 22[a]

For the director of music. To the tune
of "The Doe of the Morning."
A psalm of David.

1 My God, my God, why have you
forsaken me?[a]
Why are you so far[b] from saving me,
so far from my cries of anguish?
2 My God, I cry out by day, but you do
not answer,
by night,[c] but I find no rest.[b]
3 Yet you are enthroned as the Holy One;[d]
you are the one Israel praises.[c e]
4 In you our ancestors put their trust;
they trusted and you delivered them.
5 To you they cried out and were saved;
in you they trusted and were not put
to shame.[f]

6 But I am a worm[g] and not a man,
scorned by everyone,[h] despised[i] by
the people.

21:9 [v]Ps 50:3; La 2:2; Mal 4:1 **21:10** [w]Dt 28:18; Ps 37:28 **21:11** [x]Ps 2:1 [y]Ps 10:2 **21:12** [z]Ps 7:12-13; 18:40 **22:1** [a]Mt 27:46*; Mk 15:34* [b]Ps 10:1 **22:2** [c]Ps 42:3 **22:3** [d]Ps 99:9 [e]Dt 10:21 **22:5** [f]Isa 49:23 **22:6** [g]Job 25:6; Isa 41:14 [h]Ps 31:11 [i]Isa 49:7; 53:3 **22:7** [j]Mt 27:39, 44 [k]Mk 15:29 **22:8** [l]Ps 91:14 [m]Mt 27:43 **22:9** [n]Ps 71:6 **22:10** [o]Isa 46:3 **22:11** [p]Ps 72:12 **22:12** [q]Ps 68:30 [r]Dt 32:14 **22:13** [s]Ps 17:12 [t]Ps 35:21 **22:14** [u]Ps 31:10 [v]Job 30:16; Da 5:6 **22:15** [w]Ps 38:10; Jn 19:28 [x]Ps 104:29 **22:16** [y]Ps 59:6 [z]Isa 53:5; Zec 12:10; Jn 19:34

7 All who see me mock me;
they hurl insults,[j] shaking their
heads.[k]
8 "He trusts in the LORD," they say,
"let the LORD rescue him.[l]
Let him deliver him,
since he delights[m] in him."

9 Yet you brought me out of the womb;[n]
you made me trust in you, even at
my mother's breast.
10 From birth[o] I was cast on you;
from my mother's womb you have
been my God.

11 Do not be far from me,
for trouble is near
and there is no one to help.[p]

12 Many bulls[q] surround me;
strong bulls of Bashan[r] encircle me.
13 Roaring lions[s] that tear their prey
open their mouths wide[t] against me.
14 I am poured out like water,
and all my bones are out of joint.[u]
My heart has turned to wax;
it has melted[v] within me.
15 My mouth[d] is dried up like a potsherd,
and my tongue sticks to the roof of
my mouth;[w]
you lay me in the dust[x] of death.

16 Dogs[y] surround me,
a pack of villains encircles me;
they pierce[e z] my hands and my
feet.

[a] In Hebrew texts 22:1-31 is numbered 22:2-32.
[b] 2 Or *night, and am not silent* [c] 3 Or *Yet you are holy, / enthroned on the praises of Israel*
[d] 15 Probable reading of the original Hebrew text; Masoretic Text *strength* [e] 16 Dead Sea Scrolls and some manuscripts of the Masoretic Text, Septuagint and Syriac; most manuscripts of the Masoretic Text *me, / like a lion*

21:9 *furnace.* The Hebrew word (*tannur*) refers to a cooking oven (Ex 8:3; Lev 2:4; 7:9). It was constructed of earth, brick and broken pottery and was made in the shape of a bell, the top of which was open for the chimney. Fire was kindled inside the oven, distributing heat to the inside surface where the bread dough was placed for cooking. Oven heat, being more intense than an ordinary open flame (reducing fuel to very hot charcoal), served as a metaphor for destructive power (cf. Hos 7:7; Mal 4:1). Such punishment was also known to be literal. A Mesopotamian royal letter, possibly from about 600 BC, instructs a governor to throw corrupt priests into a burning oven. Such a custom, evidenced also in Da 3, undergirds the rhetorical power of the image in this psalm.
22:3 *enthroned.* See note on 2Ki 19:15.
22:9,10 *womb.* See note on 139:13.
22:12 *bulls.* Considered by ancient people to be one of the strongest and most potentially dangerous land animals. This is illustrated as early as c. 3000 BC by a slate palette from Egypt depicting a man being gored and trampled by a horned bull. *Bashan.* The high plateau region east of the Sea of Galilee; it was well known as a fertile grassland and therefore conducive to the grazing of cattle (Am 4:1).
22:13 *lions.* While lions no longer inhabit what was the land of ancient Israel, in ancient times they were not uncommon, and the danger they posed was well known (1Sa 17:34–37; Am 3:4; 5:19). In addition to their strength and speed, lions used stealth to hunt their victims and were feared for both their teeth and claws. These attributes are all illustrated in ancient Near Eastern artwork. In Assyrian royal hunts and art, animals (especially lions) symbolized both human enemies and the forces of chaos that the king ritually subdues. In this psalm, the reversal of this imagery is used to portray the afflictions of the psalmist.
22:14 *my bones are out of joint.* Strain and trauma can result in the sensation of aching joints; however, such language is a common figure of speech for suffering in Psalms, as well as in Mesopotamian laments, even describing the effects of emotional distress (cf. 42:11; see note on 38:3). A Mesopotamian lament uses similar imagery in the context of a physical illness in which joints were separated and limbs were splayed.
22:15 *potsherd.* See note on Job 2:8.
22:16 *Dogs.* See notes on 1Sa 24:14; 2Sa 3:8. *pierce.* The understanding of this Hebrew verb is problematic. Traditionally translated "pierce," this Hebrew verb occurs only

[17] All my bones are on display;
people stare[a] and gloat over me.[b]
[18] They divide my clothes among them
and cast lots[c] for my garment.

[19] But you, LORD, do not be far from me.
You are my strength; come quickly[d]
to help me.
[20] Deliver me from the sword,
my precious life[e] from the power
of the dogs.
[21] Rescue me from the mouth of the
lions;
save me from the horns of the wild
oxen.

[22] I will declare your name to my
people;
in the assembly I will praise
you.[f]

22:17 [a] Lk 23:35 [b] Lk 23:27 **22:18** [c] Mt 27:35*; Lk 23:34; Jn 19:24* **22:19** [d] Ps 70:5 **22:20** [e] Ps 35:17 **22:22** [f] Heb 2:12*

22:23 [g] Ps 86:12; 135:19 [h] Ps 33:8 **22:24** [i] Ps 69:17 [j] Heb 5:7 **22:25** [k] Ps 35:18 [l] Ecc 5:4 **22:26** [m] Ps 107:9 [n] Ps 40:16

[23] You who fear the LORD, praise him![g]
All you descendants of Jacob, honor
him!
Revere him,[h] all you descendants of
Israel!
[24] For he has not despised or scorned
the suffering of the afflicted one;
he has not hidden his face[i] from him
but has listened to his cry for help.[j]

[25] From you comes the theme of my
praise in the great assembly;[k]
before those who fear you[a] I will
fulfill my vows.[l]
[26] The poor will eat[m] and be satisfied;
those who seek the LORD will praise
him —[n]
may your hearts live forever!

[a] 25 Hebrew *him*

here, and can only be translated here as "pierce" if it is emended. As it stands, it indicates that the psalmist's hands and feet are "like a lion" (see NIV text note), which some commentators have interpreted to mean that the psalmist's hands and feet were trussed up on a stick as a captured lion would be. Unfortunately, despite all the lion hunting scenes that are preserved and described, no lion is shown being transported this way. If a verb is desirable here, a suitable candidate must be found among the related Semitic languages. The most likely one is similar to Akkadian and Syriac cognates that have the meaning "shrink" or "shrivel." Akkadian medical texts speak of a symptom in which the hands and feet are shrunken. Although Mt 27 uses several other lines from this psalm (e.g., Mt 27:35,39,43,46), Mt 27 is of no help here, because it does not refer to this verse. Since Matthew omits it, he likely did not read the psalm as referring to the piercing of hands and feet.

22:17 *my bones are on display.* In the same Mesopotamian lament cited in the note on v. 14, one finds a description of gauntness. The background to Ps 22 might be starvation (or even fasting, see note on 109:24), rather than disease, as in the Mesopotamian text; otherwise, the imagery might be stereotypical for extreme distress: "My bones are loose, covered (only) with skin" (cf. 102:5).

22:18 *cast lots for my garment.* Although Roman soldiers had the right to the clothes of convicted criminals (as the soldiers gambling by means of lots for Jesus' tunic [Mt 27:35]), there is no evidence of this for soldiers supervising executions in the OT period. Nevertheless, in this period we do know that plunder was sometimes divided by lot, so it is not difficult to understand a person's clothing being divided that way upon his demise. It should be noted, however, that Ps 22 does not indicate that those casting lots for the clothing were executioners. Inheritance procedures often used lots to divide the property among the heirs. A Mesopotamian lament indicates this as the person on his deathbed bemoans the fact that his valuables are already being divided up before he is dead.

22:24 *has not hidden his face.* See note on 13:1; cf. note on 42:2, "meet with God."

22:25 *fulfill my vows.* See note on 56:12.

22:26 *The poor will eat.* The type of offering sacrificed in fulfillment of a vow (v. 25) was a peace (or fellowship) offering, which was communal in nature (Lev 3:1 – 17; 7:11 – 21; 1Sa 11:15). Choice portions went to Yahweh and were burned on the altar, but the bulk of the animal was shared with other worshipers in the congregation at the temple. A ritual text from Ugarit (c. 1300 BC) specifies a daily peace offering of this type (Ugaritic, *shlmm* = Hebrew *shelamim*, Lev 3:1), of which all may eat. What this type of offering meant for Israelites is that even poor people who came to worship could partake in something to eat. They ate with the knowledge that God had answered the prayer of the one fulfilling the vow, bringing praise to God.

Assyrian panel of dogs attacking an animal, Nineveh, 645 to 635 BC. "Deliver me from the sword, my precious life from the power of the dogs" (Ps 22:20).

Kim Walton. The British Museum.

[27] All the ends of the earth[o]
will remember and turn to the LORD,
and all the families of the nations
will bow down before him,[p]
[28] for dominion belongs to the LORD[q]
and he rules over the nations.

[29] All the rich[r] of the earth will feast and
worship;
all who go down to the dust[s] will
kneel before him—
those who cannot keep themselves
alive.
[30] Posterity[t] will serve him;
future generations will be told about
the Lord.
[31] They will proclaim his righteousness,
declaring to a people yet unborn:[u]
He has done it!

Psalm 23

A psalm of David.

[1] The LORD is my shepherd,[v] I lack
nothing.[w]
[2] He makes me lie down in green
pastures,
he leads me beside quiet waters,[x]
[3] he refreshes my soul.[y]
He guides me along the right
paths[z]
for his name's sake.
[4] Even though I walk
through the darkest valley,[a][a]
I will fear no evil,[b]
for you are with me;[c]
your rod and your staff,
they comfort me.

[5] You prepare a table before me
in the presence of my enemies.
You anoint my head with oil;[d]
my cup[e] overflows.
[6] Surely your goodness and love will
follow me
all the days of my life,
and I will dwell in the house of the
LORD
forever.

[a] 4 Or *the valley of the shadow of death*

22:27 [o] Ps 2:8 [p] Ps 86:9 **22:28** [q] Ps 47:7-8 **22:29** [r] Ps 45:12 [s] Isa 26:19 **22:30** [t] Ps 102:28 **22:31** [u] Ps 78:6 **23:1** [v] Isa 40:11; Jn 10:11; 1Pe 2:25 [w] Php 4:19 **23:2** [x] Eze 34:14; Rev 7:17 **23:3** [y] Ps 19:7 [z] Ps 5:8; 85:13 **23:4** [a] Job 10:21-22 [b] Ps 3:6; 27:1 [c] Isa 43:2 **23:5** [d] Ps 92:10 [e] Ps 16:5

23:1 *shepherd.* A metaphor describing the authority and care exercised by a deity or a king who represents the gods. Marduk was the chief god in Babylonia for much of its history, and a standard hymn of praise concludes by extolling his care for the weak like a benevolent shepherd. Concerning Shamash, the Mesopotamian sun-god, a hymn identifies him as the shepherd and herdsman of all creatures. An Egyptian hymn praises the sun-god as the "Brave Protector who tends his flocks." But the image not only suggested protection, but was also an affirmation of the authority to rule (cf. 2Sa 5:2; 1Ch 11:2). A coronation prayer for the Assyrian king Ashurbanipal asks that he may rule as their (the Assyrians') shepherd. Thus, the metaphor of shepherd was a royal one, with connotations of strong leadership but tender care. One ancient Sumerian wisdom text offers a particularly good parallel to Ps 23 when it identifies a man's god as one who, as a shepherd, finds good pasturage for him.
23:2 *green pastures ... quiet waters.* Sheep in the Levant grazed on the fertile grass produced by rain. In the summer and autumn they fed on weeds and stubble left over from harvest. Like camels, sheep can go long periods of time without water and then drink as much as 2.5 gallons (9 liters). In contrast to goats, which are quite independent, sheep depend upon the shepherd to find pasture and water for them. Shepherds also provided shelter, medication, and aid in birthing. In sum, sheep were virtually helpless without the shepherd. In an Old Babylonian text, King Ammiditana claims that the god Ea gave him the wisdom to shepherd his people. He continues the metaphor by saying that he provides them with fine pastures and watering places, and makes them lie down in safe pastures.
23:4 *darkest valley.* That is, the "shadow of death" (see NIV text note; see also the articles "Death and Sheol," p. 833; "Death and the Underworld," p. 907). *your rod and your staff.* The rod was a club worn at the belt, while the staff was a walking implement that doubled as a weapon in a time of need (1Sa 17:35) and guided and controlled the sheep. These were traditional tools of the shepherd as is shown already in a cylinder seal inscription of the third millennium BC.
23:5 *prepare a table.* To set out food was a gesture of hospitality (Ge 18:1–8; Ex 2:18–20). To do so in front of someone (enemies) would publicly establish the right relationship that exists between host (in this case God) and the guest (the psalmist). Perhaps the image of Yahweh as a protective shepherd-king continues here (cf. 2Sa 9:7; 2Ki 25:27–30). *anoint ... with oil.* Olive oil could be used to treat dry or cracked skin, so it was a sign of hospitality to offer oil to visitors. A text from an Aramaic speaking community in Egypt (c. 300 BC and related culturally to Jews) uses the word for oil to speak of invigorating an old man. In a diplomatic letter from the Assyrian king Ashurbanipal (c. 650 BC) to vassal tribes in Arabia, he boasts of his good treatment of them expressed by putting oil on their heads as an act of friendliness. Thus, the psalmist is refreshed by being in God's hospitable presence.
23:6 *the house of the LORD.* Used as a term for the temple (which is very clear in 27:4), but never for the heavenly dwelling place of God. *forever.* This term could be confusing in regard to dwelling in the temple "forever," but the Hebrew says only "for length of days," i.e., for extended periods (cf. La 5:20). If the translation "dwell" (following the Septuagint, the pre-Christian Greek translation of the OT) is correct, then it would suggest a priestly office for the psalmist, for priests were the only inhabitants of the temple precinct. If, instead, we should follow the Hebrew text by translating this "I will return to the house of the LORD," we would find here the anticipation of enjoying many future opportunities to worship at the temple ("time and again"). The Babylonian king Neriglissar expresses to his god that he wants to be where he (his god) is forever. Another text requests, "May I stand before you forever in worship and devotion." The Hymn to Marduk requests that the worshiper may stand before the deity forever in prayer, supplication and entreaty. In the third millennium BC, Sumerian worshipers tried to accomplish this objective by placing statuettes of themselves in the posture of prayer in the temple. In this way they would be continuously represented in the temple. Consequently, we can see that this sentiment was commonly expressed in the ancient world, regardless of which God was being worshiped.

Psalm 24

Of David. A psalm.

[1]The earth is the LORD's,[f] and everything
in it,
the world, and all who live in it;[g]
[2]for he founded it on the seas
and established it on the waters.

[3]Who may ascend the mountain[h] of the
LORD?
Who may stand in his holy place?[i]
[4]The one who has clean hands[j] and a
pure heart,[k]
who does not trust in an idol
or swear by a false god.[a]

[5]They will receive blessing from the LORD
and vindication from God their
Savior.
[6]Such is the generation of those who
seek him,
who seek your face,[l] God of Jacob.[b,c]

[7]Lift up your heads, you gates;[m]
be lifted up, you ancient doors,
that the King of glory[n] may come in.
[8]Who is this King of glory?
The LORD strong and mighty,
the LORD mighty in battle.[o]
[9]Lift up your heads, you gates;
lift them up, you ancient doors,
that the King of glory may come in.
[10]Who is he, this King of glory?
The LORD Almighty—
he is the King of glory.

24:1 [f]Ex 9:29; Job 41:11; Ps 89:11 [g]1Co 10:26* **24:3** [h]Ps 2:6 [i]Ps 15:1; 65:4 **24:4** [j]Job 17:9 [k]Mt 5:8 **24:6** [l]Ps 27:8 **24:7** [m]Isa 26:2 [n]Ps 97:6; 1Co 2:8 **24:8** [o]Ps 76:3-6

Psalm 25[d]

Of David.

[1]In you, LORD my God,
I put my trust.[p]

[2]I trust in you;[q]
do not let me be put to shame,
nor let my enemies triumph over me.
[3]No one who hopes in you
will ever be put to shame,[r]
but shame will come on those
who are treacherous without cause.

[4]Show me your ways, LORD,
teach me your paths.[s]
[5]Guide me in your truth and teach me,
for you are God my Savior,
and my hope is in you all day long.
[6]Remember, LORD, your great mercy and
love,[t]
for they are from of old.
[7]Do not remember the sins of my youth[u]
and my rebellious ways;
according to your love[v] remember me,
for you, LORD, are good.

[8]Good and upright[w] is the LORD;
therefore he instructs[x] sinners in his
ways.

25:1 [p]Ps 86:4 **25:2** [q]Ps 41:11 **25:3** [r]Isa 49:23 **25:4** [s]Ex 33:13 **25:6** [t]Ps 103:17; Isa 63:7, 15 **25:7** [u]Job 13:26; Jer 3:25 [v]Ps 51:1 **25:8** [w]Ps 92:15 [x]Ps 32:8

[a] 4 Or *swear falsely* [b] 6 Two Hebrew manuscripts and Syriac (see also Septuagint); most Hebrew manuscripts *face, Jacob* [c] 6 The Hebrew has *Selah* (a word of uncertain meaning) here and at the end of verse 10. [d] This psalm is an acrostic poem, the verses of which begin with the successive letters of the Hebrew alphabet.

24:2 *founded it on the seas.* In the Babylonian perception of the cosmos, the earth's foundation is on what is called the *apsu.* This is a primordial watery region that is under the jurisdiction of the very important deity Enki/Ea. From the standpoint of physical geography, it represents the water table that surfaces, e.g., in marshes and springs, and is associated with the sweet-water cosmic seas and rivers. In *Enuma Elish*, one of Marduk's names, Agilima, identifies him as the one who built the earth above the water and established the upper regions. Passages such as this show us that the Israelites thought about the shape of the world the same way that their neighbors did (see the article "Cosmic Geography," p. 836). The Bible is not proposing a new way to think about the cosmos—it is insisting that Yahweh is the one who created, sustains and controls the cosmos, regardless of how the shape of the cosmos is defined.
24:4 *does not trust.* This expression means to "nurse an appetite" for something. It here refers, physiologically, to the throat, and thereby the meaning arrives at appetite or desire. In a number of contexts the same expression is used with God as the object (see Ps 25:1; 86:4; 143:8). *idol.* The Hebrew term is related to the word for "emptiness" or "vanity." Other Biblical writers use the term "no-gods" for idols (e.g., Jer 5:7).
24:7 *Lift up your heads, you gates … you ancient doors.* In the Hymn to Shamash, the Babylonian sun-god, various parts of the temple are said to rejoice over Shamash, including the gateways and entrances. A Nabonidus text refers to the gates of the temple being open wide for Shamash to enter. These would occur in the context of regular processions of the statue of the deity into his temple. If the "head" of the gates refers to an architectural feature, it would most likely be the beam or projection across the top of the gates that served as a cornice. This was a common feature in Egyptian and Mesopotamian architecture, and the Akkadian word for it, *kululu*, also refers to a headdress or turban. The idea that these would be lifted off the posts of the gates to allow something large to pass through is ingenious, but not persuasive, in that the usual design of gates would not have unencumbered cornices that could be so easily moved. The alternative, that the lifting of the heads is metaphoric, is, for the moment, more likely. In Ugaritic literature, the gods lower their heads when they are being humbled; they raise up their heads when they have reason to rejoice.
24:8 *mighty in battle.* See the article "Divine Warfare," p. 365.
25:2 *put to shame.* In ancient texts, a common expression that sums up the emotions of defeat is "shame." An Assyrian prayer to the god Nabu begs the god not to allow his faithful worshiper to experience shame in the assembly. Similarly, promises of deliverance are expressed in terms of not allowing the pious one to come to shame.
25:7 *sins of my youth.* The rashness of youthful behavior is proverbial in all cultures and is generally met with special patience and leniency by society. Like this verse, Mesopotamian laments speak of the "sins of the youth" with hope on the part of the worshiper that the deity will be merciful.

PSALM 25

HONOR-SHAME CULTURES

While honor and shame are issues common to human society and individual experience, various cultures exhibit different degrees to which these issues are important. Evidence from the ancient Near East indicates that these were relatively important factors related to social status, even between different deities. Social prestige was often experienced through acts of deference received from others (e.g., Ge 37:7 – 8; 41:43). It might come from vocational excellence (e.g., 1Sa 16:17 – 22; Pr 22:29), military exploits (e.g., 1Sa 18:6 – 7) or other meritorious actions (e.g., Ru 3:11). Perhaps the most common avenue was through material prosperity, in large measure because success was viewed as a sign of divine favor. An Old Babylonian letter makes explicit the connection between a god's favor and prosperity: "Because the god has accepted your prayers, you are now gentlemen and men of property; all your affairs have prospered."

Shame, on the other hand, was society's way of enforcing control through punishment and sanction. It might involve "official" shaming, when promoted through proper legal or political channels, such as public punishment and humiliation (e.g., Dt 25:1 – 10; 2Sa 10:1 – 5), or in an extreme case such as war, the defeated were exposed to naked exploitation (Isa 20:1 – 5). There was also "informal" shaming, to which suffering people might be subjected even if innocent of any wrongdoing. This is frequently the complaint in Biblical psalms of lament and in prayers from Mesopotamia, and it included a variety of verbal (e.g., Ps 22:7; 35:15 – 16; 42:10; Job 12:4; see note on Ps 41:5 – 6) and physical abuses (e.g., Job 16:10; 17:6), as well as social isolation (see note on Ps 31:11).

If the basic assumption were that prosperity meant divine favor, then the opposite principle of retribution also applied; if fortunes reversed, it meant divine disapproval. Since society presumed it a religious duty to shame the individual as punishment, the psalmists cried out for God to demonstrate the individual's innocence by deliverance from distress. ◆

Victory stele of Sargon showing shameful treatment of prisoners as a way to enforce control.

Jill Walton. The Louvre.

[9]He guides[y] the humble in what is right
and teaches them[z] his way.
[10]All the ways of the LORD are loving and
faithful[a]
toward those who keep the demands
of his covenant.[b]
[11]For the sake of your name,[c] LORD,
forgive my iniquity, though it is
great.

[12]Who, then, are those who fear the
LORD?
He will instruct them in the ways[d]
they should choose.[a]
[13]They will spend their days in
prosperity,[e]
and their descendants will inherit
the land.[f]
[14]The LORD confides[g] in those who fear
him;
he makes his covenant known[h] to
them.
[15]My eyes are ever on the LORD,[i]
for only he will release my feet from
the snare.

[16]Turn to me[j] and be gracious to me,
for I am lonely and afflicted.
[17]Relieve the troubles of my heart
and free me from my anguish.[k]
[18]Look on my affliction and my distress[l]
and take away all my sins.
[19]See how numerous are my enemies[m]
and how fiercely they hate me!

[20]Guard my life[n] and rescue me;
do not let me be put to shame,
for I take refuge in you.
[21]May integrity[o] and uprightness protect
me,
because my hope, LORD,[b] is in you.

[22]Deliver Israel,[p] O God,
from all their troubles!

Psalm 26

Of David.

[1]Vindicate me, LORD,
for I have led a blameless life;[q]
I have trusted[r] in the LORD
and have not faltered.[s]
[2]Test me,[t] LORD, and try me,
examine my heart and my mind;[u]
[3]for I have always been mindful of your
unfailing love
and have lived[v] in reliance on your
faithfulness.

[4]I do not sit[w] with the deceitful,
nor do I associate with hypocrites.
[5]I abhor[x] the assembly of evildoers
and refuse to sit with the wicked.
[6]I wash my hands in innocence,[y]
and go about your altar, LORD,
[7]proclaiming aloud your praise
and telling of all your wonderful
deeds.[z]

[8]LORD, I love[a] the house where you
live,
the place where your glory dwells.
[9]Do not take away my soul along with
sinners,
my life with those who are
bloodthirsty,[b]
[10]in whose hands are wicked schemes,
whose right hands are full of bribes.[c]
[11]I lead a blameless life;
deliver me[d] and be merciful to me.

[12]My feet stand on level ground;[e]
in the great congregation[f] I will
praise the LORD.

Psalm 27

Of David.

[1]The LORD is my light[g] and my
salvation[h] —
whom shall I fear?
The LORD is the stronghold of my life —
of whom shall I be afraid?[i]

[2]When the wicked advance against me
to devour[c] me,
it is my enemies and my foes
who will stumble and fall.[j]
[3]Though an army besiege me,
my heart will not fear;[k]
though war break out against me,
even then I will be confident.[l]

25:9 [y] Ps 23:3 [z] Ps 27:11 **25:10** [a] Ps 40:11 [b] Ps 103:18 **25:11** [c] Ps 31:3; 79:9 **25:12** [d] Ps 37:23 **25:13** [e] Pr 19:23 [f] Ps 37:11 **25:14** [g] Pr 3:32 [h] Jn 7:17 **25:15** [i] Ps 141:8 **25:16** [j] Ps 69:16 **25:17** [k] Ps 107:6 **25:18** [l] 2Sa 16:12 **25:19** [m] Ps 3:1 **25:20** [n] Ps 86:2 **25:21** [o] Ps 41:12 **25:22** [p] Ps 130:8 **26:1** [q] Ps 7:8; Pr 20:7 [r] Ps 28:7 [s] 2Ki 20:3; Heb 10:23

26:2 [t] Ps 17:3 [u] Ps 7:9 **26:3** [v] 2Ki 20:3 **26:4** [w] Ps 1:1 **26:5** [x] Ps 31:6; 139:21 **26:6** [y] Ps 73:13 **26:7** [z] Ps 9:1 **26:8** [a] Ps 27:4 **26:9** [b] Ps 28:3 **26:10** [c] 1Sa 8:3 **26:11** [d] Ps 69:18 **26:12** [e] Ps 27:11; 40:2 [f] Ps 22:22 **27:1** [g] Isa 60:19 [h] Ex 15:2 [i] Ps 118:6 **27:2** [j] Ps 9:3; 14:4 **27:3** [k] Ps 3:6 [l] Job 4:6

[a] 12 Or *ways he chooses* [b] 21 Septuagint; Hebrew does not have LORD. [c] 2 Or *slander*

25:15 *snare.* See notes on 124:7; 140:5.
26:2 *Test me.* See note on 19:7.
26:6–8 *altar … house.* These terms indicate that a temple setting is in view, perhaps where the psalmist hopes for the vindication of judicial innocence before the assembly of worshipers (vv. 1,11–12; see note on 17:2). One of the functions of the high priest using the Urim and Thummim was to determine difficult cases (Ex 28:30; Dt 17:8–9).
26:6 *I wash my hands.* In the tabernacle and in Solomon's temple there was a basin of water for priests to wash (Ex 30:17–21; 1Ki 7:23–26; 2Ch 4:6). The psalmist's reference to washing might allude to a similar ritual for any worshiper circulating in the court of worship. Evidence suggests that ritual washings were customary in temples from Phoenicia on the Mediterranean coast to Susa, east of Mesopotamia.
27:1 *stronghold.* Fortifications in the ancient Near East are known from before 5000 BC, as soon as rival, settled communities competed for resources, necessitating military structures for defense. If a city had adequate supplies of food and water to endure a lengthy siege, it might withstand an attack indefinitely (Samaria fell after three years, 2Ki 17:5).

4 One thing[m] I ask from the LORD,
this only do I seek:
that I may dwell in the house of the
LORD
all the days of my life,[n]
to gaze on the beauty of the LORD
and to seek him in his temple.
5 For in the day of trouble
he will keep me safe in his
dwelling;
he will hide me[o] in the shelter of
his sacred tent
and set me high upon a rock.[p]

6 Then my head will be exalted[q]
above the enemies who surround
me;
at his sacred tent I will sacrifice[r] with
shouts of joy;
I will sing and make music to the
LORD.

7 Hear my voice when I call, LORD;
be merciful to me and answer me.[s]
8 My heart says of you, "Seek his face!"
Your face, LORD, I will seek.
9 Do not hide your face[t] from me,
do not turn your servant away in
anger;
you have been my helper.
Do not reject me or forsake me,
God my Savior.
10 Though my father and mother forsake
me,
the LORD will receive me.
11 Teach me your way, LORD;
lead me in a straight path[u]
because of my oppressors.
12 Do not turn me over to the desire of
my foes,
for false witnesses[v] rise up against
me,
spouting malicious accusations.

13 I remain confident of this:
I will see the goodness of the LORD[w]
in the land of the living.[x]
14 Wait[y] for the LORD;
be strong and take heart
and wait for the LORD.

27:4 [m]Ps 90:17 [n]Ps 23:6; 26:8 **27:5** [o]Ps 17:8; 31:20 [p]Ps 40:2 **27:6** [q]Ps 3:3 [r]Ps 107:22 **27:7** [s]Ps 13:3 **27:9** [t]Ps 69:17 **27:11** [u]Ps 5:8; 25:4; 86:11 **27:12** [v]Mt 26:60; Ac 9:1 **27:13** [w]Ps 31:19 [x]Jer 11:19; Eze 26:20 **27:14** [y]Ps 40:1

Psalm 28

Of David.

1 To you, LORD, I call;
you are my Rock,
do not turn a deaf ear to me.
For if you remain silent,[z]
I will be like those who go down
to the pit.[a]
2 Hear my cry for mercy[b]
as I call to you for help,
as I lift up my hands
toward your Most Holy Place.[c]

3 Do not drag me away with the
wicked,
with those who do evil,
who speak cordially with their
neighbors
but harbor malice in their hearts.[d]
4 Repay them for their deeds
and for their evil work;
repay them for what their hands have
done[e]
and bring back on them what they
deserve.[f]

5 Because they have no regard for the
deeds of the LORD
and what his hands have done,[g]
he will tear them down
and never build them up again.
6 Praise be to the LORD,
for he has heard my cry for mercy.
7 The LORD is my strength[h] and my
shield;
my heart trusts[i] in him, and he
helps me.
My heart leaps for joy,
and with my song I praise him.[j]

8 The LORD is the strength of his
people,
a fortress of salvation for his
anointed one.[k]
9 Save your people and bless your
inheritance;[l]
be their shepherd[m] and carry them[n]
forever.

28:1 [z]Ps 83:1 [a]Ps 88:4 **28:2** [b]Ps 138:2; 140:6 [c]Ps 5:7 **28:3** [d]Ps 12:2; Ps 26:9; Jer 9:8 **28:4** [e]2Ti 4:14; Rev 22:12 [f]Rev 18:6 **28:5** [g]Isa 5:12 **28:7** [h]Ps 18:1 [i]Ps 13:5 [j]Ps 40:3; 69:30 **28:8** [k]Ps 20:6 **28:9** [l]Dt 9:29; Ezr 1:4 [m]Isa 40:11 [n]Dt 1:31; 32:11

27:4 *all the days of my life.* Pious Mesopotamian worshipers expressed the same longing for continuous presence in the temple (see note on 23:6). This is illustrated in a Babylonian incantation prayer for deliverance from illness: "May I stand before you forever in worship, prayer, and devotion."
27:9 *hide your face.* See note on 13:1.
27:10 *Though my father and mother forsake me.* While social isolation, even from one's family, is a common theme of laments (see note on 31:11), this expression may allude to the physical loss of parents due to death, which at an emotional level is experienced as abandonment. A parallel from "The Babylonian Theodicy" might help clarify the distress: "I was the youngest child when fate claimed (my) father / My mother who bore me departed to the land of no return / My father and mother left me, and with no one my guardian!"
28:2 *I lift up my hands.* Among the postures of worship, lifting hands in prayer is commonly mentioned and portrayed pictographically in ancient Near Eastern cultures. Mesopotamians possessed an entire category of prayers named "prayers with raised hands." The meaning of the gesture is submission (as it can also be for us) and hopeful appeal. This is illustrated in Egyptian art, which depicts people bringing tribute to the divine pharaoh with upraised hand and also imploring an Egyptian royal servant for favor.
28:8 *anointed one.* See note on 1Sa 2:10.

Psalm 29

A psalm of David.

1 Ascribe to the LORD,[o] you heavenly
beings,
ascribe to the LORD glory[p] and strength.
2 Ascribe to the LORD the glory due his
name;
worship the LORD in the splendor of
his[a] holiness.[q]

3 The voice[r] of the LORD is over the
waters;
the God of glory thunders,[s]
the LORD thunders over the
mighty waters.
4 The voice of the LORD is powerful;[t]
the voice of the LORD is
majestic.

29:1 [o] 1Ch 16:28 [p] Ps 96:7-9 **29:2** [q] 2Ch 20:21 **29:3** [r] Job 37:5 [s] Ps 18:13 **29:4** [t] Ps 68:33

[a] 2 Or *LORD with the splendor of*

Ps 29 The myths of the Canaanite god Baal provide important background for appreciating the message of this psalm. While speculative claims that Ps 29 is actually an adaptation of a Canaanite hymn to Baal overstate the evidence (see the article "Psalm 29: A Canaanite Hymn?" p. 93), numerous phrases and ideas in Ps 29 seem to allude to the Baal Cycle, beginning with the reference to a deity giving "voice" in the form of thunder. Baal, as storm-god, spoke with thunder and lightning (cf. v. 7). Ps 29 refers to the "voice of the LORD" seven times, which may allude to the proverbial seven thunders and lightnings of Baal. The imagery throughout these verses describes a mighty storm that forms over the waters of the Mediterranean Sea, sweeps inland across the forested mountains of Lebanon in the north, and rolls on to the Desert of Kadesh.
29:1 *heavenly beings.* Lit. "sons of gods," which refers to the supernatural beings who inhabit the heavenly realm. In 89:5–7 the same Hebrew expression ("sons of gods") is also translated "heavenly beings" and is found in poetic parallel with the "assembly … council of the holy ones," who praise Yahweh in the heavenly realm. In the ancient Near Eastern world view, the universe was inhabited by divine beings (gods, goddesses and lesser spirits) and human beings. The realm of divine beings was thought to be organized like a human royal court, with a chief god presiding and the others comprising his council. The "council" in the ancient world met to render judgments concerning the world of people. In Ps 29 the heavenly beings are called on to acknowledge the superiority and majesty of Yahweh. Typically in the ancient world the gods of the council each had their autonomy, though they did ascribe greatness to the head of the council (e.g., to Marduk in *Enuma Elish*). See the article "Divine Council," p. 615.
29:3 *the mighty waters.* Lit. "the many waters," an expression referring to what is unruly in creation (see note on 93:3–4; see also the article "Chaos Monsters," p. 953), and the sea was the epitome of such chaotic forces. In the Baal Cycle, the enemy sea-god may also be called "god of many waters." Generally hymnic literature would not be launching an argument about which god was dominant. Each god would have been extolled for their particular powers and jurisdiction, because ancient Near Eastern people did not tend to argue about the gods (except in matters of political and military supremacy). The God of Israel, however, is a jealous God and insistent on his supremacy. Since the Israelites were often inclined to worship other gods alongside Yahweh or even instead of Yahweh, there would be more possibility that they would be affirming Yahweh's jurisdictions and activities rather than the place given to other gods. Even so, this does not mean that every statement of Yahweh's supremacy is a direct polemic against other gods.

PSALM 29

Psalm 29: A Canaanite Hymn?

Many of the images in Ps 29 mirror those found in the Ugaritic Baal Cycle, showing that the hymnic traditions and rhetoric were held in common across the ancient world (see notes on Ps 74:13–14). Because of the high concentration of such images in Ps 29, as well as other similarities in poetic style to Canaanite literature, some scholars have suggested a direct borrowing from a Canaanite hymn to Baal. Such a conclusion, however, is unnecessary since the imagery and poetic style is very typical of literature from Late Bronze/Iron Age Levant (ancient Israel to Syria). Since there is insufficient evidence to suggest literary borrowing from a known Canaanite hymn, it is more likely that the similarities simply reflect common traditions. Nevertheless, such comparison offers important evidence that the Israelite psalmists were well acquainted with the hymnic styles of their neighbors and used those same styles, just as our praise music today echoes the musical styles current in our culture. ◆

[5]The voice of the LORD breaks the cedars;
the LORD breaks in pieces the cedars of Lebanon.[u]
[6]He makes Lebanon leap[v] like a calf,
Sirion[a w] like a young wild ox.
[7]The voice of the LORD strikes with flashes of lightning.
[8]The voice of the LORD shakes the desert;
the LORD shakes the Desert of Kadesh.[x]
[9]The voice of the LORD twists the oaks[b]
and strips the forests bare.
And in his temple all cry, "Glory!"[y]
[10]The LORD sits enthroned over the flood;[z]
the LORD is enthroned as King forever.[a]
[11]The LORD gives strength to his people;[b]
the LORD blesses his people with peace.[c]

29:5 [u] Jdg 9:15 **29:6** [v] Ps 114:4 [w] Dt 3:9 **29:8** [x] Nu 13:26 **29:9** [y] Ps 26:8 **29:10** [z] Ge 6:17 [a] Ps 10:16 **29:11** [b] Ps 28:8 [c] Ps 37:11

Psalm 30[c]

A psalm. A song. For the dedication of the temple.[d] Of David.

[1]I will exalt you, LORD,
for you lifted me out of the depths
and did not let my enemies gloat over me.[d]
[2]LORD my God, I called to you for help,[e]
and you healed me.[f]
[3]You, LORD, brought me up from the realm of the dead;
you spared me from going down to the pit.[g]
[4]Sing the praises of the LORD, you his faithful people;[h]
praise his holy name.[i]
[5]For his anger[j] lasts only a moment,
but his favor lasts a lifetime;
weeping may stay for the night,
but rejoicing comes in the morning.[k]

30:1 [d] Ps 25:2; 28:9 **30:2** [e] Ps 88:13 [f] Ps 6:2 **30:3** [g] Ps 28:1; 86:13 **30:4** [h] Ps 149:1 [i] Ps 97:12 **30:5** [j] Ps 103:9 [k] 2Co 4:17

[a] *6* That is, Mount Hermon [b] *9* Or *LORD makes the deer give birth* [c] In Hebrew texts 30:1-12 is numbered 30:2-13. [d] Title: Or *palace*

29:5 *cedars of Lebanon.* These forested mountains were famous throughout the ancient Near East as the best source of stout timber for construction. Kings from Egypt to Mesopotamia would boast that they gathered lumber for building projects from faraway Lebanon. Tiglath-Pileser I claims to have marched to Mount Lebanon, where he cut down cedar beams for his temple-building projects. The venture to Lebanon by the Egyptian official Wenamun was prompted by his quest for great timber. Even David and Solomon looked to these forests as the best source of timber for the royal palace and Yahweh's temple (2Sa 5:11; 1Ki 5:6–9). In the Baal Cycle, cedars from Lebanon and Sirion are the materials for Baal's palace. Ps 29:9 speaks of the oaks twisting and the forests being stripped bare. These stalwart trees shatter before the power of God.

29:6 *Sirion.* Another name for Mount Hermon (Dt 3:9) in the mountain range immediately inland from the coastal mountains of Lebanon. Hence Lebanon and Sirion are coupled together poetically in both the Baal Cycle and here. At an elevation of 9,100 feet (2,775 meters), Sirion was among the highest mountains in the geographic vicinity of Israel. These mighty mountain ranges quake when God speaks, being likened to powerful young calves and oxen skipping about (cf. 114:4).

29:7 *lightning.* Commonly viewed as a divine weapon (v. 3; 18:12; 97:2–5). Baal was depicted in Canaanite art with a lightning bolt in his hand, but Ps 29 stresses that it is Yahweh who can strike with the power of lightning.

29:8 *Desert of Kadesh.* The most familiar reference to Kadesh in the OT is the southern desert site (Kadesh Barnea), where the Israelites camped during their wilderness journey in the Sinai peninsula (Nu 13:26; Dt 1:19,46). If this location is in view, then the imagery of Ps 29 tracks the storm from the mountains in the north to the desert regions south of Judah. However, another possible referent is the region near Qadesh north of Damascus on the Orontes River. This fits well with the other northern geographic references in Ps 29, and this possible location, "wilderness of Kadesh" (*mdbr kdsh*), is known from a Ugaritic text, fitting with the other allusions in the psalm to these traditions. In this case, the more general translation of the Hebrew word used in this verse (*midbar*, "wilderness") is in view.

29:10 *enthroned over the flood … as King.* A sculptured scene from the temple of Shamash on a tablet from the Neo-Babylonian king Nabu-apla-idinna shows Shamash, the sun-god, residing on a throne under a cosmic mountain and a number of wavy lines that are considered to represent the cosmic ocean. The scene is remarkably like Yahweh sitting enthroned over the flood (or better, the celestial sea, see note on 104:3). In contrast to the Hebrew word *tehom* (Ge 1:2), which represents the cosmic waters on the earth, this word, *mabbul*, represents the cosmic waters in the heavens, where rain comes from. In Ge 6–8 it is the *mabbul* that comes upon the earth in Noah's time. Shamshi-Adad V refers to the god Ninurta as the exalted lord who rides on the Deluge. The imagery of Ps 29 combines to express the majestic power of Yahweh, so, in conclusion, the psalmist returns to the scene of his heavenly court. The Hebrew word translated "temple" in v. 9 is the Hebrew word for a "palace," and when the palace happens to be that of a deity, it is a "temple." In the Baal Cycle, the victory over the cosmic waters earns for the god of the thunderstorm both kingship and the right to have a palace-temple

Yahweh's power not only exceeds that of the many "waters" (v. 3), his kingship over the flood ascribes to Yahweh the highest possible sovereignty. Having taken up royal residence in his temple, Yahweh himself is at rest. On this basis the psalmist expresses confidence that Yahweh can give peace to his people in the midst of any imaginable chaos (v. 11).

30:3 *spared me from going down to the pit.* In a Babylonian composition, the god Marduk is reported as bringing restoration to one of his followers, setting him on his feet and giving him life by rescuing him from the pit. See the articles "Death and Sheol," p. 833; "Death and the Underworld," p. 907.

[6]When I felt secure, I said,
"I will never be shaken."
[7]LORD, when you favored me,
you made my royal mountain[a]
stand firm;
but when you hid your face,[l]
I was dismayed.

[8]To you, LORD, I called;
to the Lord I cried for mercy:
[9]"What is gained if I am silenced,
if I go down to the pit?
Will the dust praise you?
Will it proclaim your faithfulness?[m]
[10]Hear, LORD, and be merciful
to me;
LORD, be my help."

[11]You turned my wailing into
dancing;
you removed my sackcloth and
clothed me with joy,[n]
[12]that my heart may sing your praises
and not be silent.
LORD my God, I will praise[o] you
forever.[p]

30:7 [l]Dt 31:17; Ps 104:29 **30:9** [m]Ps 6:5 **30:11** [n]Ps 4:7; Jer 31:4, 13 **30:12** [o]Ps 16:9 [p]Ps 44:8 **31:2** [q]Ps 18:2 **31:3** [r]Ps 18:2 [s]Ps 23:3

Psalm 31[b]

31:1-4pp — Ps 71:1-3

For the director of music. A psalm of David.

[1]In you, LORD, I have taken refuge;
let me never be put to shame;
deliver me in your righteousness.
[2]Turn your ear to me,
come quickly to my rescue;
be my rock of refuge,[q]
a strong fortress to save me.
[3]Since you are my rock and my fortress,[r]
for the sake of your name[s] lead and
guide me.

[a] 7 That is, Mount Zion [b] In Hebrew texts 31:1-24 is numbered 31:2-25.

30:9 *What is gained . . . ?* See note on 88:10.

PSALM 30:3

Death and the Underworld

In Egypt, as early as the fourth millennium BC, burial goods evidence belief in an afterlife. Funerary practices developed into elaborate customs of burial, accompanied by ongoing food offerings, to maintain an enjoyable life in the next world. At death, the individual stood before the god of the underworld, Osiris, and the confessions of the heart were weighed against the standard of justice (*maat*; see note on Ps 85:10). Failure of character resulted in torture, but one judged "true of voice" was admitted into a joyous afterlife. The Egyptian "Book of the Dead" consists of a series of magical spells buried with the deceased person to help him or her overcome obstacles to a successful transition to life in the underworld.

Mesopotamian belief was not so optimistic. Upon death, Mesopotamians thought that the individual became a sort of ghost, but there was no judgment and no joyful existence possible. The underworld was a gloomy "land of no return," partitioned from the land of the living by a series of gates and described in one text as a place with no light and only dust and clay for food. Other texts offer some hope for food and fresh water if provided by surviving family members in ongoing funerary rituals. But without proper burial and maintenance, the ghost was doomed to wander without rest. The Hittite conception was very similar. The ghosts of the dead descended to an underworld beneath the subterranean waters.

Ancient Israelites shared views of death and the underworld more in common with Mesopotamia than with Egypt. The afterlife was an uncertain state of existence as a shadowy image of the former, living self (*rephaim*, "shades" [ESV] or "spirits" [NIV] in Isa 14:9; 26:14; "the dead" in Job 26:5; Ps 88:10). This same term (Ugaritic *rp'um*) is used in Ugaritic texts for the deceased ancestors of kings who return from the underworld to celebrate royal banquets. But unlike the departed kings of Ugarit,

continued on next page

those designated by this term in the OT have no power or ability to return to the realm of the living (see note on 106:28). The realm of the dead, called "Sheol," was located in the lowermost region of the earth, below the subterranean waters (Job 26:5, hence "depths" in Ps 139:8) and at the root of the mountains (Dt 32:22; Jnh 2:2–6). Ugaritic texts refer to the "shades" as descending into the earth (Ugaritic *ʾars* = Hebrew *erets*). Death contrasts with the "land of the living" (Ps 27:13; 116:9). Because burial was associated with decomposition in an earthen grave, one finds metaphors such as "pit" (Hebrew *bor* in Ps 30:3; 88:4,6), "decay" (Hebrew *shahat* in Ps 16:10; 49:9) or "Destruction" (Hebrew *abaddon*, personified in Ps 88:11). In moments of most extreme distress, even the righteous despaired in fear, viewing death as a hopeless end (Job 17:10–16; Ps 88:3–5). ◆

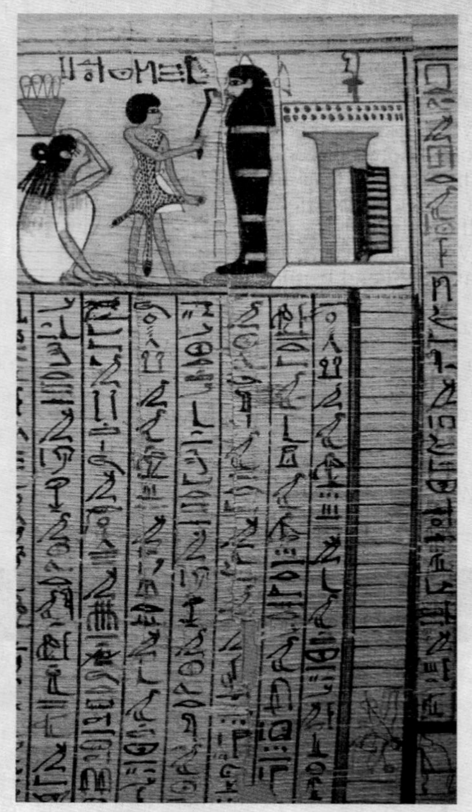

Gate to the ladder down into the underworld; from the Book of the Dead of the scribe Nebqed, Egypt, fourteenth century BC.

[4] Keep me free from the trap that is set
for me,
for you are my refuge.[t]
[5] Into your hands I commit my spirit;[u]
deliver me, LORD, my faithful God.

[6] I hate those who cling to worthless
idols;
as for me, I trust in the LORD.[v]
[7] I will be glad and rejoice in your love,
for you saw my affliction[w]
and knew the anguish[x] of my
soul.
[8] You have not given me into the hands[y]
of the enemy
but have set my feet in a spacious
place.

[9] Be merciful to me, LORD, for I am in
distress;
my eyes grow weak with sorrow,[z]
my soul and body with grief.
[10] My life is consumed by anguish
and my years by groaning;[a]
my strength fails because of my affliction,[a]
and my bones grow weak.[b]
[11] Because of all my enemies,
I am the utter contempt of my
neighbors[c]
and an object of dread to my closest
friends—
those who see me on the street flee
from me.

31:4 [t] Ps 25:15 **31:5** [u] Lk 23:46; Ac 7:59 **31:6** [v] Jnh 2:8 **31:7** [w] Ps 90:14 [x] Ps 10:14; Jn 10:27 **31:8** [y] Dt 32:30 **31:9** [z] Ps 6:7 **31:10** [a] Ps 13:2 [b] Ps 38:3; 39:11 **31:11** [c] Job 19:13; Ps 38:11; 64:8; Isa 53:4

[a] 10 Or *guilt*

31:6 *worthless idols.* See notes on 96:4–5; 135:15; see also the article "Making an Idol," p. 1010.
31:10 *my bones grow weak.* See note on 22:14.
31:11 *object of dread to my closest friends.* It is possible in cases of suffering, especially in a culture that associates such affliction with divine punishment, that even friends might withdraw. Whether or not this literally happened in each circumstance behind a psalm is not relevant, since expressions of this type became stereotypical language in psalms of suffering (cf. 41:5–6; 69:8; see the article "Honor-Shame Cultures," p. 902). In a classic example of the suffering worshiper in Mesopotamian texts, one describes how

[12]I am forgotten as though I were dead;[d]
I have become like broken pottery.
[13]For I hear many whispering,
"Terror on every side!"[e]
They conspire against me
and plot to take my life.[f]

[14]But I trust[g] in you, LORD;
I say, "You are my God."
[15]My times[h] are in your hands;
deliver me from the hands of my enemies,
from those who pursue me.
[16]Let your face shine[i] on your servant;
save me in your unfailing love.
[17]Let me not be put to shame,[j] LORD,
for I have cried out to you;
but let the wicked be put to shame
and be silent[k] in the realm of the dead.
[18]Let their lying lips[l] be silenced,
for with pride and contempt
they speak arrogantly[m] against the righteous.

[19]How abundant are the good things[n]
that you have stored up for those who fear you,
that you bestow in the sight of all,[o]
on those who take refuge in you.
[20]In the shelter of your presence you hide[p] them
from all human intrigues;[q]
you keep them safe in your dwelling
from accusing tongues.

[21]Praise be to the LORD,
for he showed me the wonders of his love[r]
when I was in a city under siege.[s]
[22]In my alarm[t] I said,
"I am cut off from your sight!"
Yet you heard my cry[u] for mercy
when I called to you for help.

[23]Love the LORD, all his faithful people![v]
The LORD preserves those who are true to him,[w]
but the proud he pays back[x] in full.
[24]Be strong and take heart,[y]
all you who hope in the LORD.

Psalm 32

Of David. A *maskil*.[a]

[1]Blessed is the one
whose transgressions are forgiven,
whose sins are covered.[z]
[2]Blessed is the one
whose sin the LORD does not count against them[a]
and in whose spirit is no deceit.[b]

[3]When I kept silent,
my bones wasted away[c]
through my groaning all day long.
[4]For day and night
your hand was heavy[d] on me;
my strength was sapped
as in the heat of summer.[b]

[5]Then I acknowledged my sin to you
and did not cover up my iniquity.
I said, "I will confess[e]
my transgressions[f] to the LORD."
And you forgave
the guilt of my sin.[g]

[6]Therefore let all the faithful pray to you
while you may be found;[h]
surely the rising of the mighty waters
will not reach them.[i]
[7]You are my hiding place;
you will protect me from trouble[j]
and surround me with songs of deliverance.[k]

[8]I will instruct[l] you and teach you in the way you should go;
I will counsel you with my loving eye on[m] you.

31:12 [d]Ps 88:4 **31:13** [e]Jer 20:3, 10; La 2:22 [f]Mt 27:1 **31:14** [g]Ps 140:6 **31:15** [h]Job 24:1; Ps 143:9 **31:16** [i]Nu 6:25; Ps 4:6 **31:17** [j]Ps 25:2-3 [k]Ps 115:17 **31:18** [l]Ps 120:2 [m]Ps 94:4 **31:19** [n]Ro 11:22 [o]Isa 64:4 **31:20** [p]Ps 27:5 [q]Job 5:21 **31:21** [r]Ps 17:7 [s]1Sa 23:7 **31:22** [t]Ps 116:11 [u]La 3:54 **31:23** [v]Ps 34:9 [w]Ps 145:20 [x]Ps 94:2 **31:24** [y]Ps 27:14 **32:1** [z]Ps 85:2 **32:2** [a]Ro 4:7-8*; 2Co 5:19 [b]Jn 1:47 **32:3** [c]Ps 31:10 **32:4** [d]Job 33:7 **32:5** [e]Pr 28:13 [f]Ps 103:12 [g]Lev 26:40 **32:6** [h]Ps 69:13; Isa 55:6 [i]Isa 43:2 **32:7** [j]Ps 9:9 [k]Ex 15:1 **32:8** [l]Ps 25:8 [m]Ps 33:18

[a] Title: Probably a literary or musical term [b] *4* The Hebrew has *Selah* (a word of uncertain meaning) here and at the end of verses 5 and 7.

his family and friends turned against him. Egyptian texts addressing the experience of suffering utilize the same motif, as illustrated in "The Dispute Between a Man and His Ba" ("Ba" is comparable to one's immaterial "soul"). In both Israel and the ancient Near East, a suffering person may lose friends because the friends assume he is suffering because he has angered a god—and no one wants to become collateral damage through associating with a recognized offender.

31:16 *Let your face shine.* See notes on 80:3,7,19; 84:11. The negative side of this image is expressed in v. 22 (see note on 13:1).

32:3 *my bones wasted away.* See note on 22:14.

32:4 *your hand was heavy on me.* While not all suffering is caused by divine discipline (see note on 38:2), Ps 32 addresses one such case. Mesopotamian laments often dwell on this theme. In one poem, the worshiper recognizes the god Marduk's punishment and states: "Heavy was his hand upon me." Similarly, in an Egyptian hymn dating about 1250 BC, the worshiper notes that even as he lay on his deathbed because of Amun's wrath, he looked for the god's mercy. A royal Hittite prayer, perhaps a generic template for such laments, appeals to the sun-god to reveal the sin that the worshiper presumes to be the cause of his illness and to be merciful.

32:6 *mighty waters.* Carries overtones of chaos (see the article "Chaos Monsters," p. 953) and could symbolize God's acts of judgment (Eze 26:19).

32:8 *I will instruct you.* It is possible that these are God's words to the chastened psalmist. However, in psalms that celebrate deliverance from trial, it is common to find words of instruction by the psalmist to the congregation, since others can learn through the psalmist's experience (cf. 25:8–15; 34:11; 51:13). This feature is illustrated in Mesopotamian texts as well. The suffering worshiper in the "Poem of the Righteous Sufferer" proclaims that he

[9]Do not be like the horse or the mule,
which have no understanding
but must be controlled by bit and bridle[n]
or they will not come to you.
[10]Many are the woes of the wicked,[o]
but the LORD's unfailing love
surrounds the one who trusts[p] in him.

[11]Rejoice in the LORD[q] and be glad, you righteous;
sing, all you who are upright in heart!

Psalm 33

[1]Sing joyfully to the LORD, you righteous;
it is fitting[r] for the upright[s] to praise him.
[2]Praise the LORD with the harp;
make music to him on the ten-stringed lyre.[t]
[3]Sing to him a new song;[u]
play skillfully, and shout for joy.
[4]For the word of the LORD is right[v] and true;
he is faithful in all he does.
[5]The LORD loves righteousness and justice;[w]
the earth is full of his unfailing love.[x]
[6]By the word[y] of the LORD the heavens were made,
their starry host by the breath of his mouth.
[7]He gathers the waters of the sea into jars[a];
he puts the deep into storehouses.
[8]Let all the earth fear the LORD;
let all the people of the world revere him.[z]
[9]For he spoke, and it came to be;
he commanded,[a] and it stood firm.
[10]The LORD foils the plans of the nations;[b]
he thwarts the purposes of the peoples.
[11]But the plans of the LORD stand firm forever,
the purposes[c] of his heart through all generations.

[12]Blessed is the nation whose God is the LORD,[d]
the people he chose[e] for his inheritance.
[13]From heaven the LORD looks down
and sees all mankind;[f]
[14]from his dwelling place[g] he watches
all who live on earth—
[15]he who forms[h] the hearts of all,
who considers everything they do.[i]
[16]No king is saved by the size of his army;[j]
no warrior escapes by his great strength.
[17]A horse[k] is a vain hope for deliverance;
despite all its great strength it cannot save.
[18]But the eyes[l] of the LORD are on those who fear him,
on those whose hope is in his unfailing love,[m]
[19]to deliver them from death
and keep them alive in famine.[n]

[20]We wait[o] in hope for the LORD;
he is our help and our shield.
[21]In him our hearts rejoice,[p]
for we trust in his holy name.
[22]May your unfailing love be with us, LORD,
even as we put our hope in you.

Psalm 34[b,c]

Of David. When he pretended to be insane before Abimelek, who drove him away, and he left.

[1]I will extol the LORD at all times;[q]
his praise will always be on my lips.
[2]I will glory[r] in the LORD;
let the afflicted hear and rejoice.[s]
[3]Glorify the LORD with me;
let us exalt[t] his name together.
[4]I sought the LORD,[u] and he answered me;
he delivered me from all my fears.
[5]Those who look to him are radiant;[v]
their faces are never covered with shame.[w]

32:9 [n]Pr 26:3 **32:10** [o]Ro 2:9 [p]Pr 16:20 **32:11** [q]Ps 64:10 **33:1** [r]Ps 147:1 [s]Ps 32:11 **33:2** [t]Ps 92:3 **33:3** [u]Ps 96:1 **33:4** [v]Ps 19:8 **33:5** [w]Ps 11:7 [x]Ps 119:64 **33:6** [y]Heb 11:3 **33:8** [z]Ps 67:7; 96:9 **33:9** [a]Ge 1:3; Ps 148:5 **33:10** [b]Isa 8:10 **33:11** [c]Job 23:13 **33:12** [d]Ps 144:15 [e]Ex 19:5; Dt 7:6 **33:13** [f]Job 28:24; Ps 11:4 **33:14** [g]1Ki 8:39 **33:15** [h]Job 10:8 [i]Jer 32:19 **33:16** [j]Ps 44:6 **33:17** [k]Ps 20:7; Pr 21:31 **33:18** [l]Job 36:7; Ps 34:15 [m]Ps 147:11 **33:19** [n]Job 5:20 **33:20** [o]Ps 130:6 **33:21** [p]Zec 10:7; Jn 16:22 **34:1** [q]Ps 71:6; Eph 5:20 **34:2** [r]Jer 9:24; 1Co 1:31 [s]Ps 119:74 **34:3** [t]Lk 1:46 **34:4** [u]Mt 7:7 **34:5** [v]Ps 36:9 [w]Ps 25:3

[a] *7* Or *sea as into a heap* [b] This psalm is an acrostic poem, the verses of which begin with the successive letters of the Hebrew alphabet. [c] In Hebrew texts 34:1-22 is numbered 34:2-23.

will teach people of the kindness of Marduk, who had responded to his prayer and restored him to favor. Later in the poem the speaker advises that anyone who has done wrong should learn from him.
33:2 *harp ... lyre.* See the articles "Lyre," p. 488; "Music and Musicians," p. 524.
33:8 *Let all the earth fear.* A similar logic calling for awesome fear of the Creator is illustrated regarding the Egyptian god Ptah, who is feared as a god with absolute control and whose utterances cannot be bypassed. Because of the creative might of Yahweh, the psalmist insists that not only Israel but all the world must worship him.
33:16 – 17 *No king is saved by the size of his army ... A horse ... cannot save.* See note on 20:7.
33:19 *keep them alive.* For ancient Near Easterners, life and death were in the hands of their gods. For example, the Egyptian creator-god Ptah had power to grant life to the one who followed the moral order and to assign death to the wrongdoer.
34:5 *radiant ... shame.* The metaphor of seeing God

[6]This poor man called, and the LORD
heard him;
he saved him out of all his troubles.
[7]The angel of the LORD[x] encamps
around those who fear him,
and he delivers them.

[8]Taste and see that the LORD is good;[y]
blessed is the one who takes refuge[z]
in him.
[9]Fear the LORD, you his holy people,
for those who fear him lack
nothing.[a]
[10]The lions may grow weak and hungry,
but those who seek the LORD lack no
good thing.[b]
[11]Come, my children, listen to me;
I will teach you[c] the fear of the LORD.
[12]Whoever of you loves life[d]
and desires to see many good days,
[13]keep your tongue from evil
and your lips from telling lies.[e]
[14]Turn from evil and do good;[f]
seek peace[g] and pursue it.

[15]The eyes of the LORD[h] are on the
righteous,[i]
and his ears are attentive to their cry;
[16]but the face of the LORD is against[j]
those who do evil,[k]
to blot out their name[l] from the
earth.

[17]The righteous cry out, and the LORD
hears[m] them;
he delivers them from all their
troubles.
[18]The LORD is close[n] to the
brokenhearted[o]
and saves those who are crushed in
spirit.

[19]The righteous person may have many
troubles,[p]
but the LORD delivers him from them
all;[q]
[20]he protects all his bones,
not one of them will be broken.[r]

[21]Evil will slay the wicked;[s]
the foes of the righteous will be
condemned.

34:7 [x]2Ki 6:17; Da 6:22 **34:8** [y]1Pe 2:3 [z]Ps 2:12 **34:9** [a]Ps 23:1 **34:10** [b]Ps 84:11 **34:11** [c]Ps 32:8 **34:12** [d]1Pe 3:10 **34:13** [e]1Pe 2:22 **34:14** [f]Ps 37:27 [g]Heb 12:14 **34:15** [h]Ps 33:18 [i]Job 36:7 **34:16** [j]Lev 17:10; Jer 44:11 [k]1Pe 3:10-12* [l]Pr 10:7 **34:17** [m]Ps 145:19 **34:18** [n]Ps 145:18 [o]Isa 57:15 **34:19** [p]ver 17 [q]ver 4,6; Pr 24:16 **34:20** [r]Jn 19:36* **34:21** [s]Ps 94:23

34:22 [t]1Ki 1:29; Ps 71:23 **35:1** [u]Ps 43:1 **35:2** [v]Ps 62:2 **35:4** [w]Ps 70:2 **35:5** [x]Job 21:18; Ps 1:4; Isa 29:5 **35:8** [y]1Th 5:3 [z]Ps 9:15 **35:9** [a]Lk 1:47 [b]Isa 61:10 **35:10** [c]Ex 15:11 [d]Ps 18:17 [e]Ps 37:14 **35:11** [f]Ps 27:12

[22]The LORD will rescue[t] his servants;
no one who takes refuge in him will
be condemned.

Psalm 35

Of David.

[1]Contend, LORD, with those who
contend with me;
fight[u] against those who fight
against me.
[2]Take up shield and armor;
arise[v] and come to my aid.
[3]Brandish spear and javelin[a]
against those who pursue me.
Say to me,
"I am your salvation."

[4]May those who seek my life
be disgraced[w] and put to shame;
may those who plot my ruin
be turned back in dismay.
[5]May they be like chaff[x] before the
wind,
with the angel of the LORD driving
them away;
[6]may their path be dark and slippery,
with the angel of the LORD pursuing
them.

[7]Since they hid their net for me without
cause
and without cause dug a pit for me,
[8]may ruin overtake them by surprise —[y]
may the net they hid entangle them,
may they fall into the pit,[z] to their
ruin.
[9]Then my soul will rejoice[a] in the LORD
and delight in his salvation.[b]
[10]My whole being will exclaim,
"Who is like you,[c] LORD?
You rescue the poor from those too
strong[d] for them,
the poor and needy[e] from those who
rob them."

[11]Ruthless witnesses[f] come forward;
they question me on things I know
nothing about.

[a] 3 Or *and block the way*

draws upon the feelings associated with basking in the sun (see notes on 4:6; 42:2; 67:1; 80:3,7,19; 84:11). Conversely, shame results in a fallen countenance (see note on 25:2).
35:2 *shield and armor.* They represent the two extremes in personal defensive equipment. Respectively, they refer to a small, round shield and a large, full-length, body shield; the latter most likely carried by an aide.
35:3 *spear and javelin.* They represent the full range of offensive weaponry (cf. v. 2 and note). The Hebrew root (*sgr*) translated "javelin" occurs nowhere else as a weapon in the OT. Herodotus refers to a Scythian double axe (Greek *sagaris*), and the Dead Sea Scrolls use the root for the handle of a lance. In the latter case, the text simply speaks of two uses for the same piece of equipment. The long wooden handle can be used to parry and deliver blows as a staff, while the pointed end is used for the finishing blow. There are numerous depictions of these and other Iron Age pieces of military equipment on wall reliefs at the Assyrian cities of Nineveh and Calah (Nimrud).
35:5 *chaff.* Cut grain stalks were gathered on a threshing floor for crushing in order to separate the kernels of grain from the husk and stalk (chaff). After threshing, the pile was tossed into the air, allowing the denser grain to drop to the threshing floor and the lighter chaff to blow away with the wind.
35:7 *net.* See notes on 124:7; 140:5.

12 They repay me evil for good[g]
and leave me like one bereaved.
13 Yet when they were ill, I put on sackcloth
and humbled myself with fasting.[h]
When my prayers returned to me unanswered,
14 I went about mourning
as though for my friend or brother.
I bowed my head in grief
as though weeping for my mother.
15 But when I stumbled, they gathered in glee;
assailants gathered against me
without my knowledge.
They slandered[i] me without ceasing.
16 Like the ungodly they maliciously mocked;[a]
they gnashed their teeth[j] at me.
17 How long,[k] Lord, will you look on?
Rescue me from their ravages,
my precious life[l] from these lions.
18 I will give you thanks in the great assembly;[m]
among the throngs I will praise you.[n]
19 Do not let those gloat over me
who are my enemies without cause;
do not let those who hate me without reason[o]
maliciously wink the eye.[p]
20 They do not speak peaceably,
but devise false accusations
against those who live quietly in the land.
21 They sneer[q] at me and say, "Aha! Aha![r]
With our own eyes we have seen it."
22 LORD, you have seen[s] this; do not be silent.
Do not be far[t] from me, Lord.
23 Awake,[u] and rise to my defense!
Contend for me, my God and Lord.
24 Vindicate me in your righteousness, LORD my God;
do not let them gloat over me.
25 Do not let them think, "Aha, just what we wanted!"
or say, "We have swallowed him up."[v]

26 May all who gloat over my distress
be put to shame[w] and confusion;
may all who exalt themselves over me[x]
be clothed with shame and disgrace.
27 May those who delight in my vindication[y]
shout for joy[z] and gladness;
may they always say, "The LORD be exalted,
who delights[a] in the well-being of his servant."
28 My tongue will proclaim your righteousness,[b]
your praises all day long.

Psalm 36[b]

For the director of music. Of David the servant of the LORD.

1 I have a message from God in my heart
concerning the sinfulness of the wicked:[c]
There is no fear of God
before their eyes.[c]
2 In their own eyes they flatter themselves
too much to detect or hate their sin.
3 The words of their mouths[d] are wicked and deceitful;
they fail to act wisely[e] or do good.[f]
4 Even on their beds they plot evil;[g]
they commit themselves to a sinful course[h]
and do not reject what is wrong.[i]
5 Your love, LORD, reaches to the heavens,
your faithfulness to the skies.
6 Your righteousness is like the highest mountains,
your justice like the great deep.[j]
You, LORD, preserve both people and animals.
7 How priceless is your unfailing love, O God!
People take refuge in the shadow of your wings.[k]
8 They feast on the abundance of your house;[l]
you give them drink from your river[m] of delights.

35:12 [g] Jn 10:32 **35:13** [h] Job 30:25; Ps 69:10 **35:15** [i] Job 30:1,8 **35:16** [j] Job 16:9; La 2:16 **35:17** [k] Hab 1:13 [l] Ps 22:20 **35:18** [m] Ps 22:25 [n] Ps 22:22 **35:19** [o] Ps 38:19; 69:4; Jn 15:25* [p] Ps 13:4; Pr 6:13 **35:21** [q] Ps 22:13 [r] Ps 40:15 **35:22** [s] Ex 3:7 [t] Ps 10:1; 28:1 **35:23** [u] Ps 44:23 **35:25** [v] La 2:16 **35:26** [w] Ps 40:14; 109:29 [x] Ps 38:16 **35:27** [y] Ps 9:4 [z] Ps 32:11 [a] Ps 40:16; 147:11 **35:28** [b] Ps 51:14 **36:1** [c] Ro 3:18* **36:3** [d] Ps 10:7 [e] Ps 94:8 [f] Jer 4:22 **36:4** [g] Pr 4:16; Mic 2:1 [h] Isa 65:2 [i] Ps 52:3; Ro 12:9 **36:6** [j] Job 11:8; Ps 77:19; Ro 11:33 **36:7** [k] Ru 2:12; Ps 17:8 **36:8** [l] Ps 65:4 [m] Job 20:17; Rev 22:1

[a] 16 Septuagint; Hebrew may mean *Like an ungodly circle of mockers,* [b] In Hebrew texts 36:1-12 is numbered 36:2-13. [c] 1 Or *A message from God: The transgression of the wicked / resides in their hearts.*

36:7 *shadow of your wings.* This image can convey two ideas: (1) Swift freedom of motion in the heavenly realm, and so it is a fitting image for deities and angelic creatures. Ugaritic myth portrays the goddess Anat as raising her wings for flight. (2) The protective covering offered by the wings of a mother bird—the image used in this psalm. Assyrian prophets used this image to promise divine protection to the king. In the context of physical danger from enemies, the goddess Ishtar encourages Esarhaddon by reminding him that she raised him between her wings, and would therefore assure his success. Egyptian art also portrays the king surrounded by the protective covering of a deity's wings.

36:8 *river of delights.* Since the word translated "delights" has the same root letters as Eden, there is possibly a reference to the waters flowing out of paradise in this phrase. The association between ancient Near Eastern temples and spring waters is well attested. In fact, some temples

[9]For with you is the fountain of life;[n]
in your light[o] we see light.
[10]Continue your love to those who know
you,
your righteousness to the upright in
heart.
[11]May the foot of the proud not come
against me,
nor the hand of the wicked drive me
away.
[12]See how the evildoers lie fallen —
thrown down, not able to rise![p]

Psalm 37[a]

Of David.

[1]Do not fret because of those who are
evil
or be envious[q] of those who do
wrong;[r]
[2]for like the grass they will soon wither,
like green plants they will soon die
away.[s]
[3]Trust in the LORD and do good;
dwell in the land[t] and enjoy safe
pasture.[u]
[4]Take delight[v] in the LORD,
and he will give you the desires of
your heart.

[5]Commit your way to the LORD;
trust in him[w] and he will do this:
[6]He will make your righteous reward[x]
shine like the dawn,[y]
your vindication like the noonday
sun.

[7]Be still[z] before the LORD
and wait patiently[a] for him;
do not fret when people succeed in
their ways,
when they carry out their wicked
schemes.

[8]Refrain from anger[b] and turn from
wrath;
do not fret — it leads only to evil.
[9]For those who are evil will be
destroyed,
but those who hope in the LORD will
inherit the land.[c]

[10]A little while, and the wicked will be
no more;[d]
though you look for them, they will
not be found.
[11]But the meek will inherit the land[e]
and enjoy peace and prosperity.

[12]The wicked plot against the righteous
and gnash their teeth[f] at them;
[13]but the Lord laughs at the wicked,
for he knows their day is coming.[g]

[14]The wicked draw the sword
and bend the bow[h]
to bring down the poor and needy,[i]
to slay those whose ways are
upright.
[15]But their swords will pierce their own
hearts,[j]
and their bows will be broken.

[16]Better the little that the righteous have
than the wealth[k] of many wicked;
[17]for the power of the wicked will be
broken,[l]
but the LORD upholds the righteous.

[18]The blameless spend their days under
the LORD's care,[m]
and their inheritance will endure
forever.
[19]In times of disaster they will not wither;
in days of famine they will enjoy
plenty.

[20]But the wicked will perish:
Though the LORD's enemies are like
the flowers of the field,
they will be consumed, they will go
up in smoke.[n]

[21]The wicked borrow and do not repay,
but the righteous give generously;[o]

36:9 [n] Jer 2:13 [o] 1Pe 2:9 **36:12** [p] Ps 140:10 **37:1** [q] Pr 23:17-18 [r] Ps 73:3 **37:2** [s] Ps 90:6 **37:3** [t] Dt 30:20 [u] Isa 40:11; Jn 10:9 **37:4** [v] Isa 58:14 **37:5** [w] Ps 4:5; Ps 55:22; Pr 16:3; 1Pe 5:7 **37:6** [x] Mic 7:9 [y] Job 11:17 **37:7** [z] Ps 62:5; La 3:26 [a] Ps 40:1 **37:8** [b] Eph 4:31; Col 3:8 **37:9** [c] Isa 57:13; 60:21 **37:10** [d] Job 7:10; 24:24 **37:11** [e] Mt 5:5 **37:12** [f] Ps 35:16 **37:13** [g] 1Sa 26:10; Ps 2:4 **37:14** [h] Ps 11:2 [i] Ps 35:10 **37:15** [j] Ps 9:16 **37:16** [k] Pr 15:16 **37:17** [l] Job 38:15; Ps 10:15 **37:18** [m] Ps 1:6 **37:20** [n] Ps 102:3 **37:21** [o] Ps 112:5

[a] This psalm is an acrostic poem, the stanzas of which begin with the successive letters of the Hebrew alphabet.

in Mesopotamia, Egypt and in the Ugaritic Baal Cycle were considered to have been founded upon springs (likened to the primeval waters), which sometimes flowed from the building itself. This would explain the parallel between God's house in the first part of the verse and these rivers (Eze 47).
36:9 *fountain of life.* See note on 87:7.
37:3 – 4 These verses echo the thought of Pr 3:5 – 6. The foundational importance of this wisdom theme in Near Eastern thought is highlighted by the fact that a comparable proverb was chosen for the sole text of a Mesopotamian cylinder seal (used by a private individual to "sign" documents and mark ownership). The owner expresses that he conscientiously sought the god and that such an attitude will mean that he will lack for nothing.
37:4 *desires of your heart.* In Akkadian texts, the attaining of one's desires concerns receiving a favorable omen concerning either intended activities or needs, such as illness or oppression, from which one seeks deliverance. One text reports that when the individual prayed to the gods he was granted his desire. If the Israelite concept has any similarity, the desire referred to here is not just any desire, but particularly the desire that concerns the psalmist in this prayer (which is articulated in v. 6; see 20:4, where the context is a request for one's plans for relieving distress to succeed).
37:7 *Be still.* See note on 46:10.
37:16 This common advice (cf. Pr 15:16; 16:8) is reflected in the Egyptian "Instruction of Amenemope": "Better is a bushel given you by the god, than five thousand through wrongdoing."

[22]those the LORD blesses will inherit the land,
but those he curses[p] will be destroyed.

[23]The LORD makes firm the steps[q]
of the one who delights[r] in him;
[24]though he may stumble, he will not fall,[s]
for the LORD upholds[t] him with his hand.

[25]I was young and now I am old,
yet I have never seen the righteous forsaken[u]
or their children begging bread.
[26]They are always generous and lend freely;
their children will be a blessing.[a][v]
[27]Turn from evil and do good;[w]
then you will dwell in the land forever.
[28]For the LORD loves the just
and will not forsake his faithful ones.

Wrongdoers will be completely destroyed[b];
the offspring of the wicked will perish.[x]
[29]The righteous will inherit the land[y]
and dwell in it forever.

[30]The mouths of the righteous utter wisdom,
and their tongues speak what is just.
[31]The law of their God is in their hearts;[z]
their feet do not slip.[a]

[32]The wicked lie in wait[b] for the righteous,
intent on putting them to death;
[33]but the LORD will not leave them in the power of the wicked
or let them be condemned when brought to trial.[c]

[34]Hope in the LORD[d]
and keep his way.
He will exalt you to inherit the land;
when the wicked are destroyed, you will see[e] it.

[35]I have seen a wicked and ruthless man
flourishing[f] like a luxuriant native tree,
[36]but he soon passed away and was no more;
though I looked for him, he could not be found.[g]

[37]Consider the blameless, observe the upright;
a future awaits those who seek peace.[c][h]
[38]But all sinners will be destroyed;
there will be no future[d] for the wicked.[i]

[39]The salvation[j] of the righteous comes from the LORD;
he is their stronghold in time of trouble.[k]
[40]The LORD helps[l] them and delivers[m] them;
he delivers them from the wicked and saves them,
because they take refuge in him.

Psalm 38[e]

A psalm of David. A petition.

[1]LORD, do not rebuke me in your anger
or discipline me in your wrath.[n]
[2]Your arrows[o] have pierced me,
and your hand has come down on me.

37:22 [p]Job 5:3; Pr 3:33 **37:23** [q]1Sa 2:9 [r]Ps 147:11 **37:24** [s]Pr 24:16 [t]Ps 145:14; 147:6 **37:25** [u]Heb 13:5 **37:26** [v]Ps 147:13 **37:27** [w]Ps 34:14 **37:28** [x]Ps 21:10; Isa 14:20 **37:29** [y]ver 9; Pr 2:21 **37:31** [z]Dt 6:6; Ps 40:8; Isa 51:7 [a]ver 23 **37:32** [b]Ps 10:8 **37:33** [c]Ps 109:31; 2Pe 2:9 **37:34** [d]Ps 27:14 [e]Ps 52:6 **37:35** [f]Job 5:3 **37:36** [g]Job 20:5 **37:37** [h]Isa 57:1-2 **37:38** [i]Ps 1:4 **37:39** [j]Ps 3:8 [k]Ps 9:9 **37:40** [l]1Ch 5:20 [m]Isa 31:5 **38:1** [n]Ps 6:1 **38:2** [o]Job 6:4; Ps 32:4

[a] 26 Or *freely; / the names of their children will be used in blessings* (see Gen. 48:20); or *freely; / others will see that their children are blessed* [b] 28 See Septuagint; Hebrew *They will be protected forever* [c] 37 Or *upright; / those who seek peace will have posterity* [d] 38 Or *posterity* [e] In Hebrew texts 38:1-22 is numbered 38:2-23.

37:28 *offspring ... will perish.* In ancient Near Eastern culture, a fate worse than death was to witness the tragic death of one's children. This concept is more than just an extension of the natural feelings one has toward one's offspring. The most meaningful afterlife a person had in the ancient world was found in the idea that their line continued in the land of the living. In that way, the deceased not only joined the community of the ancestors that had died, but, more important, continued to have a place in the community of descendants that survived. Community extended beyond the land of the living. A curse on an Aramaic tomb inscription warns that the offspring of anyone disturbing the deceased would perish. Zedekiah's fate was aggravated by the slaughter of his sons before his eyes (2Ki 25:7).

37:34 *Hope in the LORD.* This admonition is based upon trust that God will judge the wicked, and therefore personal vengeance is wrong. This thought lies behind the Egyptian proverb stating that a person is better off not to take matters into his own hand but to wait and hope and see how his god acts on his behalf. Mesopotamian wisdom warns that the speaker of evil will be accountable to Shamash (the god of justice). Nevertheless, vengeance is differentiated from justice. The gods carried out both, and humans were responsible for executing justice, but were not to carry out vengeance.

37:35 – 36 *flourishing like a luxuriant native tree, but he soon passed away.* Egyptian wisdom observed the temporary success of evil men using the same metaphor when it described an angry worshiper in the temple as like a tree growing indoors. It may flourish for a brief time, but then will be destroyed.

38:2 *your hand ... on me.* The ancients did not assume that all illness was personal punishment by the gods. For example, a letter from an advisor to the Assyrian king Esarhaddon encourages the king that his illness is not due

3 Because of your wrath there is no
health in my body;
there is no soundness in my bones[p]
because of my sin.
4 My guilt has overwhelmed me
like a burden too heavy to bear.[q]

5 My wounds fester and are loathsome
because of my sinful folly.[r]
6 I am bowed down and brought very
low;
all day long I go about mourning.[s]
7 My back is filled with searing pain;[t]
there is no health in my body.
8 I am feeble and utterly crushed;
I groan[u] in anguish of heart.

9 All my longings lie open before you,
Lord;
my sighing[v] is not hidden from you.
10 My heart pounds, my strength fails[w]
me;
even the light has gone from my
eyes.[x]
11 My friends and companions avoid me
because of my wounds;[y]
my neighbors stay far away.
12 Those who want to kill me set their
traps,[z]
those who would harm me talk of
my ruin;[a]
all day long they scheme and lie.[b]

13 I am like the deaf, who cannot hear,
like the mute, who cannot speak;
14 I have become like one who does not
hear,
whose mouth can offer no reply.
15 LORD, I wait[c] for you;
you will answer,[d] Lord my God.
16 For I said, "Do not let them gloat[e]
or exalt themselves over me when
my feet slip."[f]

17 For I am about to fall,
and my pain is ever with me.
18 I confess my iniquity;[g]
I am troubled by my sin.
19 Many have become my enemies[h]
without cause[a];
those who hate me without reason[i]
are numerous.
20 Those who repay my good with evil[j]
lodge accusations against me,
though I seek only to do what is
good.

21 LORD, do not forsake me;
do not be far[k] from me, my God.
22 Come quickly to help me,[l]
my Lord and my Savior.[m]

Psalm 39[b]

For the director of music. For Jeduthun.
A psalm of David.

1 I said, "I will watch my ways[n]
and keep my tongue from sin;[o]
I will put a muzzle on my mouth
while in the presence of the
wicked."
2 So I remained utterly silent,[p]
not even saying anything good.
But my anguish increased;
3 my heart grew hot within me.
While I meditated, the fire burned;
then I spoke with my tongue:

4 "Show me, LORD, my life's end
and the number of my days;[q]
let me know how fleeting my life is.[r]
5 You have made my days[s] a mere
handbreadth;
the span of my years is as nothing
before you.
Everyone is but a breath,[t]
even those who seem secure.[c]

6 "Surely everyone goes around like a
mere phantom;[u]
in vain they rush about,[v] heaping up
wealth
without knowing whose it will
finally be.[w]

7 "But now, Lord, what do I look for?
My hope is in you.[x]
8 Save me[y] from all my transgressions;[z]
do not make me the scorn of fools.

[a] *19* One Dead Sea Scrolls manuscript; Masoretic Text *my vigorous enemies* [b] In Hebrew texts 39:1-13 is numbered 39:2-14. [c] *5* The Hebrew has *Selah* (a word of uncertain meaning) here and at the end of verse 11.

38:3 [p] Ps 6:2; Isa 1:6 **38:4** [q] Ezr 9:6 **38:5** [r] Ps 69:5 **38:6** [s] Job 30:28; Ps 35:14; 42:9 **38:7** [t] Ps 102:3 **38:8** [u] Ps 22:1 **38:9** [v] Job 3:24; Ps 6:6; 10:17 **38:10** [w] Ps 31:10 [x] Ps 6:7 **38:11** [y] Ps 31:11 **38:12** [z] Ps 140:5 [a] Ps 35:4; 54:3 [b] Ps 35:20 **38:15** [c] Ps 39:7 [d] Ps 17:6 **38:16** [e] Ps 35:26 [f] Ps 13:4 **38:18** [g] Ps 32:5 **38:19** [h] Ps 18:17 [i] Ps 35:19 **38:20** [j] Ps 35:12; 1Jn 3:12 **38:21** [k] Ps 35:22 **38:22** [l] Ps 40:13 [m] Ps 27:1 **39:1** [n] 1Ki 2:4 [o] Job 2:10; Jas 3:2 **39:2** [p] Ps 38:13 **39:4** [q] Ps 90:12 [r] Ps 103:14 **39:5** [s] Ps 89:45 [t] Ps 62:9 **39:6** [u] 1Pe 1:24 [v] Ps 127:2 [w] Lk 12:20 **39:7** [x] Ps 38:15 **39:8** [y] Ps 51:9 [z] Ps 44:13

to divine wrath but is only a disease of the season that many others are also suffering and from which all have recovered. On a different occasion, however, an advisor identifies the king's illness as the work of the gods. However, here the psalmist is aware that the cause is divine discipline (see notes on 32:4; 91:3). Israelites thought about illness in much the same way as their neighbors as they sought balance between what we would call natural or supernatural causes.

38:3 *no health.* Physical illness stemming from divine discipline is a common theme in Biblical psalms as well as in ancient Mesopotamian laments. Ps 38 is perhaps the most descriptive of the psalms in terms of detailed physical symptoms. However, the language of physical suffering is so stereotypical that it is hazardous to guess specific clinical diseases. Some symptoms are closely associated with mental distress. The ancients were not trying to identify the pathological origin of symptoms. For example, a letter between an Assyrian king and his advisor describes a fever as one that lingers in the bones. This description is true to the experience of bodily aches and pains from fever. The general nature of these descriptions allows the poems to be used for a wide range of experiences by a later worshiper, either ancient or modern.

39:4 *number of my days.* See note on 139:16.

[9]I was silent; I would not open my mouth,[a]
for you are the one who has done this.
[10]Remove your scourge from me;
I am overcome by the blow of your hand.[b]
[11]When you rebuke[c] and discipline anyone for their sin,
you consume their wealth like a moth[d] —
surely everyone is but a breath.

[12]"Hear my prayer, LORD,
listen to my cry for help;
do not be deaf to my weeping.
I dwell with you as a foreigner,[e]
a stranger,[f] as all my ancestors were.
[13]Look away from me, that I may enjoy life again
before I depart and am no more."[g]

Psalm 40[a]

40:13-17pp — Ps 70:1-5

For the director of music. Of David. A psalm.

[1]I waited patiently[h] for the LORD;
he turned to me and heard my cry.[i]
[2]He lifted me out of the slimy pit,
out of the mud and mire;[j]
he set my feet on a rock[k]
and gave me a firm place to stand.
[3]He put a new song[l] in my mouth,
a hymn of praise to our God.
Many will see and fear the LORD
and put their trust in him.

[4]Blessed is the one[m]
who trusts in the LORD,[n]
who does not look to the proud,
to those who turn aside to false gods.[b]
[5]Many, LORD my God,
are the wonders[o] you have done,
the things you planned for us.
None can compare[p] with you;
were I to speak and tell of your deeds,
they would be too many to declare.

[6]Sacrifice and offering you did not desire —[q]
but my ears you have opened[c] —
burnt offerings[r] and sin offerings[d]
you did not require.
[7]Then I said, "Here I am, I have come —
it is written about me in the scroll.[e]
[8]I desire to do your will,[s] my God;
your law is within my heart."[t]

[9]I proclaim your saving acts in the great assembly;[u]
I do not seal my lips, LORD,
as you know.[v]
[10]I do not hide your righteousness in my heart;
I speak of your faithfulness[w] and your saving help.
I do not conceal your love and your faithfulness
from the great assembly.[x]

[11]Do not withhold your mercy from me, LORD;
may your love[y] and faithfulness[z] always protect me.
[12]For troubles[a] without number surround me;
my sins have overtaken me, and I cannot see.[b]
They are more than the hairs of my head,[c]
and my heart fails[d] within me.
[13]Be pleased to save me, LORD;
come quickly, LORD, to help me.[e]

[14]May all who want to take my life
be put to shame and confusion;
may all who desire my ruin[f]
be turned back in disgrace.
[15]May those who say to me, "Aha! Aha!"
be appalled at their own shame.
[16]But may all who seek you
rejoice and be glad in you;
may those who long for your saving help always say,
"The LORD is great!"[g]

[17]But as for me, I am poor and needy;
may the Lord think of me.
You are my help and my deliverer;
you are my God, do not delay.[h]

39:9 [a] Job 2:10 **39:10** [b] Job 9:34; Ps 32:4 **39:11** [c] 2Pe 2:16 [d] Job 13:28 **39:12** [e] 1Pe 2:11 [f] Heb 11:13 **39:13** [g] Job 10:21; 14:10 **40:1** [h] Ps 27:14 [i] Ps 34:15 **40:2** [j] Ps 69:14 [k] Ps 27:5 **40:3** [l] Ps 33:3 **40:4** [m] Ps 34:8 [n] Ps 84:12 **40:5** [o] Ps 136:4 [p] Ps 139:18; Isa 55:8 **40:6** [q] 1Sa 15:22; Am 5:22 [r] Isa 1:11 **40:8** [s] Jn 4:34 [t] Ps 37:31 **40:9** [u] Ps 22:25 [v] Jos 22:22; Ps 119:13 **40:10** [w] Ps 89:1 [x] Ac 20:20 **40:11** [y] Pr 20:28 [z] Ps 43:3 **40:12** [a] Ps 116:3 [b] Ps 38:4 [c] Ps 69:4 [d] Ps 73:26 **40:13** [e] Ps 70:1 **40:14** [f] Ps 35:4 **40:16** [g] Ps 35:27 **40:17** [h] Ps 70:5

[a] In Hebrew texts 40:1-17 is numbered 40:2-18. [b] 4 Or *to lies* [c] 6 Hebrew; some Septuagint manuscripts *but a body you have prepared for me* [d] 6 Or *purification offerings* [e] 7 Or *come / with the scroll written for me*

39:11 *moth.* In an age dependent largely on woolen clothes, the potential of moths for destruction was readily apparent. Moths lay their eggs in wool, which hatch into larva that eat the material. Not even the most enduring commodity, precious metals, can endure under God's judgment.
40:6 *Sacrifice.* See note on 51:16 – 17; see also the article "Sin and Sacrifice in the Ancient Near East," p. 932.
40:7 *scroll.* Mesopotamian texts express the idea that the gods decreed an individual's lot in life as well as the special calling of kings to service (see note on 138:8). A prayer of the Assyrian king Sennacherib (c. 700 BC) wishes that the god Assur, who holds the "Tablet of Destinies," would decree good health and a successful reign for the king (see notes on 139:2 – 4,7 – 10 and especially 139:16). Prophetic decrees concerning the divine call on the Assyrian king were recorded on clay tablets. The Hebrew language, on the other hand, was written on either leather or papyrus scrolls for official archives, and the "scroll" of this verse could be royal laws similar to Dt 17:14 – 20 or prophetic decrees such as in Ps 2; 110.

Psalm 41[a]

For the director of music. A psalm of David.

1 Blessed are those who have regard for
the weak;[i]
the LORD delivers them in times of
trouble.
2 The LORD protects and preserves
them —
they are counted among the blessed
in the land —[j]
he does not give them over to the
desire of their foes.[k]
3 The LORD sustains them on their
sickbed
and restores them from their bed of
illness.

4 I said, "Have mercy[l] on me, LORD;
heal me, for I have sinned[m] against
you."
5 My enemies say of me in malice,
"When will he die and his name
perish?[n]"
6 When one of them comes to see me,
he speaks falsely,[o] while his heart
gathers slander;[p]
then he goes out and spreads it
around.

7 All my enemies whisper together[q]
against me;
they imagine the worst for me,
saying,
8 "A vile disease has afflicted him;
he will never get up from the place
where he lies."
9 Even my close friend,[r]
someone I trusted,
one who shared my bread,
has turned[b] against me.[s]
10 But may you have mercy on me, LORD;
raise me up,[t] that I may repay them.
11 I know that you are pleased with me,[u]
for my enemy does not triumph
over me.[v]
12 Because of my integrity you uphold me[w]
and set me in your presence forever.[x]

13 Praise be to the LORD, the God of
Israel,[y]
from everlasting to everlasting.
Amen and Amen.[z]

41:1 [i] Ps 82:3-4; Pr 14:21 **41:2** [j] Ps 37:22 [k] Ps 27:12 **41:4** [l] Ps 6:2 [m] Ps 51:4 **41:5** [n] Ps 38:12 **41:6** [o] Ps 12:2 [p] Pr 26:24 **41:7** [q] Ps 56:5; 71:10-11 **41:9** [r] 2Sa 15:12; Ps 55:12
[s] Job 19:19; Ps 55:20; Mt 26:23; Jn 13:18* **41:10** [t] Ps 3:3 **41:11** [u] Ps 147:11 [v] Ps 25:2 **41:12** [w] Ps 37:17 [x] Job 36:7 **41:13** [y] Ps 72:18 [z] Ps 89:52; 106:48 **42:1** [a] Ps 119:131 **42:2** [b] Ps 63:1 [c] Jer 10:10 [d] Ps 43:4 **42:3** [e] Ps 80:5 [f] Ps 79:10

BOOK II

Psalms 42 – 72

Psalm 42[c,d]

For the director of music. A *maskil*[e] of the Sons of Korah.

1 As the deer pants for streams of water,
so my soul pants[a] for you, my God.
2 My soul thirsts[b] for God, for the living
God.[c]
When can I go[d] and meet with God?
3 My tears[e] have been my food
day and night,
while people say to me all day long,
"Where is your God?"[f]

[a] In Hebrew texts 41:1-13 is numbered 41:2-14. [b] 9 Hebrew *has lifted up his heel* [c] In many Hebrew manuscripts Psalms 42 and 43 constitute one psalm. [d] In Hebrew texts 42:1-11 is numbered 42:2-12. [e] Title: Probably a literary or musical term

41:4 *heal me.* See notes on 32:4; 38:2.
41:5 – 6 *enemies … slander.* One of the stereotypical themes of lament psalms is the social rejection and oppression that come upon the sufferer. The Mesopotamian "Poem of the Righteous Sufferer" describes the court intrigue that surrounded the afflicted with plots, slander and lies. This type of conspiracy makes sense in the political context of high society in which this psalm might have originated. However, social adversity is a common plight of average people as well, so this language functions at an emotional level for everyone, regardless of social status.
41:9 *Even my close friend … turned against me.* See note on 31:11.
42:1 *deer.* A common artistic image found on many seal impressions from the Biblical period in Israel. In Judah, there was an apparent artistic preference for depicting does, especially in poses bent over lapping or grazing. This may be an expression of the same religious symbolism reflected in this verse. The longing of deer for water was proverbial in the land of Canaan, as illustrated in a text from Ugarit (c. 1350 BC) that refers to craving for a pool of water "like a hind" (Ugaritic *aylt* = Hebrew *'yl*).
42:2 *soul.* Within the Hebrew OT, the word is *nephesh.* It refers to the "self" or to "a living being" (see Ge 2:7), but not to the "immortal soul" familiar to many in Christian theology. There is no intimation of the *nephesh* surviving after one's death. The word is related to Akkadian *napašu,* referring to the neck or throat and by extension to one's breath. There is no differentiation in the Hebrew usage between the body and the life principle, and therefore in passages like 1Ki 19:4, *nephesh* is used to mean "life." The body's energy or life force can be drained by a pouring out of the soul (v. 4; 1Sa 1:15), as it is in this lament. In Egyptian thinking, the *"ba"* is the animate vital force and is portrayed as a human-headed bird. It is separated from the body at death and is considered immortal. Its place is in heaven rather than in the netherworld, to which the body is consigned. Egyptian literature preserves a composition entitled "The Dispute Between a Man and His Ba," which is a discussion of the feasibility of suicide. In contrast, the *"ka"* is more like the shadow of what is left of the person after he has died. It inhabits the funerary statue and receives the offerings to the dead, and is therefore more like the spirit of the dead. In Mesopotamia this spirit is called the *etemmu,* which receives offerings and must be appeased. It is often associated with a ghost. The other element of one's being in Mesopotamia is called the *zaqiqu,* which appears to be closest to the soul. Like the *etemmu,* it also survives death, but little else is written about it. In Israelite terminology, the spirit of the dead is called *elohim* (see notes on 1Sa 28:7,13; see

4 These things I remember
as I pour out my soul:
how I used to go to the house of God[g]
under the protection of the Mighty One[a]
with shouts of joy and praise[h]
among the festive throng.

5 Why, my soul, are you downcast?[i]
Why so disturbed within me?
Put your hope in God,[j]
for I will yet praise him,
my Savior[k] and my God.

6 My soul is downcast within me;
therefore I will remember you
from the land of the Jordan,
the heights of Hermon—from Mount Mizar.
7 Deep calls to deep
in the roar of your waterfalls;
all your waves and breakers
have swept over me.[l]

8 By day the LORD directs his love,[m]
at night[n] his song[o] is with me—
a prayer to the God of my life.

9 I say to God my Rock,
"Why have you forgotten me?
Why must I go about mourning,[p]
oppressed by the enemy?"
10 My bones suffer mortal agony
as my foes taunt me,
saying to me all day long,
"Where is your God?"

11 Why, my soul, are you downcast?
Why so disturbed within me?
Put your hope in God,
for I will yet praise him,
my Savior and my God.[q]

Psalm 43[b]

1 Vindicate me, my God,
and plead my cause[r]
against an unfaithful nation.
Rescue me from those who are
deceitful and wicked.[s]
2 You are God my stronghold.
Why have you rejected[t] me?
Why must I go about mourning,
oppressed by the enemy?[u]
3 Send me your light[v] and your faithful care,
let them lead me;
let them bring me to your holy mountain,[w]
to the place where you dwell.[x]
4 Then I will go to the altar[y] of God,
to God, my joy and my delight.
I will praise you with the lyre,[z]
O God, my God.

5 Why, my soul, are you downcast?
Why so disturbed within me?
Put your hope in God,
for I will yet praise him,
my Savior and my God.[a]

Psalm 44[c]

For the director of music. Of the Sons of Korah. A *maskil*.[d]

1 We have heard it with our ears, O God;
our ancestors have told us[b]
what you did in their days,
in days long ago.
2 With your hand you drove out[c] the nations
and planted[d] our ancestors;
you crushed the peoples
and made our ancestors flourish.[e]
3 It was not by their sword[f] that they
won the land,
nor did their arm bring them victory;
it was your right hand, your arm,[g]
and the light of your face, for you
loved[h] them.

4 You are my King[i] and my God,
who decrees[e] victories for Jacob.
5 Through you we push back our
enemies;
through your name we trample[j] our
foes.

42:4 [g] Isa 30:29 [h] Ps 100:4 **42:5** [i] Ps 38:6; 77:3 [j] La 3:24 [k] Ps 44:3 **42:7** [l] Ps 88:7; Jnh 2:3 **42:8** [m] Ps 57:3 [n] Job 35:10 [o] Ps 63:6; 149:5 **42:9** [p] Ps 38:6 **42:11** [q] Ps 43:5 **43:1** [r] 1Sa 24:15; Ps 26:1; 35:1 [s] Ps 5:6 **43:2** [t] Ps 44:9

[u] Ps 42:9 **43:3** [v] Ps 36:9 [w] Ps 42:4 [x] Ps 84:1 **43:4** [y] Ps 26:6 [z] Ps 33:2 **43:5** [a] Ps 42:6 **44:1** [b] Ex 12:26; Ps 78:3 **44:2** [c] Ps 78:55 [d] Ex 15:17 [e] Ps 80:9 **44:3** [f] Dt 8:17; Jos 24:12 [g] Ps 77:15 [h] Dt 4:37; 7:7-8 **44:4** [i] Ps 74:12 **44:5** [j] Ps 108:13

[a] *4* See Septuagint and Syriac; the meaning of the Hebrew for this line is uncertain. [b] In many Hebrew manuscripts Psalms 42 and 43 constitute one psalm. [c] In Hebrew texts 44:1-26 is numbered 44:2-27. [d] Title: Probably a literary or musical term [e] *4* Septuagint, Aquila and Syriac; Hebrew *King, O God; / command*

also the articles "Consulting a 'Spirit,'" p. 508; "Death and Sheol," p. 833; "Death and the Underworld," p. 907). *meet with God.* Lit. "see the face of God." This imagery refers to the refreshment and deliverance one can find when God is present and attentive to the psalmist's need (see note on 4:6). A letter written by a Canaanite vassal king to his overlord, the Egyptian pharaoh, expresses hope to see the face of the king. The privilege of meeting face to face with a deity is frequently illustrated in Mesopotamian and Egyptian art. Typically, an individual is led by a lesser god or personal deity to stand before the throne of a greater god from whom the worshiper seeks favor. In Ps 42, seeing God is linked with the experience of his presence in the tabernacle or temple (see v. 4; 43:3; 63:2).

42:4 *among the festive throng.* See note on 68:24.
42:6 *Hermon.* See note on 133:3. The abundant rains on Mount Hermon supply the Jordan River, which in one northern locale cascades in the breathtaking Banias waterfall. *Mizar.* Its location is uncertain. The name means "the little hill," and therefore it may refer to a specific peak in the Hermon range. However, this would depend upon the geographic perspective and poetic intent of the writer. It is quite possible that the psalmist is referring to Mount Hermon as "little," in terms of its sacredness, in comparison to Yahweh's holy hill, Zion (43:3).
42:10 *My bones suffer.* See note on 22:14.
43:3 *holy mountain.* See note on 48:1–2.
43:4 *lyre.* See the article "Music and Musicians," p. 524.

6 I put no trust in my bow,[k]
my sword does not bring me victory;
7 but you give us victory[l] over our enemies,
you put our adversaries to shame.[m]
8 In God we make our boast[n] all day long,
and we will praise your name forever.[a][o]

9 But now you have rejected[p] and humbled us;
you no longer go out with our armies.[q]
10 You made us retreat[r] before the enemy,
and our adversaries have plundered us.
11 You gave us up to be devoured like sheep[s]
and have scattered us among the nations.[t]
12 You sold your people for a pittance,[u]
gaining nothing from their sale.
13 You have made us a reproach to our neighbors,[v]
the scorn[w] and derision of those around us.

44:6 [k] Ps 33:16 **44:7** [l] Ps 136:24 [m] Ps 53:5 **44:8** [n] Ps 34:2 [o] Ps 30:12 **44:9** [p] Ps 74:1 [q] Ps 60:1, 10 **44:10** [r] Lev 26:17; Jos 7:8; Ps 89:41 **44:11** [s] Ro 8:36 [t] Dt 4:27; 28:64; Ps 106:27 **44:12** [u] Isa 52:3; Jer 15:13 **44:13** [v] Ps 79:4; 80:6 [w] Dt 28:37

[a] 8 The Hebrew has *Selah* (a word of uncertain meaning) here.

44:6 *I put no trust in my bow.* This is an indication that it is the king speaking for the community ("we," v. 1). This affirmation of trust in Yahweh alone is an important theme in psalms involving the king (see note on 20:7).
44:11 *scattered us among the nations.* A consequence of defeat in battle was deportation of captives to be slaves in a foreign land (see notes on 107:3; 147:3). In the "Lament Over the Destruction of Ur," the patron goddess of the city laments that her daughters and sons were carried off as captives.
44:12 *You sold your people.* When the Hittite king Arnuwanda (c. 1350 BC) decries the abandonment of the people by their gods in war, he lists the various classes of people carried off to slavery; as a result, he reports that there is no longer a return of offerings or worship in the temple for the benefit of the gods.

PSALM 44

Community Laments in the Ancient Near East

Most of the psalms in the OT are prayers of an individual or prayers offered on behalf of an individual. However, many are hymns calling the congregation to praise, and a number record prayer for a community that is suffering or in distress. This last group is called "community laments" Some examples include Ps 44; 60; 74; 79; 80; 83; 85; 90; 94; 123; 126; 137. Songs of community lament have a long history in Mesopotamia, beginning with laments over the destruction of holy cities as early as the third millennium BC (see the article "City Laments," p. 951). Compositions similar to these earliest city laments became detached from their original historical setting and were used centuries later for other occasions on specific days of the temple worship calendar. One lament over the destruction of Sumer by the Gutians near the end of the third millennium BC was recast and used nearly 2,000 years later for any situation involving enemies from the northern or eastern frontier. The importance of this example is to illustrate the freedom in ancient Near Eastern cultures to reuse older songs in new contexts, applying words crafted in the original situation to a new setting. Most often, OT community laments originated in the midst of a military crisis (e.g., Jos 7:7 – 9; 2Ch 20:5 – 12). Ps 44, 60 and 83 allude to such circumstances. However, the emotional themes of these psalms lend themselves to any distressful situation in which God's people find themselves.

Community laments concerned the people as a whole, often expressed with the plural "we." However, the song was sung by a representative of the community, perhaps a king, priest or prophet, so the singular "I" appears at times, even in a lament that also uses "we" (e.g., Ps 44). A Hittite community lament over the destruction wrought

continued on next page

by an enemy is spoken by the king (Arnuwanda, c. 1350 BC) in the singular ("I") but also includes "we," in this case including his wife, the queen, as they lament how the gods plundered their land. Military disaster was not the only occasion for community lament. The Hittite laments include a series of prayers offered by King Mursili II (c. 1300 BC) concerning a plague that struck the land. One might compare the anguish over death that dominates the communal lament in Ps 90. ◆

A Hittite community lament over the destruction wrought by an enemy, spoken by King Arnuwanda, c. 1350 BC.

14 You have made us a byword among the
nations;
the peoples shake their heads[x] at us.
15 I live in disgrace all day long,
and my face is covered with shame
16 at the taunts of those who reproach
and revile[y] me,
because of the enemy, who is bent
on revenge.
17 All this came upon us,
though we had not forgotten[z] you;
we had not been false to your
covenant.
18 Our hearts had not turned[a] back;
our feet had not strayed from your
path.
19 But you crushed[b] us and made us a
haunt for jackals;
you covered us over with deep
darkness.[c]
20 If we had forgotten[d] the name of our God
or spread out our hands to a foreign
god,[e]
21 would not God have discovered it,
since he knows the secrets of the
heart?[f]

44:14 [x] Ps 109:25; Jer 24:9
44:16 [y] Ps 74:10
44:17 [z] Ps 78:7, 57; Da 9:13
44:18 [a] Job 23:11
44:19 [b] Ps 51:8 [c] Job 3:5
44:20 [d] Ps 78:11 [e] Dt 6:14; Ps 81:9
44:21 [f] Ps 139:1-2; Jer 17:10

44:19 *a haunt for jackals.* One of the images used in Mesopotamian city laments is the habitation of the fallen city by wild animals, as in the Lament Over the Destruction of Ur, where the city now has foxholes.
44:20 *forgotten the name.* A deity's name, like Yahweh, is often associated with that god's power and essential being (Ex 3:13–14; Isa 9:6). In Jer 23:27, the false prophets plan to remove God's name from the people's memory so they will be enticed to follow Baal. See note on Dt 12:5. Failure to invoke the name of Yahweh as their God is a violation of the covenant and is cause for God to punish the people (1Sa 12:9). *spread out our hands.* This posture of worship and prayer is illustrated in ancient Near Eastern iconography, perhaps symbolizing the desire to receive from the deity. Egyptian art in the tomb of the fourteenth-century BC pharaoh Horemheb depicts fugitives of famine seeking aid by lifting their spread hands toward one of his officials. Some of the petitioners have thrown themselves to the ground (cf. v. 25).

22 Yet for your sake we face death all day
long;
we are considered as sheep to be
slaughtered.[g]
23 Awake,[h] Lord! Why do you sleep?[i]
Rouse yourself! Do not reject us
forever.[j]
24 Why do you hide your face[k]
and forget our misery and
oppression?[l]
25 We are brought down to the dust;[m]
our bodies cling to the ground.
26 Rise up[n] and help us;
rescue[o] us because of your unfailing
love.

Psalm 45[a]

For the director of music. To the tune of "Lilies." Of the Sons of Korah. A *maskil.*[b] A wedding song.

1 My heart is stirred by a noble theme
as I recite my verses for the king;
my tongue is the pen of a skillful
writer.
2 You are the most excellent of men
and your lips have been anointed
with grace,[p]
since God has blessed you
forever.
3 Gird your sword[q] on your side, you
mighty one;[r]
clothe yourself with splendor and
majesty.
4 In your majesty ride forth
victoriously[s]
in the cause of truth, humility
and justice;
let your right hand achieve awesome
deeds.
5 Let your sharp arrows pierce the hearts
of the king's enemies;
let the nations fall beneath your
feet.

44:22 [g] Isa 53:7; Ro 8:36* **44:23** [h] Ps 7:6 [i] Ps 78:65 [j] Ps 77:7 **44:24** [k] Job 13:24 [l] Ps 42:9 **44:25** [m] Ps 119:25 **44:26** [n] Ps 35:2 [o] Ps 25:22 **45:2** [p] Lk 4:22 **45:3** [q] Heb 4:12; Rev 1:16 [r] Isa 9:6 **45:4** [s] Rev 6:2

[a] In Hebrew texts 45:1-17 is numbered 45:2-18.
[b] Title: Probably a literary or musical term

44:23 *Awake, Lord!* The psalmist does not, of course, think that Yahweh needs waking (121:4). Rather, he is using a metaphor to call on God to arise for action (78:65). The painful cry of desperation can lead to honest outbursts. An Egyptian work lamenting the downfall of society utilizes the same image for their chief deity, the sun-god, as people wonder whether he is asleep since his power has not been revealed. Elijah used this metaphor to taunt the prophets of Baal on Mount Carmel (1Ki 18:27). The intimacy of the psalmist with God, whom he addresses directly in such a manner, is striking.

45:1 *verses for the king.* Psalms directed to the king rather than to the deity are common in the ancient Near East, but this is the only example in the book of Psalms. Like the Egyptian Marriage Stele of Rameses the Great, the marriage portrayed in this psalm is the result of military strength—it represents a political alliance that is desirable because of the king's military victories. *pen of a skillful writer.* The scribe was one of the most respected professionals in the ancient world. One scribal exercise in Egypt boasts of how the profession of scribe is superior to all others. The Sumerian and Akkadian scribes wrote: "The scribal art is the mother of the eloquent." A fifth-century BC Aramaic wisdom text opens with the claim of the author to be a "wise and experienced scribe" ("experienced" [*mahir*] is the same word as "skillful" in this verse; cf. Ezr 7:6). In Mesopotamia, scribes wrote on clay tablets or wax boards by pressing their stylus into the soft writing medium to make the marks, and in Egypt scribes used a brush to paint on papyrus or other writing surface. Similar to the Egyptians, Israelite scribes wrote on papyrus or leather using an ink pen, which was rather like a thin brush (a pointed reed split on the end to retain ink). Scribes and sages were the official storytellers for the kings of the ancient Near East. Their command of the traditions and their association with the royal bureaucracy made it appropriate that they perform songs and stories that reminded the people of the king's role to feed and protect the land as God's political agent. Thus, during the New Year's festival in Babylon, the *Enuma Elish* (a creation epic) was recounted, representatives from other cities came to give their homage to the king, and a sacred procession wound its way through the streets of the city to the great temple of Marduk, the patron god of Babylon. When Nehemiah the scribe performs a covenant renewal ceremony, he reads the people the law, reminding them of their sacred story (Ne 8:1–13). In Ps 45:1, the poet likens the composition and oral performance of this song (his "tongue") to the "pen" of a skillful scribe, a song of beauty befitting the occasion of the king's wedding. See the article "Scrolls in the Ancient World," p. 1286.

45:2 *your lips.* Ancient descriptions of kings emphasized their grandeur and eloquence of speech. One pharaoh is described as "a master of wisdom, excellent in counsel, brilliant in his use of words." Since most communication was oral rather than written, eloquence was highly valued.

45:3–4 *Gird your sword … ride forth victoriously.* The king in both Mesopotamia and Egypt was the guardian of divine order on earth. A well-ordered society ("truth, humility and justice," v. 4) depended on a valiant king. Therefore, his prowess as a warrior was essential to carrying out his duty, and any ideal portrait of the king presented him in military splendor. This is graphically portrayed in the palace reliefs of Ashurbanipal, who is shown conquering enemies on his chariot ("ride forth victoriously," v. 4), both human and animal, thereby bringing order to the kingdom. An Egyptian royal text from about 1900 BC presents the king as one who brought order to the kingdom by his military might, assigning everything its role, subduing threats (e.g., lions and crocodiles) and defeating enemies. The imagery of a royal warrior in Ps 45 is parallel to descriptions of a divine warrior (see note on Ps 18:7), which reinforces the metaphor of the king in v. 6 as God's representative, especially in his "splendor and majesty" (v. 3; cf. 21:5 with 96:6; 104:1; 145:5). This fearsome aura is a common description of kings on military campaign. The Assyrian king Sennacherib (c. 700 BC) reported that his enemies were overwhelmed by the terrors of the splendors of his sovereignty. His son Esarhaddon (c. 680 BC) described how the god Nergal bestowed on him "awesome radiance and splendor." A similar manner of speech was used in Egypt. Pharaoh Rameses II (c. 1270 BC) likens his fury and aura in combat to that of the gods.

45:5 *nations fall beneath your feet.* See note on 110:1.

[6] Your throne, O God,[a] will last for ever
and ever;[t]
a scepter of justice will be the
scepter of your kingdom.
[7] You love righteousness[u] and hate
wickedness;
therefore God, your God, has set you
above your companions
by anointing[v] you with the oil of
joy.[w]
[8] All your robes are fragrant[x] with myrrh
and aloes and cassia;
from palaces adorned with ivory
the music of the strings makes you
glad.
[9] Daughters of kings[y] are among your
honored women;
at your right hand[z] is the royal bride
in gold of Ophir.

45:6 [t] Ps 93:2; 98:9 **45:7** [u] Ps 33:5 [v] Isa 61:1 [w] Ps 21:6; Heb 1:8-9* **45:8** [x] SS 1:3 **45:9** [y] SS 6:8 [z] 1Ki 2:19
45:10 [a] Dt 21:13 **45:11** [b] Ps 95:6 [c] Isa 54:5 **45:12** [d] Ps 22:29; Isa 49:23 **45:13** [e] Isa 61:10 **45:14** [f] SS 1:4

[10] Listen, daughter, and pay careful
attention:
Forget your people[a] and your father's
house.
[11] Let the king be enthralled by your
beauty;
honor[b] him, for he is your lord.[c]
[12] The city of Tyre will come with a gift,[b][d]
people of wealth will seek your
favor.
[13] All glorious[e] is the princess within her
chamber;
her gown is interwoven with gold.
[14] In embroidered garments she is led to
the king;[f]
her virgin companions follow her—
those brought to be with her.

[a] *6* Here the king is addressed as God's representative.
[b] *12* Or *A Tyrian robe is among the gifts*

45:6 *Your throne, O God.* The NIV capitalizes "God," suggesting that the psalmist turns the address to God at this point. However, throughout the context, the king is the addressee. In what sense can the king be called "god"? By virtue of his divine appointment, the king in the ancient Near East stood before his subjects as a representative of the divine realm. An Assyrian official reminds his king of the proverb that identifies man as a shadow of god, while the king is the perfect likeness of the god. The Egyptian king Seti I (c. 1300 BC) addressed the future rulers of Egypt as those counted among the gods. Egyptian texts often referred to the king as "god." While the king of Egypt was thought to be divine, this was not the case in Mesopotamia or Israel. In Israel the king was "adopted" as God's son (see note on 2:7). In fact, the term "gods" (Hebrew *elohim*) is used of priests who functioned as judges in the Israelite temple judicial system (Ex 21:6; 22:8–9; see note on Ps 82:6). *a scepter of justice.* As God's representative, the king was responsible to enact justice for the benefit of his land (see note on Ps 72; see also the articles "Enthronement in the Ancient Near East," p. 925; "Coronation Hymns in the Ancient Near East," p. 949). The throne was the seat from which the king dispensed justice, and the close relationship between throne, scepter and justice is illustrated in an Ugaritic text using the same terms found in this verse ("seat [*ks'*, "throne"] of kingship" coupled with "judgeship" [or "scepter of your kingdom"]). Here we can see that the Israelite ideal of kingship is parallel to that which is common in the ancient world.
45:7 *love righteousness and hate wickedness.* Pairing together these two ideas is common in ancient texts extolling ideal virtue (cf. Am 5:15). The empowerment to act on God's behalf is symbolized by "anointing, which was part of the ritual on such a joyful occasion. *anointing you with the oil of joy.* Middle Assyrian laws feature the bride being anointed by the father of the bridegroom as part of the wedding ceremony, but in this psalm, the anointing is still part of the kingship (rather than the wedding) section, and it represents God anointing the king to his position (see notes on 1Sa 2:10; 10:1).
45:8 *myrrh.* Used in oil as well as dried for incense, it is an oily resin from the branches of a tree native to Arabia. *aloes.* From trees native to East Africa and India. *cassia.* Produced by steaming the leaves of a tree from as far away as East Asia. Not only are perfumes appropriate for such a special occasion as a wedding (cf. Est 2:12), but because they are precious trade commodities, the mention of these spices stresses the success and prosperity of the king. *adorned with ivory.* The walls and furnishings of rich homes and palaces were inlaid with ivory decorations (1Ki 22:39; Am 3:15; 6:4). These were intricately designed and displayed the most sophisticated craftsmanship in the ancient world. The Assyrian king Sennacherib (c. 700 BC) boasted of the palace he built in his capital city of Nineveh as a palace of ivory that had no rival. The expression used in this Akkadian text—"palace of ivory" (*ekal shin*)—is parallel to the Hebrew of this verse (*hekal shen*). The adornment of the king's attire and the splendor of his royal abode was matched by the beauty of his bride, adorned in the "gold of Ophir" (see notes on 1Ki 9:28; 1Ch 29:4).
45:10 *Forget your people.* The usual marriage custom was for a bride to leave her parent's house to join her husband, often residing in or near his home. One Sumerian bridal song bids the young woman to regard her father and mother as "strangers" in order to join her groom in his household. A text from the northern Mesopotamian city of Emar, which may reflect broader wedding customs, describes the rituals for consecrating a high priestess in marriage to the storm-god. In the ceremony, the new priestess is adorned with jewelry (cf. Isa 61:10) and special attire as she proceeds from her father's house with maidens to the temple of her god-groom. It is of interest that a ceremonial weapon is carried in this procession, even as military symbols are part of the king's attire in Ps 45. The accompaniment of maidens is mentioned in other Mesopotamian texts as well. However, aside from cultural parallels regarding wedding customs, this psalm has little in common with the so-called Sacred Marriage texts of Mesopotamia, which celebrate a religious union between the king and a goddess.
45:12 *Tyre.* A prominent merchant city on the coast of Phoenicia, it was associated with the epitome of wealth (Eze 27:1–33), so the magnitude of honor is underscored by the lavish gifts given the bridal couple.
45:13–14 *her gown is interwoven with gold ... embroidered garments.* Clothing was a status marker in the ancient world. The princess-bride in this psalm is dressed in the richest garments. Like the young bride in Eze 16:10–13, she wears elaborately embroidered robes, probably dyed with Phoenician purple. Adding to the majesty of her ensemble is gold stitching. It would have been impossible to create a durable thread made from gold, but gold dust could have been encrusted into the thread and the

15 Led in with joy and gladness,
they enter the palace of the king.

16 Your sons will take the place of your fathers;
you will make them princes throughout the land.

17 I will perpetuate your memory through all generations;[g]
therefore the nations will praise you[h]
for ever and ever.

Psalm 46[a]

For the director of music. Of the Sons of Korah. According to *alamoth*.[b] A song.

1 God is our refuge[i] and strength,
an ever-present[j] help in trouble.
2 Therefore we will not fear,[k] though the earth give way[l]
and the mountains fall[m] into the heart of the sea,
3 though its waters roar[n] and foam
and the mountains quake with their surging.[c]

4 There is a river whose streams make glad the city of God,[o]
the holy place where the Most High dwells.
5 God is within her,[p] she will not fall;
God will help[q] her at break of day.
6 Nations[r] are in uproar, kingdoms[s] fall;
he lifts his voice, the earth melts.[t]

7 The LORD Almighty is with us;[u]
the God of Jacob is our fortress.[v]

8 Come and see what the LORD has done,[w]
the desolations[x] he has brought on the earth.
9 He makes wars[y] cease
to the ends of the earth.
He breaks the bow[z] and shatters the spear;
he burns the shields[d] with fire.[a]
10 He says, "Be still, and know that I am God;[b]
I will be exalted[c] among the nations,
I will be exalted in the earth."

45:17 [g] Mal 1:11 [h] Ps 138:4 **46:1** [i] Ps 9:9; 14:6 [j] Dt 4:7 **46:2** [k] Ps 23:4 [l] Ps 82:5 [m] Ps 18:7 **46:3** [n] Ps 93:3 **46:4** [o] Ps 48:1, 8; Isa 60:14 **46:5** [p] Isa 12:6; Eze 43:7 [q] Ps 37:40 **46:6** [r] Ps 2:1 [s] Ps 68:32 [t] Mic 1:4 **46:7** [u] 2Ch 13:12 [v] Ps 9:9 **46:8** [w] Ps 66:5 [x] Isa 61:4 **46:9** [y] Isa 2:4 [z] Ps 76:3 [a] Eze 39:9 **46:10** [b] Ps 100:3 [c] Isa 2:11

[a] In Hebrew texts 46:1-11 is numbered 46:2-12. [b] Title: Probably a musical term [c] 3 The Hebrew has *Selah* (a word of uncertain meaning) here and at the end of verses 7 and 11. [d] 9 Or *chariots*

garment to give it this added touch of wealth. Ex 39:3 explains the process by which gold was worked into each thread used to weave a garment.

45:16 *Your sons.* The success of a king's dynasty depended on the royal couple's ability to produce heirs. This was an important part of divine blessing expressed in prophetic promises to kings (see note on 132:11). Assyrian prophets announced to the king that his son and grandson would rule as kings. The royal residence as a place where generations of princes are born is illustrated in a description by the Assyrian king Ashurbanipal when he recalls that his grandfather and father had ruled there.

46:2 *the earth give way . . . mountains fall into the . . . sea.* In OT cosmic geography, the earth was thought to be set upon pillars that reached to the bottom of the subterranean ocean, where the mountains were rooted as well (see the article "Cosmic Geography," p. 836). The word picture here of the earth and its mountains collapsing into the sea is equivalent to an undoing of this fundamental structure of creation, separation of land and sea (Ge 1:9–10). The ancient Israelites appreciated fully the destructive potential of earthquakes (v. 3; Am 1:1; 8:8), so the allusions in this psalm are not purely cosmological. The psalmist imagines the most catastrophic disaster that might challenge the faith of those trusting in God.

46:3 *waters roar.* Keeping with the imagery of creation being undone, the psalmist describes the sea as violent water, a concept that is parallel to "Yamm," the chaos sea monster of Ugaritic mythology (see the article "Chaos Monsters," p. 953).

46:4 *a river whose streams.* Though the Hebrew word "river" can also refer to the destructive cosmic waters, here "river" is qualified by the word "stream," which connotes peaceful, controlled, life-giving water (1:3; Pr 21:1; Isa 32:2). In Ugaritic myth, the mountain palace of the chief god El is located at "the source of the rivers," where one appeals for favor. A portrait of the city of Nineveh depicts channels of water flowing through the garden area of the temple (cf. 65:9; see notes on 87:7; Eze 47:1–12).

46:5 *she will not fall.* In the theology of Sumerian city laments (see the article "City Laments," p. 951), as long as the city deity resided in his or her temple, the city was invulnerable to attack. The "Lament Over the Destruction of Ur" speaks of the god's temple within the city as "the lofty, untouchable mountain." After abandonment, the city is destroyed, and the god's consort stands outside the city to watch its destruction (cf. Eze 10).

46:6 *uproar.* Using the same Hebrew word for the roaring of the sea in v. 3, the psalmist refers to the threat of enemy nations. Hence, the nations are likened to the forces of chaos. Associating enemy nations with conditions of chaos is illustrated also in the Egyptian Prophecies of Neferti (c. 1960 BC). In a reversal on chaos, however, the psalmist depicts the "fall" of these kingdoms with the same Hebrew word that he used for the "fall" of the mountains in v. 2. The threat of chaos alluded to in the imagery of vv. 2–3 is turned on the nations themselves, who would rise up like the sea against God's city.

46:9 *wars cease.* Because God has subjugated all enemies. This reflects the political dominance of God on behalf of his people more than it does a utopian setting. When a new king came to the throne in a kingdom that had vassals, it was common for the vassals to test the strength and resolve of the new king as they looked for an opportunity to break free. Others might actually try to invade and take control before the new king could get established. In this psalm, the kingdom is intact and secure by the hand of God. God has brought rest to his people by resolving all unrest throughout the kingdom. Such "rest" was the goal of kings and gods in the ancient world and was the desire of people who wanted to establish order in their lives.

46:10 This verse might record a direct speech from God given to a temple priest or prophet (see note on 50:7). However, because of its brevity, this verse is more likely a citation of a well-known prophetic saying (cf. Hab 2:20). The force of this command is probably directed to the worshiping community; the people are encouraged in

11 The LORD Almighty is with us;
the God of Jacob is our fortress.

Psalm 47[a]

For the director of music. Of the Sons of Korah. A psalm.

1 Clap your hands,[d] all you nations;
shout to God with cries of joy.[e]
2 For the LORD Most High is awesome,[f]
the great King[g] over all the earth.
3 He subdued[h] nations under us,
peoples under our feet.
4 He chose our inheritance[i] for us,
the pride of Jacob, whom he loved.[b]
5 God has ascended amid shouts of joy,
the LORD amid the sounding of trumpets.[j]
6 Sing praises[k] to God, sing praises;
sing praises to our King, sing praises.
7 For God is the King of all the earth;[l]
sing to him a psalm[m] of praise.
8 God reigns[n] over the nations;
God is seated on his holy throne.
9 The nobles of the nations assemble
as the people of the God of Abraham,
for the kings[c] of the earth belong to God;[o]
he is greatly exalted.[p]

Psalm 48[d]

A song. A psalm of the Sons of Korah.

1 Great is the LORD,[q] and most worthy of praise,
in the city of our God,[r] his holy mountain.[s]
2 Beautiful[t] in its loftiness,
the joy of the whole earth,
like the heights of Zaphon[e] is Mount Zion,
the city of the Great King.[u]
3 God is in her citadels;
he has shown himself to be her fortress.[v]

47:1 [d] Ps 98:8; Isa 55:12 [e] Ps 106:47 **47:2** [f] Dt 7:21 [g] Mal 1:14 **47:3** [h] Ps 18:39, 47 **47:4** [i] 1Pe 1:4 **47:5** [j] Ps 68:33; 98:6 **47:6** [k] Ps 68:4; 89:18 **47:7** [l] Zec 14:9 [m] Col 3:16 **47:8** [n] 1Ch 16:31 **47:9** [o] Ps 72:11; 89:18 [p] Ps 97:9 **48:1** [q] Ps 96:4 [r] Ps 46:4 [s] Isa 2:2-3; Mic 4:1; Zec 8:3 **48:2** [t] Ps 50:2; La 2:15 [u] Mt 5:35 **48:3** [v] Ps 46:7

[a] In Hebrew texts 47:1-9 is numbered 47:2-10. [b] 4 The Hebrew has *Selah* (a word of uncertain meaning) here. [c] 9 Or *shields* [d] In Hebrew texts 48:1-14 is numbered 48:2-15. [e] 2 *Zaphon* was the most sacred mountain of the Canaanites.

the context to rest in God's power to save them from warfare (cf. 37:7). In this respect, it is similar to the command of the Assyrian prophet to King Esarhaddon (c. 680 BC), who was encouraged at the end of a civil war to rest in the help of his goddess Ishtar. *Be still.* Silence before God shows reverence, as illustrated in the Assyrian Hymn to Marduk, in which the other gods bow in silence before him. The term does not suggest meditation, but trust that lacks fear or anxiety.

47:1 *Clap your hands.* In accompaniment to music and dance, people would clap their hands in festive processions. A relief of the Assyrian king Ashurbanipal (c. 645 BC) shows men, women and children following the musicians and clapping their hands in a procession to celebrate the enthronement of an ally after victory over the Elamites.

47:2 *the great King.* See notes on 97:5; 99:1.

47:3 *subdued nations.* Because "chose our inheritance" is in the next verse, the historical allusion is to the conquest under Joshua, when God delivered the land of Canaan to Israel as an inheritance (see note on 105:11). *under our feet.* The placement of enemies under foot is a common theme in ancient Near Eastern texts (see note on 110:1). The coronation inscription of Pharaoh Horemheb (c. 1300 BC) equates the placement of the foreign nations under the king's feet with assigning to him the land of his rightful rule.

47:5 *God has ascended.* This is likely an allusion to a procession up to the holy mountain where God's temple and throne were located (see notes on 48:1–2; 68:24). *trumpets.* Here, refers to the ram's horn blown on special occasions (see note on Jos 6:4).

48:1–2 *his holy mountain ... Mount Zion.* In ancient Canaan, the highest mountains, particularly those in the north, were considered sacred places and appropriate locations for temples, since the top was the closest contact point between the earth and the heavens (see the articles "Hymns to Holy Cities," p. 927; "Sacred Space," p. 964). This tradition is best illustrated in mythic texts (dating c. 1300 BC) discovered at a northern coastal city of Canaan known as Ugarit. In these texts, the major deities—El, Baal and Anat—each had its own sacred mountain for a home. When Jeroboam built a temple site in northern Israel to rival the temple in Jerusalem (1Ki 12:25–33), he chose the city of Dan because it was located on the flanks of Mount Hermon, a sacred site left over from the Canaanites and the idolatrous Danites of the judges period (Jdg 18). The Hittites, who lived in the mountainous region of what is today Turkey, often depicted their gods standing on the tops of mountains.

The most striking parallel to Ps 48:2 is in the tradition about Baal, whose mountain was "Zaphon" (Ugaritic *spn* = Hebrew *spn*). The texts describe Mount Zaphon as Baal's "beautiful hill," "inheritance," "holy mountain," "lovely, mighty mountain." This background helps explain the importance of God's mountain in the OT. Such a prominent location was expected for any deity's dwelling. So the temple was on a prominent hilltop in Jerusalem, in some texts called "Mount Zion" (e.g., Ps 48:2,11; 74:2; 78:68), the Lord's "holy mountain" (Ps 43:3; 48:1; 87:1; 99:9). Even Jerusalem itself was located at higher elevation than much of the surrounding region. While the Hebrew word translated "Zaphon" can mean the direction "north," the parallel to the Baal Cycle is striking. An association between Yahweh and mountains is illustrated in other texts. Israel's experience meeting God at Mount Sinai (Ex 19–34) left an impression, so that Biblical texts speak of Yahweh coming from mountains in the south (e.g., Dt 33:2; Hab 3:3). In this way, the psalmist is using theological images that are current in the ancient world to praise Yahweh—even though Yahweh is quite different from the other gods.

48:3 *citadels ... fortress.* The psalmist associates God's presence in the city with protection (cf. 46:5). A fortified city would have exterior walls that constituted the first line of defense. Within these walls, the palace and temple complex would be fortified further as a position

PSALM 47:5–8

Enthronement in the Ancient Near East

One of the most important ceremonies in the ancient Near East was the ritual of enthronement of a king and the investiture of that person with his symbols of office. This can be seen in the investment of Marduk with his royal insignia in the *Enuma Elish* (a creation epic). Marduk is named king and then given his scepter, throne, robes and weapons by the other gods. This ritual is mirrored in the coronation practice in Assyria in which all court officials surrendered the symbols of office, resigning so that the king could decide whether to reappoint them to their duties. In Mesopotamia, enthronement is also tied to the majesty and power of the gods since it is believed that "kingship descended from on high." In the prologue to the Code of Hammurapi, e.g., the king of Babylon states that the gods called him by name and installed him to carry out their commands on earth, including the restoration of cities, the purification of sacred rites, and the establishment of "truth and justice as the declaration of the land." During the Babylonian New Year's festival (Akitu), the granting of power to the king had to be reinvested in his person, so an enthronement ritual was reenacted. Many scholars assume that Israel used psalms like this one in their own enthronement festival (for Yahweh and his king), but no positive proof has yet come forth to confirm that hypothesis. ◆

4 When the kings joined forces,
when they advanced together,[w]
5 they saw her and were astounded;
they fled in terror.[x]
6 Trembling seized them there,
pain like that of a woman in labor.
7 You destroyed them like ships of Tarshish
shattered by an east wind.[y]
8 As we have heard,
so we have seen
in the city of the LORD Almighty,
in the city of our God:
God makes her secure
forever.[a z]

9 Within your temple, O God,
we meditate on your unfailing
love.[a]
10 Like your name,[b] O God,
your praise reaches to the ends
of the earth;[c]
your right hand is filled with
righteousness.
11 Mount Zion rejoices,
the villages of Judah are
glad
because of your judgments.[d]

48:4 [w] 2Sa 10:1-19 **48:5** [x] Ex 15:16 **48:7** [y] Jer 18:17; Eze 27:26 **48:8** [z] Ps 87:5

48:9 [a] Ps 26:3 **48:10** [b] Dt 28:58; Jos 7:9 [c] Isa 41:10 **48:11** [d] Ps 97:8

[a] *8* The Hebrew has *Selah* (a word of uncertain meaning) here.

of defense in the event that the walls were breached (1Ki 16:18). The word picture here is that Yahweh in his temple is the ultimate defense for the city. Most people in the ancient world believed that their gods would defend their cities and protect them from harm. But in most other places their beliefs were based on the idea that the people gained that protection from their gods by consistently meeting the needs of their gods through rituals. In this view the gods needed the people and when the people cared for those needs, the gods protected them. Yahweh, in contrast, has no needs. He cares for his people as a response to their covenant faithfulness and as a reflection of his love for them.

48:7 *destroyed ... like ships of Tarshish.* The psalmist recalls some event from the city's collective memory when Yahweh intervened to deliver the city, perhaps similar to the destruction of Sennacherib's army (2Ki 19:32–36). The vulnerability of an army attacking Jerusalem is likened to ships bound for Tarshish that are destroyed in a great storm. Travel to Tarshish—a distant, if unknown, place in the western Mediterranean—was a hazardous sea voyage (Eze 27:25–26).

48:9 *Within your temple.* Unlike the kings who fled away at the sight of God's power (vv. 4–7), the Israelite pilgrims gain great comfort from the majesty of God's presence at Zion, because that is where his deliverance comes from. "Within" in this case may be simply entrance into Jerusalem (Mount Zion) or the temple mount complex, since

[12] Walk about Zion, go around her,
count her towers,
[13] consider well her ramparts,
view her citadels,[e]
that you may tell of them
to the next generation.[f]

[14] For this God is our God for ever and ever;
he will be our guide[g] even to the end.

Psalm 49[a]

For the director of music. Of the Sons of Korah. A psalm.

[1] Hear this, all you peoples;[h]
listen, all who live in this world,[i]
[2] both low and high,
rich and poor alike:
[3] My mouth will speak words of wisdom;[j]
the meditation of my heart will give you understanding.[k]
[4] I will turn my ear to a proverb;[l]
with the harp I will expound my riddle:[m]

[5] Why should I fear[n] when evil days come,
when wicked deceivers surround me—
[6] those who trust in their wealth[o]
and boast of their great riches?
[7] No one can redeem the life of another
or give to God a ransom for them—
[8] the ransom for a life is costly,
no payment is ever enough—[p]
[9] so that they should live on[q] forever
and not see decay.
[10] For all can see that the wise die,[r]
that the foolish and the senseless also perish,
leaving their wealth to others.[s]

48:13 [e] ver 3; Ps 122:7 [f] Ps 78:6 **48:14** [g] Ps 23:4 **49:1** [h] Ps 78:1 [i] Ps 33:8 **49:3** [j] Ps 37:30 [k] Ps 119:130 **49:4** [l] Ps 78:2 [m] Nu 12:8 **49:5** [n] Ps 23:4 **49:6** [o] Job 31:24 **49:8** [p] Mt 16:26 **49:9** [q] Ps 22:29; 89:48 **49:10** [r] Ecc 2:16 [s] Ecc 2:18, 21

[a] In Hebrew texts 49:1-20 is numbered 49:2-21.

pilgrims would not be allowed access to the inner precincts of the temple itself. *unfailing love.* Hebrew *hesed* is a legal term employed in connection with the covenant; it indicates a sense of fulfillment on their part and is the basis for their fervent worship.

48:12–13 *towers . . . ramparts . . . citadels.* The basic architecture of a fortified city functioned as its defense system and also served as a form of monumental display of the physical power of the state. *towers.* Placed at regular intervals within the wall system and dominated each gate. *ramparts.* Ranged as high as 40 feet (12 meters)—as at Tell Dan—and were set between the towers, often in an offset-inset pattern that provided more angles for arrows and for other missiles dropped or thrown by the defenders. *citadels.* Within the city, a citadel would be constructed as the strong point in case the city walls were breached. Since it was usually constructed at a high elevation, the citadel tower could also serve as a link in the signal fire system used to communicate between cities.

48:12 *Walk about Zion.* An imaginary tour in a city and praise for its features and life within its walls are a feature of ancient Near Eastern city hymns (see the article "Hymns to Holy Cities," p. 927). The Assyrian "Hymn to the City of Arbela" praises the city as being as lofty as the heavens and with foundations as firm as the heavens. The "Hymn to the City of Assur" cites the obvious prosperity of the city as praiseworthy. Here, the psalmist invites anyone to marvel at the splendor of Jerusalem, because it evokes praise of Yahweh who built it (v. 14).

49:1 *all you peoples.* While some psalms address all of humanity based on the kingship of Yahweh (see note on 97:5), here the psalmist calls out in the name of wisdom (cf. 78:1–2). The rhetorically universal appeal of wisdom (v. 3) is demonstrated by the internationally shared forms and content of wisdom literature across the ancient Near East. Since piety is not foreign to wisdom, even among the other nations, the merger of the two in the religious devotion of a psalmist is natural. In an Egyptian prayer to the scribal-god Thoth, the worshiper makes the acquisition of wisdom the central theme.

49:4 *proverb.* The Hebrew term is *mashal.* It has a wide range of meanings depending upon context: "parable" (Eze 17:2), poem (Nu 21:27), prophetic "message" (Nu 23:7). In this case, as in Pr 10:1, it refers to an instruction from God to the people, warning them, but relying on the universality of a wisdom theme so that all peoples (v. 1) can be addressed, not just the Israelites. It may also be compared to the "taunt" in Hab 2:6 that speaks with scorn of the Assyrian aggressors' loss of their ill-gotten wealth. *with the harp.* The measured parallelism of the verse would be aided in its rhythm by the strumming of a harp or zither. This might be compared to the musician employed by Elisha when he speaks a prophetic message (2Ki 3:15). A similar occurrence also appears in "The Report of Wenamun," an Egyptian text in which a musician and a prophet are paired. Certainly words of praise were chanted or sung to the sound of lyre and harp (92:1–3). It would be natural for minstrels and storytellers to recite the mighty acts of God and of Israel's heroes to the sound of music (Jdg 5:11).

49:7–9 *No one can . . . live on forever.* The quest for immortality was a vital concern in ancient Near Eastern culture. One of the earliest literary stories, the Gilgamesh Epic (a composition perhaps c. 1800 BC from sources originating in the third millennium BC), features this quest as its central, unifying theme. After the death of his friend Enkidu, Gilgamesh seeks counsel from the Mesopotamian flood hero, who with his wife are the only humans ever granted immortality by the gods. Gilgamesh is told that their circumstances were unique and that there is no one who can convene the assembly of the gods to grant him the immortality he seeks. In the Ugaritic Aqhat Legend (c. 1300 BC), King Aqhat declines a deceptive offer of eternal life by the goddess Anat, asserting that he will die as everyone does. See notes on 90:3,10.

49:10–11 *the wise die . . . Their tombs will remain.* The reality that death overcomes everyone regardless of their station in life is reflected in the Egyptian Harpers' Songs that adorned tombs in the New Kingdom period (c. 1550–1100 BC). One harpist's song observes that the dead have built their mansions throughout life and then rest in them. It urges people to build well so that their name might endure. Another song mentions the enduring reputation of the famous Egyptian wise man Imhotep, who designed the first pyramid; yet the song adds that even his tomb no longer remains. See the article "Harpers' Songs," p. 1076.

PSALM 48

HYMNS TO HOLY CITIES

From the earliest records of Mesopotamia, cities were associated with particular patron deities. For example, in the prologue to his famous law collection, Hammurapi (c. 1750 BC) declares how he built up various cities and the temples of the deities who in particular dwelled there. So close was the association between city and deity, that the city seal incorporated the name of the patron deity. The same notion held true for ancient Egypt. Different creation accounts emerged from major cities of Egypt extolling the role of the primary god worshiped in each respective city. From the founding of the nation of Israel, Yahweh's intention was to establish a holy city in which he would dwell (Dt 12:5). After various temporary locations, Jerusalem was chosen, and there David and Solomon built the permanent temple (Ps 78:60,68 – 69; 132:1 – 18). The temple, as well as the city in which it was located, became theologically the center of the created world.

Because of the close link between city, temple and deity, hymns were composed in Mesopotamia and Egypt exalting the city as a beautiful dwelling place alongside praise for the god or goddess whose temple was located there. In this practice, the psalmist is doing the same as the hymn writers throughout the ancient world. Many of the themes included in such hymns are similar to those found in the "songs of Zion" (Ps 137:3) in the book of Psalms (Ps 46; 48; 84; 87; 122). These psalms include (1) the city and its temple as the dwelling place of God; (2) the grandeur of the city's location, gates and walls; (3) the foundation of the city "in heaven"; (4) a place of security; (5) the good fortune of its inhabitants; and (6) wishes for prayer and blessing on the city. See also the articles "City Laments," p. 951; "Sacred Space," p. 964. ◆

Jerusalem, the Holy City.

[11]Their tombs will remain their houses[a]
forever,
their dwellings for endless generations,
though they had[b] named[t] lands after
themselves.

[12]People, despite their wealth, do not
endure;
they are like the beasts that perish.

[13]This is the fate of those who trust in
themselves,[u]
and of their followers, who approve
their sayings.[c]

[14]They are like sheep and are destined to
die;[v]
death will be their shepherd
(but the upright will prevail[w] over
them in the morning).
Their forms will decay in the grave,
far from their princely mansions.

[15]But God will redeem me from the
realm of the dead;[x]
he will surely take me to himself.[y]

[16]Do not be overawed when others grow
rich,
when the splendor of their houses
increases;

[17]for they will take nothing with them
when they die,
their splendor will not descend with
them.[z]

[18]Though while they live they count
themselves blessed — [a]
and people praise you when you
prosper —

[19]they will join those who have gone
before them,[b]
who will never again see the light[c]
of life.

[20]People who have wealth but lack
understanding
are like the beasts that perish.[d]

Psalm 50

A psalm of Asaph.

[1]The Mighty One, God, the LORD,[e]
speaks and summons the earth
from the rising of the sun to where
it sets.[f]

[2]From Zion, perfect in beauty,[g]
God shines forth.[h]

[3]Our God comes[i]
and will not be silent;
a fire devours before him,[j]
and around him a tempest
rages.

49:11 [t]Ge 4:17; Dt 3:14 **49:13** [u]Lk 12:20 **49:14** [v]Job 24:19; Ps 9:17 [w]Da 7:18; Mal 4:3; 1Co 6:2; Rev 2:26 **49:15** [x]Ps 56:13; Hos 13:14 [y]Ps 73:24 **49:17** [z]Ps 17:14; 1Ti 6:7 **49:18** [a]Dt 29:19; Lk 12:19 **49:19** [b]Ge 15:15 [c]Job 33:30 **49:20** [d]Ecc 3:19 **50:1** [e]Jos 22:22 [f]Ps 113:3 **50:2** [g]Ps 48:2 [h]Dt 33:2; Ps 80:1 **50:3** [i]Ps 96:13 [j]Ps 97:3; Da 7:10

[a] *11* Septuagint and Syriac; Hebrew *In their thoughts their houses will remain* [b] *11* Or *generations, / for they have* [c] *13* The Hebrew has *Selah* (a word of uncertain meaning) here and at the end of verse 15.

49:14 *Their forms will decay.* The common observation that the human body decayed to dust in the grave gave rise to imagery of the earth swallowing and consuming a corpse. Corresponding to this, Canaanite mythology described the god Mot ("Death," Ugaritic *mt* = Hebrew *mwt*) in terms of an opening in the earth that "swallowed" and "consumed."

49:15 *take me to himself.* Like the Mesopotamian culture with whom they shared a number of their religious and social ideas, the Israelites throughout most of the OT period did not have a concept of a resurrection from the dead, a last judgment or an afterlife of reward or punishment (see the articles "Death and Sheol," p. 833; "Death and the Underworld," p. 907). This only becomes evident in Judaism in the postexilic period, as exemplified by Da 12:2. Thus, in this context the psalmist is contrasting the fate of the psalmist's enemies, for whom there will be no escape from the grave, and the psalmist's own hope of redemption by Yahweh. It is unlikely that the writer is referring, as some have suggested, to escape from death altogether in the manner of Enoch (Ge 5:24) or Elijah (2Ki 2:11). The NIV's inclusion of the phrase "to himself" has been added by the NIV translators to try to make sense of an awkward expression. The concept of God "taking" a person as a reference to saving his life is preferable and can be seen clearly in 18:16, where the NIV translates the same phrase as "took hold of me."

50 title *Asaph.* May be an abbreviation for the "sons of Asaph" and thus a reference to one of the temple choirs or their repertoire of music. In Ezr 2:41, the musicians who returned to Israel with Ezra were "descendants of Asaph." According to the list of temple musicians in 1Ch 6:39, Asaph was appointed by David to serve in Jerusalem's worship space as Heman's associate.

50:1 – 4 Two images are conflated in the opening verses of this psalm. The first description of God in these verses recalls his appearance in a storm on Mount Sinai, when he spoke the words of the covenant to which the psalmist alludes throughout this psalm (Ex 19 – 24). It connotes the terrifying manifestation of a divine warrior (in Dt 33:2, Yahweh "shone forth" with his army of holy angels; see notes on Ps 18:7 – 12). This notion of radiant splendor and awe-inspiring sheen surrounding a deity is a common Mesopotamian expression. In the *Enuma Elish* (a creation epic), when the god Marduk waged war against the forces of chaos, his head "was covered with terrifying auras," a description also used of the fierce dragons he opposed. This same description was frequently used of Assyrian kings in battle. Sennacherib speaks of overwhelming Hezekiah with his terrifying splendor. The important point of this imagery for Ps 50 is that when God calls people together to speak his word or exercise judgment, his authority is backed by his awesome nature.

The second image is connected to God as lawgiver and judge. A relief at the top of the seven-foot-high (two-meter-high) diorite pillar containing a copy of the Code of Hammurapi depicts the Babylonian sun-god Shamash seated on his throne with Hammurapi standing before him. In the prologue that follows, the king accepts the responsibility to make justice prevail in the land and to rise like the sun-god Shamash over all humankind. He becomes the god's judicial representative for the Babylonian Empire. Shamash's role as divine judge is also found in Akkadian prayers for forgiveness. The Egyptian Great Hymn to Aten, composed for the court of the pharaoh Akhenaten in the fourteenth century BC, contains creation imagery very similar to that

[4] He summons the heavens above,
and the earth,[k] that he may judge
his people:
[5] "Gather to me this consecrated
people,[l]
who made a covenant[m] with me by
sacrifice."
[6] And the heavens proclaim[n] his
righteousness,
for he is a God of justice.[a,b][o]

[7] "Listen, my people, and I will speak;
I will testify[p] against you, Israel:
I am God, your God.[q]
[8] I bring no charges against you
concerning your sacrifices
or concerning your burnt offerings,[r]
which are ever before me.
[9] I have no need of a bull[s] from your
stall
or of goats from your pens,
[10] for every animal of the forest is mine,
and the cattle on a thousand hills.[t]
[11] I know every bird in the mountains,
and the insects in the fields are
mine.
[12] If I were hungry I would not tell you,
for the world[u] is mine, and all that
is in it.
[13] Do I eat the flesh of bulls
or drink the blood of goats?

[14] "Sacrifice thank offerings[v] to God,
fulfill your vows[w] to the Most High,
[15] and call[x] on me in the day of trouble;
I will deliver you, and you will
honor[y] me."

[16] But to the wicked person, God says:

"What right have you to recite my laws
or take my covenant on your lips?[z]
[17] You hate my instruction
and cast my words behind[a] you.
[18] When you see a thief, you join[b] with
him;
you throw in your lot with adulterers.
[19] You use your mouth for evil
and harness your tongue to deceit.[c]
[20] You sit and testify against your brother[d]
and slander your own mother's son.
[21] When you did these things and I kept
silent,[e]
you thought I was exactly[c] like you.
But I now arraign you
and set my accusations[f] before you.

[22] "Consider this, you who forget God,[g]
or I will tear you to pieces, with no
one to rescue you:[h]
[23] Those who sacrifice thank offerings
honor me,
and to the blameless[d] I will show my
salvation.[i]"

50:4 [k] Dt 4:26; Isa 1:2 **50:5** [l] Ps 30:4 [m] Ex 24:7 **50:6** [n] Ps 89:5 [o] Ps 75:7 **50:7** [p] Ps 81:8 [q] Ex 20:2 **50:8** [r] Ps 40:6; Hos 6:6 **50:9** [s] Ps 69:31 **50:10** [t] Ps 104:24 **50:12** [u] Ex 19:5 **50:14** [v] Heb 13:15 [w] Dt 23:21 **50:15** [x] Ps 81:7 [y] Ps 22:23 **50:16** [z] Isa 29:13 **50:17** [a] Ne 9:26; Ro 2:21-22 **50:18** [b] Ro 1:32; 1Ti 5:22 **50:19** [c] Ps 10:7; 52:2 **50:20** [d] Mt 10:21 **50:21** [e] Ecc 8:11; Isa 42:14 [f] Ps 90:8 **50:22** [g] Job 8:13; Ps 9:17 [h] Ps 7:2 **50:23** [i] Ps 91:16

[a] *6* With a different word division of the Hebrew; Masoretic Text *for God himself is judge* [b] *6* The Hebrew has *Selah* (a word of uncertain meaning) here. [c] *21* Or *thought the 'I AM' was* [d] *23* Probable reading of the original Hebrew text; the meaning of the Masoretic Text for this phrase is uncertain.

in this psalm. This is especially the case with regard to a sense of order and universality as the god's glory enriches the land.

50:4 *He summons the heavens ... and the earth.* In the ancient Near East, covenants between people were sworn before deities, who then served as witnesses to bind the agreement. Sometimes elements of nature were also invoked, including heaven and earth (Dt 4:26). Perhaps for Israel, where these elements were not deified, the stability and relative eternality of the heavens and the earth rendered them fit symbols for the durability of the covenant obligations. This rhetorical device is used by OT prophets (Dt 32:1; Isa 1:2).

50:5 *made a covenant ... by sacrifice.* Accompanying the oaths that bound a covenant, the agreement was also ratified by sacrifice (Ge 31:44–54; Ex 24:3–8). This custom was common in the ancient Near East, illustrated by an eighth-century BC Aramaic covenant from Syria in which animals were cut in half.

50:7 *Listen, my people.* Ps 50 is a prophetic speech introduced by the description of God's appearance (vv. 1–4) and continued with the speech formula in v. 16. Such prophetic words are not uncommon in psalms (cf. 2:6–9; 12:5; 60:6–8; 75:2–10; 81:6–16; 82:1–8; 89:19–37; 91:14–16; 95:7b–11; 110:1–7; 132:11–18). So one might conclude that prophetic ministry was active in the Israelite temple, as it was among Israel's neighbors, with parts of prophetic speeches recorded in psalms (see the article "Prophets and Prophecy," p. 1110). The prophetic address used in this verse is similar to the form used by temple prophets in Assyria (seventh century BC): "Listen, O Assyrians!" It echoes OT prophetic calls (cf. Isa 1:10; 28:14; 48:1; Jer 2:4; 10:1; Am 3:1; 4:1; Mic 3:1,9).

50:8 *burnt offerings.* See note on 51:16–17; see also the article "Sin and Sacrifice in the Ancient Near East," p. 932.

50:13 *Do I eat ...?* Among Israel's neighbors, part of the concept of an offering was that it fed the gods. Mesopotamian and Egyptian hymns credit the chief god with providing agricultural produce as meals for other gods. In Mesopotamian myth, humans were created to bear the labor of tending orchards and fields that provide food for offerings. Priests were largely occupied with the care and feeding of the gods. One of the best illustrations of this is found in the Mesopotamian flood story recounted in the Gilgamesh Epic. During the flood, when no humans were upon land to make offerings, the gods became hungry. Consequently, after the flood waters receded and the Mesopotamian "Noah" built an altar for sacrifices, the gods smelled the aroma of the sacrifice and gathered like flies around him. The Canaanites also held this view of their gods and sacrifices. The god Baal is the one who fattens gods and men—i.e., he provides fertility for crops and livestock that become offerings. In the Ugaritic royal stories, the Kirta epic and the Aqhat Legend, the sacrifices of the king to the gods are called "food."

The OT perspective is also that sacrifices and drink offerings are food for God (Lev 3:11,16; Nu 28:2; Jdg 9:13). However, unlike Mesopotamian texts, such as the flood story in the Gilgamesh Epic, which indicate the actual dependence of gods upon sacrificial offerings, Ps 50 categorically denies this notion. Rather, according to the psalmist, sacrifices were symbolic meals that allowed

Psalm 51[a]

For the director of music. A psalm of David. When the prophet Nathan came to him after David had committed adultery with Bathsheba.

[1] Have mercy on me, O God,
according to your unfailing love;
according to your great compassion
blot out[j] my transgressions.[k]
[2] Wash away[l] all my iniquity
and cleanse[m] me from my sin.

[3] For I know my transgressions,
and my sin is always before me.[n]
[4] Against you, you only, have
I sinned
and done what is evil in your
sight;[o]
so you are right in your verdict
and justified when you judge.[p]
[5] Surely I was sinful[q] at birth,
sinful from the time my mother
conceived me.
[6] Yet you desired faithfulness even in the
womb;
you taught me wisdom[r] in that
secret place.[s]

[7] Cleanse me with hyssop,[t] and I will be
clean;
wash me, and I will be whiter than
snow.[u]
[8] Let me hear joy and gladness;[v]
let the bones you have crushed rejoice.
[9] Hide your face from my sins[w]
and blot out all my iniquity.

[10] Create in me a pure heart,[x] O God,
and renew a steadfast spirit
within me.[y]

51:1 [j] Ac 3:19 [k] Isa 43:25; Col 2:14 **51:2** [l] 1Jn 1:9 [m] Heb 9:14 **51:3** [n] Isa 59:12 **51:4** [o] Ge 20:6; Lk 15:21 [p] Ro 3:4* **51:5** [q] Job 14:4 **51:6** [r] Pr 2:6 [s] Ps 15:2 **51:7** [t] Lev 14:4; Heb 9:19 [u] Isa 1:18 **51:8** [v] Isa 35:10 **51:9** [w] Jer 16:17 **51:10** [x] Ps 78:37; Ac 15:9 [y] Eze 18:31

[a] In Hebrew texts 51:1-19 is numbered 51:3-21.

worshipers the opportunity to give something to God and enhance fellowship, as well as provide a means of atonement. This emphasis is evident in v. 14, which commands the sacrifice of "thank offerings" as a fulfillment of vows (see note on 56:12). See the articles "Great Symbiosis," p. 186; "Sin and Sacrifice in the Ancient Near East," p. 932.

51:1 *Have mercy.* Feeling the need for forgiveness and pleading for mercy are universal experiences among humans who fear their God or gods. Many parallels exist in Mesopotamian, Egyptian and Hittite literature, but the distinction is that here the psalmist's plea is based on a belief in Yahweh's moral expectations that have been laid out in the Torah rather than on simply the whims of a deity (see notes on 14:3; 25:7; 32:4; 145:16; see also the article "Sin and Sacrifice in the Ancient Near East," p. 932).

51:3 *I know my transgressions.* In the ancient Near East, individuals typically claimed that they were mystified concerning what they could possibly have done to offend the gods. Several factors contributed to this ignorance: (1) the gods of the ancient Near East had offered no permanent revelation of themselves that might be used as a guide; (2) the gods were not characterized as acting consistently from one day to the next, making it difficult to assess one's standing in any given circumstance; and (3) offenses often took the form of neglecting rituals of which the guilty individual was not even aware. As a result, in Babylonian penitential literature (Akkadian *shigu*), e.g., the offender sometimes simply accepts blame for a vast range of sins, hoping in the process to confess to whatever has offended the god. However, at other times, he lists offenses and asserts that he is well aware of his sins. In the Hittite Prayers of Mursili, confession of one's guilt is the step toward reconciliation with his lord. In Israel, the Mosaic Law was clear enough and offenses could be clearly identified.

51:4 *Against you, you only, have I sinned.* If David is identifying Yahweh alone as the one sinned against, whom else is he ruling out with the phrase "you only"? Certainly he has wronged Bathsheba and Uriah (see title; see also 2Sa 11). It is important to notice that in the context the issue concerns who has a right to pass judgment and carry out sentence (v. 4b). In Israel, the family of the murder victim had a right to blood vengeance, and there were always political enemies who would be happy to stylize themselves as the arm of God's justice against a wayward king. Perhaps by this statement David is limiting his acknowledgment of culpability so that only Yahweh has the right of punishment.

51:5 *sinful at birth.* The observation that humans fail from the moment life begins was proverbial in Mesopotamia. In a lament over illness, a Sumerian worshiper confesses that a sinless child has never been born—no one is perfect. The individual continues by appealing to the confession of forgotten sins and those committed unwittingly (see the article "Sin and Sacrifice in the Ancient Near East," p. 932). A similar Sumerian prayer expresses that everyone has sinned against their god. The ideology in these texts is not identical to the standard Christian doctrine of original sin, in that nothing connects the origin of sin or guilt to a first human pair.

51:6 *in the womb ... in that secret place.* Based on the birth image in the previous verse, it is likely that this verse refers to obtaining knowledge while still within the womb. The penitent person thus acknowledges that his sin cannot be excused for lack of knowledge. He is aware, even from the womb, of what is right behavior, and he has failed to obey what he knows to be lawful (v. 3). A similar image of prenatal learning is found in the Egyptian Great Hymn to Aten. The writer repeatedly praises the god for supplying all that is necessary for human survival, even within the womb. To counter human nature's tendency to disobey, Egyptian religious thought is filled with the need to internalize *maat*, "truth." It is described as the bread that sustains humans (as in the royal annals of Queen Hatshepsut).

51:7 *hyssop.* See note on Nu 19:6. *whiter than snow.* White is identified with purity or joy in the Biblical tradition (see note on Isa 1:18). Dark colors, especially black, are used to signify mourning or lamentation—both of which are associated with states of impurity (35:13; Zec 3:3–5). In an Assyrian prayer, the king calls on his god to "whiten" and thus free his heart from his sin of blasphemy. In Akkadian, the verb "to brighten" overlaps with the verb "to make white." In one Babylonian magical text there is a request to become as pure and bright as heaven. See note on Ecc 9:8.

51:10 *pure heart.* Having acknowledged his sinful condition from his birth, the penitent psalmist now asks God, the only power able to grant his request, to purify his "heart" (the seat of the intellect in Hebrew tradition). A Sumerian prayer of repentance also pleads for divine mercy from the gods and transformation of the sin into

[11] Do not cast me from your presence
or take your Holy Spirit[z] from me.
[12] Restore to me the joy of your
salvation[a]
and grant me a willing spirit, to
sustain me.

[13] Then I will teach transgressors your
ways,[b]
so that sinners will turn back to
you.[c]
[14] Deliver me from the guilt of
bloodshed,[d] O God,
you who are God my Savior,[e]
and my tongue will sing of your
righteousness.[f]
[15] Open my lips, Lord,[g]
and my mouth will declare your
praise.
[16] You do not delight in sacrifice,[h] or
I would bring it;
you do not take pleasure in burnt
offerings.
[17] My sacrifice, O God, is[a] a broken spirit;
a broken and contrite heart[i]
you, God, will not despise.

51:11 [z] Eph 4:30 **51:12** [a] Ps 13:5 **51:13** [b] Ac 9:21-22 [c] Ps 22:27 **51:14** [d] 2Sa 12:9 [e] Ps 25:5 [f] Ps 35:28 **51:15** [g] Ps 9:14 **51:16** [h] 1Sa 15:22; Ps 40:6 **51:17** [i] Ps 34:18 **51:18** [j] Ps 102:16; Isa 51:3 **51:19** [k] Ps 4:5 [l] Ps 66:13 [m] Ps 66:15 **52:Title** [n] 1Sa 22:9 **52:1** [o] Ps 94:4 **52:2** [p] Ps 50:19 [q] Ps 57:4

[18] May it please you to prosper Zion,[j]
to build up the walls of Jerusalem.
[19] Then you will delight in the sacrifices
of the righteous,[k]
in burnt offerings[l] offered whole;
then bulls[m] will be offered on your
altar.

Psalm 52[b]

For the director of music. A *maskil*[c] of David. When Doeg the Edomite[n] had gone to Saul and told him: "David has gone to the house of Ahimelek."

[1] Why do you boast of evil, you mighty
hero?
Why do you boast[o] all day long,
you who are a disgrace in the eyes of
God?
[2] You who practice deceit,[p]
your tongue plots destruction;
it is like a sharpened razor.[q]

[a] 17 Or *The sacrifices of God are* [b] In Hebrew texts 52:1-9 is numbered 52:3-11. [c] Title: Probably a literary or musical term

goodness. This is similar to the petition in the "Lament Over the Destruction of Ur," which calls on the goddess Nanna to insure that "every evil heart of its people be pure." The concept of regeneration or redirection is also found in Ezekiel's prophecy of a restored nation; in that prophecy God promises to "give you a new heart" (Eze 36:26).

51:11 *your Holy Spirit.* While God's spirit shows up many times in the OT text, the explicit reference to the *Holy* Spirit, used synonymously with Yahweh's presence, occurs only here and in Isa 63:10–14. To have that presence removed or to be excluded from communion with God is the ultimate punishment imaginable. On a national scale, it would be the end of the covenant relationship and the total destruction of the people (Jer 23:39; cf. Hosea's third child Lo-Ammi [which means "not my people"] in Hos 1:9). For a reigning monarch, who is God's representative, being cut off from Yahweh's voice or presence would be the signal that the monarch's dynasty has been rejected and will come to an end (see 1Sa 16:14; 28:6). The Sumerian "Prayer to Every God" also pleads that the god would not cast out his servant, presumably away from divine favor because of his transgressions. For the ancient Israelite reader, this expression would not entail an understanding of the Trinity—only that God's spirit is characterized by holiness.

51:16–17 *sacrifice ... a broken spirit.* The sacrifices prescribed in Lev 1–7 addressed only sins committed "unintentionally" or by omission of duty (Lev 4:2,13,22,27; 5:1–4,15; see Nu 15:22–29). Sins committed in a premeditated or defiant manner were not removed by these sacrifices (Nu 15:30–36). The offending individual was left at the mercy of God; and only on the Day of Atonement were all sins, even "rebellion," removed and God's wrath appeased (Lev 16:16,21,30,34). On this day, God expected an attitude of humble contrition (Lev 16:29–31). The sin of David spoken of in this psalm was premeditated (see title); therefore, no prescribed sacrifice addressed the psalmist's plight, and capital punishment would have been just. Only God's gracious forgiveness offered to the contrite sinner, realized on the Day of Atonement, was applicable for intentional sins. A Ugaritic ritual text prescribes sacrifices (Ugaritic *dbh* = Hebrew *zbh*) for sins committed due to anger, impatience or a vile attitude.

Furthermore, like Jeremiah's direct attacks on what he considered a totally corrupt cultic system in Jerusalem (Jer 6:20; 7:4; 31:31–35), the psalmist denies the value of animal sacrifice without an ethical dimension to sustain it. The Egyptian Teaching for Merikare contains this same sentiment, indicating that the character of the upright person is more desirable than the sacrifice of an evildoer They share Samuel's (1Sa 15:22) and Hosea's (Hos 6:6) argument that God desires a devout worshiper's heart and prayers, not his or her ritual pantomime (see 1Sa 15:22 and notes on Isa 1:16–17; Jer 7:9). This is also noted in Babylonian wisdom literature, where the pious are encouraged to pay daily homage "with sacrifice, prayer, and appropriate incense-offering," and it is most important to "feel solicitude of heart" toward one's god.

51:18 *build up the walls of Jerusalem.* It is a common theme in ancient Near Eastern royal records that a successful king undertakes the building of cities and temples. The Assyrian king Shalmaneser III, e.g., boasts of the rebuilding of Assur's dilapidated walls as the fruit of his victories. After capturing Jerusalem, David expanded the size of the original Canaanite city (2Sa 5:9). Further construction is recorded for Solomon (1Ki 9:24), and an extension of the walls to embrace a wider urban core was undertaken by Hezekiah (2Ch 32:5). In each case, architectural expansion is mentioned as evidence of a stable and prudent king. The figure of speech used in this verse draws upon the natural association between a king's vitality and the undertaking of monumental architecture such as fortress walls.

52:2 *tongue.* The destructive potential of the tongue and the displeasure it stirs in God is proverbial not just in OT wisdom. A well-known Egyptian proverb warns that a malicious tongue is connected to a faulty heart and is abhorred by the Egyptian gods, who hate those whose tongues deceive and cause harm.

PSALM 51:16–17

Sin and Sacrifice in the Ancient Near East

Sacrifice in the ancient Near East served several purposes. The primary purpose of sacrifice in the cultures outside of Israel was to feed the gods (see note on Ps 50:13). A second use involved preparation in rituals, e.g., in the widespread practice of divination in Mesopotamia, Syria and the Levant, where the organs of sacrificial animals were inspected to discern answers to questions asked of the gods. Slaughter of animals also accompanied rituals designed to remove evil influences caused by demons or spells. A ritual use, found in Israel as well as neighboring nations, was to inaugurate covenants by sacrifice (see note on Ps 50:5). Sacrifice also served in ritual cleansing. Particular physical conditions (e.g., a skin disease) or unavoidable actions (e.g., sex with one's spouse or physical contact with a dead relative) rendered an individual unfit for participation in religious rituals performed in sacred places (see note on Ps 51:7). In such cases, sacrifice was part of the purifying ritual. Sacrifice also played a role in temple cleansing during the Mesopotamian Akitu festival. This is somewhat similar to the temple cleansing aspect of Israel's Day of Atonement (Lev 16); but unlike the Akitu festival, Israel's Day of Atonement was also associated with the final category of sacrifice in the ancient Near East, appeasing divine anger on account of sin. The degree to which appeasement was important varied in each of the major ancient Near Eastern civilizations, but this use of sacrifice was the most relevant in the religion of Israel.

All cultures of the ancient Near East had standards of ethical behavior and social consequences for violation of these customs. However, they differed on the religious implications of such violations and the expected rituals required by the gods in order to amend wrongs. The Egyptians valued adherence to truth and justice, called "*maat*" (see note on Ps 85:10). The ideal, as reflected in the king's duty, was to advance the well-being of society and contribute to the maintenance of temple worship (see note on Ps 72; see also the articles "Enthronement in the Ancient Near East," p. 925; "Coronation Hymns in the Ancient Near East," p. 949).

While Egyptians believed in a judgment after death, there was no necessity to offer sacrifices regarding one's wrongdoing in the present life. However, prayers of thanksgiving for mercy and forgiveness have been found that accompanied thank offerings. Offerings also contributed to the care of the deceased and the gods, and they perhaps

continued on next page

[3] You love evil rather than good,
falsehood[r] rather than speaking the truth.[a]
[4] You love every harmful word,
you deceitful tongue![s]
[5] Surely God will bring you down to everlasting ruin:
He will snatch you up and pluck[t] you from your tent;
he will uproot[u] you from the land of the living.[v]
[6] The righteous will see and fear;
they will laugh[w] at you, saying,
[7] "Here now is the man
who did not make God his stronghold
but trusted in his great wealth[x]
and grew strong by destroying others!"
[8] But I am like an olive tree[y]
flourishing in the house of God;
I trust[z] in God's unfailing love
for ever and ever.

52:3 [r] Jer 9:5 **52:4** [s] Ps 120:2,3 **52:5** [t] Isa 22:19 [u] Pr 2:22 [v] Ps 27:13 **52:6** [w] Job 22:19; Ps 37:34; 40:3 **52:7** [x] Ps 49:6 **52:8** [y] Jer 11:16 [z] Ps 13:5

[a] 3 The Hebrew has *Selah* (a word of uncertain meaning) here and at the end of verse 5.

placated the ghost of the dead so that they would not disturb the well-being of the living.

If the worshiper petitioned the gods for favor, an offering might be included. Mesopotamian laws attest to a respect for life and property rights, and family responsibilities were important. Violations of these customs resulted in social consequences; but religiously speaking, offenses against the gods were primarily the failure to bring offerings for divine food or to observe other ritual requirements (see note on Ps 50:13). In the "Poem of the Righteous Sufferer," the individual laments that his misfortune is without explanation, since he has faithfully fulfilled such religious duties. In fact, the worshiper is not even certain which duties are pleasing and which are offensive to a god — nothing is intuitive with the gods.

As mentioned above, offerings of food, including meat, obtained divine favor, and animal slaughter was necessary to perform acts of divination. However, there were no sacrificial rituals or manipulation of blood for forgiveness in Mesopotamia comparable to those of the OT. Like the Mesopotamians, the Hittites possessed laws clearly delineating right and wrong behavior. One sacrificial ritual involved squirting the blood of a sacrificial animal toward the statue of the deity in the temple, and smearing blood was used in purification.

In the extant prayers of confession, however, "sins" are infractions against temples and worship practices. So, while the Hittites offered animal sacrifices for removal of sin, the offenses were presumably for these cultic failures. At Ugarit, "burnt offerings" and "peace offerings" were sacrificed, but the theological significance is unclear. Blood was not part of the ritual, as in OT sacrifices. Some evidence points to a concept of care and feeding of the gods similar to Mesopotamia, and a few texts mention "sin."

The OT places an emphasis on the necessity of blood sacrifice for removing sin, whether it be an infraction against ceremonial requirements of worship or a violation of ethical laws. For further discussion, see note on Ps 51:16 – 17. ◆

Model of man slaughtering a bull.

Kim Walton. The Oriental Institute Museum, University of Chicago.

[9]For what you have done I will always
praise you[a]
in the presence of your faithful people.
And I will hope in your name,
for your name is good.[b]

Psalm 53[a]

53:1-6pp — Ps 14:1-7

For the director of music. According to *mahalath.*[b] A *maskil*[c] of David.

[1]The fool[c] says in his heart,
"There is no God."[d]
They are corrupt, and their ways are vile;
there is no one who does good.

[2]God looks down from heaven[e]
on all mankind
to see if there are any who understand,
any who seek God.[f]
[3]Everyone has turned away, all have
become corrupt;
there is no one who does good,
not even one.[g]

52:9 [a]Ps 30:12 [b]Ps 54:6 **53:1** [c]Ps 14:1-7; Ro 3:10 [d]Ps 10:4 **53:2** [e]Ps 33:13 [f]2Ch 15:2 **53:3** [g]Ro 3:10-12*

[a] In Hebrew texts 53:1-6 is numbered 53:2-7. [b] Title: Probably a musical term [c] Title: Probably a literary or musical term

[4]Do all these evildoers know nothing?

They devour my people as though
eating bread;
they never call on God.
[5]But there they are, overwhelmed with
dread,
where there was nothing to dread.[h]
God scattered the bones[i] of those who
attacked you;
you put them to shame, for God
despised them.

[6]Oh, that salvation for Israel would
come out of Zion!
When God restores his people,
let Jacob rejoice and Israel be glad!

Psalm 54[a]

For the director of music. With stringed instruments. A *maskil*[b] of David. When the Ziphites had gone to Saul and said, "Is not David hiding among us?"

[1]Save me, O God, by your name;[j]
vindicate me by your might.[k]
[2]Hear my prayer, O God;[l]
listen to the words of my mouth.

[3]Arrogant foes are attacking me;[m]
ruthless people are trying to kill
me[n]—
people without regard for God.[c o]

[4]Surely God is my help;[p]
the Lord is the one who sustains me.[q]
[5]Let evil recoil[r] on those who slander me;
in your faithfulness[s] destroy them.

[6]I will sacrifice a freewill offering[t] to
you;
I will praise your name, LORD, for it
is good.[u]
[7]You have delivered me[v] from all my
troubles,
and my eyes have looked in triumph
on my foes.[w]

Psalm 55[d]

For the director of music. With stringed instruments. A *maskil*[b] of David.

[1]Listen to my prayer, O God,
do not ignore my plea;[x]
[2]hear me and answer me.[y]
My thoughts trouble me and I am
distraught[z]
[3]because of what my enemy is saying,
because of the threats of the wicked;
for they bring down suffering on me[a]
and assail me in their anger.[b]

[4]My heart is in anguish within me;
the terrors[c] of death have fallen
on me.
[5]Fear and trembling[d] have beset me;
horror has overwhelmed me.
[6]I said, "Oh, that I had the wings of a
dove!
I would fly away and be at rest.
[7]I would flee far away
and stay in the desert;[e]
[8]I would hurry to my place of shelter,
far from the tempest and storm.[e]"

[9]Lord, confuse the wicked, confound
their words,
for I see violence and strife[f] in the
city.
[10]Day and night they prowl about on its
walls;
malice and abuse are within it.
[11]Destructive forces[g] are at work in the
city;
threats and lies[h] never leave its
streets.

[12]If an enemy were insulting me,
I could endure it;
if a foe were rising against me,
I could hide.
[13]But it is you, a man like myself,
my companion, my close friend,[i]
[14]with whom I once enjoyed sweet
fellowship
at the house of God,[j]
as we walked about
among the worshipers.

[15]Let death take my enemies by surprise;[k]
let them go down alive to the realm
of the dead,[l]
for evil finds lodging among them.

53:5 [h]Lev 26:17 [i]Eze 6:5 **54:1** [j]Ps 20:1 [k]2Ch 20:6 **54:2** [l]Ps 5:1; 55:1 **54:3** [m]Ps 86:14 [n]Ps 40:14 [o]Ps 36:1 **54:4** [p]Ps 118:7 [q]Ps 41:12 **54:5** [r]Ps 94:23 [s]Ps 89:49; 143:12 **54:6** [t]Ps 50:14 [u]Ps 52:9 **54:7** [v]Ps 34:6 [w]Ps 59:10 **55:1** [x]Ps 27:9; 61:1

55:2 [y]Ps 66:19 [z]Ps 77:3; Isa 38:14 **55:3** [a]2Sa 16:6-8; Ps 17:9 [b]Ps 71:11 **55:4** [c]Ps 116:3 **55:5** [d]Job 21:6; Ps 119:120 **55:8** [e]Isa 4:6 **55:9** [f]Jer 6:7 **55:11** [g]Ps 5:9 [h]Ps 10:7 **55:13** [i]2Sa 15:12; Ps 41:9 **55:14** [j]Ps 42:4 **55:15** [k]Ps 64:7 [l]Nu 16:30, 33

[a] In Hebrew texts 54:1-7 is numbered 54:3-9. [b] Title: Probably a literary or musical term [c] 3 The Hebrew has *Selah* (a word of uncertain meaning) here. [d] In Hebrew texts 55:1-23 is numbered 55:2-24. [e] 7 The Hebrew has *Selah* (a word of uncertain meaning) here and in the middle of verse 19.

54:1 *vindicate me.* A person who was suffering was believed to be receiving punishment from God. Since God was considered to be just, then the punishment was considered to be deserved. The psalmist's troubles would therefore be taken as evidence of his sinfulness (see the article "Retribution Principle," p. 823). Vindication of the psalmist would then come when God intervened to turn the tables and punish the psalmist's enemies. Such action from God would proclaim the psalmist's innocence and show that he had not lost God's favor. In this sense, God is his only hope. The Eloquent Peasant, from Egyptian wisdom literature, also calls on his god-king, pharaoh, as his "last hope" and "only judge."
54:6 *freewill offering.* See note on Nu 15:3.
55:13 *my close friend.* See note on 31:11.
55:15 *go down alive to the realm of the dead.* The judgment sought by the psalmist on his enemies is an untimely death. Like the rebellious Levite Korah and his followers (Nu 16:31 – 35), they are to be swallowed up by the earth without any further opportunity to commit mis-

[16]As for me, I call to God,
and the LORD saves me.
[17]Evening,[m] morning[n] and noon
I cry out in distress,
and he hears my voice.
[18]He rescues me unharmed
from the battle waged against me,
even though many oppose me.
[19]God, who is enthroned from of old,[o]
who does not change—
he will hear[p] them and humble them,
because they have no fear of God.

[20]My companion attacks his friends;[q]
he violates his covenant.[r]
[21]His talk is smooth as butter,
yet war is in his heart;
his words are more soothing than oil,[s]
yet they are drawn swords.[t]

[22]Cast your cares on the LORD
and he will sustain you;[u]
he will never let
the righteous be shaken.[v]
[23]But you, God, will bring down the wicked
into the pit[w] of decay;
the bloodthirsty and deceitful[x]
will not live out half their days.[y]

But as for me, I trust in you.[z]

Psalm 56[a]

For the director of music. To the tune of "A Dove on Distant Oaks." Of David. A *miktam*.[b] When the Philistines had seized him in Gath.

[1]Be merciful to me, my God,
for my enemies are in hot pursuit;[a]
all day long they press their attack.
[2]My adversaries pursue me all day long;[b]
in their pride many are attacking me.[c]
[3]When I am afraid,[d] I put my trust in you.
[4] In God, whose word I praise—
in God I trust and am not afraid.
What can mere mortals do to me?[e]

[5]All day long they twist my words;[f]
all their schemes are for my ruin.
[6]They conspire,[g] they lurk,
they watch my steps,
hoping to take my life.[h]
[7]Because of their wickedness do not[c] let them escape;
in your anger, God, bring the nations down.[i]

[8]Record my misery;
list my tears on your scroll[d]—
are they not in your record?[j]
[9]Then my enemies will turn back[k]
when I call for help.[l]
By this I will know that God is for me.[m]

[10]In God, whose word I praise,
in the LORD, whose word I praise—
[11]in God I trust and am not afraid.
What can man do to me?

[12]I am under vows[n] to you, my God;
I will present my thank offerings to you.
[13]For you have delivered me from death[o]
and my feet from stumbling,
that I may walk before God
in the light of life.[p]

[a] In Hebrew texts 56:1-13 is numbered 56:2-14.
[b] Title: Probably a literary or musical term
[c] 7 Probable reading of the original Hebrew text; Masoretic Text does not have *do not*.
[d] 8 Or *misery; / put my tears in your wineskin*

55:17 [m] Ps 141:2; Ac 3:1 [n] Ps 5:3 **55:19** [o] Dt 33:27 [p] Ps 78:59 **55:20** [q] Ps 7:4 [r] Ps 89:34 **55:21** [s] Pr 5:3 [t] Ps 28:3; 57:4; 59:7 **55:22** [u] Ps 37:5; Mt 6:25-34; 1Pe 5:7 [v] Ps 37:24 **55:23** [w] Ps 73:18 [x] Ps 5:6 [y] Job 15:32; Pr 10:27 [z] Ps 25:2 **56:1** [a] Ps 57:1-3 **56:2** [b] Ps 57:3 [c] Ps 35:1 **56:3** [d] Ps 55:4-5 **56:4** [e] Ps 118:6; Heb 13:6 **56:5** [f] Ps 41:7 **56:6** [g] Ps 59:3 [h] Ps 71:10 **56:7** [i] Ps 36:12; 55:23 **56:8** [j] Mal 3:16 **56:9** [k] Ps 9:3 [l] Ps 102:2 [m] Ro 8:31 **56:12** [n] Ps 50:14 **56:13** [o] Ps 116:8 [p] Job 33:30

chief. The parallel here to "by surprise" clarifies that going alive to the realm of the dead does not mean they will not die; rather, a sudden death is requested. The image of death as an open mouth swallowing the unaware is found in the Ugaritic Baal Cycle, in which the god of the underworld, Mot, is described as a "pool luring the wild oxen" that "eats whatever it wants with both hands."
55:17 *I cry out ... he hears.* The idea of God "hearing" means that he acts (v. 16). This common figure of speech is illustrated in many ancient Near Eastern prayers and reports of deliverance (see note on 116:2). An inscription from the king of Byblos dating to the postexilic period exalts his goddess with gratitude that she heard his voice. Later in the text the same expression is parallel with the idea that the goddess made the situation "pleasant" (i.e., peaceable) for the king. In Egyptian reliefs, a series of ears on a stele portraying a god expressed the hope that the god would hear and respond.
55:20 *violates his covenant.* Related to the immediately preceding call for God to afflict the psalmist's enemies (vv. 16–19). They have apparently violated a covenant, a serious offense in ancient culture, which would have been punished by curses from God for breaking the oath taken during the covenant-making ritual.
55:21 *talk is smooth ... war is in his heart.* The hypocritical contrast between outward speech and inward intent is illustrated by an accusation found in the annals of the Assyrian king Ashurbanipal (c. 650 BC) as he speaks about an enemy who spoke in a friendly way to him even as he plotted murder in his heart.
55:23 *pit.* See the articles "Death and Sheol," p. 833; "Death and the Underworld," p. 907.
56:8 *tears.* See note on 6:6. *scroll.* Lit. "bottle" or "wineskin" (see NIV text note; see also 119:83). This intimate image portrays a container belonging to God, filled with the psalmist's sorrow.
56:12 *vows ... thank offerings.* When the psalmist feels passionately about his distress and plea, he might promise to bring an offering to God as an act of praise after God has delivered him (65:1–3; Ge 28:20–22; 1Sa 1:11). See notes on Ge 28:20,22; Lev 7:12; 27:2; Pr 7:14; see also the article "Nazirites," p. 242.

Psalm 57[a]

57:7-11pp — Ps 108:1-5

For the director of music. To the tune of "Do Not Destroy." Of David. A *miktam*.[b] When he had fled from Saul into the cave.

[1] Have mercy on me, my God, have
mercy on me,
for in you I take refuge.[q]
I will take refuge in the shadow of your
wings[r]
until the disaster has passed.[s]

[2] I cry out to God Most High,
to God, who vindicates me.[t]
[3] He sends from heaven and saves me,[u]
rebuking those who hotly pursue
me —[c][v]
God sends forth his love and his
faithfulness.[w]

[4] I am in the midst of lions;[x]
I am forced to dwell among ravenous
beasts —
men whose teeth are spears and
arrows,
whose tongues are sharp swords.[y]

[5] Be exalted, O God, above the heavens;
let your glory be over all the earth.[z]

[6] They spread a net for my feet —
I was bowed down[a] in distress.
They dug a pit[b] in my path —
but they have fallen into it
themselves.[c]

[7] My heart, O God, is steadfast,
my heart is steadfast;[d]
I will sing and make music.
[8] Awake, my soul!
Awake, harp and lyre![e]
I will awaken the dawn.

[9] I will praise you, Lord, among the
nations;
I will sing of you among the peoples.
[10] For great is your love, reaching to the
heavens;
your faithfulness reaches to the
skies.[f]

[11] Be exalted, O God, above the heavens;
let your glory be over all the earth.[g]

Psalm 58[d]

For the director of music. To the tune of "Do Not Destroy." Of David. A *miktam*.[b]

[1] Do you rulers indeed speak justly?[h]
Do you judge people with equity?
[2] No, in your heart you devise injustice,
and your hands mete out violence
on the earth.[i]

[3] Even from birth the wicked go astray;
from the womb they are wayward,
spreading lies.
[4] Their venom is like the venom of a
snake,[j]
like that of a cobra that has stopped
its ears,
[5] that will not heed the tune of the
charmer,
however skillful the enchanter may
be.

[6] Break the teeth in their mouths,
O God;[k]
LORD, tear out the fangs of those lions![l]
[7] Let them vanish like water that flows
away;[m]
when they draw the bow, let their
arrows fall short.[n]
[8] May they be like a slug that melts
away as it moves along,
like a stillborn child[o] that never sees
the sun.

[9] Before your pots can feel the heat of
the thorns[p] —
whether they be green or dry — the
wicked will be swept away.[e][q]
[10] The righteous will be glad when they
are avenged,[r]
when they dip their feet in the blood
of the wicked.[s]

57:1 [q] Ps 2:12 [r] Ps 17:8 [s] Isa 26:20 **57:2** [t] Ps 138:8 **57:3** [u] Ps 18:9, 16 [v] Ps 56:1 [w] Ps 40:11 **57:4** [x] Ps 35:17 [y] Ps 55:21; Pr 30:14 **57:5** [z] Ps 108:5 **57:6** [a] Ps 145:14 [b] Ps 35:7 [c] Ps 7:15; Pr 28:10 **57:7** [d] Ps 108:1 **57:8** [e] Ps 16:9; 30:12; 150:3 **57:10** [f] Ps 36:5; 103:11 **57:11** [g] ver 5 **58:1** [h] Ps 82:2 **58:2** [i] Ps 94:20; Mal 3:15 **58:4** [j] Ps 140:3; Ecc 10:11 **58:6** [k] Ps 3:7 [l] Job 4:10 **58:7** [m] Jos 7:5; Ps 112:10 [n] Ps 64:3 **58:8** [o] Job 3:16 **58:9** [p] Ps 118:12 [q] Pr 10:25 **58:10** [r] Ps 64:10; 91:8 [s] Ps 68:23

[a] In Hebrew texts 57:1-11 is numbered 57:2-12. [b] Title: Probably a literary or musical term [c] *3* The Hebrew has *Selah* (a word of uncertain meaning) here and at the end of verse 6. [d] In Hebrew texts 58:1-11 is numbered 58:2-12. [e] *9* The meaning of the Hebrew for this verse is uncertain.

57:1 *shadow of your wings.* See note on 36:7.
57:4 *lions.* See note on 22:13. *tongues.* See note on 52:2.
57:6 *net.* See notes on 124:7; 140:5.
57:8 *harp and lyre.* See the articles "Lyre," p. 488; "Music and Musicians," p. 524.
58:4 – 5 *cobra ... charmer.* There are magical incantations in ancient Near Eastern texts for warding off lethal attacks from a snake. One Mesopotamian text describes "serpents that cannot be conjured." In a Ugaritic text, 12 gods are summoned to offer formulas to a charmer (Ugaritic *mlhs* = Hebrew *mlhs*) for neutralizing the poison (Ugaritic *hmt* = Hebrew *hmh*) of a snake (Ugaritic *hhs* = Hebrew *hhs*). The first 11 charms are ineffective. See note on 140:3.
The metaphor is an attempt to equate the fool/wicked, who will not listen, with a cobra (a term found in both Egyptian and Ugaritic texts) who pays no attention to the snake charmer. Both cause pain and suffering even though it is unreasonable behavior. Although snakes do not have hands to cover their ears (an internal organ), the issue here has to do with unnatural, perverse actions. Along this line, the Egyptian "Instructions of Ankhsheshonq" notes that there is no point in trying to instruct a fool, who will not listen and will hate you for attempting to teach him something. Similarly, the "Instructions of Amenemope" caution that the words of fools are more dangerous than storm winds.
58:10 *dip their feet in the blood of the wicked.* The poetic imagery is relatively subdued for the violent rhetoric that

PSALM 58

Imprecations and Incantations

Psalm 58 is known as an "imprecatory" psalm because it calls down curses (imprecations) on the enemy. In the ancient Near East, such curses were enhanced or activated by magical rituals and spells, but this sort of practice would have been unacceptable in the Biblical system. Imprecatory psalms can be best understood against the background of the Retribution Principle (see the article "Retribution Principle," p. 823). Since God's justice was seen as requiring punishment proportional to the seriousness of the sin, the psalmist is calling down the curses that would be appropriate if justice were to be maintained. These are curses of the same magnitude that God pronounces on his enemies (Isa 13:15 – 16). The forceful language of this passage contains aspects of an East Semitic curse formula that relies on the deity to carry out vengeance on the enemy nations. An example of this type of indirect curse is found in the vassal treaties of the Assyrian king Esarhaddon as he calls on a host of gods to do the treaty-breaker harm. It is also employed, with the addition of ritual acts of execration, in the Aramaic Sefire Treaty that describes bows being broken with the expected result that their enemies' bows will likewise be broken. The psalmist indirectly curses by imprecation, calling on God to "laugh at them" (Ps 59:8) in their puny efforts to menace Israel. He does not employ magical incantations or execration rituals against them, but instead relies on God to render them impotent, breaking their power and their weapons of destruction (cf. Jer 49:35; 51:56; Eze 39:3). ◆

An example of a type of indirect curse is found in the vassal treaties of the Assyrian king Esarhaddon as he calls on a host of gods to do the treaty-breaker harm. Babylonian, 672 BC.

[11] Then people will say,
"Surely the righteous still are rewarded;
surely there is a God who judges the earth."[t]

Psalm 59[a]

For the director of music. To the tune of "Do Not Destroy." Of David. A *miktam*.[b] When Saul had sent men to watch David's house in order to kill him.

[1] Deliver me from my enemies, O God;[u]
be my fortress against those who are attacking me.
[2] Deliver me from evildoers
and save me from those who are after my blood.[v]

[3] See how they lie in wait for me!
Fierce men conspire[w] against me
for no offense or sin of mine, LORD.
[4] I have done no wrong, yet they are ready to attack me.[x]
Arise to help me; look on my plight!
[5] You, LORD God Almighty,
you who are the God of Israel,
rouse yourself to punish all the nations;
show no mercy to wicked traitors.[c][y]

[6] They return at evening,
snarling like dogs,[z]
and prowl about the city.
[7] See what they spew from their mouths—
the words from their lips are sharp as swords,[a]
and they think, "Who can hear us?"[b]
[8] But you laugh at them, LORD;[c]
you scoff at all those nations.[d]

[9] You are my strength, I watch for you;
you, God, are my fortress,[e]
[10] my God on whom I can rely.

God will go before me
and will let me gloat over those who slander me.
[11] But do not kill them, Lord our shield,[d][f]
or my people will forget.[g]
In your might uproot them
and bring them down.[h]
[12] For the sins of their mouths,[i]
for the words of their lips,[j]
let them be caught in their pride.[k]
For the curses and lies they utter,
[13] consume them in your wrath,
consume them till they are no more.[l]
Then it will be known to the ends of the earth
that God rules over Jacob.[m]

[14] They return at evening,
snarling like dogs,
and prowl about the city.
[15] They wander about for food[n]
and howl if not satisfied.
[16] But I will sing of your strength,[o]
in the morning[p] I will sing of your love;[q]
for you are my fortress,
my refuge in times of trouble.[r]

[17] You are my strength, I sing praise to you;
you, God, are my fortress,
my God on whom I can rely.

Psalm 60[e]

60:5-12pp — Ps 108:6-13

For the director of music. To the tune of "The Lily of the Covenant." A *miktam*[b] of David. For teaching. When he fought Aram Naharaim[f] and Aram Zobah,[g] and when Joab returned and struck down twelve thousand Edomites in the Valley of Salt.

[1] You have rejected us,[s] God, and burst upon us;
you have been angry[t]—now restore us![u]
[2] You have shaken the land[v] and torn it open;
mend its fractures,[w] for it is quaking.
[3] You have shown your people desperate times;[x]
you have given us wine that makes us stagger.[y]

58:11 [t] Ps 9:8; 18:20
59:1 [u] Ps 143:9
59:2 [v] Ps 139:19
59:3 [w] Ps 56:6
59:4 [x] Ps 35:19, 23
59:5 [y] Jer 18:23
59:6 [z] ver 14
59:7 [a] Ps 57:4 [b] Ps 10:11
59:8 [c] Ps 37:13; Pr 1:26 [d] Ps 2:4
59:9 [e] Ps 9:9; 62:2
59:11 [f] Ps 84:9 [g] Dt 4:9 [h] Ps 106:27
59:12 [i] Ps 10:7 [j] Pr 12:13 [k] Zep 3:11
59:13 [l] Ps 104:35 [m] Ps 83:18
59:15 [n] Job 15:23
59:16 [o] Ps 21:13 [p] Ps 88:13 [q] Ps 101:1 [r] Ps 46:1
60:1 [s] 2Sa 5:20; Ps 44:9 [t] Ps 79:5 [u] Ps 80:3
60:2 [v] Ps 18:7 [w] 2Ch 7:14
60:3 [x] Ps 71:20 [y] Isa 51:17; Jer 25:16

[a] In Hebrew texts 59:1-17 is numbered 59:2-18. [b] Title: Probably a literary or musical term [c] *5* The Hebrew has *Selah* (a word of uncertain meaning) here and at the end of verse 13. [d] *11* Or *sovereign* [e] In Hebrew texts 60:1-12 is numbered 60:3-14. [f] Title: That is, Arameans of Northwest Mesopotamia [g] Title: That is, Arameans of central Syria

can be found in ancient Near Eastern culture. One might compare, e.g., the graphic nature of descriptions found in Assyrian royal inscriptions (see notes on 18:38; 137:9). In a Ugaritic text, Anat wades through the blood and gore of her slain enemies. The graphic imagery reflects that these are authentic prayers of people who deeply desire God's justice to be visited on the wicked. God is willing to hear such outbursts even though, ideally, moderation, mercy and forgiveness would be commendable. The psalmist nonetheless leaves vengeance to God. Examples such as this also remind us that these psalms were not designed to be model prayers for us to draw on (though we may sometimes find them useful in that way). When the disciples asked Jesus to teach them to pray, he did not just direct them to the book of Psalms.

59:6,14 *dogs.* See notes on 1Sa 24:14; 2Sa 3:8.

60:2 *quaking.* The metaphor of an earthquake can describe any kind of catastrophe or social upheaval, here a military disaster (see note on 82:5).

60:3 *wine ... stagger.* See note on 75:8.

[4]But for those who fear you, you have
raised a banner
to be unfurled against the bow.[a]
[5]Save us and help us with your right
hand,[z]
that those you love[a] may be
delivered.
[6]God has spoken from his sanctuary:
"In triumph I will parcel out
Shechem[b]
and measure off the Valley of
Sukkoth.
[7]Gilead[c] is mine, and Manasseh is
mine;
Ephraim is my helmet,
Judah[d] is my scepter.[e]
[8]Moab is my washbasin,
on Edom I toss my sandal;
over Philistia I shout in
triumph.[f]"
[9]Who will bring me to the fortified
city?
Who will lead me to Edom?
[10]Is it not you, God, you who have now
rejected us
and no longer go out with our armies?[g]
[11]Give us aid against the enemy,
for human help is worthless.[h]
[12]With God we will gain the victory,
and he will trample down our
enemies.[i]

60:5 [z]Ps 17:7; 108:6 [a]Ps 127:2 **60:6** [b]Ge 12:6 **60:7** [c]Jos 13:31 [d]Dt 33:17 [e]Ge 49:10 **60:8** [f]2Sa 8:1 **60:10** [g]Jos 7:12; Ps 44:9; 108:11 **60:11** [h]Ps 146:3 **60:12** [i]Nu 24:18; Ps 44:5 **61:1** [j]Ps 64:1 [k]Ps 86:6 **61:2** [l]Ps 77:3 [m]Ps 18:2

Psalm 61[b]

For the director of music. With stringed instruments. Of David.

[1]Hear my cry, O God;[j]
listen to my prayer.[k]
[2]From the ends of the earth I call
to you,
I call as my heart grows faint;[l]
lead me to the rock[m] that is higher
than I.

[a] 4 The Hebrew has *Selah* (a word of uncertain meaning) here. [b] In Hebrew texts 61:1-8 is numbered 61:2-9.

60:4 *banner.* See note on SS 2:4.
60:6–8 The list of places in this prophecy name the regions under the sovereign control of Yahweh—either his agents in battle, if Israel, or his enemies whom he will defeat if they are foreign nations. Shechem was an important city in the north-central hill country of Israel, associated with patriarchal wanderings and worship (Ge 12:6; 33:18–20; 37:12), and the place of covenant renewal for the Israelites when they settled the land under Joshua (Jos 24). Since it was closely tied with Israel's presence in the land and the covenant with Yahweh, it serves here as a central reference point for Yahweh's possession of the land. Across the Jordan River from Shechem was Sukkoth, a city also associated with Jacob (Ge 33:17) and located near the valley of the Jabbok River. It was conquered by Joshua and given to the tribe of Gad, who settled in the Transjordan (Jos 13:27). Gilead is another name for this same region, and Manasseh is the tribe whose allotment included Shechem. Therefore, these first four geographic references are actually two, and they encompass the northern hill country on the west of the Jordan and the Transjordan on the east. Being just north of Moab and Edom, this region of Israel is appropriate in Yahweh's claim of possession and challenge to these foreign nations. Ephraim's tribal region was just south of Manasseh on the west side of the Jordan River, and Judah was the southernmost part of the land. The major foreign threat to Ephraim and Judah was the Mediterranean coastal region of the Philistines to the west. Thus, the list in this prophecy names the majority of the Israelite territories and their most immediate foreign enemies. The specific application of this prophecy is against Edom, east of the Dead Sea (see v. 9; see also title).
60:6 *spoken from his sanctuary.* The verses that follow quote a prophetic speech given at the tabernacle or temple (see note on 50:7). The contents of this speech may allude to a historical context described in the psalm's title, or it may be a generic prophecy of victory listing typical enemies of Israel. Its reuse in 108:6–13 demonstrates this possibility.
60:7 *helmet.* The Israelite tribes named are God's weapons, hence agents, in the war against hostile foreigners. *scepter.* Particularly appropriate to describe Judah, since this tribe was the source of the ruling dynasty of David (Ge 49:10).
60:8 *Moab is my washbasin.* May be a reference to Moab's proximity to the Dead Sea, but certainly denotes the subjugation of that nation by Yahweh (repeated in 108:9). They are forced into servanthood, being placed in a position where they must wash the feet of their master (cf. Jn 13:5). The container referred to here is usually used for cooking, but is a multipurpose pot/basin that comes in various sizes. Washbasins were typically used for ritual washing or ritual bathing. Washbasins occur in lists of fine gifts in the Amarna tablets. Despite these general comments, the precise imagery here is obscure. *on Edom I toss my sandal.* Sandals were the ordinary footwear in the ancient Near East, but they were also a symbolic item of clothing. This may have been due to the fact that land was purchased based on whatever size triangle of land someone could walk off in an hour, a day, a week or a month (1Ki 21:15–16). Land was surveyed in triangles, and a benchmark was constructed of fieldstones to serve as a boundary marker (Dt 19:14). Since they walked off the land in sandals, the sandals became the movable title to that land. Casting a sandal is a symbolic, legal gesture employed in those situations where a *levir* refuses to accept his responsibility to a widow. She in turn removes his sandal, the symbol of ownership and inheritance, and casts it at him. This signifies his loss of inheritance rights to the lands of his relative (Dt 25:9; Ru 4:7–8). Land transfers in the Nuzi tablets also involved replacing the old owner's foot on the land with that of the new owner. In this instance in the Psalms, God aggressively casts a sandal onto Edom as a gesture of conquest or the assumption of ownership of that nation's lands.
61:2 *ends of the earth.* This expression might refer to the earth's boundary with the underworld, a brush with death similar to the thought of Jnh 2:6 (see the articles "Death and Sheol," p. 833; "Death and the Underworld," p. 907). In the Mesopotamian Gilgamesh Epic, the hero travels to the horizon (the edge of the earth), where he encounters the mountain through which one descends to the underworld.

[3]For you have been my refuge,[n]
a strong tower against the foe.[o]

[4]I long to dwell[p] in your tent forever
and take refuge in the shelter of your wings.[a][q]

[5]For you, God, have heard my vows;[r]
you have given me the heritage of
those who fear your name.[s]

[6]Increase the days of the king's life,
his years for many generations.[t]
[7]May he be enthroned in God's
presence forever;[u]
appoint your love and faithfulness to
protect him.[v]

[8]Then I will ever sing in praise of your
name[w]
and fulfill my vows day after day.

Psalm 62[b]

For the director of music. For Jeduthun.
A psalm of David.

[1]Truly my soul finds rest[x] in God;
my salvation comes from him.
[2]Truly he is my rock[y] and my salvation;
he is my fortress, I will never be
shaken.

[3]How long will you assault me?
Would all of you throw me down—
this leaning wall,[z] this tottering
fence?
[4]Surely they intend to topple me
from my lofty place;
they take delight in lies.
With their mouths they bless,
but in their hearts they curse.[c][a]

[5]Yes, my soul, find rest in God;
my hope comes from him.
[6]Truly he is my rock and my salvation;
he is my fortress, I will not be
shaken.

[7]My salvation and my honor depend on
God[d];
he is my mighty rock, my refuge.[b]
[8]Trust in him at all times, you people;
pour out your hearts to him,[c]
for God is our refuge.

[9]Surely the lowborn are but a breath,[d]
the highborn are but a lie.
If weighed on a balance,[e] they are
nothing;
together they are only a breath.
[10]Do not trust in extortion
or put vain hope in stolen goods;[f]
though your riches increase,
do not set your heart on them.[g]

[11]One thing God has spoken,
two things I have heard:
"Power belongs to you, God,
[12]and with you, Lord, is unfailing
love";
and, "You reward everyone
according to what they have done."[h]

Psalm 63[e]

A psalm of David. When he was
in the Desert of Judah.

[1]You, God, are my God,
earnestly I seek you;
I thirst for you,[i]
my whole being longs for you,
in a dry and parched land
where there is no water.

[2]I have seen you in the sanctuary[j]
and beheld your power and your
glory.

61:3 [n]Ps 62:7 [o]Pr 18:10 **61:4** [p]Ps 23:6 [q]Ps 91:4 **61:5** [r]Ps 56:12 [s]Ps 86:11 **61:6** [t]Ps 21:4 **61:7** [u]Ps 41:12 [v]Ps 40:11 **61:8** [w]Ps 65:1; 71:22 **62:1** [x]Ps 33:20 **62:2** [y]Ps 89:26 **62:3** [z]Isa 30:13 **62:4** [a]Ps 28:3

62:7 [b]Ps 46:1; 85:9; Jer 3:23 **62:8** [c]1Sa 1:15; Ps 42:4; La 2:19 **62:9** [d]Ps 39:5, 11 [e]Isa 40:15 **62:10** [f]Isa 61:8 [g]Job 31:25; 1Ti 6:6-10 **62:12** [h]Job 34:11; Mt 16:27 **63:1** [i]Ps 42:2; 84:2 **63:2** [j]Ps 27:4

[a] 4 The Hebrew has *Selah* (a word of uncertain meaning) here. [b] In Hebrew texts 62:1-12 is numbered 62:2-13. [c] 4 The Hebrew has *Selah* (a word of uncertain meaning) here and at the end of verse 8. [d] 7 Or *I God Most High is my salvation and my honor* [e] In Hebrew texts 63:1-11 is numbered 63:2-12.

61:4 *tent ... wings.* The reference to God's "tent" brings to mind the winged cherubim of the tabernacle and temple (see notes on 15:1; 2Ki 19:15). However, the imagery points beyond this to the metaphor of God's protective embrace (see note on 36:7).
61:5,8 *vows.* See notes on Ge 28:20,22; Lev 7:12; 27:2; Pr 7:14; see also the article "Nazirites," p. 242.
62:4 *curse.* Unlike modern, western culture where a "curse" is nothing more than profanity, in the ancient world curses were taken very seriously (Ex 21:17). The reason is that a curse invoked a god to bring catastrophe or death upon another person. Even Israelites believed in the reality of other supernatural beings ("gods"; see note on 82:1) who would be fully capable of affecting the well-being of humans when invoked by a curse. In Mesopotamia and Ugarit, prayers and rituals were written to ward off potential injury from enemies who may have cursed the worshiper, especially through the agency of a sorcerer.
62:9 *breath.* See notes on 49:7–9; 90:3. *highborn.* As in 4:2, this Hebrew term (*beney ish*) functions as both a euphemism for the wealthy and powerful as well as a generic term for all men of influence. Both Egyptian and Babylonian texts contain similar expressions for this class of individuals. Babylonian texts, e.g., regularly make the distinction between "a gentleman" and an "ungentlemanly person"—contrasting those who were sophisticated, cultured and refined by virtue of their standing in society with those who were not.
63:2 *I have seen you.* While only priests enjoyed access to the inside of the sanctuary, the outer court was beautifully adorned with images of cherubs (in the tabernacle, at least), majestic pillars and an ever-burning altar that represented God's presence and consumed the sacrifices offered after God had answered prayer (see notes on 22:26; 56:12). In addition to the inspiring splendor of temple worship, the metaphor of "seeing God" means that the worshiper has experienced God's favor (see notes on 4:6; 42:2 ["meet with God"]), an experience in the past that gives the psalmist hope in present distress.

3 Because your love is better than life,[k]
my lips will glorify you.
4 I will praise you as long as I live,[l]
and in your name I will lift up my hands.[m]
5 I will be fully satisfied as with the richest of foods;[n]
with singing lips my mouth will praise you.

6 On my bed I remember you;
I think of you through the watches of the night.[o]
7 Because you are my help,[p]
I sing in the shadow of your wings.
8 I cling to you;
your right hand upholds me.[q]
9 Those who want to kill me will be destroyed;[r]
they will go down to the depths of the earth.[s]
10 They will be given over to the sword
and become food for jackals.

11 But the king will rejoice in God;
all who swear by God will glory in him,[t]
while the mouths of liars will be silenced.

Psalm 64[a]

For the director of music. A psalm of David.

1 Hear me, my God, as I voice my complaint;[u]
protect my life from the threat of the enemy.[v]
2 Hide me from the conspiracy of the wicked,[w]
from the plots of evildoers.
3 They sharpen their tongues like swords
and aim cruel words like deadly arrows.[x]
4 They shoot from ambush at the innocent;[y]
they shoot suddenly, without fear.[z]

5 They encourage each other in evil plans,
they talk about hiding their snares;
they say, "Who will see it[b]?"[a]
6 They plot injustice and say,
"We have devised a perfect plan!"
Surely the human mind and heart are cunning.

7 But God will shoot them with his arrows;
they will suddenly be struck down.
8 He will turn their own tongues against them[b]
and bring them to ruin;
all who see them will shake their heads[c] in scorn.
9 All people will fear;
they will proclaim the works of God
and ponder what he has done.[d]
10 The righteous will rejoice in the LORD
and take refuge in him;[e]
all the upright in heart will glory in him![f]

Psalm 65[c]

For the director of music. A psalm of David. A song.

1 Praise awaits[d] you, our God, in Zion;
to you our vows will be fulfilled.[g]
2 You who answer prayer,
to you all people will come.[h]
3 When we were overwhelmed by sins,[i]
you forgave[e] our transgressions.[j]
4 Blessed are those you choose[k]
and bring near to live in your courts!
We are filled with the good things of your house,[l]
of your holy temple.

5 You answer us with awesome and righteous deeds,
God our Savior,[m]
the hope of all the ends of the earth
and of the farthest seas,[n]
6 who formed the mountains by your power,
having armed yourself with strength,[o]
7 who stilled the roaring of the seas,[p]
the roaring of their waves,
and the turmoil of the nations.[q]
8 The whole earth is filled with awe at your wonders;
where morning dawns, where evening fades,
you call forth songs of joy.

9 You care for the land and water it;[r]
you enrich it abundantly.

63:3 [k]Ps 69:16 **63:4** [l]Ps 104:33 [m]Ps 28:2 **63:5** [n]Ps 36:8 **63:6** [o]Ps 42:8 **63:7** [p]Ps 27:9 **63:8** [q]Ps 18:35 **63:9** [r]Ps 40:14 [s]Ps 55:15 **63:11** [t]Dt 6:13; Ps 21:1; Isa 45:23 **64:1** [u]Ps 55:2 [v]Ps 140:1 **64:2** [w]Ps 56:6; 59:2 **64:3** [x]Ps 58:7 **64:4** [y]Ps 11:2 [z]Ps 55:19 **64:5** [a]Ps 10:11 **64:8** [b]Ps 9:3; Pr 18:7 [c]Ps 22:7 **64:9** [d]Jer 51:10 **64:10** [e]Ps 25:20 [f]Ps 32:11 **65:1** [g]Ps 116:18 **65:2** [h]Isa 66:23 **65:3** [i]Ps 38:4 [j]Heb 9:14 **65:4** [k]Ps 4:3; 33:12 [l]Ps 36:8 **65:5** [m]Ps 85:4 [n]Ps 107:23 **65:6** [o]Ps 93:1 **65:7** [p]Mt 8:26 [q]Isa 17:12-13 **65:9** [r]Ps 68:9-10

[a] In Hebrew texts 64:1-10 is numbered 64:2-11. [b] *5* Or *us* [c] In Hebrew texts 65:1-13 is numbered 65:2-14. [d] *1* Or *befits*; the meaning of the Hebrew for this word is uncertain. [e] *3* Or *made atonement for*

63:7 *shadow of your wings.* See note on 36:7.
63:9 *depths of the earth.* See the articles "Death and Sheol," p. 833; "Death and the Underworld," p. 907.
63:10 *food for jackals.* Lack of a proper burial meant dismemberment by wild scavengers, which, in the common thought of the ancient world, left no peace for the disembodied spirit (see notes on 141:7; 1Ki 14:11; 2Ki 9:10).
64:3 *tongues.* See note on 52:2.
64:5 *snares.* See notes on 124:7; 140:5.
65:1 *vows.* See notes on Ge 28:20,22; Lev 7:12; 27:2; Pr 7:14; see also the article "Nazirites," p. 242.
65:4 *courts.* See note on Ps 84; see also notes on 84:3; 100:4.
65:7 *seas … nations.* See notes on 93:3–4; 144:7.

The streams of God are filled with water
to provide the people with grain,[s]
for so you have ordained it.[a]
10 You drench its furrows and level its ridges;
you soften it with showers and bless its crops.
11 You crown the year with your bounty,
and your carts overflow with abundance.
12 The grasslands of the wilderness overflow;[t]
the hills are clothed with gladness.
13 The meadows are covered with flocks[u]
and the valleys are mantled with grain;[v]
they shout for joy and sing.[w]

Psalm 66

For the director of music. A song. A psalm.

1 Shout for joy to God, all the earth![x]
2 Sing the glory of his name;[y]
make his praise glorious.
3 Say to God, "How awesome are your deeds![z]
So great is your power
that your enemies cringe[a] before you.
4 All the earth bows down[b] to you;
they sing praise[c] to you,
they sing the praises of your name."[b]

5 Come and see what God has done,
his awesome deeds[d] for mankind!
6 He turned the sea into dry land,[e]
they passed through the waters on foot—
come, let us rejoice in him.
7 He rules forever[f] by his power,
his eyes watch[g] the nations—
let not the rebellious[h] rise up against him.

8 Praise[i] our God, all peoples,
let the sound of his praise be heard;
9 he has preserved our lives
and kept our feet from slipping.[j]
10 For you, God, tested us;
you refined us like silver.[k]
11 You brought us into prison
and laid burdens[l] on our backs.
12 You let people ride over our heads;[m]
we went through fire and water,
but you brought us to a place of abundance.[n]

65:9 [s]Ps 46:4; 104:14 **65:12** [t]Job 28:26 **65:13** [u]Ps 144:13 [v]Ps 72:16 [w]Ps 98:8; Isa 55:12 **66:1** [x]Ps 100:1 **66:2** [y]Ps 79:9 **66:3** [z]Ps 65:5 [a]Ps 18:44 **66:4** [b]Ps 22:27 [c]Ps 67:3 **66:5** [d]Ps 106:22 **66:6** [e]Ex 14:22 **66:7** [f]Ps 145:13 [g]Ps 11:4 [h]Ps 140:8 **66:8** [i]Ps 98:4 **66:9** [j]Ps 121:3 **66:10** [k]Ps 17:3; Isa 48:10; Zec 13:9; 1Pe 1:6-7 **66:11** [l]La 1:13 **66:12** [m]Isa 51:23 [n]Isa 43:2

66:13 [o]Ecc 5:4 **66:15** [p]Nu 6:14; Ps 51:19 **66:16** [q]Ps 34:11 [r]Ps 71:15,24 **66:18** [s]Job 36:21; Isa 1:15; Jas 4:3 **66:19** [t]Ps 116:1-2 **66:20** [u]Ps 22:24; 68:35 **67:1** [v]Nu 6:24-26; Ps 4:6 **67:2** [w]Isa 52:10 [x]Titus 2:11 **67:4** [y]Ps 96:10-13 **67:6** [z]Lev 26:4; Ps 85:12; Eze 34:27 **67:7** [a]Ps 33:8

13 I will come to your temple with burnt offerings
and fulfill my vows[o] to you—
14 vows my lips promised and my mouth spoke
when I was in trouble.
15 I will sacrifice fat animals to you
and an offering of rams;
I will offer bulls and goats.[p]

16 Come and hear,[q] all you who fear God;
let me tell[r] you what he has done for me.
17 I cried out to him with my mouth;
his praise was on my tongue.
18 If I had cherished sin in my heart,
the Lord would not have listened;[s]
19 but God has surely listened
and has heard[t] my prayer.
20 Praise be to God,
who has not rejected[u] my prayer
or withheld his love from me!

Psalm 67[c]

For the director of music. With stringed instruments. A psalm. A song.

1 May God be gracious to us and bless us
and make his face shine on us—[d][v]
2 so that your ways may be known on earth,
your salvation[w] among all nations.[x]

3 May the peoples praise you, God;
may all the peoples praise you.
4 May the nations be glad and sing for joy,
for you rule the peoples with equity[y]
and guide the nations of the earth.
5 May the peoples praise you, God;
may all the peoples praise you.

6 The land yields its harvest;[z]
God, our God, blesses us.
7 May God bless us still,
so that all the ends of the earth will fear him.[a]

[a] *9* Or *for that is how you prepare the land* [b] *4* The Hebrew has *Selah* (a word of uncertain meaning) here and at the end of verses 7 and 15. [c] In Hebrew texts 67:1-7 is numbered 67:2-8. [d] *1* The Hebrew has *Selah* (a word of uncertain meaning) here and at the end of verse 4.

65:12 *grasslands of the wilderness.* An image of fertility even in the desert. During the rainy season, the desert does support a growth of annuals and wildflowers.
66:10 *refined.* See note on Pr 17:3.
66:13–15 *offerings ... vows ... sacrifice.* See notes on Ge 28:20,22; Lev 7:12; 27:2; Pr 7:14; see also the article "Nazirites," p. 242.
67:1 *face shine on us.* This verse echoes the priestly blessing in Nu 6:24–26. Rather than "peace" (Nu 6:26), v. 2 wishes for God's deliverance of his people to be recognized by all the nations of the earth. The metaphor of the face shining in blessing is found in Ugaritic texts (see note on 4:6) and in Akkadian texts. An example of the latter is from a twelfth-century BC boundary marker invoking blessing upon the Babylonian king Nebuchadrezzar I to be indicated by the radiant shining face of his god Enlil.

Psalm 68[a]

For the director of music. Of David.
A psalm. A song.

[1] May God arise, may his enemies be
scattered;
may his foes flee[b] before him.
[2] May you blow them away like
smoke—[c]
as wax melts[d] before the fire,
may the wicked perish before God.
[3] But may the righteous be glad
and rejoice[e] before God;
may they be happy and joyful.

[4] Sing to God, sing in praise of his
name,[f]
extol him who rides on the clouds[b][g];
rejoice before him—his name is the
LORD.[h]
[5] A father to the fatherless,[i] a defender
of widows,[j]
is God in his holy dwelling.[k]
[6] God sets the lonely in families,[c][l]
he leads out the prisoners[m] with
singing;
but the rebellious live in a sun-
scorched land.[n]

[7] When you, God, went out[o] before your
people,
when you marched through the
wilderness,[d]
[8] the earth shook, the heavens poured
down rain,[p]
before God, the One of Sinai,[q]
before God, the God of Israel.
[9] You gave abundant showers,[r] O God;
you refreshed your weary
inheritance.
[10] Your people settled in it,
and from your bounty, God, you
provided[s] for the poor.

[11] The Lord announces the word,
and the women who proclaim it are
a mighty throng:
[12] "Kings and armies flee[t] in haste;
the women at home divide the
plunder.
[13] Even while you sleep among the sheep
pens,[e][u]
the wings of my dove are sheathed
with silver,
its feathers with shining gold."
[14] When the Almighty[f] scattered[v] the
kings in the land,
it was like snow fallen on Mount
Zalmon.

[15] Mount Bashan, majestic mountain,
Mount Bashan, rugged mountain,
[16] why gaze in envy, you rugged
mountain,
at the mountain where God
chooses[w] to reign,
where the LORD himself will dwell
forever?

68:1 [b] Nu 10:35; Isa 33:3 **68:2** [c] Hos 13:3 [d] Isa 9:18; Mic 1:4 **68:3** [e] Ps 32:11 **68:4** [f] Ps 66:2 [g] Dt 33:26 [h] Ex 6:3; Ps 83:18 **68:5** [i] Ps 10:14 [j] Dt 10:18 [k] Dt 26:15 **68:6** [l] Ps 113:9 [m] Ac 12:6 [n] Ps 107:34 **68:7** [o] Ex 13:21; Jdg 4:14 **68:8** [p] Jdg 5:4 [q] Ex 19:16, 18 **68:9** [r] Dt 11:11 **68:10** [s] Ps 74:19 **68:12** [t] Jos 10:16 **68:13** [u] Ge 49:14 **68:14** [v] Jos 10:10 **68:16** [w] Dt 12:5

[a] In Hebrew texts 68:1-35 is numbered 68:2-36.
[b] 4 Or *name, / prepare the way for him who rides through the deserts*
[c] 6 Or *the desolate in a homeland*
[d] 7 The Hebrew has *Selah* (a word of uncertain meaning) here and at the end of verses 19 and 32.
[e] 13 Or *the campfires;* or *the saddlebags*
[f] 14 Hebrew *Shaddai*

68:4 *rides on the clouds.* In the Ugaritic Baal Cycle, Baal is regularly referred to as the "rider of the clouds." References can be found in both the Baal Cycle and in the Aqhat Legend. This image of power over the winds and weather stands as another example of the psalmists using descriptions of the gods that were familiar in other cultures. In doing so they are asserting Yahweh's control over nature and nations (104:3; Jer 4:13)—a control elsewhere attributed to other gods.
68:6 *sets the lonely in families.* The Egyptian tale of the Eloquent Peasant provides a model for this set of responsibilities to the weak. The king in this Middle Kingdom wisdom piece is called the father to the orphan and the "mother to the motherless." Dt 24:17–22 describes laws dealing with justice for the vulnerable (see note on Dt 24:17). Ecc 4:8–9 also examines the plight of the one who is isolated, lonely and neglected. *leads out the prisoners.* In the ancient Near East, the freeing of prisoners (from debtors' prison) as an act of justice often occurred in the first or second year of a new king's reign (and then periodically after that). For example, King Ammisaduqa of the Old Babylonian period (seventeenth century BC) cancelled economic debts on behalf of Shamash. Thus, the "jubilee" in this case was primarily concerning those in debt (for either financial or legal reasons), and for the freeing of debt-slaves (see notes on Lev 25:10,39). Unlike Israel, this Babylonian edict was entirely at the whim of the monarch, and there is no evidence that it was divinely sanctioned. Historically, a proclamation of freedom is recorded by the last king of Judah, Zedekiah (Jer 34:8–10). For these and other characteristics of a just king's reign, see note on Ps 72; see also the articles "Enthronement in the Ancient Near East," p. 925; "Coronation Hymns in the Ancient Near East," p. 949.
68:13 *the wings of my dove are sheathed with silver.* There is no clear consensus on the meaning attached to a dove "sheathed with silver" and "feathers with shining gold." Some consider it a reference to the battle standards of the fleeing kings, which were topped by a dove, the symbol of the Canaanite goddess Astarte. Others see it as a reference to Israel (see other bird images in 74:19; Hos 7:11).
68:14 *Zalmon.* Because of the parallel in v. 15 with Bashan, it is unlikely that Mount Zalmon in this psalm is the same as the mountain mentioned in Jdg 9:48 near Shechem. Zalmon means "dark" or "black" and could refer to a peak shrouded in clouds. It would also require more elevation to serve as a snow-covered eminence.
68:15 *Mount Bashan.* The Bashan region, northeast of Galilee, is a fertile plateau about 2,000 feet (610 meters) in elevation. It is surrounded by extinct volcanic peaks and rolling hills with sufficient forestland to complement its cattle-raising economy (Isa 2:13; 33:9; Jer 50:19; see note on Am 4:1). *rugged mountain.* Probably refers to the hard to climb, basaltic hills in the Bashan area.
68:16 *mountain where God chooses to reign.* See notes on 48:1–2; 132:13.

17 The chariots of God are tens of
thousands
and thousands of thousands;[x]
the Lord has come from Sinai
into his sanctuary.[a]
18 When you ascended on high,
you took many captives;[y]
you received gifts from
people,[z]
even from[b] the rebellious—
that you,[c] LORD God, might dwell
there.

19 Praise be to the Lord, to God our
Savior,[a]
who daily bears our burdens.[b]
20 Our God is a God who saves;
from the Sovereign LORD comes
escape from death.[c]
21 Surely God will crush the heads[d]
of his enemies,
the hairy crowns of those who
go on in their sins.
22 The Lord says, "I will bring them from
Bashan;
I will bring them from the depths
of the sea,[e]
23 that your feet may wade in the blood
of your foes,[f]
while the tongues of your dogs[g]
have their share."

24 Your procession, God, has come into
view,
the procession of my God and King
into the sanctuary.[h]
25 In front are the singers, after them the
musicians;
with them are the young women
playing the timbrels.[i]
26 Praise God in the great congregation;
praise the LORD in the assembly
of Israel.[j]
27 There is the little tribe[k] of Benjamin,
leading them,
there the great throng of Judah's
princes,
and there the princes of Zebulun
and of Naphtali.

28 Summon your power, God[d];
show us your strength, our God, as
you have done before.
29 Because of your temple at Jerusalem
kings will bring you gifts.[l]
30 Rebuke the beast among the reeds,
the herd of bulls[m] among the calves
of the nations.
Humbled, may the beast bring bars
of silver.
Scatter the nations[n] who delight in
war.
31 Envoys will come from Egypt;[o]
Cush[e] will submit herself to God.
32 Sing to God, you kingdoms of the
earth,
sing praise to the Lord,
33 to him who rides[p] across the highest
heavens, the ancient heavens,
who thunders with mighty
voice.[q]
34 Proclaim the power[r] of God,
whose majesty is over Israel,
whose power is in the heavens.
35 You, God, are awesome in your
sanctuary;
the God of Israel gives power and
strength to his people.[s]

Praise be to God![t]

68:17 [x] Dt 33:2; Da 7:10 **68:18** [y] Jdg 5:12 [z] Eph 4:8* **68:19** [a] Ps 65:5 [b] Ps 55:22 **68:20** [c] Ps 56:13 **68:21** [d] Ps 110:5; Hab 3:13 **68:22** [e] Nu 21:33 **68:23** [f] Ps 58:10 [g] 1Ki 21:19 **68:24** [h] Ps 63:2 **68:25** [i] Jdg 11:34; 1Ch 13:8 **68:26** [j] Ps 26:12; Isa 48:1 **68:27** [k] 1Sa 9:21 **68:29** [l] Ps 72:10 **68:30** [m] Ps 22:12 [n] Ps 89:10 **68:31** [o] Isa 19:19; 45:14 **68:33** [p] Ps 18:10 [q] Ps 29:4 **68:34** [r] Ps 29:1 **68:35** [s] Ps 29:11 [t] Ps 66:20

[a] *17* Probable reading of the original Hebrew text; Masoretic Text *Lord is among them at Sinai in holiness* [b] *18* Or *gifts for people, / even* [c] *18* Or *they* [d] *28* Many Hebrew manuscripts, Septuagint and Syriac; most Hebrew manuscripts *Your God has summoned power for you* [e] *31* That is, the upper Nile region

68:18 *When you ascended on high, you took many captives … gifts.* Like the victorious Saul in 1Sa 15:7 – 15, the triumphant Yahweh is accompanied by a procession of prisoners, loot and tribute payments. A similar image can be found in the Assyrian annals of Sennacherib, who claims to have taken over 200,000 prisoners from Judah, along with their animals and other plunder. The major deities of the ancient Near East were associated with high places, so for Yahweh to "ascend" would be to return to his holy mountain (Jer 31:12), just as Baal used Mount Zaphon as his divine base of operations in the Ugaritic and Canaanite traditions (see note on 48:1 – 2).

68:23 *your feet may wade in the blood of your foes.* The poetic language attached to battle reports can at times be rather grisly. This is certainly the case with this phrase (also used in 58:10). The similar image of wading through the blood of one's enemies is also found in the Ugaritic Baal Cycle. There the goddess gleefully slaughtered whole armies, and she "waded knee-deep in the warriors' blood."

68:24 *procession … into the sanctuary.* The New Year's festival (Akitu) in ancient Babylon included a procession in which the image of the god Marduk was paraded along a "sacred highway" through the streets of the city. The god was guided by the king ("taken by the hand") up to the Esagila temple, where the image resided during the year. It was not the normal practice for this sort of procession to take place in Jerusalem, since Yahweh could not be represented by an image. However, the ark of the covenant, which functioned as an icon of God's power and presence, was brought into the city by king David and placed within the tabernacle (2Sa 6), and this is what may be celebrated in this psalm.

68:30 *beast among the reeds.* Probably refers to the hippopotamus or the crocodile. Both were major hazards along the shores of the Nile River in Egypt. The tomb paintings from Beni Hasan include a number of scenes in which fishermen work while a crocodile lurks in the reeds nearby, or in which papyrus boats are used to hunt this dangerous reptile. Politically, the image is most likely a reference to Egypt.

68:33 *rides across the highest heavens.* See note on v. 4.

Psalm 69[a]

For the director of music. To the tune of "Lilies." Of David.

1 Save me, O God,
for the waters have come up to my neck.[u]
2 I sink in the miry depths,[v]
where there is no foothold.
I have come into the deep waters;
the floods engulf me.
3 I am worn out calling for help;[w]
my throat is parched.
My eyes fail,[x]
looking for my God.
4 Those who hate me without reason[y]
outnumber the hairs of my head;
many are my enemies without cause,[z]
those who seek to destroy me.
I am forced to restore
what I did not steal.

5 You, God, know my folly;[a]
my guilt is not hidden from you.[b]
6 Lord, the LORD Almighty,
may those who hope in you
not be disgraced because of me;
God of Israel,
may those who seek you
not be put to shame because of me.
7 For I endure scorn for your sake,[c]
and shame covers my face.[d]
8 I am a foreigner to my own family,
a stranger to my own mother's children;[e]
9 for zeal for your house consumes me,[f]
and the insults of those who insult you fall on me.[g]
10 When I weep and fast,[h]
I must endure scorn;
11 when I put on sackcloth,[i]
people make sport of me.
12 Those who sit at the gate mock me,
and I am the song of the drunkards.[j]

13 But I pray to you, LORD,
in the time of your favor;[k]
in your great love,[l] O God,
answer me with your sure salvation.
14 Rescue me from the mire,
do not let me sink;
deliver me from those who hate me,
from the deep waters.[m]
15 Do not let the floodwaters[n] engulf me
or the depths swallow me up[o]
or the pit close its mouth over me.

16 Answer me, LORD, out of the goodness of your love;[p]
in your great mercy turn to me.
17 Do not hide your face[q] from your servant;
answer me quickly, for I am in trouble.[r]
18 Come near and rescue me;
deliver[s] me because of my foes.

19 You know how I am scorned,[t]
disgraced and shamed;
all my enemies are before you.
20 Scorn has broken my heart
and has left me helpless;
I looked for sympathy, but there was none,
for comforters,[u] but I found none.[v]
21 They put gall in my food
and gave me vinegar for my thirst.[w]

22 May the table set before them become a snare;
may it become retribution and[b] a trap.
23 May their eyes be darkened so they cannot see,
and their backs be bent forever.[x]
24 Pour out your wrath[y] on them;
let your fierce anger overtake them.
25 May their place be deserted;[z]
let there be no one to dwell in their tents.[a]
26 For they persecute those you wound
and talk about the pain of those you hurt.[b]

69:1 [u] Jnh 2:5 **69:2** [v] Ps 40:2 **69:3** [w] Ps 6:6 [x] Ps 119:82; Isa 38:14 **69:4** [y] Jn 15:25* [z] Ps 35:19; 38:19 **69:5** [a] Ps 38:5 [b] Ps 44:21 **69:7** [c] Jer 15:15 [d] Ps 44:15 **69:8** [e] Ps 31:11; Isa 53:3 **69:9** [f] Jn 2:17* [g] Ps 89:50-51; Ro 15:3* **69:10** [h] Ps 35:13 **69:11** [i] Ps 35:13 **69:12** [j] Job 30:9 **69:13** [k] Isa 49:8; 2Co 6:2 [l] Ps 51:1 **69:14** [m] ver 2; Ps 144:7 **69:15** [n] Ps 124:4-5 [o] Nu 16:33 **69:16** [p] Ps 63:3 **69:17** [q] Ps 27:9 [r] Ps 66:14 **69:18** [s] Ps 49:15 **69:19** [t] Ps 22:6 **69:20** [u] Job 16:2 [v] Isa 63:5 **69:21** [w] Mt 27:34; Mk 15:23; Jn 19:28-30 **69:23** [x] Isa 6:9-10; Ro 11:9-10* **69:24** [y] Ps 79:6 **69:25** [z] Mt 23:38 [a] Ac 1:20* **69:26** [b] Isa 53:4; Zec 1:15

[a] In Hebrew texts 69:1-36 is numbered 69:2-37.
[b] 22 Or *snare / and their fellowship become*

69:1 *waters.* Deep water was symbolic for any catastrophe of life (vv. 14–15; see note on 93:3–4).
69:8 *foreigner to my own family.* Scorn from close relatives and friends is a stereotypical theme in individual laments, expressing the depth of anguish (see note on 31:11). Though even today we would feel the weight of such estrangement, it is greatly multiplied in cultures in which a person's identity is bound up in their place and role in the clan.
69:10 *fast.* See note on Est 4:16.
69:11 *sackcloth.* See the article "Mourning," p. 828.
69:19 *I am scorned.* The Israelites believed that if God were to be considered just, rewards and punishments in this life would be proportional to the righteousness or wickedness of the individual. See the article "Retribution Principle," p. 823. Consequently, someone who was suffering either from illness or catastrophe, or even at the hands of someone's actions against them, their very suffering would stand as evidence of their guilt and result in scorn.
69:21 *gall.* In some contexts, this word refers to poison (e.g., snake venom in Dt 32:33), whereas on other occasions it refers to something bitter. This would match the parallel with "vinegar." In the former usage it could lead to almost certain death, while in the latter usage it may be understood as some kind of sedative. Presumably, the fast of mourning (v. 10) would be broken with food brought to the sufferer by comforters (e.g., 2Sa 3:35). In this case, however, instead of comfort and nourishment, the mourner receives just the opposite—poison (compare Amos's charge that justice has been transformed into poison in Am 6:12).

27 Charge them with crime upon crime;[c]
do not let them share in your
salvation.[d]
28 May they be blotted out of the book of
life[e]
and not be listed with the righteous.[f]
29 But as for me, afflicted and in pain —
may your salvation, God, protect
me.[g]

30 I will praise God's name in song[h]
and glorify him[i] with thanksgiving.
31 This will please the LORD more than
an ox,
more than a bull with its horns and
hooves.[j]
32 The poor will see and be glad[k] —
you who seek God, may your hearts
live![l]
33 The LORD hears the needy[m]
and does not despise his captive
people.

34 Let heaven and earth praise him,
the seas and all that move in
them,[n]
35 for God will save Zion[o]
and rebuild the cities of Judah.[p]
Then people will settle there and
possess it;
36 the children of his servants will
inherit it,
and those who love his name will
dwell there.[q]

Psalm 70[a]

70:1-5pp — Ps 40:13-17

For the director of music. Of David. A petition.

1 Hasten, O God, to save me;
come quickly, LORD, to help me.[r]

2 May those who want to take my life[s]
be put to shame and confusion;
may all who desire my ruin
be turned back in disgrace.[t]
3 May those who say to me, "Aha! Aha!"
turn back because of their shame.
4 But may all who seek you
rejoice and be glad in you;
may those who long for your saving
help always say,
"The LORD is great!"

5 But as for me, I am poor and needy;[u]
come quickly to me,[v] O God.
You are my help and my deliverer;
LORD, do not delay.

Psalm 71

71:1-3pp — Ps 31:1-4

1 In you, LORD, I have taken refuge;
let me never be put to shame.[w]
2 In your righteousness, rescue me and
deliver me;
turn your ear[x] to me and save me.
3 Be my rock of refuge,
to which I can always go;
give the command to save me,
for you are my rock and my
fortress.[y]
4 Deliver me, my God, from the hand of
the wicked,[z]
from the grasp of those who are evil
and cruel.

5 For you have been my hope, Sovereign
LORD,
my confidence[a] since my youth.
6 From birth[b] I have relied on you;
you brought me forth from my
mother's womb.[c]
I will ever praise[d] you.
7 I have become a sign[e] to many;
you are my strong refuge.[f]
8 My mouth[g] is filled with your praise,
declaring your splendor[h] all day
long.

9 Do not cast[i] me away when I am
old;[j]
do not forsake me when my strength
is gone.
10 For my enemies speak against me;
those who wait to kill[k] me conspire[l]
together.

69:27 [c] Ne 4:5 [d] Ps 109:14; Isa 26:10 **69:28** [e] Ex 32:32-33; Lk 10:20; Php 4:3 [f] Eze 13:9 **69:29** [g] Ps 59:1; 70:5 **69:30** [h] Ps 28:7 [i] Ps 34:3 **69:31** [j] Ps 50:9-13 **69:32** [k] Ps 34:2 [l] Ps 22:26 **69:33** [m] Ps 12:5; 68:6 **69:34** [n] Ps 96:11; 148:1; Isa 44:23; 49:13; 55:12 **69:35** [o] Ob 1:17 [p] Ps 51:18; Isa 44:26 **69:36** [q] Ps 37:29; 102:28 **70:1** [r] Ps 40:13 **70:2** [s] Ps 35:4 [t] Ps 35:26 **70:5** [u] Ps 40:17 [v] Ps 141:1 **71:1** [w] Ps 25:2-3; 31:1 **71:2** [x] Ps 17:6 **71:3** [y] Ps 18:2; 31:2-3; 44:4 **71:4** [z] Ps 140:4 **71:5** [a] Job 4:6; Jer 17:7 **71:6** [b] Ps 22:10 [c] Ps 22:9; Isa 46:3 [d] Ps 9:1; 34:1; 52:9; 119:164; 145:2 **71:7** [e] Isa 8:18; 1Co 4:9 [f] 2Sa 22:3; Ps 61:3 **71:8** [g] Ps 51:15; 63:5 [h] Ps 35:28; 96:6; 104:1 **71:9** [i] Ps 51:11 [j] ver 18; Ps 92:14; Isa 46:4 **71:10** [k] Ps 10:8; 59:3; Pr 1:18 [l] Ps 31:13; 56:6; Mt 12:14

[a] In Hebrew texts 70:1-5 is numbered 70:2-6.

69:28 *blotted out of the book of life.* The metaphor of divine scribal activity is known in Mesopotamia, usually in expressions of hope that the deity would inscribe one's name for long life in a heavenly tablet. In the Sumerian Hymn to Nungal, the goddess discusses her justice as she punishes the wicked and brings mercy to those who deserve it. She claims to hold in her hands the tablets of life, on which she writes down the names of the just. Here, the psalmist wishes the opposite for his enemies (see the article "Imprecations and Incantations," p. 937).
69:31 *horns and hooves.* Indicates a full-grown bull (cf. Mic 6:6), an expensive sacrificial animal, which is ritually pure according to the Holiness Code (i.e., Lev 17:1 — 26:46; see also Lev 11:3 – 8).

Ps 70 This psalm parallels the wording of 40:13 – 17 (see the article "Repeated Psalms," p. 990).
71:7 *sign.* The use of the Hebrew term *mopet* is indicative of an extraordinary event that serves as a sign of God's power, and in this case judgment or punishment (compare the curses in Dt 28:45 – 46). This technical term appears often in the narrative of the plagues in Egypt (e.g., Ex 7:3 ["wonders"]; 11:9 ["wonders"]), and is used to signal a coming event (1Ki 13:3,5). The term does not necessarily designate something supernatural as opposed to natural (i.e., a "miracle"). In the ancient world, people did not consider anything truly "natural" — God was involved in everything and therefore "miracle" was a meaningless designation.

11 They say, "God has forsaken him;
pursue him and seize him,
for no one will rescue[m] him."
12 Do not be far[n] from me, my God;
come quickly, God, to help[o] me.
13 May my accusers perish in shame;
may those who want to harm me
be covered with scorn and
disgrace.[p]

14 As for me, I will always have hope;[q]
I will praise you more and more.
15 My mouth will tell[r] of your righteous
deeds,
of your saving acts all day long—
though I know not how to relate
them all.
16 I will come and proclaim your mighty
acts,[s] Sovereign LORD;
I will proclaim your righteous deeds,
yours alone.
17 Since my youth, God, you have taught[t]
me,
and to this day I declare your
marvelous deeds.[u]
18 Even when I am old and gray,[v]
do not forsake me, my God,
till I declare your power to the next
generation,
your mighty acts to all who are to
come.[w]

19 Your righteousness, God, reaches to
the heavens,[x]
you who have done great things.[y]
Who is like you, God?[z]
20 Though you have made me see
troubles,[a]
many and bitter,
you will restore[b] my life again;
from the depths of the earth
you will again bring me up.
21 You will increase my honor[c]
and comfort[d] me once more.

22 I will praise you with the harp[e]
for your faithfulness, my God;
I will sing praise to you with the lyre,[f]
Holy One of Israel.[g]
23 My lips will shout for joy
when I sing praise to you—
I whom you have delivered.[h]
24 My tongue will tell of your righteous
acts
all day long,[i]
for those who wanted to harm me[j]
have been put to shame and confusion.

71:11 [m] Ps 7:2 **71:12** [n] Ps 35:22; 38:21 [o] Ps 38:22; 70:1 **71:13** [p] ver 24 **71:14** [q] Ps 130:7 **71:15** [r] Ps 35:28; 40:5 **71:16** [s] Ps 106:2 **71:17** [t] Dt 4:5 [u] Ps 26:7 **71:18** [v] ver 9 [w] Ps 22:30, 31; 78:4 **71:19** [x] Ps 36:5; 57:10 [y] Ps 126:2; Lk 1:49 [z] Ps 35:10 **71:20** [a] Ps 60:3 [b] Hos 6:2 **71:21** [c] Ps 18:35 [d] Ps 23:4; 86:17; Isa 12:1; 49:13 **71:22** [e] Ps 33:2 [f] Ps 92:3; 144:9 [g] 2Ki 19:22 **71:23** [h] Ps 103:4 **71:24** [i] Ps 35:28 [j] ver 13 **72:2** [k] Isa 9:7; 11:4-5; 32:1 **72:4** [l] Isa 11:4

Psalm 72

Of Solomon.

1 Endow the king with your justice,
O God,
the royal son with your
righteousness.
2 May he judge your people in
righteousness,[k]
your afflicted ones with justice.

3 May the mountains bring prosperity to
the people,
the hills the fruit of righteousness.
4 May he defend the afflicted among the
people
and save the children of the needy;[l]
may he crush the oppressor.
5 May he endure[a] as long as the sun,
as long as the moon, through all
generations.

[a] 5 Septuagint; Hebrew *You will be feared*

71:20 *depths of the earth.* See the articles "Death and Sheol," p. 833; "Death and the Underworld," p. 907.
71:22 *harp … lyre.* See the articles "Lyre," p. 488; "Music and Musicians," p. 524.
Ps 72 Woven together throughout Ps 72 are the themes of justice, peace and domestic prosperity. In the prologue to the Code of Hammurapi, and especially in the epilogue, the king boasts that his just rule also brings peace and prosperity to the cities of his realm. Immediately following the prayer for justice in "Ashurbanipal's Coronation Hymn," the priest asks that the king's dominion might also be characterized by prosperity (abundance of grain; cf. v. 16) and "peace" (Assyrian *salimu* is akin to the Hebrew *salom* in v. 3 [NIV "prosperity"]).

Injustice resulted in social chaos (see note on 94:20). In Egyptian thought, the execution of justice by the king expels chaos from creation, bringing harmony and order to the land. Thus, in both Mesopotamia and Egypt, people set their hope on the king for justice and prosperity. In Egypt, this revolved around a pharaoh who participated in the company of the gods and mediated divine blessing to humanity, but this hope never focused beyond the currently living king, except very late in Egyptian history (c. 300 BC), when expectations arose among some that a king would arise to restore the former glory of Egypt. Similarly, Mesopotamians did not conceive of a future king who would usher in an ideal age. People considered only their contemporary king as the agent of the gods who ideally maintained a prosperous social order. In contrast, in the OT one finds a progressively developing theme of hope for a future, worldwide kingdom ruled by a Davidic king on behalf of Yahweh.
72:4 *defend the afflicted.* Care for the weak members of society is the practical test of a just and good government throughout the ancient Near East, as claimed by Hammurapi (see note on Ps 72; see also the article "Coronation Hymns in the Ancient Near East," p. 949). In the Ugaritic Kirta epic, King Kirta is rebuked for failure to "pursue the widow's case," "take up the wretched's claim," "expel the poor's oppressor" and "feed the orphan." In the Egyptian "Teaching for Merikare," the king is exhorted, "Do justice, then you endure on earth; / Calm the weeper, don't oppress the widow."
72:5 *May he endure.* Along with the hope for justice and prosperity, Ps 72 anticipates a long reign. This strikes another parallel with "Ashurbanipal's Coronation Hymn," in which the priest prays that the god Assur would "lengthen your days and years." *as long as the sun … moon.*

6 May he be like rain[m] falling on a mown
field,
like showers watering the earth.
7 In his days may the righteous flourish[n]
and prosperity abound till the moon
is no more.

8 May he rule from sea to sea
and from the River[a][o] to the ends of
the earth.[p]
9 May the desert tribes bow before him
and his enemies lick the dust.
10 May the kings of Tarshish and of
distant shores
bring tribute to him.
May the kings of Sheba[q] and Seba
present him gifts.[r]
11 May all kings bow down to him
and all nations serve him.

12 For he will deliver the needy who cry
out,
the afflicted who have no one to help.
13 He will take pity on the weak and the
needy
and save the needy from death.
14 He will rescue[s] them from oppression
and violence,
for precious[t] is their blood in his
sight.

15 Long may he live!
May gold from Sheba[u] be given him.
May people ever pray for him
and bless him all day long.
16 May grain abound throughout the
land;
on the tops of the hills may it sway.
May the crops flourish like Lebanon[v]
and thrive[b] like the grass of the
field.
17 May his name endure forever;[w]
may it continue as long as the sun.[x]

[a] *8* That is, the Euphrates [b] *16* Probable reading of the original Hebrew text; Masoretic Text *Lebanon, / from the city*

72:6 [m] Dt 32:2; Hos 6:3 **72:7** [n] Ps 92:12; Isa 2:4 **72:8** [o] Ex 23:31 [p] Zec 9:10 **72:10** [q] Ge 10:7 [r] 2Ch 9:24 **72:14** [s] Ps 69:18 [t] 1Sa 26:21; Ps 116:15 **72:15** [u] Isa 60:6 **72:16** [v] Ps 104:16 **72:17** [w] Ex 3:15 [x] Ps 89:36

These metaphors of an enduring reign are common in royal literature (see note on 89:36–37). A Phoenician royal servant named Azatiwata wished his good name to be remembered "forever like the name of the sun and the moon" (cf. v. 17; 89:36–37).

72:6 *May he be like rain.* In an agriculturally based society, rain is essential to a prosperous economy. "Ashurbanipal's Coronation Hymn" asks that in his years there may be constant rain from the heavens. In Ps 72, the king himself is likened to these precious waters that bring life to the earth. This theme occurs again in v. 16, where prayer is offered for abundant grain, like the vegetation that flourishes on the well-watered mountains of Lebanon.

72:8 *from sea to sea.* Frequently in poetry, the author uses two extremes to express the totality of everything in between (a figure of speech called "merism"). In royal literature, it was used to stress the unlimited extent of a king's dominion over geographic space and time. There may be an allusion in this verse to the geographic perspective of the ancient Near East that the earth was surrounded by the sea (see note on 24:2). Thus, "sea to sea" meant across the entire world. *the River.* Here it may refer to the Euphrates River (cf. 1Ki 4:21); but if a more universal view is intended, it could be understood as synonymous with the "sea" (i.e., the cosmic ocean viewed as a current of water, like a river, encircling the earth; see the article "Cosmic Geography," p. 836). If this viewpoint is maintained, then in this verse the phrases "sea to sea" and "River to the ends of the earth" are parallel expressions for the distance from one end of the world to the other. The peoples named in Ps 72—those of Tarshish, Sheba and Seba (v. 10)—represent the most remote and hostile places. From the farthest reaches of the Mediterranean Sea in the west to the coastal shores to the south (the Red Sea), and including the desert in between (v. 9), all people will submit to the king, and the most distant nations will bring tribute to him. This is yet another way of expressing the geographic expanse of the king's dominion from "sea to sea" (i.e., the Mediterranean Sea and the Red Sea, parts of the great ocean that surrounded the earth). Anticipation of an extensive kingdom in Ps 72 has a counterpart in "Ashurbanipal's Coronation Hymn" as well: "Spread your land wide at your feet."

72:9 *desert tribes.* Desert bands created havoc even for the mighty Assyrian Empire, necessitating repeated campaigns against them in order to keep trade routes open. This text is generally emended from the Hebrew *tsiyyim* ("desert dweller") to *tsarayw* ("his foes"). If the original reading is retained, then it could relate back to the use of "Cush" (the desert region of Ethiopia) in 68:31 as a geographic term for the "ends of the earth" and thus follow the coronation promise in v. 8.

72:10 *Tarshish … Sheba and Seba.* In order to indicate the extent of the king's power, rulers from throughout the world come to him with gifts. Thus, Tarshish, associated with the islands and nations in the western Mediterranean, represents all points to the west (see notes on Isa 23:1; 60:9). Sheba is identified with southern Arabia (Yemen) and the Sabean kingdom (see note on Isa 60:6). Sheba's location is still disputed, although some place it in Ethiopia or along the northwest Arabian incense road (Isa 43:3).

72:12–14 It is standard in ancient Near Eastern literature to portray the king as lawgiver (cf. Pr 29:14) and defender of the weak (an attribute of God in 35:10). The Egyptian tale of the "Eloquent Peasant" states that the king's duty is to "father the orphan." The coronation hymn of the Ur III king Ur-Nammu describes him as the "sustainer of Ur." In the prologue of the Code of Hammurapi, Hammurapi of Babylon is given the task by the gods to "promote the welfare of the people" and "cause justice to prevail in the land," so that "the strong might not oppress the weak." In all of these we can see that the rhetoric related to kingship in Israel follows similar lines to that found throughout the ancient Near East.

72:15 *Long may he live!* "Ashurbanipal's Coronation Hymn" asks the deities to give the king a long reign. Stereotypical interjections were used in Egyptian inscriptions, asking life for the king (e.g., "given life, duration, dominion, may he live like Re"). Length of life for a just king meant enduring peace and a good life for his people. *gold from Sheba.* While there are gold resources on the Arabian peninsula (the most likely location of Sheba), the maritime trade that took place in the Red Sea would have channeled some of the famous gold resources of Nubia (south of Egypt) through Sheba (Eze 27:22). Gold was customarily part of the tribute paid to great kings (see 2Ki 18:14–16 and Sennacherib's corresponding record of this tribute).

PSALM 72

Coronation Hymns in the Ancient Near East

There is a good deal of evidence to indicate that in the civilizations of ancient Mesopotamia kingship was viewed as a gift from the gods. The prologue to the Code of Hammurapi contains a statement that the king has been proclaimed "the shepherd" by the god Enlil, and that it is his task to "cause justice to prevail in the land." During the Akitu New Year's festival, the king was reinvested with his powers of office. This would have included a great procession and mass celebration. The Ur III texts from about 2000 BC contain hymns composed for these occasions, celebrating the coronation of king Ur-Nammu. These compositions contain a set of statements that chronicle the stages of the investiture ritual, including the "pressing of the holy scepter" into the king's hand. These verses are to be sung by or for the king, proclaiming his god-given duties as lawgiver and the constructor of canals that bring fertility to the land. There is an answering litany by the priests containing the king's titles and affirming him as "king of Ur." ◆

Investiture scene from Mari.
Kim Walton. The Louvre.

Then all nations will be blessed
through him,[a]
and they will call him blessed.[y]

18 Praise be to the LORD God, the God
of Israel,[z]
who alone does marvelous
deeds.[a]
19 Praise be to his glorious name
forever;
may the whole earth be filled with
his glory.[b]
Amen and Amen.[c]

20 This concludes the prayers of David
son of Jesse.

72:17 [y] Ge 12:3; Lk 1:48 **72:18** [z] 1Ch 29:10; Ps 41:13; 106:48 [a] Job 5:9 **72:19** [b] Nu 14:21; Ne 9:5 [c] Ps 41:13

73:1 [d] Mt 5:8

BOOK III

Psalms 73 – 89

Psalm 73

A psalm of Asaph.

1 Surely God is good to Israel,
to those who are pure in
heart.[d]

2 But as for me, my feet had almost
slipped;
I had nearly lost my foothold.

[a] 17 Or *will use his name in blessings* (see Gen. 48:20)

[3] For I envied[e] the arrogant
when I saw the prosperity of the wicked.[f]

[4] They have no struggles;
their bodies are healthy and strong.[a]
[5] They are free[g] from common human burdens;
they are not plagued by human ills.
[6] Therefore pride is their necklace;[h]
they clothe themselves with violence.[i]
[7] From their callous hearts[j] comes iniquity[b];
their evil imaginations have no limits.
[8] They scoff, and speak with malice;
with arrogance[k] they threaten oppression.
[9] Their mouths lay claim to heaven,
and their tongues take possession of the earth.
[10] Therefore their people turn to them
and drink up waters in abundance.[c]
[11] They say, "How would God know?
Does the Most High know anything?"

[12] This is what the wicked are like—
always free of care, they go on amassing wealth.[l]

[13] Surely in vain[m] I have kept my heart pure
and have washed my hands in innocence.[n]
[14] All day long I have been afflicted,
and every morning brings new punishments.

[15] If I had spoken out like that,
I would have betrayed your children.
[16] When I tried to understand[o] all this,
it troubled me deeply
[17] till I entered the sanctuary[p] of God;
then I understood their final destiny.[q]

[18] Surely you place them on slippery ground;[r]
you cast them down to ruin.

73:3 [e] Ps 37:1; Pr 23:17 [f] Job 21:7; Jer 12:1 **73:5** [g] Job 21:9 **73:6** [h] Ge 41:42 [i] Ps 109:18 **73:7** [j] Ps 17:10 **73:8** [k] Ps 17:10; Jude 16 **73:12** [l] Ps 49:6 **73:13** [m] Job 21:15; 34:9 [n] Ps 26:6 **73:16** [o] Ecc 8:17 **73:17** [p] Ps 77:13 [q] Ps 37:38 **73:18** [r] Ps 35:6

73:19 [s] Isa 47:11 **73:20** [t] Job 20:8 [u] Ps 78:65 **73:22** [v] Ps 49:10; 92:6 [w] Ecc 3:18 **73:24** [x] Ps 48:14 [y] Ps 32:8 **73:25** [z] Php 3:8 **73:26** [a] Ps 84:2 [b] Ps 40:12 **73:27** [c] Ps 119:155 **73:28** [d] Heb 10:22; Jas 4:8 [e] Ps 40:5 **74:1** [f] Dt 29:20; Ps 44:23 [g] Ps 79:13; 95:7; 100:3

[19] How suddenly[s] are they destroyed,
completely swept away by terrors!
[20] They are like a dream[t] when one awakes;[u]
when you arise, Lord,
you will despise them as fantasies.

[21] When my heart was grieved
and my spirit embittered,
[22] I was senseless[v] and ignorant;
I was a brute beast[w] before you.

[23] Yet I am always with you;
you hold me by my right hand.
[24] You guide[x] me with your counsel,[y]
and afterward you will take me into glory.
[25] Whom have I in heaven but you?
And earth has nothing I desire besides you.[z]
[26] My flesh and my heart[a] may fail,[b]
but God is the strength of my heart
and my portion forever.

[27] Those who are far from you will perish;[c]
you destroy all who are unfaithful to you.
[28] But as for me, it is good to be near God.[d]
I have made the Sovereign LORD my refuge;
I will tell of all your deeds.[e]

Psalm 74

A *maskil*[d] of Asaph.

[1] O God, why have you rejected us forever?[f]
Why does your anger smolder
against the sheep of your pasture?[g]

[a] 4 With a different word division of the Hebrew; Masoretic Text *struggles at their death; / their bodies are healthy* [b] 7 Syriac (see also Septuagint); Hebrew *Their eyes bulge with fat* [c] 10 The meaning of the Hebrew for this verse is uncertain. [d] Title: Probably a literary or musical term

73:9 *heaven ... earth.* A common figure of speech called a "merism" occurs when two opposites are mentioned to express the whole. The pairing of the words "heaven" and "earth" is common in the OT (e.g., 96:11; Ge 1:1; Dt 32:1; Job 20:27; 38:33), but a parallel using the pairing of "lips" and "tongue" appears in the Baal Cycle, when the god of death, Mot, threatens to swallow Baal by opening his mouth so wide that one lip touches heaven and the other touches earth, and the tongue touches the stars. In this verse, "heaven" and "earth" are paired to suggest that the wicked have extended their ownership (and power) to control everything.

73:24 *take me into glory.* The NIV's inclusion of the word "into" is totally interpretive, not being found in the Hebrew text. The concept of God "taking" a person as a reference to saving his life can be seen clearly in 18:16, where the NIV translates the same phrase as "took hold of me." The word "glory" is never used in Hebrew as a synonym for heaven, and here refers to an "honorable" resolution to the psalmist's crisis. His difficulties have brought him shame because suffering was considered a sign of sin and God's displeasure (see the articles "Retribution Principle," p. 823; "Death and the Underworld," p. 907). This psalm therefore expresses the hope that God will take action that will save the psalmist's life and restore his honor. Honor and shame were key issues in the cultures of the ancient Near East (see the article "Honor-Shame Cultures," p. 902), including Israel, where identity was found in one's status in the clan and in the community.

74:1 *sheep of your pasture.* This is a common metaphor in city laments. The deity is like a shepherd who has dwelt in a hut (i.e., the temple) within the sheepfold (i.e., the city).

PSALM 74

City Laments

In Mesopotamia, the destruction of a holy city and its temple and the anticipation or hope for its rebuilding gave rise to hymns called "city laments," which bear similarity to Ps 74; 79 (see also the articles "Community Laments in the Ancient Near East," p. 919; "Hymns to Holy Cities," p. 927). One of the earliest such compositions, the "Lament Over the Destruction of Ur" (c. 2000 BC), arose shortly after the destruction of the city when efforts were being made to rebuild its ruins. Designated a "harp lament" by the ancient composer, it probably accompanied the rituals associated with the restoration of the temple. The first part consists of a complaint by the patron goddess of the city; it rehearses the decision of the gods to destroy the city, describes details of the siege and slaughter of the inhabitants, and replays the painful cry of the goddess at that time. The second part is a prayer by the survivors to curse the enemy, whose onslaught is likened to a storm, and to ask for the city's restoration. The purpose of these laments appears to have been to appease and console the angry deity by shifting blame onto the enemy perpetrators and the council of the gods. Thus, no further wrath would accrue when the holy site was desecrated in the rebuilding process. Numerous themes and images are shared with the Biblical psalms (see notes on Ps 74 and 79), but some important differences remain. The Biblical psalms do not feature the words of God in lament for Jerusalem or his temple or any appeal to lesser deities for help. Rather than function to ward off further wrath, Ps 74 and Ps 79 complain that Yahweh should intervene to restore his holy city. Nothing on earth could be more symbolic of the restoration of God's rule and blessing on his people (see the article "Sacred Space," p. 964); and for this the psalmist longed and prayed. ◆

Lamentation over the ruins of Ur, c. 1800 BC.

[2]Remember the nation you purchased[h]
long ago,[i]
the people of your inheritance,
whom you redeemed[j]—
Mount Zion, where you dwelt.[k]
[3]Turn your steps toward these
everlasting ruins,
all this destruction the enemy has
brought on the sanctuary.

[4]Your foes roared[l] in the place where
you met with us;
they set up their standards[m] as
signs.
[5]They behaved like men wielding axes
to cut through a thicket of trees.[n]
[6]They smashed all the carved[o]
paneling
with their axes and hatchets.
[7]They burned your sanctuary to the
ground;
they defiled the dwelling place of
your Name.
[8]They said in their hearts, "We will
crush[p] them completely!"
They burned every place where God
was worshiped in the land.

[9]We are given no signs from God;
no prophets[q] are left,
and none of us knows how long this
will be.

[10]How long will the enemy mock you,
God?
Will the foe revile[r] your name
forever?
[11]Why do you hold back your hand,
your right hand?[s]
Take it from the folds of your
garment and destroy them!

[12]But God is my King[t] from long ago;
he brings salvation on the earth.

[13]It was you who split open the sea[u]
by your power;
you broke the heads of the monster[v]
in the waters.
[14]It was you who crushed the heads
of Leviathan
and gave it as food to the creatures
of the desert.
[15]It was you who opened up springs[w]
and streams;
you dried up[x] the ever-flowing
rivers.
[16]The day is yours, and yours also the
night;
you established the sun and
moon.[y]
[17]It was you who set all the boundaries[z]
of the earth;
you made both summer and
winter.[a]

74:2 [h]Ex 15:16 [i]Dt 32:7 [j]Ex 15:13 [k]Ps 68:16 **74:4** [l]La 2:7 [m]Nu 2:2 **74:5** [n]Jer 46:22 **74:6** [o]1Ki 6:18 **74:8** [p]Ps 83:4 **74:9** [q]1Sa 3:1

74:10 [r]Ps 44:16 **74:11** [s]La 2:3 **74:12** [t]Ps 44:4 **74:13** [u]Ex 14:21 [v]Isa 51:9; Eze 29:3 **74:15** [w]Ex 17:6; Nu 20:11 [x]Jos 2:10; 3:13 **74:16** [y]Ge 1:16; Ps 136:7-9 **74:17** [z]Dt 32:8; Ac 17:26 [a]Ge 8:22

Abandonment of the city is tantamount to abandoning the people, who are like sheep (cf. 83:12).

74:2 *where you dwelt.* In Sumerian city laments, it is only after a deity has abandoned his or her city that it is vulnerable to attack. See note on 46:5; see also the articles "Enthronement in the Ancient Near East," p. 925; "Hymns to Holy Cities," p. 927.

74:3 *destruction ... brought on the sanctuary.* The destruction of Jerusalem and the temple (586 BC), described in 2Ki 25:8–17, lies at the heart of this psalm. While there are no extra-Biblical descriptions of this event, the Babylonian Chronicle does record the capture of Jerusalem and the deportation of the king of Judah (Jehoiachin) 11 years earlier in 597 BC (2Ki 24:8–17), at which time the temple treasures were plundered.

74:4 *standards.* The Hebrew word can refer to a military banner with insignia to distinguish different troop units (see note on Nu 1:52; see also note on SS 2:4, where a different Hebrew word is used for the same object). Because these insignia bore symbols of foreign gods, raising them at the site of the temple was particularly sacrilegious (cf. v. 10).

74:6 *smashed ... with their axes.* The Lament Over the Destruction of Ur draws on the same image one might expect of such destruction: into the temple "big copper axes chewed." Other lines describe the fires that consumed buildings and people alike. These graphic images stir deep feelings for the tragedy. *carved paneling.* It is difficult to determine whether this refers to carved panels in the temple or to engravings on some of the bronze or gold pieces connected to the temple. What is clear is that the intricate artwork that embellished this temple (as many others in the ancient world) was being ruthlessly destroyed.

74:8 *every place where God was worshiped.* It is not likely the psalmist would lament the destruction of illegitimate places of worship, whether within the temple complex or at various sites throughout the land (2Ki 21:1–6; 23:1–20). Perhaps these were simply special meeting places for prayer. In cities and villages of the ancient Near East, local shrines other than central, regional temple complexes accommodated the needs of the common people. Even at times when orthodox worship prevailed in Jerusalem, one might expect multiple gathering places that did not necessarily provide for sacrifices or other unauthorized rituals in competition with the Jerusalem temple. Unfortunately, the only places for religious gathering that would leave a clear trace in the archaeological record are those with illicit features such as altars or figurines.

74:13 *split open the sea.* There is nothing in this psalm to suggest that reference is being made to the dividing of the Red Sea. The context concerns instead the cosmic battle with the sea that is referred to many times in Psalms. The Hebrew verb used here is used only here in this form, making precision somewhat difficult. If splitting is intended, it may be parallel to Marduk's splitting of Tiamat (sea) that is recounted in *Enuma Elish.* Others have translated it as a reference to the churning of the sea that sometimes precedes such battles (see note on Da 7:2–3). See the article "Chaos Monsters," p. 953.

74:14 *Leviathan.* Often identified as a crocodile; crocodiles were found mostly in Egypt (where it symbolized kingly power and greatness), but also sparsely in Palestine. However, the multiple heads here and the fiery breath in Job 41:19–21 make the crocodile identification difficult. Alternatively, Leviathan has been depicted as a sea monster—one of the chaos creatures well known in the ancient world (see the article "Leviathan," p. 874).

PSALM 74:13 – 14

CHAOS MONSTERS

In order to underscore the power of God to intervene if he so chooses, the psalmist alludes to a well-known myth in the ancient Near East about the triumph of a god over the sea serpent. The closest neighbors to ancient Israel that preserved this myth were the Canaanites, whose religion is best represented by the texts from Ugarit (c. 1300 BC). In the Ugaritic Baal Cycle, Baal defeats the sea-god Yamm (Ugaritic *ym* = Hebrew *yam*, "sea") and thereby earns the title "king" together with the right to a palace-temple (see the article "Psalm 29: A Canaanite Hymn?" p. 905). The epic refers to Yamm using the same names and imagery as those in Ps 74:13 – 14: "When you killed Litan (Ugaritic *ltn* = Hebrew *lwtyn*, "Leviathan"), the Fleeing Serpent, annihilated the Twisty Serpent, The Potentate with Seven Heads." Yahweh and Baal both conquer the "Sea," also called "Litan/Leviathan." In the Baal Cycle, the sea is portrayed as a multiheaded serpent, corresponding to the "heads" (plural) in Ps 74:13. Yamm is also called by the same name ("monster") used of Yahweh's opponent (Ugaritic *tnn* = Hebrew *taninim*). A Ugaritic magical text might also describe the scattering of Yamm's corpse in the desert (cf. Ps 74:14), although the Ugaritic text is too difficult to decipher at this point for anyone to be certain of this meaning.

The use of the Baal Cycle as an analogy to illustrate the power of Yahweh can be found in other OT passages. Isaiah describes Yahweh's final victory over evil in terms of slaying "Leviathan ... the monster [*taninim*] of the sea" (Isa 27:1). To describe the serpent, Isaiah also uses the same two adjectives that are used in the Ugaritic Baal Cycle: "fleeing" / "gliding" (Hebrew *brh*) and "twisting" / "coiling" (Hebrew *qltn*). Job 3:8 and Job 41:1 – 34 refer to Leviathan, and Job 7:12 equates the sea (*yam*) with the monster (*tannin*). Other Biblical texts combine allusions to this myth with another name for the sea monster: "Rahab" (Job 9:13; 26:12 – 13; Ps 89:9 – 10; Isa 51:9 – 10). The name "Rahab" is used as a derogatory name for Egypt (Ps 87:4;

Cylinder seal depicts seven-headed monster with flames coming off its back. This is representative of some of the chaos monsters of the Ancient Near East.

Courtesy of the Oriental Institute Museum

continued on next page

Isa 30:7). Isaiah, e.g., explicitly associated the exodus with Yahweh's victory over the sea monster, Rahab (Isa 51:9 – 10), suggesting a connection with the parting of the Red Sea. Probably, the psalmist's use of this mythic imagery in connection with God's salvation "from long ago" (Ps 74:12) also alludes in part to the exodus deliverance. However, the mention of the sun and moon, the emergence of land, and the seasons in Ps 74:15 – 17 (for "ever-flowing rivers" in Ps 74:15, see note on Ps 93:3 – 4) suggests that the psalmist has in mind the molding of all creation as a demonstration of God's supreme power. While the Baal Cycle does not connect Baal's triumph with creation, similar images in Egypt and Mesopotamia do. The Egyptian wisdom text called the "Teaching for Merikare" speaks of the well-being of mankind, tended by the god who created sky and earth and "subdued the water monster."

The Egyptian sun-god, on his sailing journey each night across the waters of the underworld, defeats a serpent who is threatening the order of creation and therefore the potential for afterlife. One Mesopotamian account of creation features the god Marduk rising to kingship through his defeat of the ocean-goddess (cf. Ps 89:9 – 10). Another Mesopotamian text advances the reputation of the god Nergal by reporting his battle against an ocean dragon.

Other evidence for shared knowledge of the Baal Cycle in Mesopotamia includes a prophetic text from Mari (c. 1800 BC), which reports a speech of the god Adad (i.e., Baal) who "fought with the Sea" (cf. Ps 89:9 – 10). Numerous iconographical images from Mesopotamia of battles between a god and a multiheaded dragon have survived. In Akkadian literature there is a creature named *bashmu* that is described as having six tongues and seven mouths. In one text *bashmu* is named alongside other fabulous creatures, including one with two heads and one with seven heads. The latter is also pictured on a cylinder seal. This seal shows four of the heads hanging limp while the battle continues with the remaining three. In Ps 104:26, the creature is a mere plaything of Yahweh (see note there).

All of this demonstrates that even though God was revealing himself to Israel as very different from the gods of the ancient world, he did not hesitate to use similar metaphors and images to do so. His own activity is described in these culturally embedded ways and makes reference to known mythology to engage the Israelite audience through familiar ideas. However, for Yahweh, imagery of defeating chaos creatures constitutes literary allusions rather than cosmic history. Yahweh did not have to battle chaos creatures in order to bring order to the cosmos. Finally, it should be noted that these chaos creatures are not inherently evil, so this is not a battle of good versus evil. These accounts instead reflect Yahweh's triumph of bringing order in the face of nonorder or disorder. ◆

18 Remember how the enemy has mocked you, LORD,
how foolish people[b] have reviled your name.
19 Do not hand over the life of your dove to wild beasts;
do not forget the lives of your afflicted[c] people forever.
20 Have regard for your covenant,[d]
because haunts of violence fill the dark places of the land.
21 Do not let the oppressed[e] retreat in disgrace;
may the poor and needy[f] praise your name.
22 Rise up, O God, and defend your cause;
remember how fools[g] mock you all day long.
23 Do not ignore the clamor of your adversaries,[h]
the uproar of your enemies, which rises continually.

74:18 [b] Dt 32:6; Ps 39:8 **74:19** [c] Ps 9:18 **74:20** [d] Ge 17:7; Ps 106:45 **74:21** [e] Ps 103:6 [f] Ps 35:10 **74:22** [g] Ps 53:1 **74:23** [h] Ps 65:7 **75:1** [i] Ps 145:18 [j] Ps 44:1; 71:16

Psalm 75[a]

For the director of music. To the tune of "Do Not Destroy." A psalm of Asaph. A song.

1 We praise you, God,
we praise you, for your Name is near;[i]
people tell of your wonderful deeds.[j]

[a] In Hebrew texts 75:1-10 is numbered 75:2-11.

[2] You say, "I choose the appointed
time;
it is I who judge with equity.
[3] When the earth and all its people
quake,[k]
it is I who hold its pillars[l] firm.[a]
[4] To the arrogant I say, 'Boast no more,'
and to the wicked, 'Do not lift up
your horns.[b][m]
[5] Do not lift your horns against heaven;
do not speak so defiantly.' "
[6] No one from the east or the west
or from the desert can exalt
themselves.
[7] It is God who judges:[n]
He brings one down, he exalts
another.[o]
[8] In the hand of the LORD is a cup
full of foaming wine mixed[p] with
spices;
he pours it out, and all the wicked of
the earth
drink it down to its very dregs.[q]

[9] As for me, I will declare[r] this forever;
I will sing praise to the God of
Jacob,
[10] who says, "I will cut off the horns of
all the wicked,
but the horns of the righteous will
be lifted up."[s]

Psalm 76[c]

For the director of music. With stringed instruments. A psalm of Asaph. A song.

[1] God is renowned in Judah;
in Israel his name is great.
[2] His tent is in Salem,[t]
his dwelling place in Zion.
[3] There he broke the flashing arrows,
the shields and the swords, the
weapons of war.[d][u]

[4] You are radiant with light,
more majestic than mountains rich
with game.
[5] The valiant lie plundered,
they sleep their last sleep;[v]
not one of the warriors
can lift his hands.
[6] At your rebuke, God of Jacob,
both horse and chariot[w] lie still.

[7] It is you alone who are to be
feared.[x]
Who can stand[y] before you when
you are angry?[z]
[8] From heaven you pronounced
judgment,
and the land feared[a] and was
quiet—
[9] when you, God, rose up to judge,[b]
to save all the afflicted of the land.
[10] Surely your wrath against mankind
brings you praise,[c]
and the survivors of your wrath are
restrained.[e]

[11] Make vows to the LORD your God and
fulfill them;[d]
let all the neighboring lands
bring gifts[e] to the One to be feared.
[12] He breaks the spirit of rulers;
he is feared by the kings of the
earth.

75:3 [k] Isa 24:19 [l] 1Sa 2:8 **75:4** [m] Zec 1:21 **75:7** [n] Ps 50:6 [o] 1Sa 2:7; Ps 147:6; Da 2:21 **75:8** [p] Pr 23:30 [q] Job 21:20; Jer 25:15 **75:9** [r] Ps 40:10 **75:10** [s] Ps 89:17; 92:10; 148:14 **76:2** [t] Ge 14:18

76:3 [u] Ps 46:9 **76:5** [v] Ps 13:3 **76:6** [w] Ex 15:1 **76:7** [x] 1Ch 16:25 [y] Ezr 9:15; Rev 6:17 [z] Ps 2:5; Na 1:6 **76:8** [a] 1Ch 16:30; 2Ch 20:29-30 **76:9** [b] Ps 9:8 **76:10** [c] Ex 9:16; Ro 9:17 **76:11** [d] Ps 50:14; Ecc 5:4-5 [e] 2Ch 32:23; Ps 68:29

[a] 3 The Hebrew has *Selah* (a word of uncertain meaning) here. [b] 4 *Horns* here symbolize strength; also in verses 5 and 10. [c] In Hebrew texts 76:1-12 is numbered 76:2-13. [d] 3 The Hebrew has *Selah* (a word of uncertain meaning) here and at the end of verse 9. [e] 10 Or *Surely the wrath of mankind brings you praise, / and with the remainder of wrath you arm yourself*

75:2 *appointed time.* The Hebrew word might be any agreed upon assembly place (Jos 8:14) or specified time (Ex 9:5). The prophet Habakkuk uses this term for God's chosen time of judgment (Hab 2:3), and in Ps 102:13 God's time for intervention is simultaneously a time of deliverance for his people. However, it also commonly refers to the assembled festivals of the religious calendar occurring three time a year: Passover and Unleavened Bread in the spring and the Festival of Tabernacles/Booths in the fall (Ex 23:15; Lev 23:2; see the article "Pilgrim Psalms," p. 1003). Given the worship setting of Ps 75 and its identification as prophetic speech (see note on 50:7), the backdrop for this psalm may be a judgment/salvation speech delivered on the occasion of such a religious gathering (cf. 50:5; 81:3,8; 95:6–9).
75:3 *pillars.* See note on 104:5; see also the article "Cosmic Geography," p. 836. Here the metaphor of "pillars" extends to the social order, as the following context suggests (see notes on 11:3; 82:5).
75:4 *horns.* Symbols of strength and therefore a basis for boasting (see note on 18:2).
75:8 *cup full of foaming wine.* When wine ferments, it produces froth from the released gases, so the metaphor perhaps suggests a particularly well-fermented product. The word picture is expanded with the description "mixed." At times, wine was mixed with water; but spices were often used to increase the pungency of the drink (SS 8:2). The allure and potentially damaging effect is described in Pr 23:29–35, so it serves as a fitting metaphor of judgment (60:3; Isa 51:17; Jer 25:15,27). *dregs.* The sediment-laden portions at the bottom of the jar.
76:2 *Salem.* This is an abbreviated form of the name Jerusalem, identified as such because of the parallelism with "Zion" in this verse. Jerusalem means "peace." The same abbreviation is used in Ge 14:18 as the royal city of Melchizedek, who met Abraham after Abraham's return from the war against the five kings. This psalm, which celebrates Yahweh's protection of Jerusalem, is closely related to the "songs of Zion" (see the article "Hymns to Holy Cities," p. 927).
76:3 *he broke … weapons of war.* Ps 76 alludes to a siege of Jerusalem broken by the intervention of Yahweh. It is not clearly identifiable with any known battle in OT history, but one like Sennacherib's siege of Jerusalem in 701 BC (2Ki 18:17—19:37) would match the description in the psalm.

Psalm 77[a]

For the director of music. For Jeduthun.
Of Asaph. A psalm.

1 I cried out to God[f] for help;
I cried out to God to hear me.
2 When I was in distress,[g] I sought the
Lord;
at night I stretched out untiring
hands,[h]
and I would not be comforted.[i]

3 I remembered you, God, and I groaned;
I meditated, and my spirit grew
faint.[b][j]
4 You kept my eyes from closing;
I was too troubled to speak.
5 I thought about the former days,[k]
the years of long ago;
6 I remembered my songs in the night.
My heart meditated and my spirit
asked:

7 "Will the Lord reject forever?
Will he never show his favor[l]
again?
8 Has his unfailing love vanished
forever?
Has his promise[m] failed for all time?
9 Has God forgotten to be merciful?[n]
Has he in anger withheld his
compassion?[o]"

10 Then I thought, "To this I will appeal:
the years when the Most High
stretched out his right hand.[p]
11 I will remember the deeds of the LORD;
yes, I will remember your miracles[q]
of long ago.
12 I will consider all your works
and meditate on all your mighty
deeds."

13 Your ways, God, are holy.
What god is as great as our God?[r]

77:1 [f]Ps 3:4 **77:2** [g]Ps 50:15; Isa 26:9, 16 [h]Job 11:13 [i]Ge 37:35 **77:3** [j]Ps 143:4 **77:5** [k]Dt 32:7; Ps 44:1; 143:5; Isa 51:9 **77:7** [l]Ps 85:1 **77:8** [m]2Pe 3:9 **77:9** [n]Ps 25:6; 40:11; 51:1 [o]Isa 49:15 **77:10** [p]Ps 31:22 **77:11** [q]Ps 143:5 **77:13** [r]Ex 15:11; Ps 71:19; 86:8

77:15 [s]Ex 6:6; Dt 9:29 **77:16** [t]Ex 14:21, 28; Hab 3:8 [u]Ps 114:4; Hab 3:10 **77:17** [v]Jdg 5:4 **77:18** [w]Jdg 5:4 **77:19** [x]Hab 3:15 **77:20** [y]Ex 13:21 [z]Ps 78:52; Isa 63:11 **78:1** [a]Isa 51:4; 55:3 **78:2** [b]Ps 49:4; Mt 13:35* **78:3** [c]Ps 44:1

14 You are the God who performs
miracles;
you display your power among the
peoples.
15 With your mighty arm you redeemed
your people,[s]
the descendants of Jacob and
Joseph.

16 The waters[t] saw you, God,
the waters saw you and writhed;[u]
the very depths were convulsed.
17 The clouds poured down water,[v]
the heavens resounded with
thunder;
your arrows flashed back and forth.
18 Your thunder was heard in the
whirlwind,
your lightning lit up the world;
the earth trembled and quaked.[w]
19 Your path led through the sea,[x]
your way through the mighty
waters,
though your footprints were not
seen.

20 You led your people[y] like a flock[z]
by the hand of Moses and Aaron.

Psalm 78

A *maskil*[c] of Asaph.

1 My people, hear my teaching;[a]
listen to the words of my mouth.
2 I will open my mouth with a
parable;[b]
I will utter hidden things, things
from of old—
3 things we have heard and known,
things our ancestors have told us.[c]

[a] In Hebrew texts 77:1-20 is numbered 77:2-21.
[b] 3 The Hebrew has *Selah* (a word of uncertain meaning) here and at the end of verses 9 and 15.
[c] Title: Probably a literary or musical term

77:16 *The waters saw you.* The psalms speak of the exodus in terms of a cosmic battle between Yahweh and unruly personified forces, such as turbulent waters, which in other ancient Near Eastern texts are hostile gods and goddesses (see the article "Chaos Monsters," p. 953).
77:17–18 *thunder ... lightning.* These natural phenomena, together with the earthquake (v. 18), are commonly associated with the appearance of a divine warrior (see the article "Divine Warfare," p. 365). Strictly speaking, the meteorological events described here happened during the exodus plagues (Ex 9:23–24), and the earthquake was an added phenomenon when Yahweh appeared on Mount Sinai (Ex 19:16–19). However, these descriptions converge in this psalm's poetic depiction of Yahweh, the divine warrior, throwing back the unruly waters of the sea during Israel's escape from the Egyptian army (Ex 15:3; see Ps 106:7 and the article "The Red Sea," p. 132).
77:19 *the sea.* See notes on Ge 1:2; Job 7:12; see also the article "Chaos Monsters," p. 953. *footprints.* The gods and goddesses of the other nations in the Near East were portrayed in various animal and human forms. Of interest is the discovery of giant footprints carved into the threshold of a temple at ʻAin Dara in Syria (tenth to eighth century BC). The footprints symbolize the deity stepping from the entrance into the inner sanctuary. Israel's God revealed himself only in the cloud and pillar of fire (Ex 40:38).
78:2 *parable.* Wisdom themes are not foreign to hymnic literature such as psalms (see note on 49:1). In the most basic sense, a "parable" is a comparison between two things, but the term is used more broadly for any saying that reflects upon the concerns of wisdom (see 49:4, where it is translated "proverb" and is echoed by the word "riddle"; see also note there). Here the concern is passing on to children the lessons of the fathers (Pr 1:8). A similar value is expressed in the Egyptian "Instruction of Ptahhotep," in which it is noted that fathers pass instruction on to their children generation after generation by their actions as well as their words.

[4] We will not hide them from
their descendants;[d]
we will tell the next
generation
the praiseworthy deeds[e] of the
LORD,
his power, and the wonders
he has done.
[5] He decreed statutes[f] for Jacob[g]
and established the law in
Israel,
which he commanded our
ancestors
to teach their children,
[6] so the next generation would
know them,
even the children yet to be
born,[h]
and they in turn would tell
their children.
[7] Then they would put their trust
in God
and would not forget[i] his
deeds
but would keep his
commands.[j]
[8] They would not be like their
ancestors[k]—
a stubborn[l] and rebellious[m]
generation,
whose hearts were not loyal to
God,
whose spirits were not
faithful to him.
[9] The men of Ephraim, though
armed with bows,[n]
turned back on the day of
battle;[o]
[10] they did not keep God's
covenant[p]
and refused to live by his law.
[11] They forgot what he had done,[q]
the wonders he had shown them.
[12] He did miracles[r] in the sight of their
ancestors
in the land of Egypt,[s] in the region of
Zoan.[t]
[13] He divided the sea[u] and led them
through;
he made the water stand up like a
wall.[v]
[14] He guided them with the cloud by day
and with light from the fire all
night.[w]

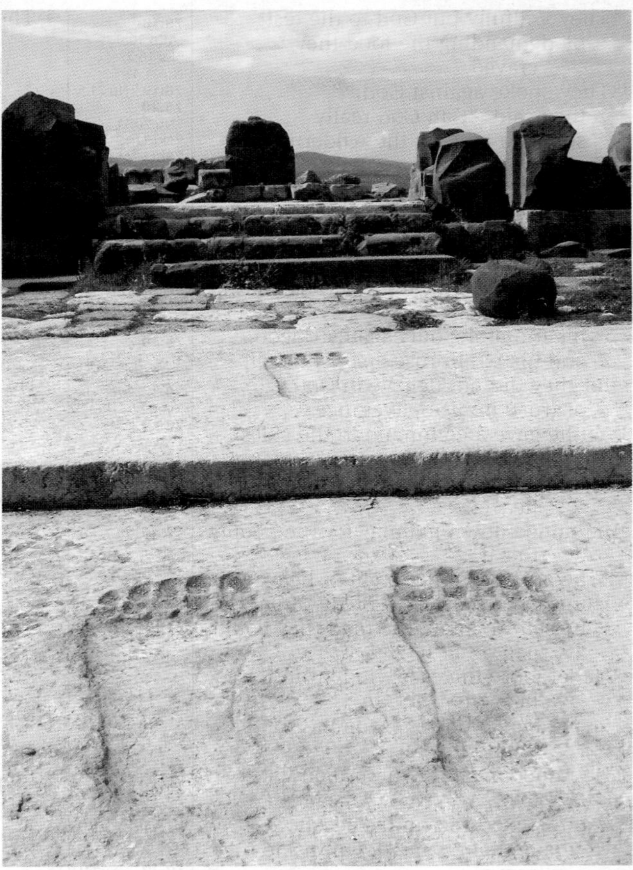

Giant footprints carved into the threshold of a temple at Ain Dara in Syria (tenth to eighth century BC). See note on Ps 77:19.
Kathryn Hooge

[15] He split the rocks[x] in the wilderness
and gave them water as abundant
as the seas;
[16] he brought streams out of a rocky
crag
and made water flow down like
rivers.
[17] But they continued to sin[y] against him,
rebelling in the wilderness against
the Most High.

78:4 [d] Dt 11:19 [e] Ps 26:7; 71:17 **78:5** [f] Ps 19:7; 81:5 [g] Ps 147:19 **78:6** [h] Ps 22:31; 102:18 **78:7** [i] Dt 6:12 [j] Dt 5:29 **78:8** [k] 2Ch 30:7 [l] Ex 32:9 [m] ver 37; Isa 30:9 **78:9** [n] ver 57; 1Ch 12:2 [o] Jdg 20:39 **78:10** [p] 2Ki 17:15 **78:11** [q] Ps 106:13

78:12 [r] Ps 106:22 [s] Ex 7-12 [t] Nu 13:22 **78:13** [u] Ex 14:21; Ps 136:13 [v] Ex 15:8 **78:14** [w] Ex 13:21; Ps 105:39 **78:15** [x] Nu 20:11; 1Co 10:4 **78:17** [y] Dt 9:22; Isa 63:10; Heb 3:16

78:9 *men of Ephraim.* Ephraim's tribe was the dominant group among the northern tribes of Israel, so the name "Ephraim" was synonymous with the whole group of northern Israel. When addressing the northern kingdom, the prophet Hosea uses Ephraim's name for the whole (e.g., Hos 5:3; 6:4; 7:1; 10:6; 11:12). Ps 78 is concerned with the downfall of the northern kingdom and the transfer of prominence to Judah as the place of God's dwelling (vv. 59–60,67–68). The use of "Ephraim" at this early point in the psalm (v. 9) signals this emphasis in the psalmist's historical allusions and admonitions from the past.
78:12 *Zoan.* The Egyptian city of Djanet, which the Greeks called Tanis. It became the capital city of the delta region in the Twenty-First Dynasty (twelfth century BC). It is in the area where the Israelites were settled in Egypt at the time of Moses.

18 They willfully put God to the test[z]
by demanding the food they craved.[a]
19 They spoke against God;[b]
they said, "Can God really
spread a table in the wilderness?
20 True, he struck the rock,
and water gushed out,[c]
streams flowed abundantly,
but can he also give us bread?
Can he supply meat[d] for his people?"
21 When the LORD heard them, he was furious;
his fire broke out[e] against Jacob,
and his wrath rose against Israel,
22 for they did not believe in God
or trust[f] in his deliverance.
23 Yet he gave a command to the skies above
and opened the doors of the heavens;[g]
24 he rained down manna[h] for the people to eat,
he gave them the grain of heaven.
25 Human beings ate the bread of angels;
he sent them all the food they could eat.
26 He let loose the east wind[i] from the heavens
and by his power made the south wind blow.
27 He rained meat down on them like dust,
birds like sand on the seashore.
28 He made them come down inside their camp,
all around their tents.
29 They ate till they were gorged—[j]
he had given them what they craved.
30 But before they turned from what they craved,
even while the food was still in their mouths,[k]
31 God's anger rose against them;
he put to death the sturdiest[l] among them,
cutting down the young men of Israel.
32 In spite of all this, they kept on sinning;
in spite of his wonders,[m] they did not believe.[n]
33 So he ended their days in futility[o]
and their years in terror.
34 Whenever God slew them, they would seek[p] him;
they eagerly turned to him again.

78:18 [z] 1Co 10:9 [a] Ex 16:2; Nu 11:4 **78:19** [b] Nu 21:5 **78:20** [c] Nu 20:11 [d] Nu 11:18 **78:21** [e] Nu 11:1 **78:22** [f] Dt 1:32; Heb 3:19 **78:23** [g] Ge 7:11; Mal 3:10 **78:24** [h] Ex 16:4; Jn 6:31* **78:26** [i] Nu 11:31 **78:29** [j] Nu 11:20 **78:30** [k] Nu 11:33 **78:31** [l] Isa 10:16 **78:32** [m] ver 11 [n] ver 22 **78:33** [o] Nu 14:29,35 **78:34** [p] Hos 5:15

35 They remembered that God was their Rock,[q]
that God Most High was their Redeemer.[r]
36 But then they would flatter him with their mouths,[s]
lying to him with their tongues;
37 their hearts were not loyal[t] to him,
they were not faithful to his covenant.
38 Yet he was merciful;[u]
he forgave[v] their iniquities[w]
and did not destroy them.
Time after time he restrained his anger
and did not stir up his full wrath.
39 He remembered that they were but flesh,[x]
a passing breeze[y] that does not return.
40 How often they rebelled[z] against him
in the wilderness[a]
and grieved him[b] in the wasteland!
41 Again and again they put God to the test;[c]
they vexed the Holy One of Israel.[d]
42 They did not remember his power—
the day he redeemed them from the oppressor,
43 the day he displayed his signs in Egypt,
his wonders in the region of Zoan.
44 He turned their river into blood;[e]
they could not drink from their streams.
45 He sent swarms of flies[f] that devoured them,
and frogs[g] that devastated them.
46 He gave their crops to the grasshopper,
their produce to the locust.[h]
47 He destroyed their vines with hail[i]
and their sycamore-figs with sleet.
48 He gave over their cattle to the hail,
their livestock[j] to bolts of lightning.
49 He unleashed against them his hot anger,[k]
his wrath, indignation and hostility—
a band of destroying angels.
50 He prepared a path for his anger;
he did not spare them from death
but gave them over to the plague.
51 He struck down all the firstborn of Egypt,[l]
the firstfruits of manhood in the tents of Ham.[m]
52 But he brought his people out like a flock;[n]
he led them like sheep through the wilderness.

78:35 [q] Dt 32:4 [r] Dt 9:26 **78:36** [s] Eze 33:31 **78:37** [t] ver 8; Ac 8:21 **78:38** [u] Ex 34:6 [v] Isa 48:10 [w] Nu 14:18,20 **78:39** [x] Ge 6:3; Ps 103:14 [y] Job 7:7; Jas 4:14 **78:40** [z] Heb 3:16 [a] Ps 95:8; 106:14 [b] Eph 4:30 **78:41** [c] Nu 14:22 [d] 2Ki 19:22; Ps 89:18 **78:44** [e] Ex 7:20-21; Ps 105:29 **78:45** [f] Ex 8:24; Ps 105:31 [g] Ex 8:2,6 **78:46** [h] Ex 10:13 **78:47** [i] Ex 9:23; Ps 105:32 **78:48** [j] Ex 9:25 **78:49** [k] Ex 15:7 **78:51** [l] Ex 12:29; Ps 135:8 [m] Ps 105:23; 106:22 **78:52** [n] Ps 77:20

78:44–48 *blood … flies … frogs … locust … hail … livestock.* See notes on Ex 7:20; 8:3; 10:4; see also the article "Interpreting the Plagues," p. 122.

78:51 *Ham.* See note on 105:23.

53 He guided them safely, so they were
unafraid;
but the sea engulfed[o] their enemies.[p]
54 And so he brought them to the border
of his holy land,
to the hill country his right hand[q]
had taken.
55 He drove out nations[r] before them
and allotted their lands to them as
an inheritance;[s]
he settled the tribes of Israel in their
homes.

56 But they put God to the test
and rebelled against the Most High;
they did not keep his statutes.
57 Like their ancestors[t] they were disloyal
and faithless,
as unreliable as a faulty bow.[u]
58 They angered him[v] with their high
places;[w]
they aroused his jealousy with their
idols.[x]
59 When God heard them, he was
furious;
he rejected Israel[y] completely.
60 He abandoned the tabernacle of
Shiloh,[z]
the tent he had set up among
humans.
61 He sent the ark of his might[a] into
captivity,[b]
his splendor into the hands of the
enemy.
62 He gave his people over to the sword;
he was furious with his inheritance.
63 Fire consumed[c] their young men,
and their young women had no
wedding songs;[d]
64 their priests were put to the sword,[e]
and their widows could not weep.
65 Then the Lord awoke as from sleep,[f]
as a warrior wakes from the stupor
of wine.
66 He beat back his enemies;
he put them to everlasting shame.[g]

78:53 [o] Ex 14:28 [p] Ps 106:10
78:54 [q] Ex 15:17; Ps 44:3
78:55 [r] Ps 44:2 [s] Jos 13:7
78:57 [t] Eze 20:27 [u] Hos 7:16
78:58 [v] Jdg 2:12 [w] Lev 26:30 [x] Ex 20:4; Dt 32:21
78:59 [y] Dt 32:19
78:60 [z] Jos 18:1
78:61 [a] Ps 132:8 [b] 1Sa 4:17
78:63 [c] Nu 11:1 [d] Jer 7:34; 16:9
78:64 [e] 1Sa 4:17; 22:18
78:65 [f] Ps 44:23
78:66 [g] 1Sa 5:6
78:68 [h] Ps 87:2
78:70 [i] 1Sa 16:1
78:71 [j] 2Sa 5:2; Ps 28:9
78:72 [k] 1Ki 9:4
79:1 [l] Ps 74:2 [m] 2Ki 25:9
79:2 [n] Dt 28:26; Jer 7:33
79:3 [o] Jer 16:4
79:4 [p] Ps 44:13; 80:6
79:5 [q] Ps 74:10 [r] Ps 74:1; 85:5 [s] Dt 29:20; Ps 89:46; Zep 3:8

67 Then he rejected the tents of Joseph,
he did not choose the tribe of
Ephraim;
68 but he chose the tribe of Judah,
Mount Zion,[h] which he loved.
69 He built his sanctuary like the heights,
like the earth that he established
forever.
70 He chose David[i] his servant
and took him from the sheep pens;
71 from tending the sheep he brought
him
to be the shepherd[j] of his people
Jacob,
of Israel his inheritance.
72 And David shepherded them with
integrity of heart;[k]
with skillful hands he led them.

Psalm 79

A psalm of Asaph.

1 O God, the nations have invaded your
inheritance;[l]
they have defiled your holy temple,
they have reduced Jerusalem to
rubble.[m]
2 They have left the dead bodies of your
servants
as food for the birds of the sky,
the flesh of your own people for
the animals of the wild.[n]
3 They have poured out blood like
water
all around Jerusalem,
and there is no one to bury the
dead.[o]
4 We are objects of contempt to our
neighbors,
of scorn and derision to those
around us.[p]

5 How long,[q] LORD? Will you be angry[r]
forever?
How long will your jealousy burn
like fire?[s]

78:58 *high places.* See notes on 1Ki 3:2; 11:7; 2Ch 1:3.
78:60 *tabernacle of Shiloh.* See notes on Jdg 18:31; 1Sa 1:3,9.
78:69 *He built his sanctuary.* The theme that gods are ultimately the builders of their own temples is frequently associated in the ancient Near East with the notion that such a temple is rooted in the cosmic realm (either in the realm below the earth's surface or in heaven). This is a poetic way of affirming its secure and enduring qualities. See the article "Architecture of the Temple," p. 572.
78:71 *shepherd.* See note on 23:1. The Assyrian king Ashurnasirpal (c. 1050 BC) identifies the goddess Ishtar as the one who took him from the mountains and named him to be shepherd of the peoples.
Ps 79 The historical event referred to in this psalm is the destruction of Jerusalem by the Babylonian army in 586 BC (see note on 74:3). Ps 79 is similar in several ways to city laments known from ancient Mesopotamia (see the article "City Laments," p. 951).
79:2 *dead bodies … as food for the birds … the animals.* In the Gilgamesh Epic, the guardian monster of the cedar forest, Huwawa, tells Gilgamesh that he should have given his flesh to be eaten by birds of prey and scavengers. For exposure of corpses, see notes on 1Ki 14:11; 2Ki 9:10. A common feature of city laments is the graphic description of the fate of the city's inhabitants. The "Lament Over the Destruction of Ur" reports corpses were piled up by the city gates and that the dead littered the ground like potsherds.
79:5 *How long … ?* This question occurs nearly 20 times in Psalms, usually in connection with a lament psalm. It is found also in Mesopotamia, as the Sumerian "Lament Over the Destruction of Sumer and Ur" asks, "How long will the eye of the enemy be cast on me?"

[6]Pour out your wrath[t] on the nations
that do not acknowledge[u] you,
on the kingdoms
that do not call on your name;[v]
[7]for they have devoured Jacob
and devastated his homeland.

[8]Do not hold against us the sins of past generations;[w]
may your mercy come quickly to meet us,
for we are in desperate need.[x]
[9]Help us,[y] God our Savior,
for the glory of your name;
deliver us and forgive our sins
for your name's sake.[z]
[10]Why should the nations say,
"Where is their God?"[a]
Before our eyes, make known among the nations
that you avenge[b] the outpoured blood of your servants.
[11]May the groans of the prisoners come before you;
with your strong arm preserve those condemned to die.
[12]Pay back into the laps[c] of our neighbors seven times[d]
the contempt they have hurled at you, Lord.
[13]Then we your people, the sheep of your pasture,[e]
will praise you forever;[f]
from generation to generation
we will proclaim your praise.

Psalm 80[a]

For the director of music. To the tune of "The Lilies of the Covenant." Of Asaph. A psalm.

[1]Hear us, Shepherd of Israel,
you who lead Joseph like a flock.[g]
You who sit enthroned between the cherubim,[h]
shine forth [2]before Ephraim,
Benjamin and Manasseh.[i]
Awaken[j] your might;
come and save us.

[3]Restore[k] us,[l] O God;
make your face shine on us,
that we may be saved.

[4]How long, LORD God Almighty,
will your anger smolder
against the prayers of your people?
[5]You have fed them with the bread of tears;
you have made them drink tears by the bowlful.[m]
[6]You have made us an object of derision[b] to our neighbors,
and our enemies mock us.[n]

[7]Restore us, God Almighty;
make your face shine on us,
that we may be saved.

[8]You transplanted a vine[o] from Egypt;
you drove out[p] the nations and planted it.
[9]You cleared the ground for it,
and it took root and filled the land.
[10]The mountains were covered with its shade,
the mighty cedars with its branches.
[11]Its branches reached as far as the Sea,[c]
its shoots as far as the River.[d][q]

[12]Why have you broken down its walls[r]
so that all who pass by pick its grapes?

79:6 [t]Ps 69:24; Rev 16:1 [u]Jer 10:25; 2Th 1:8 [v]Ps 14:4 **79:8** [w]Isa 64:9 [x]Ps 116:6; 142:6 **79:9** [y]2Ch 14:11 [z]Ps 25:11; 31:3; Jer 14:7 **79:10** [a]Ps 42:10 [b]Ps 94:1 **79:12** [c]Isa 65:6; Jer 32:18 [d]Ge 4:15 **79:13** [e]Ps 74:1; 95:7 [f]Ps 44:8 **80:1** [g]Ps 77:20 [h]Ex 25:22 **80:2** [i]Nu 2:18-24 [j]Ps 35:23 **80:3** [k]Ps 85:4; La 5:21 [l]Nu 6:25 **80:5** [m]Ps 42:3; Isa 30:20 **80:6** [n]Ps 79:4 **80:8** [o]Isa 5:1-2; Jer 2:21 [p]Jos 13:6; Ac 7:45 **80:11** [q]Ps 72:8 **80:12** [r]Ps 89:40; Isa 5:5

[a] In Hebrew texts 80:1-19 is numbered 80:2-20.
[b] 6 Probable reading of the original Hebrew text; Masoretic Text *contention* [c] 11 Probably the Mediterranean [d] 11 That is, the Euphrates

79:6 *Pour out your wrath.* While city laments such as the "Lament Over the Destruction of Ur" acknowledge that the destruction was the result of a divine decision, they also contain a section calling for divine retribution on the enemy who showed no limit in their rampage.
79:13 *we … will praise you.* A concluding vow in a city lament is the portrait of praise that will result if the city is restored. The "Lament Over the Destruction of Ur" closes with the hope that the city of the god Nanna might be restored so that praises and rituals can be renewed.
80:1 *Shepherd.* See note on Ps 23:1. *enthroned between the cherubim.* See note on 2Ki 19:15.
80:3,7,19 *make your face shine on us.* This refrain finds an echo in v. 14, where God's act of restoration is parallel to looking down from heaven and watching in a protective manner. Therefore, the metaphor of shining is probably similar to the image of God as the sun (see note on 84:11).
80:4 *God Almighty.* This Hebrew expression has traditionally been translated "God of hosts," or when coupled with the divine name Yahweh, "LORD of hosts." The word for "hosts" is associated with armies (Jdg 4:2; 1Ki 2:5; Isa 34:2). By extension, the same word refers to the "army" of heavenly beings whom Yahweh commands for his service. The psalmist calls for God to intervene militarily on behalf of his people, utilizing his heavenly army on their behalf (see 59:5).
Rashap, the Ugaritic god of war, is called in one text "Rashap of the Army" (Ugaritic *sb'* = Hebrew *sb'*, "host"). It is also possible that there is a connection between the imagery of God as a shining sun (vv. 3,7,19) and his ability to intervene with his heavenly "host/army." A conceptual parallel might be found in a letter from a Canaanite king to the Egyptian pharaoh (c. 1350 BC). The Canaanite king has readied his troops for battle to serve the sun-god, Pharaoh, whom he calls "sun of thousands." A related letter uses the image for Pharaoh as the sun "over thousands" shining forth over the horizon to muster troops.
80:5 *bread of tears.* The trauma was so long and severe, it was as though the people's daily bread was their hardship, a metaphor known from Mesopotamian texts as well.
80:11 *Sea … River.* Given the geographic description, they are likely references to the Mediterranean Sea and

[13]Boars from the forest ravage[s] it,
and insects from the fields feed on it.
[14]Return to us, God Almighty!
Look down from heaven and see![t]
Watch over this vine,
[15] the root your right hand has planted,
the son[a] you have raised up for yourself.

[16]Your vine is cut down, it is burned with fire;
at your rebuke[u] your people perish.
[17]Let your hand rest on the man at your right hand,
the son of man you have raised up for yourself.
[18]Then we will not turn away from you;
revive us, and we will call on your name.

[19]Restore us, LORD God Almighty;
make your face shine on us,
that we may be saved.

Psalm 81[b]

For the director of music. According to *gittith*.[c] Of Asaph.

[1]Sing for joy to God our strength;
shout aloud to the God of Jacob![v]
[2]Begin the music, strike the timbrel,[w]
play the melodious harp[x] and lyre.

[3]Sound the ram's horn at the New Moon,
and when the moon is full, on the day of our festival;
[4]this is a decree for Israel,
an ordinance of the God of Jacob.
[5]When God went out against Egypt,[y]
he established it as a statute for Joseph.

I heard an unknown voice say:[z]

[6]"I removed the burden from their shoulders;[a]
their hands were set free from the basket.
[7]In your distress you called[b] and I rescued you,
I answered[c] you out of a thundercloud;
I tested you at the waters of Meribah.[d][d]
[8]Hear me, my people,[e] and I will warn you—
if you would only listen to me, Israel!
[9]You shall have no foreign god[f] among you;
you shall not worship any god other than me.
[10]I am the LORD your God,
who brought you up out of Egypt.[g]
Open wide your mouth and I will fill[h] it.

[11]"But my people would not listen to me;
Israel would not submit to me.[i]
[12]So I gave them over[j] to their stubborn hearts
to follow their own devices.

[13]"If my people would only listen to me,[k]
if Israel would only follow my ways,
[14]how quickly I would subdue[l] their enemies
and turn my hand against[m] their foes!
[15]Those who hate the LORD would cringe before him,
and their punishment would last forever.
[16]But you would be fed with the finest of wheat;[n]
with honey from the rock I would satisfy you."

80:13 [s]Jer 5:6 **80:14** [t]Isa 63:15 **80:16** [u]Ps 39:11; 76:6 **81:1** [v]Ps 66:1 **81:2** [w]Ex 15:20 [x]Ps 92:3 **81:5** [y]Ex 11:4 [z]Ps 114:1 **81:6** [a]Isa 9:4 **81:7** [b]Ex 2:23; Ps 50:15 [c]Ex 19:19 [d]Ex 17:7 **81:8** [e]Ps 50:7 **81:9** [f]Ex 20:3; Dt 32:12; Isa 43:12 **81:10** [g]Ex 20:2 [h]Ps 107:9 **81:11** [i]Ex 32:1-6 **81:12** [j]Ac 7:42; Ro 1:24 **81:13** [k]Dt 5:29; Isa 48:18 **81:14** [l]Ps 47:3 [m]Am 1:8 **81:16** [n]Dt 32:14

[a] *15* Or *branch* [b] In Hebrew texts 81:1-16 is numbered 81:2-17. [c] Title: Probably a musical term [d] *7* The Hebrew has *Selah* (a word of uncertain meaning) here.

the Euphrates River, respectively, though they potentially may be references to the cosmic waters. (In the end this is a difference without a distinction, since the Mediterranean and the Euphrates were part of the cosmic waters.)

80:13 *Boars.* Not only vicious, powerful animals in the wild, but also unclean for eating (Lev 11:7; Dt 14:8, translated "pig" in both verses). Therefore, the irony of the image is that an unclean animal is destroying the food of God's people.

81:2 *music.* See the article "Music and Musicians," p. 524.

81:3 *New Moon ... festival.* The designation New Moon, i.e., the first day of the month, combined with the description "when the moon is full," the 14th day, points to the autumn religious festival. This festival opened on the 1st day of the 7th month (Sept./Oct.) with a trumpet call for a sacred assembly. It included the Day of Atonement on the 10th day and culminated with the week-long Festival of Tabernacles, which began on the 15th day (Lev 23:23–44; Nu 29:1–40). See the article "Pilgrim Psalms," p. 1003.

81:5 *unknown voice.* See note on 114:1.

81:6 This verse begins the words of the Lord spoken by a prophet at the festival. Prophetic ministry during temple worship was probably common. Assyrian temple prophets served at covenant renewal festivals. See note on 50:7.

81:7 *thundercloud ... Meribah.* There was thunder at Mount Sinai (Ex 19:16–24), but it is hard to see how that was an act of rescue, and Meribah—where Yahweh gave water from the rock (Ex 17:1–7)—preceded it. It is therefore more likely that the thundercloud is seen as the weapon of the divine warrior, Yahweh, who delivered Israel from Egypt (the same Hebrew term is used in Isa 29:6 [NIV "thunder"]).

81:16 *honey from the rock.* While most honey spoken of in the OT is the syrup from the date palm, mention of the rock here suggests bees' honey from honeycombs in the rocks.

Psalm 82

A psalm of Asaph.

1 God presides in the great assembly;
he renders judgment[o] among the "gods":
2 "How long will you[a] defend the unjust
and show partiality[p] to the wicked?[b][q]
3 Defend the weak and the fatherless;[r]
uphold the cause of the poor[s] and the oppressed.
4 Rescue the weak and the needy;
deliver them from the hand of the wicked.

5 "The 'gods' know nothing, they understand nothing.[t]
They walk about in darkness;[u]
all the foundations[v] of the earth are shaken.

6 "I said, 'You are "gods";[w]
you are all sons of the Most High.'
7 But you will die[x] like mere mortals;
you will fall like every other ruler."

8 Rise up,[y] O God, judge the earth,
for all the nations are your inheritance.[z]

82:1 [o] Ps 58:11; Isa 3:13 **82:2** [p] Dt 1:17 [q] Ps 58:1-2; Pr 18:5 **82:3** [r] Dt 24:17 [s] Jer 22:16 **82:5** [t] Ps 14:4; Mic 3:1 [u] Isa 59:9 [v] Ps 11:3 **82:6** [w] Jn 10:34* **82:7** [x] Ps 49:12; Eze 31:14 **82:8** [y] Ps 12:5 [z] Ps 2:8; Rev 11:15

83:1 [a] Ps 28:1; 35:22 **83:2** [b] Ps 2:1; Isa 17:12 [c] Jdg 8:28; Ps 81:15 **83:3** [d] Ps 31:13 **83:4** [e] Est 3:6 [f] Jer 11:19 **83:5** [g] Ps 2:2 **83:6** [h] Ps 137:7 [i] 2Ch 20:1 [j] Ge 25:16 **83:7** [k] Jos 13:5 [l] Eze 27:3 **83:8** [m] Dt 2:9 **83:9** [n] Jdg 7:1-23 [o] Jdg 4:23-24

Psalm 83[c]

A song. A psalm of Asaph.

1 O God, do not remain silent;[a]
do not turn a deaf ear,
do not stand aloof, O God.
2 See how your enemies growl,[b]
how your foes rear their heads.[c]
3 With cunning they conspire[d] against your people;
they plot against those you cherish.
4 "Come," they say, "let us destroy[e] them as a nation,
so that Israel's name is remembered[f] no more."

5 With one mind they plot together;[g]
they form an alliance against you—
6 the tents of Edom[h] and the Ishmaelites,
of Moab[i] and the Hagrites,[j]
7 Byblos,[k] Ammon and Amalek,
Philistia, with the people of Tyre.[l]
8 Even Assyria has joined them
to reinforce Lot's descendants.[b][m]

9 Do to them as you did to Midian,[n]
as you did to Sisera and Jabin at the river Kishon,[o]

[a] *2* The Hebrew is plural. [b] *2,8* The Hebrew has *Selah* (a word of uncertain meaning) here. [c] In Hebrew texts 83:1-18 is numbered 83:2-19.

82:1 *great assembly.* This Hebrew expression can be rendered more lit. "assembly of God" or "divine assembly" (cf. NASB: "congregation"; NRSV and ESV: "divine council"). Yahweh, the God of Israel, stands at the head of an assembly of heavenly beings, which in OT texts are usually called "gods" or "sons of god" (see note on 29:1). The concept of a divine council was also well known among Israel's Canaanite neighbors and in the religion of Mesopotamia (see the article "Divine Council," p. 615).

In the Baal Cycle (see note on Ps 29; see also the article "Psalm 29: A Canaanite Hymn?" p. 905), the god Yamm sends messengers who stand before the chief god El and the rest of the gods and goddesses assembled together to render a judgment on Yamm's request. Likewise, the assembly of the gods in Mesopotamia met to determine the fate of kings and peoples.

82:5 *foundations of the earth.* While this concept usually refers to the divine ordering of creation (see notes on 24:2; 104:5; see also the article "Cosmic Geography," p. 836), it is also used as a metaphor for social order, as it appears in 75:3 as well (see note on 11:3). In the ancient world, people did not differentiate clearly between social order and cosmic order. They were seen as two sides of the same coin. In the myth Enki and Inanna, a list of the foundations of order includes cosmic elements, social and cultural institutions and abstractions of behavior. Threats to order at any of these levels can ripple out into the others.

82:6 *I said, 'You are "gods."'* Throughout this psalm, God speaks through the words of a temple prophet (see note on 50:7). God is rendering a verdict of destruction on the heavenly beings who have transgressed the divinely ordained social order. An important aspect of the ancient viewpoint here is that human rulers make decisions that mirror the actions of the "gods." *gods.* This term is used both of supernatural beings and of the human rulers who are their agents (see note on 45:6). Therefore, divine retribution reaches into both the human and the heavenly realms in order to vindicate the victims of injustice and oppression (see the article "Imprecations and Incantations," p. 937).

83:5–8 The reference to Assyria (v. 8) points to the general period of Assyria's westward expansion (c. 750–700 BC), although no specific event known outside this psalm corresponds to this list of nations. The number of nations, ten, might suggest a stereotypical list of enemies. Mention of the Assyrian Empire at the end punctuates the list of nine other enemies. From the earliest times, Egyptian scribes used the term "Nine Bows" to refer to nine nations in the region of Egypt, at times including Egypt itself. Over time, the convention changed so that the specific nations listed were immediate enemies of the Egyptian king. The nations listed often described a circle around Egypt, although they were not always in geographic order. The number of nations named also varied at times. For example, the list of "Nine Bows" on Merneptah's Stele (c. 1207 BC) numbered only eight, including Israel.

Edom, Moab and Ammon were kingdoms southeast, east and northeast of the Dead Sea, respectively (Moab and Ammon being descendants of Lot, v. 8). Ishmaelites and Hagrites were Bedouin tribes in the Arabian desert east of Canaan, and Amalek refers to tribes located to the south. Gebal might refer to a city in Phoenicia (northwest of ancient Israel); however, there is evidence of the existence of a "Gebal" in the region of Edom, which better corresponds with the other places immediately before and after this name in the list. Philistia bordered Israel and Judah on the west and Tyre was a major city in Phoenicia to the northwest. Assyria controlled territories to the north and northeast. Conceptually, the list of nations portrays enemies surrounding Israel and Judah on all sides.

83:9 *Midian ... Sisera and Jabin.* During the judges period, God intervened to help Gideon defeat the Midianites

[10]who perished at Endor
and became like dung[p] on the ground.
[11]Make their nobles like Oreb and Zeeb,[q]
all their princes like Zebah and Zalmunna,[r]
[12]who said, "Let us take possession[s]
of the pasturelands of God."

[13]Make them like tumbleweed, my God,
like chaff[t] before the wind.
[14]As fire consumes the forest
or a flame sets the mountains ablaze,[u]
[15]so pursue them with your tempest
and terrify them with your storm.[v]
[16]Cover their faces with shame,[w] LORD,
so that they will seek your name.

[17]May they ever be ashamed and dismayed;
may they perish in disgrace.[x]
[18]Let them know that you, whose name is the LORD—
that you alone are the Most High
over all the earth.[y]

Psalm 84[a]

For the director of music. According to *gittith*.[b] Of the Sons of Korah. A psalm.

[1]How lovely is your dwelling place,[z]
LORD Almighty!
[2]My soul yearns,[a] even faints,
for the courts of the LORD;
my heart and my flesh cry out
for the living God.
[3]Even the sparrow has found a home,
and the swallow a nest for herself,
where she may have her young—
a place near your altar,[b]
LORD Almighty, my King and my God.[c]
[4]Blessed are those who dwell in your house;
they are ever praising you.[c]

[5]Blessed are those whose strength[d] is in you,
whose hearts are set on pilgrimage.[e]
[6]As they pass through the Valley of Baka,
they make it a place of springs;
the autumn[f] rains also cover it with pools.[d]
[7]They go from strength to strength,[g]
till each appears[h] before God in Zion.

[8]Hear my prayer, LORD God Almighty;
listen to me, God of Jacob.

83:10 [p] Zep 1:17 **83:11** [q] Jdg 7:25 [r] Jdg 8:12,21 **83:12** [s] 2Ch 20:11 **83:13** [t] Ps 35:5; Isa 17:13 **83:14** [u] Dt 32:22; Isa 9:18 **83:15** [v] Job 9:17 **83:16** [w] Ps 109:29; 132:18 **83:17** [x] Ps 35:4 **83:18** [y] Ps 59:13 **84:1** [z] Ps 27:4; 43:3; 132:5 **84:2** [a] Ps 42:1-2 **84:3** [b] Ps 43:4 [c] Ps 5:2 **84:5** [d] Ps 81:1 [e] Jer 31:6 **84:6** [f] Joel 2:23 **84:7** [g] Pr 4:18 [h] Dt 16:16

[a] In Hebrew texts 84:1-12 is numbered 84:2-13. [b] Title: Probably a musical term [c] *4* The Hebrew has *Selah* (a word of uncertain meaning) here and at the end of verse 8. [d] *6* Or *blessings*

(Jdg 6–7), a tribal group later associated with the Ishmaelites. About this same time, Sisera and Jabin, from Hazor to the north of Israel, were defeated by Deborah and Barak (Jdg 4–5). By selecting these examples, the psalmist alludes to famous victories in geographic regions corresponding to the list of enemies in vv. 5–8.

83:10 *Endor.* Not mentioned in the account of these battles in Judges (see previous note), but it is in the vicinity of both of them. The eastern end of the Jezreel Valley is about 10 miles (16 kilometers) wide from north to south. The north end is blocked off by Mount Tabor, while the south end is blocked off by Mount Gilboa. The ten-mile (16-meter) stretch between the two is broken into two passes by the smaller hill of Moreh. Endor is located in the middle of the northern pass, between the hill of Moreh, where the battle of Midian took place, and Mount Tabor, where Deborah and Barak mustered their troops.

83:11 *Oreb and Zeeb ... Zebah and Zalmunna.* Nobles killed in Gideon's battle against the Midianites (Jdg 7:25; 8:3,12,21).

83:18 *you alone are the Most High.* In the ancient world, the *existence* of a god was understood in terms of its effective *activity* as a god. A being who was inactive, ineffectual, incompetent or lacking power or authority was not a god. This statement identifies Yahweh as the only being justifiably classified as a god. See the article "Monotheism, Monolatry and Henotheism," p. 308.

Ps 84 Hymns that extol holy cities and their temples are known from the ancient Near East (see the article "Hymns to Holy Cities," p. 927). Ps 84 concentrates on the delights of a visit to Jerusalem and its temple where God dwelt. The language of "courts" (vv. 2,10) is consistent with the view of a temple as the "palace" of God (see note on 100:4). A similar sentiment is illustrated in an Egyptian prayer from c. 1200 BC in which a religious pilgrim lingers in the temple court.

84:3 *a home ... near your altar.* While the Most Holy Place, containing the ark of God's presence, was the most sacred place in the temple, it was accessible only to the high priest (Lev 16:1–2), and the altar of incense, which was within the Holy Place, could only be approached by a priest (2Ch 26:16–18). Therefore, the altar of sacrifice in the temple court was the most important center of activity for the average worshiper. The psalmist marvels at the good fortune of even a small bird to have a nest so near, probably tucked into a niche somewhere on the structure of the sanctuary itself overlooking the court and altar. Even more blessed are the priests who have the privilege of living in the temple compound (v. 4).

84:4 *those who dwell in your house.* Being constantly in deity's presence is considered a privilege to be longed for throughout the ancient Near East. The Babylonian king Neriglissar expresses to his god that he wants to be where his god is forever. Another text requests that the king might stand before the god forever in adoration. The Hymn to Marduk requests that the worshiper may stand before the deity forever in prayer, supplication and entreaty. In the third millennium BC, Sumerian worshipers tried to accomplish this objective by placing statuettes of themselves in the posture of prayer in the temple. In this way they would be continuously represented in the temple.

84:6 *Valley of Baka.* If this is a reference to a geographic location, it is obscure. The word Baka means "weeping," but this would also be difficult to understand. The alternative suggestion is that the word describes a tree, particularly, the balsam (see note on 2Sa 5:23–24). None of these help locate the valley or identify its significance.

PSALM 84

SACRED SPACE

When the patriarch Jacob encountered the Lord, he recognized the "special" nature of the place where that meeting took place (Ge 28:11 – 22). Similarly, Moses' experience confirmed how a divine visitation set apart (made "holy") the actual space around God's presence (Ex 3:5; 19:10 – 13), and the ongoing presence of God in the midst of Israel necessitated special provision to protect the sanctity of the place of his dwelling (Ex 29:43 – 45; 40:34 – 35). The most enduring location of this sacred presence was Solomon's temple (1Ki 8:10 – 13). Wherever God touches earth, there is a nexus, a connection point, between the realm of heaven and earth; and the temple served as such a point for ancient Israel (1Ki 8:27 – 30). This notion of sacred space was shared among Israel's neighbors as well, and temples were regarded as the center of the cosmos, where heaven, earth and, in some views, the underworld met. In the Mesopotamian Creation Epic, founding the temple at Babylon as a waypoint for the gods between heaven and earth was among the first acts of Marduk.

Various creation stories from Egypt originated in cities whose temples were built where the gods were believed to have evolved into the constituent parts of the cosmos. When building temples, the Egyptians filled the ground for the foundation with clean sand in order to preserve the sanctity of the building site. Once geographic space was considered sacred, successive temple projects were built over top of older ones, and in some cases remodeling involved digging back down to "virgin soil" in order to reset foundation stones. Temple architecture also marked the degrees of sacredness, from the most inner sanctuary to the outside perimeter walls of the temple compound (see note on Ps 100:4). In this way, the cosmic symbolism of sacred space was protected.

For Solomon's temple, the symbolism of a garden, guarded by gates and cherubim, suggested a portal for entry into heaven; and the large tank of water, called the "Sea" (1Ki 7:23), may have symbolized the cosmic ocean over which Yahweh presided as king (Ps 29:3; 93:1 – 5). For ancient Israelites, then, it was as though the stability of the cosmos (and certainly their nation) was bound together with Yahweh's temple. Visiting the temple was to gain a glimpse of the habitation of God on earth, the center of

continued on next page

9 Look on our shield,[a][i] O God;
look with favor on your anointed
one.[j]

10 Better is one day in your courts
than a thousand elsewhere;
I would rather be a doorkeeper[k] in the
house of my God
than dwell in the tents of the
wicked.

11 For the LORD God is a sun[l] and shield;[m]
the LORD bestows favor and honor;
no good thing does he withhold[n]
from those whose walk is blameless.

12 LORD Almighty,
blessed[o] is the one who trusts
in you.

Psalm 85[b]

For the director of music.
Of the Sons of Korah.
A psalm.

1 You, LORD, showed favor to your land;
you restored the fortunes[p] of Jacob.

84:9 [i] Ps 59:11 [j] 1Sa 16:6; Ps 2:2; 132:17 **84:10** [k] 1Ch 23:5 **84:11** [l] Isa 60:19; Rev 21:23 [m] Ge 15:1 [n] Ps 34:10 **84:12** [o] Ps 2:12 **85:1** [p] Ps 14:7; Jer 30:18; Eze 39:25

[a] 9 Or *sovereign* [b] In Hebrew texts 85:1-13 is numbered 85:2-14.

84:9 *our shield.* As in 89:18, the king is identified with the shield as an image of protection (see note on 3:3). *your anointed one.* See note on 1Sa 2:10.
84:10 *doorkeeper.* See note on 1Ch 9:17.
84:11 *sun and shield.* Both offer protection. For the shield that is obvious, but we would not necessarily think of the sun in those terms. Nonetheless, Assyrian kings use the metaphor of their protection spreading over the land like the rays of the sun.

power and rule in the world. Even more cherished was the privilege of the priests who could dwell within the temple compound. Everything about the temple, its architecture and symbolism, conveyed a sense of awe, beauty, glory and majesty of the Creator and King of the universe. See the articles "Ziggurats," p. 30; "Stairway to Heaven," p. 67; "Architecture of the Temple," p. 572; "Temples and Sacred Space," p. 724. ◆

A relief of a shrine marked by fish and boats; perhaps to Ea, the water god. Khorsabad, palace of Sargon II, 721 to 705 BC. The notion of sacred space was shared among Israel's neighbors, and temples were regarded as the center of the cosmos.

Kim Walton. The Oriental Institute Museum, University of Chicago.

2 You forgave[q] the iniquity[r] of your
people
and covered all their sins.[a]
3 You set aside all your wrath[s]
and turned from your fierce
anger.[t]

4 Restore[u] us again, God our Savior,
and put away your displeasure
toward us.
5 Will you be angry with us forever?[v]
Will you prolong your anger through
all generations?
6 Will you not revive[w] us again,
that your people may rejoice in
you?

7 Show us your unfailing love,
LORD,
and grant us your salvation.

8 I will listen to what God the LORD
says;
he promises peace[x] to his people,
his faithful servants—
but let them not turn to folly.
9 Surely his salvation[y] is near those who
fear him,
that his glory[z] may dwell in our
land.

85:2 [q] Nu 14:19 [r] Ps 78:38 **85:3** [s] Ps 106:23 [t] Ex 32:12; Dt 13:17; Ps 78:38; Jnh 3:9 **85:4** [u] Ps 80:3,7 **85:5** [v] Ps 79:5 **85:6** [w] Ps 80:18; Hab 3:2 **85:8** [x] Zec 9:10 **85:9** [y] Isa 46:13 [z] Zec 2:5

[a] 2 The Hebrew has *Selah* (a word of uncertain meaning) here.

85:8 *I will listen.* May refer to a prophet in the temple waiting for a message from God, which in this psalm would comprise vv. 9–13 (see note on 50:7). Prophets were often thought to receive their messages by being allowed to listen in at the divine council (see the article "Divine Council," p. 615.

10 Love and faithfulness[a] meet together;
righteousness[b] and peace kiss each other.
11 Faithfulness springs forth from the earth,
and righteousness[c] looks down from heaven.
12 The LORD will indeed give what is good,[d]
and our land will yield[e] its harvest.
13 Righteousness goes before him
and prepares the way for his steps.

Psalm 86

A prayer of David.

1 Hear me, LORD, and answer[f] me,
for I am poor and needy.
2 Guard my life, for I am faithful to you;
save your servant who trusts in you.[g]
You are my God; 3 have mercy[h] on me, Lord,
for I call[i] to you all day long.
4 Bring joy to your servant, Lord,
for I put my trust[j] in you.

5 You, Lord, are forgiving and good,
abounding in love[k] to all who call to you.
6 Hear my prayer, LORD;
listen to my cry for mercy.
7 When I am in distress,[l] I call to you,
because you answer me.

8 Among the gods there is none like you,[m] Lord;
no deeds can compare with yours.
9 All the nations you have made
will come and worship[n] before you, Lord;
they will bring glory[o] to your name.
10 For you are great and do marvelous deeds;[p]
you alone[q] are God.

11 Teach me your way,[r] LORD,
that I may rely on your faithfulness;
give me an undivided[s] heart,
that I may fear your name.
12 I will praise you, Lord my God, with all my heart;
I will glorify your name forever.
13 For great is your love toward me;
you have delivered me from the depths,
from the realm of the dead.

14 Arrogant foes are attacking me, O God;
ruthless people are trying to kill me—
they have no regard for you.[t]
15 But you, Lord, are a compassionate and gracious[u] God,
slow to anger, abounding in love and faithfulness.[v]
16 Turn to me and have mercy on me;
show your strength in behalf of your servant;
save me, because I serve you
just as my mother did.[w]
17 Give me a sign of your goodness,
that my enemies may see it and be put to shame,
for you, LORD, have helped me and comforted me.

85:10 [a] Ps 89:14; Pr 3:3 [b] Ps 72:2-3; Isa 32:17 **85:11** [c] Isa 45:8 **85:12** [d] Ps 84:11; Jas 1:17 [e] Lev 26:4; Ps 67:6; Zec 8:12 **86:1** [f] Ps 17:6 **86:2** [g] Ps 25:2; 31:14 **86:3** [h] Ps 4:1; 57:1 [i] Ps 88:9 **86:4** [j] Ps 25:1; 143:8 **86:5** [k] Ex 34:6; Ne 9:17; Ps 103:8; 145:8; Joel 2:13; Jnh 4:2 **86:7** [l] Ps 50:15 **86:8** [m] Ex 15:11; Dt 3:24; Ps 89:6 **86:9** [n] Ps 66:4; Rev 15:4 [o] Isa 43:7 **86:10** [p] Ps 72:18 [q] Dt 6:4; Mk 12:29; 1Co 8:4 **86:11** [r] Ps 25:5 [s] Jer 32:39 **86:14** [t] Ps 54:3 **86:15** [u] Ps 103:8 [v] Ex 34:6; Ne 9:17; Joel 2:13 **86:16** [w] Ps 116:16

85:10 *righteousness and peace.* Peace is what people experience in the absence of fear. It results when righteousness prevails (Isa 32:16–17). A similar pairing of these two concepts was shared by the Egyptians, who expressed the combination with one word: *maat.* For the Egyptians, *maat* was the natural order of the universe, "the way things ought to be." It could be translated "order" or "justice," so it embraced social justice leading to prosperous life for the community. A good illustration of this is found in the speeches of the "Eloquent Peasant," in which a peasant appeals for justice from a local magistrate. His poem links the execution of social "justice" (*maat*) with the "fair wind" that accompanies a smooth and prosperous sail on the sea. When chaos plagues Egyptian society, it is due to the absence of *maat* in the king's rule. In this verse, righteousness and peace "kiss" when God blesses his people. See note on Ps 72.

86:8 *none like you.* In ancient Near Eastern hymns, proclaiming the incomparability of a god or goddess is well attested. Whichever of the great gods a person was worshiping would be the "greatest" at that particular moment of worship. For example, in one hymn the Assyrian king Ashurbanipal (c. 650 BC) calls his national god, Assur, "lord of the gods" and "surpassing" all other gods, who themselves cannot fully comprehend him. In another hymn, he proclaims Marduk as the most high and most powerful, whose deeds make him lord of the gods. At the same time, he claims that the goddess Ishtar has "no equal among the great gods." Some expressions of worship to the Egyptian sun-god declare his incomparability: "one without parallel," "the one of surpassing power" relative to the other gods, "who conceals himself from all the gods … there is no comprehending him."

Consequently, we can see that such expressions are not solely associated with monotheism, though they comport well with it. Even the statement "you alone are God" (v. 10) has to be understood in the context of how the Israelites and their neighbors thought about the gods (see note on 83:18).

86:17 *Give me a sign.* Perhaps this request is best understood as an expectation of prophetic response in the context of worship (see note on 50:7). The demonstration of God's favor by some visible or tangible form would vindicate the psalmist in the sight of his enemies. This concept is illustrated in a letter from a Canaanite king to Pharaoh (c. 1350 BC). The king expresses his wish for a gift from Pharaoh as a visible symbol that he enjoys Pharaoh's favor: "bestow a gift upon his servant so that our enemies may see (it) and be humiliated."

Psalm 87

Of the Sons of Korah. A psalm. A song.

1 He has founded his city on the holy
mountain.
2 The LORD loves the gates of Zion[x]
more than all the other dwellings of
Jacob.

3 Glorious things are said of you,
city of God:[a][y]
4 "I will record Rahab[b][z] and Babylon
among those who acknowledge me —
Philistia too, and Tyre[a], along with
Cush[c] —
and will say, 'This one was born in
Zion.' "[d][b]
5 Indeed, of Zion it will be said,
"This one and that one were born in
her,
and the Most High himself will
establish her."
6 The LORD will write in the register[c] of
the peoples:
"This one was born in Zion."

7 As they make music[d] they will sing,
"All my fountains[e] are in you."

Psalm 88[e]

A song. A psalm of the Sons of Korah.
For the director of music. According
to *mahalath leannoth*.[f] A *maskil*[g]
of Heman the Ezrahite.

1 LORD, you are the God who saves me;[f]
day and night I cry out[g] to you.
2 May my prayer come before you;
turn your ear to my cry.
3 I am overwhelmed with troubles
and my life draws near to death.[h]
4 I am counted among those who go
down to the pit;[i]
I am like one without strength.
5 I am set apart with the dead,
like the slain who lie in the
grave,
whom you remember no more,
who are cut off[j] from your care.

6 You have put me in the lowest pit,
in the darkest depths.[k]
7 Your wrath lies heavily on me;
you have overwhelmed me with
all your waves.[h][l]
8 You have taken from me my closest
friends[m]
and have made me repulsive to
them.
I am confined[n] and cannot escape;
9 my eyes[o] are dim with grief.

I call[p] to you, LORD, every day;
I spread out my hands[q] to you.

87:2 [x] Ps 78:68
87:3 [y] Ps 46:4; Isa 60:1
87:4 [z] Job 9:13 [a] Ps 45:12 [b] Isa 19:25
87:6 [c] Ps 69:28; Isa 4:3; Eze 13:9
87:7 [d] Ps 149:3 [e] Ps 36:9
88:1 [f] Ps 51:14 [g] Ps 22:2; 27:9; Lk 18:7
88:3 [h] Ps 107:18, 26
88:4 [i] Ps 28:1
88:5 [j] Ps 31:22; Isa 53:8
88:6 [k] Ps 69:15; La 3:55
88:7 [l] Ps 42:7
88:8 [m] Job 19:13; Ps 31:11 [n] Jer 32:2
88:9 [o] Ps 38:10 [p] Ps 86:3 [q] Job 11:13; Ps 143:6

[a] *3* The Hebrew has *Selah* (a word of uncertain meaning) here and at the end of verse 6. [b] *4* A poetic name for Egypt [c] *4* That is, the upper Nile region [d] *4* Or *"I will record concerning those who acknowledge me: / 'This one was born in Zion.' / Hear this, Rahab and Babylon, / and you too, Philistia, Tyre and Cush."* [e] In Hebrew texts 88:1-18 is numbered 88:2-19. [f] Title: Possibly a tune, "The Suffering of Affliction" [g] Title: Probably a literary or musical term [h] *7* The Hebrew has *Selah* (a word of uncertain meaning) here and at the end of verse 10.

87:1 *founded his city on the holy mountain.* In OT thought, Jerusalem (also called "Zion," v. 2) was at the center of God's kingdom and the world. For the importance of holy cities and mountains in ancient Near Eastern religion, see applicable notes on Ps 48; see also the article "Hymns to Holy Cities," p. 927. The psalmist here marvels at the stability of Jerusalem resulting from Yahweh's presence in his temple, which has become the anchor point for the entire cosmos (see the article "Sacred Space," p. 964). This thought is similar to a Babylonian hymn in praise of the god Nabu's temple at Borsippa, described as having a summit that reaches the clouds, while its roots penetrate into the netherworld.
87:4 *Rahab.* Its identification is not clear. In some contexts, the name refers to the chaos serpent (see the article "Chaos Monsters," p. 953). However, the names of mythical monsters can be used symbolically for an enemy nation, and here "Rahab" is another name for Egypt (see Isa 30:7), the great empire to Israel's southwest. *Babylon.* One of the oldest and most highly esteemed cities in Mesopotamia (Ge 10:10); it is representative of the peoples from this region of the ancient Near East. *Philistia … Tyre … Cush.* No historical situation needs to be sought here, because the text is simply listing some of the nations that will be counted among those who acknowledge Yahweh (whether politically or spiritually). The list in this verse includes the great powers, Egypt (Rahab) and Babylon, the near neighbors, Philistia (southwest) and Tyre (northwest), and the distant nation Cush (i.e., Nubia), south of Egypt).

87:6 *register of the peoples.* In the ancient world, royal estate cities typically housed the administration (composed largely of relatives of the king), and their citizens enjoyed certain privileges, including exemption from taxation, corvée labor, military duty and imprisonment, as well as being beneficiaries of the most beautiful and elaborate building projects. Such privileges (Akkadian *kidinnutu*) were enjoyed, e.g., by Babylonian cities such as Nippur, Sippar and Borsippa based on their statuses as religious centers rather than as political capitals. Political capitals such as Nineveh and Babylon also were endowed with similar status. It is presumed that records would be kept to identify those who enjoyed such privileges. In this verse the psalmist alludes to the privileged status of those born in Zion.
87:7 *my fountains.* A common image in ancient Near Eastern art is a deity holding a vessel from which waters flow, bringing blessing to the worshipers. Perhaps this lyric, sung by converts to the God of Zion, alludes to the idea that the dwelling place of God is the origin of all that blesses life (see note on 46:4).
88 title *Heman the Ezrahite.* Along with Ethan (see Ps 89 title), Heman is listed as one of the famous wise men in Solomon's time (1Ki 4:31) and was appointed one of the Levitical musicians during the time of David (1Ch 15:17,19).
88:3 – 7,11 See the articles "Death and Sheol," p. 833; "Death and the Underworld," p. 907.

[10]Do you show your wonders to the
dead?
Do their spirits rise up and praise
you?[r]
[11]Is your love declared in the grave,
your faithfulness[s] in Destruction[a]?
[12]Are your wonders known in the place
of darkness,
or your righteous deeds in the land
of oblivion?

[13]But I cry to you for help,[t] LORD;
in the morning[u] my prayer comes
before you.[v]
[14]Why, LORD, do you reject[w] me
and hide your face[x] from me?
[15]From my youth I have suffered and
been close to death;
I have borne your terrors[y] and am in
despair.
[16]Your wrath has swept over me;
your terrors have destroyed me.
[17]All day long they surround me like a
flood;[z]
they have completely engulfed me.
[18]You have taken from me friend[a] and
neighbor—
darkness is my closest friend.

Psalm 89[b]

A *maskil*[c] of Ethan the Ezrahite.

[1]I will sing[b] of the LORD's great love
forever;
with my mouth I will make your
faithfulness known[c]
through all generations.
[2]I will declare that your love stands firm
forever,
that you have established your
faithfulness in heaven itself.[d]

88:10 [r]Ps 6:5
88:11 [s]Ps 30:9
88:13 [t]Ps 30:2
[u]Ps 5:3
[v]Ps 119:147
88:14 [w]Ps 43:2
[x]Job 13:24;
Ps 13:1
88:15 [y]Job 6:4
88:17
[z]Ps 22:16;
124:4
88:18 [a]ver 8;
Job 19:13;
Ps 38:11
89:1 [b]Ps 59:16;
Ps 101:1
[c]Ps 36:5; 40:10
89:2 [d]Ps 36:5
89:4 [e]2Sa 7:12-
16; 1Ki 8:16;
Ps 132:11-12;
Isa 9:7; Lk 1:33
89:5 [f]Ps 19:1
89:6 [g]Ps 113:5
89:7 [h]Ps 47:2
89:8 [i]Ps 71:19
89:9 [j]Ps 65:7
89:10 [k]Ps 87:4
[l]Ps 68:1
89:11
[m]1Ch 29:11;
Ps 24:1 [n]Ge 1:1
89:12
[o]Jos 19:22
[p]Dt 3:8;
Jos 12:1
[q]Ps 98:8

[3]You said, "I have made a covenant
with my chosen one,
I have sworn to David my servant,
[4]'I will establish your line forever
and make your throne firm through
all generations.' "[d][e]
[5]The heavens[f] praise your wonders,
LORD,
your faithfulness too, in the
assembly of the holy ones.
[6]For who in the skies above can
compare with the LORD?
Who is like the LORD among the
heavenly beings?[g]
[7]In the council of the holy ones God is
greatly feared;
he is more awesome than all who
surround him.[h]
[8]Who is like you,[i] LORD God Almighty?
You, LORD, are mighty, and your
faithfulness surrounds you.
[9]You rule over the surging sea;
when its waves mount up, you still
them.[j]
[10]You crushed Rahab[k] like one of the
slain;
with your strong arm you scattered[l]
your enemies.
[11]The heavens are yours, and yours also
the earth;[m]
you founded the world and all that
is in it.[n]
[12]You created the north and the south;
Tabor[o] and Hermon[p] sing for joy[q] at
your name.

[a] *11* Hebrew *Abaddon* [b] In Hebrew texts 89:1-52 is numbered 89:2-53. [c] Title: Probably a literary or musical term [d] *4* The Hebrew has *Selah* (a word of uncertain meaning) here and at the end of verses 37, 45 and 48.

88:10 *Do their spirits rise up and praise you?* The glorification of God's name on earth comes through the praises of his people (22:3, lit. "enthroned on the praises of Israel" [ESV, NASB]). Conversely, the dead contribute nothing in this regard. This notion forms the basis of a natural appeal to God for intervention. A similar plea is echoed in a Mesopotamian prayer to Marduk observing that the god has no profit from one who has turned to clay or dust. This very human perspective is also evident in Hittite laments.
89:3 *I have made a covenant ... sworn to David.* The theme of God's covenant with David is introduced in vv. 3 – 4 and expanded in the prophetic proclamation that begins in v. 19. David and his descendants were chosen by Yahweh to rule on the throne over the people of Israel (132:11 – 12; 2Sa 7). The covenant announced in these prophetic speeches promises unconditionally that David's dynasty would always be the rightful heirs to the throne. However, individual descendants who did not follow God's laws could be removed from kingship. Unconditional and conditional elements are compatible in ancient Near Eastern treaties and wills, with wording similar to that of Ps 89; 132; 2Sa 7. A great king might grant to a loyal subject certain guarantees of property. The property would always belong to the family; however, in the future any disloyal individual could be disciplined by the great king and lose their right to the land. However, the land remains in the possession of the family line. While the form of these royal grants is not an exact parallel with the Davidic covenant, the similar language illustrates how unconditional and conditional themes might work in compatible fashion in the same document. Another important feature of these covenants was the family terminology (see notes on Ps 2).
89:6 *among the heavenly beings.* See the article "Divine Council," p. 615.
89:9 – 10 *You rule over the surging sea ... crushed Rahab.* See the article "Chaos Monsters," p. 953.
89:12 *You created the north and the south.* A poetic way of saying the same thing as v. 11 (i.e., God created everything) by naming two extremities in order to include everything in between. A similar use of these two compass points can be found in Eze 20:47; 21:4. *north.* The Hebrew word (*tsaphon*) is perhaps significant in that the same Hebrew word is the name of a high mountain in Syria to the north of Israel: Zaphon. Although Yahweh's dwelling is most often associated with Mount Zion in Jerusalem, his presence is sometimes attached to other high mountains, like

13 Your arm is endowed with power;
your hand is strong, your right hand
exalted.
14 Righteousness and justice are the
foundation of your throne;[r]
love and faithfulness go before you.
15 Blessed are those who have learned to
acclaim you,
who walk in the light[s] of your
presence, LORD.
16 They rejoice in your name[t] all day
long;
they celebrate your righteousness.
17 For you are their glory and strength,
and by your favor you exalt our
horn.[a][u]
18 Indeed, our shield[b] belongs to the
LORD,
our king[v] to the Holy One of Israel.

19 Once you spoke in a vision,
to your faithful people you said:
"I have bestowed strength on a
warrior;
I have raised up a young man from
among the people.
20 I have found David[w] my servant;[x]
with my sacred oil I have anointed[y]
him.
21 My hand will sustain him;
surely my arm will strengthen him.[z]
22 The enemy will not get the better of
him;
the wicked will not oppress[a] him.

89:14 [r] Ps 97:2
89:15 [s] Ps 44:3
89:16 [t] Ps 105:3
89:17 [u] Ps 75:10; 92:10; 148:14
89:18 [v] Ps 47:9
89:20 [w] Ac 13:22 [x] Ps 78:70 [y] 1Sa 16:1, 12
89:21 [z] Ps 18:35
89:22 [a] 2Sa 7:10
89:23 [b] Ps 18:40 [c] 2Sa 7:9
89:24 [d] 2Sa 7:15
89:25 [e] Ps 72:8
89:26 [f] 2Sa 7:14 [g] 2Sa 22:47
89:27 [h] Col 1:18 [i] Nu 24:7 [j] Rev 1:5; 19:16
89:28 [k] ver 33-34; Isa 55:3
89:29 [l] ver 4, 36; Dt 11:21; Jer 33:17
89:32 [m] 2Sa 7:14
89:33 [n] 2Sa 7:15
89:34 [o] Nu 23:19

23 I will crush his foes before him[b]
and strike down his adversaries.[c]
24 My faithful love will be with him,[d]
and through my name his horn[c] will
be exalted.
25 I will set his hand over the sea,
his right hand over the rivers.[e]
26 He will call out to me, 'You are my
Father,[f]
my God, the Rock my Savior.'[g]
27 And I will appoint him to be my
firstborn,[h]
the most exalted[i] of the kings[j] of the
earth.
28 I will maintain my love to him forever,
and my covenant with him will
never fail.[k]
29 I will establish his line forever,
his throne as long as the heavens
endure.[l]

30 "If his sons forsake my law
and do not follow my statutes,
31 if they violate my decrees
and fail to keep my commands,
32 I will punish their sin with the rod,
their iniquity with flogging;[m]
33 but I will not take my love from him,[n]
nor will I ever betray my
faithfulness.
34 I will not violate my covenant
or alter what my lips have uttered.[o]

[a] *17 Horn* here symbolizes strong one. [b] *18* Or *sovereign* [c] *24 Horn* here symbolizes strength.

Zaphon (see note on 48:1–2). *south.* Also the place of Yahweh's mountain dwelling (Mount Sinai/Paran, Dt 33:2). In the ancient Near East, gods were often associated with high places, especially mountains, and worshiped there. Canaanite myth placed Baal's palace on Mount Zaphon. Mount Tabor and Mount Hermon in northern Israel were likewise ancient worship sites.

89:14 *Righteousness and justice.* Frequently depicted on the pedestal of Egyptian thrones is the hieroglyph for justice (*maat*, see note on 85:10), conveying the importance of this value to the rule of a good king. See note on Ps 72.

89:18 *shield.* A symbol of protection; here it is an image for the king, to whom the people have looked for their security (see notes on 3:3; 84:9,11). The people affirm their dependence on the king and ultimately on the Lord, to whom the king belongs; however, this psalm laments the king's downfall.

89:19–37 Many of the expressions in these verses (see also Ps 2; 110; 132) are similar to divine words of affirmation found in Assyrian royal prophecy, in which the god sustains the king, crushes his enemies, and establishes his house. Throughout the ancient Near East, prophetic oracles offered great assurance to the king, supported his authority in the eyes of the people, and functioned to solidify the relationship between the deity, the king and the people. In Psalms, it is also the case that these prophetic words are supportive of the king, in contrast to the prophetic books of the OT, in which the prophets often took a critical stance against the king.

89:19 *vision.* This word indicates that the ideas expressed in the following verses originated from prophetic speech (cf. Isa 1:1; Hos 12:10). The royal promises to David and his descendants began with the prophet Nathan (2Sa 7), through whom Yahweh announced his covenant, and are found in other prophetic psalms (Ps 2; 110; 132:11–18). Such prophetic oracles were sometimes uttered in a temple setting, which fits well the background of the psalms, and here, the use of the Hebrew term *hesidim* ("faithful people") refers to the community gathered for worship (also in 30:4; 52:9; 145:10; 149:1; and "consecrated people" in 50:5).

89:20 *I have anointed him.* See notes on 1Sa 2:10; 10:1.

89:24 *horn.* See note on 18:2.

89:27 *I will appoint him to be my firstborn.* As the eldest son in a family, the "firstborn" had customary right to a major share of the inheritance (Dt 21:15–17) and took leadership of the family clan upon the father's death (see the article "Inheritance Rights and Birthrights," p. 62). In the ancient Near East, the custom for royal succession was that the eldest son would be the next king. However, exceptions are known and sometimes led to internal political turmoil. For example, Ardi-Mulissi, the eldest living son of Sennacherib (704–681 BC), was replaced by Esarhaddon, a younger son, as the heir to the throne (see the article "The Death of Sennacherib," p. 661). The former assassinated his father and civil war ensued. Similarly, political tension resulted from David's selection of Solomon over an older brother for succession (see 1Ki 1). Against this backdrop, we might conclude that if the Davidic king is "firstborn" heir of the Creator of the world, then he is also the preeminent king ("most exalted," v. 27) over all world rulers.

35 Once for all, I have sworn by my
holiness—
and I will not lie to David—
36 that his line will continue forever
and his throne endure before me
like the sun;
37 it will be established forever like the
moon,
the faithful witness in the sky."

38 But you have rejected,[p] you have
spurned,
you have been very angry with your
anointed one.
39 You have renounced the covenant with
your servant
and have defiled his crown in the
dust.[q]
40 You have broken through all his
walls[r]
and reduced his strongholds[s]
to ruins.
41 All who pass by have plundered
him;
he has become the scorn of his
neighbors.[t]
42 You have exalted the right hand of his
foes;
you have made all his enemies
rejoice.[u]
43 Indeed, you have turned back the edge
of his sword
and have not supported him in
battle.[v]
44 You have put an end to his splendor
and cast his throne to the ground.
45 You have cut short the days of his
youth;
you have covered him with a mantle
of shame.[w]

46 How long, LORD? Will you hide yourself
forever?
How long will your wrath burn like
fire?[x]
47 Remember how fleeting is my life.[y]
For what futility you have created all
humanity!
48 Who can live and not see death,
or who can escape the power of the
grave?[z]
49 Lord, where is your former great love,
which in your faithfulness you swore
to David?

89:38 [p] Dt 32:19; 1Ch 28:9; Ps 44:9 **89:39** [q] La 5:16 **89:40** [r] Ps 80:12 [s] La 2:2 **89:41** [t] Ps 44:13 **89:42** [u] Ps 13:2; 80:6 **89:43** [v] Ps 44:10 **89:45** [w] Ps 44:15; 109:29 **89:46** [x] Ps 79:5 **89:47** [y] Job 7:7; Ps 39:5 **89:48** [z] Ps 22:29; 49:9

89:50 [a] Ps 69:19 **89:51** [b] Ps 74:10 **89:52** [c] Ps 41:13; 72:19 **90:1** [d] Dt 33:27; Eze 11:16 **90:2** [e] Job 15:7; Pr 8:25 [f] Ps 102:24-27 **90:3** [g] Ge 3:19; Job 34:15 **90:4** [h] 2Pe 3:8 **90:5** [i] Ps 73:20; Isa 40:6 **90:6** [j] Mt 6:30; Jas 1:10 **90:8** [k] Ps 19:12 **90:9** [l] Ps 78:33

50 Remember, Lord, how your servant
has[a] been mocked,[a]
how I bear in my heart the taunts of
all the nations,
51 the taunts with which your enemies,
LORD, have mocked,
with which they have mocked every
step of your anointed one.[b]

52 Praise be to the LORD forever!
Amen and Amen.[c]

BOOK IV

Psalms 90–106

Psalm 90

A prayer of Moses the man of God.

1 Lord, you have been our dwelling
place[d]
throughout all generations.
2 Before the mountains were born[e]
or you brought forth the whole
world,
from everlasting to everlasting you
are God.[f]

3 You turn people back to dust,
saying, "Return to dust, you
mortals."[g]
4 A thousand years in your sight
are like a day that has just gone by,
or like a watch in the night.[h]
5 Yet you sweep people away[i] in the
sleep of death—
they are like the new grass of the
morning:
6 In the morning it springs up new,
but by evening it is dry and
withered.[j]

7 We are consumed by your anger
and terrified by your indignation.
8 You have set our iniquities before
you,
our secret sins[k] in the light of your
presence.
9 All our days pass away under your
wrath;
we finish our years with a moan.[l]

[a] 50 *Or your servants have*

89:36–37 *his throne endure ... like the sun ... like the moon.* Because of their enduring presence in the universe, the imagery of sun and moon were used in royal inscriptions for the stability of a king's dynasty. A letter to the Assyrian king Esarhaddon (c. 670 BC) expresses the wish that his kingship and that of his descendants might be established as firmly as the moon and sun. In Ps 89, they are likened to witnesses to the covenant, thereby ensuring its validity for all time.
90:3 *Return to dust.* Death is decreed. According to Mesopotamian myth, the chief god Enlil became annoyed by the noise stemming from the ever-growing human population. After the flood, which was sent by the gods to wipe out humanity and thus alleviate the noise, population growth was limited by withholding immortality from humankind. In the Gilgamesh Epic, the god Enki describes how after the flood the gods swore that people should not have eternal life. The psalmist recognizes that divine judgment and death are the result of sin (v. 8). *dust.* See note on 104:29–30.

[10]Our days may come to seventy years,
or eighty, if our strength endures;
yet the best of them are but trouble and sorrow,
for they quickly pass, and we fly away.[m]
[11]If only we knew the power of your anger!
Your wrath is as great as the fear that is your due.[n]
[12]Teach us to number our days,[o]
that we may gain a heart of wisdom.[p]
[13]Relent, LORD! How long[q] will it be?
Have compassion on your servants.[r]
[14]Satisfy[s] us in the morning with your unfailing love,
that we may sing for joy[t] and be glad all our days.[u]
[15]Make us glad for as many days as you have afflicted us,
for as many years as we have seen trouble.
[16]May your deeds be shown to your servants,
your splendor to their children.[v]
[17]May the favor[a] of the Lord our God rest on us;
establish the work of our hands for us—
yes, establish the work of our hands.[w]

90:10 [m]Job 20:8 **90:11** [n]Ps 76:7 **90:12** [o]Ps 39:4 [p]Dt 32:29 **90:13** [q]Ps 6:3 [r]Dt 32:36; Ps 135:14 **90:14** [s]Ps 103:5 [t]Ps 85:6 [u]Ps 31:7 **90:16** [v]Ps 44:1; Hab 3:2 **90:17** [w]Isa 26:12

Psalm 91

[1]Whoever dwells in the shelter[x] of the Most High
will rest in the shadow[y] of the Almighty.[b]
[2]I will say of the LORD, "He is my refuge[z] and my fortress,
my God, in whom I trust."
[3]Surely he will save you
from the fowler's snare[a]
and from the deadly pestilence.[b]
[4]He will cover you with his feathers,
and under his wings you will find refuge;[c]
his faithfulness will be your shield[d] and rampart.
[5]You will not fear[e] the terror of night,
nor the arrow that flies by day,
[6]nor the pestilence that stalks in the darkness,
nor the plague that destroys at midday.
[7]A thousand may fall at your side,
ten thousand at your right hand,
but it will not come near you.
[8]You will only observe with your eyes
and see the punishment of the wicked.[f]
[9]If you say, "The LORD is my refuge,"
and you make the Most High your dwelling,

91:1 [x]Ps 31:20 [y]Ps 17:8 **91:2** [z]Ps 142:5 **91:3** [a]Ps 124:7; Pr 6:5 [b]1Ki 8:37 **91:4** [c]Ps 17:8 [d]Ps 35:2 **91:5** [e]Job 5:21 **91:8** [f]Ps 37:34; 58:10; Mal 1:5

[a] *17* Or *beauty* [b] *1* Hebrew *Shaddai*

90:10 *seventy years.* As early as 100 BC, the Apocryphal Book of Jubilees (Jubilees 23:15) contrasts the preflood life spans approaching 1,000 years (v. 4) with the post-flood expectancy of 70 years (here). A similar chronological schema is preserved in the Sumerian King List, which records the reigns of kings in the tens of thousands of years before the flood, but diminishing to hundreds of years and then tens of years after the flood.

On the basis of human skeletal remains, anthropologists have estimated the life span of people living in Canaan during Biblical times. A little over 40 percent reached adulthood (20–49 years of age) and nearly 10 percent lived beyond 50 years. Ancient Egyptian tradition idealized the maximum age as 110, as Pharaoh Amenmesses (c. 1200 BC) hoped, since that was the destiny of the righteous man. But more realistically, Egyptian tradition also set the prime of life between 40 and 60 years. Mesopotamian expectations set 40 years as "prime" with 90 years as a maximum. Records show that scribes and even many slaves lived 60 to 80 years. The mother of the Babylonian king Nabonidus lived 104 years. These cultural norms all accord with the expectation of the psalmist.

90:17 *establish the work.* Not only did ancient Israelites recognize the ephemeral nature of life and human endeavor (vv. 3–6; Ecc 2:11,16; Isa 40:6–7), but a similar humility marked Mesopotamian thought. A Mesopotamian wisdom text that treats the transitory nature of life states that humans as well as their achievements do not last. The text goes on to admonish the reader to attend to his god. In this verse, a confident trust breaks through that God is able to make human efforts count for good.

91:1 *the shadow of the Almighty.* The shadow offers protection and is usually referred to as the "shadow of your wings" (36:7; see note there).

91:3 *fowler's snare.* See notes on 124:7; 140:5. *pestilence.* Usually translated "plague" in the NIV, this Hebrew word refers to acts of God's judgment, which may include disease, but more broadly includes any disaster with fatal consequences (cf. Jer 27:13; Eze 33:27). Some commentators associate pestilence with demonic forces, which fits the imagery of a pestilence that "stalks" (v. 6). Indeed, this word and its synonym, "plague" (v. 6), are coupled with a word that is also the name of a deity of pestilence, war and the underworld in ancient Near Eastern texts: "Rashaph" (Hebrew *resheph*, see Dt 32:24; Hab 3:5 [both translated "pestilence"]). In the ancient world, all of these issues were understood as interrelated.

91:4 *under his wings.* See note on 36:7.

91:5–6 *terror of night ... the darkness.* The darkness of night creates an inherently more dangerous setting; and perhaps due to the intensification of fever at night, illness in particular was feared. A nighttime prayer from Mesopotamia to the god Nusku implores the god to dispel the fears connected with the night (e.g., demons, wicked people) and to appoint to him a "watcher of well-being and life" to guard him until daybreak.

91:6 *pestilence.* See note on v. 3.

10 no harm[g] will overtake you,
no disaster will come near your tent.
11 For he will command his angels[h]
concerning you
to guard you in all your ways;[i]
12 they will lift you up in their hands,
so that you will not strike your foot
against a stone.[j]
13 You will tread on the lion and the cobra;
you will trample the great lion and
the serpent.[k]

14 "Because he[a] loves me," says the LORD,
"I will rescue him;
I will protect him, for he
acknowledges my name.
15 He will call on me, and I will answer
him;
I will be with him in trouble,
I will deliver him and honor him.[l]
16 With long life[m] I will satisfy him
and show him my salvation.[n]"

Psalm 92[b]

A psalm. A song. For the Sabbath day.

1 It is good to praise the LORD
and make music to your name,[o]
O Most High,[p]
2 proclaiming your love in the morning[q]
and your faithfulness at night,
3 to the music of the ten-stringed lyre
and the melody of the harp.[r]

4 For you make me glad by your deeds,
LORD;
I sing for joy at what your hands
have done.[s]
5 How great are your works,[t] LORD,
how profound your thoughts![u]
6 Senseless people[v] do not know,
fools do not understand,
7 that though the wicked spring up
like grass
and all evildoers flourish,
they will be destroyed forever.

8 But you, LORD, are forever exalted.

9 For surely your enemies, LORD,
surely your enemies will
perish;
all evildoers will be scattered.[w]
10 You have exalted my horn[c][x] like
that of a wild ox;
fine oils[y] have been poured on me.
11 My eyes have seen the defeat of my
adversaries;
my ears have heard the rout of my
wicked foes.[z]

12 The righteous will flourish like a palm
tree,
they will grow like a cedar of
Lebanon;[a]

[a] *14* That is, probably the king [b] In Hebrew texts 92:1-15 is numbered 92:2-16. [c] *10* *Horn* here symbolizes strength.

91:10 [g] Pr 12:21 **91:11** [h] Heb 1:14 [i] Ps 34:7 **91:12** [j] Mt 4:6*; Lk 4:10-11* **91:13** [k] Da 6:22; Lk 10:19 **91:15** [l] 1Sa 2:30; Ps 50:15; Jn 12:26 **91:16** [m] Dt 6:2; Ps 21:4 [n] Ps 50:23 **92:1** [o] Ps 147:1 [p] Ps 135:3 **92:2** [q] Ps 89:1 **92:3** [r] 1Sa 10:5; Ne 12:27; Ps 33:2 **92:4** [s] Ps 8:6; 143:5 **92:5** [t] Rev 15:3 [u] Ps 40:5; 139:17; Isa 28:29; Ro 11:33 **92:6** [v] Ps 73:22 **92:9** [w] Ps 68:1; 89:10 **92:10** [x] Ps 89:17 [y] Ps 23:5 **92:11** [z] Ps 54:7; 91:8 **92:12** [a] Ps 1:3; 52:8; Jer 17:8; Hos 14:6

91:11 *angels ... to guard you.* In the ancient Near East, it was, of course, deities rather than angels who served as guardians. Mesopotamians believed that personal gods or family gods offered special care and protection that the great cosmic or national deities would not be bothered with. The Akkadian texts also speak of guardians of well-being and health, as well as guardian spirits. These spirits were assigned to an individual by the deity just as here. The protection that was expected in the ancient Near East was against demonic powers that were believed to be the cause of illness and trouble. Related to that was the danger of magical spells and hexes that could be pronounced against someone. The Israelites undoubtedly believed in the reality of the demon world, and many Israelites would not have successfully divorced their thinking from the magical perspectives of their neighbors. Nevertheless, the psalmist does not typically understand the problems he faces in those terms. While the OT offers no evidence for personal, guardian spirits such as those implied in the Mesopotamian texts or affirmed in some Christian traditions ("guardian angels"), Ps 91 does express confidence that Yahweh sends servants from the heavenly realm to aid his people in time of need (see note on 103:20).
91:13 *cobra ... serpent.* See notes on 58:4–5; 140:3.
91:14 *I will rescue him.* The previous verses are words of encouragement on behalf of the worshiper; beginning in v. 14, however, God himself speaks. Prophetic speech in the context of worship was not uncommon to ancient Israel, and it is preserved in some psalms (see note on 50:7). The original setting for most psalms is a matter of speculation. While the first performance of this psalm might have been addressed, e.g., to a king preparing for battle (see note on Ps 20), its preservation and subsequent use was for anyone seeking protection from God. Such reapplication of original compositions is attested across the ancient Near East (see the articles "Community Laments in the Ancient Near East," p. 919; "Repeated Psalms," p. 990). In this case, the original prophetic promise becomes a word of encouragement that God is sovereign over any danger and able to come to the aid of his people. This is not unlike contemporary use of any prophetic text from which a timeless principle is drawn for general application.
92 title *A psalm. A song. For the Sabbath day.* This is the only psalm that is designated for the Sabbath. There is little indication in the OT of any special worship ceremonies on the Sabbath. It has been suggested that this psalm accompanied the daily offerings on the Sabbath.
92:1,3 *music.* See the article "Music and Musicians," p. 524.
92:3 *lyre.* See the articles "Lyre," p. 488; "Music and Musicians," p. 524.
92:10 *horn.* See notes on 18:2; 132:17. *oils ... poured on me.* See note on 23:5.
92:12 *palm tree.* Reaching heights of 70 feet (21 meters) and living up to 200 years, the date-palm tree was a conspicuous sight of fertility along waterways in the arid climate of the ancient Near East. *cedar of Lebanon.* The rain-drenched, mountainous regions to the north of Israel were famous for towering cedar forests (see notes on 29:5; 2Sa 5:11; 1Ki 5:6; 6:15). Appreciation for the beauty and shade of trees led to the planting of groves in palace compounds. Solomon even simulated a forest by incorporating a high concentration of cedar beams into his palace (1Ki 7:2–4). There were no such groves in the court of the

Cedar of Lebanon. "The righteous will flourish like a palm tree, they will grow like a cedar of Lebanon" (Ps 92:12).

[13]planted in the house of the LORD,
they will flourish in the courts of our God.[b]
[14]They will still bear fruit[c] in old age,
they will stay fresh and green,
[15]proclaiming, "The LORD is upright;
he is my Rock, and there is no wickedness in him.[d]"

Psalm 93

[1]The LORD reigns,[e] he is robed in majesty;[f]
the LORD is robed in majesty and armed with strength;[g]
indeed, the world is established, firm and secure.[h]
[2]Your throne was established long ago;
you are from all eternity.[i]
[3]The seas[j] have lifted up, LORD,
the seas have lifted up their voice;
the seas have lifted up their pounding waves.
[4]Mightier than the thunder[k] of the great waters,
mightier than the breakers of the sea —
the LORD on high is mighty.

[5]Your statutes, LORD, stand firm;
holiness[l] adorns your house
for endless days.

Psalm 94

[1]The LORD is a God who avenges.[m]
O God who avenges, shine forth.[n]

92:13 [b]Ps 100:4 **92:14** [c]Jn 15:2 **92:15** [d]Job 34:10 **93:1** [e]Ps 97:1 [f]Ps 104:1 [g]Ps 65:6 [h]Ps 96:10 **93:2** [i]Ps 45:6 **93:3** [j]Ps 96:11 **93:4** [k]Ps 65:7 **93:5** [l]Ps 29:2 **94:1** [m]Na 1:2; Ro 12:19 [n]Ps 80:1

temple, but the metaphor drawn from royal architecture was meaningful in the context of Yahweh's temple court.
93:1 *The LORD reigns.* See note on 99:1. *world is established, firm and secure.* See notes on 24:2; 104:5.
93:2 *Your throne was established.* See note on 29:10; see also the article "Enthronement in the Ancient Near East," p. 925.
93:3–4 *The seas ... the great waters.* The link between defeating the sea, the paramount representation of nonorder, and attaining kingship, the primary human mechanism of order, was common in the ancient Near East. The Babylonian Creation Epic, in which Marduk defeats the sea, concludes with the admonition for people to sing the song of Marduk's victory over Tiamat (the sea) and his ascension to kingship over the gods. In the Ugaritic Baal Cycle, the god battles the sea in order to gain control of chaos and earn the right to be king. See the article "Chaos Monsters," p. 953.
94:1–2 *shine forth ... Rise up, Judge.* In Mesopotamia and Egypt, the sun-god was viewed as the god of justice.

2 Rise up, Judge[o] of the earth;
pay back[p] to the proud what they deserve.
3 How long, LORD, will the wicked,
how long will the wicked be jubilant?

4 They pour out arrogant[q] words;
all the evildoers are full of boasting.[r]
5 They crush your people,[s] LORD;
they oppress your inheritance.
6 They slay the widow and the foreigner;
they murder the fatherless.
7 They say, "The LORD does not see;[t]
the God of Jacob takes no notice."

8 Take notice, you senseless ones[u] among the people;
you fools, when will you become wise?
9 Does he who fashioned the ear not hear?
Does he who formed the eye not see?[v]
10 Does he who disciplines nations not punish?
Does he who teaches[w] mankind lack knowledge?
11 The LORD knows all human plans;
he knows that they are futile.[x]

12 Blessed is the one you discipline,[y] LORD,
the one you teach[z] from your law;
13 you grant them relief from days of trouble,
till a pit[a] is dug for the wicked.
14 For the LORD will not reject his people;[b]
he will never forsake his inheritance.
15 Judgment will again be founded on righteousness,[c]
and all the upright in heart will follow it.

16 Who will rise up[d] for me against the wicked?
Who will take a stand for me against evildoers?[e]
17 Unless the LORD had given me help,[f]
I would soon have dwelt in the silence of death.
18 When I said, "My foot is slipping,[g]"
your unfailing love, LORD, supported me.
19 When anxiety was great within me,
your consolation brought me joy.

20 Can a corrupt throne be allied with you—
a throne that brings on misery by its decrees?[h]
21 The wicked band together[i] against the righteous
and condemn the innocent[j] to death.
22 But the LORD has become my fortress,
and my God the rock in whom I take refuge.[k]
23 He will repay[l] them for their sins
and destroy them for their wickedness;
the LORD our God will destroy them.

Psalm 95

1 Come, let us sing for joy to the LORD;
let us shout aloud[m] to the Rock[n] of our salvation.
2 Let us come before him[o] with thanksgiving
and extol him with music[p] and song.

3 For the LORD is the great God,[q]
the great King above all gods.[r]
4 In his hand are the depths of the earth,
and the mountain peaks belong to him.
5 The sea is his, for he made it,
and his hands formed the dry land.[s]

94:2 [o] Ge 18:25 [p] Ps 31:23
94:4 [q] Ps 31:18 [r] Ps 52:1
94:5 [s] Isa 3:15
94:7 [t] Job 22:14; Ps 10:11
94:8 [u] Ps 92:6
94:9 [v] Ex 4:11; Pr 20:12
94:10 [w] Job 35:11; Isa 28:26
94:11 [x] 1Co 3:20*
94:12 [y] Job 5:17; Heb 12:5 [z] Dt 8:3
94:13 [a] Ps 55:23
94:14 [b] 1Sa 12:22; Ps 37:28; Ro 11:2
94:15 [c] Ps 97:2
94:16 [d] Nu 10:35; Ps 17:13 [e] Ps 59:2
94:17 [f] Ps 124:2
94:18 [g] Ps 38:16
94:20 [h] Ps 58:2
94:21 [i] Ps 56:6 [j] Ps 106:38; Pr 17:15, 26
94:22 [k] Ps 18:2; 59:9
94:23 [l] Ps 7:16
95:1 [m] Ps 81:1 [n] 2Sa 22:47
95:2 [o] Mic 6:6 [p] Ps 81:2; Eph 5:19
95:3 [q] Ps 48:1; 145:3 [r] Ps 96:4; 97:9
95:5 [s] Ge 1:9; Ps 146:6

Using a similar metaphor of the sun's penetrating rays, the psalmist appeals to Yahweh for justice (see notes on 19:7; 84:11).

94:20 *corrupt throne.* Corrupt government is a great evil to citizens of any community, and the value of justice extended universally. The Mesopotamian text Advice to a Prince warns of divine retribution for any king who oppresses his subjects. The god would bring chaos and devastation. The text continues with threats to advisors or officers who likewise fail to heed justice, and it applies these warnings for the benefit of specific cities in Mesopotamia. We therefore see that justice was a primary concern throughout the ancient world.

95:1 *let us sing.* See notes on Ps 149.

95:3 *King above all gods.* The supremacy of one deity over all other gods in the divine council is a prominent theme in ancient Near Eastern religions. In the Babylonian story of the exaltation of Marduk (the Creation Epic), Marduk's reward for defeating the gods of chaos was kingship over all the gods. Together they prostrated themselves and declared him their king. When the Assyrian Empire controlled Babylon, the chief god of Assyria, Assur, was regarded as supreme. The Assyrian king Ashurbanipal (c. 650 BC) declared in his Hymn to Assur his intention to magnify this king of the gods. After Baal's defeat of Yamm, the goddess Athirat argues that Baal should have his own palace: "Our king is the Mightiest Baal, our ruler, with none above him." The Hymn to Osiris, an Egyptian god, opens with the words: "Hail to you, Osiris, lord of eternity, king of the gods." Yahweh's superiority to other gods suggests his ability to give Israel victory over the other nations. See the article "Divine Council," p. 615.

95:4 *depths of the earth.* The word "depths" refers to something inaccessible to be searched or explored (cf. Job 38:16). In this verse, the "depths of the earth" are set in contrast to the highest mountain tops. In OT geography, the lower-most recesses of the earth were thought to be rooted in the deep sea (see the article "Cosmic Geography," p. 836).

6 Come, let us bow down[t] in worship,
let us kneel[u] before the LORD our Maker;[v]
7 for he is our God
and we are the people of his pasture,[w]
the flock under his care.

Today, if only you would hear his voice,
8 "Do not harden your hearts as you did at Meribah,[a][x]
as you did that day at Massah[b] in the wilderness,
9 where your ancestors tested[y] me;
they tried me, though they had seen what I did.
10 For forty years[z] I was angry with that generation;
I said, 'They are a people whose hearts go astray,
and they have not known my ways.'
11 So I declared on oath[a] in my anger,
'They shall never enter my rest.' "[b]

Psalm 96

96:1-13pp — 1Ch 16:23-33

1 Sing to the LORD[c] a new song;
sing to the LORD, all the earth.
2 Sing to the LORD, praise his name;
proclaim his salvation[d] day after day.
3 Declare his glory among the nations,
his marvelous deeds among all peoples.

4 For great is the LORD and most worthy of praise;[e]
he is to be feared[f] above all gods.[g]
5 For all the gods of the nations are idols,
but the LORD made the heavens.[h]

95:6 [t] Php 2:10 [u] 2Ch 6:13 [v] Ps 100:3; 149:2; Isa 17:7; Da 6:10-11; Hos 8:14
95:7 [w] Ps 74:1; 79:13
95:8 [x] Ex 17:7
95:9 [y] Nu 14:22; Ps 78:18; 1Co 10:9
95:10 [z] Ac 7:36; Heb 3:17
95:11 [a] Nu 14:23 [b] Dt 1:35; Heb 4:3*
96:1 [c] 1Ch 16:23
96:2 [d] Ps 71:15
96:4 [e] Ps 18:3; 145:3 [f] Ps 89:7 [g] Ps 95:3
96:5 [h] Ps 115:15
96:6 [i] Ps 29:1
96:7 [j] Ps 29:1 [k] Ps 22:27
96:8 [l] Ps 45:12; 72:10
96:9 [m] Ps 29:2 [n] Ps 114:7 [o] Ps 33:8
96:10 [p] Ps 97:1 [q] Ps 93:1 [r] Ps 67:4
96:11 [s] Ps 97:1; 98:7; Isa 49:13
96:12 [t] Isa 44:23 [u] Ps 65:13
96:13 [v] Rev 19:11
97:1 [w] Ps 96:10 [x] Ps 96:11

6 Splendor and majesty are before him;
strength and glory[i] are in his sanctuary.

7 Ascribe to the LORD,[j] all you families of nations,[k]
ascribe to the LORD glory and strength.
8 Ascribe to the LORD the glory due his name;
bring an offering[l] and come into his courts.
9 Worship the LORD in the splendor of his[c] holiness;[m]
tremble[n] before him, all the earth.[o]
10 Say among the nations, "The LORD reigns.[p]"
The world is firmly established, it cannot be moved;[q]
he will judge the peoples with equity.[r]

11 Let the heavens rejoice, let the earth be glad;[s]
let the sea resound, and all that is in it.
12 Let the fields be jubilant, and everything in them;
let all the trees of the forest[t] sing for joy.[u]
13 Let all creation rejoice before the LORD,
for he comes,
he comes to judge[v] the earth.
He will judge the world in righteousness
and the peoples in his faithfulness.

Psalm 97

1 The LORD reigns,[w] let the earth be glad;[x]
let the distant shores rejoice.

[a] 8 *Meribah* means *quarreling.* [b] 8 *Massah* means *testing.* [c] 9 Or *LORD with the splendor of*

95:6 *bow down in worship.* To prostrate oneself, a common description of homage in the ancient world. One Egyptian portrait shows subservient people moving through three different postures in homage — standing with hands raised, kneeling and lying prostrate.
95:7 *people of his pasture.* The ideal king in the ancient Near East was likened to a shepherd, an image of care and protection, a function of the gods whom the king represents (see note on Ps 23:1). The picture here is even more intimate, because Yahweh, the king (v. 3), is also viewed as one who created his people by his own hand. One Egyptian wisdom text refers to humanity as god's "cattle" for whom he provides (see note on 104:29 – 30).
95:8 *Meribah.* Means "strife" (translated "quarreling" in Ge 13:8). It refers to a place in the wilderness, "Rephidim," exact location unknown. Here the exodus generation quarreled against Moses over the lack of water (Ex 17:1 – 7). *Massah.* Related to the word "tested" in v. 9; it is another name given to the same location in recognition that Israel put Yahweh to the test as their provider (Ex 17:2,7). At the same time, the Israelites were themselves being tested by Yahweh for their fidelity, which was one of the general purposes of the trials in the wilderness (81:7; Dt 8:2).
96:1 *a new song.* Several times the OT records the creation of new music. This was common after military victories (e.g., Ex 15:1; Jdg 5:1; 1Sa 18:6 – 7). Ps 45, e.g., originated as a wedding tribute (45:1); and when the ark was brought to Jerusalem, David commissioned a "new song" (v. 1; 1Ch 16:7). Ps 96, or at least its first edition, originated from this context (compare Ps 96 with 1Ch 16:23 – 33). Any fresh experience of God might offer an occasion for the composition of a "new song."
96:4 – 5 *feared above all gods … idols.* Some psalms indicate that, in the heavenly realm, divine (supernatural) beings do exist, but they are inferior in every way to Israel's God, Yahweh, who exists in a class of his own (see notes on 29:1; 82:1; 86:8; 95:3). Hence, they are not really "gods" worthy of worship, as the other nations understand them to be. Because of this, the psalmist uses a derogatory Hebrew word for "idol," meaning "useless" or "vain." See the article "Divine Council," p. 615.
96:10 *The LORD reigns.* See note on 99:1.
97:1 *The LORD reigns.* See note on 99:1.

[2]Clouds and thick darkness[y] surround
him;
righteousness and justice are the
foundation of his throne.[z]
[3]Fire[a] goes before[b] him
and consumes[c] his foes on every
side.
[4]His lightning lights up the world;
the earth sees and trembles.[d]
[5]The mountains melt[e] like wax before
the LORD,
before the Lord of all the earth.[f]
[6]The heavens proclaim his
righteousness,[g]
and all peoples see his glory.[h]

[7]All who worship images[i] are put to
shame,[j]
those who boast in idols —
worship him,[k] all you gods!

[8]Zion hears and rejoices
and the villages of Judah are glad
because of your judgments,[l] LORD.
[9]For you, LORD, are the Most High over
all the earth;[m]
you are exalted[n] far above all gods.
[10]Let those who love the LORD hate
evil,[o]
for he guards the lives of his faithful
ones[p]
and delivers[q] them from the hand of
the wicked.[r]
[11]Light shines[a][s] on the righteous
and joy on the upright in heart.
[12]Rejoice in the LORD, you who are
righteous,
and praise his holy name.[t]

97:2 [y]Ex 19:9; Ps 18:11 [z]Ps 89:14 **97:3** [a]Da 7:10 [b]Hab 3:5 [c]Ps 18:8 **97:4** [d]Ps 104:32 **97:5** [e]Ps 46:2, 6; Mic 1:4 [f]Jos 3:11 **97:6** [g]Ps 50:6 [h]Ps 19:1 **97:7** [i]Lev 26:1 [j]Jer 10:14 [k]Heb 1:6 **97:8** [l]Ps 48:11 **97:9** [m]Ps 83:18; 95:3 [n]Ex 18:11 **97:10** [o]Ps 34:14; Am 5:15; Ro 12:9 [p]Pr 2:8 [q]Da 3:28 [r]Ps 37:40; Jer 15:21 **97:11** [s]Job 22:28 **97:12** [t]Ps 30:4

98:1 [u]Ps 96:1 [v]Ps 96:3 [w]Ex 15:6 [x]Isa 52:10 **98:2** [y]Isa 52:10 **98:3** [z]Lk 1:54 **98:4** [a]Isa 44:23 **98:5** [b]Ps 92:3 [c]Isa 51:3 **98:6** [d]Nu 10:10 [e]Ps 47:7 **98:7** [f]Ps 24:1 **98:8** [g]Isa 55:12

Psalm 98

A psalm.

[1]Sing to the LORD a new song,[u]
for he has done marvelous
things;[v]
his right hand[w] and his holy arm[x]
have worked salvation for him.
[2]The LORD has made his salvation
known[y]
and revealed his righteousness to
the nations.
[3]He has remembered[z] his love
and his faithfulness to Israel;
all the ends of the earth have seen
the salvation of our God.

[4]Shout for joy[a] to the LORD, all the
earth,
burst into jubilant song with
music;
[5]make music to the LORD with the
harp,[b]
with the harp and the sound of
singing,[c]
[6]with trumpets[d] and the blast of the
ram's horn —
shout for joy before the LORD, the
King.[e]

[7]Let the sea resound, and everything
in it,
the world, and all who live in it.[f]
[8]Let the rivers clap their hands,
let the mountains[g] sing together
for joy;

[a] *11* One Hebrew manuscript and ancient versions (see also 112:4); most Hebrew manuscripts *Light is sown*

97:2 *Clouds and thick darkness surround him.* The image of a rampant God storming through the heavens in a cloud chariot is a common one (68:4; 104:3; Jer 4:13). Such descriptions of storm theophany may be found in the texts that speak of the Ugaritic god Baal. In both the Aqhat Legend and the Baal Cycle, Baal is referred to as the "rider of the clouds" (see note on Job 37:2–5). Baal's attributes — commanding the storms, unleashing the lightning, and rushing to war as a divine warrior — even appear in the Egyptian Amarna letters. The characteristics of Yahweh as creator, fertility god and divine warrior share a great deal in common with these earlier epics. One of the ways that Yahweh presents himself as the sole divine power for the Israelites is by assuming the titles and powers of the other ancient Near Eastern gods.
97:5 *mountains melt like wax before the LORD.* Similar to a Hebrew inscription found at a trading post in the southern desert of Judah (Kuntillet Ajrud, c. 800 BC). While the words for the deity in that inscription are used of Canaanite deities, they are also generic terms for "god" (*el*) and "lord" (*baal*), and they therefore could refer to the God of Israel. *Lord of all the earth.* In v. 7, the psalmist will denounce the status of the gods of the nations; and if Israel's God is truly the only God, then he reigns over the territories and nations of these "gods." The concept of Yahweh's universal rule is affirmed in a cave inscription, possibly carved by refugees of the Babylonian invasions (c. 600 BC, or perhaps c. 700 BC, which would date to the Assyrian crisis): "Yahweh is the god of the whole earth." This is an expression of hope and faith that Yahweh will prove stronger than the gods of the other nations. A dedication inscription of a southern Mesopotamian king (Ishbi-Erra, c. 2000 BC) begins: "For the god Enlil, lord of the foreign lands." Over a millennium later, when Assyria was supreme in northern Mesopotamia, their chief god Assur was proclaimed "the lord of the lands." Egyptian ideals of their universal god find clearest expression during the reign of Akhenaten, who advanced the sun disk as sole god by declaring him Lord of all the earth.
97:7 *images ... idols ... gods.* See notes on 96:4–5; 135:15; see also the article "Making an Idol," p. 1010. For the "gods" worshiping Yahweh, see note on 29:1.
98:1 *holy arm.* See note on Ex 6:1.
98:5 *harp ... singing.* See the article "Music and Musicians," p. 524.
98:6 *trumpets ... ram's horn.* See note on Jos 6:4.
98:8 *rivers clap ... mountains sing.* It is not unusual for the Bible to personify the forces of nature, but it does not embody them with personality, as was the practice in the rest of the ancient Near East. In Mesopotamia, Canaan and Egypt, the forces of nature were manifestations of individual deities who had jurisdiction over that realm of nature and who were integrated into it.

[9]let them sing before the LORD,
for he comes to judge the earth.
He will judge the world in
righteousness
and the peoples with equity.[h]

Psalm 99

[1]The LORD reigns,[i]
let the nations tremble;
he sits enthroned between the
cherubim,[j]
let the earth shake.
[2]Great is the LORD[k] in Zion;
he is exalted[l] over all the nations.
[3]Let them praise your great and
awesome name[m]—
he is holy.
[4]The King is mighty, he loves justice[n]—
you have established equity;[o]
in Jacob you have done
what is just and right.
[5]Exalt[p] the LORD our God
and worship at his footstool;
he is holy.
[6]Moses[q] and Aaron were among his
priests,
Samuel[r] was among those who
called on his name;
they called on the LORD
and he answered[s] them.
[7]He spoke to them from the pillar of
cloud;[t]
they kept his statutes and the
decrees he gave them.
[8]LORD our God,
you answered them;
you were to Israel a forgiving God,[u]
though you punished their
misdeeds.[a]
[9]Exalt the LORD our God
and worship at his holy mountain,
for the LORD our God is holy.

Psalm 100

A psalm. For giving grateful praise.

[1]Shout for joy[v] to the LORD, all the
earth.
[2] Worship the LORD with gladness;
come before him[w] with joyful songs.
[3]Know that the LORD is God.[x]
It is he who made us,[y] and we are
his[b];
we are his people, the sheep of his
pasture.[z]
[4]Enter his gates with thanksgiving
and his courts with praise;
give thanks to him and praise his
name.[a]

98:9 [h] Ps 96:10 **99:1** [i] Ps 97:1 [j] Ex 25:22 **99:2** [k] Ps 48:1 [l] Ps 97:9; 113:4 **99:3** [m] Ps 76:1 **99:4** [n] Ps 11:7 [o] Ps 98:9 **99:5** [p] Ps 132:7 **99:6** [q] Ex 24:6 [r] Jer 15:1 [s] 1Sa 7:9 **99:7** [t] Ex 33:9 **99:8** [u] Nu 14:20 **100:1** [v] Ps 98:4 **100:2** [w] Ps 95:2 **100:3** [x] Ps 46:10 [y] Job 10:3 [z] Ps 74:1; Eze 34:31 **100:4** [a] Ps 116:17

[a] 8 Or *God, / an avenger of the wrongs done to them*
[b] 3 Or *and not we ourselves*

98:9 *equity.* The Hebrew term here is comparable to that used in Mesopotamia for the declaration of release from debts. In the ancient Near East the freeing of prisoners (from debtors' prison) as an act of justice often occurred in the first or second year of a new king's reign (and then periodically after that). The Old Babylonian period king Ammisaduqa (seventeenth century BC), e.g., cancelled economic debts on behalf of Shamash. One of the ways to bring justice was to bring relief to those who were suffering under debt (usually by no fault of their own).
99:1 *The LORD reigns.* Another way this phrase can be translated is "The LORD is king!" (NRSV; JPS). In these terms, the psalmist echoes the sorts of claims that resound throughout the praise literature of the ancient Near East. The Babylonian Creation Epic declares, "Marduk is king." In the historical context in which the Creation Epic was composed, this affirmed at the same time the kingship of Marduk over other gods as well as the corresponding rise to power of Babylon. A similar ideology was at work in Assyria. At the coronation of the Assyrian king Ashurbanipal, the national god was acclaimed with the words "Assur is king—indeed Assur is king!" This claim was part of the Assyrian view that united Assyria's growing imperial aspirations with its belief in the supremacy of the national god, Assur, over other deities. In fact, an Assyrian version of the Creation Epic substituted Assur's name for Marduk's in an assertion of the former's precedence over the latter. When Egyptians marked the deceased pharaoh's transfiguration into the form of the god Osiris, a hymn repeatedly addressed him with the title "Osiris the King." *enthroned between the cherubim.* See note on 2Ki 19:15.
99:5 *footstool.* See note on Ex 25:16.
100:3 *sheep of his pasture.* See note on 95:7.
100:4 *Enter his gates … courts.* The temple of God was viewed as his palace. Consequently, its architecture featured walls, gates and courtyards, as would the citadel or palace complex of any king. Though the core design was given by God to Moses when the portable shrine, or tabernacle, was constructed for worship during Israel's journey from Egypt to their homeland, the architecture was not unique. In fact, it replicated what could be found in the ancient world. It featured a fenced, outer courtyard, which surrounded the tabernacle (Ex 27:9–19). The tabernacle was a tent that consisted of two rooms, the Holy Place (an entry court) and the "Most Holy Place," where the ark (the footstool of God's throne) was set (Ex 25:10–22; 26:30–34; see note on Ex 25:16). The more permanent temple built by Solomon followed this basic design, but it was integrated into a larger citadel structure (1Ki 6:1–38; cf. Solomon's palace, 1Ki 7:9–12). This threefold pattern of an outside court with an inside entry court leading to an inner sanctuary was typical of temple complexes throughout the ancient Near East. The temple at Tell Tayinat in Syria (c. 800 BC) offers a close look at a plan similar to Solomon's temple. Two large pillars flank an entry porch leading into a main hall with a second, smaller room further inside that housed the image of the deity. Another Syrian temple (Tell 'Ain Dara) from about the time of Solomon featured a large court in the front, with pillars on the entry porch and two (or perhaps three) inner rooms, with many decorations of winged cherubs and palm designs. In theory, with this design the large outside courtyard of Solomon's temple was accessible to any worshiper, hence the call to worship: "Enter … his courts with praise." See the article "Architecture of the Temple," p. 572.

[5]For the LORD is good[b] and his love
endures forever;[c]
his faithfulness[d] continues through
all generations.

Psalm 101

Of David. A psalm.

[1]I will sing of your love[e] and justice;
to you, LORD, I will sing praise.
[2]I will be careful to lead a blameless
life —
when will you come to me?

I will conduct the affairs of my house
with a blameless heart.
[3]I will not look with approval
on anything that is vile.[f]

I hate what faithless people do;[g]
I will have no part in it.
[4]The perverse of heart[h] shall be far from
me;
I will have nothing to do with what
is evil.

[5]Whoever slanders their neighbor[i] in
secret,
I will put to silence;
whoever has haughty eyes[j] and a
proud heart,
I will not tolerate.

[6]My eyes will be on the faithful in the
land,
that they may dwell with me;
the one whose walk is blameless[k]
will minister to me.
[7]No one who practices deceit
will dwell in my house;
no one who speaks falsely
will stand in my presence.
[8]Every morning[l] I will put to silence
all the wicked[m] in the land;
I will cut off every evildoer[n]
from the city of the LORD.[o]

100:5 [b]1Ch 16:34; Ps 25:8 [c]Ezr 3:11; Ps 106:1 [d]Ps 119:90
101:1 [e]Ps 51:14; 89:1; 145:7
101:3 [f]Dt 15:9 [g]Ps 40:4
101:4 [h]Pr 11:20
101:5 [i]Ps 50:20 [j]Ps 10:5; Pr 6:17
101:6 [k]Ps 119:1
101:8 [l]Jer 21:12 [m]Ps 75:10 [n]Ps 118:10-12 [o]Ps 46:4

Psalm 102[a]

A prayer of an afflicted person
who has grown weak and pours out
a lament before the LORD.

[1]Hear my prayer, LORD;
let my cry for help[p] come to you.
[2]Do not hide your face[q] from me
when I am in distress.
Turn your ear to me;
when I call, answer me quickly.

[3]For my days vanish like smoke;[r]
my bones burn like glowing
embers.
[4]My heart is blighted and withered
like grass;[s]
I forget to eat my food.
[5]In my distress I groan aloud
and am reduced to skin and bones.
[6]I am like a desert owl,[t]
like an owl among the ruins.
[7]I lie awake;[u] I have become
like a bird alone[v] on a roof.
[8]All day long my enemies taunt me;
those who rail against me use my
name as a curse.
[9]For I eat ashes as my food
and mingle my drink with tears[w]
[10]because of your great wrath,[x]
for you have taken me up and
thrown me aside.
[11]My days are like the evening shadow;[y]
I wither away like grass.

[12]But you, LORD, sit enthroned forever;[z]
your renown endures[a] through all
generations.
[13]You will arise and have compassion[b]
on Zion,
for it is time to show favor to her;
the appointed time has come.
[14]For her stones are dear to your
servants;
her very dust moves them to pity.

102:1 [p]Ex 2:23
102:2 [q]Ps 69:17
102:3 [r]Jas 4:14
102:4 [s]Ps 37:2
102:6 [t]Job 30:29; Isa 34:11
102:7 [u]Ps 77:4 [v]Ps 38:11
102:9 [w]Ps 42:3
102:10 [x]Ps 38:3
102:11 [y]Job 14:2
102:12 [z]Ps 9:7 [a]Ps 135:13
102:13 [b]Isa 60:10

[a] In Hebrew texts 102:1-28 is numbered 102:2-29.

101:1 *I will.* This psalm records the vow of a king, as though he were taking an oath of office. This backdrop is evident from the references to government ministers (v. 6) and the responsibility for the overall welfare of the holy city (v. 8). In this context, the commitment of the psalmist to maintain justice is first and foremost an expression of royal duty to God for good government (see note on Ps 72). *love and justice.* The Hebrew word for "love" (*hesed*) stresses fidelity, which is here coupled with "justice," highlighting the attributes of God that the king will emulate. These characteristics marked the virtuous king throughout the ancient Near East (see notes on Ps 72; 72:4).

101:6 *the one whose walk is blameless will minister.* The king in Israel employed officials of the court to execute the responsibilities of government (2Sa 8:15 – 18; 20:23 – 26; 1Ki 4:1 – 6; 1Ch 18:14 – 17), and the righteousness of his rule depended upon their effectiveness (2Sa 8:15). One Neo-Assyrian letter illustrates the connection between the king's justice and his officials, indicating his charge to them that they should render careful justice in each case they hear. In Egypt, officials such as the vizier were responsible, as agents of the king, to ensure the maintenance of cosmic order and justice. Pharaoh Horemheb (c. 1300 BC) claims that he chose men of discretion and good character, who were loyal to the throne and had good insight into human nature. Therefore, the integrity of government officials was of supreme importance, and an Egyptian tomb painting from the mid-fourteenth century BC portrays the pharaoh holding his scepter in one hand and extending the other to dispense rewards to faithful servants.

102:2 *hide your face.* See note on 13:1.

102:3 *my bones burn.* See note on 38:3.

102:5 *skin and bones.* See note on 22:17.

102:12 *enthroned.* See note on 2Ki 19:15.

15 The nations will fear[c] the name of the
LORD,
all the kings[d] of the earth will revere
your glory.
16 For the LORD will rebuild Zion
and appear in his glory.[e]
17 He will respond to the prayer[f] of the
destitute;
he will not despise their plea.

18 Let this be written[g] for a future
generation,
that a people not yet created[h] may
praise the LORD:
19 "The LORD looked down[i] from his
sanctuary on high,
from heaven he viewed the earth,
20 to hear the groans of the prisoners[j]
and release those condemned to
death."
21 So the name of the LORD will be
declared[k] in Zion
and his praise in Jerusalem
22 when the peoples and the kingdoms
assemble to worship the LORD.

23 In the course of my life[a] he broke my
strength;
he cut short my days.
24 So I said:
"Do not take me away, my God, in the
midst of my days;
your years go on[l] through all
generations.
25 In the beginning[m] you laid the
foundations of the earth,
and the heavens are the work of
your hands.
26 They will perish,[n] but you remain;
they will all wear out like a
garment.
Like clothing you will change
them
and they will be discarded.
27 But you remain the same,[o]
and your years will never end.

102:15 [c] 1Ki 8:43 [d] Ps 138:4
102:16 [e] Isa 60:1-2
102:17 [f] Ne 1:6
102:18 [g] Ro 15:4 [h] Ps 22:31
102:19 [i] Dt 26:15
102:20 [j] Ps 79:11
102:21 [k] Ps 22:22
102:24 [l] Ps 90:2; Isa 38:10
102:25 [m] Ge 1:1; Heb 1:10-12*
102:26 [n] Isa 34:4; Mt 24:35; 2Pe 3:7-10; Rev 20:11
102:27 [o] Mal 3:6; Heb 13:8; Jas 1:17
102:28 [p] Ps 69:36 [q] Ps 89:4
103:1 [r] Ps 104:1
103:3 [s] Ps 130:8 [t] Ex 15:26
103:5 [u] Isa 40:31
103:7 [v] Ps 99:7; 147:19 [w] Ex 33:13 [x] Ps 106:22
103:8 [y] Ex 34:6; Ps 86:15; Jas 5:11
103:9 [z] Ps 30:5; Isa 57:16; Jer 3:5, 12; Mic 7:18
103:10 [a] Ezr 9:13
103:11 [b] Ps 57:10
103:12 [c] 2Sa 12:13

28 The children of your servants[p] will live
in your presence;
their descendants[q] will be
established before you."

Psalm 103

Of David.

1 Praise the LORD, my soul;[r]
all my inmost being, praise his holy
name.
2 Praise the LORD, my soul,
and forget not all his benefits—
3 who forgives all your sins[s]
and heals[t] all your diseases,
4 who redeems your life from the pit
and crowns you with love and
compassion,
5 who satisfies your desires with good
things
so that your youth is renewed like
the eagle's.[u]

6 The LORD works righteousness
and justice for all the oppressed.

7 He made known[v] his ways[w] to Moses,
his deeds[x] to the people of Israel:
8 The LORD is compassionate and
gracious,[y]
slow to anger, abounding in love.
9 He will not always accuse,
nor will he harbor his anger
forever;[z]
10 he does not treat us as our sins
deserve[a]
or repay us according to our
iniquities.
11 For as high as the heavens are above
the earth,
so great is his love[b] for those who
fear him;
12 as far as the east is from the west,
so far has he removed our
transgressions[c] from us.

[a] 23 Or *By his power*

102:19 *sanctuary on high.* It is unclear whether an earthly temple was viewed in the ancient Near East as a physical replica of a heavenly temple in which the deity dwelt, or whether it was actually one and the same that existed simultaneously in both realms. Nevertheless, ancient people did conceive of a heavenly court where the divine council met (see the article "Divine Council," p. 615), so the earthly temple symbolized the heavenly abode and was a touch point for the divine presence on earth (see the article "Sacred Space," p. 964). The idea that God's sanctuary is ultimately in heaven, not on earth, assures the psalmist that God oversees all events on earth and can deliver when he chooses (cf. 11:3–4). The monument upon which Hammurapi engraved his laws is decorated with a portrait of Shamash, the god of justice, enthroned in the heavens (see note on 19:7).
103:3 *forgives all your sins.* See notes on Ps 51. *heals all your diseases.* See notes on 38:2,3.
103:4 *the pit.* See the articles "Death and Sheol," p. 833; "Death and the Underworld," p. 907.
103:5 *eagle's.* Identifying exact species of birds in the Bible is often difficult. Whether or not one wishes to classify some varieties of vultures with eagles, the behavior of these birds that underlies the metaphor is the same. Eagles, with six-foot (about two-meter) wingspans, soar effortlessly for long periods of time; therefore, the ancients would marvel at their endurance and use this observation for comparison to the sustaining strength that comes from the Lord.
103:12 *east ... west.* In the ancient Near East, the four compass directions were oriented facing east rather than north as it is in modern times. The Hebrew word for "east" means "place of rising" (of the sun; 104:22). Another word for "east" also means "before, in front." Facing the orientation of the rising sun, the Mediterranean Sea is behind, hence the words "sea" and "behind" were used for "west."

[13]As a father has compassion[d] on his
children,
so the LORD has compassion on
those who fear him;
[14]for he knows how we are formed,[e]
he remembers that we are dust.
[15]The life of mortals is like grass,[f]
they flourish like a flower[g] of the
field;
[16]the wind blows[h] over it and it is gone,
and its place[i] remembers it no more.
[17]But from everlasting to everlasting
the LORD's love is with those who
fear him,
and his righteousness with their
children's children—
[18]with those who keep his covenant
and remember to obey his precepts.[j]
[19]The LORD has established his throne in
heaven,
and his kingdom rules[k] over all.
[20]Praise the LORD, you his angels,[l]
you mighty ones[m] who do his bidding,
who obey his word.
[21]Praise the LORD, all his heavenly
hosts,[n]
you his servants who do his
will.
[22]Praise the LORD, all his works[o]
everywhere in his dominion.

Praise the LORD, my soul.

Psalm 104

[1]Praise the LORD, my soul.[p]

LORD my God, you are very great;
you are clothed with splendor and
majesty.

[2]The LORD wraps[q] himself in light as
with a garment;
he stretches out the heavens[r] like
a tent
[3] and lays the beams[s] of his upper
chambers on their waters.
He makes the clouds[t] his chariot
and rides on the wings of the
wind.[u]

103:13 [d]Mal 3:17 **103:14** [e]Isa 29:16 **103:15** [f]Ps 90:5 [g]Job 14:2; Jas 1:10; 1Pe 1:24 **103:16** [h]Isa 40:7 [i]Job 7:10 **103:18** [j]Dt 7:9 **103:19** [k]Ps 47:2 **103:20** [l]Ps 148:2; Heb 1:14 [m]Ps 29:1 **103:21** [n]1Ki 22:19 **103:22** [o]Ps 145:10 **104:1** [p]Ps 103:22 **104:2** [q]Da 7:9 [r]Isa 40:22 **104:3** [s]Am 9:6 [t]Isa 19:1 [u]Ps 18:10

The words for "right" (hand) and "left" (hand) also meant "south" and "north," respectively. Another expression for "west," used in this verse, was related to the word for evening (i.e., the setting sun). Thus, the metaphor here takes the two most distant points imaginable, sunrise ("east") and sunset ("west") to express the casting away of sin. This contrast of east and west is also found in an Egyptian hymn to Amun, in which the deity is being praised for his judgment of the guilty. As a result of the god's discernment, the guilty is assigned to the East, and the righteous to the West.

103:14 *he knows how we are formed.* The various accounts of human origins in the literature of the ancient Near East feature various materials: clay, dust, blood (of a god), spit, etc.—all expressing something important about human nature. In a Mesopotamian creation story, Enki, god of wisdom, designs a purpose for humanity, which is fashioned from clay. He does this as a result of pondering the nature of humanity, demonstrating that the ingredient of clay reflects what humans essentially are. Enki's purpose is that humanity would relieve the minor gods of work. Further, he assigns useful roles in society to people whose bodies are disabled in some manner (see note on 8:4). The point of the psalmist is that Yahweh's knowledge of the ephemeral nature of humanity moves him to compassionate love and forgiveness (vv. 12–13).

103:20 *angels.* Lit. "messengers." Their identity is clarified by the designation "mighty ones." They are further described in 89:5–7 as participants in the divine council (see the article "Divine Council," p. 615). The idea that supernatural servants attend to the will of a deity is also known from the Baal Cycle. In the preparations for battle between the Ugaritic god Baal and the sea-god Yamm, "messengers" (Ugaritic *ml'ak* = Hebrew *malak* here) are dispatched between the two deities. Baal enlists the services of a lesser deity to forge a weapon with which to defeat Yamm and to help him build his palace. After Yamm's defeat, Baal dispatches messengers—called "gods" (Ugaritic *'ilm*; cf. Hebrew *elim*, 29:1; see the note on 91:11)—to the goddess Anat. This latter reference helps illustrate the terminology in the OT wherein "angels" are called "gods" (82:1), members of the "assembly/council of the holy ones" (89:5,7), and "heavenly beings" (29:1; 89:6).

104:2 *wraps himself in light.* The psalmist begins to expand what he means by "splendor and majesty" (v. 1). The intense light of the sun provides a common image for ancient Near Eastern hymns, especially emphasizing the provision of the deity for his people. The Hymn to Shamash (the sun-god) describes his radiance as spreading like a net over the earth, and it couples this illumination with the god's shepherding role. In Mesopotamia, the gods were considered to be characterized by a fierce shining (Akkadian *melammu*). They sometimes conferred this on the king as well. However, given the Egyptian associations in the psalm, it is more likely that we should understand the imagery in light of its Egyptian context. The Egyptian Great Hymn to Aten (see the article "The Great Hymn to Aten," p. 982) stresses the sun-god's provision for his creatures. These common cultural associations are found in the OT, a fitting metaphor in a psalm extolling God's care over his creation (see note on 84:11; cf. Dt 33:13–14; Mal 4:2, as well as the benefits of a godly king in 2Sa 23:3–4). Furthermore, light has the connotation of something beautiful and dazzling (Eze 1:4). The Aten is the sun disk and is often pictured with its rays of light shining forth. *stretches out the heavens like a tent.* The ancients probably perceived the sky (heavens) as a dome above the earth (see the article "Cosmic Geography," p. 836).

104:3 *beams of his upper chambers.* The imagery used here has more connections with what we know from the world of Mesopotamia. In the ancient world, there were several levels of heavens, and they were understood as having floors, walls and roofs (see the article "The 'Vault' and the 'Water Above,'" p. 6). In Mesopotamian texts (e.g., *Enuma Elish*), the waters of the heavens are made from one half of Tiamat's body when Marduk defeats her and sets up the cosmos. These waters are identified with the highest level of the heavens, Anu's heaven (Anu was the ancient chief deity, before Enlil or Marduk). If this imagery is being used, Yahweh is seen as inhabiting the highest heavens, the beams being the roof beams of the upper

4 He makes winds his messengers,[a][v]
flames of fire[w] his servants.

5 He set the earth[x] on its foundations;
it can never be moved.
6 You covered it[y] with the watery depths[z]
as with a garment;
the waters stood above the
mountains.
7 But at your rebuke[a] the waters fled,
at the sound of your thunder they
took to flight;
8 they flowed over the mountains,
they went down into the valleys,
to the place you assigned[b] for them.
9 You set a boundary they cannot cross;
never again will they cover the earth.

10 He makes springs[c] pour water into the
ravines;
it flows between the mountains.
11 They give water to all the beasts of the
field;
the wild donkeys quench their thirst.
12 The birds of the sky[d] nest by the
waters;
they sing among the branches.
13 He waters the mountains[e] from his
upper chambers;
the land is satisfied by the fruit of
his work.
14 He makes grass grow[f] for the cattle,
and plants for people to cultivate—
bringing forth food[g] from the earth:
15 wine[h] that gladdens human hearts,
oil[i] to make their faces shine,
and bread that sustains their hearts.

104:4 [v] Ps 148:8; Heb 1:7*; [w] 2Ki 2:11 **104:5** [x] Job 26:7; Ps 24:1-2 **104:6** [y] Ge 7:19 [z] Ge 1:2 **104:7** [a] Ps 18:15 **104:8** [b] Ps 33:7 **104:10** [c] Ps 107:33; Isa 41:18 **104:12** [d] Mt 8:20 **104:13** [e] Ps 147:8; Jer 10:13 **104:14** [f] Job 38:27; Ps 147:8; [g] Ge 1:30; Job 28:5 **104:15** [h] Jdg 9:13 [i] Ps 23:5; 92:10; Lk 7:46 **104:17** [j] ver 12 **104:18** [k] Pr 30:26 **104:19** [l] Ge 1:14 [m] Ps 19:6 **104:20** [n] Isa 45:7 [o] Ps 74:16 [p] Ps 50:10 **104:21** [q] Job 38:39; Ps 145:15; Joel 1:20 **104:22** [r] Job 37:8 **104:23** [s] Ge 3:19 **104:24** [t] Ps 40:5 [u] Pr 3:19 **104:25** [v] Ps 69:34

16 The trees of the LORD are well watered,
the cedars of Lebanon that he
planted.
17 There the birds[j] make their nests;
the stork has its home in the
junipers.
18 The high mountains belong to the wild
goats;
the crags are a refuge for the hyrax.[k]

19 He made the moon to mark the
seasons,[l]
and the sun[m] knows when to go
down.
20 You bring darkness,[n] it becomes night,[o]
and all the beasts of the forest[p]
prowl.
21 The lions roar for their prey
and seek their food from God.[q]
22 The sun rises, and they steal away;
they return and lie down in their
dens.[r]
23 Then people go out to their work,[s]
to their labor until evening.

24 How many are your works,[t] LORD!
In wisdom you made[u] them all;
the earth is full of your creatures.
25 There is the sea,[v] vast and spacious,
teeming with creatures beyond
number—
living things both large and small.
26 There the ships[w] go to and fro,
and Leviathan,[x] which you formed
to frolic there.

[a] 4 Or *angels*

104:26 [w] Ps 107:23; Eze 27:9 [x] Job 41:1

story of his dwelling. In the Mesopotamian texts, the cella of the chief god (Marduk) is in the middle heavens, but the description of Anu's abode in the highest heavens likewise presupposes a cella. See the article "Cosmic Geography," p. 836. *on their waters.* Since substantial water came from the clouds of the sky (i.e., heavens; cf. 148:4; Ge 7:11), the ancient viewpoint included a heavenly ocean and openings in the vault over the earth as a source for these waters (see the articles "The 'Vault' and 'Water Above,'" p. 6; "Cosmic Geography," p. 836. *clouds his chariot.* See notes on 97:2; Job 37:2–5.

104:4 *winds ... flames of fire.* This poetic imagery describes the servants of Yahweh, who are elsewhere identified with angelic, divine beings (see notes on 29:1; 82:1; 91:11; 103:20).

104:5 *earth on its foundations.* OT geography orients the earth upon a foundation of pillars that were established by God (75:3; 1Sa 2:8; Job 38:4). In this way, he keeps the earth stable on the subterranean ocean (see note on 24:2), upon which it might otherwise toss to and fro. The Genesis creation account, as well as the flood account (a re-creation), speak of the land emerging from the "deep" (Ge 1:2,10; 7:11; 8:2). Egyptian geography also views the earth as a disk floating on the subterranean waters, the embodiment of the god Nun. See the article "Cosmic Geography," p. 836.

104:9 *set a boundary.* With their ever constant wave action hammering at the shoreline, the seas constituted an ongoing threat to the stability of the inhabited land (see notes on 24:2; 93:3–4). The potential for destruction is underscored most graphically in the Biblical flood account and its Mesopotamian counterparts. The Mesopotamian texts allude to the danger of the sea, which is kept in check by "bolts" or "locks" set against their encroachment on land (cf. Job 38:8–11). The tides themselves suggest that boundaries are set and that the waves reach them, then retreat.

104:19 *the moon ... the sun.* In the Mesopotamian account of Marduk's creative work, he arranged the seasons of the year and the relation between the sun and moon. In the Egyptian Great Hymn to Aten, the deity is praised because he has fashioned the seasons and the sky.

104:26 *Leviathan.* Elsewhere in the OT "Leviathan" is the fearful sea monster whom Yahweh subdues to secure the safety of his people and his creation (see note on Job 3:8; see also the articles "Identification of Behemoth and Leviathan," p. 871; "Leviathan," p. 874; "Chaos Monsters," p. 953). In this verse, however, Leviathan is portrayed as merely another one of God's marvelous creatures, likened to an object of entertainment. Even as the OT authors drew imagery from the culture of their time, they did so in a way that repurposed the belief system of the pagan world around them. The rule of Yahweh over his creation might be expressed using the cultural images of a chaos conflict, but this is no real challenge to his ultimate sovereignty, as this playful description of Leviathan demonstrates.

27 All creatures look to you
to give them their food[y] at the
proper time.
28 When you give it to them,
they gather it up;
when you open your hand,
they are satisfied[z] with good
things.
29 When you hide your face,[a]
they are terrified;
when you take away their breath,
they die and return to the dust.[b]
30 When you send your Spirit,
they are created,
and you renew the face of the
ground.

104:27 [y] Job 36:31; Ps 136:25; 145:15; 147:9
104:28 [z] Ps 145:16
104:29 [a] Dt 31:17 [b] Job 34:14; Ecc 12:7

104:28 *open your hand.* The imagery of God giving good gifts with an open hand is also seen in Egyptian reliefs depicting the worship of Aten, the deified sun disk. The sun disk is portrayed with numerous arms reaching from it, each one with a hand at the end of it symbolizing the giving of blessings and favor.
104:29–30 *return to the dust ... you send your Spirit.* Both man and beast, viewed in Ps 104 as joint recipients

PSALM 104

THE GREAT HYMN TO ATEN

Under the reign of the Egyptian pharaoh Akhenaten (c. 1350 BC), the state-sponsored religion of Egypt turned momentarily toward the exclusive worship of the sun disk as the sole god (see note on Ps 86:8). One hymn originating during this time, the Great Hymn to Aten, is similar in striking ways to certain verses in Ps 104. For example, lines ii 7—iii 10 of the Great Hymn to Aten speak of the lion leaving its den at dark, then the dawn rises and people take up their work (cf. Ps 104:20–23); lines iv 8–11 refer to ships going upstream and downstream and fish darting about (cf. Ps 104:25–26); lines vii 1–8, referring to the creation of humankind, cattle and every sort of small beast, are introduced with the proclamation "How various are the things you have created, and they are all mysterious in the sight" (cf. Ps 104:24). These and other similarities have led scholars to speculate about the possible relationship between the two texts, with Biblical scholars and Egyptologists both affirming and denying any literary connection. This is perhaps the most striking example, though a number of others exist, of the ways in which Israelite psalmists tended to echo the same sort of praise language that was current in the world in which they lived. ◆

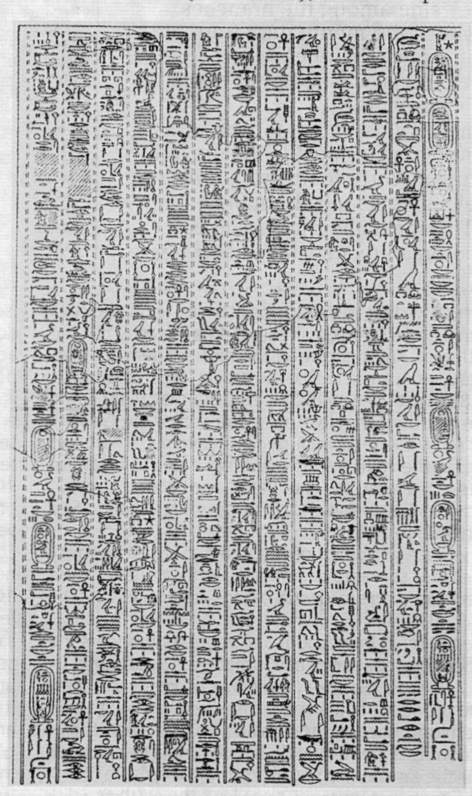

Great Hymn to Aten.
Wikimedia Commons

[31] May the glory of the LORD endure forever;
may the LORD rejoice in his works[c]—
[32] he who looks at the earth, and it trembles,[d]
who touches the mountains,[e] and they smoke.[f]

[33] I will sing[g] to the LORD all my life;
I will sing praise to my God as long as I live.
[34] May my meditation be pleasing to him,
as I rejoice[h] in the LORD.
[35] But may sinners vanish[i] from the earth
and the wicked be no more.
Praise the LORD, my soul.

Praise the LORD.[a][j]

Artist's rendition of Israel's cosmic geography.

Jonathan Walton

Psalm 105

105:1-15pp — 1Ch 16:8-22

[1] Give praise to the LORD,[k] proclaim his name;[l]
make known among the nations what he has done.
[2] Sing to him,[m] sing praise to him;
tell of all his wonderful acts.
[3] Glory in his holy name;
let the hearts of those who seek the LORD rejoice.
[4] Look to the LORD and his strength;
seek his face[n] always.

[5] Remember the wonders[o] he has done,
his miracles, and the judgments he pronounced,[p]
[6] you his servants, the descendants of Abraham,[q]
his chosen[r] ones, the children of Jacob.
[7] He is the LORD our God;
his judgments are in all the earth.

[8] He remembers his covenant[s] forever,
the promise he made, for a thousand generations,
[9] the covenant he made with Abraham,[t]
the oath he swore to Isaac.
[10] He confirmed it[u] to Jacob as a decree,
to Israel as an everlasting covenant:

104:31 [c]Ge 1:31 **104:32** [d]Ps 97:4 [e]Ex 19:18 [f]Ps 144:5 **104:33** [g]Ps 63:4 **104:34** [h]Ps 9:2 **104:35** [i]Ps 37:38 [j]Ps 105:45; 106:48 **105:1** [k]1Ch 16:34 [l]Ps 99:6

[a] 35 Hebrew *Hallelu Yah*; in the Septuagint this line stands at the beginning of Psalm 105.

105:2 [m]Ps 96:1 **105:4** [n]Ps 27:8 **105:5** [o]Ps 40:5 [p]Ps 77:11 **105:6** [q]ver 42 [r]Ps 106:5 **105:8** [s]Ps 106:45; Lk 1:72 **105:9** [t]Ge 12:7; 17:2; 22:16-18; Gal 3:15-18 **105:10** [u]Ge 28:13-15

of God's good provision, originated from the ground (Ge 2:7,19). In OT thought, the force that animates them with life is their "breath," a gift from God that is withdrawn at death, leaving only the earth-like material (Ge 2:7; 3:19; 6:17). However, life is renewed on earth by the creative work of God's Spirit (v. 30; or possibly "breath," cf. 33:6). Similar to this thought is the Egyptian "Memphite Theology" of creation, which describes the ongoing animation of humanity and animals through the active will of the god Ptah (see notes on 33:8,19). An Egyptian wisdom text states: "Well tended is mankind—god's cattle, he made sky and earth for their sake, he subdued the water monster, he made breath for their noses to live, they are his images, who came from his body" (see notes on 8:4,5,6; 139:13). This last expression differs from another Egyptian account in which humanity came from the tears of the sun-god. The Mesopotamian view differs even more, in that humanity was created out of a mixture of clay and the blood of a slain rebel-god (see note on 103:14).

104:32 *the earth ... it trembles ... mountains ... they smoke.* The glory of God is revealed in what OT scholars refer to as a "theophany" (appearance of God). This manifestation of God's glory was first expressed on Mount Sinai (Ex 19), and the imagery is associated with God's awesome power as a warrior (see notes on Ps 18:7,8). Israelites experienced earthquakes due to the existence of a major fault line along the Jordan Valley. They were not as likely to experience volcanoes, though some existed in the region. Ararat is one of the active volcanoes in the Fertile Crescent (but it has not had an eruption since 1840). Additionally, there are several volcanoes in Syria, and quite a few along the southern rim of Turkey. Most significantly, the Aegean features half a dozen volcano sites, including at least one that had an eruption during the OT period (Santorini, 1650 BC).

11 "To you I will give the land of Canaan[v]
as the portion you will inherit."

12 When they were but few in number,[w]
few indeed, and strangers in it,[x]
13 they wandered from nation to nation,
from one kingdom to another.
14 He allowed no one to oppress[y] them;
for their sake he rebuked kings:[z]
15 "Do not touch[a] my anointed ones;
do my prophets no harm."

16 He called down famine[b] on the land
and destroyed all their supplies of food;
17 and he sent a man before them—
Joseph, sold as a slave.[c]
18 They bruised his feet with shackles,[d]
his neck was put in irons,
19 till what he foretold[e] came to pass,
till the word of the LORD proved him true.
20 The king sent and released him,
the ruler of peoples set him free.[f]
21 He made him master of his household,
ruler over all he possessed,
22 to instruct his princes[g] as he pleased
and teach his elders wisdom.

23 Then Israel entered Egypt;[h]
Jacob resided as a foreigner in the land of Ham.
24 The LORD made his people very fruitful;
he made them too numerous[i] for their foes,
25 whose hearts he turned[j] to hate his people,
to conspire[k] against his servants.
26 He sent Moses[l] his servant,
and Aaron, whom he had chosen.[m]
27 They performed[n] his signs among them,
his wonders in the land of Ham.
28 He sent darkness[o] and made the land dark—
for had they not rebelled against his words?
29 He turned their waters into blood,[p]
causing their fish to die.[q]
30 Their land teemed with frogs,[r]
which went up into the bedrooms of their rulers.
31 He spoke, and there came swarms of flies,[s]
and gnats[t] throughout their country.
32 He turned their rain into hail,[u]
with lightning throughout their land;
33 he struck down their vines[v] and fig trees
and shattered the trees of their country.
34 He spoke, and the locusts came,[w]
grasshoppers without number;
35 they ate up every green thing in their land,
ate up the produce of their soil.
36 Then he struck down all the firstborn[x] in their land,
the firstfruits of all their manhood.
37 He brought out Israel, laden with silver and gold,[y]
and from among their tribes no one faltered.
38 Egypt was glad when they left,
because dread of Israel[z] had fallen on them.

39 He spread out a cloud[a] as a covering,
and a fire to give light at night.[b]
40 They asked,[c] and he brought them quail;[d]
he fed them well with the bread of heaven.[e]
41 He opened the rock,[f] and water gushed out;
it flowed like a river in the desert.

42 For he remembered his holy promise[g]
given to his servant Abraham.
43 He brought out his people with rejoicing,[h]
his chosen ones with shouts of joy;
44 he gave them the lands of the nations,[i]
and they fell heir to what others had toiled for—
45 that they might keep his precepts
and observe his laws.[j]

Praise the LORD.[a]

Psalm 106

106:1,47-48pp — 1Ch 16:34-36

1 Praise the LORD.[b]

Give thanks to the LORD, for he is good;[k]
his love endures forever.

[a] *45* Hebrew *Hallelu Yah* [b] *1* Hebrew *Hallelu Yah;* also in verse 48

105:11 [v]Ge 13:15; 15:18 **105:12** [w]Ge 34:30; Dt 7:7 [x]Ge 23:4; Heb 11:9 **105:14** [y]Ge 35:5 [z]Ge 12:17-20 **105:15** [a]Ge 26:11 **105:16** [b]Ge 41:54; Lev 26:26; Isa 3:1; Eze 4:16 **105:17** [c]Ge 37:28; 45:5; Ac 7:9 **105:18** [d]Ge 40:15 **105:19** [e]Ge 40:20-22 **105:20** [f]Ge 41:14 **105:22** [g]Ge 41:43-44 **105:23** [h]Ge 46:6; Ac 13:17 **105:24** [i]Ex 1:7,9 **105:25** [j]Ex 4:21 [k]Ex 1:6-10; Ac 7:19 **105:26** [l]Ex 3:10 [m]Nu 16:5; 17:5-8 **105:27** [n]Ex 7:8-12:51 **105:28** [o]Ex 10:22 **105:29** [p]Ps 78:44 [q]Ex 7:21 **105:30** [r]Ex 8:2,6 **105:31** [s]Ex 8:21-24 [t]Ex 8:16-18 **105:32** [u]Ex 9:22-25 **105:33** [v]Ps 78:47 **105:34** [w]Ex 10:4, 12-15 **105:36** [x]Ex 12:29 **105:37** [y]Ex 12:35 **105:38** [z]Ex 12:33; 15:16 **105:39** [a]Ex 13:21 [b]Ne 9:12; Ps 78:14 **105:40** [c]Ps 78:18, 24 [d]Ex 16:13 [e]Jn 6:31 **105:41** [f]Ex 17:6; Nu 20:11; Ps 78:15-16; 1Co 10:4 **105:42** [g]Ge 15:13-16 **105:43** [h]Ex 15:1-18; Ps 106:12 **105:44** [i]Jos 13:6-7 **105:45** [j]Dt 4:40; 6:21-24 **106:1** [k]Ps 100:5; 105:1

105:11 *the land of Canaan.* See note on Ex 3:8; see also the article "Canaan's Borders," p. 289.
105:18 *shackles ... irons.* The shackles around the ankles chaining the feet together are clear enough. Since the other instrument goes around the neck, it must be an iron collar. These were at times used to link prisoners together. Assyrian reliefs from the ninth and eighth centuries BC depict captives being transported or laboring with wooden yokes around their necks.
105:23 *land of Ham.* According to the list of nations in Ge 10:6–20, the descendants of Ham included the people who came to inhabit Egypt (Ge 10:6,13).
105:28–36 *darkness ... blood ... frogs ... flies ... gnats ... hail ... locusts ... firstborn.* See notes on Ex 7:20; 8:3; 10:4,21,22; see also the article "Interpreting the Plagues," p. 122.

2 Who can proclaim the mighty acts[l] of the LORD
or fully declare his praise?
3 Blessed are those who act justly,
who always do what is right.[m]

4 Remember me,[n] LORD, when you show favor to your people,
come to my aid when you save them,
5 that I may enjoy the prosperity[o] of your chosen ones,
that I may share in the joy[p] of your nation
and join your inheritance in giving praise.

6 We have sinned,[q] even as our ancestors did;
we have done wrong and acted wickedly.
7 When our ancestors were in Egypt,
they gave no thought to your miracles;
they did not remember[r] your many kindnesses,
and they rebelled by the sea,[s] the Red Sea.[a]
8 Yet he saved them for his name's sake,[t]
to make his mighty power known.
9 He rebuked[u] the Red Sea, and it dried up;[v]
he led them through[w] the depths as through a desert.
10 He saved them[x] from the hand of the foe;
from the hand of the enemy he redeemed them.[y]
11 The waters covered[z] their adversaries;
not one of them survived.
12 Then they believed his promises
and sang his praise.[a]

13 But they soon forgot[b] what he had done
and did not wait for his plan to unfold.
14 In the desert they gave in to their craving;
in the wilderness they put God to the test.[c]

106:2 [l] Ps 145:4, 12 **106:3** [m] Ps 15:2 **106:4** [n] Ps 119:132 **106:5** [o] Ps 1:3 [p] Ps 118:15 **106:6** [q] Da 9:5 **106:7** [r] Ps 78:11, 42 [s] Ex 14:11-12 **106:8** [t] Ex 9:16 **106:9** [u] Ps 18:15 [v] Ex 14:21; Na 1:4 [w] Isa 63:11-14 **106:10** [x] Ex 14:30 [y] Ps 107:2 **106:11** [z] Ex 14:28; 15:5 **106:12** [a] Ex 15:1-21 **106:13** [b] Ex 15:24 **106:14** [c] 1Co 10:9

106:15 [d] Nu 11:31 [e] Isa 10:16 **106:16** [f] Nu 16:1-3 **106:17** [g] Dt 11:6 **106:18** [h] Nu 16:35 **106:19** [i] Ex 32:4 **106:20** [j] Jer 2:11; Ro 1:23 **106:21** [k] Ps 78:11 [l] Dt 10:21 **106:22** [m] Ps 105:27 **106:23** [n] Ex 32:10 [o] Ex 32:11-14 **106:24** [p] Dt 8:7; Eze 20:6 [q] Heb 3:18-19 **106:25** [r] Nu 14:2 **106:26** [s] Eze 20:15; Heb 3:11 [t] Nu 14:28-35 **106:27** [u] Lev 26:33; Ps 44:11 **106:28** [v] Nu 25:2-3; Hos 9:10

15 So he gave them[d] what they asked for,
but sent a wasting disease[e] among them.

16 In the camp they grew envious[f] of Moses
and of Aaron, who was consecrated to the LORD.
17 The earth opened[g] up and swallowed Dathan;
it buried the company of Abiram.
18 Fire blazed[h] among their followers;
a flame consumed the wicked.
19 At Horeb they made a calf[i]
and worshiped an idol cast from metal.
20 They exchanged their glorious God[j]
for an image of a bull, which eats grass.
21 They forgot the God[k] who saved them,
who had done great things[l] in Egypt,
22 miracles in the land of Ham[m]
and awesome deeds by the Red Sea.
23 So he said he would destroy[n] them—
had not Moses, his chosen one,
stood in the breach[o] before him
to keep his wrath from destroying them.

24 Then they despised the pleasant land;[p]
they did not believe[q] his promise.
25 They grumbled[r] in their tents
and did not obey the LORD.
26 So he swore[s] to them with uplifted hand
that he would make them fall in the wilderness,[t]
27 make their descendants fall among the nations
and scatter[u] them throughout the lands.

28 They yoked themselves to the Baal of Peor[v]
and ate sacrifices offered to lifeless gods;
29 they aroused the LORD's anger by their wicked deeds,
and a plague broke out among them.

[a] 7 Or *the Sea of Reeds*; also in verses 9 and 22

106:7 *the Red Sea.* See the article "The Red Sea," p. 132.
106:19 *Horeb.* See the article "Mount Sinai," p. 144. *calf.* See the article "The Golden Calf," p. 167.
106:20 *image of a bull.* See the article "The Golden Calf," p. 167.
106:22 *land of Ham.* See note on 105:23.
106:28 *Baal of Peor.* See note on Nu 25:3. *ate sacrifices offered to lifeless gods.* With some types of sacrifices, part of the sacrificial animal was offered on the altar to the god, and the rest was consumed in a communal meal by the worshipers (see note on 22:26). This symbolized a union between worshipers and with the deity to whom they sacrificed (cf. Ge 31:53–54). In the case of Baal of Peor, the communal sacrifice with the Moabites also involved the Israelites in the worship of the Moabite gods and feasting with them (Nu 25:2–3); they "yoked themselves" (cf. 50:5). The NIV translation "sacrifices offered to lifeless gods" corresponds to the view that the gods and idols of other peoples are in reality dead things (Lev 26:30). However, this phrase can be translated more lit. "sacrifices of the dead," possibly alluding to some sort of mourning custom (Dt 26:14). Offerings devoted to the deceased were customary in Egypt and Mesopotamia, but these were not necessarily integral to worship of the gods, except in the case of the deceased pharaoh. Rituals from Mari (c. 1800 BC) and Ugarit incorporate sacrifices to gods in the context of a feast at which deceased kings were thought to be present.

30 But Phinehas stood up and intervened,
and the plague was checked.[w]
31 This was credited to him[x] as righteousness
for endless generations to come.
32 By the waters of Meribah[y] they angered the LORD,
and trouble came to Moses because of them;
33 for they rebelled against the Spirit of God,
and rash words came from Moses' lips.[a z]

34 They did not destroy[a] the peoples
as the LORD had commanded[b] them,
35 but they mingled[c] with the nations
and adopted their customs.
36 They worshiped their idols,[d]
which became a snare to them.
37 They sacrificed their sons[e]
and their daughters to false gods.
38 They shed innocent blood,
the blood of their sons[f] and daughters,
whom they sacrificed to the idols of Canaan,
and the land was desecrated by their blood.
39 They defiled themselves[g] by what they did;
by their deeds they prostituted[h] themselves.

40 Therefore the LORD was angry[i] with his people
and abhorred his inheritance.[j]
41 He gave them into the hands[k] of the nations,
and their foes ruled over them.

[a] 33 Or *against his spirit, / and rash words came from his lips*

106:30 [w] Nu 25:8 **106:31** [x] Nu 25:11-13 **106:32** [y] Nu 20:2-13; Ps 81:7 **106:33** [z] Nu 20:8-12 **106:34** [a] Jdg 1:21 [b] Dt 7:16 **106:35** [c] Jdg 3:5-6 **106:36** [d] Jdg 2:12 **106:37** [e] 2Ki 16:3; 17:17 **106:38** [f] Nu 35:33 **106:39** [g] Eze 20:18 [h] Lev 17:7; Nu 15:39 **106:40** [i] Jdg 2:14; Ps 78:59 [j] Dt 9:29 **106:41** [k] Jdg 2:14; Ne 9:27

106:32 *waters of Meribah.* See note on 95:8.
106:37 *sacrificed their sons and their daughters.* See notes on Lev 20:2; 1Ki 11:5; 2Ki 3:27; 16:3; Jer 7:31.

PSALM 106:37

Demons in the Old Testament

Little is known about the Israelite view of malevolent spirits, popularly called "demons" in contemporary usage. In addition to the Hebrew word *shed*, translated "false gods" in Ps 106:37, the OT has a Hebrew word *sair*, translated in the NIV as "goat idols" (Lev 17:7; 2Ch 11:15; see the NIV text note on Lev 17:7). Some suggest that the use of *sair* also refers to demons in Isa 13:21; 34:14 (NIV "wild goats"). This same Hebrew word refers to an actual goat in Ge 37:31 and frequently in texts prescribing a goat for sacrifice (e.g., Lev 4:23; Nu 7:16). The overlap in terms can be understood if the Israelites thought of malevolent spirits as normally inhabiting the hostile desert, where creatures such as wild goats were native. Some of the earliest Mesopotamian art might offer a parallel to Israelite conceptions of malevolent spirits as goats. Among the Sumerians, one demon takes the form of an ibex—the wild goat well-known in Israel. Early Sumerian art (early third millennium BC) also depicts the composite figure of a bull-man, sometimes locked in combat with a human hero, representing an evil force of some kind. Closer to the Biblical imagery is a Late Babylonian (first millennium BC) commentary on an exorcism that describes two malevolent spirits as having the faces of goats. Egyptians also portrayed malevolent, lesser spirits in human and animal form.

This is all conjecture about how Israelites might have visualized such beings. Unfortunately, their function within the religion of Israel is equally unclear. Mesopotamians associated malevolent spirits with very specific illnesses and personal misfortune, and

continued on next page

[42]Their enemies oppressed them
and subjected them to their power.
[43]Many times he delivered them,
but they were bent on rebellion[l]
and they wasted away in their sin.
[44]Yet he took note of their distress
when he heard their cry;[m]
[45]for their sake he remembered his
covenant[n]
and out of his great love[o] he relented.
[46]He caused all who held them captive
to show them mercy.[p]

[47]Save us, LORD our God,
and gather us[q] from the nations,
that we may give thanks to your holy
name
and glory in your praise.

[48]Praise be to the LORD, the God of Israel,
from everlasting to everlasting.
Let all the people say, "Amen!"[r]
Praise the LORD.

106:43 [l]Jdg 2:16-19 **106:44** [m]Jdg 3:9; 10:10 **106:45** [n]Lev 26:42; Ps 105:8 [o]Jdg 2:18 **106:46** [p]Ezr 9:9; Jer 42:12 **106:47** [q]Ps 147:2 **106:48** [r]Ps 41:13

BOOK V

Psalms 107 – 150

Psalm 107

[1]Give thanks to the LORD,[s] for he is
good;
his love endures forever.

[2]Let the redeemed[t] of the LORD tell
their story—
those he redeemed from the hand
of the foe,
[3]those he gathered[u] from the lands,
from east and west, from north
and south.[a]

[4]Some wandered in desert[v]
wastelands,
finding no way to a city where they
could settle.

107:1 [s]Ps 106:1 **107:2** [t]Ps 106:10 **107:3** [u]Ps 106:47; Isa 43:5-6 **107:4** [v]Nu 14:33; 32:13

[a] 3 Hebrew *north and the sea*

106:47 *gather us from the nations.* See note on 107:3.
107:3 *those he gathered from the lands.* This verse might celebrate the gathering of the people after exile in Mesopotamia and Egypt (cf. 126:1). The curses of Dt 28:63 – 68

they named them accordingly. However, there are no indications in the OT as to how demons were thought to interface with the human realm. Israelites sacrificed to such beings, and perhaps physical images of them were involved (see Lev 17:7 and NIV text note; 2Ch 11:15; Ps 106:28). It is possible that Yahweh employed malevolent spirits to afflict judgment (1Sa 16:14; 1Ki 22:21 – 22); but here the general word for "spirit" is used, so the identity of the spirit within the ranks of the divine council is unknown. In later Judaism, a more elaborate theology of angels and demons developed, but the classifications assumed in contemporary Christianity were largely unknown in OT times. ◆

Impression of Akkadian Cylinder Seal recovered in Ur, 2300 to 2100 BC. Early Sumerian art (early third millennium BC) also depicts the composite figure of a bull-man, sometimes locked in combat with a human hero, representing an evil force of some kind.

5 They were hungry and thirsty,
and their lives ebbed away.
6 Then they cried out[w] to the LORD in their trouble,
and he delivered them from their distress.
7 He led them by a straight way[x]
to a city where they could settle.
8 Let them give thanks to the LORD for his unfailing love
and his wonderful deeds for mankind,
9 for he satisfies[y] the thirsty
and fills the hungry with good things.[z]

10 Some sat in darkness,[a] in utter darkness,
prisoners suffering in iron chains,[b]
11 because they rebelled[c] against God's commands
and despised the plans[d] of the Most High.
12 So he subjected them to bitter labor;
they stumbled, and there was no one to help.[e]
13 Then they cried to the LORD in their trouble,
and he saved them from their distress.
14 He brought them out of darkness, the utter darkness,
and broke away their chains.[f]
15 Let them give thanks to the LORD for his unfailing love
and his wonderful deeds for mankind,
16 for he breaks down gates of bronze
and cuts through bars of iron.

17 Some became fools through their rebellious ways
and suffered affliction[g] because of their iniquities.
18 They loathed all food[h]
and drew near the gates of death.[i]
19 Then they cried to the LORD in their trouble,
and he saved them from their distress.
20 He sent out his word[j] and healed them;[k]
he rescued[l] them from the grave.[m]
21 Let them give thanks to the LORD for his unfailing love
and his wonderful deeds for mankind.
22 Let them sacrifice thank offerings[n]
and tell of his works[o] with songs of joy.

23 Some went out on the sea in ships;
they were merchants on the mighty waters.
24 They saw the works of the LORD,
his wonderful deeds in the deep.

107:6 [w]Ps 50:15 **107:7** [x]Ezr 8:21 **107:9** [y]Ps 22:26; Lk 1:53 [z]Ps 34:10 **107:10** [a]Lk 1:79 [b]Job 36:8 **107:11** [c]Ps 106:7; La 3:42 [d]2Ch 36:16 **107:12** [e]Ps 22:11 **107:14** [f]Ps 116:16; Lk 13:16; Ac 12:7 **107:17** [g]Isa 65:6-7; La 3:39 **107:18** [h]Job 33:20 [i]Job 33:22; Ps 9:13; 88:3 **107:20** [j]Mt 8:8 [k]Ps 103:3 [l]Job 33:28 [m]Ps 30:3; 49:15 **107:22** [n]Lev 7:12; Ps 50:14; 116:17 [o]Ps 9:11; 73:28; 118:17

warn of exile from the land, which would take the form of deportation as prisoners by conquering nations. This consequence of foreign attack was common in the ancient Near East. A record of Iahdun-Lim, king of Mari (c. 186 BC), reports concerning his conquest of the city of Haman that he took the population away as plunder. The Egyptian king Amenhotep II (c. 1420 BC) boasts of bringing thousands of captives back to Memphis as spoils of war from his campaigns against Syria-Palestine.

The northern kingdom of Israel suffered deportation to Assyria (2Ki 15:29; 17:6,23), first by Tiglath-Pileser III (c. 732 BC), who in one account claims to have deported 13,520 people. Then, Shalmaneser V, by the hand of Sargon II, carried off another 27,280 inhabitants of Samaria (c. 722 BC). Sennacherib reports having deported over 200,000 captives from Judah in his 701 BC campaign.

The southern kingdom of Judah experienced its final fate in the years from 605 to 586 BC, when the Babylonians deported masses from the southern kingdom, with others fleeing to Egypt and elsewhere (2Ki 24–25; Jer 41:17–18; 43:4–7; 52:15,28). A Babylonian prayer addresses the gods Shamash and Marduk as able to gather scattered, captured or exiled people. See note on 147:3.

107:10 *prisoners suffering.* Ps 107 appears to draw from four different situations of life in which God delivered his people. Prisons in ancient Israel were used primarily for temporary detention pending trial (Lev 24:10–12), housing forced labor (Jdg 16:21), unjust captivity for economic "collateral" (2Ki 4:1) or isolation of a political prisoner (Jer 52:11).

Release from prison in 107:14 may allude particularly to the exile (vv. 3,11), though many deportees were simply resettled in a foreign land to build a new life for themselves. Others, however, probably those of higher social rank who might be capable of leading an insurrection, were imprisoned. King Jehoiachin illustrates the case of one who was carried off to Babylon (2Ki 24:15) and later released from prison conditions (2Ki 25:27–30). A ration list from the palace of Babylon names Jehoiachin and his sons, who were there under house arrest. While Jehoiachin never returned to the land of Judah, others did.

While release of prisoners became a noteworthy act of deliverance in the history of Israel, this sort of action was probably typical of what was expected of ancient Near Eastern deities, as illustrated in the Hymn to Shamash, in which the god is praised for showing havens to those who have fled and roads back home to those who are lost, and for giving freedom to imprisoned, displaced people. This can also be an attribute of justice for release of those wrongly imprisoned.

107:16 *gates of bronze … bars of iron.* The Greek historian Herodotus described Babylon as having "one hundred gates in the circuit of the wall, all of bronze with bronze uprights and lintels." Large gates adorned with bronze bands featuring reliefs have been excavated at the Assyrian-period site of Balawat, giving a glimpse of what the Babylonian walls may have been like. Gates were locked by means of a bar slid across the gateway, and iron would obviously be the most difficult material to break.

107:18 *gates of death.* See the articles "Death and Sheol," p. 833; "Death and the Underworld," p. 907.

107:23–30 The Babylonian Hymn to Shamash also has a section in which Shamash is seen as rescuing merchants (and their goods) from storms at sea. However, it does not speak of Shamash either sending the waves or stilling the storm (cf. vv. 25.29), only of watching over the traveler and saving his life.

[25] For he spoke[p] and stirred up a
tempest[q]
that lifted high the waves.[r]
[26] They mounted up to the heavens and
went down to the depths;
in their peril their courage melted[s]
away.
[27] They reeled and staggered like
drunkards;
they were at their wits' end.
[28] Then they cried out to the LORD in their
trouble,
and he brought them out of their
distress.
[29] He stilled the storm[t] to a whisper;
the waves[u] of the sea[a] were hushed.
[30] They were glad when it grew calm,
and he guided them to their desired
haven.
[31] Let them give thanks to the LORD for
his unfailing love
and his wonderful deeds for
mankind.
[32] Let them exalt him in the assembly[v] of
the people
and praise him in the council of the
elders.

[33] He turned rivers into a desert,[w]
flowing springs into thirsty
ground,
[34] and fruitful land into a salt waste,[x]
because of the wickedness of those
who lived there.
[35] He turned the desert into pools of
water[y]
and the parched ground into flowing
springs;
[36] there he brought the hungry to live,
and they founded a city where they
could settle.
[37] They sowed fields and planted
vineyards[z]
that yielded a fruitful harvest;
[38] he blessed them, and their numbers
greatly increased,[a]
and he did not let their herds
diminish.

[39] Then their numbers decreased,[b] and
they were humbled
by oppression, calamity and
sorrow;
[40] he who pours contempt on nobles[c]
made them wander in a trackless
waste.[d]
[41] But he lifted the needy[e] out of their
affliction
and increased their families like
flocks.
[42] The upright see and rejoice,[f]
but all the wicked shut their mouths.[g]

[43] Let the one who is wise[h] heed these
things
and ponder the loving deeds[i] of the
LORD.

Psalm 108[b]

108:1-5pp — Ps 57:7-11
108:6-13pp — Ps 60:5-12

A song. A psalm of David.

[1] My heart, O God, is steadfast;
I will sing and make music with all
my soul.
[2] Awake, harp and lyre!
I will awaken the dawn.
[3] I will praise you, LORD, among the
nations;
I will sing of you among the peoples.
[4] For great is your love, higher than the
heavens;
your faithfulness reaches to the
skies.
[5] Be exalted, O God, above the heavens;
let your glory be over all the earth.[j]

[6] Save us and help us with your right
hand,
that those you love may be
delivered.
[7] God has spoken from his sanctuary:
"In triumph I will parcel out
Shechem
and measure off the Valley of
Sukkoth.
[8] Gilead is mine, Manasseh is mine;
Ephraim is my helmet,
Judah[k] is my scepter.
[9] Moab is my washbasin,
on Edom I toss my sandal;
over Philistia I shout in triumph."

[10] Who will bring me to the fortified city?
Who will lead me to Edom?
[11] Is it not you, God, you who have
rejected us
and no longer go out with our
armies?[l]

107:25 [p] Ps 105:31 [q] Jnh 1:4 [r] Ps 93:3 **107:26** [s] Ps 22:14 **107:29** [t] Mt 8:26 [u] Ps 89:9 **107:32** [v] Ps 22:22, 25; 35:18 **107:33** [w] 1Ki 17:1; Ps 74:15 **107:34** [x] Ge 13:10; 14:3; 19:25 **107:35** [y] Ps 114:8; Isa 41:18 **107:37** [z] Isa 65:21 **107:38** [a] Ge 12:2; 17:16, 20; Ex 1:7 **107:39** [b] 2Ki 10:32; Eze 5:12 **107:40** [c] Job 12:21 [d] Job 12:24 **107:41** [e] 1Sa 2:8; Ps 113:7-9 **107:42** [f] Job 22:19 [g] Job 5:16; Ps 63:11; Ro 3:19 **107:43** [h] Jer 9:12; Hos 14:9 [i] Ps 64:9 **108:5** [j] Ps 57:5 **108:8** [k] Ge 49:10 **108:11** [l] Ps 44:9

[a] 29 Dead Sea Scrolls; Masoretic Text / *their waves*
[b] In Hebrew texts 108:1-13 is numbered 108:2-14.

107:29 *stilled the storm*. See the article "Chaos Monsters," p. 953.
107:33 – 35 In the world-upside-down motif, all that is considered most consistent and reliable is jeopardized. The concept can be applied to the cosmic realm (sun growing dark), the natural realm (mountains being leveled), the political realm (empires being overthrown), the social realm (poor becoming rich) or the animal realm (lion and lamb together). These represent upsetting the boundaries usually associated with order. It is often used in prophetic literature in connection with the day of the Lord and coming judgment. The Babylonian Epic of Irra is roughly similar, in that it describes a reversal of Marduk's creation of order out of the original primeval chaos.

PSALM 108

Repeated Psalms

Psalm 108 is a composite from Ps 57:7 – 11 and Ps 60:5 – 12 (see notes on Ps 60:6,8). The editing of hymns to create new worship songs for new settings is also illustrated by comparing 1Ch 16:7 – 36 with Ps 105:1 – 15; 96:1 – 13; 106:47 – 48, as well as Ps 115:4 – 11 with Ps 135:15 – 20.

An example from prophetic texts is Isa 2:2 – 5 and Mic 4:1 – 5. The reuse of older material in new compositions is well attested in Mesopotamian literature, and it is probably only the limited sample of older Mesopotamian hymns that leaves us without good examples from this genre. Similarly in Egypt, well-crafted compositions were put to use in multiple forms. ◆

12 Give us aid against the enemy,
for human help is worthless.
13 With God we will gain the victory,
and he will trample down our enemies.

Psalm 109

For the director of music.
Of David. A psalm.

1 My God, whom I praise,
do not remain silent,[m]
2 for people who are wicked and deceitful
have opened their mouths against me;
they have spoken against me with lying tongues.[n]
3 With words of hatred[o] they surround me;
they attack me without cause.[p]
4 In return for my friendship they accuse me,
but I am a man of prayer.[q]
5 They repay me evil for good,[r]
and hatred for my friendship.

6 Appoint someone evil to oppose my enemy;
let an accuser[s] stand at his right hand.
7 When he is tried, let him be found guilty,
and may his prayers condemn[t] him.
8 May his days be few;
may another take his place[u] of leadership.
9 May his children be fatherless
and his wife a widow.[v]
10 May his children be wandering beggars;
may they be driven[a] from their ruined homes.
11 May a creditor seize all he has;
may strangers plunder the fruits of his labor.[w]
12 May no one extend kindness to him
or take pity[x] on his fatherless children.
13 May his descendants be cut off,[y]
their names blotted out[z] from the next generation.
14 May the iniquity of his fathers[a] be remembered before the LORD;
may the sin of his mother never be blotted out.
15 May their sins always remain before the LORD,
that he may blot out their name[b] from the earth.

16 For he never thought of doing a kindness,
but hounded to death the poor
and the needy[c] and the brokenhearted.[d]

109:1 [m] Ps 83:1 **109:2** [n] Ps 52:4; 120:2 **109:3** [o] Ps 69:4 [p] Ps 35:7; Jn 15:25 **109:4** [q] Ps 69:13 **109:5** [r] Ps 35:12; 38:20 **109:6** [s] Zec 3:1 **109:7** [t] Pr 28:9 **109:8** [u] Ac 1:20* **109:9** [v] Ex 22:24 **109:11** [w] Job 5:5 **109:12** [x] Isa 9:17 **109:13** [y] Job 18:19; Ps 37:28 [z] Pr 10:7 **109:14** [a] Ex 20:5; Ne 4:5; Jer 18:23 **109:15** [b] Job 18:17; Ps 34:16 **109:16** [c] Ps 37:14, 32 [d] Ps 34:18

[a] 10 Septuagint; Hebrew *sought*

Ps 109 For imprecations, see the article "Imprecations and Incantations," p. 937.
109:7 *prayers condemn him.* From the context it could be concluded that this refers to a petitionary prayer in a courtroom situation. Such prayers could be accompanied by oaths of innocence (such as Job's in Job 31). If the party were not truly innocent, such an oath would be a basis for divine punishment.

4 The LORD has sworn
and will not change his mind:[a]
"You are a priest forever,[b]
in the order of Melchizedek.[c]"
5 The Lord is at your right hand[a];[d]
he will crush kings[e] on the day of
his wrath.[f]
6 He will judge the nations,[g] heaping up
the dead[h]
and crushing the rulers[i] of the whole
earth.
7 He will drink from a brook along the
way,[b]
and so he will lift his head high.[j]

Psalm 111[c]

1 Praise the LORD.[d]

I will extol the LORD with all my heart
in the council of the upright and in
the assembly.
2 Great are the works[k] of the LORD;
they are pondered by all who delight
in them.
3 Glorious and majestic are his deeds,
and his righteousness endures
forever.
4 He has caused his wonders to be
remembered;
the LORD is gracious and
compassionate.[l]
5 He provides food[m] for those who fear
him;
he remembers his covenant forever.
6 He has shown his people the power of
his works,
giving them the lands of other
nations.
7 The works of his hands are faithful and
just;
all his precepts are trustworthy.[n]
8 They are established for ever[o] and ever,
enacted in faithfulness and
uprightness.
9 He provided redemption[p] for his
people;
he ordained his covenant forever—
holy and awesome[q] is his name.
10 The fear of the LORD is the beginning of
wisdom;[r]
all who follow his precepts have
good understanding.[s]
To him belongs eternal praise.[t]

Psalm 112[c]

1 Praise the LORD.[d]

Blessed are those who fear the LORD,[u]
who find great delight[v] in his
commands.
2 Their children will be mighty in the
land;
the generation of the upright will be
blessed.

110:4 [a] Nu 23:19 [b] Heb 5:6*; 7:21* [c] Heb 7:15-17* **110:5** [d] Ps 16:8 [e] Ps 2:12 [f] Ps 2:5; Ro 2:5 **110:6** [g] Isa 2:4 [h] Isa 66:24 [i] Ps 68:21 **110:7** [j] Ps 27:6 **111:2** [k] Ps 92:5; 143:5 **111:4** [l] Ps 103:8 **111:5** [m] Mt 6:26, 31-33 **111:7** [n] Ps 19:7; Rev 15:3 **111:8** [o] Isa 40:8; Mt 5:18 **111:9** [p] Lk 1:68 [q] Ps 99:3; Lk 1:49 **111:10** [r] Pr 9:10 [s] Ecc 12:13 [t] Ps 145:2 **112:1** [u] Ps 128:1 [v] Ps 119:14, 16, 47, 92

[a] 5 Or *My lord is at your right hand, LORD* [b] 7 The meaning of the Hebrew for this clause is uncertain. [c] This psalm is an acrostic poem, the lines of which begin with the successive letters of the Hebrew alphabet. [d] 1 Hebrew *Hallelu Yah*

of subjects dancing in celebration at the king's victorious return. Like that Egyptian text, this verse celebrates the king's military brilliance with images of majestic splendor and youthful prowess.
110:4 *will not change his mind.* A similar denial of duplicity accompanies a divine promise in an Assyrian royal prophecy in which the god insists to have spoken truly without lies (which was followed by a promise of victory). *a priest forever.* In Egypt and Mesopotamia, the king was regarded as a priest who was ultimately responsible for the support of temple worship and on special occasions participated in priestly duties (cf. 2Sa 6; 1Ki 8). Like the royal prophecy in Ps 110, Assyrian royal prophecies called the king to his priestly responsibility. Royal priesthood was also the custom among Canaanite peoples. By alluding to the ancient precedent of a priestly king in Canaanite Jerusalem (see Melchizedek in the note on Ge 14:18), this psalm confers upon the Davidic king in Jerusalem a priestly title without usurping the prerogatives that belong to the Levitical priests.
110:5 *The Lord is at your right hand.* A common metaphor of protection in Mesopotamian literature was the claim that a deity was stationed before, behind or at the (particularly right) side of an individual. Prophetic assurances that the deity would be alongside the king in battle were part of Assyrian royal prophecies. Ninurta, the god of battle, would be at the king's right and left side and subdue his enemies under his foot. *crush kings.* The promise of destruction of the king's enemies and foreign rulers is a predominant feature of these Assyrian prophecies.
110:7 *He will drink from a brook.* The reference to "he" in v. 7 changes from the Lord (vv. 5–6) to the king. While awkward in English style, such changes in reference can be seen in Assyrian royal prophecy, as well as in Biblical Hebrew. Some have suggested that the king drinking from the brook alludes to the coronation ritual in which the king was anointed by the spring of Gihon, which was located in the Kidron Valley below the city of Jerusalem (cf. 1Ki 1:38–39,45). This may have been a water purification ritual during the coronation, similar to what was practiced in Egypt; but the lifting of the head in this verse suggests that the symbolism involved granting strength to the king for victory. *lift his head high.* A sign of invincibility, which is illustrated in the coronation inscription concerning the Sumerian king Shulgi.
111:10 *The fear of the LORD.* The citation of familiar sayings is natural in the composition of great literature and music, a technique well known in Mesopotamia. For example, one text used in the worship of Marduk actually cites the source of the phrase: "It is said in Enuma Elish: When heaven and earth were not created, Assur came into being." Here the psalmist punctuates his opening directive to praise God (v. 1) by citing at the close of his psalm the foundational slogan of wisdom (Job 28:28; Pr 1:7; Ecc 12:13). The nexus between the two themes is revealed in the contemplation of God's works (v. 3).
112:2 *Their children will be mighty.* See notes on 127:1,4–5.

17 He loved to pronounce a curse—
may it come back on him.[e]
He found no pleasure in blessing—
may it be far from him.
18 He wore cursing[f] as his garment;
it entered into his body like
water,[g]
into his bones like oil.
19 May it be like a cloak wrapped about
him,
like a belt tied forever around him.
20 May this be the LORD's payment[h] to
my accusers,
to those who speak evil[i] of me.

21 But you, Sovereign LORD,
help me for your name's sake;[j]
out of the goodness of your love,[k]
deliver me.
22 For I am poor and needy,
and my heart is wounded within me.
23 I fade away like an evening shadow;[l]
I am shaken off like a locust.
24 My knees give[m] way from fasting;
my body is thin and gaunt.
25 I am an object of scorn[n] to my
accusers;
when they see me, they shake their
heads.[o]

26 Help me,[p] LORD my God;
save me according to your unfailing
love.
27 Let them know[q] that it is your hand,
that you, LORD, have done it.
28 While they curse,[r] may you bless;
may those who attack me be put to
shame,
but may your servant rejoice.[s]
29 May my accusers be clothed with
disgrace
and wrapped in shame[t] as in a cloak.
30 With my mouth I will greatly extol the
LORD;
in the great throng[u] of worshipers
I will praise him.
31 For he stands at the right hand[v] of the
needy,
to save their lives from those who
would condemn them.

109:17 [e] Pr 14:14; Eze 35:6 **109:18** [f] Ps 73:6 [g] Nu 5:22 **109:20** [h] Ps 94:23; 2Ti 4:14 [i] Ps 71:10 **109:21** [j] Ps 79:9 [k] Ps 69:16 **109:23** [l] Ps 102:11 **109:24** [m] Heb 12:12 **109:25** [n] Ps 22:6 [o] Mt 27:39; Mk 15:29 **109:26** [p] Ps 119:86 **109:27** [q] Job 37:7 **109:28** [r] 2Sa 16:12 [s] Isa 65:14 **109:29** [t] Ps 35:26; 132:18 **109:30** [u] Ps 35:18; 111:1 **109:31** [v] Ps 16:8; 73:23; 121:5 **110:1** [w] Mt 22:44*; Mk 12:36*; Lk 20:42*; Ac 2:34* [x] 1Co 15:25 **110:2** [y] Ps 45:6 **110:3** [z] Jdg 5:2; Ps 96:9

Psalm 110

Of David. A psalm.

1 The LORD says[w] to my lord:[a]
"Sit at my right hand
until I make your enemies
a footstool for your feet."[x]
2 The LORD will extend your mighty
scepter[y] from Zion, saying,
"Rule in the midst of your enemies!"
3 Your troops will be willing
on your day of battle.
Arrayed in holy splendor,[z]
your young men will come to you
like dew from the morning's womb.[b]

[a] *1* Or *Lord* [b] *3* The meaning of the Hebrew for this sentence is uncertain.

109:17 *a curse.* See note on 62:4.
109:24 *fasting.* Religious fasting is little attested in the ancient Near East outside of the Bible; it generally occurs in the context of mourning. In the OT the religious use of fasting is often in connection with making a request before God. Presumably, the principle is that the importance of the request causes an individual to be so concerned about their spiritual condition that physical necessities fade into the background. In this sense the act of fasting is designed as a process leading to purification and humbling oneself before God (69:10).
109:31 *right hand.* See note on 110:5.
Ps 110 This psalm is a prophetic oracle concerning the king that was probably delivered in the Jerusalem temple. The opening introduction is similar to what is found in Assyrian royal prophecy that was likely delivered in temple worship at the king's enthronement: "The word of Ishtar of Arbela to Esarhaddon." Thus, in the context of the psalm, the speaker is not the king (e.g., David) but the prophet delivering a message to the king. In Israel, prophetic oracles spoken on the coronation day provided important divine support for the king's authority. Several themes are parallel between Ps 110 and Assyrian enthronement prophecy: (1) legitimation of kingship, (2) promised destruction of enemies, (3) presence of loyal supporters and (4) priesthood of the king.

Divine authorization was also the custom in Egypt, where the pattern of coronation appears close to that described in 1Ki 1:32–35; 2Ki 11:4–21. First, the Egyptian king was elected by divine decree in the temple (in 1Ki 1, the temple had not yet been built, but the anointing took place at the tabernacle, God's temporary shrine [1Ki 1:39]). This was followed by a procession to the palace, where enthronement took place. See the article "Enthronement in the Ancient Near East," p. 925.
110:1 *Sit at my right hand.* Close physical proximity, especially at the "right" hand, is a metaphor of privileged relationship and even legal heir (45:9; 80:17; 1Ki 2:19). Esarhaddon was said to place his son Ashurbanipal, who was to succeed him as king in Assyria, at his right hand and his son Shamash-shum-ukin, who was to take the secondary status of king in Babylon, at his left. The coronation text for the Egyptian king Horemheb describes him as being presented to the gods under the embrace of the god Horus, and Egyptian art depicts him seated at Horus's right side. *I make your enemies a footstool.* Assyrian royal prophecy promises that the deity will place the king's enemies under his feet. An inscription on the throne pedestal of the Assyrian king Shalmaneser III (c. 850 BC) identifies him as a valiant king who with the help of his god had succeeded in putting all lands under his feet like a footstool. Egyptian art also shows the newly enthroned king with his feet upon a footstool with enemy nations inside, and coronation inscriptions speak of enemy nations under the king's feet. Other reliefs from Egypt and Mesopotamia portray the king with his foot on the neck or head of prostrate foes. Thus, in Ps 110, the Lord promises that the enemies of the Davidic king will be subject to him.
110:3 *Your troops ... your young men.* An Egyptian royal text might offer a parallel to this difficult verse as it speaks

PSALMS 111; 112

Acrostic Psalms

An "acrostic" is a literary device in which each new line of a poem begins with a different letter, arranged so that the whole series of letters conveys something meaningful. In all of the acrostic psalms of the OT, these letters follow the order of the Hebrew alphabet. However, much more elaborate messages can be expressed. For example, in Ashurbanipal's (Assyrian king, c. 650 BC) Hymn to Marduk and Zarpanitu, the sequence of Akkadian signs that begin each set of lines spells an entire sentence: "I am Assurbanipal, who has called out to you: give me life, Marduk, and I will praise you!"

Egyptian examples offer numerical sequences or complex messages that involve both horizontal and vertical patterns. They are more dependent on puns to accomplish their stylistic objective. Acrostics depend on writing, and therefore would not be composed orally. Likewise, they are intended to be read, not just heard, because of the importance of the visual element. Because of this, we come to understand that only a limited audience would appreciate the formal elements. This is especially clear in the Babylonian examples, where a variable sign needs to be read with one value in the poem, but with a different value in the acrostic. Some of the Babylonian examples also contain a pattern in the last sign of each line. Another variation is found in those examples where the acrostic is repeated each stanza. Nevertheless, in the case of the Hebrew alphabetic acrostics, the alphabetic element could serve as a mnemonic device.

Ps 111 and Ps 112 are both acrostics of the Hebrew alphabet, which helps pair these psalms together in a way that they complement each other in the themes and expressions mirrored by these adjacent psalms. Ps 9 and Ps 10 each contain half of the Hebrew alphabet, so unified, they form an acrostic of the whole. Acrostics can serve, then, to suggest that the meaning of the whole is greater than the sum of the parts. Ps 25, 34, 37, 119 and 145 are also acrostics of the Hebrew alphabet. Perhaps those acrostics simply ornament each psalm with an aesthetic beauty that complements the message. ◆

Cuneiform tablet containing a portion of Assurbanipal's Hymn to Marduk. This is an acrostic prayer. The first letter of each section forms the sentence, "I am Ashurbanipal who calls on you. Give me life, Marduk, I will glorify you."

Kim Walton. The British Museum.

[3]Wealth and riches are in their houses,
and their righteousness endures
forever.
[4]Even in darkness light dawns[w] for the
upright,
for those who are gracious and
compassionate and righteous.[x]
[5]Good will come to those who are
generous and lend freely,[y]
who conduct their affairs with justice.

[6]Surely the righteous will never be
shaken;
they will be remembered[z] forever.
[7]They will have no fear of bad news;
their hearts are steadfast,[a] trusting in
the LORD.
[8]Their hearts are secure, they will have
no fear;
in the end they will look in triumph
on their foes.[b]
[9]They have freely scattered their gifts to
the poor,[c]
their righteousness endures forever;
their horn[a] will be lifted[d] high in
honor.

[10]The wicked will see[e] and be vexed,
they will gnash their teeth[f] and
waste away;[g]
the longings of the wicked will come
to nothing.[h]

Psalm 113

[1]Praise the LORD.[b]

Praise the LORD, you his servants;[i]
praise the name of the LORD.
[2]Let the name of the LORD be praised,
both now and forevermore.[j]
[3]From the rising of the sun[k] to the place
where it sets,
the name of the LORD is to be
praised.

[4]The LORD is exalted[l] over all the
nations,
his glory above the heavens.[m]
[5]Who is like the LORD our God,[n]
the One who sits enthroned[o] on
high,
[6]who stoops down to look[p]
on the heavens and the earth?

[7]He raises the poor[q] from the dust
and lifts the needy[r] from the ash
heap;
[8]he seats them[s] with princes,
with the princes of his people.
[9]He settles the childless[t] woman in her
home
as a happy mother of children.

Praise the LORD.

Psalm 114

[1]When Israel came out of Egypt,[u]
Jacob from a people of foreign
tongue,
[2]Judah became God's sanctuary,
Israel his dominion.

[3]The sea looked and fled,[v]
the Jordan turned back;[w]

112:4 [w]Job 11:17 [x]Ps 97:11 **112:5** [y]Ps 37:21,26 **112:6** [z]Pr 10:7 **112:7** [a]Ps 57:7; Pr 1:33 **112:8** [b]Ps 59:10 **112:9** [c]2Co 9:9* [d]Ps 75:10 **112:10** [e]Ps 86:17 [f]Ps 37:12 [g]Ps 58:7-8 [h]Pr 11:7 **113:1** [i]Ps 135:1 **113:2** [j]Da 2:20 **113:3** [k]Isa 59:19; Mal 1:11 **113:4** [l]Ps 99:2 [m]Ps 8:1; 97:9 **113:5** [n]Ps 89:6 [o]Ps 103:19 **113:6** [p]Ps 11:4; 138:6; Isa 57:15 **113:7** [q]1Sa 2:8 [r]Ps 107:41 **113:8** [s]Job 36:7 **113:9** [t]1Sa 2:5; Ps 68:6; Isa 54:1 **114:1** [u]Ex 13:3 **114:3** [v]Ex 14:21; Ps 77:16 [w]Jos 3:16

[a] 9 *Horn* here symbolizes dignity. [b] 1 Hebrew *Hallelu Yah*; also in verse 9

112:5 *generous.* A generous spirit was a virtue across the ancient Near East. Tomb inscriptions from as early as Sixth-Dynasty Egypt (c. 2200 BC) bear as part of the epithet "I gave bread to the hungry, clothing to the naked." An early Mesopotamian wisdom collection exhorts, "Do not despise the miserable ... Give food to eat, beer to drink." Protecting the interest of the poor and upholding equal justice was enshrined in the earliest law collections of Mesopotamia.

112:9 *horn will be lifted.* See notes on 18:2; 132:17.

113:6 *who stoops down to look.* One ancient view of the universe imagined the throne of the highest god perched atop the heavens, which in turn formed a dome over the flat disk of the earth. See the article "Cosmic Geography," p. 836.

113:7 *He raises the poor.* This echoes the praise of 1Sa 2:8, which also associates God's rule over creation with his compassion to help the poor. The importance of this attribute for a deity is reflected in the Hymn to Nanaya (c. 720 BC), an Assyrian goddess who in her mercy reverses the destitution of the poor by giving abundance (see note on 145:14).

113:9 *settles the childless woman.* In the ancient Near East, conception and childbirth were sometimes accompanied by elaborate rituals of magic intended to ensure their success. Other magical rites were performed to protect newborn children from being snatched by the evil demon Lamashtu. In ancient Israel, clay figurines of the fertility goddess and other symbols associated with her were common. Their precise ritual function is unknown, but their ubiquity in the archaeological record demonstrates the anxiety felt regarding childbearing. It is therefore understandable that Yahweh is seen as the one who grants children, though here with no appeal to magical words or acts.

114:1 *foreign tongue.* The language of the Israelites, who at the exodus were delivered from bondage in Egypt, was likely a forerunner of Hebrew, which in turn was part of the larger family of Semitic languages. These languages had many common vocabulary words and similar grammatical constructions, and had some overlap with Egyptian, though it was not a Semitic language. Nevertheless, they were not mutually understandable (Ge 42:23).

114:2 *Judah ... God's sanctuary.* This reflects a temple as state imagery. God's throne was in the temple just as the king's throne was in his palace. God and king reigned over the country from their respective thrones. This concept goes all the way back into earliest recorded history as the temples served as the earliest administrative centers for the state. In this way it can be seen that the two lines of this verse are parallel in that the sanctuary is the central feature in the "dominion" (kingdom).

114:3–7 Similar to the crossing of the Red Sea at the exodus, the Jordan River was also crossed by a miraculous turning back of the waters (Jos 3–4). This event is

4 the mountains leaped like rams,
the hills like lambs.

5 Why was it, sea, that you fled?
Why, Jordan, did you turn back?
6 Why, mountains, did you leap like
rams,
you hills, like lambs?

7 Tremble, earth,[x] at the presence of the
Lord,
at the presence of the God of Jacob,
8 who turned the rock into a pool,
the hard rock into springs of water.[y]

Psalm 115

115:4-11pp — Ps 135:15-20

1 Not to us, LORD, not to us
but to your name be the glory,[z]
because of your love and
faithfulness.

2 Why do the nations say,
"Where is their God?"[a]
3 Our God is in heaven;[b]
he does whatever pleases him.[c]
4 But their idols are silver and gold,
made by human hands.[d]
5 They have mouths, but cannot speak,[e]
eyes, but cannot see.
6 They have ears, but cannot hear,
noses, but cannot smell.
7 They have hands, but cannot feel,
feet, but cannot walk,
nor can they utter a sound with their
throats.
8 Those who make them will be like
them,
and so will all who trust in them.

9 All you Israelites, trust in the LORD—
he is their help and shield.
10 House of Aaron,[f] trust in the LORD—
he is their help and shield.
11 You who fear him, trust in the LORD—
he is their help and shield.

12 The LORD remembers us and will
bless us:
He will bless his people Israel,
he will bless the house of Aaron,
13 he will bless those who fear[g] the
LORD—
small and great alike.

14 May the LORD cause you to flourish,[h]
both you and your children.
15 May you be blessed by the LORD,
the Maker of heaven[i] and earth.

16 The highest heavens belong to the
LORD,[j]
but the earth he has given[k] to
mankind.
17 It is not the dead[l] who praise the LORD,
those who go down to the place of
silence;
18 it is we who extol the LORD,
both now and forevermore.[m]

Praise the LORD.[a]

Psalm 116

1 I love the LORD,[n] for he heard my
voice;
he heard my cry[o] for mercy.
2 Because he turned his ear[p] to me,
I will call on him as long as I live.

3 The cords of death[q] entangled me,
the anguish of the grave came over
me;
I was overcome by distress and
sorrow.
4 Then I called on the name[r] of the LORD:
"LORD, save me![s]"

5 The LORD is gracious and righteous;[t]
our God is full of compassion.
6 The LORD protects the unwary;
when I was brought low,[u] he saved
me.

7 Return to your rest,[v] my soul,
for the LORD has been good[w] to you.

8 For you, LORD, have delivered me[x] from
death,
my eyes from tears,
my feet from stumbling,
9 that I may walk before the LORD
in the land of the living.[y]

114:7 [x] Ps 96:9
114:8 [y] Ex 17:6; Nu 20:11; Ps 107:35
115:1 [z] Ps 96:8; Isa 48:11; Eze 36:32
115:2 [a] Ps 42:3; 79:10
115:3 [b] Ps 103:19 [c] Ps 135:6; Da 4:35
115:4 [d] Dt 4:28; Jer 10:3-5
115:5 [e] Jer 10:5
115:10 [f] Ps 118:3
115:13 [g] Ps 128:1,4
115:14 [h] Dt 1:11
115:15 [i] Ge 1:1; 14:19; Ps 96:5
115:16 [j] Ps 89:11 [k] Ps 8:6-8
115:17 [l] Ps 6:5; 88:10-12; Isa 38:18
115:18 [m] Ps 113:2; Da 2:20
116:1 [n] Ps 18:1 [o] Ps 66:19
116:2 [p] Ps 40:1
116:3 [q] Ps 18:4-5
116:4 [r] Ps 118:5 [s] Ps 22:20
116:5 [t] Ezr 9:15; Ne 9:8; Ps 103:8; 145:17
116:6 [u] Ps 19:7; 79:8
116:7 [v] Jer 6:16; Mt 11:29 [w] Ps 13:6
116:8 [x] Ps 56:13
116:9 [y] Ps 27:13

[a] 18 Hebrew *Hallelu Yah*

described poetically using imagery of a cosmic warrior (see the article "Chaos Monsters," p. 953).
114:4 *mountains leaped.* In the Ugaritic tale concerning the building of Baal's palace, his enthronement is preceded by his voice thundering forth, with the result that the high places of the earth leap or quake. Similarly, in the Hymn to Marduk, the god's thundering voice makes the earth quake. The Hebrew verb translated "leaped" is often thought to describe a frolicking or gamboling type of motion, but it is more likely the undulating appearance of a flock of sheep or goats moving along a path. This would be an appropriate image to describe the heaving of the earth in an earthquake.
115:4 *idols.* See note on 135:15; see also the article "Making an Idol," p. 1010.
115:17 *the dead.* See note on 88:10; see also the articles "Death and Sheol," p. 833; "Death and the Underworld," p. 907.
116:1 *heard my voice.* See note on 55:17.
116:2 *turned his ear.* This is a common metaphor for God responding to a plea. It is graphically illustrated on Egyptian offering tablets that feature carvings of the deity's ears. Some of these depict the worshiper in a position of praise or prayer in front of the ears, with an inscribed prayer accompanying the art.

10 I trusted[z] in the LORD when I said,
"I am greatly afflicted";
11 in my alarm I said,
"Everyone is a liar."[a]

12 What shall I return to the LORD
for all his goodness to me?

13 I will lift up the cup of salvation
and call on the name[b] of the LORD.
14 I will fulfill my vows[c] to the LORD
in the presence of all his people.

15 Precious in the sight[d] of the LORD
is the death of his faithful servants.
16 Truly I am your servant, LORD;[e]
I serve you just as my mother did;[f]
you have freed me from my chains.

17 I will sacrifice a thank offering[g] to you
and call on the name of the LORD.
18 I will fulfill my vows to the LORD
in the presence of all his people,
19 in the courts[h] of the house of the
LORD—
in your midst, Jerusalem.

Praise the LORD.[a]

Psalm 117

1 Praise the LORD, all you nations;[i]
extol him, all you peoples.
2 For great is his love toward us,
and the faithfulness of the LORD[j]
endures forever.

Praise the LORD.[a]

Psalm 118

1 Give thanks to the LORD,[k] for he is
good;
his love endures forever.[l]

2 Let Israel say:[m]
"His love endures forever."
3 Let the house of Aaron say:
"His love endures forever."
4 Let those who fear the LORD say:
"His love endures forever."

5 When hard pressed,[n] I cried to the
LORD;
he brought me into a spacious
place.[o]
6 The LORD is with me;[p] I will not be
afraid.
What can mere mortals do
to me?[q]
7 The LORD is with me; he is my
helper.[r]
I look in triumph on my enemies.[s]

8 It is better to take refuge in the LORD[t]
than to trust in humans.[u]
9 It is better to take refuge in the LORD
than to trust in princes.[v]
10 All the nations surrounded me,
but in the name of the LORD I cut
them down.[w]
11 They surrounded me[x] on every side,[y]
but in the name of the LORD I cut
them down.
12 They swarmed around me like bees,[z]
but they were consumed as quickly
as burning thorns;[a]
in the name of the LORD I cut them
down.
13 I was pushed back and about to fall,
but the LORD helped me.[b]
14 The LORD is my strength[c] and my
defense[b];
he has become my salvation.[d]

15 Shouts of joy[e] and victory
resound in the tents of the
righteous:
"The LORD's right hand[f] has done
mighty things!
16 The LORD's right hand is lifted high;
the LORD's right hand has done
mighty things!"
17 I will not die[g] but live,
and will proclaim[h] what the LORD
has done.
18 The LORD has chastened me severely,
but he has not given me over to
death.[i]

116:10 [z] 2Co 4:13* **116:11** [a] Ro 3:4 **116:13** [b] Ps 16:5; 80:18 **116:14** [c] Ps 22:25; Jnh 2:9 **116:15** [d] Ps 72:14 **116:16** [e] Ps 119:125; 143:12 [f] Ps 86:16 **116:17** [g] Lev 7:12; Ps 50:14 **116:19** [h] Ps 96:8; 135:2 **117:1** [i] Ro 15:11* **117:2** [j] Ps 100:5 **118:1** [k] 1Ch 16:8 [l] Ps 106:1; 136:1 **118:2** [m] Ps 115:9 **118:5** [n] Ps 120:1 [o] Ps 18:19 **118:6** [p] Heb 13:6* [q] Ps 27:1; 56:4 **118:7** [r] Ps 54:4 [s] Ps 59:10 **118:8** [t] Ps 40:4 [u] Jer 17:5 **118:9** [v] Ps 146:3 **118:10** [w] Ps 18:40 **118:11** [x] Ps 88:17 [y] Ps 3:6 **118:12** [z] Dt 1:44 [a] Ps 58:9 **118:13** [b] Ps 86:17; 140:4 **118:14** [c] Ex 15:2 [d] Isa 12:2 **118:15** [e] Ps 68:3 [f] Ps 89:13 **118:17** [g] Ps 6:5; Hab 1:12 [h] Ex 15:6; Ps 73:28 **118:18** [i] 2Co 6:9

[a] *19,2* Hebrew *Hallelu Yah* [b] *14* Or *song*

116:13 *cup of salvation.* The connection in this context to the payment of vows in the temple (v. 14) suggests that a libation is being poured out as a testimony is given of God's goodness and protection. Libations were a common form of thanksgiving in the ancient world, as depicted on Egyptian, Phoenician and Mesopotamian reliefs. The libation represents the deliverance (salvation) afforded by deity and also accomplishes deliverance from the vow.
116:14 *fulfill my vows.* Vows are voluntary, conditional agreements that are common in most of the cultures of the ancient Near East, including Hittite, Ugaritic, Mesopotamian and, less often, Egyptian. In the ancient world the most common context for a vow was when a request was being made to deity. The condition would typically involve God's provision or protection while that which was vowed was usually a gift to deity. The gift would most frequently take the form of a sacrifice, but other types of gifts to the sanctuary or priests would be options. Fulfillment of a vow could usually be accomplished at the sanctuary and was a public act. In Ugaritic literature King Keret makes a vow in requesting a wife who could produce offspring. In return he offered gold and silver corresponding to his bride's weight.
117:1 *Praise the LORD.* This command to the congregation (a plural imperative) is a formulaic opening and frequent closing for hymns (Ps 111 – 113; 134 – 135; 146 – 150). A similar formal device can be seen in Egyptian hymns with the interjection "Hail!" However, the Egyptian interjection does not carry the same meaning as does the Hebrew expression, which invokes the congregation to join the worshiper in praise.
118:8 – 9 *trust in humans . . . princes.* See note on 146:3.

[19] Open for me the gates[j] of the
righteous;
I will enter and give thanks to the
LORD.
[20] This is the gate of the LORD
through which the righteous may
enter.[k]
[21] I will give you thanks, for you
answered me;[l]
you have become my salvation.

[22] The stone the builders rejected
has become the cornerstone;[m]
[23] the LORD has done this,
and it is marvelous in our eyes.
[24] The LORD has done it this very day;
let us rejoice today and be glad.

[25] LORD, save us!
LORD, grant us success!

[26] Blessed is he who comes[n] in the name
of the LORD.
From the house of the LORD we bless
you.[a]
[27] The LORD is God,
and he has made his light shine[o] on
us.
With boughs in hand, join in the festal
procession
up[b] to the horns of the altar.

[28] You are my God, and I will praise you;
you are my God,[p] and I will exalt[q]
you.

[29] Give thanks to the LORD, for he is good;
his love endures forever.

118:19 [j] Isa 26:2 **118:20** [k] Ps 24:7; Isa 35:8; Rev 22:14 **118:21** [l] Ps 116:1 **118:22** [m] Mt 21:42; Mk 12:10; Lk 20:17*; Ac 4:11*; 1Pe 2:7* **118:26** [n] Mt 21:9*; Mk 11:9*; Lk 13:35*; 19:38*; Jn 12:13* **118:27** [o] 1Pe 2:9 **118:28** [p] Isa 25:1 [q] Ex 15:2

119:1 [r] Ps 128:1 **119:2** [s] Dt 6:5 **119:3** [t] 1Jn 3:9; 5:18 **119:9** [u] 2Ch 6:16 **119:10** [v] 2Ch 15:15 [w] ver 21, 118

Psalm 119[c]

א Aleph

[1] Blessed are those whose ways are
blameless,
who walk[r] according to the law of
the LORD.
[2] Blessed are those who keep his
statutes
and seek him with all their heart—[s]
[3] they do no wrong[t]
but follow his ways.
[4] You have laid down precepts
that are to be fully obeyed.
[5] Oh, that my ways were steadfast
in obeying your decrees!
[6] Then I would not be put to shame
when I consider all your commands.
[7] I will praise you with an upright heart
as I learn your righteous laws.
[8] I will obey your decrees;
do not utterly forsake me.

ב Beth

[9] How can a young person stay on the
path of purity?
By living according to your word.[u]
[10] I seek you with all my heart;[v]
do not let me stray from your
commands.[w]

[a] 26 The Hebrew is plural. [b] 27 Or *Bind the festal sacrifice with ropes / and take it* [c] This psalm is an acrostic poem, the stanzas of which begin with successive letters of the Hebrew alphabet; moreover, the verses of each stanza begin with the same letter of the Hebrew alphabet.

118:19 *gates of the righteous.* See note on 100:4.
118:22 *cornerstone.* Houses in Canaan usually consisted of several courses (rows) of stone as a foundation, upon which the mud brick walls were constructed. Stone pillars served to support roofing and, in some cases, a second story, with wooden beams as cross members. Wealthier homes show the use of "ashlar masonry," in which the stone was dressed into rectangular blocks. Large homes could reach several stories, with stone foundation walls several feet (1.5 m to 2.5 m) thick, sometimes filled with earthen debris, to support the heavier superstructure. There is archaeological evidence of the use of wooden beams between rows of stone either for structural shape or decoration (cf. 1Ki 6:36; 7:12). In walls constructed of undressed field stones, builders utilized ashlar masonry to provide stability at points along a wall, laying rectangular stones the length of the wall ("stretchers"), alternated with others set perpendicular ("headers"). Other public buildings show similar technique. Special care was taken to select a larger and better cut stone in order to stabilize the intersection of two walls at a corner (cf. Job 38:6; Isa 28:16). Foundation and top course stones at these points were particularly important, and the phrase translated "cornerstone" (lit. "head of the corner") could refer to either.
118:27 *festal procession.* To represent the abundance and lushness of the land, Israelites were instructed to celebrate the Festival of Tabernacles by waving and decorating their booths with fruit (citron) as well as leaves and branches from willow and palm trees. The festal occasion probably included dancing and processions carrying bundles of the leafy branches. In this way, the people acknowledged the abundance provided by God and communally celebrated the visible fulfillment of the covenant. Ancient Near Eastern texts also describe the itineraries of priestly processions. These differed in that they took the images of gods, along with their various divine accoutrements, from one town to another within a kingdom. This allowed the god to visit shrines, make inspection tours of facilities owned by the principal temple community, and participate in annual festivals outside the capital. These sacred processions paraded the images and symbols of the gods through the city streets to their shrines, where sacrifices, sacred dancing and other cultic activities would take place.
119:2 *Blessed are those who keep his statutes.* Keeping law was a serious religious matter in the ancient Near East. Hammurapi points to Shamash, the god of justice, for the authorization of his collection of Babylonian laws, and he concludes with blessings for those who honor the stipulations of the law. If a future king heeded the pronouncements, his reign would be long and he would enhance the well-being of his people. Curses would be upon the one who desecrated the monument upon which the laws were recorded or who failed to observe them (cf. v. 21). At the heart of Hammurapi's concern, however, is the longevity of his monument (and thus his legacy as lawgiver), whereas the psalmist longs to keep God's law as a means of glorifying God (see also vv. 7,12,164,171,175).

11 I have hidden your word in my heart[x]
that I might not sin against you.
12 Praise be to you, LORD;
teach me your decrees.[y]
13 With my lips I recount
all the laws that come from your
mouth.[z]
14 I rejoice in following your statutes
as one rejoices in great riches.
15 I meditate on your precepts[a]
and consider your ways.
16 I delight[b] in your decrees;
I will not neglect your word.

ג Gimel

17 Be good to your servant[c] while I live,
that I may obey your word.
18 Open my eyes that I may see
wonderful things in your law.
19 I am a stranger on earth;[d]
do not hide your commands from
me.
20 My soul is consumed[e] with longing
for your laws[f] at all times.
21 You rebuke the arrogant, who are
accursed,
those who stray[g] from your
commands.
22 Remove from me their scorn[h] and
contempt,
for I keep your statutes.
23 Though rulers sit together and slander
me,
your servant will meditate on your
decrees.
24 Your statutes are my delight;
they are my counselors.

ד Daleth

25 I am laid low in the dust;[i]
preserve my life[j] according to your
word.
26 I gave an account of my ways and you
answered me;
teach me your decrees.[k]
27 Cause me to understand the way of
your precepts,
that I may meditate on your
wonderful deeds.[l]
28 My soul is weary with sorrow;[m]
strengthen me[n] according to your
word.
29 Keep me from deceitful ways;
be gracious to me and teach me your
law.
30 I have chosen the way of faithfulness;
I have set my heart on your laws.
31 I hold fast[o] to your statutes, LORD;
do not let me be put to shame.
32 I run in the path of your commands,
for you have broadened my
understanding.

ה He

33 Teach me,[p] LORD, the way of your decrees,
that I may follow it to the end.[a]
34 Give me understanding, so that I may
keep your law
and obey it with all my heart.
35 Direct me in the path of your
commands,
for there I find delight.
36 Turn my heart[q] toward your statutes
and not toward selfish gain.[r]
37 Turn my eyes away from worthless
things;
preserve my life[s] according to your
word.[b]
38 Fulfill your promise[t] to your servant,
so that you may be feared.
39 Take away the disgrace I dread,
for your laws are good.
40 How I long[u] for your precepts!
In your righteousness preserve my
life.

ו Waw

41 May your unfailing love come to me,
LORD,
your salvation, according to your
promise;
42 then I can answer[v] anyone who
taunts me,
for I trust in your word.
43 Never take your word of truth from my
mouth,
for I have put my hope in your laws.
44 I will always obey your law,
for ever and ever.
45 I will walk about in freedom,
for I have sought out your precepts.
46 I will speak of your statutes before
kings[w]
and will not be put to shame,
47 for I delight in your commands
because I love them.
48 I reach out for your commands, which
I love,
that I may meditate on your decrees.

ז Zayin

49 Remember your word to your servant,
for you have given me hope.
50 My comfort in my suffering is this:
Your promise preserves my life.[x]
51 The arrogant mock me[y] unmercifully,
but I do not turn[z] from your law.
52 I remember,[a] LORD, your ancient laws,
and I find comfort in them.
53 Indignation grips me[b] because of the
wicked,
who have forsaken your law.[c]

119:11 [x] Ps 37:31; Lk 2:19,51 **119:12** [y] ver 26 **119:13** [z] Ps 40:9 **119:15** [a] Ps 1:2 **119:16** [b] Ps 1:2 **119:17** [c] Ps 13:6; 116:7 **119:19** [d] 1Ch 29:15; Ps 39:12; 2Co 5:6; Heb 11:13 **119:20** [e] Ps 42:2; 84:2 [f] Ps 63:1 **119:21** [g] ver 10 **119:22** [h] Ps 39:8 **119:25** [i] Ps 44:25 [j] Ps 143:11 **119:26** [k] Ps 25:4; 27:11; 86:11 **119:27** [l] Ps 145:5 **119:28** [m] Ps 107:26 [n] Ps 20:2; 1Pe 5:10 **119:31** [o] Dt 11:22

119:33 [p] ver 12 **119:36** [q] 1Ki 8:58 [r] Eze 33:31; Mk 7:21-22; Lk 12:15; Heb 13:5 **119:37** [s] Ps 71:20; Isa 33:15 **119:38** [t] 2Sa 7:25 **119:40** [u] ver 20 **119:42** [v] Pr 27:11 **119:46** [w] Mt 10:18; Ac 26:1-2 **119:50** [x] Ro 15:4 **119:51** [y] Jer 20:7 [z] ver 157; Job 23:11; Ps 44:18 **119:52** [a] Ps 103:18 **119:53** [b] Ezr 9:3 [c] Ps 89:30

[a] *33* Or *follow it for its reward* [b] *37* Two manuscripts of the Masoretic Text and Dead Sea Scrolls; most manuscripts of the Masoretic Text *life in your way*

54 Your decrees are the theme of my song
wherever I lodge.
55 In the night, LORD, I remember[d] your
name,
that I may keep your law.
56 This has been my practice:
I obey your precepts.

ח Heth

57 You are my portion,[e] LORD;
I have promised to obey your words.
58 I have sought your face with all my
heart;
be gracious to me[f] according to your
promise.[g]
59 I have considered my ways[h]
and have turned my steps to your
statutes.
60 I will hasten and not delay
to obey your commands.
61 Though the wicked bind me with
ropes,
I will not forget[i] your law.
62 At midnight[j] I rise to give you thanks
for your righteous laws.
63 I am a friend to all who fear you,[k]
to all who follow your precepts.
64 The earth is filled with your love,[l]
LORD;
teach me your decrees.

ט Teth

65 Do good to your servant
according to your word, LORD.
66 Teach me knowledge and good
judgment,
for I trust your commands.
67 Before I was afflicted I went astray,[m]
but now I obey your word.
68 You are good,[n] and what you do is
good;
teach me your decrees.[o]
69 Though the arrogant have smeared me
with lies,[p]
I keep your precepts with all my
heart.
70 Their hearts are callous[q] and unfeeling,
but I delight in your law.
71 It was good for me to be afflicted
so that I might learn your decrees.
72 The law from your mouth is more
precious to me
than thousands of pieces of silver
and gold.[r]

119:55 [d]Ps 63:6 **119:57** [e]Ps 16:5; La 3:24 **119:58** [f]1Ki 13:6 [g]ver 41 **119:59** [h]Lk 15:17-18 **119:61** [i]Ps 140:5 **119:62** [j]Ac 16:25 **119:63** [k]Ps 101:6-7 **119:64** [l]Ps 33:5 **119:67** [m]Jer 31:18-19; Heb 12:11 **119:68** [n]Ps 106:1; 107:1; Mt 19:17 [o]ver 12 **119:69** [p]Job 13:4; Ps 109:2 **119:70** [q]Ps 17:10; Isa 6:10; Ac 28:27 **119:72** [r]Ps 19:10; Pr 8:10-11, 19

119:73 [s]Job 10:8; Ps 100:3; 138:8; 139:13-16 **119:74** [t]Ps 34:2 **119:75** [u]Heb 12:5-11 **119:77** [v]ver 41 **119:78** [w]Jer 50:32 [x]ver 86, 161 **119:81** [y]Ps 84:2 **119:82** [z]Ps 69:3; La 2:11 **119:84** [a]Ps 39:4; Rev 6:10 **119:85** [b]Ps 35:7; Jer 18:20, 22 **119:86** [c]Ps 35:19 [d]Ps 109:26 [e]ver 78 **119:87** [f]Isa 58:2 **119:89** [g]Mt 24:34-35; 1Pe 1:25

י Yodh

73 Your hands made me[s] and formed me;
give me understanding to learn your
commands.
74 May those who fear you rejoice[t] when
they see me,
for I have put my hope in your word.
75 I know, LORD, that your laws are
righteous,
and that in faithfulness[u] you have
afflicted me.
76 May your unfailing love be my comfort,
according to your promise to your
servant.
77 Let your compassion[v] come to me that
I may live,
for your law is my delight.
78 May the arrogant[w] be put to shame for
wronging me without cause;[x]
but I will meditate on your precepts.
79 May those who fear you turn to me,
those who understand your statutes.
80 May I wholeheartedly follow your
decrees,
that I may not be put to shame.

כ Kaph

81 My soul faints[y] with longing for your
salvation,
but I have put my hope in your
word.
82 My eyes fail,[z] looking for your promise;
I say, "When will you comfort me?"
83 Though I am like a wineskin in the
smoke,
I do not forget your decrees.
84 How long[a] must your servant wait?
When will you punish my
persecutors?
85 The arrogant dig pits[b] to trap me,
contrary to your law.
86 All your commands are trustworthy;[c]
help me,[d] for I am being persecuted
without cause.[e]
87 They almost wiped me from the earth,
but I have not forsaken[f] your
precepts.
88 In your unfailing love preserve my life,
that I may obey the statutes of your
mouth.

ל Lamedh

89 Your word, LORD, is eternal;[g]
it stands firm in the heavens.

119:72 *thousands.* The measure of silver and gold is not specified in the Hebrew text; but this lack of detail underscores the point that the value is incalculable. In a similar fashion, Solomon left the bronze objects contributed to the temple unweighed because there were so many (1Ki 7:47). The most common weight of metal currency was the silver shekel, and 10 shekels might be regarded as an annual salary (Jdg 17:10). Other measures, such as the talent or mina, were larger (50 shekels per mina and 3,000 shekels per talent). The total weight in gold paid to Solomon as tribute each year was 666 talents (1Ki 10:14). By any measure, then, "thousands" of pieces of gold and silver would be an unimaginable fortune.

90 Your faithfulness[h] continues through
all generations;
you established the earth, and it
endures.[i]
91 Your laws endure[j] to this day,
for all things serve you.
92 If your law had not been my delight,
I would have perished in my
affliction.
93 I will never forget your precepts,
for by them you have preserved my
life.
94 Save me, for I am yours;
I have sought out your precepts.
95 The wicked are waiting to destroy me,
but I will ponder your statutes.
96 To all perfection I see a limit,
but your commands are boundless.

מ Mem

97 Oh, how I love your law!
I meditate[k] on it all day long.
98 Your commands are always with me
and make me wiser[l] than my
enemies.
99 I have more insight than all my
teachers,
for I meditate on your statutes.
100 I have more understanding than the
elders,
for I obey your precepts.[m]
101 I have kept my feet[n] from every evil
path
so that I might obey your word.
102 I have not departed from your laws,
for you yourself have taught me.
103 How sweet are your words to my taste,
sweeter than honey[o] to my mouth![p]
104 I gain understanding from your
precepts;
therefore I hate every wrong path.[q]

נ Nun

105 Your word is a lamp for my feet,
a light[r] on my path.
106 I have taken an oath[s] and confirmed it,
that I will follow your righteous
laws.
107 I have suffered much;
preserve my life, LORD, according to
your word.
108 Accept, LORD, the willing praise of my
mouth,[t]
and teach me your laws.

119:90 [h] Ps 36:5 [i] Ps 148:6; Ecc 1:4 **119:91** [j] Jer 33:25 **119:97** [k] Ps 1:2 **119:98** [l] Dt 4:6 **119:100** [m] Job 32:7-9 **119:101** [n] Pr 1:15 **119:103** [o] Ps 19:10; Pr 8:11 [p] Pr 24:13-14 **119:104** [q] ver 128 **119:105** [r] Pr 6:23 **119:106** [s] Ne 10:29 **119:108** [t] Hos 14:2; Heb 13:15

119:109 [u] Jdg 12:3; Job 13:14 **119:110** [v] Ps 140:5; 141:9 [w] ver 10 **119:112** [x] ver 33 **119:113** [y] Jas 1:8 **119:114** [z] Ps 32:7; 91:1 [a] ver 74 **119:115** [b] Ps 6:8; 139:19; Mt 7:23 **119:116** [c] Ps 54:4 [d] Ps 25:2; Ro 5:5; 9:33 **119:119** [e] Eze 22:18, 19 **119:120** [f] Hab 3:16 **119:122** [g] Job 17:3 **119:123** [h] ver 82 **119:124** [i] ver 12 **119:125** [j] Ps 116:16

109 Though I constantly take my life in my
hands,[u]
I will not forget your law.
110 The wicked have set a snare[v] for me,
but I have not strayed[w] from your
precepts.
111 Your statutes are my heritage forever;
they are the joy of my heart.
112 My heart is set on keeping your
decrees
to the very end.[a][x]

ס Samekh

113 I hate double-minded people,[y]
but I love your law.
114 You are my refuge and my shield;[z]
I have put my hope[a] in your word.
115 Away from me,[b] you evildoers,
that I may keep the commands of
my God!
116 Sustain me,[c] my God, according to
your promise, and I will live;
do not let my hopes be dashed.[d]
117 Uphold me, and I will be delivered;
I will always have regard for your
decrees.
118 You reject all who stray from your
decrees,
for their delusions come to nothing.
119 All the wicked of the earth you discard
like dross;[e]
therefore I love your statutes.
120 My flesh trembles[f] in fear of you;
I stand in awe of your laws.

ע Ayin

121 I have done what is righteous and
just;
do not leave me to my oppressors.
122 Ensure your servant's well-being;[g]
do not let the arrogant oppress me.
123 My eyes fail, looking for your
salvation,
looking for your righteous promise.[h]
124 Deal with your servant according to
your love
and teach me your decrees.[i]
125 I am your servant;[j] give me
discernment
that I may understand your statutes.
126 It is time for you to act, LORD;
your law is being broken.

[a] 112 Or *decrees / for their enduring reward*

119:105 *lamp.* In OT times, lamps were made of clay in the shape of a shallow cup or saucer that was pinched on one edge to support a wick. They were not carried outside for travel, lest oil spill out of the open top; rather, they were used indoors or in a cave, where not even moonlight illumined the darkness. By extension, this custom served as a metaphor for help to find one's way in any situation. In a culture for which the night held many terrors (91:5), the light of a lamp meant safety (18:28). An Assyrian prophecy refers to the goddess Ishtar shining light from a lamp (Akkadian *nūru* = Hebrew *ner*) upon King Esarhaddon in order to see and protect him (cf. Job 29:2–3). In this verse it is God's word that provides certainty—and in this sense, security—to the choices of the psalmist who is in distress (vv. 133–135).

127 Because I love your commands
more than gold,[k] more than pure gold,
128 and because I consider all your precepts right,
I hate every wrong path.[l]

פ Pe

129 Your statutes are wonderful;
therefore I obey them.
130 The unfolding of your words gives light;[m]
it gives understanding to the simple.[n]
131 I open my mouth and pant,[o]
longing for your commands.[p]
132 Turn to me and have mercy[q] on me,
as you always do to those who love your name.
133 Direct my footsteps according to your word;[r]
let no sin rule[s] over me.
134 Redeem me from human oppression,[t]
that I may obey your precepts.
135 Make your face shine[u] on your servant
and teach me your decrees.
136 Streams of tears[v] flow from my eyes,
for your law is not obeyed.[w]

צ Tsadhe

137 You are righteous,[x] LORD,
and your laws are right.[y]
138 The statutes you have laid down are righteous;[z]
they are fully trustworthy.
139 My zeal wears me out,[a]
for my enemies ignore your words.
140 Your promises have been thoroughly tested,[b]
and your servant loves them.
141 Though I am lowly and despised,[c]
I do not forget your precepts.
142 Your righteousness is everlasting
and your law is true.[d]
143 Trouble and distress have come upon me,
but your commands give me delight.
144 Your statutes are always righteous;
give me understanding[e] that I may live.

ק Qoph

145 I call with all my heart; answer me, LORD,
and I will obey your decrees.
146 I call out to you; save me
and I will keep your statutes.
147 I rise before dawn[f] and cry for help;
I have put my hope in your word.
148 My eyes stay open through the watches of the night,[g]
that I may meditate on your promises.
149 Hear my voice in accordance with your love;
preserve my life, LORD, according to your laws.
150 Those who devise wicked schemes are near,
but they are far from your law.
151 Yet you are near,[h] LORD,
and all your commands are true.[i]
152 Long ago I learned from your statutes
that you established them to last forever.[j]

ר Resh

153 Look on my suffering[k] and deliver me,
for I have not forgotten[l] your law.
154 Defend my cause[m] and redeem me;[n]
preserve my life according to your promise.
155 Salvation is far from the wicked,
for they do not seek out[o] your decrees.
156 Your compassion, LORD, is great;
preserve my life[p] according to your laws.
157 Many are the foes who persecute me,[q]
but I have not turned from your statutes.
158 I look on the faithless with loathing,[r]
for they do not obey your word.
159 See how I love your precepts;
preserve my life, LORD, in accordance with your love.
160 All your words are true;
all your righteous laws are eternal.

ש Sin and Shin

161 Rulers persecute me[s] without cause,
but my heart trembles at your word.
162 I rejoice in your promise
like one who finds great spoil.[t]
163 I hate and detest falsehood
but I love your law.
164 Seven times a day I praise you
for your righteous laws.
165 Great peace[u] have those who love your law,
and nothing can make them stumble.
166 I wait for your salvation,[v] LORD,
and I follow your commands.
167 I obey your statutes,
for I love them greatly.
168 I obey your precepts and your statutes,
for all my ways are known[w] to you.

119:127 [k] Ps 19:10
119:128 [l] ver 104, 163
119:130 [m] Pr 6:23 [n] Ps 19:7
119:131 [o] Ps 42:1 [p] ver 20
119:132 [q] Ps 25:16; 106:4
119:133 [r] Ps 17:5 [s] Ps 19:13; Ro 6:12
119:134 [t] Ps 142:6; Lk 1:74
119:135 [u] Nu 6:25; Ps 4:6
119:136 [v] Jer 9:1, 18 [w] Eze 9:4
119:137 [x] Ezr 9:15; Jer 12:1 [y] Ne 9:13
119:138 [z] Ps 19:7
119:139 [a] Ps 69:9; Jn 2:17
119:140 [b] Ps 12:6
119:141 [c] Ps 22:6
119:142 [d] Ps 19:7
119:144 [e] Ps 19:9
119:147 [f] Ps 5:3; 57:8; 108:2
119:148 [g] Ps 63:6
119:151 [h] Ps 34:18; 145:18 [i] ver 142
119:152 [j] Lk 21:33
119:153 [k] La 5:1 [l] Pr 3:1
119:154 [m] Mic 7:9 [n] 1Sa 24:15
119:155 [o] Job 5:4
119:156 [p] 2Sa 24:14
119:157 [q] Ps 7:1
119:158 [r] Ps 139:21
119:161 [s] 1Sa 24:11
119:162 [t] 1Sa 30:16
119:165 [u] Pr 3:2; Isa 26:3, 12; 32:17
119:166 [v] Ge 49:18
119:168 [w] Pr 5:21

ת Taw

[169]May my cry come[x] before you, LORD;
give me understanding according to your word.
[170]May my supplication come[y] before you;
deliver me[z] according to your promise.
[171]May my lips overflow with praise,[a]
for you teach me[b] your decrees.
[172]May my tongue sing of your word,
for all your commands are righteous.
[173]May your hand be ready to help[c] me,
for I have chosen[d] your precepts.
[174]I long for your salvation,[e] LORD,
and your law gives me delight.
[175]Let me live[f] that I may praise you,
and may your laws sustain me.
[176]I have strayed like a lost sheep.[g]
Seek your servant,
for I have not forgotten your commands.

Psalm 120

A song of ascents.

[1]I call on the LORD in my distress,[h]
and he answers me.
[2]Save me, LORD,
from lying lips[i]
and from deceitful tongues.[j]
[3]What will he do to you,
and what more besides,
you deceitful tongue?
[4]He will punish you with a warrior's sharp arrows,[k]
with burning coals of the broom bush.
[5]Woe to me that I dwell in Meshek,
that I live among the tents of Kedar![l]
[6]Too long have I lived
among those who hate peace.
[7]I am for peace;
but when I speak, they are for war.

Psalm 121

A song of ascents.

[1]I lift up my eyes to the mountains—
where does my help come from?
[2]My help comes from the LORD,
the Maker of heaven and earth.[m]
[3]He will not let your foot slip—
he who watches over you will not slumber;
[4]indeed, he who watches over Israel
will neither slumber nor sleep.
[5]The LORD watches over[n] you—
the LORD is your shade at your right hand;
[6]the sun[o] will not harm you by day,
nor the moon by night.
[7]The LORD will keep you from all harm[p]—
he will watch over your life;
[8]the LORD will watch over your coming and going
both now and forevermore.[q]

119:169 [x]Ps 18:6 **119:170** [y]Ps 28:2 [z]Ps 31:2 **119:171** [a]Ps 51:15 [b]Ps 94:12 **119:173** [c]Ps 37:24 [d]Jos 24:22 **119:174** [e]ver 166 **119:175** [f]Isa 55:3 **119:176** [g]Isa 53:6 **120:1** [h]Ps 102:2; Jnh 2:2 **120:2** [i]Pr 12:22 [j]Ps 52:4 **120:4** [k]Ps 45:5 **120:5** [l]Ge 25:13; Jer 49:28 **121:2** [m]Ps 115:15; 124:8 **121:5** [n]Isa 25:4 **121:6** [o]Ps 91:5; Isa 49:10; Rev 7:16 **121:7** [p]Ps 41:2; 91:10-12 **121:8** [q]Dt 28:6

120:4 *burning coals of the broom bush.* The trunk of the broom bush provided hard wood that made excellent charcoal.
120:5 *Meshek.* A central Anatolian kingdom conquered by Sargon II of Assyria and invaded by the Cimmerians from southern Russia. It is thought that they were incorporated under Lydian control after the conclusion of the Cimmerian wars. They are known to the Assyrians as Mushku and to Herodotus as the Moschi. At the end of the eighth century BC, the king of Mushku was Mita, known to the Greeks as Midas, the king with the golden touch. His tomb has been identified at Gordion and excavated. *Kedar.* The second son of Ishmael (Ge 25:13) and the name of a tribe that flourished from the eighth to the fourth centuries BC. The tribe is known from Assyrian and Late Babylonian texts as Qadar. The personal names of the Kedarites appear to have been related to the southern branch of the Semitic languages. These tribal peoples were based in the Arabian peninsula and often made their way into the Levant via the Sinai. They functioned as sheep breeders and caravanners at least as late as the Hellenistic period. Since Meshek and Kedar are in opposite directions from Israel, they are probably paired as representatives of remote and barbaric places.
121:1 *to the mountains.* It is possible that looking to the mountains evokes images of danger and difficulty, especially the rugged terrain of the hill country on approach to Jerusalem, where robbers lurked. At such times, the psalmist looks to Yahweh for protection. On the other hand, the "mountains" might be a figure of speech for the location of Jerusalem, situated on a hill in the southern mountain range of Israel, where God inhabits his temple (see note on 125:2). Looking to the mountains, then, is a search for divine help, similar in spirit to 123:1. For an Israelite living at a distance from Jerusalem or traveling there, looking toward the hills of Jerusalem would be "looking up" toward God's abode, his or her only source of help (125:2).
121:4 *sleep.* See note on 44:23.
121:6 *sun … moon.* The oppressive heat of the sun is a common human experience (see also Isa 49:10; Jnh 4:8). Whether or not the ancients thought that special dangers were posed by the moon is unknown (i.e., "moonstruck," also "lunacy"). Mesopotamian medical texts diagnose some illnesses in association with the "hand of the moon god," but this is not unique to this deity, and other gods and goddesses are named more frequently in this regard. One text mentions the moon-god (Sin) and the sun-god (Shamash) together in conjunction with the same illness. Even if the psalmist would have been disinclined to acknowledge the real potency of these foreign gods, this verse addresses any anxiety that might haunt the pilgrim. Most likely, the mention of the moon balances the parallelism with the sun, which extends the potential harms to include all dangers of the night, as well as of the day. The main danger with the moon in both ancient and classical times is in the connection made between the moon and what we know as epilepsy (cf. Mt 4:24).

PSALMS 120 – 134

Pilgrim Psalms

Psalms 120 – 134 are unified as a subcollection of the Psalter by the common title "A song of ascents." The background to this title has several interpretations. The Hebrew word translated "ascents" is related to the verb "to go up." Since the Jerusalem temple is geographically situated on a hilltop in the south-central mountain region of Israel, going to Jerusalem involved an "ascent." In Ezr 7:9, Ezra refers to his "journey" from Babylon to Jerusalem using this Hebrew word (using the verb in Ezr 2:1), so one interpretation is that this term recalls the return of captives from exile in Babylon. Perhaps the most common view is that pilgrims on their journey to Jerusalem for one of the three annual agricultural festivals sang these songs in anticipation of the festivities (Ex 23:14 – 17; 34:18 – 24; Lev 23:4 – 44; Dt 16:1 – 17). The imagery of Ps 126:5 – 6; 127:2; 128:2; 129:6 – 8; 132:15 might allude to agricultural harvests.

The Hebrew word translated "ascents" can mean "steps" and was used by Ezekiel to refer to the temple staircase (Eze 40:22,31). Later Jewish tradition suggests that these 15 songs were sung by Levites at the Festival of Tabernacles as they stood on each of the 15 steps leading to the main court of the second temple. This latter interpretation does not exclude a possible early use of these songs during pilgrimages to the annual festivals. Assuming that these psalms were used in conjunction with the great pilgrim festivals, they express a strong longing in anticipation of worship in Jerusalem. The heartfelt love for worship at God's temple is similar in spirit to the words of an Egyptian text practiced by scribes expressing their deep desire to see the holy city of the god Ptah in Memphis. ◆

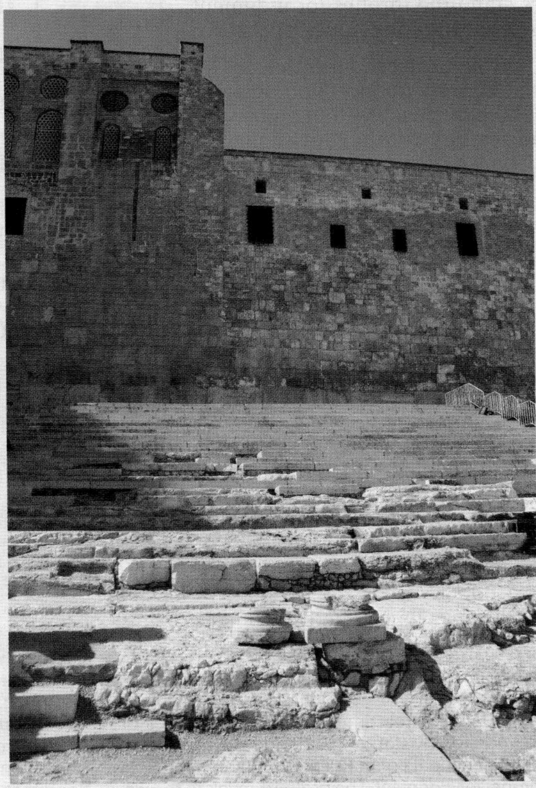

Southern steps to the Temple Mount. Ps 120 – 134 are unified as a subcollection of the Psalter by the common title "A song of ascents." The Hebrew word translated "ascents" can mean "steps," and was used by Ezekiel to refer to the temple staircase (Eze 40:22,31).

Kim Walton

Psalm 122

A song of ascents. Of David.

1 I rejoiced with those who said to me,
"Let us go to the house of the LORD."
2 Our feet are standing
in your gates, Jerusalem.

3 Jerusalem is built like a city
that is closely compacted together.
4 That is where the tribes go up—
the tribes of the LORD—
to praise the name of the LORD
according to the statute given to Israel.
5 There stand the thrones for judgment,
the thrones of the house of David.

6 Pray for the peace of Jerusalem:
"May those who love[r] you be secure.
7 May there be peace within your walls
and security within your citadels."
8 For the sake of my family and friends,
I will say, "Peace be within you."
9 For the sake of the house of the LORD our God,
I will seek your prosperity.[s]

Psalm 123

A song of ascents.

1 I lift up my eyes to you,
to you who sit enthroned[t] in heaven.
2 As the eyes of slaves look to the hand of their master,
as the eyes of a female slave look to the hand of her mistress,
so our eyes look to the LORD[u] our God,
till he shows us his mercy.
3 Have mercy on us, LORD, have mercy on us,
for we have endured no end of contempt.
4 We have endured no end
of ridicule from the arrogant,
of contempt from the proud.

Psalm 124

A song of ascents. Of David.

1 If the LORD had not been on our side—
let Israel say[v]—
2 if the LORD had not been on our side
when people attacked us,
3 they would have swallowed us alive
when their anger flared against us;
4 the flood would have engulfed us,
the torrent would have swept over us,
5 the raging waters
would have swept us away.

6 Praise be to the LORD,
who has not let us be torn by their teeth.
7 We have escaped like a bird
from the fowler's snare;[w]
the snare has been broken,
and we have escaped.
8 Our help is in the name of the LORD,
the Maker of heaven[x] and earth.

Psalm 125

A song of ascents.

1 Those who trust in the LORD are like Mount Zion,
which cannot be shaken[y] but endures forever.
2 As the mountains surround Jerusalem,
so the LORD surrounds[z] his people
both now and forevermore.

122:6 [r] Ps 51:18 **122:9** [s] Ne 2:10 **123:1** [t] Ps 11:4; 121:1; 141:8 **123:2** [u] Ps 25:15

124:1 [v] Ps 129:1 **124:7** [w] Ps 91:3; Pr 6:5 **124:8** [x] Ge 1:1; Ps 121:2; 134:3 **125:1** [y] Ps 46:5 **125:2** [z] Ps 121:8; Zec 2:4-5

122:2 *Jerusalem.* See the article "Hymns to Holy Cities," p. 927.
122:4 *tribes go up.* Three times a year all the males of Israel were required by statute to attend festivals in Jerusalem (see the article "Pilgrim Psalms," p. 1003).
122:5 *thrones for judgment.* The psalmist revels in the virtues of the city of Jerusalem, and one test of the quality of any community is its judicial system. A "throne" was a seat of authority where justice was dispensed (see the article "Enthronement in the Ancient Near East," p. 925). The city gates were places in ancient Israel where judicial matters were often settled (Dt 21:19; 22:15,24; 25:7; Ru 4:1–11; 2Sa 15:2), and archaeological excavations at the northern Israelite city of Dan have uncovered a throne platform at the entrance to the city where a magistrate possibly would have sat to render judgment. It would be likely that such seats of justice were in place at Jerusalem's gates, which would serve the needs of pilgrims on their annual visits to the city (see notes on Job 5:4; 29:7).
123:1 *lift up my eyes.* A natural attitude of prayer. At Ugarit, a city to the north of the land of Israel (c. 1300 BC) that shared common features with Canaanite and Israelite cultures, a prayer for help during a time of siege instructs worshipers to "lift your eyes to Baal."
124:4 *torrent.* Lit. "wadi," which can be a perennial stream, but more often refers to a dry riverbed that fills with water only during rain. A sudden rain storm can cause a flash flood that sweeps treacherously down the canyon.
124:7 *fowler's snare.* Remnants of an Egyptian bird snare have been found that enable reconstruction of its mechanism and operation. A circular net was held flat on the ground by two semicircular bows framing the circumference and hinged across the middle. A bird, lured by bait set at the middle of the net, would be caught when the two sides of the circle sprang upward to close around the bird. A variety of other netting systems were also employed (see note on 140:5).
125:1 *Mount Zion ... cannot be shaken.* See note on 46:5.
125:2 *mountains surround Jerusalem.* Jerusalem was built on a hill in the southern mountain range of Israel, and the temple was located at its crest (called Mount Zion, see note on 48:1–2). However, other hills exist in the surrounding area, some even higher than the temple mount. The psalmist uses this geographic image as a metaphor of Yahweh's protection.

3 The scepter of the wicked will not
remain[a]
over the land allotted to the
righteous,
for then the righteous might use
their hands to do evil.[b]
4 LORD, do good[c] to those who are good,
to those who are upright in heart.[d]
5 But those who turn[e] to crooked ways[f]
the LORD will banish with the
evildoers.

Peace be on Israel.[g]

Psalm 126

A song of ascents.

1 When the LORD restored[h] the fortunes
of[a] Zion,
we were like those who dreamed.[b]
2 Our mouths were filled with laughter,
our tongues with songs of joy.[i]
Then it was said among the nations,
"The LORD has done great things[j]
for them."
3 The LORD has done great things
for us,
and we are filled with joy.[k]

4 Restore our fortunes,[c] LORD,
like streams in the Negev.[l]
5 Those who sow with tears
will reap with songs of joy.[m]
6 Those who go out weeping,
carrying seed to sow,
will return with songs of joy,
carrying sheaves with them.

125:3 [a] Ps 89:22; Pr 22:8; Isa 14:5 [b] 1Sa 24:10; Ps 55:20 **125:4** [c] Ps 119:68 [d] Ps 7:10; 36:10; 94:15 **125:5** [e] Job 23:11 [f] Pr 2:15; Isa 59:8 [g] Ps 128:6 **126:1** [h] Ps 85:1; Hos 6:11 **126:2** [i] Job 8:21; Ps 51:14 [j] Ps 71:19 **126:3** [k] Isa 25:9 **126:4** [l] Isa 35:6; 43:19 **126:5** [m] Isa 35:10 **127:1** [n] Ps 78:69 [o] Ps 121:4 **127:2** [p] Ge 3:17 [q] Job 11:18 **127:3** [r] Ge 33:5 **127:5** [s] Pr 27:11 **128:1** [t] Ps 112:1 [u] Ps 119:1-3 **128:2** [v] Isa 3:10 [w] Ecc 8:12 **128:3** [x] Eze 19:10 [y] Ps 52:8; 144:12

Psalm 127

A song of ascents. Of Solomon.

1 Unless the LORD builds[n] the house,
the builders labor in vain.
Unless the LORD watches[o] over the city,
the guards stand watch in vain.
2 In vain you rise early
and stay up late,
toiling for food[p] to eat—
for he grants sleep[q] to[d] those he loves.

3 Children are a heritage from the LORD,
offspring a reward[r] from him.
4 Like arrows in the hands of a warrior
are children born in one's youth.
5 Blessed is the man
whose quiver is full of them.
They will not be put to shame
when they contend with their
opponents[s] in court.

Psalm 128

A song of ascents.

1 Blessed are all who fear the LORD,[t]
who walk in obedience to him.[u]
2 You will eat the fruit of your labor;[v]
blessings and prosperity[w] will be
yours.
3 Your wife will be like a fruitful vine[x]
within your house;
your children will be like olive shoots[y]
around your table.

[a] 1 Or *LORD brought back the captives to* [b] 1 Or *those restored to health* [c] 4 Or *Bring back our captives* [d] 2 Or *eat— / for while they sleep he provides for*

126:1 *restored the fortunes of Zion.* After the Persian king Cyrus conquered Babylon in 539 BC, he issued a proclamation allowing captive peoples, including Israelites, to return to their homelands and rebuild their cities and temples (2Ch 36:22–23; Ezr 1:1–11; 3:7). A document referred to as the Cyrus Cylinder records such a decree, though the Israelites are not explicitly included. Isaiah attributes Cyrus's proclamation to the sovereign providence of Yahweh (Isa 44:24—45:4). The psalmist states that the effect upon the returnees was dreamlike. See notes on 107:3; 147:3.

126:4 *streams in the Negev.* The wadis of Palestine are similar to overflowing rivers in the rainy season. However, they have little or no water during the summer season, precisely the time when water is most needed. In the Negev, the arid desert region south of Jerusalem, the periodic flooding of these wadis brought relief and life.

127:1 *house.* In OT usage, the Hebrew word can be used of a physical structure or of a family. This double meaning appears in Nathan's prophecy to David regarding the future temple and David's own future dynasty (2Sa 7:5,11b–12). The psalmist draws upon the same wordplay here, since "house" is parallel to "city" in v. 1 and is also echoed in the second half of the psalm as "children" (vv. 3,4). In either case, the Lord's help is the decisive factor in success. These are fundamental concerns for any society. Numerous Mesopotamian texts refer to the crucial role of deities in the building of a city. Prayers and incantations also recognized the necessity of divine help in procreation (see note on 113:9). The joining of these two themes is illustrated as well in the Sumerian Hymn to Nisaba. Neither houses nor cities can be built without the aid of the goddess Nisaba.

127:4–5 *arrows ... quiver.* Archery units were the most critical component of an ancient army, useful on foot, horseback (eventually), and as part of the chariot corps. The psalmist's choice of arrows as a metaphor is appropriate to the analogy of multiple children, but it also underscores the thought that the growth of the next generation is vital to the future well-being of both city and society.

128:3 *fruitful vine.* The metaphor of a vine is used for a wife, both for its connotations as a delectable fruit (SS 7:8) and for suggestions of fertility (Ge 49:22; Isa 5:1). *olive shoots.* A olive tree was versatile, useful for its wood, leaves and oil, but it also symbolized well-being (e.g., Ge 8:11) and splendor (e.g., Hos 14:6). It tenaciously produces new shoots even after being cut down. The size of the typical family in ancient Israel is difficult to estimate, but some studies suggest that an average number of live births might be four with a 50 percent mortality rate. Mesopotamians worshiped the birth-goddess Ninmah, to whom they would pray for posterity. For an Israelite, this was not just the natural hope that any human family would have, it was also related to the covenant blessings of family.

[4] Yes, this will be the blessing
for the man who fears the LORD.

[5] May the LORD bless you from Zion;[z]
may you see the prosperity of
Jerusalem
all the days of your life.

[6] May you live to see your children's
children —[a]
peace be on Israel.[b]

Psalm 129

A song of ascents.

[1] "They have greatly oppressed me from
my youth,"[c]
let Israel say;[d]

[2] "they have greatly oppressed me from
my youth,
but they have not gained the victory[e]
over me.

[3] Plowmen have plowed my back
and made their furrows long.

[4] But the LORD is righteous;[f]
he has cut me free from the cords of
the wicked."

[5] May all who hate Zion[g]
be turned back in shame.[h]

[6] May they be like grass on the roof,
which withers[i] before it can grow;

[7] a reaper cannot fill his hands with it,
nor one who gathers fill his arms.

[8] May those who pass by not say to
them,
"The blessing of the LORD be on you;
we bless you[j] in the name of the
LORD."

Psalm 130

A song of ascents.

[1] Out of the depths[k] I cry to you, LORD;

[2] Lord, hear my voice.[l]
Let your ears be attentive[m]
to my cry for mercy.

128:5 [z] Ps 20:2; 134:3 **128:6** [a] Ge 50:23; Job 42:16 [b] Ps 125:5 **129:1** [c] Ps 88:15; Hos 2:15 [d] Ps 124:1 **129:2** [e] Mt 16:18 **129:4** [f] Ps 119:137 **129:5** [g] Mic 4:11 [h] Ps 71:13 **129:6** [i] Ps 37:2 **129:8** [j] Ru 2:4; Ps 118:26 **130:1** [k] Ps 42:7; 69:2; La 3:55 **130:2** [l] Ps 28:2 [m] 2Ch 6:40; Ps 64:1

128:6 *children's children.* Seeing one's grandchildren was considered a blessing (Ge 48:11); living to see great-grandchildren was exceptional (Job 42:16). The tomb inscription of a non-Israelite priest who lived in Syria around 700 BC states: "On the day I died ... with my eyes I beheld children of the fourth generation." The psalmist measures a successful life in similar terms.

129:6 *grass on the roof.* Houses in ancient Israel were designed with flat roofs that served as major living and sleeping areas (1Sa 9:25 – 26; 2Sa 11:2). They were constructed of timber beams spanning the roof, crosshatched with branches, and covered with mud and perhaps a plaster top coat. Seeds would naturally settle and germinate in this material, but the root system would not find an adequate soil base, and new growth would soon whither.

130:1 *depths.* Deep waters, whether they be the ocean or a flood, suggested life-threatening danger to the ancient Israelite. The same Hebrew word is used in 69:2,14 in conjunction with "deep [ocean] waters" (cf. Jnh 2:3) and in Isa 51:9 – 10 with the chaos monster Rahab (see the article "Chaos Monsters," p. 953).

A modern farmer plows his field. Scripture often speaks in agricultural metaphors (Ps 129:3).

[3]If you, LORD, kept a record of sins,
Lord, who could stand?[n]
[4]But with you there is forgiveness,[o]
so that we can, with reverence,
serve you.[p]

[5]I wait for the LORD,[q] my whole being
waits,
and in his word[r] I put my hope.
[6]I wait for the Lord
more than watchmen[s] wait for the
morning,
more than watchmen wait for the
morning.[t]

[7]Israel, put your hope[u] in the LORD,
for with the LORD is unfailing
love
and with him is full redemption.
[8]He himself will redeem[v] Israel
from all their sins.

Psalm 131

A song of ascents. Of David.

[1]My heart is not proud,[w] LORD,
my eyes are not haughty;
I do not concern myself with great
matters
or things too wonderful for me.
[2]But I have calmed and quieted
myself,
I am like a weaned child with its
mother;
like a weaned child I am content.[x]
[3]Israel, put your hope[y] in the LORD
both now and forevermore.

130:3 [n] Ps 76:7; 143:2 **130:4** [o] Ex 34:7; Isa 55:7; Jer 33:8 [p] 1Ki 8:40 **130:5** [q] Ps 27:14; 33:20; Isa 8:17 [r] Ps 119:81 **130:6** [s] Ps 63:6 [t] Ps 119:147 **130:7** [u] Ps 131:3 **130:8** [v] Lk 1:68 **131:1** [w] Ps 101:5; Ro 12:16 **131:2** [x] Mt 18:3; 1Co 14:20 **131:3** [y] Ps 130:7

132:2 [z] Ge 49:24 **132:5** [a] Ac 7:46 **132:6** [b] 1Sa 17:12 [c] 1Sa 7:2 **132:7** [d] Ps 5:7 [e] Ps 99:5 **132:8** [f] Nu 10:35; Ps 78:61 **132:9** [g] Job 29:14; Isa 61:3, 10 **132:11** [h] Ps 89:3-4, 35

Psalm 132

132:8-10pp — 2Ch 6:41-42

A song of ascents.

[1]LORD, remember David
and all his self-denial.

[2]He swore an oath to the LORD,
he made a vow to the Mighty One of
Jacob:[z]
[3]"I will not enter my house
or go to my bed,
[4]I will allow no sleep to my eyes
or slumber to my eyelids,
[5]till I find a place[a] for the LORD,
a dwelling for the Mighty One of
Jacob."

[6]We heard it in Ephrathah,[b]
we came upon it in the fields of Jaar:[a][c]
[7]"Let us go to his dwelling place,[d]
let us worship at his footstool,[e]
saying,
[8]'Arise, LORD,[f] and come to your resting
place,
you and the ark of your might.
[9]May your priests be clothed with your
righteousness;[g]
may your faithful people sing for joy.'"

[10]For the sake of your servant David,
do not reject your anointed one.

[11]The LORD swore an oath to David,[h]
a sure oath he will not revoke:

[a] 6 Or *heard of it in Ephrathah, / we found it in the fields of Jearim.* (See 1 Chron. 13:5,6) (And no quotation marks around verses 7-9)

131:2 *weaned child.* Mothers nursed children as long as three years (1Sa 1:22–24). After weaning, the child would still be dependent, but in a quieter, less demanding manner than that of the infant who nurses.

132:1 *self-denial.* The opening prayer (vv. 1–10) recalls the commitment of David to establish a permanent place of worship for Yahweh, which is described in 1Ch 22:14 ("pains") using another form of the same Hebrew word for "self-denial" here. The labor of kings to build and restore worship shrines is a common theme in ancient Near East literature, and a favorable response from the deity is often associated with such acts of piety. Here, David's faithfulness is the basis of prayer for his dynasty.

132:4 *I will allow no sleep to my eyes.* This part of David's vow is similar to what was spoken concerning the Sumerian king Gudea in his temple project a thousand years before David's time. Zeal for the building project prevented his sleep. A statue of Gudea was placed in the completed temple with an inscription to remind the god of Gudea's work.

132:6 *Ephrathah.* David's homeland around Bethlehem (Ru 4:11; Mic 5:2), where he and his troops launched an expedition to locate the ark in the fields of Jaar and bring it to a permanent resting place of worship in Jerusalem (2Sa 6:1 — 7:1). *Jaar.* Probably an abbreviated reference to Kiriath Jearim, which was located over 10 miles (16 kilometers) to the northwest of Bethlehem (1Sa 6:21 — 7:1).

132:7–8 *footstool … the ark of your might.* See note on Ex 25:16.

132:10 *your anointed one.* For the king as "anointed," see notes on 1Sa 2:10; 10:1. David's anointed predecessor, King Saul, was rejected for unfaithfulness to God (1Sa 10:1; 13:13–14). Such warnings came through prophets, both in the OT and elsewhere in the ancient Near East. A letter containing a prophecy to Zimri-Lim, king of Mari, illustrates the threat of losing one's throne by action of the god. The god indicates that he can take away the throne of the king and he can restore it again — all based on whether the king fulfills the desire of the god. He can give lands as well as take them away. The psalmist prays for Yahweh's favor upon David's dynasty, but based on sure promises revealed in the prophetic speech that follows (vv. 11–18).

132:11 *The LORD swore an oath.* In the case of David, Yahweh made a prophetic promise that David's descendants would always be the rightful heirs to the throne (110:4; 2Sa 7:4–16; see notes on 89:3,19–37). Assyrian prophets spoke promises from the goddess Ishtar that she would secure King Esarhaddon on the throne of Assyria, extending this to his son and grandson. The Assyrian prophets also announced a covenant of kingship between the Assyrian gods and Esarhaddon, similar in some ways to the covenant promises announced through the prophet Nathan in 2Sa 7. The Assyrian prophecies were part of a

"One of your own descendants[i]
I will place on your throne.
12 If your sons keep my covenant
and the statutes I teach them,
then their sons will sit
on your throne[j] for ever and ever."
13 For the LORD has chosen Zion,[k]
he has desired it for his dwelling, saying,
14 "This is my resting place for ever and ever;[l]
here I will sit enthroned, for I have desired it.
15 I will bless her with abundant provisions;
her poor I will satisfy with food.[m]
16 I will clothe her priests[n] with salvation,
and her faithful people will ever sing for joy.
17 "Here I will make a horn[a] grow[o] for David
and set up a lamp[p] for my anointed one.
18 I will clothe his enemies with shame,[q]
but his head will be adorned with a radiant crown."

132:11 [i] 2Sa 7:12 **132:12** [j] Lk 1:32; Ac 2:30 **132:13** [k] Ps 48:1-2 **132:14** [l] Ps 68:16 **132:15** [m] Ps 107:9; 147:14 **132:16** [n] 2Ch 6:41 **132:17** [o] Eze 29:21; Lk 1:69 [p] 1Ki 11:36; 2Ch 21:7 **132:18** [q] Ps 35:26; 109:29 **133:1** [r] Ge 13:8; Heb 13:1 **133:2** [s] Ex 30:25 **133:3** [t] Dt 4:48 [u] Lev 25:21; Dt 28:8 [v] Ps 42:8

Psalm 133

A song of ascents. Of David.

1 How good and pleasant it is
when God's people live together[r] in unity!
2 It is like precious oil poured on the head,[s]
running down on the beard,
running down on Aaron's beard,
down on the collar of his robe.
3 It is as if the dew of Hermon[t]
were falling on Mount Zion.
For there the LORD bestows his blessing,[u]
even life forevermore.[v]

[a] *17 Horn* here symbolizes strong one, that is, king.

covenantal ceremony involving a "tablet of the covenant" (Akkadian *tuppi adê*), the Assyrian word for "covenant" being related to the Hebrew word translated "statutes" (*edut*) in 132:12 (see note on 2:7).

132:12 *If your sons keep my covenant.* While God's promises to the Davidic dynasty were unconditional, the enjoyment of a secure throne for any individual descendant of David was conditioned upon his keeping the law of God. The balance between unconditional promise and conditions for obedience is illustrated in ancient Near Eastern treaties (see notes on 89:3,27).

132:13 *the LORD has chosen Zion.* When the Assyrian king Tukulti-Ninurta I sought divine authorization to work on a temple of the god Assur, he asked whether Assur loved his mountain, Ebih. In vv. 13 – 14, the psalmist speaks of Yahweh's delight in choosing Mount Zion in Jerusalem as his dwelling place. In the ancient world, kingship and temple worship were closely related in the social system. Royal palace and temple complexes were frequently adjacent in city plans, so the welfare of the one was intimately connected with that of the other. The prophetic speech in vv. 11 – 18 reflects this close relationship between David's dynasty and his royal city, Jerusalem, where Yahweh chose to dwell in the temple.

132:14 *resting place ... enthroned.* In the ancient Near East, temples were viewed as the resting place of deity. When the gods were described as "resting" in their temples, they were seen as being enthroned in the base of operations from which they controlled the cosmos. "Rest" was the opposite of "unrest," and it represented stability and security for the people, the land and the cosmos. It expressed the god's engagement in the rule of the cosmos rather than the disengagement of relaxation. Israelites maintained the same ideology with regard to Yahweh. The temple was his resting place as he sat on his (invisible) throne in the Most Holy Place, with his feet on the footstool (the ark). "Resting" is the same as "sitting enthroned" over the ordered and stable kingdom and cosmos that he has established and maintains.

132:17 *horn.* Associated with bulls, so with this image Yahweh promises to strengthen the dynasty of David (see note on 18:2). *lamp.* The ongoing flame of a lamp points back to the promise that David's heirs would always have royal status (cf. 18:28; 1Ki 11:36; 2Ki 8:19). A proverbial expression in Mesopotamia utilized the metaphor of a fireplace; the presence or absence of fire in the family fireplace symbolized the perpetuity or cessation of offspring to carry on the family line.

133:2 *oil poured on the head.* Anointing with oil was used to symbolize God's authorization and empowerment of a king (see notes on 1Sa 2:10; 10:1) or other representative, such as a priest, for divine service. *Aaron's beard ... collar of his robe.* The ritual that set apart Aaron and his sons for priestly service involved pouring oil on their heads and garments (Ex 29:1,7,21,29; Lev 8:2,12). This "sacred anointing oil" (Ex 30:25) consisted of a mixture of oil and four spices (myrrh, cinnamon, calamus and cassia [Ex 30:23 – 24]) uniquely combined by the special skills of a perfumer (Ex 31:1 – 3,11; 37:29; 1Sa 8:13). People of the ancient Near East, from all levels of society, used aromatic oils for medical, cosmetic, ritual and magical purposes. In manufacture, perfumers transferred the fragrant properties of flowers and spices to an oil by either pressing the ingredients in linen or by steeping them in cold or hot animal fat. This product would in turn be mixed with some variety of vegetable oil (e.g., olive or sesame seed), then stored in ceramic or stone vessels for application. Sometimes multiple stages of processing brought a variety of ingredients together. For some highly refined perfumes, production could take months. The metaphor in Ps 133 draws upon associations of perfumed oil with joy, refreshment and well-being to describe unity within the covenant community (cf. Pr 27:9; see note on Ps 23:5).

133:3 *dew.* The Hebrew word can refer to condensation (e.g., Job 29:19) or light rain (e.g., Dt 32:2; 33:28; Pr 3:20). *Hermon.* One of the highest peaks in Israel's northern mountain region, it was well watered by rain, snow and dew, making it cool and lush (Jer 18:14). Vegetation in the dryer regions of southern Israel, where Jerusalem and Mount Zion were located, depended on dew and what little rain it received. Thus, for the temple mount (Mount Zion) to experience the dew of Mount Hermon pictures conditions of refreshment.

Psalm 134

A song of ascents.

1 Praise the LORD, all you servants[w] of
the LORD
who minister by night[x] in the house
of the LORD.
2 Lift up your hands[y] in the sanctuary
and praise the LORD.

3 May the LORD bless you from Zion,[z]
he who is the Maker of heaven[a] and
earth.

Psalm 135

135:15-20pp — Ps 115:4-11

1 Praise the LORD.[a]
Praise the name of the LORD;
praise him, you servants[b] of the
LORD,
2 you who minister in the house[c] of the
LORD,
in the courts[d] of the house of our
God.
3 Praise the LORD, for the LORD is good;[e]
sing praise to his name, for that is
pleasant.[f]
4 For the LORD has chosen Jacob[g] to be
his own,
Israel to be his treasured
possession.[h]

5 I know that the LORD is great,[i]
that our Lord is greater than all
gods.[j]
6 The LORD does whatever pleases him,[k]
in the heavens and on the earth,
in the seas and all their depths.

134:1 [w] Ps 135:1-2 [x] 1Ch 9:33 **134:2** [y] Ps 28:2; 1Ti 2:8 **134:3** [z] Ps 128:5 [a] Ps 124:8 **135:1** [b] Ps 113:1; 134:1 **135:2** [c] Lk 2:37 [d] Ps 116:19 **135:3** [e] Ps 119:68 [f] Ps 147:1 **135:4** [g] Dt 10:15; 1Pe 2:9 [h] Ex 19:5; Dt 7:6 **135:5** [i] Ps 48:1 [j] Ps 97:9 **135:6** [k] Ps 115:3

135:7 [l] Jer 10:13; Zec 10:1 [m] Job 28:25 [n] Job 38:22 **135:8** [o] Ex 12:12; Ps 78:51 **135:9** [p] Dt 6:22 [q] Ps 136:10-15 **135:10** [r] Nu 21:21-25; Ps 136:17-21 **135:11** [s] Nu 21:21 [t] Jos 12:7-24 **135:12** [u] Ps 78:55 **135:13** [v] Ex 3:15 [w] Ps 102:12 **135:14** [x] Dt 32:36

7 He makes clouds rise from the ends of
the earth;
he sends lightning with the rain[l]
and brings out the wind[m] from his
storehouses.[n]

8 He struck down the firstborn[o] of
Egypt,
the firstborn of people and
animals.
9 He sent his signs[p] and wonders into
your midst, Egypt,
against Pharaoh and all his
servants.[q]
10 He struck down many[r] nations
and killed mighty kings—
11 Sihon[s] king of the Amorites,
Og king of Bashan,
and all the kings of Canaan[t]—
12 and he gave their land as an
inheritance,[u]
an inheritance to his people Israel.
13 Your name, LORD, endures forever,[v]
your renown,[w] LORD, through all
generations.
14 For the LORD will vindicate his people
and have compassion on his
servants.[x]
15 The idols of the nations are silver and
gold,
made by human hands.
16 They have mouths, but cannot speak,
eyes, but cannot see.
17 They have ears, but cannot hear,
nor is there breath in their mouths.
18 Those who make them will be like
them,
and so will all who trust in them.

a 1 Hebrew *Hallelu Yah*; also in verses 3 and 21

134:1 *minister by night.* Priests and Levites served in the temple at all hours of the day and night. Evening duties included keeping the lampstand lit and the sacrifices burning, as well as guarding the gates (Ex 27:21; Lev 6:9; 1Ch 9:22–27). *minister.* More lit. "stand" (ESV; NRSV). This metaphoric use of the word "to stand" is common in the OT for a posture of ready service before a king or God (David was in Saul's "service" [1Sa 16:21–22]; angels await orders before Yahweh [1Ki 22:19–21]). This posture is illustrated by the many statues of standing worshipers that were placed in Mesopotamian temples. These representations typically show hands folded in front, representing a "self-binding" or surrender before the deity. Another gesture—that of the hands lifted up—is emphasized in v. 2 (see note on 28:2).

134:2 *Lift up your hands.* See note on 28:2. *in the sanctuary.* See note on 100:4.

135:7 *clouds … lightning … wind.* Associated with the storm-gods of Canaan and Mesopotamia (see notes on 29:7; 104:3,4). The god Baal is beckoned as one armed with clouds, winds, lightning bolts, and rains. This imagery is associated with the divine warrior, common to both Israel and her neighbors, the basis for the victories recalled in vv. 10–12. The terminology also conveys something of how the Israelites and their neighbors thought about weather systems. In the Sumerian composition entitled "Enki and the Ordering of the World," Ishkur, the weather-god, opens the gates of heaven. *from the ends of the earth.* This was the way Mesopotamians understood the origin of clouds. In Mesopotamian cosmology, the "ends of the earth" refers to the horizon. This is where the gates of heaven are located, because the sun is seen as setting there as it goes through the gates of heaven. *wind from his storehouses.* See the article "Cosmic Geography," p. 836.

135:8 *He struck down the firstborn of Egypt.* See Ex 11.

135:15 *idols of the nations.* OT law prohibits the manufacture of images of Yahweh, the god of Israel (Ex 20:4,23; Dt 4:15–19; 5:8). This was a unique religious custom, since all other ancient Near Eastern religions used statues and various other symbols to represent their gods in worship. People believed that a statue contained the personality of the god it represented; in effect, the statue was a manifestation of the deity among the people. In a Mesopotamian text, the god Marduk claims that the wood of his cult statue is "the flesh of the gods," which is adorned with precious metals and gems. But the psalmist declares that these idols are really nothing more than human crafts, a denial of the claims made about idols.

PSALM 135:15–18

Making an Idol

While objects representing deities were common in the ancient world, only statues created under carefully prescribed conditions and with proper rituals were regarded as real images that the deity inhabited. Some images were made of stone, cast of solid metal or molded from clay; however, the primary statues of deities that dominated the temples were usually carved of wood and covered with a thin layer of gold or silver and adorned with precious stones and elegant clothing. The Assyrian king Esarhaddon commissioned a major restoration of temples and images. For the creation of cult statues, he brought carpenters, goldsmiths, metalworkers and stonecutters—all skilled artisans knowledgeable in the mysteries—into the temple, and he decorated their images with ornaments and jewelry.

The ritual that brought the image to life was referred to as the "mouth washing," which possibly paralleled the work done by a midwife to clean the breathing passage of a newborn. It required the priest to whisper into the ear of the statue and to open its eyes to see and its mouth to breath. The ritual states, "This statue without its mouth opened cannot smell incense, cannot eat food, nor drink water." Then the priest swore an oath that he did not make the statue. The Egyptians, likewise, had a ritual called "Opening the Mouth and the Eyes," which operated with different actions and beliefs, but was performed to quicken the manufactured image into a living representation of the deity. Similar to the Mesopotamian ritual, the priests disavowed any hand in its manufacture. Priests in both Mesopotamia and Egypt daily attended to the statues—washing, clothing and feeding them as though they were living gods. Praise was offered to their hearing, and priests or prophets would convey messages purportedly spoken by these gods. ◆

[19] All you Israelites, praise the LORD;
house of Aaron, praise the LORD;
[20] house of Levi, praise the LORD;
you who fear him, praise the LORD.
[21] Praise be to the LORD from Zion,[y]
to him who dwells in Jerusalem.

Praise the LORD.

Psalm 136

[1] Give thanks to the LORD, for he is good.[z]
His love endures forever.[a]
[2] Give thanks to the God of gods.[b]
His love endures forever.
[3] Give thanks to the Lord of lords:
His love endures forever.

[4] to him who alone does great wonders,[c]
His love endures forever.
[5] who by his understanding[d] made the heavens,[e]
His love endures forever.
[6] who spread out the earth[f] upon the waters,[g]
His love endures forever.
[7] who made the great lights[h]—
His love endures forever.
[8] the sun to govern[i] the day,
His love endures forever.
[9] the moon and stars to govern the night;
His love endures forever.

[10] to him who struck down the firstborn[j] of Egypt
His love endures forever.
[11] and brought Israel out[k] from among them
His love endures forever.

135:21 [y]Ps 134:3 **136:1** [z]Ps 106:1 [a]1Ch 16:34; 2Ch 20:21 **136:2** [b]Dt 10:17 **136:4** [c]Ps 72:18 **136:5** [d]Pr 3:19; Jer 51:15 [e]Ge 1:1 **136:6** [f]Ge 1:9; Jer 10:12 [g]Ps 24:2 **136:7** [h]Ge 1:14, 16 **136:8** [i]Ge 1:16 **136:10** [j]Ex 12:29; Ps 135:8 **136:11** [k]Ex 6:6; 12:51

136:1 *Give thanks.* This phrase (a single word in Hebrew) implies acknowledgment to God for specific acts of deliverance, and its utterance accompanied the peace/fellowship offering (see notes on 22:26; 51:16–17; see also the article "Sin and Sacrifice in the Ancient Near East," p. 932).
136:6 *earth upon the waters.* See the article "Cosmic Geography," p. 836.

[12] with a mighty hand and outstretched
arm;[l]
His love endures forever.
[13] to him who divided the Red Sea[a][m]
asunder
His love endures forever.
[14] and brought Israel through[n] the midst
of it,
His love endures forever.
[15] but swept Pharaoh and his army into
the Red Sea;[o]
His love endures forever.

[16] to him who led his people through the
wilderness;[p]
His love endures forever.

[17] to him who struck down great kings,[q]
His love endures forever.
[18] and killed mighty kings[r] —
His love endures forever.
[19] Sihon king of the Amorites[s]
His love endures forever.
[20] and Og king of Bashan —
His love endures forever.
[21] and gave their land[t] as an inheritance,
His love endures forever.
[22] an inheritance to his servant Israel.
His love endures forever.

[23] He remembered us[u] in our low estate
His love endures forever.
[24] and freed us from our enemies.[v]
His love endures forever.
[25] He gives food[w] to every creature.
His love endures forever.
[26] Give thanks to the God of heaven.
His love endures forever.

136:12 [l] Dt 4:34; Ps 44:3 **136:13** [m] Ex 14:21; Ps 78:13 **136:14** [n] Ex 14:22 **136:15** [o] Ex 14:27; Ps 135:9 **136:16** [p] Ex 13:18 **136:17** [q] Ps 135:9-12 **136:18** [r] Dt 29:7 **136:19** [s] Nu 21:21-25 **136:21** [t] Jos 12:1 **136:23** [u] Ps 113:7 **136:24** [v] Ps 107:2 **136:25** [w] Ps 104:27; 145:15

Psalm 137

[1] By the rivers of Babylon[x] we sat and
wept[y]
when we remembered Zion.
[2] There on the poplars
we hung our harps,
[3] for there our captors asked us for
songs,
our tormentors demanded[z] songs of
joy;
they said, "Sing us one of the songs
of Zion!"

[4] How can we sing the songs of the LORD
while in a foreign land?
[5] If I forget you, Jerusalem,
may my right hand forget its skill.
[6] May my tongue cling to the roof[a] of my
mouth
if I do not remember you,
if I do not consider Jerusalem
my highest joy.

[7] Remember, LORD, what the Edomites[b]
did
on the day Jerusalem fell.[c]
"Tear it down," they cried,
"tear it down to its foundations!"
[8] Daughter Babylon, doomed to
destruction,[d]
happy is the one who repays you
according to what you have done
to us.
[9] Happy is the one who seizes your
infants
and dashes them[e] against the rocks.

137:1 [x] Eze 1:1, 3 [y] Ne 1:4 **137:3** [z] Ps 80:6 **137:6** [a] Eze 3:26 **137:7** [b] Jer 49:7; La 4:21-22; Eze 25:12 [c] Ob 1:11 **137:8** [d] Isa 13:1, 19; Jer 25:12, 26; Jer 50:15; Rev 18:6 **137:9** [e] 2Ki 8:12; Isa 13:16

[a] 13 Or *the Sea of Reeds*; also in verse 15

137:1 *rivers of Babylon.* The city of Babylon was built on the banks of the Euphrates River; however, the heartland of the Babylonian Empire embraced both the Euphrates and Tigris River systems, as well as countless canals dug for navigation and irrigation. It was in this region that many exiles from the final downfall of Judah were settled (see note on 107:3).
137:2 *poplars.* This tall tree is common along the banks and waterways of the Euphrates River, although the same word might also refer to a type of willow. *harps.* See the article "Music and Musicians," p. 924.
137:3 *songs of Zion.* See the article "Hymns to Holy Cities," p. 927.
137:7 *Edomites.* Descendants of Jacob's brother Esau, who settled the region southeast of the Dead Sea (Ge 36:1 – 8); these tribes eventually became traditional enemies of Israel (Ps 60:9; Nu 20:14 – 21; 2Sa 8:13 – 14; 2Ch 20:2,10). They were part of the mercenary forces that destroyed Jerusalem at the time of the Babylonian invasion (586 BC; see Ob 10 – 11). Diplomatic relations during this time of crisis were complicated, with alliances forming and dissolving as each nation sought its own advantage (2Ki 24:2; Jer 27:1 – 7). No extant texts outside the Bible attest to a Babylonian-Edomite alliance, but a military letter possibly dating to this time refers to an order from the king of Judah that troops be moved in the southlands in order to defend against the Edomites.
137:8 *Daughter Babylon.* The term "daughter" can refer to the people who reside in the named location (cf. Isa 47:1; Zep 3:14).
137:9 The dark realities of warfare in the ancient Near East often doomed the innocent to destruction. While soldiers and men were often subject to dismemberment and impalement, women and children might also be ravished and slaughtered (Hos 10:14; see note on Ps 79:2). Pregnant women might be lacerated in order to extract the fruit of their wombs, and infants were smashed on the ground (2Ki 8:12; Hos 13:16; Am 1:13; Na 3:10) — all to eliminate the next generation as well as the present one. The psalmist is borrowing imagery from prophetic descriptions of judgment announced against Babylon for the atrocities it committed against Jerusalem (Isa 13:16; Jer 6:11; 51:56). The use of such language is a graphic description of the cruelty of warfare in the ancient Near East (see note on Ps 18:38) The Persian conquest of Babylon in 539 BC was a peaceful takeover, but the city was razed by the Persian king Xerxes in response to a revolt in 482 BC. Under subsequent rulers, efforts were put into rebuilding from time to time, but Babylon never fully recovered, fell into decay, and was virtually abandoned by about 100 BC. See the article "Imprecations and Incantations," p. 937.

Psalm 138

Of David.

1 I will praise you, LORD, with all my heart;
before the "gods"[f] I will sing your praise.
2 I will bow down toward your holy temple[g]
and will praise your name
for your unfailing love and your faithfulness,
for you have so exalted your solemn decree
that it surpasses your fame.[h]
3 When I called, you answered me;
you greatly emboldened me.

4 May all the kings of the earth[i] praise you, LORD,
when they hear what you have decreed.
5 May they sing of the ways of the LORD,
for the glory of the LORD is great.

6 Though the LORD is exalted, he looks kindly on the lowly;[j]
though lofty, he sees them[k] from afar.
7 Though I walk[l] in the midst of trouble,
you preserve my life.
You stretch out your hand against the anger of my foes;[m]
with your right hand[n] you save me.[o]
8 The LORD will vindicate[p] me;
your love, LORD, endures forever—
do not abandon the works of your hands.[q]

138:1 [f] Ps 95:3; 96:4
138:2 [g] 1Ki 8:29; Ps 5:7; 28:2 [h] Isa 42:21
138:4 [i] Ps 102:15
138:6 [j] Ps 113:6; Isa 57:15 [k] Pr 3:34; Jas 4:6
138:7 [l] Ps 23:4 [m] Jer 51:25 [n] Ps 20:6 [o] Ps 71:20
138:8 [p] Ps 57:2; Php 1:6 [q] Job 10:3,8; 14:15
139:1 [r] Ps 17:3 [s] Jer 12:3
139:2 [t] 2Ki 19:27 [u] Mt 9:4; Jn 2:24
139:3 [v] Job 31:4
139:4 [w] Heb 4:13
139:5 [x] Ps 34:7
139:6 [y] Job 42:3; Ro 11:33
139:7 [z] Jer 23:24; Jnh 1:3
139:8 [a] Am 9:2-3 [b] Pr 15:11

Psalm 139

For the director of music.
Of David. A psalm.

1 You have searched me,[r] LORD,
and you know[s] me.
2 You know when I sit and when I rise;[t]
you perceive my thoughts[u] from afar.
3 You discern my going out and my lying down;
you are familiar with all my ways.[v]
4 Before a word is on my tongue
you, LORD, know it completely.[w]
5 You hem me in[x] behind and before,
and you lay your hand upon me.
6 Such knowledge is too wonderful for me,
too lofty[y] for me to attain.

7 Where can I go from your Spirit?
Where can I flee[z] from your presence?
8 If I go up to the heavens,[a] you are there;
if I make my bed[b] in the depths, you are there.

138:1 *before the "gods."* See the article "Divine Council," p. 615.
138:2 *name.* Refers to the reputation of God's character. Some similarity of thought exists between this psalm and the exaltation of Marduk. After Marduk answered the call to deliver his kindred gods from destruction, they declared Marduk's kingship over all the gods, acclaimed his 50 names and decreed that "his word is truth, what he says is not changed." By virtue of the fact that Yahweh delivered the psalmist (v. 3), he has exalted Yahweh's name and "decree"; so the psalmist declares God's right to receive homage from the psalmist and all kings (v. 4).
138:8 *vindicate me.* There existed in Mesopotamian religion the belief that the deities decreed the fate of individuals, often decided in the council of gods and goddesses (see 139:16). Ashurbanipal praised Assur as the "determiner of fates" and proclaimed that his own "fate" was to exercise kingship and restore the shrines of the gods. The guidance of the gods was necessary for the success of anyone's undertaking. The gods could also decree evil intentions for someone.
139:2–4 *You know … perceive … discern … know.* It is not unusual in the ancient world for it to be implied that gods or kings know everything, or that there are no limits to their knowledge. King Nabonidus claimed to be wise, knowing everything and seeing hidden things (cf. 2Sa 14:19). In most cases, however, this is little more than patronization. While there is no reason to see this psalm in that light, it should be recognized that the context is judicial rather than theological. Yahweh is being addressed as the judge who is in possession of all the information for judging the psalmist's case wisely and fairly. In Babylonian literature, Shamash is praised as one who (as the sun-god) sees all the lands, but he is also said to know their intentions and see their footprints. It is more common for the gods to be attributed boundless wisdom.
139:7–10 *Where can I go … from your presence? you are there … you are there … even there.* It is difficult to distinguish the idea of having access to every place from the idea of being simultaneously in all places. The former is all that is demanded from the words of the psalmist, and is likewise the norm in the ancient Near East. Since the sun-god is usually the god of justice, and there is nowhere his light does not shine, he sees all (cf. vv. 11–12). Even the netherworld was known to him, because the sun was believed to traverse the netherworld during the night as he moved from the western horizon to the east to rise again. As a result, the divine judge would again (see note on vv. 2–4) have all the information needed. Nothing could have been done secretly. There is no concept in the ancient Near East or in the OT of deity being in every place simultaneously in the way that omnipresence is construed in Christian theology, though this does not negate the legitimacy of that theology as it later developed.
139:8 *depths.* This Hebrew word is traditionally translated "Sheol," the underworld of the dead (see the articles "Death and Sheol," p. 833; "Death and the Underworld," p. 907). In addition to the terrestrial world of human existence, there were two other realms: the heavens and the underworld (see the article "Cosmic Geography," p. 836). This conception accords with one of the common Mesopotamian presentations of the universe consisting of the heavens above and the underworld beneath. In a Mesopotamian hymn to the goddess Gula and her consort, the

[9]If I rise on the wings of the dawn,
if I settle on the far side of the sea,
[10]even there your hand will guide me,[c]
your right hand will hold me fast.
[11]If I say, "Surely the darkness will hide me
and the light become night around me,"
[12]even the darkness will not be dark[d] to you;
the night will shine like the day,
for darkness is as light to you.

[13]For you created my inmost being;[e]
you knit me together[f] in my mother's womb.
[14]I praise you because I am fearfully and wonderfully made;
your works are wonderful,[g]
I know that full well.
[15]My frame was not hidden from you
when I was made in the secret place,
when I was woven together[h] in the depths of the earth.[i]
[16]Your eyes saw my unformed body;
all the days ordained for me were written in your book
before one of them came to be.
[17]How precious to me are your thoughts,[a] God![j]
How vast is the sum of them!
[18]Were I to count them,
they would outnumber the grains of sand—
when I awake, I am still with you.

[19]If only you, God, would slay the wicked![k]
Away from me,[l] you who are bloodthirsty!
[20]They speak of you with evil intent;
your adversaries misuse your name.[m]
[21]Do I not hate those[n] who hate you, LORD,
and abhor those who are in rebellion against you?
[22]I have nothing but hatred for them;
I count them my enemies.
[23]Search me,[o] God, and know my heart;[p]
test me and know my anxious thoughts.
[24]See if there is any offensive way in me,
and lead me[q] in the way everlasting.

139:10 [c]Ps 23:3 **139:12** [d]Job 34:22; Da 2:22 **139:13** [e]Ps 119:73 [f]Job 10:11 **139:14** [g]Ps 40:5 **139:15** [h]Job 10:11 [i]Ps 63:9 **139:17** [j]Ps 40:5 **139:19** [k]Isa 11:4 [l]Ps 119:115 **139:20** [m]Jude 15 **139:21** [n]2Ch 19:2; Ps 31:6; 119:113; 119:158 **139:23** [o]Job 31:6; Ps 26:2 [p]Jer 11:20 **139:24** [q]Ps 5:8; 143:10; Pr 15:9 **140:1** [r]Ps 17:13 [s]Ps 18:48 **140:2** [t]Ps 36:4; 56:6

Psalm 140[b]

For the director of music. A psalm of David.

[1]Rescue me,[r] LORD, from evildoers;
protect me from the violent,[s]
[2]who devise evil plans[t] in their hearts
and stir up war every day.

[a] 17 Or *How amazing are your thoughts concerning me*
[b] In Hebrew texts 140:1-13 is numbered 140:2-14.

god is described as one "who examines the heights of heaven, who investigates the bottom of the netherworld." The Mesopotamian "Poem of the Righteous Sufferer" laments: "In good times people speak of going up to heaven. When they become worried they mutter about going down to the underworld." A Canaanite king writes to Pharaoh, his overlord, about his ultimate dependence on the Egyptian king: "Should we go up into the sky, or should we go down into the netherworld, our head is in your hand." Similarly, the psalmist affirms that God is present in every conceivable domain.

139:9 This verse may be adopting solar terminology (rising on the dawn = east; setting on the far side of the sea = west). It is not unusual for the heavenly bodies (or the gods that are associated with them) to be portrayed with wings, but the phrase "wings of the dawn" does not occur in Akkadian. In Egyptian hymns, when the sun set, it descended into the underworld of the dead in order to bring light there as well. The directions of rising and setting suggest that the psalmist is identifying himself with the movement of the sun and continues to refer to God's access to the world of the living as well as the world of the dead.

139:13 *knit me together.* The creation of the individual by a deity was a known concept in Mesopotamia and Egypt, as well as in Israel. In the Egyptian Great Hymn to Aten (see the article "The Great Hymn to Aten," p. 982), the writer declares that the god creates the seed in women, and shapes fluids into human beings. In another Egyptian image, they imagined the god Khnum fashioning body parts on a potter's wheel.

Mesopotamian myth focuses on the creation of human beings in general (see note on 103:14), but in royal theology one sees an emphasis on personal creation of the individual king. The Assyrian king Ashurbanipal (c. 650 BC) states in a hymn that he has been created by the hands of the great gods. In another text, the god Nabu indicates that he was the creator of Ashurbanipal's body. The significance of these affirmations is to bolster confidence in the protective care of the gods for Ashurbanipal, whom they uniquely created. But this personal touch also extended to more ordinary people, as evidenced in a scribe's prayer in which he claims to have been "begotten" and "created" by the god. A similar point is being made in this psalm.

139:15 *depths of the earth.* This is poetic language for the unseen realm of the womb, which is like the hidden recesses of the earth (see the articles "Death and Sheol," p. 833; "Cosmic Geography," p. 836; "Death and the Underworld," p. 907).

139:16 *days ordained for me.* Along with the concept of the individual person's creation (see note on v. 13), the Mesopotamians affirmed the related idea that the days of life were ordained by the gods (see note on 69:28). In the Gilgamesh Epic, the Mesopotamian flood hero, Utnapishtim, tells Gilgamesh that it is the great gods in assembly who decree the days of life and death, but they do not disclose to any individual when their death will take place. According to Mesopotamian thought, the decisions of the divine assembly were recorded on a "Tablet of Destinies," which possibly included the course of life for each person. This was not an unalterable "fate" as in Greek myth, but it set forth the will of the gods. When a person died, it was said that he "went to his fate." On the other hand, one who dies on "a day not his fate" suffered a premature death.

139:23 *Search me.* See note on 19:7.

[3] They make their tongues as sharp as[u] a
 serpent's;
 the poison of vipers[v] is on their lips.[a]
[4] Keep me safe,[w] LORD, from the hands
 of the wicked;[x]
 protect me from the violent,
 who devise ways to trip my feet.
[5] The arrogant have hidden a snare for
 me;
 they have spread out the cords of
 their net
 and have set traps[y] for me along my
 path.

[6] I say to the LORD, "You are my God."[z]
 Hear, LORD, my cry for mercy.[a]

140:3 [u] Ps 57:4 [v] Ps 58:4; Jas 3:8 **140:4** [w] Ps 141:9 [x] Ps 71:4 **140:5** [y] Ps 31:4; 35:7 **140:6** [z] Ps 16:2 [a] Ps 116:1; 143:1 **140:7** [b] Ps 28:8 **140:8** [c] Ps 10:2-3 **140:9** [d] Ps 7:16 **140:10** [e] Ps 11:6; 21:9

[7] Sovereign LORD,[b] my strong deliverer,
 you shield my head in the day of
 battle.
[8] Do not grant the wicked[c] their desires,
 LORD;
 do not let their plans succeed.
[9] Those who surround me proudly rear
 their heads;
 may the mischief of their lips engulf
 them.[d]
[10] May burning coals fall on them;
 may they be thrown into the fire,[e]
 into miry pits, never to rise.

[a] 3 The Hebrew has *Selah* (a word of uncertain meaning) here and at the end of verses 5 and 8.

140:3 *poison of vipers.* There are over 20 species of poisonous snakes in the region around Israel. The word "serpent's" is generic. The exact identification of the word translated "vipers" is unknown, since the word only occurs here; it is probably not a spider, as one tradition has suggested, because of the parallelism with "serpent's." The association between a biting snake and the action of its tongue is illustrated in a Mesopotamian snake bite incantation. This association makes the snake a particularly good metaphor for lethally dangerous speech. The Hebrew word for poison also means "heat," which is a common image for poisonous bites. See note on 58:4 – 5. **140:5** *snare … net … traps.* The ancients used a variety of netting systems. One technique was simply to throw a net over the bird or animal (Eze 32:3). Another type involved spreading the net on the ground and using a cord to draw the net around the prey (Pr 1:17). Egyptian art depicts such a system, where rectangular-shaped nets are placed on the ground alongside one another and drawn together over the birds. A net might also be erected vertically and the animal driven into it. For a "snare" that employed a trigger mechanism, see note on 124:7. Another metaphor that may be present here is found in the ancient Near Eastern expression of magical hexes and incantations as being snares or nets that can bind a person.
140:10 *burning coals … fire.* Literal and metaphoric catastrophes that the ancients regarded appropriate for enemies. The curse section of a treaty between the Assyrian king Esarhaddon (c. 680 BC) and his vassals warns that burning coals rather than dew will rain on the disobedient vassal's land. An Assyrian prophecy during the reign of the same king reports that the god Assur rained upon his enemies "fire of heaven." Concerning the fate of a rebellious brother, the Assyrian king Ashurbanipal (c. 650 BC) reports that the gods threw him into a burning conflagration (he had died when the palace burned). *miry pits.* This

Relief depicting a variety of trapping tools, 645 to 635 BC, Nineveh. See note on Ps 140:5.

Kim Walton. The British Museum.

[11] May slanderers not be established in
the land;
may disaster hunt down the
violent.[f]

[12] I know that the LORD secures justice
for the poor
and upholds the cause[g] of the
needy.[h]

[13] Surely the righteous will praise your
name,[i]
and the upright will live[j] in your
presence.

Psalm 141

A psalm of David.

[1] I call to you, LORD, come quickly[k]
to me;
hear me[l] when I call to you.

[2] May my prayer be set before you like
incense;[m]
may the lifting up of my hands[n] be
like the evening sacrifice.[o]

[3] Set a guard over my mouth, LORD;
keep watch over the door of my
lips.

[4] Do not let my heart be drawn to
what is evil
so that I take part in wicked
deeds
along with those who are evildoers;
do not let me eat their delicacies.[p]

[5] Let a righteous man strike me — that is
a kindness;
let him rebuke me[q] — that is oil on
my head.[r]
My head will not refuse it,
for my prayer will still be against
the deeds of evildoers.

[6] Their rulers will be thrown down from
the cliffs,
and the wicked will learn that my
words were well spoken.

140:11 [f] Ps 34:21
140:12 [g] Ps 9:4 [h] Ps 35:10
140:13 [i] Ps 97:12 [j] Ps 11:7
141:1 [k] Ps 22:19; 70:5 [l] Ps 143:1
141:2 [m] Rev 5:8; 8:3 [n] 1Ti 2:8 [o] Ex 29:39,41
141:4 [p] Pr 23:6
141:5 [q] Pr 9:8 [r] Ps 23:5
141:7 [s] Ps 53:5
141:8 [t] Ps 25:15 [u] Ps 2:12
141:9 [v] Ps 140:4 [w] Ps 38:12
141:10 [x] Ps 35:8
142:1 [y] Ps 30:8
142:2 [z] Isa 26:16
142:3 [a] Ps 140:5; 143:4,7
142:4 [b] Ps 31:11; Jer 30:17
142:5 [c] Ps 46:1 [d] Ps 16:5 [e] Ps 27:13
142:6 [f] Ps 17:1 [g] Ps 79:8; 116:6

[7] They will say, "As one plows and
breaks up the earth,
so our bones have been scattered at
the mouth[s] of the grave."

[8] But my eyes are fixed[t] on you,
Sovereign LORD;
in you I take refuge[u] — do not give
me over to death.

[9] Keep me safe[v] from the traps set by
evildoers,
from the snares[w] they have laid for
me.

[10] Let the wicked fall[x] into their own
nets,
while I pass by in safety.

Psalm 142[a]

A *maskil*[b] of David. When he was
in the cave. A prayer.

[1] I cry aloud to the LORD;
I lift up my voice to the LORD for
mercy.[y]

[2] I pour out before him my complaint;[z]
before him I tell my trouble.

[3] When my spirit grows faint[a] within
me,
it is you who watch over my way.
In the path where I walk
people have hidden a snare for me.

[4] Look and see, there is no one at my
right hand;
no one is concerned for me.
I have no refuge;
no one cares[b] for my life.

[5] I cry to you, LORD;
I say, "You are my refuge,[c]
my portion[d] in the land of the
living."[e]

[6] Listen to my cry,[f]
for I am in desperate need;[g]

[a] In Hebrew texts 142:1-7 is numbered 142:2-8.
[b] Title: Probably a literary or musical term

Hebrew word is used only here in the OT. It appears to be related to a Ugaritic word for chasm or abyss (Ugaritic *mhmrt* = Hebrew *mahamor*). In the Ugaritic Baal Cycle, the god Baal is swallowed by Mot, the god of death, and Baal's descent down Mot's throat is likened to going into the "abyss" (*mhmrt*). The word is associated with water, hence the NIV's adjective "miry."

141:7 *plows.* Just after the first rains of the autumn season, the ground was soft enough for plowing. An iron point (or a set of two points) fixed to a stick for handling was pulled by oxen to break the soil. This loosening caused rocks to surface, which is perhaps the word picture behind the metaphor of this verse. Instead of an undisturbed burial, this verse pictures bones scattered at a grave, like rocks spread across the field. Disturbing the bones of those buried or destroying corpses was a severe infliction of torment upon their disembodied spirits (see the articles "Death and Sheol," p. 833; "Death and the Underworld," p. 907). Therefore, Ashurbanipal speaks of punishment of his enemies by taking their bones out of Babylon and scattering them outside the city. He also boasts of opening the graves of past kings of his enemies and carting off their bones "to inflict unrest upon their ghosts."

141:9 – 10 *traps … snares … nets.* See note on 140:5.

142 title *in the cave.* During the time that David was fleeing from Saul, he spent a lot of time in caves (e.g., 1Sa 22 – 26). The Judean wilderness, where David spent his fugitive years, has abundant caves scattered throughout the region.

142:5 *land of the living.* In ancient thought, the earth was divided into the two realms: (1) the surface, where people lived and (2) the underworld, which was the abode of the dead (see the articles "Death and Sheol," p. 833; "Death and the Underworld," p. 907).

rescue me from those who pursue me,
for they are too strong for me.
7 Set me free from my prison,[h]
that I may praise your name.
Then the righteous will gather about me
because of your goodness to me.[i]

Psalm 143

A psalm of David.

1 LORD, hear my prayer,
listen to my cry for mercy;[j]
in your faithfulness[k] and righteousness[l]
come to my relief.
2 Do not bring your servant into judgment,
for no one living is righteous[m] before you.
3 The enemy pursues me,
he crushes me to the ground;
he makes me dwell in the darkness
like those long dead.
4 So my spirit grows faint within me;
my heart within me is dismayed.[n]
5 I remember[o] the days of long ago;
I meditate on all your works
and consider what your hands have done.
6 I spread out my hands[p] to you;
I thirst for you like a parched land.[a]
7 Answer me quickly,[q] LORD;
my spirit fails.
Do not hide your face[r] from me
or I will be like those who go down to the pit.
8 Let the morning bring me word of your unfailing love,[s]
for I have put my trust in you.
Show me the way[t] I should go,
for to you I entrust my life.[u]
9 Rescue me from my enemies,[v] LORD,
for I hide myself in you.
10 Teach me to do your will,
for you are my God;
may your good Spirit
lead[w] me on level ground.

11 For your name's sake, LORD, preserve my life;[x]
in your righteousness,[y] bring me out of trouble.
12 In your unfailing love, silence my enemies;
destroy all my foes,[z]
for I am your servant.[a]

Psalm 144

Of David.

1 Praise be to the LORD my Rock,[b]
who trains my hands for war,
my fingers for battle.
2 He is my loving God and my fortress,[c]
my stronghold and my deliverer,
my shield,[d] in whom I take refuge,
who subdues peoples[b] under me.

3 LORD, what are human beings[e] that you care for them,
mere mortals that you think of them?
4 They are like a breath;
their days are like a fleeting shadow.[f]
5 Part your heavens,[g] LORD, and come down;
touch the mountains, so that they smoke.[h]
6 Send forth lightning and scatter the enemy;
shoot your arrows[i] and rout them.

142:7 [h] Ps 146:7 [i] Ps 13:6
143:1 [j] Ps 140:6 [k] Ps 89:1-2 [l] Ps 71:2
143:2 [m] Ps 14:3; Ecc 7:20; Ro 3:20
143:4 [n] Ps 142:3
143:5 [o] Ps 77:6
143:6 [p] Ps 63:1; 88:9
143:7 [q] Ps 69:17 [r] Ps 27:9; 28:1
143:8 [s] Ps 46:5; 90:14 [t] Ps 27:11 [u] Ps 25:1-2
143:9 [v] Ps 31:15
143:10 [w] Ne 9:20; Ps 23:3; 25:4-5
143:11 [x] Ps 119:25 [y] Ps 31:1
143:12 [z] Ps 52:5; 54:5 [a] Ps 116:16
144:1 [b] Ps 18:2, 34
144:2 [c] Ps 59:9; 91:2 [d] Ps 84:9
144:3 [e] Ps 8:4; Heb 2:6
144:4 [f] Ps 39:11; 102:11
144:5 [g] Ps 18:9; Isa 64:1 [h] Ps 104:32
144:6 [i] Ps 7:12-13; 18:14

[a] 6 The Hebrew has *Selah* (a word of uncertain meaning) here. [b] 2 Many manuscripts of the Masoretic Text, Dead Sea Scrolls, Aquila, Jerome and Syriac; most manuscripts of the Masoretic Text *subdues my people*

142:7 *prison.* Cisterns or pits were sometimes used as temporary prisons (Ge 37:24–25; Jer 38:6). As a place in the ground, often shut off from light (Isa 42:7), the picture of a cistern was used metaphorically for the underworld of the dead (cf. "pit" in Isa 14:15 and "dungeon" in Isa 24:22). In view of the contrast with "land of the living" (v. 5), the psalmist invites his audience to imagine his potential death as confinement in a dark, subterranean prison (143:3).
143:6 *spread out my hands.* See note on 44:20.
143:7 *pit.* See note on 142:7; see also the articles "Death and Sheol," p. 833; "Death and the Underworld," p. 907.
143:10 *lead me on level ground.* The roads of the ancient Near East were for the most part unpaved (except for a few roads in the Late Assyrian period). Although unpaved, those that were intended for wheeled transport (called "wagon roads" in the Nuzi tablets) had to be staked out, leveled and consistently maintained. However, very few texts describe the construction and maintenance of these roads. Roads for heavy transport were somewhat rare, and were primarily along the trade routes. Thus, a vassal king complained to the king of Mari that he had to arrive at the Syrian capital by a roundabout route along a major highway. Assyrian kings rarely boasted of their road constructions, as it appeared to be the duty of the local populations. In a treaty text Esarhaddon commands that when his son succeeds him, the vassal must submit to him and "smooth his way in every respect." In a hymn to the goddess Gula, the deity says that she makes straight the path of one who seeks her ways. Mountain travel was notoriously difficult, and when kings do boast of road construction, it is when they sponsored the cutting of a mountain road. Nebuchadnezzar II claimed: "I cut through steep mountains, I split rocks, opened passages, constructed a straight road."
144:1 *Rock.* See note on 18:2. *trains my hands for war.* See note on 18:32.
144:2 *fortress.* See note on 18:2. *shield.* See note on 3:3.
144:5–6 See note on 18:7–15.
144:5 For the Lord as a divine warrior, see note on 18:7.
144:6 *lightning.* See notes on 18:8,12. *arrows.* See note on 18:14.

7 Reach down your hand from on
high;
deliver me and rescue me
from the mighty waters,[j]
from the hands of foreigners[k]
8 whose mouths are full of lies,[l]
whose right hands are deceitful.

9 I will sing a new song to you, my
God;
on the ten-stringed lyre[m] I will
make music to you,
10 to the One who gives victory to
kings,
who delivers his servant David.[n]

From the deadly sword 11 deliver me;
rescue me from the hands of
foreigners
whose mouths are full of lies,
whose right hands are deceitful.[o]

12 Then our sons in their youth
will be like well-nurtured plants,[p]
and our daughters will be like
pillars
carved to adorn a palace.
13 Our barns will be filled
with every kind of provision.
Our sheep will increase by thousands,
by tens of thousands in our
fields;
14 our oxen will draw heavy loads.[a]
There will be no breaching of walls,
no going into captivity,
no cry of distress in our streets.
15 Blessed is the people[q] of whom this
is true;
blessed is the people whose God is
the LORD.

144:7 [j] Ps 69:2 [k] Ps 18:44 **144:8** [l] Ps 12:2 **144:9** [m] Ps 33:2-3 **144:10** [n] Ps 18:50 **144:11** [o] Ps 12:2; Isa 44:20 **144:12** [p] Ps 128:3 **144:15** [q] Ps 33:12

145:1 [r] Ps 30:1; 34:1 [s] Ps 5:2 **145:2** [t] Ps 71:6 **145:3** [u] Job 5:9; Ps 147:5; Ro 11:33 **145:4** [v] Isa 38:19 **145:5** [w] Ps 119:27 **145:6** [x] Ps 66:3 [y] Dt 32:3 **145:7** [z] Isa 63:7 [a] Ps 51:14 **145:8** [b] Ps 86:15 [c] Ex 34:6; Nu 14:18

Psalm 145[b]

A psalm of praise. Of David.

1 I will exalt you,[r] my God the King;[s]
I will praise your name for ever
and ever.
2 Every day I will praise[t] you
and extol your name for ever and
ever.

3 Great is the LORD and most worthy
of praise;
his greatness no one can
fathom.[u]
4 One generation[v] commends your
works to another;
they tell of your mighty acts.
5 They speak of the glorious splendor
of your majesty—
and I will meditate on your
wonderful works.[c][w]
6 They tell of the power of your
awesome works—[x]
and I will proclaim[y] your great
deeds.
7 They celebrate your abundant
goodness[z]
and joyfully sing of your
righteousness.[a]

8 The LORD is gracious and
compassionate,[b]
slow to anger and rich in love.[c]

[a] 14 Or *our chieftains will be firmly established* [b] This psalm is an acrostic poem, the verses of which (including verse 13b) begin with the successive letters of the Hebrew alphabet. [c] 5 Dead Sea Scrolls and Syriac (see also Septuagint); Masoretic Text *On the glorious splendor of your majesty / and on your wonderful works I will meditate*

144:7 *mighty waters.* See note on 18:16; see also the article "Chaos Monsters," p. 953. Here the unruly forces are foreign enemies.
144:9 *new song.* See note on 96:1. *ten-stringed lyre.* See the articles "Lyre," p. 488; "Music and Musicians," p. 524.
144:12 *well-nurtured plants…pillars.* The royal interest of this psalm in conjunction with the reference to a palace might conjure an image of flourishing civic projects. The splendor of a palace and city was enhanced by ornamental gardens. The Assyrian king Sennacherib (c. 700 BC) boasted that he adorned the city of Nineveh with a "great park" containing all kinds of herbs and fruit trees, and that he allotted plots of land for the people to plant orchards. In addition, he developed an elaborate irrigation system to keep the plantings lush. Similarly, fine architecture was a credit to any monarch who experienced success in his reign. Sennacherib spoke of the elaborate portico of his palace with copper and cedar pillars to support the grand doors. Such pillars were sometimes carved in human shape. This psalm draws on such images to describe the blessing of offspring who flourish as the most important pride of any community (see notes on 127:1,4–5).
144:13 *Our barns will be filled.* Continuing the description of a prosperous society (see note on v. 12), the psalmist speaks of agricultural fertility. Verses 12–13 allude to social conditions arising from covenant blessing (Dt 28:1–14) in contrast with those of a curse (Dt 28:15–19). Azatiwata, a Hittite official (c. 700 BC), prayed for blessing upon his own city measured in terms of children, grain and livestock, similar to Ps 144. These are the three most important components of life for people in an agriculturally based society.
144:14 *breaching of walls.* Wall carvings from Assyrian palaces illustrate the work of soldiers in siege engines that ram and claw at a city's defensive structures in order to penetrate the walls (see the article "Siege Warfare," p. 1157). Once inside, the invading army could slaughter inhabitants and take captive the survivors. In addition to community blessings and curses, Dt 28:63–68 speaks of exile and captivity as the ultimate consequence of Israel's breaking covenant with God. The practice of deporting a conquered people from their native land and resettling them in a foreign country was well known in the ancient Near East (see note on 107:3). Because such scattering and resettlement disrupted the social cohesion and stability, this policy was intended to prevent further rebellion of the conquered people against their overlord. If the hope of the king in this psalm is realized, his subjects will enjoy the blessings of quite the opposite future: a society that is at peace and enjoying the fruits of prosperity.
145:5 *glorious splendor.* See note on 104:2.

9 The LORD is good[d] to all;
he has compassion on all he has made.
10 All your works praise you,[e] LORD;
your faithful people extol you.[f]
11 They tell of the glory of your kingdom
and speak of your might,
12 so that all people may know of your mighty acts[g]
and the glorious splendor of your kingdom.
13 Your kingdom is an everlasting kingdom,[h]
and your dominion endures through all generations.

The LORD is trustworthy in all he promises
and faithful in all he does.[a]
14 The LORD upholds[i] all who fall
and lifts up all[j] who are bowed down.
15 The eyes of all look to you,
and you give them their food[k] at the proper time.
16 You open your hand
and satisfy the desires[l] of every living thing.

17 The LORD is righteous in all his ways
and faithful in all he does.
18 The LORD is near[m] to all who call on him,[n]
to all who call on him in truth.
19 He fulfills the desires[o] of those who fear him;
he hears their cry[p] and saves them.
20 The LORD watches over all who love him,[q]
but all the wicked he will destroy.[r]

21 My mouth will speak[s] in praise of the LORD.
Let every creature[t] praise his holy name
for ever and ever.

Psalm 146

1 Praise the LORD.[b]

Praise the LORD,[u] my soul.

2 I will praise the LORD all my life;[v]
I will sing praise to my God as long as I live.
3 Do not put your trust in princes,[w]
in human beings,[x] who cannot save.
4 When their spirit departs, they return to the ground;[y]
on that very day their plans come to nothing.[z]
5 Blessed are those[a] whose help[b] is the God of Jacob,
whose hope is in the LORD their God.

6 He is the Maker of heaven[c] and earth,
the sea, and everything in them—
he remains faithful[d] forever.
7 He upholds the cause of the oppressed[e]
and gives food to the hungry.[f]
The LORD sets prisoners free,[g]
8 the LORD gives sight to the blind,[h]

[a] *13* One manuscript of the Masoretic Text, Dead Sea Scrolls and Syriac (see also Septuagint); most manuscripts of the Masoretic Text do not have the last two lines of verse 13. [b] *1* Hebrew *Hallelu Yah*; also in verse 10

145:9 [d] Ps 100:5
145:10 [e] Ps 19:1 [f] Ps 68:26
145:12 [g] Ps 105:1
145:13 [h] 1Ti 1:17; 2Pe 1:11
145:14 [i] Ps 37:24 [j] Ps 146:8
145:15 [k] Ps 104:27; 136:25
145:16 [l] Ps 104:28
145:18 [m] Dt 4:7 [n] Jn 4:24
145:19 [o] Ps 37:4 [p] Pr 15:29
145:20 [q] Ps 31:23; 97:10 [r] Ps 9:5
145:21 [s] Ps 71:8 [t] Ps 65:2
146:1 [u] Ps 103:1
146:2 [v] Ps 104:33
146:3 [w] Ps 118:9 [x] Isa 2:22
146:4 [y] Ps 104:29; Ecc 12:7 [z] Ps 33:10; 1Co 2:6
146:5 [a] Ps 144:15; Jer 17:7 [b] Ps 71:5
146:6 [c] Ps 115:15; Ac 14:15; Rev 14:7 [d] Ps 117:2
146:7 [e] Ps 103:6 [f] Ps 107:9 [g] Ps 68:6
146:8 [h] Mt 9:30

145:13 *everlasting kingdom.* A parallel idea is found in the words of the servant-deity Kothar wa-Hasis to Baal urging him to assume eternal kingship. The Ugaritic expressions "eternal kingship" and "your [rule from] generation to generation" are cognate to the Hebrew "everlasting kingdom" and "all generations," respectively. A comparable expression is used in Akkadian as well, illustrated in a decree to build an Akitu house (used to house the god temporarily in the New Year's festival) for a god that would last for generations. In Biblical usage, these expressions can simply mean a lifetime or an indefinitely long time into the future (e.g., 112:6; Ex 17:16; 1Sa 27:12), but in contexts regarding divine rule, the rhetorical force stresses endless time (cf. both terms in Ex 3:15 regarding the endurance of God's name). In a letter to Esarhaddon, one of his administrators expresses the hope that Nabu and Marduk might give the king everlasting years, a just scepter and an everlasting throne.
145:14 *lifts up all who are bowed down.* This benevolent attitude was expected of any good god in ancient Near Eastern culture. The Hymn to Marduk concludes with the recognition that he is the one who raises up the weak and guides the meek. He brings protection and recovery from illness The psalmist, of course, recognizes Yahweh as the one who accomplishes these things.
145:16 *satisfy the desires.* In the ancient Near East, the gods had created people to provide for the needs of the gods. If people did that, the gods had to ensure that the people were protected from enemies and that their crops grew. Desires for safety and sufficient food were thus satisfied by the gods. In a challenge between the Canaanite gods Baal and Mot, Baal contests Mot's claim that he reigns by virtue of his ability to satisfy the people of the earth. Closer in tone to Ps 145 is the Hymn to Marduk, which praises the god out of "sweetness" of the thought of him who provides the produce of the earth; however, the ultimate purpose is to provide offerings for the gods, which the ensuing lines of the Marduk hymn indicate. In Israelite thinking, Yahweh had no needs, and his provision for his people was part of his covenant relationship with them. Their faithfulness to the covenant assured the blessings of the covenant, which would satisfy their desires.
146:3 *Do not put your trust in princes.* The goddess Ishtar admonishes the Assyrian king Esarhaddon similarly: "Do not trust in man." The young Esarhaddon had recently attained the throne after a civil war, and the instability of such a situation would have led to dependence on military leaders and other officials of court. In Ps 146, the psalmist warns against the temptation to place hope in any human, who ultimately has no control over his own destiny let alone the welfare of others.
146:4 *When their spirit departs.* See note on 104:29–30.
146:7 *He upholds the cause of the oppressed.* The psalmist lists a series of actions that demonstrate the Lord's dis-

the LORD lifts up those who are bowed
down,
the LORD loves the righteous.
9 The LORD watches over the foreigner
and sustains the fatherless and the
widow,[i]
but he frustrates the ways of the
wicked.

10 The LORD reigns[j] forever,
your God, O Zion, for all
generations.

Praise the LORD.

Psalm 147

1 Praise the LORD.[a]

How good it is to sing praises to our
God,
how pleasant[k] and fitting to praise
him![l]

2 The LORD builds up Jerusalem;[m]
he gathers the exiles[n] of Israel.
3 He heals the brokenhearted
and binds up their wounds.
4 He determines the number of the
stars[o]
and calls them each by name.

5 Great is our Lord[p] and mighty in
power;
his understanding has no limit.[q]
6 The LORD sustains the humble[r]
but casts the wicked to the ground.

7 Sing to the LORD[s] with grateful praise;
make music to our God on the harp.

8 He covers the sky with clouds;
he supplies the earth with rain[t]
and makes grass grow[u] on the hills.
9 He provides food[v] for the cattle
and for the young ravens[w] when
they call.

10 His pleasure is not in the strength[x] of
the horse,[y]
nor his delight in the legs of the
warrior;
11 the LORD delights in those who fear
him,
who put their hope in his unfailing
love.

12 Extol the LORD, Jerusalem;
praise your God, Zion.

13 He strengthens the bars of your gates
and blesses your people within you.

146:9 [i]Ex 22:22; Dt 10:18; Ps 68:5 **146:10** [j]Ex 15:18; Ps 10:16 **147:1** [k]Ps 135:3 [l]Ps 33:1 **147:2** [m]Ps 102:16 [n]Dt 30:3 **147:4** [o]Isa 40:26 **147:5** [p]Ps 48:1 [q]Isa 40:28 **147:6** [r]Ps 146:8-9 **147:7** [s]Ps 33:3 **147:8** [t]Job 38:26 [u]Ps 104:14 **147:9** [v]Ps 104:27-28; Mt 6:26 [w]Job 38:41 **147:10** [x]1Sa 16:7 [y]Ps 33:16-17

[a] 1 Hebrew *Hallelu Yah;* also in verse 20

position to help the oppressed. These can be correlated to comments in other psalms: "gives food to the hungry" (v. 7; see note on 145:16); "sets prisoners free" (v. 7; see notes on 107:3,10); "lifts up those who are bowed down" (v. 8; see notes on 113:7;145:14). The duty of any human king to defend the widow and orphan is well known in the ancient Near East (see notes on 72:4,12–14), and the same assumption would apply to any deity.

147:3 *He heals the brokenhearted.* The trauma of exile was a painful reality for many war-torn peoples in the ancient Near East (see note on 107:3). Restoration of people's suffering from exile was a concern in both Mesopotamian and Israelite religion. The need for emotional healing and restored personal relationships is expressed in a Babylonian prayer to the gods Shamash and Marduk in which the worshiper indicates the sadness of the passing years of captivity and his longing that his unhappiness be relieved.

147:4 *determines the number of the stars.* Because of its importance in divining the will of the gods, Mesopotamian astronomy attained a high degree of precision and sophistication. Interpreting divine messages from the position of the stars was comparable to reading a text inscribed on a tablet. Indeed, the stars and constellations were called "heavenly writing." The interpretive tradition dates from the third millennium BC, and by the mid-second millennium, scribes were copying detailed lists of predictive omens based upon astronomical observations, which reached a sophisticated literary form in the first millennium.

The Babylonian Creation Epic credits the god Marduk with setting the stars and constellations of the gods into place in the heavens (see notes on 104:2,19). That text uses technical terminology found in an astrological omen list organized according to the paths of particular stars in the astronomical calendar. Based upon the positions of stars relative to one another, Babylonian scholars predicted events on earth; e.g., "If the moon is surrounded by a halo and the Pleiades stand in it: in that year, women will give birth to male children." As effective representations of the gods, stars also played a role in magical rituals to invoke divine help. While astrological application to individual destinies at birth appear in the Old Babylonian period, only late in the first millennium BC did this concept become more developed (i.e., into personal horoscopes).

Egyptian religion portrays the stars embodied in Nut, the sky-goddess (see the article "Cosmic Geography," p. 836), with stellar maps painted on the ceilings of tombs and the lids of coffins from the third millennium BC. However, even though astronomy was important for calculating the Egyptian calendar, it did not develop into a science of prediction as it did in Babylon. Stellar maps did not correspond to real astronomy; rather, the depiction of stars and constellations was symbolic within the Egyptian religion of the afterlife, in which the deceased joined the divine stars of the sky. Only in the late first millennium BC do Egyptian texts attest to astronomical omens borrowed from Babylon and the development of horoscopes in a late Egyptian tradition.

147:8 *covers the sky with clouds.* While Canaanites worshiped Baal as the god of the clouds and rain (see notes on 97:2; Job 37:2–5), his Mesopotamian equivalent was known as Adad. A prayer to Adad calls upon him as the one who forms clouds in the heaven and rains down abundance, and another prayer describes the resulting joy of the mountains and meadows that have become green. The psalmists routinely use the same kinds of metaphors, descriptors and activities to describe Yahweh that Israel's neighbors use to describe their gods. Israel does not, therefore, have a unique theological rhetoric, but it has one that is familiar throughout their world.

147:10 *not in the strength of the horse.* See note on 20:7.

[14] He grants peace[z] to your borders
and satisfies you[a] with the finest
of wheat.

[15] He sends his command[b] to the
earth;
his word runs swiftly.
[16] He spreads the snow[c] like wool
and scatters the frost[d] like ashes.
[17] He hurls down his hail like pebbles.
Who can withstand his icy blast?
[18] He sends his word[e] and melts them;
he stirs up his breezes, and the
waters flow.

[19] He has revealed his word to Jacob,
his laws and decrees[f] to Israel.
[20] He has done this for no other
nation;[g]
they do not know his laws.[a]

Praise the LORD.

Psalm 148

[1] Praise the LORD.[b]

Praise the LORD from the heavens;
praise him in the heights above.
[2] Praise him, all his angels;[h]
praise him, all his heavenly hosts.
[3] Praise him, sun and moon;
praise him, all you shining stars.
[4] Praise him, you highest heavens
and you waters above the skies.[i]

[5] Let them praise the name of the
LORD,
for at his command[j] they were
created,
[6] and he established them for ever and
ever—
he issued a decree[k] that will never
pass away.

[7] Praise the LORD from the earth,
you great sea creatures[l] and all
ocean depths,
[8] lightning and hail, snow and clouds,
stormy winds that do his bidding,[m]
[9] you mountains and all hills,[n]
fruit trees and all cedars,
[10] wild animals and all cattle,
small creatures and flying birds,
[11] kings of the earth and all nations,
you princes and all rulers on earth,
[12] young men and women,
old men and children.

[13] Let them praise the name of the LORD,[o]
for his name alone is exalted;
his splendor is above the earth and
the heavens.[p]
[14] And he has raised up for his people a
horn,[c][q]
the praise of all his faithful servants,
of Israel, the people close to his
heart.

Praise the LORD.

Psalm 149

[1] Praise the LORD.[d][r]

Sing to the LORD a new song,
his praise in the assembly[s] of his
faithful people.

[2] Let Israel rejoice in their Maker;[t]
let the people of Zion be glad in
their King.[u]
[3] Let them praise his name with dancing
and make music to him with timbrel
and harp.[v]

147:14 [z] Isa 60:17-18 [a] Ps 132:15
147:15 [b] Job 37:12
147:16 [c] Job 37:6 [d] Job 38:29
147:18 [e] Ps 33:9
147:19 [f] Dt 33:4; Mal 4:4
147:20 [g] Dt 4:7-8, 32-34
148:2 [h] Ps 103:20
148:4 [i] Ge 1:7; 1Ki 8:27
148:5 [j] Ge 1:1, 6; Ps 33:6,9
148:6 [k] Job 38:33; Ps 89:37; Jer 33:25
148:7 [l] Ps 74:13-14
148:8 [m] Ps 147:15-18
148:9 [n] Isa 44:23; 49:13; 55:12
148:13 [o] Isa 12:4 [p] Ps 8:1; 113:4
148:14 [q] Ps 75:10
149:1 [r] Ps 33:2 [s] Ps 35:18
149:2 [t] Ps 95:6 [u] Ps 47:6; Zec 9:9
149:3 [v] Ps 81:2; 150:4

[a] *20* Masoretic Text; Dead Sea Scrolls and Septuagint *nation; / he has not made his laws known to them*
[b] *1* Hebrew *Hallelu Yah*; also in verse 14 [c] *14 Horn* here symbolizes strength. [d] *1* Hebrew *Hallelu Yah*; also in verse 9

147:16 *snow.* See note on 148:8.
148:2 *all his angels.* In Mesopotamian and Egyptian hymns, other deities are sometimes called upon to praise the god or goddess of the hymn. The Assyrian king Ashurbanipal (c. 650 BC), e.g., calls on all the gods to bear testimony to the greatness of Marduk. In an Egyptian hymn to Amun, Amun is hailed as one to whom the gods give praise, the creator who brought light to the world.
148:3 *sun and moon.* See notes on 19:1–2; 104:19.
148:4 *waters above the skies.* See note on 104:3.
148:7 *sea creatures…depths.* See the article "Chaos Monsters," p. 953.
148:8 *snow.* Snowfall in the southern regions of Israel is unusual, occurring about once every five years in Jerusalem, which is in the hill country, in contrast to the low coastal plain or the Jordan Valley, where snow is extremely rare. However, in the mountainous north and eastern plateaus, snow falls every winter and in places can remain throughout the winter and perhaps year round on Mount Hermon (cf. Jer 18:14). In ancient times, snow and ice were marvels of creation (see Job 37:5–6; 38:22), as were lightning and hail, which were understood to originate from the divine realm.
148:14 *raised up…a horn.* See notes on 18:2;132:17.
149:3 *dancing.* Scenes of dancing from pottery and engraved stone are known from the Near East as early as the fourth millennium BC. Egyptian iconography portrays dancers participating in festive religious processions. The god Baal Marqod (lit. "Lord of the Dance") is known from Phoenicia. While rare, depictions of dancing have also been found at archaeological sites in Israel dating to the Biblical period.

Much of the dancing that is attested in the ancient world takes place in religious contexts, though both Mesopotamian and Egyptian sources frequently depict dancers involved in entertainment. The dancing connected to festivals would probably resemble folk dancing of today, featuring the coordinated movements of a group of dancers. At other times the dances could more resemble ballet, where a scene or a drama is acted out. Single dancers usually performed either whirling, squatting, leaping, hopping-type dances or acrobatics approximating a modern gymnast's routine. Dancers sometimes performed either scantily clad or in the nude. In religious contexts, the participating officials (i.e., priests and administration) at times danced, not just the professionals. In one Hittite ritual this

[4] For the LORD takes delight[w] in his
people;
he crowns the humble with
victory.[x]
[5] Let his faithful people rejoice[y] in
this honor
and sing for joy on their beds.[z]

[6] May the praise of God be in their
mouths[a]
and a double-edged[b] sword in their
hands,
[7] to inflict vengeance on the nations
and punishment on the peoples,
[8] to bind their kings with fetters,
their nobles with shackles of iron,
[9] to carry out the sentence written
against them —[c]
this is the glory of all his faithful
people.[d]

Praise the LORD.

149:4 [w] Ps 35:27 [x] Ps 132:16 **149:5** [y] Ps 132:16 [z] Job 35:10 **149:6** [a] Ps 66:17 [b] Heb 4:12; Rev 1:16 **149:9** [c] Dt 7:1; Eze 28:26 [d] Ps 148:14

Psalm 150

[1] Praise the LORD.[a]

Praise God in his sanctuary;[e]
praise him in his mighty heavens.[f]
[2] Praise him for his acts of power;[g]
praise him for his surpassing
greatness.[h]
[3] Praise him with the sounding of the
trumpet,
praise him with the harp and lyre,[i]
[4] praise him with timbrel and dancing,[j]
praise him with the strings[k] and
pipe,
[5] praise him with the clash of cymbals,[l]
praise him with resounding cymbals.

[6] Let everything[m] that has breath praise
the LORD.

Praise the LORD.

150:1 [e] Ps 102:19 [f] Ps 19:1 **150:2** [g] Dt 3:24 [h] Ps 145:5-6 **150:3** [i] Ps 149:3 **150:4** [j] Ex 15:20 [k] Isa 38:20 **150:5** [l] 1Ch 13:8; 15:16 **150:6** [m] Ps 145:21

[a] *1* Hebrew *Hallelu Yah;* also in verse 6

specifically included the queen. There are no known examples of dancing kings.

The OT attests to the importance of dance in ancient Israel. After Yahweh's victory over the Egyptians at the crossing of the Red Sea (see the article "The Red Sea," p. 132), Miriam and the other women led Israel's worship with tambourine playing and dance (Ex 15:20). Victory dances are also described in 1Sa 18:6–7 (cf. Ex 15:19–21; 1Sa 21:11; 29:5). Celebrations of God's goodness were accompanied by dance, such as at a harvest festival (Jer 31:4–5; cf. Jdg 21:21). Finally, when David brought the ark of God to Jerusalem, he led the procession with dancing, accompanied by six musical instruments (2Sa 6:5,14). See notes on 1Sa 18:6; 2Sa 6:14.

149:6 *praise ... and a double-edged sword.* The coupling of these two seemingly incongruous ideas is understandable against a historical background such as the rebuilding of Jerusalem after the exile. Nehemiah was commissioned by both God and the king of Persia to rebuild the walls of Jerusalem, yet he and his fellow Jews lived and worked under constant danger of military attack from the surrounding nations (Ne 4). There is no explicit link between the historical setting of Nehemiah and the origin of Ps 149; however, it illustrates how war and worship might be compatible under a theocracy (cf. Ne 4:14,20). Furthermore, warfare in the ancient world was often construed as related to the activity of the gods (a divine warrior leading the army, see the article "Divine Warfare," p. 365) and was surrounded with rituals. The army divisions went out under the banner of their god, and they prayed to the god for support and praised him for victory. Consequently it would not be unusual for praise and weapons to appear in the same context. *double-edged sword.* The Hebrew terminology refers to a sword of two mouths. In the Late Bronze Age (Joshua's time), the standard sword was curved like a sickle, with the sharp edge on the outside of the curve. This shape is considered responsible for the development of the idiom "the mouth of the sword." It is possible that the idiom was retained even when the shape of the sword evolved, and a two-edged sword could be referred to as "two-mouthed," despite the loss of the shape that determined the idiom. Others, trying to retain the association between language and physical shape, have suggested a double-sided axe, though in that case the word translated "sword" here would have to be understood more broadly as "blade," a difficult (though not impossible) extension.

149:8 *fetters ... shackles.* Though the Hebrew terms used here are not the typical ones, it is likely that the former were wrist cuffs chaining the hands together, while the latter went around the ankles to chain the feet together (as is clear in 105:18). Iron was used for these by the Assyrians as early as the eighth century BC.

150:3 *trumpet.* See note on Jos 6:4. *harp and lyre.* See the articles "Lyre," p. 488; "Music and Musicians," p. 524.

150:4 *timbrel.* See the article "Music and Musicians," p. 524. *dancing.* See note on 149:3. *strings.* The Hebrew term corresponds to words in related languages meaning "hair" or "string"; therefore, it probably refers generically to stringed instruments. *pipe.* The identification of this instrument is uncertain. It may be flutelike, but some evidence points to a stringed instrument.

150:5 *cymbals.* The Hebrew term is related to the verb "to resonate" or "to ring," and with ancient sources it is commonly understood as "cymbal." Cymbals are well attested in the ancient Near East, being made of bronze and so enduring the ravages of time until discovered by modern archaeologists. They are of two different sizes, the smaller averaging about three inches (7.5 centimeters) in diameter and the larger approximately six inches (15 centimeters). The difference between cymbals implied in the words "clash" and "resounding" may allude to these two types (higher and lower pitch), or it could refer to the different manners in which cymbals can be played (single clash or allowed to resonate). See the article "Music and Musicians," p. 524.

WISDOM AND HYMNIC LITERATURE

PROVERBS

Proverbs is an anthology of wisdom sayings. While the main superscription associates the book with Solomon (1:1), elsewhere we find contributions by anonymous sages (22:17), Agur (30:1), King Lemuel's mother (31:1), and the men of Hezekiah (25:1). However, it is Solomon who is featured — being mentioned not only in the main superscription but also in 10:1; 25:1.

We observe in the historical texts of the Bible an international context to wisdom. Once realized, it is not such a shock to see just how much of Israelite wisdom is shared with Egyptian, Mesopotamian and Aramaic wisdom texts. The wisdom found in the book of Proverbs is often discovered also in ancient Near Eastern wisdom. The modern comparative study of Proverbs began in earnest with the publication of the "Instruction of Amenemope."

As more Egyptian wisdom has been published and analyzed, it has become clear that even if there is something of a special relationship between Proverbs and Amenemope, other ancient Near Eastern texts share many of the same values and principles as Proverbs and Amenemope. This is true not just of other Egyptian texts but also of Mesopotamian and especially Aramaic texts.

KEY CONCEPTS

- Proverbs are general statements that affirm godly values and virtues.
- There are two ways, and the way of wisdom is to be chosen over the path to destruction.
- Wisdom is the foundation of a godly life.
- We show wisdom in the way we speak and the way we interact with others.

This is not to deny that there are also differences between the values expressed by the Bible and those by the surrounding wisdom literature. But apart from numerous points of detail, the fundamental difference between Biblical and ancient Near Eastern wisdom is the ultimate motivation for behaving in a wise manner: namely, fear of Yahweh, the true God. ◆

Purpose and Theme

1 The proverbs of Solomon[a] son of David, king of Israel:[b]

[2] for gaining wisdom and instruction;
for understanding words of insight;
[3] for receiving instruction in prudent behavior,
doing what is right and just and fair;
[4] for giving prudence to those who are simple,[a][c]
knowledge and discretion[d] to the young—
[5] let the wise listen and add to their learning,[e]
and let the discerning get guidance—
[6] for understanding proverbs and parables,[f]
the sayings and riddles[g] of the wise.[b]

[7] The fear of the LORD[h] is the beginning of knowledge,
but fools[c] despise wisdom and instruction.

Prologue: Exhortations to Embrace Wisdom

Warning Against the Invitation of Sinful Men

[8] Listen, my son,[i] to your father's instruction
and do not forsake your mother's teaching.[j]
[9] They are a garland to grace your head
and a chain to adorn your neck.[k]

1:1 [a] 1Ki 4:29-34 [b] Pr 10:1; 25:1; Ecc 1:1 **1:4** [c] Pr 8:5 [d] Pr 2:10-11; 8:12 **1:5** [e] Pr 9:9 **1:6** [f] Ps 49:4; 78:2 [g] Nu 12:8 **1:7** [h] Job 28:28; Ps 111:10; Pr 9:10; 15:33; Ecc 12:13 **1:8** [i] Pr 4:1 [j] Pr 6:20 **1:9** [k] Pr 4:1-9

[a] *4* The Hebrew word rendered *simple* in Proverbs denotes a person who is gullible, without moral direction and inclined to evil. [b] *6* Or *understanding a proverb, namely, a parable, / and the sayings of the wise, their riddles* [c] *7* The Hebrew words rendered *fool* in Proverbs, and often elsewhere in the Old Testament, denote a person who is morally deficient.

1:1 *proverbs of Solomon.* Solomon's reign is described in the books of Kings and Chronicles. His were years of unprecedented and rarely surpassed success and prosperity for Israel. Solomon inherited a united kingdom won by the wars of his father David. The beginning of his reign was peaceful, with no significant internal or external threats. Such a time was right for productive and positive international contact, including that between wisdom teachers.

The Historical Books describe Solomon's wisdom as having a divine origin. In response to the king's piety (1Ki 3:1–15), God allowed him to choose a gift. Rather than wealth or honor, Solomon asks him for wisdom, and God grants it to him. Indeed, God was so pleased with his choice that he also gives him honor and wealth. The narrative that follows tells stories about the exercise of this divinely granted wisdom (1Ki 3:16–28).

In general, every king was aware of the need for wisdom in order to govern well, though it was not always set above other priorities the way that it should have been. It would be easy for success to be measured by the criteria inherent in one's personal ambitions. In contrast, wisdom is a quality that will pursue the good of the people and look to establish successful domestic and international policies.

Parallels to Biblical proverbs are found throughout the literature of the ancient Near East for the entire OT period. In fact, some of the earliest literary texts are proverbs dating to well over a millennium before Solomon. On one hand this is no surprise, since Solomon is identified as a collector of wise sayings. On the other, similarities do not suggest borrowing, since wisdom was common currency in the ancient world as it remains today, and observations about life take on similar parameters and stimulate similar analogies and insights.

1:6 *proverbs and parables ... riddles.* This verse lists three of the many types of wisdom writings. The proverb (Hebrew *mashal*) is an aphorism, a short statement often consisting of contrasting parallel lines. It is generally moral-laden and always didactic in character. Parables are extended contrast pieces that in narrative form both tell a story and require the audience to see a double or hidden meaning (see notes on 2Sa 12:1–4,6). Although there are no riddles in the book of Proverbs, they were apparently common enough as a form of intellectual game (see Jdg 14:12–14). *riddles.* In the OT this Hebrew term appears only in Proverbs and comes from a root that is usually translated "scornful" or "cynical." This may be an attempt to downgrade riddles as true wisdom sayings.

1:8 *my son.* Egyptian instructions are often addressed as advice to a son from a father. The book of Proverbs, particularly chs. 1–9, also presents admonitions of the father to the son. Even so, though the Egyptian instructions mention the father-son dynamic in the prologue, reference to father and son does not work itself into the advice section of the text as it does in Proverbs (e.g., vv. 8,10,15; 2:1; 3:1,11,21; 4:1,10,20). In addition, other Semitic practical wisdom texts are similar to the book of Proverbs, not just Egyptian wisdom. Other examples include the Aramaic *Words of Ahiqar* (lines 82, 96, 127, 129, 149), as well as Akkadian and Sumerian (admittedly non-Semitic) wisdom. Even so, all the Near Eastern traditions clearly place their practical wisdom in the setting of father and son. This leads to the debate as to the exact nature of the relationship. Is it biological, or is the language a metaphor for a professional relationship, i.e., of a teacher and an apprentice? Often the two probably coincided, with the biological son succeeding the father in his profession. Egyptian instruction seems the most consistently focused on profession, but even there its teaching often articulates principles that are useful for getting along in life generally. The wisdom of Proverbs is a mixture of family, professional and scribal advice. However, there is no doubt but that the father-son dynamic is often biological. Adding support to this viewpoint is the appearance of the mother, rare to be sure, along with the father in the instruction of their son (v. 8; 6:20; 31:1). *your mother's teaching.* While the book of Proverbs is similar to other ancient Near Eastern texts in that it consists of a father's instruction to his son, it gives a larger role to the mother in her son's education. An exception is found in the conclusion of Dua-Kheti's teaching for his son Pepi in The Satire of the Trades. To be sure, only Lemuel's mother actually speaks in the book of Proverbs (31:1–9), but the fact that the father speaks of the teaching of his wife is significant.

1:9 *garland ... chain.* The words of the father and mother, which embody the wisdom of the society, can become a decorative wreath for the son's head and a chain or necklace of office. Just as a champion is adorned with a

PROVERBS 1:8

Sages in the Ancient Near East

The tradition of sages who expound on the wisdom of ancient cultures is a longstanding one in the ancient Near East. The manner employed in such wisdom pieces as the "Instruction of Ptahhotep" and the "Instruction of Amenemope" suggests that there were wisdom schools in ancient Egypt and Mesopotamia. The "sage" functioned as the students' "father," conveying the substance of their culture's store of wisdom and standing as a source upon which to draw precedents. The *Words of Ahiqar*, from eighth-century BC Assyria, may indicate that some of these sages also were attached in some way to the palace bureaucracy, perhaps as members of the scribal class. The "words" of the sages included essays on personal deportment and etiquette in a variety of social situations. Their sayings also include short statements giving advice on political and diplomatic affairs. In this way they transmitted a form of cultural memory, as well as a sense of their society's basic values. ◆

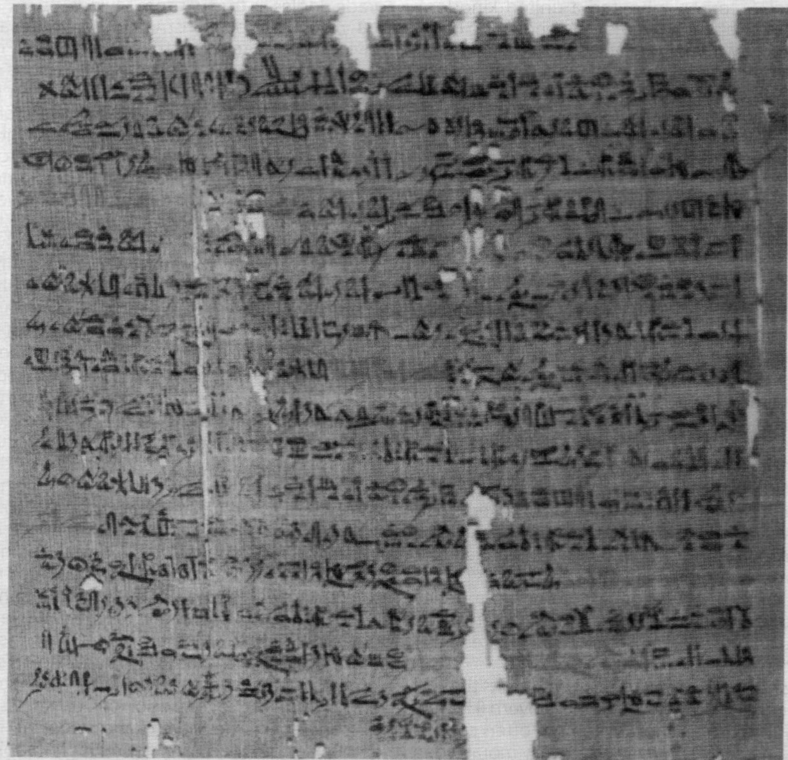

Late Eighteenth Dynasty papyrus of "Instruction of Ptahhotep."

PROVERBS 1

What Does It Mean for a Proverb to Be True?

The first important point to establish is that a proverb by definition is a generalization. A generalization is considered useful when it is *usually* true. A generalization is not a guarantee or a promise. We know that this is the case with English proverbs. For instance, we consider the proverbial statement, "Crime doesn't pay," to be true. Does that mean that there is never an instance in which crime pays? Of course not. The adage is a generalization, and we accept it as that when we recognize it as a proverbial saying. Biblical proverbs work in much the same way.

Sometimes proverbs seem to present contradictory perspectives. In English consider these pairs:

"Birds of a feather flock together."	"Opposites attract."
"Too many cooks spoil the broth."	"Two heads are better than one."
"He who hesitates is lost."	"Look before you leap."

Is only one in each set true? It would be better to recognize that each is true in given situations. In other words, sometimes wisdom would counsel, "Look before you leap," whereas in other situations wisdom would recognize that "he who hesitates is lost." Both are true when wisely applied to the situation at hand.

The OT has a similar example. In Pr 26:4 – 5, the advice is first given to restrain from answering a fool according to his folly, lest you become like him. The very next verse turns it around and says that a fool *should* be answered according to his folly so that he will not become wise in his own eyes. Again, we would have to conclude that both are true. The wise person would know which advice would be best to follow in any given situation.

These observations imply that proverbs not only teach wisdom, but require a certain level of wisdom to be used successfully. Wise words must be wisely used by wise people in order to result in wisdom. Proverbs says as much when it observes that "like the useless legs of one who is lame is a proverb in the mouth of a fool" (Pr 26:7), and that "like a thornbush in a drunkard's hand is a proverb in the mouth of a fool" (Pr 26:9).

How then is one expected to gain wisdom if it takes wisdom to learn wisdom? It must be taught by one who is already wise. In this way, we can understand the setting of proverbs as wisdom that is taught. It is a curriculum that is not meant as a self-study program. In some senses, it could be compared to a catechism, in that it provides a framework for introducing and remembering important lessons.

How then are proverbs true, authoritative revelation from God? First, we must ask what would make a proverb false. One way would be if it were to propose its teaching based on a misguided value. Examples of these are found in the ancient Near East: "Do the wish of the one present; slander the one not present" and "The man who does not sacrifice to his god can make the god run after him like a dog." In our modern context, any proverb that promoted multiplying sexual partners or affirmed that the pursuit of money or power should have highest priority would be considered false (e.g., "A deaf husband and a blind wife are always a happy couple," and "Don't offer me advice; give me money.") These are false because the values they espouse are worldly and flawed. A true proverb, then, is not one that describes a result that is always guaranteed without exception, but one that will move the student toward the development of godly values. Divine inspiration can be credited with guiding the

continued on next page

author in selecting already composed proverbs for inclusion. Any that were original compositions devised by the Biblical authors would have resulted from inspiration in the traditional ways.

There remain, however, some proverbs that run counter to our sensibilities or that we would consider unacceptable to our modern way of thinking. A number of proverbs, e.g., make derogatory statements about women (e.g., Pr 11:22; 21:9,19; 27:15–16; 30:20). Does this give us cause to label the book chauvinistic? Perhaps a few additional observations will be helpful: (1) There are many more derogatory statements made about men than about women (e.g., Pr 10:10; 14:17; 16:28; 18:13; 19:3,15,24; 20:6,19; 21:24–26; 29:22), not to mention that many of the negative characters of the book, such as the fool and the sluggard, are consistently male. (2) We must admit that there are negative characteristics of both women and men that are legitimate targets of proverbial sayings. (3) The book frequently praises wives (e.g., Pr 18:22; 19:14; 31:10–31), compares women favorably in contrast to men (e.g., Pr 11:16), and puts mothers and fathers on an equal plane (e.g., Pr 23:22; 30:17). There is nothing here to compromise the truth of these proverbs.

A second area of controversy has focused on the method of disciplining children by beating them with a rod (Pr 13:24; 22:15; 23:13–14; 29:15). It should be noted first of all that the rod was the most extreme form of child discipline and therefore could be used in Proverbs for rhetorical effect. Proverbs at times use hyperbole to make their point. Pr 23:1–2, e.g., tells the glutton to put a knife to his throat when he dines with a ruler. Second, it should be noted that using a stick for discipline was widely accepted in the ancient world as appropriate to some circumstances. The Aramaic *Words of Ahiqar* from seventh-century BC Assyria contain a proverb very similar to Pr 23:13–14: "Withhold not your son from the rod, else you will not be able to save [him from wickedness]. If I smite you, my son, you will not die, but if I leave you to your own heart [you will not live]." Finally, the balance can be seen in Pr 19:18–19, where discipline results in hope, not in physical jeopardy, and the man who is acting out of temper must be dealt with severely. Abusing children is never condoned, but effective discipline is consistently called for even to the point of inflicting low threshold physical pain when necessary.

We must be careful to interpret proverbs without falling prey to any misconceptions about what they are or about what they seek to accomplish. They promote virtues, expose vices, and advance wisdom as a means of character development that is founded on the fear of the Lord. ◆

10 My son, if sinful men entice[l] you,
do not give in[m] to them.[n]
11 If they say, "Come along with us;
let's lie in wait[o] for innocent blood,
let's ambush some harmless soul;
12 let's swallow them alive, like the grave,
and whole, like those who go down
to the pit;[p]
13 we will get all sorts of valuable things
and fill our houses with plunder;
14 cast lots with us;
we will all share the loot"—
15 my son, do not go along with them,
do not set foot[q] on their paths;[r]
16 for their feet rush into evil,
they are swift to shed blood.[s]

1:10 [l] Ge 39:7 [m] Dt 13:8 [n] Pr 16:29; Eph 5:11 **1:11** [o] Ps 10:8 **1:12** [p] Ps 28:1 **1:15** [q] Ps 119:101 [r] Ps 1:1; Pr 4:14 **1:16** [s] Pr 6:18; Isa 59:7

garland of victory and a newly appointed official is given the chain and vestments of his office, so too is the attentive son assured of prosperity and a stable life (Pr 4:1–6). As Ptahhotep says, "The wise follow their teacher's advice [and] consequently their projects do not fail." In Egyptian literature Ma'at, the goddess associated with wisdom, truth and justice, provides a garland of victory to the gods and is worn as a chain around the neck of various officials.
1:12 *let's swallow them alive.* The metaphor of swallowing for destruction and death probably derives from the Canaanite picture of the god Mot ("Death"), who performs his ghastly task by swallowing his victims. Baal's death at the hands of Mot is described as Mot's swallowing him "like an olive-cake." *grave.* This Hebrew term (*sheol*) is the most frequently used term for the place people go after they die. Often it refers simply to the grave, as here, though the grave is often seen as a portal to the netherworld (see the articles "Death and Sheol," p. 833; "Death and the Underworld," p. 907).
1:15 *do not go along with them.* The Egyptian Papyrus Insinger also counsels against joining in with evil fools. See also Pr 13:20.

[17] How useless to spread a net
where every bird can see it!
[18] These men lie in wait for their own blood;
they ambush only themselves!
[19] Such are the paths of all who go after
ill-gotten gain;
it takes away the life of those who
get it.[t]

Wisdom's Rebuke

[20] Out in the open wisdom calls aloud,[u]
she raises her voice in the public
square;
[21] on top of the wall[a] she cries out,
at the city gate she makes her
speech:

[22] "How long will you who are simple[v]
love your simple ways?
How long will mockers delight in
mockery
and fools hate knowledge?
[23] Repent at my rebuke!
Then I will pour out my thoughts to
you,

1:19 [t] Pr 15:27 **1:20** [u] Pr 8:1; 9:1-3, 13-15 **1:22** [v] Pr 8:5; 9:4, 16

[a] *21* Septuagint; Hebrew / *at noisy street corners*

1:20 *wisdom ... she.* Wisdom is personified as a woman here for the first time in the book. The fullest development of this metaphor is found in 8:1 — 9:6 (see note on 8:12). Much discussion has taken place concerning her identity and background. Many see her description as connected to an ancient Near Eastern goddess, whether Asherah, Ishtar, Isis, or Ma'at. One can make the strongest case for the latter, since Ma'at, like wisdom, refers to the order of creation, truth and justice. Often Ma'at appears to be no more than an abstract concept, but occasionally she appears as a goddess, though not one that has been given a developed personality in Egyptian literature. Most likely, Wisdom should be treated as a poetic personification.

PROVERBS 1

WHAT IS A PROVERB?

As is the case in modern conversations, proverbs function as a colloquial means of getting a point across. They are considered ancient wisdom that must be considered seriously (1Sa 24:13). When the English proverb "A penny saved is a penny earned" is quoted, the speaker is advocating the wisdom of personal thrift. In the same way, when Ezekiel quotes the proverb "Like mother, like daughter" (Eze 16:44), he is condemning Jerusalem for following in the evil footsteps of her "mother" Samaria (compare Jer 3:6 – 11 for this theme, but using "sister" as the kinship term). Ezekiel also used proverbs to signal a change in policy or fortunes. In Eze 18:2 – 3, e.g., the prophet quotes a proverb that on its surface simply acknowledges the well-known fact that a person who sees another person eat something sour will experience a similar reaction. In Israel, however, the proverb had been used to indicate the legal idea of corporate responsibility in which a son was held responsible for the sins of his father (see Ex 20:5). Now, Ezekiel states no person will be punished for anyone's sins but his or her own, and thus people "will no longer quote this proverb in Israel" (Eze 18:3).

Naturally, a proverb is only as useful as the context in which it is spoken. Thus, the writer of Proverbs notes that "like the useless legs of one who is lame is a proverb in the mouth of a fool" (Pr 26:7). This is a common saying in other wisdom literature. The "Instructions of Ankhsheshonq" warn that "fools cannot tell teaching from insult," and the "Instruction of Amenemope" states that one should not "take counsel with fools" since their words "blow like a storm" and are without substance. It is clear then that proverbs were not simply phrases to be memorized that anyone could understand. Their instruction needed to be unpacked and expounded by a wise teacher. It is like a curriculum that assumes the presence of a teacher to accomplish its aims.

Proverbs often motivate people to the best type of behavior and attitudes. Those actions it characterizes as wise often are accompanied by reward, and those that it characterizes as foolish are said to result in punishment. Indeed, the ultimate reward

continued on next page

for wise behavior is life and for foolish behavior is death. However, these rewards and punishments are often misunderstood by modern readers, who take them as promises. The proverb form is not in the business of giving out guarantees.

For instance, consider Pr 22:6: "Start children off on the way they should go, and even when they are old they will not turn from it." This proverb offers strong motivation for a parent to provide proper education. "The way they should go" would be defined by the values and principles in the rest of the book of Proverbs. But what exactly does the second part of the proverb tell us? Again, proverbs do not give promises; rather, they tell us what is the best course to a desired end, all things being equal. Of course, children are more likely to be godly if they are trained in such a way. But it may also be the case that other factors enter in. Perhaps the child will fall in with a bad peer group against the advice of the parents (Pr 1:8–19). The parents should nonetheless follow the advice of Pr 22:6 and increase the likelihood that their children will stay on the right path. ◆

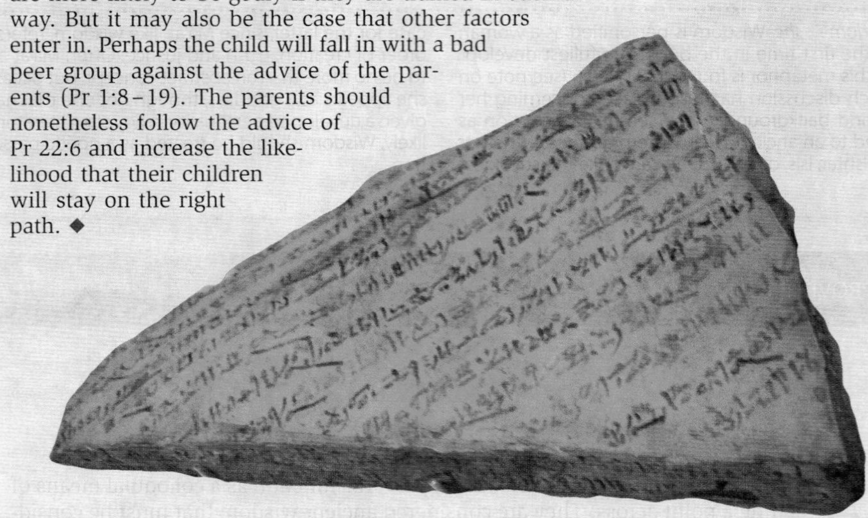

"Menna's Lament" deals with a headstrong child who ignores his father's advice. Proverbs provides strong motivation for a parent to provide proper education (Pr 22:6).

Kim Walton. The Oriental Institute Museum, University of Chicago.

I will make known to you my
 teachings.
24 But since you refuse to listen when
 I call[w]
and no one pays attention when
 I stretch out my hand,
25 since you disregard all my
 advice
and do not accept my rebuke,
26 I in turn will laugh[x] when disaster
 strikes you;
I will mock when calamity overtakes
 you[y]—
27 when calamity overtakes you like a
 storm,
when disaster sweeps over you like
 a whirlwind,
when distress and trouble
 overwhelm you.

28 "Then they will call to me but I will
 not answer;[z]
they will look for me but will not
 find me,[a]
29 since they hated knowledge
 and did not choose to fear the LORD.[b]
30 Since they would not accept my advice
 and spurned my rebuke,[c]
31 they will eat the fruit of their ways
 and be filled with the fruit of their
 schemes.[d]
32 For the waywardness of the simple will
 kill them,
and the complacency of fools will
 destroy them;[e]
33 but whoever listens to me will live in
 safety[f]
and be at ease, without fear of
 harm."[g]

1:24 [w] Isa 65:12; 66:4; Jer 7:13; Zec 7:11 **1:26** [x] Ps 2:4 [y] Pr 6:15; 10:24 **1:28** [z] 1Sa 8:18; Isa 1:15; Jer 11:11; Mic 3:4 [a] Job 27:9; Pr 8:17; Eze 8:18; Zec 7:13 **1:29** [b] Job 21:14 **1:30** [c] ver 25; Ps 81:11 **1:31** [d] Job 4:8; Pr 14:14; Isa 3:11; Jer 6:19 **1:32** [e] Jer 2:19 **1:33** [f] Ps 25:12; Pr 3:23 [g] Ps 112:8

THE WISE SON ACCORDING TO PROVERBS: AN OUTLINE

I. HIS CHARACTER

- A. He Is Teachable, Not Intractable
  1. He receives and loves instruction (18:15; 19:20)
  2. He grows in wisdom (1:5; 9:9; 10:14)
- B. He Is Righteous, Not Wicked
  1. He fears the Lord (1:7; 14:16; see below under relationship to the Lord)
  2. He hates what is false (13:5)
  3. He shuns evil (3:7; 14:16; 16:6)
  4. He does what is righteous (2:20)
  5. He speaks the truth (22:21)
- C. He Is Humble, Not Proud (15:33)
- D. He Is Self-controlled, Not Rash
  1. His temperament
     - a. He is self-controlled (29:11)
     - b. He has a calm spirit (17:27)
     - c. He is slow to become angry (29:8,11)
  2. His actions
     - a. He is cautious, not rash (19:2)
     - b. He thinks before he acts (13:16; 14:8)
     - c. He thinks before he speaks (12:23; 15:2)
- E. He Is Forgiving, Not Vindictive
  1. He is patient (19:11)
  2. He is concerned about goodwill/peace (14:9)
  3. He forgives those who wrong him (10:12; 17:9)
  4. He is not vindictive (20:22; 24:29)

II. HIS RELATIONSHIPS

- A. To the Lord
  1. He fears the Lord (9:10; 14:16; 15:33)
  2. He trusts in the Lord (3:5; 16:3,20)
  3. He is ever mindful of the Lord (3:6)
  4. He chooses the Lord's way/wisdom (8:10–11; 17:24)
  5. He submits to the Lord's discipline (1:2–3; 3:11)
  6. He confesses his sin to the Lord (28:13)
- B. To His Family
  1. To his parents
     - a. He respects them (17:6; contrast 30:17)
     - b. He listens to them (23:22; cf. 1:8; 4:1)
     - c. He seeks to bring them honor and joy
       - (1) By being wise (10:1; 15:20; 29:3)
       - (2) By being righteous (23:24)
       - (3) By being diligent (10:5)
  2. To his wife
     - a. He appreciates her
       - (1) As a gift from the Lord (18:22; 19:14)
       - (2) As his crowning glory (12:4; 31:10–31)
     - b. He praises her (31:28)
     - c. He trusts her (31:11)
     - d. He is faithful to her (5:15–20)
  3. To his children
     - a. He loves them (3:12; 13:24)
     - b. He is concerned about them (1:8—9:18)
     - c. He trains them (22:6)
       - (1) Reasons for training them
         - (a) Own peace of mind and joy (29:17)
         - (b) Child's honor and well-being (1:8–9; 4:9; 19:18; 23:13–14)
       - (2) By teaching/instructing them (1:10; chs. 5–7; 28:7; cf. 4:1–9)
       - (3) By disciplining them
         - (a) By verbal correction (13:1)
         - (b) By physical discipline (13:24; 23:13–14)
     - d. He provides for their
       - (1) Physical needs (21:20; cf. 27:23–27)
       - (2) Spiritual heritage (14:26; 20:7)
- C. To His Friends and Neighbors
  1. To his friends
     - a. He values them (27:10)
     - b. He is constant to them (17:17; 18:24)
     - c. He gives them counsel (27:9,17; cf. 27:6; 28:23)
  2. To his neighbors
     - a. He fulfills his obligations to them (3:27–28)
     - b. He strives for peace with them (3:29–30)
     - c. He does not outstay his welcome (25:17)
     - d. He does not deceive or mislead them (16:29; 26:18–19)

III. HIS WORDS

- A. The Power and Limitations of His Words
  1. Their power
     - a. The power of life and death (12:6; 13:14; 15:4; 18:21)
     - b. The power to heal or to wound (11:9,11; 12:18; 15:4,30; 16:24)
  2. Their limitations
     - a. Cannot substitute for deeds (14:23)
     - b. Cannot alter the facts (26:23–26)
     - c. Cannot compel response (29:19)
- B. The Character of His Words
  1. They are honest, not false (12:22; 16:13)
  2. They are few, not many (10:19)
     - a. Not boastful (27:2)
     - b. Not argumentative (17:14)
     - c. Not contentious (29:9)
     - d. Not a slanderer
       - (1) Revealing secrets (11:13; 20:19)
       - (2) Spreading gossip (10:18; 26:20–22)
  3. They are calm, not emotional
     - a. Rational (15:28; 17:27)
     - b. Gentle and peaceful (15:1,18)
     - c. Persuasive (25:15)
  4. They are apt, not untimely (15:23; 25:11)
- C. The Source of His Words
  1. His heart/character (compare 4:23 with Mt 12:33–35)
     - a. Positively, he is righteous (cf. 10:11; 13:14)
     - b. Negatively, he is not
       - (1) Proud (13:10; cf. 6:16–19)
       - (2) Hateful (26:24,28)
  2. His companions (13:20; 27:17)

Moral Benefits of Wisdom

2 My son, if you accept my words
and store up my commands within
you,
2 turning your ear to wisdom
and applying your heart to
understanding[h] —
3 indeed, if you call out for insight
and cry aloud for understanding,
4 and if you look for it as for silver
and search for it as for hidden
treasure,[i]
5 then you will understand the fear of
the LORD
and find the knowledge of God.[j]
6 For the LORD gives wisdom;[k]
from his mouth come knowledge
and understanding.
7 He holds success in store for the upright,
he is a shield[l] to those whose walk is
blameless,[m]
8 for he guards the course of the just
and protects the way of his faithful
ones.[n]

9 Then you will understand what is right
and just
and fair — every good path.
10 For wisdom will enter your heart,[o]
and knowledge will be pleasant to
your soul.
11 Discretion will protect you,
and understanding will guard you.[p]

12 Wisdom will save you from the ways
of wicked men,
from men whose words are perverse,
13 who have left the straight paths
to walk in dark ways,[q]
14 who delight in doing wrong
and rejoice in the perverseness of
evil,[r]
15 whose paths are crooked[s]
and who are devious in their
ways.[t]

16 Wisdom will save you also from the
adulterous woman,[u]
from the wayward woman with her
seductive words,
17 who has left the partner of her youth
and ignored the covenant she made
before God.[a][v]
18 Surely her house leads down to death
and her paths to the spirits of the
dead.[w]
19 None who go to her return
or attain the paths of life.[x]

20 Thus you will walk in the ways of the
good
and keep to the paths of the
righteous.
21 For the upright will live in the land,[y]
and the blameless will remain in it;
22 but the wicked will be cut off from the
land,[z]
and the unfaithful will be torn
from it.[a]

Wisdom Bestows Well-Being

3 My son, do not forget my teaching,[b]
but keep my commands in your
heart,
2 for they will prolong your life many
years[c]
and bring you peace and prosperity.

3 Let love and faithfulness never leave
you;
bind them around your neck,
write them on the tablet of your
heart.[d]

2:2 [h] Pr 22:17 **2:4** [i] Job 3:21; Pr 3:14; Mt 13:44 **2:5** [j] Pr 1:7 **2:6** [k] 1Ki 3:9, 12; Jas 1:5 **2:7** [l] Pr 30:5-6 [m] Ps 84:11 **2:8** [n] 1Sa 2:9; Ps 66:9 **2:10** [o] Pr 14:33 **2:11** [p] Pr 4:6; 6:22 **2:13** [q] Pr 4:19; Jn 3:19 **2:14** [r] Pr 10:23; Jer 11:15 **2:15** [s] Ps 125:5 [t] Pr 21:8 **2:16** [u] Pr 5:1-6; 6:20-29; 7:5-27 **2:17** [v] Mal 2:14 **2:18** [w] Pr 7:27 **2:19** [x] Ecc 7:26 **2:21** [y] Ps 37:29 **2:22** [z] Job 18:17; Ps 37:38 [a] Dt 28:63; Pr 10:30 **3:1** [b] Pr 4:5 **3:2** [c] Pr 4:10 **3:3** [d] Ex 13:9; Pr 6:21; 7:3; 2Co 3:3

[a] 17 Or *covenant of her God*

2:4 *as for silver ... as for hidden treasure.* The comparison between wisdom and the value of various types of riches (cf. 3:14–15; 8:10,19; Job 28) is also attested in Egyptian wisdom, as exemplified by the "Instruction of Ptahhotep": "Good speech is more hidden than greenstone (emeralds), Yet may be found among the maids at the grindstones" (lines 58–59, AEL.1.63).

2:16 *adulterous woman.* Lit. "strange" woman. *wayward woman.* Lit. "foreign" woman. For a full discussion of these terms, see the article "The 'Strange' and 'Foreign' Woman," p. 1036.

2:19 *None who go to her return.* The "strange woman" (see previous note) often, as here, takes on mythological proportions. Her house leads to death, and none who go to her return, implying that they are consigned permanently to the realm of the dead. The description of the netherworld as a "land of no return" is reminiscent of Akkadian mythology. In the Assyrian *Descent of Ishtar* and in the description of the so-called House of Death found in the Gilgamesh Epic, the realm of the dead is called "the house that none who have entered it leave" and "the road from which there is no way back."

3:3 *bind them around your neck.* The demand to bind something on one's neck is not found outside of Proverbs (but see also 6:21; 7:3 admonishes the son to bind the father's commands on his finger). However, the language reminds the reader of Dt 6:4–9, which includes a command to the people to tie the law on their hands and bind them on their foreheads. Perhaps the neck is here mentioned because disobedience is elsewhere described as a stiffening of the neck (e.g., Jer 7:26; 17:23). *tablet of your heart.* In the ancient world, writing was often done on tablets. While in Mesopotamia writing tablets were normally made of clay, in the OT the term probably refers to wooden boards covered with wax (though the Ten Commandments were written on two stone tablets; Ex 24:12). The metaphor of the heart as a tablet (not a tablet worn on a cord over the heart as some would have it) on which one writes the law, of course, points to an internalization of God's commands in one's life, so that not only one's actions but also one's motives are pure (see also Pr 7:3; Jer 31:33). The only other place where writing on the heart is specifically mentioned is Jer 17:1, where it is said that Judah's sin is inscribed on their hearts.

[4]Then you will win favor and a good
name
in the sight of God and man.[e]

[5]Trust in the LORD[f] with all your heart
and lean not on your own
understanding;
[6]in all your ways submit to him,
and he will make your paths[g]
straight.[a h]

[7]Do not be wise in your own eyes;[i]
fear the LORD and shun evil.[j]
[8]This will bring health to your body[k]
and nourishment to your bones.[l]

[9]Honor the LORD with your wealth,
with the firstfruits[m] of all your
crops;
[10]then your barns will be filled[n] to
overflowing,
and your vats will brim over with
new wine.[o]

[11]My son, do not despise the LORD's
discipline,[p]
and do not resent his rebuke,
[12]because the LORD disciplines those he
loves,[q]
as a father the son he delights in.[b r]

[13]Blessed are those who find wisdom,
those who gain understanding,
[14]for she is more profitable than silver
and yields better returns than gold.[s]
[15]She is more precious than rubies;[t]
nothing you desire can compare with
her.[u]
[16]Long life is in her right hand;
in her left hand are riches and
honor.[v]
[17]Her ways are pleasant ways,
and all her paths are peace.[w]
[18]She is a tree of life[x] to those who take
hold of her;
those who hold her fast will be
blessed.

[19]By wisdom the LORD laid the earth's
foundations,[y]
by understanding he set the
heavens[z] in place;
[20]by his knowledge the watery depths
were divided,
and the clouds let drop the dew.

[21]My son, do not let wisdom and
understanding out of your
sight,[a]
preserve sound judgment and
discretion;
[22]they will be life for you,
an ornament to grace your neck.[b]
[23]Then you will go on your way in safety,
and your foot will not stumble.[c]
[24]When you lie down,[d] you will not be
afraid;
when you lie down, your sleep[e] will
be sweet.
[25]Have no fear of sudden disaster
or of the ruin that overtakes the
wicked,
[26]for the LORD will be at your side
and will keep your foot[f] from being
snared.

[27]Do not withhold good from those to
whom it is due,
when it is in your power to act.

[a] *6* Or *will direct your paths* [b] *12* Hebrew; Septuagint *loves, / and he chastens everyone he accepts as his child*

3:4 [e] 1Sa 2:26; Lk 2:52 **3:5** [f] Ps 37:3, 5 **3:6** [g] 1Ch 28:9 [h] Pr 16:3; Isa 45:13 **3:7** [i] Ro 12:16 [j] Job 1:1; Pr 16:6 **3:8** [k] Pr 4:22 [l] Job 21:24 **3:9** [m] Ex 22:29; 23:19; Dt 26:1-15 **3:10** [n] Dt 28:8 [o] Joel 2:24 **3:11** [p] Job 5:17 **3:12** [q] Pr 13:24; Rev 3:19 [r] Dt 8:5; Heb 12:5-6* **3:14** [s] Job 28:15; Pr 8:19; 16:16 **3:15** [t] Job 28:18 [u] Pr 8:11 **3:16** [v] Pr 8:18 **3:17** [w] Pr 16:7; Mt 11:28-30 **3:18** [x] Ge 2:9; Pr 11:30; Rev 2:7 **3:19** [y] Ps 104:24 [z] Pr 8:27-29 **3:21** [a] Pr 4:20-22 **3:22** [b] Pr 1:8-9 **3:23** [c] Ps 37:24; Pr 4:12 **3:24** [d] Lev 26:6; Ps 3:5 [e] Job 11:18 **3:26** [f] 1Sa 2:9

3:6 *make your paths straight.* Trusting the Lord makes life's journey much easier. The metaphor of the deity straightening one's path is found in Babylonian literature in the hymn to the goddess Gula, the goddess of healing, who is identified as the one who gives life to faithful followers and makes a straight path for those who seek her ways. For Israelites this metaphor is particularly meaningful since much of Israel is hilly and rocky, giving travelers a great appreciation for smooth paths on level terrain.
3:15 *more precious than rubies.* While both rubies and sapphires are forms of the mineral corundum, which consists primarily of aluminum oxide, rubies are much rarer and therefore considered more precious. The Egyptian sage Ptahhotep also compares true wisdom with rare gems (emeralds), adding weight to such analogies. Diamonds were not known in the ancient world.
3:18 *tree of life.* The immediate background of this image is the tree of life in the Garden of Eden (Ge 2). Those who embrace wisdom are like those who embrace the tree of life; i.e., wisdom is the source of life in all its fullness. A symbol commonly referred to as the "tree of life" by modern scholars is well attested in ancient Mesopotamian art, though no textual evidence identifies it as such. It is more appropriate to identify it as a "cosmic tree"—a tree located in the center of the world that links the cosmic realms.
3:19 *By wisdom the LORD laid the earth's foundations.* It is not unprecedented that creation is said to be the product of a deity's wisdom. In the "Memphite Theology," the Egyptian god Ptah is said to produce the world through his heart and tongue, standing for his wisdom and his speech. According to the sages, the creative act, in order to fully demonstrate God's presence and concern, is followed by an ongoing and sustaining of the structures of the heavens and the earth.
3:20 *watery depths.* Hebrew *tehom,* which refers to the primordial cosmic ocean. In the Babylonian Creation Epic, *Enuma Elish,* the goddess representing this cosmic ocean, Tiamat, is divided in half by Marduk to make the waters above and the waters below. See note on Ge 1:2; see also the articles "The 'Vault' and 'Water Above,'" p. 6; "Cosmic Geography," p. 836.
3:27 *Do not withhold good.* Generosity to the poor is a common theme in ancient Near Eastern wisdom literature. Typical is the following quote from the Egyptian "Instruction of Any," but similar sentiments are found in the Babylonian *Counsels of Wisdom,* as well as the Egyptian "Instruction of Ptahhotep" and "Instructions of Ankhsheshonq": "Do not eat bread while another stands by, Without extending your hand to him."

28 Do not say to your neighbor,
"Come back tomorrow and I'll give it to you"—
when you already have it with you.[g]
29 Do not plot harm against your neighbor,
who lives trustfully near you.
30 Do not accuse anyone for no reason—
when they have done you no harm.

31 Do not envy[h] the violent
or choose any of their ways.

32 For the LORD detests the perverse[i]
but takes the upright into his confidence.[j]
33 The LORD's curse[k] is on the house of the wicked,[l]
but he blesses the home of the righteous.[m]
34 He mocks proud mockers
but shows favor to the humble[n] and oppressed.
35 The wise inherit honor,
but fools get only shame.

Get Wisdom at Any Cost

4 Listen, my sons,[o] to a father's instruction;
pay attention and gain understanding.
2 I give you sound learning,
so do not forsake my teaching.
3 For I too was a son to my father,
still tender, and cherished by my mother.
4 Then he taught me, and he said to me,
"Take hold of my words with all your heart;
keep my commands, and you will live.[p]
5 Get wisdom,[q] get understanding;
do not forget my words or turn away from them.
6 Do not forsake wisdom, and she will protect you;[r]
love her, and she will watch over you.
7 The beginning of wisdom is this: Get[a] wisdom.
Though it cost all[s] you have,[b] get understanding.[t]
8 Cherish her, and she will exalt you;
embrace her, and she will honor you.[u]
9 She will give you a garland to grace your head
and present you with a glorious crown.[v]"

10 Listen, my son, accept what I say,
and the years of your life will be many.[w]
11 I instruct[x] you in the way of wisdom
and lead you along straight paths.
12 When you walk, your steps will not be hampered;
when you run, you will not stumble.[y]
13 Hold on to instruction, do not let it go;
guard it well, for it is your life.[z]
14 Do not set foot on the path of the wicked
or walk in the way of evildoers.[a]
15 Avoid it, do not travel on it;
turn from it and go on your way.
16 For they cannot rest until they do evil;[b]
they are robbed of sleep till they make someone stumble.
17 They eat the bread of wickedness
and drink the wine of violence.

18 The path of the righteous[c] is like the morning sun,
shining ever brighter till the full light of day.[d]
19 But the way of the wicked is like deep darkness;[e]
they do not know what makes them stumble.

20 My son, pay attention to what I say;
turn your ear to my words.[f]
21 Do not let them out of your sight,[g]
keep them within your heart;
22 for they are life to those who find them
and health to one's whole body.[h]
23 Above all else, guard your heart,
for everything you do flows from it.[i]

3:28 [g] Lev 19:13; Dt 24:15 **3:31** [h] Ps 37:1; Pr 24:1-2 **3:32** [i] Pr 11:20 [j] Job 29:4; Ps 25:14 **3:33** [k] Dt 11:28; Mal 2:2 [l] Zec 5:4 [m] Ps 1:3 **3:34** [n] Jas 4:6*; 1Pe 5:5* **4:1** [o] Pr 1:8 **4:4** [p] Pr 7:2 **4:5** [q] Pr 16:16 **4:6** [r] 2Th 2:10 **4:7** [s] Mt 13:44-46 [t] Pr 23:23

4:8 [u] 1Sa 2:30; Pr 3:18 **4:9** [v] Pr 1:8-9 **4:10** [w] Pr 3:2 **4:11** [x] 1Sa 12:23 **4:12** [y] Job 18:7; Pr 3:23 **4:13** [z] Pr 3:22 **4:14** [a] Ps 1:1; Pr 1:15 **4:16** [b] Ps 36:4; Mic 2:1 **4:18** [c] Isa 26:7 [d] 2Sa 23:4; Da 12:3; Mt 5:14; Php 2:15 **4:19** [e] Job 18:5; Pr 2:13; Isa 59:9-10; Jn 12:35 **4:20** [f] Pr 5:1 **4:21** [g] Pr 3:21; 7:1-2 **4:22** [h] Pr 3:8; 12:18 **4:23** [i] Mt 12:34; Lk 6:45

[a] 7 Or *Wisdom is supreme; therefore get* [b] 7 Or *wisdom. / Whatever else you get*

3:32 *the LORD detests.* See note on 15:8.
4:4 *he taught me.* Throughout chs. 1–9 the father teaches his son. In the present discourse, we learn that the father himself was the recipient of teaching from his father. The family is thus the locus of wisdom teaching, but, then again, the family also provides the context for learning the law of God (Dt 6) as well as the meaningful events of the past (Ps 78:5–8).
4:9 *garland … crown.* The image of a marriage feast is given substance with the bestowing of the traditional symbols of union by the bride (wisdom) on her groom (protégé). In this case, marriage symbolism of the "glorious crown" (cf. Isa 61:10) could be compared with the fragrant bridal garments in SS 4:11. In the metaphoric sense, it could also be paralleled with Isa 28:5, where God becomes a "glorious crown, a beautiful wreath" for the Israelites.
4:17 *the bread of wickedness … the wine of violence.* The food and drink of the wicked are their very acts. Their evil sustains them. The metaphor of ingesting food and drink is used to indicate their deeply engrained wickedness. The "Instruction of Ptahhotep" uses similar language: "He lives on what others die on; distortion of speech is his bread; he is 'a dead man who is alive every day.'"
4:23 *heart.* It is a common tradition in the ancient Near East for the heart to be the seat of the intellect (cf. 14:33) and the source of stability for one who would adhere to

PROVERBS 4:1

Ancient Near Eastern Wisdom Literature

Egyptian Wisdom

The main genre of wisdom, and the one closest to the Biblical book of Proverbs, is called in Egyptian *sby3t*, a word often translated "instruction." These texts appear as early as the Old Kingdom (2715 – 2170 BC) and down to the latest periods of Egyptian history.

Kagemmi: Though brief, the significance of the "Instruction of Kagemmi" is that it is one of the oldest examples of the genre, most likely coming from the Fifth or Sixth Dynasty of the Old Kingdom period. Kagemmi was the recipient of these instructions that emphasizes proper behavior in the area of speech and table etiquette. At the end of the text, it is mentioned that Kagemmi becomes a vizier during the reign of King Sneferu.

Ptahhotep: The "Instruction of Ptahhotep" is a much longer but still early example of the genre. Ptahhotep is said to be vizier under King Izezi of the Fifth Dynasty, but Egyptologists judge that the "Instruction of Ptahhotep" is more likely to be a product of the Sixth Dynasty. Its 37 maxims promote the ideal of a quiet, contented man of humility over against a heated, anxious, striving man. The composition begins with a prologue that names Ptahhotep the speaker and his son the recipient, with the purpose being to instruct the ignorant in knowledge and excellent discourse.

Merikare: Coming from late in the First Intermediate Period (the Ninth or Tenth Dynasty), the "Teaching for Merikare" is the first example of a royal Instruction.

Any: Any was a mid-level bureaucrat in the court of Queen Nefertari, the wife of Ahmose, one of the early New Kingdom pharaohs (Eighteenth Dynasty). It treats a variety of topics, many of which are similar to those found in Proverbs, such as promiscuous women, honesty in commerce, silence, overindulgence, and generosity. The text ends with a unique epilogue, recording that Any's son at first rejects his father's counsel, but after his father confronts him, he ultimately accepts his teaching.

Amenemope: The "Instruction of Amenemope" is the Instruction text most often compared to Proverbs, and indeed it shares many themes and even some more specific parallels, as is pointed out throughout the study notes in this Biblical book. The original exemplar of this composition is likely from sometime between the tenth and sixth centuries BC. Other partial copies of this popular composition are now known, none clearly older. Even so, most scholars today would date the writing of the text to the twelfth century BC. The speaker is Amenemope, who is named "Overseer of Grains," a mid-level government official, and he is addressing his remarks to his son, Hor-em-maa-kheru. After a lengthy prologue that gives the purpose of the composition, the advice section is divided into 30 chapters.

Ankhsheshonq: This text is written in Demotic, the late cursive form of Egyptian, dated to the first century BC, but there are reasons to believe it comes from

continued on next page

the Ptolemaic period a century or two earlier. The prologue introduces the unique setting for Ankhsheshonq's advice to his son. He is writing from prison, where the pharaoh sent him for not revealing a thwarted plot against the pharaoh's life. The style of Ankhsheshonq's advice is a bit different in that it is formulated in short prose statements rather than the longer maxims of earlier Instructions. Sometimes the short maxims are bundled together by topic, but there is still a rather random kind of structure.

Papyrus Insinger: The last text of our survey is known from a papyrus from the first century AD, though again the composition is likely Ptolemaic. Like the "Instruction of Ankhsheshonq," these texts are single-line prose sentences, but unlike the earlier text, there is a definite thematic arrangement, complete with headings.

Mesopotamian Wisdom

Mesopotamian wisdom is among the earliest literary writing in Sumerian. The Akkadians, Babylonians and Assyrians do not have much by way of material that is comparable to Proverbs. The following sampling discusses three texts that are most obviously comparable to the material in the Biblical book of Proverbs.

Sumerian Proverbs. Recent study has shown that Sumerian proverb collections go back to the Early Dynastic period III (2600 – 2550 BC) and that they continued in use, being cited in the Sumerian language in Akkadian literature, even after Sumerian was no longer spoken. Most of the texts come from the Old Babylonian period. These texts were translated into Akkadian, being found in Ashurbanipal's library in the seventh century. The proverbs' major topics of concern include routines of a woman's life, the nature of family relationships, handling legal proceedings, the ways of good men as well as liars, and dealings with the palace and temple.

The "Instructions of Shuruppak" and the Counsels of Wisdom. Besides lists of proverbs, Sumerian also attests an instruction not only similar to the Egyptian "Instructions" described above but also similar to Pr 1 – 9. This is the "Instructions of Shuruppak," named after the father of the famous sage Ziusudra, who survived the flood. Its earliest attestation is from the Early Dynastic period (specifically the twenty-sixth century BC). The text contains the instructions of Shuruppak to Ziusudra his son, and it speaks to many of the subjects of wisdom instructions from other Near Eastern cultures, including Proverbs. Akkadian also attests a version of this composition as well as another text called the *Counsels of Wisdom*, in which a father teaches a son.

Aramaic Wisdom

The *Words of Ahiqar*, written in Aramaic, is a story set in the Neo-Assyrian period. Ahiqar is a wise man to King Sennacherib. Ahiqar is betrayed by his nephew, Nadin, whom Ahiqar raised, and Nadin turns the king against Ahiqar. The king sends one of his military henchmen to kill Ahiqar, but since the wise man had earlier given the soldier advice that saved his life, they plan a ruse. They take a beggar and burn him beyond recognition and pass him off as Ahiqar. Ahiqar goes into hiding. Time passes and the Egyptians bring a problem to Sennacherib, who then wishes his old wise man was around to deal with the issue. The henchman considers this an opportune time to tell the king about the ruse, and Ahiqar is restored to the king's good graces. Ahiqar then beats Nadin, and the instructions that follow this narrative beginning to the text constitute the lengthy didactic portion of the composition. ◆

24 Keep your mouth free of perversity;
keep corrupt talk far from your lips.
25 Let your eyes look straight ahead;
fix your gaze directly before you.
26 Give careful thought to the[a] paths for
your feet[j]
and be steadfast in all your ways.
27 Do not turn to the right or the left;[k]
keep your foot from evil.

Warning Against Adultery

5 My son, pay attention to my
wisdom,
turn your ear to my words[l] of
insight,
2 that you may maintain discretion
and your lips may preserve
knowledge.
3 For the lips of the adulterous woman
drip honey,
and her speech is smoother than
oil;[m]
4 but in the end she is bitter as gall,[n]
sharp as a double-edged sword.
5 Her feet go down to death;
her steps lead straight to the grave.[o]
6 She gives no thought to the way of
life;
her paths wander aimlessly, but she
does not know it.[p]

7 Now then, my sons, listen[q] to me;
do not turn aside from what I say.
8 Keep to a path far from her,[r]
do not go near the door of her
house,
9 lest you lose your honor to others
and your dignity[b] to one who is
cruel,
10 lest strangers feast on your wealth
and your toil enrich the house of
another.
11 At the end of your life you will groan,
when your flesh and body are spent.

4:26 [j] Heb 12:13* **4:27** [k] Dt 5:32; 28:14 **5:1** [l] Pr 4:20; 22:17 **5:3** [m] Ps 55:21; Pr 2:16; 7:5 **5:4** [n] Ecc 7:26 **5:5** [o] Pr 7:26-27 **5:6** [p] Pr 30:20 **5:7** [q] Pr 7:24 **5:8** [r] Pr 7:1-27 **5:12** [s] Pr 1:29; 12:1 **5:18** [t] SS 4:12-15 [u] Ecc 9:9; Mal 2:14 **5:19** [v] SS 2:9; 4:5 **5:21** [w] Ps 119:168; Hos 7:2 [x] Job 14:16; Job 31:4; 34:21; Pr 15:3; Jer 16:17; 32:19; Heb 4:13 **5:22** [y] Ps 9:16 [z] Nu 32:23; Ps 7:15-16; Pr 1:31-32 **5:23** [a] Job 4:21; 36:12 **6:1** [b] Pr 17:18 [c] Pr 11:15; 22:26-27

12 You will say, "How I hated discipline!
How my heart spurned correction![s]
13 I would not obey my teachers
or turn my ear to my instructors.
14 And I was soon in serious trouble
in the assembly of God's people."

15 Drink water from your own cistern,
running water from your own
well.
16 Should your springs overflow in the
streets,
your streams of water in the public
squares?
17 Let them be yours alone,
never to be shared with strangers.
18 May your fountain[t] be blessed,
and may you rejoice in the wife of
your youth.[u]
19 A loving doe, a graceful deer[v]—
may her breasts satisfy you always,
may you ever be intoxicated with
her love.
20 Why, my son, be intoxicated with
another man's wife?
Why embrace the bosom of a
wayward woman?

21 For your ways are in full view[w] of the
LORD,
and he examines all your paths.[x]
22 The evil deeds of the wicked ensnare
them;[y]
the cords of their sins hold them
fast.[z]
23 For lack of discipline they will die,[a]
led astray by their own great folly.

Warnings Against Folly

6 My son, if you have put up security
for your neighbor,[b]
if you have shaken hands in pledge[c]
for a stranger,

[a] 26 Or *Make level* [b] 9 Or *years*

a just and wise life (cf. 1Ki 3:5 – 9). In Egyptian religious thought, the heart (*ib*) is distinguished from the soul (*ba*) and is considered the very essence of a person's being. It is the heart that is weighed in the balance of truth when a deceased individual is examined by the gods Anubis and Thoth. The "Book of the Dead" provides spells to protect and strengthen the heart as preparation for this ordeal. In the Egyptian "Complaints of Khakheperresonb," the main speaker dialogues with his heart, which is the center of his emotions, intellect and will. Indeed, one might recognize in this composition how the heart may well be described as the place from which everything flows, as in this verse.

In the ancient world, people had no knowledge of the physiology of the brain (and likewise no knowledge of the physiology of the kidney or liver). All of the functions that we associate with the brain, they tended to attach to the various entrails, the heart being most prominent among them because blood (the essence of life) obviously flowed through the heart, and a dead person's heart stopped beating. Thus, the heart is the center of intellect, emotions, will and belief.

6:1 *if you have put up security for your neighbor.* A frequent theme covered by the book of Proverbs is advice pertaining to the giving of loans or the securing of debts (e.g., 11:15; 17:18; 20:16; 22:26; 27:13). The teaching is consistent: Do not give loans or secure debts. To understand this teaching, we need to put it in a broader context. In the first place, interest-bearing loans to fellow Israelites are forbidden (Ex 22:25). It was possible to give interest-bearing loans to foreigners (Dt 23:20), but if the word "stranger" (Hebrew *zar*) implies "foreigner" here, then even these types of loans are discouraged.

Ancient Near Eastern law collections (the Laws of Eshnunna and the Code of Hammurapi) have laws regulating the giving and receiving of loans. Ancient Egyptian wisdom literature (the "Instructions of Ankhsheshonq") gives advice to borrowers and lenders alike. People are advised to borrow money at interest for real estate investment, marrying or celebrating special

PROVERBS 5

THE "STRANGE" AND "FOREIGN" WOMAN

The father often warns the son to avoid the "strange" woman (translated "adulterous" in Pr 5:3; 7:5; 22:14; 23:27) and "foreign" woman (translated "wayward" in 5:20; 6:24; 7:5; 23:27). But what makes the strange woman strange, the foreign woman foreign? The Hebrew words for "strange" (*zara*) and "foreign" (*nokriya*) may be understood in a variety of ways. However, it is unlikely that foreign in parallel with strange would be used to indicate a non-Israelite woman. The strangeness of this woman is seen in her willingness to operate outside the bounds of moral, legal and customary restraints — an idea that is developed further in the following chapters. This lack of restraint is described in Pr 2:17 as a failure to honor her commitments to the "partner of her youth" as well as to the "covenant she made before God." The first line of this verse thus accuses her of not sustaining her marriage vows, since the words "partner of her youth" refer to her own marriage. And by committing adultery, she is breaking her covenant with God. The fact that she is described as having been in a covenant with God is further support for the view that this woman is an Israelite temptress, not an ethnically foreign one. And a temptress she is. Her primary strategy for seducing the man is through her flattering speech and secondarily through physical attraction. ◆

The Ur-Nammu law code of 57 laws including family law, which would speak to the "strange" woman's actions.

[2] you have been trapped by what
you said,
ensnared by the words of your
mouth.
[3] So do this, my son, to free
yourself,
since you have fallen into your
neighbor's hands:
Go — to the point of exhaustion —[a]
and give your neighbor no
rest!
[4] Allow no sleep to your eyes,
no slumber to your
eyelids.[d]

6:4 [d] Ps 132:4

[a] 3 Or *Go and humble yourself,*

events, but not to raise their standard of living. Cautions about lending money include making sure that the lenders have obtained security and that they are careful not to trust too highly the one to whom they are lending money.

A text that specifically warns against becoming surety or a guarantor of another is found in the "Instructions of Shuruppak" (l. 19), where it is observed that if you become the guarantor for someone else's loan, they will have some control over you.

5 Free yourself, like a gazelle from the
hand of the hunter,
like a bird from the snare of the
fowler.[e]

6 Go to the ant, you sluggard;[f]
consider its ways and be wise!
7 It has no commander,
no overseer or ruler,
8 yet it stores its provisions in summer
and gathers its food at harvest.[g]

9 How long will you lie there, you
sluggard?[h]
When will you get up from your
sleep?
10 A little sleep, a little slumber,
a little folding of the hands to
rest[i] —
11 and poverty[j] will come on you like a
thief
and scarcity like an armed man.

12 A troublemaker and a villain,
who goes about with a corrupt
mouth,
13 who winks maliciously with his
eye,[k]
signals with his feet
and motions with his fingers,
14 who plots evil[l] with deceit in his
heart —
he always stirs up conflict.[m]
15 Therefore disaster will overtake him in
an instant;
he will suddenly be destroyed —
without remedy.[n]

16 There are six things the LORD hates,
seven that are detestable to him:
17 haughty eyes,
a lying tongue,[o]
hands that shed innocent blood,[p]
18 a heart that devises wicked
schemes,
feet that are quick to rush into
evil,[q]
19 a false witness[r] who pours out lies
and a person who stirs up conflict
in the community.[s]

Warning Against Adultery

20 My son, keep your father's command
and do not forsake your mother's
teaching.[t]
21 Bind them always on your heart;
fasten them around your neck.[u]
22 When you walk, they will guide you;
when you sleep, they will watch
over you;
when you awake, they will speak to
you.
23 For this command is a lamp,
this teaching is a light,[v]
and correction and instruction
are the way to life,
24 keeping you from your neighbor's wife,
from the smooth talk of a wayward
woman.[w]
25 Do not lust in your heart after her
beauty
or let her captivate you with her
eyes.
26 For a prostitute can be had for a loaf of
bread,
but another man's wife preys on
your very life.[x]
27 Can a man scoop fire into his lap
without his clothes being burned?
28 Can a man walk on hot coals
without his feet being scorched?
29 So is he who sleeps[y] with another
man's wife;[z]
no one who touches her will go
unpunished.

30 People do not despise a thief if he
steals
to satisfy his hunger when he is
starving.
31 Yet if he is caught, he must pay
sevenfold,[a]
though it costs him all the wealth of
his house.
32 But a man who commits adultery[b] has
no sense;[c]
whoever does so destroys himself.
33 Blows and disgrace are his lot,
and his shame will never[d] be wiped
away.
34 For jealousy[e] arouses a husband's
fury,[f]
and he will show no mercy when he
takes revenge.
35 He will not accept any compensation;
he will refuse a bribe, however great
it is.[g]

6:5 [e] Ps 91:3 **6:6** [f] Pr 20:4 **6:8** [g] Pr 10:4 **6:9** [h] Pr 24:30-34 **6:10** [i] Pr 24:33 **6:11** [j] Pr 24:30-34 **6:13** [k] Ps 35:19 **6:14** [l] Mic 2:1 [m] ver 16-19 **6:15** [n] 2Ch 36:16 **6:17** [o] Ps 120:2; Pr 12:22 [p] Dt 19:10; Isa 1:15; 59:7 **6:18** [q] Ge 6:5 **6:19** [r] Ps 27:12 [s] ver 12-15 **6:20** [t] Pr 1:8

6:21 [u] Pr 3:3; 7:1-3 **6:23** [v] Ps 19:8; 119:105 **6:24** [w] Pr 2:16; 7:5 **6:26** [x] Pr 7:22-23; 29:3 **6:29** [y] Ex 20:14 [z] Pr 2:16-19; 5:8 **6:31** [a] Ex 22:1-14 **6:32** [b] Ex 20:14 [c] Pr 7:7; 9:4, 16 **6:33** [d] Pr 5:9-14 **6:34** [e] Nu 5:14 [f] Ge 34:7 **6:35** [g] Job 31:9-11; SS 8:7

6:6 *ant.* Examination of the creatures of nature provides both good and bad examples of behavior. The ant is proclaimed the paragon of hard work and foresightedness (cf. 30:25), storing food for the future. Yet another aspect of their character is noted in an Amarna letter, which states that the ant, despite its small size, is willing to defend itself when provoked.
6:9 *you sluggard.* See note on 12:24.
6:13 *winks ... signals ... motions.* This verse enigmatically talks about body language. It accuses those who wink their eye, signal with their feet and motion with their fingers of being scoundrels. While these gestures may simply be a sign of restlessness that results in bad behavior, another alternative is that they are related to ancient practices of sorcery, referring to ways of putting a hex on another person.
6:17 *lying tongue.* See note on 10:18.

Warning Against the Adulterous Woman

7 My son,[h] keep my words
and store up my commands within you.
2 Keep my commands and you will live;[i]
guard my teachings as the apple of your eye.
3 Bind them on your fingers;
write them on the tablet of your heart.[j]
4 Say to wisdom, "You are my sister,"
and to insight, "You are my relative."
5 They will keep you from the adulterous woman,
from the wayward woman with her seductive words.[k]

6 At the window of my house
I looked down through the lattice.
7 I saw among the simple,
I noticed among the young men,
a youth who had no sense.[l]
8 He was going down the street near her corner,
walking along in the direction of her house
9 at twilight,[m] as the day was fading,
as the dark of night set in.

10 Then out came a woman to meet him,
dressed like a prostitute and with crafty intent.
11 (She is unruly[n] and defiant,
her feet never stay at home;
12 now in the street, now in the squares,
at every corner she lurks.)[o]
13 She took hold of him[p] and kissed him
and with a brazen face she said:[q]

14 "Today I fulfilled my vows,
and I have food from my fellowship offering[r] at home.
15 So I came out to meet you;
I looked for you and have found you!
16 I have covered my bed
with colored linens from Egypt.
17 I have perfumed my bed[s]
with myrrh,[t] aloes and cinnamon.
18 Come, let's drink deeply of love till morning;
let's enjoy ourselves with love![u]
19 My husband is not at home;
he has gone on a long journey.
20 He took his purse filled with money
and will not be home till full moon."

21 With persuasive words she led him astray;
she seduced him with her smooth talk.[v]
22 All at once he followed her
like an ox going to the slaughter,
like a deer[a] stepping into a noose[b][w]

7:1 [h] Pr 1:8; 2:1 **7:2** [i] Pr 4:4 **7:3** [j] Dt 6:8; Pr 3:3 **7:5** [k] ver 21; Job 31:9; Pr 2:16; 6:24 **7:7** [l] Pr 1:22; 6:32 **7:9** [m] Job 24:15 **7:11** [n] Pr 9:13; 1Ti 5:13 **7:12** [o] Pr 8:1-36; 23:26-28 **7:13** [p] Ge 39:12 [q] Pr 1:20 **7:14** [r] Lev 7:11-18 **7:17** [s] Est 1:6; Isa 57:7; Eze 23:41; Am 6:4 [t] Ge 37:25 **7:18** [u] Ge 39:7 **7:21** [v] Pr 5:3 **7:22** [w] Job 18:10

[a] 22 Syriac (see also Septuagint); Hebrew *fool*
[b] 22 The meaning of the Hebrew for this line is uncertain.

7:3 *tablet of your heart.* See note on 3:3.
7:4 *my sister.* The reference to Woman Wisdom as "sister" must be understood in the context of ancient Near Eastern and Biblical love poetry ("my sister, my bride"; SS 4:9), where the "sister" is actually the beloved. In other words, the father encourages his son to make Woman Wisdom his lover, his wife. One Egyptian love poem begins: "One alone is (my) sister, having no peer: more gracious than all other women."
7:8,12 *corner.* Babylonian texts speak of small open-air shrines or niches on street corners or courtyards. One text says that there were 180 of them in the city of Babylon to the goddess Ishtar. Each of these shrines featured a raised structure with an altar on the top, and they seem to have been frequented primarily by women. In this sense, the word "corner" may refer to what is basically a cultic niche—a small, half-enclosed shrine where a small image would have stood.
7:13 *brazen face.* Compare the stance and attitude of the "brazen prostitute" in Eze 16:30. The Hebrew term here translated "brazen" is more often rendered as "strong" (e.g., Ps 52:7) or "oppressive" (e.g., Jdg 6:2), but it can also take on the connotation of impudence, i.e., to "put up a bold front" (e.g., Pr 21:29; Ecc 7:19). This latter translation fits the context of the adulterous woman who lies in wait for her victims and confidently invites them into her perfumed chambers. It also can be compared to the wife in the Code of Hammurapi who is "not circumspect" and "disparages her husband."
7:14 *fellowship offering.* While some entertain the possibility that this type of offering is associated with a pagan ritual in which the woman engages in cultic prostitution as well as the offering of sacrifice, it is best to understand this offering in the light of Lev 3; 7:11–21. The fellowship offering is one that emphasizes communion between the worshiper and God, as well as between fellow worshipers. The meat must be eaten on the same day as the sacrifice. Therefore, it seems that the woman is trying to entice the man not only with her body but also with a delicious meal. Her acts accentuate the sinfulness of her behavior, adding the misuse of holy things (the sacrifice) to adultery.
7:16 *colored linens from Egypt.* One of the most important trade items produced in Egypt was linen (Eze 27:7). Royal and personal texts contain mention of its production from flax thread and its use as a medium of exchange or barter. One Eleventh Dynasty text (First Intermediate Period, about the time of the patriarchs) describes how a farmer used cloth woven from flax harvested on his land to pay rent. Colored cloth, which required the additional step of dyeing in its manufacturing process, would have been costly, and in the case of the adulterous woman it served as both a sign of wealth and as a brightly colored enticement to enter her chamber.
7:17 *myrrh, aloes and cinnamon.* These spices are familiar also in SS 4:14, where they describe the woman's garden, a euphemism for her private sexual parts. These spices would have been imported from exotic places like Arabia and India.

23 till an arrow pierces[x] his liver,
like a bird darting into a snare,
little knowing it will cost him his life.[y]

24 Now then, my sons, listen[z] to me;
pay attention to what I say.
25 Do not let your heart turn to her ways
or stray into her paths.[a]
26 Many are the victims she has brought down;
her slain are a mighty throng.
27 Her house is a highway to the grave,
leading down to the chambers of death.[b]

Wisdom's Call

8 Does not wisdom call out?[c]
Does not understanding raise her voice?
2 At the highest point along the way,
where the paths meet, she takes her stand;
3 beside the gate leading into the city,
at the entrance, she cries aloud:[d]
4 "To you, O people, I call out;
I raise my voice to all mankind.
5 You who are simple,[e] gain prudence;[f]
you who are foolish, set your hearts on it.[a]
6 Listen, for I have trustworthy things to say;
I open my lips to speak what is right.
7 My mouth speaks what is true,[g]
for my lips detest wickedness.
8 All the words of my mouth are just;
none of them is crooked or perverse.
9 To the discerning all of them are right;
they are upright to those who have found knowledge.
10 Choose my instruction instead of silver,
knowledge rather than choice gold,[h]
11 for wisdom is more precious[i] than rubies,
and nothing you desire can compare with her.[j]

12 "I, wisdom, dwell together with prudence;
I possess knowledge and discretion.[k]
13 To fear the LORD is to hate evil;[l]
I hate[m] pride and arrogance,
evil behavior and perverse speech.
14 Counsel and sound judgment are mine;
I have insight, I have power.[n]
15 By me kings reign
and rulers[o] issue decrees that are just;
16 by me princes govern,
and nobles — all who rule on earth.[b]
17 I love those who love me,[p]
and those who seek me find me.[q]
18 With me are riches and honor,[r]
enduring wealth and prosperity.[s]
19 My fruit is better than fine gold;
what I yield surpasses choice silver.[t]
20 I walk in the way of righteousness,
along the paths of justice,
21 bestowing a rich inheritance on those who love me
and making their treasuries full.[u]

22 "The LORD brought me forth as the first of his works,[c,d]
before his deeds of old;
23 I was formed long ages ago,
at the very beginning, when the world came to be.
24 When there were no watery depths,
I was given birth,
when there were no springs overflowing with water;[v]

7:23 [x] Job 15:22; 16:13 [y] Pr 6:26; Ecc 7:26; 9:12 **7:24** [z] Pr 1:8-9; 5:7; 8:32 **7:25** [a] Pr 5:7-8 **7:27** [b] Pr 2:18; 5:5; 9:18; Rev 22:15 **8:1** [c] Pr 1:20; 9:3 **8:3** [d] Job 29:7 **8:5** [e] Pr 1:22 [f] Pr 1:4 **8:7** [g] Ps 37:30; Jn 8:14 **8:10** [h] Pr 3:14-15 **8:11** [i] Job 28:17-19 [j] Pr 3:13-15 **8:12** [k] Pr 1:4 **8:13** [l] Pr 16:6 [m] Jer 44:4 **8:14** [n] Pr 21:22; Ecc 7:19 **8:15** [o] Da 2:21; Ro 13:1 **8:17** [p] 1Sa 2:30; Ps 91:14; Jn 14:21-24 [q] Pr 1:28; Jas 1:5 **8:18** [r] Pr 3:16 [s] Dt 8:18; Mt 6:33 **8:19** [t] Pr 3:13-14; 10:20 **8:21** [u] Pr 24:4 **8:24** [v] Ge 7:11

[a] 5 Septuagint; Hebrew *foolish, instruct your minds* [b] 16 Some Hebrew manuscripts and Septuagint; other Hebrew manuscripts *all righteous rulers* [c] 22 Or *way*; or *dominion* [d] 22 Or *The LORD possessed me at the beginning of his work*; or *The LORD brought me forth at the beginning of his work*

7:23 *arrow pierces his liver.* Egyptian tomb paintings often depict the deceased noble hunting in the marshlands. Beaters frighten the fowl to break from cover, and in their terror a hail of arrows from the hunters unexpectedly meets them. The unsuspecting character of the adulterous woman's victim suggests this same attitude of preoccupation or obliviousness to the real danger he faces. *liver.* Considered among the most vital organs, so is mentioned as the target here.
8:2 *At the highest point.* See note on 9:3.
8:3 *the gate.* A pivotal point in an ancient Near Eastern city. It was the place where people went in and went out of the city. It was a place where the elders met and commerce took place. In other words, it was a public location through which most of the inhabitants of the city would pass. Thus, someone, like Woman Wisdom, speaking near the gate would attract a substantial audience. See notes on Job 5:4; 29:7.
8:11 *more precious than rubies.* See note on 3:15.
8:12 *I, wisdom.* The rest of ch. 8 contains the autobiography of Woman Wisdom. We learn about her character and her actions. At the end (vv. 32 – 36), she gives advice to the "children" (v. 32) who listen to her. In form, this self-description followed by advice follows the structure of other fictionalized autobiographies known in Hebrew (the Teacher's speech in Ecc 1:12 — 12:8), Akkadian (the Cuthean Legend of Naram-Sin, the Adad-Guppi autobiography, and the Sin of Sargon text), and Aramaic (*Words of Ahiqar*) that end with advice.
8:15 *By me kings reign.* The idea that good kings are guided by wisdom may be found in the Historical Books of the Bible (see the description of Solomon in 1Ki 1 – 4) as well as in ancient Near Eastern texts. In terms of the latter, a few of the instruction texts are the advice of a royal father to his son and successor (e.g., "Teaching for Merikare").
8:24 *When there were no watery depths.* This verse must be understood based on the background of ancient Near Eastern creation accounts that presume a primordial watery mass from which the dry land is separated. In Egypt, creation is thought to emanate from the Nun, or watery abyss (see note on Ps 104:5). In Mesopotamia and

PROVERBS 8

What Is Wisdom?

We often think of wisdom as intelligence, but we would be mistaken to bring that definition to this literature. When we look at the vast number of topics covered under the heading of "wisdom," it is easy to despair of finding common ground, for the heading covers artisan skills, scientific knowledge, etiquette, philosophy, psychology, politics, sociology and jurisprudence, just to name a few. Furthermore, the text insists on more than one occasion that the "fear of the LORD" is the beginning or foundation of wisdom (Pr 1:7; 9:10; 15:33). Does this suggest that none of those disciplines could be successfully engaged without fear of the Lord?

As we consider the way that people thought in the ancient world, perhaps we can best capture the Biblical way of understanding all of this by thinking in terms of worldview integration. In the ancient world, including Israel, *order* was an important value. Creation brought order to the cosmos; law brought order to society; etiquette brought order to human relationships; politics brought order to governance and authority. Ancient wisdom can then be understood as the pursuit of understanding and preserving order in the world. Wisdom is present when order is perceived, pursued and preserved. The people of the day wanted their worldview to fit together like a puzzle — fully integrated, with each piece placed in proper relation to the others. They saw the fear of the Lord as the keystone to this integration process. To "fear the LORD" means to take his person and role seriously. Order in the cosmos could only be understood through acknowledgment of the One who brought order. Order could only be preserved in society and in life by understanding God's requirements and expectations. In this way, wisdom can be seen to transcend the basic knowledge or skill related to particular disciplines.

A fool (or any of the other synonyms used to describe such a person) was one who brought disorder into any of the pertinent realms by their behavior or thinking. Furthermore, a fool would be one who did not fear the Lord and therefore tried to find coherence in something or someone else — usually themselves. ◆

25 before the mountains were settled
in place,
before the hills, I was given birth,[w]
26 before he made the world or its
fields
or any of the dust of the earth.[x]
27 I was there when he set the heavens in
place,[y]
when he marked out the horizon on
the face of the deep,
28 when he established the clouds above
and fixed securely the fountains of
the deep,
29 when he gave the sea its boundary[z]
so the waters would not overstep
his command,[a]
and when he marked out the
foundations of the earth.[b]
30 Then I was constantly[a] at his side.[c]
I was filled with delight day after
day,
rejoicing always in his presence,
31 rejoicing in his whole world
and delighting in mankind.[d]

8:25 [w] Job 15:7
8:26 [x] Ps 90:2
8:27 [y] Pr 3:19
8:29 [z] Ge 1:9; Job 38:10; Ps 16:6 [a] Ps 104:9 [b] Job 38:5
8:30 [c] Jn 1:1-3
8:31 [d] Ps 16:3; 104:1-30

[a] 30 Or *was the artisan*; or *was a little child*

Canaan, the creator-god (Marduk and Baal, respectively) defeat the god of the sea (Tiamat and Yamm, respectively) and by bounding their waters create the dry land (see the articles "Baal," p. 600; "Chaos Monsters," p. 953). In Ge 1 the original mass, described as formless and void (Hebrew *tohu wabohu*), is a watery mass from which the dry ground is separated on the second day (see notes on Ge 1:2,9; see also the article "The 'Vault' and 'Water Above,'" p. 6).
8:29 *when he gave the sea its boundary.* This language is reminiscent of the Babylonian Creation Epic, the *Enuma Elish*. After defeating Tiamat, the god of the sea, Marduk creates borders for her water, pushing it back in order to provide space for land (see the article "Cosmic Geography," p. 836).

32 "Now then, my children, listen to me;
blessed are[e] those who keep my ways.[f]
33 Listen to my instruction and be wise;
do not disregard it.
34 Blessed are those who listen[g] to me,
watching daily at my doors,
waiting at my doorway.
35 For those who find me[h] find life
and receive favor from the LORD.[i]
36 But those who fail to find me harm themselves;[j]
all who hate me love death."

Invitations of Wisdom and Folly

9 Wisdom has built[k] her house;
she has set up[a] its seven pillars.
2 She has prepared her meat and mixed her wine;
she has also set her table.[l]
3 She has sent out her servants, and she calls[m]
from the highest point of the city,[n]
4 "Let all who are simple come to my house!"
To those who have no sense[o] she says,
5 "Come, eat my food
and drink the wine I have mixed.[p]
6 Leave your simple ways and you will live;[q]
walk in the way of insight."

7 Whoever corrects a mocker invites insults;
whoever rebukes the wicked incurs abuse.[r]
8 Do not rebuke mockers[s] or they will hate you;
rebuke the wise and they will love you.[t]
9 Instruct the wise and they will be wiser still;
teach the righteous and they will add to their learning.[u]

8:32 [e] Lk 11:28 [f] Ps 119:1-2 **8:34** [g] Pr 3:13, 18 **8:35** [h] Pr 3:13-18 [i] Pr 12:2 **8:36** [j] Pr 15:32 **9:1** [k] Eph 2:20-22; 1Pe 2:5 **9:2** [l] Lk 14:16-23 **9:3** [m] Pr 8:1-3 [n] ver 14 **9:4** [o] Pr 6:32 **9:5** [p] Isa 55:1 **9:6** [q] Pr 8:35 **9:7** [r] Pr 23:9 **9:8** [s] Pr 15:12 [t] Ps 141:5 **9:9** [u] Pr 1:5,7

[a] *1* Septuagint, Syriac and Targum; Hebrew *has hewn out*

9:1 *seven pillars.* Many theories have been put forward to explain the significance of the seven pillars of Wisdom's house. Some interpret the significance of the number seven as indicating the seven planets known at the time; others take it as a reference to the seven creation days. However, the simplest and best explanation is to take the number seven in its typical symbolic sense, i.e., as indicating completeness. We are to picture a beautiful, large house. One ancient hymn to the god Enki (god of wisdom) may offer another connection of interest. A Sumerian hymn by Ishme-Dagan (Isin period, about 2000 BC) makes reference to seven-fold wisdom granted by Enki to the king.

9:3 *highest point of the city.* This location of Wisdom's house is extremely significant to understanding whom she represents. In the ancient Near East, the only building allowed to occupy the acropolis is the temple. This does not divinize wisdom, but expresses that God is the source of wisdom.

9:8 *Do not rebuke mockers.* A similar insight concerning dealing with mockers is provided by the Egyptian "Instructions of Ankhsheshonq" (7.4–5): "Do not instruct a fool, lest he hate you. Do not instruct him who will not listen to you."

A temple at Luxor with two sets of seven pillars. See note on Pr 9:1.

PROVERBS 8–9

EDUCATION AND SAGES IN THE ANCIENT NEAR EAST

The book of Proverbs is a book of instruction. A father teaches his son to follow in the way of wisdom and to avoid the way of folly. The metaphoric description of Lady Wisdom is that of a teacher as well. She desires to instruct her hearers in the way that leads to life.

The didactic nature of Proverbs and particularly its description of the wisdom teacher or sage raise the question of the status of the sage and education in ancient Israel. This question can only be approached in the context of the broader ancient Near East.

The clearest evidence for education and the role of the sage comes from Mesopotamia. From there we have educational tablets and literary compositions that talk about the life and formation of a young scribe. Indeed, the school has a name, the E-DUB-BA-(A), which means either "house (or 'room') of the tablet." Daniel was subjected to a Babylonian education while in exile in the court of Nebuchadnezzar (Da 1), where he learned the language and literature of the Babylonians. In Egypt too there is an old, long and distinguished tradition of education and the role of the sage in society. The Aramaic text *Words of Ahiqar* illustrates what is found elsewhere: scribes under the employ of the royal court.

The picture is not so clear in ancient Israel, and scholars debate whether or not there were ancient schools and whether or not the sage was a professional designation. That there was some form of education is clear; the question is whether the schools were institutions connected to the court or the temple, or whether education took place in the context of the family. After all, there is no mention of schools until the intertestamental period, when the *bet Midrash* is mentioned in the Apocryphal book of Sirach (see Sirach 51:23). However, it has also been pointed out that educational-type texts (so-called abecedaries) have been recovered that should be dated to the latter part of the monarchy. No one doubts that writing was taught; the question is in what kind of context. That the sage was a professional designation seems clear from its use in the Historical Books (the roles of royal advisors like Jonadab [2Sa 13]; Hushai and Ahithophel [2Sa 15–17]) and in the Prophets (e.g., Jer 18:18), but this does not mean that the title is always used in such a way.

The instructions found in the book of Proverbs have a diverse background: court, family, scribal, and perhaps even religious. For now the question of the social place of the use of Proverbs will have to remain an open-ended question, though the ancient tradition of schools in Mesopotamia and Egypt may invite speculation. ◆

10 The fear of the LORD[v] is the beginning
of wisdom,
and knowledge of the Holy One is
understanding.
11 For through wisdom[a] your days will be
many,
and years will be added to your life.[w]
12 If you are wise, your wisdom will
reward you;
if you are a mocker, you alone will
suffer.

13 Folly is an unruly woman;[x]
she is simple and knows nothing.[y]
14 She sits at the door of her house,
on a seat at the highest point of the
city,[z]
15 calling out to those who pass by,
who go straight on their way,
16 "Let all who are simple come to my
house!"
To those who have no sense she says,
17 "Stolen water is sweet;
food eaten in secret is delicious![a]"
18 But little do they know that the dead
are there,
that her guests are deep in the realm
of the dead.[b]

Proverbs of Solomon

10 The proverbs of Solomon:[c]

A wise son brings joy to his father,[d]
but a foolish son brings grief to his
mother.

2 Ill-gotten treasures have no lasting value,[e]
but righteousness delivers from
death.[f]

3 The LORD does not let the righteous go
hungry,[g]
but he thwarts the craving of the
wicked.

4 Lazy hands make for poverty,[h]
but diligent hands bring wealth.[i]

5 He who gathers crops in summer is a
prudent son,
but he who sleeps during harvest is
a disgraceful son.

6 Blessings crown the head of the
righteous,
but violence overwhelms the mouth
of the wicked.[b][j]

7 The name of the righteous[k] is used in
blessings,[c]
but the name of the wicked[l] will
rot.[m]

8 The wise in heart accept commands,
but a chattering fool comes to
ruin.[n]

9 Whoever walks in integrity[o] walks
securely,[p]
but whoever takes crooked paths
will be found out.[q]

10 Whoever winks maliciously[r] causes
grief,
and a chattering fool comes to ruin.

11 The mouth of the righteous is a
fountain of life,[s]
but the mouth of the wicked
conceals violence.[t]

9:10 [v] Job 28:28; Pr 1:7 **9:11** [w] Pr 3:16; 10:27 **9:13** [x] Pr 7:11 [y] Pr 5:6 **9:14** [z] ver 3 **9:17** [a] Pr 20:17 **9:18** [b] Pr 2:18; 7:26-27 **10:1** [c] Pr 1:1 [d] Pr 15:20; 29:3 **10:2** [e] Pr 21:6 [f] Pr 11:4, 19
10:3 [g] Mt 6:25-34 **10:4** [h] Pr 19:15 [i] Pr 12:24; 13:4; 21:5 **10:6** [j] ver 8, 11, 14 **10:7** [k] Ps 112:6 [l] Ps 109:13 [m] Ps 9:6 **10:8** [n] Mt 7:24-27 **10:9** [o] Isa 33:15 [p] Ps 23:4 [q] Pr 28:18 **10:10** [r] Ps 35:19 **10:11** [s] Ps 37:30; Pr 13:12, 14, 19 [t] ver 6

[a] *11* Septuagint, Syriac and Targum; Hebrew *me*
[b] *6* Or *righteous, / but the mouth of the wicked conceals violence*
[c] *7* See Gen. 48:20.

9:14 *highest point of the city.* See note on v. 3. Surprisingly, Woman Folly's house is also described as located at the highest point of the city, the location occupied by a temple in the ancient Near East. Thus Folly, like Wisdom, is associated with deity. In this case, she represents all the false gods and goddesses that attracted Israelites away from the true God. Thus, the choice between Wisdom and Folly is, among other things, a choice between true and false religion.
9:18 *the dead.* Here and 21:16 do not use the typical Hebrew word, but translate the Hebrew *rephaim.* In 2:18, the same Hebrew word is rendered "the spirits of the dead." Though the Hebrew word is much discussed, there is little agreement about its exact meaning. In 2:18, since *rephaim* stands in parallel to death (*mawet*), there is no doubt that the *rephaim* are deceased persons. Outside of Proverbs, this Hebrew term is used in Job 26:5; Ps 88:10; Isa 14:9; 26:14,19. This list omits occurrences in prose contexts, which raise other issues. The usual understanding of the *rephaim* as "shades" who dwell in the underworld seems correct, particularly in light of the Isaiah passages. See notes on Job 26:5; Isa 14:9.
10:4 *Lazy hands.* See note on 12:24.
10:5 *gathers crops.* Amenemope has similar advice, though expressed in connection with planting rather than harvesting, observing that plowing fields will result eventually in bread to eat.
10:6 *Blessings ... but violence.* See the article "Retribution Principle," p. 823.
10:10 *winks maliciously.* The word "maliciously" is interpretive here, and the other occurrences of this phrase include both eyes, so winking is unlikely. This eye gesture may simply be a reference to a secret signal (see 6:13; 16:30). Some have further suggested that the gesture has a magical significance, like putting a hex on someone; see note on 6:13. An alternative is suggested by the Akkadian omen-wisdom that contains a series of omens related to the eyes. One of them asserts that if a person closes his eyes he will speak falsehood. It is uncertain whether this refers to frequent blinking, or squinting the eyes shut while talking.
10:11 *fountain of life.* As the Egyptian sage Amenemope states: abundant life is to be found in wise action and speech, but "fools who talk publicly in the temple are like a tree planted indoors," which withers and dies for lack of light and is burned or cast away as trash. On the other hand, "the wise who are reserved are like a tree planted in a garden," which bears sweet fruit, provides shade and flourishes "in the garden forever."

12 Hatred stirs up conflict,
but love covers over all wrongs.[u]

13 Wisdom is found on the lips of the discerning,[v]
but a rod is for the back of one who has no sense.[w]

14 The wise store up knowledge,
but the mouth of a fool invites ruin.[x]

15 The wealth of the rich is their fortified city,[y]
but poverty is the ruin of the poor.[z]

16 The wages of the righteous is life,
but the earnings of the wicked are sin and death.[a]

17 Whoever heeds discipline shows the way to life,[b]
but whoever ignores correction leads others astray.

18 Whoever conceals hatred with lying lips
and spreads slander is a fool.

19 Sin is not ended by multiplying words,
but the prudent hold their tongues.[c]

20 The tongue of the righteous is choice silver,
but the heart of the wicked is of little value.

21 The lips of the righteous nourish many,
but fools die for lack of sense.[d]

22 The blessing of the LORD brings wealth,[e]
without painful toil for it.

23 A fool finds pleasure in wicked schemes,[f]
but a person of understanding delights in wisdom.

10:12 [u] Pr 17:9; 1Co 13:4-7; 1Pe 4:8 **10:13** [v] ver 31 [w] Pr 26:3 **10:14** [x] Pr 18:6,7 **10:15** [y] Pr 18:11 [z] Pr 19:7 **10:16** [a] Pr 11:18-19 **10:17** [b] Pr 6:23 **10:19** [c] Pr 17:28; Ecc 5:3; Jas 1:19; 3:2-12 **10:21** [d] Pr 5:22-23; Hos 4:1, 6, 14 **10:22** [e] Ge 24:35; Ps 37:22 **10:23** [f] Pr 2:14; 15:21

10:24 [g] Isa 66:4 [h] Ps 145:17-19; Mt 5:6; 1Jn 5:14-15 **10:25** [i] Ps 15:5 [j] Pr 12:3, 7; Mt 7:24-27 **10:26** [k] Pr 26:6 **10:27** [l] Pr 9:10-11 [m] Job 15:32 **10:28** [n] Job 8:13; Pr 11:7 **10:29** [o] Pr 21:15 **10:30** [p] Ps 37:9, 28-29; Pr 2:20-22 **10:31** [q] Ps 37:30 **10:32** [r] Ecc 10:12 **11:1** [s] Lev 19:36; Dt 25:13-16; Pr 20:10, 23 [t] Pr 16:11 **11:2** [u] Pr 16:18 [v] Pr 18:12; 29:23

24 What the wicked dread[g] will overtake them;
what the righteous desire will be granted.[h]

25 When the storm has swept by, the wicked are gone,
but the righteous stand firm[i] forever.[j]

26 As vinegar to the teeth and smoke to the eyes,
so are sluggards to those who send them.[k]

27 The fear of the LORD adds length to life,[l]
but the years of the wicked are cut short.[m]

28 The prospect of the righteous is joy,
but the hopes of the wicked come to nothing.[n]

29 The way of the LORD is a refuge for the blameless,
but it is the ruin of those who do evil.[o]

30 The righteous will never be uprooted,
but the wicked will not remain in the land.[p]

31 From the mouth of the righteous comes the fruit of wisdom,[q]
but a perverse tongue will be silenced.

32 The lips of the righteous know what finds favor,[r]
but the mouth of the wicked only what is perverse.

11 The LORD detests dishonest scales,[s]
but accurate weights find favor with him.[t]

2 When pride comes, then comes disgrace,[u]
but with humility comes wisdom.[v]

10:18 *lying lips.* The sages roundly and frequently condemn false speech. Lies destroy relationships and cause all kinds of havoc. Proverbs is not alone in promoting truth in speech. Examples of similar teaching from the broader Near East advise not to speak falsely since that displeases the gods.

10:27 *The fear of the LORD adds length to life.* The idea that religious piety lengthens life may be found in other ancient Near Eastern texts, as illustrated by the Sumerian "Instructions of Ur-Ninurta": "The man who knows fear of god … days will be added to his days" (lines 19, 26). But in the larger ancient world, this fear of god resulted in conscientious performance of ritual. Since the gods were believed to have needs, people who faithfully supplied those needs through ritual would be favored and protected, thus resulting in their long life. In contrast, Israelite faithfulness and fear of the Lord was demonstrated in covenant loyalty.

11:1 *The LORD detests.* See note on 15:8. *dishonest scales.* The scale described here was composed of two plates suspended from a bar of some sort. On one plate was a premeasured weight (lit. "stone" [Hebrew *eben*]), over against which the product would be balanced. Such a system could be fraudulently manipulated in a variety of ways, including falsely labeling the weight. The language of the proverb echoes legal portions of the Pentateuch (Lev 19:35–37; Dt 25:13–15) as well as prophetic indictments relating to justice (Eze 45:10; Hos 12:7–8; Am 8:5; Mic 6:11). The "Instruction of Amenemope" commits two chapters condemning the practice of altering weights, and the Babylonian "Hymn to Shamash," the god of the sun and justice, condemns those involved in fraudulent practices connected to weights and balances.

11:2 *pride.* The late Egyptian Papyrus Insinger says this about those with excessive pride: "There is he who is arrogant, and he makes a stench in the street" (27.17). Pride was often the result of a sense of self-importance. The cultures of the ancient world found greater value in the community and the clan than in the individual, so the vaunting on oneself was considered a negative trait.

[3] The integrity of the upright guides
them,
but the unfaithful are destroyed by
their duplicity.[w]

[4] Wealth is worthless in the day of
wrath,[x]
but righteousness delivers from death.[y]

[5] The righteousness of the blameless
makes their paths straight,
but the wicked are brought down by
their own wickedness.[z]

[6] The righteousness of the upright
delivers them,
but the unfaithful are trapped by evil
desires.

[7] Hopes placed in mortals die with them;
all the promise of[a] their power
comes to nothing.[a]

[8] The righteous person is rescued from
trouble,
and it falls on the wicked instead.[b]

[9] With their mouths the godless destroy
their neighbors,
but through knowledge the righteous
escape.

[10] When the righteous prosper, the city
rejoices;[c]
when the wicked perish, there are
shouts of joy.

[11] Through the blessing of the upright a
city is exalted,
but by the mouth of the wicked it is
destroyed.[d]

[12] Whoever derides their neighbor has no
sense,[e]
but the one who has understanding
holds their tongue.

[13] A gossip betrays a confidence,[f]
but a trustworthy person keeps a
secret.

[14] For lack of guidance a nation falls,[g]
but victory is won through many
advisers.[h]

[15] Whoever puts up security[i] for a
stranger will surely suffer,
but whoever refuses to shake hands
in pledge is safe.

11:3 [w] Pr 13:6
11:4 [x] Eze 7:19; Zep 1:18 [y] Ge 7:1; Pr 10:2
11:5 [z] Pr 5:21-23
11:7 [a] Pr 10:28
11:8 [b] Pr 21:18
11:10 [c] Pr 28:12
11:11 [d] Pr 29:8
11:12 [e] Pr 14:21
11:13 [f] Lev 19:16; Pr 20:19; 1Ti 5:13
11:14 [g] Pr 20:18 [h] Pr 15:22; 24:6
11:15 [i] Pr 6:1

[16] A kindhearted woman gains honor,[j]
but ruthless men gain only wealth.

[17] Those who are kind benefit
themselves,
but the cruel bring ruin on themselves.

[18] A wicked person earns deceptive
wages,
but the one who sows righteousness
reaps a sure reward.[k]

[19] Truly the righteous attain life,
but whoever pursues evil finds
death.

[20] The LORD detests those whose hearts
are perverse,
but he delights in those whose ways
are blameless.[l]

[21] Be sure of this: The wicked will not go
unpunished,
but those who are righteous will go
free.[m]

[22] Like a gold ring in a pig's snout
is a beautiful woman who shows no
discretion.

[23] The desire of the righteous ends only
in good,
but the hope of the wicked only in
wrath.

[24] One person gives freely, yet gains even
more;
another withholds unduly, but
comes to poverty.

[25] A generous person will prosper;
whoever refreshes others will be
refreshed.[n]

[26] People curse the one who hoards grain,
but they pray God's blessing on the
one who is willing to sell.

[27] Whoever seeks good finds favor,
but evil comes to one who searches
for it.[o]

[28] Those who trust in their riches will
fall,[p]
but the righteous will thrive like a
green leaf.[q]

11:16 [j] Pr 31:31
11:18 [k] Hos 10:12-13
11:20 [l] 1Ch 29:17; Ps 119:1; Pr 12:2,22
11:21 [m] Pr 16:5
11:25 [n] Mt 5:7; 2Co 9:6-9
11:27 [o] Est 7:10; Ps 7:15-16
11:28 [p] Job 31:24-28; Ps 49:6; 52:7; Mk 10:25; 1Ti 6:17 [q] Ps 1:3; 92:12-14; Jer 17:8

[a] 7 Two Hebrew manuscripts; most Hebrew manuscripts, Vulgate, Syriac and Targum *When the wicked die, their hope perishes; / all they expected from*

11:11 Wisdom has social repercussions, as does folly, since it is identified with wickedness in Proverbs. Wisdom (the result of order and the fear of the Lord) brings joy to the city, because it unites people and they prosper. Folly (the result of disorder) brings grief, because it tears people apart and they languish. The Assyrian sage Ahiqar agrees with this, though his Saying 75 speaks to only the latter point: "[The city] of the wicked will be swept away in the day of storm, and its gates will fall into ruin; for the spoil [of the wicked shall perish]."
11:12 *holds their tongue.* See note on 12:13; 29:20.
11:13 *gossip.* Those who speak ill about others behind their backs in order to ruin their reputation are fools according to Proverbs, and they will come to a bad end, since they fracture the structure of society. Ptahhotep refers to gossip as the "spouting of the hot-bellied."
11:15 *puts up security for a stranger.* See note on 6:1.
11:20 *The LORD detests.* See note on 15:8.

29 Whoever brings ruin on their family
will inherit only wind,
and the fool will be servant to the
wise.[r]

30 The fruit of the righteous is a tree of
life,[s]
and the one who is wise saves lives.

31 If the righteous receive their due[t] on
earth,
how much more the ungodly and the
sinner!

12 Whoever loves discipline loves
knowledge,
but whoever hates correction is
stupid.[u]

2 Good people obtain favor from the LORD,
but he condemns those who devise
wicked schemes.

3 No one can be established through
wickedness,
but the righteous cannot be
uprooted.[v]

4 A wife of noble character is her
husband's crown,
but a disgraceful wife is like decay in
his bones.[w]

5 The plans of the righteous are just,
but the advice of the wicked is
deceitful.

6 The words of the wicked lie in wait for
blood,
but the speech of the upright rescues
them.[x]

7 The wicked are overthrown and are no
more,[y]
but the house of the righteous stands
firm.[z]

8 A person is praised according to their
prudence,
and one with a warped mind is
despised.

9 Better to be a nobody and yet have a
servant
than pretend to be somebody and
have no food.

10 The righteous care for the needs of
their animals,
but the kindest acts of the wicked
are cruel.

11 Those who work their land will have
abundant food,
but those who chase fantasies have
no sense.[a]

12 The wicked desire the stronghold of
evildoers,
but the root of the righteous endures.

13 Evildoers are trapped by their sinful
talk,[b]
and so the innocent escape trouble.[c]

14 From the fruit of their lips people are
filled with good things,[d]
and the work of their hands brings
them reward.[e]

15 The way of fools seems right to them,[f]
but the wise listen to advice.

16 Fools show their annoyance at once,
but the prudent overlook an insult.[g]

17 An honest witness tells the truth,
but a false witness tells lies.[h]

18 The words of the reckless pierce like
swords,[i]
but the tongue of the wise brings
healing.[j]

19 Truthful lips endure forever,
but a lying tongue lasts only a
moment.

20 Deceit is in the hearts of those who
plot evil,
but those who promote peace have
joy.

21 No harm overtakes the righteous,[k]
but the wicked have their fill of
trouble.

22 The LORD detests lying lips,[l]
but he delights in people who are
trustworthy.[m]

23 The prudent keep their knowledge to
themselves,[n]
but a fool's heart blurts out folly.

11:29 [r] Pr 14:19 **11:30** [s] Jas 5:20 **11:31** [t] Pr 13:21; Jer 25:29; 1Pe 4:18 **12:1** [u] Pr 9:7-9; 15:5, 10, 12, 32 **12:3** [v] Pr 10:25 **12:4** [w] Pr 14:30 **12:6** [x] Pr 14:3 **12:7** [y] Ps 37:36 [z] Pr 10:25

12:11 [a] Pr 28:19 **12:13** [b] Pr 18:7 [c] Pr 21:23; 2Pe 2:9 **12:14** [d] Pr 13:2; 15:23; 18:20 [e] Isa 3:10-11 **12:15** [f] Pr 14:12; 16:2, 25; Lk 18:11 **12:16** [g] Pr 29:11 **12:17** [h] Pr 14:5, 25 **12:18** [i] Ps 57:4 [j] Pr 15:4 **12:21** [k] Ps 91:10 **12:22** [l] Pr 6:17; Rev 22:15 [m] Pr 11:20 **12:23** [n] Pr 10:14; 13:16

11:29 *will inherit only wind.* Those who disturb the tranquility of their family will have no prosperity. A similar thought is expressed in a Sumerian proverb: "An unjust heir who does not support a wife, who does not support a son, is not raised to prosperity." On the flip side of the same truth, Ankhsheshonq advises: "Serve your mother and father, that you may go and prosper."
11:30 *tree of life.* See note on 3:18.
12:13 *trapped by their sinful talk.* Proverbs frequently teaches that foolish speech has dire consequences and inevitably results in disorder. In some proverbs, as here, the nature of the speech is not specified, but on other occasions it is described as lying, gossip, slander, rumor and other socially destructive behaviors. Egyptian sages also recognized the connection between evil speech and negative results. A good example is from Any: "A man may be ruined by his tongue, Beware and you will do well."
12:17 *false witness.* See note on 10:18 for lying in general. The Egyptian "Instruction of Amenemope" specifically condemns falsehood (perjury) in the courtroom.
12:19 *lying tongue.* See note on 10:18.
12:22 *The LORD detests.* See note on 15:8. *lying lips.* See note on 10:18.

24 Diligent hands will rule,
but laziness ends in forced labor.[o]

25 Anxiety weighs down the heart,[p]
but a kind word cheers it up.

26 The righteous choose their friends carefully,
but the way of the wicked leads them astray.

27 The lazy do not roast[a] any game,
but the diligent feed on the riches of the hunt.

28 In the way of righteousness there is life;[q]
along that path is immortality.

13 A wise son heeds his father's instruction,
but a mocker does not respond to rebukes.[r]

2 From the fruit of their lips people enjoy good things,[s]
but the unfaithful have an appetite for violence.

3 Those who guard their lips[t] preserve their lives,[u]
but those who speak rashly will come to ruin.[v]

4 A sluggard's appetite is never filled,
but the desires of the diligent are fully satisfied.

5 The righteous hate what is false,
but the wicked make themselves a stench
and bring shame on themselves.

6 Righteousness guards the person of integrity,
but wickedness overthrows the sinner.[w]

7 One person pretends to be rich, yet has nothing;
another pretends to be poor, yet has great wealth.[x]

8 A person's riches may ransom their life,
but the poor cannot respond to threatening rebukes.

9 The light of the righteous shines brightly,
but the lamp of the wicked is snuffed out.[y]

10 Where there is strife, there is pride,
but wisdom is found in those who take advice.

11 Dishonest money dwindles away,[z]
but whoever gathers money little by little makes it grow.

12 Hope deferred makes the heart sick,
but a longing fulfilled is a tree of life.

13 Whoever scorns instruction will pay for it,[a]
but whoever respects a command is rewarded.

14 The teaching of the wise is a fountain of life,[b]
turning a person from the snares of death.[c]

15 Good judgment wins favor,
but the way of the unfaithful leads to their destruction.[b]

16 All who are prudent act with[c] knowledge,
but fools expose their folly.[d]

17 A wicked messenger falls into trouble,
but a trustworthy envoy brings healing.[e]

18 Whoever disregards discipline comes to poverty and shame,
but whoever heeds correction is honored.[f]

12:24 [o] Pr 10:4 **12:25** [p] Pr 15:13; Isa 50:4 **12:28** [q] Dt 30:15 **13:1** [r] Pr 10:1 **13:2** [s] Pr 12:14 **13:3** [t] Jas 3:2 [u] Pr 21:23 [v] Pr 18:7,20-21 **13:6** [w] Pr 11:3,5 **13:7** [x] 2Co 6:10 **13:9** [y] Job 18:5; Pr 4:18-19; 24:20 **13:11** [z] Pr 10:2 **13:13** [a] Nu 15:31; 2Ch 36:16 **13:14** [b] Pr 10:11 [c] Pr 14:27 **13:16** [d] Pr 12:23 **13:17** [e] Pr 25:13 **13:18** [f] Pr 15:5, 31-32

[a] *27* The meaning of the Hebrew for this word is uncertain. [b] *15* Septuagint and Syriac; the meaning of the Hebrew for this phrase is uncertain. [c] *16* Or *prudent protect themselves through*

12:24 *Diligent hands … but laziness.* One of the single most important themes in the book of Proverbs contrasts lazy people with the diligent. The sages considered laziness a preeminent type of folly that results in destitution. In a culture in which one's contribution to the community and clan were of great importance, laziness was among the greatest of flaws. Indeed, the Biblical sages are often at their satirical best when describing the lazy in bed like a door turning on its hinges (26:14) or refusing to go outside for fear of being attacked by a lion (26:13). *rule.* Hard workers will find themselves in positions of importance, and the lazy will be their slaves. The Egyptian "Instruction of Any" states the same principle: "He who is slack amounts to nothing, Honored is the man who's active."
12:25 *Anxiety weighs down the heart.* Worry debilitates a person. It can lead to depression and even illness. The Egyptian Papyrus Insinger observes that worry can lead to sickness or even to death. The Biblical proverb here looks to the "kind word" as an antidote, though the Israelites would not have disagreed with the Egyptian text that reminds that the god gives patience to the wise, while the ungodly are left to their own resources and flounder.
12:27 *lazy.* See note on v. 24.
13:3 *guard their lips.* Self-control in speech is a highly desired trait according to both Biblical and Egyptian sages. A narrative example of how careful speech comes to a person's aid may be observed in the Egyptian tale of the "Eloquent Peasant," in which an uneducated man comes before the king to make a plea for a favorable judgment and acquits himself so well in his speech that his request is granted.
13:4 *sluggard's.* See note on 12:24.
13:12 *tree of life.* See note on 3:18.
13:17 *wicked messenger.* Government, military, commerce, and even personal communication all depended on messengers. While writing letters was known in the ancient world, much communication took place orally. In the case of written letters or oral communications, the

19 A longing fulfilled is sweet to the soul,
but fools detest turning from evil.

20 Walk with the wise and become wise,
for a companion of fools suffers harm.[g]

21 Trouble pursues the sinner,
but the righteous[h] are rewarded with good things.

22 A good person leaves an inheritance
for their children's children,
but a sinner's wealth is stored up for the righteous.[i]

23 An unplowed field produces food for the poor,
but injustice sweeps it away.

24 Whoever spares the rod hates their children,
but the one who loves their children
is careful to discipline them.[j]

25 The righteous eat to their hearts' content,
but the stomach of the wicked goes hungry.[k]

14 The wise woman builds her house,[l]
but with her own hands the foolish one tears hers down.

2 Whoever fears the LORD walks uprightly,
but those who despise him are devious in their ways.

3 A fool's mouth lashes out with pride,
but the lips of the wise protect them.[m]

4 Where there are no oxen, the manger is empty,
but from the strength of an ox come abundant harvests.

5 An honest witness does not deceive,
but a false witness pours out lies.[n]

6 The mocker seeks wisdom and finds none,
but knowledge comes easily to the discerning.

7 Stay away from a fool,
for you will not find knowledge on their lips.

8 The wisdom of the prudent is to give thought to their ways,
but the folly of fools is deception.[o]

9 Fools mock at making amends for sin,
but goodwill is found among the upright.

10 Each heart knows its own bitterness,
and no one else can share its joy.

11 The house of the wicked will be destroyed,
but the tent of the upright will flourish.[p]

12 There is a way that appears to be right,[q]
but in the end it leads to death.[r]

13 Even in laughter[s] the heart may ache,
and rejoicing may end in grief.

14 The faithless will be fully repaid for their ways,[t]
and the good rewarded for theirs.[u]

15 The simple believe anything,
but the prudent give thought to their steps.

16 The wise fear the LORD and shun evil,[v]
but a fool is hotheaded and yet feels secure.

17 A quick-tempered person does foolish things,[w]
and the one who devises evil schemes is hated.

18 The simple inherit folly,
but the prudent are crowned with knowledge.

13:20 [g] Pr 15:31 **13:21** [h] Ps 32:10 **13:22** [i] Job 27:17; Ecc 2:26 **13:24** [j] Pr 19:18; 22:15; 23:13-14; 29:15, 17; Heb 12:7 **13:25** [k] Ps 34:10; Pr 10:3 **14:1** [l] Pr 24:3 **14:3** [m] Pr 12:6 **14:5** [n] Pr 6:19; 12:17

14:8 [o] ver 24 **14:11** [p] Pr 3:33; 12:7 **14:12** [q] Pr 12:15 [r] Pr 16:25 **14:13** [s] Ecc 2:2 **14:14** [t] Pr 1:31 [u] Pr 12:14 **14:16** [v] Pr 22:3 **14:17** [w] ver 29

delivery depended on messengers (see note on Ge 16:7). A wicked messenger would be one who did not deliver the message, lost it or delayed its reception. In the case of an oral message, a wicked messenger might forget what to say or even intentionally change the message from what its author desired. Ankhsheshonq gives advice as to the type of person to send on a particular job: "Do not send a low woman on a business of yours; she will go after her own. Do not send a wise man in a small matter when a big matter is waiting. Do not send a fool in a big matter when there is a wise man whom you can send."

13:20 *companion of fools.* The sage realizes that one's peers exercise tremendous influence on a person. If one falls in with evil people, then it is likely that that person will do evil themselves (1:8 – 19). On the other hand, associating with the wise provides good role models, as well as excellent instruction. The "Instructions of Ankhsheshonq" observe that if you befriend a fool, you are a fool, but it is wise to befriend a wise person.

13:24 *rod.* There was a real concern in ancient legal (e.g., Sumerian Law Code; Ex 20:12) and wisdom writings to teach children to honor and obey their parents. For instance, the Assyrian sage Ahiqar makes the familiar statement that to "spare the rod is to spoil the child." He also notes that those "who do not honor their parents' name are cursed for their evil by Shamash, the god of justice." The parents' responsibility for their children is also a concern. The Egyptian "Instructions of Ankhsheshonq" points out that "the children of fools wander in the streets, but the children of the wise are at their parents' sides" (compare the legal injunction regarding the rebellious son in Dt 21:18 – 21).

14:5 *false witness.* See notes on 10:18; 12:17.

14:11 *house of the wicked.* See note on 11:11.

[19] Evildoers will bow down in the
presence of the good,
and the wicked at the gates of the
righteous.[x]

[20] The poor are shunned even by their
neighbors,
but the rich have many friends.[y]

[21] It is a sin to despise one's neighbor,[z]
but blessed is the one who is kind to
the needy.[a]

[22] Do not those who plot evil go astray?
But those who plan what is good
find[a] love and faithfulness.

[23] All hard work brings a profit,
but mere talk leads only to poverty.

[24] The wealth of the wise is their crown,
but the folly of fools yields folly.

[25] A truthful witness saves lives,
but a false witness is deceitful.[b]

[26] Whoever fears the LORD has a secure
fortress,[c]
and for their children it will be a
refuge.

[27] The fear of the LORD is a fountain of
life,
turning a person from the snares of
death.[d]

[28] A large population is a king's glory,
but without subjects a prince is
ruined.

[29] Whoever is patient has great
understanding,
but one who is quick-tempered
displays folly.[e]

[30] A heart at peace gives life to the body,
but envy rots the bones.[f]

[31] Whoever oppresses the poor shows
contempt for their Maker,[g]
but whoever is kind to the needy
honors God.

14:19 [x] Pr 11:29
14:20 [y] Pr 19:4,7
14:21 [z] Pr 11:12 [a] Ps 41:1; Pr 19:17
14:25 [b] ver 5
14:26 [c] Pr 18:10; 19:23; Isa 33:6
14:27 [d] Pr 13:14
14:29 [e] Ecc 7:8-9; Jas 1:19
14:30 [f] Pr 12:4
14:31 [g] Pr 17:5
14:32 [h] Pr 6:15 [i] Job 13:15; 2Ti 4:18
14:33 [j] Pr 2:6-10
14:34 [k] Pr 11:11
14:35 [l] Mt 24:45-51; 25:14-30
15:1 [m] Pr 25:15
15:2 [n] Pr 12:23
15:3 [o] 2Ch 16:9 [p] Job 31:4; Heb 4:13 [q] Job 34:21; Jer 16:17
15:5 [r] Pr 13:1
15:6 [s] Pr 8:21
15:8 [t] Pr 21:27; Isa 1:11; Jer 6:20 [u] ver 29

[32] When calamity comes, the wicked are
brought down,[h]
but even in death the righteous seek
refuge in God.[i]

[33] Wisdom reposes in the heart of the
discerning[j]
and even among fools she lets
herself be known.[b]

[34] Righteousness exalts a nation,[k]
but sin condemns any people.

[35] A king delights in a wise servant,
but a shameful servant arouses his
fury.[l]

15 A gentle answer turns away wrath,[m]
but a harsh word stirs up anger.

[2] The tongue of the wise adorns
knowledge,
but the mouth of the fool gushes
folly.[n]

[3] The eyes[o] of the LORD are everywhere,[p]
keeping watch on the wicked and
the good.[q]

[4] The soothing tongue is a tree of life,
but a perverse tongue crushes the
spirit.

[5] A fool spurns a parent's discipline,
but whoever heeds correction shows
prudence.[r]

[6] The house of the righteous contains
great treasure,[s]
but the income of the wicked brings
ruin.

[7] The lips of the wise spread knowledge,
but the hearts of fools are not
upright.

[8] The LORD detests the sacrifice of the
wicked,[t]
but the prayer of the upright pleases
him.[u]

[a] 22 Or *show* [b] 33 Hebrew; Septuagint and Syriac *discerning / but in the heart of fools she is not known*

14:19 *bow down ... at the gates.* In this instance, gates refer to the household gates of the righteous, not the city gates (compare the obeisance of the king's servants at the king's gate in Est 3:2). In that sense, therefore, the parallelism of the verse indicates that the evil doers will be forced to show subservience to the righteous, becoming their servants. A similar case in which due respect is granted by those who had previously taken no notice of their "new masters" is found in Moses' prediction in Ex 11:8 that the Egyptian officials would "bow low to me."
14:23 *hard work.* See note on 12:24.
14:25 *false witness.* See note on 12:17.
14:31 *Whoever oppresses the poor.* Ptahhotep also instructs his reader not to engage in exploitation of the poor by attacking him just because he is weaker. Amenemope adds that any benefit you may gain will be less than satisfying.
15:1 *turns away wrath.* In the "Instruction of Any," it is understood that gentle words lead to peace, while a harsh word just makes things worse.
15:4 *tree of life.* See note on 3:18.
15:8 *The LORD detests.* Lit. "abomination of the LORD." This Hebrew phrase occurs frequently in the book (here; vv. 9,26; 3:32; 6:16; 11:1,20; 12:22; 16:5; 17:15; 20:10,23) and indicates the utmost divine censure against something. The intention of describing actions or attitudes that are an abomination to the Lord is to advise strongly against them. We have a similar phenomenon in the Sumerian proverbs that describe various actions such as serving beer with unwashed hands as an abomination of the sun-god Utu.

[9] The LORD detests the way of the wicked,
but he loves those who pursue righteousness.[v]

[10] Stern discipline awaits anyone who leaves the path;
the one who hates correction will die.[w]

[11] Death and Destruction[a] lie open before the LORD[x] —
how much more do human hearts![y]

[12] Mockers resent correction,[z]
so they avoid the wise.

[13] A happy heart makes the face cheerful,
but heartache crushes the spirit.[a]

[14] The discerning heart seeks knowledge,[b]
but the mouth of a fool feeds on folly.

[15] All the days of the oppressed are wretched,
but the cheerful heart has a continual feast.[c]

[16] Better a little with the fear of the LORD
than great wealth with turmoil.[d]

[17] Better a small serving of vegetables with love
than a fattened calf with hatred.[e]

[18] A hot-tempered person stirs up conflict,[f]
but the one who is patient calms a quarrel.[g]

[19] The way of the sluggard is blocked with thorns,[h]
but the path of the upright is a highway.

[20] A wise son brings joy to his father,[i]
but a foolish man despises his mother.

[21] Folly brings joy to one who has no sense,[j]
but whoever has understanding keeps a straight course.

[22] Plans fail for lack of counsel,
but with many advisers they succeed.[k]

[23] A person finds joy in giving an apt reply[l] —
and how good is a timely word![m]

[24] The path of life leads upward for the prudent
to keep them from going down to the realm of the dead.

[25] The LORD tears down the house of the proud,[n]
but he sets the widow's boundary stones in place.[o]

[26] The LORD detests the thoughts of the wicked,[p]
but gracious words are pure in his sight.

15:9 [v] Pr 21:21; 1Ti 6:11 **15:10** [w] Pr 1:31-32; 5:12 **15:11** [x] Job 26:6; Ps 139:8 [y] 2Ch 6:30; Ps 44:21 **15:12** [z] Am 5:10 **15:13** [a] Pr 12:25; 17:22; 18:14 **15:14** [b] Pr 18:15 **15:15** [c] ver 13 **15:16** [d] Ps 37:16-17; Pr 16:8; 1Ti 6:6 **15:17** [e] Pr 17:1 **15:18** [f] Pr 26:21 [g] Ge 13:8

15:19 [h] Pr 22:5 **15:20** [i] Pr 10:1 **15:21** [j] Pr 10:23 **15:22** [k] Pr 11:14 **15:23** [l] Pr 12:14 [m] Pr 25:11 **15:25** [n] Pr 12:7 [o] Dt 19:14; Ps 68:5-6; Pr 23:10-11 **15:26** [p] Pr 6:16

[a] *11* Hebrew *Abaddon*

15:11 *Death and Destruction.* Hebrew *"Sheol"* and *"Abaddon,"* names that relate to the grave and the netherworld (see the articles "Death and Sheol," p. 833; "Death and the Underworld," p. 907). For Death (*Sheol*), see note on 1:12, where the same Hebrew word is translated "grave." *Abaddon* is clearly a derivative of the Hebrew verb *abad* ("to destroy") and in parallel with *Sheol* stands for the place of destruction, though the nature of the destruction is never specified, and is another name for the grave and the netherworld. The NIV rightly capitalizes the words, because here they are personified. In this way, the proverb is reminiscent of Canaanite mythology, where Death is represented by the god Mot, who at one point in the mythic narrative overwhelms even Baal, the chief god of the pantheon. The Biblical text is not saying that a god like Mot actually exists. Even though Baal ultimately is revivified, the Biblical proverb shows the Lord's superiority when it says that Death and Destruction lie open before him. Personification, treating an inanimate object or a concept as if it were animate, must be carefully differentiated from identification — i.e., death can be personified without actually being identified as a personal entity.
15:16 *Better … than.* Proverbs uses the "better-than" proverb form in order to express relative values. While wealth is considered a good thing, and even a gift of Yahweh when acquired honestly, it is not the most important thing by far. If a decision must be made between wealth or a right relationship with God, or between having much or having love and peace, then the latter of each pair is far better. See 16:16. Amenemope expresses a similar value also using the better-than form as he contrasts poverty in the hand of God as better than great stores of wealth.
15:17 *Better … than.* See note on v. 16. *vegetables … a fattened calf.* Most people in the ancient world did not have meat as a regular part of their diet. Grains and vegetables were the subsistence foods. This verse refers to greens and contrasts them to the most luxurious of meals (a "fattened calf" was used only in great celebrations or cultic contexts). The teachings of Amenemope also use this type of saying: "Better is a single loaf and a happy heart than all the riches in the world and sorrow."
15:18 This proverb contrasts the hothead and the calm person. Egyptian wisdom uses this dichotomy almost as often as Biblical proverbs use the distinction between the wise and the foolish. So, e.g., Amenemope warns against befriending the hothead, and Any warns against provoking conflicts, which can be accomplished by exercising patience rather than provocation.
15:19 *sluggard.* See note on 12:24.
15:23 *timely word.* Timing is everything in the world of wisdom. One must know the proper time to say the right thing. Ankhsheshonq puts it this way: "Do not say something when it is not the time for it."
15:24 *realm of the dead.* The Hebrew word for this phrase is translated "grave" in 1:12 (see note there).
15:25 *boundary stones.* See note on 23:10.
15:26 *The LORD detests.* See note on v. 8.

CHARACTER TRAITS IN PROVERBS

TRAITS TO BE PROMOTED	
avoidance of strife	20:3
compassion for animals	12:10
contentment	13:25; 14:30; 15:27
diligence	6:6–13; 12:24,27; 13:4
faithful love	20:6
faithfulness	3:5–6; 5:15–17; 25:13; 28:20
generosity	21:26; 22:9
honesty	16:11; 24:26
humility	11:2; 16:19; 25:6–7; 29:23
integrity	11:3; 25:26; 28:18
kindness to others	11:16–17
kindness to enemies	25:21–22
leadership	30:19–31
loyalty	19:22
nobility	12:4; 31:10,29
patience	15:18; 16:32
peacefulness	16:7
praiseworthiness	27:21
righteousness	4:26–27; 11:5–6,30; 12:28; 13:6; 29:2
self-control	17:27; 25:28; 29:11
strength and honor	20:29
strength in adversity	24:10
teachableness	15:31
truthfulness	12:19,22; 23:23

TRAITS TO BE AVOIDED	
anger	29:22
antisocial behavior	18:1
beauty without discretion	11:22
blaming God	19:3
dishonesty	24:28
greed	28:25
hatred	29:27
hot temper	19:19; 29:22
immorality	6:20–35
inappropriate desire	27:7
injustice	22:16
jealousy	27:4
lack of mercy	21:13
laziness	6:6–11; 18:9; 19:15; 20:4; 24:30–34; 26:13–15
maliciousness	6:27
meddling	26:17; 30:10
pride	15:5; 16:18; 21:4,24; 29:23; 30:13
quarrelsomeness	26:21
self-conceit	26:12,16
self-deceit	28:11
self-glory	25:27
self-righteousness	30:12
social disruption	19:10
stubbornness	29:1
unfaithfulness	25:19
unneighborliness	3:27–30
vengeance	24:28–29
wickedness	21:10
wicked scheming	16:30

[27]The greedy bring ruin to their households,
but the one who hates bribes will live.[q]

[28]The heart of the righteous weighs its answers,[r]
but the mouth of the wicked gushes evil.

[29]The LORD is far from the wicked,
but he hears the prayer of the righteous.[s]

[30]Light in a messenger's eyes brings joy to the heart,
and good news gives health to the bones.

[31]Whoever heeds life-giving correction
will be at home among the wise.[t]

[32]Those who disregard discipline despise themselves,[u]
but the one who heeds correction gains understanding.

[33]Wisdom's instruction is to fear the LORD,[v]
and humility comes before honor.[w]

16 To humans belong the plans of the heart,
but from the LORD comes the proper answer of the tongue.[x]

[2]All a person's ways seem pure to them,
but motives are weighed by the LORD.[y]

[3]Commit to the LORD whatever you do,
and he will establish your plans.[z]

[4]The LORD works out everything to its proper end[a]—
even the wicked for a day of disaster.[b]

15:27 [q]Ex 23:8; Isa 33:15 **15:28** [r]1Pe 3:15 **15:29** [s]Ps 145:18-19 **15:31** [t]ver 5 **15:32** [u]Pr 1:7 **15:33** [v]Pr 1:7 [w]Pr 18:12 **16:1** [x]Pr 19:21 **16:2** [y]Pr 21:2 **16:3** [z]Ps 37:5-6; Pr 3:5-6 **16:4** [a]Isa 43:7 [b]Ro 9:22

16:5 [c]Pr 6:16 [d]Pr 11:20-21 **16:6** [e]Pr 14:16 **16:8** [f]Ps 37:16 **16:9** [g]Jer 10:23 **16:11** [h]Pr 11:1 **16:12** [i]Pr 25:5 **16:13** [j]Pr 14:35 **16:14** [k]Pr 19:12 **16:15** [l]Job 29:24

[5]The LORD detests all the proud of heart.[c]
Be sure of this: They will not go unpunished.[d]

[6]Through love and faithfulness sin is atoned for;
through the fear of the LORD evil is avoided.[e]

[7]When the LORD takes pleasure in anyone's way,
he causes their enemies to make peace with them.

[8]Better a little with righteousness
than much gain[f] with injustice.

[9]In their hearts humans plan their course,
but the LORD establishes their steps.[g]

[10]The lips of a king speak as an oracle,
and his mouth does not betray justice.

[11]Honest scales and balances belong to the LORD;
all the weights in the bag are of his making.[h]

[12]Kings detest wrongdoing,
for a throne is established through righteousness.[i]

[13]Kings take pleasure in honest lips;
they value the one who speaks what is right.[j]

[14]A king's wrath is a messenger of death,[k]
but the wise will appease it.

[15]When a king's face brightens, it means life;[l]
his favor is like a rain cloud in spring.

15:28 *mouth of the wicked gushes evil.* See note on 29:20.
16:2 *motives are weighed by the LORD.* Here human self-perception is judged in the light of the Lord's perception. The proverb speaks to our ability to deceive ourselves concerning our righteousness. Proverbs often denigrates those who are wise in their own eyes (3:7; 12:15; 26:5,12; 30:12). The observation invites profound reflection on our motives, since God is the final arbiter of whether a path is right or wrong. This is not a function of human beings. An analogy exists between Yahweh measuring (or weighing) the "spirits," and the Egyptian god Thoth weighing the heart of the dead person against the balance of Ma'at (truth and justice) in order to determine whether the deceased will enter into the afterlife.
16:5 *The LORD detests.* See note on 15:8.
16:8 *Better ... than.* See note on 15:16.
16:9 *plan their course.* See note on 19:21.
16:10 *oracle.* The Hebrew (*qesem*) is a word that is usually connected with divination. Thus, the proverb is hard to understand, because of the apparently positive reference to it on the lips of the king. *Qesem* is frequently condemned in other parts of the OT (e.g., Dt 18:10; 1Sa 15:23; 2Ki 17:17), because it is associated with pagan divination practices. Nonetheless, there are positive instances of divination elsewhere in the OT (though, admittedly, the word *qesem* is not found in these contexts), most notably in the use of the Urim and Thummim (see the article "Urim and Thummim," p. 162). Without a fuller context, it is difficult to determine with precision how *qesem* is used here. It was the priests, e.g., who manipulated the Urim and Thummim, but perhaps the king was the one who was responsible for announcing the decision (cf. 1Sa 23:1–8). If so, then perhaps the issue of justice concerns a proper presentation of the oracular decision that would have come from God. It further could point to a legal context for such an oracular decision. The temptation might be for the king to hedge the decision in the interests of his own policies, and thus the statement could also be understood as a kind of warning or prohibition. The wise king will not pervert the legal verdict rendered by the divinely inspired lot. See the articles "Magic," p. 326; "Practice of Magic," p. 627.
16:11 *Honest scales.* See note on 11:1.
16:14 The sage warns against provoking a king. After all, the king has the power of life and death. The *Tale of Ahiqar*

16 How much better to get wisdom than gold,
to get insight rather than silver![m]

17 The highway of the upright avoids evil;
those who guard their ways preserve their lives.

18 Pride goes before destruction,
a haughty spirit before a fall.[n]

19 Better to be lowly in spirit along with the oppressed
than to share plunder with the proud.

20 Whoever gives heed to instruction prospers,[a]
and blessed is the one who trusts in the LORD.[o]

21 The wise in heart are called discerning,
and gracious words promote instruction.[b][p]

22 Prudence is a fountain of life to the prudent,[q]
but folly brings punishment to fools.

23 The hearts of the wise make their mouths prudent,
and their lips promote instruction.[c]

24 Gracious words are a honeycomb,
sweet to the soul and healing to the bones.[r]

25 There is a way that appears to be right,[s]
but in the end it leads to death.[t]

26 The appetite of laborers works for them;
their hunger drives them on.

27 A scoundrel plots evil,
and on their lips it is like a scorching fire.[u]

28 A perverse person stirs up conflict,[v]
and a gossip separates close friends.[w]

29 A violent person entices their neighbor
and leads them down a path that is not good.[x]

30 Whoever winks with their eye is plotting perversity;
whoever purses their lips is bent on evil.

31 Gray hair is a crown of splendor;[y]
it is attained in the way of righteousness.

32 Better a patient person than a warrior,
one with self-control than one who takes a city.

33 The lot is cast into the lap,
but its every decision is from the LORD.[z]

17 Better a dry crust with peace and quiet
than a house full of feasting, with strife.[a]

2 A prudent servant will rule over a disgraceful son
and will share the inheritance as one of the family.

3 The crucible for silver and the furnace for gold,[b]
but the LORD tests the heart.[c]

4 A wicked person listens to deceitful lips;
a liar pays attention to a destructive tongue.

16:16 [m] Pr 8:10, 19 16:18 [n] Pr 11:2; 18:12 16:20 [o] Ps 2:12; 34:8; Pr 19:8; Jer 17:7 16:21 [p] ver 23 16:22 [q] Pr 13:14 16:24 [r] Pr 24:13-14 16:25 [s] Pr 12:15 [t] Pr 14:12 16:27 [u] Jas 3:6

16:28 [v] Pr 15:18 [w] Pr 17:9 16:29 [x] Pr 1:10; 12:26 16:31 [y] Pr 20:29 16:33 [z] Pr 18:18; 29:26 17:1 [a] Pr 15:16, 17 17:3 [b] Pr 27:21 [c] 1Ch 29:17; Ps 26:2; Jer 17:10

[a] 20 Or *whoever speaks prudently finds what is good*
[b] 21 Or *words make a person persuasive*
[c] 23 Or *prudent / and make their lips persuasive*

begins with a narrative about how the Assyrian king orders the death of Ahiqar, his wise man, based on the anger instigated by a false report filed by Ahiqar's nephew Nadin. His observations about the danger in angering a king come from his own personal experience.

16:16 *better ... than.* See note on 15:16.

16:28 *gossip.* See note on 11:13.

16:33 *lot.* The last proverb of ch. 16 returns to a theme from the beginning of the chapter (vv. 1–3,9). The point is that God is the final arbiter of the future. Human beings may attempt to find out what the future holds, but they should know that it is God who determines it. The OT approved at least one type of divination, the Urim and Thummim, and the principle behind this proverb certainly applied to it. The reason why the determinations of the Urim and Thummim were followed by leaders like David (1Sa 23:1–6) is because it was known that God determined what they would indicate (see the article "Urim and Thummim," p. 162). See also the NT use of lots in Ac 1:26. Careful study of Greek and Akkadian lot casting, as well as a close look at associated verbs, leads to the conclusion that lots are placed in a receptacle and then shaken until one comes out. Typically such lot casting was done before a deity.

17:1 *Better ... than.* See note on 15:16.

17:3 *The crucible for silver and the furnace for gold.* Gold and silver may be refined in a graphite crucible. Gold melts at a temperature of 1,948°F (1,064°C) and sterling silver at 1640°F (893°C). An additional 338°F (170°C) is necessary to allow the metal to be poured without freezing, but it also cannot be so hot that a destructive crystalline structure forms or alloys are dissipated before the metal cools. It is also important to avoid oxygen infiltration as much as possible during the melting process so that the structure of the metal will not become porous. The refining process requires expertise and an intimate knowledge of the tools and metals involved. As such it is an apt metaphor for God's testing of the heart (compare the "weighing of the heart" in the judgment of the soul in Egyptian religious tradition; see the article "The Hardening of Pharaoh's Heart," p. 124).

17:4 *liar.* See note on 10:18.

5 Whoever mocks the poor shows
contempt for their Maker;[d]
whoever gloats over disaster[e] will
not go unpunished.[f]

6 Children's children[g] are a crown to the
aged,
and parents are the pride of their
children.

7 Eloquent lips are unsuited to a godless
fool—
how much worse lying lips to a ruler!

8 A bribe is seen as a charm by the one
who gives it;
they think success will come at
every turn.

9 Whoever would foster love covers over
an offense,[h]
but whoever repeats the matter
separates close friends.[i]

10 A rebuke impresses a discerning person
more than a hundred lashes a fool.

11 Evildoers foster rebellion against God;
the messenger of death will be sent
against them.

12 Better to meet a bear robbed of her
cubs
than a fool bent on folly.

13 Evil will never leave the house
of one who pays back evil[j] for good.

14 Starting a quarrel is like breaching a
dam;
so drop the matter before a dispute
breaks out.[k]

15 Acquitting the guilty and condemning
the innocent[l] —
the LORD detests them both.[m]

16 Why should fools have money in hand
to buy wisdom,
when they are not able to
understand it?[n]

17 A friend loves at all times,
and a brother is born for a time of
adversity.

18 One who has no sense shakes hands in
pledge
and puts up security for a neighbor.[o]

19 Whoever loves a quarrel loves sin;
whoever builds a high gate invites
destruction.

20 One whose heart is corrupt does not
prosper;
one whose tongue is perverse falls
into trouble.

21 To have a fool for a child brings grief;
there is no joy for the parent of a
godless fool.[p]

22 A cheerful heart is good medicine,
but a crushed spirit dries up the
bones.[q]

23 The wicked accept bribes[r] in secret
to pervert the course of justice.

24 A discerning person keeps wisdom in
view,
but a fool's eyes[s] wander to the ends
of the earth.

25 A foolish son brings grief to his father
and bitterness to the mother who
bore him.[t]

26 If imposing a fine on the innocent is
not good,[u]
surely to flog honest officials is not
right.

27 The one who has knowledge uses
words with restraint,
and whoever has understanding is
even-tempered.[v]

28 Even fools are thought wise if they
keep silent,
and discerning if they hold their
tongues.[w]

17:5 [d] Pr 14:31 [e] Job 31:29 [f] Ob 1:12 **17:6** [g] Pr 13:22 **17:9** [h] Pr 10:12 [i] Pr 16:28 **17:13** [j] Ps 109:4-5; Jer 18:20 **17:14** [k] Pr 20:3 **17:15** [l] Pr 18:5 [m] Ex 23:6-7; Isa 5:23 **17:16** [n] Pr 23:23 **17:18** [o] Pr 6:1-5; 11:15; 22:26-27 **17:21** [p] Pr 10:1 **17:22** [q] Ps 22:15; Pr 15:13 **17:23** [r] Ex 23:8 **17:24** [s] Ecc 2:14 **17:25** [t] Pr 10:1 **17:26** [u] Pr 18:5 **17:27** [v] Pr 14:29; Jas 1:19 **17:28** [w] Job 13:5

17:5 *Whoever mocks the poor.* Some proverbs mock the lazy who end up poor (6:6–11; 10:4–5), but it is their slothfulness that is being ridiculed, not their poverty. Proverbs is aware that there are other reasons, including social injustice, that lead to poverty (e.g., 13:23). We can cite similar ideas from the ancient Near East. Amenemope warns not to laugh at the blind or the lame. In the same vein, in Mesopotamia it was considered wrong to sneer at the unfortunate or those who were downtrodden.
17:6 *children are a crown to the aged.* Descendants are a blessing to parents and grandparents. The "Instruction of Any" express a similar idea: "Happy is the man whose people are many, he is saluted on account of his progeny."
17:8 *bribe.* See note on v. 23.
17:15 *the LORD detests.* See note on 15:8.
17:17 *friend.* See note on 27:10.
17:23 *bribes.* The teaching of Proverbs about bribes at first seems contradictory. A number of passages, including the present one, are negative about bribes. Similarly, Amenemope commands: "Don't accept the gift of a powerful man, And deprive the weak for his sake." However, other passages in Proverbs suggest that bribes are acceptable and even advisable (e.g., 18:16). Just like with a timely word, it depends on the circumstance. If a bribe is used to circumvent justice, then it is evil. If the bribe is used to open doors for a good purpose, then it is appropriate.
17:27 *uses words with restraint.* The wise know how to use words appropriately and with great self-control. They know that speaking too much will lead to trouble. The wisdom of the ancient Near East shares this understanding as it paints a picture of the wise person as one who knows when to be silent. Ptahhotep, e.g., advises that silence is better than chatter and that one should only speak up when they have something positive to contribute.
17:28 *keep silent.* See note on v. 27.

18 An unfriendly person pursues
selfish ends
and against all sound judgment
starts quarrels.

[2] Fools find no pleasure in
understanding
but delight in airing their own
opinions.[x]

[3] When wickedness comes, so does
contempt,
and with shame comes reproach.

[4] The words of the mouth are deep
waters,
but the fountain of wisdom is a
rushing stream.

[5] It is not good to be partial to the
wicked[y]
and so deprive the innocent of
justice.[z]

[6] The lips of fools bring them strife,
and their mouths invite a beating.

[7] The mouths of fools are their undoing,
and their lips are a snare[a] to their
very lives.[b]

[8] The words of a gossip are like choice
morsels;
they go down to the inmost parts.[c]

[9] One who is slack in his work
is brother to one who destroys.[d]

[10] The name of the LORD is a fortified
tower;[e]
the righteous run to it and are safe.

[11] The wealth of the rich is their fortified
city;[f]
they imagine it a wall too high to
scale.

[12] Before a downfall the heart is
haughty,
but humility comes before honor.[g]

[13] To answer before listening—
that is folly and shame.[h]

[14] The human spirit can endure in
sickness,
but a crushed spirit who can
bear?[i]

[15] The heart of the discerning acquires
knowledge,[j]
for the ears of the wise seek it out.

[16] A gift[k] opens the way
and ushers the giver into the
presence of the great.

[17] In a lawsuit the first to speak seems
right,
until someone comes forward and
cross-examines.

[18] Casting the lot settles disputes[l]
and keeps strong opponents apart.

[19] A brother wronged is more unyielding
than a fortified city;
disputes are like the barred gates of
a citadel.

[20] From the fruit of their mouth a
person's stomach is filled;
with the harvest of their lips they are
satisfied.[m]

[21] The tongue has the power of life and
death,
and those who love it will eat its
fruit.[n]

[22] He who finds a wife finds what is good[o]
and receives favor from the LORD.[p]

[23] The poor plead for mercy,
but the rich answer harshly.

[24] One who has unreliable friends soon
comes to ruin,
but there is a friend who sticks
closer than a brother.[q]

19 Better the poor whose walk is
blameless
than a fool whose lips are perverse.[r]

[2] Desire without knowledge is not
good—
how much more will hasty feet miss
the way![s]

[3] A person's own folly leads to their
ruin,
yet their heart rages against the
LORD.

[4] Wealth attracts many friends,
but even the closest friend of the
poor person deserts them.[t]

[5] A false witness[u] will not go
unpunished,
and whoever pours out lies will not
go free.[v]

[6] Many curry favor with a ruler,[w]
and everyone is the friend of one
who gives gifts.[x]

[7] The poor are shunned by all their
relatives—
how much more do their friends
avoid them!

18:2 [x] Pr 12:23 **18:5** [y] Lev 19:15; Pr 24:23-25; 28:21 [z] Ps 82:2; Pr 17:15 **18:7** [a] Ps 140:9 [b] Ps 64:8; Pr 10:14; 12:13; 13:3; Ecc 10:12 **18:8** [c] Pr 26:22 **18:9** [d] Pr 28:24 **18:10** [e] 2Sa 22:3; Ps 61:3 **18:11** [f] Pr 10:15 **18:12** [g] Pr 11:2; 15:33; 16:18 **18:13** [h] Pr 20:25; Jn 7:51 **18:14** [i] Pr 15:13; 17:22 **18:15** [j] Pr 15:14 **18:16** [k] Ge 32:20 **18:18** [l] Pr 16:33 **18:20** [m] Pr 12:14 **18:21** [n] Pr 13:2-3; Mt 12:37 **18:22** [o] Pr 12:4 [p] Pr 19:14; 31:10 **18:24** [q] Pr 17:17; Jn 15:13-15 **19:1** [r] Pr 28:6 **19:2** [s] Pr 29:20 **19:4** [t] Pr 14:20 **19:5** [u] Ex 23:1 [v] Dt 19:19; Pr 21:28 **19:6** [w] Pr 29:26 [x] Pr 17:8; 18:16

18:8 *gossip.* See note on 11:13.
18:9 *slack.* See note on 12:24.
18:16 *gift.* See note on 17:23.
18:18 *Casting the lot.* See note on 16:33.
19:5,9 *false witness.* See note on 12:17.

Though the poor pursue them with
pleading,
they are nowhere to be found.[a][y]

8 The one who gets wisdom loves life;
the one who cherishes
understanding will soon
prosper.[z]

9 A false witness will not go unpunished,
and whoever pours out lies will
perish.[a]

10 It is not fitting for a fool[b] to live in
luxury—
how much worse for a slave to rule
over princes![c]

11 A person's wisdom yields patience;[d]
it is to one's glory to overlook an
offense.

12 A king's rage is like the roar of a lion,
but his favor is like dew[e] on the
grass.[f]

13 A foolish child is a father's ruin,[g]
and a quarrelsome wife is like
the constant dripping of a leaky
roof.[h]

14 Houses and wealth are inherited from
parents,[i]
but a prudent wife is from the LORD.[j]

15 Laziness brings on deep sleep,
and the shiftless go hungry.[k]

16 Whoever keeps commandments keeps
their life,
but whoever shows contempt for
their ways will die.[l]

17 Whoever is kind to the poor lends to
the LORD,
and he will reward them for what
they have done.[m]

18 Discipline your children, for in that
there is hope;
do not be a willing party to their
death.[n]

19 A hot-tempered person must pay the
penalty;
rescue them, and you will have to do
it again.

20 Listen to advice and accept discipline,[o]
and at the end you will be counted
among the wise.[p]

21 Many are the plans in a person's heart,
but it is the LORD's purpose that
prevails.[q]

22 What a person desires is unfailing
love[b];
better to be poor than a liar.

23 The fear of the LORD leads to life;
then one rests content, untouched
by trouble.[r]

24 A sluggard buries his hand in the dish;
he will not even bring it back to his
mouth![s]

25 Flog a mocker, and the simple will
learn prudence;
rebuke the discerning, and they will
gain knowledge.[t]

26 Whoever robs their father and drives
out their mother[u]
is a child who brings shame and
disgrace.

27 Stop listening to instruction, my son,
and you will stray from the words of
knowledge.

28 A corrupt witness mocks at justice,
and the mouth of the wicked gulps
down evil.[v]

29 Penalties are prepared for mockers,
and beatings for the backs of fools.[w]

20

Wine is a mocker and beer a
brawler;
whoever is led astray by them is not
wise.[x]

19:7 [y] ver 4; Ps 38:11 **19:8** [z] Pr 16:20 **19:9** [a] ver 5 **19:10** [b] Pr 26:1 [c] Pr 30:21-23; Ecc 10:5-7 **19:11** [d] Pr 16:32 **19:12** [e] Ps 133:3 [f] Pr 16:14-15 **19:13** [g] Pr 10:1 [h] Pr 21:9 **19:14** [i] 2Co 12:14 [j] Pr 18:22 **19:15** [k] Pr 6:9; 10:4 **19:16** [l] Pr 16:17; Lk 10:28 **19:17** [m] Mt 10:42; 2Co 9:6-8 **19:18** [n] Pr 13:24; 23:13-14 **19:20** [o] Pr 4:1 [p] Pr 12:15 **19:21** [q] Ps 33:11; Pr 16:9; Isa 14:24,27 **19:23** [r] Ps 25:13; Pr 12:21; 1Ti 4:8 **19:24** [s] Pr 26:15 **19:25** [t] Pr 9:9; 21:11 **19:26** [u] Pr 28:24 **19:28** [v] Job 15:16 **19:29** [w] Pr 26:3 **20:1** [x] Pr 31:4

[a] 7 The meaning of the Hebrew for this sentence is uncertain. [b] 22 Or *Greed is a person's shame*

19:11 *it is to one's glory to overlook an offense.* If one is offended, he has two choices: (1) confront the offender or (2) ignore the offense. The latter is recommended. If a person acts as if an offense has not happened, then there will be no further provocation or conflict. In maxim 29, Ptahhotep teaches the same strategy of being willing to overlook an offense.
19:12 *king's rage.* See note on 16:14.
19:15 *Laziness.* See note on 12:24.
19:18 *Discipline your children.* See note on 13:24.
19:21 *LORD's purpose.* According to Proverbs, human beings should make plans for the future, but they should do so with the awareness that their plans may be overridden by God's purpose. Such an attitude engenders humility. This is also a well-attested teaching in ancient Near Eastern wisdom, as exemplified by Amenemope who observes that human words are one thing, but the deeds of god may go a different direction.
19:28 *corrupt witness.* See notes on 10:18 and 12:17.
20:1 *beer a brawler.* Beer and strong drinks are ancient beverages. We know that both Egyptians and Mesopotamians produced alcohol. Indeed, we have beer recipes and even a hymn to the beer god from the latter. In Israel wine was the beverage of choice. Beer was not popular perhaps due to the lack of natural resources to make it readily available. Wisdom literature urges against over-consumption. To exercise wisdom, one must be in possession of all one's faculties and alcohol tends to blur one's senses and one's judgment. Thus, Ankhsheshonq puts it plainly and even advises that Pharaoh's business should not be discussed when drinking beer. But Any has the most extensive teaching. In his instruction he notes

2 A king's wrath strikes terror like the
roar of a lion;[y]
those who anger him forfeit their
lives.[z]
3 It is to one's honor to avoid strife,
but every fool is quick to quarrel.[a]
4 Sluggards do not plow in season;
so at harvest time they look but find
nothing.
5 The purposes of a person's heart are
deep waters,
but one who has insight draws them
out.
6 Many claim to have unfailing love,
but a faithful person who can find?[b]
7 The righteous lead blameless lives;
blessed are their children after them.[c]
8 When a king sits on his throne to
judge,
he winnows out all evil with his
eyes.[d]
9 Who can say, "I have kept my heart
pure;
I am clean and without sin"?[e]
10 Differing weights and differing
measures—
the LORD detests them both.[f]
11 Even small children are known by their
actions,
so is their conduct really pure[g] and
upright?
12 Ears that hear and eyes that see—
the LORD has made them both.[h]
13 Do not love sleep or you will grow
poor;[i]
stay awake and you will have food
to spare.
14 "It's no good, it's no good!" says the
buyer—
then goes off and boasts about the
purchase.
15 Gold there is, and rubies in abundance,
but lips that speak knowledge are a
rare jewel.
16 Take the garment of one who puts up
security for a stranger;
hold it in pledge[j] if it is done for an
outsider.[k]
17 Food gained by fraud tastes sweet,[l]
but one ends up with a mouth full of
gravel.
18 Plans are established by seeking
advice;
so if you wage war, obtain
guidance.[m]
19 A gossip betrays a confidence;[n]
so avoid anyone who talks too
much.
20 If someone curses their father or
mother,[o]
their lamp will be snuffed out in
pitch darkness.[p]
21 An inheritance claimed too soon
will not be blessed at the end.
22 Do not say, "I'll pay you back for this
wrong!"[q]
Wait for the LORD, and he will
avenge you.[r]
23 The LORD detests differing
weights,
and dishonest scales do not
please him.[s]
24 A person's steps are directed by the
LORD.
How then can anyone understand
their own way?[t]
25 It is a trap to dedicate something
rashly
and only later to consider one's
vows.[u]
26 A wise king winnows out the wicked;
he drives the threshing wheel over
them.[v]
27 The human spirit is[a] the lamp of the
LORD
that sheds light on one's inmost
being.

20:2 [y] Pr 19:12 [z] Pr 8:36 **20:3** [a] Pr 17:14 **20:6** [b] Ps 12:1 **20:7** [c] Ps 37:25-26; 112:2 **20:8** [d] ver 26; Pr 25:4-5 **20:9** [e] 1Ki 8:46; Ecc 7:20; 1Jn 1:8 **20:10** [f] ver 23; Pr 11:1 **20:11** [g] Mt 7:16 **20:12** [h] Ps 94:9 **20:13** [i] Pr 6:11; 19:15 **20:16** [j] Ex 22:26 [k] Pr 27:13 **20:17** [l] Pr 9:17 **20:18** [m] Pr 11:14; 24:6 **20:19** [n] Pr 11:13 **20:20** [o] Pr 30:11 [p] Ex 21:17; Job 18:5 **20:22** [q] Pr 24:29 [r] Ro 12:19 **20:23** [s] ver 10 **20:24** [t] Jer 10:23 **20:25** [u] Ecc 5:2, 4-5 **20:26** [v] ver 8

[a] 27 Or *A person's words are*

the consequences of drunkenness including evil speech, unawareness of what you are saying, possibility of injury when you fall, and rejection by friends who find you in a drunken stupor.
20:2 *king's wrath.* See note on 16:14.
20:4 *Sluggards.* See note on 12:24.
20:10 *Differing weights . . . measures.* See note on 11:1. *the LORD detests.* See note on 15:8.
20:13 *Do not love sleep.* See note on Job 22:6.
20:16 *Take the garment.* See note on 27:13.
20:22 *Wait for the LORD.* When people are hurt or offended, often the first reaction is to seek revenge. This desire often increases the offended person's anxiety and if successful may well trigger a cycle of hurt, as each party tries to get the best of the other. This proverb recommends a better way: let it go, and expect that God will take care of the situation. Christian readers will recognize the same idea behind Paul's teaching: "Do not take revenge, my dear friends, but leave room for God's wrath, for it is written: 'It is mine to avenge; I will repay,' says the Lord" (Ro 12:19). The "Instruction of Any" has similar advice; he recommends that you leave your attacker in the hands of the deity.
20:23 *differing weights.* See note on 11:1.

[28] Love and faithfulness keep a king
safe;
through love his throne is made
secure.[w]

[29] The glory of young men is their
strength,
gray hair the splendor of the old.[x]

[30] Blows and wounds scrub[y] away evil,
and beatings purge the inmost
being.

21 In the LORD's hand the king's heart
is a stream of water
that he channels toward all who
please him.

[2] A person may think their own ways are
right,
but the LORD weighs the heart.[z]

[3] To do what is right and just
is more acceptable to the LORD than
sacrifice.[a]

[4] Haughty eyes[b] and a proud heart—
the unplowed field of the wicked—
produce sin.

[5] The plans of the diligent lead to profit[c]
as surely as haste leads to poverty.

[6] A fortune made by a lying tongue
is a fleeting vapor and a deadly
snare.[a][d]

[7] The violence of the wicked will drag
them away,
for they refuse to do what is right.

[8] The way of the guilty is devious,[e]
but the conduct of the innocent is
upright.

[9] Better to live on a corner of the roof
than share a house with a
quarrelsome wife.[f]

[10] The wicked crave evil;
their neighbors get no mercy from
them.

[11] When a mocker is punished, the
simple gain wisdom;
by paying attention to the wise they
get knowledge.[g]

20:28 [w] Pr 29:14
20:29 [x] Pr 16:31
20:30 [y] Pr 22:15
21:2 [z] Pr 16:2; 24:12; Lk 16:15
21:3 [a] 1Sa 15:22; Pr 15:8; Isa 1:11; Hos 6:6; Mic 6:6-8
21:4 [b] Pr 6:17
21:5 [c] Pr 10:4; 28:22
21:6 [d] 2Pe 2:3
21:8 [e] Pr 2:15
21:9 [f] Pr 25:24
21:11 [g] Pr 19:25
21:12 [h] Pr 14:11
21:13 [i] Mt 18:30-34; Jas 2:13
21:14 [j] Pr 18:16; 19:6
21:15 [k] Pr 10:29
21:16 [l] Ps 49:14
21:17 [m] Pr 23:20-21, 29-35
21:18 [n] Pr 11:8; Isa 43:3
21:19 [o] ver 9
21:21 [p] Mt 5:6
21:22 [q] Ecc 9:15-16
21:23 [r] Jas 3:2 [s] Pr 12:13; 13:3

[12] The Righteous One[b] takes note of the
house of the wicked
and brings the wicked to ruin.[h]

[13] Whoever shuts their ears to the cry of
the poor
will also cry out and not be
answered.[i]

[14] A gift given in secret soothes
anger,
and a bribe concealed in the cloak
pacifies great wrath.[j]

[15] When justice is done, it brings joy to
the righteous
but terror to evildoers.[k]

[16] Whoever strays from the path of
prudence
comes to rest in the company of the
dead.[l]

[17] Whoever loves pleasure will become
poor;
whoever loves wine and olive oil
will never be rich.[m]

[18] The wicked become a ransom[n] for the
righteous,
and the unfaithful for the upright.

[19] Better to live in a desert
than with a quarrelsome and
nagging wife.[o]

[20] The wise store up choice food and
olive oil,
but fools gulp theirs down.

[21] Whoever pursues righteousness and
love
finds life, prosperity[c] and honor.[p]

[22] One who is wise can go up against the
city of the mighty[q]
and pull down the stronghold in
which they trust.

[23] Those who guard their mouths[r] and
their tongues
keep themselves from calamity.[s]

[a] *6* Some Hebrew manuscripts, Septuagint and Vulgate; most Hebrew manuscripts *vapor for those who seek death* [b] *12* Or *The righteous person* [c] *21* Or *righteousness*

21:1 *channels.* In the ancient Near East, irrigation ditches were dug to extend a river or lake's capability to fertilize soil. These were human-made channels that directed the water to where people needed it. It represents power and control over the use of water. To say that the king's heart is "a stream of water that [the LORD] channels" indicates that the Lord is in control of even the most powerful human beings on earth.
21:2 *the LORD weighs the heart.* See note on 16:2.
21:6 *lying tongue.* See note on 10:18.
21:9 *corner of the roof.* The "better-than" sayings provide a contrast or extreme that is preferable to contact with evil or with the disagreeable. The corner of a roof or a cramped attic chamber (see 1Ki 17:19) would be an uncomfortable perch, but its dangers or its inaccessibility might ward the sufferer from an even more unpleasant contact with a nagging wife (Pr 21:19; 25:24).
21:14 *gift.* See note on 17:23.
21:16 *the dead.* See note on 9:18.
21:17 *whoever loves wine and olive oil will never be rich.* Proverbs gives many reasons for poverty: laziness (12:24), injustice (13:23) and now overindulgence. The Egyptian sages noticed the same connection and Papyrus Insinger observes that the glutton runs the risk of poverty.

24 The proud and arrogant person[t] —
"Mocker" is his name —
behaves with insolent fury.

25 The craving of a sluggard will be the death of him,[u]
because his hands refuse to work.
26 All day long he craves for more,
but the righteous give without sparing.[v]

27 The sacrifice of the wicked is detestable[w] —
how much more so when brought with evil intent![x]

28 A false witness will perish,[y]
but a careful listener will testify successfully.

29 The wicked put up a bold front,
but the upright give thought to their ways.

30 There is no wisdom,[z] no insight, no plan
that can succeed against the LORD.[a]

31 The horse is made ready for the day of battle,
but victory rests with the LORD.[b]

22 A good name is more desirable than great riches;
to be esteemed is better than silver or gold.[c]

2 Rich and poor have this in common:
The LORD is the Maker of them all.[d]

3 The prudent see danger and take refuge,[e]
but the simple keep going and pay the penalty.[f]

4 Humility is the fear of the LORD;
its wages are riches and honor and life.

5 In the paths of the wicked are snares and pitfalls,[g]
but those who would preserve their life stay far from them.

6 Start children off on the way they should go,[h]
and even when they are old they will not turn from it.

7 The rich rule over the poor,
and the borrower is slave to the lender.

8 Whoever sows injustice reaps calamity,[i]
and the rod they wield in fury will be broken.[j]

9 The generous will themselves be blessed,[k]
for they share their food with the poor.[l]

10 Drive out the mocker, and out goes strife;
quarrels and insults are ended.[m]

11 One who loves a pure heart and who speaks with grace
will have the king for a friend.[n]

12 The eyes of the LORD keep watch over knowledge,
but he frustrates the words of the unfaithful.

13 The sluggard says, "There's a lion outside![o]
I'll be killed in the public square!"

14 The mouth of an adulterous woman is a deep pit;[p]
a man who is under the LORD's wrath falls into it.[q]

15 Folly is bound up in the heart of a child,
but the rod of discipline will drive it far away.[r]

16 One who oppresses the poor to increase his wealth
and one who gives gifts to the rich —
both come to poverty.

Thirty Sayings of the Wise

Saying 1

17 Pay attention and turn your ear to the sayings of the wise;[s]
apply your heart to what I teach,
18 for it is pleasing when you keep them in your heart
and have all of them ready on your lips.
19 So that your trust may be in the LORD,
I teach you today, even you.

21:24 [t] Ps 1:1; Pr 1:22; Isa 16:6; Jer 48:29 **21:25** [u] Pr 13:4 **21:26** [v] Ps 37:26; Mt 5:42; Eph 4:28 **21:27** [w] Isa 66:3; Jer 6:20; Am 5:22 [x] Pr 15:8 **21:28** [y] Pr 19:5 **21:30** [z] Jer 9:23 [a] Isa 8:10; Ac 5:39 **21:31** [b] Ps 3:8; 33:12-19; Isa 31:1 **22:1** [c] Ecc 7:1 **22:2** [d] Job 31:15 **22:3** [e] Pr 14:16 [f] Pr 27:12 **22:5** [g] Pr 15:19 **22:6** [h] Eph 6:4

22:8 [i] Job 4:8 [j] Ps 125:3 **22:9** [k] 2Co 9:6 [l] Pr 19:17 **22:10** [m] Pr 18:6; 26:20 **22:11** [n] Pr 16:13; Mt 5:8 **22:13** [o] Pr 26:13 **22:14** [p] Pr 2:16; 5:3-5; 7:5; 23:27 [q] Ecc 7:26 **22:15** [r] Pr 13:24; 23:14 **22:17** [s] Pr 5:1

21:28 *false witness.* See note on 12:17.
22:1 *more desirable than … better than.* See note on 15:16.
22:9 *generous.* See note on 3:27.
22:15 *Folly is bound up in the heart of a child.* Ankhsheshonq agrees that the natural disposition of youth is wickedness: "When a youth who has been taught thinks, thinking of wrong is what he does." For the idea that the young require physical discipline to grow wise, see note on 13:24.

22:18 *keep them in your heart.* This is not the usual Hebrew word for heart. The Hebrew word here is *beten* rather than *leb*, and it is more naturally translated "belly" or "stomach." The NIV appropriately translates the word in an idiom that modern English readers will understand, but by doing so it obscures the connection with Amenemope's observation that when sayings of the wise are kept in your belly, they stand as a doorpost to the heart.

[20]Have I not written thirty sayings for
you,
sayings of counsel and knowledge,
[21]teaching you to be honest and to speak
the truth,[t]
so that you bring back truthful reports
to those you serve?

Saying 2

[22]Do not exploit the poor[u] because they
are poor
and do not crush the needy in
court,[v]
[23]for the LORD will take up their case[w]
and will exact life for life.[x]

Saying 3

[24]Do not make friends with a hot-
tempered person,
do not associate with one easily
angered,
[25]or you may learn their ways
and get yourself ensnared.[y]

Saying 4

[26]Do not be one who shakes hands in
pledge[z]
or puts up security for debts;
[27]if you lack the means to pay,
your very bed will be snatched from
under you.[a]

Saying 5

[28]Do not move an ancient boundary stone[b]
set up by your ancestors.

Saying 6

[29]Do you see someone skilled in their
work?
They will serve[c] before kings;
they will not serve before officials of
low rank.

22:21 [t]Lk 1:3-4; 1Pe 3:15 **22:22** [u]Zec 7:10 [v]Ex 23:6; Mal 3:5 **22:23** [w]Ps 12:5 [x]1Sa 25:39; Pr 23:10-11 **22:25** [y]1Co 15:33 **22:26** [z]Pr 11:15 **22:27** [a]Pr 17:18 **22:28** [b]Dt 19:14; Pr 23:10 **22:29** [c]Ge 41:46

22:20 *thirty sayings.* A portion of the book of Proverbs (22:17—24:22) seems to imitate, at least in part, the literary structure of the Egyptian "Instruction of Amenemope." Amenemope contains 30 chapters following a lengthy prologue. This fact has encouraged Bible translators to make a minor emendation to the Hebrew text from a word that means "formerly" (*shilshom*) to the word that means "thirty" (*sheloshim*). There is some dispute among scholars on the identification of the 30 units within the Biblical text, since there are breaks in the sections that may indicate unrelated segments (see "my son" diversions at 23:15,19,26). Also against the connection, the NIV had to slightly emend the text to arrive at 30, and had to provide the noun sayings so that there would be something that there were 30 of. Beyond this difficulty is the fact that the 30 sections in Proverbs would each be only a few verses long (4–6 lines), while the 30 chapters in Amenemope average 12–16 lines in length. The closest parallels between Amenemope and Proverbs come to an end at 23:11, and the remaining units have close ties to other pieces of wisdom literature, including the *Words of Ahiqar.* This may indicate a general familiarity with Amenemope and other wisdom literature, but a measure of literary independence on the part of the Biblical writer or wisdom school.
22:22 *Do not exploit the poor.* See note on 14:31.
22:24 *a hot-tempered person.* Amenemope also counsels avoidance of a hothead.
22:26 *shakes hands in pledge.* See note on 6:1. Shaking hands on an agreement is not attested clearly in the ancient Near Eastern texts or iconography. The nearest portrayal from the ancient Near East can be seen on the relief on the throne dais of Shalmaneser III, where the king and his vassal Marduk-zakir-shumi look like they are shaking hands, though here it seems to be a gesture of submission.
22:28 *boundary stone.* See note on 23:10.
22:29 This proverb states that those who work hard and with skill will succeed in their careers. They will work for

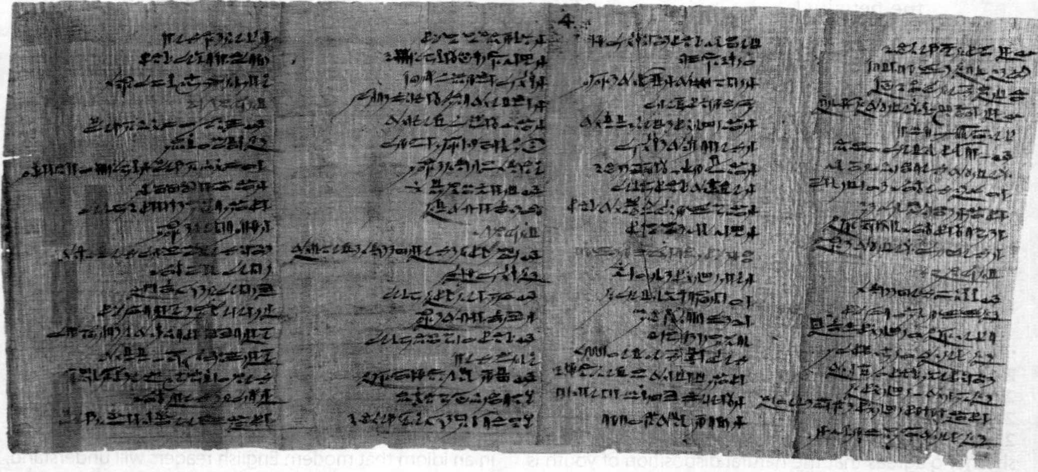

Papyrus from the "Instruction of Amenemope," Egyptian, c. 1000 BC. The manner employed in this wisdom piece suggests that there were wisdom schools in ancient Egypt.

Saying 7

23 When you sit to dine with a ruler,
note well what[a] is before you,
2 and put a knife to your throat
if you are given to gluttony.
3 Do not crave his delicacies,[d]
for that food is deceptive.

Saying 8

4 Do not wear yourself out to get rich;
do not trust your own cleverness.
5 Cast but a glance at riches, and they are gone,
for they will surely sprout wings
and fly off to the sky like an eagle.[e]

Saying 9

6 Do not eat the food of a begrudging host,
do not crave his delicacies;[f]
7 for he is the kind of person
who is always thinking about the cost.[b]
"Eat and drink," he says to you,
but his heart is not with you.
8 You will vomit up the little you have eaten
and will have wasted your compliments.

Saying 10

9 Do not speak to fools,
for they will scorn your prudent words.[g]

Saying 11

10 Do not move an ancient boundary stone[h]
or encroach on the fields of the fatherless,
11 for their Defender[i] is strong;
he will take up their case against you.[j]

Saying 12

12 Apply your heart to instruction
and your ears to words of knowledge.

Saying 13

13 Do not withhold discipline from a child;
if you punish them with the rod,
they will not die.
14 Punish them with the rod
and save them from death.

Saying 14

15 My son, if your heart is wise,
then my heart will be glad indeed;
16 my inmost being will rejoice
when your lips speak what is right.[k]

Saying 15

17 Do not let your heart envy[l] sinners,
but always be zealous for the fear of the LORD.
18 There is surely a future hope for you,
and your hope will not be cut off.[m]

Saying 16

19 Listen, my son, and be wise,
and set your heart on the right path:
20 Do not join those who drink too much wine[n]
or gorge themselves on meat,
21 for drunkards and gluttons become poor,[o]
and drowsiness clothes them in rags.

Saying 17

22 Listen to your father, who gave you life,
and do not despise your mother
when she is old.[p]

23:3 [d] ver 6-8
23:5 [e] Pr 27:24
23:6 [f] Ps 141:4
23:9 [g] Pr 1:7; 9:7; Mt 7:6
23:10 [h] Dt 19:14; Pr 22:28
23:11 [i] Job 19:25 [j] Pr 22:22-23
23:16 [k] ver 24; Pr 27:11
23:17 [l] Ps 37:1; Pr 28:14
23:18 [m] Ps 9:18; Pr 24:14, 19-20
23:20 [n] Isa 5:11, 22; Ro 13:13; Eph 5:18
23:21 [o] Pr 21:17
23:22 [p] Lev 19:32; Pr 1:8; 30:17; Eph 6:1-2

[a] 1 Or *who* [b] 7 Or *for as he thinks within himself, / so he is*; or *for as he puts on a feast, / so he is*

---

the most powerful and influential people in society, while those who are not diligent will spend their careers working for people on the lower end of the social stratum. We might compare a statement found in the final chapter of Amenemope in which a skilled scribe is seen to be worthy of promotion in the court.

23:1 *When you … dine with a ruler.* Egyptian wisdom texts often have rules concerning etiquette that give warning to the dangers of dining in the presence of a powerful superior. These include being content with what is set before you and exercising restraint (especially regarding favorite food).

23:4–5 This saying is often taken to be the closest to its parallel in the "Instruction of Amenemope," which advises people to be content with the wealth they have; anything that is gained illegitimately will quickly be gone. Though the Egyptian text is more extensive than the saying here, the similar sentiment, as well as the image of the flying bird to capture the idea of the transience of wealth, is striking. Even with these parallels, it is by no means definite that any kind of direct borrowing was involved in the composition of either piece. One could imagine that the proverbs developed independently or that both texts are dependent on another, yet unknown text or texts.

23:10 *boundary stone.* In the ancient Near East, stones were used to mark property boundaries. Archaeology has revealed Mesopotamian boundary stones (known as *kudurru*), on which inscriptions indicate ownership. To move a boundary stone was to steal land and was strictly forbidden.

23:13 This proverb encourages parents to exercise physical discipline on young children in order to move them from their natural state of folly (see 22:15 and note) to wisdom. The same idea is found in *Words of Ahiqar*, Saying 4, but it is addressed directly to the son: "If I beat you, my son, you will not die; but if I leave you alone, [you will not live]."

23:21 *drunkards and gluttons become poor.* See notes on 20:1; 21:17.

23 Buy the truth and do not sell it —
wisdom, instruction and insight as well.[q]
24 The father of a righteous child has great joy;
a man who fathers a wise son rejoices in him.[r]
25 May your father and mother rejoice;
may she who gave you birth be joyful!

Saying 18

26 My son,[s] give me your heart
and let your eyes delight in my ways,[t]
27 for an adulterous woman is a deep pit,[u]
and a wayward wife is a narrow well.
28 Like a bandit she lies in wait[v]
and multiplies the unfaithful among men.

Saying 19

29 Who has woe? Who has sorrow?
Who has strife? Who has complaints?
Who has needless bruises? Who has bloodshot eyes?
30 Those who linger over wine,[w]
who go to sample bowls of mixed wine.
31 Do not gaze at wine when it is red,
when it sparkles in the cup,
when it goes down smoothly!
32 In the end it bites like a snake
and poisons like a viper.
33 Your eyes will see strange sights,
and your mind will imagine confusing things.
34 You will be like one sleeping on the high seas,
lying on top of the rigging.
35 "They hit me," you will say, "but I'm not hurt!
They beat me, but I don't feel it!
When will I wake up
so I can find another drink?"

Saying 20

24 Do not envy[x] the wicked,
do not desire their company;

2 for their hearts plot violence,
and their lips talk about making trouble.[y]

Saying 21

3 By wisdom a house is built,[z]
and through understanding it is established;
4 through knowledge its rooms are filled
with rare and beautiful treasures.[a]

Saying 22

5 The wise prevail through great power,
and those who have knowledge muster their strength.
6 Surely you need guidance to wage war,
and victory is won through many advisers.[b]

Saying 23

7 Wisdom is too high for fools;
in the assembly at the gate they must not open their mouths.

Saying 24

8 Whoever plots evil
will be known as a schemer.
9 The schemes of folly are sin,
and people detest a mocker.

Saying 25

10 If you falter in a time of trouble,
how small is your strength![c]
11 Rescue those being led away to death;
hold back those staggering toward slaughter.[d]
12 If you say, "But we knew nothing about this,"
does not he who weighs[e] the heart perceive it?
Does not he who guards your life know it?
Will he not repay everyone according to what they have done?[f]

Saying 26

13 Eat honey, my son, for it is good;
honey from the comb is sweet to your taste.

23:23 [q] Pr 4:7 **23:24** [r] ver 15-16; Pr 10:1; 15:20 **23:26** [s] Pr 3:1; 5:1-6 [t] Ps 18:21; Pr 4:4 **23:27** [u] Pr 22:14 **23:28** [v] Pr 7:11-12; Ecc 7:26 **23:30** [w] Ps 75:8; Isa 5:11; Eph 5:18 **24:1** [x] Ps 37:1; 73:3; Pr 3:31-32; 23:17-18 **24:2** [y] Ps 10:7 **24:3** [z] Pr 14:1 **24:4** [a] Pr 8:21 **24:6** [b] Pr 11:14; 20:18; Lk 14:31 **24:10** [c] Job 4:5; Jer 51:46; Heb 12:3 **24:11** [d] Ps 82:4; Isa 58:6-7 **24:12** [e] Pr 21:2 [f] Job 34:11; Ps 62:12; Ro 2:6*

23:29 *Who has bloodshot eyes?* See note on 20:1.
23:30 *mixed wine.* The alcoholic potency of the wine, normally mixed with water, is enhanced with the addition of honey or pepper to create a type of "spiced wine." As in 20:1, the fool is the one who overindulges in wine. Drunkenness runs counter to the wisdom tradition. For instance, the Greek custom of the "symposium," or drinking party, regulated the amount of wine consumed, so that rational discourse was possible and a general atmosphere was maintained in which the celebrants could freely release their cares and display their talents in song and poetry.
23:31 *Do not gaze at wine when it is red.* It is not clear whether there is some fascination with the color red that was thought to be a further inducement to overindulge in strong drink (as is suggested by the reading of the Septuagint, the pre-Christian Greek translation of the OT) or whether there is a translation problem. *sparkles … goes down smoothly.* The sparkling nature of the wine may indicate a particularly potent vintage that is smooth to the palate (see SS 7:9) or it may be related to a term for wine in the Ugaritic Baal Cycle. The Egyptian "Instruction of Any" likewise includes warnings that drunkenness leads to careless speech, bodily harm, rejection by friends and loss of senses.
24:13 *honey … honey from the comb.* The wisdom writer here follows a tradition found in both Ps 19:10 and Eze 3:3 in which God's words/laws are equated with wisdom and

14 Know also that wisdom is like honey
for you:
If you find it, there is a future hope
for you,
and your hope will not be cut off.[g]

Saying 27

15 Do not lurk like a thief near the house
of the righteous,
do not plunder their dwelling place;
16 for though the righteous fall seven
times, they rise again,
but the wicked stumble when
calamity strikes.[h]

Saying 28

17 Do not gloat[i] when your enemy falls;
when they stumble, do not let your
heart rejoice,[j]
18 or the LORD will see and disapprove
and turn his wrath away from them.

Saying 29

19 Do not fret[k] because of evildoers
or be envious of the wicked,
20 for the evildoer has no future hope,
and the lamp of the wicked will be
snuffed out.[l]

Saying 30

21 Fear the LORD and the king,[m] my son,
and do not join with rebellious
officials,
22 for those two will send sudden
destruction on them,
and who knows what calamities
they can bring?

Further Sayings of the Wise

23 These also are sayings of the wise:[n]

To show partiality[o] in judging is not
good:[p]
24 Whoever says to the guilty, "You are
innocent,"[q]
will be cursed by peoples and
denounced by nations.
25 But it will go well with those who
convict the guilty,
and rich blessing will come on them.

26 An honest answer
is like a kiss on the lips.

27 Put your outdoor work in order
and get your fields ready;
after that, build your house.

28 Do not testify against your neighbor
without cause[r] —
would you use your lips to mislead?
29 Do not say, "I'll do to them as they
have done to me;
I'll pay them back for what they
did."[s]

30 I went past the field of a sluggard,[t]
past the vineyard of someone who
has no sense;
31 thorns had come up everywhere,
the ground was covered with weeds,
and the stone wall was in ruins.
32 I applied my heart to what I observed
and learned a lesson from what I
saw:
33 A little sleep, a little slumber,
a little folding of the hands to
rest[u] —
34 and poverty will come on you like a
thief
and scarcity like an armed man.[v]

More Proverbs of Solomon

25 These are more proverbs[w] of Solomon, compiled by the men of Hezekiah king of Judah:[x]

2 It is the glory of God to conceal a
matter;
to search out a matter is the glory of
kings.[y]
3 As the heavens are high and the earth
is deep,
so the hearts of kings are
unsearchable.

24:14 [g] Ps 119:103; Pr 16:24; 23:18 **24:16** [h] Job 5:19; Ps 34:19; Mic 7:8 **24:17** [i] Ob 1:12 [j] Job 31:29 **24:19** [k] Ps 37:1 **24:20** [l] Job 18:5; Pr 13:9; 23:17-18 **24:21** [m] Ro 13:1-5; 1Pe 2:17 **24:23** [n] Pr 1:6 [o] Lev 19:15 [p] Pr 28:21 **24:24** [q] Pr 17:15 **24:28** [r] Ps 7:4; Pr 25:18; Eph 4:25 **24:29** [s] Pr 20:22; Mt 5:38-41; Ro 12:17 **24:30** [t] Pr 6:6-11; 26:13-16 **24:33** [u] Pr 6:10 **24:34** [v] Pr 10:4; Ecc 10:18 **25:1** [w] 1Ki 4:32 [x] Pr 1:1 **25:2** [y] Pr 16:10-15

are therefore to be desired, much like one desires the sweetness of honey. In most OT texts, honey represents a natural resource, probably the syrup of the date rather than bees' honey. Evidence of bee domestication in Israel has been found at Tel Rehov, and both Hittites and Canaanites used bee honey in their sacrifices. In the Bible, honey occurs in lists with other agricultural products (2Ch 31:5). Here the reference to the honeycomb specifies the product as bees' honey. Note also that honey from the comb would be the freshest and tastiest kind. Akkadian texts also use honey figuratively as they speak of praise being sweeter than honey or wine.

24:28 *Do not testify against your neighbor without cause.* See note on 12:17.

24:29 *I'll pay them back for what they did.* See note on 20:22. Amenemope also teaches against vengeance and urges responding with silence and patience for the god to respond.

25:1 *men of Hezekiah.* This is the fifth section title (see also 1:1; 10:1; 22:17–21; 24:23) within the book. It begins another section of Solomonic proverbs (implying that what comes before is not Solomonic) that continues through the end of ch. 29, but this time, others are said to be involved. The mystery of the verse has to do with the nature of the involvement of the men of Hezekiah. It is likely that, along with other acts of reform and renewal of worship following the destruction of the northern kingdom in 722 BC, Hezekiah also initiated more care in the transmission of sacred literature. National crisis is a time for reflection, and perhaps Hezekiah attempted to gain God's favor by having traditional wisdom sayings recorded and disseminated (compare the *Words of Ahiqar,* a guide to

A well-tended vineyard stands in contrast to the one mentioned in Pr 24:30 – 31.
www.HolyLandPhotos.org

4 Remove the dross from the silver,
and a silversmith can produce a vessel;
5 remove wicked officials from the king's presence,[z]
and his throne will be established[a] through righteousness.[b]
6 Do not exalt yourself in the king's presence,
and do not claim a place among his great men;
7 it is better for him to say to you, "Come up here,"[c]
than for him to humiliate you before his nobles.

What you have seen with your eyes
8 do not bring[a] hastily to court,
for what will you do in the end
if your neighbor puts you to shame?[d]

9 If you take your neighbor to court,
do not betray another's confidence,
10 or the one who hears it may shame you
and the charge against you will stand.

11 Like apples[b] of gold in settings of silver[e]
is a ruling rightly given.
12 Like an earring of gold or an ornament of fine gold
is the rebuke of a wise judge to a listening ear.[f]
13 Like a snow-cooled drink at harvest time
is a trustworthy messenger to the one who sends him;
he refreshes the spirit of his master.[g]

25:5 [z] Pr 20:8 [a] 2Sa 7:13 [b] Pr 16:12; 29:14 **25:7** [c] Lk 14:7-10 **25:8** [d] Mt 5:25-26 **25:11** [e] ver 12; Pr 15:23 **25:12** [f] ver 11; Ps 141:5; Pr 13:18; 15:31 **25:13** [g] Pr 10:26; 13:17

[a] 7,8 Or *nobles / on whom you had set your eyes.* / [8] *Do not go* [b] *11* Or possibly *apricots*

proper behavior, presented to the king of Assyria as a means of his returning to royal favor). However, the rather general reference to "men of Hezekiah" does not allow us to be more specific in identifying who exactly they are. The text suggests that Hezekiah had court-sponsored sages who gathered and compiled wisdom sayings.

25:4 *dross.* Impurities removed during the refining process. See note on 17:3.

25:8 *do not bring hastily to court.* Amenemope also advises against bringing a charge too quickly, especially if the evidence is not strong.

25:9 *do not betray another's confidence.* According to Proverbs, such an act will ruin one's reputation. This principle is similar to that of one saying in the *Words of Ahiqar* that advises that if you reveal secrets to your friends, your reputation as one being able to hold confidences will be ruined.

25:11 *apples of gold in settings of silver.* The writer here uses the simile of a finely worked piece of jewelry, whose craftsman has been able to balance a golden piece of fruit amidst an intricately designed silver setting. The delicacy of this decorative device draws the eye, just as a right ruling or a clever saying touches the mind. *apples.* Some have suggested that the fruit named here is an apricot rather than an apple, but it makes no difference to the imagery.

25:13 *messenger.* See note on 13:17. Good messengers bring relief to those who send them, just like a cool drink

14 Like clouds and wind without rain
is one who boasts of gifts never given.

15 Through patience a ruler can be persuaded,[h]
and a gentle tongue can break a bone.[i]
16 If you find honey, eat just enough —
too much of it, and you will vomit.[j]
17 Seldom set foot in your neighbor's house —
too much of you, and they will hate you.

18 Like a club or a sword or a sharp arrow
is one who gives false testimony against a neighbor.[k]
19 Like a broken tooth or a lame foot
is reliance on the unfaithful in a time of trouble.
20 Like one who takes away a garment on a cold day,
or like vinegar poured on a wound,
is one who sings songs to a heavy heart.

21 If your enemy is hungry, give him food to eat;
if he is thirsty, give him water to drink.
22 In doing this, you will heap burning coals[l] on his head,
and the LORD will reward you.[m]

23 Like a north wind that brings unexpected rain
is a sly tongue — which provokes a horrified look.

24 Better to live on a corner of the roof
than share a house with a quarrelsome wife.[n]

25 Like cold water to a weary soul
is good news from a distant land.[o]
26 Like a muddied spring or a polluted well
are the righteous who give way to the wicked.

27 It is not good to eat too much honey,[p]
nor is it honorable to search out matters that are too deep.[q]

28 Like a city whose walls are broken through
is a person who lacks self-control.

26 Like snow in summer or rain[r] in harvest,
honor is not fitting for a fool.[s]
2 Like a fluttering sparrow or a darting swallow,
an undeserved curse does not come to rest.[t]
3 A whip for the horse, a bridle for the donkey,[u]
and a rod for the backs of fools![v]
4 Do not answer a fool according to his folly,
or you yourself will be just like him.[w]
5 Answer a fool according to his folly,
or he will be wise in his own eyes.[x]
6 Sending a message by the hands of a fool[y]
is like cutting off one's feet or drinking poison.
7 Like the useless legs of one who is lame
is a proverb in the mouth of a fool.[z]
8 Like tying a stone in a sling
is the giving of honor to a fool.[a]
9 Like a thornbush in a drunkard's hand
is a proverb in the mouth of a fool.[b]

25:15 [h] Ecc 10:4 [i] Pr 15:1 **25:16** [j] ver 27 **25:18** [k] Ps 57:4; Pr 12:18 **25:22** [l] Ps 18:8 [m] 2Sa 16:12; 2Ch 28:15; Mt 5:44; Ro 12:20* **25:24** [n] Pr 21:9
25:25 [o] Pr 15:30 **25:27** [p] ver 16 [q] Pr 27:2; Mt 23:12 **26:1** [r] 1Sa 12:17 [s] ver 8; Pr 19:10 **26:2** [t] Nu 23:8; Dt 23:5 **26:3** [u] Ps 32:9 [v] Pr 10:13 **26:4** [w] ver 5; Isa 36:21 **26:5** [x] ver 4; Pr 3:7 **26:6** [y] Pr 10:26 **26:7** [z] ver 9 **26:8** [a] ver 1 **26:9** [b] ver 7

brings relief to those who harvest during the hot spring and late summer months.
25:14 *gifts.* See note on 17:23.
25:18 *false testimony.* See note on 12:17.
25:22 *heap burning coals on his head.* The "Instruction of Amenemope" also advises the wise person to shame fools or their enemies by pulling them out of deep water and by feeding them one's bread until they are so full that they are ashamed. Similarly, the "Precepts and Admonitions" in Babylonian wisdom literature states that the wise man should not "return evil to the man who disputes with you" and should, in fact, "smile on your adversary." This is surely the direction this proverb goes, but the metaphor of heaping burning coals on the head remains elusive. Cultural phenomena that may offer some explanation include the following: (1) There was an Egyptian ritual (mentioned in a late demotic text from the third century BC) in which a man apparently gave public evidence of his penitence by carrying a pan of burning charcoal on his head when he went to ask forgiveness of the one he had offended. (2) In the Middle Assyrian laws there is an example of a punishment in which hot asphalt was poured on the offender's head. Both of these have difficulties. The first is in a late text and the action referred to has been variously interpreted. The second is hot tar, not coals, and is a punishment much like tarring (and feathering) in more recent history. At this point, no ancient texts help clarify the imagery used here.
25:23 *north wind.* In Israel, a north wind typically brings fair weather, not rain, hence the sense of something unexpected happening. But some scholars have suggested that this proverb had its origin in Egypt, where the north wind does bring the rain off the Mediterranean (5 – 10 inches [12 – 24 centimeters] per year in the delta).
25:24 *corner of the roof.* See note on 21:9.
26:1 *snow . . . rain.* Snow never occurs in the summer in Israel, and rain is an extremely rare event during the harvests of spring and summer. The Mediterranean climate of Syria and Canaan brings rain and cooler temperatures (below freezing in the higher elevations, as at Jerusalem) during the winter months (Oct. to Feb.) and the remainder of the year is dry, with only an occasional shower. Thus, this statement is like many in ancient wisdom literature (e.g., Amenemope and Ankhsheshonq) in which the fool is described as "unteachable" and dishonorable. As Ahiqar notes, there is no point in sending the Bedouin to the sea, as it is not his natural habitat.
26:6 *Sending a message.* See note on 25:13.

[10]Like an archer who wounds at random
is one who hires a fool or any
passer-by.
[11]As a dog returns to its vomit,[c]
so fools repeat their folly.[d]
[12]Do you see a person wise in their own
eyes?[e]
There is more hope for a fool than
for them.[f]

[13]A sluggard says,[g] "There's a lion in the
road,
a fierce lion roaming the streets!"[h]
[14]As a door turns on its hinges,
so a sluggard turns on his bed.[i]
[15]A sluggard buries his hand in the dish;
he is too lazy to bring it back to his
mouth.[j]
[16]A sluggard is wiser in his own eyes
than seven people who answer
discreetly.

[17]Like one who grabs a stray dog by the
ears
is someone who rushes into a
quarrel not their own.

[18]Like a maniac shooting
flaming arrows of death
[19]is one who deceives their neighbor
and says, "I was only joking!"

[20]Without wood a fire goes out;
without a gossip a quarrel dies down.[k]
[21]As charcoal to embers and as wood to
fire,
so is a quarrelsome person for
kindling strife.[l]
[22]The words of a gossip are like choice
morsels;
they go down to the inmost parts.[m]

[23]Like a coating of silver dross on
earthenware
are fervent[a] lips with an evil heart.
[24]Enemies disguise themselves with their
lips,[n]
but in their hearts they harbor deceit.[o]
[25]Though their speech is charming,[p] do
not believe them,
for seven abominations fill their
hearts.[q]
[26]Their malice may be concealed by
deception,
but their wickedness will be exposed
in the assembly.
[27]Whoever digs a pit[r] will fall into it;[s]
if someone rolls a stone, it will roll
back on them.[t]
[28]A lying tongue hates those it hurts,
and a flattering mouth[u] works
ruin.

27 Do not boast[v] about tomorrow,
for you do not know what a day
may bring.[w]

[2]Let someone else praise you, and not
your own mouth;
an outsider, and not your own lips.[x]

[3]Stone is heavy and sand[y] a burden,
but a fool's provocation is heavier
than both.

[4]Anger is cruel and fury overwhelming,
but who can stand before jealousy?[z]

[5]Better is open rebuke
than hidden love.

[6]Wounds from a friend can be trusted,
but an enemy multiplies kisses.[a]

[7]One who is full loathes honey from the
comb,
but to the hungry even what is bitter
tastes sweet.

[8]Like a bird that flees its nest[b]
is anyone who flees from home.

[9]Perfume[c] and incense bring joy to the
heart,
and the pleasantness of a friend
springs from their heartfelt advice.

26:11 [c]2Pe 2:22* [d]Ex 8:15; Ps 85:8 **26:12** [e]Pr 3:7 [f]Pr 29:20 **26:13** [g]Pr 6:6-11; 24:30-34 [h]Pr 22:13 **26:14** [i]Pr 6:9 **26:15** [j]Pr 19:24 **26:20** [k]Pr 22:10 **26:21** [l]Pr 14:17; 15:18 **26:22** [m]Pr 18:8 **26:24** [n]Ps 31:18 [o]Ps 41:6; Pr 10:18; 12:20 **26:25** [p]Ps 28:3 [q]Jer 9:4-8 **26:27** [r]Ps 7:15 [s]Est 6:13 [t]Est 2:23; 7:9; Ps 35:8; 141:10; Pr 28:10; 29:6; Isa 50:11 **26:28** [u]Ps 12:3; Pr 29:5 **27:1** [v]1Ki 20:11 [w]Mt 6:34; Lk 12:19-20; Jas 4:13-16 **27:2** [x]Pr 25:27 **27:3** [y]Job 6:3 **27:4** [z]Nu 5:14 **27:6** [a]Ps 141:5; Pr 28:23 **27:8** [b]Isa 16:2 **27:9** [c]Est 2:12; Ps 45:8

[a] 23 Hebrew; Septuagint *smooth*

26:13 *sluggard.* See note on 12:24.
26:16 *seven people.* It has been suggested that this is a reference to the famed seven sages (referring to either the *apkallu* or the *ummanu*) that brought civilization and wisdom to the world in Mesopotamian lore. The seven *apkallu* came before the flood, and the seven *ummanu*, the counterparts of the *apkallu*, came after the flood. This is possible, but one would expect a definite article ("the seven") if it were the case.
26:22 *gossip.* See note on 11:13.
26:23 *coating of silver dross.* While a glaze may be applied to pottery as decoration, it may also hide flaws and thus cheat the one who purchases the pot. Similarly, a coating of silver dross, made of adulterated, oxidized metal, may initially look good, but will quickly tarnish or flake off. Thus the "fervent" (or "smooth" [see NIV text note]) lips of a scoundrel may attempt to cover his hatred and malice with deceitful words.
26:24 *lips ... hearts.* An Akkadian proverb draws the same distinction, observing that a man may speak friendly words with his lips, but have a heart full of murder. The incantation series Shurpu speaks of one whose speech is straightforward, but whose heart is devious.
27:9 *Perfume and incense.* Various pungent scents were part of the Israelite's everyday life. Perfumes were concocted and incense burned to cover some of the more offensive smells, to enhance one's sexual attractiveness (e.g., Est 2:12; SS 1:12; cf. thirteenth-century BC Egyptian Love Songs), and to serve as an offering to God (Ex 30:34–38). Among the most common were frankincense, myrrh, saffron and mixtures of cinnamon, cassia and olive oil (see notes on Ps 45:8; 133:2; SS 3:6). Such a pleasant fragrance is an apt parallel with a friend's wise advice, since a person's wise counsel makes it desirable to be around them, just as pleasant aromas would.

10 Do not forsake your friend or a friend
of your family,
and do not go to your relative's house
when disaster[d] strikes you —
better a neighbor nearby than a
relative far away.
11 Be wise, my son, and bring joy to my
heart;[e]
then I can answer anyone who treats
me with contempt.[f]
12 The prudent see danger and take refuge,
but the simple keep going and pay
the penalty.[g]
13 Take the garment of one who puts up
security for a stranger;
hold it in pledge if it is done for an
outsider.[h]
14 If anyone loudly blesses their neighbor
early in the morning,
it will be taken as a curse.
15 A quarrelsome wife is like the dripping[i]
of a leaky roof in a rainstorm;
16 restraining her is like restraining the
wind
or grasping oil with the hand.
17 As iron sharpens iron,
so one person sharpens another.
18 The one who guards a fig tree will eat
its fruit,[j]
and whoever protects their master
will be honored.[k]
19 As water reflects the face,
so one's life reflects the heart.[a]
20 Death and Destruction[b] are never
satisfied,[l]
and neither are human eyes.[m]
21 The crucible for silver and the furnace
for gold,[n]
but people are tested by their praise.
22 Though you grind a fool in a mortar,
grinding them like grain with a
pestle,
you will not remove their folly from
them.

27:10 [d] Pr 17:17; 18:24
27:11 [e] Pr 10:1; 23:15-16 [f] Ge 24:60
27:12 [g] Pr 22:3
27:13 [h] Pr 20:16
27:15 [i] Est 1:18; Pr 19:13
27:18 [j] 1Co 9:7 [k] Lk 19:12-27
27:20 [l] Pr 30:15-16; Hab 2:5 [m] Ecc 1:8; 6:7
27:21 [n] Pr 17:3

23 Be sure you know the condition of
your flocks,[o]
give careful attention to your
herds;
24 for riches do not endure forever,[p]
and a crown is not secure for all
generations.
25 When the hay is removed and new
growth appears
and the grass from the hills is
gathered in,
26 the lambs will provide you with
clothing,
and the goats with the price of a
field.
27 You will have plenty of goats' milk
to feed your family
and to nourish your female
servants.

28 The wicked flee[q] though no one
pursues,[r]
but the righteous are as bold as a
lion.[s]
2 When a country is rebellious, it has
many rulers,
but a ruler with discernment and
knowledge maintains order.
3 A ruler[c] who oppresses the poor
is like a driving rain that leaves no
crops.
4 Those who forsake instruction praise
the wicked,
but those who heed it resist them.
5 Evildoers do not understand what is
right,
but those who seek the LORD
understand it fully.
6 Better the poor whose walk is
blameless
than the rich whose ways are
perverse.[t]
7 A discerning son heeds instruction,
but a companion of gluttons
disgraces his father.[u]

27:23 [o] Pr 12:10
27:24 [p] Pr 23:5
28:1 [q] 2Ki 7:7 [r] Lev 26:17; Ps 53:5 [s] Ps 138:3
28:6 [t] Pr 19:1
28:7 [u] Pr 23:19-21

[a] 19 *Or so others reflect your heart back to you*
[b] 20 Hebrew *Abaddon*
[c] 3 *Or A poor person*

27:10 *do not go to your relative's house.* While some proverbs suggest that a friend is equivalent to a relative in an emergency and that both will prove helpful (17:17), the present proverb actually prefers a neighbor over a relative at such a time. Perhaps the explanation is that friends are associated with a person by choice and affection, whereas a brother has no say. However, still, one might think that particularly in an ancient society a relative would help even if they did not like the person. Perhaps the key to understanding this verse is the last line, which mentions that the relative lives at a distance. Perhaps the friend is someone close and the brother far away. But, again, ancient society was not as mobile as modern society, so one wonders how often relatives would be split by such great distance. In any case, such a thought is not without parallel in the ancient Near East, since Ankhsheshonq advises that is it preferable to go to a friend rather than a brother when there are difficult circumstances. Sometimes relationship with a relative can be rancorous or antagonistic, and some relatives (e.g., a brother) might even have vested interests to be realized should you be ruined or die.

27:20 *Death and Destruction.* See note on 15:11.

27:21 *crucible … furnace.* See note on 17:3.

28:6 *Better … than.* See note on 15:16.

8 Whoever increases wealth by taking
interest[v] or profit from the poor
amasses it for another,[w] who will be
kind to the poor.[x]

9 If anyone turns a deaf ear to my
instruction,
even their prayers are detestable.[y]

10 Whoever leads the upright along an
evil path
will fall into their own trap,[z]
but the blameless will receive a good
inheritance.

11 The rich are wise in their own eyes;
one who is poor and discerning sees
how deluded they are.

12 When the righteous triumph, there is
great elation;[a]
but when the wicked rise to power,
people go into hiding.[b]

13 Whoever conceals their sins[c] does not
prosper,
but the one who confesses and
renounces them finds mercy.[d]

14 Blessed is the one who always
trembles before God,
but whoever hardens their heart falls
into trouble.

15 Like a roaring lion or a charging bear
is a wicked ruler over a helpless
people.

16 A tyrannical ruler practices extortion,
but one who hates ill-gotten gain
will enjoy a long reign.

17 Anyone tormented by the guilt of
murder
will seek refuge[e] in the grave;
let no one hold them back.

18 The one whose walk is blameless is
kept safe,
but the one whose ways are perverse
will fall[f] into the pit.[a]

19 Those who work their land will have
abundant food,
but those who chase fantasies will
have their fill of poverty.[g]

20 A faithful person will be richly blessed,
but one eager to get rich will not go
unpunished.[h]

21 To show partiality is not good[i] —
yet a person will do wrong for a
piece of bread.[j]

22 The stingy are eager to get rich
and are unaware that poverty awaits
them.[k]

23 Whoever rebukes a person will in the
end gain favor
rather than one who has a flattering
tongue.[l]

24 Whoever robs their father or mother[m]
and says, "It's not wrong,"
is partner to one who destroys.[n]

25 The greedy stir up conflict,
but those who trust in the LORD[o] will
prosper.

26 Those who trust in themselves are fools,[p]
but those who walk in wisdom are
kept safe.

27 Those who give to the poor will lack
nothing,[q]
but those who close their eyes to
them receive many curses.

28 When the wicked rise to power, people
go into hiding;[r]
but when the wicked perish, the
righteous thrive.

29

Whoever remains stiff-necked
after many rebukes
will suddenly be destroyed —
without remedy.[s]

2 When the righteous thrive, the people
rejoice;[t]
when the wicked rule, the people
groan.[u]

3 A man who loves wisdom brings joy to
his father,[v]
but a companion of prostitutes
squanders his wealth.[w]

4 By justice a king gives a country
stability,[x]
but those who are greedy for[b] bribes
tear it down.

5 Those who flatter their neighbors
are spreading nets for their feet.

6 Evildoers are snared by their own sin,[y]
but the righteous shout for joy and
are glad.

7 The righteous care about justice for the
poor,[z]
but the wicked have no such
concern.

28:8 [v] Ex 18:21 [w] Job 27:17; Pr 13:22 [x] Ps 112:9; Pr 14:31; Lk 14:12-14 **28:9** [y] Ps 66:18; 109:7; Pr 15:8; Isa 1:13 **28:10** [z] Pr 26:27 **28:12** [a] 2Ki 11:20 [b] Pr 11:10; 29:2 **28:13** [c] Job 31:33 [d] Ps 32:1-5; 1Jn 1:9 **28:17** [e] Ge 9:6 **28:18** [f] Pr 10:9 **28:19** [g] Pr 12:11 **28:20** [h] ver 22; Pr 10:6; 1Ti 6:9 **28:21** [i] Pr 18:5 [j] Eze 13:19 **28:22** [k] ver 20; Pr 23:6 **28:23** [l] Pr 27:5-6 **28:24** [m] Pr 19:26 [n] Pr 18:9 **28:25** [o] Pr 29:25 **28:26** [p] Ps 4:5; Pr 3:5 **28:27** [q] Dt 15:7; 24:19; Pr 19:17; 22:9 **28:28** [r] ver 12 **29:1** [s] 2Ch 36:16; Pr 6:15 **29:2** [t] Est 8:15 [u] Pr 28:12 **29:3** [v] Pr 10:1 [w] Pr 5:8-10; Lk 15:11-32 **29:4** [x] Pr 8:15-16 **29:6** [y] Ecc 9:12 **29:7** [z] Job 29:16; Ps 41:1; Pr 31:8-9

[a] 18 Syriac (see Septuagint); Hebrew *into one* [b] 4 Or *who give*

28:8 *interest or profit.* Charging interest to fellow Israelites was against the law (Ex 22:25; Dt 23:20). It was lawful to charge interest to non-Israelites, but nothing in this proverb indicates that that is in view. While there are no other cultures that evidence interest-free loans, ancient law codes like the Code of Hammurapi do regulate the amount of interest that a creditor may charge.

8 Mockers stir up a city,
but the wise turn away anger.[a]

9 If a wise person goes to court with a fool,
the fool rages and scoffs, and there is no peace.

10 The bloodthirsty hate a person of integrity
and seek to kill the upright.[b]

11 Fools give full vent to their rage,
but the wise bring calm in the end.[c]

12 If a ruler listens to lies,
all his officials become wicked.

13 The poor and the oppressor have this in common:
The LORD gives sight to the eyes of both.[d]

14 If a king judges the poor with fairness,
his throne will be established forever.[e]

15 A rod and a reprimand impart wisdom,
but a child left undisciplined disgraces its mother.[f]

16 When the wicked thrive, so does sin,
but the righteous will see their downfall.[g]

17 Discipline your children, and they will give you peace;
they will bring you the delights you desire.[h]

18 Where there is no revelation, people cast off restraint;
but blessed is the one who heeds wisdom's instruction.[i]

29:8 [a] Pr 11:11; 16:14 **29:10** [b] 1Jn 3:12 **29:11** [c] Pr 12:16; 19:11 **29:13** [d] Pr 22:2; Mt 5:45 **29:14** [e] Ps 72:1-5; Pr 16:12 **29:15** [f] Pr 10:1; 13:24; 17:21,25 **29:16** [g] Ps 37:35-36; 58:10; 91:8; 92:11 **29:17** [h] ver 15; Pr 10:1 **29:18** [i] Ps 1:1-2; 119:1-2; Jn 13:17

29:20 [j] Pr 26:12; Jas 1:19 **29:22** [k] Pr 14:17; 15:18; 26:21 **29:23** [l] Pr 11:2; 15:33; 16:18; Isa 66:2; Mt 23:12 **29:24** [m] Lev 5:1 **29:25** [n] Pr 28:25 **29:26** [o] Pr 19:6 **29:27** [p] ver 10

19 Servants cannot be corrected by mere words;
though they understand, they will not respond.

20 Do you see someone who speaks in haste?
There is more hope for a fool than for them.[j]

21 A servant pampered from youth
will turn out to be insolent.

22 An angry person stirs up conflict,
and a hot-tempered person commits many sins.[k]

23 Pride brings a person low,
but the lowly in spirit gain honor.[l]

24 The accomplices of thieves are their own enemies;
they are put under oath and dare not testify.[m]

25 Fear of man will prove to be a snare,
but whoever trusts in the LORD[n] is kept safe.

26 Many seek an audience with a ruler,[o]
but it is from the LORD that one gets justice.

27 The righteous detest the dishonest;
the wicked detest the upright.[p]

Sayings of Agur

30 The sayings of Agur son of Jakeh—an inspired utterance.

This man's utterance to Ithiel:

"I am weary, God,
but I can prevail.[a]

[a] 1 With a different word division of the Hebrew; Masoretic Text *utterance to Ithiel, / to Ithiel and Ukal:*

29:11 *Fools give full vent to their rage.* Uncontrolled anger can be extremely destructive, even if it is justified by an attack of some sort. If a person does not guard the expression of their anger, then it can harm them even further. Papyrus Insinger also counsels a watch over one's anger, observing that great anger creates a stench around a person.
29:15 *rod.* See note on 13:24.
29:17 *Discipline your children.* See notes on 13:24; 23:13.
29:19 *Servants cannot be corrected by mere words.* The sages operated by the principle that wisdom was not an inherent human quality—to the contrary, they considered the fear of the Lord the beginning of wisdom. Their teaching implied that people in their natural state were naive or foolish and that it took work to become wise. They also taught that some people were harder to educate than others. Here, we see that "servants" were thought by the wise to be particularly difficult to train. It was not that they were not intelligent enough to understand intellectually what they were being told. The second line affirms that they do understand but says that they do not respond. This likely indicates a lack of desire to carry out the commands of the master. It appears that they needed something more to motivate them (perhaps fear of the rod? [see note on 13:24]). Papyrus Insinger makes a similar point, observing that the servant will only obey if the master has some means of discipline at hand.
29:20 *someone who speaks in haste.* Proverbs often warns against speaking too hastily. One should think before speaking, rather than impulsively blurting out the first thing that comes to mind. Ankhsheshonq warns against blurting out whatever comes to mind. Ptahhotep advises deliberation in speech to ensure that what is said matters.
29:23 *Pride.* See note on 11:2.
30:1 *Agur son of Jakeh.* We know nothing further about this man, since neither he nor his father, Jakeh, are mentioned anywhere else. We also know nothing about Ithiel and Ukal (see NIV text note), who are named as the recipients of Agur's wisdom. Indeed, there are questions about the proper translation of some verses in Pr 30. *inspired utterance.* The Hebrew word may alternatively identify the tribe from which Agur comes ("Massa"). This may then be connected to the name of a tribe in Arabia related to the Ishmaelites mentioned in Ge 25:14; 1Ch 1:30. If so, then we have here the words of an Arabian wise man.

2 Surely I am only a brute, not a man;
I do not have human understanding.
3 I have not learned wisdom,
nor have I attained to the knowledge
of the Holy One.[q]
4 Who has gone up[r] to heaven and come
down?
Whose hands[s] have gathered up the
wind?
Who has wrapped up the waters[t] in a
cloak?[u]
Who has established all the ends of
the earth?
What is his name,[v] and what is the
name of his son?
Surely you know!

5 "Every word of God is flawless;[w]
he is a shield[x] to those who take
refuge in him.
6 Do not add[y] to his words,
or he will rebuke you and prove you
a liar.

7 "Two things I ask of you, LORD;
do not refuse me before I die:
8 Keep falsehood and lies far from me;
give me neither poverty nor riches,
but give me only my daily bread.[z]
9 Otherwise, I may have too much and
disown[a] you
and say, 'Who is the LORD?'[b]
Or I may become poor and steal,
and so dishonor the name of my
God.[c]

10 "Do not slander a servant to their
master,
or they will curse you, and you will
pay for it.

11 "There are those who curse their
fathers
and do not bless their mothers;[d]
12 those who are pure in their own eyes[e]
and yet are not cleansed of their
filth;[f]
13 those whose eyes are ever so haughty,[g]
whose glances are so disdainful;
14 those whose teeth[h] are swords
and whose jaws are set with knives[i]
to devour[j] the poor[k] from the earth
and the needy from among
mankind.[l]

15 "The leech has two daughters.
'Give! Give!' they cry.

"There are three things that are never
satisfied,[m]
four that never say, 'Enough!':
16 the grave,[n] the barren womb,
land, which is never satisfied with
water,
and fire, which never says, 'Enough!'

17 "The eye that mocks[o] a father,
that scorns an aged mother,
will be pecked out by the ravens of the
valley,
will be eaten by the vultures.[p]

18 "There are three things that are too
amazing for me,
four that I do not understand:
19 the way of an eagle in the sky,
the way of a snake on a rock,
the way of a ship on the high seas,
and the way of a man with a young
woman.

20 "This is the way of an adulterous
woman:
She eats and wipes her mouth
and says, 'I've done nothing wrong.'[q]

21 "Under three things the earth trembles,
under four it cannot bear up:
22 a servant who becomes king,[r]
a godless fool who gets plenty
to eat,
23 a contemptible woman who gets
married,
and a servant who displaces her
mistress.

24 "Four things on earth are small,
yet they are extremely wise:
25 Ants are creatures of little strength,
yet they store up their food in the
summer;[s]
26 hyraxes[t] are creatures of little power,
yet they make their home in the
crags;

30:3 [q] Pr 9:10 **30:4** [r] Ps 24:1-2; Jn 3:13; Eph 4:7-10 [s] Ps 104:3; Isa 40:12 [t] Job 26:8; 38:8-9 [u] Ge 1:2 [v] Rev 19:12 **30:5** [w] Ps 12:6; 18:30 [x] Ge 15:1; Ps 84:11 **30:6** [y] Dt 4:2; 12:32; Rev 22:18 **30:8** [z] Mt 6:11 **30:9** [a] Jos 24:27; Isa 1:4; 59:13 [b] Dt 6:12; 8:10-14; Hos 13:6 [c] Dt 8:12 **30:11** [d] Pr 20:20 **30:12** [e] Pr 16:2; Lk 18:11 [f] Jer 2:23, 35 **30:13** [g] 2Sa 22:28; Job 41:34; Ps 131:1; Pr 6:17 **30:14** [h] Job 4:11; 29:17; Ps 3:7 [i] Ps 57:4 [j] Job 24:9; Ps 14:4 [k] Am 8:4; Mic 2:2 [l] Job 19:22 **30:15** [m] Pr 27:20 **30:16** [n] Pr 27:20; Isa 5:14; 14:9, 11; Hab 2:5 **30:17** [o] Dt 21:18-21; Pr 23:22 [p] Job 15:23 **30:20** [q] Pr 5:6 **30:22** [r] Pr 19:10; 29:2 **30:25** [s] Pr 6:6-8 **30:26** [t] Ps 104:18

30:8 *Keep falsehood and lies far from me.* See note on 10:18.
30:16 *the grave.* See note on 1:12. *the barren womb.* If a woman could not have a child, the consequences were dire. Even today, couples are often saddened by an inability to have children, but in antiquity the stakes were even higher. After all, who would take care of an aging couple if there were no children? A widow without sons would be particularly vulnerable in a patriarchal society without social structures like health plans or nursing homes. One need only think of the anxieties surrounding childbirth in the Genesis patriarchal narratives (e.g., Ge 30:1) to get a sense of the issue. It was also not uncommon in the ancient world to believe that one's felicity in the afterlife was dependent on care by those who were still in the land of the living. Thus, barrenness destined one to continued difficulties in the afterlife.
30:21 – 23 This numerical proverb describes a topsy-turvy world. Similar negative thoughts about a topsy-turvy world may be found in the Admonitions of Ipu-Wer and apocalyptic texts like Isa 24:2 and the Akkadian Marduk Prophecy and Shulgi Prophecy. All of these portray a situation in which order has been disrupted, and we should recall that order is what wisdom pursues in the ancient Near East.
30:25 *Ants.* See note on 6:6.

[27] locusts[u] have no king,
yet they advance together in ranks;
[28] a lizard can be caught with the hand,
yet it is found in kings' palaces.

[29] "There are three things that are stately in their stride,
four that move with stately bearing:
[30] a lion, mighty among beasts,
who retreats before nothing;
[31] a strutting rooster, a he-goat,
and a king secure against revolt.[a]

[32] "If you play the fool and exalt yourself,
or if you plan evil,
clap your hand over your mouth![v]
[33] For as churning cream produces butter,
and as twisting the nose produces blood,
so stirring up anger produces strife."

Sayings of King Lemuel

31 The sayings[w] of King Lemuel—an inspired utterance his mother taught him.

[2] Listen, my son! Listen, son of my womb!
Listen, my son, the answer to my prayers![x]
[3] Do not spend your strength[b] on women,
your vigor on those who ruin kings.[y]

[4] It is not for kings, Lemuel—
it is not for kings to drink wine,[z]
not for rulers to crave beer,
[5] lest they drink[a] and forget what has been decreed,[b]
and deprive all the oppressed of their rights.
[6] Let beer be for those who are perishing,
wine[c] for those who are in anguish!
[7] Let them drink[d] and forget their poverty
and remember their misery no more.

[8] Speak[e] up for those who cannot speak for themselves,
for the rights of all who are destitute.
[9] Speak up and judge fairly;
defend the rights of the poor and needy.[f]

Epilogue: The Wife of Noble Character

[10][c] A wife of noble character[g] who can find?[h]
She is worth far more than rubies.
[11] Her husband[i] has full confidence in her
and lacks nothing of value.[j]
[12] She brings him good, not harm,
all the days of her life.
[13] She selects wool and flax
and works with eager hands.[k]
[14] She is like the merchant ships,
bringing her food from afar.
[15] She gets up while it is still night;
she provides food for her family
and portions for her female servants.
[16] She considers a field and buys it;
out of her earnings she plants a vineyard.

30:27 [u] Ex 10:4 **30:32** [v] Job 21:5; 29:9 **31:1** [w] Pr 22:17 **31:2** [x] Jdg 11:30; Isa 49:15 **31:3** [y] Dt 17:17; 1Ki 11:3; Ne 13:26; Pr 5:1-14 **31:4** [z] Pr 20:1; Ecc 10:16-17; Isa 5:22 **31:5** [a] 1Ki 16:9 [b] Pr 16:12; Hos 4:11

31:6 [c] Ge 14:18 **31:7** [d] Est 1:10 **31:8** [e] 1Sa 19:4; Job 29:12-17 **31:9** [f] Lev 19:15; Dt 1:16; Pr 24:23; 29:7; Isa 1:17; Jer 22:16 **31:10** [g] Ru 3:11; Pr 12:4; 18:22 [h] Pr 8:35; 19:14 **31:11** [i] Ge 2:18 [j] Pr 12:4 **31:13** [k] 1Ti 2:9-10

[a] *31* The meaning of the Hebrew for this phrase is uncertain. [b] *3* Or *wealth* [c] *10* Verses 10-31 are an acrostic poem, the verses of which begin with the successive letters of the Hebrew alphabet.

31:1 *King Lemuel.* As with Agur (see note on 30:1), we have no Biblical or extra-Biblical mention of such a king. *inspired utterance.* As with Agur, this Hebrew term may be a reference to the king's tribal affiliation (see note on 30:1). If Lemuel is from the tribe of Massa, then he would be an Arabian leader. *mother.* Note that it is his mother who teaches him here (see note on 1:8). The fact that this is a royal instruction, i.e., from a queen to her son, makes it similar to the Egyptian "Instruction of King Amenemhet" and the "Teaching for Merikare," as well as the Akkadian Advice to a Prince, though in the latter the teacher is the queen mother.
31:4 *not for rulers to crave beer.* See note on 20:1.
31:10–31 The book of Proverbs ends with an extensive description of the "wife of noble character" (v. 10). As we read this description, we see that it recapitulates much that has been said earlier about the good wife as opposed to the evil woman (5:15–20; 12:4; 18:22). Furthermore, if we read this description in the light of what was earlier said about the Woman Wisdom (1:20–33; 8:1–36; 9:1–8), we can see that this noble woman is a human reflection of the Woman Wisdom, who represents God's wisdom and even God himself. In essence, she embodies godly wisdom.

It is interesting to note that in many editions of the Hebrew canon, the book of Proverbs is then followed by Ruth, who is called a "woman of noble character" (Ru 3:11), and then by the Song of Songs, in which the woman plays the leading role in pursuit of the love relationship with the man.

There really is nothing quite like this poem in ancient Near Eastern literature, though there are some other more prosaic statements about the value of a good woman and advice about how to treat her. Ptahhotep urges men to love their wives and provide for them even as he counsels to keep them housebound, away from places of power. The "Instruction of Any" suggests that an efficient wife be given free rein in the home so that husband and wife can avoid strife.
31:10 *worth far more than rubies.* See note on 3:15.
31:16–24 The Code of Hammurapi contains several laws regulating the activities of Babylonian women who operate inns or taverns. However, this may not be construed in the same light as having the ability to buy a field or sell finely dyed and woven garments as a professional seamstress. The idealized picture in this proverb of how a woman might demonstrate wisdom in the various pursuits of life goes beyond anything that the Biblical

[17]She sets about her work vigorously;
her arms are strong for her tasks.
[18]She sees that her trading is profitable,
and her lamp does not go out at night.
[19]In her hand she holds the distaff
and grasps the spindle with her fingers.
[20]She opens her arms to the poor
and extends her hands to the needy.[l]
[21]When it snows, she has no fear for her household;
for all of them are clothed in scarlet.
[22]She makes coverings for her bed;
she is clothed in fine linen and purple.
[23]Her husband is respected at the city gate,
where he takes his seat among the elders[m] of the land.
[24]She makes linen garments and sells them,
and supplies the merchants with sashes.
[25]She is clothed with strength and dignity;
she can laugh at the days to come.
[26]She speaks with wisdom,
and faithful instruction is on her tongue.[n]
[27]She watches over the affairs of her household
and does not eat the bread of idleness.
[28]Her children arise and call her blessed;
her husband also, and he praises her:
[29]"Many women do noble things,
but you surpass them all."
[30]Charm is deceptive, and beauty is fleeting;
but a woman who fears the LORD is to be praised.
[31]Honor her for all that her hands have done,
and let her works bring her praise[o] at the city gate.

31:20 [l]Dt 15:11; Eph 4:28; Heb 13:16 **31:23** [m]Ex 3:16; Ru 4:1, 11; Pr 12:4 **31:26** [n]Pr 10:31 **31:31** [o]Pr 11:16

text elsewhere suggests is open to women. Ordinarily, they did not have the legal standing to purchase land, although they certainly worked hard with their families to cultivate it and deal with its produce. The one industry mentioned in ancient Near Eastern texts that is open to female enterprise was weaving, and this may be the model for all the other activities.
31:19 *distaff ... spindle.* Both of these Hebrew terms appear only here in the Bible. However, the context suggests that the translation is appropriate and that these are simply technical terms related to the task of spinning and weaving. There is a sense of intense activity performed by a determined woman willing to "roll up her sleeves" and produce large quantities of woven goods for both her family and for merchants to sell for her.
31:21 *scarlet.* See note on Ex 25:4. A red or purple dye would have been expensive and reserved for the wealthy.
31:22 *fine linen.* A sheet of fine linen would have been a valuable and desirable commodity, to be used as a bed covering or cut into smaller pieces for garments (see Jdg 14:12–13; Isa 3:23). *purple.* This dye, made from the glandular fluid of sea mollusks, would have been quite expensive; in this context, it is a symbol of the prosperity that the ideal wife brings to her household.
31:23 *city gate.* The traditional place for the city elders to gather to do business (cf. Lot in Sodom's gate in Ge 19:1) and to hear legal arguments (Ru 4:1–4). See notes on 8:3; Job 5:4; 29:7. *elders.* Old Babylonian records note their legal role in judging land disputes, hearing the taking of oaths, and serving as witnesses to various transactions.

WISDOM AND HYMNIC LITERATURE

ECCLESIASTES

Historical Setting

Although the text itself implies that Solomon is the author of Ecclesiastes, another alternative is that this is offered in the book as only one of many personae adopted by the sage throughout the book. The Hebrew term *Qoheleth* (translated "the Teacher") suggests one who aggregates something. It could refer to disciples gathered under his instruction, philosophical sayings/conversations, or even various vantage points (i.e., a composite of profiles). Linguistic analysis suggests to many that the final form of the book is a product of the Persian period or even the Hellenistic period, but it is well attested in the ancient world that books compiled at late dates preserve information that had been circulating for centuries.

Literary Setting

Ecclesiastes clearly fits in the broad category of "wisdom" literature. It is familiar with and interacts with the teachings of the sages. Beyond that, its closest analogies in ancient literature are the reflections on death and on its significance for how we should live that occur in various kinds of literature. This focus on death is most clearly seen in the Egyptian Harpers' Songs, and indeed there are many parallels between Ecclesiastes and the Harpers' Songs described in the study notes in this Biblical book. Other ancient texts, most notably the Gilgamesh Epic, have similar reflections on mortality. Ecclesiastes, however, is neither a Harpers' Song nor an epic poem; one could reasonably argue that it is in a class by itself. ◆

KEY CONCEPTS

- We should not expect to find "meaning" in life or to experience self-fulfillment in life apart from following God.
- The author is talking not about what should be pursued in a faith/covenant context but about what should not be pursued from a worldly perspective.
- We are to enjoy life's good times as gifts from God's hand and to accept adversity.

Everything Is Meaningless

1 The words of the Teacher,[a][a] son of David, king in Jerusalem:[b]

[2] "Meaningless! Meaningless!"
says the Teacher.
"Utterly meaningless!
Everything is meaningless."[c]

[3] What do people gain from all their labors
at which they toil under the sun?[d]
[4] Generations come and generations go,
but the earth remains forever.[e]
[5] The sun rises and the sun sets,
and hurries back to where it rises.[f]
[6] The wind blows to the south
and turns to the north;
round and round it goes,
ever returning on its course.
[7] All streams flow into the sea,
yet the sea is never full.
To the place the streams come from,
there they return again.[g]
[8] All things are wearisome,
more than one can say.
The eye never has enough of seeing,[h]
nor the ear its fill of hearing.
[9] What has been will be again,
what has been done will be done again;[i]
there is nothing new under the sun.
[10] Is there anything of which one can say,
"Look! This is something new"?
It was here already, long ago;
it was here before our time.
[11] No one remembers the former generations,
and even those yet to come
will not be remembered
by those who follow them.[j]

Wisdom Is Meaningless

[12] I, the Teacher,[k] was king over Israel in
Jerusalem. [13] I applied my mind to study
and to explore by wisdom all that is done
under the heavens. What a heavy burden
God has laid on mankind![l] [14] I have seen
all the things that are done under the sun;
all of them are meaningless, a chasing after the wind.[m]

[15] What is crooked cannot be straightened;[n]
what is lacking cannot be counted.

[16] I said to myself, "Look, I have increased in wisdom more than anyone
who has ruled over Jerusalem before me;[o]
I have experienced much of wisdom and
knowledge." [17] Then I applied myself to
the understanding of wisdom,[p] and also
of madness and folly,[q] but I learned that
this, too, is a chasing after the wind.

[18] For with much wisdom comes much sorrow;
the more knowledge, the more grief.[r]

1:1 [a] ver 12; Ecc 7:27; 12:10 [b] Pr 1:1 **1:2** [c] Ps 39:5-6; 62:9; 144:4; Ecc 12:8; Ro 8:20-21 **1:3** [d] Ecc 2:11, 22; 3:9; 5:15-16 **1:4** [e] Ps 104:5; 119:90 **1:5** [f] Ps 19:5-6 **1:7** [g] Job 36:28 **1:8** [h] Pr 27:20 **1:9** [i] Ecc 2:12; 3:15 **1:11** [j] Ecc 2:16 **1:12** [k] ver 1 **1:13** [l] Ge 3:17; Ecc 3:10 **1:14** [m] Ecc 2:11, 17 **1:15** [n] Ecc 7:13 **1:16** [o] 1Ki 3:12; 4:30; Ecc 2:9 **1:17** [p] Ecc 7:23 [q] Ecc 2:3, 12; 7:25 **1:18** [r] Ecc 2:23; 12:12

[a] *1* Or *the leader of the assembly*; also in verses 2 and 12

1:2 *Meaningless!* The Hebrew term signifies "a mere breath." The theme of futility is found in numerous literary pieces in the second millennium BC. It is expressed in Gilgamesh's affirmation that whatever mankind does is "wind." The same word used by Gilgamesh is used in other texts to describe the way the world was regulated by the gods. The theme is worked out by discussing how all of the great deeds of the heroes of old amounted to nothing.

Modern readers are inclined to read statements like this through the lens of existential pessimism, amounting to a statement meaning "life is not worth living." If the Teacher is prefiguring stoicism, however, his point is not so much on the "lack of meaning in everything that is" and more on "meaning is found elsewhere." The stoic objective is not existential despair, but the devaluing of things to which most (nonphilosophers) assign value, so that the real value of really valuable things (virtue and philosophy for stoics, fear of the Lord for Ecclesiastes) can be properly demonstrated. An adequate English word for translating this concept is elusive, but it is the opposite of ultimate self-fulfillment.

1:6 *The wind blows.* The monotony of the cycles of nature is a metaphor for the failure of human activity to accomplish anything, as each generation arises and then goes to its death. This sentiment appears in the Egyptian Harpers' Songs as well: "Water flows downstream, the north wind blows upstream [since in Egypt the Nile flows north to the Mediterranean], and likewise everybody goes to his hour."

1:8 *All things are wearisome, more than one can say.* More lit. "All things are weary; no one is able to speak." This sentiment—that there is nothing new to report and no new maxims to give—strongly echoes the "Complaints of Khakheperresonb," an Egyptian text composed in the Middle Kingdom period (c. 2055–1650 BC). In this text, the sage laments, "Would I had unknown phrases, / maxims that are strange, / Novel untried words, / Void of repetitions; / Not maxims of past speech, / Spoken by the ancestors." He further insists that "One who has spoken should not speak," in a manner reminiscent of Ecclesiastes' claim that no one is able to speak.

1:9 *there is nothing new under the sun.* For Khakheperresonb (see previous note), all that people do under the sun is a mere "imitation of the past."

1:11 *No one remembers the former generations.* This outlook rejects what seems to have been an obsession with ancient Near Eastern monarchs: the desire to create eternal monuments that would preserve their names through all generations. Of course, any educated Israelite would have known of the great stone inscriptions of Egyptian pharaohs. Perhaps the futility of this quest was already evident. There had already been examples of Egyptian monuments being buried in the sands, and not a few pharaohs had simply chiseled out the names of predecessors, as Thutmose III had done with many of Hatshepsut's inscriptions. An Egyptian text known as "Berlin Papyrus 3024" laments that those "who build in granite and who hew out chambers in pyramids" are soon forgotten, and one of the Egyptian Harpers' Songs wryly observes that even those who were once gods (i.e., the pharaohs) lie forgotten in their tombs.

ECCLESIASTES 1:12—2:11

FICTIONAL ROYAL BIOGRAPHY

Today Ecc 1:12—2:11 is widely regarded as an example of "fictional royal autobiography," i.e., of a genre in which a writer fictively assumes the identity of a long-dead king. Several examples of this genre are found in the Akkadian texts; a few of the more complete such texts are the Sargon Birth Legend, Idrimi, Kurigalzu, and the Cuthean Legend of Naram-Sin.

In the case of Ecc 2, the assumption is that the anonymous author of Ecclesiastes assumed the identity of Solomon in order to speak as though he had been fabulously rich, and thus lend authority to his words when speaking on the subject of wealth. This assumption is open to challenge, however. Known examples of fictional autobiography bear little literary resemblance to Ecc 1:12—2:11.

First, Akkadian fictional autobiography tends to be propagandistic in nature; i.e., the story serves to promote some political or cultic program. The Sargon Birth Legend was apparently composed in order to legitimate the accession to the throne of his namesake, Sargon II (who may have been a usurper). Kurigalzu is a donation text; it claims that the king made donations to shrines and concludes with a curse on whoever undoes his work. Its obvious function is to legitimate a shrine by claiming ancient, royal authority for it. The Naram-Sin text draws lessons from the king's story to make the political point that later rulers should focus on domestic issues and turn away from imperialistic adventures. A few texts give putative prophecies that attempt to legitimate either a royal policy or a shrine. The moral ruminations of Ecc 2 can hardly be described as "propagandistic" after the manner of the above Akkadian texts.

Second, fictional autobiography tends to be narrative; i.e., it tells a story and thus is truly autobiography-like (pseudodonation texts and prophecies lack narrative structure, but they should probably not be called "autobiographies"). The Sargon Birth Legend, i.e., contains a brief narrative of how Sargon's mother, a high priestess, became pregnant, bore him in secret, put him in a reed basket and set him adrift on a river. A water-drawer found him and adopted him. The Idrimi text includes an extensive history of the wars of the king. The Cuthean Legend of Naram-Sin likewise contains accounts of the battles of the king, his commands to his soldiers and the taking of omens. By contrast, Ecc 2 is not narrative ("I built houses" [Ecc 2:4] does not tell a story; it is merely an assertion that the author was rich). In short, although many scholars use the Akkadian texts to identify the genre of Ecc 1:12—2:11, there are reasons to consider this inappropriate. ◆

Sargon Birth Legend, Assyrian, seventh century BC.

ECCLESIASTES 1

HARPERS' SONGS

"Harpers' Songs," a genre of ancient Egyptian music, were performed at funerary banquets. These songs have been found in tomb inscriptions from Egypt and are generally placed beside a portrait of a man playing a harp or lute. In orthodox Egyptian religion, the harper is to sing of the bliss of the deceased, who now resides in the realm of Osiris. Several "heretic" Harpers' Songs, however, question the idea of a blissful afterlife and urge people to enjoy the life they now have, before it is too late. There are 13 known heretic Harpers' Songs, with 12 from Thebes. Along with the Gilgamesh Epic, these songs give us the closest literary parallels to Ecclesiastes. ◆

Egyptian harpists, c. 1250 BC.
National Museum of Antiquities, Leiden, CC-BY

Pleasures Are Meaningless

2 I said to myself, "Come now, I will test
you with pleasure[s] to find out what is
good." But that also proved to be meaningless. 2"Laughter,"[t] I said, "is madness.
And what does pleasure accomplish?" 3I
tried cheering myself with wine,[u] and embracing folly[v]—my mind still guiding me
with wisdom. I wanted to see what was
good for people to do under the heavens
during the few days of their lives.
4I undertook great projects: I built houses for myself[w] and planted vineyards.[x] 5I
made gardens and parks and planted
all kinds of fruit trees in them. 6I made
reservoirs to water groves of flourishing
trees. 7I bought male and female slaves
and had other slaves who were born in
my house. I also owned more herds and
flocks than anyone in Jerusalem before
me. 8I amassed silver and gold[y] for myself,
and the treasure of kings and provinces. I
acquired male and female singers,[z] and a
harem[a] as well—the delights of a man's
heart. 9I became greater by far than anyone in Jerusalem before me.[a] In all this my
wisdom stayed with me.

10I denied myself nothing my eyes desired;
I refused my heart no pleasure.
My heart took delight in all my labor,
and this was the reward for all my
toil.

2:1 [s] Ecc 7:4; 8:15; Lk 12:19 **2:2** [t] Pr 14:13; Ecc 7:6 **2:3** [u] ver 24-25; Ecc 3:12-13 [v] Ecc 1:17 **2:4** [w] 1Ki 7:1-12 [x] SS 8:11 **2:8** [y] 1Ki 9:28; 10:10, 14, 21 [z] 2Sa 19:35 **2:9** [a] 1Ch 29:25; Ecc 1:16

[a] 8 The meaning of the Hebrew for this phrase is uncertain.

2:8 *harem.* The Hebrew term here is usually taken as a designation for concubines. However, although that would not be an unusual claim for a king to make, the word is obscure and occurs only here, so its meaning is uncertain (see NIV text note). An alternative suggestion is that the Hebrew word should be translated "treasure chests."

11 Yet when I surveyed all that my hands
had done
and what I had toiled to achieve,
everything was meaningless, a chasing
after the wind;[b]
nothing was gained under the sun.[c]

Wisdom and Folly Are Meaningless

12 Then I turned my thoughts to consider
wisdom,
and also madness and folly.[d]
What more can the king's successor do
than what has already been done?[e]
13 I saw that wisdom[f] is better than folly,[g]
just as light is better than darkness.
14 The wise have eyes in their heads,
while the fool walks in the darkness;
but I came to realize
that the same fate overtakes them
both.[h]

15 Then I said to myself,

"The fate of the fool will overtake me
also.
What then do I gain by being wise?"[i]
I said to myself,
"This too is meaningless."
16 For the wise, like the fool, will not be
long remembered;
the days have already come when
both have been forgotten.[j]
Like the fool, the wise too must die!

Toil Is Meaningless

17 So I hated life, because the work that
is done under the sun was grievous to me.
All of it is meaningless, a chasing after
the wind.[k] 18 I hated all the things I had
toiled for under the sun, because I must
leave them to the one who comes after
me.[l] 19 And who knows whether that person will be wise or foolish? Yet they will
have control over all the fruit of my toil
into which I have poured my effort and
skill under the sun. This too is meaningless. 20 So my heart began to despair over
all my toilsome labor under the sun. 21 For
a person may labor with wisdom, knowledge and skill, and then they must leave all
they own to another who has not toiled for
it. This too is meaningless and a great misfortune. 22 What do people get for all the
toil and anxious striving with which they
labor under the sun?[m] 23 All their days their
work is grief and pain;[n] even at night their
minds do not rest. This too is meaningless.
24 A person can do nothing better than
to eat and drink[o] and find satisfaction in
their own toil.[p] This too, I see, is from
the hand of God,[q] 25 for without him, who
can eat or find enjoyment? 26 To the person who pleases him, God gives wisdom,
knowledge and happiness, but to the sinner he gives the task of gathering and storing up wealth[r] to hand it over to the one
who pleases God.[s] This too is meaningless, a chasing after the wind.

A Time for Everything

3 There is a time[t] for everything,
and a season for every activity under
the heavens:

2 a time to be born and a time to die,
a time to plant and a time to uproot,
3 a time to kill and a time to heal,
a time to tear down and a time to
build,
4 a time to weep and a time to laugh,
a time to mourn and a time to
dance,
5 a time to scatter stones and a time to
gather them,
a time to embrace and a time to
refrain from embracing,
6 a time to search and a time to give
up,
a time to keep and a time to throw
away,
7 a time to tear and a time to mend,
a time to be silent[u] and a time to
speak,
8 a time to love and a time to hate,
a time for war and a time for peace.

9 What do workers gain from their toil?[v]
10 I have seen the burden God has laid on
the human race.[w] 11 He has made everything beautiful in its time.[x] He has also

2:11 [b] Ecc 1:14 [c] Ecc 1:3 **2:12** [d] Ecc 1:17 [e] Ecc 1:9; 7:25 **2:13** [f] Ecc 7:19; 9:18 [g] Ecc 7:11-12 **2:14** [h] Ps 49:10; Pr 17:24; Ecc 3:19; 6:6; 7:2; 9:3, 11-12 **2:15** [i] Ecc 6:8 **2:16** [j] Ecc 1:11; 9:5 **2:17** [k] Ecc 4:2 **2:18** [l] Ps 39:6; 49:10 **2:22** [m] Ecc 1:3; 3:9 **2:23** [n] Job 5:7; 14:1; Ecc 1:18 **2:24** [o] Ecc 8:15; 1Co 15:32 [p] Ecc 3:22 [q] Ecc 3:12-13; 5:17-19; 9:7-10 **2:26** [r] Job 27:17 [s] Pr 13:22 **3:1** [t] ver 11, 17; Ecc 8:6 **3:7** [u] Am 5:13 **3:9** [v] Ecc 1:3 **3:10** [w] Ecc 1:13 **3:11** [x] ver 1

2:18 *I hated all the things I had toiled for under the sun.* Ecclesiastes laments that the wealth people acquire in their lifetimes of hard labor is simply passed on to others, who may be incompetent or unworthy of the bequest (vv. 18 – 26). This idea also has parallels in the Egyptian Harpers' Songs: "Their property has been given to others. They are gone." A common claim about ancient Near Eastern culture is that they believed that one in some sense lived on via the lives of their children, such that to die childless was considered a great calamity. There is some truth in this, as indicated by the Israelite concern to keep real property within a single family line, but one should not assume that ancient peoples were unable to reflect critically on such notions.

3:1 *a time for everything.* In further reflections on human mortality, Ecclesiastes asserts that because we are creatures of time and occasion, we must live in harmony with the ebb and flow of life (vv. 1 – 8). Any attempt to find a philosophy of time or of history in these verses should be abandoned; this text is about coming to terms with the realities of life, not about cyclical versus linear time or such notions.

3:5 *scatter stones … gather them.* Stones were cleared away from a field so that it could be used for agricultural purposes. The gathered stones were sometimes set up as boundaries between fields. The scattering of such stones would suggest land claims being dissolved or altered.

Egyptian dancers, tomb of Antefoker, Thebes, c. 1950 BC. "A time to mourn and a time to dance" (Ecc 3:4).
Wikimedia Commons

set eternity in the human heart; yet[a] no
one can fathom[y] what God has done from
beginning to end.[z] 12 I know that there is
nothing better for people than to be happy and to do good while they live. 13 That
each of them may eat and drink,[a] and
find satisfaction[b] in all their toil — this
is the gift of God.[c] 14 I know that everything God does will endure forever; nothing can be added to it and nothing taken
from it. God does it so that people will
fear him.[d]

15 Whatever is has already been,[e]
and what will be has been before;[f]
and God will call the past to
account.[b]

16 And I saw something else under the
sun:

In the place of judgment — wickedness
was there,
in the place of justice — wickedness
was there.

17 I said to myself,

"God will bring into judgment[g]
both the righteous and the wicked,
for there will be a time for every
activity,
a time to judge every deed."[h]

18 I also said to myself, "As for humans,
God tests them so that they may see that
they are like the animals.[i] 19 Surely the fate
of human beings[j] is like that of the animals; the same fate awaits them both: As
one dies, so dies the other. All have the
same breath[c]; humans have no advantage
over animals. Everything is meaningless.
20 All go to the same place; all come from
dust, and to dust all return.[k] 21 Who knows
if the human spirit rises upward[l] and if
the spirit of the animal goes down into the
earth?"

22 So I saw that there is nothing better
for a person than to enjoy their work,[m] because that is their lot.[n] For who can bring
them to see what will happen after them?

Oppression, Toil, Friendlessness

4 Again I looked and saw all the oppression[o] that was taking place under the
sun:

3:11 [y] Job 11:7; Ecc 8:17 [z] Job 28:23; Ro 11:33 **3:13** [a] Ecc 2:3 [b] Ps 34:12 [c] Dt 12:7, 18; Ecc 2:24; 5:19 **3:14** [d] Job 23:15; Ecc 5:7; 7:18; 8:12-13; Jas 1:17 **3:15** [e] Ecc 6:10 [f] Ecc 1:9 **3:17** [g] Job 19:29; Ecc 11:9; Mt 16:27; Ro 2:6-8; 2Th 1:6-7 [h] ver 1 **3:18** [i] Ps 73:22 **3:19** [j] Ecc 2:14 **3:20** [k] Ge 2:7; 3:19; Job 34:15 **3:21** [l] Ecc 12:7 **3:22** [m] Ecc 2:24; 5:18 [n] Job 31:2 **4:1** [o] Ps 12:5; Ecc 3:16

[a] 11 Or *also placed ignorance in the human heart, so that* [b] 15 Or *God calls back the past* [c] 19 Or *spirit*

3:19 *the fate of human beings is like that of the animals.* Some scholars are struck by the use of the term "fate" (Hebrew *miqreh*) here and suggest that it is comparable to the Greek terms *moira* ("fate") and *tyche* ("luck"). This, in turn, implies that Ecclesiastes was influenced by Hellenistic thinking. However, *miqreh* shows no influence from Hellenistic culture. The Greek Moirai ("Fates") are goddesses (whereas *miqreh* is not), and *miqreh* is used in Ecclesiastes not for luck or even for predestined fate, but simply for one's final destiny, i.e., death (v. 19; 2:14,15; 9:2,3). The rejection of immortality in these verses has echoes in the Harpers' Songs of Egypt. We should add that Ecclesiastes here challenges the kind of afterlife envisioned in something like official Egyptian theology, which in effect denied the significance of death. Ideas that eventually became a part of Christian theology of afterlife were not yet developed in this time.

I saw the tears of the oppressed—
and they have no comforter;
power was on the side of their
oppressors—
and they have no comforter.[p]
2 And I declared that the dead,[q]
who had already died,
are happier than the living,
who are still alive.[r]
3 But better than both
is the one who has never been born,[s]
who has not seen the evil
that is done under the sun.[t]

4 And I saw that all toil and all achievement spring from one person's envy of another. This too is meaningless, a chasing
after the wind.[u]

5 Fools fold their hands[v]
and ruin themselves.
6 Better one handful with tranquillity
than two handfuls with toil[w]
and chasing after the wind.

7 Again I saw something meaningless
under the sun:

8 There was a man all alone;
he had neither son nor brother.
There was no end to his toil,
yet his eyes were not content[x] with
his wealth.
"For whom am I toiling," he asked,
"and why am I depriving myself of
enjoyment?"
This too is meaningless—
a miserable business!

9 Two are better than one,
because they have a good return for
their labor:
10 If either of them falls down,
one can help the other up.
But pity anyone who falls
and has no one to help them up.

4:1 [p] La 1:16
4:2 [q] Jer 20:17-18; 22:10
[r] Job 3:17; 10:18
4:3 [s] Job 3:16; Ecc 6:3
[t] Job 3:22
4:4 [u] Ecc 1:14
4:5 [v] Pr 6:10
4:6 [w] Pr 15:16-17; 16:8
4:8 [x] Pr 27:20

11 Also, if two lie down together, they will
keep warm.
But how can one keep warm alone?
12 Though one may be overpowered,
two can defend themselves.
A cord of three strands is not quickly
broken.

Advancement Is Meaningless

13 Better a poor but wise youth than an
old but foolish king who no longer knows
how to heed a warning. 14 The youth may
have come from prison to the kingship, or
he may have been born in poverty within his kingdom. 15 I saw that all who lived
and walked under the sun followed the
youth, the king's successor. 16 There was
no end to all the people who were before
them. But those who came later were not
pleased with the successor. This too is
meaningless, a chasing after the wind.

Fulfill Your Vow to God

5 [a] Guard your steps when you go to the
house of God. Go near to listen rather than to offer the sacrifice of fools, who
do not know that they do wrong.

2 Do not be quick with your mouth,
do not be hasty in your heart
to utter anything before God.[y]
God is in heaven
and you are on earth,
so let your words be few.[z]
3 A dream[a] comes when there are many
cares,
and many words mark the speech of
a fool.[b]

4 When you make a vow to God, do not
delay to fulfill it.[c] He has no pleasure in
fools; fulfill your vow.[d] 5 It is better not to

[a] In Hebrew texts 5:1 is numbered 4:17, and 5:2-20 is numbered 5:1-19.

5:2 [y] Jdg 11:35
[z] Job 6:24; Pr 10:19; 20:25
5:3 [a] Job 20:8
[b] Ecc 10:14
5:4 [c] Dt 23:21; Jdg 11:35; Ps 119:60
[d] Nu 30:2; Ps 66:13-14; 76:11

4:12 *A cord of three strands.* This has a remarkable parallel in the Gilgamesh Epic, in which Gilgamesh encourages his friend Enkidu about the value of friendship: "Two men will not die; the towed boat will not sink, / a towrope of three strands cannot be cut." Both texts speak of the security that two can offer one another and then use the analogy of a three-stranded rope.
5:1 *Guard your steps when you go to the house of God.* The Egyptian "Instruction of Ptahhotep" similarly warns against speaking rashly, and a Ugaritic inscription speaks of a fool who thoughtlessly offers prayers to his god without an appropriate sense of guilt.
5:2 *God is in heaven and you are on earth.* Scholars have noticed that this is somewhat similar to a passage in the Gilgamesh Epic, in which Enkidu tries to dissuade Gilgamesh from entering the perilous Cedar Forest, and Gilgamesh replies, "Who, my friend, can scale he[aven]? / Only the gods [live] forever under the sun. / As for mankind, numbered are their days; / Whatever they achieve is but wind!" His point is that since we are mortal, we might as well grab what glory we can get. Gilgamesh's words express the pagan ideal: mortals are doomed to suffering and death, but they can give value to their lives through heroism. Ecclesiastes begins with the same premise, but moves in a different direction: Mortals are weak and perishing, and this should drive them to understand the real meaning of the fear of God.
5:3 Dreams in the ancient world were thought to offer information from the divine realm, and were therefore taken seriously. Some dreams, those given to prophets and kings, were considered a means of divine revelation. Most dreams, however, ordinary dreams of common people, were believed to contain omens that communicated information about what the gods were doing. The information that came through dreams was not believed to be irreversible, but could be a cause for concern, if not alarm. This verse would therefore best be read, "As a dream is accompanied by many worries, so a fool's speech comes with many words."
5:4 *vow to God.* Information concerning vows can be found in most of the cultures of the ancient Near East,

make a vow than to make one and not
fulfill it.[e] 6 Do not let your mouth lead you
into sin. And do not protest to the temple
messenger, "My vow was a mistake." Why
should God be angry at what you say and
destroy the work of your hands? 7 Much
dreaming and many words are meaningless. Therefore fear God.[f]

Riches Are Meaningless

8 If you see the poor oppressed[g] in a district, and justice and rights denied, do not
be surprised at such things; for one official
is eyed by a higher one, and over them
both are others higher still. 9 The increase
from the land is taken by all; the king himself profits from the fields.

10 Whoever loves money never has
enough;
whoever loves wealth is never
satisfied with their income.
This too is meaningless.

11 As goods increase,
so do those who consume them.
And what benefit are they to the owners
except to feast their eyes on them?

12 The sleep of a laborer is sweet,
whether they eat little or much,
but as for the rich, their abundance
permits them no sleep.[h]

13 I have seen a grievous evil under the
sun:[i]

wealth hoarded to the harm of its
owners,
14 or wealth lost through some
misfortune,
so that when they have children
there is nothing left for them to
inherit.

5:5 [e] Nu 30:2-4; Pr 20:25; Jnh 2:9; Ac 5:4 **5:7** [f] Ecc 3:14; 12:13 **5:8** [g] Ps 12:5; Ecc 4:1 **5:12** [h] Job 20:20 **5:13** [i] Ecc 6:1-2

5:15 [j] Job 1:21 [k] Ps 49:17; 1Ti 6:7 [l] Ecc 1:3 **5:16** [m] Pr 11:29; Ecc 1:3 **5:18** [n] Ecc 2:3 [o] Ecc 2:10, 24 **5:19** [p] 1Ch 29:12; 2Ch 1:12 [q] Ecc 6:2 [r] Job 31:2 [s] Ecc 2:24; 3:13 **5:20** [t] Dt 12:7, 18 **6:2** [u] Ps 17:14; Ecc 5:19 [v] Ecc 5:13 **6:3** [w] Job 3:16; Ecc 4:3 [x] Job 3:3

15 Everyone comes naked from their
mother's womb,
and as everyone comes, so they
depart.[j]
They take nothing from their toil[k]
that they can carry in their hands.[l]

16 This too is a grievous evil:

As everyone comes, so they depart,
and what do they gain,
since they toil for the wind?[m]
17 All their days they eat in darkness,
with great frustration, affliction and
anger.

18 This is what I have observed to be
good: that it is appropriate for a person
to eat, to drink[n] and to find satisfaction in
their toilsome labor[o] under the sun during
the few days of life God has given them—
for this is their lot. 19 Moreover, when God
gives someone wealth and possessions,[p]
and the ability to enjoy them,[q] to accept
their lot[r] and be happy in their toil—this
is a gift of God.[s] 20 They seldom reflect on
the days of their life, because God keeps
them occupied with gladness of heart.[t]

6 I have seen another evil under the
sun, and it weighs heavily on mankind: 2 God gives some people wealth,
possessions and honor, so that they lack
nothing their hearts desire, but God does
not grant them the ability to enjoy them,[u]
and strangers enjoy them instead. This is
meaningless, a grievous evil.[v]
3 A man may have a hundred children
and live many years; yet no matter how
long he lives, if he cannot enjoy his prosperity and does not receive proper burial, I
say that a stillborn[w] child is better off than
he.[x] 4 It comes without meaning, it departs
in darkness, and in darkness its name is

---

including Hittite, Ugaritic, Mesopotamian and, less often, Egyptian. Vows are voluntary agreements made with deity. The vows would typically be conditional and accompany a petition made to a deity. They were commitments to God in which the worshiper promised to undertake a certain action (generally of a ritual nature) if God answered their request. The swearing of an oath was considered a very serious matter in ancient Israel as well as throughout the ancient world. An oath is always sworn in the name of a god, which places a heavy responsibility on the swearer to carry out its stipulations, since he would be liable to divine, as well as human, retribution if he did not. Oaths were used in legal proceedings (see note on Ex 22:11) and for political treaties and covenants (see note on Dt 6:13).

5:6 *temple messenger.* There is no other Biblical reference to this office, but presumably it refers to a temple official whose job was to make sure that worshipers had fulfilled their vows.

5:13–17 The ideas presented here are similar to those in a late second-millennium BC text from Emar, a site on the Euphrates River in Syria. In the text, a father advises his son to be frugal and prudent, so as to acquire wealth. The son responds that humans, like the beasts, must die, and he wonders what value his father's possessions will be to him when he dies. He says, "Father, you have built a house. You made [its entrance] high, with a storeroom ten cubits large." The son's point is that hoarding does not make for a happy life as death approaches.

5:17 *eat in darkness.* If one works in the fields from sunrise to sundown, then both breakfast and supper are eaten in the dark.

6:3 *does not receive proper burial.* Many ancient peoples believed that the spirit of a person who did not receive proper burial wandered restlessly. An old Sumerian poem of Gilgamesh says, "'Did you see the one whose shade has no one to make funerary offerings?' 'I saw him. / He eats scrapings from the pot and crusts of bread thrown away in the street.'" Such notions do not seem to be present here in Ecclesiastes, however. Instead, the main concern is the simple lack of dignity and propriety in not receiving a funeral or not having children who care enough to bury you.

ECCLESIASTES 5–6

HELLENISTIC PHILOSOPHY AND ECCLESIASTES

A number of scholars attempt to demonstrate that Ecclesiastes has been influenced by Greek literature. The focus on God's will in Ecclesiastes, e.g., is said to reflect an awareness of teachings on determinism from the Stoic philosopher Cleanthes. These comparisons to Greek texts, however, are always abstract in nature, because there are no convincing literary parallels to Ecclesiastes; i.e., one can only argue that Ecclesiastes has some ideas that are similar to those of certain Hellenistic thinkers, but this hardly makes the case that the author of Ecclesiastes knew the Stoic texts. One Greek work that does wrestle with human mortality and suffering is Hesiod's *Works and Days*, but this book is so unlike Ecclesiastes that an attempt to link the two is far-fetched. There is no compelling reason to believe that Ecclesiastes is influenced by Greek literature. ◆

shrouded. 5Though it never saw the sun or
knew anything, it has more rest than does
that man— 6even if he lives a thousand
years twice over but fails to enjoy his prosperity. Do not all go to the same place?

7Everyone's toil is for their mouth,
 yet their appetite is never satisfied.[y]
8What advantage have the wise over
 fools?[z]
What do the poor gain
 by knowing how to conduct
 themselves before others?
9Better what the eye sees
 than the roving of the appetite.
This too is meaningless,
 a chasing after the wind.[a]

10Whatever exists has already been
 named,
 and what humanity is has been
 known;
no one can contend
 with someone who is stronger.
11The more the words,
 the less the meaning,
 and how does that profit anyone?

12For who knows what is good for a person in life, during the few and meaningless days[b] they pass through like a shadow?[c] Who can tell them what will happen
under the sun after they are gone?

Wisdom

7 A good name is better than fine
 perfume,[d]
 and the day of death better than the
 day of birth.
2It is better to go to a house of
 mourning
 than to go to a house of feasting,
for death[e] is the destiny[f] of everyone;
 the living should take this to heart.
3Frustration is better than laughter,[g]
 because a sad face is good for the
 heart.
4The heart of the wise is in the house of
 mourning,
 but the heart of fools is in the house
 of pleasure.[h]
5It is better to heed the rebuke[i] of a
 wise person
 than to listen to the song of fools.
6Like the crackling of thorns[j] under the
 pot,
 so is the laughter[k] of fools.
 This too is meaningless.

6:7 [y]Pr 16:26; 27:20 **6:8** [z]Ecc 2:15 **6:9** [a]Ecc 1:14 **6:12** [b]Job 10:20 [c]Job 14:2; Ps 39:6; Jas 4:14 **7:1** [d]Pr 22:1; SS 1:3 **7:2** [e]Pr 11:19 [f]Ps 90:12 **7:3** [g]Pr 14:13 **7:4** [h]Ecc 2:1; Jer 16:8 **7:5** [i]Ps 141:5; Pr 13:18; 15:31-32 **7:6** [j]Ps 58:9; 118:12 [k]Ecc 2:2

6:6 *all go to the same place.* See the articles "Death and Sheol," p. 833; "Death and the Underworld," p. 907.
7:1 *fine perfume.* Banqueters in the ancient world were often treated by a generous host to fine oils that would be used to anoint their foreheads. An Assyrian text from Esarhaddon's reign describes how he "drenched the foreheads" of his guests at a royal banquet with "choicest oils."
7:6 *crackling of thorns under the pot.* The thin wood of thornbushes produces a lot of noise that draws attention as it bursts quickly into flame. However, it makes very poor firewood, since it has no lasting heat or sustained cooking ability.

[7]Extortion turns a wise person into
a fool,
and a bribe[l] corrupts the heart.

[8]The end of a matter is better than
its beginning,
and patience[m] is better than
pride.

[9]Do not be quickly provoked[n] in your
spirit,
for anger resides in the lap of
fools.

[10]Do not say, "Why were the old days
better than these?"
For it is not wise to ask such
questions.

[11]Wisdom, like an inheritance, is a good
thing[o]
and benefits those who see the
sun.[p]
[12]Wisdom is a shelter
as money is a shelter,
but the advantage of knowledge is
this:
Wisdom preserves those who
have it.

[13]Consider what God has done:[q]

Who can straighten
what he has made crooked?[r]
[14]When times are good, be happy;
but when times are bad, consider
this:
God has made the one
as well as the other.
Therefore, no one can discover
anything about their future.

[15]In this meaningless life[s] of mine I have
seen both of these:

the righteous perishing in their
righteousness,
and the wicked living long in their
wickedness.[t]

[16]Do not be overrighteous,
neither be overwise—
why destroy yourself?
[17]Do not be overwicked,
and do not be a fool—
why die before your time?[u]
[18]It is good to grasp the one
and not let go of the other.
Whoever fears God[v] will avoid all
extremes.[a]

[19]Wisdom[w] makes one wise person more
powerful[x]
than ten rulers in a city.
[20]Indeed, there is no one on earth who is
righteous,[y]
no one who does what is right and
never sins.[z]

[21]Do not pay attention to every word
people say,
or you[a] may hear your servant
cursing you—
[22]for you know in your heart
that many times you yourself have
cursed others.

[23]All this I tested by wisdom and I said,

"I am determined to be wise"[b]—
but this was beyond me.
[24]Whatever exists is far off and most
profound—
who can discover it?[c]
[25]So I turned my mind to understand,
to investigate and to search out
wisdom and the scheme of
things[d]
and to understand the stupidity
of wickedness
and the madness of folly.[e]

[26]I find more bitter than death
the woman who is a
snare,[f]

7:7 [l] Ex 18:21; 23:8; Dt 16:19 **7:8** [m] Pr 14:29; Gal 5:22; Eph 4:2 **7:9** [n] Mt 5:22; Pr 14:17; Jas 1:19 **7:11** [o] Pr 8:10-11; Ecc 2:13 [p] Ecc 11:7 **7:13** [q] Ecc 2:24 [r] Ecc 1:15 **7:15** [s] Job 7:7 [t] Ecc 8:12-14; Jer 12:1 **7:17** [u] Job 15:32; Ps 55:23 **7:18** [v] Ecc 3:14 **7:19** [w] Ecc 2:13 [x] Ecc 9:13-18 **7:20** [y] Ps 14:3 [z] 1Ki 8:46; 2Ch 6:36; Pr 20:9; Ro 3:23 **7:21** [a] Pr 30:10 **7:23** [b] Ecc 1:17; Ro 1:22 **7:24** [c] Job 28:12 **7:25** [d] Job 28:3 [e] Ecc 1:17 **7:26** [f] Ex 10:7; Jdg 14:15

[a] 18 Or *will follow them both*

7:13 *straighten what he has made crooked.* In the ancient Near East, the pious were constantly baffled about what the gods were doing and why they were doing it. In a Sumerian "Hymn to Enlil," the poet says, "Your immensely clever deeds are dismaying, their meaning is a twisted thread that cannot be separated."

7:14 *When times are good, be happy.* It may strike us as odd that acute awareness of the brevity and severity of life should prompt us to enjoy ourselves when the opportunity presents itself, but this is a major feature of the Egyptian Harpers' Songs as well. *When times are good.* Lit. "On a good day." The expression "a good day" is used in the Harpers' Songs to describe a time when things are going well and one ought to have some fun. At the same time, Ecclesiastes is not simply repeating the maxims of Egyptian wisdom. The focus on enjoying life in the context of patient submission to the circumstances in which God puts us ("God has made the one as well as the other") is distinctive to Ecclesiastes.

7:16 *Do not be overrighteous, neither be overwise.* This attitude is in contrast with much of the advice of the classic wisdom teaching of the ancient world, which taught precisely that prudence and piety does protect us from harm. In the service of most of the gods, rituals satisfied the needs of the gods, and that was all that mattered. The gods could not be overfed, and there was no such thing as too much care of them. The Egyptian "Instruction of Any," e.g., says, "Observe the feast of your god, / And repeat its season, / your god is angry if it is neglected." It would be a mistake, however, to take Ecclesiastes simply as a cynical piece of antiwisdom. The exhortations here stem from a conviction that all persons are sinful (vv. 22,29) and that all attempts to impress God with personal piety fail. Also, Ecclesiastes drives the reader to a more profound understanding of the fear of God than that reflected in the external piety of the Egyptian admonition.

whose heart is a trap
and whose hands are chains.
The man who pleases God will escape her,
but the sinner she will ensnare.[g]

27 "Look," says the Teacher,[a h] "this is what I have discovered:

"Adding one thing to another to discover the scheme of things—
28 while I was still searching
but not finding—
I found one upright man among a thousand,
but not one upright woman[i] among them all.
29 This only have I found:
God created mankind upright,
but they have gone in search of many schemes."

8

Who is like the wise?
Who knows the explanation of things?
A person's wisdom brightens their face
and changes its hard appearance.

Obey the King

2 Obey the king's command, I say, because you took an oath before God. 3 Do
not be in a hurry to leave the king's presence.[j] Do not stand up for a bad cause, for
he will do whatever he pleases. 4 Since a
king's word is supreme, who can say to
him, "What are you doing?[k]"

5 Whoever obeys his command will come to no harm,
and the wise heart will know the proper time and procedure.
6 For there is a proper time and procedure for every matter,[l]
though a person may be weighed down by misery.
7 Since no one knows the future,
who can tell someone else what is to come?
8 As no one has power over the wind to contain it,
so[b] no one has power over the time of their death.
As no one is discharged in time of war,
so wickedness will not release those who practice it.

9 All this I saw, as I applied my mind to
everything done under the sun. There is
a time when a man lords it over others to
his own[c] hurt. 10 Then too, I saw the wicked buried[m]—those who used to come and
go from the holy place and receive praise[d]
in the city where they did this. This too is
meaningless.

11 When the sentence for a crime is not
quickly carried out, people's hearts are
filled with schemes to do wrong. 12 Although a wicked person who commits
a hundred crimes may live a long time,
I know that it will go better[n] with those
who fear God,[o] who are reverent before
him.[p] 13 Yet because the wicked do not fear
God,[q] it will not go well with them, and
their days[r] will not lengthen like a shadow.

14 There is something else meaningless
that occurs on earth: the righteous who
get what the wicked deserve, and the
wicked who get what the righteous deserve.[s] This too, I say, is meaningless.[t]
15 So I commend the enjoyment of life[u], because there is nothing better for a person
under the sun than to eat and drink[v] and
be glad.[w] Then joy will accompany them
in their toil all the days of the life God has
given them under the sun.

16 When I applied my mind to know
wisdom[x] and to observe the labor that is
done on earth[y]—people getting no sleep
day or night— 17 then I saw all that God
has done.[z] No one can comprehend what
goes on under the sun. Despite all their
efforts to search it out, no one can discover its meaning. Even if the wise claim
they know, they cannot really comprehend it.[a]

7:26 [g] Pr 2:16-19; 5:3-5; 7:23; 22:14 **7:27** [h] Ecc 1:1 **7:28** [i] 1Ki 11:3 **8:3** [j] Ecc 10:4 **8:4** [k] Job 9:12; Est 1:19; Da 4:35 **8:6** [l] Ecc 3:1 **8:10** [m] Ecc 1:11 **8:12** [n] Dt 12:28; Ps 37:11, 18-19; Pr 1:32-33; Isa 3:10-11 [o] Ex 1:20 [p] Ecc 3:14 **8:13** [q] Ecc 3:14; Isa 3:11 [r] Dt 4:40; Job 5:26; Ps 34:12; Isa 65:20 **8:14** [s] Job 21:7; Ps 73:14; Mal 3:15 [t] Ecc 7:15 **8:15** [u] Ps 42:8 [v] Ex 32:6; Ecc 2:3 [w] Ecc 2:24; 3:12-13; 5:18; 9:7 **8:16** [x] Ecc 1:17 [y] Ecc 1:13 **8:17** [z] Job 28:3 [a] Job 5:9; 28:23; Ecc 3:11; Ro 11:33

[a] 27 Or *the leader of the assembly* [b] 8 Or *over the human spirit to retain it, / and so* [c] 9 Or *to their* [d] 10 Some Hebrew manuscripts and Septuagint (Aquila); most Hebrew manuscripts *and are forgotten*

8:2–3 Advice concerning how to conduct oneself as a courtier is expected in wisdom literature, since its primary function was training future palace functionaries. Ecc 8 exhorts the reader to be properly submissive to authorities. Similar exhortations to obedience and proper decorum before rulers can be found in other ancient literature. The "Instruction of Ptahhotep," e.g., teaches: "If you are in the audience chamber, / Stand and sit in accordance with your position, / Which was given to you on the first day. / Do not exceed (your duty), for it will result in your being turned back." Ecclesiastes by no means supposes that government always works properly (vv. 11,14), but even so, it exhorts people to behave respectfully toward authority, since it is both safe before the king (v. 3) and right before God (the "oath" of v. 2).

8:11 *sentence for a crime.* Israel shared a common legal tradition with the rest of the ancient Near East concerning criminal punishment. The most common penalties in the Bible were stoning, death by fire, and mutilation. Ancient Near Eastern sources (e.g., the Code of Hammurapi and the Middle Assyrian Laws) occasionally mention the methods of punishment, which included drowning, mutilation and impalement. Imprisonment was not used as a punishment for crime, though there were debtors' prisons and political prisoners. Additionally, prisons would be used to detain those awaiting trial.

A Common Destiny for All

9 So I reflected on all this and concluded that the righteous and the wise and
what they do are in God's hands, but no
one knows whether love or hate awaits
them.[b] 2All share a common destiny — the
righteous and the wicked, the good and
the bad,[a] the clean and the unclean, those
who offer sacrifices and those who do not.

As it is with the good,
so with the sinful;
as it is with those who take oaths,
so with those who are afraid to take
them.[c]

3This is the evil in everything that happens under the sun: The same destiny
overtakes all.[d] The hearts of people, moreover, are full of evil and there is madness
in their hearts while they live,[e] and afterward they join the dead.[f] 4Anyone who is
among the living has hope[b] — even a live
dog is better off than a dead lion!

5For the living know that they will
die,
but the dead know nothing;[g]
they have no further reward,
and even their name[h] is forgotten.[i]
6Their love, their hate
and their jealousy have long since
vanished;
never again will they have a part
in anything that happens under
the sun.[j]

7Go, eat your food with gladness, and
drink your wine[k] with a joyful heart,[l] for
God has already approved what you do.
8Always be clothed in white,[m] and always
anoint your head with oil. 9Enjoy life with
your wife,[n] whom you love, all the days
of this meaningless life that God has giv-
en you under the sun — all your meaningless days. For this is your lot[o] in life
and in your toilsome labor under the sun.
10Whatever[p] your hand finds to do, do it
with all your might,[q] for in the realm of
the dead,[r] where you are going, there is
neither working nor planning nor knowledge nor wisdom.[s]

11I have seen something else under the
sun:

The race is not to the swift
or the battle to the strong,[t]
nor does food come to the wise[u]
or wealth to the brilliant
or favor to the learned;
but time and chance[v] happen to them
all.[w]

12Moreover, no one knows when their
hour will come:

As fish are caught in a cruel net,
or birds are taken in a snare,
so people are trapped by evil times[x]
that fall unexpectedly upon them.[y]

9:1 [b] Dt 33:3; Job 12:10; Ecc 10:14 **9:2** [c] Job 9:22; Ecc 2:14; 6:6; 7:2 **9:3** [d] Job 9:22; Ecc 2:14 [e] Jer 11:8; 13:10; 16:12; 17:9 [f] Job 21:26 **9:5** [g] Job 14:21 [h] Ps 9:6 [i] Ecc 1:11; 2:16; Isa 26:14 **9:6** [j] Job 21:21 **9:7** [k] Nu 6:20 [l] Ecc 2:24; 8:15 **9:8** [m] Ps 23:5; Rev 3:4 **9:9** [n] Pr 5:18 [o] Job 31:2 **9:10** [p] 1Sa 10:7 [q] Ecc 11:6; Ro 12:11; Col 3:23 [r] Nu 16:33 [s] Ecc 2:24 **9:11** [t] Am 2:14-15 [u] Job 32:13; Isa 47:10; Jer 9:23 [v] Ecc 2:14 [w] Dt 8:18 **9:12** [x] Pr 29:6 [y] Ps 73:22; Ecc 2:14; 8:7

[a] 2 Septuagint (Aquila), Vulgate and Syriac; Hebrew does not have *and the bad.* [b] 4 Or *What then is to be chosen? With all who live, there is hope*

9:5 *reward.* The Hebrew term probably refers to the benefits of life, in which the dead cannot partake. The dead cannot enjoy any of the things that are considered blessings in this life. Beyond that, this also indicates the Israelite belief that there was no heavenly reward for a life of faith or good works. They believed that God's justice was carried out in this life rather than accounts being settled in the afterlife. See the articles "Death and Sheol," p. 833; "Death and the Underworld," p. 907.

9:7 – 9 These verses include some of the most remarkable parallels between a Scriptural text and other ancient Near Eastern texts found anywhere in the Bible. The "Song from the Tomb of King Intef," from the Egyptian Harpers' Songs, confronts human mortality and offers the following advice: "Put myrrh on your head, / Dress in fine linen, / Anoint yourself with oils fit for a god!" Another of the Harpers' Songs, "Neferhotep I," has similar advice: "Take fine perfumes pleasing to your nostrils, with garlands, lotuses, and berries at your breast, with your sister, who is in your heart, happy at your side" ("sister" here refers to one's wife). Another strikingly similar text is in the Old Babylonian Gilgamesh Epic, where the hero laments over mortality to an ale-wife, and she gives him this advice: "When the gods created mankind, / For mankind they established death, / Life they kept for themselves. / You, Gilgamesh, let your belly be full, / Keep enjoying yourself, day and night! / Every day make merry, / Dance and play day and night! / Let your clothes be clean! / Let your head be washed, may you be bathed in water! / Gaze on the little one who holds your hand! / Let a wife enjoy your repeated embrace!" Our three different sources — Babylonian, Egyptian and Israelite — have essentially the same message: "In light of the brevity of life, enjoy yourself!" This, of itself, may not be too remarkable, but the specific nature and sequence of the advice (feasting, wearing clean clothes, anointing with oils and perfumes, and enjoying one's wife) suggests a common wisdom tradition.

9:8 *clothed in white.* Scholars have understood the color white to symbolize purity, festivity or elevated social status. In both Egypt (*Story of Sinuhe*) and Mesopotamia (Gilgamesh Epic), clean or bright garments conveyed a sense of well-being. In addition, the hot Middle Eastern climate favors the wearing of white clothes to reflect the heat.

9:11 *chance.* In ancient Near Eastern belief, fate was written on tablets, and those who controlled them controlled the destiny of the universe. If they were in the wrong hands, there was chaos in the world. In one Mesopotamian myth, a chaos creature (Anzu) stole the tablets of fate, which caused quite a stir within the divine community until he was killed. The Israelite concept of fate or chance was different than that of Mesopotamia. Instead of viewing something as a random happening (Fate), they would consider it simply an unexpected event (serendipity). "Time" and "Chance" are not presented here as two separate contingencies, but as a single factor. A "well-timed coincidence" can occur in any situation, and alter what would have been considered an assured outcome.

9:12 *fish are caught … birds are taken.* Although Ishmael and Esau were known as hunters, hunting was not a typical vocation in Israel except to confront hunger or the pre-

Wisdom Better Than Folly

13I also saw under the sun this example of wisdom[z] that greatly impressed me:
14There was once a small city with only
a few people in it. And a powerful king
came against it, surrounded it and built
huge siege works against it. 15Now there
lived in that city a man poor but wise, and
he saved the city by his wisdom. But nobody remembered that poor man.[a] 16So I
said, "Wisdom is better than strength."
But the poor man's wisdom is despised,
and his words are no longer heeded.[b]

17 The quiet words of the wise are more
to be heeded
than the shouts of a ruler of fools.
18 Wisdom[c] is better than weapons of
war,
but one sinner destroys much good.

10 As dead flies give perfume a bad
smell,
so a little folly[d] outweighs wisdom
and honor.
2 The heart of the wise inclines to the
right,
but the heart of the fool to the left.
3 Even as fools walk along the road,
they lack sense
and show everyone[e] how stupid they
are.
4 If a ruler's anger rises against you,
do not leave your post;[f]
calmness can lay great offenses to
rest.[g]

5 There is an evil I have seen under the
sun,
the sort of error that arises from a
ruler:
6 Fools are put in many high positions,[h]
while the rich occupy the low
ones.
7 I have seen slaves on horseback,
while princes go on foot like
slaves.[i]

8 Whoever digs a pit may fall into it;[j]
whoever breaks through a wall
may be bitten by a snake.[k]
9 Whoever quarries stones may be
injured by them;
whoever splits logs may be
endangered by them.[l]

10 If the ax is dull
and its edge unsharpened,
more strength is needed,
but skill will bring success.

11 If a snake bites before it is charmed,
the charmer receives no fee.[m]

12 Words from the mouth of the wise are
gracious,[n]
but fools are consumed by their
own lips.[o]
13 At the beginning their words are
folly;
at the end they are wicked
madness—
14 and fools multiply words.[p]

9:13 [z] 2Sa 20:22 **9:15** [a] Ge 40:14; Ecc 1:11; 2:16; 4:13 **9:16** [b] Pr 21:22; Ecc 7:19 **9:18** [c] ver 16 **10:1** [d] Pr 13:16; 18:2 **10:3** [e] Pr 13:16; 18:2 **10:4** [f] Ecc 8:3 [g] Pr 16:14; 25:15 **10:6** [h] Pr 29:2 **10:7** [i] Pr 19:10 **10:8** [j] Ps 7:15; 57:6; Pr 26:27 [k] Est 2:23; Ps 9:16; Am 5:19 **10:9** [l] Pr 26:27 **10:11** [m] Ps 58:5; Isa 3:3 **10:12** [n] Pr 10:32 [o] Pr 10:14; 14:3; 15:2; 18:7 **10:14** [p] Pr 15:2; Ecc 5:3; 6:12; 8:7

dominance of wild animals that caused danger to flocks. In both Assyria and Egypt, however, there are numerous wall reliefs depicting royal hunting scenes. Hunting is also implied for Solomon's court (1Ki 4:23). Fishing, like hunting, was not mentioned as recreational in ancient Israel. The book of Job describes fishing by spear or harpoon (Job 41:7) or by hook (Job 41:1–2; see also Isa 19:8). Like hunting, fishing was often the basis of metaphors, primarily as a figure of God's judgment on individuals or nations.

10:2 *right ... left.* While there is no doubt that the right side was considered the place of honor and the most protected position, there is no indication that there was something negative or inherently weak or evil connected to the left side, either in the ancient Near East or Israel. It was secondary in honor and an unexpected direction from which to attack. The fool chose the path of vulnerability and lower status.

10:7 *slaves on horseback ... princes go on foot.* Aspects of this passage have interesting parallels in the Egyptian texts. As Ecclesiastes complains of slaves on horseback, so the "Complaints of Khakheperresonb" declares, "He who used to give commands is (now) one to whom commands are given." The Admonitions of Ipu-wer similarly complains, "Indeed, princes are hungry and perish, / Servants are served." These Egyptian texts are not in all respects the same as Ecclesiastes; they tend to focus on the general lawlessness in society during times of political instability in Egypt, whereas Ecclesiastes is concerned more universally with the absurdities of human life. Still, both reflect a common way of describing a world gone wrong.

10:8 *digs a pit.* Designed to catch a large animal. With that purpose in mind, the pit was disguised, therefore making it possible that one could stumble into it himself. *breaks through a wall.* When a stone wall was dismantled, or when a breach was made in a wall for a gate, a farmer could unwittingly disturb a snake who had taken up residence among the cool stones.

10:9 *quarries stones.* The quarrying of rocks referred to here is probably not that done by professionals, because the other activities in vv. 8–9 are all normal agrarian activities. The verb is used for quarrying, but is also used in more general contexts that deal with uprooting or taking something out. Alternatively, then, this line could refer to a farmer clearing stones from his field. Injury could come from dropped rocks, hernias or scraped arms. *splits logs.* The dangers inherent in splitting logs are easily recognizable. The ax head could fly off the handle or glance off the wood and result in serious injury.

10:11 *charmed.* The Hebrew word should not evoke cartoon-like images of swaying serpents hypnotized by pipe-playing swamis. Instead it refers to snakes against which incantations are ineffective. Snake charming was well known in both Mesopotamia and Egypt. Often the practice apparently served a religious purpose; a famous artifact from Crete is the "Minoan Snake Goddess," a figurine dating to c. 1600 BC, depicting a woman holding aloft two snakes. She is apparently a priestess or goddess. Here in Ecclesiastes, however, snake charming is not a religious function, but a matter of personal safety.

No one knows what is coming—
who can tell someone else what will
happen after them?[q]

15 The toil of fools wearies them;
they do not know the way to town.

16 Woe to the land whose king was a
servant[a][r]
and whose princes feast in the
morning.

17 Blessed is the land whose king is of
noble birth
and whose princes eat at a proper
time—
for strength and not for drunkenness.[s]

18 Through laziness, the rafters sag;
because of idle hands, the house
leaks.[t]

19 A feast is made for laughter,
wine[u] makes life merry,
and money is the answer for
everything.

20 Do not revile the king[v] even in your
thoughts,
or curse the rich in your bedroom,
because a bird in the sky may carry
your words,
and a bird on the wing may report
what you say.

Invest in Many Ventures

11 Ship[w] your grain across the sea;
after many days you may receive
a return.[x]

2 Invest in seven ventures, yes, in eight;
you do not know what disaster may
come upon the land.

3 If clouds are full of water,
they pour rain on the earth.
Whether a tree falls to the south or to
the north,
in the place where it falls, there it
will lie.

10:14 [q] Ecc 9:1
10:16 [r] Isa 3:4-5, 12
10:17 [s] Dt 14:26; 1Sa 25:36; Pr 31:4
10:18 [t] Pr 20:4; 24:30-34
10:19 [u] Ge 14:18; Jdg 9:13
10:20 [v] Ex 22:28
11:1 [w] ver 6; Isa 32:20; Hos 10:12 [x] Dt 24:19; Pr 19:17; Mt 10:42

4 Whoever watches the wind will not
plant;
whoever looks at the clouds will not
reap.

5 As you do not know the path of the
wind,
or how the body is formed[b] in a
mother's womb,[z]
so you cannot understand the work
of God,
the Maker of all things.

6 Sow your seed in the morning,
and at evening let your hands
not be idle,[a]
for you do not know which will
succeed,
whether this or that,
or whether both will do equally
well.

Remember Your Creator While Young

7 Light is sweet,
and it pleases the eyes to see the
sun.[b]

8 However many years anyone may
live,
let them enjoy them all.
But let them remember[c] the days of
darkness,
for there will be many.
Everything to come is
meaningless.

9 You who are young, be happy while
you are young,
and let your heart give you joy in
the days of your youth.
Follow the ways of your heart
and whatever your eyes see,
but know that for all these
things
God will bring you into
judgment.[d]

11:5 [y] Jn 3:8-10 [z] Ps 139:14-16
11:6 [a] Ecc 9:10
11:7 [b] Ecc 7:11
11:8 [c] Ecc 12:1
11:9 [d] Job 19:29; Ecc 2:24; 3:17; 12:14; Ro 14:10

[a] 16 *Or king is a child* [b] 5 *Or know how life (or the spirit) / enters the body being formed*

10:20 *a bird in the sky may carry your words.* Stories of "little birds" who told secrets are found in Aristophanes' *The Birds*, a classical Greek comedy, and in the Hittite *Tale of Elkuhirsa*. The *Words of Ahiqar* assert that a word is like a bird and that one who releases it lacks sense.

11:1 *Ship your grain across the sea.* There is debate about the meaning of this injunction. In context, it appears to encourage trade and commerce: One should diversify the investment in seven or eight directions (v. 2) in the certainty that eventually one's investments will come back ("return," v. 1). Other translations use some iteration of "Cast your bread upon the waters, for you will find it after many days" (ESV, NKJV; cf. KJV, NASB), which brings with it an interesting alternative interpretation. Akkadian texts on beer making have prompted the suggestion that Ecc 11:1 actually refers to brewing practices. These Akkadian texts indicate that dates and a type of bread were "thrown" into the "water" during the process of mixing ingredients for beer. In this interpretation, "you will find it" would mean that the bread will come back to you as beer; and in v. 2, "give a portion to seven" (ESV, KJV; cf. NASB, NKJV) would mean that you should share the beer with others so that in lean times the others will reciprocate. On the other hand, some argue that Ecc 11:1 refers to charitable giving by pointing to similar language in the "Instructions of Ankhsheshonq," an Egyptian wisdom text from between the third and first centuries BC: "Do a good deed and throw it in the water; when it dries you will find it." For all this, the actual context of Ecc 11:1 strongly suggests that it is concerned with trade rather than either beer making or charity.

11:9 *Follow the ways of your heart.* The exhortation that we should "be happy" in the context of facing the reality of death is similar to the message of the Harpers' Songs. For example, the "Song from the Tomb of King Intef," after mourning the fact that those who have built monuments

10 So then, banish anxiety[e] from your
heart
and cast off the troubles of your
body,
for youth and vigor are meaningless.[f]

12 Remember[g] your Creator
in the days of your youth,
before the days of trouble[h] come
and the years approach when you
will say,
"I find no pleasure in them"—
2 before the sun and the light
and the moon and the stars grow
dark,
and the clouds return after the rain;
3 when the keepers of the house tremble,
and the strong men stoop,
when the grinders cease because they
are few,
and those looking through the
windows grow dim;
4 when the doors to the street are closed
and the sound of grinding fades;
when people rise up at the sound of
birds,
but all their songs grow faint;[i]
5 when people are afraid of heights
and of dangers in the streets;
when the almond tree blossoms
and the grasshopper drags itself
along
and desire no longer is stirred.
Then people go to their eternal home[j]
and mourners[k] go about the streets.

6 Remember him—before the silver cord
is severed,
and the golden bowl is broken;
before the pitcher is shattered at the
spring,
and the wheel broken at the well,
7 and the dust returns[l] to the ground it
came from,
and the spirit returns to God[m] who
gave it.[n]

8 "Meaningless! Meaningless!" says the
Teacher.[a]
"Everything is meaningless![o]"

11:10 [e] Ps 94:19 [f] Ecc 2:24 **12:1** [g] Ecc 11:8 [h] 2Sa 19:35 **12:4** [i] Jer 25:10 **12:5** [j] Job 17:13; 10:21 [k] Jer 9:17; Am 5:16 **12:7** [l] Ge 3:19; Job 34:15; Ps 146:4 [m] Ecc 3:21 [n] Job 20:8; Zec 12:1 **12:8** [o] Ecc 1:2 **12:9** [p] 1Ki 4:32 **12:10** [q] Pr 22:20-21 **12:11** [r] Ezr 9:8 **12:12** [s] Ecc 1:18 **12:13** [t] Dt 4:2; 10:12 [u] Mic 6:8 **12:14** [v] Ecc 3:17 [w] Mt 10:26; 1Co 4:5

The Conclusion of the Matter

9 Not only was the Teacher wise, but he
also imparted knowledge to the people.
He pondered and searched out and set
in order many proverbs.[p] 10 The Teacher
searched to find just the right words, and
what he wrote was upright and true.[q]
11 The words of the wise are like goads,
their collected sayings like firmly embedded nails[r]—given by one shepherd.[b] 12 Be
warned, my son, of anything in addition
to them.

Of making many books there is no end,
and much study wearies the body.[s]

13 Now all has been heard;
here is the conclusion of the matter:
Fear God and keep his
commandments,[t]
for this is the duty of all mankind.[u]
14 For God will bring every deed into
judgment,[v]
including every hidden thing,[w]
whether it is good or evil.

[a] 8 Or *the leader of the assembly*; also in verses 9 and 10
[b] 11 Or *Shepherd*

before us are now silent in their crumbling tombs, urges the audience: "Hence rejoice in your heart! / Forgetfulness profits you, follow your heart as long as you live!" Similar teaching is found in the "Instruction of Ptahhotep" from the Middle Kingdom period of Egypt: "Follow your heart as long as you live, / Do no more than is required, / do not shorten the time of 'follow-the-heart.'" The similarity of the Egyptian and Biblical exhortations to "be happy" and "follow" the heart is striking, although the Bible is distinctive for linking this concept to a fear of God.

12:3 *keepers of the house.* Could refer to male servants, common as house slaves throughout the ancient Near East, but often they were people in authority (such as Joseph's role in Potiphar's house, Ge 39:2–4).

12:1–14 Ecclesiastes concludes with several exhortations to fear God in the face of our mortality (vv. 1,6,13–14).

12:1–7 Ch. 12 includes one of the most memorable passages in the book, the allegory of death as a failing household (vv. 1–7). Egyptian "Berlin Papyrus 3024" likewise has a poem on the end of life; it is named for its refrain, "Death is before me today." It looks upon death as a release from suffering: "Death is before me today / Like a sick man's recovery, / Like going outdoors after confinement." One verse is similar to Ecc 12:5 in describing death as a return "home." It reads, "Death is before me today / Like a man's longing to see his home / When he has spent many years in captivity." The apparent optimism about death in these lines is misleading. They reflect the weariness and pain of the aged dying, for whom death is a relief. Ecc 12:1–7 metaphorically describes the suffering and weakness of the body as death draws near.

12:9–14 Ecclesiastes ends with an epilogue reasserting both a balanced view of the importance of wisdom (vv. 9–12) and the main point of the book: one should fear God (vv. 13–14). The use of an epilogue in a wisdom text is also known from Egyptian literature; epilogues appear, e.g., in the "Instruction of Ptahhotep" and the "Instruction of Any." As such, there is no reason to regard the conclusion to Ecclesiastes as a secondary addition to the text, as a number of scholars do, or to see it as a "correction" or contradiction of the gloomy realism of the rest of the book.

WISDOM AND HYMNIC LITERATURE

SONG OF SONGS

The Song of Songs is self-evidently love poetry, notwithstanding the desire of people to convert it into something else. In this regard, it is unique within the Bible. Being love poetry from an ancient land, it uses imagery that is often lost on us and that can be better understood in light of archaeological discoveries. Also, the Song follows the conventions of ancient poetry, and comparisons or analogies for interpreting it are best taken from other ancient Near Eastern love songs, not modern love poetry.

KEY CONCEPTS

- Love and sex are powerful forces in our lives.
- Wisdom will result in discipline and an understanding of appropriate timing in love.

Historical Setting

The current consensus among scholars is that Song of Songs comes from the postexilic period, even though 1:1 suggests that it comes from the time of Solomon. The primary argument for dating the text so late is that certain vocabulary appears to come from a later period in Biblical history. At the same time, we must realize that in the ancient world much of what eventually became literature circulated orally for centuries. Two main arguments can be produced for linking material in the Song to the age of Solomon. First, Song of Songs has strong similarities to Egyptian love poetry from the latter part of the second millennium BC (see the article "Egyptian Love Poetry," p. 1090). It is easier to account for these similarities in the age of Solomon than in the postexilic period. Second, 6:4 suggests that at the time of writing, Tirzah was one of the two grand cities of Israel (comparable to Jerusalem). This best fits an early first-millennium BC date (see note on 6:4). Even so, the Song itself is love poetry and thus "timeless." It is not a historical text and can be interpreted without giving great regard to the time of its composition.

Literary Setting

The Song is a series of short songs sung by a male singer, a female singer and a female chorus. Together, the songs more or less episodically describe the love of a man and woman. It would not be correct to call this a drama — it is lyric poetry and not a play. Although made up of a series of individual songs that are sung by various combinations of the three performers (such as a solo by the woman, a duet by the man and woman, a chorus song, etc.), the songs together are a unified opus that focuses on a major event of life: love and marriage. The presence of the wisdom saying in 8:6 – 7 suggests that these songs have been gathered together as illustrations of the power of love and sex. Their inherent power suggests that love and sex both need to be understood and managed wisely. ◆

1

Solomon's Song of Songs.[a]

She[a]

[2]Let him kiss me with the kisses of his
mouth—
for your love[b] is more delightful
than wine.
[3]Pleasing is the fragrance of your
perfumes;[c]
your name[d] is like perfume poured
out.
No wonder the young women[e] love
you!
[4]Take me away with you—let us
hurry!
Let the king bring me into his
chambers.[f]

Friends

We rejoice and delight in you[b];
we will praise your love more than
wine.

She

How right they are to adore you!

[5]Dark am I, yet lovely,[g]
daughters of Jerusalem,[h]
dark like the tents of Kedar,
like the tent curtains of Solomon.[c]
[6]Do not stare at me because I am
dark,
because I am darkened by the sun.
My mother's sons were angry
with me
and made me take care of the
vineyards;[i]
my own vineyard I had to neglect.
[7]Tell me, you whom I love,
where you graze your flock
and where you rest your sheep[j] at
midday.
Why should I be like a veiled woman
beside the flocks of your friends?

Friends

[8]If you do not know, most beautiful of
women,[k]
follow the tracks of the sheep
and graze your young goats
by the tents of the shepherds.

He

[9]I liken you, my darling, to a mare
among Pharaoh's chariot horses.[l]
[10]Your cheeks[m] are beautiful with
earrings,
your neck with strings of jewels.[n]
[11]We will make you earrings of gold,
studded with silver.

She

[12]While the king was at his table,
my perfume spread its fragrance.[o]
[13]My beloved is to me a sachet of
myrrh
resting between my breasts.
[14]My beloved is to me a cluster of
henna[p] blossoms
from the vineyards of En Gedi.[q]

1:1 [a] 1Ki 4:32 **1:2** [b] SS 4:10 **1:3** [c] SS 4:10 [d] Ecc 7:1 [e] Ps 45:14 **1:4** [f] Ps 45:15 **1:5** [g] SS 2:14; 4:3 [h] SS 2:7; 5:8; 5:16 **1:6** [i] Ps 69:8; SS 8:12 **1:7** [j] SS 3:1-4; Isa 13:20 **1:8** [k] SS 5:9; 6:1 **1:9** [l] 2Ch 1:17 **1:10** [m] SS 5:13 [n] Isa 61:10 **1:12** [o] SS 4:11-14 **1:14** [p] SS 4:13 [q] 1Sa 23:29

[a] The main male and female speakers (identified primarily on the basis of the gender of the relevant Hebrew forms) are indicated by the captions *He* and *She* respectively. The words of others are marked *Friends*. In some instances the divisions and their captions are debatable. [b] *4* The Hebrew is masculine singular. [c] *5* Or *Salma*

1:2 *Let him kiss me.* A kiss on the lips was a passionate expression throughout the Near East, though Egyptians touched noses instead. *wine.* The comparison of the man's love to wine is analogous to a stock metaphor of Egyptian love poetry, in which lovemaking is compared to pomegranate wine or to beer (an analogy used by a female singer in Papyrus Harris 500 in reference to her beloved's caresses). The Egyptians knew wine, but they favored beer. By contrast, Israelites preferred wine, and no word for beer occurs in Biblical Hebrew.
1:5 *Dark am I.* In the ancient world, fair skin was preferred to dark skin for class reasons (rather than racial reasons). Since the vast majority of the people were yeoman farmers, dark skin was common, whereas fair skin was exotic; sun-darkened skin marked one as a peasant rather than a member of the aristocracy. A male singer in Papyrus Chester Beatty I declares that his love is "shining, precious, white of skin"—more in accord with ancient standards of beauty than is the lady of Song of Songs. *Kedar.* Among the most powerful of the northern Arabian Bedouin tribal groups; they are tied to the genealogy of Ishmael in Ge 25:13. Their tents consisted of a three-sided pavilion made of animal skins or woven fabric. The black color would have come from the use of black goat hair.
1:7 *like a veiled woman.* This assertion has prompted a number of interpreters to suggest on the basis of Ge 38:14 that the woman does not want to look like a prostitute. More likely she refers to disguising herself so that she can covertly be with her lover.
1:8 *the tents of the shepherds.* The shepherd motif has clear parallels in ancient Near Eastern poetry; e.g., in a Middle Babylonian text about the goddess Ishtar and her lover, Tammuz, the goddess refers to Tammuz as a shepherd.
1:9 *I liken you, my darling, to a mare.* The comparison of the woman to a mare illustrates how a search for historical explanations can mislead. Recently, some interpreters have suggested that this line is to be elucidated by an ancient military tactic of sending an estrus mare out among the chariots of an opposing army with the intent that the horses' excitement would throw the enemy's battle lines into confusion. In fact, there is no suggestion of a battle or of excitement of that kind here. The real point seems to be simply that she is beautifully adorned in jewelry (v. 10) in a manner reminiscent of the extravagant trappings of the pharaoh's horses. In Egyptian artwork, such as in the tomb of Tutankhamun, one can see horses with elaborate bridles and headgear.
1:14 *henna blossoms.* Henna is a flowering shrub, *Lawsonia inermis L.*, with fragrant white blossoms. The leaves and twigs produce a red, yellow or orange dye that was used to color the hair and other parts of the body.

SONG OF SONGS 1

Egyptian Love Poetry

The Egyptian love songs contain the closest parallels from ancient texts to the Song of Songs. The Egyptian songs were composed in the Nineteenth and Twentieth Dynasties (c. thirteenth–twelfth centuries BC). Texts include the following:

- Papyrus Harris 500. This is made up of three collections.

  Collection A. This is a fairly erotic collection in which a man and woman sing of their love for each other in a series of short songs similar to the Song of Songs.

  Collection B. This is a series of songs in which a girl describes how her heart has been ensnared by her beloved.

  Collection C. This is another series of songs sung by a female solo, in which she sings of how her heart has belonged to her lover ever since she lay with him.

- The Cairo Love Songs. These were found written on a vase.

  A man and woman sing of their love for each other. The man has to cross a river to get to her, and he is carried across as if by magic.

  A boy sings songs in which he, in a very adolescent manner, pines to be near the girl of his dreams. For example, he wishes he were a laundryman so that he could touch her clothes.

- The Turin Love Song. This is a curious collection in which a group of trees sing about the love between a young man and woman.

- The Papyrus Chester Beatty I Songs. This papyrus has several kinds of texts, including three love-song collections.

  Group A. A man and woman sing of their love to each other. In one song, the man describes the beauty of his beloved in a manner similar to SS 6:4–7.

  Group B. A woman sings of her desire for her beloved to come to her.

  Group C. The Nakhtsobek Songs are about a young man who became ensnared in the pleasures of a prostitute. It, like Song of Songs, has three singing parts: a man, a woman and a female chorus. The Nakhtsobek chorus appears to represent the girls of a brothel, who sing of how delightful will be the man's night with the prostitute. The solo woman represents a prostitute who has enticed the man, and she sings of how boldly she went and took him. The man's first song tells of how he is captured by the charms of the lady, but in his second song he finds the door to her barred. She will not receive him again until he comes with sufficient payment. The man vows to bring an extravagant number of gifts to ensure that the way to her is always open. In short, the songs tell of how a young man became emotionally and financially enslaved by a prostitute. There is no narrative or drama here, but the songs together form a coherent work that focuses on a single episode in life: the entrapment of a young man by a prostitute.

Song of Songs in similar fashion uses the various singing parts to give us a picture of the lives of a man and a woman. It deals with mature love, not prostitution or adolescent infatuation, but is similar to the Nakhtsobek Songs in structural conception. Individual songs work together to give the audience a coherent, if highly poetic, interpretation of the joy and significance of sexual love. ◆

SONG OF SONGS 1

MESOPOTAMIAN LOVE POETRY

Mesopotamia has produced a fair amount of love poetry, but no collections directly analogous to the Egyptian texts or the Song of Songs. Also, the Mesopotamian songs are usually religious, singing about the love affairs of the gods, whereas the Song of Songs and the Egyptian texts are secular. Examples of Mesopotamian love poetry include:

- Songs of the goddess Inanna (Ishtar) and her lover Dumuzi (Tammuz). There are several such songs; two examples are:
  - "The Woman's Oath." Dumuzi and Inanna sing of their love for each other.
  - "Love by the Light of the Moon." Inanna, by trickery, persuades her mother Ningal to acquiesce to the sexual union of Inanna and Dumuzi.
- "Love Lyrics of Nabu and Tashmetu." A song of the love between the god Nabu and his consort, Tashmetu. It makes heavy use of the garden metaphor for the female body, as does Song of Songs. ◆

Babylonian love poem, eighteenth century BC: "My beloved knows my heart / My beloved is sweet as honey / She is as fragrant to the nose as wine / The fruit of my feelings."

The Schøyen Collection, Oslo and London, MS 2866, www.schoyencollection.com

He

[15] How beautiful[r] you are, my darling!
Oh, how beautiful!
Your eyes are doves.[s]

She

[16] How handsome you are, my beloved!
Oh, how charming!
And our bed is verdant.

He

[17] The beams of our house are cedars;[t]
our rafters are firs.

She[a]

2 I am a rose[b][u] of Sharon,[v]
a lily[w] of the valleys.

1:15 [r] SS 4:7 [s] SS 2:14; 4:1; 5:2, 12; 6:9
1:17 [t] 1Ki 6:9
2:1 [u] Isa 35:1 [v] S 1Ch 27:29 [w] SS 5:13; Hos 14:5

[a] Or *He* [b] *1* Probably a member of the crocus family

1:15 *Your eyes are doves.* Doves figure prominently on seals and other iconography as a symbol of lovemaking or seduction. They are sometimes understood as messengers of love. A Syrian cylinder seal from c. 1750 BC shows a goddess disrobing before a god as a sign of her willingness to engage in sexual procreation, and doves hover over her head. Similar uses of the dove can be found in artwork from Assyria, Mitanni and classical Greece. This may tell us that the phrase "your eyes are doves" means that her eyes are sexually attractive and provocative.

2:1 *rose of Sharon.* While the exact flower referred to here is unknown, a likely choice would be the *Polyanthus narcissus,* which grows in the hills and moist valleys of the Sharon Plain. They have been found as offerings in Hellenistic tombs in Egypt.

He

2 Like a lily among thorns
is my darling among the young women.

She

3 Like an apple[a] tree among the trees of the forest
is my beloved[x] among the young men.
I delight[y] to sit in his shade,
and his fruit is sweet to my taste.[z]
4 Let him lead me to the banquet hall,[a]
and let his banner[b] over me be love.
5 Strengthen me with raisins,
refresh me with apples,[c]
for I am faint with love.[d]
6 His left arm is under my head,
and his right arm embraces me.[e]
7 Daughters of Jerusalem, I charge you[f]
by the gazelles and by the does of the field:
Do not arouse or awaken love
until it so desires.[g]

8 Listen! My beloved!
Look! Here he comes,
leaping across the mountains,
bounding over the hills.[h]
9 My beloved is like a gazelle[i] or a young stag.[j]
Look! There he stands behind our wall,
gazing through the windows,
peering through the lattice.
10 My beloved spoke and said to me,
"Arise, my darling,
my beautiful one, come with me.
11 See! The winter is past;
the rains are over and gone.
12 Flowers appear on the earth;
the season of singing has come,
the cooing of doves
is heard in our land.
13 The fig tree forms its early fruit;[k]
the blossoming[l] vines spread their fragrance.
Arise, come, my darling;
my beautiful one, come with me."

He

14 My dove[m] in the clefts of the rock,
in the hiding places on the mountainside,
show me your face,
let me hear your voice;
for your voice is sweet,
and your face is lovely.[n]
15 Catch for us the foxes,[o]
the little foxes
that ruin the vineyards,[p]
our vineyards that are in bloom.[q]

2:3 [x] SS 1:14 [y] SS 1:4 [z] SS 4:16 **2:4** [a] Est 1:11 [b] Nu 1:52 **2:5** [c] SS 7:8 [d] SS 5:8 **2:6** [e] SS 8:3 **2:7** [f] SS 5:8 [g] SS 3:5; 8:4 **2:8** [h] ver 17; SS 8:14 **2:9** [i] 2Sa 2:18 [j] ver 17; SS 8:14 **2:13** [k] Isa 28:4; Jer 24:2; Hos 9:10; Mic 7:1; Na 3:12 [l] SS 7:12 **2:14** [m] Ge 8:8; SS 1:15 [n] SS 1:5; 8:13 **2:15** [o] Jdg 15:4 [p] SS 1:6 [q] SS 7:12

[a] 3 Or possibly *apricot*; here and elsewhere in Song of Songs

2:3 *Like an apple tree among the trees of the forest.* Some interpreters argue that the apple was unknown in ancient Israel and so translate this as "apricot." However, apples were known both in Mesopotamia and in the classical world, and there is no reason to deny that Israelites knew of the fruit. One aspect of this simile is obvious: all other men are forest trees in the woman's eyes, but her beloved is an apple tree, i.e., a tree that gives delicious fruit in contrast to a barren, ordinary tree. Apples were also understood as aphrodisiacs in Assyrian incantations.

2:4 *his banner over me be love.* The translation of the Hebrew word *degel* as "banner" is uncertain; this phrase may be better translated "his intent toward me be love." In either case, setting a standard as a symbol of possession or expressing intent to carry out an action arrives at the same objective: to make love to his beloved.

2:9 *My beloved is like a gazelle or a young stag.* The same language is used in the Papyrus Chester Beatty I songs, where the Egyptian girl sings to her beloved, "O that you came to your sister swiftly, / like a bounding gazelle in the wild." The image brings out her vision of the man as both powerful and graceful. Gazelles and does are often portrayed as the companions of the goddess of love in ancient Near Eastern art. *gazing through the windows.* Carved ivories found in excavations of the Iron Age levels at Samaria and Nimrud include the motif of "the woman at the window." This may be associated with the Phoenician goddess Astarte, who was identified with a cult of sacred prostitution (see the adulterous woman's spying through the window in Pr 7:6; see also 2Ki 9). In this case, however, it is the impatient man who periodically glances through the window to see when his lover will be ready to admit him.

2:12 *The season of singing has come.* The ancient versions took the Hebrew in v. 12 to mean, "the season of pruning has come," unlike the NIV's "season of singing." The issue is the meaning of the word *zamir,* which can mean either "song" or "pruning." Some modern interpreters say that it cannot mean "pruning" since the song has already indicated that it is spring; they argue that the pruning was done in winter. The term *zamir* ("pruning") also appears in the Gezer Calendar, a small Hebrew inscription on a piece of limestone. It dates to around 925 BC and appears to be a schoolboy's writing exercise that describes the agricultural year in ancient Israel. This inscription, compared to Isa 18:5, suggests that the Israelites continued pruning into the springtime, which would invalidate the argument that there was no pruning in spring.

2:15 *Catch for us the foxes.* The image of the foxes is highly ambiguous and has given rise to an enormous number of speculative interpretations (that the foxes are lustful boys, that the foxes represent the cunning of young lovers, etc.). Ancient parallels may be of help to us. As this text does, Aristophanes asserts that foxes commonly get into the vineyards and eat the grapes (*Knights* 1075–77). Similar comments can be found in Plato (*Republic* 365c) and Aristotle (*History of Animals* 488b.1). Images on classical pottery indicate that fox hunting was not a serious sport but more of a game for young people; perhaps they made play of the necessary task of chasing foxes from the vineyards. If so, the appeal simply speaks of one of the joys of springtime for young people and is not meant to be grist for imaginative interpreters.

She

16 My beloved is mine and I am his;[r]
he browses among the lilies.[s]
17 Until the day breaks
and the shadows flee,[t]
turn, my beloved,[u]
and be like a gazelle
or like a young stag[v]
on the rugged hills.[a][w]

3 All night long on my bed
I looked[x] for the one my heart loves;
I looked for him but did not find him.
2 I will get up now and go about the city,
through its streets and squares;
I will search for the one my heart loves.
So I looked for him but did not find him.
3 The watchmen found me
as they made their rounds in the city.[y]
"Have you seen the one my heart loves?"
4 Scarcely had I passed them
when I found the one my heart loves.
I held him and would not let him go
till I had brought him to my mother's house,[z]
to the room of the one who conceived me.[a]
5 Daughters of Jerusalem, I charge you[b]
by the gazelles and by the does of the field:
Do not arouse or awaken love
until it so desires.[c]

6 Who is this coming up from the wilderness[d]
like a column of smoke,
perfumed with myrrh[e] and incense
made from all the spices[f] of the merchant?
7 Look! It is Solomon's carriage,
escorted by sixty warriors,[g]
the noblest of Israel,
8 all of them wearing the sword,
all experienced in battle,
each with his sword at his side,
prepared for the terrors of the night.[h]
9 King Solomon made for himself the carriage;
he made it of wood from Lebanon.
10 Its posts he made of silver,
its base of gold.
Its seat was upholstered with purple,
its interior inlaid with love.
Daughters of Jerusalem, 11 come out,
and look, you daughters of Zion.[i]
Look[b] on King Solomon wearing a crown,
the crown with which his mother crowned him
on the day of his wedding,
the day his heart rejoiced.[j]

2:16 [r] SS 7:10 [s] SS 4:5; 6:3 **2:17** [t] SS 4:6 [u] SS 1:14 [v] ver 9 [w] ver 8 **3:1** [x] SS 5:6; Isa 26:9 **3:3** [y] SS 5:7 **3:4** [z] SS 8:2 [a] SS 6:9 **3:5** [b] SS 2:7 [c] SS 8:4 **3:6** [d] SS 8:5 [e] SS 1:13; 4:6,14 [f] Ex 30:34 **3:7** [g] 1Sa 8:11 **3:8** [h] Job 15:22; Ps 91:5 **3:11** [i] Isa 4:4 [j] Isa 62:5

[a] 17 Or *the hills of Bether* [b] 10,11 Or *interior lovingly inlaid / by the daughters of Jerusalem. / [11]Come out, you daughters of Zion, / and look*

2:16 *lilies.* May be lotus flowers, which were symbols of fertility and sensuality in Egypt and Canaan.

3:1–5 There are an enormous number of interpretations of this difficult text, in which the woman seeks her beloved in the city streets, encounters the guards and then suddenly finds her beloved. From a literary standpoint, the woman's action is a "quest," a tale in which the hero goes out in search of some prized possession. The closest parallel in the Bible to this text is personified Wisdom's metaphoric search for a young man who will embrace her teachings (Pr 7:10–13; 8:1–4). The most famous quest of ancient Near Eastern literature is that of Gilgamesh, who sought the plant of eternal youth after the death of his friend Enkidu. Near Eastern myths do have stories of goddesses who went in search of their perished lovers in the netherworld (Ishtar seeking Tammuz, or Anat seeking Baal). A famous quest in classical mythology is that of Orpheus, who went to Hades in hopes of bringing back his wife, Eurydice. Against all these parallels, the woman of the Song of Songs is not seeking someone who will accept her teachings, and this passage does not deal with death. Still, the fact that it is the woman who seeks the man (rather than the reverse) suggests that she is the central figure in the Song of Songs.

3:6–11 This section describes the coming of the woman (in v. 6 the word "this" in "Who is this ...?" is feminine and therefore designates a woman). Her arrival is most extravagant, as clouds of incense go up with her procession, and she herself is perfumed.

3:6 *perfumed with myrrh and incense.* Peoples of the ancient world highly valued fragrances, perfumes and anointing oils. A curious Egyptian banqueting custom was to imbed a cone of wax with fragrances and then place the wax on top of the head. As the evening progressed, body heat would melt the wax, which, running down the sides of the head, would release its aroma. Apart from the fact that the fragrances were pleasing, they also served hygienic or health-related purposes; e.g., anointing the scalp with oils killed lice. Most perfumes and incenses came from plant sources such as frankincense, myrrh, nard, saffron, aloes and calamus. None of these is indigenous to Palestine; they had to be imported from Iran, Arabia, India and elsewhere. For this reason, perfumes were extravagantly expensive (see Jn 12:3–5). Fragrances were obtained in a variety of ways, depending on the nature of the plant source (be it a root, flower, bark secretion or something else), but often the raw material was either distilled or in some way pressed or crushed.

3:7–11 Numerous interpretations of this text have been proposed, but it appears most likely that this is an Israelite wedding scene in which the bride is being carried in a litter or palanquin (not a "carriage," v. 7) to the wedding ceremony, where the groom stands wearing a ceremonial crown or garland (v. 11). The Talmud indicates that brides came to a wedding in a palanquin, and that both the bride and groom wore ceremonial crowns (in the Babylonian Talmud see *Sotah* 49a)—until such practices were interrupted by the wars against Rome. The "sixty warriors" (v. 7) are probably the friends of the groom serving as escorts or honor guards for the bride (as at Samson's wedding). The text indicates the grandeur of the wedding by elaborating on the exquisite workmanship of the palanquin (vv. 9–10).

He

4 How beautiful you are, my darling!
Oh, how beautiful!
Your eyes behind your veil are doves.[k]
Your hair is like a flock of goats
descending from the hills of Gilead.[l]
2 Your teeth are like a flock of sheep just shorn,
coming up from the washing.
Each has its twin;
not one of them is alone.[m]
3 Your lips are like a scarlet ribbon;
your mouth[n] is lovely.
Your temples behind your veil
are like the halves of a pomegranate.[o]
4 Your neck is like the tower[p] of David,
built with courses of stone[a];
on it hang a thousand shields,[q]
all of them shields of warriors.
5 Your breasts[r] are like two fawns,
like twin fawns of a gazelle[s]
that browse among the lilies.[t]
6 Until the day breaks
and the shadows flee,[u]
I will go to the mountain of myrrh[v]
and to the hill of incense.
7 You are altogether beautiful,[w] my darling;
there is no flaw in you.

8 Come with me from Lebanon, my bride,[x]
come with me from Lebanon.
Descend from the crest of Amana,
from the top of Senir,[y] the summit of Hermon,[z]
from the lions' dens
and the mountain haunts of leopards.

4:1 [k] SS 1:15; 5:12 [l] SS 6:5; Mic 7:14 **4:2** [m] SS 6:6 **4:3** [n] SS 5:16 [o] SS 6:7 **4:4** [p] SS 7:4 [q] Eze 27:10 **4:5** [r] SS 7:3 [s] Pr 5:19 [t] SS 2:16; 6:2-3 **4:6** [u] SS 2:17 [v] ver 14 **4:7** [w] SS 1:15 **4:8** [x] SS 5:1 [y] Dt 3:9 [z] 1Ch 5:23

Eighteenth-century BC fertility goddess from Mari with a neck like a tower (SS 4:4).

National Museum, Aleppo, Syria/Bridgeman Images

9 You have stolen my heart, my sister, my bride;
you have stolen my heart
with one glance of your eyes,
with one jewel of your necklace.[a]
10 How delightful[b] is your love[c], my sister, my bride!
How much more pleasing is your love than wine,

4:9 [a] Ge 41:42 **4:10** [b] SS 7:6 [c] SS 1:2

[a] *4* The meaning of the Hebrew for this phrase is uncertain.

4:1 – 15 A song that describes in detail the beauty of one's beloved is referred to as the genre of *wasf,* and the Song of Songs has several such pieces. Here, the man sings of the woman's eyes, hair, face, neck and breasts before he interrupts the description of her beauty to call for her to come with him (v. 8). Such poetry is found also in the Egyptian love songs. For example, in the Papyrus Chester Beatty I texts, a young man sings of his beloved, "Lovely the look of her eyes, / Sweet the speech of her lips, / She has not a word too much. / Upright neck, shining breast, / Hair true lapis lazuli." In contrast to the Song of Songs, however, the Egyptian texts use language that is fairly straightforward. The metaphors of the Song of Songs — a neck "like the tower of David" (v. 4) or breasts "like twin fawns" (v. 5) — are both provocative and enigmatic.
4:4 *tower of David.* According to the fashion described in the Egyptian Love Songs and depicted in art, a long neck was a characteristic of a beautiful woman. Thus a comparison with a tall, well-built tower serves as a compliment. In addition to the shape, a tower represented the pride and glory of a city. This is the imagery also used for the neck in the Bible (e.g., Ps 75:5). *on it hang a thousand shields.* The metaphor of a woman's adorned neck continues by comparing jewels and necklaces to the shields used to decorate a structure (cf. 1Ki 10:16 – 17). In Ezekiel's lament over Tyre (Eze 27), he describes how shields were hung on the city walls to add to its beauty (Eze 27:10 – 11).
4:8 In a surprising move, the man describes the woman almost as a goddess. *Amana … Senir … Hermon.* The mountains mentioned here are in Lebanon, north of Israel ("Hermon" and "Senir" are actually the same mountain), and they were the highest mountains in the region. The Gilgamesh Epic speaks of the mountains of Lebanon as the throne of the goddess Ishtar. Still, it would not be correct to assume that the man actually is singing to a goddess or that this text is a fragment of a hymn. A modern man might call the woman of his dreams an "angel" and not mean it literally. The words suggest that to the man, the woman in all her beauty is both powerful and aloof. *lions' … leopards.* These animals are often the companions of goddesses, particularly Ishtar, the Mesopotamian goddess of love. In Egypt Hathor is sometimes portrayed as a lioness, as is Sekhmet.

and the fragrance of your perfume
more than any spice!
11 Your lips drop sweetness as the
honeycomb, my bride;
milk and honey are under your
tongue.[d]
The fragrance of your garments
is like the fragrance of Lebanon.[e]
12 You are a garden locked up, my sister,
my bride;
you are a spring enclosed, a sealed
fountain.[f]
13 Your plants are an orchard of
pomegranates[g]
with choice fruits,
with henna[h] and nard,
14 nard and saffron,
calamus and cinnamon,[i]
with every kind of incense tree,
with myrrh[j] and aloes
and all the finest spices.[k]
15 You are[a] a garden fountain,
a well of flowing water
streaming down from Lebanon.

She

16 Awake, north wind,
and come, south wind!
Blow on my garden,
that its fragrance may spread
everywhere.
Let my beloved come into his garden
and taste its choice fruits.[l]

He

5 I have come into my garden, my
sister, my bride;[m]
I have gathered my myrrh with my
spice.
I have eaten my honeycomb and my
honey;
I have drunk my wine and my milk.[n]

Friends

Eat, friends, and drink;
drink your fill of love.

She

2 I slept but my heart was awake.
Listen! My beloved is knocking:
"Open to me, my sister, my darling,
my dove, my flawless[o] one.[p]
My head is drenched with dew,
my hair with the dampness of the
night."
3 I have taken off my robe—
must I put it on again?
I have washed my feet—
must I soil them again?
4 My beloved thrust his hand through
the latch-opening;
my heart began to pound for him.
5 I arose to open for my beloved,
and my hands dripped with myrrh,[q]
my fingers with flowing myrrh,
on the handles of the bolt.
6 I opened for my beloved,[r]
but my beloved had left; he was
gone.[s]
My heart sank at his departure.[b]
I looked[t] for him but did not find him.
I called him but he did not answer.
7 The watchmen found me
as they made their rounds in the
city.[u]

4:11 [d] Ps 19:10; SS 5:1 [e] Hos 14:6 **4:12** [f] Pr 5:15-18 **4:13** [g] SS 6:11; 7:12 [h] SS 1:14 **4:14** [i] Ex 30:23 [j] SS 3:6 [k] SS 1:12 **4:16** [l] SS 2:3; 5:1 **5:1** [m] SS 4:8 [n] SS 4:11; Isa 55:1 **5:2** [o] SS 4:7 [p] SS 6:9 **5:5** [q] ver 13 **5:6** [r] SS 6:1 [s] SS 6:2 [t] SS 3:1 **5:7** [u] SS 3:3

[a] 15 Or *I am* (spoken by *She*) [b] 6 Or *heart had gone out to him when he spoke*

4:12 *You are a garden locked up, my sister, my bride.* Both the use of the term "sister" as a term of endearment and the description of the woman as a garden have parallels in the Egyptian texts. Papyrus Harris 500 has the following lines sung by the woman: "I am your sister, your best one; / I belong to you like this plot of ground / That I planted with flowers / And sweet smelling herbs." In these contexts, "sister" is simply an affectionate term analogous to "sweetheart" in English; it is not literal and should not be linked to sibling marriage either in the pharaoh's household or among the gods (in the Egyptian love poetry, it is clear that the lovers are not related; see also SS 8:1). The Biblical account is distinctive for describing the woman as a garden that is "locked up." This suggests that they have not yet consummated their marriage and that she is still a virgin.

5:2–8 These verses are among the most enigmatic and controversial texts in the entire book. A principal issue here is whether or not this text actually describes the sexual union of the man and woman, or whether his departure suggests that they did not have a union. The line "My beloved thrust his hand through the latch-opening" (v. 4) appears to be a euphemism for sexual intercourse. The term "hand" is used in both the Bible and other ancient Near Eastern literature to refer to the male member. It has this significance in Isa 57:8 ("naked bodies"),10 ("strength"), as well as in the Qumran Manual of Discipline (1 QS 7:13). "Hand" also has this significance in Sumerian, Ugaritic and Egyptian texts. In the Egyptian Papyrus Harris 500, after the woman declares that she is like a garden for her beloved, she sings, "Pleasant is the canal within it, / which your hand scooped out." In that text, her body is a garden, the "canal" is her genitals, and his "hand" is his sexual member. The similarity to the language of the Song of Songs is striking. But if sexual union has taken place, what is the meaning of the departure of the man (v. 6) and the molestation of the woman by the watchmen of the city (v. 7)? The departure (like everything else in this passage) is not to be taken literally. The man's disappearance is probably the woman's perspective on the event, i.e., the man has been abrupt in his termination of the union and has not given her the kind of intimacy she desires. The violence of the watchmen suggests the violence of the loss of virginity. In Biblical language, a city can be called a "virgin," meaning that it is securely protected (e.g., Isa 47:1). The watchmen of a city are its protectors, and here represent the woman's virginity. Despite the metaphoric usage here, the metaphor, as expected, derives from real life: there was a small opening in the door that someone could reach through to get to the latch or lock. If there was a lock, the person would have to reach through with a key.

They beat me, they bruised me;
they took away my cloak,
those watchmen of the walls!
8 Daughters of Jerusalem, I charge
you[v] —
if you find my beloved,
what will you tell him?
Tell him I am faint with love.[w]

Friends

9 How is your beloved better than
others,
most beautiful of women?[x]
How is your beloved better than
others,
that you so charge us?

She

10 My beloved is radiant and ruddy,
outstanding among ten thousand.[y]
11 His head is purest gold;
his hair is wavy
and black as a raven.
12 His eyes are like doves[z]
by the water streams,
washed in milk,[a]
mounted like jewels.
13 His cheeks[b] are like beds of spice[c]
yielding perfume.
His lips are like lilies[d]
dripping with myrrh.
14 His arms are rods of gold
set with topaz.
His body is like polished ivory
decorated with lapis lazuli.[e]
15 His legs are pillars of marble
set on bases of pure gold.
His appearance is like Lebanon,[f]
choice as its cedars.

5:8 [v] SS 2:7; 3:5 [w] SS 2:5
5:9 [x] SS 1:8; 6:1
5:10 [y] Ps 45:2
5:12 [z] SS 1:15; 4:1 [a] Ge 49:12
5:13 [b] SS 1:10 [c] SS 6:2 [d] SS 2:1
5:14 [e] Job 28:6
5:15 [f] 1Ki 4:33; SS 7:4

16 His mouth[g] is sweetness itself;
he is altogether lovely.
This is my beloved,[h] this is my friend,
daughters of Jerusalem.[i]

Friends

6 Where has your beloved[j] gone,
most beautiful of women?[k]
Which way did your beloved turn,
that we may look for him
with you?

She

2 My beloved has gone[l] down to his
garden,[m]
to the beds of spices,[n]
to browse in the gardens
and to gather lilies.
3 I am my beloved's and my beloved is
mine;[o]
he browses among the lilies.[p]

He

4 You are as beautiful as Tirzah,[q]
my darling,
as lovely as Jerusalem,[r]
as majestic as troops with
banners.[s]
5 Turn your eyes from me;
they overwhelm me.
Your hair is like a flock of goats
descending from Gilead.[t]
6 Your teeth are like a flock of sheep
coming up from the washing.
Each has its twin,
not one of them is missing.[u]
7 Your temples behind your veil[v]
are like the halves of a
pomegranate.[w]

5:16 [g] SS 4:3 [h] SS 7:9 [i] SS 1:5
6:1 [j] SS 5:6 [k] SS 1:8
6:2 [l] SS 5:6 [m] SS 4:12 [n] SS 5:13
6:3 [o] SS 7:10 [p] SS 2:16
6:4 [q] Jos 12:24 [r] Ps 48:2; 50:2 [s] ver 10
6:5 [t] SS 4:1
6:6 [u] SS 4:2
6:7 [v] Ge 24:65 [w] SS 4:3

5:13 *lilies.* The Hebrew word probably refers specifically to the lotus (which is a variety of lily), and the Hebrew word is probably borrowed from Egyptian. Egyptian and Phoenician art regularly portray the lotus in artwork, and a lotus pattern is routinely used for the capitals of Egyptian stone pillars. In Solomon's temple complex, the column capitals and the great metal "Sea" undoubtedly had a lotus pattern (1Ki 7:19–26). The Egyptians considered the lotus a symbol of life, and they made a type of bread from the cluster at the center of the flower. Homer famously sings of the magical power of the lotus in his account of the land of the lotus-eaters (*Odyssey* 9). In describing his lips as lotuses, she associates him with an object of awe and beauty, and she likely means that his kisses are enchanting and invigorating.

5:15 *pillars of marble.* Now it is the woman's turn to describe her lover in flamboyant terms. A similar portrayal of perfect physical symmetry can be found in the description of the Babylonian god Marduk in the *Enuma Elish* creation epic.

6:2 *My beloved has gone down to his garden.* Ancient Israelites placed their settlements on hilltops with the gardens in the valleys below, and someone heading to a garden would naturally go downward. Thus, going down relates to the realities of Israelite life.

6:4 *You are as beautiful as Tirzah ... as lovely as Jerusalem.* The woman is compared to these two cities, apparently the most magnificent in Israel, Jerusalem to the south and Tirzah to the north. *Tirzah.* Its ruins are at Tell el-Far'ah. Evidence for settlement is found here from various periods in the Neolithic, the Early Bronze Age, the Middle Bronze Age and the Iron Age. The city there at the time of Solomon represents a high point in the history of the site. Tirzah in this phase was an elaborately planned urban center with abundant pottery, ashlar (cut stone) construction (see note on Ps 118:22), an offset-inset city wall, a large public place and shrine near the city gate, and a type of house construction not normally seen in Israel. It may have been the administrative center for the district of Ephraim in the time of Solomon. The city may have been sacked during the incursion of Sheshonq (Biblical Shishak, see notes on 1Ki 14:25,26), and it was apparently Jeroboam's capital city (1Ki 14:12–17). Omri laid siege to the city; this resulted in the palace being burned to the ground (1Ki 16:17–18). Omri moved the capital to Samaria, and Tirzah declined to insignificance. In the postexilic period it was a ruin. This suggests either that the Song of Songs was composed when Tirzah was in its glory days and a rival to Jerusalem, or that it reflects on the distant past of a once-glorious city.

8 Sixty queens[x] there may be,
and eighty concubines,[y]
and virgins beyond number;
9 but my dove,[z] my perfect one,[a] is
unique,
the only daughter of her mother,
the favorite of the one who bore
her.[b]
The young women saw her and called
her blessed;
the queens and concubines praised
her.

Friends

10 Who is this that appears like the
dawn,
fair as the moon, bright as the sun,
majestic as the stars in procession?

He

11 I went down to the grove of nut trees
to look at the new growth in the
valley,
to see if the vines had budded
or the pomegranates were in
bloom.[c]
12 Before I realized it,
my desire set me among the royal
chariots of my people.[a]

Friends

13 Come back, come back, O Shulammite;
come back, come back, that we may
gaze on you!

He

Why would you gaze on the
Shulammite
as on the dance[d] of Mahanaim?[b]

6:8 [x] Ps 45:9 [y] Ge 22:24 **6:9** [z] SS 1:15 [a] SS 5:2 [b] SS 3:4 **6:11** [c] SS 7:12 **6:13** [d] Ex 15:20 **7:1** [e] Ps 45:13

7 [c] How beautiful your sandaled
feet,
O prince's[e] daughter!
Your graceful legs are like jewels,
the work of an artist's hands.
2 Your navel is a rounded goblet
that never lacks blended wine.
Your waist is a mound of wheat
encircled by lilies.
3 Your breasts[f] are like two fawns,
like twin fawns of a gazelle.
4 Your neck is like an ivory tower.[g]
Your eyes are the pools of Heshbon[h]
by the gate of Bath Rabbim.
Your nose is like the tower of
Lebanon[i]
looking toward Damascus.
5 Your head crowns you like Mount
Carmel.[j]
Your hair is like royal tapestry;
the king is held captive by its
tresses.
6 How beautiful[k] you are and how
pleasing,
my love, with your delights![l]
7 Your stature is like that of the palm,
and your breasts[m] like clusters of
fruit.
8 I said, "I will climb the palm tree;
I will take hold of its fruit."
May your breasts be like clusters of
grapes on the vine,
the fragrance of your breath like
apples,[n]
9 and your mouth like the best wine.

7:3 [f] SS 4:5 **7:4** [g] Ps 144:12; SS 4:4 [h] Nu 21:26 [i] SS 5:15 **7:5** [j] Isa 35:2 **7:6** [k] SS 1:15 [l] SS 4:10 **7:7** [m] SS 4:5 **7:8** [n] SS 2:5

[a] 12 Or *among the chariots of Amminadab*; or *among the chariots of the people of the prince* [b] 13 In Hebrew texts this verse (6:13) is numbered 7:1. [c] In Hebrew texts 7:1-13 is numbered 7:2-14.

6:12 *chariots.* This verse is obscure, but it is possible that the chariot, as in the love literature from the ancient Near East, is a metaphor for marriage. When Ishtar proposes marriage to Gilgamesh, she uses the metaphor of the chariot to do so, and in the "Love Lyrics of Nabu and Tashmetu" the man offers to provide a chariot for the woman, and her response indicates that there had been a suggestion of a sexual encounter. Nevertheless, it remains uncertain as to how this metaphor would work among the other difficult elements of this verse (e.g., chariots being plural and modified with the name Amminadab [see NIV text note]).

6:13b *the Shulammite.* Since a definite article precedes the name Shulammite, it is probably an epithet, such as "perfect one," not a personal name. Origin of the name may be based on a connection with the Mesopotamian goddess Shulmanitu or Sala. It is unlikely that the name refers to an inhabitant of Shunem, since the woman is so closely associated with Jerusalem in the Song of Songs. *dance of Mahanaim.* The meaning of this is disputed, as illustrated by the NIV's decision to transliterate the Hebrew "Mahanaim" rather than translate it. Dance was certainly well known in ancient Israel, but most of the examples we have refer to women (not men) dancing (see notes on 1Sa 18:6; 2Sa 6:14; Ps 149:3). Specific examples include the celebratory dancing of Miriam and the women at the Red Sea (Ex 15:20), of Jephthah's daughter (Jdg 11:34) and of the women who celebrated victories in David's time (1Sa 18:6). Jdg 21:21 tells us that women danced at an annual festival at Shiloh. On the other hand, we do have the example of David's dance (2Sa 6:14–16), and there is a clay plaque found at Tell Dan that has a depiction of a man dancing and playing a lute-like instrument. Thus, dancing was not exclusively done by women. In SS 6:13, however, the man seems to be referring to an elaborate dance conducted by two companies of women ("Mahanaim" can be translated "two companies"). The point is that the chorus should not stare at the woman as if she were putting on a show.

7:4 *the pools of Heshbon.* Heshbon was a city in Transjordan, west of the Dead Sea, at a site now called Tell Hesban. The remains of several pools have been found there, although we cannot be sure to which, if any of these, the Song is referring. *tower of Lebanon.* Location unknown.

7:7 *the palm ... clusters of fruit.* The date palm was (and remains) a highly valued tree in the Near East. It had many uses (e.g., its fronds were used in weaving baskets), and its fruit is sweet. The tree is sometimes associated with fertility goddesses in ancient artwork, and the clusters of its fruit somewhat resemble a woman's breast. As such, it here represents the pleasures that the woman gives.

She

May the wine go straight to my
beloved,[o]
flowing gently over lips and
teeth.[a]
10 I belong to my beloved,
and his desire[p] is for me.[q]
11 Come, my beloved, let us go to
the countryside,
let us spend the night in the
villages.[b]
12 Let us go early to the
vineyards[r]
to see if the vines have
budded,[s]
if their blossoms[t] have opened,
and if the pomegranates[u] are
in bloom[v]—
there I will give you my love.
13 The mandrakes[w] send out their
fragrance,
and at our door is every
delicacy,
both new and old,
that I have stored up for
you, my beloved.[x]

8 If only you were to me like a
brother,
who was nursed at my
mother's breasts!
Then, if I found you outside,
I would kiss you,
and no one would despise
me.
2 I would lead you
and bring you to my mother's
house[y]—
she who has taught me.
I would give you spiced wine to
drink,
the nectar of my pomegranates.
3 His left arm is under my head
and his right arm embraces me.[z]
4 Daughters of Jerusalem, I charge
you:
Do not arouse or awaken love
until it so desires.[a]

An Egyptian woman holds mandrakes (SS 7:13) in her right hand, Amarna, 1335 BC.

Kim Walton. The Neues Museum, Berlin.

Friends

5 Who is this coming up from the
wilderness[b]
leaning on her beloved?

She

Under the apple tree I roused you;
there your mother conceived[c] you,
there she who was in labor gave you
birth.

7:9 [o] SS 5:16 **7:10** [p] Ps 45:11 [q] SS 2:16; 6:3 **7:12** [r] SS 1:6 [s] SS 2:15 [t] SS 2:13 [u] SS 4:13 [v] SS 6:11 **7:13** [w] Ge 30:14 [x] SS 4:16 **8:2** [y] SS 3:4 **8:3** [z] SS 2:6 **8:4** [a] SS 2:7; 3:5 **8:5** [b] SS 3:6 [c] SS 3:4

[a] 9 Septuagint, Aquila, Vulgate and Syriac; Hebrew *lips of sleepers* [b] 11 Or *the henna bushes*

7:13 *mandrakes ... their fragrance.* Similar to ginseng, the mandrake has a root that can resemble a human form. It produces a pungent odor and can be used as a narcotic. From ancient times, an enormous amount of lore and superstition has been associated with the plant. The fragrance of the fruit of the mandrake was thought to be an aphrodisiac. In Egyptian artwork, women hold the fruit under their noses or the noses of their husbands, apparently as a preparation for love-play. The Cairo Love Songs also allude to the erotic power of the mandrake, as does Ge 30:14–15.

8:1 *brother.* A common term of endearment for a woman to use of her lover in the ancient Near East. Here, however, the woman wishes her beloved actually *were* her brother so that she could kiss him in public. She does not, and we should not, push the point to absurdity (she would not want to make love to her brother). The main point is simply that she wishes she did not have to hide her affection for him. It appears that in ancient Israel, as in many traditional societies, any public display of affection between man and woman was forbidden, even if they were married. The exception would be a kiss or holding hands among close family members, where it would be understood that no sexual relationship existed. Thus, the woman simply wishes she had more freedom to show how much she loves her beloved. In a somewhat analogous manner, the female singer in the Papyrus Chester Beatty I songs longs to be able to show affection to her "brother," but she is held back by the watchful eyes of society.

[6]Place me like a seal over your heart,
like a seal on your arm;
for love[d] is as strong as death,
its jealousy[a][e] unyielding as the grave.
It burns like blazing fire,
like a mighty flame.[b]
[7]Many waters cannot quench love;
rivers cannot sweep it away.
If one were to give
all the wealth of one's house for love,
it[c] would be utterly scorned.[f]

Friends

[8]We have a little sister,
and her breasts are not yet grown.
What shall we do for our sister
on the day she is spoken for?
[9]If she is a wall,
we will build towers of silver on her.
If she is a door,
we will enclose her with panels of cedar.

She

[10]I am a wall,
and my breasts are like towers.
Thus I have become in his eyes
like one bringing contentment.
[11]Solomon had a vineyard[g] in Baal Hamon;
he let out his vineyard to tenants.
Each was to bring for its fruit
a thousand shekels[d][h] of silver.
[12]But my own vineyard[i] is mine to give;
the thousand shekels are for you, Solomon,
and two hundred[e] are for those who tend its fruit.

He

[13]You who dwell in the gardens
with friends in attendance,
let me hear your voice!

She

[14]Come away, my beloved,
and be like a gazelle[j]
or like a young stag[k]
on the spice-laden mountains.[l]

8:6 [d] SS 1:2 [e] Nu 5:14 **8:7** [f] Pr 6:35 **8:11** [g] Ecc 2:4 [h] Isa 7:23 **8:12** [i] SS 1:6 **8:14** [j] Pr 5:19 [k] SS 2:9 [l] SS 2:8, 17

[a] *6* Or *ardor* [b] *6* Or *fire, / like the very flame of the* LORD [c] *7* Or *he* [d] *11* That is, about 25 pounds or about 12 kilograms; also in verse 12 [e] *12* That is, about 5 pounds or about 2.3 kilograms

8:6 *Place me like a seal over your heart.* The "seal" was typically a piece of clay with a stamp on it that identified the owner of whatever was sealed (see note on 1Ki 21:8). The woman's point is that she has possession of the man's heart, and no one else should be allowed in. The seal metaphor occurs in both Egyptian and Mesopotamian literature. In an Egyptian song, the wish is expressed for the lover to be a seal ring on his beloved's finger, and in Mesopotamia it refers to the wearing of a cylinder seal—"you placed him like a seal around your neck."
8:11 *Baal Hamon.* No place called Baal Hamon ("lord of uproar" or even "husband of a mob") is known to us, and no effort to identify such a location can be called successful.

OLD TESTAMENT

ORACLES OF THE PROPHETS

GOD'S PLAN ANNOUNCED THROUGH THE PROPHETS

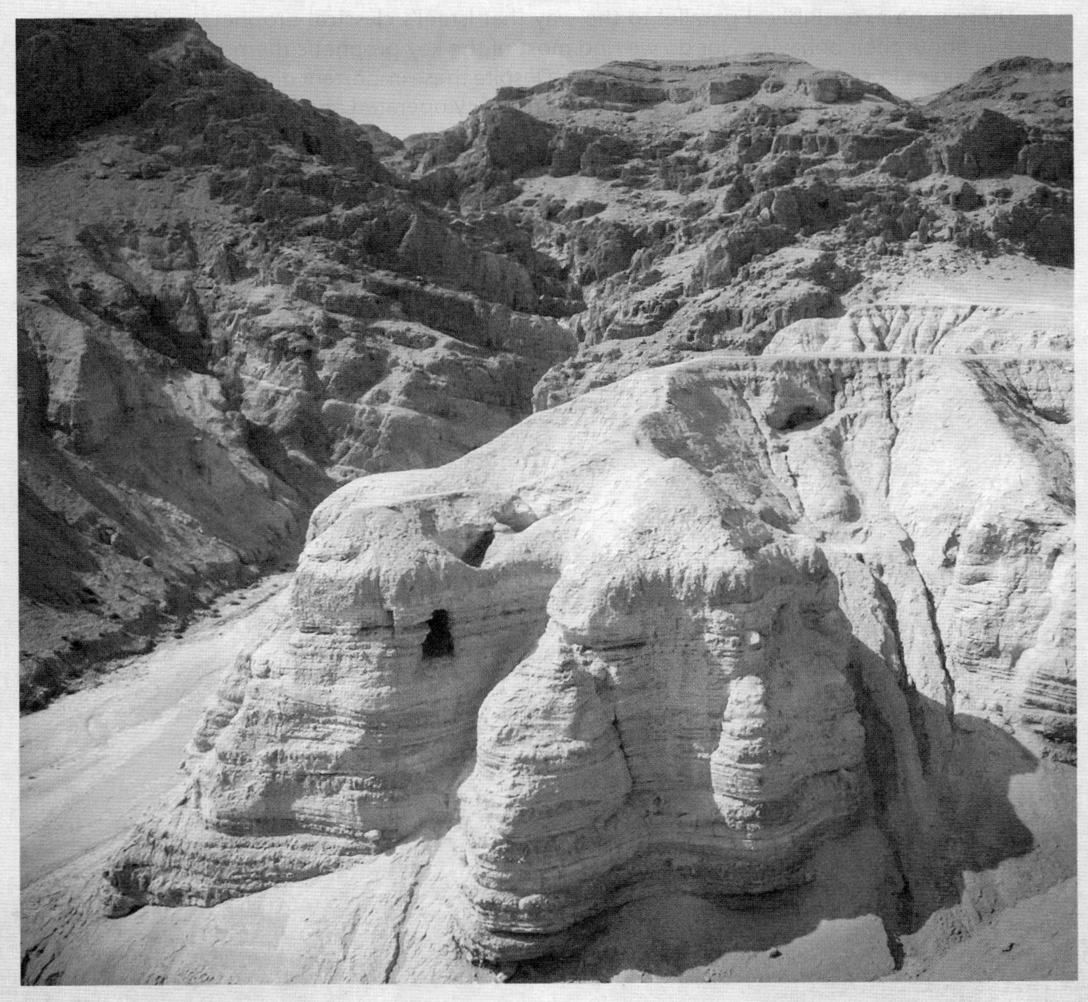

Introduction to the Oracles of the Prophets

One of the most distinctive literary genres of the OT is the prophetic literature. Since prophecy concerns the communication of messages from God to man, it is easy to conclude that such activity can only occur with a God who is real, active and intent on revealing himself. Consequently, Christians today would be naturally inclined to think that Israel was the only nation to experience prophecy because Yahweh is the only God who fills those qualifications. Nevertheless, even the Bible shows us that such is not the case; e.g., Elijah has to oppose the prophets of Baal and Asherah during the reign of Ahab (1Ki 18).

Texts mostly from Mesopotamia also confirm that prophets were active in the rest of the ancient world. The largest corpus of material comes from the eighteenth-century BC kingdom of Mari. About 50 letters to the king from administrators of outlying districts report on prophetic messages that were delivered to them to send to the king. A smaller corpus is available from Assyria in the seventh century BC. But there are no collections of oracles of particular prophets such as those found in Isaiah. The prophets of Mari and Assyria are more like the prophets we read about in the books of Kings and Chronicles: they appear on the scene to deliver a message to the king concerning what he should do to please the deity.

There is no extra-Biblical parallel to the way that Israel's classical prophets addressed the people about their behavior. Nor do we find most of the key prophetic themes addressed (e.g., impending exile, coming king, future kingdom). Despite these important differences, we can learn much from these texts about the way Israelite prophecy operated and how it was perceived by the contemporary audience. ◆

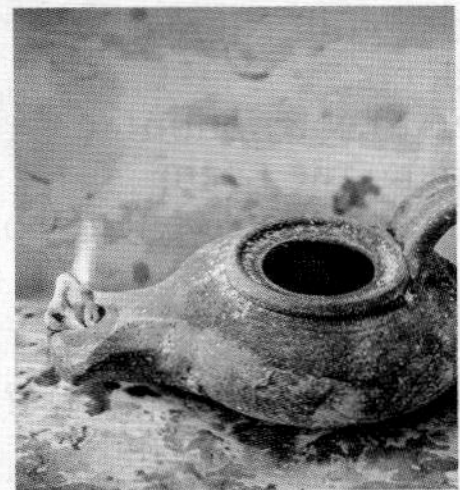

ORACLES OF THE PROPHETS

ISAIAH

Historical Setting

Isaiah prophesied during the latter half of the eighth century BC during the reign of four named kings (1:1). His prophecies did not simply concern his own era, however; they anticipated both horrifying and hopeful events in Judah's future. The prophecies describe a period of destruction and exile: many of the people would be deported far away from their own land, and the land itself would be ravaged and destroyed (586 BC). Some of the book of Isaiah addresses the situation of exile (chs. 40–55). This is not the end, however, since the exiles would return and the cities would be rebuilt (c. 535 BC). Other sections of the book seem to be directed toward this later situation (chs. 56–66).

KEY CONCEPTS

- Kings who trusted alliances brought on disaster, while kings who trusted in God experienced deliverance.
- Prophecy is not simply prediction of the future; it is God's revelation of himself, his requirements and his plan.
- It is important to have confidence in God's plan and trust him to carry it out.

Composition

The compositional history of Isaiah is debated, with numerous competing views as to the number of authors and the time of composition. There is no reason to doubt that Isaiah son of Amoz (1:1) is the authority figure whose words launch this collection and whose authority pervades it. Since the historical scope of the prophecy covers a period of over two centuries, it is possible that Isaiah's voice was joined by the voices of others who eventually compiled his words, though Isaiah's God-given prophetic gift could easily have allowed him to view these historical vistas himself. Even if other voices were joined to his, they clearly have all been subsumed under the authority of Isaiah.

We have come to understand that the main medium for prophets was oral proclamation. Though their prophecies (or some of them) may have been recorded from the start, others may have been preserved orally for a significant amount of time before being committed to writing. Writing of the prophetic books would in many cases bring conclusion to the communication and transmission process rather than stand at the beginning of the process. Prophets began by speaking rather than by writing. Many of them may not have personally written at all, their words only having been compiled at some later date. Even in such a scenario, however, these would still be considered the words of the prophet that had been passed down accurately. ◆

1 The vision[a] concerning Judah and Jerusalem[b] that Isaiah son of Amoz saw[c] during the reigns of Uzziah,[d] Jotham, Ahaz[e] and Hezekiah, kings of Judah.

A Rebellious Nation

2 Hear me, you heavens! Listen, earth!
For the LORD has spoken:[f]
"I reared children and brought
them up,
but they have rebelled[g] against me.
3 The ox knows its master,
the donkey its owner's manger,
but Israel does not know,[h]
my people do not understand."

4 Woe to the sinful nation,
a people whose guilt is great,
a brood of evildoers,[i]
children given to corruption!
They have forsaken the LORD;
they have spurned the Holy One[j] of
Israel
and turned their backs on him.

5 Why should you be beaten anymore?
Why do you persist in rebellion?[k]

1:1 [a] Nu 12:6 [b] Isa 40:9 [c] Isa 2:1 [d] 2Ch 26:22 [e] 2Ki 16:1 **1:2** [f] Mic 1:2 [g] Isa 30:1,9; 65:2 **1:3** [h] Jer 8:7; 9:3,6 **1:4** [i] Isa 14:20 [j] Isa 5:19,24 **1:5** [k] Isa 31:6

1:1 *The vision.* Most prophecies begin with a self-identification that can contain elements such as the type of literature, the identity of the prophet and the time period. These are indications that they contain actual messages to a real audience addressing real-life issues they were facing. "Vision" is a form of divine revelation that did not necessarily involve the physical eyes, since here it involves primarily words rather than images (cf. 2:1). Both prophets of Yahweh and pagan prophets experienced them. In Mesopotamia, even laypeople, both men and women, received visions or dreams from their gods. *Judah and Jerusalem.* After the split of the nation of Israel into two parts following the reign of Solomon: The northern nation was known as "Israel" or "Ephraim" (after its main tribe), with its capital in Samaria. The southern nation was "Judah" (after the main tribe occupying the area), with its capital in Jerusalem, which was also the site of the national religious shrine, the temple of Yahweh. *Isaiah son of Amoz.* In the ancient Near East a father's name commonly distinguished people with the same first name (cf. "Johnson"—son of John). This at times extended several generations, especially if an earlier ancestor had some claim to fame. Sometimes an earlier ancestor rather than the biological parent was used as an identifier. In this case, we have no specific information. *during the reigns of Uzziah … Hezekiah.* In 6:1 the commissioning of Isaiah is placed in the year Uzziah died, about 739 BC. Here it is indicated that Isaiah's prophetic ministry continued into the time of Hezekiah, at least until after the siege of Jerusalem by Sennacherib in 701 BC. This was a tumultuous half century that witnessed the rise and dominance of the Neo-Assyrian Empire, which was eventually responsible for the northern kingdom invasion, the fall of Samaria and the massive destruction in Judah. *kings of Judah.* Many OT prophecies give their date in relation to either an important event or the kings who ruled during a particular period. Similarly, in Mesopotamia documents are dated by using names of important officials, one of whose name was associated with each year. The OT is often more general, simply providing the reigns, though at times a specific year identification is given (see "The Challenging Chronology of the Kings of Israel and Judah," p. 596).
1:2 *Hear me, you heavens! Listen, earth!* Ancient Near Eastern covenants include witnesses to testify regarding covenant breach or obedience and to bring about the required punishment or blessing. They also heard the indictment in a lawsuit brought against a covenant breaker. These witnesses among Israel's neighbors included deities and elements of nature, such as heaven and earth (e.g., here; Dt 4:26; 30:19; 31:28) and things like mountains, rivers, sea and clouds.

Isaiah starts out his prophecy strong, issuing a summons to participate in a lawsuit against his people. This literary form, called a *rib*, is more specifically a suit against covenant breakers, with Israel and Judah often named as defendants (e.g., 3:13). The various personae in the suit show that it is heavily weighted against the defendant: Israel. The plaintiff is Yahweh, since it is his covenant that the defendant broke. The prosecuting attorney is the prophet, who de jure represents Yahweh. There is no defense attorney, and witnesses ("the heavens" and the "earth") are called either to testify to the wrongdoing or to observe the outcome of the trial. The judge, jury ("jury" in our way of thinking only, as there was nothing similar to a modern-day jury in the ancient world) and the one who carries out the punishment is Yahweh.
1:3 *The ox knows its master, the donkey its owner's manger.* Knowledgeable animals are commonly used in proverbial sayings. In their natural, untutored state, they know how to live and flourish in their environment. Egyptian wisdom acknowledges a dog as one recognizing its food source. This contrasts with human beings, according to Isaiah, who seemingly lack this basic survival instinct, turning against the very Creator and the order of his created universe. A Hurro-Hittite wisdom text has a deer irrationally turning against the source of its provisions, but the writer explicitly acknowledges that he is writing metaphorically of human beings: "It is not a deer, but a human." *Israel.* Deriving from the new name God conferred on Jacob (Ge 32:28), "Israel" came to designate the people of all 12 tribes descended from him. When the nation divided after the reign of Solomon, the northern kingdom used that name, while the southern kingdom was known as Judah. But the term could still refer to Judah, as it does here. It is therefore necessary to be careful in determining who "Israel" refers to, with context being the most important factor.
1:4 *sinful nation.* National sin is known of not only Israel but also her neighbors. The eighth-century BC Mesopotamian epic "Erra and Ishum" speaks of national destruction following a societal shift away from justice and righteousness in which families fail to care about one another's welfare. Divine abandonment of God's people follows their abandoning his established order. Famous city destructions in the ancient world are generally seen as a result of divine abandonment, which was usually either blamed on the violations the king had committed or accepted simply as being decreed by fate. *turned their backs.* An insulting sign of lack of interest and abandonment, in marked contrast to turning one's face toward someone in attention or obedience. Queen Hatshepsut showed dedication to her god by stating that she did not turn her back on her god. Merneptah in the Merneptah Stele claimed that he was able to conquer Libya because the protective god Seth "turned his back upon their chief."

Your whole head is injured,
your whole heart afflicted.[l]
6 From the sole of your foot to the top of your head
there is no soundness[m] —
only wounds and welts
and open sores,
not cleansed or bandaged[n]
or soothed with olive oil.[o]

7 Your country is desolate,[p]
your cities burned with fire;
your fields are being stripped by foreigners
right before you,
laid waste as when overthrown by strangers.
8 Daughter Zion is left
like a shelter in a vineyard,
like a hut[q] in a cucumber field,
like a city under siege.

9 Unless the LORD Almighty
had left us some survivors,[r]
we would have become like Sodom,
we would have been like Gomorrah.[s]

10 Hear the word of the LORD,[t]
you rulers of Sodom;[u]
listen to the instruction[v] of our God,
you people of Gomorrah!
11 "The multitude of your sacrifices —
what are they to me?" says the LORD.
"I have more than enough of burnt offerings,
of rams and the fat of fattened animals;[w]
I have no pleasure
in the blood of bulls[x] and lambs and goats.[y]
12 When you come to appear before me,
who has asked this of you,[z]
this trampling of my courts?

1:5 [l] Isa 33:6, 24
1:6 [m] Ps 38:3 [n] Isa 30:26; Jer 8:22 [o] Lk 10:34
1:7 [p] Lev 26:34
1:8 [q] Job 27:18
1:9 [r] Isa 10:20-22; 37:4, 31-32 [s] Ge 19:24; Ro 9:29*
1:10 [t] Isa 28:14 [u] Isa 3:9; Eze 16:49; Ro 9:29; Rev 11:8 [v] Isa 8:20
1:11 [w] Ps 50:8 [x] Jer 6:20 [y] 1Sa 15:22; Mal 1:10
1:12 [z] Ex 23:17

1:6 *not cleansed or bandaged or soothed with olive oil.* These procedures aided healing for injuries. Oil was an important element for wound treatment. While treatment of maladies is less frequently mentioned than their diagnosis, an Old Babylonian letter requests two measures of oil to treat and bandage a dog bite. An Akkadian text prescribes a treatment of bathing and anointing with oil. In Mesopotamia most oil was derived from the sesame seed, whereas in Israel it was derived from olives.

1:7 *fields … stripped … laid waste.* The devastation of the land was a natural consequence of invasion. Invading armies often lacked an adequate supply line and therefore expected to live off the land they were invading. What they didn't use for their own purposes, they destroyed. Not only were the crops burned, but the trampling of the land often crippled the agricultural prospects for several seasons afterward. Sometimes a land that was being attacked would even burn its own crops so that the enemy would not have the use of the food the people had worked so hard to grow. The elements included in this threat of divine destruction are typical. A well-known section of the Mesopotamian myth "Erra and Ishum" (from eighth-century BC Babylon) describes Erra's destructive intentions as including: devastating cities and making them a wilderness; destroying mountains, cattle and produce; wiping out the population; putting a fool on the throne; bringing a plague of wild beasts; and leveling the royal palace.

1:8 *Daughter Zion.* Zion was the original fortified mountain city that David conquered and claimed for his own. Jerusalem grew around this fortress. Common ancient Near Eastern practice was that smaller, unfortified cities or "suburbs" grew in proximity to a fortified location. If the surrounding areas, commonly called "daughters" of the fortress in the Bible, were attacked, inhabitants took refuge behind the walls of the fortress. Here Jerusalem is described as a daughter of Zion. *like a shelter … like a hut.* Field workers at times found protection from the elements in temporary shelters (10:29) in their fields, using them in order to remain close by during times of intense agricultural activity, but also to provide protection for the ripening crops (4:6). When they were no longer needed because the harvest season was finished, they were abandoned to fall apart. Jerusalem and Zion, the center of Israel's civil and religious life and a symbol of its national existence, will, in its punishment, become like a temporary lean-to, crumbling because it fills no further function, a non-guardian of a nonexistent crop. *like a city under siege.* Cities were generally fortified to protect against foreign incursion. Attackers had to find a way either to get in or to get the people out. The latter was accomplished by laying siege, surrounding the city (29:3), and not allowing anyone to enter or leave. Ashurbanipal (seventh century BC) describes his siege of Tyre as strangling their food supply. During the Amarna period (fourteenth century BC), the Canaanite ruler of Megiddo complained to the pharaoh about attacks by the king of Shechem. They were not able to leave the city to harvest their crops. This ultimately led either to capitulation or to disease, starvation and death by thirst. The Hittites and Egyptians used the same tactics.

1:9 *like Sodom … like Gomorrah.* Sodom and Gomorrah were prototypical bad cities in the OT because of their wickedness and subsequent destruction by an angry God (Ge 18:16 — 19:29). Jerusalem, God's covenant city, because of her equivalent evil (Isa 1:10), will be wiped out like them, exemplifying a covenant breaker's destruction (Dt 29:23).

1:11 *sacrifices … offerings.* Creation traditions in Egypt and Mesopotamia portrayed humanity as servants or cattle of the gods. Specifically, they were to provide food for the gods, relieving them of having to look after themselves. The means for doing so was sacrifice, at times identified as "food for the gods." Official Yahwism denied this function to Israel's sacrificial system, rarely describing the altar as God's "table," since he did not eat. A "table" was common in Mesopotamian ritual practice, as when King Rimush is said to have established daily offerings for the "table of Shamash." Israelites frequently forgot that God was not actually fed through sacrifice and sought to manipulate him through such offerings. It is this misuse of ritual that Isaiah and Amos condemn (e.g., Am 4:4 – 5).

1:12 *trampling of my courts.* The court was an open space enclosed by walls, surrounding or within a building; thus it had limited access. It was part of the palace and of the temple. In the case of religious sites, entry was restricted to those bringing offerings since this was a holy place. At times, the courts could be populated with worshipers. Illicit entry even into the outer court of the sanctuary defiled it, resulting in a severe punishment.

ISAIAH 1:1

The Historical Background of Isaiah

In the beginning of this period, Israel was controlled by Assyria, a major world power. Assyria's capital, Nineveh (modern-day Mosul in Iraq), was on the Tigris River, but Assyria's empire in this period stretched from what is now Iran as far west as Egypt. Lying across major land routes between Assyria and Egypt, Israel felt repeatedly the horrors of war and destruction.

Just prior to the period of Isaiah, there arose a succession of three Assyrian kings who were weaker and less aggressive than their predecessors, so Israel and Judah had enjoyed relative peace and prosperity. This came to an abrupt end in 745 BC when a new and powerful king gained the Assyrian throne. Tiglath-Pileser III (745 – 727 BC; 2Ki 15:29; cf. 2Ki 15:19, where he is called Pul) reinvigorated Assyrian expansion and aggression until the end of the Assyrian Empire, which occurred late in the following century. With Tiglath-Pileser's rise to power, the northern kingdom of Israel faced more imminent external pressure. Jeroboam II, Israel's king, had just died, and his dynasty was brought to an end by the assassination of his son Zechariah (2Ki 15:8 – 12), which was then followed by a rapid succession of multiple rulers, likely influenced by the Assyrian pressure (2Ki 15:19).

Judah's king Uzziah also died (740 BC; Isa 6:1), but his passing, though traumatic, was expected since he had been suffering from an incapacitating skin disease for some time and his son, Jotham, was effectively ruling in his place (2Ki 15:5). Jotham's reign was not seriously affected by Assyria directly; however, it was, ironically, affected by an alliance between Judah's sister nation, Israel (under Israel's king Pekah), and Israel's northern neighbor Aram (under Rezin) (2Ki 15:37). Israel and Aram allied against Judah, perhaps wanting Judah to join their coalition against Assyria, though their actual motives are unstated. They were too small to oppose Assyria on their own. Judah's refusal to join the Israel-Aram coalition led to the confrontation known as the Syro-Ephraimite War (2Ki 16:5 – 9; 2Ch 28:5 – 21; Isa 6 – 7), which particularly affected Ahaz, Jotham's son. Ahaz wavered back and forth as to whether to side with Assyria, which was strong and brutal, or Israel and Aram, which were stronger than Judah and also close by. He finally opted for a pro-Assyrian policy, against the urgings of Isaiah (Isa 7:7 – 9), and bribed Tiglath-Pileser to leave him alone and instead deal with the opposing alliance, which Tiglath-Pileser did in 734 – 732 BC (2Ki 16:7 – 9).

When Tiglath-Pileser died in 727 BC, his subjects, including Hoshea king of Israel, asserted their independence. Tiglath-Pileser's son and heir, Shalmaneser V (726 – 722 BC), soon reestablished control, and in 724 turned his attention to Israel, besieging its capital, Samaria (2Ki 17). It fell to Assyria in 722, with the deportation of many of its inhabitants. At about this time, Shalmaneser V died and was replaced by Sargon II, who claims to have made the final defeat of Samaria, though he could have just been responsible for the final mopping-up operations. Sargon also came against rebellions in the area at other times during his reign (e.g., Isa 20). More urgent, since they were closer to home, were the pressures from Babylonia under Marduk-apla-iddina (Marduk-Baladan, Isa 39:1), from Chaldea in southern Babylon.

Ahaz's son Hezekiah (sole reign: 715 – 697 BC, though he had coregencies with Ahaz [729 – 715] and Manasseh [697 – 686]) followed Ahaz on the throne, though Hezekiah did not follow Ahaz's foreign policy, since Hezekiah was strongly anti-Assyrian.

continued on next page

ANCIENT NEAR EASTERN MONARCHS: 750–530 BC*

DATE*	EGYPT	ASSYRIA	BABYLONIA	PERSIA
750	23rd Dynasty	Tiglath-Pileser III (745–727)		
725	24th Dynasty	Shalmaneser V (726–722)		
		Sargon II (722–705)		
	25th Dynasty			
700	Shabako (716–702)	Sennacherib (704–681)		
	Tirhakah (685–664)	Esarhaddon (680–669)		
675		Ashurbanipal (668–627)		
650				
625			Nabopolassar (626–605)	
600	Necho II (610–594)		Nebuchadnezzar (605–562)	
	Psammetichus II (594–589)			
	Hophra/Apries (589–570)			
575	Amasis (570–526)			
			Amel-Marduk (562–560)	
550			Neriglissar (560–556)	
			Cyrus (550–530)	
			Nabonidus (556–539)	
525				Cambyses (530–522)

* All dates are BC and are those of the kings' reigns.

Even so, Hezekiah apparently did not join a coalition against Assyria spearheaded by Philistia in 715–713 BC, which was short-lived, with the Philistine capital, Ashdod, destroyed (Isa 14:28–31; 20:1–6). Subduing his opponents to the west, Sargon turned to the south, soundly defeating Babylon in 710, but he was soon thereafter killed in battle. Again rebellion broke out among Assyria's vassals, including Babylonia under Marduk-apla-iddina/Marduk-Baladan (perhaps Isa 39:1 fits here) and Judah under Hezekiah in alliance with Philistia, Edom and Moab, apparently with Egyptian encouragement. Sargon's successor, Sennacherib (704–681), proved able and reestablished control over Babylon and then turned in his third campaign against Hezekiah and the west in 701. Sennacherib captured much of Judah, but he was able to take neither Hezekiah nor Jerusalem, possibly holding off due to payment of tribute.

Manasseh, Hezekiah's son, returned to Assyrian subservience under Sennacherib and Sennacherib's able son Esarhaddon (680–669 BC). Since Egypt had been instrumental in fomenting repeated rebellions, Assyria turned its military attention toward Egypt, going as far as destroying Thebes in 663 under the leadership of Ashurbanipal (668–627), Esarhaddon's son.

Pressures continued to rise against Assyria, not only from Egypt and Babylon, but also from the Indo-Aryans from the north, including the Medes. Upon Ashurbanipal's death, his successors were unable to maintain control, with Babylonia gaining self-rule in 626 BC under Nabopolassar. Joining with the Medes, Babylonia brought Assyria

continued on next page

to its knees, destroying its capital, Nineveh, in 612 BC and destroying the Assyrian Empire in 609.

During this period of weakness, Josiah (640–609 BC) won Judah's independence and reestablished worship of Israel's God. Josiah's son Jehoiakim was an Egyptian vassal, but in 605 the Babylonian ruler Nebuchadnezzar defeated the Egyptians at Carchemish. Jehoiakim changed his allegiance but soon rebelled, and he died during a Babylonian siege, leaving a desperate situation for his son Jehoiachin. At age 18, Jehoiachin was faced with an overwhelming force surrounding his city, which fell three months later, with the young king taken into exile. Babylon enthroned its own puppet king, Mattaniah (Jehoiachin's uncle), renaming him Zedekiah, thus showing complete control over him. The prophet Jeremiah warned Zedekiah that any defiance of Babylon was futile, since God himself was turning against his own wayward people. Zedekiah did not heed, so after a two-year siege, Jerusalem fell in July 586 BC. King Zedekiah was blinded and taken into exile, along with many of the people, and the temple and other important building were destroyed, as were the very walls of the city. Babylon then placed Gedaliah, who was not even of royal birth, over Judah as governor. This looked like the end of God's own people.

This was not the case, however, since the Neo-Babylonian Empire was itself short-lived. After its strongest and longest ruling king, Nebuchadnezzar (605–562 BC), died, three inferior monarchs reigned, but in the meantime a coalition was forming in the east between the Medes and the Persians. Under the able leadership of Cyrus, their armies moved in and brought the Neo-Babylonian Empire to an end in 539 BC. This had a direct impact on the Judahite exiles, since the Persians exercised a different foreign policy than the Assyrians and Babylonians. The latter took leading citizens of a captured nation into exile far away from their homes in order to lower the chances of them trying to liberate their country. Persia had the opposite policy, leaving them in their homes, or, in the case of Judah, allowing them to return to their native land if they so desired.

Not every Israelite in Babylonian exile took advantage of the opportunity to return to Judah (Ezr 2:64–65 numbers the returnees at 49,897). Life in Babylon and Persia was economically good for many, allowing some to reach high office (e.g., Esther) and live in relative comfort. A return to Judah, on the other hand, was difficult, as they faced hostile neighbors and the daunting task of rebuilding. The latter chapters in Isaiah apparently offer encouragement to such returnees. ◆

13 Stop bringing meaningless offerings![a]
Your incense[b] is detestable to me.
New Moons, Sabbaths and
convocations[c] —
I cannot bear your worthless
assemblies.
14 Your New Moon feasts and your
appointed festivals[d]
I hate with all my being.
They have become a burden to me;
I am weary[e] of bearing them.
15 When you spread out your hands in
prayer,
I hide[f] my eyes from you;
even when you offer many prayers,
I am not listening.

Your hands are full of blood![g]

1:13 [a] Isa 66:3 [b] Jer 7:9 [c] 1Ch 23:31 **1:14** [d] Lev 23:1-44; Nu 28:11-29:39; Isa 29:1 [e] Isa 7:13; 43:22, 24 **1:15** [f] Isa 8:17; 59:2; Mic 3:4 [g] Isa 59:3

1:13 *incense.* See 17:8. Part of Israel's sacrificial ritual was burning incense, made from various aromatic herbs, spices and resins (Ex 30:34–38; see note on Nu 16:7; cf. notes on Pr 27:9; SS 3:6). Among other ritual uses, it was burned on a special altar just in front of the entrance to the Most Holy Place in the tabernacle and temple. Apart from its function to provide a smoke screen for the presence of Yahweh, it muted the stench caused by slaughtering the sacrificial animals. *New Moons, Sabbaths and convocations.* Israel and other nations used a lunar calendar of about 28 days rather than our solar calendar. The turn of the new moon, marking a new month, was thus ritually important not only for Israel, but also for her neighbors. The Akkadian Atrahasis epic speaks of special activities revolving around the seven-day cycle. Ugarit records special rituals on that day, and Emar in north Syria had an annual New Moon festival lasting several days. In Israel, work was to cease and there were special offerings on these occasions (see notes on Nu 28:11; 1Sa 20:5; 2Ki 4:23).

1:15 *spread out your hands in prayer.* The same action accompanies some prayers and incantations in Akkadian literature, and one kind of prayer is called a "raising of

16 Wash and make yourselves clean.
Take your evil deeds out of my sight;[h]
stop doing wrong.[i]
17 Learn to do right; seek justice.[j]
Defend the oppressed.[a]
Take up the cause of the fatherless;[k]
plead the case of the widow.

18 "Come now, let us settle the matter,"[l]
says the LORD.
"Though your sins are like scarlet,
they shall be as white as snow;[m]
though they are red as crimson,
they shall be like wool.
19 If you are willing and obedient,
you will eat the good things of the land;[n]
20 but if you resist and rebel,
you will be devoured by the sword."[o]
For the mouth of the LORD
has spoken.[p]

21 See how the faithful city
has become a prostitute![q]
She once was full of justice;
righteousness used to dwell in her—
but now murderers!
22 Your silver has become dross,
your choice wine is diluted with water.

1:16 [h] Isa 52:11 [i] Isa 55:7; Jer 25:5 **1:17** [j] Zep 2:3 [k] Ps 82:3 **1:18** [l] Isa 41:1; 43:9,26 [m] Ps 51:7; Rev 7:14 **1:19** [n] Dt 30:15-16; Isa 55:2 **1:20** [o] Isa 3:25; 65:12 [p] Isa 34:16; 40:5; 58:14; Mic 4:4 **1:21** [q] Isa 57:3-9; Jer 2:20

[a] 17 Or *justice. / Correct the oppressor*

the hands" (*nish qate*). King Keret does this in the Ugaritic Keret epic. He brings sacrificial material to a high place and raises his hands heavenward. The action symbolizes supplication to a deity viewed as being "on high." Symbolic actions are used in many areas of life—religious (like here), relational (such as shaking hands today), and legal. The fact that these symbolize an inner or interpersonal reality is significant. *I hide my eyes … I am not listening.* The motif of the frustrated supplicant is well known in ancient literature. As an example, in the "Prayer to Every God" found in Ashurbanipal's library at Nineveh, the supplicant goes through a sequence of asking forgiveness from every deity for every offense he can imagine. He then laments that despite his contrition, no deity is willing to take him by the hand or stand by his side—no one hears him. From the standpoint of deity, a work like the "Lament Over the Destruction of Ur" reports that Anu and Enlil had determined not to heed the petitions for deliverance, but were determined to carry out their plans for destruction.

1:16 *Wash and make yourselves clean.* In addition to physical cleanliness, washing has symbolic meaning on the ritual level, since it is part of many sacrificial ceremonies. One Ugaritic purification rite describes the officiant washing his hands before offering a sacrifice. The Babylonian king Marduk-Baladan describes himself in a brick stamp as "king with clean hands," apparently indicating that he was suitable to rule. This is appropriate since Shamash, the god who enthrones and guides kings, "approves of clean hands." In an Akkadian cultic conflict text, after a fierce battle a king bathed himself in water, possibly with the dual purpose of physical and ritual cleansing.

1:17 Doing justice would be a basic requirement that any god would have for any people. In fact, the instruction given here could not be more formulaic. These are considered the responsibilities that any civilized society would have. Establishing justice and defending the vulnerable are the hallmarks of a successful king (see note on Ps 72; see also the articles "Enthronement in the Ancient Near East," p. 925; and "Coronation Hymns in the Ancient Near East," p. 949). The only difference between Israel and the rest of the ancient world in this area would concern how these responsibilities related to spiritual obligations. In the ancient Near East, the gods had the responsibility of maintaining justice. Part of that came to them for pragmatic reasons: oppressed people would be inclined to bother the gods with their continuous (annoying?) requests for relief. Furthermore, if injustice and violence ran rampant in society, people would not be free to make their gifts to the temple. More foundationally, it was believed that justice was built into the fabric of the cosmos, the laws of which were under the guardianship of the gods. The difference in the Israelite worldview was that in their belief, justice was built into the very character of God, and it was an attribute, not just a stewardship. Mesopotamians had the spiritual obligation to please the gods. This was accomplished primarily by rituals, but also by not "rocking the boat" of civilization.

1:18 *scarlet … white … red as crimson.* Even the cheapest dyes were likely not used regularly by the common folk for their everyday clothing, since these dyes were associated with luxury. White material, in contrast to that which is dyed, is in its pure, "clean" state, and the adjective also describes wool in Akkadian texts. In the Neo-Assyrian Marduk's Ordeal, the dead wear multicolored wool dyed that way by his red blood. In the Bible, the whiteness of snow is sometimes compared with a dreaded skin disease, so the color does not always indicate the positive notion, as it does here. There is a stark contrast between red and white in Mesopotamia as well. A ritual meant to avert evil refers to a red goat that will never become white. Both cases concern separation from evil. At the same time, red is never a symbol of evil in either the Bible or the ancient Near East.

1:21–23 *faithful city … prostitute … murderers … rebels … thieves.* If a king is supposed to maintain social order (see note on v. 17), social disintegration is a frightening prospect (59:3–8). In this case the turmoil has completely reversed the desired order. The Egyptian Prophecies of Neferti (early twentieth century BC) describe similar horrors.

1:22 *silver … dross.* Fine metals such as silver must be separated from base metals such as lead sulfide, in which they are usually suspended when found in their natural state. The process, called cupellation, heats the lead to 900–1000°F (482–539°C) in a small crucible (a cupel) made from bone ash. Most of the lead and other base metals oxidize because of the heat and are absorbed into the cupel, leaving purer silver or gold. Often this did not result in the purity necessary to work the metal, so further refinement was necessary. The metal was reheated, with impurities rising to the surface, where they could be skimmed off and discarded. The useless discard of the smelting process is the "dross." Another possible interpretation is that there was a mishap in the smelting process, and the pure and base metals did not separate sufficiently, so one was left with a useless slag, which is the dross. Only the purified metal (v. 25) could be worked to produce such things as fine jewelry. In this verse Isaiah offers a metaphor addressing the need for Israel to be purified. *choice wine is diluted with water.* The exact nature of this intoxicating drink is unclear, though the Hebrew term usually relates to an Akkadian word for a kind of beer. Beer was made from grain, mainly barley and wheat, or even dates—a staple in Mesopotamia and Egypt, where

ISAIAH 1

PROPHETS AND PROPHECY

In the OT, prophecy is a message from God; more precisely, a proclamation of God's perspective and plan. A prophet is best understood as a spokesperson for deity — a mouthpiece for God, though not a passive one. During the major periods of Biblical prophecy, the prophets arose in times of crisis and need. As the times of crisis came more frequently and were more serious, the prophets took on a greater prominence in the Biblical record. Beginning in the eighth century BC, prophecies were recorded and preserved, and they sooner or later found their way into the Biblical canon. The prophets from the eighth through the fifth centuries BC whose oracles are so preserved are called the "classical prophets," and they have their own distinctive characteristics. The prophets from before that time are referred to as the "preclassical prophets."

Evidence of the existence of a prophetic institution has been found throughout the ancient Near East. Among the Mari tablets from the eighteenth century BC, about 50 texts have been found in which local officials wrote to the king (Zimri-Lim) to inform him of prophecies that had been pronounced in their districts concerning him. Another group of prophecies came from the Neo-Assyrian Empire during the days of Esarhaddon and Ashurbanipal.

Despite some general similarities, there are clear differences between the prophetic traditions of Israel and those of the rest of the ancient Near East. In the prophecies from the ancient Near East the king was the one addressed, rather than the people as a whole. The messages generally concerned ritual activity, military matters or building projects. Sometimes the messages encouraged the king in particular activities (which is especially true of the Neo-Assyrian examples), while at other times they could be quite critical. Frequently the prophets of the ancient Near East received their messages through dreams, visions or trances, though at other times the mode of revelation is not stated. A variety of deities was represented by these prophets in the extant literature.

The Biblical prophets would not have thought of themselves as people who predicted the future; they simply engaged in proclaiming the plan of God, whether that pertained to past, present or future. They were champions of the covenant who called God's people Israel back to faithfulness. The general belief was that the prophet had access to the divine council and got to listen in on the deliberations there, and they carried messages for the people that conveyed reports from those deliberations. ◆

23 Your rulers are rebels,
partners with thieves;
they all love bribes[r]
and chase after gifts.
They do not defend the cause of the
fatherless;
the widow's case does not come
before them.[s]
24 Therefore the Lord, the LORD Almighty,
the Mighty One of Israel, declares:
"Ah! I will vent my wrath on my foes
and avenge[t] myself on my enemies.

1:23 [r] Ex 23:8 [s] Isa 10:2; Jer 5:28; Eze 22:6-7; Zec 7:10 **1:24** [t] Isa 35:4; 59:17; 61:2; 63:4

grapes for wine were harder to come by. Beer was also made in Israel, as evidenced by a brewery at Tel Goren, near En Gedi. Its intoxicating power was proverbial, with an Egyptian lover expressing his "high" from his lover's kisses rather than from beer.

1:23 *bribes.* This may be overplaying the term, which could be a gratuity proffered in order that a case might be moved up in priority so it could be heard in an overcrowded court docket — not that the verdict might be swayed through payment. *gifts.* The specific term can be an innocuous greeting gift, somewhat like modern hostess gifts. *fatherless … widow's case.* A major aspect of Israelite legal tradition involves making provision for groups classified as weak or poor: widows, orphans and the resident foreigner (Ex 22:22; Dt 10:18 – 19; 24:17 – 21). Concern for the needy is evident in Mesopotamian legal collections as early as the mid-third millennium BC, and generally addresses protection of rights and guarantee of justice in the courts. Based on very

[25] I will turn my hand against you;[a]
I will thoroughly purge away your dross
and remove all your impurities.[u]
[26] I will restore your leaders as in days of old,[v]
your rulers as at the beginning.
Afterward you will be called
the City of Righteousness,[w]
the Faithful City.[x]"
[27] Zion will be delivered with justice,
her penitent ones with righteousness.[y]
[28] But rebels and sinners will both be broken,
and those who forsake the LORD will perish.[z]
[29] "You will be ashamed because of the sacred oaks[a]
in which you have delighted;
you will be disgraced because of the gardens[b]
that you have chosen.
[30] You will be like an oak with fading leaves,
like a garden without water.
[31] The mighty man will become tinder
and his work a spark;
both will burn together,
with no one to quench the fire.[c]"

1:25 [u] Eze 22:22; Mal 3:3 **1:26** [v] Jer 33:7, 11 [w] Isa 33:5; 62:1; Zec 8:3 [x] Isa 60:14; 62:2 **1:27** [y] Isa 35:10; 62:12; 63:4 **1:28** [z] Ps 9:5; Isa 24:20; 66:24; 2Th 1:8-9 **1:29** [a] Isa 57:5 [b] Isa 65:3; 66:17 **1:31** [c] Isa 5:24; 9:18-19; 26:11; 33:14; 66:15-16,24 **2:1** [d] Isa 1:1 **2:2** [e] Isa 27:13; 56:7; 66:20; Mic 4:7

The Mountain of the LORD

2:1-4pp — Mic 4:1-3

2 This is what Isaiah son of Amoz saw concerning Judah and Jerusalem:[d]

[2] In the last days

the mountain[e] of the LORD's temple
will be established
as the highest of the mountains;
it will be exalted above the hills,
and all nations will stream to it.

[3] Many peoples will come and say,

"Come, let us go up to the mountain of the LORD,
to the temple of the God of Jacob.

[a] 25 That is, against Jerusalem

early statements in the prologues of the Ur-Nammu Code and the Code of Hammurapi, it is clear that kings considered it part of their role as wise rulers to protect the rights of the poor, the widow and the orphan (see notes on Ps 72; Isa 1:17; see also the articles "Enthronement in the Ancient Near East," p. 925; "Coronation Hymns in the Ancient Near East," p. 949). Similarly, in the Egyptian tale of the "Eloquent Peasant," the plaintiff begins by identifying his judge as the father of the orphan, the husband of the widow. This reflects a universal concern that the vulnerable classes be provided for throughout the ancient Near East.

1:28 *broken.* Breaking people as a punishment or in defeat is a common literary metaphor (8:15; 28:13). The Egyptians frequently wrote the names of their enemies on pieces of pottery or on clay figurines that they then smashed, which symbolized the metaphoric "breaking" of their enemies and invoked a curse upon them. Like the names that were broken, people prayed that the gods would work through sympathetic magic to break those named.

1:29 *sacred oaks … gardens.* Green trees and watered gardens were rare and special places among those living in (semi-)arid conditions like those found in the ancient Near East. Ashurnasirpal II boasted of collecting and planting many exotic trees and plants in his garden in Calah/Nimrud, while Nebuchadnezzar II of Babylon was proud of his terraced ("hanging") palace gardens, which were among the seven wonders of the ancient world. These were places not only of relaxation but also of worship, since gardens, sacred trees and groves were important in Canaanite and Mesopotamian popular religion. Part of the royal funerary rites seems to take place in the royal garden, and trees in particular seem to be imbued with life, not only for pagan neighbors of Israel, but even at creation. Israel herself is seduced by this cult of life and fertility and condemned for succumbing (57:5).

Trees even become objects of worship either in their own right or as symbols of a deity. Seals and scarabs found in Israel show people kneeling and also raising their hands in worship before trees. One Egyptian scene depicts a life-giving divine tree with a female breast suckling a human; in another it offers a kneeling worshiper a tray of food.

Trees were also associated with the goddess Asherah, whose cultic tree symbol is associated with Yahweh in an enigmatic inscription from Kuntillet Ajrud, an Iron Age II site in Sinai: "Yahweh of Samaria and his asherah" (see note on 44:24); there is an accompanying picture of two ibexes nibbling from a tree. This clearly illuminates syncretism among the Israelites, whose worship in gardens (65:3; 66:17) and groves God will turn to nothing by withholding water from them both (v. 30).

2:2 *mountain of the LORD's temple … highest of the mountains … exalted.* Jerusalem is situated high in the hill country of eastern Israel and physically looks down on the surrounding terrain. Visitors had to go up to visit it and within it had to climb even more to get to the temple, which overlooked the rest of the city. Israel's neighbors also associated sanctuaries and divine worship with mountains. In Ugaritic texts, Mount Zaphon is the place of Baal's mountain palace, and El, the chief Canaanite god, also resided on a mountain. The Sumerian king Gudea recorded his temple building activities in the late third millennium BC and spoke of making the temple with its head high in the mountains — indeed, it is said to grow high like a mountain range. The city of Babylon is also to be raised to the sky. See note on Ps 48:1 – 2. *all nations will stream to it.* Texts as early as 2000 BC speak of the universal appeal that will characterize a new temple. Temples are where prophecies are given to decide legal disputes and where one can inquire of the deity regarding courses of action that should be taken. It is not unusual for foreign people, even kings, to travel great distances to consult a deity. Gudea also envisions visitors from afar. If a god displays wisdom and power, all who hear will receive benefit.

2:3 – 4 *let us go up … He will teach us … He will judge … and will settle disputes.* In a prophecy concerning Ashurbanipal when he was yet crown prince, it was proclaimed that all the nations would come up to him and that he would rule over them and judge between them. In terms similar to those in Isaiah, guidance for life and decision making come from the great king, who is modeled after the Ashur, the ideal king.

He will teach us his ways,
so that we may walk in his paths."
The law[f] will go out from Zion,
the word of the LORD from Jerusalem.[g]
4 He will judge between the nations
and will settle disputes for many peoples.
They will beat their swords into plowshares
and their spears into pruning hooks.[h]
Nation will not take up sword against nation,[i]
nor will they train for war anymore.
5 Come, descendants of Jacob,[j]
let us walk in the light[k] of the LORD.

The Day of the LORD

6 You, LORD, have abandoned[l] your people,
the descendants of Jacob.
They are full of superstitions from the East;
they practice divination like the Philistines[m]
and embrace[n] pagan customs.[o]
7 Their land is full of silver and gold;
there is no end to their treasures.
Their land is full of horses;[p]
there is no end to their chariots.[q]
8 Their land is full of idols;[r]
they bow down to the work of their hands,
to what their fingers[s] have made.
9 So people will be brought low[t]
and everyone humbled[u] —
do not forgive them.[a][v]
10 Go into the rocks, hide in the ground
from the fearful presence of the LORD
and the splendor of his majesty![w]

2:3 [f] Isa 51:4,7 [g] Lk 24:47 **2:4** [h] Joel 3:10 [i] Ps 46:9; Isa 9:5; 11:6-9; 32:18; Hos 2:18; Zec 9:10 **2:5** [j] Isa 58:1 [k] Isa 60:1, 19-20; 1Jn 1:5,7 **2:6** [l] Dt 31:17 [m] 2Ki 1:2 [n] Pr 6:1 [o] 2Ki 16:7 **2:7** [p] Dt 17:16 [q] Isa 31:1; Mic 5:10 **2:8** [r] Isa 10:9-11 [s] Isa 17:8 **2:9** [t] Ps 62:9 [u] Isa 5:15 [v] Ne 4:5 **2:10** [w] 2Th 1:9; Rev 6:15-16

[a] 9 Or *not raise them up*

2:4 *beat their swords into plowshares.* Beating here has the connotation of breaking into pieces. When swords are broken, the resultant pieces of metal can be used to strengthen and sharpen the wooden tips of plow blades, called shares. They were used to loosen the soil, scratching out a furrow in which to plant. *spears into pruning hooks.* Spears could have straight or curved blades. When broken they could yield smaller, handheld tools resembling a sickle. These could be sharpened and used as small, curved knives to trim grape vines (18:5). Since God will resolve international disputes, weapons can be put to more peaceful and productive use.

2:6 *superstitions ... divination.* People desire to hear from the divine, especially as regards the future, and so seek revelation in a number of different ways. In Israel, God regularly revealed himself through his prophets in the form of visions, dreams, etc. He also responded to queries through other, less common means such as casting lots (e.g., Jos 18–19; 1Sa 14:41–42; Ac 1:26). The latter, using physical, mechanical means to question a god, is common among Israel's neighbors, and is called "divination." It comes in numerous forms and is strongly condemned as unsuitable for Israel, whose God is not to be so manipulated (e.g., Dt 18:9–14). See notes on Ge 30:27; Dt 18:10; 1Sa 28:7; see also the articles "Balaam," p. 268; "Magic," p. 326; "Consulting a 'Spirit,'" p. 508; "Practice of Magic," p. 627; "Extispicy," p. 650.

Three forms of divination are mentioned in Eze 21:21: When a Babylonian king needs to decide which direction to take, it is said that "he will cast lots with arrows, he will consult his idols, he will examine the liver." A divination technique called rhabdomancy uses arrows or sticks that are thrown to the ground, and an interpretation is made depending on how they fall (see Hos 4:12). Idol consultation used a type of household god (Hebrew *teraphim*; Ge 31:19,34,35; Zec 10:2), which was somehow expected to speak. Very common in Mesopotamia is hepatoscopy or extispicy, the examination of animal entrails, in particular the liver. They would be carefully inspected by trained priests, who would check for abnormalities. These would indicate some communication from the god regarding the future course of events. In order to stop Israel from misusing animal livers in such a way, part of the liver taken from animal sacrifices was to be completely burned (e.g., Ex 29:13).

Other types of divination were also used. In necromancy one consulted with the dead, such as when Saul consulted Samuel through a medium at Endor (1Sa 28:8–19; see notes on 1Sa 28:7; 2Ki 21:6; see also the article "Consulting a 'Spirit,'" p. 508). Mesopotamia was also the source for the practice of astrology, consultation of the heavenly bodies (see Isa 47:13; Jer 10:2; Mt 2:9). In hydromancy, people interpreted the patterns of oil placed on water in a cup or bowl (e.g., Ge 44:5,15), much like reading tea leaves today. In a practice not referred to in the Bible, Mesopotamian and Canaanite priests also inferred meaning from abnormal animal and human births.

Though Scripture condemns these practices, this is not because they do not work. There is supernatural power in the occult, but it is not open to followers of the true God. Israel depends on God's self-revelation rather than manipulating nature to find out secrets (see note on 7:11).

On an individual level, a reason to know the future was to be able take action against any evil that might be coming. Incantations and magic charms were used for protection against these. For Israel, the power to protect and heal did not lie in magic or in human strength, but in God, who welcomed prayer and was ready to protect and save (e.g., Jos 10:6; 1Sa 10:19).

2:7 *horses ... chariots.* Assyrian chariots were large, carrying four men, and pulled by four horses. The chariotry corps and cavalry represented the cutting edge of military technology. Vast economic resources were required to import the horses, build the chariots, and train the horsemen and charioteers (for an indication of the expense, see 1Ki 10:29). Assyrian military supremacy was dependent on the horses and even the kings worried about the supply of horses and gathering the necessary fodder to care for the horses. Careful census figures were kept of the types of horses available and horses were often collected in tribute or captured in raids. Reliefs show great care taken with the horses, and the army on campaign traveled with principal mounts as well as remounts for the cavalry. See notes on Dt 11:4; Jos 11:6; Jdg 1:19; see also the article "All the King's Horses," p. 720.

2:8 *idols ... what their fingers have made.* See the article "Making an Idol," p. 1010.

2:10 *the fearful presence of the LORD ... splendor.* Israel's God, Yahweh, is without physical body and form and so

[11]The eyes of the arrogant will be humbled
and human pride[x] brought low;
the LORD alone will be exalted in that day.
[12]The LORD Almighty has a day in store
for all the proud and lofty,
for all that is exalted[y]
(and they will be humbled),[z]
[13]for all the cedars of Lebanon, tall and lofty,
and all the oaks of Bashan,[a]
[14]for all the towering mountains
and all the high hills,[b]
[15]for every lofty tower
and every fortified wall,[c]
[16]for every trading ship[a][d]
and every stately vessel.
[17]The arrogance of man will be brought low
and human pride humbled;
the LORD alone will be exalted in that day,[e]
[18] and the idols will totally disappear.[f]
[19]People will flee to caves in the rocks
and to holes in the ground
from the fearful presence of the LORD
and the splendor of his majesty,
when he rises to shake the earth.[g]
[20]In that day people will throw away
to the moles and bats[h]
their idols of silver and idols of gold,
which they made to worship.
[21]They will flee to caverns in the rocks
and to the overhanging crags
from the fearful presence of the LORD
and the splendor of his majesty,
when he rises to shake the earth.[i]
[22]Stop trusting in mere humans,[j]
who have but a breath in their nostrils.
Why hold them in esteem?[k]

Judgment on Jerusalem and Judah

3 See now, the Lord,
the LORD Almighty,
is about to take from Jerusalem and Judah
both supply and support:
all supplies of food[l] and all supplies of water,[m]
2 the hero and the warrior,[n]
the judge and the prophet,
the diviner and the elder,[o]

2:11 [x]Isa 5:15; 37:23 **2:12** [y]Isa 24:4, 21; Mal 4:1 [z]Job 40:11 **2:13** [a]Zec 11:2 **2:14** [b]Isa 30:25; 40:4 **2:15** [c]Isa 25:2, 12 **2:16** [d]1Ki 10:22 **2:17** [e]ver 11 **2:18** [f]Isa 21:9 **2:19** [g]Heb 12:26 **2:20** [h]Lev 11:19 **2:21** [i]ver 19 **2:22** [j]Ps 146:3; Jer 17:5 [k]Ps 8:4; 144:3; Isa 40:15; Jas 4:14 **3:1** [l]Lev 26:26 [m]Isa 5:13; Eze 4:16 **3:2** [n]Eze 17:13 [o]2Ki 24:14; Isa 9:14-15

[a] 16 Hebrew *every ship of Tarshish*

is not visible. He has, however, a divine aura or radiance, his "glory," which is apparent to the human eye (see the article "Glory," p. 178). Medieval paintings used a halo to depict this (a circle of light above or behind the head to signify sacred persons, or, alternatively, the full-body glow [called a mandorla or aureole], symbolizing divine status). Egyptian art used the sun disk over the head of several of their deities to indicate their divine status. Akkadian texts refer to the (*pulhu*) *melammu*, the (fear-causing) radiance that characterized not only deities but also other awe-inspiring beings such as demons and kings. Several accounts of royal battles refer to this terror transferred to the king (and his army), overwhelming the enemy and leading to their defeat. Adadnirari III, e.g., describes his campaign against the Hittites in the early eighth century BC in terms of their submission to his fearful splendor.
2:13 *cedars of Lebanon.* See notes on 2Sa 5:11; 1Ki 5:6; 6:15. *Bashan.* See note on Nu 21:33.
2:15 *fortified wall.* City fortifications were necessary in the ancient Near East in order to protect inhabitants against marauders. It was a matter of pride for a city to be fortified. Built of stamped earth, brick or stone, the walls of this period were solid and could be massive, with towers placed periodically along them. In some cases, there were both inner and outer protective walls (26:1). At Lachish, the outer wall was almost 10 feet (3 meters) thick, and the inner wall was almost 20 feet (6 meters) thick. At Khorsabad, the fortress of Sargon II, the city wall was 46 feet (14 meters) thick and almost 40 feet (12 meters) high; at Nineveh among Sennacherib's building projects was a wall that could have been as much as 75 feet (23 meters) tall, though the exact height is difficult to determine, since no walls are found completely intact and height was usually measured by brick courses.
2:16 *trading ship.* Lit. "ships of Tarshish," merchant ships that carried heavy cargo (see notes on 23:1; 60:9; 1Ki 10:22; 2Ch 8:18). They were probably single-mast vessels with a single row of oars. Shipping was not among Israel's major trades, since she had few good ports, though it had some role even early in her history (cf. Jdg 5:17). Solomon established a Red Sea port at Ezion Geber in cooperation with Hiram of Tyre (see note on 1Ki 9:26). Shipping played a more major role in Ugarit, farther up the Mediterranean coast in the area of Tyre, where there is a contract for ships rented to another king. Warships were larger and could have several decks and oar banks. Both add to the prestige and wealth of their owner nations, but their pride will be brought down by God.
2:18 *idols will totally disappear.* A disappearing personal god strikes its worshiper with despair, since help is no longer available. Antagonistic gods need to be repulsed, however, which is done by means of incantations and amulets. A seventh-century BC amulet from Syria seeks to repel a warrior-god named Sasm with the anticipated result that he will pass away and never come back.
2:19 *caves in the rocks ... holes.* The powerful strongholds (v. 15) will be ineffective, and people will take up living in unnatural conditions. *shake the earth.* The awe-inspiring coming of God (v. 10) causes not only people but also nature to quake in terror. His coming, called a theophany, is often accompanied by earth-shaking phenomena. Assyrian kings associate the same convulsion with their coming.
2:20 *moles and bats.* Ineffective idols will be discarded to be with unclean rodents. The Sumerian poetess Enheduanna, in a third-millennium BC text, exalts the goddess Inanna, before whom none of the other gods are able to stand. Rather, they flutter like bats as they flee. Lifeless idols will flee to crannies before the all-powerful God, just as the other gods do before Inanna.
2:21 *shake the earth.* See note on v. 19.
3:1 *take ... all supplies of food and ... water.* See note on 1:8.
3:2–3 The list of leadership resources here is fairly extensive, covering the military, clan leadership, religious

3 the captain of fifty and the man of
rank,
the counselor, skilled craftsman and
clever enchanter.

4 "I will make mere youths their
officials;
children will rule over them."[p]

5 People will oppress each other —
man against man, neighbor against
neighbor.[q]
The young will rise up against the old,
the nobody against the honored.

6 A man will seize one of his brothers
in his father's house, and say,
"You have a cloak, you be our leader;
take charge of this heap of ruins!"
7 But in that day he will cry out,
"I have no remedy.[r]
I have no food or clothing in my
house;
do not make me the leader of the
people."

8 Jerusalem staggers,
Judah is falling;[s]
their words[t] and deeds are against the
LORD,
defying[u] his glorious presence.
9 The look on their faces testifies against
them;
they parade their sin like Sodom;[v]
they do not hide it.
Woe to them!
They have brought disaster[w] upon
themselves.

10 Tell the righteous it will be well[x] with
them,
for they will enjoy the fruit of their
deeds.[y]
11 Woe to the wicked!
Disaster[z] is upon them!
They will be paid back
for what their hands have done.

12 Youths[a] oppress my people,
women rule over them.
My people, your guides lead you
astray;[b]
they turn you from the path.

13 The LORD takes his place in court;
he rises to judge[c] the people.
14 The LORD enters into judgment[d]
against the elders and leaders of his
people:
"It is you who have ruined my
vineyard;
the plunder[e] from the poor is in your
houses.
15 What do you mean by crushing my
people[f]
and grinding the faces of the poor?"
declares the Lord,
the LORD Almighty.

16 The LORD says,
"The women of Zion[g] are haughty,
walking along with outstretched necks,
flirting with their eyes,
strutting along with swaying hips,
with ornaments jingling on their
ankles.
17 Therefore the Lord will bring sores
on the heads of the women of
Zion;
the LORD will make their scalps
bald."

3:4 [p] Ecc 10:16 *fn* **3:5** [q] Isa 9:19; Jer 9:8; Mic 7:2,6 **3:7** [r] Eze 34:4; Hos 5:13 **3:8** [s] Isa 1:7 [t] Isa 9:15, 17 [u] Ps 73:9, 11 **3:9** [v] Ge 13:13 [w] Pr 8:36; Ro 6:23 **3:10** [x] Dt 28:1-14 [y] Ps 128:2 **3:11** [z] Dt 28:15-68 **3:12** [a] ver 4 [b] Isa 9:16 **3:13** [c] Mic 6:2 **3:14** [d] Job 22:4 [e] Job 24:9; Jas 2:6 **3:15** [f] Ps 94:5 **3:16** [g] SS 3:11

personnel (both legitimate and illegitimate) and political advisors. All of these, considered to supply leadership support for the people, whether officially or in a clandestine manner, will be removed and replaced by unexpected leaders (v. 4).

3:2 *diviner.* An illegitimate source of divine revelation used by Israel's pagan neighbors but forbidden for her (see notes on 2:6; Ge 30:27; Dt 18:10; see also the articles "Balaam," p. 268; "Magic," p. 326; "Practice of Magic," p. 627).

3:3 *enchanter.* Or "whisperer." They were also unacceptable in Israel, but were still found among the people charming snakes (Ecc 10:11).

3:6 *cloak.* Or robe, the outer garment used to cover oneself. This could indicate that people were so destitute that the last one having all of his clothes left would be chosen leader. This is also a soldier's garment (9:5); it could have been fringed and embroidered, as were robes of various social classes and nationalities as shown on the Black Obelisk of Shalmaneser III. This, then, could be a call for leadership from anyone who had some evidence of being able to offer it, even if only through their official-looking garments.

3:13 *The LORD takes his place ... rises to judge.* Numerous pictures of ancient Near Eastern deities show them seated while receiving worship. When standing, the deities are more aggressive, often with weapons as instruments of judgment.

3:15 *crushing my people and grinding the faces.* Ashurnasirpal II describes Tukulti-Ninurta II using similar terms. A Middle Babylonian boundary stone includes a curse that anyone who moves the boundary stone might have their descendants crushed. The metaphor of military defeat is also depicted literally, with the king actually walking on his defeated enemies.

3:16 *haughty ... outstretched necks ... ornaments jingling on their ankles.* Pictorial representation of common folk is rare in the period of the Bible, since the upper classes receive more attention. Commoners probably wore little personal adornment. Others used greater finery, including solid bronze rings placed on the ankle. The outstretched neck could be simply a prideful posture, or it could have been caused by wearing numerous necklaces, physically forcing the outstretched posture.

3:17 *bald.* Baldness, especially among women, was not customary, and most wore well-coifed hair. Shaving all or part of the head of someone was a sign of disrespect (7:20) or mourning (15:2). A special haircut also seemed to be the mark of a slave, as noted in the Code of Hammurapi. The formally prim and proper upper-class women will be either humiliated or enslaved.

Various robes and hems shown on the Black Obelisk of Shalmaneser III, Assyrian, 858 to 824 BC. See note on Isa 3:6.

18 In that day the Lord will snatch away
their finery: the bangles and headbands
and crescent necklaces,[h] 19 the earrings
and bracelets and veils, 20 the headdresses[i] and anklets and sashes, the perfume
bottles and charms, 21 the signet rings and
nose rings, 22 the fine robes and the capes
and cloaks, the purses 23 and mirrors, and
the linen garments and tiaras and shawls.

24 Instead of fragrance[j] there will be a
stench;
instead of a sash,[k] a rope;
instead of well-dressed hair, baldness;[l]
instead of fine clothing, sackcloth;[m]
instead of beauty,[n] branding.
25 Your men will fall by the sword,[o]
your warriors in battle.
26 The gates of Zion will lament and
mourn;[p]
destitute, she will sit on the ground.[q]

4 1 In that day seven women
will take hold of one man[r]
and say, "We will eat our own food[s]
and provide our own clothes;

3:18 [h] Jdg 8:21
3:20 [i] Ex 39:28
3:24 [j] Est 2:12
[k] Pr 31:24
[l] Isa 22:12
[m] La 2:10; Eze 27:30-31
[n] 1Pe 3:3
3:25 [o] Isa 1:20
3:26 [p] Jer 14:2
[q] La 2:10
4:1 [r] Isa 13:12
[s] 2Th 3:12

3:18–23 These verses give the most extensive list of personal adornment in the Bible. Some terms are rare and not at all clearly understood. "Finery" (v. 18) is the general term, encompassing the list that follows, referring first to jewelry (vv. 18–21) and then to clothing (vv. 22–23).
3:18 *bangles.* The ankle bracelets mentioned in v. 16. *headbands.* Ornaments resembling or representing the sun, showing Egyptian influence. They are common in Israelite seals. *crescent necklaces.* Like the moon, possibly showing influence from the moon-god of Harran or from the Canaanites at Ugarit.
3:19 *earrings.* Lit. "drops," indicating their pendant shape; worn by men and women.
3:20 *headdresses.* Or turbans; were worn by Israel and her neighbors. *perfume bottles.* It is hard to imagine these serving as an item of clothing, so they are possibly a type of amulet, paralleling the "charms" mentioned next (cf. the same root, "whispering," in v. 3 ["enchanter"]). These items have been found in excavations.
3:21 *signet rings.* Or seal rings; used by some officials as a symbol of authority and worn on the finger. They left an impression when pressed into a clay writing tablet (see note on 1Ki 21:8). Other rings were worn in the nose.
3:24 *well-dressed hair.* Hair not only distinguished individuals, as it does to today, but ethnic groups could be discerned by their differing hairstyles. Elaborate hairstyles were worn by gods and leaders in Mesopotamia and Egypt. Nice hair was prized, as shown by a text describing someone as "provided with beautiful hair." Included among other gifts in a letter from Amarna were "29 silver ladles, with boxwood and ebony handles, which are for curling hair." *baldness.* See note on v. 17.
3:26 *sit on the ground.* Extreme emotion is debilitating, affecting the ability to stand. Utnapishtim experienced this when he saw the destruction of his fellow human beings after the flood in the Babylonian Gilgamesh Epic. He said, "Consequently I crouched, I sat down, I wept."
4:1 *seven women will take hold of one man.* One of the unfortunate results of war is the depletion of the male population, resulting in a higher ratio of women to men. In the ancient world, women were under the care of various men during their lives—first their fathers, then their husbands, then their sons. If these were lost through death or divorce, the woman and her children were placed in a precarious position, not the least reason being that land, the major resource of an agricultural people,

only let us be called by your name.
Take away our disgrace!"[t]

The Branch of the LORD

[2]In that day the Branch of the LORD[u] will
be beautiful and glorious, and the fruit[v]
of the land will be the pride and glory of
the survivors in Israel. [3]Those who are
left in Zion, who remain[w] in Jerusalem,
will be called holy,[x] all who are recorded[y]
among the living in Jerusalem. [4]The Lord
will wash away the filth[z] of the women of
Zion; he will cleanse the bloodstains[a] from
Jerusalem by a spirit[a] of judgment[b] and a
spirit[a] of fire.[c] [5]Then the LORD will create
over all of Mount Zion and over those who
assemble there a cloud of smoke by day
and a glow of flaming fire by night;[d] over
everything the glory[be] will be a canopy. [6]It
will be a shelter[f] and shade from the heat
of the day, and a refuge[g] and hiding place
from the storm and rain.

4:1 [t]Ge 30:23 **4:2** [u]Isa 11:1-5; 53:2; Jer 23:5-6; Zec 3:8; 6:12 [v]Ps 72:16 **4:3** [w]Ro 11:5 [x]Isa 52:1; 60:21 [y]Lk 10:20 **4:4** [z]Isa 3:24 [a]Isa 1:15 [b]Isa 28:6 [c]Isa 1:31; Mt 3:11 **4:5** [d]Ex 13:21 [e]Isa 60:1 **4:6** [f]Ps 27:5 [g]Isa 25:4

5:1 [h]Ps 80:8-9 **5:2** [i]Jer 2:21 [j]Mt 21:19; Mk 11:13; Lk 13:6 **5:3** [k]Mt 21:40 **5:4** [l]2Ch 36:15; Jer 2:5-7; Mic 6:3-4; Mt 23:37

The Song of the Vineyard

5 I will sing for the one I love
a song about his vineyard:[h]
My loved one had a vineyard
on a fertile hillside.
[2]He dug it up and cleared it of stones
and planted it with the choicest vines.[i]
He built a watchtower in it
and cut out a winepress as well.
Then he looked for a crop of good
grapes,
but it yielded only bad fruit.[j]

[3]"Now you dwellers in Jerusalem and
people of Judah,
judge between me and my vineyard.[k]
[4]What more could have been done for
my vineyard
than I have done for it?[l]
When I looked for good grapes,
why did it yield only bad?

[a] 4 Or *the Spirit* [b] 5 Or *over all the glory there*

was traditionally held by the man. Without a man and the sustenance supplied by the association with him, life was in jeopardy. This economic need is not the case here, however, since the women will provide their own provisions, apparently willing to bypass the traditional bride-price. *seven.* A significant number in the Bible, indicating completeness (e.g., 11:15; 30:26). One indication of this is that the symbol for seven in Akkadian also means "totality." This number also seems to represent an unspecified high number, as today we might say, "I told you a hundred times." Akkadian incantations parallel this use, e.g., when speaking of "seven young men and seven young women," and Inanna is given "seven divine attributes." *disgrace.* Points toward a societal rather than an economic lack. This word occurs in the context of rape, an unfortunate concomitant of war. The women are seeking either protection from such violation or a return of status to women who have already been raped and so humiliated — a state shared by a woman who was widowed (54:4).

4:3 *recorded among the living.* The righteous followers of God are inscribed in a book of life. This concept is also known in Mesopotamian thought, but instead of a book we read of a "Tablet of Destinies" (cf. 46:10), which contained the destiny of everything and was given by Tiamat to her general Kingu. In a prayer to Nabu (who subsequently controlled the tablets), Nebuchadnezzar II prays that his days be extended and that he experience old age. In the Babylonian "Poem of the Righteous Sufferer," the sufferer in the end receives several blessings, including being reckoned among the living.

4:5 *cloud of smoke by day and a glow of flaming fire by night.* God's protection and guidance were marked by these two elements when Israel departed from Egypt (Ex 13:21 – 22), and they will be restored to Israel's survivors in the eschatological day of the Lord. The powerful radiance of Mesopotamian gods (cf. 2:10; see note there) is also associated with fire, smoke and cloud. In Ugaritic literature, several times the term translated in Hebrew as "cloud" is used of a divine messenger or herald, a representative of a god.

5:1 *a song about his vineyard.* Vineyards were common in the agricultural life of Israel, with evidence of them from the ancient Near East as early as the third millennium BC. While grapes were necessary for wine production, many steps were needed to produce the final product. Isa 5 describes several of these. The rocky hill country of Israel had to be cleared of rocks and were also often terraced; the collected rocks reduced erosion caused by water runoff and retained moisture for the vines. Some of the rocks could also be used for walls surrounding the vineyards, for watchtowers from which guards could protect against marauders, and also for huts in which workers could sleep. Planting was done from cuttings rather than from seeds, and the growing plants needed to be carefully tended and pruned. Even with this careful tending, it took several seasons before usable grapes could be harvested. After harvest, the grapes were placed in baskets and carried to the winepress. These were either built or hewn out of the rock, sometimes in the vineyard itself or else some distance away. The grapes were trodden underfoot in order to release their juice, which flowed to a lower section of the press, where it was collected. It was then placed in jars for fermenting. Vintners experienced this labor firsthand. They were thus attentive to Isaiah's message and would have reacted with disgust at the news of the "bad" grapes (v. 2) after all of the effort expended. Their astonishment would have been magnified when they realized that the presentation was allegorical and that they themselves were the useless vineyard. *My loved one.* One expects to hear of the writer's human beloved, but instead sees an agricultural reference. A lover compared to a garden is familiar (e.g., SS 4:12 — 5:1), and the same comparison is found in Sumerian and Akkadian texts. A collection of the first lines of Akkadian poems identifies three such texts: (1) "she seeks the beautiful garden of your [to a male] charms"; (2) "the lover-king goes down to the garden"; and (3) "the chief gardener of the pleasure garden." The Egyptian Ptahhotep (mid-third millennium BC) instructed his son to love his wife appropriately because "she is a profitable field for her lord." Akkadian letters from the king of Byblos, Rib-Hadda, found at Amarna in Egypt, contain a proverb that compares a woman to a field four times.

5:2 *watchtower.* In order to guard from marauders or scavengers, watchtowers were built. The concept of guarding has a sexual nuance in Akkadian, where it refers to protecting one's chastity. This nuance fits well in this lover's metaphor.

ISAIAH 5

ALLEGORY

Symbolic stories are not rare in the Bible, occurring as fables or parables. They can hide a meaning that might be dangerous to state literally, such as preaching against Rome in the guise of Babylon (Rev 17:5). They can evoke emotions more readily through metaphor than through literality (e.g., the two adulterous sisters in Eze 23). Such stories can draw clear word pictures from the daily life of the hearers. There is continued discussion about whether Isa 5 should be categorized as a parable or an allegory, the distinction being how broad a comparison is intended by the tale. Parables are known from ancient Near Eastern literature as early as the Sumerian period, and a few are available from the Neo-Assyrian period. The metaphor of a city as an unproductive plant is known from the Mesopotamian epic "Erra and Ishum" (known copies date to the eighth century BC) in which Marduk laments Babylon. He says that he filled it with seeds like a pinecone but no fruit came from it, and he planted it like an orchard but never tasted its fruit. See notes on Eze 17. ◆

This vineyard with a watchtower reflects the one mentioned in Isa 5:1 – 2.
www.HolyLandPhotos.org

5 Now I will tell you
what I am going to do to my
vineyard:
I will take away its hedge,
and it will be destroyed;
I will break down its wall,[m]
and it will be trampled.[n]
6 I will make it a wasteland,
neither pruned nor cultivated,
and briers and thorns[o] will grow
there.
I will command the clouds
not to rain on it."

7 The vineyard[p] of the LORD Almighty
is the nation of Israel,
and the people of Judah
are the vines he delighted in.
And he looked for justice,[q] but saw
bloodshed;
for righteousness, but heard cries of
distress.

5:5 [m] Ps 80:12 [n] Isa 28:3, 18; La 1:15; Lk 21:24
5:6 [o] Isa 7:23, 24; Heb 6:8
5:7 [p] Ps 80:8 [q] Isa 59:15

Woes and Judgments

8 Woe[r] to you who add house to house
and join field to field[s]
till no space is left
and you live alone in the land.

9 The LORD Almighty has declared in my hearing:[t]

"Surely the great houses will become
desolate,[u]
the fine mansions left without
occupants.
10 A ten-acre vineyard will produce only a
bath[a] of wine;
a homer[b] of seed will yield only an
ephah[c] of grain."[v]
11 Woe to those who rise early in the
morning
to run after their drinks,
who stay up late at night
till they are inflamed with wine.[w]
12 They have harps and lyres at their
banquets,
pipes and timbrels and wine,
but they have no regard[x] for the deeds
of the LORD,
no respect for the work of his
hands.[y]
13 Therefore my people will go into
exile[z]
for lack of understanding;[a]
those of high rank will die of hunger
and the common people will be
parched with thirst.
14 Therefore Death[b] expands its jaws,
opening wide its mouth;[c]
into it will descend their nobles and
masses
with all their brawlers and
revelers.
15 So people will be brought low[d]
and everyone humbled,[e]
the eyes of the arrogant[f] humbled.
16 But the LORD Almighty will be exalted
by his justice,[g]

5:8 [r] Jer 22:13 [s] Mic 2:2; Hab 2:9-12 **5:9** [t] Isa 22:14 [u] Isa 6:11-12; Mt 23:38 **5:10** [v] Lev 26:26 **5:11** [w] Pr 23:29-30 **5:12** [x] Job 34:27 [y] Ps 28:5; Am 6:5-6 **5:13** [z] Hos 4:6 [a] Isa 1:3; Hos 4:6 **5:14** [b] Pr 30:16 [c] Nu 16:30 **5:15** [d] Isa 10:33 [e] Isa 2:9 [f] Isa 2:11 **5:16** [g] Isa 28:17; 30:18; 33:5; 61:8

[a] *10* That is, about 6 gallons or about 22 liters
[b] *10* That is, probably about 360 pounds or about 160 kilograms
[c] *10* That is, probably about 36 pounds or about 16 kilograms

5:8 *till no space is left.* Landowners regularly seek to expand their holdings, but this has dire consequences in an agricultural society in which family land is not only the place where you live but also the source of your food supply. To protect people from losing this vital resource, laws such as the Year of Jubilee were enacted (see Lev 25:8–55 and notes), by which land was to be returned to its original owners every 50 years. While using different legal mechanisms, Akkadian law also protected the unfettered disaffection of land outside the family or tribal unit. One means for this was public disclosure of a pending sale. A Middle Assyrian law states that one who purchased a field or house in Ashur would have to give public notice of his intention three times over the period of a month so that anyone with claims would have a chance to step forward. Lacking a response, the purchase could be finalized.

Expansion of real estate holdings in the ancient world was usually at someone else's expense. Bad harvests over several seasons could necessitate giving up ownership of property in order to pay off or work off debt. In Israel this was an economic crisis as well as a theological one. Since God had given them the land as a benefit of the covenant, each family considered its land holdings as its little share in the covenant. Therefore, what otherwise would be a financial tragedy (often with an oppressive dimension) served also to deprive someone of their part in the covenant. Additionally, the decision-making body in any community was comprised of landowners. The individual who obtained all the land rights in the community would have the power to do whatever he wanted.

5:10 Several terms in this verse refer to Hebrew measurements. *ten-acre.* Lit. "ten-yoke," where a "yoke" is the amount of land a single pair of oxen can plow in a day, though the exact size is unknown. This would be a fairly large vineyard; most translations (arbitrarily) take it as ten acres (four hectares). *bath.* A liquid measure that equals the "ephah," a dry measure for grain. The bath is about six gallons (22 liters), and the ephah is about 3/5 bushel (22 liters). *homer.* Lit. "donkey load," the amount of grain a donkey can carry, i.e., one-tenth of an ephah. A vineyard would typically be expected to yield at least 1,000 gallons of wine per acre (9,350 liters per hectare). Harvests of grain in irrigated areas across the ancient Near East yielded a normal seed-to-crop ratio of about 1:10 (though higher yields are attested in the literature). Therefore a homer of seed would usually be expected to yield ten homers of grain. In this verse the ratio is reversed as 10:1 (an ephah is about one-tenth of a homer). The yields represented here, then, are meager fractions of that normally expected.

5:11 *inflamed with wine.* Carousing and inebriation, following too much consumption of the results of the good fruit from the vine, are not good. The Bible elsewhere condemns it (Pr 20:1). The Egyptian "Instruction of Any" (c. 1100 BC) also warns that indulging in drinking beer could lead to "evil speech." Banquets with drinking were well known, ranging from the Persian period (Est 1:8) back to creation, according to the Akkadian *Enuma Elish*, in which a divine gathering is portrayed as a drinking party.

5:12 *harps and lyres . . . pipes and timbrels.* See the articles "Lyre," p. 488; "Music and Musicians," p. 524.

5:13 *my people will go into exile.* The customary foreign policy of both Assyria and Babylonia was to deport the rulers and leading citizens of conquered states, exiling them far away from their home. One study places the number of exiles dispersed throughout the Assyrian Empire during the Neo-Assyrian period at over 1.2 million. A result of this policy was the depletion of power at home as well as separating leaders from bases for resistance in their native land so they would be less likely to rebel against their overlords. Deporting entire families also aided resettlement in the new land, lessening the draw home.

Assyria did this to the northern nation of Israel (722–721 BC), as Babylonia did to Judah (605, 597 and 586 BC). To avoid Babylonian wrath for killing Judah's figurehead governor, Gedaliah, people from Judah voluntarily exiled themselves to Egypt in 581 BC. Such deportation is evident not only textually, including names mentioned indicating people of different ethnic origin, but also on reliefs on the walls of some palaces.

5:14 *Death.* Lit. *Sheol*, the netherworld, the place of the dead. See the articles "Death and Sheol," p. 833; "Death and the Underworld," p. 907.

ISAIAH 5:7

WORDPLAY

Plays on meaning and sounds, called paronomasia, appear to be linguistic universals, engaging the human sense of play. Sound play is generally language specific, not immediately clear in another, unrelated language. An example in Isa 5:7 is words using similar sounding consonants (alliteration) and vowels (assonance) placed near each other but in contrast to each other. In Isa 5:7 God looks for "justice" (*mishpat*), but finds "bloodshed" (*mishpah*). He seeks "righteousness" (*tsedaqa*), but gets "cries of distress" (*tseaqa*). Someone has suggested an English equivalent: "He sought equity, but found iniquity, a righteous nation, but instead, lamentation."

Wordplays like this capture the attention and imagination of the audience. Israel's neighbors used these as well. The Akkadian *Enuma Elish* describes Marduk: *nakhlapta aplukhti pulkhati khalipa* ("an armor garment, he was clothed with terror"). Similar wordplays have been discovered in Egyptian, Sumerian and Ugaritic literature. ◆

The Akkadian Enuma Elish (tablet 4).

Z. Radovan/www.BibleLandPictures.com

and the holy God will be proved
holy[h] by his righteous acts.
17 Then sheep will graze as in their own
pasture;[i]
lambs will feed[a] among the ruins of
the rich.

18 Woe to those who draw sin along with
cords of deceit,
and wickedness[j] as with cart
ropes,
19 to those who say, "Let God hurry;
let him hasten his work
so we may see it.
The plan of the Holy One of Israel —
let it approach, let it come into
view,
so we may know it."[k]
20 Woe to those who call evil good
and good evil,
who put darkness for light
and light for darkness,[l]
who put bitter for sweet
and sweet for bitter.[m]
21 Woe to those who are wise in their
own eyes[n]
and clever in their own sight.

5:16 [h] Isa 29:23 **5:17** [i] Isa 7:25; Zep 2:6, 14 **5:18** [j] Isa 59:4-8; Jer 23:14 **5:19** [k] Jer 17:15; Eze 12:22; 2Pe 3:4 **5:20** [l] Mt 6:22-23; Lk 11:34-35 [m] Am 5:7 **5:21** [n] Pr 3:7; Ro 12:16; 1Co 3:18-20

[a] 17 Septuagint; Hebrew / *strangers will eat*

5:18 *draw sin along with cords of deceit.* One draws along behind those things over which one has control. This is shown in numerous reliefs of bound and joined prisoners being led away. Ironically, at this point in their history, all that Isaiah's audience can parade after themselves as their greatest achievement is their sin.

22 Woe to those who are heroes at
drinking wine[o]
and champions at mixing drinks,
23 who acquit the guilty for a bribe,[p]
but deny justice[q] to the innocent.[r]
24 Therefore, as tongues of fire lick up
straw
and as dry grass sinks down in the
flames,
so their roots will decay[s]
and their flowers blow away like
dust;
for they have rejected the law of the
LORD Almighty
and spurned the word[t] of the Holy
One of Israel.
25 Therefore the LORD's anger[u] burns
against his people;
his hand is raised and he strikes
them down.
The mountains shake,
and the dead bodies are like refuse[v]
in the streets.

Yet for all this, his anger is not turned
away,[w]
his hand is still upraised.[x]

26 He lifts up a banner for the distant
nations,
he whistles[y] for those at the ends of
the earth.[z]
Here they come,
swiftly and speedily!
27 Not one of them grows tired or
stumbles,
not one slumbers or sleeps;
not a belt is loosened at the waist,[a]
not a sandal strap is broken.[b]
28 Their arrows are sharp,[c]
all their bows[d] are strung;
their horses' hooves seem like flint,
their chariot wheels like a
whirlwind.
29 Their roar is like that of the lion,[e]
they roar like young lions;
they growl as they seize[f] their prey
and carry it off with no one to rescue.[g]
30 In that day they will roar over it
like the roaring of the sea.[h]
And if one looks at the land,
there is only darkness and distress;[i]
even the sun will be darkened[j] by
clouds.

Isaiah's Commission

6 In the year that King Uzziah[k] died,[l]
I saw the Lord,[m] high and exalted,
seated on a throne;[n] and the train of his

5:22 [o] Pr 23:20 **5:23** [p] Ex 23:8 [q] Isa 10:2 [r] Ps 94:21; Jas 5:6 **5:24** [s] Job 18:16 [t] Isa 8:6; 30:9, 12 **5:25** [u] 2Ki 22:13 [v] 2Ki 9:37 [w] Jer 4:8; Da 9:16 [x] Isa 9:12, 17, 21; 10:4 **5:26** [y] Isa 7:18; Zec 10:8 [z] Dt 28:49; Isa 13:5; 18:3 **5:27** [a] Job 12:18 [b] Joel 2:7-8 **5:28** [c] Ps 45:5 [d] Ps 7:12 **5:29** [e] Jer 51:38; Zep 3:3; Zec 11:3 [f] Isa 10:6; 49:24-25 [g] Isa 42:22; Mic 5:8 **5:30** [h] Lk 21:25 [i] Isa 8:22; Jer 4:23-28 [j] Joel 2:10 **6:1** [k] 2Ch 26:22, 23 [l] 2Ki 15:7 [m] Jn 12:41 [n] Rev 4:2

5:22 *heroes ... champions.* Two military terms are used satirically, since the only opponent conquered is alcohol. *wine.* A common beverage in the area, made from grapes, honey or dates. *mixing drinks.* Drinks could be flavored by adding herbs and spices. Intoxicants were often consumed through a long, straw-like tube, which also served as a strainer.
5:23 *bribe.* A major role for a national leader was to establish justice for those unable to secure it for themselves, i.e., the weak and the disenfranchised (see note on 1:23 ["fatherless ... widow's case"]). For this reason, law codes were common. *deny justice.* When those charged with administering the law are corrupt, basing their decisions on their own economic advantage rather than on justice, they pervert justice. Because bribery makes the entire enterprise of governance problematic, it is dealt with harshly.
5:25 *dead bodies are like refuse in the streets.* The lack of a proper burial was scandalous in Israel and among her neighbors—a sign of disrespect for the departed (see notes on 1Ki 14:11; 2Ki 9:10; Ecc 6:3).
5:26 *banner.* Or standard; used as a means of calling out an army of a particular territory or indicating the place where a muster was taking place or a camp was located. It often featured an insignia of the tribe or division. *whistles.* The Hebrew can also refer to a hiss (see 7:18).
5:27 *not a belt is loosened at the waist, not a sandal strap is broken.* Preparation for battle or for work is exemplified by one's clothing being in good repair and functioning properly. In the Egyptian *Tale of Two Brothers*, when Anubis finishes engaging in battle and other work, he takes off his sandals and clothes and discards his staff and weapons. This suggests a possible military connotation for the Isaiah passage.
5:28 *arrows.* Made from reeds tipped with stone, bone or metal. *bows.* Composite bows, so called because they were formed of several materials, possibly originated in Assyria and were curved, which allowed arrows to fly greater distance. *horses' hooves.* Shoeing of horses was not practiced, so some terrain was difficult for them; however, they developed hard hoofs. See note on 2:7. *chariot wheels.* See note on 2:7.
5:29 *roar ... of the lion.* The ferocity and roar of lions proverbially inspires fear. They are shown roaring in numerous Israelite seal impressions and in other representations. They are pictured as mauling unfortunate prey and are themselves prey of mighty hunters. A hero is shown in his power holding a lion.
6:1 *Uzziah.* Also called Azariah (e.g., see 2Ki 14:21 and NIV text note), he became the tenth king of Judah after the assassination of his father, Amaziah, though they probably shared the throne while Amaziah was a prisoner of war. Uzziah, in turn, shared the throne with his son Jotham after being infected with leprosy, which perhaps led to his death. Leprosy made Uzziah ritually unclean and therefore unable to fulfill any public duties. Grief in Judah must have been great since Uzziah was the only king whom many, including Isaiah, knew, since his reign was so long (792–740 BC). The anguish could well have been exacerbated by fear, since just prior to Uzziah's death in 742 BC, the great Assyrian king Tiglath-Pileser III had ascended his throne (745 BC), reviving the waning Neo-Assyrian Empire. He turned his attention to Israel and the west, starting with military campaigns in 743 BC. In one such campaign he encountered "[Azr]iau (Azariah) of Judah," leading some to suggest that Uzziah/Azariah was the opponent mentioned by Tiglath-Pileser. Fear at this juncture in Israel's history provided opportunity for a prophet to be heard, as it did in the reign of Ahaz in Isa 7. *Lord.* See note on v. 3 ("LORD"). *high and exalted.* In a hierarchy of power and authority, God is followed by the king, with the people falling below them. We use this

robe filled the temple. [2]Above him were
seraphim,[o] each with six wings: With two
wings they covered their faces, with two
they covered their feet,[p] and with two they
were flying. [3]And they were calling to one
another:

"Holy, holy, holy is the LORD Almighty;
the whole earth is full of his glory."[q]

[4]At the sound of their voices the doorposts
and thresholds shook and the temple was
filled with smoke.

6:2 [o] Rev 4:8 [p] Eze 1:11
6:3 [q] Ps 72:19; Rev 4:8

KINGS OF JUDAH	
Amaziah	796 – 767 BC
Uzziah (Azariah)	(791) – 740/39 BC
Jotham	(750) – 732/731 BC
Ahaz	(744 / 743) – 716 / 715 BC
Hezekiah	716 / 715 – 687 / 686 BC
Manasseh	(696 / 695) – 642 / 641 BC
Amon	642 / 641 – 640 / 639 BC
Josiah	640 / 639 – 609 BC
Jehoahaz	609 BC
Jehoiakim	609 – 597 BC
Jehoiachin	597 BC
Zedekiah	597 – 587 BC

extended spatial meaning of the term when we speak of someone "moving up the ladder." It is also used of God in relation to the rest of creation. It can also have a literal meaning, where something is physically raised. This physical representation of God's metaphoric superiority is meant here, reflecting the practice of standing the divine image on a dais or pedestal in its temple. The description of the temple in Jerusalem suggests that the floor of the Most Holy Place was raised since its internal height is ten cubits less than that of the temple proper. An important Babylonian temple to the national god Marduk was named Esagila, meaning "house whose head is high." *train of his robe.* The common mode of male dress was an outer robe, which generally fell between the knee and the ankle but did not have a train per se. The Hebrew term for "train" is also translated as "hems," the very edges of his garments, which were sufficient in themselves to fill the temple. This graphically illustrates the power, majesty and size of God. The anthropomorphic picture of his garments and, in that, their farthest extremity dwarfs the physical reality of the temple, Israel's grandest architectural production. Whether Isaiah's vision refers to the physical structure he knows in Jerusalem or to a heavenly temple, the greatness of God is overpowering. A temple at ʿAin Dara (Syria) from this period has gigantic footprints carved into the pavement striding into the temple — another way to convey the colossal size of the deity who was worshiped there. The hem not only was part of the magnificent garment, but it also could play a legal role, symbolically and legally representing a person in Mesopotamian legal documents. Most of the writing needed to be done by scribes, since this skill was beyond most people, including royalty. The person legally bound by the documented agreement needed to sign it, even though that person could not read. Whereas today one might use an "X," during that period one could "sign" by leaving an impression either of one's thumbnail or of the fringe at the hem of one's robe. It was a means of personal identification. Although this passage does not concern a legal situation, by using this symbolism, God was closely associating himself with his temple in Jerusalem. The hem also had legal implications in West Semitic texts from Isaiah's period. At that time, "seizing the hem" of a god acknowledged one's submission, so this relationship was still possible to Israel since at least the hem was accessible to them. All of these data points show that the mention of the hem here is not just a comment about a random piece of a garment — the hem concerns status and identity. *temple.* The Hebrew word used here is not the common Hebrew phrase translated "house of Yahweh"; it is a rare word of Mesopotamian origin. Originating among the non-Semitic Sumerians, the term was borrowed by the Semitic speakers of Akkadian in Mesopotamia and by Hebrew speakers. The term can be used to indicate either of two "great houses" — that of the king (as in "palace"; e.g., 13:22; 39:7) and that of God (as in "temple"; e.g., 44:28; 66:6). The ambiguity of the word does well here since Yahweh is portrayed as both God and King.

6:2 *seraphim, each with six wings.* Seraphim are one of two types of heavenly beings mentioned by Isaiah, the other being "cherubim" (37:16). The latter, having a single pair of wings, are associated closely with the throne (presumably as guardians), while the seraphim are flying above it. The term for "seraphim" lit. means "burning," which has led some to associate them with lightning, but seraphim are associated elsewhere not with fire but with serpents (14:29; 30:6), possibly alluding to the metaphoric burn of venom. The serpents that bit the Israelites in the wilderness are called "seraphim" (Nu 21:6 – 9).

The ancient Near East does know of serpents associated with both divinity and royalty. A ninth-century BC tablet from Sippar shows a two-headed serpent-man, Mush-igimin ("two-faced serpent"), who was the chief constable of Shamash, the sun-god. In Egyptian art, part of the crown of the pharaoh is a uraeus, a black-necked cobra. Seraphim are also found in numerous seals, often winged, though those having six wings are rare; most have four wings. A number of these have been found in Israel, so these figures were familiar to Isaiah and his readers.

6:3 *Holy, holy, holy.* Repetition in Hebrew, as in other languages, provides emphasis — in this case, of the superlative holiness of God. Akkadian priests also used threefold repetition in some incantations, with magical words calling for divine action. Some of these repetitions were in the context of the "mouth-washing" ritual (cf. v. 7). Holiness is not an attribute associated with gods in other cultures of the ancient world. *LORD.* The personal name of the God of Israel is "Yahweh" (Hebrew *YHWH*), occurring over 460 times in Isaiah. Its exact pronunciation is uncertain, since Jews who worried about breaking the command against misusing God's name ceased using it orally by the Second Temple period. Instead, they substituted the Hebrew term for "Lord" (*adonay*, used in v. 1). Most English Bibles have maintained this legalistic avoidance of the divine name, but show its presence in the original through writing it in small capital letters (i.e., "LORD," as here in v. 3). See the article "God's Name," p. 112.

ISAIAH 6:1

DATING METHODS

Old Testament writers did not have the luxury of one fixed point in time from which to date events; they therefore dated occurrences in their texts as they related to other important events in the memory or tradition of their audience—perhaps a noteworthy natural phenomenon (e.g., the earthquake in Am 1:1) or a memorable historical occasion, such as the death of a king (Isa 6:1; 14:28) or a military attack (Isa 20:1). This convention is called "relative dating" since it relates one event to another in sequence. A contemporary example might be saying that something happened "three years ago."

Relative dating makes it difficult to correlate one such system with another. In Isa 6:1, to what year in our BC/AD system does "the year that King Uzziah died" correspond? One of the ways to accomplish this correlation is by finding "synchronisms," events involving two groups that are known from within each group. Such a correlation (which does not provide an exact date) was Israel's paying tribute to Assyria. That event is mentioned in records of both of the kings involved, Menahem of Israel (2Ki 15:19) and Tiglath-Pileser III (called "Pul" in 2Ki 15:19) of Assyria. These synchronisms, of which there are several between Israel/Judah and Mesopotamia, as well as between Israel/Judah and Egypt and between Egypt and Mesopotamia, serve as anchors, binding together separate relative dating systems.

The next step to accurate dating is helped by the detailed records kept by the Egyptians. For them, the exact moment that the star Sirius appeared in a certain position marked the beginning of the agricultural year. Their records noted these dates, and modern astronomers have determined that the star follows a cycle of 1,460 years. Putting the Egyptian records together with the astronomical data allows us to relate events in those records to our dating system.

Assyrian records also help in this way. The Assyrians collected the names for each year in what is called the Eponym List, which provides a relative chronology. An anchor point to other chronological systems, resulting in a more absolute chronology, is provided in the Eponym List by reference to a solar eclipse, which has been identified astronomically as occurring in 763 BC. ◆

5"Woe to me!" I cried. "I am ruined! For I
am a man of unclean lips, and I live among
a people of unclean lips,[r] and my eyes have
seen the King,[s] the LORD Almighty."
6Then one of the seraphim flew to me
with a live coal in his hand, which he had
taken with tongs from the altar. 7With it
he touched my mouth and said, "See, this
has touched your lips;[t] your guilt is taken
away and your sin atoned for.[u]"

6:5 [r] Jer 9:3-8 [s] Jer 51:57
6:7 [t] Jer 1:9 [u] 1Jn 1:7

6:5 *Woe to me!* Statements using "woe" are common expressions of affliction and trouble in Isaiah (3:9,11; 24:16) and elsewhere in the OT. In this verse it is brought forth by the realization of the distance between the holy God and the unclean prophet. Israel's neighbors also used similar woe formulae—e.g., when woe is called on those responsible for the death of Aqhat in the Ugaritic Aqhat Legend, or when Sargon inflicts wartime violence.
6:7 *touched my mouth.* Upon his encounter with the holy God, Isaiah realizes that he himself is ritually unclean. As such, he cannot join in voicing God's praise. He is also disqualified from proclaiming God's message to his people if the very instrument of his ministry as a prophet, his speech, is polluted by impurity. Isaiah's ritual purification comes through cauterization by a coal from the temple's incense altar. Ritual purification of the mouth as practiced in Mesopotamia is known through a number of *miš pî* ("mouth-washing") texts. This was most frequently performed on cult statues in preparation for their installation in a temple, where they became objects of worship and revelation, their mouths having been prepared. Part of the ritual called for threefold repetitions of spoken incantations (cf. v. 6) and multiple washing rituals, in contrast to the single purification of Isaiah. The purification resulting from the rituals are similar, though the instruments bringing it about (a live coal versus water)

[8]Then I heard the voice[v] of the Lord saying, "Whom shall I send? And who will
go for us?"
  And I said, "Here am I. Send me!"
  [9]He said, "Go[w] and tell this people:
"'Be ever hearing, but never
    understanding;
  be ever seeing, but never perceiving.'[x]
[10]Make the heart of this people
    calloused;[y]
  make their ears dull
  and close their eyes.[a]
Otherwise they might see with their
    eyes,
  hear with their ears,[z]
  understand with their hearts,
and turn and be healed."[a]

[11]Then I said, "For how long, Lord?"[b]
And he answered:

"Until the cities lie ruined[c]
  and without inhabitant,
until the houses are left deserted
  and the fields ruined and ravaged,
[12]until the LORD has sent everyone far
    away[d]
  and the land is utterly forsaken.[e]
[13]And though a tenth remains[f] in the
    land,
  it will again be laid waste.

6:8 [v] Ac 9:4 **6:9** [w] Eze 3:11 [x] Mt 13:15*; Lk 8:10* **6:10** [y] Dt 32:15; Ps 119:70 [z] Jer 5:21 [a] Mt 13:13-15; Mk 4:12*; Ac 28:26-27* **6:11** [b] Ps 79:5 [c] Lev 26:31 **6:12** [d] Dt 28:64 [e] Jer 4:29 **6:13** [f] Isa 1:9

[a] *9,10* Hebrew; Septuagint *'You will be ever hearing, but never understanding; / you will be ever seeing, but never perceiving.' / [10]This people's heart has become calloused; / they hardly hear with their ears, / and they have closed their eyes*

are different. One parallel is suggestive for the Isaiah context, since the special incantation priest had his mouth cleansed in order to make his presentation of the divine will more clear. In both cases, the instrument of revelation must be pure. Egypt also provides a parallel when contact by a fiery serpent rod (cf. the seraphim of v. 2) opens or purifies the mouth. Whichever society provides background for Isaiah's purification, a procedure is necessary before he can enter into the presence of a holy God. The unclean cannot be in the divine presence. Since prophets were commonly believed to receive their messages by listening in on the divine council (see the articles "Divine Council," p. 615; "Prophets and Prophecy," p. 1110), they would have to have a pure status. *your sin [is] atoned for.* Atonement, or the ritual removal of impurity caused by sin or other means, is a main theme in Leviticus (cf. Lev 22:14; 27:9; 47:11). The cognate verb in Akkadian also indicates purification and cleansing, both literally, such as brushing one's teeth, and in the cult, such as purifying a temple through rituals or magic. One Akkadian ritual series is named "burning" (*šurpu*), since fire plays a central role in it. Various spoken incantations and burning numerous objects resulting in smoke (cf. v. 4) comprise the key rituals. The second tablet of this ritual provides for purification from numerous transgressions involving the mouth (e.g., eating taboo things, evil speech, contempt, lying, etc.), but no specific mention is made of purifying the lips.

6:8 *Whom shall I send? And who will go for us?* Incantation texts seek divine intervention against some type of malady. Numerous Akkadian incantations ask which deity should be the one called to present the case for assistance. They concern the interaction between the divine and human realms through the use of a messenger, much as the discussion does in Isaiah. The deity says, "Whom shall I send and whom shall I order?" *us.* Several places in the OT where plural forms refer to Israel's sole God have raised questions: Is God one or several? The same plural form is also used by rulers (e.g., Ge 26:10,16; 2Sa 24:14), either referring to themselves through the "royal 'we'" (*pluralis majestatis*) or else including their royal retinue. Israel's neighbors envisioned a heavenly council of deities surrounding the heavenly throne. These are known from Ugarit, Byblos and Mesopotamia. Israelite orthodoxy acknowledged only one God, but lesser, semidivine beings are found in his presence—not as advisors or exercising authority over him, but as his servants. Based on this information, God's speaking with his retinue is a possibility here. See the article "Divine Council," p. 615.

6:9 *Go and tell.* In the ancient Near East, messengers were important as a means of contact between a ruler and others, including his subjects and other rulers. They served administrative, business and diplomatic functions. They were at times carefully selected and acted with the authority of the one who sent them (see, e.g., Nu 22:15, where the messengers were themselves royalty). They were to be trustworthy in passing on the charge entrusted to them and usually were commissioned to deliver their messages orally, which were often accompanied by written texts, such as letters. In the Egyptian tale of Wenamun's journey to Phoenicia, he is sent as Amon's messenger.

Some suggest that the prophets were messengers not coming solely from God but rather delivering the message of a divine council. In the ancient Near Eastern world, this was a collection of the gods who met together to decide matters, such as in the Babylonian creation account in which the council commissioned Marduk to battle Tiamat and then elevated him to chief among the gods. There are hints of such a council in the OT as well; while there is only one God, there are other supernatural beings (see the article "Divine Council," p. 615).

Among Israel's neighbors, gods also used messengers to pass along their instructions. At times they sent other deities, but they also used humans. This is common in epic texts, but also in other genres. In an Akkadian incantation a deity asks a familiar question: "Whom may I send?" (cf. v. 8). The reason for messengers was that the message would be heard and responded to, not the opposite, as was expected of Isaiah's message (vv. 9–11).

6:10 *make their ears dull and close their eyes.* Isaiah's prophetic role was to call the people to repentance and back to a relationship with God. This is impossible if the people cannot receive the message. Nonfunctioning organs have several interpretations. In the Akkadian "Poem of the Righteous Sufferer," physical debility seems to come from a supernatural attack of some kind. Among the physical symptoms, the sufferer says that as attentive as he is, his eyes and ears are not functioning. In a Sumerian prayer, similar symptoms arise when a penitent realizes that he has sinned (cf. vv. 5–7). For him, a scribe, it is his hand and mouth, the tools of his trade, that are useless. Another suggestion is that the symptoms are to parallel those of the dumb idols Israel too often worships. Instead of maintaining allegiance with a living and responsive God, they turn to sightless, deaf idols for aid (44:18). In this way, God warns that Israel will become like what they worship.

6:12 *sent everyone far away.* See note on 5:13.

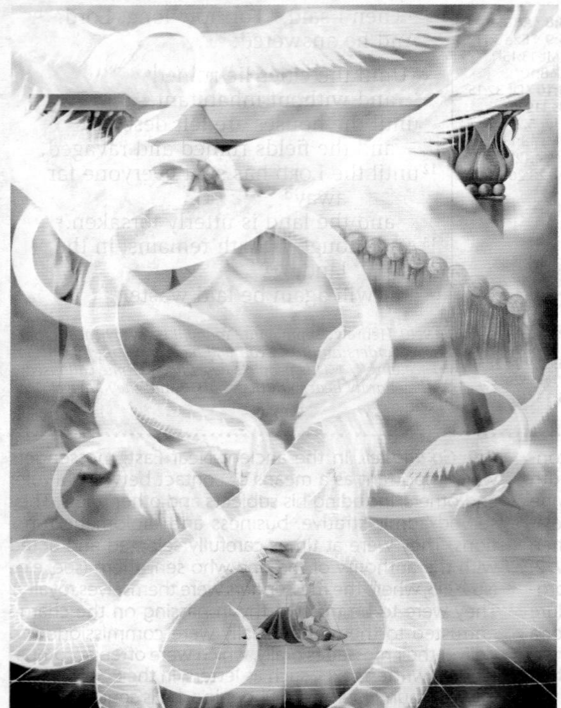

An artist's rendition of Isaiah's throne room vision. Isaiah had a vision of Yahweh in the temple. He was so huge that just the train of his robe filled it. The seraphim, here interpreted as flying serpents (explained in note on 6:2), accompanied Yahweh with proclamations of his holiness. One is shown taking a coal from the altar to purify Isaiah's lips. The scene is obscured by the smoke that filled the temple as the doorposts and threshold trembled.

Jonathan Walton

But as the terebinth and oak
leave stumps when they are cut
down,
so the holy seed will be the stump in
the land."[g]

The Sign of Immanuel

7 When Ahaz son of Jotham, the son of
Uzziah, was king of Judah, King Rezin[h]
of Aram[i] and Pekah[j] son of Remaliah king
of Israel marched up to fight against Jerusalem, but they could not overpower it.
[2]Now the house of David[k] was told,
"Aram has allied itself with[a] Ephraim[l]"; so
the hearts of Ahaz and his people were
shaken, as the trees of the forest are shak-
en by the wind.
[3]Then the LORD said to Isaiah, "Go out,
you and your son Shear-Jashub,[b] to meet
Ahaz at the end of the aqueduct of the Upper Pool, on the road to the Launderer's
Field.[m] [4]Say to him, 'Be careful, keep calm[n]
and don't be afraid.[o] Do not lose heart[p] because of these two smoldering stubs[q] of
firewood—because of the fierce anger[r] of
Rezin and Aram and of the son of Remaliah. [5]Aram, Ephraim and Remaliah's son
have plotted your ruin, saying, [6]"Let us invade Judah; let us tear it apart and divide
it among ourselves, and make the son of
Tabeel king over it." [7]Yet this is what the
Sovereign LORD says:

"'It will not take place,
it will not happen,[s]
[8]for the head of Aram is Damascus,[t]
and the head of Damascus is only
Rezin.
Within sixty-five years
Ephraim will be too shattered[u] to be
a people.
[9]The head of Ephraim is Samaria,
and the head of Samaria is only
Remaliah's son.
If you do not stand firm in your faith,[v]
you will not stand at all.'"[w]

6:13 [g] Job 14:7 **7:1** [h] 2Ki 15:37 [i] 2Ch 28:5 [j] 2Ki 15:25 **7:2** [k] ver 13; Isa 22:22

[a] 2 Or *has set up camp in* [b] 3 *Shear-Jashub* means *a remnant will return.*

[l] Isa 9:9 **7:3** [m] 2Ki 18:17; Isa 36:2 **7:4** [n] Isa 30:15 [o] Isa 35:4 [p] Dt 20:3 [q] Zec 3:2 [r] Isa 10:24 **7:7** [s] Isa 8:10; Ac 4:25 **7:8** [t] Ge 14:15 [u] Isa 17:1-3 **7:9** [v] 2Ch 20:20 [w] Isa 8:6-8; 30:12-14

7:3 *aqueduct of the Upper Pool.* The existence of an "upper" pool, apparently outside the city walls to the north, suggests a "lower" one, mentioned in Isa 22:9, perhaps within the walls and thus more secure during siege conditions. The aqueduct apparently carried water to the Upper Pool. Water was a major problem for Jerusalem throughout her history, and identification of the various elements of her water system is a matter of some debate. It appears that the king is here inspecting the water supply of the city, which would soon be under siege. See the article "Hezekiah's Tunnel," p. 663. *Launderer's Field.* Washing and working new cloth is called "fulling," which leads to many translations identifying this as the "Fuller's Field." It rid the material of natural oils before it could be used and was an important part of cloth preparation. The place where it was done seems well known, since it is the site of two important meetings (here; 36:2; cf. 2Ki 18:17).

7:4 *Be careful.* Lachish in Judah has produced several letters from the first quarter of the sixth century BC. One speaks of sending a letter of Tobyahu, servant of the king, which came to Shallum son of Yada from "the prophet" saying, "Beware." Exactly who is warning whom is unclear, but it appears to involve a confrontation between prophet and king, though in Isaiah the message is encouraging, which might not be the case in Lachish.

7:5–6 *son of Remaliah ... son of Tabeel.* Two people are shown little respect, since only their father's name is given. They are Pekah, called simply "son of Remaliah," and another who is called simply "son of Tabeel." The name is Aramaic, so it may indicate someone who had pro-Aram/Syria sympathies, i.e., someone who would oppose Judah and side with Judah's enemies in this Syro-Ephraimite conflict (see the article "Syro-Ephraimite War," p. 1125). Another possibility is that it refers to Tubail/Ethbaal, the king of Tyre who paid tribute to Assyria, along with Rezin, in about 738 BC. One of the two enemies will take over Judah for himself.

7:8 *sixty-five years.* Since the events of this story take

10Again the LORD spoke to Ahaz, 11"Ask
the LORD your God for a sign, whether
in the deepest depths or in the highest
heights."
12But Ahaz said, "I will not ask; I will
not put the LORD to the test."
13Then Isaiah said, "Hear now, you
house of David! Is it not enough to try the
patience of humans? Will you try the patience of my God[x] also? 14Therefore the
Lord himself will give you[a] a sign: The
virgin[b] will conceive and give birth to a

7:13 [x] Isa 25:1

[a] 14 The Hebrew is plural. [b] 14 Or *young woman*

place about 735 BC, the 65-year period ends in 670 BC, which is a puzzling date since the Assyrians captured Israel's capital, Samaria, and ended its monarchy 15 years later in 722 BC, with its people exiled and foreigners transplanted into its territory. Nevertheless, 669 BC is the year that Esarhaddon, king of Assyria and son of Sennacherib, died and was succeeded by his son, Ashurbanipal, who completed the deportation activities begun here (Ezr 4:10).

7:11 *Ask ... for a sign.* Seeking revelation or confirmation from the divine is common in the ancient Near East. In the OT signs could look back as reminders of what was (55:13) or proof of what was said (Ex 3:12), or they could point forward as a portent of what was to be (Isa 8:18). Omens were signs commonly used in the Near East, though they were unacceptable for Israel. Through them a skilled interpreter sought to analyze some natural phenomenon to determine the message from the gods (see notes on 2:6; Ge 30:27; Dt 18:10; see also the articles "Balaam," p. 268; "Magic," p. 326; "Practice of Magic," p. 627).

7:13 *house of David.* While earlier kings were referred to dismissively simply by their father's name (v. 6), here Ahaz is identified only by his family line: he is a Davidic descendant, as were all the kings of Judah. It was a great and perpetual line (2Ch 21:7), but Ahaz was not representing it well in this instance. The phrase also occurs in extra-Biblical texts. An eighth-century BC Aramaic inscription found at Tell Dan mentions "the house of David."

7:14 *The virgin will ... give birth to a son.* Annunciations of birth, heralding such an important event through supernatural means, are not rare. Hagar heard of Ishmael's birth (Ge 16:11), as did Manoah's wife of the birth of Samson (Jdg 13:3,5). A bilingual Akkadian-Sumerian psalm dedicated to Assur is broken, but it may refer to a supernatural "virgin" birth of Tukulti-Ninurta I. It speaks of one who was begotten by the god Enlil and placed in a maiden,

ISAIAH 7:1

SYRO-EPHRAIMITE WAR

Rezin (known as Rah/qyanu from Akkadian texts, *rdyn* in Aramaic) was an Aramean (Syrian) king who was dethroned when his nation was incorporated into the Assyrian Empire in 732 BC. He had been paying tribute to Assyria for some time, as a list of vassals dated from the reign of Tiglath-Pileser III (called "Pul" in 2Ki 15:19; 745–727 BC) shows. In order to forestall incorporation, Rezin joined Pekah, son of Remaliah (Isa 7:4–5; 8:6) and king of Israel from c. 737–732 BC, to oppose Assyria. Rezin, Pekah and Hoshea (Pekah's son and successor after Pekah was killed by the Assyrians), pressured Jotham, king of Judah (c. 750–732 BC), to join their anti-Assyrian coalition (2Ki 15:29,37), but Jotham refused. To present a united front against their common enemy, Aram/Syria and Israel (called "Ephraim," the name of its major tribe, in Isa 7:2,4) united against Judah, now led by Ahaz (732–715 BC), to force their cooperation. This attack by Aram/Syria and Israel against Judah is called the Syro-Ephraimite War.

Having been earlier concerned with rebellions in other parts of his empire, in 734 BC Tiglath-Pileser turned his attention to his holdings along the Mediterranean, where he campaigned for several years. A list of year names of his reign designates 734 BC and 732 BC as being the years he campaigned against Philistia and Damascus (Aram/Syria's capital), respectively. Judah, rightly perceiving the overwhelming superiority of Assyria over any western alliance, took the part of discretion (or cowardice) and did not join the alliance. In fact, Judah allied itself with Assyria, paying Assyria tribute. This is acknowledged in an inscription of Tiglath-Pileser dated 727 BC. The Assyrian army soon crushed the alliance. The entire episode proved theologically vexing to Israel and Judah: Does one follow logic or the direction of God? ◆

son,[y] and[a] will call him Immanuel.[bz] 15He will be eating curds and honey[a] when he knows enough to reject the wrong and choose the right, 16for before the boy knows[b] enough to reject the wrong and choose the right, the land of the two kings you dread will be laid waste.[c] 17The LORD will bring on you and on your people and on the house of your father a time unlike any since Ephraim broke away[d] from Judah—he will bring the king of Assyria.[e]"

Assyria, the LORD's Instrument

18In that day the LORD will whistle[f] for flies from the Nile delta in Egypt and for bees from the land of Assyria.[g] 19They will all come and settle in the steep ravines and in the crevices[h] in the rocks, on all the thornbushes and at all the water holes. 20In that day the Lord will use[i] a razor hired from beyond the Euphrates River—the king of Assyria[j]—to shave your head and private parts, and to cut off your beard also. 21In that day, a person will keep alive a young cow and two goats. 22And because of the abundance of the milk they give, there will be curds to eat. All who remain in the land will eat curds and honey. 23In that day, in every place where there were a thousand vines worth a thousand silver shekels,[c] there will be only briers and thorns.[k] 24Hunters will go there with bow and arrow, for the land will be covered with briers and thorns. 25As for all the hills once cultivated by the hoe, you will no longer go there for fear of the briers and thorns; they will become places where cattle are turned loose and where sheep run.[l]

Isaiah and His Children as Signs

8 The LORD said to me, "Take a large scroll[m] and write on it with an ordinary pen: Maher-Shalal-Hash-Baz."[dn] 2So I called in Uriah[o] the priest and Zechariah

7:14 [y] Lk 1:31 [z] Isa 8:8, 10; Mt 1:23* **7:15** [a] ver 22 **7:16** [b] Isa 8:4 [c] Isa 17:3; Hos 5:9, 13; Am 1:3-5 **7:17** [d] 1Ki 12:16 [e] 2Ch 28:20 **7:18** [f] Isa 5:26 [g] Isa 13:5 **7:19** [h] Isa 2:19 **7:20** [i] Isa 10:15 [j] Isa 8:7; 10:5 **7:23** [k] Isa 5:6 **7:25** [l] Isa 5:17 **8:1** [m] Isa 30:8; Hab 2:2 [n] ver 3; Hab 2:2 **8:2** [o] 2Ki 16:10

[a] *14* Masoretic Text; Dead Sea Scrolls *son, and he* or *son, and they* [b] *14* *Immanuel* means *God with us.*
[c] *23* That is, about 25 pounds or about 12 kilograms
[d] *1* *Maher-Shalal-Hash-Baz* means *quick to the plunder, swift to the spoil;* also in verse 3.

so that she gave birth to the king. This concept can be seen as early as Sumerian literature; there it is said that the god Ningirsu rejoiced over Eannatum, who was said to have been implanted in the womb by the god Ningirsu. A Canaanite text has the exact Ugaritic equivalent of this birth announcement, saying of the moon-goddess Nikkal, "Behold, the young woman will bear a son." The baby remains unnamed in that text, the main focus of which is the marriage of two lovers more than the identity of their offspring. These demonstrate that the rhetoric here was familiar in the ancient Near East, particularly in birth announcements, and generally concerned royalty. *call him.* In ancient Israel, naming had more significance than it does today, when names are usually chosen for reasons of sound, popularity or association with a family member. Hebrew names have meanings that are transparent to those who understand the language, with the significance of this meaning tied to the birth event or some other aspect of life. For example, Benjamin, meaning "son of the right [hand]" (a position of honor) was so renamed by his father, Jacob; his original name, Ben-Oni, meaning "son of my pain," was given by his mother Rachel, who was dying in childbirth (Ge 35:19). Benjamin was much more propitious for the life of the child than was Ben-Oni. In Egypt, the pharaohs were given portentous names, usually five, when they ascended the throne (cf. 9:6). *Immanuel.* Meaning "God is with us," this name is similar to one found on several Israelite seal impressions: "Yahweh is with us."

7:15 *curds.* Milk in Israel was mainly from goats and could be consumed straight or processed. One of the processing means was pressing or churning, which produced what is translated "curds" here, though it more likely refers to something like yogurt or butter, since curds are formed from coagulation. "Ghee" is a possible translation, for, like the related word in Akkadian, it refers to refining and clarifying butter for longer "shelf life." Mesopotamians used ghee for food and medicine as well as in religious rituals. A number of texts associate this milk product with honey. *honey.* Usually made from pressing dates or grapes, although wild honey from bees was also used. Evidence of domestication of the honeybee exists in Iron Age Israel. An Egyptian relief from the mid-third millennium BC shows containers of bee honey. Shamash-resha-utsur, an eighth-century BC ruler of the area of Suhu in the Middle Euphrates, claims that he brought honeybees down from the mountain, something never before achieved. Honey is also used for food and medicine (as a poultice or ingested) and for rituals in conjunction with ghee. Both could keep well, so they were important for people on the move, as well as being enjoyable condiments for everyone who could find them.

7:20 *shave your head ... cut off your beard.* From wall reliefs from the period of the OT one can see that men from Israel and Syria had pointed, goatee-type beards, while the Assyrians had full, bushy beards. This is in contrast to the Egyptians, whose men were generally clean shaven, except for an artificial bound beard on the end of the chin. Involuntary shaving was an insult for those whose society favored beards and was at times done to prisoners of war. Sennacherib wrote of defeated enemy warriors: "I cut off their beards." Mourners also shaved themselves (15:2). In Isaiah, all the hair was shaven, including that of the "private parts." See the article "Shaving in the Ancient World," p. 1340. Here shaving is used metaphorically and ironically, since the razor used against Israel is one she had "hired" to protect her in the first place.

8:1 *scroll.* See the articles "Books and Literacy," p. 666; "Scrolls in the Ancient World" p. 1286. *ordinary pen.* The term for this tool is used only one other time in the OT: Ex 32:4 ("tool"), where it is used in the manufacture of the golden calf. It is therefore assumed to be some sort of drill or chisel. Ex 32:16 uses the verbal root related to this noun ("engraved") to describe the inscription of the Ten Commandments on the tablets. Cylinder seal artisans used drills, including a "fine drill." The word translated "ordinary" here, when modifying a person, refers to their fragile mortality. Perhaps here the use of a fragile drill is intended to suggest high quality workmanship.

8:2 *Uriah.* Chief priest at the time and in charge of anything to be placed in the sanctuary. A Hebrew ostracon, probably dating from the late seventh or early sixth cen-

ISAIAH 7:16

Israel and Aram Destroyed

To understand the history leading up to the demise of the "two kings" in Isa 7:16, it is important to see the relationship of the kings to one another.

ISRAELITE KINGS	KINGS OF JUDAH	ASSYRIAN KINGS
Menahem (752–742*)	Azariah/Uzziah (791–740/39)	
Pekahiah (742–740)	Jotham (750–732/31)	
Pekah (740–732**)	Ahaz (744/43–716/15)	Tiglath-Pileser III (745–727)
Hoshea (732–722)		Shalmaneser V (727–722)
		Sargon II (722–705)
	Hezekiah (716/15–687/86)	Sennacherib (705–681)

* All dates are BC and include coregencies.
** Includes his reign in Transjordan, where he had a rival government (752–740 BC).

Tiglath-Pileser III moved west with his armies on several occasions. In 737 BC he received tribute from Rezin of Damascus (cf. Isa 7:1) and Menahem of Samaria (2Ki 15:19). When Pekah faced this army, which took several of his cities (2Ki 15:29), he apparently did not capitulate to them, because pro-Assyrian Hoshea assassinated him and took the throne (2Ki 15:30). Hoshea continued his pro-Assyrian stance, ruling as an Assyrian vassal until he turned to Egypt for help, which proved his undoing. Shalmaneser V attacked him, and Samaria fell in 722 BC (2Ki 17:3 – 23).

In this way, the "two kings" Ahaz feared, Pekah and Rezin, disappeared from the scene through the agency of Assyria, the tool God used to answer Ahaz's prayer. This was not in Israel's best interest, however, since they would soon observe that the Assyrian cure was worse than the Syro-Ephraimite threat.

Assyria under Tiglath-Pileser III flourished and expanded in what is known as the Neo – Assyrian Empire. He campaigned to the south, subduing Babylonia, and then to the west, against Syria and her allies. For a time, the empire stretched even into Egypt. In its height, the Assyrians were able to besiege and capture Samaria, ending the Israelite monarchy and exiling its leading citizens (2Ki 17:24 – 41). While Judah became a vassal nation, it did not suffer the same fate as Israel did under the Assyrians.

Several of Assyria's kings are known from the Biblical texts, as well as from their own inscriptions. They include: Tiglath-Pileser III, Shalmaneser V (2Ki 17:3 – 4; 18:9), Sargon II (Isa 20:1), Sennacherib (Isa 36:1; 37:9,17,21,37), Esarhaddon (2Ki 19:37; Ezr 4:2; Isa 37:38) and Ashurbanipal (Ezr 4:10). They were known throughout the area for their ferocity and cruelty, with a mighty army that trampled over its weaker neighbors, often torturing and killing their defeated leaders and leading citizens. ◆

son of Jeberekiah as reliable witnesses
for me. 3 Then I made love to the prophetess, and she conceived and gave birth
to a son. And the LORD said to me, "Name
him Maher-Shalal-Hash-Baz. 4 For before
the boy knows[p] how to say 'My father' or
'My mother,' the wealth of Damascus and
the plunder of Samaria will be carried off
by the king of Assyria.[q]"
5 The LORD spoke to me again:

6 "Because this people has rejected[r]
the gently flowing waters of Shiloah[s]
and rejoices over Rezin
and the son of Remaliah,[t]
7 therefore the Lord is about to bring
against them
the mighty floodwaters[u] of the
Euphrates —
the king of Assyria[v] with all his
pomp.
It will overflow all its channels,
run over all its banks
8 and sweep on into Judah, swirling over
it,
passing through it and reaching up
to the neck.
Its outspread wings will cover the
breadth of your land,
Immanuel[a]!"[w]

9 Raise the war cry,[b][x] you nations, and
be shattered!
Listen, all you distant lands.
Prepare[y] for battle, and be shattered!
Prepare for battle, and be shattered!
10 Devise your strategy, but it will be
thwarted;[z]
propose your plan, but it will not
stand,[a]
for God is with us.[c][b]

11 This is what the LORD says to me with
his strong hand upon me,[c] warning me not
to follow[d] the way of this people:

12 "Do not call conspiracy[e]
everything this people calls a
conspiracy;
do not fear what they fear,
and do not dread it.[f]
13 The LORD Almighty is the one you are
to regard as holy,[g]
he is the one you are to fear,
he is the one you are to dread.[h]
14 He will be a holy place;[i]
for both Israel and Judah he will be
a stone that causes people to stumble
and a rock that makes them fall.[j]

8:4 [p] Isa 7:16 [q] Isa 7:8 **8:6** [r] Isa 5:24 [s] Jn 9:7 [t] Isa 7:1 **8:7** [u] Isa 17:12-13 [v] Isa 7:20 **8:8** [w] Isa 7:14
8:9 [x] Isa 17:12-13 [y] Joel 3:9 **8:10** [z] Job 5:12 [a] Isa 7:7 [b] Isa 7:14; Ro 8:31 **8:11** [c] Eze 3:14 [d] Eze 2:8 **8:12** [e] Isa 7:2; 30:1 [f] 1Pe 3:14* **8:13** [g] Nu 20:12 [h] Isa 29:23 **8:14** [i] Isa 4:6; Eze 11:16 [j] Lk 2:34; Ro 9:33*; 1Pe 2:8*

[a] 8 *Immanuel* means *God with us.* [b] 9 Or *Do your worst* [c] 10 Hebrew *Immanuel*

tury BC and found in the area immediately south of the temple mount in Jerusalem, lists a number of names. Though broken, the last legible one is of an Uriyahu/Uriah. *reliable witnesses.* Important, official documents in the ancient world were not only sealed but also witnessed by reliable folk whose names were inscribed toward the end of the tablet. They are indicated in Akkadian texts by the designation "in the presence of X," their signature assuring that the one who claimed to have produced the document did indeed do so. Contracts are serious undertakings, such as one for a delivery of straw having seven witnesses. The presence of two such witnesses here indicates some sort of official document, whether a marriage contract (v. 3) or some other record of a significant naming.

8:3 *prophetess.* Although all of the writing prophets in Israel were male, females also fulfilled a prophetic role. Prophetesses are mentioned in letters concerning prophecies from nineteenth-century BC Mari in north Syria, and numerous women are named as oracle-givers, though not always designated as "prophets," in seventh-century BC prophecies concerning the Assyrian kings Esarhaddon and Ashurbanipal.

8:6 *the gently flowing waters of Shiloah.* Lying in the hills, Jerusalem had a limited water supply in the form of springs, mainly the Gihon. Water needed to be directed from them to neighboring parts of the city by aqueducts or tunnels. Hezekiah, Ahaz's son and successor, cut a tunnel from the Gihon Spring (see the article "Hezekiah's Tunnel," p. 663), but this verse cannot refer to that channel, since that was later; moreover, that tunnel was of such a pitch that the water would not be called "gently flowing." An earlier Siloam, or Shiloah, channel carried water from Gihon down the eastern side of Jerusalem and irrigated the Kidron Valley. Its lower pitch allowed the water it carried to flow more gently.

8:7 – 8 *floodwaters ... overflow all its channels ... sweep on into Judah, swirling over it.* Flooding can metaphorically describe overwhelming military force that cannot be held in check. The same metaphor was used in Mesopotamia, where flooding was damaging rather than providing necessary irrigation, as it did in Egypt. Flooding is personified as an overwhelming force in the Sumerian "Curse of Agade"" from the early second millennium BC: "The rampant Flood who knows no rival."

The Old Babylonian king Naram-Sin describes his foe in flood-like terms — leveling cities, tells and temples. Ashurnasirpal II (883 – 859 BC) describes himself as "an impetuous flood," and Shalmaneser III (858 – 824 BC) describes his onslaught on his opponents in similar terms, comparing himself to the storm-god Adad.

8:7 *the Euphrates.* While the Jordan River was important for Israel because of its geographic location in the land, the river par excellence was the Euphrates. On several occasions it is called "the River" (e.g., Ps 72:8; 80:11). The army of the Assyrians, whose homeland was along the more eastern Tigris River, needed to cross the more westerly Euphrates River to approach Israel.

8:8 *Immanuel.* Means "God is with us"; it was a propitious name in 7:14 and is here applied to the nation of Judah as a whole. Some see vv. 9 – 10 as applying the term again to Judah, but the context may rather suggest that vv. 9 – 10 are taunting words of the arrogant Assyrian army. Sennacherib's officers used similar words to dispirit Jerusalem when it was under siege, claiming that the gods of other nations had been unable to save them, implying that they were now with Assyria (2Ch 32:17). Mesopotamian rulers regularly claimed the favor of the gods.

8:14 *stone that causes people to stumble.* An Aramaic inscription from this period speaks of Panammuwa bringing a gift to Tiglath-Pileser III, who made him king after he killed the "stone of destruction" from the house of his

And for the people of Jerusalem he
will be
a trap and a snare.[k]
15 Many of them will stumble;[l]
they will fall and be broken,
they will be snared and captured."
16 Bind up this testimony of warning
and seal[m] up God's instruction
among my disciples.
17 I will wait[n] for the LORD,
who is hiding[o] his face from the
descendants of Jacob.
I will put my trust in him.

18 Here am I, and the children the LORD
has given me.[p] We are signs[q] and symbols
in Israel from the LORD Almighty, who
dwells on Mount Zion.[r]

The Darkness Turns to Light

19 When someone tells you to consult[s]
mediums and spiritists, who whisper and
mutter,[t] should not a people inquire of
their God? Why consult the dead on behalf
of the living? 20 Consult God's instruction[u]
and the testimony of warning. If anyone
does not speak according to this word,
they have no light[v] of dawn. 21 Distressed
and hungry, they will roam through the
land; when they are famished, they will
become enraged and, looking upward, will
curse[w] their king and their God. 22 Then
they will look toward the earth and see
only distress and darkness and fearful
gloom, and they will be thrust into utter
darkness.[x]

9 [a] Nevertheless, there will be no more
gloom for those who were in distress.
In the past he humbled the land of Zebulun and the land of Naphtali,[y] but in the
future he will honor Galilee of the nations,
by the Way of the Sea, beyond the Jordan —

2 The people walking in darkness
have seen a great light;[z]
on those living in the land of deep
darkness[a]
a light has dawned.[b]
3 You have enlarged the nation
and increased their joy;
they rejoice before you
as people rejoice at the harvest,
as warriors rejoice
when dividing the plunder.

8:14 [k] Isa 24:17-18 **8:15** [l] Isa 28:13; 59:10; Lk 20:18; Ro 9:32 **8:16** [m] Isa 29:11-12 **8:17** [n] Hab 2:3 [o] Dt 31:17; Isa 54:8 **8:18** [p] Heb 2:13* [q] Lk 2:34 [r] Ps 9:11 **8:19** [s] 1Sa 28:8 [t] Isa 29:4 **8:20** [u] Isa 1:10; Lk 16:29 [v] Mic 3:6 **8:21** [w] Rev 16:11 **8:22** [x] ver 20; Isa 5:30 **9:1** [y] 2Ki 15:29 **9:2** [z] Eph 5:8 [a] Lk 1:79 [b] Mt 4:15-16*

[a] In Hebrew texts 9:1 is numbered 8:23, and 9:2-21 is numbered 9:1-20.

father. This apparently refers to Panammuwa's predecessor on the throne, using terms that impugn his legitimacy. Travelers on a journey were impeded by uncleared roads (62:10), metaphorically referring to rebel leadership impeding legitimate rule. *snare.* See notes on Ps 124:7; 140:5.

8:16 *seal up.* Scrolls could be sealed either by tying a string around them and sealing the knot with clay, or by placing them in a jar and sealing the cover. The clay or the seal around the lid would be impressed with the owner's seal. Mesopotamia used cylinder seals, Egypt used scarab seals, and Syria-Palestine used stamp seals. Tablets would be sealed inside a clay envelope, which would be impressed with the owner's seal. The seals were intended to vouchsafe the integrity of the contents. They warned against tampering and, if intact, attested to the authenticity of the document. See note on 1Ki 21:8.

8:18 *We are signs and symbols.* A Mesopotamian practice views people, especially newborns, as signs or omens. The person or some abnormality they have are indicative, as seen in at least two omen collections: *Shumma izbu*, "If a fetal anomaly ..." and *Shumma alu*, "If a city ..." Isaiah chides his fellows for ignoring the signs from God standing before them and instead consulting pagan sources.

8:19 *consult the dead.* Necromancy, consulting the dead, has already been condemned by Isaiah (2:6; see 29:4). Here some of its participants are identified. "Mediums" (those who consult the ghost) or perhaps the spirits of the dead could use living people and be consulted for esoteric knowledge (19:3; see note on 1Sa 28:7; see also the article "Consulting a 'Spirit,'" p. 508). A similar Sumerian term in the Gilgamesh Epic indicates a hole into the netherworld from which a divine spirit could issue. Mesopotamian texts refer to those who "bring up" the shades of the dead. A Sumerian proverb speaks of offerings to the dead, and archaeological evidence of such offerings for the dead indicates awareness of them even in Israel.

8:21 *hungry ... famished.* See note on v. 22.

8:22 *distress and darkness and fearful gloom.* An omen from Ugarit also associates the appearance of trouble (here "distress") with famine (cf. v. 21). It is found in a list of birth omens. These are based on events in human experience that in the past have happened subsequent to an irregular birth and so are likely to follow a similar birth anomaly in the future. Famine was often the result of inadequate rainfall, resulting in greatly diminished crop yields. Inability to find adequate food could result in widespread death or population dispersion to areas better supplied (see note on 9:20).

9:1 *the land of Zebulun and the land of Naphtali.* Zebulun and Naphtali lay in the area of Galilee astride a major highway through Israel from the north. They therefore were among the first people to be attacked from the north, such as that upon Pekah under Tiglath-Pileser III in 733 BC (2Ki 15:29). When Tiglath-Pileser had conquered the region, he left only the hill country of Ephraim to Israel, making the rest into three of the provinces of his empire: (1) The Mediterranean coastal area was the province of Duru, named after the city Dor on the coast, where Assyrian archaeological remains have been found. This "Way of the Sea" may refer to a route farther north toward Tyre, running from Abel Beth Maakah westward (seaward) toward Janoah. (2) Magiddu, named for one of its major cities, Megiddo, included "Galilee of the nations." (3) Gal'azi (Gilead, 2Ki 15:29) was in Transjordan ("beyond the Jordan").

9:2 *great light ... a light has dawned.* A major Assyrian deity was Shamash, the sun-god, the source of light. Hammurapi describes himself as "solar disk of the city of Babylon, who spreads light over the lands of Sumer and Akkad," thus assuming the illuminating role of his patron, Shamash. The Egyptians and Canaanites also had important solar deities. For Israel, light symbolizes the presence of God.

[4]For as in the day of Midian's defeat,[c]
you have shattered
the yoke[d] that burdens them,
the bar across their shoulders,[e]
the rod of their oppressor.[f]
[5]Every warrior's boot used in battle
and every garment rolled in blood
will be destined for burning,[g]
will be fuel for the fire.
[6]For to us a child is born,[h]
to us a son is given,[i]
and the government[j] will be on his
shoulders.
And he will be called
Wonderful Counselor,[k] Mighty God,[l]
Everlasting Father, Prince of Peace.[m]
[7]Of the greatness of his government and
peace
there will be no end.[n]
He will reign on David's throne
and over his kingdom,
establishing and upholding it
with justice[o] and righteousness
from that time on and forever.
The zeal[p] of the LORD Almighty
will accomplish this.

9:4 [c]Jdg 7:25 [d]Isa 14:25 [e]Isa 10:27 [f]Isa 14:4; 49:26; 51:13; 54:14 **9:5** [g]Isa 2:4 **9:6** [h]Isa 53:2; Lk 2:11 [i]Jn 3:16 [j]Mt 28:18 [k]Isa 28:29 [l]Isa 10:21; 11:2 [m]Isa 26:3, 12; 66:12 **9:7** [n]Da 2:44; Lk 1:33 [o]Isa 11:4; 16:5; 32:1, 16 [p]Isa 37:32; 59:17

The LORD's Anger Against Israel

[8]The Lord has sent a message against
Jacob;
it will fall on Israel.
[9]All the people will know it —

9:4 *Midian's defeat.* Midian, related to Israel through one of Abraham's wives (Ge 25:1 – 2), was a nomadic people without a fixed geographic location. The episode of their defeat at the hand of the Israelites is most likely when Gideon was able to defeat the Midianite army with only 300 men (Jdg 7). Here, as then, it is ultimately Yahweh who is the victor (Isa 7:14 – 17). *yoke.* Joins a pair of draft animals at the shoulders in order for them to be able to pull in unison. It could also join together people used as draft animals. It is a common Biblical metaphor for heavy service, especially to foreign powers. Liberation from such oppression is expressed by breaking the yoke. The same metaphor is common in the ancient Near East. In a text from the middle second-millennium BC Amarna, a leader vows that he has the yoke of his lord on his neck. Eighth-century BC Assyrian rulers used the same image; Esarhaddon (680 – 669 BC) speaks of imposing his yoke on conquered peoples. Freedom from domination was achieved in a similar manner: "Let us break the yoke." When one is under the yoke of a beneficent being, it can be to one's advantage, for the god provides the needs of such a faithful individual. The non-Semitic Hittites in Asia Minor used the metaphor as well, so it was well at home in Israel's literary and sociological environment. *the rod.* Can also be translated "scepter"; it is that borne by an oppressing ruler. It could be used for aggressive purposes or simply held as a symbol of the leader's potential power. Breaking it symbolizes the loss of that power.
9:5 *boot.* This is the only occurrence of this word in the OT, but the term in Akkadian indicates sandals or shoes. Many soldiers are shown barefoot or with sandals, though some wear higher boots. These and their outer garments, bloodied in battle, are here banned from Israelite reuse, but were to be destroyed by fire. The bloody aftermath of battle is accentuated by an Ugaritic reference to the goddess Anat, who kills so many opponents that she wades through the knee-deep blood and gore of her enemies.
9:6 *a son is given.* The birth of a son was viewed as a matter of rejoicing in ordinary circumstances. Having a royal son to assume the throne was even more important. Panammuwa I, a Syrian king in the mid-eighth century BC, wrote an Aramaic document stating a blessing on whichever of his sons succeeded in following him to his throne. The Assyrian Esarhaddon enacted a treaty with vassals to ensure that they recognized his desire that his son, Ashurbanipal, succeed him to the throne. *he will be called.* See the article "Names in the Old Testament Period," p. 1132. *Wonderful Counselor, Mighty God, Everlasting Father, Prince of Peace.* Whether chosen by this ruler for himself (supported by the Hebrew form of the verb "will be called") or by another on his behalf, the names are auspicious for his reign. Some suggest parallels with the Egyptian practice of a five-part royal title, though only four are listed here. The Ugaritic king Niqmepa had four titles: master of justice, he who builds a (royal) house/dynasty, royal guardian, royal builder, while Mesopotamian kings employed numerous titles or epithets. Although not all are used of one ruler, they include, "counselor," "(very) strong/mighty," "mighty, heroic," "eternal/everlasting," "father," "prince" and "one who quiets, brings peace." Therefore, the concepts applied to Isaiah's ruler are well represented in their literary environment. For this series of names being one long compound name, see the article "Names in the Old Testament Period," p. 1132. *Mighty God, Everlasting Father.* An undated seal impression in Phoenician, Ammonite or Hebrew belongs to a man named Abi'ad, "eternal father." Each of these names by themselves might suggest divine names. However, they should be recognized as the theophoric element in a compound name, thus making a statement about God, as many Hebrew names do (see the article "Names in the Old Testament Period," p. 1132).
9:7 *the greatness of his government and peace.* It is the last of the royal titles of v. 6 ("Prince of Peace") that is highlighted through this phrase. "Peace" denotes more than just a lack of war; it encompasses well-being, safety and plenty, along with good relationships with one's brother, neighbor and God (e.g., 27:5). It is a longed-for end of one's life as well as an anticipated goal of Israel's settlement of the land after years of wandering (Lev 26:6). It refers to existence without fear. The Mesopotamian god Marduk is purported to prophesy of a coming ruler, one who sounds much like Nebuchadnezzar I (1124 – 1103 BC), who probably had the piece written for propaganda purposes. That prophecy of a lengthy rule of peace and plenty echoes well with that of Isaiah's Messianic vision, showing that the hope for a king who establishes peace is, unsurprisingly, a common sentiment. In another text of Nebuchadnezzar I, Marduk and other gods are described as "guardians of peace," showing that peace has royal and divine sources. *He will reign on David's throne . . . from that time on and forever.* When political stability is not a given, a long-standing throne is something that people wish for. Esarhaddon received a message from Ishtar of Arbela that his reign would be established for eternal years. It was not a statement of absolute eternity, never-ending time in an ontological sense; rather, it was a wish for a long life. This was a common blessing wished on others as well, as noted in several Amarna letters. Absolute

Ephraim and the inhabitants of
Samaria[q] —
who say with pride
and arrogance[r] of heart,
10 "The bricks have fallen down,
but we will rebuild with dressed
stone;
the fig trees have been felled,
but we will replace them with cedars."
11 But the LORD has strengthened Rezin's[s]
foes against them
and has spurred their enemies on.
12 Arameans[t] from the east and
Philistines[u] from the west
have devoured[v] Israel with open
mouth.

Yet for all this, his anger is not turned
away,
his hand is still upraised.[w]

13 But the people have not returned to
him who struck[x] them,
nor have they sought[y] the LORD
Almighty.
14 So the LORD will cut off from Israel
both head and tail,
both palm branch and reed[z] in a
single day;[a]
15 the elders[b] and dignitaries are the head,
the prophets who teach lies are the
tail.
16 Those who guide[c] this people mislead
them,
and those who are guided are led
astray.[d]
17 Therefore the Lord will take no
pleasure in the young men,[e]
nor will he pity[f] the fatherless and
widows,
for everyone is ungodly[g] and wicked,[h]
every mouth speaks folly.[i]

Yet for all this, his anger is not turned
away,
his hand is still upraised.[j]

18 Surely wickedness burns like a fire;[k]
it consumes briers and thorns,
it sets the forest thickets ablaze,[l]
so that it rolls upward in a column
of smoke.
19 By the wrath[m] of the LORD Almighty
the land will be scorched
and the people will be fuel for the fire;[n]
they will not spare one another.[o]
20 On the right they will devour,
but still be hungry;[p]
on the left they will eat,[q]
but not be satisfied.
Each will feed on the flesh of their own
offspring[a]:

9:9 [q] Isa 7:9 [r] Isa 46:12 **9:11** [s] Isa 7:8 **9:12** [t] 2Ki 16:6 [u] 2Ch 28:18 [v] Ps 79:7 [w] Isa 5:25 **9:13** [x] Jer 5:3 [y] Isa 31:1; Hos 7:7, 10 **9:14** [z] Isa 19:15 [a] Rev 18:8 **9:15** [b] Isa 3:2-3 **9:16** [c] Mt 15:14; 23:16, 24 [d] Isa 3:12 **9:17** [e] Jer 18:21 [f] Isa 27:11 [g] Isa 10:6 [h] Isa 1:4 [i] Mt 12:34 [j] Isa 5:25 **9:18** [k] Mal 4:1 [l] Ps 83:14 **9:19** [m] Isa 13:9, 13 [n] Isa 1:31 [o] Mic 7:2, 6 **9:20** [p] Lev 26:26 [q] Isa 49:26

[a] *20* Or *arm*

eternity was not a concern in the ancient world, since even most deities had a finite existence. What is in view is perpetuity either through a single lifetime or into the foreseeable future.

9:10 *bricks ... dressed stone ... fig trees ... cedars.* A broad range of quality in products available to builders is presented here, from common and ordinary to fine and rare. Cheaply available were mud bricks, which could be easily handmade from readily available material and sun-dried. Isaiah brags that this common house-building stuff will be replaced by finished, hewn ashlar stone, which has been dressed on all sides by a chisel. Requiring more work and being much more durable, these stones were also more expensive than common brick. Roof beams were generally made from the commonly available wood of the sycamore-fig, which was used in spite of its softness and lack of durability. In contrast, the speakers, in their braggadocio, purport to replace it with the harder and therefore stronger, taller and more precious cedar (cf. 2:13). This is reminiscent of the days of Solomon, who "made silver as common in Jerusalem as stones, and cedar as plentiful as sycamore-fig trees" (1Ki 10:27; 2Ch 9:27).

9:11 *Rezin's foes.* Rezin, the Aramean king of 7:1, was conquered by Assyria in the campaign of 734–732 BC (see the articles "Syro-Ephraimite War," p. 1125; "Israel and Aram Destroyed," p. 1127). Undoubtedly Assyria is the enemy noted here.

9:12 *Arameans from the east and Philistines from the west.* When Assyria campaigned in the area, it moved against all the inhabitants, including Israel, the Arameans and the Philistines. Tiglath-Pileser III lists those from whom he received tribute: Ashkelon, Judah, Damascus and Gaza. Since this verse sees Israel suffering attack from these two neighbors, this could indicate that some of their soldiers were either conscripted into the Assyrian army or were hired as mercenaries. Both are attested in Neo-Assyrian inscriptions. *his hand is still upraised.* The anthropomorphism of God's outstretched hand most often, as here, indicates anger and judgment (5:25; 23:11), though it can also bestow blessing (Dt 4:34). In the Akkadian folktale Poor Man of Nippur, the poor man greeted the mayor with his right hand and blessed him in the name of the god and the city. In iconography, the hand seems most often stretched out in blessing or supplication, though at times it indicates aggression.

9:14 *head and tail.* Being inseparable, they are known to both go the same direction. *palm branch and reed.* The "palm branch" refers to the frond-like branches that grow out of the top of the trunk. Both the frond and reed will bend in whatever direction the wind is blowing and, like the "head and tail," have no ability to act independently.

9:17 *his hand is still upraised.* See note on v. 12.

9:20 *they will devour, but still be hungry ... they will eat, but not be satisfied.* A similar description is given of two baby sons of Ilu, the chief Ugaritic god. Upon their birth, Shahru-wa-shalimu (who are personified dawn and dusk) prepare food for themselves and eat it but are never satisfied. *feed on the flesh of their own offspring.* In times of siege, when all outside supplies were cut off by the surrounding enemy, people were driven to eating the unthinkable, even their own children (see note on 2Ki 6:28). This could be metaphoric, indicative of the barbaric way people treated each other. However, there is no reason to argue that it is not literal in Isaiah. Cannibalism was one of the curses for breaking the covenant between Israel and her God (Dt 28:53–57). In the Assyrian story of the flood, the Atrahasis epic, humankind is punished by deprivation of food. This happened for so long that they began practicing

ISAIAH 9:6

NAMES IN THE OLD TESTAMENT PERIOD

In the OT names not only looked to the circumstances of birth (e.g., Jonathan means "Yahweh has given [a son]"; Reuben means "Look! A son") but could also wish a blessing (e.g., Isaiah means "Yahweh's salvation"; Immanuel means "God be/is with us"). Royal names could change when a person attained the throne. Several Israelite kings had their names changed by their overlords, showing that they were under authority of an outside power (e.g., the name of Eliakim was changed to Jehoiakim by the Egyptians, 2Ki 23:34). Others seem to have adopted their own throne name, as some have suggested for Azzariya/Azariah (meaning "Yahweh aided") adopting the name Uzziah (meaning "Yahweh is my strength"). King David was identified at his death by four titles: son of Jesse, man exalted by the Most High, anointed by Jacob's God, Israel's favorite singer (2Sa 23:1).

Sentence names in the ancient Near East. Most names in the ancient world make statements, i.e., they are self-contained sentences. Many of the statements are about a deity. One can easily recognize the deity name in names such as *Ashur*banipal, *Nebu*chadnezzar, or *Ra*meses. Anyone even casually familiar with the Bible has noticed how many Israelite names end in -iah or -el, or start with Jeho- or El-. All of these represent Israel's God. This type of name is called a theophoric name, and affirms the nature of the deity, proclaims the attributes of the deity or requests the blessing of the deity. One way to interpret the titulary of this verse is to understand it as reflecting important theophoric affirmations: The Divine Warrior is a Supernatural Planner, The Sovereign of Time is a Prince of Peace. (Note: the word "is" is not used in such constructions, as all names demonstrate).

Compound names in the ancient Near East. The name Maher-Shalal-Hash-Baz in Isa 8:1 is a compound name comprised of two parallel statements. Since Isa 9:6 proposes this child's name (singular) rather than his names (plural; the NIV translates around this by avoiding the word "name" and translating "he will be called"), an attractive option is to consider this to be just one (long and complex) compound theophoric name. Though such compound names are not the norm in the ancient Near East, Isaiah is not presenting these as common. Assyrian use of compound names can be observed in the names Tiglath-Pileser III gave to the palaces and the gates he built in Calah. The latter are named "Gates-of-Justice-Which-Give-the-Correct-Judgment-for-the-Rulers-of-the-Four-Quarters, Which-Offer-the-Yield-of-the-Mountains-and-the-Seas, Which-Admit-the-Produce-of-Mankind-Before-the-King-Their-Master." ◆

21 Manasseh will feed on Ephraim, and
Ephraim on Manasseh;
together they will turn against
Judah.[r]

Yet for all this, his anger is not turned
away,
his hand is still upraised.[s]

9:21 [r]2Ch 28:6 [s]Isa 5:25
10:1 [t]Ps 58:2
10:2 [u]Isa 3:14 [v]Isa 5:23

10 Woe to those who make unjust
laws,
to those who issue oppressive
decrees,[t]
2 to deprive[u] the poor of their rights
and withhold justice from the
oppressed of my people,[v]

cannibalism. Among the curses that Esarhaddon placed on his vassals if they should break their treaty with him was cannibalism: the flesh of sons and daughters would become their rations rather than barley.

9:21 *his hand is still upraised.* See note on v. 12.

10:1 *unjust laws … oppressive decrees.* Reference is made here not to creating a justice system, but to issuing decrees or regulations regarding specific issues. In the political climate that existed in Isaiah's time, one of the special issues that had to be addressed was the raising

making widows their prey
and robbing the fatherless.
3 What will you do on the day of reckoning,[w]
when disaster[x] comes from afar?
To whom will you run for help?[y]
Where will you leave your riches?
4 Nothing will remain but to cringe among the captives[z]
or fall among the slain.[a]

Yet for all this, his anger is not turned away,[b]
his hand is still upraised.

God's Judgment on Assyria

5 "Woe to the Assyrian,[c] the rod of my anger,
in whose hand is the club[d] of my wrath![e]
6 I send him against a godless[f] nation,
I dispatch him against a people who anger me,[g]
to seize loot and snatch plunder,[h]
and to trample them down like mud in the streets.
7 But this is not what he intends,[i]
this is not what he has in mind;
his purpose is to destroy,
to put an end to many nations.
8 'Are not my commanders[j] all kings?' he says.

10:3 [w] Job 31:14; Hos 9:7 [x] Lk 19:44 [y] Isa 20:6 **10:4** [z] Isa 24:22 [a] Isa 22:2; 34:3; 66:16 [b] Isa 5:25 **10:5** [c] Isa 14:25; Zep 2:13 [d] Jer 51:20 [e] Isa 13:3, 5, 13; 30:30; 66:14 **10:6** [f] Isa 9:17 [g] Isa 9:19 [h] Isa 5:29 **10:7** [i] Ge 50:20; Ac 4:23-28 **10:8** [j] 2Ki 18:24
10:9 [k] Ge 10:10 [l] 2Ch 35:20 [m] 2Ki 17:6 [n] 2Ki 16:9 **10:10** [o] 2Ki 19:18 **10:12** [p] Isa 28:21-22; 65:7 [q] 2Ki 19:31 [r] Jer 50:18 **10:13** [s] Isa 37:24; Da 4:30 [t] Eze 28:4 **10:14** [u] Jer 49:16; Ob 1:4 [v] Job 31:25

9 'Has not Kalno[k] fared like Carchemish?[l]
Is not Hamath like Arpad,
and Samaria[m] like Damascus?[n]
10 As my hand seized the kingdoms of the idols,[o]
kingdoms whose images excelled those of Jerusalem and Samaria—
11 shall I not deal with Jerusalem and her images
as I dealt with Samaria and her idols?' "

12 When the Lord has finished all his
work[p] against Mount Zion[q] and Jerusalem,
he will say, "I will punish the king of Assyria[r] for the willful pride of his heart and
the haughty look in his eyes. 13 For he says:
" 'By the strength of my hand I have done this,[s]
and by my wisdom, because I have understanding.
I removed the boundaries of nations,
I plundered their treasures;[t]
like a mighty one I subdued[a] their kings.
14 As one reaches into a nest,[u]
so my hand reached for the wealth[v] of the nations;

[a] 13 Or *treasures; / I subdued the mighty,*

of funds with which to pay tribute. This was generally accomplished through special tax levies, though there were always exemptions granted to either classes of people or cities that had been given sacred status. Other possible issues include the manumission of debt slaves or the disposition of property in forfeiture. Usually the claim of unjust laws was made against a ruler by his successor. The Reform Text of Uruinimgina identified oppressive practices of former days that he put a stop to. Ur-Nammu claims that he did not "impose orders" but eliminated violence and cries for justice.

10:2 *deprive the poor ... widows ... fatherless.* Hammurapi singled out "the orphan (and) the widow," while Ur-Nammu states that "the orphan was not delivered up to the rich man; the widow was not delivered up to the mighty man." King Keret from Ugarit is condemned for failing to judge the case of the widow and to care for the oppressed and the orphan. The Egyptian tale of the "Eloquent Peasant" commends someone for their caring treatment of vulnerable classes, the same ones commonly mentioned in the OT. See notes on Lev 19:15; Dt 10:18; 15:7; 24:17; see also the articles "Ancient Law Codes and Leviticus," p. 183; "Decrees and Laws," p. 301.

10:9 *Kalno ... Carchemish.* These cities represent northern Syria, with the southern city (Kalno) treated as the northern one (Carchemish) had been. *Hamath ... Arpad.* These cities represent middle Syria, again with the southern one (Hamath) having been treated like the northern one (Arpad). *Samaria ... Damascus.* These cities represent southern Syria and Palestine, with the southern city (Samaria) having been treated like the northern one (Damascus). This presents a geographic rather than a chronological sequence. This leads to a final north-south sequence with Jerusalem juxtaposed to Samaria in v. 11.

10:10–11 Jerusalem is indistinguishable from her neighbors, including Samaria, in their use of images, even though they were formally banned. The only difference mentioned is that the idols of Assyria are superior, not that Israel has disavowed them as they ought. This may indicate their relative power, since Assyria with her idols were able to subdue both Israel and Judah. Part of any ancient conquest was to take away the god images of the conquered.

Ahaz used idols, and Isaiah and his contemporaries condemn their worship (e.g., 30:22; 31:7). Archaeology has not found many idol figurines from the first millennium BC, but there are a number of seals and seal impressions from this period. Some show deities, especially from Egypt. One is inscribed "Of Abiyau, servant of Uzziah," possibly referring to King Uzziah of Judah (Isa 6:1), showing an infant Horus kneeling on lotus or papyrus plants. Another belonged to a servant of King Ahaz of Judah and has a winged sun disk, three Egyptian crowns and two uraei (Egyptian cobras) on it. It reads "Of Hezekiah, [son of] Ahaz, king of Judah." More rarely, Mesopotamian iconography is shown on a seal.

10:13–14 *I have done this ... by my wisdom ... I removed ... I plundered ... I subdued ... my hand reached ... I gathered.* The Assyrian king is condemned for his pride (v. 12). His statements are like those found in contemporary Assyrian royal inscriptions. In one inscription the Assyrian king picks up another theme found in Isaiah as he boasts of the wisdom given him by the gods.

10:13 *I removed the boundaries.* Boundaries between holdings, whether at the national or the local level, were important to maintain, as established by law (Dt 19:14; 27:17). Some boundaries were marked by stones, similar to survey markers of today, which should not be moved. This practice was used in Mesopotamia during the

as people gather abandoned eggs,
so I gathered all the countries;
not one flapped a wing,
or opened its mouth to chirp.' "

15 Does the ax raise itself above the
person who swings it,
or the saw boast against the one
who uses it?[w]
As if a rod were to wield the person
who lifts it up,
or a club[x] brandish the one who is
not wood!
16 Therefore, the Lord, the LORD Almighty,
will send a wasting disease[y] upon
his sturdy warriors;
under his pomp[z] a fire will be kindled
like a blazing flame.
17 The Light of Israel will become a fire,[a]
their Holy One[b] a flame;
in a single day it will burn and
consume
his thorns[c] and his briers.[d]
18 The splendor of his forests[e] and fertile
fields
it will completely destroy,
as when a sick person wastes away.
19 And the remaining trees of his forests
will be so few[f]
that a child could write them down.

The Remnant of Israel

20 In that day[g] the remnant of Israel,
the survivors of Jacob,
will no longer rely[h] on him
who struck them down[i]
but will truly rely[j] on the LORD,
the Holy One of Israel.
21 A remnant[k] will return,[a] a remnant of
Jacob
will return to the Mighty God.[l]
22 Though your people be like the sand
by the sea, Israel,
only a remnant will return.[m]
Destruction has been decreed,[n]
overwhelming and righteous.
23 The Lord, the LORD Almighty, will carry
out
the destruction decreed upon the
whole land.[o]

24 Therefore this is what the Lord, the
LORD Almighty, says:

"My people who live in Zion,[p]
do not be afraid of the Assyrians,
who beat[q] you with a rod
and lift up a club against you, as
Egypt did.
25 Very soon[r] my anger against you will end
and my wrath[s] will be directed to
their destruction."

26 The LORD Almighty will lash[t] them
with a whip,
as when he struck down Midian[u] at
the rock of Oreb;

10:15 [w] Isa 45:9; Ro 9:20-21 [x] ver 5 **10:16** [y] ver 18; Isa 17:4 [z] Isa 8:7 **10:17** [a] Isa 31:9 [b] Isa 37:23 [c] Nu 11:1-3 [d] Isa 9:18 **10:18** [e] 2Ki 19:23 **10:19** [f] Isa 21:17 **10:20** [g] Isa 11:10, 11 [h] 2Ki 16:7 [i] 2Ch 28:20 [j] Isa 17:7 **10:21** [k] Isa 6:13 [l] Isa 9:6 **10:22** [m] Ro 9:27-28 [n] Isa 28:22; Da 9:27 **10:23** [o] Isa 28:22; Ro 9:27-28* **10:24** [p] Ps 87:5-6 [q] Ex 5:14 **10:25** [r] Isa 17:14 [s] ver 5; Da 11:36 **10:26** [t] Isa 37:36-38 [u] Isa 9:4

[a] *21* Hebrew *shear-jashub* (see 7:3 and note); also in verse 22

Kassite period (mid-second millennium BC). More than simply delineating land holdings, they also describe their granting, along with other entitlements that provided an income for the holder. Encroachment on such entitlements was a serious business, so strong curses are placed on any who move, deface or challenge the stone and its contents (see note on Dt 19:14). Neo-Assyrian royal inscriptions frequently mention the perspective Isaiah presents here, effectively removing any boundary stones by taking over the territory of others.

10:16 *wasting disease.* "Wasting" applies to both humans and to a dry measure for such things as grain, so God here threatens the depletion of either the Assyrian people or their produce. *sturdy warriors.* Those affected are not warriors, since the term used here for "sturdy" never refers to warriors in the OT, but refers rather to fat people (17:4) or luxuriant places (Ge 27:28,39). The curses at the end of Hammurapi's law collection include invoking illness, demonic pain and incurable fever and sores. Rib-Hadda of Byblos wrote the pharaoh of his illness and attributes it to offenses against the gods. It was commonly believed that illness or disease had divine or demonic sources.

10:18 – 19 *forests ... trees.* Most of the ancient Near East was not heavily forested, so trees were valuable for building as well as for their fruit. One of Hammurapi's laws penalizes someone for tree-cutting without permission. Israel was not to destroy trees in battle (Dt 20:19). Loss of trees was one of the curses for breach of covenant (Dt 28:42). Some Assyrian conquerors prided themselves in cutting and burning their enemy's trees.

10:22 – 23 *Destruction has been decreed ... The Lord ... will carry out the destruction.* The divine decree that a city should be destroyed is a familiar motif in the ancient Near East. In the Sumerian "Lament Over the Destruction of Ur," the divine council decreed the destruction of the city. There, however, it is lamented that there is no explanation for Enlil's decree. In the Marduk Prophecy the god decrees his own removal to Hatti. The Weidner Chronicle reports that Marduk decreed the destruction of city of Babylon at the hands of the Gutians for the offenses of Naram-Sin. In the Mesopotamian epic "Erra and Ishum," Ishtar became angry and stirred up an enemy against her city of Uruk. Though there is not always a "righteous" (v. 22) reason that could be cited for the destruction, the concept presented here is very familiar.

10:24 *this is what the Lord, the LORD Almighty, says.* Since the prophet is relaying a message from his God, he often uses what is called a messenger formula (see note on 6:9; see also the article "Prophets and Prophecy," p. 1110). It is also frequent outside the Bible, with many Akkadian letters including "thus says X." *as Egypt did.* Egypt had little involvement in the affairs of Syro-Palestine during the reign of Tiglath-Pileser III, since this was a time of division and competing claims between Egypt, Nubia to the south and Libya to the west. A single incident reports that Hanun, king of Gaza, fled to Egypt for protection when Tiglath-Pileser came against his city in 734 BC. It was not until the accession of Shalmaneser V to the throne of Assyria in 727 BC that Hoshea of Israel was emboldened to approach the Egyptians for help (see note on 2Ki 17:4). The reference to Egypt here is to the time of the exodus.

10:26 *rock of Oreb.* In Jdg 7:25, two Midianite leaders,

and he will raise his staff over the
waters,[v]
as he did in Egypt.
27 In that day their burden will be lifted
from your shoulders,
their yoke[w] from your neck;[x]
the yoke will be broken
because you have grown so fat.[a]

28 They enter Aiath;
they pass through Migron;[y]
they store supplies at Mikmash.[z]
29 They go over the pass, and say,
"We will camp overnight at Geba."
Ramah[a] trembles;
Gibeah of Saul flees.
30 Cry out, Daughter Gallim![b]
Listen, Laishah!
Poor Anathoth![c]
31 Madmenah is in flight;
the people of Gebim take cover.
32 This day they will halt at Nob;[d]
they will shake their fist
at the mount of Daughter Zion,[e]
at the hill of Jerusalem.

33 See, the Lord, the LORD Almighty,
will lop off the boughs with great
power.
The lofty trees will be felled,
the tall[f] ones will be brought low.
34 He will cut down the forest thickets
with an ax;
Lebanon will fall before the Mighty
One.

The Branch From Jesse

11 A shoot will come up from the
stump of Jesse;[g]
from his roots a Branch[h] will bear
fruit.
2 The Spirit[i] of the LORD will rest on him—
the Spirit of wisdom[j] and of
understanding,
the Spirit of counsel and of might,[k]
the Spirit of the knowledge and fear
of the LORD—
3 and he will delight in the fear of the
LORD.

He will not judge by what he sees with
his eyes,[l]
or decide by what he hears with his
ears;[m]
4 but with righteousness[n] he will judge
the needy,
with justice[o] he will give decisions
for the poor[p] of the earth.
He will strike[q] the earth with the rod of
his mouth;
with the breath[r] of his lips he will
slay the wicked.
5 Righteousness will be his belt
and faithfulness[s] the sash around his
waist.[t]

6 The wolf will live with the lamb,[u]
the leopard will lie down with the
goat,

[a] 27 Hebrew; Septuagint *broken / from your shoulders*

10:26 [v] Ex 14:16
10:27 [w] Isa 9:4 [x] Isa 14:25
10:28 [y] 1Sa 14:2 [z] 1Sa 13:2
10:29 [a] Jos 18:25
10:30 [b] 1Sa 25:44 [c] Ne 11:32
10:32 [d] 1Sa 21:1 [e] Jer 6:23
10:33 [f] Am 2:9
11:1 [g] ver 10; Isa 9:7; Rev 5:5 [h] Isa 4:2
11:2 [i] Isa 42:1; 48:16; 61:1; Mt 3:16; Jn 1:32-33 [j] Eph 1:17 [k] 2Ti 1:7
11:3 [l] Jn 7:24 [m] Jn 2:25
11:4 [n] Ps 72:2 [o] Isa 9:7 [p] Isa 3:14 [q] Mal 4:6 [r] Job 4:9; 2Th 2:8
11:5 [s] Isa 25:1 [t] Eph 6:14
11:6 [u] Isa 65:25

Oreb and Zeeb, were captured by men helping Gideon. Oreb was killed at the "rock of Oreb," an unidentified site along the Jordan River.

10:27 *yoke.* See note on 9:4.

10:28–32 The 12 cities mentioned here cut a path from the north directly toward Jerusalem. This is not the itinerary followed by Sennacherib when he came against Jerusalem in 701 BC. In that campaign he cut off all the cities of the Shephelah southwest of Jerusalem, Lachish being the last, and so approached Jerusalem from that side.

10:30 *Anathoth.* This city in Benjamin reflects the name of Anath, a Canaanite goddess mentioned as early as the Mari tablets as well as those from Ugarit.

11:1–16 A beneficent and tranquil rule is also an Akkadian ideal, in spite of their bloody and brutal reality. Not only people, but also animals and plants, will benefit in a text known as the Marduk Prophecy, most likely written after the event of an actual king's reign. A letter to Ashurbanipal describes a time of justice and equity when every age and all people will enjoy fullness of health and joy.

11:1 *shoot … stump … roots.* Arboreal imagery is used to show the rebirth of a people from what looks to all outward appearances like dead growth (cf. Job 14:8). The Ugaritic Aqhat Legend speaks of Dan'el as one who had no son, or shoot/scion, like his brothers did. Tiglath-Pileser III is described as the shoot or scion of the city of Baltil (i.e., Assur) who brings justice to his people.

11:2 *The Spirit of the LORD will rest on him.* In Akkadian texts, the equivalent of the empowering Spirit of God is the awesome radiance (*melammu*) possessed by gods and at times granted to kings. It is in many ways equivalent to the "glory" (*kabod*) attributed to Israel's God (e.g., 6:3). Sennacherib credits to it his ability to subdue Hezekiah with his awe-inspiring radiance. Some reliefs from Syria and Mesopotamia show various symbols above both gods and kings, indicating some continuum between the two, not in identity but in power and enablement.

11:3–4 An Old Babylonian ruler of Der is described as a just judge who does no harm and brings justice to victims. No royal attribute is more persuasive in the description of ancient kings than that they are just. Discernment of justice is considered a divine gift, and in Mesopotamia it was exercised in particular by the gods Shamash and Adad, and in Egypt by Thoth, god of wisdom.

11:5 *belt … sash.* The same Hebrew word is used for both of these words; one is a wrap around the thighs, while the other winds between the thighs. These are the most basic articles of clothing and without them an individual would be naked.

11:6–8 Ferocious animals were a constant threat, so the elimination of this threat would be part of an ideal kingdom. In the Sumerian Myth of Enki and Ninhursag, the paradise of Dilmun is described as a pure and clean land where the lion does not kill, the wolf does not take lambs and dogs do not devour goats. Another Sumerian text, Enmerkar and the Lord of Aratta, contains an incantation concerning a day with no predators or dangerous animals. In each of these cases, the beasts will disappear. There is debate whether the Sumerian texts describe an idyllic place or just a primeval period before things received

the calf and the lion and the yearling[a]
together;
and a little child will lead them.
7 The cow will feed with the bear,
their young will lie down together,
and the lion will eat straw like
the ox.
8 The infant will play near the cobra's
den,
and the young child will put its hand
into the viper's nest.
9 They will neither harm nor destroy[v]
on all my holy mountain,
for the earth[w] will be filled with the
knowledge[x] of the LORD
as the waters cover the sea.

10 In that day the Root of Jesse will stand
as a banner[y] for the peoples; the nations[z]
will rally to him,[a] and his resting place[b]
will be glorious. 11 In that day[c] the Lord
will reach out his hand a second time to
reclaim the surviving remnant of his people from Assyria,[d] from Lower Egypt, from
Upper Egypt, from Cush,[b] from Elam,[e]
from Babylonia,[c] from Hamath and from
the islands[f] of the Mediterranean.

12 He will raise a banner for the nations
and gather the exiles of Israel;
he will assemble the scattered people[g]
of Judah
from the four quarters of the earth.
13 Ephraim's jealousy will vanish,
and Judah's enemies[d] will be
destroyed;
Ephraim will not be jealous of Judah,
nor Judah hostile toward Ephraim.[h]
14 They will swoop down on the slopes of
Philistia to the west;
together they will plunder the people
to the east.
They will subdue Edom[i] and Moab,[j]
and the Ammonites will be subject
to them.

11:9 [v] Job 5:23 [w] Ps 98:2-3; Isa 52:10 [x] Isa 45:6, 14; Hab 2:14 **11:10** [y] Jn 12:32 [z] Isa 49:23; Lk 2:32 [a] Ro 15:12* [b] Isa 14:3; 28:12; 32:17-18 **11:11** [c] Isa 10:20 [d] Isa 19:24; Hos 11:11; Mic 7:12; Zec 10:10 [e] Ge 10:22 [f] Isa 42:4, 10, 12; 66:19 **11:12** [g] Zep 3:10 **11:13** [h] Jer 3:18; Eze 37:16-17, 22; Hos 1:11 **11:14** [i] Da 11:41; Joel 3:19 [j] Isa 16:14; 25:10

11:15 [k] Isa 19:16 [l] Isa 7:20 **11:16** [m] Isa 19:23; 62:10 [n] Ex 14:26-31 **12:1** [o] Isa 25:1 **12:2** [p] Isa 26:3 [q] Ex 15:2; Ps 118:14 **12:3** [r] Jn 4:10, 14 **12:4** [s] Ps 105:1; Isa 24:15 **12:5** [t] Ex 15:1 [u] Ps 98:1

15 The LORD will dry up
the gulf of the Egyptian sea;
with a scorching wind he will sweep
his hand[k]
over the Euphrates River.[l]
He will break it up into seven
streams
so that anyone can cross over in
sandals.
16 There will be a highway[m] for the
remnant of his people
that is left from Assyria,
as there was for Israel
when they came up from Egypt.[n]

Songs of Praise

12 In that day you will say:

"I will praise[o] you, LORD.
Although you were angry with me,
your anger has turned away
and you have comforted me.
2 Surely God is my salvation;
I will trust[p] and not be afraid.
The LORD, the LORD himself, is my
strength and my defense[e];
he has become my salvation.[q]"
3 With joy you will draw water[r]
from the wells of salvation.

4 In that day you will say:

"Give praise to the LORD, proclaim his
name;[s]
make known among the nations
what he has done,
and proclaim that his name is
exalted.
5 Sing[t] to the LORD, for he has done
glorious things;[u]
let this be known to all the world.

[a] 6 Hebrew; Septuagint *lion will feed* [b] *11* That is, the upper Nile region [c] *11* Hebrew *Shinar* [d] *13* Or *hostility* [e] *2* Or *song*

their static identity. There is little evidence in Mesopotamia for a return to paradise, and evidence for such is not clear here. The context in Isaiah, however, is clearly future oriented, and none of the animal imagery relates specifically to the Genesis creation account. The "Instruction of Any," a New Kingdom Egyptian text, takes a different approach to such beasts, one closer to that in Isaiah. It spells out some of the benefits of education, which can tame even the nature of the beasts: fighting bulls that are domesticated to become like an ox, a lion that becomes docile. The animals are not removed, just their ferocity.

11:11 The places named here are not necessarily intended to represent locations of known exile for Israelites. Rather they are equivalent to the "four quarters of the earth" (v. 12). Assyria is mentioned first as the actual location of exiles, but also as a representative of the northeastern area. Egypt, to the southwest, is identified in three segments up the Nile, including the kingdom of Nubia (NIV Cush). Elam and Babylonia represent the southeastern extremes, while Hamath represents the regions to the north. Finally, the "islands" is a way of representing the areas farthest west.

11:12 *four quarters of the earth.* Assyrian kings, including those in the Neo-Assyrian period, regularly designated themselves as "king of the four quarters (of the earth)," i.e., of the entire inhabited world. These relate to the four directions of the wind. Distant lands are emphasized on a Late Babylonian world map.

11:15 *the gulf of the Egyptian sea.* Nowhere else in the OT is there mention of such a water feature as this. Most probably the event referred to is Israel's exodus from Egypt, when the power of the Red Sea was dried up for Israel to cross through (Ex 14:21–22). *break it [the Euphrates] up into seven streams.* In Mesopotamia the water supply was regulated for irrigation use by separating and diverting sluice channels from canals that drew water off from the river system. As water was diverted, the various channels slowed the flow of the water. Such control of water was also at times connected with the gods gaining control over the power of the sea in a battle over chaos.

[6] Shout aloud and sing for joy, people of Zion,
for great is the Holy One of Israel[v] among you.[w]"

A Prophecy Against Babylon

13 A prophecy against Babylon that Isaiah son of Amoz saw:

[2] Raise a banner[x] on a bare hilltop,
shout to them;
beckon to them
to enter the gates of the nobles.
[3] I have commanded those I prepared for battle;
I have summoned my warriors[y] to carry out my wrath —
those who rejoice[z] in my triumph.

[4] Listen, a noise on the mountains,
like that of a great multitude![a]
Listen, an uproar among the kingdoms,
like nations massing together!
The LORD Almighty is mustering an army for war.
[5] They come from faraway lands,
from the ends of the heavens[b] —
the LORD and the weapons of his wrath —
to destroy[c] the whole country.

[6] Wail,[d] for the day[e] of the LORD is near;
it will come like destruction from the Almighty.[a]
[7] Because of this, all hands will go limp,
every heart will melt with fear.[f]
[8] Terror[g] will seize them,
pain and anguish will grip them;
they will writhe like a woman in labor.
They will look aghast at each other,
their faces aflame.[h]
[9] See, the day of the LORD is coming
— a cruel day, with wrath and fierce anger —
to make the land desolate
and destroy the sinners within it.
[10] The stars of heaven and their constellations
will not show their light.
The rising sun[i] will be darkened[j]
and the moon will not give its light.[k]
[11] I will punish[l] the world for its evil,
the wicked for their sins.
I will put an end to the arrogance of the haughty
and will humble the pride of the ruthless.
[12] I will make people[m] scarcer than pure gold,
more rare than the gold of Ophir.
[13] Therefore I will make the heavens tremble;[n]
and the earth will shake from its place
at the wrath of the LORD Almighty,
in the day of his burning anger.

12:6 [v] Isa 49:26 [w] Zep 3:14-17 **13:2** [x] Jer 50:2; 51:27 **13:3** [y] Joel 3:11 [z] Ps 149:2 **13:4** [a] Joel 3:14 **13:5** [b] Isa 5:26 [c] Isa 24:1 **13:6** [d] Eze 30:2 [e] Isa 2:12; Joel 1:15 **13:7** [f] Eze 21:7 **13:8** [g] Isa 21:4 [h] Na 2:10 **13:10** [i] Isa 24:23 [j] Isa 5:30; Rev 8:12 [k] Eze 32:7; Mt 24:29*; Mk 13:24* **13:11** [l] Isa 3:11; 11:4; 26:21 **13:12** [m] Isa 4:1 **13:13** [n] Isa 34:4; 51:6; Hag 2:6

[a] 6 Hebrew *Shaddai*

13:2 *gates of the nobles.* Gates were prominent places in the city, since everyone had to pass through them. Often they were given ceremonial names and epithetic descriptions, similar to the description used here, apparently for its main users. See notes on Job 5:4; 29:7; Pr 8:3; 31:23.
13:6 *the day of the LORD.* A common theme in the OT Prophets. It commonly refers to a time of judgment on Israel, but it also is used of other nations facing judgment from Israel's God (see, e.g., 34:8). *Almighty.* See note on Ge 17:1; see also the article "The Name of God," p. 15.
13:10 *stars … constellations … sun … moon.* The day of the Lord will bring darkness to the cosmic light-givers of Israel's neighbors. This could be an implicit threat against their deities, since the Egyptians, Assyrians, and Canaanites worshiped the sun (as Amun-Re, Utu/Shamash and Shemesh, respectively), the moon (as Nikkal/Ningal/Nanna and Sin in Mesopotamia, Yerah in Canaan) and the stars as gods. These populations made decisions based on their worship of, consultation with, and recording of the movements of what they perceived as astral deities in the sky. As they observed, they looked for omens that would help them make these decisions. *constellations.* Specifically those associated with Orion (e.g., Sirius, the Dog Star, Am 5:8). *darkened.* Darkness often figures in curses or difficult circumstances in ancient Near Eastern reports. Sargon I (c. 2310–2273 BC) was hindered in battle by a forest that was characterized by darkness with the sun's light being dimmed. As one of the curses for breaking a covenant with him, Esarhaddon calls for the oath breakers' eyes to experience darkness. In contrast, the Assyrian gods are often described as enlightening the darkness. The gods themselves were unnerved by darkness in the Gilgamesh Epic; in the prelude to the flood, Adad, the storm-god, turned the sky to darkness.
13:11 *ruthless.* Babylonian policy toward those who rebelled against them was physically harsh, employing various atrocities such as flaying people by removing their skin. This policy was adopted from the Assyrians, whose empire preceded their own. This was not sadistic but rather an aspect of foreign policy—a form of psychological warfare that served to debilitate enemies who heard of the atrocities. This was a means of keeping vassal peoples under control through terror. Reliefs on the palace walls of Assyrian kings fulfilled the same function, filling visitors and foreign emissaries with awe and terror at the might and brutality of their overlord.
13:12 *gold of Ophir.* Particularly fine, according to the metaphor used here (see note on 1Ch 29:4). *Ophir.* Its location is disputed, though areas along the Red Sea (Saudi Arabia or East Africa) are favored. An inscription from Tel Qasile, a Philistine site in what is now Tel Aviv, is a receipt for gold of Ophir.
13:13 *heavens tremble … earth will shake.* Convulsion of heaven and earth is commonly associated with the appearance of God. It is also associated with Baal, the Canaanite storm-god, whose thunderous voice is said to make the earth shake. This would be typical of storm-gods in the ancient world and would be characteristic of theophanies.

[14]Like a hunted gazelle,
like sheep without a shepherd,[o]
they will all return to their own people,
they will flee to their native land.[p]
[15]Whoever is captured will be thrust
through;
all who are caught will fall[q] by the
sword.[r]
[16]Their infants[s] will be dashed to pieces
before their eyes;
their houses will be looted and their
wives violated.

[17]See, I will stir up[t] against them the
Medes,
who do not care for silver
and have no delight in gold.[u]
[18]Their bows will strike down the young
men;
they will have no mercy on infants,
nor will they look with compassion
on children.
[19]Babylon, the jewel of kingdoms,
the pride and glory[v] of the
Babylonians,[a]
will be overthrown[w] by God
like Sodom and Gomorrah.[x]
[20]She will never be inhabited[y]
or lived in through all generations;
there no nomads[z] will pitch their tents,
there no shepherds will rest their
flocks.
[21]But desert creatures[a] will lie there,
jackals will fill her houses;
there the owls will dwell,
and there the wild goats will leap
about.
[22]Hyenas will inhabit her strongholds,[b]
jackals[c] her luxurious palaces.
Her time is at hand,[d]
and her days will not be prolonged.

14 The LORD will have compassion[e]
on Jacob;
once again he will choose[f] Israel
and will settle them in their own
land.
Foreigners[g] will join them
and unite with the descendants of
Jacob.
[2]Nations will take them
and bring[h] them to their own place.
And Israel will take possession of the
nations[i]
and make them male and female
servants in the LORD's land.

13:14 [o] 1Ki 22:17 [p] Jer 50:16 **13:15** [q] Jer 51:4 [r] Isa 14:19; Jer 50:25 **13:16** [s] Ps 137:9 **13:17** [t] Jer 51:1 [u] Pr 6:34-35 **13:19** [v] Da 4:30 [w] Rev 14:8 [x] Ge 19:24 **13:20** [y] Isa 14:23; 34:10-15 [z] 2Ch 17:11 **13:21** [a] Rev 18:2 **13:22** [b] Isa 25:2 [c] Isa 34:13 [d] Jer 51:33 **14:1** [e] Ps 102:13; Isa 49:10, 13; 54:7-8, 10 [f] Isa 41:8; 44:1; 49:7; Zec 1:17; 2:12 [g] Eph 2:12-19 **14:2** [h] Isa 60:9 [i] Isa 49:7, 23

[a] 19 Or *Chaldeans*

13:14 *hunted gazelle.* The Assyrian king Ashurnasirpal II held a banquet as part of the inauguration of his new palace. For it he served, among other things, 1,000 spring lambs, 500 stags and 500 gazelles. Gazelle meat served a more prominent role before the domestication of meat sources, but it continued to be hunted not only for food but also for sport. The gazelle or ibex is depicted on only a few Hebrew seal impressions.
13:17 *the Medes.* Living in the northern territory of modern Iran, south of the Caspian Sea, they were descended from Japheth in the table of nations (Ge 10:2). Shalmaneser III (ninth century BC) and subsequent Assyrian kings mention the Medes in inscriptions, especially as a source of horses (see the article "All the King's Horses," p. 720). Isaiah's contemporaries, Tiglath-Pileser III and Sargon II, led numerous military campaigns into Median territory. The Medes came more to the fore in the seventh century BC, when their king Cyaxares (c. 625–585 BC), in alliance with the Chaldeans/Babylonians under Nabopolassar (626–605 BC), captured the Assyrian capital of Nineveh in 612 BC, ending the Assyrian Empire. *who do not care for silver … gold.* Sometimes attacking armies could be bought off so that they would leave without destroying those under attack (2Ki 18:13–16). This was, in fact, the purpose of tribute, which functioned on a national level like extortion payments do on a personal level. Such tribute by subject kings to their overlord is common in Akkadian texts; Esarhaddon, e.g., increases the expected payment and it was common for kings to boast of the tribute they received. The actual metals (in weighed portions) served as currency before coinage spread in use to Babylonia in the sixth century BC. The Medes are pictured as so ferocious that they cannot be satisfied with anything less than conquest.
13:19–20 *Babylon … like Sodom and Gomorrah … will never be inhabited.* Sodom and Gomorrah, lying beside the Dead (Salt) Sea, were destroyed by God (Ge 19:15–25) and thereafter symbolized utter destruction. Thorns and salty soil, rendering most plant growth impossible, were characteristics of the destroyed area. A similar destruction is wished on those who break the eighth-century BC Aramaic Sefire Treaty—invoking Hadad to sow salt on the oath breakers' land. Common royal rhetoric speaks of turning rebellious cities into ruins.
13:21 *desert creatures will lie there.* When a place is totally desolate and empty of people, the native animals can take up residence there. The eighth-century BC Aramaic Sefire Treaty has a similar curse that the city of a covenant breaker become the habitation of various desert animals. *jackals.* A unique term (NRSV "howling creatures"). *owls.* NRSV uses "ostriches," though owls are more apt to live in ruins (34:13). *wild goats.* The term can also refer to domesticated goats (Lev 4:23). As early as the Septuagint (the pre-Christian Greek translation of the OT), this Hebrew word (*seirim*) was understood in some contexts to refer to demons (Greek *daimonion*) or "goat idols" (as translated in the NIV of Lev 17:7; 2Ch 11:15). The *seirim* in those contexts are not just liminal creatures, as here in Isaiah, but appear to be objects of worship, receiving sacrifices. The case cannot be made that we must consider these to be "demons" because they fit into what we see in the ancient Near East; they most definitively do not, for not a single aspect matches up with demons as known in Mesopotamia. In Mesopotamia, demons do not receive sacrifices. When in the Bible these creatures receive sacrifices, they are being treated as gods, not as demons. Though Paul may have characterized the foreign gods as demons, with no clearly established demonology in the Hebrew Bible, it is questionable whether we can say that the Israelites believed the foreign gods to be demons. Here in Isaiah the goats appear in a list of liminal creatures and should be so considered.
13:22 *Hyenas.* See 34:13. *jackals.* An unidentified breed of canine (this Hebrew word is different than that used in v. 21; cf. 35:7; 43:20).

ISAIAH 13:1 — 14:27

NATIONS TARGETED IN ISAIAH'S PROPHECIES

During Isaiah's lifetime in the eighth century BC, Assyria was the dominant power; Babylon would play a more major role in the following centuries. Assyria was the nation that exiled Samaria and its people, and the king of Babylon, Marduk-Baladan (Marduk-apla-iddina II, 722 – 711 BC), sent envoys to Hezekiah, supporting his political aspirations against Assyria (Isa 39:1 – 8). So why does Isaiah begin with a prophecy against Babylon? While some credit this section to a much later period (e.g., the time of the fall of the Neo-Assyrian Empire during the sixth century BC), there is no compelling reason to do so, since it equally well represents the eighth-century BC situation.

A group of West Semites of unclear origin (though apparently associated with the northern Arabian peninsula) the Chaldeans/Babylonians (see Isa 13:19 – 20) settled in the swamps of lower Mesopotamia and quickly acculturated to the Assyro-Babylonian culture. More urbanized than their better-known neighbors, the Arameans, who settled a bit farther north along the Tigris River, the Chaldeans paid tribute to the Assyrian overlords, but quickly gained power over them.

In the early eighth century BC, a temporarily weakened Assyria enabled Babylonia to gain political power in the area. To thwart the threat to their southern flank, a strengthened Assyria under Tiglath-Pileser III moved in, fought against them, and assumed the Babylonian throne, uniting Assyria and Babylonia for the first time in over four centuries. They maintained a dual monarchy through the next century. It could have been this move south against Babylonia that prompted this prophecy in Isa 13:1 — 14:27. ◆

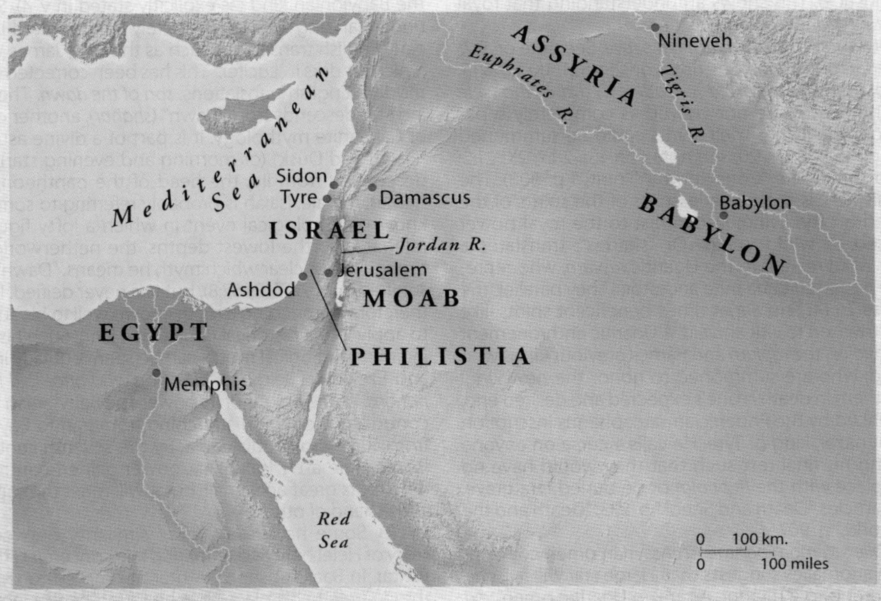

They will make captives of their captors
and rule over their oppressors.[j]

3 On the day the LORD gives you relief[k]
from your suffering and turmoil and from
the harsh labor forced on you, 4 you will
take up this taunt[l] against the king of Babylon:

How the oppressor[m] has come to an
end!
How his fury[a] has ended!
5 The LORD has broken the rod of the
wicked,[n]
the scepter of the rulers,
6 which in anger struck down peoples[o]
with unceasing blows,
and in fury subdued nations
with relentless aggression.[p]
7 All the lands are at rest and at peace;
they break into singing.[q]
8 Even the junipers[r] and the cedars of
Lebanon
gloat over you and say,
"Now that you have been laid low,
no one comes to cut us down."

9 The realm of the dead[s] below is all astir
to meet you at your coming;
it rouses the spirits of the departed to
greet you —
all those who were leaders in the
world;
it makes them rise from their
thrones —
all those who were kings over the
nations.
10 They will all respond,
they will say to you,
"You also have become weak, as we
are;
you have become like us."[t]
11 All your pomp has been brought down
to the grave,
along with the noise of your harps;
maggots are spread out beneath you
and worms[u] cover you.

12 How you have fallen[v] from heaven,
morning star,[w] son of the dawn!
You have been cast down to the
earth,
you who once laid low the nations!
13 You said in your heart,
"I will ascend[x] to the heavens;

14:2 [j] Isa 60:14; 61:5
14:3 [k] Isa 11:10
14:4 [l] Hab 2:6 [m] Isa 9:4
14:5 [n] Ps 125:3
14:6 [o] Isa 10:14 [p] Isa 47:6
14:7 [q] Ps 98:1; 126:1-3
14:8 [r] Eze 31:16
14:9 [s] Eze 32:21
14:10 [t] Eze 32:21
14:11 [u] Isa 51:8
14:12 [v] Isa 34:4; Lk 10:18 [w] 2Pe 1:19; Rev 2:28; 8:10; 9:1
14:13 [x] Da 5:23; 8:10; Mt 11:23

[a] 4 Dead Sea Scrolls, Septuagint and Syriac; the meaning of the word in the Masoretic Text is uncertain.

14:4b–21 The genre of the taunt song in these verses is based on a lament or dirge. The "taunt" (v. 4a) is a mocking speech that does not reflect actual sorrow, but rather joy at the demise of the hated ruler who is as good as dead.
14:5 *the rod … the scepter.* See note on 9:4. Shalmaneser I considered his scepter and staff to be the gift of the god Ashur (the national god of Assyria), while Tiglath-Pileser I attributed them to the god Shamash (the sun-god and god of justice). This shows an understanding that royal power was divinely given.
14:7 *All the lands are at rest and at peace.* See note on 9:7.
14:8 *cedars of Lebanon.* See notes on 2Sa 5:11; 1Ki 5:6; 6:15.
14:9 *spirits of the departed … leaders … those who were kings.* The dead were not viewed as completely separated from the living. Their spirits could be summoned back (e.g., 1Sa 28:11–20; see notes on 1Sa 28:7; 2Ki 21:6; see also the article "Consulting a 'Spirit,'" p. 508). The emphasis here is the powerlessness of the spirits of the deceased on the living, in contrast to the royal power they used to wield. *spirits.* Or "shades"; translates a Hebrew word related to the Ugaritic *rapium,* who represent the departed Canaanite ancestors. They parallel "the dead" (Isa 26:14) and are at times beneficent spirits, like Samuel, invoked to visit and aid. A Ugaritic enthronement liturgy invokes the *rapium* and names previous kings who had died, who are summoned to honor the new king. Joining them in death is one's expected and desired end, as evidenced by the Phoenician sarcophagus inscription of Eshmunazar, king of Tyre. He calls a curse on anyone disturbing his final rest such that they would have no resting place with the *Rephaim* or be buried in a grave. See the articles "Death and Sheol," p. 833; "Death and the Underworld," p. 907.
14:12 *fallen … morning star.* An Assyrian omen concerning birth anomalies suggests that a large star will fall, perhaps referring to a meteor. A broken Ugaritic omen text concerns the phenomenon of a star falling on the 30th day. *morning star.* The Hebrew (*helel*) occurs only here in the OT, though the verbal root means "shine" (13:10; Job 31:26). This "shining one" probably refers to Venus and is found also in Ugaritic mythology, with mention of "daughters of the morning star." The Vulgate translators in the fifth century AD rendered this as *"luciferos,"* also a reference to the morning star, Venus. This led interpreters centuries later to associate this passage with Satan, though it is not he who is the subject under discussion, but rather the Babylonian king (as explicitly stated in v. 4). Such an understanding was unfortunately incorporated into the early English translations such as the King James Version, which renders it "Lucifer." This has been corrected in most modern English translations. *son of the dawn.* The morning star descends from "dawn" (*shahar*), another denizen of Canaanite mythology. It is part of a divine astral pair, "Dawn and Dusk" (or morning and evening star), and is descended from Ilu, the head of the pantheon, and a human female. Isaiah is probably referring to some well-known mythological event in which a lofty figure was relegated to the lowest depths, the netherworld itself, though it is unclear which myth he means. "Dawn" is personified in the OT (Ps 57:8), but it is never deified. Isaiah is therefore historicizing a myth known well to his audience to apply it to a historical Babylonian king. Such historicizing of mythological motifs can be seen regularly in Isaiah and Ezekiel (cf., e.g., Isa 27:1). *you who once laid low the nations.* At the height of its power, the Babylonian Empire controlled the region stretching from Iran to Egypt and from Turkey to Saudi Arabia. By the seventh century BC (some time after Isaiah), its power gained control over neighbors great and small, but it will meet the same fate at the hand of others.
14:13 Some have seen some similarity between the story of Helel here and a Ugaritic tale concerning the god Athtar. In Baal's absence, Athtar attempted to sit on his throne (rule in his place), but he found he was not up to the task and subsequently took up his place in the netherworld. Though Athtar's name may have similar meaning

ISAIAH 13 – 24

PROPHECIES AGAINST FOREIGN NATIONS

International relations were often as strained in the ancient world as they are today. In the OT this is seen by the number of collections of prophecies against foreign nations (e.g., Isa 13 – 24; 34; Jer 46 – 51; Eze 25 – 32; Am 1 – 2). These foreign nations wronged God's people, so God brought judgment down on them.

Egypt had an equivalent to these Biblical prophecies in her Execration Texts. These were magical curses in which those people and nations cursed were listed on pottery bowls or clay figurines, which were then to be smashed, breaking the power of those inscribed. One of them speaks of "the Ruler of Jerusalem" and his retainers. ◆

An Egyptian execration text with curses written in hieratic script, eighteenth century BC.
Kim Walton. The Reuben and Edith Hecht Museum at the University of Haifa, Israel.

I will raise my throne[y]
above the stars of God;
I will sit enthroned on the mount of assembly,
on the utmost heights of Mount Zaphon.[a]

14 I will ascend above the tops of the clouds;
I will make myself like the Most High."[z]

14:13 [y] Eze 28:2; 2Th 2:4
14:14 [z] Isa 47:8; 2Th 2:4

[a] 13 Or *of the north*; Zaphon was the most sacred mountain of the Canaanites.

to Helel, he is not the son of Shahar (as Helel is described) nor is he thrown down after his attempt to sit on Baal's throne. Neither is the attempt itself an act of rebellion. The theme of revolt against the gods is, nevertheless, a familiar one. One of the best examples from ancient literature is the Myth of Anzu, in which a lion-bird creature attempts to steal the "Tablet of Destinies" by which the gods governed the world. Anzu decides to take supremacy of the world and the gods by stealing the tablet from the chief god, Enlil. He utters a series of "I will" statements, just as the king does here, with statements like "I will take the gods' Tablet of Destinies," "I will establish myself on the throne and wield the decrees," and "I will take command over the other gods." Boastful arrogance was typical of the antagonist in this type of account. Isaiah is using this sort of mythological motif to portray the arrogance of the human king of Babylon. *heights of Mount Zaphon.* Lit. "heights of the north" (see NIV text note). In Ugaritic texts, Saphon/Zaphon is identified with a mountain — Mount Jebel al-'Aqra or Mount Casius in classical sources (deriving from the Hittite Chazzi), which lies north of Ugarit. It is considered holy because it is capped by Baal's palace in the Ugaritic Baal Cycle and is also the site of his burial. Possibly the Baal text considers the mountain divine, though the text could equally speak of "the gods of Zaphon," a divine assembly such as that mentioned by Isaiah. The Babylonian king lays claim to divinity by establishing himself to the location of the gods.

14:14 *Most High.* Hebrew *elyon*, a title that usually describes Israel's God, sometimes in association with his name and other times on its own. Since deities are considered lofty, it is not surprising that similar titles are applied to gods of Israel's neighbors. Their supremacy is indicated spatially by several being cosmic, i.e., solar,

[15]But you are brought down to the realm
of the dead,
to the depths[a] of the pit.

[16]Those who see you stare at you,
they ponder your fate:[b]
"Is this the man who shook the earth
and made kingdoms tremble,
[17]the man who made the world a
wilderness,[c]
who overthrew its cities
and would not let his captives go
home?"

[18]All the kings of the nations lie in state,
each in his own tomb.
[19]But you are cast out[d] of your tomb
like a rejected branch;
you are covered with the slain,
with those pierced by the sword,
those who descend to the stones of
the pit.[e]
Like a corpse trampled underfoot,
20 you will not join them in burial,
for you have destroyed your land
and killed your people.

Let the offspring[f] of the wicked[g]
never be mentioned[h] again.
[21]Prepare a place to slaughter his children
for the sins of their ancestors;[i]
they are not to rise to inherit the land
and cover the earth with their cities.

[22]"I will rise up against them,"
declares the LORD Almighty.
"I will wipe out Babylon's name and
survivors,
her offspring and descendants,[j]"
declares the LORD.

[23]"I will turn her into a place for owls[k]
and into swampland;
I will sweep her with the broom of
destruction,"
declares the LORD Almighty.

[24]The LORD Almighty has sworn,[l]

"Surely, as I have planned, so it will
be,
and as I have purposed, so it will
happen.[m]
[25]I will crush the Assyrian[n] in my land;
on my mountains I will trample him
down.
His yoke[o] will be taken from my
people,
and his burden removed from their
shoulders.[p]"
[26]This is the plan[q] determined for the
whole world;
this is the hand[r] stretched out over
all nations.
[27]For the LORD Almighty has purposed,
and who can thwart him?
His hand is stretched out, and who
can turn it back?[s]

A Prophecy Against the Philistines

[28]This prophecy[t] came in the year King
Ahaz[u] died:

[29]Do not rejoice, all you Philistines,[v]
that the rod that struck you is
broken;
from the root of that snake will spring
up a viper,[w]
its fruit will be a darting, venomous
serpent.

14:15 [a] Mt 11:23; Lk 10:15 **14:16** [b] Jer 50:23 **14:17** [c] Joel 2:3 **14:19** [d] Isa 22:16-18 [e] Jer 41:7-9 **14:20** [f] Job 18:19 [g] Isa 1:4 [h] Ps 21:10 **14:21** [i] Ex 20:5; Lev 26:39 **14:22** [j] 1Ki 14:10; Job 18:19 **14:23** [k] Isa 34:11-15; Zep 2:14 **14:24** [l] Isa 45:23 [m] Ac 4:28 **14:25** [n] Isa 10:5, 12 [o] Isa 9:4 [p] Isa 10:27 **14:26** [q] Isa 23:9 [r] Ex 15:12 **14:27** [s] 2Ch 20:6; Isa 43:13; Da 4:35 **14:28** [t] Isa 13:1 [u] 2Ki 16:20 **14:29** [v] 2Ch 26:6 [w] Isa 11:8

lunar or astral deities. An Akkadian hymn title is "Exalted Ea." A Canaanite divine epithet like that used by Isaiah is "the Most High" (*ʿly*), and Baal is known as "Most High Baal." An eighth-century BC Aramaic treaty text speaks of the deities before whom the treaty is concluded, including "El" and "Elyon."

14:15 *the pit.* Initially indicating a literal pit or cistern, the Hebrew term used here metaphorically refers to the grave. The cognate Akkadian term most regularly shares the same literal meaning, though some also suggest an underworld link for it. See the articles "Death and Sheol," p. 833; "Death and the Underworld," p. 907.

14:19 – 20 *you are cast out of your tomb … you will not join them in burial.* While burial is the desired end of life, allowing a final peace, disinterment was done to move a body to a more appropriate place, as evidenced by Jacob and Joseph. Also a body could be moved within a family tomb to make room for later arrivals. Lack of a proper burial or actual removal from a grave was abhorrent (see notes on 1Ki 14:11; 2Ki 9:10; Ecc 6:3). On an Akkadian boundary stone a curse is uttered against anyone who defaces the stone that includes his corpse being cast aside with no one to see to his proper interment. This lack of final honor shows that one has reached the end of life without anyone who cares.

14:25 *trample him down.* This harsh treatment of the Assyrians is appropriate since Assyria was doing the same to its Israelite vassals. An Akkadian theodicy speaks of the wicked who trample on the powerless. *yoke.* See note on 9:4.

14:26 *the plan determined for the whole world.* See 40:8. In a monotheistic religion such as that of Israel, one could speak of a universal divine plan since there is but a single divine planner. In polytheistic religions, however, the multiplicity of deities works against a unitary divine plan; e.g., Tiamat's plan for domination was thwarted by the plan of other deities under the leadership of Marduk in the *Enuma Elish.*

Each instance of divine conflict reflects opposing divine plans. Plans could be claimed for specific cities by their gods, such as that claimed by Cyrus when he claimed that the chief god of Babylon, Marduk, had planned for him to conquer Babylon. In contrast, Yahweh, as universal Creator and Lord, can make and bring to fruition universal plans across the span of history. The gods in the ancient world devised ad hoc plans and year-by-year decreed destinies, but this never achieved the level of coherence attributed to Yahweh's plan with Israel.

14:29 *Philistines.* Philistia had been under the control of Judah during the reign of Uzziah, which took up the whole first half of the eighth century BC. They regained

30 The poorest of the poor will find pasture,
and the needy[x] will lie down in safety.[y]
But your root I will destroy by famine;[z]
it will slay[a] your survivors.
31 Wail, you gate![b] Howl, you city!
Melt away, all you Philistines!
A cloud of smoke comes from the north,[c]
and there is not a straggler in its ranks.
32 What answer shall be given
to the envoys[d] of that nation?
"The LORD has established Zion,[e]
and in her his afflicted people will find refuge.[f]"

A Prophecy Against Moab

16:6-12pp — Jer 48:29-36

15 A prophecy against Moab:[g]

Ar in Moab is ruined,[h]
destroyed in a night!
Kir in Moab is ruined,
destroyed in a night!
2 Dibon goes up to its temple,
to its high places[i] to weep;
Moab wails over Nebo and Medeba.
Every head is shaved[j]
and every beard cut off.
3 In the streets they wear sackcloth;
on the roofs and in the public squares[k]
they all wail,
prostrate with weeping.[l]
4 Heshbon and Elealeh[m] cry out,
their voices are heard all the way to Jahaz.
Therefore the armed men of Moab cry out,
and their hearts are faint.
5 My heart cries out over Moab;[n]
her fugitives flee as far as Zoar,
as far as Eglath Shelishiyah.
They go up the hill to Luhith,
weeping as they go;
on the road to Horonaim[o]
they lament their destruction.[p]
6 The waters of Nimrim are dried up[q]
and the grass is withered;[r]
the vegetation is gone
and nothing green is left.
7 So the wealth they have acquired[s] and stored up
they carry away over the Ravine of the Poplars.
8 Their outcry echoes along the border of Moab;
their wailing reaches as far as Eglaim,
their lamentation as far as Beer Elim.

14:30 [x] Isa 3:15 [y] Isa 7:21-22 [z] Isa 8:21; 9:20; 51:19 [a] Jer 25:16 **14:31** [b] Isa 3:26 [c] Jer 1:14 **14:32** [d] Isa 37:9 [e] Ps 87:2,5; Isa 44:28; 54:11 [f] Isa 4:6; Jas 2:5 **15:1** [g] Isa 11:14 [h] Jer 48:24,41 **15:2** [i] Jer 48:35 [j] Lev 21:5 **15:3** [k] Jer 48:38 [l] Isa 22:4 **15:4** [m] Nu 32:3 **15:5** [n] Jer 48:31 [o] Jer 48:3,34 [p] Jer 4:20; 48:5 **15:6** [q] Isa 19:5-7; Jer 48:34 [r] Joel 1:12 **15:7** [s] Isa 30:6; Jer 48:36

their independence during the reign of Ahaz and became the aggressor. With the rise of the Neo-Assyrian Empire, Philistia came under attack, just as the rest of the western nations did. Tiglath-Pileser III targeted Gaza in his campaign of 734 BC, and the cities of Philistia thus became tribute-paying vassals. When Sargon came to the throne, the Philistines attempted to break free of Assyria, but in 720 BC Philistia again came under attack and Gaza renewed its loyalty. In 712 BC Sargon again came west to subdue the revolt led by Ashdod. Ekron and Gath were also targeted at this time. Sennacherib's 701 BC campaign brought changes on the thrones of several of the Philistine cities, but only Ekron needed to be besieged. Through most of the eighth and seventh centuries BC, the Philistines shared the fate of their neighbors in Judah. Eventually, the Philistines were defeated and deported by Nebuchadnezzar, just as the people of Judah were. The five cities retained some degree of prominence, but the people were gradually assimilated into the general mix of the empire population by the Persian period.

15:1–4 Like many of the small Syro-Palestinian states during the eighth century BC, Moab was dominated by Assyrian hegemony over the region. Several Assyrian texts list Moabite kings paying tribute or being implicated in the periodic revolts by coalitions of these small nations (Ashdod Revolt of 713–711 BC recorded in a prism from Sargon II's reign). Since Isaiah is probably speaking during the early reign of Hezekiah, the destruction of Moabite cities is probably due to incursions by desert tribes rather than the Assyrians. It seems clear from Sennacherib's annals that Moab attempted to ingratiate herself during the 701 BC campaign that saw much of Judah devastated and Jerusalem besieged. As a result, Israelite prophets (Jer 48; Am 2:1–5) generally list Moab as an enemy nation.

The cities listed as destroyed or damaged in vv. 1–4 are all in the northern sector of Moab: Kir (Kir Hareseth in Isa 16:7) is on the upper portion of the Wadi el-Kerak and serves as the capital of the district of Ar. Nebo and Medeba are both located just east of the northern end of the Dead Sea and about 20 miles (32 kilometers) north of Dibon. Also attacked were Heshbon and Elealeh, located northeast of Nebo. The more southern cities of Dibon (20 miles [32 kilometers] north of Kir) and Jahaz were apparently not directly affected by the raiders but were in fear of future incursions.

15:2 *high places.* Canaanites (as well as Israelites, 1Ki 3:1–4) worshiped at high places, here parallel to "temple" (lit. "house"). Their exact nature is debated, but they were most likely platforms associated with sacred standing stones. The Moabite king Mesha speaks of a high place for Chemosh (Moab's national deity), which might be the destination here. *wails.* Worship has turned to mourning, as in the Lamentation Over the Destruction of Ur from a millennium earlier.

15:3 *sackcloth ... wail ... prostrate with weeping.* See the article "Mourning," p. 828.

15:5–9 The key to the line of flight for the Moabite fugitives is Zoar since all of the other sites mentioned cannot be identified (mentioned elsewhere only in the parallel text of Jer 48:3,5,34). According to Ge 14:2–3, Zoar is one of the cities of the plain. Speculation on its exact location, however, places it near Mount Nebo (Dt 34:1–3), near the northern tip of the Dead Sea as well as in the area at the southern end of the Dead Sea. Considering the apparent focus of the attack in Isa 15:1–4 around Kir and Nebo, it seems that a southern site for Zoar and these other cities would be more appropriate for a flight to safety toward Edom.

9 The waters of Dimon[a] are full of blood,
but I will bring still more upon Dimon[a] —
a lion[t] upon the fugitives of Moab
and upon those who remain in the land.

16 Send lambs[u] as tribute
to the ruler of the land,
from Sela,[v] across the desert,
to the mount of Daughter Zion.[w]
2 Like fluttering birds
pushed from the nest,[x]
so are the women of Moab
at the fords of the Arnon.[y]

3 "Make up your mind," Moab says.
"Render a decision.
Make your shadow like night —
at high noon.
Hide the fugitives,[z]
do not betray the refugees.
4 Let the Moabite fugitives stay with you;
be their shelter from the destroyer."
The oppressor[a] will come to an end,
and destruction will cease;
the aggressor will vanish from the land.
5 In love a throne[b] will be established;
in faithfulness a man will sit on it —
one from the house[b] of David[c] —
one who in judging seeks justice[d]
and speeds the cause of righteousness.
6 We have heard of Moab's[e] pride[f] —
how great is her arrogance! —
of her conceit, her pride and her insolence;
but her boasts are empty.
7 Therefore the Moabites wail,[g]
they wail together for Moab.
Lament and grieve
for the raisin cakes[h] of Kir Hareseth.[i]
8 The fields of Heshbon wither,
the vines of Sibmah also.
The rulers of the nations
have trampled down the choicest vines,
which once reached Jazer
and spread toward the desert.
Their shoots spread out
and went as far as the sea.[c]
9 So I weep,[j] as Jazer weeps,
for the vines of Sibmah.
Heshbon and Elealeh,
I drench you with tears!
The shouts of joy over your ripened fruit
and over your harvests[k] have been stilled.
10 Joy and gladness are taken away from the orchards;[l]
no one sings or shouts in the vineyards;
no one treads[m] out wine at the presses,[n]
for I have put an end to the shouting.
11 My heart laments for Moab[o] like a harp,
my inmost being[p] for Kir Hareseth.
12 When Moab appears at her high place,
she only wears herself out;
when she goes to her shrine[q] to pray,
it is to no avail.[r]

13 This is the word the LORD has already
spoken concerning Moab. 14 But now the
LORD says: "Within three years, as a servant bound by contract would count them,
Moab's splendor and all her many people
will be despised,[s] and her survivors will
be very few and feeble."[t]

A Prophecy Against Damascus

17 A prophecy against Damascus:[u]
"See, Damascus will no longer be a city
but will become a heap of ruins.[v]

15:9 [t] 2Ki 17:25
16:1 [u] 2Ki 3:4 [v] 2Ki 14:7 [w] Isa 10:32
16:2 [x] Pr 27:8 [y] Nu 21:13-14; Jer 48:20
16:3 [z] 1Ki 18:4
16:4 [a] Isa 9:4
16:5 [b] Da 7:14; Mic 4:7 [c] Lk 1:32 [d] Isa 9:7
16:6 [e] Am 2:1; Zep 2:8 [f] Ob 1:3; Zep 2:10
16:7 [g] Jer 48:20 [h] 1Ch 16:3 [i] 2Ki 3:25
16:9 [j] Isa 15:3 [k] Jer 40:12
16:10 [l] Isa 24:7-8 [m] Jdg 9:27 [n] Job 24:11
16:11 [o] Isa 15:5 [p] Isa 63:15; Hos 11:8; Php 2:1
16:12 [q] Isa 15:2 [r] 1Ki 18:29
16:14 [s] Isa 25:10; Jer 48:42 [t] Isa 21:17
17:1 [u] Ge 14:15; Jer 49:23; Ac 9:2 [v] Isa 25:2; Am 1:3; Zec 9:1

[a] 9 *Dimon*, a wordplay on *Dibon* (see verse 2), sounds like the Hebrew for *blood*. [b] 5 Hebrew *tent* [c] 8 Probably the Dead Sea

15:9 *The waters of Dimon are full of blood.* Blood flowing like, and into, a river speaks to a situation of utter destruction. A Neo-Assyrian prophecy uses the same imagery when it refers to filling a river with the blood of sacrificed enemies. Such examples of metaphors and ideas shared between the Bible and the ancient Near Eastern texts shows that the Israelites were very much a part of the ancient world.
16:1 *Send lambs as tribute.* Often tribute given from a vassal to an overlord consisted of luxury goods or money. Livestock was also levied as tribute from areas in which it was raised, such as the Persian province of Trans-Euphrates (lit. "beyond the River" [see note on Ezr 4:11]). This refers to the area west of the Euphrates, which includes the Moabite plateau, known for herds of cattle and sheep. The Moabite king had previously supplied great quantities of livestock as tribute to Israel (2Ki 3:4). *Sela.* Means "rock"; it is best known as the capital city of the Edomites (2Ki 4:7), who lived just south of Moab. This may have been the refugees' final destination, from which they contact Judah and Jerusalem. There is no known place in Moab with this name, though somewhere in its southern region fits best into the context of Isaiah. Rocky sites would be appropriately so named in both territories.
16:2 *fords of the Arnon.* The Arnon Gorge enters the Dead Sea about in the center of its eastern side. Mesha, the Moabite king, claimed to have made a military road in the Arnon, and the fords may well be where the main north-south King's Highway (see note on Nu 20:17) crossed it.
17:1 *Damascus.* The Syro-Ephraimite War (see the article "Syro-Ephraimite War," p. 1125), which raged during the middle 730s BC, ended with the Assyrian king Tiglath-Pileser III invading Syria and Israel and devastating both of these rebellious states (734–732 BC). The Syrian kingdom, ruled from Damascus by Rezin (see Isa 7:1–9), had been Israel's principal

Egyptian harvesting scene, Tomb of Unsu, c. 1550 to 1069 BC. Isa 17:5 compares the destruction of Israel to "when reapers harvest the standing grain."

[2]The cities of Aroer will be deserted
and left to flocks,[w] which will lie
down,
with no one to make them afraid.[x]
[3]The fortified city will disappear from
Ephraim,
and royal power from Damascus;
the remnant of Aram will be
like the glory[y] of the Israelites,"[z]
declares the LORD Almighty.

[4]"In that day the glory of Jacob will fade;
the fat of his body will waste[a] away.
[5]It will be as when reapers harvest the
standing grain,
gathering[b] the grain in their arms—
as when someone gleans heads of grain
in the Valley of Rephaim.
[6]Yet some gleanings will remain,[c]
as when an olive tree is beaten,[d]
leaving two or three olives on the
topmost branches,
four or five on the fruitful boughs,"
declares the LORD, the God
of Israel.

[7]In that day people will look[e] to their
Maker
and turn their eyes to the Holy One[f]
of Israel.
[8]They will not look to the altars,
the work of their hands,[g]

17:2 [w]Isa 7:21; Eze 25:5 [x]Jer 7:33; Mic 4:4 **17:3** [y]ver 4; Hos 9:11 [z]Isa 7:8, 16; 8:4 **17:4** [a]Isa 10:16 **17:5** [b]ver 11; Jer 51:33; Joel 3:13; Mt 13:30 **17:6** [c]Dt 4:27; Isa 24:13 [d]Isa 27:12 **17:7** [e]Isa 10:20 [f]Mic 7:7 **17:8** [g]Isa 2:18, 20; 30:22

political and economic rival. He had meddled in Israel and Judah's internal affairs and had encroached on their territories for over a decade. It seems apparent, however, that Rezin overstepped his bounds in leading an anti-Assyrian coalition. Assyria did not welcome a rival "Greater Syria," and the destruction of Damascus in 732 BC, as recorded in the Assyrian annals, was massive: it left hundreds of sites looking "like hills over which the flood had swept." This widespread destruction also included both the reduction of much of the city of Damascus to rubble as well as the redistribution of its territories in Syria, Transjordan and Galilee.
17:2 *Aroer.* Located on the Arnon River southeast of Dibon and just east of the King's Highway. Its fortress (which at one period measured 50 yards [45.7 meters] on each side) marked the southernmost boundary of Moab. Mesha, in his inscription, credits himself with refortifying it.
17:5 *reapers.* Grain is harvested by reapers who, while gathering the stalks in the left hand, cut them just below the grain itself with a sickle held in the right hand. This is shown in several Egyptian reliefs. *Valley of Rephaim.* Dividing the territories of Benjamin and Judah, it extending from Jerusalem to the southwest. From this passage it is evident that the valley was fertile and apparently a source of much of the provision for Jerusalem.
17:8 *Asherah poles.* See notes on Dt 7:5; 1Ki 14:23. *incense altars.* See note on Ex 30:2.

and they will have no regard for the
Asherah poles[a]
and the incense altars their fingers
have made.

9 In that day their strong cities, which
they left because of the Israelites, will be
like places abandoned to thickets and undergrowth. And all will be desolation.

10 You have forgotten[h] God your Savior;[i]
you have not remembered the Rock,
your fortress.
Therefore, though you set out the
finest plants
and plant imported vines,
11 though on the day you set them out,
you make them grow,
and on the morning[j] when you plant
them, you bring them to bud,
yet the harvest will be as nothing[k]
in the day of disease and incurable
pain.[l]

12 Woe to the many nations that rage —
they rage like the raging sea![m]
Woe to the peoples who roar —
they roar like the roaring of great
waters!
13 Although the peoples roar like the roar
of surging waters,
when he rebukes[n] them they flee[o]
far away,
driven before the wind like chaff[p] on
the hills,
like tumbleweed before a gale.[q]
14 In the evening, sudden terror!
Before the morning, they are gone![r]
This is the portion of those who
loot us,
the lot of those who plunder us.

17:10 [h]Isa 51:13 [i]Ps 68:19; Isa 12:2 **17:11** [j]Ps 90:6 [k]Hos 8:7 [l]Job 4:8 **17:12** [m]Ps 18:4; Jer 6:23; Lk 21:25 **17:13** [n]Ps 9:5 [o]Isa 13:14 [p]Isa 41:2,15-16 [q]Job 21:18 **17:14** [r]2Ki 19:35 **18:1** [s]Isa 20:3-5; Eze 30:4-5,9; Zep 2:12; 3:10 **18:2** [t]Ex 2:3 [u]Ge 10:8-9; 2Ch 12:3 [v]ver 7 **18:3** [w]Isa 5:26

A Prophecy Against Cush

18 Woe to the land of whirring
wings[b]
along the rivers of Cush,[c][s]
2 which sends envoys by sea
in papyrus[t] boats over the water.

Go, swift messengers,
to a people tall and smooth-skinned,
to a people feared far and wide,
an aggressive[u] nation of strange
speech,
whose land is divided by rivers.[v]

3 All you people of the world,
you who live on the earth,
when a banner[w] is raised on the
mountains,
you will see it,
and when a trumpet sounds,
you will hear it.

[a] *8* That is, wooden symbols of the goddess Asherah
[b] *1* Or *of locusts* [c] *1* That is, the upper Nile region

17:14 *lot.* See notes on Est 3:7; Pr 16:33.

18:1 – 7 In the OT, Cush refers to two different areas: (1) a region in Mesopotamia that may be related to the later Kassites (Ge 2:13), and (2) the territory immediately south of Egypt, the territory in view here. Translated in the Septuagint, the pre-Christian Greek translation of the OT, as "Ethiopia," Cush probably lies north and west of what we know today as Ethiopia — i.e., in what is now northern Sudan, ancient Nubia, populated by black African people.

Early in the history of Cush, its northern boundary was between the first and second Nile cataracts, though later it was pushed a bit farther south. Egypt and its neighbor to the south were constantly jockeying for power in the region. In the late eighth and early seventh centuries BC, during the Third Intermediate Period, the Twenty-Fifth (Ethiopian) Dynasty controlled Egypt and had contact with Israelite rulers (e.g., 2Ki 17:4). References to either "Egypt" or "Cush" in Isaiah most likely refer to this dynasty. They challenged Assyria's territorial expansion to the west, including Israel.

Akkadian texts refer both to Kus and to Meluhha (Nubia). In the time of Isaiah, Sargon II made several campaigns to the west against a group of anti-Assyrian allies, probably including Judah and Cush. One of his inscriptions speaks of a person named Yamani, who fled to that area of Egypt from Sargon's approaching army.

18:1 *land of whirring wings.* Locusts or other flying insects plague the Middle East (see notes on Joel 1:4,6), and another occurrence of the same Hebrew term refers to such creatures (Dt 28:42). These could be used to describe Cush, which undoubtedly suffered locust infestations, but it is curious that such a ubiquitous feature should define a distant nation. The Septuagint, the pre-Christian Greek translation of the OT, and the Targums interpret the term as a kind of boat, possibly another referent to the swiftly darting crafts of v. 2. The Egyptians, and by implication, the Cushites, used boats with sails, whose flapping would sound like the whirring of many insect wings.

18:2 *envoys.* International relations were influenced by both military encounters and diplomatic contact (see notes on 6:9; 39:7). While the former receive the greatest mention in the texts, the latter was also important in trying to maintain the peace or at least to subvert the powers of war. This type of messenger or envoy made international contact, though here in Isaiah it is unclear who the "messengers" represent or to whom they are being sent. It appears that they are to take a general, unspecified message to the world (v. 3). *tall and smooth-skinned.* Although it seems clear that Ethiopia is sending diplomatic overtures to Assyria, they would not be making the entire trip in papyrus boats. These light craft would only be suitable for the Nile. Since the Assyrians were neither tall nor smooth skinned (considering all the representations we have of short, bearded men in Assyrian reliefs), then the envoys may also be spreading the word to the Cushite people to join in the effort to unite Egypt. Herodotus's picture of "Ethiopians" as the tallest of the Africans would fit this reconstruction. *strange speech.* This unique term is a reduplicated adjective (*qaw-qaw*), meaning lit. "very strong." It may be an onomatopoetic term resembling the babbling sound of a foreign tongue, much like "barbarian" (one whose language sounds like "bar-bar"). *land is divided by rivers.* This is an apt description of Mesopotamia, the "Land of Two Rivers," the Tigris and Euphrates. However, since the envoys of the Ethiopian pharaoh Shabako, at least initially, are being sent throughout Egypt, the "rivers"

[4]This is what the LORD says to me:
"I will remain quiet and will look on
from my dwelling place,[x]
like shimmering heat in the sunshine,
like a cloud of dew[y] in the heat of
harvest."
[5]For, before the harvest, when the
blossom is gone
and the flower becomes a ripening
grape,
he will cut off the shoots with pruning
knives,
and cut down and take away the
spreading branches.[z]
[6]They will all be left to the mountain
birds of prey
and to the wild animals;[a]
the birds will feed on them all summer,
the wild animals all winter.

[7]At that time gifts will be brought to the
LORD Almighty

from a people tall and smooth-skinned,
from a people feared far and wide,
an aggressive nation of strange speech,
whose land is divided by rivers—

the gifts will be brought to Mount Zion, the
place of the Name of the LORD Almighty.[b]

18:4 [x]Isa 26:21; Hos 5:15 [y]Isa 26:19; Hos 14:5 **18:5** [z]Isa 17:10-11; Eze 17:6 **18:6** [a]Isa 56:9; Jer 7:33; Eze 32:4; 39:17 **18:7** [b]Ps 68:31 **19:1** [c]Isa 13:1; Jer 43:12 [d]Ex 12:12; Joel 3:19 [e]Ps 18:10; 104:3; Rev 1:7

A Prophecy Against Egypt

19 A prophecy[c] against Egypt:[d]

See, the LORD rides on a swift cloud[e]
and is coming to Egypt.

in this case may well be the tributaries and canals linked to the Nile River.
18:5 *pruning.* It is the wise farmer who knows the correct times of the year to cultivate and prune his vines to ensure maximum yield. The grape vines first bloom in May, and the fruit will begin to ripen by August. There are two calculated prunings: (1) as noted in the Gezer Calendar, in the fall, before the vines become dormant, the unproductive bunches from the previous year are removed, and (2) once the grapes appear, excess leaves and tendrils are cut away to encourage greater yield and even ripening. Yahweh will thus bide his time until the appropriate moment to make his pruning of the nations on earth.
18:6 The cuttings from the grape vines were often used for fuel (Eze 15:2–4), but in this example they are left as food and nesting for birds and other animals. The pruned cuttings, like the shattered nations, become little more than scattered sticks, incidentally useful through the coming seasons, but no threat to Yahweh or to Judah.
18:7 *gifts will be brought to the LORD.* Bringing gifts was a means of paying homage to a respected person. Naaman showed respect in this way to Elisha, although he refused the gifts (2Ki 5:1–19). Sometimes there is no clear demarcation between a gift and tribute, the latter deriving from some coercion such as taxation. Whichever the case for Isaiah, Israel's God is being acknowledged as sovereign, or at least being granted respect.
19:1 *Egypt.* Egypt is a divided nation during much of the eighth century BC. The nominal rule of Sheshonq's successors at Tanis was virtually ignored by the rulers over the

NATIONS AND CITIES MENTIONED IN ISAIAH

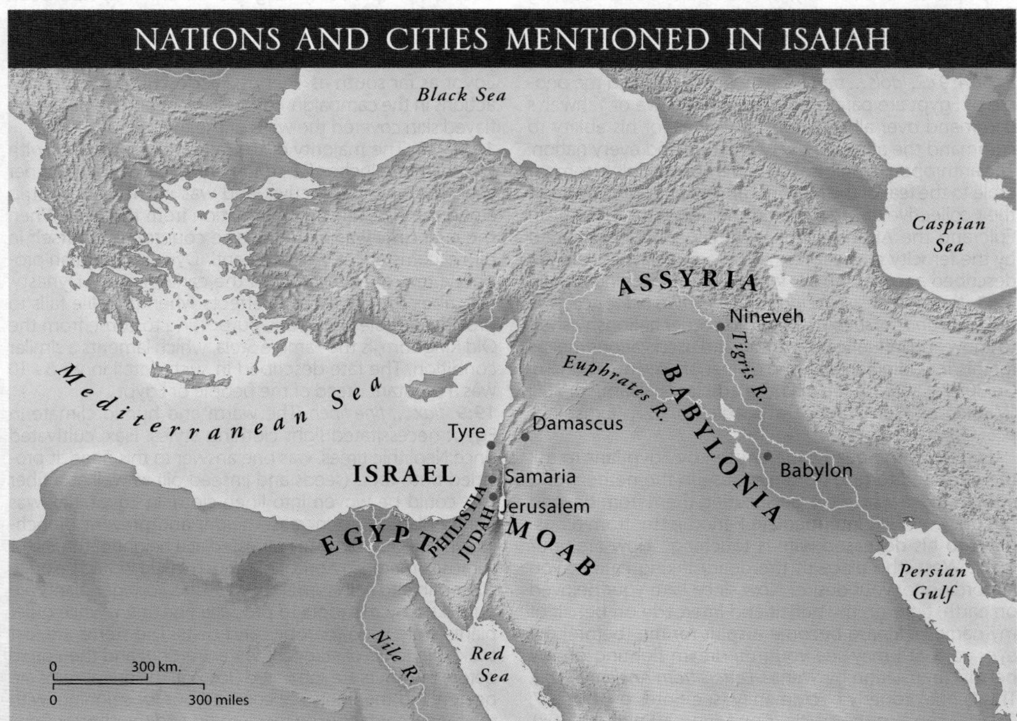

The idols of Egypt tremble before him,
and the hearts of the Egyptians melt[f]
with fear.
2 "I will stir up Egyptian against
Egyptian —
brother will fight against brother,[g]
neighbor against neighbor,
city against city,
kingdom against kingdom.[h]
3 The Egyptians will lose heart,
and I will bring their plans to
nothing;
they will consult the idols and the
spirits of the dead,
the mediums and the spiritists.[i]
4 I will hand the Egyptians over
to the power of a cruel master,
and a fierce king[j] will rule over them,"
declares the Lord, the LORD
Almighty.

19:1 [f] Jos 2:11
19:2 [g] Jdg 7:22; Mt 10:21,36 [h] 2Ch 20:23
19:3 [i] Isa 8:19; 47:13; Da 2:2,10
19:4 [j] Isa 20:4; Jer 46:26; Eze 29:19
19:5 [k] Jer 51:36
19:6 [l] Ex 7:18 [m] Isa 37:25; Eze 30:12 [n] Isa 15:6
19:7 [o] Isa 23:3
19:8 [p] Eze 47:10 [q] Hab 1:15
19:9 [r] Pr 7:16; Eze 27:7

5 The waters of the river will dry up,[k]
and the riverbed will be parched and
dry.
6 The canals will stink;[l]
the streams of Egypt will dwindle
and dry up.[m]
The reeds and rushes will wither,[n]
7 also the plants along the Nile,
at the mouth of the river.
Every sown field[o] along the Nile
will become parched, will blow
away and be no more.
8 The fishermen[p] will groan and lament,
all who cast hooks[q] into the Nile;
those who throw nets on the water
will pine away.
9 Those who work with combed flax will
despair,
the weavers of fine linen[r] will lose
hope.

south at Thebes and the patchwork of kings and chiefs around the delta region in the north. The rising threat to Egypt, represented by the expansion of Assyria under Tiglath-Pileser III after 745 BC, may have fueled the emergence of the Cushite kings Piankhy and Shabako. Their efforts to unite all Egypt were stalled for about 20 years by the rulers of Sais, who had managed to merge all of the northern territories under their leadership. The success of the Saites was aided by increased trade with the Philistines and the rest of the Levant. It was probably to the Saite king Tefnakht that many of the Assyrian border states (Philistia, Israel, Transjordan) looked for aid in their attempts to rebel. Finally, in 712 BC the Sudanese king Shabako conquered all of Egypt and once again united the country under the single rule of the Twenty-Fifth Dynasty. *rides on a swift cloud.* See notes on Job 37:2 – 5; Ps 68:4; 97:2. *idols … tremble.* The gods/idols and the people of Egypt are paralleled here in their awe of Yahweh's command over all of nature as well as for his ability to command the affairs of every creature and every nation. The anthropomorphic image of trembling idols is comparable to the fear of the Mesopotamian gods who, through their collective efforts, created the flood (the Gilgamesh Epic and the Atrahasis epic). They were overwhelmed by the ferocity of the forces they had unleashed and are described as cowering like whipped dogs behind a wall.

19:3 *they will consult the idols and the spirits of the dead, the mediums and the spiritists.* Egypt, like other nations, wished to know and influence the future and used various means for this, including dreams and divination (see notes on 2:6; Ge 30:27; Dt 18:10; see also the articles "Balaam," p. 268; "Magic," p. 326; "Practice of Magic," p. 627; "Extispicy," p. 650).

Letters to the dead were written by Egyptians to ask the departed to take up their cause in the netherworld against those who were persecuting them from beyond the grave. A First Intermediate Period letter from a husband to his deceased wife is touching: "How are you? Is the West (the place of the dead) taking care of you [according to] your desire? Now since I am your beloved on earth, fight on my behalf and intercede on behalf of my name … Please become a spirit for me [before] my eyes so that I may see you in a dream fighting on my behalf" (translation by Wente, *Letters from Ancient Egypt*). This is not properly necromancy (see notes on 1Sa 28:7; 2Ki 21:6; see also the article "Consulting a 'Spirit,'" p. 508), which was a form of divination not practiced per se in Egypt. Such consultations and supplications, says Isaiah, will be ineffective.

19:4 *cruel master … fierce king.* From an internal Egyptian perspective, this could refer to either the foreign Ethiopian ruler Piankhy (740 – 716 BC) or his brother Shabako (716 – 695 BC). The former describes his campaign to the north toward Lower Egypt to stop encroachment on his territory. In formulaic language, which could also reflect reality, he boasts that his troops undertook a great slaughter. A hand that Israel would also find harsh is that of the Assyrians, who could also be meant here. The Egyptian Osorkon IV (probably king "So" in 2Ki 17:4) had been sought for support by the last king of Israel, Hoshea, in 725 BC, an action probably not viewed favorably by Assyria. Under Ashurbanipal in 663 BC Assyria conquered Egypt as far south as Thebes. He describes some of his actions in the campaign: corpses were hung on poles and flayed skin covered the walls of the town.

19:5 – 10 The majority of the land of Egypt is arid, with less than four inches (10 centimeters) of precipitation per year. The only productive land was in the narrow strip along the Nile, relying on irrigation from the river. When the river flow was hindered, the country found itself in dire circumstances. An Eighteenth Dynasty Egyptian prophetic text of Neferti, set in the earlier Fourth Dynasty, describes the devastating effects when the Nile fails to provide. A Ptolemaic work, purporting to come from the Old Kingdom, is the Famine Stela, which laments a similar condition. The fate described in such detail in vv. 5 – 10 was a constant dread of the people of Egypt.

19:9 *flax … fine linen.* The warm and humid climate in Egypt necessitated light clothing styles. Flax, cultivated since Neolithic times, was one answer to this need. It provided both food (seeds and linseed oil) as well as a fiber that could be woven into linen cloth. In Egypt, flax was tightly planted (to increase height and prevent branching) in late October and harvested at a height of three feet (almost 1 meter) in April or May. Such a field would be quite susceptible to hail storms (Ex 9:23 – 25). Younger plants are pulled up by the roots to produce fine linen, while older plants were used for ropes and belts. The stems are first soaked in tanks of stagnant water (retting) and then dried before the fibers are separated (Jos 2:6). The dried stems are beaten and the fibers are combed out for spinning, with the longer threads used for clothing and the shorter (tow)

[10]The workers in cloth will be dejected,
and all the wage earners will be sick
at heart.
[11]The officials of Zoan[s] are nothing but
fools;
the wise counselors of Pharaoh give
senseless advice.
How can you say to Pharaoh,
"I am one of the wise men,[t]
a disciple of the ancient kings"?
[12]Where are your wise men[u] now?
Let them show you and make known
what the LORD Almighty
has planned[v] against Egypt.
[13]The officials of Zoan have become
fools,
the leaders of Memphis[w] are
deceived;
the cornerstones of her peoples
have led Egypt astray.
[14]The LORD has poured into them
a spirit of dizziness;[x]
they make Egypt stagger in all that she
does,
as a drunkard staggers around in his
vomit.
[15]There is nothing Egypt can do —
head or tail, palm branch or reed.[y]

[16]In that day the Egyptians will become
weaklings.[z] They will shudder with fear[a]
at the uplifted hand[b] that the LORD Almighty raises against them. [17]And the land
of Judah will bring terror to the Egyptians;
everyone to whom Judah is mentioned
will be terrified, because of what the LORD
Almighty is planning[c] against them.
[18]In that day five cities in Egypt will
speak the language of Canaan and swear
allegiance[d] to the LORD Almighty. One of
them will be called the City of the Sun.[a]
[19]In that day there will be an altar[e]
to the LORD in the heart of Egypt, and a

19:11 [s]Nu 13:22 [t]1Ki 4:30; Ac 7:22 **19:12** [u]1Co 1:20 [v]Isa 14:24; Ro 9:17 **19:13** [w]Jer 2:16; Eze 30:13, 16 **19:14** [x]Mt 17:17 **19:15** [y]Isa 9:14 **19:16** [z]Jer 51:30; Na 3:13 [a]Heb 10:31 [b]Isa 11:15 **19:17** [c]Isa 14:24 **19:18** [d]Zep 3:9 **19:19** [e]Jos 22:10

[a] *18* Some manuscripts of the Masoretic Text, Dead Sea Scrolls, Symmachus and Vulgate; most manuscripts of the Masoretic Text *City of Destruction*

set aside as lamp wicks (Isa 1:31, "tinder"). There were several grades of linen produced. The best set was aside for the pharaoh, the nobility and the priests. Any interruption in production would have had a ripple effect, destroying the livelihood of countless workers in the fields and factories.

19:11 *Zoan.* Usually identified with Tanis, a city on the eastern Egyptian delta about 30 miles (48 kilometers) south of the Mediterranean. It is in the area where the Israelites were settled in Egypt at the time of Moses. Zoan had become the capital of Egypt at the beginning of the Twenty-First Dynasty (1176 – 931 BC), the same period as the Israelite monarchy. Memories of official court dealings between Jerusalem and Zoan may form the basis for this reference, since the Egyptian capital was moved to Sais and Napata after 873 BC. *disciple of the ancient kings.* Because Egypt had such a long, virtually uninterrupted history, Egyptian officials faced with a crisis or an unexplained omen would chant ancient prayers and magical incantations (such as those found in the Execration Texts). Or they would consult the records of previous administrations and the "Instructions" of model officials. The cultural memories, recorded on papyrus for generations, had great authority, and the descendants of these earlier officials took great pride in being the inheritors of such wisdom (including the twenty-fifth-century BC "Instruction of Ptahhotep" and the twenty-second-century BC "Teaching for Merikare"). However, this attitude also could prevent creative or innovative decision making. Isaiah ridicules these men who pride themselves in wisdom but fail to understand how to deal with present crises.

19:13 *leaders of Memphis.* Prior to 715 BC, the delta region of Egypt was ruled by at least four rival pharaohs. The area was divided into the Tanis region (eastern delta), the region of Leontopolis (central delta), and the Saite region (western delta) — plus there were many petty kingdoms claiming independence and a portion of Egypt's ancient legacy. Mention here of Memphis (the Hebrew reads "Noph") simply ties Egypt's administrative chaos to the ancient capital city. This contrasts the irony of current anarchy with past greatness. Only after the Nubian Twenty-Fifth Dynasty arises under Shabako will Egypt once again be united under a single ruler.

19:16 *weaklings.* Some other translations: "like women." A stele of Piankhy describes him as personification of the god Horus, defeating opposing kings, designated as "bulls." The stele closes with praise to the pharaoh because he has turned bulls into women. A treaty between Ashurnirari V of Assyria and Mati'ilu of Arpad places a curse on the latter if he breaks it, with the result that his soldiers would become women.

19:18 *five cities in Egypt will … swear allegiance to the LORD.* It is impossible to identify these cities based on any historical event. Jer 44:1 does mention three cities (Migdol, Tahpanhes and Memphis) in which Israelites are dwelling, but that may have no relation to this verse. Certainly, there is evidence from the time of Solomon onward (Elephantine colony, Leontopolis) of an Israelite presence in Egypt (diplomatic and commercial). What seems most important to the statement is the very idea of Yahweh worship in Egypt, and perhaps even in a major city associated with an Egyptian god. *the language of Canaan.* Normally, when a foreign community is established in a nation it is expected that they will speak the language of that country, except among themselves. It would be difficult to do business or engage in diplomatic activity otherwise. Thus, for the Israelite languages of Hebrew or Aramaic to be spoken in Egypt would be unusual. Most likely this refers to the study of the sacred writings of the Yahwists and prayer raised to Yahweh.

19:19 *an altar to the LORD in the heart of Egypt.* The numerous Jewish residents in Egypt continued to worship their God, and so they needed shrines in which to do so. They are joined by Egyptians who, in times of crisis, will also call on Israel's God for help (v. 21). A fifth-century BC Aramaic letter from Elephantine speaks of a temple of Yaho (Yahweh) already in the sixth century BC. This shrine, which was requested to be rebuilt in this same letter, served the Jews living in Egypt. There is no evidence of a Yahwistic temple serving as a place of worship for the Egyptians, the situation envisioned here by Isaiah. *a monument to the LORD at its border.* This term designates a sacred standing stone and is viewed, either positively or negatively, as part of pagan practice. Their exact function is unclear. In Israel examples have been found from Tell Dan in the north to Arad in the south. Those in Israel are without inscription, though some found in the Sinai Desert at Serabit el-Khadem are inscribed with Egyptian hieroglyphics. An

monument[f] to the LORD at its border. 20It
will be a sign and witness to the LORD Almighty in the land of Egypt. When they
cry out to the LORD because of their oppressors, he will send them a savior and
defender, and he will rescue[g] them. 21So
the LORD will make himself known to the
Egyptians, and in that day they will acknowledge[h] the LORD. They will worship[i]
with sacrifices and grain offerings; they
will make vows to the LORD and keep
them. 22The LORD will strike[j] Egypt with a
plague; he will strike them and heal them.
They will turn[k] to the LORD, and he will
respond to their pleas and heal[l] them.

23In that day there will be a highway[m]
from Egypt to Assyria. The Assyrians will
go to Egypt and the Egyptians to Assyria. The Egyptians and Assyrians will worship[n] together. 24In that day Israel will be
the third, along with Egypt and Assyria,
a blessing[a] on the earth. 25The LORD Almighty will bless them, saying, "Blessed
be Egypt my people,[o] Assyria my handiwork,[p] and Israel my inheritance.[q]"

A Prophecy Against Egypt and Cush

20 In the year that the supreme commander,[r] sent by Sargon king of Assyria, came to Ashdod and attacked and
captured it— 2at that time the LORD spoke
through Isaiah son of Amoz.[s] He said to
him, "Take off the sackcloth[t] from your
body and the sandals[u] from your feet."
And he did so, going around stripped[v] and
barefoot.[w]

3Then the LORD said, "Just as my servant
Isaiah has gone stripped and barefoot for
three years, as a sign[x] and portent against
Egypt and Cush,[b][y] 4so the king[z] of Assyria will lead away stripped and barefoot the
Egyptian captives and Cushite exiles, young
and old, with buttocks bared—to Egypt's
shame.[a] 5Those who trusted in Cush and
boasted in Egypt[b] will be dismayed and put
to shame. 6In that day the people who live
on this coast will say, 'See what has happened to those we relied on, those we fled
to for help[c] and deliverance from the king
of Assyria! How then can we escape?[d]'"

A Prophecy Against Babylon

21 A prophecy against the Desert[e] by
the Sea:

Like whirlwinds sweeping through the
southland,[f]

19:19 [f]Ge 28:18 **19:20** [g]Isa 49:24-26 **19:21** [h]Isa 11:9 [i]Isa 56:7; Mal 1:11 **19:22** [j]Heb 12:11 [k]Isa 45:14; Hos 14:1 [l]Dt 32:39 **19:23** [m]Isa 11:16 [n]Isa 27:13 **19:25** [o]Ps 100:3 [p]Isa 29:23; 45:11; 60:21; 64:8; Eph 2:10 [q]Hos 2:23 **20:1** [r]2Ki 18:17 **20:2** [s]Isa 13:1 [t]Zec 13:4; Mt 3:4 [u]Eze 24:17, 23 [v]1Sa 19:24 [w]Mic 1:8 **20:3** [x]Isa 8:18 [y]Isa 37:9; 43:3 **20:4** [z]Isa 19:4 [a]Isa 47:3; Jer 13:22,26 **20:5** [b]2Ki 18:21; Isa 30:5 **20:6** [c]Isa 10:3 [d]Jer 30:15-17; Mt 23:33; 1Th 5:3; Heb 2:3 **21:1** [e]Isa 13:21; Jer 51:43 [f]Zec 9:14

[a] 24 Or *Assyria, whose names will be used in blessings* (see Gen. 48:20); or *Assyria, who will be seen by others as blessed* [b] 3 That is, the upper Nile region; also in verse 5

Old Aramaic stele bears an inscription indicating that it was erected by a king in honor of his god (Melqart). Here the monument is dedicated to Yahweh, the God of Israel, rather than to a pagan deity. Its location at the border could show that it is a boundary stone, set up to guard a border or even to claim it as Yahweh's territory (see 10:13; see also note on Dt 19:14).

19:21 *vows to the LORD.* Solemn promises to one's god are not only part of Israel's experience with her covenant with God (see notes on Lev 27:2; Ps 116:14), but are also evidenced among Israel's neighbors. Mesopotamian legal practice helped ascertain the truth of a claim by taking a vow before a deity. The purpose of doing such a thing in the god's presence is spelled out in an Akkadian text from Turkey, where numerous gods listed are called to be witnesses to the oath. While these can be designated "oaths of the gods," they differ from the vow made here, which is made "to," not "by," Israel's God.

20:1 *supreme commander.* This term (*tartan*) is transliterated from Akkadian (*tu/artamnu*, 2Ki 18:17). A certain Shamshu-ilu, a *turtamnu*, is described as a "great herald, [the administrator of] temples, chief of the extensive army, governor of the land of Hatti ... conqueror of the mountains in the West," so this person coming against Ashdod was of some stature. Several important officials listed in the Assyrian Eponym List have the designation *turtamnu*. *Sargon ... came to Ashdod.* The Biblical account of the Ashdod Revolt of 713–711 BC, the Assyrian records, and archaeological remains all corroborate the same events. The Philistine city revolted at the instigation of its king Azuri, and perhaps with the expectation of Egyptian support. The Assyrian annals charge him with refusing to pay tribute and fomenting rebellion among his neighbors. The Assyrian king Sargon II responded with a swift campaign that quickly suppressed their hopes for independence. He placed Azuri's younger brother, Ahimeti, on the throne, who in turn was almost immediately deposed by a usurper named Yamani. Sargon sent another expedition in 712 BC, Yamani fled to Egypt, and an Assyrian commissioner was appointed to manage Ashdod for the empire. Excavations in Stratum VIII of the city have revealed a number of mass graves under the floors. Several fragments of an Assyrian monumental stele were also found. They come from a copy of the one erected in Khorsabad, listing Sargon's conquests, including Ashdod.

20:2 *stripped and barefoot.* While nakedness was originally innocent in Genesis, it often came to denote defeat and punishment. Removal of foot coverings also indicated humiliation. The Megiddo Ivory shows two bound prisoners, naked and barefoot, being brought before a dignitary, and naked, captive leaders are being tortured in the depiction of the siege of Lachish. A Hebrew ostracon from seventh-century BC Horvat Uza includes a threat that the perpetrator of a crime will be stripped naked in judgment.

20:3 *as a sign.* For role-playing by a prophet, see Eze 4.

20:4 *Egyptian captives and Cushite exiles.* In battle, prisoners of war were common, not only in order to deplete the enemy forces but also to serve as potential hostages. Prisoners of war were considered spoils to be divided among the conquerors. They would become slaves, and it was necessary to immediately break their spirit and at the same time use them as a means of shaming their home countries or cities. Assyrian annals include lists of captives among the other items taken or in some cases impaled as an example to other rebels. Egyptian royal tomb paintings often depict lines of prisoners, bound together by the neck, marching into captivity. While these figures are not completely naked, they have been stripped of all valuables or insignias of rank.

21:1 *Desert by the Sea.* The Hebrew in this case might

an invader comes from the desert,
from a land of terror.

2 A dire[g] vision has been shown to me:
The traitor betrays,[h] the looter takes loot.
Elam,[i] attack! Media, lay siege!
I will bring to an end all the groaning she caused.

3 At this my body is racked with pain,
pangs seize me, like those of a woman in labor;[j]
I am staggered by what I hear,
I am bewildered by what I see.
4 My heart falters,
fear makes me tremble;
the twilight I longed for
has become a horror to me.

5 They set the tables,
they spread the rugs,
they eat, they drink![k]
Get up, you officers,
oil the shields!

6 This is what the Lord says to me:

"Go, post a lookout
and have him report what he sees.
7 When he sees chariots[l]
with teams of horses,
riders on donkeys
or riders on camels,
let him be alert,
fully alert."

8 And the lookout[a][m] shouted,

"Day after day, my lord, I stand on the watchtower;
every night I stay at my post.
9 Look, here comes a man in a chariot
with a team of horses.
And he gives back the answer:
'Babylon[n] has fallen,[o] has fallen!
All the images of its gods[p]
lie shattered on the ground!' "

10 My people who are crushed on the threshing floor,[q]
I tell you what I have heard
from the LORD Almighty,
from the God of Israel.

A Prophecy Against Edom

11 A prophecy against Dumah[b]:[r]
Someone calls to me from Seir,[s]
"Watchman, what is left of the night?
Watchman, what is left of the night?"

21:2 [g] Ps 60:3 [h] Isa 33:1 [i] Isa 22:6; Jer 49:34 **21:3** [j] Ps 48:6; Isa 26:17 **21:5** [k] Jer 51:39, 57; Da 5:2 **21:7** [l] ver 9 **21:8** [m] Hab 2:1 **21:9** [n] Rev 14:8 [o] Jer 51:8; Rev 18:2 [p] Isa 46:1; Jer 50:2; 51:44 **21:10** [q] Jer 51:33 **21:11** [r] Ge 25:14 [s] Ge 32:3

[a] 8 Dead Sea Scrolls and Syriac; Masoretic Text *A lion*
[b] 11 *Dumah*, a wordplay on *Edom*, means *silence* or *stillness*.

better be translated as "Wilderness by the Sea" or "swampland." Either would fit the southern portion of Mesopotamia, an area of marshes and quagmire as one gets closer to the Persian Gulf. At issue is concern for the capture of Babylon by the Assyrians in 703 BC and the expulsion of the Babylonian leader Marduk-Baladan. The anti-Assyrian party within Hezekiah's court had hoped that Babylon would be able to successfully challenge Assyria and thus give the outlying provinces like Judah an opportunity to gain their independence. These hopes were dashed with the resurgence of Assyrian power under Sennacherib. Thus this prophecy against Babylon reflects that disappointment.

21:2 *Elam ... Media.* As Israel was constantly pressed by the Mesopotamians from the east, so Mesopotamia itself experienced incursions by peoples like the Elamites and Medes from the east (present-day Iran). From their capital in Susa, the Elamites supported Marduk-Baladan's successful takeover of the Babylonian throne in 720 BC. Their help ebbed and flowed, however. By 710 BC Elam had withdrawn such aid, allowing Sargon of Assyria to take Babylon, but it sent more support in 703 BC (probably referred to here; cf. 22:6) and in 700 BC, though unsuccessfully. Elam was finally defeated by Assyria in 646 BC. The Medes joined the Babylonians to defeat Assyria in the late seventh century BC and soon thereafter expanded control into Asia Minor. The Medes themselves were soon incorporated into the Persian Empire.

21:3 *pangs ... like those of a woman in labor.* Labor pains are a common symbol of physical and mental distress and anguish (13:8; 26:17–18) and therefore serve as a ready metaphor. In the Gilgamesh Epic, when the goddess Ishtar realized the ramifications of destroying humanity, she "screamed like a woman giving birth."

21:4 *My heart falters.* Fear and suffering often present themselves metaphorically through physical manifestations such as this (see 19:1). This is because the heart, as well as other internal organs, was considered the seat of intellect and emotion in the ancient world.

21:5 *set the tables ... spread the rugs.* The apparent banquet scene portrayed here might suggest that Babylon was unprepared for the attack that will capture the city (as portrayed in Da 5). It may also refer to preparations for battle (done also by Anat, who, in the Ugaritic epic, sets up bleachers and tables for her warriors so they can watch as she slaughters her enemies) or possibly a sketching out of Babylon's defenses or its various districts prior to a siege.

21:7 *riders on donkeys or riders on camels.* Assyrian wall reliefs show soldiers riding horses in battle, including one scene where they pursue a camel rider. Camels were more regularly used as beasts of burden, as were donkeys, though at times camels were also ridden.

21:9 *Babylon has fallen.* This prophecy was fulfilled by the fall of Babylon (about two centuries after Isaiah) to a Medo-Persian alliance when Nabonidus, the last Babylonian king, lost his power base. Nabonidus was defeated by Gubaru, a former Babylonian general who had defected to the Persians, in October, 539 BC. *All the images of its gods lie shattered.* A nation's gods were supposed to protect them, leading them in military conquest. Their weakness and defeat are symbolized by their destruction. An Aramaic text from Elephantine in Egypt from 407 BC describes an attack by the Egyptians on the temple there that was razed and its pillars smashed.

21:10 *threshing floor.* See note on Ru 3:2.

21:11 *Dumah.* A wordplay on Edom (see NIV text note). During the eighth century BC, Edom was struggling to maintain its independence. The country was weakened by Judah's interest in expanding into the region: Amaziah (801–787 BC) staged a raid at the turn of the

[12]The watchman replies,
"Morning is coming, but also the
night.
If you would ask, then ask;
and come back yet again."

A Prophecy Against Arabia

[13]A prophecy[t] against Arabia:

You caravans of Dedanites,
who camp in the thickets of Arabia,
14 bring water for the thirsty;
you who live in Tema,[u]
bring food for the fugitives.
[15]They flee[v] from the sword,
from the drawn sword,
from the bent bow
and from the heat of battle.

[16]This is what the Lord says to me:
"Within one year, as a servant bound by
contract[w] would count it, all the splendor[x]
of Kedar[y] will come to an end. [17]The survivors of the archers, the warriors of Kedar,
will be few.[z]" The LORD, the God of Israel,
has spoken.

A Prophecy About Jerusalem

22 A prophecy[a] against the Valley[b] of Vision:

What troubles you now,
that you have all gone up on the
roofs,
[2]you town so full of commotion,
you city of tumult and revelry?[c]
Your slain were not killed by the
sword,
nor did they die in battle.
[3]All your leaders have fled together;
they have been captured without
using the bow.

21:13 [t]Isa 13:1 **21:14** [u]Ge 25:15 **21:15** [v]Isa 13:14 **21:16** [w]Isa 16:14 [x]Isa 17:3 [y]Ps 120:5; Isa 60:7 **21:17** [z]Isa 10:19 **22:1** [a]Isa 13:1 [b]Ps 125:2; Jer 21:13; Joel 3:2, 12, 14 **22:2** [c]Isa 32:13

century (2Ki 14:7), and his successor, Uzziah, rebuilt the port of Elath on the Gulf of Aqaba (2Ki 14:22). A further sign of Edom's weakness is its payment of tribute to the Assyrian king Adadnirari III (809–782 BC). When the Syro-Ephraimite War caused turmoil in Judah in the 730s, the Edomites regained Elath (2Ki 16:6). However, they were forced into vassalage by Tiglath-Pileser III after 732 BC and became a link in the Assyrian Empire's trade route south from Damascus to the Aqaba, called the "King's Highway" (see note on Nu 20:17). Assyrian tribute lists also demonstrate that for the rest of the century Edom remained loyal to the empire, giving little or no support to the other rebellious Palestinian vassals.

21:13 *Arabia.* Comprising territories claimed by various Bedouin tribal groups, Arabia was an area that Assyrian kings listed as a part of their empire but never truly controlled. The Arab tribes occupied the region between the southern Negev and the north-central portion of the Arabian peninsula. This could suggest a translation in this passage of "wasteland" rather than "Arabia," paralleling it with "swampland" in v. 1 (see note there). Some Arab groups engaged in caravan trade, transporting frankincense and myrrh, slaves, and dyes to both Egypt and Mesopotamia. The number of raids mentioned in various ancient texts also attest to their occasional occupation as predators on the caravan routes. Arabs appear in the records of Shalmaneser III dealing with the alliance formed against him at the battle of Qarqar in 853 BC. They continue to appear in Assyrian records down to the reign of Ashurbanipal at the end of the seventh century BC. It is also noted in the annals of Sargon II that some Arabs were forced to resettle in Palestine after the fall of Samaria in 722 BC. *Dedanites.* The Dedanite tribes used Khuraybah (modern al-'Ula) in northwest Arabia as their base of operations. Excavations have uncovered an extensive group of small satellite villages in the nearby valley of Wadi al-Qura. They operated as caravanners with contacts in Syria, Phoenicia and Palestine. During the seventh century BC they may have been part of Edom's sphere of influence and subject to Assyria's control.

21:14 *Tema.* Based on its mention in Assyrian and Aramaic inscriptions, Tema has long been identified with the oasis city of Tayma, located on the western border of the North Arabian Desert. It lies at the crossroads of three major trade routes of the "Incense Road" from southern Arabia to Syria, Mesopotamia and eastern Arabia. The riches of Tema were tapped by the emerging Mesopotamian empires of the first millennium BC. The Assyrian king Tiglath-Pileser III lists the city as one of those paying tribute in 734 BC. Along with Dedan, Tema served as a major urban center for its region during the seventh and sixth centuries BC. The Chaldean monarch Nabonidus made it his headquarters for ten years (553–543 BC) as he attempted to gain control over the incense trade.

21:16 *Kedar.* Assyrian and Neo-Babylonian texts refer to these northern Arabian tribes as Qidr, Qadr, Qeder, or Qadar. Tied to the Ishmaelites in Ge 25:13, the Kedarites functioned as sheep breeders and caravanners at least as late as the Hellenistic period. Their mention in this verse along with Tema may refer to Nabonidus's expedition to conquer the area in 553 BC. There is evidence of ties between Kedar and Tema in Babylonian economic texts. See note on Ps 120:5.

22:1 *Valley of Vision.* Based on v. 5, this is probably a reference to Jerusalem and perhaps to the Hinnom Valley (see its use in Jer 7:31–34 for divination rituals). Isaiah rebukes a people who have sought guidance from other gods and thus, despite their physical location on Mount Zion, have no true vision of events. *gone up on the roofs.* House roofs were accessible to the inhabitants, at times serving as an area for sleeping and living. They were also used as places of worship, especially of pagan deities. Sacrifices on roofs were also known in Ugarit. King Keret, having lost his family, prayed for more children and was told to sacrifice on the rooftop. Special Akkadian rituals also took place on roofs. This present passage may indicate that Israel is turning to other gods in thanks for their perceived deliverance, which in fact is not going to happen.

22:2 *you town so full of commotion.* When Sargon died in 705 BC, many of the Assyrian vassals in the west revolted, Israel's king Hezekiah among them. Hezekiah also moved against his other opponents, such as the Philistines, and sought to strengthen his own defenses. But when Sargon's successor, Sennacherib, attacked Hezekiah in 701 BC, those defenses were not the determinative factor (2Ki 19:34–36). Sennacherib's armies were able to take much of Judah according to Isa 36:1—37:38, and Sennacherib's own records refer to 46 fortified cities, as well as numerous towns, being taken. Sennacherib claims to have besieged Jerusalem, but he does not say it fell to him. This reflects the Biblical picture that shows Hezekiah being spared the humiliation of his capital falling to the enemy (2Ki 19).

All you who were caught were taken
prisoner together,
having fled while the enemy was
still far away.
4 Therefore I said, "Turn away from me;
let me weep[d] bitterly.
Do not try to console me
over the destruction of my people."[e]
5 The Lord, the LORD Almighty, has
a day
of tumult and trampling and terror[f]
in the Valley of Vision,
a day of battering down walls
and of crying out to the mountains.
6 Elam[g] takes up the quiver,[h]
with her charioteers and horses;
Kir[i] uncovers the shield.
7 Your choicest valleys are full of
chariots,
and horsemen are posted at the city
gates.[j]
8 The Lord stripped away the defenses of
Judah,
and you looked in that day
to the weapons[k] in the Palace of the
Forest.[l]
9 You saw that the walls of the City of
David
were broken through in many
places;
you stored up water
in the Lower Pool.[m]
10 You counted the buildings in
Jerusalem
and tore down houses to strengthen
the wall.
11 You built a reservoir between the two
walls[n]
for the water of the Old Pool,[o]
but you did not look to the One who
made it,
or have regard for the One who
planned it long ago.
12 The Lord, the LORD Almighty,
called you on that day
to weep[p] and to wail,
to tear out your hair[q] and put on
sackcloth.[r]
13 But see, there is joy and revelry,
slaughtering of cattle and killing of
sheep,
eating of meat and drinking of
wine![s]
"Let us eat and drink," you say,
"for tomorrow we die!"[t]

22:4 [d] Isa 15:3; Lk 19:41 [e] Jer 9:1 **22:5** [f] La 1:5 **22:6** [g] Isa 21:2 [h] Jer 49:35 [i] 2Ki 16:9 **22:7** [j] 2Ch 32:1-2 **22:8** [k] 2Ch 32:5 [l] 1Ki 7:2 **22:9** [m] 2Ch 32:4 **22:11** [n] 2Ki 25:4; Jer 39:4 [o] 2Ch 32:4
22:12 [p] Joel 2:17 [q] Mic 1:16 [r] Joel 1:13 **22:13** [s] Isa 5:22; 28:7-8; 56:12; Lk 17:26-29 [t] 1Co 15:32*

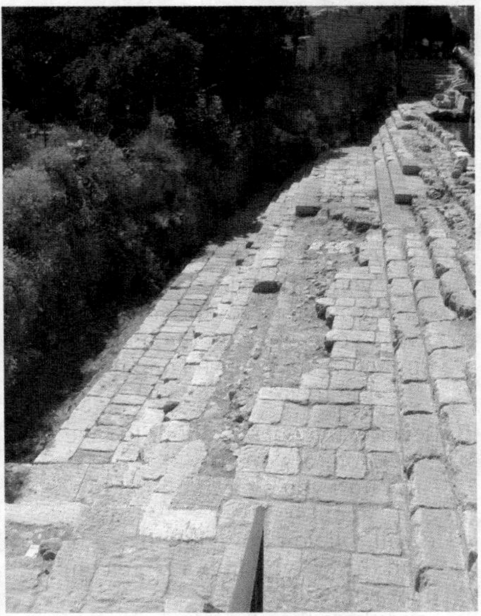

Pool of Siloam at southern end of the City of David.
Kim Walton

22:6 *Elam.* See the note on 21:2. Sennacherib regularly conscripted levees of soldiers from subject and allied peoples. Although Elam has previously supported the Babylonians and opposed Assyria, in this 701 campaign it seems clear that they have supplied a contingent of bowmen for Sennacherib's host. *Kir.* This is not the same Kir (a city) mentioned in 15:1–4. There is no consensus on the exact location of the country of Kir. Because of its association with the Arameans in Am 9:7, several attempts have been made to place it either in northern Syria or the western desert (west of the Euphrates River). Its mention here with Elam also suggests proximity to that country east of the Tigris River.
22:8 *Palace of the Forest.* See note on 1Ki 7:2 for this storehouse within the palace complex. The people hope to draw on the arsenal it contained to defend themselves against the Assyrian invaders.
22:9–11 Naturally, the defenses of Jerusalem had to be repaired and strengthened in anticipation of Assyrian efforts to take the city. There was also a need to balance the demands for more housing by the people of Judah who had fled to Jerusalem for protection and the all-important defense of the city. As a result, the area between the city's dual wall system was cleared of all temporary shelters to provide a "killing ground" should the Assyrians penetrate the outer defenses. This area was also partially flooded to make it more difficult to transverse and to add to the city's water supply.
22:9 *Lower Pool.* Jerusalem's water supply was vulnerable to enemy attack, since it lay outside the city wall and was limited in scope for an area of its size (see note on 7:3). Hezekiah sought to secure it from attack and siege. The intermittently running Gihon spring lay in the valley just east of David's city. It was joined by aqueducts and a tunnel of some 1,300 feet (400 meters) in length to other locations, including the Pool of Shiloh, the "Lower Pool" of this verse. The tunnel has an inscription above one end that details the arduous digging task. It describes two digging teams working toward each other following a circuitous route. See the article "Hezekiah's Tunnel," p. 663.
22:12 *sackcloth.* A coarse, black goat's hair fabric (50:3) worn against the skin as a sign of mourning. See the article "Mourning," p. 828.

14The LORD Almighty has revealed this
in my hearing:[u] "Till your dying day this
sin will not be atoned[v] for," says the Lord,
the LORD Almighty.

15This is what the Lord, the LORD Almighty, says:

"Go, say to this steward,
to Shebna[w] the palace administrator:
16What are you doing here and who gave
you permission
to cut out a grave[x] for yourself here,
hewing your grave on the height
and chiseling your resting place in
the rock?

17"Beware, the LORD is about to take firm
hold of you
and hurl you away, you mighty
man.
18He will roll you up tightly like a ball
and throw[y] you into a large country.
There you will die
and there the chariots you were so
proud of
will become a disgrace to your
master's house.
19I will depose you from your office,
and you will be ousted from your
position.

20"In that day I will summon my servant, Eliakim[z] son of Hilkiah. 21I will
clothe him with your robe and fasten your
sash around him and hand your authority
over to him. He will be a father to those
who live in Jerusalem and to the people
of Judah. 22I will place on his shoulder
the key[a] to the house of David;[b] what he
opens no one can shut, and what he shuts
no one can open.[c] 23I will drive him like a
peg[d] into a firm place;[e] he will become a
seat[a] of honor[f] for the house of his father.
24All the glory of his family will hang on
him: its offspring and offshoots — all its
lesser vessels, from the bowls to all the
jars.

25"In that day," declares the LORD Almighty, "the peg[g] driven into the firm
place will give way; it will be sheared off
and will fall, and the load hanging on it
will be cut down." The LORD has spoken.[h]

22:14 [u] Isa 5:9 [v] Isa 13:11; 26:21; 30:13-14; Eze 24:13 **22:15** [w] 2Ki 18:18; Isa 36:3 **22:16** [x] Mt 27:60 **22:18** [y] Isa 17:13 **22:20** [z] 2Ki 18:18; Isa 36:3 **22:22** [a] Rev 3:7 [b] Isa 7:2 [c] Job 12:14 **22:23** [d] Zec 10:4 [e] Ezr 9:8 [f] 1Sa 2:7-8; Job 36:7 **22:25** [g] ver 23 [h] Isa 46:11; Mic 4:4

[a] 23 Or *throne*

22:15 *palace administrator.* This position may have evolved from a relatively insignificant post into that of a chamberlain, in charge of all of the affairs of the palace in Uzziah's time. There is precedent for this title in Ugaritic and Phoenician texts and it would be comparable to the position of vizier in the Egyptian court. Shebna, called "palace administrator" here, is called "secretary" in 2Ki 18:18. The possibility exists that Shebna was addressed by various titles during his career, depending on his current assignment. One would expect, however, that as palace administrator he would have been the preeminent adviser and facilitator for the king. If he is referred to by a lesser title in Hezekiah's reign, then it may be surmised that he had been demoted.
22:16 *hewing ... and chiseling your resting place in the rock.* The valleys and slopes around Jerusalem contain a large number of tombs hewn from the native limestone cliffs. Among them, on the slope of Silwan, is a tomb containing a partial inscription and the title *asher al habbayit*, the same phrase used in v. 15 to describe the position once held by Shebna. The lack of a name in this inscription makes it impossible to tie it conclusively to Shebna. Isaiah's rebuke of this official is based on the extravagance of constructing an individual tomb rather than utilizing a communal cave or hewn mortuary chamber within the confines of his family holdings. These more traditional tombs included shelves for internment of the bodies, lamp niches, as well as a recessed pit for disposal of bones when the shelves were needed for fresh burials. Only the very wealthy could afford to carve an individual chamber, perhaps incorporating Phoenician or Egyptian design.
22:18 *roll ... up tightly like a ball.* An exact translation of this comparison is tentative at best, since the Hebrew term translated "roll ... up tightly" occurs only here in the Bible. The only other known case of this word is in the Canaanite Baal Cycle, where the goddess Anath is slaughtering people and their heads are piled under her like balls.
22:20 *Eliakim.* The name of this official, which means "May El establish," has been found on seal impressions from Tell Beit Mirsim, Beth Shemesh, and Ramat Rahel. He served as one who is over the house, the palace administrator, under king Hezekiah (see 36:3; 2Ki 18:18; 19:2) and therefore would be expected to affix his official seal to many documents. The seal impression containing the name Eliakim appears on a large collection of jar handles that date to the period of Hezekiah's reign. The Iron Age Lachish Stratum III, dated to 701 BC, is the most important of the sites where these handles have been found. It is likely that Eliakim's seal appears on these jars as a part of his regular duties, managing palace stores and distributing oil and wine to royal fortress sites like Lachish.
22:21 *robe.* This long tunic was worn by both genders and was also part of the priestly regalia. In the latter case, such tunics were items of value, important gifts. Correspondence regarding trade and transport of such garments is well documented in fifth-century BC Aramaic texts from the Jewish colony at Elephantine in Egypt. *father.* A leader is not regularly designated as "father" in the OT, but is so in texts of Israel's neighbors. The Phoenician king Kilamuwa in the late ninth century BC identifies himself as father to some and as mother or brother to others.
22:22 *key.* The relatively tiny locks used to secure our doors today require a very small key. However, in the Biblical period, locks were quite large and required a correspondingly large and heavy bronze or iron key (see the article "Keys and Locks," p. 414). When Eliakim is given this key, its size and probably its elaborate decoration would serve as a visible symbol of his authority to lock and unlock the rooms and gates of the palace in Jerusalem. This is also known as one of the functions of the Egyptian vizier.
22:23,25 *peg.* Eliakim's installation into office is metaphorically compared to a peg, either in the ground as a tent peg (e.g., 33:20) or on a wall, to which things may be safely attached (22:24; Eze 15:3). The metaphor highlights fixity and security, which will prove illusory.

A Prophecy Against Tyre

23 A prophecy against Tyre:[i]

Wail, you ships[j] of Tarshish![k]
For Tyre is destroyed
and left without house or harbor.
From the land of Cyprus
word has come to them.

2 Be silent, you people of the island
and you merchants of Sidon,
whom the seafarers have enriched.
3 On the great waters
came the grain of the Shihor;
the harvest of the Nile[a][l] was the
revenue of Tyre,[m]
and she became the marketplace of
the nations.

4 Be ashamed, Sidon,[n] and you fortress
of the sea,
for the sea has spoken:
"I have neither been in labor nor given
birth;
I have neither reared sons nor
brought up daughters."
5 When word comes to Egypt,
they will be in anguish at the report
from Tyre.

6 Cross over to Tarshish;
wail, you people of the island.
7 Is this your city of revelry,[o]
the old, old city,

23:1 [i] Jos 19:29; 1Ki 5:1; Jer 47:4; Eze 26,27,28; Joel 3:4-8; Am 1:9-10; Zec 9:2-4 [j] 1Ki 10:22 [k] Ge 10:4; Isa 2:16 *fn* **23:3** [l] Isa 19:7 [m] Eze 27:3 **23:4** [n] Ge 10:15, 19 **23:7** [o] Isa 22:2; 32:13

[a] 2,3 Masoretic Text; Dead Sea Scrolls *Sidon, / who cross over the sea; / your envoys* [3]*are on the great waters. / The grain of the Shihor, / the harvest of the Nile,*

23:1 – 18 The eighth century BC is a time of commercial and political expansion for the Phoenicians. A colonial empire is established, with Carthage as the principal city in the western Mediterranean (founded by Dido about 814 BC). The degree to which the Phoenicians of the island city of Tyre and of Sidon operated freely depends in this period on the extent of Assyrian influence over them. Adadnirari III (810 – 783 BC) received tribute from them, but no significant Assyrian pressure is applied until the reign of Tiglath-Pileser III (744 – 727 BC). The Assyrian king skillfully played on the fear of Tyre's expanding commercial empire to gain alliances with the city-states on Cyprus. He also forced Tyre to pay a huge amount annually (evidence of which is found in Assyrian tribute lists) to save themselves from military invasion. The wealth of Tyre was legendary (Eze 28:4 – 5; Zec 9:3); in order to defend it, Tyre's king Lulli forced the Cypriot states to submit to him. This brought on a five-year siege of Tyre by Shalmaneser V (726 – 722 BC) and his successor Sargon II (721 – 705 BC). Some attempts were made by Lulli to negotiate an end of the hostilities since the Assyrians occupied all of the Tyrian mainland. However, when Lulli again revolted at the time of Sennacherib's accession, the Assyrians forced Lulli to flee to Cyprus and installed Ittobaal over the Sidonian kingdom.

Tyre and Sidon continued to vacillate in their allegiance to Assyria after the time of Isaiah throughout the seventh century BC. In response to the Phoenician alliance with the Ethiopian Tirhakah of the Egyptian Twenty-Fifth Dynasty, Assyrian armies repeatedly invaded the coastal region around Tyre and Sidon, devastating towns and villages and placing increasing pressure on the port cities to submit to Assyrian rule. Finally, in 677 BC, Esarhaddon utterly destroyed Sidon, parading the head of its ruler, Abdimilkutte, in Nineveh. Severe diplomatic restrictions were placed on Baal I of Tyre in an effort to prevent him from aiding the Egyptians. Ashurbanipal (667 – 627 BC) also records dealing with anti-Assyrian rulers in Syro-Palestine. After crushing the Egyptians and destroying their capital at Thebes in 663 BC, Ashurbanipal installed a native Egyptian, Psammetichus I, as ruler of Lower Egypt. He then brought his army back up the coast to punish Baal I and the Phoenicians. He completely stripped Tyre of its autonomy, transforming all of Phoenicia into an Assyrian province and taking full control of the shipping trade that had been the basis of Phoenician wealth and independence. However, after Ashurbanipal's death, Tyre regained its supremacy in Mediterranean trade.

23:1 *ships of Tarshish.* The tonnage required for a merchant ship to make a profit and be seaworthy enough to ply the waters of either the Mediterranean or the Red Sea required skillful building practices. Since the "ships of Tarshish" are often mentioned in relation to trade mission (e.g., 1Ki 22:48; 2Ch 9:21), there must have been a particular type of ship involved. It is possible that they were constructed in Tarshish, but it may be that they were named for their ability to sail as far as Tarshish in the western Mediterranean. Assyrian reliefs and the bronze gate covers of Shalmaneser III from Balawat depict these ships being used for military transport as well as carrying cargoes of tribute taken from their many vassals. A relief found in the palace at Nineveh depicts the flight of Lulli, ruler of Sidon, to Cyprus. Among the ships in his fleet are tubby-looking merchantmen with a row of shields along the hull, and two levels of oarsmen (a bireme) on either side to aid the ship's movement when the sails were becalmed.

23:4 *fortress of the sea.* Tyre was originally founded around 2750 BC on a sandstone reef about 600 yards (550 meters) off the coast of southern Lebanon. Its occupied area was enlarged in the tenth century BC when Hiram I used fill to connect the older city with a nearby reef. It must have looked like a city floating on the sea to ship masters as they approached. No army was successful in capturing the city until Alexander the Great, who built a causeway from the mainland and destroyed it in 332 BC. However, Tyre was not totally self-sufficient. Its vulnerability was shown when its sister city of Ushu was captured by the Assyrians. As a result, a vassal treaty was signed in the time of Esarhaddon that reflects Tyre's capitulation even to having an Assyrian official present whenever the king read diplomatic correspondence.

23:5 *report from Tyre.* The exact time period or event described here is unclear. It could be referring to any number of events that would have dismayed the Egyptians and represented the cessation of trade and the elimination of an important political ally. Possible occasions include the Assyrian incursion into Phoenicia by Sennacherib in 701 BC or the destruction of Sidon in 677 BC by Esarhaddon. Some commentators also suggest a much later period when Sidon was conquered by the Persian king Artaxerxes III (c. 345 BC) or even Alexander the Great's capture of Tyre in 332 BC. Such a late date, however, requires either a prophetic vision of an event long after Isaiah's time or the removal of this passage completely from its Isaianic context, making it a later editor's addition.

23:6 *Tarshish.* The ambiguity in Biblical and extra-Biblical sources only indicates that Tarshish is to be found to the west of Israel. This would allow for identification with

whose feet have taken her
to settle in far-off lands?
8 Who planned this against Tyre,
the bestower of crowns,
whose merchants are princes,
whose traders are renowned in the earth?
9 The LORD Almighty planned it,
to bring down[p] her pride in all her splendor
and to humble[q] all who are renowned[r] on the earth.

10 Till[a] your land as they do along the Nile,
Daughter Tarshish,
for you no longer have a harbor.
11 The LORD has stretched out his hand[s]
over the sea
and made its kingdoms tremble.
He has given an order concerning Phoenicia
that her fortresses be destroyed.[t]
12 He said, "No more of your reveling,[u]
Virgin Daughter[v] Sidon, now crushed!

"Up, cross over to Cyprus;
even there you will find no rest."
13 Look at the land of the Babylonians,[b]
this people that is now of no account!
The Assyrians[w] have made it
a place for desert creatures;
they raised up their siege towers,
they stripped its fortresses bare
and turned it into a ruin.[x]

14 Wail, you ships of Tarshish;[y]
your fortress is destroyed!

15 At that time Tyre[z] will be forgotten for
seventy years, the span of a king's life. But
at the end of these seventy years, it will
happen to Tyre as in the song of the prostitute:

16 "Take up a harp, walk through the city,
you forgotten prostitute;
play the harp well, sing many a song,
so that you will be remembered."

17 At the end of seventy years, the LORD
will deal with Tyre. She will return to her
lucrative prostitution[a] and will ply her
trade with all the kingdoms on the face of
the earth. 18 Yet her profit and her earnings
will be set apart for the LORD;[b] they will
not be stored up or hoarded. Her profits
will go to those who live before the LORD,[c]
for abundant food and fine clothes.

The LORD's Devastation of the Earth

24 See, the LORD is going to lay waste
the earth[d]
and devastate it;
he will ruin its face
and scatter its inhabitants—
2 it will be the same
for priest as for people,[e]
for the master as for his servant,
for the mistress as for her servant,

23:9 [p] Job 40:11 [q] Isa 13:11 [r] Isa 5:13; 9:15 **23:11** [s] Ex 14:21 [t] Isa 25:2; Zec 9:3-4 **23:12** [u] Rev 18:22 [v] Isa 47:1 **23:13** [w] Isa 10:5 [x] Isa 10:7 **23:14** [y] Isa 2:16 *fn* **23:15** [z] Jer 25:22 **23:17** [a] Eze 16:26; Na 3:4; Rev 17:1 **23:18** [b] Ex 28:36; Ps 72:10 [c] Isa 60:5-9; Mic 4:13 **24:1** [d] ver 20; Isa 2:19-21; 33:9 **24:2** [e] Hos 4:9

[a] *10* Dead Sea Scrolls and some Septuagint manuscripts; Masoretic Text *Go through* [b] *13* Or *Chaldeans*

Carthage in North Africa and sites on the southeastern coast of Spain, including Tartessus. There is even some support for identifying it with Ezion Geber in the Gulf of Aqaba. After his defeat of the Egyptians in 677 BC, Esarhaddon claims in his annals to have sovereignty over Cyprus, Greece and Tarshish, i.e., the entire Phoenician commercial empire.
23:12 *Cyprus.* Lies just 76 miles (122 kilometers) off the Syrian coast. It served as a place of refuge for Phoenician kings (Lulli of Tyre escapes to Cyprus under pressure from Sargon II's Assyrian armies). This prophecy discounts it as a safe haven. If the Phoenicians lose control of Tyre and Sidon, their merchant fleet will become orphans. Their cargoes may either rot or be turned over to the Assyrians.
23:13 *The Assyrians have made [Babylon] a place for desert creatures.* For the historical background of Sennacherib's capture of Babylon in 689 BC and the exile of the Babylonian leader Marduk-Baladan, see the article "Nations Targeted in Isaiah's Prophecies," p. 1139. In this passage, the destruction of southern Mesopotamia's major city is cited as an example of Tyre's ultimate fate at the hands of the Assyrians.
23:15 *seventy years.* There are several instances in the Prophets where "seventy years" becomes a term of exile or punishment (e.g., Jer 25:12; Da 9:2; Zec 1:12). There is also a sense of completion in this number, suggesting that Tyre and the Phoenicians are in God's hands and will not be allowed to prosper again until divine judgment is fulfilled. In fact, for much of the seventh century BC Tyre will be dormant, as a succession of strong Assyrian rulers control both the city and its commercial activities. There is a brief resurgence after the destruction of Nineveh in 612 BC, but Tyre will be besieged for 13 years by the Babylonian ruler Nebuchadnezzar, severely limiting its contacts with the mainland. The Persians exercised control over the Phoenician ports as well, with Artaxerxes III burning Sidon in 345 BC after they had joined an Egyptian-inspired revolt. Tyre's destruction by Alexander the Great in 332 BC followed a seven-month siege and effectively ended the independence of the city.
23:16 This "song of the prostitute" (v. 15) describes the pitiful condition of Tyre after Yahweh's judgment of the city, which is compared to an aged prostitute who must now walk the streets singing to advertise her profession and attract customers, who no longer are willing to come to her door. The tune and coupleted lyrics were probably part of the raucous culture of Mediterranean seaports that catered to sailors on leave.
24:1 – 13 The litany of destruction found in this city lament parallels the style contained in the Sumerian Lament Over the Destruction of Ur as well as other ancient Near Eastern expressions of grief over fallen cities (see the article "City Laments," p. 951). Among the common comparisons that can be made are the descriptions of utter desolation, the fact that no person of any rank has been spared, and the failure of nature to provide what had previously nurtured the people. The Sumerian lament speaks of devastating winds, drought, famine, and bodies piled in the streets unburied. The twentieth-

ISAIAH 23:13

Siege Warfare

Assyrian siege tactics are known from inscriptions and reliefs. Supplies were first cut off from an enemy stronghold so that it would capitulate when facing starvation or death from thirst. Fortified cities were also attacked directly. For this, the attackers at times used scaling ladders. As the Lachish reliefs show, soldiers on the walls repelled such attackers by raining down on them arrows, stones or boiling liquids. An offensive priority was thus to drive the defenders off the walls. For this the Assyrians employed siege towers with battering rams in order to break through the wall. A frontal assault on thick walls took a long time, so the tower was run up with a siege ramp in order to knock off the top of the wall, which was more vulnerable.

Siege ramps were made of stone covered with tamped earth angling up the city wall. Since the towers were heavy, they would have sunk into the soft earth and become immobilized, so the ramps were topped by wooded planks to support the weight. The defenders, in the meantime, had countermeasures. Since the towers were made of wood and covered with leather for protection from archers, they were flammable. Defenders threw burning torches down on them, but the attackers doused the resultant fires with large water ladles.

When the defenders had been driven from their positions, the attackers could concentrate on the walls themselves. Rather than using a direct assault, they often used an oblique attack. Sappers or miners would tunnel under the walls, shoring up their excavations with wooden timbers. After the hole was considered large enough, it was filled with dry brush, which was then set on fire. This burned through the supporting timbers, which collapsed, bringing down the wall. The attacking forces could then easily enter the city, taking it captive. ◆

for seller as for buyer,[f]
for borrower as for lender,
for debtor as for creditor.[g]
3 The earth will be completely laid waste
and totally plundered.[h]
The LORD has spoken this word.

4 The earth dries up and withers,
the world languishes and withers,
the heavens[i] languish with the earth.
5 The earth is defiled[j] by its people;
they have disobeyed[k] the laws,
violated the statutes
and broken the everlasting covenant.
6 Therefore a curse consumes the earth;
its people must bear their guilt.
Therefore earth's inhabitants are
burned up,[l]
and very few are left.

24:2 [f]Eze 7:12 [g]Lev 25:35-37; Dt 23:19-20
24:3 [h]Isa 6:11-12
24:4 [i]Isa 2:12
24:5 [j]Ge 3:17; Nu 35:33 [k]Isa 10:6; 59:12
24:6 [l]Isa 1:31
24:7 [m]Joel 1:10-12 [n]Isa 16:8-10
24:8 [o]Isa 5:12 [p]Jer 7:34; 16:9; 25:10; Hos 2:11 [q]Rev 18:22 [r]Eze 26:13
24:9 [s]Isa 5:11, 22 [t]Isa 5:20
24:11 [u]Isa 16:10; 32:13; Jer 14:3

7 The new wine dries up and the vine
withers;[m]
all the merrymakers groan.[n]
8 The joyful timbrels[o] are stilled,
the noise[p] of the revelers has
stopped,
the joyful harp[q] is silent.[r]
9 No longer do they drink wine[s] with a
song;
the beer is bitter[t] to its drinkers.
10 The ruined city lies desolate;
the entrance to every house is
barred.
11 In the streets they cry out for wine;
all joy turns to gloom,[u]
all joyful sounds are banished from
the earth.
12 The city is left in ruins,
its gate is battered to pieces.

century BC Egyptian Prophecies of Neferti also depict a land laid bare and cursed by the disappearance of the sun and the drying up of the life-sustaining canals. The prophecies of Balaam (non-Biblical prophecies preserved in an Aramaic text found at Deir 'Alla and dating to 700 BC) describe angry gods who "lock up the heavens," turning every creature into a scavenger and forcing even princes to wear rags and priests to "smell of sweat."

[13]So will it be on the earth
and among the nations,
as when an olive tree is beaten,[v]
or as when gleanings are left after
the grape harvest.

[14]They raise their voices, they shout for
joy;[w]
from the west they acclaim the
LORD's majesty.
[15]Therefore in the east give glory[x] to the
LORD;
exalt[y] the name of the LORD, the God
of Israel,
in the islands of the sea.
[16]From the ends of the earth we hear
singing:
"Glory[z] to the Righteous One."

But I said, "I waste away, I waste
away!
Woe to me!
The treacherous betray!
With treachery the treacherous
betray![a]"
[17]Terror and pit and snare[b] await you,
people of the earth.
[18]Whoever flees at the sound of terror
will fall into a pit;
whoever climbs out of the pit
will be caught in a snare.

The floodgates of the heavens[c] are
opened,
the foundations of the earth shake.[d]
[19]The earth is broken up,
the earth is split asunder,[e]
the earth is violently shaken.
[20]The earth reels like a drunkard,[f]
it sways like a hut in the wind;
so heavy upon it is the guilt of its
rebellion[g]
that it falls — never to rise again.

[21]In that day the LORD will punish[h]
the powers in the heavens above
and the kings on the earth below.
[22]They will be herded together
like prisoners[i] bound in a dungeon;[j]
they will be shut up in prison
and be punished[a] after many days.[k]

24:13 [v]Isa 17:6 **24:14** [w]Isa 12:6 **24:15** [x]Isa 66:19 [y]Isa 25:3; Mal 1:11 **24:16** [z]Isa 28:5 [a]Isa 21:2; Jer 5:11 **24:17** [b]Jer 48:43 **24:18** [c]Ge 7:11 [d]Ps 18:7 **24:19** [e]Dt 11:6 **24:20** [f]Isa 19:14 [g]Isa 1:2, 28; 43:27 **24:21** [h]Isa 10:12 **24:22** [i]Isa 10:4 [j]Isa 42:7, 22 [k]Eze 38:8

24:23 [l]Isa 13:10 [m]Rev 22:5 [n]Heb 12:22 [o]Isa 60:19 **25:1** [p]Ps 98:1 [q]Nu 23:19 **25:2** [r]Isa 17:1 [s]Isa 17:3 [t]Isa 13:22 **25:3** [u]Isa 13:11 **25:4** [v]Isa 4:6; 17:10; 27:5; 33:16 [w]Isa 29:5; 49:25 **25:5** [x]Jer 51:55 **25:6** [y]Isa 2:2 [z]Isa 1:19; Mt 8:11; 22:4 [a]Pr 9:2 **25:7** [b]2Co 3:15-16; Eph 4:18 **25:8** [c]Hos 13:14; 1Co 15:54-55* [d]Isa 30:19; 35:10; 51:11; 65:19; Rev 7:17; 21:4

[23]The moon will be dismayed,
the sun[l] ashamed;
for the LORD Almighty will reign[m]
on Mount Zion[n] and in Jerusalem,
and before its elders — with great
glory.[o]

Praise to the LORD

25 LORD, you are my God;
I will exalt you and praise your
name,
for in perfect faithfulness
you have done wonderful things,[p]
things planned[q] long ago.
[2]You have made the city a heap of rubble,[r]
the fortified[s] town a ruin,
the foreigners' stronghold[t] a city no
more;
it will never be rebuilt.
[3]Therefore strong peoples will honor you;
cities of ruthless[u] nations will revere
you.
[4]You have been a refuge[v] for the poor,
a refuge for the needy in their
distress,
a shelter from the storm
and a shade from the heat.
For the breath of the ruthless[w]
is like a storm driving against a wall
[5] and like the heat of the desert.
You silence[x] the uproar of foreigners;
as heat is reduced by the shadow of
a cloud,
so the song of the ruthless is stilled.

[6]On this mountain[y] the LORD Almighty
will prepare
a feast[z] of rich food for all peoples,
a banquet of aged wine —
the best of meats and the finest of
wines.[a]
[7]On this mountain he will destroy
the shroud[b] that enfolds all peoples,
the sheet that covers all nations;
[8] he will swallow up death[c] forever.
The Sovereign LORD will wipe away the
tears[d]
from all faces;

[a] 22 Or *released*

24:18 *snare.* See notes on Ps 124:7; 140:5. *The floodgates of the heavens are opened.* See note on Ge 7:11; see also the article "The 'Vault' and 'Water Above,'" p. 6.
24:22 *shut up in prison.* The context may refer to imprisoned foreign kings, though they were usually executed or exiled. Thus, this phrase likely refers to "powers in the heavens" opposed to God (v. 21). Cyrus speaks of allowing the gods of Sumer and Akkad to return to their homes from their captivity under Nabonidus in Babylon (see note on 30:22 regarding imprisoned gods).
24:23 *the LORD Almighty will reign ... in Jerusalem.* People in the ancient Near East understood deities having special interest in different towns and cities. Yahweh rules in Zion just as Marduk does in Babylon. Divine ties to specific locations are physically demonstrated by the dedication of temples to them, which serve the gods in a way similar to the function of a palace for a king.
25:6 *banquet.* Royalty and people of means sponsored banquets to honor victories and special occasions. The gods also did this, especially when one of them was enthroned. Though these banquets are for the gods, the people would join in the feasting when the enthronement was celebrated annually.
25:7 – 8 *destroy the shroud ... the sheet ... he will swallow up death.* Among some of Israel's neighbors "Death" (*mwt*) was a god, and there is evidence of its personification in the OT as well (e.g., Ps 49:14). See the articles "Death and Sheol," p. 833; "Death and the Underworld," p. 907.

he will remove his people's disgrace[e]
from all the earth.
The LORD has spoken.

[9]In that day they will say,

"Surely this is our God;[f]
we trusted in him, and he saved[g] us.
This is the LORD, we trusted in him;
let us rejoice[h] and be glad in his
salvation."

[10]The hand of the LORD will rest on this
mountain;
but Moab[i] will be trampled in their
land
as straw is trampled down in the
manure.
[11]They will stretch out their hands in it,
as swimmers stretch out their hands
to swim.
God will bring down[j] their pride[k]
despite the cleverness[a] of their hands.
[12]He will bring down your high fortified
walls
and lay them low;[l]
he will bring them down to the ground,
to the very dust.

A Song of Praise

26 In that day this song will be sung in the land of Judah:

We have a strong city;[m]
God makes salvation
its walls[n] and ramparts.
[2]Open the gates
that the righteous[o] nation may enter,
the nation that keeps faith.
[3]You will keep in perfect peace
those whose minds are steadfast,
because they trust in you.
[4]Trust[p] in the LORD forever,
for the LORD, the LORD himself, is the
Rock eternal.
[5]He humbles those who dwell on high,
he lays the lofty city low;
he levels it to the ground[q]
and casts it down to the dust.
[6]Feet trample it down—
the feet of the oppressed,
the footsteps of the poor.[r]

[7]The path of the righteous is level;
you, the Upright One, make the way
of the righteous smooth.[s]
[8]Yes, LORD, walking in the way of your
laws,[b][t]
we wait for you;
your name[u] and renown
are the desire of our hearts.

[9]My soul yearns for you in the night;
in the morning my spirit longs[v] for
you.
When your judgments come upon the
earth,
the people of the world learn
righteousness.[w]
[10]But when grace is shown to the wicked,
they do not learn righteousness;
even in a land of uprightness they go
on doing evil[x]
and do not regard[y] the majesty of
the LORD.
[11]LORD, your hand is lifted high,
but they do not see[z] it.
Let them see your zeal for your people
and be put to shame;
let the fire[a] reserved for your
enemies consume them.

[12]LORD, you establish peace for us;
all that we have accomplished you
have done for us.
[13]LORD our God, other lords[b] besides you
have ruled over us,
but your name alone do we honor.[c]
[14]They are now dead,[d] they live no more;
their spirits do not rise.
You punished them and brought them
to ruin;[e]
you wiped out all memory of them.
[15]You have enlarged the nation, LORD;
you have enlarged the nation.
You have gained glory for yourself;
you have extended all the borders[f] of
the land.

[16]LORD, they came to you in their distress;[g]
when you disciplined them,
they could barely whisper a prayer.[c]
[17]As a pregnant woman about to give
birth[h]
writhes and cries out in her pain,
so were we in your presence, LORD.
[18]We were with child, we writhed in labor,
but we gave birth[i] to wind.
We have not brought salvation[j] to the
earth,
and the people of the world have not
come to life.

[19]But your dead[k] will live, LORD;
their bodies will rise—
let those who dwell in the dust
wake up and shout for joy—
your dew is like the dew of the morning;
the earth will give birth to her dead.[l]

25:8 [e] Mt 5:11; 1Pe 4:14 **25:9** [f] Isa 40:9 [g] Ps 20:5; Isa 33:22; 35:4; 49:25-26; 60:16 [h] Isa 35:2, 10 **25:10** [i] Am 2:1-3 **25:11** [j] Isa 5:25; 14:26; 16:14 [k] Job 40:12 **25:12** [l] Isa 15:1 **26:1** [m] Isa 14:32 [n] Isa 60:18 **26:2** [o] Isa 54:14; 58:8; 62:2 **26:4** [p] Isa 12:2; 50:10 **26:5** [q] Isa 25:12 **26:6** [r] Isa 3:15 **26:7** [s] Isa 42:16 **26:8** [t] Isa 56:1 [u] Isa 12:4

26:9 [v] Ps 63:1; 78:34; Isa 55:6 [w] Mt 6:33 **26:10** [x] Isa 32:6 [y] Isa 22:12-13; Hos 11:7; Jn 5:37-38; Ro 2:4 **26:11** [z] Isa 44:9, 18 [a] Heb 10:27 **26:13** [b] Isa 2:8; 10:5, 11 [c] Isa 63:7 **26:14** [d] Dt 4:28 [e] Isa 10:3 **26:15** [f] Isa 33:17 **26:16** [g] Hos 5:15 **26:17** [h] Jn 16:21 **26:18** [i] Isa 33:11; 59:4 [j] Ps 17:14 **26:19** [k] Isa 25:8; Eph 5:14 [l] Eze 37:1-14; Da 12:2

[a] *11* The meaning of the Hebrew for this word is uncertain. [b] *8* Or *judgments* [c] *16* The meaning of the Hebrew for this clause is uncertain.

26:19 *dew.* The only source of moisture in the drier parts of the year for areas of Israel. The Canaanite inhabitants of Ugarit understood it as coming from Baal. Egyptian texts describe the dew as the "tears of Horus and Thoth," containing the power of resurrection.

ISAIAH 26:19

The Old Testament Concept of Resurrection

Resurrection is most familiar in the ancient Near East in Egyptian literature, where there is an expectation that the body may be reunited with the person's *ba* (includes the mind and public persona) and *ka* (the self). This is nothing like any concept found in the OT or in Christian theology. Resurrection in the OT may be viewed in three different categories. First, there is resurrection that represents the return to life of an individual. Several OT passages refer to such an occurrence (1Ki 17:22; 2Ki 4:35; 13:21). Second, there is the doctrine of individual resurrection of the body in the afterlife; what we might call "eschatological" resurrection. Third, we could speak of a corporate resurrection: a people being brought back into existence from apparent extinction. This last is represented in Ezekiel's vision of the valley of the dry bones, where Israel is brought back to life as a nation (Eze 37). The first and third types of resurrection are demonstrably within the beliefs of ancient Israel, but the second is not so clear. Passages such as this one, and especially Da 12:1 – 2, offer the statements most easily connected to eschatological resurrection.

One important observation is that Isa 26:19 must be understood in contrast to Isa 26:14, where much of the same terminology is used. There the dead of the lords that used to exercise power over Israel are not expected to rise; rather, they have been punished and brought to ruin. Isa 26:14 then has a corporate sense to it that concerns restoration of a group to life in this world. In Isa 26:15 the author begins to contrast the prosperity brought to the nation Israel. This would lead to the conclusion that the passage is concerned with national resurrection (the third type of resurrection mentioned above), as Eze 37 is.

Da 12:1 – 2 is the only passage to speak forthrightly about differing destinies for the righteous and the wicked. But we must not jump too quickly to standard Christian

continued on next page

20 Go, my people, enter your rooms
and shut the doors[m] behind you;
hide[n] yourselves for a little while
until his wrath has passed by.[o]
21 See, the LORD is coming[p] out of his dwelling[q]
to punish[r] the people of the earth for their sins.
The earth will disclose the blood[s] shed on it;
the earth will conceal its slain no longer.

26:20 [m] Ex 12:23 [n] Ps 91:1, 4 [o] Ps 30:5; Isa 54:7-8
26:21 [p] Jude 1:14 [q] Mic 1:3 [r] Isa 13:9, 11; 30:12-14 [s] Job 16:18; Lk 11:50-51
27:1 [t] Isa 34:6; 66:16 [u] Job 3:8 [v] Ps 74:13

Deliverance of Israel

27 In that day,
the LORD will punish with his sword[t] —
his fierce, great and powerful sword —
Leviathan[u] the gliding serpent,
Leviathan the coiling serpent;
he will slay the monster[v] of the sea.
2 In that day —

27:1 *Leviathan.* See note on Job 3:8; see also the articles "Identification of Behemoth and Leviathan," p. 871; "Leviathan," p. 874; "Chaos Monsters," p. 953. Ugaritic and Canaanite myth contain detailed descriptions of a chaos beast, representing the seas or watery anarchy, in the form of a many-headed, twisting sea serpent. There is a close affinity between the description of Leviathan in Isaiah as a "coiling serpent" and the Ugaritic Baal Cycle, which speaks of how the storm-god Baal "smote Litan [i.e., Leviathan] the twisting serpent." In both cases there is a sense of the God of order and fertility vanquishing a chaos monster. Several other passages in the OT mention Leviathan, but most of them (e.g., Ps 74:14; Job 41:1 – 34) speak in terms of God's creative act that establishes control over watery chaos (personified by the sea serpent). Here, however, that struggle between order and chaos occurs at the end of time. It may be that the fall of Satan, portrayed as a seven-headed dragon in

doctrine of the resurrection. A few observations would be in order. First, Da 12:2 says "many" (NIV "multitudes") will awake, not "all"; so this is not a general resurrection. Second, Da 12:2 speaks of those who sleep in "the land of dust" (NIV "the dust of the earth"). This is the only occurrence of this phrase in the OT, but since it refers specifically to a "land" and since Sheol is often connected with dust (e.g., Job 17:16), one could deduce that it is a reference to Sheol, the netherworld (see the articles "Death and Sheol," p. 833; "Death and the Underworld," p. 907). If this is the case, both classes of individuals are to be found in Sheol. Third, the phrase translated "everlasting life" in Da 12:2 occurs only here in the OT, but similar phrases occur (in Greek) in pseudepigraphic literature such as 1 Enoch and the Sibylline Oracles. In these contexts it is equated to periods such as 500 years (1 Enoch 10:10). Fourth, we must observe that Da 12:2 conveys nothing concerning the place of resurrection; i.e., it does not speak of lasting life in heaven nor of lasting contempt in any particular locale. In fact, it does not clarify whether the resurrection to which it refers is an afterlife condition or a restoration to life on earth. Additionally, it does not indicate what criteria qualify an individual for one category or the other.

The author of Daniel anticipates that numerous individuals will be brought back to life (Da 12:2). He does not indicate whether they will be brought back to life in this world, though the OT does not speak clearly of any bodily existence in a world to come in any passage. In this resurrected life they will enjoy an extension to their life (as a reward for their faithfulness?) or will suffer ongoing humiliation (as punishment for their treachery?).

For Daniel, judgment is the prelude to the reconstitution of the nation. Da 12:1 mentions the registering of the citizens of new Israel. The resurrected righteous of Da 12:2 are not isolated individuals; they are raised to participate in this new nation. The dead apostates are raised so that their bodies can be exposed in the Valley of Ben Hinnom (cf. Jer 7:32, 19:6; see also the article "Exposure of the Dead," p. 1239).

While Da 12:1 – 3, a relatively late passage, exceeds any other statements in the OT, it remains quite basic and does not approach the fully developed doctrine of the NT. While the precise shape of Israel's doctrine is difficult to define and various interpreters arrive at vastly different conclusions, most would agree that the Israelite doctrine of resurrection should not be equated with the doctrine as eventually formulated in NT theology and in church history. ◆

"Sing about a fruitful vineyard:[w]
3 I, the LORD, watch over it;
I water[x] it continually.
I guard it day and night
so that no one may harm it.
4 I am not angry.
If only there were briers and thorns
confronting me!
I would march against them in battle;
I would set them all on fire.[y]
5 Or else let them come to me for
refuge;[z]
let them make peace[a] with me,
yes, let them make peace with me."

6 In days to come Jacob will take root,
Israel will bud and blossom[b]
and fill all the world with fruit.[c]

7 Has the LORD struck her
as he struck[d] down those who struck
her?
Has she been killed
as those were killed who killed
her?

27:2 [w] Jer 2:21
27:3 [x] Isa 58:11
27:4 [y] Isa 10:17; Mt 3:12; Heb 6:8
27:5 [z] Isa 25:4 [a] Job 22:21; Ro 5:1; 2Co 5:20
27:6 [b] Hos 14:5-6 [c] Isa 37:31
27:7 [d] Isa 37:36-38

Rev 12:3 – 9, also echoes the Ugaritic image of Litan as "the tyrant with seven heads." *monster of the sea.* See the article "Chaos Monsters," p. 953. The battle between sea and dry land is not only literally visible but also found in mythological texts. Many references place the serpent/dragon in the context of the sea. In the Ugaritic Baal Cycle, Baal confronts the sea itself (Yamm); in the Egyptian "Instruction of Merikare," a deity subdues the "water monster" as part of the creative activity; and in the Akkadian creation epic *Enuma Elish*, Tiamat, a sea goddess in dragon form, is defeated by Marduk. Here it is Yahweh who will be triumphant. While he is said to use a ferocious sword, the text highlights God's triumph over any ferocious enemy.

27:3 *I guard it.* As Yahweh guards the vineyard, so in the Ugaritic tale of Dawn and Dusk one god is called "guard of the sown," and another is "guard of the vineyard."

8 By warfare[a] and exile[e] you contend
with her—
with his fierce blast he drives her
out,
as on a day the east wind blows.
9 By this, then, will Jacob's guilt be
atoned for,
and this will be the full fruit of the
removal of his sin:[f]
When he makes all the altar stones
to be like limestone crushed to
pieces,
no Asherah poles[b][g] or incense altars
will be left standing.
10 The fortified city stands desolate,[h]
an abandoned settlement, forsaken
like the wilderness;
there the calves graze,
there they lie down;[i]
they strip its branches bare.
11 When its twigs are dry, they are broken
off
and women come and make fires
with them.
For this is a people without
understanding;[j]
so their Maker has no compassion
on them,
and their Creator[k] shows them no
favor.[l]

12 In that day the LORD will thresh from
the flowing Euphrates to the Wadi of
Egypt,[m] and you, Israel, will be gathered[n]
up one by one. 13 And in that day a great
trumpet[o] will sound. Those who were perishing in Assyria and those who were exiled in Egypt[p] will come and worship the
LORD on the holy mountain in Jerusalem.

Woe to the Leaders of Ephraim and Judah

28 Woe to that wreath, the pride of
Ephraim's[q] drunkards,
to the fading flower, his glorious
beauty,
set on the head of a fertile valley[r]—
to that city, the pride of those laid
low by wine![s]
2 See, the Lord has one who is powerful[t]
and strong.
Like a hailstorm[u] and a destructive
wind,[v]
like a driving rain and a flooding[w]
downpour,
he will throw it forcefully to the
ground.
3 That wreath, the pride of Ephraim's[x]
drunkards,
will be trampled underfoot.
4 That fading flower, his glorious beauty,
set on the head of a fertile valley,[y]
will be like figs[z] ripe before harvest—
as soon as people see them and take
them in hand,
they swallow them.

5 In that day the LORD Almighty
will be a glorious crown,[a]
a beautiful wreath
for the remnant of his people.
6 He will be a spirit of justice[b]
to the one who sits in judgment,[c]
a source of strength
to those who turn back the battle[d] at
the gate.
7 And these also stagger from wine[e]
and reel[f] from beer:
Priests[g] and prophets[h] stagger from
beer
and are befuddled with wine;
they reel from beer,
they stagger when seeing visions,[i]
they stumble when rendering
decisions.
8 All the tables are covered with vomit[j]
and there is not a spot without filth.

27:8 [e] Isa 50:1; 54:7 **27:9** [f] Ro 11:27* [g] Ex 34:13 **27:10** [h] Isa 32:14; Jer 26:6 [i] Isa 17:2 **27:11** [j] Dt 32:28; Isa 1:3; Jer 8:7 [k] Dt 32:18; Isa 43:1, 7, 15; 44:1-2, 21, 24 [l] Isa 9:17 **27:12** [m] Ge 15:18 [n] Dt 30:4; Isa 11:12; 17:6 **27:13** [o] Lev 25:9; Mt 24:31 [p] Isa 19:21, 25 **28:1** [q] ver 3; Isa 9:9 [r] ver 4 [s] Hos 7:5 **28:2** [t] Isa 40:10 [u] Isa 30:30; Eze 13:11 [v] Isa 29:6 [w] Isa 8:7 **28:3** [x] ver 1 **28:4** [y] ver 1 [z] Hos 9:10; Na 3:12 **28:5** [a] Isa 62:3 **28:6** [b] Isa 11:2-4; 32:1, 16 [c] Jn 5:30 [d] 2Ch 32:8 **28:7** [e] Isa 22:13 [f] Isa 56:10-12 [g] Isa 24:2 [h] Isa 9:15 [i] Isa 29:11; Hos 4:11 **28:8** [j] Jer 48:26

[a] *8* See Septuagint; the meaning of the Hebrew for this word is uncertain. [b] *9* That is, wooden symbols of the goddess Asherah

27:9 *limestone.* Limestone is crushed to produce a chalky substance that can be used for mortar as a liming agent in cesspits and to seal stone walls with a type of "white wash." For altar stones to be crushed in this manner is to completely extinguish their sacred nature. *Asherah poles.* See notes on Dt 7:5; 1Ki 14:23. *incense altars.* See note on Ex 30:2.
27:12 *thresh.* To separate the grain from its encasing husk (see note on Ru 3:2). *from the flowing Euphrates to the Wadi of Egypt.* This designates the idealized empire of Israel (1Ki 4:21; cf. Ge 15:18).
27:13 *trumpet.* Made out of a ram's horn and used to announce God's appearance in a theophany, to summon worshipers for holy days and ceremonies, and also to warn of an approaching enemy (see note on Jos 6:4). This particular trumpet summons exiles back to worship God in their native land.
28:1 *wreath.* While this term can refer to a garland or crown of gold or silver, as it does in Akkadian documents, here it refers to one made of a more transitory substance: flowers formed into a garland. It, like the city of Samaria for which it stands at the head of Ephraim (7:9), will soon fade away (40:6–8). Instead of being a symbol of splendor and blessing (e.g., 62:3), it will vanish before the Assyrian onslaught against Israel/Ephraim in 722 BC.
28:2 The appearance of God in self-disclosure, called a theophany, is always an event of great import. Here his power is shown not through the customary noisy thunder and trumpet blast but through the destructive power of a "destructive wind" and "driving rain." There is ambiguity of these phenomena in a marginal climate where water is desperately needed, but their excess can destroy. The deity, like the king himself, was personally involved in military activity.
28:6 *battle at the gate.* The city gate was usually the most vulnerable area of a city's defense; therefore, it needed special attention. See notes on Job 5:4; 29:7; Pr 8:3; 31:23.
28:7 *stagger from wine.* See notes on 1:22; 5:11. Alcohol use was common in the ancient Near East, so inebriation

9 "Who is it he is trying to teach?[k]
To whom is he explaining his message?
To children weaned[l] from their milk,[m]
to those just taken from the breast?
10 For it is:
Do this, do that,
a rule for this, a rule for that[a];
a little here, a little there."

11 Very well then, with foreign lips and strange tongues[n]
God will speak to this people,[o]
12 to whom he said,
"This is the resting place, let the weary rest";[p]
and, "This is the place of repose" —
but they would not listen.
13 So then, the word of the LORD to them will become:
Do this, do that,
a rule for this, a rule for that;
a little here, a little there —
so that as they go they will fall backward;
they will be injured[q] and snared and captured.[r]

14 Therefore hear the word of the LORD,[s]
you scoffers
who rule this people in Jerusalem.
15 You boast, "We have entered into a covenant with death,
with the realm of the dead we have made an agreement.
When an overwhelming scourge sweeps by,[t]
it cannot touch us,
for we have made a lie[u] our refuge
and falsehood[b] our hiding place.[v]"

16 So this is what the Sovereign LORD says:

"See, I lay a stone in Zion, a tested stone,[w]
a precious cornerstone for a sure foundation;
the one who relies on it
will never be stricken with panic.[x]
17 I will make justice[y] the measuring line
and righteousness the plumb line;[z]
hail will sweep away your refuge, the lie,
and water will overflow your hiding place.
18 Your covenant with death will be annulled;
your agreement with the realm of the dead will not stand.[a]
When the overwhelming scourge sweeps by,[b]
you will be beaten down[c] by it.
19 As often as it comes it will carry you away;[d]
morning after morning, by day and by night,
it will sweep through."

The understanding of this message will bring sheer terror.[e]
20 The bed is too short to stretch out on,
the blanket too narrow to wrap around you.[f]
21 The LORD will rise up as he did at Mount Perazim,[g]
he will rouse himself as in the Valley of Gibeon[h] —
to do his work,[i] his strange work,
and perform his task, his alien task.
22 Now stop your mocking,
or your chains will become heavier;
the Lord, the LORD Almighty, has told me
of the destruction decreed[j] against the whole land.[k]

23 Listen and hear my voice;
pay attention and hear what I say.
24 When a farmer plows for planting,
does he plow continually?
Does he keep on breaking up and working the soil?
25 When he has leveled the surface,
does he not sow caraway and scatter cumin?[l]

[a] *10* Hebrew / *sav lasav sav lasav / kav lakav kav lakav* (probably meaningless sounds mimicking the prophet's words); also in verse 13 [b] *15* Or *false gods*

28:9 [k] ver 26; Isa 30:20; 48:17; 50:4; 54:13 [l] Ps 131:2 [m] Heb 5:12-13 **28:11** [n] Isa 33:19 [o] 1Co 14:21* **28:12** [p] Isa 11:10; Mt 11:28-29 **28:13** [q] Mt 21:44 [r] Isa 8:15 **28:14** [s] Isa 1:10 **28:15** [t] ver 2, 18; Isa 8:7-8; 30:28; Da 11:22 [u] Isa 9:15 [v] Isa 29:15 **28:16** [w] Ps 118:22; Isa 8:14-15; Mt 21:42; Ac 4:11; Eph 2:20 [x] Ro 9:33*; 10:11*; 1Pe 2:6*

28:17 [y] Isa 5:16 [z] 2Ki 21:13 **28:18** [a] Isa 7:7 [b] ver 15 [c] Da 8:13 **28:19** [d] 2Ki 24:2 [e] Job 18:11 **28:20** [f] Isa 59:6 **28:21** [g] 1Ch 14:11 [h] Jos 10:10, 12; 1Ch 14:16 [i] Isa 10:12; Lk 19:41-44 **28:22** [j] Isa 10:22 [k] Isa 10:23 **28:25** [l] Mt 23:23

was sometimes seen positively and other times negatively. The Egyptian Admonitions of Ipuwer state that in times of joy, it is good when people get drunk. The "Instruction of Any" takes the opposite view, one closer to that of Isaiah, as it advises not to get drunk lest what you say gets you into trouble.

28:16 *cornerstone for a sure foundation.* See note on Ps 118:22. A building stands or falls based on the solidness of its foundation (see 44:28), and the cornerstone is what aligns and founds it. As the first stone laid, everything else needs to square to it. Laying the foundation also has important symbolism, and kings took part in a special ceremony. In Mesopotamia, foundation inscriptions often were inscribed on either bricks or tablets buried in the foundation, dedicating the building to a deity or lauding the building king. Here it is Zion, residence of God and repository of his expectations for Israel, that is to align its national life to his cornerstone and upon whose solidity the people can depend.

28:21 *Mount Perazim.* Where David defeated the Philistines (2Sa 5:20). It is near Jerusalem, and its elevation provided a tactical advantage over the enemy moving in the valley below. *Valley of Gibeon.* Joshua successfully fought the Amorites at Gibeon, which is situated on a small hill above surrounding fields near Jerusalem, a site identified with el-Jib.

28:24 *plows … breaking up and working the soil.* Since agriculture was central to the existence of most people in this period, it is well represented in texts and pictures. Plowing late in the year loosened the soil to accept seed. Some crops were seeded by throwing ("broadcasting"; e.g., dill and cumin), while others were planted more

Does he not plant wheat in its place,[a]
barley in its plot,[a]
and spelt[m] in its field?
[26]His God instructs him
and teaches him the right way.

[27]Caraway is not threshed with a sledge,
nor is the wheel of a cart rolled over cumin;
caraway is beaten out with a rod,
and cumin with a stick.
[28]Grain must be ground to make bread;
so one does not go on threshing it forever.
The wheels of a threshing cart may be rolled over it,
but one does not use horses to grind grain.
[29]All this also comes from the LORD Almighty,
whose plan is wonderful,[n]
whose wisdom is magnificent.[o]

Woe to David's City

29 Woe[p] to you, Ariel, Ariel,[q]
the city where David settled!
Add year to year
and let your cycle of festivals[r] go on.
[2]Yet I will besiege Ariel;
she will mourn and lament,[s]
she will be to me like an altar hearth.[b]
[3]I will encamp against you on all sides;
I will encircle[t] you with towers
and set up my siege works against you.
[4]Brought low, you will speak from the ground;
your speech will mumble[u] out of the dust.
Your voice will come ghostlike from the earth;
out of the dust your speech will whisper.
[5]But your many enemies will become like fine dust,
the ruthless hordes like blown chaff.[v]
Suddenly,[w] in an instant,
[6] the LORD Almighty will come
with thunder and earthquake[x] and great noise,
with windstorm and tempest and flames of a devouring fire.
[7]Then the hordes of all the nations[y] that fight against Ariel,
that attack her and her fortress and besiege her,
will be as it is with a dream,[z]
with a vision in the night—
[8]as when a hungry person dreams of eating,
but awakens[a] hungry still;
as when a thirsty person dreams of drinking,
but awakens faint and thirsty still.
So will it be with the hordes of all the nations
that fight against Mount Zion.

[9]Be stunned and amazed,
blind yourselves and be sightless;
be drunk,[b] but not from wine,[c]
stagger, but not from beer.
[10]The LORD has brought over you a deep sleep:
He has sealed your eyes[d] (the prophets);[e]
he has covered your heads (the seers).[f]

[11]For you this whole vision is nothing
but words sealed[g] in a scroll. And if you
give the scroll to someone who can read,
and say, "Read this, please," they will answer, "I can't; it is sealed." [12]Or if you give
the scroll to someone who cannot read,
and say, "Read this, please," they will answer, "I don't know how to read."

[13]The Lord says:

"These people come near to me with their mouth
and honor me with their lips,
but their hearts are far from me.[h]

28:25 [m]Ex 9:32 **28:29** [n]Isa 9:6 [o]Ro 11:33 **29:1** [p]Isa 22:12-13 [q]2Sa 5:9 [r]Isa 1:14 **29:2** [s]Isa 3:26; La 2:5 **29:3** [t]Lk 19:43-44 **29:4** [u]Isa 8:19 **29:5** [v]Isa 17:13 [w]Isa 17:14; 1Th 5:3 **29:6** [x]Mt 24:7; Mk 13:8; Lk 21:11; Rev 11:19 **29:7** [y]Mic 4:11-12; Zec 12:9 [z]Job 20:8 **29:8** [a]Ps 73:20 **29:9** [b]Isa 51:17 [c]Isa 51:21-22 **29:10** [d]Ps 69:23; Isa 6:9-10; Ro 11:8* [e]Mic 3:6 [f]1Sa 9:9 **29:11** [g]Isa 8:16; Mt 13:11; Rev 5:1-2 **29:13** [h]Eze 33:31

[a] *25* The meaning of the Hebrew for this word is uncertain. [b] *2* The Hebrew for *altar hearth* sounds like the Hebrew for *Ariel.*

carefully by seed drills to keep crop types separated from each other. An Akkadian seal shows a wooden plow being pulled by two oxen.

28:26 *His God instructs him.* Farming is here not something easily come by; rather it needs divine guidance. The Sumerians also had "farmer's instructions," which, according to its colophon, was given by Ninurta, the "farmer of Enlil," to help humans in this endeavor.

29:1,2,7 *Ariel.* Designating all or part of Jerusalem, Ariel is related to God's "altar hearth" (v. 2), which is the top of the altar on which the fire was laid. The same term appears in the Mesha Inscription, where Mesha claims to have captured and brought it back from Israel to Moab. This could be an example of metonymy, when a part, the altar surface, stands for the whole, the city in which the altar is located. Ironically, the cultic implement that should purify the people so they could worship God will itself be destroyed for its cultic perfidy.

29:3 *siege works.* See the article "Siege Warfare," p. 1157.

29:6 *the LORD Almighty will come.* See notes on 13:13; 28:2.

29:7 *besiege.* See the article "Siege Warfare," p. 1157.

29:10 *sealed your eyes ... covered your heads.* Most likely images of death here, as they are parallel to the "deep sleep" of the first line. Both phrases, however, are used only here and are therefore difficult to decipher.

29:11 *sealed in a scroll.* See notes on 8:16; 1Ki 21:8.

Their worship of me
is based on merely human rules they
have been taught.[a][i]
14 Therefore once more I will astound
these people
with wonder upon wonder;[j]
the wisdom of the wise[k] will perish,
the intelligence of the intelligent will
vanish.[l]"
15 Woe to those who go to great depths
to hide their plans from the LORD,
who do their work in darkness and think,
"Who sees us?[m] Who will know?"[n]
16 You turn things upside down,
as if the potter were thought to be
like the clay!
Shall what is formed say to the one
who formed it,
"You did not make me"?
Can the pot say to the potter,[o]
"You know nothing"?
17 In a very short time, will not Lebanon
be turned into a fertile field[p]
and the fertile field seem like a forest?[q]
18 In that day the deaf[r] will hear the
words of the scroll,
and out of gloom and darkness
the eyes of the blind will see.[s]
19 Once more the humble[t] will rejoice in
the LORD;
the needy[u] will rejoice in the Holy
One of Israel.
20 The ruthless will vanish,
the mockers[v] will disappear,
and all who have an eye for evil[w]
will be cut down—
21 those who with a word make someone
out to be guilty,
who ensnare the defender in court[x]
and with false testimony deprive the
innocent of justice.[y]

22 Therefore this is what the LORD, who
redeemed Abraham,[z] says to the descendants of Jacob:

"No longer will Jacob be ashamed;[a]
no longer will their faces grow pale.
23 When they see among them their
children,[b]
the work of my hands,[c]
they will keep my name holy;
they will acknowledge the holiness
of the Holy One of Jacob,
and will stand in awe of the God of
Israel.
24 Those who are wayward[d] in spirit will
gain understanding;[e]
those who complain will accept
instruction."[f]

29:13 [i] Mt 15:8-9*; Mk 7:6-7*; Col 2:22 **29:14** [j] Hab 1:5 [k] Jer 8:9; 49:7 [l] Isa 6:9-10; 1Co 1:19* **29:15** [m] Ps 10:11-13; 94:7; Isa 57:12 [n] Job 22:13 **29:16** [o] Isa 45:9; 64:8; Ro 9:20-21* **29:17** [p] Ps 84:6 [q] Isa 32:15 **29:18** [r] Mk 7:37 [s] Isa 32:3; 35:5; Mt 11:5 **29:19** [t] Isa 61:1; Mt 5:5; 11:29 [u] Isa 14:30; Mt 11:5; Jas 1:9; 2:5 **29:20** [v] Isa 28:22 [w] Isa 59:4; Mic 2:1 **29:21** [x] Am 5:10, 15 [y] Isa 5:23; 32:7 **29:22** [z] Isa 41:8; 63:16 [a] Isa 49:23 **29:23** [b] Isa 49:20-26 [c] Isa 19:25 **29:24** [d] Isa 28:7; Heb 5:2 [e] Isa 41:20; 60:16 [f] Isa 30:21 **30:1** [g] Isa 29:15 [h] Isa 1:2 [i] Isa 8:12 **30:2** [j] Isa 31:1 [k] Nu 27:21 [l] Isa 36:9 **30:3** [m] Isa 20:4-5; 36:6 **30:4** [n] Isa 19:11 **30:5** [o] ver 7 **30:6** [p] Ex 5:10, 21; Isa 8:22; Jer 11:4 [q] Dt 8:15 [r] Isa 15:7

Woe to the Obstinate Nation

30 "Woe[g] to the obstinate children,"[h]
declares the LORD,
"to those who carry out plans that are
not mine,
forming an alliance,[i] but not by my
Spirit,
heaping sin upon sin;
2 who go down to Egypt[j]
without consulting[k] me;
who look for help to Pharaoh's
protection,[l]
to Egypt's shade for refuge.
3 But Pharaoh's protection will be to
your shame,
Egypt's shade will bring you
disgrace.[m]
4 Though they have officials in Zoan[n]
and their envoys have arrived in
Hanes,
5 everyone will be put to shame
because of a people[o] useless to them,
who bring neither help nor advantage,
but only shame and disgrace."

6 A prophecy concerning the animals of
the Negev:

Through a land of hardship and
distress,[p]
of lions and lionesses,
of adders and darting snakes,[q]
the envoys carry their riches on
donkeys' backs,
their treasures[r] on the humps of
camels,
to that unprofitable nation,
7 to Egypt, whose help is utterly
useless.

[a] 13 Hebrew; Septuagint *They worship me in vain; / their teachings are merely human rules*

29:17 *Lebanon.* Israel's northern neighbor; it is famed for its mighty cedar forests (2:13; 14:8). These forests are the habitation of the legendary Humbaba in the Gilgamesh Epic and the destination of Wenamun to get timber in a report from late eleventh-century BC Egypt. These national symbols will be felled, leaving only a field, while the fertile fields such as those on Mount Carmel (35:2) will become forested.
30:4 *Zoan.* See note on 19:11. *Hanes.* Probably Heracleopolis, 60 miles (96 kilometers) south of Cairo and a regional capital during the Twenty-Fifth Dynasty. To seek aid, Hezekiah sent envoys to both places, but to no avail.
30:6 *animals of the Negev.* Travel through the Negev and Sinai was by donkey and camel. Dangers from lions and poisonous snakes awaited the unwary. The "adder" is literally a "burning" snake, this one having wings (see note on 6:2; 14:29), perhaps a metaphoric description of its swift, darting attack. This description might also be based on the gecko lizard, some of which can sail along on flaps of skin under their front legs (these are not poisonous, however). Esarhaddon describes a campaign against Egypt during which he encountered serpents and flying creatures.
30:7 *Rahab.* A cosmic sea creature associated with chaos. It seems to have several names or at least is asso-

Therefore I call her
Rahab the Do-Nothing.

8 Go now, write it on a tablet for them,
inscribe it on a scroll,[s]
that for the days to come
it may be an everlasting witness.
9 For these are rebellious people,
deceitful[t] children,
children unwilling to listen to the
LORD's instruction.[u]
10 They say to the seers,
"See no more visions[v]!"
and to the prophets,
"Give us no more visions of what is
right!
Tell us pleasant things,[w]
prophesy illusions.[x]
11 Leave this way,
get off this path,
and stop confronting[y] us
with the Holy One of Israel!"

12 Therefore this is what the Holy One
of Israel says:

"Because you have rejected this
message,[z]
relied on oppression[a]
and depended on deceit,
13 this sin will become for you
like a high wall,[b] cracked and
bulging,
that collapses[c] suddenly,[d] in an
instant.
14 It will break in pieces like pottery,[e]
shattered so mercilessly
that among its pieces not a fragment
will be found
for taking coals from a hearth
or scooping water out of a cistern."

15 This is what the Sovereign LORD, the
Holy One of Israel, says:

"In repentance and rest is your
salvation,
in quietness and trust[f] is your
strength,
but you would have none of it.
16 You said, 'No, we will flee on horses.'[g]
Therefore you will flee!
You said, 'We will ride off on swift
horses.'
Therefore your pursuers will be
swift!
17 A thousand will flee
at the threat of one;
at the threat of five[h]
you will all flee[i] away,
till you are left
like a flagstaff on a mountaintop,
like a banner on a hill."

18 Yet the LORD longs[j] to be gracious to you;
therefore he will rise up to show you
compassion.
For the LORD is a God of justice.[k]
Blessed are all who wait for him![l]

19 People of Zion, who live in Jerusalem,
you will weep no more.[m] How gracious he
will be when you cry for help! As soon as
he hears, he will answer[n] you. 20 Although
the Lord gives you the bread[o] of adversity

30:8 [s] Isa 8:1; Hab 2:2 **30:9** [t] Isa 28:15; 59:3-4 [u] Isa 1:10 **30:10** [v] Jer 11:21; Am 7:13 [w] 1Ki 22:8 [x] Eze 13:7; Ro 16:18 **30:11** [y] Job 21:14 **30:12** [z] Isa 5:24 [a] Isa 5:7 **30:13** [b] Ps 62:3 [c] 1Ki 20:30 [d] Isa 29:5 **30:14** [e] Ps 2:9; Jer 19:10-11 **30:15** [f] Isa 32:17 **30:16** [g] Isa 31:1,3 **30:17** [h] Lev 26:8; Jos 23:10 [i] Lev 26:36; Dt 28:25 **30:18** [j] Isa 42:14; 2Pe 3:9,15 [k] Isa 5:16 [l] Isa 25:9 **30:19** [m] Isa 60:20; 61:3 [n] Ps 50:15; Isa 58:9; 65:24; Mt 7:7-11 **30:20** [o] 1Ki 22:27

---

ciated with other mythological creatures in the OT; e.g., Leviathan, Yamm ("sea"; cf. Ps 89:9–10), and "monster" (cf. Isa 51:9). See the article "Chaos Monsters," p. 953.
30:8 *write it on a tablet … inscribe it on a scroll.* See the articles "Literacy," p. 140; "Books and Literacy," p. 666; "Scrolls in the Ancient World," p. 1286.
30:10 *seers … prophets.* "Seer" is an older term for what became known as a "prophet" (1Sa 9:9). The term here translated "prophet" is in fact "visionary" (Isa 28:15; 29:10). This term is applied to Balaam both in the Bible (Nu 24:4,16) as well as outside it. Akkadian also referred to the intermediaries between the divine and humanity by several terms. The ecstatic prophet appeared in Old Babylonian texts from Mari, but the term had decreased in use by the Neo-Assyrian period. Another term used only in Mari texts was the "answerer," though those with the title are said to come from Babylon and Syria. A later term for "seer" derives from the verb "to shout" and is used by Neo-Assyrian prophets of their divine message. Indirect messages from the gods came by visions and dreams to those designated "visionary" and "questioner." While prophets who pass messages along directly from the gods also interpret dreams and visions, not all visionaries are considered prophets. During one of Ashurbanipal's campaigns, e.g., a request is made that the goddess Ishtar would provide his troops with dreams in the night. See the article "Prophets and Prophecy," p. 1110. *no more visions.* The prophetic message was frequently unwelcome, so prophets were often silenced by force or coercion (cf. Jeremiah). The view that a prophet predicted the future could easily progress to seeing the prophet as speaking the future into being, so silencing them could be seen as averting their dire predictions. This is perhaps why Esarhaddon, a seventh-century BC king of Assyria, made his vassals swear that they would not listen to any negative reports from prophets. In addition to dealing with the prophet, other steps are called for to forestall the prophecy itself through a counterbalancing curse.
30:13–14 *a high wall, cracked and bulging … will break in pieces like pottery.* Given the extensive use of mud brick architecture throughout the ancient Near East, this must have been a common occurrence. Egyptian tomb paintings depict the process from gathering clay, water and straw to shaping the bricks in molds (see note on Ex 5:11). As the bricks weather, they erode and loose stability. If the bricks had only been sun-dried, not fire-hardened in a kiln, then they were subject to crumbling under the weight of a high wall. This would often be manifested first in cracks and bulges and eventually the entire structure would come down in an avalanche of masonry (Isa 9:10). To guard against faulty construction and increase the life of the brick walls, Hammurapi's law code provides strict punishments for careless contractors.
30:20 *the bread of adversity and the water of affliction.* The value of bread and water, the two mainstays of life, are

ISAIAH 30

Egyptian Relationships Under Hezekiah

Chafing from Assyrian domination, Hezekiah would have been tempted to turn to Egypt, the other major player of the period, for aid. When Thebes was threatened by an incursion from the west, the Egyptians accepted aid from the Ethiopian king Piankhy. Piankhy's brother and successor, Shabako, encountered Assyrian expansion toward the south. Sargon II moved as far as Philistia, where he had previously encountered and defeated the army of Osorkon IV in 720 BC. Subsequently, Egypt under Shabako developed a more conciliatory stance toward Assyria. This temporary amity could be indicated by two seal impressions of Shabako found at the Assyrian capital of Nineveh.

Shabako turned against Assyria at Sargon's death and the accession of Sargon's successor, Sennacherib. Shabako's successor, Shebitku, supported Hezekiah, who faced Assyria at Eltekeh (about 100 miles [160 kilometers] from Egypt's border), helping to fend off Assyria's capture of Judah's capital. Shebitku had brought up from Ethiopia additional troops, including his brother Tirhakah, a future king (Isa 37:9). While Judah was ultimately delivered from the immediate Assyrian threat by other means (Isa 37:36 – 37), Egypt's power was insufficient to expel Assyria completely, and so Tirhakah and his forces returned home. ◆

	EGYPTIAN PHARAOHS (LOW)	ASSYRIAN KINGS
750 BC		Ashur-nirari V 754-745
740 BC	Piankhy 747 – 716	Tiglath-pileser III 745 – 727
730 BC		Shalmaneser V 727 – 722
720 BC	Shabako 716 – 702	Sargon II 721 – 704
710 BC		Sennacherib 704 – 681
700 BC	Shebitku 702 – 690	
690 BC	Taharqa 690 – 664	
680 BC		Esarhaddon 681 – 667
670 BC	Psamtik I 664 – 610	Ashurbanipal 667 – 630
660 BC		

and the water of affliction, your teachers
will be hidden[p] no more; with your own
eyes you will see them. 21 Whether you
turn to the right or to the left, your ears
will hear a voice[q] behind you, saying,
"This is the way; walk in it." 22 Then you
will desecrate your idols[r] overlaid with silver and your images covered with gold; you will throw them away like a menstrual cloth and say to them, "Away with you!"

30:20 [p] Ps 74:9; Am 8:11 **30:21** [q] Isa 29:24 **30:22** [r] Ex 32:4

inverted. An incantation from Ugarit against sorcery uses a similar inversion with the curse "You will eat the bread of fasting."

30:22 *desecrate your idols ... and your images ... throw them away.* Destruction or removal of a cultic statue could make the attendant god depart or lose power. Esarhaddon claims in one of his campaigns that "gods and goddesses dwelling within it [the captured town] fled to heaven above like birds," while Ashurbanipal, destroying temples and statues of Susa, wrote that "their gods, their goddesses I reckoned among the phantoms." Many inscriptions record destruction or capture of the enemy's gods. *like a menstrual cloth.* There could be no more defiling substance than menstrual blood (Lev 15:19 – 23), and, for the people, no more defiling object than an idol (Dt 4:15 – 19). Here then, the idols, usually among the most precious objects in the culture, will be treated as the most disgusting piece of trash.

23 He will also send you rain[s] for the
seed you sow in the ground, and the food
that comes from the land will be rich and
plentiful. In that day your cattle will graze
in broad meadows.[t] 24 The oxen and donkeys that work the soil will eat fodder and
mash, spread out with fork[u] and shovel.
25 In the day of great slaughter, when the
towers[v] fall, streams of water will flow[w] on
every high mountain and every lofty hill.
26 The moon will shine like the sun,[x] and
the sunlight will be seven times brighter,
like the light of seven full days, when the
LORD binds up the bruises of his people
and heals[y] the wounds he inflicted.

27 See, the Name[z] of the LORD comes from
afar,
with burning anger[a] and dense
clouds of smoke;
his lips are full of wrath,[b]
and his tongue is a consuming fire.
28 His breath[c] is like a rushing torrent,
rising up to the neck.[d]
He shakes the nations in the sieve[e] of
destruction;
he places in the jaws of the peoples
a bit[f] that leads them astray.
29 And you will sing
as on the night you celebrate a holy
festival;
your hearts will rejoice
as when people playing pipes go up
to the mountain[g] of the LORD,
to the Rock of Israel.
30 The LORD will cause people to hear his
majestic voice
and will make them see his arm
coming down
with raging anger and consuming fire,
with cloudburst, thunderstorm and
hail.
31 The voice of the LORD will shatter
Assyria;[h]
with his rod he will strike[i] them down.
32 Every stroke the LORD lays on them
with his punishing club
will be to the music of timbrels and
harps,
as he fights them in battle with the
blows of his arm.[j]
33 Topheth[k] has long been prepared;
it has been made ready for the king.
Its fire pit has been made deep and wide,
with an abundance of fire and wood;
the breath of the LORD,
like a stream of burning sulfur,[l]
sets it ablaze.

Woe to Those Who Rely on Egypt

31 Woe to those who go down to
Egypt[m] for help,
who rely on horses,
who trust in the multitude of their
chariots[n]
and in the great strength of their
horsemen,
but do not look to the Holy One of
Israel,
or seek help from the LORD.[o]
2 Yet he too is wise[p] and can bring
disaster;[q]
he does not take back his words.[r]
He will rise up against that wicked
nation,[s]
against those who help evildoers.
3 But the Egyptians[t] are mere mortals
and not God;[u]
their horses are flesh and not spirit.
When the LORD stretches out his hand,[v]
those who help will stumble,
those who are helped[w] will fall;
all will perish together.

4 This is what the LORD says to me:

"As a lion[x] growls,
a great lion over its prey —
and though a whole band of shepherds
is called together against it,

30:23 [s] Isa 65:21-22 [t] Ps 65:13
30:24 [u] Mt 3:12; Lk 3:17
30:25 [v] Isa 2:15 [w] Isa 41:18
30:26 [x] Isa 24:23; 60:19-20; Rev 21:23; 22:5 [y] Dt 32:39; Isa 1:5
30:27 [z] Isa 59:19 [a] Isa 66:14 [b] Isa 10:5
30:28 [c] Isa 11:4 [d] Isa 8:8 [e] Am 9:9 [f] 2Ki 19:28; Isa 37:29
30:29 [g] Ps 42:4
30:31 [h] Isa 10:5, 12 [i] Isa 11:4
30:32 [j] Isa 11:15; Eze 32:10
30:33 [k] 2Ki 23:10 [l] Ge 19:24
31:1 [m] Dt 17:16; Isa 30:2, 5 [n] Isa 2:7 [o] Ps 20:7; Da 9:13
31:2 [p] Ro 16:27 [q] Isa 45:7 [r] Nu 23:19 [s] Isa 32:6
31:3 [t] Isa 36:9 [u] Eze 28:9; 2Th 2:4 [v] Isa 9:17, 21 [w] Isa 30:5-7
31:4 [x] Nu 24:9; Hos 11:10; Am 3:8

30:24 *eat fodder and mash, spread out with fork and shovel.* Because of the people's return to covenant obedience, even their draft animals will share in the abundance provided by God. Fodder for animals normally consisted of the remains of the chaff left by the threshing process. A common term for fodder means "small pieces of straw," which might be mixed with barley. Here, however, the livestock are fed chickpeas that had been specially prepared for them using the wooden shovel and the winnowing fork. Both of these implements helped separate the grain from the chaff and were used to create heaps.
30:28 *sieve of destruction.* The two types of sieves used by Israelite farmers gave them different results. The *kebara* (Am 9:9) had large holes that caught stones and other large objects as the worker shifted it back and forth. The sieve in this passage, the *napa*, had smaller holes and was used to separate out the smaller items from the grain through a swift up-and-down motion. This makes an excellent metaphor for God's act of judgment.
30:32 *music of timbrels and harps.* See the article "Music and Musicians," p. 524. *his arm.* The arm, especially the right arm, symbolized power and strength. See notes on Ex 6:1; Job 40:9.
30:33 *Topheth.* This was the place in the Hinnom Valley of Jerusalem where the Molek cult was practiced (see note on Jer 7:31). *burning sulfur.* Finely ground sulfur can increase the intensity and brightness of a fire. It may be this property that has made it a symbol of God's wrath, as in the case of Sodom (Ge 19:24). In this image of Assyria's funeral pyre, it magnifies the power of God to punish the enemy nation. Mixed with salt, sulfur could also rob the soil of fertility, again a sign of God's extreme displeasure.
31:4 *lion.* Among the largest carnivores in the ancient Near East, it captured the imagination for its ferocity and voracity and appeared regularly in texts and iconography. An Israelite seal on a jar handle depicts a lion attacking a gazelle, as does a late third-millennium BC Akkadian cylinder seal. Lions battle with bulls in ivories from Megiddo

it is not frightened by their shouts
or disturbed by their clamor —
so the LORD Almighty will come down[y]
to do battle on Mount Zion and on
its heights.
5 Like birds hovering overhead,
the LORD Almighty will shield[z]
Jerusalem;
he will shield it and deliver[a] it,
he will 'pass over' it and will rescue
it."

6 Return, you Israelites, to the One you
have so greatly revolted against. 7 For in
that day every one of you will reject the
idols of silver and gold[b] your sinful hands
have made.
8 "Assyria[c] will fall by no human
sword;
a sword, not of mortals, will devour[d]
them.
They will flee before the sword
and their young men will be put to
forced labor.[e]
9 Their stronghold[f] will fall because of
terror;
at the sight of the battle standard
their commanders will panic,"
declares the LORD,
whose fire[g] is in Zion,
whose furnace is in Jerusalem.

The Kingdom of Righteousness

32 See, a king[h] will reign in
righteousness
and rulers will rule with justice.[i]
2 Each one will be like a shelter[j] from
the wind
and a refuge from the storm,
like streams of water in the desert
and the shadow of a great rock in a
thirsty land.
3 Then the eyes of those who see will no
longer be closed,[k]
and the ears of those who hear will
listen.
4 The fearful heart will know and
understand,[l]
and the stammering tongue will be
fluent and clear.
5 No longer will the fool[m] be called
noble
nor the scoundrel be highly respected.
6 For fools speak folly,[n]
their hearts are bent on evil:
They practice ungodliness[o]
and spread error[p] concerning the
LORD;
the hungry they leave empty[q]
and from the thirsty they withhold
water.
7 Scoundrels use wicked methods,[r]
they make up evil schemes[s]
to destroy the poor with lies,
even when the plea of the needy[t] is
just.
8 But the noble make noble plans,
and by noble deeds[u] they stand.

The Women of Jerusalem

9 You women who are so complacent,
rise up and listen[v] to me;
you daughters who feel secure,[w]
hear what I have to say!
10 In little more than a year
you who feel secure will tremble;
the grape harvest will fail,[x]
and the harvest of fruit will not come.
11 Tremble, you complacent women;
shudder, you daughters who feel
secure!
Strip off your fine clothes[y]
and wrap yourselves in rags.
12 Beat your breasts[z] for the pleasant fields,
for the fruitful vines
13 and for the land of my people,
a land overgrown with thorns and
briers[a] —

31:4 [y] Isa 42:13
31:5 [z] Ps 91:4
[a] Isa 37:35; 38:6
31:7 [b] Isa 2:20; 30:22
31:8 [c] Isa 10:12
[d] Isa 14:25; 37:7
[e] Ge 49:15
31:9 [f] Dt 32:31, 37 [g] Isa 10:17
32:1 [h] Eze 37:24
[i] Ps 72:1-4; Isa 9:7
32:2 [j] Isa 4:6
32:3 [k] Isa 29:18
32:4 [l] Isa 29:24
32:5 [m] 1Sa 25:25
32:6 [n] Pr 19:3
[o] Isa 9:17
[p] Isa 9:16
[q] Isa 3:15
32:7 [r] Jer 5:26-28 [s] Mic 7:3
[t] Isa 61:1
32:8 [u] Pr 11:25
32:9 [v] Isa 28:23
[w] Isa 47:8; Am 6:1; Zep 2:15
32:10 [x] Isa 5:5-6; 24:7
32:11 [y] Isa 47:2
32:12 [z] Na 2:7
32:13 [a] Isa 5:6

and Lachish and attack humans in Late Bronze and Iron Age seals from Israel. Similar motifs are found in Mesopotamian, Egyptian, and Syro-Palestinian art. Pharaoh Amenemhet I claims, "I subdued lions, I captured crocodiles," while Mesopotamian kings exhibit their fearless prowess by facing them in hunting scenes. While being literal hunts, they also had metaphoric, symbolic value, identifying the king with the hunted creature over which he was master. The lion also embodied the warrior-god Ninurta.
31:8 The ultimate fate of Assyria is its annihilation as a nation by a coalition of states headed by the Chaldeans of Babylon and the Medes. The Babylonian Chronicle describes how Nineveh falls to an allied army led by Nabopolassar of Babylon and the Median ruler Cyaxares in 612 BC. The final battle, at Carchemish in 605 BC, demonstrated the ability of the Babylonian leader Nebuchadnezzar to totally demoralize the formerly invincible Assyrian shock troops and their Egyptian allies.
32:1 – 5 These verses form a reversal of the conditions faced by Isaiah in his call narrative in 6:9 – 10. What changes Israel's fortunes is the rise of a righteous king who enforces the law and maintains order. Statements such as these are part of the wisdom tradition of the ancient Near East that includes works from Egypt and Mesopotamia on the "just king." Among them is the Egyptian tale of the Eloquent Peasant, which describes a righteous king as one who is "father to the orphan" and "mother to the motherless." Similarly, the eighth-century BC Egyptian sage Ankhsheshonq states that "blessed is a city with a just ruler."
32:10 *grape harvest … harvest of fruit.* These two events could be highlighted in a metonymy, where the part represents the whole, so that the entire agricultural process will be thwarted. The time period, early fall, may indicate a time just prior to the rainy season, when marauding troops found it harder to carry out their campaigns (cf. 2Sa 11:1).
32:11 – 13 *wrap yourselves in rags … Beat your breasts … mourn.* See the article "Mourning," p. 828.

yes, mourn for all houses of merriment
and for this city of revelry.[b]
14 The fortress[c] will be abandoned,
the noisy city deserted;[d]
citadel and watchtower[e] will become a wasteland forever,
the delight of donkeys,[f] a pasture for flocks,
15 till the Spirit[g] is poured on us from on high,
and the desert becomes a fertile field,[h]
and the fertile field seems like a forest.[i]
16 The LORD's justice will dwell in the desert,
his righteousness live in the fertile field.
17 The fruit of that righteousness will be peace;[j]
its effect will be quietness and confidence[k] forever.
18 My people will live in peaceful dwelling places,
in secure homes,
in undisturbed places of rest.[l]
19 Though hail[m] flattens the forest[n]
and the city is leveled[o] completely,
20 how blessed you will be,
sowing[p] your seed by every stream,
and letting your cattle and donkeys range free.[q]

Distress and Help

33 Woe to you, destroyer,
you who have not been destroyed!
Woe to you, betrayer,
you who have not been betrayed!
When you stop destroying,
you will be destroyed;[r]
when you stop betraying,
you will be betrayed.[s]
2 LORD, be gracious to us;
we long for you.
Be our strength[t] every morning,
our salvation[u] in time of distress.
3 At the uproar of your army, the peoples flee;
when you rise up,[v] the nations scatter.
4 Your plunder, O nations, is harvested
as by young locusts;
like a swarm of locusts people
pounce on it.
5 The LORD is exalted,[w] for he dwells on high;
he will fill Zion with his justice[x] and righteousness.[y]
6 He will be the sure foundation for your times,
a rich store of salvation[z] and wisdom and knowledge;
the fear[a] of the LORD is the key to this treasure.[a]
7 Look, their brave men cry aloud in the streets;
the envoys[b] of peace weep bitterly.
8 The highways are deserted,
no travelers are on the roads.[c]
The treaty is broken,
its witnesses[b] are despised,
no one is respected.
9 The land dries up[d] and wastes away,
Lebanon[e] is ashamed and withers;[f]
Sharon is like the Arabah,
and Bashan and Carmel drop their leaves.

32:13 [b] Isa 22:2 **32:14** [c] Isa 13:22 [d] Isa 6:11; 27:10 [e] Isa 34:13 [f] Ps 104:11 **32:15** [g] Isa 11:2; Joel 2:28 [h] Ps 107:35; Isa 35:1-2 [i] Isa 29:17 **32:17** [j] Ps 119:165; Ro 14:17; Jas 3:18 [k] Isa 30:15 **32:18** [l] Hos 2:18-23 **32:19** [m] Isa 28:17; 30:30 [n] Isa 10:19; Zec 11:2 [o] Isa 24:10; 27:10 **32:20** [p] Ecc 11:1 [q] Isa 30:24 **33:1** [r] Hab 2:8; Mt 7:2 [s] Isa 21:2 **33:2** [t] Isa 40:10; 51:9; 59:16 [u] Isa 25:9 **33:3** [v] Isa 59:16-18 **33:5** [w] Ps 97:9 [x] Isa 28:6 [y] Isa 1:26 **33:6** [z] Isa 51:6 [a] Isa 11:2-3; Mt 6:33 **33:7** [b] 2Ki 18:37 **33:8** [c] Jdg 5:6; Isa 35:8 **33:9** [d] Isa 3:26 [e] Isa 2:13; 35:2 [f] Isa 24:4

[a] 6 Or *is a treasure from him* [b] 8 Dead Sea Scrolls; Masoretic Text / *the cities*

32:14 *abandoned ... deserted ... a wasteland.* In the Lament Over the Destruction of Sumer and Ur from the late third millennium BC, part of the lamented destruction is shown by the gods abandoning their temples and towns. One of the reasons for building, maintaining and provisioning temples was to maintain the support of the gods who served there (see 44:28). Should such provisioning cease, so would divine sustenance. A lack of divine support would result in the physical destruction of the city and abandonment by their inhabitants. *citadel.* This citadel refers to a section of the ridge crest southeast of the temple mount, which was part of the royal administrative area. It most likely specifies the acropolis citadel placed on this strategic height overlooking the city. This term is known from other sites, such as Dibon in the Mesha Inscription, where the Moabite king describes his fortification efforts. This area of a city needs special protection, particularly if it holds the king's residence. This hub of political life will be abandoned. *watchtower.* This Hebrew term is used only here in the Bible and is etymologically related to the "siege towers" of 23:13. Based on those discovered archaeologically, the towers usually had rectangular, heavy stone foundations not only to support their height but also to withstand attack. Towers have been found at Giloh (near Jerusalem), Ashdod, Shechem and Edom. These mighty, protective features will themselves be laid waste.
33:4 *locusts.* See note on Ex 10:4.
33:6 *the fear of the LORD.* Fear in this case is not a distressing emotion from facing pain or evil, but rather the reverence and awe before a superior. This is a desired response to one's ruler, whether divine or human. An Akkadian proverb makes this positive element clear: "Reverence gives birth to goodness." A lack of awe and reverence is undesirable, leading to destruction. Ashurbanipal executed Ahsheri, whom he describes as "one not fearing my lordship."
33:8 *treaty.* Treaties are formal agreements between two or more parties with expectations for performance from both sides, each looking after the welfare of the other. Most Biblical mentions of "covenant" or "treaty" refer to the one between Israel and her God. See the articles "Covenants," p. 143; "Decrees and Laws," p. 301; "Treaty Formats and Biblical Covenants," p. 303. *witnesses.* Those deities expected to bring about the punishments called for if the covenant was broken (1:2). In despising such gods, one is denying either their power or their interest in the treaty.
33:9 *Lebanon ... Sharon ... Bashan ... Carmel.* These four geographic areas, moving from north to south, are particularly fertile in an area surrounded by deserts.

[10]"Now will I arise,[g]" says the LORD.
"Now will I be exalted;
now will I be lifted up.
[11]You conceive[h] chaff,
you give birth[i] to straw;
your breath is a fire[j] that consumes
you.
[12]The peoples will be burned to ashes;
like cut thornbushes they will be set
ablaze.[k]"

[13]You who are far away,[l] hear[m] what I
have done;
you who are near, acknowledge my
power!
[14]The sinners in Zion are terrified;
trembling[n] grips the godless:
"Who of us can dwell with the
consuming fire?[o]
Who of us can dwell with everlasting
burning?"
[15]Those who walk righteously[p]
and speak what is right,[q]
who reject gain from extortion
and keep their hands from accepting
bribes,
who stop their ears against plots of
murder
and shut their eyes[r] against
contemplating evil —
[16]they are the ones who will dwell on
the heights,
whose refuge[s] will be the mountain
fortress.[t]
Their bread will be supplied,
and water will not fail[u] them.
[17]Your eyes will see the king[v] in his
beauty
and view a land that stretches afar.[w]
[18]In your thoughts you will ponder the
former terror:[x]
"Where is that chief officer?
Where is the one who took the
revenue?
Where is the officer in charge of the
towers?"
[19]You will see those arrogant people no
more,
people whose speech is obscure,
whose language is strange and
incomprehensible.[y]

[20]Look on Zion, the city of our festivals;
your eyes will see Jerusalem,
a peaceful abode,[z] a tent that will
not be moved;[a]
its stakes will never be pulled up,
nor any of its ropes broken.
[21]There the LORD will be our Mighty
One.
It will be like a place of broad rivers
and streams.[b]
No galley with oars will ride them,
no mighty ship will sail them.
[22]For the LORD is our judge,[c]
the LORD is our lawgiver,[d]
the LORD is our king;[e]
it is he who will save[f] us.

[23]Your rigging hangs loose:
The mast is not held secure,
the sail is not spread.

33:10 [g] Ps 12:5; Isa 2:21 **33:11** [h] Ps 7:14; Isa 59:4; Jas 1:15 [i] Isa 26:18 [j] Isa 1:31 **33:12** [k] Isa 10:17 **33:13** [l] Ps 48:10; 49:1 [m] Isa 49:1 **33:14** [n] Isa 32:11 [o] Isa 30:30; Heb 12:29 **33:15** [p] Isa 58:8 [q] Ps 15:2; 24:4 [r] Ps 119:37 **33:16** [s] Isa 25:4 [t] Isa 26:1 [u] Isa 49:10 **33:17** [v] Isa 6:5 [w] Isa 26:15 **33:18** [x] Isa 17:14 **33:19** [y] Isa 28:11; Jer 5:15 **33:20** [z] Isa 32:18 [a] Ps 46:5; 125:1-2 **33:21** [b] Isa 41:18; 48:18; 66:12 **33:22** [c] Isa 11:4 [d] Isa 2:3; Jas 4:12 [e] Ps 89:18 [f] Isa 25:9

33:18 *chief officer … the one who took the revenue … the officer in charge of the towers.* The first of these is simply a general designation ("officer"), possibly for someone associated with taxation, as is the second, the "weigher"; both of these measured incoming precious metals, coins and commodities. The third appears to be in charge of fortifications; his relationship with the former two is unclear. These are examples of administrative bureaucracy that played an important role in the administration of both court and cult among Israel's neighbors, especially those who had sizable empires.
33:19 *obscure … strange and incomprehensible.* While the Israelites undoubtedly spoke Hebrew as their home language, these foreign officials, if Assyrian, would have spoken Akkadian, or if they were from other parts of the Assyrian Empire, they would have had other home languages. Aramaic was the diplomatic, international language of the empire, with correspondence during the seventh century BC between Babylonia and Assyria taking place at least once in Aramaic. The discernible differences between dialects spoken among the Israelites (e.g., Jdg 12:5 – 6) would have been noticed by these imported officials and probably derided, if indeed Aramaic is understood here. Though not the Israelites' native tongue, Aramaic and Hebrew were closely enough allied that the Israelites could have understood either. If Akkadian is meant here, the linguistic distance between that East Semitic language and the West Semitic Hebrew would have made them mutually incomprehensible — actually removed "from hearing," as the term "obscure" here is literally translated.
33:20 *stakes.* See note on 22:23,25.
33:21 *galley with oars … ship … sail.* Though the Israelites were not a seafaring people, they did use the sea to some extent (1Ki 9:26). Israel's neighbors, both Egypt and Mesopotamia, relied more on seagoing and river vessels not only for trade but also for military activity. They used oared craft that could also have sails. An eighth-century BC Hebrew seal also shows a sailing ship, most probably on the Mediterranean or the Sea of Galilee, but Zion/Jerusalem, situated on the highlands and far from any water body sufficient to allow such craft, could not depend on them for protection.
33:22 *judge … lawgiver … king.* Various ancient Near Eastern deities fulfill these functions for different ethnic groups. Canaanite El is king for the Canaanites, and numerous Mesopotamian deities are so identified. Several Mesopotamian gods, including Adad (the storm-god) and Shamash (the sun-god), are judges. They are accredited not with dispensing laws but with acting justly and providing kings the wherewithal to promulgate just laws.
33:23 *rigging … mast … sail.* A similar boat metaphor is known from an Assyrian elegy about a woman who died in childbirth. She is described as a boat that is adrift with its mooring rope cut and the seat where the oarsman would sit broken. Here Israel is portrayed in a similar state of destitution.

Then an abundance of spoils will be
divided
and even the lame[g] will carry off
plunder.[h]
24 No one living in Zion will say, "I am
ill";[i]
and the sins of those who dwell
there will be forgiven.[j]

Judgment Against the Nations

34 Come near, you nations, and
listen;
pay attention, you peoples![k]
Let the earth[l] hear, and all that is in it,
the world, and all that comes out
of it![m]
2 The LORD is angry with all nations;
his wrath is on all their armies.
He will totally destroy[a][n] them,
he will give them over to slaughter.[o]
3 Their slain will be thrown out,
their dead bodies will stink;[p]
the mountains will be soaked with
their blood.[q]
4 All the stars in the sky will be
dissolved[r]
and the heavens rolled up[s] like a
scroll;
all the starry host will fall[t]
like withered leaves from the vine,
like shriveled figs from the fig tree.

5 My sword[u] has drunk its fill in the
heavens;
see, it descends in judgment on
Edom,[v]
the people I have totally destroyed.[w]
6 The sword of the LORD is bathed in
blood,
it is covered with fat—
the blood of lambs and goats,
fat from the kidneys of rams.
For the LORD has a sacrifice in
Bozrah
and a great slaughter in the land of
Edom.
7 And the wild oxen will fall with
them,
the bull calves and the great bulls.[x]
Their land will be drenched with
blood,
and the dust will be soaked with fat.

8 For the LORD has a day of vengeance,[y]
a year of retribution, to uphold
Zion's cause.
9 Edom's streams will be turned into
pitch,
her dust into burning sulfur;
her land will become blazing pitch!
10 It will not be quenched night or day;
its smoke will rise forever.[z]
From generation to generation it will
lie desolate;[a]
no one will ever pass through it
again.
11 The desert owl[b][b] and screech owl[b] will
possess it;
the great owl[b] and the raven will
nest there.

33:23 [g] 2Ki 7:8 [h] 2Ki 7:16 **33:24** [i] Isa 30:26 [j] Jer 50:20; 1Jn 1:7-9 **34:1** [k] Isa 41:1; 43:9 [l] Ps 49:1 [m] Dt 32:1 **34:2** [n] Isa 13:5 [o] Isa 30:25 **34:3** [p] Joel 2:20; Am 4:10 [q] ver 7; Eze 14:19; 35:6; 38:22 **34:4** [r] Isa 13:13; 2Pe 3:10 [s] Eze 32:7-8 [t] Joel 2:31; Mt 24:29*; Rev 6:13 **34:5** [u] Dt 32:41-42; Jer 46:10; Eze 21:5 [v] Am 1:11-12 [w] Isa 24:6; Mal 1:4 **34:7** [x] Ps 68:30 **34:8** [y] Isa 63:4 **34:10** [z] Rev 14:10-11; 19:3 [a] Isa 13:20; 24:1; Eze 29:12; Mal 1:3 **34:11** [b] Zep 2:14; Rev 18:2

a 2 The Hebrew term refers to the irrevocable giving over of things or persons to the LORD, often by totally destroying them; also in verse 5. *b* 11 The precise identification of these birds is uncertain.

34:4 *stars … will be dissolved … starry host will fall.* Always in command of all creation, Yahweh shows mastery over the heavens and celestial bodies, causing their brightness to be snuffed out in a reversal of creation. Prominent astral motifs in the Mesopotamian religion included the idea that the gods were given stations within the heavens and their "astral likenesses" marked the zones of the calendrical year (e.g., in the Babylonian *Enuma Elish* creation epic). In the celestial omens, the disappearing of a star or planet suggested that the related deity had suffered defeat in battle. Astral deities were considered among the most prominent and powerful of the gods. The dissolving of the stars and the fall of the starry host are therefore related. Both the natural manifestation and the deity connected to it are overcome in this act of judgment. Additionally, dream omens in Mesopotamia hold that the observation of stars falling is a bad omen. In the destruction described in the Mesopotamian epic "Erra and Ishum," Erra says that he will make planets shed their splendor and will wrench stars from the sky. *heavens rolled up like a scroll.* Most often the heavens are compared to a canopy (40:22) or a tent (Ps 104:2) that is spread over the earth. This image in Isaiah of the whole panorama of the sky being rolled up like a parchment scroll is unique in the Hebrew Bible (see the NT parallel in Rev 6:14). Additionally, the three major Babylonian gods are represented not by stars but by the sky itself. Anu is the sky-god, and the horizon is divided into three paths (connected to Anu, Enlil and Ea). Therefore, rolling up the sky is an act of judgment against the three main deities of the ancient world.
34:5 *Edom.* See notes on 21:11 ("Dumah"); Ge 36:9; Ps 137:7.
34:6 *Bozrah.* The Edomite capital on the site of what is now Buseira on the north-south King's Highway (see note on Nu 20:17) at its junction with a major east-west route some 20 miles (32 kilometers) south of the Dead Sea. Proximity to copper mines added to its wealth. It is a natural stronghold, surrounded by steep valleys. Excavations have uncovered a building with a courtyard similar to those of the Neo-Assyrian period, indicating that it was occupied during this period of Isaiah. Remains also indicate continued occupation into the Babylonian/Persian periods.
34:9 *burning sulfur.* See note on 30:33. *pitch.* The association of this Hebrew word with other, petroleum-based terms (bitumen, natural asphalt) suggests that "pitch," a tree resin, is an inappropriate translation. Smearing hot bitumen on the head of one who brought a false legal claim was a punishment in Old Babylonian texts. Here an entire land is to be so punished.
34:11 – 14 *owl … jackals … Desert creatures … wild goats.* See note on 13:21. The specific identity of each bird is unclear, but such groupings of birds and other desert animals suggest that the inhabited area will become desolate. The Lament Over the Destruction of Sumer and Ur bemoans the ruined city becoming a place not of humans but of foxholes.

God will stretch out over Edom
the measuring line of chaos
and the plumb line[c] of desolation.
12 Her nobles will have nothing there to
be called a kingdom,
all her princes[d] will vanish[e] away.
13 Thorns will overrun her citadels,
nettles and brambles her
strongholds.[f]
She will become a haunt for jackals,[g]
a home for owls.
14 Desert creatures will meet with
hyenas,[h]
and wild goats will bleat to each
other;
there the night creatures will also lie
down
and find for themselves places of
rest.
15 The owl will nest there and lay eggs,
she will hatch them, and care for her
young
under the shadow of her wings;
there also the falcons[i] will gather,
each with its mate.

16 Look in the scroll[j] of the LORD and
read:

None of these will be missing,
not one will lack her mate.
For it is his mouth[k] that has given the
order,
and his Spirit will gather them
together.
17 He allots their portions;[l]
his hand distributes them by
measure.
They will possess it forever
and dwell there from generation to
generation.[m]

Joy of the Redeemed

35 The desert[n] and the parched land
will be glad;
the wilderness will rejoice and
blossom.[o]
Like the crocus, 2 it will burst into
bloom;
it will rejoice greatly and shout for
joy.[p]
The glory of Lebanon[q] will be given
to it,
the splendor of Carmel[r] and Sharon;
they will see the glory of the LORD,
the splendor of our God.[s]

3 Strengthen the feeble hands,
steady the knees[t] that give way;
4 say to those with fearful hearts,
"Be strong, do not fear;
your God will come,
he will come with vengeance;[u]
with divine retribution
he will come to save you."

5 Then will the eyes of the blind be
opened[v]
and the ears of the deaf[w] unstopped.
6 Then will the lame[x] leap like a deer,
and the mute tongue[y] shout for joy.
Water will gush forth in the wilderness
and streams[z] in the desert.
7 The burning sand will become a pool,
the thirsty ground bubbling springs.[a]
In the haunts where jackals[b] once lay,
grass and reeds and papyrus will
grow.
8 And a highway[c] will be there;
it will be called the Way of
Holiness;[d]
it will be for those who walk on that
Way.
The unclean[e] will not journey on it;
wicked fools will not go about on it.
9 No lion[f] will be there,
nor any ravenous beast;[g]
they will not be found there.
But only the redeemed[h] will walk
there,
10 and those the LORD has rescued will
return.
They will enter Zion with singing;
everlasting joy[i] will crown their
heads.
Gladness and joy will overtake them,
and sorrow and sighing will flee away.[j]

34:11 [c] 2Ki 21:13; La 2:8 **34:12** [d] Jer 27:20; 39:6 [e] Isa 41:11-12 **34:13** [f] Isa 13:22; 32:13 [g] Ps 44:19; Jer 9:11; 10:22 **34:14** [h] Isa 13:22 **34:15** [i] Dt 14:13 **34:16** [j] Isa 30:8 [k] Isa 1:20; 58:14 **34:17** [l] Isa 17:14; Jer 13:25 [m] ver 10 **35:1** [n] Isa 27:10; 41:18-19 [o] Isa 51:3 **35:2** [p] Isa 25:9; 55:12 [q] Isa 32:15 [r] SS 7:5 [s] Isa 25:9 **35:3** [t] Job 4:4; Heb 12:12 **35:4** [u] Isa 1:24; 34:8 **35:5** [v] Mt 11:5; Jn 9:6-7 [w] Isa 29:18; 50:4 **35:6** [x] Mt 15:30; Jn 5:8-9; Ac 3:8 [y] Isa 32:4; Mt 9:32-33; 12:22; Lk 11:14 [z] Isa 41:18; Jn 7:38 **35:7** [a] Isa 49:10 [b] Isa 13:22 **35:8** [c] Isa 11:16; 33:8; Mt 7:13-14 [d] Isa 4:3; 1Pe 1:15 [e] Isa 52:1 **35:9** [f] Isa 30:6 [g] Isa 34:14 [h] Isa 51:11; 62:12; 63:4 **35:10** [i] Isa 25:9 [j] Isa 30:19; 51:11; Rev 7:17; 21:4

34:14 *night creatures.* This is the sole Biblical occurrence of the Hebrew word *lilit*. It derives from the feminine Akkadian word *lilitu*, which itself derives from Sumerian *lil* ("wind"), so in that literature this word likely refers to some wind or storm demon. In scholarly analysis it is interesting that the discussion moves from Akkadian to rabbinic and patristic literatures (where there is clear continuity). It remains possible that Isaiah refers to a spirit; but in the context, *lilit* is not acting in any of the ways that demons operate in Mesopotamia, but instead is associated with creatures (who are not spirits) in liminal areas. Without more information we must suspend further specific identification.
35:2 *Carmel.* See note on 1Ki 18:19. *Sharon.* A plain on the Mediterranean coast running about 30 miles (48 kilometers) north from the Yarkon River. It was conquered by Thutmose III and Amenhotep II, and people from there are mentioned by Mesha in the Moabite Stone. Two of its areas, Dor and Joppa, are mentioned on the fifth-century BC sarcophagus of Eshmunazar of Sidon. *the glory of the LORD.* See the article "Glory," p. 178.
35:9 *lion … ravenous beast.* See notes on 11:6–8; 31:4; Jdg 14:5.
35:10 *those the LORD has rescued.* It is in Yahweh's hand to free those held in captivity or slavery. An Akkadian text asserts, "To free the captive, Shamash, is in your power"—though more commonly this was done by a wealthy family member or by rulers. By doing this, the redeemer shows not only compassion for those suffering this fate, but also his power to be able to release them from it.

Sennacherib Threatens Jerusalem

36:1-22pp — 2Ki 18:13,17-37; 2Ch 32:9-19

36 In the fourteenth year of King Hezekiah's reign, Sennacherib[k] king of
Assyria attacked all the fortified cities of
Judah and captured them. 2Then the king
of Assyria sent his field commander with
a large army from Lachish to King Hezekiah at Jerusalem. When the commander
stopped at the aqueduct of the Upper Pool,
on the road to the Launderer's Field,[l] 3Eli-
akim[m] son of Hilkiah the palace administrator, Shebna[n] the secretary, and Joah son
of Asaph the recorder went out to him.

4The field commander said to them,
"Tell Hezekiah:

"'This is what the great king, the
king of Assyria, says: On what are
you basing this confidence of yours?
5You say you have counsel and might
for war — but you speak only empty
words. On whom are you depending,
that you rebel[o] against me? 6Look, I
know you are depending on Egypt,[p]
that splintered reed[q] of a staff, which
pierces the hand of anyone who leans
on it! Such is Pharaoh king of Egypt
to all who depend on him. 7But if
you say to me, "We are depending on
the LORD our God" — isn't he the one
whose high places and altars Hezekiah removed,[r] saying to Judah and
Jerusalem, "You must worship before
this altar"?[s]

8"'Come now, make a bargain with
my master, the king of Assyria: I will
give you two thousand horses — if
you can put riders on them! 9How
then can you repulse one officer of
the least of my master's officials, even
though you are depending on Egypt[t]
for chariots and horsemen[a]?[u] 10Fur-
thermore, have I come to attack and
destroy this land without the LORD?
The LORD himself told[v] me to march
against this country and destroy it.'"

11Then Eliakim, Shebna and Joah said
to the field commander, "Please speak to
your servants in Aramaic,[w] since we understand it. Don't speak to us in Hebrew
in the hearing of the people on the wall."

12But the commander replied, "Was it
only to your master and you that my master sent me to say these things, and not to
the people sitting on the wall — who, like
you, will have to eat their own excrement
and drink their own urine?"

13Then the commander stood and called
out in Hebrew,[x] "Hear the words of the
great king, the king of Assyria! 14This is
what the king says: Do not let Hezekiah
deceive you. He cannot deliver you! 15Do
not let Hezekiah persuade you to trust in
the LORD when he says, 'The LORD will
surely deliver us; this city will not be giv-
en into the hand of the king of Assyria.'[y]

16"Do not listen to Hezekiah. This is
what the king of Assyria says: Make peace
with me and come out to me. Then each of
you will eat fruit from your own vine and
fig tree[z] and drink water from your own
cistern,[a] 17until I come and take you to a
land like your own — a land of grain and
new wine, a land of bread and vineyards.

18"Do not let Hezekiah mislead you

36:1 [k] 2Ch 32:1
36:2 [l] Isa 7:3
36:3 [m] Isa 22:20-21 [n] 2Ki 18:18
36:5 [o] 2Ki 18:7
36:6 [p] Isa 30:2, 5 [q] Eze 29:6-7
36:7 [r] 2Ki 18:4 [s] Dt 12:2-5
36:9 [t] Isa 31:3 [u] Isa 30:2-5
36:10 [v] 1Ki 13:18
36:11 [w] Ezr 4:7
36:13 [x] 2Ch 32:18
36:15 [y] Isa 37:10
36:16 [z] 1Ki 4:25; Zec 3:10 [a] Pr 5:15

[a] 9 Or *charioteers*

36:2 *field commander.* See note on 2Ki 18:17.
36:3 *palace administrator.* See notes on 22:15; 2Ki 10:5. *secretary.* See notes on 22:15; 2Sa 8:16 – 17. *recorder.* The Hebrew (*mazkir*) is lit. "one who reminds," a secretary, an important role in palace administration. The term is used on a Moabite seal from the mid-first millennium BC. In the Assyrian Eponym List, an identification of successive years by the name and office of important officials, 741 BC is associated with Bel-Harran-Belu-Utsur, "palace herald," the equivalent of this term. See note on 2Sa 8:16 – 17.
36:4 *the great king.* A common title of Assyrian royalty, used even by Sennacherib in his own inscriptions. *king of Assyria.* The title "king of Assyria and Babylonia" is also well attested. *On what are you basing this confidence … ?* Israel is to put her trust in Yahweh, her God (8:16), but the Assyrians mock them for trusting what they view as a powerless god. Tiglath-Pileser I writes: "At the beginning of my kingship, 20,000 Mushkean men and five of their kings … trusted in their own strength … With trust in Ashur, my lord, I really inflicted a defeat on them." The Assyrian view of history was that events on earth reflected those in heaven. The Egyptians' powerlessness to aid Israel derives from the weakness of their gods, and Yahweh himself has lost power if Judah's own king can remove his shrines.
36:6 *you are depending on Egypt, that splintered reed of a staff.* A rod or staff needed strength in order to provide weight-bearing support. A reed, which is pliable, cannot supply needed support, and can supply even less support if it is broken (see 42:3). Sargon made this same claim concerning the king of Ashdod who sought to lead the kings of Palestine, Judah, Edom and Moab away from following Assyria: "To Piru, king of Egypt, a ruler unable to save them, they brought their greeting gifts [see Isa 1:23], they repeatedly pestered him (to be their) ally."
36:7 *high places and altars Hezekiah removed.* Destruction of a temple or deportation of a divine statue removed the deity's influence over that area. It meant that this god was so ineffective that he could not even look after his own interests. The Assyrian military leader claims that a king who neglects or opposes a god will suffer that god's displeasure, even as far as losing his position. Cyrus made the same claim, saying that neglecting worship led the gods to turn Babylon over to him.
36:11 *Please speak … in Aramaic.* See note on 2Ki 18:26.
36:16 *drink water from your own cistern.* Cisterns, artificial water reservoirs cut into bedrock, were important for a people without a steady and certain water supply. Public cisterns were supplemented by private ones for those of sufficient means to dig one. This propaganda promises this advantage to everyone.

when he says, 'The LORD will deliver us.' Have the gods of any nations ever delivered their lands from the hand of the king of Assyria? 19 Where are the gods of Hamath and Arpad? Where are the gods of Sepharvaim? Have they rescued Samaria from my hand? 20 Who of all the gods[b] of these countries have been able to save their lands from me? How then can the LORD deliver Jerusalem from my hand?"

21 But the people remained silent and said nothing in reply, because the king had commanded, "Do not answer him."[c]

22 Then Eliakim son of Hilkiah the palace administrator, Shebna the secretary and Joah son of Asaph the recorder went to Hezekiah, with their clothes torn, and told him what the field commander had said.

Jerusalem's Deliverance Foretold

37:1-13pp — 2Ki 19:1-13

37 When King Hezekiah heard this, he tore his clothes and put on sackcloth and went into the temple of the LORD. 2 He sent Eliakim the palace administrator, Shebna the secretary, and the leading priests, all wearing sackcloth, to the prophet Isaiah son of Amoz.[d] 3 They told him, "This is what Hezekiah says: This day is a day of distress and rebuke and disgrace, as when children come to the moment of birth[e] and there is no strength to deliver them. 4 It may be that the LORD your God will hear the words of the field commander, whom his master, the king of Assyria, has sent to ridicule the living God, and that he will rebuke him for the words the LORD your God has heard.[f] Therefore pray for the remnant[g] that still survives."

5 When King Hezekiah's officials came to Isaiah, 6 Isaiah said to them, "Tell your master, 'This is what the LORD says: Do not be afraid[h] of what you have heard — those words with which the underlings of the king of Assyria have blasphemed me. 7 Listen! When he hears a certain report,[i] I will make him want to return to his own country, and there I will have him cut down with the sword.' "

8 When the field commander heard that the king of Assyria had left Lachish, he withdrew and found the king fighting against Libnah.[j]

9 Now Sennacherib received a report[k] that Tirhakah, the king of Cush,[a] was marching out to fight against him. When he heard it, he sent messengers to Hezekiah with this word: 10 "Say to Hezekiah king of Judah: Do not let the god you depend on deceive you when he says, 'Jerusalem will not be given into the hands of the king of Assyria.'[l] 11 Surely you have heard what the kings of Assyria have done to all the countries, destroying them completely. And will you be delivered?[m] 12 Did the gods of the nations that were destroyed by my predecessors[n] deliver them — the gods of Gozan, Harran,[o] Rezeph and the people of Eden who were in Tel Assar? 13 Where is the king of Hamath or the king of Arpad? Where are the kings of Lair, Sepharvaim, Hena and Ivvah?"

Hezekiah's Prayer

37:14-20pp — 2Ki 19:14-19

14 Hezekiah received the letter from the messengers and read it. Then he went up to the temple of the LORD and spread it out before the LORD. 15 And Hezekiah prayed to the LORD: 16 "LORD Almighty, the God of Israel, enthroned between the cherubim, you alone are God[p] over all the kingdoms of the earth. You have made heaven and earth. 17 Give ear, LORD, and hear;[q] open your eyes, LORD, and see;[r] listen to all the

36:20 [b] 1Ki 20:23
36:21 [c] Pr 9:7-8; 26:4
37:2 [d] Isa 1:1
37:3 [e] Isa 26:18; 66:9; Hos 13:13
37:4 [f] Isa 36:13, 18-20 [g] Isa 1:9
37:6 [h] Isa 7:4
37:7 [i] ver 9
37:8 [j] Nu 33:20
37:9 [k] ver 7
37:10 [l] Isa 36:15
37:11 [m] Isa 36:18-20
37:12 [n] 2Ki 18:11 [o] Ge 11:31; 12:1-4; Ac 7:2
37:16 [p] Dt 10:17; Ps 86:10; 136:2-3
37:17 [q] 2Ch 6:40 [r] Da 9:18

[a] 9 That is, the upper Nile region

37:1 *tore his clothes and put on sackcloth.* See the article "Mourning," p. 828.

37:9 *Tirhakah.* Tirhakah (Taharqa) was the third king of the Twenty-Fifth Dynasty (Ethiopian). A prodigious builder during his initial years of relative peace, he also campaigned to the north, encountering Sennacherib and Esarhaddon and their armies. The latter probably viewed Egypt as the instigator of unrest among their vassals in Syro-Palestine. Tirhakah was forced to flee to Thebes, where he subsequently died.

37:12 *Rezeph.* A city on the Euphrates River north of Palmyra; a governor of Rasappa (Rezeph) is mentioned in the Assyrian Eponym List for 803 BC.

37:14 *Hezekiah … read it.* Hezekiah is said to have read, while Sennacherib is said to have heard (v. 9, NIV "received"). The relative difficulty of the writing systems of the two languages made Hebrew, with 22 letters, more accessible, while Akkadian, with hundreds of different signs, was inaccessible to most officials. Ashurbanipal is among the few rulers who could boast of bilingual literacy, reading texts both in Sumerian and Akkadian. For the most part, messengers carried communications that, while often written, were orally delivered to the recipient. See the article "Literacy," p. 140.

37:16 *enthroned between the cherubim.* Akkadian *kuribu* are protective deities represented by figures combining human, animal and bird characteristics. Such figures appear frequently in ancient Near Eastern iconography of Assyria and Syro-Palestine. They and other protective beings flanked doorways and also were carved on each side of thrones, symbolizing their protection of the enthroned ruler. Warad-Sin (1834 – 1823 BC) wrote of building his throne with a pair of protective guardians set up on either side of it. Yahweh, sitting between them, occupied the true, universal throne, superior to that of any Assyrian opponent. See note on 2Ki 19:15.

37:17 *open your eyes, LORD.* In a call for divine attention, an Aramaic treaty inscription from mid-eighth century BC Sefire, speaking to all the deities, calls: "Open your eyes to gaze upon the treaty."

words Sennacherib has sent to ridicule the
living God.
18 "It is true, LORD, that the Assyrian
kings have laid waste all these peoples
and their lands.[s] 19 They have thrown their
gods into the fire and destroyed them,[t] for
they were not gods[u] but only wood and
stone, fashioned by human hands. 20 Now,
LORD our God, deliver us from his hand,
so that all the kingdoms of the earth may
know that you, LORD, are the only God.[a][v]"

Sennacherib's Fall

37:21-38pp — 2Ki 19:20-37; 2Ch 32:20-21

21 Then Isaiah son of Amoz[w] sent a message to Hezekiah: "This is what the LORD,
the God of Israel, says: Because you have
prayed to me concerning Sennacherib king
of Assyria, 22 this is the word the LORD has
spoken against him:

"Virgin Daughter Zion
  despises and mocks you.
Daughter Jerusalem
  tosses her head[x] as you flee.
23 Who is it you have ridiculed and
  blasphemed?[y]
Against whom have you raised your
  voice
and lifted your eyes in pride?[z]
  Against the Holy One of Israel!
24 By your messengers
  you have ridiculed the Lord.
And you have said,
  'With my many chariots
I have ascended the heights of the
  mountains,
  the utmost heights of Lebanon.[a]
I have cut down its tallest cedars,
  the choicest of its junipers.
I have reached its remotest heights,
  the finest of its forests.
25 I have dug wells in foreign lands[b]
  and drunk the water there.
With the soles of my feet
  I have dried up all the streams of
  Egypt.[b]'

26 "Have you not heard?
  Long ago I ordained[c] it.
In days of old I planned[d] it;
  now I have brought it to pass,
  that you have turned fortified cities
  into piles of stone.[e]
27 Their people, drained of power,
  are dismayed and put to shame.
They are like plants in the field,
  like tender green shoots,
like grass sprouting on the roof,[f]
  scorched[c] before it grows up.

28 "But I know where you are
  and when you come and go[g]
  and how you rage[h] against me.
29 Because you rage against me
  and because your insolence[i] has
  reached my ears,
I will put my hook in your nose[j]
  and my bit in your mouth,
and I will make you return
  by the way you came.[k]

30 "This will be the sign for you, Hezekiah:

"This year you will eat what grows by
  itself,
and the second year what springs
  from that.
But in the third year sow and reap,
  plant vineyards and eat their fruit.
31 Once more a remnant of the kingdom
  of Judah
will take root below and bear fruit[l]
  above.
32 For out of Jerusalem will come a remnant,
  and out of Mount Zion a band of
  survivors.
The zeal[m] of the LORD Almighty
  will accomplish this.

33 "Therefore this is what the LORD says
concerning the king of Assyria:

"He will not enter this city
  or shoot an arrow here.
He will not come before it with shield
  or build a siege ramp against it.
34 By the way that he came he will return;[n]
  he will not enter this city,"
  declares the LORD.

37:18 [s] 2Ki 15:29; Na 2:11-12 **37:19** [t] Isa 26:14 [u] Isa 41:24,29 **37:20** [v] Ps 46:10 **37:21** [w] ver 2 **37:22** [x] Job 16:4 **37:23** [y] ver 4 [z] Isa 2:11 **37:24** [a] Isa 14:8 **37:25** [b] Dt 11:10 **37:26** [c] Ac 2:23; 4:27-28; 1Pe 2:8 [d] Isa 10:6; 25:1 [e] Isa 25:2 **37:27** [f] Ps 129:6 **37:28** [g] Ps 139:1-3 [h] Ps 2:1 **37:29** [i] Isa 10:12 [j] Isa 30:28; Eze 38:4 [k] ver 34 **37:31** [l] Isa 27:6 **37:32** [m] Isa 9:7 **37:34** [n] ver 29

[a] *20* Dead Sea Scrolls (see also 2 Kings 19:19); Masoretic Text *you alone are the LORD* [b] *25* Dead Sea Scrolls (see also 2 Kings 19:24); Masoretic Text does not have *in foreign lands.* [c] *27* Some manuscripts of the Masoretic Text, Dead Sea Scrolls and some Septuagint manuscripts (see also 2 Kings 19:26); most manuscripts of the Masoretic Text *roof / and terraced fields*

37:24 *I have ascended the heights of the mountains, the utmost heights of Lebanon. I have cut down its tallest cedars, the choicest of its junipers.* The power of conquering a distant country with its mighty trees is a motif used by Assyrian kings to glorify themselves. Shalmaneser III wrote that he went up to the Amanus Mountains (in western Syria) and "cut down cedar wood and juniper wood."

37:29 *I will put my hook in your nose and my bit in your mouth.* God will treat Assyria like recalcitrant animals, turning the tables on those who treated others similarly. Tukulti-Ninurta I stated metaphorically that he controlled a subjugated land with a bridle. This treatment is also depicted on reliefs, showing that it was literally applied to captive people in addition to animals.

37:31 *take root below and bear fruit above.* The agricultural society of Israel was aware of the relationship between good root and good fruit, often associating the two (e.g., 11:1). Curses written on a fifth-century BC Phoenician sarcophagus against any who might desecrate it include this one: "Let him have neither root below nor fruit above nor form among those living under the sun."

37:33 *siege ramp.* See the article "Siege Warfare," p. 1157.

35 "I will defend[o] this city and save it,
for my sake[p] and for the sake of
David[q] my servant!"

36 Then the angel of the LORD went out
and put to death a hundred and eighty-five
thousand in the Assyrian[r] camp. When the
people got up the next morning—there
were all the dead bodies! 37 So Sennacherib
king of Assyria broke camp and withdrew.
He returned to Nineveh[s] and stayed there.
38 One day, while he was worshiping
in the temple of his god Nisrok, his sons
Adrammelek and Sharezer killed him with
the sword, and they escaped to the land of
Ararat.[t] And Esarhaddon his son succeeded him as king.

Hezekiah's Illness

38:1-8pp — 2Ki 20:1-11; 2Ch 32:24-26

38 In those days Hezekiah became ill
and was at the point of death. The
prophet Isaiah son of Amoz[u] went to him
and said, "This is what the LORD says: Put
your house in order,[v] because you are going to die; you will not recover."
2 Hezekiah turned his face to the wall
and prayed to the LORD, 3 "Remember,
LORD, how I have walked[w] before you
faithfully and with wholehearted devotion[x] and have done what is good in your
eyes.[y]" And Hezekiah wept[z] bitterly.
4 Then the word of the LORD came to Isaiah: 5 "Go and tell Hezekiah, 'This is what
the LORD, the God of your father David,
says: I have heard your prayer and seen
your tears; I will add fifteen years[a] to your
life. 6 And I will deliver you and this city
from the hand of the king of Assyria. I will
defend[b] this city.
7 " 'This is the LORD's sign[c] to you that
the LORD will do what he has promised: 8 I
will make the shadow cast by the sun go
back the ten steps it has gone down on the
stairway of Ahaz.' " So the sunlight went
back the ten steps it had gone down.[d]

9 A writing of Hezekiah king of Judah
after his illness and recovery:

10 I said, "In the prime of my life[e]
must I go through the gates of death[f]
and be robbed of the rest of my years?[g]"
11 I said, "I will not again see the LORD himself
in the land of the living;[h]
no longer will I look on my fellow man,
or be with those who now dwell in this world.
12 Like a shepherd's tent[i] my house
has been pulled down[j] and taken from me.
Like a weaver I have rolled[k] up my life,
and he has cut me off from the loom;[l]
day and night[m] you made an end of me.

37:35 [o] Isa 31:5; 38:6 [p] Isa 43:25; 48:9,11 [q] 2Ki 20:6
37:36 [r] Isa 10:12
37:37 [s] Ge 10:11
37:38 [t] Ge 8:4; Jer 51:27
38:1 [u] Isa 37:2 [v] 2Sa 17:23
38:3 [w] Ne 13:14; Ps 26:3 [x] 1Ch 29:19 [y] Dt 6:18 [z] Ps 6:8
38:5 [a] 2Ki 18:2
38:6 [b] Isa 31:5; 37:35
38:7 [c] Isa 7:11, 14
38:8 [d] Jos 10:13
38:10 [e] Ps 102:24 [f] Ps 107:18; 2Co 1:9 [g] Job 17:11
38:11 [h] Ps 27:13; 116:9
38:12 [i] 2Co 5:1, 4; 2Pe 1:13-14 [j] Job 4:21 [k] Heb 1:12 [l] Job 7:6 [m] Ps 73:14

37:38 *Adrammelek ... killed him [Sennacherib] with the sword ... And Esarhaddon his son succeeded him as king.* Esarhaddon, Sennacherib's son and heir, writes of violent conniving to wrest away the throne by unnamed "brothers." A Babylonian chronicle records that in 681 BC on the 20th day of the month of Tebet, Sennacherib was killed by a son leading a rebellion. An Assyrian letter perhaps mentions the murderer: a son named Arad-Mullissu, a possible variation of Adrammelek. He was Sennacherib's second son, and he, after the capture and deportation of his older brother, the crown prince, would have expected to inherit the throne. Sennacherib's grooming of Esarhaddon as his successor may have enraged Arad-Mullissu enough to murder his father in hopes of gaining the throne. *land of Ararat.* Or Urartu, a mountainous region northwest of Assyria lying between Lakes Van and Urmia in what is now Armenia. Its mountains gave it some measure of protection against repeated Assyrian incursion. In the height of its power in the early eighth century BC, the kingdom of Urartu pushed west, but soon was forced back by Assyrian attacks under Tiglath-Pileser III. Urartu's relative inaccessibility and geographic distance from the centers of Assyrian power made it a suitable place for fugitives, such as Sennacherib's assassins, to seek refuge. *Esarhaddon.* Though the youngest of Sennacherib's sons, he was designated Sennacherib's heir just prior to his death. Since this was an unpopular move among his brothers, he left the area for Cilicia until after the murder of his father. He then returned and took the throne after a civil war. He led campaigns against Egypt under Tirhakah, which means he traversed Judah, but no Biblical mention is made of him turning against Judah itself. Judah under Manasseh was his vassal and provided him service. He died in 669 BC, but not before securing the position of his heir designate, Ashurbanipal, so Ashurbanipal would not have to contend with pretenders as he had.

38:1 *you are going to die; you will not recover.* A lack of parallel to this kind of statement to a king elsewhere derives from the understanding of a prophet's role. Professional prophets received a livelihood from the palace and were loath to jeopardize it. Rituals and incantations were also available to subvert the projected calamity.

38:5 *I will add fifteen years to your life.* As patrons of individuals as well as nations, gods were to look after their well-being, as people reminded them in prayers and petitions. Shalmaneser III erected a statue in honor of Adad and prayed that the god might look on the statue favorably and as a result would remove diseases from the king and grant him long life.

38:10 *gates of death.* See the articles "Death and Sheol," p. 833; "Death and the Underworld," p. 907.

38:11 *see the LORD.* Hezekiah does not view seeing the Lord as an afterlife experience. Seeing the Lord involved worshiping in the temple and enjoying the Lord's favor. See the article "The Old Testament Concept of Resurrection," p. 1160.

38:12 *shepherd's tent.* The shepherd moved frequently from place to place and therefore could break camp quickly. *rolled up ... cut me off from the loom.* The weaver worked on a horizontal loom that had the threads and material stretched on bars between stakes. When it had to be moved, the bars could simply be pulled off the stakes and rolled up. When the weaver was finished with a piece of cloth, the threads that connected the material

13I waited patiently till dawn,
but like a lion he broke[n] all my bones;[o]
day and night you made an end of me.
14I cried like a swift or thrush,
I moaned like a mourning dove.[p]
My eyes grew weak as I looked to the heavens.
I am being threatened; Lord, come to my aid!"[q]

15But what can I say?
He has spoken to me, and he himself has done this.[r]
I will walk humbly[s] all my years
because of this anguish of my soul.[t]
16Lord, by such things people live;
and my spirit finds life in them too.
You restored me to health
and let me live.[u]
17Surely it was for my benefit
that I suffered such anguish.
In your love you kept me
from the pit[v] of destruction;
you have put all my sins[w]
behind your back.[x]
18For the grave[y] cannot praise you,
death cannot sing your praise;[z]
those who go down to the pit[a]
cannot hope for your faithfulness.
19The living, the living—they praise[b] you,
as I am doing today;
parents tell their children[c]
about your faithfulness.
20The LORD will save me,
and we will sing[d] with stringed instruments[e]
all the days of our lives[f]
in the temple[g] of the LORD.

38:13 [n]Ps 51:8 [o]Job 10:16; Da 6:24 **38:14** [p]Isa 59:11 [q]Job 17:3 **38:15** [r]Ps 39:9 [s]1Ki 21:27 [t]Job 7:11 **38:16** [u]Ps 119:25 **38:17** [v]Ps 30:3 [w]Jer 31:34 [x]Isa 43:25; Mic 7:19 **38:18** [y]Ecc 9:10 [z]Ps 6:5; 88:10-11; 115:17 [a]Ps 30:9 **38:19** [b]Dt 6:7; Ps 118:17; 119:175 [c]Dt 11:19 **38:20** [d]Ps 68:25 [e]Ps 33:2 [f]Ps 116:2 [g]Ps 116:17-19

39:1 [h]2Ch 32:31 **39:2** [i]2Ch 32:31 [j]2Ki 18:15 **39:3** [k]Dt 28:49 **39:6** [l]2Ki 24:13; Jer 20:5

21Isaiah had said, "Prepare a poultice of figs and apply it to the boil, and he will recover."

22Hezekiah had asked, "What will be the sign that I will go up to the temple of the LORD?"

Envoys From Babylon

39:1-8pp — 2Ki 20:12-19

39 At that time Marduk-Baladan son of Baladan king of Babylon[h] sent Hezekiah letters and a gift, because he had heard of his illness and recovery.
2Hezekiah received the envoys[i] gladly and showed them what was in his storehouses—the silver, the gold,[j] the spices, the fine olive oil—his entire armory and everything found among his treasures. There was nothing in his palace or in all his kingdom that Hezekiah did not show them.
3Then Isaiah the prophet went to King Hezekiah and asked, "What did those men say, and where did they come from?"

"From a distant land,[k]" Hezekiah replied. "They came to me from Babylon."
4The prophet asked, "What did they see in your palace?"

"They saw everything in my palace," Hezekiah said. "There is nothing among my treasures that I did not show them."
5Then Isaiah said to Hezekiah, "Hear the word of the LORD Almighty:
6The time will surely come when everything in your palace, and all that your predecessors have stored up until this day, will be carried off to Babylon.[l] Nothing will be left, says the LORD.
7And some of your descendants, your own flesh and blood who will

to the loom had to be cut. The weaving of Hezekiah's life had been completed, and he was now to be cut loose from the land of the living. Life or history as a fabric being woven is known from Greek mythology but has not been identified in ancient Near Eastern literature.

38:20 *we will sing with stringed instruments.* The king's involvement in psalm composition is particularly well known in connection with David, but it neither began nor ended with him. As early as the end of the third millennium BC, Shulgi king of Ur was famous for his royal hymns that offered prayers for the health and welfare of the king. As late as the Roman period, Nero was a patron of the arts and considered himself a first-rate composer. The ideal king was a wise king, and music was one of the realms of wisdom.

38:21 *poultice of figs.* Figs were used medicinally in this period. Ugaritic texts describe treatments for horses using figs and malt flour. They were also used to treat human maladies.

39:1 *Marduk-Baladan.* Also known as Marduk-apla-iddina, he was king of Babylon twice: 722–710 and 705–703 BC (in between he lost his throne to Sargon II). Marduk-Baladan is called a king of Chaldea since he came from the group of Chaldean tribes taking power in Babylonia during this period. To thwart Assyrian expansion into his territory, Marduk-Baladan united Babylonian and Aramean tribes, as well as other neighbors such as the Arabs and the Elamites, by taking advantage of Assyrian political instability and maintaining independent rule until 710 BC. The yoke was not thrown off for long, since Sargon and the Assyrians wanted to control their borders. Sargon's son Sennacherib also had to contend with Marduk-Baladan, who regained his independence immediately after Sargon's death. Marduk-Baladan's military and political acumen is shown by these alliances, including the one sought here from Hezekiah. These emissaries were probably from this period and were trying to persuade him to take up the Babylonian cause against Assyria.

39:2 *received the envoys gladly.* Hezekiah would perhaps be flattered by the attention, but also would be eager to have an ally who could undermine Assyria, which currently posed the most significant threat to Judah.

39:7 *eunuchs.* See notes on 56:4; 2Ki 9:32. Some eunuchs occupied important bureaucratic positions in Assyria and Babylonia. They served in military and palace administrative roles, as well as being scribes and musicians. Tiglath-Pileser III appointed one as governor over Babylonia. From

ISAIAH 38:10 – 20

Psalm of Thanks for Healing

This genre of psalm is well known, being a natural response of gratitude for physical help. Sin-Iddinam, a king of Larsa, wrote a similar letter-prayer to his patron goddess. It begins with a salutation, identifying the god being petitioned, an element not found here, since there is only one to whom Hezekiah might pray. Then follows the writer's complaint (cf. Isa 38:10 – 12), remembering illness and danger and protesting his innocence (cf. Isa 38:13). The sufferer then prays for help (cf. Isa 38:14) by the mercy of the god. A final praise for healing in Isaiah (Isa 38:20) is paralleled by the concluding request by a rival king: "Let him live!"

Individual prayers are rare in both the Bible and its environment, since written documentation mainly concerns those with power, such as the king, as in both of these examples. ◆

A prayer letter from an Assyrian army commander to the god Shamash, asking for an oracle concerning a military campaign. The genre of the "prayer letter" was common in Sumerian and Akkadian literature. Isaiah 38:10 – 20 is also recorded as a similar "writing" or letter.

be born to you, will be taken away, and
they will become eunuchs in the palace of
the king of Babylon.[m]"
8 "The word of the LORD you have spoken is good," Hezekiah replied. For he
thought, "There will be peace and security in my lifetime.[n]"

39:7 [m] 2Ki 24:15; Da 1:1-7 **39:8** [n] 2Ch 32:26 **40:1** [o] Isa 12:1; 49:13; 51:3, 12; 52:9; 61:2; 66:13; Jer 31:13; Zep 3:14-17; 2Co 1:3 **40:2** [p] Isa 35:4

Comfort for God's People

40 Comfort, comfort[o] my people,
says your God.
2 Speak tenderly[p] to Jerusalem,
and proclaim to her

the context, this potential future is not desirable for Hezekiah's sons.
40:2 *received . . . double for all her sins.* Multifold restitution is a strong deterrent from wrongdoing. One of Hammurapi's laws against theft states: "If a man stole either an ox, sheep, donkey, pig or wooden boat, if it was either divine

that her hard service has been
completed,[q]
that her sin has been paid for,
that she has received from the LORD's
hand
double[r] for all her sins.

3 A voice of one calling:
"In the wilderness prepare
the way[s] for the LORD[a];
make straight in the desert
a highway for our God.[b][t]
4 Every valley shall be raised up,
every mountain and hill made low;
the rough ground shall become level,[u]
the rugged places a plain.
5 And the glory of the LORD will be
revealed,
and all people will see it together.[v]
For the mouth of the LORD
has spoken."[w]

6 A voice says, "Cry out."
And I said, "What shall I cry?"

"All people are like grass,[x]
and all their faithfulness is like the
flowers of the field.
7 The grass withers and the flowers fall,
because the breath[y] of the LORD
blows on them.
Surely the people are grass.
8 The grass withers and the flowers fall,
but the word[z] of our God endures
forever.[a]"

9 You who bring good news[b] to Zion,
go up on a high mountain.
You who bring good news to
Jerusalem,[c]
lift up your voice with a shout,
lift it up, do not be afraid;
say to the towns of Judah,
"Here is your God!"[c]
10 See, the Sovereign LORD comes[d] with
power,
and he rules[e] with a mighty arm.[f]
See, his reward[g] is with him,
and his recompense accompanies
him.
11 He tends his flock like a shepherd:[h]
He gathers the lambs in his arms
and carries them close to his heart;
he gently leads those that have young.

12 Who has measured the waters[i] in the
hollow of his hand,[j]
or with the breadth of his hand
marked off the heavens?[k]
Who has held the dust of the earth in a
basket,
or weighed the mountains on the
scales
and the hills in a balance?
13 Who can fathom the Spirit[d] of the LORD,
or instruct the LORD as his counselor?[l]

40:2 [q] Isa 41:11-13; 49:25 [r] Isa 61:7; Jer 16:18; Zec 9:12; Rev 18:6 **40:3** [s] Mal 3:1 [t] Mt 3:3*; Mk 1:3*; Jn 1:23* **40:4** [u] Isa 45:2, 13 **40:5** [v] Isa 52:10; Lk 3:4-6* [w] Isa 1:20; 58:14 **40:6** [x] Job 14:2 **40:7** [y] Job 41:21 **40:8** [z] Isa 55:11; 59:21 [a] Mt 5:18; 1Pe 1:24-25* **40:9** [b] Isa 52:7-10; 61:1; Ro 10:15 [c] Isa 25:9 **40:10** [d] Rev 22:7 [e] Isa 9:6-7 [f] Isa 59:16 [g] Isa 62:11; Rev 22:12 **40:11** [h] Eze 34:23; Mic 5:4; Jn 10:11 **40:12** [i] Job 38:10 [j] Pr 30:4 [k] Heb 1:10-12 **40:13** [l] Ro 11:34*; 1Co 2:16*

[a] 3 Or *A voice of one calling in the wilderness: / "Prepare the way for the LORD* [b] 3 Hebrew; Septuagint *make straight the paths of our God* [c] 9 Or *Zion, bringer of good news, / go up on a high mountain. / Jerusalem, bringer of good news* [d] 13 Or *mind*

or royal property, he shall pay thirtyfold. If it belongs to a poor man, he shall replace tenfold." In the Hittite Plague Prayers of Mursili, the king prays to avert a devastating, long-lasting plague that he suspects was caused by sin. He states that his city has already made twentyfold restitution. Israel is getting off relatively light.

40:3 *highway.* The roads of the ancient Near East were for the most part unpaved (except for a few roads in the Late Assyrian period). Although unpaved, those which were intended for wheeled transport (called "wagon roads" in the Nuzi tablets) had to be staked out, leveled and consistently maintained. However, very few texts describe the construction and maintenance of these roads. Roads for heavy transport were somewhat rare and were primarily along the trade routes. Thus, a vassal king complained to the king of Mari that he had to arrive at the Syrian capital by a roundabout route along a major highway. Assyrian kings rarely boasted of their road constructions, as they appeared to be the duty of the local populations. In a treaty text, Esarhaddon commands that when his son succeeds him the vassal must submit to him and smooth his way in every respect.

40:4 *every mountain and hill made low.* A Hittite ritual prayer uses the same terminology when describing coming deities: "Let the mountains be leveled before you (O gods)!" This refers to smoothing out the rough terrain to expedite travel.

40:5 *glory of the LORD.* See the article "Glory," p. 178.

40:8 *the word of our God endures forever.* See note on Ps 18:30.

40:9 *You who bring good news.* The good news bearer is feminine in Hebrew, like Anat, who brings good news to Baal in the Ugaritic Baal Cycle. His long-awaited house may be built just as these long-exiled people will be restored. While messengers were generally men, female messengers ("a daughter of the message") were also used in Mesopotamia.

40:10 *reward … recompense.* These Hebrew terms were probably technical words for tribute and plunder brought home by victorious warriors and kings from battle.

40:11 *shepherd.* Both rulers and deities were described as shepherds of their people in a rich and extensively used metaphor. See notes on 1Ch 11:2; Ps 23:1.

40:12 *measured the waters in the hollow of his hand.* In the Akkadian creation epic *Enuma Elish*, Marduk, after defeating the saltwater-goddess Tiamat, also looks after the freshwater-god Apsu, measuring the dimensions of his waters. Marduk is also praised in the Akkadian New Year's festival account as the one who measures the waters of the sea. The same is said of the Dog Star, Sirius. *weighed the mountains on the scales and the hills in a balance.* In the Egyptian tomb of Ay, a hymn speaks of counting of the mountains and weighing them.

40:13 – 14 The rhetorical questions in these verses are asked in such a way as to indicate that Yahweh acted alone in creation; he had no need for any outside consultants. A Sumerian poem speaks similarly of the god Enlil, who makes his own decisions with no other gods present. Usually, however, divine decisions were made in consultation with others in the divine council. This could be an individual or a group. Sometimes it is gods. See the article "Divine Council," p. 615.

[14] Whom did the LORD consult to
enlighten him,
and who taught him the right way?
Who was it that taught him
knowledge,[m]
or showed him the path of
understanding?
[15] Surely the nations are like a drop in a
bucket;
they are regarded as dust on the
scales;
he weighs the islands as though they
were fine dust.
[16] Lebanon is not sufficient for altar fires,
nor its animals[n] enough for burnt
offerings.
[17] Before him all the nations[o] are as
nothing;[p]
they are regarded by him as
worthless
and less than nothing.[q]
[18] With whom, then, will you compare
God?[r]
To what image[s] will you liken him?
[19] As for an idol,[t] a metalworker casts it,
and a goldsmith[u] overlays it with
gold[v]
and fashions silver chains for it.
[20] A person too poor to present such an
offering
selects wood that will not rot;
they look for a skilled worker
to set up an idol that will not
topple.[w]
[21] Do you not know?
Have you not heard?
Has it not been told[x] you from the
beginning?
Have you not understood[y] since the
earth was founded?[z]
[22] He sits enthroned above the circle of
the earth,
and its people are like grasshoppers.[a]
He stretches out the heavens like a
canopy,[b]
and spreads them out like a tent[c] to
live in.
[23] He brings princes[d] to naught
and reduces the rulers of this world
to nothing.[e]
[24] No sooner are they planted,
no sooner are they sown,
no sooner do they take root in the
ground,
than he blows[f] on them and they
wither,
and a whirlwind sweeps them away
like chaff.
[25] "To whom will you compare me?[g]
Or who is my equal?" says the Holy
One.
[26] Lift up your eyes and look to the
heavens:[h]
Who created[i] all these?
He who brings out the starry host[j] one
by one
and calls forth each of them by name.
Because of his great power and mighty
strength,
not one of them is missing.[k]
[27] Why do you complain, Jacob?
Why do you say, Israel,

40:14 [m] Job 21:22; Col 2:3 **40:16** [n] Ps 50:9-11; Mic 6:7; Heb 10:5-9 **40:17** [o] Isa 30:28 [p] Isa 29:7 [q] Da 4:35 **40:18** [r] Ex 8:10; 1Sa 2:2; Isa 46:5 [s] Ac 17:29 **40:19** [t] Ps 115:4 [u] Isa 41:7; Jer 10:3 [v] Isa 2:20 **40:20** [w] 1Sa 5:3 **40:21** [x] Ps 19:1; 50:6; Ac 14:17 [y] Ro 1:19 [z] Isa 48:13; 51:13 **40:22** [a] Nu 13:33; Ps 104:2; Isa 42:5 [b] Job 22:14 [c] Job 36:29 **40:23** [d] Isa 34:12 [e] Job 12:21; Ps 107:40 **40:24** [f] Isa 41:16 **40:25** [g] ver 18 **40:26** [h] Isa 51:6 [i] Ps 89:11-13; Isa 42:5 [j] Ps 147:4 [k] Isa 34:16

40:14 *right way.* The Hebrew term used here occurs most frequently with either a forensic ("judge/judgment") or procedural ("prescribed way") meaning. Here it moves beyond the realm of the court or the tabernacle courtyard to a wider understanding of decision making.

40:16 *Lebanon.* The Israelites considered that the land with the greatest forests and most varied animal life was Lebanon. In addition to supplying lumber for the temple of Solomon, the cedars of Lebanon provided sacred barges for Egypt and ships for Tyre. Moreover, the Assyrians exacted a tribute of timber from Lebanon for temple building. See notes on 2Sa 5:11; 1Ki 5:6; 6:15.

40:20 *an idol that will not topple.* A fallen representation of a god shows its lack of power and is humiliating both to it and its worshipers. Images of the gods would typically be held in place on a base by a metal peg remaining from the casting process. A third-century BC Aramaic text from Syene speaks of invaders throwing down and trampling various deities.

40:22 *the circle of the earth.* "Circle" here refers to a disc, not a sphere. The common ancient Near Eastern perspective of the heavens was like that of an inverted bowl covering the earth, itself above the primeval waters, which surmounted the underworld. In Babylonian literature, Shamash is praised as the one who suspends from the heavens the circle of the lands BWL 127:22. Likewise, in a prayer to Shamash and Adad, Adad causes it to rain on the circle of the earth Horowitz, 274,. The circle simply reflects the curvature of the horizon and thus is disk-shaped rather than a sphere (for which Hebrew uses another word). In the ancient world, the earth was consistently regarded as being circular Horowitz, 334. See the article "Cosmic Geography," p. 836. *He stretches out the heavens.* This describes an aspect of creation found also among Israel's neighbors. An Aramaic text in Demotic script from the third century BC is a ritual of service to numerous gods, the chief of which is called Mar, "Lord." He is called to return, as "you stretched out the heavens, Mar, you set the stars in place." This, like the Isaiah passage, celebrates the divine work of creation. Various understandings of the heavens existed in the ancient world, but this one suggests a tent that is raised up more than stretched out.

40:26 *He ... brings out the starry host ... and calls forth each of them by name.* In the *Enuma Elish*, the same sort of claim is made about Marduk when he established constellations (associated with the gods and their related stars) and so set up the indicators for time measurement. Interest here lies in the stars as seasonal markers (see Ge 1:16 – 18) rather than as independent objects. In the ancient world they did not know that the heavenly bodies were material objects. Mesopotamians, through their interest in omens, developed a sophisticated understanding of lunar, solar and astral cycles, including such things as eclipses, in lengthy tablet collections. See the notes on 2Ki 21:3; Ps 147:4.

"My way is hidden from the LORD;
my cause is disregarded by my God"?[l]
[28] Do you not know?
Have you not heard?[m]
The LORD is the everlasting[n] God,
the Creator of the ends of the earth.
He will not grow tired or weary,
and his understanding no one can fathom.[o]
[29] He gives strength to the weary[p]
and increases the power of the weak.
[30] Even youths grow tired and weary,
and young men[q] stumble and fall;
[31] but those who hope[r] in the LORD
will renew their strength.[s]
They will soar on wings like eagles;[t]
they will run and not grow weary,
they will walk and not be faint.[u]

The Helper of Israel

41 "Be silent[v] before me, you islands![w]
Let the nations renew their strength!
Let them come forward[x] and speak;
let us meet together[y] at the place of judgment.

[2] "Who has stirred[z] up one from the east,[a]
calling him in righteousness to his service[a]?
He hands nations over to him
and subdues kings before him.
He turns them to dust[b] with his sword,
to windblown chaff[c] with his bow.
[3] He pursues them and moves on unscathed,
by a path his feet have not traveled before.
[4] Who has done this and carried it through,
calling forth the generations from the beginning?[d]
I, the LORD—with the first of them
and with the last[e]—I am he."
[5] The islands[f] have seen it and fear;
the ends of the earth tremble.
They approach and come forward;
[6] they help each other
and say to their companions, "Be strong!"
[7] The metalworker encourages the goldsmith,[g]
and the one who smooths with the hammer
spurs on the one who strikes the anvil.
One says of the welding, "It is good."
The other nails down the idol so it will not topple.

[8] "But you, Israel, my servant,
Jacob, whom I have chosen,
you descendants of Abraham[h] my friend,[i]
[9] I took you from the ends of the earth,[j]
from its farthest corners I called you.
I said, 'You are my servant';
I have chosen[k] you and have not rejected you.
[10] So do not fear, for I am with you;[l]
do not be dismayed, for I am your God.
I will strengthen you and help[m] you;
I will uphold you with my righteous right hand.

40:27 [l] Job 27:2; Lk 18:7-8 **40:28** [m] ver 21 [n] Ps 90:2 [o] Ps 147:5; Ro 11:33 **40:29** [p] Isa 50:4; Jer 31:25 **40:30** [q] Isa 9:17; Jer 6:11; 9:21 **40:31** [r] Lk 18:1 [s] 2Co 4:16 [t] Ex 19:4; Ps 103:5 [u] 2Co 4:1; Heb 12:1-3 **41:1** [v] Hab 2:20; Zec 2:13 [w] Isa 11:11 [x] Isa 48:16 [y] Isa 1:18; 34:1; 50:8 **41:2** [z] Ezr 1:2 [a] ver 25; Isa 45:1, 13 [b] 2Sa 22:43 [c] Isa 40:24 **41:4** [d] ver 26; Isa 46:10 [e] Isa 44:6; 48:12; Rev 1:8, 17; 22:13 **41:5** [f] Eze 26:17-18 **41:7** [g] Isa 40:19 **41:8** [h] Isa 29:22; 51:2; 63:16 [i] 2Ch 20:7; Jas 2:23 **41:9** [j] Isa 11:12 [k] Dt 7:6 **41:10** [l] Jos 1:9; Isa 43:2, 5; Ro 8:31 [m] ver 13-14; Isa 44:2; 49:8

[a] 2 Or *east, / whom victory meets at every step*

40:28 *will not grow tired or weary.* In the ancient world, the gods were viewed as having human weaknesses and often were inattentive or simply unaware of events that were taking place. One result of this was that the pantheon of gods were constantly outwitting or tricking each other. When Enlil, e.g., brought on the flood to destroy humankind, Enki outwitted him by saving a remnant of humankind. However, Enki may have been tricked when he advised the human Adapa to reject the "bread of death" while in the presence of Anu, the high god. Anu subsequently gave Adapa the "bread of life," which was apparently unexpected by Enki. The gods were not indefatigable. They were in constant need of food, drink and shelter. In fact, humans were created to do the hard labor the gods preferred not to do.
41:1 *islands.* The islands or coastlands are a reference to the far-off reaches of the Mediterranean. The Hebrew word describes any place that was reached by sea travel.
41:2 *one from the east.* This must refer to Cyrus II, ruler of the Medes and Persians (44:28), the one who, in opposing Babylon, assists Israel. *windblown chaff.* During the threshing process of grain, the nutritious kernel was separated from the worthless chaff by the wind (see note on Ru 3:2). Since grain was so commonly raised in the region, this metaphor for something transitory came easily to mind. A Mesopotamian incantation against a headache wishes that the headache might be swept away and never return, like chaff swept away by the wind. The insignificance of chaff highlights the note in the Kadesh battle inscription of Rameses II in which he pays no attention to his enemies, regarding them as no more than chaff.
41:7 *nails down the idol.* See note on 40:20.
41:8 *my friend.* This phrase (lit. "my beloved") is used to describe numerous Mesopotamian rulers in relation to a deity. It was the name of several, including a ruler from the dynasty of Akkad, Naram-Sin, "the beloved of the moon god," and is part of the title and description of many others, including private individuals.
41:9 *I … have not rejected you.* Abandonment by one's god was a fearful prospect, since one depended on his personal god for help, protection and life itself. See notes on Lev 26:17; Dt 32:20.
41:10 *do not fear.* A similar word of encouragement is given several times to Esarhaddon from the goddess Ishtar of Arbela, and to Ashurbanipal by Ishtar and Ninurta. Naram-Sin similarly exhorted the readers of his stele not to fear. Such cases, like that of Isaiah, promise divine intervention on behalf of someone in trouble.

11 "All who rage[n] against you
will surely be ashamed and
disgraced;[o]
those who oppose[p] you
will be as nothing and perish.[q]
12 Though you search for your enemies,
you will not find them.[r]
Those who wage war against you
will be as nothing[s] at all.
13 For I am the LORD your God
who takes hold of your right hand[t]
and says to you, Do not fear;
I will help[u] you.
14 Do not be afraid, you worm Jacob,
little Israel, do not fear,
for I myself will help you," declares the
LORD,
your Redeemer, the Holy One of
Israel.
15 "See, I will make you into a threshing
sledge,[v]
new and sharp, with many teeth.
You will thresh the mountains and
crush them,
and reduce the hills to chaff.
16 You will winnow[w] them, the wind will
pick them up,
and a gale will blow them away.
But you will rejoice in the LORD
and glory[x] in the Holy One of Israel.

17 "The poor and needy search for water,[y]
but there is none;
their tongues are parched with thirst.
But I the LORD will answer[z] them;
I, the God of Israel, will not forsake
them.
18 I will make rivers flow[a] on barren
heights,
and springs within the valleys.
I will turn the desert[b] into pools of
water,
and the parched ground into springs.[c]
19 I will put in the desert
the cedar and the acacia, the myrtle
and the olive.
I will set junipers in the wasteland,
the fir and the cypress together,[d]
20 so that people may see and know,
may consider and understand,
that the hand of the LORD has done this,
that the Holy One of Israel has
created[e] it.

21 "Present your case," says the LORD.
"Set forth your arguments," says
Jacob's King.[f]
22 "Tell us, you idols,
what is going to happen.[g]
Tell us what the former things were,
so that we may consider them
and know their final outcome.
Or declare to us the things to come,[h]
23 tell us what the future holds,
so we may know[i] that you are gods.
Do something, whether good or bad,[j]
so that we will be dismayed and
filled with fear.
24 But you are less than nothing[k]
and your works are utterly worthless;
whoever chooses you is detestable.[l]

25 "I have stirred up one from the north,[m]
and he comes—
one from the rising sun who calls on
my name.
He treads[n] on rulers as if they were
mortar,
as if he were a potter treading the clay.
26 Who told of this from the beginning,
so we could know,
or beforehand, so we could say, 'He
was right'?
No one told of this,
no one foretold it,
no one heard any words[o] from you.

41:11 [n] Isa 17:12 [o] Isa 45:24 [p] Ex 23:22 [q] Isa 29:8 **41:12** [r] Ps 37:35-36 [s] Isa 17:14 **41:13** [t] Isa 42:6; 45:1 [u] ver 10 **41:15** [v] Mic 4:13 **41:16** [w] Jer 51:2 [x] Isa 45:25 **41:17** [y] Isa 43:20 [z] Isa 30:19 **41:18** [a] Isa 30:25 [b] Isa 43:19 [c] Isa 35:7 **41:19** [d] Isa 60:13 **41:20** [e] Job 12:9 **41:21** [f] Isa 43:15 **41:22** [g] Isa 43:9; 45:21 [h] Isa 46:10 **41:23** [i] Isa 42:9; 44:7-8; 45:3 [j] Jer 10:5 **41:24** [k] Isa 37:19; 44:9; 1Co 8:4 [l] Ps 115:8 **41:25** [m] ver 2 [n] 2Sa 22:43 **41:26** [o] Hab 2:18-19

41:11 – 16 Prophetic messages such as these were also received among Israel's neighbors. They included anticipations of favor and aid, as here, as well as woe. An undated Akkadian text speaking of putatively future kings anticipates both sorts of situations.
41:13 *I am the LORD.* A prophetic letter to Ashurbanipal begins, "I am the lord (Bel)." The deity referred to is Marduk, whom the Assyrians considered as a personification of their chief god, Ashur, who brings peace and a release from fear. A similar call to cease worry was given in letters to Ashurbanipal's father, Esarhaddon: "I am Ishtar of Arbela." The depth of care for the king indicated here is shown when Ishtar also says, "I am your father and mother. Between my wings I brought you up."
41:15 *threshing sledge.* See note on Ru 3:2.
41:16 *winnow.* See note on Ru 3:2.
41:19 The reforestation of depleted areas was done only on a minor scale in the ancient world. The Assyrian kings planted many "gardens" in their chief cities, which included hundreds of trees, but this cannot be considered full-fledged reforestation.
41:22 *former things … final outcome.* Mesopotamia used similar terms for the past ("formerly, before") and future ("that which is behind, comes after"), showing the future in relation to what had already taken place. In a sense, history was cyclical, with what happened reappearing again, as seen by analogy in seasons or successive human generations. A god encouraged Esarhaddon in an oracle by identifying himself as a skilled pilot steering a ship. The result will be that the future will be like the past in the hands of this experienced pilot.
41:25 *one from the north … one from the rising sun.* There is no contradiction here, as both statements are concerning Cyrus of Persia, who was from the east but descended upon the "rulers" (Babylon) from the north, conquering Armenia and northern Mesopotamia first. He is also said to have come "from the east" (v. 2). *mortar … clay.* This metaphor reflects on the way malleable building materials were worked prior to use. These are worked with the feet for consistency and additives, such as straw, were mixed in. These two terms indicate various types of clay.

27 I was the first to tell[p] Zion, 'Look, here
they are!'
I gave to Jerusalem a messenger of
good news.[q]
28 I look but there is no one[r]—
no one among the gods to give
counsel,[s]
no one to give answer when I ask
them.
29 See, they are all false!
Their deeds amount to nothing;[t]
their images are but wind[u] and
confusion.

The Servant of the LORD

42 "Here is my servant, whom I
uphold,
my chosen one[v] in whom I delight;
I will put my Spirit[w] on him,
and he will bring justice to the
nations.
2 He will not shout or cry out,
or raise his voice in the streets.
3 A bruised reed he will not break,
and a smoldering wick he will not
snuff out.
In faithfulness he will bring forth
justice;[x]
4 he will not falter or be discouraged
till he establishes justice on earth.
In his teaching the islands will put
their hope."[y]

5 This is what God the LORD says—
the Creator of the heavens, who
stretches them out,
who spreads out the earth with all
that springs from it,[z]
who gives breath[a] to its people,
and life to those who walk on it:
6 "I, the LORD, have called[b] you in
righteousness;[c]
I will take hold of your hand.
I will keep[d] you and will make you
to be a covenant[e] for the people
and a light for the Gentiles,[f]
7 to open eyes that are blind,[g]
to free[h] captives from prison[i]
and to release from the dungeon
those who sit in darkness.

8 "I am the LORD; that is my name![j]
I will not yield my glory to another[k]
or my praise to idols.
9 See, the former things have taken
place,
and new things I declare;
before they spring into being
I announce them to you."

41:27 [p] Isa 48:3, 16 [q] Isa 40:9 **41:28** [r] Isa 50:2; 59:16; 63:5 [s] Isa 40:13-14 **41:29** [t] ver 24 [u] Jer 5:13 **42:1** [v] Isa 43:10; Lk 9:35; 1Pe 2:4, 6 [w] Isa 11:2; Mt 3:16-17; Jn 3:34 **42:3** [x] Ps 72:2 **42:4** [y] Ge 49:10; Mt 12:18-21* **42:5** [z] Ps 24:2 [a] Ac 17:25 **42:6** [b] Isa 43:1 [c] Jer 23:6 [d] Isa 26:3 [e] Isa 49:8 [f] Lk 2:32; Ac 13:47 **42:7** [g] Isa 35:5 [h] Isa 49:9; 61:1 [i] Lk 4:19; 2Ti 2:26; Heb 2:14-15 **42:8** [j] Ex 3:15 [k] Isa 48:11

41:27 *messenger of good news.* See note on 40:9.
42:1 *my chosen one.* Divine selection is significant in the ancient world. Akkadian texts from the first millennium BC also refer to those "chosen/selected by god X." It has the connotation of election, selecting from among others for a special purpose. The specific purpose of election is not specified, but the context of royal identifications suggests this is a claim to divinely sponsored enthronement.
42:3 *A bruised reed he will not break.* An Akkadian metaphor provides a contrast to that used here. Esarhaddon brags that "with the trustworthy support of Ashur, Shamash, Nabu and Marduk ... all those not subservient to him, kings not subservient to him, he snapped like a marsh-reed, he subdued them under his feet." Such harshness of Assyrian practice on frail nations and rulers will not be evident with the servant of Yahweh. *smoldering wick.* The "wick" is lit. "flax," from whose broken fibers a wick is made. These fibers were braided together into a string or cord that trailed from the oil to the edge of the lamp, moving the oil to the lit end through capillary action. Since their purpose is to produce light, a wick that is smoldering is ordinarily quickly removed, discarded and replaced—but not under the care of this gentle ruler. In the metaphor, this refers to the way that he will care for the vulnerable.
42:5 *Creator of the heavens ... the earth ... people.* The creator gods of the ancient Near East were more limited in their range of creation. Often the cosmic elements are generated by procreation of the gods, though a creator deity may have oversight in some versions. Especially in Mesopotamian traditions, people are created by a separate deity. Egyptian traditions have more of a tendency to consolidate creative activity in one deity.
42:6 *I will keep you.* Wishes for well-being are common blessings, especially at the beginning of letters. Letters from across the ancient world include wishes of good health and that the gods may preserve and protect them.
42:7 *blind ... prison ... dungeon ... darkness.* The chiastic literary structure (*a-b / b-a*) points to the blinding darkness of imprisonment being eradicated. This sort of program that relieves the distress of those falsely imprisoned was a prominent focus of kings. Sargon wrote of freeing citizens by destroying their prison and leading them out of their captivity. The god Marduk is praised for similar activities. We know little of what prisons were like in the ancient world, but we do know that when prisons were far off or not available, pits were often used in Israel and elsewhere to hold prisoners for a temporary period of time.

While prisoners, especially those captives taken in battle, are commonly mentioned in texts and depicted on reliefs, actual prisons are rarely encountered in Israel itself, though they are known among its neighbors. In Mesopotamia, only political crimes merited imprisonment by the state. Other wrongs were between citizens and thus civil cases, and any penalties were by means of financial payment or physical punishment. Some might also be imprisoned for debt, but these would more likely be enslaved, allowing them to pay off their obligations.

Those being released here are not the violent felons found in contemporary prisons, since they would have been punished in other ways. Since punishment was more closely related to the crimes committed and was meted out quickly, there was less need for places of confinement than there is in the contemporary West. One such place was called the "house of confinement" (cognate with "prison" in 2Ki 25:27). The Sumerian Hymn to Nungal describes a prison, with a female jailer, for holding women who were awaiting trial.
42:8 *I am the LORD.* See note on 41:13.
42:9 *the former things have taken place, and new things I declare.* Among Israel's neighbors, the past was predictive of the future in the form of omens and divination. Rather than actual predictions of an unknown future,

ISAIAH 40–66

Prophecies of Consolation and Hope

Israel needed hope following destruction and exile after God abandoned Zion as a result of Israel's sins (Isa 1:7–8). Likewise, Babylonia needed encouragement after Marduk departed from Esagila, his temple in Babylon, when Assyria captured it under Sennacherib. This loss was possibly due to the previous "sin of Sargon." It was Sennacherib's son Esarhaddon whose policy it was to restore the Babylonian capital, including the statues of the gods, under his own Assyrian control, uniting the two nations. This is indicated by the statement that Marduk was at peace with the king, since his status was restored. Because the god's throne is secure, so is that of the king, and so hope is restored. ◆

Song of Praise to the LORD

10 Sing to the LORD a new song,[l]
his praise from the ends of the earth,[m]
you who go down to the sea, and all that is in it,[n]
you islands, and all who live in them.
11 Let the wilderness[o] and its towns raise their voices;
let the settlements where Kedar[p] lives rejoice.
Let the people of Sela sing for joy;
let them shout from the mountaintops.[q]
12 Let them give glory[r] to the LORD
and proclaim his praise in the islands.
13 The LORD will march out like a champion,[s]
like a warrior he will stir up his zeal;[t]
with a shout[u] he will raise the battle cry
and will triumph over his enemies.[v]

14 "For a long time I have kept silent,
I have been quiet and held myself back.
But now, like a woman in childbirth,
I cry out, I gasp and pant.
15 I will lay waste[w] the mountains and hills
and dry up all their vegetation;
I will turn rivers into islands
and dry up[x] the pools.
16 I will lead[y] the blind[z] by ways they have not known,
along unfamiliar paths I will guide them;
I will turn the darkness into light before them
and make the rough places smooth.[a]
These are the things I will do;
I will not forsake[b] them.

42:10 [l] Ps 33:3; 40:3; 98:1 [m] Isa 49:6 [n] 1Ch 16:32; Ps 96:11 **42:11** [o] Isa 32:16 [p] Isa 60:7 [q] Isa 52:7; Na 1:15 **42:12** [r] Isa 24:15 **42:13** [s] Isa 9:6 [t] Isa 26:11 [u] Hos 11:10 [v] Isa 66:14 **42:15** [w] Eze 38:20 [x] Isa 50:2; Na 1:4-6 **42:16** [y] Lk 1:78-79 [z] Isa 32:3 [a] Lk 3:5 [b] Heb 13:5

these prognostications were based on an understanding that the past would repeat itself. There is indication that the gods were thought to know the future to some extent. The god Ashur, e.g., is said to know the beginning from the end. The Hymn to Shamash is one of many pieces that also indicates that the future of humanity is established by the gods as they decree destinies. Fate or destiny is in their hands, as in an epithet for Ea, Shamash and Asaluhhi, who, by decreeing destinies, determined order for humanity. These gods, however, do not reveal their plans as Yahweh is doing here. The gods may at times give direction for future action through divination practices that receive pointed oracles, but Yahweh is offering far more.

42:11 *Kedar.* See note on 60:7. *Sela.* An Edomite capital, possibly located at the later site of Petra. Kedar and Sela represent remote areas of the desert and mountains whose people are invited to worship Yahweh.

42:13 *warrior.* Divine warriors are ubiquitous in the ancient Near East. The very creation of the world, according to the Mesopotamian *Enuma Elish* account, is a result of battle between Marduk and Tiamat. The Mesopotamian goddess Ishtar is praised as one who wields weapons and causes battle, and the god Nergal (2Ki 17:30) is the "lord of weapons." Resheph is depicted holding a club in his upraised hand, as is the Canaanite god Baal. In the Baal Cycle, Baal battles Yamm, the sea, with the use of two maces. In the same Baal account, the goddess Anat, Baal's lover, is also a bloodthirsty warrior. She is also found among the Egyptian pantheon, especially during the Nineteenth Dynasty, as holding a shield and spear. While

17 But those who trust in idols,
who say to images, 'You are our gods,'
will be turned back in utter shame.[c]

Israel Blind and Deaf

18 "Hear, you deaf;[d]
look, you blind, and see!
19 Who is blind[e] but my servant,[f]
and deaf like the messenger[g] I send?
Who is blind like the one in covenant[h] with me,
blind like the servant of the LORD?
20 You have seen many things, but you pay no attention;
your ears are open, but you do not listen."[i]
21 It pleased the LORD
for the sake of his righteousness
to make his law[j] great and glorious.
22 But this is a people plundered and looted,
all of them trapped in pits[k]
or hidden away in prisons.[l]
They have become plunder,
with no one to rescue them;
they have been made loot,
with no one to say, "Send them back."
23 Which of you will listen to this
or pay close attention[m] in time to come?
24 Who handed Jacob over to become loot,
and Israel to the plunderers?
Was it not the LORD,
against whom we have sinned?

42:17 [c] Ps 97:7; Isa 1:29; 44:11; 45:16 **42:18** [d] Isa 35:5 **42:19** [e] Isa 43:8; Eze 12:2 [f] Isa 41:8-9 [g] Isa 44:26 [h] Isa 26:3 **42:20** [i] Jer 6:10 **42:21** [j] ver 4 **42:22** [k] Isa 24:18 [l] Isa 24:22 **42:23** [m] Isa 48:18 **42:24** [n] Isa 30:15 **42:25** [o] 2Ki 25:9 [p] Isa 29:13; 47:7; 57:1, 11; Hos 7:9 **43:1** [q] ver 7 [r] Ge 32:28; Isa 44:21 [s] Isa 44:2, 6 [t] Isa 42:6; 45:3-4 **43:2** [u] Isa 8:7 [v] Dt 31:6, 8 [w] Isa 29:6; 30:27 [x] Ps 66:12; Da 3:25-27 **43:3** [y] Ex 20:2 [z] Isa 20:3 [a] Pr 21:18 **43:4** [b] Isa 63:9

For they would not follow[n] his ways;
they did not obey his law.
25 So he poured out on them his burning anger,
the violence of war.
It enveloped them in flames,[o] yet they did not understand;
it consumed them, but they did not take it to heart.[p]

Israel's Only Savior

43 But now, this is what the LORD says—
he who created you, Jacob,
he who formed[q] you, Israel:[r]
"Do not fear, for I have redeemed[s] you;
I have summoned you by name;[t]
you are mine.
2 When you pass through the waters,[u]
I will be with you;[v]
and when you pass through the rivers,
they will not sweep over you.
When you walk through the fire,[w]
you will not be burned;
the flames will not set you ablaze.[x]
3 For I am the LORD your God,[y]
the Holy One of Israel, your Savior;
I give Egypt for your ransom,
Cush[a][z] and Seba in your stead.[a]
4 Since you are precious and honored in my sight,
and because I love[b] you,
I will give people in exchange for you,
nations in exchange for your life.

[a] 3 That is, the upper Nile region

battle is not Yahweh's chief occupation, he does involve himself in it on behalf of his people. In societies such as those of Israel and her neighbors, which were regularly under military threat, having a divine battle champion was psychologically and theologically important.

42:19 *servant of the LORD.* To indicate the proper respect toward a superior, letter senders identified themselves as "your servant" in their relation with the recipient. Other texts use the term in a person's relation to a superior, such as a king. "Servant of god X" is also common in the ancient Near East. A Northwest Semitic seal reads "Belonging to Mikneiah, servant of Yahweh." So far this mention of Yahweh in such a context outside the OT is unique.

43:1 *he who formed you.* See note on 42:5. The verb connotes working and forming like a potter does the clay (e.g., Ge 2:7). In Egypt the god Khnum is seen in the same role, forming humankind, particularly the king, on a potter's wheel. He is even called "The Potter" in the "Instruction of Amenemope" because of this role. He is depicted on a relief from Luxor fashioning Amenhotep III on a potter's wheel. The situation is so bad in the Admonitions of Ipu-Wer that women are barren, expressed in terms of Khnum not fashioning because of the political and social turmoil. In Mesopotamia too, the creation epic *Enuma Elish* speaks of people created by Marduk's hands, described using a term employed elsewhere of making figurines from metal or stone. *I have summoned you by name.* In Mesopotamia, from the early Dynastic period to the Neo-Babylonian period, kings received a divine call, legitimating them in office. An inscription of Esarhaddon, e.g., reads: "Assur, the father of the gods, called my name for the rule of the land of Assur and the governorship of the lands of Sumer and Akkad," and "Nabu-apla-iddina, king of Babylon, called by Marduk," the god of Babylon.

43:2 *pass through the waters.* Baal, the Canaanite storm-god, is pictured as walking on flowing water, symbolizing his power over this force of chaos. In the Baal Cycle, he defeats the power of the water in the form of "Sea" and "River." Israel itself does not have such power and cannot on her own survive an encounter with overwhelming water. Survival can only come through the protection of her God. Water is controlled by him as its creator. This was demonstrated at the time of the exodus (Ex 14:21 – 22). The parting of the Red Sea is likely alluded to here as offering hope for their present crisis.

43:3 *I am the LORD.* See note on 41:13.

43:4 *I love you.* See note on 41:8. Mesopotamian texts record several different objects loved by the gods. The most common recipient of such divine favor is the king, with one, Naram-Sin, "beloved of the god Sin," having this as part of his name. Private individuals also have this as an element of their names. The gods are also said to love places, such as the temple Eanna that Esarhaddon describes as "beloved of my lady Ishtar." It is more difficult to document a god expressing love for a group of people.

5 Do not be afraid,[c] for I am with you;[d]
I will bring your children[e] from the east
and gather you from the west.
6 I will say to the north, 'Give them up!'
and to the south,[f] 'Do not hold them back.'
Bring my sons from afar
and my daughters[g] from the ends of the earth—
7 everyone who is called by my name,[h]
whom I created for my glory,
whom I formed and made.[i]"
8 Lead out those who have eyes but are blind,[j]
who have ears but are deaf.[k]
9 All the nations gather together[l]
and the peoples assemble.
Which of their gods foretold[m] this
and proclaimed to us the former things?
Let them bring in their witnesses to prove they were right,
so that others may hear and say, "It is true."
10 "You are my witnesses," declares the LORD,
"and my servant[n] whom I have chosen,
so that you may know and believe me
and understand that I am he.
Before me no god[o] was formed,
nor will there be one after me.
11 I, even I, am the LORD,
and apart from me there is no savior.[p]
12 I have revealed and saved and proclaimed—
I, and not some foreign god[q] among you.
You are my witnesses,[r]" declares the LORD, "that I am God.
13 Yes, and from ancient days[s] I am he.
No one can deliver out of my hand.
When I act, who can reverse it?"[t]

God's Mercy and Israel's Unfaithfulness

14 This is what the LORD says—
your Redeemer, the Holy One of Israel:
"For your sake I will send to Babylon
and bring down as fugitives[u] all the Babylonians,[a][v]
in the ships in which they took pride.
15 I am the LORD, your Holy One,
Israel's Creator, your King."

16 This is what the LORD says—
he who made a way through the sea,
a path through the mighty waters,[w]
17 who drew out[x] the chariots and horses,
the army and reinforcements together,[y]
and they lay there, never to rise again,
extinguished, snuffed out like a wick:
18 "Forget the former things;
do not dwell on the past.
19 See, I am doing a new thing![z]
Now it springs up; do you not perceive it?
I am making a way in the wilderness[a]
and streams in the wasteland.
20 The wild animals honor me,
the jackals[b] and the owls,
because I provide water[c] in the wilderness
and streams in the wasteland,
to give drink to my people, my chosen,
21 the people I formed for myself
that they may proclaim my praise.[d]

22 "Yet you have not called on me, Jacob,
you have not wearied yourselves for[b] me, Israel.[e]
23 You have not brought me sheep for burnt offerings,
nor honored[f] me with your sacrifices.[g]

[a] 14 Or *Chaldeans* [b] 22 Or *Jacob; / surely you have grown weary of*

43:5 [c] Isa 44:2 [d] Jer 30:10-11 [e] Isa 41:8 **43:6** [f] Ps 107:3 [g] 2Co 6:18 **43:7** [h] Isa 56:5; 63:19; Jas 2:7 [i] ver 1,21; Ps 100:3; Eph 2:10 **43:8** [j] Isa 6:9-10 [k] Isa 42:20; Eze 12:2 **43:9** [l] Isa 41:1 [m] Isa 41:26 **43:10** [n] Isa 41:8-9 [o] Isa 44:6,8 **43:11** [p] Isa 45:21 **43:12** [q] Dt 32:12; Ps 81:9 [r] Isa 44:8 **43:13** [s] Ps 90:2 [t] Job 9:12; Isa 14:27
43:14 [u] Isa 13:14-15 [v] Isa 23:13 **43:16** [w] Ps 77:19; Isa 11:15; 51:10 **43:17** [x] Ps 118:12; Isa 1:31 [y] Ex 14:9 **43:19** [z] 2Co 5:17; Rev 21:5 [a] Ex 17:6; Nu 20:11 **43:20** [b] Isa 13:22 [c] Isa 48:21 **43:21** [d] Ps 102:18; 1Pe 2:9 **43:22** [e] Isa 30:11 **43:23** [f] Zec 7:5-6; Mal 1:6-8 [g] Am 5:25

43:9 *bring in their witnesses.* See note on 1:2.
43:10 *Before me no god was formed, nor will there be one after me.* Ancient Near Eastern theogonies (accounts of the origins of the gods) are usually structured around generations of gods in family relationships or formed by some other physical means (see note on 42:5). Khnum, the Egyptian creator-god (see note on v. 1), is said to have fashioned gods as well as men and animals. Gods come into being not simply on an ontological level (an understanding of whether they exist metaphysically or not) but on a functional one, since they are tied with natural phenomena and thus have tasks in the physical world. Function and form came to be simultaneously. Receiving a function and a name brought a new deity into being. The latter is shown in the *Enuma Elish,* which speaks of a time when no gods were yet manifest (named) or their destinies (functions) yet decreed. Divine functions also related to spheres of influence, with some deities playing roles in heaven, others on earth, still others in the netherworld. The earthly sphere was also delineated by influence over distinct geographic areas, whether temples, towns or nations.
43:11 *I . . . am the LORD.* See note on 41:13.
43:13 *When I act, who can reverse it?* The irreversibility of God's acts is attributed to Marduk in the *Enuma Elish.* He wished supreme authority over the gods so that his decrees could not be countermanded or altered. He is then granted such authority by the other gods.
43:14 This verse is describing the defeat and capture of the Babylonians (i.e., the Chaldeans) by Cyrus. Though not found in other sources, apparently the Chaldeans unsuccessfully attempted to escape the conquest by sailing their own ships on the Euphrates River to the Persian Gulf.
43:15 *I am the LORD.* See note on 41:13.
43:17 *chariots and horses.* See note on 2:7.

I have not burdened you with grain
offerings
nor wearied you with demands[h] for
incense.[i]
24 You have not bought any fragrant
calamus[j] for me,
or lavished on me the fat of your
sacrifices.
But you have burdened me with your
sins
and wearied[k] me with your
offenses.[l]

25 "I, even I, am he who blots out
your transgressions,[m] for my own
sake,[n]
and remembers your sins no more.[o]
26 Review the past for me,
let us argue the matter together;[p]
state the case[q] for your innocence.
27 Your first father sinned;
those I sent to teach[r] you rebelled
against me.
28 So I disgraced the dignitaries of your
temple;
I consigned Jacob to destruction[a]
and Israel to scorn.[s]

Israel the Chosen

44 "But now listen, Jacob, my servant,[t]
Israel, whom I have chosen.
2 This is what the LORD says—
he who made you, who formed you
in the womb,
and who will help[u] you:
Do not be afraid, Jacob, my servant,
Jeshurun,[b][v] whom I have chosen.
3 For I will pour water[w] on the thirsty
land,
and streams on the dry ground;
I will pour out my Spirit[x] on your
offspring,
and my blessing on your
descendants.[y]
4 They will spring up like grass in a
meadow,
like poplar trees[z] by flowing
streams.[a]
5 Some will say, 'I belong to the LORD';
others will call themselves by the
name of Jacob;

43:23 [h] Jer 7:22 [i] Ex 30:35; Lev 2:1
43:24 [j] Ex 30:23 [k] Isa 1:14; 7:13 [l] Mal 2:17
43:25 [m] Ac 3:19 [n] Isa 37:35; Eze 36:22 [o] Isa 38:17; Jer 31:34
43:26 [p] Isa 1:18 [q] Isa 41:1; 50:8
43:27 [r] Isa 9:15; 28:7; Jer 5:31
43:28 [s] Jer 24:9; Eze 5:15
44:1 [t] ver 21; Jer 30:10; 46:27-28
44:2 [u] Isa 41:10 [v] Dt 32:15
44:3 [w] Joel 3:18 [x] Joel 2:28; Ac 2:17 [y] Isa 61:9; 65:23
44:4 [z] Lev 23:40 [a] Job 40:22
44:5 [b] Ex 13:9 [c] Zec 8:20-22
44:6 [d] Isa 41:21 [e] Isa 43:1 [f] Isa 41:4; Rev 1:8, 17; 22:13
44:7 [g] Isa 41:22, 26
44:8 [h] Isa 43:10 [i] Dt 4:35; 1Sa 2:2
44:9 [j] Isa 41:24
44:10 [k] Isa 41:29; Jer 10:5; Ac 19:26
44:11 [l] Isa 1:29 [m] Isa 42:17
44:12 [n] Isa 40:19; 41:6-7 [o] Jer 10:3-5; Ac 17:29

still others will write on their hand,[b]
'The LORD's,'[c]
and will take the name Israel.

The LORD, Not Idols

6 "This is what the LORD says—
Israel's King[d] and Redeemer,[e] the
LORD Almighty:
I am the first and I am the last;[f]
apart from me there is no God.
7 Who then is like me? Let him
proclaim it.
Let him declare and lay out before me
what has happened since I established
my ancient people,
and what is yet to come—
yes, let them foretell[g] what will
come.
8 Do not tremble, do not be afraid.
Did I not proclaim this and foretell it
long ago?
You are my witnesses. Is there any
God[h] besides me?
No, there is no other Rock;[i] I know
not one."

9 All who make idols are nothing,
and the things they treasure are
worthless.[j]
Those who would speak up for them
are blind;
they are ignorant, to their own
shame.
10 Who shapes a god and casts an idol,
which can profit nothing?[k]
11 People who do that will be put to
shame;[l]
such craftsmen are only human
beings.
Let them all come together and take
their stand;
they will be brought down to terror
and shame.[m]

12 The blacksmith[n] takes a tool
and works with it in the coals;
he shapes an idol with hammers,
he forges it with the might of his arm.[o]

[a] *28* The Hebrew term refers to the irrevocable giving over of things or persons to the LORD, often by totally destroying them. [b] *2* *Jeshurun* means *the upright one,* that is, Israel.

43:24 *calamus.* This is an aromatic reed or cane (Ex 30:23) used as an ingredient in recipes and rituals. The same term in Akkadian designates a sweet cane (cf. Jer 6:20).
44:2 *formed you in the womb.* Formation and care in the uterus engender praise in the Hymn to Aten, the sun-god, who supposedly creates people from sperm and makes them grow in the womb as he nourishes and soothes them. He is seen as the one who gives breath. In this way we can see that the same motifs and affirmations familiar in the ancient world were also used in Israel.
44:5 *write on their hand, 'The LORD's.'* According to the Code of Hammurapi, Babylonian slaves had a distinguishing mark of some kind, apparently in their hair. The fifth-century BC Aramaic texts from Elephantine in Egypt mention that a slave is marked with the smallest of Hebrew letters or a brand on his right hand.
44:10–17 For making idols, see note on Jer 10:3; see also the article "Making an Idol," p. 1010.
44:12 *tool.* Elsewhere, this is a woodworking tool, usually taken as an ax or chisel of some kind (e.g., Jer 10:3). In the Gezer Calendar the term is associated with flax harvest, which fits with the Ugaritic use of the word for "sickle." In this context, it seems to be something that is forged.

He gets hungry and loses his strength;
he drinks no water and grows faint.
13 The carpenter[p] measures with a line
and makes an outline with a marker;
he roughs it out with chisels
and marks it with compasses.
He shapes it in human form,[q]
human form in all its glory,
that it may dwell in a shrine.[r]
14 He cut down cedars,
or perhaps took a cypress or oak.
He let it grow among the trees of the forest,
or planted a pine, and the rain made it grow.
15 It is used as fuel[s] for burning;
some of it he takes and warms himself,
he kindles a fire and bakes bread.
But he also fashions a god and worships it;
he makes an idol and bows[t] down to it.
16 Half of the wood he burns in the fire;
over it he prepares his meal,
he roasts his meat and eats his fill.
He also warms himself and says,
"Ah! I am warm; I see the fire."
17 From the rest he makes a god, his idol;
he bows down to it and worships.
He prays[u] to it and says,
"Save[v] me! You are my god!"
18 They know nothing, they understand[w] nothing;
their eyes[x] are plastered over so they cannot see,
and their minds closed so they cannot understand.
19 No one stops to think,
no one has the knowledge or understanding[y] to say,
"Half of it I used for fuel;
I even baked bread over its coals,
I roasted meat and I ate.
Shall I make a detestable[z] thing from what is left?
Shall I bow down to a block of wood?"
20 Such a person feeds on ashes;[a] a
deluded[b] heart misleads him;
he cannot save himself, or say,
"Is not this thing in my right hand a lie?[c]"

21 "Remember[d] these things, Jacob,
for you, Israel, are my servant.
I have made you, you are my servant;[e]
Israel, I will not forget you.[f]
22 I have swept away[g] your offenses like a cloud,
your sins like the morning mist.
Return[h] to me,
for I have redeemed[i] you."

23 Sing for joy,[j] you heavens, for the LORD has done this;
shout aloud, you earth[k] beneath.
Burst into song, you mountains,[l]
you forests and all your trees,
for the LORD has redeemed Jacob,
he displays his glory[m] in Israel.

Jerusalem to Be Inhabited

24 "This is what the LORD says—
your Redeemer,[n] who formed you in the womb:

I am the LORD,
the Maker of all things,
who stretches out the heavens,[o]
who spreads out the earth by myself,
25 who foils[p] the signs of false prophets
and makes fools of diviners,[q]
who overthrows the learning of the wise[r]
and turns it into nonsense,[s]
26 who carries out the words[t] of his servants
and fulfills[u] the predictions of his messengers,

who says of Jerusalem, 'It shall be inhabited,'
of the towns of Judah, 'They shall be rebuilt,'
and of their ruins, 'I will restore them,'[v]

44:13 [p] Isa 41:7 [q] Ps 115:4-7 [r] Jdg 17:4-5 **44:15** [s] ver 19 [t] 2Ch 25:14 **44:17** [u] 1Ki 18:26 [v] Isa 45:20 **44:18** [w] Isa 1:3 [x] Isa 6:9-10 **44:19** [y] Isa 5:13; 27:11; 45:20 [z] Dt 27:15 **44:20** [a] Ps 102:9 [b] Job 15:31; Ro 1:21-23, 28; 2Th 2:11; 2Ti 3:13 [c] Isa 59:3, 4, 13; Ro 1:25 **44:21** [d] Isa 46:8; Zec 10:9 [e] ver 1-2 [f] Isa 49:15 **44:22** [g] Isa 43:25; Ac 3:19 [h] Isa 55:7 [i] 1Co 6:20 **44:23** [j] Isa 42:10 [k] Ps 148:7 [l] Ps 98:8 [m] Isa 61:3 **44:24** [n] Isa 43:14 [o] Isa 42:5 **44:25** [p] Ps 33:10 [q] Isa 47:13 [r] 1Co 1:27 [s] 2Sa 15:31; 1Co 1:19-20 **44:26** [t] Zec 1:6 [u] Isa 55:11; Mt 5:18 [v] Isa 49:8-21

44:14 *cedars ... cypress ... oak ... pine.* The identities of the cedar (see notes on 2Sa 5:11; 1Ki 5:6; 6:15) and the oak are certain. The identities of the cypress and pine are more problematic. The word translated "cypress" occurs only here and not in other cognate languages, so its interpretation is at best tentative. The word translated "pine" may be cognate with an Akkadian word for "cedar," though the exact meaning here is still uncertain.

44:24 *I am the LORD.* See note on 41:13. *spreads out the earth by myself.* Several texts from the monarchy period refer to "Yahweh and his asherah," indicating that not all Israelites held to orthodoxy. This is one reason why prophets had a message to preach. Ps 136:6 clarifies that God spreads out the earth "upon the waters." This was the regular understanding of the world in ancient times. They believed in a flat earth that had a single continent floating on the surface of the cosmic waters. *spreads.* The Hebrew verb does not refer to spreading something out as, e.g., a tablecloth or a scroll. It is most frequently used for hammering out gold or silver as an overlay. Such a verb suggests God's role in forming the diverse terrain and topography of the earth.

44:25 *makes fools of diviners.* This verse connects to the previous one in that the omens consulted by the Assyrian and Babylonian diviners were drawn from heaven and earth. In fact, major prognostications had to be confirmed by omens from both realms. Yahweh's creation of those realms indicates his control of any signs being given. Prophets were supposed to be giving messages from deity, and diviners were presumably using their arts to determine what the gods were up to by reading the omens in heaven and earth. These professionals therefore offered a constant flow of theoretically divine insight concerning the course of political events.

27 who says to the watery deep, 'Be dry,
and I will dry up your streams,'
28 who says of Cyrus,[w] 'He is my
shepherd
and will accomplish all that I please;
he will say of Jerusalem,[x] "Let it be
rebuilt,"
and of the temple,[y] "Let its
foundations be laid." '

45 "This is what the LORD says to his
anointed,
to Cyrus, whose right hand I take
hold[z] of
to subdue nations[a] before him
and to strip kings of their armor,
to open doors before him
so that gates will not be shut:
2 I will go before you
and will level[b] the mountains[a];
I will break down gates of bronze
and cut through bars of iron.[c]
3 I will give you hidden treasures,[d]
riches stored in secret places,[e]
so that you may know[f] that I am the
LORD,
the God of Israel, who summons you
by name.[g]
4 For the sake of Jacob my servant,[h]
of Israel my chosen,
I summon you by name
and bestow on you a title of honor,
though you do not acknowledge[i] me.
5 I am the LORD, and there is no other;[j]
apart from me there is no God.[k]
I will strengthen you,[l]
though you have not acknowledged me,
6 so that from the rising of the sun
to the place of its setting[m]
people may know there is none
besides me.[n]
I am the LORD, and there is no other.
7 I form the light and create darkness,
I bring prosperity and create
disaster;[o]
I, the LORD, do all these things.

8 "You heavens above, rain[p] down my
righteousness;[q]
let the clouds shower it down.

44:28 [w] 2Ch 36:22 [x] Isa 14:32 [y] Ezr 1:2-4 **45:1** [z] Ps 73:23; Isa 41:13; 42:6 [a] Jer 50:35 **45:2** [b] Isa 40:4 [c] Ps 107:16; Jer 51:30 **45:3** [d] Jer 50:37 [e] Jer 41:8 [f] Isa 41:23 [g] Ex 33:12; Isa 43:1 **45:4** [h] Isa 41:8-9 [i] Ac 17:23 **45:5** [j] Isa 44:8 [k] Ps 18:31 [l] Ps 18:39 **45:6** [m] Isa 43:5; Mal 1:11 [n] ver 5, 18 **45:7** [o] Isa 31:2; Am 3:6 **45:8** [p] Ps 72:6; Joel 3:18 [q] Ps 85:11; Isa 60:21; 61:10, 11; Hos 10:12

a 2 Dead Sea Scrolls and Septuagint; the meaning of the word in the Masoretic Text is uncertain.

44:28 *Cyrus.* Cyrus II came to the Persian throne in 559 BC. When he overthrew the Median king Astyages in 550 BC, he instituted the Persian (Achaemenid) Empire, which he ruled until his death in 530 BC. He successfully moved against Lydia in Asia Minor in 547 BC, and in 539/538 BC defeated the Babylonian Empire under Nabonidus, placing the whole of the Near East except Egypt under his control. Cyrus wrote on a clay cylinder that the chief Babylonian god, Marduk, was incensed at the lack of proper worship by Nabonidus, so the god invited Cyrus to take the throne and reestablish legitimate worship. The conquered people purportedly welcomed him in peace with greens spread before him. Among the policies Cyrus instituted was one that found a place in heart of the exiled Israelites. Cyrus decreed that exiles could return to their native lands and reestablish their religious practices. This is mentioned in the Bible (2Ch 36:22 – 23; Ezr 1:1 – 4), and also in Cyrus's own document, the Cyrus Cylinder, in which he claims that inhabitants of other lands were regathered to their home territories. *shepherd.* See notes on 1Ch 11:2; Ps 23:1. *Let its foundations be laid.* See note on Isa 28:16.
45:1 *his anointed ... Cyrus.* "Anointed" is the Hebrew term "messiah." The term developed an eschatological significance in Israel of a promised deliverer, but it is also used in its nominal and verbal forms of anointing a leader such as a priest or king (e.g., 1Sa 15:1; see notes on 1Sa 2:10; 10:1; Ps 133:2). Cyrus claims to have been placed on the Babylonian throne by the Babylonian god Marduk. Here too the Persians see themselves assuming the role of the monarchs they replace. In the same way, Cyrus could be assuming aspects of the theology and role of the Davidic monarchy, at least to the extent of reestablishing the people in their land; this includes being the anointed messiah. While not the eschatological deliverer, Cyrus is God's deliverer of the moment from Babylonian exile. *whose right hand I take hold of.* This is a well-known Akkadian idiom indicating aid and guidance. In the Cyrus Cylinder, Cyrus is said to take Marduk's hand, restoring him to prominence in the cult.
45:2 *gates of bronze.* The Greek historian Herodotus described Babylon as having "one hundred gates in the circuit of the wall, all of bronze with bronze uprights and lintels." Large bronze gates have been excavated at the Assyrian period site of Balawat, giving a glimpse of what the Babylonian walls may have been like. *bars of iron.* Gates were locked by means of a bar slid across the gateway, and iron would obviously be the most difficult to break.
45:4 *though you do not acknowledge me.* Cyrus most certainly was not a worshiper of Yahweh. In his inscriptions, his polytheism is evident. In one case he requests that all the gods pray for him to Nabu and to Marduk his lord, whom he claims to worship. Cyrus acknowledged that various gods were worshiped by different peoples, each god having control over its own people and place. In the Cyrus Cylinder, even though Marduk is the chief Babylonian deity, Cyrus describes his circumstances by acknowledging not only the work of Marduk but also that of Nabu; Cyrus also acknowledges the existence of the "gods of Sumer and Akkad, whose sanctuaries he rebuilt." Other indications suggest that Cyrus believed in Zoroastrianism — a religion based on the teachings of Zarathustra, an Iranian holy man who lived sometime in the early first millennium BC. Zoroastrianism flourished during the Achaemenid Empire in Iran (see note on Ezr 1:2; see also the article "Zoroastrianism," p. 1433). Though there is no concrete evidence for Zoroastrianism until the reigns of Darius I and his successor, Xerxes I, the names of Cyrus's children show Zoroastrian influence, and he is known to have set up a fire stand (important in Zoroastrian worship) for the king's daily ritual. In a polytheistic system, adding deities is not a theological problem. In fact, in claiming support from a new god, the theologically neutral becomes an economic and political advantage. Cyrus thus had no problem in recognizing Yahweh, though he would not have personally worshiped him, since such recognition cost nothing but gained the support of Yahweh worshipers through their tribute and allegiance. Polytheistic priests of the newly recognized god would also likely expect royal support for their religious endeavors, so they also benefited.

A priest being anointed by the gods. Khnum temple in Esna, Egypt. See note on Isa 45:1.

Olaf Tausch/Wikimedia Commons, CC BY 3.0

Let the earth open wide,
let salvation[r] spring up,
let righteousness flourish with it;
I, the LORD, have created it.

[9] "Woe to those who quarrel[s] with their Maker,
those who are nothing but potsherds
among the potsherds on the ground.
Does the clay say to the potter,[t]
'What are you making?'
Does your work say,
'The potter has no hands'?
[10] Woe to the one who says to a father,
'What have you begotten?'
or to a mother,
'What have you brought to birth?'

[11] "This is what the LORD says—
the Holy One of Israel, and its Maker:
Concerning things to come,
do you question me about my children,
or give me orders about the work of my hands?[u]

[12] It is I who made the earth
and created mankind on it.
My own hands stretched out the heavens;[v]
I marshaled their starry hosts.[w]
[13] I will raise up Cyrus[a][x] in my righteousness:
I will make all his ways straight.
He will rebuild my city
and set my exiles free,
but not for a price or reward,[y]
says the LORD Almighty."

[14] This is what the LORD says:

"The products of Egypt and the merchandise of Cush,[b]
and those tall Sabeans—
they will come over to you
and will be yours;
they will trudge behind you,
coming over to you in chains.[z]
They will bow down before you
and plead[a] with you, saying,

45:8 [r] Isa 12:3 **45:9** [s] Job 15:25 [t] Isa 29:16; Ro 9:20-21* **45:11** [u] Isa 19:25 **45:12** [v] Ge 2:1; Isa 42:5 [w] Ne 9:6 **45:13** [x] 2Ch 36:22; Isa 41:2 [y] Isa 52:3 **45:14** [z] Isa 14:1-2 [a] Jer 16:19; Zec 8:20-23

[a] *13* Hebrew *him* [b] *14* That is, the upper Nile region

45:14 *Egypt ... Cush ... Sabeans.* Egypt and Cush (see note on 18:1–7) clearly refer to Lower and Upper Egypt, respectively, while the location of the Sabeans is less clear. Josephus (*Antiquities* 2.249) looks to the tall Nubians of Ethiopia, geographically close to the others. The designation could also refer to one of two groups in the Arabian peninsula—those from Sheba in the south (Yemen) or the Saba in northwest Arabia. Darius I speaks of completing an east-west canal connecting the Nile and the Red Sea: "I am Persian; from Persia I seized Egypt; I gave the order to dig this canal from a river by name Nile which flows in Egypt to the sea which goes from Persia." This canal, shown in recent satellite images, made contact between African people and those in Arabia much closer.

'Surely God is with you,[b] and there is
no other;
there is no other god.' "

15 Truly you are a God who has been
hiding[c] himself,
the God and Savior of Israel.
16 All the makers of idols will be put to
shame and disgraced;[d]
they will go off into disgrace
together.
17 But Israel will be saved[e] by the LORD
with an everlasting salvation;[f]
you will never be put to shame or
disgraced,
to ages everlasting.

18 For this is what the LORD says —
he who created the heavens,
he is God;
he who fashioned and made the earth,
he founded it;
he did not create it to be empty,[g]
but formed it to be inhabited[h] —
he says:
"I am the LORD,
and there is no other.[i]
19 I have not spoken in secret,[j]
from somewhere in a land of
darkness;
I have not said to Jacob's descendants,[k]
'Seek me in vain.'
I, the LORD, speak the truth;
I declare what is right.[l]

20 "Gather together[m] and come;
assemble, you fugitives from the
nations.
Ignorant[n] are those who carry[o] about
idols of wood,
who pray to gods that cannot save.[p]

45:14 [b] 1Co 14:25 **45:15** [c] Ps 44:24 **45:16** [d] Isa 44:9, 11 **45:17** [e] Ro 11:26 [f] Isa 26:4 **45:18** [g] Ge 1:2 [h] Ge 1:26; Isa 42:5 [i] ver 5 **45:19** [j] Isa 48:16 [k] Isa 41:8 [l] Dt 30:11 **45:20** [m] Isa 43:9 [n] Isa 44:19 [o] Isa 46:1; Jer 10:5 [p] Isa 44:17; 46:6-7 **45:21** [q] Isa 41:22 [r] ver 5 **45:22** [s] Zec 12:10 [t] Nu 21:8-9; 2Ch 20:12 [u] Isa 49:6, 12 **45:23** [v] Ge 22:16 [w] Heb 6:13 [x] Isa 55:11 [y] Ps 63:11; Isa 19:18; Ro 14:11*; Php 2:10-11 **45:24** [z] Jer 33:16 [a] Isa 41:11 **45:25** [b] Isa 41:16 **46:1** [c] Isa 21:9; Jer 50:2; 51:44 [d] Isa 45:20 **46:2** [e] Jdg 18:17-18; 2Sa 5:21

21 Declare what is to be, present it —
let them take counsel together.
Who foretold[q] this long ago,
who declared it from the distant
past?
Was it not I, the LORD?
And there is no God apart from me,[r]
a righteous God and a Savior;
there is none but me.

22 "Turn[s] to me and be saved,[t]
all you ends of the earth;[u]
for I am God, and there is no other.
23 By myself I have sworn,[v]
my mouth has uttered in all
integrity[w]
a word that will not be revoked:[x]
Before me every knee will bow;
by me every tongue will swear.[y]
24 They will say of me, 'In the LORD alone
are deliverance[z] and strength.' "
All who have raged against him
will come to him and be put to
shame.[a]
25 But all the descendants of Israel
will find deliverance in the LORD
and will make their boast in him.[b]

Gods of Babylon

46 Bel[c] bows down, Nebo stoops low;
their idols are borne by beasts of
burden.[a]
The images that are carried[d] about are
burdensome,
a burden for the weary.
2 They stoop and bow down together;
unable to rescue the burden,
they themselves go off into
captivity.[e]

[a] 1 Or *are but beasts and cattle*

45:23 *By myself I have sworn.* Swearing an oath on the name of a god is not rare today, nor was it in the time of Isaiah. Tying an oath to a deity provides gravity to it by calling the god as witness and possible punisher if the oath is broken. Akkadian texts mention invoking a god's name in an oath, but more regularly designate an oath as "by the life of a god" or that of the king. Several letters from Lachish in Israel use as the oath formula "as Yahweh lives." But in no case does there seem to be god or king swearing by themselves, as Yahweh does here.
46:1 *Bel.* In the Akkadian language, *belu* is the equivalent to English "lord, master." This is thus a title rather than a proper name for a god. The term is used as a substitute for the name of at least two Mesopotamian gods, Shamash and Marduk. The *Enuma Elish* describes how Marduk attained this position as head of the pantheon. The Babylonian king Nebuchadnezzar had a Marduk temple, named Esagila, near his great palace in Babylon. The esteem in which Marduk/Bel was held is demonstrated by the number of Neo-Assyrian and Neo-Babylonian personal names that bore "Bel" as one element, such as the last king of Babylon, Belshazzar (Da 5:1). For a period Marduk/Bel lost his hegemony, since his statue was "kidnapped" by Sennacherib and taken to Assyria in 689 BC (see note on 36:7), where, according to the Esarhaddon Chronicle, "for 8 years of Sennacherib and 12 years of Esarhaddon, a total of 20 years, Bel dwelt in Baltil [Assur]." Marduk is probably the god referred to here (see Jer 50:2; 51:44), since it was the Babylonians whom Cyrus defeated. *Nebo.* The Hebrew rendition of the Akkadian god Nabu, the son of Marduk. He was the god of writing and wisdom, was involved in determining fate, and was a major figure in the pantheon, as shown by the number of names in which Nebu/Nabo was included (e.g., Nabopolassar, Nebuchadnezzar, and Nabonidus). *images that are carried about.* Many gods were regularly associated with animals, which at times transported them. In Egypt, the goddess Qadesh is shown being carried while standing on a lion, as are Syrian and Mesopotamian deities, including the goddess Ishtar. Some also stood on a bull, a "beast of burden." One relief shows numerous gods each being transported on different animals. Such a "divine journey" was a time of lavish celebration. While in the ancient Near East this transport seems at times a matter of honor, it can also be demeaning, as when the divine images are taken captive. Isaiah sees this as demeaning in that a lifeless, powerless idol cannot move on its own.

3 "Listen[f] to me, you descendants of
Jacob,
all the remnant of the people of
Israel,
you whom I have upheld since your
birth,
and have carried since you were
born.
4 Even to your old age and gray hairs[g]
I am he,[h] I am he who will sustain
you.
I have made you and I will carry you;
I will sustain you and I will rescue
you.
5 "With whom will you compare me or
count me equal?
To whom will you liken me that we
may be compared?[i]
6 Some pour out gold from their bags
and weigh out silver on the scales;
they hire a goldsmith[j] to make it into a
god,
and they bow down and worship it.[k]
7 They lift it to their shoulders and
carry[l] it;
they set it up in its place, and there
it stands.
From that spot it cannot move.
Even though someone cries out to it, it
cannot answer;
it cannot save[m] them from their
troubles.

8 "Remember[n] this, keep it in mind,
take it to heart, you rebels.
9 Remember the former things, those of
long ago;[o]
I am God, and there is no other;
I am God, and there is none like
me.[p]
10 I make known the end from the
beginning,
from ancient times,[q] what is still to
come.
I say, 'My purpose will stand,[r]
and I will do all that I please.'
11 From the east I summon a bird of prey;
from a far-off land, a man to fulfill
my purpose.
What I have said, that I will bring
about;
what I have planned, that I will do.
12 Listen[s] to me, you stubborn-hearted,
you who are now far from my
righteousness.[t]
13 I am bringing my righteousness near,
it is not far away;
and my salvation will not be
delayed.
I will grant salvation to Zion,
my splendor[u] to Israel.

The Fall of Babylon

47 "Go down, sit in the dust,
Virgin Daughter[v] Babylon;
sit on the ground without a throne,
queen city of the Babylonians.[a][w]
No more will you be called
tender or delicate.[x]
2 Take millstones[y] and grind[z] flour;
take off your veil.[a]
Lift up your skirts,[b] bare your legs,
and wade through the streams.

46:3 [f] ver 12 **46:4** [g] Ps 71:18 [h] Isa 43:13 **46:5** [i] Isa 40:18, 25 **46:6** [j] Isa 40:19 [k] Isa 44:17 **46:7** [l] ver 1 [m] Isa 44:17; Isa 45:20 **46:8** [n] Isa 44:21 **46:9** [o] Dt 32:7 [p] Isa 45:5, 21 **46:10** [q] Isa 45:21 [r] Pr 19:21; Ac 5:39 **46:12** [s] ver 3 [t] Ps 119:150; Isa 48:1; Jer 2:5 **46:13** [u] Isa 44:23 **47:1** [v] Isa 23:12 [w] Ps 137:8; Jer 50:42; 51:33; Zec 2:7 [x] Dt 28:56 **47:2** [y] Ex 11:5; Mt 24:41 [z] Jdg 16:21 [a] Ge 24:65 [b] Isa 32:11

[a] 1 Or *Chaldeans*; also in verse 5

46:4 *Even to your old age and gray hairs … I will carry you.* Mesopotamians referred to humans as "dark haired," while the Akkadian term for the old is "grey-haired." Long life was a desired blessing, but its accompanying infirmities were the opposite. In an Aramaic slave manumission document, one of the obligations of the freed slave is to care for his former master as a father until death.
46:6 *weigh out … on the scales.* The scales probably refer to a balance, with the Hebrew term indicating the horizontal balance beam. Things were put on one side of the balance and a known weight on the other. An Egyptian wall painting shows a human heart being weighed in this way (see note on Job 31:6). *make it into a god.* See note on Jer 10:3; see also the article "Making an Idol," p. 1010.
46:7 *They … carry it.* After an idol is made, it must be carried to its shrine to be worshiped. This sarcasm of Isaiah contrasts with the power of Israel's God, who supports his worshipers.
46:9 *I am God, and there is no other.* The Assyrians saw their god Ashur as being the god from whom all other gods derive. A proper name from the period of Isaiah is Gabbu-Ilani-Ashur, meaning "Ashur is all the gods." In the Hymn to Aten from New Kingdom Egypt, Aten is hailed as the "sole God beside whom there is none." In an environment where numerous other deities claimed power, Israel's God is not making an absolute statement of uniqueness, though he could, according to Israel's theology; rather, he is saying that the readers know his uniqueness through past experience, and this will be confirmed through future fulfillment of God's plans.
47:1 *sit on the ground without a throne.* Royal power was symbolized by a throne (cf. 6:1). Its symbolism was so powerful that Sennacherib took a portable throne along to receive homage from those whom he captured. The loss of the throne thus indicated despair and powerlessness.
47:2 *grind flour.* Grinding grain at the flour mill was one of the most menial of tasks, often done by slave girls in both Egypt and Mesopotamia. *veil.* This rare term apparently indicates a veil-like covering. In Middle Assyrian and Hittite laws, a married woman was veiled at the wedding, apparently by the husband, and veiling publicly indicates that wedding. In the Gilgamesh Epic, Gilgamesh mourns his dead friend Enkidu by covering Enkidu's face "like a bride," suggesting a bride is the paradigmatic veiled person. There is no indication from pictorial representations that veils were regularly worn in Israel or among her neighbors by married women subsequently, suggesting their use only by brides in conjunction with the ceremony itself. It is the veiling that turns the woman into a bride, according to a Middle Assyrian law: "If a man would veil his concubine, 5 (or) 6 of his companions he shall gather and he shall veil her in their presence. He shall say, 'She is (my) wife.'" This covering symbolizes the duty of care and

[3]Your nakedness[c] will be exposed
and your shame[d] uncovered.
I will take vengeance;[e]
I will spare no one."

[4]Our Redeemer—the LORD Almighty is
his name[f]—
is the Holy One of Israel.

[5]"Sit in silence, go into darkness,[g]
queen city of the Babylonians;
no more will you be called
queen of kingdoms.[h]
[6]I was angry[i] with my people
and desecrated my inheritance;
I gave them into your hand,[j]
and you showed them no mercy.
Even on the aged
you laid a very heavy yoke.
[7]You said, 'I am forever—
the eternal queen!'[k]
But you did not consider these things
or reflect[l] on what might happen.[m]

[8]"Now then, listen, you lover of pleasure,
lounging in your security[n]
and saying to yourself,
'I am, and there is none besides me.[o]
I will never be a widow[p]
or suffer the loss of children.'
[9]Both of these will overtake you
in a moment,[q] on a single day:
loss of children[r] and widowhood.
They will come upon you in full
measure,
in spite of your many sorceries[s]
and all your potent spells.[t]
[10]You have trusted[u] in your wickedness
and have said, 'No one sees me.'[v]
Your wisdom[w] and knowledge mislead[x]
you
when you say to yourself,
'I am, and there is none besides me.'
[11]Disaster will come upon you,
and you will not know how to
conjure it away.

47:3 [c]Eze 16:37; Na 3:5 [d]Isa 20:4 [e]Isa 34:8 **47:4** [f]Jer 50:34 **47:5** [g]Isa 13:10 [h]Isa 13:19 **47:6** [i]2Ch 28:9 [j]Isa 10:13 **47:7** [k]ver 5; Rev 18:7 [l]Isa 42:23,25 [m]Dt 32:29 **47:8** [n]Isa 32:9 [o]Isa 45:6; Zep 2:15 [p]Rev 18:7 **47:9** [q]Ps 73:19; 1Th 5:3; Rev 18:8-10 [r]Isa 13:18 [s]Na 3:4 [t]Rev 18:23 **47:10** [u]Ps 52:7; 62:10 [v]Isa 29:15 [w]Isa 5:21 [x]Isa 44:20

A calamity will fall upon you
that you cannot ward off with a
ransom;
a catastrophe you cannot foresee
will suddenly[y] come upon you.

[12]"Keep on, then, with your magic
spells
and with your many sorceries,[z]
which you have labored at since
childhood.
Perhaps you will succeed,
perhaps you will cause terror.
[13]All the counsel you have received has
only worn you out![a]
Let your astrologers[b] come
forward,
those stargazers who make predictions
month by month,
let them save[c] you from what is
coming upon you.
[14]Surely they are like stubble;[d]
the fire will burn them up.
They cannot even save themselves
from the power of the flame.[e]
These are not coals for warmth;
this is not a fire to sit by.
[15]That is all they are to you—
these you have dealt with
and labored[f] with since childhood.
All of them go on in their error;
there is not one that can save you.

Stubborn Israel

48 "Listen to this, you descendants
of Jacob,
you who are called by the name of
Israel
and come from the line of Judah,
you who take oaths in the name of the
LORD
and invoke[g] the God of Israel—
but not in truth[h] or righteousness—
[2]you who call yourselves citizens of the
holy city[i]

47:11 [y]1Th 5:3 **47:12** [z]ver 9 **47:13** [a]Isa 57:10; Jer 51:58 [b]Isa 44:25 [c]ver 15 **47:14** [d]Isa 5:24; Na 1:10 [e]Isa 10:17; Jer 51:30,32,58 **47:15** [f]Rev 18:11 **48:1** [g]Isa 58:2 [h]Jer 4:2 **48:2** [i]Isa 52:1

provision. The bride's unveiling by the groom in private symbolized the new intimate relationship. In contrast, a harlot was not to veil herself; her head had to remain uncovered. Unveiling such as this is the sign of an extramarital relationship, since the veil was neither placed nor removed by a husband but by the woman herself in the context of intimacy with others. Unveiling or uncovering such as this is the sign of a breach of relationship. In Old Babylonian texts from Nuzi and elsewhere, stripping and expulsion signified a divorce, in which she is stripped and driven out naked. *bare your legs.* Respectable women are generally portrayed with long skirts, so uncovered legs were considered inappropriate.

47:3 *nakedness.* Reserved for people who were poor, prisoners (20:2–4), dancing girls, or worse.

47:6 *yoke.* See note on 9:4.

47:8 *I am.* The use of "I am" would have immediately struck a chord for this Israelite audience (see the article "God's Name," p. 112), but there is no claim too arrogant for these kings to make for themselves. An Assyrian king of the ninth century, Ashurnasirpal, had a list of 11 "I am" titles for himself.

47:9 *spells.* Babylonia was famous in the ancient world for its magic and divinatory practices. Literally thousands of texts have been uncovered that deal with a multitude of subjects, including incantations that help alleviate the pain of a toothache, help a baby that is stuck in the womb, and help a mother who is barren. It appears that the common person hired an incantation priest for even the most mundane problem. The priest then came and recited a spell to either exorcise a problematic demon or other divine irritant. Incantations and magical spells were used frequently in Mesopotamia, often in close proximity with medical texts since they both concerned, among other things, the avoidance or amelioration of sickness. Incantations were intended to magically bind the supernatural powers that posed a threat. See the article "Magic," p. 326.

47:13 *astrologers . . . stargazers.* See note on 13:10.

and claim to rely[j] on the God of
Israel —
the LORD Almighty is his name:
3 I foretold the former things[k] long ago,
my mouth announced[l] them and I
made them known;
then suddenly I acted, and they
came to pass.
4 For I knew how stubborn[m] you were;
your neck muscles[n] were iron,
your forehead[o] was bronze.
5 Therefore I told you these things long
ago;
before they happened I announced
them to you
so that you could not say,
'My images brought them about;[p]
my wooden image and metal god
ordained them.'
6 You have heard these things; look at
them all.
Will you not admit them?

"From now on I will tell you of new
things,
of hidden things unknown to you.
7 They are created now, and not long
ago;
you have not heard of them before
today.
So you cannot say,
'Yes, I knew of them.'
8 You have neither heard nor
understood;
from of old your ears have not been
open.
Well do I know how treacherous you
are;
you were called a rebel[q] from birth.
9 For my own name's sake I delay my
wrath;[r]
for the sake of my praise I hold it
back from you,
so as not to destroy you completely.[s]
10 See, I have refined you, though not as
silver;
I have tested you in the furnace[t] of
affliction.
11 For my own sake,[u] for my own sake, I
do this.
How can I let myself be defamed?[v]
I will not yield my glory to another.[w]

Israel Freed

12 "Listen[x] to me, Jacob,
Israel, whom I have called:
I am he;
I am the first and I am the last.[y]
13 My own hand laid the foundations of
the earth,[z]
and my right hand spread out the
heavens;[a]
when I summon them,
they all stand up together.[b]

14 "Come together,[c] all of you, and listen:
Which of the idols has foretold these
things?
The LORD's chosen ally
will carry out his purpose[d] against
Babylon;
his arm will be against the
Babylonians.[a]
15 I, even I, have spoken;
yes, I have called[e] him.
I will bring him,
and he will succeed in his mission.

16 "Come near[f] me and listen to this:

"From the first announcement I have
not spoken in secret;[g]
at the time it happens, I am there."

And now the Sovereign LORD has sent[h]
me,
endowed with his Spirit.

17 This is what the LORD says —
your Redeemer,[i] the Holy One[j] of
Israel:
"I am the LORD your God,
who teaches you what is best for
you,
who directs[k] you in the way[l] you
should go.

48:2 [j] Isa 10:20; Mic 3:11; Ro 2:17 **48:3** [k] Isa 41:22 [l] Isa 45:21 **48:4** [m] Dt 31:27 [n] Ex 32:9; Ac 7:51 [o] Eze 3:9 **48:5** [p] Jer 44:15-18 **48:8** [q] Dt 9:7, 24; Ps 58:3 **48:9** [r] Ps 78:38; Isa 30:18 [s] Ne 9:31 **48:10** [t] 1Ki 8:51

48:11 [u] 1Sa 12:22; Isa 37:35 [v] Dt 32:27; Jer 14:7, 21; Eze 20:9, 14, 22, 44 [w] Isa 42:8 **48:12** [x] Isa 46:3 [y] Isa 41:4; Rev 1:17; 22:13 **48:13** [z] Heb 1:10-12 [a] Ex 20:11 [b] Isa 40:26 **48:14** [c] Isa 43:9 [d] Isa 46:10-11 **48:15** [e] Isa 45:1 **48:16** [f] Isa 41:1 [g] Isa 45:19 [h] Zec 2:9, 11 **48:17** [i] Isa 49:7 [j] Isa 43:14 [k] Isa 49:10 [l] Ps 32:8

[a] 14 Or *Chaldeans*; also in verse 20

48:5 *My images brought them about.* Israel's claim that God acts in history was thought to distinguish it from its neighbors, but textual evidence shows this to be otherwise. Curses of the gods called down on those who break treaties or who deface boundary stones indicate that gods are understood to work through history (see 5:25). Royal inscriptions of the gods bringing military victory through the Mesopotamian king indicate the same understanding. Deities also played a role in the political realm, as when Ashurbanipal credits them with bringing him to the throne. Prayers, both individual and corporate, indicate that both Israel and her neighbors are open to, and even expect, their gods to be responsive in personal and national history.

48:10 *refined you.* See note on 1:22. *furnace.* Smelting furnaces have been found at numerous archaeological sites. Though full metal workshops are less well known, two from the second millennium BC were found at Kanesh (Kültepe in Turkey) and another near Baghdad. Some furnaces, like one from the Late Bronze site of Tel Zeror, have nozzles on them for bellows. These were necessary because the furnaces used for smelting needed to produce higher temperatures than furnaces with solely domestic functions. A Sixth Dynasty Egyptian tomb relief shows six men blowing air into a furnace through long pipes as part of the process of refining gold. See note on Pr 17:3.

48:14 *his arm.* Cyrus's arm. *will be against the Babylonians.* See note on 44:28.

48:16 *I have not spoken in secret.* See 45:19.

48:17 *I am the LORD.* See note on 41:13.

[18]If only you had paid attention[m] to my
commands,
your peace[n] would have been like a
river,
your well-being[o] like the waves of
the sea.
[19]Your descendants would have been like
the sand,
your children like its numberless
grains;[p]
their name would never be blotted out[q]
nor destroyed from before me."

[20]Leave Babylon,
flee[r] from the Babylonians!
Announce this with shouts of joy[s]
and proclaim it.
Send it out to the ends of the earth;
say, "The LORD has redeemed[t] his
servant Jacob."
[21]They did not thirst[u] when he led them
through the deserts;
he made water flow[v] for them from
the rock;
he split the rock
and water gushed out.[w]

[22]"There is no peace," says the LORD,
"for the wicked."[x]

The Servant of the LORD

49 Listen to me, you islands;
hear this, you distant nations:
Before I was born[y] the LORD called[z] me;
from my mother's womb he has
spoken my name.
[2]He made my mouth like a sharpened
sword,[a]
in the shadow of his hand he
hid me;
he made me into a polished arrow
and concealed me in his quiver.
[3]He said to me, "You are my servant,[b]
Israel, in whom I will display my
splendor.[c]"
[4]But I said, "I have labored in vain;[d]
I have spent my strength for nothing
at all.
Yet what is due me is in the LORD's hand,
and my reward[e] is with my God."
[5]And now the LORD says—
he who formed me in the womb to
be his servant
to bring Jacob back to him
and gather Israel[f] to himself,
for I am[a] honored[g] in the eyes of the
LORD
and my God has been my strength—
[6]he says:
"It is too small a thing for you to be
my servant
to restore the tribes of Jacob
and bring back those of Israel I have
kept.
I will also make you a light for the
Gentiles,[h]
that my salvation may reach to the
ends of the earth."[i]
[7]This is what the LORD says—
the Redeemer and Holy One of
Israel[j]—
to him who was despised[k] and
abhorred by the nation,
to the servant of rulers:
"Kings[l] will see you and stand up,
princes will see and bow down,
because of the LORD, who is faithful,
the Holy One of Israel, who has
chosen you."

48:18 [m]Dt 32:29 [n]Ps 119:165; Isa 66:12 [o]Isa 45:8 **48:19** [p]Ge 22:17 [q]Isa 56:5; 66:22 **48:20** [r]Jer 50:8; 51:6, 45; Zec 2:6-7; Rev 18:4 [s]Isa 49:13 [t]Isa 52:9; 63:9 **48:21** [u]Isa 41:17 [v]Isa 30:25 [w]Ex 17:6; Nu 20:11; Ps 105:41; Isa 35:6 **48:22** [x]Isa 57:21 **49:1** [y]Isa 44:24; 46:3; Mt 1:20 [z]Isa 7:14; 9:6; 44:2; Jer 1:5; Gal 1:15 **49:2** [a]Isa 11:4; Rev 1:16
49:3 [b]Zec 3:8 [c]Isa 44:23 **49:4** [d]Isa 65:23 [e]Isa 35:4 **49:5** [f]Isa 11:12 [g]Isa 43:4 **49:6** [h]Lk 2:32 [i]Ac 13:47* **49:7** [j]Isa 48:17 [k]Ps 22:6; 69:7-9 [l]Isa 52:15

[a] 5 *Or him, / but Israel would not be gathered; / yet I will be*

48:19 *descendants … name … blotted out.* Losing the next generation and one's own honor was a serious thing. When deceased, only one's name or memory remains, and without descendants, one is soon forgotten (Jer 11:19), the family line comes to an end, and, especially for those involved in a cult of the dead, there is no one to look after the interests of the departed.
49:1 *Before I was born the LORD called me.* A prenatal call is not only important in the OT, several Mesopotamian kings make mention of it too. Ashurbanipal writes that he was called by the gods for kingship and was formed inside his mother in order to shepherd the land of Assyria. Such kings are stating that they became rulers not just because of the mighty deeds they performed but because the gods recognized their uniqueness even before birth, seeing that they were intrinsically worthy before having proven themselves in any way. *he has spoken my name.* See note on 43:1. This means more than just to recall someone. The same literal expression ("remember/invoke a name") with a deity as the subject also means "to recognize as king" in the Akkadian of this period. Nebuchadnezzar stated that Marduk named him permanently to kingship, and Cyrus claimed the same treatment (see 45:1 and note).
49:2 *mouth like a sharpened sword.* This sword imagery is also used for the prophet's word (see Jer 25:29), and God's word in the NT (e.g., Eph 6:17). Since the sword was an offensive weapon, the implication is that the word is in some sense aggressive. One of the Hebrew words for mouth also signified the term "edge," as in "edge of the sword." Thus, there may be a play on words in this verse.
49:5 *formed me in the womb.* See note on 44:2. *to bring Jacob back … and gather Israel.* Mesopotamian kings saw themselves as divinely appointed and so were delegated tasks by their deity. Often they list their achievements in the introductory section of official records. Sennacherib, e.g., starts the record of his first military campaign by identifying himself as shepherd, faithful worshiper of the gods, and one who guards right and justice, which includes coming to the aid of the needy. Restoration from exile was one of the duties of a good king (11:11; 44:28). Hammurapi, in describing his tasks in looking after Sumer and Akkad, states that he not only dug an irrigation canal but also gathered peoples who had been scattered and provided them pastures and watering places. Many Babylonian kings describe themselves as ones who gather the dispersed.

Restoration of Israel

[8]This is what the LORD says:

"In the time of my favor[m] I will
answer you,
and in the day of salvation
I will help you;[n]
I will keep[o] you and will make
you
to be a covenant for the
people,[p]
to restore the land[q]
and to reassign its desolate
inheritances,
9 to say to the captives,[r] 'Come
out,'
and to those in darkness, 'Be
free!'

"They will feed beside the roads
and find pasture on every barren
hill.[s]
10 They will neither hunger nor thirst,[t]
nor will the desert heat or the sun
beat down on them.[u]
He who has compassion[v] on them
will guide them
and lead them beside springs[w] of
water.
11 I will turn all my mountains into
roads,
and my highways[x] will be raised up.[y]
12 See, they will come from afar[z]—
some from the north, some from the
west,
some from the region of Aswan.[a]"

13 Shout for joy, you heavens;
rejoice, you earth;
burst into song, you mountains![a]
For the LORD comforts[b] his people
and will have compassion on his
afflicted ones.

14 But Zion said, "The LORD has forsaken
me,
the Lord has forgotten me."

15 "Can a mother forget the baby at her
breast
and have no compassion on the
child she has borne?
Though she may forget,
I will not forget you![c]
16 See, I have engraved[d] you on the palms
of my hands;
your walls[e] are ever before me.

Architect's drawing of the ground plan of the palace of Nur Adad in Larsa, Babylonia, 1865 to 1850 BC.

The Schøyen Collection, Oslo and London, MS 3031, www.schoyencollection.com

49:8 [m]Ps 69:13 [n]2Co 6:2* [o]Isa 26:3 [p]Isa 42:6 [q]Isa 44:26 **49:9** [r]Isa 42:7; 61:1; Lk 4:19 [s]Isa 41:18 **49:10** [t]Isa 33:16 [u]Ps 121:6; Rev 7:16 [v]Isa 14:1 [w]Isa 35:7 **49:11** [x]Isa 11:16 [y]Isa 40:4 **49:12** [z]Isa 43:5-6 **49:13** [a]Isa 44:23 [b]Isa 40:1 **49:15** [c]Isa 44:21 **49:16** [d]SS 8:6 [e]Ps 48:12-13; Isa 62:6

[a] 12 Dead Sea Scrolls; Masoretic Text *Sinim*

49:8 *restore the land.* Through neglect or war, destruction was common. Rebuilding and restoration efforts were not only necessary for the good of the country but also politically and theologically astute policies for Mesopotamian kings. The people benefited, but so did the gods, when their temples were reestablished. This type of activity provided something of an economic circularity, according to the Mesopotamian view. A god helped the king conquer a city or territory, which filled the royal treasury. Some of this revenue was in turn used to rebuild and replenish the divine sanctuaries, benefiting the gods, who would then in the future be pleased to support further expansion.
49:11 *highways.* See the note on 40:3.
49:12 *Aswan.* This militarily and commercially important site (Hebrew *sinim* [Syene], modern Aswan) is located at the first cataract of the Nile in Egypt. Just opposite on an island in the middle of the Nile was Elephantine, the site where a group of Aramaic papyrus documents from the fifth century BC were found. One of these documents claims to have been written by a scribe in Syene.
49:15 *mother.* See note on 66:13.
49:16 The mention of walls suggests that what is signified is not a mark of ownership (see note on 44:5) but rather a town plan or blueprint for the reconstructed city. No precedent is known for such an engraving on the hands, but palace plans are known. One from nineteenth-century BC Larsa shows details of walls, rooms and courtyards, while the Sumerian king Gudea had a similar plan of a temple building inscribed on the lap of one of his statues, showing even the thickness of the walls.

17 Your children hasten back,
and those who laid you waste[f]
depart from you.
18 Lift up your eyes and look around;
all your children gather[g] and come
to you.
As surely as I live,[h]" declares the LORD,
"you will wear[i] them all as
ornaments;
you will put them on, like a bride.

19 "Though you were ruined and made
desolate[j]
and your land laid waste,[k]
now you will be too small for your
people,[l]
and those who devoured you will be
far away.
20 The children born during your
bereavement
will yet say in your hearing,
'This place is too small for us;
give us more space to live in.'[m]
21 Then you will say in your heart,
'Who bore me these?
I was bereaved and barren;
I was exiled and rejected.[n]
Who brought these up?
I was left[o] all alone,
but these — where have they come
from?' "

22 This is what the Sovereign LORD says:

"See, I will beckon to the nations,
I will lift up my banner[p] to the
peoples;
they will bring your sons in their arms
and carry your daughters on their
hips.[q]
23 Kings[r] will be your foster fathers,
and their queens your nursing
mothers.[s]
They will bow down before you with
their faces to the ground;
they will lick the dust[t] at your feet.
Then you will know that I am the LORD;[u]
those who hope in me will not be
disappointed."

49:17 [f] Isa 10:6 **49:18** [g] Isa 43:5; 54:7; Isa 60:4 [h] Isa 45:23 [i] Isa 52:1 **49:19** [j] Isa 54:1, 3 [k] Isa 5:6 [l] Zec 10:10 **49:20** [m] Isa 54:1-3 **49:21** [n] Isa 5:13 [o] Isa 1:8 **49:22** [p] Isa 11:10 [q] Isa 60:4 **49:23** [r] Isa 60:3, 10-11 [s] Isa 60:16 [t] Ps 72:9 [u] Mic 7:17

49:24 [v] Mt 12:29; Lk 11:21 **49:25** [w] Isa 14:2 [x] Jer 50:33-34 [y] Isa 25:9; 35:4 **49:26** [z] Isa 9:4 [a] Isa 9:20 [b] Rev 16:6 [c] Eze 39:7 **50:1** [d] Dt 24:1; Jer 3:8; Hos 2:2 [e] Ne 5:5; Mt 18:25 [f] Dt 32:30; Isa 52:3 **50:2** [g] Isa 41:28 [h] Nu 11:23; Isa 59:1 [i] Ge 18:14 [j] Ex 14:22; Jos 3:16 **50:3** [k] Rev 6:12 **50:4** [l] Ex 4:12

24 Can plunder be taken from warriors,[v]
or captives be rescued from the
fierce[a]?

25 But this is what the LORD says:

"Yes, captives[w] will be taken from
warriors,[x]
and plunder retrieved from the
fierce;
I will contend with those who contend
with you,
and your children I will save.[y]
26 I will make your oppressors[z] eat[a] their
own flesh;
they will be drunk on their own
blood,[b] as with wine.
Then all mankind will know[c]
that I, the LORD, am your Savior,
your Redeemer, the Mighty One of
Jacob."

Israel's Sin and the Servant's Obedience

50 This is what the LORD says:

"Where is your mother's certificate of
divorce[d]
with which I sent her away?
Or to which of my creditors
did I sell[e] you?
Because of your sins you were sold;[f]
because of your transgressions your
mother was sent away.
2 When I came, why was there no one?
When I called, why was there no
one to answer?[g]
Was my arm too short[h] to deliver you?
Do I lack the strength[i] to rescue you?
By a mere rebuke I dry up the sea,[j]
I turn rivers into a desert;
their fish rot for lack of water
and die of thirst.
3 I clothe the heavens with darkness
and make sackcloth[k] its covering."

4 The Sovereign LORD has given me a
well-instructed tongue,[l]

[a] *24* Dead Sea Scrolls, Vulgate and Syriac (see also Septuagint and verse 25); Masoretic Text *righteous*

49:18 *As surely as I live.* Solemnity is added to oaths when sworn in the name of a god (see note on 45:23), but here God swears by himself, being unable to call a higher authority as witness. Egyptians used the same oath formula, placing themselves on the line if the oath should be broken. In Rameses II's Kadesh battle inscription his oath swears both by himself and his gods. *ornaments … like a bride.* The Israelite bride sometimes wore embroidered garments, jewels, a special girdle and a veil. In this passage, the bride wore an ornamental waistband. There are scores of texts from Mesopotamia that describe the exchange of gifts between two families for the purpose of marriage, but little is said of the attire of the bride or of the ceremony itself.
49:23 *I am the LORD.* See note on 41:13.

49:26 *drunk on their own blood.* The description is not of a savage conqueror but of one who has been relegated to cannibalism in order to remain alive (see note on 2Ki 6:28). One of the curses in a treaty between Assyria and Arpad calls down such a desperate plight on one who breaches the covenant. Assyrian and Babylonian inscriptions describe the plight of those reduced to such dire action during the time of siege.
50:1 *to which of my creditors did I sell you?* See 42:7. There were two main sources of slaves in the ancient Near East: the capture of foreigners through war, and economic or debt slavery with its supportive overtones. In the latter case, when someone became destitute, he could be forced to sell himself or family members into slavery in order to have the resources to survive.

to know the word that sustains the
weary.[m]
He wakens me morning by morning,[n]
wakens my ear to listen like one
being instructed.
5 The Sovereign LORD has opened my
ears;[o]
I have not been rebellious,[p]
I have not turned away.
6 I offered my back to those who
beat[q] me,
my cheeks to those who pulled out
my beard;
I did not hide my face
from mocking and spitting.[r]
7 Because the Sovereign LORD helps[s] me,
I will not be disgraced.
Therefore have I set my face like flint,[t]
and I know I will not be put to
shame.
8 He who vindicates me is near.
Who then will bring charges against
me?[u]
Let us face each other![v]
Who is my accuser?
Let him confront me!
9 It is the Sovereign LORD who helps[w] me.
Who will condemn me?
They will all wear out like a garment;
the moths[x] will eat them up.

10 Who among you fears the LORD
and obeys the word of his servant?[y]
Let the one who walks in the dark,
who has no light,
trust[z] in the name of the LORD
and rely on their God.
11 But now, all you who light fires
and provide yourselves with flaming
torches,[a]
go, walk in the light of your fires[b]
and of the torches you have set ablaze.
This is what you shall receive from my
hand:
You will lie down in torment.[c]

Everlasting Salvation for Zion

51 "Listen[d] to me, you who pursue
righteousness[e]
and who seek the LORD:
Look to the rock from which you were
cut
and to the quarry from which you
were hewn;
2 look to Abraham,[f] your father,
and to Sarah, who gave you birth.
When I called him he was only one
man,
and I blessed him and made him
many.[g]
3 The LORD will surely comfort[h] Zion
and will look with compassion on all
her ruins;[i]
he will make her deserts like Eden,[j]
her wastelands like the garden of the
LORD.
Joy and gladness[k] will be found in her,
thanksgiving and the sound of
singing.

4 "Listen to me, my people;[l]
hear me, my nation:
Instruction will go out from me;
my justice[m] will become a light to
the nations.[n]
5 My righteousness draws near speedily,
my salvation is on the way,[o]
and my arm[p] will bring justice to the
nations.
The islands will look to me
and wait in hope for my arm.
6 Lift up your eyes to the heavens,
look at the earth beneath;
the heavens will vanish like smoke,[q]
the earth will wear out like a
garment[r]
and its inhabitants die like flies.
But my salvation will last forever,
my righteousness will never fail.

7 "Hear me, you who know what is
right,[s]
you people who have taken my
instruction to heart:[t]
Do not fear the reproach of mere
mortals
or be terrified by their insults.[u]
8 For the moth will eat them up like a
garment;[v]
the worm will devour them like
wool.
But my righteousness will last forever,[w]
my salvation through all
generations."

9 Awake, awake, arm of the LORD,
clothe yourself with strength![x]
Awake, as in days gone by,
as in generations of old.[y]

50:4 [m] Mt 11:28 [n] Ps 5:3; 119:147; 143:8 **50:5** [o] Isa 35:5 [p] Mt 26:39; Jn 8:29; 14:31; 15:10; Ac 26:19; Heb 5:8 **50:6** [q] Isa 53:5; Mt 27:30; Mk 14:65; 15:19; Lk 22:63 [r] La 3:30; Mt 26:67 **50:7** [s] Isa 42:1 [t] Eze 3:8-9 **50:8** [u] Isa 43:26; Ro 8:32-34 [v] Isa 41:1 **50:9** [w] Isa 41:10 [x] Job 13:28; Isa 51:8 **50:10** [y] Isa 49:3 [z] Isa 26:4 **50:11** [a] Pr 26:18 [b] Jas 3:6 [c] Isa 65:13-15 **51:1** [d] Isa 46:3 [e] ver 7; Ps 94:15; Ro 9:30-31
51:2 [f] Isa 29:22; Ro 4:16; Heb 11:11 [g] Ge 12:2 **51:3** [h] Isa 40:1 [i] Isa 52:9 [j] Ge 2:8 [k] Isa 25:9; 66:10 **51:4** [l] Ps 50:7 [m] Isa 2:4 [n] Isa 42:4,6 **51:5** [o] Isa 46:13 [p] Isa 40:10; 63:1,5 **51:6** [q] Mt 24:35; 2Pe 3:10 [r] Ps 102:25-26 **51:7** [s] ver 1 [t] Ps 37:31 [u] Mt 5:11; Ac 5:41 **51:8** [v] Isa 50:9 [w] ver 6 **51:9** [x] Isa 52:1 [y] Dt 4:34

51:1 *the rock from which you were cut.* Stone was a common building material in Israel and was used in both dressed and undressed form. Limestone was common, shaped in the form of ashlar, which is dressed on all six sides after being hewn from a stone quarry (see note on Ps 118:22). Quarried stone is a matter of pride for Mesopotamian kings in their massive building projects, showing their power. Nebuchadnezzar writes of "a great wall from strong stones quarried from the great mountains." Zion's pride lies in the mighty foundation stones of their forefather and mother, Abraham and Sarah (v. 2).

51:9 *cut Rahab to pieces.* Complete domination is shown by dismemberment. In the Ugaritic Baal Cycle, the goddess Anat acts similarly toward her opponents, and Neo-Assyrian prophecies suggest the same. Dismemberment of victims is shown on the Assyrian Balawat gates. For Rahab, see the article "Chaos Monsters," p. 953.

Was it not you who cut Rahab to
pieces,
who pierced that monster[z] through?
10 Was it not you who dried up the sea,[a]
the waters of the great deep,
who made a road in the depths of
the sea
so that the redeemed might cross
over?
11 Those the LORD has rescued[b] will
return.
They will enter Zion with singing;
everlasting joy will crown their heads.
Gladness and joy[c] will overtake them,
and sorrow and sighing will flee
away.[d]

12 "I, even I, am he who comforts[e] you.
Who are you that you fear mere
mortals,[f]
human beings who are but grass,[g]
13 that you forget[h] the LORD your Maker,[i]
who stretches out the heavens[j]
and who lays the foundations of the
earth,
that you live in constant terror[k] every
day
because of the wrath of the oppressor,
who is bent on destruction?
For where is the wrath of the
oppressor?
14 The cowering prisoners will soon be
set free;
they will not die in their dungeon,
nor will they lack bread.[l]
15 For I am the LORD your God,
who stirs up the sea[m] so that its
waves roar—
the LORD Almighty is his name.
16 I have put my words in your mouth[n]
and covered you with the shadow of
my hand[o]—
I who set the heavens in place,
who laid the foundations of the
earth,
and who say to Zion, 'You are my
people.' "

51:9 [z] Ps 74:13 **51:10** [a] Ex 14:22 **51:11** [b] Isa 35:9 [c] Jer 33:11 [d] Rev 7:17 **51:12** [e] 2Co 1:4 [f] Ps 118:6; Isa 2:22 [g] Isa 40:6-7; 1Pe 1:24 **51:13** [h] Isa 17:10 [i] Isa 45:11 [j] Ps 104:2; Isa 48:13 [k] Isa 7:4 **51:14** [l] Isa 49:10 **51:15** [m] Jer 31:35 **51:16** [n] Dt 18:18; Isa 59:21 [o] Ex 33:22

51:17 [p] Isa 52:1 [q] Job 21:20; Rev 14:10; 16:19 [r] Ps 60:3 **51:18** [s] Ps 88:18 [t] Isa 49:21 **51:19** [u] Isa 47:9 [v] Isa 14:30 **51:20** [w] Isa 5:25; Jer 14:16 **51:21** [x] ver 17; Isa 29:9 **51:22** [y] Isa 49:25 [z] ver 17 **51:23** [a] Isa 49:26; Jer 25:15-17, 26, 28; 49:12 [b] Zec 12:2 [c] Jos 10:24

The Cup of the LORD's Wrath

17 Awake, awake![p]
Rise up, Jerusalem,
you who have drunk from the hand of
the LORD
the cup of his wrath,[q]
you who have drained to its dregs
the goblet that makes people
stagger.[r]
18 Among all the children[s] she bore
there was none to guide her;[t]
among all the children she reared
there was none to take her by the
hand.
19 These double calamities[u] have come
upon you—
who can comfort you?—
ruin and destruction, famine[v] and
sword—
who can[a] console you?
20 Your children have fainted;
they lie at every street corner,[w]
like antelope caught in a net.
They are filled with the wrath of the
LORD,
with the rebuke of your God.
21 Therefore hear this, you afflicted one,
made drunk,[x] but not with wine.
22 This is what your Sovereign LORD
says,
your God, who defends[y] his people:
"See, I have taken out of your hand
the cup[z] that made you stagger;
from that cup, the goblet of my wrath,
you will never drink again.
23 I will put it into the hands of your
tormentors,[a]
who said to you,
'Fall prostrate[b] that we may walk[c] on
you.'
And you made your back like the
ground,
like a street to be walked on."

a 19 Dead Sea Scrolls, Septuagint, Vulgate and Syriac; Masoretic Text / *how can I*

51:11 *Those the LORD has rescued will return.* The return of those dispersed through war, plague or famine is important to a nation (see 10:21). An undated Akkadian prophecy states that those scattered from a city will be reassembled. Numerous Mesopotamian kings, from Hammurapi through Marduk-Baladan II, claim restoration of the scattered as part of their legacy.
51:14 *prisoners … dungeon.* See note on 42:7.
51:15 *I am the LORD.* See note on 41:13.
51:18 *children … to take her by the hand.* In Mesopotamia as well as Israel, the eldest son received a larger inheritance than the rest of the children for the purpose of caring for the parents in their old age. The imagery here shows Jerusalem as a parent without children to take care of her in her old age.
51:20 *street corner.* Some cities in the ancient Near East show evidence of intense city planning. The norm, however, especially in the smaller towns, was a very haphazard approach in which there were few real streets but only passageways or open areas on which no homes were built. Most cities and towns featured blocks of housing tracts filled with random alleyways and dead ends with no intersecting routes. The intersections would occur when one emerged into an open square.
51:23 *Fall prostrate that we may walk on you.* Egyptian kings in the early third millennium BC are depicted as trampling over the corpses of defeated enemies. Narmer, possibly the one who unified Egypt, is seen with a mace smashing enemies and stepping over them. Likewise, the Sumerian kings from Lagash are depicted as marching over the dead bodies of their enemies. The tradition of trampling over one's enemies continued on into the first millennium BC in Assyria and Babylonia.

52 Awake, awake,[d] Zion,
clothe yourself with strength![e]
Put on your garments of splendor,[f]
Jerusalem, the holy city.[g]
The uncircumcised and defiled
will not enter you again.[h]
2 Shake off your dust;[i]
rise up, sit enthroned, Jerusalem.
Free yourself from the chains on your
neck,
Daughter Zion, now a captive.

3 For this is what the LORD says:

"You were sold for nothing,[j]
and without money[k] you will be
redeemed."

4 For this is what the Sovereign LORD
says:

"At first my people went down to
Egypt[l] to live;
lately, Assyria has oppressed them.

5 "And now what do I have here?" declares the LORD.

"For my people have been taken away
for nothing,
and those who rule them mock,[a]"
declares the LORD.
"And all day long
my name is constantly blasphemed.[m]
6 Therefore my people will know[n] my
name;
therefore in that day they will know
that it is I who foretold it.
Yes, it is I."

7 How beautiful on the mountains
are the feet of those who bring good
news,[o]
who proclaim peace,[p]
who bring good tidings,
who proclaim salvation,
who say to Zion,
"Your God reigns!"[q]
8 Listen! Your watchmen[r] lift up their
voices;
together they shout for joy.
When the LORD returns to Zion,
they will see it with their own eyes.
9 Burst into songs of joy[s] together,
you ruins[t] of Jerusalem,
for the LORD has comforted his
people,
he has redeemed Jerusalem.[u]
10 The LORD will lay bare his holy arm
in the sight of all the nations,[v]
and all the ends of the earth will see
the salvation[w] of our God.

11 Depart,[x] depart, go out from there!
Touch no unclean thing![y]
Come out from it and be pure,[z]
you who carry the articles of the
LORD's house.
12 But you will not leave in haste[a]
or go in flight;
for the LORD will go before you,[b]
the God of Israel will be your rear
guard.[c]

The Suffering and Glory of the Servant

13 See, my servant[d] will act wisely[b];
he will be raised and lifted up and
highly exalted.[e]
14 Just as there were many who were
appalled at him[c]—
his appearance was so disfigured
beyond that of any human
being
and his form marred beyond human
likeness—
15 so he will sprinkle many nations,[d]
and kings will shut their mouths
because of him.
For what they were not told, they will
see,
and what they have not heard, they
will understand.[f]

53 Who has believed our message[g]
and to whom has the arm of the
LORD been revealed?[h]

52:1 [d] Isa 51:17 [e] Isa 51:9 [f] Ex 28:2, 40; Ps 110:3; Zec 3:4 [g] Ne 11:1; Mt 4:5; Rev 21:2 [h] Na 1:15; Rev 21:27 **52:2** [i] Isa 29:4 **52:3** [j] Ps 44:12 [k] Isa 45:13 **52:4** [l] Ge 46:6 **52:5** [m] Eze 36:20; Ro 2:24* **52:6** [n] Isa 49:23 **52:7** [o] Isa 40:9; Ro 10:15* [p] Na 1:15; Eph 6:15 [q] Ps 93:1 **52:8** [r] Isa 62:6 **52:9** [s] Ps 98:4 [t] Isa 51:3 [u] Isa 48:20 **52:10** [v] Isa 66:18 [w] Ps 98:2-3; Lk 3:6 **52:11** [x] Isa 48:20 [y] Isa 1:16; 2Co 6:17* [z] 2Ti 2:19 **52:12** [a] Ex 12:11 [b] Mic 2:13 [c] Ex 14:19 **52:13** [d] Isa 42:1 [e] Isa 57:15; Php 2:9 **52:15** [f] Ro 15:21*; Eph 3:4-5 **53:1** [g] Ro 10:16* [h] Jn 12:38*

[a] 5 Dead Sea Scrolls and Vulgate; Masoretic Text *wail* [b] 13 Or *will prosper* [c] 14 Hebrew *you* [d] 15 Or *so will many nations be amazed at him* (see also Septuagint)

52:1 *The uncircumcised and defiled will not enter you again.* The culturally or religiously different are often suspect and shunned. In Egypt at the time of the patriarchs, shepherds or those with facial hair were unacceptable. Esarhaddon, after building and dedicating the temple Esharra, claims to have excluded "foreign seed" from the complex. All of these episodes could reflect xenophobia as regards the core of one's national identity.
52:7 *the feet.* While messengers often traveled by other means, some went on foot, a speedy means of transport over short distances (cf. 18:2). In Akkadian, couriers could also be called "runners" and were particularly used in military contexts. *good news.* See note on 40:9.
52:8 *When the LORD returns to Zion.* When a god departs or is removed, it is a time of mourning, but entry into a shrine is a time of celebration, since normality and order are restored. For Isaiah's audience, God is coming back home, his presence being reestablished in sacred space.
52:12 *the LORD will go before.* In the ancient Near East, one did not have to venture out alone but was preceded, guided and aided by one's god. In royal inscriptions the kings report that the gods went out before them. The great gods, including Ishtar, precede the royal army. An Aramaic Tell Dan inscription describes an unnamed ruler's confidence that even though Israel was advancing against him, he had been enthroned by his god Hadad, who went before him. *rear guard.* Isaiah's context is not military; Israel is returning to her covenant land and Yahweh is protecting from the rear as he did in the exodus (Ex 14:19).

ISAIAH 53

Substitutionary Rites

Israelites provided substitutionary atonement for wrongs ordinarily through animal sacrifice. Human substitution is much rarer. One example is the substitute king, known from Mesopotamian texts of the early second through late first millennia BC, with most examples from the time of the Assyrian king Esarhaddon (early seventh century BC). This was precipitated by an omen (generally an eclipse) that predicted the demise of the king. In order to save himself from this fate, he temporarily removed himself from the throne and enthroned an expendable substitute conscripted for that purpose.

In some cases this substitute was someone considered of no significance, and perhaps even mentally or physically impaired. He was then exalted to high status and office for as long as 100 days, though often for a shorter period. The substitute heard recitation of the evil omens, attracting them to himself. During this time, the real king was kept in relative isolation (a virtual exile) and participated in numerous purification rituals. Meanwhile, the substitute was going through the motions of being king and sitting on the throne. He was portrayed as the shepherd (a common title for Mesopotamian kings), but one could understand that he was simply a sheep about to be slaughtered. At the end of the period the substitute was put to death so that the evident design of the gods would be accomplished. The omens had suggested that it was the will of the gods to crush him. As one text puts it, he died to save the king and the crown prince, but his sacrifice is also understood to accomplish redemption for the people. The substitute king and his queen were put to death, carrying the fate of the real king upon himself. He was given a rich state funeral, an offering was made, and exorcism rituals were performed (including washings and sprinklings) so that the omens would be canceled and the days of the king could be prolonged. The substitute king and his queen were laid to rest in a royal tomb with appropriate accompanying ritual. ◆

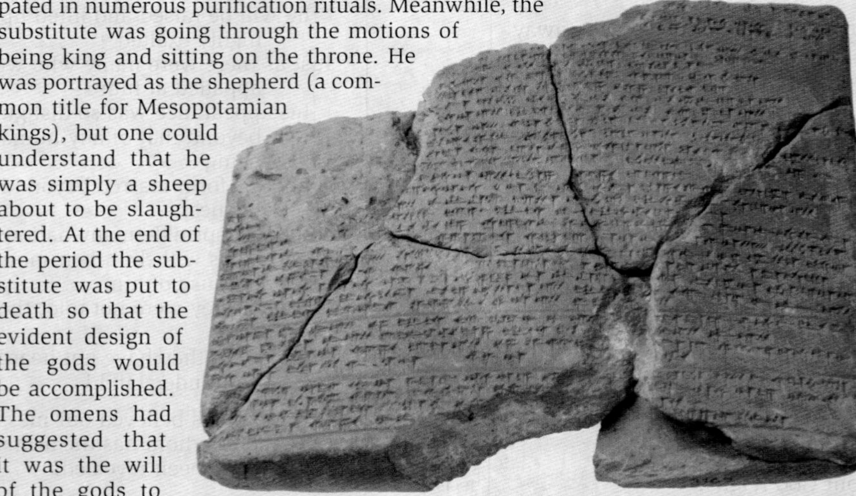

Hittite substitute king text.
Istanbul Archaeological Museum; © Dr. James C. Martin.

[2]He grew up before him like a tender
shoot,
and like a root out of dry ground.
He had no beauty or majesty to attract
us to him,
nothing in his appearance[i] that we
should desire him.
[3]He was despised and rejected by
mankind,
a man of suffering, and familiar with
pain.[j]
Like one from whom people hide their
faces
he was despised,[k] and we held him
in low esteem.

[4]Surely he took up our pain
and bore our suffering,[l]
yet we considered him punished by
God,[m]
stricken by him, and afflicted.
[5]But he was pierced for our
transgressions,[n]
he was crushed for our iniquities;
the punishment that brought us peace
was on him,
and by his wounds we are healed.[o]
[6]We all, like sheep, have gone astray,
each of us has turned to our own way;
and the LORD has laid on him
the iniquity of us all.
[7]He was oppressed and afflicted,
yet he did not open his mouth;[p]
he was led like a lamb to the slaughter,
and as a sheep before its shearers is
silent,
so he did not open his mouth.
[8]By oppression[a] and judgment he was
taken away.
Yet who of his generation protested?
For he was cut off from the land of the
living;[q]
for the transgression[r] of my people
he was punished.[b]
[9]He was assigned a grave with the
wicked,
and with the rich[s] in his death,

53:2 [i]Isa 52:14 **53:3** [j]ver 4, 10; Lk 18:31-33 [k]Ps 22:6; Jn 1:10-11 **53:4** [l]Mt 8:17* [m]Jn 19:7 **53:5** [n]Ro 4:25; 1Co 15:3; Heb 9:28 [o]1Pe 2:24-25 **53:7** [p]Mk 14:61 **53:8** [q]Da 9:26; Ac 8:32-33* [r]ver 12 **53:9** [s]Mt 27:57-60

QUOTATIONS FROM AND REFERENCES TO ISAIAH 53 IN THE NEW TESTAMENT

ISAIAH 53	NEW TESTAMENT
53:1 – 12	Lk 24:27,46; 1Pe 1:11
53:1	Jn 12:38; Ro 10:16
53:2	Mt 2:23
53:3	Mk 9:12
53:4	Mt 8:17; 1Pe 2:24
53:4 – 5	Ro 4:25
53:5	Mt 26:67; 1Pe 2:24
53:5 – 6	Ac 10:43
53:6	1Pe 2:25
53:6 – 7	Jn 1:29
53:7	Mt 26:63; 27:12,14; Mk 14:60 – 61; 15:4 – 5; 1Co 5:7; 1Pe 2:23; Rev 5:6,12; 13:8
53:7 – 8 LXX	Ac 8:32 – 33
53:8 – 9	1Co 15:3
53:9	Mt 26:24; 1Pe 2:22; 1Jn 3:5; Rev 14:5
53:11	Ro 5:19
53:12	Mt 27:38; Lk 22:37; 23:33 – 34; Heb 9:28; 1Pe 2:24

though he had done no violence,[t]
nor was any deceit in his mouth.[u]

[10]Yet it was the LORD's will[v] to crush[w]
him and cause him to suffer,[x]
and though the LORD makes[c] his life
an offering for sin,

[t]Isa 42:1-3 [u]1Pe 2:22* **53:10** [v]Isa 46:10 [w]ver 5 [x]ver 3

[a] 8 Or *From arrest* [b] 8 Or *generation considered / that he was cut off from the land of the living, / that he was punished for the transgression of my people?* [c] 10 Hebrew *though you make*

53:2 *like a tender shoot, and like a root.* Comparing people to plants is known in Egypt, where people are compared to trees who face defoliation and ultimate removal. The Akkadian language compares them to reeds and grass in their frailty and weakness.
53:4 *punished by God, stricken by him.* A blow by one's god is a serious matter. Such an expression was used in the ancient texts for illness or accident. Gods or demons were considered the ones who brought disease or injury, especially ones that came suddenly.
53:5 *by his wounds we are healed.* Ample evidence from the ancient Near East attests to the gods as the ones bringing healing, though it is associated with some gods more than others (e.g., Gula in Mesopotamian traditions). Here the substitutionary equation carries an echo of sympathetic magic whereby wounds to one brings healing to another. Sympathetic magic by wounding, however, is not typical of ancient magic/medicine.
53:7 *like a lamb to the slaughter.* Among common folks, meat was usually eaten only in ritual contexts. Consequently, this metaphor brings to mind a sacrificial scenario. The animals were too valuable alive for them to become a regular part of the diet. In an Aramaic text a metaphor occurs of a man whose enemies seek his life; the man is compared to a lamb fattened for slaughter. *as a sheep before its shearers is silent.* Ancient Near Eastern texts often describe the shearing of sheep, who characteristically underwent their lot in silence. Shearing was done annually in the spring using shears that were invented about 1000 BC. An individual could shear 20 – 30 head of sheep in a day.
53:10 *he will see his offspring and prolong his days.* With the average life expectancy of the common people

he will see his offspring[y] and prolong
his days,
and the will of the LORD will prosper
in his hand.
11 After he has suffered,[z]
he will see the light of life[a] and be
satisfied[b];
by his knowledge[c] my righteous
servant will justify[a] many,
and he will bear their iniquities.
12 Therefore I will give him a portion
among the great,[d][b]
and he will divide the spoils with
the strong,[e]
because he poured out his life unto
death,[c]
and was numbered with the
transgressors.[d]
For he bore the sin of many,
and made intercession for the
transgressors.

The Future Glory of Zion

54 "Sing, barren woman,
you who never bore a child;
burst into song, shout for joy,
you who were never in labor;
because more are the children[e] of the
desolate woman
than of her who has a husband,[f]"
says the LORD.
2 "Enlarge the place of your tent,[g]
stretch your tent curtains wide,
do not hold back;
lengthen your cords,
strengthen your stakes.[h]
3 For you will spread out to the right and
to the left;
your descendants will dispossess
nations
and settle in their desolate[i] cities.
4 "Do not be afraid; you will not be put
to shame.
Do not fear disgrace; you will not be
humiliated.
You will forget the shame of your
youth
and remember no more the reproach[j]
of your widowhood.
5 For your Maker is your husband[k]—
the LORD Almighty is his name—
the Holy One of Israel is your
Redeemer;[l]
he is called the God of all the earth.[m]
6 The LORD will call you back[n]
as if you were a wife deserted[o] and
distressed in spirit—
a wife who married young,
only to be rejected," says your God.
7 "For a brief moment[p] I abandoned you,
but with deep compassion I will
bring you back.[q]
8 In a surge of anger[r]
I hid my face from you for a
moment,
but with everlasting kindness[s]
I will have compassion on you,"
says the LORD your Redeemer.
9 "To me this is like the days of Noah,
when I swore that the waters of
Noah would never again cover
the earth.[t]
So now I have sworn not to be angry[u]
with you,
never to rebuke you again.
10 Though the mountains be shaken[v]
and the hills be removed,
yet my unfailing love for you will not
be shaken[w]
nor my covenant[x] of peace be
removed,"
says the LORD, who has compassion[y]
on you.
11 "Afflicted[z] city, lashed by storms[a] and
not comforted,[b]
I will rebuild you with stones of
turquoise,[f][c]
your foundations[d] with lapis lazuli.

53:10 [y] Ps 22:30 **53:11** [z] Jn 10:14-18 [a] Ro 5:18-19 **53:12** [b] Php 2:9 [c] Mt 26:28, 38, 39, 42 [d] Mk 15:27*; Lk 22:37*; 23:32 **54:1** [e] Isa 49:20 [f] 1Sa 2:5; Gal 4:27* **54:2** [g] Isa 49:19-20 [h] Ex 35:18; 39:40 **54:3** [i] Isa 49:19
54:4 [j] Isa 51:7 **54:5** [k] Jer 3:14 [l] Isa 48:17 [m] Isa 6:3 **54:6** [n] Isa 49:14-21 [o] Isa 50:1-2; 62:4, 12 **54:7** [p] Isa 26:20 [q] Isa 49:18 **54:8** [r] Isa 60:10 [s] ver 10 **54:9** [t] Ge 8:21 [u] Isa 12:1 **54:10** [v] Ps 46:2 [w] Isa 51:6 [x] Ps 89:34 [y] ver 8 **54:11** [z] Isa 14:32 [a] Isa 28:2; 29:6 [b] Isa 51:19 [c] 1Ch 29:2; Rev 21:18 [d] Isa 28:16; Rev 21:19-20

[a] *11* Dead Sea Scrolls (see also Septuagint); Masoretic Text does not have *the light of life.* [b] *11* Or (with Masoretic Text) [11] *He will see the fruit of his suffering / and will be satisfied* [c] *11* Or *by knowledge of him* [d] *12* Or *many* [e] *12* Or *numerous* [f] *11* The meaning of the Hebrew for this word is uncertain.

probably less than 40 years, a blessing would be to have a longer life (65:20) and offspring to provide support in one's infirmity. Esarhaddon wishes a similar blessing on any who might in the future repair the temple he rebuilt. The seventh-century BC Aramaic tomb inscription of the priest Si'gabbar indicates that this blessing can be deserved by righteous behavior.

54:1 *barren woman.* Children ensured the continuity of the clan and family and provided support for aging parents. Fertility was a matter of pride, while a barren woman was of lower socioeconomic status and thus felt shame, since it was believed that God/the gods opened or closed the womb as a response of favor or disfavor. See notes on Ge 11:30; 16:2.

54:2 *tent.* As portable accommodation, they were often used by nomads or people on the move, while settled folk dwelt in more permanent houses. The earliest listed kings in the Assyrian King List are designated as "those who live in tents." Here the tent does not symbolize transience and hardship but rather that which is easily expandable, allowing gathered abundance.

54:4 *reproach of your widowhood.* Widows were marginalized in ancient Near Eastern society, having no one to provide for and protect them and placing them low in the socioeconomic hierarchy. See note on Dt 24:17.

54:11 *turquoise.* An alternate translation is "antimony," which was used for a mortar, especially for mosaics. *lapis lazuli.* A beautiful blue stone that was highly valued in the ancient world. In a work referred to as the Uruk Prophecy, it is said that a future king will build the gates of Uruk of lapis lazuli.

12 I will make your battlements of rubies,
your gates of sparkling jewels,
and all your walls of precious stones.
13 All your children will be taught by the
LORD,[e]
and great will be their peace.[f]
14 In righteousness you will be
established:
Tyranny[g] will be far from you;
you will have nothing to fear.
Terror will be far removed;
it will not come near you.
15 If anyone does attack you, it will not
be my doing;
whoever attacks you will surrender[h]
to you.
16 "See, it is I who created the blacksmith
who fans the coals into flame
and forges a weapon fit for its work.
And it is I who have created the
destroyer to wreak havoc;
17 no weapon forged against you will
prevail,[i]
and you will refute[j] every tongue
that accuses you.
This is the heritage of the servants of
the LORD,
and this is their vindication from me,"
declares the LORD.

Invitation to the Thirsty

55 "Come, all you who are thirsty,[k]
come to the waters;
and you who have no money,
come, buy[l] and eat!
Come, buy wine and milk[m]
without money and without cost.[n]
2 Why spend money on what is not
bread,
and your labor on what does not
satisfy?[o]
Listen, listen to me, and eat what is
good,[p]
and you will delight in the richest of
fare.
3 Give ear and come to me;
listen, that you may live.[q]

54:13 [e] Jn 6:45* [f] Isa 48:18 **54:14** [g] Isa 9:4 **54:15** [h] Isa 41:11-16 **54:17** [i] Isa 29:8 [j] Isa 45:24-25 **55:1** [k] Jn 4:14; 7:37 [l] La 5:4; Mt 13:44; Rev 3:18 [m] SS 5:1 [n] Hos 14:4; Mt 10:8; Rev 21:6 **55:2** [o] Ps 22:26; Ecc 6:2; Hos 8:7 [p] Isa 1:19 **55:3** [q] Lev 18:5; Ro 10:5

[r] Isa 61:8 [s] Isa 54:8 [t] Ac 13:34* **55:4** [u] Jer 30:9; Eze 34:23-24 **55:5** [v] Isa 49:6 [w] Isa 60:9 **55:6** [x] Ps 32:6; Isa 49:8; 2Co 6:1-2 [y] Isa 65:24 **55:7** [z] Isa 32:7; 59:7 [a] Isa 44:22 [b] Isa 54:10 [c] Isa 1:18; 40:2 **55:8** [d] Isa 53:6 **55:9** [e] Ps 103:11 **55:10** [f] Isa 30:23 [g] 2Co 9:10 **55:11** [h] Isa 45:23 [i] Isa 44:26 **55:12** [j] Isa 54:10, 13

I will make an everlasting covenant[r]
with you,
my faithful love[s] promised to David.[t]
4 See, I have made him a witness to the
peoples,
a ruler and commander[u] of the
peoples.
5 Surely you will summon nations[v] you
know not,
and nations you do not know will
come running to you,
because of the LORD your God,
the Holy One of Israel,
for he has endowed you with
splendor."[w]

6 Seek the LORD while he may be found;[x]
call[y] on him while he is near.
7 Let the wicked forsake their ways
and the unrighteous their thoughts.[z]
Let them turn[a] to the LORD, and he will
have mercy[b] on them,
and to our God, for he will freely
pardon.[c]

8 "For my thoughts are not your
thoughts,
neither are your ways my ways,"[d]
declares the LORD.
9 "As the heavens are higher than the
earth,[e]
so are my ways higher than your ways
and my thoughts than your
thoughts.
10 As the rain[f] and the snow
come down from heaven,
and do not return to it
without watering the earth
and making it bud and flourish,
so that it yields seed for the sower
and bread for the eater,[g]
11 so is my word that goes out from my
mouth:
It will not return to me empty,[h]
but will accomplish what I desire
and achieve the purpose[i] for which
I sent it.
12 You will go out in joy
and be led forth in peace;[j]

54:12 *battlements.* Lit. "suns"; it most likely refers to the round, burnished shields used as crenellations along the top of the towers that flanked the gate. These are visible along the entire wall in Sennacherib's portrayal of the fortifications at Lachish (see note on Ps 84:11). *rubies.* This translation is a guess; others support "jasper." The Hebrew word is used only here and in Eze 27:16, where it is listed among exports from Aram. *gates.* Red burnished copper was popular for gates and would be plausible for these sun-like shields. The stonework of the gate area features some sort of sparkling stone. *walls.* The Hebrew is a technical term for low walls that lined the inside passage of the gateway (Eze 40:12). They are described here as being made of "precious stones," i.e., high quality stonework, perhaps with mosaics.

54:17 *servants of the LORD.* See note on 42:19.

55:8–9 In the ancient Near East the gods are often conceived of as much like people — having the same desires and whims. This is more than anthropomorphism in which the gods are thought of as having hands, eyes and feet. In Israel, Yahweh is portrayed anthropomorphically but does not have the same desires or whims as humans. Those issues aside, however, these verses talk about the way that Yahweh has plans and intentions far beyond human imagination. This is also expressed in limited ways in ancient Near Eastern texts that talk about the mind of the god as remote and impenetrable.

55:11 *my word … will not return to me empty.* See note on Ps 18:30.

the mountains and hills
will burst into song before you,
and all the trees[k] of the field
will clap their hands.[l]
13 Instead of the thornbush will grow the juniper,
and instead of briers[m] the myrtle[n] will grow.
This will be for the LORD's renown,[o]
for an everlasting sign,
that will endure forever."

Salvation for Others

56 This is what the LORD says:

"Maintain justice[p]
and do what is right,
for my salvation[q] is close at hand
and my righteousness will soon be revealed.
2 Blessed[r] is the one who does this —
the person who holds it fast,
who keeps the Sabbath[s] without desecrating it,
and keeps their hands from doing any evil."

3 Let no foreigner who is bound to the LORD say,
"The LORD will surely exclude me from his people."
And let no eunuch[t] complain,
"I am only a dry tree."

4 For this is what the LORD says:

"To the eunuchs who keep my Sabbaths,
who choose what pleases me
and hold fast to my covenant —
5 to them I will give within my temple and its walls[u]
a memorial and a name
better than sons and daughters;
I will give them an everlasting name
that will endure forever.[v]

6 And foreigners who bind themselves to the LORD
to minister[w] to him,
to love the name of the LORD,
and to be his servants,
all who keep the Sabbath[x] without desecrating it
and who hold fast to my covenant —
7 these I will bring to my holy mountain[y]
and give them joy in my house of prayer.
Their burnt offerings and sacrifices[z]
will be accepted on my altar;
for my house will be called
a house of prayer for all nations."[a][b]
8 The Sovereign LORD declares —
he who gathers the exiles of Israel:
"I will gather[c] still others to them
besides those already gathered."

God's Accusation Against the Wicked

9 Come, all you beasts of the field,[d]
come and devour, all you beasts of the forest!
10 Israel's watchmen[e] are blind,
they all lack knowledge;
they are all mute dogs,
they cannot bark;
they lie around and dream,
they love to sleep.[f]
11 They are dogs with mighty appetites;
they never have enough.
They are shepherds[g] who lack understanding;[h]
they all turn to their own way,
they seek their own gain.[i]
12 "Come," each one cries, "let me get wine!
Let us drink our fill of beer!
And tomorrow will be like today,
or even far better."[j]

57 The righteous perish,[k]
and no one takes it to heart;[l]
the devout are taken away,
and no one understands

55:12 [k] 1Ch 16:33 [l] Ps 98:8 **55:13** [m] Isa 5:6 [n] Isa 41:19 [o] Isa 63:12 **56:1** [p] Isa 1:17 [q] Ps 85:9 **56:2** [r] Ps 119:2 [s] Ex 20:8, 10; Isa 58:13 **56:3** [t] Jer 38:7 *fn*; Ac 8:27 **56:5** [u] Isa 26:1; 60:18 [v] Isa 48:19; 55:13
56:6 [w] Isa 60:7, 10; 61:5 [x] ver 2, 4 **56:7** [y] Isa 2:2 [z] Ro 12:1; Heb 13:15 [a] Mt 21:13*; Lk 19:46* [b] Mk 11:17* **56:8** [c] Isa 11:12; 60:3-11; Jn 10:16 **56:9** [d] Isa 18:6; Jer 12:9 **56:10** [e] Eze 3:17 [f] Na 3:18 **56:11** [g] Eze 34:2 [h] Isa 1:3 [i] Isa 57:17; Eze 13:19; Mic 3:11 **56:12** [j] Ps 10:6; Lk 12:18-19 **57:1** [k] Ps 12:1 [l] Isa 42:25

56:2 *Sabbath.* See note on 1:13.
56:4 *eunuchs.* This Hebrew term can at times refer simply to a court official, but it later came to refer specifically to eunuchs. Eunuchs were highly valued in government service in many varied roles during the Neo-Assyrian and Neo-Babylonian periods. The great demand for eunuchs led to young boys being included in the tribute paid to Persia so that they could be castrated and trained for government service. They had no families to distract them from their service. They were often entrusted with the care and supervision of the royal harem. Having been castrated, they posed no threat to the women of the harem and could not engender children by the harem women, children who might be mistaken for royal heirs. Eunuchs would be less likely to become involved in conspiracies because they would have no heirs to put on the throne. Assyria, Urartu and Media all made use of eunuchs in government offices.
56:9 *come and devour, all you beasts.* Wild beasts were a constant source of fear for city dwellers throughout the ancient Near East. Of course, in this passage wild beasts are a metaphor for human "beasts" who plunder and pillage city dwellers. In Assyrian texts and reliefs of this period the kings are seen hunting lions to symbolically rid the city of the scourge of wild beasts. In one case it has been suggested that the killing of 18 lions represents the 18 gates of Nineveh and the roads leading out of them. When kings killed lions in their staged lion hunts, it also symbolized their triumph over their human enemies.
56:10 *mute dogs.* In Israel dogs were held in contempt. Here they are even more useless, being unable even to warn by barking. See notes on 1Sa 24:14; 2Sa 3:8.
57:1 *heart.* Cognition and emotions are metaphorically associated with different body parts in various cultures. In Israel, strong affections are often associated with the kidneys and fear with the bowels, while particularly serious reflection and rumination take place in the heart. Such

that the righteous are taken away
to be spared from evil.[m]
2 Those who walk uprightly[n]
enter into peace;
they find rest as they lie in death.
3 "But you — come here, you children of
a sorceress,
you offspring of adulterers[o] and
prostitutes![p]
4 Who are you mocking?
At whom do you sneer
and stick out your tongue?
Are you not a brood of rebels,
the offspring of liars?
5 You burn with lust among the oaks
and under every spreading tree;[q]
you sacrifice your children[r] in the
ravines
and under the overhanging crags.
6 The idols[s] among the smooth stones of
the ravines are your portion;
indeed, they are your lot.
Yes, to them you have poured out
drink offerings[t]
and offered grain offerings.
In view of all this, should I relent?[u]
7 You have made your bed on a high and
lofty hill;[v]
there you went up to offer your
sacrifices.
8 Behind your doors and your doorposts
you have put your pagan symbols.
Forsaking me, you uncovered your bed,
you climbed into it and opened it wide;
you made a pact with those whose
beds you love,[w]
and you looked with lust on their
naked bodies.[x]
9 You went to Molek[a] with olive oil
and increased your perfumes.
You sent your ambassadors[b][y] far away;
you descended to the very realm of
the dead!

57:1 [m] 2Ki 22:20 **57:2** [n] Isa 26:7 **57:3** [o] Mt 16:4 [p] Isa 1:21 **57:5** [q] 2Ki 16:4 [r] Lev 18:21; Ps 106:37-38; Eze 16:20 **57:6** [s] Jer 3:9 [t] Jer 7:18 [u] Jer 5:9,29; 9:9 **57:7** [v] Jer 3:6; Eze 16:16 **57:8** [w] Eze 16:26; 23:7 [x] Eze 23:18 **57:9** [y] Eze 23:16,40

[a] 9 Or *to the king* [b] 9 Or *idols*

reflection and meditation are associated with the heart in Mesopotamia as well. See note on Pr 4:23. *the righteous are taken away to be spared from evil.* This verse implies that there has been a complete overturning in society, since the righteous perish as a result of disorder and unrest. A number of Babylonian wisdom texts discuss this theme. "The Babylonian Theodicy" (a text similar to the Biblical book of Job) complains that the just man suffers from all kinds of injustice, while the evil man is free to do his evil activities. The writer also complains that his personal god has done nothing to alleviate the problem. This verse offers the explanation that the righteous are not being punished with death but are being spared from evil times.

57:2 *Those who walk uprightly ... lie in death.* This offers not a hope of heaven but an escape from turmoil. Even Sheol is to be preferred over the wicked state of affairs on earth. See the articles "Death and Sheol," p. 833; "Death and the Underworld," p. 907.

57:3 *sorceress.* See note on 2:6. *adulterers.* See notes on Ex 20:14; Dt 22:22. *prostitutes.* See notes on Ge 38:15; Jdg 11:1.

57:5 *oaks ... spreading tree.* See notes on Ge 12:6; Dt 12:2. *you sacrifice your children.* See notes on Lev 20:2; 1Ki 11:5; 2Ki 3:27; 16:3; Jer 7:31.

57:6 *drink offerings ... grain offerings.* Because of a well-developed ancestor cult that pervaded much of the ancient Near East (evident, e.g., in the emphasis on the role of the male heir to care for the father's shrine in Ugaritic documents), the dead were considered to have some power to affect the living. It was believed that if libations were poured out on behalf of the dead ancestors, their spirits would then offer protection and help to those still living. In Babylon the disembodied spirit (*utukki*) or the ghost (*etemmu*) could become very dangerous if not cared for and were often the objects of incantations. Proper care for the dead would begin with proper burial and would continue with ongoing gifts and honor of the memory and name of the deceased. The firstborn was responsible for maintaining this ancestor worship and therefore inherited the family gods (often images of deceased ancestors). Such care would have been based on a belief that the spirits of the dead could communicate and had information on the future that could be of use to the living (e.g., Saul's consultation of the witch of Endor in 1Sa 28 [see notes on 1Sa 28:3,7,13; see also the article "Consulting a 'Spirit,'" p. 508]). These spirits were consulted through the efforts of priests, mediums and necromancers. This could be a dangerous practice since some spirits were considered demons and could cause great harm. While it is difficult to totally reconstruct Israelite beliefs about deceased ancestors and the afterlife, it seems clear that prior to the exile there existed a cult of the dead or ancestral worship. This is evidenced by archaeological remains: (1) standing stones (*matstsebah*), (2) channels cut into tombs for the deposit of food and drink offerings for the dead (see Dt 26:14; Ps 106:28 and notes), and (3) the importance placed on family tombs (e.g., the ancestral tomb for Abraham and his descendants at Hebron) and mourning rituals performed at these tombs (see Jer 16:5 – 7). The local and family ancestral cults were condemned by the prophets and the law.

57:7 *You have made your bed on a high and lofty hill.* High hills were where shrines were established for other deities. The reference to beds could refer to the idea that Israel's worship of these gods would be metaphorically an act of adultery against Yahweh. It is also possible that the beds refer to sexual acts performed ritually at these shrines. The sexual imagery in the following verse could support either of those possibilities.

57:8 *pagan symbols.* What these were is uncertain. They may have been symbols of the household gods (fertility figurines?) or phallic symbols of fertility. This is likely because the last line of this verse also refers to male genitalia ("naked bodies"). The Israelites also had a memorial behind their door consisting of a metal container with a portion of Scripture inside (see Dt 6:9 and note; 11:20).

57:9 *Molek.* See notes on 1Ki 11:5; Jer 7:31. *olive oil and ... perfumes.* Their use is uncertain. The olive oil may have been offerings, while the perfumes were to kindle incense offering. Another suggestion is that they were used to anoint the children that were being offered to Molek. *ambassadors ... to the very realm of the dead.* These ambassadors are those who practice necromancy, the consultation of the dead on behalf of the living. The ambassadors probably went to the shrines where the powers of the netherworld (Sheol) were venerated to seek their will by

Egyptian stele with offerings and libation presented before the god. See note on Isa 57:6.

Kim Walton. The Oriental Institute Museum, the University of Chicago.

10 You wearied yourself by such going
about,
but you would not say, 'It is
hopeless.'[z]
You found renewal of your strength,
and so you did not faint.

11 "Whom have you so dreaded and
feared[a]
that you have not been true to me,
and have neither remembered[b] me
nor taken this to heart?
Is it not because I have long been
silent[c]
that you do not fear me?
12 I will expose your righteousness and
your works,[d]
and they will not benefit you.
13 When you cry out[e] for help,
let your collection of idols save you!
The wind will carry all of them off,
a mere breath will blow them away.
But whoever takes refuge in me
will inherit the land[f]
and possess my holy mountain."[g]

57:10 [z] Jer 2:25; 18:12 **57:11** [a] Pr 29:25 [b] Jer 2:32; 3:21 [c] Ps 50:21 **57:12** [d] Isa 29:15; Mic 3:2-4,8 **57:13** [e] Jer 22:20; 30:15 [f] Ps 37:9 [g] Isa 65:9-11

57:14 [h] Isa 62:10; Jer 18:15 **57:15** [i] Isa 52:13 [j] Dt 33:27 [k] Ps 147:3 [l] Ps 34:18; 51:17; Isa 66:2 [m] Isa 61:1 **57:16** [n] Ps 85:5; 103:9; Mic 7:18 **57:17** [o] Isa 56:11 [p] Isa 1:4 **57:18** [q] Isa 30:26 [r] Isa 61:1-3 **57:19** [s] Isa 6:7; Heb 13:15 [t] Eph 2:17 [u] Ac 2:39

Comfort for the Contrite

14 And it will be said:

"Build up, build up, prepare the
road!
Remove the obstacles out of the way
of my people."[h]
15 For this is what the high and exalted[i]
One says—
he who lives forever,[j] whose name is
holy:
"I live in a high and holy place,
but also with the one who is
contrite[k] and lowly in spirit,[l]
to revive the spirit of the lowly
and to revive the heart of the
contrite.[m]
16 I will not accuse them forever,
nor will I always be angry,[n]
for then they would faint away because
of me—
the very people I have created.
17 I was enraged by their sinful greed;[o]
I punished them, and hid my face in
anger,
yet they kept on in their willful
ways.[p]
18 I have seen their ways, but I will heal[q]
them;
I will guide them and restore
comfort[r] to Israel's mourners,
19 creating praise on their lips.[s]
Peace, peace,[t] to those far and near,"[u]
says the LORD. "And I will heal
them."
20 But the wicked[v] are like the tossing
sea,
which cannot rest,
whose waves cast up mire and mud.
21 "There is no peace,"[w] says my God,
"for the wicked."[x]

True Fasting

58 "Shout it aloud,[y] do not hold
back.
Raise your voice like a trumpet.
Declare to my people their rebellion[z]
and to the descendants of Jacob
their sins.
2 For day after day they seek[a] me out;
they seem eager to know my ways,
as if they were a nation that does what
is right

57:20 [v] Job 18:5-21 **57:21** [w] Isa 59:8 [x] Isa 48:22 **58:1** [y] Isa 40:6 [z] Isa 48:8 **58:2** [a] Isa 48:1; Titus 1:16; Jas 4:8

oracular means. Molek was the god of the netherworld. See the articles "Death and Sheol," p. 833; "Death and the Underworld," p. 907.
57:13 *collection of idols.* In Ugaritic literature the term that occurs here is used to make reference to deceased spirits.
57:14 *prepare the road.* See note on 40:3.
57:20 *mire.* The Hebrew term is used only here in the OT. In Akkadian the related term designates "excrement, spittle, vomit," making the results of the work of the wicked even more abhorrent.
58:2 *seek me out.* Messages from the gods were sought through oracles (see 44:25 and note), which could come about through dreams or divination (see note on 2:6). The Israelites are seeking decisions from Yahweh that

and has not forsaken the commands
of its God.
They ask me for just decisions
and seem eager for God to come
near[b] them.
3 'Why have we fasted,'[c] they say,
'and you have not seen it?
Why have we humbled ourselves,
and you have not noticed?'[d]

"Yet on the day of your fasting, you do
as you please[e]
and exploit all your workers.
4 Your fasting ends in quarreling and
strife,[f]
and in striking each other with
wicked fists.
You cannot fast as you do today
and expect your voice to be heard[g]
on high.
5 Is this the kind of fast[h] I have chosen,
only a day for people to humble[i]
themselves?
Is it only for bowing one's head like a
reed
and for lying in sackcloth and
ashes?[j]
Is that what you call a fast,
a day acceptable to the LORD?

6 "Is not this the kind of fasting I have
chosen:
to loose the chains of injustice[k]
and untie the cords of the yoke,
to set the oppressed[l] free
and break every yoke?
7 Is it not to share your food with the
hungry[m]
and to provide the poor wanderer
with shelter[n]—
when you see the naked, to clothe[o]
them,
and not to turn away from your own
flesh and blood?[p]
8 Then your light will break forth like
the dawn,[q]

58:2 [b] Isa 29:13
58:3 [c] Lev 16:29 [d] Mal 3:14 [e] Isa 22:13; Zec 7:5-6
58:4 [f] 1Ki 21:9-13; Isa 59:6 [g] Isa 59:2
58:5 [h] Zec 7:5 [i] 1Ki 21:27 [j] Job 2:8
58:6 [k] Ne 5:10-11 [l] Jer 34:9
58:7 [m] Eze 18:16; Lk 3:11 [n] Isa 16:4; Heb 13:2 [o] Job 31:19-20; Mt 25:36 [p] Ge 29:14; Lk 10:31-32
58:8 [q] Job 11:17 [r] Isa 30:26 [s] Ex 14:19
58:9 [t] Ps 50:15 [u] Pr 6:13 [v] Ps 12:2; Isa 59:13
58:10 [w] Dt 15:7-8 [x] Isa 42:16 [y] Job 11:17
58:11 [z] Ps 107:9 [a] SS 4:15 [b] Jn 4:14
58:12 [c] Isa 49:8 [d] Isa 44:28
58:13 [e] Isa 56:2 [f] Ps 84:2, 10

and your healing[r] will quickly
appear;
then your righteousness[a] will go before
you,
and the glory of the LORD will be
your rear guard.[s]
9 Then you will call,[t] and the LORD will
answer;
you will cry for help, and he will
say: Here am I.

"If you do away with the yoke of
oppression,
with the pointing finger[u] and
malicious talk,[v]
10 and if you spend yourselves in behalf
of the hungry
and satisfy the needs of the
oppressed,[w]
then your light[x] will rise in the
darkness,
and your night will become like the
noonday.[y]
11 The LORD will guide you always;
he will satisfy your needs[z] in a sun-
scorched land
and will strengthen your frame.
You will be like a well-watered
garden,[a]
like a spring[b] whose waters never
fail.
12 Your people will rebuild the ancient
ruins[c]
and will raise up the age-old
foundations;[d]
you will be called Repairer of Broken
Walls,
Restorer of Streets with Dwellings.

13 "If you keep your feet from breaking
the Sabbath[e]
and from doing as you please on my
holy day,
if you call the Sabbath a delight[f]
and the LORD's holy day honorable,

[a] 8 Or *your righteous One*

---

would result in their receiving justice at the hands of their oppressors. These will come for Israel when they live justly so that Yahweh would be favorably disposed toward them. In the ancient Near East it was considered an expression of disfavor when the gods did not answer requests for oracles (see also 1Sa 28:6).

58:4 *fasting.* Abstention from food; it is a much rarer practice as religious ritual in ancient Near Eastern texts than in the OT. The Old Kingdom Prophecies of Neferti associate it with grief. Zoroastrianism goes as far as to condemn fasting as sinful since it weakens the body. Isaiah here condemns its misuse, not the practice per se.

58:9 *the pointing finger.* In the ancient world, pointing the finger was involved in a formal accusation (as in the Code of Hammurapi). The omen literature attaches to the gesture the power of a curse. Here it is indicative of malevolent slander.

58:12 *rebuild the ancient ruins.* See notes on 44:28; 49:8.

58:13 *Sabbath.* According to later rabbinic writings, the Sabbath in the postexilic period took on the idea of laying aside the day to worship God. The Sabbath became one of the primary means of showing loyalty to God and his statutes. In a Babylonian wisdom hymn the worshiper claims that the day of worshiping the god was a pleasure to him, a delight and joy to make music to honor the deity. The Sabbath observation has no known parallel in any of the cultures of the ancient Near East and is distinctive in that it is independent of any of the patterns or rhythms of nature; i.e., it was not celebrated on certain days of the month and was not linked to the cycles of the moon or to any other cycle of nature; it was simply observed every seventh day. Though Mesopotamians did not divide time into seven-day periods, there were particular days of the month that in their estimation were considered unlucky; these unlucky days were often seven days apart (i.e., the 7th day of the month, the 14th day of the month, etc.). In

and if you honor it by not going your
own way
and not doing as you please or
speaking idle words,
14 then you will find your joy[g] in the
LORD,
and I will cause you to ride in
triumph on the heights[h] of the
land
and to feast on the inheritance of
your father Jacob."
For the mouth of the LORD
has spoken.[i]

Sin, Confession and Redemption

59 Surely the arm of the LORD is not
too short[j] to save,
nor his ear too dull to hear.[k]
2 But your iniquities have separated
you from your God;
your sins have hidden his face from
you,
so that he will not hear.[l]
3 For your hands are stained with
blood,[m]
your fingers with guilt.
Your lips have spoken falsely,
and your tongue mutters wicked
things.
4 No one calls for justice;
no one pleads a case with integrity.
They rely on empty arguments, they
utter lies;
they conceive trouble and give birth
to evil.[n]
5 They hatch the eggs of vipers
and spin a spider's web.[o]
Whoever eats their eggs will die,
and when one is broken, an adder is
hatched.
6 Their cobwebs are useless for clothing;
they cannot cover themselves with
what they make.[p]
Their deeds are evil deeds,
and acts of violence[q] are in their
hands.
7 Their feet rush into sin;
they are swift to shed innocent blood.[r]
They pursue evil schemes;[s]
acts of violence mark their ways.[t]
8 The way of peace they do not know;
there is no justice in their paths.

58:14 [g] Job 22:26 [h] Dt 32:13 [i] Isa 1:20 **59:1** [j] Nu 11:23; Isa 50:2 [k] Isa 58:9; 65:24 **59:2** [l] Isa 1:15; 58:4 **59:3** [m] Isa 1:15 **59:4** [n] Job 15:35; Ps 7:14 **59:5** [o] Job 8:14 **59:6** [p] Isa 28:20 [q] Isa 58:4 **59:7** [r] Pr 6:17 [s] Mk 7:21-22 [t] Ro 3:15-17*

59:8 [u] Isa 57:21; Lk 1:79 **59:9** [v] Isa 5:30; 8:20 **59:10** [w] Dt 28:29 [x] Isa 8:15 [y] La 3:6 **59:11** [z] Isa 38:14; Eze 7:16 **59:12** [a] Ezr 9:6 [b] Isa 3:9 **59:13** [c] Pr 30:9; Mt 10:33; Titus 1:16 [d] Isa 5:7 [e] Mk 7:21-22 **59:14** [f] Isa 1:21 [g] Isa 48:1 **59:16** [h] Isa 41:28 [i] Ps 98:1; Isa 63:5 **59:17** [j] Eph 6:14

They have turned them into crooked
roads;
no one who walks along them will
know peace.[u]
9 So justice is far from us,
and righteousness does not reach us.
We look for light, but all is darkness;[v]
for brightness, but we walk in deep
shadows.
10 Like the blind[w] we grope along the
wall,
feeling our way like people without
eyes.
At midday we stumble[x] as if it were
twilight;
among the strong, we are like the
dead.[y]
11 We all growl like bears;
we moan mournfully like doves.[z]
We look for justice, but find none;
for deliverance, but it is far away.
12 For our offenses[a] are many in your sight,
and our sins testify[b] against us.
Our offenses are ever with us,
and we acknowledge our iniquities:
13 rebellion and treachery against the
LORD,
turning our backs[c] on our God,
inciting revolt and oppression,[d]
uttering lies[e] our hearts have
conceived.
14 So justice is driven back,
and righteousness[f] stands at a
distance;
truth[g] has stumbled in the streets,
honesty cannot enter.
15 Truth is nowhere to be found,
and whoever shuns evil becomes a
prey.
The LORD looked and was displeased
that there was no justice.
16 He saw that there was no one,[h]
he was appalled that there was no
one to intervene;
so his own arm achieved salvation[i] for
him,
and his own righteousness sustained
him.
17 He put on righteousness as his
breastplate,[j]

---

addition, a similar term was used in Babylonian texts as a full-moon day, when the king officiated at rites of reconciliation with deity, but it was not a work-free day and has little in common with the Israelite Sabbath. The legislation does not require rest as much as it stipulates cessation, interrupting the normal activities of one's occupation.
58:14 *ride … on the heights of the land.* Cities were typically built on hills because of their natural defensibility, and armies chose hills as strategic points of control. The metaphor of riding on the heights is therefore one that speaks of victory and security.

59:17 *breastplate … helmet.* Yahweh the warrior takes a stand against his people's enemies. This metaphor plays on his clothing, which was also worn by a warrior for both battle and covering. Such items are richly portrayed in reliefs and other iconography from the ancient Near East. When Marduk prepares for battle with Tiamat in the *Enuma Elish,* he is equipped mostly with weapons for attack rather than with the defensive gear referred to here. But he is said to be clothed with a cloak of awesome armor and crowned with a terrible radiance. Stone sculptures of the gods doing battle sometimes portray them

and the helmet[k] of salvation on his
head;
he put on the garments[l] of vengeance
and wrapped himself in zeal[m] as in a
cloak.
18 According to what they have done,
so will he repay
wrath to his enemies
and retribution to his foes;
he will repay the islands their due.
19 From the west,[n] people will fear the
name of the LORD,
and from the rising of the sun,[o] they
will revere his glory.
For he will come like a pent-up flood
that the breath of the LORD drives
along.[a]

20 "The Redeemer will come to Zion,
to those in Jacob who repent of their
sins,"[p]
declares the LORD.

21 "As for me, this is my covenant with
them," says the LORD. "My Spirit,[q] who is
on you, will not depart from you, and my
words that I have put in your mouth will
always be on your lips, on the lips of your
children and on the lips of their descendants — from this time on and forever,"
says the LORD.

The Glory of Zion

60 "Arise,[r] shine, for your light[s] has
come,
and the glory of the LORD rises upon
you.
2 See, darkness covers the earth
and thick darkness[t] is over the peoples,
but the LORD rises upon you
and his glory appears over you.
3 Nations[u] will come to your light,
and kings[v] to the brightness of your
dawn.

4 "Lift up your eyes and look about you:
All assemble[w] and come to you;
your sons come from afar,
and your daughters[x] are carried on
the hip.[y]
5 Then you will look and be radiant,
your heart will throb and swell with
joy;
the wealth on the seas will be brought
to you,
to you the riches of the nations will
come.
6 Herds of camels will cover your land,
young camels of Midian[z] and
Ephah.[a]
And all from Sheba[b] will come,
bearing gold and incense[c]
and proclaiming the praise[d] of the
LORD.
7 All Kedar's[e] flocks will be gathered to
you,
the rams of Nebaioth will serve you;
they will be accepted as offerings on
my altar,
and I will adorn my glorious temple.[f]

8 "Who are these[g] that fly along like
clouds,
like doves to their nests?
9 Surely the islands[h] look to me;
in the lead are the ships of Tarshish,[b][i]
bringing[j] your children from afar,
with their silver and gold,
to the honor of the LORD your God,
the Holy One of Israel,
for he has endowed you with
splendor.[k]

10 "Foreigners[l] will rebuild your walls,
and their kings[m] will serve you.
Though in anger I struck you,
in favor I will show you
compassion.[n]
11 Your gates[o] will always stand open,
they will never be shut, day or night,

59:17 [k]Eph 6:17; 1Th 5:8 [l]Isa 63:3 [m]Isa 9:7 **59:19** [n]Isa 49:12 [o]Ps 113:3 **59:20** [p]Ac 2:38-39; Ro 11:26-27* **59:21** [q]Isa 11:2; 44:3 **60:1** [r]Isa 52:2 [s]Eph 5:14 **60:2** [t]Jer 13:16; Col 1:13 **60:3** [u]Isa 45:14; Rev 21:24 [v]Isa 49:23 **60:4** [w]Isa 11:12 [x]Isa 43:6 [y]Isa 49:20-22 **60:6** [z]Ge 25:2 [a]Ge 25:4 [b]Ps 72:10 [c]Isa 43:23; Mt 2:11 [d]Isa 42:10 **60:7** [e]Ge 25:13 [f]ver 13; Hag 2:3, 7, 9 **60:8** [g]Isa 49:21 **60:9** [h]Isa 11:11 [i]Isa 2:16 *fn* [j]Isa 14:2; 43:6 [k]Isa 55:5 **60:10** [l]Isa 14:1-2 [m]Isa 49:23; Rev 21:24 [n]Isa 54:8 **60:11** [o]ver 18; Isa 62:10; Rev 21:25

[a] 19 Or *When enemies come in like a flood, / the Spirit of the LORD will put them to flight* [b] 9 Or *the trading ships*

with breastplate and helmet, but often have only weapons with no defensive armor.

60:5 *to you the riches of the nations will come.* When the Assyrians and Babylonians conquered nations, they exacted tribute that was brought to them (see notes on 10:1; 13:17; 16:1; 18:7). This is known in texts and pictured by laden people shown on palace reliefs. Now the tables are turned, with the erstwhile captives receiving tribute gifts.

60:6 *Herds of camels.* Camels were sometimes part of tribute that was brought, but they were also freight carriers for merchants; thus, those who had many camels were considered wealthy. *Midian.* A nomadic Arabian tribe that had dealings with Israel from Mosaic times (see note on 9:4). *Ephah.* Mentioned only two other times in Scripture (Ge 25:4, 1Ch 1:33); associated with Midian, possibly a clan of that tribe. It is also mentioned in the Assyrian annals of Tiglath-Pileser III. *Sheba.* A southwestern Arabian kingdom that was a great trading center known to export precious stones, gold and incense (see 1Ki 10:1 – 13; see also notes on 1Ki 10:1; Ps 72:15). This kingdom is known as Saba in native sources and in the Assyrian annals. It had a very advanced urban civilization in the first millennium BC.

60:7 Kedar (see notes on 21:16; Ps 120:5) and Nebaioth were inhabited by descendants of Ishmael (Ge 25:13; 1Ch 1:29). The area probably lies in the northwestern Arabian peninsula. Kedar (Qedar) and Nebaioth (Nabayatu) are mentioned in Akkadian texts from the Neo-Assyrian and Neo-Babylonian periods. Ashurbanipal mentions both towns in descriptions of his campaigns, and Kedar's king joined the Persians to attack Egypt during the Persian period.

60:9 *ships of Tarshish.* See note on 23:1. *Tarshish.* Its exact location is uncertain (see note on Jnh 1:3). It is also associated with silver in the seventh-century BC Hebrew Temple of the Lord ostracon.

so that people may bring you the
wealth of the nations[p] —
their kings[q] led in triumphal
procession.
12 For the nation or kingdom that will not
serve[r] you will perish;
it will be utterly ruined.

13 "The glory of Lebanon[s] will come to
you,
the juniper, the fir and the cypress
together,[t]
to adorn my sanctuary;
and I will glorify the place for my
feet.[u]
14 The children of your oppressors[v] will
come bowing before you;
all who despise you will bow down[w]
at your feet
and will call you the City of the LORD,
Zion[x] of the Holy One of Israel.

15 "Although you have been forsaken[y]
and hated,
with no one traveling[z] through,
I will make you the everlasting pride[a]
and the joy[b] of all generations.
16 You will drink the milk of nations
and be nursed[c] at royal breasts.
Then you will know that I, the LORD,
am your Savior,
your Redeemer,[d] the Mighty One of
Jacob.
17 Instead of bronze I will bring you gold,
and silver in place of iron.
Instead of wood I will bring you
bronze,
and iron in place of stones.
I will make peace your governor
and well-being your ruler.
18 No longer will violence be heard in
your land,
nor ruin or destruction within your
borders,
but you will call your walls Salvation[e]
and your gates Praise.
19 The sun will no more be your light by
day,
nor will the brightness of the moon
shine on you,
for the LORD will be your everlasting
light,[f]
and your God will be your glory.[g]
20 Your sun[h] will never set again,
and your moon will wane no more;
the LORD will be your everlasting light,
and your days of sorrow[i] will end.
21 Then all your people will be righteous[j]
and they will possess[k] the land
forever.
They are the shoot I have planted,[l]
the work of my hands,[m]
for the display of my splendor.[n]
22 The least of you will become a
thousand,
the smallest a mighty nation.
I am the LORD;
in its time I will do this swiftly."

60:11 [p] ver 5; Rev 21:26 [q] Ps 149:8 **60:12** [r] Isa 14:2 **60:13** [s] Isa 35:2 [t] Isa 41:19 [u] 1Ch 28:2; Ps 132:7 **60:14** [v] Isa 14:2 [w] Isa 49:23; Rev 3:9 [x] Heb 12:22 **60:15** [y] Isa 1:7-9; 6:12 [z] Isa 33:8 [a] Isa 4:2 [b] Isa 65:18 **60:16** [c] Isa 49:23; 66:11, 12 [d] Isa 59:20 **60:18** [e] Isa 26:1 **60:19** [f] Rev 22:5 [g] Zec 2:5; Rev 21:23 **60:20** [h] Isa 30:26 [i] Isa 35:10 **60:21** [j] Rev 21:27 [k] Ps 37:11, 22; Isa 57:13; 61:7 [l] Mt 15:13 [m] Isa 19:25; 29:23; Eph 2:10 [n] Isa 52:1 **61:1** [o] Isa 11:2 [p] Ps 45:7 [q] Mt 11:5; Lk 7:22 [r] Isa 57:15 [s] Isa 42:7; 49:9 **61:2** [t] Isa 49:8; Lk 4:18-19* [u] Isa 34:8 [v] Isa 57:18; Mt 5:4

The Year of the LORD's Favor

61 The Spirit[o] of the Sovereign LORD
is on me,
because the LORD has anointed[p] me
to proclaim good news to the poor.[q]
He has sent me to bind up[r] the
brokenhearted,
to proclaim freedom for the captives[s]
and release from darkness for the
prisoners,[a]
2 to proclaim the year of the LORD's
favor[t]
and the day of vengeance[u] of our God,
to comfort[v] all who mourn,
3 and provide for those who grieve in
Zion —

[a] 1 Hebrew; Septuagint *the blind*

60:13 *juniper.* A fragrant wood used in Mesopotamian building. Sargon roofed his royal palace with juniper beams to make it smell sweet. An Egyptian text directed to King Merikare includes juniper in the tribute of various woods from a military campaign. This reflects the same Isaianic context of tribute.

60:15 *you have been forsaken.* Divine abandonment explained the fall of cities or nations. When the deity is with the people, they flourish, but when the god leaves, they fall. Mesopotamian examples begin with third-millennium BC Sumerian texts and continue with second-millennium BC Akkadian ones. Esarhaddon, in a building description, recounts his rebuilding of Babylon, which had been destroyed because of evil within. It was precipitated because the gods and goddesses of the city went up to heaven, leaving the city to fend for itself. Abandonment by the Moabite god Chemosh is implied in the Mesha Inscription when it reports Israel's earlier victories over Moab. But abandonment is not permanent, since Chemosh and Esarhaddon's gods return, as does the God of Israel, as the end of this verse indicates.

60:22 *I am the LORD.* See note on 41:13.

61:1 *freedom for the captives and release … for the prisoners.* In the ancient Near East the freeing of prisoners (from debtors' prison) as an act of justice often occurred in the first or second year of a new king's reign (and then periodically after that). The Old Babylonian period king Ammisaduqa (seventeenth century BC) canceled economic debts on behalf of the god Shamash. Thus, the "jubilee" ("year of the LORD's favor," v. 2) in this case was primarily for those in debt (for either financial or legal reasons) and for the freeing of debt-slaves. Unlike Israel, this Babylonian edict was entirely at the whim of the monarch, and there is no evidence that it was divinely sanctioned. For an example of this as being accomplished by an ideal king, see note on 11:1 – 16. Historically, a proclamation of freedom is recorded by Zedekiah, the last king of Judah (Jer 34:8 – 10).

61:3 *oil of joy.* Anointing with oil was not only a sign of consecration for a task (v. 1) but also part of joyful feasting that took place when messengers brought good news.

to bestow on them a crown of beauty
instead of ashes,
the oil of joy
instead of mourning,
and a garment of praise
instead of a spirit of despair.
They will be called oaks of
righteousness,
a planting of the LORD
for the display of his splendor.[w]

4 They will rebuild the ancient ruins[x]
and restore the places long
devastated;
they will renew the ruined cities
that have been devastated for
generations.
5 Strangers[y] will shepherd your flocks;
foreigners will work your fields and
vineyards.
6 And you will be called priests[z] of the
LORD,
you will be named ministers of our
God.
You will feed on the wealth[a] of nations,
and in their riches you will boast.

7 Instead of your shame
you will receive a double[b] portion,
and instead of disgrace
you will rejoice in your inheritance.
And so you will inherit a double
portion in your land,
and everlasting joy will be yours.

8 "For I, the LORD, love justice;[c]
I hate robbery and wrongdoing.
In my faithfulness I will reward my
people
and make an everlasting covenant[d]
with them.
9 Their descendants will be known
among the nations
and their offspring among the
peoples.
All who see them will acknowledge
that they are a people the LORD has
blessed."

10 I delight greatly in the LORD;
my soul rejoices[e] in my God.
For he has clothed me with garments
of salvation
and arrayed me in a robe of his
righteousness,[f]
as a bridegroom adorns his head like a
priest,
and as a bride[g] adorns herself with
her jewels.
11 For as the soil makes the sprout come
up
and a garden causes seeds to grow,
so the Sovereign LORD will make
righteousness[h]
and praise spring up before all
nations.

Zion's New Name

62 For Zion's sake I will not keep
silent,
for Jerusalem's sake I will not
remain quiet,
till her vindication[i] shines out like the
dawn,
her salvation like a blazing torch.
2 The nations[j] will see your vindication,
and all kings your glory;
you will be called by a new name[k]
that the mouth of the LORD will
bestow.
3 You will be a crown[l] of splendor in the
LORD's hand,
a royal diadem in the hand of your
God.
4 No longer will they call you Deserted,[m]
or name your land Desolate.
But you will be called Hephzibah,[a]
and your land Beulah[b];
for the LORD will take delight[n] in you,
and your land will be married.[o]
5 As a young man marries a young
woman,
so will your Builder marry you;
as a bridegroom rejoices over his
bride,
so will your God rejoice[p] over you.

6 I have posted watchmen[q] on your
walls, Jerusalem;
they will never be silent day or
night.
You who call on the LORD,
give yourselves no rest,
7 and give him no rest[r] till he establishes
Jerusalem
and makes her the praise of the
earth.

[a] 4 *Hephzibah* means *my delight is in her.* [b] 4 *Beulah* means *married.*

61:3 [w] Isa 60:20-21 **61:4** [x] Isa 49:8; Eze 36:33; Am 9:14 **61:5** [y] Isa 14:1-2 **61:6** [z] Ex 19:6; 1Pe 2:5 [a] Isa 60:11 **61:7** [b] Isa 40:2; Zec 9:12 **61:8** [c] Ps 11:7; Isa 5:16 [d] Isa 55:3 **61:10** [e] Isa 25:9; Hab 3:18 [f] Ps 132:9; Isa 52:1 [g] Isa 49:18; Rev 21:2 **61:11** [h] Ps 85:11 **62:1** [i] Isa 1:26 **62:2** [j] Isa 52:10; 60:3 [k] ver 4,12 **62:3** [l] Isa 28:5; Zec 9:16; 1Th 2:19 **62:4** [m] Isa 54:6 [n] Jer 32:41; Zep 3:17 [o] Jer 3:14; Hos 2:19 **62:5** [p] Isa 65:19 **62:6** [q] Isa 52:8; Eze 3:17 **62:7** [r] Mt 15:21-28; Lk 18:1-8

61:10 *as a bride adorns herself.* See note on 49:18.
62:3 *a crown of splendor in the LORD's hand.* Deities are regularly depicted wearing crowns. Marduk's crown is described as featuring horns, using gold and lapis lazuli, and being studded with gems. An Akkadian text addressed to Bel (Marduk) identifies the city of Borsippa as the god's crown. Israel's capital city is here equated to a divine crown with its beautiful fittings.
62:4 *your land will be married.* A deity marrying a land will protect and provide for it. Akkadian deities can "marry" a king, as when an Old Akkadian king is called "husband of Ishtar" or when the same goddess offers to take Gilgamesh as her husband. But nowhere else besides Isaiah is the country itself being married to a god because in the OT this is the metaphoric language of the covenant relationship between Yahweh and Israel. Such a covenant between a god and nation has not been attested elsewhere in the ancient Near East.

8 The LORD has sworn by his right hand
and by his mighty arm:
"Never again will I give your grain[s]
as food for your enemies,
and never again will foreigners drink
the new wine
for which you have toiled;
9 but those who harvest it will eat it
and praise the LORD,
and those who gather the grapes will
drink it
in the courts of my sanctuary."

10 Pass through, pass through the gates![t]
Prepare the way for the people.
Build up, build up the highway![u]
Remove the stones.
Raise a banner[v] for the nations.

11 The LORD has made proclamation
to the ends of the earth:
"Say to Daughter Zion,[w]
'See, your Savior comes![x]
See, his reward is with him,
and his recompense accompanies
him.' "[y]
12 They will be called[z] the Holy People,[a]
the Redeemed[b] of the LORD;
and you will be called Sought After,
the City No Longer Deserted.[c]

God's Day of Vengeance and Redemption

63 Who is this coming from Edom,
from Bozrah,[d] with his garments
stained crimson?
Who is this, robed in splendor,
striding forward in the greatness of
his strength?

"It is I, proclaiming victory,
mighty to save."[e]

2 Why are your garments red,
like those of one treading the
winepress?

3 "I have trodden the winepress[f] alone;
from the nations no one was with me.
I trampled them in my anger
and trod them down in my wrath;[g]
their blood spattered my garments,[h]
and I stained all my clothing.
4 It was for me the day of vengeance;
the year for me to redeem had come.
5 I looked, but there was no one[i] to help,
I was appalled that no one gave
support;
so my own arm[j] achieved salvation
for me,
and my own wrath sustained me.[k]
6 I trampled the nations in my anger;
in my wrath I made them drunk[l]
and poured their blood[m] on the
ground."

Praise and Prayer

7 I will tell of the kindnesses[n] of the
LORD,
the deeds for which he is to be
praised,
according to all the LORD has done
for us—
yes, the many good things
he has done for Israel,
according to his compassion[o] and
many kindnesses.
8 He said, "Surely they are my people,[p]
children who will be true to me";
and so he became their Savior.
9 In all their distress he too was
distressed,
and the angel of his presence[q] saved
them.[a]
In his love and mercy he redeemed[r]
them;
he lifted them up and carried[s] them
all the days of old.
10 Yet they rebelled[t]
and grieved his Holy Spirit.[u]
So he turned and became their enemy[v]
and he himself fought against them.

11 Then his people recalled[b] the days of
old,
the days of Moses and his people—
where is he who brought them through
the sea,[w]
with the shepherd of his flock?
Where is he who set
his Holy Spirit[x] among them,
12 who sent his glorious arm of power
to be at Moses' right hand,
who divided the waters[y] before them,
to gain for himself everlasting
renown,
13 who led[z] them through the depths?
Like a horse in open country,
they did not stumble;[a]
14 like cattle that go down to the plain,
they were given rest by the Spirit of
the LORD.

62:8 [s] Dt 28:30-33; Isa 1:7; Jer 5:17 **62:10** [t] Isa 60:11 [u] Isa 11:16; 57:14 [v] Isa 11:10 **62:11** [w] Zec 9:9; Mt 21:5 [x] Rev 22:12 [y] Isa 40:10 **62:12** [z] ver 4 [a] 1Pe 2:9 [b] Isa 35:9 [c] Isa 42:16 **63:1** [d] Am 1:12 [e] Zep 3:17 **63:3** [f] Rev 14:20; 19:15 [g] Isa 22:5 [h] Rev 19:13 **63:5** [i] Isa 41:28 [j] Ps 44:3; 98:1 [k] Isa 59:16 **63:6** [l] Isa 29:9 [m] Isa 34:3 **63:7** [n] Isa 54:8 [o] Ps 51:1; Eph 2:4 **63:8** [p] Isa 51:4 **63:9** [q] Ex 33:14 [r] Dt 7:7-8 [s] Dt 1:31 **63:10** [t] Ps 78:40 [u] Ps 51:11; Ac 7:51; Eph 4:30 [v] Ps 106:40 **63:11** [w] Ex 14:22,30 [x] Nu 11:17 **63:12** [y] Ex 14:21-22; Isa 11:15 **63:13** [z] Dt 32:12 [a] Jer 31:9

[a] 9 Or *Savior* [9]*in their distress. / It was no envoy or angel / but his own presence that saved them* [b] 11 Or *But may he recall*

62:10 *Raise a banner.* A banner or ensign was a visible symbol that could be elevated to identify a person or group. While "banner" connotes some sort of flag, this more likely indicates a staff topped by an identifying emblem. Banners in ancient Israel were used for marking tribes. They appear to have been used most often in military contexts, either to rally troops together or to identify regiments of troops. In this, Israel was most certainly imitating its Near Eastern neighbors. The Assyrians used standards to identify particular regiments of troops.
63:1 *Edom.* See notes on 21:11 ("Dumah"); Ge 36:9; Ps 137:7. *Bozrah.* See note on 34:6.

This is how you guided your people
to make for yourself a glorious name.

15 Look down from heaven[b] and see,
from your lofty throne,[c] holy and glorious.
Where are your zeal[d] and your might?
Your tenderness and compassion[e]
are withheld from us.
16 But you are our Father,
though Abraham does not know us
or Israel acknowledge[f] us;
you, LORD, are our Father,
our Redeemer[g] from of old is your name.
17 Why, LORD, do you make us wander
from your ways
and harden our hearts so we do not revere[h] you?
Return[i] for the sake of your servants,
the tribes that are your inheritance.
18 For a little while your people possessed
your holy place,
but now our enemies have trampled
down your sanctuary.[j]
19 We are yours from of old;
but you have not ruled over them,
they have not been called[a] by your name.

64

[b] Oh, that you would rend the
heavens[k] and come down,[l]
that the mountains[m] would tremble
before you!
2 As when fire sets twigs ablaze
and causes water to boil,
come down to make your name known
to your enemies
and cause the nations to quake[n]
before you!
3 For when you did awesome[o] things
that we did not expect,
you came down, and the mountains
trembled before you.
4 Since ancient times no one has heard,
no ear has perceived,
no eye has seen any God besides you,
who acts on behalf of those who
wait for him.[p]
5 You come to the help of those who
gladly do right,[q]
who remember your ways.
But when we continued to sin against them,
you were angry.
How then can we be saved?
6 All of us have become like one who is unclean,
and all our righteous[r] acts are like
filthy rags;
we all shrivel up like a leaf,[s]
and like the wind our sins sweep us away.
7 No one[t] calls on your name
or strives to lay hold of you;
for you have hidden[u] your face from us
and have given us over[v] to[c] our sins.

8 Yet you, LORD, are our Father.[w]
We are the clay, you are the potter;[x]
we are all the work of your hand.
9 Do not be angry[y] beyond measure,
LORD;
do not remember our sins[z] forever.
Oh, look on us, we pray,
for we are all your people.
10 Your sacred cities have become a
wasteland;
even Zion is a wasteland, Jerusalem
a desolation.
11 Our holy and glorious temple,[a] where
our ancestors praised you,
has been burned with fire,
and all that we treasured[b] lies in ruins.
12 After all this, LORD, will you hold
yourself back?[c]
Will you keep silent[d] and punish us
beyond measure?

Judgment and Salvation

65

"I revealed myself to those who
did not ask for me;
I was found by those who did not
seek me.[e]
To a nation[f] that did not call on my name,
I said, 'Here am I, here am I.'
2 All day long I have held out my hands
to an obstinate people,[g]
who walk in ways not good,
pursuing their own imaginations[h]—
3 a people who continually provoke me
to my very face,[i]
offering sacrifices in gardens[j]
and burning incense on altars of brick;

63:15 [b] Dt 26:15; Ps 80:14 [c] Ps 123:1 [d] Isa 9:7; 26:11 [e] Jer 31:20; Hos 11:8 **63:16** [f] Job 14:21 [g] Isa 41:14; 44:6 **63:17** [h] Isa 29:13 [i] Nu 10:36 **63:18** [j] Ps 74:3-8 **64:1** [k] Ps 18:9; 144:5 [l] Mic 1:3 [m] Ex 19:18 **64:2** [n] Ps 99:1; Jer 5:22; 33:9 **64:3** [o] Ps 65:5 **64:4** [p] Isa 30:18; 1Co 2:9* **64:5** [q] Isa 26:8 **64:6** [r] Isa 46:12; 48:1 [s] Ps 90:5-6 **64:7** [t] Isa 59:4 [u] Dt 31:18; Isa 1:15; 54:8 [v] Isa 9:18 **64:8** [w] Isa 63:16 [x] Isa 29:16 **64:9** [y] Isa 57:17; 60:10 [z] Isa 43:25 **64:11** [a] Ps 74:3-7 [b] La 1:7, 10 **64:12** [c] Ps 74:10-11; Isa 42:14 [d] Ps 83:1 **65:1** [e] Hos 1:10; Ro 9:24-26; 10:20* [f] Eph 2:12 **65:2** [g] Isa 1:2, 23; Ro 10:21* [h] Ps 81:11-12; Isa 66:18 **65:3** [i] Job 1:11 [j] Isa 1:29

[a] 19 Or *We are like those you have never ruled, / like those never called* [b] In Hebrew texts 64:1 is numbered 63:19b, and 64:2-12 is numbered 64:1-11. [c] 7 Septuagint, Syriac and Targum; Hebrew *have made us melt because of*

63:16 *you, LORD, are our Father.* See notes on 9:6, 41:13.
64:4 *no eye has seen any God besides you.* See note on 46:9.
64:8 *you, LORD, are our Father.* See notes on 9:6; 41:13.
65:3 *offering sacrifices in gardens.* See note on 1:29. *altars of brick.* Most incense altars were made of limestone. This has led to the very plausible suggestion that the Hebrew word (NIV "altars of brick") can also mean "incense altars" (as it does in the inscription on a fifth-century BC limestone altar from Lachish). These were common features on the high places, where illegitimate worship took place. Alternatively, there are Babylonian rituals directed toward celestial deities that include sacrifices made on bricks.

[4]who sit among the graves
and spend their nights keeping
secret vigil;
who eat the flesh of pigs,[k]
and whose pots hold broth of impure
meat;
[5]who say, 'Keep away; don't come
near me,
for I am too sacred[l] for you!'
Such people are smoke in my nostrils,
a fire that keeps burning all day.

[6]"See, it stands written before me:
I will not keep silent[m] but will pay
back[n] in full;
I will pay it back into their laps[o]—
[7]both your sins[p] and the sins of your
ancestors,"[q]
says the LORD.
"Because they burned sacrifices on the
mountains
and defied me on the hills,[r]
I will measure into their laps
the full payment for their former
deeds."

[8]This is what the LORD says:

"As when juice is still found in a
cluster of grapes
and people say, 'Don't destroy it,
there is still a blessing in it,'
so will I do in behalf of my servants;
I will not destroy them all.
[9]I will bring forth descendants[s] from
Jacob,
and from Judah those who will
possess[t] my mountains;
my chosen people will inherit them,
and there will my servants live.[u]
[10]Sharon[v] will become a pasture for flocks,
and the Valley of Achor[w] a resting
place for herds,
for my people who seek[x] me.

65:4 [k]Lev 11:7 **65:5** [l]Mt 9:11; Lk 7:39; 18:9-12 **65:6** [m]Ps 50:3 [n]Jer 16:18 [o]Ps 79:12 **65:7** [p]Isa 22:14 [q]Ex 20:5 [r]Isa 57:7 **65:9** [s]Isa 45:19 [t]Am 9:11-15 [u]Isa 32:18 **65:10** [v]Isa 35:2 [w]Jos 7:26 [x]Isa 51:1

[11]"But as for you who forsake[y] the LORD
and forget my holy mountain,
who spread a table for Fortune
and fill bowls of mixed wine for
Destiny,
[12]I will destine you for the sword,[z]
and all of you will fall in the
slaughter;
for I called but you did not answer,[a]
I spoke but you did not listen.[b]
You did evil in my sight
and chose what displeases me."

[13]Therefore this is what the Sovereign
LORD says:

"My servants will eat,[c]
but you will go hungry;
my servants will drink,
but you will go thirsty;[d]
my servants will rejoice,
but you will be put to shame.[e]
[14]My servants will sing
out of the joy of their hearts,
but you will cry out[f]
from anguish of heart
and wail in brokenness of spirit.
[15]You will leave your name
for my chosen ones to use in their
curses;[g]
the Sovereign LORD will put you to
death,
but to his servants he will give
another name.
[16]Whoever invokes a blessing in the land
will do so by the one true God;[h]
whoever takes an oath in the land
will swear[i] by the one true God.
For the past troubles will be forgotten
and hidden from my eyes.

New Heavens and a New Earth

[17]"See, I will create
new heavens and a new earth.[j]

65:11 [y]Dt 29:24-25; Isa 1:28 **65:12** [z]Isa 27:1 [a]Pr 1:24-25; Isa 41:28; 66:4 [b]2Ch 36:15-16; Jer 7:13 **65:13** [c]Isa 1:19 [d]Isa 41:17 [e]Isa 44:9 **65:14** [f]Mt 8:12; Lk 13:28 **65:15** [g]Zec 8:13 **65:16** [h]Ps 31:5 [i]Isa 19:18 **65:17** [j]Isa 66:22; 2Pe 3:13

65:4 *who sit among the graves and spend their nights keeping secret vigil.* An Aramaic text in Demotic script also associates a grave with a vigil. Night vigils were accompanied by music. The vigil mentioned here appears to hold some sacred function beyond simply mourning by a grave. The Hebrew shows it is being done inside the grave. Secrecy indicates that it is not a generally acceptable practice, probably part of a funerary cult. *eat the flesh of pigs.* A distinctive element of orthodox Israelite religious practice was avoiding pork; thus, eating pork shows the people's religious deterioration. Even though banned, archaeological evidence indicates numerous Israelite sites with a small amount of pig remains. Pigs are rarely depicted in the ancient Near East, though there is a fourth-millennium BC seal from Luristan showing a wild pig. There is textual evidence for Egyptian abomination of pork, even for the gods, but it was by no means universally followed. Even in Egypt and Mesopotamia, where pigs were raised and eaten, they were not part of the regular offerings. An eighth-century BC Assyrian wisdom saying collection indicates that the pig is not fit for a temple since it is an abomination to the gods and considered accursed.

65:6 *it stands written before me ... I will pay it back.* Economic texts are frequent in the ancient Near East, among them numerous loan documents. Akkadian loan documents may contain any of several elements: repayment date, repayment medium, interest rate. Usually such records are written in the third person, but some are in the first person. Hebrew ostraca from Arad concerning supply allocations order that the transaction be written down.

65:11 *Fortune ... Destiny.* The proper (divine?) names used here — Gad (NIV "Fortune") and Meni (NIV "Destiny") — are obscure. Gad is attested in Canaanite and Phoenician texts, and is considered a good luck deity. Meni may have something to do with portion, and therefore some have thought that these gods may have had something to do with fate or fortune. Meni may have been the same as the Arabian goddess Manat, mentioned in the Qur'an. In the Babylonian pantheon, the god Namtar ("Destiny") was the vizier of the netherworld. Additionally Fate was at times personified and deified.

The former things will not be
remembered,[k]
nor will they come to mind.
18 But be glad and rejoice[l] forever
in what I will create,
for I will create Jerusalem to be a delight
and its people a joy.
19 I will rejoice[m] over Jerusalem
and take delight in my people;
the sound of weeping and of crying[n]
will be heard in it no more.

20 "Never again will there be in it
an infant who lives but a few days,
or an old man who does not live out
his years;[o]
the one who dies at a hundred
will be thought a mere child;
the one who fails to reach[a] a hundred
will be considered accursed.
21 They will build houses[p] and dwell in
them;
they will plant vineyards and eat
their fruit.[q]
22 No longer will they build houses and
others live in them,
or plant and others eat.
For as the days of a tree,[r]
so will be the days[s] of my people;
my chosen ones will long enjoy
the work of their hands.
23 They will not labor in vain,
nor will they bear children doomed
to misfortune;
for they will be a people blessed[t] by
the LORD,
they and their descendants[u] with
them.
24 Before they call[v] I will answer;
while they are still speaking[w] I will
hear.
25 The wolf and the lamb[x] will feed
together,
and the lion will eat straw like the ox,
and dust will be the serpent's[y] food.
They will neither harm nor destroy
on all my holy mountain,"
says the LORD.

Judgment and Hope

66 This is what the LORD says:

"Heaven is my throne,[z]
and the earth is my footstool.[a]
Where is the house[b] you will build
for me?
Where will my resting place be?
2 Has not my hand made all these
things,[c]
and so they came into being?"
declares the LORD.

"These are the ones I look on with
favor:
those who are humble and contrite
in spirit,[d]
and who tremble at my word.[e]
3 But whoever sacrifices a bull[f]
is like one who kills a person,
and whoever offers a lamb
is like one who breaks a dog's neck;
whoever makes a grain offering
is like one who presents pig's blood,
and whoever burns memorial incense[g]
is like one who worships an idol.
They have chosen their own ways,[h]
and they delight in their
abominations;
4 so I also will choose harsh treatment
for them
and will bring on them what they
dread.[i]
For when I called, no one answered,[j]
when I spoke, no one listened.
They did evil[k] in my sight
and chose what displeases me."[l]

5 Hear the word of the LORD,
you who tremble at his word:

65:17 [k]Isa 43:18; Jer 3:16 **65:18** [l]Ps 98:1-9; Isa 25:9 **65:19** [m]Isa 35:10; 62:5 [n]Isa 25:8; Rev 7:17 **65:20** [o]Ecc 8:13 **65:21** [p]Isa 32:18 [q]Isa 37:30; Am 9:14 **65:22** [r]Ps 92:12-14 [s]Ps 21:4; 91:16 **65:23** [t]Dt 28:3-12; Isa 61:9 [u]Ac 2:39 **65:24** [v]Isa 55:6 [w]Da 9:20-23; 10:12 **65:25** [x]Isa 11:6 [y]Ge 3:14; Mic 7:17

66:1 [z]Mt 23:22 [a]1Ki 8:27; Mt 5:34-35 [b]2Sa 7:7; Jn 4:20-21; Ac 7:49*; 17:24 **66:2** [c]Isa 40:26; Ac 7:50* [d]Isa 57:15; Mt 5:3-4; Lk 18:13-14 [e]Ezr 9:4 **66:3** [f]Isa 1:11 [g]Lev 2:2 [h]Isa 57:17 **66:4** [i]Pr 10:24 [j]Pr 1:24; Jer 7:13 [k]2Ki 21:2,4,6 [l]Isa 65:12

[a] 20 Or *the sinner who reaches*

66:1 *Heaven is my throne, and the earth is my footstool. Where is the house you will build for me?* In the ancient world the temple was considered the link between heaven and earth. Gods were considered to be gigantic (cf. ch. 6) and the throne room in the central sanctum in the temple was often deemed to be located in heaven as much as on earth. In this way, sacred space was perceived to exist on the cosmic level, not just the terrestrial level. The cosmic dimensions of sacred space, as expressed here, diminished any architectural splendor of the earthbound temple in comparison.

66:3 *bull … lamb … grain.* These three acceptable ritual offerings are compared to unacceptable pagan practices: killing a person, breaking a dog's neck, and presenting pig's blood. *kills a person.* At the least refers to manslaughter, but apparently here refers to human sacrifice, not of a child, but of an adult. Such sacrifices are rare in Mesopotamia, only found when the consort and retainers were buried as part of the ritual of the substitute king (see the article "Substitutionary Rites," p. 1202). During the First Dynasty in Egypt, a king was joined in his death by a retinue to serve him, though the practice was soon replaced by providing model figures and even representations of them painted on the tomb wall. *breaks a dog's neck.* Animals, including young dogs (see 56:10 – 11), were at times killed to seal a covenant. A letter from Mari concerns making such a covenant that involved killing a donkey, puppy and goat. Excavations at Tel Haror, just south of Ashkelon, have found puppy burials with the skeletons having broken necks; their significance, while suggestive, is unclear. Puppies also played a role in Hittite ritual from an earlier period. One refers to a sacrifice that is to follow defeat by an enemy that would include a man, a kid goat, a puppy and a suckling pig. *pig's blood.* Pigs, as unclean animals, were unacceptable for sacrifice in orthodox Israelite worship (see note on 65:4). A Middle Kingdom coffin text explains how, through a declaration of Ra, pork is unclean in Egypt, an abomination to the gods.

Votive plaque picturing the god Shamash seated on his heavenly throne. See note on Isa 66:1.

Kim Walton

"Your own people who hate[m] you,
and exclude you because of my name, have said,
'Let the LORD be glorified,
that we may see your joy!'
Yet they will be put to shame.[n]
6 Hear that uproar from the city,
hear that noise from the temple!
It is the sound of the LORD
repaying[o] his enemies all they deserve.

7 "Before she goes into labor,[p]
she gives birth;
before the pains come upon her,
she delivers a son.[q]
8 Who has ever heard of such things?
Who has ever seen[r] things like this?
Can a country be born in a day
or a nation be brought forth in a moment?
Yet no sooner is Zion in labor
than she gives birth to her children.
9 Do I bring to the moment of birth[s]
and not give delivery?" says the LORD.
"Do I close up the womb
when I bring to delivery?" says your God.
10 "Rejoice[t] with Jerusalem and be glad for her,
all you who love[u] her;
rejoice greatly with her,
all you who mourn over her.
11 For you will nurse[v] and be satisfied
at her comforting breasts;
you will drink deeply
and delight in her overflowing abundance."

12 For this is what the LORD says:

"I will extend peace to her like a river,[w]
and the wealth[x] of nations like a flooding stream;
you will nurse and be carried[y] on her arm
and dandled on her knees.
13 As a mother comforts her child,
so will I comfort[z] you;
and you will be comforted over Jerusalem."

14 When you see this, your heart will rejoice
and you will flourish like grass;
the hand of the LORD will be made known to his servants,
but his fury[a] will be shown to his foes.
15 See, the LORD is coming with fire,
and his chariots[b] are like a whirlwind;
he will bring down his anger with fury,
and his rebuke[c] with flames of fire.

66:5 [m] Ps 38:20; Isa 60:15 [n] Lk 13:17 **66:6** [o] Isa 65:6; Joel 3:7 **66:7** [p] Isa 54:1 [q] Rev 12:5 **66:8** [r] Isa 64:4 **66:9** [s] Isa 37:3 **66:10** [t] Dt 32:43; Ro 15:10 [u] Ps 26:8 **66:11** [v] Isa 60:16 **66:12** [w] Isa 48:18 [x] Ps 72:3; Isa 60:5; 61:6 [y] Isa 60:4 **66:13** [z] Isa 40:1; 2Co 1:4 **66:14** [a] Isa 10:5 **66:15** [b] Ps 68:17 [c] Ps 9:5

66:11 *you will nurse and be satisfied.* A blessing for those returning to Mother Jerusalem will be sufficiency of nourishment. The intimacy of a suckling child makes the imagery even more evocative. An Aramaic curse from the ninth century BC refers to the idea that many mothers will not be able to satisfy even one infant.
66:13 *As a mother.* Unlike the gods of Israel's neighbors, Yahweh is not understood as a sexual being and does not, in orthodox Israelite religious belief, have a consort (see notes on 1:29; 44:24). He is described metaphorically, however, using both male and female terms. God is called Father (see 63:16; see also notes on 9:6; 41:13). More rarely Yahweh is described using feminine metaphors (see 16:11; 46:3–4; 49:15; 54:14; 63:15–16).
66:15 *his chariots.* See note on 2:7. Marduk rides a chariot in his violent conflict with Tiamat in the *Enuma Elish.* Sennacherib speaks of himself going into battle in Ashur's chariot. Baal used clouds as his chariot, being called "charioteer of the clouds" in battle contexts. In a cultic context, Mesopotamian idols were carried in chariots or carts in some festival processions.

16 For with fire[d] and with his sword[e]
the LORD will execute judgment on
all people,
and many will be those slain by the
LORD.

17 "Those who consecrate and purify
themselves to go into the gardens,[f] following one who is among those who eat
the flesh of pigs,[g] rats and other unclean
things—they will meet their end[h] together with the one they follow," declares the
LORD.

18 "And I, because of what they have
planned and done, am about to come[a]
and gather the people of all nations and
languages, and they will come and see my
glory.

19 "I will set a sign[i] among them, and
I will send some of those who survive
to the nations—to Tarshish,[j] to the Libyans[b] and Lydians[k] (famous as archers),
to Tubal[l] and Greece, and to the distant
islands[m] that have not heard of my fame
or seen my glory.[n] They will proclaim my
glory among the nations. 20 And they will
bring all your people, from all the nations,
to my holy mountain in Jerusalem as an
offering to the LORD—on horses, in chariots and wagons, and on mules and camels," says the LORD. "They will bring them,
as the Israelites bring their grain offerings,
to the temple of the LORD in ceremonially
clean vessels.[o] 21 And I will select some of
them also to be priests[p] and Levites," says
the LORD.

22 "As the new heavens and the new
earth[q] that I make will endure before me,"
declares the LORD, "so will your name and
descendants endure.[r] 23 From one New
Moon to another and from one Sabbath[s] to
another, all mankind will come and bow
down[t] before me," says the LORD. 24 "And
they will go out and look on the dead bodies of those who rebelled against me; the
worms[u] that eat them will not die, the fire
that burns them will not be quenched,[v] and
they will be loathsome to all mankind."

66:16 [d] Isa 30:30 [e] Isa 27:1 **66:17** [f] Isa 1:29 [g] Lev 11:7 [h] Ps 37:20; Isa 1:28 **66:19** [i] Isa 11:10; 49:22 [j] Isa 2:16 [k] Eze 27:10 [l] Ge 10:2 [m] Isa 11:11 [n] 1Ch 16:24; Isa 24:15 **66:20** [o] Isa 52:11 **66:21** [p] Ex 19:6; Isa 61:6; 1Pe 2:5,9 **66:22** [q] Isa 65:17; Heb 12:26-27; 2Pe 3:13; Rev 21:1 [r] Jn 10:27-29; 1Pe 1:4-5 **66:23** [s] Eze 46:1-3 [t] Isa 19:21 **66:24** [u] Isa 14:11 [v] Isa 1:31; Mk 9:48*

[a] *18* The meaning of the Hebrew for this clause is uncertain. [b] *19* Some Septuagint manuscripts *Put* (Libyans); Hebrew *Pul*

66:23 *From one New Moon to another and from one Sabbath to another.* See note on 1:13.

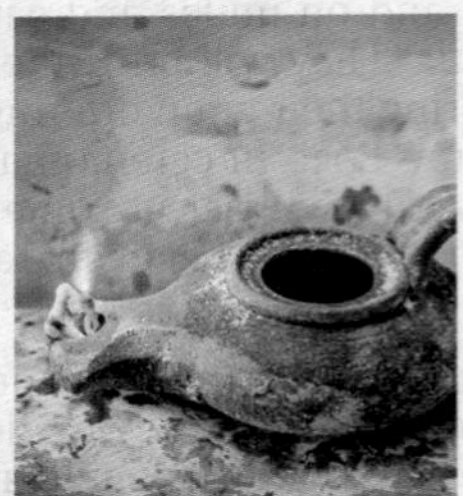

ORACLES OF THE PROPHETS

JEREMIAH

Historical Setting

The final days of Judah constitute the historical setting that sets the stage for Jeremiah's prophetic ministry. Jeremiah was born into a world of violent changes and intense power struggles. Two very significant events frame the stage upon which Jeremiah will act as God's mouthpiece. The first one can be characterized as the process by which the center of ancient Near Eastern power shifts from Assyria to Babylonia. This shift allowed Judah a certain degree of freedom, albeit short-lived, to carry out important religious and political reforms. The second event, the fall of Jerusalem, produced a profound and irreversible scar in the life and identity of ancient Israel. The political, economic, social and religious realities of the period in between these two hallmark events are the ones that surround the core of Jeremiah's prophetic activity.

KEY CONCEPTS

- The presence of the temple will not shield the people of Judah from God's judgment through the Babylonians.
- The covenant was broken and judgment (covenant curses) will come about.
- Restoration will not come for Israel until after judgment.
- The new covenant continues God's revelation of himself by providing forgiveness of sin.

Literary Setting

The literary features of the book of Jeremiah are complex. One is immediately struck by the amount of prose present in Jeremiah, whereas other prophets (e.g., Isaiah) present less prose and more poetry. Historical narrative is part of the Jeremiah prose material. The prophet also expresses his message through poetry that is powerful and full of metaphors, images and words of action. Within this poetry one encounters what has been identified as the oracles against foreign nations. To this we can add other literary features such as vision reports, symbolic actions reports, biography, confessions and laments. ◆

1 The words of Jeremiah son of Hilkiah, one of the priests at Anathoth[a] in
the territory of Benjamin. 2The word of the
LORD came to him in the thirteenth year of
the reign of Josiah son of Amon king of Judah, 3and through the reign of Jehoiakim[b]
son of Josiah king of Judah, down to the
fifth month of the eleventh year of Zedekiah[c] son of Josiah king of Judah, when the
people of Jerusalem went into exile.[d]

The Call of Jeremiah

4The word of the LORD came to me, saying,
5"Before I formed you in the womb I
knew[a][e] you,
before you were born[f] I set you apart;
I appointed you as a prophet to the
nations.[g]"

6"Alas, Sovereign LORD," I said, "I do not
know how to speak;[h] I am too young."[i]
7But the LORD said to me, "Do not say, 'I
am too young.' You must go to everyone I
send you to and say whatever I command
you. 8Do not be afraid[j] of them, for I am with
you[k] and will rescue you," declares the LORD.
9Then the LORD reached out his hand
and touched[l] my mouth and said to me, "I
have put my words in your mouth.[m] 10See,
today I appoint you over nations and kingdoms to uproot and tear down, to destroy
and overthrow, to build and to plant."[n]
11The word of the LORD came to me:
"What do you see, Jeremiah?"[o]
"I see the branch of an almond tree," I
replied.

1:1 [a] Jos 21:18; 1Ch 6:60; Jer 32:7-9 **1:3** [b] 2Ki 23:34 [c] 2Ki 24:17; Jer 39:2 [d] Jer 52:15 **1:5** [e] Ps 139:16 [f] Isa 49:1 [g] ver 10; Jer 25:15-26 **1:6** [h] Ex 4:10; 6:12 [i] 1Ki 3:7 **1:8** [j] Eze 2:6 [k] Jos 1:5; Jer 15:20 **1:9** [l] Isa 6:7 [m] Ex 4:12 **1:10** [n] Jer 18:7-10; 24:6; 31:4, 28 **1:11** [o] Jer 24:3; Am 7:8

[a] 5 Or *chose*

1:1 *Hilkiah.* Not to be identified with Jerusalem's high priest also known by this name (2Ki 22–23). *one of the priests.* Jeremiah was born into a priestly family. His father was a priest who exercised a number of responsibilities. The priests originally were in charge of guarding the sacred places set up by the Israelites throughout the country. Their main job was the preservation of sacred space. They accomplished this in many ways, performance of rituals being only one. Another important way was by instructing people in the Mosaic Law. Only by knowing the law, in all of its aspects (social, moral and ritual) could the people keep it and therefore avoid offending God such that his presence would be removed. Priests were therefore responsible for instructing worshipers with regard to purity regulations and ritual procedures. One of Jeremiah's complaints throughout his prophetic ministry is that the priests are neglecting this duty. This, of course, causes great consternation in his own family, to the point that they want Jeremiah to be silenced. *Anathoth.* A town in Benjamin populated primarily by the descendants of the rejected priest Abiathar (1Ki 2:26–27).

1:2 *thirteenth year of the reign of Josiah.* According to a widely accepted chronology, this places the beginning of Jeremiah's ministry around the year 628/627 BC. It is a critical time in Judah's history, not only because of the beginning of Josiah's reforms in 628 BC, but also because of the death of Ashurbanipal, the last successful Assyrian king, in 627 BC, and the rise of Babylon under Nabopolassar in 626 BC. Jeremiah's ministry continues until the 11th year of the reign of Zedekiah, i.e., around 587 BC. This is also the time when the Israelites are exiled for a third time to Babylon. Thus, Jeremiah's activity in Israel spans approximately 40 years. After these years Jeremiah continues to minister in exile in the land of Egypt. *Josiah.* See the article "Historical Setting of Jeremiah," p. 1222.

1:3 *Jehoiakim … Zedekiah.* See the article "Historical Setting of Jeremiah," p. 1222. *exile.* The experience of being displaced and forcibly resettled in a foreign country, where the exiles have no rights. This verse alludes to the final destruction of Jerusalem by the Babylonians and the subsequent deportation of many to Babylon. Jeremiah witnesses the terrible destruction of Jerusalem and sees with his own eyes people being dragged away into exile in Babylonia. The famous letters of the town of Lachish describe the final days of Jerusalem during the Babylonian siege. There are 18 letters sent by the captain of the garrison in Lachish, wherein one can read about the tension and suffering during the time of imminent defeat. Mesopotamian sources also describe the Babylonian attack on Jerusalem and the subsequent deportation of many of its inhabitants.

1:5 *Before I formed you in the womb.* Jeremiah was chosen and commissioned for prophetic office even before God formed him in his mother's womb. Biblical prophets such as Moses and Samuel were marked for leadership functions from the time of their birth, so in a sense one can say that they were called while in the womb. The closest Biblical example to Jeremiah's situation is the apostle Paul, who said that God had chosen and set him apart before he was born (Gal 1:15). There are writings from Egypt and Mesopotamia that exhibit similar ideas and concepts. The Egyptian god Amun said of Piankhy, a pharaoh in the eighth century BC, that he had been designated ruler when he was yet unborn; the same is said of other contemporary rulers, e.g., the Assyrian king Ashurbanipal and the Babylonian king Nabonidus. This demonstrates that this was a common sort of statement to make about important people in the ancient world. What is unique in Jeremiah's case is that the choosing by God is said to have taken place even before being *conceived* in his mother's womb. However, this may just be a matter of a slightly different nuance regarding the same theme, and one perhaps should not make too much out of the difference.

1:9 *the LORD reached out his hand and touched my mouth.* In the Hebrew Bible the outstretched hand of God often symbolizes his power. It is possible that in this context God's power is represented by this action as well as the act of placing God's words in the whole being of Jeremiah. In the experience of Isaiah, one of the seraphim touched his mouth with a burning coal, thus indicating a process of cleansing and purification not only of the mouth but of the prophet's entire being (Isa 6:6–7). *touched my mouth.* Purification of the mouth is well attested both in Egyptian and Mesopotamian contexts. Diviner priests had to undergo mouth purification before they could appear before the gods. In fact the idols were often subject to mouth-washing so that they could be recipients of a degree of sanctity. However, in the case of Jeremiah, the Lord places his words directly in the prophet's mouth without the prophet having to undergo a process of ritual purification.

1:11 *almond tree.* The Hebrew word has the same consonants as the Hebrew verb that means "to watch, be wakeful." There is an obvious play on words here that has to do with the fulfillment of God's word.

JEREMIAH 1

HISTORICAL SETTING OF JEREMIAH

The demise of the Assyrian Empire was a defining moment for the life of Judah at the end of the seventh century BC. It created a kind of power vacuum that enabled Judah to assert a degree of independence. In addition, Manasseh's extra-long reign in Judah, longer than any other king of the Davidic line, including David himself, finally came to an end in 642 BC. He had been a vassal of the Assyrian Empire and is evaluated negatively by the prophets and historians of the Bible for his influence in favor of pagan religious practices.

Manasseh was succeeded by his son Amon, who ruled only two years. It was King Josiah (640–609 BC) who was able to take advantage of this international state of affairs. Assyria was on the decline and Babylon had not yet asserted its power in the region. Thus, Josiah was able to recover political power for Judah as well as institute important religious reforms. For almost three decades Judah enjoyed a time of progress and hope. During this time, however, Babylonia started filling the vacuum left by Assyria. In 626/625 BC, Nabopolassar defeated the Assyrian army, and he founded a new dynasty in Babylon that has become known as the Neo-Babylonian Empire. This new empire lasted until 539 BC, when Babylon surrendered to the power of the Persians.

During the reign of Nabopolassar (625–605 BC), the situation in Judah remains relatively stable. Josiah leads a religious reform movement, no doubt prompted by the finding of the Book of the Law in an abandoned corner of the temple, or perhaps the scroll was part of the foundation deposit that was typically searched out during the temple restoration process. This is the approximate time when we can suppose that Jeremiah begins his preaching.

Beginning in 612 BC, matters begin to change rapidly in the overall international situation. These in turn have a direct effect on Judah's situation. Nineveh, the capital city of Assyria, is defeated by a coalition of Babylonians and Medes in 612 BC. For Assyria this means the beginning of a rapid decline toward oblivion. Only two years later, the Babylonians inflict another deadly blow on the Assyrians by taking control of Harran (610 BC). At this point, something critical takes place with respect to Judah. When Egypt sees Babylon's advance in power, it makes an attempt to help the Assyrians recover Harran. The military campaign fails miserably. The Assyrian-Egyptian coalition is defeated and Harran remains firmly in Babylonian hands. At this same time, Judah commits an unfortunate and tactical error. As the Egyptian army, led by Pharaoh Necho II (610–595 BC), marches through Israel in route to Mesopotamia, King Josiah and his army try to intercept it at Megiddo. Josiah, the one king who has embodied hope for Judah, is killed by Pharaoh Necho II, and with his death Judah's dreams and hopes dissipate into thin air. This turn of events in 609 BC no doubt affects Jeremiah and his ministry as well. The brief time of independence, growth and spiritual reform has quickly come to an end.

Pharaoh Necho II takes advantage of his victory over Judah. He immediately removes Jehoahaz, Josiah's successor, who has ruled for only three months, and he installs Eliakim, whose name is changed to Jehoiakim. This "king" serves as a puppet king under the power of the Egyptian pharaoh. This situation, as it turns out, will not last long. Once again the Egyptians make an attempt to curb Babylon's increasing power in the ancient Near East. And once again Egypt fails. Only five years after the

continued on next page

defeat at Harran in 610 BC, the Egyptians suffer a major loss at the battle of Carchemish in 605 BC. Nebuchadnezzar, who succeeds Nabopolassar that very same year, leads the Babylonian army to victory and effectively affirms Babylon's hegemony over Egypt. Nebuchadnezzar then secures his control by sundry incursions into the Syria-Palestine region.

This whole international struggle for power that has surrounded Judah leads Jehoiakim (609–598 BC) to change his loyalty back and forth between Egypt and Babylon. When Jehoiakim rebels against Babylon, Nebuchadnezzar (now king of Babylon) embarks on a military campaign and ravages Judah (598 BC). In the same time frame, Nebuchadnezzar raids the Arameans of Syria, the Moabites and the Ammonites. Jehoiakim suddenly dies and is succeeded by Jehoiachin, who rules only three months. Nebuchadnezzar has laid siege to Jerusalem, obtains the city's surrender, and exiles the Judahite king, the queen mother, along with the skilled workers of Jerusalem. Nebuchadnezzar then proceeds to place Zedekiah as king over Judah. The end of Judah and her capital city Jerusalem is in sight.

Once again, a Judahite king decides to rebel against Babylon. Zedekiah refuses to learn from the past, succumbs to pressure from the people at large, decides to align Judah with Egypt against Babylon, and withholds tribute from Nebuchadnezzar. This is a terrible mistake. Jeremiah warns against such an alliance and is immediately thrown in prison for opposing the majority opinion. Nebuchadnezzar wastes no time in dispatching his army to put a definitive end to this constant taunting on the part of a vassal and insignificant king. He first defeats all the surrounding fortified towns (as is corroborated by the Lachish letters). He then lays siege to the city of Jerusalem. This siege is temporarily lifted when the Egyptians send an army into Palestine, but there is no record of a Babylonian battle with the Egyptians at this point.

Soon thereafter the siege resumes. Hunger begins to seriously affect the Jerusalemites. Finally, in 586 BC the city wall is breached. Zedekiah, with a military escort, flees the scene. He is overtaken near Jericho by the Babylonian army and brought before Nebuchadnezzar, where he witnesses the killing of his sons, is blinded, and is bound in shackles and taken to Babylon. Soon thereafter, the Babylonian troops under the direction

CHRONOLOGY OF JEREMIAH

DATE	EVENT
686 BC	Manasseh assumes sole kingship
648 BC	Birth of Josiah
642 BC	Amon succeeds Manasseh as king
640 BC	Josiah succeeds Amon
633 BC	Josiah seeks after God (2Ch 34:3) Cyaxares becomes king of Media
628 BC	Josiah begins reforms
626 BC	Jeremiah called to be a prophet Nabopolassar becomes king of Babylonia
621 BC	Book of the Law found in the temple
612 BC	Nineveh destroyed
609 BC	Josiah slain at Megiddo Jehoahaz rules three months Jehoiakim enthroned in Jerusalem
605 BC	Babylonia defeats Egypt at Carchemish Hostages and vessels taken to Babylon Nebuchadnezzar becomes king of Babylonia
604 BC	Nebuchadnezzar returns to Judah to receive tribute
601 BC	Nebuchadnezzar defeated near Egypt
598 BC	Jehoiakim's reign ends Jehoiachin rules Dec. 9, 598, to Mar. 16, 597
597 BC	Jehoiachin deported Apr. 22 Zedekiah becomes king in Judah
588 BC	Siege of Jerusalem begins Jan. 15
587 BC	Jeremiah imprisoned (Jer 32:1–2)
586 BC	July 18, Zedekiah flees (Jer 39:4) Aug. 14, destruction begins (2Ki 25:8–10) Oct. 7, Gedaliah slain; Jews migrate to Egypt.

Adapted from *The Zondervan Encyclopedia of the Bible*: Vol. 3 by Moisés Silva. Copyright © 2009 by Zondervan, pp. 500–501. Used by permission of Zondervan.

continued on next page

of Nebuzaradan, the captain of the Babylonian imperial guard, ravage Jerusalem. The temple, the royal palace and many homes are burned and the city walls are destroyed.

This is the sad end of Judah. Jeremiah, who was thrown into this tumultuous and ever-changing stage, witnesses the fulfillment of his prophecies in a real and unusual way. He has participated actively in all of these events in that he has not been isolated from the people or from the vicissitudes of international power struggles. ◆

12The LORD said to me, "You have seen
correctly, for I am watching[a] to see that
my word is fulfilled."
13The word of the LORD came to me
again: "What do you see?"[p]

"I see a pot that is boiling," I answered. "It is tilting toward us from the north."

14The LORD said to me, "From the north
disaster will be poured out on all who live
in the land. 15I am about to summon all
the peoples of the northern kingdoms,"
declares the LORD.

"Their kings will come and set up their
thrones
in the entrance of the gates of
Jerusalem;
they will come against all her
surrounding walls
and against all the towns of Judah.[q]
16I will pronounce my judgments on my
people
because of their wickedness[r] in
forsaking me,[s]
in burning incense to other gods[t]
and in worshiping what their hands
have made.

17"Get yourself ready! Stand up and say
to them whatever I command you. Do not
be terrified[u] by them, or I will terrify you
before them. 18Today I have made you[v] a
fortified city, an iron pillar and a bronze
wall to stand against the whole land—
against the kings of Judah, its officials, its
priests and the people of the land. 19They
will fight against you but will not overcome you, for I am with you[w] and will
rescue[x] you," declares the LORD.

1:13 [p] Zec 4:2
1:15 [q] Jer 4:16; 9:11
1:16 [r] Dt 28:20 [s] Jer 17:13 [t] Jer 7:9; 19:4
1:17 [u] Eze 2:6
1:18 [v] Isa 50:7
1:19 [w] Jer 20:11 [x] ver 8
2:2 [y] Eze 16:8-14,60; Hos 2:15 [z] Dt 2:7
2:3 [a] Dt 7:6 [b] Ex 19:6 [c] Jas 1:18; Rev 14:4 [d] Isa 41:11; Jer 30:16 [e] Jer 50:7

Israel Forsakes God

2 The word of the LORD came to me:
2"Go and proclaim in the hearing of
Jerusalem:

"This is what the LORD says:

"'I remember the devotion of your
youth,[y]
how as a bride you loved me
and followed me through the
wilderness,[z]
through a land not sown.
3Israel was holy[a] to the LORD,[b]
the firstfruits[c] of his harvest;
all who devoured[d] her were held guilty,[e]
and disaster overtook them,'"
declares the LORD.

[a] 12 The Hebrew for *watching* sounds like the Hebrew for *almond tree.*

1:13 *pot that is boiling.* A boiling pot was a common sight for the prophet. The fact that it is boiling and that it is tilted toward the south indicates that danger looms in the north. *from the north.* Some consider that for Israel the north symbolized dark and mysterious powers. Indeed many of Israel's problems originated in regions located to the north. As it turned out, the final destruction of Jerusalem was caused by the Babylonians, who descended upon Israel from the north. Moreover, the city of Jerusalem was most vulnerable from the north.

1:15 *thrones in the entrance of the gates of Jerusalem.* In many of the walled cities of Israel the entrance to the city was the place where judicial decisions were rendered. Excavations in both Dan and Hazor have uncovered the podium in the gate where such thrones would have sat (though it is uncertain whether the image of a god sat on the throne or the king sat there to give judgment). See notes on Job 5:4; 29:7; Pr 8:3; 31:23.

1:18 *a fortified city, an iron pillar and a bronze wall.* These three images serve as metaphors for strength in this context as well as in other Biblical contexts (e.g., Isa 45:2). They are also present in Egyptian texts. In the Amarna letters dated to approximately the fourteenth century BC, we read that the gods and the pharaoh himself use the metaphor of a bronze wall to bestow protection on the human being. In fact, Thutmose III of Egypt used these metaphors to describe himself in such a way that he would seem invincible.

2:3 *firstfruits.* Refers to the first portion of a harvested crop, which was considered the best part and was thus to be set aside for the Lord. Dt 26:5–10 commands that Israel set apart the firstfruits of the harvest for the Lord in order to give thanks for the gift of land. According to Nu 18:12–13, this first part of the harvest could only be eaten by the priests and their families. There are no exact ancient Near Eastern parallels to firstfruits. But in the Hittite "Instructions to Priests and Temple Officials" we do have injunctions regarding offerings that belong exclusively to the gods. There are severe warnings for the priests regarding taking or withholding sacrifices

The throne/podium at the gate of Dan. "Their kings will come and set up their thrones in the entrance of the gates of Jerusalem" (Jer 1:15).

[4] Hear the word of the LORD, you
descendants of Jacob,
all you clans of Israel.

[5] This is what the LORD says:

"What fault did your ancestors find
in me,
that they strayed so far from me?
They followed worthless idols
and became worthless[f] themselves.
[6] They did not ask, 'Where is the LORD,
who brought us up out of Egypt[g]
and led us through the barren
wilderness,
through a land of deserts[h] and
ravines,[i]
a land of drought and utter darkness,
a land where no one travels and no
one lives?'
[7] I brought you into a fertile land
to eat its fruit and rich produce.[j]
But you came and defiled my land
and made my inheritance detestable.[k]
[8] The priests did not ask,
'Where is the LORD?'
Those who deal with the law did not
know me;[l]
the leaders rebelled against me.
The prophets prophesied by Baal,[m]
following worthless idols.[n]

[9] "Therefore I bring charges[o] against you
again,"
declares the LORD.
"And I will bring charges against
your children's children.
[10] Cross over to the coasts of Cyprus and
look,
send to Kedar[a] and observe closely;
see if there has ever been anything
like this:

2:5 [f] 2Ki 17:15 **2:6** [g] Hos 13:4 [h] Dt 8:15 [i] Dt 32:10 **2:7** [j] Nu 13:27; Dt 8:7-9; 11:10-12 [k] Ps 106:34-39; Jer 16:18 **2:8** [l] Jer 4:22 [m] Jer 23:13 [n] Jer 16:19 **2:9** [o] Eze 20:35-36; Mic 6:2

[a] *10* In the Syro-Arabian desert

intended for the gods. If it occurs, death is prescribed. Other items entrusted to the Hittite priests, such as silver, gold and bronze implements, belong exclusively to the gods; the priests are only stewards of these items. This is clearly similar to the firstfruits in Israel, where certain offerings and objects belong only to God.

2:8 *prophesied by Baal.* The prophets of Israel have apostatized and are invoking the Canaanite god Baal. See notes on Nu 25:3; Dt 6:14; Jdg 2:11; see also the article "Baal," p. 600.

2:10 *coasts of Cyprus.* This Hebrew phrase is often translated as "the Greek islands" or "the island of Cyprus." *Kedar.* Kedar was a son of Ishmael, the son of Abraham and Hagar (see note on Isa 60:7). The name came to designate a nomadic tribe that flourished in the Syro-Arabian desert from the eighth to the fourth centuries BC. In this context, however, Kedar in conjunction with Cyprus designates the geographic extremes of east and west. God wants messengers to go as far east and as far west as possible to find out if any other nation has changed its gods as Judah has (v. 11).

[11] Has a nation ever changed its gods?
(Yet they are not gods[p] at all.)
But my people have exchanged their
glorious[q] God
for worthless idols.
[12] Be appalled at this, you heavens,
and shudder with great horror,"
declares the LORD.
[13] "My people have committed two sins:
They have forsaken me,
the spring of living water,[r]
and have dug their own cisterns,
broken cisterns that cannot hold
water.
[14] Is Israel a servant, a slave[s] by birth?
Why then has he become plunder?
[15] Lions[t] have roared;
they have growled at him.
They have laid waste[u] his land;
his towns are burned and deserted.
[16] Also, the men of Memphis[v] and
Tahpanhes[w]
have cracked your skull.
[17] Have you not brought this on
yourselves[x]
by forsaking the LORD your God
when he led you in the way?
[18] Now why go to Egypt[y]
to drink water from the Nile[a]?[z]
And why go to Assyria
to drink water from the Euphrates?
[19] Your wickedness will punish you;
your backsliding[a] will rebuke[b]
you.
Consider then and realize
how evil and bitter[c] it is for you
when you forsake the LORD your God
and have no awe[d] of me,"
declares the Lord,
the LORD Almighty.

[20] "Long ago you broke off your yoke[e]
and tore off your bonds;
you said, 'I will not serve you!'
Indeed, on every high hill[f]
and under every spreading tree[g]
you lay down as a prostitute.
[21] I had planted[h] you like a choice vine[i]
of sound and reliable stock.

2:11 [p] Isa 37:19; Jer 16:20 [q] Ps 106:20; Ro 1:23 **2:13** [r] Ps 36:9; Jn 4:14 **2:14** [s] Ex 4:22 **2:15** [t] Jer 4:7; 50:17 [u] Isa 1:7 **2:16** [v] Isa 19:13 [w] Jer 43:7-9 **2:17** [x] Jer 4:18 **2:18** [y] Isa 30:2 [z] Jos 13:3 **2:19** [a] Jer 3:11, 22 [b] Isa 3:9; Hos 5:5 [c] Job 20:14; Am 8:10 [d] Ps 36:1 **2:20** [e] Lev 26:13 [f] Isa 57:7; Jer 17:2 [g] Dt 12:2 **2:21** [h] Ex 15:17 [i] Ps 80:8

[a] *18* Hebrew *Shihor;* that is, a branch of the Nile

2:11 *Has a nation ever changed its gods?* A rhetorical question that expects a negative answer. There is no evidence in the ancient Near East that a nation or a tribe exchanged their god or gods for other gods from other places. This is probably because in an open-ended polytheistic system such as we find in the ancient Near East, nations "adopted" other gods, which meant that they added another god to their pantheon (e.g., the Philistines adopted Dagon), which may then have eventually displaced in importance the former gods. There is no evidence, however, that they exchanged Dagon for a former Philistine deity.
2:13 *broken cisterns.* Cisterns in ancient agricultural society were dug for at least two reasons: to store grain and food, and to store rainwater. Stored rainwater was used especially during the dry season (approximately May through September). Cisterns were dug in natural rock, or the ancient Israelites at times took advantage of natural cave formations to turn them into cisterns. In many cases cisterns had to be lined with plaster to be waterproof. But in certain areas the bedrock is impermeable so that waterproofing the cistern with lime plaster was unnecessary. Cisterns could suffer cracks in the lining; therefore, water would seep out and a precious source of life was lost. Jeremiah uses the cisterns here as a metaphor to explain how Israel has abandoned Yahweh, the source of all life, and has substituted him with other gods — i.e., cracked cisterns that cannot hold water.
2:14 *Is Israel ... a slave by birth?* Another rhetorical question (see note on v. 11). The terminology here describes what in fact Israel is not, namely, a house-born slave. Other types of slaves would include those captured in war or exchanged for goods. But the text is not making that distinction. The point is that slaves are treated as property by invaders and therefore are subject to being taken as plunder.
2:15 *towns are burned.* This refers to specific campaigns of a number of Assyrian rulers who came into the Levant, including Tiglath-Pileser III (745 – 727 BC), Shalmaneser V (727 – 722 BC), Sargon II (721 – 705 BC), Sennacherib (705 – 681 BC), and Esarhaddon (681 – 669 BC). Since the Assyrians had no intention of occupying these towns, their practice was to burn them in order to warn against the cost of noncooperation.
2:16 *Memphis.* The ancient capital of Lower Egypt and hence the residence of the Egyptian kings. It is located on the west bank of the Nile River about 15 miles (24 kilometers) south of Cairo. Today it is identified with modern Mitrahineh. The Greek historian Herodotus mentions that many of Jeremiah's contemporaries fled to this city when Judah was overtaken by the Babylonians in 587 BC. During the fourth century BC, when Alexander the Great built Alexandria, Memphis permanently lost its privileged position in Egypt. *Tahpanhes.* Identified with modern Tell Defneh and known by the ancient Greeks as Daphne. It is a frontier city located in the lower delta region on the caravan route that merchants took toward Israel and Mesopotamia. During Jeremiah's time, Israelites settled there, and many sought refuge there when the Babylonians invaded Judah in 587 BC. This commercial center was built by Psammetichus I; it was an important Egyptian city for many years. *cracked your skull.* The verb translated "cracked" is problematic, and there are a number of other alternative translations for this Hebrew verb, including "shaved," which typically indicates slavery or subordination. Since there is no scholarly consensus, we cannot affirm what in this context the author is referring to, or if slavery is indicated. What seems to be clear is that the act of having one's skull cracked or head shaved suggests a change in status.
2:18 *Nile ... Euphrates.* In this context the Euphrates is mentioned as the counterpart to the Nile; both are used metaphorically to indicate military foreign aid that Israel continually tried to obtain.
2:20 *yoke.* See note on 5:5. *on every high hill and under every spreading tree.* See note on Dt 12:2.
2:21 *choice vine.* The Hebrew word used here refers to a vine of high quality that grows in the Sorek Valley, known today as the Wadi es-Sarar, located southwest of Jerusalem. This vine offers a luscious variety of deep red grapes with soft seeds. Its use here is to demonstrate that Israel, unlike Sodom, was born of good stock.

How then did you turn against me
into a corrupt,[j] wild vine?
22 Although you wash yourself with
soap
and use an abundance of cleansing
powder,
the stain of your guilt is still before
me,"
declares the Sovereign LORD.
23 "How can you say, 'I am not defiled;[k]
I have not run after the Baals'?[l]
See how you behaved in the valley;[m]
consider what you have done.
You are a swift she-camel
running[n] here and there,
24 a wild donkey[o] accustomed to the
desert,
sniffing the wind in her craving —
in her heat who can restrain her?
Any males that pursue her need not
tire themselves;
at mating time they will find her.
25 Do not run until your feet are bare
and your throat is dry.
But you said, 'It's no use!
I love foreign gods,[p]
and I must go after them.'

26 "As a thief is disgraced[q] when he is
caught,
so the people of Israel are
disgraced —
they, their kings and their officials,
their priests and their prophets.
27 They say to wood, 'You are my father,'
and to stone,[r] 'You gave me birth.'
They have turned their backs to me
and not their faces;[s]
yet when they are in trouble,[t] they say,
'Come and save us!'

2:23 [j] Isa 5:4 [k] Pr 30:12 [l] Jer 9:14 [m] Jer 7:31 [n] ver 33; Jer 31:22
2:24 [o] Jer 14:6
2:25 [p] Dt 32:16; Jer 3:13; 14:10
2:26 [q] Jer 48:27
2:27 [r] Jer 3:9 [s] Jer 18:17; 32:33 [t] Jdg 10:10; Isa 26:16

28 Where then are the gods[u] you made for
yourselves?
Let them come if they can save you
when you are in trouble![v]
For you, Judah, have as many gods
as you have towns.[w]

29 "Why do you bring charges against me?
You have all[x] rebelled against me,"
declares the LORD.
30 "In vain I punished your people;
they did not respond to correction.
Your sword has devoured your
prophets[y]
like a ravenous lion.

31 "You of this generation, consider the
word of the LORD:

"Have I been a desert to Israel
or a land of great darkness?[z]
Why do my people say, 'We are free to
roam;
we will come to you no more'?
32 Does a young woman forget her
jewelry,
a bride her wedding ornaments?
Yet my people have forgotten me,
days without number.
33 How skilled you are at pursuing love!
Even the worst of women can learn
from your ways.
34 On your clothes is found
the lifeblood[a] of the innocent poor,
though you did not catch them
breaking in.[b]
Yet in spite of all this
35 you say, 'I am innocent;
he is not angry with me.'
But I will pass judgment[c] on you
because you say, 'I have not sinned.'[d]

2:28 [u] Isa 45:20 [v] Dt 32:37 [w] 2Ki 17:29; Jer 11:13
2:29 [x] Jer 5:1; 6:13; Da 9:11
2:30 [y] Ne 9:26; Ac 7:52; 1Th 2:15
2:31 [z] Isa 45:19
2:34 [a] 2Ki 21:16 [b] Ex 22:2
2:35 [c] Jer 25:31 [d] 1Jn 1:8, 10

2:22 *soap.* A cleansing agent made by mixing the ashes of certain plants with olive oil, animal fats or water. *cleansing powder.* Most likely sodium carbonate, used as a dye or as a cleaning substance. It was imported from Egypt as there are no natural mineral deposits of this type in Israel. **2:23 – 24** *she-camel ... wild donkey.* The young female camel is unreliable. Young camels never walk in orderly fashion and run off in any direction at the slightest provocation. It is said that a young camel never takes more than three steps in any one direction. A female donkey in heat becomes the image of that which is vulgar and almost violent. She will sniff out the urine of the male donkey and then, with a loud bray, will search and chase out the male. Both animals depict Israel as being unreliable in terms of her commitments to Yahweh as well as being a nation that desperately chases after the Baals. **2:27** *wood.* In their quest for other gods, the Israelites are calling out "Father" to a piece of wood. This piece of wood (or tree or wooden pole) likely represents the Canaanite Asherah, who is the female fertility symbol (see notes on Dt 7:5; 1Ki 14:23). If so, the words are sarcastic here. Asherah is considered the mother goddess in Canaanite texts and thus should not be addressed as "father." This is another indication of the utter confusion that has overtaken the Israelites. *stone.* This term is also full of irony. Stone is the male fertility symbol. Thus, it does not have the female capacity to give birth. This male fertility symbol is connected to the Canaanite deity El, who is called "father." El is considered the head of the Ugaritic pantheon as well as the father of the gods. On a stele discovered at Ras Shamra (ancient Ugarit), El is an elderly patriarch seated on a throne with majestic presence receiving a gift from the king of Ugarit.
2:28 *have as many gods as you have towns.* Israel's neighboring countries were polytheistic; to have as many gods as towns was the norm among these nations. They generally understood their worship as being locally defined, and therefore having local patron deities was common. In this religious worldview the plurality of deities was associated with geographic locations because worshipers were required to bring their gifts to the temple. Only those who lived close could do so regularly. The gods only cared about those who could bring gifts, so each town had its own gods. See the article "Great Symbiosis," p. 186.
2:32 *jewelry.* Generally refers to ornaments of gold and silver that were considered important and a source of pride. Here it most likely describes the ornaments worn by a bride. See Eze 16:10 – 13 and notes.

36 Why do you go about so much,
changing[e] your ways?
You will be disappointed by Egypt[f]
as you were by Assyria.
37 You will also leave that place
with your hands on your head,[g]
for the LORD has rejected those you
trust;
you will not be helped[h] by them.

3 "If a man divorces[i] his wife
and she leaves him and marries
another man,
should he return to her again?
Would not the land be completely
defiled?
But you have lived as a prostitute with
many lovers[j] —
would you now return to me?"
declares the LORD.
2 "Look up to the barren heights and
see.
Is there any place where you have
not been ravished?
By the roadside[k] you sat waiting for
lovers,
sat like a nomad in the desert.
You have defiled the land[l]
with your prostitution and
wickedness.
3 Therefore the showers have been
withheld,[m]
and no spring rains[n] have fallen.
Yet you have the brazen look of a
prostitute;
you refuse to blush with shame.[o]
4 Have you not just called to me:
'My Father,[p] my friend from my youth,[q]
5 will you always be angry?[r]
Will your wrath continue forever?'
This is how you talk,
but you do all the evil you can."

Unfaithful Israel

6 During the reign of King Josiah, the
LORD said to me, "Have you seen what
faithless Israel has done? She has gone up
on every high hill and under every spreading tree[s] and has committed adultery[t]
there. 7 I thought that after she had done
all this she would return to me but she did
not, and her unfaithful sister[u] Judah saw
it. 8 I gave faithless Israel her certificate of
divorce and sent her away because of all

2:36 [e] Jer 31:22 [f] Isa 30:2,3,7 **2:37** [g] 2Sa 13:19 [h] Jer 37:7 **3:1** [i] Dt 24:1-4 [j] Jer 2:20,25; Eze 16:26,29 **3:2** [k] Ge 38:14; Eze 16:25 [l] Jer 2:7 **3:3** [m] Lev 26:19 [n] Jer 14:4 [o] Jer 6:15; 8:12; Zep 3:5 **3:4** [p] ver 19 [q] Jer 2:2 **3:5** [r] Ps 103:9; Isa 57:16 **3:6** [s] Jer 17:2 [t] Jer 2:20 **3:7** [u] Eze 16:46

2:36 *disappointed by Egypt ... by Assyria.* It is not certain whether Jeremiah is referring to specific events or to these nations in general. By at least 732 BC, both Judah and Israel entered into a vassal relationship with Assyria. However, in the end, Assyria did not protect its vassals, but destroyed them, as they did to Israel in 721 BC and to Judah in 701 BC. In both of those cases, the vassals rebelled by not paying tribute, but even Ahaz of Judah, who had aligned himself with Assyria, found that his kingdom was not safe from them. Egypt had been unable to protect its vassals against the power of Assyria or other West Asiatic kingdoms. In the end, then, neither kingdom provided the safety or security that Judah was looking for. **2:37** *hands on your head.* The custom of placing one's hands on the head was a sign of shame and humiliation (2Sa 13:19). In the broader context of the ancient Near East it seems to be a gesture that expresses deep grief and mourning. **3:1** *If a man divorces his wife ... should he return to her again?* Laws in the ancient Near East generally allowed married couples to divorce. Most laws, however, greatly favored the husband, so that the initiative to divorce usually came from the man. Even so, the man had to give up his wife's property and often had to pay an extra penalty. There are a few ancient documents that speak of a wife initiating the divorce proceedings. In general, this was discouraged; in fact, there are Old Babylonian marriage contracts that expressly forbid the wife from divorcing her husband. Jeremiah has in mind here specific divorce legislation in the Hebrew Bible, namely, Dt 24:1–4. There it states that if a man divorces his wife, he may never take her back as wife if she has married another man, regardless of whether she is widowed from her second husband. In other words, the answer to the question posed here is an unequivocal no. **3:2** *barren heights.* Though there is much debate as to the original meaning of the Hebrew term used here, one can argue on a contextual basis that here it refers to hills that have little vegetation. They may have been areas on hills that were used as lookout points. However, in this context it probably refers to worship sites that may also have been used for the fertility cults (cf. v. 21; 7:29; see notes on 1Ki 3:2; 11:7; 2Ch 1:3). *a nomad in the desert.* Nomadism was a common way of life in the ancient Near East. Groups of nonsedentary camel breeders, known as "Bedouins," were common during the first millennium BC. In earlier times, pastoral nomadism was chosen as a way of life whereby domesticated animals were exploited by being involved in seasonal movements. For many years scholars believed there was constant tension between those who chose a more sedentary town life and those who were always on the move; however, more recently evidence has shown that there was a reasonably peaceful relationship between these two groups. In the present context, "nomad" refers to either a caravan trader or a bandit who wants to take advantage of the benefits of sedentary living. **3:3** *spring rains.* These rains come in early April. This does not refer to the rainy season, which generally falls during the months of December through February. Dry farming, which is the kind of farming not dependent on irrigation (as in Babylonia) or on flooding (as in Egypt), relies heavily on the regularity of these rains. The spring rains were important for the final ripening of the crop as well as to prepare the ground for the harvest. Throughout the Hebrew Bible one can perceive how important the rain was for the Israelite farmer. Grains and vegetables planted in Israel depended on natural rainfall, both in terms of quantity and timing. **3:8** *certificate of divorce.* Apparently in certain cases of divorce, two actions were necessary: (1) a certificate or bill of divorce had to be extended to the wife, and (2) the husband had to send the wife away. The practice of extending a certificate of divorce is well attested in the ancient Near East. The major law codes, such as the Code of Hammurapi and the Laws of Eshnunna in Mesopotamia, have extensive legislation regarding divorce procedures (see note on v. 1).

her adulteries. Yet I saw that her unfaithful
sister Judah had no fear;[v] she also went
out and committed adultery. 9Because Israel's immorality mattered so little to her,
she defiled the land[w] and committed adultery with stone[x] and wood.[y] 10In spite of
all this, her unfaithful sister Judah did not
return to me with all her heart, but only in
pretense,[z]" declares the LORD.

11The LORD said to me, "Faithless Israel
is more righteous[a] than unfaithful[b] Judah.
12Go, proclaim this message toward the
north:[c]

"'Return,[d] faithless Israel,' declares the
LORD,
'I will frown on you no longer,
for I am faithful,' declares the LORD,
'I will not be angry[e] forever.
13Only acknowledge[f] your guilt—
you have rebelled against the LORD
your God,
you have scattered your favors to
foreign gods[g]
under every spreading tree,[h]
and have not obeyed[i] me,'"
declares the LORD.

14"Return,[j] faithless people," declares
the LORD, "for I am your husband. I will
choose you—one from a town and two
from a clan—and bring you to Zion.
15Then I will give you shepherds[k] after my
own heart, who will lead you with knowledge and understanding. 16In those days,
when your numbers have increased greatly in the land," declares the LORD, "people
will no longer say, 'The ark of the covenant
of the LORD.' It will never enter their minds
or be remembered;[l] it will not be missed,
nor will another one be made. 17At that
time they will call Jerusalem The Throne[m]
of the LORD, and all nations will gather in
Jerusalem to honor[n] the name of the LORD.
No longer will they follow the stubbornness of their evil hearts.[o] 18In those days
the people of Judah will join the people of
Israel,[p] and together[q] they will come from
a northern[r] land to the land[s] I gave your
ancestors as an inheritance.

19"I myself said,

"'How gladly would I treat you like my
children
and give you a pleasant land,
the most beautiful inheritance of any
nation.'
I thought you would call me 'Father'[t]
and not turn away from following me.

3:8 [v] Eze 16:47; 23:11
3:9 [w] ver 2 [x] Isa 57:6 [y] Jer 2:27
3:10 [z] Jer 12:2
3:11 [a] Eze 16:52; 23:11 [b] ver 7
3:12 [c] 2Ki 17:3-6 [d] ver 14; Jer 31:21, 22; Eze 33:11 [e] Ps 86:15
3:13 [f] Dt 30:1-3; Jer 14:20; 1Jn 1:9 [g] Jer 2:25 [h] Dt 12:2 [i] ver 25
3:14 [j] Hos 2:19
3:15 [k] Ac 20:28
3:16 [l] Isa 65:17
3:17 [m] Jer 17:12; Eze 43:7 [n] Isa 60:9 [o] Jer 11:8
3:18 [p] Hos 1:11 [q] Isa 11:13; Jer 50:4 [r] Jer 16:15; 31:8 [s] Am 9:15
3:19 [t] ver 4; Isa 63:16

20But like a woman unfaithful to her
husband,
so you, Israel, have been unfaithful
to me,"
declares the LORD.

21A cry is heard on the barren heights,[u]
the weeping and pleading of the
people of Israel,
because they have perverted their ways
and have forgotten the LORD their
God.

22"Return,[v] faithless people;
I will cure[w] you of backsliding."

"Yes, we will come to you,
for you are the LORD our God.
23Surely the idolatrous commotion on
the hills
and mountains is a deception;
surely in the LORD our God
is the salvation[x] of Israel.
24From our youth shameful[y] gods have
consumed
the fruits of our ancestors' labor—
their flocks and herds,
their sons and daughters.
25Let us lie down in our shame,[z]
and let our disgrace cover us.
We have sinned against the LORD our
God,
both we and our ancestors;
from our youth[a] till this day
we have not obeyed the LORD our
God."

4 "If you, Israel, will return,[b]
then return to me,"
declares the LORD.
"If you put your detestable idols[c] out
of my sight
and no longer go astray,
2and if in a truthful, just and righteous
way
you swear,[d] 'As surely as the LORD
lives,'[e]
then the nations will invoke blessings[f]
by him
and in him they will boast."

3This is what the LORD says to the people of Judah and to Jerusalem:

"Break up your unplowed ground[g]
and do not sow among thorns.[h]
4Circumcise yourselves to the LORD,
circumcise your hearts,[i]
you people of Judah and inhabitants
of Jerusalem,

3:21 [u] ver 2
3:22 [v] Hos 14:4 [w] Jer 33:6; Hos 6:1
3:23 [x] Ps 3:8; Jer 17:14
3:24 [y] Hos 9:10
3:25 [z] Ezr 9:6 [a] Jer 22:21
4:1 [b] Jer 3:1, 22; Joel 2:12 [c] Jer 35:15
4:2 [d] Dt 10:20; Isa 65:16 [e] Jer 12:16 [f] Ge 22:18; Gal 3:8
4:3 [g] Hos 10:12 [h] Mk 4:18
4:4 [i] Dt 10:16; Jer 9:26; Ro 2:28-29

3:9 *committed adultery with stone and wood.* This phrase is a metaphor to express what may be termed as religious or spiritual adultery (see note on 2:27). The Israelites are prone to following other gods and thus breaking their covenant with Yahweh.

4:4 *circumcise your hearts.* Though it is impossible to say when and where the practice of circumcision began, it is clear that it was not an exclusive custom of the Israelites. It was practiced by many in the ancient Near East, particularly in Egypt as early as the twenty-third century BC

or my wrath[j] will flare up and burn
like fire
because of the evil you have done—
burn with no one to quench[k] it.

Disaster From the North

5 "Announce in Judah and proclaim in
Jerusalem and say:
'Sound the trumpet throughout the
land!'
Cry aloud and say:
'Gather together!
Let us flee to the fortified cities!'[l]
6 Raise the signal to go to Zion!
Flee for safety without delay!
For I am bringing disaster from the
north,[m]
even terrible destruction."

7 A lion[n] has come out of his lair;
a destroyer of nations has set out.
He has left his place
to lay waste[o] your land.
Your towns will lie in ruins[p]
without inhabitant.
8 So put on sackcloth,[q]
lament and wail,
for the fierce anger[r] of the LORD
has not turned away from us.

9 "In that day," declares the LORD,
"the king and the officials will lose
heart,
the priests will be horrified,
and the prophets will be appalled."[s]

10 Then I said, "Alas, Sovereign LORD!
How completely you have deceived[t] this
people and Jerusalem by saying, 'You will
have peace,'[u] when the sword is at our
throats!"

11 At that time this people and Jerusalem
will be told, "A scorching wind[v] from the
barren heights in the desert blows toward
my people, but not to winnow or cleanse;
12 a wind too strong for that comes from
me. Now I pronounce my judgments[w]
against them."

13 Look! He advances like the clouds,[x]
his chariots[y] come like a whirlwind,[z]
his horses are swifter than eagles.[a]
Woe to us! We are ruined!
14 Jerusalem, wash[b] the evil from your
heart and be saved.
How long will you harbor wicked
thoughts?
15 A voice is announcing from Dan,[c]
proclaiming disaster from the hills of
Ephraim.
16 "Tell this to the nations,
proclaim concerning Jerusalem:
'A besieging army is coming from a
distant land,
raising a war cry[d] against the cities
of Judah.

4:4 [j] Zep 2:2 [k] Am 5:6
4:5 [l] Jos 10:20; Jer 8:14
4:6 [m] Jer 1:13-15; 50:3
4:7 [n] 2Ki 24:1; Jer 2:15 [o] Isa 1:7 [p] Jer 25:9
4:8 [q] Isa 22:12; Jer 6:26 [r] Jer 30:24
4:9 [s] Isa 29:9
4:10 [t] 2Th 2:11 [u] Jer 14:13
4:11 [v] Eze 17:10; Hos 13:15
4:12 [w] Jer 1:16
4:13 [x] Isa 19:1 [y] Isa 66:15 [z] Isa 5:28 [a] Dt 28:49; Hab 1:8
4:14 [b] Jas 4:8
4:15 [c] Jer 8:16
4:16 [d] Eze 21:22

(see the article "Circumcision," p. 46). What is new in Israel is the meaning and significance behind circumcision. Whereas for many cultures circumcision represented a rite of passage into a tribe or nation, for the Israelite males, circumcision became a sign of belonging to Yahweh. Here, however, Jeremiah refers to the practice in a metaphoric way to express that Israel ought to allow its will (heart) to belong totally to Yahweh. The prophet admonishes Israel to come under Yahweh's control.

4:5 *fortified cities.* Judah at different times had a number of fortified cities—cities with walls built around them to protect them against enemy invasion (see note on Isa 2:15). Some cities like Lachish had double walls. During Jeremiah's time King Josiah had rebuilt cities such as Tekoa, Arad, Azekah and even Lachish so as to make them safer. Cities or towns not fortified with walls and towers were more vulnerable to enemy attack. The Assyrian king Sennacherib (704–681 BC) boasted of having defeated and captured 46 of these fortified cities in Judah.

4:6 *signal.* The Hebrew term does not refer to an auditory sound such as the blowing of a horn that announces a state of emergency, or to a smoke or fire signal. Rather, it has to do with a flag or a visual signal. It most likely was some kind of a banner lifted by a pole to signal danger, distress and imminent danger. This was a signal for the people to try and reach the fortified cities for protection. Banners were used as signals and as standards for army troops throughout the ancient Near East (see notes on Isa 5:26; 62:10). Many had animal figures on them. A common Assyrian figure used on banners was a moon sickle mounted on a spear.

4:8 *sackcloth.* This material was used as a symbol of mourning (see the article "Mourning," p. 828). It was made out of goat or camel hair and therefore was coarse and dark in color. It was also used to make grain bags. When used in the time of mourning, it was worn around the loins and was extremely uncomfortable. Jeremiah's call to put on sackcloth and thus begin the mourning rites seems to indicate that danger and destruction are imminent.

4:11 *A scorching wind.* Probably the well-known sirocco. This wind is a hot wind from the east and can be quite destructive. *not to winnow.* Because of the strength of the sirocco, it is not useful for winnowing the grain on the threshing floor. In Israel one can find many threshing floors where the wind was used to help separate the grain from the chaff (see note on Ru 3:2). The sirocco, in contrast, carried away both the grain and the chaff. Jeremiah uses this as a metaphor to warn that God's judgment will only bring destruction. *cleanse.* Can also be translated "sift" and thus would refer to the same process of separating what is useful and valuable from what is useless.

4:15 *announcing from Dan.* Dan was the Israelite outpost farthest to the north. In fact, the boundaries of Israel were popularly expressed by the somewhat optimistic phrase "from Dan to Beersheba." During Jeremiah's time, Dan seems to have flourished despite the fact that it remained an undefended city during the seventh century BC. Because of its strategic location, it would be the first to see the approach of an enemy coming from the north. *hills of Ephraim.* South of Dan and closer to Jerusalem lays the hill country of Ephraim. It is a mountainous region that extends from Shechem to Bethel. Jeremiah uses these geographic locations in order to demonstrate that the message of danger is traveling fast across the land of Israel.

17 They surround[e] her like men guarding
a field,
because she has rebelled[f] against me,' "
declares the LORD.
18 "Your own conduct and actions[g]
have brought this on you.[h]
This is your punishment.
How bitter[i] it is!
How it pierces to the heart!"

19 Oh, my anguish, my anguish![j]
I writhe in pain.
Oh, the agony of my heart!
My heart pounds within me,
I cannot keep silent.[k]
For I have heard the sound of the
trumpet;
I have heard the battle cry.[l]
20 Disaster follows disaster;[m]
the whole land lies in ruins.
In an instant my tents[n] are destroyed,
my shelter in a moment.
21 How long must I see the battle
standard
and hear the sound of the trumpet?

22 "My people are fools;[o]
they do not know me.[p]
They are senseless children;
they have no understanding.
They are skilled in doing evil;[q]
they know not how to do good."[r]

23 I looked at the earth,
and it was formless and empty;[s]
and at the heavens,
and their light was gone.
24 I looked at the mountains,
and they were quaking;[t]
all the hills were swaying.
25 I looked, and there were no people;
every bird in the sky had flown away.[u]
26 I looked, and the fruitful land was a
desert;
all its towns lay in ruins
before the LORD, before his fierce
anger.

27 This is what the LORD says:

"The whole land will be ruined,
though I will not destroy[v] it
completely.
28 Therefore the earth will mourn[w]
and the heavens above grow dark,[x]
because I have spoken and will not
relent,[y]
I have decided and will not turn
back.[z]"

29 At the sound of horsemen and archers[a]
every town takes to flight.[b]
Some go into the thickets;
some climb up among the rocks.
All the towns are deserted;[c]
no one lives in them.

30 What are you doing,[d] you devastated
one?
Why dress yourself in scarlet
and put on jewels[e] of gold?
Why highlight your eyes with
makeup?[f]
You adorn yourself in vain.
Your lovers[g] despise you;
they want to kill you.

31 I hear a cry as of a woman in labor,[h]
a groan as of one bearing her first
child—
the cry of Daughter Zion gasping for
breath,[i]
stretching out her hands[j] and
saying,
"Alas! I am fainting;
my life is given over to murderers."

Not One Is Upright

5 "Go up and down[k] the streets of
Jerusalem,
look around and consider,
search through her squares.
If you can find but one person[l]
who deals honestly and seeks the
truth,
I will forgive[m] this city.
2 Although they say, 'As surely as the
LORD lives,'[n]
still they are swearing falsely."

4:17 [e] 2Ki 25:1, 4 [f] Jer 5:23 **4:18** [g] Ps 107:17; Isa 50:1 [h] Jer 2:17 [i] Jer 2:19 **4:19** [j] Isa 16:11; 22:4; Jer 9:10 [k] Jer 20:9 [l] Nu 10:9 **4:20** [m] Ps 42:7; Eze 7:26 [n] Jer 10:20 **4:22** [o] Jer 10:8 [p] Jer 2:8 [q] Jer 13:23; 1Co 14:20 [r] Ro 16:19 **4:23** [s] Ge 1:2 **4:24** [t] Isa 5:25; Eze 38:20 **4:25** [u] Jer 9:10; 12:4; Zep 1:3 **4:27** [v] Jer 5:10, 18; 12:12; 30:11; 46:28 **4:28** [w] Jer 12:4, 11; 14:2; Hos 4:3 [x] Isa 5:30; 50:3 [y] Nu 23:19 [z] Jer 23:20; 30:24 **4:29** [a] Jer 6:23 [b] 2Ki 25:4 [c] ver 7 **4:30** [d] Isa 10:3-4 [e] Eze 23:40 [f] 2Ki 9:30 [g] La 1:2; Eze 23:9, 22 **4:31** [h] Jer 13:21 [i] Isa 42:14 [j] Isa 1:15; La 1:17 **5:1** [k] 2Ch 16:9; Eze 22:30 [l] Ge 18:32 [m] Ge 18:24 **5:2** [n] Jer 4:2

4:23–26 Jeremiah has taken his imagery from the creation account in Ge 1:2. He describes in poetic imagery the reversion of creation back to its non-ordered stage, before God had done his work. The Mesopotamian epic "Erra and Ishum" is roughly similar in that it describes a reversal of Marduk's creation of order out of the original primeval chaos. In the world-upside-down motif, all that is considered most consistent and reliable is jeopardized. The concept can be applied to the cosmic realm (the sun growing dark), the natural realm (the mountains being leveled), the political realm (empires being overthrown), the social realm (the poor becoming rich) or the animal realm (the lion and lamb together). It is often used in prophetic literature in connection with the day of the Lord and coming judgment.
4:28 *the heavens above grow dark.* This does not necessarily refer to an eclipse. In the context of this verse together with v. 23, the darkness is associated with mourning. Not only is all creation being reversed into its original nonordered state, but the issue here seems to be that the cities are being destroyed. This destruction creates a sense of doom and darkness wherein the entire earth mourns.
4:30 *dress yourself in scarlet.* Scarlet clothing was considered the most sophisticated and elegant. Scarlet dye came from the female kermes insects (*Coccus ilicis*), which attach themselves to the leaves and branches of the kermes oak. *eyes with makeup.* The practice of lining the eyes with paint was common in the ancient Near East, particularly in Egypt. Painting the eyes makes them look larger. The eye paint, or "antinomy," most likely came from a lead sulfide, which is a dark black mineral powder.

Prisoners yoked together, Abu Simbel. The yoke was a common tool used to bind animals together and sometimes was used for human prisoners as well.

3 LORD, do not your eyes[o] look for truth?
You struck[p] them, but they felt no pain;
you crushed them, but they refused correction.[q]
They made their faces harder than stone[r]
and refused to repent.
4 I thought, "These are only the poor;
they are foolish,
for they do not know[s] the way of the LORD,
the requirements of their God.
5 So I will go to the leaders[t]
and speak to them;
surely they know the way of the LORD,
the requirements of their God."
But with one accord they too had broken off the yoke
and torn off the bonds.[u]
6 Therefore a lion from the forest will attack them,
a wolf from the desert will ravage them,
a leopard[v] will lie in wait near their towns
to tear to pieces any who venture out,
for their rebellion is great
and their backslidings many.[w]
7 "Why should I forgive you?
Your children have forsaken me
and sworn[x] by gods that are not gods.[y]
I supplied all their needs,
yet they committed adultery[z]
and thronged to the houses of prostitutes.
8 They are well-fed, lusty stallions,
each neighing for another man's wife.[a]
9 Should I not punish them for this?"[b]
declares the LORD.
"Should I not avenge myself
on such a nation as this?

10 "Go through her vineyards and ravage them,
but do not destroy them completely.[c]
Strip off her branches,
for these people do not belong to the LORD.

5:3 [o] 2Ch 16:9 [p] Isa 9:13 [q] Jer 2:30; Zep 3:2 [r] Jer 7:26; 19:15; Eze 3:8-9 **5:4** [s] Jer 8:7 **5:5** [t] Mic 3:1, 9 [u] Ps 2:3; Jer 2:20 **5:6** [v] Hos 13:7 [w] Jer 30:14 **5:7** [x] Jos 23:7; Zep 1:5 [y] Dt 32:21; Jer 2:11; Gal 4:8 [z] Nu 25:1 **5:8** [a] Jer 29:23; Eze 22:11 **5:9** [b] ver 29; Jer 9:9 **5:10** [c] Jer 4:27

5:5 *yoke.* A common instrument used in the ancient Near East to bind animals together as means for production. As time passed, it was also used to bind human prisoners as a means of control and punishment (Jer 27–28). Finally, the yoke became a symbol of control, ownership, and most often political servitude (1Ki 12:4; see note on Isa 9:4). It seems that only here and in 2:20 is "yoke" used to express the reality of Yahweh's covenant with Israel. It is more common to speak of the yoke of Egypt. However, this may be an extension of the theology of the exodus, where being freed from slavery in Egypt did not lead to unbridled freedom but to a new kind of willing bondage to Yahweh.
5:6 *lion.* Wild animals such as the lion were much more prevalent in the ancient Near East than they are in modern times. The metaphor of these wild predators representing the attack of an enemy would have been readily understood in Jeremiah's context, particularly among those who worked as shepherds. See notes on Jdg 14:5; Isa 31:4.
5:8 *lusty stallions.* Stallions, much like the female wild donkey in 2:24, cannot control their sexual appetite. Stallions do not mate for life but follow their instincts. The metaphor here describes the conduct of the Israelites.
5:10 *vineyards.* This Hebrew term is rare. Many scholars think it refers to "vine terraces." This fits the context well. In Israel there are many terraced vineyards, built in such a way so that water can be stopped from running off the slope of the hills. This guarantees that the vines will get enough moisture.

11 The people of Israel and the people of Judah
have been utterly unfaithful[d] to me,"
declares the LORD.
12 They have lied about the LORD;
they said, "He will do nothing!
No harm will come to us;[e]
we will never see sword or famine.[f]
13 The prophets[g] are but wind
and the word is not in them;
so let what they say be done to them."

14 Therefore this is what the LORD God Almighty says:

"Because the people have spoken these words,
I will make my words in your mouth[h] a fire[i]
and these people the wood it consumes.
15 People of Israel," declares the LORD,
"I am bringing a distant nation[j] against you—
an ancient and enduring nation,
a people whose language[k] you do not know,
whose speech you do not understand.
16 Their quivers are like an open grave;
all of them are mighty warriors.
17 They will devour[l] your harvests and food,
devour[m] your sons and daughters;
they will devour[n] your flocks and herds,
devour your vines and fig trees.
With the sword they will destroy
the fortified cities in which you trust.[o]

18 "Yet even in those days," declares the
LORD, "I will not destroy[p] you completely.
19 And when the people ask,[q] 'Why has the
LORD our God done all this to us?' you will
tell them, 'As you have forsaken me and
served foreign gods[r] in your own land, so
now you will serve foreigners[s] in a land
not your own.'

20 "Announce this to the descendants of Jacob
and proclaim it in Judah:
21 Hear this, you foolish and senseless people,
who have eyes[t] but do not see,
who have ears but do not hear:[u]
22 Should you not fear[v] me?" declares the LORD.
"Should you not tremble in my presence?
I made the sand a boundary for the sea,
an everlasting barrier it cannot cross.
The waves may roll, but they cannot prevail;
they may roar, but they cannot cross it.
23 But these people have stubborn and rebellious[w] hearts;
they have turned aside and gone away.
24 They do not say to themselves,
'Let us fear the LORD our God,
who gives autumn and spring rains[x] in season,
who assures us of the regular weeks of harvest.'[y]
25 Your wrongdoings have kept these away;
your sins have deprived you of good.

26 "Among my people are the wicked
who lie in wait[z] like men who snare birds
and like those who set traps to catch people.
27 Like cages full of birds,
their houses are full of deceit;[a]
they have become rich[b] and powerful
28 and have grown fat[c] and sleek.
Their evil deeds have no limit;
they do not seek justice.
They do not promote the case of the fatherless;[d]
they do not defend the just cause of the poor.[e]
29 Should I not punish them for this?"
declares the LORD.
"Should I not avenge myself
on such a nation as this?

30 "A horrible[f] and shocking thing
has happened in the land:
31 The prophets prophesy lies,[g]
the priests rule by their own authority,

5:11 [d] Jer 3:20 **5:12** [e] Jer 23:17 [f] 2Ch 36:16; Jer 14:13 **5:13** [g] Jer 14:15 **5:14** [h] Jer 1:9; Hos 6:5 [i] Jer 23:29 **5:15** [j] Dt 28:49; Isa 5:26; Jer 4:16 [k] Isa 28:11 **5:17** [l] Lev 26:16; Jer 8:16 [m] Dt 28:32; Jer 50:7, 17 [n] Dt 28:31 [o] Dt 28:33 **5:18** [p] Jer 4:27 **5:19** [q] Dt 29:24-26; 1Ki 9:9 [r] Jer 16:13 [s] Dt 28:48 **5:21** [t] Isa 6:10; Eze 12:2 [u] Mt 13:15; Mk 8:18 **5:22** [v] Dt 28:58 **5:23** [w] Dt 21:18 **5:24** [x] Ps 147:8; Joel 2:23 [y] Ge 8:22; Ac 14:17 **5:26** [z] Ps 10:8; Pr 1:11 **5:27** [a] Jer 9:6 [b] Jer 12:1 **5:28** [c] Dt 32:15 [d] Zec 7:10 [e] Isa 1:23; Jer 7:6 **5:30** [f] Jer 23:14; Hos 6:10 **5:31** [g] Eze 13:6; Mic 2:11

5:12 *They have lied about the LORD; they said, "He will do nothing!"* Certainly it was a popular prophet who offered the people the hope of peace, security and resolution of the problem. Denial is the path of least resistance. There would likewise be no shortage of prophets who saw personal gain in supporting the desires of the throne on these matters and were therefore willing to represent the best interests of the king and whatever propaganda he desired to circulate. Of the prophets known in the ancient Near East, especially from this period, few would ever offer a negative prophecy.

5:24 *autumn and spring rains.* The autumn rains are known as the early or former rains. They begin in October and run into the winter months (known as the rainy season). These rains help soften the ground for plowing in order to plant seed. This rain also helps to fill up the cisterns that have dried up over the summer months. The spring or latter rains begin in early April; these provide the needed moisture to ripen the crops for harvest (see note on 3:3).

and my people love it this way.
But what will you do in the end?

Jerusalem Under Siege

6 "Flee for safety, people of Benjamin!
Flee from Jerusalem!
Sound the trumpet in Tekoa![h]
Raise the signal over Beth Hakkerem![i]
For disaster looms out of the north,[j]
even terrible destruction.
2 I will destroy Daughter Zion,
so beautiful and delicate.
3 Shepherds[k] with their flocks will come against her;
they will pitch their tents around[l] her,
each tending his own portion."

4 "Prepare for battle against her!
Arise, let us attack at noon![m]
But, alas, the daylight is fading,
and the shadows of evening grow long.
5 So arise, let us attack at night
and destroy her fortresses!"

6 This is what the LORD Almighty says:

"Cut down the trees[n]
and build siege ramps[o] against Jerusalem.
This city must be punished;
it is filled with oppression.
7 As a well pours out its water,
so she pours out her wickedness.
Violence[p] and destruction[q] resound in her;
her sickness and wounds are ever before me.
8 Take warning, Jerusalem,
or I will turn away[r] from you
and make your land desolate
so no one can live in it."

9 This is what the LORD Almighty says:

"Let them glean the remnant of Israel
as thoroughly as a vine;
pass your hand over the branches again,
like one gathering grapes."

6:1 [h] 2Ch 11:6 [i] Ne 3:14 [j] Jer 4:6 **6:3** [k] Jer 12:10 [l] 2Ki 25:4; Lk 19:43 **6:4** [m] Jer 15:8 **6:6** [n] Dt 20:19-20 [o] Jer 32:24 **6:7** [p] Ps 55:9; Eze 7:11,23 [q] Jer 20:8 **6:8** [r] Eze 23:18; Hos 9:12

6:10 [s] Ac 7:51 [t] Jer 20:8 **6:11** [u] Jer 7:20 [v] Job 32:20; Jer 20:9 [w] Jer 9:21 **6:12** [x] Dt 28:30 [y] Jer 8:10; 38:22 [z] Isa 5:25 **6:13** [a] Isa 56:11 [b] Jer 8:10 **6:14** [c] Jer 4:10; 8:11; Eze 13:10 **6:15** [d] Jer 3:3; 8:10-12 **6:16** [e] Jer 18:15

10 To whom can I speak and give warning?
Who will listen to me?
Their ears are closed[a][s]
so they cannot hear.
The word[t] of the LORD is offensive to them;
they find no pleasure in it.
11 But I am full of the wrath[u] of the LORD,
and I cannot hold it in.[v]

"Pour it out on the children in the street
and on the young men[w] gathered together;
both husband and wife will be caught in it,
and the old, those weighed down with years.
12 Their houses will be turned over to others,[x]
together with their fields and their wives,[y]
when I stretch out my hand[z]
against those who live in the land,"
declares the LORD.
13 "From the least to the greatest,
all are greedy for gain;[a]
prophets and priests alike,
all practice deceit.[b]
14 They dress the wound of my people
as though it were not serious.
'Peace, peace,' they say,
when there is no peace.[c]
15 Are they ashamed of their detestable conduct?
No, they have no shame at all;
they do not even know how to blush.[d]
So they will fall among the fallen;
they will be brought down when I punish them,"
says the LORD.

16 This is what the LORD says:

"Stand at the crossroads and look;
ask for the ancient paths,[e]

[a] 10 Hebrew *uncircumcised*

6:1 *Tekoa.* The hometown of the prophet Amos; it was located on the road to Hebron, about ten miles (16 kilometers) south of Jerusalem. Today it is identified with Khirbet Tequa. The context here seems to point to the fact that it was on the border of arable land and at the beginning of wasteland. This suggests that Tekoa could be used as a city of refuge for those fleeing from Jerusalem. *Beth Hakkerem.* The precise location of this town is unknown. Some have identified it as Ramat Rahel, about two miles (3.2 kilometers) south of Jerusalem; however, this has not yet been proven. The meaning of its name is "house of the vineyard." The town is associated with Tekoa and Bethlehem. The church father Jerome located Beth Hakkerem on a hilltop between Jerusalem and Tekoa. If this is correct, then the town would serve as a good signal location in times of enemy attack, particularly during the time of Jeremiah. Scholars more recently have suggested that Ramat Rahel was the site of an Assyrian palace that served as a center to supervise Jerusalem, the capital city of Judah during Assyrian hegemony in the ancient Near East.

6:6 *siege ramps.* See the article "Siege Warfare," p. 1157.

6:9 *glean the remnant.* Lev 19:9–10 stipulates that landowners may not take every last bit of the harvest. In the context of Jeremiah, this metaphor has to do with severe judgment. God is allowing the Babylonians to do what the Israelites are not allowed to do in their own fields. Babylon is given permission to devastate the land of Israel. In other words, the enemy has been given clearance to "take all" and not leave anything behind.

ask where the good way[f] is, and walk
in it,
and you will find rest[g] for your souls.
But you said, 'We will not walk in it.'
17 I appointed watchmen[h] over you and
said,
'Listen to the sound of the trumpet!'
But you said, 'We will not listen.'[i]
18 Therefore hear, you nations;
you who are witnesses,
observe what will happen to them.
19 Hear, you earth:[j]
I am bringing disaster on this people,
the fruit of their schemes,[k]
because they have not listened to my
words
and have rejected my law.[l]
20 What do I care about incense from Sheba
or sweet calamus[m] from a distant
land?
Your burnt offerings are not
acceptable;[n]
your sacrifices[o] do not please me."[p]
21 Therefore this is what the LORD says:
"I will put obstacles before this people.
Parents and children alike will
stumble[q] over them;
neighbors and friends will perish."
22 This is what the LORD says:
"Look, an army is coming
from the land of the north;[r]
a great nation is being stirred up
from the ends of the earth.
23 They are armed with bow and spear;
they are cruel and show no mercy.[s]
They sound like the roaring sea
as they ride on their horses;[t]
they come like men in battle formation
to attack you, Daughter Zion."
24 We have heard reports about them,
and our hands hang limp.
Anguish[u] has gripped us,
pain like that of a woman in labor.[v]
25 Do not go out to the fields
or walk on the roads,
for the enemy has a sword,
and there is terror on every side.[w]
26 Put on sackcloth,[x] my people,
and roll in ashes;[y]
mourn with bitter wailing
as for an only son,[z]
for suddenly the destroyer
will come upon us.
27 "I have made you a tester[a] of metals
and my people the ore,
that you may observe
and test their ways.
28 They are all hardened rebels,[b]
going about to slander.[c]
They are bronze and iron;[d]
they all act corruptly.
29 The bellows blow fiercely
to burn away the lead with fire,

6:16 [f] Ps 119:3 [g] Mt 11:29 **6:17** [h] Eze 3:17 [i] Jer 11:7-8; 25:4 **6:19** [j] Isa 1:2; Jer 22:29 [k] Pr 1:31 [l] Jer 8:9 **6:20** [m] Ex 30:23 [n] Am 5:22 [o] Ps 50:8-10; Jer 7:21; Mic 6:7-8 [p] Isa 1:11 **6:21** [q] Isa 8:14 **6:22** [r] Jer 1:15; 10:22 **6:23** [s] Isa 13:18 [t] Jer 4:29 **6:24** [u] Jer 4:19 [v] Jer 4:31; 50:41-43 **6:25** [w] Jer 49:29 **6:26** [x] Jer 4:8 [y] Jer 25:34; Mic 1:10 [z] Zec 12:10 **6:27** [a] Jer 9:7 **6:28** [b] Jer 5:23 [c] Jer 9:4 [d] Eze 22:18

6:17 *the trumpet.* The *shofar* (ram's horn). See note on Jos 6:4.

6:20 *incense.* See Ex 30:34 – 38; see also note on Nu 16:7; cf. notes on Pr 27:9; SS 3:6. *Sheba.* Located in the southern Arabian peninsula (modern Yemen). Frankincense and myrrh came from this area as well as from the Far East. See note on Isa 60:6. *calamus.* This Hebrew term comes from classical sources that speak of *Calamus aromaticus* and refers to an aromatic spice cane. This spice is one of the ingredients included in the anointing oil (Ex 30:23). Perhaps this cane was imported from India. It is not to be confused with sugar cane, which spread east after the OT period.

6:23 *battle formation.* Mesopotamian military organization kept developing throughout the millennia. By the seventh century BC, partly because of previous reforms instituted by Tiglath-Pileser III of Assyria (c. 745 – 727 BC), chariots and cavalry were used as shock weapons. As time went on, the infantry gained importance alongside the chariots. There were generally three men per chariot: the driver, an archer and a shield bearer. Under King Ashurbanipal (c. 669 – 627 BC), a heavier chariot carrying four men was used.

6:26 *roll in ashes.* Sackcloth and ashes are well-known symbols of mourning both in the Biblical world and in the ancient Near East generally (see the article "Mourning," p. 828). They are also used as signs of fasting and repentance. To roll in ashes was not common, and it adds here a dynamic element to the custom (see Eze 27:30).

6:27 *tester of metals.* The Lord depicts the prophet Jeremiah as a tester of the people. In this metaphor the people are considered the ore that Jeremiah is to evaluate. The role of a metal assayer was to test the metal by smelting, a procedure that ridded metal of its impurities (see notes on Pr 17:3; Isa 48:10). In this particular case the people of Israel fail the test and are rejected.

6:28 *bronze and iron.* In the ancient world silver was extracted and assayed through a process called cupellation (see note on Isa 1:22). In the initial smelting process silver was extracted from lead ores (galena) containing less than 1% silver in a given sample. The lead was melted in shallow vessels made of porous substances such as bone ash or clay. A bellows was then used to blow air across the molten lead producing lead oxide (litharge). Some of the lead oxide was absorbed by the bone ash, while some could be skimmed off the surface. Ideally, the silver would remain. Unfortunately, this process has many potential problems. If the temperature was too high, or if the sample contained other metals (iron, copper or tin were common), the cupellation would be unsuccessful. In this situation, when the litharge was skimmed off, rather than resulting in silver extraction, what remained was tainted silver mixed with other metals, making it unusable. This unusable product is perhaps what is referred to as "dross" (Pr 25:4; Isa 1:22; see Eze 22:18 and note). Another possibility is that the text refers to the assaying process. This involved heating a sample of silver together with large amounts of lead in order to draw off the impurities. One of the possible results of the assaying process was that the quantity of lead would be insufficient to draw off the impurities, rendering the silver useless. Rather than being purified, then, the silver would be in worse shape than it was before the process. Perhaps this process is envisioned by the text and the silver becomes this useless junk.

but the refining goes on in vain;
the wicked are not purged out.
30 They are called rejected silver,
because the LORD has rejected them."[e]

False Religion Worthless

7 This is the word that came to Jeremiah
from the LORD: 2"Stand[f] at the gate of
the LORD's house and there proclaim this
message:
" 'Hear the word of the LORD, all you people of Judah who come through these gates
to worship the LORD. 3This is what the LORD
Almighty, the God of Israel, says: Reform
your ways[g] and your actions, and I will let
you live in this place. 4Do not trust in deceptive[h] words and say, "This is the temple of the LORD, the temple of the LORD, the
temple of the LORD!" 5If you really change
your ways and your actions and deal with
each other justly,[i] 6if you do not oppress the
foreigner, the fatherless or the widow and
do not shed innocent blood[j] in this place,
and if you do not follow other gods[k] to your
own harm, 7then I will let you live in this
place, in the land[l] I gave your ancestors for
ever and ever. 8But look, you are trusting in
deceptive words that are worthless.
9" 'Will you steal and murder, commit
adultery and perjury,[a] burn incense to
Baal[m] and follow other gods[n] you have not
known, 10and then come and stand before
me in this house,[o] which bears my Name,
and say, "We are safe"—safe to do all
these detestable things? 11Has this house,[p]

6:30 [e] Ps 119:119; Jer 7:29; Hos 9:17
7:2 [f] Jer 17:19
7:3 [g] Jer 18:11; 26:13
7:4 [h] Mic 3:11
7:5 [i] Jer 22:3
7:6 [j] Jer 2:34; 19:4 [k] Dt 8:19
7:7 [l] Dt 4:40
7:9 [m] Jer 11:13, 17 [n] Ex 20:3
7:10 [o] Jer 32:34; Eze 23:38-39
7:11 [p] Isa 56:7

[a] 9 Or *and swear by false gods*

7:2 *Stand at the gate.* Standing at the temple gate guaranteed a large audience for Jeremiah's proclamation. Gate areas in the ancient Near Eastern world were places where much human activity and traffic took place (see notes on Job 5:4; 29:7; Pr 8:3; 31:23). The particular area where Jeremiah stands is an area outside the temple called the "inner court." We cannot be sure which gate Jeremiah is facing, but he surely has direct contact with the majority of the temple worshipers. Jeremiah chooses this place, as well as a number of city gates (e.g., the Potsherd Gate, the Benjamin Gate), to proclaim the messages he receives from God. *worship.* Worship in the Hebrew Bible is expressed by different terms. Two Hebrew words are essential to understand Israelite worship: one means "service" and the other designates "prostration" or "bowing down." It is this second term that is used here, and generally refers to an attitude of veneration of God or of false gods. The temple was primarily a state sanctuary and thus was part of the royal estate. The temple was the "house of God," and was God's residence. It was not intended as a place of corporate worship, and worshipers were admitted in the temple courts, but not the temple itself. Sacrificial rituals were done in the courts and elsewhere. Regarding individual worship in the ancient Near East, we know that some worshipers received dreams when bowing before the image of a given deity. However, the evidence available is not explicit as to the worshiper's activity within the temple. We do know that access into the temples of Mesopotamia was restricted.

7:4 *the temple of the LORD.* The triple repetition of this phrase seems to point to some kind of magical incantation that invokes protection. Perhaps this is similar to the triple expressions that appear at the beginning of Babylonian magical texts known as Maqlû. During the time of Jeremiah the people have apparently developed a kind of blind superstition regarding the temple. At least two concepts come into play at this time. (1) As long as the temple stands on Mount Zion, popular belief is that this guarantees God's protection of Jerusalem because the temple "houses" God's presence. (2) This belief was strongly enhanced by God's intervention during the time of Hezekiah, when Jerusalem was saved from total destruction at the hands of the Assyrian king Sennacherib, who had placed the city under siege. This divine intervention helped nurture the ideology that the temple in Jerusalem was inviolable.

One can see a possible parallel here with the Mesopotamian concept of a city's patron deity. Such deities in Mesopotamia were the protectors of the temple (the house of the deity) and of the city. They were taken care of by the human population and therefore were dependent on the well-being of the city for their upkeep. As long as there was an earthly abode for the deity in a given city, the city had special protection. In the case of Israel, it seems that the influence of its neighbors, as well as the interpretation of God's divine intervention, led to the ideology known as the "inviolability of the temple," which also then meant that Jerusalem was secure. As Jeremiah is quick to point out, this is false. Yahweh, the God of Israel, has no needs—his protection of the people of Judah is connected to their keeping of the covenant not to the sacrifices they bring.

7:6 *the foreigner, the fatherless or the widow.* These three categories of persons are symbolic of the most vulnerable classes of people in the ancient Near East. Ancient law codes, such as those of Ur-Nammu and the Code of Hammurapi, show a preoccupation with protecting the rights of the poor, the widow and the orphan. See note on Lev 19:20. *do not shed innocent blood in this place.* This accusation was already mentioned in 2:34. There are explicit teachings in Deuteronomy against shedding innocent blood (Dt 19:10,13; 21:8–9). We cannot be sure what specific situation Jeremiah is referring to here. Probably the warning covers more than possible murders in the temple. We find out later that King Jehoiakim was responsible for shedding innocent blood (22:3,7). He was also responsible for killing the innocent prophet Uriah (26:20–23). These murders would have been politically motivated.

7:9 *incense.* This Hebrew term is different from the one used in 6:20 (see note there). The offering of incense to the gods is a well-attested practice in religious ritual throughout the ancient Near East. The incense offered was a mixture of spices that gave off a fragrance when placed over fire. In Mesopotamia various records mention the practice of offering incense to the gods. This custom was also part of the Israelite religious ritual. Incense could be offered as a supplement to a sacrifice. It was also burned by the priests twice a day on the altar of incense in front of the veil of the Most Holy Place. The smoke created a visual screen and the fragrance was luxurious.

7:10 *this house, which bears my Name.* In the ancient world, naming a person or an object meant having ownership and authority over that person. The Hebrew idiom "the house that bears my Name" depicts God's ownership of the temple. By placing his name on the temple, God declares he has legal rights over it and considers it

which bears my Name, become a den of
robbers[q] to you? But I have been watching![r] declares the LORD.
12"'Go now to the place in Shiloh[s] where
I first made a dwelling for my Name, and
see what I did[t] to it because of the wickedness of my people Israel. 13While you
were doing all these things, declares the
LORD, I spoke to you again and again,[u] but
you did not listen;[v] I called you, but you
did not answer.[w] 14Therefore, what I did
to Shiloh I will now do to the house that
bears my Name,[x] the temple you trust in,
the place I gave to you and your ancestors.
15I will thrust you from my presence, just
as I did all your fellow Israelites, the people of Ephraim.'[y]
16"So do not pray for this people nor offer any plea[z] or petition for them; do not
plead with me, for I will not listen to you.
17Do you not see what they are doing in
the towns of Judah and in the streets of Jerusalem? 18The children gather wood, the
fathers light the fire, and the women knead
the dough and make cakes to offer to the
Queen of Heaven.[a] They pour out drink offerings[b] to other gods to arouse[c] my anger.
19But am I the one they are provoking? declares the LORD. Are they not rather harming themselves, to their own shame?[d]
20"'Therefore this is what the Sovereign
LORD says: My anger[e] and my wrath will
be poured out on this place — on man and
beast, on the trees of the field and on the
crops of your land — and it will burn and
not be quenched.
21"'This is what the LORD Almighty, the
God of Israel, says: Go ahead, add your
burnt offerings to your other sacrifices[f]
and eat[g] the meat yourselves! 22For when
I brought your ancestors out of Egypt and
spoke to them, I did not just give them
commands about burnt offerings and sacrifices,[h] 23but I gave them this command:

7:11 [q] Mt 21:13*; Mk 11:17*; Lk 19:46* [r] Jer 29:23 **7:12** [s] Jos 18:1 [t] 1Sa 4:10-11, 22; Ps 78:60-64 **7:13** [u] 2Ch 36:15 [v] Isa 65:12 [w] Jer 35:17 **7:14** [x] 1Ki 9:7 **7:15** [y] Ps 78:67 **7:16** [z] Ex 32:10; Dt 9:14; Jer 15:1

7:18 [a] Jer 44:17-19 [b] Jer 19:13 [c] 1Ki 14:9 **7:19** [d] Jer 9:19 **7:20** [e] Jer 42:18; La 2:3-5 **7:21** [f] Isa 1:11; Am 5:21-22 [g] Hos 8:13 **7:22** [h] 1Sa 15:22; Ps 51:16; Hos 6:6

his personal property. Here God proclaims that he cares deeply for the temple and that only he should be worshiped in this place. This is equally true in the ancient Mesopotamian context. Temples were considered private residences of the deities. The presence of the deity in the temple, as in Israel, provided protection for the worshiper because the name was powerful.

7:12 *Shiloh.* Identified with modern Khirbet Seilun, located north of Bethel in the heart of Ephraim. This town served as one of the premier worship places for the Israelites from the time of Joshua until the days of Samuel. For at least some of that time, the Israelites placed the ark of the covenant and the tabernacle there, and Shiloh is where God established his name in the early years of Israel's occupation of the promised land. Archaeological excavations have shown the presence of impressive architecture that lasted until a fierce destruction that took place in the eleventh century BC, when presumably the Philistines destroyed Shiloh (cf. 1Sa 4). After this time, Shiloh never again served as the primary worship center. By Jeremiah's time, Shiloh did not have a sanctuary, though there is evidence of human occupation there well into exilic times.

7:17 *in the towns of Judah and in the streets of Jerusalem.* This is most likely an idiomatic phrase that Jeremiah uses in order to emphasize that idolatrous worship is practiced everywhere in Judah (cf. 2:28, where the prophet accuses the people of Judah of being no different from their polytheistic neighbors). This kind of statement is illustrative of the extent to which the ancient Near Eastern neighbors had an influence on the belief system of the Israelites at this time.

7:18 *cakes.* The Hebrew word is a loanword from the Akkadian language. There is considerable evidence from places such as Mari that the Babylonians used cakes in the worship of the Assyro-Babylonian goddess Ishtar. These cakes were baked over an open fire, not in an oven. A number of clay molds for cakes from the second millennium BC have been discovered in a palace kitchen at Mari. Some have a female shape and others are star-shaped. Presumably both are representative of a female goddess. *Queen of Heaven.* It is impossible to state with absolute confidence that this refers to the goddess Ishtar. Yet despite scholarly debate over the years, there is no better candidate. Ishtar is the goddess of love, sexuality and war, and there certainly was Mesopotamian influence in the worship practices of Judah, particularly from the time of King Ahaz until the reign of King Zedekiah. Ishtar is said to court the god Tammuz, who in turn dies every year along with the earth during the long dry season. Ishtar then pursues her dead partner, Tammuz, who comes to life during the wet season. Note that years later Ezekiel indicts the women of Israel for sitting at the north gate of the temple and weeping for Tammuz (Eze 8:14). Another proposed candidate from a Canaanite context is the goddess Asherah, and archaeological evidence substantiates that she was worshiped in Israel. The central issue here is that the inhabitants of Judah are worshiping the Queen of Heaven as well as Yahweh. *pour out drink offerings.* It was common practice to offer drink offerings (i.e., libations) to God in Israel (Ex 29:40; Lev 23:13,18). However, the expression here is more typical of the worship of pagan gods. There is evidence that these offerings were poured out on rooftops of houses in Jerusalem as well as on the palace rooftop.

7:20 *on man and beast, on the trees ... the crops.* The parallel between man and beast is common in Scripture (e.g., Ex 8:13 – 14). However, the addition of trees and produce is not seen elsewhere. When Enlil, the king of the gods in Mesopotamia, brought on the flood, it was leashed upon all flesh indiscriminately. The Mesopotamian epic "Erra and Ishum" also describes devastation that took both humans and animals. On the other hand, warfare tactics often targeted the produce and the trees. Trees were chopped down for the needs of the besieging army or simply as punitive deforestation. Produce was used to supply the army, trampled underfoot or intentionally destroyed in order to cripple the economy.

7:21 *eat the meat yourselves!* There is a strong sense of contempt and irony here on the part of the prophet. The whole burnt offering was meant to be consumed entirely on the altar; it was not to be eaten by the worshipers (see note on Lev 1:3). At this point, God is so disgusted with the lack of loyalty on the part of the Israelites that the offerings mean nothing to him. They are empty of meaning and commitment. Therefore the sarcastic command to eat the meat conveys the idea that the worshipers can do whatever they please. Nothing will change, nothing will be accomplished.

Obey[i] me, and I will be your God and you will be my people.[j] Walk in obedience to all I command you, that it may go well[k] with you. 24But they did not listen or pay attention;[l] instead, they followed the stubborn inclinations of their evil hearts. They went backward and not forward. 25From the time your ancestors left Egypt until now, day after day, again and again I sent you my servants the prophets.[m] 26But they did not listen to me or pay attention. They were stiff-necked and did more evil than their ancestors.'[n]

27"When you tell[o] them all this, they will not listen[p] to you; when you call to them, they will not answer. 28Therefore say to them, 'This is the nation that has not obeyed the LORD its God or responded to correction. Truth has perished; it has vanished from their lips.

29" 'Cut off[q] your hair and throw it away; take up a lament on the barren heights, for the LORD has rejected and abandoned[r] this generation that is under his wrath.

The Valley of Slaughter

30" 'The people of Judah have done evil in my eyes, declares the LORD. They have set up their detestable idols[s] in the house that bears my Name and have defiled[t] it. 31They have built the high places of Topheth[u] in the Valley of Ben Hinnom to burn their sons and daughters[v] in the fire—something I did not command, nor did it enter my mind.[w] 32So beware, the days are coming, declares the LORD, when people will no longer call it Topheth or the Valley of Ben Hinnom, but the Valley of Slaughter,[x] for they will bury[y] the dead in Topheth until there is no more room. 33Then the carcasses of this people will become food[z] for the birds and the wild animals, and there will be no one to frighten them away. 34I will bring an end to the sounds[a] of joy and gladness and to the voices of bride and bridegroom[b] in the towns of Judah and the streets of Jerusalem, for the land will become desolate.[c]

8 " 'At that time, declares the LORD, the bones of the kings and officials of Judah, the bones of the priests and prophets, and the bones of the people of Jerusalem will be removed from their graves. 2They will be exposed to the sun and the moon and all the stars of the heavens, which they have loved and served[d] and which they have followed and consulted and worshiped. They will not be gathered up or buried, but will be like dung lying on the ground. 3Wherever I banish them, all the survivors of this evil nation will prefer death to life,[e] declares the LORD Almighty.'

Sin and Punishment

4"Say to them, 'This is what the LORD says:

" 'When people fall down, do they not
get up?[f]
When someone turns away, do they
not return?
5Why then have these people turned
away?
Why does Jerusalem always turn
away?

7:23 [i] Ex 19:5 [j] Lev 26:12 [k] Ex 15:26 **7:24** [l] Ps 81:11-12; Jer 11:8 **7:25** [m] Jer 25:4 **7:26** [n] Jer 16:12 **7:27** [o] Eze 2:7 [p] Eze 3:7 **7:29** [q] Job 1:20; Isa 15:2; Mic 1:16 [r] Jer 6:30 **7:30** [s] Eze 7:20-22 [t] Jer 32:34 **7:31** [u] 2Ki 23:10 [v] Ps 106:38 [w] Jer 19:5 **7:32** [x] Jer 19:6 [y] Jer 19:11 **7:33** [z] Dt 28:26 **7:34** [a] Isa 24:8; Eze 26:13 [b] Rev 18:23 [c] Lev 26:34 **8:2** [d] 2Ki 23:5; Ac 7:42 **8:3** [e] Job 3:22; Rev 9:6 **8:4** [f] Pr 24:16

7:29 *Cut off your hair.* Both in Israel and in many places of the ancient Near East, cutting off the hair could be a sign of mourning and lament. But the expression used here is generally used to speak of the cutting of hair as part of a consecration rite to become a Nazirite (Nu 6:1–8). It seems that God is once again using irony to get his message across to the people of Judah. They may as well cut off their "consecrated" hair because their conduct in no way reflects obedience and consecration to Yahweh.
7:31 *high places of Topheth in the Valley of Ben Hinnom.* The Hinnom Valley (Jos 15:8; 18:16) has been identified with Wadi er-Rababi, which surrounds Jerusalem along the southwest. It is also referred to in the Bible as the "Valley of Ben [son of] Hinnom" (also the plural, "Valley of Benei [sons of] Hinnom"). During the monarchy in Israel, this valley became famous as the place where idolatrous practices were conducted. During Jeremiah's time this valley also became the popular place for Baal worship, which led Jeremiah to proclaim that its name would be changed to the Valley of Slaughter. "Topheth" in this context has a sinister connotation. It designates the cultic place between the Hinnom and Kidron Valleys, where children were sacrificed to the god Molek. The exact meaning of Topheth is not known, but it is generally associated with an Aramaic word that means "oven, fireplace, hearth," and is thought to signify the hearth where the child was placed. Regarding the identification of Molek and the practice of child sacrifice in Israel, there is much scholarly debate. There is now much evidence that Molek can be identified with Malik or Milku from Attartu, which suggests that Molek was a netherworld deity. *burn their sons and daughters in the fire.* Evidence for this practice outside of Scripture is rare indeed. Assyrian legal texts describe a penalty clause as "he will burn his son to Sin [a lunar deity], and his daughter to Belet-seri." The practice of human sacrifice, including children, is also illustrated from the Phoenician city of Carthage (814–146 BC). Excavations there and Jeremiah's condemnation of Topheth suggest that child sacrifice was practiced, albeit in extreme situations.
8:2 *the sun and the moon and all the stars ... they have loved and served.* The term "stars" here is often translated "host of heaven." This phrase seems to refer to a celestial army composed of the heavenly bodies in the universe. While one cannot be sure of the military connotation, it is evident that spiritual powers were attributed to these bodies that inhabited the skies. Therefore, it is not surprising that the Israelites were tempted to worship these so-called deities, who were believed to control human destiny. Long before Jeremiah, astrology was an important part of second-millennium BC Babylonia. Astral divination was perfected by the Babylonians, and during the first millennium BC the interpretation of celestial omens influenced the people of Israel to the extent that it became customary to mix astral worship with the worship of Yahweh.

Let us flee to the fortified cities[y]
and perish there!
For the LORD our God has doomed us
to perish
and given us poisoned water[z] to
drink,
because we have sinned[a] against him.
15 We hoped for peace[b]
but no good has come,
for a time of healing
but there is only terror.[c]
16 The snorting of the enemy's horses
is heard from Dan;[d]
at the neighing of their stallions
the whole land trembles.
They have come to devour
the land and everything in it,
the city and all who live there.

17 "See, I will send venomous snakes[e]
among you,
vipers that cannot be charmed,[f]
and they will bite you,"
declares the LORD.

18 You who are my Comforter[a] in sorrow,
my heart is faint[g] within me.
19 Listen to the cry of my people
from a land far away:[h]
"Is the LORD not in Zion?
Is her King no longer there?"

"Why have they aroused my anger
with their images,
with their worthless foreign idols?"[i]

20 "The harvest is past,
the summer has ended,
and we are not saved."

21 Since my people are crushed, I am
crushed;
I mourn,[j] and horror grips me.
22 Is there no balm in Gilead?[k]
Is there no physician there?
Why then is there no healing[l]
for the wound of my people?

9[b] 1 Oh, that my head were a spring of
water
and my eyes a fountain of tears!
I would weep[m] day and night
for the slain of my people.[n]
2 Oh, that I had in the desert
a lodging place for travelers,
so that I might leave my people
and go away from them;
for they are all adulterers,[o]
a crowd of unfaithful people.

3 "They make ready their tongue
like a bow, to shoot lies;[p]
it is not by truth
that they triumph[c] in the land.
They go from one sin to another;
they do not acknowledge me,"
declares the LORD.
4 "Beware of your friends;
do not trust anyone in your clan.[q]
For every one of them is a deceiver,[d r]
and every friend a slanderer.
5 Friend deceives friend,
and no one speaks the truth.
They have taught their tongues to lie;
they weary themselves with sinning.

8:14 [y] Jer 4:5; 35:11 [z] Dt 29:18; Jer 9:15; 23:15 [a] Jer 14:7,20 **8:15** [b] ver 11 [c] Jer 14:19 **8:16** [d] Jer 4:15 **8:17** [e] Nu 21:6; Dt 32:24 [f] Ps 58:5 **8:18** [g] La 5:17 **8:19** [h] Jer 9:16 [i] Dt 32:21 **8:21** [j] Jer 14:17 **8:22** [k] Ge 37:25 [l] Jer 30:12 **9:1** [m] Jer 13:17; La 2:11,18 [n] Isa 22:4 **9:2** [o] Jer 5:7-8; 23:10; Hos 4:2 **9:3** [p] Ps 64:3 **9:4** [q] Mic 7:5-6 [r] Ge 27:35

[a] *18* The meaning of the Hebrew for this word is uncertain. [b] In Hebrew texts 9:1 is numbered 8:23, and 9:2-26 is numbered 9:1-25. [c] *3* Or *lies; / they are not valiant for truth* [d] *4* Or *a deceiving Jacob*

slit open their camels, their only means of transportation, and drink blood and filthy water. Certainly if the available water was poisoned, the lives of the people under siege were profoundly threatened.

8:16 *snorting of the enemy's horses is heard from Dan.* For the strategic location and significance of Dan, see note on 4:15. This verse is hyperbolic language that is intended to elicit fear and change in the audience. *horses.* A symbol of strength. This may refer to Nebuchadnezzar's cavalry.

8:17 *vipers that cannot be charmed.* The exact species of snakes mentioned here cannot be identified. Nevertheless, it can be safely assumed that they were poisonous and deadly. This is likely a metaphor that alludes to the Babylonians invading and conquering the Israelites. Poisonous snakes are mentioned elsewhere in Scripture (Pr 23:32; Isa 11:8; 59:5). The snake is also a feared reptile in Egyptian and Mesopotamian contexts. The literature from these places includes various incantations against serpents and other dangerous crawling creatures. The prophet here declares that no incantation or ritual will prevent the enemy from biting Judah. Snake incantations were among the most common in the ancient world. *charmed.* See note on Ecc 10:11.

8:20 *The harvest is past, the summer has ended.* Most scholars agree that this statement reflects a popular proverb. *harvest.* The Hebrew term used suggests the early grain harvest, which lasts from April to June. After this time, the ingathering of fruits begins during the summer.

8:22 *balm.* An exact identification is unknown. The main candidates are a resin that comes from balsam, mastic or storax. In ancient times, resins were widely used for soothing pain and for healing. In addition, many were used as a kind of perfume to counteract the smell of wounds in a state of decay. Balm was taken from the bark of a tree drop by drop. Scholars now agree that a consistent picture emerges regarding this word for balsam: it comes from Gilead in the Transjordan, is one of the main export products of Palestine and is used as medicine. *Gilead.* Its boundaries were never well defined, and they changed often according to political and historical circumstances. It has generally been defined as the mountainous region east of the Jordan River and reaching north as far as the Yarmuk River and south as far as the Arnon River. There is strong evidence today that balm was cultivated at En Gedi, located on the west bank of the Dead Sea, as well as at Qumran, located north of En Gedi. Juglets, jars and decanters have been found there that presumably contained balm.

9:4 *Beware of your friends.* This proverb implies that no one can be trusted in times of extreme wickedness. Many centuries before his time, an Egyptian pharaoh advised his son not to have "intimates." Pharaoh Amenemhet, who died around the year 1960 BC, had experienced the betrayal of those he helped and thus told his son not to trust brother or friend.

JEREMIAH 8:1

Exposure of the Dead

Proper burial was a valued practice in the ancient Near East that was essential for the deceased person's proper entry into the netherworld. This was critical because in Mesopotamian belief the living and the dead continued in a permanent relationship and formed an ongoing community.

The cult of the dead so prevalent in the ancient Near East involved extensive preparation of the body, including washing of the body, tying the mouth shut, oiling or perfuming the body, and dressing it up in clean clothing. This concern also existed among the Israelites. Jeremiah repeatedly invokes the punishment of exposure of dead bodies through disinterment, particularly of Israelite leaders such as kings, priests and false prophets.

This kind of punishment and disturbance of the dead was also carried out by King Ashurbanipal of Assyria. In his successful eighth campaign, he desecrated the tombs of the Elamite kings and reports that in doing so he made their spirits restless and deprived them of care (i.e., offerings and libations). Jeremiah proclaims that the same desecration will happen to the tombs in Judah. ◆

They cling to deceit;[g]
they refuse to return.[h]
6 I have listened attentively,
but they do not say what is right.
None of them repent[i] of their
wickedness,
saying, "What have I done?"
Each pursues their own course[j]
like a horse charging into battle.
7 Even the stork in the sky
knows her appointed seasons,
and the dove, the swift and the thrush
observe the time of their migration.
But my people do not know[k]
the requirements of the LORD.

8 " 'How can you say, "We are wise,
for we have the law[l] of the LORD,"
when actually the lying pen of the
scribes
has handled it falsely?
9 The wise[m] will be put to shame;
they will be dismayed and trapped.
Since they have rejected the word[n] of
the LORD,
what kind of wisdom do they have?
10 Therefore I will give their wives to
other men
and their fields to new owners.[o]
From the least to the greatest,
all are greedy for gain;[p]
prophets and priests alike,
all practice deceit.
11 They dress the wound of my people
as though it were not serious.
"Peace, peace," they say,
when there is no peace.[q]
12 Are they ashamed of their detestable
conduct?
No, they have no shame[r] at all;
they do not even know how to blush.
So they will fall among the fallen;
they will be brought down when
they are punished,[s]
says the LORD.[t]

13 " 'I will take away their harvest,
declares the LORD.
There will be no grapes on the vine.[u]
There will be no figs[v] on the tree,
and their leaves will wither.[w]
What I have given them
will be taken[x] from them.[a]' "
14 Why are we sitting here?
Gather together!

8:5 [g] Jer 5:27 [h] Jer 7:24; 9:6 **8:6** [i] Rev 9:20 [j] Ps 14:1-3 **8:7** [k] Isa 1:3; Jer 5:4-5 **8:8** [l] Ro 2:17 **8:9** [m] Jer 6:15 [n] Jer 6:19 **8:10** [o] Jer 6:12 [p] Isa 56:11 **8:11** [q] Jer 6:14 **8:12** [r] Jer 3:3 [s] Ps 52:5-7; Isa 3:9 [t] Jer 6:15 **8:13** [u] Joel 1:7 [v] Lk 13:6 [w] Mt 21:19 [x] Jer 5:17

[a] *13* The meaning of the Hebrew for this sentence is uncertain.

8:14 *poisoned water to drink.* Access to drinking water was crucial to any city in the ancient world and it was provided locally (i.e., there were no regional water delivery systems). This became even more critical when a city was under siege. King Ashurbanipal of Assyria (669 – 633 BC) declared with much pride that during his military campaign into Kedar that he had cut off the only source of water, so that many died of thirst. Others were forced to

6 You[a] live in the midst of deception;[s]
in their deceit they refuse to
acknowledge me,"
declares the LORD.

7 Therefore this is what the LORD Almighty says:

"See, I will refine[t] and test[u] them,
for what else can I do
because of the sin of my people?
8 Their tongue[v] is a deadly arrow;
it speaks deceitfully.
With their mouths they all speak
cordially to their neighbors,
but in their hearts they set traps[w] for
them.
9 Should I not punish them for this?"
declares the LORD.
"Should I not avenge[x] myself
on such a nation as this?"

10 I will weep and wail for the mountains
and take up a lament concerning the
wilderness grasslands.
They are desolate and untraveled,
and the lowing of cattle is not heard.
The birds[y] have all fled
and the animals are gone.

11 "I will make Jerusalem a heap of ruins,
a haunt of jackals;[z]
and I will lay waste the towns of Judah
so no one can live there."[a]

12 Who is wise[b] enough to understand
this? Who has been instructed by the LORD
and can explain it? Why has the land been
ruined and laid waste like a desert that no
one can cross?
13 The LORD said, "It is because they
have forsaken my law, which I set before
them; they have not obeyed me or followed my law.[c] 14 Instead, they have followed[d] the stubbornness of their hearts;[e]
they have followed the Baals, as their ancestors taught them." 15 Therefore this is
what the LORD Almighty, the God of Israel, says: "See, I will make this people eat
bitter food[f] and drink poisoned water.[g] 16 I
will scatter them among nations[h] that neither they nor their ancestors have known,[i]
and I will pursue them with the sword[j] until I have made an end of them."[k]

17 This is what the LORD Almighty says:

"Consider now! Call for the wailing
women[l] to come;
send for the most skillful of them.
18 Let them come quickly
and wail over us
till our eyes overflow with tears
and water streams from our
eyelids.[m]
19 The sound of wailing is heard from
Zion:
'How ruined[n] we are!
How great is our shame!
We must leave our land
because our houses are in ruins.' "

20 Now, you women, hear the word of the
LORD;
open your ears to the words of his
mouth.
Teach your daughters how to wail;
teach one another a lament.[o]
21 Death has climbed in through our
windows
and has entered our fortresses;
it has removed the children from the
streets
and the young men[p] from the public
squares.

22 Say, "This is what the LORD declares:

" 'Dead bodies will lie
like dung[q] on the open field,
like cut grain behind the reaper,
with no one to gather them.' "

[a] 6 That is, Jeremiah (the Hebrew is singular)

9:6 [s] Jer 5:27 **9:7** [t] Isa 1:25 [u] Jer 6:27 **9:8** [v] ver 3 [w] Jer 5:26 **9:9** [x] Jer 5:9,29 **9:10** [y] Jer 4:25; 12:4; Hos 4:3 **9:11** [z] Isa 34:13 [a] Isa 25:2; Jer 26:9 **9:12** [b] Ps 107:43; Hos 14:9 **9:13** [c] 2Ch 7:19; Ps 89:30-32 **9:14** [d] Jer 2:8, 23 [e] Jer 7:24 **9:15** [f] La 3:15 [g] Jer 8:14 **9:16** [h] Lev 26:33 [i] Dt 28:64 [j] Eze 5:2 [k] Jer 44:27; Eze 5:12 **9:17** [l] 2Ch 35:25; Ecc 12:5; Am 5:16 **9:18** [m] Jer 14:17 **9:19** [n] Jer 4:13 **9:20** [o] Isa 32:9-13 **9:21** [p] 2Ch 36:17 **9:22** [q] Jer 8:2

9:11 *jackals.* Known as prowlers around ruins and uninhabited areas.
9:15 *bitter food.* A metaphor for the deep suffering and death that will engulf God's people. The term used here has been traditionally identified with a desert shrub known as white wormwood (*Artemisia herba-alba*), which grows abundantly in southern Israel. It has bitter leaves used in traditional medicine. Still today certain groups living in desert areas dry the leaves to make a strong tea. In the Bible "wormwood" is used to depict sorrow (Rev 8:11).
9:17 *wailing women.* This is the only certain reference in the Bible to professional mourners. Despite this, professional mourning carried out by women was a well-known practice in the ancient Near East. The professional mourning women were hired to weep loudly, chanting well-known dirges as well as improvising at times. They did this both in the streets and in homes. Pictorial evidence of this custom can be found in Egyptian reliefs and tomb paintings, which show women and girls, along with other family members, actively lamenting the dead. There is also a tenth-century BC sarcophagus from Byblos that depicts women mourning the death of King Ahiram. These drawings depict bare-breasted women beating their chests and pulling their hair, actions that demonstrate mourning (see the article "Mourning," p. 828). The prophet Ezekiel refers to women who sit at the door of the temple of Yahweh weeping for Tammuz, a Babylonian deity (Eze 8:14). This links with a text about Ishtar's lament for Tammuz that mentions wailing men and wailing women. This custom was also prevalent in classical Greece and it is still practiced in the Middle East.
9:22–23 The lament of these verses is typical of an ancient Near Eastern lament over the defeat and destruction of a beloved city. The vocabulary and modes of expression here are similar to those used in the 2004 BC "Lament Over the Destruction of Ur," which is composed of 11 laments that contain 436 lines. The Mesopotamian city of Ur was conquered by Kindattu, ruler of Elam. The

[23]This is what the LORD says:

"Let not the wise boast of their wisdom[r]
or the strong boast of their strength[s]
or the rich boast of their riches,[t]
[24]but let the one who boasts boast[u]
about this:
that they have the understanding to
know me,
that I am the LORD,[v] who exercises
kindness,[w]
justice and righteousness[x] on earth,
for in these I delight,"
declares the LORD.

[25]"The days are coming," declares the
LORD, "when I will punish all who are circumcised only in the flesh[y]— [26]Egypt, Judah, Edom, Ammon, Moab and all who
live in the wilderness in distant places.[a][z]
For all these nations are really uncircumcised, and even the whole house of Israel
is uncircumcised in heart.[a]"

God and Idols

10:12-16pp — Jer 51:15-19

10 Hear what the LORD says to you,
people of Israel. [2]This is what the
LORD says:

"Do not learn the ways of the nations[b]
or be terrified by signs in the
heavens,
though the nations are terrified by
them.
[3]For the practices of the peoples are
worthless;
they cut a tree out of the forest,
and a craftsman[c] shapes it with his
chisel.
[4]They adorn it with silver and gold;
they fasten it with hammer and nails
so it will not totter.[d]
[5]Like a scarecrow in a cucumber field,
their idols cannot speak;[e]
they must be carried
because they cannot walk.[f]
Do not fear them;
they can do no harm
nor can they do any good."[g]

[6]No one is like you, LORD;
you are great,[h]
and your name is mighty in power.
[7]Who should not fear you,
King of the nations?[i]
This is your due.
Among all the wise leaders of the nations
and in all their kingdoms,
there is no one like you.
[8]They are all senseless and foolish;[j]
they are taught by worthless wooden
idols.
[9]Hammered silver is brought from
Tarshish
and gold from Uphaz.

9:23 [r]Ecc 9:11 [s]1Ki 20:11 [t]Eze 28:4-5 **9:24** [u]1Co 1:31*; Gal 6:14 [v]2Co 10:17* [w]Ps 51:1; Mic 7:18 [x]Ps 36:6 **9:25** [y]Ro 2:8-9 **9:26** [z]Jer 25:23 [a]Lev 26:41; Ac 7:51; Ro 2:28 **10:2** [b]Lev 20:23 **10:3** [c]Isa 40:19 **10:4** [d]Isa 41:7 **10:5** [e]1Co 12:2 [f]Ps 115:5,7 [g]Isa 41:24; 46:7 **10:6** [h]Ps 48:1 **10:7** [i]Ps 22:28; Rev 15:4 **10:8** [j]Isa 40:19; Jer 4:22

[a] 26 Or *wilderness and who clip the hair by their foreheads*

lament speaks of the city lying in ruins with bodies lying like broken pots scattered all over the city.

9:26 *uncircumcised in heart.* See note on 4:4.

10:1 – 2 *signs in the heavens.* The Israelites were surrounded by people interested in the stars. The Babylonians are said to be the originators of astronomy and astrology. The Egyptians in the south had also developed astrology to a sophisticated degree. Behind this intricate understanding of the astral bodies lies a worldview in which celestial phenomena portend signs that can have direct and often disastrous consequences on human existence. That is why many in the ancient world lived in fear of the "signs in the heavens."

Many texts from Mesopotamia illustrate this reality. Perhaps the most developed is what is known today as the *Enuma Anu Enlil*, which is a series of 70 texts from the library of Ashurbanipal in Nineveh from the seventh century BC. These texts contain omens based on the appearance of the moon-god Sin as well as on numerous eclipses. Others refer to the sun-god Shamash and meteorological phenomena related to the storm-god Adad. Other omens are based on planetary phenomena, such as first and last sightings of certain planets. The Mesopotamian astrologers recognized various constellations that are the same as many of the ones recognized today. The Mesopotamians and Egyptians lived in a state of anxiety with respect to these astral signs, which they believed held power over human existence.

10:3 *they cut a tree … a craftsman shapes it with his chisel.* The manufacture of idols was common in the ancient Near East. Images of deities were hewn out of stone, carved out of wood, modeled in clay or cast in bronze (see the article "Making an Idol," p. 1010). Some were 4 – 10 inches (10 – 25 centimeters) high; others were life-size. Here Jeremiah refers to images chiseled out of wood and then overlaid with silver and gold and clothed in blue and purple. These idols were seen as more than merely representing a deity, but at the same time they were not identified wholly with the deity. The ancient Near Eastern person worshiped the deity they believed was present in the image, not the image itself. These statues or idols were lavishly decorated with gold and silver (v. 4). Gold was the more valuable metal. It was either beaten with a hammer into thin sheets, since it is a relatively soft metal, or it was melted and cast into a given shape. Silver, by contrast, is hardly ever found pure; it had to be extracted from its ore by smelting with the help of bellows (see note on 6:28). These idols were given life status; i.e., one might say that the god became present in the idol through a specific ritual of consecration known as the opening of or washing of the mouth (see note on 1:9). Some of these deities were depicted anthropomorphically; others were not. Nevertheless they all had to be cared for in terms of food, clothing and other such needs.

10:5 *scarecrow.* This Hebrew word occurs only here in the OT. This was as close to an image that Israel was allowed to make. Thus, the "sacred" idols are diminished to the status of scarecrows, no more powerful than palm fronds twisted around a pole. They certainly inspired no fear.

10:9 *Tarshish.* Its exact identification is still a matter of debate. Josephus, the first-century Jewish historian, identified Tarshish with Tarsus in Cilicia (modern Turkey).

What the craftsman and goldsmith
have made[k]
is then dressed in blue and
purple—
all made by skilled workers.
10 But the LORD is the true God;
he is the living God, the eternal
King.
When he is angry, the earth trembles;
the nations cannot endure his
wrath.[l]

11 "Tell them this: 'These gods, who did
not make the heavens and the earth, will
perish[m] from the earth and from under the
heavens.' "[a]

12 But God made the earth by his
power;
he founded the world by his
wisdom
and stretched out the heavens[n] by
his understanding.
13 When he thunders,[o] the waters in the
heavens roar;
he makes clouds rise from the ends
of the earth.
He sends lightning with the rain[p]
and brings out the wind from his
storehouses.

14 Everyone is senseless and without
knowledge;
every goldsmith is shamed by his
idols.
The images he makes are a fraud;
they have no breath in them.
15 They are worthless,[q] the objects of
mockery;
when their judgment comes, they
will perish.
16 He who is the Portion[r] of Jacob is not
like these,
for he is the Maker of all things,[s]
including Israel, the people of his
inheritance[t]—
the LORD Almighty is his name.[u]

10:9 [k]Ps 115:4; Isa 40:19
10:10 [l]Ps 76:7
10:11 [m]Ps 96:5; Isa 2:18
10:12 [n]Ge 1:1, 8; Job 9:8; Isa 40:22
10:13 [o]Job 36:29 [p]Ps 135:7
10:15 [q]Isa 41:24; Jer 14:22
10:16 [r]Dt 32:9; Ps 119:57 [s]ver 12 [t]Ps 74:2 [u]Jer 31:35; 32:18

10:17 [v]Eze 12:3-12
10:18 [w]1Sa 25:29
10:19 [x]Jer 14:17 [y]Mic 7:9
10:20 [z]Jer 4:20 [a]Jer 31:15; La 1:5
10:21 [b]Jer 23:2
10:22 [c]Jer 9:11
10:23 [d]Pr 20:24
10:24 [e]Ps 6:1; 38:1 [f]Jer 30:11
10:25 [g]Zep 3:8 [h]Job 18:21; Ps 14:4

Coming Destruction

17 Gather up your belongings[v] to leave
the land,
you who live under siege.
18 For this is what the LORD says:
"At this time I will hurl[w] out
those who live in this land;
I will bring distress on them
so that they may be captured."

19 Woe to me because of my injury!
My wound[x] is incurable!
Yet I said to myself,
"This is my sickness, and I must
endure[y] it."
20 My tent[z] is destroyed;
all its ropes are snapped.
My children are gone from me and are
no more;[a]
no one is left now to pitch my tent
or to set up my shelter.
21 The shepherds are senseless
and do not inquire of the LORD;
so they do not prosper
and all their flock is scattered.[b]
22 Listen! The report is coming—
a great commotion from the land of
the north!
It will make the towns of Judah
desolate,
a haunt of jackals.[c]

Jeremiah's Prayer

23 LORD, I know that people's lives are not
their own;
it is not for them to direct their steps.[d]
24 Discipline me, LORD, but only in due
measure—
not in your anger,[e]
or you will reduce me to nothing.[f]
25 Pour out your wrath on the nations[g]
that do not acknowledge you,
on the peoples who do not call on
your name.[h]

[a] *11* The text of this verse is in Aramaic.

Others suggest Carthage in North Africa as a possible location, while yet others prefer Ezion Geber in the Red Sea area. Perhaps the strongest candidate is the Phoenician colony Tartessus in southern Spain, near Gibraltar. A relatively recent discovery lends credence to the identification of Tarshish with the precious metal silver. Two Hebrew ostraca were discovered that belong to the same time period (Iron Age), though of unknown provenance. One of them records the command of a king that silver from Tarshish be given to the house of Yahweh. *Uphaz.* Its exact location is unknown. Da 10:5 also mentions it as a source of gold. Some suggest that it could be Ophir, also mentioned as an important source of gold. Once again the discovery of an ostracon sheds light on this matter. An eighth-century BC sherd found at Tel Qasile (modern Tel Aviv) bears the following inscription: "Ophir gold to Beth-horon, 30 shekels." *dressed in blue and purple.* We cannot know the exact shades of these colors, but they appear to be particularly indicative of royalty and divinity. These two Hebrew terms are also used to describe the drapery of the tabernacle and temple (Ex 26:1; 2Ch 2:7). Elsewhere these colors are associated with the wealthy and powerful of society. The dyes were quite expensive and most likely came from shells or mollusks that attached themselves to rocks on the Phoenician coast. The less expensive dyes came from vegetables.

10:13 *wind from his storehouses.* This image is used elsewhere in Scripture (Dt 28:12; Ps 33:7), where the primordial rain, lightning, snow, hail and wind are in Yahweh's storehouses. These meteorological elements are often unleashed by God's breath (wind) either as divine blessing or divine judgment. They can also defeat Israel's enemies. Note that the idea of divine storehouses is not a common imagery in the ancient Near East—the metaphor is only known from the Bible.

10:22 *haunt of jackals.* See note on 9:11.

For they have devoured[i] Jacob;
they have devoured him completely
and destroyed his homeland.[j]

The Covenant Is Broken

11 This is the word that came to Jeremiah from the LORD: 2 “Listen to the
terms of this covenant and tell them to the
people of Judah and to those who live in
Jerusalem. 3 Tell them that this is what the
LORD, the God of Israel, says: ‘Cursed[k] is
the one who does not obey the terms of
this covenant— 4 the terms I commanded
your ancestors when I brought them out of
Egypt, out of the iron-smelting furnace.[l] I
said, ‘Obey[m] me and do everything I command you, and you will be my people,[n]
and I will be your God. 5 Then I will fulfill
the oath I swore[o] to your ancestors, to give
them a land flowing with milk and honey’—the land you possess today.”
I answered, “Amen, LORD.”
6 The LORD said to me, “Proclaim all these
words in the towns of Judah and in the
streets of Jerusalem: ‘Listen to the terms
of this covenant and follow[p] them. 7 From
the time I brought your ancestors up from
Egypt until today, I warned them again and
again,[q] saying, “Obey me.” 8 But they did
not listen or pay attention;[r] instead, they
followed the stubbornness of their evil
hearts. So I brought on them all the curses[s]
of the covenant I had commanded them to
follow but that they did not keep.’ ”
9 Then the LORD said to me, “There is a
conspiracy[t] among the people of Judah and
those who live in Jerusalem. 10 They have
returned to the sins of their ancestors,[u] who
refused to listen to my words. They have
followed other gods[v] to serve them. Both
Israel and Judah have broken the covenant
I made with their ancestors. 11 Therefore this
is what the LORD says: ‘I will bring on them
a disaster[w] they cannot escape. Although
they cry[x] out to me, I will not listen[y] to
them. 12 The towns of Judah and the people
of Jerusalem will go and cry out to the gods
to whom they burn incense,[z] but they will
not help them at all when disaster[a] strikes.
13 You, Judah, have as many gods as you
have towns; and the altars you have set up
to burn incense[b] to that shameful[c] god Baal
are as many as the streets of Jerusalem.’
14 “Do not pray[d] for this people or offer
any plea or petition for them, because I
will not listen[e] when they call to me in the
time of their distress.

15 “What is my beloved doing in my temple
as she, with many others, works out her evil schemes?
Can consecrated meat avert your punishment?
When you engage in your wickedness,
then you rejoice.[a]”

16 The LORD called you a thriving olive tree
with fruit beautiful in form.
But with the roar of a mighty storm
he will set it on fire,[f]
and its branches will be broken.[g]

10:25 [i] Ps 79:7; Jer 8:16 [j] Ps 79:6-7
11:3 [k] Dt 27:26; Gal 3:10
11:4 [l] Dt 4:20; 1Ki 8:51 [m] Ex 24:8 [n] Jer 7:23; 31:33
11:5 [o] Ex 13:5; Dt 7:12; Ps 105:8-11
11:6 [p] Dt 15:5; Ro 2:13; Jas 1:22
11:7 [q] 2Ch 36:15
11:8 [r] Jer 7:26 [s] Lev 26:14-43
11:9 [t] Eze 22:25
11:10 [u] Dt 9:7 [v] Jdg 2:12-13
11:11 [w] 2Ki 22:16 [x] Jer 14:12; Eze 8:18 [y] ver 14; Pr 1:28; Isa 1:15; Zec 7:13
11:12 [z] Jer 44:17 [a] Dt 32:37
11:13 [b] Jer 7:9 [c] Jer 3:24
11:14 [d] Ex 32:10 [e] ver 11
11:16 [f] Jer 21:14 [g] Isa 27:11; Ro 11:17-24

[a] 15 Or *Could consecrated meat avert your punishment? / Then you would rejoice*

11:4 *iron-smelting furnace.* This is a metaphor for Israel's experience in Egypt, where God's people endured many years of slavery (cf. also Dt 4:20). Furnaces at this time varied in size and shape and were made either of brick or stone. In this particular metaphor iron is smelted. This furnace should not be confused with a blast furnace such as is used today. Iron has a very high melting point—about 2,800°F (1,538°C). Technology available during Jeremiah's time did not allow such a high temperature. But the ancient Israelites could achieve a temperature of 2,012°F (1,100°C), which is enough to get the iron to a softer, semisolid form that can then be forged. Initially one might see a negative use of this metaphor and think only of the suffering and anguish that God's people experienced in Egypt. Yet the process of smelting is not necessarily destructive; rather, in general it is a constructive process. Therefore, one can understand the metaphor as being positive in the sense that the experience of slavery in Egypt forged a people who could endure difficult circumstances and be transformed by them.
11:5 *flowing with milk and honey.* This stereotypical phrase alludes to a fertile land and should not be taken literally. It is used in the Bible to speak of the land of Canaan in positive terms (e.g., Ex 3:8; Nu 14:8). One can suggest that this phrase was part of a ritual that expressed thanksgiving every year when the firstfruits were offered to God. The use of such a phrase was not uncommon in the ancient Near East. In an Egyptian literary text attributed to Sinuhe from the second millennium BC, the land is described in similar fashion. There it is evident that Sinuhe had a strong love for the Egyptian country. Also, the Ugaritic Baal Cycle speaks of the heavens raining olive oil and dry stream beds flowing with honey.
11:13 *altars ... to that shameful god Baal are as many as the streets of Jerusalem.* Jeremiah again resorts to hyperbole in order to give force to his argument. He claims that the people are so immersed in Baal worship that it seems that at every corner a Baal shrine exists. It is true that in the ancient Near East many towns had numerous shrines throughout the residential areas where people could stop and engage in a religious ritual. Most of these would have some kind of an altar where incense could be burned (see note on 7:9).
11:15 *consecrated meat.* Much of the meat that was consumed in Israel was connected to the sacrificial system and was therefore eaten in specified areas in the temple. Consecrated meat would refer to meat that was used under such circumstances. The irony here is that even as they sit in the temple precincts and partake of a sacral meal, they discuss their wickedness in the table conversation.
11:16 *thriving olive tree with fruit beautiful in form.* The olive tree adorned with leaves was a common sight in Israel. It is often used as a metaphor for an abundant and satisfied life. It conjures up images of health, growth, beauty and prosperity. This is how God once had defined

[17]The LORD Almighty, who planted[h] you,
has decreed disaster for you, because the
people of both Israel and Judah have done
evil and aroused my anger by burning incense to Baal.[i]

Plot Against Jeremiah

[18]Because the LORD revealed their plot to
me, I knew it, for at that time he showed
me what they were doing. [19]I had been
like a gentle lamb led to the slaughter;
I did not realize that they had plotted[j]
against me, saying,

"Let us destroy the tree and its fruit;
let us cut him off from the land of
the living,[k]
that his name be remembered[l] no
more."
[20]But you, LORD Almighty, who judge
righteously
and test the heart and mind,[m]
let me see your vengeance on them,
for to you I have committed my
cause.

[21]Therefore this is what the LORD says
about the people of Anathoth who are
threatening to kill you,[n] saying, "Do not
prophesy in the name of the LORD or you
will die[o] by our hands"— [22]therefore this
is what the LORD Almighty says: "I will
punish them. Their young men[p] will die
by the sword, their sons and daughters by
famine. [23]Not even a remnant[q] will be left
to them, because I will bring disaster on
the people of Anathoth in the year of their
punishment.[r]"

Jeremiah's Complaint

12 You are always righteous,[s] LORD,
when I bring a case before you.
Yet I would speak with you about your
justice:
Why does the way of the wicked
prosper?[t]
Why do all the faithless live at
ease?
[2]You have planted[u] them, and they have
taken root;
they grow and bear fruit.
You are always on their lips
but far from their hearts.[v]
[3]Yet you know me, LORD;
you see me and test[w] my thoughts
about you.
Drag them off like sheep to be
butchered!
Set them apart for the day of
slaughter![x]
[4]How long will the land lie parched[y]
and the grass in every field be
withered?[z]
Because those who live in it are
wicked,
the animals and birds have
perished.[a]
Moreover, the people are saying,
"He will not see what happens
to us."

God's Answer

[5]"If you have raced with men on foot
and they have worn you out,
how can you compete with horses?
If you stumble[a] in safe country,
how will you manage in the
thickets[b] by[b] the Jordan?
[6]Your relatives, members of your own
family—
even they have betrayed you;
they have raised a loud cry against
you.[c]
Do not trust them,
though they speak well of you.[d]

11:17 [h]Isa 5:2; Jer 12:2 [i]Jer 7:9 **11:19** [j]Jer 18:18; 20:10 [k]Job 28:13; Isa 53:8 [l]Ps 83:4 **11:20** [m]Ps 7:9 **11:21** [n]Jer 12:6 [o]Jer 26:8, 11; 38:4 **11:22** [p]Jer 18:21 **11:23** [q]Jer 6:9 [r]Jer 23:12 **12:1** [s]Ezr 9:15 [t]Jer 5:27-28 **12:2** [u]Jer 11:17 [v]Isa 29:13; Jer 3:10; Mt 15:8; Titus 1:16 **12:3** [w]Ps 7:9; 11:5; 139:1-4; Jer 11:20 [x]Jer 17:18 **12:4** [y]Jer 4:28 [z]Joel 1:10-12 [a]Jer 4:25; 9:10 **12:5** [b]Jer 49:19; 50:44 **12:6** [c]Pr 26:24-25; Jer 9:4 [d]Ps 12:2

[a] 5 Or *you feel secure only* [b] 5 Or *the flooding of*

Israel. This picture is also a common one in Egypt. Amenemope (second millennium BC) describes the wise as trees planted in the garden that flourish and double their yield; the fruit is sweet and the shade is pleasant. In contrast are the fools, who are characterized as trees planted indoors; they wither and are only good for burning as trash.

11:21 *Anathoth.* See note on 1:1. *threatening to kill you.* The threat on Jeremiah's life likely has its origin in Jeremiah's support of Josiah's reform, which had resulted in the village sanctuary at Anathoth being closed down. This would not sit well with Jeremiah's priestly family or with his friends. *Do not prophesy.* Known written prophecies from the ancient Near East contain mostly positive prophecies because negative ones would not generally have been preserved in writing (it was largely the court that produced the documents). Prophecy was largely an oral exercise. People in the ancient world believed that the pronouncement of the prophecy gave it efficacy. Therefore, if they could just prevent the prophet from speaking, the prophecy would lose its power. Killing Jeremiah would be one way to prevent Jeremiah's prophecy from being fulfilled.

12:4 *He will not see what happens to us.* In the ancient world it was believed that people suffered because the gods became offended and began to ignore and neglect them (see notes on Lev 26:17; Dt 32:20; Isa 60:15). The land therefore languished and the god would have no awareness of what happened to the people. His attention was elsewhere. These gods typically did not send judgment, they just withheld blessing or even took away protective spirits. This left the people vulnerable to all the worst circumstances. Here Jeremiah is also reflecting the idea that Yahweh has abandoned the people and is no longer even aware of their desperate situation.

12:5 *thickets by the Jordan.* This phrase can also be translated the "Pride of Jordan." "Thickets" translates a Hebrew word that generally means "height." The area known as the Pride of Jordan comprises the section of wooded undergrowth on either side of the Jordan River between the Sea of Galilee and the Dead Sea. It is the lowest spot in the Jordan rift, where the Jordan swells and overflows into a jungle-like thicket of reeds, bushes and trees. In this area one can find thickets of tamarisk, willow, poplar,

7 "I will forsake my house,
abandon[e] my inheritance;
I will give the one I love
into the hands of her enemies.
8 My inheritance has become to me
like a lion in the forest.
She roars at me;
therefore I hate her.[f]
9 Has not my inheritance become to me
like a speckled bird of prey
that other birds of prey surround and attack?
Go and gather all the wild beasts;
bring them to devour.[g]
10 Many shepherds[h] will ruin my vineyard
and trample down my field;
they will turn my pleasant field
into a desolate wasteland.[i]
11 It will be made a wasteland,
parched and desolate before me;[j]
the whole land will be laid waste
because there is no one who cares.
12 Over all the barren heights in the desert
destroyers will swarm,
for the sword of the LORD[k] will devour
from one end of the land to the other;[l]
no one will be safe.
13 They will sow wheat but reap thorns;
they will wear themselves out but gain nothing.[m]
They will bear the shame of their harvest
because of the LORD's fierce anger."[n]

14 This is what the LORD says: "As for all
my wicked neighbors who seize the inheritance I gave my people Israel, I will
uproot[o] them from their lands and I will
uproot the people of Judah from among
them. 15 But after I uproot them, I will
again have compassion and will bring[p]
each of them back to their own inheritance and their own country. 16 And if
they learn well the ways of my people
and swear by my name, saying, 'As surely as the LORD lives'[q]—even as they once
taught my people to swear by Baal[r]—then
they will be established among my people.[s] 17 But if any nation does not listen,
I will completely uproot and destroy[t] it,"
declares the LORD.

A Linen Belt

13 This is what the LORD said to me:
"Go and buy a linen belt and put it
around your waist, but do not let it touch
water." 2 So I bought a belt, as the LORD directed, and put it around my waist.
3 Then the word of the LORD came to me
a second time: 4 "Take the belt you bought
and are wearing around your waist, and
go now to Perath[a] and hide it there in a
crevice in the rocks." 5 So I went and hid it
at Perath, as the LORD told me.[u]
6 Many days later the LORD said to me,
"Go now to Perath and get the belt I told
you to hide there." 7 So I went to Perath
and dug up the belt and took it from the
place where I had hidden it, but now it
was ruined and completely useless.
8 Then the word of the LORD came to
me: 9 "This is what the LORD says: 'In the
same way I will ruin the pride of Judah
and the great pride[v] of Jerusalem. 10 These
wicked people, who refuse to listen to
my words, who follow the stubbornness
of their hearts[w] and go after other gods[x]

12:7 [e] Jer 7:29 **12:8** [f] Hos 9:15; Am 6:8 **12:9** [g] Isa 56:9; Jer 15:3; Eze 23:25 **12:10** [h] Jer 23:1 [i] Isa 5:1-7 **12:11** [j] ver 4; Isa 42:25; Jer 23:10 **12:12** [k] Jer 47:6 [l] Jer 3:2 **12:13** [m] Lev 26:20; Dt 28:38; Mic 6:15; Hag 1:6 [n] Jer 4:26 **12:14** [o] Zec 2:7-9 **12:15** [p] Am 9:14-15 **12:16** [q] Jer 4:2 [r] Jos 23:7 [s] Isa 49:6; Jer 3:17 **12:17** [t] Isa 60:12 **13:5** [u] Ex 40:16 **13:9** [v] Lev 26:19 **13:10** [w] Jer 11:8; 16:12 [x] Jer 9:14

[a] 4 Or possibly *to the Euphrates*; similarly in verses 5-7

oleander, cane and reeds. There is evidence that lions ruled in these forest areas until the thirteenth century AD. Other beasts inhabited this area as well, such as the wild boar, leopard, jackals, hyenas, desert rats and otters. This was a dangerous place for human beings.

12:9 *speckled bird of prey.* This is a difficult verse to understand. In fact, many scholars consider that this text does not refer to a bird at all, but to a hyena and its lair. This has support from the Septuagint (the pre-Christian Greek translation of the OT), the Talmud, and usage in other Semitic languages. Nevertheless, the evidence is not conclusive. One can still retain the reading of "bird" and understand the word "speckled" as being something negative. If so, then just as Judah has been savage toward God, she herself will now be treated as prey by her enemies. Whether one speaks of hyenas or birds of prey, the underlying issue is that Judah has behaved in such a manner that it deserves to be punished by enemies who are characterized as creatures who feast on their prey.

13:1 *linen belt.* It is impossible to know precisely which of two kinds of loincloths is intended in this context. The first option comes from a Canaanite depiction—a simple wrapper that did not pass between the legs. A second option is provided by an Egyptian depiction of Syrians wearing a garment made up of narrow strips of overlapping cloth that did pass through the legs. These garments could be made of different materials, such as leather, wool or linen. Two important aspects of this garment need to be underlined. First, this is a garment that clings to the body; it is not like a girdle worn over clothing. Second, the finest cloth mentioned here ("linen") symbolizes what Israel meant to Yahweh, particularly as Israel is remembered in 2:2–4.

13:4 *Perath.* Generally speaking, it designates the Euphrates River in Mesopotamia. The distance between Anathoth and the Euphrates River is approximately 362 miles (582 kilometers). This would mean two long, round-trip journeys for Jeremiah. Note that the other uses of "Perath" are either accompanied by the word "river" or by a qualifying term such as "Babylon" or "Carchemish." This is the only place where "Perath" occurs without any qualifier. A good alternative to the Euphrates River can be found about four miles (6.4 kilometers) northeast of Anathoth, at a site known as Parah, modern-day Khirbet Farah and the nearby spring Wadi Farah (cf. "Parah" in Jos 18:23). The short distance to Parah makes the symbolic action carried out by Jeremiah much more viable and powerful.

JEREMIAH 13

SYMBOLIC ACTION REPORT

This style of literature is common in the literary genre of prophetic literature. These symbolic action reports include the following: the Hebrew prophet is commanded to carry out a task, that behavior is then reported, and the report of said task then is followed by an interpretation. In Jeremiah's case we have a number of situations that qualify as this kind of symbolic action report in which the prophetic message is accompanied by an illustrative action. Jeremiah is commanded to take and bury a loin cloth (Jer 13:1 – 11), to smash a clay jar (Jer 19:10 – 14), to wear an ox yoke (Jer 27:2), to buy a field (Jer 32:1 – 15) and to bury large stones (Jer 43:8), among others. There is also a symbolic action that takes place in the visionary world: Jeremiah is commanded to take a cup from the hand of Yahweh that is filled with Yahweh's wrath (Jer 25:15 – 29).

Ezekiel, a younger contemporary of Jeremiah, also uses this medium frequently. His sign acts include making a map of Jerusalem on a brick (Eze 4:1 – 3), lying on his side (Eze 4:4 – 8), eating exiles' rations (Eze 4:9 – 17), and shaving his hair (Eze 5:1 – 12), just to name a few.

Symbolic action reports are present in other ancient Near Eastern contexts. Prophets in the ancient Near East, particularly from Mari in Mesopotamia, sometimes accompanied their prophecies with a symbolic action. In texts discovered at Mari, we have a letter from Yaqqim-Adad, the governor of the city of Saggaratum, sent to King Zimri-Lim (c. 1775 – 1761 BC). In that letter Yaqqim-Adad reports that the prophet asked for a live lamb, tore it apart and ate its raw meat in public. In this way the prophet warned that a pestilence would break out in the land. ◆

to serve and worship them, will be like
this belt — completely useless! 11For as a
belt is bound around the waist, so I bound
all the people of Israel and all the people
of Judah to me,' declares the LORD, 'to be
my people for my renown[y] and praise and
honor.[z] But they have not listened.'[a]

Wineskins

12"Say to them: 'This is what the LORD,
the God of Israel, says: Every wineskin
should be filled with wine.' And if they say
to you, 'Don't we know that every wineskin should be filled with wine?' 13then tell
them, 'This is what the LORD says: I am going to fill with drunkenness[b] all who live
in this land, including the kings who sit on
David's throne, the priests, the prophets
and all those living in Jerusalem. 14I will
smash them one against the other, parents
and children alike, declares the LORD. I will
allow no pity or mercy or compassion[c] to
keep me from destroying[d] them.'"

Threat of Captivity

15Hear and pay attention,
do not be arrogant,
for the LORD has spoken.
16Give glory[e] to the LORD your God
before he brings the darkness,
before your feet stumble[f]
on the darkening hills.
You hope for light,
but he will turn it to utter darkness
and change it to deep gloom.[g]
17If you do not listen,[h]
I will weep in secret
because of your pride;
my eyes will weep bitterly,
overflowing with tears,[i]

13:11 [y] Jer 32:20; 33:9 [z] Ex 19:5-6 [a] Jer 7:26
13:13 [b] Ps 60:3; 75:8; Isa 51:17; 63:6; Jer 51:57
13:14 [c] Jer 16:5 [d] Dt 29:20; Eze 5:10
13:16 [e] Jos 7:19 [f] Jer 23:12 [g] Isa 59:9
13:17 [h] Mal 2:2 [i] Jer 9:1

13:12 *wineskin.* There is much discussion as to whether this Hebrew term is not better translated "jar," "jug," or "wine flask," and ample evidence exists to support such a translation. However, changing the image does not solve the matter of interpreting this difficult verse. We suggest Jeremiah is perhaps quoting a proverb to catch the audience's attention. He says something that really does not mean anything or is noncommunicative, and this serves to jolt the audience out of their apathy.

because the LORD's flock[j] will be
taken captive.[k]

18 Say to the king and to the queen
mother,
"Come down from your thrones,
for your glorious crowns
will fall from your heads."
19 The cities in the Negev will be shut up,
and there will be no one to open
them.
All Judah[l] will be carried into exile,
carried completely away.

20 Look up and see
those who are coming from the
north.[m]
Where is the flock[n] that was entrusted
to you,
the sheep of which you boasted?
21 What will you say when the LORD sets
over you
those you cultivated as your special
allies?[o]
Will not pain grip you
like that of a woman in labor?[p]
22 And if you ask yourself,
"Why has this happened to me?"—
it is because of your many sins[q]
that your skirts have been torn off
and your body mistreated.[r]
23 Can an Ethiopian[a] change his skin
or a leopard its spots?
Neither can you do good
who are accustomed to doing evil.

24 "I will scatter you like chaff[s]
driven by the desert wind.[t]
25 This is your lot,
the portion[u] I have decreed for you,"
declares the LORD,
"because you have forgotten me
and trusted in false gods.
26 I will pull up your skirts over your face
that your shame may be seen[v]—
27 your adulteries and lustful neighings,
your shameless prostitution![w]
I have seen your detestable acts
on the hills and in the fields.[x]

13:17 [j] Ps 80:1; Jer 23:1 [k] Jer 14:18 **13:19** [l] Jer 20:4; 52:30 **13:20** [m] Jer 6:22; Hab 1:6 [n] Jer 23:2 **13:21** [o] Jer 38:22 [p] Jer 4:31 **13:22** [q] Jer 9:2-6; 16:10-12 [r] Eze 16:37; Na 3:5-6 **13:24** [s] Ps 1:4 [t] Lev 26:33 **13:25** [u] Job 20:29; Mt 24:51 **13:26** [v] La 1:8; Eze 16:37; Hos 2:10 **13:27** [w] Jer 2:20 [x] Eze 6:13

[a] *23* Hebrew *Cushite* (probably a person from the upper Nile region)

13:18 *queen mother.* The queen mother often exercised considerable power. With respect to this verse, the queen mother likely refers to Nehushta, the mother of the young King Jehoiachin (2Ki 24:8). Jehoiachin occupied the throne for three months before he was taken into captivity by the Babylonians in 597 BC. Evidence is lacking as to whether the power and office of the queen mother was strictly defined and institutionalized. Nevertheless we know from many Mesopotamian, Egyptian and Hittite sources that the role of the queen mother was important. The wife of Zimri-Lim, king of Mari during the second millennium BC, was influential with respect to administrative details. Likewise, Naqia-Zakutu, wife of Sennacherib, king of Assyria (705–681 BC), was instrumental in securing the accession of her son Esarhaddon (681–669 BC). This role seems to have gained power particularly when the son or grandson of the queen was named king at an early age and the husband of the queen had already died. In Judah, we surmise that a queen mother could be removed from "office." In 1Ki 15:13 we read that queen mother Maakah was removed by her grandson Asa, king of Judah, because of her cultic offenses. Clearly this queen mother had high rank and official prerogatives. There is little evidence for such an office in the northern kingdom of Israel, though the names of at least two queen mothers—Zeruah (1Ki 11:26) and Jezebel (2Ki 9:22)—have been preserved. See note on 1Ki 2:19. *crowns.* The royal crown in Judah was most likely a gold circlet or diadem worn over a turban and adorned with a precious stone or stones. In the ancient Near Eastern context many different types of headdress were worn by the kings. A common one in Assyria was a conical-shaped cap that was embroidered and also decorated with precious stones. The Old Babylonian royal headgear was more of a rounded cap, whereas the Neo-Babylonian one was a cap that came to a point at the top. Egypt used crowns of varying shapes and forms, though all of them symbolized royal authority. In Jeremiah's context this verse suggests that the time has come when King Jehoiachin (who ruled for three months in 598–597 BC) and his mother will have to relinquish the crown.

13:19 *Negev.* This term normally referred to the large desert area south of Judah. In this context, however, it likely denotes the portion of southern Judah dotted with towns and garrisons running from Bethlehem to Beersheba, with Hebron in the middle. It is unclear to what extent these cities came under attack by Babylon in 597 BC, but the ostraca from Arad suggest that Edom posed a threat to them.

13:23 *Can an Ethiopian change his skin ...?* An Ethiopian is an inhabitant of Cush, a term that designates an area south of Egypt that corresponds primarily to modern-day Sudan and perhaps portions of modern-day Ethiopia. The question asked by the prophet here is obviously a rhetorical question. But a possible answer to the question may be found in an ancient Egyptian text from the fifth century BC known as the "Instructions of Onchsheshonqy," which indicates that no Nubian (i.e., Cushite) can lay off his skin. The answer to the question, implicit in the formulation of the question, is that it is absolutely impossible for such a thing to happen. *a leopard its spots?* This is a parallel question to the previous one. Once again the impossibility of something taking place is phrased by means of a rhetorical question. A similar kind of impossibility is expressed in a text of Aramaic proverbs known as the *Words of Ahiqar.* These texts come from a Jewish community that lived for a time in Egypt around the fifth century BC. One of these didactic texts contains a conversation between a leopard and a goat in which the leopard offers to give his skin to the goat so that it can keep warm. The goat replies that the leopard's real intention is to take away the goat's skin.

13:26 *pull up your skirts over your face that your shame may be seen.* This is a powerful and somewhat violent description of what will happen to Judah. This does not refer to women being taken into captivity, nor does it refer to Judah not being able to see because its face is covered. Rather, God will uncover Judah's nakedness before the enemy and allow the enemy to ravage her. The word "shame" here is a euphemism for private parts. God will expose Judah's private parts, thus rendering her vulnerable to the enemy.

Woe to you, Jerusalem!
  How long will you be unclean?"[y]

Drought, Famine, Sword

14 This is the word of the LORD that
came to Jeremiah concerning the
drought:

2 "Judah mourns,[z]
  her cities languish;
they wail for the land,
  and a cry goes up from Jerusalem.
3 The nobles send their servants for water;
  they go to the cisterns
  but find no water.[a]
They return with their jars unfilled;
  dismayed and despairing,
  they cover their heads.[b]
4 The ground is cracked
  because there is no rain in the land;[c]
the farmers are dismayed
  and cover their heads.
5 Even the doe in the field
  deserts her newborn fawn
  because there is no grass.[d]
6 Wild donkeys stand on the barren
    heights[e]
  and pant like jackals;
their eyes fail
  for lack of food."

7 Although our sins testify[f] against us,
  do something, LORD, for the sake of
    your name.
For we have often rebelled;[g]
  we have sinned[h] against you.
8 You who are the hope[i] of Israel,
  its Savior in times of distress,
why are you like a stranger in the land,
  like a traveler who stays only a
    night?
9 Why are you like a man taken by
    surprise,
  like a warrior powerless to save?[j]
You are among[k] us, LORD,
  and we bear your name;[l]
  do not forsake us!

10 This is what the LORD says about this
people:

"They greatly love to wander;
  they do not restrain their feet.[m]

13:27 [y] Hos 8:5
14:2 [z] Isa 3:26; Jer 8:21
14:3 [a] 2Ki 18:31; Job 6:19-20 [b] 2Sa 15:30
14:4 [c] Jer 3:3
14:5 [d] Isa 15:6
14:6 [e] Job 39:5-6; Jer 2:24
14:7 [f] Hos 5:5 [g] Jer 5:6 [h] Jer 8:14
14:8 [i] Jer 17:13
14:9 [j] Isa 50:2 [k] Jer 8:19 [l] Isa 63:19; Jer 15:16
14:10 [m] Ps 119:101; Jer 2:25 [n] Jer 6:20; Am 5:22 [o] Hos 9:9 [p] Jer 44:21-23; Hos 8:13
14:11 [q] Ex 32:10
14:12 [r] Isa 1:15; Jer 11:11 [s] Jer 7:21 [t] Jer 6:20
14:13 [u] Jer 5:12
14:14 [v] Jer 27:14 [w] Jer 23:21, 32 [x] Jer 23:16 [y] Eze 12:24
14:15 [z] Eze 14:9 [a] Jer 5:12-13
14:16 [b] Ps 79:3 [c] Jer 7:33 [d] Pr 1:31
14:17 [e] Jer 9:1 [f] Jer 8:21
14:18 [g] Eze 7:15
14:19 [h] Jer 7:29

So the LORD does not accept[n] them;
  he will now remember[o] their
    wickedness
  and punish them for their sins."[p]

11 Then the LORD said to me, "Do not
pray[q] for the well-being of this people.
12 Although they fast, I will not listen to
their cry;[r] though they offer burnt offerings[s] and grain offerings, I will not accept[t]
them. Instead, I will destroy them with the
sword, famine and plague."
13 But I said, "Alas, Sovereign LORD! The
prophets keep telling them, 'You will not
see the sword or suffer famine.[u] Indeed, I
will give you lasting peace in this place.'"
14 Then the LORD said to me, "The
prophets are prophesying lies[v] in my
name. I have not sent[w] them or appointed
them or spoken to them. They are prophesying to you false visions,[x] divinations,[y]
idolatries[a] and the delusions of their own
minds. 15 Therefore this is what the LORD
says about the prophets who are prophesying in my name: I did not send them,
yet they are saying, 'No sword or famine
will touch this land.' Those same prophets will perish[z] by sword and famine.[a]
16 And the people they are prophesying to
will be thrown out into the streets of Jerusalem because of the famine and sword.
There will be no one to bury[b] them, their
wives, their sons and their daughters.[c] I
will pour out on them the calamity they
deserve.[d]

17 "Speak this word to them:

" 'Let my eyes overflow with tears[e]
  night and day without ceasing;
for the Virgin Daughter, my people,
  has suffered a grievous wound,
  a crushing blow.[f]
18 If I go into the country,
  I see those slain by the sword;
if I go into the city,
  I see the ravages of famine.[g]
Both prophet and priest
  have gone to a land they know not.' "

19 Have you rejected Judah completely?[h]
  Do you despise Zion?

[a] 14 Or *visions, worthless divinations*

14:3 *cisterns.* See note on 2:13.
14:6 *jackals.* See note on 9:11.
14:12 *fast.* There was only one annual national day of fasting in Israel instituted by OT law, namely, the fasting done on the Day of Atonement, primarily as a sign of repentance. But voluntary fasting was done in a variety of circumstances, either individually or nationally. Realities such as drought, famine, sickness, death, imminent enemy invasion, or other life-threatening circumstances led the people of Israel to practice fasting. Such fasting, of course, was intended to influence God to intervene on their behalf. Fasting was often accompanied by other behavior such as lying on the ground, putting on sackcloth and ashes, weeping, tearing of clothes, and, last but not least, prayer. Fasting was often done in the context of mourning (see notes on 2:37; 4:8; see also the article "Mourning," p. 828). In ancient Near Eastern society, fasting was not as prevalent as in Israel. A reading of texts such as the "Curse of Agade," the Gilgamesh Epic, and the Ugaritic Baal Cycle shows that fasting generally took place only in the context of mourning.

Why have you afflicted us
so that we cannot be healed?[i]
We hoped for peace
but no good has come,
for a time of healing
but there is only terror.[j]
20 We acknowledge our wickedness, LORD,
and the guilt of our ancestors;
we have indeed sinned[k] against you.
21 For the sake of your name[l] do not
despise us;
do not dishonor your glorious
throne.[m]
Remember your covenant with us
and do not break it.
22 Do any of the worthless idols of the
nations bring rain?[n]
Do the skies themselves send down
showers?
No, it is you, LORD our God.
Therefore our hope is in you,
for you are the one who does all
this.

15

Then the LORD said to me: "Even if
Moses[o] and Samuel[p] were to stand
before me, my heart would not go out to
this people.[q] Send them away from my
presence![r] Let them go! 2 And if they ask
you, 'Where shall we go?' tell them, 'This
is what the LORD says:

" 'Those destined for death, to death;
those for the sword, to the sword;[s]
those for starvation, to starvation;[t]
those for captivity, to captivity.'[u]

3 "I will send four kinds of destroyers[v]
against them," declares the LORD, "the
sword to kill and the dogs to drag away
and the birds[w] and the wild animals to devour and destroy.[x] 4 I will make them abhorrent[y] to all the kingdoms of the earth[z]
because of what Manasseh[a] son of Hezekiah king of Judah did in Jerusalem.

5 "Who will have pity[b] on you,
Jerusalem?
Who will mourn for you?
Who will stop to ask how you are?
6 You have rejected[c] me," declares the
LORD.
"You keep on backsliding.
So I will reach out[d] and destroy you;
I am tired of holding back.
7 I will winnow them with a winnowing
fork
at the city gates of the land.
I will bring bereavement and
destruction on my people,[e]
for they have not changed their
ways.
8 I will make their widows more
numerous
than the sand of the sea.
At midday I will bring a destroyer[f]
against the mothers of their young
men;

14:19 [i] Jer 30:12-13 [j] Jer 8:15 **14:20** [k] Da 9:7-8 **14:21** [l] ver 7 [m] Jer 3:17 **14:22** [n] Ps 135:7 **15:1** [o] Ex 32:11; Nu 14:13-20 [p] 1Sa 7:9 [q] Jer 7:16; Eze 14:14,20 [r] 2Ki 17:20 **15:2** [s] Jer 43:11 [t] Jer 14:12 [u] Rev 13:10 **15:3** [v] Lev 26:16 [w] Dt 28:26 [x] Lev 26:22; Eze 14:21 **15:4** [y] Jer 24:9; 29:18 [z] Dt 28:25 [a] 2Ki 21:2; 23:26-27 **15:5** [b] Isa 51:19; Jer 13:14; 21:7; Na 3:7 **15:6** [c] Jer 6:19; 7:24 [d] Zep 1:4 **15:7** [e] Jer 18:21 **15:8** [f] Jer 6:4

14:22 *Do … idols … bring rain? Do the skies … send down showers?* Like most people from the ancient Near East, the Israelites viewed seasonal climate as coming from the four winds, which were derived from the four corners of the earth. God not only controlled the winds, but created them. The north wind was associated with cold conditions, dispersing rain and snow. The south wind was at times the bringer of the sirocco (see note on 4:11). The east wind brought a dry wind from the wilderness. The west wind came in from the Mediterranean Sea and was described as the "father of rain." It is clear in this verse that the common Israelite would have thought it absolutely ridiculous to imagine that the skies rained all by themselves. As in the rest of the ancient Near East, the Israelites believed that weather did not happen independent of deity.
15:4 *because of what Manasseh … did.* The mention of Manasseh's actions in this context is ominous. This king occupied the throne of Judah more years than did even King David, the founder of the Davidic dynasty. Manasseh encouraged the people to engage in idolatrous practices and even ordered the reconstruction of many pagan cultic centers that his own father, Hezekiah, had destroyed. This elicited the anger of the prophets like Jeremiah. Consequently, according to the prophets of the Hebrew Bible, the fall and final destruction of Jerusalem and the kingdom of Judah was caused primarily by the rebellious leadership and aberrant behavior of Manasseh.
15:7 *winnow them with a winnowing fork.* Once grain is harvested in Israel, it is threshed and then winnowed. This is done by throwing the harvested grain into the air with a winnowing fork so that the heavier grains fall to the threshing floor while the chaff is blown away by the gentle wind. Based on winnowing forks still in use during the nineteenth and twentieth centuries in Palestine and Syria, one can suggest that the fork used in antiquity was made out of wood, was about six feet (1.8 meters) tall, and had five or six prongs. Jeremiah here uses the process of winnowing as a metaphor for judgment and destruction. This idea is perhaps intensified by the use of the word "fork," which in Hebrew is derived from a verbal root that means "to scatter." In the minds of the hearers, this term may conjure up the idea of dispersion and exile, which in fact is what the Israelites experienced. In the Ugaritic Baal Cycle, winnowing is also used as a metaphor of punishment. In this case Mot, the god of death, cries against Baal, saying that because of Baal, Mot has lost face and has been cut up with a sword, burnt with fire, ground with a millstone and winnowed with a sieve. In other texts, the goddess Anat, who longs for Baal, seizes Mot, splits him with a sword, and winnows him with a sieve.
15:8 *midday.* Noon was considered the most secure time of the day. Most battles began at daybreak so as to take advantage of as much daylight as possible. In the present case (see also 6:4), the enemy is so confident that it can attack at any time. They can let half the day go by and still be sure of victory. To attack at noon would be a total surprise, so the use of "midday" here expresses the idea of unexpectedness. The enemy of Israel will launch a surprise attack at the most unexpected time of the day. *destroyer.* Represents the Chaldean army, which is being prepared by God to attack his people. This is not the same word as used for the destroying angel in the Passover episode (Ex 12:23), but it is used of the military operations conducted by the Lord in Jer 47:4; 51:55.

JEREMIAH 16:4

Proper Burial

Proper burial was an important value in ancient Israel as well as in the entire ancient Near East (see the article "Exposure of the Dead," p. 1239). When the prophet wants to speak of judgment and punishment, he threatens the people with the exposure of dead bodies — either by denying proper burial or by malicious disinterment.

In many cases lack of a proper burial was considered a curse, which contained three elements: (1) the body will be left unburied; (2) it will serve as food for the birds and the beasts; (3) it will be refuse on the face of the earth. A popular belief was that a person who was not interred properly remained restless until he or she was properly laid to rest. This is illustrated by a text in the Gilgamesh Epic, where the question is asked regarding the state of a corpse that is cast out into the open steppe. The answer given is that the spirit of that corpse finds no rest in the netherworld. In the vassal treaties of Esarhaddon, king of Assyria (681–669 BC), one finds curses that mention the threat of filling up the plains with corpses whose flesh will be food for eagles and vultures.

In addition to proper burial, it was considered important to fulfill certain mourning rites on behalf of the dead. This may have been influenced by forms of ancestor cult worship prevalent in the ancient Near East. This is illustrated by certain Ugaritic texts. Even though Leviticus expressly prohibits certain rites, it is evident that the Israelites did practice mourning rites such as rending garments, putting on sackcloth, shaving the hair, and even cutting the body (see the article "Mourning," p. 828). They also took part in a sort of death-cult banquet known as the *marzeah* (see note on Jer 16:5). ◆

because I have withdrawn my blessing,
my love and my pity from this people," declares the LORD. 6"Both high and low will
die in this land.[j] They will not be buried
or mourned, and no one will cut[k] themselves or shave[l] their head for the dead.
7No one will offer food to comfort those
who mourn[m] for the dead — not even for a
father or a mother — nor will anyone give
them a drink to console them.
8"And do not enter a house where there
is feasting and sit down to eat and drink.[n]
9For this is what the LORD Almighty, the
God of Israel, says: Before your eyes and
in your days I will bring an end to the
sounds[o] of joy and gladness and to the
voices of bride and bridegroom in this
place.[p]
10"When you tell these people all this
and they ask you, 'Why has the LORD decreed such a great disaster against us?
What wrong have we done? What sin have
we committed against the LORD our God?'[q]
11then say to them, 'It is because your ancestors forsook me,' declares the LORD,
'and followed other gods and served and
worshiped them. They forsook me and did
not keep my law.[r] 12But you have behaved

16:6 [j] Eze 9:5-6 [k] Lev 19:28 [l] Jer 41:5; 47:5 **16:7** [m] Eze 24:17; Hos 9:4 **16:8** [n] Ecc 7:2-4; Jer 15:17 **16:9** [o] Isa 24:8; Eze 26:13; Hos 2:11 [p] Rev 18:23 **16:10** [q] Dt 29:24; Jer 5:19 **16:11** [r] Dt 29:25-26; 1Ki 9:9; Ps 106:35-43; Jer 22:9

joyful moment or for the mourning of the dead. Though we cannot be sure what was involved in this Israelite practice, funerary rites tend to remain the same over centuries. We do know that God forbade Jeremiah to participate in these banquets as well as in other social activities such as getting married or even participating in marriage ceremonies.

16:6 *no one will cut themselves or shave their head for the dead.* The Torah prohibited the Israelites to engage in these mourning rites (Lev 19:27–28; Dt 14:1). Yet there is ample evidence that they were practiced in Israel (Isa 22:12; Am 8:10). The reason for this kind of behavior may be due to a belief in the powers held by the spirits of the dead. *cut themselves.* slashing one's body was part of Baal worship (cf. the confrontation between Elijah and the prophets of Baal in 1Ki 18:28). See note on Jer 7:29. *shave.* Studies have shown that shaving rites are flexible and can function in different ways: as a rite of separation (Nu 8:7; Dt 21:12), as a rite of aggregation (Lev 13:33; 14:8–9), and as a purification process in certain ritual contexts (Lev 14:8–9). Each case must be analyzed separately. But the underlying similarity is that shaving signals a change in status and serves to publicly announce that change.

suddenly I will bring down on them
anguish and terror.
9 The mother of seven will grow faint[g]
and breathe her last.
Her sun will set while it is still day;
she will be disgraced and
humiliated.
I will put the survivors to the sword[h]
before their enemies,"
declares the LORD.

10 Alas, my mother, that you gave me
birth,[i]
a man with whom the whole land
strives and contends![j]
I have neither lent[k] nor borrowed,
yet everyone curses me.
11 The LORD said,

"Surely I will deliver you[l] for a good
purpose;
surely I will make your enemies
plead[m] with you
in times of disaster and times of
distress.

12 "Can a man break iron—
iron from the north[n]—or bronze?

13 "Your wealth and your treasures
I will give as plunder, without charge,[o]
because of all your sins
throughout your country.[p]
14 I will enslave you to your enemies
in[a] a land you do not know,[q]
for my anger will kindle a fire[r]
that will burn against you."

15 LORD, you understand;
remember me and care for me.
Avenge me on my persecutors.[s]
You are long-suffering—do not take
me away;
think of how I suffer reproach for
your sake.[t]
16 When your words came, I ate[u] them;
they were my joy and my heart's
delight,[v]
for I bear your name,[w]
LORD God Almighty.
17 I never sat[x] in the company of revelers,
never made merry with them;
I sat alone because your hand was
on me
and you had filled me with
indignation.
18 Why is my pain unending
and my wound grievous and
incurable?[y]
You are to me like a deceptive brook,
like a spring that fails.[z]

19 Therefore this is what the LORD says:

"If you repent, I will restore you
that you may serve[a] me;
if you utter worthy, not worthless,
words,
you will be my spokesman.
Let this people turn to you,
but you must not turn to them.
20 I will make you a wall to this people,
a fortified wall of bronze;
they will fight against you
but will not overcome you,
for I am with you
to rescue and save you,"[b]
declares the LORD.
21 "I will save you from the hands of the
wicked
and deliver[c] you from the grasp of
the cruel."[d]

Day of Disaster

16 Then the word of the LORD came
to me: 2 "You must not marry[e] and
have sons or daughters in this place." 3 For
this is what the LORD says about the sons
and daughters born in this land and about
the women who are their mothers and the
men who are their fathers:[f] 4 "They will
die of deadly diseases. They will not be
mourned or buried[g] but will be like dung
lying on the ground.[h] They will perish by
sword and famine, and their dead bodies
will become food for the birds and the
wild animals."[i]
5 For this is what the LORD says: "Do not
enter a house where there is a funeral meal;
do not go to mourn or show sympathy,

[a] 14 Some Hebrew manuscripts, Septuagint and Syriac (see also 17:4); most Hebrew manuscripts *I will cause your enemies to bring you / into*

15:9 [g] 1Sa 2:5 [h] Jer 21:7 **15:10** [i] Job 3:1 [j] Jer 1:19 [k] Lev 25:36 **15:11** [l] Jer 40:4 [m] Jer 21:1-2; 37:3; 42:1-3 **15:12** [n] Jer 28:14 **15:13** [o] Ps 44:12 [p] Jer 17:3 **15:14** [q] Dt 28:36; Jer 16:13 [r] Dt 32:22; Ps 21:9 **15:15** [s] Jer 12:3 [t] Ps 69:7-9 **15:16** [u] Eze 3:3; Rev 10:10 [v] Ps 119:72, 103 [w] Jer 14:9 **15:17** [x] Ps 1:1; 26:4-5; Jer 16:8 **15:18** [y] Jer 30:15; Mic 1:9 [z] Job 6:15 **15:19** [a] Zec 3:7 **15:20** [b] Jer 20:11; Eze 3:8 **15:21** [c] Jer 50:34 [d] Ge 48:16 **16:2** [e] 1Co 7:26-27 **16:3** [f] Jer 6:21 **16:4** [g] Jer 25:33 [h] Ps 83:10; Jer 9:22 [i] Ps 79:1-3; Jer 15:3; 34:20

15:12 It seems that here iron represents the enemy, while the prophet Jeremiah is characterized by iron and bronze. The suggestion is that the enemy (iron) cannot prevail over a much stronger Jeremiah (iron-bronze). *iron from the north.* Most likely refers to a high grade Pontus iron. Pontus is located in northeast Asia Minor on the Black Sea (part of Hittite country). Already in the thirteenth century BC Shalmaneser I, the king of Assyria (1264–1234 BC), mentions the Hittite Empire as a good source of iron.
15:20 *a fortified wall of bronze.* Excavations at Balawat (ancient Imgur-Enlil), a palace located about ten miles (16 kilometers) from Nimrud, show that Shalmaneser III, king of Assyria (858–824 BC), erected gates capped with bronze. The bronze bands are decorated in relief by hammering from behind.
16:5 *funeral meal.* This Hebrew term (*marzeah*) occurs in only one other place in the Hebrew Bible (Am 6:7 ["feasting"]). However, its cognates in other ancient Near Eastern languages and cultures are well known. In an Ugaritic text that speaks of El's divine feast, the term denotes a banquet where excess drinking and feasting were the norm. That text, others from Elephantine (Egypt), and inscriptions in Punic, Nabatean and Palmyrene (though from different time periods) suggest that *marzeah* describes an institution of sorts or an association of members who periodically dedicate themselves to feasting and drinking either for a

more wickedly than your ancestors.[s] See
how all of you are following the stubbornness of your evil hearts[t] instead of obeying
me. 13So I will throw you out of this land
into a land neither you nor your ancestors
have known,[u] and there you will serve
other gods[v] day and night, for I will show
you no favor.'[w]

14"However, the days are coming," declares the LORD, "when it will no longer
be said, 'As surely as the LORD lives, who
brought the Israelites up out of Egypt,'[x]
15but it will be said, 'As surely as the LORD
lives, who brought the Israelites up out of
the land of the north and out of all the
countries where he had banished them.'[y]
For I will restore[z] them to the land I gave
their ancestors.

16"But now I will send for many fishermen," declares the LORD, "and they will
catch them.[a] After that I will send for
many hunters, and they will hunt[b] them
down on every mountain and hill and
from the crevices of the rocks.[c] 17My eyes
are on all their ways; they are not hidden[d]
from me, nor is their sin concealed from
my eyes.[e] 18I will repay them double[f] for
their wickedness and their sin, because
they have defiled my land[g] with the lifeless forms of their vile images and have
filled my inheritance with their detestable
idols."

19LORD, my strength and my fortress,
my refuge in time of distress,
to you the nations will come[h]
from the ends of the earth and say,
"Our ancestors possessed nothing but
false gods,[i]
worthless idols that did them no
good.
20Do people make their own gods?
Yes, but they are not gods!"[j]

21"Therefore I will teach them—
this time I will teach them
my power and might.
Then they will know
that my name is the LORD.

17 "Judah's sin is engraved with an
iron tool,[k]
inscribed with a flint point,
on the tablets of their hearts[l]
and on the horns of their altars.
2Even their children remember
their altars and Asherah poles[a][m]
beside the spreading trees
and on the high hills.[n]
3My mountain in the land
and your[b] wealth and all your
treasures
I will give away as plunder,[o]
together with your high places,[p]
because of sin throughout your
country.[q]
4Through your own fault you will lose
the inheritance[r] I gave you.
I will enslave you to your enemies[s]
in a land[t] you do not know,
for you have kindled my anger,
and it will burn[u] forever."

5This is what the LORD says:

"Cursed is the one who trusts in man,[v]
who draws strength from mere flesh
and whose heart turns away from
the LORD.
6That person will be like a bush in the
wastelands;
they will not see prosperity when it
comes.
They will dwell in the parched places
of the desert,
in a salt[w] land where no one lives.

16:12 [s]Jer 7:26 [t]Ecc 9:3; Jer 13:10 **16:13** [u]Dt 28:36; Jer 5:19 [v]Dt 4:28 [w]Jer 15:5 **16:14** [x]Dt 15:15; Jer 23:7-8 **16:15** [y]Isa 11:11; Jer 23:8 [z]Jer 24:6 **16:16** [a]Am 4:2; Hab 1:14-15 [b]Am 9:3; Mic 7:2 [c]1Sa 26:20 **16:17** [d]1Co 4:5; Heb 4:13 [e]Pr 15:3 **16:18** [f]Isa 40:2; Rev 18:6 [g]Nu 35:34; Jer 2:7 **16:19** [h]Isa 2:2; Jer 3:17 [i]Ps 4:2 **16:20** [j]Ps 115:4-7; Isa 37:19; Jer 2:11

17:1 [k]Job 19:24 [l]Pr 3:3; 2Co 3:3 **17:2** [m]2Ch 24:18 [n]Jer 2:20 **17:3** [o]2Ki 24:13 [p]Jer 26:18; Mic 3:12 [q]Jer 15:13 **17:4** [r]La 5:2 [s]Dt 28:48; Jer 12:7 [t]Jer 16:13 [u]Jer 7:20; 15:14 **17:5** [v]Isa 2:22; 30:1-3 **17:6** [w]Dt 29:23; Job 39:6

[a] 2 That is, wooden symbols of the goddess Asherah
[b] 2,3 Or *hills / 3and the mountains of the land. / Your*

16:20 *they are not gods!* See notes on 10:3; 14:22.
17:1 *iron tool.* The Hebrew term used here should not be confused with the one mentioned in 8:8, which speaks of writing with ink on papyrus. The instrument noted here is a stylus used to engrave metal and stone. *flint point.* Some think this is not a separate tool but the hard stone attached to the iron tool. What seems clear is the prophet's intention. He compares Israel's heart to an extremely hard surface such as metal or stone. These were used as writing surfaces in antiquity. *horns of their altars.* Refers to four protrusions that arise at the four corners of many ancient altars (Ex 27:1–2), though their significance or use is unknown. Altars of this kind have been found both in Canaanite and wider ancient Near Eastern contexts. Some consider that these projections may have been used to help in binding the victim and in securing the wood to the altar. In certain cases the horns served as a kind of protective device for a person accused of murder. That person could grasp on to the horns and receive a measure of protection from accusers, though it did not always work this way (1Ki 2:28–32). The prophet Amos, in order to illustrate the reality of imminent destruction, speaks of the horns of the altar being cut off and falling to the ground (Am 3:14).
17:2 *Asherah poles.* These are most probably wooden poles, though they could also refer to live trees. They represent the Canaanite mother-goddess Asherah, who is the symbol of fertility (see note on 2:27). Though these were forbidden for the Israelites, they often mixed worship of Yahweh with other ancient fertility symbols. Asherah poles were often placed alongside altars that were designated for the worship of Yahweh (see notes on Dt 7:5; 1Ki 14:23). *high hills.* See note on Dt 12:2.
17:6 *wastelands.* The Arabah, an area in Israel that comprises the area south of the Sea of Galilee on both sides of the Jordan River, continuing south beyond the Dead Sea, and extending southwest toward the head of the Gulf of Aqaba. Most of this region lies below sea level, and thus it is a depression that lies between two sections of higher ground. *salt land.* Land that is completely barren, such as what is found in the vicinity of the Dead Sea. Land whose level of salinity is high is useless for agriculture,

7 "But blessed is the one who trusts[x] in
the LORD,
whose confidence is in him.
8 They will be like a tree planted by the
water
that sends out its roots by the
stream.
It does not fear when heat comes;
its leaves are always green.
It has no worries in a year of drought[y]
and never fails to bear fruit."[z]

9 The heart[a] is deceitful above all things
and beyond cure.
Who can understand it?

10 "I the LORD search the heart[b]
and examine the mind,[c]
to reward[d] each person according to
their conduct,
according to what their deeds
deserve."[e]

11 Like a partridge that hatches eggs it did
not lay
are those who gain riches by unjust
means.
When their lives are half gone, their
riches will desert them,
and in the end they will prove to be
fools.[f]

12 A glorious throne,[g] exalted from the
beginning,
is the place of our sanctuary.
13 LORD, you are the hope[h] of Israel;
all who forsake[i] you will be put to
shame.
Those who turn away from you will be
written in the dust
because they have forsaken the
LORD,
the spring of living water.
14 Heal me, LORD, and I will be healed;
save me and I will be saved,
for you are the one I praise.[j]
15 They keep saying to me,
"Where is the word of the LORD?
Let it now be fulfilled!"[k]
16 I have not run away from being your
shepherd;
you know I have not desired the day
of despair.
What passes my lips is open before
you.
17 Do not be a terror[l] to me;
you are my refuge[m] in the day of
disaster.
18 Let my persecutors be put to shame,
but keep me from shame;
let them be terrified,
but keep me from terror.
Bring on them the day of disaster;
destroy them with double
destruction.[n]

Keeping the Sabbath Day Holy

19 This is what the LORD said to me:
"Go and stand at the Gate of the People,[a]
through which the kings of Judah go in
and out; stand also at all the other gates of
Jerusalem.[o] 20 Say to them, 'Hear the word
of the LORD, you kings of Judah and all
people of Judah and everyone living in Jerusalem[p] who come through these gates.[q]
21 This is what the LORD says: Be careful

17:7 [x] Ps 34:8; 40:4; Pr 16:20 **17:8** [y] Jer 14:1-6 [z] Ps 1:3; 92:12-14 **17:9** [a] Ecc 9:3; Mt 13:15; Mk 7:21-22 **17:10** [b] 1Sa 16:7; Rev 2:23 [c] Ps 17:3; 139:23; Jer 11:20; 20:12; Ro 8:27 [d] Ps 62:12; Jer 32:19 [e] Ro 2:6 **17:11** [f] Lk 12:20 **17:12** [g] Jer 3:17 **17:13** [h] Jer 14:8 [i] Isa 1:28; Jer 2:17 **17:14** [j] Ps 109:1 **17:15** [k] Isa 5:19; 2Pe 3:4 **17:17** [l] Ps 88:15-16 [m] Jer 16:19; Na 1:7 **17:18** [n] Ps 35:1-8 **17:19** [o] Jer 7:2; 26:2 **17:20** [p] Jer 19:3 [q] Jer 22:2

[a] 19 Or *Army*

which conjures up memories of Sodom and Gomorrah (Ge 19:24–26). In the Tigris-Euphrates region, a process of progressive salinity took place between the third and second millennium BC. This meant that as time went on, the percentage of salinity in the vicinity of the Persian Gulf was so great that the soil was no longer suitable for agriculture and had to be abandoned.

17:11 The translation of this verse is difficult, and there is no scholarly consensus regarding the exact meaning of the verbs used in the first line of this proverb. *partridge.* In the region of Palestine, the partridge lays eggs in shallow nests on exposed ground, making the eggs vulnerable to predators, which either eat them or crush them. Both male and female partridges sit on the eggs that the female has laid. There are at least two kinds of partridges Jeremiah may have had in mind: the black francolin partridge, which inhabits the marshy areas of Israel, Syria and Jordan; and the sand partridge, which lives in desert and semidesert regions of Israel, Jordan and the Sinai peninsula. The meaning of the proverb in this verse depends considerably on the translation. Perhaps the idea is the danger of complacency. The partridges, male and female, watch over the eggs but can never be sure all of them will hatch because of the precarious situation wherein they are laid. The same is true of the man who gains riches through unjust means.

17:13 *the LORD, the spring of living water.* "Living" water refers to running water in contrast to stagnant or contaminated water that gathers in cisterns or pools.

17:19 *Gate of the People.* Lit. "Gate of the Sons of the People." The exact location of this gate cannot be determined. "Sons of the People" is somewhat confusing. In other contexts this expression characterizes the common people. But here it speaks of the kings of Judah going in and out of this gate. Some have suggested that it may refer to one of the temple gates, comparing this passage to 7:1–12. Perhaps the most significant concept is that Jeremiah, as a prophet, goes to where the people are. He does not wait in a temple or expect the people to approach him. *other gates of Jerusalem.* During this time Jerusalem had many outer gates, as well as inner gates that protected the temple. On other occasions Jeremiah was sent to the Potsherd Gate (19:1–2) and the Temple Gate (7:1–12). The gates of the city of Jerusalem were busy places where people passed through continuously, bringing in merchandise or going to the gate areas to purchase things. These areas were also used to discuss and decide civil and legal cases in the city (see notes on Job 5:4; 29:7; Pr 8:3; 31:23). It is difficult to ascertain how many gates existed during Jeremiah's time. In Nehemiah's time, at least 11 gates are mentioned by name.

not to carry a load on the Sabbath[r] day
or bring it through the gates of Jerusalem.
22Do not bring a load out of your houses or
do any work on the Sabbath, but keep the
Sabbath day holy, as I commanded your
ancestors.[s] 23Yet they did not listen or pay
attention;[t] they were stiff-necked[u] and
would not listen or respond to discipline.[v]
24But if you are careful to obey me, declares the LORD, and bring no load through
the gates of this city on the Sabbath, but
keep the Sabbath day holy by not doing
any work on it, 25then kings who sit on
David's throne[w] will come through the
gates of this city with their officials. They
and their officials will come riding in chariots and on horses, accompanied by the
men of Judah and those living in Jerusalem, and this city will be inhabited forever. 26People will come from the towns
of Judah and the villages around Jerusalem, from the territory of Benjamin and
the western foothills, from the hill country
and the Negev,[x] bringing burnt offerings
and sacrifices, grain offerings and incense,
and bringing thank offerings to the house
of the LORD. 27But if you do not obey[y] me
to keep the Sabbath day holy by not carrying any load as you come through the
gates of Jerusalem on the Sabbath day,
then I will kindle an unquenchable fire[z] in
the gates of Jerusalem that will consume
her fortresses.' "[a]

17:21 [r] Nu 15:32-36; Ne 13:15-21; Jn 5:10
17:22 [s] Ex 20:8; 31:13; Isa 56:2-6; Eze 20:12
17:23 [t] Jer 7:26 [u] Jer 19:15 [v] Jer 7:28
17:25 [w] 2Sa 7:13; Isa 9:7; Jer 22:2, 4; Lk 1:32
17:26 [x] Jer 32:44; 33:13; Zec 7:7
17:27 [y] Jer 22:5 [z] Jer 7:20 [a] 2Ki 25:9; Am 2:5

At the Potter's House

18 This is the word that came to Jeremiah from the LORD: 2"Go down
to the potter's house, and there I will give
you my message." 3So I went down to the
potter's house, and I saw him working at
the wheel. 4But the pot he was shaping
from the clay was marred in his hands;
so the potter formed it into another pot,
shaping it as seemed best to him.
5Then the word of the LORD came to me.
6He said, "Can I not do with you, Israel, as

Model of potter at work. See note on Jer 18:2.

Kim Walton. The Oriental Institute Museum, University of Chicago.

this potter does?" declares the LORD. "Like
clay[b] in the hand of the potter, so are you
in my hand, Israel. 7If at any time I announce that a nation or kingdom is to be
uprooted,[c] torn down and destroyed, 8and
if that nation I warned repents of its evil,
then I will relent[d] and not inflict on it the
disaster[e] I had planned. 9And if at another

18:6 [b] Isa 45:9; Ro 9:20-21
18:7 [c] Jer 1:10
18:8 [d] Jer 26:13; Jnh 3:8-10 [e] Eze 18:21; Hos 11:8-9

17:26 The regions mentioned in this verse provide a kind of panoramic view of Judah's territory. *the territory of Benjamin.* Just north of Jerusalem. Benjamin and Judah are the two tribes that make up the southern kingdom of Israel. *the western foothills.* The Shephelah (Lowlands); they lie to the west and southwest of Jerusalem, going as far as the Philistine plains. *the hill country.* Goes a bit to the north of Jerusalem and mostly south, including the Hebron heights. *the Negev.* Lies farther south than the "hill country"; it is that arid desert land where Beersheba and other boundary towns are found.

18:2 *potter's house.* This image is a familiar one for Jeremiah. If we judge from the amount of pottery pieces lying all over archaeological sites in Israel, pottery was a well-known craft. In the ancient Near East, handmade pottery was crafted as early as 8500 BC, which corresponds to the Neolithic period (c. 9000–4300 BC). Pottery is a valuable instrument in helping archaeologists date historical events as well as archaeological discoveries. The kind of clay, the shape, decoration, kinds of handles and colors are all used to develop a chronology and dating system. The potter's house, or workshop, must have been a rather large place. It included various instruments as well as different areas of work. It had to have a potter's wheel, a space for treading, a kiln, a field for storing vessels and a dump for those pieces the potter discarded. The potter also needed a good source of water, which could be either a nearby stream or cistern.

18:3 *wheel.* Lit. "two stones." Excavations done at places such as Tel Miqne-Ekron have turned up seventh-century BC wheels made out of stone. The potter's wheel has been in existence since approximately the fourth millennium BC. In Jeremiah's time there were two varieties: a slow wheel, or tournette, and a fast wheel. The one

time I announce that a nation or kingdom
is to be built[f] up and planted, 10and if it
does evil[g] in my sight and does not obey
me, then I will reconsider[h] the good I had
intended to do for it.

11"Now therefore say to the people of
Judah and those living in Jerusalem, 'This
is what the LORD says: Look! I am preparing a disaster[i] for you and devising a
plan against you. So turn[j] from your evil
ways,[k] each one of you, and reform your
ways and your actions.' 12But they will reply, 'It's no use.[l] We will continue with
our own plans; we will all follow the stubbornness of our evil hearts.' "

13Therefore this is what the LORD says:

"Inquire among the nations:
Who has ever heard anything like
this?[m]
A most horrible[n] thing has been done
by Virgin Israel.
14Does the snow of Lebanon
ever vanish from its rocky slopes?
Do its cool waters from distant sources
ever stop flowing?[a]
15Yet my people have forgotten me;
they burn incense to worthless
idols,[o]
which made them stumble in their
ways,
in the ancient paths.[p]
They made them walk in byways,
on roads not built up.[q]
16Their land will be an object of horror[r]
and of lasting scorn;[s]
all who pass by will be appalled
and will shake their heads.[t]
17Like a wind[u] from the east,
I will scatter them before their
enemies;
I will show them my back and not my
face[v]
in the day of their disaster."

18They said, "Come, let's make plans[w]
against Jeremiah; for the teaching of the
law by the priest[x] will not cease, nor will
counsel from the wise, nor the word from
the prophets.[y] So come, let's attack him
with our tongues[z] and pay no attention to
anything he says."

19Listen to me, LORD;
hear what my accusers are saying!
20Should good be repaid with evil?
Yet they have dug a pit[a] for me.
Remember that I stood before you
and spoke in their behalf[b]
to turn your wrath away from them.
21So give their children over to famine;[c]
hand them over to the power of the
sword.
Let their wives be made childless and
widows;[d]
let their men be put to death,
their young men slain by the sword
in battle.
22Let a cry[e] be heard from their houses
when you suddenly bring invaders
against them,

18:9 [f] Jer 1:10; 31:28 **18:10** [g] Eze 33:18 [h] 1Sa 2:29-30 **18:11** [i] Jer 4:6 [j] 2Ki 17:13; Isa 1:16-19 [k] Jer 7:3 **18:12** [l] Isa 57:10; Jer 2:25 **18:13** [m] Isa 66:8; Jer 2:10 [n] Jer 5:30 **18:15** [o] Jer 10:15 [p] Jer 6:16 [q] Isa 57:14; 62:10 **18:16** [r] Jer 25:9 [s] Jer 19:8 [t] Ps 22:7 **18:17** [u] Jer 13:24 [v] Jer 2:27 **18:18** [w] Jer 11:19 [x] Mal 2:7 [y] Jer 5:13 [z] Ps 52:2 **18:20** [a] Ps 35:7; 57:6 [b] Ps 106:23 **18:21** [c] Jer 11:22 [d] Ps 109:9 **18:22** [e] Jer 6:26

[a] 14 The meaning of the Hebrew for this sentence is uncertain.

mentioned in this context is most likely the fast wheel. It consists of two disks or stones joined by a vertical axis. The lower one functions like a flywheel and is spun by the potter's feet. (In Sirach 38:29 we read, "So it is with the potter, sitting at his work, turning the wheel with his feet" [NEB].) This causes the upper disk or stone to rotate as well. The clay is placed on the upper disk and is shaped by the hands of the potter. As explained in this parable, often during the process of "throwing" the clay, some defect appears either in the nature of the clay or in the design of the object. The potter then squeezes the developing object into a shapeless mass of clay and begins the process of creating the clay vessel over again.

18:13 *Virgin Israel.* This title is used only two other times in Jeremiah (31:4,21; cf. 14:17). Outside of Jeremiah it appears only once more in the Prophets, in Am 5:2. This term designates the entire people of God, and in this context it seems to be used in an ironic sense. The term "virgin" here most likely describes a young woman of marriageable age who is still under the legal supervision of her father. In Ugaritic texts, a cognate term is used as an epithet of the goddess Anat. In some texts she is referred to as the virgin warrior and the valiant widow. We cannot be sure exactly what this means, but it does not refer to virginity in the modern sense of the word, for according to the Ugaritic texts Anat has had sexual intercourse on more than one occasion.

18:14 *snow of Lebanon.* Probably refers to the range of high mountains in the Anti-Lebanon range. Many of these mountains are snowcapped most of the year. The highest mountain in Lebanon is called Qurnat as-Sawda, and the snow does not melt away on this mountain until late August.

18:15 *roads not built up.* A paved road was one that was built up. Paving was an expensive undertaking. In Babylon, dirt and gravel were used to build up the roadbed. Then bricks were laid in asphalt to form a foundation. Finally, limestone slabs were laid on top, and the crevices again were filled with asphalt. This process was only affordable on the most prominent streets in a city. Excavated examples occur in Palestine as early as the Middle Bronze period. Cobblestone streets using pebbles and pottery shards set in clay were the norm. Sometimes they were coated with a lime plaster. There is no evidence of paved country roads during this period. Even an unpaved road, however, could be built up with dirt so that water flowed off it to the sides. The alternative was a road that had simply been traveled often enough to cut a path. These were etched into the terrain and tended to gather water and become mud holes.

18:20 *pit.* Used as a trap to catch animals. Many of these were dug in the desert in order to trap game. However, archaeological excavations show that pits were dug for other uses as well: storing pottery, burying garbage, and making temporary kinds of prisons. This term may be used in a figurative sense here.

for they have dug a pit to capture me
and have hidden snares[f] for my feet.
23 But you, LORD, know
all their plots to kill[g] me.
Do not forgive[h] their crimes
or blot out their sins from your sight.
Let them be overthrown before you;
deal with them in the time of your
anger.

19 This is what the LORD says: "Go
and buy a clay jar from a potter.[i]
Take along some of the elders[j] of the people and of the priests 2 and go out to the
Valley of Ben Hinnom,[k] near the entrance
of the Potsherd Gate. There proclaim the
words I tell you, 3 and say, 'Hear the word
of the LORD, you kings[l] of Judah and people of Jerusalem. This is what the LORD
Almighty, the God of Israel, says: Listen! I
am going to bring a disaster[m] on this place
that will make the ears of everyone who
hears of it tingle.[n] 4 For they have forsaken[o]
me and made this a place of foreign gods;
they have burned incense[p] in it to gods
that neither they nor their ancestors nor
the kings of Judah ever knew, and they
have filled this place with the blood of the
innocent.[q] 5 They have built the high places of Baal to burn their children[r] in the
fire as offerings to Baal — something I did
not command or mention, nor did it enter
my mind.[s] 6 So beware, the days are coming, declares the LORD, when people will
no longer call this place Topheth or the
Valley of Ben Hinnom,[t] but the Valley of
Slaughter.[u]

7 " 'In this place I will ruin[a] the plans of
Judah and Jerusalem. I will make them
fall by the sword before their enemies,[v] at
the hands of those who want to kill them,
and I will give their carcasses[w] as food[x]
to the birds and the wild animals. 8 I will
devastate this city and make it an object
of horror and scorn;[y] all who pass by will
be appalled and will scoff because of all its
wounds. 9 I will make them eat[z] the flesh
of their sons and daughters, and they will
eat one another's flesh because their enemies[a] will press the siege so hard against
them to destroy them.'
10 "Then break the jar[b] while those who
go with you are watching, 11 and say to
them, 'This is what the LORD Almighty
says: I will smash[c] this nation and this
city just as this potter's jar is smashed
and cannot be repaired. They will bury[d]
the dead in Topheth until there is no more
room. 12 This is what I will do to this place
and to those who live here, declares the
LORD. I will make this city like Topheth.
13 The houses[e] in Jerusalem and those of
the kings of Judah will be defiled like this
place, Topheth — all the houses where
they burned incense on the roofs to all the
starry hosts[f] and poured out drink offerings[g] to other gods.' "
14 Jeremiah then returned from Topheth,
where the LORD had sent him to prophesy,
and stood in the court[h] of the LORD's temple and said to all the people, 15 "This is
what the LORD Almighty, the God of Israel,

18:22 [f] Ps 140:5 **18:23** [g] Jer 11:21 [h] Ps 109:14 **19:1** [i] Jer 18:2 [j] Nu 11:17 **19:2** [k] Jos 15:8 **19:3** [l] Jer 17:20 [m] Jer 6:19 [n] 1Sa 3:11 **19:4** [o] Dt 28:20; Isa 65:11 [p] Lev 18:21 [q] 2Ki 21:16; Jer 2:34 **19:5** [r] Lev 18:21; Ps 106:37-38 [s] Jer 7:31; 32:35 **19:6** [t] Jos 15:8 [u] Jer 7:32 **19:7** [v] Lev 26:17; Dt 28:25 [w] Jer 16:4; 34:20 [x] Ps 79:2 **19:8** [y] Jer 18:16 **19:9** [z] Lev 26:29; Dt 28:49-57; La 4:10 [a] Isa 9:20 **19:10** [b] ver 1 **19:11** [c] Ps 2:9; Isa 30:14 [d] Jer 7:32 **19:13** [e] Jer 32:29; 52:13 [f] Dt 4:19; Ac 7:42 [g] Jer 7:18; Eze 20:28 **19:14** [h] 2Ch 20:5; Jer 26:2

[a] 7 The Hebrew for *ruin* sounds like the Hebrew for *jar* (see verses 1 and 10).

19:1 *jar.* Hebrew *baqbuq*, which helps in identifying the kind of jar or earthenware jug referred to here. Most scholars agree that the jug Jeremiah buys is an expensive, ring-burnished decanter that functions as a carafe. It is 4–10 inches (10–25 centimeters) high and has a heavy body with a narrow neck. The handle is attached to the neck and rim. It is used for storing liquids, and its distinctive narrow neck emits a gurgling sound. The term *baqbuq* sounds much like the gurgling sound of liquid coming out of the jug.

19:2 *Valley of Ben Hinnom.* This is one of the valleys that surrounds Jerusalem. It is located on the south side of the city and joins the Kidron Valley at the southeastern corner of the city (see note on 7:31).

19:9 *eat the flesh of their sons and daughters.* Both in Israel and in the ancient Near Eastern context, eating human flesh was only done under dire circumstances. Scripture testifies that in the cities of Samaria (2Ki 6:26–29) and Jerusalem (La 2:20; 4:10) during times of siege or famine, human flesh was eaten (see notes on 2Ki 6:28; Isa 9:20). Josephus writes that such atrocities also occurred during the Roman siege of Jerusalem. A similar curse to the one recorded here in Jeremiah can be found in the Vassal Treaties of Esarhaddon, king of Assyria (681–669 BC).

19:11 *just as this potter's jar is smashed.* The imagery here is one of destruction for the Israelites and their capital city, Jerusalem. This kind of image was common in the ancient Near East. In Egypt during the Middle Kingdom period (c. 2106–1786 BC), the Egyptians practiced magical cursing against their present or potential enemies by inscribing pottery bowls with the names of their enemies and then smashing them. This served as poignant symbolic action, similar to Jeremiah's actions here. In the "Lament Over the Destruction of Sumer and Ur," the people who are defeated are described as being smashed as if they were clay potsherds.

19:13 *burned incense on the roofs to all the starry hosts.* The roofs of houses in the ancient Near East were flat and were used as living spaces. The roof served as a natural place to offer incense as an act of worship (see 32:29; Zep 1:5). In Tablet III of the Assyrian version of the Gilgamesh Epic, Ninsun (the mother of Gilgamesh) goes up to the roof to offer incense to the sun-god, Shamash. This same practice seems to be alluded to in the Keret epic from Ugarit, which probably comes from the thirteenth century BC. In 2Ki 23:12 Josiah tears down altars that previous kings erected on the rooftops of houses. Further evidence of this practice is found in excavations carried out at Ashkelon, which brought to light the results of the Philistine city's destruction at the hands of Nebuchadnezzar, king of Babylon, in 604 BC. Archaeologists have discovered remnants of incense burners that at one time were located on house roofs.

says: 'Listen! I am going to bring on this
city and all the villages around it every disaster I pronounced against them, because
they were stiff-necked[i] and would not listen to my words.' "

Jeremiah and Pashhur

20 When the priest Pashhur son of Immer,[j] the official[k] in charge of the
temple of the LORD, heard Jeremiah prophesying these things, 2 he had Jeremiah the
prophet beaten[l] and put in the stocks[m] at
the Upper Gate of Benjamin[n] at the LORD's
temple. 3 The next day, when Pashhur released him from the stocks, Jeremiah said
to him, "The LORD's name for you is not
Pashhur, but Terror on Every Side.[o] 4 For
this is what the LORD says: 'I will make you
a terror to yourself and to all your friends;
with your own eyes[p] you will see them
fall by the sword of their enemies. I will
give[q] all Judah into the hands of the king
of Babylon, who will carry[r] them away to
Babylon or put them to the sword. 5 I will
deliver all the wealth[s] of this city into the
hands of their enemies — all its products,
all its valuables and all the treasures of the
kings of Judah. They will take it away[t] as
plunder and carry it off to Babylon. 6 And
you, Pashhur, and all who live in your
house will go into exile to Babylon. There
you will die and be buried, you and all
your friends to whom you have prophesied[u] lies.' "

Jeremiah's Complaint

7 You deceived[a] me, LORD, and I was
deceived[a];
you overpowered me and
prevailed.
I am ridiculed all day long;
everyone mocks me.
8 Whenever I speak, I cry out
proclaiming violence and
destruction.[v]
So the word of the LORD has brought
me
insult and reproach[w] all day long.
9 But if I say, "I will not mention his
word
or speak anymore in his name,"
his word is in my heart like a fire,[x]
a fire shut up in my bones.
I am weary of holding it in;[y]
indeed, I cannot.
10 I hear many whispering,
"Terror[z] on every side!
Denounce[a] him! Let's denounce him!"
All my friends[b]
are waiting for me to slip,[c] saying,
"Perhaps he will be deceived;
then we will prevail[d] over him
and take our revenge on him."
11 But the LORD[e] is with me like a mighty
warrior;
so my persecutors[f] will stumble and
not prevail.[g]
They will fail and be thoroughly
disgraced;[h]
their dishonor will never be
forgotten.
12 LORD Almighty, you who examine the
righteous
and probe the heart and mind,[i]
let me see your vengeance[j] on them,
for to you I have committed[k] my
cause.
13 Sing to the LORD!
Give praise to the LORD!
He rescues[l] the life of the needy
from the hands of the wicked.

19:15 [i] Ne 9:16; Jer 7:26; 17:23
20:1 [j] 1Ch 24:14 [k] 2Ki 25:18
20:2 [l] Jer 1:19 [m] Job 13:27 [n] Jer 37:13; 38:7; Zec 14:10
20:3 [o] ver 10
20:4 [p] Jer 29:21 [q] Jer 21:10 [r] Jer 52:27
20:5 [s] Jer 17:3 [t] 2Ki 20:17
20:6 [u] Jer 14:15; La 2:14
20:8 [v] Jer 6:7 [w] 2Ch 36:16; Jer 6:10
20:9 [x] Ps 39:3 [y] Job 32:18-20; Ac 4:20
20:10 [z] Ps 31:13; Jer 6:25 [a] Isa 29:21 [b] Ps 41:9 [c] Lk 11:53-54 [d] 1Ki 19:2
20:11 [e] Jer 1:8; Ro 8:31 [f] Jer 17:18 [g] Jer 15:20 [h] Jer 23:40
20:12 [i] Jer 17:10 [j] Ps 54:7; 59:10 [k] Ps 62:8; Jer 11:20
20:13 [l] Ps 35:10

[a] 7 Or *persuaded*

20:1 *Pashhur.* Jeremiah refers to more than one Pashhur (21:1; 38:1). The name probably had its origin in Egypt (meaning Son of Horus) and would have been common in Jeremiah's time. The Pashhur mentioned here is chief officer in the temple in Jerusalem, which makes him second in rank to the high priest. The name has been found inscribed on an ostracon discovered at the Arad sanctuary. It also appears in an ostracon dated to the eighth or seventh century BC from Aroer.
20:2 *stocks.* The meaning of the Hebrew term is uncertain. This term also appears in 29:26 and seemingly derives from the linguistic root that means "to turn, change, distort." Presumably this instrument of punishment was used to hold the body in a bent or stooped position. But in 2Ch 16:10 the same term is translated "prison" (lit. "house of stocks"). This suggests that the term may refer to a prison or guardhouse rather than to a kind of torture device. *Upper Gate of Benjamin.* Not to be confused with the city's other gate named the Benjamin Gate (37:13; 38:7). The Upper Gate may have been a temple gate located at the north of the city. Some suggest that it may be the same as the "New Gate" (26:10; 36:10).
20:4 *king of Babylon.* This is the first mention of Babylon and its king in Jeremiah. The foe of the north is no longer a mystery. This prophecy is not dated, so we do not know how it fits into the events of the time. Historically speaking, Babylon had not been a major player in the ancient Near Eastern power struggle since about the middle of the second millennium BC. Its rise to power did not happen until the battle of Carchemish in 605 BC, when Egypt was decisively defeated and Assyria ceased to exist as a nation.
20:11 *mighty warrior.* It was common in the ancient Near East to view the gods as cofighters in important battles. Victories in battles are often attributed to the gods. See the article "Divine Warfare," p. 365.
20:12 *heart and mind.* Lit. "kidneys and heart." In ancient Hebrew anthropology, the "kidneys" were considered to be the seat of emotions, affection and hidden motives. This is equivalent to the popular concept of heart today. Note that in Hebrew thought, "heart" is the center of the person's will or mind (see note on Isa 57:1). In Ugaritic texts the kidneys seem to have the ability to instruct; in Mesopotamian texts that function is more associated with the liver.

[14]Cursed be the day I was born![m]
May the day my mother bore me not
be blessed!
[15]Cursed be the man who brought my
father the news,
who made him very glad, saying,
"A child is born to you — a son!"
[16]May that man be like the towns[n]
the LORD overthrew without pity.
May he hear wailing in the morning,
a battle cry at noon.
[17]For he did not kill me in the womb,[o]
with my mother as my grave,
her womb enlarged forever.
[18]Why did I ever come out of the womb
to see trouble and sorrow
and to end my days in shame?[p]

God Rejects Zedekiah's Request

21 The word came to Jeremiah from
the LORD when King Zedekiah[q] sent
to him Pashhur[r] son of Malkijah and the
priest Zephaniah[s] son of Maaseiah. They
said: [2]"Inquire[t] now of the LORD for us because Nebuchadnezzar[a][u] king of Babylon
is attacking us. Perhaps the LORD will perform wonders[v] for us as in times past so
that he will withdraw from us."
[3]But Jeremiah answered them, "Tell
Zedekiah, [4]'This is what the LORD, the God
of Israel, says: I am about to turn[w] against
you the weapons of war that are in your
hands, which you are using to fight the
king of Babylon and the Babylonians[b] who
are outside the wall besieging[x] you. And I
will gather them inside this city. [5]I myself
will fight against you with an outstretched
hand[y] and a mighty arm in furious anger
and in great wrath. [6]I will strike down
those who live in this city — both man
and beast — and they will die of a terrible plague.[z] [7]After that, declares the LORD,
I will give Zedekiah[a] king of Judah, his
officials and the people in this city who
survive the plague, sword and famine, into
the hands of Nebuchadnezzar king of Babylon[b] and to their enemies who want to
kill them. He will put them to the sword;
he will show them no mercy or pity or
compassion.'[c]
[8]"Furthermore, tell the people, 'This is
what the LORD says: See, I am setting before you the way of life and the way of
death. [9]Whoever stays in this city will die
by the sword, famine or plague.[d] But whoever goes out and surrenders to the Babylonians who are besieging you will live;

20:14 [m]Job 3:3; Jer 15:10 **20:16** [n]Ge 19:25 **20:17** [o]Job 10:18-19 **20:18** [p]Ps 90:9 **21:1** [q]2Ki 24:18; Jer 52:1 [r]Jer 38:1 [s]2Ki 25:18; Jer 29:25; 37:3 **21:2** [t]Jer 37:3, 7 [u]2Ki 25:1 [v]Ps 44:1-4; Jer 32:17 **21:4** [w]Jer 32:5 [x]Jer 37:8-10 **21:5** [y]Jer 6:12 **21:6** [z]Jer 14:12 **21:7** [a]2Ki 25:7; Jer 52:9 [b]Jer 37:17; 39:5 [c]2Ch 36:17; Eze 7:9; Hab 1:6 **21:9** [d]Jer 14:12

[a] 2 Hebrew *Nebuchadrezzar,* of which *Nebuchadnezzar* is a variant; here and often in Jeremiah and Ezekiel
[b] 4 Or *Chaldeans*; also in verse 9

20:14 *Cursed be the day I was born!* In the Mesopotamian epic "Erra and Ishum" the governor of the city that is being destroyed is portrayed as expressing to his mother a wish that he had been stillborn or obstructed in the womb so that he would not have been born to this destiny. See note on Job 3:1.

21:1 *Zedekiah.* His original name was Mattaniah. Nebuchadnezzar, the king of Babylon, changed Mattaniah's name to Zedekiah. Once he conquered Jerusalem and exiled King Jehoiachin, along with his queen mother, Nebuchadnezzar placed Zedekiah as king over Judah. By changing Mattaniah's name Nebuchadnezzar in effect stated that he had ownership and authority over Zedekiah. The action of naming somebody or something in the ancient Near East implies power over that individual. Zedekiah was only 21 years old when he was placed on the throne. He ruled for about 11 years (597 – 586 BC). At the end of his rule, Jerusalem was defeated again by Nebuchadnezzar, and Judah as an independent nation came to an end. Zedekiah is known to have been a weak and incompetent king. See the article "Historical Setting of Jeremiah," p. 1222. *the priest Zephaniah son of Maaseiah.* This priest is an associate to Seraiah and perhaps is the successor to Pashhur son of Immer, who placed Jeremiah in the stocks (see notes on 20:1 – 2). After the fall of Jerusalem, Zephaniah and Seraiah are taken together with others before Nebuchadnezzar at Riblah. There he executes both of them. The name Zephaniah has turned up in ostraca from various places such as Arad and Jerusalem. It has also been found on jar stamps from Lachish that date to the eighth and seventh centuries BC.

21:2 *Nebuchadnezzar.* This is the first time he is mentioned in Jeremiah. He ruled in Babylon during what is called the Neo-Babylonian period (c. 626 – 539 BC). In the Hebrew Scriptures, "Babylon" and "Babylonians" are sometimes termed "Chaldea" and "Chaldeans" (e.g., Eze 23:14 – 16). The Chaldeans are the Babylonians who ruled during the Neo-Babylonian period. Nebuchadnezzar (605 – 562 BC), along with his father Nabopolassar (626 – 605 BC), was most instrumental in bringing the Babylonian Empire to its maximum expression of power. The Babylonians were able to overcome the Assyrians in 612 BC by defeating Nineveh and were also able to curb Egypt's power so that Egypt's army had to remain within its boundaries and not attempt to control Syria and Israel. *attacking us.* Nebuchadnezzar comes to attack Jerusalem because the incompetent king Zedekiah has decided to withhold tribute and place his trust in an Egyptian pharaoh. Nebuchadnezzar does not tolerate this kind of ambivalence. After defeating a number of surrounding towns, Nebuchadnezzar and his army lay siege to Jerusalem and by 587/586 categorically defeat and conquer it, just as Jeremiah has announced.

21:4 *besieging you.* A city that is victim of a siege experiences tremendous anguish and despair. When the food supplies are gone from within the city, there is no possibility of going outside the city to get food, nor is there any chance that food can be brought in. Thus, famine begins to break out within the city walls. This is aggravated by the fact that many people who normally live outside the city walls crowd into the city, creating a greater need for food and space. The situation becomes extremely critical when a water source is cut off. Exceptional cities like Jerusalem and Megiddo had camouflaged tunnels that went from within the city to the water source. This certainly helped for a period of time. However, sooner or later these were discovered, and once deep thirst is installed within the city, defeat and sure death are near. See the article "Siege Warfare," p. 1157.

they will escape with their lives.[e] 10I have
determined to do this city harm[f] and not
good, declares the LORD. It will be given
into the hands[g] of the king of Babylon,
and he will destroy it with fire.'[h]

11"Moreover, say to the royal house[i] of
Judah, 'Hear the word of the LORD. 12This
is what the LORD says to you, house of
David:

"'Administer justice[j] every morning;
rescue from the hand of the
oppressor
the one who has been robbed,
or my wrath will break out and burn
like fire
because of the evil you have done—
burn with no one to quench[k] it.
13I am against[l] you, Jerusalem,
you who live above this valley[m]
on the rocky plateau, declares the
LORD—
you who say, "Who can come against us?
Who can enter our refuge?"[n]
14I will punish you as your deeds[o]
deserve,
declares the LORD.
I will kindle a fire[p] in your forests[q]
that will consume everything around
you.'"

Judgment Against Wicked Kings

22 This is what the LORD says: "Go
down to the palace of the king of
Judah and proclaim this message there:
2'Hear the word of the LORD to you, king of
Judah, you who sit on David's throne[r]—
you, your officials and your people who
come through these gates.[s] 3This is what
the LORD says: Do what is just[t] and right.
Rescue from the hand of the oppressor[u]
the one who has been robbed. Do no
wrong or violence to the foreigner, the fatherless or the widow,[v] and do not shed
innocent blood in this place. 4For if you
are careful to carry out these commands,
then kings[w] who sit on David's throne
will come through the gates of this palace,
riding in chariots and on horses, accompanied by their officials and their people.
5But if you do not obey[x] these commands,
declares the LORD, I swear[y] by myself that
this palace will become a ruin.'"

6For this is what the LORD says about the
palace of the king of Judah:

"Though you are like Gilead to me,
like the summit of Lebanon,
I will surely make you like a
wasteland,[z]
like towns not inhabited.
7I will send destroyers[a] against you,
each man with his weapons,
and they will cut[b] up your fine cedar
beams
and throw them into the fire.

8"People from many nations will pass
by this city and will ask one another,
'Why has the LORD done such a thing to
this great city?'[c] 9And the answer will be:
'Because they have forsaken the covenant
of the LORD their God and have worshiped
and served other gods.[d]'"

10Do not weep for the dead[e] king or
mourn[f] his loss;
rather, weep bitterly for him who is
exiled,
because he will never return
nor see his native land again.

11For this is what the LORD says about Shallum[a][g] son of Josiah, who succeeded his
father as king of Judah but has gone from
this place: "He will never return. 12He will
die[h] in the place where they have led him
captive; he will not see this land again."

13"Woe to him who builds[i] his palace by
unrighteousness,
his upper rooms by injustice,

21:9 [e] Jer 38:2, 17; 39:18; 45:5 **21:10** [f] Jer 44:11, 27; Am 9:4 [g] Jer 32:28; 38:2-3 [h] Jer 52:13 **21:11** [i] Jer 13:18 **21:12** [j] Jer 22:3 [k] Isa 1:31 **21:13** [l] Eze 13:8 [m] Ps 125:2 [n] Jer 49:4; Ob 1:3-4 **21:14** [o] Isa 3:10-11 [p] 2Ch 36:19; Jer 52:13 [q] Eze 20:47 **22:2** [r] Jer 17:25; Lk 1:32 [s] Jer 17:20 **22:3** [t] Mic 6:8; Zec 7:9 [u] Ps 72:4; Jer 21:12 [v] Ex 22:22

22:4 [w] Jer 17:25 **22:5** [x] Jer 17:27 [y] Heb 6:13 **22:6** [z] Mic 3:12 **22:7** [a] Jer 4:7 [b] Isa 10:34 **22:8** [c] Dt 29:25-26; 1Ki 9:8-9; Jer 16:10-11 **22:9** [d] 2Ki 22:17; 2Ch 34:25 **22:10** [e] Ecc 4:2 [f] ver 18 **22:11** [g] 2Ki 23:31 **22:12** [h] 2Ki 23:34 **22:13** [i] Mic 3:10; Hab 2:9

[a] 11 Also called *Jehoahaz*

21:14 *forests.* This Hebrew term most likely refers not to literal forests of trees that surround the city of Jerusalem but to royal buildings within Jerusalem. 1Ki 7:1 – 12 describes a royal palace that was decorated with so much cedar that it was named the "Palace of the Forest of Lebanon (1Ki 7:2). This image of destruction is again repeated in Jer 22:6 – 7,20 – 23.

22:3 *Do what is just and right ... to the foreigner, the fatherless or the widow.* See notes on Lev 19:15; Dt 10:18; 15:7; 24:17.

22:5 *this palace will become a ruin.* The same kind of situation and similar language can be found in a text from approximately the eighth century BC. The various tablets that are used to reconstruct this text (the Mesopotamian epic "Erra and Ishum") come from Assyria and Babylonia. Erra, also known as Nergal, is the god who has authority over both wild and domestic animals. At one point he threatens to unleash wild animals from the mountains and surrounding areas so they can devastate and ravage the city. The city will then become a ruin.

22:6 *Gilead.* It was on the east side of the Jordan River. The northern limits of Gilead were vague, and the east was bounded by desert. *summit of Lebanon.* Refers to its forests (see Zec 10:10). Both Gilead and Lebanon were known for the lush productivity of their forests.

22:7 *fine cedar.* See notes on v. 6; 21:14; 2Sa 5:11; 1Ki 5:6; 6:15.

22:10 *him who is exiled.* The king of Judah referred to here is most likely Shallum, the son of Josiah. Shallum took the throne name Jehoahaz. The prophet is advising the people not to mourn Josiah anymore, but to mourn the exiled king, Jehoahaz, who will no longer see the homeland. Jehoahaz ruled only three months (609 BC). He was exiled by Pharaoh Necho II to Egypt, where Jehoahaz died. His death is considered much more disgraceful than his father's death in battle at the hand of the Egyptians.

22:13 *builds his palace.* This may be a reference to a rebuild-

making his own people work for
nothing,
not paying[j] them for their labor.
14 He says, 'I will build myself a great
palace[k]
with spacious upper rooms.'
So he makes large windows in it,
panels it with cedar[l]
and decorates it in red.
15 "Does it make you a king
to have more and more cedar?
Did not your father have food and
drink?
He did what was right and just,[m]
so all went well[n] with him.
16 He defended the cause of the poor and
needy,[o]
and so all went well.
Is that not what it means to know me?"
declares the LORD.
17 "But your eyes and your heart
are set only on dishonest gain,
on shedding innocent blood[p]
and on oppression and extortion."

18 Therefore this is what the LORD says
about Jehoiakim son of Josiah king of Judah:

"They will not mourn for him:
'Alas, my brother! Alas, my sister!'
They will not mourn for him:
'Alas, my master! Alas, his
splendor!'
19 He will have the burial of a donkey—
dragged away and thrown[q]
outside the gates of Jerusalem."

20 "Go up to Lebanon and cry out,
let your voice be heard in Bashan,
cry out from Abarim,[r]
for all your allies are crushed.
21 I warned you when you felt secure,
but you said, 'I will not listen!'
This has been your way from your youth;[s]
you have not obeyed[t] me.
22 The wind will drive all your shepherds
away,
and your allies will go into exile.
Then you will be ashamed and
disgraced
because of all your wickedness.
23 You who live in 'Lebanon,[a]'
who are nestled in cedar buildings,
how you will groan when pangs come
upon you,
pain[u] like that of a woman in labor!

24 "As surely as I live," declares the LORD,
"even if you, Jehoiachin[b][v] son of Jehoiakim king of Judah, were a signet ring on
my right hand, I would still pull you off. 25 I
will deliver[w] you into the hands of those
who want to kill you, those you fear—Nebuchadnezzar king of Babylon and the Babylonians.[c] 26 I will hurl[x] you and the mother
who gave you birth into another country,
where neither of you was born, and there
you both will die. 27 You will never come
back to the land you long to return to."

28 Is this man Jehoiachin a despised,
broken pot,[y]
an object no one wants?
Why will he and his children be
hurled[z] out,
cast into a land[a] they do not know?

22:13 [j] Lev 19:13; Jas 5:4 **22:14** [k] Isa 5:8-9 [l] 2Sa 7:2 **22:15** [m] 2Ki 23:25 [n] Ps 128:2; Isa 3:10 **22:16** [o] Ps 72:1-4, 12-13 **22:17** [p] 2Ki 24:4 **22:19** [q] Jer 36:30 **22:20** [r] Nu 27:12 **22:21** [s] Jer 3:25; 32:30 [t] Jer 7:23-28 **22:23** [u] Jer 4:31 **22:24** [v] 2Ki 24:6,8; Jer 37:1 **22:25** [w] 2Ki 24:16; Jer 34:20 **22:26** [x] 2Ki 24:8; 2Ch 36:10 **22:28** [y] Ps 31:12; Jer 48:38; Hos 8:8 [z] Jer 15:1 [a] Jer 17:4

[a] 23 That is, the palace in Jerusalem (see 1 Kings 7:2)
[b] 24 Hebrew *Koniah,* a variant of *Jehoiachin*; also in verse 28 [c] 25 Or *Chaldeans*

ing and enlargement of Solomon's palace by Jehoiakim, or it may refer to another palace altogether. At Ramat Rahel a number of structures have been found possibly dating to the time of Jehoiakim. There, a large collection of stamped jar handles bearing the phrase, "belonging to the king" have been found from this period. *people work for nothing.* Since the king needed to pay a heavy tribute to Egypt, he may have engaged in forced labor for the project. Forced labor without compensation is reminiscent of practices during Solomon's time (see note on 1Ki 5:13) and of practices periodically observed in both Egypt and Babylonia as a form of taxation (see notes on Jos 16:10; 1Ch 20:3).

22:14 *panels it with cedar.* Cedar paneling was considered the most luxurious and expensive material that could be used. It was used almost exclusively in palaces and temples. *red.* This Hebrew word is also used in Eze 23:14. The red paint comes from either red oxide or from red ocher (hematite). The use of the red color seems to have been prevalent in Mesopotamian decoration of important buildings. An example of this can be seen at Tel Barsip in an Assyrian provincial palace dated to the eighth or seventh century BC. This palace had wall decorations painted on them with various colors, including bright red.

22:18 *Jehoiakim.* See the article "Historical Setting of Jeremiah," p. 1222.

22:19 *burial of a donkey.* Jeremiah is so upset with King Jehoiakim because of his ridiculous architectural projects and his lack of justice that Jeremiah prophesies a most dishonorable burial for the king. In fact, it is no burial at all, for dead donkeys generally received no burial. Not receiving a proper burial was a terrible curse both in Israel and in the ancient Near East in general (see notes on 1Ki 14:11; 2Ki 9:10; Ecc 6:3; see also the articles "Exposure of the Dead," p. 1239; "Proper Burial," p. 1252).

22:20 *Lebanon.* Here it is indicative of the mountainous region far to the north. This is different from the expression used in v. 23, where Lebanon is a metaphor for the cedar-paneled palace in Jerusalem. *Bashan.* In the Transjordan highlands north of Gilead; this is also a mountainous region (see note on Nu 21:33). *Abarim.* A Moabite mountain region that lies to the southeast; this range includes Mount Nebo (Dt 32:49). Though these three geographic areas may or may not refer to places of mourning, it seems clear that they are intended to demonstrate that Jerusalem's lament will be heard everywhere.

22:24 *signet ring.* See note on Isa 3:21. When Yahweh pulls off Jehoiachin's signet ring, it is a sign of rejection. Yahweh does not accept or validate the king's authority.

29 O land,[b] land, land,
hear the word of the LORD!
30 This is what the LORD says:
"Record this man as if childless,[c]
a man who will not prosper[d] in his
lifetime,
for none of his offspring will prosper,
none will sit on the throne[e] of
David
or rule anymore in Judah."

The Righteous Branch

23 "Woe to the shepherds[f] who are
destroying and scattering[g] the
sheep of my pasture!"[h] declares the LORD.
2 Therefore this is what the LORD, the God
of Israel, says to the shepherds who tend
my people: "Because you have scattered
my flock and driven them away and have
not bestowed care on them, I will bestow
punishment on you for the evil[i] you have
done," declares the LORD. 3 "I myself will
gather the remnant[j] of my flock out of all
the countries where I have driven them
and will bring them back to their pasture,
where they will be fruitful and increase
in number. 4 I will place shepherds[k] over
them who will tend them, and they will no
longer be afraid[l] or terrified, nor will any
be missing,[m]" declares the LORD.

5 "The days are coming," declares the
LORD,
"when I will raise up for David[a] a
righteous Branch,[n]
a King who will reign[o] wisely
and do what is just and right[p] in the
land.
6 In his days Judah will be saved
and Israel will live in safety.
This is the name[q] by which he will be
called:
The LORD Our Righteous Savior.[r]

7 "So then, the days are coming," declares
the LORD, "when people will no longer say,
'As surely as the LORD lives, who brought
the Israelites up out of Egypt,'[s] 8 but they
will say, 'As surely as the LORD lives, who
brought the descendants of Israel up out
of the land of the north and out of all the
countries where he had banished them.'
Then they will live in their own land."[t]

22:29 [b] Jer 6:19; Mic 1:2
22:30 [c] 1Ch 3:18; Mt 1:12 [d] Jer 10:21 [e] Ps 94:20
23:1 [f] Jer 10:21; Eze 34:1-10; Zec 11:15-17 [g] Isa 56:11 [h] Eze 34:31
23:2 [i] Jer 21:12
23:3 [j] Isa 11:10-12; Jer 32:37; Eze 34:11-16
23:4 [k] Jer 3:15; 31:10; Eze 34:23 [l] Jer 30:10; 46:27-28 [m] Jn 6:39
23:5 [n] Isa 4:2 [o] Isa 9:7 [p] Isa 11:1; Zec 6:12
23:6 [q] Jer 33:16; Mt 1:21-23 [r] Ro 3:21-22; 1Co 1:30
23:7 [s] Jer 16:14
23:8 [t] Isa 43:5-6; Am 9:14-15
23:9 [u] Jer 20:8-9
23:10 [v] Jer 9:2 [w] Ps 107:34; Jer 9:10 [x] Hos 4:2-3
23:11 [y] Jer 6:13; 8:10; Zep 3:4 [z] Jer 7:10
23:12 [a] Ps 35:6; Jer 13:16 [b] Jer 11:23
23:13 [c] Jer 2:8
23:14 [d] Jer 5:30 [e] Jer 29:23 [f] Eze 13:22 [g] Ge 18:20 [h] Isa 1:9-10; Jer 20:16

Lying Prophets

9 Concerning the prophets:

My heart is broken within me;
all my bones tremble.
I am like a drunken man,
like a strong man overcome by wine,
because of the LORD
and his holy words.[u]
10 The land is full of adulterers;[v]
because of the curse[b] the land lies
parched
and the pastures[w] in the wilderness
are withered.[x]
The prophets follow an evil course
and use their power unjustly.

11 "Both prophet and priest are godless;[y]
even in my temple[z] I find their
wickedness,"
declares the LORD.
12 "Therefore their path will become
slippery;[a]
they will be banished to darkness
and there they will fall.
I will bring disaster on them
in the year they are punished,[b]"
declares the LORD.

13 "Among the prophets of Samaria
I saw this repulsive thing:
They prophesied by Baal[c]
and led my people Israel astray.
14 And among the prophets of Jerusalem
I have seen something horrible:[d]
They commit adultery and live a lie.[e]
They strengthen the hands of
evildoers,[f]
so that not one of them turns from
their wickedness.
They are all like Sodom[g] to me;
the people of Jerusalem are like
Gomorrah."[h]

15 Therefore this is what the LORD Almighty says concerning the prophets:

[a] 5 *Or up from David's line* [b] 10 *Or because of these things*

23:5 *Branch.* This Hebrew term appears in the Messianic passages such as Zec 3:8; 6:12, attributed to Zerubbabel. Most consider it a technical term referring to a rightful heir of an established dynastic line — in Israel, a future Davidic king who would restore the monarchy. A similar usage has been found in a Phoenician votive inscription honoring Melqart found on Cyprus and dating to the early third century BC. There it refers to a legitimate "branch" of the Ptolemaic dynasty of Egypt. The Dead Sea Scrolls from Qumran do not use the term in a Messianic sense, but the kingship sense does occur in Ugaritic and Assyrian texts. Tiglath-Pileser III is described as the shoot, or scion, of the city of Baltil (i.e., Assur) who brings justice to his people. *a King who will … do what is just and right.* A parallel is found in the reform declarations commonly made by Babylonian kings. Zedekiah issued such a proclamation in 588 BC (see note on 34:8).

23:13 *prophets of Samaria … prophesied by Baal.* It is difficult to identify these prophets of Samaria. Perhaps Jeremiah has in mind the prophets of Baal who were so active during Ahab's reign (874–853 BC). Alternatively, when the Assyrians exiled many of the Israelites of the northern kingdom, they brought in other peoples to mix in with the remaining population. This would have created fertile ground for syncretistic religious ideas and practices.

"I will make them eat bitter food
and drink poisoned water,[i]
because from the prophets of
Jerusalem
ungodliness has spread throughout
the land."

16 This is what the LORD Almighty says:

"Do not listen[j] to what the prophets
are prophesying to you;
they fill you with false hopes.
They speak visions[k] from their own
minds,
not from the mouth[l] of the LORD.
17 They keep saying to those who
despise me,
'The LORD says: You will have
peace.'[m]
And to all who follow the
stubbornness[n] of their hearts
they say, 'No harm[o] will come to
you.'
18 But which of them has stood in the
council of the LORD
to see or to hear his word?
Who has listened and heard his
word?
19 See, the storm[p] of the LORD
will burst out in wrath,
a whirlwind swirling down
on the heads of the wicked.
20 The anger[q] of the LORD will not turn
back[r]
until he fully accomplishes
the purposes of his heart.
In days to come
you will understand it clearly.
21 I did not send[s] these prophets,
yet they have run with their message;
I did not speak to them,
yet they have prophesied.
22 But if they had stood in my council,
they would have proclaimed my
words to my people
and would have turned[t] them from
their evil ways
and from their evil deeds.

23 "Am I only a God nearby,[u]"
declares the LORD,
"and not a God far away?
24 Who can hide[v] in secret places
so that I cannot see them?"
declares the LORD.
"Do not I fill heaven and earth?"[w]
declares the LORD.

25 "I have heard what the prophets say
who prophesy lies[x] in my name. They say,
'I had a dream![y] I had a dream!' 26 How
long will this continue in the hearts of
these lying prophets, who prophesy the
delusions[z] of their own minds? 27 They
think the dreams they tell one another will
make my people forget[a] my name, just as
their ancestors forgot[b] my name through
Baal worship. 28 Let the prophet who has a
dream recount the dream, but let the one
who has my word speak it faithfully. For
what has straw to do with grain?" declares
the LORD. 29 "Is not my word like fire," declares the LORD, "and like a hammer that
breaks a rock in pieces?

30 "Therefore," declares the LORD, "I am
against[d] the prophets[e] who steal from
one another words supposedly from me.
31 Yes," declares the LORD, "I am against the
prophets who wag their own tongues and
yet declare, 'The LORD declares.'[f] 32 Indeed,
I am against those who prophesy false
dreams,[g]" declares the LORD. "They tell
them and lead my people astray with their
reckless lies, yet I did not send or appoint
them. They do not benefit[h] these people in
the least," declares the LORD.

False Prophecy

33 "When these people, or a prophet or
a priest, ask you, 'What is the message[i]

23:15 [i] Jer 8:14; 9:15 **23:16** [j] Jer 27:9-10, 14; Mt 7:15 [k] Jer 14:14 [l] Jer 9:20 **23:17** [m] Jer 8:11 [n] Jer 13:10 [o] Jer 5:12; Am 9:10; Mic 3:11 **23:19** [p] Jer 25:32; 30:23 **23:20** [q] 2Ki 23:26 [r] Jer 30:24 **23:21** [s] Jer 14:14; 27:15 **23:22** [t] Jer 25:5; Zec 1:4 **23:23** [u] Ps 139:1-10 **23:24** [v] Job 22:12-14 [w] 1Ki 8:27 **23:25** [x] Jer 14:14 [y] ver 28, 32; Jer 29:8 **23:26** [z] 1Ti 4:1-2 **23:27** [a] Dt 13:1-3; Jer 29:8 [b] Jdg 3:7; 8:33-34 **23:29** [c] Jer 5:14 **23:30** [d] Ps 34:16 [e] Dt 18:20; Jer 14:15 **23:31** [f] ver 17 **23:32** [g] ver 25 [h] Jer 7:8; La 2:14 **23:33** [i] Mal 1:1

23:18 *council of the LORD.* There are two ways to read this phrase. First, it may refer to the prophets who stood in God's presence to receive a divine message. We know that earlier Jeremiah stood in such a council (18:20). But there the issue seems to refer to those who are not true prophets and who deceive the people. To stand in the council of the Lord is to serve as a kind of royal messenger who has been transported to the council of the Lord by way of a vision (Isa 6:1 – 8). It is the true prophet who has been privileged with this opportunity and been given the responsibility to proclaim the word of the Lord. Second, it may be understood in light of other Biblical texts and in the context of Mesopotamian religious texts. The idea of a council or assembly of the gods is found early in Mesopotamian literature. See the article "Divine Council," p. 615.
23:19 *storm.* The Hebrew term refers to a kind of swirling wind accompanied by rain. It may even refer to a kind of tornado, though these are rare and occur only near the coast. The kind of storm wind mentioned here was common during the rainy season. Both this wind and the sirocco (see note on 4:11) are metaphors for destruction, devastation and punishment in the Hebrew Bible.
23:23 *a God nearby ... a God far away.* "Nearby" and "far away" may combine the aspects of a locally involved patron deity and a powerful cosmic deity, respectively. Few gods in the ancient world would have been believed to fit this profile.
23:25 *I had a dream!* Dreams were one of the standard means for receiving messages from a god in the ancient Near East (see Jacob in Ge 28:12; Joseph in Ge 37:5 – 11; Nebuchadnezzar in Da 2; 4). Dreams appear in Old Babylonian omen texts along with the reports of the examination of sheep livers; anomalies in the weather, in births or in animals; and other presumed signs of divine will. These portents were taken quite seriously and studied. The professional priesthood in both Mesopotamia and Egypt included instruction in the interpretation of dreams and other omens (see note on Da 2:6).

from the LORD?' say to them, 'What message? I will forsake[j] you, declares the LORD.'
34If a prophet or a priest or anyone else
claims, 'This is a message[k] from the LORD,'
I will punish[l] them and their household.
35This is what each of you keeps saying
to your friends and other Israelites: 'What
is the LORD's answer?'[m] or 'What has the
LORD spoken?' 36But you must not mention
'a message from the LORD' again, because
each one's word becomes their own message. So you distort[n] the words of the living
God, the LORD Almighty, our God. 37This is
what you keep saying to a prophet: 'What
is the LORD's answer to you?' or 'What has
the LORD spoken?' 38Although you claim,
'This is a message from the LORD,' this is
what the LORD says: You used the words,
'This is a message from the LORD,' even
though I told you that you must not claim,
'This is a message from the LORD.' 39There-
fore, I will surely forget you and cast[o] you
out of my presence along with the city I
gave to you and your ancestors. 40I will
bring on you everlasting disgrace[p]—everlasting shame that will not be forgotten."

Two Baskets of Figs

24 After Jehoiachin[a][q] son of Jehoiakim king of Judah and the officials,
the skilled workers and the artisans of Judah were carried into exile from Jerusalem to Babylon by Nebuchadnezzar king
of Babylon, the LORD showed me two baskets of figs[r] placed in front of the temple of
the LORD. 2One basket had very good figs,
like those that ripen early; the other basket had very bad[s] figs, so bad they could
not be eaten.

3Then the LORD asked me, "What do you
see,[t] Jeremiah?"

"Figs," I answered. "The good ones are
very good, but the bad ones are so bad
they cannot be eaten."

23:33 [j] ver 39
23:34 [k] La 2:14 [l] Zec 13:3
23:35 [m] Jer 33:3; 42:4
23:36 [n] Gal 1:7-8; 2Pe 3:16
23:39 [o] Jer 7:15
23:40 [p] Jer 20:11; Eze 5:14-15
24:1 [q] 2Ki 24:16; 2Ch 36:9; Jer 29:2 [r] Am 8:1-2
24:2 [s] Isa 5:4
24:3 [t] Jer 1:11; Am 8:2

The Babylonian Chronicle, 605 to 594 BC, mentions the exile of Jehoiachin.

4Then the word of the LORD came to me:
5"This is what the LORD, the God of Israel, says: 'Like these good figs, I regard as
good the exiles from Judah, whom I sent
away from this place to the land of the
Babylonians.[b] 6My eyes will watch over
them for their good, and I will bring them
back[u] to this land. I will build[v] them up
and not tear them down; I will plant them
and not uproot them. 7I will give them
a heart to know me, that I am the LORD.
They will be my people,[w] and I will be
their God, for they will return[x] to me with
all their heart.[y]

24:6 [u] Jer 29:10; Eze 11:17 [v] Jer 33:7; 42:10
24:7 [w] Isa 51:16; Jer 31:33; Heb 8:10 [x] Jer 32:40 [y] Eze 11:19

[a] *1* Hebrew *Jeconiah,* a variant of *Jehoiachin*
[b] *5* Or *Chaldeans*

24:1 *Jehoiachin.* Also called Jeconiah and Coniah, he was the king of Judah whom Nebuchadnezzar captured when Jerusalem was defeated by the Babylonians in 597 BC. Jehoiachin became king at the age of 18 and ruled for three months. Nebuchadnezzar exiled Jehoiachin along with his mother, wives, officials, craftsmen, smiths and others. While in Babylon Jehoiachin was well taken care of. In a Babylonian text from that time we read that "Yaukin, king of Judah and his five sons received rations." At some point Jehoiachin was thrown in prison, but later (561 or 560 BC) he was released from prison by King Awel-Marduk (562–560 BC). This Babylonian king gave Jehoiachin a place of privilege and allowed him to eat at the royal table. This may have generated unwarranted Messianic expectations among the Israelites. *Nebuchadnezzar.* See note on 21:2; see also the article "Historical Setting of Jeremiah," p. 1222. *baskets.* The Hebrew word is generally the word for a cooking pot—a deep, round-bottomed, two-handled receptacle. *figs.* They are rich in sugar and were essential to a good diet in antiquity. They were eaten fresh or dried, pressed into cakes, or preserved. They were also used for medicinal purposes, particularly as a laxative and a tonic (see note on 2Ki 20:7).
24:2–10 In this vision, which is similar to the visions of the almond branch and the boiling pot (1:11–16), Jeremiah sees two baskets of figs in front of the temple. The good figs in the one basket symbolize the Israelites exiled to Babylon in 597 BC. These will turn back to the Lord and be able to return to their homeland. The bad figs in the other basket symbolize those who have resisted Nebuchadnezzar and stayed behind in Jerusalem, including King Zedekiah and his officials. This vision contradicts the popular notion held in Jerusalem that those who stayed in the city were the privileged ones.
24:2 *ripen early.* The fig tree produces two annual crops. The first one generally takes place in May and early June; the second one, which comes under the category of "summer fruits," takes place in August-September.

Tomb painting in Nebamun's estate garden depicts a woman gathering figs. Thebes, Egypt, c. 1350 BC.

Kim Walton. The British Museum.

8" 'But like the bad[z] figs, which are so
bad they cannot be eaten,' says the LORD,
'so will I deal with Zedekiah king of Judah, his officials[a] and the survivors[b] from
Jerusalem, whether they remain in this
land or live in Egypt.[c] 9I will make them
abhorrent[d] and an offense to all the kingdoms of the earth, a reproach and a byword,[e] a curse[af] and an object of ridicule,
wherever I banish[g] them. 10I will send the
sword,[h] famine and plague[i] against them
until they are destroyed from the land I
gave to them and their ancestors.' "

Seventy Years of Captivity

25 The word came to Jeremiah concerning all the people of Judah in
the fourth year of Jehoiakim[j] son of Josiah king of Judah, which was the first year
of Nebuchadnezzar[k] king of Babylon. 2So
Jeremiah the prophet said to all the people
of Judah[l] and to all those living in Jerusalem: 3For twenty-three years — from the
thirteenth year of Josiah[m] son of Amon
king of Judah until this very day — the
word of the LORD has come to me and I
have spoken to you again and again,[n] but
you have not listened.[o]
4And though the LORD has sent all his
servants the prophets[p] to you again and
again, you have not listened or paid any
attention. 5They said, "Turn now, each of
you, from your evil ways and your evil
practices, and you can stay in the land the

24:8 [z] Jer 29:17 [a] Jer 39:6 [b] Jer 39:9 [c] Jer 44:1, 26 **24:9** [d] Jer 15:4; 34:17 [e] Dt 28:25; 1Ki 9:7 [f] Jer 29:18 [g] Dt 28:37 **24:10** [h] Isa 51:19 [i] Jer 27:8 **25:1** [j] 2Ki 24:2; Jer 36:1 [k] 2Ki 24:1 **25:2** [l] Jer 18:11 **25:3** [m] Jer 1:2 [n] Jer 11:7; 26:5 [o] Jer 7:26 **25:4** [p] Jer 7:25

[a] 9 That is, their names will be used in cursing (see 29:22); or, others will see that they are cursed.

24:8 *Zedekiah.* See note on 21:1; see also the article "Historical Setting of Jeremiah," p. 1222.
25:1 *fourth year of Jehoiakim ... which was the first year of Nebuchadnezzar.* Determining the exact date of the fourth year of the reign of Jehoiakim and synchronizing it with the first year of Nebuchadnezzar requires knowing how chronology worked in the ancient Near East. This has to do with what is known as the accession year of a king to the throne. Jehoiakim's accession period is most likely from about September, 609 BC to April, 608 BC; thus, "the fourth year of Jehoiakim" can be either 605 or 604 BC. This date needs to be coordinated with "the first year of Nebuchadnezzar." According to the historical texts from Babylonia, Nebuchadnezzar began his reign in September, 605 BC and his accession period went from that date until March-April, 604 BC. Therefore, his first year of rule would not have begun until April, 604 BC. On this basis, the date recorded in this verse is 604 BC. This was an

LORD gave to you and your ancestors for
ever and ever. 6 Do not follow other gods[q]
to serve and worship them; do not arouse
my anger with what your hands have
made. Then I will not harm you."
7 "But you did not listen to me," declares
the LORD, "and you have aroused my anger with what your hands have made,[r] and
you have brought harm[s] to yourselves."
8 Therefore the LORD Almighty says this:
"Because you have not listened to my
words, 9 I will summon[t] all the peoples of
the north[u] and my servant[v] Nebuchadnezzar king of Babylon," declares the LORD,
"and I will bring them against this land
and its inhabitants and against all the
surrounding nations. I will completely
destroy[a] them and make them an object
of horror and scorn,[w] and an everlasting
ruin. 10 I will banish from them the sounds[x]
of joy and gladness, the voices of bride
and bridegroom,[y] the sound of millstones[z]
and the light of the lamp.[a] 11 This whole
country will become a desolate wasteland,[b] and these nations will serve the
king of Babylon seventy years.[c]
12 "But when the seventy years[d] are fulfilled, I will punish the king of Babylon
and his nation, the land of the Babylonians,[b] for their guilt," declares the LORD,
"and will make it desolate[e] forever. 13 I will
bring on that land all the things I have spoken against it, all that are written in this
book and prophesied by Jeremiah against
all the nations. 14 They themselves will
be enslaved[f] by many nations[g] and great
kings; I will repay[h] them according to their
deeds and the work of their hands."

The Cup of God's Wrath

15 This is what the LORD, the God of Israel, said to me: "Take from my hand this
cup[i] filled with the wine of my wrath and
make all the nations to whom I send you
drink it. 16 When they drink it, they will
stagger[j] and go mad[k] because of the sword
I will send among them."
17 So I took the cup from the LORD's
hand and made all the nations to whom
he sent[l] me drink it: 18 Jerusalem and the
towns of Judah, its kings and officials, to
make them a ruin and an object of horror
and scorn, a curse[c][m] — as they are today;[n]
19 Pharaoh king of Egypt, his attendants,
his officials and all his people, 20 and all
the foreign people there; all the kings of

25:6 [q] Dt 8:19 **25:7** [r] Dt 32:21 [s] 2Ki 21:15 **25:9** [t] Isa 13:3-5 [u] Jer 1:15 [v] Jer 27:6 [w] Jer 18:16 **25:10** [x] Isa 24:8; Eze 26:13 [y] Jer 7:34 [z] Ecc 12:3-4 [a] Rev 18:22-23 **25:11** [b] Jer 4:26-27; 12:11-12 [c] 2Ch 36:21 **25:12** [d] Jer 29:10 [e] Isa 13:19-22; 14:22-23 **25:14** [f] Jer 27:7 [g] Jer 50:9; 51:27-28 [h] Jer 51:6 **25:15** [i] Isa 51:17; Ps 75:8; Rev 14:10 **25:16** [j] Na 3:11 [k] Jer 51:7 **25:17** [l] Jer 1:10 **25:18** [m] Jer 24:9 [n] Jer 44:22

[a] *9* The Hebrew term refers to the irrevocable giving over of things or persons to the LORD, often by totally destroying them. [b] *12* Or *Chaldeans* [c] *18* That is, their names to be used in cursing (see 29:22); or, to be seen by others as cursed

important year since it was immediately after Nebuchadnezzar defeated the Egyptians in the battle of Carchemish (see note on 20:4; see also the article "Historical Setting of Jeremiah," p. 1222). This meant that Syria and Palestine were now much easier prey for the Babylonian army.

25:9 *my servant Nebuchadnezzar.* This kind of language sometimes misleads people to think that at this point Nebuchadnezzar is a worshiper of Yahweh. However, this is not the case. At different times in Biblical history the enemies of Israel who came to carry out God's judgment on Israel are called God's servants, insofar as they were fulfilling God's plan by punishing Israel; in no way is it indicative of a heart turned toward Yahweh. Note too that Cyrus, who was not exactly an enemy but who had power over the Israelites, is also seen in this light (Isa 44:28 — 45:1).

25:10 *the sound of millstones and the light of the lamp.* The grinding of flour was done with millstones. Without this activity, daily sustenance was jeopardized. If one encountered a town with no sound coming from millstones, it meant something was radically wrong. Life was at stake. One generally heard the sound of millstones in the morning, announcing the coming of another day of life. The absence of that sound was considered a curse in the ancient Near East. A vassal treaty of Esarhaddon king of Assyria (681 – 669 BC) contains a curse that threatens the vassal with the cessation of the sound of the grinding stone. The millstone and the lamp together symbolize domestic life in its regular daily cycle. The millstone is heard in the mornings, and the lamp burns at night. The presence of both signals joy because normality prevails. Their absence speaks of danger, devastation and death.

25:11 *seventy years.* As with many numbers in the Hebrew Bible, 70 should be understood for its rhetorical value rather than as a simple quantification. In the ancient Near East this number is stereotyped and refers to an approximate time span. In Ps 90:10, e.g., it is used as the number of years for a full life. In Isaiah we read that Tyre will be forgotten for 70 years (Isa 23:15 – 17). This same 70-year motif appears in an Esarhaddon (king of Assyria 681 – 669 BC) inscription that speaks of a period of 70 years in which Babylon will lie destroyed. The number 70 can also make reference to a specific span of time. The period of 70 years was approximately from the destruction of the temple in 587 BC to its rededication in about 515 BC. It also represents the amount of time from the initial subjugation of Israel under Nebuchadnezzar in 605 BC to the return from exile by Cyrus's decree in 535 BC.

25:15 *cup filled with the wine of my wrath.* Jeremiah receives another vision with a special divine message. A possible scenario is of a banquet with all the nations present. Jeremiah is the cupbearer and takes the wine of wrath from Yahweh and serves it to the nations. The cup mentioned here is a drinking vessel made out of clay and usually overlaid with gold or silver for royal use (it could also be a receptacle more like a shallow wine bowl).

25:19 – 26 These verses describe the various nations to whom Jeremiah will give the cup filled with the wine of God's wrath. Beginning in Egypt (v. 19), Jeremiah proceeds to cover a wide geographic region. After Egypt the cup is given to all the kings of Uz (v. 20). The exact location of Uz is still a matter of dispute; it most likely refers to a place in northwest Arabia between Dedan and Edom, even though in the Hebrew Bible it is also associated with other locations, such as Syria and Edom (Ge 10:23; 36:28).

From Uz, Jeremiah goes on to the coastal area to cover the Philistine cities such as Ashkelon, Gaza, Ekron and Ashdod (v. 20). Gath, an important Philistine city, is missing from this list, perhaps because it was destroyed years earlier in 711 BC by the Assyrian king Sargon II (721 – 705 BC). Jeremiah then moves on to the Transjordan, where he

Uz;[o] all the kings of the Philistines (those
of Ashkelon,[p] Gaza, Ekron, and the people
left at Ashdod); 21 Edom, Moab and Ammon;[q] 22 all the kings of Tyre and Sidon;[r]
the kings of the coastlands[s] across the sea;
23 Dedan, Tema, Buz and all who are in distant places[a];[t] 24 all the kings of Arabia[u] and
all the kings of the foreign people who live
in the wilderness; 25 all the kings of Zimri, Elam[v] and Media; 26 and all the kings
of the north,[w] near and far, one after the
other — all the kingdoms on the face of the
earth. And after all of them, the king of
Sheshak[b][x] will drink it too.
27 "Then tell them, 'This is what the LORD
Almighty, the God of Israel, says: Drink,
get drunk[y] and vomit, and fall to rise no
more because of the sword[z] I will send
among you.' 28 But if they refuse to take the
cup from your hand and drink, tell them,
'This is what the LORD Almighty says: You
must drink it! 29 See, I am beginning to
bring disaster[a] on the city that bears my
Name,[b] and will you indeed go unpunished?[c] You will not go unpunished, for I
am calling down a sword on all[d] who live
on the earth, declares the LORD Almighty.'
30 "Now prophesy all these words against
them and say to them:

" 'The LORD will roar[e] from on high;
he will thunder[f] from his holy
dwelling
and roar mightily against his land.
He will shout like those who tread the
grapes,
shout against all who live on the
earth.
31 The tumult will resound to the ends of
the earth,
for the LORD will bring charges[g]
against the nations;
he will bring judgment on all mankind
and put the wicked to the sword,' "
declares the LORD.

32 This is what the LORD Almighty says:

"Look! Disaster is spreading
from nation to nation;[h]
a mighty storm[i] is rising
from the ends of the earth."

33 At that time those slain[j] by the LORD will
be everywhere — from one end of the earth
to the other. They will not be mourned or
gathered[k] up or buried,[l] but will be like
dung lying on the ground.

34 Weep and wail, you shepherds;
roll[m] in the dust, you leaders of the
flock.
For your time to be slaughtered[n] has
come;
you will fall like the best of the rams.[c]
35 The shepherds will have nowhere to
flee,
the leaders of the flock no place to
escape.[o]
36 Hear the cry of the shepherds,
the wailing of the leaders of the flock,
for the LORD is destroying their
pasture.
37 The peaceful meadows will be laid
waste
because of the fierce anger of the LORD.
38 Like a lion[p] he will leave his lair,
and their land will become desolate
because of the sword[d] of the oppressor
and because of the LORD's fierce
anger.

25:20 [o] Job 1:1 [p] Jer 47:5
25:21 [q] Jer 49:1
25:22 [r] Jer 47:4 [s] Jer 31:10
25:23 [t] Jer 9:26; 49:32
25:24 [u] 2Ch 9:14
25:25 [v] Ge 10:22
25:26 [w] Jer 50:3,9 [x] Jer 51:41
25:27 [y] ver 16, 28; Hab 2:16 [z] Eze 21:4
25:29 [a] Jer 13:12-14 [b] 1Pe 4:17 [c] Pr 11:31 [d] ver 30-31
25:30 [e] Isa 16:10; 42:13 [f] Joel 3:16; Am 1:2
25:31 [g] Hos 4:1; Joel 3:2; Mic 6:2
25:32 [h] Isa 34:2 [i] Jer 23:19
25:33 [j] Isa 66:16; Eze 39:17-20 [k] Jer 16:4 [l] Ps 79:3
25:34 [m] Jer 6:26 [n] Isa 34:6; Jer 50:27
25:35 [o] Job 11:20
25:38 [p] Jer 4:7

[a] 23 Or *who clip the hair by their foreheads*
[b] 26 *Sheshak* is a cryptogram for Babylon.
[c] 34 Septuagint; Hebrew *fall and be shattered like fine pottery*
[d] 38 Some Hebrew manuscripts and Septuagint (see also 46:16 and 50:16); most Hebrew manuscripts *anger*

goes from south to north, encountering Edom, Moab and Ammon (v. 21). He then returns to the coastline north of the Philistine cities to cover Phoenicia, including the cities of Tyre and Sidon (v. 22).

We cannot be absolutely sure who the "kings of the coastlands across the sea" are (v. 22). They could be the kings of the island of Cyprus and other islands in the Mediterranean. But they could also include Carthage in North Africa and islands off the coast of Spain. This judgment may be an extension of the one reserved for Phoenicia. Jeremiah proceeds south, across northern Arabia to the caravan centers of Dedan, Tema (an oasis) and Buz (v. 23). From here Jeremiah travels to Zimri (whose location is unknown), Elam and Media (v. 25), which are located in southwest Iran. Since not every place can be mentioned, Jeremiah concludes with "all the kingdoms on the face of the earth" (v. 26). This summary excludes Babylon, which will be considered in the next sentence.

25:26 *the king of Sheshak.* The king of Babylon; he is the last to drink from the cup of God's wrath. "Sheshak" spells "Babylon" using a code called *atbash*, which interchanges the letters of a name with an equivalent one in the Hebrew alphabet. It works like this: The last letter of the Hebrew alphabet is substituted by the first; the penultimate is substituted by the second, and so on. If this were done in English, the letter *z* would be represented by the letter *a*, the letter *y* would be substituted by the letter *b*, etc. If one takes the consonants of the name Sheshak (*sh-sh-k*) and uses the code described here, one ends up with *b-b-l*. The combination of these three consonants yields the name Babylon. A similar case occurs in 51:1, where the *atbash* ("Leb Kamai") is used for Chaldea (see the NIV text note on 51:1). The purpose of *atbash* is to hide the identity of an enemy. This kind of a cipher could not be used in Akkadian (the language of Mesopotamia), for that language is based not on an alphabet but on a system of syllables.

25:30 *shout like those who tread the grapes.* Treading grapes was done by foot. This usually took place at the end of a harvest season and was generally associated with celebration and tumult. Those who treaded grapes sang loudly and shouted as they worked. This singing was often accompanied by musicians. There are pictures of Egyptian men treading grapes who are accompanied by musicians.

Jeremiah Threatened With Death

26 Early in the reign of Jehoiakim[q] son
of Josiah king of Judah, this word
came from the LORD: 2"This is what the
LORD says: Stand in the courtyard[r] of the
LORD's house and speak to all the people
of the towns of Judah who come to worship in the house of the LORD. Tell[s] them
everything I command you; do not omit[t]
a word. 3Perhaps they will listen and each
will turn[u] from their evil ways. Then I will
relent[v] and not inflict on them the disaster
I was planning because of the evil they
have done. 4Say to them, 'This is what the
LORD says: If you do not listen[w] to me and
follow my law,[x] which I have set before
you, 5and if you do not listen to the words
of my servants the prophets, whom I have
sent to you again and again (though you
have not listened[y]), 6then I will make this
house like Shiloh[z] and this city a curse[a][a]
among all the nations of the earth.' "

7The priests, the prophets and all the
people heard Jeremiah speak these words
in the house of the LORD. 8But as soon
as Jeremiah finished telling all the people everything the LORD had commanded
him to say, the priests, the prophets and
all the people seized him and said, "You
must die! 9Why do you prophesy in the
LORD's name that this house will be like
Shiloh and this city will be desolate and
deserted?"[b] And all the people crowded around Jeremiah in the house of the
LORD.

10When the officials of Judah heard
about these things, they went up from
the royal palace to the house of the LORD
and took their places at the entrance of
the New Gate of the LORD's house. 11Then
the priests and the prophets said to the
officials and all the people, "This man
should be sentenced to death[c] because he
has prophesied against this city. You have
heard it with your own ears!"

12Then Jeremiah said to all the officials[d]
and all the people: "The LORD sent me to
prophesy[e] against this house and this city
all the things you have heard.[f] 13Now reform[g] your ways and your actions and
obey the LORD your God. Then the LORD
will relent and not bring the disaster he
has pronounced against you. 14As for me,
I am in your hands;[h] do with me whatever
you think is good and right. 15Be assured,
however, that if you put me to death, you
will bring the guilt of innocent blood on
yourselves and on this city and on those
who live in it, for in truth the LORD has
sent me to you to speak all these words in
your hearing."

16Then the officials[i] and all the people
said to the priests and the prophets, "This
man should not be sentenced to death![j] He
has spoken to us in the name of the LORD
our God."

17Some of the elders of the land stepped
forward and said to the entire assembly
of people, 18"Micah[k] of Moresheth prophesied in the days of Hezekiah king of Judah. He told all the people of Judah, 'This
is what the LORD Almighty says:

> " 'Zion[l] will be plowed like a field,
> Jerusalem will become a heap of
> rubble,[m]
> the temple hill[n] a mound overgrown
> with thickets.'[b][o]

[a] 6 That is, its name will be used in cursing (see 29:22); or, others will see that it is cursed. [b] 18 Micah 3:12

26:1 [q] 2Ki 23:36 **26:2** [r] Jer 19:14 [s] Jer 1:17; Mt 28:20; Ac 20:27 [t] Dt 4:2 **26:3** [u] Jer 36:7 [v] Jer 18:8 **26:4** [w] Lev 26:14 [x] 1Ki 9:6 **26:5** [y] Jer 25:4 **26:6** [z] Jos 18:1 [a] 2Ki 22:19 **26:9** [b] Jer 9:11 **26:11** [c] Dt 18:20; Jer 18:23; 38:4; Mt 26:66; Ac 6:11 **26:12** [d] Jer 1:18 [e] Am 7:15; Ac 4:18-20; 5:29 [f] ver 2, 15 **26:13** [g] Jer 7:5; Joel 2:12-14 **26:14** [h] Jer 38:5 **26:16** [i] Ac 23:9 [j] Ac 5:34-39; 23:29 **26:18** [k] Mic 1:1 [l] Isa 2:3 [m] Ne 4:2; Jer 9:11 [n] Mic 4:1; Zec 8:3 [o] Jer 17:3

26:1 *Early in the reign of Jehoiakim.* Since Jehoiakim's accession year was from about September, 609 BC to April, 608 BC (see note on 25:1), his first complete regnal year began in April, 608 BC. Mesopotamia used a post-dating accession year system, in which the accession year is not counted as the first year of rule. Egypt, for most of its history, used a non-accession year system, whereby there was no accession year computed. The first year of rule began the day the pharaoh took office. Israel began with the non-accession system but later on (under influence of Assyrian and Babylonian rule) adopted the accession year system, as here.
26:6 *Shiloh.* See note on 7:12.
26:8 *You must die!* When Jeremiah finishes speaking the word he has received from God, the priests, the prophets and all the people seize him and threaten his life. One senses the power of the spoken word here. Jeremiah's opponents take his words seriously. This is because in the ancient Near East not only is the prophet the channel for divine messages but in the act of speaking the message the prophet unleashes the divine action. Therefore, if the prophet has said something that the authorities or the ones in power dislike, they will want to silence him. King Esarhaddon of Assyria (681 – 669 BC) gave written instructions to his vassals that if they heard of an evil plan that would go against the authorities — whether it be from family, friends, prophet, ecstatic, dream interpreter, or any other — they were to report it immediately.
26:18 *Moresheth.* The hometown of the prophet Micah. It is located near the Philistine town of Gath. In fact, in Mic 1:14 it is called "Moresheth Gath." It has been identified with modern-day Tell Judeideh, which is a site in the low western hills. It is only about six miles (9.6 kilometers) northeast of Lachish. Excavations at this site have brought to light remains from the time of Micah (c. 737 – 699 BC) and Jeremiah (c. 627 – 580 BC). *Hezekiah king of Judah.* He ruled over Judah primarily during the last quarter of the eighth century BC, about 100 years before the time of Jeremiah. He came to the throne when he was 25 years old. Hezekiah instituted a religious reform in Judah, getting rid of the "high places" and the "sacred stones" (2Ki 18:4; see note there) that were forbidden by Deuteronomic law; he also launched a campaign to refurbish the temple. Politically speaking, Hezekiah sought independence from Assyria. This led to a military response by the Assyrian king and his army. In the so-called annals of Sennacherib, we read that this Assyrian king (705 – 681 BC) launched a military campaign against Judah. Sennacherib had laid siege

19“Did Hezekiah king of Judah or anyone else in Judah put him to death? Did not Hezekiah[p] fear the LORD and seek his favor? And did not the LORD relent,[q] so that he did not bring the disaster[r] he pronounced against them? We are about to bring a terrible disaster[s] on ourselves!”

20(Now Uriah son of Shemaiah from Kiriath Jearim[t] was another man who prophesied in the name of the LORD; he prophesied the same things against this city and this land as Jeremiah did. 21When King Jehoiakim[u] and all his officers and officials heard his words, the king was determined to put him to death. But Uriah heard of it and fled[v] in fear to Egypt. 22King Jehoiakim, however, sent Elnathan[w] son of Akbor to Egypt, along with some other men. 23They brought Uriah out of Egypt and took him to King Jehoiakim, who had him struck down with a sword and his body thrown into the burial place of the common people.)

24Furthermore, Ahikam[x] son of Shaphan supported Jeremiah, and so he was not handed over to the people to be put to death.

Judah to Serve Nebuchadnezzar

27 Early in the reign of Zedekiah[a][y] son of Josiah king of Judah, this word came to Jeremiah from the LORD: 2This is what the LORD said to me: “Make a yoke[z] out of straps and crossbars and put it on your neck. 3Then send word to the kings of Edom, Moab, Ammon,[a] Tyre and Sidon through the envoys who have come to Jerusalem to Zedekiah king of Judah. 4Give them a message for their masters and say, ‘This is what the LORD Almighty, the God of Israel, says: “Tell this to your masters: 5With my great power and outstretched arm[b] I made the earth and its people and the animals that are on it, and I give[c] it to anyone I please. 6Now I will give all your countries into the hands of my servant[d] Nebuchadnezzar[e] king of Babylon; I will make even the wild animals subject to him.[f] 7All nations will serve[g] him and his son and his grandson until the time[h] for his land comes; then many nations and great kings will subjugate[i] him.

8“ ‘ “If, however, any nation or kingdom will not serve Nebuchadnezzar king of Babylon or bow its neck under his yoke, I will punish that nation with the sword, famine and plague, declares the LORD, until I destroy it by his hand. 9So do not listen to your prophets, your diviners, your interpreters of dreams, your mediums[j] or your sorcerers who tell you, ‘You will not serve

26:19 [p] 2Ch 32:24-26; Isa 37:14-20 [q] Ex 32:14; 2Sa 24:16 [r] Jer 44:7 [s] Hab 2:10
26:20 [t] Jos 9:17
26:21 [u] 1Ki 19:2 [v] Mt 10:23
26:22 [w] Jer 36:12,25
26:24 [x] 2Ki 22:12
27:1 [y] 2Ch 36:11
27:2 [z] Jer 28:10,13
27:3 [a] Jer 25:21
27:5 [b] Dt 9:29 [c] Ps 115:16
27:6 [d] Jer 25:9 [e] Jer 21:7; Eze 29:18-20 [f] Jer 28:14; Da 2:37-38
27:7 [g] 2Ch 36:20 [h] Jer 25:12 [i] Jer 25:14; Da 5:28
27:9 [j] Dt 18:11

[a] *1* A few Hebrew manuscripts and Syriac (see also 27:3,12 and 28:1); most Hebrew manuscripts *Jehoiakim* (Most Septuagint manuscripts do not have this verse.)

---

to 46 of Hezekiah’s strong cities. The text then goes on to say that Sennacherib made Hezekiah a prisoner in his city “like a bird in a cage.” See 2Ki 18.

26:20 *Uriah son of Shemaiah.* The name of this prophet was common in Judah during this time. It shows up repeatedly on ostraca (such as those at Lachish) and seals.

26:23 *burial place of the common people.* We cannot be sure if Uriah is left unburied (see note on 22:19). But we do know that he was placed without proper ceremony in a less-than-desirable location. According to 2Ki 23:6 the burial grounds for the common people were located in the Kidron Valley, the area between the temple and the Mount of Olives. This area contains graves to this day.

27:1 *Early in the reign of Zedekiah.* The Hebrew Masoretic text, which is the “standard” text used for most translations of the Hebrew Bible, has “Jehoiakim” here. But Zedekiah is mentioned in the rest of the chapter. In ch. 28 the narrator says that “in ... that same year, the fourth year” of Zedekiah’s reign (28:1), a confrontation between Hananiah and Jeremiah takes place. Based on these facts, it is possible that in 27:1 the name “Jehoiakim” should read “Zedekiah” and that the phrase “early in the reign” designates Zedekiah’s fourth year in power. See note on 21:1; see also the article “Historical Setting of Jeremiah,” p. 1222.

27:2 *yoke.* This yoke that Jeremiah wears is most likely not the entire yoke placed on oxen in antiquity but only the collar formed by the cords and yoke pegs. See note on 5:5.

27:3 *Edom, Moab, Ammon, Tyre and Sidon.* Envoys from these five neighboring nations come to Jerusalem to conspire with Zedekiah against Nebuchadnezzar king of Babylon. A domestic rebellion that took place in Babylon against Nebuchadnezzar in 595–594 BC may have sparked hopes that these smaller nations could get rid of the Babylonian yoke. Note that Egypt does not participate in this meeting; this may be one of the reasons this rebellion never materializes. Another possible reason may be that the king heeds Jeremiah’s advice to submit to Babylonia willingly.

27:5 *outstretched arm.* See notes on Ex 6:1; Job 40:9.

27:6 *my servant Nebuchadnezzar.* See note on 25:9. *Nebuchadnezzar.* See note on 21:2. *make even the wild animals subject to him.* The yoke symbolizes the subjection of domesticated animals. In this prophetic text, even the wild animals will be placed under the power of the Babylonian king. There are numerous Assyrian reliefs from the time of King Ashurbanipal (669–633 BC) that depict the hunting and subduing of wild animals such as lions and onagers. These are intended metaphorically to demonstrate the king’s victories over his enemies.

27:9 *your prophets, your diviners, your interpreters of dreams, your mediums or your sorcerers.* Jeremiah addresses those who represent these professions who are not residing in Jerusalem but in the neighboring nations. *prophets.* Those responsible to speak, proclaim and articulate the message received directly from the deity (see the article “Prophets and Prophecy,” p. 1110). *diviners.* Those involved not so much in predicting the future but in the process of prognostication by reading omens, shaking arrows, casting lots and examining the entrails of sacrificial animals. They do this in order to advise the king. *dreams.* Accepted as a medium for divine revelation (see note on 23:25). *mediums.* We do not have specific information that distinguishes them from sorcerers or diviners, though presumably they are responsible for making contact with the dead. *sorcerers.* Those more identified with magic,

the king of Babylon.' 10They prophesy lies[k]
to you that will only serve to remove you
far from your lands; I will banish you and
you will perish. 11But if any nation will
bow its neck under the yoke[l] of the king
of Babylon and serve him, I will let that
nation remain in its own land to till it and
to live there, declares the LORD."'"

12I gave the same message to Zedekiah
king of Judah. I said, "Bow your neck under the yoke of the king of Babylon; serve
him and his people, and you will live.
13Why will you and your people die[m] by
the sword, famine and plague with which
the LORD has threatened any nation that
will not serve the king of Babylon? 14Do
not listen to the words of the prophets
who say to you, 'You will not serve the
king of Babylon,' for they are prophesying lies[n] to you. 15'I have not sent[o] them,'
declares the LORD. 'They are prophesying
lies in my name.[p] Therefore, I will banish
you and you will perish,[q] both you and
the prophets who prophesy to you.'"

16Then I said to the priests and all these
people, "This is what the LORD says: Do
not listen to the prophets who say, 'Very
soon now the articles[r] from the LORD's
house will be brought back from Babylon.'
They are prophesying lies to you. 17Do not
listen to them. Serve the king of Babylon,
and you will live. Why should this city become a ruin? 18If they are prophets and
have the word of the LORD, let them plead[s]
with the LORD Almighty that the articles
remaining in the house of the LORD and
in the palace of the king of Judah and in
Jerusalem not be taken to Babylon. 19For
this is what the LORD Almighty says about
the pillars, the bronze Sea,[t] the movable
stands and the other articles[u] that are left
in this city, 20which Nebuchadnezzar king
of Babylon did not take away when he
carried[v] Jehoiachin[a][w] son of Jehoiakim
king of Judah into exile from Jerusalem
to Babylon, along with all the nobles of
Judah and Jerusalem— 21yes, this is what
the LORD Almighty, the God of Israel, says
about the things that are left in the house
of the LORD and in the palace of the king
of Judah and in Jerusalem: 22'They will be
taken[x] to Babylon and there they will remain until the day[y] I come for them,' declares the LORD. 'Then I will bring[z] them
back and restore them to this place.'"

The False Prophet Hananiah

28 In the fifth month of that same
year, the fourth year, early in the
reign of Zedekiah[a] king of Judah, the
prophet Hananiah son of Azzur, who was
from Gibeon,[b] said to me in the house of
the LORD in the presence of the priests and
all the people: 2"This is what the LORD
Almighty, the God of Israel, says: 'I will
break the yoke[c] of the king of Babylon.
3Within two years I will bring back to this
place all the articles[d] of the LORD's house
that Nebuchadnezzar king of Babylon removed from here and took to Babylon. 4I
will also bring back to this place Jehoiachin[a][e] son of Jehoiakim king of Judah and
all the other exiles from Judah who went
to Babylon,' declares the LORD, 'for I will
break the yoke of the king of Babylon.'"

5Then the prophet Jeremiah replied to
the prophet Hananiah before the priests
and all the people who were standing in
the house of the LORD. 6He said, "Amen!
May the LORD do so! May the LORD fulfill
the words you have prophesied by bringing the articles of the LORD's house and
all the exiles back to this place from Babylon. 7Nevertheless, listen to what I have

27:10 [k]Jer 23:25
27:11 [l]Jer 21:9
27:13 [m]Eze 18:31
27:14 [n]Jer 14:14
27:15 [o]Jer 23:21 [p]Jer 29:9 [q]Jer 6:15
27:16 [r]2Ki 24:13; 2Ch 36:7, 10; Jer 28:3; Da 1:2
27:18 [s]1Sa 7:8
27:19 [t]2Ki 25:13 [u]Jer 52:17-23
27:20 [v]2Ch 36:10; Jer 24:1 [w]Jer 22:24
27:22 [x]2Ki 25:13 [y]2Ch 36:21 [z]Ezr 1:7; 7:19
28:1 [a]Jer 27:1, 3 [b]Jos 9:3
28:2 [c]Jer 27:12
28:3 [d]2Ki 24:13
28:4 [e]Jer 22:24-27

[a] 20,4 Hebrew *Jeconiah,* a variant of *Jehoiachin*

incantations and spells (see note on Isa 47:9). For further information on these professions, see note on Isa 2:6.

27:16 *articles from the LORD's house.* Most likely refers to the furnishings that belonged to the temple. Nebuchadnezzar king of Babylon had looted the temple when he defeated Jerusalem in 597 BC, taking its most valuable gold vessels (2Ki 24:13). Other accessories were carried off 11 years later (see 2Ch 4 for a list of the temple's furnishings). Prophets such as Hananiah raised the hopes of priests and others by saying that the vessels would soon be returned.

27:19 *the pillars.* Most likely the two bronze pillars placed at the entrance of the vestibule of Solomon's temple (see note on 1Ki 7:15–22), called Jakin and Boaz (1Ki 7:21). *the bronze Sea.* This was a large bronze basin that was probably placed in the courtyard of Solomon's temple (see note on 1Ki 7:23–26). *movable stands.* These were smaller basins probably used to wash sacrificial animals (see note on 1Ki 7:27–37).

27:20 *Jehoiachin.* See notes on 13:18; 24:1.

27:22 *They will be taken to Babylon.* In the ancient Near East, when an army defeated an enemy, they generally destroyed as much as they could. But it was also common procedure to loot the temple and take away sacred objects. This happened to Jerusalem when it was defeated by Nebuchadnezzar.

28:1 *early in the reign of Zedekiah.* Though there is some question as to the exact time frame mentioned here (see notes on 21:1; 27:1), most agree this event occurred in 594–593 BC. This verse also mentions that it takes place "in the fifth month." The reason for mentioning this fact may be that Hananiah's death happens in the seventh month of the same year (v. 17). *Hananiah son of Azzur.* Hananiah is a prophet who represents the Jerusalem prophets, who are against Jeremiah and his message. As with previous names mentioned, Hananiah is a common name in Judah at this time. *Gibeon.* A Benjamite town located close to Anathoth, Jeremiah's hometown. It is identified with el-Jib, which lies about six miles (9.6 kilometers) north of Jerusalem. Much like Anathoth, Gibeon was a priestly town and a major cultic site (see note on 2Ch 1:3).

to say in your hearing and in the hearing of all the people: 8From early times
the prophets who preceded you and me
have prophesied war, disaster and plague[f]
against many countries and great kingdoms. 9But the prophet who prophesies
peace will be recognized as one truly sent
by the LORD only if his prediction comes
true.[g]"

10Then the prophet Hananiah took the
yoke[h] off the neck of the prophet Jeremiah and broke it, 11and he said[i] before all
the people, "This is what the LORD says:
'In the same way I will break the yoke of
Nebuchadnezzar king of Babylon off the
neck of all the nations within two years.'"
At this, the prophet Jeremiah went on his
way.

12After the prophet Hananiah had broken the yoke off the neck of the prophet
Jeremiah, the word of the LORD came to
Jeremiah: 13"Go and tell Hananiah, 'This
is what the LORD says: You have broken a
wooden yoke, but in its place you will get
a yoke of iron. 14This is what the LORD Almighty, the God of Israel, says: I will put
an iron yoke[j] on the necks of all these nations to make them serve[k] Nebuchadnezzar king of Babylon, and they will serve
him. I will even give him control over the
wild animals.[l]'"

15Then the prophet Jeremiah said to
Hananiah the prophet, "Listen, Hananiah!
The LORD has not sent[m] you, yet you have
persuaded this nation to trust in lies.[n]
16Therefore this is what the LORD says: 'I
am about to remove you from the face of
the earth.[o] This very year you are going to
die, because you have preached rebellion[p]
against the LORD.'"

17In the seventh month of that same
year, Hananiah the prophet died.

A Letter to the Exiles

29 This is the text of the letter that the
prophet Jeremiah sent from Jeru-
salem to the surviving elders among the
exiles and to the priests, the prophets and
all the other people Nebuchadnezzar had
carried into exile from Jerusalem to Babylon.[q] 2(This was after King Jehoiachin[a][r]
and the queen mother, the court officials
and the leaders of Judah and Jerusalem,
the skilled workers and the artisans had
gone into exile from Jerusalem.) 3He entrusted the letter to Elasah son of Shaphan
and to Gemariah son of Hilkiah, whom
Zedekiah king of Judah sent to King Nebuchadnezzar in Babylon. It said:

4This is what the LORD Almighty,
the God of Israel, says to all those I
carried[s] into exile from Jerusalem to
Babylon: 5"Build[t] houses and settle
down; plant gardens and eat what
they produce. 6Marry and have sons
and daughters; find wives for your
sons and give your daughters in marriage, so that they too may have sons
and daughters. Increase in number
there; do not decrease. 7Also, seek
the peace and prosperity of the city
to which I have carried you into exile.

28:8 [f]Lev 26:14-17; Isa 5:5-7 **28:9** [g]Dt 18:22 **28:10** [h]Jer 27:2 **28:11** [i]Jer 14:14; 27:10 **28:14** [j]Dt 28:48 [k]Jer 25:11 [l]Jer 27:6 **28:15** [m]Jer 29:31 [n]Jer 20:6; 29:21; La 2:14; Eze 13:6 **28:16** [o]Ge 7:4 [p]Dt 13:5; Jer 29:32 **29:1** [q]2Ch 36:10 **29:2** [r]2Ki 24:12; Jer 22:24-28 **29:4** [s]Jer 24:5 **29:5** [t]ver 28

[a] 2 Hebrew *Jeconiah,* a variant of *Jehoiachin*

28:10 *broke it.* Since Jeremiah only used the yoke collar formed by the cords and yoke pegs (see note on 27:2), what is being broken are the yoke pegs that hold the yoke in place on either side of the neck of the ox. Given the language that is used both here and in ch. 27 regarding the yoke, it is unlikely that the crossbar of the yoke was broken.

28:13 *yoke of iron.* The mention of replacing the broken "wooden yoke" with an iron yoke certainly has dramatic effect. This obviously points toward a much harsher kind of servitude that will be imposed on Judah. This kind of metaphor is reminiscent of the curse articulated in Dt 28:47–48: "Because you did not serve the LORD your God joyfully ... you will serve the enemies the LORD sends against you. He will put an iron yoke on your neck until he has destroyed you." It should be clarified that a literal iron yoke would not have been at all practical because of its excessive weight.

28:14 *control over the wild animals.* See note on 27:6.

29:1 *letter.* This Hebrew term can refer to any document no matter what it is written on. Here it likely refers to a letter written on papyrus. It would be rolled into a scroll and then sealed. Jeremiah sends this letter to those who were exiled to Babylon in 597 BC. The letter is carried from Jerusalem to Babylon by a traveling merchant or a Babylonian messenger. We have ample evidence of this custom in the ancient Near East. Nineteen letters discovered at Lachish and dated approximately from 589 to 586 BC serve as a good illustration of the practice of writing and sending letters at this time. *Nebuchadnezzar.* See note on 21:2; see also the article "Historical Setting of Jeremiah," p. 1222. *exile.* The defeat of Jerusalem in 597 BC and the exile of the city's leaders are recorded in various historical documents from Judah (e.g., 2Ki 24:10–17) and Mesopotamia (e.g., the Babylonian Chronicle). See notes on 2Ki 15:29; Isa 5:13.

29:2 *Jehoiachin.* See notes on 13:18; 24:1. *queen mother.* See note on 13:18. *the skilled workers and the artisans.* Cf. 24:1. They would be useful to Nebuchadnezzar in Babylon. They represent a class of people economically well positioned in society. They were also able to assist in building projects that were very important to the Babylonian king. Moreover, the absence of these people in Judah weakened Judah's possibilities of gaining independence. Deporting important members of a society was not practiced only by the Babylonian kings. Earlier the Assyrian kings Esarhaddon (681–669 BC) and Ashurbanipal (669–633 BC) exiled skilled workers from Egypt. In a text known as "The Prisms of Esarhaddon and Ashurbanipal," there is a long list of deported workers such as physicians, coppersmiths, goldsmiths, cart wrights, bakers, fishermen, and many others.

29:3 *Zedekiah.* See note on 21:1; see also the article "Historical Setting of Jeremiah," p. 1222.

Pray[u] to the LORD for it, because if it
prospers, you too will prosper." 8Yes,
this is what the LORD Almighty, the
God of Israel, says: "Do not let the
prophets and diviners among you
deceive[v] you. Do not listen to the
dreams you encourage them to have.[w]
9They are prophesying lies[x] to you in
my name. I have not sent them," declares the LORD.
10This is what the LORD says:
"When seventy years[y] are completed
for Babylon, I will come to you and
fulfill my good promise to bring you
back[z] to this place. 11For I know the
plans[a] I have for you," declares the
LORD, "plans to prosper you and not
to harm you, plans to give you hope
and a future. 12Then you will call on
me and come and pray to me, and I
will listen[b] to you. 13You will seek[c]
me and find me when you seek me
with all your heart.[d] 14I will be found
by you," declares the LORD, "and will
bring you back[e] from captivity.[a] I will
gather you from all the nations and
places where I have banished you,"
declares the LORD, "and will bring you
back to the place from which I carried
you into exile."[f]
15You may say, "The LORD has
raised up prophets for us in Babylon," 16but this is what the LORD
says about the king who sits on
David's throne and all the people
who remain in this city, your fellow
citizens who did not go with you
into exile— 17yes, this is what the
LORD Almighty says: "I will send the
sword, famine and plague[g] against
them and I will make them like figs[h]
that are so bad they cannot be eaten.
18I will pursue them with the sword,
famine and plague and will make
them abhorrent[i] to all the kingdoms
of the earth, a curse[b] and an object
of horror,[j] of scorn and reproach,
among all the nations where I drive
them. 19For they have not listened
to my words,"[k] declares the LORD,
"words that I sent to them again and
again by my servants the prophets.[l]
And you exiles have not listened either," declares the LORD.
20Therefore, hear the word of the
LORD, all you exiles whom I have
sent[m] away from Jerusalem to Babylon. 21This is what the LORD Almighty, the God of Israel, says about
Ahab son of Kolaiah and Zedekiah
son of Maaseiah, who are prophesying lies[n] to you in my name: "I will
deliver them into the hands of Nebuchadnezzar king of Babylon, and he
will put them to death before your
very eyes. 22Because of them, all the
exiles from Judah who are in Babylon
will use this curse: 'May the LORD
treat you like Zedekiah and Ahab,
whom the king of Babylon burned[o] in
the fire.' 23For they have done outrageous things in Israel; they have committed adultery[p] with their neighbors'
wives, and in my name they have uttered lies—which I did not authorize.
I know[q] it and am a witness to it,"
declares the LORD.

Message to Shemaiah

24Tell Shemaiah the Nehelamite, 25"This
is what the LORD Almighty, the God of Israel, says: You sent letters in your own
name to all the people in Jerusalem, to the
priest Zephaniah[r] son of Maaseiah, and to
all the other priests. You said to Zephaniah, 26'The LORD has appointed you priest
in place of Jehoiada to be in charge of the
house of the LORD; you should put any
maniac[s] who acts like a prophet into the
stocks[t] and neck-irons. 27So why have you
not reprimanded Jeremiah from Anathoth,
who poses as a prophet among you? 28He
has sent this message[u] to us in Babylon:
It will be a long time.[v] Therefore build[w]
houses and settle down; plant gardens and
eat what they produce.' "
29Zephaniah the priest, however, read
the letter to Jeremiah the prophet. 30Then
the word of the LORD came to Jeremiah:
31"Send this message to all the exiles:
'This is what the LORD says about Shemaiah[x] the Nehelamite: Because Shemaiah
has prophesied to you, even though I did
not send[y] him, and has persuaded you to
trust in lies, 32this is what the LORD says:
I will surely punish Shemaiah the Nehelamite and his descendants.[z] He will have
no one left among this people, nor will
he see the good[a] things I will do for my
people, declares the LORD, because he has
preached rebellion[b] against me.' "

29:7 [u] Ezr 6:10; 1Ti 2:1-2
29:8 [v] Jer 37:9 [w] Jer 23:27
29:9 [x] Jer 14:14; 27:15
29:10 [y] 2Ch 36:21; Jer 25:12; Da 9:2 [z] Jer 21:22
29:11 [a] Ps 40:5
29:12 [b] Ps 145:19
29:13 [c] Mt 7:7 [d] Dt 4:29; Jer 24:7
29:14 [e] Dt 30:3; Jer 30:3 [f] Jer 23:3-4
29:17 [g] Jer 27:8 [h] Jer 24:8-10
29:18 [i] Jer 15:4 [j] Dt 28:25; Jer 42:18
29:19 [k] Jer 6:19 [l] Jer 25:4
29:20 [m] Jer 24:5
29:21 [n] ver 9; Jer 14:14
29:22 [o] Da 3:6
29:23 [p] Jer 23:14 [q] Heb 4:13
29:25 [r] 2Ki 25:18; Jer 21:1
29:26 [s] 2Ki 9:11; Hos 9:7; Jn 10:20 [t] Jer 20:2
29:28 [u] ver 1 [v] ver 10 [w] ver 5
29:31 [x] ver 24 [y] Jer 14:14; 28:15
29:32 [z] 1Sa 2:30-33 [a] ver 10 [b] Jer 28:16

[a] 14 Or *will restore your fortunes* [b] 18 That is, their names will be used in cursing (see verse 22); or, others will see that they are cursed.

29:10 *When seventy years are completed.* See note on 25:11.
29:26 *stocks.* See note on 20:2. *neck-irons.* This Hebrew term only occurs once in the Hebrew Bible, and its meaning is not clear. The translation "neck-iron" comes from a cognate term in Jewish Aramaic. Given our speculation regarding the meaning of "stocks" in 20:2 (see note there), we can suggest that a neck-iron is also a restraining device that would serve to display, punish and humiliate a prisoner.

Restoration of Israel

30 This is the word that came to Jeremiah from the LORD: 2"This is what
the LORD, the God of Israel, says: 'Write[c] in
a book all the words I have spoken to you.
3The days are coming,' declares the LORD,
'when I will bring[d] my people Israel and
Judah back from captivity[a] and restore[e]
them to the land I gave their ancestors to
possess,' says the LORD."
4These are the words the LORD spoke
concerning Israel and Judah: 5"This is
what the LORD says:

"'Cries of fear[f] are heard—
terror, not peace.
6Ask and see:
Can a man bear children?
Then why do I see every strong man
with his hands on his stomach like a
woman in labor,[g]
every face turned deathly pale?
7How awful that day[h] will be!
No other will be like it.
It will be a time of trouble[i] for Jacob,
but he will be saved[j] out of it.

8"'In that day,' declares the LORD
Almighty,
'I will break the yoke[k] off their necks
and will tear off their bonds;
no longer will foreigners enslave
them.[l]
9Instead, they will serve the LORD their
God
and David[m] their king,[n]
whom I will raise up for them.
10"'So do not be afraid,[o] Jacob my
servant;[p]
do not be dismayed, Israel,'
declares the LORD.
'I will surely save[q] you out of a distant
place,
your descendants from the land of
their exile.
Jacob will again have peace and
security,[r]
and no one will make him afraid.
11I am with you and will save you,'
declares the LORD.
'Though I completely destroy all the
nations
among which I scatter you,
I will not completely destroy[s] you.
I will discipline[t] you but only in due
measure;
I will not let you go entirely
unpunished.'[u]

12"This is what the LORD says:

"'Your wound is incurable,
your injury beyond healing.[v]
13There is no one to plead your cause,
no remedy for your sore,
no healing[w] for you.
14All your allies[x] have forgotten you;
they care nothing for you.
I have struck you as an enemy[y] would
and punished you as would the cruel,[z]
because your guilt is so great
and your sins[a] so many.
15Why do you cry out over your wound,
your pain that has no cure?
Because of your great guilt and many
sins
I have done these things to you.

16"'But all who devour[b] you will be
devoured;
all your enemies will go into exile.[c]

30:2 [c] Isa 30:8 **30:3** [d] Jer 29:14 [e] Jer 16:15 **30:5** [f] Jer 6:25 **30:6** [g] Jer 4:31 **30:7** [h] Isa 2:12; Joel 2:11 [i] Zep 1:15 [j] ver 10 **30:8** [k] Isa 9:4 [l] Eze 34:27 **30:9** [m] Isa 55:3-4; Lk 1:69; Ac 2:30; 13:23 [n] Eze 34:23-24; 37:24; Hos 3:5 **30:10** [o] Isa 43:5; Jer 46:27-28 [p] Isa 44:2 [q] Jer 29:14 [r] Isa 35:9 **30:11** [s] Jer 4:27; 46:28 [t] Jer 10:24 [u] Am 9:8 **30:12** [v] Jer 15:18 **30:13** [w] Jer 8:22; 14:19; 46:11 **30:14** [x] Jer 22:20; La 1:2 [y] Job 13:24 [z] Job 30:21 [a] Jer 5:6 **30:16** [b] Isa 33:1; Jer 2:3; 10:25 [c] Isa 14:2; Joel 3:4-8

[a] 3 Or *will restore the fortunes of my people Israel and Judah*

30:2 *book.* The Hebrew word (translated "letter" in 29:1) is not a book in the modern sense of the word, but refers to any document whatever its form. Given the time period and the geographic context of this written record, this most likely refers to a scroll (see the article "Scrolls in the Ancient World," p. 1286).

30:12 *Your wound is incurable.* This expression seems to be a common curse both in the Hebrew Bible and in Mesopotamia. According to Dt 28, if the people of God disobey the stipulations of their covenant, they will suffer the kind of punishment Egyptians experienced at the time of the exodus. In fact, there will be no cure for the sickness that will plague them (Dt 28:27). A similar situation is described in the Code of Hammurapi (c. 1792–1750 BC), where a curse is pronounced to the effect that a person might be smitten with an incurable malady, which no physician is able to understand.

30:14 *All your allies.* Jehoiakim of Judah had been put on the throne by the Egyptians in 609 BC, and he remained loyal to them until Nebuchadnezzar's domination made that impossible. After the fall of Ashkelon to Nebuchadnezzar in 604, Jehoiakim paid tribute to Babylon for a few years. But when Nebuchadnezzar failed in his attempted invasion of Egypt in 601, Jehoiakim again sided with Egypt and stopped sending the yearly tribute east. Thus in 597 when Nebuchadnezzar undertook his punitive raid against Jerusalem, Egypt was the principal ally on whom Judah relied. Later that year, Nebuchadnezzar put Zedekiah on the throne. Zedekiah almost immediately began meeting with a coalition of the small western states to stand together against Nebuchadnezzar (see note on 27:3). In 595 BC, a new pharaoh, Psammetichus II, took the throne of Egypt. He enjoyed an early military success against the Nubians in the south, and one papyrus reports that his success was celebrated with a victory tour in Palestine. Therefore, though Egypt was not the instigator of the alliance, there was cause to expect their support against Babylon. It is uncertain which nations were actually part of the alliance when it finally took shape. As it turned out, Egypt's army was routed in their confrontation with the Babylonians in 588 BC (see note on 37:5), and it would appear, based on Ps 137:7, that allies such as the Edomites threw their support to Babylon when it became clear that Jerusalem was about to fall. Only Ammon and Tyre of the western states became objects of Nebuchadnezzar's wrath.

Those who plunder[d] you will be
plundered;
all who make spoil of you I will
despoil.
17 But I will restore you to health
and heal your wounds,'
declares the LORD,
'because you are called an outcast,[e]
Zion for whom no one cares.'

18 "This is what the LORD says:

" 'I will restore the fortunes[f] of Jacob's
tents
and have compassion[g] on his
dwellings;
the city will be rebuilt[h] on her ruins,
and the palace will stand in its
proper place.
19 From them will come songs[i] of
thanksgiving[j]
and the sound of rejoicing.[k]
I will add to their numbers,[l]
and they will not be decreased;
I will bring them honor,[m]
and they will not be disdained.
20 Their children[n] will be as in days of
old,
and their community will be
established[o] before me;
I will punish all who oppress them.
21 Their leader[p] will be one of their
own;
their ruler will arise from among
them.
I will bring him near[q] and he will
come close to me —
for who is he who will devote
himself
to be close to me?'
declares the LORD.
22 " 'So you will be my people,
and I will be your God.' "

23 See, the storm[r] of the LORD
will burst out in wrath,
a driving wind swirling down
on the heads of the wicked.
24 The fierce anger[s] of the LORD will not
turn back[t]
until he fully accomplishes
the purposes of his heart.
In days to come
you will understand[u] this.

30:16 [d] Jer 50:10
30:17 [e] Jer 33:24
30:18 [f] ver 3; Jer 31:23 [g] Ps 102:13 [h] Jer 31:4,24,38
30:19 [i] Isa 35:10; 51:11 [j] Isa 51:3 [k] Ps 126:1-2; Jer 31:4 [l] Jer 33:22 [m] Isa 60:9
30:20 [n] Isa 54:13; Jer 31:17 [o] Isa 54:14
30:21 [p] ver 9 [q] Nu 16:5
30:23 [r] Jer 23:19
30:24 [s] Jer 4:8 [t] Jer 4:28 [u] Jer 23:19-20

31:1 [v] Jer 30:22
31:2 [w] Nu 14:20 [x] Ex 33:14
31:3 [y] Dt 4:37 [z] Hos 11:4
31:4 [a] Jer 30:19
31:5 [b] Jer 50:19 [c] Isa 65:21; Am 9:14
31:6 [d] Isa 2:3; Jer 50:4-5; Mic 4:2
31:7 [e] Dt 28:13; Isa 61:9 [f] Ps 14:7; 28:9 [g] Isa 37:31
31:8 [h] Jer 3:18; 23:8 [i] Dt 30:4; Eze 34:12-14 [j] Isa 42:16 [k] Eze 34:16; Mic 4:6
31:9 [l] Ps 126:5 [m] Isa 63:13 [n] Isa 49:11

31 "At that time," declares the LORD, "I will be the God[v] of all the families of Israel, and they will be my people."

2 This is what the LORD says:

"The people who survive the sword
will find favor[w] in the wilderness;
I will come to give rest[x] to Israel."

3 The LORD appeared to us in the past,[a]
saying:

"I have loved[y] you with an everlasting
love;
I have drawn[z] you with unfailing
kindness.
4 I will build you up again,
and you, Virgin Israel, will be
rebuilt.
Again you will take up your timbrels
and go out to dance with the joyful.[a]
5 Again you will plant vineyards
on the hills of Samaria;[b]
the farmers will plant them
and enjoy their fruit.[c]
6 There will be a day when watchmen
cry out
on the hills of Ephraim,
'Come, let us go up to Zion,
to the LORD our God.' "[d]

7 This is what the LORD says:

"Sing with joy for Jacob;
shout for the foremost[e] of the
nations.
Make your praises heard, and say,
'LORD, save[f] your people,
the remnant[g] of Israel.'
8 See, I will bring them from the land of
the north[h]
and gather[i] them from the ends of
the earth.
Among them will be the blind[j] and the
lame,[k]
expectant mothers and women in
labor;
a great throng will return.
9 They will come with weeping;[l]
they will pray as I bring them back.
I will lead[m] them beside streams of
water
on a level[n] path where they will not
stumble,

[a] 3 Or *LORD has appeared to us from afar*

30:23 *storm.* See note on 23:19.
31:4 *Virgin Israel.* In this case the personification of Israel does not appear to be with ironic overtones. See note on 18:13. *timbrels.* See the article "Music and Musicians," p. 524.
31:8 *gather them from the ends of the earth.* This stock phrase alludes to the dispersion of God's people. "From the ends of the earth" is a phrase similar to the one found in Isa 41:9 (cf. Isa 43:5–6; cf. also Isa 11:11, where a number of nations are mentioned, such as Assyria, Lower Egypt, Upper Egypt, Cush, Elam, Babylonia, Hamath, and the islands of the Mediterranean). *the ends of the earth.* Refers to the farthest corners of the earth as it was known at that time. It is also common to find that rulers in Mesopotamia are described as having dominion over the four corners of the earth.
31:9 *beside streams of water.* Israel is full of streams, but they are not always full of water. Rainfall is generally limited to the months of October through February. For the rest of the year, these "wadis" (stream beds) are dry, and thus they are often used as walking paths.

because I am Israel's father,[o]
and Ephraim is my firstborn son.

10 "Hear the word of the LORD, you nations;
proclaim it in distant coastlands:[p]
'He who scattered Israel will gather[q] them
and will watch over his flock like a shepherd.'[r]
11 For the LORD will deliver Jacob
and redeem[s] them from the hand of those stronger[t] than they.
12 They will come and shout for joy on the heights[u] of Zion;
they will rejoice in the bounty[v] of the LORD —
the grain, the new wine and the olive oil,[w]
the young of the flocks and herds.
They will be like a well-watered garden,[x]
and they will sorrow[y] no more.
13 Then young women will dance and be glad,
young men and old as well.
I will turn their mourning[z] into gladness;
I will give them comfort and joy[a] instead of sorrow.
14 I will satisfy[b] the priests with abundance,
and my people will be filled with my bounty,"
declares the LORD.

15 This is what the LORD says:

"A voice is heard in Ramah,[c]
mourning and great weeping,
Rachel weeping for her children
and refusing to be comforted,[d]
because they are no more."[e]

16 This is what the LORD says:

"Restrain your voice from weeping
and your eyes from tears,[f]
for your work will be rewarded,[g]"
declares the LORD.
"They will return[h] from the land of the enemy.
17 So there is hope for your descendants,"
declares the LORD.
"Your children will return to their own land.

18 "I have surely heard Ephraim's moaning:
'You disciplined[i] me like an unruly calf,[j]
and I have been disciplined.
Restore[k] me, and I will return,
because you are the LORD my God.
19 After I strayed,[l]
I repented;
after I came to understand,
I beat[m] my breast.
I was ashamed and humiliated
because I bore the disgrace of my youth.'
20 Is not Ephraim my dear son,
the child in whom I delight?
Though I often speak against him,
I still remember[n] him.
Therefore my heart yearns for him;
I have great compassion[o] for him,"
declares the LORD.

21 "Set up road signs;
put up guideposts.
Take note of the highway,[p]
the road that you take.
Return,[q] Virgin[r] Israel,
return to your towns.
22 How long will you wander,[s]
unfaithful[t] Daughter Israel?

31:9 [o] Ex 4:22; Jer 3:4 **31:10** [p] Isa 66:19; Jer 25:22 [q] Jer 50:19 [r] Isa 40:11; Eze 34:12 **31:11** [s] Isa 44:23; 48:20 [t] Ps 142:6 **31:12** [u] Eze 17:23; Mic 4:1 [v] Joel 3:18 [w] Hos 2:21-22 [x] Isa 58:11 [y] Isa 65:19; Jn 16:22; Rev 7:17 **31:13** [z] Isa 61:3 [a] Ps 30:11; Isa 51:11 **31:14** [b] ver 25 **31:15** [c] Jos 18:25 [d] Ge 37:35 [e] Jer 10:20; Mt 2:17-18*

31:16 [f] Isa 25:8; 30:19 [g] Ru 2:12 [h] Jer 30:3; Eze 11:17 **31:18** [i] Job 5:17 [j] Hos 4:16 [k] Ps 80:3 **31:19** [l] Eze 36:31 [m] Eze 21:12; Lk 18:13 **31:20** [n] Hos 4:4; 11:8 [o] Isa 55:7; 63:15; Mic 7:18 **31:21** [p] Jer 50:5 [q] Isa 52:11 [r] ver 4 **31:22** [s] Jer 2:23 **31:22** [t] Jer 3:6

31:10 *distant coastlands.* In different contexts this stock phrase can refer to the Greek islands (2:10), Crete (47:4), Phoenician colonies, or Cyprus (25:22). But in this context, in addition to all of these places, the phrase seems somewhat akin to "the ends of the earth" (v. 8) in that it refers to the outer limits of the then-known world. Such areas are indicated on a small clay tablet known as the Babylonian world map dating to about this time. It pictures a disk-shaped landmass surrounded by the distant outlying regions.
31:12 *the grain, the new wine and the olive oil.* These three products are the principal staples of life in Palestine. They form a kind of triadic formula throughout Deuteronomy (Dt 7:13; 11:14; 12:17; 14:23; 18:4; 28:51; see also Hos 2:8,22). *grain.* Can refer either to wheat or barley — the main field crops in Biblical times. The harvest of these crops extended over a period of seven weeks.
31:15 *Ramah.* Means "heights"; it is a matter of much debate as to whether the term here refers to a specific place or to any elevation. There was a town by this name, and it is generally identified with modern er-Ram, located about four miles (6.4 kilometers) north of Jerusalem. Others identify it with modern Ramallah, which lies about 7.5 miles (12 kilometers) north of Jerusalem. Ramah became famous during the time of the judges in Israel, for both Deborah and Samuel were associated with the place (Jdg 4:5; 1Sa 1:19). The situation of anguish at Ramah may be due to its strategic location. After the destruction of Jerusalem, Ramah may have served as a kind of staging place for those prisoners taken into exile. The connection between Ramah and Rachel is a matter of scholarly debate. One possible explanation hinges on the location of Rachel's tomb. If indeed it lies in the vicinity of Ramah, in the place known as Zelzah, then the connection seems logical.
31:19 *breast.* The Hebrew word is better rendered "thigh." The action of hitting one's thigh in Israel was a sign of pain, repentance or sorrow (Eze 21:12). The same kind of expression seems to have been used in the second millennium BC in Mesopotamia. In a text known as the *Descent of Ishtar,* we find the expression "she struck her thigh and bit her finger." In the context, this action expresses pain and disgust.
31:21 *Virgin Israel.* See note on 18:13.

The LORD will create a new thing on
earth —
the woman will return to[a] the man."

[23]This is what the LORD Almighty, the
God of Israel, says: "When I bring them
back from captivity,[b][u] the people in the
land of Judah and in its towns will once
again use these words: 'The LORD bless
you, you prosperous city,[v] you sacred
mountain.'[w] [24]People will live[x] together
in Judah and all its towns — farmers and
those who move about with their flocks.
[25]I will refresh the weary and satisfy the
faint."[y]

[26]At this I awoke[z] and looked around.
My sleep had been pleasant to me.

[27]"The days are coming," declares the
LORD, "when I will plant[a] the kingdoms
of Israel and Judah with the offspring of
people and of animals. [28]Just as I watched
over them to uproot and tear down, and
to overthrow, destroy and bring disaster,[b]
so I will watch over them to build and
to plant,"[c] declares the LORD. [29]"In those
days people will no longer say,

'The parents[d] have eaten sour grapes,
and the children's teeth are set on
edge.'[e]

[30]Instead, everyone will die for their own
sin;[f] whoever eats sour grapes — their own
teeth will be set on edge.

[31]"The days are coming," declares the
LORD,
"when I will make a new covenant[g]
with the people of Israel
and with the people of Judah.
[32]It will not be like the covenant[h]
I made with their ancestors[i]
when I took them by the hand
to lead them out of Egypt,
because they broke my covenant,
though I was a husband to[c] them,[d]"
declares the LORD.
[33]"This is the covenant I will make with
the people of Israel
after that time," declares the LORD.
"I will put my law in their minds
and write it on their hearts.[j]
I will be their God,
and they will be my people.[k]
[34]No longer will they teach[l] their
neighbor,
or say to one another, 'Know the LORD,'
because they will all know[m] me,
from the least of them to the
greatest,"
declares the LORD.
"For I will forgive[n] their wickedness
and will remember their sins[o] no
more."

[35]This is what the LORD says,

he who appoints[p] the sun
to shine by day,
who decrees the moon and stars
to shine by night,[q]

31:23 [u]Jer 30:18 [v]Isa 1:26 [w]Ps 48:1; Zec 8:3 **31:24** [x]Zec 8:4-8 **31:25** [y]Jn 4:14 **31:26** [z]Zec 4:1 **31:27** [a]Eze 36:9-11; Hos 2:23 **31:28** [b]Jer 18:8; 44:27 [c]Jer 1:10 **31:29** [d]La 5:7 [e]Eze 18:2 **31:30** [f]Isa 3:11; Gal 6:7 **31:31** [g]Jer 32:40; Eze 37:26; Lk 22:20; Heb 8:8-12*; 10:16-17 **31:32** [h]Ex 24:8 [i]Dt 5:3 **31:33** [j]2Co 3:3 [k]Jer 24:7; Heb 10:16 **31:34** [l]1Jn 2:27 [m]Jn 6:45 [n]Isa 54:13; Jer 33:8; 50:20 [o]Mic 7:19; Ro 11:27; Heb 10:17* **31:35** [p]Ps 136:7-9 [q]Ge 1:16

[a] 22 Or *will protect* [b] 23 Or *I restore their fortunes* [c] 32 Hebrew; Septuagint and Syriac / *and I turned away from* [d] 32 Or *was their master*

31:23 *sacred mountain.* This is an honorific title for the city of Jerusalem (see especially Ps 2:6; 15:1; 43:3; Isa 11:9; 27:13; 56:7; 66:20). It was customary in the ancient Near East to consider that a deity's residence was on a mountain height. It was considered an expression of that god's sovereignty and role as dispenser of fertility. As such, the heavenly residence (temple) should be modeled by the earthly temple. Jerusalem lies on an elevated place surrounded by valleys, and thus it was natural to consider it the dwelling place of God.

31:29 *The parents have eaten sour grapes.* This was a well-known proverb in Jeremiah's time, probably repeated many times both in Judah and among the exiles in Babylon. The idea of corporate responsibility for sin and the possibility that children pay for the sin of previous generations finds an interesting parallel in a Neo-Assyrian prayer in which the supplicant seeks release from the effect of sins committed by grandparents, parents or even siblings.

31:33 *write it on their hearts.* The idea of writing divine revelation on the human heart was not a strange image for the ancient inhabitant of Judah because of the practice of extispicy in the surrounding cultures. Extispicy is the practice whereby diviners seek an answer to a question posed to a deity by examining the appearance of the entrails of a specially slaughtered young ram (see the article "Extispicy," p. 650). The underlying concept is that the divine message is written on the liver, lungs, colon or heart of the animal. The appearance of the entrails is interpreted after the dissection of the carcass. The vocabulary used by Jeremiah here is similar to that used in extispicy omens found in Mesopotamian literature. Jeremiah proclaims that whereas in the past the hearts of the Israelites were inscribed with sin (see 17:1 and note), now a new covenant will be written on those hearts. In such a case the metaphor of writing on the heart suggests a context of revelation: God's law will be revealed by Israel as they live out its principles.

31:35 – 36 In Mesopotamia the "Tablet of Destinies" contained the decrees that were the foundation for all that happened on earth. The people took omens seriously because they believed that these decrees were mirrored in the heavenly bodies, in the behavior of animals and even in the entrails of animals. The assumption is that a divine decree is binding for all time. In the Babylonian creation epic *Enuma Elish,* the gods proclaim that Marduk's "word shall not be challenged" and his "decree shall not be altered." Similarly, in the wisdom sayings of the Egyptian Amenemope about justice, he states that "judgment belongs to the divine assembly, verdicts are sealed by divine decree." In the Ugaritic Baal Cycle, the goddess Anat, in her attempt to flatter the chief god El, tells him that his "decrees are wise" and his "wisdom endures forever." Occasionally, a text will refer to a god's decree as "evil," as in the Atrahasis epic (a flood story), but still these commands are carried out because of the lordship the ancient gods are said to have over creation. For the reigns of kings related to the endurance of the cosmos, see note on Ps 89:36 – 37.

who stirs up the sea
so that its waves roar —
the LORD Almighty is his name:[r]
36 "Only if these decrees[s] vanish from my
sight,"
declares the LORD,
"will Israel[t] ever cease
being a nation before me."

37 This is what the LORD says:

"Only if the heavens above can be
measured[u]
and the foundations of the earth
below be searched out
will I reject[v] all the descendants of
Israel
because of all they have done,"
declares the LORD.

38 "The days are coming," declares the
LORD, "when this city will be rebuilt[w] for
me from the Tower of Hananel[x] to the
Corner Gate.[y] 39 The measuring line will
stretch from there straight to the hill of
Gareb and then turn to Goah. 40 The whole
valley[z] where dead bodies[a] and ashes are
thrown, and all the terraces out to the Kidron Valley[b] on the east as far as the corner
of the Horse Gate,[c] will be holy[d] to the
LORD. The city will never again be uprooted or demolished."

31:35 [r] Jer 10:16 **31:36** [s] Isa 54:9-10; Jer 33:20-26 [t] Ps 89:36-37 **31:37** [u] Jer 33:22 [v] Jer 33:24-26; Ro 11:1-5 **31:38** [w] Jer 30:18 [x] Ne 3:1 [y] 2Ki 14:13; Zec 14:10 **31:40** [z] Jer 7:31-32 [a] Jer 8:2 [b] 2Sa 15:23; Jn 18:1 [c] 2Ki 11:16 [d] Joel 3:17; Zec 14:21 **32:1** [e] 2Ki 25:1 [f] Jer 25:1; 39:1 **32:2** [g] Ne 3:25; Jer 37:21 **32:3** [h] Jer 26:8-9 [i] ver 28; Jer 34:2-3 **32:4** [j] Jer 38:18, 23; 39:5-7; 52:9 **32:5** [k] Jer 39:7; Eze 12:13

Jeremiah Buys a Field

32 This is the word that came to Jeremiah from the LORD in the tenth[e]
year of Zedekiah king of Judah, which
was the eighteenth[f] year of Nebuchadnezzar. 2 The army of the king of Babylon was
then besieging Jerusalem, and Jeremiah
the prophet was confined in the courtyard
of the guard[g] in the royal palace of Judah.
3 Now Zedekiah king of Judah had imprisoned him there, saying, "Why do you
prophesy[h] as you do? You say, 'This is
what the LORD says: I am about to give
this city into the hands of the king of Babylon, and he will capture[i] it. 4 Zedekiah
king of Judah will not escape[j] the Babylonians[a] but will certainly be given into
the hands of the king of Babylon, and will
speak with him face to face and see him
with his own eyes. 5 He will take[k] Zedekiah to Babylon, where he will remain until
I deal with him, declares the LORD. If you

[a] 4 Or *Chaldeans*; also in verses 5, 24, 25, 28, 29 and 43

31:37 While Yahweh is capable of measuring the heavens (see note on Isa 40:12) and is intimately familiar with the foundations of the earth, these are beyond the reach of any human endeavor. The various creation epics from Mesopotamia (the Atrahasis epic, the *Enuma Elish*) describe the establishment of the heavens and the earth, the ordering of the universe and the charges given to each god to regulate his/her sphere of influence. Thus the knowledge of the heavens and the nether regions belongs only to the divine. There is no instance in which any human succeeds in quests to gain such knowledge (the heroes Gilgamesh and Adapa come the closest, but they are limited by their mortality). The mysteries and prerogatives of election are exclusive to Yahweh just as the mysteries and prerogatives of the cosmos are.

31:38 – 40 These verses are a kind of description of the boundaries of Jerusalem. It is suggested that these reflect the boundaries as they existed in Nehemiah's time, though there is no scholarly consensus as to the extent of Nehemiah's Jerusalem.

31:38 *Tower of Hananel.* Seems to have been located at the northwest corner of the temple complex. This probably is the area where the Babylonians breached the fortifications to enter into the city. This tower was later replaced by the Antonia Fortress of Herod. *Corner Gate.* On the west or northwest side of the city. It was probably located about 180 yards (165 meters) west of the Ephraim Gate and thus at approximately the same place where the present Jaffa Gate is situated. This means that here we have the rebuilding of the northwest side of the city.

31:39 *hill of Gareb … turn to Goah.* In this description of the boundaries of Jerusalem (see note on vv. 38 – 40), the walking tour takes us counterclockwise toward the south. The exact locations of the two hills mentioned here are not known. Given the information we do have, Gareb is probably on the southwest and Goah on the southeast of the city. This places Goah somewhere in the Valley of Ben Hinnom (see notes on 7:31; 19:2).

31:40 *Kidron Valley.* See note on 2Ki 23:4. *Horse Gate.* On the east wall of the city and therefore toward the northern end of the Kidron Valley. There is some doubt as to whether this gate was situated directly east of the southeast corner of the temple complex, or whether it was farther south. It is presumed that horses would have come through this gate into the palace. This is also the gate where Athaliah was killed (2Ki 11:16).

32:1 *tenth year of Zedekiah … eighteenth year of Nebuchadnezzar.* Once again we face a difficult chronological problem (see note on 25:1). We have already explained the different dating systems used in the ancient Near East and how Israel seems to have changed its custom under Babylonian rule (see note on 26:1). By means of synchronistic chronology it seems likely that the 10th year of Zedekiah and the 18th year of Nebuchadnezzar is 587 BC. It must be admitted that difficulties remain in trying to solve the chronological mysteries present in the ancient Near Eastern dating systems.

32:2 *besieging Jerusalem.* The siege of Jerusalem is described in detail in chs. 37 – 38. The mention of the siege here probably refers to the final siege begun in February, 587 BC. The initial siege may have started as early as 588. However, Egypt attempted a final attack against Babylon in order to curb Babylon's invasion and thus forced a temporary lifting of the siege on Jerusalem. Once the Babylonians effectively controlled this Egyptian resurgence, they pressed fully against Jerusalem. The city fell about a year later. *courtyard of the guard.* Situated within the premises of the king's palace. Jeremiah is in protective custody but enjoys a great degree of freedom. He is able to conduct a business transaction (i.e., the purchase of property), preach and receive visitors. These quarters are much more comfortable than the vaulted cell in a dungeon (see note on 37:16) or the empty cistern (see note on 38:6) — confinement situations that Jeremiah later experiences.

fight against the Babylonians, you will not
succeed.' "[l]
[6]Jeremiah said, "The word of the LORD
came to me: [7]Hanamel son of Shallum
your uncle is going to come to you and
say, 'Buy my field at Anathoth, because as
nearest relative it is your right and duty[m]
to buy it.'
[8]"Then, just as the LORD had said, my
cousin Hanamel came to me in the courtyard of the guard and said, 'Buy my field
at Anathoth in the territory of Benjamin.

32:5 [l]Jer 21:4
32:7 [m]Lev 25:24-25; Ru 4:3-4; Mt 27:10*

32:7 *Anathoth.* See note on 1:1. *as nearest relative it is your right and duty to buy it.* According to Israelite law, land belonged to the family and was not to be bought or sold as an investment commodity. We do not know for sure why Jeremiah's cousin Hanamel is forced to sell his property. He no doubt belongs to the same priestly family as Jeremiah. Hanamel may have become poor because of the political and economic conditions in Judah at this time. But he may have wanted to get rid of property since at this time it would have little value because of the Babylonian siege. Regardless of the reason, a next of kin has the privilege and duty of buying the property so that it remains in the extended family (Lev 25:25 – 31; see note on Lev 25:25). We suspect that Hanamel first offers it to other family members, who have first rights, but they decide not to purchase land under Babylonian control. When it is offered to Jeremiah, he immediately becomes what is known in Biblical tradition as the "redeemer." He "redeems" the land so that it will remain in the family. Needless to say, this is a ridiculous time to buy property. But the prophet of God follows through with his responsibility as a member of the covenant community.
32:8 *courtyard of the guard.* See note on v. 2.

JEREMIAH 32:10

Title Deeds in the Ancient Near East

In the ancient Near East, two copies of a deed were written up on papyrus or parchment. A single sheet was used — the top half for the main copy and the bottom half for the duplicate copy. The top half was rolled, signed, sealed and designated as "the sealed deed of purchase." The copy (the bottom half) was kept open so that it could be used for future reference if needed. The sealing was done as a precautionary measure so that the original deed could not be altered or tampered with, and thus there could be no questions regarding the original text.

The practice of writing up duplicate copies is illustrated by documents found at Elephantine in Egypt. These documents come from the fifth century BC and are written in Aramaic and Greek by members of a Jewish community that settled there after Jerusalem was destroyed by the Babylonians.

In transactions in Ugarit from the fourteenth to twelfth centuries BC, many land purchases followed the same procedure seen in Jer 32. Witnesses were present at the signing and the document was sealed. ◆

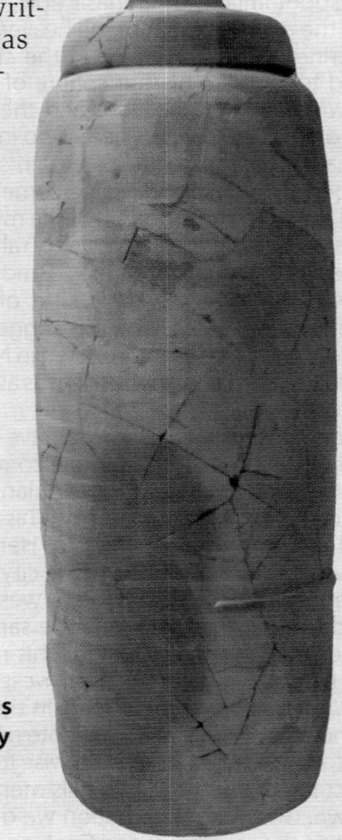

Pottery jar from Qumran. Baruch (Jer 32:12) was to place the sealed and unsealed deeds in a clay jar, similar to this one.

Kim Walton. The Oriental Institute Museum, University of Chicago.

Since it is your right to redeem it and possess it, buy it for yourself.'
"I knew that this was the word of the
LORD; 9so I bought the field at Anathoth
from my cousin Hanamel and weighed
out for him seventeen shekels[a] of silver.[n]
10I signed and sealed the deed, had it witnessed,[o] and weighed out the silver on the
scales. 11I took the deed of purchase — the
sealed copy containing the terms and conditions, as well as the unsealed copy —
12and I gave this deed to Baruch[p] son of
Neriah,[q] the son of Mahseiah, in the presence of my cousin Hanamel and of the
witnesses who had signed the deed and
of all the Jews sitting in the courtyard of
the guard.
13"In their presence I gave Baruch these
instructions: 14'This is what the LORD Almighty, the God of Israel, says: Take these
documents, both the sealed and unsealed
copies of the deed of purchase, and put
them in a clay jar so they will last a long
time. 15For this is what the LORD Almighty,
the God of Israel, says: Houses, fields and
vineyards will again be bought in this
land.'[r]
16"After I had given the deed of purchase to Baruch son of Neriah, I prayed
to the LORD:

17"Ah, Sovereign LORD,[s] you have
made the heavens and the earth by
your great power and outstretched
arm.[t] Nothing is too hard[u] for you.
18You show love[v] to thousands but
bring the punishment for the parents'
sins into the laps of their children[w]
after them. Great and mighty God,
whose name is the LORD Almighty,[x]
19great are your purposes and mighty
are your deeds.[y] Your eyes are open
to the ways of all mankind;[z] you reward each person according to their
conduct and as their deeds deserve.[a]
20You performed signs and wonders
in Egypt[b] and have continued them to
this day, in Israel and among all mankind, and have gained the renown
that is still yours. 21You brought your
people Israel out of Egypt with signs
and wonders, by a mighty hand[c] and
an outstretched arm and with great
terror.[d] 22You gave them this land you
had sworn to give their ancestors, a
land flowing with milk and honey.[e]
23They came in and took possession[f]
of it, but they did not obey you or follow your law;[g] they did not do what
you commanded them to do. So you
brought all this disaster[h] on them.
24"See how the siege ramps are
built up to take the city. Because of
the sword, famine and plague,[i] the
city will be given into the hands of
the Babylonians who are attacking it.
What you said[j] has happened, as you
now see. 25And though the city will
be given into the hands of the Babylonians, you, Sovereign LORD, say
to me, 'Buy the field with silver and
have the transaction witnessed.'"

26Then the word of the LORD came to
Jeremiah: 27"I am the LORD, the God of all
mankind.[k] Is anything too hard for me?
28Therefore this is what the LORD says: I
am about to give this city into the hands
of the Babylonians and to Nebuchadnezzar[l] king of Babylon, who will capture it.[m]
29The Babylonians who are attacking this
city will come in and set it on fire; they
will burn it down,[n] along with the houses[o]

32:9 [n] Ge 23:16 **32:10** [o] Ru 4:9 **32:12** [p] ver 16; Jer 36:4; 43:3,6; 45:1 [q] Jer 51:59 **32:15** [r] ver 43-44; Jer 30:18; Am 9:14-15 **32:17** [s] Jer 1:6 [t] 2Ki 19:15; Ps 102:25 [u] Mt 19:26 **32:18** [v] Dt 5:10 [w] Ex 20:5 [x] Jer 10:16 **32:19** [y] Isa 28:29 [z] Pr 5:21; Jer 16:17 [a] Jer 17:10; Mt 16:27 **32:20** [b] Ex 9:16 **32:21** [c] Ex 6:6; 1Ch 17:21; Da 9:15 [d] Dt 26:8 **32:22** [e] Ex 3:8; Jer 11:5 **32:23** [f] Ps 44:2; 78:54-55 [g] Ne 9:26; Jer 11:8 [h] Da 9:14 **32:24** [i] Jer 14:12 [j] Dt 4:25-26; Jos 23:15-16 **32:27** [k] Nu 16:22 **32:28** [l] 2Ch 36:17 [m] ver 3 **32:29** [n] 2Ch 36:19; Jer 21:10; 37:8,10; 52:13 [o] Jer 19:13

[a] 9 That is, about 7 ounces or about 200 grams

32:9 *weighed out.* Balances to measure weights were used early in the development of civilization. Archaeological excavations reveal that the Egyptians developed balances and used them much more than did the Mesopotamians. These balances originally consisted of two pans suspended by cords from a beam that in turn was suspended by a cord in its center. These were then improved by placing a standard in the center. Before coinage was introduced in the mid-seventh century BC in Asia Minor, monetary value was determined by weighing ingots or scraps of precious metals on these balances. *seventeen shekels of silver.* During the seventh century BC, silver was used in the ancient Near East as a mode of payment. An average Israelite shekel weighed about 11.5 grams (0.4 ounces). Thus, the price of Hanamel's field was approximately 200 grams (7 ounces) of silver. This would be the equivalent of about a year and a half of income for the regular laborer. We should not speculate on the price of the land purchased. We do not know current values of property, nor do we know the size of the field Jeremiah purchases. Presumably land values would have been depressed because of the siege against Jerusalem and its imminent destruction.

32:10 *signed and sealed the deed.* A land transaction was basically carried out in four steps: writing the document, signature of witnesses, sealing the document and storing the document. (On ancient deeds, see the article "Title Deeds in the Ancient Near East," p. 1278.) Baruch, the scribe, was to place the sealed and unsealed deeds in a clay jar (vv. 11 – 14); this would serve somewhat as a modern safety deposit box. This storage custom is illustrated by the many documents found near Qumran. The well-known Dead Sea Scrolls were stored in clay jars. In addition, these leather scrolls were wrapped in linen cloth for further protection.

32:12 *Baruch son of Neriah, the son of Mahseiah.* This is the first mention of Baruch in Jeremiah (see note on 36:4). Here his responsibilities are to write, tie up and seal Jeremiah's deed of purchase, and then protect it by placing it in a clay jar.

32:22 *flowing with milk and honey.* See notes on 11:5; Ex 3:8.

32:24 *siege ramps.* See the article "Siege Warfare," p. 1157.

32:29 *burning incense on the roofs.* See note on 19:13.

where the people aroused my anger by
burning incense on the roofs to Baal and
by pouring out drink offerings[p] to other
gods.
30"The people of Israel and Judah have
done nothing but evil in my sight from
their youth;[q] indeed, the people of Israel have done nothing but arouse my anger[r] with what their hands have made,[s]
declares the LORD. 31From the day it was
built until now, this city has so aroused
my anger and wrath that I must remove[t]
it from my sight. 32The people of Israel
and Judah have provoked me by all the
evil[u] they have done — they, their kings
and officials, their priests and prophets,
the people of Judah and those living in
Jerusalem. 33They turned their backs[v] to
me and not their faces; though I taught[w]
them again and again, they would not listen or respond to discipline. 34They set up
their vile images in the house that bears
my Name and defiled[x] it. 35They built
high places for Baal in the Valley of Ben
Hinnom to sacrifice their sons and daughters to Molek,[y] though I never commanded — nor did it enter my mind[z] — that they
should do such a detestable thing and so
make Judah sin.
36"You are saying about this city, 'By the
sword, famine and plague[a] it will be given
into the hands of the king of Babylon'; but
this is what the LORD, the God of Israel,
says: 37I will surely gather[b] them from all
the lands where I banish them in my furious anger and great wrath; I will bring
them back to this place and let them live
in safety.[c] 38They will be my people,[d] and
I will be their God. 39I will give them singleness[e] of heart and action, so that they
will always fear me and that all will then
go well for them and for their children after them. 40I will make an everlasting covenant[f] with them: I will never stop doing
good to them, and I will inspire them to
fear me, so that they will never turn away
from me.[g] 41I will rejoice in doing them
good[h] and will assuredly plant[i] them in
this land with all my heart and soul.
42"This is what the LORD says: As I have
brought all this great calamity on this people, so I will give them all the prosperity I
have promised[j] them. 43Once more fields
will be bought[k] in this land of which you
say, 'It is a desolate waste, without people or animals, for it has been given into
the hands of the Babylonians.' 44Fields will
be bought for silver, and deeds[l] will be
signed, sealed and witnessed in the territory of Benjamin, in the villages around Jerusalem, in the towns of Judah and in the
towns of the hill country, of the western
foothills and of the Negev,[m] because I will
restore[n] their fortunes,[a] declares the LORD."

Promise of Restoration

33 While Jeremiah was still confined
in the courtyard[o] of the guard, the
word of the LORD came to him a second
time: 2"This is what the LORD says, he who
made the earth,[p] the LORD who formed it
and established it — the LORD is his name:[q]
3'Call[r] to me and I will answer you and tell
you great and unsearchable things you do
not know.' 4For this is what the LORD, the
God of Israel, says about the houses in this
city and the royal palaces of Judah that
have been torn down to be used against
the siege[s] ramps[t] and the sword 5in the
fight with the Babylonians[b]: 'They will be
filled with the dead bodies of the people
I will slay in my anger and wrath.[u] I will
hide my face[v] from this city because of all
its wickedness.
6" 'Nevertheless, I will bring health and
healing to it; I will heal my people and
will let them enjoy abundant peace and
security. 7I will bring Judah[w] and Israel back from captivity[c][x] and will rebuild
them as they were before.[y] 8I will cleanse[z]
them from all the sin they have committed

32:29 [p] Jer 44:18
32:30 [q] Jer 22:21 [r] Jer 8:19 [s] Jer 25:7
32:31 [t] 2Ki 23:27; 24:3
32:32 [u] Isa 1:4-6; Da 9:8
32:33 [v] Jer 2:27; Eze 8:16 [w] Jer 7:13
32:34 [x] Jer 7:30
32:35 [y] Lev 18:21 [z] Jer 7:31; 19:5
32:36 [a] ver 24
32:37 [b] Jer 23:3,6 [c] Dt 30:3; Eze 34:28
32:38 [d] Jer 24:7; 2Co 6:16*
32:39 [e] Eze 11:19
32:40 [f] Isa 55:3 [g] Jer 24:7
32:41 [h] Dt 30:9 [i] Jer 24:6; 31:28; Am 9:15
32:42 [j] Jer 31:28
32:43 [k] ver 15
32:44 [l] ver 10 [m] Jer 17:26 [n] Jer 33:7, 11, 26
33:1 [o] Jer 32:2-3; 37:21; 38:28
33:2 [p] Jer 10:16 [q] Ex 3:15; 15:3
33:3 [r] Isa 55:6; Jer 29:12
33:4 [s] Eze 4:2 [t] Jer 32:24; Hab 1:10
33:5 [u] Jer 21:4-7 [v] Isa 8:17
33:7 [w] Jer 32:44 [x] Jer 30:3; Am 9:14 [y] Isa 1:26
33:8 [z] Heb 9:13-14

[a] 44 Or *will bring them back from captivity*
[b] 5 Or *Chaldeans*
[c] 7 Or *will restore the fortunes of Judah and Israel*

32:35 *sacrifice their sons and daughters.* See notes on 7:31; Lev 20:2; 1Ki 11:5; 2Ki 3:27; 16:3.

33:4 – 5 The Hebrew text of these verses is difficult to understand, partly because of technical terms not common in the Hebrew Bible. Whatever we may say regarding these verses will be provisional and based on some archaeological discoveries, particularly at Lachish and Jerusalem.

It was common at this time to build houses either into the wall of the city or right next to it. It is known that those who lived "in the wall" were generally the poor people, who by default lived in the most dangerous and vulnerable place of the city. In this context one can suggest that these houses were considered by the powerful in the city to be "disposable," so that they were torn down to defend against the siege ramps built up by the enemy on the outside of the city wall (see the article "Siege Warfare," p. 1157). It may well be the case that some of these houses were also used as army barracks, makeshift hospitals and burial places. Most burial places were outside of the city, but the enemy had control of the surroundings at this point.

Evidence from excavations at Lachish suggests that a counter-ramp was built inside the city in order to strengthen the walls against the Assyrian ramp constructed outside the city wall. This inside ramp was about 120 yards (110 meters) long and rose up over the original wall to a height of 3 yards (2.75 meters). Excavations at Jerusalem also suggest that the Babylonians built a siege ramp on the eastern slope that overlooked the Kidron Valley. The Babylonians probably availed themselves of precarious houses built on the outside terraces of the city wall.

against me and will forgive[a] all their sins
of rebellion against me. 9Then this city will
bring me renown, joy, praise[b] and honor[c]
before all nations on earth that hear of all
the good things I do for it; and they will be
in awe and will tremble at the abundant
prosperity and peace I provide for it.'

10"This is what the LORD says: 'You say
about this place, "It is a desolate waste,
without people or animals."[d] Yet in the
towns of Judah and the streets of Jerusalem that are deserted, inhabited by neither
people nor animals, there will be heard
once more 11the sounds of joy and gladness,[e] the voices of bride and bridegroom,
and the voices of those who bring thank
offerings[f] to the house of the LORD, saying,

"Give thanks to the LORD Almighty,
for the LORD is good;[g]
his love endures forever."[h]

For I will restore the fortunes of the land
as they were before,' says the LORD.

12"This is what the LORD Almighty says:
'In this place, desolate[i] and without people or animals—in all its towns there will
again be pastures for shepherds to rest their
flocks.[j] 13In the towns of the hill country,
of the western foothills and of the Negev,[k]
in the territory of Benjamin, in the villages
around Jerusalem and in the towns of Judah, flocks will again pass under the hand[l]
of the one who counts them,' says the LORD.

14" 'The days are coming,' declares the
LORD, 'when I will fulfill the good prom-
ise[m] I made to the people of Israel and
Judah.

15" 'In those days and at that time
I will make a righteous[n] Branch[o]
sprout from David's line;
he will do what is just and right in
the land.
16In those days Judah will be saved[p]
and Jerusalem will live in safety.
This is the name by which it[a] will be
called:
The LORD Our Righteous Savior.'[q]

17For this is what the LORD says: 'David
will never fail[r] to have a man to sit on the
throne of Israel, 18nor will the Levitical[s]
priests ever fail to have a man to stand
before me continually to offer burnt offerings, to burn grain offerings and to present
sacrifices.[t]' "

19The word of the LORD came to Jeremiah: 20"This is what the LORD says: 'If you
can break my covenant with the day[u] and
my covenant with the night, so that day
and night no longer come at their appointed time, 21then my covenant[v] with David
my servant—and my covenant with the
Levites who are priests ministering before me—can be broken and David will
no longer have a descendant to reign on
his throne.[w] 22I will make the descendants
of David my servant and the Levites who
minister before me as countless[x] as the
stars in the sky and as measureless as the
sand on the seashore.' "

23The word of the LORD came to Jeremiah: 24"Have you not noticed that these
people are saying, 'The LORD has rejected the two kingdoms[b][y] he chose'? So they
despise[z] my people and no longer regard
them as a nation.[a] 25This is what the LORD
says: 'If I have not made my covenant with
day and night[b] and established the laws of
heaven and earth,[c] 26then I will reject[d] the
descendants of Jacob[e] and David my servant and will not choose one of his sons
to rule over the descendants of Abraham,
Isaac and Jacob. For I will restore their fortunes[c][f] and have compassion on them.' "

Warning to Zedekiah

34 While Nebuchadnezzar king of
Babylon and all his army and all
the kingdoms and peoples[g] in the empire
he ruled were fighting against Jerusalem[h]
and all its surrounding towns, this word
came to Jeremiah from the LORD: 2"This is
what the LORD, the God of Israel, says: Go
to Zedekiah[i] king of Judah and tell him,
'This is what the LORD says: I am about
to give this city into the hands of the king
of Babylon, and he will burn it down.[j]
3You will not escape from his grasp but

33:8 a Jer 31:34; Mic 7:18; Zec 13:1 **33:9** b Jer 13:11 c Isa 62:7; Jer 3:17 **33:10** d Jer 32:43 **33:11** e Isa 51:3 f Lev 7:12 g 1Ch 16:8; Ps 136:1 h 1Ch 16:34; 2Ch 5:13; Ps 100:4-5 **33:12** i Jer 32:43 j Isa 65:10; Eze 34:11-15 **33:13** k Jer 17:26 l Lev 27:32 **33:14** m Jer 29:10 **33:15** n Ps 72:2 o Isa 4:2; 11:1; Jer 23:5 **33:16** p Isa 45:17 q 1Co 1:30 **33:17** r 2Sa 7:13; 1Ki 2:4; Ps 89:29-37; Lk 1:33 **33:18** s Dt 18:1 t Heb 13:15 **33:20** u Ps 89:36 **33:21** v Ps 89:34 w 2Ch 7:18 **33:22** x Ge 15:5 **33:24** y Eze 37:22 z Ne 4:4 a Jer 30:17 **33:25** b Jer 31:35-36 c Ps 74:16-17 **33:26** d Jer 31:37 e Isa 14:1 f ver 7 **34:1** g Jer 27:7 h 2Ki 25:1; Jer 39:1 **34:2** i 2Ch 36:11 j ver 22; Jer 32:29; 37:8

[a] 16 Or *he* [b] 24 Or *families* [c] 26 Or *will bring them back from captivity*

33:13 *towns of the hill country.* They provide a panoramic view of the land (see note on 17:26).
33:15 *Branch.* See note on 23:5.
34:1–7 It is difficult to date precisely the events narrated in vv. 1–7. Obviously a siege on Jerusalem is in process. One chronology suggests that the siege began as early as the summer of 588 BC. But it is also possible that it did not begin until 587. Another matter to consider is whether the events here happen before the Egyptian advance against the Babylonian army, which caused a temporary lifting of the siege, or after this reprieve for Jerusalem (see note on 32:2). The best one can suggest, based on the tenor of the passage, is that these events take place toward the end of the siege when Zedekiah and the people of Jerusalem are getting desperate.
34:1 *all the kingdoms ... were fighting against Jerusalem.* Babylon had conquered many nations by this time. It was customary for a victor to obligate the defeated nations to sign a treaty whereby they would lend military help to the sovereign nation whenever it was needed (see note on Dt 6:5). It is evident in this text that Nebuchadnezzar had enlisted support from all his vassal kings to fight against Jerusalem. Jerusalem by itself did not stand a chance against such a powerful enemy force.

will surely be captured and given into his
hands.[k] You will see the king of Babylon
with your own eyes, and he will speak
with you face to face. And you will go to
Babylon.
4"'Yet hear the LORD's promise to you,
Zedekiah king of Judah. This is what the
LORD says concerning you: You will not
die by the sword; 5you will die peacefully.
As people made a funeral fire[l] in honor
of your predecessors, the kings who ruled
before you, so they will make a fire in
your honor and lament, "Alas,[m] master!"
I myself make this promise, declares the
LORD.'"

34:3 [k] 2Ki 25:7; Jer 21:7; 32:4
34:5 [l] 2Ch 16:14; 21:19 [m] Jer 22:18
34:7 [n] Jos 10:3 [o] Jos 10:10; 2Ch 11:9
34:8 [p] 2Ki 11:17 [q] Ex 21:2; Lev 25:10,39-41; Ne 5:5-8

6Then Jeremiah the prophet told all this
to Zedekiah king of Judah, in Jerusalem,
7while the army of the king of Babylon
was fighting against Jerusalem and the
other cities of Judah that were still holding
out — Lachish[n] and Azekah.[o] These were
the only fortified cities left in Judah.

Freedom for Slaves

8The word came to Jeremiah from the
LORD after King Zedekiah had made a covenant with all the people[p] in Jerusalem to
proclaim freedom[q] for the slaves. 9Every-
one was to free their Hebrew slaves, both
male and female; no one was to hold a

34:5 *funeral fire.* This funeral rite must not be confused with cremation of a body, nor is this burning done in order to mask odors coming from a diseased or partially decayed body. The practice described here may be associated with a custom that can be archaeologically corroborated from around the middle of the eighth century BC. It involved the building of an artificial mound over the ground (called a tumulus). This tumulus was shaped like a truncated cone with a flat top and steep slopes. The ones found and excavated on the ridges west of Jerusalem were 20 feet (6 meters) high and 150 feet (45.7 meters) in diameter. It seems as if these tumuli were used to burn incense and perfumes as a ritual that accompanied the body's internment. This was done most likely to honor the wealthy and royalty. It was also practiced among the Assyrian kings (see note on 2Ch 16:14).

34:7 *Lachish.* One of the most important cities in Judah during the seventh and early sixth centuries BC. It was one of two fortified cities that guarded the Shephelah (lowlands) border. See notes on 2Ki 14:19; 18:14. *Azekah.* A fortress city much like Lachish. The site is located about 11 miles (17.7 kilometers) north of Lachish and 18 miles (29 kilometers) southwest of Jerusalem.

34:8 *proclaim freedom for the slaves.* King Zedekiah (597 – 586 BC) initiates a covenant with the inhabitants of Judah in which he proclaims the release of all Hebrew slaves. Initially one is tempted to associate this action with the Jubilee Year release legislated in Lev 25:39 – 46 (or the Sabbatical Year release legislated in Ex 21:2 – 6; Dt 15:2 – 3). Though this may be true, it is also possible that this release during the Babylonian siege is intended to add numbers to the army in this time of national emergency. Slaves were normally not drafted into the army. Releasing them under conditions of siege made them eligible for being drafted. In an interesting letter from Mari dated to about 1765 BC, King Hammurapi declares the general release of slaves and merchants in order to strengthen his army when Babylon is under enemy attack.

Aerial view of Lachish.

Relief of the siege of Lachish.

fellow Hebrew in bondage.[r] [10]So all the officials and people who entered into this
covenant agreed that they would free their
male and female slaves and no longer hold
them in bondage. They agreed, and set
them free. [11]But afterward they changed
their minds and took back the slaves they
had freed and enslaved them again.
[12]Then the word of the LORD came to
Jeremiah: [13]"This is what the LORD, the
God of Israel, says: I made a covenant
with your ancestors[s] when I brought them
out of Egypt, out of the land of slavery.
I said, [14]'Every seventh year each
of you must free any fellow Hebrews who have sold themselves
to you. After they have served
you six years, you must let them
go free.'[a][t] Your ancestors, however, did not listen to me or pay
attention[u] to me. [15]Recently you
repented and did what is right in
my sight: Each of you proclaimed
freedom to your own people.[v]
You even made a covenant before me in the house that bears
my Name.[w] [16]But now you have
turned around[x] and profaned[y]
my name; each of you has taken
back the male and female slaves
you had set free to go where they
wished. You have forced them to
become your slaves again.
[17]"Therefore this is what the
LORD says: You have not obeyed
me; you have not proclaimed
freedom to your own people. So I
now proclaim 'freedom' for you,[z]
declares the LORD — 'freedom'
to fall by the sword, plague and
famine. I will make you abhorrent
to all the kingdoms of the earth.[a]
[18]Those who have violated my
covenant and have not fulfilled
the terms of the covenant they
made before me, I will treat like
the calf they cut in two and then
walked between its pieces.[b] [19]The
leaders of Judah and Jerusalem,
the court officials,[c] the priests and all the
people of the land who walked between
the pieces of the calf, [20]I will deliver[d] into
the hands of their enemies who want to
kill them.[e] Their dead bodies will become
food for the birds and the wild animals.[f]
[21]"I will deliver Zedekiah[g] king of Judah and his officials[h] into the hands of
their enemies who want to kill them, to

34:9 [r]Lev 25:39-46 **34:13** [s]Ex 24:8 **34:14** [t]Ex 21:2 [u]Dt 15:12; 2Ki 17:14 **34:15** [v]ver 8 [w]Jer 7:10-11; 32:34 **34:16** [x]Eze 3:20; 18:24 [y]Ex 20:7; Lev 19:12 **34:17** [z]Mt 7:2; Gal 6:7 [a]Dt 28:25,64; Jer 29:18

[a] *14* Deut. 15:12

34:18 [b]Ge 15:10 **34:19** [c]Zep 3:3-4 **34:20** [d]Jer 21:7 [e]Jer 11:21 [f]Dt 28:26; Jer 7:33; 19:7 **34:21** [g]Jer 32:4 [h]Jer 39:6; 52:24-27

34:14 *Every seventh year each of you must free any fellow Hebrews.* While this text seems to refer specifically to the Sabbatical Year legislation present in the Torah (Ex 21:2–6; Dt 15:2–3), which is different from the Jubilee Year (Lev 25:39–55), we cannot be sure of the connection between these two regulations in the Torah. In the Sabbatical Year legislation, any Hebrew slave who works for a period of six years is eligible to be freed in the seventh year. Note too that Zedekiah's proclamation of freedom in the previous verses does not seem to be connected to the Sabbatical Year because he proclaims freedom for all slaves during the same year, irrespective of the number of years they have worked as slaves.

34:18 *the calf they cut in two.* The ritual of severing an animal's body as part of a covenant-making ceremony is found only here and in Ge 15:9–10 (see the article "Ratifying the Covenant," p. 42). Ancient Near Eastern parallels from the Old Babylonian Mari letters and the eighth-century BC Aramaic text of the Sefire Treaty between Abban and Yarimlim both describe cutting an animal in two. The symbolic aspect of this type of sacrifice is to provide a graphic picture of what would happen to the covenant breaker. When the landowners of Judah took back their debt-slaves after the Egyptian invasion had temporarily lifted the siege of Jerusalem, they broke their solemn oath to Yahweh and laid themselves open to horrendous punishment.

34:21 *army of the king of Babylon, which has withdrawn*

the army of the king of Babylon, which
has withdrawn[i] from you. 22I am going to
give the order, declares the LORD, and I
will bring them back to this city. They will
fight against it, take[j] it and burn[k] it down.
And I will lay waste the towns of Judah so
no one can live there."

The Rekabites

35 This is the word that came to Jeremiah from the LORD during the
reign of Jehoiakim[l] son of Josiah king of
Judah: 2"Go to the Rekabite[m] family and
invite them to come to one of the side
rooms[n] of the house of the LORD and give
them wine to drink."
3So I went to get Jaazaniah son of Jeremiah, the son of Habazziniah, and his
brothers and all his sons — the whole family of the Rekabites. 4I brought them into
the house of the LORD, into the room of the
sons of Hanan son of Igdaliah the man of
God.[o] It was next to the room of the officials, which was over that of Maaseiah son
of Shallum[p] the doorkeeper.[q] 5Then I set
bowls full of wine and some cups before
the Rekabites and said to them, "Drink
some wine."
6But they replied, "We do not drink
wine, because our forefather Jehonadab[a][r]
son of Rekab gave us this command: 'Neither you nor your descendants must ever
drink wine.[s] 7Also you must never build
houses, sow seed or plant vineyards; you
must never have any of these things, but
must always live in tents.[t] Then you will
live a long time in the land[u] where you
are nomads.' 8We have obeyed everything our forefather[v] Jehonadab son of
Rekab commanded us. Neither we nor
our wives nor our sons and daughters
have ever drunk wine 9or built houses to
live in or had vineyards, fields or crops.[w]
10We have lived in tents and have fully
obeyed everything our forefather Jehonadab commanded us. 11But when Nebuchadnezzar king of Babylon invaded[x] this
land, we said, 'Come, we must go to Jerusalem[y] to escape the Babylonian[b] and
Aramean armies.' So we have remained
in Jerusalem."
12Then the word of the LORD came to Jeremiah, saying: 13"This is what the LORD Almighty, the God of Israel, says: Go and tell
the people of Judah and those living in Jerusalem, 'Will you not learn a lesson[z] and
obey my words?' declares the LORD. 14'Jehonadab son of Rekab ordered his descendants not to drink wine and this command
has been kept. To this day they do not drink
wine, because they obey their forefather's
command. But I have spoken to you again
and again,[a] yet you have not obeyed[b] me.
15Again and again I sent all my servants
the prophets[c] to you. They said, "Each of
you must turn[d] from your wicked ways and
reform[e] your actions; do not follow other
gods to serve them. Then you will live in
the land[f] I have given to you and your ancestors." But you have not paid attention
or listened[g] to me. 16The descendants of Jehonadab son of Rekab have carried out the
command their forefather[h] gave them, but
these people have not obeyed me.'
17"Therefore this is what the LORD God
Almighty, the God of Israel, says: 'Listen!
I am going to bring on Judah and on everyone living in Jerusalem every disaster[i]
I pronounced against them. I spoke to
them, but they did not listen;[j] I called to
them, but they did not answer.' "[k]
18Then Jeremiah said to the family of
the Rekabites, "This is what the LORD Almighty, the God of Israel, says: 'You have
obeyed the command of your forefather
Jehonadab and have followed all his instructions and have done everything he
ordered.' 19Therefore this is what the LORD
Almighty, the God of Israel, says: 'Jehonadab son of Rekab will never fail[l] to have a
descendant to serve[m] me.' "

Jehoiakim Burns Jeremiah's Scroll

36 In the fourth year of Jehoiakim[n]
son of Josiah king of Judah, this
word came to Jeremiah from the LORD:

34:21 [i] Jer 37:5 **34:22** [j] Jer 39:1-2 [k] Jer 39:8 **35:1** [l] 2Ch 36:5 **35:2** [m] 2Ki 10:15; 1Ch 2:55 [n] 1Ki 6:5 **35:4** [o] Dt 33:1 [p] 1Ch 9:19 [q] 2Ki 12:9 **35:6** [r] 2Ki 10:15 [s] Lev 10:9; Nu 6:2-4; Lk 1:15 **35:7** [t] Heb 11:9 [u] Ex 20:12; Eph 6:2-3 **35:8** [v] Pr 1:8; Col 3:20 **35:9** [w] 1Ti 6:6 **35:11** [x] 2Ki 24:1 [y] Jer 8:14

35:13 [z] Jer 6:10; 32:33 **35:14** [a] Jer 7:13; 25:3 [b] Isa 30:9 **35:15** [c] Jer 7:25 [d] Jer 26:3 [e] Isa 1:16-17; Jer 4:1; 18:11; Eze 18:30 [f] Jer 25:5 [g] Jer 7:26 **35:16** [h] Mal 1:6 **35:17** [i] Jos 23:15; Jer 21:4-7 [j] Pr 1:24; Ro 10:21 [k] Isa 65:12; 66:4; Jer 7:13 **35:19** [l] Jer 33:17 [m] Jer 15:19 **36:1** [n] 2Ch 36:5

[a] *6* Hebrew *Jonadab*, a variant of *Jehonadab*; here and often in this chapter [b] *11* Or *Chaldean*

from you. This certainly refers to the Egyptian incursion into Canaan in order to limit Babylon's power in the area. The Babylonians are forced to lift the siege temporarily (see note on 37:5), but Jerusalem's fate is sealed.
35:2 *one of the side rooms of the house of the LORD.* The temple was surrounded by an outside construction on three sides — a building that had three slight stories alongside three of the walls of the temple. The lower story was similar to the rooms that flanked certain temples in Egypt and Mesopotamia. This building was under the jurisdiction of the Levitical priests (1Ch 23:27 – 28). These chambers were living and working quarters for priests who were responsible for different functions within the temple. *give them wine.* We can surmise that Jeremiah takes the Rekabites to the room of the sons of Hanan (v. 4) because that is where they store the wine.
35:11 *Aramean armies.* In the eleventh to ninth centuries BC, the Arameans were present all along the Euphrates from Babylon to Carchemish. As such they posed a constant problem to the Assyrian Empire. During the time of Jeremiah, the Aramean army was under the control of Nebuchadnezzar and had to support the Babylonian king's needs. Shortly after Nebuchadnezzar's rise to power in Babylon, he moved into Syria practically unopposed to exact tribute and to punish rebellious towns and territories.
36:1 *fourth year of Jehoiakim.* Coincides with Nebuchadnezzar's first year, which places the writing of the scroll (v. 2) in 605 BC. This year was a critical one for the entire

JEREMIAH 35

The Rekabite Family

What we know about the clan of the Rekabites comes only from this text. According to the information here, they formed a kind of subculture within the Israelite society, and they claimed to be following the instructions of their ancestor Jehonadab son of Rekab. This ancestor was a zealous supporter of Jehu, who had invited Rekab to witness the final extermination of Ahab's royal house and the violent purge of Baal worship (2Ki 10:15 – 27). One Biblical source traces their origins to the Kenites (1Ch 2:55), which in turn leads us to the possibility that they were originally a guild of craftsmen dedicated to working with metal.

For many years scholars assumed, based on Jer 35, that the Rekabites lived a nomadic or seminomadic life free from alcohol. According to the instructions of Jehonadab, the Rekabites were not to build houses but had to live in tents — rules that seem to constitute the essence of nomadism. In this sense they would indeed be considered a subculture in that there was generally conflict between those who chose a nomadic or seminomadic lifestyle and those who chose a more settled existence based on an agricultural way of life.

More recently, however, scholars have offered alternative suggestions as to the lifestyle of the Rekabites. Some of the suggestions are:

1. They actually resided in permanent settlements in the hills of Judah.
2. They were a guild of itinerant craftsmen who made chariots and weaponry.
3. They were prophets who linked up with the itinerant lifestyle of Elijah.

In the final analysis, whether the Rekabites were a nomadic group or not, this is not what concerns Jeremiah. The prophet does not appeal to them because he endorses their lifestyle. Rather, he presents them as an example of true obedience and faithfulness. They have shown that they have been much more obedient and faithful to their ancestor Jehonadab than Judah has been to Yahweh.

This is why Jeremiah lifts them up as an example for Judah. The Rekabites receive a promise from Jeremiah (Jer 35:19), and it is worthy of note that a descendant of the Rekabites is mentioned as one who helps in the rebuilding of Jerusalem (Ne 3:14). This may or may not be evidence that the Rekabites survive the Babylonian exile. ◆

2 "Take a scroll[o] and write on it all the
words I have spoken to you concerning Israel, Judah and all the other nations from
the time I began speaking to you in the
reign of Josiah[p] till now. 3 Perhaps[q] when
the people of Judah hear[r] about every
disaster I plan to inflict on them, they will
each turn[s] from their wicked ways; then
I will forgive[t] their wickedness and their
sin."

36:2 [o] Ex 17:14; Jer 30:2; Hab 2:2 [p] Jer 1:2; 25:3 **36:3** [q] ver 7; Eze 12:3 [r] Mk 4:12 [s] Jer 26:3; Jnh 3:8; Ac 3:19 [t] Jer 18:8

ancient Near East. In this year, just before his accession to the throne, Nebuchadnezzar decisively defeated Pharaoh Necho II and the Egyptian army at Carchemish. The balance of power in the region shifted in favor of the Babylonians, and this opened the way for Babylon to begin subjugating Syria and Palestine (2Ki 24:7). During 604 BC, presumably the year when the scroll was read, Nebuchadnezzar demanded submission and tribute of all the states in Syria and Palestine. Apparently, the only city that rebelled was Ashkelon. This rebellion cost Ashkelon more than it ever imagined. Its citizens had hoped to get support from Egypt, but that never materialized. The Philistine city was defeated and utterly destroyed. It became a heap of ruins (Jer 47:5 – 7). There is archaeological evidence that the city was thoroughly burned, and a complete skeleton of one of the victims was found lying amid the burned debris. By 592 BC a number of exiled skilled laborers from Ashkelon were living and working in Babylon. These events certainly had an effect on the inhabitants of Judah, and it is in the midst of this context that Jeremiah dictates the material that is to be copied onto a scroll by the scribe Baruch.

36:2 *Take a scroll and write.* This is the only time that

JEREMIAH 36:2

Scrolls in the Ancient World

Scrolls in the ancient world were generally made of parchment or papyrus. Parchment was made of animal skins processed so that they became adequate writing materials. A papyrus scroll was made from the stalk of a papyrus plant, an aquatic plant common in Egypt. Papyrus was being used in Egypt from around 3000 BC. The dry climate in Egypt favored the preservation of papyri documents. This was not the case in Israel, however, where the climate was detrimental to the preservation of papyri.

In Mesopotamia the preferred medium was a clay tablet. These tablets could be preserved by firing them in an oven. Many have survived the aggressive climate conditions of Mesopotamia because enemies set fire to the cities where they were stored and thereby preserved them.

The oldest Hebrew papyrus found thus far is a document that can be dated to the late eighth or early seventh century BC. It was found near Wadi Murabba'at, which is in the vicinity of the Dead Sea. It must be remembered that most of the Dead Sea Scrolls discovered in the vicinity of the famous settlement called Qumran were written on parchment. Both papyri and parchment were expensive writing materials.

Jeremiah informs us of the practice of using a scribe to inscribe prophecies on either papyrus or parchment. In Jer 36 Jeremiah dictates the contents of the prophecy to a professional scribe named Baruch. We cannot know for sure whether Jeremiah used papyrus or parchment for writing material. ◆

MUR 17, the earliest Hebrew papyrus found, seventh century BC.

Courtesy Israel Antiquities Authority; Photographer: Shai Halevi

4So Jeremiah called Baruch[u] son of Neriah, and while Jeremiah dictated[v] all the
words the LORD had spoken to him, Baruch wrote them on the scroll.[w] 5Then Jeremiah told Baruch, "I am restricted; I am
not allowed to go to the LORD's temple.
6So you go to the house of the LORD on a
day of fasting[x] and read to the people from
the scroll the words of the LORD that you
wrote as I dictated. Read them to all the
people of Judah who come in from their
towns. 7Perhaps they will bring their petition before the LORD and will each turn[y]
from their wicked ways, for the anger[z] and
wrath pronounced against this people by
the LORD are great."
8Baruch son of Neriah did everything
Jeremiah the prophet told him to do; at
the LORD's temple he read the words of the
LORD from the scroll.
9In the ninth month[a]
of the fifth year of Je-
hoiakim son of Josiah
king of Judah, a time
of fasting[b] before the
LORD was proclaimed
for all the people in Jerusalem and those
who had come from the towns of Judah.
10From the room of Gemariah son of Shaphan the secretary,[c] which was in the upper courtyard at the entrance of the New
Gate[d] of the temple, Baruch read to all the
people at the LORD's temple the words of
Jeremiah from the scroll.
11When Micaiah son of Gemariah, the
son of Shaphan, heard all the words of the
LORD from the scroll, 12he went down to
the secretary's room in the royal palace,
where all the officials were sitting: Elishama the secretary, Delaiah son of Shemaiah, Elnathan[e] son of Akbor, Gemariah son
of Shaphan, Zedekiah son of Hananiah,
and all the other officials. 13After Micaiah
told them everything he had heard Baruch
read to the people from the scroll, 14all the
officials sent Jehudi[f] son of Nethaniah, the
son of Shelemiah, the son of Cushi, to say
to Baruch, "Bring the scroll from which
you have read to the people and come." So
Baruch son of Neriah went to them with
the scroll in his hand. 15They said to him,
"Sit down, please, and read it to us."

36:4 [u] Jer 32:12 [v] ver 18 [w] Eze 2:9 **36:6** [x] ver 9 **36:7** [y] Jer 26:3 [z] Dt 31:17 **36:9** [a] ver 22 [b] 2Ch 20:3 **36:10** [c] Jer 52:25 [d] Jer 26:10 **36:12** [e] Jer 26:22 **36:14** [f] ver 21

Wooden scribal palette, sixteenth century BC, with two wells containing red and black pigment. The slot for pens is grooved to allow insertion of the cover, only part of which remains.

the Hebrew Bible talks about the process of writing prophetic words on a scroll. These words are intended for public reading. We cannot be sure whether this is the first time that Jeremiah's words are recorded on a scroll. Most of his proclamations, as well as those of other Hebrew prophets, were first issued orally. The final process of when and how the words of the prophets are committed to writing is still a matter of debate. The Hebrew text here uses two words for what is translated "scroll." This may be a technical term that designates a special kind of scroll. We can assume that this scroll is made either of pasted papyrus or sewn skins, both of which were used for writing in Israel at this time (see note on 30:2; see also the article "Scrolls in the Ancient World," p. 1286). This kind of scroll may have been used only for important documents.

36:4 *Baruch.* Jeremiah employs the services of a professional scribe named Baruch. This person has traditionally been considered a scribe of importance, perhaps even a royal scribe. His seal impression has been found among bullae belonging to royal officials. Based on this finding, it is assumed that Baruch was an official scribe and not simply Jeremiah's personal scribe. The Jewish historian Josephus writes that Baruch came from a distinguished family and was a capable scribe who knew his native tongue well.

36:6 *a day of fasting.* We have no evidence that in preexilic times in Israel there were any fixed days of fasting, with the possible exception of the Day of Atonement (cf. Lev 16:29,31). Any days of public fasting during Jeremiah's time, then, were the result of specific situations that merited such a practice. Fasts in the ancient Near East could be called in the face of national emergencies such as a military defeat or threat, the death of a king, a plague, a drought or a military siege. Thus, the reason for an upcoming public fast day here is most likely the military incursion of Babylonian forces in the region of Judah. Jeremiah chooses such a day since he can expect a bigger audience and perhaps a more receptive one because of the fear of military attack.

36:9 *ninth month.* The month Kislev, which corresponds to our November–December. *fifth year of Jehoiakim.* 604 BC. If this is the time when a public fast is called for, the reason may have been the devastating attack Nebuchadnezzar carried out against Ashkelon (see note on v. 1). This would signal a terrible threat to Jerusalem, and it would be natural for a public fast of mourning to be held at this time.

36:10 *the room of … the secretary, which was in the upper courtyard at the entrance of the New Gate.* The various rooms that surrounded the temple served different functions (see note on 35:2). This verse provides a lot of detail, though the exact locations of the secretary's room, the upper courtyard, and the New Gate are still unknown. According to some, the New Gate was perhaps located to the south of the inner court of the temple, which served as a connection to the royal residence. As to the secretary's room one can speculate that it led to the "great court" since it was from that room that Baruch reads Jeremiah's scroll in the hearing of all the people.

So Baruch read it to them. [16]When they
heard all these words, they looked at each
other in fear and said to Baruch, "We must
report all these words to the king." [17]Then
they asked Baruch, "Tell us, how did you
come to write all this? Did Jeremiah dictate it?"
[18]"Yes," Baruch replied, "he dictated[g] all
these words to me, and I wrote them in
ink on the scroll."
[19]Then the officials said to Baruch, "You
and Jeremiah, go and hide.[h] Don't let anyone know where you are."
[20]After they put the scroll in the room of
Elishama the secretary, they went to the
king in the courtyard and reported everything to him. [21]The king sent Jehudi[i] to get
the scroll, and Jehudi brought it from the
room of Elishama the secretary and read
it to the king[j] and all the officials standing
beside him. [22]It was the ninth month and
the king was sitting in the winter apartment,[k] with a fire burning in the firepot
in front of him. [23]Whenever Jehudi had
read three or four columns of the scroll,
the king cut them off with a scribe's knife
and threw them into the firepot, until the
entire scroll was burned in the fire.[l] [24]The
king and all his attendants who heard all
these words showed no fear,[m] nor did they
tear their clothes.[n] [25]Even though Elnathan, Delaiah and Gemariah urged the king
not to burn the scroll, he would not listen
to them. [26]Instead, the king commanded
Jerahmeel, a son of the king, Seraiah son
of Azriel and Shelemiah son of Abdeel to
arrest[o] Baruch the scribe and Jeremiah the
prophet. But the LORD had hidden[p] them.

36:18 [g] ver 4
36:19 [h] 1Ki 17:3
36:21 [i] ver 14
[j] 2Ki 22:10
36:22
[k] Am 3:15
36:23 [l] 1Ki 22:8
36:24 [m] Ps 36:1
[n] Ge 37:29; 2Ki 22:11; Isa 37:1
36:26
[o] Mt 23:34
[p] Jer 15:21

[27]After the king burned the scroll containing the words that Baruch had written
at Jeremiah's dictation,[q] the word of the
LORD came to Jeremiah: [28]"Take another
scroll and write on it all the words that
were on the first scroll, which Jehoiakim
king of Judah burned up. [29]Also tell Jehoiakim king of Judah, 'This is what the
LORD says: You burned that scroll and said,
"Why did you write on it that the king of
Babylon would certainly come and destroy
this land and wipe from it[r] both man and
beast?" [30]Therefore this is what the LORD
says about Jehoiakim king of Judah: He
will have no one to sit on the throne of David; his body will be thrown out[s] and exposed to the heat by day and the frost by
night. [31]I will punish him and his children
and his attendants for their wickedness;
I will bring on them and those living in
Jerusalem and the people of Judah every
disaster[t] I pronounced against them, because they have not listened.'"
[32]So Jeremiah took another scroll and
gave it to the scribe Baruch son of Neriah,
and as Jeremiah dictated,[u] Baruch wrote[v]
on it all the words of the scroll that Jehoiakim king of Judah had burned[w] in the
fire. And many similar words were added
to them.

Jeremiah in Prison

37 Zedekiah[x] son of Josiah was made
king[y] of Judah by Nebuchadnezzar
king of Babylon; he reigned in place of Jehoiachin[a][z] son of Jehoiakim. [2]Neither he
nor his attendants nor the people of the

36:27 [q] ver 4
36:29
[r] Isa 30:10
36:30
[s] Jer 22:19
36:31 [t] Pr 29:1
36:32 [u] ver 4
[v] Ex 34:1
[w] ver 23
37:1 [x] 2Ki 24:17
[y] Eze 17:13
[z] 2Ki 24:8, 12; 2Ch 36:10; Jer 22:24

[a] 1 Hebrew *Koniah,* a variant of *Jehoiachin*

36:16 *We must report all these words to the king.* Prophecies that represented a threat to the kingdom had to be brought to the king's attention, but that is not a job that anyone would want to do. Excavations at Mari, a city on the Euphrates, have brought to light archives that contain numerous examples of oracular speech that date from the eighteenth century BC. If the prophecies proclaimed by the prophets at Mari had implications for state affairs, they were written on clay tablets and reported to the king. This document was often accompanied by a hem of the prophet's clothing to serve as a kind of guarantee of authenticity. Once again the role of the scribe was critical. He was the one who wrote down the message received by the prophet through a dream or some ecstatic experience.
36:22 *firepot.* The Hebrew term seems to be an Egyptian loanword that means "brazier." This kind of stove was a common feature in the king's palace. There were two kinds, one made out of clay and the other made out of metal. The ones in the palace were probably made out of metal. This brazier would be a convenient instrument for burning a scroll.
36:23 *columns.* The Hebrew word usually means "door" and is also used for a manuscript column in one of the Lachish letters. The origin of this transfer of meaning from "door" to "column" in a scroll may come from writing boards. A group of 16 writing boards made out of ivory were found in the Assyrian city of Nimrud from the Neo-Assyrian period (750–625 BC). Such boards were hinged pieces of hard material (here ivory, but often wood) that open and shut like a book. Inside were shallow compartments filled with wax for writing. Thus each side of the writing board that would contain a column of writing was like a door. *scroll.* It was likely made out of papyrus rather than animal skin parchment. A king would not likely have endured the strong odor of burning animal skin. *scribe's knife.* A small knife used for cutting papyri. In this case the knife most likely belongs to Jehudi. *until the entire scroll was burned in the fire.* Upon hearing the words of Jeremiah written on the scroll, the king of Judah becomes upset. He does not like what he hears. In Hebrew culture words are considered to have the power to bring things to pass. By eliminating the words, by burning them in a ritual of sorts, King Jehoiakim seeks to annul the reality that the text proclaims. It is interesting to compare this with the warnings in the vassal treaties of Esarhaddon, king of Assyria (681–669 BC). There are severe instructions to the vassals with respect to the clay tablets on which the treaty stipulations are written. Any attempt to destroy them and thus nullify the agreement would activate a curse.
36:30 *his body will be thrown out and exposed.* See note on 22:19.
37:1 *Zedekiah . . . was made king of Judah by Nebuchadnez-*

land paid any attention[a] to the words the
LORD had spoken through Jeremiah the
prophet.
3King Zedekiah, however, sent Jehukal
son of Shelemiah with the priest Zephaniah[b] son of Maaseiah to Jeremiah the
prophet with this message: "Please pray[c]
to the LORD our God for us."
4Now Jeremiah was free to come and
go among the people, for he had not yet
been put in prison.[d] 5Pharaoh's army had
marched out of Egypt,[e] and when the Babylonians[a] who were besieging Jerusalem
heard the report about them, they withdrew[f] from Jerusalem.[g]
6Then the word of the LORD came to
Jeremiah the prophet: 7"This is what the
LORD, the God of Israel, says: Tell the king
of Judah, who sent you to inquire[h] of me,
'Pharaoh's army, which has marched out
to support you, will go back to its own
land, to Egypt.[i] 8Then the Babylonians will
return and attack this city; they will capture it and burn[j] it down.'
9"This is what the LORD says: Do not
deceive[k] yourselves, thinking, 'The Babylonians will surely leave us.' They will
not! 10Even if you were to defeat the entire Babylonian[b] army that is attacking you
and only wounded men were left in their
tents, they would come out and burn this
city down."
11After the Babylonian army had withdrawn[l] from Jerusalem because of Pharaoh's army, 12Jeremiah started to leave the
city to go to the territory of Benjamin to
get his share of the property[m] among the
people there. 13But when he reached the
Benjamin Gate, the captain of the guard,
whose name was Irijah son of Shelemiah,
the son of Hananiah, arrested him and
said, "You are deserting to the Babylonians!"
14"That's not true!" Jeremiah said. "I
am not deserting to the Babylonians." But
Irijah would not listen to him; instead, he
arrested[n] Jeremiah and brought him to the
officials. 15They were angry with Jeremiah and had him beaten[o] and imprisoned
in the house[p] of Jonathan the secretary,
which they had made into a prison.
16Jeremiah was put into a vaulted cell
in a dungeon, where he remained a long
time. 17Then King Zedekiah sent for him

37:2 [a] 2Ki 24:19; 2Ch 36:12, 14 **37:3** [b] Jer 29:25; 52:24 [c] 1Ki 13:6; Jer 21:1-2; 42:2 **37:4** [d] ver 15; Jer 32:2 **37:5** [e] Eze 17:15 [f] Jer 34:21 [g] 2Ki 24:7 **37:7** [h] 2Ki 22:18 [i] Jer 2:36; La 4:17 **37:8** [j] Jer 34:22; 39:8 **37:9** [k] Jer 29:8 **37:11** [l] ver 5 **37:12** [m] Jer 32:9 **37:14** [n] Jer 40:4 **37:15** [o] Jer 20:2 [p] Jer 38:26

[a] *5* Or *Chaldeans*; also in verses 8, 9, 13 and 14
[b] *10* Or *Chaldean*; also in verse 11

zar. King Jehoiakim was succeeded by Jehoiachin during the Babylonian siege of Jerusalem. The city was defeated three months later in 597 BC, and his reign quickly came to an end (see note on 24:1). At this point Nebuchadnezzar places Mattaniah, Jehoiachin's uncle, on the throne. In order to further demonstrate his power and authority over Mattaniah, Nebuchadnezzar changes his name to Zedekiah (see note on 21:1). Zedekiah rules Judah under the watchful eye of Nebuchadnezzar from 597 – 586 BC, when Jerusalem is destroyed by the Babylonian army. See the article "Historical Setting of Jeremiah," p. 1222.

37:5 *they withdrew from Jerusalem.* Jerusalem is under siege by the Babylonians. In 589 BC, after the death of Psammetichus II, a new pharaoh named Apries (called Hophra in 44:30) rises to power in Egypt. This pharaoh is ambitious but totally incompetent. According to Eze 17:15, Judah sends a request to Apries early in his reign, soliciting military aid to fight off the Babylonians. This request is perhaps corroborated by one of the Lachish letters, in which there is mention of a commander from Judah who goes down to Egypt. Apries responds to this request and dispatches an army into Judah, which effectively forces the Babylonians to withdraw their suffocating siege on Jerusalem. There seems to be no record of any battle taking place between the Egyptians and Babylonians at this time. Perhaps the mere presence of the Egyptian army in Judah's territory forces the Babylonian withdrawal. There is a text, however, from the so-called annals of Nebuchadnezzar that may refer to a battle. The military conflict between Babylon and Egypt ends in a standstill, with heavy losses on both sides. This may have given Zedekiah and his people some hope. However, history tells us that it is short-lived.

37:13 *Benjamin Gate.* The location of this gate and its exact identification are still a matter of speculation. The fact that Jeremiah goes through this gate on his way to Anathoth, which is to the north-northeast of Jerusalem (see note on 1:1), suggests that this gate opens up toward the northeast. This means that it is not far from the temple courts. Some scholars identify this gate with the Gate of the People (see 17:19 and note), the gate kings used. The Benjamin Gate has been identified with different gates mentioned in postexilic texts, such as the Inspection Gate (Ne 3:31) and the Sheep Gate (Ne 3:32). Others identify it with the Upper Gate of Benjamin (Jer 20:2). What we can say is that Zedekiah uses it as a place to conduct official business (38:7). See notes on Job 5:4; 29:7; Pr 8:3; 31:23.

37:15 *house … made into a prison.* Generally speaking, formal prisons were not part of the societies in the ancient Near East. This was because "prisons," understood as places of confinement, were not used to punish a person. They were merely used as places of detainment, where a person would be held until a decision was reached regarding his case. The person was either set free, put to death or left to die. Thus, "prisons" in this sense often were chambers in temples, royal palaces and private homes. Some prisoners were placed in granaries, silos or storerooms. In the Mesopotamian Hymn to Nungal, we read that a person was imprisoned in a holding cell in a temple. So-called prisons at Mari, in Mesopotamia, during the second millennium BC were not so different from regular dwelling places. These examples show us that what is stated in Jeremiah is not uncommon at all. *Jonathan the secretary.* Though we know nothing of him, we can suggest that he is a royal scribe, since he has a kind of prison right in his house.

37:16 *vaulted cell in a dungeon.* It is difficult to know exactly what this cell looked like. One of the Hebrew terms used here is rare and used only in this context in the Hebrew Bible. Presumably, from what Jeremiah says in v. 20, this was an uncomfortable and life-threatening place. Based on a comparison with the empty water cistern where Jeremiah sunk in the mud (38:6), one can

and had him brought to the palace, where
he asked[q] him privately,[r] "Is there any
word from the LORD?"
"Yes," Jeremiah replied, "you will be
delivered[s] into the hands of the king of
Babylon."
18 Then Jeremiah said to King Zedekiah,
"What crime[t] have I committed against you
or your attendants or this people, that you
have put me in prison? 19 Where are your
prophets who prophesied to you, 'The king
of Babylon will not attack you or this land'?
20 But now, my lord the king, please listen.
Let me bring my petition before you: Do
not send me back to the house of Jonathan
the secretary, or I will die there."
21 King Zedekiah then gave orders for
Jeremiah to be placed in the courtyard of
the guard and given a loaf of bread from
the street of the bakers each day until all
the bread[u] in the city was gone.[v] So Jeremiah remained in the courtyard of the
guard.[w]

Jeremiah Thrown Into a Cistern

38 Shephatiah son of Mattan, Gedaliah son of Pashhur, Jehukal[a][x] son of
Shelemiah, and Pashhur son of Malkijah
heard what Jeremiah was telling all the
people when he said, 2 "This is what the
LORD says: 'Whoever stays in this city will
die by the sword, famine or plague,[y] but
whoever goes over to the Babylonians[b]
will live. They will escape with their lives;
they will live.'[z] 3 And this is what the LORD
says: 'This city will certainly be given into
the hands of the army of the king of Babylon, who will capture it.' "[a]

4 Then the officials[b] said to the king,
"This man should be put to death.[c] He is
discouraging the soldiers who are left in
this city, as well as all the people, by the
things he is saying to them. This man is
not seeking the good of these people but
their ruin."
5 "He is in your hands," King Zedekiah
answered. "The king can do nothing to oppose you."
6 So they took Jeremiah and put him into
the cistern of Malkijah, the king's son,
which was in the courtyard of the guard.[d]
They lowered Jeremiah by ropes into the
cistern; it had no water in it, only mud,
and Jeremiah sank down into the mud.
7 But Ebed-Melek,[e] a Cushite,[c] an official[d][f] in the royal palace, heard that they
had put Jeremiah into the cistern. While
the king was sitting in the Benjamin Gate,[g]
8 Ebed-Melek went out of the palace and
said to him, 9 "My lord the king, these
men have acted wickedly in all they have
done to Jeremiah the prophet. They have
thrown him into a cistern, where he will
starve to death when there is no longer
any bread[h] in the city."
10 Then the king commanded Ebed-Melek the Cushite, "Take thirty men from
here with you and lift Jeremiah the prophet out of the cistern before he dies."
11 So Ebed-Melek took the men with
him and went to a room under the treasury in the palace. He took some old rags
and worn-out clothes from there and let

37:17 [q] Jer 15:11 [r] Jer 38:16 [s] Jer 21:7 **37:18** [t] 1Sa 26:18; Jn 10:32; Ac 25:8 **37:21** [u] Isa 33:16; Jer 38:9 [v] 2Ki 25:3; Jer 52:6 [w] Jer 32:2; 38:6, 13, 28 **38:1** [x] Jer 37:3 **38:2** [y] Jer 34:17 [z] Jer 21:9; 39:18; 45:5 **38:3** [a] Jer 21:4, 10; 32:3 **38:4** [b] Jer 36:12 [c] Jer 26:11 **38:6** [d] Jer 37:21 **38:7** [e] Jer 39:16 [f] Ac 8:27 [g] Job 29:7 **38:9** [h] Jer 37:21

[a] *1* Hebrew *Jukal,* a variant of *Jehukal* [b] *2* Or *Chaldeans;* also in verses 18, 19 and 23 [c] *7* Probably from the upper Nile region [d] *7* Or *a eunuch*

suggest that this was an underground dungeon that was part of the house. If this place was in good condition, it may have been used originally to store grain.
37:21 *a loaf of bread.* The custom of handing out a ration of bread is illustrated by an ostracon from Arad that most likely dates from the late seventh to early sixth centuries BC. That letter contains an order authorizing the commanding officer at Arad to hand out rations to the soldiers under his command. Each soldier would have received about the equivalent of one loaf of bread per day. *the street of the bakers.* It was customary in antiquity to cluster together craftsmen of the same type in defined districts or in the same quarter. This was especially true in Mesopotamia. In Israel there was a defined district where cloth was bleached (Isa 7:3) and a section for the potters (Jer 18:2; cf. 1Ki 20:34).
38:6 *the cistern . . . had no water in it, only mud.* An empty cistern during a time of enemy siege may indicate that matters are critical in Jerusalem at this time. Cisterns full of rainwater were important for the survival of the people during times of siege because people were unable to leave the city to get water from springs or wells that were usually situated outside of the city walls. Some cisterns were bottle-shaped, about three yards (2.75 meters) wide and five yards (4.5 meters) deep. They would be covered with a stone placed over the small opening at the top. Other cisterns were bell-shaped, about three yards wide (2.75 meters) and four yards (3.7 meters) deep. Still others, like the ones at Qumran, where the Dead Sea Scrolls were discovered, had steps leading into them. Cisterns could be carved out of natural rock or converted from cave formations. Some cisterns had to be lined with plaster to make them waterproof. Others were carved into what is called Cenomanian limestone, which is impermeable and therefore needed no additional treatment to hold water. Cisterns were also used to store grain and food (see note on 2:13). Jeremiah was lowered into a water cistern that was empty, but the bottom had a considerable layer of sediment turned into mud, which in and of itself was life threatening.
38:7 *Ebed-Melek.* This official's Hebrew name means "servant of the king." Having received a Hebrew name suggests the possibility that this Cushite official had come north as a slave. *official.* This Hebrew term is generally understood as "eunuch" (see note on Isa 39:7). We cannot state for sure whether this term designates Ebed-Melek's physical condition or his capacity as a royal official. *the king was sitting in the Benjamin Gate.* Legal and civil decision making in Israel took place at the city gate (see notes on Job 5:4; 29:7; Pr 8:3; 31:23). *Benjamin Gate.* See note on 37:13.

them down with ropes to Jeremiah in the cistern. 12Ebed-Melek the Cushite said to Jeremiah, "Put these old rags and worn-out clothes under your arms to pad the ropes." Jeremiah did so, 13and they pulled him up with the ropes and lifted him out of the cistern. And Jeremiah remained in the courtyard of the guard.[i]

Zedekiah Questions Jeremiah Again

14Then King Zedekiah sent for Jeremiah the prophet and had him brought to the third entrance to the temple of the LORD. "I am going to ask you something," the king said to Jeremiah. "Do not hide[j] anything from me."

15Jeremiah said to Zedekiah, "If I give you an answer, will you not kill me? Even if I did give you counsel, you would not listen to me."

16But King Zedekiah swore this oath secretly[k] to Jeremiah: "As surely as the LORD lives, who has given us breath,[l] I will neither kill you nor hand you over to those who want to kill you."[m]

17Then Jeremiah said to Zedekiah, "This is what the LORD God Almighty, the God of Israel, says: 'If you surrender to the officers of the king of Babylon, your life will be spared and this city will not be burned down; you and your family will live.[n] 18But if you will not surrender to the officers of the king of Babylon, this city will be given into the hands[o] of the Babylonians and they will burn[p] it down; you yourself will not escape[q] from them.' "

19King Zedekiah said to Jeremiah, "I am afraid[r] of the Jews who have gone over[s] to the Babylonians, for the Babylonians may hand me over to them and they will mistreat me."

20"They will not hand you over," Jeremiah replied. "Obey[t] the LORD by doing what I tell you. Then it will go well with you, and your life[u] will be spared. 21But if you refuse to surrender, this is what the LORD has revealed to me: 22All the women[v] left in the palace of the king of Judah will be brought out to the officials of the king of Babylon. Those women will say to you:

" 'They misled you and overcame
you—
those trusted friends of yours.
Your feet are sunk in the mud;
your friends have deserted you.'

23"All your wives and children[w] will be brought out to the Babylonians. You yourself will not escape from their hands but will be captured[x] by the king of Babylon; and this city will[a] be burned down."

24Then Zedekiah said to Jeremiah, "Do not let anyone know about this conversation, or you may die. 25If the officials hear that I talked with you, and they come to you and say, 'Tell us what you said to the king and what the king said to you; do not hide it from us or we will kill you,' 26then tell them, 'I was pleading with the king not to send me back to Jonathan's house[y] to die there.' "

27All the officials did come to Jeremiah and question him, and he told them everything the king had ordered him to say. So they said no more to him, for no one had heard his conversation with the king.

28And Jeremiah remained in the courtyard of the guard[z] until the day Jerusalem was captured.

The Fall of Jerusalem

39:1-10pp — 2Ki 25:1-12; Jer 52:4-16

39 This is how Jerusalem was taken: 1In the ninth year of Zedekiah king of Judah, in the tenth month, Nebuchadnezzar king of Babylon marched against Jerusalem with his whole army and laid siege[a] to it. 2And on the ninth day of the fourth month of Zedekiah's eleventh year, the city wall was broken through. 3Then all the officials[b] of the king of Babylon came

38:13 [i] Jer 37:21
38:14 [j] 1Sa 3:17
38:16 [k] Jer 37:17 [l] Isa 42:5; 57:16 [m] ver 4
38:17 [n] 2Ki 24:12; Jer 21:9
38:18 [o] ver 3; Jer 34:3 [p] Jer 37:8 [q] Jer 24:8; 32:4
38:19 [r] Isa 51:12; Jn 12:42 [s] Jer 39:9
38:20 [t] Jer 11:4 [u] Isa 55:3
38:22 [v] Jer 6:12
38:23 [w] 2Ki 25:6 [x] Jer 41:10
38:26 [y] Jer 37:15
38:28 [z] Jer 37:21; 39:14
39:1 [a] 2Ki 25:1; Jer 52:4; Eze 24:2
39:3 [b] Jer 21:4

[a] 23 Or *and you will cause this city to*

38:14 *third entrance to the temple.* This entrance to the temple in Jerusalem is mentioned only here. Its location is unknown. The most that we can suggest at this point is that it is a private place and thus can be considered as the king's private entrance into the temple.

38:23 *All your wives and children will be brought out to the Babylonians.* When a nation or city was conquered in the ancient Near East, the defeated were vulnerable to the whims and appetites of the victors. The Babylonians normally exiled the best of society, thus depriving them of their land, identity, religion and sense of worth. Others were raped, tortured and killed. There are reliefs from the time of Shalmaneser III of Assyria (858 – 824 BC) that show women and children being marched away.

39:1 *ninth year of Zedekiah.* Once again the matter of chronology is difficult (cf. notes on 25:1; 32:1). Some scholars prefer a chronology that places the beginning of the Babylonian siege in 587 BC. Other scholars argue for 588. The different dates are the result of different calendars. Some believe that at this time Judah was using the Babylonian calendar, in which a new year begins in March – April (the month of Nisan/Aviv), whereas others believe that the older Israelite calendar was still in use, in which a new year begins in September – October (the month of Tishri/Ethanim). Following the 588 BC view, the siege begins approximately in January (the month of Tebeth) of 588 BC. As to when the wall of Jerusalem is finally breached, the same chronological problems apply. But if we use 588 as the beginning of the siege, the wall is breached in July (the month of Tammuz) of 586 BC. This tragic event takes place during the 11th year of Zedekiah, which can be synchronized with the 18th year of Nebuchadnezzar.

39:3 *Middle Gate.* Mentioned only here in the Hebrew Bible. Scholars have offered numerous identifications.

Babylonian cuneiform tablet mentioning Nebo-Sarsekim, 595 BC. See note on Jer 39:3.

and took seats in the Middle Gate: Nergal-Sharezer of Samgar, Nebo-Sarsekim a chief officer, Nergal-Sharezer a high official and all the other officials of the king of Babylon.
4 When Zedekiah king of Judah and all the soldiers saw them, they fled; they left the city at night by way of the king's garden, through the gate between the two walls, and headed toward the Arabah.[a]
5 But the Babylonian[b] army pursued them and overtook Zedekiah[c] in the plains of Jericho. They captured him and took him to Nebuchadnezzar king of Babylon at Riblah[d] in the land of Hamath, where he pronounced sentence on him.
6 There at Riblah the king of Babylon slaughtered the sons of Zedekiah before his eyes and

39:5 [c] Jer 32:4 [d] 2Ki 23:33

[a] 4 Or *the Jordan Valley* [b] 5 Or *Chaldean*

Some suggest it is the same as the Fish Gate (see Ne 3:3 and note). Others identify it with a gate in the center of the city. More recent excavations conducted within the Jewish Quarter of the Old City of Jerusalem suggest that the Middle Gate was situated in the middle of the northern defense wall. If so, the Middle Gate can be seen today at the "Israelite Tower," also located in the Jewish Quarter of the Old City. This gate, which faces north, coincides with the suggestion that the Babylonian attack came from the north, as most attacks on Jerusalem did because that is where the city was most vulnerable (see note on 1:13). It is at this gate that the Babylonian officials who claim victory take their seats to send a clear signal to a defeated Judah that they are now in charge. *Nebo-Sarsekim a chief officer.* Recently (July, 2007), a very small cuneiform tablet that is stored in the British Museum seems to have shed light on this person. The tiny tablet has been dated to c. 595 BC, which is eight to nine years before the destruction of Jerusalem. The name on the tablet is written as Nabu-sharrussum-ukin, and this person is described as the "chief eunuch" of Nebuchadnezzar II, king of Babylon. The cuneiform tablet informs us that Nabu-sharrussum-ukin presented a gold offering of almost two pounds (900 grams) to a temple in Babylon. The person mentioned in this cuneiform tablet could very well be the same person that is mentioned in this verse of Jeremiah.

39:4 *they fled ... toward the Arabah.* When Zedekiah king of Judah becomes aware that the city of Jerusalem has fallen to the Babylonians, he flees the city along with his court officials. Note that Zedekiah flees from the south side of the city, most likely because the Babylonians have attacked from the north. *the king's garden.* Location unknown. *gate between the two walls.* The identity of this gate is unknown. As with other gates mentioned in Jeremiah, this one also has been identified with different gates mentioned elsewhere in the Hebrew Bible. Some have suggested this is the Fountain Gate (see Ne 2:14 and note), while others suggest the Dung Gate (see note on Ne 3:1 – 32). *between the two walls.* The double wall is most likely the result of Hezekiah's earlier construction of a second wall to protect Jerusalem against an Assyrian attack (Isa 22:9 – 11). *the Arabah.* Generally speaking, the Arabah refers to the Jordan Valley, although technically it is the rift valley that extends from the Sea of Galilee to the Gulf of Aqaba (see note on 17:6). In this case, the name designates the semidesert area south of Jericho. Zedekiah is probably hoping to cross over the Jordan River into Moab or Ammon and seek protection there.

39:5 *Riblah.* Strategically placed on the cross section of

also killed all the nobles of Judah. 7 Then he put out Zedekiah's eyes[e] and bound him with bronze shackles to take him to Babylon.[f]

8 The Babylonians[a] set fire[g] to the royal palace and the houses of the people and broke down the walls[h] of Jerusalem. 9 Nebuzaradan commander of the imperial guard carried into exile to Babylon the people who remained in the city, along with those who had gone over to him, and the rest of the people.[i] 10 But Nebuzaradan the commander of the guard left behind in the land of Judah some of the poor people, who owned nothing; and at that time he gave them vineyards and fields.

11 Now Nebuchadnezzar king of Babylon had given these orders about Jeremiah through Nebuzaradan commander of the imperial guard: 12 "Take him and look after him; don't harm[j] him but do for him whatever he asks." 13 So Nebuzaradan the commander of the guard, Nebushazban a chief officer, Nergal-Sharezer a high official and all the other officers of the king of Babylon 14 sent and had Jeremiah taken out of the courtyard of the guard.[k] They turned him over to Gedaliah son of Ahikam,[l] the son of Shaphan, to take him back to his home. So he remained among his own people.[m]

15 While Jeremiah had been confined in the courtyard of the guard, the word of the LORD came to him: 16 "Go and tell Ebed-Melek[n] the Cushite, 'This is what the LORD Almighty, the God of Israel, says: I am about to fulfill my words against this city — words concerning disaster,[o] not prosperity. At that time they will be fulfilled before your eyes. 17 But I will rescue[p] you on that day, declares the LORD; you will not be given into the hands of those you fear. 18 I will save you; you will not fall by the sword[q] but will escape with your life,[r] because you trust[s] in me, declares the LORD.' "

39:7 [e] Eze 12:13 [f] Jer 32:5 **39:8** [g] Jer 38:18 [h] Ne 1:3 **39:9** [i] Jer 40:1 **39:12** [j] Pr 16:7; 1Pe 3:13 **39:14** [k] Jer 38:28 [l] 2Ki 22:12 [m] Jer 40:5 **39:16** [n] Jer 38:7 [o] Jer 21:10; Da 9:12 **39:17** [p] Ps 41:1-2 **39:18** [q] Jer 45:5 [r] Jer 21:9; 38:2 [s] Jer 17:7 **40:2** [t] Jer 50:7 **40:3** [u] Da 9:11 [v] Dt 29:24-28; Ro 2:5-9 **40:4** [w] Ge 13:9; Jer 39:11-12 **40:5** [x] 2Ki 25:22

Jeremiah Freed

40 The word came to Jeremiah from the LORD after Nebuzaradan commander of the imperial guard had released him at Ramah. He had found Jeremiah bound in chains among all the captives from Jerusalem and Judah who were being carried into exile to Babylon. 2 When the commander of the guard found Jeremiah, he said to him, "The LORD your God decreed this disaster for this place.[t] 3 And now the LORD has brought it about; he has done just as he said he would. All this happened because you people sinned[u] against the LORD and did not obey[v] him. 4 But today I am freeing you from the chains on your wrists. Come with me to Babylon, if you like, and I will look after you; but if you do not want to, then don't come. Look, the whole country lies before you; go wherever you please."[w] 5 However, before Jeremiah turned to go,[b] Nebuzaradan added, "Go back to Gedaliah[x] son

[a] 8 Or *Chaldeans* [b] 5 Or *Jeremiah answered*

military highways that run from Egypt to Mesopotamia. Pharaoh Necho II used Riblah in 609 BC, when King Jehoahaz of Judah was brought before him and was subsequently taken away to Egypt in chains (2Ki 23:33). He also used this city as his base in preparation for the battle of Carchemish in 605 BC. Even before this time, the Assyrians had used the city as a military outpost. Nebuchadnezzar used Riblah as his military headquarters while laying siege against Jerusalem.

39:7 *put out Zedekiah's eyes.* The practice of blinding a captured enemy, as well as slaves, was relatively common in the ancient Near East. Slaves were often blinded in just one eye so that they could continue working. *bound him with bronze shackles.* The use of shackles or chains to bind prisoners is illustrated by bas-reliefs from the palace of the Assyrian king Ashurbanipal (669 – 633 BC). Egyptian prisoners are depicted being marched away from Thebes with their feet in chains and their hands tied. Samson too was bound by bronze shackles after being blinded by his Philistine enemies (Jdg 16:21).

39:9 *carried into exile.* The first (great) exile of the Jews to Babylonia occurred in 597 BC; at that time 3,023 persons were carried away (52:28). This verse narrates a second (lesser) exile, which takes place in 587/586 BC; only 832 persons are exiled to Babylonia (52:29). In 605 BC, another 745 were taken. These represent the most qualified people of Israelite society. The practice of exiling people from a defeated nation began much earlier with the Assyrian kings (see notes on 2Ki 15:29; Isa 5:13).

39:10 *the poor people ... he gave ... vineyards and fields.* The Babylonian king did not take the poor of Israelite society to Babylonia, for they were of no use to the Babylonian kingdom. And since they have no resources, they do not represent any threat to Babylon. The Babylonian king gives land to the landless of Israel and in this way begins a process of redistribution of the land.

40:1 *Ramah.* See note on 31:15. In this context, Ramah is used as a holding place for the deported prisoners from Judah. It is located on the road that leads north toward Syria and then on to Babylon.

40:5 *Gedaliah son of Ahikam, the son of Shaphan.* Nebuchadnezzar's newly appointed governor of Judah, Gedaliah, is mentioned with a double patronym. Gedaliah belongs to an important scribal family that has a longstanding relationship with Jeremiah. Shaphan was one of the persons present when the Book of the Law was found in the temple during Josiah's reform (2Ki 22:3 – 14). Shaphan's son Ahikam was instrumental in providing protection to Jeremiah when Jeremiah's life was threatened (Jer 26:24). Thus, it would only be natural for Jeremiah to live under the protection of Gedaliah, the newly appointed governor. Gedaliah sets up his headquarters at Mizpah (v. 6), the new capital of what has become a Babylonian province, since Jerusalem is now uninhabitable. At the beginning of his mandate, Gedaliah is somewhat successful at implementing a process of restoring Judah's economy and reconstructing a beaten and weakened society.

of Ahikam, the son of Shaphan, whom
the king of Babylon has appointed over
the towns of Judah, and live with him
among the people, or go anywhere else
you please."[y]
Then the commander gave him provisions and a present and let him go. 6So
Jeremiah went to Gedaliah son of Ahikam
at Mizpah[z] and stayed with him among the
people who were left behind in the land.

Gedaliah Assassinated

40:7-9; 41:1-3pp — 2Ki 25:22-26

7When all the army officers and their
men who were still in the open country
heard that the king of Babylon had appointed Gedaliah son of Ahikam as governor over the land and had put him in
charge of the men, women and children
who were the poorest[a] in the land and who
had not been carried into exile to Babylon,
8they came to Gedaliah at Mizpah[b] — Ishmael[c] son of Nethaniah, Johanan and Jonathan the sons of Kareah, Seraiah son of
Tanhumeth, the sons of Ephai the Netophathite,[d] and Jaazaniah[a] the son of the Maakathite,[e] and their men. 9Gedaliah son of
Ahikam, the son of Shaphan, took an oath
to reassure them and their men. "Do not
be afraid to serve[f] the Babylonians,[b]" he
said. "Settle down in the land and serve
the king of Babylon, and it will go well
with you.[g] 10I myself will stay at Mizpah[h]
to represent you before the Babylonians
who come to us, but you are to harvest the
wine, summer fruit and olive oil, and put
them in your storage jars, and live in the
towns you have taken over."[i]
11When all the Jews in Moab,[j] Ammon,
Edom and all the other countries heard
that the king of Babylon had left a remnant in Judah and had appointed Gedaliah son of Ahikam, the son of Shaphan,
as governor over them, 12they all came
back to the land of Judah, to Gedaliah at
Mizpah, from all the countries where they
had been scattered.[k] And they harvested
an abundance of wine and summer fruit.
13Johanan son of Kareah and all the
army officers still in the open country
came to Gedaliah at Mizpah[l] 14and said to
him, "Don't you know that Baalis king of
the Ammonites[m] has sent Ishmael son of
Nethaniah to take your life?" But Gedaliah
son of Ahikam did not believe them.
15Then Johanan son of Kareah said privately to Gedaliah in Mizpah, "Let me go
and kill Ishmael son of Nethaniah, and no
one will know it. Why should he take your
life and cause all the Jews who are gathered around you to be scattered and the
remnant of Judah to perish?"
16But Gedaliah son of Ahikam said to
Johanan son of Kareah, "Don't do such a
thing! What you are saying about Ishmael
is not true."

41 In the seventh month Ishmael[n] son
of Nethaniah, the son of Elishama,
who was of royal blood and had been one
of the king's officers, came with ten men
to Gedaliah son of Ahikam at Mizpah.
While they were eating together there,
2Ishmael[o] son of Nethaniah and the ten
men who were with him got up and struck
down Gedaliah son of Ahikam, the son of
Shaphan, with the sword, killing the one
whom the king of Babylon had appointed[p]
as governor over the land.[q] 3Ishmael also
killed all the men of Judah who were with
Gedaliah at Mizpah, as well as the Babylonian[c] soldiers who were there.
4The day after Gedaliah's assassination,
before anyone knew about it, 5eighty men
who had shaved off their beards,[r] torn

40:5 [y]Jer 39:14 **40:6** [z]Jdg 20:1; 1Sa 7:5-17 **40:7** [a]Jer 39:10 **40:8** [b]ver 13 [c]ver 14; Jer 41:1,2 [d]2Sa 23:28 [e]Dt 3:14 **40:9** [f]Jer 27:11 [g]Jer 38:20 **40:10** [h]ver 6 [i]Dt 1:39 **40:11** [j]Nu 25:1
40:12 [k]Jer 43:5 **40:13** [l]ver 8 **40:14** [m]2Sa 10:1-19; Jer 25:21; 41:10 **41:1** [n]Jer 40:8 **41:2** [o]Ps 41:9; 109:5 [p]Jer 40:5 [q]2Sa 3:27; 20:9-10 **41:5** [r]Lev 19:27

[a] 8 Hebrew *Jezaniah,* a variant of *Jaazaniah*
[b] 9 Or *Chaldeans;* also in verse 10
[c] 3 Or *Chaldean*

40:10 *harvest the wine, summer fruit and olive oil.* Jerusalem fell in July of 586 BC. This is just before grapes, olives, figs, dates and other fruits are ready to be harvested.
40:14 *Baalis king of the Ammonites.* This king appears only here in the Hebrew Bible. We know little about him. He may have been present at the Jerusalem political gathering (594–593 BC), when a number of kings got together to plan a rebellion against Babylon — a conspiracy that never materialized (see notes on 27:3; 30:14). Baalis may also have supported Gedaliah's opponents, who represented the Davidic family's claim to the throne. But perhaps he wanted to destabilize the process of reconstruction initiated in Mizpah, so that Judah would not represent any threat to Ammon in the near future. In any case, he evidently participates in a plot to kill Gedaliah, the governor Nebuchadnezzar king of Babylon has placed to rule over what remained of Judah. In recent years an Ammonite seal has been discovered at Tell el-'Umeiri that bears the name of Baalis. This site is located about eight miles (almost 13 kilometers) southwest of Amman, Jordan. This is the first extra-Biblical information available to us regarding this Ammonite king.
41:1 *seventh month.* Tishri/Ethanim, which is the equivalent to September–October. No year is given here. Though some scholars consider that the events narrated here happened three to five years after the fall of Jerusalem, others suggest it happened within the same year as the fall of the city (i.e., 586 BC). If so, then Gedaliah would have ruled only two to three months before his assassination. The month of Tishri/Ethanim is the month when the Feast of Booths was celebrated. At this time many of the inhabitants of Judah who were left behind by the Babylonians would celebrate the Festival of Tabernacles (Booths), a festival clearly associated with the agricultural life of Israel. This would have been a good time for Ishmael and his group to approach the town of Mizpah without being noticed.
41:5 *shaved off their beards, torn their clothes and cut themselves.* These are clear and common signs of mourning (see the article "Mourning," p. 828). *bringing grain offerings*

their clothes and cut themselves came
from Shechem,[s] Shiloh[t] and Samaria,[u]
bringing grain offerings and incense with
them to the house of the LORD.[v] 6Ishmael
son of Nethaniah went out from Mizpah to
meet them, weeping[w] as he went. When
he met them, he said, "Come to Gedaliah son of Ahikam." 7When they went into
the city, Ishmael son of Nethaniah and the
men who were with him slaughtered them
and threw them into a cistern. 8But ten
of them said to Ishmael, "Don't kill us!
We have wheat and barley, olive oil and
honey, hidden in a field."[x] So he let them
alone and did not kill them with the others. 9Now the cistern where he threw all
the bodies of the men he had killed along
with Gedaliah was the one King Asa[y] had
made as part of his defense[z] against Baasha[a] king of Israel. Ishmael son of Nethaniah filled it with the dead.
10Ishmael made captives of all the rest
of the people[b] who were in Mizpah — the
king's daughters along with all the others
who were left there, over whom Nebuzaradan commander of the imperial guard
had appointed Gedaliah son of Ahikam.
Ishmael son of Nethaniah took them captive and set out to cross over to the Ammonites.[c]
11When Johanan[d] son of Kareah and
all the army officers who were with him
heard about all the crimes Ishmael son of
Nethaniah had committed, 12they took all
their men and went to fight Ishmael son of
Nethaniah. They caught up with him near
the great pool[e] in Gibeon. 13When all the
people[f] Ishmael had with him saw Johanan son of Kareah and the army officers
who were with him, they were glad. 14All
the people Ishmael had taken captive at
Mizpah turned and went over to Johanan
son of Kareah. 15But Ishmael son of Nethaniah and eight of his men escaped[g] from
Johanan and fled to the Ammonites.

Flight to Egypt

16Then Johanan son of Kareah and all
the army officers who were with him led
away all the people of Mizpah who had
survived,[h] whom Johanan had recovered
from Ishmael son of Nethaniah after Ishmael had assassinated Gedaliah son of
Ahikam — the soldiers, women, children
and court officials he had recovered from
Gibeon. 17And they went on, stopping at
Geruth Kimham[i] near Bethlehem on their
way to Egypt[j] 18to escape the Babylonians.[a] They were afraid[k] of them because
Ishmael son of Nethaniah had killed Gedaliah[l] son of Ahikam, whom the king of
Babylon had appointed as governor over
the land.

42 Then all the army officers, including Johanan[m] son of Kareah and
Jezaniah[b] son of Hoshaiah, and all the
people from the least to the greatest[n] approached 2Jeremiah the prophet and said
to him, "Please hear our petition and
pray[o] to the LORD your God for this entire remnant.[p] For as you now see, though
we were once many, now only a few[q] are
left. 3Pray that the LORD your God will
tell us where we should go and what we
should do."[r]
4"I have heard you," replied Jeremiah
the prophet. "I will certainly pray[s] to the
LORD your God as you have requested; I
will tell you everything the LORD says and
will keep nothing back from you."[t]
5Then they said to Jeremiah, "May the
LORD be a true and faithful witness[u] against

41:5 [s]Ge 33:18; Jdg 9:1-57; 1Ki 12:1 [t]Jos 18:1 [u]1Ki 16:24 [v]2Ki 25:9 **41:6** [w]2Sa 3:16 **41:8** [x]Isa 45:3 **41:9** [y]1Ki 15:22; 2Ch 16:6 [z]Jdg 6:2 [a]2Ch 16:1 **41:10** [b]Jer 40:7, 12 [c]Jer 40:14 **41:11** [d]Jer 40:8 **41:12** [e]2Sa 2:13 **41:13** [f]ver 10 **41:15** [g]Job 21:30; Pr 28:17 **41:16** [h]Jer 43:4 **41:17** [i]2Sa 19:37 [j]Jer 42:14 **41:18** [k]Isa 51:12; Jer 42:16; Lk 12:4-5 [l]Jer 40:5 **42:1** [m]Jer 40:13; 41:11 [n]Jer 6:13; 44:12 **42:2** [o]Jer 36:7; Ac 8:24; Jas 5:16 [p]Isa 1:9 [q]Lev 26:22; La 1:1 **42:3** [r]Ps 86:11; Pr 3:6 **42:4** [s]Ex 8:29; 1Sa 12:23 [t]1Ki 22:14; 1Sa 3:17 **42:5** [u]Ge 31:50

[a] *18* Or *Chaldeans* [b] *1* Hebrew; Septuagint (see also 43:2) *Azariah*

and incense. With Jerusalem and its temple destroyed, it seems curious that pilgrims would be on their way to make sacrifices there. Considering the places from which these pilgrims are coming (Shechem, Shiloh and Samaria), all of which have been cultic and political centers, their journey may have overtones of an attempted restoration of Jerusalem. It may be that they even were planning to perform cultic rituals to purify the destroyed temple and thus restore its usefulness (compare the restoration by Josiah in 2Ch 34:8, see note on 2Ch 24:4–14). Considering the number of destroyed shrines throughout the ancient Near East, there must have been proscribed rituals designed to cleanse them and prepare them to be used once again. Evidence of this is found in the Assyrian annals of Esarhaddon, which describe how Marduk allowed Babylon and its temples to be destroyed and restored.

41:12 *great pool in Gibeon.* If the party is trying to get to Ammonite territory, Gibeon is in the wrong direction. The most direct way to Ammon from Mizpah does not go through Gibeon. From Mizpah one would go north to Bethel and then connect with a major road that goes east toward Jericho and the Jordan Valley. Gibeon is about three miles (4.8 kilometers) southwest of Mizpah. This means that Ishmael and his group head in almost the opposite direction of Ammon. However, Ishmael probably would try to deceive his pursuers. Furthermore, he may have been planning on taking an alternative route that goes southeast from Gibeon to Jerusalem, where he could then take the Ascent of Adumim down to the Jordan Valley. One should not expect a fugitive to follow what would be considered the most normal route.

41:17 *Geruth Kimham.* Probably the name of a small town or village located near Bethlehem. "Geruth" appears only here in the Hebrew Bible. Its exact meaning is unknown, though it most likely refers to a kind of lodging place, fief or habitation. The name of this village can presumably be traced to the Kimham of 2Sa 19:38–41, who had the honor of escorting King David across the Jordan on his way back to Jerusalem. Kimham was of the house of Barzillai, a wealthy man from Gilead. According to 1Ki 2:7 he received a royal pension. Presumably, therefore, he received a portion of land from David that was near Bethlehem. This place eventually becomes known as Geruth Kimham.

us if we do not act in accordance with everything the LORD your God sends you to tell
us. 6Whether it is favorable or unfavorable,
we will obey the LORD our God, to whom we
are sending you, so that it will go well[v] with
us, for we will obey[w] the LORD our God."
7Ten days later the word of the LORD
came to Jeremiah. 8So he called together
Johanan son of Kareah and all the army
officers[x] who were with him and all the
people from the least to the greatest. 9He
said to them, "This is what the LORD, the
God of Israel, to whom you sent me to
present your petition, says:[y] 10'If you stay
in this land, I will build[z] you up and not
tear you down; I will plant[a] you and not
uproot you,[b] for I have relented concerning the disaster I have inflicted on you.[c]
11Do not be afraid of the king of Babylon,[d]
whom you now fear.[e] Do not be afraid of
him, declares the LORD, for I am with you
and will save[f] you and deliver you from
his hands.[g] 12I will show you compassion
so that he will have compassion on you
and restore you to your land.'[h]
13"However, if you say, 'We will not
stay in this land,' and so disobey[i] the LORD
your God, 14and if you say, 'No, we will go
and live in Egypt,[j] where we will not see
war or hear the trumpet or be hungry for
bread,' 15then hear the word of the LORD,
you remnant of Judah. This is what the
LORD Almighty, the God of Israel, says: 'If
you are determined to go to Egypt and you
do go to settle there, 16then the sword[k] you
fear will overtake you there, and the famine you dread will follow you into Egypt,
and there you will die. 17Indeed, all who
are determined to go to Egypt to settle
there will die by the sword, famine and
plague;[l] not one of them will survive or
escape the disaster I will bring on them.'
18This is what the LORD Almighty, the God
of Israel, says: 'As my anger and wrath[m]
have been poured out on those who lived
in Jerusalem,[n] so will my wrath be poured
out on you when you go to Egypt. You
will be a curse[a] and an object of horror,[o] a
curse[a] and an object of reproach; you will
never see this place again.'[p]
19"Remnant of Judah, the LORD has told
you, 'Do not go to Egypt.'[q] Be sure of this:
I warn you today 20that you made a fatal mistake when you sent me to the LORD
your God and said, 'Pray to the LORD our
God for us; tell us everything he says and
we will do it.'[r] 21I have told you today, but
you still have not obeyed the LORD your
God in all he sent me to tell you.[s] 22So
now, be sure of this: You will die by the
sword, famine and plague[t] in the place
where you want to go to settle."[u]

43 When Jeremiah had finished telling the people all the words of the
LORD their God—everything the LORD had
sent him to tell them[v]— 2Azariah son of
Hoshaiah and Johanan[w] son of Kareah
and all the arrogant men said to Jeremiah,
"You are lying! The LORD our God has not
sent you to say, 'You must not go to Egypt
to settle there.' 3But Baruch son of Neriah
is inciting you against us to hand us over
to the Babylonians,[b] so they may kill us or
carry us into exile to Babylon."[x]
4So Johanan son of Kareah and all the
army officers and all the people disobeyed
the LORD's command[y] to stay in the land
of Judah.[z] 5Instead, Johanan son of Kareah and all the army officers led away all
the remnant of Judah who had come back
to live in the land of Judah from all the
nations where they had been scattered.[a]
6They also led away all those whom Nebuzaradan commander of the imperial guard
had left with Gedaliah son of Ahikam, the
son of Shaphan—the men, the women,
the children and the king's daughters. And
they took Jeremiah the prophet and Baruch son of Neriah along with them. 7So
they entered Egypt in disobedience to the
LORD and went as far as Tahpanhes.[b]

[a] *18* That is, your name will be used in cursing (see 29:22); or, others will see that you are cursed.
[b] *3* Or *Chaldeans*

42:6 [v] Dt 5:29; 6:3; Jer 7:23 [w] Ex 24:7; Jos 24:24 **42:8** [x] ver 1 **42:9** [y] 2Ki 22:15 **42:10** [z] Jer 24:6 [a] Jer 31:28 [b] Eze 36:36 [c] Jer 18:8 **42:11** [d] Jer 27:11 [e] Nu 14:9 [f] Isa 43:5 [g] Jer 1:8; Ro 8:31 **42:12** [h] Ps 106:44-46 **42:13** [i] Jer 44:16 **42:14** [j] Nu 11:4-5 **42:16** [k] Eze 11:8 **42:17** [l] ver 22; Jer 44:13 **42:18** [m] Dt 29:18-20; Jer 7:20 [n] 2Ch 36:19; Jer 39:1-9 [o] Jer 29:18 [p] Jer 22:10 **42:19** [q] Dt 17:16; Isa 30:7 **42:20** [r] ver 2 **42:21** [s] Eze 2:7; Zec 7:11-12 **42:22** [t] ver 17; Eze 6:11 [u] Hos 9:6 **43:1** [v] Jer 26:8; 42:9-22 **43:2** [w] Jer 42:1 **43:3** [x] Jer 38:4 **43:4** [y] Jer 42:5-6 [z] Jer 42:10 **43:5** [a] Jer 40:12 **43:7** [b] Jer 2:16; 44:1

42:10 *I have relented.* In the Mesopotamian epic "Erra and Ishum," Marduk abandons his shrine in Babylon to allow Erra, a destructive god, to bring judgment on the people of the city. When the destruction has been carried out, Marduk is full of grief for the city of his dwelling. Yahweh's grief is over the destruction that Jerusalem brought on herself; he is not having second thoughts, wishing that he had not acted the way that he did. There is much that is different between the Israelite and Babylonian material, but the motif of a deity grieving over destruction that he himself has brought or allowed is an element common to both. In earlier Sumerian literature, a similar motif is reflected when deities abandon a city for which the divine council has decreed destruction.

43:7 *they entered Egypt.* This event can be defined as the Egyptian Diaspora. It is generally considered to be less significant for the future of Judaism than the Babylonian Diaspora. Though perhaps a number of Israelites fled to Egypt during the Assyrian period (cf. Isa 11:11), the main settlement of Jews takes place at this time. *Tahpanhes.* See note on 2:16. Tahpanhes is a desert site bordering on the Sinai peninsula and is located about 11 miles (17.7 kilometers) west of the present-day Suez Canal. Excavations have demonstrated that its main period of occupation took place in the seventh century BC. At that time Psammetichus I (664–610 BC) placed a group of Greek mercenaries to protect the area. Because of its strategic location on the main commercial road that led to Palestine, it would be natural for a group of Judahites to settle there. According to the pseudepigraphal text known as The Lives of the Prophets, Jeremiah was stoned to death and buried at Tahpanhes.

8 In Tahpanhes[c] the word of the LORD came to Jeremiah: 9 "While the Jews are watching, take some large stones with you and bury them in clay in the brick pavement at the entrance to Pharaoh's palace in Tahpanhes. 10 Then say to them, 'This is what the LORD Almighty, the God of Israel, says: I will send for my servant[d] Nebuchadnezzar king of Babylon, and I will set his throne over these stones I have buried here; he will spread his royal canopy above them. 11 He will come and attack Egypt,[e] bringing death to those destined for death, captivity to those destined for captivity, and the sword to those destined for the sword.[f] 12 He will set fire to the temples of the gods[g] of Egypt; he will burn their temples and take their gods captive. As a shepherd picks[h] his garment clean of lice, so he will pick Egypt clean and depart. 13 There in the temple of the sun[a] in Egypt he will demolish the sacred pillars and will burn down the temples of the gods of Egypt.' "

Disaster Because of Idolatry

44 This word came to Jeremiah concerning all the Jews living in Lower Egypt—in Migdol,[i] Tahpanhes[j] and Memphis[k]—and in Upper Egypt:[l] 2 "This is what the LORD Almighty, the God of Israel, says: You saw the great disaster I brought on Jerusalem and on all the towns of Judah. Today they lie deserted and in ruins[m] 3 because of the evil they have done. They aroused my anger by burning incense to and worshiping other gods[n] that neither they nor you nor your ancestors[o] ever knew. 4 Again and again[p] I sent my servants the prophets,[q] who said, 'Do not do this detestable thing that I hate!' 5 But they did not listen or pay attention; they did not turn from their wickedness or stop burning incense to other gods.[r] 6 Therefore, my fierce anger was poured out; it raged against the towns of Judah and the streets of Jerusalem and made them the desolate ruins they are today.

7 "Now this is what the LORD God Almighty, the God of Israel, says: Why bring such great disaster[s] on yourselves by cutting off from Judah the men and women,[t] the children and infants, and so leave yourselves without a remnant? 8 Why arouse my anger with what your hands have made,[u] burning incense to other gods in Egypt, where you have come to live?[v] You will destroy yourselves and make yourselves a curse[b] and an object of reproach[w] among all the nations on earth. 9 Have you forgotten the wickedness committed by your ancestors and by the kings and queens of Judah and the wickedness committed by you and your wives in the land of Judah and the streets of Jerusalem?[x] 10 To this day they have not humbled themselves or shown reverence, nor have they followed my law[y] and the decrees I set before you and your ancestors.[z]

11 "Therefore this is what the LORD Almighty, the God of Israel, says: I am determined to bring disaster[a] on you and to destroy all Judah. 12 I will take away the

43:8 [c] Jer 2:16
43:10 [d] Isa 44:28; Jer 25:9; 27:6
43:11 [e] Jer 46:13-26; Eze 29:19-20 [f] Jer 15:2; 44:13; Zec 11:9
43:12 [g] Jer 46:25; Eze 30:13 [h] Ps 104:2; 109:18-19
44:1 [i] Ex 14:2 [j] Jer 43:7,8 [k] Isa 19:13 [l] Isa 11:11; Jer 46:14
44:2 [m] Isa 6:11; Jer 9:11; 34:22
44:3 [n] ver 8; Dt 13:6-11; 29:26 [o] Dt 32:17; Jer 19:4
44:4 [p] Jer 7:13 [q] Jer 7:25; 25:4; 26:5
44:5 [r] Jer 11:8-10
44:7 [s] Jer 26:19 [t] Jer 51:22
44:8 [u] Jer 25:6-7 [v] 1Co 10:22 [w] Jer 42:18
44:9 [x] ver 17,21
44:10 [y] Jos 1:7 [z] 1Ki 9:6-9
44:11 [a] Jer 21:10; Am 9:4

[a] 13 Or *in Heliopolis* [b] 8 That is, your name will be used in cursing (see 29:22); or, others will see that you are cursed; also in verse 12; similarly in verse 22.

43:10 *my servant Nebuchadnezzar.* See note on 25:9.
43:11 *He will come and attack Egypt.* We know little of Nebuchadnezzar's final years and possible military incursions into Egypt. Both Jeremiah and Ezekiel fully expected Babylonia to invade Egypt. There is a questionable reference to an attack against Egypt by Nebuchadnezzar in the writings of Josephus, who writes that during the 23rd year of Nebuchadnezzar (582 BC), the Babylonian king first attacked the Ammonites and Moabites, then invaded Egypt. If this indeed happened, it would have coincided approximately with the time that the Jewish group arrived at Tahpanhes. In addition to this source, there are some fragmentary Babylonian texts that suggest that in Nebuchadnezzar's 37th year (c. 568 BC) he attacked Egypt. Amasis II was the pharaoh in Egypt at this time. Scholars by and large agree that Nebuchadnezzar was not able to conquer Egypt at this time. Nevertheless, he may well have caused much damage to the military outposts populated by Jewish exiles.
43:13 *temple of the sun.* This phrase translates a Hebrew expression that normally designates a place-name. Here it obviously points toward a place in Egypt. Most agree that Jeremiah uses this term to designate the Egyptian city of Heliopolis (Biblical "On" [cf. Ge 41:45]). The site of this city is presently in a northeast suburb of Cairo. Heliopolis was the center for the worship of the sun-god Ra and an important political and cult center in Egypt. *sacred pillars.* Also called sacred stones, they were erected in Israel for a variety of reasons. They could be used as memorials to a person who had died (Ge 35:20), as a kind of marker at the entrance of a sanctuary (Ex 26:32,37), and as pagan objects of worship (Ex 23:24; see note on 1Ki 14:23). In the Egyptian context, this term refers to what is known as an "obelisk"—a sacred monument native to ancient Egypt, considered to have originated in the cult center of Heliopolis. The destruction of such a sacred object at the hands of the Babylonians would have represented a disgrace for the Egyptians.
44:1 *Migdol.* The Hebrew term has a West Semitic origin and means "tower, fortress." The Egyptians borrowed it and used it both as a noun and as a proper name. As a place-name it was used for various military outposts that served to protect Egypt's boundaries. In Jeremiah Migdol denotes an Egyptian border town that lies about 25 miles (40 kilometers) northeast of Tahpanhes (see notes on 2:16 and 43:7). *Tahpanhes.* See note on 43:7. *Memphis.* See note on 2:16. *Upper Egypt.* The Hebrew term here is *patros*, the equivalent of the Egyptian *Patoris*, meaning "South Land." It is a place-name that encompasses the area south of the delta in Upper Egypt. Assyrian texts from the time of Esarhaddon (681–669 BC) indicate that Esarhaddon conquered Egypt, Paturisi and Nubia.

remnant[b] of Judah who were determined
to go to Egypt to settle there. They will all
perish in Egypt; they will fall by the sword
or die from famine. From the least to the
greatest, they will die by sword or famine.[c]
They will become a curse and an object of
horror, a curse and an object of reproach.[d]
13 I will punish those who live in Egypt
with the sword, famine and plague,[e] as I
punished Jerusalem. 14 None of the remnant of Judah who have gone to live in
Egypt will escape or survive to return to
the land of Judah, to which they long to
return and live; none will return except a
few fugitives."[f]
15 Then all the men who knew that their
wives were burning incense to other gods,
along with all the women who were present — a large assembly — and all the people living in Lower and Upper Egypt, said
to Jeremiah, 16 "We will not listen[g] to the
message you have spoken to us in the
name of the LORD! 17 We will certainly do
everything we said we would:[h] We will
burn incense to the Queen of Heaven[i] and
will pour out drink offerings to her just
as we and our ancestors, our kings and
our officials did in the towns of Judah and
in the streets of Jerusalem. At that time
we had plenty of food and were well off
and suffered no harm.[j] 18 But ever since we
stopped burning incense to the Queen of
Heaven and pouring out drink offerings to
her, we have had nothing and have been
perishing by sword and famine.[k]"
19 The women added, "When we burned
incense to the Queen of Heaven[l] and
poured out drink offerings to her, did not
our husbands know that we were making
cakes impressed with her image and pouring out drink offerings to her?"
20 Then Jeremiah said to all the people,
both men and women, who were answering him, 21 "Did not the LORD remember[m]
and call to mind the incense[n] burned in
the towns of Judah and the streets of Jerusalem[o] by you and your ancestors,[p] your
kings and your officials and the people of
the land? 22 When the LORD could no longer endure your wicked actions and the
detestable things you did, your land became a curse[q] and a desolate waste without inhabitants, as it is today.[r] 23 Because
you have burned incense and have sinned
against the LORD and have not obeyed him
or followed his law or his decrees or his
stipulations, this disaster[s] has come upon
you, as you now see."[t]
24 Then Jeremiah said to all the people, including the women,[u] "Hear the
word of the LORD, all you people of Judah in Egypt.[v] 25 This is what the LORD Almighty, the God of Israel, says: You and
your wives have done what you said you
would do when you promised, 'We will
certainly carry out the vows we made to
burn incense and pour out drink offerings
to the Queen of Heaven.'[w]
"Go ahead then, do what you promised!
Keep your vows![x] 26 But hear the word of
the LORD, all you Jews living in Egypt: 'I
swear[y] by my great name,' says the LORD,
'that no one from Judah living anywhere
in Egypt will ever again invoke my name
or swear, "As surely as the Sovereign LORD
lives."[z] 27 For I am watching over them for
harm,[a] not for good; the Jews in Egypt
will perish by sword and famine until
they are all destroyed. 28 Those who escape the sword and return to the land of
Judah from Egypt will be very few.[b] Then
the whole remnant of Judah who came to
live in Egypt will know whose word will
stand — mine or theirs.[c]
29 " 'This will be the sign to you that I
will punish you in this place,' declares
the LORD, 'so that you will know that my
threats of harm against you will surely
stand.'[d] 30 This is what the LORD says: 'I am
going to deliver Pharaoh[e] Hophra king of
Egypt into the hands of his enemies who
want to kill him, just as I gave Zedekiah[f]

44:12 [b] ver 7 [c] Isa 1:28 [d] Jer 29:18; 42:15-18
44:13 [e] Jer 42:17
44:14 [f] ver 28; Jer 22:24-27; Ro 9:27
44:16 [g] Jer 11:8-10
44:17 [h] Dt 23:23 [i] ver 25; Jer 7:18 [j] Hos 2:5-13
44:18 [k] Mal 3:13-15
44:19 [l] Jer 7:18
44:21 [m] Isa 64:9; Jer 14:10 [n] Jer 11:13 [o] ver 9 [p] Ps 79:8
44:22 [q] Jer 25:18 [r] Ge 19:13; Ps 107:33-34
44:23 [s] Jer 40:2 [t] 1Ki 9:9; Jer 7:13-15; Da 9:11-12
44:24 [u] ver 15 [v] Jer 43:7
44:25 [w] ver 17 [x] Eze 20:39
44:26 [y] Ge 22:16; Isa 48:1; Heb 6:13-17 [z] Dt 32:40; Ps 50:16
44:27 [a] Jer 31:28
44:28 [b] ver 13-14; Isa 10:19 [c] ver 17, 25-26
44:29 [d] Pr 19:21
44:30 [e] Jer 46:26; Eze 30:21 [f] 2Ki 25:1-7

44:15 *Lower and Upper Egypt.* These geographic designations are influenced by the fact that the Nile River flows north. Hence, Upper Egypt refers to the southern portion of Egypt, whereas Lower Egypt designates the northern region that encompasses the delta all the way to the region of Memphis. In this context, the geographic location for the various Jewish settlements in Egypt is given in general terms. We can perhaps assume that places such as Memphis, Tahpanhes and Migdol are included in this description.
44:17 *Queen of Heaven.* This deity perhaps has its origin in the Babylonian-Assyrian deity Ishtar (see note on 7:18). She is known in Palestine as the goddess Asherah. Her presence in Egypt is now confirmed by an Aramaic papyrus discovered at Hermopolis in the delta region of Egypt, dated to the fifth century BC.
44:19 *When we burned incense.* See note on 19:13. In this case the Jewish women, far from being loyal to Yahweh, argue that when they worshiped the Queen of Heaven, they were well off and did not suffer hunger and violence. *incense.* See notes on 6:20; 7:9. *poured our drink offerings.* See note on 7:18. *cakes impressed with her image.* It is likely that the use of offering cakes shaped in the goddess's image is a practice borrowed from Mesopotamia, where such molds have been found. *cakes.* The Hebrew word (*kawwanim*) is a loanword from Akkadian *kamanu*, a type of sweet cake associated with the cult of Ishtar. They were baked in ashes and often were sweetened with honey or figs. The ritual texts describing *eshsheshu* festivals in Mesopotamian cities include both meat and cake offerings.
44:30 *Pharaoh Hophra king of Egypt.* "Hophra" is the Biblical name given to Pharaoh Apries (see note on 37:5) of the Twenty-Sixth (Saite) Dynasty in Egypt. Apries succeeded Psammetichus II and ruled Egypt from 589 – 570 BC. In

king of Judah into the hands of Nebuchadnezzar king of Babylon, the enemy who wanted to kill him.’ ”[g]

A Message to Baruch

45 When Baruch[h] son of Neriah wrote on a scroll the words Jeremiah the prophet dictated in the fourth year of Jehoiakim[i] son of Josiah king of Judah, Jeremiah said this to Baruch: 2“This is what the LORD, the God of Israel, says to you, Baruch: 3You said, ‘Woe to me! The LORD has added sorrow to my pain; I am worn out with groaning[j] and find no rest.’ 4But the LORD has told me to say to you, ‘This is what the LORD says: I will overthrow what I have built and uproot what I have planted,[k] throughout the earth.[l] 5Should you then seek great things for yourself? Do not seek them.[m] For I will bring disaster on all people, declares the LORD, but wherever you go I will let you escape with your life.’ ”[n]

44:30 [g] Jer 39:5 **45:1** [h] Jer 32:12; 36:4, 18, 32 [i] 2Ch 36:5 **45:3** [j] Ps 69:3 **45:4** [k] Jer 11:17 [l] Isa 5:5-7; Jer 18:7-10 **45:5** [m] Mt 6:25-27, 33 [n] Jer 21:9; 38:2; 39:18

46:1 [o] Jer 1:10; 25:15-38 **46:2** [p] 2Ki 23:29 [q] 2Ch 35:20 [r] Jer 45:1 **46:3** [s] Isa 21:5; Jer 51:11-12 **46:4** [t] Eze 21:9-11 [u] 1Sa 17:5, 38; 2Ch 26:14; Ne 4:16

A Message About Egypt

46 This is the word of the LORD that came to Jeremiah the prophet concerning the nations:[o]

2Concerning Egypt:

This is the message against the army of Pharaoh Necho[p] king of Egypt, which was defeated at Carchemish[q] on the Euphrates River by Nebuchadnezzar king of Babylon in the fourth year of Jehoiakim[r] son of Josiah king of Judah:

3“Prepare your shields,[s] both large and small,
and march out for battle!
4Harness the horses,
mount the steeds!
Take your positions
with helmets on!
Polish[t] your spears,
put on your armor![u]

Jeremiah Hophra is portrayed as the Egyptian king who opposed Nebuchadnezzar before Jerusalem fell. This resulted in a violent retaliation from the Neo-Babylonian Empire. After failing in his first attempt to thwart Babylon's advance into Palestine, Hophra led a naval operation against Phoenicia with the same purpose — to check Babylon's advance against Judah and later into Egypt. After this, he focused his efforts on setting up and maintaining the military outposts to protect Egypt. He also allowed Jewish refugees to settle at various locations in Egypt. During his final years as king, Hophra showed a sad lack of judgment. He relied too heavily on foreign mercenary troops who did not respond as he expected. Classical sources such as Herodotus and Diodorus report that Apries was assassinated in a military coup led by his successor, Amasis II, who ruled from about 570 – 526 BC. A slightly different version records that Amasis, realizing how much Apries was loathed by the people, turned Apries over to the people, who then strangled him. For possible military incursions by Nebuchadnezzar into Egypt during this time, see note on 43:11.

45:1 *fourth year of Jehoiakim.* Identified with the year 605 BC (see note on 36:1). This was an important year in terms of power shifts in the ancient Near East. It was the year when Yahweh instructed Jeremiah to write the first scroll. It was also the year that the Babylonians defeated the Egyptians at Carchemish. The Egyptians had come to the aid of the Assyrians, but they were met head-on by the Babylonians. The defeat of the Egyptians at the battle of Carchemish signaled the end of the Assyrian Empire.

46:1 *concerning the nations.* Ch. 46 begins a section in Jeremiah defined as the "Messages Against the Nations" (chs. 46 – 51). This is a distinct literary genre within the Prophets. A particular feature of such oracles against the nations is that they are rarely pronounced in the presence of the foreign nations. Furthermore, even though they are directed against the foreign nations, these oracles are primarily intended for Israelite ears.

46:2 *Pharaoh Necho.* Pharaoh Necho II was part of the Twenty-Sixth (Saite) Dynasty in Egypt (664 – 525 BC); he ruled from 610 – 595 BC. At the beginning of his rule much was changing in Mesopotamia. The powerful Assyrian Empire had suffered two deadly blows. Nineveh was defeated by the Babylonians and Medes in 612 BC, and two years later the Assyrians suffered another defeat at Harran. In light of this, Necho II decided to venture north through Palestine in order to provide help to the Assyrians. On the way he killed Josiah king of Judah at the battle of Megiddo in 609 BC (2Ch 35:20 – 24). This turned out to be a devastating blow to the inhabitants of Judah. Necho II then attempted to aid the Assyrians by establishing himself at Carchemish. However, in 605 BC, during the famous battle of Carchemish, the Babylonian army defeated the Egyptians, sending them back to Egypt. Shortly thereafter, the Babylonians continued to conquer southward until they had control over all Palestine, right to the border of Egypt.

46:3 *shields, both large and small.* Most ancient Near Eastern soldiers were armed with shields for protection. At least two types of shields were used by Israelite warriors. The small one was round and rather light. It served as a buckler, was generally held in the left hand, and was often used to protect the face. This type of shield can be seen in the Lachish relief and is frequently mentioned in the Hebrew Bible. Egyptian soldiers also used a small shield. These were rounded at the top and rectangular at the bottom. Unfortunately, most shields in the ancient Near East were made of perishable materials such as wood covered with skin or wickerwork and leather, so they have not been preserved for archaeologists to find. The larger shield could be of different shapes: rectangular, oblong or figure eight. These protected the entire body, particularly from spears, lances and arrows. They were used often in siege warfare to protect the archers. It was a heavier shield that did not allow for quick maneuverability. This meant that some foot soldiers were aided by a shield bearer, who stood by his side. There are a number of reliefs that show King Ashurbanipal of Assyria (669 – 627 BC) at war in which one can see these larger shields, both oblong and rectangular.

46:4 *Harness the horses, mount the steeds!* There is no conclusive evidence that the Egyptian army used cavalry at this time (seventh century BC). But Assyrian and Babylonian armies had been using chariots and cavalry already in the tenth century BC. There are numerous reliefs from the time of King Ashurnasirpal II (884 – 858 BC) on that depict Assyrian armies with both chariots and cavalry. By the time of Tiglath-Pileser III (745 – 727 BC), cavalry became much more important in Mesopotamian

JEREMIAH 46

Oracles Against Foreign Nations

The book of Jeremiah includes six chapters of messages that are directed to foreign nations (Jer 46 – 51). These "oracles," as far as we can determine, were never proclaimed in the presence of those nations considered to be Israel's enemies. In fact, though directed to the foreign nations, it is clear that these oracles were also intended for Israel's ears. This literary device is also present in somewhat varied forms in the literary legacy left by Mesopotamian and Egyptian "prophets" and "scribes."

In Mesopotamia we often find oracles against other nations in the form of curses. This is quite common, e.g., in the Vassal Treaties of Esarhaddon (see note on Jer 19:9), where the sovereign king promises terrible punishment and destruction against the vassal who disobeys or rebels. With respect to an oracle received through divine revelation, we have documents from Mari that date as early as the second millennium BC that illustrate this practice. One of the prophetic texts from Mari constitutes a revelation against a foreign enemy. In addition to this text, we can point to two other texts that are perhaps even more pertinent. These texts from Mari clearly contain oracles of judgment against Eshnunna. In fact the texts contain warnings against "trusting in the peacemaking of the man of Eshnunna." In another so-called prophetic text from Mari, the message is directed toward a wide geographic area including Sippar, a central Babylonian city, and Halab/Aleppo in the west.

In Egypt we have literary examples that combine the "oracle against foreign nations" with a "symbolic action report." There are texts that describe the process whereby Egyptians inscribed on pottery bowls the names of their enemies. The magical incantation that followed involved smashing the pottery bowls to pieces (see notes on Jer 19:11). There is no doubt that Jeremiah's literary text is well at home in the wider ancient Near Eastern context. ◆

[5] What do I see?
They are terrified,
they are retreating,
their warriors are defeated.
They flee[v] in haste
without looking back,
and there is terror[w] on every side,"
declares the LORD.
[6] "The swift cannot flee[x]
nor the strong escape.
In the north by the River Euphrates
they stumble and fall.[y]
[7] "Who is this that rises like the Nile,
like rivers of surging waters?[z]
[8] Egypt rises like the Nile,
like rivers of surging waters.
She says, 'I will rise and cover the earth;
I will destroy cities and their people.'
[9] Charge, you horses!
Drive furiously, you charioteers![a]
March on, you warriors — men of Cush[a]
and Put who carry shields,
men of Lydia[b] who draw the bow.

46:5 [v] ver 21 [w] Jer 49:29 **46:6** [x] Isa 30:16 [y] ver 12, 16; Da 11:19 **46:7** [z] Jer 47:2 **46:9** [a] Jer 47:3 [b] Isa 66:19

[a] *9* That is, the upper Nile region

armies. Sometime later, during the reign of Ashurbanipal (669 – 627 BC), horses were also used for hunting lions and onagers. The intensive use of cavalry may have given the Assyrians and Babylonians a decided military advantage over the Egyptians. *Take your positions with helmets on!* Helmets in the ancient Near East were usually made of leather or metal and were used as defensive headgear. Goliath wore a bronze helmet (1Sa 17:5,38). The helmets had different shapes: round, cone-shaped, and with flaps to cover the cheek and ears. Reliefs from Assyria show their warriors wearing cone-shaped helmets.

46:9 *Cush.* The Biblical name for ancient Ethiopia — an area south of Egypt that corresponds to modern-day Sudan and perhaps includes Ethiopia as well. It was inhabited by non-Egyptians. It was also identified from early times as Nubia. See note on Isa 18:1 – 7. Cush, Put and Lydia

10 But that day[c] belongs to the Lord, the
LORD Almighty—
a day of vengeance, for vengeance
on his foes.
The sword will devour[d] till it is
satisfied,
till it has quenched its thirst with
blood.
For the Lord, the LORD Almighty, will
offer sacrifice[e]
in the land of the north by the River
Euphrates.

11 "Go up to Gilead and get balm,[f]
Virgin[g] Daughter Egypt.
But you try many medicines in vain;
there is no healing[h] for you.
12 The nations will hear of your shame;
your cries will fill the earth.
One warrior will stumble over
another;
both will fall[i] down together."

13 This is the message the LORD spoke to
Jeremiah the prophet about the coming of
Nebuchadnezzar king of Babylon to attack
Egypt:[j]

14 "Announce this in Egypt, and proclaim
it in Migdol;
proclaim it also in Memphis and
Tahpanhes:[k]
'Take your positions and get ready,
for the sword devours those around
you.'
15 Why will your warriors be laid low?
They cannot stand, for the LORD will
push them down.[l]
16 They will stumble[m] repeatedly;
they will fall[n] over each other.
They will say, 'Get up, let us go back
to our own people and our native
lands,
away from the sword of the
oppressor.'
17 There they will exclaim,
'Pharaoh king of Egypt is only a loud
noise;
he has missed his opportunity.[o]'

18 "As surely as I live," declares the
King,[p]
whose name is the LORD Almighty,
"one will come who is like Tabor[q]
among the mountains,
like Carmel[r] by the sea.
19 Pack your belongings for exile,[s]
you who live in Egypt,
for Memphis will be laid waste
and lie in ruins without inhabitant.

20 "Egypt is a beautiful heifer,
but a gadfly is coming
against her from the north.[t]
21 The mercenaries[u] in her ranks
are like fattened calves.
They too will turn and flee[v] together,
they will not stand their ground,
for the day[w] of disaster is coming upon
them,
the time for them to be punished.
22 Egypt will hiss like a fleeing serpent
as the enemy advances in force;
they will come against her with axes,
like men who cut down trees.

46:10 [c] Joel 1:15 [d] Dt 32:42 [e] Zep 1:7 **46:11** [f] Jer 8:22 [g] Isa 47:1 [h] Jer 30:13; Mic 1:9 **46:12** [i] Isa 19:4; Na 3:8-10 **46:13** [j] Isa 19:1 **46:14** [k] Jer 43:8 **46:15** [l] Isa 66:15-16 **46:16** [m] Lev 26:37 [n] ver 6 **46:17** [o] Isa 19:11-16 **46:18** [p] Jer 48:15 [q] Jos 19:22 [r] 1Ki 18:42 **46:19** [s] Isa 20:4 **46:20** [t] ver 24; Jer 47:2 **46:21** [u] 2Ki 7:6 [v] ver 5 [w] Ps 37:13

represent mercenary contingents who participated in the Egyptian army and thus served as reminders of past political and military events in Egypt's history. A Nubian named Shabako founded the Nubian (Cushite) dynasty (eighth to seventh centuries BC), also known as the Twenty-Fifth Dynasty in Egypt. The third king of that dynasty (Tirhakah) sent an army to aid Hezekiah in his struggle against Sennacherib king of Assyria (704–681 BC). This surge in power is perhaps the reason why Cush receives a prominent place in this message for Egypt. *Put.* Its identity cannot be known with certainty, but it is generally identified as Libya on the basis of the translation of Put in the Septuagint (the pre-Christian Greek translation of the OT) and in the Vulgate, as well as Old Persian inscriptions. Put and Cush are listed in the table of nations in Ge 10 as sons of Ham and brothers of Egypt (Ge 10:6). *Lydia.* Identified with the Ludites of Ge 10:13. We suggest that Lydia here refers to the Lydia in Asia Minor. History tells us that Psammetichus of the Egyptian Saite Dynasty received help from Gyges, king of Lydia, to resist the Assyrian army during the first half of the seventh century BC. Since then, Lydian mercenaries were present in Egypt.

46:11 *Go up to Gilead and get balm.* See note on 8:22.

46:13 *Nebuchadnezzar ... to attack Egypt.* See note on 43:11.

46:14 *Migdol.* See note on 44:1. *Memphis.* See note on 2:16. *Tahpanhes.* See note on 43:7.

46:18 *Tabor.* This important mountain is located in the northeast corner of the Jezreel Valley, which is the southern limit of lower Galilee. Mount Tabor's importance lay mainly in its location. Placed on the edge of the Jezreel Valley, it was a constant witness to north-south commercial and military movements. When the Egyptians fled south after being defeated by the Babylonians, they most likely passed through the Jezreel Valley and therefore were in full view of Mount Tabor. *Carmel.* This mountain is located on the Mediterranean Sea just to the west of the present port of Haifa. See note on 1Ki 18:19.

46:19 *Memphis.* See note on 2:16.

46:20 *gadfly.* The Hebrew term is used only here in the Hebrew Bible. It is generally understood to designate a horsefly or gadfly (*Tabanus bovinus*). A Ugaritic cognate verb means "to gnaw, bite, rip off." Thus, this insect seems to be one that stings cattle, since Egypt is described as a "heifer" in the previous line. Babylon is compared to a gadfly that will come from the north to bite, sting and inflict injury on Egypt.

46:22 *like men who cut down trees.* The image conveyed here is one of destruction. The enemy from the north comes with axes to destroy not only a forest but also the nation. Assyrian bas-reliefs show chariots that carried up to four soldiers armed with bows, arrows and sometimes axes. The evidence suggests that particularly Neo-Assyrian kings customarily destroyed the orchards of their enemies. This seems to have been part of their military strategy. One must admit, however, that Egypt is not known for its forests.

23 They will chop down her forest,"
declares the LORD,
"dense though it be.
They are more numerous than locusts,[x]
they cannot be counted.
24 Daughter Egypt will be put to shame,
given into the hands of the people of
the north.[y]"

25 The LORD Almighty, the God of Israel, says: "I am about to bring punishment
on Amon god of Thebes,[z] on Pharaoh, on
Egypt and her gods[a] and her kings, and on
those who rely[b] on Pharaoh. 26 I will give
them into the hands[c] of those who want
to kill them — Nebuchadnezzar king[d] of
Babylon and his officers. Later, however,
Egypt will be inhabited[e] as in times past,"
declares the LORD.

27 "Do not be afraid,[f] Jacob my servant;
do not be dismayed, Israel.
I will surely save you out of a distant
place,
your descendants from the land of
their exile.[g]
Jacob will again have peace and
security,
and no one will make him afraid.
28 Do not be afraid, Jacob my servant,
for I am with you,"[h] declares the LORD.
"Though I completely destroy[i] all the
nations
among which I scatter you,
I will not completely destroy you.
I will discipline you but only in due
measure;
I will not let you go entirely
unpunished."

A Message About the Philistines

47 This is the word of the LORD that
came to Jeremiah the prophet concerning the Philistines before Pharaoh attacked Gaza:[j]

2 This is what the LORD says:

"See how the waters are rising in the
north;[k]
they will become an overflowing
torrent.
They will overflow the land and
everything in it,
the towns and those who live in
them.
The people will cry out;
all who dwell in the land will wail
3 at the sound of the hooves of galloping
steeds,
at the noise of enemy chariots
and the rumble of their wheels.
Parents will not turn to help their
children;
their hands will hang limp.
4 For the day has come
to destroy all the Philistines
and to remove all survivors
who could help Tyre[l] and Sidon.[m]

46:23 [x] Jdg 7:12 **46:24** [y] Jer 1:15 **46:25** [z] Eze 30:14; Na 3:8 [a] Jer 43:12 [b] Isa 20:6 **46:26** [c] Jer 44:30 [d] Eze 32:11 [e] Eze 29:11-16 **46:27** [f] Isa 41:13; 43:5 [g] Isa 11:11; Jer 50:19 **46:28** [h] Isa 8:9-10 [i] Jer 4:27

47:1 [j] Ge 10:19; Am 1:6; Zec 9:5-7 **47:2** [k] Isa 8:7; 14:31 **47:4** [l] Am 1:9-10; Zec 9:2-4 [m] Jer 25:22

46:25 *Amon god of Thebes.* Thebes is the Greek name that refers to a city the Egyptians called Waset. It was the most important city in Egypt after Memphis and was located on the Nile River 438 miles (705 kilometers) south of the Mediterranean and 140 miles (225 kilometers) north of Elephantine (see note on 43:7). It served as the capital city of Egypt from the Middle Kingdom (c. 2100 BC) up until the Assyrian invasion led by Ashurbanipal (c. 663/661 BC). In Egyptian texts Thebes is referred to as "the city of Amun." This is evidence that in the early stages, the most important god of Thebes and, by extension, of Egypt was Amun. This god was known as the "Hidden One." He was manifested in the wind, whose origin and destination cannot be known. Amun was also the mysterious source of life in human beings and animals. As time progressed and as the Egyptians acknowledged more and more the power in the sun, a fusion took place between the sun-god Ra and the god of life and breath, Amun. It was conveniently argued that they were one and the same; the result was the god Amun-Ra. The famous temple of Karnak at Thebes was dedicated to Amun-Ra, who became the head of the Egyptian pantheon at the beginning of the New Kingdom (c. 1550 BC).

47:1 *Pharaoh attacked Gaza.* Nebuchadnezzar began his move toward invading Egypt in early 601 BC. However, the investing of Palestine, including the acceptance of Jehoiakim's pledge of loyalty to Babylonian rule, required some delays that prevented any direct move against Egyptian territory until November of that year. Perhaps the king hoped to make as easy a conquest of Egypt as had Ashurbanipal in 663. Since that time, however, the Saite pharaohs of the Twenty-Sixth Dynasty had concentrated much of their efforts and wealth on building several lines of defense along the Gaza road as well as farther south. This was designed to prevent an army from making either a direct march along the Sinai's Mediterranean coast or inland across the desert. When, according to Herodotus, Nebuchadnezzar's army is defeated at the Egyptian fortress of Migdol on the eastern branch of the Nile delta, Necho II's forces pursued him north and captured Gaza. They held it for two years until Nebuchadnezzar once again campaigned in Palestine.

47:2 *waters are rising in the north.* This is reminiscent of the image Jeremiah saw when he was called to be a prophet. At that time he saw a boiling pot "tilting toward us from the north" (see 1:13 and note). It is obvious from these images that danger looms in the north; in this case the threat is against the Philistines. It is also clear that the reference is to Babylon. Jeremiah is using a common image in the ancient Near East. When treaties were drawn up, they included a series of curses that promised punishment for any violation of that treaty. One of those punishments was the flooding of the land. In the Vassal Treaties of Esarhaddon, the king of Assyria (681 – 669 BC) threatens the vassal with the curse that a flood would rise and bring devastation. In light of this curse, we can better understand Jeremiah's oracle that speaks of waters rising in the north.

47:4 *Tyre and Sidon.* These are two Phoenician seaports that lie to the north of the Philistine cities in what is Lebanon today. Tyre was the principal seaport on the Phoenician coast (see note on Ne 13:16). It was built partly on

The LORD is about to destroy the
Philistines,[n]
the remnant from the coasts of
Caphtor.[a][o]
5 Gaza will shave[p] her head in
mourning;
Ashkelon[q] will be silenced.
You remnant on the plain,
how long will you cut yourselves?
6 " 'Alas, sword[r] of the LORD,
how long till you rest?
Return to your sheath;
cease and be still.'
7 But how can it rest
when the LORD has commanded it,
when he has ordered it
to attack Ashkelon and the coast?"

A Message About Moab

48:29-36pp — Isa 16:6-12

48 Concerning Moab:

This is what the LORD Almighty, the God of Israel, says:

"Woe to Nebo,[s] for it will be ruined.
Kiriathaim[t] will be disgraced and
captured;
the stronghold[b] will be disgraced
and shattered.
2 Moab will be praised[u] no more;
in Heshbon[c][v] people will plot her
downfall:
'Come, let us put an end to that
nation.'
You, the people of Madmen,[d] will also
be silenced;
the sword will pursue you.
3 Cries of anguish arise from Horonaim,[w]
cries of great havoc and destruction.
4 Moab will be broken;
her little ones will cry out.[e]
5 They go up the hill to Luhith,[x]
weeping bitterly as they go;
on the road down to Horonaim
anguished cries over the destruction
are heard.
6 Flee! Run for your lives;
become like a bush[f] in the desert.[y]
7 Since you trust in your deeds and
riches,
you too will be taken captive,
and Chemosh[z] will go into exile,[a]
together with his priests and
officials.
8 The destroyer will come against every
town,
and not a town will escape.
The valley will be ruined
and the plateau destroyed,
because the LORD has spoken.

47:4 [n] Ge 10:14; Joel 3:4 [o] Dt 2:23 **47:5** [p] Jer 41:5; Mic 1:16 [q] Jer 25:20 **47:6** [r] Jer 12:12 **48:1** [s] Nu 32:38 [t] Nu 32:37 **48:2** [u] Isa 16:14 [v] Nu 21:25 **48:3** [w] Isa 15:5 **48:5** [x] Isa 15:5 **48:6** [y] Jer 17:6 **48:7** [z] Nu 21:29 [a] Isa 46:1-2; Jer 49:3

[a] 4 That is, Crete [b] 1 Or *captured; / Misgab* [c] 2 The Hebrew for *Heshbon* sounds like the Hebrew for *plot.* [d] 2 The name of the Moabite town Madmen sounds like the Hebrew for *be silenced.* [e] 4 Hebrew; Septuagint / *proclaim it to Zoar* [f] 6 Or *like Aroer*

the mainland and partly on an island and was a thriving commercial and cultural center. Sidon was located about 25 miles (40 kilometers) north of Tyre. Sidon served at times as the capital city of Phoenicia and was fortified by a strong wall; it had two harbors protected by a few small islands and a breakwater (see note on Isa 23:1 – 18). We cannot be sure about the connection between Philistia and Phoenicia. Most scholars speculate that there was both a political and a commercial relationship between them. In the city of Ashkelon there is archaeological evidence from the destruction level caused by Nebuchadnezzar that includes numerous artifacts from Phoenicia. *coasts of Caphtor.* Am 9:7 refers to Caphtor as the place of origin of the Philistines. Documents from Mari and Ugarit also mention Caphtor, as do certain Egyptian and Greek texts. On this basis scholars favor identifying Caphtor with Crete. A few still consider that Caphtor should be identified with Cappadocia, which is an inland area in Asia Minor.

47:5 *shave her head ... cut yourselves.* These practices pertain to mourning rites observed in the ancient Near East (see the article "Mourning," p. 828). *Ashkelon.* It is one of the largest archaeological sites in Israel, covering approximately 150 acres (60.75 hectares). It was occupied from about 2000 BC to AD 1500 by many different cultures — Canaanite, Philistine, Phoenician, Roman, Byzantine, Islamic, and Crusader. It is located about 12 miles (19 kilometers) north of Gaza and ten miles (16 kilometers) south of Ashdod on the coastal highway. During most of the Iron Age (1200 – 586 BC) this beautiful coastal city was under the control of the Philistines. The document known as the Babylonian Chronicle states clearly that Ashkelon was destroyed by King Nebuchadnezzar (605 – 562 BC) in 604. For the destruction of Ashkelon, see note on 36:1.

48:1 *Moab.* See note on Isa 15:1 – 4; see also the article "Moab," p. 450. *Nebo.* Generally associated with the mountain where Moses stood to view the promised land. In this context, however, the reference is to a nearby city associated with the mountain. It is most commonly identified with Khirbet Muhaiyat, a town about three miles (4.8 kilometers) northwest of Medeba and five miles (8 kilometers) southwest of Heshbon. The town may have been settled originally by a group of Babylonian origin since "Nebo" is the name of an important Babylonian deity (Nabu). The Moabite Stone of King Mesha, dated to about the mid-ninth century BC, speaks of the town of Nebo coming under Moabite domination and having some kind of cultic worship of Yahweh at the time Mesha captured it for Moab. *Kiriathaim.* The exact location of this town that King Mesha of Moab claims to have built is unknown. One of the sites proposed is Khirbet el-Qureiya. This site is located about six miles (9.7 kilometers) west of Medeba. If this identification is correct, then Kiriathaim is close to Nebo.

48:2 *Heshbon.* Its identification is still uncertain, but it is usually identified with modern Hesban located in northern Moab. This site is located about 5 miles (8 kilometers) northeast of Mount Nebo and 34 miles (55 kilometers) east of Jerusalem. Though settled by the Israelite tribe of Reuben, by the seventh century BC it was under Moabite control. This town is not mentioned in the Moabite Stone. Pottery and ostraca dated to the time of Jeremiah suggest that during his time Heshbon was under Ammonite rule.

48:7 *Chemosh.* See notes on Nu 21:29; Jdg 11:24; Ru 1:16; 2Ki 23:13.

9 Put salt on Moab,
for she will be laid waste[a];
her towns will become desolate,
with no one to live in them.

10 "A curse on anyone who is lax in doing
the LORD's work!
A curse on anyone who keeps their
sword[b] from bloodshed![c]

11 "Moab has been at rest[d] from youth,
like wine left on its dregs,[e]
not poured from one jar to another—
she has not gone into exile.
So she tastes as she did,
and her aroma is unchanged.
12 But days are coming,"
declares the LORD,
"when I will send men who pour from
pitchers,
and they will pour her out;
they will empty her pitchers
and smash her jars.
13 Then Moab will be ashamed[f] of
Chemosh,
as Israel was ashamed
when they trusted in Bethel.

14 "How can you say, 'We are warriors,[g]
men valiant in battle'?
15 Moab will be destroyed and her towns
invaded;
her finest young men will go down
in the slaughter,[h]"
declares the King,[i] whose name is
the LORD Almighty.[j]

16 "The fall of Moab is at hand;[k]
her calamity will come quickly.
17 Mourn for her, all who live around her,
all who know her fame;
say, 'How broken is the mighty scepter,
how broken the glorious staff!'

18 "Come down from your glory
and sit on the parched ground,[l]
you inhabitants of Daughter Dibon,[m]
for the one who destroys Moab
will come up against you
and ruin your fortified cities.[n]
19 Stand by the road and watch,
you who live in Aroer.[o]
Ask the man fleeing and the woman
escaping,
ask them, 'What has happened?'
20 Moab is disgraced, for she is shattered.
Wail[p] and cry out!
Announce by the Arnon[q]
that Moab is destroyed.
21 Judgment has come to the plateau—
to Holon, Jahzah[r] and Mephaath,[s]
22 to Dibon,[t] Nebo and Beth
Diblathaim,
23 to Kiriathaim, Beth Gamul and Beth
Meon,[u]
24 to Kerioth[v] and Bozrah—
to all the towns of Moab, far and near.
25 Moab's horn[bw] is cut off;
her arm[x] is broken,"
declares the LORD.

48:10 [b] Jer 47:6 [c] 1Ki 20:42; 2Ki 13:15-19 **48:11** [d] Zec 1:15 [e] Zep 1:12 **48:13** [f] Hos 10:6 **48:14** [g] Ps 33:16 **48:15** [h] Jer 50:27 [i] Jer 46:18 [j] Jer 51:57 **48:16** [k] Isa 13:22 **48:18** [l] Isa 47:1 [m] Nu 21:30; Jos 13:9 [n] ver 8 **48:19** [o] Dt 2:36 **48:20** [p] Isa 16:7 [q] Nu 21:13 **48:21** [r] Nu 21:23; Isa 15:4 [s] Jos 13:18 **48:22** [t] Jos 13:9, 17 **48:23** [u] Jos 13:17 **48:24** [v] Am 2:2 **48:25** [w] Ps 75:10 [x] Ps 10:15; Eze 30:21

[a] 9 Or *Give wings to Moab, / for she will fly away*
[b] 25 *Horn* here symbolizes strength.

48:9 *Put salt on Moab.* The translation of this verse is difficult and remains a matter of debate. The term translated "salt" is based on a Ugaritic parallel. If this translation is correct, we can appeal to ancient Near Eastern texts that illustrate this practice, as well as some examples from the OT—e.g., Abimelek scattered salt over the ground of the city of Shechem after he destroyed it (Jdg 9:45). Tiglath-Pileser I (1115–1076 BC) of Assyria is also known for scattering salt over the ruins of a conquered city.
48:11 *wine left on its dregs.* After the grapes have been trod, the resulting juice was poured into large storage jars (about 10 gallons or 37 liters) and they were sealed with clay, leaving only a small vent hole to bleed off the fermentation gases. The fermentation process was allowed to continue for 40 days, as the wine lay with its dregs or lees. *poured from one jar to another.* For the process of wine-making to be completed, the wine must be poured out from the original jars into fresh ones. When this process is carried out, the dregs are strained out. This is done so that the fermentation process can be completed and the wine can then age over time. The transferring of the wine from a state where it is resting on the dregs implies movement and separation.
48:13 *trusted in Bethel.* Whereas in most places in the Hebrew Bible Bethel is a place name, here in all probability it refers to a West Semitic deity. The parallelism with Chemosh in the previous line seems to require a deity. "Bethel" appears in many personal names and as the name of a deity in other ancient Near Eastern texts. Beginning as early as the Assyrian period, we find that the deity Bethel is mentioned in a seventh-century BC treaty between Esarhaddon (681–669 BC) and Baal of Tyre, in which we read of Bethel and of Anath-Bethel.
48:16 *fall of Moab.* There is little evidence available for a Babylonian invasion of Moab. Josephus writes that Babylon invaded both Moab and Ammon about five years after the destruction of Jerusalem. This would place the Babylonian oppression over Moab at about 582/581 BC. We have no other inscriptional evidence to support this claim.
48:18 *Dibon.* Located about two miles (3.2 kilometers) north of the Arnon River. It served as the capital city of Moab while Mesha was king in the ninth century BC.
48:19 *Aroer.* Located about 1.25 miles (2 kilometers) southeast of Dibon. It is one of several Aroers in Palestine; this one is on the Arnon River and is a fortress that guards the King's Highway.
48:20 *Arnon.* The Arnon River was the traditional northern boundary of Moab (see note on 48:1). This river flows through the central Moabite mountains and empties into the Dead Sea south of Aroer. During short periods of time the Moabites extended the boundary as far as Heshbon.
48:25 *horn.* In the ancient Near East it is often used as a metaphor of strength and power. Along with the image of "arm" (Ps 44:3) or "outstretched arm" (Ps 136:12, with reference to Yahweh's arm), "horn" occurs in Psalms as that which symbolizes strength (see note on Ps 18:2). Based on Egyptian, Greek and Latin literature, some scholars suggest that horn here should be understood as "bow." They suggest that it has to do with one of the materials

26 "Make her drunk,[y]
for she has defied the LORD.
Let Moab wallow in her vomit;
let her be an object of ridicule.
27 Was not Israel the object of your
ridicule?[z]
Was she caught among thieves,
that you shake your head[a] in scorn[b]
whenever you speak of her?
28 Abandon your towns and dwell among
the rocks,
you who live in Moab.
Be like a dove[c] that makes its nest
at the mouth of a cave.[d]

29 "We have heard of Moab's pride[e] —
how great is her arrogance! —
of her insolence, her pride, her conceit
and the haughtiness of her heart.
30 I know her insolence but it is futile,"
declares the LORD,
"and her boasts accomplish nothing.
31 Therefore I wail[f] over Moab,
for all Moab I cry out,
I moan for the people of Kir
Hareseth.[g]
32 I weep for you, as Jazer weeps,
you vines of Sibmah.[h]
Your branches spread as far as the
sea[a];
they reached as far as[b] Jazer.
The destroyer has fallen
on your ripened fruit and grapes.
33 Joy and gladness are gone
from the orchards and fields of
Moab.
I have stopped the flow of wine[i] from
the presses;
no one treads them with shouts of
joy.[j]
Although there are shouts,
they are not shouts of joy.

34 "The sound of their cry rises
from Heshbon to Elealeh[k] and
Jahaz,[l]
from Zoar[m] as far as Horonaim[n] and
Eglath Shelishiyah,
for even the waters of Nimrim are
dried up.[o]
35 In Moab I will put an end
to those who make offerings on the
high places[p]
and burn incense[q] to their gods,"
declares the LORD.

36 "So my heart laments[r] for Moab like
the music of a pipe;
it laments like a pipe for the people
of Kir Hareseth.
The wealth they acquired[s] is gone.
37 Every head is shaved[t]
and every beard cut off;
every hand is slashed
and every waist is covered with
sackcloth.[u]
38 On all the roofs in Moab
and in the public squares
there is nothing but mourning,
for I have broken Moab
like a jar[v] that no one wants,"
declares the LORD.
39 "How shattered she is! How they wail!
How Moab turns her back in shame!
Moab has become an object of
ridicule,
an object of horror to all those
around her."

40 This is what the LORD says:

"Look! An eagle is swooping[w] down,
spreading its wings[x] over Moab.
41 Kerioth[c] will be captured
and the strongholds taken.
In that day the hearts of Moab's
warriors
will be like the heart of a woman in
labor.[y]
42 Moab will be destroyed[z] as a nation[a]
because she defied[b] the LORD.
43 Terror and pit and snare[c] await you,
you people of Moab,"
declares the LORD.
44 "Whoever flees[d] from the terror
will fall into a pit,
whoever climbs out of the pit
will be caught in a snare;

48:26 [y] Jer 25:16,27 **48:27** [z] Jer 2:26 [a] Job 16:4; Jer 18:16 [b] Mic 7:8-10 **48:28** [c] Ps 55:6-7 [d] Jdg 6:2 **48:29** [e] Job 40:12; Isa 16:6 **48:31** [f] Isa 15:5-8 [g] 2Ki 3:25 **48:32** [h] Isa 16:8-9 **48:33** [i] Isa 16:10 [j] Joel 1:12 **48:34** [k] Nu 32:3 [l] Isa 15:4 [m] Ge 13:10 [n] Isa 15:5 [o] Isa 15:6 **48:35** [p] Isa 15:2; 16:12 [q] Jer 11:13 **48:36** [r] Isa 16:11 [s] Isa 15:7 **48:37** [t] Isa 15:2; Jer 41:5 [u] Ge 37:34 **48:38** [v] Jer 22:28 **48:40** [w] Dt 28:49; Hab 1:8 [x] Isa 8:8 **48:41** [y] Isa 21:3 **48:42** [z] Ps 83:4; Isa 16:14 [a] ver 2 [b] ver 26 **48:43** [c] Isa 24:17 **48:44** [d] 1Ki 19:17; Isa 24:18

[a] *32* Probably the Dead Sea [b] *32* Two Hebrew manuscripts and Septuagint; most Hebrew manuscripts *as far as the Sea of* [c] *41* Or *The cities*

used to construct the composite bow. If this is considered along with the statements in 49:35 ("I will break the bow of Elam") and Hos 1:5 ("I will break Israel's bow"), one can support the idea of understanding "bow" in this context.
48:28 *like a dove.* The Moabites are compared to doves that build their nests in places difficult to reach. The Moabites are to flee the comforts of settled living in the city and become fugitives who flee from danger and have to live in rock clefts and crevices. The Arnon Gorge, with its caves, crevices and high cliffs, most likely provides the background to this statement.
48:31 *Kir Hareseth.* This city perhaps served as a capital city of ancient Moab. It is identified with modern-day Kerak, which sits atop a mountain about 3,000 feet (915 meters) above sea level. It is 16 miles (25.7 kilometers) south of the Arnon River and 11 miles (17.7 kilometers) east of the Dead Sea.
48:37 Each of the actions described here are common mourning practices in the ancient Near East. See the article "Mourning," p. 828.
48:41 *Kerioth.* The Hebrew term can also be translated "the cities" (see the NIV text note). Despite this possibility, it is also possible to understand a place-name here that refers to a fortified town in Moab. The prophet Amos speaks of the "fortresses of Kerioth" (Am 2:2). Though Kerioth has not been identified with certainty, a possible candidate is el-Qereiyat, located northwest of Dibon.

for I will bring on Moab
the year[e] of her punishment,"
declares the LORD.

45 "In the shadow of Heshbon
the fugitives stand helpless,
for a fire has gone out from Heshbon,
a blaze from the midst of Sihon;[f]
it burns the foreheads of Moab,
the skulls[g] of the noisy boasters.
46 Woe to you, Moab![h]
The people of Chemosh are
destroyed;
your sons are taken into exile
and your daughters into captivity.

47 "Yet I will restore[i] the fortunes of Moab
in days to come,"
declares the LORD.

Here ends the judgment on Moab.

A Message About Ammon

49 Concerning the Ammonites:[j]
This is what the LORD says:

"Has Israel no sons?
Has Israel no heir?
Why then has Molek[a] taken possession
of Gad?
Why do his people live in its towns?
2 But the days are coming,"
declares the LORD,
"when I will sound the battle cry[k]
against Rabbah[l] of the Ammonites;
it will become a mound of ruins,
and its surrounding villages will be
set on fire.
Then Israel will drive out
those who drove her out,[m]"
says the LORD.
3 "Wail, Heshbon, for Ai[n] is destroyed!
Cry out, you inhabitants of Rabbah!
Put on sackcloth and mourn;
rush here and there inside the walls,
for Molek will go into exile,[o]
together with his priests and
officials.
4 Why do you boast of your valleys,
boast of your valleys so fruitful?
Unfaithful Daughter Ammon,
you trust in your riches[p] and say,
'Who will attack me?'[q]
5 I will bring terror on you
from all those around you,"
declares the Lord,
the LORD Almighty.
"Every one of you will be driven away,
and no one will gather the fugitives.

6 "Yet afterward, I will restore[r] the
fortunes of the Ammonites,"
declares the LORD.

A Message About Edom

49:9-10pp — Ob 5-6
49:14-16pp — Ob 1-4

7 Concerning Edom:[s]

This is what the LORD Almighty says:

"Is there no longer wisdom in Teman?[t]
Has counsel perished from the
prudent?
Has their wisdom decayed?

48:44 [e] Jer 11:23 **48:45** [f] Nu 21:21,26-28 [g] Nu 24:17 **48:46** [h] Nu 21:29 **48:47** [i] Jer 12:15; 49:6,39 **49:1** [j] Am 1:13; Zep 2:8-9 **49:2** [k] Jer 4:19 [l] Dt 3:11 [m] Isa 14:2; Eze 21:28-32; 25:2-11 **49:3** [n] Jos 8:28 [o] Jer 48:7 **49:4** [p] Jer 9:23; 1Ti 6:17 [q] Jer 21:13 **49:6** [r] ver 39; Jer 48:47 **49:7** [s] Ge 25:30; Eze 25:12 [t] Ge 36:11, 15,34

[a] 1 Or *their king*; also in verse 3

48:45 *Sihon.* Probably the name of the king of the Amorites, whose capital city was Heshbon. This would be the same Sihon who was defeated by Moses and the Israelites prior to their entry into the promised land (Nu 21:21–31). Most of the towns mentioned previously in ch. 48 would have been under this king's control at one time or another. Perhaps the name Sihon is being applied to the territory that King Sihon once ruled.
49:1 *Ammonites.* A tribal group that lived just to the north of Moab in the Transjordan region (see note on Dt 2:19). The capital city was Rabbah (see note on v. 2). The kingdom of Ammon came under the control of the Babylonians during the sixth century BC. This situation was perhaps precipitated because of Ammonite complicity in the murder of Gedaliah, who was appointed by the Babylonians as governor of Judah (see note on 40:14). The Babylonians conquered Ammon, but retained the Ammonite king. Though some have argued that after the Babylonian destruction the Ammonites continued to inhabit the area, more recent studies indicate that only a few remained after this defeat. *Molek.* See notes on 7:31; 1Ki 11:5.
49:2 *Rabbah.* The capital city of the Ammonite tribal group. It is also known as "Rabbah of the children of Ammon." Rabbah has been identified as Jebel Qalʿah (modern Citadel Hill), which sits in the middle of the modern city of Amman, Jordan, 25 miles (40 kilometers) east of the Jordan River. This city was also strategically located on commercial crossroads that went north-south and east-west.
49:3 *Heshbon.* Jeremiah obviously considers Heshbon as being important for both Moab and Ammon. Since both countries will suffer destruction, Heshbon is mentioned in both messages (see note on 48:2). *Ai.* This Ai must be distinguished from the more well-known Ai located east of Bethel, across the Jordan River from Ammon. The location of the Ai mentioned here is still uncertain. The name in Hebrew means "heap of ruins." There is a modern town named Ai in the Kerak region that is about 1.25 miles (2 kilometers) southeast of Kathrabba, Jordan. It is possible that Jeremiah has this town in mind, or he may have used the name to conjure up the image of a heap or ruins. *Rabbah.* See note on v. 2. *sackcloth.* See note on 4:8; see also the article "Mourning," p. 828.
49:7 *Edom.* Located on a high plateau that sits about 6,600 feet (2,012 meters) above sea level. It is a rugged mountainous region that extended approximately from the River Zered in the north to the Gulf of Aqaba in the south. It extends from the Arabah Valley in the west to the Syrian-Arabian Desert in the east. See notes on Ge 36:9; Ps 137:7; Isa 21:11 ("Dumah"). *Teman.* It can mean "south" or "southland" in Hebrew; it is also a proper name, as attested in Ob 9. It seems to refer both to a city and to a region. In this context we suggest that it designates the northeast region of Edom, whose capital city was Bozrah (see note on v. 13).

8 Turn and flee, hide in deep caves,
you who live in Dedan,[u]
for I will bring disaster on Esau
at the time when I punish him.
9 If grape pickers came to you,
would they not leave a few grapes?
If thieves came during the night,
would they not steal only as much
as they wanted?
10 But I will strip Esau bare;
I will uncover his hiding places,
so that he cannot conceal himself.
His armed men are destroyed,
also his allies and neighbors,
so there is no one[v] to say,
11 'Leave your fatherless children;[w] I will
keep them alive.
Your widows too can depend on me.'"

12 This is what the LORD says: "If those
who do not deserve to drink the cup[x] must
drink it, why should you go unpunished?[y]
You will not go unpunished, but must drink
it. 13 I swear[z] by myself," declares the LORD,
"that Bozrah[a] will become a ruin and a
curse,[a] an object of horror and reproach;
and all its towns will be in ruins forever."

14 I have heard a message from the LORD;
an envoy was sent to the nations to
say,
"Assemble yourselves to attack it!
Rise up for battle!"

15 "Now I will make you small among the
nations,
despised by mankind.
16 The terror you inspire
and the pride of your heart have
deceived you,
you who live in the clefts of the rocks,
who occupy the heights of the hill.
Though you build your nest[b] as high
as the eagle's,
from there I will bring you down,"
declares the LORD.
17 "Edom will become an object of horror;[c]
all who pass by will be appalled and
will scoff
because of all its wounds.[d]
18 As Sodom and Gomorrah[e] were
overthrown,
along with their neighboring towns,"
says the LORD,
"so no one will live there;
no people will dwell[f] in it.

19 "Like a lion coming up from Jordan's
thickets[g]
to a rich pastureland,
I will chase Edom from its land in an
instant.
Who is the chosen one I will appoint
for this?
Who is like me and who can challenge
me?[h]
And what shepherd can stand
against me?"

20 Therefore, hear what the LORD has
planned against Edom,
what he has purposed[i] against those
who live in Teman:
The young of the flock[j] will be dragged
away;
their pasture will be appalled at their
fate.
21 At the sound of their fall the earth will
tremble;[k]
their cry[l] will resound to the Red
Sea.[b]
22 Look! An eagle will soar and swoop[m]
down,
spreading its wings over Bozrah.
In that day the hearts of Edom's
warriors
will be like the heart of a woman in
labor.[n]

A Message About Damascus

23 Concerning Damascus:[o]

"Hamath[p] and Arpad[q] are dismayed,
for they have heard bad news.
They are disheartened,
troubled like[c] the restless sea.[r]

49:8 [u] Jer 25:23 **49:10** [v] Mal 1:2-5 **49:11** [w] Hos 14:3 **49:12** [x] Jer 25:15 [y] Jer 25:28-29 **49:13** [z] Ge 22:16 [a] Ge 36:33; Isa 34:6 **49:16** [b] Job 39:27; Am 9:2 **49:17** [c] ver 13 [d] Jer 50:13; Eze 35:7 **49:18** [e] Ge 19:24; Dt 29:23 [f] ver 33 **49:19** [g] Jer 12:5 [h] Jer 50:44 **49:20** [i] Isa 14:27 [j] Jer 50:45 **49:21** [k] Eze 26:15 [l] Jer 50:46; Eze 26:18 **49:22** [m] Hos 8:1 [n] Isa 13:8; Jer 48:40-41 **49:23** [o] Ge 14:15; 2Ch 16:2; Ac 9:2 [p] Isa 10:9; Am 6:2; Zec 9:2 [q] 2Ki 18:34 [r] Ge 49:4; Isa 57:20

[a] *13* That is, its name will be used in cursing (see 29:22); or, others will see that it is cursed. [b] *21* Or *the Sea of Reeds* [c] *23* Hebrew *on* or *by*

49:8 *Dedan.* Dedan has been identified with a site called al-Khuraybah, next to modern al-'Ula, which is located about 50 miles (80 kilometers) southwest of modern Teima. It is an important northwestern Arabian oasis. Dedan was primarily known for its involvement in caravan trade. It was the merchants and caravan traders that drew the anger of the Hebrew prophets (Isa 21:13 and Eze 38:13).

49:13 *Bozrah.* A capital city of Edom, it is identified with a mountain site near Buseira in modern Jordan. Located about 20 miles (32 kilometers) southeast of the Dead Sea, Bozrah was strategically located at the crossroads of the King's Highway, which goes north-south, and another major east-west commercial road. It was a fortified town that covered about 19 acres (7.7 hectares). The town was fortified with a wall and had a significant administrative center. All evidence uncovered dates Bozrah to the Late Iron Age. There is also evidence of destruction of public buildings by fire. Presumably Nebuchadnezzar was responsible for this, though some suggest that there is no concluding proof for such a supposition. The evidence also suggests that after this destructive fire, Bozrah was abandoned.

49:23 *Damascus.* The capital city of Aram (Syria) from about the tenth to the eighth centuries BC. In this context the name represents the entire nation. Damascus was a constant threat to the northern kingdom of Israel until it was defeated by Tiglath-Pileser III of Assyria in 732 BC. This Assyrian king declares in a building inscription from this time period that he destroyed 592 towns of the 16 districts of the country of Damascus. Damascus remained

[24]Damascus has become feeble,
she has turned to flee
and panic has gripped her;
anguish and pain have seized her,
pain like that of a woman in labor.
[25]Why has the city of renown not been
abandoned,
the town in which I delight?
[26]Surely, her young men will fall in the
streets;
all her soldiers will be silenced[s] in
that day,"
declares the LORD Almighty.
[27]"I will set fire[t] to the walls of
Damascus;
it will consume the fortresses of Ben-
Hadad.[u]"

A Message About Kedar and Hazor

[28]Concerning Kedar[v] and the kingdoms
of Hazor, which Nebuchadnezzar king of
Babylon attacked:

This is what the LORD says:

"Arise, and attack Kedar
and destroy the people of the East.[w]
[29]Their tents and their flocks will be
taken;
their shelters will be carried off
with all their goods and camels.
People will shout to them,
'Terror[x] on every side!'
[30]"Flee quickly away!
Stay in deep caves, you who live in
Hazor,"
declares the LORD.
"Nebuchadnezzar king of Babylon has
plotted against you;
he has devised a plan against you.
[31]"Arise and attack a nation at ease,
which lives in confidence,"
declares the LORD,
"a nation that has neither gates nor
bars;[y]
its people live far from danger.
[32]Their camels will become plunder,
and their large herds will be spoils of
war.
I will scatter to the winds those who
are in distant places[a][z]
and will bring disaster on them from
every side,"
declares the LORD.
[33]"Hazor will become a haunt of jackals,
a desolate[a] place forever.
No one will live there;
no people will dwell[b] in it."

A Message About Elam

[34]This is the word of the LORD that came
to Jeremiah the prophet concerning Elam,[c]

49:26 [s]Jer 50:30 **49:27** [t]Jer 43:12; Am 1:4 [u]1Ki 15:18 **49:28** [v]Ge 25:13 [w]Jdg 6:3 **49:29** [x]Jer 6:25; 46:5 **49:31** [y]Eze 38:11 **49:32** [z]Jer 9:26 **49:33** [a]Jer 10:22 [b]ver 18; Jer 51:37 **49:34** [c]Ge 10:22

[a] 32 Or *who clip the hair by their foreheads*

under Assyrian control until the middle of the seventh century BC. With the collapse of the Assyrian Empire in the late seventh century BC, Damascus seems to have gained a degree of independence that was short-lived. After the Babylonians defeated the Egyptians in the battle of Carchemish in 605 BC, effectively sealing Assyria's fate, Damascus came under Babylonian control. By 599–598 BC the Syrian army joined the Babylonian army to begin a series of attacks on Judah (2Ki 24:2). *Hamath.* An ancient city in Syria identified with modern Hama, located 209 miles (336 kilometers) north of Damascus on the east bank of the Orontes River. This city in antiquity was the center of an independent kingdom. As with Judah and the other states in the Syro-Palestinian area, Hamath fell under the oppression of the Assyrians. Tiglath-Pileser III conquered Hamath in 740 BC. Later on, Sargon II (721–705 BC) destroyed the city completely; this same king had destroyed Samaria a year earlier. Years later Pharaoh Necho occupied the "land of Hamath," before the battle of Carchemish (see note on 46:2; see also the article "Historical Setting of Jeremiah," p. 1222). The Babylonian Chronicle reports that Nebuchadnezzar intercepted the Egyptians at Hamath as they fled from Carchemish in 605 BC. *Arpad.* This city is identified with modern Tell Rif'at, which is located about 22 miles (35 kilometers) north of Aleppo. It is an Aramean city in northwestern Syria. Archaeological excavations show Assyrian presence in Arpad during the seventh century BC and Neo-Babylonian presence during the sixth century BC. Both in the Hebrew Bible and in Assyrian documents Arpad and Hamath are mentioned together.

49:27 *Ben-Hadad.* The name of at least two rulers of Damascus. However, during Jeremiah's time no king by that name ruled in Damascus. The expression "fortresses of Ben-Hadad" must be understood in the same way as one understands the "house of Omri" to refer to the northern kingdom of Israel, or the "house of David" to refer to the united kingdom of Israel. Ben-Hadad here is synonymous with the Syrian royal house.

49:28 *Kedar.* Designates a group of nomadic Arabian tribes (see note on 2:10). This tribal group is mentioned often in Mesopotamian texts from different periods, such as Assyrian annals that come from the times of Tiglath-Pileser III (745–727 BC), Sargon II (721–705 BC), Sennacherib (704–681 BC) and Esarhaddon (681–669 BC). This group of tribes suffered the military incursions of both Assyrian and Babylonian armies. In fact, they caused trouble for Nebuchadnezzar king of Babylon, which in turn provoked a Babylonian attack on the Arabian tribes. *Hazor.* Here does not refer to the well-known city that lies just north of the Sea of Galilee but most likely refers to a region inhabited by the *hazerim*, a group of desert tribesmen who lived east and southeast of Palestine.

49:33 *haunt of jackals.* Jeremiah uses this expression to portray a context of absolute desolation and devastation (see note on 9:11). The irony is that the king of Babylon will transform a desert region into an even more desolate place. This language of devastation is common throughout the ancient Near East. In a Sumerian text that had its origins in the third millennium BC known as the "Lament Over the Destruction of Sumer and Ur," vocabulary such as abandoned, haunted, destroyed, piled corpses, melted away and ravaged is used over and over again.

49:34 *Elam.* Located in the fertile hill country east of the Tigris River. It lay opposite southern Babylonia and occupied what is known as Iran today. Susa was its capital and

early in the reign of Zedekiah[d] king of Judah:

[35]This is what the LORD Almighty says:

"See, I will break the bow[e] of Elam,
the mainstay of their might.
[36]I will bring against Elam the four winds[f]
from the four quarters of heaven;
I will scatter them to the four winds,
and there will not be a nation
where Elam's exiles do not go.
[37]I will shatter Elam before their foes,
before those who want to kill them;
I will bring disaster on them,
even my fierce anger,"[g]
declares the LORD.
"I will pursue them with the sword[h]
until I have made an end of them.
[38]I will set my throne in Elam
and destroy her king and officials,"
declares the LORD.
[39]"Yet I will restore[i] the fortunes of Elam
in days to come,"
declares the LORD.

49:34 [d] 2Ki 24:18
49:35 [e] Isa 22:6
49:36 [f] ver 32
49:37 [g] Jer 30:24 [h] Jer 9:16
49:39 [i] Jer 48:47

A Message About Babylon

51:15-19pp — Jer 10:12-16

50 This is the word the LORD spoke
through Jeremiah the prophet concerning Babylon[j] and the land of the Babylonians[a]:

[2]"Announce and proclaim[k] among the nations,
lift up a banner and proclaim it;
keep nothing back, but say,
'Babylon will be captured;[l]
Bel[m] will be put to shame,
Marduk[n] filled with terror.
Her images will be put to shame
and her idols filled with terror.'
[3]A nation from the north will attack her
and lay waste her land.
No one will live[o] in it;
both people and animals[p] will flee away.

[4]"In those days, at that time,"
declares the LORD,

50:1 [j] Ge 10:10; Isa 13:1
50:2 [k] Jer 4:16 [l] Jer 51:31 [m] Isa 46:1 [n] Jer 51:47
50:3 [o] ver 13; Isa 14:22-23 [p] Zep 1:3

[a] 1 Or *Chaldeans*; also in verses 8, 25, 35 and 45

most important city. The Elamites and the ancient Medes occupied this territory during the seventh century BC. They were known as skilled archers. From the seventh century BC on they were in constant conflict with the Assyrians. In 645 BC Ashurbanipal decisively defeated the Elamites, but by 612 BC Assyria had collapsed and Elam came under the control of the Medes. We have no extra-Biblical evidence of Elam's existence as a nation during the Neo-Babylonian period. Jeremiah is the only Hebrew prophet to pronounce a prophecy against this faraway country.

49:36 *the four winds.* The metaphor of strong winds sent by the deity is one of total judgment and destruction. There are similar expressions in the "Lament Over the Destruction of Ur," a text probably composed in the late third or early second millennium BC. In that text we read of the god Enlil unleashing the burning, evil winds that will devastate the land.

50:1 *Babylon.* The capital city of Babylonia. The city of Babylon was located in antiquity on the Euphrates River, about 55 miles (88 kilometers) south of modern-day Baghdad, Iraq, close to the modern town of Hilla. The ancient city straddled this river and was connected by a stone bridge. It covered about three square miles (7.8 square kilometers).

Babylon was also the name given to the entire southern region of Mesopotamia that lies between the Euphrates and Tigris Rivers and goes to the Persian Gulf. During Jeremiah's time, this area was also known as Chaldea. The Chaldeans are primarily associated with the Babylonians who lived during what is known as the Neo-Babylonian Empire (625 – 539 BC). Though Babylon already existed during the third millennium BC, it did not gain importance until the time of King Hammurapi (1792 – 1750 BC) during the First Dynasty of Babylon.

Babylon's time of greatest power and achievement took place during the reign of King Nebuchadnezzar (605 – 562 BC). During his reign Jerusalem was destroyed and many of its inhabitants were exiled to Babylonia. Nebuchadnezzar is famous for his building projects. He built a special temple to the god Marduk, as well as a large outer wall with a moat in front of the wall to protect the city. Nebuchadnezzar is also famous for the Ishtar Gate that he erected and decorated lavishly, which stood at the entrance of the city. He speaks of himself as a great builder and leader of the country.

Babylon's glory days came to an end when it was defeated by Cyrus, king of Persia, in 539 BC. This defeat was accomplished with relatively little killing, destruction or looting. Records tell us that Cyrus was aided by a group of unhappy priests of the chief god Marduk and by Babylonians who opposed the way King Nabonidus (556 – 539 BC) was leading the country.

50:2 *Bel ... Marduk.* The Hebrew term *bel* is a cognate of the Akkadian *belu*, which essentially means "lord." It is also related to the Canaanite *baal*, which also means "lord." At some point during the second millennium BC, the title Bel was transferred to the Babylonian chief deity, Marduk (see note on Isa 46:1). Until that time it had been reserved for the Sumerian storm-god Enlil, who was the chief god of the Akkadian pantheon. However, with the rise of the city of Babylon to prominence in Mesopotamia, particularly during the Neo-Babylonian period (625 – 539 BC), the Babylonian patron deity Marduk became known as Bel Marduk. In this context it is clear that Bel and Marduk are one and the same deity. Jeremiah's comments regarding Marduk's shame may have been fulfilled in the time of King Nabonidus (556 – 539 BC), who was not loyal to Marduk to the point of leaving Marduk out of the New Year's procession. This process of loss of power and status was completed with the Persian defeat of the city of Babylon.

50:3 *nation from the north.* This is reminiscent of the vision that was part of Jeremiah's call (see note on 1:13), where a foe from the north (Babylon) would come to destroy Jerusalem. The matter now is turned around 180 degrees. Babylon itself will be attacked from the north. As it turns out, Babylon too seems to have been most vulnerable from the north. Her defeat came at the hands of a coalition of Persians and Medes, who came from the north.

"the people of Israel and the people of
Judah together[q]
will go in tears[r] to seek[s] the LORD
their God.
5 They will ask the way to Zion
and turn their faces toward it.
They will come[t] and bind themselves
to the LORD
in an everlasting covenant[u]
that will not be forgotten.

6 "My people have been lost sheep;[v]
their shepherds have led them
astray
and caused them to roam on the
mountains.
They wandered over mountain and
hill[w]
and forgot their own resting place.[x]
7 Whoever found them devoured them;
their enemies said, 'We are not
guilty,[y]
for they sinned against the LORD, their
verdant pasture,
the LORD, the hope[z] of their
ancestors.'

8 "Flee[a] out of Babylon;
leave the land of the Babylonians,
and be like the goats that lead the
flock.
9 For I will stir up and bring against
Babylon
an alliance of great nations from the
land of the north.
They will take up their positions
against her,
and from the north she will be
captured.
Their arrows will be like skilled
warriors
who do not return empty-handed.
10 So Babylonia[a] will be plundered;
all who plunder her will have their
fill,"
declares the LORD.

11 "Because you rejoice and are glad,
you who pillage my inheritance,[b]
because you frolic like a heifer
threshing grain
and neigh like stallions,
12 your mother will be greatly ashamed;
she who gave you birth will be
disgraced.
She will be the least of the nations —
a wilderness, a dry land, a desert.
13 Because of the LORD's anger she will
not be inhabited
but will be completely desolate.
All who pass Babylon will be appalled;
they will scoff[c] because of all her
wounds.[d]

14 "Take up your positions around Babylon,
all you who draw the bow.[e]
Shoot at her! Spare no arrows,
for she has sinned against the LORD.

50:4 [q] Jer 3:18; Hos 1:11 [r] Ezr 3:12; Jer 31:9 [s] Hos 3:5 **50:5** [t] Jer 33:7 [u] Isa 55:3; Jer 32:40; Heb 8:6-10 **50:6** [v] Isa 53:6; Mt 9:36; 10:6 [w] Jer 3:6; Eze 34:6 [x] ver 19 **50:7** [y] Jer 2:3 [z] Jer 14:8 **50:8** [a] Isa 48:20; Jer 51:6; Rev 18:4 **50:11** [b] Isa 47:6 **50:13** [c] Jer 18:16 [d] Jer 49:17 **50:14** [e] ver 29, 42

[a] 10 Or *Chaldea*

NATIONS AND CITIES UNDER JUDGMENT IN JEREMIAH

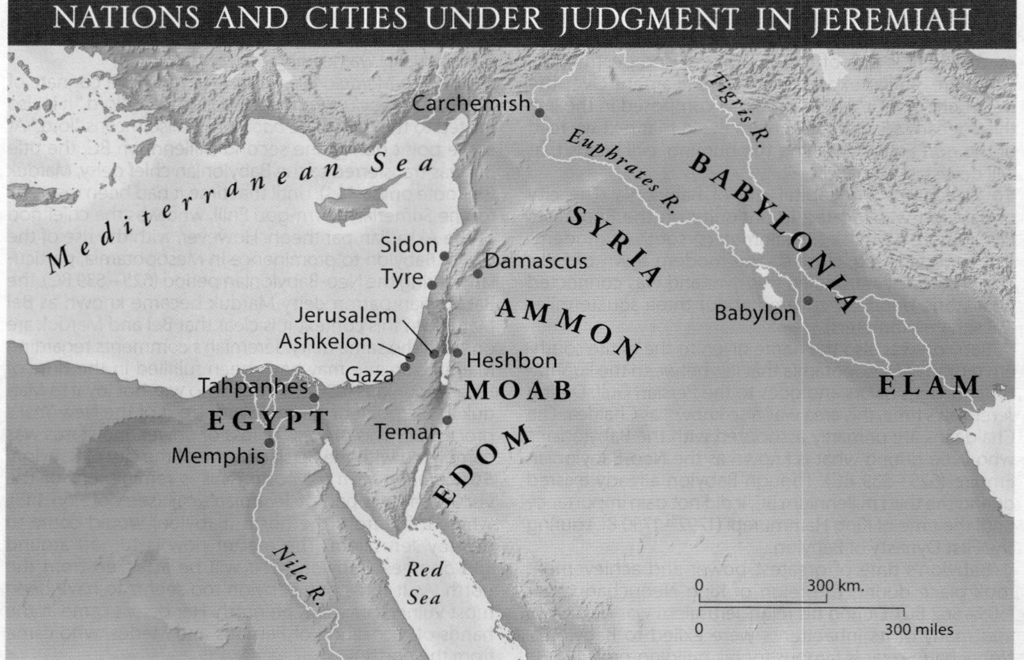

15 Shout[f] against her on every side!
She surrenders, her towers fall,
her walls[g] are torn down.
Since this is the vengeance[h] of the LORD,
take vengeance on her;
do to her[i] as she has done to others.
16 Cut off from Babylon the sower,
and the reaper with his sickle at harvest.
Because of the sword[j] of the oppressor
let everyone return to their own people,[k]
let everyone flee to their own land.[l]

17 "Israel is a scattered flock
that lions[m] have chased away.
The first to devour them
was the king[n] of Assyria;
the last to crush their bones
was Nebuchadnezzar[o] king[p] of Babylon."

18 Therefore this is what the LORD Almighty, the God of Israel, says:
"I will punish the king of Babylon and his land
as I punished the king[q] of Assyria.[r]
19 But I will bring[s] Israel back to their own pasture,
and they will graze on Carmel and Bashan;
their appetite will be satisfied
on the hills[t] of Ephraim and Gilead.
20 In those days, at that time,"
declares the LORD,
"search will be made for Israel's guilt,
but there will be none,
and for the sins[u] of Judah,
but none will be found,
for I will forgive[v] the remnant[w] I spare.
21 "Attack the land of Merathaim
and those who live in Pekod.[x]
Pursue, kill and completely destroy[a] them,"
declares the LORD.
"Do everything I have commanded you.
22 The noise[y] of battle is in the land,
the noise of great destruction!
23 How broken and shattered
is the hammer of the whole earth!
How desolate[z] is Babylon
among the nations!
24 I set a trap[a] for you, Babylon,
and you were caught before you knew it;
you were found and captured[b]
because you opposed[c] the LORD.
25 The LORD has opened his arsenal
and brought out the weapons[d] of his wrath,
for the Sovereign LORD Almighty has work to do
in the land of the Babylonians.[e]
26 Come against her from afar.
Break open her granaries;
pile her up like heaps of grain.
Completely destroy[f] her
and leave her no remnant.
27 Kill all her young bulls;
let them go down to the slaughter!
Woe to them! For their day has come,
the time for them to be punished.
28 Listen to the fugitives and refugees
from Babylon
declaring in Zion[g]
how the LORD our God has taken vengeance,[h]
vengeance for his temple.

29 "Summon archers against Babylon,
all those who draw the bow.[i]

50:15 [f] Jer 51:14 [g] Jer 51:44, 58 [h] Jer 51:6 [i] Ps 137:8; Rev 18:6 **50:16** [j] Jer 25:38 [k] Isa 13:14 [l] Jer 51:9 **50:17** [m] Jer 2:15 [n] 2Ki 17:6 [o] 2Ki 24:10, 14 [p] 2Ki 25:7 **50:18** [q] Isa 10:12 [r] Eze 31:3 **50:19** [s] Jer 31:10; Eze 34:13 [t] Jer 31:5; 33:12 **50:20** [u] Mic 7:18, 19 [v] Jer 31:34 [w] Isa 1:9 **50:21** [x] Eze 23:23 **50:22** [y] Jer 4:19-21; 51:54 **50:23** [z] Isa 14:16 **50:24** [a] Da 5:30-31 [b] Jer 51:31 [c] Job 9:4 **50:25** [d] Isa 13:5 [e] Jer 51:25, 55 **50:26** [f] Isa 14:22-23 **50:28** [g] Isa 48:20; Jer 51:10 [h] ver 15 **50:29** [i] ver 14

[a] *21* The Hebrew term refers to the irrevocable giving over of things or persons to the LORD, often by totally destroying them; also in verse 26.

50:19 *Carmel and Bashan ... Ephraim and Gilead.* Jeremiah speaks here of the restoration of Israel by mentioning four non-Babylonian sites known for possessing not only the richest pastureland in all of Israel but also the best vineyards and agricultural fields. *Carmel.* Situated on the Mediterranean coast, it designates a region of hills covered with dense vegetation (see note on 46:18). *Bashan.* The northeastern region in the Transjordan area known for its fertile soil and impressive oak trees (see note on 22:20). *Ephraim.* Also known as the northern kingdom of Israel, it is known for its fertile soil and for possessing ideal conditions for the cultivation of grapes and various other products such as wheat, fruit and vegetables (see note on 4:15). *Gilead.* It is known for its medicinal plants (see notes on 8:22; 22:6).

50:21 *Merathaim.* This term is a derogatory name that Jeremiah uses for Babylon. This Hebrew word means "double rebellion." However, the use of this term here is most likely intended as a wordplay on the Akkadian term *marratum*, which literally means "bitter," as in salt water, and which designates the region in southern Babylonia where the Tigris and Euphrates Rivers converge at the mouth of the Persian Gulf. This is a marshy area where the river waters mix in with the salt water of the Persian Gulf. This certainly is an appropriate meaning and image for this prophecy of doom for the Babylonians. They too will suffer in bitterness—the same kind of bitterness they inflicted on so many other peoples. *Pekod.* The name of an important Aramean tribe that settled along the east bank of the lower Tigris River. The name also denotes this region where the tribe lived, which is centered between the sealand in the south and the Diyala River in the north. In Babylonian sources this tribe is known by the name of Pukudu, who are mentioned along with their governor in "The Court of Nebuchadnezzar" document. Pekod and Merathaim together represent the entire nation of Babylonia. The Hebrew term for Pekod can mean "to punish," which means that Jeremiah is once again using a play on words. The entire nation of Babylonia will be punished for its atrocities and will suffer in bitterness.

Encamp all around her;
let no one escape.
Repay[j] her for her deeds;[k]
do to her as she has done.
For she has defied[l] the LORD,
the Holy One of Israel.
30 Therefore, her young men[m] will fall in the streets;
all her soldiers will be silenced in that day,"
declares the LORD.
31 "See, I am against[n] you, you arrogant one,"
declares the Lord, the LORD Almighty,
"for your day has come,
the time for you to be punished.
32 The arrogant one will stumble and fall
and no one will help her up;
I will kindle a fire[o] in her towns
that will consume all who are around her."

33 This is what the LORD Almighty says:

"The people of Israel are oppressed,[p]
and the people of Judah as well.
All their captors hold them fast,
refusing to let them go.[q]
34 Yet their Redeemer is strong;
the LORD Almighty[r] is his name.
He will vigorously defend their cause[s]
so that he may bring rest[t] to their land,
but unrest to those who live in Babylon.

35 "A sword[u] against the Babylonians!"
declares the LORD—
"against those who live in Babylon
and against her officials and wise[v] men!
36 A sword against her false prophets!
They will become fools.
A sword against her warriors![w]
They will be filled with terror.
37 A sword against her horses and chariots[x]
and all the foreigners in her ranks!
They will become weaklings.[y]
A sword against her treasures!
They will be plundered.
38 A drought on[a] her waters!
They will dry[z] up.
For it is a land of idols,[a]
idols that will go mad with terror.

39 "So desert creatures and hyenas will live there,
and there the owl will dwell.
It will never again be inhabited
or lived in from generation to generation.[b]
40 As I overthrew Sodom and Gomorrah[c]
along with their neighboring towns,"
declares the LORD,
"so no one will live there;
no people will dwell in it.

41 "Look! An army is coming from the north;[d]
a great nation and many kings
are being stirred up from the ends of the earth.[e]
42 They are armed with bows[f] and spears;
they are cruel and without mercy.[g]
They sound like the roaring sea[h]
as they ride on their horses;
they come like men in battle formation
to attack you, Daughter Babylon.[i]
43 The king of Babylon has heard reports about them,
and his hands hang limp.
Anguish has gripped him,
pain like that of a woman in labor.
44 Like a lion coming up from Jordan's thickets
to a rich pastureland,
I will chase Babylon from its land in an instant.
Who is the chosen[j] one I will appoint for this?
Who is like me and who can challenge me?[k]
And what shepherd can stand against me?"

45 Therefore, hear what the LORD has planned against Babylon,

50:29 [j] Rev 18:6 [k] Jer 51:56 [l] Isa 47:10 **50:30** [m] Isa 13:18; Jer 49:26 **50:31** [n] Jer 21:13 **50:32** [o] Jer 21:14; 49:27 **50:33** [p] Isa 58:6 [q] Isa 14:17 **50:34** [r] Jer 51:19 [s] Jer 15:21; 51:36 [t] Isa 14:7 **50:35** [u] Jer 47:6 [v] Da 5:7 **50:36** [w] Jer 49:22 **50:37** [x] Jer 51:21 [y] Jer 51:30; Na 3:13

50:38 [z] Jer 51:36 [a] ver 2 **50:39** [b] Isa 13:19-22; 34:13-15; Jer 51:37; Rev 18:2 **50:40** [c] Ge 19:24 **50:41** [d] Jer 6:22 [e] Isa 13:4; Jer 51:22-28 **50:42** [f] ver 14 [g] Isa 13:18 [h] Isa 5:30 [i] Jer 6:23 **50:44** [j] Nu 16:5 [k] Job 41:10; Isa 46:9; Jer 49:19

[a] 38 Or *A sword against*

50:43 *The king of Babylon has heard reports.* This description seems to fits the situation that surrounded King Nabonidus (556–539 BC), the last king of the Neo-Babylonian Empire. He was a dedicated worshiper of the moon-god Sin. This created a number of problems for the Babylonian priests of the sun-god Marduk, who became unhappy with Nabonidus.

The Babylonian king neglected Babylon, to the point of restoring a sanctuary to the god Sin at Harran. He then spent ten years in his Arabian capital at Teima, leaving his son Belshazzar as regent in Babylon. By the time Nabonidus returned, he was close to 70 years old. He made a weak attempt at restoring worship and loyalty to the god Marduk, the patron deity of Babylonia. He also sought to fortify the city of Babylon, along with outlying areas, for he knew by then that the Persians were on the move.

All of this proved to be too little too late. He no longer had the support of the political or religious leadership of Babylon, who by this time welcomed the invasion of the Persians. Cyrus king of Persia (539–530 BC) advanced against Babylon in 539 BC. Cyrus defeated resistance forces at Opis and Sippar, and then entered Babylon, apparently without doing battle (see note on v. 1), on Oct. 13, 539 BC. It is possible, however, to view the defeat of Babylon as the end of a long period of violent border battles, including bloody battles at Opis and Sippar. Nabonidus may have been taken away to Persia, where he would have lived his last days.

what he has purposed[l] against the
land of the Babylonians:
The young of the flock will be dragged
away;
their pasture will be appalled at their
fate.
46 At the sound of Babylon's capture the
earth will tremble;
its cry[m] will resound among the
nations.

51

This is what the LORD says:

"See, I will stir up the spirit of a
destroyer
against Babylon and the people of
Leb Kamai.[a]
2 I will send foreigners to Babylon
to winnow[n] her and to devastate her
land;
they will oppose her on every side
in the day of her disaster.
3 Let not the archer string his bow,[o]
nor let him put on his armor.[p]
Do not spare her young men;
completely destroy[b] her army.
4 They will fall[q] down slain in Babylon,[c]
fatally wounded in her streets.[r]
5 For Israel and Judah have not been
forsaken[s]
by their God, the LORD Almighty,
though their land[d] is full of guilt[t]
before the Holy One of Israel.

6 "Flee[u] from Babylon!
Run for your lives!
Do not be destroyed because of her
sins.[v]
It is time for the LORD's vengeance;[w]
he will repay[x] her what she
deserves.
7 Babylon was a gold cup[y] in the LORD's
hand;
she made the whole earth drunk.
The nations drank her wine;
therefore they have now gone mad.
8 Babylon will suddenly fall[z] and be
broken.
Wail over her!
Get balm[a] for her pain;
perhaps she can be healed.

9 " 'We would have healed Babylon,
but she cannot be healed;
let us leave[b] her and each go to our
own land,
for her judgment[c] reaches to the skies,
it rises as high as the heavens.'

10 " 'The LORD has vindicated[d] us;
come, let us tell in Zion
what the LORD our God has done.'[e]

11 "Sharpen the arrows,[f]
take up the shields![g]
The LORD has stirred up the kings of
the Medes,[h]
because his purpose[i] is to destroy
Babylon.
The LORD will take vengeance,
vengeance for his temple.[j]
12 Lift up a banner against the walls of
Babylon!
Reinforce the guard,
station the watchmen,
prepare an ambush!
The LORD will carry out his purpose,
his decree against the people of
Babylon.
13 You who live by many waters[k]
and are rich in treasures,[l]
your end has come,
the time for you to be destroyed.
14 The LORD Almighty has sworn by
himself:[m]
I will surely fill you with troops, as
with a swarm of locusts,[n]
and they will shout[o] in triumph over
you.

50:45 [l] Ps 33:11; Isa 14:24; Jer 51:11 **50:46** [m] Rev 18:9-10 **51:2** [n] Isa 41:16; Jer 15:7; Mt 3:12 **51:3** [o] Jer 50:29 [p] Jer 46:4 **51:4** [q] Isa 13:15 [r] Jer 49:26; 50:30 **51:5** [s] Isa 54:6-8 [t] Hos 4:1 **51:6** [u] Jer 50:8 [v] Nu 16:26; Rev 18:4 [w] Jer 50:15 [x] Jer 25:14 **51:7** [y] Jer 25:15-16; Rev 14:8-10; 17:4

51:8 [z] Isa 21:9; Rev 14:8 [a] Jer 46:11 **51:9** [b] Isa 13:14; Jer 50:16 [c] Rev 18:4-5 **51:10** [d] Mic 7:9 [e] Jer 50:28 **51:11** [f] Jer 50:9 [g] Jer 46:4 [h] ver 28 [i] Jer 50:45 [j] Jer 50:28 **51:13** [k] Rev 17:1, 15 [l] Isa 45:3; Hab 2:9 **51:14** [m] Am 6:8 [n] ver 27; Na 3:15 [o] Jer 50:15

[a] 1 *Leb Kamai* is a cryptogram for Chaldea, that is, Babylonia. [b] 3 The Hebrew term refers to the irrevocable giving over of things or persons to the LORD, often by totally destroying them. [c] 4 Or *Chaldea* [d] 5 Or *Almighty, / and the land of the Babylonians*

51:1 *Leb Kamai.* Means lit. "the heart of those who rise against me." But though this may be part of what Jeremiah wants to communicate, there is something else behind this name. This is a cryptogram known as *atbash* (see note on 25:26). In this case Leb Kamai is used to disguise the name Caldea. The equivalent transliterated Hebrew letters work as follows: *lbqmy* (Leb Kamai) is equal to *ksdym* (Caldea). Jeremiah writes this perhaps in order to provoke Babylon.
51:8 *Get balm for her pain.* This metaphor describes somebody who is deathly ill. Babylon is personified as a patient near death (cf. the parallel with Judah's situation described in 30:12 – 15). The request for balm as medicine is understandable in this context. The Mesopotamian prescription texts inform us that most of the medical treatment practiced in Babylon consisted of herbal remedies. *balm.* See note on 8:22.
51:11 *kings of the Medes.* The Medes were originally a federation of Indo-European tribes that migrated into the highlands east of Babylonia, in present-day northwestern Iran (see note on Isa 13:17). They came to this area in the early Iron Age (c. 1200 BC) and became a kingdom in the eighth century BC with the capital in the ancient city of Ecbatana. In 614 BC, they attacked Ashur. Two years later, the Medes, led by their king Cyaxares, joined the Babylonians and defeated the Neo-Assyrian capital of Nineveh. This enabled them to expand their territory westward to the Halys River. By the end of the seventh century BC, Media had positioned itself as one of the four principal powers of the ancient Near East, along with Babylonia, Lydia and Egypt. By the middle of the sixth century BC, Cyrus the Great, by defeating Astyages, king of Media, with one stroke brought the Medes under the control of the Persian Empire. As far as the documentation that is available, both written and otherwise, we do not know of an independent Median attack on Babylon.

15 "He made the earth by his power;
he founded the world by his wisdom
and stretched[p] out the heavens by
his understanding.
16 When he thunders,[q] the waters in the
heavens roar;
he makes clouds rise from the ends
of the earth.
He sends lightning with the rain
and brings out the wind from his
storehouses.[r]
17 "Everyone is senseless and without
knowledge;
every goldsmith is shamed by his
idols.
The images he makes are a fraud;[s]
they have no breath in them.
18 They are worthless,[t] the objects of
mockery;
when their judgment comes, they
will perish.
19 He who is the Portion of Jacob is not
like these,
for he is the Maker of all things,
including the people of his
inheritance —
the LORD Almighty is his name.

20 "You are my war club,[u]
my weapon for battle —
with you I shatter[v] nations,
with you I destroy kingdoms,
21 with you I shatter horse and rider,[w]
with you I shatter chariot and driver,
22 with you I shatter man and woman,
with you I shatter old man and
youth,
with you I shatter young man and
young woman,[x]
23 with you I shatter shepherd and flock,
with you I shatter farmer and oxen,
with you I shatter governors and
officials.[y]

51:15 [p]Ge 1:1; Job 9:8; Ps 104:2 **51:16** [q]Ps 18:11-13 [r]Ps 135:7; Jnh 1:4 **51:17** [s]Isa 44:20; Hab 2:18-19 **51:18** [t]Jer 18:15 **51:20** [u]Isa 10:5 [v]Mic 4:13 **51:21** [w]Ex 15:1 **51:22** [x]2Ch 36:17; Isa 13:17-18 **51:23** [y]ver 57

51:24 [z]Jer 50:15 **51:25** [a]Zec 4:7 **51:26** [b]ver 29; Isa 13:19-22; Jer 50:12 **51:27** [c]Isa 13:2; Jer 50:2 [d]Jer 25:14 [e]Ge 8:4 [f]Ge 10:3 **51:28** [g]ver 11 **51:29** [h]ver 43; Isa 13:20 **51:30** [i]Jer 50:36

24 "Before your eyes I will repay[z] Babylon and all who live in Babylonia[a] for all the wrong they have done in Zion," declares the LORD.

25 "I am against you, you destroying
mountain,
you who destroy the whole earth,"
declares the LORD.
"I will stretch out my hand against you,
roll you off the cliffs,
and make you a burned-out
mountain.[a]
26 No rock will be taken from you for a
cornerstone,
nor any stone for a foundation,
for you will be desolate[b] forever,"
declares the LORD.

27 "Lift up a banner[c] in the land!
Blow the trumpet among the nations!
Prepare the nations for battle against
her;
summon against her these
kingdoms:[d]
Ararat,[e] Minni and Ashkenaz.[f]
Appoint a commander against her;
send up horses like a swarm of
locusts.
28 Prepare the nations for battle against
her —
the kings of the Medes,[g]
their governors and all their officials,
and all the countries they rule.
29 The land trembles and writhes,
for the LORD's purposes against
Babylon stand —
to lay waste the land of Babylon
so that no one will live there.[h]
30 Babylon's warriors[i] have stopped
fighting;
they remain in their strongholds.

[a] 24 Or *Chaldea*; also in verse 35

51:27 *Ararat.* One of three northern nations, along with Minni and Ashkenaz, mentioned by Jeremiah that wielded significant military power. The territory denoted by Ararat is found in Assyrian cuneiform texts, where it is called Urartu. It encompasses a large territory in east Anatolia (eastern Asia Minor, i.e., Turkey) near Lake Van (see note on Isa 37:38). It rose to power in the ninth century BC, when Assyria was weak, and it was able to hold its own until the sixth century BC. Urartu suffered a significant defeat at the hands of the Assyrian king Sargon II in 714 BC. After this defeat, Urartian royal inscriptions became much less abundant. Early in the sixth century BC, Urartu was first defeated by a coalition of Medes and Scythians (585 BC) and then was passed over to the Persians when they defeated the Medes. The Urartian kings, particularly in the early period (mid-ninth century BC), were constantly involved in building projects. They are known for their outstanding stone-working abilities. *Minni.* A second military power (in addition to Ararat) summoned by Yahweh to punish the Babylonians. They are to be identified with the Manneans, who lived north of Assyria and just south of Lake Urmia in present-day northwest Iran. This is the only mention of them in the OT. Just as Judah was caught between the Mesopotamian and Egyptian powers, Minni was caught between the conquering wishes of Assyria and Urartu (Ararat). The attested history of the Manneans begins with the reign of the Assyrian king Shalmaneser III (858 – 824 BC) and ends with the fall of the Assyrian Empire. At that time they were brought under Median control and were eventually absorbed by the Persian Empire. *Ashkenaz.* A territory north of Ararat and Minni between the Black and Caspian Seas. Its people are referred to as the *Ishkuzas* in Assyrian texts but are known as Scythians in classical sources. These ancient nomads were fierce warriors who were also good horse breeders. They spoke an Indo-European language, and by the sixth century BC first came under the power of the Median Empire and later, like the Urartians and the Manneans, were absorbed by the Persians. Ashkenaz was perhaps the only real threat to Babylon of the three nations mentioned.

51:28 *kings of the Medes.* See note on v. 11.

Their strength is exhausted;
they have become weaklings.[j]
Her dwellings are set on fire;
the bars[k] of her gates are broken.
31 One courier[l] follows another
and messenger follows messenger
to announce to the king of Babylon
that his entire city is captured,
32 the river crossings seized,
the marshes set on fire,
and the soldiers terrified.[m]"

33 This is what the LORD Almighty, the God of Israel, says:

"Daughter Babylon is like a threshing floor[n]
at the time it is trampled;
the time to harvest[o] her will soon come."

34 "Nebuchadnezzar[p] king of Babylon has devoured us,
he has thrown us into confusion,
he has made us an empty jar.
Like a serpent he has swallowed us
and filled his stomach with our delicacies,
and then has spewed us out.
35 May the violence done to our flesh[a] be on Babylon,"
say the inhabitants of Zion.
"May our blood be on those who live in Babylonia,"
says Jerusalem.[q]

36 Therefore this is what the LORD says:

"See, I will defend your cause[r]
and avenge[s] you;
I will dry up[t] her sea
and make her springs dry.
37 Babylon will be a heap of ruins,
a haunt[u] of jackals,
an object of horror and scorn,
a place where no one lives.[v]
38 Her people all roar like young lions,
they growl like lion cubs.
39 But while they are aroused,
I will set out a feast for them
and make them drunk,
so that they shout with laughter —
then sleep forever and not awake,"
declares the LORD.[w]
40 "I will bring them down
like lambs to the slaughter,
like rams and goats.

41 "How Sheshak[b][x] will be captured,[y]
the boast of the whole earth seized!
How desolate Babylon will be
among the nations!
42 The sea will rise over Babylon;
its roaring waves[z] will cover her.
43 Her towns will be desolate,
a dry and desert land,
a land where no one lives,
through which no one travels.[a]
44 I will punish Bel[b] in Babylon
and make him spew out[c] what he has swallowed.
The nations will no longer stream to him.
And the wall[d] of Babylon will fall.

45 "Come out[e] of her, my people!
Run[f] for your lives!
Run from the fierce anger of the LORD.
46 Do not lose heart or be afraid[g]
when rumors[h] are heard in the land;
one rumor comes this year, another the next,
rumors of violence in the land
and of ruler against ruler.
47 For the time will surely come
when I will punish the idols[i] of Babylon;
her whole land will be disgraced[j]
and her slain will all lie fallen within her.
48 Then heaven and earth and all that is in them
will shout[k] for joy over Babylon,

[a] 35 Or *done to us and to our children* [b] 41 *Sheshak* is a cryptogram for Babylon.

51:30 [j] Isa 19:16 [k] Isa 45:2; La 2:9; Na 3:13 **51:31** [l] 2Sa 18:19-31 **51:32** [m] Jer 50:36 **51:33** [n] Isa 21:10 [o] Isa 17:5; Hos 6:11 **51:34** [p] Jer 50:17 **51:35** [q] ver 24; Ps 137:8 **51:36** [r] Ps 140:12; Jer 50:34; La 3:58 [s] ver 6; Ro 12:19 [t] Jer 50:38 **51:37** [u] Isa 13:22; Rev 18:2 [v] Jer 50:13,39 **51:39** [w] ver 57 **51:41** [x] Jer 25:26 [y] Isa 13:19 **51:42** [z] Isa 8:7 **51:43** [a] ver 29, 62; Isa 13:20; Jer 2:6 **51:44** [b] Isa 46:1 [c] ver 34 [d] ver 58; Jer 50:15 **51:45** [e] Rev 18:4 [f] ver 6; Isa 48:20; Jer 50:8 **51:46** [g] Jer 46:27 [h] 2Ki 19:7 **51:47** [i] ver 52; Isa 46:1-2; Jer 50:2 [j] Jer 50:12 **51:48** [k] Isa 44:23; Rev 18:20

51:32 *river crossings seized.* Military objectives always include control of the fords of streams and rivers (see Jdg 3:28; 12:5). In this way, communication lines are cut, armies can no longer take the most direct route and are prevented from flanking an enemy force. One of the major fords across the Tigris River came under the control of the Persians when they took the city of Opis a few weeks before Babylon fell. They took Sippar on the Euphrates River just a few days later. By the possession of these two cities, the Persians could effectively cut off any supplies coming down either the Tigris or Euphrates. It would have been extremely demoralizing to the Babylonians to hear that they were becoming increasingly isolated from their allies as well as the towns and villages that supplied their food and raw materials. This report might well be compared to the progressively negative reports chronicled in the Lachish letters during Nebuchadnezzar's 598 BC campaign in Judah. *marshes set on fire.* In addition to the wall systems, towers and other typical defensive installations, Babylon was also protected by a number of ditches and pools, designed to slow or stop enemy advance to the city. Within these pools or bordering them were canebrakes. If these were set on fire, they would have added to the sense of peril for the city's inhabitants, and the smoke would have masked enemy movements and intensified the breathing difficulties for the people downwind. The fires would also have flushed out any sentries or advance troops that the Babylonians might have stationed along these water obstructions.

51:37 *haunt of jackals.* See note on 49:33.

51:41 *Sheshak.* This is a cryptogram for Babylon (see note on 25:26).

51:44 *Bel.* A Babylonian deity (see note on 50:2).

for out of the north[l]
destroyers will attack her,"
declares the LORD.

49 "Babylon must fall because of Israel's
slain,
just as the slain in all the earth
have fallen because of Babylon.[m]
50 You who have escaped the sword,
leave[n] and do not linger!
Remember[o] the LORD in a distant land,
and call to mind Jerusalem."

51 "We are disgraced,[p]
for we have been insulted
and shame covers our faces,
because foreigners have entered
the holy places of the LORD's house."[q]

52 "But days are coming," declares the
LORD,
"when I will punish her idols,[r]
and throughout her land
the wounded will groan.
53 Even if Babylon ascends to the
heavens[s]
and fortifies her lofty stronghold,
I will send destroyers[t] against her,"
declares the LORD.

54 "The sound of a cry comes from
Babylon,
the sound of great destruction[u]
from the land of the Babylonians.[a]
55 The LORD will destroy Babylon;
he will silence her noisy din.
Waves[v] of enemies will rage like great
waters;
the roar of their voices will resound.
56 A destroyer[w] will come against
Babylon;
her warriors will be captured,
and their bows will be broken.[x]
For the LORD is a God of retribution;
he will repay[y] in full.
57 I will make her officials and wise men
drunk,
her governors, officers and warriors
as well;
they will sleep[z] forever and not
awake,"
declares the King,[a] whose name is
the LORD Almighty.

51:48 [l] ver 11
51:49 [m] Ps 137:8; Jer 50:29
51:50 [n] ver 45 [o] Ps 137:6
51:51 [p] Ps 44:13-16; 79:4 [q] La 1:10
51:52 [r] ver 47
51:53 [s] Ge 11:4; Isa 14:13-14 [t] Jer 49:16
51:54 [u] Jer 50:22
51:55 [v] Ps 18:4
51:56 [w] ver 48 [x] Ps 46:9 [y] ver 6; Ps 94:1-2; Hab 2:8
51:57 [z] Ps 76:5; Jer 25:27 [a] Jer 46:18; 48:15
51:58 [b] ver 44 [c] ver 64 [d] Hab 2:13
51:59 [e] Jer 36:4 [f] Jer 52:1 [g] Jer 28:1
51:60 [h] Jer 30:2; 36:2
51:62 [i] Isa 13:20; Jer 50:13,39
51:64 [j] ver 58 [k] Job 31:40
52:1 [l] 2Ki 24:17 [m] Jos 10:29; 2Ki 8:22
52:2 [n] Jer 36:30
52:3 [o] Isa 3:1 [p] Eze 17:12-16
52:4 [q] Zec 8:19 [r] 2Ki 25:1-7; Jer 39:1

58 This is what the LORD Almighty says:

"Babylon's thick wall[b] will be leveled
and her high gates set on fire;
the peoples[c] exhaust themselves for
nothing,
the nations' labor is only fuel for the
flames."[d]

59 This is the message Jeremiah the
prophet gave to the staff officer Seraiah
son of Neriah,[e] the son of Mahseiah, when
he went to Babylon with Zedekiah[f] king
of Judah in the fourth[g] year of his reign.
60 Jeremiah had written on a scroll[h] about
all the disasters that would come upon
Babylon — all that had been recorded concerning Babylon. 61 He said to Seraiah,
"When you get to Babylon, see that you
read all these words aloud. 62 Then say,
'LORD, you have said you will destroy this
place, so that neither people nor animals
will live in it; it will be desolate[i] forever.'
63 When you finish reading this scroll, tie a
stone to it and throw it into the Euphrates.
64 Then say, 'So will Babylon sink to rise no
more because of the disaster I will bring
on her. And her people[j] will fall.'"

The words of Jeremiah end[k] here.

The Fall of Jerusalem

52:1-3pp — 2Ki 24:18-20; 2Ch 36:11-16
52:4-16pp — Jer 39:1-10
52:4-21pp — 2Ki 25:1-21; 2Ch 36:17-20

52 Zedekiah[l] was twenty-one years
old when he became king, and he
reigned in Jerusalem eleven years. His
mother's name was Hamutal daughter
of Jeremiah; she was from Libnah.[m] 2 He
did evil in the eyes of the LORD, just as
Jehoiakim[n] had done. 3 It was because of
the LORD's anger that all this happened to
Jerusalem and Judah,[o] and in the end he
thrust them from his presence.

Now Zedekiah rebelled[p] against the
king of Babylon.

4 So in the ninth year of Zedekiah's reign,
on the tenth[q] day of the tenth month, Nebuchadnezzar king of Babylon marched
against Jerusalem[r] with his whole army.

[a] 54 Or *Chaldeans*

51:58 *Babylon's thick wall will be leveled.* The city of Babylon was surrounded by two large, thick walls. This kind of construction is referred to as a casemate wall. The inner wall of the city of Babylon was about 21 feet (6.4 meters) thick, while the outer wall measured about 12 feet (3.7 meters) thick. These walls were not made of stone, as in Israel, but were built with bricks. Clay is a natural and common commodity in the region. The older inner wall was made of sunbaked brick. Nebuchadnezzar built a new system of walls farther to the south and east out of baked bricks. He also had a protective moat dug around the wall and filled it with water, and he enhanced the security with a system of artificial lakes and flooded areas. There were a number of gates along the wall. The most famous gate is the Ishtar Gate, enameled in brilliant blue and decorated with lions and dragons. The walls were fortified with 250 towers. Jeremiah declares that even this impressive defensive structure and system would not be enough to stop the enemy. We know from historical sources that the Persians invaded Babylon without engaging in battle (see notes on 50:1,43).

52:1 *Zedekiah ... reigned in Jerusalem eleven years.* See note on 21:1; see also the article "Historical Setting of Jeremiah," p. 1222.

They encamped outside the city and built
siege works all around it.[s] 5The city was
kept under siege until the eleventh year of
King Zedekiah.
6By the ninth day of the fourth month
the famine in the city had become so severe that there was no food for the people to eat.[t] 7Then the city wall was broken
through, and the whole army fled. They
left the city at night through the gate between the two walls near the king's garden, though the Babylonians[a] were surrounding the city. They fled toward the
Arabah,[b] 8but the Babylonian[c] army pursued King Zedekiah and overtook him in
the plains of Jericho. All his soldiers were
separated from him and scattered, 9and he
was captured.[u]
He was taken to the king of Babylon at
Riblah[v] in the land of Hamath,[w] where
he pronounced sentence on him. 10There
at Riblah the king of Babylon killed the
sons[x] of Zedekiah before his eyes; he also
killed all the officials of Judah. 11Then he
put out Zedekiah's eyes, bound him with
bronze shackles and took him to Babylon,
where he put him in prison till the day of
his death.[y]
12On the tenth day of the fifth[z] month,
in the nineteenth year of Nebuchadnezzar
king of Babylon, Nebuzaradan[a] commander of the imperial guard, who served the
king of Babylon, came to Jerusalem. 13He
set fire[b] to the temple[c] of the LORD, the
royal palace and all the houses of Jerusalem. Every important building he burned
down. 14The whole Babylonian army, under the commander of the imperial guard,
broke down all the walls[d] around Jerusalem. 15Nebuzaradan the commander of the
guard carried into exile some of the poorest people and those who remained in the
city, along with the rest of the craftsmen[d]
and those who had deserted to the king of
Babylon. 16But Nebuzaradan left behind[e]
the rest of the poorest people of the land
to work the vineyards and fields.
17The Babylonians broke up the bronze
pillars,[f] the movable stands[g] and the
bronze Sea[h] that were at the temple of the
LORD and they carried all the bronze to
Babylon.[i] 18They also took away the pots,
shovels, wick trimmers, sprinkling bowls,
dishes and all the bronze articles used in
the temple service.[j] 19The commander of
the imperial guard took away the basins,
censers,[k] sprinkling bowls, pots, lampstands, dishes and bowls used for drink
offerings — all that were made of pure gold
or silver.
20The bronze from the two pillars, the
Sea and the twelve bronze bulls under
it, and the movable stands, which King
Solomon had made for the temple of the
LORD, was more than could be weighed.[l]
21Each pillar was eighteen cubits high and
twelve cubits in circumference[e]; each was
four fingers thick, and hollow.[m] 22The
bronze capital[n] on top of one pillar was
five cubits[f] high and was decorated with
a network and pomegranates of bronze all
around. The other pillar, with its pomegranates, was similar. 23There were ninety-six pomegranates on the sides; the total
number of pomegranates[o] above the surrounding network was a hundred.
24The commander of the guard took as
prisoners Seraiah[p] the chief priest, Zephaniah[q] the priest next in rank and the three
doorkeepers. 25Of those still in the city, he
took the officer in charge of the fighting
men, and seven royal advisers. He also
took the secretary who was chief officer
in charge of conscripting the people of the
land, sixty of whom were found in the

52:4 [s] Eze 24:1-2 **52:6** [t] Isa 3:1 **52:9** [u] Jer 32:4 [v] Nu 34:11 [w] Nu 13:21 **52:10** [x] Jer 22:30 **52:11** [y] Eze 12:13 **52:12** [z] Zec 7:5; 8:19 [a] Jer 39:9 **52:13** [b] 2Ch 36:19; Ps 74:8; La 2:6 [c] Ps 79:1; Mic 3:12 **52:14** [d] Ne 1:3 **52:16** [e] Jer 40:6

52:17 [f] 1Ki 7:15 [g] 1Ki 7:27-37 [h] 1Ki 7:23 [i] Jer 27:19-22 **52:18** [j] Ex 27:3; 1Ki 7:45 **52:19** [k] 1Ki 7:50 **52:20** [l] 1Ki 7:47 **52:21** [m] 1Ki 7:15 **52:22** [n] 1Ki 7:16 **52:23** [o] 1Ki 7:20 **52:24** [p] 2Ki 25:18 [q] Jer 21:1; 37:3

[a] *7* Or *Chaldeans*; also in verse 17 [b] *7* Or *the Jordan Valley* [c] *8* Or *Chaldean*; also in verse 14 [d] *15* Or *the populace* [e] *21* That is, about 27 feet high and 18 feet in circumference or about 8.1 meters high and 5.4 meters in circumference [f] *22* That is, about 7 1/2 feet or about 2.3 meters

52:7 *Then the city wall was broken through.* See "Historical Setting of Jeremiah," p. 1222. The Babylonian army had systematically defeated all the surrounding fortified towns of Judah. Nebuchadnezzar now advanced against Jerusalem. During its final siege, the king and his army seem to have built a siege wall rather than a siege ramp. A text from Esarhaddon king of Assyria (681 – 669 BC) uses a cognate Assyrian term to speak of a siege wall. In this historical record Esarhaddon claims that his soldiers climbed over the siege wall to do battle. As the Babylonian army was finishing the siege wall, famine weakened and demoralized the inhabitants of Jerusalem (see the article "Siege Warfare," p. 1157). When the Babylonians were able to pass through or over the protective wall of Jerusalem, the Judahite army fled along with King Zedekiah and his bodyguard. They fled south and east, hoping to cross the Jordan River into Moab or Ammon to seek protection (see note on 39:4).

52:12 *Nebuzaradan commander of the imperial guard.* The title of this commander means lit. "chief of the cooks." This person is also known to us from a text called "The Court of Nebuchadnezzar," in which he is also listed as the chief cook. He seems to have been responsible for food distribution, for organizing the exile and for destroying Jerusalem. The common practice among Babylonian and Assyrian armies was to burn down the major public buildings, which included the temple and the protective walls surrounding the city. There is evidence of this burning during 586 BC. The "Burnt House" in the so-called house of Ahiel is one example of the destruction by fire led by Nebuzaradan.
52:18 We have no extra-Biblical sources that list the number of items plundered from Jerusalem by the Babylonians. The list here no doubt reflects the one found in 1Ki 7:13 – 51. It would be impossible for the writer to have access to a formal list of plundered items, assuming that one was written up at all.

Ruins at Babylon.
Dr. James C. Martin, Baker Photo Archive.

city. 26 Nebuzaradan[r] the commander took
them all and brought them to the king of
Babylon at Riblah. 27 There at Riblah, in
the land of Hamath, the king had them
executed.

So Judah went into captivity, away[s] from
her land. 28 This is the number of the people
Nebuchadnezzar carried into exile:[t]

in the seventh year, 3,023 Jews;
29 in Nebuchadnezzar's eighteenth year,
832 people from Jerusalem;
30 in his twenty-third year,
745 Jews taken into exile by Nebuzaradan the commander of the imperial guard.
There were 4,600 people in all.

52:26 [r] ver 12
52:27 [s] Jer 20:4
52:28 [t] 2Ki 24:14-16; 2Ch 36:20
52:33 [u] 2Sa 9:7
52:34 [v] 2Sa 9:10

Jehoiachin Released

52:31-34pp — 2Ki 25:27-30

31 In the thirty-seventh year of the exile
of Jehoiachin king of Judah, in the year
Awel-Marduk became king of Babylon, on
the twenty-fifth day of the twelfth month,
he released Jehoiachin king of Judah and
freed him from prison. 32 He spoke kindly
to him and gave him a seat of honor higher than those of the other kings who were
with him in Babylon. 33 So Jehoiachin put
aside his prison clothes and for the rest of
his life ate regularly at the king's table.[u]
34 Day by day the king of Babylon gave Jehoiachin a regular allowance[v] as long as
he lived, till the day of his death.

52:28 *This is the number of the people … carried into exile.* The exile of the Judahites to Babylon took place in three stages. The numbers listed here would seem to include only adult men, to the exclusion of women and children (who no doubt were carried off to Babylon as well). A total of 4,600 adult men were carried away to Babylon. These represented the most qualified and skilled people of the land of Palestine, but not a large percentage of the total population.

52:31 *Jehoiachin.* He had been in exile for 37 years. At this time he is released from prison and given a place of honor beside Awel-Marduk, the king of Babylon (562 – 560 BC). Jehoiachin's release occurs about 561/560 BC. See notes on 13:18; 24:1. The Biblical text also implies there were other exiled kings in Babylonia. The document known as "The Court of Nebuchadnezzar" mentions the kings of Tyre, Gaza, Sidon, Arvad, Ashdod and others. *Awel-Marduk.* In Hebrew the name can mean "Foolish Marduk." This may be a pejorative way of referring to the Babylonian king. His Babylonian name is Amel-Marduk, which means "man of Marduk." He was the son and successor of Nebuchadnezzar. He only ruled for two years and was assassinated by Neriglissar, who took over the throne and ruled from 560 – 556 BC.

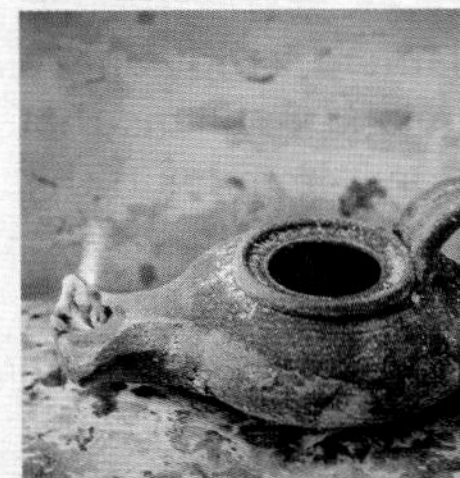

ORACLES OF THE PROPHETS

LAMENTATIONS

The book of Lamentations in the English Bible takes its name from the Greek and Latin versions, which translate the Hebrew *qinoth* "dirges, laments." The Hebrew Bible names a book by the first word or phrase. Lamentations is one of the "megilloth," or five scrolls that are read during various of the annual festivals. Lamentations has traditionally been read in observation of *Tish b'av* (ninth of the month 'Av), the anniversary of the destruction of Jerusalem. While *Tish b'av* is a later development, it is a likely extension of the communal mourning over Jerusalem reflected in Jer 41:5; Zec 7:3 – 5; 8:19.

KEY CONCEPTS

- Lament targets not only one's situation but also one's spiritual condition.
- Any circumstance in life can provide an opportunity to know God better.

Historical Setting

Lamentations focuses on the trauma experienced by the kingdom of Judah at the hands of Nebuchadnezzar and the Babylonians. In 604 BC Nebuchadnezzar's military confronted the western states, and Babylonian power was brought to bear on Judah. In less than a decade the devastation of Judah had begun with the first deportation.

Typical of ancient Near Eastern warfare, if time permitted, cities fortified as Jerusalem was were often "softened" by siege warfare. This protracted strangulation of a city deprived the defenders and citizenry of food and often of water. Thirst and starvation would decimate the besieged population. Though from an earlier period, the art and inscriptions of the Assyrian palaces provide insight into the horrors of the siege. They also show the intensity of devastation once the defenses were broken down.

There was no theory of "separation of church and state" in the ancient Near East. The city-state was viewed as the realm of a patron deity. Palace and temple were intimately connected functionally and were often closely situated physically. One implication of this view is that in order to vanquish a city-state, not only must the military be defeated and the royal court put out of commission (either by killing the king or rendering him unfit to reign — often by mutilation), but the temple and its accoutrements were to be looted and put out of commission. Putting the god under submission was just as important as putting the king and his military under submission.

When the kingdom of Judah fell to the Babylonian Empire (586 BC), the temple and the palace were destroyed, along with the rest of the capital city, and the leadership and much of the population were carried away captive. This devastation was not merely sociopolitical, it was also deeply theological and spiritual.

Literary Setting

The poetry of lament is quite common in the Hebrew Bible. The lament is not only a complaint but also a profound request for help. The prophet Jeremiah proclaims that people ought to engage in lamentation because Jerusalem's destruction is imminent. This kind of lamentation that is characterized by strong, passionate language and pathos is also present in Mesopotamian literature. In the "Lament Over the Destruction of Sumer and Ur," the language and anguish expressed is much like that present in this lament over Jerusalem. Suffering and desolation capture the hearts of the inhabitants, who make earnest pleas to God/gods. In addition, just as God is depicted as suffering over the destruction of the chosen city of Jerusalem in Lamentations, the Mesopotamian gods also grieve and weep over the devastation of a favorite city. ◆

1 [a] How deserted lies the city,
once so full of people!
How like a widow[a] is she,
who once was great[b] among the
nations!
She who was queen among the
provinces
has now become a slave.[c]

2 Bitterly she weeps[d] at night,
tears are on her cheeks.
Among all her lovers[e]
there is no one to comfort her.
All her friends have betrayed[f] her;
they have become her enemies.[g]

3 After affliction and harsh labor,
Judah has gone into exile.[h]
She dwells among the nations;
she finds no resting place.[i]
All who pursue her have overtaken her
in the midst of her distress.

4 The roads to Zion mourn,
for no one comes to her appointed
festivals.
All her gateways are desolate,[j]
her priests groan,
her young women grieve,
and she is in bitter anguish.[k]

5 Her foes have become her masters;
her enemies are at ease.
The LORD has brought her grief[l]
because of her many sins.
Her children have gone into exile,[m]
captive before the foe.

6 All the splendor has departed
from Daughter Zion.[n]
Her princes are like deer
that find no pasture;
in weakness they have fled
before the pursuer.

7 In the days of her affliction and
wandering
Jerusalem remembers all the
treasures
that were hers in days of old.
When her people fell into enemy hands,
there was no one to help her.[o]
Her enemies looked at her
and laughed at her destruction.

8 Jerusalem has sinned[p] greatly
and so has become unclean.
All who honored her despise her,
for they have all seen her naked;[q]
she herself groans[r]
and turns away.

9 Her filthiness clung to her skirts;
she did not consider her future.[s]
Her fall[t] was astounding;
there was none to comfort[u] her.
"Look, LORD, on my affliction,[v]
for the enemy has triumphed."

10 The enemy laid hands
on all her treasures;[w]
she saw pagan nations
enter her sanctuary[x] —
those you had forbidden[y]
to enter your assembly.

11 All her people groan[z]
as they search for bread;[a]

1:1 [a] Isa 47:8 [b] 1Ki 4:21 [c] Isa 3:26; Jer 40:9 **1:2** [d] Ps 6:6 [e] Jer 3:1 [f] Jer 4:30; Mic 7:5 [g] ver 16 **1:3** [h] Jer 13:19 [i] Dt 28:65 **1:4** [j] Jer 9:11 [k] Joel 1:8-13 **1:5** [l] Jer 30:15 [m] Jer 39:9; 52:28-30 **1:6** [n] Jer 13:18 **1:7** [o] Jer 37:7; La 4:17 **1:8** [p] ver 20; Isa 59:2-13 [q] Jer 13:22, 26 [r] ver 21, 22 **1:9** [s] Dt 32:28-29; Isa 47:7; Eze 24:13 [t] Jer 13:18 [u] Ecc 4:1; Jer 16:7 [v] Ps 25:18 **1:10** [w] Isa 64:11 [x] Ps 74:7-8; Jer 51:51 [y] Dt 23:3 **1:11** [z] Ps 38:8 [a] Jer 52:6

[a] This chapter is an acrostic poem, the verses of which begin with the successive letters of the Hebrew alphabet.

1:1 *the city.* Jerusalem. Why would the destruction of Jerusalem be such a momentous event? First, there is the general significance of a city in the ancient Near East. Up to the time of the fall of Jerusalem the economy of the region was pastoral-agrarian. However, there is ample evidence of "permanent" settlements inhabited by people engaged in a variety of pursuits other than farming by the fourth millennium BC. The material remains of these cities indicate they were centers of security, crafts, trade and religion.

Second, there was the sense of security that cities tended to offer. The terrain of Judah offered a degree of natural security. The Dead Sea and wilderness offered protection to the east. The relatively steep ascent and deep v-shaped canyons to the west presented an impediment to invading forces. In addition to these natural defenses, fortification of a city like Jerusalem provided a measure of security for the surrounding population as well. By the time of the united monarchy in Israel there was a fairly well-developed administrative structure.

Third, and perhaps the most significant, there is the spiritual factor. Dt 12:5 indicates that God would "choose [a place] from among all [Israel's] tribes to put his Name there for his dwelling." This claim established the spiritual and theological significance of a particular place. By bringing the ark of the covenant to Jerusalem, David made Jerusalem the spiritual center. Under David and Solomon Jerusalem also became the economic capital of Israel. Later, Isaiah would call Jerusalem the "holy city" (Isa 52:1). Throughout the Psalms and the Prophets, "Zion" represents the Lord's presence. It was common for cities in the ancient Near East to have patron deities who were seen as the real king.

When the kingdom of Judah fell to the Babylonian Empire (586 BC), the temple and the palace were destroyed, along with the rest of the capital city and the leadership, and much of the population was carried away captive. This devastation was not merely sociopolitical, it was deeply theological and spiritual as well.

1:4 *appointed festivals.* There were three pilgrimage festivals in the Israelite calendar: the Festival of Unleavened Bread (which includes Passover), the Festival of Weeks (or Harvest or Pentecost) and the Festival of Tabernacles (or Booths or Ingathering). See the article "Festivals," p. 220. Under normal circumstances, the roads would be filled with pilgrims traveling to Jerusalem during these times. They were occasions for joy and celebration. In troubled times, few would take the risk, and now there is no city or temple to come to. The phrase indicates the city has ceased to function.

1:8 *unclean.* See note on Lev 21:1; see also the article "Unclean Food," p. 197.

they barter their treasures for food
to keep themselves alive.
"Look, LORD, and consider,
for I am despised."

12 "Is it nothing to you, all you who pass by?[b]
Look around and see.
Is any suffering like my suffering[c]
that was inflicted on me,
that the LORD brought on me
in the day of his fierce anger?[d]

13 "From on high he sent fire,
sent it down into my bones.[e]
He spread a net for my feet
and turned me back.
He made me desolate,[f]
faint[g] all the day long.

14 "My sins have been bound into a yoke[a];[h]
by his hands they were woven together.
They have been hung on my neck,
and the Lord has sapped my strength.
He has given me into the hands[i]
of those I cannot withstand.

15 "The Lord has rejected
all the warriors in my midst;[j]
he has summoned an army[k]
against me
to[b] crush my young men.[l]
In his winepress the Lord has trampled
Virgin Daughter Judah.

16 "This is why I weep
and my eyes overflow with tears.[m]
No one is near to comfort[n] me,
no one to restore my spirit.
My children are destitute
because the enemy has prevailed."[o]

17 Zion stretches out her hands,[p]
but there is no one to comfort her.
The LORD has decreed for Jacob
that his neighbors become his foes;
Jerusalem has become
an unclean thing among them.

18 "The LORD is righteous,
yet I rebelled[q] against his command.
Listen, all you peoples;
look on my suffering.[r]
My young men and young women
have gone into exile.[s]

19 "I called to my allies
but they betrayed me.
My priests and my elders
perished[t] in the city

1:12 [b] Jer 18:16 [c] ver 18 [d] Isa 13:13; Jer 30:24 **1:13** [e] Job 30:30 [f] Jer 44:6 [g] Hab 3:16 **1:14** [h] Dt 28:48; Isa 47:6 [i] Jer 32:5 **1:15** [j] Jer 37:10 [k] Isa 41:2 [l] Isa 28:18; Jer 18:21 **1:16** [m] La 2:11, 18; 3:48-49 [n] Ps 69:20; Ecc 4:1 [o] ver 2; Jer 13:17; 14:17 **1:17** [p] Jer 4:31 **1:18** [q] 1Sa 12:14 [r] ver 12 [s] Dt 28:32,41 **1:19** [t] Jer 14:15; La 2:20

[a] 14 Most Hebrew manuscripts; many Hebrew manuscripts and Septuagint *He kept watch over my sins* [b] 15 Or *has set a time for me / when he will*

1:15 *winepress.* It accommodated a load of grapes as well as space for the persons who would tread the juice out of the grapes with bare feet. The juice would flow through a drain channel into large earthen jars, where it would ferment into wine. The fact that wine making was such a common and visible part of the culture provided speakers and writers with rich metaphors their audience would easily understand. While the winepress provides a number of positive metaphors, here the emphasis is on the trampling and crushing aspects.

LAMENTATIONS 1

NEO-SUMERIAN LAMENTS

The Neo-Sumerian laments that we do have come from the Old Babylonian period (c. 2000 – 1530 BC). The distinctive Sumerian city laments include three "major" compositions: the "Lament Over the Destruction of Ur," the "Lament Over the Destruction of Sumer and Ur," and the "Lament Over the Destruction of Nippur." Other city laments include the "Lament Over the Destruction of Sumer and Uruk," and the "Lament Over the Destruction of Eridu." These share the following characteristics: a literary treatment of the destruction of a significant city, the treatment of the destruction and restoration of a sanctuary, the treatment of decisions by deity(ies) that resulted in abandonment, and the treatment of efforts of the royal court to rebuild. ◆

Lachish captives being led into exile.

while they searched for food
to keep themselves alive.

20 "See, LORD, how distressed[u] I am!
I am in torment[v] within,
and in my heart I am disturbed,
for I have been most rebellious.
Outside, the sword bereaves;
inside, there is only death.[w]

21 "People have heard my groaning,[x]
but there is no one to comfort me.[y]
All my enemies have heard of my distress;
they rejoice[z] at what you have done.
May you bring the day[a] you have announced
so they may become like me.

22 "Let all their wickedness come before you;
deal with them
as you have dealt with me
because of all my sins.[b]
My groans are many
and my heart is faint."

2[a] How the Lord has covered Daughter Zion
with the cloud of his anger[b]![c]
He has hurled down the splendor of Israel
from heaven to earth;
he has not remembered his footstool[d]
in the day of his anger.

2 Without pity[e] the Lord has swallowed[f] up
all the dwellings of Jacob;
in his wrath he has torn down
the strongholds[g] of Daughter Judah.
He has brought her kingdom and its princes
down to the ground[h] in dishonor.

3 In fierce anger he has cut off
every horn[c,d][i] of Israel.
He has withdrawn his right hand[j]
at the approach of the enemy.
He has burned in Jacob like a flaming fire
that consumes everything around it.[k]

4 Like an enemy he has strung his bow;[l]
his right hand is ready.

1:20 [u] Jer 4:19 [v] La 2:11 [w] Dt 32:25; Eze 7:15 **1:21** [x] ver 8 [y] ver 4 [z] La 2:15 [a] Isa 47:11; Jer 30:16 **1:22** [b] Ne 4:5 **2:1** [c] La 3:44 [d] Ps 99:5; 132:7 **2:2** [e] La 3:43 [f] Ps 21:9 [g] Ps 89:39-40; Mic 5:11 [h] Isa 25:12 **2:3** [i] Ps 75:5, 10 [j] Ps 74:11 [k] Isa 42:25; Jer 21:4-5, 14 **2:4** [l] Job 16:13; La 3:12-13

[a] This chapter is an acrostic poem, the verses of which begin with the successive letters of the Hebrew alphabet. [b] 1 Or *How the Lord in his anger / has treated Daughter Zion with contempt* [c] 3 Or *off / all the strength*; or *every king* [d] 3 *Horn* here symbolizes strength.

2:1 *footstool.* In Assyrian sources the imagery of establishing a royal throne and footstool in a city-state represents the sovereign's presence and authority (see Ps 99:5). In Ps 132:7 it refers to the temple. In 1Ch 28:2 it is used in parallel with the ark of the covenant. In this text Yahweh has withdrawn his presence (see note on Eze 10:18; see also the article "Esarhaddon's Inscription Concerning Babylon," p. 1346).
2:3 *right hand.* See note on Ps 16:8.

Like a foe he has slain
all who were pleasing to the eye;[m]
he has poured out his wrath like fire[n]
on the tent of Daughter Zion.

5 The Lord is like an enemy;[o]
he has swallowed up Israel.
He has swallowed up all her palaces
and destroyed her strongholds.[p]
He has multiplied mourning and
lamentation
for Daughter Judah.[q]

6 He has laid waste his dwelling like a
garden;
he has destroyed his place of
meeting.[r]
The LORD has made Zion forget
her appointed festivals and her
Sabbaths;[s]
in his fierce anger he has spurned
both king and priest.[t]

7 The Lord has rejected his altar
and abandoned his sanctuary.
He has given the walls of her
palaces[u]
into the hands of the enemy;
they have raised a shout in the house
of the LORD
as on the day of an appointed
festival.

8 The LORD determined to tear down
the wall around Daughter Zion.
He stretched out a measuring line[v]
and did not withhold his hand from
destroying.
He made ramparts and walls lament;
together they wasted away.[w]

9 Her gates[x] have sunk into the ground;
their bars he has broken and
destroyed.

2:4 [m] Eze 24:16, 25 [n] Isa 42:25; Jer 7:20 **2:5** [o] Jer 30:14 [p] ver 2 [q] Jer 9:17-20 **2:6** [r] Jer 52:13 [s] La 1:4; Zep 3:18 [t] La 4:16 **2:7** [u] Ps 74:7-8; Isa 64:11; Jer 33:4-5 **2:8** [v] 2Ki 21:13; Isa 34:11 [w] Isa 3:26 **2:9** [x] Ne 1:3

Her king and her princes are exiled[y]
among the nations,
the law[z] is no more,
and her prophets no longer find
visions[a] from the LORD.

10 The elders of Daughter Zion
sit on the ground in silence;
they have sprinkled dust on their
heads[b]
and put on sackcloth.[c]
The young women of Jerusalem
have bowed their heads to the
ground.[d]

11 My eyes fail from weeping,[e]
I am in torment within[f];
my heart is poured out[g] on the ground
because my people are destroyed,
because children and infants faint[h]
in the streets of the city.

12 They say to their mothers,
"Where is bread and wine?"
as they faint like the wounded
in the streets of the city,
as their lives ebb away
in their mothers' arms.[i]

13 What can I say for you?
With what can I compare you,
Daughter Jerusalem?
To what can I liken you,
that I may comfort you,
Virgin Daughter Zion?[j]
Your wound is as deep as the sea.[k]
Who can heal you?

14 The visions of your prophets
were false and worthless;
they did not expose your sin
to ward off your captivity.[l]
The prophecies they gave you
were false and misleading.[m]

[y] Dt 28:36; 2Ki 24:15 [z] 2Ch 15:3 [a] Jer 14:14 **2:10** [b] Job 2:12 [c] Isa 15:3 [d] Job 2:13; Isa 3:26 **2:11** [e] La 1:16; 3:48-51 [f] La 1:20 [g] ver 19; Ps 22:14 [h] La 4:4 **2:12** [i] La 4:4 **2:13** [j] Isa 37:22 [k] Jer 14:17; La 1:12 **2:14** [l] Isa 58:1 [m] Jer 2:8; 23:25-32, 33-40; 29:9; Eze 13:3; 22:28

2:6 *dwelling.* The Hebrew word refers not to a substantial shelter (cf. Jnh 4:5) but to a hut intended for temporary cover. The same imagery is used in the early second-millennium BC "Lament Over the Destruction of Ur," where the speaker laments that his sturdy and righteous house has caved in as if it were a garden hut.
2:8 *wall.* The city wall itself provided a barrier from the enemy as well as a protected platform from which the city's defenders could fire on the enemy. *measuring line.* Used to determine the area of land holdings, where boundaries were drawn, and what territory belonged to which landholder (private or city) — but none of these explain the connection to the walls and ramparts in this verse. From the use of this metaphor in 2Ki 21:13 and Isa 34:11, it can be assumed that it represents a typical action connected with military conquest. A besieging army would not have the leisure to do such measuring during the battle, so this must refer to the demolition phase. It was rare for city walls to be totally demolished, and from Nehemiah we know that Jerusalem's wall was not totally demolished. However, many sections of the wall may suffer damage due to siege machines, battering rams and sapping operations. Plumb lines would have been used to help determine segments of wall that were no longer stable, and the measuring line would have been used to delineate how much of which sections would need to come down. *ramparts.* A rampart or outer wall served to protect the main city wall from threat of battering rams and to impede a frontal assault. In some cases, the rampart may be nothing more than a mound raised to encircle the city. It may be faced with a stone glacis.
2:11 *eyes fail from weeping.* The imagery the poet uses here is consistent with that used elsewhere in the Hebrew Bible and pervasively in literature from neighboring cultures. Emotions were commonly understood psychosomatically, as integral to the person. Distressing situations were understood to have physical implications as well as emotional impact. At its core, distress impacts the gut (*meeh*, "intestines"; NIV "within") and *kabed* ("liver"; NIV "heart") and then expresses itself through the eyes, which flow with tears. And as the tears flow, vision is impaired — the eyes "fail" — and one's strength flows out.

15 All who pass your way
clap their hands at you;[n]
they scoff[o] and shake their heads
at Daughter Jerusalem:
"Is this the city that was called
the perfection of beauty,[p]
the joy of the whole earth?"[q]
16 All your enemies open their mouths
wide against you;[r]
they scoff and gnash their teeth[s]
and say, "We have swallowed her
up.[t]
This is the day we have waited for;
we have lived to see it."
17 The LORD has done what he planned;
he has fulfilled his word,
which he decreed long ago.[u]
He has overthrown you without
pity,[v]
he has let the enemy gloat over
you,
he has exalted the horn[a] of your
foes.[w]
18 The hearts of the people
cry out to the Lord.[x]
You walls of Daughter Zion,
let your tears[y] flow like a river
day and night;[z]
give yourself no relief,
your eyes no rest.[a]
19 Arise, cry out in the night,
as the watches of the night begin;
pour out your heart[b] like water
in the presence of the Lord.[c]
Lift up your hands to him
for the lives of your children,
who faint[d] from hunger
at every street corner.
20 "Look, LORD, and consider:
Whom have you ever treated like
this?
Should women eat their offspring,[e]
the children they have cared for?[f]
Should priest and prophet be killed[g]
in the sanctuary of the Lord?
21 "Young and old lie together
in the dust of the streets;
my young men and young women
have fallen by the sword.[h]
You have slain them in the day of your
anger;
you have slaughtered them without
pity.[i]
22 "As you summon to a feast day,
so you summoned against me
terrors[j] on every side.
In the day of the LORD's anger
no one escaped or survived;
those I cared for and reared[k]
my enemy has destroyed."

3[b] I am the man who has seen
affliction
by the rod of the LORD's wrath.[l]
2 He has driven me away and made me
walk
in darkness[m] rather than light;
3 indeed, he has turned his hand against
me[n]
again and again, all day long.
4 He has made my skin and my flesh
grow old
and has broken my bones.[o]
5 He has besieged me and surrounded
me
with bitterness[p] and hardship.[q]
6 He has made me dwell in darkness
like those long dead.[r]
7 He has walled me in so I cannot
escape;[s]
he has weighed me down with
chains.[t]

2:15 [n] Eze 25:6 [o] Jer 19:8 [p] Ps 50:2 [q] Ps 48:2 **2:16** [r] Ps 56:2; La 3:46 [s] Job 16:9 [t] Ps 35:25 **2:17** [u] Dt 28:15-45 [v] ver 2; Eze 5:11 [w] Ps 89:42 **2:18** [x] Ps 119:145 [y] La 1:16 [z] Jer 9:1 [a] La 3:49 **2:19** [b] 1Sa 1:15; Ps 62:8 [c] Isa 26:9 [d] Isa 51:20 **2:20** [e] Dt 28:53; Jer 19:9 [f] La 4:10 [g] Ps 78:64; Jer 14:15 **2:21** [h] 2Ch 36:17; Ps 78:62-63; Jer 6:11 [i] Jer 13:14; La 3:43; Zec 11:6 **2:22** [j] Ps 31:13; Jer 6:25 [k] Hos 9:13 **3:1** [l] Job 19:21; Ps 88:7 **3:2** [m] Jer 4:23 **3:3** [n] Isa 5:25 **3:4** [o] Ps 51:8; Isa 38:13; Jer 50:17 **3:5** [p] ver 19 [q] Jer 23:15 **3:6** [r] Ps 88:5-6 **3:7** [s] Job 3:23 [t] Jer 40:4

[a] 17 *Horn* here symbolizes strength. [b] This chapter is an acrostic poem; the verses of each stanza begin with the successive letters of the Hebrew alphabet, and the verses within each stanza begin with the same letter.

2:15 *clap their hands.* Gestures and body language take on different meanings in different cultures. In current Western society, clapping hands can be used to show appreciation, to summon subordinates or children, to get someone's attention, to accompany music or to express frustration (one clap). There were also several functions in the ancient world. Clapping could be used in praise (Ps 47:1) or applause (2Ki 11:12), but in this verse a different verb is used. The verb used here designates a gesture of anger or derision (cf. Nu 24:10 ["struck … together"]; Job 27:23 ["claps … in derision"]). Variations may exist in the precise movement involved: compare the different significations in Western culture of (1) striking the palms together parallel to the body on a horizontal plain (applause); (2) slapping the palms together in a roughly vertical movement (frustration); and (3) striking the palms together perpendicular to the body while alternating which hand is on top and which is on bottom (as if knocking the dust off). It is unclear precisely what motion is conveyed here.

2:19 *watches of the night.* Hebrew reckoning of time divided the night into three four-hour "watches": first watch, middle watch and morning watch. These would be determined by observing the position of circumpolar stars.

2:20 *women eat their offspring.* Cannibalism is a standard element of curses in Assyrian treaties of the seventh century BC. It was the last resort in times of impending starvation. This level of desperation could occur in times of severe famine (as illustrated in the Atrahasis epic) or could be the result of siege (as during Ashurbanipal's siege of Babylon, about 650 BC) when the food supply had become depleted, as anticipated in the treaty texts. Siege warfare was common in the ancient world, so this may not have been as rare an occasion as might be presumed (see the article "Siege Warfare," p. 1157).

8 Even when I call out or cry for help,
he shuts out my prayer.[u]
9 He has barred my way with blocks of stone;
he has made my paths crooked.[v]
10 Like a bear lying in wait,
like a lion in hiding,
11 he dragged me from the path and mangled[w] me
and left me without help.
12 He drew his bow[x]
and made me the target[y] for his arrows.[z]

13 He pierced my heart
with arrows from his quiver.[a]
14 I became the laughingstock[b] of all my people;
they mock me in song[c] all day long.
15 He has filled me with bitter herbs
and given me gall to drink.[d]

16 He has broken my teeth with gravel;[e]
he has trampled me in the dust.
17 I have been deprived of peace;
I have forgotten what prosperity is.
18 So I say, "My splendor is gone
and all that I had hoped from the LORD."[f]

19 I remember my affliction and my wandering,
the bitterness and the gall.
20 I well remember them,
and my soul is downcast[g] within me.[h]
21 Yet this I call to mind
and therefore I have hope:

22 Because of the LORD's great love we are not consumed,
for his compassions never fail.[i]
23 They are new every morning;
great is your faithfulness.[j]
24 I say to myself, "The LORD is my portion;[k]
therefore I will wait for him."

25 The LORD is good to those whose hope is in him,
to the one who seeks him;[l]
26 it is good to wait quietly
for the salvation of the LORD.[m]

3:8 [u] Job 30:20; Ps 22:2
3:9 [v] Isa 63:17; Hos 2:6
3:11 [w] Hos 6:1
3:12 [x] La 2:4 [y] Job 7:20 [z] Ps 7:12-13; 38:2
3:13 [a] Job 6:4
3:14 [b] Jer 20:7 [c] Job 30:9
3:15 [d] Jer 9:15
3:16 [e] Pr 20:17
3:18 [f] Job 17:15
3:20 [g] Ps 42:5 [h] Ps 42:11
3:22 [i] Ps 78:38; Mal 3:6
3:23 [j] Zep 3:5
3:24 [k] Ps 16:5
3:25 [l] Isa 25:9; 30:18
3:26 [m] Ps 37:7; 40:1

27 It is good for a man to bear the yoke
while he is young.

28 Let him sit alone in silence,[n]
for the LORD has laid it on him.
29 Let him bury his face in the dust—
there may yet be hope.[o]
30 Let him offer his cheek to one who would strike him,[p]
and let him be filled with disgrace.

31 For no one is cast off
by the Lord forever.[q]
32 Though he brings grief, he will show compassion,
so great is his unfailing love.[r]
33 For he does not willingly bring affliction
or grief to anyone.[s]

34 To crush underfoot
all prisoners in the land,
35 to deny people their rights
before the Most High,
36 to deprive them of justice—
would not the Lord see such things?[t]

37 Who can speak and have it happen
if the Lord has not decreed it?[u]
38 Is it not from the mouth of the Most High
that both calamities and good things come?[v]
39 Why should the living complain
when punished for their sins?[w]

40 Let us examine our ways and test them,[x]
and let us return to the LORD.[y]
41 Let us lift up our hearts and our hands
to God in heaven,[z] and say:
42 "We have sinned and rebelled[a]
and you have not forgiven.[b]

43 "You have covered yourself with anger
and pursued us;
you have slain without pity.[c]
44 You have covered yourself with a cloud[d]
so that no prayer[e] can get through.
45 You have made us scum[f] and refuse
among the nations.

3:28 [n] Jer 15:17
3:29 [o] Jer 31:17
3:30 [p] Job 16:10; Isa 50:6
3:31 [q] Ps 94:14; Isa 54:7
3:32 [r] Ps 78:38; Hos 11:8
3:33 [s] Eze 33:11
3:36 [t] Jer 22:3; Hab 1:13
3:37 [u] Ps 33:9-11
3:38 [v] Job 2:10; Isa 45:7; Jer 32:42
3:39 [w] Jer 30:15; Mic 7:9
3:40 [x] 2Co 13:5 [y] Ps 119:59; 139:23-24
3:41 [z] Ps 25:1; 28:2
3:42 [a] Da 9:5 [b] Jer 5:7-9
3:43 [c] La 2:2, 17,21
3:44 [d] Ps 97:2 [e] ver 8
3:45 [f] 1Co 4:13

3:15 *bitter herbs.* This Hebrew word occurs elsewhere only in the Passover passages. *gall.* Wormwood; it is a bitter-tasting shrub used for medicinal purposes and also occasionally to brew a strong tea. Both "bitter herbs" and "gall" serve here as a metaphor for bitterness.
3:16 *broken my teeth with gravel.* The second phrase of the verse suggests that the teeth were broken by shoving the face hard into the gravel rather than forcing someone to chew gravel.
3:27 *yoke.* The term is used in both Hebrew and other texts from the ancient Near East to refer to the beam apparatus that hitched two animals together to pull a plow or vehicle and as a metaphor for submission.
3:34 *crush underfoot.* See note on 2:1. Ps 68:21 presents Israel's victorious, sovereign Lord as one who will "crush the heads of his enemies." The Victory Stele of Naram-Sin depicts the enemy being crushed underfoot. Amenhotep II is depicted with his enemies underfoot. A pair of Tutankhamun's sandals found in his tomb depict a pair of bound enemies—one Asiatic, one Nubian—on the insole, providing opportunity to continually "crush underfoot" his enemies.

46 "All our enemies have opened their
mouths
wide against us.[g]
47 We have suffered terror and pitfalls,[h]
ruin and destruction.[i]"
48 Streams of tears flow from my eyes[j]
because my people are destroyed.[k]

49 My eyes will flow unceasingly,
without relief,[l]
50 until the LORD looks down
from heaven and sees.[m]
51 What I see brings grief to my soul
because of all the women of my city.

52 Those who were my enemies without
cause
hunted me like a bird.[n]
53 They tried to end my life in a pit[o]
and threw stones at me;
54 the waters closed over my head,[p]
and I thought I was about to perish.

55 I called on your name, LORD,
from the depths of the pit.[q]
56 You heard my plea:[r] "Do not close your
ears
to my cry for relief."
57 You came near when I called you,
and you said, "Do not fear."[s]

58 You, Lord, took up my case;[t]
you redeemed my life.[u]
59 LORD, you have seen the wrong done
to me.[v]
Uphold my cause!
60 You have seen the depth of their
vengeance,
all their plots against me.[w]

61 LORD, you have heard their insults,
all their plots against me—
62 what my enemies whisper and
mutter
against me all day long.[x]
63 Look at them! Sitting or standing,
they mock me in their songs.
64 Pay them back what they deserve,
LORD,
for what their hands have done.[y]
65 Put a veil over their hearts,[z]
and may your curse be on them!
66 Pursue them in anger and destroy
them
from under the heavens of the
LORD.

4 [a] How the gold has lost its luster,
the fine gold become dull!
The sacred gems are scattered
at every street corner.[a]

2 How the precious children of Zion,
once worth their weight in gold,
are now considered as pots of clay,
the work of a potter's hands!

3 Even jackals offer their breasts
to nurse their young,
but my people have become heartless
like ostriches in the desert.[b]

4 Because of thirst the infant's tongue
sticks to the roof of its mouth;[c]
the children beg for bread,
but no one gives it to them.[d]

5 Those who once ate delicacies
are destitute in the streets.
Those brought up in royal purple[e]
now lie on ash heaps.[f]

[a] This chapter is an acrostic poem, the verses of which begin with the successive letters of the Hebrew alphabet.

3:46 [g] La 2:16 **3:47** [h] Jer 48:43 [i] Isa 24:17-18; 51:19 **3:48** [j] La 1:16 [k] La 2:11 **3:49** [l] Jer 14:17 **3:50** [m] Isa 63:15 **3:52** [n] Ps 35:7 **3:53** [o] Jer 37:16 **3:54** [p] Ps 69:2; Jnh 2:3-5 **3:55** [q] Ps 130:1; Jnh 2:2 **3:56** [r] Ps 55:1 **3:57** [s] Isa 41:10 **3:58** [t] Jer 51:36 [u] Ps 34:22; Jer 50:34 **3:59** [v] Jer 18:19-20 **3:60** [w] Jer 11:20; 18:18 **3:62** [x] Eze 36:3 **3:64** [y] Ps 28:4 **3:65** [z] Isa 6:10 **4:1** [a] Eze 7:19 **4:3** [b] Job 39:16 **4:4** [c] Ps 22:15 [d] La 2:11,12 **4:5** [e] Jer 6:2 [f] Am 6:3-7

3:48–49 *tears flow from my eyes ... My eyes will flow.* See note on 2:11.
3:53 *pit.* The Hebrew term here is the common word for cistern. Cisterns were particularly significant in the mountainous topography and semiarid climate of the region of Judah (see note on Jer 38:6). Water was at a premium. Great effort was made to conserve rain water and run-off. The "first audience" of these poems would have a mental picture of pits carved into the limestone of the Judahite mountains. The interiors of their cisterns were plastered over to prevent water loss. A stone lid was placed over the opening to prevent debris from entering the cistern and to inhibit evaporation. Having one's own cistern was a source of security and a sign of independence. However, cisterns were not always full of water. When not maintained or in times of drought their contents turned to mud and slime. Officials of King Zedekiah's court pursue their stated intent to put Jeremiah to death by lowering him into an unused cistern. There he was left to die of starvation and hypothermia. By extension, "going down into the pit (cistern)" became a euphemism for "death." Jeremiah reports that at least on occasion cisterns proved to be convenient places to stash cadavers. *stones.* The Hebrew word is singular ("stone"). The NIV translators interpret the term as a collective noun indicating that death by stoning was attempted. In the setting, however, the "first audience" may have pictured the stone lid being placed over the cistern, sealing in the captives and leading to a slimy, cold death by hypothermia.
4:3 *ostriches.* There is still controversy over whether "ostriches" is the proper translation of this Hebrew word. Ostriches occur in hunting scenes in Egyptian paintings as well as on cylinder seals, and they inhabited many regions of the ancient Near East. The alternative translation preferred by some is "eagle-owl." The ostrich identification would correspond with the inattention to the young attributed to the ostrich (a different Hebrew word) in Job 39:13–16. Casual observation could make the ostrich appear heartless since it lays its eggs in the sand and often leaves the nest to hunt for food.
4:5 *purple.* Or "scarlet" (Hebrew *tola* rather than the more commonly used *argaman*). *Tola* refers to the color produced by dye made from the insect *Kermes ilicis* (formerly known as *Coccus ilicis*) rather than to the color derived from the murex snail. Its use was restricted to the ceremonial garments of only the highest ranking civil and religious leaders.

6 The punishment of my people
is greater than that of Sodom,[g]
which was overthrown in a moment
without a hand turned to help her.

7 Their princes were brighter than snow
and whiter than milk,
their bodies more ruddy than rubies,
their appearance like lapis lazuli.

8 But now they are blacker[h] than soot;
they are not recognized in the
streets.
Their skin has shriveled on their
bones;[i]
it has become as dry as a stick.

9 Those killed by the sword are better off
than those who die of famine;
racked with hunger, they waste away
for lack of food from the field.[j]

10 With their own hands compassionate
women
have cooked their own children,[k]
who became their food
when my people were destroyed.

11 The LORD has given full vent to his
wrath;
he has poured out his fierce anger.
He kindled a fire[l] in Zion
that consumed her foundations.[m]

12 The kings of the earth did not believe,
nor did any of the peoples of the
world,
that enemies and foes could enter
the gates of Jerusalem.[n]

13 But it happened because of the sins of
her prophets
and the iniquities of her priests,[o]
who shed within her
the blood of the righteous.

14 Now they grope through the streets
as if they were blind.[p]
They are so defiled with blood[q]
that no one dares to touch their
garments.

15 "Go away! You are unclean!" people
cry to them.
"Away! Away! Don't touch us!"
When they flee and wander about,
people among the nations say,
"They can stay here no longer."[r]

16 The LORD himself has scattered
them;
he no longer watches over them.[s]
The priests are shown no honor,
the elders[t] no favor.

17 Moreover, our eyes failed,
looking in vain[u] for help;[v]
from our towers we watched
for a nation[w] that could not
save us.

18 People stalked us at every step,
so we could not walk in our
streets.
Our end was near, our days were
numbered,
for our end had come.[x]

19 Our pursuers were swifter
than eagles[y] in the sky;
they chased us[z] over the mountains
and lay in wait for us in the desert.

20 The LORD's anointed,[a] our very life
breath,
was caught in their traps.[b]

4:6 [g] Ge 19:25 **4:8** [h] Job 30:28 [i] Ps 102:3-5 **4:9** [j] Jer 15:2; 16:4 **4:10** [k] Lev 26:29; Dt 28:53-57; Jer 19:9; La 2:20; Eze 5:10 **4:11** [l] Jer 17:27 [m] Dt 32:22; Jer 7:20; Eze 22:31 **4:12** [n] 1Ki 9:9; Jer 21:13 **4:13** [o] Jer 5:31; 6:13; Eze 22:28; Mic 3:11

4:14 [p] Isa 59:10 [q] Jer 2:34; 19:4 **4:15** [r] Lev 13:46 **4:16** [s] Isa 9:14-16 [t] La 5:12 **4:17** [u] Isa 20:5; Eze 29:16 [v] La 1:7 [w] Jer 37:7 **4:18** [x] Eze 7:2-12; Am 8:2 **4:19** [y] Dt 28:49 [z] Isa 5:26-28 **4:20** [a] 2Sa 19:21 [b] Jer 39:5; Eze 12:12-13; 19:4,8

4:8 – 10 The siege Nebuchadnezzar laid against Jerusalem (2Ki 25:1 – 3) lasted a year and a half. Siege was one of the tactics used in the ancient Near East to subdue a city (see the article "Siege Warfare," p. 1157). The population was cut off from the source of their food until their resistance broke. The Arameans used this tactic against Israel's capital city, Samaria. The severity of the famine coupled with the resolute resistance of the besieged occasioned some in the population to resort to cannibalism (see note on Jer 19:9).
4:17 *looking in vain for help.* When Nebuchadnezzar undertook his punitive raid against Jerusalem in 597 BC, Egypt was the principal ally on whom Judah relied. Later that year, Nebuchadnezzar put Zedekiah on the throne. Zedekiah almost immediately began meeting with a coalition of the small western states to stand together against Nebuchadnezzar (see note on Jer 27:3). In 595 BC, a new pharaoh, Psammetichus II, took the throne of Egypt. He enjoyed an early military success against the Nubians in the south, and one papyrus reports that his success was celebrated with a victory tour in Palestine. There was cause to expect his support against Babylon. It is uncertain which nations were actually part of the alliance when it finally took shape. As it turned out, Egypt's army was routed in their confrontation with the Babylonians in 588 BC (see Jer 37:5 – 7), and it would appear, based on Ps 137:7, that allies such as the Edomites threw their support to Babylon when it became clear that Jerusalem was about to fall.
4:19 *mountains.* From the perspective of the people of Judah, especially those of Jerusalem, the Judahite mountains represented a measure of security. Up to this time, the great battlefields of history were either down along the coastal plain and broad valleys of the foothills or up north in the Jezreel Valley and the Beth Shan Valley. If the enemy did ascend into the mountains, the central Benjamin plateau, about 5 miles (8 kilometers) north of Jerusalem, provided a suitable battlefield. But rugged terrain around Jerusalem was hard for invading armies to negotiate. *desert.* The Desert of Judah was harder than even the mountains were for invading armies to negotiate. This was where David fled for refuge from Saul. But the poet's point is that these natural defenses were inadequate this time.
4:20 *The LORD's anointed, our very life breath.* The poet refers here to the Davidic king who ideally reigned under Yahweh, Israel's ultimate and proper sovereign. In Israel, while the king represented authority, administered jus-

We thought that under his shadow
we would live among the nations.

[21] Rejoice and be glad, Daughter Edom,
you who live in the land of Uz.
But to you also the cup[c] will be
passed;
you will be drunk and stripped
naked.[d]
[22] Your punishment will end, Daughter
Zion;[e]
he will not prolong your exile.
But he will punish your sin, Daughter
Edom,
and expose your wickedness.[f]

5 Remember, LORD, what has happened
to us;
look, and see our disgrace.[g]
[2] Our inheritance[h] has been turned over
to strangers,
our homes[i] to foreigners.
[3] We have become fatherless,
our mothers are widows.[j]
[4] We must buy the water we drink;
our wood can be had only at a
price.[k]
[5] Those who pursue us are at our
heels;
we are weary[l] and find no rest.
[6] We submitted to Egypt and Assyria[m]
to get enough bread.
[7] Our ancestors sinned and are no
more,
and we bear their punishment.[n]
[8] Slaves[o] rule over us,
and there is no one to free us from
their hands.[p]

4:21 [c] Jer 25:15 [d] Isa 34:6-10; Am 1:11-12; Ob 1:16 **4:22** [e] Isa 40:2; Jer 33:8 [f] Ps 137:7; Mal 1:4 **5:1** [g] Ps 44:13-16; 89:50 **5:2** [h] Ps 79:1 [i] Zep 1:13 **5:3** [j] Jer 15:8; 18:21 **5:4** [k] Isa 3:1 **5:5** [l] Ne 9:37 **5:6** [m] Hos 9:3 **5:7** [n] Jer 14:20; 16:12 **5:8** [o] Ne 5:15 [p] Zec 11:6

tice, exercised mercy, and provided protection, he was always subject to Yahweh. There is indication in the larger culture of the ancient Near East that the king is god incarnate. By the time of the pyramids, the Egyptian pharaoh was referred to as god. The divine king was seen as the one on whom subjects depended for life and livelihood. Sesostris III (c.1878–1843 BC) is referred to as "he who gives breath to his subjects." Early Mesopotamian texts use similar expressions. The poet here expresses that the promised and anointed king, the representative of Yahweh—Israel's breath of life—had been taken away. *under his shadow.* The Hebrews perceived Yahweh as Protector and often used the metaphor of shadow (see note on Ps 91:1) or shade (Ps 121:5). Similarly, both Egyptian and Mesopotamian texts refer to the king/god as a "shadow," implying protector. In the *Report of Wenamun*, describing an Egyptian official's trip to Byblos in what is now Lebanon, it is claimed for Wenamun that "the shadow of Pharaoh [referring to the Phoenician prince]—life, prosperity, health!—your lord has fallen on you!" What these disparate cultures share in common is a connection between the concept of king and the concept of deity and the notion that God/king is the source of life and security.

4:21 *Edom.* See note on Jer 49:7. Edom had become an Assyrian vassal state in the reign of Tiglath-Pileser III and continued under their rule until the death of Ashurbanipal a century later. It is likely that they submitted themselves to Nebuchadnezzar's rule in 605 BC. Although some Judahite refugees may have found shelter in Edom, they apparently remained passive as Jerusalem was destroyed (see Ps 137:7; Ob 11). The Babylonian campaign against Ammon and Moab in 594 BC seems not to have affected Edom. It is likely that they remained unscathed until the time of Nabonidus's campaign in 552 BC. *Uz.* The homeland of Job (Job 1:1); it is identified with Edom and northwest Arabia in Esau's genealogy (Ge 36:28).

5:2 *Our inheritance has been turned over to strangers.* The poet laments the loss of this inheritance, an external indication of the breakdown of the covenant relationship. Inheritance and property rights were significant issues in the ancient Near East, but they were especially important in Israel (see the article "Land Grants," p. 361). The significance of property and inheritance rights in the ancient Near East is illustrated by the Vassal Treaties of Esarhaddon, which include among its curses: "May your sons not have authority over your house, but a foreign enemy divide your possessions."

5:6 *submitted.* Lit. "gave hand," which has sometimes been idiomatically rendered "shook hands," but more likely refers to a gesture formalizing surrender to foreign sovereignty. The Assyrian king Shalmaneser III, e.g., is pictured on a throne dais, dressed in royal attire, shaking hands with Marduk-zakir-shumi mentioned in the text inscribed on the dais. In one of the Amarna letters, Yapahu, prince of Gezer, complains that his brother has "given his two hands to the chief of the 'Apiru.' And now the [land of ...] anna is hostile to me." The implication is that Yapahu's brother has made an alliance with the enemy. In Hezekiah's call to Israel and Judah to return to Yahweh and celebrate the Passover, he calls on the people to renew their allegiance, lit. "give a hand" (NIV "submit"), to Yahweh (2Ch 30:8). *Egypt and Assyria.* From the beginning of the seventh century BC, Judah had been under Assyrian control. Manasseh was a loyal vassal for most of his 55 years. During the time of Josiah, Judah experienced a glimpse of independence as the mantle was shifting from Assyria to Babylon. During that interim, Egypt began to exercise more control in the region. Jehoiakim, the son of Josiah, had been put on the throne by the Egyptians in 609 BC, and he remained loyal to them until Nebuchadnezzar's domination made that impossible. After the fall of Ashkelon to Nebuchadnezzar in 604, Jehoiakim paid tribute to Babylon for a few years. But when Nebuchadnezzar failed in his attempted invasion of Egypt in 601, Jehoiakim again sided with Egypt and stopped sending the yearly tribute east. Thus, in 597 when Nebuchadnezzar undertook his punitive raid against Jerusalem, Egypt was the principal ally on whom Judah relied. It can fairly be said, then, that Judah had been totally dependent on Egypt and Assyria—and that reliance went back a century or more.

5:7 *Our ancestors sinned ... we bear their punishment.* The idea that the poet and his generation bore some measure of guilt previously incurred by their forebears is based on the covenant stipulation, "I, the LORD your God, am a jealous God, punishing the children for the sin of the parents to the third and fourth generation of those who hate me" (Ex 20:5; Dt 5:9; cf. Ex 34:7; Nu 14:18,33). It is reflected in the proverbial "sour grapes" saying (see Jer 31:29; Eze 18:2 and notes), albeit from a different perspective. It is important to note, however, that the poet understands that the cause of the calamity is also the result of his own sin and that of his contemporaries (1:20a).

[9] We get our bread at the risk of our
lives
because of the sword in the desert.
[10] Our skin is hot as an oven,
feverish from hunger.[q]
[11] Women have been violated[r] in Zion,
and virgins in the towns of Judah.
[12] Princes have been hung up by their
hands;
elders are shown no respect.[s]
[13] Young men toil at the millstones;
boys stagger under loads of wood.
[14] The elders are gone from the city gate;
the young men have stopped their
music.[t]
[15] Joy is gone from our hearts;
our dancing has turned to
mourning.[u]
[16] The crown[v] has fallen from our head.
Woe to us, for we have sinned![w]

5:10 [q] La 4:8-9
5:11 [r] Zec 14:2
5:12 [s] La 4:16
5:14 [t] Isa 24:8; Jer 7:34
5:15 [u] Jer 25:10
5:16 [v] Ps 89:39 [w] Isa 3:11

5:12 *Princes have been hung up by their hands.* The Hebrew text is ambiguous regarding whether the princes are hung at the hands of the enemy or are hung suspended from their own hands. There is no precedent for the latter. *hung.* Generally done after execution had taken place. Victims were usually "hung" by being impaled. The practice was most commonly used on rebellion leaders or members of the royal house (1Sa 31:10). The practice of impaling the bodies of their defeated enemies was commonly used by armies in the ancient Near East. The Assyrians, e.g., considered it a psychological ploy and a terror tactic (as depicted on the walls of their royal palaces). See note on Est 2:23.
5:13 *toil at the millstones.* Grinding grain into flour was usually done with millstones and was the job of the lowest members of society. One of the basic "appliances" of any ancient household would have been the hand mill (called a saddle quern), which had two stones for grinding: a lower stone with a concave surface and a loaf-shaped upper stone. The daily chore of grinding grain into flour involved sliding the upper stone over the grain spread on the lower stone. Larger milling houses often served as prison workhouses in Mesopotamia, but each prisoner still used a hand mill for grinding. The palace at Ebla had a room containing 16 hand mills inferred to be a place where prisoners ground grain. Grinding houses used prisoners of war, criminals and those who had defaulted on their debts. *loads of wood.* Wood was a constant necessity for keeping the fires of the kitchens supplied. The palace, temple and upper class employed the services of slave labor to man the system. Even children were capable of helping transport and distribute the wood.
5:16 *crown.* Crowns are worn by royalty as a symbol of their status and authority. As a result, the word was extended to refer to the abstract concept of the dignity and honor that are the natural accompaniments of status and authority. In this passage the reference is not to an actual crown that Israel wore but to the dignity and honor.

Wooden model of Egyptian woman grinding grain, 2134 to 1991 BC. See note on La 5:13.
Wikimedia Commons

Relief of mourning captives.

Kim Walton, British Museum

[17]Because of this our hearts[x] are faint,
because of these things our eyes[y]
grow dim
[18]for Mount Zion, which lies desolate,[z]
with jackals prowling over it.

[19]You, LORD, reign forever;
your throne endures[a] from
generation to generation.

[20]Why do you always forget us?[b]
Why do you forsake us so long?
[21]Restore[c] us to yourself, LORD, that we
may return;
renew our days as of old
[22]unless you have utterly rejected us
and are angry with us beyond
measure.[d]

5:17 [x] Isa 1:5 [y] Ps 6:7 **5:18** [z] Mic 3:12 **5:19** [a] Ps 45:6; 102:12, 24-27 **5:20** [b] Ps 13:1; 44:24 **5:21** [c] Ps 80:3 **5:22** [d] Isa 64:9

5:21 *Restore us.* At or near the end of each of the classic Mesopotamian city laments an appeal for restoration is made to deity (see the article "City Laments," p. 951). In the various laments the appeal is voiced either by the citizens or by a lower-level deity. The Ur lament includes a brief appeal to "undo the sins"; it also requests, "May every heart of its people be pure before thee! May the heart of those who dwell in the land be good before thee!" On the other hand, the laments over Sumer and Ur and over Eridu do not include this sort of confession/petition.

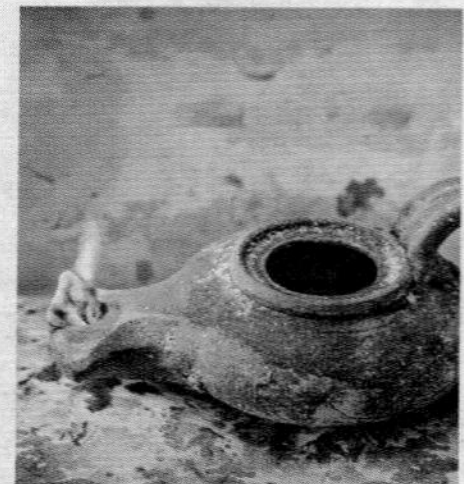

ORACLES OF THE PROPHETS

EZEKIEL

The book of Ezekiel's testimony unequivocally presents itself as having been delivered in exile during the Babylonian captivity. Based upon the dating formulas in 1:2 and 40:1, Ezekiel's prophecies extend for approximately 20 years (593 – 571 BC). The prophet himself, however, had been in Babylonia since 605 BC, the date of the first deportation of the Jerusalem elite into exile. Ezekiel considers himself part of the community-in-exile. He views events in Judah from afar, described only by way of numerous visions and probably from personal memory of the last days of the Davidic dynasty. In 33:21, in the 12th year of his exile, he receives news of the fall of Jerusalem from a fugitive.

KEY CONCEPTS

- The people of Israel will be reborn.
- God will return to again dwell among his people.
- There will be a new covenant between God and his people.
- Israel will know that Yahweh is God.

Ezekiel went into exile with between 8,000 and 10,000 others — the nobility, artisans, priests and religious personnel — who had been sent to Babylonia with King Jehoiachin during the first deportation (2Ki 24:14 – 16). He was a victim of a common policy of the Assyrians and the Babylonians: the practice of selective deportations. By removing political, spiritual and economic leadership, the Babylonians aimed to break down national resistance, prevent any possibility of revolt, and bolster the economy and military machine of the conqueror's homeland.

The recovery of the Akkadian background of the book of Ezekiel can increase our understanding of a number of expressions, themes and motifs — many of which have been misunderstood, gratuitously emended, completely overlooked, or termed "obscure." It appears that the Biblical writer has woven into his creation images, terms and idioms taken from his contemporary religious, legal, social and political reality. For example, Ezekiel's description contains a reminiscence of the Mesopotamian Ishtar festival. Exiled in Babylonia, Ezekiel could not have failed to be confronted with the grandiose and in many respects obscene Ishtar festival. Shocked by the practices he discovered in Mesopotamia, he draws heavily on the Ishtar cult as the epitome of idolatrous and religious straying of the nation.

Ezekiel also frequently uses imagery that is known from the Mesopotamian epic "Erra and Ishum," a literary piece that was popular in Babylonia during the time the exiles were living there. Knowledge of the literature of Babylonia helps us understand allusions, both subtle and blatant, that are woven throughout the book. ◆

Ezekiel's Inaugural Vision

1 In my thirtieth year, in the fourth
month on the fifth day, while I was
among the exiles[a] by the Kebar River, the
heavens were opened[b] and I saw visions[c]
of God.
2 On the fifth of the month — it was the
fifth year of the exile of King Jehoiachin[d] —
3 the word of the LORD came to Ezekiel the
priest, the son of Buzi, by the Kebar River
in the land of the Babylonians.[a] There the
hand of the LORD was on him.[e]
4 I looked, and I saw a windstorm coming out of the north[f] — an immense cloud
with flashing lightning and surrounded by
brilliant light. The center of the fire looked
like glowing metal,[g] 5 and in the fire was
what looked like four living creatures.[h] In
appearance their form was human,[i] 6 but
each of them had four faces[j] and four
wings. 7 Their legs were straight; their feet
were like those of a calf and gleamed like
burnished bronze.[k] 8 Under their wings on
their four sides they had human hands.[l]
All four of them had faces and wings, 9 and
the wings of one touched the wings of another. Each one went straight ahead; they
did not turn as they moved.[m]
10 Their faces looked like this: Each of
the four had the face of a human being,
and on the right side each had the face
of a lion, and on the left the face of an
ox; each also had the face of an eagle.[n]

1:1 [a] Eze 11:24-25 [b] Mt 3:16; Ac 7:56 [c] Ex 24:10 **1:2** [d] 2Ki 24:15 **1:3** [e] 2Ki 3:15; Eze 3:14,22 **1:4** [f] Jer 1:14 [g] Eze 8:2 **1:5** [h] Rev 4:6 [i] ver 26 **1:6** [j] Eze 10:14 **1:7** [k] Da 10:6; Rev 1:15 **1:8** [l] Eze 10:8 **1:9** [m] Eze 10:22 **1:10** [n] Eze 10:14; Rev 4:7

[a] 3 Or *Chaldeans*

1:1 *Kebar River.* Ezekiel and his compatriots in exile have settled in the vicinity of the Kebar Canal, one of the many branches of an elaborate irrigation system that distributed water from the Euphrates River throughout the city and its environs. *I saw visions.* Apocalyptic literature is characterized by visions filled with the imagery sometimes associated with God's manifold powers as creator. A divine messenger usually interprets the message that is conveyed to the prophet (see Rev 1:1 – 3). There are some pieces of Akkadian literature that show prototypes of some of the characteristics of Biblical apocalyptic, but nothing that is very close. Apocalyptic literature is most recognizable in its use of rich symbolism that draws heavily on mythological motifs. In prophetic literature, the symbols are rarely interpreted. Often the visions themselves do not symbolically represent a foretold happening, but serve as occasions for a message concerning what God is going to do. Most scholars now consider Ezekiel's prophetic visions as being influential on later apocalyptic literature (see Da 7 – 12; Zec 8 – 14); e.g., his vision of God enthroned in a shining chariot has been incorporated into Da 10:5 – 6, as well as the pseudepigraphal book of 1 Enoch 14:18. See the article "Apocalyptic Literature," p. 1554.

1:2 *exile of King Jehoiachin.* The name Jehoiachin appears in a Babylonian ration list dating from the 10th to the 35th year of the reign of Nebuchadnezzar II (595 – 569 BC). While in Babylonian exile at the court of Nebuchadnezzar, Jehoiachin retained the royal title "the king of the land of Judah" and, together with his five sons, received generous food rations. From the Babylonian point of view, therefore, not only was Jehoiachin in exile, but he was still considered by his conquerors as the legitimate king of Judah. Zedekiah was merely the "regent prince" in Jerusalem, and this is how Ezekiel consistently refers to Zedekiah. He never uses the term "king" when speaking of Zedekiah. Nebuchadnezzar's successor, Amel-Marduk (Biblical Awel-Marduk) continued to treat Jehoiachin kindly. In 561 BC he removed Jehoiachin from prison and made him live in his palace, where Jehoiachin was given special rank among his fellow exiled kings (2Ki 25:27 – 30; Jer 52:31 – 34).

1:3 *Babylonians.* In Ezekiel the Hebrew name "Chaldeans" is interchanged with "Babylonians" (12:13; 23:14,23). The term "Chaldeans" designates one of the several Aramean tribes that had settled into southern Babylonia in the early part of the first millennium BC. In 625 BC one of their leaders, Nabopolassar, succeeded in gaining Babylon independence from Assyria. Nebuchadnezzar II was the second monarch in this Neo-Babylonian (i.e., Chaldean) dynasty. See the article "Historical Setting of Jeremiah," p. 1222.

1:4 *glowing metal.* This Hebrew term occurs in the Bible only in Ezekiel (here; v. 27; 8:2). It is related to an Akkadian word meaning "amber," a brilliant semiprecious stone used in the fabrication of divine statues. It served to enhance the shine of the eyes of the statue or to give an impression of radiance by reflecting light. Thus a Neo-Babylonian religious text uses this term to describe the outward appearance of the glowing face of the god Nergal.

1:5 *four living creatures.* It seems that in the elaboration of his vision Ezekiel takes as a model the gigantic composite creatures well known in Assyrian and Babylonian iconographic and glyptic art. These hybrid creatures protected the entrance into temples or palaces. The colossal Assyrian composite creatures unearthed during archaeological excavations provide a fitting example. They have been excavated at the site of ancient Nimrud, where they guarded the doorways to the palace of Ashurnasirpal II (883 – 859 BC). One of these is a winged bull with a human head; another has the body of a lion. Ezekiel consistently repeats the expression "looked like" (e.g., vv. 4,5,10,22,26,27), indicating his unwillingness to commit himself to the substantial identity of the seen with the compared. It looked "like" fire, living creatures, a human being, but these buffer terms indicate that this is only a "vision." This is the sort of language regularly used in reports of dreams and visions.

1:10 *Each of the four had the face of a human being ... a lion ... an ox ... an eagle.* The head of the animal should in some way recall the qualities attributed to the divinity itself. *human being.* The most dignified and noble of all creatures, being created in the image of God and ruling over all the other creatures (Ge 1:28; Ps 8). *lion.* Symbolizes royalty, strength and courage both in the Bible and in the ancient Near Eastern world (Jdg 14:18; 2Sa 1:23; 17:10). *eagle.* The swiftest and the most high-flying of birds (Dt 28:49; Isa 40:31; Jer 48:40). *ox.* The most frequent symbol of fertility. It was the emblematic animal of the northwest Semitic storm-god Adad, the one who brought rain and with it renewed fertility of the land (Ps 106:19 – 20). These four, furthermore, particularly represent the categories of terrestrial creatures: humans, wild animals, domestic animals, birds.

In Mesopotamia it is lesser divinities like guardian genii that are portrayed in composite form, including winged biped or quadrupeds with human faces. Two tiny bronze figurines from Ischali dating from Old Babylonian times show a god and a goddess, each with four identical human faces conveying the idea of all-observing potency. Two-faced gods, so-called Janus figures, however, are

Artist's rendition of Ezekiel's vision.
Jonathan Walton

11 Such were their faces. They each had
two wings[o] spreading out upward, each
wing touching that of the creature on either side; and each had two other wings
covering its body. 12 Each one went straight
ahead. Wherever the spirit would go, they
would go, without turning as they
went. 13 The appearance of the living creatures was like burning coals
of fire or like torches. Fire moved
back and forth among the creatures;
it was bright, and lightning[p] flashed
out of it. 14 The creatures sped back
and forth like flashes of lightning.[q]
15 As I looked at the living creatures, I saw a wheel on the ground
beside each creature with its four
faces. 16 This was the appearance
and structure of the wheels: They
sparkled like topaz,[r] and all four
looked alike. Each appeared to be
made like a wheel intersecting a
wheel. 17 As they moved, they would
go in any one of the four directions
the creatures faced; the wheels did
not change direction[s] as the creatures went. 18 Their rims were high
and awesome, and all four rims
were full of eyes[t] all around.
19 When the living creatures
moved, the wheels beside them
moved; and when the living creatures rose from the ground, the
wheels also rose. 20 Wherever the
spirit would go, they would go,[u]
and the wheels would rise along
with them, because the spirit of the
living creatures was in the wheels.
21 When the creatures moved, they
also moved; when the creatures
stood still, they also stood still; and
when the creatures rose from the
ground, the wheels rose along with
them, because the spirit of the living creatures was in the wheels.[v]
22 Spread out above the heads of the living creatures was what looked something

1:11 [o] Isa 6:2 **1:13** [p] Rev 4:5 **1:14** [q] Ps 29:7 **1:16** [r] Eze 10:9-11; Da 10:6 **1:17** [s] ver 9 **1:18** [t] Eze 10:12; Rev 4:6 **1:20** [u] ver 12 **1:21** [v] Eze 10:17

more common in Mesopotamia. The major difference between the prophet's vision and Mesopotamian parallels is that Ezekiel's creatures have four different faces; for that we have no known analogues.

1:15 – 18 Naturally, a chariot with wheels facing all four directions could not travel effectively in any direction. However, the purpose of the image is found in its symbolic value of attention to all the corners of the world — God's omnipresence. In addition, the chariot is actually upheld on the outstretched wings of God's four-faced creatures and flies through the air. There is, however, a sense of motion implicit in having the wheels in place. This is based on a comparison with the winged-bull figures that guarded entranceways in Assyrian palaces. Many of them have a fifth leg to suggest that though the figure is frozen in the relief, it is actually dynamic and in motion. Assyrian art also provides examples of wheeled chariots with high rims and multiple spokes that may be the origin of this image in Ezekiel. The wheels in Assyrian chariots of this time sometimes feature thick rims made up of concentric bands as well as spokes. The depiction of a "wheel intersecting a wheel" (v. 16) may thus represent a greater stability for the chariot, as multiple axles and tires do for modern trucks.

1:18 *all four rims were full of eyes.* The eyes with which the rims of the wheels are inlaid may signify constant divine watchfulness. Rims full of eyes are comparable to the many "eye stones" that adorned the tiaras of the Assyrians' divine statues. Alternatively, some of the depictions of chariots of this time period used the technology of creating a tread for the wooden chariot wheels by driving metal studs into the wheels all around the circumference.

1:22 *a vault, sparkling like crystal.* Above the heads of the four creatures is a platform sparkling like crystal or ice. Ancient Near Eastern glyptic art and sculpture contain images of winged creatures holding up a pillar, a throne, or a platform. In the seventh-century BC Assyrian palace at Nineveh, miniature sphinxes served as column bases. Similarly, a twelfth-century BC Phoenician wheeled cult stand depicts a human-faced, lion-bodied, winged figure. Its wings and head appear to be holding up one side of the stand. More significantly, first millennium BC

like a vault,[w] sparkling like crystal, and
awesome. 23 Under the vault their wings
were stretched out one toward the other,
and each had two wings covering its body.
24 When the creatures moved, I heard the
sound of their wings, like the roar of rushing waters, like the voice[x] of the Almighty,[a]
like the tumult of an army.[y] When they
stood still, they lowered their wings.
25 Then there came a voice from above
the vault over their heads as they stood
with lowered wings. 26 Above the vault
over their heads was what looked like a
throne of lapis lazuli,[z] and high above on
the throne was a figure like that of a man.[a]
27 I saw that from what appeared to be his
waist up he looked like glowing metal, as
if full of fire, and that from there down
he looked like fire; and brilliant light surrounded him.[b] 28 Like the appearance of a
rainbow[c] in the clouds on a rainy day, so
was the radiance around him.[d]

1:22 [w] Eze 10:1 **1:24** [x] Eze 10:5; 43:2; Da 10:6; Rev 1:15; 19:6 [y] 2Ki 7:6
1:26 [z] Ex 24:10; Eze 10:1 [a] Rev 1:13 **1:27** [b] Eze 8:2 **1:28** [c] Ge 9:13; Rev 10:1 [d] Rev 4:2

[a] 24 Hebrew *Shaddai*

Mesopotamian texts speak of three levels of the heavens, each of which feature pavements of different colored stone. The lower heavens are said to have a platform of jasper, usually associated with a glassy, translucent or opaque appearance. In those texts, the pavement of the middle heavens is lapis lazuli (see note on Isa 54:11) and holds up the dais of the god Bel (i.e., Marduk).

1:26 *throne.* The image of a deity's throne in procession is well known in the ancient Near East. Engraved cylinder seals from the end of the third millennium BC show a deity standing in a four-wheeled chariot/cart drawn by a composite quadruped with a lion's head and wings. Assyrian reliefs show wheeled thrones for both kings and gods that also feature poles for bearers to use to carry the throne. *lapis lazuli.* See note on Isa 54:11.

1:27 *glowing metal.* See note on v. 4. *brilliant light.* The figure sitting on the throne is surrounded with splendor. The brilliant light stands for a numinous quality that seems to reflect a major literary and iconographic feature of Mesopotamian culture, the so-called *melammu,* radiance or divine effulgence surrounding beings or sacred objects that have divine power (see the article "Glory," p. 178).

EZEKIEL 1

ARAMAIC

The Aramaic language was increasingly becoming the trade and diplomatic language of the last days of the Babylonian Empire in the sixth century BC. Ezekiel's extended stay in Babylonian exile accounts for the unusually high proportion of Aramaic and Akkadian words in his book and the numerous images and themes that have their background in his land of exile. Ezekiel is truly a product of his time and of his environment. As attested many times in the past, the literati and intellectual leadership of any age succeed in finding common meeting grounds despite political, social or religious pressures intended to keep them separate. It is therefore conceivable that Ezekiel was able to converse with Babylonian scribes and religious leaders in Aramaic, acquiring knowledge of Akkadian literature, or at least its main themes, motifs and metaphors. ◆

This seventh-century BC funerary stele has a carved scene and an inscription in Aramaic, Neirab.

Kim Walton. The Louvre.

This was the appearance of the likeness
of the glory[e] of the LORD. When I saw it,
I fell facedown,[f] and I heard the voice of
one speaking.

Ezekiel's Call to Be a Prophet

2 He said to me, "Son of man,[a] stand[g]
up on your feet and I will speak to
you." 2 As he spoke, the Spirit came into
me and raised me[h] to my feet, and I heard
him speaking to me.
3 He said: "Son of man, I am sending you
to the Israelites, to a rebellious nation that
has rebelled against me; they and their ancestors have been in revolt against me to
this very day.[i] 4 The people to whom I am
sending you are obstinate and stubborn.[j]
Say to them, 'This is what the Sovereign
LORD says.' 5 And whether they listen or
fail to listen[k] — for they are a rebellious
people[l] — they will know that a prophet
has been among them.[m] 6 And you, son of
man, do not be afraid[n] of them or their
words. Do not be afraid, though briers
and thorns[o] are all around you and you
live among scorpions. Do not be afraid
of what they say or be terrified by them,
though they are a rebellious people.[p] 7 You
must speak my words to them, whether
they listen or fail to listen, for they are rebellious.[q] 8 But you, son of man, listen to
what I say to you. Do not rebel like that
rebellious people;[r] open your mouth and
eat[s] what I give you."
9 Then I looked, and I saw a hand[t]
stretched out to me. In it was a scroll,
10 which he unrolled before me. On both
sides of it were written words of lament
and mourning and woe.[u]

3 And he said to me, "Son of man, eat
what is before you, eat this scroll; then
go and speak to the people of Israel." 2 So
I opened my mouth, and he gave me the
scroll to eat.
3 Then he said to me, "Son of man, eat
this scroll I am giving you and fill your
stomach with it." So I ate[v] it, and it tasted
as sweet as honey[w] in my mouth.
4 He then said to me: "Son of man, go
now to the people of Israel and speak my
words to them. 5 You are not being sent to
a people of obscure speech and strange
language,[x] but to the people of Israel —
6 not to many peoples of obscure speech
and strange language, whose words you
cannot understand. Surely if I had sent
you to them, they would have listened to
you.[y] 7 But the people of Israel are not willing to listen to you because they are not
willing to listen to me, for all the Israelites

1:28 [e] Eze 8:4 [f] Eze 3:23; Da 8:17; Rev 1:17
2:1 [g] Da 10:11
2:2 [h] Eze 3:24; Da 8:18
2:3 [i] Jer 3:25; Eze 20:8-24
2:4 [j] Eze 3:7
2:5 [k] Eze 3:11 [l] Eze 3:27 [m] Eze 33:33
2:6 [n] Jer 1:8, 17 [o] Isa 9:18; Mic 7:4 [p] Eze 3:9
2:7 [q] Jer 1:7; Eze 3:10-11
2:8 [r] Isa 50:5 [s] Jer 15:16; Rev 10:9
2:9 [t] Eze 8:3
2:10 [u] Rev 8:13
3:3 [v] Jer 15:16 [w] Ps 19:10; Ps 119:103; Rev 10:9-10
3:5 [x] Isa 28:11; Jnh 1:2
3:6 [y] Mt 11:21-23

[a] 1 The Hebrew phrase *ben adam* means *human being.* The phrase *son of man* is retained as a form of address here and throughout Ezekiel because of its possible association with "Son of Man" in the New Testament.

2:1 *Son of man.* The prophet is addressed 92 times with the expression "son of man." In Hebrew it refers to a "son of humankind" and therefore refers to him as a mortal. The collective word has an underlying note of helplessness and frailty. In contrast to other prophets (see, e.g., Jer 1:11; 24:3; Am 7:8; 8:2), the Lord speaks to Ezekiel without using his name (the name "Ezekiel" occurs only twice in the book). Ezekiel is called this in order to underline his mortal nature among the divine beings who often fill the scene and speak to him. Ezekiel's call to prophetic service is described in ancient royal court language. *stand up.* Having been brought into the presence of a king, a person would signify subjection with the gesture of prostration and would not dare to rise unless authorized to do so by the king.

2:4 *This is what the Sovereign LORD says.* This is the prophetic adaptation of the "messenger formula." Numerous letters in Mari, El-Amarna, and the ancient Near East start in the following manner: "To my lord say: 'Thus says so and so.'" With this formula, messengers began their verbatim delivery of messages. This expression is found 129 times in Ezekiel, a frequency matched only by Jeremiah. Precisely because these two prophets were challenged by their contemporaries, they insist on the fact that they have been commissioned to speak by and on behalf of the Sovereign Lord.

2:6 *briers and thorns ... scorpions.* The metaphors used in this verse seem to reflect Babylonian influence, in which case they should not be interpreted as threats to Ezekiel but as symbols of protection. In a Neo-Babylonian collection of incantations the speaker describes his inviolability in a similar way by describing himself as a thornbush or the stinger of a scorpion. This understanding of such metaphors is confirmed by the fact that this statement occurs at the very point where Biblical call narratives place the promise of divine presence for the commissioning of the prophet.

2:10 *On both sides ... were written words of lament and mourning and woe.* Scrolls were made out of papyrus or leather. A relief of Sennacherib now in the British Museum shows two scribes, one with two wooden writing boards covered with beeswax and hinged as a diptych and another with a papyrus or leather scroll recording plunder. Since the scroll mentioned by Ezekiel is written on both sides, it is presumably made out of papyrus and not leather. Only around the first century AD did the quality of skin sufficiently improve to allow writing on both sides. Following the custom of that time, the content of the scroll is summarized on the outside of the rolled document with three ominous words, each of which spells disaster: lament, mourning, and woe. The title of the document sets the tone of Ezekiel's ministry.

3:3 *So I ate it.* The notion of ingestion as a means of appropriating the divine word has been compared with the practice of ingesting magical inscriptions as found on Greco-Egyptian papyri. The important thing is not the act of swallowing the scroll but the memorization of its particularly difficult content. An anthropological study of the pedagogical system of Palestinian rabbis points out the importance of memorable gestures in the act of learning. "Chewing" of the scroll corresponds to an act of memorization and thorough appropriation of its verbal content. In the light of these analogies Ezekiel's "eating of the scroll" should be understood as an act of memorization and not necessarily as a literal ingestion of a papyrus scroll.

are hardened and obstinate.[z] 8But I will
make you as unyielding and hardened as
they are.[a] 9I will make your forehead like
the hardest stone, harder than flint. Do
not be afraid of them or terrified by them,
though they are a rebellious people.[b]”
10And he said to me, “Son of man, listen
carefully and take to heart all the words
I speak to you. 11Go now to your people
in exile and speak to them. Say to them,
‘This is what the Sovereign LORD says,’
whether they listen or fail to listen.[c]”
12Then the Spirit lifted me up,[d] and I
heard behind me a loud rumbling sound
as the glory of the LORD rose from the
place where it was standing.[a] 13It was
the sound of the wings of the living creatures brushing against each other and the
sound of the wheels beside them, a loud
rumbling sound.[e] 14The Spirit then lifted
me up and took me away, and I went in
bitterness and in the anger of my spirit,
with the strong hand of the LORD on me.
15I came to the exiles who lived at Tel Aviv
near the Kebar River.[f] And there, where
they were living, I sat among them for sev-
en days[g]—deeply distressed.

Ezekiel's Task as Watchman

16At the end of seven days the word of
the LORD came to me:[h] 17“Son of man, I
have made you a watchman[i] for the people of Israel; so hear the word I speak and
give them warning from me. 18When I say
to a wicked person, ‘You will surely die,’
and you do not warn them or speak out
to dissuade them from their evil ways in
order to save their life, that wicked person will die for[b] their sin, and I will hold
you accountable for their blood.[j] 19But if
you do warn the wicked person and they
do not turn from their wickedness or from
their evil ways, they will die for their sin;
but you will have saved yourself.[k]
20“Again, when a righteous person
turns from their righteousness and does
evil, and I put a stumbling block before
them, they will die. Since you did not
warn them, they will die for their sin.
The righteous things that person did will
not be remembered, and I will hold you
accountable for their blood.[l] 21But if you
do warn the righteous person not to sin
and they do not sin, they will surely live
because they took warning, and you will
have saved yourself.[m]”
22The hand of the LORD[n] was on me
there, and he said to me, “Get up and go[o]
out to the plain,[p] and there I will speak
to you.” 23So I got up and went out to
the plain. And the glory of the LORD was
standing there, like the glory I had seen
by the Kebar River,[q] and I fell facedown.[r]
24Then the Spirit came into me and
raised me[s] to my feet. He spoke to me
and said: “Go, shut yourself inside your
house. 25And you, son of man, they will
tie with ropes; you will be bound so that
you cannot go out among the people.[t] 26I
will make your tongue stick to the roof
of your mouth so that you will be silent
and unable to rebuke them, for they are a

3:7 [z] Eze 2:4; Jn 15:20-23
3:8 [a] Jer 1:18
3:9 [b] Isa 50:7; Eze 2:6; Mic 3:8
3:11 [c] Eze 2:4-5,7
3:12 [d] Eze 8:3; Ac 8:39
3:13 [e] Eze 1:24; 10:5,16-17
3:15 [f] Ps 137:1 [g] Job 2:13
3:16 [h] Jer 42:7
3:17 [i] Isa 52:8; Jer 6:17; Eze 33:7-9
3:18 [j] ver 20; Eze 33:6
3:19 [k] 2Ki 17:13; Eze 14:14,20; Ac 18:6; 20:26; 1Ti 4:14-16
3:20 [l] Ps 125:5; Eze 18:24; 33:12,18
3:21 [m] Ac 20:31
3:22 [n] Eze 1:3 [o] Ac 9:6 [p] Eze 8:4
3:23 [q] Eze 1:1 [r] Eze 1:28
3:24 [s] Eze 2:2
3:25 [t] Eze 4:8

[a] *12* Probable reading of the original Hebrew text; Masoretic Text *sound—may the glory of the LORD be praised from his place* [b] *18* Or *in*; also in verses 19 and 20

3:9 *I will make your forehead like the hardest stone, harder than flint.* This verse focuses on the toughness and perseverance with which the prophet is equipped in order to withstand his audience's hostility and defiance. The threefold repetition of the root *hzq* ("to harden") is probably a wordplay on the prophet's name, Ezekiel (*yehezkel*), meaning "God toughens."

3:15 *Tel Aviv.* A Mesopotamian place-name. The phrase denotes what remains of a settlement after having been swept by the flood, i.e., a deluge-ruined heap. The expression occurs in the epilogue of the Code of Hammurapi, where the king invokes curses on the ruler who disregards his precepts. In his annals, the Assyrian king Tiglath-Pileser III (744–727 BC) boasts how he wrought havoc on enemy cities by making them like the ruin after a flood.

Tel Aviv may have been applied to the present site in the aftermath of the Chaldean destruction of the region around Nippur prior to the arrival of the exiles from Judah. In an effort to rebuild the local economy, a Babylonian administrator may have settled the Hebrew exiles on that site. A wordplay may be implied here, indicating a new beginning for Ezekiel's compatriots in their land of exile after the flood-like storm of destruction destroyed Jerusalem and their homeland.

3:22 *The hand of the LORD was on me.* Cf. 8:1; 37:1. The reference to the Lord's hand coming on Ezekiel compares with the equivalent expression in the Akkadian composition (*Ludlul bel nemeqi* 3.1: "I will praise the lord of wisdom") also known as the "Poem of the Righteous Sufferer," where Marduk's hand was heavy on the one who suffered. In this way the prophet describes the urgency, pressure and compulsion by which he is overwhelmed by divine presence. In the rest of the Bible, God's hand is a manifestation of divine power (e.g., Ex 9:3; Dt 2:15; 1Sa 5:9; Isa 41:20).

3:24–26 *shut yourself inside your house … you will be bound … you will be silent.* The significance of Ezekiel's initial confinement may be found in extra-Biblical analogues. His experience of the inability to speak should be interpreted within its ancient Near Eastern milieu. Most elements describing Ezekiel's confinement occur in Akkadian "medical" incantation texts: "the hand of god" on an individual, "seizure of the mouth," and "binding of the limbs" with ropes. Ezekiel's experience of confinement, binding and speechlessness is part of the description of his commissioning into a specific prophetic office. These elements should probably be taken as symbolic and stereotypical. Taken at face value, Ezekiel's speechlessness lasts more than seven years, from one week after his inaugural vision (v. 16; 1:3) to the day he receives the news of Jerusalem's fall (33:21–22).

rebellious people.[u] 27But when I speak to
you, I will open your mouth and you shall
say to them, 'This is what the Sovereign
LORD says.'[v] Whoever will listen let them
listen, and whoever will refuse let them
refuse; for they are a rebellious people.[w]

Siege of Jerusalem Symbolized

4 "Now, son of man, take a block of
clay, put it in front of you and draw
the city of Jerusalem on it. 2Then lay siege
to it: Erect siege works against it, build a
ramp[x] up to it, set up camps against it and
put battering rams around it.[y] 3Then take
an iron pan, place it as an iron wall between you and the city and turn your face
toward it. It will be under siege, and you
shall besiege it. This will be a sign[z] to the
people of Israel.[a]
4"Then lie on your left side and put the
sin of the people of Israel upon yourself.[a]
You are to bear their sin for the number of
days you lie on your side. 5I have assigned
you the same number of days as the years
of their sin. So for 390 days you will bear
the sin of the people of Israel.
6"After you have finished this, lie down
again, this time on your right side, and
bear the sin of the people of Judah. I have
assigned you 40 days, a day for each year.[b]
7Turn your face toward the siege of Jerusalem and with bared arm prophesy against
her. 8I will tie you up with ropes so that
you cannot turn from one side to the other until you have finished the days of your
siege.[c]
9"Take wheat and barley, beans and
lentils, millet and spelt;[d] put them in a
storage jar and use them to make bread
for yourself. You are to eat it during the
390 days you lie on your side. 10Weigh out
twenty shekels[b] of food to eat each day
and eat it at set times. 11Also measure out
a sixth of a hin[c] of water and drink it at set
times. 12Eat the food as you would a loaf
of barley bread; bake it in the sight of the
people, using human excrement[e] for fuel."
13The LORD said, "In this way the people
of Israel will eat defiled food among the
nations where I will drive them."[f]
14Then I said, "Not so, Sovereign LORD![g]
I have never defiled myself. From my
youth until now I have never eaten anything found dead[h] or torn by wild animals. No impure meat has ever entered
my mouth.[i]"
15"Very well," he said, "I will let you
bake your bread over cow dung instead of
human excrement."
16He then said to me: "Son of man, I
am about to cut off[j] the food supply in
Jerusalem. The people will eat rationed
food in anxiety and drink rationed water
in despair,[k] 17for food and water will be
scarce. They will be appalled at the sight

3:26 [u] Eze 2:5; 24:27; 33:22 **3:27** [v] ver 11 [w] Eze 12:3; 24:27; 33:22 **4:2** [x] Jer 6:6 [y] Eze 21:22 **4:3** [z] Isa 8:18; 20:3; Eze 12:3-6; 24:24,27 [a] Jer 39:1 **4:6** [b] Nu 14:34; Da 9:24-26; 12:11-12

4:8 [c] Eze 3:25 **4:9** [d] Isa 28:25 **4:12** [e] Isa 36:12 **4:13** [f] Hos 9:3 **4:14** [g] Jer 1:6; Eze 9:8; 20:49 [h] Lev 11:39 [i] Ex 22:31; Dt 14:3; Ac 10:14 **4:16** [j] Ps 105:16; Eze 5:16 [k] ver 10-11; Lev 26:26; Isa 3:1; Eze 12:19

[a] *4* Or *upon your side* [b] *10* That is, about 8 ounces or about 230 grams [c] *11* That is, about 2/3 quart or about 0.6 liter

4:1 *take a block of clay ... draw the city of Jerusalem on it.* Local Babylonian coloring is evident in the use of the term for a sun-dried brick (NIV "block of clay"), on which the prophet is to draw the map of Jerusalem. This would be an unusual action in Judah. Such maps, however, were common in the Neo-Babylonian Empire. Numerous depictions of Mesopotamian cities have been found drawn on clay tablets. The maps of Mesopotamian cities, however, do not depict a siege situation. While Ezekiel uses a Babylonian practice of drawing maps on clay tablets, here again he gives it a new meaning. While the image communicates typical representations, Ezekiel provides it with an oral explanation ("this is Jerusalem," 5:5), giving it specific historical relevance.

4:2 *lay siege to it.* See the article "Siege Warfare," p. 1157.

4:3 *an iron wall.* Iron in earlier periods was counted among the precious metals. Although more commonly used in the sixth century BC, it still would have been considered a prized object because of its strength and durability. Since Ezekiel is directing the symbolic siege, he must represent God. The iron wall is then understood to be the barrier between God and the people of Jerusalem. It signals that they may expect no help in the coming siege from the divine warrior Yahweh.

4:9 *wheat and barley, beans and lentils, millet and spelt.* All these products were found in Mesopotamia. Among the names of the cereals enumerated some words, such as "millet," occur only here in the Bible. Millet required irrigation in the land of Israel. It was more common in Mesopotamia because of the abundance of water and irrigation channels. The mixture of these grains is intended not as some exotic Babylonian recipe but as a siege diet. A Talmudic anecdote recounts an experiment in which these elements were combined to make bread. The product was so disgusting that not even a dog would eat it. Under siege, however, famished humans eat food that even dogs refuse to eat.

4:10 *twenty shekels of food to eat each day.* This is about eight ounces (230 grams) of food per day (barely a handful), about eight to ten times less than normal daily food intake. The allotment of water too is severely reduced (v. 11). This description announces the scarcity of food in besieged Jerusalem.

4:12 – 15 The typical fuel in areas like Mesopotamia and Palestine was dried animal dung or cakes made from the waste pulp of crushed olives. Trees were too precious to be cut for cooking and warming. Ezekiel, however, is horrified when God commands him to cook using human dung (v. 12), an unclean substance that must be buried away from human habitation (Dt 23:12 – 14). As a priest this act would defile him, and he simply cannot bring himself to obey (v. 14). Thus God compromises by allowing him to cook over cow dung (v. 15).

4:16 *cut off the food supply.* This language is influenced by the "covenant curses" of Lev 26; Dt 29:20, which will befall the people who persist in breaking the alliance with God. The scarcity of food is a hallmark of these curses. In these images, Ezekiel's contemporaries would recognize that the prophet is referring to the outworking of a curse. The ninth-century BC bilingual (Aramaic and Akkadian) Tell Fakhariyah Inscription from northern Mesopotamia states a similar curse expressed as scarcity of food.

of each other and will waste away because of[a] their sin.[l]

God’s Razor of Judgment

5 “Now, son of man, take a sharp sword and use it as a barber’s razor[m] to shave[n] your head and your beard.[o] Then take a set of scales and divide up the hair. [2]When the days of your siege come to an end, burn a third of the hair inside the city. Take a third and strike it with the sword all around the city. And scatter a third to the wind. For I will pursue them with drawn sword.[p] [3]But take a few hairs and tuck them away in the folds of your garment.[q] [4]Again, take a few of these and throw them into the fire and burn them up. A fire will spread from there to all Israel.

[5]“This is what the Sovereign LORD says: This is Jerusalem, which I have set in the center of the nations, with countries all around her. [6]Yet in her wickedness she has rebelled against my laws and decrees more than the nations and countries around her. She has rejected my laws and has not followed my decrees.[r]

[7]“Therefore this is what the Sovereign LORD says: You have been more unruly than the nations around you and have not followed my decrees or kept my laws. You have not even[b] conformed to the standards of the nations around you.[s]

[8]“Therefore this is what the Sovereign LORD says: I myself am against you, Jerusalem, and I will inflict punishment on you in the sight of the nations.[t] [9]Because of all your detestable idols, I will do to you what I have never done before and will never do again.[u] [10]Therefore in your midst parents will eat their children, and children will eat their parents.[v] I will inflict punishment on you and will scatter all your survivors to the winds.[w] [11]Therefore as surely as I live, declares the Sovereign LORD, because you have defiled my sanctuary with all your vile images[x] and detestable practices,[y] I myself will shave you; I will not look on you with pity or spare you.[z] [12]A third of your people will die of the plague or perish by famine inside you; a third will fall by the sword outside your walls; and a third I will scatter to the winds and pursue with drawn sword.[a]

4:17 [l]Lev 26:39; Eze 24:23; 33:10
5:1 [m]Isa 7:20 [n]Eze 44:20 [o]Lev 21:5
5:2 [p]ver 12; Lev 26:33
5:3 [q]Jer 39:10
5:6 [r]Jer 11:10; Eze 16:47-51; Zec 7:11
5:7 [s]2Ch 33:9; Jer 2:10-11; Eze 16:47
5:8 [t]Eze 15:7
5:9 [u]Da 9:12; Mt 24:21
5:10 [v]Lev 26:29; La 2:20 [w]Lev 26:33; Ps 44:11; Eze 12:14; Zec 2:6
5:11 [x]Eze 7:20 [y]2Ch 36:14; Eze 8:6 [z]Eze 7:4,9
5:12 [a]ver 2, 17; Jer 15:2; 21:9; Eze 6:11-12; 12:14

[a] *17* Or *away in* [b] *7* Most Hebrew manuscripts; some Hebrew manuscripts and Syriac *You have*

5:1 *take a sharp sword … shave your head and your beard.* A sword would have been an awkward instrument to shave the beard and head. Though “sword” is the usual translation of this Hebrew word, it can be used for other sharp implements, including axes, daggers and chisels (cf. 26:9 [“weapons”]; Jos 5:2 [“knives”]). In Ugaritic, an implement described by this word is used to carve roast meat. A general-purpose translation like “blade” would be preferable. *barber’s razor.* The word translated “barber” corresponds to an Akkadian term. Ezekiel borrows it either directly from Akkadian or from Aramaic, which is more probable, the latter having become the new common tongue of that time. Other Biblical texts use more indigenous terms in order to express the action of “shaving” and the instrument called a “razor” (Nu 8:7; Isa 7:20). Only in Ezekiel does one find the unique mention of a “barber’s razor” (expressed with a foreign word). The prophet may be referring to an implement well attested in Mesopotamian society of his time and foreign to traditional Israelite economy. See the article “Shaving in the Ancient World,” p. 1340.
5:2–4 Cutting or shaving the hair is most often associated with rituals of mourning (Isa 15:2). However, when a Nazirite vow has been completed, the law commands that the hair that has been dedicated during the period of the vow is to be cut and placed as a sacrifice in the fire (Nu 6:18). Hair (along with blood) was one of the main representatives in ancient thinking of a person’s life essence. As such it was often an ingredient in sympathetic magic. This is evident, e.g., in the practice of sending along a lock of the presumed prophet’s hair when the prophecies were sent to the king of Mari. The hair would be used in divination to determine whether the prophet’s message would be accepted as valid.
5:5 *center of the nations.* See note on 38:12.
5:7 *unruly.* This Hebrew term (“unruly, noisy crowd, tumult, clamor”) has also a metaphoric meaning of “insolent noise, hubris, rebellion.” The NIV mostly translates it with “crowd” or “horde,” which is only one of its meanings. It misses a prominent feature of Ezekiel’s message: the Lord’s wrath against the excessive “clamor” of certain groups.

This particular way of speaking can be clarified in the light of a prominent motif in Mesopotamian literature. In the Atrahasis epic, an eighteenth-century BC Babylonian story of the great flood, the terms “noise” and “clamor” are a recurring theme describing how the human race multiplied and became a “noisy crowd.” Their “uproar” is an expression of their rebellion and defiance of divinely imposed limits. Enlil, the supreme god of the divine council, decides to send the great flood so that the “insolent noise” of the humans may stop.

The same literary motif is found in the Old Babylonian Cuthean Legend of Naram-Sin. Several lines describe how the invaders destroy the cities of the Mesopotamian plain by trampling its tumult. Furthermore, “noise” and “clamor” are seen as metaphors for human wicked behavior, describing not merely noise but rather cries of rebellion.

The ninth-century BC Mesopotamian epic “Erra and Ishum” speaks of the “clamor” of the inhabitants of Babylonia that becomes unbearable to Erra, the god of plague and war, who then decides to destroy them (Erra I 40). It seems, therefore, that in Ezekiel this term is not used in a private or esoteric way; rather, it points to a sophisticated writer who has adapted to his purpose a prominent motif of Akkadian literature.
5:10 *parents will eat their children, and children will eat their parents.* According to Lev 26:29, the standard curse of covenant violators is cannibalism, where parents eat their children. Ezekiel caps this by stating a hitherto unheard of patricidal cannibalism, where children eat their parents. Ancient Near Eastern texts attest to the practice of cannibalism during sieges. See note on La 4:8–10.

EZEKIEL 5:1 – 4

Shaving in the Ancient World

Ezekiel's symbolic action of shaving is comparable to a ritual act found in the Babylonian apotropaic *namburbi* texts, though this may be more akin to the remnant saved (Eze 5:3) than the destruction (Eze 5:1 – 2). This ritual in which a man is shaved and his hair gathered into a pot is performed in connection with a catastrophe like an earthquake. Shaving part of the head occurs in the context of punishment by the court alongside flogging in the Code of Hammurapi.

According to Eze 5:1 – 2, having shaved himself, Ezekiel is ordered to weigh out his hair on a set of scales and divide it into three equal parts. A Babylonian incantation text also speaks of a man's hair being weighed as an item of identification. This comparison suggests that the act of weighing hair was practiced in Ezekiel's Babylonian environment. The use of a set of scales intimates to those who grasp the meaning of this sign-act performance that the judgment that the Lord metes out is not haphazard but deliberate and carefully measured.

Manipulation of parts of the body like shaving (or circumcision and laceration) is common to many cultures. According to social anthropologists such manipulation functions to distinguish individuals and to communicate status distinctions. In Nu 8:7 the Levites shave their whole bodies. This act marks their symbolic submission to divine authority.

In the case of Ezekiel and his elaborate symbolic act, one can argue that the shaving indicates a change in the status of the Israelites from free individuals to captives submitted to their Babylonian conquerors. The shaving serves as a public, temporary marker of this status change. ◆

Painting from the tomb of Userhet shows barbers at work, c. 1438 to 1312 BC.

Egypt, Luxor, West Thebes, Sheik el Gurnak. Tomb of Usirhat, barber, details from fresco. (New Kingdom, Dynasty XVIII)/De Agostini Picture Library/ G. Dagli Orti/Bridgeman Images

[13]"Then my anger will cease and my
wrath[b] against them will subside, and I
will be avenged.[c] And when I have spent
my wrath on them, they will know that I
the LORD have spoken in my zeal.

[14]"I will make you a ruin and a reproach among the nations around you, in
the sight of all who pass by.[d] [15]You will
be a reproach and a taunt, a warning and
an object of horror to the nations around
you when I inflict punishment on you in
anger and in wrath and with stinging rebuke.[e] I the LORD have spoken.[f] [16]When I
shoot at you with my deadly and destructive arrows of famine, I will shoot to destroy you. I will bring more and more famine upon you and cut off your supply of
food.[g] [17]I will send famine and wild beasts
against you, and they will leave you childless. Plague and bloodshed[h] will sweep
through you, and I will bring the sword
against you. I the LORD have spoken.[i]"

Doom for the Mountains of Israel

6 The word of the LORD came to me:
[2]"Son of man, set your face against
the mountains[j] of Israel; prophesy against
them [3]and say: 'You mountains of Israel, hear the word of the Sovereign LORD.
This is what the Sovereign LORD says to
the mountains and hills, to the ravines
and valleys:[k] I am about to bring a sword
against you, and I will destroy your high
places.[l] [4]Your altars will be demolished
and your incense altars[m] will be smashed;
and I will slay your people in front of your
idols. [5]I will lay the dead bodies of the Israelites in front of their idols, and I will
scatter your bones[n] around your altars.
[6]Wherever you live, the towns will be laid
waste and the high places demolished, so
that your altars will be laid waste and devastated, your idols[o] smashed and ruined,
your incense altars[p] broken down, and
what you have made wiped out.[q] [7]Your
people will fall slain among you, and you
will know that I am the LORD.

[8]" 'But I will spare some, for some of
you will escape[r] the sword when you are
scattered among the lands and nations.[s]
[9]Then in the nations where they have
been carried captive, those who escape
will remember me—how I have been
grieved[t] by their adulterous hearts, which
have turned away from me, and by their
eyes, which have lusted after their idols.[u]
They will loathe themselves for the evil
they have done and for all their detestable practices.[v] [10]And they will know that
I am the LORD; I did not threaten in vain to
bring this calamity on them.

[11]" 'This is what the Sovereign LORD says:
Strike your hands together and stamp your
feet and cry out "Alas!" because of all the
wicked and detestable practices of the people of Israel, for they will fall by the sword,
famine and plague.[w] [12]One who is far

Canaanite incense altar, Taanach, thirteenth to twelfth centuries BC. Incense altars (Eze 6:4) were made of baked clay, about two feet high, and usually inscribed with animal figures and idols of Canaanite gods.

5:13 [b]Eze 21:17; 36:6 [c]Isa 1:24
5:14 [d]Lev 26:32; Ne 2:17; Ps 74:3-10; 79:1-4
5:15 [e]1Ki 9:7; Jer 22:8-9; 24:9 [f]Eze 25:17
5:16 [g]Dt 32:24
5:17 [h]Eze 38:22 [i]Eze 14:21
6:2 [j]Eze 36:1
6:3 [k]Eze 36:4 [l]Lev 26:30
6:4 [m]2Ch 14:5
6:5 [n]Jer 8:1-2
6:6 [o]Mic 1:7; Zec 13:2 [p]Lev 26:30 [q]Isa 6:11; Eze 5:14
6:8 [r]Jer 44:28 [s]Isa 6:13; Jer 44:14; Eze 12:16; 14:22
6:9 [t]Ps 78:40; Isa 7:13 [u]Eze 20:7, 24 [v]Eze 20:43; 36:31
6:11 [w]Eze 5:12; 21:14, 17; 25:6

6:3 *high places.* See notes on 1Ki 3:2; 11:7; 2Ch 1:3.
6:4 *idols.* The Hebrew term (*gillulim*) used here is one of the key terms in Ezekiel, and it therefore merits particular attention. It is one of the terms the prophet favors to designate pagan gods or idols. Out of its 49 occurrences in the OT, it occurs 39 times in Ezekiel. The term represents an outrageous manner of designating pagan idols as dung. It seems to be a specially coined term of derision treating pagan idols as "dung-gods."
6:5 See note on Jer 22:19.
6:11 *Strike your hands.* Gestures and body language take on different meanings in different cultures. In current western society, clapping hands can be used to show appreciation, to summon subordinates or children, to get someone's attention, to accompany music, or to express frustration (one clap). There were also several functions in the ancient world. Clapping could be used in praise (Ps 47:1) or applause (2Ki 11:12), or as a gesture

away will die of the plague, and one who
is near will fall by the sword, and anyone
who survives and is spared will die of famine. So will I pour out my wrath on them.[x]
13And they will know that I am the LORD,
when their people lie slain among their
idols around their altars, on every high hill
and on all the mountaintops, under every
spreading tree and every leafy oak[y]—places where they offered fragrant incense to
all their idols.[z] 14And I will stretch out my
hand[a] against them and make the land a
desolate waste from the desert to Diblah[a]—
wherever they live. Then they will know
that I am the LORD.[b]' "

The End Has Come

7 The word of the LORD came to me:
2"Son of man, this is what the Sovereign LORD says to the land of Israel:

" 'The end![c] The end has come
    upon the four corners[d] of the land!
3The end is now upon you,
    and I will unleash my anger against
        you.
I will judge you according to your
        conduct
    and repay you for all your detestable
        practices.
4I will not look on you with pity;[e]
    I will not spare you.
I will surely repay you for your
        conduct
    and for the detestable practices
        among you.
" 'Then you will know that I am the LORD.'

5"This is what the Sovereign LORD says:

" 'Disaster![f] Unheard-of[b] disaster!
    See, it comes!
6The end has come!
    The end has come!
It has roused itself against you.
    See, it comes!
7Doom has come upon you,
    upon you who dwell in the land.
The time has come! The day is near![g]
    There is panic, not joy, on the
        mountains.
8I am about to pour out my wrath[h]
        on you
    and spend my anger against you.
I will judge you according to your
        conduct
    and repay you for all your detestable
        practices.[i]
9I will not look on you with pity;
    I will not spare you.
I will repay you for your conduct
    and for the detestable practices
        among you.

" 'Then you will know that it is I the LORD
who strikes you.

10" 'See, the day!
    See, it comes!
Doom has burst forth,
    the rod[j] has budded,
    arrogance has blossomed!
11Violence has arisen,[c]
    a rod to punish the wicked.
None of the people will be left,
    none of that crowd—
none of their wealth,
    nothing of value.[k]
12The time has come!
    The day has arrived!
Let not the buyer rejoice
    nor the seller grieve,
    for my wrath is on the whole
        crowd.[l]
13The seller will not recover
    the property that was sold—
    as long as both buyer and seller live.
For the vision concerning the whole
        crowd
    will not be reversed.
Because of their sins, not one of them
    will preserve their life.[m]

[a] *14* Most Hebrew manuscripts; a few Hebrew manuscripts *Riblah* [b] *5* Most Hebrew manuscripts; some Hebrew manuscripts and Syriac *Disaster after*
[c] *11* Or *The violent one has become*

6:12 [x] Eze 5:12
6:13 [y] Isa 57:5 [z] 1Ki 14:23; Jer 2:20; Eze 20:28; Hos 4:13
6:14 [a] Isa 5:25 [b] Eze 14:13
7:2 [c] Am 8:2, 10 [d] Rev 7:1; 20:8
7:4 [e] Eze 5:11
7:5 [f] 2Ki 21:12
7:7 [g] Eze 12:23; Zep 1:14
7:8 [h] Isa 42:25; Eze 9:8; 14:19; Na 1:6 [i] Eze 20:8, 21; 36:19
7:10 [j] Ps 89:32; Isa 10:5
7:11 [k] Jer 16:6; Zep 1:18
7:12 [l] ver 7; Isa 5:13-14; Eze 30:3
7:13 [m] Lev 25:24-28

---

of anger or derision (Nu 24:10; Job 27:23). Variations may exist in the precise movement involved: compare the different significations in Western culture of (1) striking the palms together parallel to the body on a horizontal plain (applause); (2) slapping the palms together in a roughly vertical movement (frustration); and (3) striking the palms together perpendicular to the body while alternating which hand is on top and which is on bottom (as if knocking the dust off). *stamp your feet.* Often a sign of frustration or anger, as in the Ugaritic Aqhat Legend. In that tale the hero refuses to give his bow to the goddess Anat, telling her hunting weapons are for men. She is so angry that she violently stamps her foot and goes off in a rush to seek revenge from the gods. *cry out "Alas!"* An exclamation of frustration that reinforces this scene of impending divine punishment. In this verse Ezekiel is instructed by God to perform a series of symbolic gestures (clapping, stomping his foot, and crying out "Alas!") that display God's wrath.

7:10 *the day.* Like prophets who have preceded him, Ezekiel refers to the coming of the "day of the LORD." The first prophet in the Bible to have mentioned this day of doom was Amos (Am 5:18–20).

7:13 *The seller will not recover the property.* The extent of the doom pronounced upon the nation is such that even the Jubilee Year will not be celebrated (see note on Lev 25:10). Ordinarily, property that has been sold to satisfy debts could be redeemed during the Jubilee, thereby restoring the grants of lands that were first made after the conquest (the Code of Hammurapi contains similar clauses regarding redemption of land). Now the "divine lease" has been revoked and there will be no economic advantage for buyer or seller in the age of destruction to come.

14 " 'They have blown the trumpet,
they have made all things ready,
but no one will go into battle,
for my wrath is on the whole crowd.
15 Outside is the sword;
inside are plague and famine.
Those in the country
will die by the sword;
those in the city
will be devoured by famine and
plague.[n]
16 The fugitives who escape
will flee to the mountains.
Like doves[o] of the valleys,
they will all moan,
each for their own sins.[p]
17 Every hand will go limp;[q]
every leg will be wet with urine.
18 They will put on sackcloth
and be clothed with terror.[r]
Every face will be covered with shame,
and every head will be shaved.[s]
19 " 'They will throw their silver into the
streets,
and their gold will be treated as a
thing unclean.
Their silver and gold
will not be able to deliver them
in the day of the LORD's wrath.[t]
It will not satisfy their hunger
or fill their stomachs,
for it has caused them to stumble[u]
into sin.[v]
20 They took pride in their beautiful
jewelry
and used it to make their detestable
idols.
They made it into vile images;[w]
therefore I will make it a thing
unclean for them.
21 I will give their wealth as plunder to
foreigners
and as loot to the wicked of the earth,
who will defile it.[x]
22 I will turn my face[y] away from the
people,
and robbers will desecrate the place
I treasure.
They will enter it
and will defile it.

23 " 'Prepare chains!
For the land is full of bloodshed,[z]
and the city is full of violence.
24 I will bring the most wicked of nations
to take possession of their houses.
I will put an end to the pride of the
mighty,
and their sanctuaries[a] will be
desecrated.[b]
25 When terror comes,
they will seek peace in vain.[c]
26 Calamity upon calamity[d] will come,
and rumor upon rumor.
They will go searching for a vision
from the prophet,
priestly instruction in the law will
cease,
the counsel of the elders will come
to an end.[e]
27 The king will mourn,
the prince will be clothed with
despair,[f]
and the hands of the people of the
land will tremble.
I will deal with them according to their
conduct,[g]
and by their own standards I will
judge them.

" 'Then they will know that I am the
LORD.[h]' "

7:15 [n] Dt 32:25; Jer 14:18; La 1:20; Eze 5:12 7:16 [o] Isa 59:11 [p] Ezr 9:15; Eze 6:8 7:17 [q] Isa 13:7; Eze 21:7; 22:14 7:18 [r] Ps 55:5 [s] Isa 15:2-3; Eze 27:31; Am 8:10 7:19 [t] Eze 13:5; Zep 1:7, 18 [u] Eze 14:3 [v] Pr 11:4 7:20 [w] Jer 7:30 7:21 [x] 2Ki 24:13 7:22 [y] Eze 39:23-24 7:23 [z] 2Ki 21:16 7:24 [a] Eze 24:21 [b] 2Ch 7:20; Eze 28:7 7:25 [c] Eze 13:10, 16 7:26 [d] Jer 4:20 [e] Isa 47:11; Eze 20:1-3; Mic 3:6 7:27 [f] Ps 109:19; Eze 26:16 [g] Eze 18:20 [h] ver 4 8:1 [i] Eze 14:1 [j] Eze 33:31 [k] Eze 1:1-3 8:2 [l] Eze 1:4, 26-27

Idolatry in the Temple

8 In the sixth year, in the sixth month on
the fifth day, while I was sitting in my
house and the elders[i] of Judah were sitting
before[j] me, the hand of the Sovereign LORD
came on me there.[k] 2 I looked, and I saw a
figure like that of a man.[a] From what appeared to be his waist down he was like
fire, and from there up his appearance was
as bright as glowing metal.[l] 3 He stretched
out what looked like a hand and took me
by the hair of my head. The Spirit lifted

[a] 2 Or *saw a fiery figure*

7:17 *Every hand will go limp.* Represents a nonverbal expression of failed strength or loss of courage. *every leg will be wet with urine.* Indicates the loss of bladder control that occurs in a moment of extreme crisis. The prophet's words recall a Neo-Assyrian description of fleeing enemies: "Their hearts beat like that of a fledgling dove chased away, they passed hot urine." Urine would be visible on the legs of soldiers because their skirts were knee high.
8:1 *the hand of the Sovereign LORD came on me.* See note on 3:22.
8:2 *glowing metal.* See note on 1:4.
8:3 *took me by the hair of my head.* The vision of the departure of the glory of the Lord from the Jerusalem temple reflects formal elements of a definite type of vision known in Akkadian literature. A shining figure that had the appearance of fire took Ezekiel by the lock of his hair. A similar expression is found in "The Vision of the Netherworld by an Assyrian Crown Prince." The tablet comes from Ashur and is dated around 670 BC. The composition describes how an Assyrian prince (perhaps Ashurbanipal), for unknown reasons, wishes to see the netherworld. To this end he sacrifices to Ereshkigal, the queen of the netherworld, and prays to her and to Erra/Nergal, her consort. His request is granted, and in a dream he receives a vision of the netherworld. He sees Erra/Nergal as a shining figure with lightning flashing from his arms. Erra/Nergal then takes the prince by the hair and carries him. The same expression occurs in the Mesopotamian myth *Nergal and Ereshkigal*, where it is said that Nergal seized Ereshkigal by her hair.

me up[m] between earth and heaven and in visions of God he took me to Jerusalem, to the entrance of the north gate of the inner court, where the idol that provokes to jealousy[n] stood. 4And there before me was the glory[o] of the God of Israel, as in the vision I had seen in the plain.[p]

5Then he said to me, "Son of man, look toward the north." So I looked, and in the entrance north of the gate of the altar I saw this idol[q] of jealousy.

6And he said to me, "Son of man, do you see what they are doing — the utterly detestable[r] things the Israelites are doing here, things that will drive me far from my sanctuary? But you will see things that are even more detestable."

7Then he brought me to the entrance to the court. I looked, and I saw a hole in the wall. 8He said to me, "Son of man, now dig into the wall." So I dug into the wall and saw a doorway there.

9And he said to me, "Go in and see the wicked and detestable things they are doing here." 10So I went in and looked, and I saw portrayed all over the walls all kinds of crawling things and unclean animals and all the idols of Israel.[s] 11In front of them stood seventy elders of Israel, and Jaazaniah son of Shaphan was standing among them. Each had a censer[t] in his hand, and a fragrant cloud of incense[u] was rising.

12He said to me, "Son of man, have you seen what the elders of Israel are doing in the darkness, each at the shrine of his own idol? They say, 'The LORD does not see[v] us; the LORD has forsaken the land.' " 13Again, he said, "You will see them doing things that are even more detestable."

14Then he brought me to the entrance of the north gate of the house of the LORD, and I saw women sitting there, mourning the god Tammuz. 15He said to me, "Do you see this, son of man? You will see things that are even more detestable than this."

16He then brought me into the inner court of the house of the LORD, and there at the entrance to the temple, between the portico and the altar,[w] were about twenty-five men. With their backs toward the temple of the LORD and their faces toward the east, they were bowing down to the sun in the east.[x]

17He said to me, "Have you seen this, son of man? Is it a trivial matter for the people of Judah to do the detestable things they are doing here? Must they also fill the land with violence[y] and continually arouse my anger?[z] Look at them putting the branch to their nose! 18Therefore I will deal with them in anger; I will not look on them with pity[a] or spare them. Although they shout in my ears, I will not listen[b] to them."

Judgment on the Idolaters

9 Then I heard him call out in a loud voice, "Bring near those who are appointed to execute judgment on the city, each with a weapon in his hand." 2And I saw six men coming from the direction of

8:3 [m] Eze 3:12; 11:1 [n] Ex 20:5; Dt 32:16 **8:4** [o] Eze 1:28 [p] Eze 3:22 **8:5** [q] Ps 78:58; Jer 32:34 **8:6** [r] Eze 5:11 **8:10** [s] Ex 20:4 **8:11** [t] Nu 16:17 [u] Nu 16:35

8:12 [v] Ps 10:11; Isa 29:15; Eze 9:9 **8:16** [w] Joel 2:17 [x] Dt 4:19; 17:3; Job 31:28; Jer 2:27; Eze 11:1, 12 **8:17** [y] Eze 9:9 [z] Eze 16:26 **8:18** [a] Eze 9:10; 24:14 [b] Isa 1:15; Jer 11:11; Mic 3:4; Zec 7:13

8:5 *idol.* The Hebrew word used here is an unusual one that is thought to be a loanword from Phoenician or Canaanite. The same word is used to describe the image of Asherah that Manasseh set up in the temple complex (2Ch 33:7, 15). Though this should not be considered the same image, it could easily be another Asherah. Any image that was the object of worship would provoke Yahweh's jealousy according to the second commandment of the Decalogue.

8:10 *crawling things and unclean animals.* The images portrayed on the inner wall of one of the rooms at the entrance to the palace court (v. 7) may be pictorial representations of unclean animals that are worshiped by "the seventy elders of Israel" (v. 11), perhaps similar to the representations of serpents, crocodiles, beetles, baboons and lions that appear in the many versions of the Egyptian "Book of the Dead." Another suggestion compares the wall decorations with animal motifs to those found in Mesopotamian houses, which were decorated with different colored species of ants and cockroaches. These animal motifs had apotropaic purposes, as confirmed by omen texts mentioning reptiles, lizards, scorpions, cockroaches and beetles that might be encountered both inside the house and on its walls.

8:14 *mourning the god Tammuz.* It is generally admitted that this refers to a Mesopotamian rite of lamenting over the god Dumuzi/Tammuz. This is the only reference to Tammuz in the Bible. In the Mesopotamian myth *Descent of Ishtar,* Tammuz is Ishtar's lover, whom she betrays and sends to the netherworld to take her place, thus putting into effect his cyclic resurrection. This was a Mesopotamian way of explaining the seasons. While Tammuz was in the netherworld, the vegetation on earth was dying, dried up by the sun. In this verse Ezekiel is describing some elements of religious syncretism taking place among the people of Judah.

8:16 *bowing down to the sun in the east.* Official evidence of sun worship in ancient Israel seems to be tied primarily to the reign of Manasseh. The horses and chariots of the sun that he set up were destroyed by Josiah as he cleansed the temple complex of foreign religious influence (see note on 2Ki 21:3). Place-names such as Beth Shemesh (Jos 15:10), En Shemesh (Jos 15:7) and Mount Heres (Jdg 1:35) also attest to the popularity of sun worship. Perhaps it is not coincidental that ch. 8 is dated to the time of the autumn equinox, when the sun would be at the angle to shine directly into the temple at sunrise. While Egypt, Canaan and Mesopotamia all had sun-gods (Amun-Ra, Shemesh and Shamash, respectively), it is more likely that this is syncretistic worship of Yahweh as a sun-god. This would complete the series of scenes that portrayed Canaanite worship (v. 5), Egyptian worship (vv. 10 – 11), Mesopotamian worship (v. 14), and syncretistic worship of Yahweh (v. 16).

9:2 *six men ... each with a deadly weapon in his hand.* In Eze 9, the prophet sees the coming of God's six agents

the upper gate, which faces north, each
with a deadly weapon in his hand. With
them was a man clothed in linen[c] who had
a writing kit at his side. They came in and
stood beside the bronze altar.
3Now the glory[d] of the God of Israel
went up from above the cherubim,[e] where
it had been, and moved to the threshold
of the temple. Then the LORD called to the
man clothed in linen who had the writing kit at his side 4and said to him, "Go
throughout the city of Jerusalem and put
a mark[f] on the foreheads of those who
grieve and lament[g] over all the detestable
things that are done in it.[h]"
5As I listened, he said to the others, "Follow him through the city and kill, without
showing pity[i] or compassion. 6Slaughter
the old men, the young men and wom-
en, the mothers and children, but do not
touch anyone who has the mark. Begin at
my sanctuary." So they began with the old
men[j] who were in front of the temple.[k]
7Then he said to them, "Defile the
temple and fill the courts with the slain.
Go!" So they went out and began killing
throughout the city. 8While they were killing and I was left alone, I fell facedown,[l]
crying out, "Alas, Sovereign LORD! Are you
going to destroy the entire remnant of Israel in this outpouring of your wrath on
Jerusalem?[m]"
9He answered me, "The sin of the people
of Israel and Judah is exceedingly great;
the land is full of bloodshed and the city is
full of injustice.[n] They say, 'The LORD has
forsaken the land; the LORD does not see.'[o]
10So I will not look on them with pity[p] or
spare them, but I will bring down on their
own heads what they have done.[q]"
11Then the man in linen with the writing
kit at his side brought back word, saying,
"I have done as you commanded."

God's Glory Departs From the Temple

10 I looked, and I saw the likeness of
a throne[r] of lapis lazuli[s] above the
vault[t] that was over the heads of the cherubim. 2The LORD said to the man clothed
in linen,[u] "Go in among the wheels[v]

9:2 [c] Lev 16:4; Eze 10:2; Rev 15:6 **9:3** [d] Eze 10:4 [e] Eze 11:22 **9:4** [f] Ex 12:7; 2Co 1:22; Rev 7:3; 9:4 [g] Ps 119:136; Jer 13:17; Eze 21:6 [h] Ps 119:53 **9:5** [i] Eze 5:11 **9:6** [j] Eze 8:11-13, 16 [k] 2Ch 36:17; Jer 25:29; 1Pe 4:17 **9:8** [l] Jos 7:6 [m] Eze 11:13; Am 7:1-6 **9:9** [n] Eze 22:29 [o] Job 22:13; Eze 8:12 **9:10** [p] Eze 7:4; 8:18 [q] Isa 65:6; Eze 11:21 **10:1** [r] Rev 4:2 [s] Ex 24:10 [t] Eze 1:22 **10:2** [u] Eze 9:2 [v] Eze 1:15

of judgment, accompanied by a recorder. In the Mesopotamian epic "Erra and Ishum," the god of plague and war has at his service seven executioners called "the Seven" ([d]Sebetti). They are his weapons of destruction that march at his side. In both Ezekiel and the Mesopotamian epic "Erra and Ishum" the seven executioners are employed to implement divine judgment. In Ezekiel they turn against the idolaters and those who commit abominations, while in the Mesopotamian epic "Erra and Ishum" they turn against humans, who are accused of having neglected the worship of Erra and Marduk, patron god of Babylon—i.e., of having committed religious offenses. "The Seven" in the Mesopotamian epic "Erra and Ishum" and the seven executioners in Eze 9 are not free to act as they please. Their activity is controlled and directed by a superior power—Erra or Yahweh, respectively. What makes this comparison pertinent is the fact that "the Seven" are invoked whenever a treaty is concluded between two parties. *man ... who had a writing kit.* The motif of a divine record-keeper is found in the Gilgamesh Epic, where Belet-seri kneels before Ereshkigal (the queen of the underworld in Akkadian belief) and reads out the names of mortals who will die. But the scribal writing kit carried by the man here would evoke the image of Nabu, the god of scribes and the scribe of the gods. Nabu was one of the most popular Babylonian gods of the period, as is demonstrated by his appearance in so many of Babylonian names (e.g., Nebuchadnezzar). He is the one who keeps the accounts on the tablet of life, just as the scribal personage here in Ezekiel is doing. *bronze altar.* Part of the furnishings of the original temple complex created by Solomon (see note on Ex 27:1). It had sat in front of the temple between the new altar and the temple, and had then been moved to the north side to make room for the idolatrous altar erected by Ahaz (2Ki 16:14; see note on 2Ki 16:15).

9:4 *mark on the foreheads.* Here we find another literary motif that ch. 9 shares with Akkadian literature (see previous note). The writing down of names or the marking of certain individuals can on certain occasions be an ominous process. According to the Gilgamesh Epic, on periodic occasions the gods made lists that determined who among the humans was to live and who was to die. It refers to Belet-seri, recorder of the netherworld, who reads a tablet, presumably with a list of names, before Ereshkigal, the queen of the netherworld. In Hebrew the "mark" is a *taw* sign. The protective sign *taw,* the last letter of the alphabet written in paleo-Hebrew script, represents two intersecting diagonal lines, the shape of an *X,* and resembles a cross. It was compared to the magical diagonal lines written on the tablets of the Mesopotamian epic "Erra and Ishum" that prevented any tampering with the text written on them. Its purpose here is merely to discriminate the good people from the rest of the population.

10:2 *cherubim.* Eze 10 echoes some elements from the previous texts. The four living creatures of ch. 1 are called "cherubim" here in Eze 10. Modern scholars have compared these creatures with the winged sphinxes and other composite quadrupeds pictured as supporting the throne of ancient Near Eastern kings or serving as pedestals of gods. That Ezekiel does not immediately identify the creatures as cherubim indicates that some difference sets them apart from the Mesopotamian sanctuary images, though he doesn't give further specification.

Comparable is the early disk-wheeled divine chariot with a god standing in it. The Lord too is said to ride in a chariot (Isa 66:15; Hab 3:8). In the vision of divine judgment in Da 7:9, God's throne is equipped with wheels. Related to this image is one in which "bull-men" support a "stool" on which the symbol of a god rests, or one in which a four-winged "eagle-man" with upraised arms supports a divine symbol over his head. Perhaps even more apt is the high-backed, wheeled sedan chair of the Assyrian king Ashurnasirpal II (883–859 BC), depicted on the bronze gate found at Balawat.

The role of the cherubim and of the different winged creatures is to delimit sacred space. On account of their holiness, neither the Israelite God nor the ancient Near Eastern divinities can be directly approached. Access is guarded and protected by the cherubim creatures. They indicate that one is approaching holy ground.

EZEKIEL 10

Esarhaddon's Inscription Concerning Babylon

In his Neo-Assyrian inscription, Esarhaddon (681 – 669 BC) recounts how his father, Sennacherib, had to destroy Babylon on account of three major offenses:

1. Political offenses: treason and perjury by using the gold from the Esagila temple to buy military help from the Elamites against Assyria.
2. Moral and social offenses: lies, oppression and corruption.
3. Religious offenses: they stole the property of Marduk's temple and incurred his wrath.

Marduk consequently sent an inundation like the great flood and destroyed his temple Esagila in Babylon, and the gods fled.

This was accompanied by the Assyrian spoliation of divine images from their temples. It was meant to portray the abandonment of the enemy's gods in submission to the superior power of the invader's god.

The Akkadian accounts of the departure of the divinity from its temple display several links with Ezekiel's vision of the Lord's departure:

1. They assume a symbiotic relationship between deity, land and people, analogous to the association of the Lord, Jerusalem and the Israelites.
2. They attribute divine abandonment directly to the wrath of the patron god.
3. The divine wrath was precipitated by the wickedness of the deity's subjects, expressed in both cultic and moral misdeeds.
4. The god's departure often coincides with the enemy army moving in and destroying the city.

One of Esarhaddon's numerous inscriptions describing his restoration of Babylon.

Kim Walton. The British Museum.

For Ezekiel's compatriots in exile, the exposure of the sin of the people, the expression of the divine wrath, and finally the Lord's abandonment of his temple and his city has a familiar ring. The prophet does not, however, rationalize the defeat of Jerusalem as a capitulation of Yahweh to the supreme might of the Babylonian god Marduk. He grounds the defeat instead in Yahweh's holiness. The social, political, economic and religious wrongdoings of Jerusalem's population are incompatible with Yahweh's ethics. Therefore God's glory departs from the midst of his people. ◆

beneath the cherubim. Fill[w] your hands
with burning coals from among the cherubim and scatter them over the city." And
as I watched, he went in.
3 Now the cherubim were standing on
the south side of the temple when the
man went in, and a cloud filled the inner
court. 4 Then the glory of the LORD[x] rose
from above the cherubim and moved to
the threshold of the temple. The cloud
filled the temple, and the court was full of
the radiance of the glory of the LORD. 5 The
sound of the wings of the cherubim could
be heard as far away as the outer court,
like the voice[y] of God Almighty[a] when he
speaks.
6 When the LORD commanded the man in
linen, "Take fire from among the wheels,
from among the cherubim," the man went
in and stood beside a wheel. 7 Then one
of the cherubim reached out his hand to
the fire that was among them. He took up
some of it and put it into the hands of the
man in linen, who took it and went out.
8 (Under the wings of the cherubim could
be seen what looked like human hands.)[z]
9 I looked, and I saw beside the cherubim four wheels, one beside each of the
cherubim; the wheels sparkled like topaz.[a] 10 As for their appearance, the four of
them looked alike; each was like a wheel
intersecting a wheel. 11 As they moved,
they would go in any one of the four directions the cherubim faced; the wheels
did not turn about[b] as the cherubim went.
The cherubim went in whatever direction
the head faced, without turning as they
went. 12 Their entire bodies, including their
backs, their hands and their wings, were
completely full of eyes,[b] as were their four
wheels.[c] 13 I heard the wheels being called
"the whirling wheels." 14 Each of the cherubim[d] had four faces:[e] One face was that
of a cherub, the second the face of a human being, the third the face of a lion, and
the fourth the face of an eagle.[f]
15 Then the cherubim rose upward.
These were the living creatures[g] I had
seen by the Kebar River. 16 When the cherubim moved, the wheels beside them
moved; and when the cherubim spread
their wings to rise from the ground, the
wheels did not leave their side. 17 When
the cherubim stood still, they also stood
still; and when the cherubim rose, they
rose with them, because the spirit of the
living creatures was in them.[h]
18 Then the glory of the LORD departed
from over the threshold of the temple and
stopped above the cherubim.[i] 19 While I
watched, the cherubim spread their wings
and rose from the ground, and as they
went, the wheels went with them.[j] They
stopped at the entrance of the east gate of
the LORD's house, and the glory of the God
of Israel was above them.
20 These were the living creatures I had
seen beneath the God of Israel by the Kebar River,[k] and I realized that they were
cherubim. 21 Each had four faces[l] and four
wings,[m] and under their wings was what
looked like human hands. 22 Their faces
had the same appearance as those I had
seen by the Kebar River. Each one went
straight ahead.

God's Sure Judgment on Jerusalem

11 Then the Spirit lifted me up and
brought me to the gate of the house
of the LORD that faces east. There at the
entrance of the gate were twenty-five men,
and I saw among them Jaazaniah son of

10:2 [w] Rev 8:5
10:4 [x] Eze 1:28; 9:3
10:5 [y] Job 40:9; Eze 1:24
10:8 [z] Eze 1:8
10:9 [a] Eze 1:15-16; Rev 21:20
10:12 [b] Rev 4:6-8 [c] Eze 1:15-21
10:14 [d] 1Ki 7:36 [e] Eze 1:6 [f] Eze 1:10; Rev 4:7
10:15 [g] Eze 1:3,5
10:17 [h] Eze 1:20-21
10:18 [i] Ps 18:10
10:19 [j] Eze 11:1, 22
10:20 [k] Eze 1:1
10:21 [l] Eze 41:18 [m] Eze 1:6

[a] 5 Hebrew *El-Shaddai* [b] 11 Or *aside*

10:4 *the radiance of the glory of the LORD.* See notes on 1:27; Ex 13:21; see also the article "Glory," p. 178.
10:9 *topaz.* Reflects the light and provides a sense of translucent brilliance.
10:12 *full of eyes.* See note on 1:18.
10:14 *four faces.* See note on 1:10.
10:15 *Kebar River.* See note on 1:1.
10:18 *the glory of the LORD departed.* Here Ezekiel is echoing one of the major literary and religious themes of ancient Near Eastern literature: the theme of divine abandonment or the stories of gods forsaking their temples. It is found already in Sumerian texts as an attempt to explain a city's misfortune. The five Sumerian city laments, dating from 2000–1800 BC, mention the fear of the people and the disaster that falls on the city when the deity abandons its shrine, leaves its statue, and departs to the heavens. The people felt bereaved and abandoned with no protection (see note on Jer 12:4). In Neo-Assyrian and Neo-Babylonian times the motif is widely used in the service of a political propaganda. The divine abandonment is the rationale of choice adopted by Assyrian scribes as they attempt to account for the human capture of divine images from the perspective of divine will. See the article "Esarhaddon's Inscription Concerning Babylon," p. 1346. *the threshold.* Entranceways have great symbolic significance in the Biblical world. They serve as a place of judgment (Dt 22:20–21) as well as a legal site where acts of submission and worship may take place (1Sa 5:4; Eze 46:1–2). They also mark the point of entry and exit from a private home, or, as in Ezekiel, from the realm of sacred space to the secular world.
10:19 *east gate.* This would be the gate of the outer court of the temple. While the temple complex had an east-west orientation, it is unclear how closely tied to this sacred precincts were the buildings and courtyards of the royal palace. It is possible that the gate Ezekiel is referring to in this case is one of those that connected the temple and the palace. If this is the case, then its significance is heightened as Yahweh prepares to abandon both the religious community as well as the secular authorities to their fate.
11:1–12 Ezekiel refutes the claims of Jerusalem's new rulers that they have created a safe haven in the city for the people. He turns this around, transforming the pot

Azzur and Pelatiah son of Benaiah, leaders of the people.[n] 2The LORD said to me,
"Son of man, these are the men who are
plotting evil and giving wicked advice in
this city. 3They say, 'Haven't our houses
been recently rebuilt? This city is a pot,[o]
and we are the meat in it.'[p] 4Therefore
prophesy[q] against them; prophesy, son of
man."
5Then the Spirit of the LORD came on
me, and he told me to say: "This is what
the LORD says: That is what you are saying, you leaders in Israel, but I know what
is going through your mind.[r] 6You have
killed many people in this city and filled
its streets with the dead.[s]
7"Therefore this is what the Sovereign
LORD says: The bodies you have thrown
there are the meat and this city is the pot,
but I will drive you out of it.[t] 8You fear the
sword, and the sword is what I will bring
against you, declares the Sovereign LORD.[u]
9I will drive you out of the city and deliver you into the hands[v] of foreigners and
inflict punishment on you.[w] 10You will fall
by the sword, and I will execute judgment
on you at the borders of Israel.[x] Then you
will know that I am the LORD. 11This city
will not be a pot[y] for you, nor will you be
the meat in it; I will execute judgment on
you at the borders of Israel. 12And you will
know that I am the LORD, for you have not
followed my decrees[z] or kept my laws but
have conformed to the standards of the
nations around you.[a]"
13Now as I was prophesying, Pelatiah[b]
son of Benaiah died. Then I fell facedown
and cried out in a loud voice, "Alas, Sovereign LORD! Will you completely destroy
the remnant of Israel?[c]"

The Promise of Israel's Return

14The word of the LORD came to me:
15"Son of man, the people of Jerusalem
have said of your fellow exiles and all the
other Israelites, 'They are far away from
the LORD; this land was given to us as our
possession.'[d]
16"Therefore say: 'This is what the Sovereign LORD says: Although I sent them
far away among the nations and scattered
them among the countries, yet for a little
while I have been a sanctuary[e] for them in
the countries where they have gone.'
17"Therefore say: 'This is what the Sovereign LORD says: I will gather you from
the nations and bring you back from the
countries where you have been scattered,
and I will give you back the land of Israel
again.'[f]
18"They will return to it and remove all
its vile images[g] and detestable idols.[h] 19I
will give them an undivided heart[i] and put
a new spirit in them; I will remove from
them their heart of stone[j] and give them a
heart of flesh.[k] 20Then they will follow my
decrees and be careful to keep my laws.[l]
They will be my people, and I will be their
God.[m] 21But as for those whose hearts are
devoted to their vile images and detestable idols, I will bring down on their own
heads what they have done, declares the
Sovereign LORD.[n]"
22Then the cherubim, with the wheels
beside them, spread their wings, and
the glory of the God of Israel was above

11:1 [n] Eze 8:16; 10:19; 43:4-5 **11:3** [o] Jer 1:13; Eze 24:3 [p] ver 7, 11 **11:4** [q] Eze 3:4, 17 **11:5** [r] Jer 17:10 **11:6** [s] Eze 7:23; 22:6 **11:7** [t] Eze 24:3-13; Mic 3:2-3 **11:8** [u] Pr 10:24 **11:9** [v] Ps 106:41 [w] Dt 28:36; Eze 5:8 **11:10** [x] 2Ki 14:25 **11:11** [y] ver 3 **11:12** [z] Lev 18:4; Eze 18:9 [a] Eze 8:10 **11:13** [b] ver 1 [c] Eze 9:8 **11:15** [d] Eze 33:24 **11:16** [e] Ps 90:1; 91:9; Isa 8:14 **11:17** [f] Jer 3:18; 24:5-6; Eze 28:25; 34:13 **11:18** [g] Eze 5:11 [h] Eze 37:23 **11:19** [i] Jer 32:39 [j] Zec 7:12 [k] Eze 18:31; 36:26; 2Co 3:3 **11:20** [l] Ps 105:45 [m] Eze 14:11; 36:26-28 **11:21** [n] Eze 9:10; 16:43

(Jerusalem) from a tightly sealed storage jar into a cooking pot in which the people (see Mic 3:3) and their false rulers will be broiled over the flame of Yahweh's anger (compare Eze 22:18 – 22).

11:13 *Pelatiah son of Benaiah died.* The name Pelatiah means "The Lord is my deliverance," or "The Lord's remnant." This name seems to have enjoyed great popularity near the end of Judah's history. Its meaning reflects the longing of the people for divine intervention on their behalf. Since this man bearing such a significant name has just died, the prophet immediately grasps the name as a portent of the coming disaster: Pelatiah son of Benaiah ("the Lord has built up") has died. He has symbolized the hope of Jerusalem, but that hope has become futile. With his death the hope of the city dies.

11:17 *I will gather you.* The idea of the powerful and generous ruler who gathers a dispersed people is a major ancient Near Eastern motif that appears with great frequency in Mesopotamian literature. The expression "to gather the dispersed" originated in Sumerian royal inscriptions commemorating the reestablishment of a stable rule after the Ur III political and economic disaster and in connection with several building projects, where it frequently appears in stereotypical expressions like "to establish in their dwellings the scattered countries" and "to make return to their place its [i.e., the city's] scattered peoples." While the king usually gathers the dispersed, in one Sumerian prayer this action is attributed to a god. This feature parallels Biblical usage of the expression.

11:19 *heart of stone.* This concept had a couple of associations in the ancient world, mostly from Egypt. First of all, in Egyptian beliefs, it was the heart that was weighed in judgment to determine whether or not the afterlife could be attained. If it was weighed down with guilt and sin, the results could be disastrous (see the article "The Hardening of Pharaoh's Heart," p. 124). A heart of stone would be a heavy heart. More important is the imagery connected to the mummification process. The heart was preserved in the mummy, but a stone carved in the shape of a dung beetle was placed on top of the heart. This stone had spells on it because Egyptians believed that the heart might betray the individual when he came to judgment and thereby jeopardize his attainment of the afterlife. In Egypt, the scarab beetle was the symbol of eternal life. By placing it inside the mummy by the heart, they believed they were securing the renewal of the person's life and vitality. In contrast, Yahweh is going to bring his people back to life by returning to them hearts of flesh that will not betray them. The imagery of an unhardened heart would be apt in that vv. 17 – 20 suggest a new exodus and a new covenant.

them.[o] 23The glory[p] of the LORD went up from within the city and stopped above the mountain[q] east of it. 24The Spirit[r] lifted me up and brought me to the exiles in Babylonia[a] in the vision[s] given by the Spirit of God.

Then the vision I had seen went up from me, 25and I told the exiles everything the LORD had shown me.[t]

The Exile Symbolized

12 The word of the LORD came to me: 2"Son of man, you are living among a rebellious people. They have eyes to see but do not see and ears to hear but do not hear, for they are a rebellious people.[u]

3"Therefore, son of man, pack your belongings for exile and in the daytime, as they watch, set out and go from where you are to another place. Perhaps[v] they will understand,[w] though they are a rebellious people.[x] 4During the daytime, while they watch, bring out your belongings packed for exile. Then in the evening, while they are watching, go out like those who go into exile.[y] 5While they watch, dig through the wall and take your belongings out through it. 6Put them on your shoulder as they are watching and carry them out at dusk. Cover your face so that you cannot see the land, for I have made you a sign[z] to the Israelites."

7So I did as I was commanded.[a] During the day I brought out my things packed for exile. Then in the evening I dug through the wall with my hands. I took my belongings out at dusk, carrying them on my shoulders while they watched.

8In the morning the word of the LORD came to me: 9"Son of man, did not the Israelites, that rebellious people, ask you, 'What are you doing?'[b]

10"Say to them, 'This is what the Sovereign LORD says: This prophecy concerns the prince in Jerusalem and all the Israelites who are there.' 11Say to them, 'I am a sign to you.'

"As I have done, so it will be done to them. They will go into exile as captives.[c]

12"The prince among them will put his things on his shoulder at dusk[d] and leave, and a hole will be dug in the wall for him to go through. He will cover his face so that he cannot see the land.[e] 13I will spread my net[f] for him, and he will be caught in my snare;[g] I will bring him to Babylonia, the land of the Chaldeans, but he will not see[h] it, and there he will die.[i] 14I will scatter to the winds all those around him—his staff and all his troops—and I will pursue them with drawn sword.[j]

15"They will know that I am the LORD, when I disperse them among the nations and scatter them through the countries. 16But I will spare a few of them from the sword, famine and plague, so that in the nations where they go they may acknowledge all their detestable practices. Then they will know that I am the LORD.[k]"

17The word of the LORD came to me: 18"Son of man, tremble as you eat your food,[l] and shudder in fear as you drink your water. 19Say to the people of the land: 'This is what the Sovereign LORD says about those living in Jerusalem and in the land of Israel: They will eat their food in anxiety and drink their water in despair, for their land will be stripped of everything[m] in it because of the violence of all who live there.[n] 20The inhabited towns will be laid waste and the land will be desolate. Then you will know that I am the LORD.[o]' "

[a] 24 Or *Chaldea*

11:22 [o] Eze 10:19 **11:23** [p] Eze 8:4; 10:4 [q] Zec 14:4 **11:24** [r] Eze 8:3 [s] 2Co 12:2-4 **11:25** [t] Eze 3:4, 11 **12:2** [u] Isa 6:10; Eze 2:6-8; Mt 13:15 **12:3** [v] Jer 36:3 [w] Jer 26:3 [x] 2Ti 2:25-26 **12:4** [y] ver 12; Jer 39:4 **12:6** [z] ver 12; Isa 8:18; 20:3; Eze 4:3; 24:24 **12:7** [a] Eze 24:18; 37:10 **12:9** [b] Eze 17:12; 20:49; 24:19 **12:11** [c] 2Ki 25:7; Jer 15:2; 52:15 **12:12** [d] Jer 39:4 [e] Jer 52:7 **12:13** [f] Eze 17:20; 19:8; Hos 7:12 [g] Isa 24:17-18 [h] Jer 39:7 [i] Jer 52:11; Eze 17:16 **12:14** [j] 2Ki 25:5; Eze 5:10, 12 **12:16** [k] Jer 22:8-9; Eze 6:8-10; 14:22 **12:18** [l] La 5:9; Eze 4:16 **12:19** [m] Eze 6:6-14; Mic 7:13; Zec 7:14 [n] Eze 4:16; 23:33 **12:20** [o] Isa 7:23-24; Jer 4:7

11:23 *mountain east.* The Mount of Olives. From here one can look down on the temple mount and the city. From a vantage point in Jerusalem, this would be the limit of how far one could look to the east. Whether the implication is that God is going to sit outside the city and watch (compare Jnh 4:5), or whether it is from here that he returns to heaven (it is the traditional site of the ascension of Christ as well, though NT support is slight) is uncertain.

12:4 *packed for exile.* In this sign-act Ezekiel is to pack an exile's knapsack in preparation for a long journey. The article in question is often represented on Neo-Assyrian monumental reliefs celebrating the victories of Assyrian kings that portray captives being led away in procession with large bags slung over their shoulders. The knapsack must have contained the barest necessities.

12:5 *dig through the wall.* As depicted in Assyrian reliefs, when a city is besieged a number of different measures are used to breach its defenses. Among these is undermining or drilling through the city walls (see the article "Siege Warfare," p. 1157). Since Ezekiel is digging from the outside of the wall inward, he takes on the role of the Babylonians, who are working at God's command to break through into the city.

12:12 *prince.* Ezekiel's antipathy toward the last king of Jerusalem and the fundamentally antidynastic stance in his judgment prophecies is expressed in his preference for the term "prince" instead of "king." *cover his face.* This has been variously interpreted as an expression of grief or an allusion to Zedekiah's blinding that occurred when the Babylonians captured the city. The key to the interpretation lies not in the covering of the eyes but in the reference to not seeing the land. This motif of not seeing the land as punishment appears in ancient Near Eastern curses.

12:18 *tremble as you eat … shudder in fear as you drink.* Since eating and drinking are the most basic activities of daily life, the mood at the table often reflects current conditions. At the Passover, the Israelites were to eat their meal "in haste" (Ex 12:11) as a reflection of their readiness to leave. Here the anxiety betrays the threat they are living under.

There Will Be No Delay

21 The word of the LORD came to me:
22 “Son of man, what is this proverb you
have in the land of Israel: ‘The days go
by and every vision comes to nothing’?[p]
23 Say to them, ‘This is what the Sovereign
LORD says: I am going to put an end to this
proverb, and they will no longer quote it
in Israel.’ Say to them, ‘The days are near
when every vision will be fulfilled.[q] 24 For
there will be no more false visions or flattering divinations[r] among the people of
Israel. 25 But I the LORD will speak what I
will, and it shall be fulfilled without delay.
For in your days, you rebellious people, I
will fulfill whatever I say, declares the Sovereign LORD.[s]’ ”
26 The word of the LORD came to me:
27 “Son of man, the Israelites are saying,
‘The vision he sees is for many years from
now, and he prophesies about the distant
future.’[t]
28 “Therefore say to them, ‘This is what
the Sovereign LORD says: None of my
words will be delayed any longer; whatever I say will be fulfilled, declares the Sovereign LORD.’ ”

False Prophets Condemned

13 The word of the LORD came to me:
2 “Son of man, prophesy against the
prophets of Israel who are now prophesying. Say to those who prophesy out of
their own imagination: ‘Hear the word
of the LORD![u] 3 This is what the Sovereign
LORD says: Woe to the foolish[a] prophets[v]
who follow their own spirit and have seen
nothing![w] 4 Your prophets, Israel, are like
jackals among ruins. 5 You have not gone
up to the breaches in the wall to repair[x]
it for the people of Israel so that it will
stand firm in the battle on the day of the
LORD.[y] 6 Their visions are false and their
divinations a lie. Even though the LORD
has not sent them, they say, “The LORD
declares,” and expect him to fulfill their
words.[z] 7 Have you not seen false visions
and uttered lying divinations when you
say, “The LORD declares,” though I have
not spoken?
8 “ ‘Therefore this is what the Sovereign
LORD says: Because of your false words
and lying visions, I am against you, declares the Sovereign LORD. 9 My hand will
be against the prophets who see false visions and utter lying divinations. They
will not belong to the council of my people
or be listed in the records[a] of Israel, nor
will they enter the land of Israel. Then you
will know that I am the Sovereign LORD.[b]
10 “ ‘Because they lead my people astray,[c]
saying, “Peace,” when there is no peace,
and because, when a flimsy wall is built,
they cover it with whitewash,[d] 11 therefore
tell those who cover it with whitewash
that it is going to fall. Rain will come in
torrents, and I will send hailstones hur-
tling down, and violent winds will burst
forth.[e] 12 When the wall collapses, will
people not ask you, “Where is the whitewash you covered it with?”
13 “ ‘Therefore this is what the Sovereign
LORD says: In my wrath I will unleash a violent wind, and in my anger hailstones[f] and
torrents of rain will fall with destructive
fury.[g] 14 I will tear down the wall you have
covered with whitewash and will level it
to the ground so that its foundation[h] will
be laid bare. When it[b] falls,[i] you will be
destroyed in it; and you will know that I
am the LORD. 15 So I will pour out my wrath
against the wall and against those who covered it with whitewash. I will say to you,
“The wall is gone and so are those who
whitewashed it, 16 those prophets of Israel

[a] 3 Or *wicked* [b] 14 Or *the city*

12:22 [p] Eze 11:3; Am 6:3; 2Pe 3:4 **12:23** [q] Ps 37:13; Joel 2:1; Zep 1:14 **12:24** [r] Jer 14:14; Eze 13:23; Zec 13:2-4 **12:25** [s] Isa 14:24; Hab 1:5 **12:27** [t] Da 10:14 **13:2** [u] ver 17; Jer 23:16; 37:19 **13:3** [v] La 2:14 [w] Jer 23:25-32 **13:5** [x] Isa 58:12; Eze 22:30 [y] Eze 7:19 **13:6** [z] Jer 28:15; Eze 22:28 **13:9** [a] Jer 17:13 [b] Eze 20:38 **13:10** [c] Jer 50:6 [d] Eze 7:25; 22:28 **13:11** [e] Eze 38:22 **13:13** [f] Rev 11:19; 16:21 [g] Ex 9:25; Isa 30:30 **13:14** [h] Mic 1:6 [i] Jer 6:15

12:24 *flattering divinations.* See note on Isa 2:6.
13:10 *flimsy wall … cover it with whitewash.* Ezekiel uses an analogy similar to that in Jer 6:14; 8:11. In both, the prophet's reality is covered up and people delude themselves into believing that a wound is not serious or a wall is sturdy. It reflects the tendency to hide structural problems with cosmetic solutions. Mesopotamian law codes also deal with unscrupulous builders and homeowners who neglect repairs or attempt to hide unsafe workmanship.
13:11 *hailstones.* This expression occurs only in Ezekiel (see also v.13; 38:22). All three uses of this expression appear in contexts in which God will use them together with other elements of nature as implements of punishment and destruction. Ezekiel uses it alongside of rain and wind, so a meteorological phenomenon must be intended, though hail is ice, not stone. The Hebrew term seems to echo a cognate Akkadian term pertaining to a type of stone (perhaps steatite) that can be carved and transformed into objects such as kitchen utensils. Overall, however, it may refer more to the color of a common stone rather than a geological classification. In Babylonia this stone was used for the fabrication of everyday objects like bowls, spindles and flasks. In Akkadian the word was never used for meteorological phenomena, so it is more likely that in Ezekiel it is a metaphoric expression comparing hail to stones of a certain color.
13:13 *violent wind.* In Mesopotamian laments over the ruin of major cities like Ur, Eridu, Lagash and Nippur dating from Old Babylonian times, the storm or tempestuous wind is mentioned as the main symbol of divine punishment and destruction. The "Lament Over the Destruction of Sumer and Ur" describes the destruction as an onslaught of a violent storm. *hailstones.* See note on v. 11.
13:14 *wall … covered with whitewash.* See note on v. 10. *its foundation will be laid bare.* God's wrath is so strong that the symbolic wall constructed of deceptive prophecy is to be totally razed to its bare foundations. Its foundation will be seen for what it is: self-interest and self-advancement rather than the word of God. Foundations usually consisted of a few courses of stone laid in trenches.

who prophesied to Jerusalem and saw visions of peace for her when there was no peace, declares the Sovereign LORD.[j]” ’

17“Now, son of man, set your face against the daughters[k] of your people who prophesy out of their own imagination. Prophesy against them[l] 18and say, ‘This is what the Sovereign LORD says: Woe to the women who sew magic charms on all their wrists and make veils of various lengths for their heads in order to ensnare people. Will you ensnare the lives of my people but preserve your own? 19You have profaned[m] me among my people for a few handfuls of barley and scraps of bread. By lying to my people, who listen to lies, you have killed those who should not have died and have spared those who should not live.[n]

20“ ‘Therefore this is what the Sovereign LORD says: I am against your magic charms with which you ensnare people like birds and I will tear them from your arms; I will set free the people that you ensnare like birds. 21I will tear off your veils and save my people from your hands, and they will no longer fall prey to your power. Then you will know that I am the LORD.[o] 22Because you disheartened the righteous with your lies, when I had brought them no grief, and because you encouraged the wicked not to turn from their evil ways and so save their lives,[p] 23therefore you will no longer see false visions or practice divination.[q] I will save my people from your hands. And then you will know that I am the LORD.[r]’ ”

Idolaters Condemned

14 Some of the elders of Israel came to me and sat down in front of me.[s] 2Then the word of the LORD came to me: 3“Son of man, these men have set up idols in their hearts and put wicked stumbling blocks[t] before their faces. Should I let them inquire of me at all?[u] 4Therefore speak to them and tell them, ‘This is what the Sovereign LORD says: When any of the Israelites set up idols in their hearts and put a wicked stumbling block before their faces and then go to a prophet, I the LORD will answer them myself in keeping with their great idolatry. 5I will do this to recapture the hearts of the people of Israel, who have all deserted[v] me for their idols.’[w]

6“Therefore say to the people of Israel, ‘This is what the Sovereign LORD says: Repent! Turn from your idols and renounce all your detestable practices![x]

7“ ‘When any of the Israelites or any foreigner[y] residing in Israel separate themselves from me and set up idols in their hearts and put a wicked stumbling block before their faces and then go to a prophet to inquire of me, I the LORD will answer them myself. 8I will set my face against[z] them and make them an example and a byword.[a] I will remove them from my people. Then you will know that I am the LORD.

9“ ‘And if the prophet[b] is enticed[c] to utter a prophecy, I the LORD have enticed that prophet, and I will stretch out my hand against him and destroy him from among my people Israel.[d] 10They will bear their guilt — the prophet will be as guilty as the one who consults him. 11Then the people of Israel will no longer stray[e] from me, nor will they defile themselves anymore with all their sins. They will be my people, and I will be their God, declares the Sovereign LORD.[f]’ ”

Jerusalem’s Judgment Inescapable

12The word of the LORD came to me: 13“Son of man, if a country sins against me

13:16 [j]Isa 57:21; Jer 6:14 **13:17** [k]Rev 2:20 [l]ver 2 **13:19** [m]Eze 20:39; 22:26 [n]Pr 28:21 **13:21** [o]Ps 91:3 **13:22** [p]Jer 23:14; Eze 33:14-16 **13:23** [q]ver 6; Eze 12:24 [r]Mic 3:6 **14:1** [s]Eze 8:1; 20:1 **14:3** [t]ver 7; Eze 7:19 [u]Isa 1:15; Eze 20:31 **14:5** [v]Zec 11:8 [w]Jer 2:11 **14:6** [x]Isa 2:20; 30:22 **14:7** [y]Ex 12:48; 20:10 **14:8** [z]Eze 15:7 [a]Eze 5:15 **14:9** [b]Jer 14:15 [c]Jer 4:10 [d]1Ki 22:23 **14:11** [e]Eze 48:11 [f]Eze 11:19-20; 37:23

13:18 *sew magic charms on all their wrists.* This practice is a bit uncertain since the Hebrew term only appears in this chapter (vv. 18,20). It is possible that it relates to Akkadian "binding magic." Babylonian incantation texts describe how persons wishing to bind others to their will made bands that they wore on their arms or wrists, empowering them with an oath. Perhaps these false female prophets were employing something similar or perhaps Ezekiel is simply comparing their influence to a practice known to him from Babylonia. *veils of various lengths.* The women involved in magical practices are making veils. The meaning of the term is uncertain. It differs from the usual Hebrew words for veils and therefore suggests a special kind of veil used in magical practices. The Babylonian series of incantations called Maqlû refers to calling on gods of the night and refers to the night as a "veiled bride" (Tablet I, 1 – 2), the female counterpart of the gods of darkness presiding over witchcraft.

14:1 *elders.* The mention of the elders of Israel also occurs in 8:1; 20:1,3. This group's existence and status were rooted in preexilic Judahite social structures. Although King Jehoiachin and members of his court were also in Babylonian exile, they seem not to have exercised any authority over the exiled Judahites. Rather, the exiles were governed in the traditional manner by the heads of the clans, referred to as the "family heads" (Ezr 1:5; 8:1; Ne 12:22,23) or "heads of the families" (Ezr 2:68; 4:2; Ne 7:70,71). These leaders are referred to in Aramaic as "elders of the Jews." The Jews in exile were not the only social group to have been organized in this manner. A document from the time of the Persian king Cambyses (529 BC) records an exact counterpart for the colony of Egyptian exiles near Babylon in its reference to the assembly of the elders of the Egyptians.

14:3,4,7 *idols in their hearts.* The Hebrew expression specifies that they have set idols *upon* their hearts. One possible interpretation understands this expression as indicating that the Israelites are wearing amulets of gods on their chests. It was a widespread custom among the Babylonians to wear all kinds of amulets around their neck and on their chest beneath their clothes. In light of such use, Ezekiel is likely reacting to some practices that the Israelites in exile have been adopting from their hosts.

by being unfaithful and I stretch out my
hand against it to cut off its food supply[g]
and send famine upon it and kill its people and their animals,[h] 14even if these three
men — Noah,[i] Daniel[a][j] and Job[k] — were in
it, they could save only themselves by their
righteousness,[l] declares the Sovereign LORD.
15"Or if I send wild beasts[m] through
that country and they leave it childless
and it becomes desolate so that no one
can pass through it because of the beasts,[n]
16as surely as I live, declares the Sovereign LORD, even if these three men were
in it, they could not save their own sons
or daughters. They alone would be saved,
but the land would be desolate.[o]
17"Or if I bring a sword[p] against that
country and say, 'Let the sword pass
throughout the land,' and I kill its people
and their animals,[q] 18as surely as I live,
declares the Sovereign LORD, even if these
three men were in it, they could not save
their own sons or daughters. They alone
would be saved.
19"Or if I send a plague into that land
and pour out my wrath[r] on it through
bloodshed, killing its people and their animals,[s] 20as surely as I live, declares the
Sovereign LORD, even if Noah, Daniel and
Job were in it, they could save neither son
nor daughter. They would save only themselves by their righteousness.[t]
21"For this is what the Sovereign LORD
says: How much worse will it be when I
send against Jerusalem my four dreadful
judgments — sword and famine and wild
beasts and plague — to kill its men and
their animals![u] 22Yet there will be some
survivors — sons and daughters who will
be brought out of it.[v] They will come to
you, and when you see their conduct[w] and
their actions, you will be consoled regarding the disaster I have brought on Jerusalem — every disaster I have brought on it.
23You will be consoled when you see their
conduct and their actions, for you will
know that I have done nothing in it without cause, declares the Sovereign LORD.[x]"

Jerusalem as a Useless Vine

15 The word of the LORD came to me:
2"Son of man, how is the wood of a
vine[y] different from that of a branch from
any of the trees in the forest? 3Is wood ever
taken from it to make anything useful? Do
they make pegs from it to hang things on?
4And after it is thrown on the fire as fuel
and the fire burns both ends and chars
the middle, is it then useful for anything?[z]
5If it was not useful for anything when it
was whole, how much less can it be made
into something useful when the fire has
burned it and it is charred?
6"Therefore this is what the Sovereign
LORD says: As I have given the wood of the
vine among the trees of the forest as fuel
for the fire, so will I treat the people living
in Jerusalem. 7I will set my face against[a]
them. Although they have come out of the
fire, the fire will yet consume them. And

[a] *14* Or *Danel,* a man of renown in ancient literature; also in verse 20

14:13 [g] Lev 26:26 [h] Eze 5:16; 6:14; 15:8 **14:14** [i] Ge 6:8 [j] ver 20; Eze 28:3; Da 1:6; 6:13 [k] Job 1:1 [l] Job 42:9; Jer 15:1; Eze 18:20 **14:15** [m] Eze 5:17 [n] Lev 26:22 **14:16** [o] Eze 18:20 **14:17** [p] Lev 26:25; Eze 5:12; 21:3-4 [q] Eze 25:13; Zep 1:3 **14:19** [r] Eze 7:8 [s] Eze 38:22 **14:20** [t] ver 14 **14:21** [u] Jer 15:3; Eze 5:17; 33:27; Am 4:6-10; Rev 6:8 **14:22** [v] Eze 12:16 [w] Eze 20:43 **14:23** [x] Jer 22:8-9 **15:2** [y] Isa 5:1-7; Jer 2:21; Hos 10:1 **15:4** [z] Eze 19:14; Jn 15:6 **15:7** [a] Ps 34:16; Eze 14:8

14:14 *Noah, Daniel and Job.* The Biblical Noah and Job are paragons of virtue from eras long ago. They are not considered to be Israelites. Moreover, the spelling of Daniel here (*dnl*) differs from the Hebrew spelling of the prophet Daniel (*dnyl*) and is usually taken as a reference to another ancient Gentile of old — hence the aptness of comparing the king of Tyre to him (28:3).

In the Ugaritic texts, the father of the hero Aqhat is a king, Dan'el, who is described as the righteous ruler "who judges the cause of the widow and adjudicates the case of the fatherless." This is a stock phrase that describes a righteous ruler *par excellence.* Dan'el is an upright man who prays to god and gives righteous judgment. The memory of an ancient righteous man named Dan'el is part of the common tradition in the ancient Near East. He has become an emblematic figure and we may see a reference to him here in Ezekiel.

The context favors such an understanding. The point of Ezekiel's invectives is that Israel has become more wicked and worse than the nations and countries around her. In 5:6 – 7, Israel is accused of not even conforming to the standards of the nations around her. Even if the three noble Gentiles of old — Noah, Dan'el and Job — would intercede for Israel, they could not revert the judgment God ordained for the wayward and rebellious nation. Accepting a reference to Ugaritic Dan'el in this verse makes Ezekiel's invective even more poignant and squares well with the rest of his message.

15:2 – 8 Like the song of the vineyard in Isa 5:1 – 6, Ezekiel also uses the vine as a metaphor for Judah (see also 17:5 – 10). In each case, the uselessness of the vine versus a branch or a tree well rooted is the justification for its destruction. A similar image appears in an Egyptian wisdom piece, the "Instruction of Amenemope." There too a plant that serves as the metaphor for fools who speak without thinking is uprooted, burned and destroyed because it soon withers and has no value once uprooted. The metaphor of a city as an unproductive plant is known from the Mesopotamian epic "Erra and Ishum" (known copies date to the eighth century BC) in which Marduk laments Babylon. He says that he filled it with seeds like a pinecone but no fruit came from it, and he planted it like an orchard but never tasted its fruit.

15:7 *Although they have come out of the fire, the fire will yet consume them.* Refers to events related to the fall of Jerusalem and its aftermath. The first burning refers to the siege of Jerusalem in Zedekiah's time (2Ki 25:1 – 4). The second burning adds a judgment that the people will face after the fall of Jerusalem. Many of the inhabitants who remained behind after 587 BC took up residence at Mizpah or returned to their home villages while Gedaliah served as governor at Mizpah. After the Judahite rebels murdered Gedaliah, they were subjected to more Chaldean/Babylonian wrath and punishment by dispersion (2Ki 25:22 – 26; Jer 40:7 — 43:7).

when I set my face against them, you will
know that I am the LORD.[b] 8I will make
the land desolate[c] because they have been
unfaithful,[d] declares the Sovereign LORD."

Jerusalem as an Adulterous Wife

16 The word of the LORD came to me:
2"Son of man, confront Jerusalem
with her detestable practices[e] 3and say,
'This is what the Sovereign LORD says to
Jerusalem: Your ancestry[f] and birth were
in the land of the Canaanites; your father
was an Amorite and your mother a Hittite.[g] 4On the day you were born[h] your
cord was not cut, nor were you washed
with water to make you clean, nor were
you rubbed with salt or wrapped in cloths.
5No one looked on you with pity or had
compassion enough to do any of these
things for you. Rather, you were thrown
out into the open field, for on the day you
were born you were despised.

6" 'Then I passed by and saw you kicking about in your blood, and as you lay
there in your blood I said to you, "Live!"[a][i]
7I made you grow[j] like a plant of the field.
You grew and developed and entered puberty. Your breasts had formed and your
hair had grown, yet you were stark naked.[k]

8" 'Later I passed by, and when I looked
at you and saw that you were old enough
for love, I spread the corner of my garment[l]
over you and covered your naked body. I
gave you my solemn oath and entered into
a covenant with you, declares the Sovereign LORD, and you became mine.[m]

9" 'I bathed you with water and washed[n]
the blood from you and put ointments on
you. 10I clothed you with an embroidered[o]
dress and put sandals of fine leather on

15:7 [b] Isa 24:18; Am 9:1-4 **15:8** [c] Eze 14:13 [d] Eze 17:20 **16:2** [e] Eze 20:4; 22:2 **16:3** [f] Eze 21:30 [g] ver 45 **16:4** [h] Hos 2:3 **16:6** [i] Ex 19:4 **16:7** [j] Dt 1:10 [k] Ex 1:7 **16:8** [l] Ru 3:9 [m] Jer 2:2; Hos 2:7, 19-20 **16:9** [n] Ru 3:3 **16:10** [o] Ex 26:36

[a] 6 A few Hebrew manuscripts, Septuagint and Syriac; most Hebrew manuscripts repeat *and as you lay there in your blood I said to you, "Live!"*

16:2 *confront Jerusalem.* That the allegory in ch. 16 is intended as an invective is clear from the imperative with which it starts. *her.* The ancient Near Eastern custom of personifying cities as female and married to the patron deity may have influenced Ezekiel in presenting Jerusalem as a woman. The accusation of religious straying of the people of Jerusalem is expressed through the description of the shameless acts of a brazen prostitute (v. 30), which draws some of its imagery from Canaanite practices but also contains a reminiscence of the Mesopotamian Ishtar festival. Exiled in Babylonia, Ezekiel could not have failed to be confronted with the grandiose and, in many respects, obscene Ishtar festival. He seems to draw heavily on the Ishtar cult as the epitome of idolatrous and religious straying of his own nation.

16:4 All of the actions described here would ordinarily be those of the midwife. She would cut and tie off the umbilical cord, rinse the placenta off the newborn, clean the baby's skin with salt water, and finally wrap it in a blanket. The child would then be presented to the parents to be named. However, in this case the child is not accepted as a member of the household and instead is left in a field, where its fate is left up to God. The role of the midwife in preparing the birthing room and caring for the newborn is often attributed to deity in the ancient world—especially in metaphors. In a segment of the Babylonian Atrahasis epic, the fertility goddess Mami is the midwife of the gods who brings humanity into being. In the Egyptian Great Hymn to Aten, the sun-god presides as midwife over the lands of Egypt each morning. The midwife rituals involved provide for both the physical needs of the child as well as a symbolic transference from the realm of the womb to the living world.

16:5 *thrown out into the open field.* Both classical and ancient Near Eastern sources make mention of infanticide. Graphic evidence of this has been found in recent excavations at Ashkelon. The bodies of a hundred infants were uncovered that had been disposed of in a sewer drain dating to the Roman-Byzantine period. Infanticide was usually employed to dispose of female or malformed children. This was done as a means of either population control or economic necessity since many villages barely were able to feed and care for healthy children and adults. The fact that the infant was "thrown out" into a field has legal implications as well. The parents are renouncing all legal claims to the child and leaving it up to God and/or another person to "adopt" and thus save the child's life. Among the examples of this practice are Moses' exposure in the Nile (Ex 2:1–10) and the birth legend of Sargon of Akkad.

16:6 *in your blood.* This expression corresponds to an Akkadian adoption formula: "in birth fluid and blood." One Neo-Babylonian Akkadian text describes an adoption procedure as abandoning a child still covered in his amniotic fluid and birth blood and giving him to the wet nurse. Interpreted in the light of ancient Near Eastern texts, the Hebrew expression signifies a formal declaration of adoption. Whoever takes a child while "in its blood" acquires full legal right to it. The Code of Hammurapi indicates that a child so adopted may never be reclaimed by the birth parents.

16:7 This verse speaks of a young maiden having reached the age of marriageability: her breasts are formed and her pubic hair has grown. These references should be taken as conventional tokens of marriageability in the ancient Near East, as attested by an almost identical text found in an Inanna/Ishtar hymn.

16:9 *I bathed you with water … and put ointments on you.* Marriage in ancient Mesopotamia, like marriage in ancient Israel, included ceremonies and rites. Bathing and anointing are part of a wedding ceremony in Old Babylonian and Middle Assyrian texts, as indicated as early as Sumerian sacred marriage texts.

16:10 *embroidered dress.* Among the bridal gifts is embroidered cloth for her gown. Only the finest cloth was embroidered, and it was considered a prize in war (Jdg 5:30) as well as a luxury item suitable for trade with other countries (Eze 27:16). On a more practical level, both the Code of Hammurapi and the Laws of Lipit-Ishtar from Mesopotamia list oil, grain and clothing as the items that husbands are required to supply their wives. *sandals of fine leather.* Ordinary sandals were made from woven fibrous material and secured with leather thongs (Isa 5:27). Footwear entirely made of leather would be a luxury and a signifier of both wealth and power. Fine leather sandals are represented on the panels of the Black Obelisk of Shalmaneser III (ninth century BC) and on wall paintings from the time of the Assyrian king Sargon II (721–705 BC).

you. I dressed you in fine linen[p] and covered you with costly garments.[q] 11 I adorned you with jewelry:[r] I put bracelets[s] on your arms and a necklace[t] around your neck, 12 and I put a ring on your nose,[u] earrings on your ears and a beautiful crown[v] on your head. 13 So you were adorned with gold and silver; your clothes were of fine linen and costly fabric and embroidered cloth. Your food was honey, olive oil[w] and the finest flour. You became very beautiful and rose to be a queen.[x] 14 And your fame[y] spread among the nations on account of your beauty,[z] because the splendor I had given you made your beauty perfect, declares the Sovereign LORD.

15 " 'But you trusted in your beauty and used your fame to become a prostitute. You lavished your favors on anyone who passed by[a] and your beauty became his.[b] 16 You took some of your garments to make gaudy high places, where you carried on your prostitution.[c] You went to him, and he possessed your beauty.[*a*] 17 You also took the fine jewelry I gave you, the jewelry made of my gold and silver, and you made for yourself male idols and engaged in prostitution with them.[d] 18 And you took your embroidered clothes to put on them, and you offered my oil and incense before them. 19 Also the food I provided for you — the flour, olive oil and honey I gave you to eat — you offered as fragrant incense before them. That is what happened, declares the Sovereign LORD.[e]

20 " 'And you took your sons and daughters[f] whom you bore to me[g] and sacrificed them as food to the idols. Was your prostitution not enough?[h] 21 You slaughtered my children and sacrificed them to the idols.[i] 22 In all your detestable practices and your prostitution you did not remember the days of your youth,[j] when you were naked and bare, kicking about in your blood.[k]

23 " 'Woe! Woe to you, declares the Sovereign LORD. In addition to all your other wickedness, 24 you built a mound for yourself and made a lofty shrine[l] in every public square.[m] 25 At every street corner you built your lofty shrines and degraded your beauty, spreading your legs with increasing promiscuity to anyone who passed by.[n] 26 You engaged in prostitution with the Egyptians, your neighbors with large genitals, and aroused my anger[o] with your increasing promiscuity.[p] 27 So I stretched out my hand[q] against you and reduced your territory; I gave you over to the greed of your enemies, the daughters of the Philistines,[r] who were shocked by your lewd conduct. 28 You engaged in prostitution with the Assyrians[s] too, because you were insatiable; and even after that, you still were not satisfied. 29 Then you increased your promiscuity to include Babylonia,[*b*t] a land of merchants, but even with this you were not satisfied.

30 " 'I am filled with fury against you,[*c*] declares the Sovereign LORD, when you do all these things, acting like a brazen prostitute![u] 31 When you built your mounds at every street corner and made your lofty shrines[v] in every public square, you were unlike a prostitute, because you scorned payment.

32 " 'You adulterous wife! You prefer strangers to your own husband! 33 All prostitutes receive gifts, but you give gifts[w] to all your lovers, bribing them to come to you from everywhere for your illicit favors.[x] 34 So in your prostitution you are the opposite of others; no one runs after you for your favors. You are the very opposite, for you give payment and none is given to you.

a 16 The meaning of the Hebrew for this sentence is uncertain. *b* 29 Or *Chaldea* *c* 30 Or *How feverish is your heart,*

16:10 [p] Eze 27:16 [q] ver 18
16:11 [r] Eze 23:40 [s] Isa 3:19; Eze 23:42 [t] Ge 41:42
16:12 [u] Isa 3:21 [v] Isa 28:5; Jer 13:18
16:13 [w] 1Sa 10:1 [x] Dt 32:13-14; 1Ki 4:21
16:14 [y] 1Ki 10:24 [z] La 2:15
16:15 [a] ver 25 [b] Isa 57:8; Jer 2:20; Eze 23:3; 27:3
16:16 [c] 2Ki 23:7
16:17 [d] Eze 7:20
16:19 [e] Hos 2:8
16:20 [f] Jer 7:31 [g] Ex 13:2 [h] Ps 106:37-38; Isa 57:5; Eze 23:37
16:21 [i] 2Ki 17:17; Jer 19:5
16:22 [j] Jer 2:2; Hos 11:1 [k] ver 6
16:24 [l] ver 31; Isa 57:7 [m] Ps 78:58; Jer 2:20; 3:2; Eze 20:28
16:25 [n] ver 15; Pr 9:14
16:26 [o] Eze 8:17 [p] Eze 20:8; 23:19-21
16:27 [q] Eze 20:33 [r] 2Ch 28:18
16:28 [s] 2Ki 16:7
16:29 [t] Eze 23:14-17
16:30 [u] Jer 3:3
16:31 [v] ver 24
16:33 [w] Isa 30:6; 57:9 [x] Hos 8:9-10

16:11 – 12 *bracelets ... necklace ... ring on your nose ... earrings ... crown.* The full array of jewelry provided by the husband consists of many of the types of jewelry regularly used to adorn a woman's body and head (compare the more complete list in Isa 3:18 – 23). Like the bride gifts for Rebekah (Ge 24:22), there are arm bracelets, possibly with animal heads at each end. The necklace may have been a strand of beads or linked metal rings similar to those in Assyrian reliefs or the Nimrud ivories depicting royal Assyrian women. Her nose ring again follows the style of Rebekah's adornment (Ge 24:22), and her earrings were probably ovoid loops inserted into pierced ears. Most striking of all is the golden crown, or tiara, on her head; it completes the ensemble of a ruler's wife and has parallels in both Egyptian and Assyrian art.
16:15 *prostitute.* See notes on Ge 38:15; Jdg 11:1.
16:21 *slaughtered my children and sacrificed them to the idols.* See notes on Lev 20:2; 1Ki 11:5; 2Ki 3:27; 16:3; Jer 7:31.
16:24 *mound ... lofty shrine in every public square.* These places of idolatrous worship were also erected "at every street corner" (v. 31). *mound.* The Hebrew term means something rounded, thus possibly an artificially constructed elevation on which cultic actions were performed. This word is attested in Ugaritic and in Mari Akkadian literature. It designates the base or the pedestal on which was placed the stone statue (baetylus) representing one of the divinities.
16:28 – 29 *You engaged in prostitution ... you were not satisfied.* The woman who incarnates the city of Jerusalem is so restless and dissatisfied that she roams the squares looking for new lovers. She is unable to achieve her role of a wife and a mother. She kills her children and abandons her husband.

Such a description may suggest to Israelites in Babylon the goddess Inanna, the patroness of prostitutes. As in this portrayal of Jerusalem, she is a restless and a perpetually dissatisfied goddess who abandons her lovers one after another.

35“ ‘Therefore, you prostitute, hear the
word of the LORD! 36This is what the Sovereign LORD says: Because you poured out
your lust and exposed your naked body
in your promiscuity with your lovers, and
because of all your detestable idols, and
because you gave them your children’s
blood,[y] 37therefore I am going to gather all
your lovers, with whom you found pleasure, those you loved as well as those you
hated. I will gather them against you from
all around and will strip you in front of
them, and they will see you stark naked.[z]
38I will sentence you to the punishment
of women who commit adultery and who
shed blood;[a] I will bring on you the blood
vengeance of my wrath and jealous anger.[b]
39Then I will deliver you into the hands of
your lovers, and they will tear down your
mounds and destroy your lofty shrines.
They will strip you of your clothes and
take your fine jewelry and leave you stark
naked.[c] 40They will bring a mob against
you, who will stone[d] you and hack you to
pieces with their swords. 41They will burn
down[e] your houses and inflict punishment
on you in the sight of many women.[f] I will
put a stop[g] to your prostitution, and you
will no longer pay your lovers. 42Then my
wrath against you will subside and my
jealous anger will turn away from you; I
will be calm and no longer angry.[h]
43“ ‘Because you did not remember[i] the
days of your youth but enraged me with
all these things, I will surely bring down[j]
on your head what you have done, declares the Sovereign LORD. Did you not
add lewdness to all your other detestable
practices?[k]
44“ ‘Everyone who quotes proverbs will
quote this proverb about you: “Like mother, like daughter.” 45You are a true daughter of your mother, who despised her husband and her children; and you are a true
sister of your sisters, who despised their
husbands and their children. Your mother
was a Hittite and your father an Amorite.[l]
46Your older sister was Samaria, who lived
to the north of you with her daughters;
and your younger sister, who lived to the
south of you with her daughters, was Sodom.[m] 47You not only followed their ways
and copied their detestable practices, but
in all your ways you soon became more
depraved than they.[n] 48As surely as I live,
declares the Sovereign LORD, your sister
Sodom and her daughters never did what
you and your daughters have done.[o]
49“ ‘Now this was the sin of your sister
Sodom:[p] She and her daughters were arrogant,[q] overfed and unconcerned; they did
not help the poor and needy.[r] 50They were
haughty and did detestable things before
me. Therefore I did away with them as
you have seen.[s] 51Samaria did not commit
half the sins you did. You have done more
detestable things than they, and have
made your sisters seem righteous by all
these things you have done.[t] 52Bear your
disgrace, for you have furnished some

16:36 [y] Jer 19:5; Eze 23:10 **16:37** [z] Jer 13:22 **16:38** [a] Eze 23:45 [b] Lev 20:10; Eze 23:25 **16:39** [c] Eze 23:26; Hos 2:3 **16:40** [d] Jn 8:5, 7 **16:41** [e] Dt 13:16 [f] Eze 23:10 [g] Eze 23:27, 48 **16:42** [h] Isa 54:9; Eze 5:13; 39:29 **16:43** [i] Ps 78:42 [j] Eze 22:31 [k] ver 22; Eze 11:21 **16:45** [l] Eze 23:2 **16:46** [m] Ge 13:10-13; Eze 23:4 **16:47** [n] 2Ki 21:9; Eze 5:7 **16:48** [o] Mt 10:15; 11:23-24 **16:49** [p] Ge 13:13 [q] Ps 138:6 [r] Eze 18:7, 12, 16; Lk 12:16-20 **16:50** [s] Ge 18:20-21; 19:5 **16:51** [t] Jer 3:8-11

16:36 *you … exposed your naked body in your promiscuity with your lovers.* This verse is part of a series of graphic descriptions of the sexual parts of both the harlot Jerusalem and her lovers. *you poured out your lust.* Has sexual connotations in the same vein as the verses speaking of a woman spreading her legs to passersby (v. 25), of the Egyptians with their large genitals (v. 26), and the baring of pudenda (vv. 36 – 37). These expressions go hand in hand with the reference to lewdness (vv. 27,43,58), whoredom and nudity (vv. 7,22,39). Such details can be understood in the light of comparative texts related to the Ishtar festival and the liturgical texts sung in her honor. In one of the songs sung by the cultic singer, the sexual parts of the goddess Ishtar were praised. Unbridled licentiousness was part of Ishtar's festival, and Ezekiel's sexual imagery is probably a reflection of the orgiastic aspects of the Ishtar's cult he witnessed in the land of his exile.

16:39 *mounds … lofty shrines.* See note on v. 24. *strip you … leave you … naked.* Ezekiel, who has taken over the marriage metaphor from Hosea, discusses in detail the punishment descending on an adulteress (v. 38; 23:45). In Isa 47:2 – 3, where Babylon is depicted as a whore, her private parts are also uncovered as punishment for her transgressions. In Na 3:5 the city of Nineveh is presented as an unchaste woman who will be uncovered on account of her many promiscuous acts. With the act of stripping, the husband is not only humiliating his wife in public but is also signifying symbolically that he brings to an end the commitments he has been bound to since the commencement of the marriage. According to parallel ancient Near Eastern texts, the public stripping of one's wife represented a nonverbal gesture signifying a divorce. The act of stripping naked an adulterous wife is paralleled by a Middle Babylonian text from Hana and a text from Nuzi. In the Hana text, a woman who wished to divorce her husband must leave the house naked. The standard phrase runs "to strip off the garment and to drive out naked." The parallels not only illustrate what was apparently a widespread custom but also suggest that this treatment inflicted on the wife was intended, in addition to shaming her, to emphasize her sudden lack of economic security.

16:45 *Your mother was a Hittite and your father an Amorite.* Ezekiel's reference is not only to these Canaanite peoples but also to the intermarriage that must have taken place over the centuries between them and the Israelites.

16:46 *Samaria … Sodom.* The warning is quite clear here. Both Samaria, the capital of the northern kingdom of Israel, and Sodom were destroyed by God for being corrupt (Ge 19:12 – 25; 2Ki 17:5 – 18). The reference to Samaria as the older or "big" sister may refer to its relative importance as the capital of ten tribes. It was constructed by Omri (1Ki 16:24) in the ninth century BC and thus was much "younger" than even David's Jerusalem. God may have chosen Sodom simply because of the tradition of its destruction (Am 4:11). As a city, it probably predated Jerusalem's founding, but it was probably smaller in terms of size given the ease with which it is said to have been captured in Ge 14:8 – 11.

justification for your sisters. Because your
sins were more vile than theirs, they appear more righteous than you. So then, be
ashamed and bear your disgrace, for you
have made your sisters appear righteous.
53“ ‘However, I will restore[u] the fortunes
of Sodom and her daughters and of Samaria and her daughters, and your fortunes
along with them, 54so that you may bear
your disgrace[v] and be ashamed of all you
have done in giving them comfort. 55And
your sisters, Sodom with her daughters
and Samaria with her daughters, will return to what they were before; and you
and your daughters will return to what
you were before.[w] 56You would not even
mention your sister Sodom in the day of
your pride, 57before your wickedness was
uncovered. Even so, you are now scorned
by the daughters of Edom[a][x] and all her
neighbors and the daughters of the Philistines — all those around you who despise
you. 58You will bear the consequences of
your lewdness and your detestable practices, declares the LORD.[y]
59“ ‘This is what the Sovereign LORD
says: I will deal with you as you deserve,
because you have despised my oath by
breaking the covenant.[z] 60Yet I will remember the covenant I made with you in
the days of your youth, and I will establish
an everlasting covenant[a] with you. 61Then
you will remember your ways and be
ashamed[b] when you receive your sisters,
both those who are older than you and
those who are younger. I will give them to
you as daughters, but not on the basis of
my covenant with you. 62So I will establish
my covenant with you, and you will know
that I am the LORD.[c] 63Then, when I make
atonement[d] for you for all you have done,
you will remember and be ashamed and
never again open your mouth[e] because of
your humiliation, declares the Sovereign
LORD.[f] ’ ”

Two Eagles and a Vine

17 The word of the LORD came to me:
2“Son of man, set forth an allegory
and tell it to the Israelites as a parable.[g]
3Say to them, ‘This is what the Sovereign
LORD says: A great eagle[h] with powerful
wings, long feathers and full plumage of
varied colors came to Lebanon.[i] Taking
hold of the top of a cedar, 4he broke off
its topmost shoot and carried it away to a
land of merchants, where he planted it in
a city of traders.
5“ ‘He took one of the seedlings of the
land and put it in fertile soil. He planted
it like a willow by abundant water,[j] 6and
it sprouted and became a low, spreading
vine. Its branches turned toward him, but
its roots remained under it. So it became a
vine and produced branches and put out
leafy boughs.
7“ ‘But there was another great eagle
with powerful wings and full plumage.
The vine now sent out its roots toward
him from the plot where it was planted

16:53 [u] Isa 19:24-25 **16:54** [v] Jer 2:26; Eze 14:22 **16:55** [w] Mal 3:4 **16:57** [x] 2Ki 16:6 **16:58** [y] Eze 23:49 **16:59** [z] Eze 17:19 **16:60** [a] Jer 32:40; Eze 37:26 **16:61** [b] Eze 20:43 **16:62** [c] Jer 24:7; Eze 20:37,43-44; Hos 2:19-20 **16:63** [d] Ps 65:3; 79:9 [e] Ro 3:19 [f] Ps 39:9; Da 9:7-8 **17:2** [g] Eze 20:49 **17:3** [h] Hos 8:1 [i] Jer 22:23 **17:5** [j] Dt 8:7-9; Isa 44:4

[a] *57* Many Hebrew manuscripts and Syriac; most Hebrew manuscripts, Septuagint and Vulgate *Aram*

16:57 *Edom.* See note on Jer 49:7. Given the apparent alliance between the Edomites and the Chaldeans/Babylonians at the time of Jerusalem's siege (see Ps 137:7), the Edomites would be in a position to gloat over or even loot Judah once the Babylonians had conquered the capital. *Philistines.* During the seventh century BC they vacillated between antagonism and alliance with the Babylonians. Ashkelon, e.g., was sacked and burned by Nebuchadnezzar in 604 BC. In any case, Jerusalem's capture in 597 and destruction in 587 would have been the basis upon which other states could chide the people of Jerusalem, considering that city to be the new Sodom and evidence of God's righteous anger against a corrupt and disobedient nation.
16:60 *Yet I will remember the covenant I made with you.* The enduring covenant of which the Lord speaks resumes the initial marriage metaphor with which ch. 16 began. In ch. 16 the pendulum swings metaphorically from abandoned child of suspect parentage to princess bride with the Lord as groom, from royal wedding to prostitution, and from disgraceful conduct of an unfaithful wife to an everlasting covenant. The covenant stands here for marriage (as in Pr 2:17; Mal 2:14). The marital metaphor implies children, who attest to the love of the parents, guarantee the future of a nation, and ensure the continuation of the parental love.
17:1 – 24 Ezekiel uses a riddle of two eagles and a vine to refer to the relations of the kings of Judah to the kings of Babylon and Egypt.
17:3 *A great eagle with powerful wings.* The eagle is the symbol of royal strength and splendor. The Assyrian king Sennacherib (704 – 681 BC) calls the eagle "the prince of birds." In the ancient Near East the eagle was also a common military symbol seen on ensigns as early as Old Babylonian times and as late as the Persian and Roman periods. Kings in battle were often described as eagles with outstretched wings. Another Assyrian king, Esarhaddon (681 – 669 BC), boasts of spreading his eagle-like pinions to destroy enemies. A near contemporary of Ezekiel, the prophet Habakkuk described the attack of the Babylonians in a similar manner: "They fly like an eagle swooping to devour" (Hab 1:8). Here the great eagle most likely refers to Nebuchadnezzar, the king of Babylon.
17:4 *broke off … carried it away … planted it.* Transplanted cedars were a feature of Assyrian royal gardens. Tiglath-Pileser I (1115 – 1077 BC) and Ashurnasirpal II (883 – 859 BC) transplanted cedars from Lebanon and a series of other trees to their royal cities. This well-known feature of Mesopotamian kings who tended their royal gardens is metaphorically applied to Nebuchadnezzar, who arrived in Jerusalem (called "Lebanon" in v. 3) ten years earlier in 597 BC. *topmost shoot.* King Jehoiachin, who, after a three-month reign, was carried away captive to Babylon, the "city of traders," along with his family, other members of Judahite nobility, and the prophet Ezekiel. Nebuchadnezzar appointed Jehoiachin's uncle Mattaniah (renamed Zedekiah) in Jehoiachin's place to secure the loyalty of the throne of Judah to the Babylonians.

and stretched out its branches to him for
water.[k] 8 It had been planted in good soil
by abundant water so that it would produce branches, bear fruit and become a
splendid vine.'
9 "Say to them, 'This is what the Sovereign LORD says: Will it thrive? Will it not
be uprooted and stripped of its fruit so that
it withers? All its new growth will wither.
It will not take a strong arm or many people to pull it up by the roots. 10 It has been
planted,[l] but will it thrive? Will it not wither
completely when the east wind strikes it—
wither away in the plot where it grew?' "
11 Then the word of the LORD came to me:
12 "Say to this rebellious people, 'Do you
not know what these things mean?[m]' Say
to them: 'The king of Babylon went to Jerusalem and carried off her king and her nobles,[n] bringing them back with him to Babylon.[o] 13 Then he took a member of the royal
family and made a treaty with him, putting
him under oath.[p] He also carried away the
leading men of the land, 14 so that the kingdom would be brought low,[q] unable to rise
again, surviving only by keeping his treaty. 15 But the king rebelled[r] against him by
sending his envoys to Egypt to get horses
and a large army.[s] Will he succeed? Will
he who does such things escape? Will he
break the treaty and yet escape?[t]
16 " 'As surely as I live, declares the Sovereign LORD, he shall die[u] in Babylon,
in the land of the king who put him on
the throne, whose oath he despised and
whose treaty he broke.[v] 17 Pharaoh[w] with
his mighty army and great horde will be
of no help to him in war, when ramps[x]
are built and siege works erected to destroy many lives.[y] 18 He despised the oath
by breaking the covenant. Because he had
given his hand in pledge[z] and yet did all
these things, he shall not escape.
19 " 'Therefore this is what the Sovereign
LORD says: As surely as I live, I will repay
him for despising my oath and breaking
my covenant.[a] 20 I will spread my net[b] for
him, and he will be caught in my snare.
I will bring him to Babylon and execute
judgment[c] on him there because he was
unfaithful to me. 21 All his choice troops
will fall by the sword,[d] and the survivors[e]
will be scattered to the winds.[f] Then you
will know that I the LORD have spoken.
22 " 'This is what the Sovereign LORD
says: I myself will take a shoot from the
very top of a cedar and plant it; I will
break off a tender sprig from its topmost
shoots and plant it on a high and lofty
mountain.[g] 23 On the mountain heights of
Israel I will plant it; it will produce branches and bear fruit and become a splendid
cedar. Birds of every kind will nest in it;
they will find shelter in the shade of its

17:7 [k] Eze 31:4
17:10 [l] Hos 13:15
17:12 [m] Eze 12:9 [n] 2Ki 24:15 [o] Eze 24:19
17:13 [p] 2Ch 36:13
17:14 [q] Eze 29:14
17:15 [r] Jer 52:3 [s] Dt 17:16 [t] Jer 34:3; 38:18
17:16 [u] Jer 52:11; Eze 12:13 [v] 2Ki 24:17
17:17 [w] Jer 37:7 [x] Eze 4:2 [y] Isa 36:6; Jer 37:5; Eze 29:6-7
17:18 [z] 1Ch 29:24
17:19 [a] Eze 16:59
17:20 [b] Eze 12:13; 32:3 [c] Jer 2:35; Eze 20:36
17:21 [d] Eze 12:14 [e] 2Ki 25:11 [f] 2Ki 25:5
17:22 [g] Jer 23:5; Eze 20:40; 36:1, 36; 37:22

17:13 *a member of the royal family.* Zedekiah; this description recognizes him as a member of the Davidic dynasty. The expression has an exact Akkadian counterpart, underlining the legitimacy of a king in contrast to a usurper, who was called "a son of nobody." *made a treaty ... putting him under oath.* These phrases derive from the realm of suzerainty treaties and loyalty oaths. These too have exact Akkadian counterparts. The use of such specific political terminology from the sphere of international treaties calls attention to Ezekiel's main contention: Zedekiah's breach of the vassal treaty with the Babylonian king Nebuchadnezzar.

17:15 *king rebelled.* Zedekiah's breaking away from Nebuchadnezzar appears to have coincided with the accession of Psammetichus II (595–589 BC) as king of Egypt. A papyrus from El Hibeh refers to a visit of the pharaoh to Syria-Palestine in his fourth year (591 BC) officially as a religious pilgrimage to Byblos. To conduct a pilgrimage under the nose of the Chaldean/Babylonian overlords carried with it a challenge to Babylonian suzerainty, which was not lost on the local rulers of the region. During the Babylonian siege of Jerusalem, Judah looked to Psammetichus II's successor, Hophra (589–570 BC), for help—but to no avail (Jer 37:5–7). Egypt did not take up arms to defend its former ally. Zedekiah's pro-Egyptian policy was not a last-minute strategy concocted out of desperation but was a long-lasting tendency of the Jerusalem nobility that both Jeremiah and Ezekiel denounced as fundamentally wrong and hopeless.

17:19 The invective of this verse is addressed against King Zedekiah, who broke the vassal treaty with the king of Babylon, Nebuchadnezzar. Here the prophecies concerning the breach of vassal loyalty have been "radicalized" in a unique way by presenting the offense against the king of Babylon as an offense against the Lord. Some scholars argue that according to the Babylonian practice of covenant making, the vassals had to swear by their own divinities. As implied by 2Ch 36:13, the God of Israel was presumably appealed to by both Zedekiah and Nebuchadnezzar as a witness in the vassal oaths between them. Consequently, the Lord turns against the oath and treaty breaker, Zedekiah. Hittite practice normally required vassals to swear by the gods of both nations. Assyrian practice ignored the gods of the vassals, while the later Babylonians had vassals swear by their own gods.

According to 2Ki 24:17, the king of Babylon "made Mattaniah, Jehoiachin's uncle, king in his place and changed his name to Zedekiah." Both Mattaniah and Zedekiah are Yahwistic names (iah = Yah, short for Yahweh, i.e., the Lord). While his old name means "Gift of Yahweh," the new one means "Righteousness of Yahweh." Since this name was given him by his Babylonian overlord, one might assume that Nebuchadnezzar made the new king of Judah swear by the "righteousness" of the Lord that he would remain true to his word. Zedekiah, however, acted as a traitor toward his Babylonian overlord in contrast to the meaning of the new name given to him.

17:20 *spread my net.* The mention of the net as the Lord's weapon echoes a major ancient Near Eastern iconographic and literary motif. The net is the weapon that the gods used in punishing political perjury. Nets and snares are also used in metaphors for magical hexes that exercise power over their victims.

17:23 *a splendid cedar ... Birds ... will find shelter.* The concept of the cosmic tree or the "one tree" is common to many peoples and traditions. It stands as a representation

Stele of the Vultures depicts prisoners in a net, twenty-fifth century BC. The mention of the net as the Lord's weapon (Eze 17:20) echoes this motif.

Kim Walton. The Louvre.

branches.[h] [24]All the trees of the forest[i] will
know that I the LORD bring down the tall
tree and make the low tree grow tall. I dry
up the green tree and make the dry tree
flourish.

"'I the LORD have spoken, and I will
do it.[j]'"

The One Who Sins Will Die

18 The word of the LORD came to me:
[2]"What do you people mean by quoting this proverb about the land of Israel:

"'The parents eat sour grapes,
and the children's teeth are set on edge'?[k]

[3]"As surely as I live, declares the Sovereign LORD, you will no longer quote this
proverb in Israel. [4]For everyone belongs to
me, the parent as well as the child—both
alike belong to me. The one who sins is
the one who will die.[l]

[5]"Suppose there is a righteous man
who does what is just and right.
[6]He does not eat at the mountain[m] shrines
or look to the idols[n] of Israel.
He does not defile his neighbor's wife
or have sexual relations with a woman during her period.
[7]He does not oppress[o] anyone,
but returns what he took in pledge[p] for a loan.
He does not commit robbery
but gives his food to the hungry
and provides clothing for the naked.[q]

17:23 [h]Ps 92:12; Isa 2:2; Eze 31:6; Da 4:12; Hos 14:5-7; Mt 13:32 **17:24** [i]Ps 96:12 [j]Eze 19:12; 21:26; 22:14; Am 9:11 **18:2** [k]Isa 3:15; Jer 31:29; La 5:7 **18:4** [l]ver 20; Isa 42:5; Ro 6:23 **18:6** [m]Eze 22:9 [n]Dt 4:19; Eze 6:13; 20:24 **18:7** [o]Ex 22:21 [p]Ex 22:26; Dt 24:12 [q]Dt 15:11; Mt 25:36

of beauty and fertility, drawing its sustenance from the waters of the earth and providing shelter and food to all creatures that shelter under its boughs. Its symmetry and stability provide in ancient Near Eastern sources a check against death and a promise of the continuance of existence. Thus in Assyrian art is found a stylized "tree of life" that may have represented the role of the king to care for his people (see note on Da 4:10–12).

18:2 *The parents eat sour grapes, and the children's teeth are set on edge.* In ch. 18 Ezekiel discusses the traditional belief in corporate guilt and responsibility. The doctrine of divine retribution or nemesis held that children would be punished for the crimes of their parents. The doctrine of transgenerational transmission of guilt is expressed in the second commandment of the Decalogue: "I, the LORD your God, am a jealous God, punishing the children for the sin of the parents to the third and fourth generation of those who hate me" (Ex 20:5). A similar idea is found in ancient Near Eastern texts. Faced with a plague that was affecting the people of his land, the fourteenth-century BC Hittite king Mursili II indicates in a prayer to the storm-god that though his father had sinned, he was innocent. He then acknowledges, however, that the father's sin falls upon the son, and so he is suffering for his father's sin.

The Bible interprets the fall of Jerusalem in the same manner. The removal of King Jehoiakim is described as an act of divine retribution "because of the sins of Manasseh" (2Ki 24:3), Jehoiakim's dynastic ancestor. The idea of collective responsibility is found in the Hittite Laws, in which it is stated that the punishment for disobeying the order of the king will involve the culprit, the perpetrator of the offense, but also his entire household. It indicates that he and his whole family must be killed, so that there will be no continuance of his line.

A distinction must be retained between the reality that the choices made by one generation may bring continuing troubles for successive generations and the legal restriction that punishment for a specific crime by a parent should not be carried out on a child. For example, some Babylonian indications are that if a person caused the death of another's son, his own son should be put to death. This is a different matter from recognizing that there are ongoing consequences for bad choices.

18:5–9 Ezekiel's list of virtues and vices seems to have arisen in priestly and temple circles. There are several Egyptian parallels of such lists that were inscribed at the entrances to temples containing most of the cataloged sins found in Ezekiel's list. Such lists were intended to inculcate Egyptian priests with virtue and devotion.

18:6 *eat at the mountain shrines.* Presumably, this is a charge of idolatry at local high places. Unfortunately, there is no parallel from Biblical or ancient Near Eastern law to help illumine this practice. It might be compared to the giving of Jerusalem's children as food to the gods (16:20) and to the charge that the people of Judah are willing to worship "on every high hill" (6:13; Jer 2:20) throughout the land. A similar condemnation of the use of hilltop shrines by the people of Israel can be found in Hos 4:13. *idols of Israel.* It would appear that Ezekiel is using a stock phrase coined during the late monarchy or perhaps during the

[8]He does not lend to them at interest
or take a profit from them.[r]
He withholds his hand from doing
wrong
and judges fairly[s] between two parties.
[9]He follows my decrees
and faithfully keeps my laws.
That man is righteous;[t]
he will surely live,[u]
declares the Sovereign LORD.

[10]"Suppose he has a violent son, who
sheds blood[v] or does any of these other
things[a] [11](though the father has done none
of them):

"He eats at the mountain shrines.
He defiles his neighbor's wife.
[12]He oppresses the poor[w] and needy.
He commits robbery.
He does not return what he took in
pledge.
He looks to the idols.
He does detestable things.[x]
[13]He lends at interest and takes a profit.[y]

Will such a man live? He will not! Because
he has done all these detestable things, he
is to be put to death; his blood will be on
his own head.[z]
[14]"But suppose this son has a son who
sees all the sins his father commits, and
though he sees them, he does not do such
things:[a]

[15]"He does not eat at the mountain
shrines
or look to the idols of Israel.
He does not defile his neighbor's wife.
[16]He does not oppress anyone
or require a pledge for a loan.
He does not commit robbery
but gives his food to the hungry
and provides clothing for the naked.[b]
[17]He withholds his hand from
mistreating the poor
and takes no interest or profit from
them.
He keeps my laws and follows my
decrees.

He will not die for his father's sin; he will
surely live. [18]But his father will die for
his own sin, because he practiced extortion, robbed his brother and did what was
wrong among his people.

[19]"Yet you ask, 'Why does the son not
share the guilt of his father?' Since the son
has done what is just and right and has
been careful to keep all my decrees, he
will surely live.[c] [20]The one who sins is the
one who will die. The child will not share
the guilt of the parent, nor will the parent
share the guilt of the child. The righteousness of the righteous will be credited to
them, and the wickedness of the wicked
will be charged against them.[d]
[21]"But if a wicked person turns away
from all the sins they have committed and
keeps all my decrees and does what is
just and right, that person will surely live;
they will not die.[e] [22]None of the offenses
they have committed will be remembered
against them. Because of the righteous
things they have done, they will live.[f]
[23]Do I take any pleasure in the death of
the wicked? declares the Sovereign LORD.
Rather, am I not pleased[g] when they turn
from their ways and live?[h]
[24]"But if a righteous person turns from
their righteousness and commits sin and
does the same detestable things the wicked person does, will they live? None of the
righteous things that person has done will
be remembered. Because of the unfaithfulness they are guilty of and because of the
sins they have committed, they will die.[i]
[25]"Yet you say, 'The way of the Lord is
not just.' Hear, you Israelites: Is my way
unjust?[j] Is it not your ways that are unjust? [26]If a righteous person turns from
their righteousness and commits sin, they
will die for it; because of the sin they have
committed they will die. [27]But if a wicked person turns away from the wickedness they have committed and does what
is just and right, they will save their life.[k]
[28]Because they consider all the offenses
they have committed and turn away from
them, that person will surely live; they
will not die. [29]Yet the Israelites say, 'The
way of the Lord is not just.' Are my ways
unjust, people of Israel? Is it not your ways
that are unjust?
[30]"Therefore, you Israelites, I will judge
each of you according to your own ways,
declares the Sovereign LORD. Repent![l] Turn
away from all your offenses; then sin will

[a] 10 Or *things to a brother*

18:8 [r]Ex 22:25; Lev 25:35-37; Dt 23:19-20 [s]Zec 8:16 **18:9** [t]Hab 2:4 [u]Lev 18:5; Eze 20:11; Am 5:4 **18:10** [v]Ex 21:12 **18:12** [w]Am 4:1 [x]2Ki 21:11; Isa 59:6-7; Jer 22:17; Eze 8:6, 17 **18:13** [y]Ex 22:25 [z]Eze 33:4-5 **18:14** [a]2Ch 34:21; Pr 23:24 **18:16** [b]Ps 41:1; Isa 58:10 **18:19** [c]Ex 20:5; Dt 5:9; Jer 15:4; Zec 1:3-6 **18:20** [d]Dt 24:16; 1Ki 8:32; 2Ki 14:6; Isa 3:11; Mt 16:27; Ro 2:9 **18:21** [e]Eze 33:12, 19 **18:22** [f]Ps 18:20-24; Isa 43:25; Mic 7:19 **18:23** [g]Ps 147:11 [h]Eze 33:11; 1Ti 2:4 **18:24** [i]1Sa 15:11; 2Ch 24:17-20; Eze 3:20; 20:27; 2Pe 2:20-22 **18:25** [j]Ge 18:25; Jer 12:1; Eze 33:17; Zep 3:5; Mal 2:17; 3:13-15 **18:27** [k]Isa 1:18 **18:30** [l]Mt 3:2

exile for the extreme impurity associated with idol worship. His language is intentionally vulgar as it characterizes the idols in the crudest possible way: they are best likened to feces or stools of excrement (see note on 6:4).
18:8 *lend ... at interest.* Consistent with Biblical law, Ezekiel considers the practice of charging interest on a loan an unrighteous act (see notes on Lev 25:36; Dt 23:19–20; Pr 6:1; 28:8).
18:20 *The one who sins is the one who will die.* While the social structure of the ancient Near East was primarily oriented toward the group (tribe, clan, family), there is a strand of individual responsibility that appears in literary and philosophical works. Among the examples of this is a statement in the Gilgamesh Epic. The Mesopotamian god Ea berates the chief god Enlil for bringing on the great flood without just cause, insisting that the sinner is the one who should be punished for his own sin.

not be your downfall.[m] 31 Rid yourselves of
all the offenses you have committed, and
get a new heart[n] and a new spirit. Why will
you die, people of Israel?[o] 32 For I take no
pleasure in the death of anyone, declares
the Sovereign LORD. Repent and live![p]

A Lament Over Israel's Princes

19 "Take up a lament[q] concerning the
princes[r] of Israel 2 and say:

"'What a lioness was your mother
among the lions!
She lay down among them
and reared her cubs.
3 She brought up one of her cubs,
and he became a strong lion.
He learned to tear the prey
and he became a man-eater.
4 The nations heard about him,
and he was trapped in their pit.
They led him with hooks
to the land of Egypt.[s]

5 "'When she saw her hope unfulfilled,
her expectation gone,
she took another of her cubs
and made him a strong lion.[t]
6 He prowled among the lions,
for he was now a strong lion.
He learned to tear the prey
and he became a man-eater.[u]
7 He broke down[a] their strongholds
and devastated[v] their towns.
The land and all who were in it
were terrified by his roaring.
8 Then the nations[w] came against him,
those from regions round about.
They spread their net for him,
and he was trapped in their pit.[x]
9 With hooks they pulled him into a cage
and brought him to the king of
Babylon.[y]

18:30 [m] Eze 7:3; 33:20; Hos 12:6 **18:31** [n] Ps 51:10 [o] Isa 1:16-17; Eze 11:19; 36:26 **18:32** [p] Eze 33:11 **19:1** [q] Eze 26:17; 27:2,32 [r] 2Ki 24:6 **19:4** [s] 2Ki 23:33-34; 2Ch 36:4 **19:5** [t] 2Ki 23:34 **19:6** [u] 2Ki 24:9; 2Ch 36:9 **19:7** [v] Eze 30:12 **19:8** [w] 2Ki 24:2 [x] 2Ki 24:11 **19:9** [y] 2Ch 36:6

They put him in prison,
so his roar was heard no longer
on the mountains of Israel.[z]

10 "'Your mother was like a vine in your
vineyard[b]
planted by the water;
it was fruitful and full of branches
because of abundant water.[a]
11 Its branches were strong,
fit for a ruler's scepter.
It towered high
above the thick foliage,
conspicuous for its height
and for its many branches.[b]
12 But it was uprooted[c] in fury
and thrown to the ground.
The east wind made it shrivel,
it was stripped of its fruit;
its strong branches withered
and fire consumed them.[d]
13 Now it is planted in the desert,[e]
in a dry and thirsty land.[f]
14 Fire spread from one of its main[c]
branches
and consumed[g] its fruit.
No strong branch is left on it
fit for a ruler's scepter.'[h]

"This is a lament and is to be used as a
lament."

Rebellious Israel Purged

20 In the seventh year, in the fifth
month on the tenth day, some of
the elders of Israel came to inquire of the
LORD, and they sat down in front of me.[i]
2 Then the word of the LORD came to me:
3 "Son of man, speak to the elders of Israel
and say to them, 'This is what the Sover-

[z] 2Ki 24:15 **19:10** [a] Ps 80:8-11 **19:11** [b] Eze 31:3; Da 4:11 **19:12** [c] Eze 17:10 [d] Isa 27:11; Eze 28:17; Hos 13:15 **19:13** [e] Eze 20:35 [f] Hos 2:3 **19:14** [g] Eze 20:47 [h] Eze 15:4 **20:1** [i] Eze 8:1

[a] *7* Targum (see Septuagint); Hebrew *He knew*
[b] *10* Two Hebrew manuscripts; most Hebrew manuscripts *your blood*
[c] *14* Or *from under its*

19:3 *a strong lion ... became a man-eater.* In ch. 19, by using the special genre of a dirge, Ezekiel evokes the melancholic atmosphere of a lament over the rulers of Israel and Judah presented as lions. The lion was a common symbol for royalty in the ancient Near East.
19:4 *he was trapped in their pit.* Lion hunting was one of the favorite sports of many kings in the ancient Near East. The method of using a pit to capture a lion reflects ancient lion-hunting techniques. An eighteenth-century BC letter from northern Syria describes how once the lion was trapped in the pit, wood was thrown into it and set on fire, thus killing the lion.
19:9 *cage.* This Hebrew word occurs only here in the Bible and is a loanword from Akkadian. Though originally thought to be a cage for transporting war prisoners, it is now certain that both the Akkadian word and its Hebrew counterpart denote a "neck-stock" or "(wooden) collar" used to transport both animals (lions) and prisoners of war. A comment from Ashurbanipal's annals illustrates the use of this device for both humans and animals as it talks about putting a pillory on a captive's neck together with a bear and a dog at the gate of Nineveh.
20:1 *seventh year ... fifth month ... tenth day.* Based on the year in which Jehoiachin and his court were taken into Babylonian exile, this date formula would correlate to Aug. 15, 591 BC. It is possible that it could refer to 593 if one were counting from the beginning of the year that Jehoiachin became king in Jerusalem. *inquire of the LORD.* Messages were sought in troubled times. In Babylonian religious practice the occurrence of an omen might lead someone to go to a prophet or priest to ask for an interpretation. At other times, it may be a historical event that would make it desirable to have a word from God. It may be that the elders hoped to demonstrate their trust in Yahweh by this act. However, there is also evidence in Jeremiah of representatives of the king seeking out the prophet and virtually ordering him to speak a message of salvation for Jerusalem (Jer 21:1 – 2). There is no indication in the text what may have motivated this visit to Ezekiel. Since his speech goes back to the wilderness situation and makes frequent reference to Israel's early history with Egypt, it may well be a potential agreement between Egypt's pharaoh Psammetichus II and Judah's king Zedekiah that prompted concern among the elders.

eign LORD says: Have you come to inquire[j]
of me? As surely as I live, I will not let
you inquire of me, declares the Sovereign
LORD.[k]’
4“Will you judge them? Will you judge
them, son of man? Then confront them
with the detestable practices of their ancestors[l] 5and say to them: ‘This is what the
Sovereign LORD says: On the day I chose[m]
Israel, I swore with uplifted hand to the
descendants of Jacob and revealed myself to them in Egypt. With uplifted hand I
said to them, “I am the LORD your God.[n]”
6On that day I swore to them that I would
bring them out of Egypt into a land I had
searched out for them, a land flowing with
milk and honey,[o] the most beautiful of all
lands.[p] 7And I said to them, “Each of you,
get rid of the vile images[q] you have set
your eyes on, and do not defile yourselves
with the idols of Egypt. I am the LORD your
God.[r]”
8“ ‘But they rebelled against me and
would not listen to me; they did not get rid
of the vile images they had set their eyes
on, nor did they forsake the idols of Egypt.[s]
So I said I would pour out my wrath on
them and spend my anger against them
in Egypt.[t] 9But for the sake of my name,
I brought them out of Egypt.[u] I did it to
keep my name from being profaned in
the eyes of the nations among whom they
lived and in whose sight I had revealed
myself to the Israelites. 10Therefore I led
them out of Egypt and brought them into
the wilderness.[v] 11I gave them my decrees
and made known to them my laws, by
which the person who obeys them will
live.[w] 12Also I gave them my Sabbaths as
a sign[x] between us, so they would know
that I the LORD made them holy.
13“ ‘Yet the people of Israel rebelled[y]
against me in the wilderness. They did not
follow my decrees but rejected my laws—
by which the person who obeys them
will live—and they utterly desecrated my
Sabbaths. So I said I would pour out my
wrath[z] on them and destroy them in the
wilderness.[a] 14But for the sake of my name
I did what would keep it from being profaned in the eyes of the nations in whose
sight I had brought them out.[b] 15Also with
uplifted hand I swore to them in the wilderness that I would not bring them into
the land I had given them—a land flowing
with milk and honey, the most beautiful
of all lands[c]— 16because they rejected my
laws and did not follow my decrees and
desecrated my Sabbaths. For their hearts[d]
were devoted to their idols.[e] 17Yet I looked
on them with pity and did not destroy
them or put an end to them in the wilderness. 18I said to their children in the
wilderness, “Do not follow the statutes
of your parents[f] or keep their laws or defile yourselves with their idols. 19I am the
LORD your God;[g] follow my decrees and
be careful to keep my laws.[h] 20Keep my
Sabbaths holy, that they may be a sign between us. Then you will know that I am
the LORD your God.[i]”
21“ ‘But the children rebelled against me:
They did not follow my decrees, they were
not careful to keep my laws, of which I
said, “The person who obeys them will
live by them,” and they desecrated my
Sabbaths. So I said I would pour out my
wrath on them and spend my anger against
them in the wilderness. 22But I withheld[j]
my hand, and for the sake of my name I
did what would keep it from being profaned in the eyes of the nations in whose
sight I had brought them out. 23Also with
uplifted hand I swore to them in the wilderness that I would disperse them among
the nations and scatter[k] them through the
countries, 24because they had not obeyed
my laws but had rejected my decrees and
desecrated my Sabbaths,[l] and their eyes
lusted after[m] their parents’ idols.[n] 25So I
gave[o] them other statutes that were not
good and laws through which they could
not live;[p] 26I defiled them through their
gifts—the sacrifice of every firstborn—
that I might fill them with horror so they
would know that I am the LORD.[q]’
27“Therefore, son of man, speak to the
people of Israel and say to them, ‘This
is what the Sovereign LORD says: In this
also your ancestors blasphemed[r] me by

20:3 [j] Eze 14:3 [k] Mic 3:7
20:4 [l] Eze 16:2; 22:2; Mt 23:32
20:5 [m] Dt 7:6 [n] Ex 6:7
20:6 [o] Ex 3:8; Jer 32:22 [p] Dt 8:7; Ps 48:2; Da 8:9
20:7 [q] Ex 20:4 [r] Ex 20:2; Lev 18:3; Dt 29:18
20:8 [s] Eze 7:8 [t] Isa 63:10
20:9 [u] Eze 36:22; 39:7
20:10 [v] Ex 13:18
20:11 [w] Lev 18:5; Dt 4:7-8; Ro 10:5
20:12 [x] Ex 31:13
20:13 [y] Ps 78:40 [z] Dt 9:8 [a] Nu 14:29; Ps 95:8-10; Isa 56:6
20:14 [b] Eze 36:23
20:15 [c] Ps 95:11; 106:26
20:16 [d] Nu 15:39 [e] Am 5:26
20:18 [f] Zec 1:4
20:19 [g] Ex 20:2 [h] Dt 5:32-33; 6:1-2; 8:1; 11:1; 12:1
20:20 [i] Jer 17:22
20:22 [j] Ps 78:38
20:23 [k] Lev 26:33; Dt 28:64
20:24 [l] ver 13 [m] Eze 6:9 [n] ver 16
20:25 [o] Ps 81:12 [p] 2Th 2:11
20:26 [q] 2Ki 17:17
20:27 [r] Ro 2:24

It is believed that Psammetichus made overtures to Zedekiah in 592 BC.

20:5 *swore with uplifted hand.* There are many references in the Bible to taking an oath by raising up a hand to heaven (e.g., Dt 32:40; Da 12:7). Ezekiel uses the phrase ten times with God being the one to take an oath by raising his hand. Since God has no need to raise a hand toward himself, we can assume that it is just being used here as a stock phrase for making an oath.

20:6 *flowing with milk and honey.* See notes on Ex 3:8; Jer 11:5.

20:25 *statutes ... laws.* The Hebrew terms used here are extremely important to a proper understanding of Ezekiel's controversial statement. This is not a reference to the law given at Mount Sinai, and the Hebrew word *torah* is not used. The Hebrew word the NIV translates "statutes" is the same Hebrew word that is translated "decrees" in v. 24 except that in v. 24 it is feminine (as usual) rather than masculine (as here). The Hebrew word the NIV translates "laws" is the word for God's judicial decisions. The consequence of Israel's unfaithfulness, then, was that God decreed events that were not in their favor, and he made judicial decisions that threatened their survival. This resulted in God's use of forces that devastate Israel such as war, famine, plague, foreign armies.

being unfaithful to me:[s] 28When I brought
them into the land[t] I had sworn to give
them and they saw any high hill or any
leafy tree, there they offered their sacrifices, made offerings that aroused my anger, presented their fragrant incense and
poured out their drink offerings.[u] 29Then I
said to them: What is this high place you
go to?' " (It is called Bamah[a] to this day.)

Rebellious Israel Renewed

30"Therefore say to the Israelites: 'This
is what the Sovereign LORD says: Will you
defile yourselves[v] the way your ancestors did and lust after their vile images?[w]
31When you offer your gifts—the sacrifice
of your children[x] in the fire—you continue to defile yourselves with all your idols
to this day. Am I to let you inquire of me,
you Israelites? As surely as I live, declares
the Sovereign LORD, I will not let you inquire of me.[y]
32" 'You say, "We want to be like the nations, like the peoples of the world, who
serve wood and stone." But what you have
in mind will never happen. 33As surely as
I live, declares the Sovereign LORD, I will
reign over you with a mighty hand and
an outstretched arm and with outpoured
wrath.[z] 34I will bring you from the nations[a]
and gather you from the countries where
you have been scattered—with a mighty
hand and an outstretched arm and with
outpoured wrath.[b] 35I will bring you into
the wilderness of the nations and there,
face to face, I will execute judgment[c] upon
you. 36As I judged your ancestors in the
wilderness of the land of Egypt, so I will
judge you, declares the Sovereign LORD.[d]
37I will take note of you as you pass under my rod,[e] and I will bring you into the
bond of the covenant.[f] 38I will purge[g] you
of those who revolt and rebel against me.
Although I will bring them out of the land
where they are living, yet they will not enter the land of Israel. Then you will know
that I am the LORD.[h]
39" 'As for you, people of Israel, this is
what the Sovereign LORD says: Go and
serve your idols,[i] every one of you! But
afterward you will surely listen to me and
no longer profane my holy name with
your gifts and idols.[j] 40For on my holy
mountain, the high mountain of Israel,
declares the Sovereign LORD, there in the
land all the people of Israel will serve me,
and there I will accept them. There I will
require your offerings[k] and your choice
gifts,[b] along with all your holy sacrifices.[l] 41I will accept you as fragrant incense
when I bring you out from the nations and
gather you from the countries where you
have been scattered, and I will be proved
holy[m] through you in the sight of the nations.[n] 42Then you will know that I am the
LORD,[o] when I bring you into the land of
Israel,[p] the land I had sworn with uplifted hand to give to your ancestors. 43There
you will remember your conduct and all
the actions by which you have defiled
yourselves, and you will loathe yourselves
for all the evil you have done.[q] 44You will
know that I am the LORD, when I deal with
you for my name's sake[r] and not according to your evil ways and your corrupt
practices, you people of Israel, declares
the Sovereign LORD.[s]' "

Prophecy Against the South

45The word of the LORD came to me:
46"Son of man, set your face toward
the south; preach against the south and
prophesy against[t] the forest of the southland.[u] 47Say to the southern forest: 'Hear
the word of the LORD. This is what the Sovereign LORD says: I am about to set fire to
you, and it will consume all your trees,
both green and dry. The blazing flame
will not be quenched, and every face from
south to north will be scorched by it.[v]
48Everyone will see that I the LORD have
kindled it; it will not be quenched.[w]' "
49Then I said, "Sovereign LORD, they are
saying of me, 'Isn't he just telling parables?[x]' "[c]

Babylon as God's Sword of Judgment

21 [d] The word of the LORD came to
me: 2"Son of man, set your face
against Jerusalem and preach against the
sanctuary. Prophesy against[y] the land of
Israel 3and say to her: 'This is what the
LORD says: I am against you.[z] I will draw
my sword from its sheath and cut off from
you both the righteous and the wicked.[a]
4Because I am going to cut off the righ-

[a] *29* Bamah means *high place.* [b] *40* Or *and the gifts of your firstfruits* [c] *49* In Hebrew texts 20:45-49 is numbered 21:1-5. [d] In Hebrew texts 21:1-32 is numbered 21:6-37.

20:27 [s] Eze 18:24
20:28 [t] Ps 78:55, 58 [u] Eze 6:13
20:30 [v] ver 43 [w] Jer 16:12
20:31 [x] Eze 16:20 [y] Ps 106:37-39; Jer 7:31
20:33 [z] Jer 21:5
20:34 [a] 2Co 6:17* [b] Isa 27:12-13; Jer 44:6; La 2:4
20:35 [c] Jer 2:35
20:36 [d] Nu 11:1-35; 1Co 10:5-10
20:37 [e] Lev 27:32; Jer 33:13 [f] Eze 16:62
20:38 [g] Eze 34:17-22; Am 9:9-10 [h] Ps 95:11; Jer 44:14; Eze 13:9; Mal 3:3; Heb 4:3
20:39 [i] Jer 44:25 [j] Isa 1:13; Eze 43:7; Am 4:4
20:40 [k] Isa 60:7 [l] Isa 56:7; Mal 3:4
20:41 [m] Eze 28:25; 36:23 [n] Eze 11:17
20:42 [o] Eze 38:23 [p] Eze 34:13; 36:24
20:43 [q] Eze 6:9; 16:61; Hos 5:15
20:44 [r] Eze 36:22 [s] Eze 24:24
20:46 [t] Eze 21:2; Am 7:16 [u] Isa 30:6; Jer 13:19
20:47 [v] Isa 9:18-19; 13:8; Jer 21:14
20:48 [w] Jer 7:20
20:49 [x] Mt 13:13; Jn 16:25
21:2 [y] Eze 20:46
21:3 [z] Jer 21:13 [a] ver 9-11; Job 9:22

20:47 *set fire to you.* This verse describes the kind of phenomenon that the Babylonians of Ezekiel's time attributed to Erra, the god of fire, plague and destruction, and to Erra's lieutenant, Ishum.

21:3 *I will draw my sword.* As early as the end of the third millennium BC, the invasion of armies is interpreted as the intentional actions of a patron deity who has been angered by the behavior of the people (e.g., the Gutian invasion that brought an end to the Empire of Agade in the "Curse of Agade"). In Mesopotamia this traditional theology is represented also in Cyrus's rhetoric concerning the overthrow of the Babylonians because of Marduk's displeasure with Nabonidus.

21:4 *cut off the righteous and the wicked.* The announce-

Burning of conquered cities (Eze 20:47) was common in the ancient world and archaeologists can often easily detect the burn layer like this one at Hazor.
Kim Walton

teous and the wicked, my sword will be
unsheathed against everyone from south
to north.[b] 5Then all people will know that
I the LORD have drawn my sword from its
sheath; it will not return[c] again.'[d]
6"Therefore groan, son of man! Groan
before them with broken heart and bitter
grief.[e] 7And when they ask you, 'Why are
you groaning?' you shall say, 'Because of
the news that is coming. Every heart will
melt with fear and every hand go limp;[f]
every spirit will become faint and every
leg will be wet with urine.' It is coming! It
will surely take place, declares the Sovereign LORD."
8The word of the LORD came to me:

21:4 [b]Eze 20:47
21:5 [c]ver 30
[d]Na 1:9
21:6 [e]Isa 22:4
21:7 [f]Eze 22:14; 7:17
21:10 [g]Ps 110:5-6; Isa 34:5-6
21:11 [h]Jer 46:4

9"Son of man, prophesy and say, 'This is
what the Lord says:

"'A sword, a sword,
sharpened and polished —
10sharpened for the slaughter,[g]
polished to flash like lightning!

"'Shall we rejoice in the scepter of my
royal son? The sword despises every such
stick.

11"'The sword is appointed to be
polished,[h]
to be grasped with the hand;
it is sharpened and polished,
made ready for the hand of the slayer.

ment that both righteous and wicked will be cut off reflects the intensity of the divine judgment. The statement rules out any hope for Judah and Jerusalem. Since historical reality does not confirm total destruction of the population of Judah by Nebuchadnezzar, this hyperbole may be seen as a deliberate rhetorical device intended to shock his audience and to awaken them out of their spiritual lethargy. The same inclusion of the righteous with the wicked occurs in the Mesopotamian epic "Erra and Ishum," describing the result of indiscriminate destruction that befell the inhabitants of Babylon. Erra himself admits that he made no distinction between the righteous and the wicked. Yet in Babylon too a remnant was left, allowing the city to continue to live.

21:9 *sword.* While this term occurs no fewer than 89 times in Ezekiel as one of the principal key words of the book, the greater part of ch. 21 is dedicated to this term, where it occurs 15 times. Therefore ch. 21 is usually called the song of the sword. The Mesopotamian epic "Erra and Ishum" describes a similar event to the one described in Ezekiel. It deals with the destruction of the city of Babylon on account of the cultic and social crimes of its inhabitants. The agent of destruction is Erra's lieutenant, Ishum, who incarnates the ravaging effect of fire. This composition first addresses him as "torch" and then as "sword." In Ezekiel's song of the sword, where he identifies fire with the sword, the prophet appears to have adopted a Babylonian literary motif for his own rhetorical purposes.

12 Cry out and wail, son of man,
for it is against my people;
it is against all the princes of Israel.
They are thrown to the sword
along with my people.
Therefore beat your breast.[i]

13 " 'Testing will surely come. And what
if even the scepter, which the sword despises, does not continue? declares the
Sovereign LORD.'

14 "So then, son of man, prophesy
and strike your hands[j] together.
Let the sword strike twice,
even three times.
It is a sword for slaughter —
a sword for great slaughter,
closing in on them from every side.[k]
15 So that hearts may melt with fear[l]
and the fallen be many,
I have stationed the sword for
slaughter[a]
at all their gates.
Look! It is forged to strike like
lightning,
it is grasped for slaughter.[m]
16 Slash to the right, you sword,
then to the left,
wherever your blade is turned.
17 I too will strike my hands[n] together,
and my wrath[o] will subside.
I the LORD have spoken."

18 The word of the LORD came to me:
19 "Son of man, mark out two roads for the
sword of the king of Babylon to take, both
starting from the same country. Make a
signpost where the road branches off to the
city. 20 Mark out one road for the sword to
come against Rabbah of the Ammonites[p]
and another against Judah and fortified
Jerusalem. 21 For the king of Babylon will
stop at the fork in the road, at the junction
of the two roads, to seek an omen: He will
cast lots[q] with arrows, he will consult his
idols, he will examine the liver.[r] 22 Into his
right hand will come the lot for Jerusalem,
where he is to set up battering rams, to
give the command to slaughter, to sound
the battle cry, to set battering rams against
the gates, to build a ramp and to erect siege
works.[s] 23 It will seem like a false omen to
those who have sworn allegiance to him,
but he will remind[t] them of their guilt and
take them captive.

24 "Therefore this is what the Sovereign LORD says: 'Because you people have
brought to mind your guilt by your open
rebellion, revealing your sins in all that
you do — because you have done this, you
will be taken captive.

25 " 'You profane and wicked prince of Israel, whose day has come, whose time of
punishment has reached its climax,[u] 26 this
is what the Sovereign LORD says: Take off
the turban, remove the crown.[v] It will not
be as it was: The lowly will be exalted and
the exalted will be brought low.[w] 27 A ruin!
A ruin! I will make it a ruin! The crown
will not be restored until he to whom it
rightfully belongs shall come; to him I will
give it.'[x]

28 "And you, son of man, prophesy and
say, 'This is what the Sovereign LORD says
about the Ammonites[y] and their insults:

21:12 [i] Jer 31:19 **21:14** [j] Nu 24:10 [k] Eze 6:11; 30:24 **21:15** [l] 2Sa 17:10 [m] Ps 22:14 **21:17** [n] ver 14; Eze 22:13 [o] Eze 5:13 **21:20** [p] Dt 3:11; Jer 49:2; Am 1:14 **21:21** [q] Pr 16:33 [r] Nu 22:7; 23:23 **21:22** [s] Eze 4:2; 26:9 **21:23** [t] Nu 5:15 **21:25** [u] Eze 35:5 **21:26** [v] Jer 13:18 [w] Ps 75:7; Eze 17:24 **21:27** [x] Ps 2:6; Jer 23:5-6; Eze 37:24; Hag 2:21-22 **21:28** [y] Zep 2:8

[a] *15* Septuagint; the meaning of the Hebrew for this word is uncertain.

21:21 According to v. 20, Nebuchadnezzar hesitated at Damascus, wondering whether to attack Rabbah of the Ammonites or Jerusalem in Judah. As was customary in ancient Near Eastern war campaigns, he resolved the issue by using divinatory techniques to determine which route to take. In v. 21, he applies three methods of divination: (1) He shakes the arrows, a practice known as belomancy or rhabdomancy, which consists of tossing inscribed arrows and drawing one, as one would draw a lot, on the assumption that the selected arrow shows the advice of the gods (see note on 2Ki 13:15 – 19). (2) He consults his idols, here called the *teraphim.* While the term *teraphim* occurs only 15 times in the OT, the scholarly bibliography on these objects is voluminous without completely dissipating the mystery that surrounds their exact use. They are associated with the protecting and counseling spirits of the ancestors to whom one turns for advice when faced with a difficult decision (see the article "Household Gods," p. 72). (3) He examines the liver of a sacrificial animal, a common form of Mesopotamian divination called hepatoscopy (see the article "Extispicy," p. 650). Clay models of livers have been found at a great many archaeological sites in the Near East, confirming their widespread use in antiquity. One found in Babylon is mapped into more than 50 sections and punctuated by special interpretative marks.

21:26 *turban ... crown.* Based on descriptions in Mesopotamian texts and artistic renderings on Assyrian palace walls, it seems that the "crown" of a king was in fact more like a turban. A cloth was wound around the head several times and it in turn was encrusted with jewels and golden ornaments and elaborately embroidered with symbols of the king's majesty. Ezekiel, in calling for Zedekiah to remove his headgear, is commanding the king to relinquish his primary symbol of power because he no longer deserves to wear it. *The lowly will be exalted and the exalted will be brought low.* This statement is not a call simply for a change in the occupant of the throne of Jerusalem, where Zedekiah replaces Jehoiachin. The prophet uses a well-known topos of ancient Near Eastern literature, announcing a wholesale revolution and a radical social upheaval that serves as a corrective affecting all strata of Judahite society.

21:28 *polished to consume.* The Hebrew is an idiomatic expression "to open the mouth in murder." This unusual expression reflects the manner in which the ancients spoke about the sword as a devouring animal. It is part of an important literary and iconographic motif present in the ancient Near East and reflected in the Bible. The sword is seen as having a mouth, as in another common Biblical expression: "to put to the mouth of the sword." The sword is often presented under the metaphor of a devouring

" 'A sword,[z] a sword,
drawn for the slaughter,
polished to consume
and to flash like lightning!
29 Despite false visions concerning you
and lying divinations about you,
it will be laid on the necks
of the wicked who are to be slain,
whose day has come,
whose time of punishment has
reached its climax.[a]
30 " 'Let the sword return to its sheath.[b]
In the place where you were created,
in the land of your ancestry,[c]
I will judge you.
31 I will pour out my wrath on you
and breathe out my fiery anger[d]
against you;
I will deliver you into the hands of
brutal men,
men skilled in destruction.[e]
32 You will be fuel for the fire,[f]
your blood will be shed in your land,
you will be remembered[g] no more;
for I the LORD have spoken.' "

Judgment on Jerusalem's Sins

22 The word of the LORD came to me:
2 "Son of man, will you judge her? Will
you judge this city of bloodshed?[h] Then confront her with all her detestable practices[i]
3 and say: 'This is what the Sovereign LORD
says: You city that brings on herself doom
by shedding blood[j] in her midst and defiles
herself by making idols, 4 you have become
guilty because of the blood you have shed[k]
and have become defiled by the idols you
have made. You have brought your days
to a close, and the end of your years has
come.[l] Therefore I will make you an object
of scorn to the nations and a laughingstock
to all the countries.[m] 5 Those who are near
and those who are far away will mock you,
you infamous city, full of turmoil.
6 " 'See how each of the princes of Israel who are in you uses his power to shed
blood.[n] 7 In you they have treated father and
mother with contempt;[o] in you they have
oppressed the foreigner and mistreated the
fatherless and the widow.[p] 8 You have despised my holy things and desecrated my
Sabbaths.[q] 9 In you are slanderers[r] who are
bent on shedding blood; in you are those
who eat at the mountain shrines[s] and commit lewd acts.[t] 10 In you are those who dishonor their father's bed; in you are those
who violate women during their period,
when they are ceremonially unclean.[u] 11 In
you one man commits a detestable offense
with his neighbor's wife, another shamefully defiles his daughter-in-law,[v] and another
violates his sister,[w] his own father's daughter. 12 In you are people who accept bribes[x]
to shed blood; you take interest and make a
profit from the poor. You extort unjust gain
from your neighbors.[y] And you have forgotten me, declares the Sovereign LORD.
13 " 'I will surely strike my hands[z] together at the unjust gain[a] you have made and
at the blood[b] you have shed in your midst.
14 Will your courage endure or your hands
be strong in the day I deal with you? I the
LORD have spoken,[c] and I will do it.[d] 15 I will
disperse you among the nations and scatter[e] you through the countries; and I will
put an end to your uncleanness.[f] 16 When
you have been defiled[a] in the eyes of the
nations, you will know that I am the LORD.' "
17 Then the word of the LORD came to
me: 18 "Son of man, the people of Israel
have become dross[g] to me; all of them are
the copper, tin, iron and lead left inside
a furnace. They are but the dross of silver.[h] 19 Therefore this is what the Sovereign
LORD says: 'Because you have all become
dross, I will gather you into Jerusalem.
20 As silver, copper, iron, lead and tin are
gathered into a furnace to be melted with
a fiery blast, so will I gather you in my anger and my wrath and put you inside the
city and melt you.[i] 21 I will gather you and I
will blow on you with my fiery wrath, and
you will be melted inside her. 22 As silver is
melted[j] in a furnace, so you will be melted
inside her, and you will know that I the
LORD have poured out my wrath on you.' "[k]

21:28 [z] Jer 12:12 **21:29** [a] ver 25; Eze 22:28; 35:5 **21:30** [b] Jer 47:6 [c] Eze 16:3 **21:31** [d] Eze 22:20-21 [e] Jer 51:20-23 **21:32** [f] Mal 4:1 [g] Eze 25:10 **22:2** [h] Eze 24:6, 9; Na 3:1 [i] Eze 16:2 **22:3** [j] ver 6, 13, 27; Eze 23:37, 45 **22:4** [k] 2Ki 21:16 [l] Eze 21:25 [m] Eze 5:14 **22:6** [n] Isa 1:23 **22:7** [o] Dt 5:16; 27:16 [p] Ex 22:21-22 **22:8** [q] Eze 23:38-39 **22:9** [r] Lev 19:16 [s] Eze 18:11 [t] Hos 4:10, 14 **22:10** [u] Lev 18:8, 19 **22:11** [v] Lev 18:15 [w] Lev 18:9; 2Sa 13:14 **22:12** [x] Dt 27:25; Mic 7:3 [y] Lev 19:13 **22:13** [z] Eze 21:17 [a] Isa 33:15 [b] ver 3 **22:14** [c] Eze 24:14 [d] Eze 17:24; 21:7 **22:15** [e] Dt 4:27; Zec 7:14 [f] Eze 23:27 **22:18** [g] Ps 119:119; Isa 1:22 [h] Jer 6:28-30 **22:20** [i] Mal 3:2 **22:22** [j] Isa 1:25 [k] Eze 20:8, 33

[a] 16 Or *When I have allotted you your inheritance*

---

monster that "eats" flesh and "drinks" blood (see Dt 32:42; 2Sa 2:26; Jer 46:10). A similar conception of the sword is found in Akkadian texts such as the vassal treaties of Esarhaddon (680–669 BC) and numerous Egyptian texts. This idiomatic expression finds its explanation in the evidence of archaeology. In excavations throughout the Middle East swords and battle axes have been found in which the blade is represented as the tongue sticking out of the open, ravenous mouth of a lion or a dragon, which constitutes the base of the sword hilt or the handle of the ax.

22:7 *treated father and mother with contempt ... oppressed the foreigner and mistreated the fatherless and the widow.* The particular responsibility of the king to prevent the abuse of parents and the helpless is a requirement of just rule in the ancient Near East. See notes on Lev 19:15; Dt 10:18; 15:7; 24:17; Ps 72:4,12–14.

22:18 *dross.* In the smelting process, silver is separated from lead and other alloyed metals (copper, tin and iron) through a two-stage process. During the second stage, after all vestiges of sulfur have been removed, the silver is liquefied and the lead dross floats on the surface, allowing it to be skimmed off. Ezekiel's metaphor suggests a further purification of Judah is necessary (i.e., the exilic experience) so that the dross of its lawless, covenant-breaking nature can be removed by God's hot wrath (see Mal 3:1–4). See note on Jer 6:28.

23 Again the word of the LORD came to me: 24 "Son of man, say to the land, 'You are a land that has not been cleansed or rained on in the day of wrath.'[l] 25 There is a conspiracy[m] of her princes[a] within her like a roaring lion tearing its prey; they devour people,[n] take treasures and precious things and make many widows[o] within her. 26 Her priests do violence to my law[p] and profane my holy things; they do not distinguish between the holy and the common;[q] they teach that there is no difference between the unclean and the clean;[r] and they shut their eyes to the keeping of my Sabbaths, so that I am profaned among them.[s] 27 Her officials within her are like wolves tearing their prey; they shed blood and kill people to make unjust gain.[t] 28 Her prophets whitewash[u] these deeds for them by false visions and lying divinations. They say, 'This is what the Sovereign LORD says'—when the LORD has not spoken.[v] 29 The people of the land practice extortion and commit robbery; they oppress the poor and needy and mistreat the foreigner,[w] denying them justice.[x]

30 "I looked for someone among them who would build up the wall[y] and stand before me in the gap on behalf of the land so I would not have to destroy it, but I found no one.[z] 31 So I will pour out my wrath on them and consume them with my fiery anger, bringing down[a] on their own heads all they have done, declares the Sovereign LORD.[b]"

Two Adulterous Sisters

23 The word of the LORD came to me: 2 "Son of man, there were two women, daughters of the same mother.[c] 3 They became prostitutes in Egypt,[d] engaging in prostitution[e] from their youth. In that land their breasts were fondled and their virgin bosoms caressed. 4 The older was named Oholah, and her sister was Oholibah. They were mine and gave birth to sons and daughters. Oholah is Samaria, and Oholibah is Jerusalem.

5 "Oholah engaged in prostitution while she was still mine; and she lusted after her lovers, the Assyrians[f]—warriors[g] 6 clothed in blue, governors and commanders, all of them handsome young men, and mounted horsemen. 7 She gave herself as a prostitute to all the elite of the Assyrians and defiled herself with all the idols of everyone she lusted after.[h] 8 She did not give up the prostitution she began in Egypt,[i] when during her youth men slept with her, caressed her virgin bosom and poured out their lust on her.[j]

9 "Therefore I delivered her into the hands[k] of her lovers, the Assyrians, for whom she lusted.[l] 10 They stripped[m] her naked, took away her sons and daughters and killed her with the sword. She became a byword among women,[n] and punishment was inflicted on her.[o]

11 "Her sister Oholibah saw this, yet in her lust and prostitution she was more depraved than her sister.[p] 12 She too lusted after the Assyrians—governors and commanders, warriors in full dress, mounted horsemen, all handsome young men.[q] 13 I saw that she too defiled herself; both of them went the same way.

14 "But she carried her prostitution still further. She saw men portrayed on a wall,[r]

22:24 [l] Eze 24:13
22:25 [m] Jer 11:9 [n] Hos 6:9 [o] Jer 15:8
22:26 [p] Mal 2:7-8 [q] Eze 44:23 [r] Lev 10:10 [s] 1Sa 2:12-17; Jer 2:8,26; Hag 2:11-14
22:27 [t] Isa 1:23
22:28 [u] Eze 13:10 [v] Eze 13:2,6-7
22:29 [w] Ex 22:21; 23:9 [x] Isa 5:7
22:30 [y] Eze 13:5 [z] Ps 106:23; Jer 5:1
22:31 [a] Eze 16:43 [b] Eze 7:8-9; 9:10; Ro 2:8
23:2 [c] Jer 3:7; Eze 16:45
23:3 [d] Jos 24:14 [e] Lev 17:7
23:5 [f] 2Ki 16:7; Hos 5:13 [g] Hos 8:9
23:7 [h] Hos 5:3; 6:10
23:8 [i] Ex 32:4 [j] Eze 16:15
23:9 [k] 2Ki 18:11 [l] Hos 11:5
23:10 [m] Hos 2:10 [n] Eze 16:41 [o] Eze 16:36
23:11 [p] Jer 3:8-11; Eze 16:51
23:12 [q] 2Ki 16:7-15; 2Ch 28:16
23:14 [r] Eze 8:10

[a] *25* Septuagint; Hebrew *prophets*

22:24 *not ... rained on in the day of wrath.* In the Babylonian Mesopotamian epic "Erra and Ishum" one finds a unique reference in Akkadian literature of the city of Sippar being spared the great flood. Some have argued that this singular reference to the day of wrath in connection with the great flood in Ezekiel may stem from the awareness of Ezekiel and the exiles in Babylon of the Mesopotamian epic "Erra and Ishum," a work that perhaps dates to the eighth century BC (at the earliest). Numerous points of contact exist between the Mesopotamian epic "Erra and Ishum" and the book of Ezekiel by way of allusions and motifs. There is an additional similarity concerning the way in which the literary motif of the preservation from the great flood is used in the Mesopotamian epic "Erra and Ishum" and in Ezekiel. In the former, the god Marduk tells Erra that the city of Sippar has been spared the deluge. The city survived that great calamity, but it did not escape a subsequent destruction provoked by Erra and Ishum, whose name means "Fire." Here in Eze 22:24, the land of Israel had been spared the rains of the great flood in the day of wrath. The evildoers, however, will not be spared the subsequent destruction by fire: "So I [the LORD] will pour my wrath on them and consume them with my fiery anger" (v. 31).

23:5 *warriors.* Or "guardsmen"; the Hebrew term corresponds to the Akkadian word for "bodyguard." Shortly after the fall of the northern kingdom, some Israelite warriors were integrated into the Assyrian military forces. In an Assyrian document from that time, this same term is applied to a man with an Israelite name.

23:6 *clothed in blue.* Assyrian warriors, colorfully attired, are pictured on Assyrian reliefs. *mounted horsemen.* Since the time of Ashurnasirpal II (883–859 BC), organized cavalry became important as the chief assault force of the Assyrian army.

23:7 *prostitute to all the elite of the Assyrians.* Under the metaphor of Oholah's prostitution, the prophet castigates Israel's political alliances. The northern kingdom's "liaison" with Assyria began with the tribute Jehu paid to Shalmaneser III in 841 BC (see the article "Omri and Jehu in History," p. 632). Jehu's grandson Joash paid tribute to Adadnirari III (796 BC), who perhaps delivered him from Aramean oppression (2Ki 13:5). After Tiglath-Pileser III conquered Hamath (738 BC), the Assyrian annals mention Menahem of Samaria among the western kinglets who paid him tribute. This prolonged relationship with the Assyrians was of no avail, however, since they destroyed Samaria in 722 BC and deported most of its population.

23:14 *men portrayed on a wall.* One of the standard means of decorating the walls of Mesopotamian palace

figures of Chaldeans[a] portrayed in red,[s]
15with belts around their waists and flowing turbans on their heads; all of them
looked like Babylonian chariot officers,
natives of Chaldea.[b] 16As soon as she
saw them, she lusted after them and sent
messengers to them in Chaldea. 17Then
the Babylonians came to her, to the bed
of love, and in their lust they defiled her.
After she had been defiled by them, she
turned away from them in disgust. 18When
she carried on her prostitution openly and
exposed her naked body, I turned away[t]
from her in disgust, just as I had turned
away from her sister.[u] 19Yet she became
more and more promiscuous as she recalled the days of her youth, when she
was a prostitute in Egypt. 20There she lusted after her lovers, whose genitals were
like those of donkeys and whose emission
was like that of horses. 21So you longed for
the lewdness of your youth, when in Egypt
your bosom was caressed and your young
breasts fondled.[c][v]

22"Therefore, Oholibah, this is what the
Sovereign LORD says: I will stir up your
lovers against you, those you turned away
from in disgust, and I will bring them
against you from every side[w]— 23the Babylonians[x] and all the Chaldeans, the men
of Pekod[y] and Shoa and Koa, and all the
Assyrians with them, handsome young
men, all of them governors and commanders, chariot officers and men of high rank,
all mounted on horses.[z] 24They will come
against you with weapons,[d] chariots and
wagons[a] and with a throng of people; they
will take up positions against you on every side with large and small shields and
with helmets. I will turn you over to them
for punishment,[b] and they will punish you
according to their standards. 25I will direct
my jealous anger against you, and they
will deal with you in fury. They will cut
off your noses and your ears, and those
of you who are left will fall by the sword.
They will take away your sons and daughters,[c] and those of you who are left will be
consumed by fire.[d] 26They will also strip[e]
you of your clothes and take your fine jewelry.[f] 27So I will put a stop[g] to the lewdness
and prostitution you began in Egypt. You
will not look on these things with longing
or remember Egypt anymore.

28"For this is what the Sovereign LORD
says: I am about to deliver you into the
hands[h] of those you hate, to those you
turned away from in disgust. 29They will
deal with you in hatred and take away everything you have worked for. They will
leave you stark naked, and the shame of
your prostitution will be exposed. Your
lewdness and promiscuity[i] 30have brought
this on you, because you lusted after the
nations and defiled yourself with their
idols.[j] 31You have gone the way of your sister; so I will put her cup[k] into your hand.[l]

32"This is what the Sovereign LORD says:

"You will drink your sister's cup,
a cup large and deep;
it will bring scorn and derision,
for it holds so much.[m]
33You will be filled with drunkenness
and sorrow,
the cup of ruin and desolation,
the cup of your sister Samaria.[n]
34You will drink it[o] and drain it dry
and chew on its pieces—
and you will tear your breasts.

23:14 [s]Jer 22:14
23:18 [t]Ps 78:59; 106:40; Jer 6:8 [u]Jer 12:8; Am 5:21
23:21 [v]Eze 16:26
23:22 [w]Eze 16:37
23:23 [x]2Ki 20:14-18 [y]Jer 50:21 [z]2Ki 24:2
23:24 [a]Jer 47:3; Eze 26:7, 10; Na 2:4 [b]Jer 39:5-6
23:25 [c]ver 47 [d]Eze 20:47-48
23:26 [e]Jer 13:22 [f]Isa 3:18-23; Eze 16:39
23:27 [g]Eze 16:41
23:28 [h]Jer 34:20
23:29 [i]Dt 28:48
23:30 [j]Eze 6:9
23:31 [k]Jer 25:15 [l]2Ki 21:13
23:32 [m]Ps 60:3; Isa 51:17; Jer 25:15
23:33 [n]Jer 25:15-16
23:34 [o]Ps 75:8; Isa 51:17

[a] *14* Or *Babylonians* [b] *15* Or *Babylonia*; also in verse 16 [c] *21* Syriac (see also verse 3); Hebrew *caressed because of your young breasts* [d] *24* The meaning of the Hebrew for this word is uncertain.

gates and walls was with the figures of soldiers, kings and symbolic beasts (such as the dragons on the Ishtar Gate in Babylon). The Assyrian palace in Nineveh has preserved scenes of siege warfare, hunting, and royal and divine figures. Much of what we know about the appearance, clothing and military techniques and weapons come from these reliefs. Although much of the paint has now worn away, it is evident that these figures were once brightly colored, in some cases larger than life size, and undoubtedly intimidating to subject peoples. Such power by association might have also been enticing to the leaders of Judah, as Ezekiel suggests.

23:15 *chariot officers.* Assyrian and Babylonian chariots generally carried three men: (1) a driver; (2) the commander, who wielded bow and spear; and (3) a shield-bearer, who also handed weapons to the commander as needed. The Akkadian term for chariot officers is *shalshu*; this may be a cognate for Hebrew *shalishim*, which is used here (the Hebrew root makes it likely that there is some connection to "three"). An alternative suggestion is that the term refers to an officer of the third rank.

23:23 This verse enumerates a series of invaders, instruments of God's judgment on Israel. *Pekod.* See note on Jer 50:21. They are mentioned several times in the inscriptions of Tiglath-Pileser III (745–727 BC) and Sargon II 721–705 BC). The name is found listed in "The Court of Nebuchadnezzar" document, which mentions the names of 11 senior officials who acted as district officials of Babylonia, simply designated by their tribal association. *Shoa and Koa.* Identified with Aramean tribes called Sutû and Qutu in Akkadian literature. In the ninth-century BC Babylonian Mesopotamian epic "Erra and Ishum," the Sutû and Qutu are the principal invaders coming down from the mountains and attacking various cities in the Mesopotamian valley. The presence of these Aramean tribes in the Northwest Semitic region is attested since the time of Mari (eighteenth century BC).

23:25 *cut off your noses and your ears.* In the ancient Near East this was done to a variety of subordinates who broke faith, such as Egyptian officials who were false to their commission or slaves who received stolen goods from their master's wife (while the thieving wife's nose or ears may also have been cut off). An adulteress's nose could be cut off at her husband's wish.

I have spoken, declares the Sovereign LORD.

35“Therefore this is what the
Sovereign LORD says: Since you
have forgotten[p] me and turned
your back on me,[q] you must bear
the consequences of your lewdness
and prostitution.”

36The LORD said to me: “Son of
man, will you judge Oholah and
Oholibah? Then confront[r] them
with their detestable practices,[s]
37for they have committed adultery and blood is on their hands.
They committed adultery with
their idols; they even sacrificed
their children, whom they bore to
me, as food for them.[t] 38They have
also done this to me: At that same
time they defiled my sanctuary and
desecrated my Sabbaths. 39On the
very day they sacrificed their children to their idols, they entered my
sanctuary and desecrated[u] it. That
is what they did in my house.[v]

40“They even sent messengers
for men who came from far away,[w]
and when they arrived you bathed
yourself for them, applied eye
makeup[x] and put on your jewelry.[y] 41You sat on an elegant couch,[z]
with a table[a] spread before it on
which you had placed the incense
and olive oil that belonged to me.

42“The noise of a carefree crowd
was around her; drunkards were
brought from the desert along
with men from the rabble, and
they put bracelets[b] on the wrists
of the woman and her sister and
beautiful crowns on their heads.[c] 43Then I
said about the one worn out by adultery,
‘Now let them use her as a prostitute,[d] for
that is all she is.’ 44And they slept with her.
As men sleep with a prostitute, so they
slept with those lewd women, Oholah and
Oholibah. 45But righteous judges will sentence them to the punishment of women
who commit adultery and shed blood, because they are adulterous and blood is on
their hands.[e]

Tomb painting of Nefertari showing eye makeup (Eze 23:40), 1298 to 1235 BC.

Wikimedia Commons

46“This is what the Sovereign LORD says:
Bring a mob[f] against them and give them
over to terror and plunder. 47The mob
will stone them and cut them down with
their swords; they will kill their sons and
daughters and burn[g] down their houses.[h]

48“So I will put an end to lewdness in

23:35 [p]Isa 17:10; Jer 3:21 [q]1Ki 14:9 **23:36** [r]Eze 16:2 [s]Isa 58:1; Eze 22:2; Mic 3:8 **23:37** [t]Eze 16:36 **23:39** [u]2Ki 21:4 [v]Jer 7:10 **23:40** [w]Isa 57:9 [x]2Ki 9:30 [y]Jer 4:30; Eze 16:13-19 **23:41** [z]Est 1:6; Pr 7:17; Am 6:4 [a]Isa 65:11; Eze 44:16 **23:42** [b]Ge 24:30 [c]Eze 16:11-12 **23:43** [d]ver 3 **23:45** [e]Lev 20:10; Eze 16:38; Hos 6:5 **23:46** [f]Eze 16:40 **23:47** [g]2Ch 36:19 [h]2Ch 36:17; Eze 16:40-41

23:40 *eye makeup.* Women throughout the ancient Near East regularly enlarged and darkened their eyes with a mixture of olive oil and malachite (green) or galena (black) (see note on 2Ki 9:30). Babylonian sources mention eye paint that included stibnite (antimony trisulfide). Decorated palettes were used to grind the ore and mix it for application. These palettes have been found at many Iron II sites in Israel, including Megiddo.

23:41 *elegant couch.* The adulteress Jerusalem is portrayed in much the same light as the prostitute in Pr 7:10 – 23. Both seduce their lovers with an inviting couch, incense and persuasive words. Prior to the Hellenistic period, all references to the couch are associated with a sleeping chamber (see 2Sa 4:7; Ps 6:6), not the banqueting room. *incense and olive oil.* As part of the anticipated sexual activity, the adulteress Jerusalem has perfumed her bed chamber with incense (SS 1:3; 4:10; see note on SS 3:6) and has sweet smelling oils at hand for anointing their hair and bodies (Est 2:12). Similar images are found in the Cairo Love Songs discovered by archaeologists in the Karnak temple complex in Luxor (Biblical Thebes).

you tell us what these things have to do
with us?[a] Why are you acting like this?"
20 So I said to them, "The word of the
LORD came to me: 21 Say to the people of
Israel, 'This is what the Sovereign LORD
says: I am about to desecrate my sanctuary — the stronghold in which you take
pride, the delight of your eyes,[b] the object
of your affection. The sons and daughters[c]
you left behind will fall by the sword.[d]
22 And you will do as I have done. You will
not cover your mustache and beard or eat
the customary food of mourners.[e] 23 You
will keep your turbans on your heads and
your sandals on your feet. You will not
mourn[f] or weep but will waste away because of[a] your sins and groan among yourselves.[g] 24 Ezekiel will be a sign[h] to you;
you will do just as he has done. When this
happens, you will know that I am the Sovereign LORD.'
25 "And you, son of man, on the day
I take away their stronghold, their joy
and glory, the delight of their eyes, their
heart's desire, and their sons and daughters[i] as well — 26 on that day a fugitive will
come to tell you[j] the news. 27 At that time
your mouth will be opened; you will speak
with him and will no longer be silent. So
you will be a sign to them, and they will
know that I am the LORD.[k]"

A Prophecy Against Ammon

25 The word of the LORD came to me:
2 "Son of man, set your face against
the Ammonites[l] and prophesy against
them.[m] 3 Say to them, 'Hear the word of the
Sovereign LORD. This is what the Sovereign
LORD says: Because you said "Aha![n]" over
my sanctuary when it was desecrated and
over the land of Israel when it was laid
waste and over the people of Judah when
they went into exile,[o] 4 therefore I am going
to give you to the people of the East[p] as a
possession. They will set up their camps
and pitch their tents among you; they will
eat your fruit and drink your milk.[q] 5 I will
turn Rabbah[r] into a pasture for camels and
Ammon into a resting place for sheep.[s]
Then you will know that I am the LORD.
6 For this is what the Sovereign LORD says:
Because you have clapped your hands and
stamped your feet, rejoicing with all the
malice of your heart against the land of Israel,[t] 7 therefore I will stretch out my hand[u]
against you and give you as plunder to the
nations. I will wipe you out from among
the nations and exterminate you from the
countries. I will destroy[v] you, and you will
know that I am the LORD.[w]' "

A Prophecy Against Moab

8 "This is what the Sovereign LORD says:
'Because Moab[x] and Seir said, "Look,
Judah has become like all the other nations," 9 therefore I will expose the flank
of Moab, beginning at its frontier towns —
Beth Jeshimoth[y], Baal Meon[z] and Kiriathaim[a] — the glory of that land. 10 I will give
Moab along with the Ammonites to the
people of the East as a possession, so that
the Ammonites will not be remembered[b]
among the nations; 11 and I will inflict punishment on Moab. Then they will know
that I am the LORD.' "

A Prophecy Against Edom

12 "This is what the Sovereign LORD
says: 'Because Edom[c] took revenge on Judah and became very guilty by doing so,

24:19 [a] Eze 12:9; 37:18 **24:21** [b] Ps 27:4 [c] Eze 23:25 [d] Jer 7:14, 15; Eze 23:47 **24:22** [e] Jer 16:7 **24:23** [f] Job 27:15 [g] Ps 78:64 **24:24** [h] Isa 20:3; Eze 4:3; 12:11 **24:25** [i] Jer 11:22 **24:26** [j] 1Sa 4:12; Job 1:15-19 **24:27** [k] Eze 3:26; 33:22 **25:2** [l] Eze 21:28; Zep 2:8-9 [m] Jer 49:1-6 **25:3** [n] Eze 26:2; 36:2 [o] Pr 17:5 **25:4** [p] Jdg 6:3 [q] Dt 28:33, 51; Jdg 6:33 **25:5** [r] Dt 3:11; Eze 21:20 [s] Isa 17:2 **25:6** [t] Ob 1:12; Zep 2:8 **25:7** [u] Zep 1:4 [v] Eze 21:31 [w] Am 1:14-15 **25:8** [x] Jer 48:1; Am 2:1 **25:9** [y] Nu 33:49 [z] Nu 32:3; Jos 13:17 [a] Nu 32:37; Jos 13:19 **25:10** [b] Eze 21:32 **25:12** [c] 2Ch 28:17

[a] 23 Or *away in*

24:22 *You will not cover your mustache and beard or eat the customary food of mourners.* Here (and in v. 17) Ezekiel exhorts the exiled Judahites not to mourn for the fall of Jerusalem and its temple. The breakdown of mourning rites in the face of universal grief is portrayed in a passage from the ancient Egyptian Prophecies of Neferti, which describes the collapse of the social order of the Old Kingdom and extreme introversion of the grief-stricken people. In that context mourning is absent in the face of denial and a concern for oneself. If this offers any direction, Ezekiel is not commanding the people not to mourn (his own lack of mourning was the response to God's instructions) but is saying that, in fact, the people will not mourn. The Judahite survivors in exile will be able only to groan in self-absorbed, inward-turned grief.
25:4 *people of the East.* In this prophecy against Ammon, Judah's neighbor across the Jordan River, southeast of Jerusalem, the expression "people of the East" refers to tent-dwelling Arabic nomads of the Syro-Arabian desert. Their incursions were a constant threat to the settled populations on which they bordered. In Jer 49:28 (see note there), they are identified with the Arab tribe of the Kedarites, who were in turn destroyed by Nebuchadnezzar in the sixth century BC. *milk.* Represents a staple food of nomadic herdsmen. In the Egyptian *Story of Sinuhe*, while exiled among nomadic Bedouin tribes, the Egyptian official was supplied with "milk in every (kind of) cooking." The standard benediction is that one should enjoy the fruit of one's own labors/vineyards (Ps 128:2; Isa 3:10). In this case, however, what has been worked for will become the property of invaders (cf. Eze 23:29).
25:5 *Rabbah.* See note on Jer 49:2.
25:8 *Moab.* Among the states represented at Zedekiah's strategy meeting in 597 BC (Jer 27:3). Although it apparently survived and served as a place of refuge for Judahites fleeing Nebuchadnezzar's destruction of Jerusalem in 587, its role as potential troublemaker in the region was not forgotten. Josephus records a later campaign by the Babylonian king in 582 – 581 BC to reduce both Ammon and Moab. There is not sufficient evidence to demonstrate how effective this campaign actually was, but, like Ammon, the nation of Moab probably survived to become a part of the Persian Empire at the end of the sixth century BC.
25:12 *Edom.* See note on Jer 49:7. It apparently stayed neutral or pro-Babylonian (Ps 137:7) during the conflicts

the land, that all women may take warning and not imitate you.[i] 49You will suffer
the penalty for your lewdness and bear
the consequences of your sins of idolatry.
Then you will know that I am the Sovereign LORD.[j]"

Jerusalem as a Cooking Pot

24 In the ninth year, in the tenth
month on the tenth day, the word
of the LORD came to me:[k] 2"Son of man,
record this date, this very date, because
the king of Babylon has laid siege to Jerusalem this very day.[l] 3Tell this rebellious
people[m] a parable[n] and say to them: 'This
is what the Sovereign LORD says:

" 'Put on the cooking pot;[o] put it on
and pour water into it.
4Put into it the pieces of meat,
all the choice pieces—the leg and
the shoulder.
Fill it with the best of these bones;
5 take the pick of the flock.[p]
Pile wood beneath it for the bones;
bring it to a boil
and cook the bones in it.[q]

6" 'For this is what the Sovereign LORD says:

" 'Woe to the city of bloodshed,[r]
to the pot now encrusted,
whose deposit will not go away!
Take the meat out piece by piece
in whatever order[s] it comes.

7" 'For the blood she shed is in her
midst:
She poured it on the bare rock;
she did not pour it on the ground,
where the dust would cover it.[t]
8To stir up wrath and take revenge
I put her blood on the bare rock,
so that it would not be covered.

9" 'Therefore this is what the Sovereign
LORD says:

" 'Woe to the city of bloodshed!
I, too, will pile the wood high.
10So heap on the wood
and kindle the fire.
Cook the meat well,
mixing in the spices;
and let the bones be charred.
11Then set the empty pot on the coals
till it becomes hot and its copper
glows,
so that its impurities may be melted
and its deposit burned away.[u]
12It has frustrated all efforts;
its heavy deposit has not been
removed,
not even by fire.

13" 'Now your impurity is lewdness. Because I tried to cleanse you but you would
not be cleansed from your impurity, you
will not be clean again until my wrath
against you has subsided.[v]

14" 'I the LORD have spoken. The time
has come for me to act. I will not hold
back; I will not have pity, nor will I relent. You will be judged according to your
conduct and your actions,[w] declares the
Sovereign LORD.[x]' "

Ezekiel's Wife Dies

15The word of the LORD came to me:
16"Son of man, with one blow I am about
to take away from you the delight of your
eyes. Yet do not lament or weep or shed
any tears.[y] 17Groan quietly; do not mourn
for the dead. Keep your turban fastened
and your sandals on your feet; do not cover your mustache and beard or eat the customary food of mourners.[z]"

18So I spoke to the people in the morning, and in the evening my wife died. The
next morning I did as I had been commanded.

19Then the people asked me, "Won't

23:48 [i] 2Pe 2:6 **23:49** [j] Eze 7:4; 9:10; 20:38 **24:1** [k] Eze 8:1 **24:2** [l] 2Ki 25:1; Jer 39:1; 52:4 **24:3** [m] Isa 1:2; Eze 2:3,6 [n] Eze 17:2; 20:49 [o] Jer 1:13; Eze 11:3 **24:5** [p] Jer 52:10 [q] Jer 52:24-27 **24:6** [r] Eze 22:2 [s] Ob 1:11; Na 3:10 **24:7** [t] Lev 17:13 **24:11** [u] Jer 21:10; Eze 22:15 **24:13** [v] Jer 6:28-30; Eze 16:42; 22:24 **24:14** [w] Eze 36:19 [x] Eze 18:30 **24:16** [y] Jer 13:17; 16:5; 22:10 **24:17** [z] Jer 16:7

24:1 *ninth year … tenth month … tenth day.* Basing his dating scheme on the accession year for Zedekiah (596 BC), then the date for the beginning of siege of Jerusalem by Nebuchadnezzar's army would be Jan. 5, 587 BC; alternatively, this has been reckoned as Jan. 15, 588.
24:3 *cooking pot.* Usually a wide-mouthed ceramic jar, though here it is made of copper (v. 11). When manufactured for temple use the vessel would be made of silver or gold. Available in various sizes, they could be used over a fire if placed on a platform or tripod of stones, as in the narrative in 2Ki 4:38. For the use of a cooking pot as part of a prophetic message, see Jeremiah's "pot that is boiling" in Jer 1:13.
24:6 *pot now encrusted.* Ezekiel probably describes not the pot itself but the contents of the pot ("choice" pieces of meat, v. 4) as tainted or diseased. *in whatever order it comes.* The casting of the lot would be done to decide which pieces would be reserved for special use (perhaps to be gifts to the temple). But in this analogy, though they were choice pieces of meat, they had gone bad and were not eligible for holy use.
24:10 *spices.* In recipes from eighteenth-century BC Babylonia, seasonings for meat dishes and stews included salt as well as onions, leeks, mint and garlic. In these ancient preparations, the cooks added distinctive flavor with anise, coriander, cumin and dill. Given the metaphoric nature of this meal, the well-cooked meat may even refer to bodies of the people being prepared for burial with spices. *let the bones be charred.* The meat is cooked so thoroughly that it easily comes off the bones. The bones then are broken so that the marrow will mix with the other ingredients and add flavor to the broth. Once this has been poured off, what remains is a virtually useless mass of carbonized bits. For easy disposal they will be burned so completely that they literally fall apart and can be scattered over the refuge heap (cf. 22:15). A thorough job of either purification or destruction could be drawn from this metaphor, though the context favors the former (v. 11).

Tomb wall showing a funeral procession. Saqqara, 1550 to 1292 BC. See note on Eze 24:22.

[13]therefore this is what the Sovereign LORD
says: I will stretch out my hand against
Edom and kill both man and beast.[d] I
will lay it waste, and from Teman to Dedan[e] they will fall by the sword. [14]I will
take vengeance on Edom by the hand of
my people Israel, and they will deal with
Edom in accordance with my anger[f] and
my wrath; they will know my vengeance,
declares the Sovereign LORD.' "

A Prophecy Against Philistia

[15]"This is what the Sovereign LORD
says: 'Because the Philistines[g] acted in
vengeance and took revenge with malice
in their hearts, and with ancient hostility
sought to destroy Judah, [16]therefore this is
what the Sovereign LORD says: I am about
to stretch out my hand against the Philistines,[h] and I will wipe out the Kerethites[i]
and destroy those remaining along the
coast. [17]I will carry out great vengeance
on them and punish them in my wrath.
Then they will know that I am the LORD,
when I take vengeance on them.' "

A Prophecy Against Tyre

26 In the eleventh month of the
twelfth[a] year, on the first day of the
month, the word of the LORD came to me:
[2]"Son of man, because Tyre[j] has said of Jerusalem, 'Aha![k] The gate to the nations is

25:13 [d]Eze 29:8 [e]Jer 25:23 **25:14** [f]Eze 35:11 **25:15** [g]2Ch 28:18 **25:16** [h]Jer 47:1-7 [i]1Sa 30:14; Zep 2:4-5 **26:2** [j]2Sa 5:11; Isa 23 [k]Eze 25:3

[a] *1* Probable reading of the original Hebrew text; Masoretic Text does not have *month of the twelfth.*

that lead to the destruction of Jerusalem. Jer 40:11 does indicate that Edom accepted Judahite refugees after 587 BC. Nebuchadnezzar apparently did not extend his Transjordanian campaign of 582 BC as far as Edom, but his successor, Nabonidus, records in the Nabonidus Chronicle a siege of the Edomite city of Bozrah in 552 BC. Archaeological excavations at Buseira and at Tell el-Kheleifeh indicate destruction levels during this period followed by a quick rebuilding and a resumption of economic activity along the southern range of the King's Highway.

25:13 *Teman.* See note Jer 49:7. *Dedan.* See notes on Isa 21:13; Jer 49:8.

25:15 *Philistines.* The omission of the cities of Philistia from the list of states represented at Zedekiah's meeting in 597 BC (Jer 27:3) suggests that this area was firmly in the control of the Babylonians at that time. This region had been badly weakened by the late seventh-century BC campaigns of Pharaoh Psammetichus I as Assyrian control waned there (see Jer 25:20; Zep 2:4). The sons of the king of Ashkelon, an important city in Philistia, are recorded in Babylonian ration lists dating to 592 BC, indicating their hostage status. When the Philistine states joined in the Judahite revolt of 588, Nebuchadnezzar deported them and apparently settled them near Nippur. By the Persian period, little of the indigenous Philistine population remained in Philistia.

25:16 *Kerethites.* Ezekiel creates a poetic parallelism between Philistines and Kerethites, but it is still unclear whether these two peoples were actually related ethnically or historically. The Kerethites are most often associated with the island of Crete, and it would appear these people became mercenaries shortly after their migration to the southern coast of Palestine near Gaza (see 1Sa 30:14; 2Sa 8:18). See notes on 2Sa 8:18; 1Ki 1:38; 2Ki 11:4.

broken, and its doors have swung open to
me; now that she lies in ruins I will prosper,’ 3therefore this is what the Sovereign
LORD says: I am against you, Tyre, and I
will bring many nations against you, like
the sea[l] casting up its waves. 4They will
destroy[m] the walls of Tyre[n] and pull down
her towers; I will scrape away her rubble
and make her a bare rock. 5Out in the sea[o]
she will become a place to spread fishnets,
for I have spoken, declares the Sovereign
LORD. She will become plunder[p] for the
nations, 6and her settlements on the mainland will be ravaged by the sword. Then
they will know that I am the LORD.

7“For this is what the Sovereign LORD
says: From the north I am going to bring
against Tyre Nebuchadnezzar[a][q] king of
Babylon, king of kings,[r] with horses and
chariots,[s] with horsemen and a great
army. 8He will ravage your settlements on
the mainland with the sword; he will set
up siege works[t] against you, build a ramp[u]
up to your walls and raise his shields
against you. 9He will direct the blows of
his battering rams against your walls and
demolish your towers with his weapons.
10His horses will be so many that they will
cover you with dust. Your walls will tremble at the noise of the warhorses, wagons
and chariots[v] when he enters your gates
as men enter a city whose walls have
been broken through. 11The hooves[w] of
his horses will trample all your streets; he
will kill your people with the sword, and
your strong pillars[x] will fall to the ground.[y]
12They will plunder your wealth and loot
your merchandise; they will break down
your walls and demolish your fine houses
and throw your stones, timber and rubble
into the sea.[z] 13I will put an end[a] to your
noisy songs, and the music of your harps[b]
will be heard no more.[c] 14I will make you a
bare rock, and you will become a place to
spread fishnets. You will never be rebuilt,[d]
for I the LORD have spoken, declares the
Sovereign LORD.

26:3 [l] Isa 5:30; Jer 50:42; 51:42 **26:4** [m] Isa 23:1, 11 [n] Am 1:10 **26:5** [o] Eze 27:32 [p] Eze 29:19 **26:7** [q] Jer 27:6 [r] Ezr 7:12; Da 2:37 [s] Eze 23:24; Na 2:3-4 **26:8** [t] Jer 6:6 [u] Eze 21:22 **26:10** [v] Jer 4:13 **26:11** [w] Isa 5:28 [x] Jer 43:13 [y] Isa 26:5 **26:12** [z] Isa 23:8; Eze 27:3-27; 28:8 **26:13** [a] Jer 7:34 [b] Isa 14:11 [c] Jer 25:10; Rev 18:22 **26:14** [d] Job 12:14; Mal 1:4
26:15 [e] Eze 27:35 [f] Jer 49:21 **26:16** [g] Job 8:22 [h] Hos 11:10 [i] Eze 32:10 **26:17** [j] Eze 19:1; 27:32 [k] Isa 14:12 **26:18** [l] Isa 23:5; 41:5; Eze 27:35 **26:19** [m] Isa 8:7-8 **26:20** [n] Eze 32:18; Am 9:2; Jnh 2:2,6 [o] Eze 32:24,30 **26:21** [p] Eze 27:36; 28:19; Rev 18:21 **27:3** [q] ver 33

15“This is what the Sovereign LORD says
to Tyre: Will not the coastlands[e] tremble[f]
at the sound of your fall, when the wounded groan and the slaughter takes place in
you? 16Then all the princes of the coast will
step down from their thrones and lay aside
their robes and take off their embroidered
garments. Clothed[g] with terror, they will sit
on the ground, trembling[h] every moment,
appalled[i] at you. 17Then they will take up
a lament[j] concerning you and say to you:

“ ‘How you are destroyed, city of
  renown,
  peopled by men of the sea!
You were a power on the seas,
  you and your citizens;
you put your terror
  on all who lived there.[k]
18Now the coastlands tremble
  on the day of your fall;
the islands in the sea
  are terrified at your collapse.’[l]

19“This is what the Sovereign LORD says:
When I make you a desolate city, like cities no longer inhabited, and when I bring
the ocean depths over you and its vast
waters cover you,[m] 20then I will bring you
down with those who go down to the pit,[n]
to the people of long ago. I will make you
dwell in the earth below, as in ancient ruins, with those who go down to the pit,
and you will not return or take your place[b]
in the land of the living.[o] 21I will bring you
to a horrible end and you will be no more.
You will be sought, but you will never
again be found, declares the Sovereign
LORD.”[p]

A Lament Over Tyre

27 The word of the LORD came to me:
2“Son of man, take up a lament concerning Tyre. 3Say to Tyre, situated at the
gateway to the sea,[q] merchant of peoples

[a] *7* Hebrew *Nebuchadrezzar,* of which *Nebuchadnezzar* is a variant; here and often in Ezekiel and Jeremiah
[b] *20* Septuagint; Hebrew *return, and I will give glory*

26:4 *Tyre.* The island capital of Phoenicia (present-day Lebanon). See notes on Isa 23:1 – 18; Jer 47:4.

26:7 *Nebuchadnezzar.* His correct Hebrew name is Nebuchadrezzar (see NIV text note), reflecting his Akkadian name *Nabû-kuddura-usur* ("[the god] Nabû, protect the eldest son (or heir)!"). Spelling his name Nebuchadnezzar is a disobliging pun on the name of this king who destroyed Jerusalem. This spelling with a *nun* instead of a *resh* presupposes Akkadian *Nabû-kudana-usur* ("Nabû, protect the mule!"). The mule, being a hybrid animal, is incapable of producing offspring. This scurrilous etymology, therefore, expresses the opposite of what was intended with the original meaning of the name (see the article "Names in the Old Testament Period," p. 1132). Moreover, the absence of a descendant was a notorious curse in Assyrian treaties and ancient Near Eastern curse formulas. In Ezekiel, however, the Babylonians in general are portrayed in a positive light, for they are in the service of the Lord's plan to punish Judah and other nations. *king of kings.* A title frequently applied to Assyrian kings. The Babylonians must have copied this practice from their Assyrian predecessors, just as the Persians did some time later.

26:8 – 9 This description of the stages of the siege is the most detailed one in the Bible and is based on the repeated experience of victims of Assyrian and Babylonian attacks. See the article "Siege Warfare," p. 1157.

27:2 *lament.* A technical term for a dirge sung at the death of an individual (as in 19:1 for the princes of Israel) or after the destruction of a city and its people (as here). The book of Lamentations represents such a lament over the fall of Jerusalem. Beginning with Old Babylonian

on many coasts, 'This is what the Sovereign LORD says:

"'You say, Tyre,
"I am perfect in beauty.[r]"
[4] Your domain was on the high seas;
your builders brought your beauty to perfection.
[5] They made all your timbers
of juniper from Senir[a];[s]
they took a cedar from Lebanon
to make a mast for you.
[6] Of oaks[t] from Bashan
they made your oars;
of cypress wood[b] from the coasts of Cyprus[u]
they made your deck, adorned with ivory.
[7] Fine embroidered linen from Egypt was your sail
and served as your banner;

27:3 [r] Eze 28:2
27:5 [s] Dt 3:9
27:6 [t] Nu 21:33; Jer 22:20; Zec 11:2 [u] Ge 10:4; Isa 23:12

[a] 5 That is, Mount Hermon [b] 6 Targum; the Masoretic Text has a different division of the consonants.

times, the Mesopotamian literary tradition produced a specific genre of lengthy city laments (see the article "City Laments," p. 951). Five major city laments over the destruction of cities such as Ur, Uruk and Eridu are extant.

27:4 *Your domain was on the high seas.* Tyre was a maritime power. An Assyrian relief dating from the time of Sennacherib depicts Phoenician ships and a city, probably Tyre. A parallel Akkadian phrase is similarly used for the location of Tyre.

27:5 *Senir.* According to Dt 3:9, Mount Senir is the Amorite name for Mount Hermon, the southernmost spur of the Anti-Lebanon range lying to the east of the Beqaa Valley. It is mentioned in Assyrian inscriptions as Saniru. Senir and Hermon are placed side by side in 1Ch 5:23; SS 4:8.

27:6 *Cyprus.* Hebrew *Kittim*, which is equated with Kittion, an important Phoenician colony in southeast Cyprus. Cyprus trees still abound in the forests of Cyprus.

27:7 *Elishah.* The location of the islands of Elishah is uncertain. Elishah was a son of Javan in Ge 10:4. It was known as a Tyrian colony famous for its dyes. Elishah is probably the Alashiya of the Amarna tablets, usually designated as Cyprus. Seven Amarna tablets mention a king of Alashiya who wrote letters to the Egyptian monarchs in the thirteenth century BC.

NATIONS AND CITIES UNDER JUDGMENT IN EZEKIEL

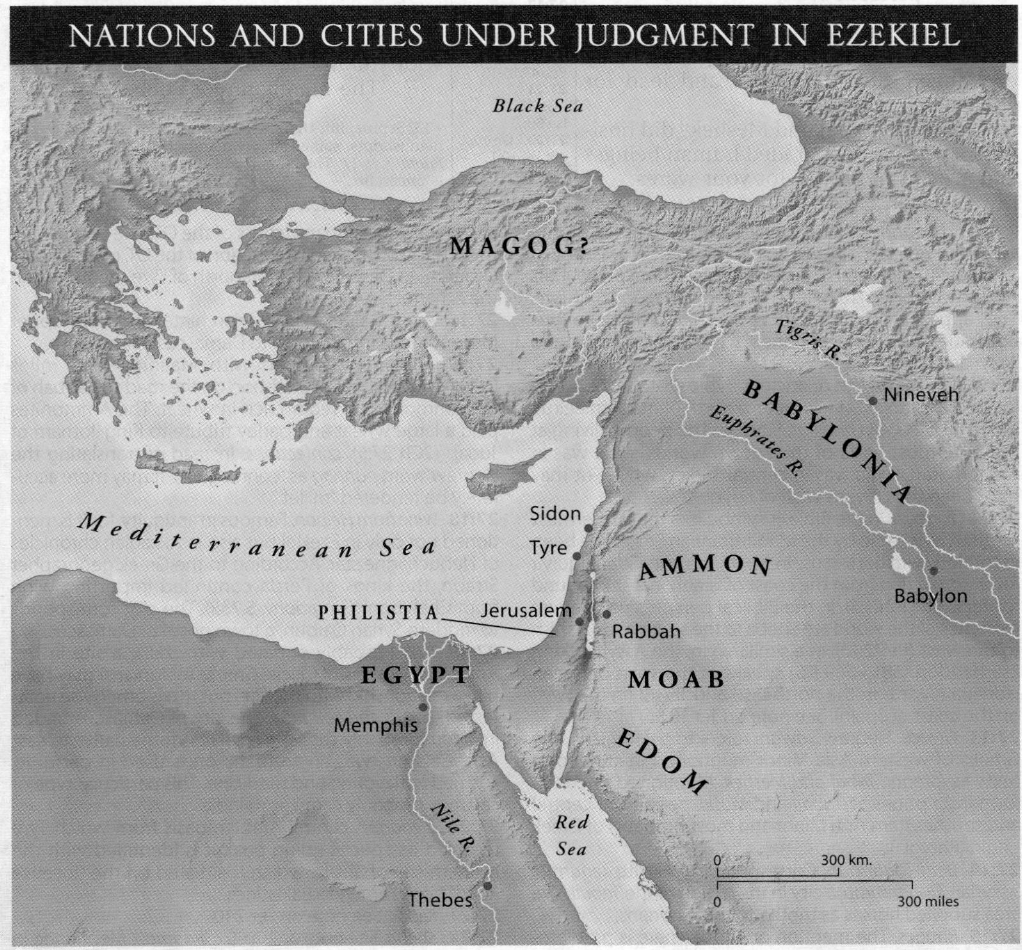

your awnings were of blue and purple[v]
from the coasts of Elishah.
8 Men of Sidon and Arvad[w] were your
oarsmen;
your skilled men, Tyre, were aboard
as your sailors.[x]
9 Veteran craftsmen of Byblos[y] were on
board
as shipwrights to caulk your seams.
All the ships of the sea and their sailors
came alongside to trade for your wares.

10 " 'Men of Persia,[z] Lydia and Put[a]
served as soldiers in your army.
They hung their shields and helmets
on your walls,
bringing you splendor.
11 Men of Arvad and Helek
guarded your walls on every side;
men of Gammad
were in your towers.
They hung their shields around your
walls;
they brought your beauty to
perfection.

12 " 'Tarshish[b] did business with you because of your great wealth of goods;[c] they
exchanged silver, iron, tin and lead for
your merchandise.
13 " 'Greece, Tubal and Meshek[d] did business with you; they traded human beings[e]
and articles of bronze for your wares.
14 " 'Men of Beth Togarmah[f] exchanged
chariot horses, cavalry horses and mules
for your merchandise.
15 " 'The men of Rhodes[a][g] traded with
you, and many coastlands[h] were your
customers; they paid you with ivory[i] tusks
and ebony.
16 " 'Aram[b][j] did business with you because of your many products; they exchanged turquoise,[k] purple fabric, embroidered work, fine linen, coral and rubies
for your merchandise.
17 " 'Judah and Israel traded with you;
they exchanged wheat from Minnith[l] and
confections,[c] honey, olive oil and balm for
your wares.
18 " 'Damascus[m] did business with you
because of your many products and great
wealth of goods. They offered wine from
Helbon, wool from Zahar 19 and casks of
wine from Izal in exchange for your wares:
wrought iron, cassia and calamus.
20 " 'Dedan traded in saddle blankets
with you.
21 " 'Arabia and all the princes of Kedar[n]
were your customers; they did business
with you in lambs, rams and goats.
22 " 'The merchants of Sheba[o] and Raa-

27:7 [v] Ex 25:4; Jer 10:9 **27:8** [w] Ge 10:18 [x] 1Ki 9:27 **27:9** [y] Jos 13:5; 1Ki 5:18 **27:10** [z] Eze 38:5 [a] Eze 30:5 **27:12** [b] Ge 10:4 [c] ver 18,33 **27:13** [d] Ge 10:2; Isa 66:19; Eze 38:2 [e] Rev 18:13 **27:14** [f] Ge 10:3; Eze 38:6 **27:15** [g] Ge 10:7 [h] Jer 25:22 [i] 1Ki 10:22; Rev 18:12 **27:16** [j] Jdg 10:6; Isa 7:1-8 [k] Eze 28:13 **27:17** [l] Jdg 11:33 **27:18** [m] Ge 14:15; Eze 47:16-18 **27:21** [n] Ge 25:13; Isa 60:7 **27:22** [o] Ge 10:7, 28; 1Ki 10:1-2; Isa 60:6

[a] *15* Septuagint; Hebrew *Dedan* [b] *16* Most Hebrew manuscripts; some Hebrew manuscripts and Syriac *Edom* [c] *17* The meaning of the Hebrew for this word is uncertain.

27:8 *Sidon and Arvad.* Phoenician cities that lay on the Mediterranean coast north of Tyre. Sidon was about 25 miles (40 kilometers) north of Tyre (see note on Jer 47:4). Arvad was about 110 miles (177 kilometers) north of Tyre. They appear at this time to have been subordinate to Tyre. Both cities are often mentioned in the Amarna letters and Assyrian annals.
27:9 *Byblos.* The site of ancient Byblos (Arabic *Gebeil*) is located 25.5 miles (41 kilometers) north of modern Beirut.
27:10 *Persia, Lydia and Put.* Signifies the peoples living at the outermost parts of the known world. Persia was in western Iran, Lydia was in central Turkey, while Put may have been the Libyans west of Egypt.
27:12 *Tarshish.* In the Bible, it symbolizes the farthermost location reachable by the Mediterranean Sea. It has been identified with Tartessus, in Spain, on the Guadalquivir River. Jonah fled from the coast of Israel on a ship bound for Tarshish (Jnh 1:3). In the Biblical perspective, the two extremes of the world are Sheba to the south and Tarshish to the west (Ps 72:10). In a similar vein, the Assyrian king Esarhaddon (681 – 669 BC) speaks of the span between Iadnana (Cyprus in the northeast) and Tarsisi (in the west on the coast of Spain). See note on Jer 10:9.
27:13 *Greece.* Hebrew *yawan*; refers to the Ionians, the Greeks of western Asia Minor mentioned in cuneiform texts as *Iamani. Tubal and Meshek.* Mentioned in cuneiform inscriptions as *Tabali* and *Muški*, peoples of central and southeastern Asia Minor and most probably of Greek origin (Phrygia).
27:14 *Beth Togarmah.* Corresponds to Hittite *Tegarma*, Assyrian *Til-garimmu*, a city in the region of the *Tabali*. The area supplied horses as tribute to the Assyrians.
27:15 *Rhodes.* The mention of Rhodes here is problematic in the earliest manuscripts of the OT. The Septuagint, the pre-Christian Greek translation of the OT, reads Dedan. Others read Danuna, a region north of Tyre mentioned in the Amarna letters.
27:16 *Aram.* Refers to the Syrian hinterland from Upper Mesopotamia in the north to Damascus in the south.
27:17 *Minnith.* Identified with Maanith, four miles (6.4 kilometers) out of Heshbon on the road to Rabbah of the Ammonites, a region rich in wheat. The Ammonites paid a large wheat and barley tribute to King Jotham of Judah (2Ch 27:5). *confections.* Instead of translating the Hebrew word *pannag* as "confections," it may more accurately be rendered "millet."
27:18 *wine from Helbon.* Famous in antiquity, for it is mentioned not only in Ezekiel but also in Akkadian chronicles of Nebuchadnezzar. According to the Greek geographer Strabo, the kings of Persia continued importing wine from Chalybon (*Geography*, 5.735). The city corresponds to modern Syrian Qalbun, a town north of Damascus.
27:19 *Izal.* Probably equated with Izalla, a site in the Anatolian foothills of Cilicia. Greeks (or Ionians) may have had a relationship with the site, but this is otherwise unattested. *cassia and calamus.* The city of Damascus traded in *qiddu* (probably cassia), a costly perfume native to east Asia. Calamus was an aromatic grass used in perfume, cosmetics, flavoring and medicine. This particular type of calamus probably came from India.
27:20 *Dedan.* A central Arabian oasis from which Tyre received its special riding gear. It is identified with the modern site of al-Ula, which is situated on the "Incense Road" from Yemen to Palestine.
27:21 *Kedar.* See note on Jer 2:10.
27:22 *Sheba.* See note on Isa 60:6. *Raamah.* Mentioned in

mah traded with you; for your merchandise they exchanged the finest of all kinds
of spices[p] and precious stones, and gold.
23“ ‘Harran,[q] Kanneh and Eden[r] and merchants of Sheba, Ashur and Kilmad traded
with you. 24In your marketplace they traded
with you beautiful garments, blue fabric,
embroidered work and multicolored rugs
with cords twisted and tightly knotted.

25“ ‘The ships of Tarshish[s] serve
as carriers for your wares.
You are filled with heavy cargo
as you sail the sea.
26Your oarsmen take you
out to the high seas.
But the east wind[t] will break you to
pieces
far out at sea.
27Your wealth,[u] merchandise and wares,
your mariners, sailors and
shipwrights,
your merchants and all your soldiers,
and everyone else on board
will sink into the heart of the sea
on the day of your shipwreck.
28The shorelands will quake[v]
when your sailors cry out.
29All who handle the oars
will abandon their ships;
the mariners and all the sailors
will stand on the shore.
30They will raise their voice
and cry bitterly over you;
they will sprinkle dust[w] on their heads
and roll[x] in ashes.[y]
31They will shave their heads because
of you
and will put on sackcloth.

27:22 [p]Ge 43:11 **27:23** [q]2Ki 19:12 [r]Isa 37:12 **27:25** [s]Isa 2:16 *fn* **27:26** [t]Ps 48:7; Jer 18:17 **27:27** [u]Pr 11:4 **27:28** [v]Eze 26:15 **27:30** [w]2Sa 1:2 [x]Jer 6:26 [y]Rev 18:18-19

27:31 [z]Isa 16:9 [a]Isa 22:12; Eze 7:18 **27:32** [b]Eze 26:17 **27:33** [c]ver 12; Eze 28:4-5 **27:34** [d]Zec 9:4 **27:35** [e]Eze 26:15 **27:36** [f]Jer 18:16; 19:8; 49:17; 50:13; Zep 2:15 [g]Ps 37:10, 36; Eze 26:21 **28:2** [h]Isa 14:13

They will weep[z] over you with anguish
of soul
and with bitter mourning.[a]
32As they wail and mourn over you,
they will take up a lament[b]
concerning you:
“Who was ever silenced like Tyre,
surrounded by the sea?”
33When your merchandise went out on
the seas,
you satisfied many nations;
with your great wealth[c] and your
wares
you enriched the kings of the
earth.
34Now you are shattered by the sea
in the depths of the waters;
your wares and all your company
have gone down with you.[d]
35All who live in the coastlands[e]
are appalled at you;
their kings shudder with horror
and their faces are distorted with
fear.
36The merchants among the nations
scoff at you;[f]
you have come to a horrible end
and will be no more.[g]’ ”

A Prophecy Against the King of Tyre

28 The word of the LORD came to me:
2“Son of man, say to the ruler of
Tyre, ‘This is what the Sovereign LORD
says:

“ ‘In the pride of your heart
you say, “I am a god;
I sit on the throne[h] of a god
in the heart of the seas.”

the OT only in conjunction with Sheba. It may be associated with Rgmt (the vowels of the ancient name are not certain), a city in the district of Najran in central Arabia.

27:23 *Harran, Kanneh and Eden ... Sheba, Ashur and Kilmad.* All of these areas were in the north and east of Tyre. *Harran.* Situated on the Balikh River in Upper Mesopotamia. *Kanneh.* Probably Assyrian Kannu, the location of which is unknown. *Eden.* Bit Adini, an Aramean state west of the Balikh River in Syria. *Sheba.* See note on Isa 60:6. *Ashur.* The name of the old capital city of Assyria, as well as the name of the primary god of Assyria. *Kilmad.* Otherwise unknown.

27:24 The merchandise listed here is very rare and exotic. Many of the words are attested only here in Scripture. Cognates with Akkadian have somewhat helped in shedding light on their meaning.

27:25 *ships of Tarshish.* Although the note on v. 12 denotes a specific region for Tarshish (i.e., Spain), the designation “ships of Tarshish” seems to imply a Phoenician provenience similar to what is found in Isa 23:1 – 18 (see note on Isa 23:1). Thus, they may have been ships bound for Tarshish.

27:30 *sprinkle dust on their heads and roll in ashes.* See the article “Mourning,” p. 828.

28:2 *I am a god; I sit on the throne of a god in the heart of the seas.* Apparently the king of Tyre had a role in the ritual of the “Awakening of Melqart,” the chief god of Tyre (*mlk qrt,* “king of the city”), in which the king was attributed divine status. Second-century AD Roman author Aelian reports that the Tyrian Phoenician royal dynasty claimed descent from the gods (*Varia Historia,* 14.30). Moreover, this verse seems to allude to a sea-girt divine abode, a prominent motif of ancient Near Eastern literature. The Ugaritic god El has his abode at the mouth of the rivers, i.e., “at the sources of the floods, in the midst of the Headwaters of the Two Oceans.”

In Sumerian texts, the gods of creation, Enki and Ninhursag, dwell on the paradisiacal island of Dilmun, which is situated at the junction of two seas. In Arabic the region is called Bahrain, which means “two seas.” The same motif was later applied to the city of Eridu in southern Mesopotamia, located at the mouth of the Tigris and Euphrates Rivers and not far away from Nippur, where Ezekiel is stationed.

The Greek historian Xenophon (c. 430 – 354 BC) mentions that in the Persian period royal palaces were built at river sources (*Anabasis,* 1.4.7,10), implying that kings attempted to imitate gods in their choice of the location for their dwellings. In applying this ancient motif to the king of Tyre, who boasts of sitting on such a divine throne chosen by the gods, Ezekiel castigates this expression of hubris.

But you are a mere mortal and not a god,
though you think you are as wise as a god.[i]
3 Are you wiser than Daniel[a]?[j]
Is no secret hidden from you?
4 By your wisdom and understanding
you have gained wealth for yourself
and amassed gold and silver
in your treasuries.[k]
5 By your great skill in trading
you have increased your wealth,
and because of your wealth
your heart has grown proud.[l]

6 " 'Therefore this is what the Sovereign LORD says:

" 'Because you think you are wise,
as wise as a god,
7 I am going to bring foreigners against you,
the most ruthless of nations;[m]
they will draw their swords against your beauty and wisdom
and pierce your shining splendor.
8 They will bring you down to the pit,[n]
and you will die a violent death
in the heart of the seas.[o]
9 Will you then say, "I am a god,"
in the presence of those who kill you?
You will be but a mortal, not a god,
in the hands of those who slay you.
10 You will die the death of the uncircumcised[p]
at the hands of foreigners.

I have spoken, declares the Sovereign LORD.' "

11 The word of the LORD came to me:
12 "Son of man, take up a lament[q] concerning the king of Tyre and say to him: 'This is what the Sovereign LORD says:

" 'You were the seal of perfection,
full of wisdom and perfect in beauty.[r]
13 You were in Eden,[s]
the garden of God;[t]
every precious stone adorned you:
carnelian, chrysolite and emerald,
topaz, onyx and jasper,
lapis lazuli, turquoise[u] and beryl.[b]
Your settings and mountings[c] were made of gold;
on the day you were created they were prepared.
14 You were anointed[v] as a guardian cherub,[w]
for so I ordained you.

28:2 [i] Ps 9:20; 82:6-7; Isa 31:3; 2Th 2:4 **28:3** [j] Da 1:20; 5:11-12 **28:4** [k] Zec 9:3 **28:5** [l] Job 31:25; Ps 52:7; 62:10; Hos 12:8; 13:6 **28:7** [m] Eze 30:11; 31:12; 32:12; Hab 1:6 **28:8** [n] Eze 32:30 [o] Eze 27:27 **28:10** [p] Eze 31:18; 32:19,24 **28:12** [q] Eze 19:1 [r] Eze 27:2-4 **28:13** [s] Ge 2:8 [t] Eze 31:8-9 [u] Eze 27:16 **28:14** [v] Ex 30:26; 40:9 [w] Ex 25:17-20

[a] *3* Or *Danel*, a man of renown in ancient literature
[b] *13* The precise identification of some of these precious stones is uncertain. [c] *13* The meaning of the Hebrew for this phrase is uncertain.

28:3 *Daniel.* The Hebrew spelling (*dnl*) suggests a person other than the prophet Daniel (Hebrew *dnyl*) (see note on 14:14). It is widely accepted that a reference is made here to the Ugaritic Dan'el, renowned for his justice, who by Ezekiel's time had acquired the aura of the great sage of the past. A counter argument favoring the Israelite Daniel, a contemporary of Ezekiel, is that Dan'el is not distinguished by his wisdom in the known literature.
28:5 *because of your wealth your heart has grown proud.* Tyre's commercial affluence has gone to its head. The inhabitants of the city are guilty of hubris and are going to be struck down in reprisal. The message is reinforced with a wordplay, a technique that exerted much influence on the ear of ancient Near Eastern hearers. Tyre's pretension of divine prerogatives is an act of profanation against deity.
28:7 *shining splendor.* A king's shining splendor or radiance points to a concept well documented in ancient Near Eastern literature. The sanctity of a king is often said to be manifest by an awe-inspiring radiance or an aura characteristic of deities and divine beings. The Mesopotamians used the Akkadian term *melammu* ("awe-inspiring luminosity") in order to describe this concept (see the article "Glory," p. 178).
28:10 *die the death of the uncircumcised.* To be uncircumcised was a disgrace to the circumcised Israelites (Ge 34:14) and Egyptians. This descriptor is not uncommon in the ancient world. For example, one text describes princes from the northern shores of Egypt as being uncircumcised. The term used is *motey*, a word occurring only here that can mean either "impure" or "uncircumcised." The text says that the various lords from the north could not enter the royal palace because they were uncircumcised and they ate fish, both features seen as an abomination by the pharaoh. The Egyptians, who practiced circumcision like the Israelites, counted the killed uncircumcised enemy soldiers by cutting off their private parts (cf. 1Sa 18:25–27). Contrary to the Philistines, the Phoenicians of Tyre and Sidon practiced circumcision as attested by Herodotus, who records their assertion that they adopted it from the Egyptians (*Histories* 2.104). The expression would therefore be as insulting to the Tyrian as to an Israelite.
28:13 *Eden, the garden of God.* This is one of the few references to Eden outside of the early chapters of Genesis (see also Eze 31). It is clearly understood as a garden, though v. 16 also understands it as a mountain. It is clearly portrayed as sacred space as God's presence is evidenced. No parallel images are known in the rest of the ancient world. Interpreters have come to a variety of conclusions about the force of the metaphor here developed concerning this individual. *every precious stone adorned you: carnelian, chrysolite and emerald, topaz, onyx and jasper, lapis lazuli, turquoise and beryl.* In the ninth tablet of the Gilgamesh Epic, the hero leaves Uruk in search of the immortal Utnapishtim, the Babylonian Noah. Pressing on to the end of the world, he comes to the mountains where the sun sets and rises and to the tunnel under the mountains. Gilgamesh reaches the far end of the tunnel just in time, before the sun can catch up with him, and he finds himself in a garden of jewels, where the immortal survivor of the flood lives. Such parallels only offer partial similarity to the description of the paradise-like garden in the Bible.
28:14 *guardian cherub … walked among the fiery stones.* The growing collection of Phoenician ivories attests to the prominence of the cherub motif in Phoenician art and iconography. Especially noteworthy is the carving of a king-cherub whose face appears to be the portrait of the king and under whose feet are seen alternating patterns of stylized tulip flower gardens and mountains.

EZEKIEL 28:11 – 19

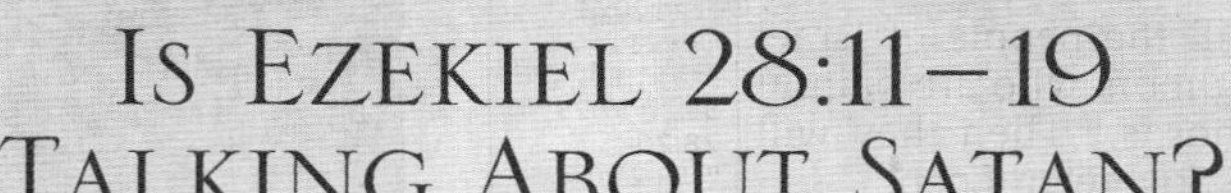

Is Ezekiel 28:11–19 Talking About Satan?

In the history of interpretation some have construed this passage as referring to Satan's fall. Satan is not referred to in this passage, and he is never identified in the Bible as either having been a cherub (a guardian of sacred space, not an angel) or as having a role in the Garden of Eden. The passage tells us who it is talking about (Eze 28:12), and the background available makes perfect sense of that identification and the metaphoric analogies that the text uses. Sound interpretation calls on us to refrain from adding ideas into the text that are not there. Instead, when we enter the world of the Israelite author and audience we can fill gaps in our understanding with information that the cultural context provides. ◆

You were on the holy mount of God;
you walked among the fiery stones.
15 You were blameless in your ways
from the day you were created
till wickedness was found in you.
16 Through your widespread trade
you were filled with violence,[x]
and you sinned.
So I drove you in disgrace from the
mount of God,
and I expelled you, guardian
cherub,[y]
from among the fiery stones.
17 Your heart became proud[z]
on account of your beauty,
and you corrupted your wisdom
because of your splendor.
So I threw you to the earth;
I made a spectacle of you before
kings.
18 By your many sins and dishonest
trade
you have desecrated your
sanctuaries.
So I made a fire come out from you,
and it consumed you,
and I reduced you to ashes[a] on the
ground
in the sight of all who were
watching.
19 All the nations who knew you
are appalled at you;
you have come to a horrible end
and will be no more.[b]' "

A Prophecy Against Sidon

20 The word of the LORD came to me:
21 "Son of man, set your face against[c] Sidon;[d] prophesy against her 22 and say:
'This is what the Sovereign LORD says:

" 'I am against you, Sidon,
and among you I will display my
glory.[e]
You will know that I am the LORD,
when I inflict punishment[f] on you
and within you am proved to be
holy.

28:16 [x] Hab 2:17 [y] Ge 3:24 **28:17** [z] Eze 31:10 **28:18** [a] Mal 4:3 **28:19** [b] Jer 51:64; Eze 26:21; 27:36 **28:21** [c] Eze 6:2 [d] Ge 10:15; Jer 25:22 **28:22** [e] Eze 39:13 [f] Eze 30:19

28:18 *desecrated your sanctuaries.* In Ezekiel, the temple of Israel is desecrated when it is despoiled by the Babylonians (7:21 – 22). Something can also be "desecrated" by failure to treat its property as holy. In this verse the prince is being charged with pillaging sanctuary treasuries or misappropriating temple funds, whether of Tyre or of surrounding territories.

28:21 *Sidon.* This great trading city had been defeated and its king, Luli, had been deposed by the Assyrian king Sennacherib in 701 BC for joining an anti-Assyrian coalition. Under Abdimilkutte, Sidon again revolted against Esarhaddon of Assyria in 677 BC. The city was destroyed to its foundations and its king was beheaded. The Assyrians rebuilt the city and named it Kar-Asarhaddon, which became the center of Assyria's administration of the area. In Jer 27:3, envoys from Sidon were included in the conspirators that met in Jerusalem in 594 BC. A few years later Sidon was forced to submit to Nebuchadnezzar of Babylon and many of its people were deported. There is no record of this, but some Sidonian exiles are known from the city of Uruk in Babylonia in this period. Herodotus reports that in 588 BC the Egyptians fought against Sidon in an attempt to gain control of the Phoenician coast, but it is likely that Sidon was already a Babylonian vassal at this time.

23 I will send a plague upon you
and make blood flow in your streets.
The slain will fall within you,
with the sword against you on every side.
Then you will know that I am the LORD.[g]

24 " 'No longer will the people of Israel have malicious neighbors who are painful briers and sharp thorns.[h] Then they will know that I am the Sovereign LORD.

25 " 'This is what the Sovereign LORD says: When I gather[i] the people of Israel from the nations where they have been scattered,[j] I will be proved holy[k] through them in the sight of the nations. Then they will live in their own land, which I gave
to my servant Jacob.[l]
26 They will live there in safety[m] and will build houses and plant vineyards; they will live in safety when I inflict punishment on all their neighbors who maligned them. Then they will know that I am the LORD their God.[n]' "

28:23 [g] Eze 38:22
28:24 [h] Nu 33:55; Jos 23:13; Eze 2:6
28:25 [i] Ps 106:47; Jer 32:37 [j] Isa 11:12 [k] Eze 20:41 [l] Jer 23:8; Eze 11:17; 34:27; 37:25
28:26 [m] Jer 23:6 [n] Isa 65:21; Jer 32:15; Eze 38:8; Am 9:14-15
29:1 [o] ver 17; Eze 26:1
29:2 [p] Jer 25:19 [q] Isa 19:1-17; Jer 46:2; Eze 30:1-26; 31:1-18; 32:1-32
29:3 [r] Jer 44:30 [s] Ps 74:13; Isa 27:1; Eze 32:2
29:4 [t] 2Ki 19:28 [u] Eze 38:4

A Prophecy Against Egypt

Judgment on Pharaoh

29 In the tenth year, in the tenth month on the twelfth day, the word of the LORD came to me:[o]
2 "Son of man, set your face against Pharaoh king of Egypt[p] and prophesy against him and
against all Egypt.[q]
3 Speak to him and say: 'This is what the Sovereign LORD says:

" 'I am against you, Pharaoh[r] king of Egypt,
you great monster[s] lying among your streams.
You say, "The Nile belongs to me;
I made it for myself."
4 But I will put hooks[t] in your jaws
and make the fish of your streams stick to your scales.
I will pull you out from among your streams,
with all the fish sticking to your scales.[u]

Esarhaddon stele (671 BC) depicting ropes that seem to end in a ring that goes through the lips of the prisoners (Eze 29:4).

5 I will leave you in the desert,
you and all the fish of your streams.
You will fall on the open field
and not be gathered or picked up.
I will give you as food
to the beasts of the earth and the birds of the sky.[v]

29:5 [v] Jer 7:33; 34:20; Eze 32:4-6; 39:4

29:1 *tenth year ... tenth month ... twelfth day.* When compared to the date given in 24:1, this appears to be one year later; however, it has often been concluded by commentators that the notation in 24:1 is made in accordance with a nonaccession-year system rather than an accession-year system (see notes on 24:1; Jer 26:1; Da 2:1). If this is so, this prophecy occurs only two days after the siege of Jerusalem has begun. This is more likely because the Egyptian response to the siege took place that first summer.

29:3 *great monster lying among your streams.* This appears on the surface to refer to a crocodile (see "scales" in v. 4). Crocodiles populated the Nile and so make an appropriate image, but they were also on the periphery of the conjunction with chaos creatures, which would also be suitable imagery here.

29:4 *hooks in your jaws.* Herodotus (*History*, 2.70) describes the procedure of catching a crocodile in the Nile: "The hunter baits a hook with a chine of pork, and lets it float into the middle of the river; he himself stays on the bank with a young live pig, which he beats. Hearing the cries of the pig, the crocodile goes after the sound, and meets the chine, which it swallows; then the hunter pulls the line." In this context, however, even if Pharaoh is equated with the crocodile, the "great monster" crouching in the Nile (v. 3), the focus of the verse is on the manner of leading prisoners with hooks in their mouths or jaws. This is a practice portrayed in Assyrian reliefs as a means of humiliating captives and taking them into exile.

29:5 *I will give you as food to the beasts of the earth and the birds of the sky.* In this prophetic oracle, the scat-

6Then all who live in Egypt will know that
I am the LORD.

" 'You have been a staff of reed[w] for
the people of Israel. 7When they grasped
you with their hands, you splintered[x] and
you tore open their shoulders; when they
leaned on you, you broke and their backs
were wrenched.[a][y]

8" 'Therefore this is what the Sovereign
LORD says: I will bring a sword against you
and kill both man and beast.[z] 9Egypt will
become a desolate wasteland. Then they
will know that I am the LORD.

" 'Because you said, "The Nile is mine; I
made it,[a]" 10therefore I am against you and
against your streams, and I will make the
land of Egypt a ruin and a desolate waste
from Migdol to Aswan,[b] as far as the border of Cush.[b] 11The foot of neither man
nor beast will pass through it; no one will
live there for forty years.[c] 12I will make the
land of Egypt desolate among devastated
lands, and her cities will lie desolate forty years among ruined cities. And I will
disperse the Egyptians among the nations
and scatter them through the countries.[d]

29:6 [w] 2Ki 18:21; Isa 36:6 **29:7** [x] Isa 36:6 [y] Eze 17:15-17 **29:8** [z] Eze 14:17; 32:11-13 **29:9** [a] Eze 30:7-8, 13-19 **29:10** [b] Eze 30:6 **29:11** [c] Eze 32:13 **29:12** [d] Jer 46:19; Eze 30:7, 23, 26

29:14 [e] Eze 30:14 [f] Eze 17:14 **29:15** [g] Zec 10:11 **29:16** [h] Isa 36:4, 6 [i] Isa 30:2; Hos 8:13 **29:17** [j] Eze 24:1 **29:18** [k] Jer 27:6; Eze 26:7-8 [l] Jer 48:37

13" 'Yet this is what the Sovereign LORD
says: At the end of forty years I will gather
the Egyptians from the nations where they
were scattered. 14I will bring them back
from captivity and return them to Upper
Egypt,[e] the land of their ancestry. There
they will be a lowly[f] kingdom. 15It will be
the lowliest of kingdoms and will never
again exalt itself above the other nations.[g]
I will make it so weak that it will never
again rule over the nations. 16Egypt will
no longer be a source of confidence[h] for
the people of Israel but will be a reminder of their sin in turning to her for help.
Then they will know that I am the Sovereign LORD.[i]' "

Nebuchadnezzar's Reward

17In the twenty-seventh year, in the first
month on the first day, the word of the
LORD came to me:[j] 18"Son of man, Nebuchadnezzar[k] king of Babylon drove his
army in a hard campaign against Tyre;
every head was rubbed bare[l] and every

[a] *7* Syriac (see also Septuagint and Vulgate); Hebrew *and you caused their backs to stand* [b] *10* That is, the upper Nile region

tered, exposed corpses suffer the ultimate disgrace: they are eaten by animals, a common threat in ancient Near Eastern curses. The Assyrian king Esarhaddon tells of not properly burying his enemies but instead allowing wild animals to devour them. Not to have a proper burial implied that the descendants could not perform the usual religious duties for their dead ancestors. The person left to die in disgrace became a roaming spirit unable to find rest. What Ezekiel is announcing in this verse would have been frightening for his hearers. One of the fundamental duties of the descendants was to honor their ancestors. See note on Jer 22:19.

29:6 *staff of reed.* In 720 BC, Sargon II of Assyria characterized the pharaoh as "a king who cannot save," although he had been "bribed" by a coalition of little states. Sargon had to put down a rebellion that began in Philistine Ashdod together with Judah and other allies. In the time of Ezekiel, King Jehoiakim was raised to the throne of Judah by Pharaoh Necho (2Ki 23:34). He rebelled against his new Babylonian overlord, Nebuchadnezzar, hoping for Egyptian support that never came. In the last days of Judah, Pharaoh Hophra dispatched an army to relieve besieged Jerusalem. The intervention proved futile as he retreated without even engaging a battle with the Babylonians. Isa 36:6 calls the Egyptians a "splintered reed of a staff." For Judah, Egypt incarnates betrayed promises and disappointed hopes. Such an attitude of betrayal is universally condemned in ancient literature.

29:10 *Migdol.* See note on Jer 44:1. It appears in the exodus story (Ex 14:2). *Aswan.* Means "market, trading post." It is the ancient southern border of Egypt and corresponds to modern Aswan, at the first cataract of the Nile (see note on Isa 49:12). Beyond it lay Cush, the Egyptian designation of territory south of Egypt.

29:11 *forty years.* A rhetorical way of talking about a period of one generation. The Israelites had a 40-year period of wandering in the desert (Nu 14:33). In Northwest Semitic texts it also designates a period of temporary national punishment. King Mesha of Moab gives 40 years as the length of Israelite occupation of part of his land during the time of his god's anger.

29:14 *Upper Egypt.* Upper Egypt (or the land of Pathros) designated all of Egypt south of Memphis. An ancient Egyptian tradition asserted that the nation had originated in the south, in Upper Egypt. Esarhaddon of Assyria claimed to be the king of Musur (northern Egypt) and Paturisi (Pathros). The table of nations in Ge 10:14 (see also 1Ch 1:12) treats "Pathrusites" (people of Upper Egypt) as descendants of "Egypt" (*mitsrayim*, Lower Egypt).

29:18 *hard campaign against Tyre.* The complete destruction of the city of Tyre prophesied in ch. 27 did not come to pass under Nebuchadnezzar. In Ezekiel's time Nebuchadnezzar blockaded the city and severely curtailed Tyre's trade. The siege lasted 13 years (Josephus, *Against Apion* 1.156). In the end the two sides must have come to a compromise. King Ethbaal III of Tyre was deposed. He probably corresponds to "the king of Tyre" who appears among other royal captives deported to Babylon in "The Court of Nebuchadnezzar" document. A Babylonian royal high commissioner was appointed over the town. The city, however, remained intact and was not even subjected to habitual looting. The kind of thorough destruction of Tyre as described in this chapter was achieved only by Alexander the Great in 332 BC. Alexander's soldiers worked for seven months to build a causeway linking the island with the coast. Whereas Alexander usually treated his prisoners fairly humanely, he made a hideous example of Tyre. Alexander's final attack on the city was said to have cost 8,000 Tyrians their lives. Moreover, crosses were hewn for 2,000 male citizens and set up along the shores of the land. According to the sources, 30,000 women, children and older people were sold into slavery, though we cannot say whether that is hyperbole. Alexander was not only taking a town but also destroying a myth. The world would learn that the Phoenician lords of the sea had been vanquished by him, the lord of the earth, and that there were no other demigods but the demigod Alexander of Macedonia. *no reward.* Soldiers usually received plunder in the form of

shoulder made raw. Yet he and his army
got no reward from the campaign he led
against Tyre. 19 Therefore this is what the
Sovereign LORD says: I am going to give
Egypt to Nebuchadnezzar king of Babylon,
and he will carry off its wealth. He will loot
and plunder the land as pay for his army.[m]
20 I have given him Egypt as a reward for
his efforts because he and his army did it
for me, declares the Sovereign LORD.[n]
21 "On that day I will make a horn[a][o]
grow for the Israelites, and I will open
your mouth[p] among them. Then they will
know that I am the LORD.[q]"

A Lament Over Egypt

30 The word of the LORD came to me:
2 "Son of man, prophesy and say:
'This is what the Sovereign LORD says:

" 'Wail[r] and say,
"Alas for that day!"
3 For the day is near,[s]
the day of the LORD[t] is near —
a day of clouds,
a time of doom for the nations.
4 A sword will come against Egypt,
and anguish will come upon Cush.[b]
When the slain fall in Egypt,
her wealth will be carried away
and her foundations torn down.[u]

29:19 [m] Jer 43:10-13; Eze 30:4, 10, 24-25
29:20 [n] Isa 10:6-7; 45:1; Jer 25:9
29:21 [o] Ps 132:17 [p] Eze 33:22 [q] Eze 24:27
30:2 [r] Isa 13:6
30:3 [s] Eze 7:7; Joel 2:1, 11; Ob 1:15 [t] ver 18; Eze 7:12, 19
30:4 [u] Eze 29:19
30:5 [v] Eze 27:10 [w] Jer 25:20
30:6 [x] Eze 29:10
30:7 [y] Eze 29:12
30:9 [z] Isa 18:1-2 [a] Isa 23:5 [b] Eze 32:9-10
30:10 [c] Eze 29:19

5 Cush and Libya,[v] Lydia and all Arabia,
Kub and the people[w] of the covenant land
will fall by the sword along with Egypt.
6 " 'This is what the LORD says:

" 'The allies of Egypt will fall
and her proud strength will fail.
From Migdol to Aswan[x]
they will fall by the sword within her,
declares the Sovereign LORD.
7 " 'They will be desolate
among desolate lands,
and their cities will lie
among ruined cities.[y]
8 Then they will know that I am the LORD,
when I set fire to Egypt
and all her helpers are crushed.

9 " 'On that day messengers will go out
from me in ships to frighten Cush[z] out of
her complacency. Anguish[a] will take hold
of them on the day of Egypt's doom, for it
is sure to come.[b]

10 " 'This is what the Sovereign LORD says:

" 'I will put an end to the hordes of
Egypt
by the hand of Nebuchadnezzar king
of Babylon.[c]

[a] *21 Horn* here symbolizes strength. [b] *4* That is, the upper Nile region; also in verses 5 and 9

persons, animals and possessions. However, Tyre was able to get an exemption from destruction by yielding to Babylon. Thus, there was no pillaging of the city.
29:19 *I . . . give Egypt to Nebuchadnezzar.* God is promising Nebuchadnezzar the land of Egypt as compensation for his failure in plundering Tyre. Both in the Bible and in the ancient Near Eastern texts, plunder is represented as a gift from the national deity (cf. Dt 20:14). Neo-Assyrian royal inscriptions, referring to the enlargement of the Review Palace at Nineveh, state that it was used for storing battle equipment as well as goods plundered from the enemy by the power of the god Assur. Closer to ancient Israel, king Hazael of Damascus states in an Old Aramaic inscription dating from the end of the ninth century BC that the plunder he captured was given to him by his national god Hadad. *He will loot and plunder.* It was inevitable that Nebuchadnezzar would eventually have to invade and attempt to conquer Egypt. The Medes had united the territory east of the Tigris, effectively cutting Babylon off from direct trade with the east, and the Egyptians, with their Phoenician allies, were constantly causing political and commercial problems in the west and along the Arabian trade routes. An extended siege (13 years according to the fourth-century BC Greek historian Menander) bottled up Tyre and devastated much of Phoenicia (584 – 571 BC). A fragmentary portion of Nebuchadnezzar's annals from his 37th year, Herodotus and Eze 29:19 – 21 refers to the invasion of Egypt in 568 BC, but no details are given other than victories over desert tribes. It is likely that some Babylonian garrisons were installed in the fortresses of the Sinai following this campaign.
29:21 *horn.* The horns of an animal were considered tokens of their power, and thus were a figure of strength. Many of the deities of Mesopotamia were depicted with horns. Thus, making a horn to sprout signifies a return of Israel's power. Additionally, it must be noted that occasionally the crowns of kings also often featured horns, and a horn could therefore refer more specifically to a king.
30:5 *Cush and Libya, Lydia.* Jer 46:9 lists Cush, Put (i.e., Libya) and Lydia in the same order as foreign components of Pharaoh Necho's army at the battle of Carchemish. From extra-Biblical sources it is known that the army of the Saite dynasty comprised, besides Egyptians, Greeks, Ionians, Rhodians, Carians, Libyans, Phoenicians and Jewish mercenaries. In the campaign of Psammetichus II against Nubia (591 BC), Carian, Ionian, Rhodian and Phoenician soldiers commemorated their involvement in the event by inscribing their names on the colossus of Rameses II at Abu Simbel. *the people of the covenant land.* A case can be made for this being a treaty of mutual assistance concluded between Zedekiah (17:15) and the Saite Egypt. Several sources point to Jewish mercenaries in Egyptian military campaigns. The second-century BC Letter of Aristeas speaks of Psammetichus I having dispatched confederate Jewish troops to fight against the king of the Ethiopians.
30:9 *ships.* This Hebrew term (an Egyptian loanword) refers to military boats, not reed boats or merchant ships. *frighten Cush.* Nubia (called "Cush" here) felt that having Egypt as a buffer zone offered a certain amount of protection from any of the powers from the east that would arise. Though the Egyptian pharaoh, Psammetichus II, campaigned against Nubia in 593 BC, it is not attack from Egypt that is threatened in this passage. The Persian king Cambyses invaded Nubia in 525 BC, and from that time it was counted as part of the Persian Empire. Nubians served as mercenaries in the Persian army.
30:10 – 11 *Nebuchadnezzar . . . and his army . . . against Egypt.* See note on 29:19.

Nilometer (marks in wall) measures the depth of the Nile at Elephantine. Egyptian agriculture depended on the annual inundation of the Nile, so if it were to dry out (Eze 30:12), it would create a national crisis. In ancient times they were aware of their dependence on the inundation and devised measuring devices to keep their records.

11 He and his army — the most ruthless of
nations[d] —
will be brought in to destroy the
land.
They will draw their swords against
Egypt
and fill the land with the slain.
12 I will dry up[e] the waters of the Nile[f]
and sell the land to an evil nation;
by the hand of foreigners
I will lay waste the land and
everything in it.
I the LORD have spoken.

13 " 'This is what the Sovereign LORD says:

" 'I will destroy the idols[g]
and put an end to the images in
Memphis.[h]
No longer will there be a prince in
Egypt,[i]
and I will spread fear throughout the
land.
14 I will lay[j] waste Upper Egypt,
set fire to Zoan[k]
and inflict punishment on Thebes.[l]
15 I will pour out my wrath on Pelusium,
the stronghold of Egypt,
and wipe out the hordes of Thebes.
16 I will set fire to Egypt;
Pelusium will writhe in agony.
Thebes will be taken by storm;
Memphis will be in constant distress.
17 The young men of Heliopolis[m] and
Bubastis
will fall by the sword,
and the cities themselves will go into
captivity.

30:11 [d] Eze 28:7 **30:12** [e] Isa 19:6 [f] Eze 29:9 **30:13** [g] Jer 43:12 [h] Isa 19:13 [i] Zec 10:11 **30:14** [j] Eze 29:14 [k] Ps 78:12,43 [l] Jer 46:25 **30:17** [m] Ge 41:45

30:12 *sell.* In the ancient world the concept of selling something did not emphasize getting money for it, as it might in today's economy; rather, the emphasis was on the transfer of ownership. In Akkadian the word for "sell" is also the word for "give." Ru 4:3 – 5 also shows flexibility in the use of this Hebrew term (see "selling" in Ru 4:3). As a result, it is not pertinent to ask what Yahweh is receiving in return. That is not the issue. He is transferring possession of the land from Egypt to Babylon.
30:13 *Memphis.* The royal residence during this period and the center of the cult of the god Ptah, a creator deity and patron of the craft guilds. It was the city in which kings were enthroned.
30:14 *Upper Egypt.* See note on 29:14. *Zoan.* An important administrative center in the eighth and seventh centuries BC. See note on Isa 19:11. *Thebes.* The chief city of Upper (southern) Egypt.
30:15 *Pelusium.* Sin, usually identified with Pelusium, was an important fortress town in the northeast frontier of the delta region. It held a strategic position in Egypt's defense against invaders from western Asia.
30:17 *Heliopolis.* Aven (Hellenized as Heliopolis, "city of the sun-god") was at the apex of the Nile delta region, just north of the city of Cairo. It normally appears in Hebrew as On (see Ge 41:45,50). *Bubastis.* Pi-beset (Hellenized as Bubastis) was a town in the Nile delta region. It is modern

18 Dark will be the day at Tahpanhes
when I break the yoke of Egypt;[n]
there her proud strength will come
to an end.
She will be covered with clouds,
and her villages will go into
captivity.[o]
19 So I will inflict punishment on Egypt,
and they will know that I am the
LORD.' "

Pharaoh's Arms Are Broken

20 In the eleventh year, in the first month
on the seventh day, the word of the LORD
came to me:[p] 21 "Son of man, I have broken the arm[q] of Pharaoh king of Egypt.
It has not been bound up to be healed[r]
or put in a splint so that it may become
strong enough to hold a sword. 22 Therefore this is what the Sovereign LORD says:
I am against Pharaoh king of Egypt.[s] I will
break both his arms, the good arm as well
as the broken one, and make the sword fall
from his hand.[t] 23 I will disperse the Egyptians among the nations and scatter them
through the countries.[u] 24 I will strengthen[v]
the arms of the king of Babylon and put
my sword[w] in his hand, but I will break
the arms of Pharaoh, and he will groan
before him like a mortally wounded man.
25 I will strengthen the arms of the king of
Babylon, but the arms of Pharaoh will fall
limp. Then they will know that I am the
LORD, when I put my sword into the hand
of the king of Babylon and he brandishes
it against Egypt. 26 I will disperse the Egyptians among the nations and scatter them
through the countries. Then they will
know that I am the LORD.[x]"

30:18 [n] Lev 26:13 [o] ver 3 **30:20** [p] Eze 26:1; 29:17; 31:1 **30:21** [q] Jer 48:25 [r] Jer 30:13; 46:11 **30:22** [s] Jer 46:25 [t] Ps 37:17 **30:23** [u] Eze 29:12 **30:24** [v] Zec 10:6, 12 [w] Eze 21:14; Zep 2:12 **30:26** [x] Eze 29:12 **31:1** [y] Jer 52:5 [z] Eze 30:20 **31:3** [a] Isa 10:34

Pharaoh as a Felled Cedar of Lebanon

31 In the eleventh year,[y] in the third
month on the first day, the word
of the LORD came to me:[z] 2 "Son of man,
say to Pharaoh king of Egypt and to his
hordes:

" 'Who can be compared with you in
majesty?
3 Consider Assyria, once a cedar in
Lebanon,
with beautiful branches
overshadowing the forest;
it towered on high,
its top above the thick foliage.[a]
4 The waters nourished it,
deep springs made it grow tall;
their streams flowed
all around its base

Tell Basta, located 35 miles (8 kilometers) south of Cairo on the Tanitic branch of the Nile. It was the residence of Sheshonq (Biblical Shishak), a powerful monarch of the Twenty-Second Dynasty in the tenth century BC.

30:18 *Tahpanhes.* Tahpanhes was an outpost in the eastern delta region of the Nile, bordering the Sinai. It was later known as Daphne by the Greeks, who inhabited the outpost as mercenaries by the seventh century BC. The Greek historian Herodotus states that Daphne was one of three outposts set up by the Egyptians to stop the Assyrian invasion. The Judahites in flight from the Babylonians may have stopped there in the early sixth century BC.

30:20 *eleventh year ... first month ... seventh day.* Apr. 29, 587 BC.

30:21 *broken the arm of Pharaoh.* A scene from the reign of Amenhotep II depicts the pharaoh holding locks of his enemy in one hand and the other hand poised to bludgeon the man. The scene is common in Egypt, and in this case includes an accompanying inscription identifying the pharaoh as a god whose arm is great. The figure of the broken arm of the pharaoh may be an ironic echo of royal epithets from the Saite dynasty. Hophra, the pharaoh of Ezekiel's time, uses as a royal epithet the expression "possessor of a strong arm." This title was the second formal name of his tutelary.

31:1 *eleventh year ... third month ... first day.* June 21, 587 BC, nearly two months after the date mentioned in 30:20. Since there is no firm information concerning the date of the Egyptian interference, it is difficult to relate this prophecy to the timing of the event.

31:2 *Pharaoh.* As in 29:3, Ezekiel is probably addressing the office of pharaoh in general. Hophra was the reigning monarch in 587 BC.

31:3 – 17 The power of the Assyrian state waxed and waned for nearly three centuries (c. 900 – 612 BC). At its height its geographic range was enormous, ranging from Iran in the east to central Egypt, central Anatolia, and Cyprus in the west. It covered much of the Arabian Desert in the south, and ranged as far north as modern day Armenia. In Ezekiel's time it had passed off the scene rather recently (about 20 years earlier), so it served as a perfect image of a long-standing super power that had crumbled to nothing.

31:3 – 14 The tree used for the metaphor here is the cedar, a well-known ancient Near Eastern symbol of majesty (see notes on 2Sa 5:11; 1Ki 5:6; 6:15). It was used for the construction of many important palaces and temples. Egyptian, Assyrian and Babylonian kings all recount how they cut down the cedars of Lebanon in order to construct their mighty edifices. The myth of a cosmic tree is also found in Mesopotamian contexts. Its roots are fed by the great subterranean ocean and its top merges with the clouds, and thus it binds together the heavens, the earth and the netherworld. The Sumerian Gilgamesh Epic has a motif of a great tree offering shelter to animals. The Sumerian goddess Inanna discovered the sacred cosmic tree on the banks of the Euphrates and transplanted it in her sacred garden at Uruk, where it attracted the mythical Anzu (a birdlike chaos creature), a snake, and Lilith (an evil demon). In the Mesopotamian epic "Erra and Ishum," Marduk speaks of the *meshu* tree, whose roots reach down through the oceans to the netherworld and whose top is above the heavens. In Assyrian contexts, the motif of a sacred tree is also well-known. Some have called it a tree of life, and some also associate it with this world tree. It is often flanked by animals or by human or divine figures. A winged disk is typically centrally located over the top of the tree. The king is represented as the human personification of this tree. The tree is thought to represent the divine world order, but textual discussion of it is lacking. As is often the case in Ezekiel, this mythical motif is transformed to a political image.

and sent their channels
to all the trees of the field.
5 So it towered higher
than all the trees of the field;
its boughs increased
and its branches grew long,
spreading because of abundant
waters.[b]
6 All the birds of the sky
nested in its boughs,
all the animals of the wild
gave birth under its branches;
all the great nations
lived in its shade.[c]
7 It was majestic in beauty,
with its spreading boughs,
for its roots went down
to abundant waters.
8 The cedars[d] in the garden of God
could not rival it,
nor could the junipers
equal its boughs,
nor could the plane trees
compare with its branches—
no tree in the garden of God
could match its beauty.[e]
9 I made it beautiful
with abundant branches,
the envy of all the trees of Eden[f]
in the garden of God.[g]

10 " 'Therefore this is what the Sovereign
LORD says: Because the great cedar towered over the thick foliage, and because it
was proud[h] of its height, 11 I gave it into the
hands of the ruler of the nations, for him
to deal with according to its wickedness.
I cast it aside,[i] 12 and the most ruthless of
foreign nations[j] cut it down and left it. Its
boughs fell on the mountains and in all
the valleys;[k] its branches lay broken in all
the ravines of the land. All the nations of
the earth came out from under its shade
and left it.[l] 13 All the birds settled on the
fallen tree, and all the wild animals lived
among its branches.[m] 14 Therefore no other trees by the waters are ever to tower
proudly on high, lifting their tops above
the thick foliage. No other trees so well-
watered are ever to reach such a height;
they are all destined for death,[n] for the
earth below, among mortals who go down
to the realm of the dead.[o]

15 " 'This is what the Sovereign LORD
says: On the day it was brought down to
the realm of the dead I covered the deep
springs with mourning for it; I held back
its streams, and its abundant waters were
restrained. Because of it I clothed Lebanon
with gloom, and all the trees of the field
withered away. 16 I made the nations tremble[p] at the sound of its fall when I brought
it down to the realm of the dead to be with
those who go down to the pit. Then all
the trees[q] of Eden, the choicest and best
of Lebanon, the well-watered trees, were
consoled[r] in the earth below.[s] 17 They too,
like the great cedar, had gone down to the
realm of the dead, to those killed by the
sword,[t] along with the armed men who
lived in its shade among the nations.

18 " 'Which of the trees of Eden can be
compared with you in splendor and majesty? Yet you, too, will be brought down
with the trees of Eden to the earth below;
you will lie among the uncircumcised,[u]
with those killed by the sword.

" 'This is Pharaoh and all his hordes, declares the Sovereign LORD.' "

A Lament Over Pharaoh

32 In the twelfth year, in the twelfth
month on the first day, the word of
the LORD came to me:[v] 2 "Son of man, take
up a lament[w] concerning Pharaoh king of
Egypt and say to him:

31:5 [b] Eze 17:5 **31:6** [c] Eze 17:23; Mt 13:32 **31:8** [d] Ps 80:10 [e] Ge 2:8-9 **31:9** [f] Ge 2:8 [g] Ge 13:10; Eze 28:13 **31:10** [h] Isa 14:13-14; Eze 28:17 **31:11** [i] Da 5:20 **31:12** [j] Eze 28:7 [k] Eze 32:5; 35:8 [l] Eze 32:11-12; Da 4:14 **31:13** [m] Isa 18:6; Eze 29:5; 32:4 **31:14** [n] Ps 82:7 [o] Ps 63:9; Eze 26:20; 32:24 **31:16** [p] Eze 26:15 [q] Isa 14:8 [r] Eze 14:22; 32:31 [s] Isa 14:15; Eze 32:18 **31:17** [t] Ps 9:17 **31:18** [u] Jer 9:26; Eze 32:19,21 **32:1** [v] Eze 31:1; 33:21 **32:2** [w] Eze 19:1; 27:2

31:8 *garden of God.* Identified as Eden here; however, it is not invoking the image of a utopian home that humans had been driven out of. Unlike the paradise motif in the Bible, the Mesopotamian garden of the gods was not a paradise that humans had occupied and then lost, but it was the beautiful protected property of the gods that humans trespassed at their peril. Such was the cedar forest that Gilgamesh and his companion Enkidu gained access to when they defeated the divinely appointed guardian of the forest, Huwawa. These gardens, like the royal gardens of this period, were wooded parks featuring beautiful and exotic trees. This description is also appropriate for the Biblical Eden.

31:12 *cut it down.* The fall of the great Assyrian Empire has been described by modern scholars as a "historical scandal." It was at its height in the early seventh century BC, when it successfully conquered Egypt. However, a great civil war in 652–648 BC showed the inherent weakness of the huge state. After the devastation of the civil war, Assyria quickly weakened. By the end of Ashurbanipal's reign (either 631 or 627 BC) all economic and other textual sources disappear from Nineveh, the Assyrian capital. By 626 BC the Chaldeans of Babylonia had declared their independence. Within 14 years all of the major Assyrian cities had been destroyed, the monarchy had fled to Harran in Syria, and the army was in chaos. The Assyrians may have participated in the battle of Carchemish against Nebuchadnezzar but were never heard from again. Thus, within the 40 or so years after the great civil war, Assyria had been consigned to oblivion.

31:15–16 *Lebanon ... Eden.* This comparison draws together the Biblical motif of Eden, as the protected property of Yahweh, and the Mesopotamian motif of the cedar forest, as the protected property of the gods. See note on v. 8.

32:1 *twelfth year ... twelfth month ... first day.* Mar. 3, 585 BC, a few months after the report of the fall of Jerusalem had reached Ezekiel.

32:2 *like a lion.* The Egyptian pharaohs compared themselves with the lion. Seti I (1318–1301 BC) attacked a fortified palace and on the wall of the temple in Karnak describes himself as victor who prevailed over them like

"'You are like a lion[x] among the nations;
you are like a monster in the seas
thrashing about in your streams,
churning the water with your feet
and muddying the streams.[y]

3"'This is what the Sovereign LORD says:

"'With a great throng of people
I will cast my net over you,
and they will haul you up in my net.[z]
4I will throw you on the land
and hurl you on the open field.
I will let all the birds of the sky settle on you
and all the animals of the wild gorge themselves on you.[a]
5I will spread your flesh on the mountains
and fill the valleys[b] with your remains.
6I will drench the land with your flowing blood[c]
all the way to the mountains,
and the ravines will be filled with your flesh.
7When I snuff you out, I will cover the heavens
and darken their stars;
I will cover the sun with a cloud,
and the moon will not give its light.[d]
8All the shining lights in the heavens
I will darken over you;
I will bring darkness over your land,
declares the Sovereign LORD.
9I will trouble the hearts of many peoples
when I bring about your destruction
among the nations,
among[a] lands you have not known.
10I will cause many peoples to be appalled at you,
and their kings will shudder with horror because of you
when I brandish my sword before them.
On the day[e] of your downfall
each of them will tremble
every moment for his life.[f]

11"'For this is what the Sovereign LORD says:

32:2 [x]Eze 19:3, 6; Na 2:11-13 [y]Eze 29:3; 34:18 **32:3** [z]Eze 12:13 **32:4** [a]Isa 18:6; Eze 31:12-13 **32:5** [b]Eze 31:12 **32:6** [c]Isa 34:3 **32:7** [d]Isa 13:10; 34:4; Eze 30:3; Joel 2:2, 31; 3:15; Mt 24:29; Rev 8:12 **32:10** [e]Jer 46:10 [f]Eze 26:16; 27:35

[a] 9 Hebrew; Septuagint *bring you into captivity among the nations, / to*

a fierce lion. Rameses III (1195 – 1164 BC) describes his battle against the Sea Peoples (i.e., the Philistines) in a similar vein. *monster in the seas.* The monster in this case is not located in the Nile River but "in the seas." This reference is probably to the cosmic monsters destroyed by God (see the article "Chaos Monsters," p. 953). In the Bible, as well as in the ancient Near East, the sea represents chaos and nonorder, as do the sea monsters (i.e., chaos creatures) that live there. The obvious physical struggle between the sea and the land, as well as the fierce, seemingly unstoppable energy displayed by the savage sea, gave rise to cosmic myths in the ancient Near East. The *Enuma Elish* creation epic from Babylon describes how Marduk vanquishes Tiamat while this goddess of watery chaos is in the form of a dragon. Much of the Baal Cycle in Ugaritic legend involves Baal's struggle against his rival Yamm, the god of the sea. Similarly, the Baal Cycle claims that both Anat and Baal conquered Litan, the seven-headed dragon, and thus gained mastery over the seas. In Ps 104:26 (see note there), Yahweh is said to play with Leviathan (see the article "Leviathan," p. 874), and in Job 41:1 – 11, God challenges Job to show his control over Leviathan as God does. The kingdoms represented by these beasts are therefore associated with the forces of chaos that bring disorder to God's world and need to be overcome (see notes on Da 7). The imagery of this chapter demonstrates that Ezekiel and his audience were familiar with the mythological literature from the culture they now lived in. For Ezekiel allusions to this imagery — sometimes blatant, other times subtle — serve as a framework for his prophetic message. The parallel between lion and monster (i.e., dragon) seems strange to us, but it was not at all unusual in Ezekiel's world. The famous Ishtar Gate in Babylon and the procession way leading up to it used glazed bricks to create alternating images of lions and dragons. Additionally, in the mythological traditions of Mesopotamia, a composite creature that combined lion and dragon features was common. This is especially true of Labbu in the Labbu Myth. From as early as the beginning of the second millennium BC, kings used lion and dragon in parallel to describe themselves. *churning the water … muddying the streams.* This description indicates a typical mythical scene in which the churning of the cosmic ocean disturbs the creatures (often sea monsters), who represent the forces of chaos and nonorder. In the *Enuma Elish* creation epic, the sky-god, Anu, creates the four winds that stir up the deep and its goddess, Tiamat. Here it is the monster who churns up the sea with the threat that chaos will bring disorder to the world.

32:3 *haul you up in my net.* In both "Erra and Ishum" and *Enuma Elish*, the creature representing the forces of chaos (Anzu and Tiamat, respectively) are captured in a net.

32:4 *all the birds … and all the animals … gorge themselves on you.* In the Labbu Myth, Labbu is described as a monster that is 50 miles (80 kilometers) long and a mile (1.6 kilometers) wide.

32:5 – 6 In his description of carnage and destruction, Ezekiel uses some stereotypical formulations and literary motifs found in Assyrian cuneiform inscriptions. Kings such as Tiglath-Pileser I (1115 – 1077 BC) and Ashurnasirpal I (1049 – 1031 BC) claim to have piled up corpses and dyed the mountains red with blood. In Tiglath-Pileser's inscription, as in vv. 5 – 6, one finds the three terms of "mountains" (v. 5), hollows ("ravines," v. 6), and plains ("valleys," v. 5). As in the Assyrian formulas, body and blood may be either in highland or lowland (vv. 5 – 6; 6:3; 31:12; 35:8; 36:4,6). In describing scenes of carnage, Ezekiel seems to follow a well-established ancient Near Eastern literary pattern. Besides these links with the language of royal inscriptions, in the Labbu Myth, the blood of the slain monster is said to flow for three years and three months.

32:7 – 8 These cosmic effects reflect the world-upside-down motif that is well known in the ancient world (see notes on Ps 107:33 – 35; Jer 4:23 – 26). It additionally strikes at the heart of the Egyptian religion that features the sun-god most prominently.

"'The sword of the king of Babylon[g]
will come against you.
12 I will cause your hordes to fall
by the swords of mighty men—
the most ruthless of all nations.[h]
They will shatter the pride of Egypt,
and all her hordes will be
overthrown.[i]
13 I will destroy all her cattle
from beside abundant waters
no longer to be stirred by the foot of
man
or muddied by the hooves of cattle.[j]
14 Then I will let her waters settle
and make her streams flow like oil,
declares the Sovereign LORD.
15 When I make Egypt desolate
and strip the land of everything in it,
when I strike down all who live there,
then they will know that I am the
LORD.[k]'

16 "This is the lament[l] they will chant
for her. The daughters of the nations will
chant it; for Egypt and all her hordes they
will chant it, declares the Sovereign LORD."

Egypt's Descent Into the Realm of the Dead

17 In the twelfth year, on the fifteenth
day of the month, the word of the LORD
came to me:[m] 18 "Son of man, wail for
the hordes of Egypt and consign[n] to the
earth below both her and the daughters of
mighty nations, along with those who go
down to the pit.[o] 19 Say to them, 'Are you
more favored than others? Go down and
be laid among the uncircumcised.'[p] 20 They
will fall among those killed by the sword.
The sword is drawn; let her be dragged[q]
off with all her hordes. 21 From within the
realm of the dead[r] the mighty leaders will
say of Egypt and her allies, 'They have
come down and they lie with the uncircumcised, with those killed by the sword.'
22 "Assyria is there with her whole army;
she is surrounded by the graves of all her
slain, all who have fallen by the sword.
23 Their graves are in the depths of the pit[s]
and her army lies around her grave. All
who had spread terror in the land of the
living are slain, fallen by the sword.
24 "Elam[t] is there, with all her hordes
around her grave. All of them are slain,
fallen by the sword.[u] All who had spread
terror in the land of the living[v] went down
uncircumcised to the earth below. They
bear their shame with those who go down
to the pit.[w] 25 A bed is made for her among
the slain, with all her hordes around her
grave. All of them are uncircumcised,
killed by the sword. Because their terror
had spread in the land of the living, they
bear their shame with those who go down
to the pit; they are laid among the slain.
26 "Meshek and Tubal[x] are there, with
all their hordes around their graves. All
of them are uncircumcised, killed by the
sword because they spread their terror in

32:11 [g] Jer 46:26 **32:12** [h] Eze 28:7 [i] Eze 31:11-12 **32:13** [j] Eze 29:8, 11 **32:15** [k] Ex 7:5; 14:4, 18; Ps 107:33-34; Eze 6:7 **32:16** [l] 2Sa 1:17; 2Ch 35:25; Eze 26:17 **32:17** [m] ver 1 **32:18** [n] Jer 1:10 [o] Eze 31:14, 16; Mic 1:8 **32:19** [p] ver 29-30; Eze 28:10; 31:18 **32:20** [q] Ps 28:3 **32:21** [r] Isa 14:9 **32:23** [s] Isa 14:15 **32:24** [t] Ge 10:22 [u] Jer 49:37 [v] Job 28:13 [w] Eze 26:20 **32:26** [x] Ge 10:2; Eze 27:13

32:17 *twelfth year … fifteenth day.* Mar. 17, 585 BC, two weeks later than the date mentioned in 32:1.
32:19 *laid among the uncircumcised.* Egyptian priests and kings were circumcised. The disdain the Israelites felt for the uncircumcised is well attested in the Bible (Ge 34:14; Jdg 14:3). This verse reflects the view that Egypt's rulers felt the same. To be buried among the uncircumcised was an additional affront, adding insult to injury.
32:20 *They will fall among those killed by the sword.* Pharaoh and his hordes will die on the battlefield and be subject to ignominy. Battle-fallen corpses were stripped, plundered and sometimes beheaded by the victors. Ancient Near Eastern reliefs often depict naked and headless bodies. Their remains were buried in mass graves (39:11–16).
32:22–30 The nations listed in vv. 22–30 all suffered significant devastation. Ezekiel probably has in mind the final defeat and destruction of the Assyrian Empire at the end of the sixth century BC. The Assyrian armies were destroyed at the battle of Carchemish by Nebuchadnezzar of Babylon. Thus, the imagery sees that the final end of Assyria is in Sheol, the "realm of the dead" (v. 21).
32:24 *Elam.* It, with its capital Susa, was located on the Iranian plateau. It was devastated by the Assyrian king Ashurbanipal during a two-year campaign (647–646 BC). Ashurbanipal boasts of having devastated Elam to such a degree that the country returned to its original condition of wild, uninhabited land. The beasts could roam freely, unafraid of humans, who were no more. In the mid-sixth century BC, Elam was absorbed in the empire of the Medes and Persians.
32:26 *Meshek and Tubal.* At the end of the eighth century BC, these two Anatolian kingdoms were ravaged by internal warfare, conquered by Sargon II of Assyria, and invaded by the Cimmerians (from what is today southern Russia). Unfortunately, little of their history survives from the seventh and early sixth centuries BC. It is thought that Meshek and Tubal were incorporated under Lydian control after the conclusion of the Cimmerian wars. In the spring of 585 BC, the Lydians are at war with the Medes (see note on v. 1; see the article "Gog, of the Land of Magog," p. 1394). Meshek and Tubal are mentioned again in the Persian period as separate ethnic identities. They are known to the Assyrians as Mushku (central Anatolia) and Tabal (eastern Anatolia) and to Herodotus as Moschi and Tibarenoi (subject states of the Persian Empire). At the end of the eighth century, the king of Mushku was Mita, known to the Greeks as Midas, the king with the golden touch. His tomb has been identified at Gordion and excavated. *hordes around their graves.* Ezekiel's tour of the netherworld resembles a similar description found in "The Vision of the Netherworld by an Assyrian Crown Prince." In this cuneiform composition from Ashur dating from around 670 BC, an Assyrian prince in his dream tours the netherworld during a night vision. He sees 15 different underworld divinities and describes each one in great detail. The Assyrian prince is sent back to earth with a specific mission: to proclaim to the living what he had seen. It therefore seems that in his vision of the netherworld, Ezekiel draws on a well-established ancient Near Eastern genre: descriptions of the denizens of the netherworld and the prophetic commissioning of warning the living

the land of the living. 27 But they do not lie with the fallen warriors of old,[a] who went down to the realm of the dead with their weapons of war — their swords placed under their heads and their shields[b] resting on their bones — though these warriors also had terrorized the land of the living.

28 "You too, Pharaoh, will be broken and will lie among the uncircumcised, with those killed by the sword.

29 "Edom[y] is there, her kings and all her princes; despite their power, they are laid with those killed by the sword. They lie with the uncircumcised, with those who go down to the pit.[z]

30 "All the princes of the north[a] and all the Sidonians[b] are there; they went down with the slain in disgrace despite the terror caused by their power. They lie uncircumcised with those killed by the sword and bear their shame with those who go down to the pit.

31 "Pharaoh — he and all his army — will see them and he will be consoled[c] for all his hordes that were killed by the sword, declares the Sovereign LORD. 32 Although I had him spread terror in the land of the living, Pharaoh and all his hordes will be laid among the uncircumcised, with those killed by the sword, declares the Sovereign LORD."

Renewal of Ezekiel's Call as Watchman

33 The word of the LORD came to me: 2 "Son of man, speak to your people and say to them: 'When I bring the sword[d] against a land, and the people of the land choose one of their men and make him their watchman,[e] 3 and he sees the sword coming against the land and blows the trumpet[f] to warn the people, 4 then if anyone hears the trumpet but does not heed the warning[g] and the sword comes and takes their life, their blood will be on their own head.[h] 5 Since they heard the sound of the trumpet but did not heed the warning, their blood will be on their own head. If they had heeded the warning, they would have saved themselves. 6 But if the watchman sees the sword coming and does not blow the trumpet to warn the people and the sword comes and takes someone's life, that person's life will be taken because of their sin, but I will hold the watchman accountable for their blood.'[i]

7 "Son of man, I have made you a watchman for the people of Israel; so hear the word I speak and give them warning from me.[j] 8 When I say to the wicked, 'You wicked person, you will surely die,[k]' and you do not speak out to dissuade them from their ways, that wicked person will die for[c] their sin, and I will hold you accountable for their blood.[l] 9 But if you do warn the wicked person to turn from their ways and they do not do so, they will die for their sin, though you yourself will be saved.[m]

10 "Son of man, say to the Israelites, 'This is what you are saying: "Our offenses and sins weigh us down, and we are wasting away[n] because of[d] them. How then can we live?[o]"' 11 Say to them, 'As surely as I live, declares the Sovereign LORD, I take

32:29 [y] Isa 34:5-15; Jer 49:7; Eze 35:15; Ob 1:1 [z] Eze 25:12-14 **32:30** [a] Jer 25:26; Eze 38:6; 39:2 [b] Jer 25:22; Eze 28:21 **32:31** [c] Eze 14:22; 31:16 **33:2** [d] Jer 12:12 [e] Eze 3:11 **33:3** [f] Hos 8:1 **33:4** [g] 2Ch 25:16 [h] Jer 6:17; Eze 18:13; Zec 1:4; Ac 18:6 **33:6** [i] Eze 3:18 **33:7** [j] Jer 26:2; Eze 3:17 **33:8** [k] ver 14 [l] Eze 18:4 **33:9** [m] Eze 3:17-19 **33:10** [n] Eze 24:23 [o] Lev 26:39; Eze 4:17

[a] *27* Septuagint; Hebrew *warriors who were uncircumcised* [b] *27* Probable reading of the original Hebrew text; Masoretic Text *punishment* [c] *8* Or *in;* also in verse 9 [d] *10* Or *away in*

about the frightening conditions that reign there. Contrary to the polytheistic description of the netherworld in the Assyrian text, in Ezekiel's vision of the realm of the dead, there are no distinctive divinities charged with managing the realm.

32:27 *swords placed under their heads.* In the netherworld the dead warriors lay down their swords, insignia of their power. In the Gilgamesh Epic, the dead kings also have to lay down their crowns. There Enkidu describes what he sees in the netherworld, the House of Darkness, the abode of Irkalla: "In the House of Dust, which I entered, I looked at [rulers], their crowns put away" (7.4.40 – 41).

32:29 *Edom.* A Semitic-speaking neighbor of Judah, it was south and east of the Dead Sea (see note on Jer 49:7). In the eighth century BC Edom fell under the control of the Assyrians, as noted in the annals of Tiglath-Pileser III (745 – 727 BC), and continued under their rule until the death of Ashurbanipal a century later. During that time the Edomites were often conscripted into the Assyrian armies, and thus they figure often in the annals. During the Babylonian period Edom evidently sided with the great empire, although there are not extra-Biblical records to verify this. It is likely that they submitted themselves to Nebuchadnezzar's rule in 605 BC. Although some Judahite refugees may have found shelter in Edom, it apparently remained passive as Jerusalem was destroyed (see Ps 137:7; Ob 11). The Babylonian campaign against Ammon and Moab in 594 BC seems not to have affected Edom. It is likely that they remained unscathed until the time of Nabonidus's campaign in 552 BC.

32:30 *princes of the north.* Most likely Aramean rulers or sheiks. There were a number of hostile Aramean kingdoms north of Israel/Judah, the largest was centered in Damascus.

33:2 *watchman.* He stands at the place in the city where he has the most strategic view of the surroundings and watches for any approaching enemy army. He either reports by word of mouth or by trumpet. His task is simply to sound the alarm of the approaching enemy. He is absolved of responsibility if the city dwellers refuse to heed his call. Ezekiel's portrayal of himself as prophetic watchman is similar to Isaiah's (Isa 21:6 – 9) and Jeremiah's charges (Jer 6:17). Though no similar label has been found attached to prophets in the ancient Near East, the concept is familiar enough. The prophets were expected to be able to warn the king of impending situations (in military or cultic realms) that might jeopardize his person or the stability of his kingdom. The spiritual sense used in vv. 2 – 20 is picked up (probably from Ezekiel) in the Dead Sea Scrolls sectarian documents where the leader of the community is on the lookout for the judgment of God.

33:3 *trumpet.* See note on Jos 6:4.

no pleasure in the death of the wicked,
but rather that they turn from their ways
and live.[p] Turn! Turn from your evil ways!
Why will you die, people of Israel?'[q]
12"Therefore, son of man, say to your
people, 'If someone who is righteous disobeys, that person's former righteousness
will count for nothing. And if someone
who is wicked repents, that person's former wickedness will not bring condemnation. The righteous person who sins will
not be allowed to live even though they
were formerly righteous.'[r] 13If I tell a righteous person that they will surely live, but
then they trust in their righteousness and
do evil, none of the righteous things that
person has done will be remembered; they
will die for the evil they have done.[s] 14And
if I say to a wicked person, 'You will surely die,' but they then turn away from their
sin and do what is just[t] and right— 15if
they give back what they took in pledge
for a loan, return what they have stolen,[u]
follow the decrees that give life, and do
no evil—that person will surely live; they
will not die.[v] 16None of the sins that person has committed will be remembered
against them. They have done what is just
and right; they will surely live.[w]
17"Yet your people say, 'The way of the
Lord is not just.' But it is their way that is
not just. 18If a righteous person turns from
their righteousness and does evil, they will
die for it.[x] 19And if a wicked person turns
away from their wickedness and does
what is just and right, they will live by doing so. 20Yet you Israelites say, 'The way of
the Lord is not just.' But I will judge each
of you according to your own ways."

Jerusalem's Fall Explained

21In the twelfth year of our exile, in the
tenth month on the fifth day, a man who
had escaped[y] from Jerusalem came to me
and said, "The city has fallen![z]" 22Now the
evening before the man arrived, the hand
of the LORD was on me,[a] and he opened
my mouth[b] before the man came to me
in the morning. So my mouth was opened
and I was no longer silent.[c]
23Then the word of the LORD came to me:
24"Son of man, the people living in those
ruins[d] in the land of Israel are saying,
'Abraham was only one man, yet he possessed the land. But we are many; surely
the land has been given to us as our possession.'[e] 25Therefore say to them, 'This is
what the Sovereign LORD says: Since you
eat meat with the blood[f] still in it and look
to your idols and shed blood, should you
then possess the land?[g] 26You rely on your
sword, you do detestable things, and each
of you defiles his neighbor's wife.[h] Should
you then possess the land?'
27"Say this to them: 'This is what the
Sovereign LORD says: As surely as I live,
those who are left in the ruins will fall by
the sword, those out in the country I will
give to the wild animals to be devoured,
and those in strongholds and caves will
die of a plague.[i] 28I will make the land a
desolate waste, and her proud strength
will come to an end, and the mountains of
Israel will become desolate so that no one
will cross them. 29Then they will know
that I am the LORD, when I have made the
land a desolate waste because of all the
detestable things they have done.'
30"As for you, son of man, your people
are talking together about you by the walls
and at the doors of the houses, saying to
each other, 'Come and hear the message
that has come from the LORD.' 31My people come to you, as they usually do, and
sit before[j] you to hear your words, but
they do not put them into practice. Their
mouths speak of love, but their hearts are
greedy for unjust gain.[k] 32Indeed, to them

33:11 [p] Eze 18:32; 2Pe 3:9 [q] Eze 18:23
33:12 [r] 2Ch 7:14; Eze 3:20
33:13 [s] Eze 18:24; Heb 10:38; 2Pe 2:20-21
33:14 [t] Eze 18:27
33:15 [u] Ex 22:1-4; Lev 6:2-5 [v] Eze 20:11; Lk 19:8
33:16 [w] Isa 43:25; Eze 18:22
33:18 [x] Eze 3:20; Eze 18:26
33:21 [y] Eze 24:26 [z] 2Ki 25:4, 10; Jer 39:1-2; Eze 32:1
33:22 [a] Eze 1:3 [b] Lk 1:64 [c] Eze 3:26-27; 24:27
33:24 [d] Eze 36:4 [e] Isa 51:2; Jer 40:7; Eze 11:15; Ac 7:5
33:25 [f] Ge 9:4; Dt 12:16 [g] Jer 7:9-10; Eze 22:6, 27
33:26 [h] Eze 22:11
33:27 [i] 1Sa 13:6; Isa 2:19; Jer 42:22; Eze 39:4
33:31 [j] Eze 8:1 [k] Ps 78:36-37; Isa 29:13; Eze 22:27; Mt 13:22; 1Jn 3:18

33:15 *pledge for a loan.* Pledges for loans were customary throughout the ancient Near East. Thousands of loan contracts have been uncovered from Mesopotamia, showing that it was quite an ordinary procedure. At Terqa in Middle Bronze Age Syria, a certain Puzurum made a loan at the local temple of the sun-god Shamash. He retained one half of a cuneiform contract, while the temple (functioning in this case as a bank) retained the other. Thus, the half retained by the temple functioned as a receipt. When Puzurum paid off the loan, the temple returned to him the temple's half of the contract. The return of a pledge by a repentant wicked person suggests that an oppressive debt situation was resolved with the debt being forgiven.
33:21 *twelfth year ... tenth month ... fifth day.* Jan. 19, 585 BC. It is about five months after the fall of Jerusalem. *a man who had escaped from Jerusalem.* Most commentaries agree that this is not a fugitive, or even a refugee, but one of the survivors who has been brought captive to Babylon with the first wave of exiles from the destruction.
33:25 *you eat meat with the blood still in it.* Although every major translation uses the same phrase in this verse, in context it should read "you eat over the blood," referring to a pagan rite mentioned in Lev 19:26 (see note there) and formally banned as a form of divination. Documents from the second and first millennia BC attest to a similar practice throughout the ancient Near East. A pit or a hole was dug in order to call up the spirits of the netherworld. The diviner poured libations around the pit and sacrificed an animal. Its blood was poured into the pit and the spirits of the netherworld were invoked.
33:27 *wild animals.* They were a constant source of fear for city dwellers throughout the ancient Near East. In Assyrian texts and reliefs of this period the kings are seen hunting lions to symbolically rid the city of the scourge of wild beasts. Sometimes invading armies were represented metaphorically as wild beasts.
33:32 *love songs.* Love (or erotic) songs had long been sources of entertainment for city dwellers. The itinerant

you are nothing more than one who sings
love songs with a beautiful voice and plays
an instrument well, for they hear your
words but do not put them into practice.[l]
33“When all this comes true — and it
surely will — then they will know that a
prophet has been among them.[m]”

The LORD Will Be Israel’s Shepherd

34 The word of the LORD came to me:
2“Son of man, prophesy against the
shepherds of Israel; prophesy and say to
them: ‘This is what the Sovereign LORD
says: Woe to you shepherds of Israel who
only take care of yourselves! Should not
shepherds take care of the flock?[n] 3You eat
the curds, clothe yourselves with the wool
and slaughter the choice animals, but you
do not take care of the flock.[o] 4You have
not strengthened the weak or healed the
sick or bound up the injured. You have
not brought back the strays or searched
for the lost. You have ruled them harshly
and brutally.[p] 5So they were scattered because there was no shepherd,[q] and when
they were scattered they became food for
all the wild animals.[r] 6My sheep wandered
over all the mountains and on every high
hill. They were scattered over the whole
earth, and no one searched or looked for
them.[s]
7“ ‘Therefore, you shepherds, hear the
word of the LORD: 8As surely as I live, declares the Sovereign LORD, because my
flock lacks a shepherd and so has been
plundered and has become food for all the
wild animals, and because my shepherds
did not search for my flock but cared
for themselves rather than for my flock,
9therefore, you shepherds, hear the word
of the LORD: 10This is what the Sovereign
LORD says: I am against[t] the shepherds and
will hold them accountable for my flock.
I will remove them from tending the flock
so that the shepherds can no longer feed
themselves. I will rescue[u] my flock from
their mouths, and it will no longer be food
for them.[v]
11“ ‘For this is what the Sovereign LORD
says: I myself will search for my sheep and
look after them. 12As a shepherd[w] looks
after his scattered flock when he is with
them, so will I look after my sheep. I will
rescue them from all the places where
they were scattered on a day of clouds and
darkness.[x] 13I will bring them out from the
nations and gather them from the countries, and I will bring them into their own
land. I will pasture them on the mountains
of Israel, in the ravines and in all the settlements in the land.[y] 14I will tend them in
a good pasture, and the mountain heights

33:32 [l] Mk 6:20 **33:33** [m] 1Sa 3:20; Jer 28:9; Eze 2:5 **34:2** [n] Ps 78:70-72; Isa 40:11; Jer 3:15; 23:1; Mic 3:11; Jn 10:11; 21:15-17 **34:3** [o] Isa 56:11; Eze 22:27; Zec 11:16 **34:4** [p] Zec 11:15-17 **34:5** [q] Nu 27:17 [r] ver 28; Isa 56:9 **34:6** [s] Ps 142:4; 1Pe 2:25 **34:10** [t] Jer 21:13 [u] Ps 72:14 [v] 1Sa 2:29-30; Zec 10:3 **34:12** [w] Isa 40:11; Jer 31:10; Lk 19:10 [x] Eze 30:3 **34:13** [y] Jer 23:3

singer of songs traveled from town to town, entertaining the people. Many of these songs were eventually written down in the cuneiform record. Portions of the Gilgamesh Epic may well have been sung to the city dwellers in Sumer in much the same way that Homer’s *Iliad* and *Odyssey* were sung by traveling poets before being written down centuries later. Love songs are connected to ritual marriage texts (the Tammuz liturgy) in Sumerian times and were popular in Egypt during the second half of the second millennium BC (Eighteenth and Nineteenth Dynasties). It is a severe indictment that the people have reduced the role of the messenger of God to mere entertainment.

34:2 *shepherds of Israel.* The association of kingship with shepherding is a typical ancient Near Eastern manner of viewing monarchy. Royal authority belonged to God or the gods; the king exercised it on behalf of the gods. The sheep belonged to the divine ruler; the king was the earthly caretaker. The people as a flock were given in trust, and eventually the king was called to account for his exercise of the office of shepherd. The judgment against the shepherds of Israel in ch. 34 indicates that Israelite kings often came up short in meeting the demands of their divine commissioning as shepherds of their people. See notes on 1Ch 11:2; Ps 23:1.

34:3 The three staple by-products of sheep and goats (goats’ milk/curds, sheep’s wool, meat) are used here to extend the metaphor of the leaders gleaning all the benefits but not fulfilling their responsibilities. Royal and priestly administrations were of necessity supported by the population through taxations of various sorts, but it was expected that the population would in turn benefit rather than be exploited.

34:4 Verse 3 concerned the privileges of the shepherd (see previous note). Verse 4 turns to the neglected responsibilities. The metaphor goes beyond the normal responsibilities of making sure that the sheep are protected and fed. Instead it focuses on the remedial duties, caring for the sick and finding the lost. These equate to the need for kings to bring about justice for alienated and disenfranchised people such as the widow and orphan (see notes on Ps 72; Isa 1:17; see also the articles “Enthronement in the Ancient Near East,” p. 925; “Coronation Hymns in the Ancient Near East,” p. 949).

34:12 *I look after my sheep.* The portrayal of the Lord in the role of a shepherd follows a common Near Eastern notion of deities, such as the Semitic sun-god Shamash, functioning as shepherds over their people. This perception is also reflected in divine epithets, such as Marduk being “the shepherd of the people,” and Akkadian personal names like “Marduk has shepherded me” and “Shamash is my shepherd.” All of this readily brings to mind the imagery of Ps 23. The idea of the God of Israel being a shepherd of his people goes back to the time of the nomadic existence of the patriarchs, who, like Jacob, acknowledged God as “my shepherd all my life” (Ge 48:15).

34:13 *I will … gather them from the countries.* The imagery of gathering the people of Israel from among the countries where they have been scattered has a long history in the ancient Near Eastern royal ideology. In the prologue to his law code, the Babylonian king Hammurapi (1792 – 1750 BC) boasts of being the one who gathers together the scattered people of Isin, a city in southern Mesopotamia. He further declares concerning other parts of Mesopotamia that he gathered scattered populations and pastured them with blessing and prosperity. To gather the scattered people is the prerogative of the patron deity of a city or nation. It is a symbol of recovered prosperity and security. See note on 11:17.

of Israel[z] will be their grazing land. There
they will lie down in good grazing land,
and there they will feed in a rich pasture[a] on the mountains of Israel.[b] 15 I myself will tend my sheep and have them
lie down, declares the Sovereign LORD.[c]
16 I will search for the lost and bring back
the strays. I will bind up the injured and
strengthen the weak,[d] but the sleek and
the strong I will destroy. I will shepherd
the flock with justice.[e]

17 " 'As for you, my flock, this is what the
Sovereign LORD says: I will judge between
one sheep and another, and between rams
and goats.[f] 18 Is it not enough for you to
feed on the good pasture? Must you also
trample the rest of your pasture with your
feet? Is it not enough for you to drink clear
water? Must you also muddy the rest with
your feet? 19 Must my flock feed on what
you have trampled and drink what you
have muddied with your feet?

20 " 'Therefore this is what the Sovereign
LORD says to them: See, I myself will judge
between the fat sheep and the lean sheep.
21 Because you shove with flank and shoulder, butting all the weak sheep with your
horns[g] until you have driven them away,
22 I will save my flock, and they will no
longer be plundered. I will judge between
one sheep and another.[h] 23 I will place over
them one shepherd, my servant David,
and he will tend[i] them; he will tend them
and be their shepherd. 24 I the LORD will
be their God,[j] and my servant David will
be prince among them. I the LORD have
spoken.[k]

25 " 'I will make a covenant of peace with
them and rid the land of savage beasts[l]
so that they may live in the wilderness
and sleep in the forests in safety.[m] 26 I will
make them and the places surrounding my
hill a blessing.[a][n] I will send down showers
in season;[o] there will be showers of blessing.[p] 27 The trees will yield their fruit and
the ground will yield its crops; the people will be secure in their land. They will
know that I am the LORD, when I break the
bars of their yoke[q] and rescue them from
the hands of those who enslaved them.[r]
28 They will no longer be plundered by
the nations, nor will wild animals devour
them. They will live in safety, and no one
will make them afraid.[s] 29 I will provide for
them a land renowned[t] for its crops, and
they will no longer be victims of famine[u]
in the land or bear the scorn[v] of the nations.[w] 30 Then they will know that I, the
LORD their God, am with them and that
they, the Israelites, are my people, declares
the Sovereign LORD.[x] 31 You are my sheep,
the sheep of my pasture,[y] and I am your
God, declares the Sovereign LORD.' "

A Prophecy Against Edom

35 The word of the LORD came to me:
2 "Son of man, set your face against
Mount Seir; prophesy against it 3 and say:
'This is what the Sovereign LORD says: I am
against you, Mount Seir, and I will stretch
out my hand[z] against you and make you
a desolate waste.[a] 4 I will turn your towns
into ruins and you will be desolate. Then
you will know that I am the LORD.[b]

5 " 'Because you harbored an ancient
hostility and delivered the Israelites over
to the sword at the time of their calamity, the time their punishment reached its
climax,[c] 6 therefore as surely as I live, declares the Sovereign LORD, I will give you
over to bloodshed and it will pursue you.[d]
Since you did not hate bloodshed, bloodshed will pursue you. 7 I will make Mount
Seir a desolate waste and cut off from it all
who come and go. 8 I will fill your mountains with the slain; those killed by the
sword will fall on your hills and in your
valleys and in all your ravines.[e] 9 I will
make you desolate forever; your towns
will not be inhabited. Then you will know
that I am the LORD.[f]

10 " 'Because you have said, "These two

[a] 26 Or *I will cause them and the places surrounding my hill to be named in blessings* (see Gen. 48:20); or *I will cause them and the places surrounding my hill to be seen as blessed*

34:14 [z] Eze 20:40 [a] Ps 23:2 [b] Eze 36:29-30 **34:15** [c] Ps 23:1-2 **34:16** [d] Mic 4:6 [e] Isa 10:16; Lk 5:32 **34:17** [f] Mt 25:32-33 **34:21** [g] Dt 33:17 **34:22** [h] Ps 72:12-14; Jer 23:2-3 **34:23** [i] Isa 40:11 **34:24** [j] Eze 36:28 [k] Jer 30:9 **34:25** [l] Lev 26:6 [m] Isa 11:6-9; Hos 2:18 **34:26** [n] Ge 12:2 [o] Ps 68:9 [p] Dt 11:13-15; Isa 44:3

34:27 [q] Lev 26:13 [r] Jer 30:8 **34:28** [s] Jer 30:10; Eze 39:26 **34:29** [t] Isa 4:2 [u] Eze 36:29 [v] Eze 36:6 [w] Eze 36:15 **34:30** [x] Eze 14:11; 37:27 **34:31** [y] Ps 100:3; Jer 23:1 **35:3** [z] Jer 6:12 [a] Eze 25:12-14 **35:4** [b] ver 9 **35:5** [c] Ps 137:7; Eze 21:29 **35:6** [d] Isa 63:2-6 **35:8** [e] Eze 31:12 **35:9** [f] Jer 49:13

34:23 *I will place over them one shepherd, my servant David.* Ezekiel's hope of a divinely appointed king in the context of national restoration agrees with a common Near Eastern pattern of restoration prophecies. The Akkadian Marduk Prophecy ends with an announcement of restoration and predicts the arrival of "a king of Babylon." The latter will preside over the renewal of the city and of its population. Other Akkadian prophecies announce the arrival of a series of kings, bearers of renewal. In these prophecies, however, no names of kings are given. They are usually referred to with generic terms like "king" or "prince." Nevertheless, in some prophecies there are enough circumstantial details to identify the kings in question. In a piece of Babylonian literature called the Dynastic Prophecy, behind the archaic title "King of Elam" one can identify the Persian king Cjebelyrus.

35:2 *Mount Seir.* The ancient name of the mountainous region south of the Dead Sea on both sides of the Rift Valley running south to the Gulf of Aqaba. The name Seir is found in the fourteenth-century BC Amarna letters from Egypt. According to Scripture, the mountains of Seir were occupied first by the Horites (Dt 2:12,22), who were later displaced by the Edomites. Seir became synonymous with the entire country of Edom.

35:5 *ancient hostility.* This verse addresses the longstanding dissension between Edom and Israel. Elsewhere in Scripture the Edomites are said to cheer when Nebuchadnezzar I destroyed Jerusalem (e.g., Ps 137; Joel 3:19; Ob 1 – 14). This is the only text that implies that the Edomites played an active role in the conquest.

nations and countries will be ours and
we will take possession[g] of them,” even
though I the LORD was there, 11therefore
as surely as I live, declares the Sovereign LORD, I will treat you in accordance
with the anger[h] and jealousy you showed
in your hatred of them and I will make
myself known among them when I judge
you.[i] 12Then you will know that I the LORD
have heard all the contemptible things
you have said against the mountains of
Israel. You said, “They have been laid
waste and have been given over to us to
devour.[j]” 13You boasted against me and
spoke against me without restraint, and
I heard it.[k] 14This is what the Sovereign
LORD says: While the whole earth rejoices, I will make you desolate.[l] 15Because
you rejoiced[m] when the inheritance of Israel became desolate, that is how I will
treat you. You will be desolate, Mount
Seir,[n] you and all of Edom.[o] Then they
will know that I am the LORD.’ ”

Hope for the Mountains of Israel

36 “Son of man, prophesy to the
mountains of Israel and say, ‘Mountains of Israel, hear the word of the LORD.
2This is what the Sovereign LORD says: The
enemy said of you, “Aha![p] The ancient
heights[q] have become our possession.[r]” ’
3Therefore prophesy and say, ‘This is what
the Sovereign LORD says: Because they ravaged and crushed you from every side so
that you became the possession of the rest
of the nations and the object of people’s
malicious talk and slander,[s] 4therefore,
mountains of Israel, hear the word of the
Sovereign LORD: This is what the Sovereign
LORD says to the mountains and hills, to
the ravines and valleys,[t] to the desolate ruins and the deserted towns that have been
plundered and ridiculed by the rest of the
nations around you[u]— 5this is what the
Sovereign LORD says: In my burning zeal
I have spoken against the rest of the nations, and against all Edom, for with glee
and with malice in their hearts they made
my land their own possession so that they
might plunder its pastureland.’[v] 6Therefore
prophesy concerning the land of Israel and
say to the mountains and hills, to the ravines and valleys: ‘This is what the Sovereign LORD says: I speak in my jealous
wrath because you have suffered the scorn
of the nations.[w] 7Therefore this is what the
Sovereign LORD says: I swear with uplifted
hand that the nations around you will also
suffer scorn.

8“ ‘But you, mountains of Israel, will
produce branches and fruit[x] for my people Israel, for they will soon come home.
9I am concerned for you and will look on
you with favor; you will be plowed and
sown, 10and I will cause many people to
live on you—yes, all of Israel. The towns
will be inhabited and the ruins rebuilt.[y]
11I will increase the number of people
and animals living on you, and they will
be fruitful and become numerous. I will
settle people on you as in the past[z] and
will make you prosper more than before.[a]
Then you will know that I am the LORD. 12I
will cause people, my people Israel, to live
on you. They will possess you, and you
will be their inheritance;[b] you will never
again deprive them of their children.

13“ ‘This is what the Sovereign LORD
says: Because some say to you, “You devour people[c] and deprive your nation
of its children,” 14therefore you will no
longer devour people or make your nation childless, declares the Sovereign
LORD. 15No longer will I make you hear
the taunts of the nations, and no longer
will you suffer the scorn of the peoples or
cause your nation to fall, declares the Sovereign LORD.[d]’ ”

Israel’s Restoration Assured

16Again the word of the LORD came to
me: 17“Son of man, when the people of Israel were living in their own land, they defiled it by their conduct and their actions.
Their conduct was like a woman’s monthly uncleanness in my sight.[e] 18So I poured
out[f] my wrath on them because they had
shed blood in the land and because they
had defiled it with their idols. 19I dispersed them among the nations, and they
were scattered[g] through the countries; I
judged them according to their conduct
and their actions.[h] 20And wherever they
went among the nations they profaned[i]
my holy name, for it was said of them,
‘These are the LORD’s people, and yet they
had to leave his land.’[j] 21I had concern for
my holy name, which the people of Israel
profaned among the nations where they
had gone.[k]

22“Therefore say to the Israelites, ‘This
is what the Sovereign LORD says: It is
not for your sake, people of Israel, that I
am going to do these things, but for the
sake of my holy name, which you have
profaned[l] among the nations where you
have gone.[m] 23I will show the holiness of
my great name, which has been profaned
among the nations, the name you have
profaned among them. Then the nations
will know that I am the LORD, declares the
Sovereign LORD, when I am proved holy[n]
through you before their eyes.[o]

24“ ‘For I will take you out of the nations; I will gather you from all the countries and bring you back into your own

35:10 [g] Ps 83:12; Eze 36:2, 5
35:11 [h] Eze 25:14 [i] Ps 9:16; Mt 7:2
35:12 [j] Jer 50:7
35:13 [k] Da 11:36
35:14 [l] Jer 51:48
35:15 [m] Ob 1:12 [n] ver 3 [o] Isa 34:5-6, 11; Jer 50:11-13; La 4:21
36:2 [p] Eze 25:3 [q] Dt 32:13 [r] Eze 35:10
36:3 [s] Ps 44:13-14
36:4 [t] Eze 6:3 [u] Dt 11:11; Ps 79:4; Eze 34:28
36:5 [v] Jer 50:11; Eze 25:12-14; 35:10, 15
36:6 [w] Ps 123:3-4; Eze 34:29
36:8 [x] Isa 27:6
36:10 [y] ver 33; Isa 49:17-23
36:11 [z] Mic 7:14 [a] Jer 31:28; Eze 16:55
36:12 [b] Eze 47:14, 22
36:13 [c] Nu 13:32
36:15 [d] Ps 89:50-51; Eze 34:29
36:17 [e] Jer 2:7
36:18 [f] 2Ch 34:21
36:19 [g] Dt 28:64 [h] Eze 39:24
36:20 [i] Ro 2:24 [j] Isa 52:5; Jer 33:24; Eze 12:16
36:21 [k] Ps 74:18; Isa 48:9
36:22 [l] Ro 2:24* [m] Ps 106:8
36:23 [n] Eze 20:41 [o] Ps 126:2; Isa 5:16

land.[p] 25 I will sprinkle[q] clean water on
you, and you will be clean; I will cleanse[r]
you from all your impurities and from all
your idols.[s] 26 I will give you a new heart[t]
and put a new spirit in you; I will remove
from you your heart of stone and give
you a heart of flesh.[u] 27 And I will put my
Spirit[v] in you and move you to follow my
decrees and be careful to keep my laws.
28 Then you will live in the land I gave
your ancestors; you will be my people,[w]
and I will be your God.[x] 29 I will save you
from all your uncleanness. I will call for
the grain and make it plentiful and will
not bring famine[y] upon you. 30 I will increase the fruit of the trees and the crops
of the field, so that you will no longer suffer disgrace among the nations because of
famine.[z] 31 Then you will remember your
evil ways and wicked deeds, and you will
loathe yourselves for your sins and detestable practices.[a] 32 I want you to know that
I am not doing this for your sake, declares
the Sovereign LORD. Be ashamed and disgraced for your conduct, people of Israel![b]
33 " 'This is what the Sovereign LORD
says: On the day I cleanse you from all
your sins, I will resettle your towns, and
the ruins will be rebuilt. 34 The desolate land will be cultivated instead of lying desolate in the sight of all who pass
through it. 35 They will say, "This land that
was laid waste has become like the garden
of Eden;[c] the cities that were lying in ruins, desolate and destroyed, are now fortified and inhabited.[d]" 36 Then the nations
around you that remain will know that I
the LORD have rebuilt what was destroyed
and have replanted what was desolate. I
the LORD have spoken, and I will do it.'[e]
37 "This is what the Sovereign LORD says:
Once again I will yield to Israel's plea and
do this for them: I will make their people
as numerous as sheep, 38 as numerous as
the flocks for offerings[f] at Jerusalem during her appointed festivals. So will the ruined cities be filled with flocks of people.
Then they will know that I am the LORD."

The Valley of Dry Bones

37 The hand of the LORD was on me,[g]
and he brought me out by the Spir-
it[h] of the LORD and set me in the middle of
a valley;[i] it was full of bones.[j] 2 He led me
back and forth among them, and I saw a
great many bones on the floor of the valley, bones that were very dry. 3 He asked
me, "Son of man, can these bones live?"
I said, "Sovereign LORD, you alone
know.[k]"
4 Then he said to me, "Prophesy to these
bones and say to them, 'Dry bones, hear
the word of the LORD![l] 5 This is what the
Sovereign LORD says to these bones: I will
make breath[a] enter you, and you will
come to life.[m] 6 I will attach tendons to you
and make flesh come upon you and cover
you with skin; I will put breath in you,
and you will come to life. Then you will
know that I am the LORD.[n]' "
7 So I prophesied as I was commanded. And as I was prophesying, there was
a noise, a rattling sound, and the bones
came together, bone to bone. 8 I looked,
and tendons and flesh appeared on them
and skin covered them, but there was no
breath in them.
9 Then he said to me, "Prophesy to the
breath;[o] prophesy, son of man, and say to
it, 'This is what the Sovereign LORD says:
Come, breath, from the four winds and
breathe into these slain, that they may
live.' " 10 So I prophesied as he commanded
me, and breath entered them; they came
to life and stood up on their feet—a vast
army.[p]
11 Then he said to me: "Son of man,
these bones are the people of Israel. They
say, 'Our bones are dried up and our
hope is gone; we are cut off.'[q] 12 Therefore

[a] 5 The Hebrew for this word can also mean *wind* or *spirit* (see verses 6-14).

36:24 [p] Eze 34:13; 37:21 **36:25** [q] Heb 9:13; 10:22 [r] Ps 51:2, 7 [s] Zec 13:2 **36:26** [t] Jer 24:7 [u] Ps 51:10; Eze 11:19 **36:27** [v] Eze 37:14 **36:28** [w] Jer 30:22 [x] Eze 14:11; 37:14, 27 **36:29** [y] Eze 34:29 **36:30** [z] Lev 26:4-5; Eze 34:27; Hos 2:21-22 **36:31** [a] Eze 6:9; 20:43 **36:32** [b] Dt 9:5 **36:35** [c] Joel 2:3 [d] Isa 51:3 **36:36** [e] Eze 17:22; 22:14; 37:14; 39:27-28 **36:38** [f] 1Ki 8:63; 2Ch 35:7-9

37:1 [g] Eze 1:3; 8:3 [h] Eze 11:24; Lk 4:1; Ac 8:39 [i] Jer 7:32 [j] Jer 8:2; Eze 40:1 **37:3** [k] Dt 32:39; 1Sa 2:6; Isa 26:19 **37:4** [l] Jer 22:29 **37:5** [m] Ge 2:7; Ps 104:29-30 **37:6** [n] Eze 38:23; Joel 2:27; 3:17 **37:9** [o] Ps 104:30 **37:10** [p] Rev 11:11 **37:11** [q] La 3:54

36:25 *clean.* The Hebrew term occurs three times in this verse. It serves to underline the action that the Lord will perform in order to cleanse his people and their land from defilement. Both ancient Israel and ancient Near Eastern societies attest to the use of water as a means of ritual purification. In Ex 29:4, water is used in the consecration of priests and Levites (cf. Nu 8:7). Lev 16:4,24,26 describes the ablutions of the high priest on the Day of Atonement. A Neo-Babylonian tablet describes the purification of a temple in Babylon with the use of water.

36:26 *heart.* Considered the seat of the mind and its will, or inclinations (see note on Jer 20:12). *heart of stone.* See notes on 11:19; Isa 6:9–10; see also the article "The Hardening of Pharaoh's Heart," p. 124.

37:1 *The hand of the LORD was on me.* See note on 3:22.

37:1–2 *valley ... full of bones.* The large amount of bones described here implies it was the scene of a major catastrophe. The depiction of a large number of corpses that were denied a proper burial is reminiscent of many battle scenes and descriptions of battle scenes found in the earliest periods of Mesopotamian and Egyptian history. Furthermore, the Assyrian annals describe the destruction of Assyria's enemies in similar terms. A typical ancient Near Eastern curse has the corpse of the cursed victim exposed to the elements.

37:9 *the four winds.* "The breath" will blow on the bones in the valley and bring them to life. The source of this breath is "the four winds," meaning "the four directions." In both Hebrew and Akkadian the expression stands for the division of the world into four quadrants, a typical ancient Near Eastern manner of speaking of the world in its totality.

37:12,13 *open your graves and bring you up from them.* The concept of resurrection was known in some parts of

prophesy and say to them: 'This is what
the Sovereign LORD says: My people, I am
going to open your graves and bring you
up from them; I will bring you back to
the land of Israel.[r] 13Then you, my people, will know that I am the LORD, when I
open your graves and bring you up from
them. 14I will put my Spirit[s] in you and
you will live, and I will settle you in your
own land. Then you will know that I the
LORD have spoken, and I have done it, declares the LORD.[t]' "

One Nation Under One King

15The word of the LORD came to me:
16"Son of man, take a stick of wood and
write on it, 'Belonging to Judah and the Israelites[u] associated with him.[v]' Then take
another stick of wood, and write on it,
'Belonging to Joseph (that is, to Ephraim)
and all the Israelites associated with him.'
17Join them together into one stick so that
they will become one in your hand.[w]
18"When your people ask you, 'Won't
you tell us what you mean by this?'[x] 19say
to them, 'This is what the Sovereign LORD
says: I am going to take the stick of Joseph—which is in Ephraim's hand—and
of the Israelite tribes associated with him,
and join it to Judah's stick. I will make
them into a single stick of wood, and they
will become one in my hand.'[y] 20Hold before their eyes the sticks you have written
on 21and say to them, 'This is what the
Sovereign LORD says: I will take the Israelites out of the nations where they have
gone. I will gather them from all around
and bring them back into their own land.[z]
22I will make them one nation in the land,
on the mountains of Israel. There will be
one king over all of them and they will
never again be two nations or be divided
into two kingdoms.[a] 23They will no longer
defile[b] themselves with their idols and vile
images or with any of their offenses, for I
will save them from all their sinful backsliding,[a] and I will cleanse them. They will
be my people, and I will be their God.[c]
24" 'My servant David[d] will be king over
them, and they will all have one shepherd.[e] They will follow my laws and be
careful to keep my decrees.[f] 25They will
live in the land I gave to my servant Jacob, the land where your ancestors lived.[g]
They and their children and their children's children will live there forever,[h]
and David my servant will be their prince
forever.[i] 26I will make a covenant of peace[j]
with them; it will be an everlasting covenant. I will establish them and increase
their numbers,[k] and I will put my sanctuary among them forever.[l] 27My dwelling
place[m] will be with them; I will be their
God, and they will be my people.[n] 28Then
the nations will know that I the LORD make
Israel holy,[o] when my sanctuary is among
them forever.' "

The LORD's Great Victory Over the Nations

38 The word of the LORD came to me:
2"Son of man, set your face against
Gog, of the land of Magog,[p] the chief
prince of[b] Meshek and Tubal;[q] prophesy
against him 3and say: 'This is what the
Sovereign LORD says: I am against you,
Gog, chief prince of[c] Meshek and Tubal.[r]
4I will turn you around, put hooks[s] in your

[a] 23 Many Hebrew manuscripts (see also Septuagint); most Hebrew manuscripts *all their dwelling places where they sinned* [b] 2 Or *the prince of Rosh,* [c] 3 Or *Gog, prince of Rosh,*

37:12 [r] Dt 32:39; 1Sa 2:6; Isa 26:19; Hos 13:14; Am 9:14-15
37:14 [s] Joel 2:28-29 [t] Eze 36:27-28,36
37:16 [u] 1Ki 12:20; 2Ch 10:17-19 [v] Nu 17:2-3; 2Ch 15:9
37:17 [w] ver 24; Isa 11:13; Jer 50:4; Hos 1:11
37:18 [x] Eze 24:19
37:19 [y] Zec 10:6
37:21 [z] Isa 43:5-6; Eze 36:24; 39:27
37:22 [a] Isa 11:13; Jer 3:18; Hos 1:11
37:23 [b] Eze 36:25; 43:7 [c] Eze 11:18; 36:28
37:24 [d] Hos 3:5 [e] Isa 40:11; Eze 34:23 [f] Ps 78:70-71
37:25 [g] Eze 28:25 [h] Am 9:15 [i] Isa 11:1
37:26 [j] Isa 55:3 [k] Jer 30:19 [l] Eze 16:62
37:27 [m] Lev 26:11; Jn 1:14 [n] 2Co 6:16*
37:28 [o] Ex 31:13; Eze 20:12
38:2 [p] Ge 10:2 [q] Rev 20:8
38:3 [r] Eze 39:1
38:4 [s] 2Ki 19:28

---

the ancient Near East. The Egyptians believed that some of the deceased rose as stars and took their places in the heavens. In general, the only awakening that took place in the ancient worldview was the calling up of spirits of the dead (which is not permanent and not a bodily presence) or the awakening of the fertility gods of nature cycles. These fertility gods died annually when the agricultural cycle came to an end, and they "wintered" in the netherworld. Then they were ritually awakened in the spring. None of this bears any resemblance to a theological doctrine of resurrection that is first hinted at in Da 12:2. Occasional revivifications or indications of national return to life as found in this passage are not representative of a doctrine of resurrection. See the article "The Old Testament Concept of Resurrection," p. 1160.

37:16 *take a stick of wood and write on it.* It is likely, since this wood is being written on, that Ezekiel is using two wooden tablets. It was a common practice to use wooden boards coated with a beeswax concoction for the writing of messages that were formal but did not need to be archived and preserved. See the article "Literacy," p. 140.

37:24 *My servant David will be king ... They will follow my laws.* The Ptolemaic Demotic Chronicle attempts to explain Egyptian history from 404 BC to the time of its composition through the operation of the law of divine retribution (see the article "Retribution Principle," p. 823). Only the kings (the pharaohs of the Twenty-Seventh to the Thirtieth Dynasties) who lived in accordance with the will of the gods prospered. Catastrophes, destructions of cities, and foreign invasions were explained as the consequence of disobedience to the will of the gods. Deliverance from such evils, however, is prophesied in the form of an ideal king from Heracleopolis who will fulfill the divine law and thereby embody the ideal of perfect and just rule. At 3:16 in that chronicle one reads, "Rejoice over the ruler who will be; for he will not forsake the law." Both Ezekiel and the Egyptian text envisage the arrival of a new ruler whose reign will be characterized by scrupulous respect of religious and social laws.

38:2 *Meshek and Tubal.* See note on 32:26.

38:4 *hooks in your jaws.* The Assyrians typically put hooks in the jaws of defeated enemies, either for the purposes of humiliation or to deport them to other lands. This practice is often described in their annals and graphically depicted in their wall reliefs. Esarhaddon is depicted on a stele from Zinjirli in Syria as leading Baal of Tyre and Tirhakah

jaws and bring you out with your whole
army — your horses, your horsemen fully
armed, and a great horde with large and
small shields, all of them brandishing their
swords.[t] 5Persia, Cush[a][u] and Put[v] will be
with them, all with shields and helmets,
6also Gomer[w] with all its troops, and Beth
Togarmah[x] from the far north with all its
troops — the many nations with you.
7" 'Get ready; be prepared,[y] you and all
the hordes gathered about you, and take
command of them. 8After many days[z] you
will be called to arms. In future years you
will invade a land that has recovered from
war, whose people were gathered from
many nations[a] to the mountains of Israel,
which had long been desolate. They had
been brought out from the nations, and
now all of them live in safety.[b] 9You and
all your troops and the many nations with
you will go up, advancing like a storm;[c]
you will be like a cloud[d] covering the land.
10" 'This is what the Sovereign LORD
says: On that day thoughts will come into
your mind and you will devise an evil
scheme.[e] 11You will say, "I will invade a
land of unwalled villages; I will attack a
peaceful and unsuspecting people — all
of them living without walls and without
gates and bars.[f] 12I will plunder and loot
and turn my hand against the resettled ruins and the people gathered from the nations, rich in livestock and goods, living
at the center of the land.[b]" 13Sheba[g] and
Dedan and the merchants of Tarshish and
all her villages[c] will say to you, "Have you
come to plunder? Have you gathered your
hordes to loot, to carry off silver and gold,
to take away livestock and goods and to
seize much plunder?[h]" '
14"Therefore, son of man, prophesy and
say to Gog: 'This is what the Sovereign
LORD says: In that day, when my people Israel are living in safety,[i] will you not take
notice of it? 15You will come from your
place in the far north, you and many nations with you, all of them riding on horses,
a great horde, a mighty army.[j] 16You will advance against my people Israel like a cloud[k]
that covers the land. In days to come, Gog,
I will bring you against my land, so that the
nations may know me when I am proved
holy through you before their eyes.[l]
17" 'This is what the Sovereign LORD
says: You are the one I spoke of in former days by my servants the prophets
of Israel. At that time they prophesied
for years that I would bring you against
them. 18This is what will happen in that
day: When Gog attacks the land of Israel,
my hot anger will be aroused, declares

38:4 [t] Eze 29:4; Da 11:40 **38:5** [u] Ge 10:6 [v] Eze 27:10 **38:6** [w] Ge 10:2 [x] Eze 27:14 **38:7** [y] Isa 8:9 **38:8** [z] Isa 24:22 [a] Isa 11:11 [b] Jer 23:6 **38:9** [c] Isa 28:2 [d] Jer 4:13; Joel 2:2 **38:10** [e] Ps 36:4; Mic 2:1 **38:11** [f] Jer 49:31; Zec 2:4 **38:13** [g] Eze 27:22 [h] Isa 10:6; Jer 15:13 **38:14** [i] ver 8; Zec 2:5 **38:15** [j] Eze 39:2 **38:16** [k] ver 9 [l] Isa 29:23; Eze 39:21

[a] *5* That is, the upper Nile region [b] *12* The Hebrew for this phrase means *the navel of the earth.* [c] *13* Or *her strong lions*

of Egypt by a rope tied to a ring through their lips. Ashurbanipal claims to have pierced the cheeks of Uate (king of Ishmael) with a sharp-edged tool and put a ring in his jaw. *large and small shields.* Body shields and hand shields, respectively (see notes on Ps 3:3; Jer 46:3).

38:5 *Persia, Cush and Put.* See the article "Gog, of the Land of Magog," p. 1394.

38:6 *Gomer.* Equated with the Gimirrai of the Assyrian annals and the Cimmerians of Greek sources. In Homer's *Odyssey* they lived on the north shore of the Black Sea. They attacked the kingdom of Urartu from the north and caused problems for the Assyrians in the eighth century BC. Sargon died in battle against them in Tubal. They appear to have been driven through the Caucasus Mountains into Anatolia according to Herodotus. They came to be involved with the Anatolian kingdom of Lydia in the seventh century BC. They overran the Phrygians and sacked the capital at Gordion, the royal seat of the famous King Midas in 676. In 644 they overthrew Sardis, the capital of the Lydian state. This was when Gyges met his death. During Ezekiel's time the Cimmerians had been driven out of Lydia by Alyattes. They later came under the control of the Medes. *Beth Togarmah.* Most likely the capital city of Kammanu, a central Anatolian kingdom. It was known in Hittite sources as Tegaramara and in Assyrian sources as Til-garimmu.

38:11 *unwalled villages.* This Hebrew term is used also in Est 9:19 ("villages"); Zec 2:4 ("city without walls"). Unlike fortified cities, they have normally been defined as rural settlements without walls, bars or gates. They are defenseless and vulnerable.

38:12 *center of the land.* Lit. "navel of the earth." Jerusalem's situation in the center of the nations reflects her theological significance as the centerpiece of God's actions in the world and the object of God's covenant care. This motif of "the navel of the earth" occurs in Sumerian and Akkadian literature under the term "Bond of Heaven and Earth," applied to the temples at Nippur, Larsa and Sippar, or "Bond of the Lands," applied to Babylon. A circular sixth-century BC map of the world from Babylon locates this city in the center, surrounded by neighbors, some positioned irrespective of their actual location.

38:13 *Sheba.* This kingdom was a great trading center in southwestern Arabia that exported precious stones, gold and incense (see note on Isa 60:6). This kingdom is known as Saba in native sources and in the Assyrian annals. It had a very advanced urban civilization in the first millennium BC. *Dedan.* A central Arabian oasis where Tyre received its special riding gear. It is identified with the modern site of al-'Ula, which is situated on the "Incense Road" from Yemen to Palestine. *merchants of Tarshish.* In this context they appear to represent merchant peoples who did their trade on the overland routes across the Arabian Desert to Sheba and Dedan, and on to the Mediterranean Sea.

38:17 *by my servants the prophets.* Lit. "of whom I spoke by the hand of my servants." An almost exact parallel is found in the eighth-century BC Aramaic Zakkur Inscription, where the god Baal Shamayim speaks by the hand of seers and messengers. Both the Hebrew and the Aramaic idioms mean "by the agency of."

38:18 – 21 The correlation between divine anger (v. 18) and calamities of cosmic proportions (vv. 19 – 21) is found in Neo-Assyrian texts. These were neither apocalyptic nor eschatological predictions but simply stereotypical literary descriptions of major political upheavals affecting

EZEKIEL 38:2

Gog, of the Land of Magog

The name "Gog" seems to derive from Gyges, the name of the king of Lydia in Asia Minor, mentioned in several inscriptions of Ashurbanipal (668–631 BC). Gyges has a legendary reputation of having invented coinage (Herodotus, *Histories* 1.813). The name "Magog" recurs in Eze 39:6 as the name of a people. It is found again in the table of nations in Ge 10:2 and its parallel 1Ch 1:5, where Magog is identified as the second son of Japheth (i.e., the ancestor of the Greek tribes), alongside other Indo-European ethnic groups like Gomer, Madai, Javan, Tubal, Meshek and Tiras. Josephus (*Antiquities* 1.123) identified Magog with the Scythians. Magog is often interpreted as a contraction of an original Akkadian *mat Gugi* ("land of Gog") and as referring to the territory of Lydia in western Anatolia.

Ezekiel makes use of genuine ethnic names that recur in the enumeration of peoples who traded with Tyre (Eze 27:13). Meshek is the Assyrian Mushku, which under Sargon II designated Phrygia, in Asia Minor. Tubal is the Assyrian Tabal, the region between the Halys River and the Taurus Mountains. Gomer is the Assyrian *Gimirri*, the Cimmerians of the Greeks, who in the seventh century BC raided all Anatolia. The Akkadian column of Darius's Behistun inscription renders Persian *Saka* (Scythian) with *Gimairaia*.

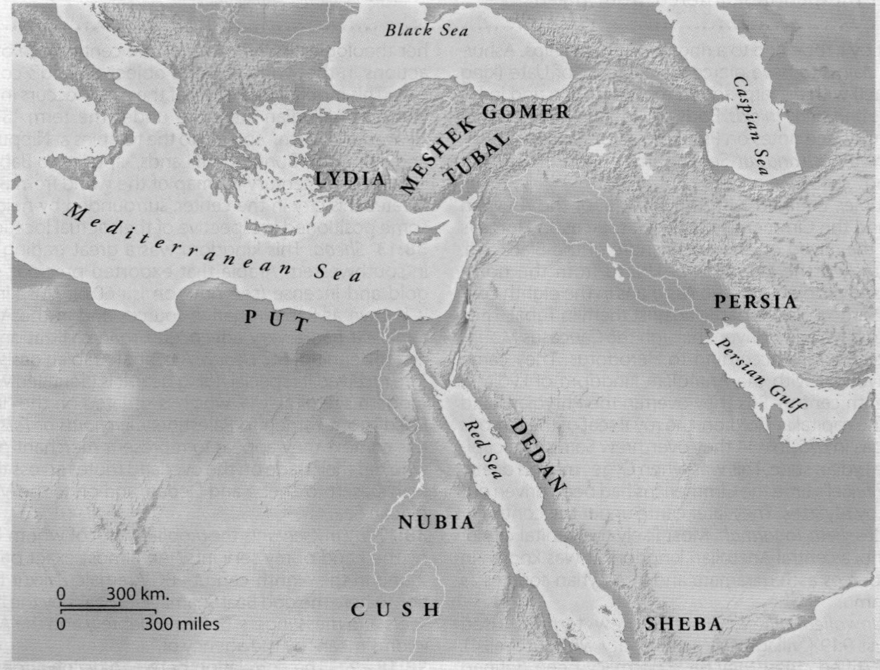

Territories in Eze 38.

continued on next page

The Old Babylonian "Cuthean Legend of Naram-Sin," copied in Neo-Assyrian times, has been compared with Ezekiel's Gog prophecy. The following parallels have been pointed out:

1. In both, the invading horde is set apart by God/the gods in a remote area of the north.
2. In both, this area lies in Anatolia.
3. In both, the horde is led by several princes under the supreme command of one of them.
4. In both, a historical royal name is utilized without regard for actual history.
5. In both, the horde goes out for a long march of plunder and devastation.
6. In both, the horde is constituted of many peoples.

This parallel suggests that Ezekiel is using an ancient Near Eastern literary cliché in order to designate the invading hordes. The names in Ezekiel's list form a geographic pattern: Meshek, Tubal, Gomer and Beth Togarmah (Eze 38:2,6) represent the northern extreme of the world known to Israel, while Persia, Cush and Put (Eze 38:5) represent the eastern and southern extreme — suggesting that the whole neighboring world is involved in this attack against Israel. A similar rhetorical strategy occurs in a Neo-Assyrian inscription of Sargon II.

It is often suggested that this prophecy may include an example of cryptography, one of the techniques elaborated by the Mesopotamian scribes and adopted by the later rabbinic Midrash. Written backward, Magog (*m-g-g*) becomes Gagam (*g-g-m*). Applying the procedure of cryptic writing, where each letter of the Hebrew alphabet is replaced by the preceding one, the result is Babel or Babylon (*b-b-l*). The use of cryptography or coded messages is well documented in Mesopotamian texts.

The recognition of the technique of cryptography in Eze 38:2 – 6 would result in understanding this prophecy as being directed against Babylonia, the only major nation that is absent from Ezekiel's prophecy. It is particularly significant that this kind of cryptography is amply attested in Babylonian incantations.

Eze 38 – 39 could be perceived as containing some incantatory elements announcing the doom over the Babylonians and other enemies of Judah who destroyed Jerusalem and plundered the remaining population. Ezekiel may have used some ancient names of peoples who lived in the seventh century BC in order to create a cipher for Babylon. ◆

the Sovereign LORD. [19]In my zeal and fiery wrath I declare that at that time there
shall be a great earthquake in the land of
Israel.[m] [20]The fish in the sea, the birds in
the sky, the beasts of the field, every creature that moves along the ground, and all
the people on the face of the earth will
tremble at my presence. The mountains
will be overturned, the cliffs will crum-
ble and every wall will fall to the ground.[n]
[21]I will summon a sword[o] against Gog on
all my mountains, declares the Sovereign
LORD. Every man's sword will be against
his brother.[p] [22]I will execute judgment[q]
on him with plague and bloodshed; I will
pour down torrents of rain, hailstones[r]
and burning sulfur on him and on his
troops and on the many nations with him.
[23]And so I will show my greatness and my
holiness, and I will make myself known in
the sight of many nations. Then they will
know that I am the LORD.[s]'

38:19 [m]Ps 18:7; Eze 5:13; Hag 2:6,21 **38:20** [n]Hos 4:3; Na 1:5 **38:21** [o]Eze 14:17 [p]1Sa 14:20; 2Ch 20:23; Hag 2:22 **38:22** [q]Isa 66:16; Jer 25:31 [r]Ps 18:12; Rev 16:21 **38:23** [s]Eze 36:23

Mesopotamia. After enumerating a series of evils perpetrated by the Babylonians, the annals of Esarhaddon describe Marduk's anger and the result that all balance and order (including the courses of the stars) was disrupted; flooding turned cities into wasteland.

38:19 *great earthquake in the land of Israel.* This appears to be a cosmic earthquake, similar to ones described in Ex 19; Jdg 5:4 – 5; Ps 68:8 – 9; 114; Isa 30:27 – 28; Hab 3:3 – 7 (see note on 1Sa 14:15). This type of imagery is also found in the annals of Esarhaddon of Assyria. The Levant was prone to earthquakes, but Israel is on the edge of the zone that has its center in Anatolia. The well-known, historical quakes occurred in 760 and 31 BC. In the Christian era, the region has averaged about one major quake per century.

38:22 *hailstones.* See note on 13:11. The occurrence of hailstones as divine judgment in conquest accounts is

39 "Son of man, prophesy against Gog
and say: 'This is what the Sovereign LORD says: I am against you, Gog,
chief prince of[a] Meshek and Tubal.[t] 2 I will
turn you around and drag you along. I will
bring you from the far north and send you
against the mountains of Israel. 3 Then I
will strike your bow[u] from your left hand
and make your arrows[v] drop from your
right hand. 4 On the mountains of Israel you will fall, you and all your troops
and the nations with you. I will give you
as food to all kinds of carrion birds and
to the wild animals.[w] 5 You will fall in the
open field, for I have spoken, declares the
Sovereign LORD. 6 I will send fire[x] on Magog and on those who live in safety in the
coastlands,[y] and they will know that I am
the LORD.

7 " 'I will make known my holy name
among my people Israel. I will no longer
let my holy name be profaned,[z] and the
nations will know that I the LORD am the
Holy One in Israel.[a] 8 It is coming! It will
surely take place, declares the Sovereign
LORD. This is the day I have spoken of.

9 " 'Then those who live in the towns
of Israel will go out and use the weapons for fuel and burn them up — the small
and large shields, the bows and arrows,
the war clubs and spears. For seven years
they will use them for fuel.[b] 10 They will
not need to gather wood from the fields or
cut it from the forests, because they will
use the weapons for fuel. And they will
plunder those who plundered them and
loot those who looted them, declares the
Sovereign LORD.[c]

11 " 'On that day I will give Gog a burial place in Israel, in the valley of those
who travel east of the Sea. It will block the
way of travelers, because Gog and all his
hordes will be buried there. So it will be
called the Valley of Hamon Gog.[b][d]

12 " 'For seven months the Israelites will
be burying them in order to cleanse the
land.[e] 13 All the people of the land will
bury them, and the day I display my glory[f] will be a memorable day for them, declares the Sovereign LORD. 14 People will
be continually employed in cleansing the
land. They will spread out across the land
and, along with others, they will bury any
bodies that are lying on the ground.

" 'After the seven months they will carry
out a more detailed search. 15 As they go
through the land, anyone who sees a human bone will leave a marker beside it until the gravediggers bury it in the Valley of
Hamon Gog, 16 near a town called Hamonah.[c] And so they will cleanse the land.'

17 "Son of man, this is what the Sovereign LORD says: Call out to every kind of
bird[g] and all the wild animals: 'Assemble
and come together from all around to the
sacrifice I am preparing for you, the great
sacrifice on the mountains of Israel. There
you will eat flesh and drink blood. 18 You
will eat the flesh of mighty men and drink
the blood of the princes of the earth as

39:1 [t] Eze 38:2,3 **39:3** [u] Hos 1:5 [v] Ps 76:3 **39:4** [w] ver 17-20; Eze 29:5; 33:27 **39:6** [x] Eze 30:8; Am 1:4 [y] Jer 25:22 **39:7** [z] Ex 20:7 [a] Isa 12:6; Eze 36:16,23 **39:9** [b] Ps 46:9 **39:10** [c] Isa 14:2; 33:1; Hab 2:8 **39:11** [d] Eze 38:2 **39:12** [e] Dt 21:23 **39:13** [f] Eze 28:22 **39:17** [g] Rev 19:17

[a] *1* Or *Gog, prince of Rosh,* [b] *11 Hamon Gog* means *hordes of Gog.* [c] *16 Hamonah* means *horde.*

not unique. In a letter to his god (Assur), Sargon of Assyria reports that in his campaign against Urartu (714 BC) the god Adad stormed against his enemies with "stones from heaven" and so annihilated them. This battle included a coalition that fled through the passes and valleys pursued by Sargon, with the enemy king hiding at last in the clefts of a mountain. *burning sulfur.* Brimstone; it is a yellow crystalline substance that ignites in air and is often found in volcanic regions. See note on Isa 30:33. It has no connection with hailstones except they were both calamities that would befall the area.

39:9 *use the weapons for fuel.* Passages that speak of the destruction of weapons of war usually focus on using them for practical and beneficial purposes. The wooden parts could be burned in place of firewood, as here (this sometimes extended even to the clothing, as in Isa 9:5), and the metal parts could be recycled into agricultural use (Isa 2:4; Mic 4:3).

39:11 *burial place.* An absolute identification is uncertain. Scholars have identified it as the "Valley of Travelers" or, based upon an Ugaritic parallel, "those who have passed on." The latter makes the most sense. Gog has desired to be identified with the great kings of old; now he is, since they are all dead. Ugaritic texts refer to a group called the Rephaim, who are beings of the netherworld (see note on Isa 14:9). *Valley of Hamon Gog.* The dead bodies of the defeated army that invaded the land and people of Israel will be buried in the valley that means "hordes of Gog." This valley appears to play on the name of a valley next to Jerusalem, the Valley of Hinnom, notorious for the child sacrifices performed there (see notes on Lev 20:2; 1Ki 11:5; 2Ki 3:27; 16:3; Jer 7:31). The explanatory note in v. 16 adds a clue in the localization of the burial ground for the enemies of the Lord and Israel. The association of the term *hamon* ("clamor, hubris") with Jerusalem in three earlier judgment prophecies is especially instructive. The form Hamonah (v. 16) is linked with 7:12 (NIV "the whole crowd"), where *hamona* had functioned as shorthand for all of Jerusalem's riotous, defiant and wicked behavior. In 5:7, the prophet denounced Jerusalem's *hamon*, which exceeded the tumult and wickedness of all surrounding nations. Some of these nations appear in 23:40–42, bringing their own depraved and boisterous ways into the city of Jerusalem, at her invitation. Hamonah therefore stands for the capital of Judah in a skillful unfolding of the divine judgment on Jerusalem and the nations.

39:16 *Hamonah.* See previous note.

39:17 *Call out to every kind of bird and all the wild animals ... come ... eat flesh.* The practice of throwing bodies out into the open to be eaten by wild animals is well attested in ancient Near Eastern texts. This treatment amounts to a curse. This punishment is applied in particular to those who have broken treaties. In the light of these parallels, the punishment God inflicts on the nations that have invaded the land of Israel should probably be seen as an outworking of a curse in retribution for a broken agreement, i.e., a betrayal of a pact of nonaggression.

if they were rams and lambs, goats and
bulls — all of them fattened animals from
Bashan.[h] 19At the sacrifice I am preparing
for you, you will eat fat till you are glutted
and drink blood till you are drunk. 20At my
table you will eat your fill of horses and
riders, mighty men and soldiers of every
kind,' declares the Sovereign LORD.[i]
21"I will display my glory among the
nations, and all the nations will see the
punishment I inflict and the hand I lay on
them.[j] 22From that day forward the people
of Israel will know that I am the LORD their
God. 23And the nations will know that the
people of Israel went into exile for their
sin, because they were unfaithful to me.
So I hid my face from them and handed
them over to their enemies, and they all
fell by the sword.[k] 24I dealt with them according to their uncleanness and their offenses, and I hid my face from them.[l]
25"Therefore this is what the Sovereign
LORD says: I will now restore the fortunes
of Jacob[a][m] and will have compassion[n] on
all the people of Israel, and I will be zealous for my holy name.[o] 26They will forget
their shame and all the unfaithfulness they
showed toward me when they lived in
safety[p] in their land with no one to make
them afraid.[q] 27When I have brought them
back from the nations and have gathered
them from the countries of their enemies,
I will be proved holy through them in the
sight of many nations.[r] 28Then they will
know that I am the LORD their God, for
though I sent them into exile among the
nations, I will gather them to their own
land, not leaving any behind. 29I will no
longer hide my face from them, for I will
pour out my Spirit[s] on the people of Israel,
declares the Sovereign LORD."

The Temple Area Restored

40 In the twenty-fifth year of our exile,
at the beginning of the year, on the
tenth of the month, in the fourteenth year
after the fall of the city[t] — on that very day
the hand of the LORD was on me[u] and he
took me there. 2In visions[v] of God he took
me to the land of Israel and set me on a
very high mountain,[w] on whose south side
were some buildings that looked like a city.
3He took me there, and I saw a man whose
appearance was like bronze;[x] he was
standing in the gateway with a linen cord
and a measuring rod[y] in his hand. 4The
man said to me, "Son of man, look carefully and listen closely and pay attention to
everything I am going to show you, for that
is why you have been brought here. Tell[z]
the people of Israel everything you see.[a]"

The East Gate to the Outer Court

5I saw a wall completely surrounding
the temple area. The length of the measuring rod in the man's hand was six long
cubits,[b] each of which was a cubit and a
handbreadth. He measured[b] the wall; it
was one measuring rod thick and one rod
high.

39:18 [h] Ps 22:12; Jer 51:40
39:20 [i] Rev 19:17-18
39:21 [j] Ex 9:16; Isa 37:20; Eze 38:16
39:23 [k] Isa 1:15; 59:2; Jer 22:8-9; 44:23
39:24 [l] Jer 2:17, 19; 4:18; Eze 36:19
39:25 [m] Jer 33:7; Eze 34:13 [n] Jer 30:18 [o] Isa 27:12-13
39:26 [p] 1Ki 4:25 [q] Isa 17:2; Eze 34:28; Mic 4:4
39:27 [r] Eze 36:23-24; 37:21; 38:16
39:29 [s] Joel 2:28; Ac 2:17
40:1 [t] 2Ki 25:7; Jer 39:1-10; 52:4-11; Eze 33:21 [u] Eze 1:3
40:2 [v] Da 7:1, 7 [w] Eze 17:22; Rev 21:10
40:3 [x] Eze 1:7; Da 10:6; Rev 1:15 [y] Eze 47:3; Zec 2:1-2; Rev 11:1; 21:15
40:4 [z] Jer 26:2 [a] Eze 44:5
40:5 [b] Eze 42:20

[a] *25* Or *now bring Jacob back from captivity* [b] *5* That is, about 11 feet or about 3.2 meters; also in verse 12. The long cubit of about 21 inches or about 53 centimeters is the basic unit of measurement of length throughout chapters 40 – 48.

39:23 *I hid my face.* The anthropomorphic notion of the Lord hiding his face occurs three times in ch. 39 (vv. 23,24,29) and heightens God's involvement in Israel's fate. In Ezekiel, the nation's disaster is expressed with a typical expression found in numerous ancient Near Eastern texts. The origin of the expression is found in ancient court language for looking favorably or unfavorably on someone. For a king to turn his face from a subject spelled disaster. The hiding of the face therefore appropriately describes the disposition of the deity, as in a Neo-Babylonian text entitled "A Prayer of Lamentation to Ishtar." The person praying expresses the feeling of being abandoned by the divinity and wonders whether the god is angry and has turned her face away.
39:25 *restore the fortunes of Jacob.* The idiomatic expression "to restore the fortunes" encountered earlier in 16:53 (where "Sodom" is a reference to Jerusalem) and in 29:14 (with reference to Egypt) represents a technical reference to a model of restoration. It indicates the Lord's reversal of his judgment. The same expression occurs in the eighth-century BC Aramaic Sefire Stele III.
40:1 *tenth of the month.* The time of the year is described as the "beginning of the year," similar to an Akkadian equivalent. The present vision is thus dated to the tenth day of Nisan/Aviv in the "twenty-fifth year of [the] exile," or Apr. 28, 573 BC. In the Israelite calendar, this was the beginning of Passover activities. The lamb was to be chosen on this day and slaughtered on the 14th day of the month.
40:3 *a linen cord.* May be similar to the "measuring line," which was used to measure the city in Zec 2:1. Thus, it appears that it was used for extremely long distances. *measuring rod.* Used to measure short distances. Some have argued that the stele of Ur-Nammu of the Sumerian city of Ur shows a similar representation.
40:5 *temple.* While ch. 39 ended with the description of the Lord's victory against Gog and its hordes who invaded the land of Israel, ch. 40 begins with the description of the new temple for the Lord. This sequence is significant. It follows a similar pattern found in ancient Near Eastern literature. The Babylonian creation epic *Enuma Elish* first describes how the patron god of Babylon defeated the forces of chaos symbolized by Tiamat. From her body Marduk creates the heaven and earth, and then the council of the gods decides to create humans to serve the gods. The latter action is followed almost immediately by the construction of Marduk's temple, Esagila, as a suitable place for him to reside in his city of Babylon. Similarly, in the Ugaritic literature, the god Baal earns the right to his own temple on Mount Zaphon (i.e., Mount in the North) by his victory over the forces of decay and chaos symbolized by the god Mot, whose very name means "death." This vision of Ezekiel's can be best understood when compared to the accounts of temples and temple building in the ancient

6Then he went to the east gate.[c] He
climbed its steps and measured the threshold of the gate; it was one rod deep. 7The
alcoves[d] for the guards were one rod long
and one rod wide, and the projecting
walls between the alcoves were five cubits[a] thick. And the threshold of the gate
next to the portico facing the temple was
one rod deep.
8Then he measured the portico of the
gateway; 9it[b] was eight cubits[c] deep and its
jambs were two cubits[d] thick. The portico
of the gateway faced the temple.
10Inside the east gate were three alcoves
on each side; the three had the same measurements, and the faces of the projecting
walls on each side had the same measurements. 11Then he measured the width of
the entrance of the gateway; it was ten
cubits and its length was thirteen cubits.[e]
12In front of each alcove was a wall one
cubit high, and the alcoves were six cubits square. 13Then he measured the gateway from the top of the rear wall of one
alcove to the top of the opposite one; the
distance was twenty-five cubits[f] from one
parapet opening to the opposite one. 14He
measured along the faces of the projecting walls all around the inside of the gateway — sixty cubits.[g] The measurement
was up to the portico[h] facing the courtyard.[i][e] 15The distance from the entrance
of the gateway to the far end of its portico was fifty cubits.[j] 16The alcoves and the
projecting walls inside the gateway were
surmounted by narrow parapet openings
all around, as was the portico; the openings all around faced inward. The faces of
the projecting walls were decorated with
palm trees.[f]

The Outer Court

17Then he brought me into the outer
court.[g] There I saw some rooms and a pavement that had been constructed all around
the court; there were thirty rooms[h] along
the pavement.[i] 18It abutted the sides of the
gateways and was as wide as they were
long; this was the lower pavement. 19Then
he measured the distance from the inside of
the lower gateway to the outside of the inner court;[j] it was a hundred cubits[k][k] on the
east side as well as on the north.

The North Gate

20Then he measured the length and
width of the north gate, leading into the
outer court. 21Its alcoves[l] — three on each
side — its projecting walls and its portico
had the same measurements as those of
the first gateway. It was fifty cubits long
and twenty-five cubits wide. 22Its openings, its portico[m] and its palm tree dec-

40:6 [c] Eze 8:16 **40:7** [d] ver 36 **40:14** [e] Ex 27:9
40:16 [f] ver 21-22; 2Ch 3:5; Eze 41:26 **40:17** [g] Rev 11:2 [h] Eze 41:6 [i] Eze 42:1 **40:19** [j] Eze 46:1 [k] ver 23,27 **40:21** [l] ver 7 **40:22** [m] ver 49

[a] *7* That is, about 8 3/4 feet or about 2.7 meters; also in verse 48 [b] *8,9* Many Hebrew manuscripts, Septuagint, Vulgate and Syriac; most Hebrew manuscripts *gateway facing the temple; it was one rod deep. 9Then he measured the portico of the gateway; it* [c] *9* That is, about 14 feet or about 4.2 meters [d] *9* That is, about 3 1/2 feet or about 1 meter [e] *11* That is, about 18 feet wide and 23 feet long or about 5.3 meters wide and 6.9 meters long [f] *13* That is, about 44 feet or about 13 meters; also in verses 21, 25, 29, 30, 33 and 36 [g] *14* That is, about 105 feet or about 32 meters [h] *14* Septuagint; Hebrew *projecting wall* [i] *14* The meaning of the Hebrew for this verse is uncertain. [j] *15* That is, about 88 feet or about 27 meters; also in verses 21, 25, 29, 33 and 36 [k] *19* That is, about 175 feet or about 53 meters; also in verses 23, 27 and 47

world as well as against the account in the book of Kings. *six long cubits.* The normal cubit (six handbreadths) has been estimated at 18 inches (45 centimeters), and the long cubit (seven handbreadths) here at about 21 inches (53 centimeters). The rod mentioned by Ezekiel was about six long cubits, or 11 feet (3.2 meters) long.

40:6 – 16 The size and design of the gateway shows its great importance in the temple complex. The jambs were decorated with palm fronds, presumably similar to those in Solomon's temple (1Ki 6:29 – 36). These types of fortified installations were built for military, not religious, purposes. Later in Ezekiel we are told that the gates were to be manned by the Levites, who guarded the sacred places in the temple. The overall design of the gatehouse is typical of a number of preexilic Palestinian city gates from Megiddo, Hazor and Gezer. While these gates are typical of city gates, they are much more extensive than would be usually found with temples. See notes on Job 5:4; 29:7; Pr 8:3; 31:23.

This structure was clearly a "guardhouse." According to vv. 13,15 it measured 50 cubits (88 feet or 27 meters) by 25 cubits (44 feet or 13 meters). It compares to the guardrooms of Solomon's temple (1Ki 14:28), although their size is not mentioned. Of nearly 20 Iron Age gate systems excavated in Israel, this would be larger than most. The gates at Dan, Megiddo and Lachish are 80 – 100 feet (24.4 – 30.5 meters) wide (compared to the 44 feet or 13 meters of this gate). But those gates are larger than most, and the average gate runs closer to the width of the gate described here. The depth of this gate, however, is on the large size (88 feet or 27 meters). One of the deepest excavated gates is at Lachish; it is nearly 82 feet (25 meters). The descriptions and measurements of the chambers are comparable to Iron Age gates.

40:6 *east gate.* The gate through which Yahweh's glory would make its entry (43:1 – 4). Similarly, God's glory had left the temple through the same gate (10:19). Since temples tended to be oriented toward the east, this would be the most important gate.

40:17 – 19 With the addition of information from 42:6, the outer court had a group of rooms that may have been used by worshipers as eating and meeting places during the periods of religious events. The rooms were pillared porticos. The size of the rooms is not given. The area did contain a raised pavement of about 100 cubits (about 175 feet or 53 meters). The Hebrew term for "pavement" is a rare word. In Est 1:6 the term represents a mosaic floor inlaid with precious stones.

40:20 – 27 The north and south gates have the same features as those of the east gate: recesses, jambs, niches, a vestibule and palm decorations. The measurements of the three gates are also identical. See note on vv. 6 – 16.

EZEKIEL'S TEMPLE

Ezekiel uses a long or "royal" cubit, about 21 inches or 53 centimeters ("cubit and a handbreadth," Eze 40:5) as opposed to the standard Hebrew cubit of about 18 inches or 45 centimeters.

Scripture describes a floor plan but provides few height dimensions. This artwork shows an upward projection of the temple over the floor plan. This temple existed only in a vision of Ezekiel (Eze 40:2) and was never actually built as were the temples of Solomon, Zerubbabel and Herod, but some premillennial interpreters believe that it will be built in the future.

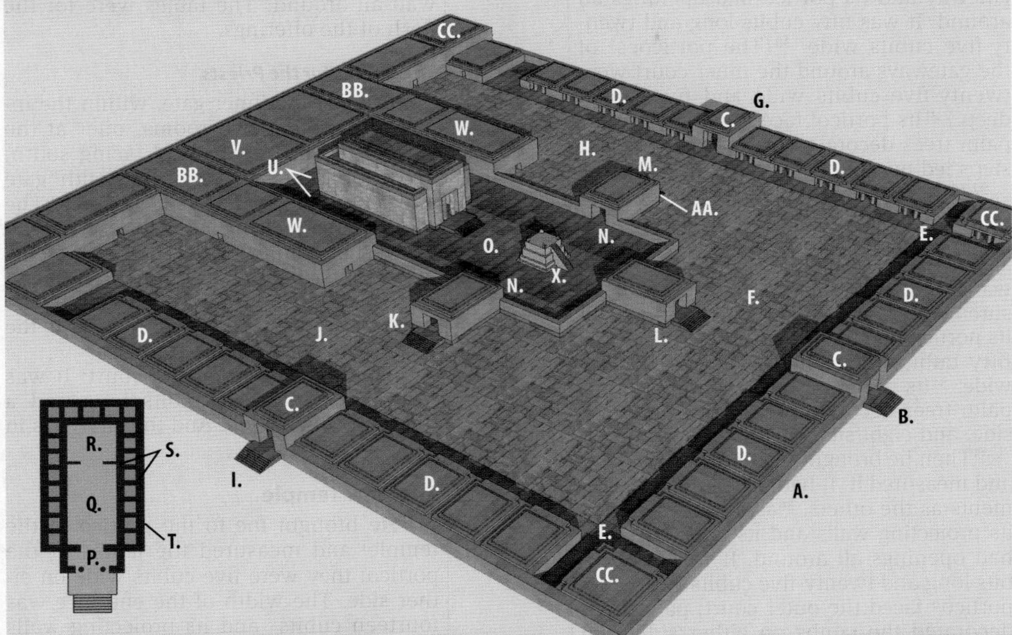

A. Wall (40:5,16–20)
B. East gate (40:6–14,16)
C. Portico (40:8)
D. Outer court (40:17)
E. Pavement (40:17)
F. East inner court (40:19)
G. North gate (40:20–22)
H. North inner court (40:23)
I. South gate (40:24–26)
J. South inner court (40:27)
K. Gateway (40:28–31)
L. Gateway (40:32–34)
M. Gateway (40:35–38)
N. Priests' rooms (40:44–45)
O. Court (40:47)
P. Temple portico (40:48–49)
Q. Outer sanctuary (41:1–2)
R. Most Holy Place (41:3–4)
S. Temple walls (41:5–7,9,11)
T. Base (41:8)
U. Open area (41:10)
V. West building (41:12)
W. Priests' rooms (42:1–10)
X. Altar (43:13–17)
AA. Rooms for preparing sacrifices (40:39–43)
BB. Ovens (46:19–20)
CC. Kitchens (46:21–24)

orations had the same measurements as
those of the gate facing east. Seven steps
led up to it, with its portico opposite them.
23There was a gate to the inner court facing the north gate, just as there was on
the east. He measured from one gate to
the opposite one; it was a hundred cubits.[n]

The South Gate

24Then he led me to the south side and
I saw the south gate. He measured its
jambs and its portico, and they had the
same measurements as the others. 25The
gateway and its portico had narrow openings all around, like the openings of the
others. It was fifty cubits long and twenty-five cubits wide.[o] 26Seven steps led
up to it, with its portico opposite them;
it had palm tree decorations on the faces of the projecting walls on each side.[p]
27The inner court[q] also had a gate facing
south, and he measured from this gate to

40:23 [n] ver 19
40:25 [o] ver 33
40:26 [p] ver 22
40:27 [q] ver 32

40:26 *palm tree decorations.* They were not only artistically beautiful but also reminiscent of Solomon's temple (1Ki 6:29–36). These types of decorations were common in Iron Age Palestine, particularly in connection with temple facades.

the outer gate on the south side; it was a hundred cubits.

The Gates to the Inner Court

28 Then he brought me into the inner court through the south gate, and he measured the south gate; it had the same measurements[r] as the others. 29 Its alcoves, its projecting walls and its portico had the same measurements as the others. The gateway and its portico had openings all around. It was fifty cubits long and twenty-five cubits wide. 30 (The porticoes[s] of the gateways around the inner court were twenty-five cubits wide and five cubits deep.) 31 Its portico[t] faced the outer court; palm trees decorated its jambs, and eight steps led up to it.

32 Then he brought me to the inner court on the east side, and he measured the gateway; it had the same measurements as the others. 33 Its alcoves, its projecting walls and its portico had the same measurements as the others. The gateway and its portico had openings all around. It was fifty cubits long and twenty-five cubits wide. 34 Its portico[u] faced the outer court; palm trees decorated the jambs on either side, and eight steps led up to it.

35 Then he brought me to the north gate[v] and measured it. It had the same measurements as the others, 36 as did its alcoves,[w] its projecting walls and its portico, and it had openings all around. It was fifty cubits long and twenty-five cubits wide. 37 Its portico[a] faced the outer court; palm trees decorated the jambs on either side, and eight steps led up to it.

The Rooms for Preparing Sacrifices

38 A room with a doorway was by the portico in each of the inner gateways, where the burnt offerings[x] were washed. 39 In the portico of the gateway were two tables on each side, on which the burnt offerings,[y] sin offerings[b][z] and guilt offerings[a] were slaughtered. 40 By the outside wall of the portico of the gateway, near the steps at the entrance of the north gateway were two tables, and on the other side of the steps were two tables. 41 So there were four tables on one side of the gateway and four on the other — eight tables in all — on which the sacrifices were slaughtered. 42 There were also four tables of dressed stone[b] for the burnt offerings, each a cubit and a half long, a cubit and a half wide and a cubit high.[c] On them were placed the utensils for slaughtering the burnt offerings and the other sacrifices.[c] 43 And double-pronged hooks, each a handbreadth[d] long, were attached to the wall all around. The tables were for the flesh of the offerings.

The Rooms for the Priests

44 Outside the inner gate, within the inner court, were two rooms, one[e] at the side of the north gate and facing south, and another at the side of the south[f] gate and facing north. 45 He said to me, "The room facing south is for the priests who guard the temple,[d] 46 and the room facing north[e] is for the priests who guard the altar.[f] These are the sons of Zadok,[g] who are the only Levites who may draw near to the LORD to minister before him.[h]"

47 Then he measured the court: It was square — a hundred cubits long and a hundred cubits wide. And the altar was in front of the temple.

The New Temple

48 He brought me to the portico of the temple[i] and measured the jambs of the portico; they were five cubits wide on either side. The width of the entrance was fourteen cubits[g] and its projecting walls were[h] three cubits[i] wide on either side. 49 The portico[j] was twenty cubits[j] wide, and twelve[k] cubits[l] from front to back. It was reached by a flight of stairs,[m] and there were pillars[k] on each side of the jambs.

40:28 [r] ver 35 **40:30** [s] ver 21 **40:31** [t] ver 22 **40:34** [u] ver 22 **40:35** [v] Eze 44:4; 47:2 **40:36** [w] ver 7 **40:38** [x] 2Ch 4:6; Eze 42:13 **40:39** [y] Eze 46:2 [z] Lev 4:3,28 [a] Lev 7:1

40:42 [b] Ex 20:25 [c] ver 39 **40:45** [d] 1Ch 9:23 **40:46** [e] Eze 42:13 [f] Nu 18:5 [g] 1Ki 2:35 [h] Nu 16:5; Eze 43:19; 44:15; 45:4; 48:11 **40:48** [i] 1Ki 6:2 **40:49** [j] ver 22; 1Ki 6:3 [k] 1Ki 7:15

[a] *37* Septuagint (see also verses 31 and 34); Hebrew *jambs* [b] *39* Or *purification offerings* [c] *42* That is, about 2 2/3 feet long and wide and 21 inches high or about 80 centimeters long and wide and 53 centimeters high [d] *43* That is, about 3 1/2 inches or about 9 centimeters [e] *44* Septuagint; Hebrew *were rooms for singers, which were* [f] *44* Septuagint; Hebrew *east* [g] *48* That is, about 25 feet or about 7.4 meters [h] *48* Septuagint; Hebrew *entrance was* [i] *48* That is, about 5 1/4 feet or about 1.6 meters [j] *49* That is, about 35 feet or about 11 meters [k] *49* Septuagint; Hebrew *eleven* [l] *49* That is, about 21 feet or about 6.4 meters [m] *49* Hebrew; Septuagint *Ten steps led up to it*

40:28 – 37 The inner court gates were mirror images of the outer gates (see note on vv. 6 – 16). The inner courtyard backed up to the wall on the western side, with a structure between the wall and the back of the temple. That is why there were no western gates.
40:39 *burnt offerings.* See Lev 1 and notes. *sin offerings.* See Lev 4 and notes. *guilt offerings.* See Lev 5:14 – 19 and notes.
40:43 *double-pronged hooks.* These hooks on the walls have traditionally been interpreted as being used to hang utensils. A more recent interpretation argues that they were niches or ledges for the storage of the utensils, much like what is described in the Dead Sea Scrolls (Temple Scroll, 30:13).
40:47 The inner court was a perfect square, 100 cubits (about 175 feet or 53 meters) on each side. This is about 2/3 acre (1/4 hectare). Since the temple, as sacred space, was considered the center of order in the cosmos, symmetry and proportions were important. See the articles "Temples and Sacred Space," p. 724; "Sacred Space," p. 964.
40:49 *portico.* See note on 1Ki 6:3.

41 Then the man brought me to
the main hall[l] and measured the
jambs; the width of the jambs was six cubits[a] on each side.[b] 2The entrance was ten
cubits[c] wide, and the projecting walls on
each side of it were five cubits[d] wide. He
also measured the main hall; it was forty
cubits long and twenty cubits wide.[e][m]
3Then he went into the inner sanctuary
and measured the jambs of the entrance;
each was two cubits[f] wide. The entrance
was six cubits wide, and the projecting
walls on each side of it were seven cubits[g]
wide. 4And he measured the length of the
inner sanctuary; it was twenty cubits, and
its width was twenty cubits across the end
of the main hall.[n] He said to me, "This is
the Most Holy Place.[o]"
5Then he measured the wall of the temple; it was six cubits thick, and each side
room around the temple was four cubits[h]
wide. 6The side rooms were on three levels, one above another, thirty[p] on each level. There were ledges all around the wall
of the temple to serve as supports for the
side rooms, so that the supports were not
inserted into the wall of the temple.[q] 7The
side rooms all around the temple were
wider at each successive level. The structure surrounding the temple was built in
ascending stages, so that the rooms wid-
ened as one went upward. A stairway[r]
went up from the lowest floor to the top
floor through the middle floor.
8I saw that the temple had a raised base
all around it, forming the foundation of
the side rooms. It was the length of the
rod, six long cubits. 9The outer wall of the
side rooms was five cubits thick. The open
area between the side rooms of the temple
10and the priests' rooms was twenty cubits wide all around the temple. 11There
were entrances to the side rooms from the
open area, one on the north and another
on the south; and the base adjoining the
open area was five cubits wide all around.
12The building facing the temple courtyard on the west side was seventy cubits[i]
wide. The wall of the building was five
cubits thick all around, and its length was
ninety cubits.[j]
13Then he measured the temple; it was
a hundred cubits[k] long, and the temple
courtyard and the building with its walls
were also a hundred cubits long. 14The
width of the temple courtyard on the east,
including the front of the temple, was a
hundred cubits.[s]
15Then he measured the length of the
building facing the courtyard at the rear of
the temple, including its galleries[t] on each
side; it was a hundred cubits.
The main hall, the inner sanctuary and
the portico facing the court, 16as well
as the thresholds and the narrow windows[u] and galleries around the three of
them — everything beyond and including
the threshold was covered with wood. The
floor, the wall up to the windows, and the
windows were covered.[v] 17In the space
above the outside of the entrance to the
inner sanctuary and on the walls at regular intervals all around the inner and outer
sanctuary 18were carved[w] cherubim[x] and
palm trees.[y] Palm trees alternated with
cherubim. Each cherub had two faces:[z]
19the face of a human being toward the

41:1 [l] ver 23
41:2 [m] 2Ch 3:3
41:4 [n] 1Ki 6:20 [o] Ex 26:33; Heb 9:3-8
41:6 [p] Eze 40:17 [q] 1Ki 6:5
41:7 [r] 1Ki 6:8
41:14 [s] Eze 40:47
41:15 [t] Eze 42:3
41:16 [u] 1Ki 6:4 [v] ver 25-26; 1Ki 6:15; Eze 42:3
41:18 [w] 1Ki 6:18 [x] Ex 37:7; 2Ch 3:7 [y] 1Ki 6:29; 7:36 [z] Eze 10:21

[a] *1* That is, about 11 feet or about 3.2 meters; also in verses 3, 5 and 8 [b] *1* One Hebrew manuscript and Septuagint; most Hebrew manuscripts *side, the width of the tent* [c] *2* That is, about 18 feet or about 5.3 meters [d] *2* That is, about 8 3/4 feet or about 2.7 meters; also in verses 9, 11 and 12 [e] *2* That is, about 70 feet long and 35 feet wide or about 21 meters long and 11 meters wide [f] *3* That is, about 3 1/2 feet or about 1.1 meters; also in verse 22 [g] *3* That is, about 12 feet or about 3.7 meters [h] *5* That is, about 7 feet or about 2.1 meters [i] *12* That is, about 123 feet or about 37 meters [j] *12* That is, about 158 feet or about 48 meters [k] *13* That is, about 175 feet or about 53 meters; also in verses 14 and 15

41:5 – 11 Ezekiel describes here the auxiliary structures of the temple. There are a number of technical architectural expressions discussed in this section, many of which have uncertain meanings. Much of the description, however, is reminiscent of that found in 1Ki 6:5 – 8 concerning Solomon's temple. Although Ezekiel sketches the auxiliary structures around the temple, he does not describe their function, nor does the author of 1 Kings. Similar single and multistoried rooms from Egyptian religious centers imply that they were used as storehouses for temple treasures. Temples built by Merneptah and Rameses II (thirteenth century BC) had storage spaces three to four times larger than the temple itself. This was also common in Mesopotamia.

41:13 – 14 Both Solomon's temple and the temple of Ezekiel consisted of three rooms. The dimensions of the holy room and the great hall in both temples are identical.

41:15 *the building facing the courtyard at the rear of the temple.* The identification and function of this building are primarily determined by understanding the obscure Hebrew term used for "galleries" or "ledges." These galleries appeared on the outside of the structure. They either came in threes or were three levels. They could be seen from both the inner and outer courts. Some have concluded that these functioned as galleries or walkways (or both).

41:16 *narrow windows.* They were probably set high in the walls above the level of the annex rooms, similar to Solomon's temple (1Ki 6:29 – 35).

41:17 – 20 The palm and cherub imagery is clearly reminiscent of Solomon's temple (1Ki 6:29 – 36). However, these cherubim have only a human and a lion head, unlike the four faces of the cherubim in Solomon's temple (Eze 10:14). These were no longer freestanding structures, but were carved into the walls, which is most likely why there were fewer heads. The figures are flanked by the palm imagery, a common motif on ivories and other art forms. The same imagery is seen on ivory carvings from Arslan Tash in first millennium BC Syria and from a scene painted on storage jars from Iron Age Kuntillet Ajrud in Palestine.

palm tree on one side and the face of a lion toward the palm tree on the other. They were carved all around the whole temple.[a] 20From the floor to the area above the entrance, cherubim and palm trees were carved on the wall of the main hall.

21The main hall[b] had a rectangular doorframe, and the one at the front of the Most Holy Place was similar. 22There was a wooden altar[c] three cubits[a] high and two cubits square[b]; its corners, its base[c] and its sides were of wood. The man said to me, "This is the table[d] that is before the LORD." 23Both the main hall[e] and the Most Holy Place had double doors.[f] 24Each door had two leaves—two hinged leaves[g] for each door. 25And on the doors of the main hall were carved cherubim and palm trees like those carved on the walls, and there was a wooden overhang on the front of the portico. 26On the sidewalls of the portico were narrow windows with palm trees carved on each side. The side rooms of the temple also had overhangs.[h]

The Rooms for the Priests

42 Then the man led me northward into the outer court and brought me to the rooms[i] opposite the temple courtyard[j] and opposite the outer wall on the north side.[k] 2The building whose door faced north was a hundred cubits long and fifty cubits wide.[d] 3Both in the section twenty cubits[e] from the inner court and in the section opposite the pavement of the outer court, gallery[l] faced gallery at the three levels.[m] 4In front of the rooms was an inner passageway ten cubits wide and a hundred cubits[f] long.[g] Their doors were on the north.[n] 5Now the upper rooms were narrower, for the galleries took more space from them than from the rooms on the lower and middle floors of the building. 6The rooms on the top floor had no pillars, as the courts had; so they were smaller in floor space than those on the lower and middle floors. 7There was an outer wall parallel to the rooms and the outer court; it extended in front of the rooms for fifty cubits. 8While the row of rooms on the side next to the outer court was fifty cubits long, the row on the side nearest the sanctuary was a hundred cubits long. 9The lower rooms had an entrance[o] on the east side as one enters them from the outer court.

10On the south side[h] along the length of the wall of the outer court, adjoining the temple courtyard and opposite the outer wall, were rooms[p] 11with a passageway in front of them. These were like the rooms on the north; they had the same length and width, with similar exits and dimensions. Similar to the doorways on the north 12were the doorways of the rooms on the south. There was a doorway at the beginning of the passageway that was parallel to the corresponding wall extending eastward, by which one enters the rooms.

13Then he said to me, "The north[q] and south rooms facing the temple courtyard are the priests' rooms, where the priests who approach the LORD will eat the most holy offerings. There they will put the most holy offerings—the grain offerings, the sin offerings[i][r] and the guilt offerings[s]—for the place is holy.[t] 14Once the priests enter the holy precincts, they are not to go into the outer court until they leave behind the garments[u] in which they minister, for these are holy. They are to put on other clothes before they go near the places that are for the people.[v]"

15When he had finished measuring what was inside the temple area, he led me out by the east gate[w] and measured the area all around: 16He measured the east side with the measuring rod; it was five hundred cubits.[j,k] 17He measured the north side; it was five hundred cubits[l] by the measuring rod. 18He measured the south side; it was five hundred cubits by the measuring rod. 19Then he turned to the west side and measured; it was five hundred cubits by the measuring rod. 20So he measured[x] the area on all four sides. It had a wall around it,[y] five hundred cubits long and five hundred cubits wide,[z] to separate the holy from the common.[a]

God's Glory Returns to the Temple

43 Then the man brought me to the gate facing east,[b] 2and I saw the glory of the God of Israel coming from the

41:19 [a]Eze 10:14 **41:21** [b]ver 1 **41:22** [c]Ex 30:1 [d]Ex 25:23; Eze 23:41; 44:16; Mal 1:7, 12 **41:23** [e]ver 1 [f]1Ki 6:32 **41:24** [g]1Ki 6:34 **41:26** [h]ver 15-16; Eze 40:16 **42:1** [i]ver 13 [j]Eze 41:12-14 [k]Eze 40:17 **42:3** [l]Eze 41:15 [m]Eze 41:16 **42:4** [n]Eze 46:19 **42:9** [o]Eze 44:5; 46:19

42:10 [p]ver 1 **42:13** [q]Eze 40:46 [r]Lev 10:17; 6:25 [s]Lev 14:13 [t]Ex 29:31; Lev 6:29; 7:6; 10:12-13; Nu 18:9-10 **42:14** [u]Eze 44:19 [v]Ex 29:9; Lev 8:7-9 **42:15** [w]Eze 43:1 **42:20** [x]Eze 40:5 [y]Zec 2:5 [z]Eze 45:2; Rev 21:16 [a]Eze 22:26 **43:1** [b]Eze 10:19; 42:15; 44:1; 46:1

[a] 22 That is, about 5 1/4 feet or about 1.5 meters
[b] 22 Septuagint; Hebrew *long* [c] 22 Septuagint; Hebrew *length* [d] 2 That is, about 175 feet long and 88 feet wide or about 53 meters long and 27 meters wide
[e] 3 That is, about 35 feet or about 11 meters
[f] 4 Septuagint and Syriac; Hebrew *and one cubit*
[g] 4 That is, about 18 feet wide and 175 feet long or about 5.3 meters wide and 53 meters long
[h] 10 Septuagint; Hebrew *Eastward*
[i] 13 Or *purification offerings* [j] 16 See Septuagint of verse 17; Hebrew *rods*; also in verses 18 and 19.
[k] 16 Five hundred cubits equal about 875 feet or about 265 meters; also in verses 17, 18 and 19.
[l] 17 Septuagint; Hebrew *rods*

42:13 *priests' rooms.* Though little is known of the priests' rooms in Solomon's temple, they were well known in Babylonia. In the Babylonian temple complex this was a room in which the priestly vestments and the costly garments of the statues of deities were stored. These vestments were highly valued because of the gold and silver objects used to decorate the garments. Goldsmiths received official permission to enter into these rooms in order to work on the vestments of the priests and the divine images.

east. His voice was like the roar of rushing
waters,[c] and the land was radiant with his
glory.[d] 3 The vision I saw was like the vision I had seen when he[a] came to destroy
the city and like the visions I had seen
by the Kebar River, and I fell facedown.
4 The glory[e] of the LORD entered the temple
through the gate facing east.[f] 5 Then the
Spirit[g] lifted me up[h] and brought me into
the inner court, and the glory of the LORD
filled the temple.
6 While the man was standing beside
me, I heard someone speaking to me
from inside the temple. 7 He said: "Son of
man, this is the place of my throne and
the place for the soles of my feet. This is
where I will live among the Israelites forever. The people of Israel will never again
defile my holy name—neither they nor
their kings—by their prostitution and the
funeral offerings[b] for their kings at their
death.[c][i] 8 When they placed their threshold
next to my threshold and their doorposts
beside my doorposts, with only a wall between me and them, they defiled my holy
name by their detestable practices. So I destroyed them in my anger. 9 Now let them
put away from me their prostitution and
the funeral offerings for their kings, and I
will live among them forever.[j]
10 "Son of man, describe the temple to
the people of Israel, that they may be
ashamed[k] of their sins. Let them consider
its perfection, 11 and if they are ashamed of
all they have done, make known to them
the design of the temple—its arrangement, its exits and entrances—its whole
design and all its regulations[d] and laws.
Write these down before them so that they
may be faithful to its design and follow all
its regulations.[l]
12 "This is the law of the temple: All the
surrounding area[m] on top of the mountain
will be most holy. Such is the law of the
temple.

The Great Altar Restored

13 "These are the measurements of the
altar[n] in long cubits,[e] that cubit being a
cubit and a handbreadth: Its gutter is a
cubit deep and a cubit wide, with a rim
of one span[f] around the edge. And this is
the height of the altar: 14 From the gutter
on the ground up to the lower ledge that
goes around the altar it is two cubits high,
and the ledge is a cubit wide.[g] From this
lower ledge to the upper ledge that goes
around the altar it is four cubits high, and
that ledge is also a cubit wide.[h] 15 Above
that, the altar hearth is four cubits high,
and four horns[o] project upward from the
hearth. 16 The altar hearth is square, twelve
cubits[i] long and twelve cubits wide. 17 The
upper ledge also is square, fourteen cubits[j]
long and fourteen cubits wide. All around
the altar is a gutter of one cubit with a
rim of half a cubit.[f] The steps[p] of the altar
face east."
18 Then he said to me, "Son of man, this
is what the Sovereign LORD says: These
will be the regulations for sacrificing burnt
offerings[q] and splashing blood[r] against the

43:2 [c] Rev 1:15 [d] Isa 6:3; Eze 11:23; Rev 18:1
43:4 [e] Eze 1:28 [f] Eze 10:19
43:5 [g] Eze 11:24 [h] Eze 3:12; 8:3
43:7 [i] Lev 26:30
43:9 [j] Eze 37:26-28
43:10 [k] Eze 16:61
43:11 [l] Eze 44:5
43:12 [m] Eze 40:2
43:13 [n] 2Ch 4:1
43:15 [o] Ex 27:2
43:17 [p] Ex 20:26
43:18 [q] Ex 40:29 [r] Lev 1:5, 11; Heb 9:21-22

[a] *3* Some Hebrew manuscripts and Vulgate; most Hebrew manuscripts *I* [b] *7* Or *the memorial monuments*; also in verse 9 [c] *7* Or *their high places* [d] *11* Some Hebrew manuscripts and Septuagint; most Hebrew manuscripts *regulations and its whole design* [e] *13* That is, about 21 inches or about 53 centimeters; also in verses 14 and 17. The long cubit is the basic unit for linear measurement throughout Ezekiel 40–48. [f] *13,17* That is, about 11 inches or about 27 centimeters [g] *14* That is, about 3 1/2 feet high and 1 3/4 feet wide or about 105 centimeters high and 53 centimeters wide [h] *14* That is, about 7 feet high and 1 3/4 feet wide or about 2.1 meters high and 53 centimeters wide [i] *16* That is, about 21 feet or about 6.4 meters [j] *17* That is, about 25 feet or about 7.4 meters

43:3 *Kebar River.* See note on 1:1.
43:4 *The glory of the LORD entered the temple through the gate facing east.* In ancient Near Eastern rituals and texts, the gates are important in association with the entry of the god into the temple. In a Neo-Assyrian building ritual for opening a new gate in a building, first the new gate is to be purified before the gods can enter the building. The importance of the gate as a place of the god's entry into the temple is expressed as well in Anatolian and Syrian iconography.
43:7 *this is ... the place for the soles of my feet.* In the passageway from the portico to the entrance hall of the tenth-century BC 'Ain Dara temple in northern Syria, a pair of enormous bare footprints is carved in the floor, followed by a single footprint beyond. Another single footprint is carved on the threshold between the entrance hall and the next hall. If these dimensions were translated into height, the individual would be over 60 feet (18 meters) tall. These footprints undoubtedly represent the deity to whom the temple was dedicated, probably Baal Hadad, striding into his abode, walking toward the throne room. Ezekiel's reference to the soles of Yahweh's feet resembles this ancient Near Eastern tradition of deities entering their temples and leaving the trace of their passage as footprints in the temple floor. *funeral offerings for their kings.* The terminology here refers to a pagan cult of the dead, similar to that of Lev 26:30 (see NIV text note there). Ezekiel probably had in mind a veneration of the spirits of Israel's royal ancestors, much like a cult of the royal dead at Ugarit. Whether the kings were considered deified at either place is not clear.
43:8 *threshold ... doorposts.* The statement here in v. 8 corresponds with the description of Solomon's temple in 1 Kings. The original temple was built as one element of the entire Solomonic palace complex. Only a wall separated the temple and palace, and they bordered "threshold to threshold, and doorpost to doorpost."
43:13–17 Although the technical vocabulary for the altar is similar to that found in Akkadian, the altar of Ezekiel is most similar to that of Solomon's temple (1Ki 2:28; 2Ch 4:1). The length of the sides is similar in both cases, while the horns were a common motif in altars in the Levant. Though the altar is large, it is not as large as Solomon's and is comparable to those archaeology has uncovered.

altar when it is built: 19You are to give a
young bull[s] as a sin offering[a] to the Levitical priests of the family of Zadok,[t] who
come near[u] to minister before me, declares
the Sovereign LORD. 20You are to take some
of its blood and put it on the four horns
of the altar and on the four corners of the
upper ledge[v] and all around the rim, and
so purify the altar[w] and make atonement
for it. 21You are to take the bull for the sin
offering and burn it in the designated part
of the temple area outside the sanctuary.[x]
22"On the second day you are to offer a
male goat without defect for a sin offering,
and the altar is to be purified as it was purified with the bull. 23When you have finished purifying it, you are to offer a young
bull and a ram from the flock, both without defect.[y] 24You are to offer them before
the LORD, and the priests are to sprinkle
salt[z] on them and sacrifice them as a burnt
offering to the LORD.
25"For seven days[a] you are to provide a
male goat daily for a sin offering; you are
also to provide a young bull and a ram
from the flock, both without defect.[b] 26For
seven days they are to make atonement for
the altar and cleanse it; thus they will dedicate it. 27At the end of these days, from
the eighth day[c] on, the priests are to present your burnt offerings and fellowship
offerings[d] on the altar. Then I will accept
you, declares the Sovereign LORD."

The Priesthood Restored

44 Then the man brought me back
to the outer gate of the sanctuary,
the one facing east,[e] and it was shut. 2The
LORD said to me, "This gate is to remain
shut. It must not be opened; no one may
enter through it.[f] It is to remain shut because the LORD, the God of Israel, has entered through it. 3The prince himself is the
only one who may sit inside the gateway
to eat in the presence[g] of the LORD. He is to
enter by way of the portico of the gateway
and go out the same way.[h]"
4Then the man brought me by way of
the north gate to the front of the temple.
I looked and saw the glory of the LORD
filling the temple[i] of the LORD, and I fell
facedown.[j]
5The LORD said to me, "Son of man, look
carefully, listen closely and give attention
to everything I tell you concerning all the
regulations and instructions regarding the
temple of the LORD. Give attention to the entrance to the temple and all the exits of the
sanctuary.[k] 6Say to rebellious Israel,[l] 'This
is what the Sovereign LORD says: Enough
of your detestable practices, people of Israel! 7In addition to all your other detestable
practices, you brought foreigners uncircumcised in heart[m] and flesh into my sanctuary,
desecrating my temple while you offered
me food, fat and blood, and you broke my
covenant.[n] 8Instead of carrying out your
duty in regard to my holy things, you put
others in charge of my sanctuary.[o] 9This is
what the Sovereign LORD says: No foreigner
uncircumcised in heart and flesh is to enter
my sanctuary, not even the foreigners who
live among the Israelites.[p]
10" 'The Levites who went far from me
when Israel went astray[q] and who wandered from me after their idols must bear
the consequences of their sin.[r] 11They may
serve in my sanctuary, having charge of
the gates of the temple and serving in it;
they may slaughter the burnt offerings[s]

43:19 [s] Lev 4:3; Eze 45:18-19 [t] Eze 44:15 [u] Nu 16:40; Eze 40:46 **43:20** [v] ver 17 [w] Lev 16:19 **43:21** [x] Ex 29:14; Heb 13:11 **43:23** [y] Ex 29:1 **43:24** [z] Lev 2:13; Mk 9:49-50 **43:25** [a] Lev 8:33 [b] Ex 29:37 **43:27** [c] Lev 9:1 [d] Lev 17:5 **44:1** [e] Eze 43:1 **44:2** [f] Eze 43:4-5

44:3 [g] Ex 24:9-11 [h] Eze 46:2,8 **44:4** [i] Isa 6:4; Rev 15:8 [j] Eze 1:28; 3:23 **44:5** [k] Eze 40:4; 43:10-11 **44:6** [l] Eze 3:9 **44:7** [m] Lev 26:41 [n] Ge 17:14; Ex 12:48; Lev 22:25 **44:8** [o] Lev 22:2; Nu 18:7 **44:9** [p] Joel 3:17; Zec 14:21 **44:10** [q] 2Ki 23:8 [r] Nu 18:23 **44:11** [s] 2Ch 29:34

[a] 19 Or *purification offering*; also in verses 21, 22 and 25

43:19 *family of Zadok.* Zadok was the representative of Aaron's line who served as high priest during the reigns of David and Solomon. In the postexilic community the sons of Zadok had the altar duties reserved for them, while the Levites had less significant duties than before. The Zadokites held the high priesthood until the time of the Greek ruler Antiochus IV (175 – 164 BC). In fact, some have supposed that the Dead Sea Scrolls community may have been formed in response to the end of the Zadokite priesthood.
43:24 *sprinkle salt on them.* The reference here is to a "covenant of salt" (see note on Lev 2:13). The preservative qualities of salt made it a symbol of the permanence of the covenant relationship. Thus, the addition of salt was a reminder of God's covenant.
43:25,26 *seven days.* In the ancient Near East generally and in Israel particularly, seven-day installation and dedication services are common.
44:1 – 2 *the outer gate … facing east … is to remain shut.* The Sacred Gate of the city of Babylon was the gate through which the procession of Marduk (the primary god of the city) and other deities passed and returned again. Like the east gate described by Ezekiel, the Sacred Gate was apparently opened for God to pass through and was shut at all other times.
44:3 *prince.* In this context he is a religious figure who is responsible for eating his sacrificial meals before the Lord in the sacred (east) gate. Earlier in Ezekiel the term was used for the role of a Davidic figure (e.g., 34:24, 37:25). Here he has no royal or political role to play, only a role inside the temple precincts. He has no access through the east gate that is reserved for divine use; he only has an act to perform there. It is clear that he is not serving a priestly function, for he is not allowed to actually step inside the inner court. *portico of the gateway.* The prince was able to enter the gate structure through the portico (or vestibule) of the gateway, meaning that he had already come into the courtyard through another gate and entered the eastern gateway from the inside. He stood by the post of the gate, which enabled him to see the cultic activity of the priests.
44:8 *others in charge.* Foreigners had been recruited for temple service, probably as temple guards, perhaps since the time of Manasseh and Amon. Neo-Babylonian and Phoenician records appear to affirm the probability of the installation of foreigners in this type of temple service.

and sacrifices for the people and stand before the people and serve them.[t] 12But because they served them in the presence of their idols and made the people of Israel fall into sin, therefore I have sworn with uplifted hand[u] that they must bear the consequences of their sin, declares the Sovereign LORD.[v] 13They are not to come near to serve me as priests or come near any of my holy things or my most holy offerings; they must bear the shame[w] of their detestable practices.[x] 14And I will appoint them to guard the temple for all the work that is to be done in it.[y]

15"'But the Levitical priests, who are descendants of Zadok and who guarded my sanctuary when the Israelites went astray from me, are to come near to minister before me; they are to stand before me to offer sacrifices of fat and blood, declares the Sovereign LORD.[z] 16They alone are to enter my sanctuary; they alone are to come near my table[a] to minister before me and serve me as guards.[b]

17"'When they enter the gates of the inner court, they are to wear linen clothes;[c] they must not wear any woolen garment while ministering at the gates of the inner court or inside the temple. 18They are to wear linen turbans[d] on their heads and linen undergarments[e] around their waists. They must not wear anything that makes them perspire.[f] 19When they go out into the outer court where the people are, they are to take off the clothes they have been ministering in and are to leave them in the sacred rooms, and put on other clothes, so that the people are not consecrated[g] through contact with their garments.[h]

20"'They must not shave their heads or let their hair grow long, but they are to keep the hair of their heads trimmed.[i] 21No priest is to drink wine when he enters the inner court.[j] 22They must not marry widows or divorced women; they may marry only virgins of Israelite descent or widows of priests.[k] 23They are to teach my people the difference between the holy and the common[l] and show them how to distinguish between the unclean and the clean.[m]

24"'In any dispute, the priests are to serve as judges[n] and decide it according to my ordinances. They are to keep my laws and my decrees for all my appointed festivals, and they are to keep my Sabbaths holy.[o]

25"'A priest must not defile himself by going near a dead person; however, if the dead person was his father or mother, son or daughter, brother or unmarried sister, then he may defile himself.[p] 26After he is cleansed, he must wait seven days.[q] 27On the day he goes into the inner court of the sanctuary to minister in the sanctuary, he is to offer a sin offering[a] for himself, declares the Sovereign LORD.

28"'I am to be the only inheritance[r] the priests have. You are to give them no possession in Israel; I will be their possession. 29They will eat the grain offerings, the sin offerings and the guilt offerings; and everything in Israel devoted[b] to the LORD[s] will belong to them.[t] 30The best of all the firstfruits[u] and of all your special gifts will belong to the priests. You are to give them the first portion of your ground meal[v] so that a blessing[w] may rest on your household.[x] 31The priests must not eat anything, whether bird or animal, found dead or torn by wild animals.[y]

[a] 27 Or *purification offering*; also in verse 29
[b] 29 The Hebrew term refers to the irrevocable giving over of things or persons to the LORD.

44:11 [t] Nu 3:5-37; 16:9; 1Ch 26:12-19 **44:12** [u] Ps 106:26 [v] 2Ki 16:10-16 **44:13** [w] Eze 16:61 [x] Nu 18:3 **44:14** [y] Nu 18:4; 1Ch 23:28-32 **44:15** [z] Jer 33:18; Eze 40:46; Zec 3:7 **44:16** [a] Eze 41:22 [b] Nu 18:5 **44:17** [c] Ex 39:27-28; Rev 19:8 **44:18** [d] Ex 28:39; Isa 3:20 [e] Ex 28:42 [f] Lev 16:4 **44:19** [g] Lev 6:27; Eze 46:20 [h] Lev 6:10-11; Eze 42:14 **44:20** [i] Lev 21:5; Nu 6:5 **44:21** [j] Lev 10:9 **44:22** [k] Lev 21:7 **44:23** [l] Eze 22:26 [m] Mal 2:7 **44:24** [n] Dt 17:8-9; 1Ch 23:4 [o] 2Ch 19:8 **44:25** [p] Lev 21:1-4 **44:26** [q] Nu 19:14 **44:28** [r] Nu 18:20; Dt 10:9; 18:1-2; Jos 13:33 **44:29** [s] Lev 27:21 [t] Nu 18:9,14 **44:30** [u] Nu 18:12-13 [v] Nu 15:18-21 [w] Mal 3:10 [x] Ne 10:35-37 **44:31** [y] Ex 22:31; Lev 22:8

44:14 *guard the temple.* Implies guarding not just the gates of the temple but the entire temple complex. They were also responsible for caring for the temple and its grounds, and they supervised activities on the temple grounds. See note on 1Ch 9:17.

44:17 *wear linen clothes ... not wear any woolen garment.* The reason for the prohibition of wool appears to be a practical one. Wool was more likely to cause one to sweat. Since all bodily excretions caused defilement, steps needed to be taken to prevent their occurrence in the temple complex. This appears also to be the case in Egypt, where, according to Herodotus and the Roman writer Lucian, linen was also used in the material for priestly garments. Herodotus adds that the Egyptian priests consistently washed their linen garments.

44:19 *sacred rooms.* See note on 42:13.

44:20 *must not shave their heads.* Shaving the head bald or letting the hair grow very long was most likely forbidden because of the pagan customs associating it with Canaanite cults of the dead. The taboo has its inspiration from Lev 21:5.

44:21 *No priest is to drink wine when he enters the inner court.* This prohibition has its parallel in Lev 10:9. Though pagan cultic intoxication was well known, e.g., from the Babylonian creation epic *Enuma Elish*, it is most likely that the prohibition was to make sure that the priest had control of his faculties (see note on Isa 28:7).

44:22 The explicit prohibition concerning the priest and marriage comes from Lev 21:7,13 – 15 (see note on Lev 21:7). It appears from Lev 21:15 that the concern was for the dilution of the purity of the priestly line, although Ezekiel does not mention the reason for the prohibition.

44:29 – 30 Although these verses provide the physical sustenance for the priests, there is more. The priests were actually invited to eat Yahweh's food. For more information, see Nu 18:8 – 19 and notes. They were also authorized to eat the *herem*, i.e., every irredeemable devoted thing. These items were evidently those designated for any use, except that which was prescribed for the cult.

Israel Fully Restored

45 “ ‘When you allot the land as an
inheritance,[z] you are to present to
the LORD a portion of the land as a sacred
district, 25,000 cubits[a] long and 20,000[b]
cubits[c] wide; the entire area will be holy.[a]
2 Of this, a section 500 cubits[d] square[b] is
to be for the sanctuary, with 50 cubits[e]
around it for open land. 3 In the sacred
district, measure off a section 25,000 cubits long and 10,000 cubits[f] wide. In it will
be the sanctuary, the Most Holy Place. 4 It
will be the sacred portion of the land for
the priests,[c] who minister in the sanctuary
and who draw near to minister before the
LORD. It will be a place for their houses
as well as a holy place for the sanctuary.[d]
5 An area 25,000 cubits long and 10,000 cubits wide will belong to the Levites, who
serve in the temple, as their possession for
towns to live in.[g][e]
6 “ ‘You are to give the city as its property an area 5,000 cubits[h] wide and 25,000
cubits long, adjoining the sacred portion;
it will belong to all Israel.[f]
7 “ ‘The prince will have the land bordering each side of the area formed by the
sacred district and the property of the city.
It will extend westward from the west side
and eastward from the east side, running
lengthwise from the western to the eastern border parallel to one of the tribal portions.[g] 8 This land will be his possession
in Israel. And my princes will no longer
oppress my people but will allow the people of Israel to possess the land according
to their tribes.[h]
9 “ ‘This is what the Sovereign LORD says:
You have gone far enough, princes of Israel! Give up your violence and oppression and do what is just and right.[i] Stop
dispossessing my people, declares the
Sovereign LORD. 10 You are to use accurate
scales,[j] an accurate ephah[i][k] and an accurate bath.[j] 11 The ephah[l] and the bath are
to be the same size, the bath containing
a tenth of a homer and the ephah a tenth
of a homer; the homer is to be the standard measure for both. 12 The shekel[k] is to
consist of twenty gerahs.[m] Twenty shekels
plus twenty-five shekels plus fifteen shekels equal one mina.[l]
13 “ ‘This is the special gift you are to offer: a sixth of an ephah[m] from each homer
of wheat and a sixth of an ephah[n] from
each homer of barley. 14 The prescribed
portion of olive oil, measured by the bath,
is a tenth of a bath[o] from each cor (which
consists of ten baths or one homer, for ten
baths are equivalent to a homer). 15 Also
one sheep is to be taken from every flock
of two hundred from the well-watered pastures of Israel. These will be used for the
grain offerings, burnt offerings[n] and fellowship offerings to make atonement[o] for
the people, declares the Sovereign LORD.
16 All the people of the land will be required to give this special offering to the

45:1 [z] Eze 47:21-22 [a] Eze 48:8-9, 29 **45:2** [b] Eze 42:20 **45:4** [c] Eze 40:46 [d] Eze 48:10-11 **45:5** [e] Eze 48:13 **45:6** [f] Eze 48:15-18 **45:7** [g] Eze 48:21 **45:8** [h] Nu 26:53; Eze 46:18 **45:9** [i] Jer 22:3; Zec 7:9-10; 8:16 **45:10** [j] Dt 25:15; Pr 11:1; Am 8:4-6; Mic 6:10-11 [k] Lev 19:36 **45:11** [l] Isa 5:10 **45:12** [m] Ex 30:13; Lev 27:25; Nu 3:47 **45:15** [n] Lev 1:4 [o] Lev 6:30

[a] *1* That is, about 8 miles or about 13 kilometers; also in verses 3, 5 and 6 [b] *1* Septuagint (see also verses 3 and 5 and 48:9); Hebrew *10,000* [c] *1* That is, about 6 1/2 miles or about 11 kilometers [d] *2* That is, about 875 feet or about 265 meters [e] *2* That is, about 88 feet or about 27 meters [f] *3* That is, about 3 1/3 miles or about 5.3 kilometers; also in verse 5 [g] *5* Septuagint; Hebrew *temple; they will have as their possession 20 rooms* [h] *6* That is, about 1 2/3 miles or about 2.7 kilometers [i] *10* An ephah was a dry measure having the capacity of about 3/5 bushel or about 22 liters. [j] *10* A bath was a liquid measure equaling about 6 gallons or about 22 liters. [k] *12* A shekel weighed about 2/5 ounce or about 12 grams. [l] *12* That is, 60 shekels; the common mina was 50 shekels. Sixty shekels were about 1 1/2 pounds or about 690 grams. [m] *13* That is, probably about 6 pounds or about 2.7 kilograms [n] *13* That is, probably about 5 pounds or about 2.3 kilograms [o] *14* That is, about 2 1/2 quarts or about 2.2 liters

45:1 *sacred district.* Land reserved for use by the God of the temple area. Ezekiel portrays the land as a gift that was returned to the divine benefactor. As early as the early fourth millennium BC, the city of Uruk in southern Mesopotamia had sacred districts in the center of its town. In ancient Mesopotamia, the sacred districts were separated by retaining walls for the structure or a large citadel wall surrounded the entire sacred precinct. Access to sacred precincts was limited and strict standards were maintained regarding who could enter on what occasions. This is a continuation of the sacred compass idea that was established in Israel when the tabernacle was set up in the wilderness period (see notes on Nu 18:1,3; the also the articles "Temples and Sacred Space," p. 724; "Sacred Space," p. 964).

45:2 – 6 The larger consecrated area was about 8 miles (13 kilometers) long and 6.5 miles (10.5 kilometers) wide, an area of over 50 square miles (130 square kilometers). This could be compared to the approximately 620 square miles (1,600 square kilometers) of the entire district of Yehud (what had included Judah) under Persian rule. One half of this area (the center of the area) was reserved for the priests and sanctuary. One other area, 8 miles (13 kilometers) by 3 miles (5 kilometers), was reserved for the city, which was most likely Jerusalem, although the name is not given. If this design were superimposed on the land of Israel, it would encompass a large central segment of the tribal allotment of Judah. The territorial scheme shows the relative importance of the officials of the state, depending upon their placement near the center, where there was the closest access to God.

45:7 *prince.* See note on 44:3.

45:10 *accurate scales.* In an economy that did not have standardized weights and measures, traders were often tempted to cheat by falsifying the balances and measurements, often by using improper weights and false bottoms and other ways to alter the sizes of vessels. The two-armed balance scales were used to weigh out goods in Israel. *ephah.* A dry standard used for measuring grain; it equaled about 3/5 bushel (22 liters). *bath.* A liquid standard used for measuring oil, wine and water; it was about six gallons (22 liters). Both an ephah and a bath are one tenth of a homer (v. 11).

prince in Israel. 17 It will be the duty of the prince to provide the burnt offerings, grain offerings and drink offerings at the festivals, the New Moons and the Sabbaths[p]—at all the appointed festivals of Israel. He will provide the sin offerings,[a] grain offerings, burnt offerings and fellowship offerings to make atonement for the Israelites.[q]

18 " 'This is what the Sovereign LORD says: In the first month[r] on the first day you are to take a young bull without defects[s] and purify the sanctuary.[t] 19 The priest is to take some of the blood of the sin offering and put it on the doorposts of the temple, on the four corners of the upper ledge[u] of the altar[v] and on the gateposts of the inner court. 20 You are to do the same on the seventh day of the month for anyone who sins unintentionally[w] or through ignorance; so you are to make atonement for the temple.

21 " 'In the first month on the fourteenth day you are to observe the Passover,[x] a festival lasting seven days, during which you shall eat bread made without yeast. 22 On that day the prince is to provide a bull as a sin offering for himself and for all the people of the land.[y] 23 Every day during the seven days of the festival he is to provide seven bulls and seven rams[z] without defect as a burnt offering to the LORD, and a male goat for a sin offering.[a] 24 He is to provide as a grain offering[b] an ephah for each bull and an ephah for each ram, along with a hin[b] of olive oil for each ephah.[c]

25 " 'During the seven days of the festival,[d] which begins in the seventh month on the fifteenth day, he is to make the same provision for sin offerings, burnt offerings, grain offerings and oil.[e]

46 " 'This is what the Sovereign LORD says: The gate of the inner court[f] facing east[g] is to be shut on the six working days, but on the Sabbath day and on the day of the New Moon[h] it is to be opened. 2 The prince is to enter from the outside through the portico[i] of the gateway and stand by the gatepost. The priests are to sacrifice his burnt offering and his fellowship offerings. He is to bow down in worship at the threshold of the gateway and then go out, but the gate will not be shut until evening.[j] 3 On the Sabbaths and New Moons the people of the land are to worship in the presence of the LORD at the entrance of that gateway.[k] 4 The burnt offering the prince brings to the LORD on the Sabbath day is to be six male lambs and a ram, all without defect. 5 The grain offering given with the ram is to be an ephah,[c] and the grain offering with the lambs is to be

45:17 [p] Lev 23:38; Isa 66:23 [q] 1Ki 8:62; 2Ch 31:3; Eze 46:4-12 **45:18** [r] Ex 12:2 [s] Lev 22:20; Heb 9:14 [t] Lev 16:16, 33 **45:19** [u] Eze 43:17 [v] Lev 16:18-19; Eze 43:20 **45:20** [w] Lev 4:27 **45:21** [x] Ex 12:11; Lev 23:5-6 **45:22** [y] Lev 4:14 **45:23** [z] Job 42:8 [a] Nu 28:16-25 **45:24** [b] Nu 28:12-13 [c] Eze 46:5-7 **45:25** [d] Dt 16:13 [e] Lev 23:34-43; Nu 29:12-38 **46:1** [f] Eze 40:19 [g] 1Ch 9:18 [h] ver 6; Isa 66:23 **46:2** [i] ver 8 [j] ver 12; Eze 44:3 **46:3** [k] Lk 1:10

[a] *17* Or *purification offerings*; also in verses 19, 22, 23 and 25 [b] *24* That is, about 1 gallon or about 3.8 liters [c] *5* That is, probably about 35 pounds or about 16 kilograms; also in verses 7 and 11

45:17 *prince.* Here the prince is seen in a royal role. Typically in the ancient Near East the king was the one who provided the sacrifices for the festival rituals. This can be observed in Biblical texts as well as in the nations surrounding Israel. At the large public festivals, the general population often played the role of audience while the leaders of the people (court and temple) took center stage. The pageantry could be grandiose and the largesse of the king was made evident.

45:18 – 20 The ritual described here has all the earmarks of a purification ceremony to dedicate the new sanctuary. These were typically seven-day affairs that assured that the holy place and holy objects were ready for use. It marked the beginning of the operation of the sanctuary.

45:21 – 25 In Ezekiel's formulation, Passover takes on a different look than the traditional observance established in Ex 11 – 12. Originally Passover was established as a family-oriented festival in which the head of the household served a priestly role and the home served as the location of the festivities. The related Festival of Unleavened Bread had gradually merged with Passover, as is indicated here as well. In the Passover celebrations carried out by Hezekiah (2Ch 30) and Josiah (2Ch 35), there was a more national and centralized aspect to the observance, but that is even more the case here in Ezekiel.

46:1 *the day of the New Moon.* Keyed to their use of a lunar calendar, ancient Israel marked the first day of the month, with its "new moon" phase, as a festival day (every 29 – 30 days). Like the Sabbath, all work was to cease (Am 8:5), and sacrifices were to be made (Nu 28:11 – 15). In the monarchy period, the king became a prominent figure in these celebrations. The festival continued to be observed in the postexilic period as well (Ezr 3:5; Ne 10:33). New moon festivals were also prominent in Mesopotamia from late in the third millennium BC to the Neo-Babylonian period in the middle of the first millennium BC. The cult of the moon was widespread throughout the ancient Near East, and moon deities figured prominently in mythological texts. Although the Israelites were forbidden to worship any heavenly bodies (including the lunar cult: e.g., Dt 23:5; Jer 8:2), they were allowed to celebrate the first of the month with trumpets and burnt offerings.

46:2 *prince is to enter.* See note on 44:3.

46:3 *On the Sabbaths and New Moons the people ... are to worship.* This is one of the few explicit references in the OT to worship on the Sabbath. It is usually only spoken of in terms of prohibited activities. Many of Israel's festivals featured "holy convocations" but such are never mandated for the Sabbath. Here it is also interesting to note that the temple is the focal point for this Sabbath worship. Temples served as gathering places when public sacred rituals were being performed (at events designated as holy convocations). One must be careful not to associate too closely our worship in church on Sunday with Israel's acts of worship at the temple on the Sabbath. The differences are both profuse and profound. For example, a church is where God's people ("the church") gather for corporate worship. The temple hosted worship activities, but it was not generally large enough to hold many people. People performed their rituals and left. A temple was the actual residence of the deity and was therefore sacred space, whereas a church is simply a place that is sacred when God's people, in whom the presence of Christ dwells, are present.

as much as he pleases, along with a hin[a] of olive oil for each ephah.[l] 6On the day of the New Moon[m] he is to offer a young bull, six lambs and a ram, all without defect. 7He is to provide as a grain offering one ephah with the bull, one ephah with the ram, and with the lambs as much as he wants to give, along with a hin of oil for each ephah.[n] 8When the prince enters, he is to go in through the portico[o] of the gateway, and he is to come out the same way.[p]

9" 'When the people of the land come before the LORD at the appointed festivals,[q] whoever enters by the north gate to worship is to go out the south gate; and whoever enters by the south gate is to go out the north gate. No one is to return through the gate by which they entered, but each is to go out the opposite gate. 10The prince is to be among them, going in when they go in and going out when they go out.[r] 11At the feasts and the appointed festivals, the grain offering is to be an ephah with a bull, an ephah with a ram, and with the lambs as much as he pleases, along with a hin of oil for each ephah.[s]

12" 'When the prince provides[t] a freewill offering[u] to the LORD—whether a burnt offering or fellowship offerings—the gate facing east is to be opened for him. He shall offer his burnt offering or his fellowship offerings as he does on the Sabbath day. Then he shall go out, and after he has gone out, the gate will be shut.[v]

13" 'Every day you are to provide a year-old lamb without defect for a burnt offering to the LORD; morning by morning you shall provide it.[w] 14You are also to provide with it morning by morning a grain offering, consisting of a sixth of an ephah[b] with a third of a hin[c] of oil to moisten the flour. The presenting of this grain offering to the LORD is a lasting ordinance.[x] 15So the lamb and the grain offering and the oil shall be provided morning by morning for a regular[y] burnt offering.[z]

16" 'This is what the Sovereign LORD says: If the prince makes a gift from his inheritance to one of his sons, it will also belong to his descendants; it is to be their property by inheritance.[a] 17If, however, he makes a gift from his inheritance to one of his servants, the servant may keep it until the year of freedom;[b] then it will revert to the prince. His inheritance belongs to his sons only; it is theirs. 18The prince must not take any of the inheritance[c] of the people, driving them off their property. He is to give his sons their inheritance out of his own property, so that not one of my people will be separated from their property.' "

19Then the man brought me through the entrance[d] at the side of the gate to the sacred rooms facing north, which belonged to the priests, and showed me a place at the western end. 20He said to me, "This is the place where the priests are to cook the guilt offering and the sin offering[d] and bake the grain offering, to avoid bringing them into the outer court and consecrating[e] the people."[f]

21He then brought me to the outer court and led me around to its four corners, and I saw in each corner another court. 22In the four corners of the outer court were enclosed[e] courts, forty cubits long and thirty cubits wide;[f] each of the courts in the four corners was the same size. 23Around the inside of each of the four courts was a ledge of stone, with places for fire built all around under the ledge. 24He said to me, "These are the kitchens where those who minister at the temple are to cook the sacrifices of the people."

The River From the Temple

47 The man brought me back to the entrance to the temple, and I saw water[g] coming out from under the threshold of the temple toward the east (for the temple faced east). The water was coming down from under the south side of the temple, south of the altar.[h] 2He then brought me out through the north gate

46:5 [l] ver 11; Eze 45:24 **46:6** [m] ver 1; Nu 10:10 **46:7** [n] Eze 45:24 **46:8** [o] ver 2 [p] Eze 44:3 **46:9** [q] Ex 23:14; 34:20 **46:10** [r] 2Sa 6:14-15; Ps 42:4 **46:11** [s] ver 5 **46:12** [t] Eze 45:17 [u] Lev 7:16 [v] ver 2 **46:13** [w] Ex 29:38; Nu 28:3 **46:14** [x] Da 8:11 **46:15** [y] Ex 29:42 [z] Ex 29:38; Nu 28:5-6 **46:16** [a] 2Ch 21:3 **46:17** [b] Lev 25:10 **46:18** [c] Lev 25:23; Eze 45:8; Mic 2:1-2 **46:19** [d] Eze 42:9 **46:20** [e] Lev 6:27 [f] Zec 14:20 **47:1** [g] Isa 55:1 [h] Ps 46:4; Joel 3:18; Rev 22:1

[a] *5* That is, about 1 gallon or about 3.8 liters; also in verses 7 and 11 [b] *14* That is, probably about 6 pounds or about 2.7 kilograms [c] *14* That is, about 1 1/2 quarts or about 1.3 liters [d] *20* Or *purification offering* [e] *22* The meaning of the Hebrew for this word is uncertain. [f] *22* That is, about 70 feet long and 53 feet wide or about 21 meters long and 16 meters wide

46:9 The instruction to enter and exit by opposite gates appears to simply regulate the congestion on occasions of great crowds in the temple and to ensure the orderly flow of people. The temple area is to represent the epitome of orderliness, including even the traffic pattern. Anything that is uncontrolled or reflects confusion has no place.
46:19–24 A good number of temples in the ancient Near East were attached to kitchens. These have been found at Ur, Tell Asmar, and Terqa in Mesopotamia, and at Karnak in Egypt. Many of the kitchen complexes were larger than the temple it serviced. 2Ch 35:11–13 implies the existence of kitchens associated with Solomon's temple.
47:1 *water coming out ... of the temple.* The association between ancient Near Eastern temples and spring waters is well attested. In fact, some temples in Mesopotamia, Egypt and in the Ugaritic Baal Cycle were considered founded upon springs (likened to the primeval waters), sometimes flowing from the building itself. Thus, the symbolic cosmic mountain (temple) stood upon the symbolic primeval waters (spring). See note on v. 2.
47:2 *trickling.* The Hebrew verb is related to the noun *pak*, which means "vase." The initial source of water is quite limited, as if water was pouring from a narrow gullet of a jar or a vase. This detail is important. It shows that Ezekiel

and led me around the outside to the outer
gate facing east, and the water was trickling from the south side.
3As the man went eastward with a
measuring line[i] in his hand, he measured
off a thousand cubits[a] and then led me
through water that was ankle-deep. 4He
measured off another thousand cubits
and led me through water that was knee-
deep. He measured off another thousand
and led me through water that was up to
the waist. 5He measured off another thousand, but now it was a river that I could
not cross, because the water had risen and
was deep enough to swim in — a river that
no one could cross.[j] 6He asked me, "Son of
man, do you see this?"
Then he led me back to the bank of the
river. 7When I arrived there, I saw a great
number of trees on each side of the river.[k]
8He said to me, "This water flows toward
the eastern region and goes down into the
Arabah,[b][l] where it enters the Dead Sea.
When it empties into the sea, the salty
water there becomes fresh.[m] 9Swarms of
living creatures will live wherever the river flows. There will be large numbers of
fish, because this water flows there and
makes the salt water fresh; so where the
river flows everything will live.[n] 10Fisher-
men[o] will stand along the shore; from En
Gedi[p] to En Eglaim there will be places for
spreading nets.[q] The fish will be of many
kinds[r] — like the fish of the Mediterranean Sea.[s] 11But the swamps and marshes
will not become fresh; they will be left for
salt.[t] 12Fruit trees of all kinds will grow on
both banks of the river.[u] Their leaves will
not wither, nor will their fruit[v] fail. Every
month they will bear fruit, because the
water from the sanctuary flows to them.
Their fruit will serve for food and their
leaves for healing.[w]"

47:3 [i] Eze 40:3 **47:5** [j] Isa 11:9; Hab 2:14 **47:7** [k] ver 12; Rev 22:2 **47:8** [l] Dt 3:17; Jos 3:16 [m] Isa 41:18 **47:9** [n] Isa 12:3; 55:1; Jn 4:14; 7:37-38 **47:10** [o] Mt 4:19 [p] Jos 15:62 [q] Eze 26:5 [r] Ps 104:25; Mt 13:47 [s] Nu 34:6 **47:11** [t] Dt 29:23 **47:12** [u] ver 7; Rev 22:2 [v] Ps 1:3 [w] Ge 2:9; Jer 17:8 **47:13** [x] Nu 34:2-12 [y] Ge 48:5 **47:14** [z] Ge 12:7; Dt 1:8; Eze 20:5-6 **47:15** [a] Eze 48:1 **47:16** [b] 2Sa 8:8 [c] Nu 13:21; Eze 48:1 **47:17** [d] Eze 48:1

The Boundaries of the Land

13This is what the Sovereign LORD says:
"These are the boundaries[x] of the land
that you will divide among the twelve
tribes of Israel as their inheritance, with
two portions for Joseph.[y] 14You are to divide it equally among them. Because I
swore with uplifted hand to give it to your
ancestors, this land will become your inheritance.[z]

15"This is to be the boundary of the land:

"On the north side it will run from the
Mediterranean Sea by the Hethlon
road[a] past Lebo Hamath to Zedad,
16Berothah[c][b] and Sibraim (which lies
on the border between Damascus and
Hamath),[c] as far as Hazer Hattikon,
which is on the border of Hauran.
17The boundary will extend from the
sea to Hazar Enan,[d] along the northern border of Damascus, with the
border of Hamath to the north. This
will be the northern boundary.[d]
18"On the east side the boundary will
run between Hauran and Damascus,

[a] *3* That is, about 1,700 feet or about 530 meters
[b] *8* Or *the Jordan Valley* [c] *15,16* See Septuagint and 48:1; Hebrew *road to go into Zedad, 16Hamath, Berothah.*
[d] *17* Hebrew *Enon,* a variant of *Enan*

was probably inspired by a common decoration found in numerous ancient Near Eastern temples: the motif of the flowing vase. For example, in northern Syria, on the site of eighteenth-century BC Mari, a statue of a goddess with a flowing vase was discovered. Closer in time, divine guardian figures of the temple of Nabu are each portrayed as holding vases with water coming forth.

47:9 *Swarms of living creatures will live wherever the river flows. There will be large numbers of fish, because this water flows there and makes the salt water fresh.* The reference to the original Hebrew is essential here in order to correctly understand Ezekiel's description of the miraculous torrent that will produce an ecological renewal of the Dead Sea and the entire desert region south of Jerusalem. In designating the water the Hebrew uses the dual (*nahalayim*) "two rivers," or "two streams." Here again one recognizes the ancient Near Eastern background of Ezekiel's vision. In iconographic representations of gods with a flowing vase, one often finds two rivers flowing from the vase that the divinities hold in their hands. In Mesopotamia the two streams are supposed to represent the Tigris and Euphrates Rivers. In Ishtar's temple in Uruk, dating from the fourteenth century BC, there is an entire wall made out of colored bricks that represent a series of gods and goddesses holding a vase with rivers represented as spirals flowing and encompassing the entire temple. In Mari in one of the palace halls a color painting was found with several details that make it particularly pertinent for a comparison with Ezekiel. In the upper register, the goddess Ishtar hands over to King Zimri-Lim a measuring rod and a cord, symbolizing the king's activity in rebuilding temples. In the lower register, two goddesses hold a flowing vase in their hands from which streams flow with fish swimming up and down the streams. Several elements found on this eighteenth-century BC painting appear in Ezekiel: a linen cord and a measuring rod (40:3), flowing streams abounding with fish (47:9–10) and a symbol of vegetation (either a palm tree or an ear of corn), corresponding to the trees that grow along the flowing streams in Ezekiel (47:12).

47:12 *Their leaves will not wither, nor will their fruit fail ... Their fruit will serve for food and their leaves for healing.* The combining of flowing streams with a tree of healing appears in a seventh-century BC Sumerian-Akkadian incantation from Ashurbanipal's library. By reciting this short text the incantation priest would attempt to heal a sick man who appealed to him for help. As is well known, Gilgamesh sets out in his quest for immortality to the place where Utnapishtim lives, "at the mouth [source] of two rivers." There he obtains the plant of immortality, allowing "the old man to grow young (again)" (Gilgamesh Epic, 11.195–96). In both Ezekiel and in Akkadian literature, the tree of immortality, with leaves that never wither, is associated with an ideal setting of a paradise-like sanctuary.

BOUNDARIES OF THE LAND IN EZEKIEL'S VISION

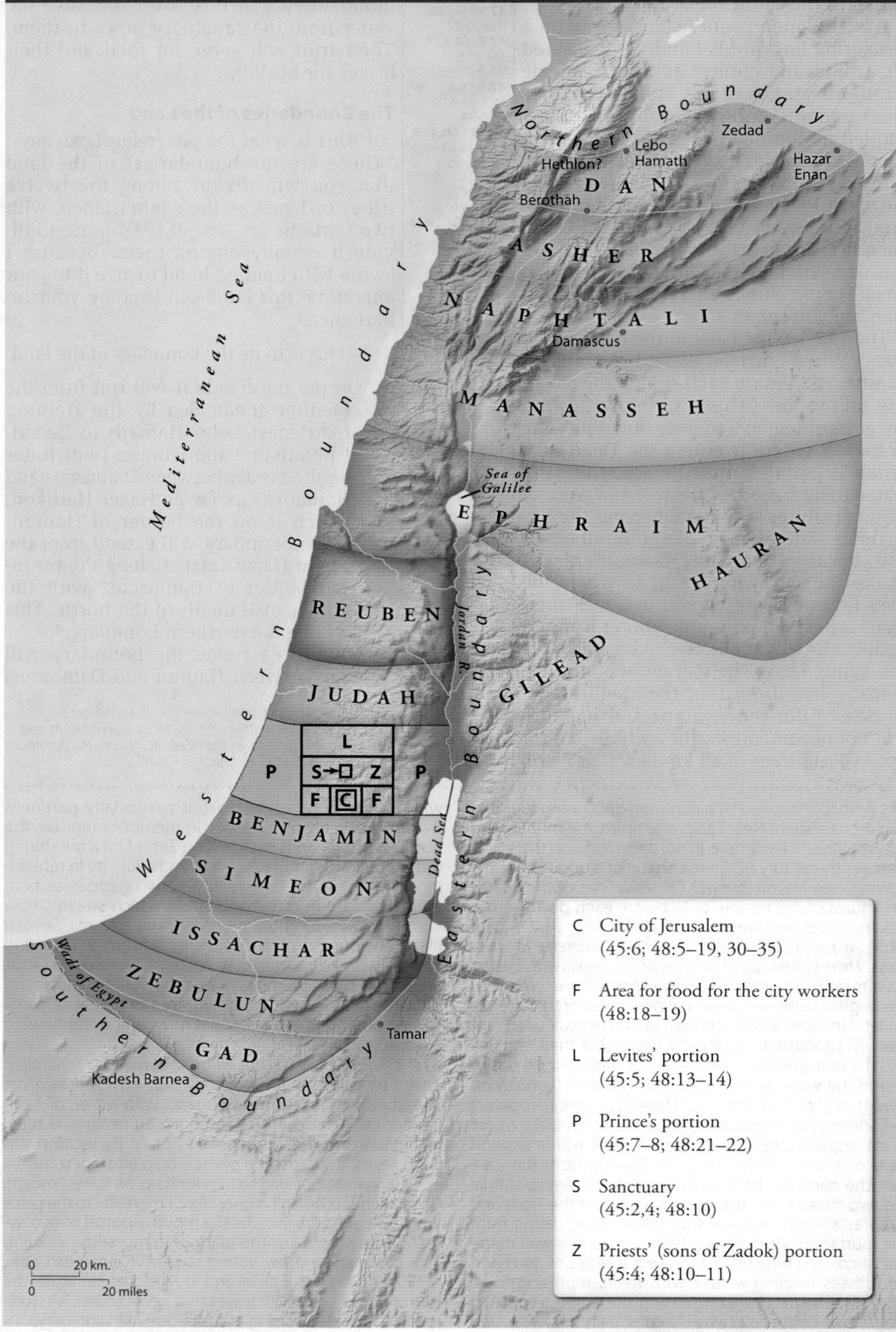

Northern Boundary
Zedad
Lebo Hamath
Hethlon?
Hazar Enan
DAN
Berothah
ASHER
NAPHTALI
Damascus
MANASSEH
Sea of Galilee
EPHRAIM
HAURAN
Mediterranean Sea
Western Boundary
REUBEN
Jordan R.
Eastern Boundary
GILEAD
JUDAH
L
P
S→□
Z
P
F
C
F
BENJAMIN
Dead Sea
SIMEON
ISSACHAR
Wadi of Egypt
ZEBULUN
Tamar
GAD
Kadesh Barnea
Southern Boundary

C City of Jerusalem (45:6; 48:5–19, 30–35)

F Area for food for the city workers (48:18–19)

L Levites' portion (45:5; 48:13–14)

P Prince's portion (45:7–8; 48:21–22)

S Sanctuary (45:2,4; 48:10)

Z Priests' (sons of Zadok) portion (45:4; 48:10–11)

0 20 km.
0 20 miles

along the Jordan between Gilead and
the land of Israel, to the Dead Sea and
as far as Tamar.[a] This will be the eastern boundary.
19 "On the south side it will run from
Tamar as far as the waters of Meribah Kadesh,[e] then along the Wadi
of Egypt[f] to the Mediterranean Sea.[g]
This will be the southern boundary.
20 "On the west side, the Mediterranean
Sea will be the boundary to a point
opposite Lebo Hamath.[h] This will be
the western boundary.[i]

21 "You are to distribute this land among
yourselves according to the tribes of Israel. 22 You are to allot it as an inheritance
for yourselves and for the foreigners[j] residing among you and who have children.
You are to consider them as native-born
Israelites; along with you they are to be
allotted an inheritance among the tribes
of Israel.[k] 23 In whatever tribe a foreigner
resides, there you are to give them their
inheritance," declares the Sovereign LORD.

The Division of the Land

48 "These are the tribes, listed by
name: At the northern frontier,
Dan[l] will have one portion; it will follow
the Hethlon road[m] to Lebo Hamath;[n] Hazar Enan and the northern border of Damascus next to Hamath will be part of its
border from the east side to the west side.
2 "Asher[o] will have one portion; it will
border the territory of Dan from east to
west.
3 "Naphtali[p] will have one portion; it
will border the territory of Asher from east
to west.
4 "Manasseh[q] will have one portion; it
will border the territory of Naphtali from
east to west.
5 "Ephraim[r] will have one portion; it will
border the territory of Manasseh[s] from
east to west.[t]
6 "Reuben[u] will have one portion; it will
border the territory of Ephraim from east
to west.

47:19 [e] Dt 32:51 [f] Isa 27:12 [g] Eze 48:28 **47:20** [h] Eze 48:1 [i] Nu 34:6 **47:22** [j] Isa 14:1 [k] Nu 26:55-56; Isa 56:6-7; Ro 10:12; Eph 2:12-16; 3:6; Col 3:11 **48:1** [l] Ge 30:6 [m] Eze 47:15-17 [n] Eze 47:20 **48:2** [o] Jos 19:24-31 **48:3** [p] Jos 19:32-39 **48:4** [q] Jos 17:1-11 **48:5** [r] Jos 16:5-9 [s] Jos 17:7-10 [t] Jos 17:17 **48:6** [u] Jos 13:15-21

48:7 [v] Jos 15:1-63 **48:8** [w] ver 21 **48:9** [x] Eze 45:1 **48:10** [y] ver 21; Eze 45:3-4 **48:11** [z] 2Sa 8:17 [a] Lev 8:35 [b] Eze 14:11; 44:15 **48:13** [c] Eze 45:5 **48:14** [d] Lev 25:34; 27:10,28

7 "Judah[v] will have one portion; it will
border the territory of Reuben from east
to west.
8 "Bordering the territory of Judah from
east to west will be the portion you are to
present as a special gift. It will be 25,000
cubits[b] wide, and its length from east to
west will equal one of the tribal portions;
the sanctuary will be in the center of it.[w]
9 "The special portion you are to offer
to the LORD will be 25,000 cubits long
and 10,000 cubits[c] wide.[x] 10 This will be
the sacred portion for the priests. It will
be 25,000 cubits long on the north side,
10,000 cubits wide on the west side,
10,000 cubits wide on the east side and
25,000 cubits long on the south side. In
the center of it will be the sanctuary of the
LORD.[y] 11 This will be for the consecrated
priests, the Zadokites,[z] who were faithful
in serving me[a] and did not go astray as
the Levites did when the Israelites went
astray.[b] 12 It will be a special gift to them
from the sacred portion of the land, a most
holy portion, bordering the territory of the
Levites.
13 "Alongside the territory of the priests,
the Levites will have an allotment 25,000
cubits long and 10,000 cubits wide. Its
total length will be 25,000 cubits and its
width 10,000 cubits.[c] 14 They must not
sell or exchange any of it. This is the best
of the land and must not pass into other
hands, because it is holy to the LORD.[d]
15 "The remaining area, 5,000 cubits[d]
wide and 25,000 cubits long, will be for
the common use of the city, for houses and for pastureland. The city will be
in the center of it 16 and will have these
measurements: the north side 4,500 cubits,[e] the south side 4,500 cubits, the east

[a] *18* See Syriac; Hebrew *Israel. You will measure to the Dead Sea.* [b] *8* That is, about 8 miles or about 13 kilometers; also in verses 9, 10, 13, 15, 20 and 21 [c] *9* That is, about 3 1/3 miles or about 5.3 kilometers; also in verses 10, 13 and 18 [d] *15* That is, about 1 2/3 miles or about 2.7 kilometers [e] *16* That is, about 1 1/2 miles or about 2.4 kilometers; also in verses 30, 32, 33 and 34

48:1 – 7 Israel's tribal allotments here in Ezekiel follow the premonarchical order of excluding the Levites and cutting the tribe of Joseph in half (Ephraim and Manasseh) in order to keep the number of allotments to 12. However, they show little concern for historical realities. As with ch. 47, the territory east of the Jordan is overlooked. Further, the east-west boundaries run in contrast to the natural physical landscape, which is defined by north-south lines. The tribal allotments are identical to one another in size and also respect the traditional genealogical relationships among the tribes, discriminating between the descendants of Jacob's wives and his handmaidens. Judah and Benjamin, however, retain their close proximity to the sanctuary.

48:15 *The city will be in the center of it.* In ch. 48 Ezekiel describes the new city and the allotment of land to each tribe. Although the city is square, the length of each side is mentioned separately; the north, south, east and west sides are all 4,500 cubits (1.5 miles or 2.4 kilometers). In the Gilgamesh Epic, one finds a similar description of the dimensions of the city of Uruk. These dimensions have been interpreted as representing the Mesopotamian ideal of a well-proportioned city. The measurements given by Ezekiel and the disposition of the new city of Jerusalem surrounded with areas for houses and pasturelands, with each tribe receiving a specific "portion" of land and priests being allotted a "sacred portion" (v. 10), may also be seen as a vision of an ideal distribution of space in the new temple and the new city.

side 4,500 cubits, and the west
side 4,500 cubits.[e] 17The pastureland for the city will be 250
cubits[a] on the north, 250 cubits
on the south, 250 cubits on the
east, and 250 cubits on the west.
18What remains of the area, bordering on the sacred portion
and running the length of it,
will be 10,000 cubits on the east
side and 10,000 cubits on the
west side. Its produce will supply food for the workers of the
city.[f] 19The workers from the city
who farm it will come from all
the tribes of Israel. 20The entire
portion will be a square, 25,000
cubits on each side. As a special
gift you will set aside the sacred
portion, along with the property
of the city.

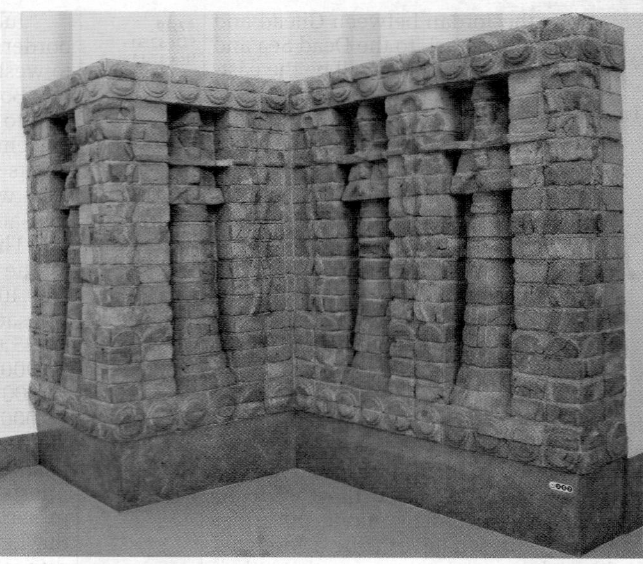

The façade of the Temple of Inanna from Uruk shows water flowing from the temple just as Ezekiel describes it in Eze 47:1.
Kim Walton, Vorderasiatisches Museum.

21"What remains on both sides
of the area formed by the sacred
portion and the property of the
city will belong to the prince. It
will extend eastward from the
25,000 cubits of the sacred portion to the eastern border, and westward
from the 25,000 cubits to the western border. Both these areas running the length
of the tribal portions will belong to the
prince, and the sacred portion with the
temple sanctuary will be in the center of
them.[g] 22So the property of the Levites and
the property of the city will lie in the center of the area that belongs to the prince.
The area belonging to the prince will lie
between the border of Judah and the border of Benjamin.
23"As for the rest of the tribes: Benjamin[h] will have one portion; it will extend
from the east side to the west side.
24"Simeon[i] will have one portion; it will
border the territory of Benjamin from east
to west.
25"Issachar[j] will have one portion; it will
border the territory of Simeon from east
to west.
26"Zebulun[k] will have one portion; it
will border the territory of Issachar from
east to west.
27"Gad[l] will have one portion; it will
border the territory of Zebulun from east
to west.
28"The southern boundary of Gad will
run south from Tamar[m] to the waters of
Meribah Kadesh, then along the Wadi of
Egypt to the Mediterranean Sea.[n]
29"This is the land you are to allot as
an inheritance to the tribes of Israel, and
these will be their portions," declares the
Sovereign LORD.

The Gates of the New City

30"These will be the exits of the city: Beginning on the north side, which is 4,500
cubits long, 31the gates of the city will be
named after the tribes of Israel. The three
gates on the north side will be the gate of
Reuben, the gate of Judah and the gate
of Levi.
32"On the east side, which is 4,500 cubits long, will be three gates: the gate of
Joseph, the gate of Benjamin and the gate
of Dan.
33"On the south side, which measures
4,500 cubits, will be three gates: the gate
of Simeon, the gate of Issachar and the
gate of Zebulun.
34"On the west side, which is 4,500 cubits long, will be three gates: the gate of
Gad, the gate of Asher and the gate of
Naphtali.
35"The distance all around will be
18,000 cubits.[b]
"And the name of the city from that time
on will be:

THE LORD IS THERE.[o]"

48:16 [e] Rev 21:16 **48:18** [f] Eze 45:6 **48:21** [g] ver 8, 10; Eze 45:7 **48:23** [h] Jos 18:11-28 **48:24** [i] Ge 29:33; Jos 19:1-9 **48:25** [j] Jos 19:17-23 **48:26** [k] Jos 19:10-16 **48:27** [l] Jos 13:24-28 **48:28** [m] Ge 14:7 [n] Eze 47:19 **48:35** [o] Isa 12:6; 24:23; Jer 3:17; 14:9; 33:16; Joel 3:21; Zec 2:10; Rev 21:3

[a] *17* That is, about 440 feet or about 135 meters
[b] *35* That is, about 6 miles or about 9.5 kilometers

48:31 *gates … named after the tribes of Israel.* In cities of the ancient world, such as Babylon, the gates were often named after the gods. It is not unusual, however, for gates to be named for where they lead to. This was the more common practice in Israel.

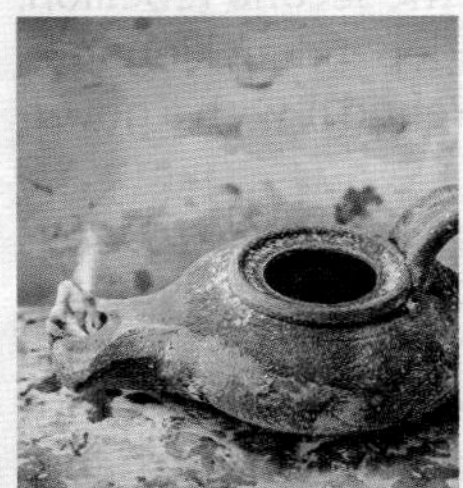

ORACLES OF THE PROPHETS

DANIEL

Historical Setting

The setting of the book of Daniel covers much of the Neo-Babylonian Empire and the early years of the Persian Empire. From the mid-eighth century BC, Assyria was the dominant power in the ancient Near East. By the time of Ashurbanipal's death in 627 BC, Assyria had slipped into decline. An internal struggle for the throne after his death was exploited by Nabopolassar, a Chaldean prince from southern Mesopotamia. He marched on Babylon, defeated an Assyrian army outside the city, and captured it, declaring himself king of Babylon in 626. Assyrian attempts to oust him failed. Soon the Medes, from the east, joined the Babylonians in attacking Assyria. Egypt supported Assyria and sent an army to help. The combined armies repelled attacks by Nabopolassar in 616 and 615. In 614 the Medes captured Ashur, the ancient Assyrian capital, and in 612 Nineveh, the current capital, fell to a combined Babylonian-Median assault. The Assyrian army retreated to Harran on the Euphrates, but it was expelled from there by the Babylonians in 610. When a combined Assyrian-Egyptian army failed to retake Harran in 609, Assyrian power was finished.

KEY CONCEPTS

- Daniel uses his training to develop knowledge and skills that God in turn draws on to use Daniel in his service.
- Even the most powerful and successful kings the world has known acknowledge the sovereignty of Yahweh.

Judah had been an Assyrian vassal for over a century. The decline of Assyria enabled King Josiah to institute religious reform. Since this involved removing the trappings of the worship of Assyrian gods from the temple, it amounted to a declaration of independence. Probably because he did not want to exchange Assyrian domination for Egyptian, Josiah opposed Pharaoh Necho II when he went to Assyria's aid in 609 BC. Josiah was killed in battle at Megiddo (2Ki 23:29 – 30). The Judahites put his younger son Jehoahaz on the throne but, on his return from Harran, Necho replaced Jehoahaz with his older brother Jehoiakim (2Ki 23:31 – 35). The Egyptians tried to prevent the Babylonians from crossing the Euphrates, but in 605 they were defeated at Carchemish by an army under crown prince Nebuchadnezzar. They soon suffered another crushing defeat by him at Hamath in Syria, after which Syria and Palestine, including Judah, came under Babylonian control. Shortly after the battle Nabopolassar died and Nebuchadnezzar became king of Babylon. He left Jehoiakim on the throne of Judah but, according to Da 1, he took plunder and captives from Jerusalem to Babylon. Daniel and his friends were among the captives.

They were joined there by other captives from Judah during the turbulent final years of Judah's existence, which involved two rebellions against Babylon. Both rebellions were crushed by Nebuchadnezzar, one in 597 BC and the other in 587. After the second rebellion, Jerusalem and its temple were destroyed and Judah ceased to be an independent kingdom. It was incorporated into the Babylonian Empire as a province (called "Yehud"), with a governor appointed by the Babylonians (2Ki 25:22).

The Neo-Babylonian Empire declined after Nebuchadnezzar's death, weakened by court intrigues. In 556 BC Nabonidus, who was from a noble family but not the royal line, seized the throne. His devotion to Sin, the moon-god, and various religious innovations resulted in friction with the powerful priests of Marduk in Babylon, as well as the populace of the city. This may have been one reason why he moved his residence to the oasis of Tema in Arabia. He probably also wanted to control the lucrative trade along the Arabian caravan routes. During his absence crown prince Belshazzar was regent in Babylon.

The Medes annexed the northern and eastern portions of the Assyrian Empire when it collapsed. As Babylonia's power declined, Media's increased, and Media became a serious rival power. Early in Nabonidus's reign, Cyrus, vassal king of Anshan in Persia, rebelled against his Median overlord, Astyages. By 550 BC he had captured the Median capital, Ecbatana, and dethroned Astyages. Cyrus rapidly extended his empire to the north and east. As the threat from Cyrus grew, Nabonidus returned to Babylon. In 539 BC Cyrus defeated a Babylonian army at Opis on the Tigris. Soon afterward his general, Gubaru, entered Babylon unopposed. When Cyrus arrived a few weeks later, many Babylonians welcomed him as a liberator. In 538 Cyrus issued a decree allowing Jews to return to Jerusalem, take back the temple vessels looted by Nebuchadnezzar, and restore their community and worship there. This was part of his general policy of respecting the customs of his subject peoples.

The Persian Empire continued for just over 200 years before collapsing under the onslaught of Alexander the Great. This event and its aftermath are the subject of the visions in Da 7 – 12 (see notes there).

Literary Setting

Daniel contains two different kinds of material. Chs. 1 – 6 contain stories about Daniel and his companions. The rest of the book contains accounts of visions experienced and recounted by Daniel. Both of these types of literature are paralleled in the ancient Near East.

Though the book occasionally has Daniel speaking in the first person, the narratives are largely third person. Daniel is not named as the author. While there is no reason to question the authenticity of the accounts in the book, the fact that many narrative traditions were preserved orally, perhaps even for centuries before being committed to writing, results in uncertainty concerning when and by whom the book was compiled. ◆

Daniel's Training in Babylon

1 In the third year of the reign of Jehoiakim king of Judah, Nebuchadnez-
zar[a] king of Babylon came to Jerusalem
and besieged it.[b] 2 And the Lord delivered
Jehoiakim king of Judah into his hand,
along with some of the articles from the
temple of God. These he carried off to the
temple of his god in Babylonia[a] and put in
the treasure house of his god.[c]

3 Then the king ordered Ashpenaz,
chief of his court officials, to bring into
the king's service some of the Israelites
from the royal family and the nobility[d] —
4 young men without any physical defect,
handsome, showing aptitude for every
kind of learning, well informed, quick
to understand, and qualified to serve in
the king's palace. He was to teach them

1:1 [a] 2Ki 24:1 [b] 2Ch 36:6 **1:2** [c] 2Ch 36:7; Jer 27:19-20; Zec 5:5-11 **1:3** [d] 2Ki 20:18; 24:15; Isa 39:7

[a] 2 Hebrew *Shinar*

1:1 *Jehoiakim.* A king of Judah, he was a son of Josiah who was put on the throne by the Egyptian pharaoh Necho as he attempted to exercise control over Syria-Palestine. When Josiah was killed in battle, the people had enthroned his son Jehoahaz, who represented an anti-Egyptian faction. This situation lasted for three months (while Necho was busy at Harran). Then Necho deposed Jehoahaz and sent him off as a captive to Egypt. Pro-Egyptian Jehoiakim was then placed on the throne with the expectation that he would be a loyal Egyptian vassal. The situation changed dramatically when Nebuchadnezzar gained control of the region following the fall of Carchemish. Jehoiakim played the role of reluctant Babylonian vassal for several years, but after Nebuchadnezzar's failure to invade Egypt in 601 BC, Jehoiakim again broke with Babylon and sought the support of Egypt in his rebellion. This disloyalty eventually proved fatal and led to the Babylonian siege of Jerusalem in 597 BC (see notes on 2Ki 24:1,10). *Nebuchadnezzar.* Nebuchadnezzar II (605 – 562 BC) was the second ruler of the Chaldean kingdom centered at Babylon that ruled the ancient Near East for nearly a century. He was the son of Nabopolassar, a Chaldean who declared independence from Assyria in 626 BC. In his long reign of 43 years, Nebuchadnezzar pacified Egypt (though he was unsuccessful in conquering it) and literally rebuilt the city of Babylon, which had suffered destruction at the hands of the Assyrians. In fact, most of the city of Babylon that has been uncovered by modern excavators was from Nebuchadnezzar's reign. Thus, the Chaldean kingdom was primarily his creation, and it crumbled only a generation after his death. This great king was remembered in many cultural traditions, including sources from Greece (who knew him as a great builder) and Israel.

1:2 *articles from the temple.* They were made of valuable metals and therefore were desirable plunder. There was also symbolic value in taking them. For most people in the ancient Near East, taking these articles would have demonstrated the superiority of the gods of Babylonia over the God of Israel. Plundering the temple showed that the god of that temple was weak. *the temple of his god.* The patron deity of Babylon and head of its pantheon was Marduk. He was the son of Enki, one of the ancient triad of Mesopotamian gods. The Babylonian creation epic *Enuma Elish* recounts how Marduk gained supremacy in the pantheon after defeating the monsters of chaos and creating the world. This myth was formulated to legitimate the elevation of Marduk to his supreme position sometime during the second millennium BC. Nabopolassar was a devotee of Nabu, Marduk's son, as the naming of Nabopolassar's son Nebuchadnezzar indicates. Nebuchadnezzar seems to have made Marduk his personal god since most of his inscriptions invoke him. Nebuchadnezzar, continuing work begun by Nabopolassar, restored the ancient ziggurat, or stepped temple-tower, of Babylon, named Etemenanki ("the building which is the foundation of heaven and earth") and the associated temple of Marduk, called Esagila ("the temple that raises its head"). These buildings dominated the city, with the temple-tower rising to about 300 feet (90 meters).

1:4 *serve in the king's palace.* The training the young men were scheduled to receive was intended to prepare them for royal service. As courtiers, they might serve as scribes, advisors, sages, diplomats, provincial governors or attendants to members of the royal household, just to name a few possibilities. In seventh-century BC letters to Assyrian kings, the five principal classes of scholarly experts serving the king were: astrologer/scribe, diviner, exorcist (this term is used to describe those compared to Daniel and his friends in v. 20), physician, and chanter of lamentations. It would not be unusual for an individual to be trained in a number of these disciplines. Training foreigners for these positions was expected to result in the assimilation of the best and brightest of the next generation. Their skills would then benefit the Babylonians rather than the enemies of the Babylonians. *the language and literature of the Babylonians.* Babylonian and Assyrian are dialects of Akkadian, a Semitic language like Aramaic and Hebrew. While the language itself would not have been unusually difficult to learn, the system used to write it was. It required learning hundreds of symbols and the rules for using them correctly. This was done by first copying simple exercises set by the teacher. As the student progressed, he would move on to copying important literary texts. Many of these were religious in nature. The learning process was therefore also an induction into the worldview and culture of Babylonia. Though the use of wax-covered wooden writing boards was common as a temporary medium, the standard writing material in Mesopotamia was a tablet of clay, which was readily available. When moist these tablets were written on using a stylus, which was usually cut from a reed; the tablets were then dried in the sun. The stylus made wedge-shaped marks. Modern scholars call this writing "cuneiform," from the Latin word for a wedge (*cuneus*). Several wedge-shaped marks were combined to form a specific "sign." The writing system was not alphabetic, like that used to write English, Hebrew or Aramaic, but was syllabic. A syllable is a combination of a vowel and consonant(s), such as "ud," "du," or "dug." Because of the number of possible combinations, a syllabic writing system needs many more signs than the number of letters used for an alphabet. About 600 distinct cuneiform signs are known. The syllabic signs used to write Akkadian were originally designed by the Sumerians to record their language. The Sumerians lived in southern Babylonia before the Semitic people who spoke Akkadian migrated into the region. Sumerian is not a Semitic language and is quite different in nature from Akkadian. As a result, the system was not ideal for writing Akkadian. This contributed to its complexity when used to write it. *Babylonians.* The Hebrew word used here (*kasdim*) is translated "Chaldeans." Outside of Daniel it is used in the OT of the people of Babylonia in general. Chaldea appears in Assyrian inscriptions from the ninth century BC on as

the language and literature of the Babylonians.[a] 5The king assigned them a daily
amount of food and wine[e] from the king's
table. They were to be trained for three
years, and after that they were to enter the
king's service.[f]
6Among those who were chosen were
some from Judah: Daniel,[g] Hananiah,
Mishael and Azariah. 7The chief official
gave them new names: to Daniel, the
name Belteshazzar;[h] to Hananiah, Shadrach; to Mishael, Meshach; and to Azariah, Abednego.[i]
8But Daniel resolved not to defile[j] him-

1:5 [e] ver 8, 10 [f] ver 19 **1:6** [g] Eze 14:14 **1:7** [h] Da 4:8; 5:12 [i] Da 2:49; 3:12 **1:8** [j] Eze 4:13-14

[a] 4 Or *Chaldeans*

the name of a region in southern Babylonia inhabited by several interrelated tribes. Both Biblical and classical sources call Nabopolassar's dynasty "Chaldean," but there is no clear evidence that they were ethnically Chaldean. The term "Chaldean" has ethnic connotations in 5:30; 9:1; and it may here as well. In every other occurrence in Daniel, it denotes a "professional" group among the wise men. Elsewhere this meaning is first found in Herodotus in the fifth century BC, where the Chaldeans are priests of the god Bel. By Hellenistic times the term "Chaldean" came to mean specifically "astrologer." If the term has its professional meaning here in Daniel, it may imply that Daniel and his companions were trained specifically in the literature used by diviners.

1:5 *food.* The Hebrew (*pat-bag*) is borrowed from Persian. It does not signify any particular kind of food. It was often barley and oil, and sometimes meat. *from the king's table.* Many people were assigned daily rations from the king's table: courtiers, officials, artisans, foreign dignitaries — basically those who were considered to be in some way part of the king's household. Those receiving such rations were expected to show loyalty to the king in return. A group of tablets excavated in the southern palace at Babylon show that King Jehoiachin of Judah and his five sons received rations of oil from the royal stores. These tablets cover the years from 592/1 – 569/8 BC. When Nebuchadnezzar besieged Jerusalem, Jehoiachin submitted to him, and he, his family and various others of his household were taken as captives to Babylon (2Ki 24:12). *trained for three years.* This seems to have been the usual length of training for a competent scribe. In the literature available from the Old Babylonian period, training included the language and literature areas mentioned in the note on v. 4 as well as mathematics and music. For a diviner, it is expected that the training period was longer, but precise indications in the literature are lacking.

1:7 *new names.* Changing someone's name was one way in which a conqueror expressed his authority. When Nebuchadnezzar made Mattaniah, Jehoiachin's uncle, king in his place, Nebuchadnezzar changed Mattaniah's name to Zedekiah (2Ki 24:17). Pharaoh Necho behaved similarly (2Ki 23:34). In both cases the new names were Hebrew names. The fact that Daniel and his companions are given Babylonian names is another indication of the intention that they should be assimilated into Babylonian culture.

1:8 *defile himself with the royal food and wine.* There have been extensive discussions and a variety of suggestions

DANIEL 1

STORIES ABOUT COURTIERS

Stories about courtiers were popular in the ancient Near East. Several are known from ancient Egypt, the best known being the stories of Sinuhe and Wenamun. Within the OT there are the stories of Esther (with the subplot of the story of the courtier Mordecai) and Joseph (Ge 37 – 50). In several of these stories the courtier, like Daniel, is living in a foreign court.

Scholars recognize two main types of stories about courtiers, both of which occur in Daniel. One is the conflict story, in which the hero's life is endangered, usually because of a conspiracy by other courtiers (Da 3; 6). The other is the contest story, in which the hero solves a problem that other courtiers cannot and so proves his superiority (Da 1; 2; 4; 5).

Many of the stories were intended to edify the readers as well as entertain them. Imaginative storytelling is an effective teaching method. The stories in Daniel are certainly intended to convey theological and moral truths. The stories about courtiers in the service of foreign kings seem also to have had the purpose of encouraging the conquered people to maintain their sense of identity and worth. In the case of Daniel and his companions, the issue of identity centers on faithfulness to the God of Israel. They are held up as models of how faithful Jews should live in exile in Babylon. ◆

self with the royal food and wine, and
he asked the chief official for permission
not to defile himself this way. 9 Now God
had caused the official to show favor[k]
and compassion[l] to Daniel, 10 but the official told Daniel, "I am afraid of my lord
the king, who has assigned your[a] food
and drink. Why should he see you looking worse than the other young men your
age? The king would then have my head
because of you."
11 Daniel then said to the guard whom
the chief official had appointed over
Daniel, Hananiah, Mishael and Azariah,
12 "Please test your servants for ten days:
Give us nothing but vegetables to eat and
water to drink. 13 Then compare our appearance with that of the young men who
eat the royal food, and treat your servants
in accordance with what you see." 14 So
he agreed to this and tested them for ten
days.
15 At the end of the ten days they looked
healthier and better nourished than any of
the young men who ate the royal food.[m]
16 So the guard took away their choice food
and the wine they were to drink and gave
them vegetables instead.[n]
17 To these four young men God gave
knowledge and understanding[o] of all
kinds of literature and learning.[p] And Daniel could understand visions and dreams
of all kinds.[q]
18 At the end of the time[r] set by the king
to bring them into his service, the chief
official presented them to Nebuchadnezzar. 19 The king talked with them, and he
found none equal to Daniel, Hananiah,
Mishael and Azariah; so they entered the
king's service.[s] 20 In every matter of wisdom and understanding about which the
king questioned them, he found them ten

1:9 [k] Ge 39:21; Pr 16:7 [l] 1Ki 8:50; Ps 106:46
1:15 [m] Ex 23:25
1:16 [n] ver 12-13
1:17 [o] 1Ki 3:12 [p] Da 2:23; Jas 1:5 [q] Da 2:19,30; 7:1; 8:1
1:18 [r] ver 5
1:19 [s] Ge 41:46

[a] *10* The Hebrew for *your* and *you* in this verse is plural.

regarding the reasons why Daniel and his friends refused the king's food. Most work on the assumption that the contrast is between meat and vegetables (see notes on vv. 5,12). Others have noted that Daniel's decision may be based on his reluctance to show allegiance to the king by sharing his food, but that would hold no matter what the young men ate. Others believe that it has to do with Jewish dietary laws (kosher), which would likely have rendered certain meat unclean. But improper storage or preparation could render other food unclean as well. Furthermore, the Jewish dietary laws did not prohibit wine. Another approach suggests the problem is with meat offered to idols. The finest meats were undoubtedly supplied to the palace from the temples, where the meat had been offered before idols (and the wine poured out in libations before the gods), but any food could easily have come through the same route. The decision certainly has nothing to do with vegetarianism or avoidance of rich foods for nutritional purposes (see 10:3). There are numerous examples in intertestamental literature (e.g., Tobit, Judith, Jubilees) of Jews seeing the necessity of refraining from food served by Gentiles. It is not so much something in the food that defiles as much as it is the total program of assimilation. At this point the Babylonian government is exercising control over every aspect of their lives. They have little means to resist the forces of assimilation that are controlling them. They seize on one of the few areas in which they can still exercise choice as an opportunity to preserve their distinct identity.

1:12 *vegetables.* The Hebrew word generally refers to the seeds used for animal feed, fodder or planting. In neither Akkadian nor Hebrew is it used to describe human food. But the text does not suggest that they are being provided with a restaurant-style prepared and served meal. To eat "from the king's table" (v. 5) meant only that they were provided rations at the expense of the royal budget. It is well known that military rations consisted of measured amounts of grain that the soldiers then used to prepare their meals. Cereal grains could be ground, mashed and cooked in water to produce a porridge. This could therefore involve the same amount of ration as referred to in v. 5 but prepared by themselves rather than in the king's kitchens.

1:17 *visions and dreams.* It is not always easy to distinguish between visions and dreams. Ecstatic experience, like that of the Hebrew prophets, including visions and auditions (hearing a divine voice), had only a marginal place in Mesopotamian religion. Dreams had a significant, though secondary, role in Mesopotamian divination. There were specialist diviners trained in interpreting dreams, which were considered to be communications from the gods. This verse and v. 20 suggest that Daniel and his companions were trained specifically in the literature and skills of the Mesopotamian diviners. The Mesopotamians believed that the gods communicated messages to them in various ways. It was the diviner's task to obtain and interpret these messages or omens. The different forms of divinatory practice can be roughly divided into three types: (1) The study of unsolicited omens. This involved observing various forms of natural phenomena, such as astronomical and meteorological events, the behavior of animals, and abnormal births. (2) The obtaining of omens by using various techniques for asking a question of the god(s) and obtaining an answer. Some of the techniques used were dropping oil on water and observing the shapes formed, burning incense and observing the shapes made by the smoke, and sacrificing an animal and observing its entrails, especially the liver. (3) The use of human "mediums." Prophecy was not common in Mesopotamia, being attested mainly from its western fringes, such as at Mari. Dream interpretation was more widespread. Necromancy (i.e., consultation of the dead by means of a human medium) was also practiced.

From the second millennium BC on a considerable amount of Akkadian literature developed around omens. Collections of different types of omens were made. Instruction manuals were written. Diviners' reports were recorded. Various rituals and prayers related to divination were written down. Different forms of divination were popular at various times and places. In the first millennium BC the study of animal entrails, abnormal births, and astronomical phenomena (the origins of modern astrology) were particularly popular.

1:20 *magicians.* The term used here is of Egyptian origin (Ge 41:8,24; Ex 7:11,22). Egyptians were considered particularly skilled at dream interpretation, and Egyptian interpreters were employed at the Assyrian court. The term could, no doubt, be applied to all dream interpreters,

times better than all the magicians and enchanters in his whole kingdom.[t]
21 And Daniel remained there until the
first year of King Cyrus.[u]

Nebuchadnezzar's Dream

2 In the second year of his reign, Nebuchadnezzar had dreams;[v] his mind was
troubled[w] and he could not sleep.[x] 2 So the
king summoned the magicians,[y] enchanters, sorcerers[z] and astrologers[a][a] to tell him
what he had dreamed.[b] When they came
in and stood before the king, 3 he said to
them, "I have had a dream that troubles[c]
me and I want to know what it means.[b]"
4 Then the astrologers answered the
king,[c][d] "May the king live forever![e] Tell
your servants the dream, and we will interpret it."

1:20 [t] 1Ki 4:30; Da 2:13,28
1:21 [u] Da 6:28; 10:1
2:1 [v] Job 33:15,18; Da 4:5 [w] Ge 41:8 [x] Est 6:1; Da 6:18
2:2 [y] Ge 41:8 [z] Ex 7:11 [a] ver 10; Da 5:7 [b] Da 4:6
2:3 [c] Da 4:5
2:4 [d] Ezr 4:7 [e] Da 3:9; 5:10
2:5 [f] ver 12 [g] Ezr 6:11; Da 3:29
2:6 [h] ver 48; Da 5:7,16

5 The king replied to the astrologers,
"This is what I have firmly decided: If you
do not tell me what my dream was and
interpret it, I will have you cut into pieces[f] and your houses turned into piles of
rubble.[g] 6 But if you tell me the dream and
explain it, you will receive from me gifts
and rewards and great honor.[h] So tell me
the dream and interpret it for me."
7 Once more they replied, "Let the king
tell his servants the dream, and we will
interpret it."
8 Then the king answered, "I am certain that you are trying to gain time, because you realize that this is what I have

[a] 2 Or *Chaldeans*; also in verses 4, 5 and 10
[b] 3 Or *was*
[c] 4 At this point the Hebrew text has *in Aramaic*, indicating that the text from here through the end of chapter 7 is in Aramaic.

whatever their ethnic origin. *enchanters.* The term used here is of Akkadian origin and refers to "incantation priests." Their general task was to ward off the effects of threatening omens by performing the appropriate rituals. This often included reciting incantations. One specialty of these priests was "health care" in the sense of observing a sick person's symptoms and other relevant factors (such as the time when the symptom occurred) and then deciding on the likely outcome of the illness and the appropriate ritual(s) to perform to deal with it. Maybe the use of "magicians" and "enchanters" makes the point that Daniel and his companions surpassed both the foreign and native wise men at the court.

1:21 *first year of King Cyrus.* Presumably this refers to the first year of Cyrus's reign over Babylon, which began in October 539 BC.

2:1 *second year of his reign.* Nebuchadnezzar came to the throne in September 605 BC. Under the Babylonian "accession year" dating, his first year began in spring 604, and his second year ran from spring 603 to spring 602. The Babylonian Chronicle for this year is badly broken, but refers to some significant military activity. *Nebuchadnezzar had dreams.* In the ancient Near East dreams were considered one of the ways in which the gods communicated with humans. Since kings were believed to stand in a special relationship to the gods, their dreams were of particular importance. Several reports of dreams are found in royal inscriptions from Egypt and Mesopotamia. Nebuchadnezzar's dream is an example of a *symbolic dream*, the meaning of which is not obvious and needs to be interpreted. Until this was done, he would not know whether it foretold good or ill. Dreams played only a secondary role in Mesopotamian divination. They were more important in the reigns of some kings than others, perhaps a reflection of the king's personal piety. Dreams were thought to be messages from the gods brought by a spirit messenger whose Akkadian name was Zaqiqu. Basically two types of dream were recognized as communications from the gods. In *message dreams* a divine being spoke directly to the dreamer, so that interpretation was not needed. A *symbolic dream* involved the dreamer seeing or experiencing something, the meaning of which was not obvious; thus, interpretation was needed. All known records of this kind of dream come from Sumerian or Babylonian sources rather than from Assyrian ones. Interpretation could be done in one of two ways. *Deductive interpretation* relied on consultation of collections of dream omens (called "dream books"), which contained lists of things that might occur in dreams and assigned meanings to each one. *Intuitive interpretation* depended simply on the wisdom and insight of the interpreter. There is no evidence of a specific group of professionals who devoted themselves wholly to dream interpretation. Instead, this was done by priests, both male and female, who were competent in several types of divination. When a dream presaged something bad, there were rituals that could be performed to prevent the calamity from happening. This is one reason why it was important to discover the meaning of a dream as soon as possible.

2:2 *magicians.* See note on 1:20. *enchanters.* See note on 1:20. *sorcerers.* Practitioners who are condemned a number of times in the OT (Ex 22:18; Dt 18:10; Mal 3:5). The Hebrew word for them is closely related to an Akkadian term for people skilled in charms and incantations, some of which would have been used to avert the calamity presaged in a dream. *astrologers.* This same Hebrew term is translated "Babylonians" in 1:4. The fact that slightly different lists of "experts" are given in vv. 10,27 indicates that the lists are simply meant to represent the range of such people at the court, not name all of them.

2:4 *answered the king.* At this point and continuing through the end of ch. 7, the language of the book of Daniel changes from Hebrew to Aramaic (see NIV text note). Aramaic was the international language used throughout the multilingual Babylonian Empire and beyond. Hebrew and Aramaic belong to the Semitic language family and use the same alphabet. They look much the same when written down.

2:5 *I will have you cut into pieces and your houses turned into piles of rubble.* Dismembering people as a punishment is attested in ancient Mesopotamia. Compare this threat with that of Darius in Ezr 6:11.

2:6 *tell me the dream and explain it.* A dream was thought to have its effect whether or not the dreamer could remember its details on waking. To forget a dream was itself a bad omen, indicating the anger of the dreamer's personal god. Nebuchadnezzar may have forgotten the details of his dream, but it is also possible that he was testing his diviners to try to ensure a genuine interpretation of what he thought might be a particularly important dream. Kings did not always trust their "experts." On at least one occasion Sennacherib separated diviners into groups to reduce collusion and ensure a reliable interpretation of an omen.

firmly decided: [9]If you do not tell me the dream, there is only one penalty[i] for you. You have conspired to tell me misleading and wicked things, hoping the situation will change. So then, tell me the dream, and I will know that you can interpret it for me."[j]

[10]The astrologers answered the king, "There is no one on earth who can do what the king asks! No king, however great and mighty, has ever asked such a thing of any magician or enchanter or astrologer.[k] [11]What the king asks is too difficult. No one can reveal it to the king except the gods,[l] and they do not live among humans."

[12]This made the king so angry and furious[m] that he ordered the execution[n] of all the wise men of Babylon. [13]So the decree was issued to put the wise men to death, and men were sent to look for Daniel and his friends to put them to death.[o]

[14]When Arioch, the commander of the king's guard, had gone out to put to death the wise men of Babylon, Daniel spoke to him with wisdom and tact. [15]He asked the

2:9 [i]Est 4:11 [j]Isa 41:22-24 **2:10** [k]ver 27 **2:11** [l]Da 5:11 **2:12** [m]Da 3:13, 19 [n]ver 5 **2:13** [o]Da 1:20

2:11 *What the king asks is too difficult.* It was part of the diviner's art to interpret dreams by either deductive or inductive means (see note on v. 1), but the diviner had no means for discovering what the dream itself had been. It was believed that the gods communicated through dreams, and the experts believed that the gods would reveal to them the interpretation of the dreams through their use of the resources available to them. There was no precedent for the gods revealing the dream itself.

2:12 *he ordered the execution of all the wise men.* There are partial parallels to this angry outburst and threat by Nebuchadnezzar in Saul's massacre of the priests at Nob (1Sa 22:13 – 19) because they had helped David. In secular history, a parallel exists in Darius's massacre of the Magi because one of them had usurped the throne. A closer parallel is Xerxes' beheading of the engineers who built a bridge that was destroyed in a storm, since it was a case of punishing failed "experts."

2:14 *commander of the king's guard.* This is the official title of an important functionary whose duties were sometimes unsavory. When Jerusalem fell to the Babylonians, the commander in charge of methodically destroying and dismantling the city and disposing of captives either by execution or deportation carried this title (2Ki 25:8). It is similar to the title held by Potiphar in Ge 37:36. The terminology suggests something like "chief cook," but like some of our contemporary government titles (e.g., "party whip"), the office must be understood by examining its function, not its title.

DANIEL 2:1

THE BABYLONIAN CHRONICLE

Two surviving tablets of the Babylonian Chronicle record events in the first 11 years of Nebuchadnezzar's reign. The entry for the seventh year refers to the capture of Jerusalem in 597 BC in response to Jehoiakim's rebellion after the failure of a Babylonian attempt to invade Egypt in 701. Nebuchadnezzar replaced Jehoiachin, who had succeeded his father before the siege of the city, with Zedekiah (2Ki 24:1 - 17). The date of the capture of Jerusalem is Mar. 15/16, 597 BC according to our calendar. ◆

THE LAST KINGS OF JUDAH	
Josiah	639–609*
Jehoahaz	609
Jehoiakim	609–598
Jehoiachin	598–597
Zedekiah	597–587

*All dates are BC and those of the kings' reigns.

THE NEO-BABYLONIAN KINGS	
Nabopolassar	626–605*
Nebuchadnezzar II	605–562
Amel-Marduk	562–560
Neriglissar	560–556
Labashi-Marduk	556
Nabonidus	556–539

*All dates are BC and those of the kings' reigns.

king's officer, "Why did the king issue such
a harsh decree?" Arioch then explained the
matter to Daniel. 16 At this, Daniel went in
to the king and asked for time, so that he
might interpret the dream for him.
17 Then Daniel returned to his house and
explained the matter to his friends Hananiah, Mishael and Azariah.[p] 18 He urged
them to plead for mercy[q] from the God of
heaven concerning this mystery,[r] so that
he and his friends might not be executed
with the rest of the wise men of Babylon.
19 During the night the mystery[s] was revealed to Daniel in a vision.[t] Then Daniel
praised the God of heaven 20 and said:

"Praise be to the name of God for ever
and ever;[u]
wisdom and power[v] are his.
21 He changes times and seasons;[w]
he deposes[x] kings and raises up
others.
He gives wisdom[y] to the wise
and knowledge to the discerning.
22 He reveals deep and hidden things;[z]
he knows what lies in darkness,[a]
and light[b] dwells with him.
23 I thank and praise you, God of my
ancestors:[c]
You have given me wisdom[d] and
power,
you have made known to me what we
asked of you,
you have made known to us the
dream of the king."

Daniel Interprets the Dream

24 Then Daniel went to Arioch,[e] whom
the king had appointed to execute the wise
men of Babylon, and said to him, "Do not
execute the wise men of Babylon. Take me
to the king, and I will interpret his dream
for him."
25 Arioch took Daniel to the king at once
and said, "I have found a man among the
exiles from Judah[f] who can tell the king
what his dream means."
26 The king asked Daniel (also called Belteshazzar),[g] "Are you able to tell me what
I saw in my dream and interpret it?"
27 Daniel replied, "No wise man, enchanter, magician or diviner can explain to
the king the mystery he has asked about,[h]
28 but there is a God in heaven who reveals
mysteries.[i] He has shown King Nebuchadnezzar what will happen in days to come.[j]
Your dream and the visions that passed
through your mind[k] as you were lying in
bed are these:
29 "As Your Majesty was lying there, your
mind turned to things to come, and the
revealer of mysteries showed you what is
going to happen. 30 As for me, this mystery has been revealed[l] to me, not because
I have greater wisdom than anyone else
alive, but so that Your Majesty may know
the interpretation and that you may understand what went through your mind.
31 "Your Majesty looked, and there before
you stood a large statue—an enormous,
dazzling statue,[m] awesome in appearance.
32 The head of the statue was made of pure
gold, its chest and arms of silver, its belly
and thighs of bronze, 33 its legs of iron, its
feet partly of iron and partly of baked clay.
34 While you were watching, a rock was cut
out, but not by human hands.[n] It struck
the statue on its feet of iron and clay and

2:17 [p] Da 1:6
2:18 [q] Isa 37:4 [r] Jer 33:3
2:19 [s] ver 28 [t] Job 33:15; Da 1:17
2:20 [u] Ps 113:2; 145:1-2 [v] Jer 32:19
2:21 [w] Da 7:25 [x] Job 12:19; Ps 75:6-7 [y] Jas 1:5
2:22 [z] Job 12:22; Ps 25:14; Da 5:11 [a] Ps 139:11-12; Jer 23:24; Heb 4:13 [b] Isa 45:7; Jas 1:17
2:23 [c] Ex 3:15 [d] Da 1:17
2:24 [e] ver 14
2:25 [f] Da 1:6; 5:13; 6:13
2:26 [g] Da 1:7
2:27 [h] ver 10
2:28 [i] Ge 40:8; Am 4:13 [j] Ge 49:1; Da 10:14 [k] Da 4:5
2:30 [l] Isa 45:3; Da 1:17; Am 4:13
2:31 [m] Hab 1:7
2:34 [n] Zec 4:6

2:18 *the God of heaven.* This title for God is found in Ge 24:3,7. Its other uses in the OT are in postexilic books, especially Chronicles, Ezra and Nehemiah. Persian documents use it of Ahura Mazda, the good god of Zoroastrianism (see the article "Zoroastrianism," p. 1433). It is used to refer to the God of Israel in the papyri written by the Jewish colonists at Elephantine in Egypt. Clearly it was an epithet for God that was acceptable to both Jews and non-Jews.
2:27 *wise man.* In Daniel this is a general term for an expert in various forms of divination. This "mantic wisdom" is different from the "instructional wisdom" of "the wise" spoken of in the book of Proverbs (e.g., Pr 1:5; 3:35; 9:9). *enchanter.* See note on 1:20. *magician.* See note on 1:20. *diviner.* This term comes from a verb that means "to cut," hence "to determine." It may mean "fate determiner"—i.e., a person who foretells someone's fate. The use of the word in the Qumran scrolls, however, suggests the meaning "exorcist."
2:31 *a large statue.* The appearance of colossal figures, often the statue of a deity, is fairly common in dream reports from the ancient Near East. Pharaoh Merneptah saw a giant statue of the god Ptah, who gave Merneptah permission to fight the Libyans. The Sumerian ruler Gudea saw a huge figure in a dream. In one dream reported in the reign of the Assyrian emperor Ashurbanipal, an inscription on the pedestal of a statue of the god Sin foretold the failure of a rebellion. Apparently it was not only rulers who had such dreams. One of the motifs listed in the Babylonian "dream book" is the appearance of a god's statue. What Nebuchadnezzar sees in his dream differs from these in that the figure represents the course of history.
2:32 *The head of the statue was made of pure gold.* No major statues of gods from first-millennium BC Mesopotamia have yet been discovered. A number of divine images from the second millennium BC have been recovered, and some are made of a combination of materials. One example from Ugarit is a bronze figure of a god, the head of which was covered with gold and the body with silver. Another is made from five materials: electrum, gold, silver, bronze and steatite. King Esarhaddon of Assyria boasts of a statue of himself made of gold, silver and copper that was placed before the gods to constantly request well-being for him. Since idols were often "dressed," it is possible that it was the parts that were visible that were covered with precious metals (or perhaps the metals were used in crafting the clothing of the statue).
2:33 *its feet partly of iron and partly of baked clay.* It is not clear what this means. It has been suggested that the reference is to iron inlaid with terra cotta.

smashed them.[o] 35Then the iron, the clay,
the bronze, the silver and the gold were
all broken to pieces and became like chaff
on a threshing floor in the summer. The
wind swept them away[p] without leaving
a trace. But the rock that struck the statue
became a huge mountain[q] and filled the
whole earth.
36"This was the dream, and now we will
interpret it to the king. 37Your Majesty, you
are the king of kings.[r] The God of heaven
has given you dominion[s] and power and
might and glory; 38in your hands he has
placed all mankind and the beasts of the
field and the birds in the sky. Wherever
they live, he has made you ruler over them
all.[t] You are that head of gold.
39"After you, another kingdom will arise,
inferior to yours. Next, a third kingdom,
one of bronze, will rule over the whole
earth. 40Finally, there will be a fourth kingdom, strong as iron — for iron breaks and
smashes everything — and as iron breaks
things to pieces, so it will crush and break
all the others.[u] 41Just as you saw that the
feet and toes were partly of baked clay
and partly of iron, so this will be a divided kingdom; yet it will have some of the
strength of iron in it, even as you saw iron
mixed with clay. 42As the toes were partly
iron and partly clay, so this kingdom will
be partly strong and partly brittle. 43And
just as you saw the iron mixed with baked
clay, so the people will be a mixture and
will not remain united, any more than iron
mixes with clay.
44"In the time of those kings, the God
of heaven will set up a kingdom that will
never be destroyed, nor will it be left to
another people. It will crush[v] all those
kingdoms[w] and bring them to an end,

2:34 [o] ver 44-45; Ps 2:9; Isa 60:12; Da 8:25
2:35 [p] Ps 1:4; 37:10; Isa 17:13 [q] Isa 2:3; Mic 4:1
2:37 [r] Eze 26:7 [s] Jer 27:7
2:38 [t] Jer 27:6; Da 4:21-22
2:40 [u] Da 7:7, 23
2:44 [v] Ps 2:9; 1Co 15:24 [w] Isa 60:12

Artist's rendition of Nebuchadnezzar's vision (Da 2:19).
Jonathan Walton

2:40 *Finally, there will be a fourth kingdom.* The division of a period of history into four empires or four ages, sometimes symbolized by four metals, has a number of parallels in ancient and classical literature. Two Zoroastrian texts speak of four ages symbolized by four metals: gold, silver, steel and "iron mixed" (the exact meaning of this is unclear). These texts are known only from thirteenth-century AD copies, but the material in them is much older. It is unlikely to be any older than the third century BC because the rulers of the final age seem to be Alexander the Great and his successors. A portion of Sibylline Oracle 4, which probably dates to the third century BC, speaks of four world empires: Assyrian, Median, Persian and Macedonian. These empires are not linked with any metals. A later addition adds Rome as a fifth empire. The sequence of empires reflects the experience of that part of the eastern Mediterranean world, perhaps part of Asia Minor, that passed directly from Assyrian rule to Median rule. In his *Works and Days* the eighth-century BC Greek poet Hesiod divides history into five eras. Four are characterized by metals in the sequence gold, silver, bronze and iron. Between the bronze and iron eras, Hesiod inserts the era of the Greek heroes, but he does not link it to any metal. This sequence of metals seems to rest on the historical memory of the transition from the Bronze Age to the Iron Age, since of the era symbolized by bronze the poet says, "Of bronze were their implements: there was no black iron." The Latin poet Ovid adopted this four-metal scheme, without the era of heroes, in his *Metamorphoses* (late first century BC). Hesiod's scheme seems to have been well known throughout the eastern Mediterranean world. It may be reflected in the imagery of Nebuchadnezzar's dream, which follows it with the addition of the admixture of clay with iron in the feet. Nebuchadnezzar, probably representing the whole Babylonian Empire, is identified with the head of gold. Identification of the rest of the sequence depends on evidence drawn from Da 7–8.

2:44 *but it will itself endure forever.* A Babylonian text known as the Uruk Prophecy describes the rise and fall of a series of kings. Concerning the last king mentioned it says not only that he will rule in Uruk but that his dynasty will be established forever. According to one possible interpretation of the text, this king is Nebuchadnezzar. This statement seems to turn into prophecy what is sometimes requested in royal prayers. Nabonidus, e.g., prays that his dynasty would be established forever.

but it will itself endure forever.[x] 45This
is the meaning of the vision of the rock[y]
cut out of a mountain, but not by human
hands[z]—a rock that broke the iron, the
bronze, the clay, the silver and the gold
to pieces.
"The great God has shown the king
what will take place in the future. The
dream is true and its interpretation is
trustworthy."
46Then King Nebuchadnezzar fell prostrate[a] before Daniel and paid him honor
and ordered that an offering[b] and incense
be presented to him. 47The king said to
Daniel, "Surely your God is the God of
gods[c] and the Lord of kings[d] and a revealer of mysteries,[e] for you were able to reveal this mystery."
48Then the king placed Daniel in a high
position and lavished many gifts on him.
He made him ruler over the entire province of Babylon and placed him in charge
of all its wise men.[f] 49Moreover, at Daniel's
request the king appointed Shadrach, Meshach and Abednego administrators over
the province of Babylon,[g] while Daniel
himself remained at the royal court.

The Image of Gold and the Blazing Furnace

3 King Nebuchadnezzar made an image[h]
of gold, sixty cubits high and six cubits
wide,[a] and set it up on the plain of Dura
in the province of Babylon. 2He then summoned the satraps, prefects, governors, advisers, treasurers, judges, magistrates and
all the other provincial officials[i] to come to
the dedication of the image he had set up.
3So the satraps, prefects, governors, advisers, treasurers, judges, magistrates and all

2:44 [x] Ps 145:13; Isa 9:7; Da 4:34; 6:26; 7:14, 27; Mic 4:7, 13; Lk 1:33
2:45 [y] Isa 28:16 [z] Da 8:25
2:46 [a] Da 8:17; Ac 10:25 [b] Ac 14:13
2:47 [c] Da 11:36 [d] Da 4:25 [e] ver 22, 28
2:48 [f] ver 6; Da 4:9; 5:11
2:49 [g] Da 1:7
3:1 [h] Isa 46:6; Jer 16:20; Hab 2:19
3:2 [i] ver 27; Da 6:7

[a] *1* That is, about 90 feet high and 9 feet wide or about 27 meters high and 2.7 meters wide

2:46 *presented.* This verb usually is used in Hebrew for pouring out libations. But neither the (grain) offering nor the incense that are mentioned here can be poured out in libations. The text here, however, continues to be in Aramaic, in which the verb means "provided." This makes Nebuchadnezzar's treatment of Daniel a bit more understandable, as he provides Daniel with the materials with which Daniel can make an appropriate offering to his God.
2:48 *ruler over the entire province of Babylon.* The empire was divided into provinces, or satrapies, of which Babylon was one. Daniel is exalted to high office in the province, but that vague description finds definition in the next statement that clarifies the nature of this high office: he is made prefect over the wise men. This is more likely a ranking within his guild rather than an administrative position in the civil government.
3:1 *an image.* The image is never positively identified as the image of a deity, though v. 28 could easily suggest it. If the image was a divine image, it would be odd that the name of the deity was not given and even more unusual that it was set up in an open area rather than associated with a temple. Part of the care of the gods was to house and feed them, and such maintenance could not easily be kept up in an open location. If it is not the image of a god, it becomes more difficult to understand the three friends' refusal to participate in its service or worship (v. 28; see note on Ex 20:4). The other main alternative is to see it as an image of the king. But there was no prohibition against bowing down before kings as an act of respect. Additionally, images of kings during the Assyrian and Babylonian periods were usually made to be put in temples to stand before the deity requesting the well-being of the king. Typically, then, they represented the king to the god, not to the people. Perhaps the best alternative is to understand the event in the context of the Assyrian practice of erecting steles or statues (often in inaccessible places) that commemorate a king's rule. While these were intended to exalt the king, the reliefs on the Balawat gates demonstrate that offerings were made before these representations. In the scene portrayed on the gates, the king himself is present, but the offerings are made to the stele. In this way the king is given the honors that are generally given to the gods, but by personally distancing himself, he does not make himself equal to the gods. Such rituals were used as occasions for provincial territories to take loyalty oaths. This would make sense here in light of the suggestion in the dream of ch. 2 that the Babylonian kingdom would have a limited time of rule. In Assyrian practice, the weapon of Ashur (perhaps even a battle standard) was set up for ceremonies in which vassal kings entered into loyalty oaths. Failure to participate would suggest insubordination, whereas participation would signify the acceptance of the deity's (and king's) sovereignty. The three friends are not being asked to worship a deity, but they are being asked to participate in rituals that honor the king in ways similar to how the gods were treated (though the king is not being viewed as deity). Their interpretation causes them to consider this bowing down to be forbidden by their law, and they feel strongly enough about that that they are willing to risk their lives. *sixty cubits high and six cubits wide.* That is, about 90 feet (27.5 meters) high and 9 feet (2.75 meters) wide. These proportions are odd since the height to width ratio for a normal human figure is about five to one. It may be that part of the height was a pedestal, though one would expect the pedestal to be wider than the image in order to provide the structure with stability. Another possibility is that it was a partially sculptured stele. Although such a stele would not normally be described as an "image," there is an example of the Aramaic word used here being used of such a stele. *Dura.* The Akkadian word *dûru* means "a walled place." Several towns were named Der, and "Dur-" was a common element in place-names, making it impossible to locate the "plain of Dura" with any certainty.
3:2 *summoned.* As mentioned in the note on v. 1, it is likely that the occasion for this gathering was for the taking of a loyalty oath. A century earlier it is known that Assyrian king Ashurbanipal gathered his chief officials together in Babylon to take a loyalty oath. A letter has been preserved from one of the officials who was out of town and therefore made arrangements to take the oath in the presence of the palace overseer. The letter specifically mentions that when he took the oath he was surrounded by the images of the gods. *satraps.* A Persian term borrowed into Aramaic as early as the sixth century BC for the ruler of a province. *prefects, governors.* Both are Semitic titles for the two levels of subordinates to the satraps. *advisors, treasurers, judges, magistrates.* These are Persian loanwords whose translation is very tentative. The list of officials appears to be in rank order.

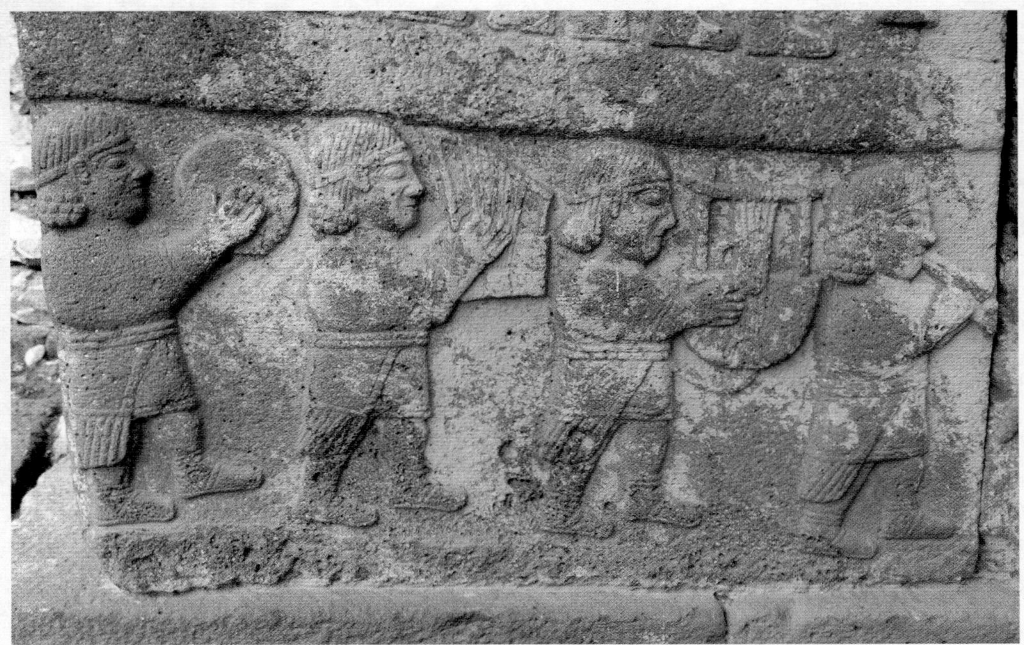

Eighth-century BC orthostat from Karatepe, Turkey, showing musicians playing their instruments: a drum, harps or lyres and flute. These are some of the instruments mentioned in Da 3:5.

the other provincial officials assembled for
the dedication of the image that King Nebuchadnezzar had set up, and they stood
before it.
4Then the herald loudly proclaimed,
"Nations and peoples of every language,[j]
this is what you are commanded to do:
5As soon as you hear the sound of the
horn, flute, zither, lyre, harp, pipe and all
kinds of music, you must fall down and
worship the image of gold that King Nebuchadnezzar has set up.[k] 6Whoever does
not fall down and worship will immediately be thrown into a blazing furnace."[l]
7Therefore, as soon as they heard the
sound of the horn, flute, zither, lyre, harp
and all kinds of music, all the nations and
peoples of every language fell down and
worshiped the image of gold that King
Nebuchadnezzar had set up.[m]
8At this time some astrologers[a][n] came
forward and denounced the Jews. 9They
said to King Nebuchadnezzar, "May the
king live forever![o] 10Your Majesty has issued a decree[p] that everyone who hears
the sound of the horn, flute, zither, lyre,
harp, pipe and all kinds of music must
fall down and worship the image of gold,[q]

3:4 [j] Da 4:1; 6:25
3:5 [k] ver 10, 15
3:6 [l] ver 11, 15, 21; Jer 29:22; Da 6:7; Mt 13:42, 50; Rev 13:15
3:7 [m] ver 5
3:8 [n] Da 2:10
3:9 [o] Ne 2:3; Da 5:10; 6:6
3:10 [p] Da 6:12 [q] ver 4-6

[a] *8* Or *Chaldeans*

3:5 The names of several of these instruments are Greek, but there had been enough contact with Greece even by the sixth century BC that this is not unusual. Nebuchadnezzar was known to make use of foreign musicians, as shown in the rations lists. These lists also attest to the presence of some Greeks in Babylon. *horn.* A wind instrument that, judging by the word used, is an animal's horn rather than a metal trumpet. *flute.* A wind instrument of the variety that is played by blowing through the end. *zither.* A stringed instrument whose name is borrowed from Greek. It is known from Homer's writings (eighth century BC) and is a type of lyre. There were a wide variety of lyres in the ancient world, but there are no early attestations of the zither or dulcimer. *lyre.* A stringed instrument whose name occurs as a foreign word in Greek. It is probably a harp. *harp.* A stringed instrument that is most likely a different style of lyre. *pipe.* This is the most difficult of the instruments to identify. Suggestions have ranged from bagpipes to double flute to percussion. It is a Greek loanword into Aramaic, and it happens also to come into English as "symphony."

3:6 *thrown into a blazing furnace.* Death by burning is referred to occasionally during the Assyrian, Babylonian, Persian and Greek Empires. Most notably, a letter from a Mesopotamian king dating to the sixth century BC instructs a governor to throw corrupt priests into a burning oven. No clear details are given about the furnace. Verses 22–23 may indicate that it had an opening at the top through which the victims were thrown into the fire, and there seems to have been a door or opening in the side through which Nebuchadnezzar could see into it (v. 25). It was probably constructed not for the purpose of punishment but for the making of the image, which would have required melting and casting the metal, or for other construction work.

[11]and that whoever does not fall down and worship will be thrown into a blazing furnace. [12]But there are some Jews whom you have set over the affairs of the province of Babylon — Shadrach, Meshach and Abednego[r] — who pay no attention[s] to you, Your Majesty. They neither serve your gods nor worship the image of gold you have set up."[t]

[13]Furious[u] with rage, Nebuchadnezzar summoned Shadrach, Meshach and Abednego. So these men were brought before the king, [14]and Nebuchadnezzar said to them, "Is it true, Shadrach, Meshach and Abednego, that you do not serve my gods[v] or worship the image[w] of gold I have set up? [15]Now when you hear the sound of the horn, flute, zither, lyre, harp, pipe and all kinds of music, if you are ready to fall down and worship the image I made, very good. But if you do not worship it, you will be thrown immediately into a blazing furnace. Then what god[x] will be able to rescue[y] you from my hand?"

[16]Shadrach, Meshach and Abednego[z] replied to him, "King Nebuchadnezzar, we do not need to defend ourselves before you in this matter. [17]If we are thrown into the blazing furnace, the God we serve is able to deliver[a] us from it, and he will deliver[b] us[a] from Your Majesty's hand. [18]But even if he does not, we want you to know, Your Majesty, that we will not serve your gods or worship the image of gold you have set up.[c]"

[19]Then Nebuchadnezzar was furious with Shadrach, Meshach and Abednego, and his attitude toward them changed. He ordered the furnace heated seven[d] times hotter than usual [20]and commanded some of the strongest soldiers in his army to tie up Shadrach, Meshach and Abednego and throw them into the blazing furnace. [21]So these men, wearing their robes, trousers, turbans and other clothes, were bound and thrown into the blazing furnace. [22]The king's command was so urgent and the furnace so hot that the flames of the fire killed the soldiers who took up Shadrach, Meshach and Abednego,[e] [23]and these three men, firmly tied, fell into the blazing furnace.

[24]Then King Nebuchadnezzar leaped to his feet in amazement and asked his advisers, "Weren't there three men that we tied up and threw into the fire?"

They replied, "Certainly, Your Majesty."

[25]He said, "Look! I see four men walking around in the fire, unbound and unharmed, and the fourth looks like a son of the gods."

[26]Nebuchadnezzar then approached the opening of the blazing furnace and shouted, "Shadrach, Meshach and Abednego, servants of the Most High God,[f] come out! Come here!"

So Shadrach, Meshach and Abednego came out of the fire, [27]and the satraps, prefects, governors and royal advisers[g] crowded around them.[h] They saw that the fire[i] had not harmed their bodies, nor was a hair of their heads singed; their robes were not scorched, and there was no smell of fire on them.

[28]Then Nebuchadnezzar said, "Praise be to the God of Shadrach, Meshach and Abednego, who has sent his angel[j] and rescued his servants! They trusted[k] in him and defied the king's command and were willing to give up their lives rather than serve or worship any god except their own God.[l] [29]Therefore I decree[m] that the people of any nation or language who say anything against the God of Shadrach, Meshach and Abednego be cut into pieces and their houses be turned into piles of rubble,[n] for no other god can save[o] in this way."

[30]Then the king promoted Shadrach, Meshach and Abednego in the province of Babylon.[p]

Nebuchadnezzar's Dream of a Tree

4 [b] King Nebuchadnezzar,

To the nations and peoples of every language,[q] who live in all the earth:

3:12 [r] Da 2:49 [s] Da 6:13 [t] Est 3:3 **3:13** [u] Da 2:12 **3:14** [v] Isa 46:1; Jer 50:2 [w] ver 1 **3:15** [x] Isa 36:18-20 [y] Ex 5:2; 2Ch 32:15 **3:16** [z] Da 1:7 **3:17** [a] Ps 27:1-2 [b] Job 5:19; Jer 1:8 **3:18** [c] ver 28; Jos 24:15 **3:19** [d] Lev 26:18-28 **3:22** [e] Da 1:7 **3:26** [f] Da 4:2,34 **3:27** [g] ver 2 [h] Isa 43:2; Heb 11:32-34 [i] Da 6:23 **3:28** [j] Ps 34:7; Da 6:22; Ac 5:19 [k] Job 13:15; Ps 26:1; 84:12; Jer 17:7 [l] ver 18 **3:29** [m] Da 6:26 [n] Ezr 6:11 [o] Da 6:27 **3:30** [p] Da 2:49 **4:1** [q] Da 3:4

[a] 17 Or *If the God we serve is able to deliver us, then he will deliver us from the blazing furnace and* [b] In Aramaic texts 4:1-3 is numbered 3:31-33, and 4:4-37 is numbered 4:1-34.

3:19 *seven times hotter.* This is hyperbole. The brick kilns of the time normally operated at around 1650°F (900°C). With the technology available it would not have been possible even to double this temperature.

3:25 *a son of the gods.* This is a common expression in Semitic languages for a supernatural being. A polytheist like Nebuchadnezzar would use it for a member of the pantheon of gods. Recognition of a figure as divine would normally be predicated on either the clothing (especially a horned helmet) or what the Babylonians referred to as a *melammu*, a divine glow around the being.

4:1 – 2 A proclamation such as this would typically be recorded on a stele and set up in a prominent place. Sometimes copies would be made and circulated around, such as was done with Darius's Behistun inscription. Many of the elements of this proclamation are common to royal inscriptions or to Aramaic letters, though it is unusual for a king to be so vulnerable as here.

4:1 *King Nebuchadnezzar, To the nations and peoples of every language.* This form of opening is common in Aramaic letters of the Persian period and is also found in Neo-Babylonian letters. A Biblical example is Ezr 7:12. *May you prosper greatly!* The great majority of Aramaic letters follow the opening with a greeting involving some form of the Aramaic root *shlm* ("peace, well-being, prosperity"), as here.

May you prosper greatly![r]
2 It is my pleasure to tell you about
the miraculous signs[s] and wonders
that the Most High God[t] has performed for me.

3 How great are his signs,
how mighty his wonders![u]
His kingdom is an eternal kingdom;
his dominion endures[v] from
generation to generation.

4 I, Nebuchadnezzar, was at home
in my palace, contented[w] and prosperous. 5 I had a dream[x] that made
me afraid. As I was lying in bed,
the images and visions that passed
through my mind[y] terrified me. 6 So I
commanded that all the wise men of
Babylon be brought before me to interpret[z] the dream for me. 7 When the
magicians,[a] enchanters, astrologers[a]
and diviners[b] came, I told them the
dream, but they could not interpret it
for me.[c] 8 Finally, Daniel came into my
presence and I told him the dream.
(He is called Belteshazzar,[d] after the
name of my god, and the spirit of the
holy gods[e] is in him.)
9 I said, "Belteshazzar, chief[f] of the
magicians, I know that the spirit of
the holy gods[g] is in you, and no mystery is too difficult for you. Here is
my dream; interpret it for me. 10 These
are the visions I saw while lying in
bed:[h] I looked, and there before me
stood a tree in the middle of the land.
Its height was enormous.[i] 11 The tree
grew large and strong and its top
touched the sky; it was visible to the
ends of the earth. 12 Its leaves were
beautiful, its fruit abundant, and on
it was food for all. Under it the wild
animals found shelter, and the birds
lived in its branches;[j] from it every
creature was fed.
13 "In the visions I saw while lying
in bed,[k] I looked, and there before me
was a holy one,[l] a messenger,[b] coming down from heaven. 14 He called
in a loud voice: 'Cut down the tree
and trim off its branches; strip off its
leaves and scatter its fruit. Let the
animals flee from under it and the
birds from its branches.[m] 15 But let the
stump and its roots, bound with iron
and bronze, remain in the ground, in
the grass of the field.

" 'Let him be drenched with the
dew of heaven, and let him live with
the animals among the plants of the
earth. 16 Let his mind be changed from
that of a man and let him be given the
mind of an animal, till seven times[c]
pass by for him.[n]
17 " 'The decision is announced by
messengers, the holy ones declare the
verdict, so that the living may know
that the Most High[o] is sovereign[p] over

4:1 [r] Da 6:25
4:2 [s] Ps 74:9 [t] Da 3:26
4:3 [u] Ps 105:27; Da 6:27 [v] Da 2:44
4:4 [w] Ps 30:6
4:5 [x] Da 2:1 [y] Da 2:28
4:6 [z] Da 2:2
4:7 [a] Ge 41:8 [b] Isa 44:25; Da 2:2 [c] Da 2:10
4:8 [d] Da 1:7 [e] Da 5:11, 14
4:9 [f] Da 2:48 [g] Da 5:11-12
4:10 [h] ver 5 [i] Eze 31:3-4
4:12 [j] Eze 17:23; Mt 13:32
4:13 [k] Da 7:1 [l] ver 23; Dt 33:2; Da 8:13
4:14 [m] Eze 31:12; Mt 3:10
4:16 [n] ver 23, 32
4:17 [o] ver 2, 25; Ps 83:18 [p] Jer 27:5-7; Da 2:21; 5:18-21

[a] *7* Or *Chaldeans* [b] *13* Or *watchman*; also in verses 17 and 23 [c] *16* Or *years*; also in verses 23, 25 and 32

4:4 *I, Nebuchadnezzar.* The use of "I" and the content of what follows give what began as a letter similarity to two other forms of Akkadian literature. The first is the *fictional Akkadian autobiography* (an example is the "Cuthean Legend of Naram-Sin"). This also tells of a king's act of pride (failing to heed the gods' instructions given through omens) that leads to disaster and repentance. It was published for the benefit of others — in the case of Naram-Sin, other kings. The other form of literature is the *dream report* (see notes on 1:17; 2:1).

4:10 – 12 The concept of the cosmic tree in the center of the world is a common motif in the ancient Near East. It is also used in Eze 31 (see note on Eze 31:3 – 14). Its roots are fed by the great subterranean ocean and its top merges with the clouds, and thus binds together the heavens, the earth, and the netherworld. In the Mesopotamian epic "Erra and Ishum," Marduk speaks of the meshu tree whose roots reach down through the oceans to the netherworld and whose top is above the heavens. In the Sumerian epic Lugalbanda and Enmerkar, the "eagle-tree" has a similar role. In Assyrian contexts, the motif of a sacred tree is also well known. Some have called it a tree of life, and some also associate it with this world tree. It is often flanked by animals or by human or divine figures. A winged disk is typically centrally located over the top of the tree. The king is represented as the human personification of this tree. The tree is thought to represent the divine world order, but textual discussion of it is lacking.

4:13 *messenger.* The Aramaic noun used here means "one who is awake, a watcher." The "Watchers" are widely attested in Jewish literature of the Hellenistic and early Roman period. The best-known example is "The Book of Watchers" in 1 Enoch 1 – 36, where the term usually refers to the fallen angels. However, even in 1 Enoch the term is used of the (good) archangel Raphael (1 Enoch 22:6) and of the four archangels (1 Enoch 20:1). There is no evidence outside Daniel of the word "watcher" being used in this specialized way of heavenly beings before the third century BC, though Mesopotamian religion included the idea of a variety of protecting deities or angels.

4:15 *the stump and its roots, bound with iron and bronze.* It is difficult to determine whether it is a part of the tree that is bound with iron, or whether it is the king. If it is the tree, the text indicates that its taproot should be bound (not the stump). While trees are sometimes gilded with metal bands in ancient Mesopotamia, there is no case of treating a stump that way, much less a taproot. *dew of heaven.* In Babylonian texts, dew is considered to come down from the stars of heaven and is sometimes seen as the mechanism by which the stars bring either sickness or healing.

4:16 *Let his mind be changed.* See note on v. 33. *seven times.* This may mean seven years, but there is no firm basis for this. The word for "times" means a definite period, though one that can be of any length. Omens sometimes had a set time over which their effects could take place, which could be of various lengths.

all kingdoms on earth and gives them
to anyone he wishes and sets over
them the lowliest[q] of people.'
18 "This is the dream that I, King
Nebuchadnezzar, had. Now, Belteshazzar, tell me what it means, for
none of the wise men in my kingdom
can interpret it for me.[r] But you can,[s]
because the spirit of the holy gods is
in you."[t]

Daniel Interprets the Dream

19 Then Daniel (also called Belteshazzar) was greatly perplexed for
a time, and his thoughts terrified[u]
him. So the king said, "Belteshazzar,
do not let the dream or its meaning
alarm you."
Belteshazzar answered, "My lord,
if only the dream applied to your enemies and its meaning to your adversaries! 20 The tree you saw, which
grew large and strong, with its top
touching the sky, visible to the whole
earth, 21 with beautiful leaves and
abundant fruit, providing food for all,
giving shelter to the wild animals, and
having nesting places in its branches

4:17 [q] Da 11:21 **4:18** [r] Ge 41:8; Da 5:8, 15 [s] Ge 41:15 [t] ver 7-9
4:19 [u] Da 7:15, 28; 8:27; 10:16-17

THE NEO-BABYLONIAN EMPIRE 626–539 BC

The Babylonians, while continuing the militaristic tradition of Assyria, created an astonishing renaissance of Sumero-Akkadian civilization. Led by Nebuchadnezzar (605–562 BC), the Neo-Babylonian Empire carried out a building program of canals and monuments that was ambitious in the extreme.

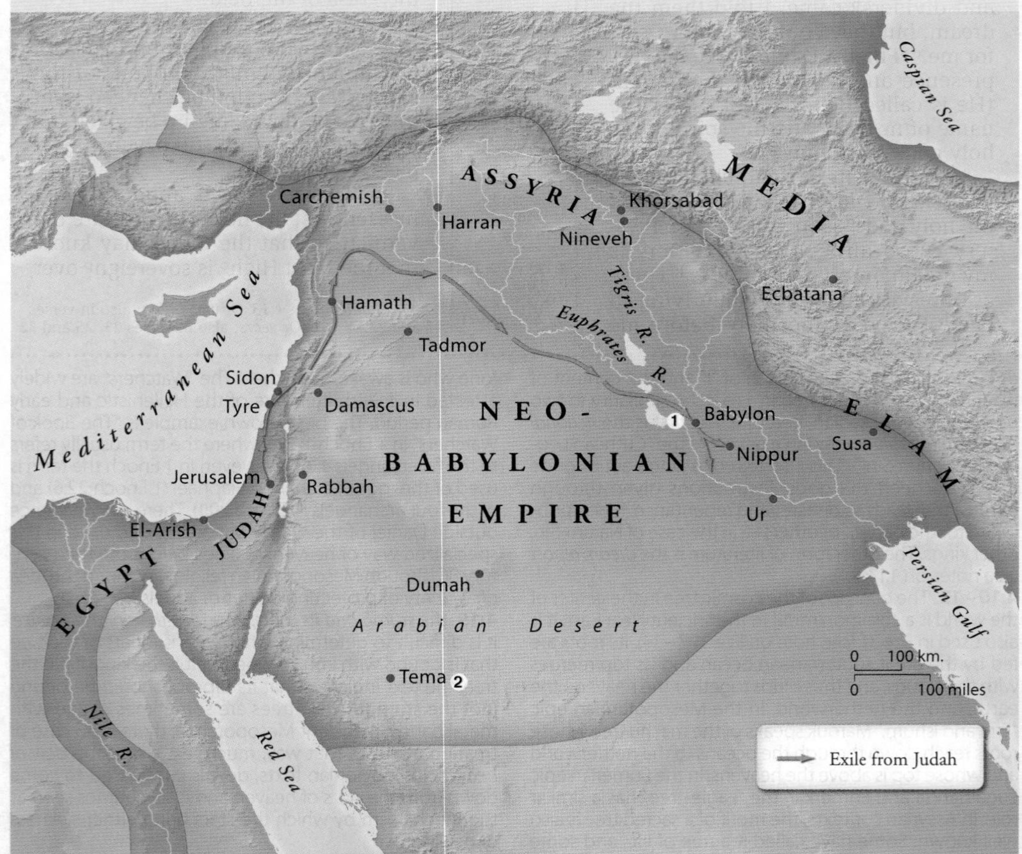

1 Early Greek and Roman authors rhapsodized about the capital city astride the Euphrates. A four-horse chariot could turn atop the high hundred-gated walls. Babylon also boasted one of the world's seven wonders, the famed hanging gardens, as well as a stepped temple-tower 295 feet high and, according to Herodotus, several colossal gold statues weighing many tons.

2 Discoveries of inscriptions in clay have shown that the last king of Babylonia, Nabonidus, absented himself at Tema in Arabia while Belshazzar acted as regent in the capital (see ch. 5).

for the birds — 22Your Majesty, you
are that tree![v] You have become great
and strong; your greatness has grown
until it reaches the sky, and your dominion extends to distant parts of the
earth.[w]
23"Your Majesty saw a holy one,[x] a
messenger, coming down from heav-
en and saying, 'Cut down the tree and
destroy it, but leave the stump, bound
with iron and bronze, in the grass of
the field, while its roots remain in the
ground. Let him be drenched with the
dew of heaven; let him live with the
wild animals, until seven times pass
by for him.'[y]
24"This is the interpretation, Your
Majesty, and this is the decree[z] the
Most High has issued against my lord
the king: 25You will be driven away
from people and will live with the wild
animals; you will eat grass like the ox
and be drenched with the dew of heav-
en. Seven times will pass by for you
until you acknowledge that the Most
High[a] is sovereign over all kingdoms
on earth and gives them to anyone he
wishes.[b] 26The command to leave the
stump of the tree with its roots[c] means
that your kingdom will be restored
to you when you acknowledge that
Heaven rules.[d] 27Therefore, Your Majesty, be pleased to accept my advice:
Renounce your sins by doing what is
right, and your wickedness by being
kind to the oppressed.[e] It may be that
then your prosperity will continue.[f]"

The Dream Is Fulfilled

28All this happened[g] to King Nebuchadnezzar. 29Twelve months later,
as the king was walking on the roof
of the royal palace of Babylon, 30he
said, "Is not this the great Babylon I
have built as the royal residence, by
my mighty power and for the glory of
my majesty?"[h]
31Even as the words were on his
lips, a voice came from heaven, "This
is what is decreed for you, King Nebuchadnezzar: Your royal authority has
been taken from you. 32You will be
driven away from people and will live
with the wild animals; you will eat
grass like the ox. Seven times will
pass by for you until you acknowledge that the Most High is sovereign
over all kingdoms on earth and gives
them to anyone he wishes."
33Immediately what had been said
about Nebuchadnezzar was fulfilled.
He was driven away from people and
ate grass like the ox. His body was
drenched with the dew of heaven until his hair grew like the feathers of
an eagle and his nails like the claws
of a bird.[i]
34At the end of that time, I, Nebuchadnezzar, raised my eyes toward
heaven, and my sanity was restored.
Then I praised the Most High; I honored and glorified him who lives forever.[j]

His dominion is an eternal dominion;
his kingdom endures from
generation to generation.[k]
35All the peoples of the earth
are regarded as nothing.[l]
He does as he pleases[m]
with the powers of heaven
and the peoples of the earth.

4:22 [v] 2Sa 12:7 [w] Jer 27:7; Da 2:37-38; 5:18-19 **4:23** [x] ver 13 [y] Da 5:21 **4:24** [z] Job 40:12; Ps 107:40 **4:25** [a] ver 17; Ps 83:18 [b] Jer 27:5; Da 5:21 **4:26** [c] ver 15 [d] Da 2:37 **4:27** [e] Isa 55:6-7 [f] 1Ki 21:29; Ps 41:3; Eze 18:22 **4:28** [g] Nu 23:19 **4:30** [h] Isa 37:24-25; Da 5:20; Hab 2:4 **4:33** [i] Da 5:20-21 **4:34** [j] Da 12:7; Rev 4:10 [k] Ps 145:13; Da 2:44; 5:21; 6:26; Lk 1:33 **4:35** [l] Isa 40:17 [m] Ps 115:3; 135:6

4:22 *Your Majesty, you are that tree!* The ancient Near Eastern king was sometimes identified with the tree of life (see note on vv. 10–12), as he was the source of protection and sustenance for his people. Also, there are what seem to be anthropomorphic depictions of the Assyrian sacred tree, thus drawing together the cosmic tree of the dream with the king's identification as the tree.
4:30 *the great Babylon I have built.* Nebuchadnezzar carried out major building works in Babylon. The Euphrates was channeled into a number of canals passing through the city. He embellished the major streets, especially the great Procession Way along which the images of the gods were drawn at festivals. Moreover, he did major work on the religious buildings of the city (see note on 1:2). According to later historians, he built a luxurious palace with its hanging (terraced) gardens, which was identified as one of the seven wonders of the ancient world, though recent studies by scholars have suggested that it was actually Sennacherib's building in Nineveh that was mistaken as Nebuchadnezzar's in Babylon. Regardless, his building activity was extensive and legendary.
4:33 What is said about Nebuchadnezzar's condition here and in v. 16 is often identified by modern interpreters as zooanthropy, a psychological disorder in which a person thinks they have become an animal and behave accordingly. An alternative sees the change that happened to Nebuchadnezzar as that which is also described as happening to the hero in the *Tale of Ahiqar*: "The hair on my head had grown to my shoulders, and my beard reached my breast; and my body was fouled with dust and my nails were grown like eagles." There are also parallels with what is said of the wild, animal-like creature Enkidu in the Gilgamesh Epic who is described as hairy, unclothed and eating grass before he became "civilized" as a human being. It is therefore possible that the description of Nebuchadnezzar is intended to present him as an exile from civilized human society. Very few surviving Babylonian sources give information about the last 30 years of Nebuchadnezzar's life. A fragmentary cuneiform text seems to refer to some mental disorder afflicting Nebuchadnezzar and perhaps his neglecting and leaving Babylon, maybe putting his son Amel-Marduk (Biblical Awel-Marduk) in charge for a while, and then of his repentance for neglect of the worship of the gods. Unfortunately the text is too fragmentary for any firm conclusions to be drawn.

DANIEL 4:33

The Tale of Ahiqar

Ahiqar was a high official in the courts of the Assyrian kings Sennacherib (704–681 BC) and Esarhaddon (680–669), and renowned for his wisdom and skill. Having no son, he adopted his nephew Nadin and trained him to be his successor. Nadin was a scoundrel and plotted against his uncle, convincing Esarhaddon that Ahiqar should be executed for treason. When the king's officer came to carry out the sentence, Ahiqar was able to remind him that he had once saved the officer's life in a similar situation. The officer hid Ahiqar in his own house and executed a eunuch in Ahiqar's place.

Hearing of Ahiqar's "death," the king of Egypt sent Esarhaddon a challenge. If he could send someone to Egypt to successfully fulfill a particular, difficult task, Assyria would receive Egypt's revenue for three years; if he could not, then Egypt would receive a similar sum from Assyria. Just when Esarhaddon was afraid he would lose the challenge, the officer revealed that Ahiqar was alive. Ahiqar was immediately sent to Egypt, where he succeeded in the task, to general amazement. When he returned with great wealth, he promptly settled accounts with Nadin, who was beaten to death. There is evidence that someone called Ahiqar held high office during the reign of Esarhaddon. ◆

DANIEL 4:34–35

The Prayer of Nabonidus

An Aramaic text from Qumran, usually referred to as the Prayer of Nabonidus, has some similarities to the story in Da 4. In this text, written in the first person, Nabonidus is afflicted with some disease for seven years, a Jewish diviner is involved in his restoration, and the king writes a letter to honor God. The scroll preserves no mention of comparison to a beast, though some interpreters have reconstructed a line to include such a reference. Although some see reference to a dream in a piece of the fragment, others reject this on good philological grounds. There are notable differences between the Qumran and Biblical texts: the king's name is different, the disease is different, the Jewish diviner is not named, there is no report of a dream and its interpretation. What relationship there might be between the two texts is unclear. The fragmentary state of the Qumran text adds to the uncertainty. The scroll connects the seven-year illness with Nabonidus's well-known stay in Tema, which has the advantage of offering a historical anchor to the king's absence (attributed to illness). This may suggest that in the Qumran community they had associated the tradition of Da 4 with Nabonidus rather than with Nebuchadnezzar. ◆

No one can hold back his hand
or say to him: "What have you done?"[n]

[36]At the same time that my sanity
was restored, my honor and splendor
were returned to me for the glory of
my kingdom.[o] My advisers and nobles sought me out, and I was restored to my throne and became even
greater than before. [37]Now I, Nebuchadnezzar, praise and exalt and glorify the King of heaven, because everything he does is right and all his
ways are just.[p] And those who walk
in pride he is able to humble.[q]

The Writing on the Wall

5 King Belshazzar gave a great banquet[r]
for a thousand of his nobles and drank
wine with them. [2]While Belshazzar was
drinking his wine, he gave orders to bring
in the gold and silver goblets[s] that Nebuchadnezzar his father[a] had taken from the
temple in Jerusalem, so that the king and
his nobles, his wives and his concubines
might drink from them.[t] [3]So they brought
in the gold goblets that had been taken
from the temple of God in Jerusalem, and
the king and his nobles, his wives and his
concubines drank from them. [4]As they
drank the wine, they praised the gods of
gold and silver, of bronze, iron, wood and
stone.[u]

[5]Suddenly the fingers of a human hand
appeared and wrote on the plaster of the

4:35 [n]Isa 45:9; Ro 9:20 **4:36** [o]Pr 22:4 **4:37** [p]Dt 32:4; Ps 33:4-5 [q]Ex 18:11; Job 40:11-12; Da 5:20,23 **5:1** [r]Est 1:3 **5:2** [s]2Ki 24:13; Jer 52:19 [t]Est 1:7; Da 1:2 **5:4** [u]Ps 135:15-18; Hab 2:19; Rev 9:20

[a] 2 Or *ancestor*; or *predecessor*; also in verses 11, 13 and 18

5:1 *King Belshazzar.* The son of Nabonidus, the last king of Babylon. He acted as regent in Babylon while Nabonidus spent ten years in Tema in Arabia. Because Belshazzar did not enjoy full royal prerogatives and was not given the title "king" in Babylonian records, it has been argued that calling him "king" here is inaccurate. A bilingual ninth-century BC inscription throws light on this issue. In the Assyrian text the ruler of Guzan is called "governor," whereas in the Aramaic text he is styled "king." This suggests that the Aramaic term "king" (*mlk*) had a wider meaning or was used more loosely than the Akkadian term (*sharru*) and that it is not wrong to use it of Belshazzar. *gave a great banquet.* This story records the final downfall of the Neo-Babylonian Empire in mid-October 539 BC. There are a number of accounts of the fall of Babylon (the first three in contemporary ancient Near Eastern sources, the last three in later classical sources), which differ in some details. (1) The Cyrus Cylinder says that Cyrus entered Babylon unopposed and captured Nabonidus. (2) The Babylonian Chronicle says that Nabonidus fled following a revolt against him in Babylonia and Cyrus's capture of Sippar without a fight. He was later captured when he returned to Babylon. Cyrus entered Babylon without a battle. (3) The Dynastic Prophecy seems to say that Cyrus sent Nabonidus into exile. (4) Berossus says that Cyrus captured Babylon while Nabonidus was besieged in Borsippa. Nabonidus then surrendered and was sent into exile in Carmania. (5) Herodotus says that Cyrus captured Babylon by temporarily diverting the course of the Euphrates when the Babylonians were feasting and dancing. His troops waded along the riverbed, where the river passed through the city walls. (6) Xenophon says much the same, adding that the Persians took the city at night and that Gobryas, one of Cyrus's generals, killed the Babylonian king, a riotous, indulgent, cruel and godless young man. The king said to have been killed by Cyrus's general Gobryas may have been Belshazzar. *banquet.* This banquet is taking place in mid-October (15th of Tashritu) 539 BC. In the past few days the Persians had taken the city of Opis (50 miles [80 kilometers] north on the Tigris) in a bloody battle, and then crossed over to the Euphrates, where the city of Sippar surrendered without a fight on the 14th of Tashritu. It is likely that Babylon has received word of these events and that Belshazzar knows that the Persian army is on the march toward Babylon. Some sources indicate that Nabonidus had been with the army at Opis and fled when the city fell. When Nabonidus was captured, it was in Babylon, but the texts are unclear about when he arrived. Berossus (a third-century BC Chaldean historian, quoted by Josephus) claims that he was trapped in the city of Borsippa (about 17 miles [27 kilometers] south of Babylon). In light of all of this, it appears that the banquet represents one final gathering before the momentous events that are about to transpire. Herodotus refers to a festival celebration that was taking place when the city fell. There is no reason to think, however, that the banquet reflects Belshazzar's pessimism about the outcome. Babylon was a defensible city, and the Babylonians believed their gods to be strong.

5:2 *the gold and silver goblets ... from the temple in Jerusalem.* See note on 1:2. These goblets had probably not been melted down because they were recognized as sacred objects. In v. 23 Daniel condemns Belshazzar for putting sacred vessels to profane use and for using vessels dedicated to the Most High God to worship idols. *Nebuchadnezzar his father.* Belshazzar was the eldest son of Nabonidus. As early as Herodotus in the fifth century BC, Nebuchadnezzar and Nabonidus are given the same name in Greek (Labynetos). Daniel may be following the same tradition as Herodotus. Alternatively, Nabonidus might have married one of Nebuchadnezzar's daughters, making Belshazzar Nebuchadnezzar's grandson. In the Semitic languages "father" and "son" can be used of more distant forebears and descendants. Another possibility is suggested by the inscription on the Black Obelisk of Shalmaneser III. In this artifact Jehu, a king of Israel, is called "son of Omri" even though he had no blood relationship to him. He is simply being designated as the successor to a well-known king.

5:4 *praised the gods.* Belshazzar and his administration are well aware that the empire hangs by a thread and that the next several days will be of utmost significance. They are hoping that their gods will bring victory for them, as they had in the days of Nebuchadnezzar's great conquests. To that end, they are "toasting the gods" and celebrating their past victories. It is also possible, though not explicitly stated, that libations were poured out to the gods from these vessels. They are making their supplications not only to Marduk, the patron of Babylon, but to the gods of other cities of the region whose images had been gathered into Babylon during these troubled times.

5:5 *a human hand.* A lifeless, detached hand would have suggested a defeated enemy. Casualty counts were made by cutting off the right hands of all of the dead (recall the broken-off hands of Dagon in 1Sa 5:3–4). By drinking from the vessels, the Babylonians were recalling the defeat of

wall, near the lampstand in the royal
palace. The king watched the hand as it
wrote. 6His face turned pale and he was
so frightened[v] that his legs became weak[w]
and his knees were knocking.
7The king summoned the enchanters,
astrologers[a] and diviners.[x] Then he said
to these wise[y] men of Babylon, "Whoever reads this writing and tells me what it
means will be clothed in purple and have
a gold chain placed around his neck,[z] and
he will be made the third highest ruler in
the kingdom."[a]
8Then all the king's wise men came in,
but they could not read the writing or tell
the king what it meant.[b] 9So King Belshazzar became even more terrified[c] and his face
grew more pale. His nobles were baffled.
10The queen,[b] hearing the voices of the
king and his nobles, came into the banquet
hall. "May the king live forever!"[d] she said.
"Don't be alarmed! Don't look so pale!
11There is a man in your kingdom who has
the spirit of the holy gods[e] in him. In the
time of your father he was found to have
insight and intelligence and wisdom[f] like
that of the gods. Your father, King Nebuchadnezzar, appointed him chief of the magicians, enchanters, astrologers and diviners.[g] 12He did this because Daniel, whom
the king called Belteshazzar,[h] was found
to have a keen mind and knowledge and
understanding, and also the ability to interpret dreams, explain riddles and solve difficult problems.[i] Call for Daniel, and he will
tell you what the writing means."
13So Daniel was brought before the
king, and the king said to him, "Are you
Daniel, one of the exiles my father the
king brought from Judah?[j] 14I have heard
that the spirit of the gods is in you and
that you have insight, intelligence and out-

5:6 [v] Da 4:5 [w] Eze 7:17
5:7 [x] Isa 44:25 [y] Da 4:6-7 [z] Ge 41:42 [a] Da 2:5-6,48; 6:2-3
5:8 [b] Da 2:10, 27
5:9 [c] Isa 21:4
5:10 [d] Da 3:9
5:11 [e] Da 4:8-9, 19 [f] ver 14; Da 1:17 [g] Da 2:47-48
5:12 [h] Da 1:7 [i] ver 14-16; Da 6:3
5:13 [j] Da 6:13
5:17 [k] 2Ki 5:16
5:18 [l] Jer 27:7; Da 2:37-38
5:19 [m] Da 2:12-13; 3:6
5:20 [n] Da 4:30 [o] Jer 13:18 [p] Job 40:12; Isa 14:13-15
5:21 [q] Eze 17:24 [r] Da 4:16-17,35
5:22 [s] Ex 10:3; 2Ch 33:23

standing wisdom. 15The wise men and enchanters were brought before me to read
this writing and tell me what it means, but
they could not explain it. 16Now I have
heard that you are able to give interpretations and to solve difficult problems. If
you can read this writing and tell me what
it means, you will be clothed in purple
and have a gold chain placed around your
neck, and you will be made the third highest ruler in the kingdom."
17Then Daniel answered the king, "You
may keep your gifts for yourself and give
your rewards to someone else.[k] Nevertheless, I will read the writing for the king
and tell him what it means.
18"Your Majesty, the Most High God
gave your father Nebuchadnezzar sovereignty and greatness and glory and splendor.[l] 19Because of the high position he
gave him, all the nations and peoples of
every language dreaded and feared him.
Those the king wanted to put to death,
he put to death;[m] those he wanted to
spare, he spared; those he wanted to promote, he promoted; and those he wanted to humble, he humbled. 20But when
his heart became arrogant and hardened
with pride,[n] he was deposed from his royal throne and stripped[o] of his glory.[p] 21He
was driven away from people and given
the mind of an animal; he lived with the
wild donkeys and ate grass like the ox;
and his body was drenched with the dew
of heaven, until he acknowledged that the
Most High God is sovereign[q] over all kingdoms on earth and sets over them anyone
he wishes.[r]
22"But you, Belshazzar, his son,[c] have
not humbled[s] yourself, though you knew

[a] 7 Or *Chaldeans*; also in verse 11 [b] 10 Or *queen mother* [c] 22 Or *descendant*; or *successor*

Yahweh (perhaps along with other gods and nations), but this is no lifeless, severed hand of a dead god. It is quite animated and has a message to give. The effect might be similar if the head of a decapitated victim began to speak. *wrote on the plaster of the wall, near the lampstand.* This is a curious detail since one might have expected plaster all around the room that would be illuminated by many lampstands. The excavation of the throne room in Babylon can offer some explanation. The hall was 170 feet (51.8 meters) by 55 feet (16.75 meters); it was entered through three spacious courtyards that led the way from the entrance just inside the Ishtar Gate. Some of the wall space was covered with blue enameled brick, while other parts were plaster. The word used for lampstand is an unusual one and may be a Persian loanword. As such it likely represents a distinct, singular lampstand, perhaps of a special type.

5:7 *clothed in purple and have a gold chain placed around his neck.* Marks of honor and royal approval (Ge 41:42; Est 8:15). Purple clothing was made using an expensive dye and was normally only worn by royalty. The chain may have been an insignia of office. *third highest ruler.* This may indicate being ranked only behind Belshazzar and his father, Nabonidus—though the term used may represent the title of a high official.

5:8 *they could not read the writing.* Some have suggested that the writing was in code or an unusual language, but nothing in the text suggests this. Aramaic, like Hebrew, was written without vowels and sometimes without word divisions. Thus, the writing on the wall may have consisted of a string of nine consonants (*mn'tqlprs*). Uncertainty about word division and vowels would be enough to baffle the wise men and leave them unable to say what it meant.

5:10 *queen.* That she can enter the king's presence unbidden and that her memory goes back beyond that of Belshazzar suggests that the "queen" is the queen mother. Also, she seems to be a different person from any of Belshazzar's wives noted in vv. 2–3. In ancient Near Eastern courts the queen mother was often an influential figure. Nabonidus's mother (Belshazzar's grandmother), Adad-Guppi, was a very influential person and the quintessential queen mother. Her 104 years, however, had come to a close about 546 BC, so she was no longer alive at this time. Nabonidus's wife, Belshazzar's mother, identified by Herodotus as Nitocris, is more likely referred to here.

The Nabonidus cylinder inscription from Ur, 555 to 539 BC, names Belshazzar (Da 5:1).

all this. 23 Instead, you have set yourself up
against[t] the Lord of heaven. You had the
goblets from his temple brought to you,
and you and your nobles, your wives and
your concubines drank wine from them.
You praised the gods of silver and gold,
of bronze, iron, wood and stone, which
cannot see or hear or understand.[u] But
you did not honor the God who holds in
his hand your life[v] and all your ways.[w]
24 Therefore he sent the hand that wrote
the inscription.
25 "This is the inscription that was written:

MENE, MENE, TEKEL, PARSIN

26 "Here is what these words mean:

Mene[a]: God has numbered the
days[x] of your reign and
brought it to an end.[y]

27 *Tekel*[b]: You have been weighed
on the scales and found
wanting.[z]
28 *Peres*[c]: Your kingdom is divided
and given to the Medes[a] and
Persians."[b]

29 Then at Belshazzar's command, Daniel was clothed in purple, a gold chain
was placed around his neck, and he was
proclaimed the third highest ruler in the
kingdom.
30 That very night Belshazzar,[c] king of
the Babylonians,[d] was slain,[d] 31 and Darius[e] the Mede took over the kingdom, at
the age of sixty-two.[e]

5:23 [t] Jer 50:29 [u] Ps 115:4-8; Hab 2:19 [v] Job 12:10 [w] Job 31:4; Jer 10:23 **5:26** [x] Jer 27:7 [y] Isa 13:6 **5:27** [z] Ps 62:9 **5:28** [a] Isa 13:17 [b] Da 6:28 **5:30** [c] ver 1 [d] Isa 21:9; Jer 51:31 **5:31** [e] Da 6:1; 9:1

[a] 26 *Mene* can mean *numbered* or *mina* (a unit of money). [b] 27 *Tekel* can mean *weighed* or *shekel.* [c] 28 *Peres* (the singular of *Parsin*) can mean *divided* or *Persia* or *a half mina* or *a half shekel.* [d] 30 Or *Chaldeans* [e] 31 In Aramaic texts this verse (5:31) is numbered 6:1.

5:25 *MENE, MENE, TEKEL, PARSIN.* Initially Daniel reads the writing as the names of standard Babylonian weights: the "mina," the "shekel," and the "peres" (*parsin* is a form meaning "two peres"). Archaeologists have found weights with these names inscribed on them. The mina was 60 times the weight of the shekel in Babylonia but 50 times the shekel in Palestine. The name "peres" often means a half mina but can mean a half shekel. Alternatively, the words can be taken as verbs for weighing and assessing. As such their significance extends beyond the commercial realm, as scales and weights were also used to depict divine evaluation and judgment (as in the Egyptian "Book of the Dead"). Daniel appears to have used both noun and verb forms in his interpretation. Wordplay was a common means used to interpret omens in this period. It also would be ironic that the last term, *peres*, also sounds like the word for the Persians.

5:27 *weighed on the scales.* The imagery of the scales may have had an astronomical connotation. Babylon fell on the 16th of the Babylonian month Teshrit. Babylonians traditionally linked this month with the constellation of The Scales (the one we call Libra). Its annual appearance in the night sky for the first time was associated with the middle of the month. The court astrologers would know this and would have seen it as confirmation of Daniel's interpretation of the omen.

5:31 *Darius the Mede.* All extra-Biblical sources say that Cyrus II of Persia captured Babylon (539 BC). No historical king named Darius is known until Darius I of Persia, who ruled from 522–486 BC. There have been various suggestions identifying Darius the Mede with a known historical figure. One popular suggestion identifies Darius with Ugbaru (Gobryas in Greek), the general who captured Babylon on Cyrus's behalf. He was governor of Gutium in Media. However, it is now clear that he died only three weeks after capturing the city, and there is no

Daniel in the Den of Lions

6 [a] It pleased Darius[f] to appoint 120 satraps[g] to rule throughout the king-
dom, [2]with three administrators over
them, one of whom was Daniel.[h] The
satraps were made accountable[i] to them
so that the king might not suffer loss.
[3]Now Daniel so distinguished himself
among the administrators and the satraps
by his exceptional qualities that the king
planned to set him over the whole kingdom.[j] [4]At this, the administrators and the
satraps tried to find grounds for charges
against Daniel in his conduct of government affairs, but they were unable to do
so. They could find no corruption in him,
because he was trustworthy and neither
corrupt nor negligent. [5]Finally these men
said, "We will never find any basis for
charges against this man Daniel unless it
has something to do with the law of his
God."[k]

[6]So these administrators and satraps
went as a group to the king and said:
"May King Darius live forever![l] [7]The royal
administrators, prefects, satraps, advisers
and governors[m] have all agreed that the
king should issue an edict and enforce
the decree that anyone who prays to any
god or human being during the next thirty
days, except to you, Your Majesty, shall be
thrown into the lions' den.[n] [8]Now, Your
Majesty, issue the decree and put it in
writing so that it cannot be altered — in
accordance with the law of the Medes and
Persians, which cannot be repealed."[o] [9]So
King Darius put the decree in writing.

[10]Now when Daniel learned that the decree had been published, he went home
to his upstairs room where the windows
opened toward[p] Jerusalem. Three times
a day he got down on his knees[q] and
prayed, giving thanks to his God, just as
he had done before.[r] [11]Then these men
went as a group and found Daniel praying
and asking God for help. [12]So they went to
the king and spoke to him about his royal
decree: "Did you not publish a decree that
during the next thirty days anyone who
prays to any god or human being except to
you, Your Majesty, would be thrown into
the lions' den?"

The king answered, "The decree
stands — in accordance with the law of
the Medes and Persians, which cannot be
repealed."[s]

[13]Then they said to the king, "Daniel,

6:1 [f] Da 5:31 [g] Est 1:1 **6:2** [h] Da 2:48-49 [i] Ezr 4:22 **6:3** [j] Ge 41:41; Est 10:3; Da 5:12-14 **6:5** [k] Ac 24:13-16 **6:6** [l] Ne 2:3; Da 2:4 **6:7** [m] Da 3:2 [n] Ps 59:3; 64:2-6; Da 3:6 **6:8** [o] Est 1:19 **6:10** [p] 1Ki 8:48-49 [q] Ps 95:6 [r] Ac 5:29 **6:12** [s] Est 1:19; Da 3:8-12

[a] In Aramaic texts 6:1-28 is numbered 6:2-29.

evidence that he was given the title "king," as Darius is in Da 6:6. Another suggestion identifies Darius with a governor of Babylon and Beyond the River (the area west of the Euphrates) called Gubaru. But it is now clear that he was not appointed to this post until four years after the capture of Babylon. The most likely suggestion, though it too has problems, takes Darius the Mede as an alternative name for Cyrus the Persian, who was about 62 years old when Babylon fell (see note on 6:28).

6:1 *satraps.* The main administrative division of the Persian Empire was the satrapy. The number of satrapies with their ruling satraps varied with time but was usually in the 20s. Greek writers used the term "satrap" of various Persian royal officials as well as of the governors of the satrapies. This, presumably, is the case here.

6:7 *edict ... decree.* The content and implications of this decree have caused much debate. There is no evidence that the Persian kings were ever inclined to deify themselves. This leads some to suggest that the decree simply made the king the sole representative of the deity for the period of 30 days. All prayers to God or the gods would need to be channeled through him. We could speculate that the king accepts such a suggestion to address the struggle in Persia between the advocates of pure Zoroastrianism (see the article "Zoroastrianism," p. 1433) and the supporters of the traditional Persian religion who advocated a syncretistic form of religion, which the Magi seem to have favored. The decree could be seen as a stand against syncretism, with the king representing Ahura Mazda. Given that Persian rulers had a tolerant attitude to the religions of their subject peoples, Darius probably intended the decree to apply to the Persian population alone. Daniel fell afoul of it because he was a very senior Persian official. *den.* The Aramaic word used means "pit." The pit envisaged in this story seems to be an underground cavity with a relatively small hole at the top that could be covered by a large stone. Although this particular form of punishment is not mentioned elsewhere, in earlier Assyrian texts, oath breakers were put into cages of wild animals set up in the city square to be publicly devoured, and the Persian kings used some horrible forms of execution.

6:8 *the law of the Medes and Persians ... cannot be repealed.* This concept can be traced far back in literature, particularly with reference to the gods, whose decrees were unchangeable; however, no specific attestation has been documented outside of the books of Daniel and Esther (Est 1:19; 8:8). Nonetheless, a tradition at least as early as the time of Hammurapi (eighteenth century BC) recognized that a judge could not change a decision that had been made. In this sense, we may be dealing with a ruling rather than a law. Greek sources conflict with one another; Herodotus indicates significant freedom on the part of Persian kings to change their minds, while Diodorus Siculus cites an instance where Darius III could not do so. Certainly no lower official could countermand the decrees of the Persian king, and the king himself may have thought it too humiliating to go back and reconsider something he had already decreed. Royal code of honor would have made it out of the question for the king to rescind an order.

6:10 *windows opened toward Jerusalem.* The practice of praying facing the temple in Jerusalem is mentioned in the OT only in 1Ki 8:22 – 54; Ps 5:7. *Three times a day.* Prayer at "evening, morning and noon" is mentioned in Ps 55:17, but it is not clear whether this was a generally accepted practice. 1Ch 23:30 refers only to morning and evening prayers in the temple. *down on his knees.* The OT refers to both standing (1Ch 23:30; Ne 9:2,5) and kneeling (1Ki 8:54; Ezr 9:5) in prayer. Daniel's practice of prayer probably reflects a custom that grew up among the Jewish exiles in the eastern Diaspora.

DANIEL 6:7

ZOROASTRIANISM

There is considerable debate about the origins, teachings and history of Zoroastrianism in Persia. This is partly because the surviving Zoroastrian texts are limited and were not written down until about the sixth century AD. By that time the religion had undergone considerable development and change.

Most scholars date Zarathushtra (called Zoroaster by the Greeks), the originator of the religion, to 1200 – 1000 BC, though some argue for earlier or later dates. He came from a cattle-herding background, probably in northeastern Iran. He preached the worship of Ahura Mazda, "the wise lord." It is unclear whether he advocated monotheism or dualism. He did preach an ethical dualism, teaching that everyone must choose between righteousness and the lie, and that people will be ultimately judged by whether their good deeds outweigh their evil deeds. Fire is central in Zoroastrian rituals because it is the symbol of Ahura Mazda and of light and truth.

Whether or not Zoroaster taught monotheism, Zoroastrianism became dualistic in its teaching. According to its religious texts there are two primordial, uncreated spirits — a good spirit (Ahura Mazda) and an evil spirit (Angra Mainyu or Ahriman). These are in conflict, and God (Ahura Mazda) will only triumph over the evil one (Angra Mainyu) in the end with the help of humans who choose his side in the struggle.

Precisely when Zoroastrianism began to be accepted by the Persian rulers is a hotly debated issue. Initially it seems to have been opposed by the Magi, the influential hereditary priests of the old, polytheistic religion of the Medes and Persians. The Magi, probably originally a priestly Median tribe, became influential at the Persian court from the time of Cyrus II. Eventually they seem to have promoted a syncretistic religion that combined elements of the old religion with Zoroastrianism.

Following the Islamic conquest of Iran in the seventh century AD, the Zoroastrians were subjected to persecution. The majority fled to the area around Bombay in India, where they were given the name "Parsees/Parsis" (Persians). Today the Parsees of India are the main surviving community of Zoroastrians. There are small communities in Pakistan and Iran and in several other countries to which Parsees have migrated. ◆

who is one of the exiles from Judah,[t] pays
no attention[u] to you, Your Majesty, or to
the decree you put in writing. He still prays
three times a day." 14When the king heard
this, he was greatly distressed;[v] he was determined to rescue Daniel and made every
effort until sundown to save him.

15Then the men went as a group to King
Darius and said to him, "Remember, Your
Majesty, that according to the law of the
Medes and Persians no decree or edict that
the king issues can be changed."[w]

16So the king gave the order, and they
brought Daniel and threw him into the lions' den.[x] The king said to Daniel, "May
your God, whom you serve continually,
rescue[y] you!"

17A stone was brought and placed over
the mouth of the den, and the king sealed[z]
it with his own signet ring and with the
rings of his nobles, so that Daniel's situation might not be changed. 18Then the
king returned to his palace and spent the
night without eating[a] and without any entertainment being brought to him. And he
could not sleep.[b]

6:13 [t] Da 2:25; 5:13 [u] Est 3:8; Da 3:12
6:14 [v] Mk 6:26
6:15 [w] Est 8:8
6:16 [x] ver 7 [y] Job 5:19; Ps 37:39-40
6:17 [z] Mt 27:66
6:18 [a] 2Sa 12:17 [b] Est 6:1; Da 2:1

6:17 *the king sealed it with his own signet ring.* There were three kinds of seals in use in the ancient Near East: cylinder seals, stamp seals and signet rings. The signet ring tended to be used for more personal business. The stone closing the pit was sealed in some way with several different seals to prevent it being tampered with in the night. Possibly a cord or cloth was fastened across the rock using clay, into which the seals were impressed.

19At the first light of dawn, the king got
up and hurried to the lions' den. 20When
he came near the den, he called to Daniel
in an anguished voice, "Daniel, servant of
the living God, has your God, whom you
serve continually, been able to rescue you
from the lions?"[c]
21Daniel answered, "May the king live
forever![d] 22My God sent his angel,[e] and he
shut the mouths of the lions.[f] They have
not hurt me, because I was found innocent
in his sight.[g] Nor have I ever done any
wrong before you, Your Majesty."
23The king was overjoyed and gave
orders to lift Daniel out of the den. And
when Daniel was lifted from the den, no
wound[h] was found on him, because he
had trusted[i] in his God.
24At the king's command, the men who
had falsely accused Daniel were brought in
and thrown into the lions' den,[j] along with
their wives and children.[k] And before they
reached the floor of the den, the lions overpowered them and crushed all their bones.[l]
25Then King Darius wrote to all the nations and peoples of every language in all
the earth:

"May you prosper greatly![m]

26"I issue a decree that in every part
of my kingdom people must fear and
reverence the God of Daniel.[n]

"For he is the living God
and he endures forever;
his kingdom will not be destroyed,
his dominion will never end.[o]
27He rescues and he saves;
he performs signs and
wonders[p]
in the heavens and on the
earth.
He has rescued Daniel
from the power of the lions."[q]

28So Daniel prospered during the reign
of Darius and the reign of Cyrus[a][r] the Persian.

Daniel's Dream of Four Beasts

7 In the first year of Belshazzar[s] king of
Babylon, Daniel had a dream, and visions passed through his mind[t] as he was

6:20 [c]Da 3:17 **6:21** [d]Da 2:4 **6:22** [e]Da 3:28 [f]Ps 91:11-13; Heb 11:33 [g]Ac 12:11; 2Ti 4:17 **6:23** [h]Da 3:27 [i]1Ch 5:20 **6:24** [j]Dt 19:18-19; Est 7:9-10; Ps 54:5 [k]Dt 24:16; 2Ki 14:6 [l]Isa 38:13 **6:25** [m]Da 4:1 **6:26** [n]Ps 99:1-3; Da 3:29 [o]Da 2:44; 4:34 **6:27** [p]Da 4:3 [q]ver 22 **6:28** [r]2Ch 36:22; Da 1:21 **7:1** [s]Da 5:1 [t]Da 1:17

[a] 28 Or *Darius, that is, the reign of Cyrus*

6:19–23 This passage describes innocence by ordeal. "Ordeal" describes a judicial situation in which the accused is placed in the hand of God using some mechanism, generally one that will put the accused in jeopardy. If the deity intervenes to protect the accused from harm, the verdict is innocent. Most trials by ordeal in the ancient Near East involve dangers such as water, fire or poison. When the accused is exposed to these threats, they are in effect being assumed guilty until the deity declares otherwise by action on their behalf.
6:24 *along with their wives and children.* This is an unusually severe form of punishment. When a high-ranking official and close associate of Darius I was judged guilty of revolt against him, Darius had most of the man's family executed with him. It would also be logical that the king would not want to leave family members of the executed alive to foment rebellion or conspire against him.
6:28 *the reign of Darius and the reign of Cyrus.* This can also be translated "the reign of Darius, that is, the reign of Cyrus" (see NIV text note). Note the similar construction in 1Ch 5:26: "Pul king of Assyria (that is, Tiglath-Pileser king of Assyria)." Kings in the ancient Near East usually had more than one "throne name." *the Persian.* Since Cyrus took over the Median Empire and had a Median mother, he could also be called "the Mede," even "king of the Medes."
7:1 *the first year of Belshazzar king of Babylon.* This year is presumably the first year of Belshazzar's regency. The "Verse Account of Nabonidus" says that when Nabonidus

DANIEL 6:28

THE CYRUS CYLINDER

This barrel-shaped clay cylinder (see photo, p. xxviii) with a cuneiform inscription was buried in a "foundation deposit" to commemorate building work done in Babylon by Cyrus. It was found during excavations in 1879. It records the Persian capture of Babylon "without any battle," and in the concluding section it records Cyrus's policy regarding the peoples whom the Babylonians had taken captive. Ezr 1:1–3; 6:3–5 tell us how this policy was applied to the Judahite captives in Babylon. ◆

lying in bed. He wrote[u] down the substance of his dream.
2Daniel said: "In my vision at night I
looked, and there before me were the four
winds of heaven[v] churning up the great
sea. 3Four great beasts,[w] each different
from the others, came up out of the sea.
4"The first was like a lion,[x] and it had
the wings of an eagle.[y] I watched until its
wings were torn off and it was lifted from
the ground so that it stood on two feet like
a human being, and the mind of a human
was given to it.
5"And there before me was a second
beast, which looked like a bear. It was
raised up on one of its sides, and it had
three ribs in its mouth between its teeth. It
was told, 'Get up and eat your fill of flesh!'[z]
6"After that, I looked, and there before
me was another beast, one that looked
like a leopard.[a] And on its back it had four
wings like those of a bird. This beast had
four heads, and it was given authority to
rule.
7"After that, in my vision at night I
looked, and there before me was a fourth
beast — terrifying and frightening and
very powerful. It had large iron[b] teeth;
it crushed and devoured its victims and
trampled underfoot whatever was left. It
was different from all the former beasts,
and it had ten horns.[c]

7:1 [u] Jer 36:4 **7:2** [v] Rev 7:1 **7:3** [w] Rev 13:1 **7:4** [x] Jer 4:7 [y] Eze 17:3 **7:5** [z] Da 2:39 **7:6** [a] Rev 13:2 **7:7** [b] Da 2:40 [c] Rev 12:3

went to Tema, he "entrusted the kingship" to Belshazzar. According to his own inscriptions, Nabonidus spent ten years in Tema, so the first year of the regency cannot be later than 550/549 BC. The Chronicle for Nabonidus's seventh year (549 BC) mentions Belshazzar as regent in Babylon, but the accounts of the earlier years are broken or missing, so it is not possible to say for certain when the regency began. In any case the dating means that Daniel's vision in ch. 7 took place before the events of chs. 5 – 6.

7:2 – 3 *the four winds of heaven churning up the great sea. Four great beasts ... came up out of the sea.* The phrase "the four winds (of heaven)" is common in Akkadian literature. Outside Daniel, the only occurrences in the Hebrew Bible are in Jer 49:36; Eze 37:9; Zec 2:6. All these, like Daniel, have a Babylonian connection. Jeremiah was addressing Elam at a time when it and Judah were under Babylonian rule; Ezekiel prophesied in Babylon; Zechariah was with a group of Jews who had returned from exile there. The imagery of strange monsters in a turbulent sea is reminiscent of the Babylonian creation epic *Enuma Elish*, in which a turbulent sea and weird monsters represent the forces of chaos. These forces, led by the goddess Tiamat (who has the form of a dragon in the story), have to be defeated by Marduk, the god of Babylon, before he can create the ordered world. Among the weapons he takes for the battle with Tiamat are the four winds.

7:3 – 8 In the Babylonian omen series called *Shumma izbu*, which Daniel would have been well aware of from his training, various birth abnormalities are recorded along with what sort of event they forecast. Several of the descriptions of the beasts in Daniel's visions can also be found in the *Shumma izbu* series. Some of the common elements in the descriptions include: raised up on one side (cf. v. 5), multiple heads (cf. v. 6), and multiple horns (cf. v. 7). Most of the observations of abnormalities were made of domesticated species, a large proportion being sheep and goats. Some of the abnormalities are described by comparison to various wild beasts. There are examples of sheep giving birth to lambs that (in some way) resemble a wolf, a fox, a tiger, a lion, a bear, or a leopard. In ch. 7 Daniel is observing these abnormalities not in reality but in a dream (v. 2), thus combining two important omen mechanisms (dreams and odd births). The "dream books" (see note on 2:1) often feature ominological information (celestial or extispicy omens) being viewed in dreams and carrying the same significance as if they were viewed in reality. Being familiar with both literatures, Daniel would have been inclined to interpret the dream along the lines suggested in the *izbu* omens. The omen interpretations often concerned political events, e.g., "the prince will take the land of his enemy." Nevertheless, Daniel's dream goes well beyond the *izbu* omens. The descriptions suggest that he does see fearsome chaos beasts rather than simply sheep or goats with odd characteristics. Additionally, many of the features of Daniel's beasts are neither found nor expected in *izbu* omens, e.g., wings and iron teeth. For this reason it is also important to understand the nature of some of the mythological imagery that pertains to the dream. A number of different mythological sources offer similarities to the beast imagery used by Daniel. A seventh-century BC Akkadian piece called "A Vision of the Netherworld" includes 15 divine beings in the forms of various hybrid beasts. Following that, Nergal, king of the netherworld, is seen seated on his throne; he identifies himself as the son of the king of the gods. There are many significant differences between this vision and Daniel's vision, but the similarities in imagery are helpful background.

7:3 *out of the sea.* In the Bible and in the ancient Near East, the sea represents chaos and disorder, as do the sea monsters that live there (see the article "Chaos Monsters," p. 953).

7:4 *lion ... wings of an eagle.* Winged figures are common in the art and sculpture of Mesopotamia. Winged bulls and winged lions, both with human heads, flanked thrones and entryways in Assyria, Babylon and Persia. Winged human figures (wearing headdresses with horns) are known as early as the eighth century BC and stood guard at Cyrus's palace in Pasargadae. Winged creatures also figure in dreams. Herodotus reports a dream that Cyrus had just a few days before his death in which he saw Darius (then a young man) with wings that overshadowed Asia and Europe. In the Myth of Anzu (see next note), Anzu is defeated by having his wings plucked. This motif is also significant in the story of Etana, who helps an eagle whose wings have been plucked.

7:7 *a fourth beast.* In the Myth of Anzu, a composite creature (Anzu) steals the "Tablet of Destinies," which comprised a sort of constitution of the cosmos. The goddess Mami, the most ancient of deities who created all the gods, is called forth. She is asked to send her son, Ninurta, to battle Anzu. The god Ninurta defeats the monster and recovers the "Tablet of Destinies." Ninurta (who is also known for his defeat of other beasts, e.g., the bull-man in the sea, the six-headed ram, and the seven-headed serpent) then is granted dominion and glory. There are certainly many differences with Da 7, and there should be no thought that the Myth of Anzu figures prominently here. Those who would have been familiar with the Myth of Anzu, however, would likely have seen echoes of it in this vision. The myth has roots as early as the beginning of the second millennium BC but is principally known from mid-first-millennium

8 "While I was thinking about the horns,
there before me was another horn, a little[d] one, which came up among them; and
three of the first horns were uprooted before it. This horn had eyes like the eyes of
a human being[e] and a mouth that spoke
boastfully.[f]
9 "As I looked,

"thrones were set in place,
 and the Ancient of Days took his seat.
His clothing was as white as snow;
 the hair of his head was white like
 wool.[g]
His throne was flaming with fire,
 and its wheels[h] were all ablaze.
10 A river of fire[i] was flowing,
 coming out from before him.[j]
Thousands upon thousands attended
 him;
ten thousand times ten thousand
 stood before him.
The court was seated,
 and the books[k] were opened.

11 "Then I continued to watch because of
the boastful words the horn was speaking.
I kept looking until the beast was slain
and its body destroyed and thrown into
the blazing fire.[l] 12 (The other beasts had
been stripped of their authority, but were
allowed to live for a period of time.)
13 "In my vision at night I looked, and
there before me was one like a son of
man,[a][m] coming with the clouds of heav-
en.[n] He approached the Ancient of Days
and was led into his presence. 14 He was
given authority,[o] glory and sovereign power; all nations and peoples of every language worshiped him.[p] His dominion is
an everlasting dominion that will not pass
away, and his kingdom is one that will
never be destroyed.[q]

The Interpretation of the Dream

15 "I, Daniel, was troubled in spirit, and
the visions that passed through my mind
disturbed me.[r] 16 I approached one of those
standing there and asked him the meaning
of all this.
"So he told me and gave me the interpretation[s] of these things: 17 "The four great
beasts are four kings that will rise from the

7:8 [d] Da 8:9 [e] Rev 9:7 [f] Ps 12:3; Rev 13:5-6 **7:9** [g] Rev 1:14 [h] Eze 1:15; 10:6 **7:10** [i] Ps 50:3; 97:3; Isa 30:27 [j] Dt 33:2; Ps 68:17; Rev 5:11 [k] Rev 20:11-15 **7:11** [l] Rev 19:20 **7:13** [m] Mt 8:20*; Rev 1:13* [n] Mt 24:30; Rev 1:7 **7:14** [o] Mt 28:18 [p] Ps 72:11; 102:22; 1Co 15:27; Eph 1:22 [q] Da 2:44; Heb 12:28; Rev 11:15 **7:15** [r] Da 4:19 **7:16** [s] Da 8:16; 9:22; Zec 1:9

[a] *13* The Aramaic phrase *bar enash* means *human being.* The phrase *son of man* is retained here because of its use in the New Testament as a title of Jesus, probably based largely on this verse.

Babylonian texts. One ninth-century BC relief inscription from Nimrud pictures Ninurta fighting a beast with lion's legs but standing upright on eagle's feet. The beast is feathered and has two wings, lion paws for hands with sharp, extended claws, a gaping mouth with fierce teeth, and two horns. It is thought to be a depiction of Anzu. *ten horns.* It was common in Mesopotamia for gods (and occasionally kings) to wear crowns featuring protruding or embossed horns. Sometimes the sets of horns were stacked one upon another in tiers. The winged lion from Ashurnasirpal's palace has a conical crown on its human head with three pairs of tiered horns embossed on it. Another interesting connection is that in the creation epic *Enuma Elish*, Tiamat is the fearsome beast that the hero of the gods has to defeat. To help her, Tiamat creates 11 monsters that must also be defeated. Here also the fourth beast is associated with 11 horns (the ten plus the little horn).

7:9 *the Ancient of Days.* In Canaanite mythology the head of the pantheon is El, who is depicted as an aged person. Among his titles are "judge," "father" and a phrase that is usually taken to mean "father of years." This suggests that Daniel is using imagery and descriptions that would have been well known to his audience. *His throne was flaming with fire, and its wheels were all ablaze.* The immediate background here is probably Ezekiel's vision of God's fiery chariot throne (Eze 1; 10). A more general background may be the chariots or carts used to carry the images of deities in processions in the ancient Near East.

7:10 *the books were opened.* Record keeping of various kinds was common in ancient royal courts. There are numerous references in 1 – 2 Kings to "the book of the annals of the kings of Israel/Judah" (e.g., 1Ki 14:19,29). Est 6:1 refers to "the book of the chronicles" that recorded events in the reign of the Persian king. No doubt these records were similar to the Assyrian and Babylonian Chronicles. Records were also kept of royal decisions and decrees (Ezr 6:1 – 5).

7:13 *one like a son of man.* In Aramaic and Hebrew the phrase "son of man" is simply a common expression to describe someone or something as human or humanlike. In Ezekiel, God often addresses the prophet as "son of man" to emphasize his humanness (e.g., Eze 2:6). *coming with the clouds of heaven.* In ancient Near Eastern literature clouds are often associated with the appearances of deities. In the OT it is Yahweh, the God of Israel, who rides on the clouds as his chariot (Ps 104:3; Isa 19:1). In Canaanite mythology Baal, the son of El, is described as "rider/charioteer of the clouds." After doing battle with, and defeating, Yamm/Sea, Baal is promised an everlasting kingdom and eternal dominion. Some scholars see echoes of this story in Da 7:9 – 14. Others argue for a background in Mesopotamian cosmic conflict myths (such as the creation epic *Enuma Elish* and the Myth of Anzu), which depict a deity (Marduk and Ninurta, respectively) defeating the representative of chaos (Tiamat and Anzu, respectively) and regaining authority and dominion for the gods and for himself. Daniel's vision has no conflict between the "one like a son of man" and the beasts. The interpretation in vv. 17 – 27, however, makes it clear that the "one like a son of man" in some way represents "the holy people of the Most High" (vv. 18,22), who are in conflict with the "little horn" that arises out of the fourth beast (v. 8).

7:16 *one of those standing there.* Interpreting angels appear in Ezekiel and Zechariah. They are common in apocalyptic literature from the OT on. They do not appear in Mesopotamian literature.

7:17 *four kings.* See the note on 2:40 concerning the four kingdoms motif in ancient literature. In 2:38 the Babylonian Empire is identified as the first kingdom. Nebuchadnezzar's experience in ch. 4 is echoed in the description of the first beast; this suggests that the first beast represents the Babylonian Empire. If the "little" horn in chs. 7 – 8 stands for the same king, then the fourth beast represents the Macedonian Empire of Alexander

DANIEL 7–8

Dreams and Dream Reports

The experience Daniel reports in Da 7 is called both a "dream" and "visions" (Da 7:1). Dreams were an important form of divination in the ancient Near East, and what are called "dream reports" were presented in a standard pattern that Da 7–8 follow. It is notable that of all the various methods of divination used in the ancient Near East, only dreams are regarded as acceptable in the OT. One reason for this may be that in most of the other methods, the diviner takes the initiative (e.g., by pouring oil on water and observing the shape of the drops or by sacrificing a sheep and examining its liver) and so might be seen as coercing the deity to get an answer. In the case of dreams, the deity can be seen as taking the initiative.

There are two things about the interpretation of the dreams/visions in Daniel that differ from what was generally the case in the ancient Near East. A diviner would normally interpret a dream by consulting a book of "dream omens" in which the significance of different things and events that might be seen in a dream were recorded, presumably partly based on past experience. In Da 2 and Da 4, Daniel does not do this but relies on God to give him the interpretation. In Da 7–8 the interpretation is given by an angelic figure. These two features emphasise that these are genuine revelations from the God of Israel.

The pattern of dream reports in ancient Egypt, Greece and Mesopotamia is quite uniform from the third millennium BC to the end of the first millennium BC. It is as follows, showing how Da 7–8 fits it:

Introduction	7:1	8:1
Report of the dream	7:2–27	8:2–25
Closure of the dream	7:28a	8:26
Reaction of the dreamer	7:28b	8:27

Da 7–8 are examples of "symbolic visions." These were a feature of Hebrew prophecy from as early as Amos (c. 760 BC). However, whereas in earlier prophets (e.g., Jer 1; 24; Am 7–8) the symbolism is quite simple, in Daniel it is quite complex. It is important to realize that the symbolism in these visions is not simply a form of "code" that is "cracked" (e.g., when it is said that the goat in Da 8 represents the Greek Empire). As we shall see, the symbols used have deep cultural roots so that, to those who are aware of them, they have a significance and "feel" that goes beyond the intellectual level. A modern equivalent might be the significance that their country's flag has for many people (so that "burning the flag" becomes an emotive political act) or the significance that the jersey of a football team has for an ardent fan (who will pay a lot to buy a replica in order to wear it proudly as a statement of allegiance). The cultural significance of the symbols gives the visions additional meanings that are lost on those who are unaware of them and who therefore concentrate simply on the "surface" identification of the meaning of the symbols. Symbolic visions like this are common in Jewish and Christian apocalypses from about 250 BC to about AD 250—the book of Revelation in the NT being a good example.

The two visions that make up Da 9 and Da 10–12 do not have the "dream report" structure, nor are they symbolic visions. They are "epiphany visions" in which a supernatural being appears and conveys a verbal message. In their form and content they have no clear parallel elsewhere in the OT. The content is a fairly detailed survey of history, presented in short, enigmatic phrases. Da 8:23–25 shares these characteristics. In Da 10–12 there is an illuminating parallel in the so-called Akkadian Prophecies (see the article "Daniel and the Akkadian Prophecies," p. 1449). ◆

earth. 18But the holy people of the Most High will receive the kingdom and will possess it forever — yes, for ever and ever.'[t]

19"Then I wanted to know the meaning of the fourth beast, which was different from all the others and most terrifying, with its iron teeth and bronze claws — the beast that crushed and devoured its victims and trampled underfoot whatever was left. 20I also wanted to know about the ten horns on its head and about the other horn that came up, before which three of them fell — the horn that looked more imposing than the others and that had eyes and a mouth that spoke boastfully. 21As I watched, this horn was waging war against the holy people and defeating them,[u] 22until the Ancient of Days came and pronounced judgment in favor of the holy people of the Most High, and the time came when they possessed the kingdom.

23"He gave me this explanation: 'The fourth beast is a fourth kingdom that will appear on earth. It will be different from all the other kingdoms and will devour the whole earth, trampling it down and crushing it.[v] 24The ten horns[w] are ten kings who will come from this kingdom. After them another king will arise, different from the earlier ones; he will subdue three kings. 25He will speak against the Most High[x] and oppress his holy people and try to change the set times[y] and the laws. The holy people will be delivered into his hands for a time, times and half a time.[a][z]

26" 'But the court will sit, and his power will be taken away and completely destroyed forever. 27Then the sovereignty, power and greatness of all the kingdoms under heaven will be handed over to the holy people of the Most High. His kingdom will be an everlasting[a] kingdom, and all rulers will worship[b] and obey him.'

28"This is the end of the matter. I, Daniel, was deeply troubled[c] by my thoughts, and my face turned pale, but I kept the matter to myself."

Daniel's Vision of a Ram and a Goat

8 In the third year of King Belshazzar's reign, I, Daniel, had a vision, after the one that had already appeared to me. 2In my vision I saw myself in the citadel of Susa[d] in the province of Elam;[e] in the vision I was beside the Ulai Canal. 3I looked up,[f] and there before me was a ram with

7:18 [t] Isa 60:12-14; Rev 2:26; 20:4 **7:21** [u] Rev 13:7 **7:23** [v] Da 2:40 **7:24** [w] Rev 17:12 **7:25** [x] Isa 37:23; Da 11:36 [y] Da 2:21 [z] Da 8:24; 12:7; Rev 12:14 **7:27** [a] Da 2:44; 4:34; Lk 1:33; Rev 11:15; 22:5 [b] Ps 22:27; 72:11; 86:9 **7:28** [c] Da 4:19 **8:2** [d] Est 1:2 [e] Ge 10:22 **8:3** [f] Da 10:5

[a] 25 Or *for a year, two years and half a year*

the Great. There is, however, much debate about the identification of the four kings.

7:18 *the holy people of the Most High.* The Aramaic text here introduces "the holy ones of the Most High." In the OT "holy ones" nearly always refers to heavenly beings. The only undisputed use of it to refer to humans is Ps 34:9. The term "holy ones" occurs in the literature written by the sectarians at Qumran and always refers to angels or heavenly beings. The same is true of fragments of Aramaic texts, mainly of the Enochic literature, found at Qumran. In other Jewish literature "holy ones" refers to angels in Wisdom of Solomon 5:5; 10:10 but to humans in Wisdom of Solomon 18:9; 3 Maccabees 6:9; its use in 1 Maccabees 1:46 is unclear. The NIV translates the text as "holy people," thereby illustrating the fact that scholars are divided over whether "the holy ones of the Most High" in the Aramaic text of Daniel refers to heavenly beings or to the Jews.

7:24 *ten kings.* At least on this point the text makes it clear that the ten horns represent ten kingdoms/kings. There are ten kingdoms that spring from Alexander's Empire: Ptolemaic Egypt, Seleucia, Macedon, Pergamum, Pontus, Bithynia, Cappadocia, Armenia, Parthia and Bactria. Yet others believe that the ten are successors to the Roman Empire and, as such, may be still future. There is no agreement as to the identity of these ten kings.

7:25 *He will ... try to change the set times and the laws.* In Mesopotamian literature the times and laws are controlled by the cosmic decrees embodied in the "Tablet of Destinies." These are held by the assembly of the gods or by the chief god on its behalf. In some stories they are misappropriated. In the creation epic *Enuma Elish*, they are given to Kingu, leader of the renegade gods who support Tiamat. In the Myth of Anzu, the monster Anzu steals them and threatens to use them, thus endangering the stability of the cosmos. Those who identify the little horn of v. 8 and 8:9 with Antiochus IV Epiphanes see here a reference to his persecution of the Jews from 167 to 164 BC. During this persecution he prohibited the keeping of the Sabbath and other Jewish festivals and commanded that copies of the Torah be destroyed (1 Maccabees 1:44–61). *time, times and half a time.* The word used here for "time" is the same word translated "times" in 4:16 (see note there). The word "times" is simply a plural and does not necessarily suggest two times. The Babylonians were very sophisticated mathematicians, and early on the gods had been represented numerically (Sin = 30; Ishtar = 15). Furthermore, the gods, with their numerical valuations and planetary associations, figured in the astronomical terminology by which the cyclic movements in the heavens were used in calendrical calculations. All of these factors make it very difficult to unpack the significance of this phrase.

7:27 *the holy people of the Most High.* A strict rendering of the Aramaic is "the people of the holy ones of the Most High." A text from Qumran contains the phrase "the people of the holy ones of the covenant," who are clearly the same as "your people Israel." In 12:7 "the holy people" who suffer are clearly "your people" (i.e., the Jews) of 12:1.

8:1 *third year of King Belshazzar's reign.* Likely either 550 or 547 BC. See note on 7:1.

8:2 *Susa.* The capital of the territory of Elam, some 200 miles (320 kilometers) from Babylon. The city will later become the royal residence of the Achaemenid kings of Persia, so it is a suitable locale for the vision. *Ulai Canal.* An artificial canal on the north side of the city of Susa that was closely associated with Susa both in cuneiform and classical sources. Though Daniel could have actually made the journey, it is more likely that he is transported in a vision, as Ezekiel sometimes experiences.

8:3–4 *ram.* In later literature (the first several centuries AD), the signs of the zodiac are associated with countries, and the ram is associated with Persia. There is no

two horns, standing beside the canal, and
the horns were long. One of the horns was
longer than the other but grew up later. 4 I
watched the ram as it charged toward the
west and the north and the south. No animal could stand against it, and none could
rescue from its power. It did as it pleased[g]
and became great.
5 As I was thinking about this, suddenly a goat with a prominent horn between
its eyes came from the west, crossing the
whole earth without touching the ground.
6 It came toward the two-horned ram I
had seen standing beside the canal and
charged at it in great rage. 7 I saw it attack the ram furiously, striking the ram
and shattering its two horns. The ram
was powerless to stand against it; the goat
knocked it to the ground and trampled on
it,[h] and none could rescue the ram from its
power. 8 The goat became very great, but at
the height of its power the large horn was
broken off,[i] and in its place four prominent horns grew up toward the four winds
of heaven.[j]
9 Out of one of them came another horn,
which started small but grew in power to
the south and to the east and toward the
Beautiful Land.[k] 10 It grew until it reached[l]
the host of the heavens, and it threw some
of the starry host down to the earth[m] and
trampled[n] on them. 11 It set itself up to be
as great as the commander of the army
of the LORD;[o] it took away the daily sacrifice[p] from the LORD, and his sanctuary
was thrown down.[q] 12 Because of rebellion,
the LORD's people[a] and the daily sacrifice
were given over to it. It prospered in everything it did, and truth was thrown to
the ground.
13 Then I heard a holy one[r] speaking, and
another holy one said to him, "How long
will it take for the vision to be fulfilled[s]—
the vision concerning the daily sacrifice,
the rebellion that causes desolation, the
surrender of the sanctuary and the trampling underfoot[t] of the LORD's people?"

8:4 [g] Da 11:3,16 **8:7** [h] Da 7:7 **8:8** [i] 2Ch 26:16-21; Da 5:20 [j] Da 7:2; Rev 7:1 **8:9** [k] Da 11:16 **8:10** [l] Isa 14:13 [m] Rev 12:4 [n] Da 7:7 **8:11** [o] Da 11:36-37 [p] Eze 46:13-14 [q] Da 11:31; 12:11

8:13 [r] Da 4:23 [s] Da 12:6 [t] Lk 21:24; Rev 11:2

Tetradrachm with portrait of Alexander adorned with the ram's horn of the Egyptian god Amun. Greek, 305 to 281 BC. Some scholars believe that the goat with a prominent horn (Da 8:5) represents the coming of Alexander the Great.

[a] 12 Or *rebellion, the armies*

evidence, however, that such an association was made as early as the book of Daniel. The concept of the zodiac has its origin in the intertestamental period. *a ram with two horns.* The interpretation in v. 20 makes it clear that the ram with two horns is the combined Medo-Persian Empire. The later and longer horn represents the Persians. Cyrus II (the Great) of Persia began his reign in 559 BC as a vassal of the Medes. In 550 he rebelled and defeated the Median king Astyages, creating a single Medo-Persian Empire. By 546 he had gained control of the kingdom of Lydia and much of Asia Minor. In 539 he conquered Babylon. Eventually the empire expanded north and west into Greece and west and south through Syria and Palestine to Egypt.

8:5 *a goat with a prominent horn.* As the interpretation in v. 21 makes clear, this goat represents the coming of Alexander the Great. Between 334 and 331 BC Alexander won a series of battles against Darius III of Persia and became ruler of an empire that stretched from Greece to India. Note that in the OT, the goat is regarded as a stronger animal than the ram (see Jer 50:8).

8:8 *the large horn was broken off.* At the height of his power, Alexander died of a fever in Babylon in 323 BC. *four prominent horns grew up toward the four winds of heaven.* After Alexander's death his empire was eventually divided between four of his generals (see note on v. 22; see also the article "Greek History," p. 1440). Their realms did not correspond to the four compass points, but "the four winds of heaven" is an Akkadian idiom (see note on 7:2).

8:9 *another horn, which started small.* In view of what is said in the following verses, there is general agreement that this horn is a symbol for the Seleucid ruler Antiochus IV Epiphanes. *grew in power to the south and to the east.* Antiochus IV campaigned in Egypt to the south (1 Maccabees 1:16–20) and against the Parthians to the east (1 Maccabees 3:27–37). *Beautiful Land.* Israel (see Da 11:16,41).

8:10 *the host of the heavens ... the starry host.* In the ancient Near East this referred to the assembly of the gods, many of whom were represented by celestial bodies (whether planets or stars). The Bible sometimes uses the phrase to refer to the illegitimate worship of these deities (see note on 2Ki 21:3). On other occasions, the phrase is used for Yahweh's angelic council (see the article "Divine Council," p. 615). Finally, it can refer simply to the stars with no personalities behind them (Isa 40:26). In the destruction described in the Mesopotamian epic "Erra and Ishum," Erra says that he will make planets shed their splendor and will wrench stars from the sky. Here the starry host represent one side in the cosmic battle and fall temporarily victim to the evil horn, thus suggesting they are some of God's minions.

8:11 *daily sacrifice.* The Hebrew word used is taken from the word "regular" in the phrase "regular burnt offering" in Nu 28:3,10 and elsewhere. It probably refers to the regular morning and evening sacrifices in the temple.

DANIEL 8

GREEK HISTORY

The king represented by the large horn (Da 8:8,21) is undisputed: Alexander the Great, whose Greek army swept away the Persian Empire between 335 and 331 BC. When Alexander died suddenly in 323 at the age of 33, the two who could claim ancestral right to the kingdom (illegitimate half-brother, Philip Arrideus; and son of Alexander and Roxane, Alexander IV, born two months after his father's death) were installed as figureheads while the operation of the kingdom was entrusted to three experienced officers: Antipater (viceroy of Macedon), Perdiccas (head of the armies), and Craterus (in charge of the treasury and advisor to Arrideus). By 321 BC these three regents sufficiently antagonized one another that a battle was instigated by a fourth player, Ptolemy, who had been given a position of authority in Egypt. Craterus was killed in battle, and Perdiccas was assassinated in a mutiny by several of his generals, one of whom was Seleucus.

Meanwhile Antipater took the lead and placed a friend, Antigonus, in Perdiccas's position. In 319 BC Antipater died an old man, and despite his appointment of another, within two years his son, Cassander, had gained control of Macedonia and most of the territory of Greece. In the summer of 317, those opposing Cassander executed Philip Arrideus. Alexander IV and his mother, Roxane, were placed under house arrest and effectively deposed, though they were not executed until 310. The three who ruled were now Cassander in the west, Ptolemy in Egypt, and Antigonus in the east. As Antigonus sought to solidify his control of the east, he attempted to dominate Seleucus (now governor of Babylon) who, in 315, exposed Antigonus's schemes for power to the other leaders: Ptolemy, Cassander and Lysimachus (governor of Thrace). Battles continued to be enjoined until 311, when Antigonus compromised for peace with Ptolemy, Cassander and Lysimachus, leaving Seleucus isolated but in control of Babylonia.

By 309 BC, Ptolemy decided to move against Antigonus, but he pushed too far and

continued on next page

14 He said to me, "It will take 2,300 evenings and mornings; then the sanctuary
will be reconsecrated."[u]

The Interpretation of the Vision

15 While I, Daniel, was watching the vision[v] and trying to understand it, there
before me stood one who looked like a
man.[w] 16 And I heard a man's voice from
the Ulai calling, "Gabriel,[x] tell this man
the meaning of the vision."
17 As he came near the place where I was
standing, I was terrified and fell prostrate.[y]
"Son of man,"[a] he said to me, "understand
that the vision concerns the time of the
end."[z]
18 While he was speaking to me, I was in
a deep sleep, with my face to the ground.[a]

8:14 [u] Da 12:11-12 **8:15** [v] ver 1 [w] Da 10:16-18 **8:16** [x] Da 9:21; Lk 1:19 **8:17** [y] Eze 1:28; Da 2:46; Rev 1:17 [z] Hab 2:3 **8:18** [a] Da 10:9

[a] *17* The Hebrew phrase *ben adam* means *human being.* The phrase *son of man* is retained as a form of address here because of its possible association with "Son of Man" in the New Testament.

8:14 *2,300 evenings and mornings.* Many commentators think the "evenings and mornings" refer to the offerings of the daily sacrifice (see v. 11 and note), making the period 1,150 days or about three years and two months. Antiochus had pagan sacrifices offered in the temple on the 15th of Kislev, 167 BC, and the Jews reconsecrated the temple on the 25th of Kislev, 164 BC (1 Maccabees 1:54; 4:52–54), but Antiochus had stopped Jewish rituals sometime before the 15th of Kislev (1 Maccabees 1:44–51). Others, taking the period as 2,300 days, have suggested it is the period between the removal of the high priest Onias III from office in 171 BC and the rededication of the temple. It may be that the number has a symbolic or rhetorical meaning that is now not clear to us.

8:16 *Gabriel.* This is the first time an angel is named in the Bible. The name means "man of God." In 1 Enoch 9:1, Gabriel and Michael (cf. Da 10:13) are listed among four archangels, and they are listed among seven archangels in 1 Enoch 20:1–7. In the latter reference Gabriel is said to be in charge of "Paradise." He is also included among the archangels in the War Scroll from the Dead Sea Scrolls of Qumran. In Lk 1:19 Gabriel brings the message of the

ended up in 306 under the attack of Antigonus and his son Demetrius. Antigonus's invasion of Egypt failed and in 305 Ptolemy, along with Cassander, Seleucus and Lysimachus (most likely to be identified as the four horns of Da 8:22), declared themselves the successor kings to Alexander. Yet it was still four more years until Antigonus was killed in the battle of Ipsus in 301 BC. Cassander died only three years later (298 BC) and Demetrius continued to cause trouble, but the division of the empire into four parts represents the fallout of this 20-year succession struggle. ◆

Mosaic of Alexander the Great, c. 100 BC.
Wikimedia Commons

Then he touched me and raised me to my
feet.[b]
19He said: "I am going to tell you what
will happen later in the time of wrath, because the vision concerns the appointed
time of the end.[a][c] 20The two-horned ram
that you saw represents the kings of Media
and Persia. 21The shaggy goat is the king
of Greece,[d] and the large horn between
its eyes is the first king.[e] 22The four horns
that replaced the one that was broken off
represent four kingdoms that will emerge
from his nation but will not have the same
power.

23"In the latter part of their reign, when
rebels have become completely wicked, a
fierce-looking king, a master of intrigue,
will arise. 24He will become very strong,
but not by his own power. He will cause
astounding devastation and will succeed
in whatever he does. He will destroy those
who are mighty, the holy people.[f] 25He will
cause deceit to prosper, and he will consider himself superior. When they feel secure, he will destroy many and take his
stand against the Prince of princes.[g] Yet

8:18 [b] Eze 2:2; Da 10:16-18 **8:19** [c] Hab 2:3 **8:21** [d] Da 10:20 [e] Da 11:3 **8:24** [f] Da 7:25; 11:36 **8:25** [g] Da 11:36

[a] 19 *Or because the end will be at the appointed time*

birth of John the Baptist to his father, Zechariah, and in Lk 1:26 – 38 Gabriel relates Jesus' impending birth to Mary. In the polytheistic religions of the ancient world, the messengers of the gods usually came from the lower ranks of the gods themselves, such as Hermes in Greek mythology.
8:22 *four kingdoms.* The four kingdoms that eventually arose out of Alexander's empire were: (1) Macedonia and Greece, ruled by Cassander, (2) Thrace and Asia Minor, ruled by Lysimachus, (3) northern Syria, Mesopotamia and regions to the east, ruled by Seleucus, (4) southern Syria, Palestine and Egypt, ruled by Ptolemy.
8:23 *a fierce-looking king.* This is Antiochus IV Epiphanes, who ruled from 175 to 164 BC. See 11:21 – 39 and notes.
8:25 *Yet he will be destroyed, but not by human power.* This refers to Antiochus's untimely death by disease in late 164 BC. See note on 11:40.

ALEXANDER’S EMPIRE

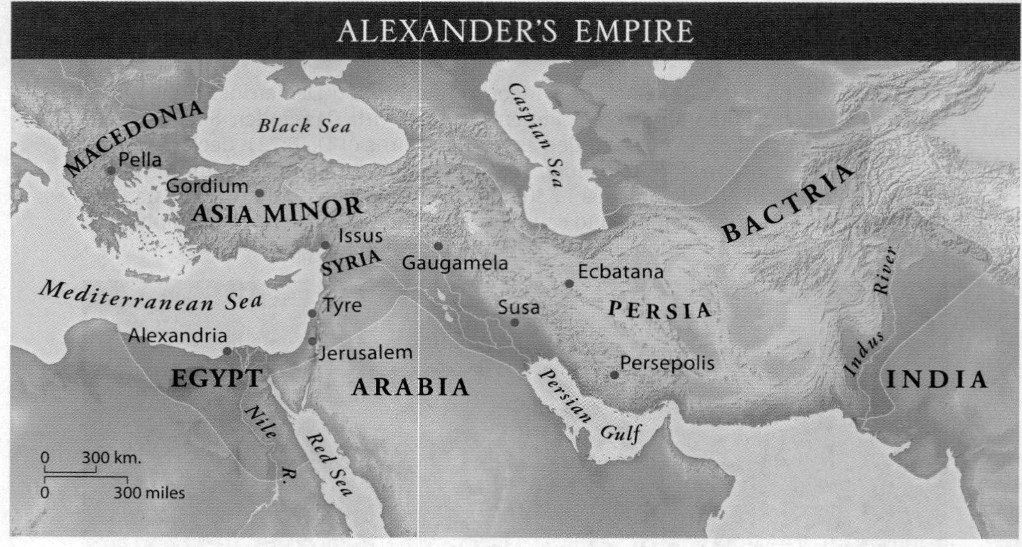

he will be destroyed, but not by human
power.[h]
26“The vision of the evenings and mornings that has been given you is true,[i] but
seal[j] up the vision, for it concerns the distant future.”[k]
27I, Daniel, was worn out. I lay exhausted for several days. Then I got up and
went about the king’s business.[l] I was appalled[m] by the vision; it was beyond understanding.

Daniel’s Prayer

9 In the first year of Darius[n] son of Xerxes[a] (a Mede by descent), who was
made ruler over the Babylonian[b] kingdom— 2in the first year of his reign, I,
Daniel, understood from the Scriptures,
according to the word of the LORD given to
Jeremiah the prophet, that the desolation
of Jerusalem would last seventy[o] years.
3So I turned to the Lord God and pleaded
with him in prayer and petition, in fasting,
and in sackcloth and ashes.[p]
4I prayed to the LORD my God and confessed:

“Lord, the great and awesome
God,[q] who keeps his covenant of
love[r] with those who love him and
keep his commandments, 5we have
sinned and done wrong.[s] We have
been wicked and have rebelled; we
have turned away[t] from your commands and laws.[u] 6We have not listened to your servants the prophets,[v]
who spoke in your name to our kings,
our princes and our ancestors, and to
all the people of the land.
7“Lord, you are righteous, but this
day we are covered with shame[w]—
the people of Judah and the inhabitants of Jerusalem and all Israel,
both near and far, in all the countries
where you have scattered[x] us because
of our unfaithfulness to you.[y] 8We
and our kings, our princes and our
ancestors are covered with shame,
LORD, because we have sinned against
you. 9The Lord our God is merciful
and forgiving,[z] even though we have
rebelled against him;[a] 10we have not

8:25 [h] Da 2:34; 11:21
8:26 [i] Da 10:1 [j] Rev 22:10 [k] Da 10:14
8:27 [l] Da 2:48 [m] Da 7:28
9:1 [n] Da 5:31
9:2 [o] 2Ch 36:21; Jer 29:10; Zec 7:5
9:3 [p] Ne 1:4; Jer 29:12
9:4 [q] Dt 7:21 [r] Dt 7:9
9:5 [s] Ps 106:6 [t] Isa 53:6 [u] ver 11; La 1:20
9:6 [v] 2Ch 36:16; Jer 44:5
9:7 [w] Ps 44:15 [x] Dt 4:27; Am 9:9 [y] Jer 3:25
9:9 [z] Ps 130:4 [a] Ne 9:17; Jer 14:7

[a] *1* Hebrew *Ahasuerus* [b] *1* Or *Chaldean*

9:1 *first year of Darius son of Xerxes.* If Darius is another name for Cyrus (see note on 6:28), this is 539 BC. Cyrus’s father was not Xerxes but Cambyses. However, there is evidence that “Xerxes” was a Persian dynastic throne name; thus, it could have been applied to any of Cyrus’s forebears who are known to us by other names. Alternatively, the Hebrew name translated as “Xerxes” may represent the name of Cyrus’s maternal great-grandfather, Cyaxares. He was significant because he led the Median forces involved in the destruction of the Assyrian Empire.

9:2 *the word of the LORD given to Jeremiah.* The significance of the date line (v. 1) is that it refers to the time of Babylon’s downfall, an appropriate time for Jewish exiles to take note of Jeremiah’s prophecies about this event. Jeremiah declared that Babylon’s dominance would last 70 years (Jer 25:11–12) and that only after this time would the Jews return from exile (Jer 29:10). Jeremiah may have used the figure 70 as a round number, indicating a lifetime (Ps 90:10; Isa 23:15).

9:3 *in fasting, and in sackcloth and ashes.* In the OT the combination of fasting, sackcloth and ashes (or dust) is an expression of grief because of some calamity (Est 4:1–3) or penitence (Ne 9:1; Isa 58:5). The practice is also known in Canaan and Mesopotamia (Jnh 3:5–9). See the article “Mourning,” p. 828.

obeyed the LORD our God or kept the
laws he gave us through his servants
the prophets.[b] 11 All Israel has transgressed your law and turned away,
refusing to obey you.
"Therefore the curses and sworn
judgments written in the Law of Moses, the servant of God, have been
poured out on us, because we have
sinned[c] against you. 12 You have fulfilled[d] the words spoken against us
and against our rulers by bringing
on us great disaster. Under the whole
heaven nothing has ever been done
like what has been done to Jerusalem.[e] 13 Just as it is written in the Law
of Moses, all this disaster has come
on us, yet we have not sought the favor of the LORD our God by turning
from our sins and giving attention to
your truth.[f] 14 The LORD did not hesitate to bring the disaster[g] on us, for
the LORD our God is righteous in everything he does; yet we have not
obeyed him.[h]
15 "Now, Lord our God, who
brought your people out of Egypt
with a mighty hand[i] and who made
for yourself a name[j] that endures to
this day, we have sinned, we have
done wrong. 16 Lord, in keeping with
all your righteous acts,[k] turn away
your anger and your wrath from Jerusalem,[l] your city, your holy hill.[m] Our
sins and the iniquities of our ancestors have made Jerusalem and your
people an object of scorn[n] to all those
around us.

9:10 [b] 2Ki 17:13-15; 18:12 **9:11** [c] Isa 1:4-6; Jer 8:5-10 **9:12** [d] Isa 44:26; Zec 1:6 [e] Jer 44:2-6; Eze 5:9 **9:13** [f] Isa 9:13; Jer 2:30 **9:14** [g] Jer 44:27 [h] Ne 9:33 **9:15** [i] Jer 32:21 [j] Ne 9:10 **9:16** [k] Ps 31:1 [l] Jer 32:32 [m] Zec 8:3 [n] Eze 5:14 **9:17** [o] Nu 6:24-26; Ps 80:19 **9:18** [p] Ps 80:14 [q] Isa 37:17; Jer 7:10-12; 25:29 **9:19** [r] Ps 44:23 **9:20** [s] ver 3; Ps 145:18; Isa 58:9 **9:21** [t] Da 8:16; Lk 1:19 [u] Ex 29:39 **9:23** [v] Da 10:19; Lk 1:28 [w] Da 10:11-12; Mt 24:15 **9:24** [x] Isa 53:10 [y] Isa 56:1

17 "Now, our God, hear the prayers
and petitions of your servant. For
your sake, Lord, look with favor[o] on
your desolate sanctuary. 18 Give ear,
our God, and hear; open your eyes
and see[p] the desolation of the city
that bears your Name.[q] We do not
make requests of you because we are
righteous, but because of your great
mercy. 19 Lord, listen! Lord, forgive![r]
Lord, hear and act! For your sake, my
God, do not delay, because your city
and your people bear your Name."

The Seventy "Sevens"

20 While I was speaking and praying,
confessing my sin and the sin of my people Israel and making my request to the
LORD my God for his holy hill[s] — 21 while I
was still in prayer, Gabriel,[t] the man I had
seen in the earlier vision, came to me in
swift flight about the time of the evening
sacrifice.[u] 22 He instructed me and said
to me, "Daniel, I have now come to give
you insight and understanding. 23 As soon
as you began to pray, a word went out,
which I have come to tell you, for you are
highly esteemed.[v] Therefore, consider the
word and understand the vision:[w]
24 "Seventy 'sevens'[a] are decreed for
your people and your holy city to finish[b] transgression, to put an end to sin,
to atone[x] for wickedness, to bring in everlasting righteousness,[y] to seal up vision
and prophecy and to anoint the Most Holy
Place.[c]

[a] 24 Or *'weeks'*; also in verses 25 and 26
[b] 24 Or *restrain* [c] 24 Or *the most holy One*

9:17 *your desolate sanctuary.* The Babylonians destroyed Jerusalem and the temple in 587 BC, so the temple had been in a ruined state for nearly 50 years.
9:21 *in swift flight.* Only here in the OT is a divine messenger/angel (as distinct from the seraphim of Isa 6) said to fly. There is no indication here that this is winged flight, especially since Gabriel is called a "man." Because the Hebrew expression here is unclear, some scholars think it refers to "weariness," not "flight." 1 Enoch 61:1 contains the earliest Jewish reference to winged angels. *the time of the evening sacrifice.* The Israelite day ended at sundown, about 6:00 p.m. The evening sacrifice took place in the late afternoon, around 4:00 p.m.
9:24 *Seventy 'sevens.'* Analogy with the "seven sabbath years" in Lev 25:8 (meaning 49 years) leads most commentators to take this to mean "seventy weeks of years." Seven years was the sabbatical year cycle, in the last year of which the land was to be left fallow (Lev 25:3–4). Seven sabbatical year cycles led up to the Year of Jubilee, when slaves were freed, debts remitted, and land returned to its original owners (Lev 25). Seventy sabbatical cycles equals ten Jubilee cycles. In the following verses special attention is paid to the first Jubilee cycle (v. 25, "seven 'sevens'") and to the final sabbatical cycle (v. 27), suggesting that these numbers carry a symbolic significance. This is supported by several verbal and thematic links between Daniel's prayer and Lev 26:27–45, a passage warning of a period of divine wrath measured in sabbatical cycles, and the apparent understanding of Jeremiah's 70 years in terms of sabbatical cycles in 2Ch 36:20–21. The symbolic use of weeks and Jubilee cycles is found in intertestamental Jewish literature. The Apocalypse of Weeks in 1 Enoch 91; 93 divides history into ten weeks, divided into segments of seven and three weeks. In the Testament of Levi 16–18, history covers a span of 70 weeks. The Book of Jubilees structures the whole of history by periods of ten Jubilees. There are also examples of the symbolic use of seven and multiples of seven (including time periods) in Babylonian and Ugaritic literature. These symbolic schemas are intended not as strict chronologies but as a way of expressing the significance of history. This has been referred to as chronography and needs to be distinguished from chronology. *seal up vision and prophecy.* See note on 12:4. *anoint the Most Holy Place.* The consecration ceremony that involves anointing and purification of the Most Holy Place in Ex 29 (especially vv. 36–37) is sufficient background for understanding this statement. The desecration of the Most Holy Place requires its purification. Assyrian temple inscriptions also refer to the anointing of a temple that is to be repaired and restored by a future prince.

25 "Know and understand this: From
the time the word goes out to restore and
rebuild[z] Jerusalem until the Anointed
One,[a][a] the ruler, comes, there will be sev-
en 'sevens,' and sixty-two 'sevens.' It will
be rebuilt with streets and a trench, but
in times of trouble. 26 After the sixty-two
'sevens,' the Anointed One will be put to
death[b] and will have nothing.[b] The people
of the ruler who will come will destroy the
city and the sanctuary. The end will come
like a flood:[c] War will continue until the
end, and desolations have been decreed.
27 He will confirm a covenant with many
for one 'seven.'[c] In the middle of the 'sev-
en'[c] he will put an end to sacrifice and
offering. And at the temple[d] he will set up
an abomination that causes desolation,
until the end that is decreed[d] is poured
out on him.[e]"[f]

Daniel's Vision of a Man

10 1 In the third year of Cyrus[e] king of
Persia, a revelation was given to
Daniel (who was called Belteshazzar).[f]
Its message was true[g] and it concerned a
great war.[g] The understanding of the message came to him in a vision.
2 At that time I, Daniel, mourned[h] for
three weeks. 3 I ate no choice food; no
meat or wine touched my lips; and I used
no lotions at all until the three weeks were
over.
4 On the twenty-fourth day of the first
month, as I was standing on the bank of
the great river, the Tigris,[i] 5 I looked up and
there before me was a man dressed in lin-
en,[j] with a belt of fine gold[k] from Uphaz
around his waist. 6 His body was like topaz, his face like lightning,[l] his eyes like
flaming torches,[m] his arms and legs like
the gleam of burnished bronze,[n] and his
voice like the sound of a multitude.
7 I, Daniel, was the only one who saw

9:25 [z] Ezr 4:24 [a] Jn 4:25 **9:26** [b] Isa 53:8 [c] Na 1:8 **9:27** [d] Isa 10:22 **10:1** [e] Da 1:21 [f] Da 1:7 [g] Da 8:26 **10:2** [h] Ezr 9:4 **10:4** [i] Ge 2:14 **10:5** [j] Eze 9:2; Rev 15:6 [k] Jer 10:9 **10:6** [l] Mt 17:2 [m] Rev 19:12 [n] Rev 1:15

[a] 25 Or *an anointed one*; also in verse 26
[b] 26 Or *death and will have no one*; or *death, but not for himself*
[c] 27 Or *'week'*
[d] 27 Septuagint and Theodotion; Hebrew *wing*
[e] 27 Or *it*
[f] 27 Or *And one who causes desolation will come upon the wing of the abominable temple, until the end that is decreed is poured out on the desolated city*
[g] 1 Or *true and burdensome*

9:25 *the word goes out to restore and rebuild Jerusalem.* Various suggestions have been made regarding the identification of this decree: Cyrus's decree recorded in Ezr 1:1 – 4 (539 BC), Darius's decree recorded in Ezr 6:1 – 12 (521 BC), Artaxerxes' decree recorded in Ezr 7:12 – 26 (458 BC), or Artaxerxes' warrant given to Nehemiah in Ne 2:7 – 8 (445 BC). Because the Hebrew here simply says "word" and does not use one of the specific terms for a royal decree, it may well refer to a prophetic "word of the LORD," such as Jeremiah's prophecies about 70 years in Jer 25:12 (605 BC) or Jer 29:10 (597 BC) or his prophecies of restoration in Jer 30:18 – 22; 31:38 – 40 (586 BC). *the Anointed One.* As the NIV text note recognizes, the noun is indefinite in the Hebrew text ("*an* anointed one"). The term "*the* Messiah" does not occur in the Prophets as a technical term for the ideal, future Davidic king. Both priests and kings were anointed when installed in their office in ancient Israel. The punctuation of the Hebrew and the separation out of two periods of time suggest that the figure referred to in this verse may be one of those involved in the return from exile. Suggestions are Cyrus (called "his [the LORD's] anointed" in Isa 45:1), Joshua the high priest, or Zerubbabel the governor (both called "anointed" in Zec 4:14). *streets.* The Hebrew word refers to the public squares where people met to do the commercial and civic business of the city. *trench.* Refers to a dry moat that was often part of a city's defenses. The combination of "streets" and a "trench" then indicates that Jerusalem will again be a place of security and prosperity, providing all of the civic functions of a smoothly operating urban center.

9:26 *the Anointed One.* As in v. 25 (see note there), the noun is indefinite. Assuming a separation between the two time periods (see note on v. 25), this "Anointed One" is often identified with the high priest Onias III. His murder by Antiochus IV in 171 BC (referred to in 11:22) led to a seven-year period of persecution in Judah, which included the desecration of the temple in 167 BC.

9:27 *an abomination that causes desolation.* The Hebrew word for "desolation" (*shomem*) is probably a play on the Aramaic title *Baal Shamem* ("lord of heaven"), which was used to refer to the Greek god Olympian Zeus. Antiochus IV dedicated the Jerusalem temple to this god (2 Maccabees 6:2). This desecration perpetrated by Antiochus served as a prototype for all future desecrations. Even in the sixth century BC, however, this concept had precedent. In a work called the "Verse Account of Nabonidus," the priests of Marduk list the offenses of Nabonidus that purportedly led to Marduk's overthrow of Nabonidus in favor of the Persian king Cyrus. Among the accusations are that Nabonidus built an abomination, a work of unholiness (a statue of the god Nanna placed in the temple of Marduk), and ordered an end to the most important rituals.

10:1 *third year of Cyrus.* With regard to his rule over Babylon, this was 537 BC. *Cyrus.* See note on 8:4.

10:3 *I ate no choice food.* In Jewish apocalyptic literature fasting is a preparation for receiving a revelation. Ezra (2 Esdras 5:13) and Baruch (2 Baruch 9:2; 12:5; 20:5 – 6; 47:2) fast for seven days prior to receiving revelations. The fast is not always total. On two occasions Ezra abstains from meat and wine, eating only wild plants (2 Esdras 9:24; 12:51). *I used no lotions.* Perfumed oils were the ancient equivalent of deodorant. Anointing with them was particularly associated with gladness and feasting (Ecc 9:8), and so it was not done during a period of mourning (2Sa 14:2; Isa 61:3).

10:5 – 6 White linen is the typical clothing for priests as well as for supernatural operatives (Eze 9 – 10). The gold waistband is lavishly impressive, but most of the description focuses on the physical features of the man (usually identified as Gabriel). The five features described (a body like topaz, a face like lightning, eyes like torches, limbs like bronze, and a voice like a multitude) can also be found in the descriptions of the creatures that bear the chariot throne in Eze 1. There the general appearance of the vehicle is compared to fire and lightning (Eze 1:4), the wheels by which the creatures stand are compared to topaz (Eze 1:16), the legs of the creatures are like burnished bronze (Eze 1:7, "feet"). All of the same Hebrew terms are

the vision; those who were with me did not see it,[o] but such terror overwhelmed them that they fled and hid themselves. 8 So I was left alone,[p] gazing at this great vision; I had no strength left,[q] my face turned deathly pale and I was helpless.[r] 9 Then I heard him speaking, and as I listened to him, I fell into a deep sleep, my face to the ground.[s]

10 A hand touched me[t] and set me trembling on my hands and knees.[u] 11 He said, "Daniel, you who are highly esteemed,[v] consider carefully the words I am about to speak to you, and stand up,[w] for I have now been sent to you." And when he said this to me, I stood up trembling.

12 Then he continued, "Do not be afraid, Daniel. Since the first day that you set your mind to gain understanding and to humble[x] yourself before your God, your words were heard, and I have come in response to them.[y] 13 But the prince of the Persian kingdom resisted me twenty-one days. Then Michael,[z] one of the chief princes, came to help me, because I was detained there with the king of Persia. 14 Now I have come to explain[a] to you what will happen to your people in the future, for the vision concerns a time yet to come.[b]"

15 While he was saying this to me, I bowed with my face toward the ground and was speechless.[c] 16 Then one who looked like a man[a] touched my lips, and I opened my mouth and began to speak.[d] I said to the one standing before me, "I am overcome with anguish[e] because of the vision, my lord, and I feel very weak. 17 How can I, your servant, talk with you, my lord? My strength is gone and I can hardly breathe."[f]

18 Again the one who looked like a man touched[g] me and gave me strength. 19 "Do not be afraid, you who are highly esteemed," he said. "Peace![h] Be strong now; be strong."[i]

When he spoke to me, I was strengthened and said, "Speak, my lord, since you have given me strength."[j]

20 So he said, "Do you know why I have come to you? Soon I will return to fight against the prince of Persia, and when I go, the prince of Greece[k] will come; 21 but first I will tell you what is written in the Book of Truth.[l] (No one supports me against them except Michael,[m] your prince.

11 1 And in the first year of Darius[n] the Mede, I took my stand to support and protect him.)

The Kings of the South and the North

2 "Now then, I tell you the truth:[o] Three more kings will arise in Persia, and then a fourth, who will be far richer than all the others. When he has gained power by his wealth, he will stir up everyone against the kingdom of Greece.[p] 3 Then a mighty king will arise, who will rule with great power and do as he pleases.[q] 4 After he has arisen, his empire will be broken up and parceled out toward the four winds of

10:7 [o] 2Ki 6:17-20; Ac 9:7 **10:8** [p] Ge 32:24 [q] Da 8:27 [r] Hab 3:16 **10:9** [s] Da 8:18 **10:10** [t] Jer 1:9 [u] Rev 1:17 **10:11** [v] Da 9:23 [w] Eze 2:1 **10:12** [x] Da 9:3 [y] Da 9:20 **10:13** [z] ver 21; Da 12:1; Jude 1:9 **10:14** [a] Da 9:22 [b] Da 2:28; 8:26; Hab 2:3 **10:15** [c] Eze 24:27; Lk 1:20 **10:16** [d] Isa 6:7; Jer 1:9; Da 8:15-18 [e] Isa 21:3 **10:17** [f] Da 4:19 **10:18** [g] ver 16 **10:19** [h] Jdg 6:23; Isa 35:4 [i] Jos 1:9 [j] Isa 6:1-8 **10:20** [k] Da 8:21; 11:2 **10:21** [l] Da 11:2 [m] ver 13; Jude 1:9 **11:1** [n] Da 5:31 **11:2** [o] Da 10:21 [p] Da 10:20 **11:3** [q] Da 8:4, 21

[a] *16* Most manuscripts of the Masoretic Text; one manuscript of the Masoretic Text, Dead Sea Scrolls and Septuagint *Then something that looked like a human hand*

used. In Eze 1 the sound of the creatures' wings were like an army (Eze 1:24), whereas the angel in Daniel has a voice that sounds like a multitude. Daniel is clear, however, that his visitor had the appearance of a man rather than the composite beasts seen by Ezekiel. In the Babylonian wisdom composition entitled *Ludlul bel nemeqi*, the sufferer, after a long period of suffering and mourning, has a dream in which he sees an impressive young man (both in physique and attire) standing over him, resulting in his body being numbed. The individual's message is not preserved, but it is generally assumed that it had to do with approaching deliverance.

10:13 *the prince of the Persian kingdom.* The prince is a member of the divine council. He is not evil, only antagonistic to Michael (Israel) which is to be expected because the political conflict between nations is always recapitulated by the gods. Yahweh has abandoned Israel (Eze 10 and evidenced by Michael now representing them, cf. Ex 33:2 – 3) and is now supporting Cyrus, king of Persia. The princes of Persia (and Greece) do not oppose Yahweh, only Michael. The significance of this passage is not that Yahweh's will is being thwarted by powerful evil agents but that Yahweh's return to Israel (envisioned by Ezekiel) has not yet occurred and is not imminent, as Daniel hopes. Persia will be replaced by Greece before Michael is replaced by Yahweh and the exile is ended. *Michael.* There are no names given for angels in earlier literature (see note on 8:16). Michael becomes a much more familiar figure in the Qumran literature and in the intertestamental literature, primarily the book of Enoch. Michael is considered the guardian of the people of Israel.

10:21 *the Book of Truth.* This presumably contains the course of history that is to be revealed (11:2). It can be compared with the "heavenly tablets" revealed to Enoch (1 Enoch 93:2), which contained the account of future history, and with the Babylonian "Tablet of Destinies" (see note on 7:25)

11:2 *Three more kings will arise in Persia, and then a fourth.* Scholars disagree as to whether "the fourth" means the fourth in the series beginning with Cyrus or a fourth following the three after Cyrus. Also, there were more than five rulers of the Persian Empire. The most obvious candidate for the fourth king is Xerxes I because he was very wealthy and invaded Greece. The wording "three … then a fourth" is an idiom used in Hebrew wisdom sayings (e.g., Pr 30:15 – 31) and by Am 1 – 2 in prophecies of judgment. It seems to indicate a totality of examples. If this idiom is being used here, it would be summarizing the nature of the Persian kings as rulers who amass wealth and provoke conflict with the Greeks.

11:3 *a mighty king.* Alexander the Great, who succeeded to the throne of Macedonia in 336 BC. See note on 8:5.

11:4 *his empire will be broken up … It will not go to his descendants.* See note on 8:8. *the four winds.* Alexander died in 323 BC and a 20-year struggle for succession ensued that eventually led to a four-way division of the

heaven.[r] It will not go to his descendants,
nor will it have the power he exercised,
because his empire will be uprooted and
given to others.
5 "The king of the South will become
strong, but one of his commanders will
become even stronger than he and will
rule his own kingdom with great power.
6 After some years, they will become allies.
The daughter of the king of the South will

11:4 [r] Da 7:2; 8:22

empire (see the article "Greek History," p. 1440). Two of those divisions were in the Aegean region (Cassander had Greece and Macedonia; Lysimachus had Thrace), while the other two divided up the Near East (Ptolemy had Egypt and Palestine; Seleucus had Syria, Mesopotamia and Persia). The Ptolemaic line is going to be represented by the "king of the South" (v. 5), while the Seleucid line will be represented by the "king of the North" (v. 7).
11:5 *The king of the South.* Ptolemy I Soter (305–285). The text will now focus on the two kingdoms (Ptolemaic Egypt and Seleucia) that flanked Palestine. Ptolemy was a power broker and instigator during much of the 20-year succession struggle (playing a significant role as early as 321 BC), but Seleucus emerged as the stronger party with the largest kingdom. Ptolemy's military action in 321 broke up the original group that had assumed power after Alexander's death. One of his few failures came in 309 BC when he attempted to move against Antigonus (Seleucus's predecessor). By 306 it was clear that he had overextended himself, and he had to fall back and regroup. Still, in 306 BC he was able to declare himself king of Egypt. *one of his commanders.* Seleucus I Nicator (312–280 BC). After Alexander died, Perdiccas became head of the armies, and Seleucus was one of his generals. He was among the group that assassinated Perdiccas. Seleucus briefly gained control of Babylon but was forced to flee when Perdiccas's successor, Antigonus, moved against him in 316. Seleucus then served as a general for Ptolemy from 316–312 BC. They fought together against Antigonus at the battle of Gaza. After Antigonus's defeat at Gaza, Seleucus regained control of Babylon, which became the center of his power. Verses 4–5 cover the period from Alexander's death through the reigns of the first kings of the two empires, about 40 years.
11:6 *After some years, they will become allies.* The text now moves forward about 40 years. These years had witnessed the First and Second Syrian Wars (274–271 BC and 260–253 BC, respectively), which were fought mostly over the control of the trade routes, ports and natural

PTOLEMIES AND SELEUCIDS

Soon after the death of Alexander the Great in 323 BC, his generals divided his empire into four parts, two of which—Egypt and Syria—were under the rule of the Ptolemies and Seleucids respectively. The Holy Land was controlled from Egypt by the Ptolemaic dynasty from 323 to 198, and was subsequently governed by the Seleucids of Syria from 198 to 142.

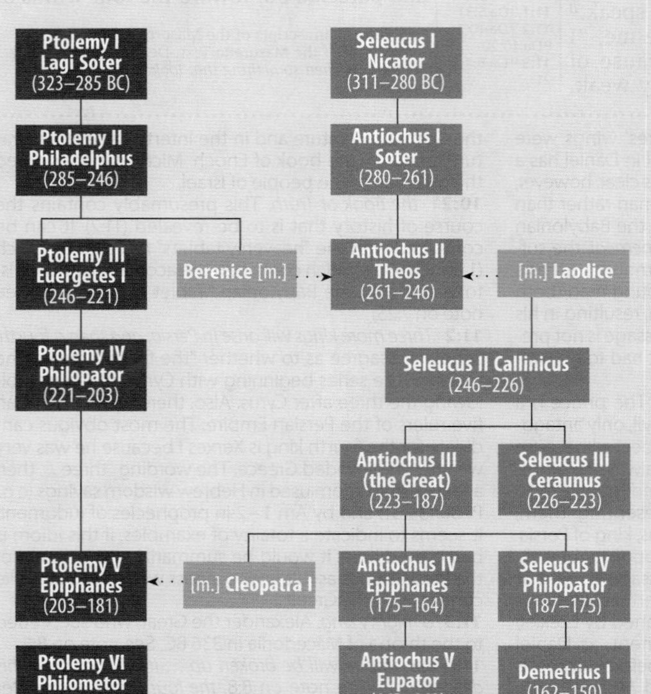

The Diadochi, as the successors of Alexander were called, struggled bitterly for power over his domain. At first Ptolemy I seized his own satrapy, Egypt and North Africa, which had splendid resources and natural defense capabilities. Seleucus gained Syria and Mesopotamia, and by 301 Lysimachus held Thrace and Asia Minor while Cassander ruled Macedon. The situation changed again by 277, when only three major Hellenistic kingdoms stabilized in Egypt, in Syria, and in Macedonia under the Antigonids (277–168). Each continued until the eventual triumph of Rome.

Daniel 11 treats the "king of the South" and the "king of the North," describing their conflicts, wars and alliances. Their hostility toward the people of God culminated in the "abomination that causes desolation" (11:31), identified historically with the reign of Antiochus IV Epiphanes (175–164). The Maccabean revolt followed, leading eventually to the founding of the Hasmonean dynasty.

Continued political rivalries in Judea brought the intervention of the Roman general Pompey in 63 BC. This event signaled the end of Jewish political independence, except for periods of brief autonomy during the ill-fated revolts of the first and second Christian centuries.

go to the king of the North to make an
alliance, but she will not retain her power, and he and his power[a] will not last. In
those days she will be betrayed, together
with her royal escort and her father[b] and
the one who supported her.
[7]“One from her family line will arise to
take her place. He will attack the forces of
the king of the North[s] and enter his fortress; he will fight against them and be
victorious. [8]He will also seize their gods,[t]
their metal images and their valuable articles of silver and gold and carry them off
to Egypt.[u] For some years he will leave the

11:7 [s] ver 6
11:8 [t] Isa 37:19; 46:1-2
[u] Jer 43:12

[a] 6 Or *offspring* [b] 6 Or *child* (see Vulgate and Syriac)

resources of Syria. In the aftermath of the second war there was interest in peace, and the text now focuses on this pivotal moment in history. *daughter of the king of the South.* Berenice, the daughter of Ptolemy II Philadelphus (285 – 246 BC). She was sent (with an entourage) by her father about 252 BC to marry the Seleucid king Antiochus II Theos (261 – 246 BC), thereby establishing an alliance between their kingdoms. The alliance would give Ptolemy control of Syria and Antiochus control of Asia Minor. *she will be betrayed.* The fragile relationship held for a couple of years, and Berenice had a child, but a former wife of Antiochus, Laodice, whose sons had been cut off from succession, allegedly poisoned Antiochus and consequently had Berenice and her son (along with many from her entourage) murdered. Ptolemy II also had died in that year. Needless to say, the alliance crumbled and the next 50 years were full of tumultuous warfare between the two kingdoms.

11:7 *One from her family line.* Ptolemy III Euergetes (246 – 221 BC). Upon hearing of the death of Antiochus, Berenice had summoned her brother (who had acceded to the throne in Egypt) to intervene in Syria in order to support her son’s claim to the throne. He was unable to secure control of Syria before the murder of his nephew and sister (see previous note). In 245 BC (the Third Syrian War), Ptolemy III pressed his invasion of Seleucia and successfully attacked the Syrian capitals of Antioch (on the Orontes River) and Seleucia (this is Seleucia Pieria in Syria) and took much plunder. The cities were quickly recovered by Seleucus II after Ptolemy returned to Egypt.

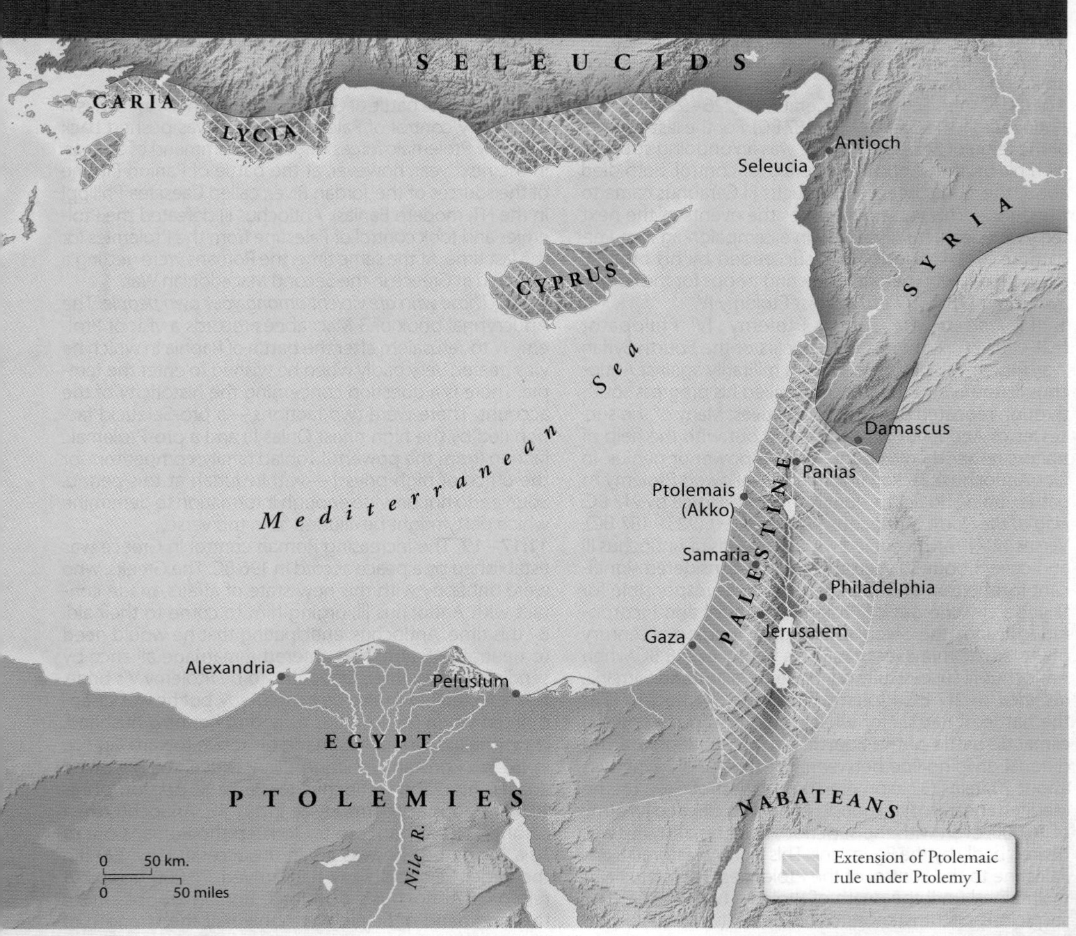

king of the North alone. 9Then the king
of the North will invade the realm of the
king of the South but will retreat to his
own country. 10His sons will prepare for
war and assemble a great army, which will
sweep on like an irresistible flood[v] and
carry the battle as far as his fortress.
11"Then the king of the South will march
out in a rage and fight against the king of
the North, who will raise a large army, but
it will be defeated.[w] 12When the army is
carried off, the king of the South will be
filled with pride and will slaughter many
thousands, yet he will not remain triumphant. 13For the king of the North will
muster another army, larger than the first;
and after several years, he will advance
with a huge army fully equipped.
14"In those times many will rise against
the king of the South. Those who are violent among your own people will rebel
in fulfillment of the vision, but without
success. 15Then the king of the North will
come and build up siege ramps[x] and will
capture a fortified city. The forces of the
South will be powerless to resist; even
their best troops will not have the strength
to stand. 16The invader will do as he pleases;[y] no one will be able to stand against
him.[z] He will establish himself in the
Beautiful Land and will have the power
to destroy it.[a] 17He will determine to come
with the might of his entire kingdom and
will make an alliance with the king of the
South. And he will give him a daughter in
marriage in order to overthrow the kingdom, but his plans[a] will not succeed[b] or
help him. 18Then he will turn his attention
to the coastlands[c] and will take many of
them, but a commander will put an end

11:10 [v] Isa 8:8; Jer 46:8; Da 9:26 **11:11** [w] Da 8:7-8 **11:15** [x] Eze 4:2 **11:16** [y] Da 8:4 [z] Jos 1:5; Da 8:7 [a] Da 8:9 **11:17** [b] Ps 20:4 **11:18** [c] Isa 66:19; Jer 25:22

[a] *17* Or *but she*

11:9 *the king of the North.* Seleucus II Callinicus (246 – 226 BC), Laodice's son, emerged the beneficiary of all of the treachery and intrigue of his mother. *will invade ... but will retreat.* In 243 BC he attempted to gain control of southern Syria and Palestine. Not only was he unsuccessful, but the momentum turned against him and he ended up losing territory.

11:10 *His sons.* Seleucus III Ceraunus (226 – 223 BC) and Antiochus III (the Great) (223 – 187 BC). For the last 15 years of the reign of Seleucus II, there was an ongoing struggle with his brother, Antiochus Hierax, for control. Both died about the same time, and Seleucus III Ceraunus came to the throne. This verse telescopes the events of the next ten years. Seleucus III is killed in a campaign against Pergamum in Asia Minor. He is succeeded by his brother, Antiochus III, who begins mustering troops for the Fourth Syrian War (221 – 217 BC) against Ptolemy IV.

11:11 *king of the South.* Ptolemy IV Philopator (221 – 203 BC). For most of the years of the Fourth Syrian War, Ptolemy IV had little success militarily against Antiochus III (the Great) and only forestalled his progress south through repeated diplomatic initiatives. Many of the successes of Antiochus III were carried out with the help of traitors rather than through military power or genius. In fact Antiochus's lackadaisical tactics allowed Ptolemy to gather, train and field a significant armed force by 217 BC. *king of the North.* Antiochus III (the Great) (223 – 187 BC). Verses 12 – 19 are occupied with the deeds of Antiochus III and cover about 30 years. His reign is considered significant for the text of Daniel because he is responsible for taking Palestine out of Ptolemaic control and incorporating it into the Seleucid kingdom, ending a century of Ptolemaic rule over Israel. This began in 218 BC when Antiochus III successfully penetrated Galilee and Samaria. *defeated.* In 217 BC, Ptolemy IV engaged Antiochus III at the battle of Raphia for what would turn out to be the climactic battle of the Fourth Syrian War. Raphia, a traditional dividing line between Palestine and Egypt, was about 20 miles (32 kilometers) southwest of Gaza on the Mediterranean coast. Though Antiochus claimed an army of 70,000, even with the superior size of his army, he was beaten badly by the Egyptians. This victory restored Syro-Palestine to the control of the Ptolemies. This status was maintained until the death of Ptolemy IV in 203 BC. The suspicious circumstances of his death (while still in his 30s) brought his six-year-old son, Ptolemy V Epiphanes (204 – 180 BC) to the throne of Egypt.

11:13 *another army, larger than the first.* Taking the opportunity of the conflict over who was in charge after the death of Ptolemy IV (see previous note), Antiochus III allied with Philip V of Macedon to initiate the Fifth Syrian War (202 – 200 BC).

11:14 – 16 The battle of Gaza in 201 BC gained Antiochus III temporary control of Palestine, but he was pushed back again by Ptolemaic forces under the command of Scopas. In the next year, however, at the battle of Panion (at one of the sources of the Jordan River; called Caesarea Philippi in the NT, modern Banias), Antiochus III defeated the Ptolemies and took control of Palestine from the Ptolemies for the last time. At the same time, the Romans were getting a foothold in Greece in the Second Macedonian War.

11:14 *Those who are violent among your own people.* The Apocryphal book of 3 Maccabees records a visit of Ptolemy IV to Jerusalem after the battle of Raphia in which he was treated very badly when he wished to enter the temple. There is a question concerning the historicity of the account. There were two factions — a pro-Seleucid faction (led by the high priest Onias II) and a pro-Ptolemaic faction (from the powerful Tobiad family, competitors for the office of high priest) — within Judah at this period. Sources do not provide enough information to determine which party might be alluded to in this verse.

11:17 – 19 The increasing Roman control in Greece was established by a peace accord in 196 BC. The Greeks, who were unhappy with this new state of affairs, made contact with Antiochus III, urging him to come to their aid. By this time, Antiochus, anticipating that he would need to neutralize Egypt, had entered a marriage alliance by sending his daughter, Cleopatra, to be Ptolemy V's bride. He expected her to also be a useful spy, but he was disappointed when her loyalties turned to her new husband. Nevertheless, Antiochus made his move toward Greece in 192 BC. Constantly shifting alliances eventually worked against him, and Antiochus lost a large portion of his 10,000 troops at Thermopylae in 191 BC. Antiochus then resorted to sea battle to try to keep the Romans out of Asia Minor, but he was again unsuccessful. By 190 BC, the larger Seleucid army had arrived, 75,000 troops to reinforce Antiochus's positions. Roman troops under the command of Scipio were only half the strength of

DANIEL 11

Daniel and the Akkadian Prophecies

The long, enigmatically expressed survey of history in Da 11 has no analogy elsewhere in the OT. There is, however, some similarity between Da 8:23 – 25; 11:3 – 45 and a group of texts known as the Akkadian Prophecies.

There are five "core texts" (the Marduk Prophecy, the Shulgi Prophecy, the Dynastic Prophecy, the Uruk Prophecy, and Text A) and at least two others that have some similarity to them. All five texts are presented as prophecies that take the form of concise surveys of a series of rulers' reigns. The rulers are not named but are referred to as "a king/prince" or as "king of X." In most cases plausible correlations can be made between the rulers and events alluded to in the texts and known historical rulers and events.

These texts have been recognized as a form of propagandist interpretation of history composed during the reign of the last king mentioned, and in some cases they are intended to legitimate his reign. If this is the case, they come from various dates between the twelfth century BC (the Marduk Prophecy) and the third century BC (the Dynastic Prophecy). There is a literary relationship between these prophecies and the omen texts, especially astronomical omens. This raises the possibility that they might have been included in the kind of literature that Daniel studied (see note on Da 7:3 – 8).

There are significant points of similarity in literary style between Da 11 and these prophecies, such as the concise listing of the events of kings' reigns, the use of enigmatic phraseology, and the phrase "(after him) a king shall arise." It is possible, then, that Daniel uses a recognized literary form but adapts it for his own use. In particular, it is used not to legitimate the last king mentioned but to declare his inevitable demise. More generally, it is used to express the sovereignty of the God of Israel over history. The noted similarities would not be sufficient to demonstrate that Daniel is also written after the fact. ◆

to his insolence and will turn his insolence back on him.[d] 19 After this, he will
turn back toward the fortresses of his own
country but will stumble and fall,[e] to be
seen no more.[f]
20 "His successor will send out a tax collector to maintain the royal splendor.[g] In a
few years, however, he will be destroyed,
yet not in anger or in battle.
21 "He will be succeeded by a contemptible[h] person who has not been given the
honor of royalty.[i] He will invade the kingdom when its people feel secure, and he
will seize it through intrigue. 22 Then an

11:18 [d] Hos 12:14 **11:19** [e] Ps 27:2 [f] Ps 37:36; Eze 26:21 **11:20** [g] Isa 60:17 **11:21** [h] Da 4:17 [i] Da 8:25

Antiochus's army when the forces met at Magnesia (about 50 miles [80 kilometers] north of Ephesus). Yet due to lack of training and tactical errors on the part of the Seleucid army, Antiochus was defeated and much of his army was slaughtered. The terms of surrender were humiliating, devastating and accepted without argument.

11:20 *His successor.* Seleucus IV Philopator (187 – 175 BC). This son of Antiochus III had a relatively peaceful reign and appears to maintain favorable relations with Jerusalem. The exception alluded to in this verse was when he dispatched one of his chief officials, Heliodorus, to Jerusalem to seize funds that were reported either to be in excess of what was needed or being hoarded by anti-Seleucid factions. Before the high priest Onias III could get to Antioch to appeal the decision and offer explanation, Seleucus was assassinated in a plot carried out by Heliodorus, with Seleucus IV's brother, Antiochus IV, suspected by historians of complicity.

11:21 *contemptible person.* Antiochus IV Epiphanes (175 – 164 BC). He was the brother of Seleucus IV, had been in Rome as a political hostage, and was just returning (he had gotten as far as Athens) when the assassination of his brother took place. One of his goals was to convert Jerusalem into a center for Greek culture and help the

overwhelming army will be swept away before him; both it and a prince of the covenant will be destroyed.[j] 23 After coming to an agreement with him, he will act deceitfully,[k] and with only a few people he will rise to power. 24 When the richest provinces feel secure, he will invade them and will achieve what neither his fathers nor his forefathers did. He will distribute plunder, loot and wealth among his followers.[l] He will plot the overthrow of fortresses — but only for a time.

25 "With a large army he will stir up his strength and courage against the king of the South. The king of the South will wage war with a large and very powerful army, but he will not be able to stand because of the plots devised against him. 26 Those who eat from the king's provisions will try to destroy him; his army will be swept away, and many will fall in battle. 27 The two kings, with their hearts bent on evil,[m] will sit at the same table and lie[n] to each other, but to no avail, because an end will still come at the appointed time.[o] 28 The king of the North will return to his own country with great wealth, but his heart will be set against the holy covenant. He will take action against it and then return to his own country.

29 "At the appointed time he will invade the South again, but this time the outcome will be different from what it was before. 30 Ships of the western coastlands[p] will oppose him, and he will lose heart. Then he will turn back and vent his fury against the holy covenant. He will return and show favor to those who forsake the holy covenant.

31 "His armed forces will rise up to desecrate the temple fortress and will abolish the daily sacrifice. Then they will set up

11:22 [j] Da 8:10-11
11:23 [k] Da 8:25
11:24 [l] Ne 9:25
11:27 [m] Ps 64:6 [n] Ps 12:2; Jer 9:5 [o] Hab 2:3
11:30 [p] Ge 10:4

Jews make the transition to becoming Greek citizens with Greek ways. The intrigues that he became involved in were many, but certainly the main one concerning Jerusalem was how he handled the high priesthood (see next note). The text calls him "contemptible," and indeed he was. His title "Epiphanes" means "god manifest" — but the people preferred "Epimanes," i.e., "Madman." While he was certainly a member of the royal line, the throne should have gone to Seleucus's son, Demetrius (who instead was taking Antiochus IV's place as hostage in Rome). Another intrigue concerned the throne. He set up a coregency with another nephew (a minor), who a few years later was murdered.

11:22 *an overwhelming army.* In some way represents the opponents to Antiochus's reign. This could include internal political opponents, Jewish antagonists, and/or foreign opposition such as that which develops in Egypt. *prince of the covenant.* The high priest Onias III was detained by Antiochus IV; in the interim, Onias's brother Jason conspired to usurp Onias's position. He paid a considerable sum to Antiochus and offered to be cooperative in the Hellenization of Judah (promotion of Greek culture at the expense of Jewish practices). Three years later Menelaus, with the probable support of the Tobiads, paid a larger sum and, the precedent having been established, was awarded the office over Jason. According to 2 Maccabees, Onias was murdered about 171 BC. Many identify him as the "prince of the covenant" referred to in this verse, but others attach that title to Ptolemy VI (see note on v. 25).

11:25 *king of the South.* Ptolemy VI Philometor (181 – 146 BC). *will not be able to stand because of the plots devised against him.* Ptolemy VI was young when he came to the throne and was aided by two officials, Eulaeus and Lenaeus, who stirred up antagonism against Syria with the intention of undermining Ptolemy. Prompted by Egypt's growing animosity, and perhaps even in response to Egypt's military action, Antiochus's dreams of adding Egypt to his kingdom were finally acted on in 169 BC (the First Egyptian War). Antiochus succeeded in capturing the city of Memphis and securing the surrender of Ptolemy VI. The humiliation of Ptolemy in the First Egyptian War is thought to have been the result of bad advice given by his two advisors. After Antiochus's successful siege of Memphis, the citizens of Alexandria defied him by making Ptolemy's younger brother king. Antiochus took immediate steps to break their revolt but was unable to take Alexandria. As soon as he returned to Syria, Ptolemy VI disavowed any loyalty to Antiochus and his coregency with his brother was reinstated.

11:27 *two kings.* Antiochus IV and Ptolemy VI.

11:28 *against the holy covenant.* Roman, Greek and Jewish sources differ with regard to the details at this point. There is no question that on his return from Egypt, Antiochus raided the temple treasury, most likely to secure additional funds for his continuing military activities. The sources disagree about whether this incident took place after the First Egyptian War (September 169 BC), or after the Second Egyptian War (168 BC).

11:29 – 30 In the spring of 168 BC, Antiochus again had to besiege Memphis, and he did so successfully, taking control of Lower Egypt. As he again prepared to lay siege against a weakened Alexandria, he actually had himself crowned king of Egypt. But there was a difference this time. Egypt had appealed to Rome for help, and Rome's ships ("ships of the western coastlands," v. 30) arrived as Antiochus approached Alexandria. Roman consul Gaius Popillius Laenas met him by the walls of Alexandria and commanded Antiochus to leave Egypt. When Antiochus replied that he had to consult with his advisors, the Roman consul drew a circle in the dirt around the king and insisted that he give his answer before stepping out of the circle. A humiliated Antiochus conceded to Roman authority and straggled toward home, looking for a way to vent his misery. This was probably in July 168 BC.

11:30 *he will turn back and vent his fury against the holy covenant.* A rumor that Antiochus IV had been killed in Egypt prompted Jason (see note on v. 22) to attack Jerusalem in an attempt to oust Menelaus as high priest. Jason killed many in the city, but he failed to take full control of it and fled to Ammon. When Antiochus heard of the trouble in Jerusalem, he assumed that the city was in revolt and moved to deal with it. The exact course of events is unclear. A Syrian force entered the city, perhaps by subterfuge, and slaughtered many. It was probably at this time that a citadel, called the Akra, occupied by Syrian troops was established near the temple mount to protect the pro-Hellenists in the city.

11:31 *His armed forces will rise up to desecrate the temple*

44But reports from the east and the north
will alarm him, and he will set out in a
great rage to destroy and annihilate many.
45He will pitch his royal tents between the
seas at[a] the beautiful holy mountain. Yet
he will come to his end, and no one will
help him.

The End Times

12 "At that time Michael,[g] the great
prince who protects your people,
will arise. There will be a time of distress[h]
such as has not happened from the beginning of nations until then. But at that
time your people—everyone whose name
is found written in the book[i]—will be delivered.[j] 2Multitudes who sleep in the dust
of the earth will awake: some to everlasting life, others to shame and everlasting
contempt.[k] 3Those who are wise[b][l] will
shine[m] like the brightness of the heavens,
and those who lead many to righteousness, like the stars for ever and ever.[n] 4But
you, Daniel, roll up and seal[o] the words
of the scroll until the time of the end.[p]
Many will go here and there to increase
knowledge."

5Then I, Daniel, looked, and there before me stood two others, one on this bank
of the river and one on the opposite bank.[q]
6One of them said to the man clothed in
linen,[r] who was above the waters of the
river, "How long will it be before these astonishing things are fulfilled?"[s]
7The man clothed in linen, who was
above the waters of the river, lifted his
right hand and his left hand toward heav-
en, and I heard him swear by him who
lives forever,[t] saying, "It will be for a
time, times and half a time.[c][u] When the
power of the holy people[v] has been finally broken, all these things will be completed.[w]"

8I heard, but I did not understand. So I
asked, "My lord, what will the outcome of
all this be?"

12:1 [g] Da 10:13 [h] Da 9:12; Mt 24:21; Mk 13:19; Rev 16:18 [i] Ex 32:32; Ps 56:8 [j] Jer 30:7 **12:2** [k] Isa 26:19; Mt 25:46; Jn 5:28-29 **12:3** [l] Da 11:33 [m] Mt 13:43; Jn 5:35 [n] 1Co 15:42 **12:4** [o] Isa 8:16 [p] ver 9, 13; Rev 22:10 **12:5** [q] Da 10:4 **12:6** [r] Eze 9:2 [s] Da 8:13 **12:7** [t] Rev 10:5-6 [u] Da 7:25 [v] Da 8:24 [w] Lk 21:24; Rev 10:7

[a] 45 Or *the sea and* [b] 3 Or *who impart wisdom*
[c] 7 Or *a year, two years and half a year*

those rulers who deify themselves and oppose God and his people.

12:1 *Michael.* See note on 10:13. *the book.* This appears to be a reference to the book of life. In Ex 32:32–34 Moses is willing to be blotted out of the book, an action that would result in his death. Yahweh replies that the one who sins is wiped out from the book. The metaphor is of a ledger that contains a list of the living. This is comparable to the book that contains the names of those destined for death that Enkidu sees in his dream of the netherworld in the Gilgamesh Epic. When someone's sins mandate judgment, their name is blotted out, thus leading to their death. This draws a connection between the book of life and the book of judgment. Here the book still pertains to continued life because those recorded will be delivered from the persecution. Here it is not yet conceived of as a book of eternal life.

12:2 *Multitudes who sleep in the dust of the earth will awake.* Any consideration of resurrection is going to be founded in concepts of the afterlife, so we have to begin there. There are several different concepts of afterlife that are evidenced in the ancient Near East. The most fundamental concept is continued existence in a grave-like netherworld, where there is no differentiation in the treatment of the righteous and the wicked. The Israelites called this place Sheol (see note on Isa 14:9; see also the articles "Death and Sheol," p. 833; "Death and the Underworld," p. 907), and they believed that it allowed for no interaction with God. In Canaan and Mesopotamia there were netherworld deities who governed this realm. In Egypt the netherworld existence is more congenial for those who pass the judgment and enter its confines. Those who are not approved are devoured. None of these concepts include the idea of resurrection out of the netherworld. In general, the only awakening that took place in the ancient worldview was the calling up of spirits of the dead (which is not permanent and not a bodily presence) or the awakening of the fertility gods of nature cycles. These died annually when the agricultural cycle came to an end, they "wintered" in the netherworld, and they were ritually awakened in the spring. None of this bears any resemblance to a theological doctrine of resurrection. Likewise not comparable are the occasional revivifications (when an individual is restored to life) or the indications of national return to life (Ezekiel's dry bones).

Nevertheless, just as Jeremiah was the backdrop of Da 11, Ezekiel may form the backdrop for this section of Da 12. In Ezekiel's vision of the dry bones (Eze 37), the nation of Israel in its entirety would be restored to life. Daniel may be further distinguishing that the nation will be restored as Ezekiel said—but while many would be restored to life, others would be doomed to contempt and shame. This recognizes the factions among the Jews observed in Da 11 (Torah loyalists versus Hellenizers).

The modern Christian doctrine about resurrection includes six elements: (1) it is individual, not national; (2) it is material, not spiritual; (3) it is universal, not isolated; (4) it is outside of the netherworld; (5) it is permanent immortality; and (6) it draws distinctions between the righteous and the wicked. Zoroastrianism (see the article "Zoroastrianism," p. 1433) appears to have all of these elements, but the nature of the sources makes it difficult to determine how early the Persians developed these concepts. Only the last is set forth clearly in Daniel. See the article "The Old Testament Concept of Resurrection," p. 1160.

12:3 *shine like the brightness of the heavens ... like the stars.* Stars and angels are associated by the fact that both are referred to as the host of heaven (see note on 8:10). It was current in Greek thinking, as well as in intertestamental apocalyptic literature, that the righteous become stars or angels. Daniel only speaks of comparison, not identification.

12:4 *roll up and seal the words of the scroll.* Akkadian texts sometimes contain a "secrecy colophon"—a note at the end saying that the contents of the text are to be kept secret and only divulged to those with the right to know them. The Dynastic Prophecy has such a colophon: "A secret of the great gods. You may show it to the initiated, but to the uninitiated you must not show it."

12:7 *a time, times and half a time.* See note on 7:25.

the abomination that causes desolation.[q]
32 With flattery he will corrupt those who
have violated the covenant, but the people
who know their God will firmly resist[r] him.
33 "Those who are wise will instruct[s]
many, though for a time they will fall by
the sword or be burned or captured or
plundered.[t] 34 When they fall, they will receive a little help, and many who are not
sincere[u] will join them. 35 Some of the wise
will stumble, so that they may be refined,[v]
purified and made spotless until the time
of the end, for it will still come at the appointed time.

The King Who Exalts Himself

36 "The king will do as he pleases. He
will exalt and magnify himself above every god and will say unheard-of things[w]
against the God of gods.[x] He will be successful until the time of wrath[y] is completed, for what has been determined must
take place. 37 He will show no regard for
the gods of his ancestors or for the one
desired by women, nor will he regard any
god, but will exalt himself above them all.
38 Instead of them, he will honor a god of
fortresses; a god unknown to his ancestors
he will honor with gold and silver, with
precious stones and costly gifts. 39 He will
attack the mightiest fortresses with the
help of a foreign god and will greatly hon-
or those who acknowledge him. He will
make them rulers over many people and
will distribute the land at a price.[a]
40 "At the time of the end the king of
the South[z] will engage him in battle,
and the king of the North will storm[a]
out against him with chariots and cavalry and a great fleet of ships. He will invade many countries and sweep through
them like a flood.[b] 41 He will also invade
the Beautiful Land. Many countries will
fall, but Edom,[c] Moab[d] and the leaders of
Ammon will be delivered from his hand.
42 He will extend his power over many
countries; Egypt will not escape. 43 He will
gain control of the treasures of gold and
silver and all the riches of Egypt,[e] with
the Libyans[f] and Cushites[b] in submission.

11:31 [q] Da 8:11-13; 9:27; Mt 24:15*; Mk 13:14* **11:32** [r] Mic 5:7-9 **11:33** [s] Mal 2:7 [t] Mt 24:9; Jn 16:2; Heb 11:32-38 **11:34** [u] Mt 7:15; Ro 16:18 **11:35** [v] Ps 78:38; Da 12:10; Zec 13:9; Jn 15:2 **11:36** [w] Rev 13:5-6 [x] Dt 10:17; Isa 14:13-14; Da 7:25; 8:11-12,25; 2Th 2:4 [y] Isa 10:25; 26:20 **11:40** [z] Isa 21:1 [a] Isa 5:28 [b] Eze 38:4 **11:41** [c] Isa 11:14 [d] Jer 48:47 **11:43** [e] Eze 30:4 [f] 2Ch 12:3; Na 3:9

[a] 39 Or *land for a reward* [b] 43 That is, people from the upper Nile region

fortress and will abolish the daily sacrifice. To conservative Jews the presence of the Akra, with its Syrian garrison (see note on v. 30), desecrated the holy city of Jerusalem. Worse was to come. Antiochus IV made an edict proscribing the traditional Jewish religious practices on pain of death. The regular sacrifices in the temple were stopped. Observance of the Sabbath and other festivals, circumcision, and the food laws were banned. Copies of the Torah were searched for and destroyed. *the abomination that causes desolation.* 1 Maccabees 1:54 says that on the 15th of Kislev, 167 BC, "they erected a desolating sacrilege upon the altar of burnt offering." This is usually taken to be an idol of Olympian Zeus (see note on 9:27).

11:32 *the people who know their God will firmly resist him.* Many Jews at least acquiesced to Antiochus IV's policies. Others refused to desert their religion. Opposition took various forms, from passive disobedience to armed revolt. The main organized rebellion was led by the Hasmoneans. When a Syrian envoy came to their town of Modein to enforce Antiochus's edict, the head of the family, a priest named Mattathias, killed the envoy. The family fled and became the rallying point for other rebels. Judas, one of Mattathias's five sons, became the military commander and gained the nickname "Maccabeus" ("hammer") because of the defeats he inflicted on the Syrian forces sent against the rebels. In December 164 BC, about three years after the desecration of the temple, Judas regained control of Jerusalem, purified the temple, and resumed the sacrifices. This event is not recorded in Da 11.

11:33 *fall by the sword or be burned or captured or plundered.* The persecution of faithful Jews by Antiochus IV's agents and collaborators is described vividly in 1 Maccabees 1–2; 2 Maccabees 6–7.

11:34 *a little help.* What this refers to is unclear. Many take it as a reference to the Maccabees, whose military actions are seen as less important than the more fundamental refusal to desert the Jewish religious practices. Because the Maccabees took action against apostate Jews, some may have joined them out of fear, not principle.

11:35 *the wise.* These people are no doubt Jews well versed in the Hebrew Scriptures. There has been much inconclusive debate about whether they can be identified with any particular known group of Jews.

11:36 *He will exalt and magnify himself above every god.* The inscriptions on Antiochus IV's coins provide a background to this verse. The early coins have the simple inscription "of King Antiochus." This gradually expands to "of King Antiochus, God Manifest, Victory-Bringer," which is found on coins from 169 BC on. Alexander the Great and his successors were given some divine honors, but Antiochus IV was the first to use the epithet "God" on his coins, and by adding "Manifest" ("Epiphanes") he strengthened the claim to identification with the deity. "Victory-Bringer" was one of the epithets used of Zeus. Antiochus's contemporaries recognized his arrogance and some gave him the nickname "Epimanes" ("Madman") in place of "Epiphanes." If Antiochus is the subject of vv. 36–39, they provide a general evaluation of his character and policies.

11:37 *the gods of his ancestors.* The Seleucids had traditionally worshiped Apollo as their patron god. *the one desired by women.* Probably the god Adonis, whose worship was popular in Egypt. Antiochus IV promoted the worship of Olympian Zeus.

11:38 *a god of fortresses.* This may be Zeus, worshiped as Baal Shamem by the Syrian troops in the Akra in Jerusalem (see note on v. 30).

11:40 *At the time of the end.* The final verses of ch. 11 have perplexed commentators for centuries. They seem to continue the story of Antiochus IV and recount his downfall and death, but what they say does not correspond to what is known of Antiochus IV's final years. The accounts we have of his final campaign and death differ among themselves, but they agree that Antiochus embarked on a campaign in Persia, failed in an attempt to rob a temple, and died an untimely death, apparently due to a sudden illness. Many interpreters see here a reference to the distant future, with Antiochus becoming a prototype of

Daniel would have been locked in the enclosure where lions were kept in captivity for royal hunts. Here a lion is being released for the Assyrian king to hunt.

Baker photo archive, Dr. James C. Martin, British Museum.

9He replied, "Go your way, Daniel, because the words are rolled up and sealed until the time of the end.[x] 10Many will be purified, made spotless and refined,[y] but the wicked will continue to be wicked.[z] None of the wicked will understand, but those who are wise will understand.[a]

11"From the time that the daily sacrifice is abolished and the abomination that causes desolation[b] is set up, there will be 1,290 days. 12Blessed is the one who waits[c] for and reaches the end of the 1,335 days.[d]

13"As for you, go your way till the end. You will rest,[e] and then at the end of the days you will rise to receive your allotted inheritance.[f]"

12:9 [x]ver 4 **12:10** [y]Da 11:35 [z]Isa 32:7; Rev 22:11 **12:10** [a]Hos 14:9 **12:11** [b]Da 8:11; 9:27; Mt 24:15*; Mk 13:14* **12:12** [c]Isa 30:18 [d]Da 8:14 **12:13** [e]Isa 57:2 [f]Ps 16:5; Rev 14:13

12:11 – 12 *1,290 days ... 1,335 days.* No one has suggested a satisfactory explanation for these two time periods. Attempts have been made to relate them to the time lapses between different pairs of significant events during Antiochus IV's persecution of the Jews, but the evidence is too limited for this to be done with any certainty. Various calendars were in use at the time. Some were based on a lunar year of 354 days, some on a solar year of 364 days, and others on a luni-solar year of 360 days. Each had to employ corrections of various kinds to keep it in line with the true solar year of just over 365 days. Attempts have been made to explain the different figures in Daniel as different ways of reckoning three and a half solar years according to different calendars. It may simply be that the numbers have a symbolic significance that is now lost to us.

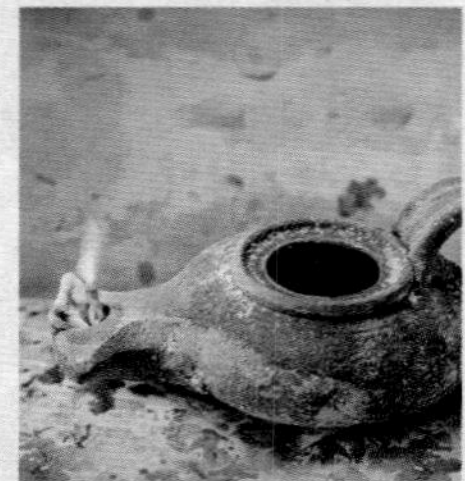

ORACLES OF THE PROPHETS

HOSEA

Extra-Biblical evidence complements and supplements what 2Ki 14:23 – 29 already tells us about life in Israel under Jeroboam II, king over Hosea the public prophet. The scenario painted there reflects the time before Tiglath-Pileser III took the throne of Assyria late in the spring of 745 BC. During Jeroboam's reign, Assyria had had little influence in Israel, but Syria, Israel's neighbor and traditional rival to the north, had been in recurring conflict. Syria's losses were economically and militarily advantageous for Israel, allowing Jeroboam II to reclaim strategic territory to the north and east.

The economic windfall created a buffer zone that helped the elite in Israel accumulate the wealth that they badly abused, as Amos and Hosea eloquently remind us. Such abuse of wealth might be reflected in the archaeological record at the former capital city of Tirzah (Tell el-Farah [North]; see 1Ki 15:33; 16:8). There in Stratum III, dating to the eighth century BC, were found solidly built, stately four-room houses in the neighborhood immediately south of an administrative headquarters, while farther to the south was a cluster of four-roomed houses that were very poorly built and shabbily aligned. Samaria had a large cluster of impressive building complexes outside the city (especially to the south toward Shechem), which possibly suggests a similar gap between the socioeconomic classes.

KEY CONCEPTS

- Loving God and being compassionate and merciful to those around you are the values most desired by God.
- Israel is guilty of syncretism and injustice.
- The key theme of the prophets concerns whether the people will respond to God's warnings and instructions.

History, especially as it relates to the other kings of Israel, sheds further light on Hosea's time. The murder of Jeroboam II's son, Zechariah, spelled an end not only to the Jehu dynasty (the longest in Israel's history) but also to any semblance of political stability in Israel. From then on, as one short-lived, illegitimate king replaced another, all that reigned with consistency was chaos itself. And it could not have come at a worse time for Israel. Starting with the kingdom of Urartu near Turkey in the north (743 – 740 BC) and moving progressively southward over an additional three campaigns (in 738, 734, 733 – 732 BC), the Assyrian king Tiglath-Pileser III, a brilliant military strategist, systematically mobilized his army against the entire eastern Mediterranean seaboard in order to quell rebellions and redirect needed goods along trade routes to Assyria.

Assyria's foreign policy in effect allowed kingdoms like Israel three main options: (1) submit voluntarily and pay tribute; (2) be conquered and pay tribute as an independent puppet state; or (3) be conquered and pay tribute as a full-fledged province of Assyria, complete with an Assyrian overseer. Israel graduated from option one to option two under Tiglath-Pileser III (campaigns of 738 and 732, respectively) and to option three later under Sargon II (722).

Each of these three stages of Israel's subjugation is attested in Assyrian sources. Records of Tiglath-Pileser found on slabs at Calah record Menahem of Israel (745 – 737 BC) paying voluntary tribute. The Assyrian king's annals also record Israel's ill-fated final king, Hoshea, being installed as a puppet king (in keeping with option two). And finally came option three. Annals from stone slabs and inscriptions on walls at Khorsabad contain the Assyrian king Sargon II's boast of besieging and conquering Samaria, carrying away exiles, and installing one of his own officers to rule there. ◆

1 The word of the LORD that came to
Hosea son of Beeri during the reigns
of Uzziah, Jotham, Ahaz and Hezekiah,
kings of Judah,[a] and during the reign of
Jeroboam[b] son of Jehoash[a] king of Israel:[c]

Hosea's Wife and Children

2 When the LORD began to speak through
Hosea, the LORD said to him, "Go, marry a promiscuous[d] woman and have children with her, for like an adulterous wife
this land is guilty of unfaithfulness[e] to the
LORD." 3 So he married Gomer daughter of
Diblaim, and she conceived and bore him
a son.
4 Then the LORD said to Hosea, "Call him
Jezreel,[f] because I will soon punish the
house of Jehu for the massacre at Jezreel,
and I will put an end to the kingdom of Israel. 5 In that day I will break Israel's bow
in the Valley of Jezreel.[g]"
6 Gomer[h] conceived again and gave birth
to a daughter. Then the LORD said to Hosea, "Call her Lo-Ruhamah (which means
"not loved"), for I will no longer show
love to Israel,[i] that I should at all forgive
them. 7 Yet I will show love to Judah; and
I will save them—not by bow,[j] sword or
battle, or by horses and horsemen, but I,
the LORD their God,[k] will save them."
8 After she had weaned Lo-Ruhamah,
Gomer had another son. 9 Then the LORD
said, "Call him Lo-Ammi (which means
"not my people"), for you are not my people, and I am not your God.[b]
10 "Yet the Israelites will be like the sand
on the seashore, which cannot be measured or counted.[l] In the place where it
was said to them, 'You are not my people,'
they will be called 'children of the living
God.'[m] 11 The people of Judah and the people of Israel will come together;[n] they will
appoint one leader[o] and will come up out
of the land,[p] for great will be the day of
Jezreel.[c]

1:1 [a] Isa 1:1; Mic 1:1 [b] 2Ki 13:13 [c] Am 1:1 **1:2** [d] Jer 3:1; Hos 2:2,5; 3:1 [e] Dt 31:16; Jer 3:14; Eze 23:3-21; Hos 5:3 **1:4** [f] 2Ki 10:1-14; Hos 2:22 **1:5** [g] 2Ki 15:29 **1:6** [h] ver 3 [i] Hos 2:4 **1:7** [j] Ps 44:6 [k] Zec 4:6 **1:10** [l] Ge 22:17; Jer 33:22 [m] ver 9; Ro 9:26* **1:11** [n] Isa 11:12, 13 [o] Jer 23:5-8 [p] Eze 37:15-28

[a] *1* Hebrew *Joash,* a variant of *Jehoash* [b] *9* Or *your I AM* [c] *11* In Hebrew texts 1:10,11 is numbered 2:1,2.

1:1 *during the reigns of Uzziah ... Jeroboam.* Hosea prophesied from as early as the time of the Israelite king Jeroboam II (786–745 BC) to as late as the reign of the Judahite king Hezekiah (725–686 BC; 715–687 BC as sole king). His prophetic ministry thus lasted 20–45 years. Most if not all of it took place before the conquest of Samaria by the Assyrians in 722 BC. It is odd that a book about a prophet from the northern kingdom of Israel ministering within the kingdom of Israel begins by mentioning the kings of Judah prior to the king of Israel. This suggests that the message of the book in its final form was directed primarily to the southern kingdom of Judah and at a later period when Hosea's preaching had become famous for its divine authority and abiding relevancy.

1:2 *Go, marry a promiscuous woman.* The following background information serves to supplement the debates found in other commentaries, including whether Gomer was promiscuous before (as is more likely), or only after, her marriage to Hosea. First, the Hebrew word rendered by the NIV as "promiscuous" is not a technical term for a prostitute; it is rather a general term describing the promiscuous sexual behavior of a woman who is either betrothed or married. Its scope of meaning can nonetheless include the sexual behavior of a prostitute as well (see Na 3:4, where both "wanton lust" and "prostitution" translate the same Hebrew word). Regarding the possibility of her involvement in prostitution, we must rule out for lack of evidence any notion that Hosea's wife was likely involved in what is normally meant by "sacred prostitution"—i.e., prostitution at a temple where the sex act was done imitatively to conjure up fertility among the gods. Second, the Hebrew syntax of the phrase in which "promiscuous" occurs *can* (and usually does) describe the *present* behavior of the woman, thereby favoring the notion that Gomer was promiscuous at the time Hosea married her. Thirdly, the Hebrew directive draws especial attention to the implications of the command for the person who receives the command, suggesting in this case that the Lord knew that he was asking Hosea to do something ominous, at personal cost. And finally, assuming, as we should, that Hosea was asked to marry an unchaste person, one remaining moral issue is certain: given the great moral offense that would otherwise apply to Gomer's first husband, Hosea married a woman whose husband was no longer on the scene. Gomer was thus likely a prostitute, or else a promiscuous divorcee or widow. And since the legitimacy of Gomer's children pre-Hosea is questioned (see next segment of this note) she was most likely a prostitute. *and have children with her.* Other translations (NASB, KJV, NKJV) carry the sense that Hosea is being asked to take Gomer's children, born before her marriage to Hosea, and adopt them as his own. In support of this idea, in 2:1 the three "sign-children" (two boys and a girl) are told to speak to their "sisters" (note the plural) as well as to their "brothers." A face-value reading of these plurals suggests that Jezreel, Lo-Ruhamah and Lo-Ammi were recent additions to what we today would call a blended family. It is doubtful that Hosea intended us to explore the situation of Gomer's older children beyond the significance attached to their names. In their real lives, however, these children had more than their names to distance them from their father. In Mesopotamia and Israel, inheritance of property, as well as one's status in society, were normally passed on from father to son. A child's uncertain paternity could disqualify him or her for these vital benefits. Hosea implies that the same dubious status applies to the Israelites in relation to God their Father. Owing to their mother's wantonness, any children Gomer had before marrying Hosea, as well as Lo-Ruhamah and Lo-Ammi who came later, faced financial insecurity and deprivation of inheritance rights were Hosea to have pressed the issue.

1:4 *Jezreel.* The name has significance, as does the location it denotes. Jezreel can mean both "God scatters" (with negative connotations) and "God sows" (with positive connotations, including the bestowal of fertility). The wordplay also worked because, even more than in English, the Hebrew word "Jezreel" sounds much like "Israel" and was thus used by Hosea to denote Israel (2:22). The town of Jezreel (modern-day Zer'in), a secondary capital of Israel, was the site for the overzealous coup d'état of Jehu in which Joram, Jezebel, all of Ahab's sons, and also Ahaziah king of Judah were assassinated (2Ki 9–10).

2 [a] "Say of your brothers, 'My people,'
and of your sisters, 'My loved one.'[q]

Israel Punished and Restored

2 "Rebuke your mother,[r] rebuke her,
for she is not my wife,
and I am not her husband.
Let her remove the adulterous[s] look
from her face
and the unfaithfulness from between
her breasts.
3 Otherwise I will strip her naked
and make her as bare as on the day
she was born;[t]
I will make her like a desert,[u]
turn her into a parched land,
and slay her with thirst.
4 I will not show my love to her
children,[v]
because they are the children of
adultery.
5 Their mother has been unfaithful
and has conceived them in disgrace.
She said, 'I will go after my lovers,[w]
who give me my food and my water,
my wool and my linen, my olive oil
and my drink.'[x]
6 Therefore I will block her path with
thornbushes;
I will wall her in so that she cannot
find her way.[y]
7 She will chase after her lovers but not
catch them;
she will look for them but not find
them.[z]
Then she will say,
'I will go back to my husband as at
first,[a]
for then I was better off[b] than now.'
8 She has not acknowledged[c] that I was
the one
who gave her the grain, the new
wine and oil,
who lavished on her the silver and
gold —
which they used for Baal.[d]

9 "Therefore I will take away my grain[e]
when it ripens,
and my new wine[f] when it is ready.
I will take back my wool and my
linen,
intended to cover her naked body.
10 So now I will expose her lewdness
before the eyes of her lovers;
no one will take her out of my
hands.[g]
11 I will stop[h] all her celebrations:
her yearly festivals, her New
Moons,
her Sabbath days — all her appointed
festivals.[i]
12 I will ruin her vines[j] and her fig trees,
which she said were her pay from
her lovers;

2:1 [q] ver 23 **2:2** [r] ver 5; Isa 50:1; Hos 1:2 [s] Eze 23:45 **2:3** [t] Eze 16:4, 22 [u] Isa 32:13-14 **2:4** [v] Eze 8:18 **2:5** [w] Jer 3:6 [x] Jer 44:17-18 **2:6** [y] Job 3:23; 19:8; La 3:9 **2:7** [z] Hos 5:13 [a] Jer 2:2; 3:1 [b] Eze 16:8 **2:8** [c] Isa 1:3 [d] Eze 16:15-19; Hos 8:4 **2:9** [e] Hos 8:7 [f] Hos 9:2 **2:10** [g] Eze 16:37 **2:11** [h] Jer 7:34 [i] Isa 1:14; Jer 16:9; Hos 3:4; Am 8:10 **2:12** [j] Isa 7:23; Jer 8:13

[a] In Hebrew texts 2:1-23 is numbered 2:3-25.

2:2 *she is not my wife, and I am not her husband.* Several ancient Near Eastern parallels indicate that Hosea is here alluding to the legal language of an actual statement of divorce. According to Mesopotamian cuneiform sources, a person effected a divorce by saying, "You are not my wife." Similarly, within the Egyptian Jewish community of the fifth century BC on the island of Elephantine, a husband or wife could make a statement in repudiation of the marriage by standing up in a congregation and saying, "I hated [personal name], my husband/wife." Likely excepting when there were solid grounds for the divorce, such as adultery, the dismissing party would be obligated to pay the other "money of hatred" (which varied from a modest to a fair sum). The dowry in such a case always reverted to the wife. Moreover, the wife was entitled to go wherever she desired, including back to the home of her father. Such practices are attested widely in the ancient world.
2:3 *strip her naked.* Several documents, including wills that were found in the town of Nuzi, refer to this type of treatment of a wife who abandons her husband to live with another man. It is typically the children who perform this legal act. It is intended to humiliate and perhaps served as an instrument of divorce, though in cases where the husband has already died, it is related to property rights.
2:5,8 Both the Code of Hammurapi and the Middle Assyrian Laws contain lists of items that a husband must by law supply his wife for her daily maintenance. These include grain, oil, wool and clothing. These staples formed the basis of the economy of the ancient Near East and were the symbols of fertility granted to the people by God (Jer 31:12). Thus, within the marriage metaphor employed by Hosea, the providing of these items represented God's fulfillment of the covenant agreement. However, Israel's choice is to take "lovers" (i.e., other gods), worship them and give them presents of gold and silver instead of acknowledging Yahweh's gifts (cf. Eze 16:13 – 19). Israel credited the fertility gods such as Baal for the provision of these needs.
2:12 *vines and … fig trees … her pay from her lovers.* The Egyptian "Love Songs" of Papyrus Harris 500 mention the giving of a jug of sweet mandrake wine as a lover's present. Such gifts would have been common as an expression of endearment or affection, but the term for payment here is the one used to mean the fee of a prostitute rather than the offering to a lover. This draws the metaphor of Israel/Gomer's infidelity back into focus. The use of vines and fig trees also strikes at another source of wealth and festivity in ancient Israel. There could be no celebration without these important products that were harvested in August and September. *wild animals will devour them.* The eighth-century BC Aramaic inscription from Deir 'Alla that contains the prophecy of Balaam and the twentieth-century BC Egyptian Prophecies of Neferti both describe an abandoned land in which strange and ravenous animals forage for food. Ravaging wild beasts were considered one of the typical scourges that a deity would send as punishment. As early as the Gilgamesh Epic in Mesopotamia, the god Ea had reprimanded Enlil for using something as dramatic as a flood rather than sending lions to ravage the people. The gods used wild beasts along with disease, drought and famine to reduce the human population. A common threat connected to negative omens in the Assyrian period was that lions and

HOSEA 2:8

THE BAAL IN HOSEA

"Baal" is not the personal name of a god in Hosea; generally in the OT, the word translated "Baal" in English is the title of a particular god. A preferable rendering to "Baal" would thus be "the Master" or the like (compare the way we unhesitatingly use the title "the Lord," knowing it refers to Yahweh).

When used, as it is here, with reference to a god worshiped in the northern kingdom of Israel, the "Baal" is most likely a title for one specific major Phoenician-type Baal deity. This deity was likely the same as the one introduced by Queen Jezebel in the time of King Ahab (1Ki 16:31 – 32; 21:25 – 26) in the previous century. As the seventh-century BC treaty between King Esarhaddon of Assyria and Ethbaal of Tyre illustrates by its use of "Baal" with a number of gods, there were plenty of Baals to choose from. This treaty mentions two of the more likely candidates for the "Baal" against whom Hosea is writing and with whom Yahweh was likely being confused.

1. *Baal-Shamem.* A prominent, widely attested god, this "Lord of the heavens" is mentioned in several Phoenician and Aramaic texts throughout the first millennium BC and on to the fourth century AD. His identity and character are debated. He has been variously identified with the gods Hadad, Athtar and El (given here in order of likeliness). A supreme weather-god (often ranking chief among gods), he comes to be associated with the sun. He was regularly invoked in times of drought. If Baal-Shamem is the "Baal" of Hosea, passages with divine action involving the sun or rain (Hos 6:3 – 4), divine supremacy, the god's wisdom, etc. are potentially brought into particular relief.

2. *Melqart.* The "Baal of Tyre," whose name literally means "king of the city," has affinities with the netherworldly Nergal, as well as with Greek Heracles (Roman Hercules). He had a cultic affinity with royal ancestors and was widely known as a heroic protector of cities. His death and resurrection were elaborately celebrated in a ritual involving fire. Although his identity as a weather-god is not clear, it can readily be inferred. Mentioned in many ancient sources, Melqart was looked to as a source of prosperity and fertility. If Melqart is the "Baal" of Hosea, passages pertaining to possible veneration of kings or the dead, child sacrifice, resurrection (especially Hos 6:2; 13:1), and protection of the city are potentially brought into particular relief.

continued on next page

I will make them a thicket,[k]
and wild animals will devour them.[l]
[13] I will punish her for the days
she burned incense to the Baals;[m]
she decked herself with rings and jewelry,[n]
and went after her lovers,[o]
but me she forgot,[p]"
declares the LORD.

[14] "Therefore I am now going to allure her;
I will lead her into the wilderness
and speak tenderly to her.
[15] There I will give her back her vineyards,
and will make the Valley of Achor[a][q]
a door of hope.

2:12 [k] Isa 5:6 [l] Hos 13:8 **2:13** [m] Hos 11:2 [n] Eze 16:17 [o] Hos 4:13 [p] Hos 4:6; 8:14; 13:6 **2:15** [q] Jos 7:24, 26

[a] *15* *Achor* means *trouble.*

wolves would rage through the land. In like manner devastation by wild animals was one of the curses invoked for treaty violation. The image here is one of the chaos that results when civilization falls apart (see Dt 32:23 – 25 for an example of God cursing the land and its produce). **2:15** *Valley of Achor.* When Achan violated the ban during the capture of Jericho, he and his entire family were stoned to death in what came to be known as the Valley of Achor (Jos 7:25 – 26). The site is located on Judah's northern tribal border (Jos 15:7), modern El Buquê'ah. Hosea's mention of the "Valley of Trouble" (see NIV text note) is an attempt to demonstrate that if even such an ill-fated place can be transformed, then so can Gomer/Israel's relationship with Hosea/Yahweh.

In addition to these gods it is important to include the Canaanite god Baal known from the Ugaritic texts. This is so because of the possibility (even likelihood) that his character influenced most if not all conceptions of the various Baal-type deities of the region in the early first millennium BC. That Baal, also known as Hadad, is the most active god in the Ugaritic texts, despite technically being accountable to the chief god El. He is a storm-god *par excellence*, so much so that the fertility of the land depends on him bringing rain and staying alive despite the battles he is portrayed as having in the literature with his chief rivals Yamm ("Sea") and Mot ("Death"). Whereas his primary consort at Ugarit is Anat, in later Syria-Palestine it appears to be Astarte. Titles of Baal include "rider of the clouds," "mighty Baal," and "the prince, Baal (or lord) of the earth."

Finally, a word should be said about the "Baals" in the plural (Hos 2:13,17; 11:2). The term applies most often in the OT to illicit gods in general. Where gender is important, the term applies to male gods. In Hosea, "the Baals" are likely either (1) the retinue of whomever the "Baal" refers to or (2) gods of lesser importance with whom the "Baal" was in some other way associated. This grouping together of gods under the title "the Baals" is somewhat analogous to the catchall category of gods mentioned at the end of a Phoenician inscription from Karatepe in eastern Turkey (ancient Cilicia) and roughly contemporaneous with Hosea. It ends with a curse by king Azatiwata that individual gods, as well as the entire group of the sons of God, should wipe out anyone who defaces the monument by removing Azatiwata's name. ◆

Hadad statue, 775 BC. Baal-Shamem has been sometimes identified with the god Hadad.

Kim Walton. The Pergamon Museum, Berlin.

There she will respond[a][r] as in the days
of her youth,[s]
as in the day she came up out of
Egypt.[t]

16 "In that day," declares the LORD,
"you will call me 'my husband';
you will no longer call me 'my master.[b]'
17 I will remove the names of the Baals
from her lips;[u]
no longer will their names be invoked.[v]
18 In that day I will make a covenant for
them
with the beasts of the field, the birds
in the sky
and the creatures that move along
the ground.[w]
Bow and sword and battle
I will abolish[x] from the land,
so that all may lie down in safety.[y]
19 I will betroth[z] you to me forever;
I will betroth you in[c] righteousness
and justice,[a]
in[c] love and compassion.

2:15 [r] Ex 15:1-18 [s] Jer 2:2 [t] Hos 12:9 **2:17** [u] Ex 23:13; Ps 16:4 [v] Jos 23:7

2:18 [w] Job 5:22 [x] Isa 2:4 [y] Jer 23:6; Eze 34:25 **2:19** [z] Isa 62:4 [a] Isa 1:27

[a] 15 Or *sing* [b] 16 Hebrew *baal* [c] 19 Or *with*

2:19 *I will betroth you in righteousness and justice.* It is best to follow the NIV text note, which renders the Hebrew preposition as "with" instead of "in." The just, righteous and loving attributes of God are thus a (re-)betrothal gift. This must be a re-betrothal and not a flashback to Hosea's first occasion of marriage. This is because according to ancient Near Eastern custom, were this the first time of marriage for the bride, the gifts would have gone to the

20 I will betroth you in[a] faithfulness,
and you will acknowledge[b] the LORD.

21 "In that day I will respond,"
declares the LORD—
"I will respond[c] to the skies,
and they will respond to the earth;
22 and the earth will respond to the grain,
the new wine and the olive oil,[d]
and they will respond to Jezreel.[b]
23 I will plant[e] her for myself in the land;
I will show my love to the one I
called 'Not my loved one.[c]'[f]
I will say to those called 'Not my
people,[d]' 'You are my people';[g]
and they will say, 'You are my God.[h]'"

Hosea's Reconciliation With His Wife

3 The LORD said to me, "Go, show your
love to your wife again, though she is
loved by another man and is an adulteress.[i] Love her as the LORD loves the Israelites, though they turn to other gods and
love the sacred raisin cakes.[j]"
2 So I bought her for fifteen shekels[e] of silver and about a homer and a lethek[f] of barley. 3 Then I told her, "You are to live with
me many days; you must not be a prostitute or be intimate with any man, and I will
behave the same way toward you."
4 For the Israelites will live many days
without king or prince,[k] without sacrifice[l]
or sacred stones, without ephod or household gods.[m] 5 Afterward the Israelites will
return and seek the LORD their God and
David their king.[n] They will come trembling to the LORD and to his blessings in
the last days.[o]

The Charge Against Israel

4 Hear the word of the LORD, you
Israelites,
because the LORD has a charge to
bring
against you who live in the land:
"There is no faithfulness, no love,
no acknowledgment[p] of God in the
land.
2 There is only cursing,[g] lying[q] and
murder,[r]
stealing[s] and adultery;
they break all bounds,
and bloodshed follows bloodshed.
3 Because of this the land dries up,[t]
and all who live in it waste away;[u]
the beasts of the field, the birds in the
sky
and the fish in the sea are swept
away.[v]

4 "But let no one bring a charge,
let no one accuse another,
for your people are like those
who bring charges against a
priest.[w]
5 You stumble[x] day and night,
and the prophets stumble with you.
So I will destroy your mother[y]—
6 my people are destroyed from lack
of knowledge.[z]

"Because you have rejected knowledge,
I also reject you as my priests;
because you have ignored the law[a] of
your God,
I also will ignore your children.
7 The more priests there were,
the more they sinned against me;
they exchanged their glorious God[h][b]
for something disgraceful.[c]
8 They feed on the sins of my people
and relish their wickedness.[d]
9 And it will be: Like people, like
priests.[e]

2:20 [b] Jer 31:34; Hos 6:6; 13:4 **2:21** [c] Isa 55:10; Zec 8:12 **2:22** [d] Jer 31:12; Joel 2:19 **2:23** [e] Jer 31:27 [f] Hos 1:6 [g] Hos 1:10 [h] Ro 9:25*; 1Pe 2:10 **3:1** [i] Hos 1:2 [j] 2Sa 6:19 **3:4** [k] Hos 13:11 [l] Da 11:31; Hos 2:11 [m] Jdg 17:5-6; Zec 10:2 **3:5** [n] Eze 34:23-24 [o] Jer 50:4-5 **4:1** [p] Jer 7:28 **4:2** [q] Hos 7:3; 10:4 [r] Hos 6:9 [s] Hos 7:1 **4:3** [t] Jer 4:28 [u] Isa 33:9 [v] Jer 4:25; Zep 1:3 **4:4** [w] Dt 17:12; Eze 3:26 **4:5** [x] Eze 14:7 [y] Hos 2:2 **4:6** [z] Hos 2:13; Mal 2:7-8 [a] Hos 8:1, 12 **4:7** [b] Hab 2:16 [c] Hos 10:1, 6; 13:6 **4:8** [d] Isa 56:11; Mic 3:11 **4:9** [e] Isa 24:2

[a] 20 Or *with* [b] 22 *Jezreel* means *God plants.* [c] 23 Hebrew *Lo-Ruhamah* (see 1:6) [d] 23 Hebrew *Lo-Ammi* (see 1:9) [e] 2 That is, about 6 ounces or about 170 grams [f] 2 A homer and a lethek possibly weighed about 430 pounds or about 195 kilograms. [g] 2 That is, to pronounce a curse on [h] 7 Syriac (see also an ancient Hebrew scribal tradition); Masoretic Text *me; / I will exchange their glory*

father of the bride (see the article "Marriage Contracts," p. 59). In the case of a widow or divorcee who didn't live at home (which one can well imagine applied in the case of Gomer), this gift would go directly to the bride, as we see here.

3:1 *sacred raisin cakes.* See note on Jer 44:19 for the offering of sweet cakes (made from figs or dates) to the gods of Mesopotamia. There is some uncertainty in translating the Hebrew word here. Some commentators suggest that jars of wine are meant rather than compressed cakes of grapes or raisins. In either case, it is the produce of the grape harvest that is being used as an offering.

3:2 *bought her.* Given the value of the barley added to the 15 shekels of silver, one estimate would make Hosea's total outlay approximately 30 shekels. This amount is equal to the amount due as compensation for the loss of a slave in Ex 21:32. Since Gomer's situation is unclear, it is not possible to make a definite determination of why Hosea would pay out this amount. Based on Middle Assyrian Laws, however, he may be redeeming her from a legal situation from which she could not extricate herself (such as paying a debt she owed). *fifteen shekels.* About six ounces (170 grams). *a homer and a lethek.* Possibly weighed about 430 pounds (195 kilograms).

3:4 *sacred stones.* See notes on 1Ki 14:23; Jer 43:13. *ephod.* See note on 1Sa 2:18. *household gods.* See the article "Household Gods," p. 72.

4:3 *Because of this the land dries up.* Ugaritic texts serve to illustrate a belief within the culture of a connection between the welfare of an important individual, such as the king, and the welfare of the land. The occasion that precipitated El's order to inspect the land for evidence of a drought was a physical illness on the part of King Kirta. Israelites in Hosea's day may similarly have thought there to be a link between the moral failures of figures like the king, princes and priests and various problems that affected the land and its creatures.

I will punish both of them for their
ways
and repay them for their deeds.[f]

10 "They will eat but not have enough;[g]
they will engage in prostitution but
not flourish,
because they have deserted[h] the LORD
to give themselves 11 to prostitution;[i]
old wine and new wine
take away their understanding.[j]
12 My people consult a wooden idol,[k]
and a diviner's rod speaks to them.[l]
A spirit of prostitution leads them
astray;[m]
they are unfaithful to their God.
13 They sacrifice on the mountaintops
and burn offerings on the hills,
under oak,[n] poplar and terebinth,
where the shade is pleasant.[o]
Therefore your daughters turn to
prostitution[p]
and your daughters-in-law to
adultery.[q]

14 "I will not punish your daughters
when they turn to prostitution,
nor your daughters-in-law
when they commit adultery,
because the men themselves consort
with harlots[r]
and sacrifice with shrine
prostitutes —
a people without understanding will
come to ruin!

15 "Though you, Israel, commit adultery,
do not let Judah become guilty.

"Do not go to Gilgal;[s]
do not go up to Beth Aven.[a]
And do not swear, 'As surely as the
LORD lives!'
16 The Israelites are stubborn,
like a stubborn heifer.
How then can the LORD pasture them
like lambs[t] in a meadow?
17 Ephraim is joined to idols;
leave him alone!
18 Even when their drinks are gone,
they continue their prostitution;
their rulers dearly love shameful
ways.
19 A whirlwind[u] will sweep them away,
and their sacrifices will bring them
shame.[v]

4:9 [f] Jer 5:31; Hos 8:13; 9:9, 15 **4:10** [g] Lev 26:26; Mic 6:14 [h] Hos 7:14; 9:17 **4:11** [i] Hos 5:4 [j] Pr 20:1 **4:12** [k] Jer 2:27 [l] Hab 2:19 [m] Isa 44:20 **4:13** [n] Isa 1:29 [o] Jer 3:6; Hos 11:2 [p] Jer 2:20; Am 7:17 [q] Hos 2:13 **4:14** [r] ver 11 **4:15** [s] Hos 9:15; 12:11; Am 4:4 **4:16** [t] Isa 5:17; 7:25 **4:19** [u] Hos 12:1; 13:15 [v] Isa 1:29 **5:1** [w] Hos 6:9; 9:8 **5:2** [x] Hos 4:2 [y] Hos 9:15 **5:3** [z] Hos 6:10 **5:4** [a] Hos 4:11 [b] Hos 4:6 **5:5** [c] Hos 7:10 **5:6** [d] Mic 6:6-7 [e] Pr 1:28; Isa 1:15; Eze 8:6 **5:7** [f] Hos 6:7 [g] Hos 2:4 [h] Hos 2:11-12 **5:8** [i] Hos 9:9; 10:9 [j] Isa 10:29

Judgment Against Israel

5 "Hear this, you priests!
Pay attention, you Israelites!
Listen, royal house!
This judgment is against you:
You have been a snare[w] at Mizpah,
a net spread out on Tabor.
2 The rebels are knee-deep in slaughter.[x]
I will discipline all of them.[y]
3 I know all about Ephraim;
Israel is not hidden from me.
Ephraim, you have now turned to
prostitution;
Israel is corrupt.[z]

4 "Their deeds do not permit them
to return to their God.
A spirit of prostitution[a] is in their
heart;
they do not acknowledge[b] the LORD.
5 Israel's arrogance testifies[c] against
them;
the Israelites, even Ephraim, stumble
in their sin;
Judah also stumbles with them.
6 When they go with their flocks and
herds
to seek the LORD,[d]
they will not find him;
he has withdrawn[e] himself from
them.
7 They are unfaithful[f] to the LORD;
they give birth to illegitimate[g]
children.
When they celebrate their New Moon
feasts,
he will devour[b][h] their fields.
8 "Sound the trumpet in Gibeah,[i]
the horn in Ramah.[j]

[a] 15 *Beth Aven* means *house of wickedness* (a derogatory name for Bethel, which means *house of God*).
[b] 7 Or *Now their New Moon feasts / will devour them and*

4:12 *wooden idol.* Although it is possible that Hosea is referring to the practice of rhabdomancy (divining the will of the gods by casting rods or wands; see note on Isa 2:6 for a variety of forms of divination), this is more likely a reference to sacred groves or Asherah poles (see notes on Dt 7:5; 1Ki 14:23). Idols were often carved from wood (Jer 10:3–5; Hab 2:18–19), and this practice was so common in Mesopotamia that Sumerian texts refer to certain types of wood as the "flesh of the gods."
4:13 *They sacrifice on the mountaintops ... on the hills.* See notes on 1Ki 3:2; 11:7; 2Ch 1:3. *under oak, poplar and terebinth.* See notes on Ge 12:6; Dt 12:2.
4:14 *shrine prostitutes.* See notes on Ge 38:15; Dt 23:17–18.
4:15 *Beth Aven.* See NIV text note.
5:1 *snare ... net.* See notes on Ps 124:7; 140:5.
5:7 *New Moon.* While Hosea may be referring once again to the New Moon festivals that had become corrupted by Baal worship (see 2:11), the term used here can simply mean the arrival of a new month in the cycle of the lunar year. See notes on Nu 28:11; 1Sa 20:5; 2Ki 4:23.
5:8 *Gibeah ... Ramah ... Beth Aven.* There is an allusion here to a military confrontation between the northern and southern kingdoms (Ephraim and Judah, respectively) concerning the border between the two. The reference to the three cities in Benjamin (Gibeah = Jeba'; Ramah = Er-Ram; Beth Aven = Khirbet el-'Askar) suggests either that they are being invaded by Ephraim (perhaps the beginning of an attack on Jerusalem), or that their men

Raise the battle cry in Beth Aven[a];[k]
lead on, Benjamin.
9 Ephraim will be laid waste
on the day of reckoning.[l]
Among the tribes of Israel
I proclaim what is certain.[m]
10 Judah's leaders are like those
who move boundary stones.[n]
I will pour out my wrath[o] on them
like a flood of water.
11 Ephraim is oppressed,
trampled in judgment,
intent on pursuing idols.[b][p]
12 I am like a moth[q] to Ephraim,
like rot to the people of Judah.

13 "When Ephraim saw his sickness,
and Judah his sores,
then Ephraim turned to Assyria,[r]
and sent to the great king for help.[s]
But he is not able to cure[t] you,
not able to heal your sores.[u]
14 For I will be like a lion[v] to Ephraim,
like a great lion to Judah.
I will tear them to pieces and go away;
I will carry them off, with no one to
rescue them.[w]
15 Then I will return to my lair
until they have borne their guilt
and seek my face[x]—
in their misery[y]
they will earnestly seek me.[z]"

Israel Unrepentant

6 "Come, let us return to the LORD.
He has torn us to pieces[a]
but he will heal us;
he has injured us
but he will bind up our wounds.[b]
2 After two days he will revive us;[c]
on the third day he will restore us,
that we may live in his presence.
3 Let us acknowledge the LORD;
let us press on to acknowledge
him.
As surely as the sun rises,
he will appear;
he will come to us like the winter
rains,[d]
like the spring rains that water the
earth.[e]"

4 "What can I do with you, Ephraim?[f]
What can I do with you, Judah?
Your love is like the morning mist,
like the early dew that disappears.[g]
5 Therefore I cut you in pieces with my
prophets,
I killed you with the words of my
mouth[h]—
then my judgments go forth like the
sun.[c][i]
6 For I desire mercy, not sacrifice,[j]
and acknowledgment[k] of God rather
than burnt offerings.
7 As at Adam,[d] they have broken the
covenant;[l]
they were unfaithful[m] to me there.

5:8 [k] Hos 4:15
5:9 [l] Isa 37:3; Hos 9:11-17 [m] Isa 46:10; Zec 1:6
5:10 [n] Dt 19:14 [o] Eze 7:8
5:11 [p] Hos 9:16; Mic 6:16
5:12 [q] Isa 51:8
5:13 [r] Hos 7:11; 8:9 [s] Hos 10:6 [t] Hos 14:3 [u] Jer 30:12
5:14 [v] Am 3:4 [w] Mic 5:8
5:15 [x] Hos 3:5 [y] Jer 2:27 [z] Isa 64:9
6:1 [a] Hos 5:14 [b] Dt 32:39; Jer 30:17; Hos 14:4
6:2 [c] Ps 30:5
6:3 [d] Joel 2:23 [e] Ps 72:6
6:4 [f] Hos 11:8 [g] Hos 7:1; 13:3
6:5 [h] Jer 1:9-10; 23:29 [i] Heb 4:12
6:6 [j] Isa 1:11; Mt 9:13*; 12:7* [k] Hos 2:20
6:7 [l] Hos 8:1 [m] Hos 5:7

[a] 8 *Beth Aven* means *house of wickedness* (a derogatory name for Bethel, which means *house of God*). [b] 11 The meaning of the Hebrew for this word is uncertain. [c] 5 The meaning of the Hebrew for this line is uncertain. [d] 7 Or *Like Adam*; or *Like human beings*

are being called to battle by Judah (perhaps to invade Ephraim). Each of these sites guards the northern track to Judah's capital. The alarm being raised is most likely associated with a phase of the Syro-Ephraimite War of the 730s BC (see the article "Syro-Ephraimite War," p. 1125).

5:10 *move boundary stones.* See note on Dt 19:14.

5:13 *Ephraim turned to Assyria.* The destructive effects of the Syro-Ephraimite War will leave both Israel (Ephraim) and Judah exhausted and even more vulnerable to the political hegemony of the Assyrians. Realizing that their status as vassals was deteriorating, two Israelite kings—Menahem in 738 BC (2Ki 15:19–20) and later Hoshea in 732 BC (2Ki 17:3)—were forced to pay large sums to keep the Assyrians from further ravaging their country. The Assyrian annals of Tiglath-Pileser III record these tribute payments, along with those of many other small nations, being economically drained by the empire's need for funds. *great king.* The NIV differs from the Hebrew text, which reads "king (of) Yareb." It differs because there is no known king or place with this name and because the word order is backward for a king's name. The NIV option, differing only with the traditional vocalization of the Hebrew letters and not the letters themselves, arises because the expression occurs in parallelism with "the king of Assyria." Moreover, "great king" finds warrant from the Assyrian language itself, which has an expression *sharru rabu*, meaning "great king," which, when translated into the Hebrew language, would have consonants similar to what we have here in the Hebrew text. The interpretation of the NIV finds support from an Aramaic text that similarly transfers this common Assyrian expression into its own language.

6:3 *winter rains ... spring rains.* Based on the Mediterranean climate of the Middle East, Israel receives its rain twice during the year. The "winter" rains fall from December to February. As noted in the tenth-century BC Gezer calendar, this moisture softens the earth and prepares it for plowing and sowing of wheat, barley and oats. The "spring" rains come during March and April and provide the life-giving water needed for the sowing of millet and vegetable crops. It is the timing of these rains that makes the difference between a good harvest and famine. Tying Yahweh to the rains supersedes Baal's role as the rain and fertility god, and tying Yahweh to the sun supersedes the sun-gods who were often associated with justice.

6:7 *Adam.* Rather than a reference to the first man, here "Adam" is best understood as a place-name. This provides a better match with the word "there" later in the verse and also with the place-name Gilead in v. 8. Pharaoh Shishak's inscription, recorded in the temple of Amun in Karnak, mentions Adam; it was the first place Shishak captured on his way across the Jordan River to overpower King Jeroboam of Israel in the tenth century BC. Mentioned also in Jos 3:16, it is located on the east side of the Jordan River a short distance south of the point where the Jabbok River meets the Jordan River.

[8]Gilead is a city of evildoers,
stained with footprints of blood.
[9]As marauders lie in ambush for a
victim,
so do bands of priests;
they murder on the road to Shechem,
carrying out their wicked schemes.[n]
[10]I have seen a horrible[o] thing in Israel:
There Ephraim is given to
prostitution,
Israel is defiled.[p]

[11]"Also for you, Judah,
a harvest[q] is appointed.

"Whenever I would restore the
fortunes of my people,
7 [1]whenever I would heal Israel,
the sins of Ephraim are exposed
and the crimes of Samaria revealed.[r]
They practice deceit,[s]
thieves break into houses,[t]
bandits rob in the streets;
[2]but they do not realize
that I remember[u] all their evil
deeds.
Their sins engulf them;[v]
they are always before me.

[3]"They delight the king with their
wickedness,
the princes with their lies.[w]
[4]They are all adulterers,[x]
burning like an oven
whose fire the baker need not stir
from the kneading of the dough till it
rises.

6:9 [n]Jer 7:9-10; Eze 22:9; Hos 7:1 **6:10** [o]Jer 5:30 [p]Hos 5:3 **6:11** [q]Jer 51:33; Joel 3:13 **7:1** [r]Hos 6:4 [s]ver 13 [t]Hos 4:2 **7:2** [u]Jer 14:10; Hos 8:13 [v]Jer 2:19 **7:3** [w]Hos 4:2; Mic 7:3 **7:4** [x]Jer 9:2

7:5 [y]Isa 28:1,7 **7:6** [z]Ps 21:9 **7:7** [a]ver 16 **7:8** [b]ver 11; Ps 106:35; Hos 5:13 **7:9** [c]Isa 1:7; Hos 8:7 **7:10** [d]Hos 5:5 [e]Isa 9:13 **7:11** [f]Hos 11:11 [g]Hos 5:13; 12:1 **7:12** [h]Eze 12:13

[5]On the day of the festival of our king
the princes become inflamed with
wine,[y]
and he joins hands with the
mockers.
[6]Their hearts are like an oven;[z]
they approach him with intrigue.
Their passion smolders all night;
in the morning it blazes like a
flaming fire.
[7]All of them are hot as an oven;
they devour their rulers.
All their kings fall,
and none of them calls[a] on me.

[8]"Ephraim mixes[b] with the nations;
Ephraim is a flat loaf not turned
over.
[9]Foreigners sap his strength,[c]
but he does not realize it.
His hair is sprinkled with gray,
but he does not notice.
[10]Israel's arrogance testifies against
him,[d]
but despite all this
he does not return to the LORD his God
or search[e] for him.

[11]"Ephraim is like a dove,[f]
easily deceived and senseless —
now calling to Egypt,
now turning to Assyria.[g]
[12]When they go, I will throw my net[h]
over them;
I will pull them down like the birds
in the sky.

6:8–9 *Gilead ... stained with ... blood ... murder on the road to Shechem.* The event chronicled here may be Pekah's rebellion against the Israelite king Pekahiah in 736 BC (2Ki 15:25). Apparently the fighting began at Adam, with the aid of a group of Gileadites, and spread west along the Wadi Farah road into Israel as far as the city of Shechem. Apparently, Pekah's supporters were aided by priests from Bethel in their efforts to eliminate the king's officials.

7:4–8 In the light of the tumultuous nature of Israel's political scene in the 730s BC, these baking metaphors are quite apt. The oven depicted here was made of clay and was cylindrical in shape. Examples of this device have been excavated at Taanach and Megiddo. It may have been embedded into the floor or lay on it. The domed roof had a large hole covered by a door, through which the baker would first add fuel (wood, dried grass, dung, or cakes made from olive residue). Flames would escape through the hole until a hot bed of coals remained. The heat would be captured as the door was closed and would remain for many hours (enough for the bread to be kneaded and allowed to rise). Then the baker would place the slightly raised flat bread on the inner walls of the oven or amongst the coals. The metaphor plays on these mundane tasks and well-known images. The rebel forces of Pekah, fiercely "flamed" within the oven of Israel's political affairs, destroyed Pekahiah's regime in 735 BC. The resentment caused by this action smoldered as an oven holding its heat and waiting to burn those in charge. Then in 732 BC Hoshea assassinated Pekah and immediately reversed Israel's political alliances (2Ki 15:30), shifting to Assyria for help and then three years later once again seeking an Egyptian alliance (Hos 7:11). This muddled policy left Israel "half-baked," like a loaf left on the wall of the oven that had never been turned. It was burnt on one side and doughy on the other.

7:11 *Ephraim is like a dove.* The vacillating political policy of the kings of Israel is compared to the gullibility (cf. Pr 14:15) of doves who are an easy prey for the fowler's net. In addition, the dove's lack of concern over lost chicks may be compared to Israel's political amnesia with regard to Assyrian policies (see Hos 5:13). *Egypt ... Assyria.* Throughout much of his brief reign, Pekah practiced an anti-Assyrian policy and sought aid from the Egyptians. This had led to the campaign of Tiglath-Pileser III described in 2Ki 15:29 that resulted in the capture of much of the Galilee region and a deportation of Israelites to Assyria. Once Hoshea came to the throne, he initially paid tribute to the Assyrians, but then sent envoys to Egypt. Such duplicity enraged the Assyrian king Shalmaneser V, and he besieged Samaria for three years. His successor, Sargon II, then took the city in 721 BC and deported much of the Israelite population.

7:12 *throw my net over ... the birds.* There were a number of different techniques used to snare birds. Although hunters might simply use a sling, a throwing stick or a bow to take down individual fowl, the majority of instances in the Bible and in ancient art depict large flocks of birds being captured in nets or cages. The tomb of Kagemmi at

Fragment from tomb of Nebamun showing quail being caught in nets. Thebes, Egypt, c. 1350 BC. "I will throw my net over them; I will pull them down like the birds in the sky" (Hos 7:12).

When I hear them flocking together,
I will catch them.
13 Woe[i] to them,
because they have strayed[j] from me!
Destruction to them,
because they have rebelled against me!
I long to redeem them
but they speak about me[k] falsely.
14 They do not cry out to me from their hearts[l]
but wail on their beds.
They slash themselves,[a] appealing to their gods
for grain and new wine,[m]
but they turn away from me.[n]
15 I trained them and strengthened their arms,
but they plot evil[o] against me.
16 They do not turn to the Most High;
they are like a faulty bow.[p]
Their leaders will fall by the sword
because of their insolent words.
For this they will be ridiculed[q]
in the land of Egypt.[r]

Israel to Reap the Whirlwind

8 "Put the trumpet to your lips!
An eagle[s] is over the house of the Lord
because the people have broken my covenant
and rebelled against my law.[t]
2 Israel cries out to me,
'Our God, we acknowledge you!'

7:13 [i] Hos 9:12 [j] Jer 14:10; Eze 34:4-6; Hos 9:17 [k] ver 1; Mt 23:37 **7:14** [l] Jer 3:10 [m] Am 2:8 [n] Hos 13:16 **7:15** [o] Na 1:9,11
7:16 [p] Ps 78:9, 57 [q] Eze 23:32 [r] Hos 9:3 **8:1** [s] Dt 28:49; Jer 4:13 [t] Hos 4:6; 6:7

[a] 14 Some Hebrew manuscripts and Septuagint; most Hebrew manuscripts *They gather together*

Saqqarah (Sixth Dynasty Egypt) portrays the fowler using a net. Apparently some fowlers also used decoys, along with bait food, in their snares to attract the birds. Clearly, Israel's kings have been snared in the net of political ambitions cast by both of the ancient superpowers, Egypt and Assyria.

7:16 *faulty bow.* The composite bow, made from a combination of wood, horn and animal tendons (indicated in the Ugaritic Aqhat Legend), was subject to changes in weather and humidity. If it was not kept in a case, it could lose its strength and be described as unreliable or slack (Ps 78:57). The Assyrian wisdom sayings in the *Words of Ahiqar* speak of the arrows of the wicked being turned back on them, and this may also be part of Hosea's condemnation of the Israel's leaders (see Ps 64:2–7).

8:1 *trumpet.* As in 5:8, the sounding of the trumpet, or ram's horn, is a signal of approaching danger (see note on Jos 6:4). This would have set the people in motion, driving their animals into the protection of the city walls. *eagle.* The Hebrew can also mean "vulture." Hosea employs an image of a bird of prey swooping down on its victim. It seems most likely that he is referring to Assyria, once again being used as a tool of God's wrath. The hunting eagle or vulture would have been a familiar sight and they were often used in Near Eastern epic and myth, as in the Ugaritic Aqhat Legend and the Akkadian Etana myth.

3 But Israel has rejected what is good;
an enemy will pursue him.
4 They set up kings without my consent;
they choose princes without my approval.[u]
With their silver and gold
they make idols[v] for themselves
to their own destruction.
5 Samaria, throw out your calf-idol![w]
My anger burns against them.
How long will they be incapable of purity?[x]
6 They are from Israel!
This calf — a metalworker has made it;
it is not God.
It will be broken in pieces,
that calf of Samaria.

7 "They sow the wind
and reap the whirlwind.[y]
The stalk has no head;
it will produce no flour.
Were it to yield grain,
foreigners would swallow it up.[z]
8 Israel is swallowed up;[a]
now she is among the nations
like something no one wants.[b]
9 For they have gone up to Assyria
like a wild donkey wandering alone.
Ephraim has sold herself to lovers.
10 Although they have sold themselves among the nations,
I will now gather them together.[c]
They will begin to waste away[d]
under the oppression of the mighty king.

11 "Though Ephraim built many altars for sin offerings,
these have become altars for sinning.[e]
12 I wrote for them the many things of my law,
but they regarded them as something foreign.
13 Though they offer sacrifices as gifts to me,
and though they eat[f] the meat,
the LORD is not pleased with them.
Now he will remember[g] their wickedness
and punish their sins:[h]
They will return to Egypt.[i]
14 Israel has forgotten[j] their Maker
and built palaces;
Judah has fortified many towns.
But I will send fire on their cities
that will consume their fortresses."[k]

8:4 [u] Hos 13:10 [v] Hos 2:8 **8:5** [w] Hos 10:5 [x] Jer 13:27 **8:7** [y] Pr 22:8; Isa 66:15; Hos 10:12-13; Na 1:3 [z] Hos 2:9 **8:8** [a] Jer 51:34 [b] Jer 22:28 **8:10** [c] Eze 16:37; 22:20 [d] Jer 42:2 **8:11** [e] Hos 10:1; 12:11 **8:13** [f] Jer 7:21 [g] Hos 7:2 [h] Hos 4:9 [i] Hos 9:3,6 **8:14** [j] Dt 32:18; Hos 2:13 [k] Jer 17:27 **9:1** [l] Isa 22:12-13 [m] Hos 10:5 **9:2** [n] Hos 2:9 **9:3** [o] Lev 25:23 [p] Hos 8:13 [q] Eze 4:13; Hos 7:11 **9:4** [r] Jer 6:20; Hos 8:13 [s] Hag 2:13-14 **9:5** [t] Isa 10:3; Jer 5:31 [u] Hos 2:11 **9:6** [v] Isa 19:13 [w] Isa 5:6; Hos 10:8

Punishment for Israel

9 Do not rejoice, Israel;
do not be jubilant[l] like the other nations.
For you have been unfaithful[m] to your God;
you love the wages of a prostitute
at every threshing floor.
2 Threshing floors and winepresses will not feed the people;
the new wine[n] will fail them.
3 They will not remain[o] in the LORD's land;
Ephraim will return to Egypt[p]
and eat unclean food in Assyria.[q]
4 They will not pour out wine offerings to the LORD,
nor will their sacrifices please[r] him.
Such sacrifices will be to them like the bread of mourners;
all who eat them will be unclean.[s]
This food will be for themselves;
it will not come into the temple of the LORD.

5 What will you do[t] on the day of your appointed festivals,[u]
on the feast days of the LORD?
6 Even if they escape from destruction,
Egypt will gather them,
and Memphis[v] will bury them.
Their treasures of silver will be taken over by briers,
and thorns[w] will overrun their tents.

8:5 *calf-idol.* There is ample evidence of the association of Baal worship with bovine cult images or pictures of bulls (such as the zoomorphic depiction from Tell el-Asch'ari). King Jeroboam attempted to create his own shrines at Dan and Bethel as rivals to Jerusalem by using golden calves to serve as representations of God's throne (see notes on 1Ki 12:28 – 29). Hosea now condemns the golden calves placed in these shrines as a source of false worship and a reflection of the syncretism of Baal and Yahweh worship in Israel. By Hosea's time, only Bethel still remains, since Tiglath-Pileser III had conquered Dan in 733 BC and presumably destroyed the shrine there.
8:14 *palaces.* Hebrew *hekal*, perhaps a cognate of Akkadian *egal*, "big house," may mean either temple or palace. At least during Jeroboam II's early reign, there was an effort to build fortified cities and monumental buildings in Samaria and other major cities (cf. Judah in 2Ch 26:9 – 10).
9:1 *prostitute at every threshing floor.* One of the essential installations within the farming areas of Israel was the threshing floor, where harvested grain was brought for processing and distribution. It would also be the likely site for public gatherings (see 1Ki 22:10) and for harvest celebrations (Dt 16:13). See note on Ru 3:2.
9:4 *bread of mourners.* A house in mourning, having had contact with the dead, is considered unclean for seven days and must be ritually purified in order to resume normal social and religious activity (see note on Nu 19:11,14,16). During the period of their impurity, all their food, by extension, is equally contaminated. While it may be used to nourish their bodies, these meals are joyless and none of the food may be offered as a sacrifice to God (see Jer 16:7; Eze 24:17). This is how Hosea characterizes life in the coming exile.
9:6 *Memphis.* See note on Jer 2:16.

7 The days of punishment[x] are coming,
the days of reckoning are at hand.
Let Israel know this.
Because your sins[y] are so many
and your hostility so great,
the prophet is considered a fool,[z]
the inspired person a maniac.
8 The prophet, along with my God,
is the watchman over Ephraim,[a]
yet snares[a] await him on all his paths,
and hostility in the house of his God.
9 They have sunk deep into corruption,
as in the days of Gibeah.[b]
God will remember[c] their wickedness
and punish them for their sins.

10 "When I found Israel,
it was like finding grapes in the desert;
when I saw your ancestors,
it was like seeing the early fruit on
the fig tree.
But when they came to Baal Peor,[d]
they consecrated themselves to that
shameful idol[e]
and became as vile as the thing they
loved.
11 Ephraim's glory will fly away like a
bird[f]—
no birth, no pregnancy, no
conception.[g]
12 Even if they rear children,
I will bereave them of every one.
Woe[h] to them
when I turn away from them![i]
13 I have seen Ephraim, like Tyre,
planted in a pleasant place.[j]
But Ephraim will bring out
their children to the slayer."

14 Give them, LORD—
what will you give them?
Give them wombs that miscarry
and breasts that are dry.[k]

15 "Because of all their wickedness in
Gilgal,[l]
I hated them there.
Because of their sinful deeds,[m]
I will drive them out of my house.
I will no longer love them;
all their leaders are rebellious.[n]
16 Ephraim[o] is blighted,
their root is withered,
they yield no fruit.[p]
Even if they bear children,
I will slay[q] their cherished
offspring."

17 My God will reject them
because they have not obeyed[r] him;
they will be wanderers among the
nations.[s]

10 Israel was a spreading vine;[t]
he brought forth fruit for himself.
As his fruit increased,
he built more altars;[u]
as his land prospered,
he adorned his sacred stones.[v]
2 Their heart is deceitful,[w]
and now they must bear their guilt.[x]
The LORD will demolish their altars[y]
and destroy their sacred stones.[z]

3 Then they will say, "We have no king
because we did not revere the LORD.
But even if we had a king,
what could he do for us?"
4 They make many promises,
take false oaths[a]
and make agreements;[b]

9:7 [x] Isa 34:8; Jer 10:15; Mic 7:4 [y] Jer 16:18 [z] Isa 44:25; La 2:14; Eze 14:9-10 **9:8** [a] Hos 5:1 **9:9** [b] Jdg 19:16-30; Hos 5:8; 10:9 [c] Hos 8:13 **9:10** [d] Nu 25:1-5; Ps 106:28-29 [e] Jer 11:13; Hos 4:14 **9:11** [f] Hos 4:7; 10:5 [g] ver 14 **9:12** [h] Hos 7:13 [i] Dt 31:17 **9:13** [j] Eze 27:3 **9:14** [k] ver 11; Lk 23:29 **9:15** [l] Hos 4:15 [m] Hos 7:2 [n] Isa 1:23; Hos 4:9; 5:2 **9:16** [o] Hos 5:11 [p] Hos 8:7 [q] ver 12 **9:17** [r] Hos 4:10 [s] Dt 28:65; Hos 7:13 **10:1** [t] Eze 15:2 [u] 1Ki 14:23 [v] Hos 8:11; 12:11 **10:2** [w] 1Ki 18:21 [x] Hos 13:16 [y] ver 8 [z] Mic 5:13 **10:4** [a] Hos 4:2 [b] Eze 17:19; Am 5:7

[a] 8 Or *The prophet is the watchman over Ephraim, / the people of my God*

9:7 *prophet … a maniac.* There was sometimes a very fine line drawn between a person who was invested with the spirit of God (1Sa 9:6) and one who was considered to simply be insane (1Sa 21:13 – 15; 2Ki 9:11). In this case, however, Hosea's enemies attempt to discredit him by claiming his prophecies are actually just the ravings of a madman (cf. Jeremiah in Jer 29:25 – 28 and Amos in Am 7:10).
9:9 *days of Gibeah.* See Jdg 19. Clearly, this story was well enough known in Hosea's day, since he merely has to mention the name of the city to raise the specter of lawless and scandalous behavior.
9:10 *grapes in the desert … fruit on the fig tree.* There is a sense of unexpected pleasure to be found in grapes growing in the desert or ripe figs in the early part of the summer. Evidence of "grape cairns" in the Negev indicate that viticulture is possible here, and the small bunches are said to be particularly sweet. This is also the case of the small figs that ripen in May-June. They are considered such a delicacy that they are to be eaten immediately after picking (see Isa 28:4; Na 3:12). *Baal Peor.* See Nu 25:1 – 18 and notes.
9:13 *children to the slayer.* It is possible that this is an allusion to the political turmoil in which the leaders of Israel have embroiled the people and thus laid their families open to the rampaging Assyrian armies. The Sumerian "Lament Over the Destruction of Ur" describes similar events during times of siege where parents abandon their children. Another possibility is that the "slayer of children" is a demon. Among the Babylonian demons was Pashittu, who was considered a baby snatcher. This would be another way of referring to child exposure (see note on Eze 16:5).
9:15 *wickedness in Gilgal.* While Hosea's condemnation may be based on events during the conquest period or at the time of Saul's inauguration as king (1Sa 11:12 – 15), it is also possible that he is referring to a contemporary event that is not recorded elsewhere and is now unknown.
10:1 *sacred stones.* See notes on 1Ki 14:23; Jer 43:13.
10:4 *poisonous weeds.* Hebrew *rosh*; here it may be the veined henbane (*Hyoscyamus reticulatus*), which occurs in ploughed fields, especially those near steppe and desert regions. It grows to a height of two feet (60 centimeters), with hairy foliage and a yellowish, pink-veined flower. Another candidate is the Syrian scabious (*Cephalaria syriaca*), which has poisonous seeds. Shallow planting actually helps spread these plants since only the stalks are cut while their deep roots lie untouched (see Job 31:40).

therefore lawsuits spring up
like poisonous weeds in a plowed field.
[5]The people who live in Samaria fear
for the calf-idol of Beth Aven.[a][c]
Its people will mourn over it,
and so will its idolatrous priests,[d]
those who had rejoiced over its splendor,
because it is taken from them into exile.[e]
[6]It will be carried to Assyria[f]
as tribute for the great king.[g]
Ephraim will be disgraced;[h]
Israel will be ashamed of its foreign alliances.
[7]Samaria's king will be destroyed,[i]
swept away like a twig on the surface of the waters.
[8]The high places of wickedness[b][j] will be destroyed—
it is the sin of Israel.
Thorns[k] and thistles will grow up
and cover their altars.[l]
Then they will say to the mountains,
"Cover us!"
and to the hills, "Fall on us!"[m]

[9]"Since the days of Gibeah,[n] you have sinned, Israel,
and there you have remained.[c]
Will not war again overtake
the evildoers in Gibeah?
[10]When I please, I will punish[o] them;
nations will be gathered against them
to put them in bonds for their double sin.
[11]Ephraim is a trained heifer
that loves to thresh;
so I will put a yoke
on her fair neck.
I will drive Ephraim,
Judah must plow,
and Jacob must break up the ground.
[12]Sow righteousness[p] for yourselves,
reap the fruit of unfailing love,
and break up your unplowed ground;[q]
for it is time to seek[r] the LORD,
until he comes
and showers his righteousness[s] on you.
[13]But you have planted wickedness,
you have reaped evil,[t]
you have eaten the fruit of deception.
Because you have depended on your own strength
and on your many warriors,[u]
[14]the roar of battle will rise against your people,
so that all your fortresses will be devastated[v]—
as Shalman devastated Beth Arbel on the day of battle,
when mothers were dashed to the ground with their children.[w]
[15]So will it happen to you, Bethel,
because your wickedness is great.
When that day dawns,
the king of Israel will be completely destroyed.[x]

God's Love for Israel

11 "When Israel was a child, I loved him,
and out of Egypt I called my son.[y]
[2]But the more they were called,
the more they went away from me.[d]

10:5 [c]Hos 5:8 [d]2Ki 23:5 [e]Hos 8:5; 9:1, 3, 11 **10:6** [f]Hos 11:5 [g]Hos 5:13 [h]Isa 30:3; Hos 4:7 **10:7** [i]Hos 13:11 **10:8** [j]1Ki 12:28-30; Hos 4:13 [k]Hos 9:6 [l]ver 2; Isa 32:13 [m]Lk 23:30*; Rev 6:16 **10:9** [n]Hos 5:8 **10:10** [o]Eze 5:13; Hos 4:9 **10:12** [p]Pr 11:18 [q]Jer 4:3 [r]Hos 12:6 [s]Isa 45:8 **10:13** [t]Job 4:8; Hos 7:3; 11:12; Gal 6:7-8 [u]Ps 33:16 **10:14** [v]Isa 17:3 [w]Hos 13:16 **10:15** [x]ver 7 **11:1** [y]Ex 4:22; Hos 12:9, 13; 13:4; Mt 2:15*

[a] 5 *Beth Aven* means *house of wickedness* (a derogatory name for Bethel, which means *house of God*).
[b] 8 Hebrew *aven*, a reference to Beth Aven (a derogatory name for Bethel); see verse 5.
[c] 9 Or *there a stand was taken*
[d] 2 Septuagint; Hebrew *them*

10:5–6 *the calf-idol … is taken from them into exile. It will be carried to Assyria as tribute.* Hosea's prediction of a Samarian calf-idol being carried away as plunder to Assyria betrays an awareness of Assyrian practice. A relief dating to the reign of Tiglath-Pileser III (744–727 BC) shows a line of Assyrians carrying away various god-statues from vanquished areas. Rhetoric found in the speech of Sennacherib's field commander to Hezekiah at a later time suggests the Assyrians would have attributed their successful conquest to the abandonment of Israel by God (2Ki 18:19–25).

10:5 *Beth Aven.* See NIV text note.

10:11 *trained heifer … to thresh … plow … break up the ground.* It may be that young oxen were first trained to accept the yoke by putting them to work on the threshing floor. This relatively simple task, during which they had the opportunity of the reward of grazing (Dt 25:4), made them more docile (see Jer 50:11). Once they were able to easily receive direction, then a sledge could be added that would get the animals used to pulling a load (2Sa 24:22). This in turn prepared them for the more disciplined task of plowing a furrow in a virgin field. Ephraim is being compared to such an animal that enjoys the grazing but now will be yoked.

10:14 *as Shalman devastated Beth Arbel.* This apparently well-known event is unknown to modern historians. Both the individual and the place name are obscure. *Shalman.* Possibly refers to the Assyrian king Shalmaneser V, who could have traveled through a place called Arbel on his way to capture Samaria. Alternatively, it could refer to Shalmaneser III, who ruled Assyria a little more than a century earlier and wreaked havoc on Hazael of Damascus and then exacted tribute from King Jehu of Israel. He too could have passed through Arbel. And finally, it could refer to a Moabite king Salmanu, whose payment of tribute to Tiglath-Pileser III is recorded in Assyrian annals. *Beth Arbel.* There are two options on its identity: (1) Arbela on the western shore of the Sea of Galilee, mentioned in 1 Maccabees 9:2 or (2) modern-day Irbid, just across the Jordan River on the south side of the Jabbok River. *mothers were dashed to the ground with their children.* See note on 13:16.

11:1 *When Israel was a child, I loved him.* Hosea's testimony here would have provided assurance to all that God had fulfilled the parental obligation of suitable support that was a stipulation in adoptive agreements. The importance of testimony of care is well illustrated by an Old

They sacrificed to the Baals[z]
and they burned incense to images.[a]
3 It was I who taught Ephraim to walk,
taking them by the arms;[b]
but they did not realize
it was I who healed[c] them.
4 I led them with cords of human
kindness,
with ties of love.[d]
To them I was like one who lifts
a little child to the cheek,
and I bent down to feed[e] them.

5 "Will they not return to Egypt[f]
and will not Assyria[g] rule over them
because they refuse to repent?
6 A sword[h] will flash in their cities;
it will devour their false prophets
and put an end to their plans.
7 My people are determined to turn
from me.[i]
Even though they call me God Most
High,
I will by no means exalt them.

8 "How can I give you up, Ephraim?[j]
How can I hand you over, Israel?
How can I treat you like Admah?
How can I make you like Zeboyim?[k]
My heart is changed within me;
all my compassion is aroused.
9 I will not carry out my fierce anger,[l]
nor will I devastate[m] Ephraim again.
For I am God, and not a man[n]—
the Holy One among you.
I will not come against their cities.
10 They will follow the LORD;
he will roar like a lion.
When he roars,
his children will come trembling
from the west.[o]
11 They will come from Egypt,
trembling like sparrows,
from Assyria,[p] fluttering like doves.
I will settle them in their homes,"[q]
declares the LORD.

11:2 [z] Hos 2:13 [a] 2Ki 17:15; Isa 65:7; Jer 18:15 **11:3** [b] Dt 1:31; Hos 7:15 [c] Jer 30:17 **11:4** [d] Jer 31:2-3 [e] Ex 16:32; Ps 78:25 **11:5** [f] Hos 7:16 [g] Hos 10:6 **11:6** [h] Hos 13:16 **11:7** [i] Jer 3:6-7; 8:5 **11:8** [j] Hos 6:4 [k] Ge 14:8 **11:9** [l] Dt 13:17; Jer 30:11 [m] Mal 3:6 [n] Nu 23:19 **11:10** [o] Hos 6:1-3 **11:11** [p] Isa 11:11 [q] Eze 28:26

11:12 [r] Hos 4:2 **12:1** [s] Eze 17:10 [t] 2Ki 17:4 **12:2** [u] Mic 6:2 [v] Hos 4:9 **12:3** [w] Ge 25:26 [x] Ge 32:24-29 **12:4** [y] Ge 28:12-15; 35:15 **12:5** [z] Ex 3:15 **12:6** [a] Mic 6:8 [b] Hos 6:1-3; 10:12; Mic 7:7 **12:7** [c] Am 8:5 **12:8** [d] Ps 62:10; Rev 3:17 **12:9** [e] Lev 23:43; Hos 11:1

Israel's Sin

12 Ephraim has surrounded me with lies,[r]
Israel with deceit.
And Judah is unruly against God,
even against the faithful Holy One.[a]

12[b] 1 Ephraim feeds on the wind;[s]
he pursues the east wind all day
and multiplies lies and violence.
He makes a treaty with Assyria
and sends olive oil to Egypt.[t]
2 The LORD has a charge[u] to bring
against Judah;
he will punish Jacob[c] according to
his ways
and repay him according to his
deeds.[v]
3 In the womb he grasped his brother's
heel;[w]
as a man he struggled[x] with God.
4 He struggled with the angel and
overcame him;
he wept and begged for his favor.
He found him at Bethel[y]
and talked with him there—
5 the LORD God Almighty,
the LORD is his name![z]
6 But you must return to your God;
maintain love and justice,[a]
and wait for your God always.[b]

7 The merchant uses dishonest scales[c]
and loves to defraud.
8 Ephraim boasts,
"I am very rich; I have become
wealthy.[d]
With all my wealth they will not find
in me
any iniquity or sin."

9 "I have been the LORD your God
ever since you came out of Egypt;[e]

[a] *12* In Hebrew texts this verse (11:12) is numbered 12:1.
[b] In Hebrew texts 12:1-14 is numbered 12:2-15.
[c] *2* *Jacob* means *he grasps the heel,* a Hebrew idiom for *he takes advantage of* or *he deceives.*

Babylonian legal case involving adoption. In that case, testimony that a child had received parental care bolstered the claim, disputed by some, that the child was indeed the adopted son of his alleged father and was thus eligible to receive his inheritance.

11:8 *Admah … Zeboyim.* These two cities, neither of which have been positively identified by archaeologists, are traditionally included with Sodom and Gomorrah as sites of utter destruction and evidence of God's judgment (see notes on Ge 19:7; Isa 1:9).

12:1 *treaty with Assyria.* Like his predecessor Menahem, Hoshea was initially forced to pay tribute to the Assyrian king Tiglath-Pileser III. The Assyrian annals even boast that when Hoshea assassinated Pekah to take the throne of Israel, the Assyrian king "placed Hoshea as king over them." It also notes that Hoshea paid "10 talents of gold [and] 1000 (?) talents of silver" as tribute, probably to confirm his position as king in 732 BC. *sends olive oil to Egypt.* Shortly after Hoshea had accepted the role of Assyrian vassal king in Israel, he then shifted his allegiance by sending a large quantity of olive oil (one of Israel's major forms of wealth) to Egypt. This would have been a valuable commodity—especially in Egypt, where olives were not grown. Playing to both superpowers and their factions, however, would soon draw Assyrian ire and lead in 722 BC to the invasion of Israel by Shalmaneser V.

12:7 *merchant.* The Hebrew is also translated "Canaan," which at least evokes the idea of Canaanite influence. *dishonest scales.* See notes on Dt 25:13; Job 31:6; Pr 11:1. This same charge is made against unscrupulous merchants in Am 8:5. The indictment seems to be based on the idea that Israel's economic community has been corrupted by the immoral practices of its neighbors. In an economy that did not have standardized weights and measures, traders were often tempted to cheat by falsifying the balances and measurements, often by using improper weights and false bottoms and other ways to alter the sizes of vessels.

I will make you live in tents[f] again,
as in the days of your appointed festivals.
10 I spoke to the prophets,
gave them many visions
and told parables[g] through them."[h]

11 Is Gilead wicked?[i]
Its people are worthless!
Do they sacrifice bulls in Gilgal?[j]
Their altars will be like piles of stones
on a plowed field.[k]
12 Jacob fled to the country of Aram[a];[l]
Israel served to get a wife,
and to pay for her he tended sheep.[m]
13 The LORD used a prophet to bring Israel
up from Egypt,
by a prophet he cared for him.[n]
14 But Ephraim has aroused his bitter
anger;
his Lord will leave on him the guilt
of his bloodshed[o]
and will repay him for his contempt.[p]

The LORD's Anger Against Israel

13 When Ephraim spoke, people
trembled;[q]
he was exalted[r] in Israel.
But he became guilty of Baal
worship[s] and died.
2 Now they sin more and more;
they make idols for themselves from
their silver,[t]
cleverly fashioned images,
all of them the work of craftsmen.
It is said of these people,
"They offer human sacrifices!
They kiss[b] calf-idols![u]"
3 Therefore they will be like the morning
mist,
like the early dew that disappears,[v]
like chaff[w] swirling from a threshing
floor,[x]
like smoke[y] escaping through a
window.

4 "But I have been the LORD your God
ever since you came out of Egypt.[z]
You shall acknowledge no God but
me,[a]
no Savior[b] except me.
5 I cared for you in the wilderness,
in the land of burning heat.
6 When I fed them, they were satisfied;
when they were satisfied, they
became proud;
then they forgot me.[c]
7 So I will be like a lion to them,
like a leopard I will lurk by the path.
8 Like a bear robbed of her cubs,[d]
I will attack them and rip them
open;
like a lion I will devour them —
a wild animal will tear them apart.[e]

9 "You are destroyed, Israel,
because you are against me,[f] against
your helper.[g]

12:9 [f] Ne 8:17 **12:10** [g] Eze 20:49 [h] 2Ki 17:13; Jer 7:25 **12:11** [i] Hos 6:8 [j] Hos 4:15 [k] Hos 8:11 **12:12** [l] Ge 28:5 [m] Ge 29:18 **12:13** [n] Ex 13:3; Isa 63:11-14 **12:14** [o] Eze 18:13 [p] Da 11:18 **13:1** [q] Jdg 12:1 [r] Jdg 8:1 [s] Hos 11:2 **13:2** [t] Isa 46:6; Jer 10:4 [u] Isa 44:17-20 **13:3** [v] Hos 6:4 [w] Isa 17:13 [x] Da 2:35 [y] Ps 68:2 **13:4** [z] Hos 12:9 [a] Ex 20:3 [b] Isa 43:11; 45:21-22 **13:6** [c] Dt 32:12-15; Hos 2:13 **13:8** [d] 2Sa 17:8 [e] Ps 50:22 **13:9** [f] Jer 2:17-19 [g] Dt 33:29

[a] 12 That is, Northwest Mesopotamia [b] 2 Or *"Men who sacrifice / kiss*

12:10 *parables.* One of the ways that the prophet is able to convey God's message is through the use of analogies or comparative stories. The parable thus can provide a dual meaning by using everyday life scenes or images and then providing an interpretation of God's will or judgment. Cf. Nathan's parable of the ewe lamb in 2Sa 12:1 – 4 (see note there).
12:11 *Gilead ... Gilgal.* For Gilead's association with Pekah's revolt, see note on 6:8 – 9. For cultic activities at Gilgal, see notes on 9:15; Am 4:4 – 5.
12:12 *Jacob fled.* Hosea returns to a theme he first used at the beginning of ch. 12, drawing on the traditions about Jacob and using them to parallel the nation of Israel's coming plight and possible redemption. So, just as the unscrupulous Jacob was forced to flee from Palestine to Harran to escape Esau's wrath (see Ge 27 – 28), now Israel will once again be forced to "live in tents" (Hos 12:9). The new life and family Jacob/Israel finds in Aram, however, led him back to Palestine and served as the origin of the Israelite people.
13:2 *make idols.* See Isa 44:9 – 25 and notes; see also the note on Jer 10:3; see further the article "Making an Idol," p. 1010). The acquisition and use of the skills necessary to fashion these images is simply another example, according to Hosea, of Israel's intent to syncretize or corrupt its worship with false gods. *kiss calf-idols.* Kissing was the common act of submission offered to kings and gods, as attested most famously by the Black Obelisk of Shalmaneser III, on which the Israelite king Jehu is shown kissing the ground in front of the Assyrian king. Likewise, the kissing of the idol involved kissing its feet in an act of homage, submission and allegiance. Thus, e.g., in a letter from Mari, the governor of Terqa, Kibri-Dagan, recommends that Zimri-Lim, king of Mari, proceed to Terqa in order to kiss the feet of the statue of the god Dagan/Dagon.
13:3 *chaff.* See note on Ps 35:5. *threshing floor.* See note on Ru 3:2. *smoke escaping through a window.* The typical Israelite pillared house had no chimney through which the smoke of the small campfire (set in the middle of the ground floor in winter) could escape. Nor is it any longer believed that there was an open courtyard above the area where the fire was. Smoke could thus escape only through an open (front) door or else through the windows, which of course had no glass. Based on depictions from ivory plaques, windows were quite narrow slits in the walls on the second story of homes (so designed for security and for keeping cool in summer and warm in winter). *window.* Here a different Hebrew word for window is used that denotes a window specifically for allowing smoke to escape.
13:7 *lion.* See notes on Jdg 14:5; Isa 31:4; Jer 5:6. *leopard.* The idea of the leopard as a silent, stalking hunter fits God's role as the destroyer of the unprepared and the unvigilant Israel (see Jer 5:6). The cunning leopard appears in wisdom literature as well. There is a short fable about the leopard in the Assyrian *Words of Ahiqar* in which the leopard attempts to trick a goat by offering to lend the goat his coat to shelter itself from the cold. The goat escapes and calls back that the leopard was merely hoping for its hide. Leopards still inhabit some regions of Israel (En Gedi) but were not as common as lions in antiquity.

[10]Where is your king,[h] that he may save
you?
Where are your rulers in all your
towns,
of whom you said,
'Give me a king and princes'?[i]
[11]So in my anger I gave you a king,
and in my wrath I took him away.[j]
[12]The guilt of Ephraim is stored up,
his sins are kept on record.[k]
[13]Pains as of a woman in childbirth[l]
come to him,
but he is a child without wisdom;
when the time arrives,
he doesn't have the sense to come
out of the womb.[m]

[14]"I will deliver this people from the
power of the grave;[n]
I will redeem them from death.
Where, O death, are your plagues?
Where, O grave, is your destruction?[o]

"I will have no compassion,
[15] even though he thrives[p] among his
brothers.
An east wind[q] from the LORD will
come,
blowing in from the desert;
his spring will fail
and his well dry up.[r]
His storehouse will be plundered[s]
of all its treasures.
[16]The people of Samaria must bear their
guilt,[t]
because they have rebelled[u] against
their God.
They will fall by the sword;[v]
their little ones will be dashed[w] to
the ground,
their pregnant women[x] ripped
open."[a]

Repentance to Bring Blessing

14 [b] Return, Israel, to the LORD your
God.
Your sins have been your downfall![y]

[2]Take words with you
and return to the LORD.
Say to him:
"Forgive all our sins
and receive us graciously,[z]
that we may offer the fruit of our lips.[ca]
[3]Assyria cannot save us;
we will not mount warhorses.[b]
We will never again say 'Our gods'[c]
to what our own hands have made,
for in you the fatherless[d] find
compassion."

[4]"I will heal[e] their waywardness
and love them freely,[f]
for my anger has turned away from
them.
[5]I will be like the dew to Israel;
he will blossom like a lily.[g]
Like a cedar of Lebanon[h]
he will send down his roots;[i]
[6] his young shoots will grow.
His splendor will be like an olive tree,[j]
his fragrance like a cedar of
Lebanon.[k]
[7]People will dwell again in his shade;[l]
they will flourish like the grain,
they will blossom like the vine—
Israel's fame will be like the wine[m]
of Lebanon.[n]
[8]Ephraim, what more have I[d] to do with
idols?[o]
I will answer him and care for him.
I am like a flourishing juniper;
your fruitfulness comes from me."

[9]Who is wise?[p] Let them realize these
things.
Who is discerning? Let them
understand.[q]
The ways of the LORD are right;[r]
the righteous walk[s] in them,
but the rebellious stumble in them.

13:10 [h] 2Ki 17:4 [i] 1Sa 8:6; Hos 8:4 **13:11** [j] 1Ki 14:10; Hos 10:7 **13:12** [k] Dt 32:34 **13:13** [l] Isa 13:8; Mic 4:9-10 [m] Isa 66:9 **13:14** [n] Ps 49:15; Eze 37:12-13 [o] 1Co 15:55* **13:15** [p] Hos 10:1 [q] Eze 19:12 [r] Jer 51:36 [s] Jer 20:5 **13:16** [t] Hos 10:2 [u] Hos 7:14 [v] Hos 11:6 [w] 2Ki 8:12; Hos 10:14 [x] 2Ki 15:16; Isa 13:16 **14:1** [y] Hos 5:5 **14:2** [z] Mic 7:18-19 [a] Heb 13:15 **14:3** [b] Ps 33:17; Isa 31:1 [c] Hos 8:6 [d] Ps 10:14; 68:5 **14:4** [e] Hos 6:1 [f] Zep 3:17 **14:5** [g] SS 2:1 [h] Isa 35:2 [i] Job 29:19 **14:6** [j] Ps 52:8; Jer 11:16 [k] SS 4:11 **14:7** [l] Ps 91:1-4 [m] Hos 2:22 [n] Eze 17:23 **14:8** [o] ver 3 **14:9** [p] Ps 107:43 [q] Pr 10:29; Isa 1:28 [r] Ps 111:7-8; Zep 3:5; Ac 13:10 [s] Isa 26:7

[a] *16* In Hebrew texts this verse (13:16) is numbered 14:1. [b] In Hebrew texts 14:1-9 is numbered 14:2-10.
[c] *2* Or *offer our lips as sacrifices of bulls*
[d] *8* Or Hebrew; Septuagint *What more has Ephraim*

13:16 Hosea forecasts that the warfare to come will destroy the town and villages of the Israelites; not even women and children will be spared from the rampaging army as it pillages and rapes (see note on Ps 137:9). *little ones ... dashed to the ground.* It would appear that this phrase actually is a standard description of warfare's devastation. Ninth-century BC Assyrian conquest accounts speak of the burning of young boys and girls. *pregnant women ripped open.* This practice is mentioned very rarely. It is a practice attributed to Assyrian king Tiglath-Pileser I (1115–1077 BC) in a hymn praising his conquests. It is also referred to in passing in a Neo-Babylonian lament.
14:5 *dew.* Yahweh's relationship with Israel is likened to the dew, which provides the only moisture available to flowers and trees during the dry months of summer (see Isa 26:19). *lily.* It is not common in Palestine today, though it can be found in some areas. There is dispute whether it was more common in antiquity or not. *cedar of Lebanon.* See note on v. 6. *send down his roots.* God's life-giving essence ensures the fertility and virility of the nation so that it continues to grow and expand, like the massive root system of the olive tree (v. 6).
14:6 *cedar of Lebanon.* Considered the most useful of the large-growth trees in the ancient Near East. It was prized for its lumber (1Ki 6:9–10) and was a symbol of wealth in Mesopotamian literature, including the Gilgamesh Epic and the annals of many kings from the Sumerians through the Assyrians. See notes on 2Sa 5:11; 1Ki 5:6; 6:15.

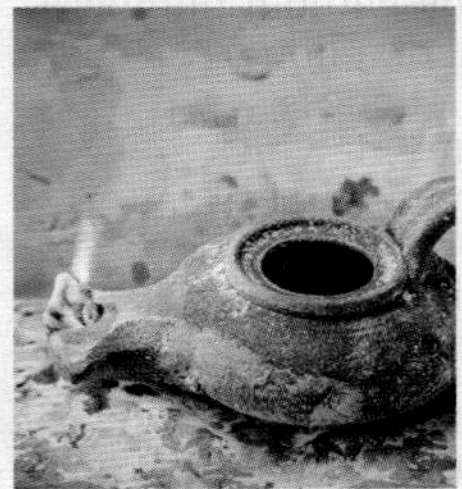

ORACLES OF THE PROPHETS

JOEL

Historical Setting

Unlike many of the prophetic books, the superscription of the book of Joel contains no historical data (i.e., mention of the reign of a particular king), nor is there any mention of the prophet in any other Biblical book. Furthermore, there are few hints in the text as to its date. The first part of the book describes an ecological crisis, while the remainder of the work provides few references to historical situations in Israel or in neighboring states. Thus, the book has been notoriously difficult to date, and opinions have greatly varied, ranging from the ninth century BC to the postexilic period, as late as the fourth century BC.

The first part of the book (1:1 — 2:27) lacks any reference to a king, has frequent statements about priests, and appears to describe active temple worship. None of these items provide conclusive evidence for a date. However, the second part of the book (2:28 — 3:21) appears to contain references to the fall of Judah, the Jewish Diaspora and a return of the exiles (e.g., 3:2,7), which suggest a postexilic time period. There are also no references to Samaria and to the northern kingdom that fell in 722 BC. Moreover, references to the Greeks (3:6) and the citing of earlier prophetic literature (Isa 2:4, referenced in Joel 3:10; Am 1:2, referenced in Joel 3:16) appear to imply a later date to the text, probably between the eighth and sixth centuries BC. The other peoples mentioned (Philistines, Sabeans, Tyrians and Sidonians) are known to have had relations with Israel throughout the early first millennium BC. There are, however, references to an invasion of Judah by locusts, etc., which, if symbolic, may be referring to the invasion of the Assyrians in 701 BC or the Chaldeans in 598 and/or 586 BC. In sum, the book of Joel does not lend itself to an easy chronological determination. ◆

KEY CONCEPTS

- Natural disasters can serve as the judgment of God, but not all who suffer the consequences should therefore be judged guilty. Such disasters draw our attention to God and stimulate us to self-examination.
- The day of judgment is to be feared, and therefore should motivate us to change our ways.
- Prophecy is more important for what it reveals about God than for what it reveals about the future. Fulfillment is sure, but the message is primary.

1 The word of the LORD that came[a] to Joel[b] son of Pethuel.

An Invasion of Locusts

[2]Hear this,[c] you elders;
listen, all who live in the land.[d]
Has anything like this ever happened
in your days
or in the days of your ancestors?[e]
[3]Tell it to your children,[f]
and let your children tell it to their
children,
and their children to the next
generation.
[4]What the locust swarm has left
the great locusts have eaten;
what the great locusts have left
the young locusts have eaten;
what the young locusts have left
other locusts[a] have eaten.[g]

[5]Wake up, you drunkards, and weep!
Wail, all you drinkers of wine;[h]
wail because of the new wine,
for it has been snatched from your
lips.
[6]A nation has invaded my land,
a mighty army without number;[i]
it has the teeth[j] of a lion,
the fangs of a lioness.
[7]It has laid waste[k] my vines
and ruined my fig trees.[l]
It has stripped off their bark
and thrown it away,
leaving their branches white.

[8]Mourn like a virgin in sackcloth[m]
grieving for the betrothed of her
youth.
[9]Grain offerings and drink offerings[n]
are cut off from the house of the
LORD.
The priests are in mourning,
those who minister before the LORD.
[10]The fields are ruined,
the ground is dried up;[o]

1:1 [a] Jer 1:2 [b] Ac 2:16 **1:2** [c] Hos 5:1 [d] Hos 4:1 [e] Joel 2:2 **1:3** [f] Ex 10:2; Ps 78:4 **1:4** [g] Dt 28:39; Na 3:15 **1:5** [h] Joel 3:3 **1:6** [i] Joel 2:2, 11, 25 [j] Rev 9:8 **1:7** [k] Isa 5:6 [l] Am 4:9 **1:8** [m] ver 13; Isa 22:12; Am 8:10 **1:9** [n] Hos 9:4; Joel 2:14, 17 **1:10** [o] Isa 24:4

[a] *4* The precise meaning of the four Hebrew words used here for locusts is uncertain.

1:2 *Hear this.* Appeals for an attentive audience are not unique to ancient Israelite literature. The goddess Inanna in the Sumerian text Enmerkar and the Lord of Aratta encourages the hero Enmerkar to listen and take heed to her advice. The same is found in the Ugaritic Baal Cycle, where Sapsu calls out to Mot (personified Death) to listen to his words. *Has anything like this ever happened . . . ?* Asking a rhetorical question concerning an unprecedented event is seen in Sumerian literature: in Dumuzi's Dream ("Since time of yore, who ever saw a sister revealing the hiding place of her brother?"), in *Inanna's Descent to the Underworld* ("Who ever saw a man find safety for his life in a house not his own?"), and in the "Curse of Agade" ("Who ever saw a king holding [his] head in [his] hands for all of seven years?"). These examples show that Israelites would have used many of the same rhetorical devices as their neighbors, demonstrating that literarily they had much in common with their cultural environment.
1:4 *locust swarm . . . great locusts . . . young locusts . . . other locusts.* Since the locusts are compared to an army in 2:4 – 9, Joel is probably describing a real locust plague that occurred. The four different Hebrew terms used here and in 2:25 appear individually or in pairs in other places in Scripture (e.g., Dt 28:38, Isa 33:4; Am 7:1). Opinion is divided as to whether these four Hebrew terms for locusts refer to different developmental phases or to different species of locust. The Mesopotamian hymn to the goddess Nanaya has interesting parallels with this verse: "The evil locust which destroys the crop/grain, the wicked dwarf-locust which dries up the orchards." The hymn was apparently composed in response to a locust infestation during the time of Sargon II. Like Joel, the hymn lists at least two types of locusts, which appear to be distinct species and not developmental stages. The migratory locust does not go through a metamorphosis as easily recognizable as that of a butterfly. Over 20 words for locust have been found in Akkadian, the language of the Assyrians and the Babylonians.
1:6 *A nation has invaded.* The locusts here in Joel are described as a "nation." Conversely, Sumerian, Ugaritic, Egyptian and Assyrian literature occasionally compare human armies to locusts. The army of Keret in the Ugaritic Keret epic is said to be as numerous as locusts. Defeated enemies during the reigns of New Kingdom monarchs Rameses II (1279 – 1212 BC) and Merneptah (1212 – 1204 BC) in Egypt are often compared to locusts. Likewise, the Assyrian annals during the reigns of Sargon II (721 – 705 BC) and Sennacherib (705 – 681 BC) compare locusts to invading armies. Comparing bees, birds and flies with a nation is also found in Homer's *Iliad*.
1:7 *vines . . . fig trees.* Locusts do not favor the plants mentioned here, so they only attack them when everything else is gone. This is an indication of the extent of the damage. Additionally, the vine and fig are signs of security and prosperity, so their devastation is symbolic of the mood among the population. *stripped off their bark.* Locusts are known not only to devour plant life but also to break off branches and strip off bark. If there is significant damage to the bark, the tree may not survive; even if it does survive, the healing process will greatly reduce its fruitfulness.
1:8 *virgin.* The Hebrew word refers to a woman who has not yet officially left the house of her father. She may still have a "husband" by contract if the bride-price has been paid, even if the marriage has not yet been consummated. The metaphor here then refers to one of the most tragic situations imaginable: the mourning of a woman who has been betrothed and is very close to marriage when she loses her husband. Such should be the depth of Israel's mourning. *sackcloth.* See the article "Mourning," p. 828.
1:9 *Grain offering and the drink offerings are cut off from the house of the LORD.* A phrase in the "Hymn to Nanaya" ("which cuts off the daily offerings of the gods and goddesses") is remarkably similar to this sentence in Joel. Both texts bemoan the fact that the locust plague has impeded the sacrificial offerings, which were fundamental to the life of the spiritual community.
1:10 – 12 Many incidents concerning the destruction of fields and orchards are noted in annals of the Neo-Assyrian kings. These acts of destruction were usually done by the Assyrians themselves on the trees, canals and meadows of their enemy, all of which were vital to the existence of states in this dry desert region. Thus, Assyrian attacks often crippled the economy of an enemy state, as it took

the grain is destroyed,
the new wine[p] is dried up,
the olive oil fails.

11 Despair, you farmers,[q]
wail, you vine growers;
grieve for the wheat and the barley,
because the harvest of the field is destroyed.[r]
12 The vine is dried up
and the fig tree is withered;
the pomegranate, the palm and the apple[a] tree—
all the trees of the field—are dried up.[s]
Surely the people's joy
is withered away.

A Call to Lamentation

13 Put on sackcloth,[t] you priests, and mourn;
wail, you who minister[u] before the altar.
Come, spend the night in sackcloth,
you who minister before my God;
for the grain offerings and drink offerings[v]
are withheld from the house of your God.
14 Declare a holy fast;[w]
call a sacred assembly.
Summon the elders
and all who live in the land
to the house of the LORD your God,
and cry out[x] to the LORD.

15 Alas for that[y] day!
For the day of the LORD[z] is near;
it will come like destruction from the Almighty.[b]
16 Has not the food been cut off[a]
before our very eyes—
joy and gladness
from the house of our God?[b]
17 The seeds are shriveled
beneath the clods.[cc]
The storehouses are in ruins,
the granaries have been broken down,
for the grain has dried up.
18 How the cattle moan!
The herds mill about
because they have no pasture;
even the flocks of sheep are suffering.

19 To you, LORD, I call,[d]
for fire[e] has devoured the pastures[f] in the wilderness
and flames have burned up all the trees of the field.
20 Even the wild animals pant for you;[g]
the streams of water have dried up[h]
and fire has devoured the pastures in the wilderness.

An Army of Locusts

2 Blow the trumpet[i] in Zion;[j]
sound the alarm on my holy hill.

Let all who live in the land tremble,
for the day of the LORD[k] is coming.
It is close at hand[l]—

1:10 [p] Hos 9:2 **1:11** [q] Jer 14:3-4; Am 5:16 [r] Isa 17:11 **1:12** [s] Hag 2:19 **1:13** [t] Jer 4:8 [u] Joel 2:17 [v] ver 9 **1:14** [w] 2Ch 20:3 [x] Jnh 3:8 **1:15** [y] Jer 30:7 [z] Isa 13:6,9; Joel 2:1,11,31
1:16 [a] Isa 3:7 [b] Dt 12:7 **1:17** [c] Isa 17:10-11 **1:19** [d] Ps 50:15 [e] Am 7:4 [f] Jer 9:10 **1:20** [g] Ps 104:21 [h] 1Ki 17:7 **2:1** [i] Jer 4:5 [j] ver 15 [k] Joel 1:15; Zep 1:14-16 [l] Ob 1:15

[a] *12* Or possibly *apricot* [b] *15* Hebrew *Shaddai* [c] *17* The meaning of the Hebrew for this word is uncertain.

years for a fruit tree to grow to maturity and as much as 20 years for a date palm to mature. Moreover, the ecological devastation wrought by the invasion would often reduce fertility. In fact, the destruction of an enemy's fruit trees was often an effective way of causing the surrender of a fortified town, whose people would then be susceptible to starvation. The locusts are thus likened to an invading army that destroys the economy of the land.
1:14 *cry out to the LORD.* It was common in the ancient Near East to see locust plagues as having been sent from a deity (see note on Ex 10:4), so the natural response was to pray for the removal of the plague. A relief from the period of Sargon II of Assyria (721–705 BC) has a person with a locust above his head in front of the deity Shamash, presumably to placate the god for the removal of a plague or to give thanksgiving for deliverance from a plague. Furthermore, the Assyrians and Babylonians employed magical incantations and omens to avert locust plagues. One Assyrian omen states, "If the inner side of the liver is curved at the spot [which indicates] devastation by locusts, there will be pestilence in the prince's country." Though the Israelites did not employ incantations and omens, they certainly did pray for relief from natural disasters such as locust plagues.
2:1 *holy hill.* Various mountains were given religious veneration in the ancient Near East. In fact, the idea of a divine residence on a mountain is common in ancient Near Eastern and Aegean mythology. Mount Zion is often mentioned in Scripture as the place God has chosen as his dwelling place (see 3:17; Ps 46; 48; 76; 87). Similarly, Mount Zaphon was the home of Baal in Ugaritic texts, where it is also described as "my mountain." In addition, Mount Olympus is well known as a divine residence in Greek literature. See notes on Ps 48:1–2; Isa 2:2. *day of the LORD.* Each year in Mesopotamia (often twice a year) there was an enthronement festival for the king of the gods (see the article "Enthronement in the Ancient Near East," p. 925). During the course of this Akitu festival, the deity determined the destiny of his subjects and reestablished order as he had done long ago when he defeated the forces of chaos. In fact, the creation epic *Enuma Elish* that recounts Marduk's defeat of Tiamat and his elevation to the head of the pantheon was read during the course of the festival. Though the texts never refer to the Akitu festival as the "Day of Marduk," there are some similarities. The "day of the LORD" refers to the occasion on which Yahweh will ascend to his throne with the purpose of binding chaos and bringing justice to the world order. The destinies of his subjects will be determined as the righteous are rewarded and the wicked suffer the consequences of their rebellion and sin. For Israel there is no firm evidence that this was represented in a regular ritual; rather, it is reflected in a historical expectation. As is often the case, then, to the extent that there is a connection,

[2] a day of darkness[m] and gloom,[n]
a day of clouds and blackness.
Like dawn spreading across the mountains
a large and mighty army[o] comes,
such as never was in ancient times[p]
nor ever will be in ages to come.

[3] Before them fire devours,
behind them a flame blazes.
Before them the land is like the garden of Eden,[q]
behind them, a desert waste[r] —
nothing escapes them.
[4] They have the appearance of horses;[s]
they gallop along like cavalry.
[5] With a noise like that of chariots[t]
they leap over the mountaintops,
like a crackling fire[u] consuming stubble,
like a mighty army drawn up for battle.

[6] At the sight of them, nations are in anguish;[v]
every face turns pale.[w]
[7] They charge like warriors;
they scale walls like soldiers.
They all march in line,
not swerving[x] from their course.
[8] They do not jostle each other;
each marches straight ahead.
They plunge through defenses
without breaking ranks.
[9] They rush upon the city;
they run along the wall.
They climb into the houses;
like thieves they enter through the windows.[y]

[10] Before them the earth shakes,[z]
the heavens tremble,
the sun and moon are darkened,[a]
and the stars no longer shine.[b]
[11] The LORD[c] thunders
at the head of his army;
his forces are beyond number,
and mighty is the army that obeys his command.
The day of the LORD is great;[d]
it is dreadful.
Who can endure it?[e]

2:2 [m] Am 5:18 [n] Da 9:12 [o] Joel 1:6 [p] Joel 1:2 **2:3** [q] Ge 2:8 [r] Ps 105:34-35 **2:4** [s] Rev 9:7 **2:5** [t] Rev 9:9 [u] Isa 5:24; 30:30 **2:6** [v] Isa 13:8 [w] Na 2:10 **2:7** [x] Isa 5:27 **2:9** [y] Jer 9:21 **2:10** [z] Ps 18:7 [a] Mt 24:29 [b] Isa 13:10; Eze 32:8 **2:11** [c] Joel 1:15 [d] Zep 1:14; Rev 18:8 [e] Eze 22:14

Rend Your Heart

[12] "Even now," declares the LORD,
"return[f] to me with all your heart,
with fasting and weeping and mourning."

[13] Rend your heart[g]
and not your garments.[h]
Return to the LORD your God,
for he is gracious and compassionate,
slow to anger and abounding in love,[i]
and he relents from sending calamity.[j]
[14] Who knows? He may turn[k] and relent
and leave behind a blessing[l] —
grain offerings and drink offerings[m]
for the LORD your God.

[15] Blow the trumpet[n] in Zion,
declare a holy fast,[o]
call a sacred assembly.[p]
[16] Gather the people,
consecrate[q] the assembly;
bring together the elders,
gather the children,
those nursing at the breast.
Let the bridegroom[r] leave his room
and the bride her chamber.
[17] Let the priests, who minister before the LORD,
weep between the portico and the altar.[s]
Let them say, "Spare your people, LORD.
Do not make your inheritance an object of scorn,[t]
a byword among the nations.
Why should they say among the peoples,
'Where is their God?[u]' "

The LORD's Answer

[18] Then the LORD was jealous[v] for his land
and took pity on his people.

[19] The LORD replied[a] to them:

2:12 [f] Jer 4:1; Hos 12:6 **2:13** [g] Ps 34:18; Isa 57:15 [h] Job 1:20 [i] Ex 34:6 [j] Jer 18:8 **2:14** [k] Jer 26:3 [l] Hag 2:19 [m] Joel 1:13 **2:15** [n] Nu 10:2 [o] Jer 36:9 [p] Joel 1:14 **2:16** [q] Ex 19:10, 22 [r] Ps 19:5 **2:17** [s] Eze 8:16; Mt 23:35 [t] Dt 9:26-29; Ps 44:13 [u] Ps 42:3 **2:18** [v] Zec 1:14

[a] *18,19* Or LORD *will be jealous . . . / and take pity . . . /* [19] *The* LORD *will reply*

Israel appears to have historicized that which elsewhere is in the realm of myth and ritual. The "day of the LORD" also has elements of theophany usually connected with the divine warrior who defeats the disruptive powers (see notes on 1Sa 14:6; 2Sa 5:24; see also the article "Divine Warfare," p. 365). Such theophanies often are accompanied by cosmic effects (see note on 1Ki 19:11). The cosmic effects often depict a world upside down (see note on Jer 4:23–26). The "day of the LORD" was a momentous day, and these are the kinds of occurrences that characteristically accompany momentous days. All of this helps our understanding of the "day of the LORD" by showing us that Israelite thinking and the prophet's communication intersect with a wide spectrum of ideas current in the culture. The originality in the Israelite literature is not that whole new matrices are being created but that known ideas are being combined and applied in unique ways.

2:17 *between the portico and the altar.* In context, this is referring to the entrance area of the temple, where access was limited to priests, and thus it served as a buffer between the people and the holy place itself. The portico (see note on 1Ki 6:3) at the front of the main hall to Solomon's temple measured 10 cubits by 20 cubits (see NIV text notes on 1Ki 6:3). Since this area was sacred, it was

"I am sending you grain, new wine
and olive oil,[w]
enough to satisfy you fully;
never again will I make you
an object of scorn[x] to the nations.

20 "I will drive the northern horde[y] far
from you,
pushing it into a parched and barren
land;
its eastern ranks will drown in the
Dead Sea
and its western ranks in the
Mediterranean Sea.
And its stench[z] will go up;
its smell will rise."

Surely he has done great things!
21 Do not be afraid,[a] land of Judah;
be glad and rejoice.
Surely the LORD has done great things![b]
22 Do not be afraid, you wild animals,
for the pastures in the wilderness are
becoming green.[c]
The trees are bearing their fruit;
the fig tree and the vine yield their
riches.[d]
23 Be glad, people of Zion,
rejoice[e] in the LORD your God,
for he has given you the autumn rains
because he is faithful.
He sends you abundant showers,
both autumn and spring rains,[f] as
before.
24 The threshing floors will be filled with
grain;
the vats will overflow[g] with new
wine[h] and oil.

2:19 [w] Jer 31:12 [x] Eze 34:29 **2:20** [y] Jer 1:14-15 [z] Isa 34:3 **2:21** [a] Isa 54:4; Zep 3:16-17 [b] Ps 126:3 **2:22** [c] Ps 65:12 [d] Joel 1:18-20 **2:23** [e] Ps 149:2; Isa 12:6; 41:16; Hab 3:18; Zec 10:7 [f] Lev 26:4 **2:24** [g] Lev 26:10; Mal 3:10 [h] Am 9:13

2:26 [i] Lev 26:5 [j] Isa 62:9 [k] Ps 126:3; Isa 25:1 **2:27** [l] Joel 3:17 **2:28** [m] Eze 39:29 **2:29** [n] 1Co 12:13; Gal 3:28 **2:30** [o] Lk 21:11 [p] Mk 13:24-25 **2:31** [q] Mt 24:29 [r] Isa 13:9-10; Mal 4:1,5

25 "I will repay you for the years the
locusts have eaten —
the great locust and the young locust,
the other locusts and the locust
swarm[a] —
my great army that I sent among you.
26 You will have plenty to eat, until you
are full,[i]
and you will praise[j] the name of the
LORD your God,
who has worked wonders[k] for you;
never again will my people be shamed.
27 Then you will know that I am in Israel,
that I am the LORD[l] your God,
and that there is no other;
never again will my people be shamed.

The Day of the LORD

28 "And afterward,
I will pour out my Spirit[m] on all
people.
Your sons and daughters will prophesy,
your old men will dream dreams,
your young men will see visions.
29 Even on my servants,[n] both men and
women,
I will pour out my Spirit in those
days.
30 I will show wonders in the heavens[o]
and on the earth,[p]
blood and fire and billows of smoke.
31 The sun will be turned to darkness[q]
and the moon to blood
before the coming of the great and
dreadful day of the LORD.[r]

[a] 25 The precise meaning of the four Hebrew words used here for locusts is uncertain.

particularly sacrilegious that 25 priests of the Lord worshiped the sun there (Eze 8:16) and that Zechariah was murdered there (2Ch 24:20–22).

2:20 *northern horde.* No doubt symbolizes the locust plague. The Assyrian "Hymn to Nanaya" (see note on 1:9) is similar in that it requests that the goddess command that the locusts disappear, similar to God removing them from the midst of Israel.

2:23 *autumn rains ... spring rains.* See note on Jer 5:24. Echoing the promises of Lev 26:3–4; Dt 11:13–15, Joel describes God's covenant loyalty toward Israel in regard to bringing rain. In contrast, the withholding of rain was seen as a sign of God's disfavor (Jer 3:3; Hos 6:3).

2:28 *pour out my Spirit.* The concept of having God's Spirit "poured out" on an individual signified election by the deity. This was done in Mesopotamia with the monarch, who was endowed with *melammu*, a word denoting the glory of the deity (see the article "Glory," p. 178). In fact, monarchs had their own *melammu*, which often, in context, meant "royal terror." Assyrian monarchs, such as Shalmaneser III and Shamshi-Adad V, described themselves in this way in their annals, especially in regard to the enemy: "I poured my *melammu* over them." Demons, and even inanimate objects, such as palaces and royal weapons, could also be endowed with this manifestation of divine presence. Moreover, the name of the Mesopotamian god of dreams, Zaqiqu, meant "wind/spirit," showing a connection, like that in Joel, between spirit and dream revelation. However, there was a darker side to this term; it also referred to phantoms or ghosts, haunted places, ruined cities (i.e., "ghost towns") or even nothingness. It is more likely that an Israelite of Joel's time would think in some of these terms rather than think of the third person of the Trinity. See note on Jdg 6:34.

2:31 *sun will be turned to darkness and the moon to blood.* This passage is no doubt describing solar and lunar eclipses, respectively, which were often considered evil omens in Mesopotamian society, portending disaster, especially to the nation or to the king. In fact, Mesopotamian kings sometimes abdicated their throne and had another sit on the throne until the eclipse (and bad omen) was over. In effect, it was hoped that the substitute king, not the true king, would thus endure the hardships associated with the eclipse (see the article "Substitutionary Rites," p. 1202).

The Neo-Assyrian kings were especially concerned about celestial observations and their explanations. Often, a new or full moon was predicted by scholars and reported to the king, especially if the omen was favorable. Interestingly, the nonoccurrence of lunar eclipses is periodically mentioned in the scholarly reports to the king, much to the relief of the monarch. However, a prediction that a lunar eclipse was probable gave the crown time to prepare for the oncoming danger. The scholars who

32 And everyone who calls
on the name of the LORD will be
saved;[s]
for on Mount Zion[t] and in Jerusalem
there will be deliverance,[u]
as the LORD has said,
even among the survivors[v]
whom the LORD calls.[a]

The Nations Judged

3 [b] "In those days and at that time,
when I restore the fortunes[w] of
Judah and Jerusalem,
2 I will gather all nations
and bring them down to the Valley
of Jehoshaphat.[c]
There I will put them on trial[x]
for what they did to my inheritance,
my people Israel,
because they scattered my people
among the nations
and divided up my land.
3 They cast lots for my people
and traded boys for prostitutes;
they sold girls for wine[y] to drink.

4 "Now what have you against me, Tyre
and Sidon[z] and all you regions of Philistia?
Are you repaying me for something I have
done? If you are paying me back, I will
swiftly and speedily return on your own
heads what you have done.[a] 5 For you took
my silver and my gold and carried off my
finest treasures to your temples.[d][b] 6 You
sold the people of Judah and Jerusalem to
the Greeks, that you might send them far
from their homeland.
7 "See, I am going to rouse them out of
the places to which you sold them,[c] and
I will return on your own heads what
you have done. 8 I will sell your sons[d] and
daughters to the people of Judah,[e] and
they will sell them to the Sabeans, a nation far away." The LORD has spoken.

9 Proclaim this among the nations:
Prepare for war![f]
Rouse the warriors![g]
Let all the fighting men draw near
and attack.
10 Beat your plowshares into swords
and your pruning hooks[h] into spears.

2:32 [s] Ac 2:17-21*; Ro 10:13* [t] Isa 46:13 [u] Ob 1:17 [v] Isa 11:11; Mic 4:7; Ro 9:27 **3:1** [w] Jer 16:15 **3:2** [x] Eze 36:5 **3:3** [y] Am 2:6 **3:4** [z] Mt 11:21 [a] Isa 34:8 **3:5** [b] 2Ch 21:16-17 **3:7** [c] Isa 43:5-6; Jer 23:8 **3:8** [d] Isa 60:14 [e] Isa 14:2 **3:9** [f] Isa 8:9 [g] Jer 46:4 **3:10** [h] Isa 2:4; Mic 4:3

[a] 32 In Hebrew texts 2:28-32 is numbered 3:1-5. [b] In Hebrew texts 3:1-21 is numbered 4:1-21.
[c] 2 *Jehoshaphat* means *the LORD judges*; also in verse 12.
[d] 5 Or *palaces*

predicted them also gave the monarch advice on how to proceed. We are not certain as to how the scholars determined the eclipse was going to happen, but the prediction was usually only a few days before the event.

Solar eclipses were rare and more difficult to predict. They were sometimes considered good omens for the king and particularly bad for his enemies, but here the connotation is negative. In one report, the time and even color of the solar eclipse was crucial to a favorable report. If it was red on the west side and rode the south wind, locusts would attack. However, if it occurred in Ziv/Iyyar (II) on the 28th day, the days of the king would be long, and the land would enjoy abundant business.

3:2 *Valley of Jehoshaphat.* Though there is no certainty as to the location of this valley, the Judahite king Jehoshaphat defeated a coalition of Moabites, Ammonites and Meunites in the vicinity of the Desert of Tekoa in the Valley of Berakah (means "blessing") (2Ch 20:20–26), which was so named because of Judah's victory.

3:4 *Tyre and Sidon ... regions of Philistia.* The historical incident referred to here is uncertain; perhaps this verse is simply referring to the common practice and reputation of these seaports. Tyre and Sidon were the leading port cities of Phoenicia from at least the late second millennium BC, controlling the sea trade routes to Egypt, Anatolia, the Aegean and beyond. The southern region of Philistia was also involved in trade in the first millennium BC.

3:6 *sold the people ... to the Greeks.* Slavery in the ancient Near East was not an economically productive institution. The palace economy was not complex enough to absorb a high number of slaves for supervision. Not until the Greco-Roman period did slavery become a powerfully viable economic force. Slaves were often foreigners who were prisoners of war, and they were often, as in the case in Joel, foreign slaves brought from abroad. They were often dedicated to the temple to serve the religious personnel. Members of the local population who went into debt were often sold into slavery, which was often temporary (until they were able to redeem themselves). Nevertheless, slave trade was a lucrative enterprise for some merchants. Slaves from Subartu in northern Mesopotamia were valued in Babylonian and Assyria in the Old Babylonian period. The Code of Hammurapi determined that the seller in many cases granted a one month "guarantee" that the slave would not run away or die. In the Neo-Assyrian period this was lengthened to 100 days. The average price of a slave in the late third millennium BC was between 10–15 shekels of silver, 20 shekels in the early second millennium BC, and 50–60 shekels in the Neo-Assyrian period. Though nothing is known for certain concerning slave trade from the coast of Canaan to the Greeks, the trading relationships between the Aegean and eastern Mediterranean in this period are well established. *Greeks.* Or Ionians (Biblical Javan, probably referring to Greek-speaking peoples from the western coast of Anatolia and the Aegean islands). They are mentioned in Assyrian sources by the eighth century BC during the reign of Sargon II (721–705 BC). Eze 27:13 also notes slave trade between Greece and Tyre in the sixth century BC.

3:8 *Sabeans.* The exact location of Sheba, or Saba, is uncertain, although it was most likely in south Arabia in present-day Yemen. However, the Saba are mentioned in Assyrian annals during the reigns of Tiglath-Pileser III (745–727 BC) and Sargon II (721–705 BC) in the vicinity of northern Arabia. It is possible that there was an expansion of the southern Sabeans to the north in this period. Sabeans are also known in the vicinity of Ethiopia in Africa.

3:10 *Beat your plowshares into swords and your pruning hooks into spears.* This is a reversal of the end of warfare described in Isa 2:2–4; Mic 4:1–4. Farmers are called up for military service and are to bring their agricultural implements, from which the blacksmith refashioned the seven-inch (17.75-centimeter) metal tip of the plowshare (or possibly a heavy hoe) into swords and pruning hooks (small knives used to remove leaves from grapevines)

Let the weakling[i] say,
"I am strong!"
11 Come quickly, all you nations from every side,
and assemble[j] there.

Bring down your warriors,[k] LORD!

12 "Let the nations be roused;
let them advance into the Valley of Jehoshaphat,
for there I will sit
to judge[l] all the nations on every side.
13 Swing the sickle,
for the harvest[m] is ripe.
Come, trample the grapes,
for the winepress[n] is full
and the vats overflow —
so great is their wickedness!"
14 Multitudes, multitudes
in the valley of decision!
For the day of the LORD[o] is near
in the valley of decision.
15 The sun and moon will be darkened,
and the stars no longer shine.
16 The LORD will roar from Zion
and thunder from Jerusalem;[p]
the earth and the heavens will tremble.[q]
But the LORD will be a refuge for his people,
a stronghold[r] for the people of Israel.

3:10 [i] Zec 12:8 **3:11** [j] Eze 38:15-16; Zep 3:8 [k] Isa 13:3 **3:12** [l] Isa 2:4 **3:13** [m] Hos 6:11; Mt 13:39; Rev 14:15-19 [n] Rev 14:20 **3:14** [o] Isa 34:2-8; Joel 1:15 **3:16** [p] Am 1:2 [q] Eze 38:19 [r] Jer 16:19

3:17 [s] Joel 2:27 [t] Isa 4:3 **3:18** [u] Ex 3:8 [v] Isa 30:25; 35:6 [w] Rev 22:1-2 [x] Eze 47:1; Am 9:13 **3:19** [y] Ob 1:10 **3:20** [z] Am 9:15 **3:21** [a] Eze 36:25

Blessings for God's People

17 "Then you will know that I, the LORD your God,[s]
dwell in Zion,[t] my holy hill.
Jerusalem will be holy;
never again will foreigners invade her.

18 "In that day the mountains will drip new wine,
and the hills will flow with milk;[u]
all the ravines of Judah will run with water.[v]
A fountain will flow out of the LORD's house[w]
and will water the valley of acacias.[a][x]
19 But Egypt will be desolate,
Edom a desert waste,
because of violence[y] done to the people of Judah,
in whose land they shed innocent blood.
20 Judah will be inhabited forever[z]
and Jerusalem through all generations.
21 Shall I leave their innocent blood unavenged?
No, I will not.[a]"

The LORD dwells in Zion!

a 18 Or *Valley of Shittim*

into spearheads. The plow was a single-furrow plow, a straight pole that was parallel to the ground, with a point or plowshare at the end. Before the Iron Age, many plowshares were made of either stone or bronze, and many have survived in archaeological excavations. The point of the plow broke up the hard ground in order to give the seeds a place to germinate during the winter months. A hoe was needed to smash the dirt clods and level the ground. At any rate, having a sharp point was crucial (see 1Sa 13:19–22).

3:15 The eighth-century BC Deir 'Alla "Plaster Inscription" describes Balaam's vision in which he saw the heavens with "dense cloud, / That darkness exists there, not brilliance." The similarity between that text and this verse lies in the contrast between the darkness and brilliance. Moreover, the Hebrew root, *nogah*, a term usually associated with the light of heavenly bodies, is also attested in the Balaam text.

3:18 *hills will flow with milk.* A number of scholars have seen parallels between various statements in Joel and Ugaritic literature from the second-millennium BC coastal Syria. One Ugaritic text depicts honey flowing in streams, while another describes Baal's return to life: "the heavens rain oil, the valleys flow with honey." These Ugaritic texts are similar to Joel in that they all reflect metaphors for prosperity. Israelites would have been reminded that there is a "land of milk and honey." *A fountain will flow out of the LORD's house.* The connection of spring waters and temples in the ancient Near East is well known from Mesopotamia and Ugarit in Syria. The temple was often associated with the waters of life that flowed from a spring within the building itself. In fact, the temple was considered as having been built upon a spring or the primeval waters of creation. The Sumerian Eninnu temple, built by Gudea of Lagash, rose up out of the primeval waters (Sumerian *apsu*), and was called the "foundation of the *apsu*." Many later-period Egyptian temples were considered a replica of the first temple fashioned on the primeval mound and the Nun, the abysmal waters. Even the Ugaritic Baal Cycle describes a temple founded upon springs, which even flowed from the building. The Mesopotamian creation epic *Enuma Elish* describes the foundation of the earth, with waters flowing from the divine Apsu. *valley of acacias.* Or Valley of Shittim (see NIV text note). Its location is not certain, but it may be the Wadi 'en-Nar, a continuation of the Kidron Valley that runs to the Dead Sea. However, it is possible that, like the Valley of Jehoshaphat (see note on v. 2), the valley of acacias has symbolic significance. Since acacias grow in dry places, the implication is that even the driest valley will have flowing water.

3:19 *shed innocent blood.* Both the Egyptians and Edomites are known to have plundered Israel in the past. The Egyptian monarchs Shishak I (1Ki 14:25–26; 2Ch 12:2–12), Osorkon I (see 2Ch 14:9–15 and note on 2Ch 14:9; 16:8) and Necho (2Ki 23:29–34) all attacked Israel (although Necho's attack in 609 BC may have been after Joel, depending upon when the book was written). The Edomites mistreated Judahite soldiers who fled from the Chaldeans/Babylonians in 586 BC, once again, perhaps later than Joel.

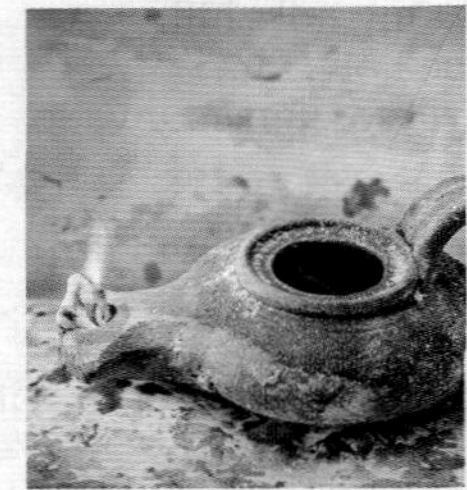

ORACLES OF THE PROPHETS

AMOS

The details of how the prophecies Amos delivered to Israel at Bethel came to be recorded remain unknown. It is impossible to determine whether he dictated his revelations to a scribe or composed them himself, or whether they were written down sometime later.

The book of Amos has traditionally been assigned to the middle or latter years of the reign of Jeroboam II (c. 760 BC). More recent historical investigation and chronological calculations have pushed the date for the writing of Amos's prophecies nearer 750 – 748 BC, just prior to the death of Jeroboam. This understanding is based on indications that the historical events alluded to in the book are reflections of a time when pro-Assyrian Israel was under assault by an anti-Assyrian coalition centered in Syro-Palestine. Amos ambiguously dated the words "he saw" (1:1) concerning Israel to the reigns of King Uzziah of Judah and King Jeroboam II of Israel. The reigns of both of these monarchs extended over a period of more than four decades. Politically and economically, both kings brought stability and prosperity to their respective kingdoms. Territorial borders were expanded through successful military conquest against foreign foes, Israel and Judah managed a peaceful coexistence and commercial enterprise and agricultural production burgeoned.

The reference to "the earthquake" (1:1) in the superscription provides little help in fixing the precise date of Amos's prophecy. Archaeological discoveries at sites like Samaria and Hazor attest such destruction by earthquake, and Zechariah's mention of the natural disaster (Zec 14:5) indicates that the tremor was long remembered in Israel. Yet attempts to pinpoint the year in which the quake occurred are highly speculative. Consequently, the time of Amos's prophetic activity is best assigned to the general time period ranging from 760 – 750 BC. ◆

KEY CONCEPTS

- Loving God and being compassionate and merciful to those around you are the values most desired by God.
- Israel is guilty of syncretism and injustice.
- The key theme of the prophets concerns whether the people will respond to God's warnings and instructions.

1 The words of Amos, one of the shepherds of Tekoa[a] — the vision he saw
concerning Israel two years before the
earthquake,[b] when Uzziah[c] was king of
Judah and Jeroboam[d] son of Jehoash[a] was
king of Israel.[e]
2 He said:

"The LORD roars[f] from Zion
and thunders from Jerusalem;[g]
the pastures of the shepherds dry up,
and the top of Carmel[h] withers."[i]

1:1 [a] 2Sa 14:2 [b] Zec 14:5 [c] 2Ch 26:23 [d] 2Ki 14:23 [e] Hos 1:1 **1:2** [f] Isa 42:13 [g] Joel 3:16 [h] Am 9:3 [i] Jer 12:4
1:3 [j] Isa 8:4; 17:1-3 [k] Am 2:6 **1:4** [l] Jer 49:27 [m] Jer 17:27 [n] 1Ki 20:1; 2Ki 6:24

Judgment on Israel's Neighbors

3 This is what the LORD says:

"For three sins of Damascus,[j]
even for four, I will not relent.[k]
Because she threshed Gilead
with sledges having iron teeth,
4 I will send fire[l] on the house of Hazael
that will consume the fortresses[m] of
Ben-Hadad.[n]

[a] *1* Hebrew *Joash,* a variant of *Jehoash*

1:1 *Amos.* Most OT characters are introduced with their patronymic ("son of...") or are at least qualified by a placename ("Micah of Moresheth," Mic 1:1). Amos is distinctive in having no further identification, but he is not unique in that sense. He is definitely not Isaiah's father (Isa 1:1) — their names differ even more in Hebrew than they do in English. His name was not uncommon in the ancient Levant; it appears on two seals from the same general area and period, and it also appears in Phoenician and Punic sources. It has a passive form and means simply "protected." *one of the shepherds.* Amos was a farmer by trade, not a professional or permanent prophet, as he later protests fiercely (7:14). However, the Hebrew word translated "shepherds" is not the usual one for someone who keeps sheep. It only occurs elsewhere in the OT in 2Ki 3:4 of King Mesha of Moab, who paid Israel an enormous tribute, and indicates someone who is a "sheep-breeder." In 7:14 "shepherd" translates a different Hebrew term that normally refers to cattle herding. So Amos probably kept a range of animals, though both Hebrew terms may be fairly general. Amos also describes himself as a dresser of "sycamore-fig trees" (7:14). This involves scraping or piercing the figs to hasten their growth and repel insects. However, sycamores grew in the western foothills and the Jordan Valley, not in Tekoa, so Amos was either a migrant worker to the former or, more probably, owned sycamore-fig groves in the latter. Either way, he was an ordinary farmer used to hard manual labor. *the earthquake.* Israel's territory lay along the geologic fault line running from Asia Minor to Africa's Great Rift Valley, so Israel was very prone to earthquakes. This one is not mentioned elsewhere (except perhaps Isa 5:25), but it must have been extremely strong, since it was cited centuries later to illustrate the upheaval of God's future appearing (Zec 14:5). This earthquake is now established in the archaeological record with evidence from excavations at Hazor, Gezer, Beersheba, and possibly Lachish, Deir 'Alla, Ashdod and Bethel. Earthquakes became a common prophetic motif of future calamity, and one is implied in Am 9:1, which uses the same Hebrew root for "shake." More important for Amos, this earthquake must have validated his ministry as a true prophet of Yahweh. *Uzziah... Jeroboam.* The kings named in Amos's date formula provide a range of time for his prophetic mission. Uzziah of Judah and Jeroboam II of Israel ruled for most of the first half of the eighth century BC. The earthquake cited here and attested by excavations at Hazor (Stratum VI) dates to approximately 760 BC. Since Amos claims not to be a professional prophet, many interpreters believe that the prophecies of this book would have covered a very short span of time rather than stretching over several decades.
1:2 *The LORD roars.* Normally it is lions that roar (as in 3:4,8). Here, the first divine comment on this complacent society was not reasoned argument but a blood-curdling leonine "roar" that withers all vegetation from lowland pasture to Mount Carmel's peak. *dry up... withers.* If literal, this suggests a devastating drought, often a mark of divine punishment, as it was for Ahab earlier (1Ki 17:1). If metaphoric, as is perhaps more likely, it is a chilling image of divine judgment (cf. Jer 25:30; Joel 3:16). Similarly the Sumerian Exaltation of Inanna acclaims: "When you roar at the earth like Thunder, no vegetation can stand up to you."
1:3 – 5 Damascus was the capital city of Israel's powerful northeastern neighbor, called both Syria (from the Greek geographic term) and, more commonly, Aram. This was often the most influential neighbor in the entire region. In building his empire David conquered it, but it regained freedom in Solomon's reign (1Ki 11:23 – 25) and was then involved in seemingly incessant warfare with Israel (e.g., 1Ki 20; 22). The Tell Dan Stele from the early divided monarchy recounts an Aramean defeat of the "House of David," while the reuse of this broken stele in a wall at Dan indicates Israelite recapture of the town.

At one point this long-running feud was suspended while Aram and Israel joined forces against the expansionist Assyrians under Shalmaneser III. The Assyrians later fought a coalition of western kings including Ahab at Qarqar (on the Orontes River in Syria) in 853 BC. They boasted of victory, but this is unlikely since they then fought repeated campaigns against similar coalitions in 849, 848 and 845 BC. Eventually the Assyrians retreated, not to reappear for another half century.

The prophets were also concerned with Aram. Elijah was to anoint Hazael (1Ki 19:15); Elisha actually did this and wept as he foresaw its terrible effect (2Ki 8:7 – 15). Hazael duly made his coup d'état and soon defeated Israel, reducing its military to ten token chariots (2Ki 13:7). However, the Assyrians then returned and subdued Aram, leaving Israel free to expand territorially and progress economically. This was the key political factor behind Israel's prosperity in the time of Amos.

Israel's northeasterly region of Gilead was often invaded by Aram (cf. 1Ki 22:3), but there is no other record of the atrocity condemned here. Since Israel had long recovered all its territory, including Gilead, this judgment must indict Aram for a former crime, which apparently consisted of driving threshing sledges over prostrate prisoners. Shortly after Amos, the Assyrian Tiglath-Pileser III boasted of the region Bit-Sha'alli, "I threshed as though with a threshing sledge."

God's judgment would fall specifically on the royal dynasty of the usurper Hazael (843 – 796 BC) and his son Ben-Hadad III (796 – 770 BC), as well as on Damascus. It would also fall on the Valley of Aven and Beth Eden, two places mentioned because of their verbal associations (see the article "Playing With Place-Names," p. 1482). The first plays on the name of a local valley ("Aven" means wickedness); the second, probably on the city-state Bit-Adini, located by the Euphrates River in the far north. With poetic justice, the Arameans would return to Kir, which Amos later cites as their place of origin (9:7). Kir was probably just north of the Persian Gulf, since elsewhere it

AMOS 1:3 — 2:3

Amos's Judgments Against Foreign Nations

Amos's judgments first address neighboring nations. Such judgments are common in Israelite prophecy (cf. Isa 13 – 23; Jer 46 – 51; Eze 25 – 32) but are rare in other ancient traditions. There is no evidence that they were ever delivered to the named recipients. Rather, they are part of the prophet's rhetorical strategy: here Amos is inviting agreement and sympathy from his immediate audience before addressing them directly.

Amos crisscrosses Israel: northeast (Damascus in Am 1:2 – 5), southwest (Gaza/Philistia in Am 1:6 – 8), northwest (Tyre in Am 1:9 – 10), and finally southeast and east (Edom, Ammon, Moab in Am 1:11 — 2:3). All these states were subdued by David and most were incorporated into his empire by treaty, though they all became independent on the death of Solomon. Their fortunes varied over the next two centuries, and by Amos's time the northern states were increasingly threatened by Assyria.

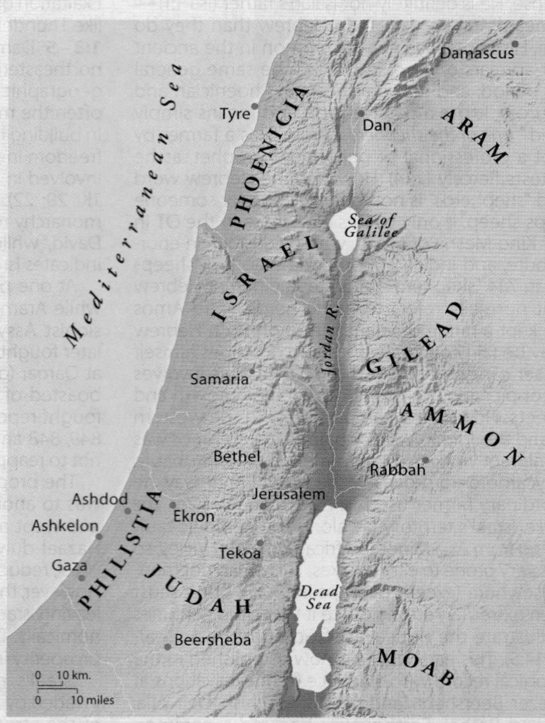

Nations and cities mentioned in Amos.

These judgments against foreign nations are very similar in form, but each is slightly different. The opening numerical statement is the same (Am 1:3,6,9,11,13; 2:1), but other aspects often vary, e.g., the number of places named, the declaration of punishment, the length of the judgment, the concluding messenger formula. This shows skillful use of elegant variation.

Except for Judah (Am 2:4 – 5), the nations are condemned for what we call "crimes against humanity." Even in ancient times certain activities were reprehensible to everyone. ◆

AMOS 1:3 — 2:6

"For Three ... Even for Four"

We sometimes use "101" to mean "a great many." We don't mean "101" literally; the number simply conveys the idea of one more than an already large figure. Ancient Semitic peoples had a similar idiom; they would give a number and then add one more, usually to convey "enough and more than enough." This pattern of "x then x + 1" can be seen in several Biblical texts, particularly wisdom books: (Job 5:19; 33:14,29; Ps 62:11; Pr 6:16; 30:15,18,21,29; Mic 5:5). Similar examples can be found in Akkadian, Hittite, Egyptian, Ugaritic, Aramaic and Greek literature; e.g., Ugaritic texts use "seven brothers, eight mother's sons." ◆

5 I will break down the gate[o] of
Damascus;
I will destroy the king who is in[a] the
Valley of Aven[b]
and the one who holds the scepter in
Beth Eden.
The people of Aram will go into exile
to Kir,[p]"
says the LORD.

6 This is what the LORD says:

"For three sins of Gaza,[q]
even for four, I will not relent.
Because she took captive whole
communities
and sold them to Edom,[r]
7 I will send fire on the walls of Gaza
that will consume her fortresses.
8 I will destroy the king[c] of Ashdod[s]
and the one who holds the scepter in
Ashkelon.
I will turn my hand[t] against Ekron,
till the last of the Philistines[u] are dead,"
says the Sovereign LORD.[v]

9 This is what the LORD says:

"For three sins of Tyre,[w]
even for four, I will not relent.
Because she sold whole communities
of captives to Edom,
disregarding a treaty of brotherhood,
10 I will send fire on the walls of Tyre
that will consume her fortresses.[x]"

11 This is what the LORD says:

"For three sins of Edom,[y]
even for four, I will not relent.
Because he pursued his brother with a
sword
and slaughtered the women of the
land,
because his anger raged continually
and his fury flamed unchecked,[z]
12 I will send fire on Teman[a]
that will consume the fortresses of
Bozrah."

1:5 [o] Jer 51:30 [p] 2Ki 16:9 **1:6** [q] 1Sa 6:17; Zep 2:4 [r] Ob 1:11 **1:8** [s] 2Ch 26:6 [t] Ps 81:14 [u] Eze 25:16 [v] Isa 14:28-32; Zep 2:4-7 **1:9** [w] 1Ki 5:1; 9:11-14; Isa 23:1-18; Jer 25:22; Joel 3:4; Mt 11:21 **1:10** [x] Zec 9:1-4 **1:11** [y] Nu 20:14-21; 2Ch 28:17; Jer 49:7-22 [z] Eze 25:12-14 **1:12** [a] Ob 1:9-10

[a] 5 Or *the inhabitants of* [b] 5 *Aven* means *wickedness.* [c] 8 Or *inhabitants*

is linked with Elam/Persia (Isa 22:6). Barely 20 years after this judgment, in 733 – 732 BC, the Assyrians duly fulfilled this prophecy (2Ki 16:9).

1:6 – 8 Gaza was probably the largest of the Philistine cities. Here it represents the whole people, with the other cities mentioned later (v. 8). Historically, the Philistines were Israel's second most powerful enemy (see notes on Ge 21:32; Jdg 3:3; Isa 14:29), and they were sometimes paired with Aram in prophetic texts (e.g., 9:7; Isa 9:12). Here the Philistines are condemned for raiding Israelite villages and enslaving their inhabitants. The victims are unnamed, and could have been either neighboring Judahites or more northerly Israelites. Such raiding for slavery was common in the ancient world. The Philistines are also condemned in Joel 3:4 – 8, where the prophet foretells God's repayment in kind. Here Edom was possibly acting as Gaza's agent to sell these unfortunate people (cf. Joel 3:8). While the Philistines' punishment is very similar to that of the Arameans, no kings are named, perhaps because their kings ruled collectively. The Assyrian advance led to the conquest of Philistia in 734 BC and the ongoing suppression of various subsequent revolts.

1:9 – 10 Tyre was an ancient maritime city, built on an island just off the Mediterranean coast about 35 miles (56 kilometers) north of the Mount Carmel headland. Founded in the third millennium BC, it is mentioned in several ancient Near Eastern sources in the third and second millennia BC and frequently in Biblical texts in the first millennium BC. Tyre and Sidon were the two main Phoenician cities, with preeminence varying through time. See notes on Isa 23:1 – 18; Jer 47:4.

1:11 – 12 For Edom, see notes on Jer 49:7; Eze 32:29. Shortly after the time of Amos, the Edomites recaptured the southern port and held it from then onward. Later,

AMOS 1:5

PLAYING WITH PLACE-NAMES

Israel's writers generally enjoyed wordplays with names, and the prophets often made puns with place-names. The longest example is Mic 1:10–15 (see notes on Mic 1:10–16; see also the chart "Proposed Dates for the Book of Micah," p. 1517). Occasionally they would change names to make a point, e.g., Bethel (meaning "House of God") is sometimes dubbed Beth Aven (meaning "House of Wickedness") (Hos 4:15; Am 4:4).

Another example of toying with names (though not used in Amos) is the so-called Atbash device. The name comes from the Hebrew consonants, ʾ, *T*, *B*, *Sh*, which are, respectively, the first, last, second, and second-to-last letters of the Hebrew alphabet (the equivalent in English is *A*, *Z*, *B*, *Y*). In this cryptic device, the letters of a name counted from the beginning of the alphabet are replaced by those counted from the end, e.g., Babylon (*BBL*) becomes Sheshak (*ShShK* [Jer 51:41]), Chaldea becomes Leb Kamai (Jer 51:1). ◆

13 This is what the LORD says:

"For three sins of Ammon,[b]
even for four, I will not relent.
Because he ripped open the pregnant
women[c] of Gilead
in order to extend his borders,
14 I will set fire to the walls of Rabbah[d]
that will consume her fortresses
amid war cries[e] on the day of battle,
amid violent winds on a stormy day.
15 Her king[a] will go into exile,
he and his officials together,"
says the LORD.

1:13 [b] Jer 49:1-6; Eze 21:28; 25:2-7 [c] Hos 13:16 **1:14** [d] Dt 3:11 [e] Am 2:2

2 This is what the LORD says:

"For three sins of Moab,
even for four, I will not relent.
Because he burned to ashes
the bones of Edom's king,
2 I will send fire on Moab
that will consume the fortresses of
Kerioth.[b]
Moab will go down in great tumult
amid war cries and the blast of the
trumpet.

[a] *15* Or / *Molek* [b] *2* Or *of her cities*

when Jerusalem fell to the Babylonians, the treachery of the Edomites and their appropriation of Judahite land was bitterly denounced (Ps 137:7; Eze 25:12–14; Ob 10–14; cf. also Joel 3:19). Edom, already featured in these judgments (Am 1:6,9), is now directly condemned for fighting its own "brother" (i.e., Israel and Judah), and doing so mercilessly. The former charge is often made elsewhere; the latter is stressed in three synonymous phrases (v. 11), making this the most emotionally charged judgment. God would destroy its two key cities: Teman, the southern capital, and Bozrah, the northern fortress town.

1:13–15 For Ammon, see note on Jer 49:1. The crime indicted here is not otherwise known, but it would fit well in the late ninth century BC, when Aram/Syria oppressed Gilead from the north (v. 3; see note on vv. 3–5), leaving Ammon unchallenged to attack from the east. Such assaults on pregnant women were occasionally featured in ancient warfare, especially when an army wanted to terrorize and decimate the local residents (see note on Hos 13:16). There are three other OT references to it, all in the ninth to eighth centuries BC. Elisha and Hosea predicted this fate for Israel itself (2Ki 8:12; Hos 13:16), and the usurper Menahem did this to a town that resisted his coup d'état in Israel's anarchic final years (2Ki 15:16). There are also two Mesopotamian references from different periods to this practice.

In punishment, the capital city of Rabbah will again be breached and its hierarchy exiled. This judgment is the first to portray noisy battle (see also 2:2) and the only one to envisage a violent storm. Tempest and whirlwind are common metaphors of battle in Akkadian sources, e.g., "I blew against the enemy like the onrush of a raging storm." They are also frequently used in connection with Yahweh in Biblical texts (2Ki 2:1; Job 38:1; Eze 1:4) and of warrior gods executing divine judgment in general.

2:1–3 For Moab, see notes on Ge 19:37–38; Dt 2:9; see also the article "Moab," p. 450. Here Moab is condemned for burning the Edomite king's bones, probably after disinterring his corpse. Cremation was virtually unknown in the Semitic world (see note on 6:10), and this act of violation was reprehensible. The implication of burning the body may be, as the Targum explains, that the ash was then used for whitewash, an ultimate humiliation. Even the dead deserved some respect. While not the Moabite capital, Kerioth (v. 2) is highlighted for punishment probably because it contained the main shrine to their chief god Chemosh, as the Mesha Stele records.

3 I will destroy her ruler[f]
and kill all her officials with him,"[g]
says the LORD.

4 This is what the LORD says:

"For three sins of Judah,[h]
even for four, I will not relent.
Because they have rejected the law[i] of
the LORD
and have not kept his decrees,[j]
because they have been led astray[k] by
false gods,[a][l]
the gods[b] their ancestors followed,[m]
5 I will send fire on Judah
that will consume the fortresses of
Jerusalem.[n]"

Judgment on Israel

6 This is what the LORD says:

"For three sins of Israel,
even for four, I will not relent.
They sell the innocent for silver,
and the needy for a pair of
sandals.[o]
7 They trample on the heads of the
poor
as on the dust of the ground
and deny justice to the oppressed.
Father and son use the same girl
and so profane my holy name.[p]
8 They lie down beside every altar
on garments taken in pledge.[q]
In the house of their god
they drink wine[r] taken as fines.

9 "Yet I destroyed the Amorites[s] before
them,
though they were tall as the cedars
and strong as the oaks.
I destroyed their fruit above
and their roots[t] below.
10 I brought you up out of Egypt[u]
and led you forty years in the
wilderness[v]
to give you the land of the Amorites.[w]

11 "I also raised up prophets[x] from among
your children
and Nazirites[y] from among your
youths.
Is this not true, people of Israel?"
declares the LORD.
12 "But you made the Nazirites drink
wine
and commanded the prophets not to
prophesy.[z]

13 "Now then, I will crush you
as a cart crushes when loaded with
grain.
14 The swift will not escape,
the strong[a] will not muster their
strength,
and the warrior will not save his life.[b]
15 The archer[c] will not stand his ground,
the fleet-footed soldier will not get
away,
and the horseman will not save his
life.

2:3 [f]Ps 2:10 [g]Isa 40:23 **2:4** [h]2Ki 17:19; Hos 12:2 [i]Jer 6:19 [j]Eze 20:24 [k]Isa 9:16 [l]Isa 28:15 [m]2Ki 22:13; Jer 16:12 **2:5** [n]Jer 17:27; Hos 8:14 **2:6** [o]Joel 3:3; Am 8:6 **2:7** [p]Am 5:11-12; 8:4 **2:8** [q]Ex 22:26 [r]Am 4:1; 6:6 **2:9** [s]Nu 21:23-26; Jos 10:12 [t]Eze 17:9; Mal 4:1 **2:10** [u]Ex 20:2; Am 3:1 [v]Dt 2:7 [w]Ex 3:8; Am 9:7 **2:11** [x]Dt 18:18; Jer 7:25 [y]Nu 6:2-3; Jdg 13:5 **2:12** [z]Isa 30:10; Jer 11:21; Am 7:12-13; Mic 2:6 **2:14** [a]Jer 9:23 [b]Ps 33:16; Isa 30:16-17 **2:15** [c]Eze 39:3

[a] 4 *Or by lies* [b] 4 *Or lies*

2:4–5 Judah was the sister kingdom of Israel, and the ancient rivalry between them doubtless engendered much applause for Amos from among the listening audience of the northern kingdom as Amos condemns his homeland. However, Judah is cited not for crimes against humanity, like the other nations, but for neglecting Yahweh's law and breaking the first commandment. Archaeological discovery gives occasional support to the Biblical portrayal of idolatry in Judah and Israel.

2:6 *For three sins of Israel, even for four.* As Amos hones in on his main target, he begins with not just one sin but several sins: enslavement, judicial corruption, sexual perversion, and economic exploitation. *sell the innocent.* May be a specific example of judicial corruption rather than the slavery condemned previously. *a pair of sandals.* Either indicates a trifling amount, refers proverbially to bypassing legal traditions enacted by sandal removal (cf. Dt 25:9; Ru 4:7), or is a mistranslation of a rare synonym for "bribe."

2:7 *use the same girl.* Does not refer to general or cultic prostitution, since the sin here is that father and son are both involved. More likely this is exploitation of female bond servants who marry into the household (Ex 21:7–11; cf. Dt 22:30) but are not given proper honor and protection.

2:8 *garments taken in pledge.* They should be returned to the poor before sunset (Ex 22:26–27; Dt 24:12–13), since they were needed as blankets.

2:11 *Nazirites.* See the article "Nazirites," p. 242. The variant "Nazirite-for-life" is not noted in legal texts but is illustrated with Samson and Samuel (Jdg 13:5–7; 1Sa 1:11). Amos probably refers to the latter and sees it as a divine calling similar to that of a prophet. This is the only reference to Nazirites as a well-known phenomenon, here in poetic parallel with prophets. Perhaps they flourished for a short period in Amos's day, possibly as a response to the corruption of society that Amos denounces. By the late postexilic period, Nazirite vows were again well known, though they were almost entirely personal vows and for limited periods. There are several instances recorded in Josephus as well as those implied in Ac 18:18; 21:23–24. The Mishnah stipulates that the Nazirite vow must last at least 30 days. There is no obvious parallel in other ancient cultures of ordinary people (i.e., those not priests or prophets) undertaking temporary or permanent restrictions for religious reasons other than personal vows.

2:14–16 *The swift … the strong … the warrior … The archer … the fleet-footed soldier … the horseman … the bravest warriors.* The entire Israelite military force is covered by this sevenfold description. The term "bravest warriors" (v. 16) probably means "charioteers," since chariots were a common feature of ancient warfare from early times in, e.g., Egypt (Ex 14:7), Canaan (Jdg 4:3), Philistines (1Sa 13:5), Israel (1Ki 10:26) and Syria (1Ki 20:20–21). However, 1Ki 20:20–21 shows that armies could also have cavalry, though it is unclear when cavalry became widespread; some 50 years later the Assyrians mocked Judah for having so few men able to ride horses. Amos declares that all these powerful forces cannot withstand divine judgment.

AMOS 2:6–8

Economic Changes and Social Classes in Eighth-Century BC Israel

In the light of political changes that took place at the beginning of the eighth century BC (Assyrian expansion and the capture of Damascus), Israel was able to widen its economic interests and restore its hegemony over a greater area of the Transjordan. In addition, both Israel and Judah will be ruled during the first half of the century by strong kings (Jeroboam II and Uzziah, respectively) with long reigns. This made it easier to establish a comprehensive economic policy that concentrated on the mass production of export items such as grain, olive oil and wine. Large areas of the Shephelah and the lowland valleys had already been given over to wheat production (2Ch 26:10). Now, in the eighth century BC, the elite were able to impose this economic policy on the small hill country farms and villages. As a result, previous agricultural strategies that attempted to distribute potential risks between herding and farming were given over to specific cash crops, and the smaller holdings of the peasant farmers, who were overburdened with debts, were enclosed into large estates. This very efficient use of the land, however, eliminated the mixed crops that had formerly been grown in the village culture and more quickly exhausted the soil. Fallowing and grazing animals on harvested fields would have been eliminated or rigidly controlled. Under this new policy, an attempt was made to increase exports to the extent that there was a real hunger problem for the peasant class, while the nobility and merchant class were able to indulge in the luxury goods supplied by their Phoenician trading partners. Thus, in addition to facing rising prices at home on basic goods, such as wheat and barley, the impoverished, former peasant farmers now found themselves forced into debt servitude or day labor. Seeing them ground under the heel of exploiting employers and cheated by greedy merchants who sold them adulterated or inferior

continued on next page

[16]Even the bravest warriors[d]
will flee naked on that day,"
declares the LORD.

Witnesses Summoned Against Israel

3 Hear this word, people of Israel, the word the LORD has spoken against you—against the whole family I brought up out of Egypt:[e]

[2]"You only have I chosen[f]
of all the families of the earth;
therefore I will punish you
for all your sins.[g]"

[3]Do two walk together
unless they have agreed to do so?
[4]Does a lion roar in the thicket
when it has no prey?[h]
Does it growl in its den
when it has caught nothing?
[5]Does a bird swoop down to a trap on
the ground
when no bait is there?
Does a trap spring up from the ground
if it has not caught anything?
[6]When a trumpet sounds in a city,
do not the people tremble?

2:16 [d]Jer 48:41 **3:1** [e]Am 2:10 **3:2** [f]Dt 7:6; Lk 12:47 [g]Jer 14:10 **3:4** [h]Ps 104:21; Hos 5:14

3:2 *chosen.* The Hebrew verb means "know." The same idiom of a god knowing a family is used in Akkadian texts to describe the care that family gods provide for their worshipers.

3:3–6 The seven rhetorical questions in these verses stress that every effect has a cause, and the seventh question makes clear that the coming disaster will be caused by the Lord. The images give cameos of ordinary life: traveling together, growling lions, bird hunting, and warning of danger.

3:6 *trumpet.* The shofar; it was made of a ram's horn and

grain for their meals, it is no wonder that Amos harangued the rich for their lack of concern for the poor. In such an atmosphere of social injustice, agricultural specialization and economic speculation, the prophet reminds the Israelites of their covenant obligations. Amos warns them that corrupt judges and dishonest businessmen can expect no mercy from an angry God. Similarly, in the twentieth-century BC Egyptian tale of the "Eloquent Peasant," we find a commoner using impressive rhetoric to admonish the pharaoh about the importance of justice. ◆

Wheat in the Huleh Valley. Eighth-century kings concentrated on the mass production of export items such as grain, olive oil and wine.

Wikimedia Commons

When disaster comes to a city,
has not the LORD caused it?[i]

7 Surely the Sovereign LORD does nothing
without revealing his plan[j]
to his servants the prophets.[k]

8 The lion has roared—
who will not fear?
The Sovereign LORD has spoken—
who can but prophesy?[l]

9 Proclaim to the fortresses of Ashdod
and to the fortresses of Egypt:
"Assemble yourselves on the
mountains of Samaria;[m]

see the great unrest within her
and the oppression among her
people."

10 "They do not know how to do right,[n]"
declares the LORD,
"who store up in their fortresses[o]
what they have plundered[p] and
looted."

11 Therefore this is what the Sovereign
LORD says:

"An enemy will overrun your land,
pull down your strongholds
and plunder your fortresses.[q]"

3:6 [i] Isa 14:24-27; 45:7 **3:7** [j] Ge 18:17; Da 9:22; Jn 15:15; Rev 10:7 [k] Jer 23:22 **3:8** [l] Jer 20:9; Jnh 1:1-3; 3:1-3; Ac 4:20 **3:9** [m] Am 4:1; 6:1 **3:10** [n] Jer 4:22; Am 5:7; 6:12 [o] Zep 1:9 [p] Hab 2:8 **3:11** [q] Am 2:5; 6:14

was used in ordinary contexts and in religious celebrations as well as to signal danger (see note on Jos 6:4).
3:11 *An enemy.* Overshadowing the preaching of Amos but unmentioned in the book is the emerging power of Assyria. Assyria had been an important empire in the fourteenth to eleventh centuries BC but then declined. In the ninth century BC it reemerged and advanced westward, to be checked by western states at Qarqar in

[12]This is what the LORD says:

"As a shepherd rescues from the lion's[r] mouth
only two leg bones or a piece of an ear,
so will the Israelites living in Samaria be rescued,
with only the head of a bed
and a piece of fabric[a] from a couch.[b][s]"

[13]"Hear this and testify[t] against the descendants of Jacob," declares the Lord, the
LORD God Almighty.

[14]"On the day I punish Israel for her sins,
I will destroy the altars of Bethel;[u]
the horns of the altar will be cut off
and fall to the ground.
[15]I will tear down the winter house[v]
along with the summer house;[w]
the houses adorned with ivory[x] will be destroyed
and the mansions will be demolished,"
declares the LORD.

3:12 [r] 1Sa 17:34 [s] Am 6:4 **3:13** [t] Eze 2:7 **3:14** [u] Am 5:5-6 **3:15** [v] Jer 36:22 [w] Jdg 3:20 [x] 1Ki 22:39

[a] *12* The meaning of the Hebrew for this phrase is uncertain. [b] *12* Or *Israelites be rescued, / those who sit in Samaria / on the edge of their beds / and in Damascus on their couches.*

853 BC. A decade later the Assyrians conducted another campaign westward and exacted tribute from Jehu, as portrayed on the Black Obelisk now in the British Museum. However, these were more raids than conquests, and they then remained beyond Israel's horizon for nearly a century. But now, in the mid-eighth century BC, they are again advancing westward. Amos sees this ominous development but doesn't name them; a little later Hosea names them repeatedly. In 722 BC Assyria conquered Samaria and exiled many Israelites (2Ki 17).

3:12 *As a shepherd rescues … two leg bones or a piece of an ear.* In Israel (Ex 22:13) and elsewhere, a shepherd was not responsible for animals devoured by wild beasts. However, he had to provide evidence, hence the need to rescue any uneaten bones and scraps. This powerful image is applied to Israel: only a few useless scraps will remain.

3:14 *altars of Bethel.* After the division of the nation of Israel into the northern kingdom of Israel and the southern kingdom of Judah, Israel's first king, Jeroboam I, built temples at Dan in the north and Bethel in the south of his new kingdom to prevent its people from traveling to Jerusalem (1Ki 12:26–30). The Dan temple faded from view, while the Bethel one became the national and royal shrine (cf. Am 7:13) and received repeated prophetic censure. This is the only reference to Bethel altars in the plural—presumably the main altar was complemented by others. *horns of the altar.* See notes on Ex 30:2; Jer 17:1.

3:15 *winter house … summer house … houses adorned with ivory … mansions.* The four types of residence mentioned here clearly include the whole range of wealthy homes, all to be swept away in divine judgment (similarly in 6:11). Ahab had a summer residence in the capital city of Samaria and a winter one in the warmer Jezreel Valley (1Ki 21:1,18). His city palace was even "adorned with ivory" (1Ki 22:39), a sign of wealth and prestige (cf. Ps 45:8, which describes a royal wedding). A century later many others had apparently followed Ahab's example of extravagance, since excavations at Samaria have revealed many fine ivory decorations that testify to a luxurious lifestyle. These display sphinxes (i.e., cherubim), palm fronds typical of Bronze Age ivories, and a variety of animal, human and other newer motifs that

AMOS 2:11

PROPHETS

Amos was chronologically the first of the "writing prophets," i.e., those whose preaching was preserved with other material in books named after them. But he was certainly not the first prophet. In the Pentateuch the term is used of Abraham, Miriam, the 70 elders, the non-Israelite Balaam, and of course Moses, the prophet *par excellence*. In the premonarchy era there were the prophetess Deborah, an unnamed prophet (1Sa 2:27), Samuel, and various groups of prophets, while in the united monarchy we read of Gad and Nathan. Then in the two centuries or so of the divided kingdoms before Amos, there was a long succession of prophets: Ahijah, Shemaiah, Jehu, Micaiah, Elijah and Elisha, as well as many unnamed individuals, and the 'sons of the prophets' with whom Elijah and Elisha associated. And of course there were many false prophets in Israel, including the prophets of Baal and Asherah.

There was great variety in all aspects of prophetic activity and life. The groups of Samuel's time prophesied in an ecstatic frenzy, which enveloped Saul when he met them. Similarly, Elisha requested the stimulus of music in order to prophesy. By

continued on next page

Israel Has Not Returned to God

4 Hear this word, you cows of Bashan[y]
on Mount Samaria,[z]
you women who oppress the poor
and crush the needy
and say to your husbands, "Bring us
some drinks![a]"
2 The Sovereign LORD has sworn by his
holiness:
"The time will surely come
when you will be taken away[b] with
hooks,
the last of you with fishhooks.[a]
3 You will each go straight out
through breaches in the wall,[c]
and you will be cast out toward
Harmon,[b]"
declares the LORD.
4 "Go to Bethel and sin;
go to Gilgal[d] and sin yet more.
Bring your sacrifices every
morning,[e]
your tithes[f] every three years.[c][g]
5 Burn leavened bread[h] as a thank
offering
and brag about your freewill
offerings[i] —

4:1 [y] Ps 22:12; Eze 39:18 [z] Am 3:9 [a] Am 2:8; 5:11; 8:6 **4:2** [b] Am 6:8 **4:3** [c] Eze 12:5 **4:4** [d] Hos 4:15 [e] Nu 28:3 [f] Dt 14:28 [g] Eze 20:39; Am 5:21-22 **4:5** [h] Lev 7:13 [i] Lev 22:18-21

[a] 2 Or *away in baskets, / the last of you in fish baskets*
[b] 3 Masoretic Text; with a different word division of the Hebrew (see Septuagint) *out, you mountain of oppression*
[c] 4 Or *days*

show both Egyptian and Syrian influences. They were probably all luxurious imports.

4:1 *cows of Bashan.* Bashan was the fertile tableland northeast of the Jordan. It was prime cattle country, and its animals were renowned. Here it is used as a stinging epithet for the capital's women, who are rich, idle, pampered and inevitably fatter than those whom they have reduced to poverty.

4:2 *hooks ... fishhooks.* The exact meaning of these two terms is uncertain. If this common translation is correct, the verse may refer to a standard form of Assyrian cruelty to captives that is depicted in many reliefs and texts. In any case, it presages humiliating treatment.

4:3 *Harmon.* Since this word occurs only here, there have been a number of suggestions on its meaning. Some scholars consider it a place-name and thus the place where the captives are exiles. Among the suggestions here are Mount Minni in Assyria (see Jer 51:27) or Hermal, near Kadesh on the Orontes River. For those who emend the text, the translation of "dung heap" for *hadmon* (exchanging a single letter) is the most likely, since it is a suitable place for the disposal of the bodies of prisoners.

4:4–5 Amos's impressive array of rhetorical devices includes sarcastic mockery. Gilgal lay in the Jordan Valley just northeast of Jericho. It became an important cult center alongside Bethel (cf. 5:5; 1Sa 7:16; Hos 4:15). The sacrifices and offerings mentioned here echo those prescribed in Lev 1–7, though the northern kingdom may have developed its own versions in its schismatic worship (cf. 1Ki 12:32–33).

4:4 *years.* Lit. "days" (see NIV text note). It may refer to (1) an otherwise unknown practice of offering tithes on the third day of pilgrimage, (2) tithes offered every few days ("three" in Hebrew sometimes means "several"), or (3) possibly the triennial tithe (cf. Dt 14:28–29; the Hebrew "days" in the plural sometimes indicates extended time). Whatever their exact rhythm, tithes, like offerings, were plentiful.

contrast, Nathan confronted David after his terrible sin with a carefully prepared story. Many of these prophets seemed to live on their own, while others seemed to share a communal life. Some lived in the country and were visited by ordinary people on "high days and holy days," while others lived in the city and were consulted by royalty.

There may have been development over time. An important aside in the Samuel story tells us that the term "prophet" replaced the older term "seer" (although "prophet" also occurs in the early accounts, and "man of God" occurs in various texts). The groups of prophets prevalent in the times of Samuel (eleventh century BC) and Elisha (ninth century BC) seem to have faded from view by the time of Amos (eighth century BC). Perhaps they offered social and spiritual responses to oppression and apostasy that were more appropriate in some periods than in others.

Recent discoveries and study have revealed much about prophets in other ancient Near Eastern societies. It is hardly surprising that they existed; any society that believes in contact between the human and the divine will inevitably have human intermediaries. This material is being increasingly studied, and one writer notes that "the more we learn about the non-Israelite version [of prophecy], the less wide the gap between it and its Israelite counterpart appears." Certainly there are many similarities of social function and oracular form. Yet certain key differences remain. Non-Israelite prophecy almost entirely lacks three important features: a sense of prophetic call, a challenge to king and people, and an ethical concern. These loom large in Biblical prophecy, not the least in Amos. ◆

AMOS 3:7

THE "SOVEREIGN LORD"

"Sovereign LORD" is Amos's favorite title for God, occurring 21 times in the book of Amos. It is literally "Lord Yahweh" (Hebrew *adonay yhwh*). However, by the late postexilic era many Jews felt that, in order not to misuse the name of Yahweh (Ex 20:7), they should not pronounce it at all. So instead they used the title "Lord" (Hebrew *adonay*) whenever they came to *yhwh* in the Hebrew text. This practice was continued when they translated their Scriptures into Greek. Thus the Septuagint (the pre-Christian Greek translation of the OT) and other translations use the Greek equivalent *kurios* (Lord) when translating the Hebrew *yhwh*. This is one reason the NT often refers to God as "Lord." Most English Bible translations have followed this precedent, representing the Hebrew *yhwh* by the word "LORD" (using small capitals to distinguish it from *adonay*, "Lord"). See the article "God's Name," p. 112.

In light of this, the compound Hebrew name *adonay yhwh* in Amos and elsewhere obviously poses a problem for translators. To read it as *adonay adonay* or to translate it as "Lord LORD" would sound odd. So when *yhwh* immediately follows *adonay*, the Jewish tradition was to read it not as a second *adonay* but as *elohim* ("God"). Many English translations follow this practice with "Lord GOD" (again using small capitals for GOD). However, the NIV takes a different line, and translates "Sovereign LORD." While this is not an exact translation, it captures something of the force of bringing the two words together. And it is very appropriate in the book of Amos, which stresses Yahweh's sovereignty. ◆

boast about them, you Israelites,
for this is what you love to do,"
declares the Sovereign LORD.

6 "I gave you empty stomachs in every city
and lack of bread in every town,
yet you have not returned to me,"
declares the LORD.[j]

7 "I also withheld rain from you
when the harvest was still three months away.
I sent rain on one town,
but withheld it from another.[k]
One field had rain;
another had none and dried up.
8 People staggered from town to town for water[l]
but did not get enough to drink,
yet you have not returned[m] to me,"
declares the LORD.[n]

9 "Many times I struck your gardens and vineyards,
destroying them with blight and mildew.[o]
Locusts devoured your fig and olive trees,[p]
yet you have not returned[q] to me,"
declares the LORD.

10 "I sent plagues[r] among you
as I did to Egypt.
I killed your young men with the sword,
along with your captured horses.
I filled your nostrils with the stench of your camps,
yet you have not returned to me,"
declares the LORD.[s]

4:6 [j] Isa 3:1; Jer 5:3; Hag 2:17 **4:7** [k] Ex 9:4, 26; Dt 11:17; 2Ch 7:13 **4:8** [l] Eze 4:16-17 [m] Jer 3:7 [n] Jer 14:4 **4:9** [o] Dt 28:22 [p] Joel 1:7 [q] Jer 3:10; Hag 2:17 **4:10** [r] Ex 9:3; Dt 28:27 [s] Isa 9:13

4:6 *empty stomachs.* Translates the Hebrew idiom "cleanness of teeth," which refers not to dental hygiene but to famine. This must have been a recent experience, sufficiently within memory to be meaningful to Amos's audience. Drought and famine have been perpetual dangers in Palestine.

4:9 *Locusts.* Locust swarms are still an occasional menace, devastating everything in their path, and are well attested elsewhere in the ancient Near East. A Mari letter from a millennium earlier complains: "On account of the locusts my district could not harvest [anything]." All the natural disasters mentioned in vv. 6–9 were clearly a divine warning.

4:10 *I killed.* Probably refers to the Syrian oppression some 50 years earlier (see note on 1:3–5), the most recent period of sustained subjugation.

11 "I overthrew some of you
as I overthrew Sodom and Gomorrah.[t]
You were like a burning stick snatched
from the fire,
yet you have not returned to me,"
declares the LORD.

12 "Therefore this is what I will do to
you, Israel,
and because I will do this to you,
Israel,
prepare to meet your God."

13 He who forms the mountains,[u]
who creates the wind,
and who reveals his thoughts[v] to
mankind,
who turns dawn to darkness,
and treads on the heights of the
earth[w] —
the LORD God Almighty is his name.[x]

A Lament and Call to Repentance

5 Hear this word, Israel, this lament[y] I
take up concerning you:

2 "Fallen is Virgin[z] Israel,
never to rise again,
deserted in her own land,
with no one to lift her up.[a]"

3 This is what the Sovereign LORD says
to Israel:

"Your city that marches out a thousand
strong
will have only a hundred left;
your town that marches out a hundred
strong
will have only ten left.[b]"

4 This is what the LORD says to Israel:

"Seek me and live;[c]
5 do not seek Bethel,
do not go to Gilgal,[d]
do not journey to Beersheba.[e]
For Gilgal will surely go into exile,
and Bethel will be reduced to
nothing.[a][f]"

6 Seek[g] the LORD and live,[h]
or he will sweep through the tribes
of Joseph like a fire;[i]
it will devour them,
and Bethel[j] will have no one to
quench it.

7 There are those who turn justice into
bitterness[k]
and cast righteousness to the
ground.

8 He who made the Pleiades and Orion,[l]
who turns midnight into dawn[m]
and darkens day into night,[n]
who calls for the waters of the sea
and pours them out over the face of
the land —
the LORD is his name.[o]
9 With a blinding flash he destroys the
stronghold
and brings the fortified city to ruin.[p]
10 There are those who hate the one who
upholds justice in court[q]
and detest the one who tells the
truth.[r]

11 You levy a straw tax on the poor[s]
and impose a tax on their grain.
Therefore, though you have built stone
mansions,[t]
you will not live in them;
though you have planted lush
vineyards,
you will not drink their wine.[u]
12 For I know how many are your
offenses
and how great your sins.

There are those who oppress the
innocent and take bribes
and deprive the poor of justice in the
courts.[v]
13 Therefore the prudent keep quiet in
such times,
for the times are evil.

14 Seek good, not evil,
that you may live.
Then the LORD God Almighty will be
with you,
just as you say he is.

4:11 [t] Ge 19:24; Jer 23:14 **4:13** [u] Ps 65:6 [v] Da 2:28 [w] Mic 1:3 [x] Isa 47:4; Am 5:8, 27; 9:6 **5:1** [y] Eze 19:1 **5:2** [z] Jer 14:17 [a] Jer 50:32; Am 8:14 **5:3** [b] Isa 6:13; Am 6:9 **5:4** [c] Isa 55:3; Jer 29:13 **5:5** [d] 1Sa 11:14; Am 4:4 [e] Am 8:14 [f] 1Sa 7:16 **5:6** [g] Isa 55:6 [h] ver 14 [i] Dt 4:24 [j] Am 3:14 **5:7** [k] Am 6:12 **5:8** [l] Job 9:9 [m] Isa 42:16 [n] Ps 104:20; Am 8:9 [o] Ps 104:6-9; Am 4:13 **5:9** [p] Mic 5:11 **5:10** [q] Isa 29:21 [r] 1Ki 22:8 **5:11** [s] Am 8:6 [t] Am 3:15 [u] Mic 6:15 **5:12** [v] Isa 5:23; Am 2:6-7

[a] 5 Hebrew *aven*, a reference to Beth Aven (a derogatory name for Bethel); see Hosea 4:15.

5:1 *lament.* Laments over death, or "funerary laments" (as distinct from psalm laments), were common in the ancient world. Well-known examples are of David for Saul and Jonathan (2Sa 1:19 – 27), and Gilgamesh for Enkidu in the Gilgamesh Epic (see note on Ps 49:7 – 9).
5:2 *Virgin.* This title might be better translated "Maiden" or "Mistress," since the analogy has more to do with youthful potential than sexual innocence. The Hebrew term means a young, reputable woman who is still under her father's protection. The title also occurs in Jer 18:13; 31:21; it is similar to the expression "Daughter X" used in the OT (e.g., 2Ki 19:21; Ps 9:14) and other ancient literature.
5:8 *Pleiades and Orion.* See note on Job 9:9.
5:11 *though you … you will not.* The curse used here is called a "futility curse" (so all of their effort and success will be futile) and could be compared to an inscription on a Babylonian boundary stone calling on the gods to see that anyone who builds a house on stolen land should have the house taken from them. *stone mansions.* Lit. "houses of dressed stone," the term used for the stone of the temple (1Ki 5:17; 6:36). In ancient Israel most dwellings were made of mud brick, and stone was only used for monumental buildings like temples and palaces, walls and gates. So individuals who could afford to build with dressed stone were very wealthy.
5:12 *courts.* Lit. "gates."

AMOS 5:12

Administration of Justice

In ancient Israel, justice was administered at the local level. The book of Deuteronomy mentions several layers of administration, of which the village elders and local judges constituted the most important. There was a court of appeal, though it is hard to know how often or how well it functioned. Various kings may have attempted to centralize and control it, but David's failure to manage it efficiently allowed Absalom to foment rebellion (2Sa 15:2 – 4). Most of the laws imply that disputes should be settled at the village level. This was far more satisfactory in a traditional society that had no police or prison system and where local knowledge was all-important.

The public area in Israelite villages was just inside the gates (see note on Am 5:12). Here the men would gather, swap stories, conduct business, and settle disputes, as is neatly illustrated in Ru 4:1. The law warns severely against partiality to either rich or poor (Lev 19:15) and against bribery and corruption (Dt 16:19 – 20), but the repeated complaint of Amos and his fellow prophets is that the rich found ways around this.

In ancient Mesopotamia justice was usually administered "at the gate" as well, though in its more centralized society there were some professional judges. However, it was equally firm against corruption. The Code of Hammurapi, section 5, stipulates: "If a judge gave a judgment . . . but later has altered his judgment . . . he shall pay twelvefold the claim which holds in that case; furthermore, they shall expel him in the assembly from his seat of judgment and he shall never again sit with the judges in a case." ◆

Gate chambers and passageway of the upper gate at Dan.

Kim Walton

15 Hate evil,[w] love good;
maintain justice in the courts.
Perhaps the LORD God Almighty will
have mercy[x]
on the remnant[y] of Joseph.
16 Therefore this is what the Lord, the
LORD God Almighty, says:

"There will be wailing[z] in all the streets
and cries of anguish in every public
square.
The farmers[a] will be summoned to weep
and the mourners to wail.
17 There will be wailing in all the
vineyards,
for I will pass through[b] your midst,"
says the LORD.[c]

The Day of the LORD

18 Woe to you who long
for the day of the LORD![d]
Why do you long for the day of the
LORD?
That day will be darkness,[e] not light.[f]
19 It will be as though a man fled from a
lion
only to meet a bear,
as though he entered his house
and rested his hand on the wall
only to have a snake bite him.[g]
20 Will not the day of the LORD be
darkness, not light—
pitch-dark, without a ray of
brightness?[h]

21 "I hate, I despise your religious festivals;[i]
your assemblies[j] are a stench to me.
22 Even though you bring me burnt
offerings and grain offerings,
I will not accept them.
Though you bring choice fellowship
offerings,
I will have no regard for them.[k]
23 Away with the noise of your songs!
I will not listen to the music of your
harps.[l]
24 But let justice[m] roll on like a river,
righteousness like a never-failing
stream![n]

25 "Did you bring me sacrifices[o] and
offerings
forty years[p] in the wilderness,
people of Israel?
26 You have lifted up the shrine of your
king,
the pedestal of your idols,
the star of your god[a]—
which you made for yourselves.
27 Therefore I will send you into exile
beyond Damascus,"
says the LORD, whose name is God
Almighty.[q]

Woe to the Complacent

6 Woe to you[r] who are complacent in
Zion,
and to you who feel secure on
Mount Samaria,
you notable men of the foremost nation,
to whom the people of Israel come![s]

5:15 [w] Ps 97:10; Ro 12:9 [x] Joel 2:14 [y] Mic 5:7,8 **5:16** [z] Jer 9:17 [a] Joel 1:11 **5:17** [b] Ex 12:12 [c] Isa 16:10; Jer 48:33 **5:18** [d] Joel 1:15 [e] Joel 2:2 [f] Isa 5:19,30; Jer 30:7 **5:19** [g] Job 20:24; Isa 24:17-18; Jer 15:2-3; 48:44 **5:20** [h] Isa 13:10; Zep 1:15 **5:21** [i] Lev 26:31 [j] Isa 1:11-16 **5:22** [k] Isa 66:3; Am 4:4; Mic 6:6-7 **5:23** [l] Am 6:5 **5:24** [m] Jer 22:3 [n] Mic 6:8 **5:25** [o] Isa 43:23 [p] Dt 32:17 **5:27** [q] Am 4:13; Ac 7:42-43* **6:1** [r] Lk 6:24 [s] Isa 32:9-11

[a] 26 Or *lifted up Sakkuth your king / and Kaiwan your idols, / your star-gods*; Septuagint *lifted up the shrine of Molek / and the star of your god Rephan, / their idols*

5:16,17 *wailing.* See the article "Mourning," p. 828.
5:18 *the day of the LORD.* We do not know when this concept originated, except that by the mid-eighth century BC it was current in Israel. As to how it originated, two views are proposed. (1) Some think it comes from the concept of "holy warfare" or "Yahweh warfare," i.e., battles conducted at God's bequest, with his aid, and often with annihilation of the enemy. The "day of the LORD" thus meant the day of victorious battle, and the phrase came to depict the expected glorious future. (2) Others trace it to a great festival in the autumn celebrating Yahweh as Israel's God and King. The "day of the LORD" thus referred to this annual event and, by extension, to the time when his rule would bring peace and prosperity to all. Neither view is certain. What is clear, however, is that Amos reversed popular expectation by proclaiming that the "day of the LORD" would bring unrelieved "pitch-dark" gloom (v. 20). Amos does this with a string of vivid metaphors in vv. 18–20—the ancient equivalent of "out of the frying pan, into the fire."
5:26 As the NIV text note reveals, this verse is difficult, with many words ambiguous. In the first pair, Sakkuth could be "shrine" or a name, and "your king" (root *m-l-k*) could be the underworld deity Molek or the Ammonite deity Milkom. In the second pair, "pedestal" could be the name Kaiwan—the Septuagint (the pre-Christian Greek translation of the OT) gives this as Rephan, the form that is then quoted in Ac 7:43. Clearly the prophet denounces idolatry, but its exact form is uncertain. One common view, reflected in the NIV text, is that the prophet condemns various cult objects: "shrine," "pedestal" and "star." Amos's contemporary Hosea also mentions various cultic accoutrements that were revered by the Israelites and of which they would soon be deprived (e.g., Hos 3:4; 8:4–6). Sometimes these were lifted up and paraded in the ancient world, as illustrated in graphic art. This fits the general context, though it is not the easiest way to read the Hebrew words. The other common view, reflected in the NIV text note and argued by many commentators, is that a form of astral worship is condemned. The word translated "shrine" is really "Sakkuth" and "pedestal" is "Kaiwan"—corrupted forms of names for the god Saturn known from various lists from Mesopotamia, Ebla and Ugarit. This implies that by this stage Israel had succumbed to the worship of heavenly bodies, as did many of its neighbors, and as did Judah a century later (cf. Josiah's reforms, 2Ki 23:5).
5:27 *exile beyond Damascus.* Since the Assyrians are never directly mentioned in Amos, it is unclear that this is what he meant when he spoke of the coming exile of the people of Israel. Using such an imprecise phrase as "beyond Damascus" is reminiscent of Jeremiah's threat "from the north" (Jer 1:14), and both simply indicate the direction of Mesopotamia as the source of the coming destruction.
6:1 *Mount Samaria.* For Amos's parallelism to work most effectively, Mount Samaria would have to also contain a

[2]Go to Kalneh[t] and look at it;
go from there to great Hamath,[u]
and then go down to Gath[v] in
Philistia.
Are they better off than[w] your two
kingdoms?
Is their land larger than yours?
[3]You put off the day of disaster
and bring near a reign of terror.[x]
[4]You lie on beds adorned with ivory
and lounge on your couches.
You dine on choice lambs
and fattened calves.[y]
[5]You strum away on your harps[z] like
David
and improvise on musical
instruments.[a]
[6]You drink wine[b] by the bowlful
and use the finest lotions,
but you do not grieve[c] over the ruin
of Joseph.

6:2 [t]Ge 10:10 [u]2Ki 18:34 [v]2Ch 26:6 [w]Na 3:8 6:3 [x]Isa 56:12; Am 9:10 6:4 [y]Eze 34:2-3; Am 3:12 6:5 [z]Isa 5:12; Am 5:23 [a]1Ch 15:16 6:6 [b]Am 2:8 [c]Eze 9:4 6:8 [d]Ge 22:16; Heb 6:13 [e]Lev 26:30 [f]Ps 47:4 [g]Am 4:2 [h]Dt 32:19 6:9 [i]Am 5:3 6:10 [j]1Sa 31:12 [k]Am 8:3

[7]Therefore you will be among the first
to go into exile;
your feasting and lounging will end.

The LORD Abhors the Pride of Israel

[8]The Sovereign LORD has sworn by himself[d] — the LORD God Almighty declares:

"I abhor[e] the pride of Jacob[f]
and detest his fortresses;
I will deliver up[g] the city
and everything in it.[h]"

[9]If ten[i] people are left in one house,
they too will die. [10]And if the relative who
comes to carry the bodies out of the house
to burn them[a][j] asks anyone who might be
hiding there, "Is anyone else with you?"
and he says, "No," then he will go on to
say, "Hush![k] We must not mention the
name of the LORD."

[a] 10 Or *to make a funeral fire in honor of the dead*

worship center, just as Mount Zion does in Jerusalem. It is likely a reference to the acropolis section of the city, where the temple and palace would be located. Considering Micah's condemnation of Samaria and its idols (Mic 1:6–7) and Isaiah's reference to "Samaria and her idols" (Isa 10:11), it seems likely that Israel's capital had a major shrine during the reign of Jeroboam II.

6:2 *Kalneh.* The capital of a late-Hittite state in north-central Syria, roughly halfway between the northeastern corner of the Mediterranean Sea and the Euphrates River. It was conquered briefly by the Assyrians under Shalmaneser III in the mid-ninth century BC (859–853 BC), but it is not mentioned again in their records until the mid-eighth century BC, in reference to reconquest in 739 BC by Tiglath-Pileser III after a revolt. *Hamath.* An important city-state on the Orontes River, roughly halfway between Kalneh to the north and Damascus to the south. Like Kalneh it was conquered by Shalmaneser III in 859 BC, but then joined the western coalition that checked the Assyrians at Qarqar in 853 BC. In the following years they lost some territory but soon recovered it. Like Kalneh it was reconquered in 739 BC, but its history immediately before this is unclear. *Gath.* One of the five chief cities of the Philistines.

There are three ways to understand these historical references. (1) Amos is referring to the defeats of these cities a century previously. Though a long time ago, they were memorable, and the lesson still valuable. (2) Amos refers to their conquest by Assyria in the immediately preceding years. While there are no extant records of this, it provides a suitable context for the revolt and reconquest in 739 BC. (3) This section comes not from "before the earthquake" (1:1) but from after 739 BC, when their defeat provided a chilling warning.

The lesson from Philistine Gath could refer to (1) possible capture by the Syrians under Hazael in a southern campaign against nearby Jerusalem in the late ninth century BC (2Ki 12:18), (2) capture by Judah under Uzziah in the first half of the eighth century BC (2Ch 26:6), or (3) capture by Tiglath-Pileser in 734 BC as the Assyrians advanced farther south.

6:4 *beds adorned with ivory.* The idea of a bed made from some exotic or luxurious material is reminiscent of king Og's iron bed in Dt 3:11 (see also Solomon's ivory throne in 2Ch 9:17–19). Sennacherib's Assyrian annals mention that Judah's king Hezekiah included a couch inlaid with ivory among his tribute items. Ivory decor was very popular at this time for inlays in furniture and for wall panels. One of the principal sources of ivory was elephant tusks, which were imported from Aram (where Syrian elephants were not yet extinct at this time).

6:5 *harps ... musical instruments.* See the article "Music and Musicians," p. 524.

6:6 *wine.* The ancient world had beer, wine and strong drink, just like today. Wine in the OT could be a sign of divine favor (Ps 104:15) and an element of true worship (Dt 14:26), but drinking to excess or in idle luxury was frequently condemned. Here "the bowlful" probably indicates excess. Ancient art shows wine served in bowls, and various excavations have uncovered such bowls. *lotions.* The use of fine oils or lotions for cosmetic, hygienic and therapeutic purposes was widespread in the ancient Near East, and in the OT oil is often coupled with wine in descriptions of pleasure (e.g., Ps 23:5). A large number of ostraca recovered from eighth-century BC Samaria record various commercial transactions and tax payments, and a dozen of these mention "refined oil."

6:7 *feasting.* The Hebrew noun *marzeah* occurs only here and in Jer 16:5, where it is linked to mourning (NIV "funeral meal"). However, the root *mrzh* occurs throughout the ancient Semitic world in reference to drinking and occasionally eating, in celebration or commiseration. The *marzeah* was often a social institution, sometimes with members and at a specified location, with elements variously of a pub, a drinking den, a London gentlemen's club, a Masonic lodge, an annual fete, and an Irish wake. It could be associated with death, as in Jer 16:5, but its primary connotation was drinking. Here it connotes feasting — soon to be abruptly ended.

6:9–10 These verses portray the horrific aftermath of destruction, describing a houseful of dead bodies being discovered by a relative. He searches for survivors but is promptly told not even to mention Yahweh's name, presumably lest further catastrophe strike.

6:10 *burn them.* Cremation was generally abhorred in Israel and beyond. The few OT exceptions concerned not normal corpse disposal but exemplary capital punishment: Achan's sin after Jericho (Jos 7:25), and serious sexual misconduct (Lev 20:14; 21:9). The men of Jabesh Gilead burned the corpses of Saul and his sons, but this

[11] For the LORD has given the command,
and he will smash the great house[l]
into pieces
and the small house into bits.[m]
[12] Do horses run on the rocky crags?
Does one plow the sea[a] with oxen?
But you have turned justice into poison[n]
and the fruit of righteousness into
bitterness[o] —
[13] you who rejoice in the conquest of Lo
Debar[b]
and say, "Did we not take Karnaim[c]
by our own strength?[p]"
[14] For the LORD God Almighty declares,
"I will stir up a nation[q] against you,
Israel,
that will oppress you all the way
from Lebo Hamath[r] to the valley of
the Arabah.[s]"

Locusts, Fire and a Plumb Line

7 This is what the Sovereign LORD
showed me:[t] He was preparing swarms
of locusts[u] after the king's share had been
harvested and just as the late crops were
coming up. [2] When they had stripped the
land clean,[v] I cried out, "Sovereign LORD,
forgive! How can Jacob survive?[w] He is so
small![x]"
[3] So the LORD relented.[y]
"This will not happen," the LORD said.[z]
[4] This is what the Sovereign LORD
showed me: The Sovereign LORD was calling for judgment by fire;[a] it dried up the
great deep and devoured[b] the land. [5] Then
I cried out, "Sovereign LORD, I beg you,
stop! How can Jacob survive? He is so
small![c]"
[6] So the LORD relented.[d]
"This will not happen either," the Sovereign LORD said.
[7] This is what he showed me: The Lord
was standing by a wall that had been built
true to plumb,[d] with a plumb line[e] in his

6:11 [l] Am 3:15 [m] Isa 55:11 **6:12** [n] Hos 10:4 [o] Am 5:7 **6:13** [p] Job 8:15; Isa 28:14-15 **6:14** [q] Jer 5:15 [r] 1Ki 8:65 [s] Am 3:11 **7:1** [t] Am 8:1 [u] Joel 1:4 **7:2** [v] Ex 10:15 [w] Isa 37:4 [x] Eze 11:13 **7:3** [y] Dt 32:36; Jer 26:19; Jnh 3:10 [z] Hos 11:8 **7:4** [a] Isa 66:16 [b] Dt 32:22 **7:5** [c] ver 1-2; Joel 2:17 **7:6** [d] Jnh 3:10

[a] 12 With a different word division of the Hebrew; Masoretic Text *plow there* [b] 13 *Lo Debar* means *nothing.* [c] 13 *Karnaim* means *horns; horn* here symbolizes strength. [d] 7 The meaning of the Hebrew for this phrase is uncertain. [e] 7 The meaning of the Hebrew for this phrase is uncertain; also in verse 8.

was respectful, partial (since they then buried the bones), and probably necessary for hygiene given the delay following their death (1Sa 31:12). Earlier in Amos (2:1), the Moabites are fiercely condemned for burning the king of Edom's bones. So here cremation may have been used as a last resort in an emergency, perhaps to avoid disease.

6:13 *Lo Debar.* A town usually located just east of the Jordan in Ammonite territory. It is mentioned in several texts, with slightly variant spellings, but here it is spelled mockingly as "Nothing" (see the article "Playing With Place-Names," p. 1482). *Karnaim.* A town north of Lo Debar in Transjordan, east of the Sea of Kinnereth (Galilee). The name means lit. "horns," a common symbol of strength. But whether the town captured was "Nothingville" or "Stronghold," the Israelites' boasting was futile.

6:14 *from Lebo Hamath to the valley of the Arabah.* Again a section ends with prediction of defeat and oppression. *Lebo Hamath.* Means "Gate of Hamath." It lay north of Damascus about halfway to Hamath itself. It is sometimes referred to as the northern edge of ideal Israel (1Ki 8:65; 1Ch 13:5), though the nation seldom reached that far. Israel captured it (and probably the towns of v. 13) during the expansion by Jeroboam II in the decades before Amos's ministry (cf. 2Ki 14:25). This will only result in more territory for Assyrian oppression. *valley of the Arabah.* Mentioned only here, it was a wadi at the northern end of the Dead Sea marking Israel's southern boundary.

7:1 *swarms of locusts.* This first vision (vv. 1–3) is of God preparing a locust swarm to devastate the country (see note on Ex 10:4). *after the king's share . . . just as the late crops were coming up.* The detail of the crops and the timing of the plague are particularly important. There were two main crops each year in ancient Israel. The first was sown in the autumn, watered by the late autumn rains and harvested in the spring. The second was sown in winter, watered by the spring rains and harvested in the early summer. The Gezer calendar gives a good summary of the agricultural year. This probably remained the pattern in later centuries, though there is no other extra-Biblical textual evidence. *share.* This Hebrew term (lit. "mowing") is used only here. This was obviously some or all of the first harvest. Whatever the proportion, it shows that the king took a significant part of the best produce in a heavy tax. The timing of the plague means that the monarchy already has its share so may remain unconcerned about the plight of the ordinary people, whose share is completely wiped out as locusts "stripped the land clean" (v. 2). Lack of rain during the long dry summer would make further crops impossible, resulting in famine and starvation.

7:2 *forgive.* This Hebrew verb is used in the OT only of divine forgiveness, e.g., following the wilderness rebellion (Nu 14:20), in Solomon's temple prayer (1Ki 8:30) and in a memorable Isaianic text (Isa 55:7). Here Amos fulfills the important OT prophetic role of interceding on behalf of the people, a role not evidenced for prophets in other cultures, where divination priests or incantation priests might more likely serve this role. His appeal is based not on Israel's repentance but implicitly on God's relationship with Israel, which would cease if the nation was wiped out.

7:4–6 This second vision develops a common motif. This fire even consumes "the great deep," the cosmic deep beneath the earth that is the source of its seas and river and is sometimes associated with the underworld.

7:7–9 The meaning of this vision is clear: Yahweh uses a handheld instrument that has some association with a wall to illustrate coming judgment. However, the Hebrew text is less clear (see note on v. 7).

7:7 *plumb line.* The Hebrew term translated "plumb line" has the same stem as the Akkadian term *annaku.* The latter was thought to mean "tin or lead," hence the interpretation as "lead weight" (i.e., plumb line). However, recent study suggests that *annaku* means specifically "tin," not lead, and tin is too light to make an effective plumb line. Various other proposals have been made concerning the meaning of the term and the nature of the vision, but none is convincing. Whatever Amos sees in Yahweh's hand, he understands it as an illustration of judgment.

hand. 8And the LORD asked me, "What do you see,[e] Amos?[f]"

"A plumb line,[g]" I replied.

Then the Lord said, "Look, I am setting a plumb line among my people Israel; I will spare them no longer.[h]

9"The high places of Isaac will be
destroyed
and the sanctuaries[i] of Israel will be
ruined;
with my sword I will rise against the
house of Jeroboam.[j]"

Amos and Amaziah

10Then Amaziah the priest of Bethel[k] sent a message to Jeroboam[l] king of Israel: "Amos is raising a conspiracy[m] against you in the very heart of Israel. The land cannot bear all his words.[n] 11For this is what Amos is saying:

" 'Jeroboam will die by the sword,
and Israel will surely go into exile,
away from their native land.' "

12Then Amaziah said to Amos, "Get out, you seer! Go back to the land of Judah. Earn your bread there and do your prophesying there.[o] 13Don't prophesy anymore at Bethel, because this is the king's sanctuary and the temple of the kingdom.[p]"

14Amos answered Amaziah, "I was neither a prophet[q] nor the son of a prophet, but I was a shepherd, and I also took care of sycamore-fig trees. 15But the LORD took me from tending the flock[r] and said to me, 'Go, prophesy to my people Israel.'[s] 16Now then, hear the word of the LORD. You say,

" 'Do not prophesy against[t] Israel,
and stop preaching against the
descendants of Isaac.'

17"Therefore this is what the LORD says:

" 'Your wife will become a prostitute[u]
in the city,
and your sons and daughters will fall
by the sword.
Your land will be measured and
divided up,
and you yourself will die in a pagan[a]
country.
And Israel will surely go into exile,
away from their native land.[v]' "

A Basket of Ripe Fruit

8 This is what the Sovereign LORD showed me: a basket of ripe fruit. 2"What do you see,[w] Amos?[x]" he asked.

"A basket of ripe fruit," I answered.

Then the LORD said to me, "The time is ripe for my people Israel; I will spare them no longer.[y]

3"In that day," declares the Sovereign LORD, "the songs in the temple will turn to wailing.[b][z] Many, many bodies — flung everywhere! Silence![a]"

4Hear this, you who trample the needy
and do away with the poor[b] of the
land,[c]

5saying,

"When will the New Moon be over
that we may sell grain,

[a] 17 Hebrew *an unclean* [b] 3 Or *"the temple singers will wail*

7:8 [e] Jer 1:11, 13 [f] Isa 28:17; La 2:8; Am 8:2 [g] 2Ki 21:13 [h] Jer 15:6; Eze 7:2-9 **7:9** [i] Lev 26:31 [j] 2Ki 15:9; Isa 63:18; Hos 10:8 **7:10** [k] 1Ki 12:32 [l] 2Ki 14:23 [m] Jer 38:4 [n] Jer 26:8-11 **7:12** [o] Mt 8:34 **7:13** [p] Am 2:12; Ac 4:18 **7:14** [q] 2Ki 2:5; 4:38 **7:15** [r] 2Sa 7:8 [s] Jer 7:1-2; Eze 2:3-4 **7:16** [t] Eze 20:46; Mic 2:6 **7:17** [u] Hos 4:13 [v] 2Ki 17:6; Eze 4:13; Hos 9:3 **8:2** [w] Jer 24:3 [x] Am 7:8 [y] Eze 7:2-9 **8:3** [z] Am 5:16 [a] Am 5:23; 6:10 **8:4** [b] Pr 30:14 [c] Ps 14:4; Am 2:7

7:10 *Amos is raising a conspiracy.* Throughout the ancient world it was believed that prophets not only proclaimed the message of deity but also in the process unleashed the divine action (see the article "Prophets and Prophecy," p. 1110). In Assyrian king Esarhaddon's instructions to his vassals, he requires that they report any improper or negative statements that may be made by anyone, but he specifically names prophets, ecstatics and dream interpreters. It is no wonder, then, that a prophet negatively disposed toward a king must somehow be controlled lest he bring about all sorts of havoc. One can perhaps understand why a king would be inclined to imprison a prophet whose very words might incite insurrection or impose doom.

7:12 *Earn your bread there.* Amaziah's charge that Amos is a professional ("for hire") prophet implies that Amaziah has no concept of any other form of prophetic ministry.

7:13 *king's sanctuary … temple of the kingdom.* These descriptions of Bethel occur only here in the OT. However, it was common for ancient Near Eastern monarchs to exercise patronage over sanctuaries; in the Jerusalem temple there was even a special entrance for the king.

7:14 *neither a prophet nor the son of a prophet.* Amos immediately responds to Amaziah's charge (see note on v. 12) by declaring that he is a farmer (see note on 1:1) called by God for a specific prophetic mission. Amos had a clear sense of divine call, something well attested in other Biblical prophets but not in prophetic texts from surrounding cultures (see the article "Prophets and Prophecy," p. 1110).

7:17 In response to Amaziah's prohibition (v. 16), Amos delivers a specific personal prophecy of destitution and death. This is similar to curses elsewhere; e.g., a treaty of the Assyrian Ashurnirari says, "May Mati'ilu become like a prostitute and his soldiers women. May they receive gifts like a prostitute in the square of the city."

8:1 – 3 In this vision Amos sees a basket of ripe fruit. The Hebrew writers loved wordplays. Here "ripe fruit" (*qayits,* usually figs) is punned with "end" (*qets*). Wordplays do not translate easily from one language to another, but the NIV does well to match "ripe fruit" with "the time is ripe." Ripe fruit normally means harvest celebration; here it presages ripeness for judgment.

8:5 As Nehemiah discovered several centuries later in Persian-period Jerusalem, the desire of merchants to conduct business sometimes makes their compliance with religious law and Sabbath regulations a matter for complaint or even circumvention (see note on Ne 10:31). There were religious festivals in surrounding cultures (see note on Ex 20:8), but only Israel was commanded to obey the Sabbath law and cease all work (Ex 31:12 – 17). This restriction on trade caused friction and apparently

and the Sabbath be ended
that we may market wheat?"—
skimping on the measure,
boosting the price
and cheating with dishonest scales,[d]
6 buying the poor with silver
and the needy for a pair of sandals,
selling even the sweepings with the
wheat.[e]

7 The LORD has sworn by himself, the
Pride of Jacob:[f] "I will never forget[g] anything they have done.

8 "Will not the land tremble[h] for this,
and all who live in it mourn?
The whole land will rise like the Nile;
it will be stirred up and then sink
like the river of Egypt.[i]

9 "In that day," declares the Sovereign
LORD,

"I will make the sun go down at noon
and darken the earth in broad
daylight.[j]
10 I will turn your religious festivals into
mourning
and all your singing into weeping.
I will make all of you wear sackcloth[k]
and shave your heads.
I will make that time like mourning for
an only son[l]
and the end of it like a bitter day.[m]

11 "The days are coming," declares the
Sovereign LORD,
"when I will send a famine through
the land—
not a famine of food or a thirst for
water,
but a famine of hearing the words of
the LORD.[n]
12 People will stagger from sea to sea
and wander from north to east,
searching for the word of the LORD,
but they will not find it.[o]

13 "In that day

"the lovely young women and strong
young men
will faint because of thirst.[p]
14 Those who swear by the sin of
Samaria—
who say, 'As surely as your god
lives, Dan,'[q]
or, 'As surely as the god[a] of
Beersheba[r] lives'—
they will fall, never to rise again.[s]"

8:5 [d] 2Ki 4:23; Ne 13:15-16; Hos 12:7; Mic 6:10-11 **8:6** [e] Am 2:6 **8:7** [f] Am 6:8 [g] Hos 8:13 **8:8** [h] Hos 4:3 [i] Ps 18:7; Jer 46:8; Am 9:5 **8:9** [j] Job 5:14; Isa 59:9-10; Jer 15:9; Am 5:8; Mic 3:6 **8:10** [k] Jer 48:37 [l] Jer 6:26; Zec 12:10 [m] Eze 7:18 **8:11** [n] 1Sa 3:1; 2Ch 15:3; Eze 7:26 **8:12** [o] Eze 20:3, 31 **8:13** [p] Isa 41:17; Hos 2:3 **8:14** [q] 1Ki 12:29 [r] Am 5:5 [s] Am 5:2

[a] 14 Hebrew *the way*

contributed to corrupt business practices as a way of "making up" the losses. *skimping … boosting … cheating.* Certainly, Amos's complaints against Israelite merchants are not unique; e.g., the charge made against merchants that they use false balances is found in the Egyptian "Instruction of Amenemope" and in a clause in the Babylonian wisdom literature. Similarly, the Code of Hammurapi contains a statement about bankers who "use a light scale to measure the grain or the silver that they lend and a heavy scale to measure the grain or the silver that they collect."

8:6 *sweepings with the wheat.* In their efforts to squeeze as much profit as possible from their holdings, grain merchants cheat the poor by selling the "husks" of the wheat. A similar charge is made in the Egyptian tale of the "Eloquent Peasant" against those who "substitute lesser for better goods." *sweepings.* This Hebrew word occurs only here, but it is related to the Hebrew word meaning "to fall" and reflects the poorest quality or that which is left over.

8:8 *rise … then sink like the river of Egypt.* Egyptian agriculture relied heavily on the annual flooding of the Nile. The waters would flood in September and recede in October, leaving a short winter period for cultivation crops. Occasionally the flood was too weak, with catastrophic results, and Egyptian texts often note "a year of low Nile" with hunger and misery. The powerful image of a rising and flooding river occurs in a variety of prophetic contexts. Here it may well be another prediction of the coming earthquake (1:1) that would convulse the solid earth as if it was water. The imagery is repeated in 9:5.

8:9 *sun go down at noon.* Since a lunar or solar eclipse was considered a portent of evil or the anger of the gods in the ancient Near East, there are many citations in the literature. Among them is the prediction by the prophet Balaam in the Deir 'Alla inscription that the divine assembly has decided to "bring darkness instead of light." Priests of the moon-god Sin in Babylonia would wear torn garments and sing dirges during an eclipse, and there are numerous letters and omen texts in Babylonian and Assyrian records referring to eclipses. Many are written to kings either warning them of a coming eclipse or assuring the monarch that they will be kept informed of the likelihood of coming occurrences. For Biblical examples, see Joel 3:15; Zec 14:6.

8:12 *from sea to sea.* Used fairly often by the Biblical writers (e.g., Ps 72:8; Zec 9:10) to distinguish east and west (from the Mediterranean west to the Dead Sea or the Jordan River). A similar expression occurs in the Karatepe Stele, where "from sunrise to sunset" (cf. Isa 45:6) is used for east to west or a sense of universality. Since it is combined here with "north to east," it is possible that it defines the southern latitudinal border of the northern kingdom. In their staggering search for water during the drought, the people will search from one end of the kingdom to the other. *from north to east.* The southern boundary has been defined in the previous line, and the western boundary is, of course, the Mediterranean. From Bethel one could still search to the Galilee region to the north, heading for places like Samaria or Dan, and to the east, whether Beth Shan or the Transjordan territory of Gilead.

8:14 *swear by.* The focus of worship is clear only for Dan, where it is "your god." For Samaria, it is "the sin" (some translations, "shame"), an unusual but understandable epithet for the "calf of Samaria" (Hos 8:6). Adding different vowels would give Ashima, but worship of this goddess was only introduced later by deportees from Hamath (2Ki 17:30). For Beersheba, the puzzling focus of worship is lit. "the way [*derek*] of Beersheba." Perhaps *derek* here does not have its common meaning "way" but is a rare homonym meaning "power."

Israel to Be Destroyed

9 I saw the Lord standing by the altar, and he said:

"Strike the tops of the pillars
so that the thresholds shake.
Bring them down on the heads[t] of all the people;
those who are left I will kill with the sword.
Not one will get away,
none will escape.
2 Though they dig down to the depths below,[u]
from there my hand will take them.
Though they climb up to the heavens above,[v]
from there I will bring them down.[w]
3 Though they hide themselves on the top of Carmel,[x]
there I will hunt them down and seize them.[y]
Though they hide from my eyes at the bottom of the sea,
there I will command the serpent to bite them.[z]
4 Though they are driven into exile by their enemies,
there I will command the sword[a] to slay them.

"I will keep my eye on them
for harm[b] and not for good.[c]"[d]

5 The Lord, the LORD Almighty —
he touches the earth and it melts,[e]
and all who live in it mourn;
the whole land rises like the Nile,
then sinks like the river of Egypt;[f]
6 he builds his lofty palace[a] in the heavens
and sets its foundation[b] on the earth;
he calls for the waters of the sea
and pours them out over the face of the land —
the LORD is his name.[g]

7 "Are not you Israelites
the same to me as the Cushites[c]?"[h]
declares the LORD.
"Did I not bring Israel up from Egypt,
the Philistines from Caphtor[d][i]
and the Arameans from Kir?[j]

8 "Surely the eyes of the Sovereign LORD
are on the sinful kingdom.
I will destroy it
from the face of the earth.
Yet I will not totally destroy
the descendants of Jacob,"
declares the LORD.[k]

9 "For I will give the command,
and I will shake the people of Israel
among all the nations

9:1 [t] Ps 68:21 9:2 [u] Ps 139:8 [v] Jer 51:53 [w] Ob 1:4 9:3 [x] Am 1:2 [y] Ps 139:8-10 [z] Jer 16:16-17 9:4 [a] Lev 26:33; Eze 5:12 [b] Jer 21:10 [c] Jer 39:16 [d] Jer 44:11 9:5 [e] Ps 46:2; Mic 1:4 [f] Am 8:8 9:6 [g] Ps 104:1-3,5-6,13; Am 5:8 9:7 [h] Isa 20:4; 43:3 [i] Dt 2:23; Jer 47:4 [j] 2Ki 16:9; Isa 22:6; Am 1:5; 2:10 9:8 [k] Jer 44:27

[a] *6* The meaning of the Hebrew for this phrase is uncertain. [b] *6* The meaning of the Hebrew for this word is uncertain. [c] *7* That is, people from the upper Nile region [d] *7* That is, Crete

9:1–4 Unlike the first four visions (7:1–3,4–6,7–9; 8:1–3), Amos here is merely a spectator as Yahweh proclaims horrendous judgment, to be enacted presumably by the Assyrians on the Bethel temple. The tops (or capitals) of the pillars supporting the roof will be smashed so violently that the building will be destroyed down to its foundations, and leaders and commoners alike will be slaughtered. The Assyrians, like most ancient conquerors, executed leaders of conquered peoples and any they deemed to be rebels. Sargon, who eventually captured Samaria, boasted regarding a rebel Hittite: "Himself I flayed; the rebels I killed in their cities and established [again] peace and harmony."
9:1 *none will escape.* Five flight scenarios are envisaged in the following verses, with two opposing pairs from the cosmic world (underworld, heavens) and the natural world (mountain, seas), and a single scenario in the human world. None of these provides escape from divine retribution. A fourteenth-century BC Amarna letter similarly affirms that neither heaven nor underworld provide escape from the Egyptian pharaoh.
9:2 *depths below.* Lit. "Sheol." Its reference to the cosmic extremity of the underworld is clear here from its parallelism with "heavens." A repeated Biblical theme is that the dead in Sheol are cut off from Yahweh and can no longer praise or petition him. However, another repeated theme reflected here is that God's authority extends even to Sheol, and nothing there is hidden from him. See the articles "Death and Sheol," p. 833; "Death and the Underworld," p. 907.
9:3 *the serpent.* Many ancient cultures envisaged a great sea monster or serpent (see the article "Chaos Monsters," p. 953). Here God would command this very creature to fulfill his purpose.
9:5 *rises … then sinks like the river of Egypt.* See note on 8:8.
9:6 *lofty palace in the heavens.* Amos's attempt to express God's complete control over all creation begins with a multistoried or many chambered sanctuary or palace in the heavens (cf. Ps 78:69; Isa 66:1). These "upper chambers" (Ps 104:3) bind together the vaults of heaven while at the same time they rest upon the waters. A precedent for these lofty chambers is found in the *Enuma Elish*, which contains a description of the building of the Esagila temple to Marduk in Babylon in which the gods "built a stage-tower as high as Apsu [= heaven]." In the Biblical and ancient Near Eastern view, the cosmos was a temple and the temple was a microcosmos.
9:7 *Cushites.* See note on Jer 46:9. *Philistines.* See notes on Ge 21:32; Jdg 3:3; Isa 14:29. *Arameans.* See notes on Dt 26:5; Jdg 3:8.
9:9 *as grain is shaken in a sieve.* The work of processing harvested grain included crushing the stalks on the threshing floor with a sled, winnowing (see note on Ru 3:2), and finally using a sieve to separate the kernels of grain from small stones and other debris. The sieve mentioned here has large holes and works best when shaken sideways and in a circular motion. This ordinarily forces the debris to the sides and allows the kernels to fall to the ground, where they can be collected (see Sirach 27:4).

as grain[l] is shaken in a sieve,[m]
and not a pebble will reach the ground.
10 All the sinners among my people
will die by the sword,
all those who say,
'Disaster will not overtake or meet us.'[n]

Israel's Restoration

11 "In that day

"I will restore David's fallen shelter —
I will repair its broken walls
and restore its ruins —
and will rebuild it as it used to be,[o]
12 so that they may possess the remnant of Edom[p]
and all the nations that bear my name,[a][q]"
declares the LORD,
who will do these things.[r]

13 "The days are coming," declares the LORD,

"when the reaper will be overtaken by the plowman[s]
and the planter by the one treading grapes.
New wine will drip from the mountains
and flow from all the hills,[t]
14 and I will bring my people Israel
back from exile.[b]

"They will rebuild the ruined cities[u]
and live in them.
They will plant vineyards and drink their wine;
they will make gardens and eat their fruit.[v]
15 I will plant[w] Israel in their own land,
never again to be uprooted
from the land I have given them,"
says the LORD your God.[x]

9:9 [l] Lk 22:31 [m] Isa 30:28 **9:10** [n] Am 6:3 **9:11** [o] Ps 80:12 **9:12** [p] Nu 24:18 [q] Isa 43:7 [r] Ac 15:16-17* **9:13** [s] Lev 26:5 [t] Joel 3:18 **9:14** [u] Isa 61:4 [v] Jer 30:18; 31:28; Eze 28:25-26 **9:15** [w] Isa 60:21 [x] Jer 24:6; Eze 34:25-28; 37:12,25

[a] *12* Hebrew; Septuagint *so that the remnant of people / and all the nations that bear my name may seek me*
[b] *14* Or *will restore the fortunes of my people Israel*

9:11 *David's fallen shelter.* This unique expression may well refer to the united monarchy that "fell" in schism on the death of Solomon. God promises to restore it "as it used to be" — the same Hebrew phrase is used by Amos's contemporary Micah ("as in days long ago," Mic 7:14) in similar reference to past prosperity.
9:12 *Edom and all the nations.* Control over bitter rival Edom (see note on 1Ki 11:14 – 17) and other neighbors represents a return to the political unity and hegemony of David's time (2Sa 8).
9:14 – 15 *They will plant vineyards ... I will plant Israel.* The obvious wordplay reinforces this wonderful concluding prophecy of agricultural replenishment and national renewal. The exile is over; the new and secure order has come.

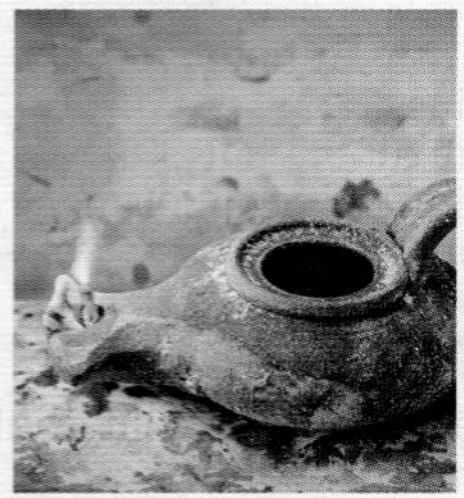

ORACLES OF THE PROPHETS

OBADIAH

Edom Outside the Bible

The earliest mentions of Edom outside the Bible occur in Egyptian inscriptions of the thirteenth century BC that give both the name Edom and the name Seir. There are no other extra-Biblical references until Assyrian kings claimed tribute from the land about 800 BC and named two kings: Qaus-Malak (c. 730 BC) and Qaus-gabri (c. 670 BC; see note on v. 3). Edom's domain sometimes extended west of the Arabah (cf. Nu 34:3). In the seventh century BC there is archaeological evidence in the form of pottery and cultic objects for Edomites living in the Negev and a record of Edomites threatening Judahites in the area (Arad Ostracon 24). In Hellenistic and Roman times, the influx of Edomites into the southern half of Judah had become so great that the region was known as Idumea.

KEY CONCEPTS

- Natural disasters (like the locust plague in Joel) can serve as the judgment of God, but not all who suffer the consequences should therefore be judged guilty. Such disasters draw our attention to God and stimulate us to self-examination.
- The day of judgment is to be feared, and therefore should motivate us to change our ways.
- Prophecy is more important for what it reveals about God than for what it reveals about the future. Fulfillment is sure, but the message is primary.

The Date of Obadiah

Dating Obadiah's prophecy is difficult. Edomite enmity is noted on various occasions throughout Israel's history (e.g., Ps 83), but a date at the time of Nebuchadnezzar's attacks is attractive. Edomites and others attacked Judah in Jehoiakim's reign (2Ki 24:2), and shortly afterward Jeremiah urged them to submit to Babylon (Jer 27:3 – 11). Many find a date after the fall of Jerusalem in 586 BC persuasive. There is no clear report of Edomites involved in that event, but Ezekiel's prophecy (Eze 35) against them suggests they may have been; Obadiah implies they at least took advantage of the event. Jeremiah's oracle against Edom (Jer 49:7 – 22) contains verses that are similar to Obadiah (compare Jer 49:14 – 16 with Ob 1b – 4; Jer 49:9 with Ob 5). Both perhaps speak of the interval between the Babylonian attacks of 597 and 587 – 586 BC. Ammon and Moab were apparently subjugated by Nebuchadnezzar shortly afterward, but Edom had a short respite. It was the last king of Babylon, Nabonidus, who probably annexed Edom in 553 BC, leaving a carving on a remote cliff not far from the capital, Bozrah (modern Buseira), to mark his triumph. Signs of destruction by fire from that time have been found in some Edomite towns, and although occupation was resumed, the kingdom of Edom had ended. Finally, others have dated Obadiah closer to 500 BC, reflecting perhaps the reference to the Edomites in Mal 1:4. ◆

Obadiah's Vision

1-4pp — Jer 49:14-16
5-6pp — Jer 49:9-10

1 The vision of Obadiah.

This is what the Sovereign LORD says
about Edom[a] —

We have heard a message from the
LORD:
An envoy[b] was sent to the nations to
say,
"Rise, let us go against her for
battle"[c] —

2 "See, I will make you small among the
nations;
you will be utterly despised.
3 The pride[d] of your heart has deceived
you,
you who live in the clefts of the
rocks[a]
and make your home on the heights,
you who say to yourself,
'Who can bring me down to the
ground?'[e]
4 Though you soar like the eagle
and make your nest[f] among the
stars,
from there I will bring you down,"[g]
declares the LORD.[h]
5 "If thieves came to you,
if robbers in the night —
oh, what a disaster awaits you! —
would they not steal only as much
as they wanted?
If grape pickers came to you,
would they not leave a few grapes?[i]
6 But how Esau will be ransacked,
his hidden treasures pillaged!
7 All your allies[j] will force you to the
border;
your friends will deceive and
overpower you;

1 [a] Isa 63:1-6; Jer 49:7-22; Eze 25:12-14; Am 1:11-12 [b] Isa 18:2 [c] Jer 6:4-5 **3** [d] Isa 16:6 [e] Isa 14:13-15; Rev 18:7 **4** [f] Hab 2:9 [g] Isa 14:13 [h] Job 20:6 **5** [i] Dt 24:21 **7** [j] Jer 30:14

[a] 3 Or *of Sela*

1 *vision.* Lit. "what is seen," the term also used to introduce the prophecies of Isaiah (Isa 1:1) and Nahum (Na 1:1). *Obadiah.* The name means the "servant" or "slave" of the Lord. He is, therefore, one who does what he is told by his master, here as an agent delivering a message. *Edom.* The principal theme of the book of Obadiah is an indictment of Edom for its crimes against Judah. The nation of Edom, located south and east of the Dead Sea, has a mixed tradition among the Israelites (see note on 1Ki 11:14 – 17). During the period of the Neo-Assyrian Empire and the Neo-Babylonian Empire (734 – 586 BC), Edom had been a vassal state. Most likely Obadiah's complaint against Edom relates to the participation of Edom in the final destruction of Jerusalem and the exile of its people by Nebuchadnezzar of Babylon in 587/586 BC, but records are unclear concerning the precise role that Edom played. *envoy.* The rare Hebrew word used here is only found in the poetical books (Pr 13:17; 25:13; Isa 18:2; 57:9). There is nothing to distinguish it from the common word for "messenger" or "angel" (see note on Ex 3:2). Throughout the ancient world, the messenger's role was essential, for there was no other means of formal communication. When nations went to war in the ancient Near East, it was necessary to call on all covenant partners and vassal states to send troops and supplies for a combined effort. Messengers would be sent to call on them to honor their treaty commitments and conscript the specified number of soldiers (see 1Sa 11:3 – 4 and the reciprocal defense pact found in the treaty between Pharaoh Rameses II and the Hittite king Hattusili III). The Mari texts even describe the practice of sending envoys to the temple of a god to inform the deity of the military situation and call on his aid in the coming conflict.

2 *small.* Nothing in Edom's history could lead it to place itself among the "great powers," even if it did control the valuable trade routes bringing incense, gold and other rarities by land and sea from southern Arabia.

3 *clefts of the rocks.* A major cause of Edom's pride is revealed. The natural cliffs and ravines edging its land provided inaccessible fortresses and made it ideal for guerrilla activity. The phrase may equally well be translated "clefts of Sela," the name of the fortress that Amaziah captured and renamed Joktheel (2Ki 14:7, cf. 2Ch 25:11 – 12). There are two possible locations for Sela. One is Umm el-Biyara, a flat-topped rock rising almost 1,000 feet (300 meters) above the Petra basin and 3,700 feet (1,130 meters) above sea level. Ruined buildings of the eighth and seventh centuries BC were excavated there, and among the finds was an imprint on clay of a king of Edom's seal. The rival candidate is another flat-topped rock near Bozrah, still called Sela, also yielding Iron Age remains.

4 *eagle.* Edom's cliffs offer ideal nests for the griffon vulture and the imperial eagle, although their numbers have fallen markedly in modern times.

5 *grapes.* Although only small quantities of grapes are grown in the area today, the Edomite vineyards were evidently renowned in Biblical times. Isaiah pictured God, having subdued the nations, as one coming from Edom and Bozrah, his clothes stained as if he had trodden the grapes there (Isa 63:1 – 6), while earlier Isaiah spoke of the devastation of the vineyards of Moab (Isa 16:7 – 10; cf. Jer 48:32). The Israelites were commanded, "Do not go over your vineyard a second time or pick up the grapes that have fallen. Leave them for the poor and the foreigner" (Lev 19:10; cf. Dt 24:21), but nothing was to be left of Edom (cf. Jer 6:9; Mic 7:1). Edom's failure to stand by its brother Jacob (Ob 10; cf. Am 1:11) and its exultation at the fall of Jerusalem condemned it to isolation and annihilation by the Babylonians.

7 *allies . . . friends.* "Allies" translates the Hebrew for "men of your covenant," while "friends" translates the Hebrew for "men of your peace." These are defined as "those who eat your bread" in solemnization of a pact or treaty (cf. Jacob and Laban [Ge 31:46,54], Joshua and the Gibeonites (Jos 9:14]). So for one partner to turn against the other was gross treachery (cf. "close friend" of Ps 41:9). Many ancient Near Eastern texts contain similar concepts. A pharaoh complained to a Syrian ruler that he had heard "you are at peace with the ruler of Qadesh and eat and drink together . . . Why are you at peace with a ruler whom (I) am fighting with?" "Peace and brotherhood" was the term used for an alliance. In the pact made by Pharaoh Rameses II and the Hittite king Hattusili III about 1259 BC, the Egyptian says of the Hittite, "He is my brother, and I am his brother. He is at peace with me, and I am at peace with him forever." A Hittite king wrote to a newly enthroned king of Babylon

OBADIAH 1

Obadiah's Audience

Obadiah, like other Hebrew prophets, condemned a foreign nation. This raises the question of his audience. Although he addressed Edom, his message was for his own people, for it is unlikely that many Edomites heard it and their language, while close to Hebrew, was not the same and probably sounded different. This prophecy, therefore, is an encouragement to God's people that their disasters were not final, that restoration would come; however, at the same time, the prophecy is a caution lest they behave in the same way as the Edomites, risking a similar punishment. See the article "Prophets and Prophecy," p. 1110. ◆

those who eat your bread[k] will set a
trap for you,[a]
but you will not detect it.
8 "In that day," declares the LORD,
"will I not destroy[l] the wise men of
Edom,
those of understanding in the
mountains of Esau?
9 Your warriors, Teman,[m] will be
terrified,
and everyone in Esau's mountains
will be cut down in the slaughter.
10 Because of the violence[n] against your
brother Jacob,[o]
you will be covered with shame;
you will be destroyed forever.[p]
11 On the day you stood aloof
while strangers carried off his wealth
and foreigners entered his gates
and cast lots[q] for Jerusalem,
you were like one of them.
12 You should not gloat over your brother
in the day of his misfortune,
nor rejoice[r] over the people of Judah
in the day of their destruction,[s]
nor boast so much
in the day of their trouble.[t]
13 You should not march through the
gates of my people
in the day of their disaster,
nor gloat over them in their calamity[u]
in the day of their disaster,
nor seize their wealth
in the day of their disaster.
14 You should not wait at the crossroads
to cut down their fugitives,
nor hand over their survivors
in the day of their trouble.

15 "The day of the LORD is near[v]
for all nations.
As you have done, it will be done to you;
your deeds[w] will return upon your
own head.
16 Just as you drank on my holy hill,
so all the nations will drink[x]
continually;
they will drink and drink
and be as if they had never been.

7 [k] Ps 41:9 **8** [l] Job 5:12; Isa 29:14 **9** [m] Ge 36:11, 34 **10** [n] Joel 3:19 [o] Ps 137:7; Am 1:11-12 [p] Eze 35:9 **11** [q] Na 3:10 **12** [r] Eze 35:15 [s] Pr 17:5 [t] Mic 4:11 **13** [u] Eze 35:5 **15** [v] Eze 30:3 [w] Jer 50:29; Hab 2:8 **16** [x] Jer 25:15; 49:12

[a] *7* The meaning of the Hebrew for this clause is uncertain.

in phrases found in many diplomatic documents: "[When your father] and I established friendly relations and became brothers, [we] spoke [as follows]: 'We are brothers. To the enemy of one another [we will be hostile and with] the friend of one another we will be friendly.'"

8 *the wise men of Edom.* The tradition of Edomite wisdom can be somewhat substantiated by the nation's association with Job, who was from Uz, which is considered by some to be in Edom, and with Job's friend, Eliphaz the Temanite (see Job 1:1; 2:11). Living on the fringe of the northern Arabian desert and benefitting from the caravan trade and accessible copper deposits, it may be that Edom was known for its business acumen or diplomatic shrewdness (see the parallel statement in Jer 49:7).

10 *brother Jacob.* Edomites were the descendants of Esau, the brother of Jacob, who in turn was the father of the Israelites. When this book pits Israel against Edom, it is logical to harken back to the enmity between the two brothers.

11 *gates.* See notes on Job 5:4; 29:7; Pr 8:3; 31:23. *cast lots.* Where a decision had to be made that could result in inequity, as with looted objects that could not be divided, throwing lots was an acceptable solution across the ancient world (Jos 18 – 19; Ps 22:18; Pr 18:18). Laws from Assyria prescribe that the eldest brother, after choosing his primary portion of the estate, should throw lots equally with his brothers for his second share.

13 *gates.* See note on v. 11.

16 *drink and drink.* From early times, drinking bouts have been popular, leading to stupefaction. Edom's enjoyment

17 But on Mount Zion will be deliverance;[y]
it will be holy,[z]
and Jacob will possess his inheritance.
18 Jacob will be a fire
and Joseph a flame;
Esau will be stubble,
and they will set him on fire and
destroy[a] him.
There will be no survivors
from Esau."
The LORD has spoken.
19 People from the Negev will occupy
the mountains of Esau,
and people from the foothills will
possess
the land of the Philistines.[b]
They will occupy the fields of Ephraim
and Samaria,[c]
and Benjamin will possess Gilead.
20 This company of Israelite exiles who
are in Canaan
will possess the land as far as
Zarephath;[d]
the exiles from Jerusalem who are in
Sepharad
will possess the towns of the
Negev.[e]
21 Deliverers will go up on[a] Mount Zion
to govern the mountains of Esau.
And the kingdom will be the
LORD's.[f]

17 [y] Am 9:11-15 [z] Isa 4:3 **18** [a] Zec 12:6 **19** [b] Isa 11:14 [c] Jer 31:5 **20** [d] 1Ki 17:9-10 [e] Jer 33:13 **21** [f] Ps 22:28; Zec 14:9, 16; Rev 11:15

[a] 21 Or *from*

of Judah's disaster, like excessive drinking, brought Edom down to the level of all other nations (cf. La 4:21).
18 *no survivors.* Powerful kings showed no mercy to rebellious vassals. Thus Assyrian kings boasted that "not a man escaped" when their troops crushed rebels who broke their oaths of loyalty. In the same way, God pronounced his verdict on nations that defied him.
19 Edom's demise, in common with the disappearance of other local enemies of God's people, would allow dispossessed Israelites to occupy their territories, moving from the Negev eastward into Edom and from the foothills westward to the Philistine cities on the coast and back into the hill country of Israel, with the small tribe of Benjamin gaining the rich pastures of Transjordanian Gilead. *the land of the Philistines.* The southwestern corner of the promised land was already in Philistine hands before Israel arrived in Canaan (Ex 13:17). They remained obstacles to Israel even after the exile (Ne 13:23–24).
20 *Zarephath.* Ten miles (16 kilometers) south of Sidon, Sarepta in Greek (Lk 4:26), modern Sarafand, lay in the northern part of the unconquered territory (Jos 13:4,6; Jdg 1:31). Throughout the days of the kings of Israel and Judah this was the land of the Phoenicians, each major city controlling the area around it, with Zarephath falling under the sway of Sidon, then of Tyre. Obadiah foresees Israelite exiles living in Canaan, at last taking the region for themselves. *Sepharad.* Possible locations for this site range from Spain to the Hesperides to western Media. These identifications are based on place-names and some textual evidence from the Neo-Assyrian period. However, the most likely site for Sepharad is Sardis in western Asia Minor. This was the Lydian capital during the Persian period and a bilingual inscription found there names the city in Aramaic with the same consonants as the Hebrew name here in Obadiah. This would be a very far distance for exiles from Jerusalem to travel, but the implication in the text is that even the most distant would return to reclaim a portion of the land.
21 *to govern.* A small kingdom could become a vassal of a greater power, retaining much of its independence so long as it was loyal. Alliance with the suzerain's enemy or other forms of rebellion would bring heavy punishment, as seen above in Egypt, and absorption of the kingdom into the suzerain's realm under a governor of his choice. When Samaria rebelled against Sargon of Assyria, e.g., Sargon captured the city, deported the inhabitants and reported, "I repopulated Samerina, making it greater than before. I brought into it people from other lands my hands had conquered. I appointed one of my officers as governor over them." That would be Edom's destiny, becoming part of the kingdom of Israel's God; Edom would become a servant of the Lord, like Obadiah.

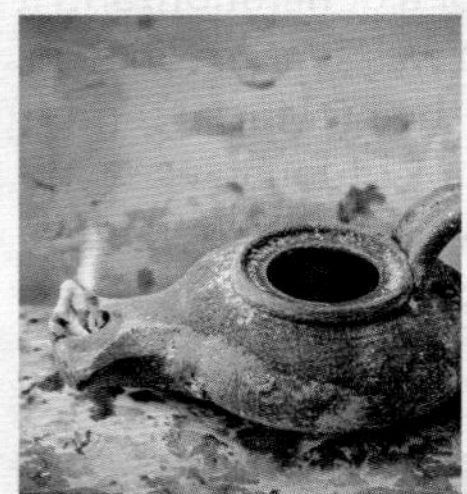

ORACLES OF THE PROPHETS

JONAH

Historical Setting

A reference to "Jonah son of Amittai" in 2Ki 14:25 places the setting for the book of Jonah between 790 and 760 BC. Jonah therefore serves in the generation just before Amos and Hosea, at the beginning of classical prophecy in Israel. During the time of Jonah, the reign of Jeroboam II (793–753 BC) achieved unparalleled prosperity and military success in the history of Israel's divided monarchy. The Arameans were the only hindrance to territorial expansion. Assyria, in a period of decline, was preoccupied with internal security. This background is important for it shows that the northern kingdom of Israel at this time was near the top, not the bottom, in the realm of international politics.

This situation was a reversal from a century earlier when, under Shalmaneser III, the Assyrian Empire had extended its control into the west, exercising authority over Aram, Israel, Judah, and many others. The end of his reign, however, saw revolt by several Assyrian centers (including Nineveh) from 826–820 BC. His son, Shamshi-Adad V, subdued the rebellion, but Assyrian control over the west weakened considerably.

Shamshi-Adad V died about 811 BC and left as heir to the throne his young son, Adadnirari III. Until the boy came of age the country was ruled by Shamshi-Adad's widow, Sammuramat, who retained extensive control until her death. Adadnirari reigned until 783 BC. His city of residence and capital was not Nineveh, but Calah. He was succeeded by three sons: Shalmaneser IV, Ashur-Dan III and Ashurnirari V, respectively. This was a period of practical anarchy. Particularly notable is the series of rebellions between 763 and 758. These were led by disaffected officials who show evidence of usurping royal prerogatives. In such a political climate, a prophecy proclaiming the imminent fall of Nineveh would be taken quite seriously.

With the accession of Tiglath-Pileser III in 745 BC, a new dynasty began that established Assyrian supremacy for a century. Tiglath-Pileser III was succeeded by Shalmaneser V, Sargon II and, finally, Sennacherib, who enlarged Nineveh and made it the capital of the Assyrian Empire more than 50 years after the time of Jonah.

KEY CONCEPTS

- Much of the significance of the book depends on understanding that the Ninevite response is superficial, yet God responds anyway.
- Jonah is put in Nineveh's shoes in order for the book to make its point about God's compassion being undeserved.
- Jonah is not a missionary; he is a prophet.
- Jonah's message is of judgment, not instruction or hope.

The importance of this information for the study of the book of Jonah is the understanding that at the time of Jonah, Assyria had not been a threat to Israel for a generation, and it would be no threat for a generation to come. In addition, when Jonah was sent to Nineveh, he was being sent not to the capital city of a vast empire but to one of the provincial centers of a struggling nation. Some would consider this evidence that the book of Jonah was written several centuries after the Assyrian Empire had come and gone by an author unfamiliar with the details of history. Preferably, it could suggest that God had chosen to send Jonah to Nineveh in anticipation of the role it would eventually play.

Literary Genre

In current trends within critical scholarship, Jonah is commonly labeled as parody or satire. The former typically lampoons a piece of literature, while the latter targets people (specific or stereotyped categories) or events, as Jonah does. Satire can be either an enactment or a written composition in which vice, folly or incompetence is held up for ridicule. The closer to reality a satire can be, the more effective it is. By definition it targets real people and tries to use the mannerisms and words that they use. Satire exaggerates reality, but by its nature is based on reality.

Satire and parody are both known in the ancient world and the Bible. The examples of parody in the ancient Near East also target entities that are considered to be historical and from which historical information may be deduced. In the realm of related satire, the Babylonian "Dialogue of Pessimism" targets a wide variety of cultural institutions. The satire in the book of Jonah targets Jonah personally as a ludicrous example of how a prophet might behave. ◆

Jonah Flees From the LORD

1 The word of the LORD came to Jonah[a]
son of Amittai:[b] 2“Go to the great city
of Nineveh[c] and preach against it, because
its wickedness has come up before me.”
3But Jonah ran[d] away from the LORD and
headed for Tarshish. He went down to Joppa,[e] where he found a ship bound for that
port. After paying the fare, he went aboard
and sailed for Tarshish to flee from the LORD.
4Then the LORD sent a great wind on the
sea, and such a violent storm arose that
the ship threatened to break up.[f] 5All the
sailors were afraid and each cried out to
his own god. And they threw the cargo
into the sea to lighten the ship.[g]
But Jonah had gone below deck, where
he lay down and fell into a deep sleep.
6The captain went to him and said, “How
can you sleep? Get up and call[h] on your
god! Maybe he will take notice of us so
that we will not perish.”[i]
7Then the sailors said to each other,
“Come, let us cast lots to find out who is
responsible for this calamity.”[j] They cast
lots and the lot fell on Jonah. 8So they
asked him, “Tell us, who is responsible for
making all this trouble for us? What kind
of work do you do? Where do you come
from? What is your country? From what
people are you?”
9He answered, “I am a Hebrew and I
worship the LORD, the God of heaven,[k]
who made the sea and the dry land.[l]”

1:1 [a] Mt 12:39-41 [b] 2Ki 14:25 **1:2** [c] Ge 10:11 **1:3** [d] Ps 139:7 [e] Jos 19:46; Ac 9:36, 43 **1:4** [f] Ps 107:23-26 **1:5** [g] Ac 27:18-19 **1:6** [h] Jnh 3:8 [i] Ps 107:28 **1:7** [j] Jos 7:10-18; 1Sa 14:42 **1:9** [k] Ac 17:24 [l] Ps 146:6

1:2 *the great city of Nineveh.* See Introduction: Historical Setting.

1:3 *Tarshish.* Some modern assessments have placed Tarshish as far west as Spain. Esarhaddon's inscriptions refer to a Tarsisi that is west of Cyprus and Greece: "All the kings from [the islands] amidst the sea—from the country Iadnana (Cyprus), as far as Tarsisi, bowed to my feet and I received heavy tribute." Early Christian sources associated "Tharsis" with Rhodes or Carthage. In Ge 10:4 Tarshish is listed along with Elishah and Kittim, both associated with parts of Cyprus. Though the location remains uncertain, it is used in texts to refer to the farthest known point in the west. The conflicting geographic indications in ancient texts suggest the possibility that it refers in a more general sense to far-off islands. In Solomon's day the ships going to Tarshish would not return for three years (1Ki 10:22). *Joppa.* The only ports along the Mediterranean coast of Israel were Joppa, Dor and Akko. Akko was at the northern limit of Israel and was often under Phoenician control. It was little used because of the prominence of Tyre a little farther north. Situated at the southern end of modern Tel Aviv, Joppa is known from ancient and classical sources throughout the Biblical period. In the second millennium BC it is one of the targets of the Egyptian campaign of Thutmose III and is referred to as an Egyptian stronghold in the Amarna letters of the mid-fourteenth century BC. In first-millennium BC Assyrian texts it is under the control of the Philistine city of Ashkelon and is conquered by Sennacherib in 701 BC. That fact, combined with the knowledge that most sea trade at this time was carried out by the Phoenicians and Egyptians, leads us to infer that the sailors on the ship would not have been Israelites. *paying the fare.* Commentators remain divided on the question of whether Jonah bought passage on the ship or hired out the ship. The Hebrew term, usually referring to hire of service, favors the latter, a much more expensive proposition. Likely Jonah would have paid in silver, but no ancient sources indicate what the cost to Jonah might have been.

1:5 *each cried out to his own god.* Working from the inference that the sailors were likely Phoenicians, we can note that in Canaanite/Phoenician belief, though the god of the sky and storm was Hadad (often referred to by the title Baal), Yamm, the god of the sea and of chaos, would be considered the most likely candidate for bringing on such a storm (notice that Jonah identifies Yahweh as God of the sea and dry land [v. 9], not the God of the storm, suggesting he was juxtaposing Yahweh to a god such as Yamm rather than a storm-god such as Baal Hadad). Archaeological evidence suggests another god of the sea whom sailors considered their protective patron. In Esarhaddon's treaty with Tyre, three deities are identified as patron gods of Phoenician sailors: Baal Shamem, Baal Malage and Baal Zaphon. The idea that some offense could have awakened Yamm and his sea creatures and brought the storm would be considered in the realm of possibility. Alternatively, they may have thought that someone had offended the sailor patron gods, who therefore had abandoned them to whatever Yamm wanted to do. Most people in the ancient Near East felt the closest relationship to be with their ancestral, patron or personal deities. Such deities would be the primary focus of personal worship but were not typically the cosmic deities able to send a storm such as this. Even though the sailors would not think that their personal deities had sent the storm, these are the deities to whom they might cry. Their hope would be that one of them might be able and willing to intervene on their behalf in the divine assembly and thus procure mercy. They are calling for assistance rather than crying out in repentance. The captain awakens Jonah so that Jonah might also call upon his own patron deity (v. 6). *they threw the cargo into the sea.* What the sailors throw overboard is most likely their supplies of food and water for the journey. If Jonah is the only passenger, there are no merchants aboard and therefore little merchandise for trade. The crew is made up of sailors, not merchants. *cargo.* The Hebrew word usually has to do with equipment or containers of various sorts. It can also refer to belongings (basic, such as ship stores) or possessions (jewelry). Different words are used to refer to trade goods.

1:7 *cast lots.* In the ancient Near East lot casting was one form of divination and was used for decision making. The process of casting lots was begun by each individual placing some identifiable marker into a container (cf. Pr 16:33, where the lot is put into a pouch above the belt). Using more specific information provided in Homer, the presumption is that the container the lots were put into was shaken up and down (as opposed to side to side) until one of the lots came out (as opposed to being drawn out by hand). In this way it can be understood that deity draws the lot out. The intention of the sailors in casting the lots was simply to get divine direction as to who could help resolve their dilemma. Thus when the lot falls on Jonah, they turn to him for information and enlightenment. Why has deity chosen him to give them understanding of their crisis? Jonah's guilt has not yet been established—only that he possesses critical information. And so, the questioning begins.

1:9 *I worship the LORD.* Yahweh is often construed in

JONAH 1:3

Ships and Seafaring in the Ancient World

Ships traveled the Mediterranean between Egypt and the Syrian coast as early as 2700 BC. Evidence comes from paintings and reliefs, models of ships dedicated to the gods, and archaeology of sunken ships. The Phoenician seagoing merchant ships of the first millennium BC had single masts and rectangular sails hung on a yardarm. They were round-bottomed, tub-shaped vessels. There was a quarterdeck toward the stern for shelter and equipment, while the cargo was stored in the bottom beneath the deck. They averaged 75 feet (almost 23 meters) long and 20 feet (6 meters) wide and were steered by a rudder mounted on the port side near the stern. The crew rarely exceeded 20, and the payload ranged from 100–500 tons (90–450 metric tons). With a favorable wind they could sail at five knots (5.75 miles per hour or 9.3 kilometers per hour) covering up to 100 nautical miles (160 kilometers) per day, although two to three knots (2.3 to 3.5 miles per hour or 3.7 to 5.6 kilometers per hour) covering 50 nautical miles (57.5 miles or 92.5 kilometers) was more common.

Winds and currents in the Mediterranean dictated that ships follow a counterclockwise route. This suggests that even if Jonah's ship were going to the western Mediterranean, it would have sailed north along the coast from Joppa to Tyre, Cyprus, Asia Minor, the Ionian Sea and on to the Straits of Gibraltar. Ships usually kept in sight of land; thus it is that when the sailors in Jonah encounter problems, they attempt to row to land (Jnh 1:13). ◆

Third-century AD sarcophagus depicts scenes from the life of Jonah.

10 This terrified them and they asked,
"What have you done?" (They knew he
was running away from the LORD, because
he had already told them so.)
11 The sea was getting rougher and
rougher. So they asked him, "What should
we do to you to make the sea calm down
for us?"
12 "Pick me up and throw me into the
sea," he replied, "and it will become calm.
I know that it is my fault that this great
storm has come upon you."[m]

1:12 [m] 2Sa 24:17; 1Ch 21:17
1:13 [n] Pr 21:30
1:14 [o] Dt 21:8 [p] Ps 115:3
1:15 [q] Ps 107:29; Lk 8:24
1:16 [r] Mk 4:41

13 Instead, the men did their best to row
back to land. But they could not, for the
sea grew even wilder than before.[n] 14 Then
they cried out to the LORD, "Please, LORD,
do not let us die for taking this man's life.
Do not hold us accountable for killing an
innocent man,[o] for you, LORD, have done
as you pleased."[p] 15 Then they took Jonah
and threw him overboard, and the raging
sea grew calm.[q] 16 At this the men greatly
feared[r] the LORD, and they offered a sacrifice to the LORD and made vows to him.

Israel as possessing the authority Canaanites attributed to their gods El and Baal. Jonah's first comment is in line with that as he identifies Yahweh as the "God of heaven." This might even relate directly to the sailors' patron, Baal Shamem ("Master of the Heavens"). In addition, however, Jonah informs the sailors that Yahweh is also understood to be the God who created "the sea and the dry land." This is not the same as calling him a sea-god. Sea-gods are those who have been given jurisdiction over the sea and whose attributes are manifested in the sea. They are not considered to be the ones who created the sea. In Jonah's confession, then, Yahweh is identified as outranking both Baal and Yamm. The sailors would understand that this was not just a standard patron deity. By v. 16 the sailors "feared the LORD," expressing how impressed they are with the display of his power. Jonah's confession that he fears Yahweh seems cliché or ironic in contrast, since Jonah did not fear sufficiently to obey.

1:10 *he had already told them.* Jonah had told them earlier that he was fleeing from his God, but that had not concerned them — that was his problem and probably not all that uncommon. Their terror now increases as they realize that Jonah's flight from a cosmic deity has put them all in jeopardy of suffering the wrath of Jonah's god along with him.

1:11 *What should we do to you . . . ?* Once Jonah's guilt has been established and the offense and the offended deity identified with confidence, the next question logically concerns appeasement. In the thinking of the ancient world, appeasement of the deity's anger was more important than repentance from sin, though if an offense had been identified, as here, it would have to be somehow rectified. Usually appeasement was accomplished by the performance of a specified ritual to soothe the heart of the deity. Here, however, the sailors ask not about performing a ritual for the deity but about doing something to Jonah. The major options would be (1) isolating him from them so that they would no longer be included in his fate or (2) performing an apotropaic ritual, i.e., a ritual to purify and/or protect Jonah from divine wrath.

1:12 *throw me into the sea.* It is interesting that Jonah chooses not only an isolation strategy but one that also would have been perceived as the most primitive of the options for appeasement. The sailors seem scandalized at what appears to be little more than human sacrifice. They attempt another strategy of isolation: rowing back to land to drop Jonah off. This is not only the more humane choice but also logical given the fact that they jettisoned their supplies and that without Jonah, they have no reason to continue the trip.

1:16 *they offered a sacrifice to the LORD and made vows to him.* Not all sacrifices were burnt sacrifices in the ancient

The old Jaffa (Joppa) port, where Jonah would have boarded the ship for Tarshish (Jnh 1:3).

JONAH 1:17

Fantastic Creatures Sent From the Gods

In the famous Babylonian Gilgamesh Epic, the two heroes, Gilgamesh and Enkidu, encounter a number of divinely appointed creatures. Huwawa is the guardian of the cedar forest that they slay in combat. Consequently, Anu is persuaded by his daughter Ishtar to send the "Bull of Heaven" against the two for this act of presumption. Later in the epic, as Gilgamesh journeys to the end of the world, he encounters the scorpion men who were the guardians of the mountains there.

Though today we consider Gilgamesh to be fanciful mythology, the people in the ancient world took it very seriously and would have considered these to be "real" creatures, though associated with the supernatural realm (as Bible readers would think of cherubim or seraphim). The Bull of Heaven is particularly interesting in that it is sent in response to the hubris of the hero, with the intention of teaching him a lesson. Jonah likewise had acted against deity (by fleeing) and was subsequently confronted by a cosmic creature ordained by deity. In the Gilgamesh Epic the Bull of Heaven is not symbolic or allegorical. It is considered real but, as a supernatural creature, would not be classed alongside any standard list of zoological specimens. A similar understanding may be possible for the "huge fish" in Jonah (Jnh 1:17). ◆

Jonah's Prayer

17 Now the LORD provided a huge fish to
swallow Jonah,[s] and Jonah was in the belly of the fish three days and three nights.

2 [a] 1 From inside the fish Jonah prayed to
the LORD his God. 2 He said:

"In my distress I called to the LORD,[t]
and he answered me.
From deep in the realm of the dead
I called for help,
and you listened to my cry.
3 You hurled me into the depths,[u]
into the very heart of the seas,
and the currents swirled about
me;

1:17 [s] Mt 12:40; 16:4; Lk 11:30 **2:2** [t] Ps 18:6; 120:1 **2:3** [u] Ps 88:6

[a] In Hebrew texts 2:1 is numbered 1:17, and 2:1-10 is numbered 2:2-11.

world. Sailors would have had some provision on the ship for offerings to the gods during their long dangerous journey. If there were any goods left on the ship, a presentation offering of grain or a libation of oil or pure water would have been appropriate. The vows would also have pertained to offering a gift to deity, whether in silver or in grain offering, as is usually the case both in the OT and the ancient world. In the Babylonian "Hymn to Shamash," those celebrating at wharf-side are portrayed in worship: "You are the one who saved them, surrounded by mighty waves, you accept from them in return their fine, clear libations. You drink their sweet beer and brew." Vows were usually conditional before the fact, but they could also be appropriate as a response to an act of deliverance. Here they reflect the sailors' gratitude at having been spared. Offering of a vow to a particular deity does not imply that other deities have been cast aside. In the polytheistic world there was ample room for unlimited numbers of deities.

1:17 *huge fish.* In Canaanite beliefs various sea monsters were associates of the sea-god Yamm, and sometimes they were even identified with him (see the article "Chaos Monsters," p. 953). If the sailors saw the fish, it is possible that they viewed it as a manifestation of the sea-god. No other texts in the ancient world refer to a chaos creature from the sea by the term "fish," but creatures that live in unknown regions (desert or sea) that we know to be real animals were at times also associated with chaos creatures. At the same time, readers familiar with Biblical narratives would be aware of common creatures acting at God's prompting (e.g., Balaam's donkey in Nu 22:21 – 41 and Elijah's ravens in 1Ki 17:2 – 6). *three days and three nights.* A person is considered truly dead after three days in the grave or netherworld. In *Inanna's Descent to the Underworld*, the goddess Inanna goes down into the netherworld and tells her servant that if she has not returned in three days, she should begin to lament for her and make petitions to the gods for her return. With this idea in mind, the three days and nights in the belly of the fish in the realm of death would be an indication that Jonah was at the threshold of death.

2:2 – 6 In Jonah's prayer we find reference to several components of Israel's cosmic geography. *Sheol* (NIV

all your waves and breakers
swept over me.[v]
4 I said, 'I have been banished
from your sight;[w]
yet I will look again
toward your holy temple.'
5 The engulfing waters threatened
me,[a]
the deep surrounded me;
seaweed was wrapped around my
head.[x]
6 To the roots of the mountains I sank
down;
the earth beneath barred me in
forever.
But you, LORD my God,
brought my life up from the pit.

7 "When my life was ebbing away,
I remembered[y] you, LORD,
and my prayer[z] rose to you,
to your holy temple.[a]

2:3 [v]Ps 42:7
2:4 [w]Ps 31:22
2:5 [x]Ps 69:1-2
2:7 [y]Ps 77:11-12 [z]2Ch 30:27
[a]Ps 11:4; 18:6
2:8 [b]2Ki 17:15; Jer 10:8
2:9 [c]Ps 50:14, 23; Hos 14:2
[d]Ecc 5:4-5
[e]Ps 3:8
3:1 [f]Jnh 1:1

8 "Those who cling to worthless idols[b]
turn away from God's love for them.
9 But I, with shouts of grateful praise,
will sacrifice[c] to you.
What I have vowed[d] I will make good.
I will say, 'Salvation[e] comes from the
LORD.' "

10 And the LORD commanded the fish,
and it vomited Jonah onto dry land.

Jonah Goes to Nineveh

3 Then the word of the LORD came to Jonah[f] a second time: 2 "Go to the great
city of Nineveh and proclaim to it the message I give you."
3 Jonah obeyed the word of the LORD and
went to Nineveh. Now Nineveh was a very
large city; it took three days to go through
it. 4 Jonah began by going a day's journey

[a] 5 Or *waters were at my throat*

"realm of the dead," v. 2) is the general term for the netherworld—the abode of the dead. *Tehom* (NIV "deep," v. 5) is a reference to the primordial waters of the chaos sea. The "roots of mountains" (v. 6) refer to foundations on which the world was believed to be anchored. These cosmic mountains held back the chaos waters, held up the sky, and were rooted in the netherworld. Parallel to the roots of the mountains is *erets* (NIV "earth," v. 6), the normal Hebrew word for land but also used as a designation for the netherworld. Finally, *shahat* (NIV "pit," v. 6) is given as yet another synonym for the netherworld. See the article "Cosmic Geography," p. 836.

2:4 *banished from your sight.* Being banished from the presence of deity implies disqualification from access to the sacred precincts of the temple. In general one had to maintain a certain level of ritual purity to have access to sacred precincts. Jonah's conclusion that he had been banished would have come not from admitting that he had disobeyed but as a conclusion that death was imminent. His deliverance by the fish would have fostered the hope that he would again appear in God's presence. It is clear from Jonah's prayer that he views the fish as his deliverance rather than punishment. *temple.* The temple is mentioned both here and in v. 7 as what Jonah prays toward and what he desires access to. It raises the intriguing question of which temple he has in mind. He prays to Yahweh, who has only one legitimate temple, in Jerusalem. Yet he is a prophet from the northern kingdom of Israel, which had rejected the Jerusalem temple in favor of the golden calf shrines in Dan and Bethel. These shrines are never referred to as temples of Yahweh, though the Israelites may have regarded them as such if the calves were viewed as escorts or pedestals of Yahweh (similar to the cherubim and ark), as is sometimes claimed. Being accepted in the temple and enjoying renewed access to God's presence would indicate being restored to favor. The context here and the offhand reference simply to the "temple" favors the Jerusalem temple as being intended.

2:6 *barred me in.* Jonah's mention of bars, even if it is figurative, refers to the ancient Near Eastern idea that there are gates to the netherworld. This coincides with the ancient worldview that the netherworld was a city with walls and gates. In Ugaritic literature the city of Mot, god of the netherworld, is *Hmry* ("the Pit"). The OT refers to a netherworld city with gates in Job 38:17; Isa 38:10. Babylonian evidence comes from a twelfth-century BC boundary marker on which is depicted the netherworld city with tall gates guarded by a serpent-like creature. Entrance to the netherworld was typically through the grave, construed as a portal of sorts. Here Jonah views himself as having arrived at the gates of the netherworld by passing through the level of the chaos waters.

2:9 *What I have vowed I will make good.* For vows in general, see note on Jdg 11:30; see also the article "Nazirites," p. 242. Since that which was vowed was usually some material gift, there is little reason to think that Jonah vowed to repent of his disobedience and to willingly take up his mission to Nineveh. More likely he has vowed a gift of thanksgiving for being delivered from what seemed to be certain death.

3:3 *went to Nineveh.* The journey to Nineveh from Joppa (where we assume the fish left Jonah) was about 550 miles (885 kilometers). Caravans usually traveled 20–25 miles (32–40 kilometers) a day, which means Jonah made the trip in about a month. *large city.* The size of Nineveh is expressed in terms of the time that it would take Jonah to carry out his assignment. He is not circling the circumference of the walls but is going to all the public places in the city to make his proclamation. His itinerary would have included many of the dozen gate areas as well as several of the temple areas. There would have been certain times during the day when significant announcements could be made.

3:4 *Forty more days and Nineveh will be overthrown.* The prophecies of the prophets of the ancient Near East are typically ones of instruction and encouragement for the king. There is some indictment (usually cultic matters left undone) but little attestation of judgment oracles against the king who is being addressed. In the only possible exception there is an oracle against Zimri-Lim: "A devouring [plague] will take place. Issue a claim against the cities that they return the sacred things. The man who has committed violence let them expel from the city." Occasionally a prophet will proclaim judgment on an enemy of the king, e.g., "Into the net which he ties, I will gather him. His city I will destroy, and his treasure, which is from ancient times, I will surely plunder." In contrast, prophecies of impending judgment are common in the OT. There

JONAH 3:4–5

Prophets Receiving a Hearing

The institution of prophecy was not something that existed only in Israel. Each country would have had prophets who spoke on behalf of deity. When Assyrian kings received prophecies, they took them very seriously, whether the prophet was known or not and whether the deity was known or not. The prophecies that are preserved from the Assyrian period date to the time of Ashurbanipal, about a century after the historical period in which Jonah is set.

Prophecy, unlike divination, did not use omens in its procedures, though sometimes divination experts offered prophecies in addition to omen interpretations. It would not matter to an official which god a prophet represented. People in the ancient world believed in an open system in which any number of gods could be active and powerful. When delegations moved from country to country to conduct diplomatic affairs, it was not unusual for diviners or prophets to be part of the delegation, giving confirmation that the negotiations had the favor of the gods of the visiting delegation. Kings were often interested in collecting all of the advice available in a given situation. There is an example of this in the Bible when Jehoshaphat asks to hear the advice of Ahab's prophets as they consider a joint military endeavor (1Ki 22:2–7).

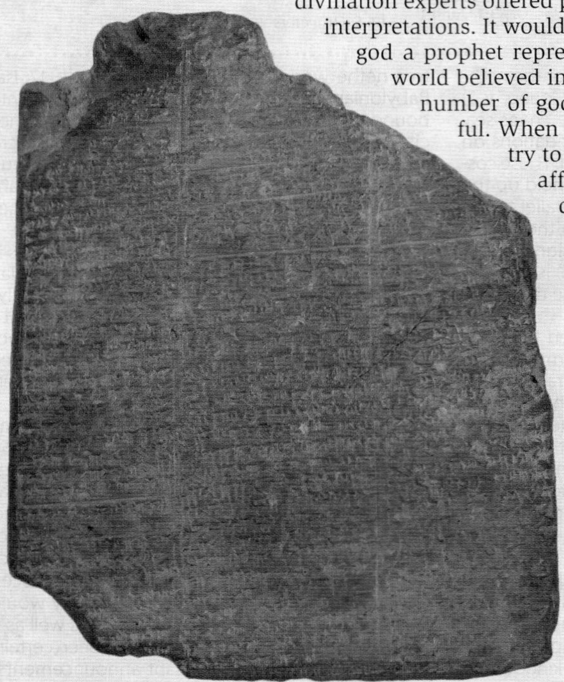

Assyrian prophecy text.

Kim Walton. The British Museum.

The fact that Jonah is a foreigner representing a deity from a distant land even tends to give greater weight to his message. He is doing them a favor and has gone to a great deal of trouble to do so. He has nothing to gain, so the idea that he is compelled by deity is the most plausible explanation. It is important to keep in mind that, contrary to popular interpretations, Jonah is not asking them to change religions or get rid of their other gods. They only have to believe that Yahweh is intending action against them and that he is capable of carrying it out. ◆

into the city, proclaiming, "Forty more
days and Nineveh will be overthrown."
5The Ninevites believed God. A fast was
proclaimed, and all of them, from the
greatest to the least, put on sackcloth.[g]
6When Jonah's warning reached the
king of Nineveh, he rose from his throne,
took off his royal robes, covered himself
with sackcloth and sat down in the dust.[h]
7This is the proclamation he issued in Nineveh:

"By the decree of the king and his nobles:

Do not let people or animals, herds
or flocks, taste anything; do not let
them eat or drink.[i] 8But let people
and animals be covered with sackcloth. Let everyone call[j] urgently on
God. Let them give up their evil ways
and their violence. 9Who knows?[k]
God may yet relent and with compassion turn[l] from his fierce anger so that
we will not perish."

10When God saw what they did and
how they turned from their evil ways, he

3:5 [g] Da 9:3; Lk 11:32 **3:6** [h] Job 2:8, 13; Eze 27:30-31 **3:7** [i] 2Ch 20:3 **3:8** [j] Ps 130:1; Jnh 1:6 **3:9** [k] 2Sa 12:22 [l] Joel 2:14

is no suggestion in this text that Jonah offered indictment (e.g., of their idolatry), instruction (e.g., in the law), encouragement or hope (e.g., for deliverance). The prophet's role should not be confused with the missionary's role. Unlike the missionary who has a message of hope (the gospel) and who comes hoping to see conversion, the prophet has whatever message God has given him and comes only to deliver it.

3:5 *The Ninevites believed God.* The text only indicates that the Ninevites believed the message of impending doom that Jonah had delivered. In the prophecy texts from Mari in the eighteenth century BC we get a glimpse of the authentication procedures. If the message came from an unknown prophet, something like the imprint of the hem of his/her garment was provided to the king for authentication of the prophecy. More important, the substance of the message would be confirmed by other divination procedures. In the divination procedures of the ancient Near East, which included prophecy, the practitioners preferred to have omens or messages confirmed through at least two different procedures. Omens could be read from the movement of the heavenly bodies, from the actions of animals or the flight of birds, or from the configurations of the entrails of sacrificial animals, just to name a few. Once it was determined to their satisfaction that this was a legitimate divine message, they would have accepted it and responded. It is likely that the Ninevites would have confirmed Jonah's message in similar ways before they responded. Ninevites would not necessarily have asked why they were going to be destroyed. The literature indicates to us that in Mesopotamia they did not think that they could know the reasons or even whether there were reasons. In the "Lament Over the Destruction of Ur," Sin, the patron deity of the city, asks why it was overthrown. The answer is given by Enlil, the head of the pantheon, that cities and dynasties were not intended to last forever, and the supremacy of Ur had run its course. Despite their acceptance of the veracity of Jonah's message and their sincere response, they are still polytheistic Assyrians ignorant of the nature of Israel's law, faith and God. *A fast was proclaimed ... put on sackcloth.* The most relevant usage of sackcloth in an Akkadian text is in an Esarhaddon inscription in which he is said to have "wrapped his body in sackcloth befitting a penitent sinner." See the article "Mourning," p. 828. Fasting is much more difficult to attest than use of sackcloth. While fasting is not detectable in religious rituals or for repentance in Mesopotamia, individuals did occasionally refrain from eating and drinking in mourning rites. In addition, there were special dietary instructions for certain days throughout the Babylonian year. Other occasions when the Mesopotamians did not eat or drink seem to be similar to the situation recorded in Ac 23:12, when a group of men vowed not to eat or drink until they had killed the apostle Paul. While these examples may be called fasting, there are no obvious spiritual or cultic connections to the act.

3:6 *king of Nineveh.* The gravest problem with the king of Assyria being called the king of Nineveh is that during the time of Jonah, the king of Assyria did not have his residence at Nineveh. Though Nineveh may have been a large and important city, it was not a royal city. Jonah would not have encountered the king of Assyria on his throne in Nineveh, because the king of Assyria did not have a throne in Nineveh. A more likely interpretation is that the "king of Nineveh" is not the king of Assyria but a governor or noble who was ruling the city/province. Concerning terminology, the Hebrew term translated "king" in Jonah (*melek*), though used throughout the OT for kings, does not pose an insuperable problem when we consider that an Assyrian official is being described. The normal Akkadian (Assyrian) word for king is *šarru*, but the bilingual Tel Fakhariyah Inscription translates the Akkadian *šaknu* ("governor") with the Aramaic *mlk*. This suggests that West Semitic languages (Aramaic and Hebrew) could use this word to refer to local ruling governors or nobles. Furthermore, the governor (*šaknu/mlk*) could rule over either the city of Nineveh or the province of Nineveh. In fact, in the *limmu* list of Assyrian notables, the designated official for the year 761 BC was Nabu-mukin-ahi, governor of the region of Nineveh.

3:7–9 The proclamation of the king details the strategies for appeasing the angry god. Aside from the rituals of sackcloth and fasting discussed above, some behavioral changes were dictated. Though Assyrians had no revelation from their gods that would equate to Israel's covenant law, they understood that justice was important to the gods for the order that it brought to society. Lawlessness would be offensive to the gods, so here they act to remedy that condition. It is possible that various rituals would have been performed to seek to appease God or protect them from destruction. To whatever extent such rituals may have been pursued, the text has no interest in them. God is responding to their humility and their repentance, not their rituals (which would have been attempts at manipulation).

3:8 *animals be covered with sackcloth.* That even animals should be adorned with the signs of repentance is not outlandish. Even today black hearses are used by funeral parlors and horses in funeral procession feature black accessories. Since sackcloth itself is not frequently attested in ancient literature, it is no surprise that we have no examples of animals being draped with it. The Apocryphal book of Judith, however, contains an example of the Jews responding in a similar way when Holofernes marched on Jerusalem (Judith 4:10–12). In addition, Herodotus notes that Persian mourning customs included cutting horses' manes, just as people shaved their heads.

3:10 *he relented.* God's action has been translated in various ways (KJV "repented"; NRSV "changed his mind"). This

relented[m] and did not bring on them the destruction[n] he had threatened.[o]

Jonah's Anger at the LORD's Compassion

4 But to Jonah this seemed very wrong, and he became angry.[p] 2 He prayed to the LORD, "Isn't this what I said, LORD, when I was still at home? That is what I tried to forestall by fleeing to Tarshish. I knew[q] that you are a gracious and compassionate God, slow to anger and abounding in love,[r] a God who relents from sending calamity.[s] 3 Now, LORD, take away my life,[t] for it is better for me to die[u] than to live."

4 But the LORD replied, "Is it right for you to be angry?"[v]

5 Jonah had gone out and sat down at a place east of the city. There he made himself a shelter, sat in its shade and waited to see what would happen to the city. 6 Then the LORD God provided a leafy plant[a] and made it grow up over Jonah to give shade for his head to ease his discomfort, and Jonah was very happy about the plant. 7 But at dawn the next day God provided a worm, which chewed the plant so that it withered.[w] 8 When the sun rose, God provided a scorching east wind, and the sun blazed on Jonah's head so that he grew faint. He wanted to die, and said, "It would be better for me to die than to live."

9 But God said to Jonah, "Is it right for you to be angry about the plant?"

"It is," he said. "And I'm so angry I wish I were dead."

10 But the LORD said, "You have been concerned about this plant, though you did not tend it or make it grow. It sprang up overnight and died overnight. 11 And should I not have concern[x] for the great city of Nineveh,[y] in which there are more than a hundred and twenty thousand people who cannot tell their right hand from their left—and also many animals?"

3:10 [m] Am 7:6 [n] Jer 18:8 [o] Ex 32:14 **4:1** [p] ver 4; Lk 15:28 **4:2** [q] Jer 20:7-8 [r] Ex 34:6; Ps 86:5, 15 [s] Joel 2:13 **4:3** [t] 1Ki 19:4 [u] Job 7:15 **4:4** [v] Mt 20:11-15 **4:7** [w] Joel 1:12 **4:11** [x] Jnh 3:10 [y] Jnh 1:2; 3:2

[a] 6 The precise identification of this plant is uncertain; also in verses 7, 9 and 10.

is one of the main passages used in discussions about whether God can change his mind. In the ancient Near East the gods were erratic and could be managed through various ritual approaches. The gods were believed to have needs, and when humans met those needs, they were attempting to soothe the god from any irritation and earn the god's goodwill. It was therefore their desired intention to induce the god to change his mind concerning how he was treating them. This mutual dependence is the fulcrum of the Assyrian religious system. See the article "Great Symbiosis," p. 186.

When the Biblical text insists that God is not one to change his mind (Nu 23:19; 1Sa 15:29, both texts using the same verb as in Jnh 3:10), it is in the context of covenant agreements, not the outcome of prophetic pronouncements (see Jer 18:8). Mesopotamians also confirm that what their gods decree cannot be altered: "What you proclaim in the assembly, An and Enlil cannot throw out; the oracles uttered on your tongue never change in heaven or earth; / A place you sanction meets no ruin; / A place you brand does not last." There is a distinction to be made then between ad hoc action, which could be impacted by "gifts" to the deity, and formal divine decrees, which could not be altered.

4:2 *gracious and compassionate … slow to anger and abounding in love … relents.* Jonah's list of five attributes is practically creedal in the OT (Ex 34:6; Ne 9:17; Ps 86:15; Joel 2:13), so it is ironic that Jonah uses them as a basis of his complaint. The gods of the ancient Near East can be described in similar terms when maintenance of justice is at issue. In a nineteenth-century BC prayer to Utu (the sun-god), the god is described as a "righteous god who loves to preserve people alive, who hears prayer, [is] long on mercy, who knows clemency, loving justice, choosing righteousness." In addition, prayers in the ancient Near East request the gods to be merciful (comparable to the Hebrew words translated "gracious" and "compassionate"), and they portray them as showing mercy to the afflicted. The god Gula, e.g., is described as "merciful and compassionate." Furthermore, the gods relent when they are appeased. So, in *Enuma Elish* 6.137 Marduk's fourth name identifies him as "furious but relenting." In contrast to the situation in Israel, people in Assyria are expected to be loyal to the gods but the gods are not typically described as being loyal toward people, though prayers ask them to be. The gods are said to "love" the king, but this is an expression of preference and favor. Jonah's list, then, does not necessarily distinguish Yahweh from how the gods of the ancient world are portrayed. The list simply represents the attributes that Jonah recognizes as assuring that his trip to Nineveh will initiate a series of inevitabilities: Jonah will give his message, Nineveh will respond (ignorantly and inadequately), God will relent.

4:8 *east wind.* The east wind was a problem in Palestine because of the desert to the east, but in Nineveh it would have been a very different situation. Because of the mountains east of the Tigris River running northwest to southeast, the prevailing winds in Mesopotamia are northwest and southeast. The east wind was named the mountain wind and usually brought rain. This verse specifies a particular type of east wind ("scorching"), but this Hebrew word is used only here so its nuance is obscure. It may be important to note that it is not the wind, but the sun, that is designated as the element that oppressed Jonah.

4:11 There is much discussion about the size of Nineveh's population. For some time the number 300,000 has been cited as the estimated population of the city and its environs in the seventh century BC. Recent estimates using a variety of documents have confirmed that such a number is reasonable. If that is so, the number 120,000 for the earlier period is not exaggerated.

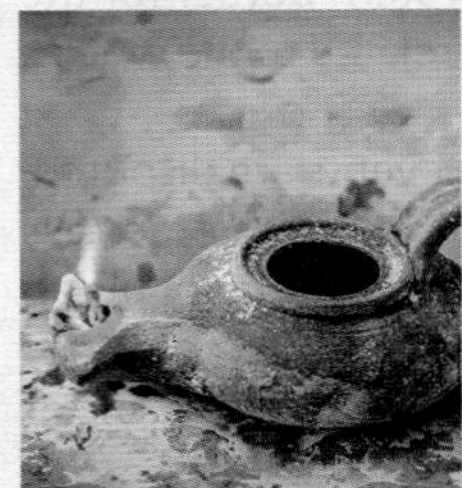

ORACLES OF THE PROPHETS

MICAH

Two anchors place Micah's activity at the end of the eighth century BC: (1) Mic 1:1 links the prophet to the Judahite kings Jotham, Ahaz and Hezekiah, whose reigns extend from (at most) 750 to 687 BC; and (2) Jer 26:18 quotes Micah and refers to Micah's proclamations as taking place "in the days of Hezekiah king of Judah," again at the end of the eighth century BC. The second half of the eighth century BC was so dynamic that even with these limits it is quite difficult to characterize the political world of Micah. For instance, Micah speaks of the devastation of the western lowlands of Judah in ch. 1, but this area was attacked as many as four times in the eighth century BC, and readings of difficult passages change depending on which of these conquests is behind his oracle. Further, Micah talks about economic justice, but the attempt to characterize this message is stymied by the sheer variety of economic relationships at the end of the eighth century BC.

KEY CONCEPTS

- Spiritual renewal begins with putting an end to one's unjust treatment of others. This is not all there is, but it is the essential first step.
- Oracles of the prophets generally fall into four categories: *indictment* (telling the people what they are doing wrong), *judgment* (indicating how God is going to respond to their sin), *instruction* (identifying what response is appropriate) and *aftermath* (outlining the hope for deliverance and restoration after the judgment).

Historical Background

The earliest dates for the context of Micah's speeches have recently been argued as beginning in 747 BC, during the early years of Jotham in Judah and the last years of Jeroboam II in Israel. Others place Micah's oracles in the context of the struggle between Israel and Judah, which culminated in the Syro-Ephraimite War (735 – 734 BC) as Damascus and Samaria fought against Jerusalem to install an anti-Assyrian ruler on the throne. Ahaz responded by inviting the Assyrian king into the region, an action that quickly resulted in the defeat of Damascus and the beginning of Assyrian hegemony in the region.

Still others place Micah's message in the days when Assyria returned to end the last vestiges of Israelite independence in an attack on Samaria that culminated in Samaria's destruction in 722 BC. According to many, this event is either predicted or recorded in Mic 1 and marks the beginning of Micah's ministry.

Finally, in 701 BC Hezekiah revolted against the Assyrians, but he was thoroughly defeated by Sennacherib's armies. Only Jerusalem survived the attacks that completely destroyed the lowlands of Judah and allowed the Philistines to dominate Judah's western border for the following century. This last event is perhaps the event most commonly related to the oracles of Micah, particularly to the events described in 1:10 – 16.

While the exact parallels between Micah's oracles and any of these events are disputed, scholars have noted that determining which of these events is behind Micah's oracles is key to understanding the details of the message of the book. The modern reader of Micah should at least be aware of the variety of ways in which different historical backgrounds have made a difference in the understanding of, and even translations of, several difficult passages in the book of Micah. ◆

1 The word of the LORD that came to Micah of Moresheth[a] during the reigns of Jotham,[b] Ahaz[c] and Hezekiah, kings of Judah[d] — the vision[e] he saw concerning Samaria and Jerusalem.

2 Hear, you peoples, all of you,[f]
listen, earth[g] and all who live in it,
that the Sovereign LORD may bear
witness[h] against you,
the Lord from his holy temple.[i]

Judgment Against Samaria and Jerusalem

3 Look! The LORD is coming from his
dwelling[j] place;
he comes down and treads on the
heights of the earth.[k]
4 The mountains melt[l] beneath him
and the valleys split apart,[m]
like wax before the fire,
like water rushing down a slope.
5 All this is because of Jacob's
transgression,
because of the sins of the people of
Israel.
What is Jacob's transgression?
Is it not Samaria?[n]
What is Judah's high place?
Is it not Jerusalem?

6 "Therefore I will make Samaria a heap
of rubble,
a place for planting vineyards.
I will pour her stones[o] into the valley
and lay bare her foundations.[p]
7 All her idols[q] will be broken to pieces;
all her temple gifts will be burned
with fire;
I will destroy all her images.[r]
Since she gathered her gifts from the
wages of prostitutes,[s]
as the wages of prostitutes they will
again be used."

Weeping and Mourning

8 Because of this I will weep[t] and wail;
I will go about barefoot and naked.

1:1 [a] Jer 26:18 [b] 1Ch 3:12 [c] 1Ch 3:13 [d] Hos 1:1 [e] Isa 1:1 **1:2** [f] Ps 50:7 [g] Jer 6:19 [h] Ge 31:50; Dt 4:26; Isa 1:2 [i] Ps 11:4 **1:3** [j] Isa 18:4 [k] Am 4:13 **1:4** [l] Ps 46:2, 6 [m] Nu 16:31; Na 1:5 **1:5** [n] Am 8:14 **1:6** [o] Am 5:11 [p] Eze 13:14 **1:7** [q] Eze 6:6 [r] Dt 9:21 [s] Dt 23:17-18 **1:8** [t] Isa 15:3

1:1 *Moresheth.* Located approximately 6 miles (9.6 kilometers) northeast of Lachish in the Shephelah, Moresheth (Tell Judeideh, about 20 miles [32 kilometers] southwest of Jerusalem) would have been one of the suburbs of the Philistine city of Gath (Tell es-Safi). After the establishment of David's kingdom, Gath served, along with Lachish, Adullam and Mareshah, as a fortified center (2Ch 11:7 – 10). All of these sites, along with countless villages, were destroyed by Sennacherib's Assyrian army in 701 BC. *Jotham, Ahaz and Hezekiah.* Their reigns cover the last half of the eighth century BC. Micah's first oracle (vv. 2 – 7), which deals with Israel's northern capital of Samaria, would date to just prior to that city's destruction by the Assyrians in 722 BC.
1:3 *coming from his dwelling place.* Magnifies the sense of majesty inherent to this theophany of Yahweh. *treads on the heights of the earth.* An expression of power used very often of vanquishing enemies (Dt 33:29; Ps 108:13). However, in this case the image is of God displaying control over creation, using the earth's mountains as stepping stones (Am 4:13). A similar image is created of the swift, mountain-hopping movements of the divine messengers in the Ugaritic Baal Cycle. Cities were typically built on hills because of their natural defensibility, and armies chose hills as strategic points of control. The metaphor of treading on the heights therefore also speaks of victory and security. Another image that may also be implied derives from the fact that the word translated "heights," besides referring to elevated terrain, often carries the idea of a cultic high place. The image of the god's feet founded on the high cultic mountains is also depicted in cylinder seals from Ugarit. So perhaps Micah also includes a subtle jibe as the venerated high places are trampled underfoot.
1:4 *The mountains melt ... the valleys split apart.* When he comes forth or calls forth from his lofty abode, all creation trembles at the sound of the Divine Warrior. A roughly contemporary inscription from Kuntillet Ajrud relates that when the god El appeared, "the mountains melted." The more vivid rendering of Micah's metaphor "like wax before the fire" aptly catches the intense reaction of creation to the appearance of Yahweh. The reaction of the valleys is not as clear. It may be that Micah pictures an earthquake with fissures appearing in the valleys (Jdg 5:4 – 5), but more likely, the image here is of the "waters below" (see Ge 1:6 – 7) gushing after having been stirred by the passing of the Almighty (Hab 3:10), with those waters making an appearance as "water rushing down a slope."
1:5 *Judah's high place.* The *bamot* of Judah are often condemned in the Former Prophets, but the irony here is that Jerusalem itself is pictured in this category. Elsewhere the *bamot* are condemned in favor of worship in Jerusalem (see note on 1Ki 3:2). The condemnation of Jerusalem, however, might make sense if this diatribe is located in the time of Ahaz, whose specific sins, according to the book of Kings, included the installation of an additional altar in the temple precinct (see 2Ki 16:10 – 16 and note), just one of several changes "in deference to the king of Assyria" (2Ki 16:18).
1:6 *Samaria.* Micah's denunciation of Samaria uses several vivid images, with the force that the thriving urban capital will be transformed into an agricultural plot, its formidable buildings nothing more than stones to be cleared for the crops. Evidence of the prosperity of Samaria is found in the excavations revealing, e.g., the extensive fortifications that defined the acropolis beginning in the days of Omri. Of additional interest, archaeologists recovered the Samaria ostraca, a series of receipts for goods delivered from the surrounding area. These receipts were probably the contribution of the estates of various nobles supplied from abroad but living in the capital. *pour her stones into the valley.* While earlier summaries of the excavations at Samaria spoke of the Assyrian destruction of Samaria around 722 BC, recent archaeologists are no longer certain if the Assyrians razed the city or whether they merely replaced its political structure and many of its inhabitants while leaving its architecture substantially intact. Some of this imagery may, while retaining the concept of destruction, also hint at ritual defilement. Isaiah speaks of the cultic "smooth stones of the ravine" (Isa 57:6) and a fifth-century BC Phoenician inscription uses the uncovering of foundations as an evidence that something has been cursed. The language here might be focused on the cursing of Samaria rather than on the disposition of its architecture.
1:8 *I.* In this verse the first-person referent appears to shift

I will howl like a jackal
and moan like an owl.
9 For Samaria's plague[u] is incurable;
it has spread to Judah.[v]
It has reached the very gate[w] of my people,
even to Jerusalem itself.
10 Tell it not in Gath[a];
weep not at all.
In Beth Ophrah[b]
roll in the dust.
11 Pass by naked[x] and in shame,
you who live in Shaphir.[c]
Those who live in Zaanan[d]
will not come out.
Beth Ezel is in mourning;
it no longer protects you.
12 Those who live in Maroth[e] writhe in pain,
waiting for relief,[y]
because disaster has come from the LORD,
even to the gate of Jerusalem.
13 You who live in Lachish,[z]
harness fast horses to the chariot.

1:9 [u] Jer 46:11 [v] 2Ki 18:13 [w] Isa 3:26 **1:11** [x] Eze 23:29 **1:12** [y] Jer 14:19 **1:13** [z] Jos 10:3

[a] *10 Gath* sounds like the Hebrew for *tell.* [b] *10 Beth Ophrah* means *house of dust.* [c] *11 Shaphir* means *pleasant.* [d] *11 Zaanan* sounds like the Hebrew for *come out.* [e] *12 Maroth* sounds like the Hebrew for *bitter.*

from Yahweh to Micah. *weep and wail ... go about barefooted and naked ... howl like a jackal ... moan like an owl.* Micah combines both the terms of mourning for death with a mimic of the desolation of exile. In the first couplet, Micah weeps and wails, using verbs that are almost always used in the context of mourning for the dead (see the article "Mourning," p. 828), in this case in anticipation of the devastation of Judah. Further, Micah strips off his clothing and shoes. While the tearing of garments is often a sign of mourning, the nakedness of the prophet seems more closely linked to the anticipation of exile (see note on Isa 20:2). The final metaphor can be related to mourning or to exile. Some propose that the jackal and the "owl" are mentioned here for their distinctive howl or piercing cry, perhaps paralleled with the cry of the mourner. The more likely connection, however, is to the jackal and the "ostrich," two animals found on the fringes of the inhabited places, signaling that Judah is to be a desolate wilderness, left to these animals. Jackals are commonly used to signify wilderness areas (Job 30:29, Isa 13:21 – 22; 34:13; 43:20), and ostrich remains have been found in excavations on the border of the wilderness (Tell Jemmeh) and in pottery representation from the southern Negev site of Qitmit.

1:9 *gate of my people.* The text makes the transition here, as in v. 5, from Samaria to the southern kingdom of Judah, characterized by Jerusalem. In one sense, the "gate" can stand as the public place for the whole city. Assyrian kings often set up memorial stones or impaled kings in front of the gate in order to reach the whole population in the most public terms possible. And they summarized times of siege by noting control over the ability to enter or exit the gate. In this particular passage, two other suggestions have been made. First, there is a textual oddity with a new character "he" (NIV "it"), mentioned as arriving at the city gate. Some have argued that this is the Divine Warrior of the first few verses who has finally arrived at his destination of judgment. Others focus on the commercial function of the gate. The commercial injustice, which Micah will later discuss, has now even infected the very marketplaces of Jerusalem.

1:10 – 16 These verses are so difficult that scholars have resorted to a host of textual emendations to make sense out of the many oddities of the text. There is, however, no solid aspect on which to build. Even if the events that are described are contemporary with Micah, which most assume, it is clear that Micah lived through several attacks on Judah. Several very different periods have been proposed as the background for this section (see the chart "Proposed Dates for the Book of Micah," p. 1517).

1:10 *Gath.* Likely Tell es-Safi, which had its power broken at the end of the ninth century BC (2Ki 12:17) and seems not to have survived the revolt of 712 BC.

1:11 – 12 *Shaphir ... Zaanan ... Beth Ezel ... Maroth.* None of these sites can be positively identified and most are entirely unknown. Given the difficulty in identifying these sites, some have seen these either as distortions of names or as even created names intended as wordplays (see the article "Playing With Place-Names," p. 1482). Shaphir (meaning "beautiful" or "pleasant") will be naked, Zaanan (sounds like the Hebrew for "come out") will not come out, Beth Ezel (perhaps has the unlikely meaning "standing place") will not stand, and Maroth (sounds like the Hebrew for "bitter") will wait for relief. These conjectured puns work in some cases (Shaphir and Zaanan) better than others (Beth Ezel and Maroth).

1:12 The translation of v. 12 is critical for understanding the surrounding text. Two distinct possibilities emerge that are related to the different possible historical contexts for all of vv. 10 – 16 (see the chart "Proposed Dates for the Book of Micah," p. 1517). The first, and most common, is the translation that is suggested by the NIV. In this case, the idea of the verse is that Maroth, like the other cities on the list, is being attacked as part of a general attack on all of lowland Judah. From this translation, the attack of Sennacherib in 701 BC would be the most logical historical background. An alternate translation reads "Surely the inhabitants of Maroth hoped for good because evil has come down from the LORD to the gates of Jerusalem." In other words, Maroth, part of Judah, is actually rooting against Jerusalem (Isa 8:6), perhaps rooting that an Israelite coalition would succeed and topple Jerusalem. Unfortunately for Maroth, not only would Jerusalem survive, but the Assyrians would soon be on the scene, threatening the Judahite lowland in concert with Jerusalem.

1:13 *Lachish.* Identified with Tell ed-Duweir, now called Tel Lachish, situated near the Wadi Ghafr — a main route from the coastal plain to the Hebron hills. Archaeological digs there have revealed (Stratum IV) a large fortified city in this period, which we may assume was constructed during the reign of Rehoboam (2Ch 11:5 – 12,23). Among the finds were an impressive city-gate complex in the southwestern wall (the city's only gate), and a palace-fort in the center of the city that was attached to a storehouse and a stable. It was to this city, then — the most important fortified city in Judah after Jerusalem — that Amaziah fled when Jerusalem was lost. *harness fast horses to the chariot.* Chariots were the shock troops of the ancient world, (see note on Isa 2:7), but their maintenance was a severe financial strain on the ancient kingdoms of the region. The Israelite Ahab stood out for his ability to muster 2,000 chariots to oppose the Assyrian Shalmaneser III at the battle of Qarqar in 853 BC. By Ahab's time, chariots regularly appear in battles as part of Israelite and Judahite forces. In Micah's discussion a century later, only a single chariot

You are where the sin of Daughter Zion
began,
for the transgressions of Israel were
found in you.
14 Therefore you will give parting gifts[a]
to Moresheth Gath.
The town of Akzib[a][b] will prove deceptive[c]
to the kings of Israel.
15 I will bring a conqueror against you
who live in Mareshah.[b][d]

1:14 [a] 2Ki 16:8 [b] Jos 15:44 [c] Jer 15:18 1:15 [d] Jos 15:44

[a] 14 *Akzib* means *deception.* [b] 15 *Mareshah* sounds like the Hebrew for *conqueror.*

is mentioned. It is not clear whether this singular reference is merely a function of his poetic speech and the whole chariot force is meant to be mobilized or whether the chariot here, rather than being part of an organized resistance, is being harnessed to flee the oncoming invasion (Am 2:14–16). *You are where the sin of Daughter Zion began.* While this is part of a vague section (see note on vv. 10–16), it is most likely related to the sins that were introduced in v. 5, perhaps related to social injustice. If the "sin" referred to is specific to these verses, however, it is likely that it refers to the chariot forces (Isa 2:7; 22:18; 31:1) or the military fortifications of Lachish diverting attention away from the real source of strength for the kingdom of Judah.

1:14–15 *Moresheth Gath … Akzib … Mareshah … Adullam.* Moresheth Gath, the probable hometown of the author, is likely Tell Judeideh. Akzib is listed in this region in the district lists of Jos 15 and has been identified with Tell el-Beidah, which does have archaeological evidence of occupation in the late eighth century BC. Mareshah (Marisa) has been conclusively identified through inscriptions as being at Tell Sandanhanna, just northeast of Lachish. Excavations there have also uncovered evidence of occupation during the late eighth century BC. Adullam (Ge 38; Jos 15; 2Ch 11) has been identified with Khirbet esh-Sheikh Madkur, although it has not been excavated. All of these cities are identified, are in the same region of the low hill country (the Shephelah), and, to the extent that they have been excavated, have yielded evidence of occupation in the late eighth century BC. One question

PROPOSED DATES FOR THE BOOK OF MICAH

DATE: c. 750 BC

Evidence:

- If Mic 1:2–16 is a unit, then this must take place before the fall of Samaria in 722 BC.
- 2Ki 15:37 refers to battles between Israel and Judah at this time.
- 2Ch 26:6–8; 28:17–18 imply that the lowlands were lost to Judah at this time.

Problems: No archaeological evidence of destruction has been found at the lowland cities that have been excavated.

Meaning: Micah describes an internal rebellion against the pro-Assyrian policies of Samaria and Jerusalem.

DATE: 735–734 BC

Evidence:

- References to "Israel" (e.g., Mic 1:14) point to a time before the fall of Samaria (722 BC).
- 2Ch 28:5–21 speaks of a great defeat of Judah at the hands of Israel and the loss of the lowlands to Philistia.
- Reference to "Gath" (Mic 1:10) points to a time before it was destroyed by Sargon in 712 BC.
- Several lowland cities were destroyed more than once in the late eighth century BC, and the first of their destructions likely dates to 735–734 BC.

Problems: Lachish is one of the major cities described in Micah (Mic 1:13), and it was destroyed in 701 BC at the hands of Sennacherib.

Meaning: Micah laments Judah's defeat at the hand of guilty Israel.

DATE: 701 BC

Evidence:

- Archaeological evidence for the destruction of the lowlands is pervasive, particularly at Lachish (2Ki 18:13–14).
- In his inscriptions, Sennacherib specifically claims to have destroyed and depopulated the specific area that Micah is describing, and in Sennacherib's reliefs, he pictures this same destruction.

Problems:

- References to Gath are a purely literary allusion.
- There is no connection to Mic 1:2–9, and no connection to the chronological sequence of Micah's prophecies.
- "Israel" (e.g., Mic 1:14) must be a generic reference to the entirety of the north and south.

Meaning: Micah laments the Assyrian conquest of the lowlands; Judah has now begun to suffer Samaria's fate. If it were clear that Micah's discussion were to be linked with Sennacherib, then one might read this phrase as a merely literary allusion to 2Sa 1:20 or, as some have done, to restore "Giloh" or some more fitting site.

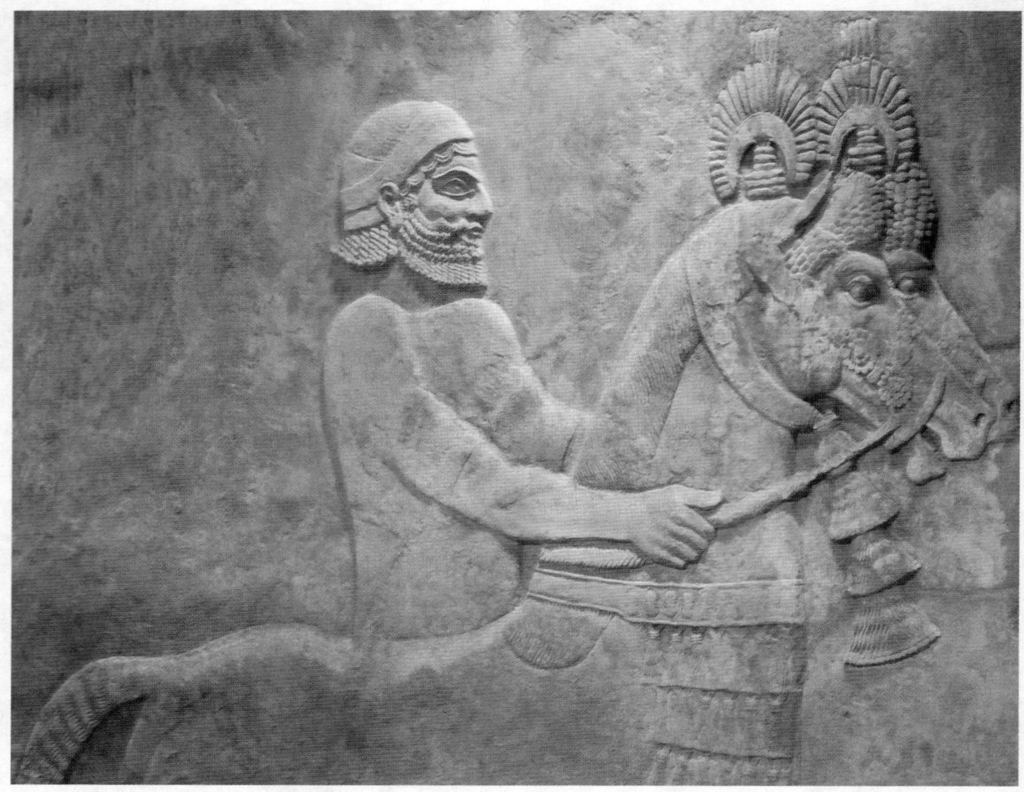

Harnessing horses (Mic 1:13).

Kim Walton. The Oriental Institute Museum, University of Chicago.

The nobles of Israel
will flee to Adullam.[e]
16 Shave[f] your head in mourning
for the children in whom you
delight;
make yourself as bald as the vulture,
for they will go from you into
exile.

1:15 [e] Jos 12:15
1:16 [f] Job 1:20

Human Plans and God's Plans

2 Woe to those who plan iniquity,
to those who plot evil on their
beds![g]
At morning's light they carry it out
because it is in their power to do it.
2 They covet fields[h] and seize them,
and houses, and take them.

2:1 [g] Ps 36:4
2:2 [h] Isa 5:8

is whether the clear identification of these cities can help to explain the location or function of the first four cities (vv. 11–12). Some have opted for a contrast: these (vv. 14–15) are lowland cities, while the earlier cities (vv. 11–12) are from the highlands. Others have opted for continuity: all the cities should be located in the lowlands. *kings of Israel ... nobles of Israel.* How these words are read depends, once again, on the historical background for this whole section (see the chart "Proposed Dates for the Book of Micah," p. 1517). This section could be translated to imply that the "parting gifts" of v. 14 and the town of Akzib will fall to the kings of Israel. The "conqueror" of v. 15 and the "nobles of Israel" could actually be the Israelite king and his army. On the other hand, if a campaign after 722 BC is preferred, then the "kings of Israel" are kings of the southern kingdom (3:8–10; 5:1–3) and the "nobles of Israel" coming to Adullam may be a reference to inhabitants of Lachish headed to exile.
1:16 *Shave your head.* A sign of mourning (Isa 15:2) among the peoples of the region. Laws banning similar, but likely different, practices occur in the prohibition of Dt 14:1. *bald as the vulture.* Its scavenging role is nicely paralleled in the desolation and destruction that Micah envisions (Hos 8:1).
2:1–5 As with the story of Ahab and Naboth (1Ki 21), an inheritance in the land was a key part of not only agricultural life but also religious participation in Israel. Because of this, selling of land was akin to renouncing the promises and protection of Yahweh. In this case, land is seized or sold, and the tribal terms hint at the greater consequences. Micah describes the hierarchy of Israelite society, a nested series of father-son relationships: *bet* = house, v. 2; *mishpahah* > *ah* = family/clan (NIV "people"), v. 3; *am* = people, v. 4; *qahal* = assembly, v. 5. See note on 5:2. For this unjust act, jeopardizing the inheritance of a neighbor, the perpetrators are to be rejected entirely from the religious community (see Dt 23). Several attempts have been made to determine the exact nature of the offending land seizure—from an economic reorganization that disenfranchised smaller landholders to some sort of military conquest—but the text is not specific on this point.

They defraud[i] people of their homes,
they rob them of their inheritance.

3 Therefore, the LORD says:

"I am planning disaster[j] against this
people,
from which you cannot save
yourselves.
You will no longer walk proudly,[k]
for it will be a time of calamity.
4 In that day people will ridicule you;
they will taunt you with this
mournful song:
'We are utterly ruined;[l]
my people's possession is divided up.
He takes it from me!
He assigns our fields to traitors.' "

5 Therefore you will have no one in the
assembly of the LORD
to divide the land[m] by lot.

False Prophets

6 "Do not prophesy," their prophets say.
"Do not prophesy about these
things;
disgrace[n] will not overtake us.[o]"
7 You descendants of Jacob, should it be
said,
"Does the LORD become[a] impatient?
Does he do such things?"

"Do not my words do good[p]
to the one whose ways are upright?[q]
8 Lately my people have risen up
like an enemy.
You strip off the rich robe
from those who pass by without a
care,
like men returning from battle.
9 You drive the women of my people
from their pleasant homes.[r]
You take away my blessing
from their children forever.
10 Get up, go away!
For this is not your resting place,[s]
because it is defiled,[t]
it is ruined, beyond all remedy.
11 If a liar and deceiver[u] comes and says,
'I will prophesy for you plenty of
wine and beer,'
that would be just the prophet for
this people![v]

Deliverance Promised

12 "I will surely gather all of you, Jacob;
I will surely bring together the
remnant[w] of Israel.
I will bring them together like sheep in
a pen,
like a flock in its pasture;
the place will throng with people.
13 The One who breaks open the way will
go up before[x] them;
they will break through the gate and
go out.
Their King will pass through before
them,
the LORD at their head."

Leaders and Prophets Rebuked

3 Then I said,

"Listen, you leaders[y] of Jacob,
you rulers of Israel.
Should you not embrace justice,
2 you who hate good and love evil;
who tear the skin from my people
and the flesh from their bones;[z]
3 who eat my people's flesh,[a]
strip off their skin
and break their bones in pieces;[b]

2:2 [i] Jer 22:17 **2:3** [j] Jer 18:11; Am 3:1-2 [k] Isa 2:12 **2:4** [l] Jer 4:13 **2:5** [m] Jos 18:4 **2:6** [n] Mic 6:16 [o] Am 2:12 **2:7** [p] Ps 119:65 [q] Ps 15:2; 84:11 **2:9** [r] Jer 10:20

2:10 [s] Dt 12:9 [t] Lev 18:25-29; Ps 106:38-39 **2:11** [u] Jer 5:31 [v] Isa 30:10 **2:12** [w] Mic 4:7; 5:7; 7:18 **2:13** [x] Isa 52:12 **3:1** [y] Jer 5:5 **3:2** [z] Ps 53:4; Eze 22:27 **3:3** [a] Ps 14:4 [b] Zep 3:3

[a] 7 Or *Is the Spirit of the LORD*

2:5 *divide the land by lot.* When the father of a family died, the landholdings were divided among the sons by lot. The Laws of Eshnunna, the Code of Hammurapi and the Middle Assyrian Laws all make reference to this situation. Given this background, Micah would be suggesting that the one who has oppressively accumulated landholdings will have no one to pass them on to. Here, however, the focus is likely more specific to Israel's covenant sense of land as divided among the tribes at the time of Joshua (Jos 18:8–10; Jdg 20–21). The oppressor and his family will not be counted among the "assembly of the LORD." In this case, Micah views Joshua's division as a narrative type of the future division of the eschatological promised land.
2:6–11 Micah, as many prophets before him, was confronted by rival prophets who supported the unjust actions of the people. In these verses, Micah defends his prophecy of judgment by noting that it is rooted in the unjust actions of the people (vv. 8–9). As in 1Ki 13 or Am 7, the false prophets described a future of blessing despite the injustice around them.
2:12–13 These verses provide a vivid picture of the king/shepherd leading the large and noisy flock of his people. The NIV translation obscures what is likely a geographic reference. The word translated as "pen" would be better translated as the proper name "Bozrah" (which, of course, means "pen"). Bozrah was the capital of ancient Edom. While many places across the valley in Transjordan were devoted to raising sheep and goats, Edom relied most exclusively on its pastoral economy. For that reason, the author here recalls the famed tumult of gathered flocks of sheep at the Edomite capital of Bozrah.
3:2–3 While human sacrifice, specifically child sacrifice, is attested not only in Israel and Judah but also in Ammon, Moab and Phoenicia (see notes on Lev 20:2; 1Ki 11:5; 2Ki 3:27; 16:3; Jer 7:31), Micah is not arguing that the rulers of Judah and Israel practiced cannibalism. Rather, he uses the distant reference to the horror of human sacrifice and combines it with the image of an everyday meal. The cooking pots of Israel and Judah were small enough that larger bones had to be broken up in order to make the common stew. The combination of human sacrifice with the mundane details of family dinner creates a particularly vivid image of the everyday cruelty of these leaders.

who chop them up like meat for the pan,
like flesh for the pot?[c]"

4 Then they will cry out to the LORD,
but he will not answer them.[d]
At that time he will hide his face[e] from them
because of the evil they have done.

5 This is what the LORD says:

"As for the prophets
who lead my people astray,[f]
they proclaim 'peace'
if they have something to eat,
but prepare to wage war against anyone
who refuses to feed them.
6 Therefore night will come over you,
without visions,
and darkness, without divination.[g]
The sun will set for the prophets,[h]
and the day will go dark for them.
7 The seers will be ashamed[i]
and the diviners disgraced.[j]
They will all cover their faces
because there is no answer from God."
8 But as for me, I am filled with power,
with the Spirit of the LORD,
and with justice and might,
to declare to Jacob his transgression,
to Israel his sin.[k]

9 Hear this, you leaders of Jacob,
you rulers of Israel,
who despise justice
and distort all that is right;[l]
10 who build[m] Zion with bloodshed,[n]
and Jerusalem with wickedness.[o]
11 Her leaders judge for a bribe,
her priests teach for a price,
and her prophets tell fortunes for money.[p]
Yet they look for the LORD's support
and say,
"Is not the LORD among us?
No disaster will come upon us."[q]
12 Therefore because of you,
Zion will be plowed like a field,
Jerusalem will become a heap of rubble,[r]
the temple hill a mound overgrown with thickets.

The Mountain of the LORD

4:1-3pp — Isa 2:1-4

4 In the last days

the mountain[s] of the LORD's temple will be established
as the highest of the mountains;
it will be exalted above the hills,[t]
and peoples will stream to it.[u]

2 Many nations will come and say,

"Come, let us go up to the mountain of the LORD,[v]
to the temple of the God of Jacob.[w]
He will teach us his ways,[x]
so that we may walk in his paths."
The law will go out from Zion,
the word of the LORD from Jerusalem.
3 He will judge between many peoples
and will settle disputes for strong nations far and wide.[y]

3:3 [c] Eze 11:7 **3:4** [d] Ps 18:41; Isa 1:15 [e] Dt 31:17 **3:5** [f] Isa 3:12; 9:16 **3:6** [g] Isa 8:19-22 [h] Isa 29:10 **3:7** [i] Mic 7:16 [j] Isa 44:25 **3:8** [k] Isa 58:1 **3:9** [l] Ps 58:1-2; Isa 1:23 **3:10** [m] Jer 22:13 [n] Hab 2:12 [o] Eze 22:27 **3:11** [p] Isa 1:23; Jer 6:13; Hos 4:8, 18 [q] Jer 7:4 **3:12** [r] Jer 26:18 **4:1** [s] Zec 8:3 [t] Eze 17:22 [u] Ps 22:27; 86:9; Jer 3:17 **4:2** [v] Jer 31:6 [w] Zec 2:11; 14:16 [x] Ps 25:8-9; Isa 54:13 **4:3** [y] Isa 11:4

3:5 *prophets who lead my people astray.* Like Balaam in Numbers, the prophets of Micah's day appear to have been offering their services to the highest bidder (v. 11). It seems to have been a typical practice, even with Israelite prophets, for the inquisitor to offer some present to the seer in return for their message (1Sa 9; 1Ki 14; 2Ki 5). At Mari, clothing and jewelry were demanded in exchange for the prophetic word, but a true prophet could still only relay the message given by the divine. Prophets went by the title *apilum* ("answerer") at Mari, referring to their role in relaying the divine answer, and Micah turns this title against such prophets with the curse that they will not supply the "answer" that they advertised (v. 7). Micah uses the language of uncleanness (as in 2:10) and mourning with his metaphor "cover their faces" (v. 7; Lev 13:45) to describe their shame.

3:12 *Jerusalem will become a heap of rubble.* Micah foretells the ruin of a capital city, just as in ch. 1. Now it is Jerusalem and its temple that are to become a "heap of rubble" (see also 1:6) because they have built Zion with "bloodshed" (3:10), likely a metaphor for iniquity in general rather than a specific reference to human sacrifice. The image of de-urbanization and abandonment is created by Micah's plow and forest language, but again, these are merely metaphors for destruction. Jeremiah quotes this prophecy and dates it to the reign of Hezekiah (Jer 26:18), but we do not know whether Hezekiah's positive response to this prophecy should be related to the deliverance of Jerusalem in 701 BC, to the decision to stay away from Assyria altogether in 712 BC, or to some earlier conflict.

4:1–5 Like Isaiah, Micah presents both positive and negative pictures of the future, both occurring "in the last days" (4:1; Isa 2:2) or "in that day" (4:6; Isa 2:11). In this vision, the abandoned "mountain" (v. 1; see 3:12) is transformed into the center of the nations (v. 1). Zion produces justice (v. 2) instead of bloodshed (3:9–11). War (1:10–16; 2:8–9) is overcome by images of peace (v. 3). The lost inheritance (2:1–2) is restored (v. 4). But the placement of vv. 1–5 immediately after ch. 3 results in a mixing of mountain metaphors. The mountain of the Lord was both a physical place, the city of Jerusalem (3:12), and a religious symbol for the rule of any god. The Canaanite god El issued binding decrees from his mountain, and Baal used his mountain as a defensive stronghold. In ch. 4, Micah first talks of a mountain in this religious sense. Yahweh's inviolable mountain, his heavenly abode, will issue decrees unopposed.

4:3 *swords into plowshares ... spears into pruning hooks.* Micah's vision rests on a visual rather than functional similarity between these items: a sword is short and straight, like a plow point; a spear is long with a blade at the end, as a type of pruning hook. Ancient plows were straight points of metal that attached to a wooden plow.

They will beat their swords into
plowshares
and their spears into pruning hooks.[z]
Nation will not take up sword against
nation,
nor will they train for war anymore.[a]
4 Everyone will sit under their own vine
and under their own fig tree,[b]
and no one will make them afraid,[c]
for the LORD Almighty has spoken.[d]
5 All the nations may walk
in the name of their gods,[e]
but we will walk in the name of the
LORD
our God for ever and ever.[f]

The LORD's Plan

6 "In that day," declares the LORD,

"I will gather the lame;
I will assemble the exiles[g]
and those I have brought to grief.[h]
7 I will make the lame my remnant,[i]
those driven away a strong nation.

4:3 [z] Joel 3:10 [a] Isa 2:4 **4:4** [b] 1Ki 4:25 [c] Lev 26:6 [d] Isa 1:20; Zec 3:10 **4:5** [e] 2Ki 17:29 [f] Jos 24:14-15; Isa 26:8; Zec 10:12 **4:6** [g] Ps 147:2 [h] Eze 34:13, 16; 37:21; Zep 3:19 **4:7** [i] Mic 2:12

The attachment of the metal and wood was specialized enough that there was no way to use a sword as a plow without considerable reworking by the smith. Similarly, the spear needed to be thoroughly reworked in order to be used as a pruning hook. This determined metallurgical effort provides the meaning for Micah's use of the metaphor: farmers would only go to such trouble if they were sure of permanent safety.

4:4 *own vine . . . own fig tree.* The vine and fig were the two most important fruits of an ancient Israelite garden. The vine, because of the length of time necessary before good grapes were produced, was often a symbol of a sedentary life. The fig was known for its sweet produce (Jdg 9:11) and, like the vine, for its pleasant shade. Like the previous metaphor (see note on v. 3), the picture of the vine and fig tree also point to long-term investment and stability.

Fragment of a tomb painting in Nebamun's estate garden with trees, c. 1350 BC, Thebes, Egypt. This fragment appears to show a pool in a garden that might have belonged to Nebamun. The pool is shown full of birds, lotus flowers and tilapia fish, while papyrus grows along the edge. Around the pool are palms, dom-palms, sycamore fig, mandrakes, and other bushes. The vine and fig (Mic 4:4) were the two most important fruits in an ancient Israelite garden.

The LORD will rule over them in Mount
 Zion
from that day and forever.[j]
8 As for you, watchtower of the flock,
 stronghold[a] of Daughter Zion,
the former dominion will be restored[k]
 to you;
kingship will come to Daughter
 Jerusalem."

9 Why do you now cry aloud—
 have you no king[b]?
Has your ruler[c] perished,
 that pain seizes you like that of a
 woman in labor?[m]
10 Writhe in agony, Daughter Zion,
 like a woman in labor,
for now you must leave the city
 to camp in the open field.
You will go to Babylon;[n]
 there you will be rescued.
There the LORD will redeem[o] you
 out of the hand of your enemies.

11 But now many nations
 are gathered against you.
They say, "Let her be defiled,
 let our eyes gloat[p] over Zion!"
12 But they do not know
 the thoughts of the LORD;
they do not understand his plan,[q]
 that he has gathered them like
 sheaves to the threshing floor.
13 "Rise and thresh, Daughter Zion,
 for I will give you horns of iron;
I will give you hooves of bronze,
 and you will break to pieces many
 nations."[r]
You will devote their ill-gotten gains to
 the LORD,
their wealth to the Lord of all the
 earth.

4:7 [j] Da 7:14; Lk 1:33; Rev 11:15 **4:8** [k] Isa 1:26 **4:9** [l] Jer 8:19 [m] Jer 30:6 **4:10** [n] 2Ki 20:18; Isa 43:14 [o] Isa 48:20 **4:11** [p] La 2:16; Ob 1:12 **4:12** [q] Isa 55:8; Ro 11:33-34

A Promised Ruler From Bethlehem

5[d] Marshal your troops now, city of
 troops,
for a siege is laid against us.
They will strike Israel's ruler
 on the cheek[s] with a rod.

2 "But you, Bethlehem[t] Ephrathah,[u]
 though you are small among the
 clans[e] of Judah,
out of you will come for me
 one who will be ruler over Israel,
whose origins are from of old,[v]
 from ancient times."[w]

3 Therefore Israel will be abandoned
 until the time when she who is in
 labor bears a son,
and the rest of his brothers return
 to join the Israelites.

4:13 [r] Da 2:44 **5:1** [s] La 3:30 **5:2** [t] Jn 7:42 [u] Ge 48:7 [v] Ps 102:25 [w] Mt 2:6*

[a] 8 Or *hill* [b] 9 Or *King* [c] 9 Or *Ruler* [d] In Hebrew texts 5:1 is numbered 4:14, and 5:2-15 is numbered 5:1-14. [e] 2 Or *rulers*

4:8 *watchtower.* Otherwise unknown as a construction in Jerusalem, but in this case it appears connected with the stronghold (lit. "Ophel"). The term "Ophel" was an architectural term denoting the acropolis on which the citadel of the city was placed. In Jerusalem, this highpoint was located at the north end of the city of David, just south of the temple mount. By emphasizing the highest, most fortified portion of the city, Micah is completing the reversal of the judgment described at the end of ch. 3.
4:10 *Babylon.* During the late eighth century BC, Babylon was not an independent power capable of threatening Israel or Judah. Rather, as in Hosea or Isa 7–11, Assyria was the dominant empire in the world. 2Ki 20:12–19, however, describes envoys from Babylon arriving in Jerusalem roughly at the end of the eighth century BC (likely in 713). These envoys may have been attempting to convince Hezekiah to join in the revolt against Assyria, which took place just a year later. While this does not explain how Micah's readers would have understood the link between Babylon and exile in the eighth century BC, it at least allows that Babylon was part of the political landscape in Micah's day.
4:12 *threshing floor.* See note on Ru 3:2.
5:1 *strike ... on the cheek.* A common Biblical idea signifying humiliation and disrespect (1Ki 22:24; Job 16:10; Ps 3:7; La 3:30). This verse is a close parallel to vv. 9,11, where Zion suffers before deliverance.
5:2 *Bethlehem Ephrathah ... small among the clans of Judah.* This reference gives insight into the ongoing clan structure of Israel in the eighth century BC. Bethlehem is located five miles (8 kilometers) south of Jerusalem and had been home to Jesse and his sons, notably David. Ephrathah is a clan name claimed by some of the inhabitants of Bethlehem. The town and clan are not equivalent, although one was often used as shorthand for the other. Understanding the relationship between town and clan can be quite difficult because of shifting clan affiliations and clans shifting between localities. The Chronicler, e.g., links the Ephrathites and Tekoa, a town east of Bethlehem. And David is repeatedly referred to as an Ephrathite (1Sa 17:12; cf. Ru 1:2; 4:11), despite the fact that he presumably had no genetic relationship to the Ephrathite line (1Ch 2:19,24; 4:5). One could join a clan/city and use its affiliation as a title without actually joining the clan itself (see Elkanah in 1Sa 1:1; 1Ch 6:23–27) or, as in David's case, one could be amalgamated into both city and clan. This reference demonstrates that the tribal organization of Judah was not obliterated by the arrival of a king. The king was merely the father of tribes, just as tribal leaders were fathers to clans, just like clan/city elders were fathers of their extended households, and the patriarch was the father of his family—and this organization persisted throughout the Israelite and Judahite monarchies. It is clear that Micah is referring to a new Davidic king here, but he could have done this merely by referring to Bethlehem. The addition of the clan name ("Ephrathah") intensifies the martial elements in this section. *clans.* Or "rulers" (see NIV text note); lit. "thousands." In the military muster, all the warriors were organized by clan, with each clan constituting a unit known as a "thousand" (regardless of their actual number). In this passage even though the "thousand" of Bethlehem, specifically the clan muster of Ephrathah, was quite weak (see Jdg 6:15), it would still win the military victory.

[4]He will stand and shepherd his flock[x]
in the strength of the LORD,
in the majesty of the name of the
LORD his God.
And they will live securely, for then his
greatness[y]
will reach to the ends of the earth.

[5]And he will be our peace[z]
when the Assyrians invade[a] our land
and march through our fortresses.
We will raise against them seven
shepherds,
even eight commanders,[b]
[6]who will rule[a] the land of Assyria with
the sword,
the land of Nimrod[c] with drawn
sword.[bd]
He will deliver us from the Assyrians
when they invade our land
and march across our borders.[e]

[7]The remnant[f] of Jacob will be
in the midst of many peoples
like dew from the LORD,
like showers on the grass,[g]
which do not wait for anyone
or depend on man.
[8]The remnant of Jacob will be among
the nations,
in the midst of many peoples,
like a lion among the beasts of the
forest,[h]
like a young lion among flocks of
sheep,
which mauls and mangles[i] as it goes,
and no one can rescue.[j]
[9]Your hand will be lifted up[k] in triumph
over your enemies,
and all your foes will be destroyed.

[10]"In that day," declares the LORD,

"I will destroy your horses from among
you
and demolish your chariots.[l]
[11]I will destroy the cities[m] of your
land
and tear down all your strongholds.[n]
[12]I will destroy your witchcraft
and you will no longer cast spells.[o]
[13]I will destroy your idols
and your sacred stones from among
you;
you will no longer bow down
to the work of your hands.[p]
[14]I will uproot from among you your
Asherah poles[cq]
when I demolish your cities.
[15]I will take vengeance[r] in anger and
wrath
on the nations that have not obeyed
me."

5:4 [x]Isa 40:11; 49:9; Eze 34:11-15, 23; Mic 7:14 [y]Isa 52:13; Lk 1:32 5:5 [z]Isa 9:6; Lk 2:14; Col 1:19-20 [a]Isa 8:7 [b]Isa 10:24-27 5:6 [c]Ge 10:8 [d]Zep 2:13 [e]Na 2:11-13 5:7 [f]Mic 2:12 [g]Isa 44:4 5:8 [h]Ge 49:9 [i]Mic 4:13; Zec 10:5 [j]Ps 50:22; Hos 5:14 5:9 [k]Ps 10:12 5:10 [l]Hos 14:3; Zec 9:10 5:11 [m]Isa 6:11 [n]Hos 10:14; Am 5:9 5:12 [o]Dt 18:10-12; Isa 2:6; 8:19 5:13 [p]Eze 6:9; Zec 13:2 5:14 [q]Ex 34:13 5:15 [r]Isa 65:12 6:1 [s]Ps 50:1; Eze 6:2 6:2 [t]Dt 32:1 [u]Hos 12:2 [v]Ps 50:7 6:3 [w]Jer 2:5 6:4 [x]Dt 7:8 [y]Ex 4:16 [z]Ps 77:20 [a]Ex 15:20

The LORD's Case Against Israel

6 Listen to what the LORD says:

"Stand up, plead my case before the
mountains;[s]
let the hills hear what you have to
say.

[2]"Hear,[t] you mountains, the LORD's
accusation;[u]
listen, you everlasting foundations of
the earth.
For the LORD has a case against his
people;
he is lodging a charge[v] against
Israel.

[3]"My people, what have I done to you?
How have I burdened[w] you? Answer
me.
[4]I brought you up out of Egypt
and redeemed you from the land of
slavery.[x]
I sent Moses[y] to lead you,
also Aaron[z] and Miriam.[a]

[a] 6 Or *crush* [b] 6 Or *Nimrod in its gates* [c] 14 That is, wooden symbols of the goddess Asherah

5:4 *shepherd his flock.* While this phrase has clear overtones to the early life of David himself, it was also a stock phrase used by Egyptian and Mesopotamian kings. See note on Eze 34:2.
5:10–15 These verses list a series of things that the ancient Israelites would have relied upon instead of Yahweh.
5:10 *horses … chariots.* The premier offensive weaponry of an eighth-century BC army (see note on Isa 2:7).
5:12–13 *witchcraft … spells … idols … sacred stones.* Micah describes various cultic measures that might have provided some confidence for the people. Micah's attempt here is not to delve into the details of these practices; rather, he mentions witchcraft and spells as a merism for all those things that might be used to tell the future. Similarly, idols and sacred stones stand for anything that might mark the presence of the divine. See note on Isa 2:6.
5:14 *Asherah poles.* See notes on Dt 7:5; 1Ki 14:23.
6:1–2 Micah depicts a courtroom, drawing on the covenant ratification language also visible in Dt 32:1. However, unlike courtroom indictments elsewhere (Isa 1; Hos 4), Micah's proceedings are unconventional. After declaring that Yahweh will indict Israel, Micah presents a justification of Yahweh rather than a critique of Israel. It is possible to link the resumptive "Listen" (lit. "Hear") of v. 9 with the "Hear" of v. 2, so that a more typical indictment follows in vv. 9–16. While it might be tempting to link Micah with everyday court or covenant proceedings based upon the language of the first verse, the succeeding verses follow no known pattern.
6:3 *what have I done to you?* This very expression, far from being a statement for the prosecution, is found as a pleading defense in the Amarna letters, which describe the weak defense of a petty prince before the mighty Egyptian pharaoh. Here, it is as if Yahweh is in the docket facing the accusations of the people. The mention of Miriam and Aaron (v. 4) is notable for its rarity outside the Pentateuch, and the reference to Shittim and Gilgal (v. 5) is simply a reference to the early events of the conquest

[5]My people, remember
what Balak[b] king of Moab plotted
and what Balaam son of Beor
answered.
Remember your journey from Shittim[c]
to Gilgal,[d]
that you may know the righteous
acts[e] of the LORD."

[6]With what shall I come before the
LORD
and bow down before the exalted
God?
Shall I come before him with burnt
offerings,
with calves a year old?[f]
[7]Will the LORD be pleased with
thousands of rams,[g]
with ten thousand rivers of olive
oil?[h]
Shall I offer my firstborn[i] for my
transgression,
the fruit of my body for the sin of
my soul?[j]
[8]He has shown you, O mortal, what is
good.
And what does the LORD require of
you?
To act justly[k] and to love mercy
and to walk humbly[a][l] with your
God.[m]

6:5 [b]Nu 22:5-6 [c]Nu 25:1 [d]Jos 5:9-10 [e]Jdg 5:11; 1Sa 12:7 6:6 [f]Ps 40:6-8; 51:16-17 6:7 [g]Isa 40:16 [h]Ps 50:8-10 [i]Lev 18:21 [j]2Ki 16:3 6:8 [k]Isa 1:17; Jer 22:3 [l]Isa 57:15 [m]Dt 10:12-13; 1Sa 15:22; Hos 6:6

6:10 [n]Eze 45:9-10; Am 3:10; 8:4-6 6:11 [o]Lev 19:36; Hos 12:7 6:12 [p]Isa 1:23 [q]Isa 3:8 [r]Jer 9:3 6:13 [s]Isa 1:7; 6:11 6:14 [t]Isa 9:20 [u]Isa 30:6

Israel's Guilt and Punishment

[9]Listen! The LORD is calling to the
city—
and to fear your name is wisdom—
"Heed the rod and the One who
appointed it.[b]
[10]Am I still to forget your ill-gotten
treasures, you wicked house,
and the short ephah,[c] which is
accursed?[n]
[11]Shall I acquit someone with dishonest
scales,[o]
with a bag of false weights?
[12]Your rich people are violent;[p]
your inhabitants are liars[q]
and their tongues speak deceitfully.[r]
[13]Therefore, I have begun to destroy[s]
you,
to ruin[d] you because of your sins.
[14]You will eat but not be satisfied;[t]
your stomach will still be empty.[e]
You will store up but save nothing,[u]
because what you save[f] I will give to
the sword.

[a] 8 Or *prudently* [b] 9 The meaning of the Hebrew for this line is uncertain. [c] 10 An ephah was a dry measure. [d] 13 Or *Therefore, I will make you ill and destroy you; / I will ruin* [e] 14 The meaning of the Hebrew for this word is uncertain. [f] 14 Or *You will press toward birth but not give birth, / and what you bring to birth*

narrative (Jos 2:1; 4:19), referring to staging areas on either side of the Jordan.

6:5 *Balaam.* See Nu 22–24; see also the article "Balaam," p. 268.

6:6–7 Micah lists a series of possible sacrifices to bring to God. Some have argued that this list is using extreme and exaggerated numbers. The reference to "thousands" and "ten thousand," e.g., is a common idiom for numbers beyond counting (1Sa 18:7). However, the sacrifices listed here were all too real to the audience, even in their quantity. The year-old animal was the common requirement for a sacrificial animal in texts of Leviticus and Numbers, representing the ideal. Solomon sacrificed flocks without number as part of the dedication of the temple recorded in 1Ki 8. Oil was both a sacrifice in itself (Ge 28:18) and a part of a number of priestly ceremonies recorded in Exodus and Leviticus. Archaeological discoveries at sacred precincts from the Bronze through Iron Ages have found sacred oil to be one of the most significant offerings. The most extreme sacrifice, however, was the offering of a child to appease the gods or to fulfill a vow. Again, this was not mere hyperbole, as both Mesha in the ninth century BC and Ahaz in Micah's own day had done this very thing—likely when both were faced with a difficult military situation.

6:8 The expectations listed here in a general sense summarize what the law called Israel to do, yet these expectations do not differ from what would have been expected of people throughout the ancient world if they desired to ensure that society operated smoothly. Consequently we can see that Micah is calling Israel to a minimal standard of behavior that is recognized as what any sensible people should do. This is the starting point for changing their direction, not a comprehensive statement of all expectations (for a more challenging list, see Dt 10:12–22).

6:10 *ephah.* A dry measure equal to about 3/5 bushel (22 liters). Just as Amos criticizes dishonest merchants for "skimping on the measure" (Am 8:5), Micah also cautions them against cheating their customers with a false ("short") measure of grain. One of the offenses listed in the Shurpu incantation series from Mesopotamia was buying by a large measure and selling by a small one.

6:11 *dishonest scales.* Just as in ch. 2, Micah describes dishonest commerce. In the eighth and seventh centuries BC, there is a marked increase in the number of inscribed weights found in the archaeological record as determining exact weights and measures, for commerce became increasingly important. In addition, archaeological strata from the eighth and seventh centuries BC show a marked increase in the amount of *Hacksilber* (a German term that refers to small fragments of silver jewelry or ingots cut or fused to a standard weight). While payment using silver by weight was not new, its use also expanded in the eighth and seventh centuries BC. The growth of impersonal exchange networks over large distances, exemplified in the Phoenician expansion, greatly increased the need for weights and measures that could be counted on by all. It should come as no surprise that the legal literature of the ancient Near East is quite concerned with upholding just weights and measurements. The "Instruction of Amenemope," e.g., includes two chapters entirely devoted to the upholding of accurate measurements. Several Mesopotamian texts are similarly clear on this point.

6:13–16 As a judgment for their violations of the covenant, God resolves to strike the people with a series of curses often called "futility curses" because inverse cause and effect characterizes them (Hos 4:10; Zep 1:13). This is a common curse form found throughout the length and breadth of ancient Near Eastern texts, from myths to land grants to vassal treaties.

15 You will plant but not harvest;[v]
you will press olives but not use the oil,
you will crush grapes but not drink the wine.[w]
16 You have observed the statutes of Omri[x]
and all the practices of Ahab's[y] house;
you have followed their traditions.[z]
Therefore I will give you over to ruin[a]
and your people to derision;
you will bear the scorn[b] of the nations.[a]"

Israel's Misery

7 What misery is mine!
I am like one who gathers summer fruit
at the gleaning of the vineyard;
there is no cluster of grapes to eat,
none of the early figs that I crave.
2 The faithful have been swept from the land;[c]
not one upright person remains.
Everyone lies in wait to shed blood;[d]
they hunt each other with nets.[e]
3 Both hands are skilled in doing evil;[f]
the ruler demands gifts,
the judge accepts bribes,
the powerful dictate what they desire—
they all conspire together.
4 The best of them is like a brier,[g]
the most upright worse than a thorn hedge.
The day God visits you has come,
the day your watchmen sound the alarm.
Now is the time of your confusion.[h]

6:15 [v] Dt 28:38; Jer 12:13 [w] Am 5:11; Zep 1:13 **6:16** [x] 1Ki 16:25 [y] 1Ki 16:29-33 [z] Jer 7:24 [a] Jer 25:9 [b] Jer 51:51 **7:2** [c] Ps 12:1 [d] Mic 3:10 [e] Jer 5:26 **7:3** [f] Pr 4:16 **7:4** [g] Eze 2:6 [h] Isa 22:5; Hos 9:7

5 Do not trust a neighbor;
put no confidence in a friend.[i]
Even with the woman who lies in your embrace
guard the words of your lips.
6 For a son dishonors his father,
a daughter rises up against her mother,[j]
a daughter-in-law against her mother-in-law—
a man's enemies are the members of his own household.[k]

7 But as for me, I watch in hope[l] for the LORD,
I wait for God my Savior;
my God will hear[m] me.

Israel Will Rise

8 Do not gloat over me,[n] my enemy!
Though I have fallen, I will rise.[o]
Though I sit in darkness,
the LORD will be my light.[p]
9 Because I have sinned against him,
I will bear the LORD's wrath,[q]
until he pleads my case
and upholds my cause.
He will bring me out into the light;
I will see his righteousness.[r]
10 Then my enemy will see it
and will be covered with shame,[s]
she who said to me,
"Where is the LORD your God?"
My eyes will see her downfall;[t]
even now she will be trampled[u] underfoot
like mire in the streets.

7:5 [i] Jer 9:4 **7:6** [j] Eze 22:7 [k] Mt 10:35-36* **7:7** [l] Ps 130:5; Isa 25:9 [m] Ps 4:3 **7:8** [n] Pr 24:17 [o] Ps 37:24; Am 9:11 [p] Isa 9:2 **7:9** [q] La 3:39-40 [r] Isa 46:13 **7:10** [s] Ps 35:26 [t] Isa 51:23 [u] Zec 10:5

[a] 16 Septuagint; Hebrew *scorn due my people*

6:16 *statutes of Omri.* The meaning of this is not clear from other Biblical texts since Omri is passed over with almost no comment by the author of Kings. This lack of comment in Kings is in stark contrast to the portrayal of Omri in ninth-century BC inscriptions. In the Mesha Stele, Omri's rule over Moab is unchallenged by even the rebellious Moabite king, and in the Black Obelisk of Shalmaneser III, Omri's name is as famous in the northern kingdom of Israel as David's was famous in the southern kingdom of Judah. Micah's reference to Omri is juxtaposed with a reference to the works of the house of Ahab. While Ahab receives much more scrutiny in Kings, the author of Kings accuses him of so many things that it is difficult to pick out one thing in particular. Several suggestions have been made, including idolatry and foreign alliances.
7:1 Micah describes a time near the end of October, at the end of the dry season. During September and early October, the summer fruits—grapes, figs, pomegranates, and finally olives—were harvested. It was a time of work but also one of celebration for the productive harvest (Dt 16:13–15). But Micah describes the time after the celebration has finished and before the appearance of the "autumn rains" (Joel 2:23), which were necessary for the sowing of new cereals. In this interlude, nothing is growing, nothing is ripening and one simply hopes through the dryness for rain.
7:3 *the ruler demands gifts, the judge accepts bribes.* It was the height of injustice when those whose sole task was to be just arbiters were now subject to bribes. The administration of justice was the very definition of the Israelite judge and king (see notes on Ps 72; Isa 1:17), but this idea was hardly unique to the Israelites. The Egyptian tale of the "Eloquent Peasant" expects the Egyptian magistrate to uphold justice and the Egyptian lord to fight corruption as a fundamental moral responsibility.
7:6 Even the basic family structure falls apart as the day of punishment arrives. The groups Micah pairs here describe the spheres of authority within the Israelite family. The father had authority over his sons and the men of his household; the mother had authority over her unmarried daughters and married daughters-in-law. In this sphere the authority of the father or mother was virtually unlimited, and to oppose such authority was a serious offense. This image likely combines rebellion as a tragic corollary of the day of punishment and rebellion as the natural reaction to injustice of the parents by children waiting for the Lord (Mt 10; Lk 12).
7:10 *mire in the streets.* In the ancient town or city, the dirt streets and alleys were the dumping ground for

[11]The day for building your walls[v] will
come,
the day for extending your
boundaries.
[12]In that day people will come to you
from Assyria and the cities of Egypt,
even from Egypt to the Euphrates
and from sea to sea
and from mountain to mountain.[w]
[13]The earth will become desolate
because of its inhabitants,
as the result of their deeds.[x]

Prayer and Praise

[14]Shepherd[y] your people with your staff,[z]
the flock of your inheritance,
which lives by itself in a forest,
in fertile pasturelands.[a]
Let them feed in Bashan and Gilead[a]
as in days long ago.

[15]"As in the days when you came out of
Egypt,
I will show them my wonders.[b]"
[16]Nations will see and be ashamed,[c]
deprived of all their power.
They will put their hands over their
mouths
and their ears will become deaf.
[17]They will lick dust like a snake,
like creatures that crawl on the
ground.
They will come trembling out of their
dens;
they will turn in fear[d] to the LORD
our God
and will be afraid of you.
[18]Who is a God like you,
who pardons sin[e] and forgives[f] the
transgression
of the remnant[g] of his inheritance?[h]
You do not stay angry[i] forever
but delight to show mercy.[j]
[19]You will again have compassion on us;
you will tread our sins underfoot
and hurl all our iniquities[k] into the
depths of the sea.[l]
[20]You will be faithful to Jacob,
and show love to Abraham,
as you pledged on oath to our ancestors[m]
in days long ago.

7:11 [v] Isa 54:11 **7:12** [w] Isa 19:23-25 **7:13** [x] Isa 3:10-11 **7:14** [y] Mic 5:4 [z] Ps 23:4 [a] Jer 50:19 **7:15** [b] Ex 3:20; Ps 78:12 **7:16** [c] Isa 26:11 **7:17** [d] Isa 25:3; 49:23; 59:19 **7:18** [e] Isa 43:25; Jer 50:20 [f] Ps 103:8-13 [g] Mic 2:12 [h] Ex 34:9 [i] Ps 103:9 [j] Jer 32:41 **7:19** [k] Isa 43:25 [l] Jer 31:34 **7:20** [m] Dt 7:8; Lk 1:72

[a] 14 Or *in the middle of Carmel*

household refuse, often including human refuse. This same "mire" could be found when the abandoned cistern was used as a garbage dump (Ps 40:2; Jer 38:7). The resulting concoction was not particularly hygienic, but it was a vivid metaphor for the destination of Micah's mocker.

7:11 *day for building your walls.* This refers not to the fortification of a city but to the reapportioning of the inheritance of the people. The "walls" in this case are the small boundary walls, often at the edges of fields or vineyards, that marked out one plot from another (Nu 22:24; Ps 80:12; Isa 5:5; Hos 2:6).

7:14 *Bashan and Gilead.* Located in the northern Transjordan, they had enough rainfall that plentiful harvests were the norm. Their mere mention brought to mind abundance and fertility in the land since these areas only failed to produce if the famine was complete (Isa 33:9). Elijah was one who took refuge in this area when famine covered the land (1Ki 17), but Micah looks further back and recalls the reaction of Reuben, Gad and Manasseh to this ideal pastureland in Nu 32.

7:17 *lick dust like a snake.* Just as the serpent was cursed in the Garden of Eden to eat dust (see Ge 3:14 and note), so also the enemy nations will also be humbled (see Ps 72:9). Since foreign nations are often depicted as serpents (Isa 14:29; Jer 8:17), this may be a further condemnation of the use of snakes as fertility symbols and deities in Mesopotamian and Egyptian religious art. In the Amarna letters, eating dirt or dust is a metaphor for suffering defeat.

7:19 *tread our sins underfoot.* Yahweh's forgiveness of Israel allows a conquest of sin in much the same way that a monarch triumphs over his enemy, treading the enemy underfoot (Ps 60:12) or placing the enemy's neck under the monarch's foot (Jos 10:24). Similar images of the activities of divine warrior gods are found in Anat slaughtering her enemies in the Ugaritic Baal Cycle and the military exploits of the Babylonian god Marduk and the Hittite god Teshub.

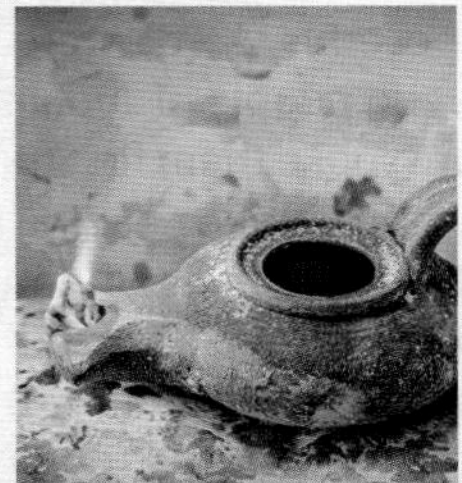

ORACLES OF THE PROPHETS

NAHUM

Historical Background

The prophecy of Nahum concerns the fall of Judah's oppressor, the Assyrian Empire, and of Nineveh, Assyria's capital city (612 BC), bringing relief for Judah. Nineveh had been a major settlement since prehistoric times, as it controlled a crossing of the Tigris River, standing on its eastern bank. Kings had built temples there to honor the goddess Ishtar (Astarte) and palaces for themselves, and Sennacherib made it his principal city in 704 BC, soon after his accession. He built himself a grand new palace on the ancient mound now called Kuyunjik and a palace for his heir at the modern Mosul site of Nebi Yunis, a shrine for the prophet Jonah that was destroyed in AD 2014. Sennacherib built a wall around the whole city of Nineveh, enclosing an area of 750 hectares (1,850 acres), with eventually 18 gates through it and a moat at some parts. Sennacherib's successors added to his buildings and continued erecting new ones. The most magnificent was the palace of Ashurbanipal, which rivaled Sennacherib's in wealth of decoration, especially stone panels carved with scenes of his triumphs in war and hunting.

This splendid city fell to the Babylonians and Medes late in the seventh century BC. The Babylonian Chronicle tablets tell how the Chaldean king Nabopolassar chased the Assyrians out of Babylonia between 626 and 616 BC, and then defeated Assyrian forces in their homeland. The Medes of Iran, commanded by Cyaxares, joined the assault and took the ancient capital of Ashur in 614 BC. Nabopolassar made an alliance with the Medes and the combined forces captured, looted and destroyed Nineveh after a three-month siege in 612 BC. The Assyrian king Sin-shar-ishkun set fire to his palace and perished in the flames, Greek sources report. Although some Assyrian forces under King Ashur-Uballit II held out in Harran and farther west with Egyptian support until 605 BC, Nineveh's glory had passed; its yoke was broken. Excavations at various points in the defenses have revealed the attempts to defend the city and the fates of some of the defenders.

KEY CONCEPTS

- The prophets arose in troubled times to declare the messages God gave them.
- The prophets at times were perplexed about what God was doing.
- Even in times of crisis and confusion, God expects his people to be faithful and trust him.
- With God, there is always reason for hope.

Message and Audience

Although Nahum addresses the Assyrians, readers should not suppose his words were directed toward them. Rather, these oracles were given to encourage the people of Judah at a time when the future appeared dark and uncertain. Whether Nahum spoke them first to an audience or wrote them down first cannot be determined, although the unique heading "the book [i.e., document] of the vision of Nahum" (Na 1: 1) may imply the latter. In Assyria at that time, when people uttered prophecies concerning the king, they were written down for transmission to him, as had happened over a millennium before in Mari. Placed in an archive, the prophecies could be checked as time passed to verify or discount their forecasts. Prophecies concerning other people may also have been put into writing and a similar situation may be supposed for Israel and Judah. ◆

1 A prophecy[a] concerning Nineveh.[b] The
book of the vision of Nahum the Elkoshite.

The LORD's Anger Against Nineveh

2 The LORD is a jealous[c] and avenging
God;
the LORD takes vengeance[d] and is
filled with wrath.
The LORD takes vengeance on his foes
and vents his wrath against his
enemies.
3 The LORD is slow to anger[e] but great in
power;
the LORD will not leave the guilty
unpunished.[f]
His way is in the whirlwind and the
storm,
and clouds[g] are the dust of his feet.
4 He rebukes the sea and dries it up;
he makes all the rivers run dry.
Bashan and Carmel[h] wither
and the blossoms of Lebanon fade.
5 The mountains quake[i] before him
and the hills melt away.[j]
The earth trembles at his presence,
the world and all who live in it.
6 Who can withstand his indignation?
Who can endure[k] his fierce anger?
His wrath is poured out like fire;[l]
the rocks are shattered[m] before
him.

1:1 [a] Isa 13:1; 19:1; Jer 23:33-34 [b] Jnh 1:2; Na 2:8; Zep 2:13 **1:2** [c] Ex 20:5 [d] Dt 32:41; Ps 94:1 **1:3** [e] Ne 9:17 [f] Ex 34:7 [g] Ps 104:3 **1:4** [h] Isa 33:9 **1:5** [i] Ex 19:18 [j] Mic 1:4 **1:6** [k] Mal 3:2 [l] Jer 10:10 [m] 1Ki 19:11

1:1 *Nineveh.* After its use here, the name of the Assyrian capital does not reappear until 2:8. In 1:8,11; 2:1, the Hebrew has feminine grammatical forms that logically refer to Nineveh and so the NIV supplies the name in those verses. In 1:14 the Hebrew has masculine pronouns, so the king of Nineveh is more likely in view. Where the city is meant, it stands for the king in particular and for all the inhabitants in general. Nineveh had been a major settlement since prehistoric times since it controlled an eastern crossing of the Tigris River. Kings had built temples there to honor the goddess Ishtar and palaces for themselves, and Sennacherib made it his principal city in 704 BC, soon after his accession. He built a wall around the whole city, enclosing an area of 1,850 acres (750 hectares), with, eventually, 18 gates through it and a moat at some parts. The enclosure was bisected by the Khosr River, a tributary of the Tigris that rose in the hills to the northeast. After unusually heavy rains, that and other streams could undermine the foundations of buildings in Nineveh, so the king installed a system of canals, aqueducts and dams to harness and control those streams for the benefit of Nineveh, the sites of the waterworks being marked with sculptures and inscriptions. Sennacherib's successors added to his buildings and continued erecting new ones. The most magnificent of these was the palace of Ashurbanipal, which rivaled Sennacherib's in wealth of decoration, especially stone panels carved with scenes of his triumphs in war and hunting. This splendid city fell to the Babylonians and Medes late in the seventh century BC. According to Greek sources, the Assyrian king Sin-shar-ishkun set fire to his palace and perished in the flames. Excavations at various points in the defenses have revealed the attempts to defend the city and the fate of some of the defenders. *Nahum.* The name means "comforted," but it may be a shortened form of Nehemiah, which means "the LORD has comforted," or Naham-el, which means "God has comforted." In Nehemiah's name, the final three letters refer to Yahweh—this is referred to as the "theophoric" element of the name. At times names were shortened by omitting the theophoric element (cf. Ahaz and Ahaziah). *the Elkoshite.* Like Amos (Am 1:1) and Micah (Mic 1:1), Nahum is identified by his hometown (Elkosh), not by his father's name. Several locations have been proposed for Elkosh, which is not mentioned anywhere else in Scripture. Possibilities include (1) an unlikely identification with Al-Kosh in northern Iraq, (2) the simplistic equation with Capernaum, which means "the village of Nahum," on the shore of the Sea of Galilee and (3) the possibility of a place in Judah. None is wholly convincing, but Nahum probably did live in Judah.

1:2 *jealous ... avenging ... vengeance.* Nahum's prophecy opens with a general declaration of the aspects of the character of Israel's God that will be central to his message. The Lord will not allow any human power to challenge his position, his name and his reputation, for which he is jealous and which is bound up with the conduct and fate of the people who bear his name. Those who try to equal or supplant him will be the objects of his vengeance; he will not leave the guilty unpunished. This verse has a form typical of ancient Semitic poetry, building from the key words of the first line to repetition and elaboration in the following lines. The Lord's attitude is comparable with the positions attributed by ancient writers to other deities who were concerned to protect their own reputations. In the "Curse of Agade," a Sumerian poem, the god Enlil, furious at a presumptuous king who had attacked the god's temple, decreed the king's downfall and the invasion of the land by a barbarian tribe. To salvage the rest of the land, the other leading gods pronounced a great curse on the king's capital city, Agade: nobody and nothing in it would function and it would never be inhabited again.

1:3–6 This description of God's power echoes many Biblical passages—from the exodus and the crossing of the Red Sea ("the sea ... dries it up," v. 4) to the theophany at Mount Sinai ("the mountains quake ... the rocks are shattered," vv. 5–6) and the crossing of the Jordan River ("the rivers run dry," v. 4)—while making the particular experiences through which Israel had known God at work into more general characteristics of him. Similar phrases occur in many poems (compare "Bashan and Carmel wither" [v. 4] with "the top of Carmel withers" [Am 1:2]), and some can be found in thirteenth-century BC poems from Ugarit in northern Syria that are applied to the god Baal. Sumerian poetry describes gods and goddesses as roaring like thunder, riding on the storm, stirring up the dust. In the Babylonian Creation Epic, when Marduk, the hero of the gods, advanced to face their enemy, Tiamat, "he mounted the terrible chariot, the unopposable Storm Demon" and at Ugarit, the god Baal is described as "rider on the clouds." In another epic poem, the fire-god Ishum attacks the land of Babylon's enemies in a mountainous region: "He raised his hand, he destroyed the mountain ... He cut away the trunks of the cedar forest, / The thicket looked as if the deluge had passed over ... he obliterated mountains and slew their wild life, / He convulsed the sea and destroyed its increase." See the article "Divine Warfare," p. 365.

1:5 *hills melt away.* This figure of judgment is echoed in a fragment of poetry written about 800 BC on the plaster of a wall in the desert caravanserai at Kuntillet Ajrud on the road from Gaza to Elath: "when God shone forth ... the mountains melted, and peaks grew weak."

7 The LORD is good,[n]
a refuge in times of trouble.
He cares for[o] those who trust in him,
8 but with an overwhelming flood
he will make an end of Nineveh;
he will pursue his foes into the
realm of darkness.

9 Whatever they plot against the LORD
he will bring[a] to an end;
trouble will not come a second time.
10 They will be entangled among thorns[p]
and drunk from their wine;
they will be consumed like dry
stubble.[b][q]
11 From you, Nineveh, has one come
forth
who plots evil against the LORD
and devises wicked plans.

12 This is what the LORD says:

"Although they have allies and are
numerous,
they will be destroyed[r] and pass
away.
Although I have afflicted you, Judah,
I will afflict you no more.[s]
13 Now I will break their yoke[t] from your
neck
and tear your shackles away."

1:7 [n] Jer 33:11 [o] Ps 1:6 **1:10** [p] 2Sa 23:6 [q] Isa 5:24; Mal 4:1 **1:12** [r] Isa 10:34 [s] Isa 54:6-8; La 3:31-32 **1:13** [t] Isa 9:4

[a] *9* Or *What do you foes plot against the LORD? / He will bring it* [b] *10* The meaning of the Hebrew for this verse is uncertain.

1:7 *He cares for.* This translation of the Hebrew verb usually rendered "to know" assumes a sense found in the Ugaritic phrase *il dydnn*, "the god who cares for me." Oracles women gave in the name of the Assyrian goddess Ishtar reassured king Esarhaddon, "I will keep you safe," "Do not be afraid, O king, I have spoken to you, I have not lied to you; I have given you faith, I will not let you be shamed," and advised him, "Do not trust human beings, lift your eyes, look to me." *trust in him.* Expressions of trust are found in Assyrian personal names, e.g., Tukulti-Ninurta ("my trust is in Ninurta") and Mutakkil-Ashur ("the one who inspires trust is Ashur").
1:10 *entangled among thorns.* If the obscure Hebrew words are correctly translated, they depict the impasse that will overtake the plotter. His road will be choked, as the Assyrian king Sargon described a route: "thorns, thistles and bush had grown over [the tracks]."
1:12 *allies.* According to the Babylonian Chronicle, Egypt and the Mannaeans of Iran (see "Minni" in Jer 51:27), were the only powers to support Assyria. Others were allies largely from fear and had no loyalty to Assyria.
1:13 *yoke.* See notes on Jer 5:5; La 3:27. Yoking conquered kings like animals pulling a plow or a chariot was a means Assyrian kings occasionally used to demean them. More often the term is a figure for control, as in Biblical texts. When he drove the Assyrians from Babylonia, after the gods had allowed the Assyrians rule there for decades, Nabopolassar (626 – 605 BC), the conqueror of Nineveh, proclaimed, "The Assyrian who had ruled Akkad [Babylonia] because of divine anger and had, with his heavy

Balawat gate showing prisoners with yokes around their necks, c. 859 to 824 BC. Assyrian kings occasionally yoked conquered peoples (Na 1:13) as a form of humiliation.

Kim Walton. The British Museum.

[14]The LORD has given a command
concerning you, Nineveh:
"You will have no descendants to
bear your name.[u]
I will destroy the images[v] and idols
that are in the temple of your gods.
I will prepare your grave,[w]
for you are vile."

[15]Look, there on the mountains,
the feet of one who brings good
news,[x]
who proclaims peace![y]
Celebrate your festivals,[z] Judah,
and fulfill your vows.
No more will the wicked invade you;[a]
they will be completely destroyed.[a]

Nineveh to Fall

2[b] An attacker[b] advances against you,
Nineveh.
Guard the fortress,
watch the road,
brace yourselves,
marshal all your strength!

[2]The LORD will restore[c] the splendor[d] of
Jacob
like the splendor of Israel,
though destroyers have laid them waste
and have ruined their vines.

[3]The shields of the soldiers are red;
the warriors are clad in scarlet.[e]
The metal on the chariots flashes
on the day they are made ready;
the spears of juniper are
brandished.[c]

[4]The chariots[f] storm through the streets,
rushing back and forth through the
squares.
They look like flaming torches;
they dart about like lightning.

1:14 [u]Isa 14:22 [v]Mic 5:13 [w]Eze 32:22-23 **1:15** [x]Isa 40:9; Ro 10:15 [y]Isa 52:7 [z]Lev 23:2-4 [a]Isa 52:1 **2:1** [b]Jer 51:20 **2:2** [c]Eze 37:23 [d]Isa 60:15 **2:3** [e]Eze 23:14-15 **2:4** [f]Jer 4:13

[a] 15 In Hebrew texts this verse (1:15) is numbered 2:1.
[b] In Hebrew texts 2:1-13 is numbered 2:2-14.
[c] 3 Hebrew; Septuagint and Syriac *ready; / the horsemen rush to and fro.*

---

yoke, oppressed the inhabitants of the country ... I removed them from Akkad and caused [the Babylonians] to throw off their yoke." *shackles.* Shackles or handcuffs of bronze or iron were also common means of securing prisoners (see note on Ps 105:18).

1:14 *Nineveh.* Probably refers to the king of Nineveh (see note on v. 1). *no descendants.* Every ancient man feared dying without a son to continue his name, for that would mean he would be forgotten (compare Absalom, 2Sa 18:18, with Abraham, Ge 15:2–3; see also Isa 53:8) and, certainly in the societies around Judah, there would be no one to perform the rites that would allow his spirit to rest peacefully in the next world. The names of Assyrian noblemen who fell out of favor were erased from their monuments, and even the names of discredited kings and gods were chipped from carvings in Egypt. *your gods.* In their heyday, Assyrian troops had carried the statues of gods from conquered places to their cities, but they rarely destroyed them, for that was, in effect, to deny the existence of the gods they represented. Now Assyria's gods would suffer that worse fate: they would be destroyed. The wealth of the temples and the statues decorated with precious metals and gems would be smashed and looted. Even Assur (the national patron god), Nabu (a favorite god), the war-god Ninurta and the great goddess Ishtar would disappear. *your grave.* A city could hardly have a grave, but the city can represent its inhabitants and, in particular, its king. Ancient people often made arrangements in advance for their burial, but that would not be the case for the people of Nineveh.

1:15 *the feet of one who brings good news.* The phrasing echoes Isa 40:9 and may point to knowledge of the earlier prophet's words or to a common saying. While horses might be used in some regions, in Israel much of the terrain was rough, so it favored runners. Messengers could be regularly employed, carrying dispatches from king to king or from merchant to merchant, or they could be athletic young men chosen for a particular occasion. Their task was often dangerous as, besides wild animals, they might face bandits or, if traveling far, the soldiers of hostile rulers on their journeys. Messengers were expected to be trustworthy, conveying their messages accurately. Although not in view here, they might carry written messages and in Hittite texts of the second millennium BC agreement between the written message and the messenger's words was the proof of authenticity. *Celebrate your festivals ... fulfill your vows.* This would only be possible in times of peace, when people could travel safely and leave their homes without fear of raiders attacking in their absence. In the Babylonian Chronicle frequent entries report the failure to hold the major annual festival marking the New Year there, usually because of war or other forms of unrest.

2:1 *fortress.* Roads led to Nineveh from every direction, so it is likely that there were watch posts, at least, beyond the city walls, although none have been identified.

2:2 *The LORD will restore ... their vines.* Destroying fruit trees was a severe action in war. When he devastated an unruly region, Sargon of Assyria said, "I cut down its extensive vines and so brought its drinking to an end."

2:3 *shields ... are red.* In Assyria it was common rhetoric to speak of cities and countrysides dyed red with the blood of enemies and the army marching through the blood of their enemies. Additionally, Isa 9:5 refers to a practice of warriors rolling their garments in blood. It would be logical, therefore, that armies would choose to wear red tunics, the decoration suggesting that they were covered with the blood of their enemies. Wall paintings uncovered in the Assyrian provincial palace at Tel Barsip on the mid-Euphrates show Assyrian soldiers of the late eighth century BC wearing red and blue tunics. Their shields are colored in concentric circles, alternately reddish brown and pale blue, but whether or not these colors are exact (they may have suffered chemical change during burial) and what they indicate are uncertain.

2:4 *squares.* Beside the palaces on their terraces, the houses of the city occupied the lower ground, with orchards and gardens interspersed among them. Some of the main streets of Nineveh were paved as part of Sennacherib's beautification of the city. Paved areas were sometimes found inside of the city gates. *torches.* Clarification of the meaning of this unique Hebrew word has come from Ugaritic texts of the thirteenth century BC. In them a related word denotes a type of blanket or fabric, and so the Hebrew expression here can be understood as bright-colored trappings on the rushing chariots. The paintings

5 Nineveh summons her picked troops,
yet they stumble[g] on their way.
They dash to the city wall;
the protective shield is put in place.
6 The river gates[h] are thrown open
and the palace collapses.
7 It is decreed[a] that Nineveh
be exiled and carried away.
Her female slaves moan[i] like doves
and beat on their breasts.[j]
8 Nineveh is like a pool
whose water is draining away.
"Stop! Stop!" they cry,
but no one turns back.
9 Plunder the silver!
Plunder the gold!
The supply is endless,
the wealth from all its treasures!
10 She is pillaged, plundered, stripped!
Hearts melt, knees give way,
bodies tremble, every face grows pale.[k]

11 Where now is the lions' den,[l]
the place where they fed their young,
where the lion and lioness went,
and the cubs, with nothing to fear?
12 The lion killed[m] enough for his cubs
and strangled the prey for his mate,
filling his lairs with the kill
and his dens with the prey.

13 "I am against[n] you,"
declares the LORD Almighty.
"I will burn up your chariots in
smoke,[o]
and the sword will devour your
young lions.
I will leave you no prey on the
earth.
The voices of your messengers
will no longer be heard."

2:5 g Jer 46:12 **2:6** h Na 3:13 **2:7** i Isa 59:11 j Isa 32:12 **2:10** k Isa 29:22 **2:11** l Isa 5:29 **2:12** m Jer 51:34 **2:13** n Jer 21:13; Na 3:5 o Ps 46:9 **3:1** p Eze 22:2; Mic 3:10

Woe to Nineveh

3 Woe to the city of blood,[p]
full of lies,
full of plunder,
never without victims!
2 The crack of whips,
the clatter of wheels,
galloping horses
and jolting chariots!
3 Charging cavalry,
flashing swords
and glittering spears!

[a] 7 The meaning of the Hebrew for this word is uncertain.

at Tel Barsip (see note on v. 3) include a royal chariot with its body colored red, and one Assyrian text refers to the chariot of a goddess decorated with colored wool.

2:5 *picked troops.* Traditionally, Babylonian and Assyrian kings relied on soldiers levied from the population in return for plots of land that they could cultivate. In the Assyrian Empire squadrons of permanent soldiers were posted in key places, and this standing army included men from subjugated regions, some from Samaria being among those listed. *protective shield.* Garrisons of cities under attack would hang shields upon the battlements for extra protection against enemy arrows and sling-stones. Sennacherib's sculpture of the siege of Lachish shows them clearly.

2:6 *river gates.* Sennacherib created an extensive network of canals to irrigate the land around Nineveh and to control waters that might endanger his extended city, with dams to provide reservoirs. By breaching the dams, the attackers could cause a surge of water along the Khosr River, weakening the walls where the river entered the city and rapidly emptying the reservoirs.

2:7 *is decreed.* The Hebrew word is a unique form and past commentators tried to explain it as the name of an Assyrian queen, Hussab. Apart from the lack of evidence for a queen of that name, the introduction of such a figure here would be odd, for the prophecy names no other person. The translation "decreed" or "established" is the most satisfactory at present, followed by the assumption that the city is supplied as the subject of the next verb, "be exiled." *be exiled.* The threat of exile hung over every small kingdom of the ancient Near East if they rejected the suzerainty of a greater power or rebelled against one. Examples are known from the third millennium BC onward of powerful kings deporting conquered populations to other parts of their realms. The Assyrian kings engaged in this policy extensively, listing the numbers of peoples they transferred from one place to another, Sennacherib accounting for over 500,000. The people of Samaria were removed to the east, and people from other regions settled in Samaria (2Ki 17:6,24). When Sennacherib attacked Judah because King Hezekiah had broken the treaty his father Ahaz had made, he records that he took away 200,150 people from Judah. Exiles were not necessarily used as slave labor. Often the promise of the Rab-shakeh to the citizens of Jerusalem became a reality (2Ki 18:31 – 32); the exiles were settled on land from which they could make a living, but they could not return to their own country. The threat of exile was not, therefore, something the people of Israel and Judah became aware of only when it happened to them, as sometimes supposed; it was an ever-present possibility. *female slaves moan like doves.* The cries of doves were often compared with the laments of mourners in Hebrew literature (Isa 38:14; 59:11), in earlier Sumerian texts (e.g., the "Curse of Agade") and in later Babylonian texts.

2:9 *Plunder.* A glimpse of the treasures of Nineveh appeared in AD 1988 – 1990, when Iraqi archaeologists opened tombs of Assyrian queens at Nimrud, ancient Calah, 25 miles (40 kilometers) south of Nineveh. Masses of golden jewelry, dishes and bowls of gold and other valuable objects lay in the vaults. For the first time, modern eyes are able to see the sort of riches that ancient texts describe and the sculptures in Assyrian palaces portray. The Babylonian Chronicle notes the "heavy plunder" Babylonian forces took in Nineveh and other places. Far more awaited the conquerors in the palaces of Nineveh, garnered from conquered kingdoms and harvested as tribute.

2:11 – 12 *lions' den … lion.* From the earliest times, Mesopotamian imagery portrayed the king killing the lion, which was a threat to domestic animals and herds. See notes on Jdg 14:5; Isa 31:4; Jer 5:6. In the underlying ideology the lions represented the fierce enemies of the king being defeated.

3:3 *Many casualties, piles of dead.* Assyrian armies had inflicted these horrors on conquered enemies. The inscriptions of Ashurnasirpal give the most frightful reports: "I captured many soldiers alive. The rest of them

Shields from Til Barsip. See note on Na 2:3.

Jill Walton. The Louvre.

Many casualties,
piles of dead,
bodies without number,
people stumbling over the corpses[q] —
4 all because of the wanton lust of a prostitute,
alluring, the mistress of sorceries,[r]
who enslaved nations by her prostitution[s]
and peoples by her witchcraft.

5 "I am against[t] you," declares the LORD Almighty.
"I will lift your skirts[u] over your face.
I will show the nations your nakedness[v]
and the kingdoms your shame.
6 I will pelt you with filth,[w]
I will treat you with contempt[x]
and make you a spectacle.[y]
7 All who see you will flee from you and say,
'Nineveh[z] is in ruins — who will mourn for her?'[a]
Where can I find anyone to comfort[b] you?"

8 Are you better than[c] Thebes,[d]
situated on the Nile,[e]
with water around her?

3:3 [q] 2Ki 19:35; Isa 34:3 **3:4** [r] Isa 47:9 [s] Isa 23:17; Eze 16:25-29 **3:5** [t] Na 2:13 [u] Jer 13:22 [v] Isa 47:3 **3:6** [w] Job 9:31 [x] 1Sa 2:30; Jer 51:37 [y] Isa 14:16 **3:7** [z] Na 1:1 [a] Jer 15:5 [b] Isa 51:19 **3:8** [c] Am 6:2 [d] Jer 46:25 [e] Isa 19:6-9

I burnt. I carried off valuable tribute from them. I built a pile of live (men and) heads before his gate. I erected on stakes 700 soldiers before their gate. I razed, destroyed (and) turned in to ruin hills the city. I burnt their adolescent boys and girls." When Sennacherib conquered Babylon, he related, "I left no one. I filled the city squares with their corpses." Relief sculptures depict Assyrian soldiers bringing the heads of their enemies for secretaries to record. In a treaty in Aramaic, the suzerain threatens to "pile corpse upon corpse" in the vassal's town should he prove unfaithful.

3:5 *nakedness.* Public exposure was a recognized punishment for a rebellious or unfaithful wife in Babylonia. In an Aramaic stele from Sefire (mid-eighth century BC), one curse should a partner be disloyal to a treaty is as follows: "[Just as a pros]ti[tute is stripped naked] so may the wives of Mati'el be stripped naked." Prisoners are shown stripped bare, humiliated and powerless in Mesopotamian pictures from the beginning of history, on seal designs of the late fourth millennium BC, and on the famous Royal Standard of Ur from about 2,500 BC — although on Assyrian sculptures only those about to be executed are naked. The Babylonian god Erra counts among the evils he inflicts on the world the following: "I shall cut off the garment from a man's body, / And I shall make the young man walk naked in the city square."

3:7 *Nineveh is in ruins.* The Babylonian Chronicle says the enemies reduced the city to "a heap of rubble," and when the Greek adventurer Xenophon passed the site some 200 years later, he was apparently unaware that Nineveh had stood there (see 1:14).

3:8 *Thebes.* Identified as the "city of Amun," ancient

The river was her defense,
the waters her wall.
9 Cush[a][f] and Egypt were her boundless strength;
Put[g] and Libya[h] were among her allies.
10 Yet she was taken captive[i]
and went into exile.
Her infants were dashed[j] to pieces
at every street corner.
Lots were cast for her nobles,
and all her great men were put in chains.
11 You too will become drunk;[k]
you will go into hiding[l]
and seek refuge from the enemy.

12 All your fortresses are like fig trees
with their first ripe fruit;
when they are shaken,
the figs[m] fall into the mouth of the eater.
13 Look at your troops —
they are all weaklings.[n]
The gates[o] of your land
are wide open to your enemies;
fire has consumed the bars of your gates.[p]

14 Draw water for the siege,[q]
strengthen your defenses![r]
Work the clay,
tread the mortar,
repair the brickwork!

3:9 [f] 2Ch 12:3 [g] Eze 27:10 [h] Eze 30:5 **3:10** [i] Isa 20:4 [j] Isa 13:16; Hos 13:16 **3:11** [k] Isa 49:26 [l] Isa 2:10 **3:12** [m] Isa 28:4 **3:13** [n] Isa 19:16; Jer 50:37 [o] Na 2:6 [p] Isa 45:2 **3:14** [q] 2Ch 32:4 [r] Na 2:1

3:15 [s] Joel 1:4 **3:17** [t] Jer 51:27 **3:18** [u] Ps 76:5-6 [v] Isa 56:10 [w] 1Ki 22:17 **3:19** [x] Jer 30:13; Mic 1:9 [y] Job 27:23; La 2:15; Zep 2:15

15 There the fire will consume you;
the sword will cut you down —
they will devour you like a swarm of locusts.
Multiply like grasshoppers,
multiply like locusts![s]
16 You have increased the number of your merchants
till they are more numerous than the stars in the sky,
but like locusts they strip the land
and then fly away.
17 Your guards are like locusts,[t]
your officials like swarms of locusts
that settle in the walls on a cold day —
but when the sun appears they fly away,
and no one knows where.

18 King of Assyria, your shepherds[b] slumber;[u]
your nobles lie down to rest.[v]
Your people are scattered[w] on the mountains
with no one to gather them.
19 Nothing can heal you;[x]
your wound is fatal.
All who hear the news about you
clap their hands[y] at your fall,
for who has not felt
your endless cruelty?

[a] *9* That is, the upper Nile region [b] *18* That is, rulers

Thebes is now occupied by modern Karnak and Luxor. Assyrian troops entered and ransacked Thebes under the command of Ashurbanipal in 663 BC, after the Egyptian pharaoh Tirhakah had died and his successor had fled from the city. Ashurbanipal's annals report the massive plunder taken back to Nineveh, including two obelisks made of electrum, weighing 2,500 talents (about 93.75 tons or 83.5 metric tons).

3:9 *Put and Libya.* Earlier commentators understood Put as the ancient Egyptian name for Somalia, Punt, from which exotic goods were brought to Egypt, but the names are not etymologically equivalent. Put is better identified with an ancient name for Libya or part of it; therefore, the expression is best understood as "Put, that is, Libya."

3:10 *Lots were cast for her nobles.* As the leaders of Egypt were forced to surrender, they were distributed as slaves, along with the rest of the loot, among the Assyrian commanders. Provisions for the division of spoils, including the casting of lots, is also found in Homer's *Iliad*, the Mari texts and Joel 3:3.

3:13 *your troops — they are all weaklings.* The idea that soldiers might become weaklings, so losing their strength to fight occurs elsewhere in the Prophets (of Egyptians in Isa 19:16; of Babylonians in Jer 50:37; 51:30) and was also used as a curse on enemies. A variation appears in an inscription of the Assyrian king Tukulti-Ninurta I (c. 1244 – 1208 BC), who prayed that the goddess Ishtar change his enemy "from a man to a woman, may she cause his manhood to dwindle away." It also appears in an inscription of Esarhaddon of Assyria (680 – 669 BC): "May Ishtar turn him from a man into a woman."

3:14 *strengthen your defenses.* Excavations in the gateways of Nineveh have revealed how the citizens tried to control entry into the city by building extra walls within them in an attempt to narrow and control passage into the city.

3:17 *officials.* Many of the officials in the Assyrian court, some of them eunuchs, were foreigners or sons of foreigners brought as hostages or deportees (cf. Daniel) and so, despite the absence of racism in Assyria, may have felt no loyalty to the Assyrian king.

3:18 *King of Assyria.* Since the date of the book of Nahum is uncertain, it is not possible to determine which king of Assyria is referred to in this final oracle. Most scholars would say that the earliest date would be shortly after the capture of Thebes in 663 BC and the terminus date would be the actual fall of Nineveh in 612 BC. It may be that Nahum was written as encouragement to the people of Judah to revolt as the Assyrian Empire began to break apart after Ashurbanipal's death in 627 BC. Alternatively, the reference may be to Sin-shar-ishkun, who was the Assyrian king when Nineveh fell. *no one to gather them.* Although a forlorn remnant of Assyria held out in Harran for a few years, the kingdom and the country lost any political power. Assyria became a province of the Babylonian and the Persian Empires, and then it disappeared.

3:19 *your wound is fatal.* When medical skills were rudimentary, any wound could prove fatal. Neither the attentions of the best physicians nor the priestly incantations, well attested among Babylonian texts, could effect a cure. A long-standing Babylonian curse prayed that the goddess of healing might put a persistent, unhealable wound or sore on the enemy's body.

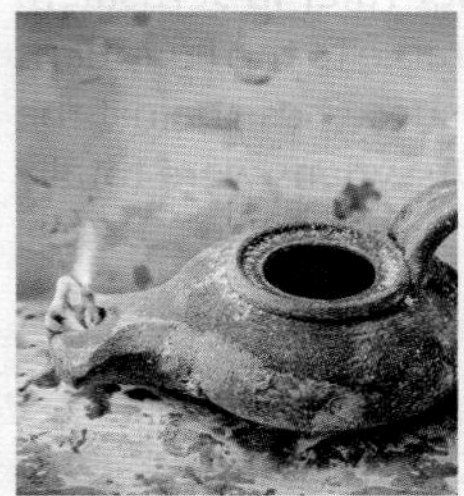

ORACLES OF THE PROPHETS

HABAKKUK

Historical Setting

We are not given the date of Habakkuk's oracle, but it anticipates the rise of the Neo-Babylonians (Chaldeans) that began as early as 625 BC and came to fruition between 612 and 605 BC. The Neo-Babylonians, or Chaldeans, only become a significant threat to Judah after the battle of Carchemish in 605, but by 597 they had captured Jerusalem and taken King Jehoiachin as a hostage (2Ki 24:10 – 14).

Political Analysis of the Seventh Century BC

Internal turmoil in Assyria in the latter half of the seventh century BC may have encouraged Judah to seek a larger political role in Syria-Palestine. Between 652 and 648 BC a power struggle occurred within the royal family pitting the emperor, Ashurbanipal, against a rebel named Shamash-shum-ukin and his allies in Babylonia, Elam and Arabia. However, no significant change occurred in Judah's political fortunes until after the death of Ashurbanipal in 627 BC, when a full pullout of Assyrian forces from Syria-Palestine took place. At that point it became clear that Assyria was not going to bring further punishment to Judah, and Habakkuk's oracles turned their attention to Babylon.

The kings of Judah (Manasseh, Amon and Josiah) during the latter part of the seventh century BC would have noted the shifting political situation. The outbreak of a civil war between Assyrian claimants to the throne (Ashur-etel-ilani and Sin-sharra-ishkun) serve as the prelude to Josiah's reform (2Ki 22 – 23; 2Ch 34 – 35) and any attempts on his part to expand Judah's territory and influence. One additional impetus is the likelihood that Josiah was at least nominally allied with the Egyptians during the period after 630 BC.

Unfortunately, Josiah is not mentioned in the Babylonian Chronicle or in any other ancient text from Mesopotamia or Egypt. The death of Josiah at Megiddo ended any further hopes of a return to political independence for Judah. An anti-Egyptian faction placed Josiah's son Jehoahaz on the throne, but after three months he

KEY CONCEPTS

- The prophets arose in troubled times to declare the messages God gave them.
- The prophets at times were perplexed about what God was doing.
- Even in times of crisis and confusion, God expects his people to be faithful and trust him.
- With God, there is always reason for hope.

was taken as a hostage — first to Riblah in central Syria and then to Egypt (2Ki 23:31 – 34). Necho II installed his brother Eliakim (renamed Jehoiakim) as puppet ruler in Jerusalem (2Ki 23:34 – 35). The political situation in Syria-Palestine remained favorable to the Egyptians for several years, with a garrison installed in Carchemish and military successes against the Babylonian king Nabopolassar in 606 BC. The last contingents of the Assyrians were totally defeated, along with their Egyptian allies, at the battle of Carchemish in 605 BC. ◆

1 The prophecy[a] that Habakkuk the prophet received.

Habakkuk's Complaint

[2]How long, LORD, must I call for help,
but you do not listen?[b]
Or cry out to you, "Violence!"
but you do not save?[c]
[3]Why do you make me look at injustice?
Why do you tolerate[d] wrongdoing?
Destruction and violence[e] are before me;
there is strife,[f] and conflict abounds.
[4]Therefore the law[g] is paralyzed,
and justice never prevails.
The wicked hem in the righteous,
so that justice is perverted.[h]

The LORD's Answer

[5]"Look at the nations and watch—
and be utterly amazed.[i]
For I am going to do something in your days
that you would not believe,
even if you were told.[j]
[6]I am raising up the Babylonians,[a][k]
that ruthless and impetuous people,
who sweep across the whole earth
to seize dwellings not their own.[l]
[7]They are a feared and dreaded people;[m]
they are a law to themselves
and promote their own honor.
[8]Their horses are swifter[n] than leopards,
fiercer than wolves at dusk.
Their cavalry gallops headlong;
their horsemen come from afar.
They fly like an eagle swooping to devour;
[9]they all come intent on violence.
Their hordes[b] advance like a desert wind
and gather prisoners[o] like sand.
[10]They mock kings
and scoff at rulers.[p]
They laugh at all fortified cities;
by building earthen ramps they capture them.
[11]Then they sweep past like the wind[q]
and go on—
guilty people, whose own strength is their god."[r]

1:1 [a]Na 1:1 **1:2** [b]Ps 13:1-2; 22:1-2 [c]Jer 14:9 **1:3** [d]ver 13 [e]Jer 20:8 [f]Ps 55:9 **1:4** [g]Ps 119:126 [h]Job 19:7; Isa 1:23; 5:20; Eze 9:9 **1:5** [i]Isa 29:9 [j]Ac 13:41* **1:6** [k]2Ki 24:2 [l]Jer 13:20 **1:7** [m]Isa 18:7; Jer 39:5-9 **1:8** [n]Jer 4:13 **1:9** [o]Hab 2:5 **1:10** [p]2Ch 36:6 **1:11** [q]Jer 4:11-12 [r]Da 4:30

[a] 6 Or *Chaldeans* [b] 9 The meaning of the Hebrew for this word is uncertain.

1:2–4 Although Habakkuk is speaking to the people of Judah in the late seventh century BC, his statements regarding social injustice are quite similar to those made by Amos to the northern kingdom of Israel in the eighth century BC. Both prophets condemn the self-indulgent and corrupt leaders of their time (see the articles "Economic Changes and Social Classes in Eighth-Century BC Israel," p. 1484; "Administration of Justice," p. 1490). Accusations of social injustice are standard fare in Egyptian wisdom literature. The authors in this genre attempt to hold the leadership of the nation to a very high standard, and feel it is essential for the survival of their culture that corruption be exposed and dealt with by the highest powers. Thus in the period of the Middle Kingdom (2050–1800 BC), a text entitled "Dispute Over Suicide" was composed to expose those social ills that had nearly destroyed Egyptian society during the recently completed First Intermediate Period (2258–2050 BC). The man who asks for the release of death through suicide complains that "everyone is a thief," "hearts are covetous" and "crimes outrage no one." Also during this time of instability, the tale of the "Eloquent Peasant" speaks of the need for Egypt's administrators to check the actions of lawmakers who "approve of robbery" and inspectors who "condone corruption." He calls on judges not to accept bribes or tolerate perjury. In the ancient Near East justice was the most basic and necessary characteristic of society. It was the job of the king to maintain justice (see notes on Ps 72; Isa 1:17). To an even greater extent, the covenant required that Israel strictly maintain justice on both a personal and societal level.

1:6 *the Babylonians.* The Chaldeans, who are first mentioned in Mesopotamian sources in the ninth century BC. Although related ethnically to the other Aramean tribes of southern Babylonia, they had a distinct tribal structure. As the Assyrian Empire began to weaken, Chaldean leaders, including Nabopolassar and Nebuchadnezzar, eventually gained their independence and established the Neo-Babylonian dynasty after 625 BC. Nebuchadnezzar inherited this powerful state in 605 BC, becoming its most famous king. He literally rebuilt the city of Babylon and solidified Babylonian control throughout the Near East, and he even attacked Egypt (albeit unsuccessfully). His long reign lasted until 562 BC. He was briefly succeeded by three descendants, who reigned a total of six years. The last king of the dynasty was Nabonidus, who had apparently been a high official during Nebuchadnezzar's reign. He reigned until 539 BC, when Babylon was captured by the Medo-Persians under Cyrus the Great.

1:9 *intent on violence.* The Assyrian annals are filled with accounts of their rampaging armies that ruthlessly smashed all opposition and took thousands of prisoners. Spear-wielding cavalry were employed as a shock force, leading the charge in battle ahead of the infantry. Their mobility was also useful in wooded country where archers were ineffective. The kings were also fond of describing themselves with bestial powers: Sennacherib "raged like a lion" as he ordered an invasion of Babylonia and set out before a mighty host "like a mighty wild ox." They also attempted to frighten their opponents with a rhetoric of intimidation, such as that used by King Sargon II, who boasted that he had "poured out his awe-inspiring radiance upon all lands," or by Ashurnasirpal II, whose enemies were said to cringe before the splendor of his weapons. This strategy has been termed the "ideology of terror." Exemplary punishments were often used to instill fear, including flaying alive, impalement, cutting off body parts and burning alive.

1:10 *earthen ramps.* See the article "Siege Warfare," p. 1157.

1:11 *strength is their god.* The ultimate indictment of the Neo-Babylonians is their utter disregard for law and the sovereignty of other nations and their rulers, and their single-minded mission to garner loot as they "sweep past like the wind" through an area, overwhelming it with their fierce horsemen and chariots. The translation

Habakkuk's Second Complaint

12 LORD, are you not from everlasting?
My God, my Holy One,[s] you[a] will never die.
You, LORD, have appointed[t] them to execute judgment;
you, my Rock, have ordained them to punish.
13 Your eyes are too pure to look on evil;
you cannot tolerate wrongdoing.[u]
Why then do you tolerate the treacherous?
Why are you silent while the wicked swallow up those more righteous than themselves?
14 You have made people like the fish in the sea,
like the sea creatures that have no ruler.
15 The wicked foe pulls all of them up with hooks,[v]
he catches them in his net,[w]
he gathers them up in his dragnet;
and so he rejoices and is glad.
16 Therefore he sacrifices to his net
and burns incense[x] to his dragnet,
for by his net he lives in luxury
and enjoys the choicest food.
17 Is he to keep on emptying his net,
destroying nations without mercy?[y]

2 I will stand at my watch[z]
and station myself on the ramparts;[a]
I will look to see what he will say[b] to me,
and what answer I am to give to this complaint.[b][c]

The LORD's Answer

2 Then the LORD replied:

"Write[d] down the revelation
and make it plain on tablets
so that a herald[c] may run with it.
3 For the revelation awaits an appointed time;
it speaks of the end[e]
and will not prove false.
Though it linger, wait[f] for it;
it[d] will certainly come
and will not delay.[g]

4 "See, the enemy is puffed up;
his desires are not upright—

1:12 [s] Isa 31:1 [t] Isa 10:6 1:13 [u] La 3:34-36 1:15 [v] Isa 19:8 [w] Jer 16:16 1:16 [x] Jer 44:8 1:17 [y] Isa 14:6; 19:8 2:1 [z] Isa 21:8 [a] Ps 48:13 [b] Ps 85:8 [c] Ps 5:3 2:2 [d] Rev 1:19 2:3 [e] Da 8:17; 10:14 [f] Ps 27:14 [g] Eze 12:25; Heb 10:37-38

Stele of victory from Susa depicts enemies caught in a net, 2371 to 2316 BC. See note on Hab 1:15.
Kim Walton. The Louvre.

[a] *12* An ancient Hebrew scribal tradition; Masoretic Text *we* [b] *1* Or *and what to answer when I am rebuked* [c] *2* Or *so that whoever reads it* [d] *3* Or *Though he linger, wait for him; / he*

of this phrase is uncertain and a number of alternatives have been suggested. If the NIV translation is retained, the charge may reflect the pain of those faced with the rapine committed by invading armies, despite the fact that Babylonian inscriptions invariably give credit for military victories to the strength provided to kings by their gods. Thus Nabopolassar extols Nabu and Marduk for aiding him to remove the Assyrian yoke from his land.

1:12 *Rock.* The use of this title as an attribute of deity is found in personal names both in the Bible (e.g., Elizur, "my God is a Rock" [Nu 1:5]) and in Amorite personal names in the Mari texts (e.g., Suri-Dagan).

1:15 *hooks ... net ... dragnet.* Nineteenth-century BC Egyptian wall paintings from Beni Hasan depict fishermen using spears, hook and line, as well as dragnets made of woven baskets (see Eze 12:13; Am 4:2). Rulers, in their propagandistic pronouncements, employed proverbs or metaphors to depict their strength. Thus they were capable of trapping their enemies like fish or birds in a net (see Hos 5:1). The use of a net filled with fish is found in the account of Pharaoh Thutmose III's victory at Megiddo. He refers to his enemies "lying prostrate like fishes in the bulge of a net." As seen in the Mari texts, the gods assist the king to overcome treacherous enemies, promising to gather Babylon "into the net" and assuring him that the ruler of Eshnunna will be collected "into a net with which I will surround him."

2:2 *Write down the revelation ... on tablets.* Like Isaiah (Isa 30:8), the prophet is commanded to write down his oracle. See the articles "Literacy," p. 140; "Books and Literacy," p. 666; "Scrolls in the Ancient World," p. 1286. *a herald may run with it.* The idea of running with a mes-

but the righteous person will live by
his faithfulness[a][h] —
5 indeed, wine[i] betrays him;
he is arrogant and never at rest.
Because he is as greedy as the grave
and like death is never satisfied,[j]
he gathers to himself all the nations
and takes captive all the peoples.

6 "Will not all of them taunt[k] him with ridicule and scorn, saying,

" 'Woe to him who piles up stolen
goods
and makes himself wealthy by
extortion![l]
How long must this go on?'
7 Will not your creditors suddenly arise?
Will they not wake up and make you
tremble?
Then you will become their prey.[m]
8 Because you have plundered many
nations,
the peoples who are left will plunder
you.[n]
For you have shed human blood;[o]
you have destroyed lands and cities
and everyone in them.

9 "Woe to him who builds[p] his house by
unjust gain,
setting his nest on high
to escape the clutches of ruin!
10 You have plotted the ruin[q] of many
peoples,
shaming[r] your own house and
forfeiting your life.
11 The stones[s] of the wall will cry out,
and the beams of the woodwork will
echo it.

12 "Woe to him who builds a city with
bloodshed[t]
and establishes a town by injustice!

2:4 [h] Ro 1:17*; Gal 3:11*; Heb 10:37-38*
2:5 [i] Pr 20:1 [j] Pr 27:20; 30:15-16
2:6 [k] Isa 14:4 [l] Am 2:8
2:7 [m] Pr 29:1
2:8 [n] Isa 33:1; Zec 2:8-9 [o] ver 17
2:9 [p] Jer 22:13
2:10 [q] Jer 26:19 [r] ver 16
2:11 [s] Jos 24:27; Lk 19:40
2:12 [t] Mic 3:10

2:13 [u] Isa 50:11 [v] Isa 47:13
2:14 [w] Nu 14:21 [x] Isa 11:9
2:16 [y] ver 10 [z] La 4:21 [a] Isa 51:22
2:17 [b] Jer 51:35 [c] Jer 50:15 [d] ver 8
2:18 [e] Jer 5:21 [f] Ps 115:4-5; Jer 10:14
2:19 [g] 1Ki 18:27

13 Has not the LORD Almighty determined
that the people's labor is only fuel
for the fire,[u]
that the nations exhaust themselves
for nothing?[v]
14 For the earth will be filled with the
knowledge of the glory[w] of the
LORD
as the waters cover the sea.[x]

15 "Woe to him who gives drink to his
neighbors,
pouring it from the wineskin till they
are drunk,
so that he can gaze on their naked
bodies!
16 You will be filled with shame[y] instead
of glory.
Now it is your turn! Drink and let
your nakedness be exposed[b]![z]
The cup[a] from the LORD's right hand is
coming around to you,
and disgrace will cover your glory.
17 The violence[b] you have done to
Lebanon will overwhelm you,
and your destruction of animals will
terrify you.[c]
For you have shed human blood;[d]
you have destroyed lands and cities
and everyone in them.

18 "Of what value is an idol[e] carved by a
craftsman?
Or an image that teaches lies?
For the one who makes it trusts in his
own creation;
he makes idols that cannot speak.[f]
19 Woe to him who says to wood, 'Come
to life!'
Or to lifeless stone, 'Wake up!'[g]

[a] 4 Or *faith* [b] 16 Masoretic Text; Dead Sea Scrolls, Aquila, Vulgate and Syriac (see also Septuagint) *and stagger*

sage suggests its urgency or importance. What is unclear is whether the one who reads the message is a "herald" (with NIV), whose task is to run from location to location reading aloud his proclamation, or whether it refers to anyone who reads the message (see NIV text note). In the former, the inscribed tablets would be entrusted to a professional. In the latter, the inscription would be set up in a public place, and as individuals would read it, they would run off to spread the news. Preference lies with the former since the text here speaks of tablets. Publicly posted inscriptions would usually be on steles. Professional messengers were a common fixture in royal courts, such as those at ancient Mari and Babylon. They were needed as "runners" to carry their lord's commands (see Jer 36:4–6 for Baruch's mission as Jeremiah's scribe and messenger).

2:18 *an image that teaches lies.* This represents Habakkuk's charge that priests and kings manipulate people by making the idol speak or pronounce an oracle in the name of the god. This is not suggesting deception. The images were believed to communicate through the oracles that were given in the practice of extispicy — reading omens from the entrails of sacrificed animals (see the article "Extispicy," p. 650). The omens, however, were the result of the interpretations of the divination experts and could therefore easily be used for manipulation.

2:19 *lifeless stone.* The archives of the Assyrian king Esarhaddon contain a text dealing with the theological problem of crafting a divine image. The king asks, "Whose right is it ... to create gods and goddesses ... Is it the right of deaf and blind human beings who are ignorant of themselves?" He then calls on the gods to send an omen to indicate when and how these images are to be created and to endow the craftsmen with divine knowledge and skill. Once an image was shaped, the rituals of mouth-washing and "opening the mouth" were initiated in Babylon to transform a fabricated object into the physical embodiment of the god. Both rituals were predicated on the belief in a divine collaboration between the gods and the craftsmen to create through "inspirational cooperation" a divine statue. The "Opening the Mouth and the Eyes" ritual also purified the image and restored its sanctity after coming into contact with impurity or an improper ritual act. See the article "Making an Idol," p. 1010.

Can it give guidance?
  It is covered with gold and silver;[h]
  there is no breath in it."
[20]The LORD is in his holy temple;[i]
  let all the earth be silent[j] before him.

Habakkuk's Prayer

3 A prayer of Habakkuk the prophet. On *shigionoth*.[a]

[2]LORD, I have heard[k] of your fame;
  I stand in awe[l] of your deeds, LORD.
Repeat[m] them in our day,
  in our time make them known;
  in wrath remember mercy.[n]

[3]God came from Teman,
  the Holy One from Mount Paran.[b]
His glory covered the heavens
  and his praise filled the earth.[o]
[4]His splendor was like the sunrise;
  rays flashed from his hand,
  where his power was hidden.
[5]Plague went before him;
  pestilence followed his steps.
[6]He stood, and shook the earth;
  he looked, and made the nations
    tremble.
The ancient mountains crumbled
  and the age-old hills collapsed[p] —
  but he marches on forever.
[7]I saw the tents of Cushan in distress,
  the dwellings of Midian[q] in
    anguish.[r]

[8]Were you angry with the rivers,[s] LORD?
  Was your wrath against the streams?
Did you rage against the sea
  when you rode your horses
  and your chariots to victory?[t]
[9]You uncovered your bow,
  you called for many arrows.[u]
You split the earth with rivers;
10 the mountains saw you and writhed.
Torrents of water swept by;
  the deep roared[v]
  and lifted its waves[w] on high.

2:19 [h]Jer 10:4 **2:20** [i]Ps 11:4 [j]Isa 41:1 **3:2** [k]Ps 44:1 [l]Ps 119:120 [m]Ps 85:6 [n]Isa 54:8 **3:3** [o]Ps 48:10 **3:6** [p]Ps 114:1-6 **3:7** [q]Jdg 7:24-25 [r]Ex 15:14 **3:8** [s]Ex 7:20 [t]Ps 68:17 **3:9** [u]Ps 7:12-13 **3:10** [v]Ps 98:7 [w]Ps 93:3

[a] *1* Probably a literary or musical term [b] *3* The Hebrew has *Selah* (a word of uncertain meaning) here and at the middle of verse 9 and at the end of verse 13.

3:1 *shigionoth.* The hymnic character of ch. 3 is expressed by the inclusion of a superscription, the use of the rubric *Selah* (see NIV text note on v. 3), and a colophon (v. 19b). While the meaning of *shigionoth* is uncertain, it is related to *shagah* ("to go astray"), suggesting a lament or possibly a song with uneven meter (see Ps 7:1). If a linguistic connection can be made with Akkadian *shegu*, then its usage, in the form *shigu*, in a prayer to Marduk indicates a sense of emotion and supplication, perhaps accompanied by a whimpering sound.
3:3 *Teman ... Mount Paran.* Teman is a place-name associated with Edom (Jer 49:7; Ob 9) and is an indicator in this text of God, (*qadosh*) "the Holy One," whose epiphany arises from the east (cf. Ps 78:26). The name also appears in the Kuntillet Ajrud inscription in association with Yahweh. This verse is the only place in the Bible where Teman and Paran are paralleled, since the former is associated with Esau (Ge 36:15) and the latter with Ishmael (Ge 21:21). The Desert of Paran generally refers to the area between Mount Sinai and the oasis of Kadesh Barnea, but its usage suggests a wider range of territory, extending to the east of the Arabah in the vicinity of Teman (see Nu 10:12; 1Sa 25:1).
3:4 *His splendor was like the sunrise.* God's "glory" is worn like a garment (see Ps 104:1). It may also be a form of divine armor; Marduk in the *Enuma Elish* is "garbed in a ghastly armored garment ... His head covered with terrifying auras." Once the obscuring clouds are swept away (compare the rays of the Aten in the Egyptian hymn that "dispel the dark"), a virtual light show accompanies God's approach, with lightning and fire streaking from his hand and obscuring any attempts to anthropomorphize or minutely describe God's visage. Evidence of the solar aspects of Yahweh worship have appeared on a 700 BC bulla inscribed with "Yaho has shown forth," as well as in personal names containing the element *zerah* ("shining forth"). Phrases similar to those in this verse occur in Babylonian hymns describing theophanies (compare "Shamash has shone forth on the foundation of heaven ... Shamash has filled the lands with his heavenly splendor").
3:5 *Plague ... pestilence.* Yahweh goes forth accompanied by a retinue of forces, including beams of light as well as the destructive elements mentioned here (cf. Dt 33:2). Some have interpreted pestilence and plague in this verse as living creatures since at least the second one is found as a divine name in Canaanite contexts. Some Ugaritic texts describe Baal as having attendants, and Akkadian texts describe Marduk accompanied by other gods who go before and behind him. A similar depiction is also found in the Mesopotamian epic "Erra and Ishum," where Erra, a god of war and plague, has seven minor deities as his companions, each of whom contributes to the devastation of the lands he chooses to attack. Similarly, in Dt 32:23 – 24 the calamities heaped on a disobedient people by Yahweh include arrows (comparable to the metaphor for the fever brought by the plague-god Rashaph), pestilence and plague.
3:7 *Cushan.* This ethnic term, possibly a subgroup of the Midianites (see notes on Ex 2:15; Nu 12:1), refers to a pastoral nomadic group, and it appears only in this text. Kushu is mentioned in Egyptian texts from the Middle Bronze Age referring to a people in the southern Transjordanian region. Habakkuk here predicts the route of the divine warrior from his holy mountain to attack the Babylonians.
3:8 *rage against the sea.* While there are some similarities in this verse to Ugaritic literature, especially in the Baal Cycle stories about Baal and his conflict with the sea-god Yamm, (see the articles "Baal," p. 600; "Chaos Monsters," p. 953) it is unlikely that there is a direct, compositional or thematic reliance on them in Habakkuk. Thus the pairing of *naharim* ("rivers") with *yam* ("sea") is only suggestive of the cosmic struggle found between the gods Baal and Yamm in Ugaritic literature. In fact the only direct parallel in Ugaritic with the word pair in Hab 3:8 is found in a nonconflict passage, and this may be an indication that the prophet is referring not to the Ugaritic cosmic battle motif but to a metaphoric usage of "river" and "sea" as traditional enemies of Yahweh in the trek from Egypt across the Red Sea and then across the Jordan River.
3:9 – 11 *bow ... arrows ... flying arrows ... flashing spear.* One common understanding of the role of the deity in the ancient Near East was that of divine warrior (see the article "Divine Warfare," p. 365).

11 Sun and moon stood still[x] in the
heavens
at the glint of your flying arrows,[y]
at the lightning of your flashing
spear.
12 In wrath you strode through the earth
and in anger you threshed[z] the nations.
13 You came out to deliver[a] your people,
to save your anointed one.
You crushed[b] the leader of the land of
wickedness,
you stripped him from head to foot.
14 With his own spear you pierced his
head
when his warriors stormed out to
scatter us,[c]
gloating as though about to devour
the wretched[d] who were in hiding.
15 You trampled the sea with your horses,
churning the great waters.[e]

16 I heard and my heart pounded,
my lips quivered at the sound;
decay crept into my bones,
and my legs trembled.
Yet I will wait patiently for the day of
calamity
to come on the nation invading us.
17 Though the fig tree does not bud
and there are no grapes on the
vines,
though the olive crop fails
and the fields produce no food,[f]
though there are no sheep in the pen
and no cattle in the stalls,[g]
18 yet I will rejoice in the LORD,[h]
I will be joyful in God my Savior.

19 The Sovereign LORD is my strength;[i]
he makes my feet like the feet of a
deer,
he enables me to tread on the
heights.[j]

For the director of music. On my
stringed instruments.

3:11 [x] Jos 10:13 [y] Ps 18:14 **3:12** [z] Isa 41:15 **3:13** [a] Ps 20:6; 28:8 [b] Ps 68:21; 110:6 **3:14** [c] Jdg 7:22 [d] Ps 64:2-5 **3:15** [e] Ex 15:8; Ps 77:19

3:17 [f] Joel 1:10-12, 18 [g] Jer 5:17 **3:18** [h] Isa 61:10; Php 4:4 **3:19** [i] Dt 33:29; Ps 46:1-5 [j] Dt 32:13; 2Sa 22:34; Ps 18:33

3:12 *you strode through the earth.* The song at this point is a call for a theophany in which Yahweh will manifest divine power to save the people. This strident characteristic of the divine warrior is found in the Akkadian phrase *alakki ili*, "the gait of a god."

3:17 *fig … grapes … olive … sheep … cattle.* The prophet provides a basic list of those products and livestock that form the basis of the ancient economy. They would have been the objects taken by rampaging armies and given as tribute and taxes, leaving the land barren.

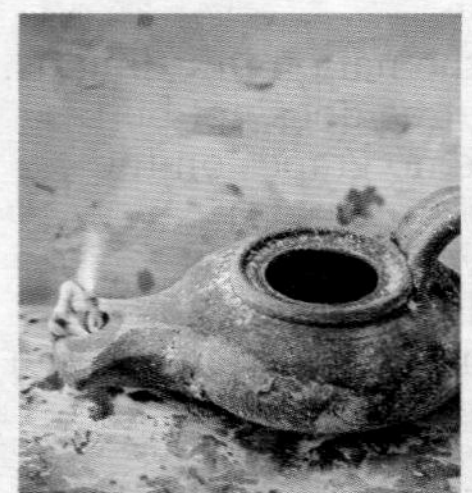

ORACLES OF THE PROPHETS

ZEPHANIAH

Historical Setting

There is Assyrian evidence that at the end of the eighth century BC and into the early seventh century BC the Judahite kings Hezekiah (715 – 687 BC) and Manasseh (687 – 642 BC) gave tribute to the Assyrian monarchs Sargon II (721 – 705 BC), Sennacherib (705 – 681 BC), Esarhaddon (681 – 668 BC) and Ashurbanipal (668 – 626 BC).

However, the political map of the ancient Near East changed dramatically during the reign of Josiah. Though there had been various rebellions against Assyria in the past (with strong participation by Hezekiah in 701 BC and by Manasseh in 652 – 648 BC), Assyria was able to quell these insurgencies and punish the offenders. Ashurbanipal, however, was unable to keep the empire unified during his whole reign. It is apparent that by 626 BC, Assyria's southern neighbor, Babylon, had declared its independence from Assyria (under the tutelage of Nabopolassar [626 – 605 BC]). Moreover, Assyria was now subject to attack from Babylon in the south and from the Medes in the northeast (modern Iran). By 612 BC, all of the major urban centers of the Assyrian core (including Nineveh) were destroyed, and only a small remnant of the Assyrian army and royal house were holed up in Harran in northern Syria (until about 609 BC).

Josiah's reform of 622/621 BC may have been, in part, a response to Assyrian weakness and the uncertainty of world events. In fact, Josiah may have been attempting to reassert Judah's independence and reclaim Davidic authority over all of Israel once again. Thus, his reform roughly coincides with the establishment of Chaldean independence from Assyria, beginning with the reign of Nabopolassar in 626 BC, with whom Josiah probably allied himself. ◆

KEY CONCEPTS

- The prophets arose in troubled times to declare the messages God gave them.
- The prophets at times were perplexed about what God was doing.
- Even in times of crisis and confusion, God expects his people to be faithful and trust him.
- With God, there is always reason for hope.

1 The word of the LORD that came to Zephaniah son of Cushi, the son of Gedaliah, the son of Amariah, the son of Hezekiah, during the reign of Josiah[a] son of Amon king of Judah:

Judgment on the Whole Earth in the Day of the LORD

2 "I will sweep away everything
from the face of the earth,"[b]
declares the LORD.
3 "I will sweep away both man and beast;
I will sweep away the birds in the sky[c]
and the fish in the sea —
and the idols that cause the wicked to stumble."[a]

"When I destroy all mankind
on the face of the earth,"[d]
declares the LORD,
4 "I will stretch out my hand[e] against Judah
and against all who live in Jerusalem.
I will destroy every remnant of Baal worship in this place,[f]
the very names of the idolatrous priests[g] —
5 those who bow down on the roofs
to worship the starry host,
those who bow down and swear by the LORD
and who also swear by Molek,[b][h]
6 those who turn back from following[i] the LORD
and neither seek[j] the LORD nor inquire[k] of him."

7 Be silent[l] before the Sovereign LORD,
for the day of the LORD[m] is near.
The LORD has prepared a sacrifice;[n]
he has consecrated those he has invited.

8 "On the day of the LORD's sacrifice
I will punish[o] the officials
and the king's sons[p]
and all those clad
in foreign clothes.
9 On that day I will punish
all who avoid stepping on the threshold,[c]

1:1 [a] 2Ki 22:1; 2Ch 34:1-35:25
1:2 [b] Ge 6:7
1:3 [c] Jer 4:25 [d] Hos 4:3
1:4 [e] Jer 6:12 [f] Mic 5:13 [g] Hos 10:5
1:5 [h] Jer 5:7
1:6 [i] Isa 1:4; Jer 2:13 [j] Isa 9:13 [k] Hos 7:7
1:7 [l] Hab 2:20; Zec 2:13 [m] ver 14; Isa 13:6 [n] Isa 34:6; Jer 46:10
1:8 [o] Isa 24:21 [p] Jer 39:6

[a] 3 The meaning of the Hebrew for this line is uncertain.
[b] 5 Hebrew *Malkam*
[c] 9 See 1 Samuel 5:5.

1:1 *Zephaniah son of.* The long genealogy in the superscription is unusual in the Prophets. Only in Jer 36:14 is there a text contemporary to Zephaniah containing a genealogy similar in length and scope. The introduction of the prophet by name establishes both authority and accountability. In Mesopotamia, it also appears that prophets were legally bound to their oracles. In fact, one prophet from Mari enclosed a clipping of his hair and the fringe of his garment (for purposes of identification) along with the message. In addition, the name of a particular prophet is attached to each of the oracles about the Assyrian king Esarhaddon. It therefore appears that there was a practice of the royal court keeping record of prophetic oracles. *Hezekiah.* Probably not the king of Judah, since the writer would most likely have made that clear to the reader. *during the reign of Josiah.* Though there are some who want to date the book as late as 200 BC, in all likelihood Zephaniah was born during the reign of Manasseh (687–642 BC). The superscription of the book gives evidence that Zephaniah prophesied in Judah during the reign of Manasseh's grandson Josiah (640–609 BC), roughly contemporary with Nahum and Jeremiah. Most scholars have argued that Zephaniah prophesied before Josiah's reform in the 18th year of his reign (c. 621 BC), as the oracles make no mention of the king himself, let alone anything about the reforms during Josiah's reign. Furthermore, the description of Nineveh's doom in 2:13–15 would probably not have been relevant after 625 BC, when Assyrian power was clearly on the wane, and certainly not after its demise in 612 BC. See Introduction: Historical Setting.

1:4 *priests.* The Hebrew term (*komer*) denotes priests of other gods in 2Ki 23:5; Hos 10:5. The term is found in cognate languages of Akkadian, Aramaic, Syriac and Ugaritic—all as general terms for priest. Josiah removed these clergy during his reforms (2Ki 23:5). *Kumru* priests are known from Akkadian texts (in the Assyrian dialect) in the early second millennium BC from Cappadocia in Anatolia and from Mari in Syria. The feminine form of the term (*kumirtu* = priestess) occurs in a seventh-century BC inscription from the Assyrian king Ashurbanipal concerning an Arabian queen. A variant of the term is also found in Aramaic for priests in the first century BC. Thus, these "idolatrous" priests could have been either priests who were servicing the shrines of Baal or apostate priests of Yahweh.

1:5 *starry host.* See note on 2Ki 21:3. *Molek.* See notes on 1Ki 11:5; Jer 7:31.

1:7 *day of the LORD.* There have been numerous attempts to equate this with ancient Near Eastern sources such as the annual Akitu festival in Assyria and Babylonia. It is certainly possible that the Israelites took the mythical festival, historicized it and applied it to Yahweh. There is no evidence that the Day of Yahweh was celebrated annually. Furthermore, the Biblical concept of the Day of Yahweh was very diverse, representing historical (i.e., military) and apocalyptic episodes. See notes on Joel 2:1; Am 5:18.

1:8 *the king's sons.* Several seals from Judah during the period of the monarchy have been found; the owner of each seal is identified as the "son of the king," a title found in variant forms in Egypt (Amarna) and Syria (Mari and Ugarit) in the second millennium BC. In these cases, the term probably refers to administrative officials, not necessarily royal descendants. *clad in foreign clothes.* Although it has been suggested that this refers to those who were willing to wear the styles of foreign peoples, it is more likely that this refers to those who dressed like priests of foreign deities. The most distinctive component of priestly attire evident from Neo-Assyrian iconography is the high-flared headdress. Based upon historical context, it makes sense to see this as an attack against Assyrian influence at the Judahite royal court. Since there are few iconographic depictions of clothing in this period, it is not certain what other clothing styles are intimated here.

1:9 *stepping on the threshold.* This judgment appears to be related to the Philistine custom in 1Sa 5:5 concerning

who fill the temple of their gods
with violence and deceit.[q]

10 "On that day,"
declares the LORD,
"a cry will go up from the Fish Gate,[r]
wailing from the New Quarter,
and a loud crash from the hills.
11 Wail,[s] you who live in the market
district[a];
all your merchants will be wiped
out,
all who trade with[b] silver will be
destroyed.[t]
12 At that time I will search Jerusalem
with lamps
and punish those who are
complacent,[u]
who are like wine left on its dregs,[v]
who think, 'The LORD will do
nothing,[w]
either good or bad.'
13 Their wealth will be plundered,[x]
their houses demolished.
Though they build houses,
they will not live in them;
though they plant vineyards,
they will not drink the wine."[y]

14 The great day of the LORD[z] is near[a]—
near and coming quickly.
The cry on the day of the LORD is
bitter;
the Mighty Warrior shouts his battle
cry.
15 That day will be a day of wrath—
a day of distress and anguish,
a day of trouble and ruin,
a day of darkness and gloom,
a day of clouds and blackness[b]—
16 a day of trumpet and battle cry[c]
against the fortified cities
and against the corner towers.[d]
17 "I will bring such distress on all
people
that they will grope about like those
who are blind,[e]
because they have sinned against the
LORD.
Their blood will be poured out[f] like
dust
and their entrails like dung.[g]
18 Neither their silver nor their gold
will be able to save them
on the day of the LORD's wrath."[h]
In the fire of his jealousy
the whole earth will be consumed,[i]
for he will make a sudden end
of all who live on the earth.[j]

Judah and Jerusalem Judged Along With the Nations

Judah Summoned to Repent

2 Gather together,[k] gather yourselves
together,
you shameful[l] nation,
2 before the decree takes effect
and that day passes like windblown
chaff,[m]
before the LORD's fierce anger[n]
comes upon you,
before the day of the LORD's wrath
comes upon you.
3 Seek[o] the LORD, all you humble of the
land,
you who do what he commands.

1:9 [q] Am 3:10 **1:10** [r] 2Ch 33:14 **1:11** [s] Jas 5:1 [t] Hos 9:6 **1:12** [u] Am 6:1 [v] Jer 48:11 [w] Eze 8:12 **1:13** [x] Jer 15:13 [y] Dt 28:30, 39; Am 5:11; Mic 6:15 **1:14** [z] ver 7; Joel 1:15 [a] Eze 7:7 **1:15** [b] Isa 22:5; Joel 2:2

1:16 [c] Jer 4:19 [d] Isa 2:15 **1:17** [e] Isa 59:10 [f] Ps 79:3 [g] Jer 9:22 **1:18** [h] Eze 7:19 [i] ver 2-3; Zep 3:8 [j] Ge 6:7 **2:1** [k] 2Ch 20:4; Joel 1:14 [l] Jer 3:3; 6:15 **2:2** [m] Isa 17:13; Hos 13:3 [n] La 4:11 **2:3** [o] Am 5:6

[a] 11 Or *the Mortar* [b] 11 Or *in*

priests of Dagon who did not "step on the threshold," probably representing a belief (unacceptable in Israel) that evil spirits congregated near the doorway and stepping on the doorsill allowed them access. Many religious structures in Syria added a raised platform that elevated (and thus protected) the object of worship from its surroundings. However, the Assyrians and others in this period more commonly buried holy objects such as apotropaic figurines under the threshold of houses, hopefully to prevent the entry of evil spirits. Moreover, one was not allowed to step on the threshold, as it was considered sacrilegious and dangerous. Either of these possibilities is plausible.

1:10 *Fish Gate.* This was a Jerusalem gate on the northern wall of the city circling the temple mount, known as early as the reign of Manasseh and mentioned during the time of Nehemiah. Tyrian merchants entered Jerusalem through that gate, bringing fish and other imported goods (cf. Ne 3:3; 13:16). Archaeological work has confirmed the Fish Gate's location in the north. *New Quarter.* Hebrew *mishneh*; it apparently refers to the new section of Jerusalem built during the reign of Hezekiah (715–686 BC; 2Ch 32:5) and repaired by Manasseh, Hezekiah's successor (2Ch 33:14). It was probably on the Western Hill of Jerusalem, west of the City of David and the temple mount and across the Tyropoeon Valley. It could have been established to shore up defenses in anticipation of Sennacherib's imminent invasion in 701 BC and the influx of refugees from the north.

1:11 *market district.* The market, or mortar, district (derived from the Hebrew word for "mortar" or "hollow place," i.e., a bowl-shaped depression) or neighborhood was probably enclosed within the city walls during Zephaniah's time, possibly located in the Tyropoeon Valley, between the New Quarter in the west and the temple mount in the east, although its precise location is uncertain. Based upon the context in Zephaniah, it was apparently a center of commercial activity.

1:13 The curse listed in this verse is similar to an eighth-century BC Aramaic inscription from Sefire and a curse from Ashurbanipal's annals against his enemies who violated the terms of his treaties. Curses were often added to any type of covenant as a component of the oath to bind the parties. Thus, those who broke the terms of the agreement were subject to the curses that were listed (e.g., Jdg 21:18; Ne 10:29). Similarly, treaties between powerful states and subject states had like terminology (i.e., the lesser state that broke the terms of an agreement was subject to the penalties listed therein).

Seek righteousness, seek humility;[p]
perhaps you will be sheltered[q]
on the day of the LORD's anger.

Philistia

4 Gaza[r] will be abandoned
and Ashkelon left in ruins.
At midday Ashdod will be emptied
and Ekron uprooted.
5 Woe to you who live by the sea,
you Kerethite[s] people;
the word of the LORD is against you,[t]
Canaan, land of the Philistines.
He says, "I will destroy you,
and none will be left."[u]
6 The land by the sea will become
pastures
having wells for shepherds
and pens for flocks.[v]
7 That land will belong
to the remnant of the people of
Judah;
there they will find pasture.
In the evening they will lie down
in the houses of Ashkelon.
The LORD their God will care for them;
he will restore their fortunes.[a][w]

Moab and Ammon

8 "I have heard the insults[x] of Moab
and the taunts of the Ammonites,
who insulted[y] my people
and made threats against their land.

2:3 [p] Ps 45:4; Am 5:14-15 [q] Ps 57:1 **2:4** [r] Am 1:6, 7-8; Zec 9:5-7 **2:5** [s] Eze 25:16 [t] Am 3:1 [u] Isa 14:30 **2:6** [v] Isa 5:17 **2:7** [w] Ps 126:4; Jer 32:44 **2:8** [x] Jer 48:27 [y] Eze 25:3

[a] 7 Or *will bring back their captives*

2:4–7 The oracle against Philistia predicts the quick destruction of Gaza, Ashkelon, Ashdod and Ekron (v. 4). Southern Philistine towns that may have been under Egyptian control, such as Gath, are not mentioned here. It is known that Sargon of Assyria claimed to have taken Gath in 712/711 BC, and there is no evidence of its rebuilding. Egypt had presumably taken this area over around the end of the reign of Ashurbanipal of Assyria, sometime after 640 BC, when the Assyrian empire was in serious decline. Thus, Egypt rushed into southern Palestine to fill a "power vacuum."

2:4 *midday.* This implies a conquest that would take half a day. This is ironic, as it took the Egyptian monarch Psammetichus I nearly 30 years to take Ashdod (c. 640–611 BC), a siege that was probably in progress while Zephaniah was prophesying. Thus, Yahweh would not make this conquest a long, drawn-out matter, but he would take the area rapidly. Esarhaddon of Assyria (681–669 BC) claims to have taken Egyptian Memphis in "half a day."

2:5 *Kerethite people.* The Kerethites were probably a subgroup of Philistines, coming from Crete (Caphtor), although this relationship is not entirely clear. They are often associated with the Pelethites, and both were used as mercenaries in David's army (1Sa 30:14; 2Sa 8:18). Apparently Philistia stayed loyal to Assyria during its weakness and attempted to block Egyptian incursions into Palestine. Herodotus notes that Psammetichus I (664–610 BC) campaigned in Philistia against Ashdod and Ashkelon.

2:7 *remnant of the people of Judah.* Josiah expanded Judahite territory into Philistia as far as the Mediterranean Sea north of Joppa according to an ostracon that shows evidence of a Judahite governor during the time of Josiah at a fortress between Ashdod and Joppa. Zephaniah may be alluding to this expansion. Archaeological excavations at Ekron give evidence of concern for exiles, as the Assyrians expanded the size of the site, constructed a new citadel tower, and rebuilt the mud brick city wall. The Assyrians evidently moved large numbers of Israelites to Ekron to work on their olive oil industry.

2:8 *Moab … Ammonites.* Little is known about the relationship of Judah to these Jordanian states in the latter half of the seventh century BC. In fact, there are a few pieces of information that may shed light on this period. Both Moab and Ammon were among nations that gave tribute to Assyria during the reigns of Sargon, Sennacherib and Esarhaddon. This verse implies that they had moved in to Judahite territory. Our understanding of the region in this period is mainly linked to Kedar, a nomadic Arabic

ZEPHANIAH 2:4–15

JUDGMENT ON THE NATIONS

These oracles probably present the theological rationale for the Josianic expansion into the Transjordan (Moab and Ammon) and Philistia, most likely because of the weakness of Assyria. Josiah's expansion is implicitly evidenced by pottery from Tel Qasile in Philistia from the seventh century BC that may be Judahite. Furthermore, Josiah spread his reforms into the former territories of the northern kingdom (2Ch 34:1–7). The four regions may refer to a worldwide theme, at least symbolically, as the four cardinal points of the compass are probably represented by these four nations. ◆

9 Therefore, as surely as I live,"
declares the LORD Almighty,
the God of Israel,
"surely Moab[z] will become like Sodom,[a]
the Ammonites[b] like Gomorrah—
a place of weeds and salt pits,
a wasteland forever.
The remnant of my people will
plunder[c] them;
the survivors of my nation will
inherit their land.[d]"

10 This is what they will get in return for
their pride,[e]
for insulting[f] and mocking
the people of the LORD Almighty.
11 The LORD will be awesome[g] to them
when he destroys all the gods[h] of the
earth.
Distant nations will bow down to him,[i]
all of them in their own lands.

Cush

12 "You Cushites,[aj] too,
will be slain by my sword.[k]"

Assyria

13 He will stretch out his hand against the
north
and destroy Assyria,
leaving Nineveh[l] utterly desolate
and dry as the desert.[m]
14 Flocks and herds will lie down there,
creatures of every kind.
The desert owl[n] and the screech owl
will roost on her columns.
Their hooting will echo through the
windows,
rubble will fill the doorways,
the beams of cedar will be exposed.

15 This is the city of revelry[o]
that lived in safety.[p]
She said to herself,
"I am the one! And there is none
besides me."[q]
What a ruin she has become,
a lair for wild beasts!
All who pass by her scoff[r]
and shake their fists.

Jerusalem

3 Woe to the city of oppressors,[s]
rebellious and defiled![t]
2 She obeys[u] no one,
she accepts no correction.[v]
She does not trust in the LORD,
she does not draw near[w] to her
God.
3 Her officials within her
are roaring lions;
her rulers are evening wolves,[x]
who leave nothing for the morning.
4 Her prophets are unprincipled;
they are treacherous people.[y]
Her priests profane the sanctuary
and do violence to the law.[z]
5 The LORD within her is righteous;
he does no wrong.[a]
Morning by morning he dispenses his
justice,
and every new day he does not fail,
yet the unrighteous know no shame.

Jerusalem Remains Unrepentant

6 "I have destroyed nations;
their strongholds are demolished.
I have left their streets deserted,
with no one passing through.

2:9 [z] Isa 15:1-16:14; Jer 48:1-47 [a] Dt 29:23 [b] Jer 49:1-6; Eze 25:1-7 [c] Isa 11:14 [d] Am 2:1-3 **2:10** [e] Isa 16:6 [f] Jer 48:27 **2:11** [g] Joel 2:11 [h] Zep 1:4 [i] Zep 3:9 **2:12** [j] Isa 18:1; 20:4 [k] Jer 46:10 **2:13** [l] Na 1:1 [m] Mic 5:6 **2:14** [n] Isa 14:23 **2:15** [o] Isa 32:9 [p] Isa 47:8 [q] Eze 28:2 [r] Na 3:19 **3:1** [s] Jer 6:6 [t] Eze 23:30 **3:2** [u] Jer 22:21 [v] Jer 7:28 [w] Ps 73:28; Jer 5:3 **3:3** [x] Eze 22:27 **3:4** [y] Jer 9:4 [z] Eze 22:26 **3:5** [a] Dt 32:4

[a] *12* That is, people from the upper Nile region

tribe known in Ge 25:13 as descendants of a son of Ishmael. Assyrian sources describe Kedarite movements into the Transjordan after 640 BC, causing warfare between the Kedarites and Assyria. Ashurbanipal (668–627 BC) claimed victories over Uate of Sumu-il (presumably Ishmael) and Kedar. Moreover, Kamashalta of Moab defeated the Arab (i.e., Kedarite) forces of Ammuladin at roughly the same time. It is likely that the strife resulting from the movement of the Kedarites into this region, coupled with the Josianic expansion, may have weakened Ammon and Moab, which is reflected in the oracles. It is interesting to note that Edom, the other Transjordanian state in the region with connections to Judah, is not mentioned here. It is probably because Edom was under Egyptian control, as was southern Philistia (see note on 2:4–7), and Egypt was not in direct conflict with Judah at this point, though that was to change after the fall of Nineveh in 612 BC.

2:11 *Distant nations … in their own lands.* A Babylonian map of the world has Babylon and nearby Mesopotamian nations in the center of a landmass, surrounded by a large body of water. Beyond the water are small lands or islands in the midst of the "sea." Perhaps Israel had a similar conceptual "map," with Israel in the center of the earth, with other coastland nations surrounding it, along with a large body of water.

2:12 *Cushites.* The historical context for this oracle is not certain, as the Ethiopian (or Cushite) dynasty of Egypt ended in 664 BC with the Assyrian conquest of Thebes. It appears to imply that the Assyrian victory was done under Yahweh's providence. Psammetichus I, the founder of the Saite (or Twenty-Sixth) Dynasty, was not allied with Judah until 616 BC. There is no evidence of Cushite (as opposed to Egyptian) troops that may have been sent to help Assyria. Zephaniah may merely be noting the passing of the Cushite dynasty of Egypt, when Tirhakah died in 663 BC, fleeing from the Assyrian conquest of Thebes.

2:13 *Assyria.* The main oppressor of Judah for a century, so an oracle against it is not the least bit surprising. The oracle sees the destruction of Nineveh and Assur (which occurred in 614–612 BC) as in the future, and thus the oracle must have been written previous to this. The destruction of Nineveh is portrayed in language similar to ancient Near Eastern treaty curses (see note on 1:13). Xenophon, in his travels in Upper Mesopotamia, noted that by 401 BC Nineveh had become desert sand.

3:3 *roaring lions … evening wolves.* Animal names were often used in a positive manner as an indication of high status or nobility in Judah and elsewhere (e.g., Ugarit). Shema, a royal official of Jeroboam II, owned a seal with a representation of a roaring lion on it. In contrast, the lion's

Their cities are laid waste;[b]
they are deserted and empty.
7 Of Jerusalem I thought,
'Surely you will fear me
and accept correction!'
Then her place of refuge[a] would not be destroyed,
nor all my punishments come upon[b] her.
But they were still eager
to act corruptly[c] in all they did.
8 Therefore wait[d] for me,"
declares the LORD,
"for the day I will stand up to testify.[c]
I have decided to assemble the nations,[e]
to gather the kingdoms
and to pour out my wrath on them—
all my fierce anger.
The whole world will be consumed[f]
by the fire of my jealous anger.

Restoration of Israel's Remnant

9 "Then I will purify the lips of the peoples,
that all of them may call[g] on the name of the LORD
and serve[h] him shoulder to shoulder.
10 From beyond the rivers of Cush[d][i]
my worshipers, my scattered people,
will bring me offerings.[j]
11 On that day you, Jerusalem, will not be put to shame[k]
for all the wrongs you have done to me,
because I will remove from you
your arrogant boasters.
Never again will you be haughty
on my holy hill.
12 But I will leave within you
the meek[l] and humble.
The remnant of Israel
will trust[m] in the name of the LORD.
13 They[n] will do no wrong;[o]
they will tell no lies.[p]
A deceitful tongue
will not be found in their mouths.
They will eat and lie down[q]
and no one will make them afraid.[r]"
14 Sing, Daughter Zion;[s]
shout aloud,[t] Israel!
Be glad and rejoice with all your heart,
Daughter Jerusalem!
15 The LORD has taken away your punishment,
he has turned back your enemy.
The LORD, the King of Israel, is with you;[u]
never again will you fear[v] any harm.
16 On that day
they will say to Jerusalem,
"Do not fear, Zion;
do not let your hands hang limp.[w]
17 The LORD your God is with you,
the Mighty Warrior who saves.[x]
He will take great delight[y] in you;
in his love he will no longer rebuke you,
but will rejoice over you with singing."

18 "I will remove from you
all who mourn over the loss of your appointed festivals,
which is a burden and reproach for you.
19 At that time I will deal
with all who oppressed you.
I will rescue the lame;
I will gather the exiles.[z]
I will give them praise[a] and honor
in every land where they have suffered shame.
20 At that time I will gather you;
at that time I will bring[b] you home.
I will give you honor[c] and praise
among all the peoples of the earth
when I restore your fortunes[e][d]
before your very eyes,"
says the LORD.

3:6 [b] Lev 26:31 **3:7** [c] Hos 9:9 **3:8** [d] Ps 27:14 [e] Joel 3:2 [f] Zep 1:18 **3:9** [g] Zep 2:11 [h] Isa 19:18 **3:10** [i] Ps 68:31 [j] Isa 60:7 **3:11** [k] Joel 2:26-27 **3:12** [l] Isa 14:32 [m] Na 1:7 **3:13** [n] Isa 10:21; Mic 4:7 [o] Ps 119:3 [p] Rev 14:5 [q] Eze 34:15; Zep 2:7 [r] Eze 34:25-28 **3:14** [s] Zec 2:10 [t] Isa 12:6 **3:15** [u] Eze 37:26-28 [v] Isa 54:14 **3:16** [w] Job 4:3; Isa 35:3-4; Heb 12:12 **3:17** [x] Isa 63:1 [y] Isa 62:4 **3:19** [z] Eze 34:16; Mic 4:6 [a] Isa 60:18 **3:20** [b] Jer 29:14; Eze 37:12 [c] Isa 56:5; 66:22 [d] Joel 3:1

[a] *7* Or *her sanctuary* [b] *7* Or *all those I appointed over* [c] *8* Septuagint and Syriac; Hebrew *will rise up to plunder* [d] *10* That is, the upper Nile region [e] *20* Or *I bring back your captives*

den is symbolic for evil courtiers of the king in Assyrian literature of the seventh century BC.

3:9 *purify the lips.* The ritual purification of the lips was common in Mesopotamian rituals and symbolized the inner purification of the person. Two Mesopotamian ritual prayers (the "Prayer of the Gods of the Night" and the Old Babylonian *baru* prayer) speak of purifying the mouth or lips, symbolic of total purity. One Mesopotamian priest states, "I am the *ashipu* of Eridu whose mouth is pure," allowing him to pronounce the incantations for the deity. In fact, it appears that "purity of mouth" in Mesopotamia was a condition for standing before the divine council, similar to Isaiah's standing before God in Isa 6 (see note on Isa 6:7). Here in Zephaniah, all of the people will now be prepared to stand before God because of their pure language (or lips).

3:10 *rivers of Cush.* Since Cush here is likely referring to what is now known as the Sudan, the rivers in question are probably the Blue and White Nile Rivers of Upper Egypt, near the second cataract of the Nile. The same phrase is used in Isa 18:1 concerning the Cushite (or Ethiopian) dynasty of Egypt (see note on Isa 18:1–7).

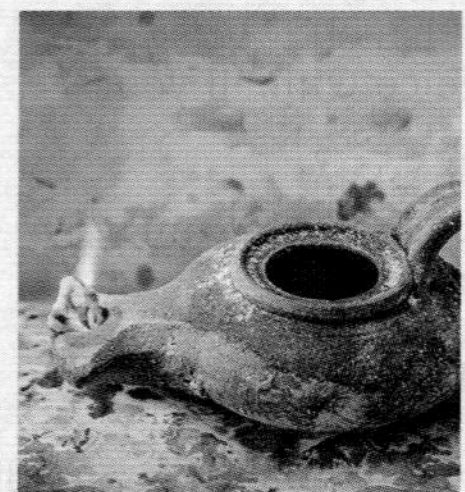

ORACLES OF THE PROPHETS

HAGGAI

Historical Setting

The present book of Haggai consists of a series of connected prophetic oracles that offer precise dates, locating the prophet's activity in the year 520 BC. Based on narratives in Ezra, the initial return of exiles to Jerusalem and the vicinity was around 538 BC. These early returnees would have faced the daunting tasks of clearing away the rubble of the destruction of Jerusalem and rebuilding homes and civic institutions. It is not hard to envision a scene in which the rebuilding of their community was physically and emotionally exhausting. While the book of Ezra notes that the rebuilding of the temple was also begun during the early years of the return, apparently completing this task in addition to addressing physical and economic needs was too much for the community to maintain. The rebuilding of the temple lagged until Haggai and his contemporary Zechariah responded to God's call to urge the completion of the temple.

Part of Haggai's task was also to help the community find a new way to understand their identity in a world in which so much had changed. Prior to the destruction of Jerusalem, Judah had an expansive territory, a king of the line of David on the throne (ensuring some measure of political and social autonomy), and a relatively prosperous economy. With the conquest of Judah by the Babylonians and the subsequent conquest of the Babylonian Empire by the Persian Empire, those who chose to return to Jerusalem found themselves in a radically different setting. No longer was the old territory of Judah maintained — now they were part of a smaller geopolitical region known as the province of Yehud. As a small portion of a much larger empire, Yehud was ruled by a "governor" appointed by the Persian king. And imperial forces were likely stationed in nearby areas, an implicit threat should the empire detect any hint of rebellion. Without territory or a king of their own, the one point of physical contact the returnees had with their past was the temple.

Haggai and his contemporary Zechariah make the case to the community of returnees that their first priority should be the restoration of the temple. By making such a clear commitment to the ongoing worship of God, blessings would flow to the community, and the future existence of the remnant of Israel would be secure. The temple was to serve as the center point to give the former exiles a new way of understanding themselves in a changed world. ◆

KEY CONCEPTS

- Spiritual restoration must precede social or political restoration.
- God's presence is the key to restoration, thus the importance of rebuilding the temple.

A Call to Build the House of the LORD

1 In the second year of King Darius,[a] on
the first day of the sixth month, the
word of the LORD came through the prophet Haggai[b] to Zerubbabel[c] son of Shealtiel,
governor[d] of Judah, and to Joshua[e] son of
Jozadak,[a][f] the high priest:
2 This is what the LORD Almighty says:
"These people say, 'The time has not yet
come to rebuild the LORD's house.'"
3 Then the word of the LORD came
through the prophet Haggai:[g] 4 "Is it a time
for you yourselves to be living in your
paneled houses,[h] while this house remains
a ruin?[i]"
5 Now this is what the LORD Almighty
says: "Give careful thought[j] to your ways.
6 You have planted much, but harvested little.[k] You eat, but never have enough. You
drink, but never have your fill. You put on
clothes, but are not warm. You earn wages,[l] only to put them in a purse with holes
in it."
7 This is what the LORD Almighty says:
"Give careful thought to your ways. 8 Go
up into the mountains and bring down
timber and build my house, so that I may
take pleasure[m] in it and be honored," says
the LORD. 9 "You expected much, but see, it
turned out to be little. What you brought
home, I blew away. Why?" declares the
LORD Almighty. "Because of my house,
which remains a ruin,[n] while each of you
is busy with your own house. 10 Therefore,
because of you the heavens have withheld their dew and the earth its crops.[o]

1:1 [a] Ezr 4:24 [b] Ezr 5:1 [c] Mt 1:12-13 [d] Ezr 5:3 [e] Ezr 2:2 [f] 1Ch 6:15; Ezr 3:2 **1:3** [g] Ezr 5:1 **1:4** [h] 2Sa 7:2 [i] ver 9; Jer 33:12 **1:5** [j] La 3:40 **1:6** [k] Dt 28:38 [l] Hag 2:16; Zec 8:10 **1:8** [m] Ps 132:13-14 **1:9** [n] ver 4 **1:10** [o] Lev 26:19; Dt 28:23

[a] *1* Hebrew *Jehozadak*, a variant of *Jozadak*; also in verses 12 and 14

1:1 *second year of King Darius.* Darius was the third king of the Persian Empire and came into power under difficult conditions, as a major rival for the throne contested Darius's rule. Cambyses, son of the empire's founder, Cyrus the Great, died under mysterious circumstances in 522 BC while in Syria. About the time of his death, a figure named Bardiya had claimed the throne in Persia. A group of Persian aristocrats joined with Darius to defeat Bardiya, but while the central portion of the empire was consumed in the question of who would succeed Cambyses, many outlying parts of the empire rebelled against Persian rule. It was not until the second year of Darius's rule that he was able to consolidate his control over the far-flung ends of the empire (from Egypt to the borders of modern India). *Zerubbabel son of Shealtiel, governor of Judah.* One of the major changes for the Jewish community in this period was the imposition of a "governor" over the community, appointed by the Persian king. Eventually under Darius the Persian Empire developed a system that broke down the empire into large regions ("satrapies"), and the satrap was the primary supervisor of the "governors" of the smaller districts ("medina"). Having a royal appointee as the primary administrator over the community underscored the lack of political self-determination of the community. While Zerubbabel bears a Babylonian name, he was in all likelihood Jewish. A Zerubbabel appears in the list of descendants of David at 1Ch 3:19, but in that list Zerubbabel is the son of Pedaiah, who was a son of Shealtiel. Numerous suggestions have been offered for this difference between genealogies, none of which has the consensus of scholars. The prophet Haggai makes it clear that Zerubbabel was the legitimate political figurehead. Zerubbabel's role in invigorating the effort to rebuild the temple is also recounted in Ezr 3. *Joshua son of Jozadak, the high priest.* This "word of the LORD" is addressed to the entire community but more directly to its primary leaders, the governor representing the political sphere and the high priest representing the religious sphere. Since the subject is the temple, both leaders needed to work jointly to insure the rebuilding, since both governmental funds and gifts for the temple would be used to pay for the effort. Joshua's lineage is more fully described in 1Ch 6:14–15, where Jozadak's father is given as Seraiah, who was high priest at the time of the destruction of Jerusalem. Seraiah was executed by Nebuchadnezzar following the sacking of the city (2Ki 25:18–21), and Jozadak, presumably Seraiah's eldest son and next in succession to the high priesthood, was taken into exile. Joshua would have been born in captivity but raised with the expectation of functioning as high priest should the temple be rebuilt.
1:2 *LORD Almighty.* Usually this Hebrew title is rendered "LORD of hosts" in English, the "hosts" representing the vast powers God has at his disposal. A classic example of this aspect of God's character can be seen in 2Ki 6:15–17. This title for God, repeatedly used in Haggai, serves as a reminder that, while the community may feel powerless in the control of a great empire, God commands unimaginable forces.
1:4 *paneled.* The Hebrew term presents some difficulty. Paneled buildings would have been extraordinary in the ancient Near East, and they certainly would have been rarely used in most private homes of this period. On the other hand, the use of "your" may indicate that the charge is intended for the governor and high priest, two high-status officials who may well have enjoyed some touches of luxury in their private dwellings. Some suggest the term has more of a sense of "finished," that the prophet's concerns here relate more to the idea that the leading officials have ensured that their personal homes be finished while not taking the steps that would have ensured that the temple (God's house) be finished.
1:6 *You earn wages, only to put them in a purse with holes.* Though coinage was introduced under the Persian Empire, it was not at all common in the region around Jerusalem until late in the empire's history. Wages in Haggai's day were likely paid in grain, and the reference to persons who earn wages may well relate to those working for the government in various public works projects. The image being offered is an intensification of the earlier phrases: not only are primary producers, farmers, unable to satisfy their basic needs, but those earning steady pay only see it eroded by higher costs for goods and services in tight market conditions.
1:8 *Go up into the mountains and bring down timber.* Indications are clear that the temple was rebuilt with cut stone (Ezr 5:8). Timber beams would be used as additional support elements and for spanning the interior for a roof. There is some ambiguity here in terms of what "mountains" the timber is to be obtained from. Structural elements for stone buildings were usually of cedar, gained from the mountains of Lebanon (1Ki 5:6–9). Some suggest the "timber" of this command relates to local resources that would be employed as scaffolding or other apparatus.

11I called for a drought[p] on the fields and the mountains, on the grain, the new wine, the olive oil and everything else the ground produces, on people and livestock, and on all the labor of your hands.[q]"

12Then Zerubbabel[r] son of Shealtiel, Joshua son of Jozadak, the high priest, and the whole remnant[s] of the people obeyed[t] the voice of the LORD their God and the message of the prophet Haggai, because the LORD their God had sent him. And the people feared[u] the LORD.

13Then Haggai, the LORD's messenger, gave this message of the LORD to the people: "I am with[v] you," declares the LORD. 14So the LORD stirred up the spirit of Zerubbabel[w] son of Shealtiel, governor of Judah, and the spirit of Joshua son of Jozadak, the high priest, and the spirit of the whole remnant[x] of the people. They came and began to work on the house of the LORD Almighty, their God, 15on the twenty-fourth day of the sixth month.[y]

The Promised Glory of the New House

2 In the second year of King Darius, 1on the twenty-first day of the seventh month, the word of the LORD came through the prophet Haggai: 2"Speak to Zerubbabel son of Shealtiel, governor of Judah, to Joshua son of Jozadak,[a] the high priest, and to the remnant of the people. Ask them, 3'Who of you is left who saw this house[z] in its former glory? How does it look to you now? Does it not seem to you like nothing?[a] 4But now be strong, Zerubbabel,' declares the LORD. 'Be strong,[b] Joshua son of Jozadak, the high priest. Be strong, all you people of the land,' declares the LORD, 'and work. For I am with[c] you,' declares the LORD Almighty. 5'This is what I covenanted with you when you came out of Egypt.[d] And my Spirit[e] remains among you. Do not fear.'

6"This is what the LORD Almighty says: 'In a little while[f] I will once more shake the heavens and the earth,[g] the sea and the dry land. 7I will shake all nations, and what is desired by all nations will come, and I will fill this house[h] with glory,' says the LORD Almighty. 8'The silver is mine and the gold is mine,' declares the LORD Almighty. 9'The glory[i] of this present house will be greater than the glory of the former house,' says the LORD Almighty. 'And in this place I will grant peace,' declares the LORD Almighty."

Blessings for a Defiled People

10On the twenty-fourth day of the ninth month,[j] in the second year of Darius, the word of the LORD came to the prophet Haggai: 11"This is what the LORD Almighty says: 'Ask the priests[k] what the law says: 12If someone carries consecrated meat in the fold of their garment, and that fold touches some bread or stew, some wine, olive oil or other food, does it become consecrated?[l]' "

The priests answered, "No."

13Then Haggai said, "If a person defiled by contact with a dead body touches one of these things, does it become defiled?"

[a] 2 Hebrew *Jehozadak*, a variant of *Jozadak*; also in verse 4

1:11 [p] Dt 28:22; 1Ki 17:1 [q] Hag 2:17 **1:12** [r] ver 1 [s] ver 14; Isa 1:9; Hag 2:2 [t] Isa 50:10 [u] Dt 31:12 **1:13** [v] Mt 28:20; Ro 8:31 **1:14** [w] Ezr 5:2 [x] ver 12 **1:15** [y] ver 1 **2:3** [z] Ezr 3:12 [a] Zec 4:10 **2:4** [b] 1Ch 28:20; Zec 8:9; Eph 6:10 [c] 2Sa 5:10; Ac 7:9 **2:5** [d] Ex 29:46 [e] Ne 9:20; Isa 63:11 **2:6** [f] Isa 10:25 [g] Heb 12:26* **2:7** [h] Isa 60:7 **2:9** [i] Ps 85:9 **2:10** [j] ver 1 **2:11** [k] Lev 10:10-11; Dt 17:8-11; Mal 2:7 **2:12** [l] Lev 6:27; Mt 23:19

1:13 *Haggai, the LORD's messenger.* The use of "messenger" here is very unusual, since the Hebrew term is not often used to refer to a prophet (Isa 42:19; 44:26 are two noteworthy parallel examples). In Jewish tradition, Haggai, Zechariah and Malachi are often grouped together. This may be due in part to Haggai's title here as well as Malachi's statement that God is sending his "messenger" to prepare the way of the Lord (Mal 3:1)—these unusual terms serving to frame the works of these three prophets. *I am with you.* In the ancient Near East, it was common for prophets to encourage the king in fulfilling important religious duties such as building temples. The god could be "with" the king or leadership by giving them success in building the temple. More important, at the completion of this project, Yahweh would be with Israel in the sense that he would again be dwelling in their midst in the temple.
1:15 *twenty-fourth day of the sixth month.* In comparing the opening date formula (v. 1) with this date, it appears the community actually acted on Haggai's message within three weeks. This would seem to suggest a fairly quick response to Haggai's word on the part of the community leadership, since allocating resources and budgeting for building materials would normally take some time.
2:3 *Who of you is left ...?* Those who may have seen the temple prior to its destruction by the Babylonians would be few in number since some 67 years have passed to this point in the narrative. The question may be intended as a rhetorical point: no one is able to compare the previous temple with the one under construction.
2:6 *I will once more shake.* Shaking is a typical expression in the ancient Near East for a manifestation of the deity. The connection of this expression with a manifestation of God, combined with Haggai's mention of the exodus in v. 5, points toward the prophet making a deliberate parallel to the self-disclosure of God to Israel at Sinai (Ex 19). So the "once more" is making a parallel between what God did for Israel at Sinai and what he will do for the postexilic community.
2:10 *twenty-fourth day of the ninth month.* The prophet is receiving a new word about two months after his last oracle. It is not clear to whom the oracle is addressed, though the use of second person plural references in what follows would suggest the community as a whole.
2:12 *consecrated meat.* Once a sacrifice is offered to God, it is considered to be set aside; it is devoted to the person of God and thus shares in God's holiness. As such there are specific rules governing who may and who may not partake of the meat (Lev 7:20). Here, the point is that other items do not automatically become holy by contact with something that is consecrated: it takes an intentional action of devoting something to God to impart holiness.

"Yes," the priests replied, "it becomes
defiled.[m]"
14Then Haggai said, " 'So it is with this
people and this nation in my sight,' declares the LORD. 'Whatever they do and
whatever they offer[n] there is defiled.
15" 'Now give careful thought[o] to this
from this day on[a] — consider how things
were before one stone was laid[p] on another in the LORD's temple.[q] 16When anyone came to a heap of twenty measures,
there were only ten. When anyone went
to a wine vat to draw fifty measures, there
were only twenty.[r] 17I struck all the work
of your hands[s] with blight,[t] mildew and
hail, yet you did not return to me,' declares
the LORD.[u] 18'From this day on, from this
twenty-fourth day of the ninth month,
give careful thought to the day when the
foundation[v] of the LORD's temple was laid.
Give careful thought: 19Is there yet any
seed left in the barn? Until now, the vine
and the fig tree, the pomegranate and the
olive tree have not borne fruit.
" 'From this day on I will bless you.' "

2:13 [m]Lev 22:4-6 **2:14** [n]Isa 1:13 **2:15** [o]Hag 1:5 [p]Ezr 3:10 [q]Ezr 4:24 **2:16** [r]Hag 1:6 **2:17** [s]Hag 1:11 [t]Dt 28:22; 1Ki 8:37; Am 4:9 [u]Am 4:6 **2:18** [v]Zec 8:9

Zerubbabel the LORD's Signet Ring

20The word of the LORD came to Haggai
a second time on the twenty-fourth day of
the month: 21"Tell Zerubbabel[w] governor of
Judah that I am going to shake the heavens and the earth. 22I will overturn royal
thrones and shatter the power of the foreign kingdoms.[x] I will overthrow chariots[y]
and their drivers; horses and their riders
will fall, each by the sword of his brother.[z]
23" 'On that day,' declares the LORD Almighty, 'I will take you, my servant[a] Zerubbabel son of Shealtiel,' declares the
LORD, 'and I will make you like my signet
ring, for I have chosen you,' declares the
LORD Almighty."

2:21 [w]Ezr 5:2 **2:22** [x]Da 2:44 [y]Mic 5:10 [z]Jdg 7:22 **2:23** [a]Isa 43:10

[a] 15 Or *to the days past*

2:16 *wine vat.* When grapes were brought in from the harvest, they were crushed and the resulting juice stored in a large vat in order for the sediments and pieces of grape to settle out. It would begin fermentation in the vat, but its final processing would occur when it was drawn off into storage jars or skins. The image here relates to the processing of the harvest for future use.

2:19 *the vine and the fig tree, the pomegranate and the olive tree.* These are all late summer crops whose harvest would be long past by the ninth month (also known as Kislev, approximately November-December). They would be dormant plants at the point of Haggai's proclamation. But the promise of the oracle is that — though at this point these crops are not currently bearing — with the restoration of the temple, the community can anticipate abundance in the coming agricultural cycle. *I will bless you.* In the ancient Near East, people believed there was a direct connection between honoring the deity and agricultural productivity. By establishing a permanent place where regular sacrifices would be offered to a god, the community could assume the honored god would respond with prosperity in the form of abundant crops. Israel shares in this perspective, seeing obedience to God as a means to economic prosperity (see, e.g., Dt 7:12 – 15).

2:22 *chariots and their drivers; horses and their riders.* One of the innovations of the Persian army was the extensive use of cavalry in battle, something no other force could match until the coming of Alexander the Great.

2:23 *my signet ring.* In the ancient Near East, a signet ring was an engraved stone bearing a mark that was unique to the individual. Such signets were used as signatures to contracts and/or legal documents or to emboss seals of scrolls, and they could be entrusted to a trusted servant.

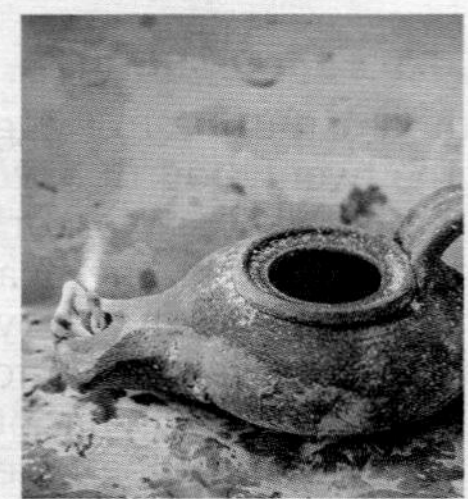

ORACLES OF THE PROPHETS

ZECHARIAH

Historical Setting

The setting for Zechariah's prophecy, like that of Haggai's, was the reign of Darius I, king of Persia (521 – 486 BC). Despite the return of the Jews from Babylonian exile, there was little evidence of the program of covenant restoration Yahweh had promised Jerusalem. Selfishness crippled community spirit, and the general mood of the period was gloomy and dismal. In fact, only a small percentage of Jewish captives had actually returned to Judah, and the city walls still lay in ruins. The temple of God remained a rubble heap, and drought and blight ravaged the land. Judah remained a Persian vassal state, and the surrounding nations continued to harass the leaders in Jerusalem and thwart their timid efforts to improve the bleak situation.

The prophet Zechariah complemented Haggai's message in calling for a spiritual revival among the people. Zechariah's ministry began just two months after Haggai's, and his last dated message was delivered in 518 BC. So Zechariah's ministry in Jerusalem probably lasted more than two years. The reference to Haggai and Zechariah in Ezr 5:1 suggests that they continued to support and encourage the people until the temple was completed and rededicated to the worship of Yahweh with the celebration of the Passover in 515 BC.

The situation in the Persian Empire is that Darius I had some difficulty securing the throne of Persia for himself after the death of Cambyses in Egypt in 522 BC. Two years of intrigue — at times bordering on civil war — had suggested to some that the empire was falling apart and that all the conquered territories might soon be free of the imperial yoke. Such was not to be the case, however, as Darius consolidated his control in 520 BC, ensuring the continued existence of the empire.

KEY CONCEPTS

- Spiritual restoration must precede social or political restoration.
- God's presence is the key to restoration, thus the importance of rebuilding the temple.

Literary Setting

One emphasis that ties all the various sections of the book together is the urgency of rebuilding the temple and the implications for completing the task. In weaving his various points around this emphasis, the prophet taps into common motifs and metaphors from temple-building accounts in the ancient Near East.

A second aspect of the literary setting is found in apocalyptic literature, in which visions figure prominently under the tutelage of angelic guides. Such literature is an expression of worldwide crisis in which good and evil are locked in a cosmic struggle. See the articles "Dreams and Temple Building in the Ancient Near East," p. 718; "Apocalyptic Literature," p. 1554; "Ancient Temple-Building Accounts and Zechariah," p. 1557. ◆

A Call to Return to the LORD

1 In the eighth month of the second year
of Darius,[a] the word of the LORD came
to the prophet Zechariah[b] son of Berekiah,[c] the son of Iddo:[d]
2 “The LORD was very angry[e] with your
ancestors. 3 Therefore tell the people: This
is what the LORD Almighty says: ‘Return to
me,’ declares the LORD Almighty, ‘and I will
return to you,’[f] says the LORD Almighty. 4 Do
not be like your ancestors,[g] to whom the
earlier prophets proclaimed: This is what
the LORD Almighty says: ‘Turn from your
evil ways[h] and your evil practices.’ But they
would not listen or pay attention to me,[i]
declares the LORD. 5 Where are your ancestors now? And the prophets, do they live
forever? 6 But did not my words and my de-

1:1 [a] Ezr 4:24; 6:15 [b] Ezr 5:1 [c] Mt 23:35; Lk 11:51 [d] ver 7; Ne 12:4
1:2 [e] 2Ch 36:16
1:3 [f] Mal 3:7; Jas 4:8
1:4 [g] 2Ch 36:15 [h] Ps 106:6 [i] 2Ch 24:19; Ps 78:8; Jer 6:17

1:1 *eighth month of the second year of Darius.* The date formula would place the message between the third and fourth oracles of Haggai in 520 BC, so Haggai would have already been active for several months prior to Zechariah's first message. This was a particularly interesting time in the political history of the Persian Empire (see note on Hag 1:1; see also the Introduction to Haggai: Historical Setting). *Iddo.* Usually if several ancestors are mentioned in a genealogical note, the last one is someone of importance. In Ne 12:4 there is an Iddo who is mentioned among the priests who returned with Zerubbabel in the first wave in 538 BC. If this is the same Iddo, it indicates that Zechariah is of a prominent family with a priestly heritage.

1:3 *Return to me ... and I will return to you.* This is a refrain very similar to the words of several otherwise unknown prophets in 2 Chronicles. Azariah, e.g., tells King Asa, "If you seek him, he will be found by you, but if you forsake him, he will forsake you" (2Ch 15:2). This suggests that a new conditionality has entered into God's relationship to Israel. Following the destruction of the kingdom of Judah, God will respond as humans make the effort, and the implication is that if the community does not make

ZECHARIAH 1

APOCALYPTIC LITERATURE

The name "apocalyptic" has traditionally been given to a particular genre of literature. Apocalyptic literature is defined by its characteristics. It has some traceable roots outside the Bible (see the article "Daniel and the Akkadian Prophecies," p. 1449), but it finds its earliest true members in OT books such as Daniel and Zechariah. In the Bible it is intricately intertwined with prophetic literature. There are over a dozen Jewish apocalyptic works from the intertestamental period, the most prominent being 4 Ezra and the books of Enoch. The book of Revelation is the NT's contribution to the genre. Other Christian apocalypses began to appear on the heels of the NT, including works like the Shepherd of Hermas, the Apocalypse of Peter and the Ascension of Isaiah. The genre was a favorite of the Gnostics, whose literature contains numerous examples.

Apocalypses feature a narrative framework and often portray an angelic interpreter or guide alongside the prophet. The angel may take the prophet on a tour of heavenly realms to convey certain realities and activities. Alternatively, the angel may unveil a future time of trouble and deliverance, though even then the focus of the literature is often more interested in affecting the present. This literature operates by means of a broad spectrum of symbols using significant numbers and mythological images. It draws heavily on both Biblical and extra-Biblical literature. It tends to schematize.

When reading apocalyptic literature, there are a couple of important guidelines to keep in mind. First, each detail does not necessarily carry symbolic significance. Even the details that do carry symbolic significance may not be transparent to us, and speculating accomplishes little. Second, it is important to remember that the apocalyptic vision is not the message itself, but rather is the vehicle or occasion for the message. So, e.g., the message of the first vision of Zechariah (Zec 1:7–17) is not that there are going to be four horses of different colors in a myrtle grove. The message is laid out very clearly in Zec 1:14–17. Apocalyptic literature is simply a medium, and in the end it is more interested in revealing God than in revealing the future. ◆

ZECHARIAH 1:1

THE HISTORICAL SETTING OF ZECHARIAH

Like his contemporary Haggai, Zechariah found himself called to challenge the postexilic community to complete the rebuilding of the temple. While the first members of the community returned to Jerusalem around 538 BC, the opening chapters of the book of Ezra suggest that they were so preoccupied by the task of rebuilding the city that they could not complete the temple. It was only due to the subsequent efforts of Zerubbabel, the governor of the province, and the ministries of Haggai and Zechariah that the temple was finished around 515 BC (Ezr 5:1; 6:15).

Although the archaeological data is fragmentary, there is enough to suggest that the exiles returned to a shattered urban landscape where considerable effort was needed simply to survive. Modern-day population estimates place the total population in the Persian period around 30,000 individuals in the area of the province of Yehud (the Persian administrative name for the district), which would represent a loss of 70 percent of the population of the region prior to the destruction of Jerusalem by the Babylonians. Jerusalem was the only significant city in the province, and much of the population lived in small, unwalled villages.

The picture overall is consistent with the tone of the prophetic messages of Haggai and Zechariah: the community was struggling to rebuild a sustainable economy, and severe limits on resources made rebuilding the temple an almost unthinkable task. For this reason, both Haggai and Zechariah needed to remind their audiences that God controlled the resources (see Hag 2:8–9; Zec 4:6–7). ◆

crees, which I commanded my servants the
prophets, overtake your ancestors?

"Then they repented and said, 'The
LORD Almighty has done to us what our
ways and practices deserve,[j] just as he determined to do.' "

The Man Among the Myrtle Trees

7On the twenty-fourth day of the eleventh month, the month of Shebat, in the
second year of Darius, the word of the
LORD came to the prophet Zechariah son
of Berekiah, the son of Iddo.

8During the night I had a vision, and
there before me was a man mounted on
a red[k] horse. He was standing among the
myrtle trees in a ravine. Behind him were
red, brown and white horses.[l]

9I asked, "What are these, my lord?"

The angel[m] who was talking with me
answered, "I will show you what they
are."

10Then the man standing among the
myrtle trees explained, "They are the ones
the LORD has sent to go throughout the
earth."[n]

1:6 [j] Jer 12:14-17; La 2:17
1:8 [k] Rev 6:4 [l] Zec 6:2-7
1:9 [m] Zec 4:1, 4-5
1:10 [n] Zec 6:5-8

the effort, God sees no obligation for him to act on the community's behalf. *LORD Almighty.* As in Haggai (e.g., Hag 1:2,5,7,9,14), this title emphasizes God's omnipotence in the face of the community's relative lack of earthly power. See note on Hag 1:2.

1:7 *twenty-fourth day of the eleventh month.* This would be Feb. 15, 519 BC. This would suggest the visions of Zechariah began just prior to Israel's marking of the New Year. In addition, some scholars believe that Darius marched to Egypt in 519 BC to secure their renewed loyalty and that the preparations of the army for this march was a source of concern for the people of Judah. They could have felt very uncertain about what demands might be made on them and how they would be treated.

1:8 *During the night I had a vision.* It was common in the ancient Near East for prophets to receive visions in the form of dreams. There are surviving accounts from Neo-Sumerian times (c. 2100–2000 BC) of scribes skilled in the interpretation of prophetic dreams, and by Assyrian times common dream motifs were interpreted by comparing them with earlier dreams. A particularly rich archive reporting of such dream oracles was recovered from the excavation of ancient Mari, and in many cases accounts of the dream are being related to the king since the dreams

11And they reported to the angel of the
LORD who was standing among the myrtle
trees, "We have gone throughout the earth
and found the whole world at rest and in
peace."[o]
12Then the angel of the LORD said, "LORD
Almighty, how long will you withhold
mercy from Jerusalem and from the towns
of Judah, which you have been angry with
these seventy[p] years?" 13So the LORD spoke
kind and comforting words to the angel
who talked with me.[q]
14Then the angel who was speaking to
me said, "Proclaim this word: This is what
the LORD Almighty says: 'I am very jealous[r] for Jerusalem and Zion, 15and I am
very angry with the nations that feel secure.[s] I was only a little angry, but they
went too far with the punishment.'[t]
16"Therefore this is what the LORD says:
'I will return[u] to Jerusalem with mercy,
and there my house will be rebuilt. And
the measuring line[v] will be stretched out
over Jerusalem,' declares the LORD Almighty.
17"Proclaim further: This is what the
LORD Almighty says: 'My towns will again
overflow with prosperity, and the LORD
will again comfort[w] Zion and choose[x] Jerusalem.' "[y]

1:11 [o] Isa 14:7
1:12 [p] Da 9:2
1:13 [q] Zec 4:1
1:14 [r] Joel 2:18; Zec 8:2
1:15 [s] Jer 48:11 [t] Ps 123:3-4; Am 1:11
1:16 [u] Zec 8:3 [v] Zec 2:1-2
1:17 [w] Isa 51:3 [x] Isa 14:1 [y] Zec 2:12

Four Horns and Four Craftsmen

18Then I looked up, and there before me
were four horns. 19I asked the angel who
was speaking to me, "What are these?"
He answered me, "These are the horns[z]
that scattered Judah, Israel and Jerusalem."
20Then the LORD showed me four craftsmen. 21I asked, "What are these coming
to do?"
He answered, "These are the horns that
scattered Judah so that no one could raise
their head, but the craftsmen have come
to terrify them and throw down these
horns of the nations who lifted up their
horns[a] against the land of Judah to scatter
its people."[a][b]

A Man With a Measuring Line

2 [b] Then I looked up, and there before
me was a man with a measuring line
in his hand. 2I asked, "Where are you going?"
He answered me, "To measure Jerusalem, to find out how wide and how long
it is."[c]
3While the angel who was speaking to
me was leaving, another angel came to

1:19 [z] Am 6:13
1:21 [a] Ps 75:4 [b] Ps 75:10
2:2 [c] Eze 40:3; Rev 21:15

[a] *21* In Hebrew texts 1:18-21 is numbered 2:1-4. [b] In Hebrew texts 2:1-13 is numbered 2:5-17.

have implications for royal policies. In one typical example, a report is sent to the king of a prophet who had a dream in which he entered a temple to Dagan and the statue of the god began to speak to him. *man mounted on a red horse.* The Persians were well known for their mounted couriers who traveled daily through the empire maintaining the most efficient communication system known in the ancient world. *myrtle trees.* They evoke the image of palace gardens. Persian kings enjoyed the parks of trees that stood beside the audience halls, and they received visitors and reports there.

1:11 *the whole world at rest and in peace.* The second year of Darius was marked by the new king's ability to finally gain control over the extensive Persian Empire (see note on Hag 1:1; see also the Introduction to Haggai: Historical Setting). With political disturbances behind him, Darius could focus his rule on organizing and extending his authority throughout the empire. Later Greek writers acclaimed Darius as a lawgiver and enlightened leader, suggesting far-sighted administrative skill. Whether attributable to Darius or not, the fact remains that the empire he commanded became one of the most diverse and peaceful political structures in antiquity.

1:12 *these seventy years.* According to the prophet Jeremiah, the exile in Babylon was to last 70 years (Jer 29:10). While it is not clear what the prophet meant by this date, the book of Ezra interprets it as marking the end of the exile with the restoration of the temple in Jerusalem (Ezr 1:1).

1:16 *measuring line.* Prior to modern times, surveying was conducted with a line or other implements of a set length (Eze 40:3). Zechariah's mention of the measuring line indicates that new construction was underway, so it was necessary for a surveyor to mark the boundaries of the property.

1:18 *four horns.* "Horn" is often used in the Bible as an image of power (Dt 33:17; 1Sa 2:1). In this case, the horns are representative of generic national powers that have caused the exile of the community. "Horn" is also a common motif for power in the ancient Near East, both as a decorative element on symbols of royal power and as a metaphor for such power. It may be that the prophet is envisioning some specific item adorned with horns, but there is nothing in the description that mandates such a specific reference.

1:20 *craftsmen.* Among the many categories of Babylonian temple personnel at the end of the sixth century BC was one designated "craftsmen" (*ummanu*). A number of different guilds were included in this group (those who worked with materials such as wood, metal, leather, gold, cloth, stone and gems, as well as those who carried out tasks such as laundering). This same term was extended to serve as a title of royal advisors believed to be supernaturally endowed. Individuals of this title are also identified as the sages who composed famous pieces of literature. In short, this term referred to various experts in the employ of the palace and temple. The Mesopotamian epic "Erra and Ishum" makes it clear that it was the *ummanu* who were responsible for crafting divine images. The Hebrew term used here can also refer to a wide range of guild workers, including those who craft images and serve the temples, but it is never clearly extended to sages or royal administrative advisors.

2:2 *measure Jerusalem.* As the process is begun for the rebuilding of the temple in Jerusalem, preparations must be made. In the ancient world temple-building was a complex undertaking replete with ritual and intended to be a joint act carried out by divine and human parties. Since the temple was sacred space, the dimensions, placement and orientation of the temple were all of great

ZECHARIAH 1:16

Ancient Temple-Building Accounts and Zechariah

The Sippar Cylinder of Nabonidus (556 – 539 BC) commemorates the rebuilding of one of the primary temples to the god Sin located in Harran. The account notes, "Ehulhul, the temple of Sin in Harran, where since the days of yore Sin, the great lord, had established his favorite residence — his heart became angry against that city and temple." The account goes on to say that Sin sent the Medes to destroy the city and the temple but then became "reconciled" with the city, and to honor Nabonidus, Sin appeared to him in a dream with Marduk, the primary god of Babylon, to command the rebuilding of the temple. When Nabonidus indicates his concern due to the city being under control of the Medes, Marduk declares that the threat will be no more. Both deities call forth Cyrus of Persia to defeat the Medes and allow Nabonidus to enter the city. So Nabonidus undertook the rebuilding "in a propitious month, on an auspicious day," which divination, probably liver omens, had revealed. The temple was completed and Nabonidus brought images of various deities from Babylon to Harran "in joy and gladness," filling the temple with fine gifts and causing Harran to appear "as brilliant as moonlight" (Sin being associated with the moon). Following the completion of this work, the king prays to Sin to bless the city and temple and to support Nabonidus's reign by conquering the king's enemies and annihilating any who were hostile to the king.

One can see how the opening of the prophet's work recalls God's earlier displeasure with the community (Zec 1:2 – 6), only to move on to the first vision in which God's intention is to see the temple rebuilt (Zec 1:7 – 17). One difference between typical temple-rebuilding texts and the prophet's message is the focus of the divine attention: while Sin and Marduk bestow favors and support to King Nabonidus, in Zechariah God's concerns are for the community at large. ◆

meet him 4and said to him: "Run, tell that
young man, 'Jerusalem will be a city without walls[d] because of the great number[e]
of people and animals in it. 5And I myself
will be a wall[f] of fire around it,' declares
the LORD, 'and I will be its glory[g] within.'

6"Come! Come! Flee from the land of
the north," declares the LORD, "for I have
scattered you to the four winds of heav-
en,"[h] declares the LORD.
7"Come, Zion! Escape, you who live in
Daughter Babylon!"[i] 8For this is what the

2:4 [d] Eze 38:11 [e] Isa 49:20; Jer 30:19; 33:22 **2:5** [f] Isa 26:1 [g] Rev 21:23 **2:6** [h] Eze 17:21 **2:7** [i] Isa 48:20

importance (see the article "Temples and Sacred Space," p. 724). Deities were called upon to give some of that information. If a temple previously existed on the site, as here, it would be important to rebuild at the same place, and measuring tools would be used to locate that place. Since the temple represented the center of order in the cosmos, it must reflect consummate order and proportioning. A survey of temple-building texts from the ancient world illustrate these concerns. The Ur-Nammu Stele depicts the various steps in temple building. As in most texts, the whole process is begun by the divine command (see 1:16). As a sign of this command, the king is given the rope and rod for measurement; these serve as his authorization to proceed. Once the measurements are complete, they then have to be confirmed by the deity.

2:4 *city without walls.* Walls were part of a defensive fortification system that protected ancient cities. In the ancient Near East a city would not exist without walls unless the residents were secure in their military power or a larger entity, such as an empire, removed the walls to ensure the urban population was well aware of its vulnerability. When Babylon attempted to rebel against Xerxes, Darius's successor, he ordered that its walls be taken down. The prophet's comment shows that either Jerusalem will grow so rapidly that there will be no time to establish the city's defenses or, more likely, there was no need for defensive works since the empire was ensuring the community's security.

2:6 *land of the north.* In Jeremiah, the north was the direction from which the enemy would come (see note on

LORD Almighty says: "After the Glorious
One has sent me against the nations that
have plundered you — for whoever touches you touches the apple of his eye[j]— 9I
will surely raise my hand against them so
that their slaves will plunder them.[a][k] Then
you will know that the LORD Almighty has
sent me.[l]
10"Shout and be glad, Daughter Zion.[m]
For I am coming,[n] and I will live among
you,"[o] declares the LORD. 11"Many nations
will be joined with the LORD in that day
and will become my people. I will live
among you and you will know that the
LORD Almighty has sent me to you. 12The
LORD will inherit[p] Judah as his portion in
the holy land and will again choose[q] Jerusalem. 13Be still[r] before the LORD, all mankind, because he has roused himself from
his holy dwelling."

Clean Garments for the High Priest

3 Then he showed me Joshua[s] the high
priest standing before the angel of the
LORD, and Satan[b][t] standing at his right side
to accuse him. 2The LORD said to Satan,
"The LORD rebuke you,[u] Satan! The LORD,
who has chosen[v] Jerusalem, rebuke you!
Is not this man a burning stick snatched
from the fire?"[w]
3Now Joshua was dressed in filthy
clothes as he stood before the angel. 4The
angel said to those who were standing before him, "Take off his filthy clothes."
Then he said to Joshua, "See, I have
taken away your sin,[x] and I will put fine
garments[y] on you."
5Then I said, "Put a clean turban[z] on his
head." So they put a clean turban on his
head and clothed him, while the angel of
the LORD stood by.
6The angel of the LORD gave this charge
to Joshua: 7"This is what the LORD Almighty says: 'If you will walk in obedience to me and keep my requirements,
then you will govern my house[a] and have
charge of my courts, and I will give you a
place among these standing here.
8" 'Listen, High Priest Joshua, you and
your associates seated before you, who
are men symbolic[b] of things to come: I am
going to bring my servant, the Branch.[c]

2:8 [j] Dt 32:10 **2:9** [k] Isa 14:2 [l] Zec 4:9 **2:10** [m] Zep 3:14 [n] Zec 9:9 [o] Lev 26:12; Zec 8:3 **2:12** [p] Dt 32:9; Ps 33:12; Jer 10:16 [q] Zec 1:17 **2:13** [r] Hab 2:20 **3:1** [s] Hag 1:1; Zec 6:11 [t] Ps 109:6 **3:2** [u] Jude 1:9 [v] Isa 14:1 [w] Am 4:11; Jude 1:23 **3:4** [x] Eze 36:25; Mic 7:18 [y] Isa 52:1; Rev 19:8 **3:5** [z] Ex 29:6 **3:7** [a] Dt 17:8-11; Eze 44:15-16 **3:8** [b] Eze 12:11 [c] Isa 4:2

[a] 8,9 Or *says after . . . eye:* 9*"I . . . plunder them."*
[b] 1 Hebrew *satan* means *adversary.*

Jer 1:13). Eventually it became clear that Babylon was that enemy from the north. Even though Babylon was located east of Jerusalem, all traffic flowed in an arc around the Syrian desert. Thus Babylonians would come into Judah from the north and Israelites would go to Babylon from the north. Now Zechariah is urging them to flee from the lands of their captors. *four winds.* See note on 6:1.

2:9 *their slaves will plunder them.* In ancient Near Eastern thought, social chaos is represented by a reversal of normal human relations. One Egyptian sage observes a reversal when those who at one time were wealthy are now begging for bread, while those who previously were beggars find themselves with plenty. The prophet Zechariah is saying that the situation will be desperate when slaves are able to plunder their masters.

3:1 *Satan.* In the Hebrew, the use of the definite article ("the") before *satan* both here and in Job 1 – 2 indicates that the author intends a noun describing a function ("adversary") rather than a personal name. As a common noun, the Hebrew word *satan* can be used to speak of either human beings (e.g., 1Sa 29:4; 1Ki 11:14) or a variety of supernatural beings (cf. the role of the angel of the Lord in Nu 22:22,32). See the article "Satan," p. 820. The ultimate focus of the accuser's contentions is God's policies. When Joshua stands in the presence of God, the adversary opposes Joshua because he is covered with the stains of his and his people's guilt. God's policy of forgiveness is therefore questioned.

3:3 *Joshua.* Joshua, the sitting high priest in this period, shared leadership in the community with Zerubbabel. Though Zerubbabel had legitimate Davidic pedigree and therefore a claim to the throne, the fact that Yehud was under Persian rule necessarily restricted his role. Zerubbabel therefore served as governor; as part of the imperial system, the governor's range of powers was very constricted. As high priest, Joshua may have enjoyed control over resources and parts of the community that a governor could not access, thus making it critical that both of these individuals cooperate on the rebuilding effort. There are no contemporary extra-Biblical references to the high priest Joshua, but in the Biblical accounts his grandfather, Seraiah, had been executed by Nebuchadnezzar when Jerusalem fell to the Babylonians (2Ki 25:18 – 21), and Joshua is therefore also likely related to Ezra (see Ezr 7:1).

3:4 *standing before him.* Since the scene features an accuser and a court setting, we can recognize a type-scene familiar from the ancient world: the heavenly court. Most ancient Near Eastern cultures believed that decisions by which the cosmos was run and human matters resolved were made in the divine council, which was made up of the principal members of the pantheon (see the article "Divine Council," p. 615).

3:5 *Put a clean turban on his head.* This is clearly an investiture scene (used in the OT and the ancient Near East to portray the elevation of someone to a new position or status, cf. Joseph, Aaron or Daniel), but the interpretive question turns on the significance of the investiture. If it were a vesting of Joshua as high priest, we might expect some reference to the various high priestly garments known from the rest of the OT. As it stands, the only specific piece of clothing referred to is the turban, and the Hebrew word used is not the same as that describing the high priestly turban. Given the larger context of temple building, an alternative that is worth considering is that the headpiece referred to here is the special headpiece used by kings in the ancient Near East to carry the ceremonial first brick for laying the foundation of temples. Numerous examples of this appear in ancient Near Eastern reliefs from the Sumerian period (e.g., the Ur-Nanshe Stele) to the Neo-Assyrian period (notably Ashurbanipal). If this is the nature of the turban here in Zechariah, Joshua is being purified and prepared for his role in the construction of the temple.

3:8 *Branch.* See note on 6:12.

9See, the stone I have set in front of Joshua! There are seven eyes[a] on that one
stone,[d] and I will engrave an inscription
on it,' says the LORD Almighty, 'and I will
remove the sin[e] of this land in a single day.
10" 'In that day each of you will invite
your neighbor to sit under your vine and
fig tree,[f]' declares the LORD Almighty."

The Gold Lampstand and the Two Olive Trees

4 Then the angel who talked with me
returned and woke[g] me up, like someone awakened from sleep.[h] 2He asked me,
"What do you see?"[i]
I answered, "I see a solid gold lampstand[j] with a bowl at the top and seven
lamps[k] on it, with seven channels to the
lamps. 3Also there are two olive trees[l] by
it, one on the right of the bowl and the
other on its left."
4I asked the angel who talked with me,
"What are these, my lord?"
5He answered, "Do you not know what
these are?"
"No, my lord," I replied.[m]
6So he said to me, "This is the word of
the LORD to Zerubbabel:[n] 'Not by might
nor by power, but by my Spirit,'[o] says the
LORD Almighty.
7"What are you, mighty mountain?
Before Zerubbabel you will become level ground.[p] Then he will bring out the
capstone[q] to shouts of 'God bless it! God
bless it!' "

3:9 [d] Isa 28:16 [e] Jer 50:20 **3:10** [f] 1Ki 4:25; Mic 4:4 **4:1** [g] Da 8:18 [h] Jer 31:26 **4:2** [i] Jer 1:13 [j] Ex 25:31; Rev 1:12 [k] Rev 4:5
4:3 [l] ver 11; Rev 11:4 **4:5** [m] Zec 1:9 **4:6** [n] Ezr 5:2 [o] Isa 11:2-4; Hos 1:7 **4:7** [p] Jer 51:25 [q] Ps 118:22

[a] 9 Or *facets*

3:9 *seven eyes on that one stone.* Since the context of Zechariah speaks of the stone that is set before Zechariah, the discussion would likely concern a foundation stone or the first brick (see note on v. 5). In this regard it should be noted that it was not uncommon in Mesopotamia to include gemstones in the foundation deposit of a temple. Consequently, we might suggest that the foundation stone is being set before Joshua, and seven precious stones are being inlaid on it. In the ancient world, facets were not yet being cut on gems, but there is evidence of gems being cut in the shape of eyes.
4:2 *solid gold lampstand with a bowl at the top and seven lamps on it, with seven channels to the lamps.* The bowl is to hold the oil to fuel the lamp, and the seven channels direct the oil to the wicks at the ends of the channels. Seven, being a number representing completeness, is an appropriate number of wicks since the lamp seems to represent God's comprehension of what is happening in the world (v. 10). Theoretically such a lamp can be envisioned, and support can be adduced using artifactual evidence. A seven-spouted lamp was found at Tell Dothan dating to the Late Bronze Age. Other finds suggest that multiple lamps were sometimes arranged around the edge of a bowl. No artifacts combine these features to illustrate the object being described here. An alternative suggestion that has been made on the basis of known artifacts is that the lamp is a kernos ring (see below). Though these terracotta vessels were typically used for libations, examples have been found in Palestine dating to the Persian period that show evidence of their use as lamps.
4:3 *two olive trees by it.* The vision described here probably concerns that which is or will be inscribed on the foundation stone. In this case the stones referred to in ch. 4 would be the same as the stones mentioned in ch. 3. The lampstand and the trees may then be evaluated in light of the iconography of the ancient Near East, where it is not uncommon for figures to be portrayed flanking a stylized representation of deity. The crescent moon emblem with upturned horns not only represents the deity but also is reminiscent of the bowl of a lamp. In these seals, the symmetry of two trees represents two worshipers, as is also the case in Zechariah's vision.
4:7 *What are you, mighty mountain? Before Zerubbabel you will become level ground.* The height on which the temple

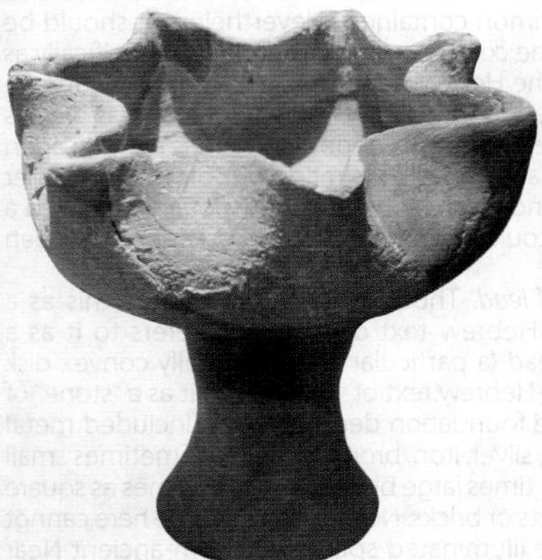

Seven-spouted lamp, tenth to ninth century BC, Tel Dan. See note on Zec 4:2.

Kernos ring, c. 2000 BC.

8Then the word of the LORD came to me:
9"The hands of Zerubbabel have laid the
foundation[r] of this temple; his hands will
also complete it.[s] Then you will know that
the LORD Almighty has sent me[t] to you.
10"Who dares despise the day of small
things,[u] since the seven eyes[v] of the LORD
that range throughout the earth will rejoice when they see the chosen capstone[a]
in the hand of Zerubbabel?"
11Then I asked the angel, "What are
these two olive trees[w] on the right and the
left of the lampstand?"
12Again I asked him, "What are these
two olive branches beside the two gold
pipes that pour out golden oil?"
13He replied, "Do you not know what
these are?"
"No, my lord," I said.
14So he said, "These are the two who
are anointed[x] to[b] serve the Lord of all the
earth."

The Flying Scroll

5 I looked again, and there before me
was a flying scroll.[y]
2He asked me, "What do you see?"
I answered, "I see a flying scroll, twenty
cubits long and ten cubits wide.[c]"
3And he said to me, "This is the curse[z]
that is going out over the whole land; for
according to what it says on one side, every thief[a] will be banished, and according
to what it says on the other, everyone who
swears falsely[b] will be banished. 4The
LORD Almighty declares, 'I will send it out,
and it will enter the house of the thief and
the house of anyone who swears falsely by
my name. It will remain in that house and
destroy it completely, both its timbers and
its stones.[c]'"

The Woman in a Basket

5Then the angel who was speaking to
me came forward and said to me, "Look
up and see what is appearing."
6I asked, "What is it?"
He replied, "It is a basket." And he added, "This is the iniquity[d] of the people
throughout the land."
7Then the cover of lead was raised, and
there in the basket sat a woman! 8He said,
"This is wickedness," and he pushed her
back into the basket and pushed its lead
cover down on it.[d]

4:9 [r] Ezr 3:11 [s] Ezr 3:8; 6:15; Zec 6:12 [t] Zec 2:9 **4:10** [u] Hag 2:3 [v] Zec 3:9; Rev 5:6 **4:11** [w] ver 3; Rev 11:4 **4:14** [x] Ex 29:7; 40:15; Da 9:24-26; Zec 3:1-7 **5:1** [y] Eze 2:9; Rev 5:1
5:3 [z] Isa 24:6; 43:28; Mal 3:9; 4:6 [a] Ex 20:15; Mal 3:8 [b] Isa 48:1 **5:4** [c] Lev 14:34-45; Hab 2:9-11; Mal 3:5 **5:8** [d] Mic 6:11

[a] *10* Or *the plumb line* [b] *14* Or *two who bring oil and* [c] *2* That is, about 30 feet long and 15 feet wide or about 9 meters long and 4.5 meters wide [d] *6* Or *appearance*

stood made hauling up construction materials difficult. The speaker is promising that with a commitment to rebuilding the temple, God will make this height seem a trivial matter. *the capstone.* In Mesopotamia, part of the rebuilding of a temple involved bringing out a stone from the earlier structure to be installed in the new building, demonstrating continuity. It may well be that this is the stone that Zerubbabel is bringing out and why it receives so much attention. If this association is accurate, as seems likely, it would be better to translate this as the foundation stone (with its importance designating it as the "premier" stone). Temple-building accounts refer both to the removal of this stone from the site so that leveling of the site could take place and to reinstalling it at the appropriate time.

5:2 *twenty cubits long and ten cubits wide.* Given the conventional size of a cubit, the dimensions given would be about 30 feet long and 15 feet wide (9 meters long and 4.5 meters wide). The fact that the prophet can report on these dimensions suggests his vision shows the scroll unrolled. The "flying" component (v. 1) would be a sign of the transitional nature of the scroll, suspended between heaven and earth, like the basket noted in v. 9.

5:3 *on one side … on the other.* Though it is not unheard of for scrolls to have writing on both sides, the terminology here suggests that two side-by-side columns of writing are intended, perhaps one column addressing each of the crimes. *every thief … everyone who swears falsely.* In the temple-building context of Zechariah's visions, these two offenses would be particularly noteworthy. As in building projects today, the project often calls for raising support from key donors before construction begins. They pledge donations that provide the backing that the project needs to proceed. In the ancient world, such pledges were supported by formal oaths to follow through, and such oaths transformed the pledged gifts into divine property. In this combination, anyone who had pledged gifts to the temple initially but then reneged on their pledges would be guilty first of swearing falsely and then of theft, for they continued to possess that which now technically belonged to deity (cf. Hag 1:4; Mal 3:8–10). The "curse" written on the scroll would bring about the destruction of not only that which had been withheld but also the house of the perpetrators.

5:6 *basket.* While ceramic vessels are the most commonly found examples of standard volume measures, there is ample evidence in narrative and artistic sources to demonstrate that baskets of woven reeds were also used as common containers. Nevertheless, it should be noted that the container is never identified specifically as a basket in the Hebrew text. Special ceremonial containers were used to transport the premier stone as well as to house the foundation deposits. There is no indication what material this basket is made out of. The container used for foundation deposits in Mesopotamia is called a *quppu* and could be either a wicker basket or a wooden chest.

5:7 *cover of lead.* Though the NIV interprets this as a "cover," the Hebrew text of this verse refers to it as a "talent" of lead (a particular weight, usually convex disk shaped); the Hebrew text of v. 8 refers to it as a "stone" of lead. Temple foundation deposits often included metal pieces (gold, silver, iron, bronze, lead) — sometimes small scraps, other times large blocks, and sometimes as square convex tablets or bricks. Nevertheless, its role here cannot presently be illuminated specifically from ancient Near Eastern materials. There is no evidence for the use of lead as a cover for any form of vessel in antiquity. *in the basket sat a woman.* The small size of the container has led to the conclusion that a figurine of a woman is in the basket. The most logical connection of figurines to temple building would be that figurine pegs were often buried next to

9Then I looked up — and there before
me were two women, with the wind in
their wings! They had wings like those of
a stork,[e] and they lifted up the basket between heaven and earth.
10"Where are they taking the basket?" I
asked the angel who was speaking to me.
11He replied, "To the country of Babylonia[a][f] to build a house[g] for it. When the
house is ready, the basket will be set there
in its place."[h]

Four Chariots

6 I looked up again, and there before me
were four chariots[i] coming out from
between two mountains — mountains of
bronze. 2The first chariot had red horses,
the second black,[j] 3the third white,[k] and
the fourth dappled — all of them powerful.
4I asked the angel who was speaking to
me, "What are these, my lord?"
5The angel answered me, "These are
the four spirits[b][l] of heaven, going out from
standing in the presence of the Lord of the
whole world. 6The one with the black
horses is going toward the north country,
the one with the white horses toward the
west,[c] and the one with the dappled horses toward the south."
7When the powerful horses went out,
they were straining to go throughout the
earth.[m] And he said, "Go throughout the
earth!" So they went throughout the earth.
8Then he called to me, "Look, those going toward the north country have given
my Spirit[d] rest[n] in the land of the north."

A Crown for Joshua

9The word of the LORD came to me:
10"Take silver and gold from the exiles
Heldai, Tobijah and Jedaiah, who have
arrived from Babylon.[o] Go the same day
to the house of Josiah son of Zephaniah. 11Take the silver and gold and make a
crown,[p] and set it on the head of the high
priest, Joshua[q] son of Jozadak.[e][r] 12Tell him
this is what the LORD Almighty says: 'Here
is the man whose name is the Branch,[s]
and he will branch out from his place and
build the temple of the LORD.[t] 13It is he
who will build the temple of the LORD, and

5:9 [e] Lev 11:19
5:11 [f] Ge 10:10 [g] Jer 29:5, 28 [h] Da 1:2
6:1 [i] ver 5
6:2 [j] Rev 6:5
6:3 [k] Rev 6:2
6:5 [l] Eze 37:9; Mt 24:31; Rev 7:1
6:7 [m] Zec 1:10
6:8 [n] Eze 5:13; 24:13
6:10 [o] Ezr 7:14-16; Jer 28:6
6:11 [p] Ps 21:3 [q] Zec 3:1 [r] Ezr 3:2
6:12 [s] Isa 4:2; Zec 3:8 [t] Ezr 3:8-10; Zec 4:6-9

[a] *11* Hebrew *Shinar* [b] *5* Or *winds* [c] *6* Or *horses after them* [d] *8* Or *spirit* [e] *11* Hebrew *Jehozadak*, a variant of *Jozadak*

the foundation deposit or beneath the door-pivot stone. Such figurines could either indicate dedication to a particular deity or represent an apotropaic (protective) deity. Unfortunately, there are numerous problems with this interpretation. Theologically, it is difficult to see why a figurine, putatively idolatrous, would be accorded the status granted here. Archaeologically, the foundation pegs are not attested anywhere near this time period. The latest examples are from about 2000 BC. Culturally, this practice is not attested in Persian contexts. Iconographically, the pegs were generally not women. Finally, contextually, the other elements in this vision (container, lead) have no connection to foundation pegs. Consequently, unless further examples were to be found in this period, this interpretation should be set aside, and no other information from the ancient Near East can inform our interpretation. In all likelihood, however, this is a figurine.

5:9 *two women.* The common assumption that these are angels cannot be sustained. In the OT angels are neither portrayed as female nor as having wings. In the broader ancient Near Eastern context, female deities are sometimes portrayed as having wings (e.g., Anat in Ugaritic literature and Ishtar in Mesopotamian literature). Most winged figures in the iconography, however, are protective spirits, which are often seen flanking gods or sacred items (such as the cosmic tree). This interpretation would fit well with the information in this context as apocalyptic imagery drawing on this iconography. *stork.* The Hebrew term seems to indicate any bird of the long-legged variety. A number of birds in this order are migratory, and at seasonal times they are present in Palestine. As with the scroll (v. 2), the flying component of the image seems to point to a transitional state between heaven and earth.

5:11 *build a house for it.* The pronoun "it" is feminine, as are the woman and the basket. Since the second part of this verse makes reference to the basket rather than the woman, the house is seen as being built for it rather than for her. This would further confirm that the "basket" should be identified as a foundation deposit that will be set in place in a temple there. *house.* A word often used for a temple.

6:1 *four chariots.* These are called the four spirits, the same terms as the "four winds" in 2:6. Ps 104:4 refers to the winds as the messengers of Yahweh, and that is the function these chariots are serving here. The horsemen in ch. 1 were comparable to the Persian courier service, but chariots were not used that way. It is unusual that a chariot should be used by a messenger, because it would only slow him down and tire his horses unnecessarily. In the ancient Near East a supernatural being in a chariot was usually transporting the deity rather than serving as a messenger (see note on 2Ki 2:11). *mountains of bronze.* It is not entirely clear what the prophet is trying to convey with this image. Some believe it is a reference to a common Mesopotamian image of the sun-god rising between two mountains, the morning light making rock appear bronze in color. Others see in the reference to bronze an allusion to fortifications, bronze being used for gateways and other defensive works. Mountains were often seen as the home of God.

6:12 *Branch.* It is not clear whom this refers to, and the Hebrew term used here is not the same Hebrew term used in Isa 11:1 to refer to a coming ruler. Scholars tend to argue two ways on the identity of this figure. (1) Given the earlier promise that Zerubbabel will be the one to complete the temple (4:9), the "Branch" is Zerubbabel, and hence the prophet anticipates a coronation of the governor as a king over an independent Judah. (2) This is a future ruler, a Messianic figure, who will benefit from the faithfulness of Joshua and the temple priesthood. There is no indication that Jerusalem at this time period could have envisioned a successful revolt against the Persian Empire since the city was unwalled and impoverished. In the broader ancient Near Eastern context, the term "branch," or terms based on similar metaphors, have been attested as technical terminology referring to the rightful heir of an established dynastic line.

he will be clothed with majesty and will
sit and rule on his throne. And he[a] will be
a priest[u] on his throne. And there will be
harmony between the two.' 14The crown
will be given to Heldai,[b] Tobijah, Jedaiah
and Hen[c] son of Zephaniah as a memorial
in the temple of the LORD. 15Those who are
far away will come and help to build the
temple of the LORD,[v] and you will know
that the LORD Almighty has sent me to
you.[w] This will happen if you diligently
obey[x] the LORD your God."

Justice and Mercy, Not Fasting

7 In the fourth year of King Darius, the
word of the LORD came to Zechariah
on the fourth day of the ninth month, the
month of Kislev.[y] 2The people of Bethel
had sent Sharezer and Regem-Melek, together with their men, to entreat[z] the LORD
3by asking the priests of the house of the
LORD Almighty and the prophets, "Should
I mourn[a] and fast in the fifth[b] month, as I
have done for so many years?"

4Then the word of the LORD Almighty
came to me: 5"Ask all the people of the
land and the priests, 'When you fasted[c]
and mourned in the fifth and seventh
months for the past seventy years, was it
really for me that you fasted? 6And when
you were eating and drinking, were you
not just feasting for yourselves? 7Are
these not the words the LORD proclaimed
through the earlier prophets[d] when Jerusalem and its surrounding towns were at
rest[e] and prosperous, and the Negev and
the western foothills[f] were settled?'"

8And the word of the LORD came again
to Zechariah: 9"This is what the LORD Almighty said: 'Administer true justice;[g]
show mercy and compassion to one another. 10Do not oppress the widow or the
fatherless, the foreigner[h] or the poor. Do
not plot evil against each other.'[i]

11"But they refused to pay attention;
stubbornly they turned their backs and
covered their ears.[j] 12They made their
hearts as hard as flint[k] and would not
listen to the law or to the words that
the LORD Almighty had sent by his Spirit
through the earlier prophets.[l] So the LORD
Almighty was very angry.[m]

13"'When I called, they did not listen;[n]
so when they called, I would not listen,'[o]
says the LORD Almighty.[p] 14'I scattered[q]
them with a whirlwind[r] among all the nations, where they were strangers. The land
they left behind them was so desolate that
no one traveled through it. This is how
they made the pleasant land desolate.[s]'"

The LORD Promises to Bless Jerusalem

8 The word of the LORD Almighty came
to me.

2This is what the LORD Almighty says:
"I am very jealous for Zion; I am burning
with jealousy for her."

3This is what the LORD says: "I will return[t] to Zion and dwell in Jerusalem.[u]
Then Jerusalem will be called the Faithful City, and the mountain of the LORD Almighty will be called the Holy Mountain."

4This is what the LORD Almighty says:
"Once again men and women of ripe old
age will sit in the streets of Jerusalem,[v]
each of them with cane in hand because
of their age. 5The city streets will be filled
with boys and girls playing there.[w]"

6This is what the LORD Almighty says:
"It may seem marvelous to the remnant of
this people at that time,[x] but will it seem
marvelous to me?[y]" declares the LORD Almighty.

7This is what the LORD Almighty says: "I
will save my people from the countries of
the east and the west.[z] 8I will bring them
back[a] to live in Jerusalem; they will be my
people,[b] and I will be faithful and righteous to them as their God."

9This is what the LORD Almighty says:
"Now hear these words, 'Let your hands
be strong[c] so that the temple may be built.'
This is also what the prophets[d] said who
were present when the foundation was
laid for the house of the LORD Almighty.
10Before that time there were no wages[e]

6:13 [u] Ps 110:4 **6:15** [v] Isa 60:10 [w] Zec 2:9-11 [x] Isa 58:12; Jer 7:23; Zec 3:7 **7:1** [y] Ne 1:1 **7:2** [z] Jer 26:19; Zec 8:21 **7:3** [a] Zec 12:12-14 [b] Jer 52:12-14; Zec 8:19 **7:5** [c] Isa 58:5 **7:7** [d] Zec 1:4 [e] Jer 22:21 [f] Jer 17:26 **7:9** [g] Zec 8:16 **7:10** [h] Ex 22:21 [i] Ex 22:22; Isa 1:17 **7:11** [j] Jer 8:5; 11:10; 17:23 **7:12** [k] Jer 17:1; Eze 11:19 [l] Ne 9:29 [m] Da 9:12 **7:13** [n] Pr 1:24 [o] Isa 1:15; Jer 11:11; 14:12; Mic 3:4 [p] Pr 1:28 **7:14** [q] Dt 4:27; 28:64-67 [r] Jer 23:19 [s] Jer 44:6 **8:3** [t] Zec 1:16 [u] Zec 2:10 **8:4** [v] Isa 65:20 **8:5** [w] Jer 30:20; 31:13 **8:6** [x] Ps 118:23; 126:1-3 [y] Jer 32:17,27 **8:7** [z] Ps 107:3; Isa 11:11; 43:5 **8:8** [a] Zec 10:10 [b] Eze 11:19-20; 36:28; Zec 2:11 **8:9** [c] Hag 2:4 [d] Ezr 5:1 **8:10** [e] Hag 1:6

[a] *13* Or *there* [b] *14* Syriac; Hebrew *Helem* [c] *14* Or *and the gracious one, the*

6:14 *Hen son of Zephaniah.* While many English translations render "Hen" as a personal name, there is good evidence to see this as a title for a temple steward, so the crown is being entrusted to several individuals, including "Josiah the steward, son of Zephaniah" (see v. 10).

7:1 *fourth day of the ninth month, the month of Kislev.* Sometime in December of 518 BC, about two years since Zechariah's opening oracle.

7:3 *fast in the fifth month.* Fasts typically marked major national disasters, of which there had been many in the recent history of Israel. Since the text provides no explanation of what these fasts in ch. 7 marked, we can only offer suggestions by matching up events with months. We know that Nebuchadnezzar's destruction of the temple took place in the fifth month (2Ki 25:8–9), and since it is the temple that is being rebuilt, it would make sense that the delegation has come to inquire about whether the fast should be continued.

7:5 *fasted ... in the fifth and seventh months.* For the fast in the fifth month, see the previous note. It is much more difficult to identify a historical event that would have occasioned a fast in the seventh month. Of the events that occurred surrounding the destruction of the temple and Jerusalem, the only one that is stated to have taken place in the seventh month is the assassination of Gedaliah (Jer 41), the governor appointed by Nebuchadnezzar after the right to kingship had been revoked.

for people or hire for animals. No one
could go about their business safely because of their enemies, since I had turned
everyone against their neighbor. 11But now
I will not deal with the remnant of this
people as I did in the past,"[f] declares the
LORD Almighty.
12"The seed will grow well, the vine will
yield its fruit,[g] the ground will produce its
crops,[h] and the heavens will drop their
dew.[i] I will give all these things as an inheritance[j] to the remnant of this people.
13Just as you, Judah and Israel, have been
a curse[a][k] among the nations, so I will save
you, and you will be a blessing.[b][l] Do not
be afraid, but let your hands be strong."
14This is what the LORD Almighty says:
"Just as I had determined to bring disaster[m] on you and showed no pity when your
ancestors angered me," says the LORD Almighty, 15"so now I have determined to do
good[n] again to Jerusalem and Judah. Do
not be afraid. 16These are the things you
are to do: Speak the truth[o] to each other, and render true and sound judgment
in your courts;[p] 17do not plot evil[q] against
each other, and do not love to swear falsely.[r] I hate all this," declares the LORD.
18The word of the LORD Almighty came
to me.
19This is what the LORD Almighty says:
"The fasts of the fourth,[s] fifth,[t] seventh[u]
and tenth[v] months will become joyful[w]
and glad occasions and happy festivals for
Judah. Therefore love truth[x] and peace."
20This is what the LORD Almighty says:
"Many peoples and the inhabitants of
many cities will yet come, 21and the inhabitants of one city will go to another and
say, 'Let us go at once to entreat[y] the LORD
and seek the LORD Almighty. I myself am
going.' 22And many peoples and powerful
nations will come to Jerusalem to seek the
LORD Almighty and to entreat him."[z]

8:11 [f] Isa 12:1
8:12 [g] Joel 2:22
[h] Ps 67:6
[i] Ge 27:28
[j] Ob 1:17
8:13 [k] Jer 42:18
[l] Ge 12:2
8:14
[m] Jer 31:28;
Eze 24:14
8:15 [n] ver 13;
Jer 29:11;
Mic 7:18-20
8:16 [o] Ps 15:2;
Eph 4:25
[p] Zec 7:9
8:17 [q] Pr 3:29
[r] Pr 6:16-19
8:19 [s] Jer 39:2
[t] Jer 52:12
[u] 2Ki 25:25
[v] Jer 52:4
[w] Ps 30:11
[x] ver 16
8:21 [y] Zec 7:2
8:22 [z] Ps 117:1;
Isa 60:3;
Zec 2:11

8:23 [a] Isa 45:14;
1Co 14:25
9:1 [b] Isa 17:1
9:2 [c] Jer 49:23
[d] Eze 28:1-19
9:3 [e] Job 27:16;
Eze 28:4
9:4 [f] Isa 23:1;
Eze 26:3-5;
28:18

23This is what the LORD Almighty says:
"In those days ten people from all languages and nations will take firm hold
of one Jew by the hem of his robe and
say, 'Let us go with you, because we have
heard that God is with you.' "[a]

Judgment on Israel's Enemies

9 A prophecy:

The word of the LORD is against the
land of Hadrak
and will come to rest on
Damascus[b] —
for the eyes of all people and all the
tribes of Israel
are on the LORD —[c]
2and on Hamath[c] too, which borders
on it,
and on Tyre[d] and Sidon, though they
are very skillful.
3Tyre has built herself a stronghold;
she has heaped up silver like dust,
and gold like the dirt of the streets.[e]
4But the Lord will take away her
possessions
and destroy her power on the sea,
and she will be consumed by fire.[f]
5Ashkelon will see it and fear;
Gaza will writhe in agony,
and Ekron too, for her hope will
wither.
Gaza will lose her king
and Ashkelon will be deserted.
6A mongrel people will occupy
Ashdod,
and I will put an end to the pride of
the Philistines.

[a] 13 That is, your name has been used in cursing (see Jer. 29:22); or, you have been regarded as under a curse.
[b] 13 Or *and your name will be used in blessings* (see Gen. 48:20); or *and you will be seen as blessed*
[c] 1 Or *Damascus. / For the eye of the LORD is on all people, / as well as on the tribes of Israel,*

8:12 *all these things as an inheritance.* It was common in the ancient Near East to connect the establishment of a temple with the coming of blessing in the form of prosperity (see note on Hag 2:19). Zechariah is expressing the same theme: that prosperity was surely coming since the community was completing the rebuilding of the temple.
8:23 *by the hem of his robe.* In the ancient Near East, grasping the hem of the robe presumes the petitioner is on his knees, so this is an action of throwing one's self completely on the mercy of the person receiving the petition.
9:1 *Hadrak.* Well known from Assyrian sources as Hatarikka (the city over which Zakkur was king), even though it is otherwise absent from the Biblical record. *Damascus.* An important administrative center in the Persian Empire, it may have been the administrative center of the Persian satrapy of which Jerusalem was part. Both Hadrak and Damascus are in the Persian satrapy of Abarnahara (meaning "across the river"), which was bordered on the east by the Syrian desert and stretched from eastern Sinai and the Gulf of Aqaba up through Syria to the west bank of the Euphrates — thus roughly covering the area of the empire of David and Solomon from earlier times.
9:3 *Tyre has built herself a stronghold.* Tyre was a growing economic center under the Persian Empire and was the focus on a major campaign by Alexander the Great, who took the city in 332 BC. Tyre was frequently the rival of Sidon, until Sidon was destroyed in 351 BC.
9:5 *Gaza will lose her king.* During the Persian Empire it appears that Gaza and the regions around it were under a "dimorphic" administration, a provincial governor representing Persian interests and a native king maintaining traditional powers. So Gaza's loss of its king would anticipate it coming more under the direct control of the empire.
9:6 *Ashdod.* The 70-acre (28-hectare) site of Ashdod is located near the coast north of Ashkelon. It had the advantage of being on the main coastal highway and close enough to the sea to have a small harbor. The city

[7] I will take the blood from their mouths,
the forbidden food from between
their teeth.
Those who are left will belong to our
God
and become a clan in Judah,
and Ekron will be like the Jebusites.
[8] But I will encamp at my temple
to guard it against marauding forces.
Never again will an oppressor overrun
my people,
for now I am keeping watch.[g]

The Coming of Zion's King

[9] Rejoice greatly, Daughter Zion!
Shout, Daughter Jerusalem!
See, your king comes to you,
righteous and victorious,[h]
lowly and riding on a donkey,
on a colt, the foal of a donkey.[i]
[10] I will take away the chariots from
Ephraim
and the warhorses from Jerusalem,
and the battle bow will be broken.[j]
He will proclaim peace to the nations.
His rule will extend from sea to sea
and from the River[a] to the ends of
the earth.[k]
[11] As for you, because of the blood of my
covenant[l] with you,
I will free your prisoners[m] from the
waterless pit.
[12] Return to your fortress,[n] you prisoners
of hope;
even now I announce that I will
restore twice as much to you.
[13] I will bend Judah as I bend my bow
and fill it with Ephraim.[o]
I will rouse your sons, Zion,
against your sons, Greece,[p]
and make you like a warrior's
sword.[q]

The Lord Will Appear

[14] Then the Lord will appear over them;[r]
his arrow will flash like lightning.[s]

9:8 [g] Isa 52:1; 54:14 **9:9** [h] Isa 9:6-7; 43:3-11; Jer 23:5-6; Zep 3:14-15; Zec 2:10 [i] Mt 21:5*; Jn 12:15* **9:10** [j] Hos 1:7; 2:18; Mic 4:3; 5:10; Zec 10:4 [k] Ps 72:8 **9:11** [l] Ex 24:8 [m] Isa 42:7 **9:12** [n] Joel 3:16 **9:13** [o] Isa 49:2 [p] Joel 3:6 [q] Jer 51:20 **9:14** [r] Isa 31:5 [s] Ps 18:14; Hab 3:11

[a] *10* That is, the Euphrates

was destroyed by Nebuchadnezzar, but it was rebuilt in the Persian period. Excavations have uncovered this settlement, though later Hellenistic building activity obliterated major sections of the Persian town.

9:7 *Ekron.* The site of Ekron (Tel Miqne in the Sorek Valley) is located about 22 miles (35 kilometers) southwest of Jerusalem and about 15 miles (24 kilometers) from the Mediterranean. The site has been extensively excavated and consists of a lower city of about 40 acres (16 hectares), an upper tell of about 10 acres (4 hectares), and an acropolis. Its main industry was the production of olive oil. Archaeological excavations attest to the massive destruction of the town by Nebuchadnezzar in the last years of the seventh century BC. Literarily, this is attested in the Aramaic Saqqarah papyrus (the "Adon" letter) in a letter from the king of Ekron to the Egyptian pharaoh requesting support. No archaeological evidence suggests that it was resettled in the Persian period. This raises the unanswerable question of why the town should be mentioned in a text a century or more after its destruction. *like the Jebusites.* The comparison of Ekron to the Jebusites most likely indicates that the people of Ekron will be absorbed into the population of Judah.

9:9 *donkey.* Though the literature does not always do so, we must distinguish between a donkey (referred to in this passage) and a mule (a hybrid between a horse and a donkey). The mule (Hebrew *pered*) is preferred over the donkey as an official royal mount. The evidence for a donkey as a royal mount is meager. In Akkadian there is an occasional passing reference to a donkey for the king to ride. A Hittite narrative called The Queen of Qanesh and the Tale of Zalpa has the 30 royal sons driving a donkey, but it does not specify that they ride them. In Ugaritic literature the goddess Athiratu rides on a donkey in one text, thus indicating it as a regal, if not royal, mount. In Biblical texts elites occasionally ride on an *ayir* (translated "colt" in this verse) or on an *aton* (translated "foal of a "donkey" in this verse and Balaam's mount in Nu 22:21 – 35). Consequently, evidence is lacking to suggest that the king in this verse is being provided with transparently royal trappings. The contrast offered by the specification of his mount is that it would be clear that this king is not coming in a military context (which would have featured a horse, mule or chariot), but he is coming in peace and humility.

9:10 *battle bow.* In Assyrian texts from the seventh century BC (Esarhaddon), deity breaking the bow of the enemy is a way of describing defeat. In this passage it appears to prevent future battle. In other Biblical texts the same concept is expressed by beating swords into plowshares (see note on Isa 2:4). *proclaim peace to the nations.* Once a king had taken control of a conquered realm, there was always the fear that he would seek to execute vengeance against those who had opposed him. It was reassuring when the new ruler would "proclaim peace." When Cyrus captured Babylon, one of his first official acts was to declare a state of peace. *from sea to sea.* Rather than referring to particular seas, such as the Mediterranean and the Dead Sea, the universal tone of the passage suggests that reference is being made to cosmic seas that encompass all the inhabited lands. See the article "Cosmic Geography," p. 836. *the River to the ends of the earth.* When "river" is used with a definite article, it is usually a name for the Euphrates. Other translations fail to include a definite article, therefore suggesting a more abstract cosmic reference. In Akkadian literature the great cosmic river is known as Apsu; it serves as a suitable contrast to the "ends of the earth." *ends of the earth.* Refers to the most distant known places.

9:13 *against your sons, Greece.* Continual expansion of Greek trade during the Persian Empire led to a wide sphere of Greek influence. At what point this influence was perceived as a potential enemy is unclear. Some think the prophet's mention is a clear reference to the campaigns of Alexander the Great, though it would be almost a century before he came onto the international scene. On several earlier occasions the Persian Empire and elements of the Greeks were in conflict, which could easily have engendered such comments.

9:14 *The Lord will appear.* Numerous elements in vv. 14 – 15 (arrow/lightning, trumpet, storms, shield) indicate that the author is using the divine warrior motif, familiar throughout the ancient world in all periods and cultures. See the article "Divine Warfare," p. 365. *storms of*

The Sovereign LORD will sound the
trumpet;
he will march in the storms[t] of the
south,
15 and the LORD Almighty will shield[u]
them.
They will destroy
and overcome with slingstones.
They will drink and roar as with wine;
they will be full like a bowl
used for sprinkling[a] the corners[v] of
the altar.
16 The LORD their God will save his
people on that day
as a shepherd saves his flock.
They will sparkle in his land
like jewels in a crown.[w]
17 How attractive and beautiful they will be!
Grain will make the young men
thrive,
and new wine the young women.

The LORD Will Care for Judah

10 Ask the LORD for rain in the
springtime;
it is the LORD who sends the
thunderstorms.
He gives showers of rain to all people,
and plants of the field to everyone.
2 The idols[x] speak deceitfully,
diviners see visions that lie;
they tell dreams that are false,
they give comfort in vain.
Therefore the people wander like sheep
oppressed for lack of a shepherd.[y]

3 "My anger burns against the
shepherds,
and I will punish the leaders;[z]
for the LORD Almighty will care
for his flock, the people of Judah,
and make them like a proud horse in
battle.
4 From Judah will come the cornerstone,
from him the tent peg,[a]
from him the battle bow,[b]
from him every ruler.
5 Together they[b] will be like warriors in
battle
trampling their enemy into the mud
of the streets.[c]
They will fight because the LORD is
with them,
and they will put the enemy
horsemen to shame.[d]

6 "I will strengthen Judah
and save the tribes of Joseph.
I will restore them
because I have compassion on them.[e]
They will be as though
I had not rejected them,
for I am the LORD their God
and I will answer[f] them.
7 The Ephraimites will become like
warriors,
and their hearts will be glad as with
wine.[g]
Their children will see it and be joyful;
their hearts will rejoice in the LORD.
8 I will signal[h] for them
and gather them in.
Surely I will redeem them;
they will be as numerous[i] as before.
9 Though I scatter them among the
peoples,
yet in distant lands they will
remember me.[j]
They and their children will survive,
and they will return.
10 I will bring them back from Egypt
and gather them from Assyria.[k]
I will bring them to Gilead[l] and
Lebanon,
and there will not be room[m] enough
for them.
11 They will pass through the sea of
trouble;
the surging sea will be subdued
and all the depths of the Nile will
dry up.[n]

9:14 [t] Isa 21:1; 66:15 **9:15** [u] Isa 37:35; Zec 12:8 [v] Ex 27:2 **9:16** [w] Isa 62:3; Jer 31:11 **10:2** [x] Eze 21:21 [y] Eze 34:5; Hos 3:4; Mt 9:36 **10:3** [z] Jer 25:34 **10:4** [a] Isa 22:23 [b] Zec 9:10

10:5 [c] 2Sa 22:43 [d] Am 2:15; Hag 2:22 **10:6** [e] Zec 8:7-8 [f] Zec 13:9 **10:7** [g] Zec 9:15 **10:8** [h] Isa 5:26 [i] Jer 33:22; Eze 36:11 **10:9** [j] Eze 6:9 **10:10** [k] Isa 11:11 [l] Jer 50:19 [m] Isa 49:19 **10:11** [n] Isa 19:5-7; 51:10

[a] 15 Or *bowl, / like* [b] 4,5 Or *ruler, all of them together. / [5]They*

the south. Israel understood God as traditionally coming from the "south" to manifest himself (Dt 33:2; Hab 3:3).
10:1 *Ask the LORD for rain.* In the ancient world national gods were not always the ones considered directly responsible for fertility. Rather, a variety of cosmic deities (e.g., storm deities) or city patrons were seen as having that jurisdiction. During the monarchy period the people needed to be reminded that it was not Baal who gave them rain, but Yahweh, their national God (cf. 1Ki 17 – 18; Hos 2:8 – 9). Zechariah includes both the warrior aspects of the storm-god (9:14 – 17) with the fertility aspects indicated here.
10:2 *idols.* The *teraphim* referred to just a few other times in Scripture (see the article "Household Gods," p. 72). *shepherd.* Though this context is not entirely clear, it was very common for kings to refer to themselves as a "shepherd" (see note on Eze 34:2), and so the prophet may be alluding to the idea that there is no king to lead this group of people.
10:4 *cornerstone.* See note on Isa 28:16. *tent peg.* Though foundation figurine pegs are known from earlier periods, their use is not attested in any context close to the time of Zechariah. The term used here is consistently used for the pegs used to drive ropes into the ground that held up tents. Thus they secure the stability of the tent, just as a cornerstone secures the stability of a building. For metaphoric usage associated with leadership, see Isa 22:23; Ezr 9:8 – 9.
10:5 *horsemen.* One of the major innovations the Persian Empire introduced into warfare was the employment of cavalry units that could swiftly outmaneuver foot soldiers.
10:11 *Assyria's pride … Egypt's scepter.* Even though the community is under the central control of a single empire, the major reference points of coercive power remained

Assyria's pride[o] will be brought down
and Egypt's scepter[p] will pass away.
12 I will strengthen them in the LORD
and in his name they will live
securely,[q]"
declares the LORD.

11 Open your doors, Lebanon,[r]
so that fire may devour your
cedars!
2 Wail, you juniper, for the cedar has fallen;
the stately trees are ruined!
Wail, oaks of Bashan;
the dense forest[s] has been cut down!
3 Listen to the wail of the shepherds;
their rich pastures are destroyed!
Listen to the roar of the lions;
the lush thicket of the Jordan is
ruined![t]

Two Shepherds

4 This is what the LORD my God says:
"Shepherd the flock marked for slaughter.
5 Their buyers slaughter them and go unpunished. Those who sell them say, 'Praise
the LORD, I am rich!' Their own shepherds
do not spare them.[u] 6 For I will no longer
have pity on the people of the land," declares the LORD. "I will give everyone into
the hands of their neighbors[v] and their
king. They will devastate the land, and I
will not rescue anyone from their hands."[w]
7 So I shepherded the flock marked for
slaughter, particularly the oppressed of the
flock. Then I took two staffs and called
one Favor and the other Union, and I
shepherded the flock. 8 In one month I got
rid of the three shepherds.
The flock detested me, and I grew weary of them 9 and said, "I will not be your
shepherd. Let the dying die, and the perishing perish.[x] Let those who are left eat
one another's flesh."
10 Then I took my staff called Favor[y] and
broke it, revoking[z] the covenant I had
made with all the nations. 11 It was revoked
on that day, and so the oppressed of the
flock who were watching me knew it was
the word of the LORD.
12 I told them, "If you think it best, give
me my pay; but if not, keep it." So they
paid me thirty pieces of silver.[a]
13 And the LORD said to me, "Throw it to
the potter"—the handsome price at which
they valued me! So I took the thirty pieces
of silver and threw them to the potter at
the house of the LORD.[b]
14 Then I broke my second staff called
Union, breaking the family bond between
Judah and Israel.
15 Then the LORD said to me, "Take again
the equipment of a foolish shepherd. 16 For
I am going to raise up a shepherd over the
land who will not care for the lost, or seek
the young, or heal the injured, or feed the
healthy, but will eat the meat of the choice
sheep, tearing off their hooves.

17 "Woe to the worthless shepherd,[c]
who deserts the flock!
May the sword strike his arm[d] and his
right eye!
May his arm be completely withered,
his right eye totally blinded!"[e]

Jerusalem's Enemies to Be Destroyed

12 A prophecy: The word of the LORD
concerning Israel.

The LORD, who stretches out the heavens,[f] who lays the foundation of the
earth,[g] and who forms the human spirit
within a person,[h] declares: 2 "I am going
to make Jerusalem a cup[i] that sends all
the surrounding peoples reeling.[j] Judah[k]
will be besieged as well as Jerusalem.

10:11 [o] Zep 2:13 [p] Eze 30:13 **10:12** [q] Mic 4:5 **11:1** [r] Eze 31:3 **11:2** [s] Isa 32:19 **11:3** [t] Jer 2:15; 50:44 **11:5** [u] Jer 50:7; Eze 34:2-3 **11:6** [v] Zec 14:13 [w] Isa 9:19-21; Jer 13:14; Mic 5:8; 7:2-6 **11:9** [x] Jer 15:2; 43:11

11:10 [y] ver 7 [z] Ps 89:39; Jer 14:21 **11:12** [a] Ex 21:32; Mt 26:15 **11:13** [b] Mt 27:9-10*; Ac 1:18-19 **11:17** [c] Jer 23:1 [d] Eze 30:21-22 [e] Jer 23:1 **12:1** [f] Isa 42:5; Jer 51:15 [g] Ps 102:25; Heb 1:10 [h] Isa 57:16 **12:2** [i] Ps 75:8 [j] Isa 51:23 [k] Zec 14:14

Assyria, which had destroyed the northern kingdom and taken away thousands (2Ki 17:5–6), and Egypt, which had received exiles from Jerusalem when it fell to the Babylonians (2Ki 25:26). In the prophet's report, Assyria and Egypt will no longer be able to prevent the return of exiles.
11:12 *thirty pieces of silver.* While this is often connected to the price of a slave who was accidentally killed (Ex 21:32), that price represents a different economic stage in Israel's history. Since the 30 pieces of silver is being paid for a wage, it is more likely that this reflects an ancient Near Eastern expression for an insultingly low wage.
11:13 Three possible explanations have been given for this verse, and it is difficult to decide between them. (1) It is likely that there was a pottery shop in the vicinity of the temple that served the temple's needs. But why would this money be thrown there? (2) The Hebrew word for potter simply means "fashioner," so some have suggested that here it refers to a metalworker who is perhaps going to make a figurine out of the silver. This may offer an explanation of why the silver is thrown here, but it requires an unusual meaning to be applied to a fairly common noun. (3) It has been observed that the Hebrew word rendered "potter" can, with very little change, be understood as "treasury." Some of the early translations take this route, and it can find some support in the NT as well (Mt 27:5–6, though Matthew also refers to the potter [Mt 27:7]). Each interpretation has its difficulties, and no information from the ancient Near East can shed light that explains the actions of the prophet.
11:16 *eat the meat.* Herds of sheep were rarely used for meat. The wool was far more valuable. A shepherd's main responsibility was to preserve the life and health of the sheep so as to vouchsafe their continued productivity. Eating the meat spoke of a shortsighted self-indulgence of undisciplined appetites rather than wise management of long-term resources. *tearing off their hooves.* May represent an attempt to persuade the owner that the sheep had been devoured by a wild animal so that the shepherd would not be held accountable (see notes on Ex 22:11; 1Sa 25:16; Am 3:12).
12:2 *cup … reeling.* The Hebrew expression "cup of reeling" is used also in Isa 51:17,22, but here in v. 2 the text

3On that day, when all the nations[l] of the
earth are gathered against her, I will make
Jerusalem an immovable rock[m] for all the
nations. All who try to move it will injure[n]
themselves. 4On that day I will strike every
horse with panic and its rider with madness," declares the LORD. "I will keep a
watchful eye over Judah, but I will blind
all the horses of the nations.[o] 5Then the
clans of Judah will say in their hearts,
'The people of Jerusalem are strong, because the LORD Almighty is their God.'
6"On that day I will make the clans of
Judah like a firepot[p] in a woodpile, like a
flaming torch among sheaves. They will
consume[q] all the surrounding peoples
right and left, but Jerusalem will remain
intact in her place.
7"The LORD will save the dwellings of
Judah first, so that the honor of the house
of David and of Jerusalem's inhabitants
may not be greater than that of Judah.[r]
8On that day the LORD will shield[s] those
who live in Jerusalem, so that the feeblest
among them will be like David, and the
house of David will be like God,[t] like the
angel of the LORD going before[u] them. 9On
that day I will set out to destroy all the nations that attack Jerusalem.[v]

Mourning for the One They Pierced

10"And I will pour out on the house
of David and the inhabitants of Jerusalem a spirit[a] of grace and supplication.[w]
They will look on[b] me, the one they have
pierced,[x] and they will mourn for him as
one mourns for an only child, and grieve
bitterly for him as one grieves for a firstborn son. 11On that day the weeping in Jerusalem will be as great as the weeping of
Hadad Rimmon in the plain of Megiddo.[y]
12The land will mourn,[z] each clan by itself, with their wives by themselves: the
clan of the house of David and their wives,
the clan of the house of Nathan and their
wives, 13the clan of the house of Levi and
their wives, the clan of Shimei and their
wives, 14and all the rest of the clans and
their wives.

Cleansing From Sin

13 "On that day a fountain[a] will be
opened to the house of David and
the inhabitants of Jerusalem, to cleanse[b]
them from sin and impurity.
2"On that day, I will banish the names
of the idols[c] from the land, and they will
be remembered no more," declares the
LORD Almighty. "I will remove both the
prophets[d] and the spirit of impurity from
the land. 3And if anyone still prophesies,
their father and mother, to whom they
were born, will say to them, 'You must
die, because you have told lies in the
LORD's name.' Then their own parents will
stab the one who prophesies.[e]
4"On that day every prophet will be
ashamed[f] of their prophetic vision. They
will not put on a prophet's garment[g] of

12:3 [l] Zec 14:2 [m] Da 2:34-35 [n] Mt 21:44 **12:4** [o] Ps 76:6 **12:6** [p] Isa 10:17-18; Zec 11:1 [q] Ob 1:18 **12:7** [r] Jer 30:18; Am 9:11 **12:8** [s] Joel 3:16; Zec 9:15 [t] Ps 82:6 [u] Mic 7:8 **12:9** [v] Zec 14:2-3 **12:10** [w] Isa 44:3; Eze 39:29; Joel 2:28-29 [x] Jn 19:34, 37*; Rev 1:7 **12:11** [y] 2Ki 23:29 **12:12** [z] Mt 24:30; Rev 1:7 **13:1** [a] Jer 17:13 [b] Ps 51:2; Heb 9:14 **13:2** [c] Ex 23:13; Eze 36:25; Hos 2:17 [d] 1Ki 22:22; Jer 23:14-15 **13:3** [e] Dt 13:6-11; 18:20; Jer 23:34; Eze 14:9 **13:4** [f] Jer 6:15; Mic 3:6-7 [g] Mt 3:4

[a] 10 Or *the Spirit* [b] 10 Or *to*

actually speaks of a bowl (*saph*) rather than a cup. It is possible that the author chose the word "bowl" in order to execute a wordplay. The Hebrew word *saph* also means "threshold." Just as the drink from a vessel could cause drunkenness and stumbling, a threshold could easily cause stumbling because a part of the threshold was raised above ground level. The threshold consisted of a large stone slab that featured sockets on each end into which the door pivots were fitted (though large gates would have separate sockets sunk into the ground). The door would close against the protruding threshold. This threshold slab could also then be the "immovable rock" in v. 3.

12:3 *immovable rock.* If the word translated "cup" in v. 2 is doing double duty as a reference to the threshold, then this would likely refer to the threshold slab (see note on v. 2). As an integral part of the gate structure, the threshold stone would probably be dislodged when the gates were destroyed. This would be a prime objective of a besieging army. Tearing down gates is mentioned in Neo-Babylonian texts, but the taking up of the threshold is not specifically referred to. A Sumerian lament over Eridu reports that the doorframe was ripped out. Akkadian texts describe the high grade of stone that was used and the function these slabs served as a foundation for both gates and walls. When Sennacherib destroyed Babylon he tore out the foundations of temples and walls and threw them into the canal. Temple thresholds were often inscribed with prayers for protection.

12:11 *the weeping of Hadad Rimmon in the plain of Megiddo.* Both Hadad and Rimmon were names for West Semitic storm-gods that some Canaanite texts relate to Baal. The only time they appear in a compound form is here. As a consequence, many have taken the "weeping" to refer to some ritual mourning festival associated with the death and return of a Canaanite deity. But it would be very strange for the prophet to be using an idolatrous ceremony to illustrate an event that causes deep sorrow. Others have noted that the "weeping" is not *over* Hadad Rimmon, so possibly the name is of a place or town. The "weeping" may be connected to the sense of loss the community experienced when Josiah was killed in battle on the plain of Megiddo, a lament that was made into a tradition (2Ch 35:24–25). Unfortunately, we do not know if the tradition was still being observed into the Persian period.

12:12–13 David and Levi are recognizable as the royal and priestly lines, respectively. Nathan and Shimei are more difficult in that there are numerous individuals in the Bible with those names. Since Nathan is one of the sons of David (2Sa 5:14) and Shimei is one of the grandsons of Levi (Nu 3:17,21), many see in these verses a reference to clans and subclans. Also of interest is the possibility that all of these clans have a relationship to Zerubbabel. He descends from David through Nathan and through Levi (Lk 3:29,31), and Zerubbabel's brother is named Shimei (1Ch 3:19).

13:4 *prophet's garment of hair.* The distinctive prophet's cloak is most likely made of animal skin and is hairy in appearance—though not all cloaks were so made. Very

hair[h] in order to deceive. 5Each will say, 'I
am not a prophet. I am a farmer; the land
has been my livelihood since my youth.[a]'[i]
6If someone asks, 'What are these wounds
on your body[b]?' they will answer, 'The
wounds I was given at the house of my
friends.'

The Shepherd Struck, the Sheep Scattered

7"Awake, sword,[j] against my shepherd,[k]
    against the man who is close to me!"
    declares the LORD Almighty.
"Strike the shepherd,
    and the sheep will be scattered,[l]
    and I will turn my hand against the
        little ones.
8In the whole land," declares the LORD,
    "two-thirds will be struck down and
        perish;
    yet one-third will be left in it.[m]
9This third I will put into the fire;[n]
    I will refine them like silver[o]
    and test them like gold.
They will call[p] on my name
    and I will answer[q] them;
I will say, 'They are my people,'[r]
    and they will say, 'The LORD is our
        God.'[s]"

The LORD Comes and Reigns

14 A day of the LORD[t] is coming, Jerusalem, when your possessions will
be plundered and divided up within your
very walls.

2I will gather all the nations to Jerusalem to fight against it; the city will be
captured, the houses ransacked, and the
women raped. Half of the city will go into
exile, but the rest of the people will not be
taken from the city.[u] 3Then the LORD will
go out and fight[v] against those nations, as
he fights on a day of battle. 4On that day
his feet will stand on the Mount of Olives,[w]
east of Jerusalem, and the Mount of Olives
will be split in two from east to west, forming a great valley, with half of the mountain moving north and half moving south.
5You will flee by my mountain valley, for
it will extend to Azel. You will flee as you
fled from the earthquake[c][x] in the days of
Uzziah king of Judah. Then the LORD my
God will come,[y] and all the holy ones with
him.[z]

6On that day there will be neither sunlight[a] nor cold, frosty darkness. 7It will be
a unique[b] day—a day known only to the
LORD—with no distinction between day
and night.[c] When evening comes, there
will be light.[d]

8On that day living water[e] will flow out
from Jerusalem, half of it east[f] to the Dead
Sea and half of it west to the Mediterranean Sea, in summer and in winter.

9The LORD will be king over the whole
earth.[g] On that day there will be one LORD,
and his name the only name.[h]

13:4 [h] 2Ki 1:8; Isa 20:2 **13:5** [i] Am 7:14 **13:7** [j] Jer 47:6 [k] Isa 40:11; 53:4; Eze 37:24 [l] Mt 26:31*; Mk 14:27* **13:8** [m] Eze 5:2-4, 12 **13:9** [n] Mal 3:2 [o] Isa 48:10; 1Pe 1:6-7 [p] Ps 50:15 [q] Zec 10:6 [r] Jer 30:22 [s] Jer 29:12 **14:1** [t] Isa 13:9; Mal 4:1 **14:2** [u] Isa 13:6; Zec 13:8 **14:3** [v] Zec 9:14-15 **14:4** [w] Eze 11:23 **14:5** [x] Am 1:1 [y] Isa 29:6; 66:15-16 [z] Mt 16:27; 25:31 **14:6** [a] Isa 13:10; Jer 4:23 **14:7** [b] Jer 30:7 [c] Rev 21:23-25; 22:5 [d] Isa 30:26 **14:8** [e] Eze 47:1-12; Jn 7:38; Rev 22:1-2 [f] Joel 2:20 **14:9** [g] Dt 6:4; Isa 45:24; Rev 11:15 [h] Eph 4:5-6

[a] 5 Or *farmer; a man sold me in my youth* [b] 6 Or *wounds between your hands* [c] 5 Or *5My mountain valley will be blocked and will extend to Azel. It will be blocked as it was blocked because of the earthquake*

---

little is said about prophetic garb in the ancient Near East, so comparison is difficult. It may be of interest that Assyrian inscriptions beginning at this period portray a few individuals wearing lion-headed cloaks. Where it can be determined, these individuals are involved in ritual activities (dance) and accompany deity. It is guessed that they may be exorcists.

13:6 *wounds.* May represent scars from past actions or active wounds that were inflicted by idolatrous prophets to enter into a prophetic state. Such actions are depicted in several places in the OT, such as the prophets of Baal cutting themselves (1Ki 18:28).

14:2 *I will gather all the nations to Jerusalem to fight against it.* The element of a cataclysmic final battle is seen by many as part of the complex of apocalyptic literature (see Introduction: Literary Setting). In this oracle, the prophet describes a battle in which all human hope would seem to be extinguished until God intervenes to directly make war upon "the nations." The primary interest of the prophet is not the battle but the result, which is God's perfect world in which God is enthroned as king over all (v. 9).

14:4 *Mount of Olives.* Located across the Kidron Valley to the east of Jerusalem. It runs north and south, and its steep ascent impedes easy movement from Jerusalem toward the east and the Jordan River and Jericho. Though the Mount of Olives is well known from the Gospels, this is the only direct reference to it in the OT. *split in two.* The concept of splitting a mountain to make a way of escape (v. 5) is not attested in the ancient Near East.

14:5 *Azel.* The Hebrew text at this point is very difficult to interpret. This may be the place-name of a location near Jerusalem that is otherwise unknown, or it may be a noun having the sense of "sides," with the new valley reaching to the sides of Mount Zion and the Mount of Olives. *earthquake in the days of Uzziah.* This appears to be a reference to the earthquake mentioned in the opening of the book of Amos (see Am 1:1 and note). There is evidence of a sizeable earthquake in Stratum VI of the excavations at Hazor, dated approximately to 760 BC.

14:6–7 The imagery of these verses take the reader all the way back to Ge 1, where God set up the functioning cosmos. The regular rotation of day and night was the most central aspect of order imposed on the cosmos. In the ancient world the orderly functioning of the cosmos was the most important focus of creative activity. Not only will the markers of time be set aside, but also the indications of weather variation.

14:8 *living water.* "Living" water refers to water that is moving rather than the still waters of shepherding imagery. As can be seen in Eze 47, living water flows from sacred space as a sign of the benevolent and fructifying presence and kingship of deity (see note on Eze 47:1). This concept is depicted in iconography throughout the ancient world. This includes mythic scenes that portray the gods in connection with flowing waters (Canaanite El, Egyptian Nun) as well as the depiction of a variety of kings and deities of a variety of ranks holding jars from which waters flow (see note on Eze 47:2).

10 The whole land, from Geba[i] to Rimmon, south of Jerusalem, will become
like the Arabah. But Jerusalem will be
raised up[j] high from the Benjamin Gate
to the site of the First Gate, to the Corner Gate, and from the Tower of Hananel
to the royal winepresses, and will remain
in its place.[k] 11 It will be inhabited; never
again will it be destroyed. Jerusalem will
be secure.[l]
12 This is the plague with which the
LORD will strike all the nations that fought
against Jerusalem: Their flesh will rot
while they are still standing on their feet,
their eyes will rot in their sockets, and
their tongues will rot in their mouths.[m]
13 On that day people will be stricken by
the LORD with great panic. They will seize
each other by the hand and attack one another.[n] 14 Judah[o] too will fight at Jerusalem. The wealth of all the surrounding nations will be collected[p]—great quantities
of gold and silver and clothing. 15 A similar
plague[q] will strike the horses and mules,
the camels and donkeys, and all the animals in those camps.
16 Then the survivors from all the nations that have attacked Jerusalem will go
up year after year to worship the King, the
LORD Almighty, and to celebrate the Festival of Tabernacles.[r] 17 If any of the peoples
of the earth do not go up to Jerusalem to
worship the King, the LORD Almighty, they
will have no rain.[s] 18 If the Egyptian people
do not go up and take part, they will have
no rain. The LORD[a] will bring on them the
plague he inflicts on the nations that do
not go up to celebrate the Festival of Tabernacles.[t] 19 This will be the punishment
of Egypt and the punishment of all the nations that do not go up to celebrate the
Festival of Tabernacles.
20 On that day HOLY TO THE LORD will be
inscribed on the bells of the horses, and
the cooking pots[u] in the LORD's house will
be like the sacred bowls[v] in front of the
altar. 21 Every pot in Jerusalem and Judah
will be holy[w] to the LORD Almighty, and
all who come to sacrifice will take some
of the pots and cook in them. And on that
day[x] there will no longer be a Canaanite[b][y]
in the house of the LORD Almighty.[z]

14:10 [i] 1Ki 15:22 [j] Jer 30:18; Am 9:11 [k] Zec 12:6 **14:11** [l] Eze 34:25-28 **14:12** [m] Lev 26:16; Dt 28:22 **14:13** [n] Zec 11:6 **14:14** [o] Zec 12:2 [p] Isa 23:18 **14:15** [q] ver 12 **14:16** [r] Isa 60:6-9 **14:17** [s] Jer 14:4; Am 4:7 **14:18** [t] ver 12 **14:20** [u] Eze 46:20 [v] Zec 9:15 **14:21** [w] Ro 14:6-7; 1Co 10:31 [x] Ne 8:10 [y] Zec 9:8 [z] Eze 44:9

[a] 18 Or *part, then the LORD* [b] 21 Or *merchant*

14:10 *from Geba to Rimmon.* Both place-names appear in the narratives of Nehemiah. Geba is related to a village in the territory of Benjamin (Ne 11:31), and Rimmon is apparently several miles/kilometers north of Beersheba (Ne 11:29). This more or less delineates the provincial boundaries of Yehud in the Persian Empire. See map, p. 780. *Arabah.* This term has both specific and general meanings. As a specific geographic designation, it refers to the arid region around the Dead Sea and south to the Gulf of Aqaba. As a general topographic designation, it refers to flat steppe land. The context of this verse demands the latter meaning.
14:12 Among the most common treatments of prominent enemies in the ancient Near East were flaying the skin, putting out the eyes, and cutting out the tongue. Here those are accomplished through "plague." These symptoms are unattested as connected to any particular plague in the ancient Near East.
14:16 *Festival of Tabernacles.* Although an enthronement festival per se is unattested in Israelite practice, it is often assumed to exist and, if it does exist, it would most logically be connected to the Festival of Tabernacles (see notes on 1Ki 12:33; Ezr 3:4). That would especially be significant in this context as the nations are expected to attend in order to acknowledge the kingship of Yahweh. Regular enthronement festivals are well known in the ancient world and it would be unusual if Israel did not have one (see the article "Enthronement in the Ancient Near East," p. 925).
14:18 *no rain.* Egypt receives very little rain, and what it receives is not essential to its productivity. Agriculture in Egypt is dependent almost entirely on the annual flooding of the Nile.
14:20 *HOLY TO THE LORD.* Something with this designation is given sacred status as part of that which is purified for service within the sacred space of the temple precinct where Yahweh's presence dwelt. In Ex 28:36–38 this was engraved on the golden plate worn by the high priest. *bells.* Although priests wore bells on their garments (Ex 28:33), this is a different Hebrew word. The Hebrew word used here may simply refer to metal discs that tinkled together. *cooking pots.* The most common of the temple vessels. *sacred bowls.* Used for the most significant ritual activities, such as transporting the blood of the sacrificed animals. Both cooking pots and sacred bowls came in a variety of shapes and sizes.

ORACLES OF THE PROPHETS

MALACHI

Historical Setting

The message of Malachi reflected conditions associated with the period of pre-Ezra decline (c. 515 – 458 BC, i.e., between the completion of the second temple to the ministry of Ezra in Jerusalem). Jerusalem, which was likely a satrapy (or province) under the rule of a Persian governor, was small, struggling and insignificant — a social and political backwater in the vast Persian Empire. The ongoing petty hostilities with the Samaritans and the burdensome vassal status to Persia contributed to the skepticism and doubt that characterized popular response to Yahweh as God. The Persians themselves were engaged in a titanic contest against the Greeks for control of the west. It was against this dismal setting that Malachi prophesied in Jerusalem as God's messenger.

KEY CONCEPTS

- God does not need the worship of his people, but he is worthy of highest honor and praise and is rightly offended when he is treated with disdain.
- The prophets cry out for God's people to respond to him and deal with their shortcomings.

Literary Setting

The obscurity of Malachi's title verse has spawned a range of opinions as to the book's author and its date of writing. The word *Malachi* is judged by some as simply being a title, "my messenger." By contrast, more traditional Biblical scholars have regarded the title "Malachi" as a proper name identifying a prophetic figure rooted in postexilic Jewish history.

It is important to recognize that the position of the book of Malachi at the end of the OT in the English Bible has little bearing on the chronological placement of the book in Jewish history. Malachi predates other OT books such as Esther, Ezra-Nehemiah and Chronicles, with the date of its writing usually assigned to a time coinciding with the work of Ezra and Nehemiah in Jerusalem (c. 450 – 400 BC). This view is based largely on the parallel descriptions of religious and social decay in the postexilic community recorded in Malachi and the books of Ezra and Nehemiah. All three confront the problems of intermarriage with foreigners, divorce, abuses associated with the priesthood, temple services, the tithe, the Sabbath, and the oppression of the poor.

Careful study of the Hebrew language of Malachi, however, reveals that the book has considerable linguistic similarities with OT writings dated to the sixth century BC rather than the fifth century BC. Based on the detailed information gleaned from this kind of technical linguistic analysis of the postexilic Prophets, we conclude that Malachi was most likely composed in Jerusalem during the very early years of religious and social decline prior to the time of Ezra the scribe (c. 500–475 BC). Persian influence on the thought and language of Malachi can be seen in the prophet's references to "a scroll of remembrance" (3:16; cf. Est 6:1; Da 7:10; 12:1) and "the sun of righteousness" (4:2). ◆

1 A prophecy:[a] The word[b] of the LORD to Israel through Malachi.[a]

Israel Doubts God's Love

2“I have loved[c] you,” says the LORD.

“But you ask, ‘How have you loved us?’

“Was not Esau Jacob's brother?” declares the LORD. “Yet I have loved Jacob,[d] 3but Esau I have hated, and I have turned his hill country into a wasteland[e] and left his inheritance to the desert jackals.[f]”

4Edom may say, “Though we have been crushed, we will rebuild[g] the ruins.”

But this is what the LORD Almighty says: “They may build, but I will demolish. They will be called the Wicked Land, a people always under the wrath of the LORD.[h] 5You will see it with your own eyes and say, ‘Great[i] is the LORD—even beyond the borders of Israel!’[j]

Breaking Covenant Through Blemished Sacrifices

6“A son honors his father, and a slave his master. If I am a father, where is the honor due me? If I am a master, where is the respect[k] due me?” says the LORD Almighty.[l]

“It is you priests who show contempt for my name.

“But you ask, ‘How have we shown contempt for your name?’

7“By offering defiled food[m] on my altar.

“But you ask, ‘How have we defiled you?’

“By saying that the LORD's table is contemptible. 8When you offer blind animals for sacrifice, is that not wrong? When you sacrifice lame or diseased animals,[n] is that not wrong? Try offering them to your governor! Would he be pleased with you? Would he accept you?” says the LORD Almighty.[o]

9“Now plead with God to be gracious to us. With such offerings[p] from your hands, will he accept you?”—says the LORD Almighty.

10“Oh, that one of you would shut the temple doors, so that you would not light useless fires on my altar! I am not pleased[q] with you,” says the LORD Almighty, “and I will accept no offering[r] from your hands. 11My name will be great among the nations, from where the sun rises to where it sets. In every place incense[s] and pure offerings will be brought to me, because my name will be great among the nations,” says the LORD Almighty.

12“But you profane it by saying, ‘The Lord's table is defiled,’ and, ‘Its food[t] is contemptible.’ 13And you say, ‘What a burden!’[u] and you sniff at it contemptuously,” says the LORD Almighty.

“When you bring injured, lame or diseased animals and offer them as sacrifices, should I accept them from your hands?” says the LORD. 14“Cursed is the cheat who has an acceptable male in his flock and vows to give it, but then sacrifices a blemished animal[v] to the Lord. For I am a great king,[w]” says the LORD Almighty, “and my name is to be feared among the nations.

Additional Warning to the Priests

2 “And now, you priests, this warning is for you.[x] 2If you do not listen, and if you do not resolve to honor my name,” says the LORD Almighty, “I will send a curse[y] on you, and I will curse your blessings. Yes, I have already cursed them, because you have not resolved to honor me.

3“Because of you I will rebuke your de-

1:1 [a] Na 1:1 [b] 1Pe 4:11
1:2 [c] Dt 4:37 [d] Ro 9:13*
1:3 [e] Isa 34:10 [f] Eze 35:3-9
1:4 [g] Isa 9:10 [h] Eze 25:12-14
1:5 [i] Ps 35:27; Mic 5:4 [j] Am 1:11-12
1:6 [k] Isa 1:2 [l] Job 5:17
1:7 [m] ver 12; Lev 21:6
1:8 [n] Lev 22:22; Dt 15:21 [o] Isa 43:23
1:9 [p] Lev 23:33-44
1:10 [q] Hos 5:6 [r] Isa 1:11-14; Jer 14:12
1:11 [s] Isa 60:6-7; Rev 8:3
1:12 [t] ver 7
1:13 [u] Isa 43:22-24
1:14 [v] Lev 22:18-21 [w] 1Ti 6:15
2:1 [x] ver 7
2:2 [y] Dt 28:20

[a] 1 *Malachi* means *my messenger.*

1:1 *Malachi.* Unlike the books of Haggai and Zechariah, the book of Malachi contains no date formulas linking the prophet's message to the reign of any particular Persian king. Malachi does make reference to the "governor" of Yehud (v. 8) and a rebuilt temple in Jerusalem (v. 10). Thus the book may be dated broadly to the period after the completion of the second temple (515 BC). It seems likely that Malachi addressed the Jews in the province of Yehud during the reign of King Darius I (522–486 BC), making Malachi a slightly later contemporary of Haggai and Zechariah.

1:3 *his hill country.* Esau's hill country is Seir (Ge 36:8–9,21), which was in the eastern Negev. The "hill country of Seir" is mentioned several times in Scripture (e.g., Ge 14:6; Dt 2:1,5; Jos 24:4). It was most likely a designation for the southern portion of the Edomite state, between the Wadi al-Ghuwayr and Ras en-Naqb.

1:4 *Edom.* See notes on Jer 49:7; Eze 32:29.

1:8 *blind...lame or diseased animals.* The prophet rebukes the people and the priests for shaming Yahweh with inferior offerings that were considered inappropriate even for the local Persian-appointed governor. The termination of temple funding from the Persian government may have prompted such behavior as a "cost-cutting" measure (see note on 3:8), but it seems more likely that the burden of cultic and imperial taxation became so heavy that compromising the temple sacrificial rituals and ignoring the tithe requirements became a pragmatic solution for maintaining the barest standards of subsistence living in the face of persistent economic depression due to drought and blight (cf. 3:14; Hag 1:6,10–11; Zec 8:12).

1:12 *Lord's table.* This expression is unique to Malachi in the OT. The context suggests the table is synonymous with the altar of burnt offering, since animal and grain sacrifices were figuratively understood as "food" for Yahweh (cf. v. 7; Lev 3:11,16). The "table" was also a symbol of fellowship in the ancient world, since the meal or "feast" was a part of the covenant ratification ceremony, the sealing of an alliance with a ceremonial meal. The prophet rebukes the people and the priests because the offering of impure sacrifices both profaned the worship of Yahweh and demonstrated contempt for their covenant relationship with him.

Edom's landscape (Mal 1:4).

scendants[a]; I will smear on your faces the
dung[z] from your festival sacrifices, and
you will be carried off with it.[a] 4And you
will know that I have sent you this warning so that my covenant with Levi[b] may
continue," says the LORD Almighty. 5"My
covenant was with him, a covenant[c] of
life and peace,[d] and I gave them to him;
this called for reverence and he revered
me and stood in awe of my name. 6True
instruction[e] was in his mouth and nothing false was found on his lips. He walked
with me in peace and uprightness, and
turned many from sin.[f]
7"For the lips of a priest[g] ought to preserve knowledge, because he is the messenger[h] of the LORD Almighty and people
seek instruction from his mouth.[i] 8But
you have turned from the way and by
your teaching have caused many to stumble;[j] you have violated the covenant with
Levi," says the LORD Almighty. 9"So I have
caused you to be despised[k] and humiliated before all the people, because you have
not followed my ways but have shown
partiality in matters of the law."

Breaking Covenant Through Divorce

10Do we not all have one Father[b]?[l] Did
not one God create us? Why do we profane the covenant[m] of our ancestors by
being unfaithful to one another?
11Judah has been unfaithful. A detestable thing has been committed in Israel
and in Jerusalem: Judah has desecrated
the sanctuary the LORD loves by marrying[n]

2:3 [z] Ex 29:14 [a] 1Ki 14:10 **2:4** [b] Nu 3:12 **2:5** [c] Dt 33:9 [d] Nu 25:12 **2:6** [e] Dt 33:10 [f] Jer 23:22; Jas 5:19-20 **2:7** [g] Jer 18:18 [h] Nu 27:21 [i] Lev 10:11 **2:8** [j] Jer 18:15 **2:9** [k] 1Sa 2:30 **2:10** [l] 1Co 8:6 [m] Ex 19:5 **2:11** [n] Ne 13:23

[a] 3 Or *will blight your grain* [b] 10 Or *father*

2:11 *marrying women who worship a foreign god.* The difficult Hebrew expression here is used in the collective sense of foreign women who had married into the Hebrew clans of Yehud (in violation of the Israelite practice of endogamy, i.e., marrying within the ethnic group [Dt 7:3–4]). The prophet recognized that in intermarriage of this sort one weds both a foreign woman and a foreign god. The gravity of the situation accounts for Malachi's unusual language in the larger disputation, insinuating that the adultery of divorcing Hebrew women and marrying foreign women was tantamount to being "unfaithful," i.e., committing idolatry (vv. 14–16). The practice of deserting and divorcing Hebrew women for the purpose of marrying non-Hebrew women was probably motivated by economics, since intermarriage was a requisite for entering the well-established mercantile guilds of postexilic Palestine already in place when the Hebrews returned from exile.

women who worship a foreign god.[o] 12As
for the man who does this, whoever he
may be, may the LORD remove[p] him from
the tents of Jacob[a]—even though he
brings an offering[q] to the LORD Almighty.
13Another thing you do: You flood the
LORD's altar with tears. You weep and wail
because he no longer looks with favor[r] on
your offerings or accepts them with pleasure from your hands. 14You ask, "Why?"
It is because the LORD is the witness between you and the wife of your youth.[s]
You have been unfaithful to her, though
she is your partner, the wife of your marriage covenant.
15Has not the one God made you?[t] You
belong to him in body and spirit. And
what does the one God seek? Godly offspring.[b][u] So be on your guard, and do not
be unfaithful to the wife of your youth.
16"The man who hates and divorces his
wife,[v]" says the LORD, the God of Israel,
"does violence to the one he should protect,"[c] says the LORD Almighty.

So be on your guard, and do not be unfaithful.

Breaking Covenant Through Injustice

17You have wearied[w] the LORD with your
words.

"How have we wearied him?" you ask.

By saying, "All who do evil are good in
the eyes of the LORD, and he is pleased
with them" or "Where is the God of justice?"

3 "I will send my messenger, who will
prepare the way before me.[x] Then suddenly the Lord you are seeking will come
to his temple; the messenger of the covenant, whom you desire, will come," says
the LORD Almighty.

2But who can endure[y] the day of his
coming? Who can stand when he appears? For he will be like a refiner's fire[z]
or a launderer's soap. 3He will sit as a refiner and purifier of silver;[a] he will purify[b]
the Levites and refine them like gold and
silver. Then the LORD will have men who
will bring offerings in righteousness, 4and
the offerings[c] of Judah and Jerusalem will
be acceptable to the LORD, as in days gone
by, as in former years.[d]

5"So I will come to put you on trial. I
will be quick to testify against sorcerers,
adulterers and perjurers,[e] against those
who defraud laborers of their wages,[f] who

2:11 [o] Ezr 9:1; Jer 3:7-9
2:12 [p] Eze 24:21 [q] Mal 1:10
2:13 [r] Jer 14:12
2:14 [s] Pr 5:18
2:15 [t] Ge 2:24; Mt 19:4-6 [u] 1Co 7:14
2:16 [v] Dt 24:1; Mt 5:31-32; 19:4-9
2:17 [w] Isa 43:24
3:1 [x] Isa 40:3; Mt 11:10*; Mk 1:2*; Lk 7:27*
3:2 [y] Eze 22:14; Rev 6:17 [z] Zec 13:9; Mt 3:10-12
3:3 [a] Da 12:10 [b] Isa 1:25
3:4 [c] 2Ch 7:12; Ps 51:19; Mal 1:11 [d] 2Ch 7:3
3:5 [e] Jer 7:9 [f] Lev 19:13; Jas 5:4

[a] 12 Or *12May the LORD remove from the tents of Jacob anyone who gives testimony in behalf of the man who does this* [b] 15 The meaning of the Hebrew for the first part of this verse is uncertain. [c] 16 Or *"I hate divorce," says the LORD, the God of Israel, "because the man who divorces his wife covers his garment with violence,"*

2:14–16 Mosaic Law permitted a man to divorce his wife for something he finds "indecent" about her (Dt 24:1). Though it is of an unspecified nature, it presumably is misconduct short of adultery, since adultery was a capital offense (Lev 20:10; cf. Mt 19:7–9). The use of the term "hates" in v. 16 is the familiar idiom for a statement of divorce in the ancient Near East. Here it indicates not God's hate of divorce (as in some translations) but that the husband has invoked the divorce proclamation by stating that he hates his wife. Malachi's enlightened view of marriage and harsh admonition against divorce apparently had little impact on the postexilic community, as evidenced by the reforms undertaken by Ezra and Nehemiah when they confronted the same abuses some five decades later (Ne 13:23–27). Documents from Elephantine, a sectarian Jewish military colony located near Aswan in Egypt, shed light on Jewish marriage and divorce practices in the Persian period. Unlike Malachi's understanding of marriage as a covenant (v. 14), the Elephantine community emphasized the contractual nature of marriage, with attention given to the pragmatic legal and economic aspects of the marriage bond (e.g., issues of bride-price, dowry, property rights and inheritance). The union resulting from the marriage contract could be dissolved by either party at will and without delineating any specific grounds for divorce.
3:1 *messenger.* See note on Isa 6:9.
3:2 *refiner's fire.* Malachi borrows from the prophets Isaiah (Isa 1:25), Jeremiah (Jer 6:29; 9:7) and Ezekiel (Eze 22:17–22) the imagery of God refining his people Israel by burning or smelting away the dross of their evil ways. A shift has been detected in the use of the metal refining motif from the destructive aspects of divine judgment in preexilic prophecy to a stress on purification in the postexilic prophets (cf. Zec 13:1). The refining and smelting of metals was accomplished in one of two types of furnaces: (1) the kiln or "blast furnace," in which there is direct contact between the fuel and the ore, yielding an oxidizing or reducing reaction, or (2) the "crucible furnace," which protects the ore or metal from direct contact with fuel of the fire or the products of its combustion and achieves separation of precious metals by means of both oxidation and amalgamation. Malachi may be referring to a metallurgy process known as cupellation. Such refinement of silver required exposure of the ores to high temperatures in a blast of the air (from a bellows) that resulted in the oxidation of unwanted metals and other impurities. The purified silver was retrieved in a cupel, or a small cup-like mold, made of a porous material like bone ash or clay. See notes on Isa 48:10; Jer 6:28; 11:4. *soap.* The Hebrew term (*borit*) occurs in the OT only here and Jer 2:22. The word describes an alkaline salt or soda powder derived from the ice plant (found in Mesopotamia but not Syro-Palestine) and used as a laundry detergent in the ancient world. Most scholars understand that Malachi appeals to the imagery of two common trades, the smelter and the fuller, or launderer, to demonstrate the pattern of divine judgment as both testing and cleansing (cf. Ps 66:10; Da 11:35; 12:10). Others interpret the expression against the backdrop of smelting metals since lye or potash may be used as a reagent in separating the dross from the precious metal. If so, then the prophet makes reference to a two-stage metallurgy process of smelting and purifying the crude lead.
3:5 *sorcerers.* The Hebrew term refers to those who practice divination or fortune telling by means of occult magic and witchcraft to influence people or events for either their own gain or that of their clients. See note on Isa 2:6.

oppress the widows[g] and the fatherless, and deprive the foreigners among you of justice, but do not fear me," says the LORD Almighty.

Breaking Covenant by Withholding Tithes

6"I the LORD do not change.[h] So you, the descendants of Jacob, are not destroyed.
7Ever since the time of your ancestors you have turned away[i] from my decrees and have not kept them. Return to me, and I will return to you,"[j] says the LORD Almighty.

"But you ask, 'How are we to return?'

8"Will a mere mortal rob God? Yet you rob me.

"But you ask, 'How are we robbing you?'

"In tithes[k] and offerings. 9You are under
a curse—your whole nation—because you are robbing me. 10Bring the whole
tithe into the storehouse,[l] that there may be food in my house. Test me in this," says the LORD Almighty, "and see if I will not throw open the floodgates[m] of heaven and pour out so much blessing that there will not be room enough to store it. 11I will prevent pests from devouring your crops, and the vines in your fields will not drop their fruit before it is ripe," says the LORD Almighty. 12"Then all the nations will call
you blessed,[n] for yours will be a delightful land,"[o] says the LORD Almighty.

3:5 [g] Ex 22:22
3:6 [h] Nu 23:19; Jas 1:17
3:7 [i] Jer 7:26; Ac 7:51 [j] Zec 1:3
3:8 [k] Ne 13:10-12
3:10 [l] Ne 13:12 [m] 2Ki 7:2
3:12 [n] Isa 61:9 [o] Isa 62:4

Israel Speaks Arrogantly Against God

13"You have spoken arrogantly[p] against me," says the LORD.

"Yet you ask, 'What have we said against you?'

14"You have said, 'It is futile[q] to serve God. What do we gain by carrying out his requirements and going about like mourners[r] before the LORD Almighty? 15But now
we call the arrogant blessed. Certainly evildoers[s] prosper, and even when they put God to the test, they get away with it.'"

The Faithful Remnant

16Then those who feared the LORD talked with each other, and the LORD listened and heard.[t] A scroll[u] of remembrance was written in his presence concerning those who feared the LORD and honored his name.

17"On the day when I act," says the LORD Almighty, "they will be my treasured possession.[v] I will spare[w] them, just as a father has compassion and spares his son who serves him. 18And you will again see
the distinction between the righteous[x] and the wicked, between those who serve God and those who do not.

3:13 [p] Mal 2:17
3:14 [q] Ps 73:13 [r] Isa 58:3
3:15 [s] Jer 7:10
3:16 [t] Ps 34:15 [u] Ps 56:8
3:17 [v] Dt 7:6 [w] Ps 103:13; Isa 26:20
3:18 [x] Ge 18:25
4:1 [y] Joel 2:31 [z] Isa 5:24; Ob 1:18

Judgment and Covenant Renewal

4[a] "Surely the day is coming;[y] it will burn like a furnace. All the arrogant and every evildoer will be stubble,[z] and

[a] In Hebrew texts 4:1-6 is numbered 3:19-24.

3:8 *tithes and offerings.* The tithe, or a tenth part, from the produce of the land (including grain, fruit, and flocks and herds) was required by Mosaic Law (Lev 27:30–33; Dt 12:6,11). The tithes were given to support the Levites "as their inheritance in return for the work they [did] while serving at the tent of meeting" (Nu 18:21; cf. Dt 14:22–29). The "offerings" may refer to the "tithe of the tithe" or the tithe-tax that the Levites were required to present as the Lord's offering (Nu 18:26). In effect, Malachi upbraids the people for not bringing their tithes to the temple and rebukes the Levitical corps for not presenting the tithe-tax to Yahweh on what they did receive. The prophet's promise of rainfall yielding an abundance of food (see note on v. 10) is contingent not upon the ritual of tithing but upon the posture of repentance that motivates the act of giving (v. 7). Distinctions between tithes and taxes were blurred in the Biblical world since collection and redistribution of resources for the maintenance of the administrative structures of society (whether civil or religious) was commonplace. The shift in Persian royal policy may have had some impact on the tithing practices of postexilic Judah, since reforms of temple funding under Xerxes meant a loss of revenue for temple cults across the empire.
3:10 *floodgates of heaven.* A poetic expression for drenching rainfall (Ge 7:11; 8:2; Isa 24:18; cf. the Septuagint, the pre-Christian Greek translation of the OT: "the sluices [or torrents] of heaven"). Some commentators draw inferences regarding Hebrew cosmology from the prophet's reference to the "windows" of heaven. Usually Malachi's language is understood as an appeal to commonly known features of ancient Near Eastern cosmology; namely, the heavenly vault above which there is water, which may fall down through openings known as windows (see the articles "The 'Vault' and 'Water Above,'" p. 6; "Cosmic Geography," p. 836.
3:16 *scroll of remembrance.* The metaphor of God as "the divine bookkeeper" is attested elsewhere in the OT (e.g., Ex 32:32; Ps 56:8; 69:28; 87:6; 139:16; Isa 4:3; 65:6; Eze 13:9). The idea of deities keeping heavenly tablets upon which were recorded the deeds and destinies of individuals and nations extends from Sumerian to Talmudic times. Malachi's divine register contrasts with that of the prophet Jeremiah, who warned that those turning away from Yahweh would be "written in the dust" (Jer 17:13; translated "registered in the underworld" in the NJB). The concept of heavenly books is also well documented in later extra-Biblical Jewish literature. A similar heavenly book containing the deeds of individuals as a record for divine judgment is also found in the Persian religion of Zoroaster (see the article "Zoroastrianism," p. 1433). Although not a heavenly book, the "book of the chronicles" mentioned in Est 6:1 offers a parallel example of a book or scroll recording the good deeds of loyal subjects. Following Persian tradition, Malachi's "scroll of remembrance" was both a catalog of names and a record of events. Yahweh's scroll was apparently an ongoing account of the words and deeds of the God-fearers in postexilic Yehud—a memorializing scroll that permits Yahweh to identify those who belong to him.
4:1 *furnace.* A fixed or portable beehive-shaped earthenware oven or stove used especially for baking bread.

the day that is coming will set them on
fire," says the LORD Almighty. "Not a root
or a branch will be left to them. 2But for
you who revere my name, the sun of righteousness[a] will rise with healing[b] in its
rays. And you will go out and frolic[c] like
well-fed calves. 3Then you will trample[d]
on the wicked; they will be ashes[e] under
the soles of your feet on the day when I
act," says the LORD Almighty.
4"Remember the law[f] of my servant Moses, the decrees and laws I gave him at
Horeb for all Israel.
5"See, I will send the prophet Elijah[g] to
you before that great and dreadful day of
the LORD comes.[h] 6He will turn the hearts
of the parents to their children,[i] and the
hearts of the children to their parents; or
else I will come and strike[j] the land with
total destruction."[k]

4:2 [a] Lk 1:78; Eph 5:14 [b] Isa 30:26 [c] Isa 35:6 **4:3** [d] Job 40:12 [e] Eze 28:18 **4:4** [f] Ps 147:19 **4:5** [g] Mt 11:14; Lk 1:17 [h] Joel 2:31 **4:6** [i] Lk 1:17 [j] Isa 11:4; Rev 19:15 [k] Zec 5:3

4:2 *sun of righteousness.* This expression is unique to Malachi in the OT. It may be a solar epithet for Yahweh or simply a figurative description of the eschatological day of the Lord (see notes on Joel 2:1; Am 5:18). It is possible that the source for Malachi's solar epithet was the winged sun disk, pervasive in ancient Near Eastern iconography (see notes on Ex 10:22; Job 31:26; 38:15; Ps 9:20; 104:2,28; Isa 2:10; 9:2; Eze 8:16; Jnh 4:2; Hab 3:4; see also the article "The Great Hymn to Aten," p. 982). This icon depicting (falcon or eagle) wings against a full sun represented the guardianship of the deity, an emblem of divine effulgence as well as protection and blessing for those peoples overshadowed by the "wings" of the deity.

4:4 *Horeb.* The place-name Horeb functions synonymously as an alternative designation for Mount Sinai (cf. Ex 33:6; 1Ki 19:8) or it may refer to the desolate region bordering Mount Sinai (e.g., Ex 17:6; Dt 1:19). See the article "Mount Sinai," p. 144.

The Time Between the Testaments

The time between the Testaments was one of ferment and change — a time of the realignment of traditional power blocs and the passing of a Near Eastern cultural tradition that had been dominant for almost 3,000 years.

In Biblical history, the approximately 400 years that separate the time of Nehemiah from the birth of Christ are known as the intertestamental period (c. 433 – 5 BC). Sometimes called the "silent" years because of the absence of prophetic revelation, they were anything but silent in terms of historical significance and cultural change. The events, literature and social forces of these years would shape the world of the NT.

History

With the Babylonian exile, Israel ceased to be an independent nation and became a minor territory in a succession of larger empires. Very little is known about the latter years of Persian domination because the Jewish historian Josephus (c. AD 37 – 100), our primary source for the intertestamental period, all but ignores them.

With Alexander the Great's acquisition of the Holy Land (332 BC), a new and more insidious threat to Israel emerged. Alexander was committed to the creation of a world united by Greek language and culture, a policy followed by his successors. This policy, called Hellenization, had a dramatic impact on the Jews.

At Alexander's death (323 BC) the empire he won was divided among his generals. Two of them founded dynasties — the Ptolemies of Egypt and the Seleucids in Syria and Mesopotamia — that would contend for control of the Holy Land for over a century.

The rule of the Ptolemies was considerate of Jewish religious sensitivities, but in 198 BC the Seleucids took control and paved the way for one of the most heroic periods in Jewish history.

The early Seleucid years were largely a continuation of the tolerant rule of the Ptolemies, but Antiochus IV Epiphanes (whose title means "God made manifest" and who ruled 175 – 164 BC) changed that when he attempted to consolidate his fading empire through a policy of radical Hellenization. While a segment of the Jewish aristocracy had already adopted Greek ways, many Jews were outraged.

Foreign Domination of Israel (722 BC—AD 135)

OLD TESTAMENT PERIOD	**The Assyrian Empire** (722 – 605 BC)
	The Babylonian Empire (605 – 539 BC)
	The Persian Empire (539 – 334 BC)
INTERTESTAMENTAL PERIOD	**The Macedonian-Greek Empire** (334 – 166 BC) • Alexander the Great (334 – 323 BC) • Ptolemaic Domination (323 – 198 BC) • Seleucid Domination (198 – 166 BC)
	Jewish Independence (166 – 63 BC) • The Maccabees • The Hasmonean Dynasty
NEW TESTAMENT PERIOD	**The Roman Empire** (63 BC – AD 135) • The Herodian Dynasty • Roman Governors • Destruction of Jerusalem (AD 70) • Second Revolt Ends the Jewish State (AD 135)

Adapted from *Four Portraits, One Jesus* by Mark L. Strauss. Copyright © 2007 by Mark L. Strauss, p. 95. Used by permission of Zondervan.

Antiochus's atrocities were aimed at the eradication of Jewish religion. He prohibited some of the central elements of Jewish practice, attempted to destroy all copies of the Torah (the Pentateuch) and required offerings to the Greek god Zeus. His crowning outrage was the erection of a statue of Zeus and the sacrificing of a pig in the Jerusalem temple itself.

Opposition to Antiochus was led by Mattathias, an elderly villager from a priestly family, and

PALESTINE OF THE MACCABEES AND HASMONEAN DYNASTY

Judea at the beginning of the revolt
Additions of Jonathan, 160–142 BC
Additions of Simon, 142–134 BC
Additions of Hyrcanus I, 134–104 BC
Additions of Aristobulus I, 104–103 BC
Additions of Alexander Jannaeus, 103–76 BC
Kingdom of Alexander Jannaeus
COELE-SYRIA
PHOENICIA
Sidon
Damascus
Tyre
Dan (Antiochia)
Paneas
Cadasa
Seleucia
Hazor
Bascama
Ptolemais
Bethsaida
Gamala
Gennesaret
Taricheae
Sea of Galilee
Dathema
Arbela
Hippus
GALILEE
Philoteria
Sepphoris
Mt. Carmel
Jezreel Valley
Dora
Mediterranean Sea
Strato's Tower
GALAADITIS
Scythopolis
Pella
SAMARIA
Jordan R.
Gerasa
Samaria
Ammathus
Mt. Gerizim
Shechem
Apollonia
Acrabeta
PEREA
Joppa
Alexandrium
Gadora
Arimathea
Apherema
Lydda
Philadelphia
Docus
Jamnia
Gazara
JUDEA
Jericho
Esbus
Azotus
Accaron
Jerusalem
Hyrcania
Samaga
PHILISTIA
Ascalon
Herodium
Medeba
Beth Zur
Machaerus
Anthedon
Marisa
Adora
Hebron
Gaza
Dead Sea
En Gedi
MOABITIS
Orda
Gerar
IDUMEA
Masada
Raphia
Beersheba
NABATEANS
Rhinocorura
Malatha
Wadi of Egypt
Petra
0 10 km.
0 10 miles

his five sons: Judas (called "Maccabeus" — probably meaning "hammerer"), Jonathan, Simon, John and Eleazar. Mattathias destroyed a Greek altar established in his village, Modein, and killed Antiochus's emissary. This triggered the Maccabean revolt, a 24-year war (166 – 142 BC) that resulted in the independence of Judah until the Romans took control in 63 BC.

The victory of Mattathias's family was a hollow one, however. With the death of his last son, Simon, the Hasmonean dynasty they founded soon evolved into an aristocratic, Hellenistic regime sometimes hard to distinguish from that of the Seleucids. During the reign of Simon's son, John Hyrcanus, the orthodox Jews who had supported the Maccabees fell out of favor. With only a few exceptions, the rest of the Hasmoneans supported the Jewish Hellenizers. The Pharisees were actually persecuted by Alexander Jannaeus (103 – 76 BC).

The Hasmonean dynasty ended when, in 63 BC, an expanding Roman empire intervened in a dynastic clash between the two sons of Jannaeus, Aristobulus II and Hyrcanus II. Pompey, the general who subdued the East for Rome, took Jerusalem after a three-month siege of the temple area, massacring priests in the performance of their duties and entering the Most Holy Place. This sacrilege began Roman rule in a way that Jews could neither forgive nor forget.

THE MACCABEAN-HASMONEAN PERIOD

SELEUCID KINGS		JEWISH LEADERS		PTOLEMAIC KINGS	
Seleucus I (Nicator)	321 – 281			Ptolemy I (Soter)	323 – 285
Antiochus I (Soter)	281 – 261				
Antiochus II (Theos)	261 – 246			Ptolemy II (Philadelphus)	285 – 246
Seleucus II (Callinicus)	246 – 225			Ptolemy III (Euergetes)	246 – 222
Seleucus III (Soter)	225 – 223			Ptolemy IV (Philopator)	221 – 205
Antiochus III (the Great)	223 – 187			Ptolemy V (Epiphanes)	204 – 180
Seleucus IV (Philopator)	187 – 175			Ptolemy VI (Philometor)	180 – 145
Antiochus IV (Epiphanes)	175 – 163	Mattathias Judas	166 166 – 160		
Antiochus V (Eupator)	163 – 162				
Demetrius I (Soter)	162 – 150	Jonathan	160 – 143		
Alexander Balas	150 – 145			Ptolemy VII (Neos Philopator)	145
Demetrius II (Nicator)	145 – 139	Simon	143 – 135	Ptolemy VII (Neos Philopator)	145
(Antiochus VI [Epiphanes Dionysus])	145 – 142			Ptolemy VIII (Euergetes II or Physcon)	145 – 116
Antiochus VII (Sidetes)	139 – 129	John Hyrcanus I	135 – 104		
Demetrius II (Nicator)	129 – 125				
Antiochus VIII (Grypus)	125/4 – 113			Ptolemy IX (Soter II or Lathyrus)	116 – 110
Antiochus IX (Philopator Cyzicenus)	113 – 111				
Antiochus VIII (Grypus)	111 – 95	Aristobulus	104 – 103	Ptolemy X (Alexander)	110 – 109 108 – 88
Seleucus VI	95 – 54	Alexander Jannaeus	103 – 76		
Antiochus X (Eusebes)	94 – 83			Ptolemy IX (Soter II or Lathyrus)	88 – 80
Tigranes, King of Armenia	83 – 69	Salome Alexandra	76 – 67	Ptolemy XI (Alexander II)	80 (20 days)
				Ptolemy XII (Philopator Philadelphus Neos Dionysus or Auletes)	80 – 51
Antiochus XIII (Asiaticus)	69 – 65	Hyrcanus II Aristobulus	67 (3 months) 67 – 63	Cleopatra VII	51 – 30

Literature

During these unhappy years of oppression and internal strife, the Jewish people produced a sizable body of literature that both recorded and addressed their era. Three of the more significant literary collections are the Septuagint, the Apocrypha and the Dead Sea Scrolls.

Septuagint. Jewish tradition says that 72 scholars, under the sponsorship of Ptolemy Philadelphus (c. 250 BC), were brought together on the island of Pharos, near Alexandria, where they produced a Greek translation of the OT in 72 days. From this tradition the Latin word for 70, "Septuagint," became the name attached to the translation. The Roman numeral for 70, LXX, is used as an abbreviation for it.

Behind that tradition lies the probability that at least the Torah (the five books of Moses) was translated into Greek c. 250 BC for the use of the Greek-speaking Jews of Alexandria. The rest of the OT and some noncanonical books were also included in the LXX before the dawning of the Christian era.

The Septuagint quickly became the Bible of the Jews outside the Holy Land who, like the Alexandrians, no longer spoke Hebrew. It would be difficult to overestimate its influence. It made the Scriptures available both to the Jews who no longer spoke their ancestral language and to the entire Greek-speaking world. It later became the Bible of the early church. Also, its widespread popularity and use contributed to the retention of the Apocrypha by some branches of Christendom.

Apocrypha. Derived from a Greek word that means "hidden," Apocrypha has acquired the meaning "false," but in a technical sense it describes a specific body of writings. This collection consists of a variety of books and additions to canonical books that, with the exception of 2 Esdras (c. AD 90), were written during the intertestamental period. Their recognition as authoritative in Roman and Eastern Christianity is the result of a complex historical process.

The limits of the Hebrew canon of the OT, also accepted by most Protestants today, were very likely established by the dawn of the second century AD. In spite of disagreements among some of the church fathers as to which books were canonical and which were not, the Apocryphal books (which were included in the Septuagint) continued in common use by most Christians until the Reformation. During this period most Protestants decided to follow the original Hebrew canon, while Rome, at the Council of Trent (1546), and more recently at the First Vatican Council (1869–70), affirmed the larger "Alexandrian" canon that includes the Apocrypha.

The Apocryphal books have retained their place primarily through the weight of ecclesiastical authority, without which they would not commend themselves as canonical literature. There is no evidence that Jesus or the apostles ever quoted any Apocryphal works as inspired Scripture. The Jewish community that produced them repudiated them, and the historical surveys in the apostolic sermons recorded in Acts completely ignore the period they cover. Even the sober, historical account of 1 Maccabees is tarnished by errors and anachronisms.

There is nothing of theological value in the Apocryphal books that cannot be duplicated in canonical Scripture. Nonetheless, this body of literature does provide a valuable source of information for the study of the intertestamental period.

Dead Sea Scrolls. In the spring of 1947 Arab shepherds chanced upon a cave in the hills overlooking the southwestern shore of the Dead Sea that contained what has been called the greatest manuscript discovery of modern times. The documents and fragments of documents found in a group of such caves, dubbed the "Dead Sea Scrolls," included OT books, a few books of the Apocrypha, apocalyptic works, pseudepigrapha (books that purport to be the work of ancient heroes of the faith) and a number of books peculiar to the sect that produced them.

Approximately a third of the documents are Biblical, with Psalms, Deuteronomy and Isaiah—the books quoted most often in the NT—occurring most frequently. One of the most remarkable finds was a complete, 24-foot-long scroll of Isaiah.

The Scrolls have made a significant contribution to the quest for a form of the OT texts most accurately reflecting the original manuscripts; they provide copies more than 1,000 years closer to the time of originals than were previously known. The understanding of Biblical Hebrew and Aramaic and knowledge of the development of Judaism between the Testaments have been increased significantly. Of great importance to readers of the Bible is the demonstration of the care with which OT texts were copied, thus providing objective evidence for the extraordinary reliability of those texts.

Social Developments

The Judaism of Jesus' day was, to a large extent, the result of changes that came about in response to the pressures of the intertestamental period.

Diaspora. The Diaspora (dispersion) of Israel begun in the exile accelerated during these years until a writer of the day could say that Jews filled every land and sea.

Jews outside the Holy Land, cut off from the temple, concentrated their religious life in the study of the Torah and the life of the synagogue (see below). The missionaries of the early church began their Gentile ministries among the Diaspora, using the Greek translation of the OT (the Septuagint).

Sadducees. In the Holy Land, the Greek world made its greatest impact through the party of the Sadducees. Made up of aristocrats, it became the temple party. Because of their position, the Sadducees had a vested interest in the status quo.

Relatively few in number, they wielded disproportionate political power and controlled the high priesthood. They rejected all religious writings except the Torah, as well as any doctrine (such as resurrection from the dead) not found in those five books.

Synagogue. During the Babylonian exile, Israel was cut off from the temple, divested of nationhood and surrounded by pagan religious practices. The nation's faith was threatened. Under these circumstances, the exiles turned their religious focus from what they had lost to what they retained — the Torah and the belief that they were God's people. They concentrated on the law rather than nationhood, on personal piety rather than sacramental rectitude and on prayer as an acceptable replacement for the sacrifices denied to them.

When they returned from the exile, they brought with them this new form of religious expression, as well as the synagogue (its center), and Judaism became a faith that could be practiced wherever the Torah could be carried. The emphases on personal piety and a relationship with God, which characterized synagogue worship, not only helped preserve Judaism but also prepared the way for the Christian gospel.

Pharisees. As the party of the synagogue, the Pharisees strove to reinterpret the law. They built a "hedge" around it to enable Jews to live righteously before God in a world that had changed drastically since the days of Moses. Although they were comparatively few in number, the Pharisees enjoyed the support of the people and influenced popular opinion as well as national policy. They were the only party to survive the destruction of the temple in AD 70 and were the spiritual progenitors of modern Judaism.

Essenes. An almost forgotten Jewish sect (but referred to by Philo and Josephus) until the discovery of the Dead Sea Scrolls, the Essenes were a small, separatist group that grew out of the conflicts of the Maccabean age. Like the Pharisees, they stressed strict legal observance, but they considered the temple priesthood corrupt and rejected much of the temple ritual and sacrificial system. Though they are mentioned by several ancient writers, the precise nature of the Essenes is still not certain, though it is widely held that the Qumran community that produced the Dead Sea Scrolls was probably an Essene group.

Because they were convinced that they were the true remnant of Israel, these Qumran sectarians had separated themselves from Judaism at large and devoted themselves to personal purity and preparation for the final war between the "Sons of Light and the Sons of Darkness." They practiced an apocalyptic faith, looking back to the contributions of their previous leader, known as "Teacher of Righteousness," and forward to the coming of two Messiahs: a priestly one from the line of Aaron and a royal one from the line of David. In the Jewish War of AD 66 – 73, the community at Qumran was destroyed, and the Essenes dropped from history.

Attempts have been made to equate aspects of the beliefs of the Qumran community with the origins of Christianity. Some have seen a prototype of Jesus in their "Teacher of Righteousness," and John the Baptist's apocalyptic message and desert lifestyle have parallels with those at Qumran. Most of these parallels, however, are superficial, and there is no hard evidence of direct contact between either Jesus or John and the Qumran community. ◆

FROM MALACHI TO CHRIST

The Persian Period
450–330 BC

For about 200 years after Nehemiah's time the Persians controlled Judah, but the Jews were allowed to carry on their religious observances and were not interfered with. During this time Judah was ruled by high priests, who answered to the Persian authorities.

The Hellenistic Period
330–166 BC

In the late fourth century BC, Alexander the Great defeated the Persians repeatedly in battle and quickly conquered the eastern Mediterranean region, including Syria, Egypt, Persia and Babylonia. Alexander believed in the superiority of Greek culture and was convinced that it was the one force that could unify the world. Alexander permitted the Jews to observe their laws and even granted them exemption from tribute or tax during their sabbath years. When he built Alexandria in Egypt, he encouraged Jews to live there. The Greek conquest prepared the way for the translation of the Hebrew Old Testament into Greek (Septuagint version), beginning c. 250 BC.

The Hasmonean Period
166–63 BC

When this historical period began, the Jews were being greatly oppressed. The Ptolemies of Egypt had been tolerant of the Jews and their religious practices, but the Seleucid rulers of Syria were determined to force Hellenism on them. Copies of the Scriptures were ordered destroyed, and laws were enforced banning circumcision and other Jewish practices. The oppressed Jews revolted, led by Judas Maccabeus.

The Roman Period
Begins in 63 BC

In the year 63 BC, Pompey, the Roman general, captured Jerusalem, and the provinces in the Holy Land became subject to Rome. The Romans ruled at times through local vassal kings and at other times through Roman governors who were appointed by the emperors. Herod the Great was ruler of that whole region at the time of Jesus' birth.

410 · **400 BC** · 390 · 380 · 370 · 360 · 350 · 340 · 330 · 320 · 310 · **300** · 290 · 280 · 270 · 260 · 250 · 240 · 230 · 220 · 210 · **200** · 190 · 180 · 170 · 160 · 150 · 140 · 130 · 120 · 110 · **100** · 90 · 80 · 70 · 60 · 50 · 40 · 30 · 20 · 10 · 10 · 20 · AD 30

Rule of Alexander the Great

Rule of the Ptolemies of Egypt

Rule of the Seleucids of Syria

Hasmonean Dynasty

Herod the Great rules as king; subject to Rome

Malachi c. 430 BC

334–323 Alexander the Great conquers the East

330–328 Alexander's years of power

320 Ptolemy (I) Soter conquers Jerusalem

311 Seleucus conquers Babylon; Seleucid dynasty begins

226 Antiochus (III) of Syria conquers the Holy Land

223–187 Antiochus becomes Seleucid ruler of Syria

198 Antiochus defeats Egypt and gains control of the Holy Land

175–164 Antiochus (IV) Epiphanes rules Syria; Judaism is prohibited

167 Mattathias and his sons rebel against Antiochus; Maccabean revolt begins

166–160 Judas Maccabeus's leadership

160–143 Jonathan is high priest

142–134 Simon becomes high priest; establishes Hasmonean dynasty (see map and essay, pp. 1572–1574)

134–104 John Hyrcanus enlarges the independent Jewish state

103 Aristobulus's rule

102–76 Alexander Janneus's rule

75–67 Rule of Salome Alexandra with Hyrcanus II as high priest

66–63 Battle between Aristobulus II and Hyrcanus II

63 Pompey invades the Holy Land; Roman rule begins

63–40 Hyrcanus II governs but is subject to Rome

40–37 Parthians conquer Jerusalem

37 Herod becomes ruler of the Holy Land

19 Herod's temple begun

4 Herod dies; Archelaus succeeds him

Key New Testament Terms

Age to come: The most basic scheme of ancient Judean belief about the future was that at some point the current age of hardship would end and God would establish a new era of peace, justice and righteousness. Jewish people generally expected Israel to be exalted over the nations in that coming age.

Already / not yet: A phrase scholars often use to summarize the early Christian perspective on God's future kingdom. Because we recognize that the coming Messiah has already come once, that Christ's resurrection is the first installment of the promised future resurrection, and that the gift of the Spirit gives us a foretaste of the future world, we can speak of an "already" dimension of the kingdom as well as looking forward to its "not yet" consummation.

Anaphora: An ancient rhetorical device in which multiple sentences or clauses begin with the same word or phrase.

Apocalypses, apocalyptic: A form of Jewish literature, developed from one line of the Biblical prophetic tradition, emphasizing visions or heavenly journeys meant to reveal divine mysteries. Some of these secrets were often about the future; thus scholars popularly apply the title to works or material that often used many symbols and that dealt with the end time. (Some other Jewish mystics may have valued revelations but downplayed the end-time references.)

Apocrypha: The usual title for books accepted in the Catholic but not Protestant canons. Most of these books appear in versions of the Septuagint (the pre-Christian Greek translation of the OT) that were widely used in the Diaspora. While most Judean Jews did not accept most of these books as part of their developing canon and the NT does not cite them with standard "Scripture" formulas, the NT contains numerous allusions to these works.

Apostle: The secular Greek term applies to messengers or ambassadors; the closest Jewish equivalent applied to agents commissioned with and backed by the authority of their senders, insofar as they kept to the content of their commission. The OT spoke of prophets being "sent" as God's messengers; the NT apparently limits the title to those commissioned with special authority (perhaps on the OT model of Moses and prophetic judges like Samuel). This includes the Twelve (Ac 6:2), but (especially in Paul's usage) also includes some others as well.

Aramaic: A Semitic language (related to Hebrew) used as an international language before Alexander's conquests brought Greek to the urban centers. Various forms of Aramaic remained widely spoken in Syria, Palestine and further east, although Greek was prevalent in most major urban centers in the eastern Mediterranean world of Jesus' day (e.g., Alexandria, Antioch and to a lesser extent, Jerusalem). Most rural Galileans spoke Aramaic, but in Lower Galilee most Aramaic speakers probably also knew Greek.

Ascetic: Self-denying; some philosophic and religious groups demanded such discipline (sometimes to display indifference to one's bodily desires and pain). Asceticism grew stronger in late antiquity than it was in the first century.

Associations: Relatively permanent social groups or clubs that shared common interests (often as guilds of workers or religious groups) and that met regularly, typically sharing a common meal. Whether or not associations or clubs were primarily cultic, they honored a patron deity and included some religious rites, such as a libation of wine at the beginning of their banquet.

Atone, atonement: Many ancient cultures believed in appeasing a deity's anger through the punishment of a substitute. Greek culture respected laying down one's life for another; some forms of Judaism (notably 4 Maccabees) emphasized that martyrs turned away God's anger against the people. NT images of atonement may relate especially to OT sin and atonement offerings, where a sacrifice's death (by the shedding of its blood) allowed a sinner to be forgiven.

Baptize, baptism: Many ancient cults practiced ceremonial washings, which are also common in the OT and Judaism; some Jewish sects (such as the people who produced the Dead Sea Scrolls) were particularly scrupulous about these washings, but others (such as Sadducees and Pharisees) also shared this emphasis. Whereas most of these washings were often repeated, one kind of immersion (apparently attested even by some first- and second-century Gentile writers) was employed for conversion, namely of Gentiles converting to Judaism (alongside male circumcision). See the article "Baptism," p. 1686.

Canon: An agreed-upon minimum of works held to be divinely authoritative as Scripture. While all Jews accepted the Pentateuch, some books remained debated in various Jewish groups. Most of Palestinian Judaism, however, accepted roughly our current OT, with some groups (such as the Qumran sectarians) varying somewhat (additional psalms; perhaps canonical status for some other authoritative works such as much of 1 Enoch; possibly excluding Esther, though this may be an argument from silence). In the Diaspora, versions of the Septuagint (the pre-Christian Greek translation of the OT) often included many books in what we call the Apocrypha. For the NT canon, see "New Testament."

Chiasm: An inverted parallel structure in which the first and last elements in a text are parallel, the second and penultimate elements are parallel, and so on (in longer chiastic structures).

Chief priests: They were prominent members of the top aristocratic priestly families, Jerusalem's ruling class. Although the OT spoke of a single "chief priest," Jewish writers by the NT period described all of the chief priestly families as "chief priests," in addition to the leading high priest.

Christ: The Greek translation of the Hebrew "Messiah" ("Anointed One"). Many Gentile readers may have simply assumed this to be Jesus' surname, since "anointed one" carried no official connotations in Greek. See "Messiah."

Church: The Greek term commonly meant "assemblies," including civic assemblies. It did not mean "called-out ones," as some modern etymological analyses suggest. It also translates the Hebrew *qahal* (the assembly of Israel) in the Septuagint (the pre-Christian Greek translation of the OT), as does the Greek term translated "synagogue." "Synagogue" and "church" both claimed the mantle of the OT "congregation" of Israel. The Qumran sectarians applied the same Hebrew term to their own assembly.

Client: In Roman society, this was a person socially dependent on a "patron." The client was expected to bestow honor and/or political support on the patron in return for economic, legal, and other assistance from the patron. When this study Bible employs the term, it is normally in this general sense rather than the narrower usage of clients who actually accompanied their patrons to political activities during much of the business day (more relevant before the rise of Rome's emperor). See "Patron."

Cynic: A particular philosophic sect known for its disdain of human culture. Apart from begging, Cynics claimed to be independent from society. Mostly urban, they lived and preached on the streets, possessing little more than a staff, cloak, a bag for begging and sometimes a cup.

Dead Sea Scrolls: Mostly pre-Christian documents found in caves near modern Khirbet Qumran. The key extra-Biblical documents seem to reflect a distinctive Jewish sect, which most (though not all) scholars identify with the Essenes (based on parallel descriptions of their wilderness community especially in Josephus and Philo). See "Qumran community."

Demon: Although Greeks used the term for both good and bad spirits (sometimes heroes, demigods or disembodied souls), most first-century Judeans applied the label to malevolent spirits, which some viewed as fallen angels and some simply as hostile personal entities. Descriptions of spirit possession in the Gospels, Josephus, and later sources resemble many experiences of spirit possession reported by anthropologists in various cultures today.

Diaspora: Jewish people living outside the Holy Land. Between Parthia and the Mediterranean world, undoubtedly more first-century Jews lived outside the land than in it; many scholars estimate that 80 percent of Jews in the NT era lived outside the Holy Land.

Diatribe: A teaching style characteristic of Stoics and some other philosophers, often using rhetorical questions and objections from imaginary critics.

Digression: A temporary change of subject; this technique is common in ancient written sources and was likely also common in ancient oratory.

Disciples: Students and adherents of various rabbinic, philosophic or rhetorical schools. Those studying at the tertiary level were most often in the latter half of their teenage years and tended to become professionals using the skills learned. They normally sought to learn from their teacher, often propagating and sometimes publishing his teachings (but respecting and accurately representing them even if they came to disagree).

Divination: Among Gentiles, the art of determining the will of the gods or the future by means of signs supposedly embedded in nature, such as unusual details in sacrificial entrails (the innards of a sacrificed animal), the flight of birds, the patterns of oil on water and other signs.

Dualism: A binary division of some sort. Moral dualism, for example, starkly divides good and evil, such as often appears in Dead Sea Scrolls that divide humanity into the people of light and the people of darkness. Both apocalyptic literature and Greek philosophers developed a cosmic dualism between heaven and earth; Jewish eschatology also divided the present age from the future age.

1 Enoch: An apocalypse, probably originally in Aramaic, deriving mostly from the second century BC. Its thinking at points resembles that of the sectarian Dead Sea Scrolls, which include Aramaic portions of it (the full text survived in Ethiopic).

Epicureans: A Greek philosophic school viewing pleasure (lack of pain) as the highest good, denying both an afterlife and traditional Greek deities. See the article "Ancient Philosophies," p. 1913.

Eschatological: Involving the end-time or ultimate future. Because Jesus has already come as well as is yet to come, some NT passages speak as if the end time has already begun (though is not yet finished); the Messiah, his kingdom and resurrection were all end-time concepts that take on meaning different from traditional Jewish expectations in light of Jesus' first coming. Other passages, however, continue to present the end (in its fullness) as a future event.

Essenes: A strict Jewish sect, at least a group of whom became monastics in the wilderness. A majority of scholars attribute most of the Dead Sea Scrolls to them. They may have numbered only a few thousand at any given time.

Eternal life: The "life of the world to come," inaugurated by the resurrection from the dead in many Jewish sources (starting with Da 12:2). As in some passages in the NT, Jewish sources sometimes abbreviate it as "life." This relates to the Jewish tradition of the contrast between the present evil age and the glorious age to come. See note on Jn 3:17 – 18.

Exorcism: The casting out of demons. Various early Jewish sources (such as in Josephus or in Ac 19:13) often claimed to effect it by foul-smelling substances, invoking the help of higher spirits or even using a so-called magic ring. Some also sought to harness or manipulate spirits through name invocation, magic formulas and charms.

4 Ezra: The non-Christian section, chs. 3 to 14, is a late first-century or early second-century AD apocalyptic work.

Freedperson: A person legally freed from slavery. Most slaves of Roman citizens themselves became citizens when freed. Manumission (freeing of slaves) was very common; sometimes slaves were manumitted as a reward for faithfulness; sometimes via purchase by another slave (who earned money on the side); sometimes, unfortunately, as a means of conserving the slaveholder's resource — that is, so the slaveholder would not have to care for aged slaves who could no longer work.

Gehenna: The Greek form of the Hebrew "Gehinnom," which Jewish sources widely applied to the place where the wicked would be tormented after death. Some Jews believed that the wicked would be instantly annihilated there; others that they would be tormented for a period of time, then either annihilated or released. Other Jewish writings reflect the view apparently dominant in the Synoptic Gospels and Revelation: namely, eternal torment.

Genre: A work's literary type (e.g., biography, song or letter). The Bible's text represents many different types of genres, and understanding which genre type the text is helps to understand the intent of the work itself.

Gentile: Someone who is not Jewish.

Gnosticism: Systems of thought that mixed elements of Christianity, Greek philosophy and often Jewish and pagan elements. In its developed form it is first documented in the early second century AD. Although the tendencies that produced it stem from an earlier period, many NT scholars today object to reading developed gnostic systems back into the NT period. Specialists in gnosticism have shown that it was never a single, cohesive movement.

Gospel: "Good news," used in a wide variety of contexts (especially involving heralds), but in the NT often alluding back to Isaiah's message of hope concerning the salvation and restoration of God's people (e.g., Isa 52:7). (This entry refers to the normal NT use of "gospel," not to the literary genre of the Gospels, on which see the Introduction to the Gospels, p. 1598.)

Grace: In inscriptions, the Greek word often involves a benefactor's free generosity; the ancient world understood praise as a proper response to such generosity. NT usage often evokes the OT idea of God's "covenant love" (though often translated differently in the Septuagint, the pre-Christian Greek translation of the OT).

Hellenistic: The blending of Greek and Near Eastern cultures following the conquests of Alexander the Great. Thus "Hellenistic Judaism" is Judaism deeply influenced by Greek culture. Most Mediterranean Judaism was influenced by Hellenism to a greater or lesser degree by the NT period.

Hermeneutics: The process toward or methods of interpretation.

Holy Spirit: Although a rare title for God's Spirit in the OT (Ps 51:11; Isa 63:10), it was (usually) one of the most common titles for the Spirit of God by NT times. Many associated the Spirit especially with prophecy (some sectarian circles also often associated the Spirit with purification), and believed that the Spirit was less widely available since the death of the prophets. Various prophets (especially Isaiah, Ezekiel and Joel) had predicted an end-time outpouring of the Spirit; the Qumran sectarians and especially the early Christians believed that the end-time Spirit was active among them. Like the Qumran sectarians, NT writings associate the Spirit both with spiritual purification (as in Eze 36:25 – 27), inspiration to prophecy and to other prophetic-type works; the NT also includes some other activities of the Spirit.

Hyperbole: Rhetorical overstatement, a common technique of ancient Jewish (and other) sages to draw attention to one's point.

Josephus: An educated first-century Jewish historian who wrote especially about Jewish history, partly to defend his people and to present them favorably to Gentiles.

Kingdom: The term normally meant "authority," "reign" or "rule." Scripture speaks of God's "kingdom" in terms of his rule over the nations. It also speaks in a special way of God's unchallenged reign in the end time (Da 2:44 – 45; 7:14,27). Jewish people in Jesus' day spoke of God reigning in the present, but usually also prayed for the consummation of this kingdom in the future. See the article "Kingdom," p. 1616.

Law: The Greek *nomos*, which is often translated as "law," often reflects the sense of the Hebrew Torah, which can include the five books of Moses, all of Scripture, or God's "instruction" and "teaching" (including but not limited to his regulations in Scripture). Jewish people celebrated the law as God's gracious gift to teach them how to live rightly.

Libation: Ritual pouring of some fluid (such as water or wine) to honor divinities or deceased persons. Greeks used libations not only in more directly cultic contexts but also before most banquets.

Maccabees: A family of priests in the second century BC. They were leaders of the Jewish revolution against the Greco-Syrian tyrant Antiochus Epiphanes, a ruler who tried to force Greek customs — including Greek religion — on Judea. Their successors (the Hasmonean dynasty) ruled Judea until the Romans helped Herod achieve power.

Magic: Practices used by people who claimed to draw on or manipulate non-human spiritual power, often for malevolent or selfish purposes. Magic frequently claimed to manipulate spirits, sometimes by using special knowledge. See the article "Magic in the New Testament," p. 1884.

Messiah: Lit. "Anointed One." Various figures were anointed in the Bible (including priests and kings), and some Jewish people (the priestly Qumran sect) expected both an "anointed" future king and an "anointed" priest. But most applied the label "Messiah" especially to the future king descended from David who would rule when God freed Israel from the rule of the nations (in the NT period, most obviously Rome). Beyond this primary feature, views diverged widely; some apparently envisioned an exalted, heavenly sort of figure, but an expectation of a warrior Messiah seems more common.

Midrash: A customary written form of Scripture exposition employed by Jewish teachers, often by reading the text in light of other texts and finding significance in every detail.

Mysteries: Greeks had various cults called "mysteries," initiation into which was a popular activity; initiates were not allowed to reveal the secrets of these groups. Jewish sources in Greek, however, use the term "mystery" in much broader ways, often for unknown divine wisdom. Some Dead Sea Scrolls speak of interpreting God's mysteries; some of these are mysteries about his kingdom (see Da 2:47).

Mystery cults: Various Greek cults entered by initiation, the details of which members had to keep secret. Cults and initiation practices differed widely among themselves. Because their rites were so secretive, our knowledge is limited. Because they were syncretistic, in later centuries they borrowed some Christian features into their own beliefs and rituals. Some cults, such as Mithraism, spread in the Roman world (especially among soldiers) only after the wide spread of Christianity there.

Narrative: A story (a form applicable to both true stories and fiction).

New Testament: The later designation for the earliest Christian documents ultimately accepted by most Christians as canonical. These works technically do not form a testament or covenant, although they often report the fulfillment of the "new covenant," a new agreement between God and humanity. Many of the works, such as the four Gospels and Paul's key letters, were already accepted as canonical Scripture by writers in the second century. Some works remained debated much longer (e.g., Hebrews and 2 Peter). Other proposed works were not accepted, including both works similar to the accepted ones (such as the Didache and 1 Clement) and those further from its message (such as Hermas). Some works discussed in modern scholarship were never (e.g., nearly all gnostic works) or barely ever (e.g., the Gospel of Thomas) considered to be canonical by mainstream Christian churches over a wide geographic range.

Old Testament: The later designation for the Hebrew Bible (along with its Aramaic works) that came to be accepted in the Jewish and Protestant canon (and the Catholic canon minus the Apocrypha). The title is a misnomer since these works technically do not form a testament or covenant (although they report covenants); common usage, however, makes this and *Tanakh* (the later Jewish label for the same works) the best descriptions available.

Papyri: Ancient business documents, personal correspondence and the like written on papyrus scrolls. People manufactured papyrus from a type of reed, but water and moisture could destroy the writing. Some papyri (e.g., most of the Dead Sea Scrolls) have survived from the Judean desert, but the vast majority of ancient papyri known today came from arid regions of Egypt.

Parable: Comparisons, often in the form of stories, often used by Jewish sages as a sort of "sermon illustration." See the article "Parables," p. 1692.

Pastoral Epistles: 1 – 2 Timothy and Titus. Paul wrote his letters to these two church leaders as pastoral exhortations; hence the term.

Patron: The socially superior person on whom clients depended. These individuals granted favors, wrote recommendation letters and so forth for their clients in return for their clients honoring them. In this general sense, this Roman role in some ways resembles the Greek role of benefactors, who bestowed favors on cities or persons in return for honor. Scholars also often use the term "patrons" simply in the modern English sense of "supporters." See "Client."

Peasants: Poor farmers who often worked the estates of rich landlords or eked out a bare living working the ground. Although under-represented in ancient literature (which comes mainly from more literate urban elites), they constituted the majority of the population of ancient Mediterranean society.

Pharisees: Although in Jesus' day no longer as politically powerful as they had been generations earlier, they remained influential in NT Jewish culture. They were reputed for their piety and meticulous interpretation of the law according to ancestral tradition. They emphasized tithing, purity rules and the future resurrection of the righteous. In Jesus' day they especially divided into two schools, that of Hillel and that of Shammai; the latter was more conservative and probably dominant before AD 70. Josephus estimates their numbers at roughly 6,000. Although some probably grew up poor, many came from wealthier families that could afford their education in the Torah and Pharisaic tradition.

Philo: A first-century Jewish philosopher who sought to articulate Judaism in a manner appealing to a Greek philosophic setting. He was highly respected in the Alexandrian Jewish community.

Pilate: Pontius Pilate was governor of Judea from AD 26 to 36; he had a contentious and sometimes violent relationship with his Judean subjects. See note on Mt 27:2.

Plato: A fourth-century BC disciple of Socrates who emphasized dualism between the "real" world of ideas and the "shadowy" material world. Later Platonists expanded some of these ideas, sometimes also mixing with them ideas from other philosophic systems.

Prophecy: Speaking God's message by inspiration (sometimes, but not necessarily even usually, involving the future). While most Jewish people by the NT period still believed that prophecy sometimes occurred, many reserved the title "prophets" for God's spokespersons in the past (in contrast to early Christian claims). See the article "Prophecy in Antiquity," p. 2009.

Proselyte: A convert to Judaism. Gentile converts were usually purified by water and males were almost always circumcised (uncircumcised "God-fearers" could involve less commitment; see note on Ac 10:2 [under *God-fearing*]).

Pseudepigrapha: A modern collection of diverse ancient Jewish works, normally by authors other than those they name, that do not belong in earlier collections (Scripture, Apocrypha, Dead Sea Scrolls, rabbinic literature). These works include, for example, 1 Enoch (mostly from the second century BC), 4 Ezra and 2 Baruch.

Pythagoreanism: A philosophic system said to be founded by the earlier sage Pythagoras. It assigned mystical significance to numbers and required of its followers abstinence from eating meat and beans, among other conditions.

Qumran community: The group that created the Dead Sea Scrolls, referred to as such because the scrolls were found at Khirbet Qumran. See "Dead Sea Scrolls."

Rabbi: A term meaning "My master," a respectful title for Jewish teachers in Semitic-speaking regions such as Judea and further east. Probably after AD 70 the title came to apply to teachers ordained in the rabbinic movement, which (according to most scholars) developed especially from Pharisaic scribes (especially the schools of Shammai and Hillel). When applied to the period of the Gospels, the notes refer to Jewish sages who were knowledgeable in the law; when to a later period, to members of the rabbinic movement. Many of their teachings are preserved in rabbinic literature.

Rabbinic literature: Collections of teachings of the rabbis, arranged from the early third century AD (like the Mishnah) through the Medieval period. Because Pharisees and rabbis highly valued tradition, the earlier (Tannaitic) sources (reporting the teachings of rabbis before the third century) are often helpful in illustrating one line of early Jewish thought.

Repentance: The term refers not merely to a "change of thinking," as some have argued. It recalls the invitation in the Biblical prophets for Israel to "turn" back to the Lord (e.g., Hos 14:1, "return"). Jewish people could also use the term for turning from individual sins. True repentance was supposed to bring change, not mere apology apart from or without interest in change.

Resurrection: The holistic Jewish hope that the dead (or at least the righteous dead) would be raised to a new bodily existence of some sort at a future time (see Da 12:2). Pharisees embraced this view, probably widely held by Judeans (except the Sadducees), but no one expected one person to rise with a new body before the end-time general resurrection. See the article "Resurrection," p. 2012.

Rhetoric: Professional public speaking, the more popular of the two forms of advanced education in the Greek and Roman world of the NT period (the other being philosophy). Some rhetoric affected urban society in general, since people regularly heard speeches in civic assemblies and even in the marketplaces. See the article "Rhetoric and Paul's Letters," p. 1986.

Sabbath: The seventh day, Hebrew *Shabbat*, on which Jewish people were to rest from work (see Ex 20:8 – 11).

Sadducees: A Jewish sect mostly aligned with Jerusalem's aristocratic priests and profiting from their position in the social order, they tried to keep peace between the Roman government and their people. They held primary control in the temple and denied Pharisaic traditions, including those beliefs about the resurrection of the dead and other beliefs about the end time. The Judean-Roman war that started in AD 66 apparently brought an end to this sect.

Samaritans: A people who claimed that they were descendants of Jacob but whom Jews considered to be of mixed blood. They worshiped Israel's God but apparently (according to our later sources) did not accept Israel's prophets or Scripture later than Moses. They insisted that Mount Gerizim, not Jerusalem, was the proper holy site for worship; Jews and Samaritans each protested the other group's holy site. Conflicts often took place at the verbal level, but the Roman military occasionally needed to intervene in violent conflicts between the groups. See the article "Samaria and Samaritans," p. 1812.

Sanhedrin: The term "sanhedrin" applied to any local senate, but in the NT it applies to the one in Jerusalem. Rome governed many of its provinces through municipal aristocracies in chief cities; Jerusalem's Sanhedrin was to handle most Judean affairs. The usually negative role of the Sanhedrin in the NT is not surprising. Josephus claims that Herod the Great eliminated his political enemies and filled the Sanhedrin with his own political supporters, whose descendants continued to dominate most of the Sanhedrin through the NT period. The high priest held highest rank in Jerusalem's Sanhedrin; although a lifelong, hereditary office in the OT period, the high priests of this period were appointed by Rome or those to whom Rome delegated authority.

Satan: Initially a title ("the satan," i.e., "the adversary" in the Hebrew of Job), but functioning as a proper name for the devil in 2 Chronicles and Zechariah, as well as in Jewish sources in the NT period (although these also use other names; e.g., "Belial"). Both Biblical and early Jewish usage treated him as a literal evil spiritual personage, although his particular appearances throughout Scripture as such are debated. Developing OT themes, early Judaism viewed Satan as accuser (cf. Zec 3:1 – 2), tempter (cf. 1Ch 21:1), and deceiver.

Savior: A title that Gentiles applied to Greek deities and "divine" rulers, but which Jewish people applied to Israel's true God, including in the Septuagint, the pre-Christian Greek translation of the OT (e.g., Isa 45:21; Hab 3:18).

Scribes: In most of the eastern Mediterranean world the title applied to anyone who wrote legal documents. Sometimes this was the only person in a village who could write proficiently. Wealthy people sometimes had their own scribes (often slaves) to whom they could dictate correspondence. Judeans and Galileans, however, apparently applied this term also to respected legal experts who could adjudicate questions of Scripture, taught boys to recite it, and handled issues requiring reading and writing. (The most respected of these men probably filled a role akin to that of rabbis in later sources.) Some, but not all, belonged to the Pharisaic party.

Septuagint: The most common forms of the pre-Christian Greek translation of the OT, widely used in the ancient Mediterranean world. It is commonly abbreviated LXX (on account of the tradition that 70 scholars produced it). Although there are variations in LXX manuscripts as in NT manuscripts, the notes in this study Bible focus on the most common readings.

Slave: Any person involved in servitude to another, but the wide range of occupations and levels of status varied far beyond the character of slavery in some subsequent societies. Thus, for example, while some slaves were highly educated and relatively well off, slavery in mines or in gladiatorial combat was a virtual death sentence. Both free peasants and field slaves had a difficult life, but many urban household slaves achieved freedom and exercised more social and economic mobility than free peasants. Slaves could be beaten and lacked some key rights available to free persons; nevertheless, many achieved freedom (see "Freedperson"). See the articles "Ancient Slavery and the Background for Philemon," p. 2134; "Slaves and Slaveholders in Ephesians 6," p. 2068.

Son of God: Jewish sources applied the title most broadly to Israel as a whole (Ex 4:22), but more specifically to the Davidic royal line (2Sa 7:14) and ultimately to the future Davidic ruler (cf. Ps 2:7; 89:27). (In the ancient Near East, a king could be viewed as a son of the deity; Scripture adopted analogous language for David's line.) The Dead Sea Scrolls also apply this title in 2Sa 7:14 to the Messiah. Polytheists had many deities who were sons of other deities; emperors were deemed sons of their normally deified predecessors.

Son of Man: A Hebrew and Aramaic idiom for "human being." When Jesus refers to himself this way he at least sometimes (and possibly often) evokes Da 7:13 – 14, where the description applies to a representative of God's suffering holy people (which is described in Da 7:25 – 27). With them, he would ultimately rule forever.

Spirit of God: See "Holy Spirit."

Stoicism: The most popular philosophic sect in the first century. Stoics allowed for continuing the popular practice of religion, although they reinterpreted its meaning for intellectuals. They emphasized that Reason ordered matter, that one's only free choice was to cooperate with rather than protest Fate, and that the universe periodically collapsed back into the primordial fire only to afterward repeat the same cycle of existence. See the article "Ancient Philosophies," p. 1913.

Synagogues: Local Jewish assembly halls used for community meetings, public prayers and the reading of Scripture (in the Diaspora, originally these were called "prayer houses"). Much of a local Jewish community would gather there on the Sabbath.

Synoptic Gospels: The Gospels of Matthew, Mark and Luke — so designated because of the substantial overlap among their narratives.

Targum: Vernacular Aramaic paraphrases of books of the Hebrew Bible. Most of our extant Targumim date much later than the NT, but sometimes they reflect older traditions. The practice of paraphrasing into the vernacular is at least as old as Ne 8:8.

Tax collectors: Hated by many Jews, they were viewed as collaborators with the occupying empire because they collected taxes for the government (apparently often at personal profit). Taxes helped fund Herod the Great's projects, including the Jerusalem temple, his palaces and various civic projects in his realm (as well as some pagan temples in Gentile areas). Taxes became so oppressive in some areas of Egypt that many peasants abandoned their property and resettled elsewhere. Some argue that many NT tax collectors were customs officials. See note on Mk 2:14.

Zealots: Jewish nationalists revolting against Rome and its lackeys. The name technically may apply especially to a particular group of such nationalists just before the war of 66 – 70, although clearly a number of other revolutionaries existed before this time. Defending his own people's reputation in the empire, Josephus portrays all the revolutionaries as mere bandits and extremists. While there is truth in his picture, those urging revolt apparently had sympathizers even among many Pharisees and some of the younger members of the high-priestly elite. In the NT period, the term "zealot" could mean simply someone who was zealous for a cause.

New Testament Chronology

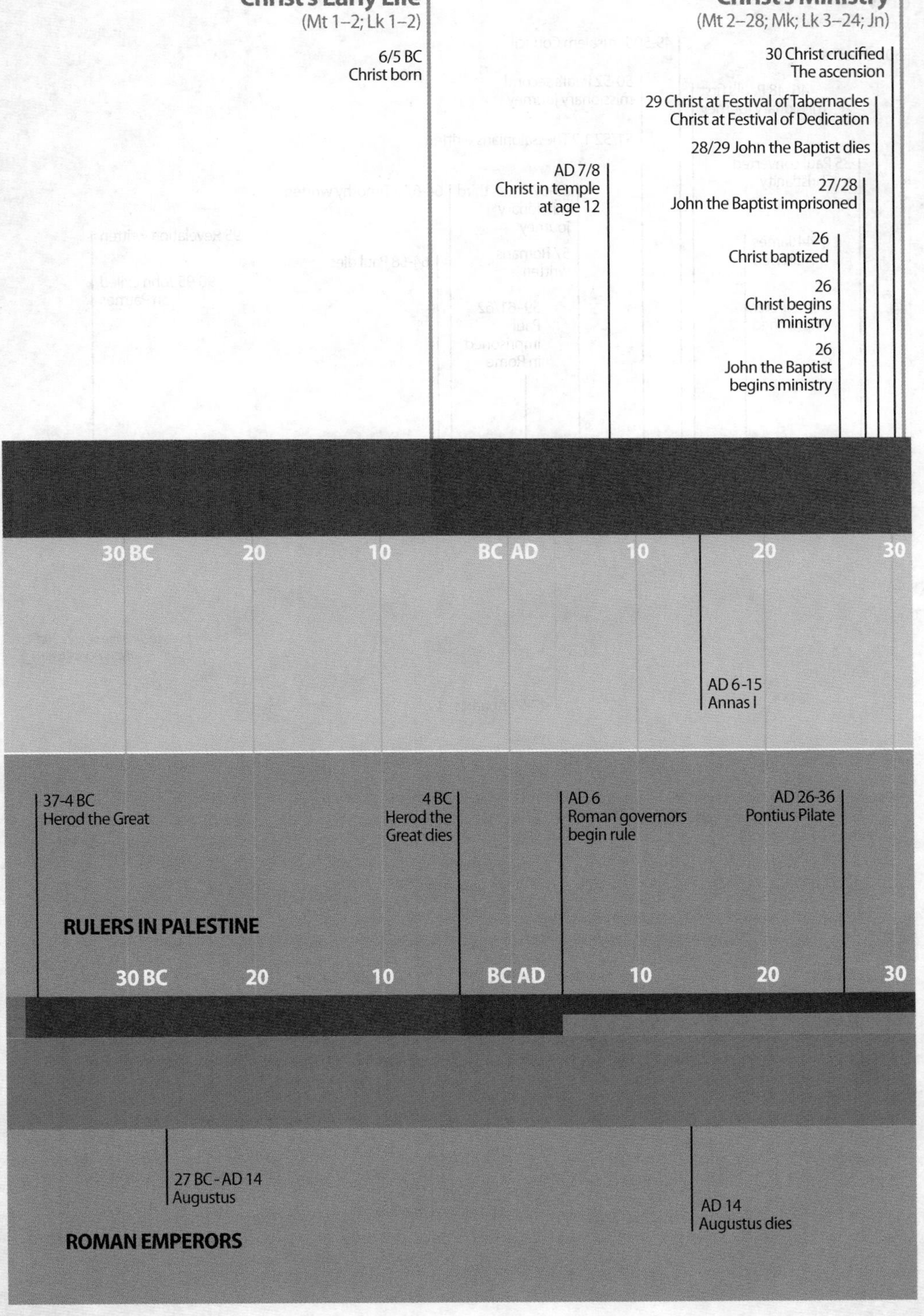

Christ's Early Life
(Mt 1–2; Lk 1–2)
6/5 BC
Christ born
AD 7/8
Christ in temple
at age 12
Christ's Ministry
(Mt 2–28; Mk; Lk 3–24; Jn)
30 Christ crucified
The ascension
29 Christ at Festival of Tabernacles
Christ at Festival of Dedication
28/29 John the Baptist dies
27/28
John the Baptist imprisoned
26
Christ baptized
26
Christ begins
ministry
26
John the Baptist
begins ministry
30 BC
20
10
BC AD
10
20
30
AD 6-15
Annas I
37-4 BC
Herod the Great
4 BC
Herod the
Great dies
AD 6
Roman governors
begin rule
AD 26-36
Pontius Pilate
RULERS IN PALESTINE
30 BC
20
10
BC AD
10
20
30
27 BC - AD 14
Augustus
AD 14
Augustus dies
ROMAN EMPERORS

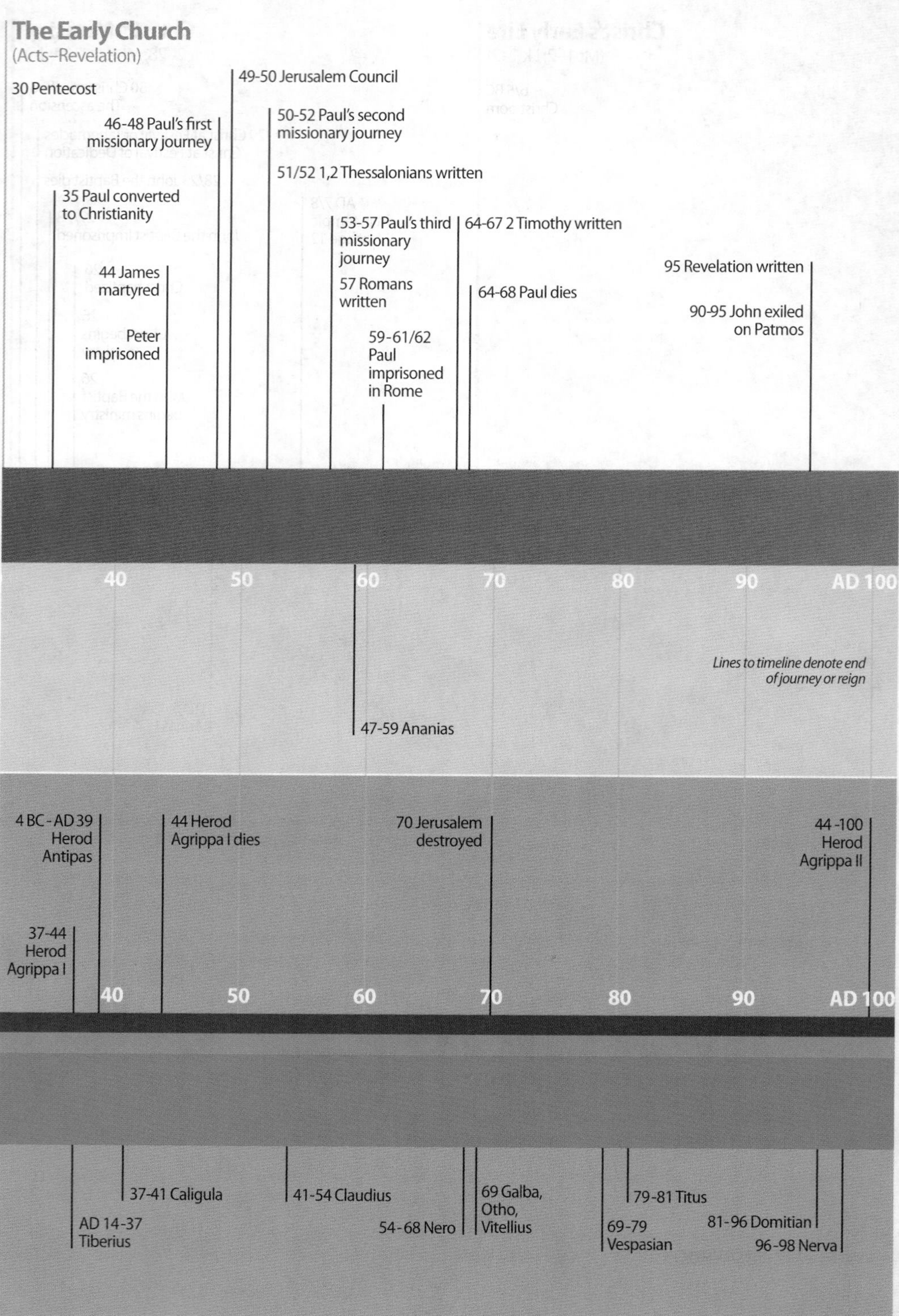
The Early Church
(Acts–Revelation)
30 Pentecost
46-48 Paul's first missionary journey
49-50 Jerusalem Council
50-52 Paul's second missionary journey
51/52 1,2 Thessalonians written
35 Paul converted to Christianity
53-57 Paul's third missionary journey
64-67 2 Timothy written
44 James martyred
95 Revelation written
57 Romans written
64-68 Paul dies
90-95 John exiled on Patmos
Peter imprisoned
59-61/62 Paul imprisoned in Rome
40
50
60
70
80
90
AD 100
Lines to timeline denote end of journey or reign
47-59 Ananias
4 BC - AD 39 Herod Antipas
44 Herod Agrippa I dies
70 Jerusalem destroyed
44 -100 Herod Agrippa II
37-44 Herod Agrippa I
40
50
60
70
80
90
AD 100
37-41 Caligula
41-54 Claudius
69 Galba, Otho, Vitellius
79-81 Titus
AD 14-37 Tiberius
54-68 Nero
69-79 Vespasian
81-96 Domitian
96-98 Nerva

NEW TESTAMENT

NEW TESTAMENT

THE GOSPELS & ACTS

ACCOUNTS OF JESUS AND THE EARLY CHURCH

Hearing the Gospels as First-Century Hearers Heard Them

Bible readers who come to the four accounts of Jesus' life typically have multiple questions about these different works. This essay seeks to address a few of the more pertinent questions that may be raised by readers based on the culturally relevant goals of this study Bible: How would the Gospels' first audience have understood these writings, historically and theologically? How reliable are their sources? Are there any other gospels besides the four in the Bible? How were the Gospels first published? In this essay, we'll examine the principles behind each of these foundational questions in turn.

The Gospels as Ancient Biographies About Jesus

As a category of literature, the Gospels are unique in the sense that they tell us the story of Someone unique. In many respects, however, they follow a form that ancient hearers and readers would have recognized. In the ancient world, a book about a recent historical person was called a *bios*, or in English, a "biography."

Modern readers should keep in mind that ancient biographies differed from typical modern biographies. First, they were shorter than most modern biographies. They varied in length, but could easily be as short as Mark's Gospel or expand to roughly double that length: as long as Matthew or Luke. Second, ancient biographies did not always start with the person's childhood (as in Matthew and Luke), but sometimes opened with a person's public activity or career (as in Mark and, after the prologue, John).

Moreover, whereas modern biographies are usually arranged chronologically, ancient biographers often arranged their material topically. Thus we should not be surprised when, for example, Matthew has some material in a different sequence than do Mark or Luke. That was expected in ancient biography, and the church fathers recognized this point. (Already in the early second century, Papias observed that Mark did not write everything in chronological order.)

Writers often paraphrased material in their own words. Thus, finding slightly different wording in different Gospels (e.g., Matthew's usual "kingdom of heaven" versus Mark's "kingdom of God") should not surprise us. Presumably to increase understanding, Luke even adapts the style of roof mentioned in Mk 2:4 to fit the style of roofs in the northern Mediterranean world where his primary audience lived (Lk 5:19).

Nevertheless, then as today, biographies were a form of *historical* writing. Biographers liked to teach moral lessons through the accounts that they wrote, but like other historians, they did so in a special way that differed from fictional sorts of writing. They could offer lessons, but they were expected to make their points by using genuine information, not by composing fiction. When writing about characters of centuries past, sometimes historians and biographers admitted that some of the information available to them might be merely legendary. When writing about characters of the past two generations, however — within living memory of eyewitnesses — they generally had very substantial information. Comparing such "recent" biographies by different writers concerning the same characters quickly reveals that ancient biographers depended on information, not free imagination, when they wrote their works.

The Point of the Gospels

The Gospels communicate historical information, but this does not mean — as some modern readers have supposed — that the Gospels do not also teach theology. The modern contrast between history and theology misunderstands how history was written in the ancient world.

Ancient historians wrote with a sense of moral responsibility: they communicated the events of the past so that readers in the present could learn positive examples to follow and negative examples to avoid. Both historians and novelists sought to communicate their stories in an engaging way, but only the former sought to do so using genuine information, and only the former normally presented models to imitate. In this period, historians and biographers, rather than novelists, used the facts of history to communicate moral, political or theological ideas or emphases. This is true of the Gospels as well. If we read them only as a matter of historical interest and not to hear what we can learn for our lives today, we miss part of the purpose of the Gospels. At the same time, the Gospels do not merely teach us moral lessons. Most of all they teach us about who Jesus is — a theological message. This characteristic is also consistent with biographies, which were first and foremost about the individuals whose stories they recount.

Above all else, the Gospels are stories about Jesus. Jesus was both hero and Lord to his early followers, and his disciples would have been expected to tell and retell the stories about him as long as they lived. Most of what is significant about most founders of movements — whether Socrates, Muhammad, or Joseph Smith — is preserved by the movements themselves, by those initially most interested in the founders. For Christians, the Gospels are of prime importance, because they help us to know better the one we also honor as our Lord.

The Gospels' Reliable Sources

Ancient tradition reports that two of the Gospels' authors were eyewitnesses of the events: Matthew and the beloved disciple of John 19:35 and 21:24. Early tradition also reports that Mark's Gospel relies heavily on Peter's eyewitness accounts.

Luke more directly tells us about potential sources for gospels in his day. Luke does not claim to be an eyewitness of Jesus' ministry itself, but his work does imply that he traveled with Paul (see note on Ac 16:10) and spent up to two years near him in Judea (Ac 21:17; 24:27; 27:1). This would have given Luke ample time to check into sources such as those he mentions. By the time Luke wrote, "many" had written about Jesus (Lk 1:1), suggesting that written gospel accounts about Jesus were already circulating within the first generation.

Luke also cites oral tradition stemming from eyewitnesses (Lk 1:2). Some readers today, especially in technology-driven cultures, doubt that disciples would have remembered detailed information for decades. Nevertheless, even in Western cultures, many families once passed on family stories orally for generations. Memory skills were no less developed in Mediterranean antiquity. Thus, for example, elementary education throughout the Mediterranean world depended heavily on memorization. Rhetorical students — those preparing for public careers — learned to deliver from memory speeches that could even be two hours in length. Traveling storytellers, often illiterate with regard to written texts, could recite entire books by heart. Thus the disciples' and others' memories could easily have preserved the most striking sayings of and stories about Jesus for the few decades before these accounts began to be preserved in writing.

In the ancient world, the practice of oral memory was most developed among disciples, advanced students of teachers or adherents of schools. Greek philosophic schools passed on the teachers' beliefs from one generation to the next. Students often rehearsed the previous day's lectures so they could repeat back the main points. In Greek schools more generally, students often took notes on their teachers' lectures and sometimes published them for the teachers. Teachers often expected their students to publish their teachings, and teachings of the founder of a school of thought often became foundational for that school's beliefs.

The range of surviving Jewish sources is more limited, but the evidence here points in the same direction as all other surviving evidence from the period. If anything, Jewish disciples were even more meticulous about preserving and passing on the sayings of their teachers than were disciples of Gentile teachers. Moreover, throughout the Roman Empire, not all disciples agreed with everything their teachers taught, but even when they disagreed they would have respectfully represented their teacher accurately. Like other disciples, Jesus' disciples would have told and retold the stories about Jesus, solidifying such accounts both in their memory and in the corporate memory of the early church.

Some scholars who grow up in societies with less-developed memory skills challenge this background, arguing that Jesus' disciples were unlike all the other disciples we read about in the same period; these scholars protest that the disciples were uneducated and illiterate. Against this premise several observations may be offered. First, texts about the disciples being "unlearned" merely mean that they lacked the training available to the elite, not that they lacked all training. Fishermen made a better living, and probably had somewhat better education, than the majority of people in Galilee (most people were peasants). Second, in many cultures memory skills are inversely proportional to literacy — that is, sometimes people who are illiterate have even stronger memories because they cannot simply refer to other sources if they forget them. Finally, ancient sources are clear that memory skills were *not* limited to the highly educated. Traveling bards who recited all of Homer's poetry by heart were generally not educated, yet few scholars in the modern West could compare with them in their capacity to memorize. This observation also holds true today; in some places even those who are illiterate can, for example, recite large sections of the Qur'an or other writings from memory.

The Gospel writers had a variety of memories, oral sources and written works on which they could draw. Normally memories and oral traditions remain most accurate in the first generation or two, within living memory of eyewitnesses who can communicate and confirm events. In antiquity, as today, writers of histories and biographies would consult eyewitnesses first and foremost. Throughout the first generation, when information about Jesus was becoming widespread, Jesus' original disciples plus his brother James remained in positions of leadership in the church (Gal 1:18 – 19; 2:9; cf. 1Co 15:5 – 7). By the time Luke wrote, he could see his purpose as merely confirming information that was already widely known (Lk 1:3 – 4).

Some scholars protest that some lines of evidence for the accuracy of oral tradition come from only limited circles. Yet almost *any* claim about evidence we can identify from antiquity is limited; only a sample of sources have survived. The evidence we do have for accurate tradition, however, is undoubtedly a representative sample. It is widespread among varied settings and virtually all points in the same direction. No responsible scholar would dismiss virtually all the contemporary evidence we do have and then argue the opposite conclusion based on silence.

Jesus' Teachings

Various ancient Jewish sages had their own distinctive teaching traits, but other forms of teaching were common among them. They commonly taught in parables very similar to those of Jesus (see the article "Parables," p. 1692); they used riddles to provoke thought; they used proverbs that often made a particular point without covering all possible exceptions or circumstances (cf. Pr 26:4 – 5); and they often used graphic hyperbole (rhetorical overstatement) to reinforce their points. Although Jesus often used the teaching techniques that were common in his day, other traits are distinctive to him, such as the phrase "*truly* I say to you." Most distinctive, of course, are passages where Jesus hints at his deity (e.g., Mt 18:20; Jn 8:58).

Because Jesus addressed especially crowds of poor Galilean farmers as he traveled from place to place, his teachings are not systematic; instead, they are often meant to provoke thought and make a point, sometimes in a graphic way that holds an audience's attention. For a modern reader to directly convert Jesus' words into rules or statements of systematic theology therefore sometimes misses their point. For example, Jesus requires caring for parents in their old age (Mk 7:9 – 13), but summons people to abandon their family responsibilities if need be to follow him (Mt 8:21 – 22 parallel to Lk 9:59 – 62; Mt 10:37 parallel to Lk 14:26). Is Jesus pro-family, or is he a home-wrecker? In fact, Jesus should come before everything else, but "hating" one's family (Lk 14:26) is *hyperbole*, merely a graphic way of making his point.

Hyperbole is common in Jesus' teaching. We recognize it in the most obvious cases: for example, ripping out one's eye as a solution to lust (Mt 5:28 – 29), swallowing a camel whole (Mt 23:24), or squeezing a camel through a needle's eye (Mk 10:25). Some suggest that it would be consistent to view some other sayings in the same way — for example, giving up one's only cloak (Mt 5:40

parallel to Lk 6:29) or treating all remarriage as adultery (Mk 10:11 – 12, the literal point being found in 10:9). Such observations and cautions are very important, but we should also be careful not to miss the *purpose* of hyperbole: to graphically underline the point being made. Thus, for example, we should not downplay Jesus' commands to give all to those in need (Mk 10:21; Lk 12:33; 14:33). Even if we do not all relinquish literally all our possessions to follow Jesus (cf. Mt 27:57; Lk 10:38; Ac 2:44 – 45; 12:12 – 13), we surrender our *ownership* of them. If Jesus is genuinely Lord of our lives, then he is Lord also of our possessions, and we must use them as wisely and as generously as he would desire. Likewise, even if we believe that treating all remarriage as adultery may go too far (Mt 5:32, 19:19), we must work hard to preserve and nurture marriages, viewing as sacred what God has joined together.

Understanding how Jesus spoke can help us understand how best to obey and apply his teachings today.

Miracle Stories

In the West, skepticism about the Gospels started especially because some Western philosophers had pronounced miracles impossible. For such scholars, the Gospels were not trustworthy because they included miracle accounts; one nineteenth-century scholar, David Strauss, thus regarded the Gospels as late and their miracle accounts as legends and myths. Strauss did so because of his philosophic assumptions, not because of evidence: in fact, one of his own friends was healed when a German Lutheran pastor prayed for him.

Historically, the argument against the Gospels' miracle reports followed this logic: miracles are not believable because respectable eyewitnesses (those known to the upper-class, elite people who made this argument) do not report them happening. Therefore if some *otherwise* reputable eyewitnesses do claim miracles happening, they are not to be believed. This is, of course, a circular argument, but it influenced many scholars who were or became skeptics in reference to the Bible. They assumed that miracle reports cannot come from eyewitnesses, because miracles cannot happen. Therefore, in their view, any reports of significant miracles do not reflect early testimony, but rather a process of legendary growth over generations (or at least decades).

Today, however, one can easily demonstrate that these assumptions about eyewitnesses are false, even in the West. Worldwide, literally hundreds of millions of people, from a wide range of denominations and church traditions, claim to have witnessed or experienced divine healing. Sources in China attribute to healing experiences millions of new Christian conversions over the course of two decades. In a survey conducted several decades ago in one large city in India, more than 10 percent of *non*-Christians claimed to have been cured when Christians prayed for them in Jesus' name.

The sorts of miracles reported by eyewitnesses today include the same range as in the Gospels. A skeptic may find other explanations for many of the cures, but it is simply impossible empirically to deny that eyewitnesses otherwise known to be reliable do claim the sorts of cures reported in the Gospels. In other words, the miracle accounts in the Gospels can reflect information from eyewitnesses, exactly as can any of the other accounts in the Gospels.

How would ancient hearers have learned from the miracle stories in the Gospels? Presumably they would have learned from them the way that ancients believed they learned from accounts of cures in Greek temples, or the way that Christians in many cultures hear the Gospels' miracle stories today: they would have experienced these accounts as invitations to faith in the power and love of Jesus, whom we as Christians believe has risen and remains alive and active today.

Lost "Gospels"?

Many people today speculate about the influence of "lost Gospels." Although this is mostly sensationalism, some early accounts of Jesus' life were undoubtedly lost. Luke mentions that "many" wrote accounts about Jesus before Luke did, but the majority of scholars believe that only one of these that he has in mind (Mark) survived intact. A majority of scholars also believe that Matthew and Luke drew on another shared source that often follows the same sequence present in these two Gospels; this document has not survived and is reconstructed merely based on where Matthew and Luke overlap. Some scholars believe that this lost document was an early collection by Matthew, focusing especially on sayings, used by Mark, Luke, and our current version of Matthew's Gospel (which incorporates also most of Mark's narrative). Other scholars reconstruct differently the sequence in which our Gospels were written, but the point remains: most of Luke's "many" sources did not survive.

Some later works have also been sometimes called gospels. Unlike the four Gospels preserved in the Bible, however, these other works date to a later timeframe for writing, no longer within living memory of the eyewitnesses. The earliest of them, often referred to as the "Gospel of Thomas," is usually dated more than 100 years after Jesus's death and resurrection and some 70 years after Mark's Gospel. (Some scholars date it even later, to 100 years after Mark.) Of all the later gospels, Thomas is the earliest and the likeliest to contain some sayings about Jesus, but scholars have not agreed on any way to discover which sayings, if any, are authentic (besides the ones already recorded in our first-century Gospels).

Thomas is usually classified as belonging to the group called "gnostic gospels," although later ones are generally far more gnostic than Thomas. These works are not really "gospels" at all, for they are not narratives about Jesus. (Comparing them with the canonical Gospels, then, is like comparing apples and oranges; they are completely different categories.) The "gnostic gospels" are usually collections of sayings that their authors claim were passed on "secretly." As most ancient Christians recognized, those who had to claim information passed on "secretly" were admitting that they had no real evidence that any of the information went back to anyone who knew Jesus. Moreover, the amorphous group of beliefs we define as Gnosticism, and thus clearly gnostic elements, do not clearly predate the second century; these works are all much later — many of them many *centuries* later. Mostly they were accepted as authoritative only in their own, small gnostic groups. In the wider church's canon lists over the next few centuries, none of them appear, with only a single exception (one reference to Thomas), whereas the canonical Gospels always appear.

Other late "gospels" are called "apocryphal gospels." These works come from the heyday of novels, in the late second and early third centuries (with many written later still). They are entertaining and sometimes edifying novels. They are not, however, true accounts about Jesus. Whereas the first-century Gospels assume ancient Galilean customs, Jewish figures of speech, and the like, these later gospels betray their own time period. Apocryphal gospels and acts contain stories of talking dogs, walking crosses, obedient bed bugs and the like; in one of them Jesus strikes dead a boy who offends him and strikes blind the boy's parents for complaining. Some ancient Christians read them, but the churches never viewed them as Scripture.

Only Matthew, Mark, Luke and John survive from the first century. Unlike the other works, they include abundant Judean and Galilean traits. By the late second century, mainstream churches from one end of the Roman Empire to the other accepted these four, and only these four, Gospels as genuine apostolic memories of Jesus. If one wishes to learn more about Jesus than what one reads in the surviving first-century Gospels, later fictions are not the best place to start. One would do better to read works that genuinely shed light on Jesus' milieu, even if they do not talk about Jesus himself. These would include, for example, collections of Jewish ideas circulating in Jesus' day, such as the book of Sirach, probably 1 Enoch, or undisputed Biblical works that are actually cited in the Gospels such as Deuteronomy, Psalms, Isaiah and Daniel.

How the Gospels First Circulated

The ancient world was vastly different from our modern world of printing presses, copy machines and electronic publishing. Most books were copied by hand, one at a time, although very popular books could be dictated to multiple scribes at once. Books were normally written on scrolls in the first century, though in the second century Christians appear to be among the first adopters (or possibly innovators) of the sort of bound volumes we use for hard-copy books today. Christians found useful this bound version, called a codex, because it allowed for more material to be included in one volume without making it too cumbersome.

Writing material was expensive; for example, a copy of the Gospel of Mark may have required the equivalent early twenty-first-century buying power of $1000 – $2000 U.S. Most people thus could not own their own copies of books. In fact, most would not have needed these copies anyway, since most people were either illiterate or only semiliterate. Although inscriptions were posted in cities with the assumption that many people could understand at least some writing, illiteracy was high. It was highest among women (due to the practices of ancient education) and in rural areas, but even many urban-dwelling men could not read, especially a work as long and detailed as a Gospel.

Most people thus *heard* the Gospels rather than *read* them for themselves. (That is why this study Bible's notes usually speak of the Gospels' first *audience* or hearers rather than their first readers.) They might hear an entire Gospel read during a church meeting, which was typically an intimate gathering in the home of one of the believers. Because many were accustomed to listening intently to stories or speeches, they would be able to follow the stories carefully. Hearing the accounts over and over, they would quickly learn much of the material by heart. Additionally, most people could not unroll multiple scrolls trying to find related passages; rather, they often quoted from memory from many different Biblical books.

Some books in antiquity were sold in book markets, but books achieved their greatest circulation when given public readings or especially when read at banquets. Persons of means who liked a book they heard could have a scribe write out a new copy for them. Because early Christians met around the Lord's Supper, they also had a banquet setting for the reading of the Gospels. The most familiar form of public reading for them, however, would have been the use of Scripture in the synagogues. Already in the second century, Christians read apostolic works as Scripture alongside the Old Testament.

Authorship of the Gospels

By the standards used to evaluate ancient works' authorship, the traditions of the Gospels' authorship are very early. This is not surprising, given the amount of work represented by each of the Gospels. Works such as the Gospels normally would require careful writing and revision, then oral presentation and further revision based on feedback.

Works as large as these were major literary undertakings, requiring so much papyrus that in terms of early twenty-first-century buying power the larger Gospels may have been worth thousands of U.S. dollars, as suggested earlier. They were not as large as elite, multivolume historical works, but were nevertheless larger works than the vast majority of people could hope to afford.

Normally in antiquity readers knew who produced such major works, whether by information on the outside of the scroll or by knowledge circulated only by word of mouth. In a work this size, authorship would be one of the last details forgotten.

Moreover, had the church in fact forgotten the authorship of the Gospels, the traditions about their authorship would likely look very different. Second-century churches in different parts of the Roman Empire would likely have come up with different speculations about authorship, probably often preferring the names of apostles favored by their own locales. Instead, the early churches throughout the Empire settled on the same authors for the Gospels (Matthew, Mark, Luke and John). Moreover, if the church were inventing names for authors, non-apostles such as Mark and Luke make little sense.

These observations suggest that the traditions about the different Gospels' authorship are very early, as Martin Hengel argued. These traditions may offer more compelling evidence for some Gospels (such as Luke) than for others (such as Matthew), but on the whole they are stronger than many critics recognize. For Christians, of course, what matters most is not the tradition of human authorship, but our confidence that God speaks to us through these texts, and that they preserve the voice of our Lord Jesus Christ. ◆

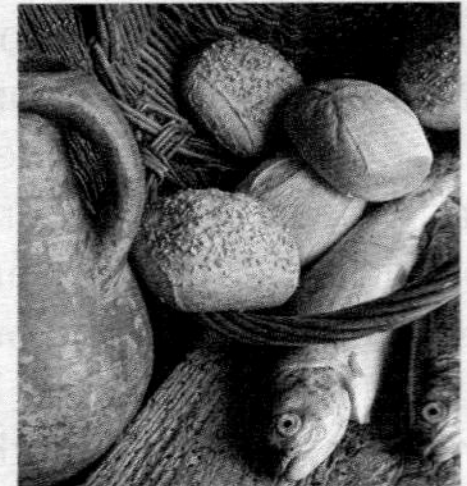

THE GOSPEL OF MATTHEW

Matthew's Position Among the Gospels

As a Gospel, Matthew is an ancient biography, and the information treated in the introduction to the Gospels in general also applies to Matthew. But just as other ancient biographies differed from one another even when they described the same person, so do the four Gospels. Of the four Gospels, Matthew is the most carefully arranged by topic and therefore lends itself most easily to a hierarchical outline. Along with John, Matthew is also an emphatically Jewish Gospel; Matthew moves in a thought world resembling that of the emerging rabbinic movement (the circle of Jewish sages and law-teachers) more than do the other Synoptic Gospels. (Our sources for rabbinic Judaism are later than the NT, but later rabbis avoided early Christian writings, so the frequent parallels — sometimes even in sayings and expressions, for which see, e.g., Mt 7:2; 18:20; 19:3, 24; 21:21; 22:2; 23:25 — presumably stem from concepts, customs and figures of speech already circulating among sages in the first century.)

QUICK GLANCE

AUTHOR:
Matthew, also called Levi

AUDIENCE:
Greek-speaking Jewish Christians

DATE:
Between AD 50 and 90, perhaps in the 70s

THEME:
Matthew presents Jesus as the Jewish Messiah sent by God to fulfill OT prophecy.

Authorship

As noted above, the traditions of the Gospels' authorship are very early. Works as large as Matthew's Gospel were major literary undertakings. As suggested for the Gospels generally, in a work this size, authorship would be one of the last matters forgotten. That observation would surely be particularly relevant for Matthew's Gospel, which seems to have enjoyed popularity right from the start. Matthew was the early second-century church's favorite and most-cited Gospel.

Some raise questions about the ancient tradition in the case of Matthew. One reason for these questions is that the earliest tradition about Matthew's Gospel (from a very early second-century church father named Papias) is that he wrote in Hebrew and that other Gospels, probably including Mark, drew on this work. Most scholars agree that our current Gospel of Matthew was not written in Hebrew, nor does it appear to be mostly translated from Hebrew. Most scholars, moreover, believe that our current Gospel of Matthew makes use of Mark's Gospel, casting doubt on Papias's apparent suggestion that Matthew wrote first (although it is possible to interpret Papias differently).

If Papias was wrong about some details, why should we trust him on others? This is a legitimate concern. Nevertheless, some other factors may mitigate the concern. First, some scholars believe that even if Papias does not properly describe our current Gospel of Matthew, he preserves some genuine information; possibly Matthew wrote a collection of Jesus' sayings (fitting the meaning of Papias's word here) in Hebrew or Aramaic, on which others (including Matthew's later Gospel in Greek) drew. Second, people are usually more apt to be correct about the simple fact of a document's authorship than about the circumstances of its writing. So even if Papias was partly or largely wrong, if he knew anything at all about these works written just a generation before him, he likely knew about their authorship.

Another objection that some raise against the traditional belief that Matthew wrote this Gospel is that Matthew, who was one of Jesus' disciples (9:9; 10:3; Mk 3:18), would not need to depend on Mark's Gospel, since Matthew was an eyewitness of most of Jesus' public ministry. Ancient approaches to eyewitness sources differed somewhat from modern approaches, however. Thus when the historian Xenophon writes an account of events in which he participated, he nevertheless depends heavily on an earlier-published work by another author, because the other work was already in wide circulation. By the same token, Matthew could have been an eyewitness and nevertheless used Mark because its wide circulation (or its association with Peter) made it a standard work. None of this proves that Matthew wrote this Gospel. It does, however, call into question the conviction with which some scholars dismiss that early tradition.

Provenance and Date

There is no consensus and no certain means of resolving Matthew's precise setting or date. Some general considerations may be relevant. Because Matthew, more than any other NT document, addresses Jewish concepts closely paralleled in the emerging rabbinic movement, the common scholarly view that he wrote from the Roman province of Syria (which included Judea and Galilee) makes good sense. Some scholars also find similarities between Matthew and other documents from early Syrian Christianity.

Because Matthew wrote in Greek, which dominated in Syria's urban centers, rather than Aramaic, which dominated in rural areas, Matthew's core audience might have been located in an urban setting. Many scholars thus suggest that Matthew writes especially for Antioch in Syria. Antioch had a large Jewish community, one of the few Jewish communities not devastated by the Judean war; it also was an early Christian center of mission to Gentiles (Ac 11:20; 13:1 – 3; Gal 2:11 – 12).

Ultimately, what we can be sure of is that Matthew wrote especially to Jewish believers in Jesus in the eastern Mediterranean world. Whatever specific "core" audience he may have envisioned, as the author of a major literary work Matthew probably hoped that his Gospel would circulate as widely as possible.

Matthew's date is also a matter of much debate. If Matthew was the first Gospel writer, he probably wrote before Jerusalem's destruction in AD 70. A larger number of scholars, however, believe that Matthew made use of Mark's Gospel, and many thus date Matthew after 70. On this view, it is not surprising that Matthew must urge his Jewish Christian audience to bring the message of the kingdom to Gentiles — many Jewish followers of Jesus at that time would have felt little love for the people who destroyed their holy city and enslaved many of their people. Nevertheless, even before 70, tensions were building toward that climax, so a similar background could be relevant on either dating.

A majority of scholars think that Matthew writes after 70 also because of allusions to the destruction of the temple and the holy city. In possible contrast to Mark's more ambiguous relationship between Jesus' warning of the temple's destruction and the promise of his return, Matthew seems to distinguish the two events (compare 24:2 – 3 with Mk 13:2 – 4). (Some also point to Mt 22:7.) Such features could well suggest a post-70 date. Nevertheless, it seems clear from the earliest sources (including some shared by and thus earlier than Matthew and Luke) that Jesus himself did predict impending judgment on the temple (23:38; Mk 13:2,14; Lk 13:35; cf. Mk 11:15 – 17).

In the end, the specific question of date may be a moot point. (Indeed, some scholars think that Matthew and/or his assistants expanded the Gospel in subsequent editions at different times.) Because the Gospels are primarily concerned with events that have already occurred in the past, the time they describe is more crucial than the time in which they wrote, although the latter is helpful for considering why the different writers emphasized some particular themes.

Background

Only rarely can scholars studying ancient documents pinpoint precise dates for those documents. One does not need to know exact dates or locations to reconstruct the general setting of such works, however.

As will be clear from the following study notes on Matthew's Gospel, Matthew addresses an audience comfortable with traditional Jewish forms of speech. For example, one need only compare Mark's pervasive "kingdom of God" with Matthew's usual "kingdom of heaven" to see that Matthew prefers traditional (and emphatically) Jewish formulations.

Because Jewish thinking took many forms in different parts of the ancient world, it is valuable to be more precise in this case. Whereas Jewish people who liked apocalyptic literature would particularly appreciate Revelation, Jews in the Diaspora would appreciate Hebrews, and groups such as the Essenes might appreciate John's Gospel, Matthew often moves in a more "rabbinic" world. That is, the views and arguments of teachers and interpreters of the law, who came to be called rabbis, are very relevant to Matthew's Gospel. Most of the sources from which we know rabbinic thought are later, but they offer numerous parallels to Matthew's ways of handling Scripture and intimate understanding of Pharisaic debates with Jesus (e.g., see notes on 19:3; 23:25 – 26). Because Jesus was himself a sage and engaged in discussion, and often debate, with Pharisaic teachers, Matthew continues to engage a world within which Jesus himself moved. ◆

The Genealogy of Jesus the Messiah

1:1-17pp — Lk 3:23-38
1:3-6pp — Ru 4:18-22
1:7-11pp — 1Ch 3:10-17

1 This is the genealogy[a] of Jesus the Messiah[b] the son of David,[a] the son of Abraham:[b]

2 Abraham was the father of Isaac,[c]
Isaac the father of Jacob,[d]
Jacob the father of Judah and his brothers,[e]
3 Judah the father of Perez and Zerah, whose mother was Tamar,[f]
Perez the father of Hezron,
Hezron the father of Ram,
4 Ram the father of Amminadab,
Amminadab the father of Nahshon,
Nahshon the father of Salmon,
5 Salmon the father of Boaz, whose mother was Rahab,
Boaz the father of Obed, whose mother was Ruth,
Obed the father of Jesse,
6 and Jesse the father of King David.[g]

David was the father of Solomon, whose mother had been Uriah's wife,[h]
7 Solomon the father of Rehoboam,
Rehoboam the father of Abijah,
Abijah the father of Asa,
8 Asa the father of Jehoshaphat,
Jehoshaphat the father of Jehoram,
Jehoram the father of Uzziah,
9 Uzziah the father of Jotham,
Jotham the father of Ahaz,
Ahaz the father of Hezekiah,
10 Hezekiah the father of Manasseh,[i]
Manasseh the father of Amon,
Amon the father of Josiah,
11 and Josiah the father of Jeconiah[c] and his brothers at the time of the exile to Babylon.[j]

12 After the exile to Babylon:
Jeconiah was the father of Shealtiel,[k]
Shealtiel the father of Zerubbabel,[l]
13 Zerubbabel the father of Abihud,
Abihud the father of Eliakim,
Eliakim the father of Azor,
14 Azor the father of Zadok,
Zadok the father of Akim,
Akim the father of Elihud,

1:1 [a] 2Sa 7:12-16; Isa 9:6,7; 11:1; Jer 23:5,6; Mt 9:27; Lk 1:32,69; Ro 1:3; Rev 22:16 [b] Ge 22:18; Gal 3:16 **1:2** [c] Ge 21:3,12 [d] Ge 25:26 [e] Ge 29:35 **1:3** [f] Ge 38:27-30 **1:6** [g] 1Sa 16:1; 17:12 [h] 2Sa 12:24 **1:10** [i] 2Ki 20:21 **1:11** [j] 2Ki 24:14-16; Jer 27:20; Da 1:1,2 **1:12** [k] 1Ch 3:17 [l] 1Ch 3:19; Ezr 3:2

[a] *1* Or *is an account of the origin* [b] *1* Or *Jesus Christ. Messiah* (Hebrew) and *Christ* (Greek) both mean *Anointed One*; also in verse 18. [c] *11* That is, Jehoiachin; also in verse 12

1:1 *genealogy of Jesus.* "The book of the genealogy" here uses the exact Greek phrase found in the Greek translation of Ge 5:1, including the Greek word from which we get our name for the book "Genesis." Similar phrases appear with other genealogies in Genesis. The phrase in Matthew functions differently, however. In Genesis, the phrase is followed by a list of the person's descendants, who depend on their ancestor for their meaning. Matthew, by contrast, lists not Jesus' descendants but his *ancestors.* Jesus is so pivotal for Israel's history that even his ancestors depend on him for their purpose and meaning.

When Jewish people spoke of the "son of David" they usually thought of David's descendant *par excellence*, the Messiah (i.e., the Davidic king; cf. 22:42). Jesus is thus the fulfillment of God's promise to raise up a king from David's line. Although Ishmaelites and others also claimed descent from Abraham, Jewish people customarily applied the title "children of Abraham" to Jewish people in particular. Matthew presents Jesus as both Israel's rightful ruler and as one identified fully with his people. Many scholars find this identification with Jesus' people's heritage also in 2:15,18; 4:1 – 11 (see applicable notes there).

1:2 *Abraham … Isaac … Jacob.* For the births of Isaac, Jacob, and Jacob's sons, see Ge 21 – 30; 35:18.

1:3 *Tamar.* Ancient genealogies often omitted women. Jewish hearers would have expected that if Matthew included any women, he would have chosen some of the famous matriarchs: Sarah, Rebekah, Leah and (outside Judah's line here) Rachel. Instead he includes four women with Gentile associations. In Ge 38, Tamar was likely a Canaanite; she had married into Judah's family but tragedy prevented her from bearing an heir in Judah's line. Unable to secure a brother-in-law to fulfill the levirate custom of providing her husband an heir through her, she deceived Judah himself into doing it. Judah, who had helped sell his brother Joseph into slavery (Ge 37:26 – 27), is confronted with his own sinfulness (Ge 38:26) and changes (Ge 44:33 – 34).

1:5 *Rahab.* Because Rahab joined Israel, it was natural for her to marry into Israel. Though not an Israelite, she hid Israel's spies on her roof, betrayed Jericho and saved her family; she contrasts with Achan of Judah, who hid loot under his tent, betrayed Israel and destroyed his family (Jos 2:1 – 21; 6:23 – 25; 7:1 – 26). Already in the book of Joshua, then, God used Rahab to show that he valued loyalty to his covenant more than ethnic background. *Ruth.* Normally Moabites were not allowed to become Israelites (Dt 23:3), but God welcomed Ruth because she followed him (Ru 1:16), and she became an ancestor of King David.

1:6 *Uriah's wife.* Matthew calls Solomon's mother not by her name (Bathsheba) but the woman who "had been Uriah's wife," his widow. Bathsheba may have been from Judah (compare her father's name in 2Sa 11:3 with 2Sa 23:34), but she had married into a Hittite family (2Sa 11:3). Thus each of the four women in Matthew's genealogy (vv. 3 – 6) is somehow closely associated with Gentiles.

1:7 – 11 The list of David's royal descendants summarizes the history of Judah until the exile (the material covered in 1 – 2 Kings and 2 Chronicles). By slight changes in orthography (used by other Jewish teachers to make theological points), Matthew evokes other elements of Israel's history as well (the Psalms and the Prophets). In his Greek text, "Asa" (vv. 7 – 8) is literally "Asaph," the name of a leader of Israel's worship (1Ch 16:5,7,37; 25:1 – 6; the superscriptions of Ps 50; 73 – 83). Likewise, in the Greek Matthew changes the name of the wicked king Amon to the name of the prophet Amos (v. 10).

1:12 *Jeconiah.* Although God judged Jeconiah (Jer 22:24,28; 24:1 ["Jehoiachin" in these vv.]), God restored his descendant Zerubbabel to leadership (e.g., Ezr 3:8; Hag 2:2,23).

1:13 – 16 Israelite genealogies could skip generations; thus Matthew lists only 11 generations from the exile before Joseph, whereas Luke lists about 20.

[15] Elihud the father of Eleazar,
Eleazar the father of Matthan,
Matthan the father of Jacob,
[16] and Jacob the father of Joseph, the
husband of Mary,[m] and Mary
was the mother of Jesus who is
called the Messiah.[n]

[17] Thus there were fourteen generations
in all from Abraham to David, fourteen

1:16 [m] Lk 1:27 [n] Mt 27:17

1:17 *fourteen generations.* Even though Matthew skips some generations, the three sets of names he has listed in this verse do not come out to exactly the same number each. Matthew is giving a rounded number, showing that at roughly equivalent intervals in Israel's history, something dramatic happened. These focal times of conspicuous divine activity surround Abraham, David, the exile, and now the coming of the Messiah, son of David (see

MATTHEW 1:1 – 17

Matthew's Genealogy

People often preserved genealogies, especially if they included some important or prominent ancestors. In Egypt, e.g., genealogies were important for determining tax status, so there were sometimes financial implications of not preserving the list of one's ancestors correctly! Among the Jewish people, priests and Levites could perform their duties only if they could demonstrate their ancestry. But no Jewish family ancestry could be more prominent than the Davidic royal line. Although Matthew's and Luke's genealogies trace Jesus' royal ancestry on Joseph's side of the family through somewhat different paths (which some attribute to levirate marriage adoptions), both emphasize that, many centuries earlier, Jesus' line proceeded from King David (cf. Ro 1:3; Rev 5:5).

Ancient Jewish genealogies had several purposes. One was often to highlight the purity of one's Israelite (or Levite, etc.) ancestry. It is thus striking that Matthew includes in his genealogy four women who had clear associations with Gentiles (see notes on Mt 1:3,5,6). These women include three ancestors of King David and the mother of King Solomon; Matthew thus highlights God's welcome for God-fearing Gentiles already in his opening paragraph, based on Israel's history.

Another purpose of *Biblical* genealogies was to provide a connection between significant generations. Genesis does not narrate the activities of every generation between Adam and Noah or between Noah and Abraham. Rather, Genesis focuses on those major figures and summarizes the time between them by listing others (see note on Mt 1:1). In the same way, Matthew lists many generations, here in schematic groups of roughly 14 each, connecting the most momentous occasions in Israel's history: Abraham, David, the exile and now the Messiah (see note on Mt 1:17).

Jewish teachers observed that one's ancestry showed God's faithfulness; some remarked that arranging all the marriages in people's ancestry was a greater miracle than the parting of the sea in Moses' day. Matthew's genealogy sets the tone of this Gospel by evoking the Biblical history of Israel. Jewish recipients familiar with Scripture would hear the names of most of these ancestors with rich nuances of how God had guided his people's history. Far from being foreign to their heritage, Jesus was its climax.

Although the genealogy does not quote Scripture, it evokes the entire Biblical narrative of Israel's history. Ancient rabbis sometimes developed wordplays by changing a letter here or there, and some scholars find such wordplays in Matthew's genealogy. In addition to Jesus being the direct heir of the royal line of David, he is the spiritual heir to the Psalms and the Prophets. Thus, these scholars note, the Greek text of Matthew's genealogy speaks of not precisely "Asa" but the psalmist Asaph (Mt 1:8) and not precisely the wicked king "Amon" but the prophet Amos (Mt 1:10). ◆

from David to the exile to Babylon, and
fourteen from the exile to the Messiah.

Joseph Accepts Jesus as His Son

18This is how the birth of Jesus the Messiah came about[a]: His mother Mary was
pledged to be married to Joseph, but before they came together, she was found to
be pregnant through the Holy Spirit.[o] 19Be-
cause Joseph her husband was faithful to
the law, and yet[b] did not want to expose
her to public disgrace, he had in mind to
divorce[p] her quietly.
20But after he had considered this, an
angel of the Lord appeared to him in a
dream and said, "Joseph son of David, do
not be afraid to take Mary home as your
wife, because what is conceived in her is
from the Holy Spirit. 21She will give birth
to a son, and you are to give him the name
Jesus,[c][q] because he will save his people
from their sins."[r]
22All this took place to fulfill what the
Lord had said through the prophet: 23"The
virgin will conceive and give birth to a
son, and they will call him Immanuel"[d][s]
(which means "God with us").
24When Joseph woke up, he did what
the angel of the Lord had commanded him
and took Mary home as his wife. 25But he
did not consummate their marriage until
she gave birth to a son. And he gave him
the name Jesus.[t]

1:18 [o] Lk 1:35
1:19 [p] Dt 24:1
1:21 [q] Lk 1:31 [r] Lk 2:11; Ac 5:31; 13:23, 28
1:23 [s] Isa 7:14; 8:8, 10
1:25 [t] ver 21

[a] *18* Or *The origin of Jesus the Messiah was like this*
[b] *19* Or *was a righteous man and*
[c] *21* *Jesus* is the Greek form of *Joshua,* which means *the LORD saves.*
[d] *23* Isaiah 7:14

note on v. 1). Some scholars point out that when "David" is spelled in Hebrew letters and calculated as numbers (Hebrew used letters also as numbers), it comes out to 14. Some other scholars attribute this to coincidence.

1:18 *before they came together.* Whenever possible, biographers of important figures reported the figures' honorable ancestry, honorable behavior of their parents, or special circumstances surrounding their birth. Those who compare Jesus' virgin birth to Greek stories about gods impregnating women, however, appeal to a milieu quite foreign to this account. In the Greek stories, the gods are many, are immoral, and impregnate women who are thus not virgins. Much more relevant are Biblical accounts of God empowering supernatural births in the OT (Ge 21:1 – 2; 25:21; 30:22; Jdg 13:3). Even among miraculous births, however, God does something new: Jesus is born not merely from someone previously unable to bear, but from a virgin.

Greek men, on average, were more than ten years older than their brides, because Greeks had a shortage of marriageable women (sources suggest that girl babies were discarded more often than boys). Jewish men, however, were usually only a few years older than their wives; both genders assumed some adult responsibilities at puberty, but men would often work a few years so they could provide financial stability for marriage. Betrothal involved a financial agreement between families. It often lasted about a year; in conservative Galilean families the couple could not be together alone before the wedding, so Joseph may not have known Mary very well.

1:19 *divorce her quietly.* More binding than modern Western engagements, betrothal could be ended only by divorce or by the death of one of the partners. Sexual unfaithfulness was grounds for divorce throughout the ancient world; both law and custom in fact required a man to divorce an unfaithful wife or fiancée. (Romans did not allow subject peoples to execute convicted persons without Roman permission in this period; although some lynchings may have occurred in secret, they were rare, so Mary likely faced divorce rather than death [see Lev 20:10].) A Jewish man who divorced a faithful wife had to refund the money she brought into the marriage (normally a gift from her father). In the case of an unfaithful wife, however, the husband could keep this money, plus he was entitled to a refund of any money he may have paid the father as a bride price. (Paying the father was the traditional Israelite custom; the father giving his daughter a monetary gift was a more recent but now widespread custom.) Joseph might thus have profited financially by divorcing Mary in front of elders, in a court setting. Instead, sensitive to her shame, he prefers a private divorce. A private divorce meant giving her a certificate of divorce, which would specify her freedom to marry someone else, in front of two or three witnesses.

1:20 *angel.* The angel of the Lord sometimes announced births (Ge 16:10; Jdg 13:3) and other events (e.g., Ge 22:15 – 18). This angel appears to Joseph especially in dreams (here; 2:13,19), a common way that God speaks in Scripture (e.g., Ge 20:3; 31:24; 1Ki 3:5), sometimes by his angel (Ge 31:11; cf. Ge 28:12). The first Joseph heard God through dreams (Ge 37:5,9). As here, divine messages often encouraged people not to fear (e.g., Ge 15:1; 21:17; 26:24; 46:3). Greeks often reported dreams about deceased persons, but in Biblical dreams God or angels are the most common speakers.

1:21 Biblical birth announcements sometimes included these elements: a woman "will bear a son" (Ge 16:11; 17:19,21; Jdg 13:3,5) "and you will call his name" (Ge 16:11; 17:19; Isa 7:14; 8:3). Jesus is the same name in Greek as Joshua, which in its earliest form (*Yehoshua*) means "God is salvation" (eventually contracted to *Yeshua*).

1:22 – 23 *to fulfill what the Lord had said through the prophet: "The virgin will conceive … and they will call him Immanuel" (which means "God with us").* In context, the son of Isa 7:14 was a sign to King Ahaz, and was probably Isaiah's own son (Isa 7:10 – 17; 8:3 – 4). Isaiah's children's names were for "signs" to Israel (Isa 8:18). Nevertheless, Isaiah's son signified not only immediate deliverance in their own time, but pointed to the ultimate deliverance with the future birth of the ultimate Davidic ruler (Isa 9:6 – 7; cf. Isa 11:1 – 5). That would be the ultimate fulfillment of the promise of "Immanuel" (Isa 7:14), "God with us": the king would himself be the "Mighty God" (Isa 9:6), a title for God elsewhere in Isaiah (Isa 10:21). Matthew has in mind the context of the entire section of Isaiah, which he again cites soon afterward (see Isa 9:1 – 2 in Mt 4:15 – 16).

1:24 *took Mary home as his wife.* If Mary's pregnancy was known, Joseph could repudiate responsibility and perhaps evade suspicion by divorcing her. By instead marrying her, Joseph assumes responsibility for the pregnancy, embracing her shame. The couple could long be a matter of village gossip. Joseph valued God's direct calling through a dream more than what others thought of him.

1:25 *did not consummate their marriage.* Joseph and Mary could not avoid physical closeness; often newly married couples lived together in a small room on top of the home

The Magi Visit the Messiah

2 After Jesus was born in Bethlehem in
Judea,[u] during the time of King Herod,[v] Magi[a] from the east came to Jerusalem 2and asked, "Where is the one who
has been born king of the Jews?[w] We saw
his star[x] when it rose and have come to
worship him."
3When King Herod heard this he was
disturbed, and all Jerusalem with him.
4When he had called together all the

2:1 [u] Lk 2:4-7 [v] Lk 1:5 **2:2** [w] Jer 23:5; Mt 27:11; Mk 15:2; Jn 1:49; 18:33-37 [x] Nu 24:17

[a] *1* Traditionally *wise men*

of the groom's parents. Most people in antiquity supposed that a man and woman together alone for even a short time (less than an hour) would give way to sexual temptation. This would be all the more the case with those who were young; young men were considered particularly prone to passion. On average Jewish men married when about 18 to 20, with their brides in their mid-teens (sometimes even as young as 12 to 14). Yet Joseph and Mary abstained from intercourse before Jesus' birth. On the first night of a wedding feast, intercourse would normally rupture the bride's hymen, and the bloody sheet could be displayed as proof that she had entered marriage as a virgin. By making love on the first night of their wedding, Joseph and Mary could have proved that she had a virgin conception. Yet God's plan was not merely a virgin conception, but a virgin birth (v. 23). Joseph and Mary chose God's honor above their own.

2:1–2 *Magi from the east came to Jerusalem.* It was common for dignitaries to come and congratulate a new ruler. Magi undoubtedly came with a significant caravan. *Magi.* These were a famous class of astrologers and dream-interpreters who served the Persian king. Their title appears in the most common Greek version of the OT only in Daniel, where it applies to Daniel's enemies; this is not surprising, since astrology, as a form of divination, was forbidden in Scripture. Yet these Magi come to worship the new king (vv. 2,11); as Matthew often emphasizes, God calls followers from unexpected places (cf. 3:9; 8:10–12; 12:41–42; 21:31).
2:2 *star.* Some scholars think this is a conjunction of the heavenly sign that Persians associated with Judea together with the one they associated with kingship. Others associate it with other reported celestial anomalies about this time.
2:3 *he was disturbed.* Although Scripture forbade astrol-

MATTHEW 2:1

Herod the Great

Herod the Great achieved power in Judea with Roman backing; he brutally suppressed all opposition. Herod was a friend of Marc Antony but, unfortunately, an enemy of Antony's mistress Cleopatra. When Octavian (Augustus) Caesar defeated Antony and Cleopatra, Herod submitted to him. Noting that he had been a loyal friend to Antony until the end, Herod promised that he would now be no less loyal to Caesar, and Caesar accepted this promise. Herod named cities for Caesar and built temples in his honor.

Ethnically Herod was an Idumean (an Edomite); his ancestors had been forcibly converted to Judaism, and he built for Jerusalem's God the ancient world's largest and most magnificent temple. Politically astute, however, Herod also built temples honoring the divine emperor Augustus and made lavish contributions to Gentile cities in or near his territory. Among his other reported politically savvy acts was the execution of members of the old Sanhedrin who opposed him; he replaced those council members instead with his own political supporters. He did not usually tolerate dissent. When some young disciples of religious teachers took down the golden eagle that Herod had erected on the temple, he had them executed.

Most of our sources about Herod focus on his acts in Jerusalem, but the character of Herod that they reveal fits what Matthew says about him. So protective was Herod of his power and so jealous of potential rivals that his more popular brother-in-law, a very young high priest, had a drowning "accident"—in a pool that archaeology shows was very shallow. When his favorite wife Mariamne, a Maccabean princess, was falsely accused of adultery he had her strangled, though he later named a tower in his palace in her honor. He executed two of his sons who were falsely accused of plotting against him. Five days before he died he executed another son (the one who had falsely framed the other two).

continued on next page

people's chief priests and teachers of the
law, he asked them where the Messiah
was to be born. 5"In Bethlehem[y] in Judea,"
they replied, "for this is what the
prophet has written:

6"'But you, Bethlehem, in the land of
Judah,
are by no means least among the
rulers of Judah;
for out of you will come a ruler
who will shepherd my people Israel.'[a]"[z]

7Then Herod called the Magi secretly
and found out from them the exact time

2:5 [y] Jn 7:42
2:6 [z] 2Sa 5:2; Mic 5:2

[a] 6 Micah 5:2,4

ogy, most of the ancient world had come to believe in astrology from the east, considered the "science" of its day. Jewish people generally doubted that the stars controlled Israel's future, but they granted that the stars predicted the Gentiles' future. It was also widely believed that comets and other heavenly signs predicted the demise of rulers; for this reason some rulers reportedly executed other members of the elite, so that the other deaths, rather than their own, could fulfill the predicted demise. Herod undoubtedly respected foreign ideas. Besides honoring Israel's God, Herod built temples for Caesar in Gentile cities.

2:4–6 *where the Messiah was to be born … in Judea … Bethlehem.* If the star specified a king born in Judea, the Magi naturally expected to find him in Jerusalem's palace. But it is Scripture that specifies the new king's exact birthplace, and for this Herod consults his own wise men. (There is a parallel to this in one Jewish tradition, in which a scribe warned Pharaoh about the birth of Moses, Israel's deliverer.) Probably most of the "chief priests and teachers of the law" (v. 4) Herod gathered were members of the Sanhedrin, Jerusalem's municipal aristocracy. Herod had reportedly killed members of the Sanhedrin that opposed him and replaced them with his own political supporters. These Bible experts know precisely where the expected king should be born: in David's hometown of Bethlehem, as prophesied in Mic 5:2. Although everyone knows the Magi's mission (vv. 2–3), there is no indication that the Bible experts join them in their quest. Knowing the Bible is not always the same thing as obeying it.

So much did Herod crave honor it is said that when he was on his deathbed he ordered many nobles arrested. He thought that if many people were executed on the day that he died, he could ensure that there would be mourning rather than celebration at the time of his death. When he died, however, the nobles were released and the people celebrated. ◆

A model of Herod's palace in Jerusalem. The towers were named after important people in Herod's life: Hippicus (a friend), Phasael (Herod's brother), and Mariamne (Herod's wife).

the star had appeared. 8He sent them to
Bethlehem and said, "Go and search carefully for the child. As soon as you find
him, report to me, so that I too may go
and worship him."
9After they had heard the king, they went
on their way, and the star they had seen
when it rose went ahead of them until it
stopped over the place where the child
was. 10When they saw the star, they were
overjoyed. 11On coming to the house, they
saw the child with his mother Mary, and
they bowed down and worshiped him.[a]
Then they opened their treasures and presented him with gifts[b] of gold, frankincense
and myrrh. 12And having been warned[c] in
a dream[d] not to go back to Herod, they returned to their country by another route.

The Escape to Egypt

13When they had gone, an angel[e] of the
Lord appeared to Joseph in a dream.[f] "Get
up," he said, "take the child and his mother and escape to Egypt. Stay there until I
tell you, for Herod is going to search for
the child to kill him."
14So he got up, took the child and his
mother during the night and left for Egypt,
15where he stayed until the death of Herod. And so was fulfilled what the Lord had
said through the prophet: "Out of Egypt I
called my son."[a][g]
16When Herod realized that he had been
outwitted by the Magi, he was furious,
and he gave orders to kill all the boys in
Bethlehem and its vicinity who were two
years old and under, in accordance with
the time he had learned from the Magi.
17Then what was said through the prophet
Jeremiah was fulfilled:

18"A voice is heard in Ramah,
weeping and great mourning,
Rachel weeping for her children
and refusing to be comforted,
because they are no more."[b][h]

The Return to Nazareth

19After Herod died, an angel of the Lord
appeared in a dream[i] to Joseph in Egypt
20and said, "Get up, take the child and his
mother and go to the land of Israel, for
those who were trying to take the child's
life are dead."
21So he got up, took the child and his
mother and went to the land of Israel.
22But when he heard that Archelaus was

2:11 [a] Isa 60:3 [b] Ps 72:10 **2:12** [c] Heb 11:7 [d] ver 13,19,22; Mt 27:19 **2:13** [e] Ac 5:19 [f] ver 12,19,22

2:15 [g] Ex 4:22,23; Hos 11:1 **2:18** [h] Jer 31:15 **2:19** [i] ver 12,13,22

[a] *15* Hosea 11:1 [b] *18* Jer. 31:15

2:8 *Bethlehem.* It is perhaps six miles (nine kilometers) from Jerusalem, perhaps not much more than a three-hour journey for the caravan.
2:11 *bowed down.* Prostration was a way that Persians venerated rulers as well as deities. Magi could be Zoroastrian dualists, but in this period may have still been polytheists (worshipers of multiple gods). *gold, frankincense and myrrh.* Frankincense and myrrh mostly came from southern Arabia and Somaliland, and thus were very expensive. People often used these spices in royal courts and other lavish settings (cf. Ps 72:10; Isa 60:6).
2:12 *warned in a dream.* Magi were known for their reported ability to interpret dreams. Because their large caravan could have been visible during the day from Herod's nearby fortress Herodium, they presumably left under cover of night. Herod would expect them to return to Jerusalem, and from there to follow a road that would take them to the north and the east. Instead, they travel southward toward Hebron, then north along a coastal road or east along a caravan route.
2:13 *Lord appeared to Joseph in a dream.* In one Jewish tradition, a dream warned Moses' father to protect him from Pharaoh. *escape to Egypt.* A large Jewish community already lived in Egypt. Alexandria, a Greek-founded city in the northern delta region of Egypt, included perhaps the largest Jewish community outside Judea and Galilee. Perhaps one-third of Alexandria was Jewish, so the family could easily find refuge there. Further, if they had means to transport safely even some of the gold and spices (v. 11) they would have means to support themselves for a long period of time.
2:15 *what the Lord had said through the prophet.* In context, Hos 11:1 describes God bringing Israel as his "son" from Egypt. The context, however, also goes on to speak of a new exodus, when God would save his people from captivity (Hos 11:5,11; on the new exodus, see also note on Mt 3:3). Because Jesus identifies with and recapitulates the history of his people (see note on 1:1), the principles in passages about the exodus, captivity (v. 18) and testing in the wilderness (4:1 – 11) apply also to him.
2:16 *gave orders to kill all the boys.* Herod acts here in keeping with what we know of his character from other sources (see the article "Herod the Great," p. 1610). The actual size of ancient Bethlehem is unclear, but some estimate perhaps 20 boys under the age of two were killed. Jewish people considered abandoning or killing babies a pagan practice, conspicuously associated with evil kings such as Antiochus IV Epiphanes. The most widely known example, however, was Pharaoh in the OT (Ex 1:16,22). In this narrative, the pagan Magi worship the true king, whereas the Jewish ruler acts like a pagan one. (For Matthew's interest in Gentiles, see the Introduction to Matthew: Provenance and Date; see also 28:19.)
2:17 – 18 Matthew quotes from Jer 31:15; Matthew undoubtedly knew that the context calls Israel God's "son" (Jer 31:20) and goes on to promise a new covenant (Jer 31:31 – 34). Jer 31:15 depicts Rachel weeping as her descendants are carried into captivity in the exile. Matthew would have known that Rachel's tomb was near Bethlehem (Ge 35:19); like Israel's exile, the slaughter of Bethlehem's infants is a tragedy, but one that could not prevent the ultimate promise of God's restoration in the new covenant.
2:20 *go to the land of Israel ... those who were trying to take the child's life are dead.* The angel's promise here evokes Ex 4:19: Moses can return to Egypt because those who sought his life have died. Jesus here is thus like Moses, Israel's deliverer — and, ominously, Judea has become like Egypt in Moses' day.
2:22 *Archelaus was reigning.* A few days before Herod died in 4 BC, Archelaus, his son by a Samaritan wife,

reigning in Judea in place of his father
Herod, he was afraid to go there. Having
been warned in a dream,[j] he withdrew
to the district of Galilee,[k] 23 and he went
and lived in a town called Nazareth.[l] So
was fulfilled[m] what was said through the
prophets, that he would be called a Nazarene.[n]

2:22 [j] ver 12, 13, 19; Mt 27:19 [k] Lk 2:39
2:23 [l] Lk 1:26; Jn 1:45, 46 [m] Mt 1:22 [n] Mk 1:24
3:1 [o] Lk 1:13, 57-66; 3:2-19

John the Baptist Prepares the Way

3:1-12pp — Mk 1:3-8; Lk 3:2-17

3 In those days John the Baptist[o] came,
preaching in the wilderness of Judea
2 and saying, "Repent, for the kingdom
of heaven[p] has come near." 3 This is he

3:2 [p] Da 2:44; Mt 4:17; 6:10; Lk 11:20; 21:31; Jn 3:3, 5; Ac 1:3, 6

became ruler. Scholars often observe that Archelaus shared his father's vices while lacking his administrative competence. Archelaus made many enemies, and his inability to keep peace during the turbulence of AD 6 led to Rome removing him and banishing him to Gaul.

2:23 *Nazareth.* Population estimates for Nazareth vary; the village proper may have contained perhaps 500 residents (smaller than Bethlehem). Nazareth was a traditional and religiously conservative Galilean town; pottery suggests that many of its residents had migrated from Judea. Ancients sometimes built arguments on wordplays, and Jewish teachers often interpreted the OT this way. Some think that Matthew plays on Jdg 13:5: he "is to be a Nazirite." Others, probably more commonly, believe that Matthew plays on Isa 11:1, which depicts the Messiah as a "Branch," in Hebrew, *nezer.* Other Biblical passages depict the Messiah as a branch (Isa 4:2; Jer 23:5; 33:15; Zec 3:8; 6:12), as do the Dead Sea Scrolls.

3:1–2 A first-century Jewish historian, Josephus, also reports that John baptized people in the wilderness, inviting them to spiritual transformation. Josephus, however, adapts his description of John to appeal to Greek readers, as he depicts the "sects" of Judea—Pharisees, Sadducees and Essenes—along the lines of Greek philosophic sects. The Gospels, however, portray John in a way more in keeping with authentic Judean prophets: a preacher of the imminent new era of God's reign. "Kingdom of heaven" was an accepted Jewish way of speaking about God's reign (cf. Da 2:44; 4:26). The wilderness was one of the few places where prophetic figures could safely draw crowds, but of course it lacked the amenities of civilization.

3:3 Matthew quotes Isa 40:3. Some Biblical prophets, including Isaiah, had prophesied a new exodus, by which God would gather his people from exile (Isa 11:16; Jer 23:7–8; Hos 2:14–15). He would establish a way through the wilderness, as he had led his people through the wilderness of old. John was a herald preparing the people for this event, and for the coming of "the Lord"—by which the Hebrew text of Isaiah referred to God himself.

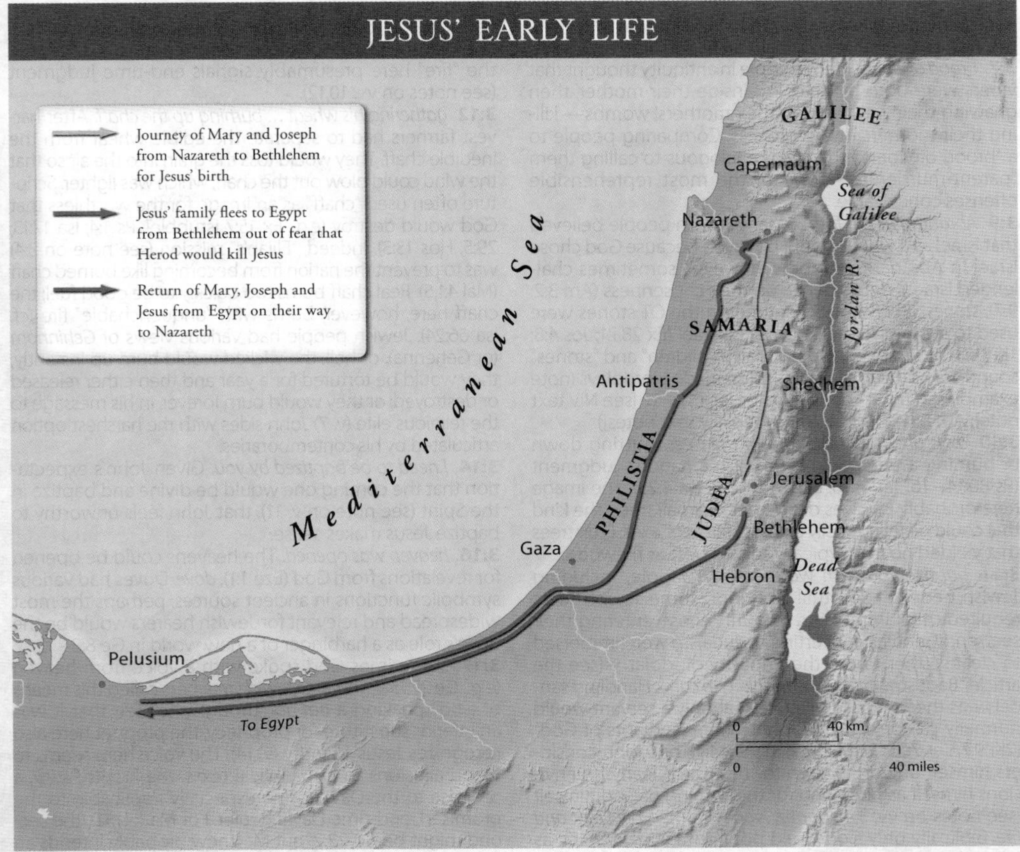

who was spoken of through the prophet
Isaiah:

"A voice of one calling in the
wilderness,
'Prepare the way for the Lord,
make straight paths for him.' "[a][q]

4John's clothes were made of camel's
hair, and he had a leather belt around
his waist.[r] His food was locusts[s] and wild
honey. 5People went out to him from Jerusalem and all Judea and the whole region
of the Jordan. 6Confessing their sins, they
were baptized by him in the Jordan River.
7But when he saw many of the Pharisees and Sadducees coming to where
he was baptizing, he said to them: "You
brood of vipers![t] Who warned you to flee
from the coming wrath?[u] 8Produce fruit
in keeping with repentance.[v] 9And do not
think you can say to yourselves, 'We have
Abraham as our father.' I tell you that out
of these stones God can raise up children
for Abraham. 10The ax is already at the
root of the trees, and every tree that does
not produce good fruit will be cut down
and thrown into the fire.[w]

11"I baptize you with[b] water for repentance. But after me comes one who is more
powerful than I, whose sandals I am not
worthy to carry. He will baptize you with[b]
the Holy Spirit[x] and fire.[y] 12His winnowing
fork is in his hand, and he will clear his
threshing floor, gathering his wheat into
the barn and burning up the chaff with
unquenchable fire."[z]

The Baptism of Jesus

3:13-17pp — Mk 1:9-11; Lk 3:21,22; Jn 1:31-34

13Then Jesus came from Galilee to the
Jordan to be baptized by John.[a] 14But John
tried to deter him, saying, "I need to be
baptized by you, and do you come to me?"
15Jesus replied, "Let it be so now; it is
proper for us to do this to fulfill all righteousness." Then John consented.
16As soon as Jesus was baptized, he
went up out of the water. At that moment
heaven was opened, and he saw the Spirit
of God[b] descending like a dove and alighting on him. 17And a voice from heaven[c]
said, "This is my Son,[d] whom I love; with
him I am well pleased."[e]

3:3 [q] Isa 40:3; Mal 3:1; Lk 1:76; Jn 1:23
3:4 [r] 2Ki 1:8 [s] Lev 11:22
3:7 [t] Mt 12:34; 23:33 [u] Ro 1:18; 1Th 1:10
3:8 [v] Ac 26:20
3:10 [w] Mt 7:19; Lk 13:6-9; Jn 15:2,6
3:11 [x] Mk 1:8 [y] Isa 4:4; Ac 2:3,4
3:12 [z] Mt 13:30
3:13 [a] Mk 1:4
3:16 [b] Isa 11:2; 42:1
3:17 [c] Mt 17:5; Jn 12:28 [d] Ps 2:7; 2Pe 1:17,18 [e] Isa 42:1; Mt 12:18; 17:5; Mk 1:11; 9:7; Lk 9:35

[a] *3* Isaiah 40:3 [b] *11* Or *in*

3:4 *leather belt.* It evokes Elijah (2Ki 1:8), who was to prepare the way for God's coming (Mal 4:5–6). See note on Mk 1:6.

3:7 *brood of vipers.* Many people in antiquity thought that vipers were born by hatching inside their mother, then gnawing their way through their mothers' wombs — killing their mothers in the process. Comparing people to a "brood of vipers," then, was analogous to calling them "parent-murderers" — one of the most reprehensible offenses conceivable.

3:9 *Abraham as our father.* Many Jewish people believed that Israel as a whole would be saved because God chose Israel in Abraham. Prophets, however, sometimes challenged Israel's dependence on their chosenness (Am 3:2; 9:7). *stones … children.* Sometimes in the OT stones were used to symbolize the 12 tribes of Israel (Ex 28:21; Jos 4:8; 1Ki 18:31). In Hebrew and Aramaic, "children" and "stones" sound very similar; prophets often made wordplays (note examples in the Hebrew texts of Jer 1:11 – 12 [see NIV text note]; Am 8:1 – 2; Mic 1:10 – 15 [see NIV text notes]).

3:10 *ax is already at the root of the trees.* Cutting down or burning a tree could symbolize a nation's judgment (Ps 80:14 – 16; Jer 11:16; Eze 31:10 – 18; Da 4:23). The image here probably involves dead trees or small trees, the kind that could be felled easily by most farmers' axes. Fruit trees that yielded no fruit typically served best as firewood.

3:11 *baptize you with water.* Many people, including Jewish people, had ritual washings; some Jewish sects required ritual immersion to purify those entering their sect, and Gentiles converting to Judaism were immersed to cleanse them from the impurity of idolatry (see the article "Baptism," p. 1686). *sandals … to carry.* Handling sandals was the sort of servile task that only a servant would normally perform; the prophets were "servants of God" (2Ki 9:7; Jer 7:25; 26:5; 29:19; 35:15; 44:4), but John considers himself unworthy even for this role. Clearly he envisions himself as preparing for the coming of God himself (see notes on vv. 3,4). *baptize you with the Holy Spirit and fire.* Biblically only God could pour out his own Spirit, as he promised to do at the time of the coming restoration (Isa 32:15; 44:3; Eze 39:29; Joel 2:28). In contrast to the Spirit, the "fire" here presumably signals end-time judgment (see notes on vv. 10,12).

3:12 *gathering his wheat … burning up the chaff.* After harvest farmers had to separate the edible wheat from the inedible chaff. They would toss the grain into the air so that the wind could blow out the chaff, which was lighter. Scripture often used "chaff" as an image for the worthless that God would destroy (e.g., Ex 15:7 [stubble]; Ps 1:4; Isa 17:13; 29:5; Hos 13:3). Indeed, "Elijah's" mission (see note on 3:4) was to prevent the nation from becoming like burned chaff (Mal 4:1,5). Real chaff burns too quickly to be good fuel; the chaff here, however, burns with "unquenchable" fire (cf. Isa 66:24). Jewish people had various views of *Gehinnom* (or Gehenna), or hell: the wicked would burn up instantly; they would be tortured for a year and then either released or destroyed; or they would burn forever. In his message to the religious elite (v. 7) John sides with the harshest option articulated by his contemporaries.

3:14 *I need to be baptized by you.* Given John's expectation that the coming one would be divine and baptize in the Spirit (see note on v. 11), that John feels unworthy to baptize Jesus makes sense.

3:16 *heaven was opened.* The heavens could be opened for revelations from God (Eze 1:1). *dove.* Doves had various symbolic functions in ancient sources; perhaps the most widespread and relevant for Jewish hearers would be the dove's role as a harbinger of a new world in Ge 8:8 – 12.

3:17 Sometimes God spoke with a voice from heaven (e.g., Ge 22:15 – 18). Later Jewish teachers called this means of God speaking a *bat qol*; though they felt that it was an inferior substitute for prophecy, the prophet here also recognizes Jesus' identity (v. 14). The voice here seems to blend allusions to two Biblical texts; the first is Ps 2:7, a promise to the Davidic line especially applicable to the promised, end-time Davidic ruler. For Mark (1:11), the second might be Ge 22:2, but Matthew probably intends an

Jesus Is Tested in the Wilderness

4:1-11pp — Mk 1:12,13; Lk 4:1-13

4 Then Jesus was led by the Spirit into
the wilderness to be tempted[a] by the
devil. 2After fasting forty days and forty nights,[f] he was hungry. 3The tempter[g] came to him and said, "If you are the
Son of God,[h] tell these stones to become
bread."
4Jesus answered, "It is written: 'Man
shall not live on bread alone, but on every word that comes from the mouth of
God.'[b]"[i]
5Then the devil took him to the holy
city[j] and had him stand on the highest
point of the temple. 6"If you are the Son of

4:2 [f] Ex 34:28; 1Ki 19:8 **4:3** [g] 1Th 3:5 [h] Mt 3:17; Jn 5:25; Ac 9:20 **4:4** [i] Dt 8:3 **4:5** [j] Ne 11:1; Da 9:24; Mt 27:53

[a] *1* The Greek for *tempted* can also mean *tested.*
[b] *4* Deut. 8:3

allusion instead to Isa 42:1, given the way Matthew translates this passage in 12:18.

4:1 *to be tempted.* In Scripture, God's servants generally faced testing before they were ready for their public ministries. Following Biblical precedent, ancient Judaism recognized the devil as tempter (cf. 1Ch 21:1), accuser (Job 1:9–11; 2:4–5; Zec 3:1) and deceiver. Jesus being led into the wilderness probably evokes Israel's experience (cf. Ex 13:18; see note on Mt 4:2). "Led," "wilderness," and being tempted or tested for "forty" periods of time all appear together in Dt 8:2; Jesus quotes Dt 8:3 in v. 4.

4:2 *fasting forty days and forty nights.* This period of fasting before Jesus' ministry recalls Moses fasting 40 days and nights before receiving the law (Ex 24:18; 34:28; cf. 2:20); Elijah also followed the same example (1Ki 19:8). Jesus being tested in the wilderness 40 days also likely recalls Israel being tested in the wilderness for 40 years (see notes on 2:15,17–18).

4:3 The tempter directly challenges or reinterprets God's words in 3:17; cf. Ge 3:1–4. Magicians sometimes claimed the power to change one substance into another. Jesus can multiply food, but trusts his Father's care (cf. v. 11; 6:11; 14:19–20).

4:4 *It is written.* A common formula for citing Scripture (already in, e.g., Jos 8:31; 2Ch 31:3; Ezr 6:18). In vv. 4–10, Jesus quotes three texts given to Israel when they were tempted in the wilderness. Here he quotes from Dt 8:3, which in context addressed Israel as God's "son" (Dt 8:5). The devil might seek to offer a different interpretation of Jesus' sonship (v. 3; cf. 3:17); Jesus, however, appeals to Scripture to define this sonship.

4:5 *highest point of the temple.* Might refer to the temple complex's southeast corner overlooking the Kidron Valley.

4:6 Later rabbis also expected that even the devil and demons knew Scripture, though the devil did not obey it. Again reframing Jesus' sonship (3:17; see note on 4:4),

JESUS' BAPTISM AND TEMPTATION

Events surrounding Jesus' baptism reveal the intense religious excitement and social ferment of the early days of John the Baptist's ministry. Herod had been cruel and rapacious; Roman military occupation was harsh. Some agitation centered around the change of governors from Gratus to Pilate in AD 26. Most of the people hoped for a religious solution to their intolerable political situation, and when they heard of a new prophet, they flocked out into the desert to hear him. The religious sect (Essenes) from Qumran professed similar doctrines of repentance and baptism. Jesus was baptized at Bethany on the other side of the Jordan (see Jn 1:28). John also baptized at "Aenon near Salim" (Jn 3:23).

For Jesus' temptation, see notes on Mt 4:1–11; Lk 4:1–13.

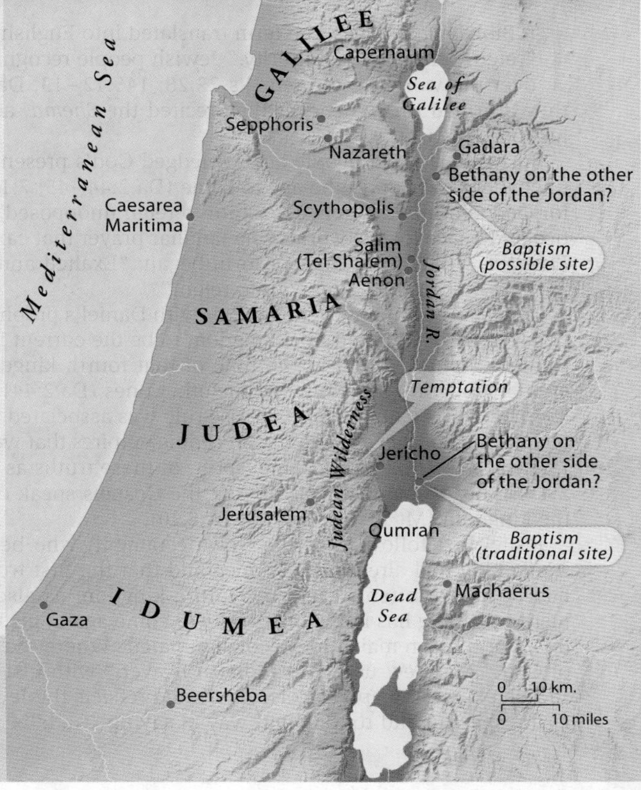

Many interpreters place John's baptismal ministry at a point on the middle reaches of the Jordan River, where trade routes converge at a natural ford not far from the modern site of Tel Shalem.

God," he said, "throw yourself down. For
it is written:

"'He will command his angels
concerning you,
and they will lift you up in their
hands,
so that you will not strike your foot
against a stone.'[a]"[k]

7Jesus answered him, "It is also written: 'Do not put the Lord your God to the
test.'[b]"[l]

8Again, the devil took him to a very
high mountain and showed him all the
kingdoms of the world and their splendor.
9"All this I will give you," he said, "if you
will bow down and worship me."
10Jesus said to him, "Away from me, Satan![m] For it is written: 'Worship the Lord
your God, and serve him only.'[c]"[n]
11Then the devil left him, and angels
came and attended him.[o]

4:6 [k] Ps 91:11,12
4:7 [l] Dt 6:16
4:10 [m] 1Ch 21:1 [n] Dt 6:13
4:11 [o] Mt 26:53; Lk 22:43; Heb 1:14

[a] *6* Psalm 91:11,12 [b] *7* Deut. 6:16 [c] *10* Deut. 6:13

the devil quotes Ps 91:11 – 12 out of context. The psalm refers to God's protection if one falls; it does not refer to jumping.
4:7 Continuing the general context of his previous quotation, Jesus quotes Dt 6:16, which in context warns against Israel's dissatisfaction with God's provision in the wilderness.
4:10 Still following the context, Jesus cites Dt 6:13, which prohibited idolatry (Dt 6:14), recognizing the one true God (Dt 6:4 – 5,12).
4:11 *angels ... attended him.* Trusting the Father rather than creating bread (vv. 3 – 4) or presuming on angels (vv. 6 – 7), Jesus here receives angelic help after his fast (cf. 26:53).

MATTHEW 4:17

Kingdom

In Biblical languages, the term translated into English as "kingdom" usually meant "reign," "rule," or "authority." Jewish people recognized that God reigned as king over the world he created (Ps 22:28; 145:12 – 13; Da 4:3,34). Some believed that they affirmed this whenever they recited the *Shema*, acknowledging that there was just one true God (Dt 6:4).

But while Jewish people acknowledged God's present rule, most looked for God's unchallenged reign in the age to come (Da 2:44 – 45; 7:14,27). Many prayed regularly for God's future kingdom — for him to reign unopposed, to fulfill his purposes of justice and peace for the world. One familiar prayer that came to be prayed daily was the *Kaddish*, which in its ancient form began: "Exalted and hallowed be his great name ... May he cause his kingdom to reign."

By Jesus' day, many were familiar with Daniel's prophecy about four kingdoms and believed the fourth and final kingdom to be the current Roman Empire (Da 2:37 – 43). Daniel prophesied that in the time of that fourth kingdom, God would establish an eternal kingdom, overthrowing the other ones (Da 2:44). This kingdom belonged to a "Son of man," a human one, whose rule was associated with the deliverance of God's people and contrasted with the preceding empires that were compared with beasts (Da 7:12 – 14,17 – 18,21 – 22). Daniel spoke of these truths as "mysteries" (Da 2:28 – 29; cf. 2:47). Thus it is not surprising that the Gospels speak of the "secret" or "secrets" of the kingdom (Mt 13:11; Mk 4:11; Lk 8:10).

Jesus' first followers in the New Testament, who believed that the coming Messianic king had already come once and that the first fruits of the future resurrection had occurred, often treated the future kingdom as also present. We recognize that just as the king has both come and will come again, his kingdom has already invaded this world but remains to be consummated. Where the other Gospels use "kingdom of God," Matthew uses "kingdom of heaven" with just four or five exceptions. This Jewish expression appears elsewhere and reflects the Jewish use of "heaven" at times as a respectful and roundabout way of saying "God." ◆

Jesus Begins to Preach

12 When Jesus heard that John had been
put in prison,[p] he withdrew to Galilee.[q]
13 Leaving Nazareth, he went and lived in
Capernaum,[r] which was by the lake in
the area of Zebulun and Naphtali — 14 to
fulfill what was said through the prophet
Isaiah:

15 "Land of Zebulun and land of
Naphtali,
the Way of the Sea, beyond the
Jordan,
Galilee of the Gentiles —
16 the people living in darkness
have seen a great light;
on those living in the land of the
shadow of death
a light has dawned."[a][s]

17 From that time on Jesus began to
preach, "Repent, for the kingdom of heav-
en[t] has come near."

Jesus Calls His First Disciples

4:18-22pp — Mk 1:16-20; Lk 5:2-11; Jn 1:35-42

18 As Jesus was walking beside the Sea
of Galilee,[u] he saw two brothers, Simon
called Peter[v] and his brother Andrew.
They were casting a net into the lake, for
they were fishermen. 19 "Come, follow
me,"[w] Jesus said, "and I will send you out
to fish for people." 20 At once they left their
nets and followed him.
21 Going on from there, he saw two other brothers, James son of Zebedee and his
brother John.[x] They were in a boat with
their father Zebedee, preparing their nets.
Jesus called them, 22 and immediately they
left the boat and their father and followed
him.

Jesus Heals the Sick

23 Jesus went throughout Galilee,[y] teaching in their synagogues,[z] proclaiming the
good news[a] of the kingdom,[b] and healing every disease and sickness among the
people.[c] 24 News about him spread all over
Syria,[d] and people brought to him all who
were ill with various diseases, those suffering severe pain, the demon-possessed,[e]
those having seizures,[f] and the paralyzed;[g]
and he healed them. 25 Large crowds from
Galilee, the Decapolis,[b] Jerusalem, Judea
and the region across the Jordan followed
him.[h]

Introduction to the Sermon on the Mount

5 Now when Jesus saw the crowds, he
went up on a mountainside and sat
down. His disciples came to him, 2 and he
began to teach them.

The Beatitudes

5:3-12pp — Lk 6:20-23

He said:

3 "Blessed are the poor in spirit,
for theirs is the kingdom of
heaven.[i]

a 16 Isaiah 9:1,2 *b* 25 That is, the Ten Cities

4:12 p Mt 14:3 q Mk 1:14 **4:13** r Mk 1:21; Lk 4:23,31; Jn 2:12; 4:46,47 **4:16** s Isa 9:1,2; Lk 2:32 **4:17** t Mt 3:2 **4:18** u Mt 15:29; Mk 7:31; Jn 6:1 v Mt 16:17,18 **4:19** w Mk 10:21, 28,52 **4:21** x Mt 20:20 **4:23** y Mk 1:39; Lk 4:15,44 z Mt 9:35; 13:54; Mk 1:21; Lk 4:15; Jn 6:59 a Mk 1:14 b Mt 3:2; Ac 20:25 c Mt 8:16; 15:30; Ac 10:38 **4:24** d Lk 2:2 e Mt 8:16,28; 9:32; 15:22; Mk 1:32; 5:15, 16,18 f Mt 17:15 g Mt 8:6; 9:2; Mk 2:3 **4:25** h Mk 3:7,8; Lk 6:17 **5:3** i ver 10,19; Mt 25:34

4:13 *Capernaum.* A fishing town of perhaps 1,000 or 2,000 on the Sea of Galilee. Jesus is never mentioned as ministering in the two largest cities in Galilee, Sepphoris or Tiberias, but Capernaum was well situated for contact with the rest of Galilee. Later sources show that Capernaum became a stronghold for Galilean followers of Jesus.
4:15 – 16 The context of the cited passage (Isa 9:1 – 2) is clearly Messianic (Isa 9:6 – 7). This passage also allows Matthew to connect Jesus again (cf. 1:3,5 – 6; 2:1 – 2) with mission to the Gentiles. Despite the historic connection with Gentiles in Galilee, however, its Jewish cities and towns observed the Law of Moses.
4:17 *the kingdom of heaven has come near.* See the article "Kingdom," p. 1616.
4:18 *they were fishermen.* Family businesses were common. Many scholars argue that commercial fishermen were better off economically than peasants, who comprised the majority of the empire's (and Galilee's) population. Most people could not usually afford meat, but fish was more available, and fishing was a major occupation on the Sea of Galilee. Note that the sea was actually a lake; only Galileans called it a sea. The Gospels' usage of this word reflects their dependence on Jesus' original Galilean setting.
4:19 *Come.* Respectable teachers usually waited for disciples to choose them; only the most radical sages were reputed to choose their own disciples. *follow me.* A disciple would come "after," or walk behind, his teacher. *fish for people.* In Scripture, God sometimes used people's backgrounds, e.g., as shepherds (Ex 3:1; 1Sa 17:15; 2Sa 5:2; Isa 63:11).
4:22 *immediately they left the boat and their father.* Leaving one's family and livelihood was a rare and serious commitment. Disciples were usually in their teens, and many of Jesus' disciples may have been in this range.
4:24 *all over Syria.* Judea and Galilee belonged to the Roman province of Syria; even Syria's major Gentile cities (such as Damascus and especially Antioch) included many Jewish residents. The Decapolis, a group of Hellenistic cities in Syria near Galilee, included such towns as Gadara, Gerasa, Hippos and Pella. The primary feature of these cities that connected them was their Hellenistic (Greek) character, but many Jewish residents lived there in this period. *all who were ill.* Sickness was pervasive and people gathered at hot springs or any place they hoped to find a cure.
4:25 *Large crowds.* That crowds would follow one reputed to work miracles is to be expected. Even hot springs with apparent curative properties drew large numbers of ailing people.
5:1 *sat down.* Senior teachers of the law would sit to explain it. Some scholars compare Jesus' teaching from a mountain here to Moses' giving the law from a mountain (cf. Ex 24:12).
5:3 Beatitudes constitute a common literary form (e.g., Ps 1:1). See note on Lk 6:20.

4 Blessed are those who mourn,
for they will be comforted.[j]
5 Blessed are the meek,
for they will inherit the earth.[k]
6 Blessed are those who hunger and
thirst for righteousness,
for they will be filled.[l]
7 Blessed are the merciful,
for they will be shown mercy.
8 Blessed are the pure in heart,[m]
for they will see God.[n]
9 Blessed are the peacemakers,
for they will be called children of
God.[o]
10 Blessed are those who are persecuted
because of righteousness,[p]
for theirs is the kingdom of heaven.

11 "Blessed are you when people insult
you,[q] persecute you and falsely say all
kinds of evil against you because of me.
12 Rejoice and be glad,[r] because great is
your reward in heaven, for in the same
way they persecuted the prophets who
were before you.[s]

Salt and Light

13 "You are the salt of the earth. But if
the salt loses its saltiness, how can it be
made salty again? It is no longer good for
anything, except to be thrown out and
trampled underfoot.[t]
14 "You are the light of the world.[u] A
town built on a hill cannot be hidden.
15 Neither do people light a lamp and put
it under a bowl. Instead they put it on its
stand, and it gives light to everyone in the
house.[v] 16 In the same way, let your light
shine before others, that they may see
your good deeds and glorify[w] your Father
in heaven.

The Fulfillment of the Law

17 "Do not think that I have come to
abolish the Law or the Prophets; I have
not come to abolish them but to fulfill
them.[x] 18 For truly I tell you, until heaven
and earth disappear, not the smallest letter, not the least stroke of a pen, will by
any means disappear from the Law until
everything is accomplished.[y] 19 Therefore
anyone who sets aside one of the least of
these commands[z] and teaches others accordingly will be called least in the kingdom of heaven, but whoever practices and
teaches these commands will be called
great in the kingdom of heaven. 20 For I tell

5:4 [j] Isa 61:2, 3; Rev 7:17
5:5 [k] Ps 37:11; Ro 4:13
5:6 [l] Isa 55:1, 2
5:8 [m] Ps 24:3, 4 [n] Heb 12:14; Rev 22:4
5:9 [o] ver 44, 45; Ro 8:14
5:10 [p] 1Pe 3:14
5:11 [q] 1Pe 4:14
5:12 [r] Ac 5:41; 1Pe 4:13, 16 [s] Mt 23:31, 37; Ac 7:52; 1Th 2:15
5:13 [t] Mk 9:50; Lk 14:34, 35
5:14 [u] Jn 8:12
5:15 [v] Mk 4:21; Lk 8:16
5:16 [w] Mt 9:8
5:17 [x] Ro 3:31
5:18 [y] Lk 16:17
5:19 [z] Jas 2:10

5:4 *those who mourn.* Repentance, whether over one's own sins or those of one's society, was often expressed in mourning. God promised future comfort to his people (Isa 40:1; 51:3; 61:2–3; 66:13).
5:5 *the meek.* Ps 37:11 promises that the meek (the humble, the lowly, those who depend on the Lord rather than themselves [cf. Ps 37:9; cf. also "poor in spirit" in Mt 5:3]) would inherit the earth. *the earth.* Although this could mean simply "the land," by Jesus' day Jewish people spoke of the righteous "inheriting the kingdom" and thus ruling the world (cf. Da 7:14).
5:8 *the pure in heart.* God would bless the "pure in heart" (Ps 73:1). God's people in the end time would "see" him.
5:9 *the peacemakers.* Some Judeans and Galileans believed that God would help them wage war against the Romans to establish God's kingdom, but Jesus assigns the kingdom instead to the meek (v. 5), those who show mercy (v. 7), those who are persecuted (v. 10), and those who make peace (v. 9).
5:10 *theirs is the kingdom of heaven.* Ancient writers sometimes bracketed off a special section of material by starting and finishing it with the same point—here, that "the kingdom of heaven" (cf. v. 3, see also the article "Kingdom," p. 1616) will be given to the righteous and humble.
5:11 *because of me.* Jewish people spoke of suffering for God's name; Jesus thus may fill a divine role here.
5:12 *persecuted the prophets.* In Scripture, prophets sometimes faced persecution; by Jesus' day, Jewish tradition highlighted this point even more.
5:13 *salt loses its saltiness.* Some commentators note that much ancient salt contained impurities, which could dissolve; but Jesus also uses a graphic image—how can true salt stop being salt? When asked what to do with unsalty salt, a later rabbi advised, "Salt it with the afterbirth of a mule." Mules are sterile and thus lack afterbirth; his point was that the question was stupid. If salt *could* lose its saltiness, what would it be useful for? Jesus compares a disciple who does not live out the values of the kingdom with unsalty salt—salt that cannot fulfill its purpose.
5:14 *light of the world.* God had called his people to be a light to the nations (Isa 42:6; 49:6), so his salvation would reach the ends of the earth (Isa 49:6). *town built on a hill.* Many ancient cities were built on hills; their lights could also make them visible against the horizon at night.
5:15 *light a lamp and put it under a bowl.* The most common oil lamps of this period were small enough to hold in the hand; placing such a lamp under a container would obscure and likely extinguish it. Invisible light was about as useful to ancient Galileans as was tasteless salt (v. 13).
5:18 *truly I tell you.* Lit. "Amen, I tell you"; "amen" normally concluded a prayer, and most scholars believe that beginning a saying this way implied distinctive authority. *smallest letter.* The smallest Hebrew letter was a *yod*, formed by a single stroke of the pen. One Jewish story recounted that the *yod* removed from Sarai's name (when it was changed to Sarah, Ge 17:15) protested to God from one generation to another, lamenting its removal from Scripture, until finally God put the *yod* back in the Bible. When Hoshea's name was changed to Joshua (Nu 13:16), a *yod* was reinserted in Scripture. "So you see," remarked Jewish teachers, "not a single *yod* can pass from God's Word." In a similar Jewish story, a *yod* protested that King Solomon was trying to remove it from Scripture; "A thousand Solomons shall be uprooted," God declared, "but not a single *yod* will pass from my Word." Such illustrations were merely graphic ways of emphasizing that all of God's Word must be respected; no part was too small to matter.
5:19 *least of these commands.* Jewish teachers sometimes spoke of the least and greatest commandments, and of people who were least and greatest in the kingdom. Normally they did not mean such statements as matters of mathematical precision, but as graphic ways of emphasizing the value of all the commandments. Thus, e.g., some later rabbis declared that the least commandment was

you that unless your righteousness surpasses that of the Pharisees and the teachers of the law, you will certainly not enter
the kingdom of heaven.

Murder

5:25,26pp — Lk 12:58,59

21 “You have heard that it was said to the
people long ago, ‘You shall not murder,[a][a]
and anyone who murders will be subject
to judgment.’ 22 But I tell you that anyone
who is angry with a brother or sister[b],[c] will
be subject to judgment.[b] Again, anyone
who says to a brother or sister, ‘Raca,’[d] is
answerable to the court.[c] And anyone who
says, ‘You fool!’ will be in danger of the
fire of hell.[d]
23 “Therefore, if you are offering your gift
at the altar and there remember that your
brother or sister has something against
you, 24 leave your gift there in front of the
altar. First go and be reconciled to them;
then come and offer your gift.
25 “Settle matters quickly with your adversary who is taking you to court. Do it
while you are still together on the way, or
your adversary may hand you over to the
judge, and the judge may hand you over
to the officer, and you may be thrown
into prison. 26 Truly I tell you, you will
not get out until you have paid the last
penny.

Adultery

27 “You have heard that it was said, ‘You
shall not commit adultery.’[e][e] 28 But I tell
you that anyone who looks at a woman
lustfully has already committed adultery
with her in his heart.[f] 29 If your right eye
causes you to stumble,[g] gouge it out and
throw it away. It is better for you to lose
one part of your body than for your whole
body to be thrown into hell. 30 And if your
right hand causes you to stumble, cut it off
and throw it away. It is better for you to
lose one part of your body than for your
whole body to go into hell.

5:21 [a] Ex 20:13; Dt 5:17 **5:22** [b] 1Jn 3:15 [c] Mt 26:59 [d] Jas 3:6

5:27 [e] Ex 20:14; Dt 5:18 **5:28** [f] Pr 6:25 **5:29** [g] Mt 18:6, 8,9; Mk 9:42-47

[a] 21 Exodus 20:13 [b] 22 The Greek word for *brother or sister* (*adelphos*) refers here to a fellow disciple, whether man or woman; also in verse 23. [c] 22 Some manuscripts *brother or sister without cause* [d] 22 An Aramaic term of contempt [e] 27 Exodus 20:14

the demand that people free a mother bird (Dt 22:7), but that whoever kept this command received life, the same reward as one who kept the greatest command, honoring father and mother (Dt 5:16). The titles of least or greatest in the kingdom are also graphic and hyperbolic. A rabbi could, e.g., praise one pupil as wiser than the entire rest of the world, and the next day praise another pupil in the same terms; such statements were graphic ways of making the point, not invitations to calculate an individual's precise merit.

5:20 *the Pharisees and the teachers of the law.* Pharisees belonged to a movement scrupulous in understanding and obeying the law according to the traditions of their predecessors (the "tradition of the elders"; see 15:2; Mk 7:3,5). Far more than the aristocratic Sadducees, Pharisees were also popular with the people and respected for their piety. They tithed meticulously, were careful about ritual purity, and at least during the dry season, they often fasted twice a week. The term for "teachers of the law" can refer even to executors of legal documents in villages, but in the Gospels it normally refers to those who were literate and formally trained in the Law of Moses, often teaching others the law. Jesus' words are again designed to shock his hearers, since Pharisees and teachers of the law would be among the people most respected for piety. But Jesus demands a deeper form of righteousness (see vv. 21 – 48).

5:21 *heard that it was said.* Sometimes Jewish teachers would say something like, "You have heard it said, but I say," meaning, "You thought it meant only this, but it actually means also this ..." (cf. 1Co 7:12). *murder.* The prohibition against murder was one of the cardinal commandments (Ex 20:13; Dt 5:17).

5:22 *anyone who is angry.* The law limited sin, but Jesus' kingdom demands go deeper; the law said, "You shall not murder," but Jesus demanded, "You shall not *want* to murder." Some other ancient teachers agreed that desiring to kill someone revealed the same sort of heart that actually could commit murder. The insult, "Raca" (essentially meaning, "empty," "devoid of value") was roughly equivalent to the common insult, "Fool." The punishments might also be equivalent, if the "judgment" and the "court" refer to the tradition, attested in later Jewish literature, of a *heavenly* court (cf. vv. 25 – 26). Jesus' word for "hell" here is a Greek rendering of *Gehinnom* (Gehenna), a place of fiery torment for the damned (see note on 3:12); by adding explicit mention of "fire," Jesus underlines the warning even more strongly. Jesus might have employed an element of hyperbole to drive home the point (cf. his use of "fools" in 23:17).

5:23 – 24 God welcomed offerings only from those who acted justly (Ge 4:4 – 7; Pr 15:8; Isa 1:11 – 17; Jer 6:20; Am 5:21 – 24).

5:26 *paid the last penny.* The term for "penny" here refers to the *quadrans*, a Roman coin equivalent to only several minutes' wages. Some think this parable uses the image of debt imprisonment, a Gentile custom forbidden in Jewish circles in this period.

5:27 *adultery.* The prohibition against adultery was one of the cardinal commandments and allowed no exceptions (Ex 20:14; Dt 5:18).

5:28 *anyone who looks at a woman lustfully.* Whereas the law merely said, "You shall not commit adultery," Jesus demanded, "You shall not *want* to commit adultery." Many ancient Jewish moralists condemned lust; some later rabbis even compared extreme lust to adultery. Jesus' warning here develops the context of the prohibition against adultery in the law: the seventh commandment prohibited adultery, but the tenth commandment warned that one should not even *covet* one's neighbor's wife (Ex 20:17; Dt 5:21). Jesus uses here the same verb as in the standard Greek translation of the tenth commandment. He refers, then, to wanting to have one's neighbor's wife. The principle, of course, extends beyond Jesus' illustration, applying to both genders and to single people, coveting one who might be someone else's spouse someday.

5:30 *cut it off.* Corporal punishment in which a member was cut off was better than capital punishment or eternal torment. Because cutting off an offending member would not necessarily end one's sin, Jesus here uses hyperbole, or rhetorical overstatement, to graphically

Divorce

31"It has been said, 'Anyone who divorces his wife must give her a certificate
of divorce.'[a][h] 32But I tell you that anyone
who divorces his wife, except for sexual
immorality, makes her the victim of adultery, and anyone who marries a divorced
woman commits adultery.[i]

Oaths

33"Again, you have heard that it was said
to the people long ago, 'Do not break your
oath,[j] but fulfill to the Lord the vows you
have made.'[k] 34But I tell you, do not swear
an oath at all:[l] either by heaven, for it is
God's throne;[m] 35or by the earth, for it is
his footstool; or by Jerusalem, for it is the
city of the Great King.[n] 36And do not swear
by your head, for you cannot make even
one hair white or black. 37All you need to
say is simply 'Yes' or 'No';[o] anything beyond this comes from the evil one.[b][p]

Eye for Eye

38"You have heard that it was said, 'Eye
for eye, and tooth for tooth.'[c][q] 39But I tell
you, do not resist an evil person. If anyone slaps you on the right cheek, turn to
them the other cheek also.[r] 40And if anyone wants to sue you and take your shirt,
hand over your coat as well. 41If anyone
forces you to go one mile, go with them
two miles. 42Give to the one who asks you,
and do not turn away from the one who
wants to borrow from you.[s]

Love for Enemies

43"You have heard that it was said,
'Love your neighbor[d][t] and hate your enemy.'[u] 44But I tell you, love your enemies
and pray for those who persecute you,[v]
45that you may be children[w] of your Father in heaven. He causes his sun to rise
on the evil and the good, and sends rain
on the righteous and the unrighteous.[x]
46If you love those who love you, what reward will you get?[y] Are not even the tax
collectors doing that? 47And if you greet
only your own people, what are you doing
more than others? Do not even pagans do
that? 48Be perfect, therefore, as your heavenly Father is perfect.[z]

5:31 [h] Dt 24:1-4
5:32 [i] Lk 16:18
5:33 [j] Lev 19:12 [k] Nu 30:2; Dt 23:21; Mt 23:16-22
5:34 [l] Jas 5:12 [m] Isa 66:1; Mt 23:22
5:35 [n] Ps 48:2
5:37 [o] Jas 5:12 [p] Mt 6:13; 13:19, 38; Jn 17:15; 2Th 3:3; 1Jn 2:13, 14; 3:12; 5:18, 19
5:38 [q] Ex 21:24; Lev 24:20; Dt 19:21
5:39 [r] Lk 6:29; Ro 12:17, 19; 1Co 6:7; 1Pe 3:9
5:42 [s] Dt 15:8; Lk 6:30
5:43 [t] Lev 19:18 [u] Dt 23:6
5:44 [v] Lk 6:27, 28; 23:34; Ac 7:60; Ro 12:14; 1Co 4:12; 1Pe 2:23
5:45 [w] ver 9 [x] Job 25:3
5:46 [y] Lk 6:32
5:48 [z] Lev 19:2; 1Pe 1:16

[a] *31* Deut. 24:1 [b] *37* Or *from evil* [c] *38* Exodus 21:24; Lev. 24:20; Deut. 19:21 [d] *43* Lev. 19:18

underline his point: one must do whatever is necessary to evade destruction. Jesus probably mentions the eye first (v. 29) because of the sin just mentioned (v. 28).

5:31 *certificate of divorce.* Cf. Dt 24:1; such a certificate allowed a wife to remarry; the key element of such certificates was the phrase, "You are now free to marry another man" (sometimes abbreviated, "You are now free").

5:32 *except for sexual immorality.* One school of Pharisees (the school of Hillel) allowed divorce for any reason; the other (the school of Shammai) allowed it only for "sexual immorality" (as here). A legal divorce permitted remarriage, but without a valid divorce, a wife's new marriage was invalid, hence adulterous. (In a Jewish legal setting the wife's divorce was more at issue than the husband's because Jewish law in principle permitted men to have multiple wives.) Jesus here depicts divorce as invalid, apart from the partner's infidelity. Because Jesus often used graphic hyperbole (see note on v. 30), offered general statements that might be qualified in some cases (see note on 1Co 7:15), and elsewhere treated the dissolution of marriage as genuine (though normally wrong; cf. Mt 19:6; Jn 4:18), some view the present statement as hyperbole. Hyperbole was meant to graphically reinforce the point, here the warning against breaking one's marriage.

5:33 *Do not break your oath.* An oath invoked a deity's witness that one was telling the truth. Here Jesus alludes to texts such as Lev 19:12; Nu 30:2; Dt 23:21–22.

5:34–35 *do not swear an oath at all.* A few radical sages and sects forbade oaths, demanding that one's integrity be so great that oaths were unnecessary. Other Jewish people sometimes tried to evade the curse incurred in broken oaths by swearing by something less than God. *heaven.* "Heaven" is God's throne and "earth" his footstool in Isa 66:1; "Jerusalem" is "the city of the Great King" in Ps 48:2.

5:36 *cannot make even one hair white or black.* People could not control signs of aging.

5:38 *Eye for eye, and tooth for tooth.* The principle of equal justice enshrined in "eye for eye" appeared widely in ancient law; although only in Israel did it apply across class lines (see note on Lev 24:20). In a number of ancient legal collections, this rule appears beside rules pertaining to being struck on the cheek (v. 39).

5:39 *slaps you on the right cheek.* The backhanded blow on the right cheek was meant primarily as an insult, a challenge to the honor of the person struck. The striker could be taken to court and fined for this offense.

5:40 *hand over your coat.* The coat was the one possession that a creditor could not legally seize from a debtor (Ex 22:26–27; Dt 24:12–13). The very poor might have only a single coat; in such cases, surrendering both the inner and outer garments might leave one naked. In this case, an element of hyperbole might be involved, and/or (as some suggest) it might include shaming one's aggressor with such extensive cooperation.

5:41 *forces you to go one mile.* Roman soldiers, viewed as members of the hostile occupying army, sometimes forced civilians to carry gear for them. Jesus envisions shocking compliance, voluntary cooperation far beyond what the soldier demands.

5:43 *hate your enemy.* The command to love one's neighbor is explicit in Lev 19:18. The command to hate enemies, while emphasized by some contemporary Jewish sects, was not explicit in Scripture, but extrapolated from pious examples there (Ps 31:6; 119:113; 139:21).

5:44 Some ancient thinkers advocated nonresistance, often on the grounds that anything that could be taken away did not really matter. Jesus' words go even deeper: to love one's enemies.

5:45 *that you may be children of your Father.* Ancient moralists, not only Jews but also some Gentiles, often urged imitation of the perfect, divine example.

5:46 *even the tax collectors.* For mainstream Galileans and Judeans, tax collectors (see note on 9:9) and Gentiles were negative examples.

5:47 *greet.* See note on 23:7,8.

5:48 *Be perfect.* Ancient speakers and writers sometimes

Giving to the Needy

6 “Be careful not to practice your righteousness in front of others to be seen
by them.[a] If you do, you will have no reward from your Father in heaven.
2“So when you give to the needy, do not
announce it with trumpets, as the hypocrites do in the synagogues and on the
streets, to be honored by others. Truly I tell
you, they have received their reward in full.
3But when you give to the needy, do not let
your left hand know what your right hand
is doing, 4so that your giving may be in secret. Then your Father, who sees what is
done in secret, will reward you.[b]

Prayer

6:9-13pp — Lk 11:2-4

5“And when you pray, do not be like the
hypocrites, for they love to pray standing[c]
in the synagogues and on the street corners
to be seen by others. Truly I tell you, they
have received their reward in full. 6But
when you pray, go into your room, close
the door and pray to your Father,[d] who is
unseen. Then your Father, who sees what
is done in secret, will reward you. 7And
when you pray, do not keep on babbling[e]
like pagans, for they think they will be
heard because of their many words.[f] 8Do
not be like them, for your Father knows
what you need[g] before you ask him.
9“This, then, is how you should pray:

“ ‘Our Father in heaven,
hallowed be your name,
10your kingdom[h] come,
your will be done,[i]
on earth as it is in heaven.
11Give us today our daily bread.[j]
12And forgive us our debts,
as we also have forgiven our debtors.[k]
13And lead us not into temptation,[a][l]
but deliver us from the evil one.[b]’[m]

14For if you forgive other people when
they sin against you, your heavenly Father
will also forgive you.[n] 15But if you do not
forgive others their sins, your Father will
not forgive your sins.[o]

6:1 [a]Mt 23:5 **6:4** [b]ver 6, 18; Col 3:23, 24 **6:5** [c]Mk 11:25; Lk 18:10-14 **6:6** [d]2Ki 4:33 **6:7** [e]Ecc 5:2 [f]1Ki 18:26-29 **6:8** [g]ver 32 **6:10** [h]Mt 3:2 [i]Mt 26:39 **6:11** [j]Pr 30:8 **6:12** [k]Mt 18:21-35 **6:13** [l]Jas 1:13 [m]Mt 5:37 **6:14** [n]Mt 18:21-35; Mk 11:25, 26; Eph 4:32; Col 3:13 **6:15** [o]Mt 18:35

[a] 13 The Greek for *temptation* can also mean *testing.*
[b] 13 Or *from evil*; some late manuscripts *one, / for yours is the kingdom and the power and the glory forever. Amen.*

concluded a section with a summary. After offering six examples, Jesus climaxes with a conclusion that encompasses all righteousness. See note on v. 45.

6:1 *Be careful not to practice your righteousness in front of others.* Ancient speakers and writers would sometimes state a thesis and then develop it with illustrations; Jesus illustrates this thesis with examples from charity (vv. 2–4), prayer (vv. 5–15), and fasting (vv. 16–18). Because sages offered riddles and statements meant to provoke thought rather than systematic outlines of their beliefs, some of a sage's statements could appear to be in tension with some of his other statements. Jesus provokes thought in the tension between 5:16 and the command here in v. 1: the difference is whom one seeks to honor. (Note that the Greek term translated “honored” in v. 2 is the same Greek term translated “glorify” in 5:16.)

6:2 *Truly I tell you.* See note on 5:18. Givers did not literally use trumpets to announce their gifts; this image is graphic hyperbole. *they have received their reward in full.* When one had been paid in full, ancient business receipts used similar language. Some scholars note that “hypocrites” means “play-actors”; by this period, though, it meant anyone acting in pretense, including for insincere religious activity (Sirach 1:29; 32:15; 33:2).

6:3 Again Jesus employs hyperbole as a graphic way to focus attention on the point (see notes on v. 2; 5:22,30,32,40).

6:6 *go into your room, close the door.* Most people lacked private rooms; this could be a closet or storeroom, probably again hyperbole (cf. 14:23; 26:36–44) to emphasize the importance of seeking only God's approval by one's religious activity.

6:7 *keep on babbling like pagans.* Gentiles sometimes piled up many names for the deities they invoked, and often appealed to deities' “obligations” to reward the petitioners' sacrifices and the like. This approach contrasts with simple dependence on one's faithful heavenly Father (v. 8).

6:8 *your Father.* In Jewish culture, a father was normally someone loving and trustworthy, on whom a child could depend for needs (cf. 7:9–11).

6:9–10 Jesus here echoes a prayer regularly recited by Jewish people, a prayer known as the *Kaddish.* Its earliest form began, “Exalted and hallowed be his great name, in the world that he created according to his will; may he cause his kingdom to reign ...” The Jewish prayer invited God's future reign to change the world; Jesus presumably intends it the same way, although for believers in Jesus the kingdom is “already/not yet” (see the article “Kingdom,” p. 1616). Scripture promised that in the future God's name would be “hallowed,” or “proved holy,” in the world (Eze 36:23; 38:23; 39:27). Even in the present, many Jewish teachers consider honoring God's name the supreme objective and profaning it the most terrible sin. *your ... your ... your.* In Greek, the word “your” is emphatic in these first three petitions of Jesus' model prayer (cf. v. 33).

6:9 *Our Father.* Some Greeks called Zeus “father”; more pervasively, Jewish people addressed God as “heavenly Father” in prayers. (On Jesus' special use of “Abba,” see note on Mk 14:36.) For dependence on one's father, see note on 6:8.

6:11 *our daily bread.* Prayer for food was one of the most common prayers in antiquity. God, who supplied daily bread to his people for 40 years in the wilderness (Dt 8:2–3), can be trusted for sustenance.

6:12 *forgive us our debts.* Scripture commanded God's people to forgive all economic debts every 7th and 50th year so that no one would be permanently impoverished. Jewish teachers, however, also recognized sins as “debts” before God (cf. 18:21–35). The sixth benediction in a regularly prayed Jewish prayer, the *Amida,* included a prayer for forgiveness; cf. also note on v. 14.

6:13 *lead us not into temptation.* A similar Jewish evening prayer meant not, “Do not let us be tempted,” but “Do not let us fail when we are tested” (cf. 26:41–42,47). The late addition, “for yours is the kingdom ...” (see NIV text note) fits the church's use of the prayer; Jewish people often added such doxologies at the close of prayers.

6:14 *your heavenly Father will also forgive you.* Some other Jewish sages also emphasized that one who wants to seek God's forgiveness must also forgive other mortals (Sirach 28:1–8).

Fasting

16“When you fast, do not look somber[p] as the hypocrites do, for they disfigure their faces to show others they are fasting. Truly I tell you, they have received their reward in full. 17But when you fast, put oil on your head and wash your face, 18so that it will not be obvious to others that you are fasting, but only to your Father, who is unseen; and your Father, who sees what is done in secret, will reward you.[q]

Treasures in Heaven

6:22,23pp — Lk 11:34-36

19“Do not store up for yourselves treasures on earth,[r] where moths and vermin destroy,[s] and where thieves break in and steal. 20But store up for yourselves treasures in heaven,[t] where moths and vermin do not destroy, and where thieves do not break in and steal.[u] 21For where your treasure is, there your heart will be also.[v]

22“The eye is the lamp of the body. If your eyes are healthy,[a] your whole body will be full of light. 23But if your eyes are unhealthy,[b] your whole body will be full of darkness. If then the light within you is darkness, how great is that darkness!

24“No one can serve two masters. Either you will hate the one and love the other, or you will be devoted to the one and despise the other. You cannot serve both God and money.[w]

Do Not Worry

6:25-33pp — Lk 12:22-31

25“Therefore I tell you, do not worry[x] about your life, what you will eat or drink; or about your body, what you will wear. Is not life more than food, and the body more than clothes? 26Look at the birds of the air; they do not sow or reap or store away in barns, and yet your heavenly Father feeds them.[y] Are you not much more valuable than they?[z] 27Can any one of you by worrying add a single hour to your life[c]?[a]

28“And why do you worry about clothes? See how the flowers of the field grow. They do not labor or spin. 29Yet I tell you that not even Solomon in all his splendor[b] was dressed like one of these. 30If that is how God clothes the grass of the field, which is here today and tomorrow is thrown into the fire, will he not much more clothe you—you of little faith?[c] 31So do not worry, saying, ‘What shall we eat?’ or ‘What shall we drink?’ or ‘What shall we wear?’ 32For the pagans run after all these things, and your heavenly Father knows that you need them.[d] 33But seek first his kingdom and his righteousness, and all these things will be given to you as well.[e] 34Therefore do not worry about tomorrow, for tomorrow will worry about itself. Each day has enough trouble of its own.

Judging Others

7:3-5pp — Lk 6:41,42

7 “Do not judge, or you too will be judged.[f] 2For in the same way you judge others, you will be judged, and with the measure you use, it will be measured to you.[g]

6:16 [p] Isa 58:5
6:18 [q] ver 4,6
6:19 [r] Pr 23:4; Heb 13:5 [s] Jas 5:2,3
6:20 [t] Mt 19:21; Lk 12:33; 18:22; 1Ti 6:19 [u] Lk 12:33
6:21 [v] Lk 12:34
6:24 [w] Lk 16:13
6:25 [x] ver 27, 28,31,34; Lk 10:41; 12:11, 22; Php 4:6; 1Pe 5:7
6:26 [y] Job 38:41; Ps 147:9 [z] Mt 10:29-31
6:27 [a] Ps 39:5
6:29 [b] 1Ki 10:4-7
6:30 [c] Mt 8:26; 14:31; 16:8
6:32 [d] ver 8
6:33 [e] Mt 19:29; Mk 10:29-30
7:1 [f] Lk 6:37; Ro 14:4, 10, 13; 1Co 4:5; Jas 4:11, 12
7:2 [g] Mk 4:24; Lk 6:38

[a] 22 The Greek for *healthy* here implies *generous*.
[b] 23 The Greek for *unhealthy* here implies *stingy*.
[c] 27 Or *single cubit to your height*

6:17 *oil ... wash.* When Jewish people fasted, they not only abstained from food, but also from washing their clothes, having intercourse, shaving, and anointing themselves. People anointed their skin with olive oil and then scraped off the oil to cleanse themselves; like many Gentiles, Judeans and Galileans often anointed their heads with oil in connection with washing (even on the Sabbath).
6:19 *moths and vermin.* Expensive clothing, counted as one expression of wealth, was susceptible to moths and vermin. *thieves.* Thieves could dig through mud-brick walls; people often kept all their money in a strongbox in their home, sometimes under the floor.
6:20–21 Jewish people sometimes spoke of heavenly rewards as treasure in heaven.
6:22 The "healthy" eye here is lit. "single," which can mean "sincere" or "genuine," but also prepares for v. 24.
6:23 *eyes are unhealthy.* Jesus plays on a familiar expression. Jewish people sometimes spoke of a "good" (NIV "healthy") eye as a generous one, and an "evil" (lit.; NIV "unhealthy") eye as a stingy one. *light ... darkness.* Because light cannot be darkness, Jesus again used shocking language to hold attention (cf. salt losing its saltiness in 5:13).
6:24 *two masters.* Sharing a slave was a rare situation; it arose, e.g., when two siblings might inherit one slave. When it did occur, the slave normally preferred one master to the other. *money.* "Mammon" (KJV) was an Aramaic designation for money or property, but here Jesus apparently personified it. (Personification was one ancient technique for communicating graphically.)
6:26 *birds of the air.* Nature had long been an interest of wise teachers (1Ki 4:33), and both Greek and Jewish sages often used lessons from nature to illustrate their points. Jewish people recognized God's providential rule over all of nature (though some denied his concern for bird nests).
6:27 *add a single hour.* Sages could use shocking or creative language to hold hearers' attention. Literally Jesus spoke of adding a "cubit" (KJV; a measurement of length; NIV "hour") to one's longevity or possibly height.
6:32 *your heavenly Father knows.* Most people in the ancient world were poor, dependent on harvests for food. Naturally, they sought basic necessities; Jesus here invites them to trust their heavenly Father enough to seek first his kingdom.
6:34 *tomorrow will worry.* "Tomorrow" may be personified in another graphic statement (see note on v. 24).
7:2 *in the same way.* In principle, many Jewish sages (and even some Greek thinkers) would have agreed with Jesus (Sirach 28:1–3). Nevertheless, following Jesus in practice requires more than agreeing with him in principle. *measure.* The need to "measure" appropriately was common in

[3]"Why do you look at the speck of sawdust in your brother's eye and pay no attention to the plank in your own eye? [4]How can you say to your brother, 'Let me take the speck out of your eye,' when all the time there is a plank in your own eye? [5]You hypocrite, first take the plank out of your own eye, and then you will see clearly to remove the speck from your brother's eye.

[6]"Do not give dogs what is sacred; do not throw your pearls to pigs. If you do, they may trample them under their feet, and turn and tear you to pieces.

Ask, Seek, Knock

7:7-11pp — Lk 11:9-13

[7]"Ask and it will be given to you;[h] seek and you will find; knock and the door will be opened to you. [8]For everyone who asks receives; the one who seeks finds;[i] and to the one who knocks, the door will be opened.

[9]"Which of you, if your son asks for bread, will give him a stone? [10]Or if he asks for a fish, will give him a snake? [11]If you, then, though you are evil, know how to give good gifts to your children, how much more will your Father in heaven give good gifts to those who ask him! [12]So in everything, do to others what you would have them do to you,[j] for this sums up the Law and the Prophets.[k]

The Narrow and Wide Gates

[13]"Enter through the narrow gate.[l] For wide is the gate and broad is the road that leads to destruction, and many enter through it. [14]But small is the gate and narrow the road that leads to life, and only a few find it.

True and False Prophets

[15]"Watch out for false prophets.[m] They come to you in sheep's clothing, but inwardly they are ferocious wolves.[n] [16]By their fruit you will recognize them.[o] Do people pick grapes from thornbushes, or figs from thistles?[p] [17]Likewise, every good tree bears good fruit, but a bad tree bears bad fruit. [18]A good tree cannot bear bad fruit, and a bad tree cannot bear good fruit. [19]Every tree that does not bear good fruit is cut down and thrown into the fire.[q] [20]Thus, by their fruit you will recognize them.

True and False Disciples

[21]"Not everyone who says to me, 'Lord, Lord,'[r] will enter the kingdom of heaven, but only the one who does the will of my Father who is in heaven.[s] [22]Many will say to me on that day,[t] 'Lord, Lord, did we not prophesy in your name and in your name drive out demons and in your name perform many miracles?'[u] [23]Then I will tell them plainly, 'I never knew you. Away from me, you evildoers!'[v]

7:7 [h] Mt 21:22; Mk 11:24; Jn 14:13, 14; 15:7, 16; 16:23, 24; Jas 1:5-8; 4:2, 3; 1Jn 3:22; 5:14, 15
7:8 [i] Pr 8:17; Jer 29:12, 13
7:12 [j] Lk 6:31 [k] Ro 13:8-10; Gal 5:14
7:13 [l] Lk 13:24
7:15 [m] Jer 23:16; Mt 24:24; Mk 13:22; Lk 6:26; 2Pe 2:1; 1Jn 4:1; Rev 16:13 [n] Ac 20:29
7:16 [o] Mt 12:33; Lk 6:44 [p] Jas 3:12
7:19 [q] Mt 3:10
7:21 [r] Hos 8:2; Mt 25:11 [s] Ro 2:13; Jas 1:22
7:22 [t] Mt 10:15 [u] 1Co 13:1-3
7:23 [v] Ps 6:8; Mt 25:12, 41; Lk 13:25-27

markets. "It is measured to one according to the measure by which one measures" was also a Jewish maxim.

7:3–5 *speck ... plank.* This graphic, hyperbolic image would likely draw laughter — and provoke thought. If a splinter endangered a person with blindness, how much more did a roof beam; ancient eye surgery was a delicate art that could result in blindness.

7:6 The meaning of this saying is debated, but some think its point is similar to Pr 23:9: "Do not speak to fools, for they will scorn your prudent words." *dogs.* Could apply to the wicked (cf. Ps 22:16,20; 59:6,14–15; Pr 26:11); Jewish people normally despised dogs as unclean scavengers (Ex 22:31). *pigs.* Unclean (Lev 11:7) and could not appreciate what was valuable (Pr 11:22).

7:7 *Ask and it will be given.* Few others, if any, encouraged such radical, childlike confidence in God's provision.

7:9–10 *bread ... fish.* Most Jewish fathers were dependable providers. Bread and fish were the basic staples of the Galilean diet.

7:11 *how much more ... !* Jewish teachers (and some Gentiles) often used analogy arguments from lesser to greater.

7:12 *do to others what you would have them do to you.* Some earlier Jewish teachers offered this principle of wisdom, recognized in many cultures (e.g., Letter of Aristeas 207; Greeks; even Confucius), though often in the negative form ("Whatever you do not want others to do to you, do not do to them," Tobit 4:15; Philo, *Hypothetica* 7.6). Later rabbis also attributed to Hillel, a sage before Jesus, the claim that this principle constituted the heart of the law (Babylonian Talmud *Shabbat* 31a). Sages sometimes appealed to common wisdom to make a point, as Jesus may be doing here.

7:13–14 *leads to destruction ... leads to life.* Greek, Roman, and Jewish writers often spoke of two ways; the choice between life and death was an ancient one (Dt 30:19). Many applied this image of the two ways to the afterlife. Many mainstream Jews felt that most Jews would be saved, but some, like Jesus, warned that most people would be lost (e.g., the later apocalyptic author of 4 Ezra 7:45–61; 8:1–3).

7:15 *sheep's clothing ... wolves.* Wolves coming disguised as sheep was a common image (even in one of Aesop's fables), though it is also graphic hyperbole: wolves do not wear clothing, and it was impossible to transform one's skin (Jer 13:23). Wolves were the most obvious and common predators of sheep, killing sheep to feed themselves; their image was often used to represent humans who would harm others. Judeans and Galileans were well aware that some prophets were false; indeed, on multiple occasions, in the decades following Jesus' ministry, alleged prophets led followers to destruction at the hands of Rome's armies.

7:16 See note on Jas 3:12.

7:21–22 Although Greek and Jewish accounts sometimes delegated judgment to an exalted human, the ultimate judge in Jewish belief was God. Some Jewish exorcists invoked Solomon's name to try to expel demons (Josephus, *Antiquities* 8.47), but the sense here may exalt Jesus more: Jewish people more often could speak of acting (e.g., 1Sa 17:45; Ps 118:11–12) or prophesying (e.g., Dt 18:22; 1 Esdras 6:1) in the name of God.

7:23 *I never knew you.* This was a recognized formula of repudiation and rejection.

The Wise and Foolish Builders

7:24-27pp — Lk 6:47-49

24 “Therefore everyone who hears these
words of mine and puts them into practice[w] is like a wise man who built his
house on the rock. 25 The rain came down,
the streams rose, and the winds blew and
beat against that house; yet it did not fall,
because it had its foundation on the rock.
26 But everyone who hears these words of
mine and does not put them into practice is like a foolish man who built his
house on sand. 27 The rain came down,
the streams rose, and the winds blew and
beat against that house, and it fell with a
great crash.”

28 When Jesus had finished saying these
things,[x] the crowds were amazed at his
teaching,[y] 29 because he taught as one who
had authority, and not as their teachers of
the law.

Jesus Heals a Man With Leprosy

8:2-4pp — Mk 1:40-44; Lk 5:12-14

8 When Jesus came down from the
mountainside, large crowds followed
him. 2 A man with leprosy[a][z] came and
knelt before him[a] and said, “Lord, if you
are willing, you can make me clean.”
3 Jesus reached out his hand and touched
the man. “I am willing,” he said. “Be
clean!” Immediately he was cleansed of
his leprosy. 4 Then Jesus said to him, “See
that you don’t tell anyone.[b] But go, show
yourself to the priest and offer the gift Moses commanded,[c] as a testimony to them.”

The Faith of the Centurion

8:5-13pp — Lk 7:1-10

5 When Jesus had entered Capernaum,
a centurion came to him, asking for help.
6 “Lord,” he said, “my servant lies at home
paralyzed, suffering terribly.”
7 Jesus said to him, “Shall I come and
heal him?”
8 The centurion replied, “Lord, I do not
deserve to have you come under my roof.
But just say the word, and my servant will
be healed.[d] 9 For I myself am a man under
authority, with soldiers under me. I tell
this one, ‘Go,’ and he goes; and that one,
‘Come,’ and he comes. I say to my servant,
‘Do this,’ and he does it.”

7:24 [w] Jas 1:22-25 **7:28** [x] Mt 11:1; 13:53; 19:1; 26:1 [y] Mt 13:54; Mk 1:22; 6:2; Lk 4:32; Jn 7:46 **8:2** [z] Lk 5:12

[a] Mt 9:18; 15:25; 18:26; 20:20 **8:4** [b] Mt 9:30; Mk 5:43; 7:36; 8:30 [c] Lev 14:2-32 **8:8** [d] Ps 107:20

a 2 The Greek word traditionally translated *leprosy* was used for various diseases affecting the skin.

7:24 – 27 Some other Jewish teachers told a similar parable, with a major difference: In their story, the foundational rock in their parables was the Torah, God’s law (*Abot de Rabbi Nathan* 24A). Here Jesus’ teaching holds the same role as God’s message in the traditional parable (cf. also the two ways in vv. 13 – 14; the principle in Pr 10:25).

7:29 *as one who had authority.* Most teachers did not want to speak on their own authority; when possible, they cited earlier authorities that supported their teaching. By contrast, Jesus declares, “Truly I tell you” (5:18), and, most offensively of all, speaks of judging (vv. 21 – 23) and ranks his message with God’s law (vv. 24 – 27). On Jesus’ authority, cf. 8:9.

8:1 — 9:38 Some scholars count ten specific miracles (not counting summaries) in chs. 8 – 9, evoking Moses’ ten major judgment signs in Egypt; others note three sets of miracle stories revealing Jesus’ authority, interspersed with the demands of Jesus’ authority for his followers. Because ancient biographies were usually arranged topically, Matthew does group many miracles in this section.

8:2 *man with leprosy.* Although a majority of scholars doubt that ancient leprosy was limited to what is called leprosy today, it included severe skin conditions that led to isolation from society (in most societies; for Jewish society, see Lev 13:1 — 14:32). Jewish tradition compared it with the uncleanness of death (cf. Nu 12:10 – 12; 2Ki 5:7), and some later teachers attributed leprosy to the leper’s sin (especially the sin of slander). Out of respect, supplicants often recognized God’s prerogative to choose, even while pleading for him to act (Ge 18:27,30 – 32; cf. 2Sa 10:12; Da 3:17 – 18).

8:3 *touched the man.* Because lepers were unclean (Lev 13:45 – 46), anyone who touched them contracted temporary ritual impurity. Jesus here touches the unclean man (cf. 9:21 – 22,25) to cure him.

8:4 *don’t tell.* Ancients respected people who did not seek their own honor. *show yourself to the priest.* A priest was required to inspect a leper who believed that he or she was cleansed, and an offering in the temple should follow (Lev 14:1 – 9).

8:5 *Capernaum.* See note on 4:13. *centurion.* Centurions commanded roughly 80 troops (not literally 100, despite the name) and were the backbone of the Roman army; often they worked their way up through the ranks to achieve their position. Roman military units were stationed in Caesarea, which was on the coast, and in Jerusalem; they consisted of auxiliary troops, mostly recruited from Syria. Matthew omits Luke’s messengers (Lk 7:3) as he elsewhere omits those of Mk 5:35 in 9:18; other ancient biographers used this technique of compression to keep focused on the main point.

8:6 *my servant.* Servants could be viewed as members of households; in this case, the servant could be the only member of or a significant part of the centurion’s household. During their 20 years of service, soldiers in the Roman army were not allowed to marry officially, although they sometimes took local concubines. Most soldiers could not easily afford servants (the average price of a slave was about a third of the best-paid legionary’s annual wages), but average centurions made some 15 times the wages of the lowest-paid soldiers.

8:7 *Shall I come . . . ?* The NIV translates Jesus’ response as a question because in Greek, the “I” here is emphatic. Jewish people were not supposed to enter the homes of unclean Gentiles (see note on Ac 10:28).

8:8 *say the word.* People in antiquity sought healing at hot springs, special shrines, sometimes through magic and occasionally through contact with holy persons. Long-distance miracles, however, were considered extraordinary; this centurion expresses special faith (v. 10).

8:9 *a man under authority.* The centurion understands how authority works: just as soldiers obey the centurion because he is backed by the authority of the empire,

10When Jesus heard this, he was amazed
and said to those following him, "Truly I
tell you, I have not found anyone in Israel
with such great faith.[e] 11I say to you that
many will come from the east and the
west,[f] and will take their places at the
feast with Abraham, Isaac and Jacob in
the kingdom of heaven.[g] 12But the subjects
of the kingdom[h] will be thrown outside,
into the darkness, where there will be
weeping and gnashing of teeth."[i]

13Then Jesus said to the centurion,
"Go! Let it be done just as you believed
it would."[j] And his servant was healed at
that moment.

Jesus Heals Many

8:14-16pp — Mk 1:29-34; Lk 4:38-41

14When Jesus came into Peter's house,
he saw Peter's mother-in-law lying in bed
with a fever. 15He touched her hand and
the fever left her, and she got up and began to wait on him.

16When evening came, many who were
demon-possessed were brought to him, and
he drove out the spirits with a word and
healed all the sick.[k] 17This was to fulfill[l] what
was spoken through the prophet Isaiah:

"He took up our infirmities
and bore our diseases."[a][m]

The Cost of Following Jesus

8:19-22pp — Lk 9:57-60

18When Jesus saw the crowd around
him, he gave orders to cross to the other
side of the lake.[n] 19Then a teacher of the
law came to him and said, "Teacher, I will
follow you wherever you go."

20Jesus replied, "Foxes have dens and
birds have nests, but the Son of Man[o] has
no place to lay his head."

21Another disciple said to him, "Lord,
first let me go and bury my father."

22But Jesus told him, "Follow me,[p] and
let the dead bury their own dead."

Jesus Calms the Storm

8:23-27pp — Mk 4:36-41; Lk 8:22-25
8:23-27Ref — Mt 14:22-33

23Then he got into the boat and his disciples followed him. 24Suddenly a furious
storm came up on the lake, so that the
waves swept over the boat. But Jesus was
sleeping. 25The disciples went and woke

8:10 [e] Mt 15:28
8:11 [f] Ps 107:3; Isa 49:12; 59:19; Mal 1:11 [g] Lk 13:29
8:12 [h] Mt 13:38 [i] Mt 13:42, 50; 22:13; 24:51; 25:30; Lk 13:28
8:13 [j] Mt 9:22
8:16 [k] Mt 4:23, 24
8:17 [l] Mt 1:22 [m] Isa 53:4
8:18 [n] Mk 4:35
8:20 [o] Da 7:13; Mt 12:8, 32, 40; 16:13, 27, 28; 17:9; 19:28; Mk 2:10; 8:31
8:22 [p] Mt 4:19

[a] *17* Isaiah 53:4 (see Septuagint)

everything will obey Jesus because he is backed by God's authority (cf. 9:6,8; 28:18).

8:11 *the east and the west.* May include Jews in the Diaspora (Isa 43:5) but given the context here presumably include also Gentiles (Isa 25:6 – 7; 56:3 – 8). *at the feast.* Jewish people expected a banquet for the righteous in God's end-time kingdom (cf. Isa 25:6).

8:12 *the subjects ... will be thrown outside.* Many believed that descent from Abraham (3:9) ensured their admittance to the feast (v. 11). Jewish sources often envisioned damnation in darkness, sometimes as a prelude to or alongside burning (e.g., 1 Enoch 10:4 – 6; 103:8). *weeping and gnashing of teeth.* People would weep over their damnation (Judith 16:17). Gnashing teeth can depict anger (Job 16:9; Ps 35:16; 37:12; 112:10) but here may reflect anguish or agony.

8:14 *Peter's mother-in-law.* It was common for households to include members of the extended family (newly married couples sometimes lived in a room atop the home of the groom's parents). Here Peter's family has probably taken in his wife's widowed mother. *fever.* Common and (in the case of malaria) often severe and recurrent.

8:16 *with a word.* Gentile exorcists often used incantations or invoked a higher spirit to drive out a lower one. Jewish exorcists sometimes used magic associated with Solomon or used smelly roots to gag spirits out. By simply expelling demons by his command, Jesus demonstrates special authority.

8:17 *took up our infirmities ... diseases.* The context of Isa 53:4 refers to the suffering servant whose death would satisfy God's demand for Israel's punishment. The context in Isaiah also suggests healing of spiritual sickness (Isa 53:5; cf. Isa 6:10; 42:18 – 19). Nevertheless, Matthew understood that Isaiah looked for a wider restoration; the promised era of restoration would also include physical restoration (Isa 35:5 – 6). While God heals people in the present age, death still continues; yet Jesus' healings in this age offer a foretaste of the promised kingdom, when God will restore people and nature permanently (Isa 35:1 – 10).

8:20 *no place to lay his head.* The proper response to a leader's warning about difficulty ahead (as in 2Sa 15:19 – 20) was to follow him anyway (2Sa 15:21 – 22).

8:21 *bury my father.* Many considered honoring parents a son's greatest obligation (e.g., Josephus *Against Apion* 2.206), and burying them was the greatest expression of that obligation (cf., e.g., Tobit 4:3 – 4; 6:15; 4 Maccabees 16:11). The obligation fell most heavily on the eldest son. To neglect this duty was unthinkable; it would make one an outcast from the extended family and dishonored in one's village, normally for the rest of one's life. But a son whose father had just died would not normally be out talking with a rabbi; on receiving news of the father's death, he would immediately see to the father's burial. Some scholars note that, "I must first bury my father" sometimes functions as a polite request for delay until the father dies — sometimes a delay of years — so the son can continue with filial obligations in the meantime. Others suggest that this son refers to secondary burial — the custom of reburying the father's bones a year after the initial burial. On either of these views, the son could be requesting a considerable delay.

8:22 *let the dead bury their own dead.* Even if the son is asking for a considerable delay (see note on v. 21), Jesus' response would be shocking; burying one's father was one of society's greatest obligations (see note on v. 21). In mainstream Jewish society, only God could claim honor above parents in such a dramatic way. Ancient sources sometimes refer to the spiritually (or socially) dead; alternatively, Jesus could refer to the physically dead, using shocking, graphic language to make his point, as he often did.

8:24 *furious storm.* The Sea of Galilee is far below sea level and surrounded by hills with deep ravines; thus sudden storms can strike it unexpectedly. Galilean fishing boats were normally small.

him, saying, "Lord, save us! We're going to drown!"

[26]He replied, "You of little faith,[q] why are you so afraid?" Then he got up and rebuked the winds and the waves, and it was completely calm.[r]

[27]The men were amazed and asked, "What kind of man is this? Even the winds and the waves obey him!"

8:26 [q] Mt 6:30 [r] Ps 65:7; 89:9; 107:29

8:28 [s] Mt 4:24

Jesus Restores Two Demon-Possessed Men

8:28-34pp — Mk 5:1-17; Lk 8:26-37

[28]When he arrived at the other side in the region of the Gadarenes,[a] two demon-possessed[s] men coming from the tombs met him. They were so violent that no

[a] 28 Some manuscripts *Gergesenes;* other manuscripts *Gerasenes*

8:26 *rebuked the winds and the waves.* Greeks had stories of gods or special heroes who could control weather, but these were legends from the distant past, not reports from within living memory of eyewitnesses, as in the Gospels. For those who knew Scripture, the one with power over the winds and waves was God.

8:28 *region of the Gadarenes.* Whereas Mark identifies the territory by the better known but more distant

MATTHEW 8:16,28–34

Demons and the Bible

Many readers assume that the belief in demons attested in Scripture the superstitious beliefs of all ancient peoples. Yet anthropologists witness possession trances in most cultures today. Demons' reality, of course, cannot be decided by archaeology. Researchers can demonstrate, however, that the notion that the New Testament writers simply reflect the prescientific views of their contemporaries is simplistic and misleading.

Demons in the Ancient Near East

Ancient Near Eastern society was awash in texts containing magical incantations and amulets intended to protect people from evil spirits (spells for defense against demons are called "apotropaic spells"). For example, one of the feared demons of Neo-Assyrian times was the lion-headed female figure Lamashtu, who was thought especially to attack pregnant women and babies. For protection women wore a necklace with a pendant of the god Pazuzu. An enormous number of apotropaic spells have survived from Babylonia, employing magical words and rituals involving plants, animal parts and other sacred objects. Even today in the eastern Mediterranean it is not uncommon to see amulets intended to ward off the "evil eye."

Bronze head of Pazuzu, for protection against the demon Lamashtu, 800–600 BC, Iraq.

Demons in Non-Biblical Jewish Literature

Ancient Jewish literature was also fascinated with magic as a means of dealing with demons. The Apocryphal book of Tobit tells the story of one "Sarah, daughter of Raguel," who had been married — and widowed on her wedding night through the

continued on next page

one could pass that way. 29"What do you
want with us,[t] Son of God?" they shouted.
"Have you come here to torture us before
the appointed time?"[u]
30Some distance from them a large herd
of pigs was feeding. 31The demons begged
Jesus, "If you drive us out, send us into
the herd of pigs."
32He said to them, "Go!" So they came
out and went into the pigs, and the whole
herd rushed down the steep bank into
the lake and died in the water. 33Those

8:29 [t]Jdg 11:12; 2Sa 16:10; 1Ki 17:18; Mk 1:24; Lk 4:34; Jn 2:4 [u]2Pe 2:4

Gerasa (for a time, the capital of the Decapolis; cf. Mk 5:1), Matthew identifies the location by the nearest significant town, Gadara. Both towns were in the area of the Decapolis. *from the tombs.* People often associated spirits with tombs.
8:29 *the appointed time.* The day of judgment, the time of their doom.
8:30 *herd of pigs.* Gadara (v. 28) is in the region of the Decapolis, the majority of whose residents were Gentiles. Jews did not rear pigs (cf. Lev 11:7).
8:32 *into the lake.* Jewish people believed that demons could be bound, sometimes beneath bodies of water; some Jews believed they could be destroyed.

intervention of the demon Asmodeus — seven times. Meanwhile Tobias, the son of the blind Tobit, journeyed to Media, where Sarah lived, traveling in the company of a man who turned out to be the angel Raphael. While Tobias was sitting by the Tigris River a fish tried to eat his foot. Raphael instructed Tobias to seize the fish and extract its gall, heart and liver. If he would burn the heart and liver in the presence of an individual afflicted by a demon, that person would be delivered. Arriving in Media, Raphael informed Tobias that he was to marry Sarah but that he could thwart the demon Asmodeus by burning the fish's liver and heart when he went in to her. Tobias safely took Sarah as his wife, after which he used the fish gall to cure his father's blindness.

The Testament of Solomon, a work from the third century AD, further illustrates the widespread belief in apotropaic magic. This is a pseudepigraphical work (one that falsely claims to have been written by a famous person of the Old Testament) attributed to Solomon. In this work Solomon received a powerful ring from the angel Michael. With it he could imprison or control demons and deliver people from affliction. For example, Solomon forced the demon Lix Tetrax to help build the temple by hurling stones up to the workers.

Demons in the Old Testament

The Old Testament is remarkably reticent about evil spirits, so much so that it seems to have no developed demonology. Even so, three facts stand out:

- There are no incantations, rituals or amulets prescribed for giving an individual protection from spirits. Considering how much of the Torah is devoted to ritual and to sacred objects, this is a remarkable omission.
- God is said to have complete authority over the spirits, which cannot operate in the world without his approval. If a "lying spirit" goes out it is only with divine consent (1Ki 22:23; cf. Job 1 – 2).
- The main concern of the Old Testament writers was that people avoid seeking to avail themselves of magical powers through contact with spirits (e.g., Dt 18:10 – 12).

Demons in the New Testament

The New Testament demonstrates two realities about evil spirits:

- Jesus has absolute power over them; this was a matter of divine authority, not magic or sorcery.
- The New Testament mocks the claims of magicians by describing their inability to deal with real spirits. The failed efforts of Simon the sorcerer (Ac 8:9 – 24) and the sons of Sceva (Ac 19:13 – 16) to obtain apostolic authority illustrate the point that the miracles of the New Testament had nothing in common with ancient magic.

Jesus had no use for demonic spirits and did not seek to employ them to do his bidding. ◆

tending the pigs ran off, went into the town and reported all this, including what had happened to the demon-possessed men. 34 Then the whole town went out to meet Jesus. And when they saw him, they pleaded with him to leave their region.[v]

Jesus Forgives and Heals a Paralyzed Man

9:2-8pp — Mk 2:3-12; Lk 5:18-26

9 Jesus stepped into a boat, crossed over and came to his own town.[w] 2 Some men brought to him a paralyzed man,[x] lying on a mat. When Jesus saw their faith,[y] he said to the man, "Take heart,[z] son; your sins are forgiven."[a]

3 At this, some of the teachers of the law said to themselves, "This fellow is blaspheming!"[b]

4 Knowing their thoughts,[c] Jesus said, "Why do you entertain evil thoughts in your hearts? 5 Which is easier: to say, 'Your sins are forgiven,' or to say, 'Get up and walk'? 6 But I want you to know that the Son of Man[d] has authority on earth to forgive sins." So he said to the paralyzed man, "Get up, take your mat and go home." 7 Then the man got up and went home. 8 When the crowd saw this, they were filled with awe; and they praised God,[e] who had given such authority to man.

The Calling of Matthew

9:9-13pp — Mk 2:14-17; Lk 5:27-32

9 As Jesus went on from there, he saw a man named Matthew sitting at the tax collector's booth. "Follow me," he told him, and Matthew got up and followed him.

10 While Jesus was having dinner at Matthew's house, many tax collectors and sinners came and ate with him and his disciples. 11 When the Pharisees saw this, they asked his disciples, "Why does your teacher eat with tax collectors and sinners?"[f]

12 On hearing this, Jesus said, "It is not the healthy who need a doctor, but the sick. 13 But go and learn what this means: 'I desire mercy, not sacrifice.'[a][g] For I have not come to call the righteous, but sinners."[h]

Jesus Questioned About Fasting

9:14-17pp — Mk 2:18-22; Lk 5:33-39

14 Then John's disciples came and asked him, "How is it that we and the Pharisees fast often,[i] but your disciples do not fast?"

15 Jesus answered, "How can the guests of the bridegroom mourn while he is with them?[j] The time will come when the bridegroom will be taken from them; then they will fast.[k]

16 "No one sews a patch of unshrunk cloth on an old garment, for the patch will pull away from the garment, making the tear worse. 17 Neither do people pour new wine into old wineskins. If they do, the skins will burst; the wine will run out and the wineskins will be ruined. No, they pour new wine into new wineskins, and both are preserved."

8:34 [v] Lk 5:8; Ac 16:39 **9:1** [w] Mt 4:13 **9:2** [x] Mt 4:24 [y] ver 22 [z] Jn 16:33 [a] Lk 7:48 **9:3** [b] Mt 26:65; Jn 10:33 **9:4** [c] Ps 94:11; Mt 12:25; Lk 6:8; 9:47; 11:17 **9:6** [d] Mt 8:20 **9:8** [e] Mt 5:16; 15:31; Lk 7:16; 13:13; 17:15; 23:47; Jn 15:8; Ac 4:21; 11:18; 21:20 **9:11** [f] Mt 11:19; Lk 5:30; 15:2; Gal 2:15 **9:13** [g] Hos 6:6; Mic 6:6-8; Mt 12:7 [h] 1Ti 1:15 **9:14** [i] Lk 18:12 **9:15** [j] Jn 3:29 [k] Ac 13:2, 3; 14:23

[a] *13* Hosea 6:6

8:34 *pleaded with him to leave.* Especially after the destruction of the pigs, Gentiles might think of Jesus as a powerful and dangerous magician. Economic interests mattered more to them than a person, as was common (cf. Ac 16:19; 19:27).
9:2 *your sins are forgiven.* Priests might perhaps pronounce God's forgiveness after atonement had occurred, but no sacrifice was offered here. The teachers of the law thus consider the pronouncement presumptuous (v. 3).
9:6 *the Son of Man has authority.* The Son of Man's authority echoes Da 7:13 – 14. Jesus has authority not merely to pronounce God's forgiveness (cf. v. 2), but to forgive — a divine prerogative!
9:9 *tax collector's booth.* Most people in the Roman Empire did not like tax collectors; Jewish people viewed them as traitors. Their job affected the poor most dramatically. In fact, when harvests were bad in Egypt, it was not unheard of for the population of an entire village to leave town and start a village somewhere else when they heard that a tax collector was coming. Some consider Matthew a customs officer charging tariffs on goods passing through. Like other tax collectors, customs officers could search possessions; customs income normally went to local governments run by elites who were cooperative with Rome. See note on Mk 2:14. *Follow me.* See note on 4:19.
9:10 *having dinner.* The term often connotes a banquet (a festive meal where people reclined), which was probably in Jesus' honor. Eating with someone established a covenant of friendship, which normally also signified approval.
9:11 *Pharisees ... tax collectors.* Later rabbis sometimes contrasted Pharisees, as the godliest Judeans one would normally meet, with tax collectors, as the most ungodly one would normally meet. Pharisees did not approve of eating with sinners, making Jesus' behavior perplexing to them.
9:12 *healthy.* Ancient speakers and writers often used sickness and physicians as moral or intellectual analogies.
9:13 *go and learn.* Jewish teachers sometimes exhorted their hearers to "go and learn," but Jesus' exhortation might seem more insulting here (cf. 12:5). *I desire mercy, not sacrifice.* Those who valued ritual sacrifices above compassion toward others missed God's heart (Hos 6:6; also quoted in Mt 12:7). In principle Pharisees, especially the school of Hillel, valued mercy — but none would have embraced sinners as Jesus did.
9:14 *How is it ...?* People in antiquity often held teachers responsible for the behavior of their disciples.
9:15 *mourn.* Fasting was often linked with mourning, whereas weddings were the supreme time for rejoicing. In fact, rabbis taught that weddings even took priority over many religious obligations.
9:17 People employed animal skins, most often goatskins, as containers for fluids. Wine expands as it ferments; still-expanding, new wine would rupture wineskins that had already been stretched by old, fermenting wine. Jesus' new order demanded a new approach.

Jesus Raises a Dead Girl and Heals a Sick Woman

9:18-26pp — Mk 5:22-43; Lk 8:41-56

18 While he was saying this, a synagogue leader came and knelt before him[l]
and said, "My daughter has just died. But
come and put your hand on her,[m] and she
will live." 19 Jesus got up and went with
him, and so did his disciples.
20 Just then a woman who had been
subject to bleeding for twelve years came
up behind him and touched the edge of
his cloak.[n] 21 She said to herself, "If I only
touch his cloak, I will be healed."
22 Jesus turned and saw her. "Take heart,
daughter," he said, "your faith has healed
you."[o] And the woman was healed at that
moment.[p]
23 When Jesus entered the synagogue
leader's house and saw the noisy crowd
and people playing pipes,[q] 24 he said, "Go
away. The girl is not dead[r] but asleep."[s]
But they laughed at him. 25 After the crowd
had been put outside, he went in and
took the girl by the hand, and she got up.
26 News of this spread through all that region.[t]

Jesus Heals the Blind and the Mute

27 As Jesus went on from there, two blind
men followed him, calling out, "Have mercy on us, Son of David!"[u]
28 When he had gone indoors, the blind
men came to him, and he asked them, "Do
you believe that I am able to do this?"
"Yes, Lord," they replied.
29 Then he touched their eyes and said,
"According to your faith let it be done
to you";[v] 30 and their sight was restored.
Jesus warned them sternly, "See that no
one knows about this."[w] 31 But they went
out and spread the news about him all
over that region.[x]
32 While they were going out, a man who
was demon-possessed[y] and could not talk[z]
was brought to Jesus. 33 And when the demon was driven out, the man who had
been mute spoke. The crowd was amazed
and said, "Nothing like this has ever been
seen in Israel."[a]
34 But the Pharisees said, "It is by the
prince of demons that he drives out demons."[b]

The Workers Are Few

35 Jesus went through all the towns and
villages, teaching in their synagogues, proclaiming the good news of the kingdom
and healing every disease and sickness.[c]
36 When he saw the crowds, he had compassion on them,[d] because they were harassed and helpless, like sheep without a
shepherd.[e] 37 Then he said to his disciples,
"The harvest[f] is plentiful but the workers
are few.[g] 38 Ask the Lord of the harvest,
therefore, to send out workers into his harvest field."

Jesus Sends Out the Twelve

10:2-4pp — Mk 3:16-19; Lk 6:14-16; Ac 1:13
10:9-15pp — Mk 6:8-11; Lk 9:3-5; 10:4-12
10:19-22pp — Mk 13:11-13; Lk 21:12-17
10:26-33pp — Lk 12:2-9
10:34,35pp — Lk 12:51-53

10 Jesus called his twelve disciples
to him and gave them authority to
drive out impure spirits[h] and to heal every
disease and sickness.

9:18 [l] Mt 8:2 [m] Mk 5:23 **9:20** [n] Mt 14:36; Mk 3:10 **9:22** [o] Mk 10:52; Lk 7:50; 17:19; 18:42 [p] Mt 15:28 **9:23** [q] 2Ch 35:25; Jer 9:17,18 **9:24** [r] Ac 20:10 [s] Jn 11:11-14 **9:26** [t] Mt 4:24 **9:27** [u] Mt 15:22; Mk 10:47; Lk 18:38-39 **9:29** [v] ver 22 **9:30** [w] Mt 8:4 **9:31** [x] ver 26; Mk 7:36 **9:32** [y] Mt 4:24 [z] Mt 12:22-24 **9:33** [a] Mk 2:12 **9:34** [b] Mt 12:24; Lk 11:15 **9:35** [c] Mt 4:23 **9:36** [d] Mt 14:14 [e] Nu 27:17; Eze 34:5, 6; Zec 10:2; Mk 6:34 **9:37** [f] Jn 4:35 [g] Lk 10:2 **10:1** [h] Mk 3:13-15; Lk 9:1

9:18 *synagogue leader.* This term encompasses different roles in different locations; a synagogue could have multiple leaders, and the title was often honorary. Generally, however, those holding this office were prominent persons of means.
9:20 *subject to bleeding.* Such a condition made someone ritually impure. Because her bleeding was long-term and intercourse was forbidden in such circumstances, she was probably divorced (if she had ever been married), fairly socially isolated, and destitute. Because anyone whose cloak she touched became ritually impure (cf. Lev 15:25 – 27), she does not announce that she is touching Jesus. This woman's faith might appear scandalous to others, but she is desperate and knows that her cure lies with Jesus and him alone. *the edge of his cloak.* May refer to Jesus' Jewish tassels (note the Greek translation in the Septuagint [the pre-Christian Greek translation of the OT]of Nu 15:38 – 39; Dt 22:12; see note on Mt 23:5).
9:23 *noisy crowd ... pipes.* Burials were conducted quickly in Judea and Galilee, so mourners gathered immediately when someone died. Professional mourners helped facilitate grieving; at least two might be present for a poor person, but a synagogue official's resources could accommodate more.
9:24 *asleep.* "Sleep" was a frequent metaphor for death in antiquity, though Jesus is also maintaining an element of privacy, as in 8:4.
9:25 *took the girl by the hand.* The touch of someone bleeding could communicate ritual impurity for one day, but touching a corpse made one impure for a week (Nu 19:11). Not ashamed to be considered unclean by others, Jesus instead makes clean those whom he touches.
9:27 *two blind men.* Biblical law mandated concern for the blind, but few professions outside of begging would be open to them. Blind men could follow Jesus' voice. *Son of David.* Implies that Jesus is the promised ruler of Israel.
9:34 *by the prince of demons.* Even in the second century, Christianity's detractors could not deny that Jesus performed miracles, but they attributed these to sorcery rather than to God. Jesus' accusers would know that the required penalty for sorcery was death (Ex 22:18).
9:36 *like sheep without a shepherd.* An OT picture of God's people (Nu 27:17; 1Ki 22:17; Eze 34:5), but God had promised to one day shepherd them himself (Eze 34:11 – 16).
9:37 – 38 Once grain was ripe, gathering it in quickly before it could spoil was an urgent task. Landowners would hire extra labor (cf. 20:1).
10:1 Disciples of teachers were like apprentices; the best could ideally carry on the teacher's work. *twelve.* See note on 19:28.

2 These are the names of the twelve
apostles: first, Simon (who is called Peter) and his brother Andrew; James son of
Zebedee, and his brother John; 3 Philip and
Bartholomew; Thomas and Matthew the
tax collector; James son of Alphaeus, and
Thaddaeus; 4 Simon the Zealot and Judas
Iscariot, who betrayed him.[i]
5 These twelve Jesus sent out with the
following instructions: "Do not go among
the Gentiles or enter any town of the Samaritans.[j] 6 Go rather to the lost sheep of
Israel.[k] 7 As you go, proclaim this message:
'The kingdom of heaven[l] has come near.'
8 Heal the sick, raise the dead, cleanse
those who have leprosy,[a] drive out demons. Freely you have received; freely
give.
9 "Do not get any gold or silver or copper
to take with you in your belts[m] — 10 no bag
for the journey or extra shirt or sandals or
a staff, for the worker is worth his keep.[n]
11 Whatever town or village you enter,
search there for some worthy person and
stay at their house until you leave. 12 As
you enter the home, give it your greeting.[o]
13 If the home is deserving, let your peace
rest on it; if it is not, let your peace return
to you. 14 If anyone will not welcome you
or listen to your words, leave that home
or town and shake the dust off your feet.[p]
15 Truly I tell you, it will be more bearable
for Sodom and Gomorrah[q] on the day of
judgment[r] than for that town.[s]
16 "I am sending you out like sheep
among wolves.[t] Therefore be as shrewd as
snakes and as innocent as doves.[u] 17 Be on
your guard; you will be handed over to
the local councils[v] and be flogged in the
synagogues.[w] 18 On my account you will
be brought before governors and kings[x]
as witnesses to them and to the Gentiles.
19 But when they arrest you, do not worry
about what to say or how to say it.[y] At that
time you will be given what to say, 20 for it
will not be you speaking, but the Spirit of
your Father[z] speaking through you.
21 "Brother will betray brother to death,
and a father his child; children will rebel
against their parents[a] and have them put

10:4 [i] Mt 26:14-16,25,47; Jn 13:2,26,27 **10:5** [j] 2Ki 17:24; Lk 9:52; Jn 4:4-26,39,40; Ac 8:5,25 **10:6** [k] Jer 50:6; Mt 15:24 **10:7** [l] Mt 3:2 **10:9** [m] Lk 22:35 **10:10** [n] 1Ti 5:18 **10:12** [o] 1Sa 25:6 **10:14** [p] Ne 5:13; Lk 10:11; Ac 13:51 **10:15** [q] 2Pe 2:6 [r] Mt 12:36; 2Pe 2:9; 1Jn 4:17 [s] Mt 11:22,24 **10:16** [t] Lk 10:3 [u] Ro 16:19 **10:17** [v] Mt 5:22 [w] Mt 23:34; Mk 13:9; Ac 5:40; 26:11 **10:18** [x] Ac 25:24-26 **10:19** [y] Ex 4:12 **10:20** [z] Ac 4:8 **10:21** [a] ver 35,36; Mic 7:6

[a] *8* The Greek word traditionally translated *leprosy* was used for various diseases affecting the skin.

10:2 *apostles.* Or "commissioned agents," those authorized by the sender's authority to bring the message. Some of the names in vv. 2 – 4 (Simon, James, John and Judas) were very common, explaining why some are given additional identifying titles.
10:5 *Gentiles … Samaritans.* Samaria bordered Galilee on the south, and Gentile cities surrounded it on the outside; Jesus' disciples are thus essentially confined to Galilee during this mission. For Samaritans, see the article "Samaria and Samaritans," p. 1812; see also applicable notes on Jn 4.
10:6 *lost sheep.* For Israel as God's lost sheep, see Isa 53:6; Jer 50:6; Eze 34:5; cf. Ps 119:176.
10:7 *proclaim this message.* Disciples normally carried on their teacher's or school's message; see 3:2; 4:17.
10:9 *in your belts.* Travelers often carried money in a pouch tied to one's belt.
10:10 *no bag for the journey.* Wandering Cynic philosophers, found in some Gentile cities, carried a bag for begging, which is prohibited here. *extra shirt.* In the poorest areas, many peasants had only a single cloak. *sandals.* Judean sandals had light straps running from between the toes to just above the ankle; unlike shoes, such sandals protected only the bottom of the foot. *staff.* Travelers used a staff for protection against robbers, snakes and other creatures, and sometimes for maintaining one's balance while walking on uneven mountain paths. Matthew's description is slightly more demanding than Mark's (Mk 6:8 – 11); ancient readers were accustomed to such minor variations in ancient historical and biographical works. Biblical prophets also had to live simply in times of widespread apostasy, not dependent on decadent society (cf., e.g., 3:1,4; 1Ki 17:4 – 6; 18:13; 2Ki 4:38; 5:15 – 16,26; 6:1).
10:11 *stay at their house.* Hospitality was one of the chief virtues in Mediterranean antiquity, and Jewish travelers could normally count on Jewish hospitality even in Diaspora cities. When Essenes (members of a strict Jewish sect) traveled, they traveled light, depending on hospitality from other Essenes.
10:12 – 13 *your greeting … let your peace rest.* The conventional Jewish greeting was *shalom,* "May it be well with you." This was a blessing, i.e., an implicit prayer to God. See note on 23:7.
10:14 *shake the dust off your feet.* Jewish people sometimes shook profane dust from their feet when entering a more holy place; some did so when leaving pagan territory to enter the Holy Land (cf. v. 15).
10:15 *Sodom and Gomorrah.* Sodom rejected God's messengers (Ge 19:4 – 5). Biblical prophets used Sodom as the epitome of wickedness, often applying the image to Israel (Dt 32:32; Isa 1:10; 3:9; Jer 23:14; Eze 16:46 – 49).
10:16 *sheep among wolves.* Ancients viewed sheep as helpless against wolves, and some Jewish teachers viewed Israel as such sheep. More unusual, Jesus says that his sheep are *sent* among wolves. *doves.* Many thought of doves as timid or weak.
10:17 *local councils … synagogues.* Priests and other elders normally judged local councils. Synagogues doubled as community centers, and disciplines could be meted out there. If they carried out beatings as in somewhat later tradition, the condemned person would be tied to a post, then given 26 lashes with a calf-leather whip across the back and 13 lashes across the chest. The number of lashes (39; cf. 2Co 11:24) was to prevent accidentally exceeding the Biblical limit of 40 (Dt 25:3).
10:18 *governors and kings.* In the Roman Empire, governors ruled most provinces. The emperor appointed his own representatives to govern provinces with legions, and appointed equestrians to control some other provinces; the senate appointed governors for provinces not directly under the emperor's control. The emperor also allowed some states to retain client kings answerable to Rome, such as Herod the Great (2:1), Aretas (2Co 11:32) and, briefly, Herod Agrippa I (Ac 12:1).
10:20 *Spirit of your Father speaking.* Scripture and Jewish tradition often associated God's Spirit with prophetic empowerment to speak God's message.
10:21 – 23 Many Jewish people expected these suffer-

to death. [22]You will be hated by everyone
because of me, but the one who stands
firm to the end will be saved.[b] [23]When you
are persecuted in one place, flee to another. Truly I tell you, you will not finish going through the towns of Israel before the
Son of Man comes.

[24]"The student is not above the teacher, nor a servant above his master.[c] [25]It is
enough for students to be like their teachers, and servants like their masters. If the
head of the house has been called Beelzebul,[d] how much more the members of his
household!

[26]"So do not be afraid of them, for there
is nothing concealed that will not be disclosed, or hidden that will not be made
known.[e] [27]What I tell you in the dark,
speak in the daylight; what is whispered
in your ear, proclaim from the roofs. [28]Do
not be afraid of those who kill the body
but cannot kill the soul. Rather, be afraid
of the One[f] who can destroy both soul
and body in hell. [29]Are not two sparrows
sold for a penny? Yet not one of them
will fall to the ground outside your Father's care.[a] [30]And even the very hairs of
your head are all numbered.[g] [31]So don't
be afraid; you are worth more than many
sparrows.[h]

[32]"Whoever acknowledges me before
others,[i] I will also acknowledge before my
Father in heaven. [33]But whoever disowns
me before others, I will disown before my
Father in heaven.[j]

[34]"Do not suppose that I have come to
bring peace to the earth. I did not come
to bring peace, but a sword. [35]For I have
come to turn

" 'a man against his father,
a daughter against her mother,
a daughter-in-law against her mother-in-law[k]—
[36] a man's enemies will be the members of his own household.'[b][l]

[37]"Anyone who loves their father or
mother more than me is not worthy of
me; anyone who loves their son or daughter more than me is not worthy of me.[m]
[38]Whoever does not take up their cross and
follow me is not worthy of me.[n] [39]Whoever
finds their life will lose it, and whoever loses their life for my sake will find it.[o]

[40]"Anyone who welcomes you welcomes me,[p] and anyone who welcomes
me welcomes the one who sent me.[q]
[41]Whoever welcomes a prophet as a
prophet will receive a prophet's reward,
and whoever welcomes a righteous person as a righteous person will receive a

10:22 [b]Mt 24:13; Mk 13:13 **10:24** [c]Lk 6:40; Jn 13:16; 15:20 **10:25** [d]Mk 3:22 **10:26** [e]Mk 4:22; Lk 8:17 **10:28** [f]Isa 8:12, 13; Heb 10:31 **10:30** [g]1Sa 14:45; 2Sa 14:11; Lk 21:18; Ac 27:34 **10:31** [h]Mt 12:12 **10:32** [i]Ro 10:9 **10:33** [j]Mk 8:38; 2Ti 2:12 **10:35** [k]ver 21 **10:36** [l]Mic 7:6 **10:37** [m]Lk 14:26 **10:38** [n]Mt 16:24; Lk 14:27 **10:39** [o]Lk 17:33; Jn 12:25 **10:40** [p]Mt 18:5; Gal 4:14 [q]Lk 9:48; Jn 12:44; 13:20

[a] *29* Or *will*; or *knowledge* [b] *36* Micah 7:6

ings of the righteous to precede the end. Although some regarded fleeing (v. 23) as dishonorable, most preferred it to dying.

10:24 *student is not above the teacher.* Apart from attending to the master's feet, disciples would ideally do for their rabbi anything a servant would do. A mature disciple could become a rabbi but was not normally considered greater than the one who schooled him.

10:25 *Beelzebul.* Because Jesus' first hearers spoke Aramaic, they may have caught a wordplay: *Beelzebul* literally means "master of the house"; it probably plays on *Baal-Zebub*, a pagan deity (2Ki 1:2 – 3,6,16). *Beelzebul* was also used with reference to Satan; cf. 12:24 – 28.

10:27 *from the roofs.* Neighbors could sometimes communicate from their flat rooftops as opposed to the narrow streets below, but their shouting, unobstructed by buildings, would be audible over a longer distance.

10:28 *kill the body.* Many Jewish people by this period distinguished the body from the identity, or soul, that persisted after death. Most Judeans affirmed the resurrection of the body as well as the persistence of the soul; the wicked would be resurrected for torment (Da 12:2).

10:29 *two sparrows … penny.* The poor could purchase sparrows, probably the cheapest meat in the market. *penny.* An *assarion*, worth less than an hour's wage for the average worker (cf. a roughly equivalent calculation in Lk 12:6).

10:30 *hairs of your head.* A promise that not a hair would fall meant that one would be completely protected (1Sa 14:45; 2Sa 14:11; 1Ki 1:52); here, no detail of care goes unnoticed by their Father (for the father image, see note on 7:9 – 10).

10:31 *more.* Jewish teachers often reasoned by means of *qal vaomer*, "How much more?" arguments. If God watches over sparrows (v. 29), he certainly watches over his children.

10:32 *acknowledges me.* Jewish teachers emphasized "acknowledging" or "confessing" God, a principle Jesus here applies to himself.

10:35 *daughter-in-law against her mother-in-law.* Because Mic 7:6 addresses grievous sins characteristic of Israel before announcing Israel's restoration, Jewish tradition sometimes applied its image of familial division to the final tribulation. Because newly married couples sometimes lived with the groom's family, daughter-in-law and mother-in-law are natural examples (more than, e.g., son-in-law).

10:37 *loves their father or mother more than me.* Many Jewish people considered the mandate to honor one's parents the greatest commandment; they accorded only God himself greater honor.

10:38 *take up their cross.* A person condemned to be executed would often carry the horizontal beam of his cross out to the site of his execution, where it would be affixed to an upright stake. Because authorities liked to make executions as public as possible, for their deterrent effect, those being led to execution were typically led naked through busy streets, exposing the condemned to public humiliation and sometimes mockery.

10:40 *welcomes me.* However one treated an agent or ambassador reflected one's feelings toward the sender; one's treatment of a prophet reflected one's treatment of God (Ex 16:8; 1Sa 8:7).

10:41 On hospitality to Jesus' agents, see note on v. 11. God would reward hospitable treatment of his prophets (e.g., 1Ki 17:12 – 16; 2Ki 4:8 – 17).

righteous person's reward. 42 And if anyone gives even a cup of cold water to one
of these little ones who is my disciple, truly I tell you, that person will certainly not
lose their reward."[r]

Jesus and John the Baptist

11:2-19pp — Lk 7:18-35

11 After Jesus had finished instructing his twelve disciples,[s] he went
on from there to teach and preach in the
towns of Galilee.[a]
2 When John, who was in prison,[t] heard
about the deeds of the Messiah, he sent
his disciples 3 to ask him, "Are you the
one who is to come,[u] or should we expect
someone else?"
4 Jesus replied, "Go back and report to
John what you hear and see: 5 The blind
receive sight, the lame walk, those who
have leprosy[b] are cleansed, the deaf hear,
the dead are raised, and the good news is
proclaimed to the poor.[v] 6 Blessed is anyone
who does not stumble on account of me."[w]
7 As John's[x] disciples were leaving, Jesus
began to speak to the crowd about John:
"What did you go out into the wilderness
to see? A reed swayed by the wind? 8 If not,
what did you go out to see? A man dressed
in fine clothes? No, those who wear fine
clothes are in kings' palaces. 9 Then what
did you go out to see? A prophet?[y] Yes, I
tell you, and more than a prophet. 10 This
is the one about whom it is written:

"'I will send my messenger ahead of you,
who will prepare your way before
you.'[c][z]

11 Truly I tell you, among those born of
women there has not risen anyone greater
than John the Baptist; yet whoever is least
in the kingdom of heaven is greater than
he. 12 From the days of John the Baptist until now, the kingdom of heaven has been
subjected to violence,[d] and violent people
have been raiding it. 13 For all the Prophets
and the Law prophesied until John. 14 And
if you are willing to accept it, he is the
Elijah who was to come.[a] 15 Whoever has
ears, let them hear.[b]
16 "To what can I compare this generation? They are like children sitting in the
marketplaces and calling out to others:

17 "'We played the pipe for you,
and you did not dance;
we sang a dirge,
and you did not mourn.'

18 For John came neither eating[c] nor drinking,[d] and they say, 'He has a demon.'

10:42 [r] Mt 25:40; Mk 9:41; Heb 6:10 **11:1** [s] Mt 7:28 **11:2** [t] Mt 14:3 **11:3** [u] Ps 118:26; Jn 11:27; Heb 10:37 **11:5** [v] Isa 35:4-6; 61:1; Lk 4:18, 19 **11:6** [w] Mt 13:21 **11:7** [x] Mt 3:1 **11:9** [y] Mt 21:26; Lk 1:76

11:10 [z] Mal 3:1; Mk 1:2 **11:14** [a] Mal 4:5; Mt 17:10-13; Mk 9:11-13; Lk 1:17; Jn 1:21 **11:15** [b] Mt 13:9, 43; Mk 4:23; Lk 14:35; Rev 2:7 **11:18** [c] Mt 3:4 [d] Lk 1:15

[a] 1 Greek *in their towns* [b] 5 The Greek word traditionally translated *leprosy* was used for various diseases affecting the skin. [c] *10* Mal. 3:1
[d] *12* Or *been forcefully advancing*

10:42 *even a cup of cold water.* The poorest person might have only water to offer, but hospitality obligations demanded sharing with a visitor what one had. Hot and weary travelers usually preferred water cold.
11:2–3 John understood that Jesus' *deeds* (such as healings) were good, but he may have been concerned that they differed from John's message of end-time outpourings of the Spirit and fire (see note on 3:11).
11:2 *in prison.* Herod Antipas imprisoned John in his Perean fortress Machaerus (14:3).
11:4–5 *report ... what you hear and see.* Jesus depicts his current mission of restoring the disabled and preaching to the poor as a foretaste of the promised coming era of restoration. He does so by borrowing language from Isa 35:5–6; 61:1. Josephus mentions two first-century prophetic figures after Jesus who each promised an end-time sign that they failed to deliver; with the possible exception of these failed leaders, no ancient workers of unusual acts besides Jesus claimed that the future kingdom was arriving in their own ministry or signs.
11:6 *Blessed.* On beatitudes, see note on 5:3. *stumble.* Often used as a metaphor for sin or falling away.
11:7 *reed.* The emblem on Antipas's coins was a reed. John's hearers would be familiar with reeds, since they grew as tall as 16 feet (5 meters) around the Jordan, where John had baptized. Reeds were used figuratively for what was weak and undependable in time of trouble (1Ki 14:15; 2Ki 18:21; 3 Maccabees 2:22).
11:8 *kings' palaces.* Herod Antipas, who imprisoned John, was only a tetrarch but was the closest to a king with palaces that Jesus' Galilean hearers might ordinarily see.
11:10 The promised messenger of Mal 3:1 may be one like Elijah (see Mal 4:5; cf. Mt 3:4 and 2Ki 1:8).
11:11 *least in the kingdom ... is greater than he.* Both Jews and Gentiles offered comparisons not only between good and bad, but also between good and better; this is clearly a case of the latter kind of comparison. Such comparisons were meant to exalt the better all the more by virtue of its superiority to something else good.
11:12 *subjected to violence.* Some Jewish people sought to establish God's kingdom by force, striking against Romans and the Jewish aristocrats who supported them. Some suggest that Jesus speaks here parabolically of spiritual warriors, who prevail in laying hold of the kingdom not with physical but with spiritual force.
11:13 *until John.* Jewish people often summarized Scripture as "the Law and the Prophets." Although some of the elite believed that prophets ceased after Malachi, most people recognized John the Baptist as a prophet (14:5; 21:26).
11:14 On John as Elijah, see note on v. 10.
11:15 *Whoever has ears.* This is the language of riddles, inviting the wise to consider the meaning. Israel was not always ready to hear (Isa 6:10; Jer 6:10; Eze 12:2).
11:16 *To what can I compare ...?* Rabbis often began parables with phrases such as this. *children.* They sometimes played games of weddings or funerals (e.g., burying a grasshopper). Here Jesus envisions spoiled children who argue inconsistently so long as they get their way.
11:17 *dance ... mourn.* Dancing was appropriate for the celebrations of weddings, and mourning for funerals. Both were community events; as funeral processions passed, e.g., bystanders were often expected to join in the procession.
11:18 *has a demon.* A prophet with a demon would be assumed a false prophet—for which the penalty was death (Dt 13:5).

19The Son of Man came eating and drinking, and they say, 'Here is a glutton and
a drunkard, a friend of tax collectors and
sinners.'[e] But wisdom is proved right by
her deeds."

Woe on Unrepentant Towns

11:21-23pp — Lk 10:13-15

20Then Jesus began to denounce the
towns in which most of his miracles had
been performed, because they did not repent. 21"Woe to you, Chorazin! Woe to
you, Bethsaida![f] For if the miracles that
were performed in you had been performed in Tyre and Sidon,[g] they would
have repented long ago in sackcloth and
ashes.[h] 22But I tell you, it will be more
bearable for Tyre and Sidon on the day of
judgment than for you.[i] 23And you, Capernaum,[j] will you be lifted to the heavens?
No, you will go down to Hades.[a][k] For if
the miracles that were performed in you
had been performed in Sodom, it would
have remained to this day. 24But I tell you
that it will be more bearable for Sodom on
the day of judgment than for you."[l]

The Father Revealed in the Son

11:25-27pp — Lk 10:21,22

25At that time Jesus said, "I praise you,
Father,[m] Lord of heaven and earth, because you have hidden these things from
the wise and learned, and revealed them
to little children.[n] 26Yes, Father, for this is
what you were pleased to do.

27"All things have been committed to
me[o] by my Father.[p] No one knows the Son
except the Father, and no one knows the
Father except the Son and those to whom
the Son chooses to reveal him.[q]

28"Come to me,[r] all you who are weary and burdened, and I will give you rest.
29Take my yoke upon you and learn from
me,[s] for I am gentle and humble in heart,
and you will find rest for your souls.[t] 30For
my yoke is easy and my burden is light."[u]

Jesus Is Lord of the Sabbath

12:1-8pp — Mk 2:23-28; Lk 6:1-5
12:9-14pp — Mk 3:1-6; Lk 6:6-11

12 At that time Jesus went through
the grainfields on the Sabbath. His
disciples were hungry and began to pick
some heads of grain[v] and eat them. 2When
the Pharisees saw this, they said to him,
"Look! Your disciples are doing what is
unlawful on the Sabbath."[w]

3He answered, "Haven't you read what
David did when he and his companions
were hungry?[x] 4He entered the house of
God, and he and his companions ate the
consecrated bread — which was not lawful
for them to do, but only for the priests.[y]
5Or haven't you read in the Law that the
priests on Sabbath duty in the temple

11:19 [e]Mt 9:11
11:21 [f]Mk 6:45; Lk 9:10; Jn 12:21
[g]Mt 15:21; Lk 6:17; Ac 12:20
[h]Jnh 3:5-9
11:22 [i]ver 24; Mt 10:15
11:23 [j]Mt 4:13
[k]Isa 14:13-15
11:24 [l]Mt 10:15
11:25 [m]Lk 22:42; Jn 11:41
[n]1Co 1:26-29
11:27 [o]Mt 28:18
[p]Jn 3:35; 13:3; 17:2 [q]Jn 10:15
11:28 [r]Jn 7:37
11:29 [s]Jn 13:15; Php 2:5; 1Pe 2:21; 1Jn 2:6
[t]Jer 6:16
11:30 [u]1Jn 5:3
12:1 [v]Dt 23:25
12:2 [w]ver 10; Lk 13:14; 14:3; Jn 5:10; 7:23; 9:16
12:3 [x]1Sa 21:6
12:4 [y]Lev 24:5,9

[a] *23* That is, the realm of the dead

11:19 *a glutton and a drunkard.* Like a false prophet, someone who is a habitual glutton and a drunkard was deemed worthy of death (Dt 21:20 – 21).
11:21 *Woe to you.* Prophets sometimes announced judgments with the form, "Woe to you ..." (e.g., Isa 29:1; Eze 16:23; Am 5:18). *Chorazin ... Bethsaida.* No one should question historically that Jesus as a prophet denounced these towns. Virtually no one outside of Galilee knew of Chorazin (about two miles [three kilometers] from Capernaum). Probably soon after Jesus' ministry, around the year 30 (though some do suggest earlier), Bethsaida began to be called Julia; although Josephus later uses both names, the Gospels use only the earlier, local name. *Tyre and Sidon.* These Phoenician cities had been objects of God's judgment (e.g., Isa 23; Eze 26 – 28); Jezebel (Ahab's wife) was from the region of Sidon (1Ki 16:31). *sackcloth and ashes.* Appropriate dress to show mourning or repentance (e.g., Jer 6:26; Da 9:3).
11:22 Cf. note on 12:39 – 42.
11:23 Jesus applies to Capernaum an image from the prophecy against Babylon in Isa 14:11 – 12.
11:29 *Take my yoke ... find rest.* Only the poorest people would use a yoke to pull their loads. When used figuratively, a yoke represented slavery or submission; Jewish teachers spoke of bearing the yoke of God's kingdom, through the yoke of the law. Only God would call the yoke of the kingdom or of the law "my yoke." A sage before Jesus' era said, "Come near me, you who are unlearned ... Get wisdom, put your neck under her yoke ... Look with your eyes: I have labored only a little and I have found for myself great rest" (Sirach 51:23 – 27). Jesus evokes such words, but whereas the earlier sage referred to wisdom's yoke, Jesus speaks of his own. Those who turned back to God's ways would find rest for their souls (Jer 6:16). Jesus' understanding of rest (v. 28) clearly differs from that of the Pharisees (12:1 – 14).
12:1 *pick some heads.* On normal days, it was legal to pick heads of grain from others' fields (Dt 23:25; cf. Ru 2:2); Pharisaic tradition, however, viewed such activity as work, and thus illegal on the Sabbath (cf. Ex 31:13 – 14; 35:2). Scripture itself prohibited preparing food on the Sabbath (Ex 16:22 – 30; 35:3), but Jewish people often feasted on the Sabbath (on food that was prepared the previous day) and Jewish tradition prohibited fasting on it. Jesus' disciples might thus pick grain if other food was unavailable.
12:2 *the Pharisees saw.* One would not normally find Pharisees in wheat fields on the Sabbath, unless they were traveling with Jesus or seeking to evaluate his activity (or perhaps they observed from afar in a town). Teachers were held responsible for their disciples' behavior.
12:3,5 *Haven't you read ... ?* Such a question would insult the learned Pharisees.
12:4 Whether David actually had with him the companions mentioned in 1Sa 21:4 – 5 or the high priest merely believed that David did, the high priest's actions show that he understood that hunger and an urgent situation took priority over ritual law.
12:5 *priests ... in the temple.* During debates about what was permissible on the Sabbath or other holy days, Jewish teachers sometimes appealed to the activity of priests in the temple on such days.

desecrate the Sabbath[z] and yet are innocent? 6 I tell you that something greater than the temple is here.[a] 7 If you had
known what these words mean, 'I desire
mercy, not sacrifice,'[a][b] you would not have
condemned the innocent. 8 For the Son of
Man[c] is Lord of the Sabbath."

9 Going on from that place, he went into
their synagogue, 10 and a man with a shriveled hand was there. Looking for a reason
to bring charges against Jesus, they asked
him, "Is it lawful to heal on the Sabbath?"[d]

11 He said to them, "If any of you has a
sheep and it falls into a pit on the Sabbath,
will you not take hold of it and lift it out?[e]
12 How much more valuable is a person
than a sheep![f] Therefore it is lawful to do
good on the Sabbath."

13 Then he said to the man, "Stretch out
your hand." So he stretched it out and it
was completely restored, just as sound as
the other. 14 But the Pharisees went out
and plotted how they might kill Jesus.[g]

God's Chosen Servant

15 Aware of this, Jesus withdrew from
that place. A large crowd followed him,
and he healed all who were ill.[h] 16 He
warned them not to tell others about him.[i]
17 This was to fulfill what was spoken
through the prophet Isaiah:

18 "Here is my servant whom I have
chosen,
the one I love, in whom I delight;[j]
I will put my Spirit on him,
and he will proclaim justice to the
nations.
19 He will not quarrel or cry out;
no one will hear his voice in the
streets.
20 A bruised reed he will not break,
and a smoldering wick he will not
snuff out,
till he has brought justice through to
victory.
21 In his name the nations will put
their hope."[b][k]

Jesus and Beelzebul

12:25-29pp — Mk 3:23-27; Lk 11:17-22

22 Then they brought him a demon-possessed man who was blind and mute, and
Jesus healed him, so that he could both talk
and see.[l] 23 All the people were astonished
and said, "Could this be the Son of David?"[m]
24 But when the Pharisees heard this, they
said, "It is only by Beelzebul,[n] the prince
of demons, that this fellow drives out demons."[o]

25 Jesus knew their thoughts[p] and said
to them, "Every kingdom divided against
itself will be ruined, and every city or
household divided against itself will not
stand. 26 If Satan[q] drives out Satan, he is
divided against himself. How then can
his kingdom stand? 27 And if I drive out
demons by Beelzebul, by whom do your
people[r] drive them out? So then, they will
be your judges. 28 But if it is by the Spirit

12:5 [z] Nu 28:9, 10; Jn 7:22,23 **12:6** [a] ver 41, 42 **12:7** [b] Hos 6:6; Mic 6:6-8; Mt 9:13 **12:8** [c] Mt 8:20 **12:10** [d] ver 2; Lk 13:14; 14:3; Jn 9:16 **12:11** [e] Lk 14:5 **12:12** [f] Mt 10:31 **12:14** [g] Mt 26:4; 27:1; Mk 3:6; Lk 6:11; Jn 5:18; 11:53 **12:15** [h] Mt 4:23 **12:16** [i] Mt 8:4 **12:18** [j] Mt 3:17 **12:21** [k] Isa 42:1-4 **12:22** [l] Mt 4:24; 9:32-33 **12:23** [m] Mt 9:27 **12:24** [n] Mk 3:22 [o] Mt 9:34 **12:25** [p] Mt 9:4 **12:26** [q] Mt 4:10 **12:27** [r] Ac 19:13

[a] 7 Hosea 6:6 [b] 21 Isaiah 42:1-4

12:6 Jesus claims to bear God's presence more than does the temple.
12:7 See note on 9:13.
12:10 In general, Jewish teachers felt that whatever one could do before the Sabbath should not be done on the Sabbath. Life-saving procedures were acceptable; other medical treatments on the Sabbath were debated.
12:11 People often dug and disguised pits to capture predators, but sometimes their own animals fell into these or natural pits. Unlike Essenes, who were stricter, Pharisees and most other people did try to help their animals out of pits on the Sabbath, sometimes using a rope.
12:12 Jewish teachers often used "How much more?" arguments; no one would have disagreed with the premise that a person is more valuable than a sheep.
12:13 *he stretched it out.* Cf. 1Ki 13:6. Technically Jesus does not apply medical treatment or even lay hands on the man; no one considered a command to stretch out one's hand as work!
12:14 The Pharisaic school of Hillel permitted prayer for the sick on the Sabbath; the dominant Pharisaic school, the school of Shammai, rejected this but did not persecute Hillelites for allowing it. Jesus, however, may have appeared a more direct threat. Later sources suggest that Pharisees would have weighed their traditions more heavily than other teachers' miracles. Nevertheless, in contrast to Jerusalem's Sadducees, Pharisees in this period normally lacked the kind of political power needed to carry out such plans against Jesus.
12:18–21 Matthew cites Isa 42:1–4. As elsewhere in this section of Isaiah (Isa 41:8; 44:1–2,21; 45:4; 49:3), the "servant" in Isa 42:1–4 is Israel; but because the servant fails in his mission (Isa 42:18–19), God raises up one within Israel to fulfill the mission and suffer on behalf of Israel (Isa 49:5–7; 52:13—53:12, especially 53:4–6,9). Jesus fulfilled this mission, though in ways that his contemporaries did not expect. Matthew translates the wording in a way that brings it into alignment with the heavenly proclamation in Mt 3:17, so that the heavenly proclamation evokes Isaiah's servant.
12:21 Those quoting a passage might end on a point they did not want to omit—here concern for the Gentiles (cf. 4:15; 28:19). The Hebrew text speaks of "coasts" or "islands," giving an example of distant peoples, but Matthew follows here the common Greek translation that captures the text's theological sense, applying it to all Gentiles.
12:23 *Son of David.* Alludes to the promised Davidic ruler (see 1:1; cf. Psalms of Solomon 17:21).
12:24 *by Beelzebul.* See note on 10:25. This is the charge of performing feats by sorcery—an activity that warranted death (e.g., Ex 22:18).
12:27 *by whom do your people drive them out?* Other Jewish people engaged in exorcism (Josephus, *Antiquities* 8.47; 4Q242 f1 3.4 in the Dead Sea Scrolls; cf. Tobit 8:3). *your people.* This phrase (lit. "your sons") could refer to disciples or apprentices.
12:28 *by the Spirit of God.* Because many Jewish people

of God that I drive out demons, then the
kingdom of God has come upon you.
29"Or again, how can anyone enter a
strong man's house and carry off his possessions unless he first ties up the strong
man? Then he can plunder his house.
30"Whoever is not with me is against
me, and whoever does not gather with me
scatters.[s] 31And so I tell you, every kind
of sin and slander can be forgiven, but
blasphemy against the Spirit will not be
forgiven.[t] 32Anyone who speaks a word
against the Son of Man will be forgiven,
but anyone who speaks against the Holy
Spirit will not be forgiven, either in this
age[u] or in the age to come.[v]
33"Make a tree good and its fruit will be
good, or make a tree bad and its fruit will
be bad, for a tree is recognized by its fruit.[w]
34You brood of vipers,[x] how can you who
are evil say anything good? For the mouth
speaks[y] what the heart is full of. 35A good
man brings good things out of the good
stored up in him, and an evil man brings
evil things out of the evil stored up in him.
36But I tell you that everyone will have to
give account on the day of judgment for
every empty word they have spoken. 37For
by your words you will be acquitted, and
by your words you will be condemned."

The Sign of Jonah

12:39-42pp — Lk 11:29-32
12:43-45pp — Lk 11:24-26

38Then some of the Pharisees and teachers of the law said to him, "Teacher, we
want to see a sign from you."[z]
39He answered, "A wicked and adulterous generation asks for a sign! But
none will be given it except the sign of
the prophet Jonah.[a] 40For as Jonah was
three days and three nights in the belly of
a huge fish,[b] so the Son of Man[c] will be
three days and three nights in the heart
of the earth.[d] 41The men of Nineveh[e] will
stand up at the judgment with this generation and condemn it; for they repented at
the preaching of Jonah,[f] and now something greater than Jonah is here. 42The
Queen of the South will rise at the judgment with this generation and condemn it;
for she came[g] from the ends of the earth
to listen to Solomon's wisdom, and now
something greater than Solomon is here.
43"When an impure spirit comes out
of a person, it goes through arid places
seeking rest and does not find it. 44Then
it says, 'I will return to the house I left.'
When it arrives, it finds the house unoccupied, swept clean and put in order. 45Then
it goes and takes with it seven other spirits
more wicked than itself, and they go in
and live there. And the final condition of
that person is worse than the first.[h] That
is how it will be with this wicked generation."

Jesus' Mother and Brothers

12:46-50pp — Mk 3:31-35; Lk 8:19-21

46While Jesus was still talking to the
crowd, his mother[i] and brothers[j] stood
outside, wanting to speak to him. 47Some-
one told him, "Your mother and brothers

12:30 [s] Mk 9:40; Lk 11:23 **12:31** [t] Mk 3:28, 29; Lk 12:10 **12:32** [u] Titus 2:12 [v] Mk 10:30; Lk 20:34, 35; Eph 1:21; Heb 6:5 **12:33** [w] Mt 7:16, 17; Lk 6:43, 44 **12:34** [x] Mt 3:7; 23:33 [y] Mt 15:18; Lk 6:45 **12:38** [z] Mt 16:1; Mk 8:11, 12; Lk 11:16; Jn 2:18; 6:30; 1Co 1:22

12:39 [a] Mt 16:4; Lk 11:29 **12:40** [b] Jnh 1:17 [c] Mt 8:20 [d] Mt 16:21 **12:41** [e] Jnh 1:2 [f] Jnh 3:5 **12:42** [g] 1Ki 10:1; 2Ch 9:1 **12:45** [h] 2Pe 2:20 **12:46** [i] Mt 1:18; 2:11, 13, 14, 20; Lk 1:43; 2:33, 34, 48, 51; Jn 2:1, 5; 19:25, 26 [j] Mt 13:55; Jn 2:12; 7:3, 5; Ac 1:14; 1Co 9:5; Gal 1:19

believed that the fullness of the Spirit had been quenched after the last Biblical prophets and would be poured out again fully only in the end time, Jesus presents his activity by the Spirit as evidence that the end-time kingdom had come upon them.

12:29 *strong man.* People understood that no one could seize a strong person's possessions (cf. Psalms of Solomon 5:3) without first tying him up; Jesus can take away what Satan possessed because Jesus first defeated him (cf. Isa 49:24–25).

12:30 *Whoever is not with me.* Among both Jews and Greeks, some recognized the principle that where opposition existed, one would be on either one side or the other. (The same principle existed in Roman party politics.)

12:32 *in this age or in the age to come.* Jewish people distinguished the present age from the promised future age of righteousness. Jewish sources often viewed deliberate sin as unforgivable (Nu 15:30–31; Dt 29:18–20); some teachers believed that even these sins could be atoned for if the sinner was repentant. The sin here appears to involve rejection even of the Spirit's clear attestation of Jesus through signs (v. 28)—perhaps implying a heart too hard to repent. (The sort of person fearful of having committed the sin is not the hard-hearted kind of person the sin addresses.)

12:34 *brood of vipers.* See note on 3:7.

12:38 *sign.* Later sources suggest that most Pharisaic teachers would have weighed their traditions more heavily than they did miracles; their reception of Jesus' signs so far has not been friendly (see v. 24).

12:39–42 *the sign of the prophet Jonah … men of Nineveh … Queen of the South.* The Ninevites apparently did not witness the sign of Jonah in the fish's belly; they repented instead through his preaching. One Jewish tradition claims that Jonah tried to avoid preaching to Ninevites lest their repentance shame Israel for failing to do likewise (*Mekilta Pisha* 1.80–82; cf. Jnh 3:10—4:2); if any of Jesus' hearers were familiar with this tradition, it would make Jesus' comparison here all the more graphic. The Gentile "Queen of the South" respected Solomon's wisdom (1Ki 10:1–13); some Jewish traditions from this period identify her as the queen of Ethiopia. In some Jewish traditions, God would render the unrepentant without excuse on the day of judgment; he would do this through the testimonies of those who repented despite better excuses. Although Jewish people expected God to vindicate Israel against the nations on the day of judgment, some later rabbinic traditions claim that repentant Gentiles would testify against unrepentant Israelites at that time.

12:43–45 Speakers often returned charges against their accusers; some have accused Jesus of acting by Satan (v. 24), but Jesus implies that it is his accusers who do so: he was driving out demons, but "this wicked generation" (v. 45) was welcoming them back in!

12:47–50 Children were obligated to honor their parents. The expected response is for Jesus to immediately

are standing outside, wanting to speak to you."

48He replied to him, "Who is my mother, and who are my brothers?" 49Pointing to his disciples, he said, "Here are my mother and my brothers. 50For whoever does the will of my Father in heaven[k] is my brother and sister and mother."

The Parable of the Sower

13:1-15pp — Mk 4:1-12; Lk 8:4-10
13:16,17pp — Lk 10:23,24
13:18-23pp — Mk 4:13-20; Lk 8:11-15

13 That same day Jesus went out of the house[l] and sat by the lake. 2Such large crowds gathered around him that he got into a boat[m] and sat in it, while all the people stood on the shore. 3Then he told them many things in parables, saying: "A farmer went out to sow his seed. 4As he was scattering the seed, some fell along the path, and the birds came and ate it up. 5Some fell on rocky places, where it did not have much soil. It sprang up quickly, because the soil was shallow. 6But when the sun came up, the plants were scorched, and they withered because they had no root. 7Other seed fell among thorns, which grew up and choked the plants. 8Still other seed fell on good soil, where it produced a crop — a hundred,[n] sixty or thirty times what was sown. 9Whoever has ears, let them hear."[o]

10The disciples came to him and asked, "Why do you speak to the people in parables?"

11He replied, "Because the knowledge of the secrets of the kingdom of heaven has been given to you,[p] but not to them. 12Whoever has will be given more, and they will have an abundance. Whoever does not have, even what they have will be taken from them.[q] 13This is why I speak to them in parables:

"Though seeing, they do not see;
  though hearing, they do not hear or understand.[r]

14In them is fulfilled the prophecy of Isaiah:

"'You will be ever hearing but never understanding;
  you will be ever seeing but never perceiving.
15For this people's heart has become calloused;
  they hardly hear with their ears,
  and they have closed their eyes.
Otherwise they might see with their eyes,
  hear with their ears,
  understand with their hearts
and turn, and I would heal them.'[a][s]

16But blessed are your eyes because they see, and your ears because they hear.[t]

12:50 [k] Jn 15:14 **13:1** [l] ver 36; Mt 9:28 **13:2** [m] Lk 5:3 **13:8** [n] Ge 26:12 **13:9** [o] Mt 11:15 **13:11** [p] Mt 11:25; 16:17; 19:11; Jn 6:65; 1Co 2:10, 14; Col 1:27; 1Jn 2:20,27 **13:12** [q] Mt 25:29; Lk 19:26 **13:13** [r] Dt 29:4; Jer 5:21; Eze 12:2 **13:15** [s] Isa 6:9, 10; Jn 12:40; Ac 28:26,27; Ro 11:8 **13:16** [t] Mt 16:17

[a] *15* Isaiah 6:9,10 (see Septuagint)

welcome his mother and brothers, but he avails himself of the occasion to illustrate a point. As often, he does so in a way that his contemporaries would have viewed as dramatic and shocking.

13:2 *got into a boat.* Pushing out from shore provided sufficient distance for Jesus' voice to carry. Galilee had many acoustic settings — including a cove near Capernaum — that could allow one's voice to carry to vast numbers of hearers.

13:3 See the article "Parables," p. 1692. Most Galileans, like most people in the Roman Empire, were rural farmers. Whereas the parables of later rabbis focus more often on royal courts, Jesus' parables most often address the agrarian settings of most of his hearers. *seed.* Some Jewish sources compare God's Word to seed.

13:4 Many ancient sources speak of plowing before sowing (which would have prevented the farmer from wasting some seed in this case!), but others clearly speak of sowing before plowing. Jesus chooses the latter method for this parable, since only God knows the different kinds of hearts among whom the Word is sown. *some fell along the path.* Paths often led through fields.

13:5 *rocky places.* Much of the soil in the Holy Land is rocky.

13:7 *thorns.* A kind of thistle is common around roads and can reach more than three feet (a meter), typically in the month of April.

13:8 The average yield of seed in ancient Israel was probably between seven and a half to tenfold. A hundredfold was a remarkably good harvest (Ge 26:12), but even thirtyfold was exceptional.

13:9 See note on 11:15.

13:10 Rabbis often used parables as sermon illustrations, but without the sermon that the parable illustrated, a parable might function instead as a riddle, in which the listener is challenged to figure out what the parable means. Disciples often asked their teachers questions, sometimes seeking understanding privately after a public lecture.

13:11 *secrets of the kingdom.* Jesus refers to special revelations about God's promised kingdom, not information that would never be known; see Da 2:28 – 30,45. Here the secrets go to those who understand (v. 23) — that is, the true disciples who remained after the crowds had gone, and thus received the interpretation from Jesus. See note on Mk 4:11.

13:12 *will be given more.* The principle that one who has can receive more worked in ancient economics; some also recognized this principle with knowledge of wisdom or the law.

13:13 – 15 Rabbis who taught in parables frequently related them to Scripture. Many passages address similar issues in Israel (e.g., Dt 29:4; Isa 42:19 – 20; 43:8; 44:18; Jer 5:21; Eze 12:2), but one key text often picked up in the NT is cited in vv. 14 – 15. In Isa 6:9 – 10, God calls Isaiah to reveal truth to Israel that Israel will not receive, until the impending judgment (Isa 6:11). Their increasing spiritual blindness was punishment for their refusal to heed what God was already speaking (cf. Isa 29:9 – 10). Those who did turn, however, would be "healed," i.e., restored (cf. Isa 53:5; Hos 11:3; 14:4).

13:16 *blessed are your eyes.* Jewish people often praised one person by uttering a beatitude over someone who knew them; the disciples are blessed because they receive revelation about Jesus and his kingdom (cf. 1Ki 10:8).

17For truly I tell you, many prophets and
righteous people longed to see what you
see[u] but did not see it, and to hear what
you hear but did not hear it.
18"Listen then to what the parable of
the sower means: 19When anyone hears
the message about the kingdom[v] and does
not understand it, the evil one[w] comes
and snatches away what was sown in
their heart. This is the seed sown along
the path. 20The seed falling on rocky
ground refers to someone who hears the
word and at once receives it with joy. 21But
since they have no root, they last only a
short time. When trouble or persecution
comes because of the word, they quickly
fall away.[x] 22The seed falling among the
thorns refers to someone who hears the
word, but the worries of this life and the
deceitfulness of wealth[y] choke the word,
making it unfruitful. 23But the seed falling on good soil refers to someone who
hears the word and understands it. This
is the one who produces a crop, yielding
a hundred, sixty or thirty times what was
sown."[z]

The Parable of the Weeds

24Jesus told them another parable: "The
kingdom of heaven is like[a] a man who
sowed good seed in his field. 25But while
everyone was sleeping, his enemy came
and sowed weeds among the wheat, and
went away. 26When the wheat sprouted
and formed heads, then the weeds also
appeared.
27"The owner's servants came to him
and said, 'Sir, didn't you sow good seed
in your field? Where then did the weeds
come from?'
28" 'An enemy did this,' he replied.
"The servants asked him, 'Do you want
us to go and pull them up?'
29" 'No,' he answered, 'because while
you are pulling the weeds, you may uproot
the wheat with them. 30Let both grow together until the harvest. At that time I will
tell the harvesters: First collect the weeds
and tie them in bundles to be burned;
then gather the wheat and bring it into
my barn.' "[b]

The Parables of the Mustard Seed and the Yeast

13:31,32pp — Mk 4:30-32
13:31-33pp — Lk 13:18-21

31He told them another parable: "The
kingdom of heaven is like[c] a mustard
seed,[d] which a man took and planted in
his field. 32Though it is the smallest of all
seeds, yet when it grows, it is the largest of
garden plants and becomes a tree, so that
the birds come and perch in its branches."[e]
33He told them still another parable:
"The kingdom of heaven is like[f] yeast that
a woman took and mixed into about sixty pounds[a] of flour[g] until it worked all
through the dough."[h]
34Jesus spoke all these things to the
crowd in parables; he did not say anything
to them without using a parable.[i] 35So was
fulfilled what was spoken through the
prophet:

"I will open my mouth in parables,
I will utter things hidden since the
creation of the world."[b][j]

The Parable of the Weeds Explained

36Then he left the crowd and went into
the house. His disciples came to him and

13:17 [u] Jn 8:56; Heb 11:13; 1Pe 1:10-12 **13:19** [v] Mt 4:23 [w] Mt 5:37 **13:21** [x] Mt 11:6 **13:22** [y] Mt 19:23; 1Ti 6:9, 10, 17 **13:23** [z] ver 8 **13:24** [a] ver 31, 33, 45, 47; Mt 18:23; 20:1; 22:2; 25:1; Mk 4:26, 30 **13:30** [b] Mt 3:12 **13:31** [c] ver 24 [d] Mt 17:20; Lk 17:6 **13:32** [e] Ps 104:12; Eze 17:23; 31:6; Da 4:12 **13:33** [f] ver 24 [g] Ge 18:6 [h] Gal 5:9 **13:34** [i] Mk 4:33; Jn 16:25 **13:35** [j] Ps 78:2; Ro 16:25, 26; 1Co 2:7; Eph 3:9; Col 1:26

[a] *33* Or about 27 kilograms [b] *35* Psalm 78:2

13:18 *what the parable ... means.* Rabbis often gave interpretations with their parables (see note on v. 10), but Jesus gives these interpretations privately (see note on v. 11).
13:24 *kingdom of heaven is like.* Jewish parables often began with, "Such-and-such is like ..."; the named subject (here, the kingdom) was compared not simply with the next noun (here, a man) but with the entire parable that followed.
13:25 *enemy came and sowed weeds.* Ancient legal sources show that feuding, rival farmers occasionally did sow poisonous plants in one another's fields.
13:26–29 The poisonous weeds here are darnel (*Lolium temulentum*), which cannot be distinguished from wheat in the early stages. Once past the early stages, however, the weeds' roots become entwined with those of the wheat. Workers thus could not uproot the darnel without damaging the wheat.
13:30 *Let both grow together.* Once the wheat was full grown and ready to be harvested, the darnel, now distinguishable from it, could be uprooted and used as cheap fuel. Laborers gathered wheat into sheaves, transporting it (often on donkeys) to a village's threshing floor, or in this case to that of this large estate. Once threshed, it would be stored in a barn.
13:31 *mustard seed.* Scholars do not all agree about which plant is in view here, but ancient sources agree in describing the mustard seed as proverbially small (v. 32). Some argue that this shrub often grew to eight to ten feet (two and a half to three meters) high around the Sea of Galilee; others that the likeliest shrub in view rarely grew to more than five feet (one and a half meters). If so, birds could only "perch" (v. 32) in its branches (not "nest," as the term might be translated); the language, however, evokes the image of a great kingdom of old that would be supplanted by God's kingdom (Da 4:12). The glorious future kingdom was already active in a hidden way in Jesus' ministry.
13:33 *yeast.* Some Jewish texts used "yeast" to symbolize evil, but it did not always mean that (Ge 19:3; Ex 12:11,39; Lev 23:17) and does not mean that here. Although bakeries might prepare large amounts of bread, Jesus refers to a Galilean housewife. The amount here is thus exorbitant: her labor would produce enough bread to feed more than 100 people.
13:35 Matthew quotes Ps 78:2, attributing it to a prophet, because the psalms were considered prophetically inspired (cf. 1Ch 25:1–6; 2Ch 29:30).

said, "Explain to us the parable[k] of the
weeds in the field."
37He answered, "The one who sowed
the good seed is the Son of Man.[l] 38The
field is the world, and the good seed
stands for the people of the kingdom. The
weeds are the people of the evil one,[m]
39and the enemy who sows them is the
devil. The harvest[n] is the end of the age,[o]
and the harvesters are angels.[p]
40"As the weeds are pulled up and
burned in the fire, so it will be at the end
of the age. 41The Son of Man[q] will send out
his angels,[r] and they will weed out of his
kingdom everything that causes sin and
all who do evil. 42They will throw them
into the blazing furnace, where there will
be weeping and gnashing of teeth.[s] 43Then
the righteous will shine like the sun[t] in
the kingdom of their Father. Whoever has
ears, let them hear.[u]

The Parables of the Hidden Treasure and the Pearl

44"The kingdom of heaven is like[v] treasure hidden in a field. When a man found
it, he hid it again, and then in his joy
went and sold all he had and bought that
field.[w]
45"Again, the kingdom of heaven is
like[x] a merchant looking for fine pearls.
46When he found one of great value, he
went away and sold everything he had
and bought it.

13:36 [k] Mt 15:15
13:37 [l] Mt 8:20
13:38 [m] Jn 8:44,45; 1Jn 3:10
13:39 [n] Joel 3:13 [o] Mt 24:3; 28:20 [p] Rev 14:15
13:41 [q] Mt 8:20 [r] Mt 24:31
13:42 [s] ver 50; Mt 8:12
13:43 [t] Da 12:3 [u] Mt 11:15
13:44 [v] ver 24 [w] Isa 55:1; Php 3:7,8
13:45 [x] ver 24
13:47 [y] ver 24 [z] Mt 22:10
13:49 [a] Mt 25:32
13:50 [b] Mt 8:12
13:53 [c] Mt 7:28
13:54 [d] Mt 4:23 [e] Mt 7:28
13:55 [f] Lk 3:23; Jn 6:42 [g] Mt 12:46

The Parable of the Net

47"Once again, the kingdom of heaven
is like[y] a net that was let down into the
lake and caught all kinds[z] of fish. 48When
it was full, the fishermen pulled it up on
the shore. Then they sat down and collected the good fish in baskets, but threw the
bad away. 49This is how it will be at the
end of the age. The angels will come and
separate the wicked from the righteous[a]
50and throw them into the blazing furnace,
where there will be weeping and gnashing
of teeth.[b]
51"Have you understood all these
things?" Jesus asked.
"Yes," they replied.
52He said to them, "Therefore every
teacher of the law who has become a disciple in the kingdom of heaven is like the
owner of a house who brings out of his
storeroom new treasures as well as old."

A Prophet Without Honor

13:54-58pp — Mk 6:1-6

53When Jesus had finished these parables,[c] he moved on from there. 54Coming
to his hometown, he began teaching the
people in their synagogue,[d] and they were
amazed.[e] "Where did this man get this
wisdom and these miraculous powers?"
they asked. 55"Isn't this the carpenter's
son?[f] Isn't his mother's[g] name Mary, and
aren't his brothers James, Joseph, Simon

13:37 *Son of Man.* See Da 7:13 – 14.
13:39 *harvest.* Some other ancient Jewish sources also apply the familiar image of harvest to the end of the age (see, e.g., 2 Baruch 70:2).
13:41 *will send out his angels.* That the Son of Man commands angels shows that he is no ordinary human figure.
13:42 *blazing furnace.* Jewish people often conceived of Gehinnom, or hell, as a place of fiery torment and/or destruction. *weeping and gnashing of teeth.* See note on 8:12.
13:43 *shine like the sun.* Developing the image of Da 12:3, as here, many Jewish sources spoke of the righteous "shining" in the future age. Cf. 17:2.
13:44 *treasure hidden.* Given widespread poverty in antiquity, it is no surprise that stories of buried treasure were popular; people sometimes stored their wealth by burying it in a strongbox, sometimes under the floor of their home. *bought that field.* Ancient title deeds to land normally specified ownership of both the land and everything in it. Here a peasant, perhaps a tenant living on and working a wealthy landowner's field, apparently finds a hoard of coins. The focus of most such stories was the finder's subsequent wealth, but Jesus emphasizes the great worth of the kingdom and the price one must be willing to pay for it.
13:45 *merchant.* Unlike the peasant noted in v. 44, this merchant is a person of means. *looking for fine pearls.* Divers gathered pearls from the Indian Ocean, Persian Gulf and Red Sea; wealthy women in Rome wore pearls in necklaces, the most expensive of which would have cost tens of millions of dollars in today's currency. Jewish teachers sometimes used expensive pearls to represent the teaching of Torah; Jesus applies it to his message about the kingdom. Ancient pearl stories often emphasize the finder's piety; Jesus instead emphasizes the value of God's kingdom (v. 46).
13:47 *net.* Jesus probably refers here not to the smaller casting net, but to a seine net, also known as a dragnet, pulled between two boats. Floaters on top of such nets kept one part of the net on the surface while sinkers allowed the bottom to gather in fish from deep below. *all kinds of fish.* Many of the more than 20 kinds of fish available in the Sea of Galilee were inedible or ritually impure, but a seine net would catch all varieties of fish.
13:52 *new treasures as well as old.* The old treasures of the OT could be employed usefully in light of the newer and fuller message of the kingdom.
13:55 *carpenter's son.* When Jesus was still a young child, the Galilean city of Sepphoris, just four miles (six kilometers) from Nazareth, was burned to the ground. Herod Antipas, tetrarch of Galilee, immediately set to rebuilding it and may have eventually made it his capital. Carpenters (the term here includes woodwork) were thus in demand during the period in which Jesus grew up, and he would have likely also learned the trade from his father. (Boys could learn trades as apprentices to anyone, but this included their fathers, and Jesus became a carpenter; Mk 6:3.) *mother's name … brothers.* "Mary" was the most popular Jewish woman's name in this period, and the names of Jesus' brothers here were also very common.

and Judas? 56 Aren't all his sisters with us? Where then did this man get all these things?" 57 And they took offense[h] at him.

But Jesus said to them, "A prophet is not without honor except in his own town and in his own home."[i]

58 And he did not do many miracles there because of their lack of faith.

John the Baptist Beheaded

14:1-12pp — Mk 6:14-29

14 At that time Herod[j] the tetrarch heard the reports about Jesus,[k] 2 and he said to his attendants, "This is John the Baptist;[l] he has risen from the dead! That is why miraculous powers are at work in him."

3 Now Herod had arrested John and bound him and put him in prison[m] because of Herodias, his brother Philip's wife,[n] 4 for John had been saying to him: "It is not lawful for you to have her."[o] 5 Herod wanted to kill John, but he was afraid of the people, because they considered John a prophet.[p]

6 On Herod's birthday the daughter of Herodias danced for the guests and pleased Herod so much 7 that he promised with an oath to give her whatever she asked. 8 Prompted by her mother, she said, "Give me here on a platter the head of John the Baptist." 9 The king was distressed, but because of his oaths and his dinner guests, he ordered that her request be granted 10 and had John beheaded[q] in the prison. 11 His head was brought in on a platter and given to the girl, who carried it to her mother. 12 John's disciples came and took his body and buried it.[r] Then they went and told Jesus.

Jesus Feeds the Five Thousand

14:13-21pp — Mk 6:32-44; Lk 9:10-17; Jn 6:1-13
14:13-21Ref — Mt 15:32-38

13 When Jesus heard what had happened, he withdrew by boat privately to a solitary place. Hearing of this, the crowds followed him on foot from the towns. 14 When Jesus landed and saw a large crowd, he had compassion on them[s] and healed their sick.[t]

15 As evening approached, the disciples came to him and said, "This is a remote place, and it's already getting late. Send the crowds away, so they can go to the villages and buy themselves some food."

16 Jesus replied, "They do not need to go away. You give them something to eat."

17 "We have here only five loaves[u] of bread and two fish," they answered.

18 "Bring them here to me," he said. 19 And he directed the people to sit down on the grass. Taking the five loaves and the two fish and looking up to heaven, he gave thanks and broke the loaves.[v] Then he gave them to the disciples, and the

13:57 [h] Jn 6:61 [i] Lk 4:24; Jn 4:44 **14:1** [j] Mk 8:15; Lk 3:1, 19; 13:31; 23:7, 8; Ac 4:27; 12:1 [k] Lk 9:7-9 **14:2** [l] Mt 3:1 **14:3** [m] Mt 4:12; 11:2 [n] Lk 3:19, 20 **14:4** [o] Lev 18:16; 20:21 **14:5** [p] Mt 11:9 **14:10** [q] Mt 17:12 **14:12** [r] Ac 8:2 **14:14** [s] Mt 9:36 [t] Mt 4:23 **14:17** [u] Mt 16:9 **14:19** [v] 1Sa 9:13; Mt 26:26; Mk 8:6; Lk 24:30; Ac 2:42; 27:35; 1Ti 4:4

13:56 *his sisters.* Ancient sources sometimes name men but not women; possibly their names were thus not available to Matthew.

13:57 Scripture noted prophets being rejected, even in their hometowns (Jer 1:1; 11:21); Jewish traditions about the prophets amplified this pattern even further.

14:1 *Herod the tetrarch.* Whereas Mark calls Herod a "king" (Mk 6:14), Luke and (usually) Matthew use the more precise "tetrarch," governor-prince of a small territory. (The term "tetrarch" no longer carried its original sense of "one-fourth" of a territory.) Herod Antipas became tetrarch of Galilee and Perea in 4 BC on the death of his father, King Herod the Great (2:19); a Samaritan wife of Herod was mother of both Antipas and Archelaus (cf. Mt 2:22).

14:3 – 5 John opposed Antipas's affair with Herodias on moral grounds, but it had also become a political embarrassment to Antipas that eventually nearly cost him his kingdom (see note on Mk 6:17). For this reason, allowing John's continuing criticism was to risk fueling further dissent within the kingdom. The first-century Jewish historian Josephus shows that John was popular with the people, and that Antipas feared the risk that this popularity posed (*Antiquities* 18.116 – 119). Political considerations about John's popularity both demanded John's arrest and delayed John's execution.

14:6 *Herod's birthday.* Birthdays remained in this period a largely Gentile custom, but Antipas and the ruling class were thoroughly Hellenized. Persons of status expected those invited to attend their birthday parties, which typically included excessive drinking. *daughter of Herodias.* Herodias's daughter Salome was probably between 12 and 14 years old, and perhaps already betrothed or married to Philip the tetrarch. Sensuous dancing was common at such parties but not for members of the royal family; the Herodian family, however, was known for such excesses.

14:7 *promised with an oath.* An oath called a deity to attest the truth of one's claim (or to punish one for dishonoring the deity's name by invoking it falsely). Ancients had stories of people regretting their oaths; rabbis could release people from oaths like this one, but to not keep his public word would be a matter of shame.

14:10 *beheaded.* Beheading was considered the most merciful form of execution, since it killed quickly (although executioners did not always succeed on the first blow).

14:11 *head was brought in on a platter.* Ancient accounts in which heads were displayed at banquets, especially to please the woman or boy for whom the banquet host was lusting, emphasize that the hosts abused their authority in a detestable manner.

14:12 *disciples came and took his body.* Bodies were more readily granted to family members. Normally the eldest son would bury someone who died, but John's disciples fulfill this role for him (for disciples as sons, see note on 23:9; Jn 13:33). This act highlights the failure of most of Jesus' male disciples in 27:55 – 60.

14:15 *they can ... buy themselves some food.* Nearby villages, with a few hundred or at most a few thousand people each, would not have had enough spare bread ready to feed more than 5,000 people (v. 21).

14:17 – 18 God often used what people had to perform wonders (Ex 4:1 – 3; 14:16; 2Ki 4:1 – 7).

14:19 The feeding miracle resembles those of Moses, Elijah, and in this case especially Elisha (2Ki 4:42 – 44).

disciples gave them to the people. [20]They all ate and were satisfied, and the disciples picked up twelve basketfuls of broken pieces that were left over. [21]The number of those who ate was about five thousand men, besides women and children.

Jesus Walks on the Water

14:22-33pp — Mk 6:45-51; Jn 6:16-21
14:34-36pp — Mk 6:53-56

[22]Immediately Jesus made the disciples get into the boat and go on ahead of him to the other side, while he dismissed the

14:20 *disciples picked up twelve basketfuls.* Ancient moralists condemned waste; cf. also use of leftovers in 2Ki 4:7,44.

14:21 *five thousand men.* The number is higher than that of most Galilean villages, including much higher than the currently estimated population of Capernaum. Ancient sources often numbered only men; Matthew thus might not know the number of women and children, but he

MATTHEW 14

Houses in the Holy Land of the First Century AD: Peter's House in Capernaum; Insulae

Housing conditions in the first-century Holy Land varied dramatically according to people's financial situations. The best preserved homes are those that were built for the upper classes and constructed with obvious craftsmanship from lasting materials. Of these, the most splendid examples are the remains of Herod the Great's lavish palaces in Jerusalem, Masada and Jericho.

These structures, along with other luxurious houses discovered in Jerusalem's upper city, reflect the stylistic conventions of contemporary Roman villas. The villa was structured around an open, colonnaded courtyard and contained a large reception room and dining area to accommodate large gatherings. Floors were covered with detailed stone mosaics, and walls were painted with frescoes. These upper-class houses and palaces in Judea also contained distinctively Jewish features, such as ritual baths alongside ordinary bathrooms, the absence of human or animal representation in mosaics and frescoes and the presence of Jewish symbols (e.g., the menorah).

Since relatively few people lived in palatial homes, many more examples of middle-class dwellings have been revealed through archaeology. An important example, discovered in Jerusalem in 1970, is known as the "burnt house." This home was completely buried with soot and ash from the destruction of the city in AD 70 and, therefore, has been well preserved. The floor plan reflects a common pattern of three medium-sized rooms, a small storage room, a small kitchen and a stepped, ritual bath built around a paved courtyard. The walls were covered with a thin layer of limestone plaster, and the floors consisted of pressed earth. Furnishings within the house included rectangular stone tables, bowls, plates, cups and cylindrical weights, one of which identifies the owner as Bar Karos.

Other significant examples of first-century houses have been unearthed in Capernaum. Excavations near the ruins of the ancient synagogue there revealed a group of approximately 12 homes constructed of black basalt rocks and small pebbles and arranged around a central courtyard containing ovens and grinding stones. These single-story dwellings had floors of beaten black earth and stairways leading to flat

continued on next page

crowd. 23 After he had dismissed them, he went up on a mountainside by himself to pray.[w] Later that night, he was there alone, 24 and the boat was already a considerable distance from land, buffeted by the waves because the wind was against it.

25 Shortly before dawn Jesus went out to them, walking on the lake. 26 When the disciples saw him walking on the lake,

14:23 [w] Lk 3:21

mentions them anyway, reminding us of the magnitude of Jesus' miracle.

14:25 *before dawn.* Literally the text speaks of the "fourth watch of the night," based on the Roman division of the night into four parts; the fourth watch refers to the final hours before dawn. Jesus was approaching them from the east, which might make his approach more visible.

14:26 *ghost.* Apparitions were usually frightening (though Josephus employs the term here translated "ghost" for angels). Jewish tradition warned of dangerous

roofs. The less-substantial roofs were probably built with tree branches covered with mud and straw (cf. Mk 2:4).

The largest of these homes attracted particular attention in that it featured a crushed limestone floor and had plastered walls filled with decorations (including flowers, pomegranates and numerous crosses) and inscriptions, which were fragmentary and in many languages: 124 in Greek, 18 in Syriac, 15 in Hebrew and 1 in Latin. Most of the inscriptions were short prayers, such as "Christ have mercy" or "Lord Jesus Christ help." Others contained the name of Peter, suggesting that this home was venerated in antiquity as a place of Christian pilgrimage and associated with the memory of Peter. Thus, this dwelling has become known as the house of Peter in Capernaum (Mt 8:14; Mk 1:29; Lk 4:38).

The lowest urban classes in many cities inhabited crowded tenement buildings called *insulae*—multistoried buildings divided into numerous apartments called *cenaculi*. The lowest floor generally contained a shop in which the proprietor also lived. The upper floors were accessed through outside staircases. The *insulae* usually lacked any system of heating, running water or sewage. Eutychus most likely fell from the third floor window of an *insula* while listening to Paul preach Christ in Troas (Ac 20:7–12). ◆

An artist's recreation of first-century houses in Capernaum. The houses were built with black basalt rocks covered with plaster and had stairs leading to flat roofs that were probably built with branches and covered with mud and straw.

they were terrified. "It's a ghost,"[x] they
said, and cried out in fear.
27 But Jesus immediately said to them:
"Take courage![y] It is I. Don't be afraid."[z]
28 "Lord, if it's you," Peter replied, "tell
me to come to you on the water."
29 "Come," he said.
Then Peter got down out of the boat,
walked on the water and came toward
Jesus. 30 But when he saw the wind, he
was afraid and, beginning to sink, cried
out, "Lord, save me!"
31 Immediately Jesus reached out his
hand and caught him. "You of little faith,"[a]
he said, "why did you doubt?"
32 And when they climbed into the boat,
the wind died down. 33 Then those who
were in the boat worshiped him, saying,
"Truly you are the Son of God."[b]
34 When they had crossed over, they landed at Gennesaret. 35 And when the men of
that place recognized Jesus, they sent word
to all the surrounding country. People
brought all their sick to him 36 and begged
him to let the sick just touch the edge of his
cloak,[c] and all who touched it were healed.

That Which Defiles

15:1-20pp — Mk 7:1-23

15 Then some Pharisees and teachers
of the law came to Jesus from Jerusalem and asked, 2 "Why do your disciples break the tradition of the elders? They
don't wash their hands before they eat!"[d]
3 Jesus replied, "And why do you break
the command of God for the sake of your
tradition? 4 For God said, 'Honor your father
and mother'[a][e] and 'Anyone who curses their
father or mother is to be put to death.'[b][f] 5 But
you say that if anyone declares that what
might have been used to help their father or
mother is 'devoted to God,' 6 they are not to
'honor their father or mother' with it. Thus
you nullify the word of God for the sake of
your tradition. 7 You hypocrites! Isaiah was
right when he prophesied about you:

8 " 'These people honor me with their lips,
but their hearts are far from me.
9 They worship me in vain;
their teachings are merely human
rules.[g]'[c][h]"

10 Jesus called the crowd to him and said,
"Listen and understand. 11 What goes into
someone's mouth does not defile them,[i]
but what comes out of their mouth, that is
what defiles them."[j]
12 Then the disciples came to him and
asked, "Do you know that the Pharisees
were offended when they heard this?"
13 He replied, "Every plant that my heavenly Father has not planted[k] will be pulled
up by the roots. 14 Leave them; they are
blind guides.[d][l] If the blind lead the blind,
both will fall into a pit."[m]

14:26 [x] Lk 24:37
14:27 [y] Mt 9:2; Ac 23:11 [z] Da 10:12; Mt 17:7; 28:10; Lk 1:13,30; 2:10; Ac 18:9; 23:11; Rev 1:17
14:31 [a] Mt 6:30
14:33 [b] Ps 2:7; Mt 4:3
14:36 [c] Mt 9:20
15:2 [d] Lk 11:38
15:4 [e] Ex 20:12; Dt 5:16; Eph 6:2 [f] Ex 21:17; Lev 20:9
15:9 [g] Col 2:20-22 [h] Isa 29:13; Mal 2:2
15:11 [i] Ac 10:14,15 [j] ver 18
15:13 [k] Isa 60:21; 61:3; Jn 15:2
15:14 [l] Mt 23:16,24; Ro 2:19 [m] Lk 6:39

[a] *4* Exodus 20:12; Deut. 5:16 [b] *4* Exodus 21:17; Lev. 20:9 [c] *9* Isaiah 29:13 [d] *14* Some manuscripts *blind guides of the blind*

night spirits. On a popular level, many Gentiles and probably a number of Jews believed in ghosts, although such a belief technically contradicted mainstream Jewish views of the afterlife (heaven or hell and future resurrection). Gentiles often believed that the ghosts of those drowned at sea hovered over the sites of their deaths.

14:27 *It is I.* Literally, Jesus says, "I am"; although this can mean, "It is I," the activity in the context supports an allusion to Jesus' deity (cf. Ex 3:14, where the same Greek phrase used in the Septuagint, the pre-Christian Greek translation of the OT, is used here also).

14:29 *walked on the water.* Peter had Biblical precedent for stepping into water with faith in the divine command (Jos 3:8,13,15 – 17), though in Exodus and Joshua the water parted rather than sustained one's weight.

14:32 *wind died down.* They would recognize God's power to calm the sea (Job 26:12; Ps 65:7; 89:9 – 10; 107:29; Jnh 1:15; Sirach 43:23).

14:34 *Gennesaret.* A plain of several square miles/kilometers that lay between Capernaum and the large city of Tiberias.

14:36 *edge of his cloak.* See note on 9:20.

15:1 *from Jerusalem.* The largest number of Pharisees and teachers of the law resided in Jerusalem.

15:2 *wash their hands.* Pharisees were particularly known for passing on and following earlier but post-Biblical traditions (see, e.g., Josephus, *Antiquities* 13.297). Washing hands before meals for the sake of maintaining ritual purity was probably originally a custom of the Jews in the Diaspora. Pharisees were known to be very meticulous regarding this practice.

15:4 Virtually all Jewish people would have agreed with the requirement to honor father and mother (Ex 20:12; Dt 5:16) and not to curse them (Ex 21:17; Lev 20:9). Many Jewish teachers considered honoring parents the greatest commandment in the law, and labored hard to fulfill this commandment. Jesus, however, points out that some of their other traditions have been used to subvert it. Like Jesus, Pharisees could suspend aspects of the law to ensure that its intention was met. Individual practice, however, does not always match the highest ideal of their group.

15:5 – 6 People could make vows by God, dedicating property for the temple. By declaring property so dedicated one prohibited others from using it; even outside the Holy Land, some teachers employed vows like these to prohibit objects from use by relatives. Although many teachers may have agreed with Jesus that people who acted in this way were abusing the system, they would not have tried to annul the vows or challenge the system.

15:8 – 9 Isa 29:13 addressed a people who valued their human traditions over Isaiah's prophetic message.

15:10 – 11 At least some rabbis agreed with this principle, but taught it only in private, lest it be abused.

15:12 *Pharisees were offended.* Offending respected people, such as the Pharisees, could create powerful social and political enemies. Most Pharisees held little direct political power, but they were highly influential with the people (especially around Jerusalem).

15:13 *pulled up.* Jesus uses the Biblical image of building up or tearing down God's people (Ps 28:5; Jer 1:10; 11:17; 18:7 – 8; 24:6; 31:4,28; 42:10; 45:4; compare Jer 12:2 with Isa 29:13).

15:14 *blind guides.* Those who were literally blind often

15Peter said, "Explain the parable to us."[n]
16"Are you still so dull?"[o] Jesus asked
them. 17"Don't you see that whatever enters the mouth goes into the stomach and
then out of the body? 18But the things that
come out of a person's mouth come from
the heart,[p] and these defile them. 19For out
of the heart come evil thoughts — murder,
adultery, sexual immorality, theft, false
testimony, slander.[q] 20These are what defile a person;[r] but eating with unwashed
hands does not defile them."

The Faith of a Canaanite Woman

15:21-28pp — Mk 7:24-30

21Leaving that place, Jesus withdrew to
the region of Tyre and Sidon.[s] 22A Canaanite woman from that vicinity came to him,
crying out, "Lord, Son of David,[t] have
mercy on me! My daughter is demon-possessed and suffering terribly."[u]
23Jesus did not answer a word. So his disciples came to him and urged him, "Send
her away, for she keeps crying out after us."
24He answered, "I was sent only to the
lost sheep of Israel."[v]
25The woman came and knelt before
him.[w] "Lord, help me!" she said.
26He replied, "It is not right to take the
children's bread and toss it to the dogs."
27"Yes it is, Lord," she said. "Even the
dogs eat the crumbs that fall from their
master's table."
28Then Jesus said to her, "Woman, you
have great faith![x] Your request is granted."
And her daughter was healed at that moment.

Jesus Feeds the Four Thousand

15:29-31pp — Mk 7:31-37
15:32-39pp — Mk 8:1-10
15:32-39Ref — Mt 14:13-21

29Jesus left there and went along the Sea
of Galilee. Then he went up on a mountainside and sat down. 30Great crowds

15:15 [n]Mt 13:36 **15:16** [o]Mt 16:9 **15:18** [p]Mt 12:34; Lk 6:45; Jas 3:6 **15:19** [q]Gal 5:19-21 **15:20** [r]Ro 14:14 **15:21** [s]Mt 11:21 **15:22** [t]Mt 9:27 [u]Mt 4:24 **15:24** [v]Mt 10:6, 23; Ro 15:8 **15:25** [w]Mt 8:2 **15:28** [x]Mt 9:22

15:30 [y]Mt 4:23 **15:31** [z]Mt 9:8 **15:32** [a]Mt 9:36 **15:36** [b]Mt 14:19 **15:37** [c]Mt 16:10 **16:1** [d]Ac 4:1 [e]Mt 12:38

came to him, bringing the lame, the blind,
the crippled, the mute and many others,
and laid them at his feet; and he healed
them.[y] 31The people were amazed when
they saw the mute speaking, the crippled
made well, the lame walking and the blind
seeing. And they praised the God of Israel.[z]
32Jesus called his disciples to him and
said, "I have compassion for these people;[a] they have already been with me three
days and have nothing to eat. I do not
want to send them away hungry, or they
may collapse on the way."
33His disciples answered, "Where could
we get enough bread in this remote place
to feed such a crowd?"
34"How many loaves do you have?"
Jesus asked.
"Seven," they replied, "and a few small
fish."
35He told the crowd to sit down on the
ground. 36Then he took the seven loaves
and the fish, and when he had given
thanks, he broke them[b] and gave them
to the disciples, and they in turn to the
people. 37They all ate and were satisfied.
Afterward the disciples picked up seven
basketfuls of broken pieces that were left
over.[c] 38The number of those who ate was
four thousand men, besides women and
children. 39After Jesus had sent the crowd
away, he got into the boat and went to the
vicinity of Magadan.

The Demand for a Sign

16:1-12pp — Mk 8:11-21

16 The Pharisees and Sadducees[d]
came to Jesus and tested him by
asking him to show them a sign from
heaven.[e]
2He replied, "When evening comes,
you say, 'It will be fair weather, for the
sky is red,' 3and in the morning, 'Today
it will be stormy, for the sky is red and
overcast.' You know how to interpret the

had someone sighted who could guide them. *pit.* For the prevalence of pits, see note on 12:11; for falling into a pit as a metaphor of judgment, see, e.g., Ps 7:15; Pr 26:27; Isa 24:18; Jer 48:43 – 44; Eze 19:4.
15:15 Disciples could ask teachers for private explanations.
15:19 *murder … slander.* Lists of vices are common in ancient literature. Two thirds of the offenses listed here are violations of the Ten Commandments (see 19:18, in the same order as here and as in Ex 20:13 – 16).
15:21 *Tyre and Sidon.* Leading cities of Phoenicia. Jezebel was from Sidonian territory, but so were a widow and her child who received healing through the ministry of Elijah (1Ki 17:8 – 24). Many dispossessed Canaanites from the Israelite conquest had moved north into Phoenician territory.
15:22 *Son of David.* Implies this Gentile's recognition that Jesus is rightful ruler of Israel.
15:26 *toss it to the dogs.* Though not used as a direct label here, when it was so used, "dog" was a harsh insult for either gender. (When used negatively, Gentiles associated dogs with dung, promiscuity, and the devouring of corpses.) Jewish people often viewed dogs as no better than rodents, and figuratively as hostile predators (e.g., Ps 22:16,20).
15:27 *dogs eat the crumbs.* Gentiles sometimes raised dogs as pets; they could clean up scraps of food left by the family. Too desperate to take offense, this woman humbles herself to seize any opportunity for healing. Many people appreciated quick-witted retorts.
16:1 *Pharisees and Sadducees.* Pharisees and Sadducees usually worked together only when they had a common mission or a common enemy they considered very dangerous. *sign from heaven.* Could mean simply a sign from God, but in this context may mean predicting a heavenly sign such as an eclipse or other phenomenon.
16:3 *how to interpret … the sky.* In the Holy Land, Mediterranean winds bringing rain from the west could yield a red sky in the morning.

appearance of the sky, but you cannot interpret the signs of the times.[a][f] 4A wicked
and adulterous generation looks for a sign,
but none will be given it except the sign
of Jonah."[g] Jesus then left them and went
away.

The Yeast of the Pharisees and Sadducees

5When they went across the lake, the
disciples forgot to take bread. 6"Be careful," Jesus said to them. "Be on your
guard against the yeast of the Pharisees
and Sadducees."[h]
7They discussed this among themselves
and said, "It is because we didn't bring
any bread."
8Aware of their discussion, Jesus asked,
"You of little faith,[i] why are you talking
among yourselves about having no bread?
9Do you still not understand? Don't you
remember the five loaves for the five thousand, and how many basketfuls you gathered?[j] 10Or the seven loaves for the four
thousand, and how many basketfuls you
gathered?[k] 11How is it you don't understand that I was not talking to you about
bread? But be on your guard against the
yeast of the Pharisees and Sadducees."
12Then they understood that he was not
telling them to guard against the yeast
used in bread, but against the teaching of
the Pharisees and Sadducees.[l]

16:3 [f] Lk 12:54-56 **16:4** [g] Mt 12:39 **16:6** [h] Lk 12:1 **16:8** [i] Mt 6:30 **16:9** [j] Mt 14:17-21 **16:10** [k] Mt 15:34-38 **16:12** [l] Ac 4:1

Peter Declares That Jesus Is the Messiah

16:13-16pp — Mk 8:27-29; Lk 9:18-20

13When Jesus came to the region of
Caesarea Philippi, he asked his disciples,
"Who do people say the Son of Man is?"
14They replied, "Some say John the Baptist;[m] others say Elijah; and still others,
Jeremiah or one of the prophets."[n]
15"But what about you?" he asked.
"Who do you say I am?"
16Simon Peter answered, "You are the
Messiah, the Son of the living God."[o]
17Jesus replied, "Blessed are you, Simon
son of Jonah, for this was not revealed to
you by flesh and blood,[p] but by my Father
in heaven. 18And I tell you that you are
Peter,[b][q] and on this rock I will build my
church,[r] and the gates of Hades[c] will not
overcome it. 19I will give you the keys[s] of
the kingdom of heaven; whatever you bind
on earth will be[d] bound in heaven, and
whatever you loose on earth will be[d] loosed
in heaven."[t] 20Then he ordered his disciples
not to tell anyone[u] that he was the Messiah.

Jesus Predicts His Death

16:21-28pp — Mk 8:31 – 9:1; Lk 9:22-27

21From that time on Jesus began to explain to his disciples that he must go to

16:14 [m] Mt 3:1; 14:2 [n] Mk 6:15; Jn 1:21 **16:16** [o] Mt 4:3; Ps 42:2; Jn 11:27; Ac 14:15; 2Co 6:16; 1Th 1:9; 1Ti 3:15; Heb 10:31; 12:22 **16:17** [p] 1Co 15:50; Gal 1:16; Eph 6:12; Heb 2:14 **16:18** [q] Jn 1:42 [r] Eph 2:20 **16:19** [s] Isa 22:22; Rev 3:7 [t] Mt 18:18; Jn 20:23 **16:20** [u] Mk 8:30

[a] *2,3* Some early manuscripts do not have *When evening comes . . . of the times.* [b] *18* The Greek word for *Peter* means *rock.* [c] *18* That is, the realm of the dead [d] *19* Or *will have been*

16:4 *the sign of Jonah.* See note on 12:39 – 42.
16:5 *forgot to take bread.* Teachers sometimes delegated to particular disciples the task of procuring food for a journey.
16:6 *yeast of the Pharisees and Sadducees.* Yeast was sometimes used as a symbol for evil, and for what spreads; since the disciples would not likely want to borrow yeast from Pharisees and Sadducees to bake new bread, they should not take Jesus literally.
16:13 *Caesarea Philippi.* A Gentile city at the northern boundary of ancient Israel (see note on Mk 8:27). That Jesus chose this site for discussing his identity with his disciples might prefigure the mission to the Gentiles (28:19).
16:16 *Son of the living God.* "Son of God" was an appropriate title for the Davidic line, especially the ultimate ruler (cf. 2Sa 7:14; Ps 2:7), as also recognized in the Qumran scrolls.
16:17 *Blessed are you, Simon.* For beatitudes, see note on 5:3; teachers sometimes pronounced blessings on students who offered wise answers. *flesh and blood.* A common way of saying, "human beings" or "mortals."
16:18 *Peter, and on this rock.* In the Greek of this period, *Petros* (Peter's name) was used interchangeably with *petra* ("rock"). Prophets and others commonly used wordplays to make a point; but while Peter may be a rock in his role of confessing Christ (v. 16), he becomes a stumbling block in his role of resisting the meaning of that confession, namely, Jesus' calling to the cross (vv. 22 – 23). Teachers and founders of schools normally expected their disciples to carry on after them and spread their movements. *church.* The Greek term was used in the Septuagint, the pre-Christian Greek translation of the OT, for the community of Israel; the Qumran sect applied the same Hebrew term behind it to their own community. *gates of Hades.* A familiar ancient expression for the realm of the dead (both in Greek literature and in the Greek translation of the Biblical gates of Sheol or of death, e.g., Job 38:17; Isa 38:10); even martyrdom (vv. 21,24) cannot stop God's plan.
16:19 *keys of the kingdom.* Palace keys were large, and an important official carried them (Isa 22:22). In contrast to those who were shutting people out of God's kingdom (23:13), those who confess Jesus as Christ (v. 16) can usher people in. *bind . . . loose.* May include disciplinary authority (see note on 18:18) but perhaps also authority to evaluate those to be admitted (cf. an officer with a similar function at Qumran). The basis for true admission is the shared confession of v. 16.
16:20 *not to tell anyone.* For the "Messianic secret," see Introduction to Mark: Messianic Secret. In Mediterranean society, the honorable man did not directly boast unless it could be justified as necessary. Some suggest that direct Messianic claims were not to be made until God had publicly vindicated the claimants. More generally, healers and leaders drew impossibly large crowds (cf. Mk 3:8 – 10), and political deliverers risked being viewed as a threat and hunted down by the Romans prematurely.
16:21 *must be killed.* Even aside from their presupposing that Jesus could not have been a prophet, the more skeptical scholars who doubt that Jesus could have foreknown his death misunderstand Jesus' milieu. No one could make a commotion in the temple and challenge the priestly elite, as Jesus did, and *not* expect to be executed.

A Roman house key that doubled as a ring. Jesus said to Peter, "I will give you the keys of the kingdom of heaven" (Mt 16:19).

Jerusalem and suffer many things[v] at the
hands of the elders, the chief priests and
the teachers of the law, and that he must
be killed and on the third day[w] be raised
to life.[x]
22Peter took him aside and began to rebuke him. "Never, Lord!" he said. "This
shall never happen to you!"
23Jesus turned and said to Peter, "Get
behind me, Satan![y] You are a stumbling
block to me; you do not have in mind the
concerns of God, but merely human concerns."
24Then Jesus said to his disciples, "Whoever wants to be my disciple must deny
themselves and take up their cross and follow me.[z] 25For whoever wants to save their
life[a] will lose it, but whoever loses their
life for me will find it.[a] 26What good will it
be for someone to gain the whole world,
yet forfeit their soul? Or what can anyone
give in exchange for their soul? 27For the
Son of Man[b] is going to come[c] in his Father's glory with his angels, and then he
will reward each person according to what
they have done.[d]
28"Truly I tell you, some who are standing here will not taste death before they
see the Son of Man coming in his kingdom."

16:21 [v]Mk 10:34; Lk 17:25 [w]Jn 2:19 [x]Mt 17:22, 23; 27:63; Mk 9:31; Lk 9:22; 18:31-33; 24:6, 7 **16:23** [y]Mt 4:10 **16:24** [z]Mt 10:38; Lk 14:27 **16:25** [a]Jn 12:25 **16:27** [b]Mt 8:20 [c]Ac 1:11 [d]Job 34:11; Ps 62:12; Jer 17:10; Ro 2:6; 2Co 5:10; Rev 22:12

The Transfiguration

17:1-8pp — Lk 9:28-36
17:1-13pp — Mk 9:2-13

17 After six days Jesus took with him
Peter, James and John the brother
of James, and led them up a high mountain by themselves. 2There he was transfigured before them. His face shone like the
sun, and his clothes became as white as
the light. 3Just then there appeared before
them Moses and Elijah, talking with Jesus.
4Peter said to Jesus, "Lord, it is good for
us to be here. If you wish, I will put up
three shelters — one for you, one for Moses and one for Elijah."
5While he was still speaking, a bright
cloud covered them, and a voice from

[a] *25* The Greek word means either *life* or *soul;* also in verse 26.

The exceptions might be if the challenger were insane, fled, or raised an army, but there is no reason to expect any of these in Jesus' case. Jesus intended to die; regarding the purpose, see notes on 20:28; 26:28 — where Jesus tells us that he died for *us.*

16:22 Messianic expectations were diverse, but usually involved the Davidic Messiah's triumph over Israel's enemies. Peter may intend encouragement, but disciples were not supposed to rebuke their teachers.

16:23 *Get behind me.* Disciples were expected to walk behind their teachers, and Jesus might allude figuratively to that posture here. *Satan.* By offering the kingdom without the cross (v. 22), Peter fills Satan's role (see 4:8 – 10; cf. 27:42 – 43). *stumbling block.* Plays on Peter's name (see note on v. 18).

16:24 *take up their cross.* Those condemned to execution would often carry the horizontal beam of their cross (the *patibulum*) out to the site of their execution, through an often hostile and mocking mob. Ironically, Jesus' disciples fail even in carrying Jesus' cross (26:69 – 75), so that his executioners have to draft a bystander to carry it (27:32).

16:25 – 26 Jewish apocalyptic writers agreed that eternal life was well worth losing one's life in this age (e.g., 1 Enoch 108:10; 2 Baruch 51:15 – 16).

16:28 *not taste death ... coming in his kingdom.* In context, the Synoptic Gospels apply this promise in the short term to the transfiguration (17:1 – 9), of which Peter, James and John were witnesses. This event points proleptically to Jesus' postresurrection reign (cf. Eph 1:19 – 23) and ultimately to his return, but these three disciples experience a foretaste.

17:1 *six days.* Might evoke Ex 24:16, the context of Moses receiving God's revelation on the mountain (Ex 24:15).

17:2 *face shone like the sun.* Although some other stories about shining people appear in antiquity, the most obvious one — and the one that would have been known to all of Matthew's audience — was Moses, transformed as he saw God's glory (Ex 34:29 – 30,35). Yet Jesus is no mere Moses (vv. 3 – 5).

17:3 *Moses and Elijah.* Elijah had been caught up to heaven alive (2Ki 2:11) and Moses was buried by God himself (Dt 34:5 – 6); a few even believed that Moses, like Elijah, had not died (e.g., *Sipre Dt* 357.10.5). More importantly, Scripture had promised the coming of Elijah (Mal 4:4 – 5) and a prophet like Moses (Dt 18:15 – 19). The disciples experience a divine revelation on the mountain just as Moses and Elijah each did at Mount Sinai.

17:4 *put up three shelters.* Because of the Festival of Tabernacles, not only field workers but all Jewish men would know how to erect temporary shelters.

17:5 *bright cloud covered them.* Recalls the cloud of glory at Sinai when God revealed himself; Jewish teachers spoke of the cloud of God's presence as the *shekinah.* On the divine voice from heaven, see note on 3:17. Here the voice adds, "Listen to him," which some see as an allusion to the promised prophet like Moses (Dt 18:15).

the cloud said, "This is my Son, whom I
love; with him I am well pleased.[e] Listen
to him!"[f]
6When the disciples heard this, they fell
facedown to the ground, terrified. 7But
Jesus came and touched them. "Get up,"
he said. "Don't be afraid."[g] 8When they
looked up, they saw no one except Jesus.
9As they were coming down the mountain, Jesus instructed them, "Don't tell
anyone[h] what you have seen, until the Son
of Man[i] has been raised from the dead."[j]
10The disciples asked him, "Why then
do the teachers of the law say that Elijah
must come first?"
11Jesus replied, "To be sure, Elijah
comes and will restore all things.[k] 12But I
tell you, Elijah has already come,[l] and they
did not recognize him, but have done to
him everything they wished.[m] In the same
way the Son of Man is going to suffer[n] at
their hands." 13Then the disciples understood that he was talking to them about
John the Baptist.

Jesus Heals a Demon-Possessed Boy

17:14-19pp — Mk 9:14-28; Lk 9:37-42

14When they came to the crowd, a man
approached Jesus and knelt before him.
15"Lord, have mercy on my son," he said.
"He has seizures[o] and is suffering greatly.
He often falls into the fire or into the water. 16I brought him to your disciples, but
they could not heal him."
17"You unbelieving and perverse generation," Jesus replied, "how long shall I stay
with you? How long shall I put up with
you? Bring the boy here to me." 18Jesus
rebuked the demon, and it came out of the
boy, and he was healed at that moment.
19Then the disciples came to Jesus in
private and asked, "Why couldn't we
drive it out?"
20He replied, "Because you have so little
faith. Truly I tell you, if you have faith[p] as
small as a mustard seed,[q] you can say to
this mountain, 'Move from here to there,'
and it will move.[r] Nothing will be impossible for you." [21][a]

Jesus Predicts His Death a Second Time

22When they came together in Galilee,
he said to them, "The Son of Man[s] is going to be delivered into the hands of men.
23They will kill him,[t] and on the third day[u]
he will be raised to life."[v] And the disciples were filled with grief.

The Temple Tax

24After Jesus and his disciples arrived
in Capernaum, the collectors of the two-
drachma temple tax[w] came to Peter and
asked, "Doesn't your teacher pay the temple tax?"
25"Yes, he does," he replied.
When Peter came into the house, Jesus
was the first to speak. "What do you
think, Simon?" he asked. "From whom
do the kings of the earth collect duty and
taxes[x] — from their own children or from
others?"
26"From others," Peter answered.
"Then the children are exempt," Jesus
said to him. 27"But so that we may not
cause offense,[y] go to the lake and throw
out your line. Take the first fish you catch;
open its mouth and you will find a four-
drachma coin. Take it and give it to them
for my tax and yours."

a 21 Some manuscripts include here words similar to Mark 9:29.

17:5 [e] Mt 3:17; 2Pe 1:17 [f] Ac 3:22,23
17:7 [g] Mt 14:27
17:9 [h] Mk 8:30 [i] Mt 8:20 [j] Mt 16:21
17:11 [k] Mal 4:6; Lk 1:16,17
17:12 [l] Mt 11:14 [m] Mt 14:3,10 [n] Mt 16:21
17:15 [o] Mt 4:24
17:20 [p] Mt 21:21 [q] Mt 13:31; Mk 11:23; Lk 17:6 [r] 1Co 13:2
17:22 [s] Mt 8:20
17:23 [t] Ac 2:23; 3:13 [u] Mt 16:21 [v] Mt 16:21
17:24 [w] Ex 30:13
17:25 [x] Mt 22:17-21; Ro 13:7
17:27 [y] Jn 6:61

17:6 *fell facedown.* A common way to humble one's self before God, and a usual response to revelations from God and sometimes angels (1Ch 21:16; Eze 1:28; 3:23; 43:3; 44:4; Da 8:17 – 18; 10:8 – 9; also in other ancient Jewish accounts). People also feared Moses when he was radiant (Ex 34:30).

17:7 *Don't be afraid.* Revealers often commanded those who fell facedown during revelations to arise or not to be afraid (Eze 2:1 – 2; Da 8:18; 10:11 – 12; also other ancient Jewish accounts). Beyond these examples, the encouragement not to be afraid is common in Biblical revelations (Ge 15:1; 21:17; 26:24; Jos 8:1; Jdg 6:23).

17:10 *Elijah must come first.* Mal 4:5 – 6 predicted Elijah's return, which was therefore widely anticipated (e.g., Sirach 48:10).

17:12 – 13 *Elijah ... John the Baptist.* Ancient peoples recognized that whereas some prophecies were literal, others were figurative. Writers also sometimes spoke of an individual as a "new" so-and-so — e.g., a "new Caesar" or a "new Alexander."

17:15 *seizures.* Although the epileptic activity here is caused by a spirit (v. 18), as many people in antiquity would expect, Matthew recognizes that not all epileptic activity involves spirits (he distinguishes the two issues in 4:24).

17:20 *mustard seed ... mountain.* Some later sources suggest that "moving mountains" was a Jewish figure of speech for doing what was considered impossible. A massive mountain was a graphic contrast to a tiny mustard seed (see note on 13:31).

17:22 – 23 See note on 16:21.

17:24 *temple tax.* Until the revolt against Rome, all Jewish adult males in the Roman Empire paid an annual two-drachma tax for the support of the Jerusalem temple. This tax yielded so much revenue that the temple authorities simply began constructing a golden vine, to which they added annually. Some Jewish sects refused to contribute to this tax, so the collectors asked Peter what Jesus' response would be. (After the temple's destruction in AD 70, Rome required Jewish people to continue to pay this tax — now to Rome.)

17:25 – 26 *their own children ... are exempt.* Tax regulations often listed those who were exempt. Conquerors charged tribute from the conquered, not from the conquerors' own people; a king's dependents were exempt from his taxes. Priests (and later rabbis) were exempted from the two-drachma tax noted here.

The Greatest in the Kingdom of Heaven

18:1-5pp — Mk 9:33-37; Lk 9:46-48

18 At that time the disciples came to
Jesus and asked, "Who, then, is the
greatest in the kingdom of heaven?"
2He called a little child to him, and
placed the child among them. 3And he
said: "Truly I tell you, unless you change
and become like little children,[z] you will
never enter the kingdom of heaven.[a]
4Therefore, whoever takes the lowly position of this child is the greatest in the kingdom of heaven.[b] 5And whoever welcomes
one such child in my name welcomes me.[c]

Causing to Stumble

6"If anyone causes one of these little ones — those who believe in me — to
stumble, it would be better for them to
have a large millstone hung around their
neck and to be drowned in the depths of
the sea.[d] 7Woe to the world because of the
things that cause people to stumble! Such
things must come, but woe to the person
through whom they come![e] 8If your hand
or your foot causes you to stumble,[f] cut it
off and throw it away. It is better for you to
enter life maimed or crippled than to have
two hands or two feet and be thrown into
eternal fire. 9And if your eye causes you to
stumble,[g] gouge it out and throw it away.
It is better for you to enter life with one
eye than to have two eyes and be thrown
into the fire of hell.[h]

The Parable of the Wandering Sheep

18:12-14pp — Lk 15:4-7

10"See that you do not despise one of
these little ones. For I tell you that their
angels[i] in heaven always see the face of
my Father in heaven. [11][a]
12"What do you think? If a man owns a
hundred sheep, and one of them wanders
away, will he not leave the ninety-nine on
the hills and go to look for the one that
wandered off? 13And if he finds it, truly
I tell you, he is happier about that one
sheep than about the ninety-nine that did
not wander off. 14In the same way your
Father in heaven is not willing that any of
these little ones should perish.

Dealing With Sin in the Church

15"If your brother or sister[b] sins,[c] go
and point out their fault,[j] just between the
two of you. If they listen to you, you have
won them over. 16But if they will not listen, take one or two others along, so that
'every matter may be established by the
testimony of two or three witnesses.'[d][k]

18:3 [z] Mt 19:14; 1Pe 2:2 [a] Mt 3:2 **18:4** [b] Mk 9:35 **18:5** [c] Mt 10:40 **18:6** [d] Mk 9:42; Lk 17:2 **18:7** [e] Lk 17:1 **18:8** [f] Mt 5:29; Mk 9:43, 45 **18:9** [g] Mt 5:29 [h] Mt 5:22 **18:10** [i] Ge 48:16; Ps 34:7; Ac 12:11, 15; Heb 1:14 **18:15** [j] Lev 19:17; Lk 17:3; Gal 6:1; Jas 5:19, 20 **18:16** [k] Nu 35:30; Dt 17:6; 19:15; Jn 8:17; 2Co 13:1; 1Ti 5:19; Heb 10:28

[a] *11* Some manuscripts include here the words of Luke 19:10. [b] *15* The Greek word for *brother or sister* (*adelphos*) refers here to a fellow disciple, whether man or woman; also in verses 21 and 35. [c] *15* Some manuscripts *sins against you* [d] *16* Deut. 19:15

18:1 *greatest in the kingdom.* Jewish teachers sometimes debated what kind of person would be greatest in the kingdom; expecting Jesus the Messiah (16:16) to soon establish his kingdom, the disciples' concerns here are less theoretical. Jewish sages praised humility, but men nevertheless often had ambition.
18:2 *little child.* In ancient society, children were powerless and often overlooked. Ancient speakers and writers typically offered powerful leaders as heroes and models for imitation.
18:3 *like little children.* Children lacked social power; they also needed to depend on their fathers or other providers (see note on 7:9–10).
18:5 *in my name.* Jesus treats powerless children as his representatives (see note on 10:40).
18:6 *large millstone hung around their neck.* Romans sometimes executed people guilty of particularly heinous crimes by drowning them, tied down with a heavy weight; Jewish people normally regarded this punishment as too inhumane. *millstone.* Used by women to grind, but the term here refers to the much larger kind of grinding stone at the community mill; grain was crushed between an upper and lower millstone. The stone was turned by donkeys (a donkey could pull more than 100 pounds [45 kilograms]); one so encumbered would sink quickly (more quickly than with the type of stone described in Jer 51:63–64; cf. 1 Enoch 48:9).
18:7 *stumble.* The law forbade placing stumbling blocks in front of those who might be hurt by them (Lev 19:14); by Jesus' day, many used the expression figuratively for what would cause someone to sin or turn from God.
18:8 *enter life maimed.* In many Jewish traditions, one would first be resurrected in the form in which one died before being fully restored (e.g., 2 Baruch 50:2–4). The righteous expected to receive back any limbs lost in God's service (e.g., 2 Maccabees 7:11; 14:46). Against many Jewish traditions, the resurrection would include the raising of the damned as well as the righteous (Da 12:2).
18:10 *their angels.* Many Jewish people believed in guardian angels (see note on Heb 1:14; also e.g., Tobit 5:22; Pseudo-Philo's *Biblical Antiquities* 11:12; 59:4; in the Tosefta see *Shabbat* 17:2–3). In Jewish tradition, the angels who saw God's face were the most powerful angels, who were typically the ones closest to God's throne.
18:12 Most people of status in the ancient Mediterranean world looked down on shepherds as lower-class, dirty or uncivilized. (Despite many Biblical examples of shepherds, ancient sources suggest that the Judean elite agreed with the high-status consensus.) One hundred was an average size for a flock. Shepherds and other herders did leave their flocks to search for missing animals; often they left them with other shepherds or herders working with them in the same vicinity (cf. Lk 2:8).
18:15 *just between the two of you.* Jesus here agrees with other Jewish teachers: Jewish ethics heavily emphasized reproving a person privately first, so they would have opportunity to make matters right without facing shame.
18:16 *take one or two others along.* Evidence needed to be collected in case the offender did not repent. The demand for at least two witnesses (Dt 17:6; 19:15) was foundational in Jewish law, especially as understood by Pharisees and Essenes.

17If they still refuse to listen, tell it to the
church;[l] and if they refuse to listen even
to the church, treat them as you would a
pagan or a tax collector.[m]
18"Truly I tell you, whatever you bind
on earth will be[a] bound in heaven, and
whatever you loose on earth will be[a]
loosed in heaven.[n]
19"Again, truly I tell you that if two of
you on earth agree about anything they
ask for, it will be done for them[o] by my
Father in heaven. 20For where two or three
gather in my name, there am I with them."

The Parable of the Unmerciful Servant

21Then Peter came to Jesus and asked,
"Lord, how many times shall I forgive my
brother or sister who sins against me?[p] Up
to seven times?"[q]
22Jesus answered, "I tell you, not seven
times, but seventy-seven times.[b][r]
23"Therefore, the kingdom of heaven is
like[s] a king who wanted to settle accounts[t]
with his servants. 24As he began the settlement, a man who owed him ten thousand bags of gold[c] was brought to him.
25Since he was not able to pay,[u] the master
ordered that he and his wife and his children and all that he had be sold[v] to repay
the debt.
26"At this the servant fell on his knees
before him.[w] 'Be patient with me,' he
begged, 'and I will pay back everything.'
27The servant's master took pity on him,
canceled the debt and let him go.
28"But when that servant went out, he
found one of his fellow servants who owed
him a hundred silver coins.[d] He grabbed
him and began to choke him. 'Pay back
what you owe me!' he demanded.
29"His fellow servant fell to his knees

18:17 [l] 1Co 6:1-6 [m] Ro 16:17; 2Th 3:6, 14 **18:18** [n] Mt 16:19; Jn 20:23 **18:19** [o] Mt 7:7 **18:21** [p] Mt 6:14 [q] Lk 17:4 **18:22** [r] Ge 4:24 **18:23** [s] Mt 13:24 [t] Mt 25:19 **18:25** [u] Lk 7:42 [v] Lev 25:39; 2Ki 4:1; Ne 5:5, 8 **18:26** [w] Mt 8:2

[a] *18* Or *will have been* [b] *22* Or *seventy times seven* [c] *24* Greek *ten thousand talents*; a talent was worth about 20 years of a day laborer's wages. [d] *28* Greek *a hundred denarii*; a denarius was the usual daily wage of a day laborer (see 20:2).

18:17 *tell it to the church.* Synagogues functioned as community centers, and thus could also double as community courts. Even outside the Holy Land, Rome allowed Jewish communities to exercise discipline within Gentile cities' minority Jewish communities. The church here functions similarly. The Greek terms translated "church" (*ekklēsia*) and "synagogue" (*synagōgē*) are both used to translate the OT term *qahal*, used for the community of God's people. If the offender still did not repent, the highest level of discipline was exclusion from the community of God's people. This discipline appears both in the Dead Sea Scrolls and in later rabbinic sources.
18:18 *bound … loosed in heaven.* The community following the above procedures (vv. 15 – 17) acts on the authority of heaven. (Later rabbis believed that their decisions based on Scripture and tradition coincided with the decrees of the heavenly court.) Later rabbis employ the terminology "binding" and "loosing" for their authority to interpret the law. Here the phrase extends to judicial decisions, reflecting the figurative application of what "binding" or "loosing" a prisoner normally meant.
18:19 *two of you on earth agree.* Although the principle that God answers prayer is broader, the two or three people in vv. 19 – 20 presumably refer to the two or three witnesses in v. 16 ("earth" and "heaven" likewise echo v. 18). Some suggest that it might be relevant that in Scripture, the witnesses were to be the first to strike the offender (Dt 17:7); here they are to pray.
18:20 *two or three gather in my name.* One familiar Jewish saying was that where two or three gathered to study God's law, God's presence was among them (in the Mishnah see *'Abot* 3:2, 6; *Mekilta Bahodesh* 11). Jewish people considered God alone omnipresent; Jesus speaks of himself here as the divine presence (cf. 1:23; 28:20).
18:21 *Up to seven times?* Although Jewish tradition valued forgiveness, some teachers allowed only three occasions for deliberate sin, since they doubted the offender's sincerity beyond that point.
18:22 *seventy-seven times.* Some scholars argue that Jesus here reverses the principle of vengeance in Ge 4:24 (77 times). Hyperbole reinforces the point.
18:23 *the kingdom of heaven is like.* See note on 13:24. *king.* A frequent figure in Jewish parables; he normally represented God. Jesus uses characteristics of a Gentile kingdom in this parable because some of the most shocking images (especially vv. 25,34) would not work in a Jewish setting. The king may resemble what we know of Ptolemaic rulers in Hellenistic, pre-Roman Egypt. Such a king would settle accounts with his tax farmers. The tax farmers are responsible to pay him the taxes for the people they are assigned to tax; they would then recoup their cost and make a profit by collecting the taxes from the people. After bad harvests or other crises, however, the tax revenue might not be available.
18:24 *ten thousand bags of gold.* Unlike many realistic details in the parable, the servant who has fallen so far in debt would shock Jesus' hearers. If the talents (translated here "bags of gold") are gold rather than silver (cf. Est 3:9), the amount this servant owes may be more than the amount of money in circulation in any petty kingdom in Jesus' day (by comparison, Herod the Great's annual tax revenue was about 800 talents). This was as much as 100 million denarii (as much as 70 or even 100 million days' wages for a peasant). Indeed, perhaps the only reason the figure is not placed even higher is that the term translated "bags of gold" here was the largest currency available, and "ten thousand" was the largest numerical designation in Greek.
18:25 *his wife and his children and all that he had be sold.* The king could not hope to recoup his losses by selling the man and his family; the most expensive slave might sell for one talent, and often this could be the price for 20 slaves. The man's property could also not match the amount mentioned in v. 24. The sale might make the angry king feel better, however. Jewish teachers forbade selling wives or children to repay debts, but this is presumably a Gentile king.
18:26 *I will pay back.* "I will repay" commonly appeared in ancient promissory notes; the promise to repay is in this case impossibly absurd.
18:27 *took pity on him.* Selling the man will not recoup the king's losses (see notes on vv. 24 – 25); in a culture valuing honor, however, showing mercy would at least serve the king's reputation for benevolence.
18:28 *hundred silver coins.* The other servant owes the merciless man perhaps nearly as little as a millionth of

and begged him, ‘Be patient with me, and
I will pay it back.’
30“But he refused. Instead, he went off
and had the man thrown into prison until
he could pay the debt. 31When the other servants saw what had happened, they
were outraged and went and told their
master everything that had happened.
32“Then the master called the servant
in. ‘You wicked servant,’ he said, ‘I canceled all that debt of yours because you
begged me to. 33Shouldn’t you have had
mercy on your fellow servant just as I had
on you?’ 34In anger his master handed him
over to the jailers to be tortured, until he
should pay back all he owed.
35“This is how my heavenly Father will
treat each of you unless you forgive your
brother or sister from your heart.”[x]

Divorce

19:1-9pp — Mk 10:1-12

19 When Jesus had finished saying
these things,[y] he left Galilee and
went into the region of Judea to the other
side of the Jordan. 2Large crowds followed
him, and he healed them[z] there.
3Some Pharisees came to him to test him.
They asked, “Is it lawful for a man to divorce his wife[a] for any and every reason?”
4“Haven’t you read,” he replied, “that
at the beginning the Creator ‘made them
male and female,’[a][b] 5and said, ‘For this reason a man will leave his father and mother
and be united to his wife, and the two will
become one flesh’[b]?[c] 6So they are no longer two, but one flesh. Therefore what God
has joined together, let no one separate.”
7“Why then,” they asked, “did Moses
command that a man give his wife a certificate of divorce and send her away?”[d]
8Jesus replied, “Moses permitted you to
divorce your wives because your hearts
were hard. But it was not this way from
the beginning. 9I tell you that anyone
who divorces his wife, except for sexual
immorality, and marries another woman
commits adultery.”[e]

18:35 [x] Mt 6:14; Jas 2:13
19:1 [y] Mt 7:28
19:2 [z] Mt 4:23
19:3 [a] Mt 5:31
19:4 [b] Ge 1:27; 5:2
19:5 [c] Ge 2:24; 1Co 6:16; Eph 5:31
19:7 [d] Dt 24:1-4; Mt 5:31
19:9 [e] Mt 5:32; Lk 16:18

[a] *4* Gen. 1:27 [b] *5* Gen. 2:24

---

what that man had owed the king. *choke him.* Ancient sources show that creditors sometimes did in fact choke their debtors when demanding payment. The fellow servant may have had no money available at that point because he too had been settling accounts with the king (v. 23). (Some suggest that the merciless man, having failed to collect sufficient tax revenue from his subjects previously, has now determined to ruthlessly exact all that is owed.)

18:30 – 33 By imprisoning his fellow servant, the merciless man not only renders him unable to repay his debt (unless friends or relatives come to his aid) but also takes him out of active service for the king, costing the king even more money! Nor will the king’s benevolence toward the merciless servant help the king’s reputation, in light of this servant’s current behavior.

18:34 *tortured.* Most Jewish hearers would have recoiled at the sound of torture, but they would have known that some Gentile rulers practiced this, sometimes to extort money from the tortured person’s friends. Seeing that this servant had fallen from the king’s favor, however, his former friends will not be so foolish politically as to come to his defense. The man will never repay his debt — and thus he will never escape.

19:3 *divorce his wife for any … reason.* Jewish teachers in general regarded divorce as tragic but the choice of the husband; they would not normally interfere. Although wealth could buy exceptions for powerful women, the usual Judean custom was that only the husband had the option of divorce. (If the husband were abusive, however, a court could force him to grant his wife a divorce.) There were two schools of thought among the Pharisees: the school of Shammai and the school of Hillel. Shammaites outnumbered Hillelites in Jesus’ day (unlike after AD 70), but various ancient sources suggest that on the question of divorce the Hillelite view probably reflected the dominant practice in the larger society (cf. Sirach 25:26; Josephus, *Antiquities* 4.253; *Life* 415, 426). Shammaites interpreted the grounds for divorce in Dt 24:1 (“something indecent about her,” emphasizing *indecent*) as a reference to the wife’s unfaithfulness; by contrast, Hillelites emphasized the word *something* and believed that a husband could divorce his wife for any cause (rendered here “for any and every reason”). Some sages recommended divorcing a disrespectful or disobedient wife (Sirach 25:25 – 26). Although few husbands would have taken advantage of the rule, Hillelites graphically claimed that a husband could divorce his wife even for burning the bread; a later Hillelite rabbi added, “or if he finds someone more beautiful” (in the Mishnah see *Gittin* 9:10; *Sipre Dt* 269.1.1).

19:4 *Haven’t you read …?* Jesus’ question would insult the Pharisees. Nevertheless, his line of argument would be hard to discredit; many other Jewish thinkers of this period found divine ideals in the creation narrative. The Qumran sectarians, e.g., used Ge 1:27 (cited here) to prohibit kings from marrying multiple wives (Damascus Document 4.20 — 5.2; Temple Scroll 56.18 – 19). For many Jewish people, the ideals of the “beginning” also foreshadowed the future kingdom.

19:5 – 6 Teachers sometimes challenged other teachers’ interpretations of verses (here some Pharisees’ understanding of Dt 24:1) by appealing to other texts that contradicted those interpretations. Jesus here appeals to Ge 2:24.

19:8 *because your hearts were hard.* Ancient teachers of the law sometimes recognized that some of Moses’ laws were concessions to human weakness. Civil laws by their nature represent not God’s ideals but merely limits on human sin (see notes on 5:22,28).

19:9 *commits adultery.* Viewing remarriage as adultery treats a first marriage as indissoluble in God’s sight. This was shocking hyperbole, however, since Jesus’ point is that marriage should not be broken, not that it never is broken (see v. 6). Shammaites allowed divorce only for grounds of unfaithfulness; Jesus sides with them as against the many others who allowed it “for any and every reason” (v. 3; see note there). (The other NT exception, in 1Co 7:15, also involves a matter beyond the believer’s control; the principle common to both passages seems to be that believers should never break their marriage covenant, but that neither are they ultimately responsible for the other partner doing so.)

10 The disciples said to him, "If this is
the situation between a husband and wife,
it is better not to marry."
11 Jesus replied, "Not everyone can accept this word, but only those to whom it
has been given.[f] 12 For there are eunuchs
who were born that way, and there are eunuchs who have been made eunuchs by
others — and there are those who choose
to live like eunuchs for the sake of the
kingdom of heaven. The one who can accept this should accept it."

The Little Children and Jesus

19:13-15pp — Mk 10:13-16; Lk 18:15-17

13 Then people brought little children to
Jesus for him to place his hands on them[g]
and pray for them. But the disciples rebuked them.
14 Jesus said, "Let the little children
come to me, and do not hinder them, for
the kingdom of heaven belongs[h] to such as
these."[i] 15 When he had placed his hands
on them, he went on from there.

The Rich and the Kingdom of God

19:16-29pp — Mk 10:17-30; Lk 18:18-30

16 Just then a man came up to Jesus and
asked, "Teacher, what good thing must I
do to get eternal life[j]?"[k]
17 "Why do you ask me about what is
good?" Jesus replied. "There is only One
who is good. If you want to enter life, keep
the commandments."[l]
18 "Which ones?" he inquired.
Jesus replied, " 'You shall not murder,
you shall not commit adultery,[m] you shall
not steal, you shall not give false testimony, 19 honor your father and mother,'[a][n] and
'love your neighbor as yourself.'[b]"[o]
20 "All these I have kept," the young man
said. "What do I still lack?"
21 Jesus answered, "If you want to be
perfect,[p] go, sell your possessions and
give to the poor,[q] and you will have treasure in heaven.[r] Then come, follow me."
22 When the young man heard this, he
went away sad, because he had great
wealth.
23 Then Jesus said to his disciples, "Truly I tell you, it is hard for someone who
is rich[s] to enter the kingdom of heaven.
24 Again I tell you, it is easier for a camel
to go through the eye of a needle than for
someone who is rich to enter the kingdom
of God."
25 When the disciples heard this, they
were greatly astonished and asked, "Who
then can be saved?"
26 Jesus looked at them and said, "With
man this is impossible, but with God all
things are possible."[t]
27 Peter answered him, "We have left everything to follow you![u] What then will
there be for us?"
28 Jesus said to them, "Truly I tell you, at
the renewal of all things, when the Son of
Man sits on his glorious throne,[v] you who
have followed me will also sit on twelve

19:11 [f] Mt 13:11; 1Co 7:7-9, 17 **19:13** [g] Mk 5:23 **19:14** [h] Mt 25:34 [i] Mt 18:3; 1Pe 2:2 **19:16** [j] Mt 25:46 [k] Lk 10:25 **19:17** [l] Lev 18:5 **19:18** [m] Jas 2:11 **19:19** [n] Ex 20:12-16; Dt 5:16-20 [o] Lev 19:18; Mt 5:43 **19:21** [p] Mt 5:48 [q] Lk 12:33; Ac 2:45; 4:34-35 [r] Mt 6:20 **19:23** [s] Mt 13:22; 1Ti 6:9, 10 **19:26** [t] Ge 18:14; Job 42:2; Jer 32:17; Zec 8:6; Lk 1:37; 18:27; Ro 4:21 **19:27** [u] Mt 4:19 **19:28** [v] Mt 20:21; 25:31

[a] *19* Exodus 20:12-16; Deut. 5:16-20 [b] *19* Lev. 19:18

19:10 *better not to marry.* Ancient marriage contracts often included a clause specifying what would happen in case of divorce. Because parents arranged many marriages, and many Galilean couples had no unchaperoned time together before marriage, the disciples fear the prospect of marriage with no escape for difficult circumstances.
19:12 *eunuchs.* Although eunuchs in Near Eastern royal courts could exercise power, Greco-Roman society often ridiculed eunuchs as effeminate or "half-men." Jewish people abhorred castration, and eunuchs were excluded from the covenant (Dt 23:1). Speaking figuratively of long-term singleness, Jesus explains that there are some "who choose to live like eunuchs for the sake of the kingdom of heaven." Apart from some Essenes, most of Jesus' Jewish contemporaries regarded marriage and rearing children as an important duty.
19:13 *place his hands on them.* A person blessed by God could lay hands on someone to pray for a blessing on them (e.g., Ge 48:14). *disciples rebuked them.* Disciples sometimes tried to protect their teachers from distractions (cf. 2Ki 4:27).
19:14 *do not hinder them.* See note on 18:5. A man of God could overrule his disciple from keeping a supplicant away (cf. 2Ki 4:27).
19:16 *eternal life.* If later Jewish sources are representative, sometimes people asked Jewish teachers how to have eternal life. Eternal life was the life of the coming age (Da 12:2), thus of the kingdom (cf. v. 23).
19:17 *keep the commandments.* God had promised Israel life if they obeyed his commandments (e.g., Lev 25:18; Dt 4:1,40; 30:19 – 20); this originally referred to long life in the promised land, but Jewish teachers by Jesus' day understood it to apply also to eternal life.
19:18 – 19 Of the six stipulations in the Ten Commandments that deal with one's neighbor (Ex 20:12 – 17), Jesus lists five (Matthew omits Mark's "defraud" [Mk 10:19], which was not specifically one of these commandments). Jesus also lists the commandment from Lev 19:18, which he treats as a summary of the law toward one's neighbor (see note on 22:39).
19:22 *he had great wealth.* Sages usually welcomed would-be disciples, but some radical teachers made harsh demands to weed out those who would not be serious, especially when prospective disciples were wealthy or arrogant. Accounts of such sages emphasize that they were not impressed by worldly status and that wealth is not what makes us important.
19:24 *camel . . . eye of a needle.* See note on Lk 18:25.
19:26 *with God all things are possible.* Scripture was clear that nothing was impossible for God (Ge 18:14; Jer 32:17,27), apart from something contrary to his character.
19:28 *at the renewal of all things.* The term translated "the renewal" was used by Stoic philosophers for the fiery destruction and restoration of the cosmos; in a Jewish setting, it refers to the promised new creation (cf. Isa 65:17; 66:22). *twelve tribes.* Most Jewish people expected God to restore the 12 tribes of Israel at the time of the end.

thrones, judging the twelve tribes of Israel.[w] 29And everyone who has left houses
or brothers or sisters or father or mother
or wife[a] or children or fields for my sake
will receive a hundred times as much and
will inherit eternal life.[x] 30But many who
are first will be last, and many who are
last will be first.[y]

The Parable of the Workers in the Vineyard

20 "For the kingdom of heaven is like[z]
a landowner who went out early in
the morning to hire workers for his vineyard.[a] 2He agreed to pay them a denarius[b]
for the day and sent them into his vineyard.
3"About nine in the morning he went
out and saw others standing in the marketplace doing nothing. 4He told them,
'You also go and work in my vineyard,
and I will pay you whatever is right.' 5So
they went.

"He went out again about noon and
about three in the afternoon and did the
same thing. 6About five in the afternoon
he went out and found still others standing around. He asked them, 'Why have
you been standing here all day long doing
nothing?'
7" 'Because no one has hired us,' they
answered.

"He said to them, 'You also go and work
in my vineyard.'
8"When evening came,[b] the owner of
the vineyard said to his foreman, 'Call the
workers and pay them their wages, beginning with the last ones hired and going on
to the first.'
9"The workers who were hired about
five in the afternoon came and each received a denarius. 10So when those came
who were hired first, they expected to receive more. But each one of them also received a denarius. 11When they received
it, they began to grumble[c] against the
landowner. 12'These who were hired last
worked only one hour,' they said, 'and
you have made them equal to us who
have borne the burden of the work and
the heat[d] of the day.'
13"But he answered one of them, 'I am
not being unfair to you, friend.[e] Didn't
you agree to work for a denarius? 14Take
your pay and go. I want to give the one
who was hired last the same as I gave you.
15Don't I have the right to do what I want
with my own money? Or are you envious
because I am generous?'[f]
16"So the last will be first, and the first
will be last."[g]

Jesus Predicts His Death a Third Time

20:17-19pp — Mk 10:32-34; Lk 18:31-33

17Now Jesus was going up to Jerusalem. On the way, he took the Twelve aside
and said to them, 18"We are going up to
Jerusalem,[h] and the Son of Man[i] will be

19:28 [w]Lk 22:28-30; Rev 3:21; 4:4; 20:4 **19:29** [x]Mt 6:33; 25:46 **19:30** [y]Mt 20:16; Mk 10:31; Lk 13:30 **20:1** [z]Mt 13:24 [a]Mt 21:28, 33 **20:8** [b]Lev 19:13; Dt 24:15
20:11 [c]Jnh 4:1 **20:12** [d]Jnh 4:8; Lk 12:55; Jas 1:11 **20:13** [e]Mt 22:12; 26:50 **20:15** [f]Dt 15:9; Mk 7:22 **20:16** [g]Mt 19:30 **20:18** [h]Lk 9:51 [i]Mt 8:20

[a] *29* Some manuscripts do not have *or wife.* [b] *2* A denarius was the usual daily wage of a day laborer.

Qumran documents even speak of a group of 12 leaders, apparently because of their expectation that God would restore the 12 tribes. Jesus was preparing for the restoration of his people and of creation.
19:30 *first will be last ... last will be first.* Many Jewish thinkers expected the coming age to reverse current fortunes: the lowly would be exalted and the exalted brought low. Most Jewish people expected that God would exalt the people of Israel and punish their Gentile oppressors.
20:1 *like a landowner.* Jewish parables often began with, "Such-and-such is like ..."; the named subject (here, *kingdom*) was compared not simply with the next noun (here, *a man*) but with the entire parable that followed. Because of God's greatness, Jewish teachers often compared him in parables to a king or landowner. *hire workers for his vineyard.* Most Galileans worked in agriculture. During harvest time, those who owned large amounts of land needed to hire many extra workers to bring in the harvest quickly so that none of it would spoil. Landless unemployed people were numerous and could be available for work as early as sunrise; shepherds and goatherds might also add their services. Most workers were hired as harvesters; a smaller number might stand watch to prevent theft, and some boys could drive the donkeys.
20:2 *denarius.* Roughly a day's normal wage.
20:3 *nine in the morning.* Lit. the "third hour" from sunrise. Others may have been finishing smaller harvests on their own land or simply arrived later than the first group. The day began at sunrise, but people might work 12 hours a day during harvest.
20:8 *pay them their wages.* Subsistence-level workers were to be paid daily so they could feed themselves and their families (Lev 19:13; Dt 24:15).
20:11 – 12 Rarely would subordinates in antiquity speak so rudely to a landowner from whom they might hope for future employment or favors. Although by their culture's standards the landowner is socially superior, they fail to greet him with a title.
20:13 – 15 Ancients valued and praised benevolence; this landowner has not wronged the complaining workers by showing extra benevolence to others. The landowner shames the complainers, showing that they are complaining about benevolence. Grace is not fair; it is generous.
20:16 *the last will be first, and the first will be last.* See note on 19:30. Ancient speakers and writers sometimes bracketed a passage by repeating at the end what they said at the beginning. With the above parable (vv. 1 – 15) some scholars compare a later rabbinic parable: a king paid a worker representing Israel, who worked particularly diligently, much more than he paid the other workers, who represented Gentiles. The parable's point was that in this world God paid Gentiles back in full for any good they did, but that Israel would be blessed forever in the world to come (*Sipra Behuqotai* 2.262.1.9). Jesus' point was quite different: God is gracious to bless all who serve him, including those who seem the most unexpected to enter his kingdom.
20:17 – 19 See note on 16:21.

delivered over to the chief priests and the teachers of the law.[j] They will condemn him to death 19and will hand him over to the Gentiles to be mocked and flogged[k] and crucified.[l] On the third day[m] he will be raised to life!"[n]

A Mother's Request

20:20-28pp — Mk 10:35-45

20Then the mother of Zebedee's sons[o] came to Jesus with her sons and, kneeling down,[p] asked a favor of him.

21"What is it you want?" he asked.

She said, "Grant that one of these two sons of mine may sit at your right and the other at your left in your kingdom."[q]

22"You don't know what you are asking," Jesus said to them. "Can you drink the cup[r] I am going to drink?"

"We can," they answered.

23Jesus said to them, "You will indeed drink from my cup,[s] but to sit at my right or left is not for me to grant. These places belong to those for whom they have been prepared by my Father."

24When the ten heard about this, they were indignant[t] with the two brothers. 25Jesus called them together and said, "You know that the rulers of the Gentiles lord it over them, and their high officials exercise authority over them. 26Not so with you. Instead, whoever wants to become great among you must be your servant,[u] 27and whoever wants to be first must be your slave— 28just as the Son of Man[v] did not come to be served, but to serve,[w] and to give his life as a ransom[x] for many."

Two Blind Men Receive Sight

20:29-34pp — Mk 10:46-52; Lk 18:35-43

29As Jesus and his disciples were leaving Jericho, a large crowd followed him. 30Two blind men were sitting by the roadside, and when they heard that Jesus was going by, they shouted, "Lord, Son of David,[y] have mercy on us!"

31The crowd rebuked them and told them to be quiet, but they shouted all the louder, "Lord, Son of David, have mercy on us!"

32Jesus stopped and called them. "What do you want me to do for you?" he asked.

33"Lord," they answered, "we want our sight."

34Jesus had compassion on them and touched their eyes. Immediately they received their sight and followed him.

Jesus Comes to Jerusalem as King

21:1-9pp — Mk 11:1-10; Lk 19:29-38
21:4-9pp — Jn 12:12-15

21 As they approached Jerusalem and came to Bethphage on the Mount of Olives,[z] Jesus sent two disciples, 2saying to them, "Go to the village ahead of you, and at once you will find a donkey tied there, with her colt by her. Untie them and bring them to me. 3If anyone says anything to you, say that the Lord needs them, and he will send them right away."

20:18 [j] Mt 16:21; 27:1,2 **20:19** [k] Mt 16:21 [l] Ac 2:23 [m] Mt 16:21 [n] Mt 16:21 **20:20** [o] Mt 4:21 [p] Mt 8:2 **20:21** [q] Mt 19:28 **20:22** [r] Isa 51:17, 22; Jer 49:12; Mt 26:39, 42; Mk 14:36; Lk 22:42; Jn 18:11 **20:23** [s] Ac 12:2; Rev 1:9 **20:24** [t] Lk 22:24, 25 **20:26** [u] Mt 23:11; Mk 9:35 **20:28** [v] Mt 8:20 [w] Lk 22:27; Jn 13:13-16; 2Co 8:9; Php 2:7 [x] Isa 53:10; Mt 26:28; 1Ti 2:6; Titus 2:14; Heb 9:28; 1Pe 1:18, 19 **20:30** [y] Mt 9:27 **21:1** [z] Mt 24:3; 26:30; Mk 14:26; Lk 19:37; 21:37; 22:39; Jn 8:1; Ac 1:12

20:20 *mother of Zebedee's sons.* Women, and especially older women, could get away with requests and demands that men could not (or might even get in trouble for).
20:22,23 *cup.* Biblical prophets used a cup to symbolize sufferings, normally as divine judgment (Isa 51:17; Jer 25:15–17; 51:7; Hab 2:16; Zec 12:2); here it applies to Jesus' painful death (26:39).
20:24 *they were indignant.* Rivalry and competition for honor were common and expected in ancient Mediterranean society.
20:25 *lord it over them.* For the pervasive emphasis on rank even among Jewish people, see notes on 23:6–7; but Gentile rulers offered a particularly obvious example, and one that Jewish people would view negatively.
20:28 *give his life as a ransom for many.* This verse recalls Isaiah's description of the suffering servant: Jesus gave "his life" (Isa 53:12) "as a ransom" (cf. Isa 53:10–11) "for many" (Isa 53:11–12). The idea of one person suffering to ransom others was understood in Jewish and many Gentile cultures; Jewish people believed that righteous martyrs could also satisfy and turn away God's wrath from their people (see especially 4 Maccabees 17:7—18:5).
20:29 *were leaving Jericho.* In Mark, they *approached* Jericho (Mk 10:46). Some point out that the OT site of Jericho had been largely abandoned, and that the new Jericho lay south of it, suggesting that Mark refers to old Jericho and Matthew to the new one. Others suggest that Matthew highlights the proximity to Jerusalem (some 17 miles [27 kilometers] farther southwest). Given the range of differences accepted in ancient biography, the difference between the two accounts here might even be considered negligible.
20:30 *Two blind men.* Matthew has two blind men whereas Mark has one (Mk 10:46). Some think that Mark highlighted only one whose name he knew (Mk 10:46), whereas Matthew knew of a second one; others suggest, on the analogy of some Jewish interpretive practices, that Matthew simply compensates for omitting another account of another blind man's healing (Mk 8:22–26). Many think that Matthew might also reuse the same story in two places where it fits relevantly (Mt 9:27–30). If so, it fits the recognition that ancient biographies were often arranged topically; because of this a biography occasionally could mention the same story in two places (in this case, topically in ch. 9 but here in ch. 20 following Mark's sequence).
21:1 *approached Jerusalem.* The Roman road from Jericho (20:29) to Jerusalem led 17 miles (27 kilometers) farther southwest and 3,000 feet (900 meters) higher. Jerusalem would become visible when travelers reached Bethphage on the Mount of Olives; officially a Jerusalem suburb, it lay on the other side of the valley of the brook Kidron.
21:3 *the Lord needs them.* Authorities could temporarily commandeer people or animals for service (see note on 5:41). Jesus uses his authority in this exceptional instance; he is a king (v. 5).

4 This took place to fulfill what was spoken through the prophet:

5 "Say to Daughter Zion,
'See, your king comes to you,
gentle and riding on a donkey,
and on a colt, the foal of a
donkey.' "[a][a]

6 The disciples went and did as Jesus
had instructed them. 7 They brought the
donkey and the colt and placed their
cloaks on them for Jesus to sit on. 8 A very
large crowd spread their cloaks[b] on the
road, while others cut branches from the
trees and spread them on the road. 9 The
crowds that went ahead of him and those
that followed shouted,

"Hosanna[b] to the Son of David!"[c]

"Blessed is he who comes in the name
of the Lord!"[cd]

"Hosanna[b] in the highest heaven!"[e]

10 When Jesus entered Jerusalem, the
whole city was stirred and asked, "Who
is this?"

11 The crowds answered, "This is Jesus,
the prophet[f] from Nazareth in Galilee."

Jesus at the Temple

21:12-16pp — Mk 11:15-18; Lk 19:45-47

12 Jesus entered the temple courts and
drove out all who were buying[g] and selling there. He overturned the tables of the
money changers[h] and the benches of those
selling doves.[i] 13 "It is written," he said to
them, " 'My house will be called a house
of prayer,'[dj] but you are making it 'a den
of robbers.'[e]"[k]

14 The blind and the lame came to him
at the temple, and he healed them.[l] 15 But
when the chief priests and the teachers of
the law saw the wonderful things he did
and the children shouting in the temple
courts, "Hosanna to the Son of David,"[m]
they were indignant.[n]

16 "Do you hear what these children are
saying?" they asked him.

21:5 [a] Isa 62:11; Zec 9:9
21:8 [b] 2Ki 9:13
21:9 [c] ver 15; Mt 9:27 [d] Ps 118:26; Mt 23:39 [e] Lk 2:14
21:11 [f] Lk 7:16, 39; 24:19; Jn 1:21, 25; 6:14; 7:40
21:12 [g] Dt 14:26 [h] Ex 30:13 [i] Lev 1:14
21:13 [j] Isa 56:7 [k] Jer 7:11
21:14 [l] Mt 4:23
21:15 [m] ver 9; Mt 9:27 [n] Lk 19:39

[a] *5* Zech. 9:9 [b] *9* A Hebrew expression meaning "Save!" which became an exclamation of praise; also in verse 15 [c] *9* Psalm 118:25,26 [d] *13* Isaiah 56:7 [e] *13* Jer. 7:11

21:5–7 Hopes for redemption ran high at Passover, and many Judeans interpreted redemption as deliverance from foreign oppression. Zec 9:9 speaks of a "lowly" king (when applied to rulers the description meant gracious, merciful); he comes as a king, but not as a warrior-conqueror. He comes not riding on a horse (cf. Est 6:8) but on a donkey (cf. 1Ki 1:33). In Zechariah, the king is said to ride on a donkey, even on a donkey colt. Unlike Mark (Mk 11:4–7), Matthew mentions the disciples bringing not only the colt but also the mother. Jewish interpreters sometimes read literally everything they could in a text, even if the parallel lines were two ways of saying the same thing. In Hebrew, however, though the mother is mentioned, the adult donkey on whom the king rides appears male (the common Greek version is more ambiguous, but Matthew apparently translates the Hebrew here). Whether or not Matthew mentions the mother because of Zechariah's wording, it is hard to imagine that the disciples would not have brought the mother; the colt was an unweaned foal, so it's unlikely to have cooperated easily without its mother's presence, perhaps in the lead. Although Matthew mentions cloaks on both animals, Jesus sat on the cloaks only on the colt.
21:8 *spread their cloaks on the road.* People could honor new kings by throwing their cloaks down where the kings would sit (v. 7) or tread; see, e.g., 2Ki 9:13. *others cut branches.* Branches were used for celebrations (Ps 118:27), though not as much at Passover as at the later Festival of Tabernacles.
21:9 The crowds would know Ps 118:25–26 by heart. It was part of the Hallel, consisting of Ps 113–118, which was sung at the Passover season (see Mt 26:30). *Hosanna.* Means, "Save!" (a cry for deliverance). *Son of David.* The title leaves no doubt that some in the crowds already think of Jesus as a Messianic figure (see note on 1:1).
21:11 *from Nazareth in Galilee.* Most of Jesus' supporters, those who knew most about him at this point, would have been Galileans.
21:12 If merely prophesying the temple's demise could stir the temple authorities to hostile action (Jer 26:11; Josephus, *Wars* 6.300–9), it is not surprising that within a week of this incident Jesus was executed. Because Passover pilgrims came from all over the ancient world and each locality had its own special currency, money changers were necessary before people could buy sacrifices in the temple. Those who traveled from far away could not bring their own sacrifices, but would have to buy sacrifices at the temple. The issue is not the service provided but the location, as v. 13 makes clear. Jesus was not interfering with the massive tourist trade or other merchants outside the temple; his concern was with the distraction in the temple courts.
21:13 *a house of prayer … 'a den of robbers.'* Isa 56:7 explained the temple's purpose: a house for prayer. Jesus charged that his people were instead making it "a den of robbers," quoting Jer 7:11. The context in Jeremiah was that God's people were committing sins, yet felt safe from God's judgment in the temple, like robbers felt safe in their dens. God thus promised that he would destroy the temple—probably an implication of Jesus as well (cf. 24:2).
21:14 *The blind and the lame came to him.* Pharisaic teachers did not require the blind or those unable to walk to come to festivals in Jerusalem; many scholars argue that some Jewish traditions also excluded them from the court of Israel in the temple. Jesus, however, takes special interest in helping them.
21:15 *chief priests and the teachers of the law.* The aristocratic priests belonged to Jerusalem's wealthy ruling class, which was responsible to keep peace for the Romans. The teachers of the law might have additional theological objections; because those referred to here may belong to the ruling council (cf. 26:57), they probably also have political objections. *Hosanna.* See note on v. 9.
21:16 *From the lips … praise.* Jesus here quotes the Greek version of Ps 8:2; the Hebrew reads "strength" instead of "praise." Jewish interpreters frequently chose the textual

"Yes," replied Jesus, "have you never
read,

" 'From the lips of children and infants
you, Lord, have called forth your
praise'[a]?"[o]

17 And he left them and went out of the
city to Bethany,[p] where he spent the night.

Jesus Curses a Fig Tree

21:18-22pp — Mk 11:12-14,20-24

18 Early in the morning, as Jesus was on
his way back to the city, he was hungry.
19 Seeing a fig tree by the road, he went up
to it but found nothing on it except leaves.
Then he said to it, "May you never bear
fruit again!" Immediately the tree withered.[q]

20 When the disciples saw this, they
were amazed. "How did the fig tree wither so quickly?" they asked.

21 Jesus replied, "Truly I tell you, if you
have faith and do not doubt,[r] not only can
you do what was done to the fig tree, but
also you can say to this mountain, 'Go,
throw yourself into the sea,' and it will
be done. 22 If you believe, you will receive
whatever you ask for[s] in prayer."

The Authority of Jesus Questioned

21:23-27pp — Mk 11:27-33; Lk 20:1-8

23 Jesus entered the temple courts, and,
while he was teaching, the chief priests
and the elders of the people came to him.
"By what authority[t] are you doing these
things?" they asked. "And who gave you
this authority?"

24 Jesus replied, "I will also ask you one
question. If you answer me, I will tell you
by what authority I am doing these things.
25 John's baptism—where did it come
from? Was it from heaven, or of human
origin?"

They discussed it among themselves
and said, "If we say, 'From heaven,' he
will ask, 'Then why didn't you believe
him?' 26 But if we say, 'Of human origin'—
we are afraid of the people, for they all
hold that John was a prophet."[u]

27 So they answered Jesus, "We don't know."

Then he said, "Neither will I tell you by
what authority I am doing these things.

The Parable of the Two Sons

28 "What do you think? There was a man
who had two sons. He went to the first
and said, 'Son, go and work today in the
vineyard.'[v]

29 " 'I will not,' he answered, but later he
changed his mind and went.

30 "Then the father went to the other son
and said the same thing. He answered, 'I
will, sir,' but he did not go.

31 "Which of the two did what his father
wanted?"

"The first," they answered.

Jesus said to them, "Truly I tell you, the
tax collectors[w] and the prostitutes[x] are entering the kingdom of God ahead of you.
32 For John came to you to show you the
way of righteousness,[y] and you did not believe him, but the tax collectors[z] and the
prostitutes[a] did. And even after you saw
this, you did not repent[b] and believe him.

The Parable of the Tenants

21:33-46pp — Mk 12:1-12; Lk 20:9-19

33 "Listen to another parable: There was
a landowner who planted[c] a vineyard. He
put a wall around it, dug a winepress in it
and built a watchtower.[d] Then he rented

21:16 [o] Ps 8:2 **21:17** [p] Mt 26:6; Mk 11:1; Lk 24:50; Jn 11:1, 18; 12:1 **21:19** [q] Isa 34:4; Jer 8:13 **21:21** [r] Mt 17:20; Lk 17:6; 1Co 13:2; Jas 1:6 **21:22** [s] Mt 7:7 **21:23** [t] Ac 4:7; 7:27 **21:26** [u] Mt 11:9; Mk 6:20 **21:28** [v] ver 33; Mt 20:1 **21:31** [w] Lk 7:29 [x] Lk 7:50 **21:32** [y] Mt 3:1-12 [z] Lk 3:12, 13; 7:29 [a] Lk 7:36-50 [b] Lk 7:30 **21:33** [c] Ps 80:8 [d] Isa 5:1-7

[a] *16* Psalm 8:2 (see Septuagint)

tradition or translation that best communicated their point. The primary language of the Sadducees was probably Greek (the dominant language of their tomb inscriptions). The psalm refers primarily to infants, but Jesus may reason: if infants, then "how much more" (see note on 7:11) other children.

21:17 *went out ... to Bethany.* Many pilgrims would arrive as much as a week early for the festival. Jerusalem's population would swell during the festival, so some visitors would lodge in nearby villages.

21:19 Passersby were welcome to take a small amount of fruit for their needs (see note on 12:1). On the reasons for the tree lacking fruit, see note on Mk 11:13. Matthew's sequence differs from Mark's, but biographies did not normally pretend to be arranged chronologically, and minor differences were common in ancient biography.

21:21 *say to this mountain.* Some later sources suggest that "moving mountains" was a Jewish figure of speech for doing what was considered impossible. Some scholars think that "*this* mountain" (emphasis added) refers to the Mount of Olives, which was within sight of the disciples (v. 1; cf. Zec 14:4).

21:23 *what authority.* The chief priests and elders exercised traditional authority over the people, supported by Rome.

21:24 *I will also ask.* Jewish teachers often countered questions with questions.

21:28–31 Jewish culture demanded that sons honor, obey and answer their fathers respectfully. Minor sons also often worked on the family's farm or learned a trade from their father.

21:28 *What do you think?* Allows for one ancient function of parables: inviting the hearers to condemn themselves from their own mouths (2Sa 12:4–7).

21:32 *the way of righteousness.* A familiar Jewish phrase for "the way of God's will" or "the right way" (e.g., Pr 8:20; 12:28; 16:31). *tax collectors.* See note on 9:9. *prostitutes.* Although Jewish texts speak of prostitution as primarily a Gentile practice, both foreign and Jewish prostitutes are attested in ancient Israel, including in Jerusalem.

21:33–34 Profits from vineyards usually did not begin to be realized until four years after planting; the owner is presumably wealthy enough to be able to afford the delay. Although many Galileans owned their own plots of land,

the vineyard to some farmers and moved
to another place.[e] 34When the harvest time
approached, he sent his servants[f] to the
tenants to collect his fruit.
35"The tenants seized his servants; they
beat one, killed another, and stoned a
third.[g] 36Then he sent other servants[h] to
them, more than the first time, and the
tenants treated them the same way. 37Last
of all, he sent his son to them. 'They will
respect my son,' he said.
38"But when the tenants saw the son,
they said to each other, 'This is the heir.[i]
Come, let's kill him[j] and take his inheritance.'[k] 39So they took him and threw him
out of the vineyard and killed him.
40"Therefore, when the owner of the
vineyard comes, what will he do to those
tenants?"
41"He will bring those wretches to a
wretched end,"[l] they replied, "and he will
rent the vineyard to other tenants,[m] who
will give him his share of the crop at harvest time."
42Jesus said to them, "Have you never
read in the Scriptures:

" 'The stone the builders rejected
has become the cornerstone;
the Lord has done this,
and it is marvelous in our eyes'[a]?[n]

43"Therefore I tell you that the kingdom of God will be taken away from you[o]
and given to a people who will produce its
fruit. 44Anyone who falls on this stone will
be broken to pieces; anyone on whom it
falls will be crushed."[b][p]
45When the chief priests and the Pharisees heard Jesus' parables, they knew he
was talking about them. 46They looked for
a way to arrest him, but they were afraid
of the crowd because the people held that
he was a prophet.[q]

The Parable of the Wedding Banquet

22:2-14Ref — Lk 14:16-24

22 Jesus spoke to them again in parables, saying: 2"The kingdom of
heaven is like[r] a king who prepared a
wedding banquet for his son. 3He sent his
servants[s] to those who had been invited to
the banquet to tell them to come, but they
refused to come.
4"Then he sent some more servants[t]
and said, 'Tell those who have been invited that I have prepared my dinner: My
oxen and fattened cattle have been butchered, and everything is ready. Come to the
wedding banquet.'
5"But they paid no attention and went
off — one to his field, another to his business. 6The rest seized his servants, mistreated them and killed them. 7The king

21:33 [e] Mt 25:14, 15
21:34 [f] Mt 22:3
21:35 [g] 2Ch 24:21; Mt 23:34, 37; Heb 11:36, 37
21:36 [h] Mt 22:4
21:38 [i] Heb 1:2 [j] Mt 12:14 [k] Ps 2:8
21:41 [l] Mt 8:11, 12 [m] Ac 13:46; 18:6; 28:28
21:42 [n] Ps 118:22, 23; Ac 4:11; 1Pe 2:7
21:43 [o] Mt 8:12
21:44 [p] Lk 2:34
21:46 [q] ver 11, 26
22:2 [r] Mt 13:24
22:3 [s] Mt 21:34
22:4 [t] Mt 21:36

[a] 42 Psalm 118:22,23 [b] 44 Some manuscripts do not have verse 44.

many landless peasants found work on larger estates. Wealthy absentee landowners were common; they usually either contracted laborers or rented their land to tenant farmers (serfs). Tenant farmers lived and worked their estates and merely paid the landowners a portion of the harvest (v. 34). Farmers used rough stone walls or hedges to keep out hungry animals; watchtowers for guards (usually huts with flat roofs) might also provide some shelter during harvest (cf. 2Ch 26:10; Isa 1:8). The arrangements for the vineyard here thus are not unusual, but together they closely follow Isa 5:2, in the context of which Israel was the vineyard (Isa 5:7). The "tenants" in v. 34 must thus be the temporary caretakers of Israel — the chief priests and the elders (vv. 23,45).

21:34 *to collect his fruit.* Contracts specified the tenants' obligations. Because tenants did not own the land they worked, they sometimes had to pay the landowners half the harvest.

21:35 *seized his servants … killed another.* Even during war, everyone in antiquity viewed the murder of unarmed messengers as treachery. Jewish people hearing the parable would think of the tradition of Israel persecuting God's prophets (cf. 5:12; 23:34).

21:37 *he sent his son.* In Jewish parables, a landowner often represented God and his son was generally Israel; here, however, it is clear that Jesus means himself as the son. Ancient hearers would have expected the landowner to seek to destroy the tenants before this point, and would regard the gesture of sending his son as naively gentle. No one has a right to complain that God is not merciful enough.

21:38 *take his inheritance.* No court would have given the inheritance to these tenants; the state would have executed them instead.

21:42 See notes on Mk 11:9, Lk 20:17.

21:43 *given to a people.* Some relate the new "nation" here to the holy nation of Ex 19:5 – 6, suggesting the people of a new exodus (1Pe 2:9).

21:44 *falls on this stone … be crushed.* Jewish teachers often linked various passages based on a common key word; Jesus thinks of other "stone" passages in addition to Ps 118:22 (cited in v. 42). One could stumble over God's stone (Isa 8:14 – 15; cf. Isa 28:16), or it could crush one (Da 2:44).

22:2 *The kingdom of heaven is like.* See note on 13:24. Many Jewish parables depict God as a king; sometimes his son represented Israel marrying the law. Here the son is presumably Jesus. *wedding banquet.* Because the size of wedding banquets displayed honor, hosts usually invited as many people as possible.

22:3 *those who had been invited … refused to come.* Refusal to accept a banquet invitation insulted the inviter; insulting a king was treason. But such invitations were normally RSVP, followed up by a second notice once the food was ready. Thus the people now refusing to come, at the second notice, had already agreed to come at the first invitation ("those who had been invited"). Their refusal now was therefore a conspicuously deliberate and provocative insult.

22:4 *oxen and fattened cattle.* A fattened calf alone could feed a village (cf. Lk 15:23); the king has made massive preparations, and the meat will spoil unless the guests come quickly.

22:6 *killed them.* All ancient readers would have agreed

was enraged. He sent his army and destroyed those murderers[u] and burned their
city.
8 "Then he said to his servants, 'The
wedding banquet is ready, but those I invited did not deserve to come. 9 So go to
the street corners[v] and invite to the banquet anyone you find.' 10 So the servants
went out into the streets and gathered all
the people they could find, the bad as well
as the good,[w] and the wedding hall was
filled with guests.
11 "But when the king came in to see the
guests, he noticed a man there who was
not wearing wedding clothes. 12 He asked,
'How did you get in here without wedding
clothes, friend[x]?' The man was speechless.
13 "Then the king told the attendants,
'Tie him hand and foot, and throw him
outside, into the darkness, where there
will be weeping and gnashing of teeth.'[y]
14 "For many are invited, but few are
chosen."[z]

Paying the Imperial Tax to Caesar

22:15-22pp — Mk 12:13-17; Lk 20:20-26

15 Then the Pharisees went out and laid
plans to trap him in his words. 16 They sent
their disciples to him along with the Herodians.[a] "Teacher," they said, "we know
that you are a man of integrity and that
you teach the way of God in accordance
with the truth. You aren't swayed by others,
because you pay no attention to who they
are. 17 Tell us then, what is your opinion? Is
it right to pay the imperial tax[a][b] to Caesar
or not?"
18 But Jesus, knowing their evil intent,
said, "You hypocrites, why are you trying
to trap me? 19 Show me the coin used for
paying the tax." They brought him a denarius, 20 and he asked them, "Whose image is this? And whose inscription?"
21 "Caesar's," they replied.
Then he said to them, "So give back to
Caesar what is Caesar's,[c] and to God what
is God's."
22 When they heard this, they were
amazed. So they left him and went away.[d]

Marriage at the Resurrection

22:23-33pp — Mk 12:18-27; Lk 20:27-40

23 That same day the Sadducees,[e] who
say there is no resurrection,[f] came to him
with a question. 24 "Teacher," they said,
"Moses told us that if a man dies without
having children, his brother must marry
the widow and raise up offspring for him.[g]
25 Now there were seven brothers among
us. The first one married and died, and
since he had no children, he left his wife
to his brother. 26 The same thing happened

22:7 [u] Lk 19:27
22:9 [v] Eze 21:21
22:10 [w] Mt 13:47,48
22:12 [x] Mt 20:13; 26:50
22:13 [y] Mt 8:12
22:14 [z] Rev 17:14
22:16 [a] Mk 3:6
22:17 [b] Mt 17:25
22:21 [c] Ro 13:7
22:22 [d] Mk 12:12
22:23 [e] Ac 4:1 [f] Ac 23:8; 1Co 15:12
22:24 [g] Dt 25:5,6

[a] *17* A special tax levied on subject peoples, not on Roman citizens

that slaughtering messengers was an offense worthy of death. By universal ancient law, heralds, or messengers, were to be exempt from any harm, even during times of war.

22:7 *burned their city.* Conquerors burned resistant cities; a generation after Jesus' ministry, Rome's army burned Jerusalem.

22:9 *invite . . . anyone you find.* The first invited guests had dishonored the king; the only way to recoup some honor is to find other guests before the food can spoil.

22:11 *not wearing wedding clothes.* In another Jewish parable possibly (but not certainly) as early as the first century, wise servants waited at a king's gate, awaiting the promised banquet; foolish servants kept laboring with soiled garments and were unprepared when his banquet was ready. Regarding the parable here in ch. 22, some scholars suggest that the host would have provided special garments; others simply note that coming to a wedding banquet in soiled clothing would insult the host. In v. 12, the king asks how the intruder made it past the servants guarding the doors; the intruder's refusal to answer may suggest that his insulting act was deliberate. If the first invited guests represent Jerusalem's leaders at Jesus' first coming, the rudely dressed man perhaps represents professed followers of Jesus unprepared for his second.

22:17 *what is your opinion?* The four questions in vv. 16 – 17,24 – 28,36,43 were the sorts of questions Jewish teachers often raised in this period. People often questioned speakers to try to embarrass them; failure to overcome the speaker would show the speaker's superiority.

22:19 – 20 *coin . . . denarius . . . image . . . inscription.* Copper coins minted in Judea omitted the emperor's image, but silver and gold coins were minted elsewhere. The most likely coin here, a silver denarius (minted at Lyon, France), bore the emperor's image and the title "Tiberius Caesar, son of the divine Augustus." Conservative Jews were supposed to avoid images; a few years earlier, Jerusalemites told Pilate that they would rather die than allow the imperial standards bearing Caesar's image into the city. Most dramatically, this coin and the attendant tax had incited a revolt a quarter century earlier. Nevertheless, it is not surprising that Jesus' interlocutors had this coin. Jews could not pay taxes without this coin; it was mandatory for poll taxes in all the empire's provinces.

22:21 *what is Caesar's . . . what is God's.* Some argue that Jesus was saying that Caesar was welcome to mere money, which bore Caesar's image. By contrast, on this view, people should surrender to God what bears *God's* image — themselves.

22:23 *who say there is no resurrection.* Pharisees, whose views were closer to the mainstream in Judea, often defended the doctrine of the future resurrection of the righteous against the Sadducees, who denied it. Pharisees believed that the Sadducees would be excluded from the life of the world to come because of the Sadducean denial of resurrection.

22:24 *must marry the widow.* Because widows could be left destitute, it was the duty of the deceased husband's brother to marry the widow in order to provide for her and to raise up offspring for the deceased (Dt 25:5 – 6). She had married into the brother's family and was therefore partly their responsibility.

22:26 *down to the seventh.* See note on Lk 20:29 – 31.

to the second and third brother, right on
down to the seventh. 27 Finally, the woman died. 28 Now then, at the resurrection,
whose wife will she be of the seven, since
all of them were married to her?"
29 Jesus replied, "You are in error because you do not know the Scriptures[h] or
the power of God. 30 At the resurrection
people will neither marry nor be given
in marriage;[i] they will be like the angels
in heaven. 31 But about the resurrection of
the dead—have you not read what God
said to you, 32 'I am the God of Abraham,
the God of Isaac, and the God of Jacob'[a]?[j]
He is not the God of the dead but of the
living."
33 When the crowds heard this, they
were astonished at his teaching.[k]

The Greatest Commandment

22:34-40pp — Mk 12:28-31

34 Hearing that Jesus had silenced the
Sadducees,[l] the Pharisees got together. 35 One of them, an expert in the law,[m]
tested him with this question: 36 "Teacher,
which is the greatest commandment in the
Law?"
37 Jesus replied: " 'Love the Lord your
God with all your heart and with all your
soul and with all your mind.'[b][n] 38 This is the
first and greatest commandment. 39 And
the second is like it: 'Love your neighbor
as yourself.'[c][o] 40 All the Law and the Prophets hang on these two commandments."[p]

Whose Son Is the Messiah?

22:41-46pp — Mk 12:35-37; Lk 20:41-44

41 While the Pharisees were gathered
together, Jesus asked them, 42 "What do
you think about the Messiah? Whose son
is he?"
"The son of David,"[q] they replied.
43 He said to them, "How is it then that
David, speaking by the Spirit, calls him
'Lord'? For he says,

44 " 'The Lord said to my Lord:
"Sit at my right hand
until I put your enemies
under your feet." '[d][r]

45 If then David calls him 'Lord,' how can
he be his son?" 46 No one could say a word
in reply, and from that day on no one
dared to ask him any more questions.[s]

A Warning Against Hypocrisy

23:1-7pp — Mk 12:38,39; Lk 20:45,46
23:37-39pp — Lk 13:34,35

23 Then Jesus said to the crowds and
to his disciples: 2 "The teachers of
the law[t] and the Pharisees sit in Moses'

22:29 [h] Jn 20:9 **22:30** [i] Mt 24:38 **22:32** [j] Ex 3:6; Ac 7:32 **22:33** [k] Mt 7:28 **22:34** [l] Ac 4:1 **22:35** [m] Lk 7:30; 10:25; 11:45; 14:3 **22:37** [n] Dt 6:5 **22:39** [o] Lev 19:18; Mt 5:43; 19:19; Gal 5:14 **22:40** [p] Mt 7:12 **22:42** [q] Mt 9:27 **22:44** [r] Ps 110:1; Ac 2:34,35; 1Co 15:25; Heb 1:13; 10:13 **22:46** [s] Mk 12:34; Lk 20:40 **23:2** [t] Ezr 7:6, 25; Ne 8:4

[a] *32* Exodus 3:6 [b] *37* Deut. 6:5 [c] *39* Lev. 19:18 [d] *44* Psalm 110:1

22:28 Saddducees were known to pose conundrums such as this to the Pharisees, seeking to illustrate what they believed were the absurd implications of belief in the resurrection.
22:29 *you do not know the Scriptures.* Although the most obvious Biblical text to which Jesus would allude could be Da 12:2, in v. 32 Jesus proves his case from the Pentateuch (the first five books of the Bible). When arguing against Sadducees, Pharisees also made a case from the Pentateuch, because that was what Sadducees would readily accept.
22:30 *neither marry nor be given in marriage.* Grooms married; fathers gave their daughters in marriage. Most Jewish people agreed that angels, who were immortal, did not propagate; the same then would be true of those resurrected to immortality.
22:31 *have you not read …* The highly educated and literate Sadducees would hear Jesus' question as an insult.
22:32 *the God of Abraham, the God of Isaac, and the God of Jacob.* Jewish prayers regularly referred to God in this way. Jesus articulates a position that many of his hearers would have accepted, namely, that the patriarchs remained alive before God. Some other Jewish intellectuals also supported this view (e.g., 4 Maccabees 7:18–19; 16:25; Philo, *Abraham* 50–55).
22:36 *greatest commandment in the Law.* Despite requiring obedience to all the commandments, Pharisaic teachers often debated among themselves which commandment was the greatest. Many, e.g., felt that the greatest was honoring one's parents. One later rabbi came closer to Jesus' view here: Rabbi Akiba thought that "Love your neighbor" (v. 39) was the greatest commandment (*Sipra Qedoshim* 4.200.3.7).
22:37 Jewish people regularly recited this passage (Dt 6:5); it provides a summary of the law, especially with regard to God.
22:39 Jesus uses Lev 19:18 as the summary for commandments regarding other people. It was common to link texts based on a common key word or phrase; Lev 19:18 here begins with the same phrase as the verse previously cited (Dt 6:5): *we'ahavta*, "you shall love." Some other thinkers linked these two commands, but to our knowledge only Jesus linked them as the greatest commandments, which became foundational for his early followers (cf. Jn 13:34–35; Ro 13:8–10; Gal 5:14; Jas 2:8).
22:40 *All the Law and the Prophets hang on these.* Others had also looked for summarizing principles of the law (e.g., Mic 6:8). See note on 7:12.
22:44 *The Lord said to my Lord.* Psalm 110:1 speaks of a ruler of the nations, a priest like Melchizedek (Ps 110:4), who is distinct from God the Father yet also called "Lord." Since Jewish people avoided pronouncing the divine name in this period, and YHWH was pronounced "lord," they would read the passage, both in Hebrew and in Greek, as "the Lord" speaking to "my Lord." *under your feet.* Subdued enemies are often depicted as being under a conqueror's feet.
22:45 *how can he be …?* Rabbis sometimes grappled with reconciling apparently contradictory positions; Jesus is not denying that the Messiah is David's descendant, a title he has not refused (9:27; 15:22; 20:30–31), but is showing that the Messiah is not *merely* like David. If David addresses this figure as "Lord," David recognizes one greater than himself, which a mere "new David" or Davidic descendant would not be.
23:2 *Moses' seat.* Many scholars identify Moses' seat with

JEWISH SECTS

PHARISEES	
Their roots can be traced to the Hasidim of the second century BC.	(1) Along with the Torah, they accepted as equally inspired and authoritative all the commands set forth in the oral traditions preserved by the rabbis.
	(2) On free will and determination, they held to a mediating view that did not allow either human free will or the sovereignty of God to cancel out the other.
	(3) They accepted a rather developed hierarchy of angels and demons.
	(4) They believed in the immortality of the soul and in reward and retribution after death.
	(5) They believed in the resurrection of the dead.
	(6) The main emphasis of their teaching was ethical rather than theological.

SADDUCEES	
They probably had their beginning during the Hasmonean period (166–63 BC). Their demise occurred c. AD 70 with the fall of Jerusalem and the destruction of the temple.	(1) They considered only the books of Moses to be canonical Scripture, denying that the oral law was authoritative and binding.
	(2) They were very exacting in Levitical purity.
	(3) They attributed everything to free will.
	(4) They argued that there is neither resurrection of the dead nor a future life.
	(5) They rejected the idea of a spiritual world, including belief in angels and demons.

ESSENES	
They probably originated among the Hasidim, along with the Pharisees, from whom they later separated (see the apocryphal book 1 Maccabees 2:42; 7:13). The Hasidim were a group of zealous Jews who took part with the Maccabeans in a revolt against the Syrians c. 165 –155 BC. A group of Essenes probably moved to Qumran c. 150 BC, where they copied scrolls and deposited them in nearby caves.	(1) They strictly observed the purity laws of the Torah.
	(2) They practiced communal ownership of property.
	(3) They had a strong sense of mutual responsibility.
	(4) Daily worship was an important feature along with daily study of their sacred scriptures.
	(5) Solemn oaths of piety and obedience had to be taken.
	(6) Sacrifices were offered on holy days and during their sacred seasons, but not at the temple, which they considered to be corrupt.
	(7) Marriage was avoided by some but was not condemned in principle.
	(8) They attributed to fate everything that happened.

ZEALOTS	
They originated during the reign of Herod the Great c. 6 BC. A group of Zealots were among the last defenders against the Romans at Masada in AD 73.	(1) They opposed payment of taxes to a pagan emperor because they believed that allegiance was due to God alone.
	(2) They were fiercely loyal to Jewish tradition.
	(3) They endorsed the use of violence as long as it accomplished a good end.
	(4) They were opposed to the influence of Greek pagan culture in the Holy Land.

seat. 3So you must be careful to do everything they tell you. But do not do what they do, for they do not practice what they preach. 4They tie up heavy, cumbersome loads and put them on other people's shoulders, but they themselves are not willing to lift a finger to move them.[u]

5"Everything they do is done for people to see:[v] They make their phylacteries[a][w] wide and the tassels on their garments[x] long; 6they love the place of honor at banquets and the most important seats in the synagogues;[y] 7they love to be greeted with respect in the marketplaces and to be called 'Rabbi' by others.[z]

8"But you are not to be called 'Rabbi,' for you have one Teacher, and you are all brothers. 9And do not call anyone on earth 'father,' for you have one Father,[a] and he is in heaven. 10Nor are you to be called instructors, for you have one Instructor, the Messiah. 11The greatest among you will be your servant.[b] 12For those who exalt themselves will be humbled, and those who humble themselves will be exalted.[c]

Seven Woes on the Teachers of the Law and the Pharisees

13"Woe to you, teachers of the law and Pharisees, you hypocrites![d] You shut the door of the kingdom of heaven in people's faces. You yourselves do not enter, nor will you let those enter who are trying to.[e] [14][b]

15"Woe to you, teachers of the law and Pharisees, you hypocrites! You travel over land and sea to win a single convert,[f] and when you have succeeded, you make them twice as much a child of hell[g] as you are.

16"Woe to you, blind guides![h] You say, 'If anyone swears by the temple, it means nothing; but anyone who swears by the gold of the temple is bound by that oath.'[i] 17You blind fools! Which is greater: the gold, or the temple that makes the gold sacred?[j] 18You also say, 'If anyone swears by the altar, it means nothing; but anyone who swears by the gift on the altar is bound by that oath.' 19You blind men! Which is greater: the gift, or the altar that makes the gift sacred?[k] 20Therefore, anyone who swears by the altar swears by it and by everything on it. 21And anyone who swears by the temple swears by it and by the one who dwells[l] in it. 22And anyone who swears by heaven swears by God's throne and by the one who sits on it.[m]

23:4 [u]Lk 11:46; Ac 15:10; Gal 6:13 **23:5** [v]Mt 6:1, 2, 5, 16 [w]Ex 13:9; Dt 6:8 [x]Nu 15:38; Dt 22:12 **23:6** [y]Lk 11:43; 14:7; 20:46 **23:7** [z]ver 8; Mk 9:5; 10:51; Jn 1:38, 49 **23:9** [a]Mal 1:6; Mt 7:11 **23:11** [b]Mt 20:26; Mk 9:35 **23:12** [c]Lk 14:11 **23:13** [d]ver 15, 23, 25, 27, 29 [e]Lk 11:52 **23:15** [f]Ac 2:11; 6:5; 13:43 [g]Mt 5:22 **23:16** [h]ver 24; Mt 15:14 [i]Mt 5:33-35 **23:17** [j]Ex 30:29 **23:19** [k]Ex 29:37 **23:21** [l]1Ki 8:13; Ps 26:8 **23:22** [m]Ps 11:4; Mt 5:34

[a] *5* That is, boxes containing Scripture verses, worn on forehead and arm [b] *14* Some manuscripts include here words similar to Mark 12:40 and Luke 20:47.

a prominent seat found in some ancient synagogues. Because such seats are not titled, however, some other scholars take "Moses' seat" here figuratively for those who would seek to take the position of Moses. Rabbis sometimes used the formula, "to sit in so-and-so's seat," to mean, "to be so-and-so's successor"; the rabbis claimed that they continued the work of Moses by expounding the law.

23:5 *They make their phylacteries wide.* Jewish people tried to practice literally the (probably figurative) command of Ex 13:9,16; Dt 6:8; 11:18; thus they made boxes with Scripture verses (*tefillin*, or phylacteries) that they strapped to their left hand and forehead during particular prayers. (The Greek term used here can also mean amulets, but the Scripture boxes seem in view; such boxes have been found by archaeologists.) *tassels ... long.* Jewish sources associate this practice with the Biblical requirement to wear blue and white tassels, or fringes (called *tzitzith*), on the corners of their garments to remind them of God's commandments (Nu 15:38 – 39; Dt 22:12). (Some later rabbis felt that God would punish more strictly the person who in prayer neglected the white threads more than someone who neglected the blue ones.) The issue here is not wearing phylacteries or tassels (cf. 9:20; 14:36), but seeking to draw honor to oneself rather than God (cf. 6:2).

23:6 *place of honor.* Throughout the Mediterranean world, people at banquets were usually seated according to their social rank; prominent members of the community thus received honor at banquets. Such preferential seating also characterized community assemblies and, in the Jewish community, synagogues. In synagogues the best seats were on the *bema*, the raised platform, where synagogues had them. In some synagogues, many people may have sat on the floor (Jas 2:3); in such synagogues, those who sat on benches around the walls had better seats (other synagogues had additional benches).

23:7,8 *Rabbi.* Social convention stipulated that social inferiors should greet superiors first; later rabbis believed that the superiors included rabbis. In this period, "rabbi" meant, "my master," a title of great honor (though it gradually came to be used with Jewish teachers' names, e.g., Rabbi Tarfon). Later rabbis trained disciples in their own traditions, passed down from their teachers, and in the Law of Moses. Although Jesus' disciples should "make disciples" (28:19), they should make disciples of Jesus and not of themselves.

23:9 *father.* People often addressed respected older men or leaders as "fathers"; the title and role were also applied to many rabbis by their disciples.

23:12 Scripture, followed by Jewish tradition, warned that the day of God's judgment would exalt the lowly and humble the proud (e.g., Isa 2:11 – 12; 5:15 – 16; Eze 21:26).

23:13 "Woes" could function as laments or mourning, but prophets often used them as creative ways to pronounce impending judgment (cf. 18:7; Isa 5:18 – 23; cf. mocking laments in Isa 15:5; 16:11; Jer 48:36; 51:8). Because Jesus speaks here of "shutting" the kingdom, cf. note on 16:19.

23:15 *win a single convert.* Many Jewish people approved of making proselytes, or converts, from Gentiles. We do not know of any concerted missions movement, however; Jesus probably uses the language of hyperbole.

23:16 *blind guides.* See note on 15:14. *oath.* See note on 5:34 – 35. To avoid the risk of breaking an oath by God's name, people began swearing by other things associated with God. Much gold decorated the temple, including a golden vine, very large in size, located high on the temple wall, to which more gold was added each year (see note on 17:24).

23:17 – 19 Tradition viewed anything placed on the altar as consecrated to God.

23:22 Heaven is God's throne, according to Isa 66:1.

23"Woe to you, teachers of the law
and Pharisees, you hypocrites! You give
a tenth[n] of your spices—mint, dill and
cumin. But you have neglected the more
important matters of the law—justice,
mercy and faithfulness.[o] You should have
practiced the latter, without neglecting the
former. 24You blind guides![p] You strain out
a gnat but swallow a camel.

25"Woe to you, teachers of the law and
Pharisees, you hypocrites! You clean the
outside of the cup and dish,[q] but inside
they are full of greed and self-indulgence.[r]
26Blind Pharisee! First clean the inside of
the cup and dish, and then the outside
also will be clean.

27"Woe to you, teachers of the law and
Pharisees, you hypocrites! You are like
whitewashed tombs,[s] which look beautiful on the outside but on the inside are
full of the bones of the dead and everything unclean. 28In the same way, on the
outside you appear to people as righteous
but on the inside you are full of hypocrisy
and wickedness.

29"Woe to you, teachers of the law
and Pharisees, you hypocrites! You build
tombs for the prophets[t] and decorate the
graves of the righteous. 30And you say, 'If
we had lived in the days of our ancestors,
we would not have taken part with them
in shedding the blood of the prophets.' 31So
you testify against yourselves that you are
the descendants of those who murdered
the prophets.[u] 32Go ahead, then, and complete[v] what your ancestors started!

33"You snakes! You brood of vipers![w]
How will you escape being condemned to
hell?[x] 34Therefore I am sending you prophets and sages and teachers. Some of them
you will kill and crucify;[y] others you will
flog in your synagogues[z] and pursue from
town to town.[a] 35And so upon you will
come all the righteous blood that has been
shed on earth, from the blood of righteous
Abel[b] to the blood of Zechariah son of Ber-

23:23 [n] Lev 27:30 [o] Mic 6:8; Lk 11:42 **23:24** [p] ver 16 **23:25** [q] Mk 7:4 [r] Lk 11:39 **23:27** [s] Lk 11:44; Ac 23:3 **23:29** [t] Lk 11:47,48 **23:31** [u] Ac 7:51-52 **23:32** [v] 1Th 2:16 **23:33** [w] Mt 3:7; 12:34 [x] Mt 5:22 **23:34** [y] 2Ch 36:15, 16; Lk 11:49 [z] Mt 10:17 [a] Mt 10:23 **23:35** [b] Ge 4:8; Heb 11:4

23:23 *tenth of your spices.* The Biblical tithe complemented other OT offerings, such as the firstborn of the flock; in most passages, it consisted of a tenth of one's agrarian produce (Lev 27:30; Ne 10:37), but sometimes also livestock (Lev 27:32; 2Ch 31:6). This was set aside to support the ministry caste (priests and Levites; Nu 18:21–28) and for a feast every third year at the central place of worship (Dt 14:23,28; 26:12). The grain was stored for distribution (Mal 3:10). Because different passages offered somewhat different details, Pharisees came up with three tithes, paying roughly 23 percent each year. Pharisees were known for their scrupulousness in tithing; if they were not certain that the farmer had already tithed the produce, they would tithe it again to be certain. Because tithes were on food, however, Pharisees in this period debated whether spices such as dill (anise), cumin, and mint counted (later rabbis decided in favor of tithing the first two but did not deem it necessary to tithe mint). The Shammaite school of Pharisees in Jesus' day rejected the need to tithe on black cumin. Jesus here speaks of a hyperbolic Pharisee, even more scrupulous than normal! Yet this Pharisee, fixated on details, missed the heart of the law (for earlier summaries of the law's heart, see Dt 10:12–13; Mic 6:8).

23:24 *gnat ... camel.* The camel was the largest animal in ancient Israel and the gnat proverbially small; Jesus uses graphic hyperbole to make his point. The law forbade drinking from a vessel in which something died (Lev 11:32–33); Pharisaic regulations excluded something as small as a gnat from such consideration, but Jesus' hyperbolic Pharisee strains out even a gnat, lest it die in his drink. The Aramaic words for *camel* and *gnat* sound almost the same; prophets sometimes used wordplays, witty puns to drive home a point (e.g., the Hebrew of Jer 1:11–12; Mic 1:10–15; see NIV text notes there).

23:25–26 *clean the outside ... clean the inside.* First-century Pharisees debated whether to cleanse the inside or outside of a cup first. Shammaites doubted that it mattered either way, but Hillelites required cleaning the inside first. Jesus appears to agree with the Hillelites here, but unlike the Pharisees he speaks figuratively about the human heart.

23:27 *whitewashed tombs.* Tombs were whitewashed to warn away Passover pilgrims coming to Jerusalem for the festival, lest they incur ritual impurity by touching a tomb. (According to Jewish tradition, if so much as their shadow touched not only a corpse but a tomb, they incurred ritual impurity for seven days.) Here Jesus speaks of whitewash as a beautifying agent to conceal corruption (Eze 13:10–15; 22:28). The Pharisees, who emphasized ritual purity, look good on the outside but whoever approaches them becomes impure.

23:29 *build tombs for the prophets.* In this period many tombs were being built in Jerusalem to honor prophetic figures.

23:31 *you are the descendants of those who murdered the prophets.* People employed the phrase "descendants of" literally but also figuratively for those who acted like their ancestors; Jesus plays on these two senses here. By identifying their ancestors as those who killed the prophets rather than as the prophets themselves (cf. 5:12), the tomb-builders show where their real allegiance lies.

23:32 *Go ahead ... !* Prophets often ironically invited people to go on sinning—and be judged (1Ki 18:27; Isa 6:9; 29:9; Jer 23:28; 44:25–26; Eze 3:27; Am 4:4–5).

23:33 *brood of vipers.* See note on 3:7. *hell.* Gehinnom (see note on 3:12).

23:34 *flog in your synagogues.* See note on 10:17.

23:35 *Abel to ... Zechariah.* According to a common arrangement of the Scriptures, Abel would have been the first martyr in the OT and Zechariah the last. Abel's blood cried out for vengeance against his killer (Ge 4:10; contrast Heb 11:4; 12:24). As Zechariah was being murdered, he cried out for vengeance (2Ch 24:22). Jewish tradition recognized that Zechariah's blood desecrated the sanctuary (on blood desecrating a sanctuary, see note on 24:15). Indeed, in one Jewish tradition, a fountain of blood spurted up from the site of his murder, inviting judgment for generations until the Babylonians conquered Jerusalem. Only then did the people plead with God to forgive them for the blood of Zechariah, and only then did the fountain stop. The saying here may conflate the Zechariah killed in 2 Chronicles with the postexilic prophet Zechariah, son of Berekiah (Zec 1:1,7). Sometimes Jewish traditions conflated figures accidentally, but sometimes they deliberately linked figures to evoke further associations

ekiah,[c] whom you murdered between the
temple and the altar.[d] 36 Truly I tell you, all
this will come on this generation.[e]
37 "Jerusalem, Jerusalem, you who kill
the prophets and stone those sent to you,[f]
how often I have longed to gather your
children together, as a hen gathers her
chicks under her wings, and you were not
willing. 38 Look, your house is left to you
desolate.[g] 39 For I tell you, you will not see
me again until you say, 'Blessed is he who
comes in the name of the Lord.'[a]"[h]

The Destruction of the Temple and Signs of the End Times

24:1-51pp — Mk 13:1-37; Lk 21:5-36

24 Jesus left the temple and was walking away when his disciples came
up to him to call his attention to its buildings. 2 "Do you see all these things?" he
asked. "Truly I tell you, not one stone here
will be left on another;[i] every one will be
thrown down."
3 As Jesus was sitting on the Mount of
Olives,[j] the disciples came to him privately. "Tell us," they said, "when will this
happen, and what will be the sign of your
coming and of the end of the age?"
4 Jesus answered: "Watch out that no
one deceives you. 5 For many will come
in my name, claiming, 'I am the Messiah,' and will deceive many.[k] 6 You will hear
of wars and rumors of wars, but see to
it that you are not alarmed. Such things
must happen, but the end is still to come.
7 Nation will rise against nation, and kingdom against kingdom.[l] There will be famines[m] and earthquakes in various places.
8 All these are the beginning of birth pains.
9 "Then you will be handed over to be
persecuted[n] and put to death,[o] and you
will be hated by all nations because of
me. 10 At that time many will turn away
from the faith and will betray and hate
each other, 11 and many false prophets[p]
will appear and deceive many people.
12 Because of the increase of wickedness,
the love of most will grow cold, 13 but the
one who stands firm to the end will be
saved.[q] 14 And this gospel of the kingdom[r]
will be preached in the whole world[s] as a
testimony to all nations, and then the end
will come.
15 "So when you see standing in the holy
place[t] 'the abomination that causes desolation,'[b][u] spoken of through the prophet Daniel — let the reader understand —

23:35 [c] Zec 1:1 [d] 2Ch 24:21
23:36 [e] Mt 10:23; 24:34
23:37 [f] 2Ch 24:21; Mt 5:12
23:38 [g] 1Ki 9:7, 8; Jer 22:5
23:39 [h] Ps 118:26; Mt 21:9
24:2 [i] Lk 19:44
24:3 [j] Mt 21:1
24:5 [k] ver 11, 23, 24; 1Jn 2:18
24:7 [l] Isa 19:2 [m] Ac 11:28
24:9 [n] Mt 10:17 [o] Jn 16:2
24:11 [p] Mt 7:15
24:13 [q] Mt 10:22
24:14 [r] Mt 4:23 [s] Lk 2:1; 4:5; Ac 11:28; 17:6; Ro 10:18; Col 1:6, 23; Rev 3:10; 16:14
24:15 [t] Ac 6:13 [u] Da 9:27; 11:31; 12:11

[a] *39* Psalm 118:26 [b] *15* Daniel 9:27; 11:31; 12:11

relevant to their point (cf. note on 1:7 – 11). Matthew sometimes cites the prophet Zechariah (Mt 21:5; 26:31; 27:9 – 10).
23:36 Guilt for murder invited judgment (Dt 21:8) and could be passed on from generation to generation until avenged (2Sa 21:1,14). *this generation.* Climactic because the ultimate murder, that of God's own Son, would be committed (cf. 21:35 – 39).
23:37 *you who kill the prophets.* Jewish tradition acknowledged and even amplified the OT record of persecuted prophets. *as a hen gathers her chicks under her wings.* In the OT and Jewish tradition, God sheltered his people under his wings (Ps 17:8; 36:7; 57:1; 61:4; 63:7; 91:4); Jesus here assumes that divine role.
23:38 *left ... desolate.* Jesus refers here to the temple's desolation (fulfilled roughly 40 years later, in AD 70) brought about by its desecration. See note on 24:15.
23:39 In Matthew, Jesus speaks of a future blessing when citing Ps 118:26, since the crowds have already offered this blessing in the past (21:9). Jesus thus agrees with the earlier Biblical prophets who offered hope for God's beloved people (e.g., Hos 14:4 – 7; Am 9:11 – 15).
24:1 *its buildings.* See next note. The majority of Jews lived outside of the Holy Land, but the temple tax (see note on 17:24) shows that they also remained loyal to the temple.
24:2 *not one stone here will be left on another; every one will be thrown down.* A small minority of Jews denounced the temple as impure and announced judgment on it or the establishment that ran it; some believed that God would send a new temple. More commonly, Jewish people affirmed that the temple was invincible. Jesus' prophecy includes, as often in his teaching, an element of hyperbole (not something writers would have invented after the temple's destruction in AD 70). Some of the stones remain (albeit in the retaining wall), not surprising in view of their massive size; one block almost 40 feet (12 meters) long weighs nearly 400 tons (360 metric tons), and some smaller ones weigh 2 – 5 tons (1.8 – 4.5 metric tons).
24:3 *sign of your coming and of the end of the age.* Some Jewish sources (especially in apocalyptic literature) were preoccupied with signs of the end. In the following discourse Jesus addresses both questions (about the temple's destruction, 24:2 – 3; and about the sign indicating his coming and the end), but he does not identify which question he is answering at a given time. This fits a prophetic pattern often found in earlier Biblical prophets (e.g., Joel seems to blend a nearer locust plague with an invasion in the later day of the Lord).
24:6 – 14 Many Jewish thinkers offered lists of sufferings, which they sometimes called the "birth pangs" of the Messiah or of the new world; these sufferings would precede the end of the age. Although these sufferings include those mentioned here (such as apostasy, wickedness, persecution and hardships), they also include some more unusual phenomena such as mutant infants. Jesus, however, will answer the question about the sign of his coming (v. 3) with a single sign *at* his coming (v. 30). In contrast to many other Jewish thinkers, he identifies the events listed here as merely "the beginning of birth pains" (v. 8) and not yet the end (v. 6), in contrast to one activity — evangelizing all nations — that precedes the end (v. 14). Most events listed here, including earthquakes, many false prophets, and the like, happened at least sometimes even before AD 70 (as well as afterward).
24:15 *abomination that causes desolation.* Some Jewish prophets inside Jerusalem kept prophesying deliverance up until the temple was destroyed; Jesus instead prophesies the truth, which is often less comfortable for us to hear. Historically, when God's people persisted in disobedience, God allowed the temple to be desecrated (an "abomination") and ultimately destroyed ("desolation"); the pattern is most obvious in Daniel (Da 8:13; 9:27; 11:31;

16then let those who are in Judea flee to
the mountains. 17Let no one on the housetop[v] go down to take anything out of the
house. 18Let no one in the field go back to
get their cloak. 19How dreadful it will be in
those days for pregnant women and nursing mothers![w] 20Pray that your flight will
not take place in winter or on the Sabbath.
21For then there will be great distress, unequaled from the beginning of the world
until now—and never to be equaled again.[x]
22"If those days had not been cut short,
no one would survive, but for the sake of
the elect[y] those days will be shortened.
23At that time if anyone says to you, 'Look,
here is the Messiah!' or, 'There he is!' do
not believe it.[z] 24For false messiahs and
false prophets will appear and perform
great signs and wonders[a] to deceive, if
possible, even the elect. 25See, I have told
you ahead of time.
26"So if anyone tells you, 'There he is,
out in the wilderness,' do not go out; or,
'Here he is, in the inner rooms,' do not
believe it. 27For as lightning[b] that comes
from the east is visible even in the west,
so will be the coming of the Son of Man.[c]
28Wherever there is a carcass, there the
vultures will gather.[d]
29"Immediately after the distress of
those days

"'the sun will be darkened,
and the moon will not give its light;
the stars will fall from the sky,
and the heavenly bodies will be
shaken.'[a][e]

[a] *29* Isaiah 13:10; 34:4

24:17 [v] 1Sa 9:25; Mt 10:27; Lk 12:3; Ac 10:9 **24:19** [w] Lk 23:29 **24:21** [x] Da 12:1; Joel 2:2 **24:22** [y] ver 24, 31 **24:23** [z] Lk 17:23; 21:8 **24:24** [a] 2Th 2:9-11; Rev 13:13 **24:27** [b] Lk 17:24 [c] Mt 8:20 **24:28** [d] Lk 17:37 **24:29** [e] Isa 13:10; 34:4; Eze 32:7; Joel 2:10, 31; Zep 1:15; Rev 6:12, 13; 8:12

12:11). Some references in Daniel sound as though they refer to the desecration that happened in the second century BC under Antiochus Epiphanes (see notes on Da 11:31 and context); according to some ancient calculations, the desecration of Da 9:27 could have happened in the first century; and the context of 12:11 sounds as if it refers to the end time. Jewish prophecy, not often preoccupied with chronology, sometimes blended similar events without regard to the different times in which they might occur (see note on v. 3). Josephus, a Jewish historian who lived through the events of AD 66–70, believed that the "abomination" referred to Jewish nationalists slaughtering priests in the temple (for bloodshed in the sanctuary desecrating it, see note on 23:35). He believed that the "desolation" was the temple's destruction three and a half years later. At that time, on the site of the temple Roman soldiers worshiped the image of Caesar that they carried on their standards, which Jewish people regarded as idols. Christian scholars debate whether the events of AD 66–70 represent the temple's final desolation.

24:16 *flee to the mountains.* During invasions, people usually crowded into walled cities for protection, but Jesus warns against that measure in this case. Jerusalem is in the Judean hill country. Large armies could not take advantage of their numbers on narrow mountain paths; here David and his supporters had evaded Saul's pursuing army, and the Maccabees had launched their guerilla warfare against invaders. Jesus' own followers, remembering his prophecy and also, according to ancient sources, instructed by their own Christian prophets, fled the city before it was too late.

24:17 *housetop.* Rooftops in this region were flat, and people engaged in various activities on their roofs, such as drying vegetables, chatting with neighbors, praying, and the like. The roof was approached by an outside staircase or ladder, so it would take extra time to enter the house after descending. Despite an element of hyperbole, Jesus is right to emphasize haste. Once Jerusalem fell into the hands of the Jewish revolutionaries, it was difficult for anyone still there to escape the city; some months after that, in AD 68, even those who did escape the city could no longer flee safely to the Romans. Syrian auxiliaries working for Rome, hearing that Judean fugitives swallowed jewels in hopes of maintaining resources after their escape from the city, intercepted the fugitives and sliced them open.

24:18 *get their cloak.* People would rise at dawn, say some prayers, and start to work in their fields. As the day grew warmer, they would leave their outer garment at the edge of the field. This garment was essential for keeping warm at night (it could double as a blanket), and was so important that it was the one item that a creditor could not seize from a debtor overnight. Yet Jesus warns his hearers to flee without it—life mattered more than even the most necessary of possessions.

24:19 *pregnant women and nursing mothers.* For these women fleeing would be particularly difficult. Mothers also could mourn the loss of small children caused by the hardship (2 Baruch 10:13–15); in fact, Josephus laments that during the siege of Jerusalem, some hungry mothers even ate their children (Josephus, *Wars* 6.208–12).

24:20 *in winter or on the Sabbath.* In Judea, winter was the rainy season, and otherwise dry creek beds could flood with water from the mountains; cold winter rains also buried some roads in mud. The Jordan River also flooded, making it harder to cross; Josephus reports that even in the spring of AD 68 Judean fugitives were trapped by the flooding Jordan and thus slaughtered by their pursuers (Josephus, *Wars* 4.433). Armies normally withdrew from battle during the winter; travel was particularly dangerous in the cold mountains (cf. v. 16). On the Sabbath Jerusalem's gates would be shut and fellow Judeans, less aware of imminent danger than were the disciples, would resist those wishing to ride animals.

24:21 *great distress.* Da 12:1 spoke of a final tribulation greater than any that preceded it. *never to be equaled again.* Cf. Joel 2:2; may suggest that Matthew expected history to continue even after the temple's destruction.

24:22 *cut short.* Might mean that the period of tribulation would not last the full number of expected days (cf. Da 12:11–13).

24:26 *out in the wilderness.* Some Jewish people expected an end-time deliverer or deliverance to take place in the wilderness (see note on 3:3).

24:27 *lightning.* Appears in ancient sources for something seen far and wide (Ps 97:4). *coming of the Son of Man.* Evokes Da 7:13–14.

24:28 *carcass ... vultures.* Greek and Roman depictions of the aftermath of battles usually included vultures picking clean unburied corpses; the same was true in Scripture (Dt 28:25–26; 1Sa 17:44; Ps 79:1–2; Eze 39:17–20).

24:29 Jesus here echoes Isa 13:10 and probably the Greek version of Isa 34:4; cf. similarly Joel 2:10,31. The passages in Isaiah graphically depict judgment on specific

30 “Then will appear the sign of the Son
of Man in heaven. And then all the peoples of the earth[a] will mourn when they
see the Son of Man coming on the clouds
of heaven,[f] with power and great glory.[b]
31 And he will send his angels[g] with a loud
trumpet call,[h] and they will gather his
elect from the four winds, from one end
of the heavens to the other.
32 “Now learn this lesson from the fig
tree: As soon as its twigs get tender and its
leaves come out, you know that summer
is near. 33 Even so, when you see all these
things, you know that it[c] is near, right at
the door.[i] 34 Truly I tell you, this generation will certainly not pass away until all
these things have happened.[j] 35 Heaven
and earth will pass away, but my words
will never pass away.[k]

The Day and Hour Unknown

24:37-39pp — Lk 17:26,27
24:45-51pp — Lk 12:42-46

36 “But about that day or hour no one
knows, not even the angels in heaven,
nor the Son,[d] but only the Father.[l] 37 As it
was in the days of Noah,[m] so it will be
at the coming of the Son of Man. 38 For in
the days before the flood, people were eating and drinking, marrying and giving in
marriage,[n] up to the day Noah entered the
ark; 39 and they knew nothing about what
would happen until the flood came and
took them all away. That is how it will be
at the coming of the Son of Man. 40 Two
men will be in the field; one will be taken
and the other left.[o] 41 Two women will be
grinding with a hand mill; one will be tak-
en and the other left.[p]
42 “Therefore keep watch, because you
do not know on what day your Lord will
come.[q] 43 But understand this: If the owner of the house had known at what time
of night the thief was coming,[r] he would
have kept watch and would not have let his
house be broken into. 44 So you also must be
ready,[s] because the Son of Man will come at
an hour when you do not expect him.
45 “Who then is the faithful and wise servant,[t] whom the master has put in charge
of the servants in his household to give
them their food at the proper time? 46 It
will be good for that servant whose master finds him doing so when he returns.[u]
47 Truly I tell you, he will put him in charge
of all his possessions.[v] 48 But suppose that
servant is wicked and says to himself, ‘My
master is staying away a long time,’ 49 and
he then begins to beat his fellow servants
and to eat and drink with drunkards.[w]
50 The master of that servant will come on
a day when he does not expect him and at
an hour he is not aware of. 51 He will cut

24:30 [f] Da 7:13; Rev 1:7 **24:31** [g] Mt 13:41 [h] Isa 27:13; Zec 9:14; 1Co 15:52; 1Th 4:16; Rev 8:2; 10:7; 11:15 **24:33** [i] Jas 5:9 **24:34** [j] Mt 16:28; 23:36 **24:35** [k] Mt 5:18 **24:36** [l] Ac 1:7 **24:37** [m] Ge 6:5; 7:6-23 **24:38** [n] Mt 22:30 **24:40** [o] Lk 17:34 **24:41** [p] Lk 17:35 **24:42** [q] Mt 25:13; Lk 12:40 **24:43** [r] Lk 12:39 **24:44** [s] 1Th 5:6 **24:45** [t] Mt 25:21,23 **24:46** [u] Rev 16:15 **24:47** [v] Mt 25:21,23 **24:49** [w] Lk 21:34

[a] *30* Or *the tribes of the land* [b] *30* See Daniel 7:13-14. [c] *33* Or *he* [d] *36* Some manuscripts do not have *nor the Son.*

---

empires but Jewish people also saw them as presaging global judgments. People in antiquity expected cosmic signs before catastrophic events such as Jerusalem's fall; Jewish apocalyptic literature expected them especially before the end.

24:30 *sign.* Some understand this as an ensign or banner (Isa 11:12; 49:22), though the term is used in other texts for heavenly signs (cf., e.g., Rev 12:1; perhaps Ac 2:19 – 20). *mourn.* Might allude to Zec 12:10. *the Son of Man coming on the clouds of heaven.* Quotes Da 7:13.

24:31 *he will send his angels.* That the Son of Man sends "his angels" indicates his deity (cf. Zec 14:5). *trumpet call.* One regularly prayed Jewish prayer expected a trumpet when God would deliver his people at the end. Trumpets were used for summons to gather and for military instructions (cf. Isa 27:12 – 13; 1Co 15:52; 1Th 4:16 – 17). *from one end of the heavens to the other.* Because people typically viewed the heavens as a dome over the earth, this would include "from the ends of the earth" (as in Mk 13:27).

24:32 *fig tree.* See note on Mk 11:13.See also note on Lk 21:29 – 30.

24:34 *this generation.* See note on 23:36; the temple was destroyed about 40 years (the rough figure often used as a Biblical generation) after Jesus promised this. The distinction between the specified timing here and the unknown timing of v. 36 may relate to the two distinct questions asked in v. 3.

24:35 *my words will never pass away.* Jesus equates his words with God's (Isa 40:8; Zec 1:5 – 6; cf. Mt 5:18).

24:36 *that day or hour.* Jewish teachers disagreed among themselves as to whether God had immutably fixed the day of redemption or whether it would depend on human cooperation. Some tried to calculate dates; others regarded such calculations as impossible. Jesus affirms that the Father knows the time (cf. Zec 14:7), though no one else did. He notes some prerequisites for the end (vv. 15,34) but also that it would catch people by surprise (vv. 37 – 44).

24:37 *days of Noah.* Jewish people often viewed the flood as prefiguring the day of judgment. Jesus warns that as the flood caught the people of Noah's day unprepared (vv. 38 – 39), so would his coming catch the final generation unprepared (for the lack of signs, see note on vv. 6 – 14).

24:38 Grooms married and fathers gave in marriage.

24:41 *hand mill.* Many Galilean homes shared a common courtyard with other families, and housewives worked together at a common millstone. The implication here is that, despite the closest of associations, one is taken (to judgment, v. 39) but the other is spared.

24:45 *wise servant.* Slaves could be entrusted with great authority; household managers were often high-level slaves.

24:48 *staying away a long time.* A common story line, appearing also in some Jewish parables, was the temptation posed when a ruler, master or husband went on a long journey. In the stories, the person often returned and caught someone unprepared (v. 50).

24:49 *eat and drink with drunkards.* Gluttony and drunkenness were often associated with squandering. A slave exploiting fellow slaves and carousing with the master's resources would be punished harshly.

24:51 *cut him to pieces.* People regarded dismemberment as a terrible punishment, often inflicted just before or after execution.

him to pieces and assign him a place with the hypocrites, where there will be weeping and gnashing of teeth.[x]

The Parable of the Ten Virgins

25 "At that time the kingdom of heaven will be like[y] ten virgins who took their lamps[z] and went out to meet the bridegroom.[a] 2Five of them were foolish and five were wise.[b] 3The foolish ones took their lamps but did not take any oil with them. 4The wise ones, however, took oil in jars along with their lamps. 5The bridegroom was a long time in coming, and they all became drowsy and fell asleep.[c]

6"At midnight the cry rang out: 'Here's the bridegroom! Come out to meet him!'

7"Then all the virgins woke up and trimmed their lamps. 8The foolish ones said to the wise, 'Give us some of your oil; our lamps are going out.'[d]

9" 'No,' they replied, 'there may not be enough for both us and you. Instead, go to those who sell oil and buy some for yourselves.'

10"But while they were on their way to buy the oil, the bridegroom arrived. The virgins who were ready went in with him to the wedding banquet.[e] And the door was shut.

11"Later the others also came. 'Lord, Lord,' they said, 'open the door for us!'

12"But he replied, 'Truly I tell you, I don't know you.'

13"Therefore keep watch, because you do not know the day or the hour.[f]

The Parable of the Bags of Gold

25:14-30Ref — Lk 19:12-27

14"Again, it will be like a man going on a journey,[g] who called his servants and entrusted his wealth to them. 15To one he gave five bags of gold, to another two bags, and to another one bag,[a] each according to his ability.[h] Then he went on his journey. 16The man who had received five bags of gold went at once and put his money to work and gained five bags more. 17So also, the one with two bags of gold gained two more. 18But the man who had received one bag went off, dug a hole in the ground and hid his master's money.

19"After a long time the master of those servants returned and settled accounts with them.[i] 20The man who had received five bags of gold brought the other five. 'Master,' he said, 'you entrusted me with five bags of gold. See, I have gained five more.'

21"His master replied, 'Well done, good and faithful servant! You have been faithful with a few things; I will put you in

[a] 15 Greek *five talents . . . two talents . . . one talent;* also throughout this parable; a talent was worth about 20 years of a day laborer's wage.

24:51 [x] Mt 8:12
25:1 [y] Mt 13:24 [z] Lk 12:35-38; Ac 20:8; Rev 4:5 [a] Rev 19:7; 21:2
25:2 [b] Mt 24:45
25:5 [c] 1Th 5:6
25:8 [d] Lk 12:35
25:10 [e] Rev 19:9
25:13 [f] Mt 24:42, 44; Mk 13:35; Lk 12:40
25:14 [g] Mt 21:33; Lk 19:12
25:15 [h] Mt 18:24, 25
25:19 [i] Mt 18:23

25:1 *ten virgins.* On the evening of a wedding, the bride and bridesmaids would wait at the bride's parents' home; the groom would then come with his entourage to escort the bride and her entourage, with music and dancing, to the site of the wedding. Because the exact timing was unpredictable, given the many preparations (and the bride's relatives haggling over the value of the gifts given them), the bridesmaids needed to stay ready. This particular groom was delayed more than usual (v. 5), but a groom would normally come after dark to escort the bride to the wedding. Women could be married in their early to mid-teens; the bridesmaids were normally virgins who would want to perform their duties well, as they hoped to find husbands themselves soon.
25:4 *their lamps.* The small lamps of this period could be held in a hand, contained only a limited amount of oil, and emitted only a limited amount of light. More likely in view here are torches, which characterized night weddings throughout the ancient Mediterranean world. In poorer villages the torches might be simple oil-soaked rags wrapped around sticks; some suggest that these sticks would need to be rewrapped every 15 minutes or so.
25:9 *may not be enough.* If the wise were to share their oil, they might all end up with too little, and the wedding procession would be ruined.
25:10 *went in with him to the wedding banquet.* For the wedding ceremony, the group would go to the groom's home (normally his parents' home); the couple was expected to consummate the marriage that night, but the wedding banquet would last for several days (often seven). The new couple would normally stay at the home of the groom's parents, sometimes in a room on top of the roof, until the groom could secure a home of his own.
25:11 *open the door.* The door could be bolted shut, but with visitors coming and going, it would not be bolted for the entirety of the wedding celebration, which might last seven days. Rather, it is bolted against them; the unwise bridesmaids' negligence has insulted the couple and the other participants in the wedding.
25:12 *I don't know you.* A form of repudiation, the purpose of this statement is to treat the hearers as strangers. Most of the community would be welcome at the feast; the five foolish virgins, however, were now alienated from their own community. As with the graphic punishment in 24:51, the severe punishment here is meant to seize the hearers' attention (see 25:13).
25:14 *entrusted his wealth to them.* See note on 24:48. High-level slaves often served as managers for household estates, so entrusting wealth to them was not unusual. Other Jewish parables have a similar story line.
25:16 *put his money to work.* Moneylending was common and was often done through temples, which normally doubled as banks because deposits were considered safe there. Since few people had capital, those who did could lend money at significant interest. Investors thus could receive five or even ten times their investment (cf. Lk 19:16–18); at the very least, they could double their investment.
25:18 *hid his master's money.* People often buried money in a strongbox to keep it safe, but it would have been safe with the bankers and also increased (in contrast to vv. 16–17).
25:21 *put you in charge of many things.* Slaves could be rewarded. Roman law allowed slaves not only to manage estates, but also to earn and hold money and receive bonuses. Some imperial freedmen even wielded more power than many aristocrats.

ONE ARRANGEMENT OF THE LIFE OF CHRIST

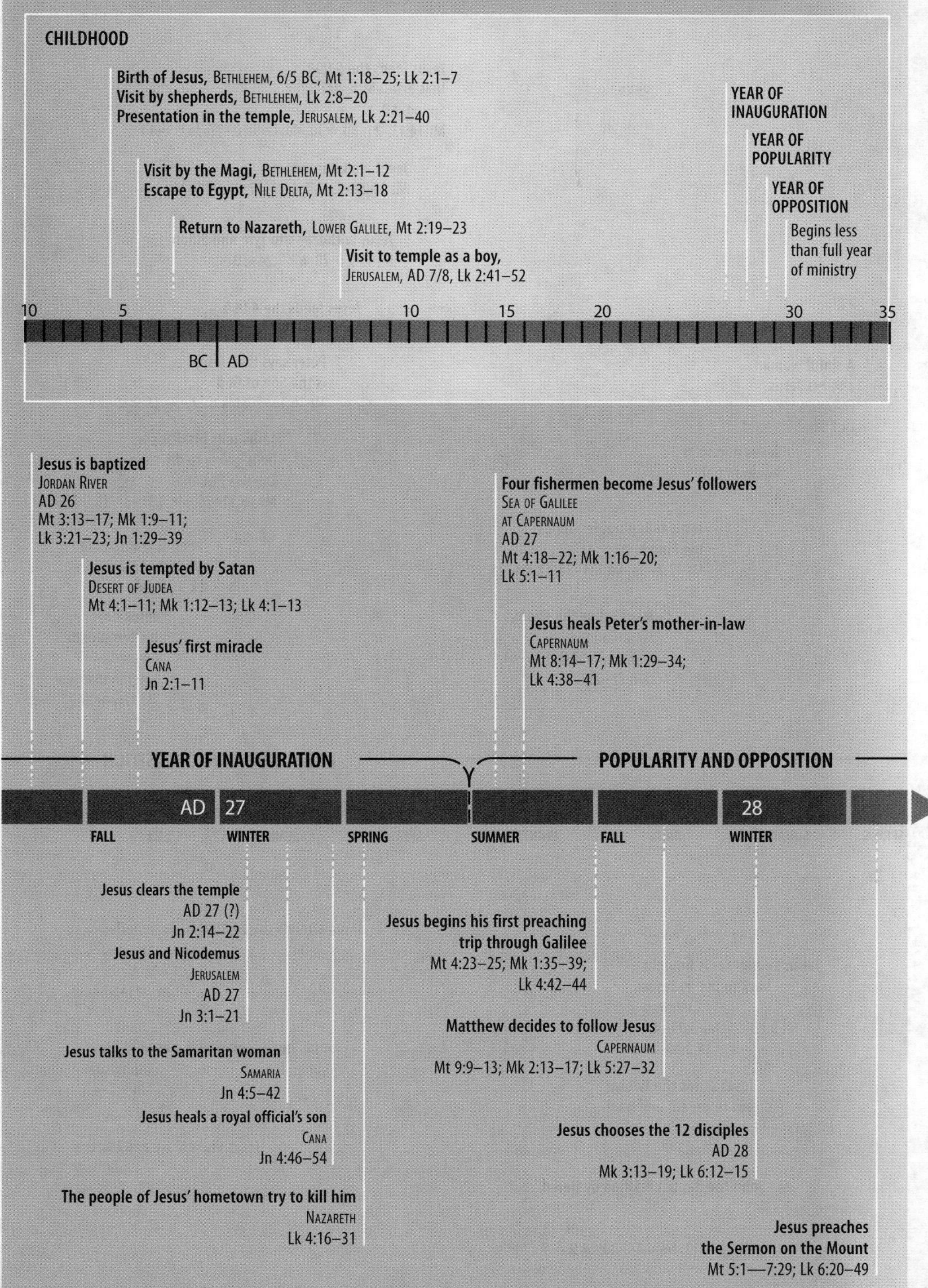
CHILDHOOD
Birth of Jesus, Bethlehem, 6/5 BC, Mt 1:18–25; Lk 2:1–7
Visit by shepherds, Bethlehem, Lk 2:8–20
Presentation in the temple, Jerusalem, Lk 2:21–40
Visit by the Magi, Bethlehem, Mt 2:1–12
Escape to Egypt, Nile Delta, Mt 2:13–18
Return to Nazareth, Lower Galilee, Mt 2:19–23
Visit to temple as a boy, Jerusalem, AD 7/8, Lk 2:41–52
YEAR OF INAUGURATION
YEAR OF POPULARITY
YEAR OF OPPOSITION
Begins less than full year of ministry
10
5
10
15
20
30
35
BC
AD
Jesus is baptized
Jordan River
AD 26
Mt 3:13–17; Mk 1:9–11; Lk 3:21–23; Jn 1:29–39
Jesus is tempted by Satan
Desert of Judea
Mt 4:1–11; Mk 1:12–13; Lk 4:1–13
Jesus' first miracle
Cana
Jn 2:1–11
Four fishermen become Jesus' followers
Sea of Galilee at Capernaum
AD 27
Mt 4:18–22; Mk 1:16–20; Lk 5:1–11
Jesus heals Peter's mother-in-law
Capernaum
Mt 8:14–17; Mk 1:29–34; Lk 4:38–41
YEAR OF INAUGURATION
POPULARITY AND OPPOSITION
AD 27
28
FALL
WINTER
SPRING
SUMMER
FALL
WINTER
Jesus clears the temple
AD 27 (?)
Jn 2:14–22
Jesus and Nicodemus
Jerusalem
AD 27
Jn 3:1–21
Jesus talks to the Samaritan woman
Samaria
Jn 4:5–42
Jesus heals a royal official's son
Cana
Jn 4:46–54
The people of Jesus' hometown try to kill him
Nazareth
Lk 4:16–31
Jesus begins his first preaching trip through Galilee
Mt 4:23–25; Mk 1:35–39; Lk 4:42–44
Matthew decides to follow Jesus
Capernaum
Mt 9:9–13; Mk 2:13–17; Lk 5:27–32
Jesus chooses the 12 disciples
AD 28
Mk 3:13–19; Lk 6:12–15
Jesus preaches the Sermon on the Mount
Mt 5:1—7:29; Lk 6:20–49

Dotted lines leading to the timeline are meant to define sequence of events only. All dates are approximate.

ONE ARRANGEMENT OF THE LIFE OF CHRIST (CONT.)

A sinful woman anoints Jesus
Capernaum
Lk 7:36–50

Jesus ministers again in Galilee
Lk 8:1–3

Jesus tells parables about the kingdom
Mt 13:1–52; Mk 4:1–34; Lk 8:4–18

Jesus calms the storm
Sea of Galilee
Mt 8:23–27; Mk 4:35–41; Lk 8:22–25

Jesus feeds the 5,000
Near Bethsaida
Spring, AD 29
Mt 14:13–21; Mk 6:30–44; Lk 9:10–17; Jn 6:1–14

Jesus walks on water
Mt 14:22–33; Mk 6:45–52; Jn 6:16–21

Jesus withdraws to Tyre and Sidon
Mt 15:21–28; Mk 7:24–30

Jesus feeds the 4,000
Mt 15:32–39; Mk 8:1–9

Peter says that Jesus is the Son of God
Mt 16:13–20; Mk 8:27–30; Lk 9:18–21

Jesus tells his disciples he is going to die soon
Caesarea Philippi
Mt 16:21–26; Mk 8:31–37; Lk 9:22–25

Jesus is transfigured
Mt 17:1–13; Mk 9:2–13; Lk 9:28–36

Jesus pays his temple tax
Capernaum
Later in that year
Mt 17:24–27

POPULARITY AND OPPOSITION

Oct. 29 | 29

SPRING **SUMMER** **FALL** **WINTER** **SPRING** **SUMMER** **FALL**

Jairus's daughter is brought back to life by Jesus
Capernaum
Mt 9:18–26; Mk 5:21–43; Lk 8:40–56

Jesus sends the Twelve out to preach and heal
Mt 9:35—11:1; Mk 6:6–13; Lk 9:1–6

John the Baptist is killed by Herod
Machaerus
AD 28
Mt 14:1–12; Mk 6:14–29; Lk 9:7–9

Jesus attends the Festival of Tabernacles
Jerusalem
October, AD 29
Jn 7:11–52

Jesus heals a man who was born blind
Jerusalem
Jn 9:1–41

Jesus visits Mary and Martha
Bethany
Lk 10:38–42

The most likely dates for Jesus' public ministry are AD 27–30; the next most likely option, however, is 30–33.

ONE ARRANGEMENT OF THE LIFE OF CHRIST (CONT.)

Jesus begins his last trip to Jerusalem
AD 30
Lk 17:11

Jesus blesses the little children
ACROSS THE JORDAN
Mt 19:13–15; Mk 10:13–16; Lk 18:15–17

Jesus talks to the rich young man
ACROSS THE JORDAN
Mt 19:16–30; Mk 10:17–31; Lk 18:18–30

Jesus again predicts his death and resurrection
NEAR THE JORDAN
Mt 20:17–19; Mk 10:32–34; Lk 18:31–34

Jesus heals blind Bartimaeus
JERICHO
Mt 20:29–34; Mk 10:46–52; Lk 18:35–43

Jesus talks to Zacchaeus
JERICHO
Lk 19:1–10

Jesus returns to Bethany to visit Mary and Martha
BETHANY
Jn 11:55—12:1

THE LAST WEEK

The "Triumphal" Entry, JERUSALEM, Sunday
Mt 21:1–11; Mk 11:1–10; Lk 19:29–44; Jn 12:12–19

Jesus curses the fig tree, Monday
Mt 21:18–19; Mk 11:12–14

Jesus clears the temple, Monday
Mt 21:12–13; Mk 11:15–18

The authority of Jesus questioned, Tuesday
Mt 21:23–27; Mk 11:27–33; Lk 20:1–8

Jesus teaches in the temple, Tuesday
Mt 21:28—23:39; Mk 12:1–44; Lk 20:9—21:4

Jesus anointed, BETHANY, Tuesday
Mt 26:6–13; Mk 14:3–9; Jn 12:2–11

The plot against Jesus, Wednesday
Mt 26:14–16; Mk 14:10–11; Lk 22:3–6

The Last Supper, Thursday
Mt 26:17–29; Mk 14:12–25; Lk 22:7–20; Jn 13:1–38

Jesus comforts the disciples, Thursday
Jn 14:1—16:33

Gethsemane, Thursday
Mt 26:36–46; Mk 14:32–42; Lk 22:40–46

Jesus' arrest and trial, Thursday night and Friday
Mt 26:47—27:26; Mk 14:43—15:15;
Lk 22:47—23:25; Jn 18:2—19:16

Jesus' crucifixion and death, GOLGOTHA, Friday
Mt 27:27–56; Mk 15:16–41;
Lk 23:26–49; Jn 19:17–30

The burial of Jesus, JOSEPH'S TOMB, Friday
Mt 27:57–66; Mk 15:42–47;
Lk 23:50–56; Jn 19:31–42

30 WINTER | SPRING | SUMMER | FALL | 31 WINTER | SPRING | SUMMER

Jesus raises Lazarus from the dead
BETHANY
Winter, AD 30
Jn 11:1–44

AFTER THE RESURRECTION

The empty tomb, JERUSALEM, Sunday
Mt 28:1–10; Mk 16:1–8; Lk 24:1–12; Jn 20:1–10

Mary Magdalene sees Jesus in the garden
JERUSALEM, Sunday
Mt 16:9–11; Jn 20:11–18

Jesus appears to the two going to Emmaus
Sunday
Mk 16:12–13; Lk 24:13–35

Jesus appears to 10 disciples
JERUSALEM, Sunday
Mk 16:14; Lk 24:36–43; Jn 20:19–25

Jesus appears to the 11 disciples
JERUSALEM, One week later
Jn 20:26–31

Jesus talks with some of his disciples
SEA OF GALILEE, One week later
Jn 21:1–25

Jesus ascends to his Father in heaven
MOUNT OF OLIVES, 40 days later
Mt 28:16–20; Mk 16:19–20; Lk 24:44–53

charge of many things.[j] Come and share your master's happiness!'

22 "The man with two bags of gold also came. 'Master,' he said, 'you entrusted me with two bags of gold; see, I have gained two more.'

23 "His master replied, 'Well done, good and faithful servant! You have been faithful with a few things; I will put you in charge of many things.[k] Come and share your master's happiness!'

24 "Then the man who had received one bag of gold came. 'Master,' he said, 'I knew that you are a hard man, harvesting where you have not sown and gathering where you have not scattered seed. 25 So I was afraid and went out and hid your gold in the ground. See, here is what belongs to you.'

26 "His master replied, 'You wicked, lazy servant! So you knew that I harvest where I have not sown and gather where I have not scattered seed? 27 Well then, you should have put my money on deposit with the bankers, so that when I returned I would have received it back with interest.

28 " 'So take the bag of gold from him and give it to the one who has ten bags. 29 For whoever has will be given more, and they will have an abundance. Whoever does not have, even what they have will be taken from them.[l] 30 And throw that worthless servant outside, into the darkness, where there will be weeping and gnashing of teeth.'[m]

The Sheep and the Goats

31 "When the Son of Man comes[n] in his glory, and all the angels with him, he will sit on his glorious throne.[o] 32 All the nations will be gathered before him, and he will separate[p] the people one from another as a shepherd separates the sheep from the goats.[q] 33 He will put the sheep on his right and the goats on his left.

34 "Then the King will say to those on his right, 'Come, you who are blessed by my Father; take your inheritance, the kingdom[r] prepared for you since the creation of the world.[s] 35 For I was hungry and you gave me something to eat, I was thirsty and you gave me something to drink, I was a stranger and you invited me in,[t] 36 I needed clothes and you clothed me,[u] I was sick and you looked after me,[v] I was in prison and you came to visit me.'[w]

37 "Then the righteous will answer him, 'Lord, when did we see you hungry and feed you, or thirsty and give you something to drink? 38 When did we see you a stranger and invite you in, or needing clothes and clothe you? 39 When did we see you sick or in prison and go to visit you?'

40 "The King will reply, 'Truly I tell you, whatever you did for one of the least of these brothers and sisters of mine, you did for me.'[x]

41 "Then he will say to those on his left, 'Depart from me,[y] you who are cursed, into the eternal fire[z] prepared for the devil and his angels.[a] 42 For I was hungry and you gave me nothing to eat, I was thirsty and you gave me nothing to drink, 43 I was a stranger and you did not invite me in, I needed clothes and you did not clothe me, I was sick and in prison and you did not look after me.'

44 "They also will answer, 'Lord, when did we see you hungry or thirsty or a

25:21 [j] ver 23; Mt 24:45,47; Lk 16:10
25:23 [k] ver 21
25:29 [l] Mt 13:12; Mk 4:25; Lk 8:18; 19:26
25:30 [m] Mt 8:12
25:31 [n] Mt 16:27; Lk 17:30 [o] Mt 19:28
25:32 [p] Mal 3:18 [q] Eze 34:17,20
25:34 [r] Mt 3:2; 5:3,10,19; 19:14; Ac 20:32; 1Co 15:50; Gal 5:21; Jas 2:5 [s] Heb 4:3; 9:26; Rev 13:8; 17:8
25:35 [t] Job 31:32; Isa 58:7; Eze 18:7; Heb 13:2
25:36 [u] Isa 58:7; Eze 18:7; Jas 2:15,16 [v] Jas 1:27 [w] 2Ti 1:16
25:40 [x] Pr 19:17; Mt 10:40,42; Heb 6:10; 13:2
25:41 [y] Mt 7:23 [z] Isa 66:24; Mt 3:12; 5:22; Mk 9:43,48; Lk 3:17; Jude 7 [a] 2Pe 2:4

25:24 *you are a hard man.* In a manner that would have shocked ancient audiences, the servant insults the master, essentially blaming his master's harsh character for his own failure to increase his master's investment.
25:31 *sit on his glorious throne.* Some Jewish texts portray God delegating judgment to subordinates (such as Abel), but usually judgment, especially on the cosmic scale depicted in this parable, belongs to God alone. In Da 7:13–14, the Son of Man receives eternal authority over all peoples; coming with angels may allude to God's coming in Zec 14:5 (where the "holy ones" were sometimes understood to be angels).
25:32 *sheep ... goats.* Sheep were considered more valuable than goats, were usually raised in greater numbers, and were much more obedient. The OT depicted as shepherds of God's people Moses and David but especially God himself; God's people were depicted as sheep. Some report that sheep and goats were typically separated at night because of the animals' differing preferences.
25:33 *his right.* Ancient culture honored the right above the left.
25:34 In other early Jewish parables, the King (here, Jesus; v. 31) almost always represents God. Jewish texts often spoke of the righteous "inheriting" the kingdom or the world to come.
25:35 The basic hospitality described here fits expectations for how agents of the kingdom should be treated (10:11,42).
25:36 *sick and you looked after me.* Visiting the sick was a common practice. Those in prison could easily die of malnutrition unless friends or family outside brought food; sometimes guards demanded bribes to convey the goods to prisoners, so a visit to a relative in prison became a potentially costly journey.
25:40 *brothers and sisters of mine.* For the meaning of Jesus' brothers and sisters, see 12:50; 23:8; for its range of meaning, see note on Ac 9:17. Some see the siblings here as the poor; the idea that how one treats the poor is how one treats God has Biblical warrant (Pr 19:17). Others see the siblings here as Jesus' agents who bring the gospel; the idea that how one treats agents of God's message is how one treats God also has Biblical warrant (see notes on 10:40–42). The latter view fits the use of similar language elsewhere in Matthew.
25:41 *the eternal fire.* See note on 3:12.

stranger or needing clothes or sick or in
prison, and did not help you?'
45"He will reply, 'Truly I tell you, whatever you did not do for one of the least of
these, you did not do for me.'[b]
46"Then they will go away to eternal
punishment, but the righteous to eternal
life.[c]"[d]

The Plot Against Jesus

26:2-5pp — Mk 14:1,2; Lk 22:1,2

26 When Jesus had finished saying all
these things,[e] he said to his disciples, 2"As you know, the Passover[f] is two
days away — and the Son of Man will be
handed over to be crucified."
3Then the chief priests and the elders of
the people assembled[g] in the palace of the
high priest, whose name was Caiaphas,[h]
4and they schemed to arrest Jesus secretly
and kill him.[i] 5"But not during the festival," they said, "or there may be a riot[j]
among the people."

Jesus Anointed at Bethany

26:6-13pp — Mk 14:3-9
26:6-13Ref — Lk 7:37,38; Jn 12:1-8

6While Jesus was in Bethany[k] in the
home of Simon the Leper, 7a woman came
to him with an alabaster jar of very expensive perfume, which she poured on his
head as he was reclining at the table.
8When the disciples saw this, they were
indignant. "Why this waste?" they asked.
9"This perfume could have been sold at a
high price and the money given to the poor."
10Aware of this, Jesus said to them,
"Why are you bothering this woman? She
has done a beautiful thing to me. 11The
poor you will always have with you,[a][l]
but you will not always have me. 12When
she poured this perfume on my body, she
did it to prepare me for burial.[m] 13Truly I
tell you, wherever this gospel is preached
throughout the world, what she has done
will also be told, in memory of her."

Judas Agrees to Betray Jesus

26:14-16pp — Mk 14:10,11; Lk 22:3-6

14Then one of the Twelve — the one
called Judas Iscariot[n] — went to the chief
priests 15and asked, "What are you willing
to give me if I deliver him over to you?" So
they counted out for him thirty pieces of
silver.[o] 16From then on Judas watched for
an opportunity to hand him over.

[a] *11* See Deut. 15:11.

25:45 [b] Pr 14:31; 17:5
25:46 [c] Mt 19:29; Jn 3:15,16,36; 17:2,3; Ro 2:7; Gal 6:8; 5:11,13, 20 [d] Da 12:2; Jn 5:29; Ac 24:15; Ro 2:7, 8; Gal 6:8
26:1 [e] Mt 7:28
26:2 [f] Jn 11:55; 13:1
26:3 [g] Ps 2:2 [h] ver 57; Jn 11:47-53; 18:13,14,24,28
26:4 [i] Mt 12:14
26:5 [j] Mt 27:24
26:6 [k] Mt 21:17
26:11 [l] Dt 15:11
26:12 [m] Jn 19:40
26:14 [n] ver 25, 47; Mt 10:4
26:15 [o] Ex 21:32; Zec 11:12

26:1 — 27:66 When biographers wrote about a person whose death was significant (e.g., a martyr), they generally devoted significant space to recounting the person's death.

26:3 *chief priests.* Although the OT spoke of a single "chief priest," Jewish writers by this period described all of the chief priestly families as "chief priests," in addition to the leading high priest. *palace of the high priest.* Even had the plans not been for an extrajudicial arrest, making plans in the high priest's home instead of the Sanhedrin's normal meeting place violated ancient protocols for justice. A Roman governor appointed Joseph Caiaphas as high priest, and he was politically savvy enough to remain in office from AD 18 to 36. (He is well documented in Josephus, and some scholars believe that his ossuary has been found.) Josephus, the Pharisees and the Essenes all report the abuse of power in this period at the hands of the aristocratic priests.

26:5 *riot.* Jerusalem's population increased fivefold during Passover, making it difficult to control the crowds; many people died by trampling when riots occurred under such conditions.

26:6 *Bethany.* A village on the Mount of Olives outside of Jerusalem; Jesus had friends there (21:17; Jn 11:1), and Jerusalem was too crowded at this season for everyone to find easy lodging within the city walls.

26:7 *alabaster jar of very expensive perfume.* Natural alabaster (here likely calcite) is translucent, sometimes banded, and can resemble white marble. Soft and easily carved, it was also easily broken. People often stored expensive ointments in alabaster flasks, but because they were sealed to keep the ointments from evaporating, they might need to be broken to release the ointment. As to the expense and the sacrifice, there is a possibility that this could have been her dowry, but it also could have been an inheritance from her father (if there were no male heirs) or her husband; or she could have been one of the rare women to have her own resources. Such long-necked containers have been found in tombs from this period near Jerusalem; people apparently lavished the ointment on deceased loved ones. This expensive perfume may have been planned for a funeral, either a future one or one canceled because of Jesus' healing ministry. Providing a guest with oil to anoint his head could be simple courtesy, but one could also anoint a king in this way (2Ki 9:6).

26:8 Ancient historians sometimes taught lessons by contrasting the behavior of different individuals. Here the woman (v. 7), disciples (v. 8) and Judas (v. 15) offer contrasting views of what Jesus is worth.

26:9 *money given to the poor.* Some pious Jews took extra consideration for the poor at festivals (cf. Tobit 2:2; in the Mishnah see Pesahim 9:11; 10:1).

26:11 Jesus alludes to Dt 15:11, the context of which requires caring for the poor (Dt 15:1 – 10). Jesus is not minimizing care for the poor but recognizes that his own honor should come before everything else.

26:12 For the use of flasks of perfume to honor the bodies of the deceased, see note on v. 7.

26:13 *throughout the world.* Other ancient writers used similar hyperbole to speak of the hope or expectation of widespread fame.

26:15 *willing to give me.* Ancient ethics abhorred those who betrayed friendship or other loyalties for money. *thirty pieces of silver.* The price of a slave specified by the law (Ex 21:32, subsequent inflation notwithstanding); it was also the wage paid to the reliable shepherd of God's people in Zec 11:12 – 13 (recalled in Mt 27:9 – 10). Each silver coin was worth four drachmas; 30 pieces of silver thus represented more than 100 days' wages for an average worker. Cf. the earlier disciple in 2Ki 5:26 – 27.

The Last Supper

26:17-19pp — Mk 14:12-16; Lk 22:7-13
26:20-24pp — Mk 14:17-21
26:26-29pp — Mk 14:22-25; Lk 22:17-20; 1Co 11:23-25

17 On the first day of the Festival of Unleavened Bread,[p] the disciples came to Jesus and asked, "Where do you want us to make preparations for you to eat the Passover?"

18 He replied, "Go into the city to a certain man and tell him, 'The Teacher says: My appointed time[q] is near. I am going to celebrate the Passover with my disciples at your house.'" 19 So the disciples did as Jesus had directed them and prepared the Passover.

20 When evening came, Jesus was reclining at the table with the Twelve. 21 And while they were eating, he said, "Truly I tell you, one of you will betray me."[r]

22 They were very sad and began to say to him one after the other, "Surely you don't mean me, Lord?"

23 Jesus replied, "The one who has dipped his hand into the bowl with me will betray me.[s] 24 The Son of Man will go just as it is written about him.[t] But woe to that man who betrays the Son of Man! It would be better for him if he had not been born."

25 Then Judas, the one who would betray him, said, "Surely you don't mean me, Rabbi?"[u]

Jesus answered, "You have said so."

26 While they were eating, Jesus took bread, and when he had given thanks, he broke it[v] and gave it to his disciples, saying, "Take and eat; this is my body."

27 Then he took a cup, and when he had given thanks, he gave it to them, saying, "Drink from it, all of you. 28 This is my blood of the[a] covenant,[w] which is poured out for many for the forgiveness of sins.[x] 29 I tell you, I will not drink from this fruit of the vine from now on until that day when I drink it new with you[y] in my Father's kingdom."

30 When they had sung a hymn, they went out to the Mount of Olives.[z]

Jesus Predicts Peter's Denial

26:31-35pp — Mk 14:27-31; Lk 22:31-34

31 Then Jesus told them, "This very night you will all fall away on account of me,[a] for it is written:

> "'I will strike the shepherd,
> and the sheep of the flock will be scattered.'[b][b]

32 But after I have risen, I will go ahead of you into Galilee."[c]

33 Peter replied, "Even if all fall away on account of you, I never will."

26:17 [p] Ex 12:18-20 **26:18** [q] Jn 7:6, 8, 30; 12:23; 13:1; 17:1 **26:21** [r] Lk 22:21-23; Jn 13:21 **26:23** [s] Ps 41:9; Jn 13:18 **26:24** [t] Isa 53; Da 9:26; Mk 9:12; Lk 24:25-27, 46; Ac 17:2, 3; 26:22, 23 **26:25** [u] Mt 23:7 **26:26** [v] Mt 14:19; 1Co 10:16 **26:28** [w] Ex 24:6-8; Heb 9:20 [x] Mt 20:28; Mk 1:4 **26:29** [y] Ac 10:41 **26:30** [z] Mt 21:1; Mk 14:26 **26:31** [a] Mt 11:6 [b] Zec 13:7; Jn 16:32 **26:32** [c] Mt 28:7, 10, 16

[a] 28 Some manuscripts *the new* [b] 31 Zech. 13:7

26:17 By this period, Passover was counted as the beginning of the Festival of Unleavened Bread. The group would need to eat Passover within the city walls (a custom based on Dt 16:7), despite the crowding. Preparing Passover required, not only finding a place, but also procuring a sacrificed lamb in the temple (unless already procured by the host) as well as bitter herbs (cf. Ex 12:8), unleavened bread and fruit. Jesus' group of disciples gathers for Passover the way a family would.
26:20 *evening.* The Passover meal was always eaten in the evening, after sundown; it had to be finished by midnight. *reclining at the table.* Although Jewish people could sit for other meals, for banquets the men reclined, like Greeks. Men supported themselves on their left elbow, leaving the right hand free to take food from the table.
26:21 *betray.* In antiquity, a disciple's behavior reflected on the teacher, and a follower's betrayal would bring shame to a leader.
26:23 *dipped … with me.* The person of highest status should dip first; if dipping *with* Jesus means at the same time, the action probably reflects disrespect. Ideally three or four people would recline on each large couch, with bowls of bitter herbs (cf. Nu 9:11) for dipping bread in front of each group. Whether or not such couches were available on this occasion, Judas was undoubtedly reclining close to Jesus (cf. Jn 13:26).
26:24 *woe to that man.* Although some Jewish people focused more on God's sovereignty and others more on human choice, most accepted both without viewing them as contradictory. *It would be better for him if he had not been born.* Widely used by both Jews and Greeks, it appears in earlier Scripture (Job 3:3 – 26; Jer 20:14 – 18).
26:26 See note on Lk 22:19.
26:27 *took a cup.* Jesus would lift the cup as he spoke about it. Tradition suggests that the wine used for Passover was red.
26:28 *my blood of the covenant.* Jesus alludes to Ex 24:8, where the first covenant with Israel was inaugurated by sacrificial blood. Because crucifixion did not require blood (though blood was shed in Jesus' case), the mention of blood highlights the sacrificial character of the death, as in Exodus. Presumably the covenant here, in contrast with Exodus, is the "new covenant" (Jer 31:31, as in Lk 22:20; 1Co 11:25), a promise celebrated in some other ancient Jewish circles. *poured out for many.* May evoke Isa 53:12 (see note on 20:28). The thought of consuming blood revolted Jewish people (e.g., Lev 17:14), but Jesus is not speaking literally.
26:29 *I will not drink … until.* Jewish people often offered vows of abstinence, promising not to partake of a particular food or drink until such-and-such a matter occurred. Because the fourth and final cup of Passover wine was drunk after the closing hymn, which occurs in v. 30, the present cup is probably the third one.
26:30 *sung a hymn.* After the meal, Jewish people would sing the remaining psalms of the Hallel. (The Hallel consisted of Ps 113 – 118, but they might sing the first several psalms earlier in the evening.) A stairway led down to the Kidron Valley, from which they would then ascend the Mount of Olives.
26:31 In its context Zec 13:7 speaks of false prophets, but the principle of sheep scattering without a shepherd is a wider one (cf. the probable allusion to Eze 34:5 in Mt 9:36), and Matthew may also be thinking of the faithful shepherd in Zec 11:9 – 13 (to which he alludes in Mt 26:15 [see note there]). The Dead Sea Scrolls also seem to apply Zec 13:7 in a more positive way (see Damascus Document 19.5 – 9).

Ancient olive trees still grow in the Garden of Gethsemane, where Jesus prayed before his arrest (Mt 26:36).

34 "Truly I tell you," Jesus answered,
"this very night, before the rooster crows,
you will disown me three times."[d]
35 But Peter declared, "Even if I have to
die with you,[e] I will never disown you."
And all the other disciples said the same.

Gethsemane

26:36-46pp — Mk 14:32-42; Lk 22:40-46

36 Then Jesus went with his disciples to
a place called Gethsemane, and he said to
them, "Sit here while I go over there and
pray." 37 He took Peter and the two sons of
Zebedee[f] along with him, and he began to
be sorrowful and troubled. 38 Then he said
to them, "My soul is overwhelmed with
sorrow[g] to the point of death. Stay here
and keep watch with me."[h]
39 Going a little farther, he fell with his
face to the ground and prayed, "My Father,
if it is possible, may this cup[i] be taken from
me. Yet not as I will, but as you will."[j]
40 Then he returned to his disciples and
found them sleeping. "Couldn't you men
keep watch with me[k] for one hour?" he
asked Peter. 41 "Watch and pray so that you
will not fall into temptation.[l] The spirit is
willing, but the flesh is weak."
42 He went away a second time and
prayed, "My Father, if it is not possible for
this cup to be taken away unless I drink it,
may your will be done."
43 When he came back, he again found
them sleeping, because their eyes were
heavy. 44 So he left them and went away
once more and prayed the third time, saying the same thing.
45 Then he returned to the disciples and
said to them, "Are you still sleeping and
resting? Look, the hour[m] has come, and
the Son of Man is delivered into the hands
of sinners. 46 Rise! Let us go! Here comes
my betrayer!"

Jesus Arrested

26:47-56pp — Mk 14:43-50; Lk 22:47-53

47 While he was still speaking, Judas, one
of the Twelve, arrived. With him was a large
crowd armed with swords and clubs, sent
from the chief priests and the elders of the

26:34 [d] ver 75; Jn 13:38 **26:35** [e] Jn 13:37 **26:37** [f] Mt 4:21 **26:38** [g] Jn 12:27 [h] ver 40,41 **26:39** [i] Mt 20:22 [j] ver 42; Ps 40:6-8; Isa 50:5; Jn 5:30; 6:38 **26:40** [k] ver 38 **26:41** [l] Mt 6:13 **26:45** [m] ver 18

26:39 *this cup.* See note on 20:22,23; cf. 26:27–28.
26:40 *sleeping.* It was customary to stay up late speaking of God's acts of redemption on the night of Passover. The disciples, who may have often stayed awake longer on other Passover nights, fall asleep on this one. *Couldn't you men keep watch with me for one hour?* People valued vigilance (for night watchmen and the like), especially when danger was near.
26:47 *armed with swords and clubs.* Armed men sent from the local elite were probably the Levite temple guards; Jerusalem's leaders had no authority over Roman soldiers. Some later Jewish traditions complained that the

people. 48Now the betrayer had arranged a
signal with them: "The one I kiss is the man;
arrest him." 49Going at once to Jesus, Judas
said, "Greetings, Rabbi!"[n] and kissed him.
50Jesus replied, "Do what you came for,
friend."[a o]

Then the men stepped forward, seized
Jesus and arrested him. 51With that, one of
Jesus' companions reached for his sword,[p]
drew it out and struck the servant of the
high priest, cutting off his ear.[q]
52"Put your sword back in its place,"
Jesus said to him, "for all who draw the
sword will die by the sword.[r] 53Do you
think I cannot call on my Father, and he
will at once put at my disposal more than
twelve legions of angels?[s] 54But how then
would the Scriptures be fulfilled[t] that say
it must happen in this way?"

55In that hour Jesus said to the crowd,
"Am I leading a rebellion, that you have
come out with swords and clubs to capture me? Every day I sat in the temple
courts teaching,[u] and you did not arrest
me. 56But this has all taken place that
the writings of the prophets might be fulfilled."[v] Then all the disciples deserted
him and fled.

26:49 [n] ver 25 **26:50** [o] Mt 20:13; 22:12 **26:51** [p] Lk 22:36,38 [q] Jn 18:10 **26:52** [r] Ge 9:6; Rev 13:10 **26:53** [s] 2Ki 6:17; Da 7:10; Mt 4:11 **26:54** [t] ver 24 **26:55** [u] Mk 12:35; Lk 21:37; Jn 7:14,28; 18:20 **26:56** [v] ver 24

[a] 50 Or *"Why have you come, friend?"*

servants of the high priest in this period used clubs when abusing people.
26:48 *kiss.* See note on Lk 22:47.
26:52 *all who draw the sword will die by the sword.* This statement of Jesus resembles a Jewish proverb; if the resemblance is not coincidence, he may be drawing on a familiar expression to make his point.
26:53 *twelve legions of angels.* A legion had about 6,000 soldiers. The entire Roman province of Syria (which included Judea) normally had only three legions altogether (Josephus *Antiquities* 17.286).

MATTHEW 26:59–68; MARK 14:55–64; LUKE 22:66–71; JOHN 18:12–24

Jesus' Trial

Ancient sources show that the inner workings of official councils, both the Sanhedrin and the Roman Senate, often became known; large bodies of people could not keep secrets from being leaked for very long.

Some have challenged the accuracy of the Gospels' trial narratives based on later rabbinic reports about the Sanhedrin. The rabbinic reports, however, are well over a century later than the Gospel reports, and the Gospel reports fit our other first-century evidence (especially Josephus) concerning how such matters were handled. Moreover, later rabbinic reports offer a Pharisaic perspective on the ideal that should have been followed; the Sanhedrin, however, was dominated by Sadducees who cared little for Pharisaic perspectives. Because this was a special night meeting of the Sanhedrin during the time of a festival, it is likely that many members were unable to attend (if they were even invited).

The members of the Sanhedrin who met to try Jesus violated ethical standards held not only by Pharisees but even by many Gentile moralists of the period. Trials were supposed to be conducted during daylight, in the normal meeting hall (in this case that was near the temple), not in the leading judge's home. Whereas Pharisees opposed hasty executions after deliberations, the Sadducees were known for harsh and often quick punishments. The most obvious breach of ethics, of course, is the presence of false and mutually contradictory witnesses. Clearly some members of the Sanhedrin present acted with legal integrity, cross-examining the witnesses, but by Pharisaic standards, the case should have been thrown out once the witnesses contradicted one another (Mk 14:59). The high priest's plan may have been simply to have a preliminary hearing to formulate a charge to bring to Pilate (cf. Mt 27:1; Mk 15:1; Lk 22:66; 23:1), the expected procedure before accusing someone before the governor.

The actions of the Sanhedrin fit what we know of the period. The Roman government usually depended on local elites to charge troublemakers. Local elites were often

continued on next page

Jesus Before the Sanhedrin

26:57-68pp — Mk 14:53-65; Jn 18:12,13,19-24

[57]Those who had arrested Jesus took him to Caiaphas[w] the high priest, where the teachers of the law and the elders had assembled. [58]But Peter followed him at a distance, right up to the courtyard of the high priest.[x] He entered and sat down with the guards[y] to see the outcome.

[59]The chief priests and the whole Sanhedrin[z] were looking for false evidence against Jesus so that they could put him to death. [60]But they did not find any, though many false witnesses[a] came forward.

Finally two[b] came forward [61]and declared, "This fellow said, 'I am able to destroy the temple of God and rebuild it in three days.' "[c]

[62]Then the high priest stood up and said to Jesus, "Are you not going to answer? What is this testimony that these men are bringing against you?" [63]But Jesus remained silent.[d]

The high priest said to him, "I charge

26:57 [w]ver 3 **26:58** [x]Jn 18:15 [y]Jn 7:32,45,46 **26:59** [z]Mt 5:22 **26:60** [a]Ps 27:12; 35:11; Ac 6:13 [b]Dt 19:15 **26:61** [c]Jn 2:19 **26:63** [d]Mt 27:12,14

26:57 *Caiaphas.* See note on v. 3.
26:60 *false witnesses.* False testimony was common in Gentile trials; some Greek rhetorical handbooks even taught people how to provide the most persuasive false witness. Jewish law heavily emphasized careful cross-examination; where witnesses contradicted one another too severely, the case should be thrown out. In a capital case, witnesses found to be false were to be executed (Dt 19:16 – 21). *two came forward.* This is significant; two was the minimum number of witnesses allowed for acceptable testimony.
26:61 *rebuild it in three days.* Some Jewish people expected God to provide a new temple. It is clear, however, that the testimony here rests on a misinterpretation of Jesus (see Jn 2:19).
26:63 *I charge you under oath.* This was a regular formula requiring people to testify. *the Messiah.* He would also be the king of the Jews; hence, Jesus' response to the high

corrupt, and all our other sources from the period (Josephus, the Dead Sea Scrolls, and Pharisaic memories) agree that the aristocratic priesthood that controlled Jerusalem abused its power against others. A generation later, the chief priests arrested a Jewish prophet for announcing judgment against the temple; they handed him over to a Roman governor, who had him beaten until (Josephus says) his bones showed (Josephus, *Wars* 6.300 – 305). Their treatment of Jesus fits their usual behavior toward those who challenged their authority. ◆

The Church of St. Peter marks the traditional location of Jesus' trial.

you under oath[e] by the living God:[f] Tell us
if you are the Messiah, the Son of God."
64 "You have said so," Jesus replied.
"But I say to all of you: From now on you
will see the Son of Man sitting at the right
hand of the Mighty One[g] and coming on
the clouds of heaven."[a][h]
65 Then the high priest tore his clothes[i]
and said, "He has spoken blasphemy!
Why do we need any more witnesses?
Look, now you have heard the blasphemy. 66 What do you think?"
"He is worthy of death,"[j] they answered.
67 Then they spit in his face and struck
him with their fists.[k] Others slapped him
68 and said, "Prophesy to us, Messiah. Who
hit you?"[l]

Peter Disowns Jesus

26:69-75pp — Mk 14:66-72; Lk 22:55-62; Jn 18:16-18,25-27

69 Now Peter was sitting out in the courtyard, and a servant girl came to him. "You
also were with Jesus of Galilee," she said.
70 But he denied it before them all. "I
don't know what you're talking about,"
he said.
71 Then he went out to the gateway,
where another servant girl saw him and
said to the people there, "This fellow was
with Jesus of Nazareth."
72 He denied it again, with an oath: "I
don't know the man!"
73 After a little while, those standing
there went up to Peter and said, "Surely
you are one of them; your accent gives
you away."
74 Then he began to call down curses, and
he swore to them, "I don't know the man!"
Immediately a rooster crowed. 75 Then
Peter remembered the word Jesus had
spoken: "Before the rooster crows, you
will disown me three times."[m] And he
went outside and wept bitterly.

Judas Hangs Himself

27 Early in the morning, all the chief
priests and the elders of the people made their plans how to have Jesus
executed.[n] 2 So they bound him, led him
away and handed him over[o] to Pilate the
governor.[p]
3 When Judas, who had betrayed him,[q]
saw that Jesus was condemned, he was
seized with remorse and returned the thirty pieces of silver[r] to the chief priests and
the elders. 4 "I have sinned," he said, "for I
have betrayed innocent blood."
"What is that to us?" they replied.
"That's your responsibility."[s]
5 So Judas threw the money into the
temple[t] and left. Then he went away and
hanged himself.[u]
6 The chief priests picked up the coins
and said, "It is against the law to put this
into the treasury, since it is blood money."
7 So they decided to use the money to buy
the potter's field as a burial place for for-

26:63 [e] Lev 5:1 [f] Mt 16:16
26:64 [g] Ps 110:1 [h] Da 7:13; Rev 1:7
26:65 [i] Mk 14:63
26:66 [j] Lev 24:16; Jn 19:7
26:67 [k] Mt 16:21; 27:30
26:68 [l] Lk 22:63-65
26:75 [m] ver 34; Jn 13:38
27:1 [n] Mt 12:14; Mk 15:1; Lk 22:66
27:2 [o] Mt 20:19 [p] Mk 15:1; Lk 13:1; Ac 3:13; 1Ti 6:13
27:3 [q] Mt 10:4 [r] Mt 26:14, 15
27:4 [s] ver 24
27:5 [t] Lk 1:9, 21 [u] Ac 1:18

[a] *64* See Psalm 110:1; Daniel 7:13.

---

priest's question would prove useful in a charge of treason (27:11). *Son of God.* A Messianic title.

26:64 *the Son of Man ... coming on the clouds of heaven.* Recalls Da 7:13. *sitting at the right hand.* Recalls Ps 110:1. Jesus used both of these passages earlier (22:44; 24:30). *Mighty One.* Here is literally "power," sometimes used in Jewish sources as a circumlocution for God.

26:65 *tore his clothes ... blasphemy.* People tore their clothes for mourning, and in Jewish tradition hearing blasphemy was a mandatory cause for mourning in this way. Later rabbis restricted blasphemy technically to cursing with God's sacred name, but most people used this term more broadly. Caiaphas can construe Jesus' words as blasphemy only if he implies that Jesus in v. 64 has associated himself with God in a way that diminishes God's honor.

26:66 According to later tradition, the high priest would ask for the verdict and (much less likely for this period and an informal hearing) members would respond from youngest to eldest.

26:67 The abuse reported here is the gravest violation of legal ethics for a trial.

26:68 They mock Jesus as a false prophet as well as Messiah.

26:72 *I don't know the man!* Regarding oaths, see notes on 5:33–35. *I don't know.* A way of repudiating someone (see note on 25:12).

26:73 *accent.* Judeans thought that Galileans did not correctly distinguish their gutturals. Judeans held prejudice against Galileans as comparatively backward; in this case, they would connect Peter with his Galilean teacher.

27:1 *Early in the morning.* Governors, like other members of the Roman elite, met clients in the morning, from sunrise until 11 a.m. Whatever else could have been on the docket, local municipal leaders would be admitted first.

27:2 *Pilate.* He was governor of Judea from AD 26 to 36; he may have remained in power to this point because Sejanus, whom many scholars think was his patron, was close to the emperor, though Pilate's position would have become tenuous after Sejanus was executed in AD 31. His relationship with the local leaders had involved conflict from the start, from bringing imperial standards into the city to redirecting money from the temple treasury. His slaughter of Samaritans proved too controversial and led to Rome removing him from office in AD 36.

27:4 *betrayed innocent blood.* God avenged innocent blood (Dt 21:8; 2Ki 24:3–4); here many share in the guilt yet try to pass it to others (see v. 24).

27:5 *hanged himself.* The penalty for false witnesses in capital cases was death (Dt 19:16–21). Many people regarded hanging as a dishonorable form of suicide (cf. 2Sa 17:23, note on Ac 16:27). Most Jewish people rejected suicide as immoral under most circumstances. In the usual ancient view, hanging himself within the temple would have desecrated it.

27:6 *blood money.* Irony was common in ancient literature, and Matthew's audience would certainly understand the irony of elite priests being more concerned with the temple's purity than with a judicial murder that was currently underway.

27:7 *potter's field.* Possibly Matthew's audience knew

eigners. 8That is why it has been called the
Field of Blood[v] to this day. 9Then what was
spoken by Jeremiah the prophet was fulfilled:[w] "They took the thirty pieces of silver, the price set on him by the people of
Israel, 10and they used them to buy the potter's field, as the Lord commanded me."[a][x]

Jesus Before Pilate

27:11-26pp — Mk 15:2-15; Lk 23:2,3,18-25;
Jn 18:29 – 19:16

11Meanwhile Jesus stood before the governor, and the governor asked him, "Are
you the king of the Jews?"[y]
"You have said so," Jesus replied.
12When he was accused by the chief
priests and the elders, he gave no answer.[z] 13Then Pilate asked him, "Don't
you hear the testimony they are bringing
against you?"[a] 14But Jesus made no reply,[b]
not even to a single charge — to the great
amazement of the governor.
15Now it was the governor's custom at
the festival to release a prisoner[c] chosen by
the crowd. 16At that time they had a well-
known prisoner whose name was Jesus[b]
Barabbas. 17So when the crowd had gathered, Pilate asked them, "Which one do
you want me to release to you: Jesus Barabbas, or Jesus who is called the Messiah?"[d]
18For he knew it was out of self-interest that
they had handed Jesus over to him.

27:8 [v]Ac 1:19
27:9 [w]Mt 1:22
27:10 [x]Zec 11:12, 13; Jer 32:6-9
27:11 [y]Mt 2:2
27:12 [z]Mt 26:63; Mk 14:61; Jn 19:9
27:13 [a]Mt 26:62
27:14 [b]Mk 14:61
27:15 [c]Jn 18:39
27:17 [d]ver 22; Mt 1:16
27:19 [e]Jn 19:13 [f]ver 24 [g]Ge 20:6; Nu 12:6; 1Ki 3:5; Job 33:14-16; Mt 1:20; 2:12, 13, 19, 22
27:20 [h]Ac 3:14
27:22 [i]Mt 1:16
27:24 [j]Mt 26:5 [k]Ps 26:6 [l]Dt 21:6-8 [m]ver 4
27:25 [n]Jos 2:19; Ac 5:28
27:26 [o]Isa 53:5; Jn 19:1

19While Pilate was sitting on the judge's
seat,[e] his wife sent him this message:
"Don't have anything to do with that innocent[f] man, for I have suffered a great
deal today in a dream[g] because of him."
20But the chief priests and the elders
persuaded the crowd to ask for Barabbas
and to have Jesus executed.[h]
21"Which of the two do you want me to
release to you?" asked the governor.
"Barabbas," they answered.
22"What shall I do, then, with Jesus
who is called the Messiah?"[i] Pilate asked.
They all answered, "Crucify him!"
23"Why? What crime has he committed?" asked Pilate.
But they shouted all the louder, "Crucify him!"
24When Pilate saw that he was getting
nowhere, but that instead an uproar[j] was
starting, he took water and washed his
hands[k] in front of the crowd. "I am innocent of this man's blood,"[l] he said. "It is
your responsibility!"[m]
25All the people answered, "His blood is
on us and on our children!"[n]
26Then he released Barabbas to them.
But he had Jesus flogged,[o] and handed
him over to be crucified.

[a] *10* See Zech. 11:12,13; Jer. 19:1-13; 32:6-9. [b] *16* Many manuscripts do not have *Jesus*; also in verse 17.

---

enough Hebrew to know that the Hebrew term for "potter" (see vv. 7,10) could be read as "treasury" by changing vowels, as ancient rabbis often did to impress a point upon their listeners.

27:9 – 10 Jewish teachers linked texts based on shared key words or phrases, and sometimes conflated similar texts so that one would read one text in light of the other. By using words from Zechariah but the name of Jeremiah, Matthew may want Biblically literate hearers to link the passages (cf. Jer 32:6 – 14, which is similar to Zec 11:12 – 13; perhaps also Jer 19:10 – 13). Zec 11:13 adds that the money was thrown to the potter "at the house of the LORD," as Matthew's audience may have realized.

27:11 *king of the Jews.* For Romans, such a charge meant treason; only the emperor could grant the title "king." In the provinces, the usual penalty for treason was death by the slow torture of crucifixion.

27:14 *made no reply.* Some accounts of Jewish martyrs included their refusal to respond to their persecutors; cf. also Isa 53:7.

27:15 *governor's custom … to release a prisoner.* Customs similar to this one existed in various locations; governors often chose to honor the precedents set by their predecessors, although no law required this practice.

27:17 A governor might not wish to appear too lenient, a weakness that his subjects might then exploit; Roman culture valued firmness. A governor's concern for order often took precedence over individual matters of justice, especially when the accused were not Roman citizens. Pilate apparently calculates that the crowd will select (cf. v. 15) Jesus, a popular Messianic figure whom Pilate deems harmless, over Barabbas, thus freeing him from the obligation to release the latter.

27:19 *judge's seat.* This seat was at Herod the Great's former palace, where Roman governors stayed when they visited Jerusalem. *in a dream.* People took dreams very seriously (see note on 1:20); God had revealed truth to Gentile officials this way (Ge 41:25; Da 2:28).

27:20 *persuaded the crowd.* Ancient literature often reports leaders swaying fickle crowds. Whereas the crowds in Galilee knew Jesus, most of those present on this occasion would have been Judeans who did not know him directly.

27:24 *washed his hands … I am innocent.* Jerusalemites had forced Pilate to back down previously. Indeed, when Pilate first became governor, under cover of night he brought into Jerusalem the standards that Jewish people regarded as idols. The crowds forced him to back down. Washing hands was a way of disclaiming responsibility for innocent blood (Dt 21:6 – 7). *It is your responsibility!* Claiming to be compelled by others did not truly relieve a leader of responsibility, however (cf. 27:4; Jer 38:5).

27:25 *His blood is on us and on our children!* Such expressions invoked curses against themselves if they were wrong (cf., e.g., Jer 42:5). Probably the judgment invited here was fulfilled in AD 70 (see note on 23:36).

27:26 *flogged, and handed him over to be crucified.* A governor pronouncing sentence would typically say something like, "You will mount the cross." Prisoners were normally stripped and publicly flogged before execution. Whereas Jewish law allowed a maximum of 39 lashes with a whip of calf leather, Roman practice allowed floggings until the flogger grew tired. A Roman soldier's *flagellum* was a leather whip embedded with bone, iron, or metal spikes at the end. The instrument of torture would slice

The Soldiers Mock Jesus

27:27-31pp — Mk 15:16-20

27Then the governor's soldiers took
Jesus into the Praetorium[p] and gathered
the whole company of soldiers around
him. 28They stripped him and put a scarlet
robe on him,[q] 29and then twisted together
a crown of thorns and set it on his head.
They put a staff in his right hand. Then
they knelt in front of him and mocked
him. "Hail, king of the Jews!" they said.[r]
30They spit on him, and took the staff and
struck him on the head again and again.[s]
31After they had mocked him, they took off
the robe and put his own clothes on him.
Then they led him away to crucify him.[t]

The Crucifixion of Jesus

27:33-44pp — Mk 15:22-32; Lk 23:33-43; Jn 19:17-24

32As they were going out,[u] they met a
man from Cyrene,[v] named Simon, and
they forced him to carry the cross.[w] 33They
came to a place called Golgotha (which
means "the place of the skull").[x] 34There
they offered Jesus wine to drink, mixed
with gall;[y] but after tasting it, he refused
to drink it. 35When they had crucified
him, they divided up his clothes by casting lots.[z] 36And sitting down, they kept
watch[a] over him there. 37Above his head
they placed the written charge against
him: THIS IS JESUS, THE KING OF THE JEWS.

38Two rebels were crucified with him,[b]
one on his right and one on his left. 39Those
who passed by hurled insults at him, shaking their heads[c] 40and saying, "You who are
going to destroy the temple and build it in
three days,[d] save yourself![e] Come down
from the cross, if you are the Son of God!"[f]
41In the same way the chief priests, the
teachers of the law and the elders mocked
him. 42"He saved others," they said, "but he
can't save himself! He's the king of Israel![g]
Let him come down now from the cross,
and we will believe[h] in him. 43He trusts in
God. Let God rescue him[i] now if he wants
him, for he said, 'I am the Son of God.'" 44In
the same way the rebels who were crucified
with him also heaped insults on him.

27:27 [p] Jn 18:28, 33; 19:9
27:28 [q] Jn 19:2
27:29 [r] Isa 53:3; Jn 19:2,3
27:30 [s] Mt 16:21; 26:67
27:31 [t] Isa 53:7
27:32 [u] Heb 13:12 [v] Ac 2:10; 6:9; 11:20; 13:1 [w] Mk 15:21; Lk 23:26
27:33 [x] Jn 19:17
27:34 [y] ver 48; Ps 69:21
27:35 [z] Ps 22:18
27:36 [a] ver 54
27:38 [b] Isa 53:12
27:39 [c] Ps 22:7; 109:25; La 2:15
27:40 [d] Mt 26:61; Jn 2:19 [e] ver 42 [f] Mt 4:3,6
27:42 [g] Jn 1:49; 12:13 [h] Jn 3:15
27:43 [i] Ps 22:8

---

open the flesh, sometimes leaving it in bloody strips or exposing sinews and bones, and occasionally killing the victim before crucifixion.

27:27 *Praetorium.* The governor's residence was in Herod the Great's former palace in the upper city of Jerusalem. Several hundred soldiers comprised the Roman cohort in Jerusalem's Antonia Fortress; the term here could imply that number or a smaller force within it.

27:28 *stripped him.* Naked crucifixion was meant to shame the victim, but other mockery and ridicule commonly accompanied execution. *scarlet.* Color gradations in Greek differed from those in modern English; the range of the term translated "purple" in Mk 15:17 and Jn 19:2 sometimes included "scarlet." Soldiers wore red cloaks, but when faded the cloak could resemble "purple," like the cloaks of Hellenistic princes.

27:29 *crown of thorns.* Hellenistic vassal princes wore garlands; soldiers may have used an available shrub such as acanthus to weave a wreath for Jesus. Imitating Hellenistic garlands, the soldiers may have intended the thorns to point especially outward, but some of the thorns would nevertheless turn inward, scraping the scalp. Scalp wounds bleed particularly profusely. *staff.* Some suggest that the staff was a bamboo cane used for military floggings. *Hail.* Equivalent to the Latin *Ave*; it was a common address to rulers. Most of Rome's soldiers in Jerusalem were Syrian auxiliaries; in many locations, Syrians and Jews often clashed. *king of the Jews.* In ridiculing Jesus in this way, the soldiers are also probably mocking Jewish people more generally.

27:30 *spit on him.* Spit was used to spite, and Jewish people deemed the spittle of Gentiles to be impure.

27:32 *Cyrene.* In North Africa included; its population included many local Libyans, resident Greeks and Jews. *Simon.* Simon was a Greek name very commonly used by Jews (because it resembled the patriarchal name Simeon). His coming to Jerusalem probably suggests that he is Jewish by faith, whatever his ethnic background. *they forced him to carry the cross.* Normally the condemned person was forced to publicly carry the horizontal beam (the *patibulum*) of his own cross out to the site of his execution. If Jesus were too weak from the beating to undertake this task, however, Rome's soldiers had the authority to draft a bystander to perform labor for them (see note on 5:41).

27:33 *the place of the skull.* The location may have earned this name because so many prisoners died there. A proposed site for the crucifixion dating back to the nineteenth century (Gordon's Calvary), deemed so partly because it was shaped like a skull at that time, is not relevant for first-century topography.

27:34 *wine to drink, mixed with gall.* Wine had pain-killing properties (Pr 31:6 – 7); many think that myrrh (Mk 15:23) also had such properties, but Matthew emphasizes instead gall. Gall was known for its bitterness and appears in Ps 69:21, a psalm of a righteous sufferer, in a context cited by the Gospels in connection with Jesus' death.

27:35 *crucified him.* Romans crucified people naked; Jewish people regarded nakedness as a special shame. Those hanging on crosses could not chase away flies from their wounds, could not restrain their bodily wastes for the hours or days it took them to finish dying, and could not protect themselves from heat or cold. Some may have died from asphyxiation, but people usually died more quickly from shock (due to blood loss) or dehydration. *divided up his clothes.* Recalls Ps 22:18, but also fits historical practice. Roman execution squads (typically about four men) had rights to whatever clothing or other personal effects remained on the prisoner. *casting lots.* Soldiers used dice and other means to gamble.

27:37 *written charge.* See note on Lk 23:38.

27:39 *shaking their heads.* See Ps 22:7. Romans preferred to crucify offenders in public places, often on major roads, where passersby would see in graphic detail what happens to those who resist Rome.

27:43 Perhaps unwittingly, Jesus' mockers virtually repeat the idea of Ps 22:8 — the Biblical words of those mocking a righteous sufferer. Their words here and in v. 40 also evoke a passage in the widely read Jewish work Wisdom of Solomon (2:18): mockers charge that if the righteous person genuinely is God's son, God will rescue him. Ironically, they speak inverted truth: in order

The Death of Jesus

27:45-56pp — Mk 15:33-41; Lk 23:44-49; Jn 19:29-30

45 From noon until three in the afternoon darkness[j] came over all the land. 46 About three in the afternoon Jesus cried out in a loud voice, *"Eli, Eli,[a] lema sabachthani?"* (which means "My God, my God, why have you forsaken me?").[b k]

47 When some of those standing there heard this, they said, "He's calling Elijah."

48 Immediately one of them ran and got a sponge. He filled it with wine vinegar,[l] put it on a staff, and offered it to Jesus to drink. 49 The rest said, "Now leave him alone. Let's see if Elijah comes to save him."

50 And when Jesus had cried out again in a loud voice, he gave up his spirit.[m]

51 At that moment the curtain of the temple[n] was torn in two from top to bottom. The earth shook, the rocks split[o] 52 and the tombs broke open. The bodies of many holy people who had died were raised to life. 53 They came out of the tombs after Jesus' resurrection and[c] went into the holy city[p] and appeared to many people.

54 When the centurion and those with him who were guarding[q] Jesus saw the earthquake and all that had happened, they were terrified, and exclaimed, "Surely he was the Son of God!"[r]

55 Many women were there, watching from a distance. They had followed Jesus from Galilee to care for his needs.[s] 56 Among them were Mary Magdalene, Mary the mother of James and Joseph,[d] and the mother of Zebedee's sons.[t]

The Burial of Jesus

27:57-61pp — Mk 15:42-47; Lk 23:50-56; Jn 19:38-42

57 As evening approached, there came a rich man from Arimathea, named Joseph, who had himself become a disciple of Jesus. 58 Going to Pilate, he asked for Jesus' body, and Pilate ordered that it be given to him. 59 Joseph took the body, wrapped it in a clean linen cloth, 60 and placed it in his own new tomb[u] that he had cut out of

27:45 [j] Am 8:9 **27:46** [k] Ps 22:1 **27:48** [l] ver 34; Ps 69:21 **27:50** [m] Jn 19:30 **27:51** [n] Ex 26:31-33; Heb 9:3, 8 [o] ver 54 **27:53** [p] Mt 4:5 **27:54** [q] ver 36 [r] Mt 4:3; 17:5 **27:55** [s] Lk 8:2, 3 **27:56** [t] Mk 15:47; Lk 24:10; Jn 19:25 **27:60** [u] Mt 27:66; 28:2; Mk 16:4

[a] 46 Some manuscripts *Eloi, Eloi* [b] 46 Psalm 22:1
[c] 53 Or *tombs, and after Jesus' resurrection they*
[d] 56 Greek *Joses,* a variant of *Joseph*

to save others, Jesus must choose not to save himself (v. 42).

27:45 *darkness.* Often appears as a judgment in the OT (e.g., Ex 10:21 – 23), including darkness at noon (Am 8:9).

27:46 Jesus quotes Ps 22:1, a prayer of a righteous sufferer that begins by expressing abandonment but goes on to celebrate God's vindication (Ps 22:22 – 24). Although Jesus prays in the vernacular Aramaic in Mark (*Eloi*), in Matthew the prayer is in Hebrew (*Eli*), as was customary in Jewish prayers (and the original psalm). The Hebrew *Eli* more readily explains how hearers thought he was calling for "Elijah" (*Eliyahu*; v. 47).

27:47 *He's calling Elijah.* See note on v. 46. Elijah was expected before the Lord's coming (Mal 4:5 – 6), but in rabbinic tradition he also was thought to act like an angel and help rabbis in need.

27:48 *wine vinegar.* Cheaper than normal wine and more readily assuaged thirst than water, it was widely used by the nonelite, including workers and soldiers. *staff.* Most Judean reeds would have worked for the purpose of the staff here (the term most frequently means "reed"). Cf. Ps 69:21, especially in conjunction with gall in v. 34.

27:51 *curtain ... was torn in two.* In later rabbinic tradition signs accompanied the death of the righteous. The veil torn here is probably the inner one; priests would be offering the afternoon/evening sacrifice at this time (cf. v. 46), so would be present in the sanctuary to witness the event. This act probably implies the departure of God's presence from the temple, prefiguring its destruction (cf. Eze 9:3; 10:4 – 18). Some believe that the point also includes new access to the Most Holy Place through Jesus' sacrifice — that access to God no longer required an intermediary (cf. Heb 6:19 – 20; 9:3; 10:19 – 20). *earth shook.* Most people viewed earthquakes as divine activity, often as judgment or as signs warning of it.

27:52 *many holy people ... were raised to life.* Gentiles could view apparitions of the dead as frightening portents of harm to follow. Jewish people might have viewed the resuscitation of numerous long-dead people as a miraculous prefiguring of the end-time resurrection, though this is the only occasion on which such an experience is recorded.

27:54 *Son of God.* Gentiles viewed many figures, especially heroes and the emperor, as sons of gods; recognizing Jesus as Jewish, the Gentile execution squad recognizes him as the son of the one true God of Israel.

27:55 *Many women were there.* Women providing financial patronage were not unusual, though the practice could be criticized by a movement's detractors. That the women followed Jesus, however, may have been viewed by many outsiders as scandalous (see note on Lk 8:2 – 3). Women were not usually subject to suspicion the way that men were; nevertheless, that Jesus was followed to the cross and tomb by women would be seen as a courageous contrast to the male disciples who were mostly in hiding.

27:56 The presence of at least two women named Mary here is not surprising; sources show that it was by far the most common name for Jewish women in this era.

27:58 *asked for Jesus' body.* Romans usually expected those executed for treason to be left for vultures or dogs. Given the sensitivities of all Jews, however (Dt 21:22 – 23), Pilate would probably grant them the body; it had been, after all, at the urging of the local elite that he had ordered Jesus executed. Yet even Jewish executions normally led to dishonorable burials, initially in a grave for public criminals (but allowing subsequent reinterment in a family tomb). Exceptions could be made, and family members would not be punished for requesting the body. For a member of the elite to request the body, however, was to take a large risk: unless acting specifically at the behest of the Sanhedrin, he could be associated with Jesus' alleged treason. Moreover, officials sometimes liked to pin such charges on members of the elite so that they could confiscate their property. Joseph thus acts courageously.

27:60 *new tomb.* When the condemned were buried at all, they normally received dishonorable burials (see note on v. 58), but Joseph insists on providing Jesus an honorable burial in the only family tomb quickly available — his

the rock. He rolled a big stone in front of
the entrance to the tomb and went away.
61 Mary Magdalene and the other Mary were
sitting there opposite the tomb.

The Guard at the Tomb

62 The next day, the one after Preparation Day, the chief priests and the Pharisees went to Pilate. 63 "Sir," they said, "we

own (cf. 1Ki 13:30–31; Isa 53:12). Many of the tombs in this area belonged to people of wealth; the entrance to such a tomb was often a disk-shaped rock, a yard/meter in diameter, requiring multiple people to move it. Such a stone lay in a groove but could not be moved from inside. The early Christian tradition of the site of the tomb is at least as old as the decade following Jesus' interment. Tradition is unanimous, and custom required, that Jesus be buried outside the city walls, but the site is *within* the expanded walls of Jerusalem from the time of AD 41–43; the site is therefore older than that. The tombs on this site (the Catholic site of the Holy Sepulchre) date to the period in question; by the second century, a pagan emperor sought to deliberately desecrate the site. (By contrast, the Garden Tomb favored by some Protestants is a recent historical guess, belongs to the wrong period, and lacks any claim to authenticity.)

27:62 *after Preparation Day.* The Sabbath—normally not

MATTHEW 27

The Location of Jesus' Tomb

According to the New Testament, Jesus was buried in a new tomb hewn out of rock (Mt 27:60; Mk 15:46; Lk 23:53) in a garden near the crucifixion site (Jn 19:41), just outside the city (Jn 19:20; Heb 13:12). In addition, the entrance was low and sealed with a stone (Mt 27:60; Mk 15:46; Jn 20:11), and on the right side it was possible to sit where the body of Jesus had lain (Mk 16:5; Jn 20:12). Based upon the Biblical description and upon other known first-century tombs, the tomb of Jesus can be reconstructed as having had a small forecourt, a low entry passage and a burial chamber with benches, or "couches," on three sides for the placement of the deceased.

There are two main contenders for the location of Jesus' tomb in the Old City of Jerusalem: the Garden Tomb, 275 yards (251 meters) north of the Damascus Gate, and the Church of the Holy Sepulchre in the Christian Quarter. The Garden Tomb, however, has no authentic ancient tradition associated with it. It was suggested as the site of Jesus' burial after the renowned British military hero Charles Gordon, while visiting Jerusalem in 1883, suggested that Calvary would have been located on a nearby hill. His identification was based on a fanciful interpretation of ancient Jerusalem as being in the shape of a skeleton, with the skull (i.e., Golgotha) positioned at a hill north of the Damascus Gate. This led to the identification of a tomb on the western side of the hill as Jesus' burial place, once referred to as Gordon's Tomb. Modern investigations of the Garden Tomb and others in the vicinity, however, indicate that they were part of a cemetery dating to the divided monarchy period rather than to the first century AD.

The Church of the Holy Sepulchre location, on the other hand, has a tradition going back to early Christian times. When the Roman emperor Hadrian rebuilt Jerusalem in AD 130/131, he constructed a temple to Jupiter and Venus over the site of the present Church of the Holy Sepulchre. In AD 325 Constantine ordered the removal of Hadrian's temple. Local Christian tradition had claimed this to be the site of Jesus' tomb, and, remarkably, when Hadrian's temple was cleared away, a tomb area was indeed discovered beneath it. Constantine had a church constructed on the site and built a small structure, or edicule, within the building to enclose the tomb itself. The present Church of the Holy Sepulchre is the continuation of Constantine's church.

In favor of the authenticity of this location is the fact that there was a continuous Christian presence in Jerusalem from Jesus' death until Constantine uncovered the tomb. This Christian community doubtless would have venerated the site of Jesus'

continued on next page

remember that while he was still alive
that deceiver said, 'After three days I will
rise again.'[v] 64So give the order for the
tomb to be made secure until the third
day. Otherwise, his disciples may come
and steal the body and tell the people
that he has been raised from the dead.
This last deception will be worse than the
first."

65"Take a guard,"[w] Pilate answered. "Go,
make the tomb as secure as you know
how." 66So they went and made the tomb
secure by putting a seal[x] on the stone[y] and
posting the guard.[z]

27:63 [v] Mt 16:21
27:65 [w] ver 66; Mt 28:11
27:66 [x] Da 6:17 [y] ver 60; Mt 28:2 [z] Mt 28:11

a day that the leaders should be doing business with the governor!

27:66 *putting a seal on the stone and posting the guard.* Because Pilate probably would not hand Roman soldiers over to the local elite, he may be granting them permission to station members of their own Levite guards there. Others suggest that they would not need permission to station their own guards and believe instead that Pilate granted a small detachment of his soldiers. The leaders themselves would not wish to incur uncleanness because of the corpse or remain near the tomb on the Sabbath.

burial, preserving the memory of the location of his tomb. Also, the site of the church was an old quarry during the time of Jesus, although at least part of it had been made into a garden (Jn 19:41). The fact that the site of the Church of the Holy Sepulchre had been a quarry implies that it was outside the walls of the city (it is today inside the Old City). This agrees with the fact that Jesus was crucified outside the walls. Within this area at least four tombs cut into the western rock face have been discovered, only one of which corresponds to the type in which Jesus was buried.

The church was destroyed in 614 and rebuilt in 626. The edicule was destroyed in 1009 by the Egyptian caliph al-Hakim Bi-Amr Allah. Contemporary accounts suggest that the southern wall, the burial couch and part of the northern wall survived this destruction. The rebuilt edicule has suffered damage and neglect over the centuries since that time, so that today it is a hodgepodge of reconstructions and repairs. Although absolute certainty is impossible, the evidence points to the Church of the Holy Sepulchre as being the actual site of Jesus' tomb. ◆

Church of the Holy Sepulchre, the location many modern scholars believe is built on the site of Jesus' tomb.

Jesus Has Risen

28:1-8pp — Mk 16:1-8; Lk 24:1-10; Jn 20:1-8

28 After the Sabbath, at dawn on the first day of the week, Mary Magdalene and the other Mary[a] went to look at the tomb.

2There was a violent earthquake,[b] for an angel[c] of the Lord came down from heaven and, going to the tomb, rolled back the stone and sat on it. 3His appearance was like lightning, and his clothes were white as snow.[d] 4The guards were so afraid of him that they shook and became like dead men.

5The angel said to the women, "Do not be afraid,[e] for I know that you are looking for Jesus, who was crucified. 6He is not here; he has risen, just as he said.[f] Come and see the place where he lay. 7Then go quickly and tell his disciples: 'He has risen from the dead and is going ahead of you into Galilee.[g] There you will see him.' Now I have told you."

8So the women hurried away from the tomb, afraid yet filled with joy, and ran to tell his disciples. 9Suddenly Jesus met them.[h] "Greetings," he said. They came to him, clasped his feet and worshiped him. 10Then Jesus said to them, "Do not be afraid. Go and tell my brothers[i] to go to Galilee; there they will see me."

The Guards' Report

11While the women were on their way, some of the guards[j] went into the city and reported to the chief priests everything that had happened. 12When the chief priests had met with the elders and devised a plan, they gave the soldiers a large sum of money, 13telling them, "You are to say, 'His disciples came during the night and stole him away while we were asleep.' 14If this report gets to the governor,[k] we will satisfy him and keep you out of trouble." 15So the soldiers took the money and did as they were instructed. And this story has been widely circulated among the Jews to this very day.

The Great Commission

16Then the eleven disciples went to Galilee, to the mountain where Jesus had told them to go.[l] 17When they saw him, they worshiped him; but some doubted. 18Then Jesus came to them and said, "All authority in heaven and on earth has been given to me.[m] 19Therefore go and make disciples of all nations,[n] baptizing them in the name of the Father and of the Son and of the Holy Spirit,[o] 20and teaching[p] them to obey everything I have commanded you. And surely I am with you[q] always, to the very end of the age."[r]

28:1 [a] Mt 27:56
28:2 [b] Mt 27:51 [c] Jn 20:12
28:3 [d] Da 10:6; Mk 9:3; Jn 20:12
28:5 [e] ver 10; Mt 14:27
28:6 [f] Mt 16:21
28:7 [g] ver 10, 16; Mt 26:32
28:9 [h] Jn 20:14-18
28:10 [i] Jn 20:17; Ro 8:29; Heb 2:11-13, 17
28:11 [j] Mt 27:65, 66
28:14 [k] Mt 27:2
28:16 [l] ver 7, 10; Mt 26:32
28:18 [m] Da 7:13, 14; Lk 10:22; Jn 3:35; 17:2; 1Co 15:27; Eph 1:20-22; Php 2:9, 10
28:19 [n] Mk 16:15, 16; Lk 24:47; Ac 1:8; 14:21 [o] Ac 2:38; 8:16; Ro 6:3, 4
28:20 [p] Ac 2:42 [q] Mt 18:20; Ac 18:10 [r] Mt 13:39

28:1 The resurrection narratives vary in length in the different Gospels; ancient writers liked to make optimal use of the entire length of their scroll, and sometimes simply ran out of room to include more detail. *at dawn.* The Sabbath technically ends at sundown on what we call Saturday night, but the women would not easily and safely find the tomb before first light.
28:2 *earthquake.* See note on 27:51. *rolled back the stone.* See note on 27:60. Humans could not easily sit on such a disk-shaped stone.
28:3 *like lightning.* Glorious angels appear in both Scripture (e.g., Da 10:5 – 6) and Jewish tradition.
28:4 *became like dead men.* A dramatic experience of the supernatural could sometimes cause one to collapse without strength (Da 10:8 – 9).
28:7 *tell his disciples.* Both Jewish and Roman law normally regarded a woman's testimony as of limited value, treating women as unstable (see, e.g., Justinian, *Institutes* 2.10.6; Josephus, *Antiquities* 4.219; in the Mishnah see *Yebamot* 15:1, 8 – 10; 16:7; *ketubbot* 1:6 – 9; in the Tosefta see *Yebamot* 14:10). It is to the women, however, that God's agents first entrust the testimony of Jesus' resurrection.
28:12 – 15 *we will satisfy him.* Bribery was illegal but extremely common; the first-century Jewish historian Josephus reports its practice both by Roman governors in Judea and the high priests.
28:13 *stole him away.* There is no reason for Matthew to mention as widely circulated a charge that was not widely circulated, yet the guards' report is not very plausible. Tomb robbers were not common in Judea, but when they did strike they looted goods, not bodies. Guards would not sleep through the commotion of someone rolling away the stone, and guards who did sleep on duty faced severe penalties — in a case such as this one, potentially death. Their implausible falsehood contrasts with the report of the women commissioned in vv. 7, 10.
28:18 *All authority.* Jesus' universal authority (going beyond the earthly authority noted in 9:6) may evoke Da 7:13 – 14; cf. Isa 9:6 – 7. His role exceeds that of any human figure in Jewish sources, including David and his royal line.
28:19 *make disciples.* Jewish teachers lectured groups of Jewish disciples, but Jesus here commissions his followers to convert and train disciples from all peoples, climaxing a theme that runs through Matthew's Gospel (see 1:3 – 6; 2:1 – 2; 4:15; 8:5 – 13; 10:15; 11:21 – 23; 12:41 – 42; 15:22 – 28; 24:14; 27:54). Although many Jewish people welcomed Gentile converts, they lacked an overt program of missionizing them, such as we find here. *baptizing them.* Jewish people used baptism when converting Gentiles, so it provided an easily understood form for expressing conversion. *name of the Father and of the Son and of the Holy Spirit.* Jewish people considered the Holy Spirit to be God's Spirit, thus divine (though not normally personal, as here); they regularly called God "Father" in many prayers; for Jesus to be listed here between the Father and the divine Spirit implies Jesus' deity.
28:20 *teaching them to obey everything.* Discipleship (v. 19) always included teaching. *with you always.* Jewish people considered only God omnipresent; Jesus thus appears here as divine (see 1:23; 18:20).

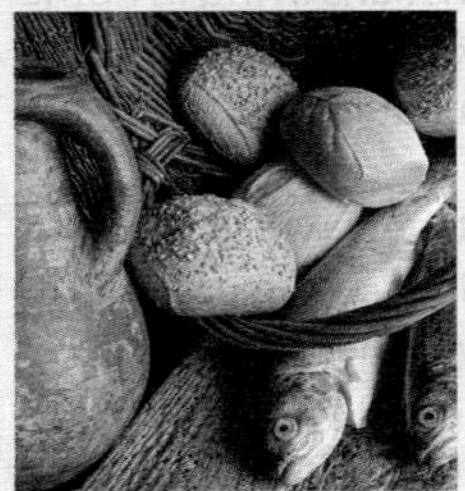

THE GOSPEL OF MARK

Background

Mark is almost exactly half the length of Matthew and Luke, suggesting standardized scroll lengths. Given the cost of ancient scrolls, Mark would have been the most affordable of the Gospels, and must have circulated widely in the first century. Matthew and Luke both considered Mark sufficiently reliable to draw heavily on this Gospel. By the second century, however, church fathers were more interested in completeness and focused more heavily on Matthew, which incorporated a majority of Mark's material.

QUICK GLANCE

AUTHOR:
John Mark

AUDIENCE:
Mostly Gentile Christians, probably in the church at Rome

DATE:
Between the mid-50s and late 60s AD

THEME:
To encourage his readers to persevere through suffering and persecution, Mark presents Jesus as the Servant-Messiah and Son of God who died as a ransom for sinners.

Authorship

That Mark wrote this Gospel represents the earliest and undisputed tradition of the church, reaching back to the early church father Papias (and thus within several decades of this Gospel's publication). This early tradition reports that Mark derived his information directly from Peter, a close eyewitness of most of the events narrated in the Gospel. Mark apparently knows Aramaic, and its influence shows up in his Greek (or in the Greek of the milieu where he grew up). Mark was a common Roman name, but in Aramaic-speaking areas of Judea it would have occurred especially among elite families. Thus the author of this Gospel could be the cousin of Barnabas who worked with Paul (Ac 12:12,25; 13:5,13; 15:37,39), including later in Rome (Col 4:10). This is probably the same Mark who also worked with Peter in Rome (1Pe 5:13), independently supporting Papias's belief about authorship.

Date

Any proposed date is based on somewhat slender evidence, though very few scholars date Mark later than AD 75, and the majority date it around 70 or as early as 64. A few have dated it even earlier, to the reign of Caligula in the 40s, though one wonders if Mark would have taken notes from Peter so early, especially if he is the same Mark who abandoned Paul in that decade (Ac 13:13). Because it encourages disciples to stand in the face of persecution, many suggest that the Gospel was written especially to encourage Christians living in Rome under Nero's persecution, which began in 64, probably the most common date offered by conservative scholars. Early Christian tradition declares that both Paul and Peter were martyred during that period of persecution in Rome.

Mark is likely the earliest of our four Gospels. Papias says that Matthew wrote first, but also says that Mark depended on Peter; some scholars think that Matthew's earlier writing refers only to a collection of Jesus' sayings compiled by Matthew rather than the later Gospel of Matthew. Because roughly 90 percent of Mark's accounts appear in some form in Matthew's Gospel, and because Mark's grammar is weaker, it seems much more likely that Matthew's Gospel drew on Mark, rather than the reverse. (The Biblical quotations in Matthew also reflect a mixture of the standard Greek translation and a different way of translating the Hebrew; by contrast, where Matthew overlaps with Mark, his quotations follow only the standard Greek translation, as Mark's quotations do.) Mark must be early enough for it to have become the standard account, despite its grammatical weaknesses; Matthew and Luke both draw on it heavily. Because there is some reason to believe that Luke writes in the 70s, a date for Mark around 64 is a reasonable proposal.

Reliability

See the Introduction to the Gospels, p. 1598. If Mark draws on the recollections of Peter, as the earliest and only tradition suggests, he had access to firsthand information. There is nothing in this Gospel that could not at least potentially come from an eyewitness, and as many scholars have persuasively argued (e.g., Richard Bauckham), the firsthand memories of Jesus' disciples undoubtedly circulated for many decades after Jesus' resurrection. Matthew and Luke, who probably wrote within two decades of Mark, had far better access to Mark's identity and sources than modern scholars do. The dependence of Matthew and Luke on Mark (according to the most common scholarly view) shows two things: first, that like good biographers they followed their sources rather than made them up; and second, they considered Mark a particularly trustworthy source. This would be especially true if, like Papias, they believed that Peter's authority stood behind it.

Messianic Secret

One theme in Mark often emphasized by modern scholars, yet already noted in the church fathers, is what scholars usually call the Messianic secret. Jesus conceals his Messiahship from the public until the conclusion of his ministry and even urges many of those healed in private to keep the healing secret (though this attempt often proves unsuccessful). A key reason for silence about the healings is that Jesus was drawing ever-increasing crowds, creating conditions difficult for personal ministry (1:45; 2:2; 3:9 – 10,20). The presence of such crowds would also draw unwelcome attention from the political elites, and premature revelation of his Messiahship would precipitate his premature execution as king of the Jews. Moreover, Jesus' Messianic title and purpose, clearly misunderstood by his own disciples, would certainly be misunderstood by the crowds. Scholars have offered some possible subsidiary motives: (1) some argue that potential Messiahs received the title only once enthroned; (2) people in antiquity viewed premature boasting negatively; (3) Biblical prophets sometimes faded into the background so their divine message could be highlighted.

Yet Jesus clearly remains the hero of Mark's Gospel; even the disciples often misunderstand him, but God's purposes are fulfilled exactly as promised. The opening proclamation of the kingdom climaxes in Jesus' crucifixion as king of the Jews, with Mark only afterward pointing his audience to the resurrection that lies beyond it. This pattern fits the hiddenness of Jesus' Messiahship. Mark knows that the kingdom will come in its fullness but recognizes that in the present it is visible only to some (4:11 – 12,30 – 32; cf. 2Co 2:15 – 16). Jesus focuses on the sick, the poor, the morally and socially marginalized, and others, rather than cultivating the favor of the powerful. Yet in the words of Paul, God reveals his power in weakness; indeed, ultimately in the epitome of human weakness: in the cross (1Co 1:18 – 25). ◆

John the Baptist Prepares the Way

1:2-8pp — Mt 3:1-11; Lk 3:2-16

1 The beginning of the good news about
Jesus the Messiah,[a] the Son of God,[b][a]
2 as it is written in Isaiah the prophet:

"I will send my messenger ahead of you,
who will prepare your way"[c][b] —
3 "a voice of one calling in the
wilderness,
'Prepare the way for the Lord,
make straight paths for him.' "[d][c]

4 And so John the Baptist[d] appeared in the
wilderness, preaching a baptism of repentance[e] for the forgiveness of sins.[f] 5 The
whole Judean countryside and all the people of Jerusalem went out to him. Confessing their sins, they were baptized by him
in the Jordan River. 6 John wore clothing
made of camel's hair, with a leather belt
around his waist, and he ate locusts[g] and
wild honey. 7 And this was his message:
"After me comes the one more powerful
than I, the straps of whose sandals I am
not worthy to stoop down and untie.[h] 8 I
baptize you with[e] water, but he will baptize you with[e] the Holy Spirit."[i]

The Baptism and Testing of Jesus

1:9-11pp — Mt 3:13-17; Lk 3:21,22
1:12,13pp — Mt 4:1-11; Lk 4:1-13

9 At that time Jesus came from Nazareth[j]
in Galilee and was baptized by John in the
Jordan. 10 Just as Jesus was coming up out
of the water, he saw heaven being torn
open and the Spirit descending on him like
a dove.[k] 11 And a voice came from heaven:
"You are my Son,[l] whom I love; with you
I am well pleased."
12 At once the Spirit sent him out into the
wilderness, 13 and he was in the wilderness

1:1 [a] Mt 4:3
1:2 [b] Mal 3:1; Mt 11:10; Lk 7:27
1:3 [c] Isa 40:3; Jn 1:23
1:4 [d] Mt 3:1 [e] Ac 13:24 [f] Lk 1:77
1:6 [g] Lev 11:22
1:7 [h] Ac 13:25
1:8 [i] Isa 44:3; Joel 2:28; Ac 1:5; 2:4; 11:16; 19:4-6
1:9 [j] Mt 2:23
1:10 [k] Jn 1:32
1:11 [l] Mt 3:17

[a] *1* Or *Jesus Christ. Messiah* (Hebrew) and *Christ* (Greek) both mean *Anointed One.* [b] *1* Some manuscripts do not have *the Son of God.* [c] *2* Mal. 3:1 [d] *3* Isaiah 40:3 [e] *8* Or *in*

1:1 *good news about Jesus the Messiah.* Especially in the context of Isaiah's message of Israel's restoration (Isa 40:3), quoted in v. 3, "good news" evokes the promised restoration (Isa 40:9; 61:1). This was good news of peace for God's people, good news of the kingdom (i.e., good news that he reigns, hence would restore his people; Isa 52:7). Thus Jesus announces good news that the time for this kingdom has drawn near (vv. 14–15).
1:2–3 In both of these Biblical quotations, one prepares the way for God himself. Although Mark quotes both Malachi (Mal 3:1 in v. 2) and Isaiah (Isa 40:3 in v. 3), he gives the name only of the more prominent prophet. He may wish to draw attention to Isaiah partly because of the connection he intends with Isaiah's context (see note on v. 1). Ancient interpreters often treated Scripture as a seamless whole and often linked texts based on a common key word, phrase, or concept (here, "prepare the way"). Malachi referred to one who would come like Elijah (Mal 4:5–6); Mark recognizes that this applies to John the Baptist (cf. v. 6; 9:11–13). The quoted verse from Isaiah also speaks of one preparing the way, and the way in the wilderness described the promised new exodus, a new era of salvation and restoration for God's people (Isa 11:16; 19:23–25; 43:16–21; 51:10–11; cf. Isa 49:8–12; 57:14). The tradition is undoubtedly Judean and thus very early, long before John's ministry in the wilderness; the Qumran community, in the desert southeast of Jerusalem, also applied Isa 40:3 to their own mission.
1:4 *wilderness.* The wilderness was a place of hardship, but it was the safest place to draw crowds. In the context of v. 3, it evokes the promised new exodus of salvation (cf. Isa 40:3; Hos 2:14). No one outside of Judea would have known to speak of someone baptizing in the Jordan (v. 5) as being in the wilderness, but the fertile area around the Jordan quickly gave way to wilderness beyond it. *baptism.* Jewish people had various ritual immersions; one, the immersion of Gentiles converting to Judaism, involved a wholesale turning to a new way of life. See the article "Baptism," p. 1686. *repentance.* Jewish people valued repentance; John here may evoke the prophets' calls to Israel to "turn" back to God (e.g., Isa 44:22; Jer 3:12,14,22; Hos 12:6; 14:1–2; Joel 2:12–13; Zec 1:3–4; Mal 3:7). *forgiveness of sins.* One of God's promises for the restoration time (Isa 43:25; 44:22; 53:5,11–12).
1:5 *Jordan River.* Because crossing the Jordan signaled entering the promised land in Jos 1:11, here it might evoke the promise of restoration. More certainly, it was the one large body of water suitable for John's mission.
1:6 *clothing made of camel's hair … a leather belt.* John's leather girdle recalls Elijah (2Ki 1:8), fitting Mark's Biblical introduction of John in v. 2. Like his location, his clothing and diet suggest a rugged lifestyle. A garment of camel's hair was a garment of sackcloth, indicating mourning, likely over the nation's sin. *locusts.* Some Jewish people ate locusts (which were kosher), but only someone who lived completely in the wilderness might be limited to such a diet. *wild honey.* Obtained after smoking wild bees from their hive.
1:7 *sandals I am not worthy to … untie.* Assisting others with their sandals was normally the sort of task that only a low-level servant would normally perform; the prophets were "servants of God" (2Ki 9:7; Jer 7:25; 26:5–6; 29:19; 35:15; 44:4), and Jesus considered John the greatest prophet (Mt 11:11) but John considers himself unworthy even for this role. The one whose way he prepares is thus none other than God himself (cf. vv. 2–3).
1:8 *baptize you with the Holy Spirit.* One promise for the time of restoration (cf. vv. 2–3) was the pouring out of God's Spirit (Isa 32:15; 44:3; Eze 39:29; Joel 2:28–29); only God himself could pour out God's Spirit (cf. v. 7).
1:9 *from Nazareth in Galilee.* Outside of their own communities, people were often named for the community they came from. By some modern estimates, Nazareth, like many Galilean villages, had only some 500 residents (although sparser habitation away from the village's center may not be counted). *baptized by John.* Being baptized "by" someone presumably meant under their supervision; given what are thought usual practices at the time, Jesus may have bent himself forward.
1:10 *heaven being torn open.* The heavens could be opened for revelations (Eze 1:1). *Spirit descending.* The Spirit's coming begins the promise of v. 8. *like a dove.* See note on Mt 3:16.
1:11 *voice came from heaven.* A heavenly voice at Isaac's sacrifice spared Isaac, Abraham's beloved son (Ge 22:2,12, especially v. 12 in the Septuagint, the pre-Christian Greek translation of the OT); God also named David's dynasty as his son (Ps 2:7). Later rabbis subordinated the value of heavenly voices to prophets in Scripture, but here the heavenly voice confirms the prophetic one (v. 3).
1:13 *forty days.* As Israel faced testing for 40 years in the wilderness, they would also pass through the wilderness

forty days, being tempted[a] by Satan.[m] He was with the wild animals, and angels attended him.

Jesus Announces the Good News

1:16-20pp — Mt 4:18-22; Lk 5:2-11; Jn 1:35-42

14 After John was put in prison, Jesus went into Galilee,[n] proclaiming the good news of God.[o] 15 "The time has come,"[p] he said. "The kingdom of God has come near. Repent and believe the good news!"[q]

Jesus Calls His First Disciples

16 As Jesus walked beside the Sea of Galilee, he saw Simon and his brother Andrew casting a net into the lake, for they were fishermen. 17 "Come, follow me," Jesus said, "and I will send you out to fish for people." 18 At once they left their nets and followed him.

19 When he had gone a little farther, he saw James son of Zebedee and his brother John in a boat, preparing their nets. 20 Without delay he called them, and they left their father Zebedee in the boat with the hired men and followed him.

Jesus Drives Out an Impure Spirit

1:21-28pp — Lk 4:31-37

21 They went to Capernaum, and when the Sabbath came, Jesus went into the synagogue and began to teach.[r] 22 The people were amazed at his teaching, because he taught them as one who had authority, not as the teachers of the law.[s] 23 Just then a man in their synagogue who was possessed by an impure spirit cried out, 24 "What do you want with us,[t] Jesus of Nazareth?[u] Have you come to destroy us? I know who you are — the Holy One of God!"[v]

25 "Be quiet!" said Jesus sternly. "Come out of him!"[w] 26 The impure spirit shook the man violently and came out of him with a shriek.[x]

27 The people were all so amazed[y] that they asked each other, "What is this? A new teaching — and with authority! He even gives orders to impure spirits and they obey him." 28 News about him spread quickly over the whole region[z] of Galilee.

Jesus Heals Many

1:29-31pp — Mt 8:14,15; Lk 4:38,39
1:32-34pp — Mt 8:16,17; Lk 4:40,41

29 As soon as they left the synagogue,[a] they went with James and John to the home of Simon and Andrew. 30 Simon's mother-in-law was in bed with a fever,

[a] *13* The Greek for *tempted* can also mean *tested.*

1:13 [m] Mt 4:10
1:14 [n] Mt 4:12
[o] Mt 4:23
1:15 [p] Gal 4:4; Eph 1:10
[q] Ac 20:21
1:21 [r] Mt 4:23; Mk 10:1
1:22 [s] Mt 7:28, 29
1:24 [t] Mt 8:29
[u] Mt 2:23; Lk 24:19; Ac 24:5
[v] Lk 1:35; Jn 6:69; Ac 3:14
1:25 [w] ver 34
1:26 [x] Mk 9:20
1:27
[y] Mk 10:24,32
1:28 [z] Mt 9:26
1:29 [a] ver 21,23

during the promised new exodus (see vv. 2–3). Here Jesus endures the testing 40 days before beginning the promised restoration. *wild animals.* Cf. protection from animals in Eze 34:25; Da 6:22.

1:14 *prison.* For John's imprisonment, see 6:17. *good news.* See note on v. 1.

1:15 *time has come ... kingdom of God has come near.* Although similar language applied to other foreordained events (e.g., Eze 7:7), in context the "time" here refers to the time of God's promised reign (e.g., Isa 52:7; cf. 49:8); "kingdom" means "reign." To be ready for that time, people needed to "repent," i.e., turn (see note on v. 4). *good news.* See also v. 14. See note on v. 1; Isa 52:7, which speaks of both "good news" and God's reign, may be especially in view here. Sometimes a theme would bracket a section, and *good news* may bracket Mark's introduction.

1:16 *Sea of Galilee.* Only local people called this lake a "sea" (as the Gospels usually call it in Greek); the usual usage in the Gospels reflects the memories of Jesus' early Galilean disciples. Fishing was a major occupation on the Sea of Galilee. Many believe that commercial fishermen, although not elite, were usually better off economically than the peasants who comprised the majority of Galileans.

1:17 *Come, follow me.* Only the most radical teachers called disciples, rather than waiting for disciples to choose them (e.g., 1Ki 19:19). *follow.* Lit. to "come after" a teacher was to take the posture of a disciple.

1:19 *preparing their nets.* Nets needed care and even periodic repair; winter was harder on them than summer.

1:20 *hired men.* A family business that employed hired servants had ample income. *followed him.* To abandon a family business, which the sons would normally expect to inherit, had dramatic implications for the family as a whole.

1:21 *Capernaum.* A fishing town; some estimate its population at about 1,500, perhaps three times that of Nazareth. *synagogue.* Archaeologists have found some of this synagogue beneath a later one constructed on the same site. Jewish people gathered in synagogues on the Sabbath to pray and study Scripture.

1:22 *teachers of the law.* These men often cited the opinions of earlier teachers.

1:23 *possessed by an impure spirit.* Although rarely, some early Jewish sources explicitly associated evil spirits with impurity.

1:24 *What do you want with us ...?* Lit. "What (is there between) us and you?" (cf. 5:7) — a phrase that emphasizes distance and often hostility between the speaker and the one addressed (Jdg 11:12; 1Ki 17:18; 2Ki 3:13; 2Ch 35:21 in the Septuagint, the pre-Christian Greek translation of the OT). *I know who you are.* In some magical texts, those trying to control spirits declare, "I know you" or "I know your name." Here the spirit might try to use such knowledge to ward off Jesus — clearly unsuccessfully.

1:26 *with a shriek.* People often expected spirits to display their departure dramatically. People often tried to expel demons through incantations or strong odors; Jesus' ability to expel demons simply by commanding them was extraordinary and invited amazement.

1:28 *spread quickly.* Villages were often close together and rumors spread rapidly.

1:29 *home of Simon and Andrew.* Some homes in Capernaum were free standing, but many were built around courtyards shared with other homes. Sometimes extended family stayed in a home together (note here Simon's brother Andrew is mentioned as an owner of the house). Newly married couples sometimes had a room on the roof of the groom's parents; because many men died in their 50s, families might also need to take in a widowed mother (v. 30).

1:30 *fever.* Fevers were common; one of the most

and they immediately told Jesus about
her. [31]So he went to her, took her hand
and helped her up.[b] The fever left her and
she began to wait on them.
[32]That evening after sunset the people
brought to Jesus all the sick and demon-
possessed.[c] [33]The whole town gathered at
the door, [34]and Jesus healed many who
had various diseases.[d] He also drove out
many demons, but he would not let the
demons speak because they knew who he
was.[e]

Jesus Prays in a Solitary Place

1:35-38pp — Lk 4:42,43

[35]Very early in the morning, while it
was still dark, Jesus got up, left the house
and went off to a solitary place, where

1:31 [b] Lk 7:14 **1:32** [c] Mt 4:24 **1:34** [d] Mt 4:23 [e] Mk 3:12; Ac 16:17, 18

common causes of fevers in the ancient Mediterranean world was malaria, which could be serious and did not normally disappear suddenly.
1:32 *after sunset.* Because one should not carry loads on the Sabbath, which it is (v. 21), people wait until sundown (Jewish people reckoned days from sundown to sundown) to bring the afflicted to Jesus. *sick and demon-possessed.* The promised restoration (see note on vv. 2–3) included healing (Isa 35:5–6). Mark's series of miracle stories could remind ancient hearers of the series of miracle accounts surrounding Elijah and Elisha (especially 1Ki 17–19; 2Ki 1–8).
1:33 *whole town.* Ancient writers often used hyperbole; some estimate Capernaum's population at roughly 1,500. *at the door.* Homes were often small, though Peter's may have been larger (fishermen could earn ample incomes).
1:35 *house.* Many people could be staying in a home at one time (see note on v. 29). *solitary place.* Most homes

MARK 1:4

Baptism

From the OT to Greek, Hittite and Egyptian temples, ritual purity and purification were important in the ancient world. Jewish people observed various ceremonial washings, and some groups, such as the Essenes, took these practices to an extreme. Some thinkers related physical purifications to spiritual or intellectual ones. Writing for a largely Gentile audience, Josephus noted that John the Baptist required inward purification by righteousness (what the Gospel writers call repentance) before the outward purification he administered (*Antiquities* 18.117).

Many Jewish people were also familiar with a sort of baptism associated with conversion, a once-for-all kind of turning. Although some have questioned whether Jewish people practiced conversion-baptism this early, it appears in various sources. Even the late first- to early second-century Stoic philosopher Epictetus mentions it (*Diatribai* 2.9.20). Later rabbis would not have borrowed the practice from Christians, and it is difficult to imagine conversion to Judaism being accepted without purification. If John the Baptist and Jesus' early followers drew on this background, they were requiring even their fellow Jews to come to God on the same terms as Gentiles. That is, everyone needed a mark of conversion, regardless of ethnic or religious background.

Granted, those joining the Essene sect were also baptized during their initiation, and this immersion also offers an analogy. But this baptism did not have the same force as that of John's baptism or that of Jesus' disciples. For the Essenes, it was simply the first of many purification rituals, and only a small component of the process of joining the sect. For John and Jesus' movement, a single, emphatic baptism itself represented a transition to the new life.

That both John and Jesus' followers baptized is significant. Because Jesus is the main connection between John the Baptist and Jesus' movement, it is hard to doubt that Jesus urged his followers to baptize (cf. Mt 28:19; Jn 4:1–2), following the model of John's baptism (cf. Ac 1:5,22). That is, it is no coincidence that both John's and Jesus' followers practiced baptism.

Jewish initiatory baptisms involved immersion; later rabbis in fact required full-body immersions to be performed naked, to guarantee that the entire body was

continued on next page

he prayed.[f] [36]Simon and his companions
went to look for him, [37]and when they
found him, they exclaimed: "Everyone is
looking for you!"
[38]Jesus replied, "Let us go somewhere
else — to the nearby villages — so I can
preach there also. That is why I have
come."[g] [39]So he traveled throughout Galilee, preaching in their synagogues[h] and
driving out demons.[i]

1:35 [f] Lk 3:21
1:38 [g] Isa 61:1
1:39 [h] Mt 4:23
[i] Mt 4:24
1:40 [j] Mk 10:17

Jesus Heals a Man With Leprosy

1:40-44pp — Mt 8:2-4; Lk 5:12-14

[40]A man with leprosy[a] came to him and
begged him on his knees,[j] "If you are willing, you can make me clean."
[41]Jesus was indignant.[b] He reached out
his hand and touched the man. "I am

[a] *40* The Greek word traditionally translated *leprosy* was used for various diseases affecting the skin.
[b] *41* Many manuscripts *Jesus was filled with compassion*

were tightly packed together; and villages along the Sea of Galilee were often close together. Finding privacy (cf. Mt 6:6), with so many people desiring attention (v. 33), required rising before others did (in that culture, normally at sunrise, which at various times of year averaged about 5:30 – 6:30 a.m.).

1:40 *leprosy.* The category of what was called leprosy in the ancient world included severe skin conditions that typically led to isolation from society (in most societies; for Jewish society, see Lev 13:1 — 14:32). Out of respect, as elsewhere in Scripture (Ge 18:27,30 – 32; cf. 2Sa 10:12; Da 3:18), this man recognized Jesus' prerogative to choose, even while pleading for him to act.

1:41 *touched the man.* Because lepers were unclean (Lev 13:45 – 46), anyone who touched them contracted temporary ritual impurity. Jesus here touches someone

covered. Nevertheless, at an early stage Christians began making other arrangements where conditions were less than ideal (*Didache* 7.1 – 3).

Water was often associated with the Spirit (e.g., Isa 44:3; Eze 36:25 – 27; Joel 2:28 – 29), allowing for a ready analogy with baptism. Because Jewish baptism of Gentiles signified these Gentiles' conversions, some associate being "baptized" in the Spirit with conversion. But because Jewish baptism also normally involved immersion, some associate being "baptized" in the Spirit with a fuller experience beyond conversion. Still others allow the phrase to focus on different nuances in different passages. ◆

Jesus was baptized by John the Baptist in the Jordan River (Mk 1:9).

willing," he said. "Be clean!" 42Immediately the leprosy left him and he was cleansed.

43Jesus sent him away at once with a strong warning: 44"See that you don't tell this to anyone.[k] But go, show yourself to the priest[l] and offer the sacrifices that Moses commanded for your cleansing,[m] as a testimony to them." 45Instead he went out and began to talk freely, spreading the news. As a result, Jesus could no longer enter a town openly but stayed outside in lonely places.[n] Yet the people still came to him from everywhere.[o]

Jesus Forgives and Heals a Paralyzed Man

2:3-12pp — Mt 9:2-8; Lk 5:18-26

2 A few days later, when Jesus again entered Capernaum, the people heard that he had come home. 2They gathered in such large numbers[p] that there was no room left, not even outside the door, and he preached the word to them. 3Some men came, bringing to him a paralyzed man,[q] carried by four of them. 4Since they could not get him to Jesus because of the crowd, they made an opening in the roof above Jesus by digging through it and then lowered the mat the man was lying on. 5When Jesus saw their faith, he said to the paralyzed man, "Son, your sins are forgiven."[r]

6Now some teachers of the law were sitting there, thinking to themselves, 7"Why does this fellow talk like that? He's blaspheming! Who can forgive sins but God alone?"[s]

8Immediately Jesus knew in his spirit that this was what they were thinking in their hearts, and he said to them, "Why are you thinking these things? 9Which is easier: to say to this paralyzed man, 'Your sins are forgiven,' or to say, 'Get up, take your mat and walk'? 10But I want you to know that the Son of Man[t] has authority on earth to forgive sins." So he said to the man, 11"I tell you, get up, take your mat and go home." 12He got up, took his mat and walked out in full view of them all. This amazed everyone and they praised God,[u] saying, "We have never seen anything like this!"[v]

Jesus Calls Levi and Eats With Sinners

2:14-17pp — Mt 9:9-13; Lk 5:27-32

13Once again Jesus went out beside the lake. A large crowd came to him,[w] and he began to teach them. 14As he walked along, he saw Levi son of Alphaeus sitting at the tax collector's booth. "Follow me,"[x] Jesus told him, and Levi got up and followed him.

15While Jesus was having dinner at Levi's house, many tax collectors and sinners were eating with him and his disciples, for there were many who followed him. 16When the teachers of the law who were Pharisees[y] saw him eating with the sinners and tax collectors, they asked his disciples: "Why does he eat with tax collectors and sinners?"[z]

1:44 [k]Mt 8:4 [l]Lev 13:49 [m]Lev 14:1-32 **1:45** [n]Lk 5:15, 16 [o]Mk 2:13; Lk 5:17; Jn 6:2 **2:2** [p]ver 13; Mk 1:45 **2:3** [q]Mt 4:24 **2:5** [r]Lk 7:48 **2:7** [s]Isa 43:25 **2:10** [t]Mt 8:20 **2:12** [u]Mt 9:8 [v]Mt 9:33 **2:13** [w]Mk 1:45; Lk 5:15; Jn 6:2 **2:14** [x]Mt 4:19 **2:16** [y]Ac 23:9 [z]Mt 9:11

unclean (cf. Mk 5:31,41) to cure him. For one Biblical precedent for healing a leper (in that case without touching him), see 2Ki 5:10 – 14.

1:44 *don't tell this to anyone.* Although men of influence often competed for honor, ancients respected people who did not seek their own honor; moreover, Jesus has already been having trouble with crowds (v. 33). *show … the priest.* See note on Mt 8:4

1:45 Where valuable medical resources are lacking, people flock to what they believe might cure them; in antiquity, e.g., including in Galilee, people flocked to hot springs hoping to be cured. News of the miraculous healings naturally prompted many to seek similar healing.

2:2 *no room left.* Most homes in Capernaum were small (see note on 1:29).

2:4 *opening in the roof.* Logs used as roof beams supported most Galilean roofs; reeds or branches were laid across these logs, then the whole was overlaid with packed mud or clay (contrast Lk 5:19). Such roofs were stable enough for walking, but one could break through them by digging. A staircase or in some cases a ladder led to the roof.

2:7 *He's blaspheming!* Although priests might pronounce God's forgiveness, only God could forgive sins (Mic 7:18). Later rabbis defined blaspheming more narrowly (cursing with the divine name, as in Lev 24:11), but the term used here can mean any demeaning speech, including speech dishonoring God.

2:8 *Jesus knew … what they were thinking.* God sometimes revealed secrets about others to prophets (e.g., 2Ki 5:26; 6:12).

2:10 *Son of Man has authority.* Echoes Da 7:13 – 14, hinting at Jesus' special identity.

2:14 *tax collector's booth.* Most people in the Roman Empire did not like tax collectors; Jewish people viewed them as traitors. For assessment purposes, tax collectors were allowed to search anything except the person of a Roman lady; any property not properly declared was subject to seizure. In Egypt, tax collectors were sometimes so brutal that they were known to beat up aged women in an attempt to learn where their tax-owing relatives were hiding. Ancient documents reveal that when harvests were bad, on occasion an entire village, hearing that a tax collector was coming, would leave town and start a village somewhere else. People sometimes paid tax collectors bribes to prevent even higher fees being extorted. Some scholars consider Levi a customs officer who would charge tariffs on goods passing through Capernaum. Such tariffs were small by themselves (often less than 3 percent) but drove up the cost of goods because they were multiplied by all the borders they passed through. Customs officers could search possessions; customs income normally went to local governments run by elites who were cooperative with Rome. Others regard Levi as collecting taxes from local residents, likely working especially for agents of Galilee's ruler, Herod Antipas.

2:16 *teachers of the law who were Pharisees.* Because Pharisees were known to be meticulous in interpreting the law, it was natural that some teachers of the law were Pharisees. Later rabbis sometimes contrasted Pharisees, as the godliest Judeans one would normally meet, with

17On hearing this, Jesus said to them, "It
is not the healthy who need a doctor, but
the sick. I have not come to call the righteous, but sinners."[a]

Jesus Questioned About Fasting

2:18-22pp — Mt 9:14-17; Lk 5:33-38

18Now John's disciples and the Pharisees were fasting.[b] Some people came and
asked Jesus, "How is it that John's disciples and the disciples of the Pharisees are
fasting, but yours are not?"
19Jesus answered, "How can the guests
of the bridegroom fast while he is with
them? They cannot, so long as they have
him with them. 20But the time will come
when the bridegroom will be taken from
them,[c] and on that day they will fast.
21"No one sews a patch of unshrunk
cloth on an old garment. Otherwise, the
new piece will pull away from the old,
making the tear worse. 22And no one pours
new wine into old wineskins. Otherwise,
the wine will burst the skins, and both the
wine and the wineskins will be ruined. No,
they pour new wine into new wineskins."

Jesus Is Lord of the Sabbath

2:23-28pp — Mt 12:1-8; Lk 6:1-5
3:1-6pp — Mt 12:9-14; Lk 6:6-11

23One Sabbath Jesus was going through
the grainfields, and as his disciples walked
along, they began to pick some heads of
grain.[d] 24The Pharisees said to him, "Look,
why are they doing what is unlawful on
the Sabbath?"[e]
25He answered, "Have you never read
what David did when he and his companions were hungry and in need? 26In the
days of Abiathar the high priest,[f] he entered the house of God and ate the consecrated bread, which is lawful only for
priests to eat.[g] And he also gave some to
his companions."[h]
27Then he said to them, "The Sabbath
was made for man,[i] not man for the Sabbath.[j] 28So the Son of Man[k] is Lord even of
the Sabbath."

Jesus Heals on the Sabbath

3 Another time Jesus went into the synagogue,[l] and a man with a shriveled
hand was there. 2Some of them were looking for a reason to accuse Jesus, so they
watched him closely[m] to see if he would
heal him on the Sabbath.[n] 3Jesus said to
the man with the shriveled hand, "Stand
up in front of everyone."
4Then Jesus asked them, "Which is lawful on the Sabbath: to do good or to do
evil, to save life or to kill?" But they remained silent.
5He looked around at them in anger
and, deeply distressed at their stubborn
hearts, said to the man, "Stretch out your

2:17 [a] Lk 19:10; 1Ti 1:15
2:18 [b] Mt 6:16-18; Ac 13:2
2:20 [c] Lk 17:22
2:23 [d] Dt 23:25
2:24 [e] Mt 12:2
2:26 [f] 1Ch 24:6; 2Sa 8:17 [g] Lev 24:5-9 [h] 1Sa 21:1-6
2:27 [i] Ex 23:12; Dt 5:14 [j] Col 2:16
2:28 [k] Mt 8:20
3:1 [l] Mt 4:23; Mk 1:21
3:2 [m] Mt 12:10 [n] Lk 14:1

---

tax collectors, as the most ungodly one would normally meet. *eat with tax collectors.* Pharisees were careful about eating habits (e.g., all food must first be tithed) and valued religiously edifying conversation. More generally, people viewed table fellowship as establishing a covenant of friendship (indeed, in one ancient story, two warriors stopped fighting each other when they discovered that their fathers had shared a meal!). By eating with sinners Jesus thus appears to endorse them. Scripture warned against spending time with the ungodly lest one be influenced by them (Ps 1:1; 119:63; Pr 13:20; 14:7; 28:7), but Jesus is influencing them rather than the reverse.

2:17 *healthy ... sick.* See note on Mt 9:12.

2:18 People in antiquity often held teachers responsible for the behavior of their disciples. *fasting.* Jewish tradition had added various fasts to Scripture, and fasting was a common expression of piety, including among Pharisees (see note on Lk 18:12).

2:19 *guests of the bridegroom fast.* Fasting was often linked with mourning, whereas weddings were considered a time for rejoicing. Many rabbis taught that weddings took priority over many religious obligations. To fast during a wedding would be to reject hospitality and fail to participate in the festivities, and so would prove offensive to the host.

2:22 *wineskins.* Ancient people used animal skins, most often goatskins, as containers for fluids. Wine expands as it ferments, so fermenting wine would have already expanded old wineskins to their limit. Filling these older, stiffer containers with still-expanding new wine would rupture them. Jesus' new order demanded a new approach.

2:23 *pick some heads of grain.* Israelite law permitted those who were hungry to pick heads of grain when passing through a field (Dt 23:25; Ru 2:2). The complication here, in the eyes of their detractors, is doing so on the Sabbath (Ex 34:21; cf. reaping in the Mishnah in *Shabbat* 7:2).

2:24 *Pharisees.* See note on Mt 12:2. Pharisees followed their traditions carefully, but even Pharisees did not always agree among themselves on which actions violated the Sabbath. Like Jesus (vv. 25 – 26), they cited Scripture to support their various positions.

2:25 *Have you never read ...?* This question would insult Pharisees, who were reputed to be meticulous in the law. See note on Mt 12:4.

2:26 *Abiathar the high priest.* Ahimelek, not his son Abiathar, was the chief priest at the exact time described. By the first century, the title "high priest" (though normally in the plural) applied to anyone in the high-priestly families, both in the NT and Josephus (e.g., *Antiquities* 20.6, 180 – 181; *Wars* 4.160, 238); Mark identifies the era by the better-known son. Nevertheless, Matthew and Luke are clearer and more precise by omitting the reference to Abiathar.

2:27 Some other Jewish sayings followed this sort of reasoning (2 Maccabees 5:19; 2 Baruch 14:18).

2:28 *Son of Man.* Because Son of Man also means "human being," Jesus' hearers on this occasion could construe him as saying (in light of v. 27) that human needs take precedence over the Sabbath. The context of Jesus' ministry, however, suggest that he is making a much more dramatic claim (see note on v. 10).

3:2 *heal him on the Sabbath.* See note on Mt 12:10.

3:5 *hand was completely restored.* For healing a withered hand, cf. 1Ki 13:6. Technically Jesus does not apply medical

hand." He stretched it out, and his hand was completely restored. 6Then the Pharisees went out and began to plot with the Herodians[o] how they might kill Jesus.[p]

Crowds Follow Jesus

3:7-12pp — Mt 12:15,16; Lk 6:17-19

7Jesus withdrew with his disciples to the lake, and a large crowd from Galilee followed.[q] 8When they heard about all he was doing, many people came to him from Judea, Jerusalem, Idumea, and the regions across the Jordan and around Tyre and Sidon.[r] 9Because of the crowd he told his disciples to have a small boat ready for him, to keep the people from crowding him. 10For he had healed many,[s] so that those with diseases were pushing forward to touch him.[t] 11Whenever the impure spirits saw him, they fell down before him and cried out, "You are the Son of God."[u] 12But he gave them strict orders not to tell others about him.[v]

Jesus Appoints the Twelve

3:16-19pp — Mt 10:2-4; Lk 6:14-16; Ac 1:13

13Jesus went up on a mountainside and called to him those he wanted, and they came to him.[w] 14He appointed twelve[a][x] that they might be with him and that he might send them out to preach 15and to have authority to drive out demons.[y] 16These are the twelve he appointed: Simon (to whom he gave the name Peter),[z] 17James son of Zebedee and his brother John (to them he gave the name Boanerges, which means "sons of thunder"), 18Andrew, Philip, Bartholomew, Matthew, Thomas, James son of Alphaeus, Thaddaeus, Simon the Zealot 19and Judas Iscariot, who betrayed him.

Jesus Accused by His Family and by Teachers of the Law

3:23-27pp — Mt 12:25-29; Lk 11:17-22
3:31-35pp — Mt 12:46-50; Lk 8:19-21

20Then Jesus entered a house, and again a crowd gathered,[a] so that he and his disciples were not even able to eat.[b] 21When his family[b] heard about this, they went to take charge of him, for they said, "He is out of his mind."[c]

22And the teachers of the law who came down from Jerusalem[d] said, "He is possessed by Beelzebul![e] By the prince of demons he is driving out demons."[f]

23So Jesus called them over to him and began to speak to them in parables:[g] "How can Satan[h] drive out Satan? 24If a kingdom is divided against itself, that kingdom cannot stand. 25If a house is divided against itself, that house cannot stand. 26And if Satan opposes himself and is divided, he cannot stand; his end has come. 27In fact, no one can enter a strong man's house without first tying him up. Then he can plunder the strong man's house.[i] 28Truly I tell you, people can be forgiven all their sins and every slander they utter, 29but whoever blasphemes against the

3:6 [o] Mt 22:16; Mk 12:13 [p] Mt 12:14 **3:7** [q] Mt 4:25 **3:8** [r] Mt 11:21 **3:10** [s] Mt 4:23 [t] Mt 9:20 **3:11** [u] Mt 4:3; Mk 1:23,24 **3:12** [v] Mt 8:4; Mk 1:24,25,34; Ac 16:17,18 **3:13** [w] Mt 5:1 **3:14** [x] Mk 6:30 **3:15** [y] Mt 10:1 **3:16** [z] Jn 1:42
3:20 [a] ver 7 [b] Mk 6:31 **3:21** [c] Jn 10:20; Ac 26:24 **3:22** [d] Mt 15:1 [e] Mt 10:25; 11:18; 12:24; Jn 7:20; 8:48, 52; 10:20 [f] Mt 9:34 **3:23** [g] Mk 4:2 [h] Mt 4:10 **3:27** [i] Isa 49:24, 25

[a] *14* Some manuscripts *twelve — designating them apostles —*   [b] *21* Or *his associates*

---

treatment or even lay hands on the man; no one considered a command to stretch out one's hand as work!

3:6 *began to plot with the Herodians.* These Pharisees are inconsistent with usual Pharisaic traditions. See note on Mt 12:14. Many Pharisees were nationalists; Herodians supported the Herodian family, who worked for Rome. Pharisees worked together with Herodians only in the most urgent circumstances.

3:8 *Idumea.* The area of Edom, forcibly converted to Judaism starting in 129 BC; Herod the Great had been from there. *regions across the Jordan.* To the east; included Perea, one of Herod Antipas's territories. *Tyre and Sidon.* Phoenician cities to the north, although some Jews lived there.

3:9 See note on 4:1.

3:14 *twelve.* The sacred number of Israel's tribes; those who saw themselves as a remnant of or renewal movement within Israel could symbolize this by choosing 12 leaders (cf. 1QS 8.1 – 2 in the Dead Sea Scrolls).

3:16 *Simon … Peter.* The Greek name Simon, which resembles the name of the Biblical patriarch Simeon, was one of the most popular Jewish male names of the period (perhaps the most popular). A special epithet or nickname would thus be helpful to distinguish different Simons (cf. v. 18). Nicknames were common; "Peter" means "rock."

3:17 *James … John.* Common Jewish names in the period (James means lit. "Jacob").

3:18 *Andrew.* A rare name. *Philip.* A common enough Greek name, sometimes used by Jewish people, including in Israel. *Matthew.* A somewhat common Jewish name. *Zealot.* Can mean simply someone noted for zeal, but at least in the next generation the title came to apply to those who expressed their zeal by fighting foreign oppressors and those viewed as collaborating with them.

3:19 *Judas Iscariot.* Although the meaning is uncertain, "Iscariot" may have meant, "man from Kerioth" (see Jos 15:25; cf. Jn 6:71).

3:21 *family … went to take charge of him.* Relatives (cf. v. 31) usually tried to hide the behavior of family members that could bring shame on the family.

3:22 *possessed.* Some in antiquity associated insanity (v. 21) with demonization. Some also thought that false teachers could speak by demons. If this association is at all in view here, it suggests a serious charge, since the penalty for leading God's people astray was death (Dt 13:5; 18:20). *Beelzebul.* Probably a corruption of the name of the pagan deity Baalzebub (2Ki 1:2 – 3; see note on Mt 10:25).

3:27 *tying him up.* Magicians sought to "bind" spirits to secure their service, but Jesus is not invoking magic. Rather he's offering a parable that shows his opposition to Satan. Delivering the strong man's (the devil's) possessions from his grasp alludes to God's promise in Isa 49:25: God would defend and deliver his people from the powerful one.

3:29 *whoever blasphemes against the Holy Spirit.* One

Holy Spirit will never be forgiven; they are
guilty of an eternal sin."[j]
30He said this because they were saying,
"He has an impure spirit."
31Then Jesus' mother and brothers arrived.[k] Standing outside, they sent someone
in to call him. 32A crowd was sitting around
him, and they told him, "Your mother and
brothers are outside looking for you."
33"Who are my mother and my brothers?" he asked.
34Then he looked at those seated in a
circle around him and said, "Here are my
mother and my brothers! 35Whoever does
God's will is my brother and sister and
mother."

The Parable of the Sower

4:1-12pp — Mt 13:1-15; Lk 8:4-10
4:13-20pp — Mt 13:18-23; Lk 8:11-15

4 Again Jesus began to teach by the
lake.[l] The crowd that gathered around
him was so large that he got into a boat
and sat in it out on the lake, while all the
people were along the shore at the water's
edge. 2He taught them many things by parables,[m] and in his teaching said: 3"Listen!
A farmer went out to sow his seed.[n] 4As
he was scattering the seed, some fell along
the path, and the birds came and ate it up.
5Some fell on rocky places, where it did
not have much soil. It sprang up quickly,
because the soil was shallow. 6But when
the sun came up, the plants were scorched,
and they withered because they had no
root. 7Other seed fell among thorns, which
grew up and choked the plants, so that
they did not bear grain. 8Still other seed
fell on good soil. It came up, grew and
produced a crop, some multiplying thirty,
some sixty, some a hundred times."[o]
9Then Jesus said, "Whoever has ears to
hear, let them hear."[p]
10When he was alone, the Twelve and
the others around him asked him about
the parables. 11He told them, "The secret
of the kingdom of God[q] has been given to
you. But to those on the outside[r] everything is said in parables 12so that,

"'they may be ever seeing but never
perceiving,
and ever hearing but never
understanding;
otherwise they might turn and be
forgiven!'[a]"[s]

13Then Jesus said to them, "Don't you
understand this parable? How then will
you understand any parable? 14The farmer
sows the word.[t] 15Some people are like seed

3:29 [j] Mt 12:31, 32; Lk 12:10
3:31 [k] ver 21
4:1 [l] Mk 2:13; 3:7
4:2 [m] ver 11; Mk 3:23
4:3 [n] ver 26
4:8 [o] Jn 15:5; Col 1:6
4:9 [p] ver 23; Mt 11:15
4:11 [q] Mt 3:2 [r] 1Co 5:12, 13; Col 4:5; 1Th 4:12; 1Ti 3:7
4:12 [s] Isa 6:9, 10; Mt 13:13-15
4:14 [t] Mk 16:20; Lk 1:2; Ac 4:31; 8:4; 16:6; 17:11; Php 1:14

[a] 12 Isaiah 6:9,10

may "blaspheme" the Spirit because the Spirit is divine (most Jewish people recognized that the Spirit was divine, though they did not identify him as a separate person within the Godhead, as some NT passages do). Attributing the Holy Spirit's work to an impure spirit (v. 30) is roughly tantamount to calling God Satan. Resorting to this tactic to deny the Spirit's clear evidence about Jesus' identity reflects impenetrable intransigence against truth, making repentance unlikely. One who genuinely repents has presumably not gone so far. *guilty of an eternal sin.* Biblical law provided atonement for most sins, but not for deliberate sins (Nu 15:30 – 31; Dt 29:18 – 20).
3:33 *my mother and my brothers.* Figurative kinship language was common in antiquity; e.g., one could call a respected older woman "mother" and call comrades or fellow members of one's ethnic group "brothers." Nevertheless, refusal to give higher priority to one's physical family would appear offensive in ancient Mediterranean culture.
4:1 *teach by the lake.* One's voice can carry to a crowd better if one is some distance away rather than surrounded by people on the same level. Some locations such as a cove near Capernaum also are thought to provide natural amplification for sound.
4:2 See the article "Parables," p. 1692.
4:4 *some fell along the path.* See note on Mt 13:4.
4:5 *rocky places.* See note on Mt 13:5.
4:7 *thorns.* The plant described here is possibly a variety of thistle that commonly thrives around roads. It can grow to a height of more than three feet (a meter) by the month of April in the Holy Land.
4:8 *some multiplying thirty, some sixty, some a hundred times.* See note on Mt 13:8.
4:9 *Whoever has ears.* This is the language of riddles, inviting the wise to consider the meaning. Israel was not always ready to hear (Isa 6:10; Jer 6:10; Eze 12:2).
4:10 *the Twelve.* In antiquity, groups were sometimes named after their original number and could retain that title as a group. *asked him.* See note on Mt 13:10.
4:11 *The secret of the kingdom.* A special revelation about God's promised kingdom, not information that would never be known; see Da 2:28 – 30,44. ("Secret" or "mystery" as divine information now being divinely revealed also appears often in the Dead Sea Scrolls.) *given to you.* Some sages made some special information available only to their closest disciples, not considering outsiders ready for it. (This was true even of some later rabbis, who felt that teachings about creation or Ezekiel's vision of God on his throne-chariot were dangerous if revealed to the unprepared.) Here the secrets go to those who "accept" it (v. 20) — i.e., the true disciples who remained after the crowds had gone, and thus received the interpretation from Jesus.
4:12 Rabbis who used parables in their teaching frequently related them to Scripture. Many OT passages speak of similar hardness of heart (e.g., Dt 29:4; Isa 42:19 – 20; 43:8; 44:18; Jer 5:21; Eze 12:2), but Jesus condenses a text in Isaiah in this parable. In Isaiah 6:9 – 10, God calls Isaiah to reveal truth to Israel that Israel will not receive, until the impending judgment (Isa 6:11). Their spiritual blindness increased as punishment for their refusal to heed what they had already heard from God (Isa 29:9 – 10).
4:13 *Don't you understand . . . ?* See note on Mt 13:18.
4:14 *the word.* Ancient Jewish sources occasionally compared God's word, the law, to seed (cf. 4 Ezra 3:20; 9:31 – 32); Jesus refers here to the message about the kingdom (v. 11).

MARK 4:2

PARABLES

In Greek, *parabolē*, i.e., "parable," can mean "comparison" or "analogy." Many scholars, however, argue that Jesus' parables especially fit the range of forms referred to by the Hebrew term *mashal*, which is sometimes translated *parabolē*, or parable, in the Septuagint, the pre-Christian Greek translation of the OT. A *mashal* could be a proverb, riddle, similitude, or other saying of the wise; the Greek version uses *parabolē* similarly (e.g., Ps 78:2; Pr 1:6). The Greek term appears nine times in Sirach, a pre-Christian book of Jewish wisdom.

Most of Jesus' parables are *story* parables, a distinctively Jewish form. Fables (cf. the plant fable in Jdg 9:8 – 15) existed in a range of cultures, including Greek culture, but most of Jesus' parables are closer to the human story parables that appear in rabbinic sources, sources that sometimes reflect earlier traditions. In earlier sources, both prophets (2Sa 12:1 – 7; Isa 5:1 – 7) and Jewish apocalyptic writers (e.g., 1 Enoch 1:2 – 3; 37 – 71) used some parables. Although later rabbinic parables are more stereotypical, they share with Jesus' parables even some standard figures (e.g., a king representing God, sometimes throwing a banquet for his son, and the like). Because most of Jesus' hearers were rural Galileans, Jesus' stories tend to be more agrarian and less addressed to the elite than were later rabbinic parables. Jesus' parables, unlike those of the rabbis, also tend to subvert traditional values, sometimes in shocking ways. Like later rabbis, Jesus apparently sometimes recycled or reapplied more traditional story lines, as Jesus' parables sometimes resemble other ancient Jewish stories.

Because later Christians such as Paul do not develop story parables, they are distinctive to Jesus in the NT. Most scholars of all persuasions thus usually deem the Gospels' parables authentic to Jesus, not the sort of sayings that some scholars believe later Christians would have invented for him. By contrast, some more skeptical scholars have doubted that the *interpretations* of parables offered by Jesus in the Gospels were really uttered by Jesus. More recent scholarship has challenged such skepticism, however. Other Jewish parables frequently have interpretations, as Jewish scholarship on parables recognizes.

It is in fact parables that *lack* interpretations that appear more unusual in antiquity. Parables were like sermon illustrations, but they often made little sense without being

continued on next page

along the path, where the word is sown.
As soon as they hear it, Satan[u] comes and
takes away the word that was sown in
them. 16Others, like seed sown on rocky
places, hear the word and at once receive it
with joy. 17But since they have no root, they
last only a short time. When trouble or persecution comes because of the word, they
quickly fall away. 18Still others, like seed
sown among thorns, hear the word; 19but
the worries of this life, the deceitfulness
of wealth[v] and the desires for other things
come in and choke the word, making it unfruitful. 20Others, like seed sown on good
soil, hear the word, accept it, and produce
a crop — some thirty, some sixty, some a
hundred times what was sown."

4:15 [u] Mt 4:10 **4:19** [v] Mt 19:23; 1Ti 6:9, 10, 17; 1Jn 2:15-17

A Lamp on a Stand

21He said to them, "Do you bring in a
lamp to put it under a bowl or a bed? Instead, don't you put it on its stand?[w] 22For
whatever is hidden is meant to be disclosed, and whatever is concealed is meant
to be brought out into the open.[x] 23If anyone has ears to hear, let them hear."[y]

4:21 [w] Mt 5:15 **4:22** [x] Jer 16:17; Mt 10:26; Lk 8:17; 12:2 **4:23** [y] ver 9; Mt 11:15

4:17 *quickly fall away.* Jewish people viewed apostasy as a terrible sin.
4:21 *lamp ... under a bowl.* The most common oil lamps of this period were small enough to hold in the hand; placing such a lamp under a container would obscure and likely extinguish it.

connected to a sermon. Because Jesus often offered the illustrations independently, interpreting the parables only privately to his disciples afterward (Mk 4:10–12), they served as riddles to the crowds, inviting the hearers to consider Jesus' point.

Some scholars have questioned Jesus' interpretations particularly in cases such as the parable of the sower, where his interpretation identifies meanings for multiple points in the parable (in this case, the four soils, the birds, and so forth). This objection arose because some interpreters, reacting against the overinterpretation of parables by earlier writers, insisted on each parable having only a single point. Often Jesus' parables do have a single main point, and many details merely contribute to the story. Comparison with other ancient Jewish parables, however, demonstrates that parables could include multiple figurative points of contact, just like the interpretations the Gospels provide for Jesus' parables. There is no historical reason, then, to question their authenticity. ◆

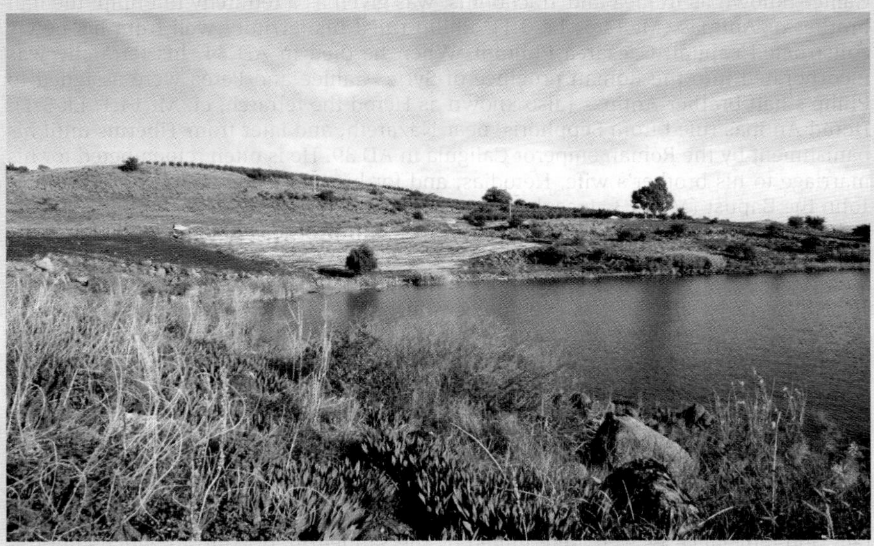

Sower's Cove, where many believe Jesus taught the parable of the sower.
www.HolyLandPhotos.org

24“Consider carefully what you hear,”
he continued. “With the measure you use,
it will be measured to you — and even
more.[z] 25Whoever has will be given more;
whoever does not have, even what they
have will be taken from them.”[a]

The Parable of the Growing Seed

26He also said, “This is what the kingdom of God is like.[b] A man scatters seed
on the ground. 27Night and day, whether he sleeps or gets up, the seed sprouts
and grows, though he does not know how.
28All by itself the soil produces grain —
first the stalk, then the head, then the full
kernel in the head. 29As soon as the grain
is ripe, he puts the sickle to it, because the
harvest has come.”[c]

The Parable of the Mustard Seed

4:30-32pp — Mt 13:31,32; Lk 13:18,19

30Again he said, “What shall we say the
kingdom of God is like,[d] or what parable
shall we use to describe it? 31It is like a

4:24 [z] Mt 7:2; Lk 6:38
4:25 [a] Mt 13:12; 25:29
4:26 [b] Mt 13:24
4:29 [c] Rev 14:15
4:30 [d] Mt 13:24

4:24 *measure you use.* Jesus uses the language of the marketplace, where grain or other substances would be weighed out for a certain amount of money, and would need to be weighed out fairly. Some Jewish texts apply the image to God's justice at the last judgment.
4:30 *What shall we say ...?* Rabbis would often introduce parables in language like this.

MARK 4 

Herod's Successors and Uneasy Relations Between Rome and Judeans

Herod's Successors

When Herod died in 4 BC, the predominantly Gentile area northeast of the Sea of Galilee, known as Ituraea and Trachonitis, was given as a tetrarchy to Philip, the half brother of Antipas (Mt 14:3; Lk 3:1). Philip ruled his territory well from his newly constructed capital, Caesarea Philippi. When he died in AD 34, his tetrarchy was incorporated into the Roman province of Syria. Galilee and Perea were assigned to Philip's half brother Antipas (also known as Herod the tetrarch, cf. Mt 14:1; Lk 3:1). Herod Antipas ruled from Sepphoris, near Nazareth, and later from Tiberius until his banishment by the Roman emperor Caligula in AD 39. He is often remembered for his marriage to his brother's wife, Herodias, and for his imprisonment and execution of John the Baptist (Mt 14:3; Josephus, *Antiquities* 18.5.1–2).

Judea and Samaria were placed under the control of Herod's son Archelaus (the full brother of Antipas and half-brother of Philip), who was given the title of ethnarch (cf. Mt 2:22). Archelaus began his reign by slaughtering 3,000 people during the Jewish Passover, and he was eventually banished for incompetence by Augustus to Gaul in 6 AD (Josephus, *Antiquities* 17.13.2). At this point Judea became a Roman province, ruled directly by a series of Roman prefects (AD 6–41) and then procurators (AD 44–66), who maintained their residence in Caesarea and at the Fortress of Antonia near the temple in Jerusalem. The most important prefecture for early Christianity was that of Pontius Pilate (AD 26–36).

The Uneasy Relations Between Rome and Judea

Under the prefects, internal Jewish affairs were governed by the high priestly aristocracy and judicial cases were determined by the Sanhedrin, or court to which later tradition assigned seventy-one members. The prefects reserved the power of the sword, or the right of capital punishment. However, Jewish leadership seems to have retained this power in cases that dealt exclusively with religious crimes, especially those having to do with the sanctity of the temple. The prefects further maintained their authority over the high priests through the power of appointment and by means of Roman custody of the high priestly garments (Josephus, *Antiquities* 20.1.1).

After a brief return to Herodian rule under Agrippa from AD 41–44 (cf. Ac 12:20–23), Judea, Samaria and Galilee were ruled by a series of procurators until the outbreak of war in AD 66. Agrippa's son reigned over a small kingdom in the north from AD 48–66 (Ac 25:13), and several later procurators are known from the New Testament, including Marcus Antonius Felix (AD 52–59; Ac 23:24) and Porcius Festus (AD 59–62; Ac 24:27), under both of whom Paul was imprisoned.

The reality of Roman control during the time of Jesus produced various reactions within Israelite society. Archaeology has revealed the large extent to which the upper classes adopted Greco-Roman customs and welcomed this new relationship. Evidence for such Hellenization can be observed in both public and private architecture, civic institutions and the widespread use of the Greek language. At the same time, Roman control generated widespread animosity and concern for the vitality of traditional Jewish values and expectations. ◆

mustard seed, which is the smallest of
all seeds on earth. 32Yet when planted, it
grows and becomes the largest of all garden plants, with such big branches that
the birds can perch in its shade."
33With many similar parables Jesus
spoke the word to them, as much as they
could understand.[e] 34He did not say anything to them without using a parable.[f]
But when he was alone with his own disciples, he explained everything.

Jesus Calms the Storm

4:35-41pp — Mt 8:18,23-27; Lk 8:22-25

35That day when evening came, he said
to his disciples, "Let us go over to the
other side." 36Leaving the crowd behind,
they took him along, just as he was, in the
boat.[g] There were also other boats with
him. 37A furious squall came up, and the
waves broke over the boat, so that it was
nearly swamped. 38Jesus was in the stern,
sleeping on a cushion. The disciples woke
him and said to him, "Teacher, don't you
care if we drown?"
39He got up, rebuked the wind and said to
the waves, "Quiet! Be still!" Then the wind
died down and it was completely calm.
40He said to his disciples, "Why are you
so afraid? Do you still have no faith?"[h]
41They were terrified and asked each
other, "Who is this? Even the wind and
the waves obey him!"

Jesus Restores a Demon-Possessed Man

5:1-17pp — Mt 8:28-34; Lk 8:26-37
5:18-20pp — Lk 8:38,39

5 They went across the lake to the region of the Gerasenes.[a] 2When Jesus
got out of the boat,[i] a man with an impure
spirit[j] came from the tombs to meet him.
3This man lived in the tombs, and no one
could bind him anymore, not even with
a chain. 4For he had often been chained
hand and foot, but he tore the chains apart
and broke the irons on his feet. No one
was strong enough to subdue him. 5Night
and day among the tombs and in the hills
he would cry out and cut himself with
stones.
6When he saw Jesus from a distance,
he ran and fell on his knees in front of
him. 7He shouted at the top of his voice,
"What do you want with me,[k] Jesus, Son
of the Most High God?[l] In God's name
don't torture me!" 8For Jesus had said to
him, "Come out of this man, you impure
spirit!"

4:33 [e] Jn 16:12
4:34 [f] Jn 16:25
4:36 [g] ver 1; Mk 3:9; 5:2,21; 6:32,45
4:40 [h] Mt 14:31; Mk 16:14
5:2 [i] Mk 4:1 [j] Mk 1:23
5:7 [k] Mt 8:29 [l] Mt 4:3; Lk 1:32; 6:35; Ac 16:17; Heb 7:1

[a] *1* Some manuscripts *Gadarenes*; other manuscripts *Gergesenes*

4:31 – 32 *mustard seed ... birds can perch.* Scholars do not all agree regarding which plant Jesus has in mind. The majority view would treat Jesus' words here as hyperbole: a tiny seed (though not literally the tiniest) yields a large perennial shrub, growing anew every spring. The shrub can often reach a height of five feet (one and a half meters) and sometimes even ten feet (three meters). If this is the plant in question, birds could normally only perch in its branches (not "nest," as the Greek term is sometimes translated). The quoted language evokes something more than a literal mustard bush: it borrows for God's kingdom the image of a great kingdom of old that would be supplanted by God's kingdom (Da 4:12). The glorious future kingdom was already active in a hidden way in Jesus' ministry.
4:33 – 34 See notes on vv. 10 – 11.
4:37 *boat.* Galilean fishing boats were usually fairly small; the surviving example is 27 feet (8.2 meters) long, 7.5 feet (2.3 meters) wide and possibly 4.3 feet (1.3 meters) deep. Such a boat was built especially of cedar planks (but supplemented with other wood, even scrap wood) with joints and nails. In addition to a mast, it had four places spread out for rowers. Rental contracts stipulated that boats were to be returned unharmed barring an act of God, such as a storm. The shape of the hills surrounding the Sea of Galilee can funnel storms onto the water; they can be sudden and devastating to small boats out in the midst of the lake.
4:38 *stern, sleeping on a cushion.* The stern was probably elevated, and thus would fill with water less quickly. If any comparison is intended with Jonah, who had to be awakened on a boat during a storm, their behavior is a contrast (cf. Jnh 1:5 – 6,12). Sleeping in security may fit faith (Ps 4:8); Greeks also respected sages who remained calm during storms.
4:41 *the wind and the waves obey him.* Jewish people understood that God controls the wind and waves (Ps 65:7; 89:9; 107:29); they did not expect it of a human being.
5:1 *region of the Gerasenes.* The Decapolis, a group of Hellenistic cities in Syria near Galilee, included such towns as Gadara (Mt 8:28) and Gerasa, Hippos and Pella. The population of the region was predominantly Gentile (cf. v. 11). Gerasa was much farther from the lake than Matthew's Gadara, but larger and thus better known to Mark's hearers (Jews and Gentiles outside the holy land and Syria). A region could be named by a town in its vicinity, even a town that is farther from the site. Some suggest instead the site of Gergesa (modern Kursi), which has a cliff and tombs in the area.
5:3 *lived in the tombs.* Jewish people regarded tombs and anything associated with the dead as impure; some associated spirits with such sites. *no one could bind him.* Superhuman strength appears in some reports of spirit possession in various cultures, occasionally even to the point of breaking restraints, as in this case. By contrast, Jesus can in some sense bind the strong man (cf. 3:27).
5:5 *cut himself with stones.* Observers in various cultures report that some of the spirit-possessed try to harm themselves or others, although in some cases they also seem immune to pain. Some participants in pagan cults were known to cut themselves as masochistic offerings to their gods (including in 1Ki 18:28), a practice that Israel's benevolent God forbade (Dt 14:1).
5:7 *What do you want with me ... ?* See note on 1:24. *Most High God.* See note on Ac 16:17. *In God's name.* The Greek term normally means to put one under oath. This language appeared sometimes in magical exorcisms or often in other magical invocations of spirits; if the demons are trying to use defensive magic against Jesus, however, they are unsuccessful.

[9]Then Jesus asked him, "What is your
name?"
"My name is Legion,"[m] he replied, "for
we are many." [10]And he begged Jesus again
and again not to send them out of the area.
[11]A large herd of pigs was feeding on
the nearby hillside. [12]The demons begged
Jesus, "Send us among the pigs; allow
us to go into them." [13]He gave them permission, and the impure spirits came out

5:9 [m] ver 15

5:9 *What is your name?* Magicians often tried to control a spirit by using its name. If the spirits attempted to magically control Jesus in v. 7, they failed; here Jesus demands their name. *Legion.* On paper, a Roman legion had a strength of 6,000 (though usually a fighting force of closer to 5,000). A legion included ten cohorts, each with six centuries, but the demons are probably simply indicating that they are many (cf. the many pigs in v. 13).

5:10 *out of the area.* Just as soldiers got attached to regions, so observers report that in some places spirits claim to be attached to locales or local cultures. Some Jewish people (as evidenced in 1 Enoch) also recognized that demons could at most plead when confronted with God's power.

5:11 *herd of pigs.* Jewish people considered pigs unclean (Lev 11:7–8).

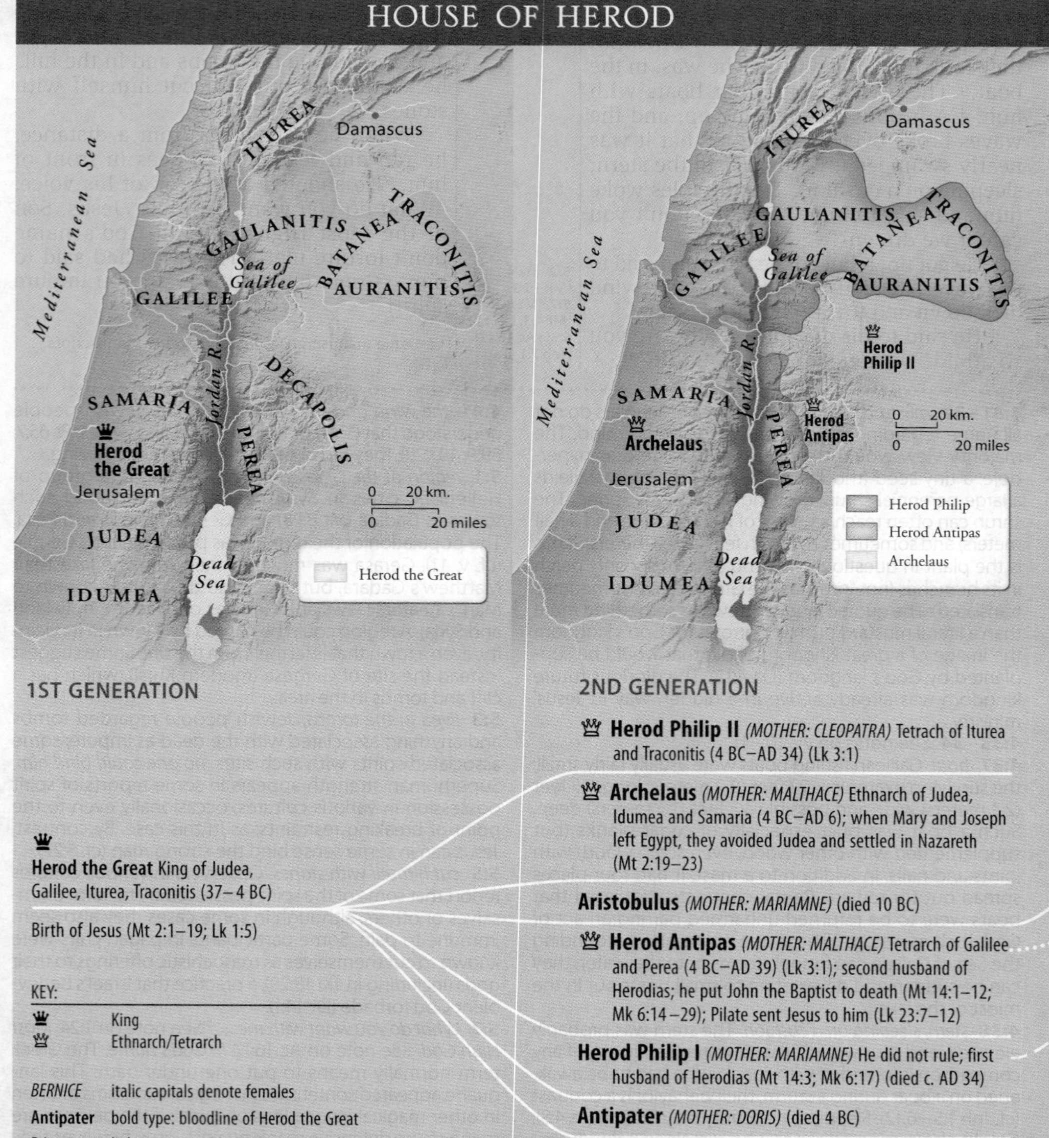

and went into the pigs. The herd, about
two thousand in number, rushed down
the steep bank into the lake and were
drowned.
14 Those tending the pigs ran off and reported this in the town and countryside,
and the people went out to see what had
happened. 15 When they came to Jesus,
they saw the man who had been possessed by the legion[n] of demons,[o] sitting
there, dressed and in his right mind; and
they were afraid. 16 Those who had seen it
told the people what had happened to the
demon-possessed man — and told about

5:15 [n] ver 9 [o] ver 16, 18; Mt 4:24

5:13 *into the lake.* Mark does not clarify the spirits' fate, but presumably they were at least somehow immobilized. *drowned.* Pigs may swim, but not indefinitely, probably especially after plunging over a steep bank. In some Jewish traditions demons could be destroyed (e.g., *Abot de Rabbi Nathan* 37A) or could be bound in an abyss (1 Enoch 88:1 – 3) or under the earth (Jubilees 5:6; 1 Enoch 10:12; 14:5) or bodies of water (Testament of Solomon 5:11; 25:7). **5:14** *Those tending the pigs.* Pigs require little oversight, but even if the herders were few, they were responsible to the owners (whether individuals or the town) for the pigs' welfare.

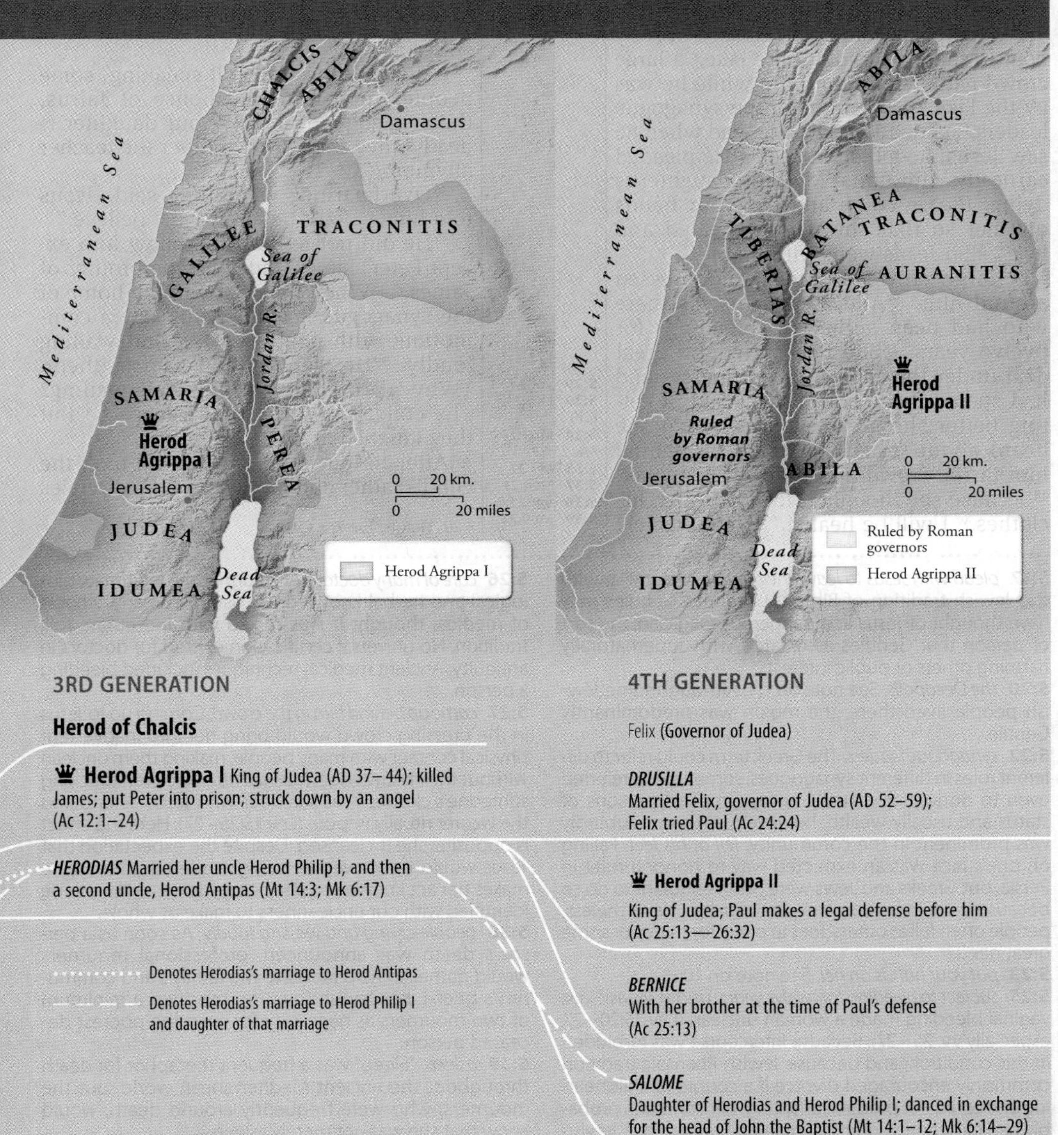

the pigs as well. 17 Then the people began to plead with Jesus to leave their region.

18 As Jesus was getting into the boat, the man who had been demon-possessed begged to go with him. 19 Jesus did not let him, but said, "Go home to your own people and tell them[p] how much the Lord has done for you, and how he has had mercy on you." 20 So the man went away and began to tell in the Decapolis[a][q] how much Jesus had done for him. And all the people were amazed.

Jesus Raises a Dead Girl and Heals a Sick Woman

5:22-43pp — Mt 9:18-26; Lk 8:41-56

21 When Jesus had again crossed over by boat to the other side of the lake,[r] a large crowd gathered around him while he was by the lake.[s] 22 Then one of the synagogue leaders,[t] named Jairus, came, and when he saw Jesus, he fell at his feet. 23 He pleaded earnestly with him, "My little daughter is dying. Please come and put your hands on[u] her so that she will be healed and live." 24 So Jesus went with him.

A large crowd followed and pressed around him. 25 And a woman was there who had been subject to bleeding[v] for twelve years. 26 She had suffered a great deal under the care of many doctors and had spent all she had, yet instead of getting better she grew worse. 27 When she heard about Jesus, she came up behind him in the crowd and touched his cloak, 28 because she thought, "If I just touch his clothes,[w] I will be healed." 29 Immediately her bleeding stopped and she felt in her body that she was freed from her suffering.[x]

30 At once Jesus realized that power[y] had gone out from him. He turned around in the crowd and asked, "Who touched my clothes?"

31 "You see the people crowding against you," his disciples answered, "and yet you can ask, 'Who touched me?' "

32 But Jesus kept looking around to see who had done it. 33 Then the woman, knowing what had happened to her, came and fell at his feet and, trembling with fear, told him the whole truth. 34 He said to her, "Daughter, your faith has healed you.[z] Go in peace[a] and be freed from your suffering."

35 While Jesus was still speaking, some people came from the house of Jairus, the synagogue leader.[b] "Your daughter is dead," they said. "Why bother the teacher anymore?"

36 Overhearing[b] what they said, Jesus told him, "Don't be afraid; just believe."

37 He did not let anyone follow him except Peter, James and John the brother of James.[c] 38 When they came to the home of the synagogue leader,[d] Jesus saw a commotion, with people crying and wailing loudly. 39 He went in and said to them, "Why all this commotion and wailing? The child is not dead but asleep."[e] 40 But they laughed at him.

After he put them all out, he took the child's father and mother and the disciples

5:19 [p] Mt 8:4
5:20 [q] Mt 4:25; Mk 7:31
5:21 [r] Mt 9:1 [s] Mk 4:1
5:22 [t] ver 35, 36, 38; Lk 13:14; Ac 13:15; 18:8, 17
5:23 [u] Mt 19:13; Mk 6:5; 7:32; 8:23; 16:18; Lk 4:40; 13:13; Ac 6:6
5:25 [v] Lev 15:25-30
5:28 [w] Mt 9:20
5:29 [x] ver 34
5:30 [y] Lk 5:17; 6:19
5:34 [z] Mt 9:22 [a] Ac 15:33
5:35 [b] ver 22
5:37 [c] Mt 4:21
5:38 [d] ver 22
5:39 [e] Mt 9:24

[a] 20 That is, the Ten Cities [b] 36 Or *Ignoring*

5:17 *plead with Jesus to leave their region.* Unfamiliar with the Jewish tradition of Biblical prophets, Gentiles may have thought of Jesus as a dangerous magician, the sort of person that Gentiles associated with supernaturally harming others or public interests.
5:20 *the Decapolis.* See note on v. 1. Although some Jewish people lived there, the region was predominantly Gentile.
5:22 *synagogue leaders.* The Greek term could refer to different roles in different synagogues; sometimes it referred even to donors. It virtually always implied persons of status and usually wealth, however; Jairus undoubtedly was prominent in the community. *fell at his feet.* Falling on one's face was an expected way to honor a ruler in Persia, but Greeks and Jews were often reluctant to do so because it could be construed as worship. Nevertheless, people often fell at others' feet to plead for mercy or some great need.
5:23 *put your hands on her.* See note on 10:13.
5:25 *subject to bleeding for twelve years.* Under Jewish law, vaginal bleeding made a woman unclean (Lev 15:20–27, especially vv. 25–27). Because intercourse was forbidden in this condition, and because Jewish Pharisaic tradition commonly encouraged divorce if a couple of childbearing age could not produce offspring, her condition probably had either prevented her marriage or ended it. Jewish women often married soon after puberty.
5:26 *care of many doctors.* Although some legitimate biological and herbal knowledge existed, in many schools of medical thought it was mixed with inaccurate folk tradition. No universal certification existed for doctors in antiquity. Ancient medical techniques included bleeding a person.
5:27 *came up behind him in the crowd.* Coming up to Jesus in the pressing crowd would bring her into inadvertent physical contact with many people, making them unclean without their knowledge. *touched his cloak.* Even touching someone's clothes — as she does with Jesus — rendered the wearer ritually impure (Lev 15:26–27). Here the effect is opposite: she is cleansed. Despite the expectation that Jesus would be viewed as being rendered unclean, he makes her act known (vv. 30–34); Jesus was willing to be identified with our uncleanness to make us whole.
5:38 *people crying and wailing loudly.* As soon as a person's death was announced, professional mourners would gather to help facilitate the family's and community's grief. Later Jewish tradition specified a minimum of two mourners as necessary for even the poorest deceased person.
5:39 *asleep.* "Sleep" was a frequent metaphor for death throughout the ancient Mediterranean world, but the mourners, who were frequently around death, would know that she was not merely asleep.

THE DECAPOLIS AND THE LANDS BEYOND THE JORDAN

1 Place east of the Jordan River where John the Baptist was baptizing (Jn 1:28). Here at Bethany on the other side of the Jordan John saw Jesus and called him the "Lamb of God" (Jn 1:29,35).

2 Philip, Andrew and Peter were from Bethsaida (see Jn 1:44; 12:21). Jesus healed a blind man here (Mk 8:22). Feeding of the 5,000 took place near here (Lk 9:10).

3 Jesus and his disciples withdrew to Caesarea Philippi (Mt 16:13; Mk 8:27), and here Peter confessed that Jesus was the Messiah (Mt 16:15–16).

4 Paul was converted near Damascus and was brought blinded into the city (Ac 9:3,8; 22:6,11).

who were with him, and went in where
the child was. 41He took her by the hand[f]
and said to her, *"Talitha koum!"* (which
means "Little girl, I say to you, get up!").[g]
42Immediately the girl stood up and began to walk around (she was twelve years
old). At this they were completely astonished. 43He gave strict orders not to let
anyone know about this,[h] and told them
to give her something to eat.

A Prophet Without Honor

6:1-6pp — Mt 13:54-58

6 Jesus left there and went to his hometown,[i] accompanied by his disciples.
2When the Sabbath came,[j] he began to
teach in the synagogue,[k] and many who
heard him were amazed.[l]

"Where did this man get these things?"
they asked. "What's this wisdom that has
been given him? What are these remarkable miracles he is performing? 3Isn't this
the carpenter? Isn't this Mary's son and
the brother of James, Joseph,[a] Judas and
Simon?[m] Aren't his sisters here with us?"
And they took offense at him.[n]

4Jesus said to them, "A prophet is not
without honor except in his own town,
among his relatives and in his own
home."[o] 5He could not do any miracles
there, except lay his hands on[p] a few sick
people and heal them. 6He was amazed at
their lack of faith.

5:41 [f]Mk 1:31 [g]Lk 7:14; Ac 9:40
5:43 [h]Mt 8:4
6:1 [i]Mt 2:23
6:2 [j]Mk 1:21 [k]Mt 4:23 [l]Mt 7:28
6:3 [m]Mt 12:46 [n]Mt 11:6; Jn 6:61
6:4 [o]Lk 4:24; Jn 4:44
6:5 [p]Mk 5:23
6:6 [q]Mt 9:35; Mk 1:39; Lk 13:22
6:7 [r]Mk 3:13 [s]Dt 17:6; Lk 10:1 [t]Mt 10:1
6:11 [u]Mt 10:14
6:12 [v]Lk 9:6
6:13 [w]Jas 5:14
6:14 [x]Mt 3:1

Jesus Sends Out the Twelve

6:7-11pp — Mt 10:1,9-14; Lk 9:1,3-5

Then Jesus went around teaching from
village to village.[q] 7Calling the Twelve to
him,[r] he began to send them out two by
two[s] and gave them authority over impure
spirits.[t]

8These were his instructions: "Take
nothing for the journey except a staff—
no bread, no bag, no money in your
belts. 9Wear sandals but not an extra
shirt. 10Whenever you enter a house, stay
there until you leave that town. 11And if
any place will not welcome you or listen
to you, leave that place and shake the
dust off your feet[u] as a testimony against
them."

12They went out and preached that people should repent.[v] 13They drove out many
demons and anointed many sick people
with oil[w] and healed them.

John the Baptist Beheaded

6:14-29pp — Mt 14:1-12
6:14-16pp — Lk 9:7-9

14King Herod heard about this, for Jesus'
name had become well known. Some were
saying,[b] "John the Baptist[x] has been raised
from the dead, and that is why miraculous
powers are at work in him."

[a] 3 Greek *Joses,* a variant of *Joseph* [b] 14 Some early manuscripts *He was saying*

5:41 *took her by the hand.* Contact with a bleeding person (vv. 28–34) could render a person impure until evening (Lev 15:21–23,27), but touching a corpse rendered one impure for a week (Nu 19:14,16). *Talitha koum!* Jesus addresses her in Aramaic, the mother tongue of most Galileans.
5:42 *twelve years old.* At this age, she had probably entered puberty and was close to the ordinary minimum age for a girl's marriage in Jewish custom. Tomb inscriptions often lament those who died too young for marriage, but there is no need for further lamentation here.
6:3 *carpenter.* See note on Mt 13:55. *Mary's son.* See note on Mt 13:55.
6:4 People normally expected support from their relatives and from fellow citizens from one's home area. Prophets, however, often faced rejection and persecution (e.g., Jer 26:20), even in their own communities (cf. Jer 1:1; 11:21).
6:7 *two by two.* In antiquity, heralds or messengers most often traveled in pairs (valuable for a message's witnesses; cf. the minimum number of witnesses in Dt 17:6; 19:15). No less important, traveling together provided greater safety.
6:8 *staff.* Travelers used a staff for protection against robbers, snakes and other creatures, and sometimes for maintaining one's balance while walking on uneven mountain paths. *no bag.* In the Gentile world, wandering Cynic philosophers, known for living simply on city streets, carried a bag for begging, which is prohibited here.
6:9 *sandals.* Judean sandals had light straps running from between the toes to just above the ankle; unlike shoes, such sandals protected only the bottom of the foot. *extra shirt.* In the poorest areas, many peasants had only a single cloak. Biblical prophets also had to live simply in times of widespread apostasy, not dependent on decadent society (cf., e.g., 1:4; 1Ki 17:2–16; 18:13; 2Ki 4:38; 5:15–19,26; 6:1).
6:10 Hospitality was one of the chief virtues in Mediterranean antiquity, and Jewish travelers could normally count on Jewish hospitality even in Diaspora cities.
6:11 *shake the dust off your feet.* Proper hospitality included offering water for guests to wash their feet; here the travelers' feet remain conspicuously unwashed. Jewish people sometimes shook profane dust from their feet when entering a more holy place (cf. Ex 3:5); some did so when leaving pagan territory to enter the Holy Land. Cf. notes on Ac 18:6; 22:23.
6:13 *anointed many sick people.* People anointed themselves in connection with washing, but a more particular sort of anointing is in view here. Many people in antiquity believed that olive oil had medicinal properties (e.g., Josephus, *Antiquities* 17.172; *Wars* 1.657); Jewish people regularly used it on sores and wounds (cf., e.g., Isa 1:6; Lk 10:34), and some anointed people for healing for a range of maladies. Anointing was also employed for consecration, however (e.g., Ex 30:30; 40:13,15; 1Sa 10:1). Because of this range of associations, oil provided an obvious symbol for healing.
6:14 *King Herod.* This member of the Herod family is Herod Antipas, son of Herod the Great (Mt 2:1) by a Samaritan wife named Malthace, and full brother of Archelaus (Josephus, *Wars* 1.562; cf. Mt 2:22). Technically, Herod Antipas was not a "king," but a tetrarch (Mt 14:1; Lk 3:1,19; 9:7)—governor of a territory (in his case, Galilee and Perea). He was from a royal family and many Galileans probably experienced him as if he were a king locally, but

15 Others said, "He is Elijah."[y]
And still others claimed, "He is a prophet,[z] like one of the prophets of long ago."[a]
16 But when Herod heard this, he said,
"John, whom I beheaded, has been raised
from the dead!"
17 For Herod himself had given orders to
have John arrested, and he had him bound
and put in prison.[b] He did this because of
Herodias, his brother Philip's wife, whom
he had married. 18 For John had been saying to Herod, "It is not lawful for you to
have your brother's wife."[c] 19 So Herodias
nursed a grudge against John and wanted to kill him. But she was not able to,
20 because Herod feared John and protected him, knowing him to be a righteous
and holy man.[d] When Herod heard John,
he was greatly puzzled[a]; yet he liked to
listen to him.
21 Finally the opportune time came. On
his birthday Herod gave a banquet[e] for his
high officials and military commanders
and the leading men of Galilee.[f] 22 When
the daughter of[b] Herodias came in and
danced, she pleased Herod and his dinner guests.
The king said to the girl, "Ask me for
anything you want, and I'll give it to you."
23 And he promised her with an oath,
"Whatever you ask I will give you, up to
half my kingdom."[g]
24 She went out and said to her mother,
"What shall I ask for?"
"The head of John the Baptist," she answered.
25 At once the girl hurried in to the king
with the request: "I want you to give me
right now the head of John the Baptist on
a platter."
26 The king was greatly distressed, but
because of his oaths and his dinner guests,
he did not want to refuse her. 27 So he immediately sent an executioner with orders
to bring John's head. The man went, beheaded John in the prison, 28 and brought

6:15 [y] Mal 4:5 [z] Mt 21:11 [a] Mt 16:14; Mk 8:28 **6:17** [b] Mt 4:12; 11:2; Lk 3:19,20 **6:18** [c] Lev 18:16; 20:21 **6:20** [d] Mt 11:9; 21:26 **6:21** [e] Est 1:3; 2:18 [f] Lk 3:1 **6:23** [g] Est 5:3, 6; 7:2

[a] 20 Some early manuscripts *he did many things*
[b] 22 Some early manuscripts *When his daughter*

ultimately his desire for the title *king* cost him his authority altogether (see note on v. 17). *raised from the dead.* The sort of resurrection rumored here is like the raisings by prophets (1Ki 17:19–24; 2Ki 4:32–37), not a permanent raising to eternal life.

6:15 *Elijah.* People expected Elijah to prepare the way for the end (Mal 4:5–6). Some Jewish people, especially among those who were aristocrats, believed that prophets in the ancient sense had ceased, though many other Jews did follow the promises of those who acted like end-time prophets.

6:17 *because of Herodias.* For political reasons, Antipas had married the daughter of the powerful Nabatean king Aretas IV (mentioned in 2Co 11:32). Herod Antipas tried to win Herodias, though she was married to Antipas's half brother Philip. When he wanted to marry Herodias, his brother's wife, however, Herodias insisted that she would not marry a polygamist, so Antipas determined to divorce the Nabatean princess. She fled to her father, and the resulting feud stirred political trouble for Antipas; many of his Perean subjects were ethnically Nabatean, with loyalties to their people. Eventually, after the events narrated here, Aretas IV vanquished Herod Antipas in battle, and Antipas's own people attributed his loss to divine judgment for Herod's wicked execution of John the Baptist. John's criticisms of Antipas's behavior were moral (Lev 18:16; 20:21), but because they were politically sensitive Antipas kept John in prison. Josephus (*Antiquities* 18.119) says that Antipas imprisoned him in his Perean fortress Machaerus, which included a dungeon. (Perea was a region across the Jordan; John's ministry had likely been active in this area.)

Ultimately, long after John's execution, Antipas's marriage to Herodias cost him his kingdom, but for different reasons. Josephus reports that Herodias was jealous that her brother, Agrippa I, became "king" of Judea (AD 41–44) whereas her new husband, Antipas, had remained merely a tetrarch since his father's death in 4 BC, nearly three decades earlier. Thus she insisted that Antipas petition the emperor for the same privileged title; when Antipas finally complied, he was banished to Gaul, where he and Herodias spent the rest of their days without a kingdom (Josephus, *Antiquities* 18.240–255).

6:18 *not lawful.* Prophets often called God's people back to God's law, in this case Lev 18:16; 20:21.

6:19 *wanted to kill him.* Herodias's behavior here fits the depiction of her character by the Jewish historian Josephus (see note on v. 17).

6:20 *liked to listen to him.* Aristocrats often liked to listen to philosophers and other speakers; Antipas showed interest in prophets (cf. Lk 23:8–9).

6:21 *birthday.* See note on Mt 14:6.

6:22 *daughter of Herodias ... danced.* Herodias's daughter Salome was probably between 12 to 14 years old, and perhaps already betrothed or married to Philip the tetrarch, when she was called on to dance. These parties often featured sensuous dancing, but typically members of the royal family were not called on to participate. The Herodian family, however, was known for such excesses.

6:23 *oath.* See note on Mt 14:7. *up to half my kingdom.* Herod's promise evokes the promise made to Esther (Est 5:3,6; 7:2), but Esther interceded for life whereas here Salome will request a prophet's death. That Antipas is intoxicated seems clear here: as a tetrarch under Rome, Antipas lacked authority to give away any of his kingdom!

6:24 *went out.* Archaeologists note that the fortress Machaerus had two banquet halls; as in Greek banquets, the men and women dined separately. Thus Salome "went out." Her mother Herodias was therefore also not present to witness her husband's behavior.

6:25 *head of John the Baptist.* On some other occasions ancient sources report powerful authorities gruesomely executing persons (usually prisoners) at banquets as a favor to someone attractive. Ancients who read these reports normally regarded the person who granted the execution as wicked and disgusting.

6:26 *because of his oaths and his dinner guests.* The ancient Mediterranean world deeply valued honor and abhorred shame; Antipas's public honor was at stake (see note on v. 23).

6:27 *beheaded John in the prison.* Because it was quick, beheading was considered the most merciful form of execution (though vv. 24–25 show that other considerations prevail here).

back his head on a platter. He presented it
to the girl, and she gave it to her mother.
29On hearing of this, John's disciples came
and took his body and laid it in a tomb.

Jesus Feeds the Five Thousand

6:32-44pp — Mt 14:13-21; Lk 9:10-17; Jn 6:5-13
6:32-44Ref — Mk 8:2-9

30The apostles[h] gathered around Jesus
and reported to him all they had done and
taught.[i] 31Then, because so many people were coming and going that they did
not even have a chance to eat,[j] he said to
them, "Come with me by yourselves to a
quiet place and get some rest."

32So they went away by themselves in
a boat[k] to a solitary place. 33But many
who saw them leaving recognized them
and ran on foot from all the towns and got
there ahead of them. 34When Jesus landed and saw a large crowd, he had compassion on them, because they were like
sheep without a shepherd.[l] So he began
teaching them many things.

35By this time it was late in the day, so
his disciples came to him. "This is a remote place," they said, "and it's already
very late. 36Send the people away so that
they can go to the surrounding countryside and villages and buy themselves
something to eat."

37But he answered, "You give them
something to eat."[m]

They said to him, "That would take
more than half a year's wages[a]! Are we to
go and spend that much on bread and give
it to them to eat?"

38"How many loaves do you have?" he
asked. "Go and see."

When they found out, they said,
"Five — and two fish."[n]

39Then Jesus directed them to have
all the people sit down in groups on the
green grass. 40So they sat down in groups
of hundreds and fifties. 41Taking the five
loaves and the two fish and looking up
to heaven, he gave thanks and broke the
loaves.[o] Then he gave them to his disciples to distribute to the people. He also
divided the two fish among them all.
42They all ate and were satisfied, 43and
the disciples picked up twelve basketfuls
of broken pieces of bread and fish. 44The
number of the men who had eaten was
five thousand.

Jesus Walks on the Water

6:45-51pp — Mt 14:22-32; Jn 6:15-21
6:53-56pp — Mt 14:34-36

45Immediately Jesus made his disciples get into the boat[p] and go on ahead of
him to Bethsaida,[q] while he dismissed the
crowd. 46After leaving them, he went up
on a mountainside to pray.[r]

47Later that night, the boat was in the
middle of the lake, and he was alone on

6:30 [h] Mt 10:2; Lk 9:10; 17:5; 22:14; 24:10; Ac 1:2,26 [i] Lk 9:10 **6:31** [j] Mk 3:20 **6:32** [k] ver 45; Mk 4:36 **6:34** [l] Mt 9:36 **6:37** [m] 2Ki 4:42-44 **6:38** [n] Mt 15:34; Mk 8:5 **6:41** [o] Mt 14:19 **6:45** [p] ver 32 [q] Mt 11:21 **6:46** [r] Lk 3:21

[a] 37 Greek *take two hundred denarii*

6:29 *John's disciples … took his body.* Sons or other next of kin would normally take responsibility for a body's burial; lacking these, a teacher's disciples could perform this filial sort of obligation. *laid it in a tomb.* On burial customs, and the reticence of some to grant burial to their executed enemies, see notes on Mt 27:58 – 60.

6:34 *sheep without a shepherd.* Scripture spoke of God's people without a leader as sheep without a shepherd (Nu 27:17; 1Ki 22:17; 2Ch 18:16; Zec 10:2; for others, cf. Isa 13:14). In such a setting, God himself might become their shepherd (Eze 34:8 – 16).

6:35 – 44 Ancient speakers and writers liked to contrast characters. Jesus' benevolent banquet here contrasts with Herod's drunken, lustful, murderous banquet in the preceding narrative.

6:35 *late in the day.* An evening meal often began shortly before (or sometimes after) sundown; although not feasible here, people would normally want to be safely home before sundown.

6:36 *villages.* Fewer than 3,000 would live even in the largest villages; most villages had only hundreds. *buy themselves something to eat.* Village markets would include bread and, around the lake, fish, although most such selling would occur before sundown. The villages in this region probably could not feed the entire crowd (see v. 44), but the disciples would at least be free from responsibility. A host should feed even the most unannounced of guests, but these were hardly normal circumstances.

6:38 *loaves … fish.* Bread was the most basic staple in the ancient Mediterranean world, but people also often ate fish, especially in fishing areas such as around the Sea of Galilee.

6:39 *green grass.* That the grass is green suggests it is springtime (Jn 6:4).

6:41 *looking up to heaven.* A familiar gesture for prayer, both among Jews (e.g., Ps 123:1; 1 Esdras 4:58) and Gentiles. *gave thanks and broke the loaves.* By this period it was a Jewish custom to thank God before one's meal; then one would divide and distribute it. The later blessing, probably already sometimes in use, included: "Blessed are you … who bring forth bread from the earth." (At some point it also became a custom to thank God after meals.) Multiplying food evokes Moses (the manna) and especially Elijah (1Ki 17:13 – 16) and Elisha (2Ki 4:3 – 7,42 – 44).

6:43 *twelve basketfuls.* Polite hosts with means served enough food for some to be left over. Nevertheless, most people disapproved of wasting resources.

6:44 *five thousand.* Many today estimate Capernaum's population between 600 and 1,500; some estimate Sepphoris's population at only 15,000, though it was one of Galilee's two largest cities. Even if these estimates were to prove low, a crowd of 5,000 (not including women and children, Mt 14:21) represents more people than most towns contained. The crowd's size indicates that Jesus was now one of the most popular figures in Galilee.

6:45 *Bethsaida.* Also known as Julias, especially after AD 30, but the Gospels, which preserve early tradition, prefer its traditional local name.

6:47 *middle of the lake.* The lake is not large (13 miles [21 kilometers] long by 8 miles [13 kilometers] wide at its widest point), and the disciples were probably crossing at a much narrower point. Nevertheless, progress was delayed by contrary winds (v. 48).

land. 48He saw the disciples straining at
the oars, because the wind was against
them. Shortly before dawn he went out to
them, walking on the lake. He was about
to pass by them, 49but when they saw him
walking on the lake, they thought he was
a ghost.[s] They cried out, 50because they all
saw him and were terrified.
Immediately he spoke to them and said,
"Take courage! It is I. Don't be afraid."[t]
51Then he climbed into the boat[u] with
them, and the wind died down.[v] They
were completely amazed, 52for they had
not understood about the loaves; their
hearts were hardened.[w]
53When they had crossed over, they
landed at Gennesaret and anchored there.[x]
54As soon as they got out of the boat, people recognized Jesus. 55They ran throughout that whole region and carried the sick
on mats to wherever they heard he was.
56And wherever he went — into villages,
towns or countryside — they placed the
sick in the marketplaces. They begged
him to let them touch even the edge of
his cloak,[y] and all who touched it were
healed.

That Which Defiles

7:1-23pp — Mt 15:1-20

7 The Pharisees and some of the teachers of the law who had come from
Jerusalem gathered around Jesus 2and
saw some of his disciples eating food
with hands that were defiled,[z] that is, unwashed. 3(The Pharisees and all the Jews
do not eat unless they give their hands a
ceremonial washing, holding to the tradition of the elders.[a] 4When they come from
the marketplace they do not eat unless
they wash. And they observe many other
traditions, such as the washing of cups,
pitchers and kettles.[a])[b]
5So the Pharisees and teachers of the
law asked Jesus, "Why don't your disciples live according to the tradition of the
elders[c] instead of eating their food with
defiled hands?"
6He replied, "Isaiah was right when he
prophesied about you hypocrites; as it is
written:

" 'These people honor me with their
lips,
but their hearts are far from me.
7They worship me in vain;
their teachings are merely human
rules.'[b][d]

8You have let go of the commands of God
and are holding on to human traditions."[e]
9And he continued, "You have a fine
way of setting aside the commands of God
in order to observe[c] your own traditions![f]
10For Moses said, 'Honor your father and
mother,'[d][g] and, 'Anyone who curses their
father or mother is to be put to death.'[e][h]
11But you say[i] that if anyone declares that
what might have been used to help their
father or mother is Corban (that is, devoted

6:49 [s] Lk 24:37 **6:50** [t] Mt 14:27 **6:51** [u] ver 32 [v] Mk 4:39 **6:52** [w] Mk 8:17-21 **6:53** [x] Jn 6:24, 25 **6:56** [y] Mt 9:20 **7:2** [z] Ac 10:14, 28; 11:8; Ro 14:14
7:3 [a] ver 5,8,9, 13; Lk 11:38 **7:4** [b] Mt 23:25; Lk 11:39 **7:5** [c] ver 3; Gal 1:14; Col 2:8 **7:7** [d] Isa 29:13 **7:8** [e] ver 3 **7:9** [f] ver 3 **7:10** [g] Ex 20:12; Dt 5:16 [h] Ex 21:17; Lev 20:9 **7:11** [i] Mt 23:16, 18

[a] 4 Some early manuscripts *pitchers, kettles and dining couches* [b] 6,7 Isaiah 29:13 [c] 9 Some manuscripts *set up* [d] 10 Exodus 20:12; Deut. 5:16 [e] 10 Exodus 21:17; Lev. 20:9

6:48 *about to pass by.* This phrase could evoke God's activity in Ex 33:22; 34:6 and applies to God also in Job 9:11, one of the same passages that refers to God treading on the sea (Job 9:8; God treads on the sea also in Ps 77:19; Hab 3:15). Together with Jesus' "I am" statement (see v. 50; translated "It is I") the narrative leaves no doubt as to Jesus' divine identity (see note on v. 50).
6:49 *ghost.* Despite widespread Jewish teachings about heaven and the future resurrection, on a popular level many people believed in ghosts and certainly spirits more generally. Some people in antiquity believed that the souls of those who died unburied at sea wandered near the site of their demise.
6:50 *It is I.* The NIV's translation is legitimate and fits the context, but the words in Greek here also mean "I am," evoking Ex 3:14 and (especially in the Greek version) Isa 41:4; 43:10; 48:12; 51:12. Together with the context of Jesus treading on waters and being "about to pass by" (v. 48), this experience reveals Jesus' deity (see note on v. 48).
6:53 *Gennesaret.* Refers either to a plain (over three miles [five kilometers] long by over one mile [one and a half kilometers] wide) on the northwest of the lake, between Capernaum and Tiberias, or to a town on the site of ancient Kinnereth (Jos 19:35). Jesus probably ministered often in this densely populated and prosperous region.
6:55 *mats.* Would be readily available; for the poor, mats could be their only beds.
7:1 *teachers of the law.* Although the Greek term translated here can mean "scribes," and many ancient villages had scribes who could write legal documents, high-level Jewish scribes were probably teachers of the law. Most Pharisees and many teachers were apparently based in Jerusalem.
7:3 *ceremonial washing.* The Jewish custom of washing hands arose after the completion of the OT, probably in the Diaspora. Mark's audience may only have known only the Diaspora practice, but the Pharisees, who were centered in Judea, were known to be particularly meticulous in this custom.
7:4 *unless they wash.* People could cleanse their hands to remove ritual impurity contracted in the public markets. They would pour water over the hands or immerse them as far as the wrist. *washing of cups, pitchers and kettles.* Pharisees developed elaborate rules for purifying vessels.
7:5 *tradition of the elders.* Pharisees were known for faithfully following their oral traditions. *defiled hands.* Public opinion judged teachers by their disciples' behavior.
7:7 *human rules.* Isa 29:13 challenged reliance on rules made by men — a warning here used to challenge Pharisaic traditions (vv. 3 – 5).
7:10 Ancient Mediterranean cultures emphasized honoring and caring for parents; Pharisees valued this practice even more highly than most.
7:11 Jewish people could vow and dedicate property to the temple (*corban* means "consecrated to God"). One could thus render property forbidden for others' use.

to God)— 12 then you no longer let them do anything for their father or mother. 13 Thus you nullify the word of God[j] by your tradition[k] that you have handed down. And you do many things like that."

14 Again Jesus called the crowd to him and said, "Listen to me, everyone, and understand this. 15 Nothing outside a person can defile them by going into them. Rather, it is what comes out of a person that defiles them." [16][a]

17 After he had left the crowd and entered the house, his disciples asked him[l] about this parable. 18 "Are you so dull?" he asked. "Don't you see that nothing that enters a person from the outside can defile them? 19 For it doesn't go into their heart but into their stomach, and then out of the body." (In saying this, Jesus declared all foods[m] clean.)[n]

20 He went on: "What comes out of a person is what defiles them. 21 For it is from within, out of a person's heart, that evil thoughts come—sexual immorality, theft, murder, 22 adultery, greed,[o] malice, deceit, lewdness, envy, slander, arrogance and folly. 23 All these evils come from inside and defile a person."

Jesus Honors a Syrophoenician Woman's Faith

7:24-30pp — Mt 15:21-28

24 Jesus left that place and went to the vicinity of Tyre.[b][p] He entered a house and did not want anyone to know it; yet he could not keep his presence secret. 25 In fact, as soon as she heard about him, a woman whose little daughter was possessed by an impure spirit[q] came and fell at his feet. 26 The woman was a Greek, born in Syrian Phoenicia. She begged Jesus to drive the demon out of her daughter.

27 "First let the children eat all they want," he told her, "for it is not right to take the children's bread and toss it to the dogs."

28 "Lord," she replied, "even the dogs under the table eat the children's crumbs."

29 Then he told her, "For such a reply, you may go; the demon has left your daughter."

30 She went home and found her child lying on the bed, and the demon gone.

Jesus Heals a Deaf and Mute Man

7:31-37pp — Mt 15:29-31

31 Then Jesus left the vicinity of Tyre[r] and went through Sidon, down to the Sea of Galilee[s] and into the region of the Decapolis.[c][t] 32 There some people brought to him a man who was deaf and could hardly talk,[u] and they begged Jesus to place his hand on[v] him.

33 After he took him aside, away from the crowd, Jesus put his fingers into the man's ears. Then he spit[w] and touched the man's tongue. 34 He looked up to heaven[x] and with a deep sigh[y] said to him, *"Ephphatha!"* (which means "Be opened!"). 35 At this, the man's ears were opened, his tongue was loosened and he began to speak plainly.[z]

7:13 [j] Heb 4:12 [k] ver 3
7:17 [l] Mk 9:28
7:19 [m] Ro 14:1-12; Col 2:16; 1Ti 4:3-5 [n] Ac 10:15
7:22 [o] Mt 20:15
7:24 [p] Mt 11:21
7:25 [q] Mt 4:24
7:31 [r] ver 24; Mt 11:21 [s] Mt 4:18 [t] Mt 4:25; Mk 5:20
7:32 [u] Mt 9:32; Lk 11:14 [v] Mk 5:23
7:33 [w] Mk 8:23
7:34 [x] Mk 6:41; Jn 11:41 [y] Mk 8:12
7:35 [z] Isa 35:5,6

[a] *16* Some manuscripts include here the words of 4:23.
[b] *24* Many early manuscripts *Tyre and Sidon*
[c] *31* That is, the Ten Cities

Some exploited the loophole that this practice created; one could dedicate for sacred use what instead should be used to care for aged parents.

7:15–19 A few other rabbis eventually offered statements similar to Jesus' in v. 15. They did so only privately to their disciples, however, since they still expected literal observance of the commandments. Even some Jews who interpreted the food laws allegorically (such as the Jewish philosopher Philo) objected when some others went so far as to reject literal observance. In v. 19 Mark construes Jesus as relaxing literal observance.

7:21–22 Ancient writers, both Jewish and Gentile, often listed vices.

7:24 *Tyre.* A major city in Syrian Phoenicia (v. 26). God answered Elijah's prayer to heal a woman's child in this region in 1Ki 17:9–24.

7:26 *born in Syrian Phoenicia.* This description distinguishes the original Phoenician homeland in Syria from Libophoenicia, the Phoenician settlements in North Africa. Since the time of Alexander, "Greeks" (including Macedonians) had constituted a ruling class of citizens; the republics of Tyre and Sidon now considered themselves Greek.

7:27 *children's bread.* Citizens of Tyre and Sidon flourished in part at the expense of the countryside, whose resources they exploited, and also needed imports from Judea. Some scholars thus suggest that, in a sense, she belonged to a class that had been taking bread that Jews and Gentiles in the outlying region could have used to feed their children. Now she must humble herself in a different situation. Most important, Jesus emphasizes the priority of Israel; humbling herself to acknowledge this priority requires transcending ancient national rivalries. *dogs.* This term was a harsh insult for either gender, but it is not used as a direct label here. Nevertheless, Jews, unlike some Gentiles, did not keep dogs as pets and typically treated them as unclean, so it is not a complimentary image.

7:28 *children's crumbs.* See note on Mt 15:27.

7:29–30 Those who persevered in insistent faith often experienced rewards (cf. such respectful insistence in, e.g., Ge 18:23–32; Ex 32:11–14; 1Ki 18:36–37; 2Ki 2:2,4,6,9; 4:28).

7:31 *Sidon.* Like Tyre (see note on v. 24), Sidon was a major city of Phoenicia. Sidon is roughly 24 miles (39 kilometers) from Tyre, so probably required the minimum of a day's travel on foot. It was known for pagan worship, but a Jewish community lived there. *the Decapolis.* See note on 5:1.

7:33 *fingers into the man's ears.* Jesus might thoughtfully communicate his intentions to the man, who was brought by others, in a makeshift sign language. *spit.* Spittle was usually deemed unclean, but it was sometimes used in medicinal, magical, and religious cures.

7:34 *Ephphatha!* Mark retains Jesus' expression in Aramaic, the dominant language in rural Galilee.

36Jesus commanded them not to tell anyone.[a] But the more he did so, the more they kept talking about it. 37People were overwhelmed with amazement. "He has done everything well," they said. "He even makes the deaf hear and the mute speak."

Jesus Feeds the Four Thousand

8:1-9pp — Mt 15:32-39
8:1-9Ref — Mk 6:32-44
8:11-21pp — Mt 16:1-12

8 During those days another large crowd gathered. Since they had nothing to eat, Jesus called his disciples to him and said, 2"I have compassion for these people;[b] they have already been with me three days and have nothing to eat. 3If I send them home hungry, they will collapse on the way, because some of them have come a long distance."

4His disciples answered, "But where in this remote place can anyone get enough bread to feed them?"

5"How many loaves do you have?" Jesus asked.

"Seven," they replied.

6He told the crowd to sit down on the ground. When he had taken the seven loaves and given thanks, he broke them and gave them to his disciples to distribute to the people, and they did so. 7They had a few small fish as well; he gave thanks for them also and told the disciples to distribute them.[c] 8The people ate and were satisfied. Afterward the disciples picked up seven basketfuls of broken pieces that were left over.[d] 9About four thousand were present. After he had sent them away, 10he got into the boat with his disciples and went to the region of Dalmanutha.

11The Pharisees came and began to question Jesus. To test him, they asked him for a sign from heaven.[e] 12He sighed deeply[f] and said, "Why does this generation ask for a sign? Truly I tell you, no sign will be given to it."

7:36 [a] Mt 8:4
8:2 [b] Mt 9:36
8:7 [c] Mt 14:19
8:8 [d] ver 20
8:11 [e] Mt 12:38
8:12 [f] Mk 7:34

13Then he left them, got back into the boat and crossed to the other side.

The Yeast of the Pharisees and Herod

14The disciples had forgotten to bring bread, except for one loaf they had with them in the boat. 15"Be careful," Jesus warned them. "Watch out for the yeast[g] of the Pharisees[h] and that of Herod."[i]

16They discussed this with one another and said, "It is because we have no bread."

17Aware of their discussion, Jesus asked them: "Why are you talking about having no bread? Do you still not see or understand? Are your hearts hardened?[j] 18Do you have eyes but fail to see, and ears but fail to hear? And don't you remember? 19When I broke the five loaves for the five thousand, how many basketfuls of pieces did you pick up?"

"Twelve,"[k] they replied.

20"And when I broke the seven loaves for the four thousand, how many basketfuls of pieces did you pick up?"

8:15 [g] 1Co 5:6-8 [h] Lk 12:1 [i] Mt 14:1; Mk 12:13
8:17 [j] Isa 6:9, 10; Mk 6:52
8:19 [k] Mt 14:20; Mk 6:41-44; Lk 9:17; Jn 6:13

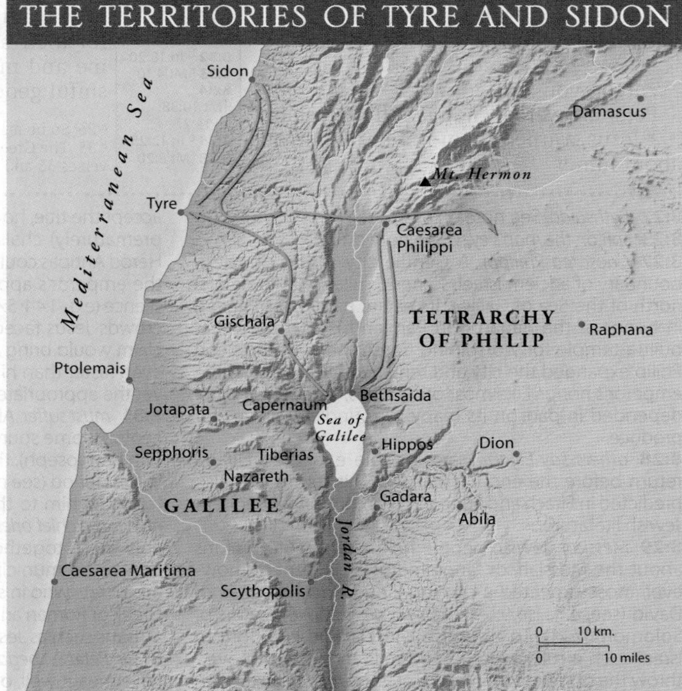

8:6 See note on 6:41.
8:7 See note on 6:38.
8:8 See note on 6:43.
8:9 See note on 6:44.
8:11 *sign from heaven.* Could mean simply one from God, or predicting a heavenly sign such as an eclipse or other phenomenon.
8:15 *yeast.* Known for spreading and pervading its sphere of influence. *Pharisees … Herod.* Pharisees and Herodians worked together only in exceptional circumstances (12:13; see note on 3:6), but they shared a common spiritual problem.
8:17 *Do you still not see …?* On spiritual blindness, see note on 4:12.

They answered, "Seven."[l]
21 He said to them, "Do you still not understand?"[m]

Jesus Heals a Blind Man at Bethsaida

22 They came to Bethsaida,[n] and some
people brought a blind man[o] and begged
Jesus to touch him. 23 He took the blind
man by the hand and led him outside the
village. When he had spit[p] on the man's
eyes and put his hands on[q] him, Jesus
asked, "Do you see anything?"
24 He looked up and said, "I see people;
they look like trees walking around."
25 Once more Jesus put his hands on the
man's eyes. Then his eyes were opened,
his sight was restored, and he saw everything clearly. 26 Jesus sent him home, saying, "Don't even go into[a] the village."

Peter Declares That Jesus Is the Messiah

8:27-29pp — Mt 16:13-16; Lk 9:18-20

27 Jesus and his disciples went on to the
villages around Caesarea Philippi. On the
way he asked them, "Who do people say
I am?"
28 They replied, "Some say John the Baptist;[r] others say Elijah;[s] and still others,
one of the prophets."
29 "But what about you?" he asked.
"Who do you say I am?"
Peter answered, "You are the Messiah."[t]
30 Jesus warned them not to tell anyone
about him.[u]

Jesus Predicts His Death

8:31 — 9:1pp — Mt 16:21-28; Lk 9:22-27

31 He then began to teach them that the
Son of Man[v] must suffer many things[w] and
be rejected by the elders, the chief priests
and the teachers of the law,[x] and that he
must be killed[y] and after three days[z] rise
again.[a] 32 He spoke plainly[b] about this, and
Peter took him aside and began to rebuke
him.
33 But when Jesus turned and looked at
his disciples, he rebuked Peter. "Get behind me, Satan!"[c] he said. "You do not
have in mind the concerns of God, but
merely human concerns."

The Way of the Cross

34 Then he called the crowd to him along
with his disciples and said: "Whoever
wants to be my disciple must deny themselves and take up their cross and follow
me.[d] 35 For whoever wants to save their
life[b] will lose it, but whoever loses their
life for me and for the gospel will save
it.[e] 36 What good is it for someone to gain
the whole world, yet forfeit their soul?
37 Or what can anyone give in exchange
for their soul? 38 If anyone is ashamed of
me and my words in this adulterous and
sinful generation, the Son of Man[f] will be

8:20 [l] ver 6-9; Mt 15:37 **8:21** [m] Mk 6:52 **8:22** [n] Mt 11:21 [o] Mk 10:46; Jn 9:1 **8:23** [p] Mk 7:33 [q] Mk 5:23 **8:28** [r] Mt 3:1 [s] Mal 4:5 **8:29** [t] Jn 6:69; 11:27 **8:30** [u] Mt 8:4; 16:20; 17:9; Mk 9:9; Lk 9:21 **8:31** [v] Mt 8:20 [w] Mt 16:21 [x] Mt 27:1,2 [y] Ac 2:23; 3:13 [z] Mt 16:21 [a] Mt 16:21 **8:32** [b] Jn 18:20 **8:33** [c] Mt 4:10 **8:34** [d] Mt 10:38; Lk 14:27 **8:35** [e] Jn 12:25 **8:38** [f] Mt 8:20

[a] 26 Some manuscripts *go and tell anyone in*
[b] 35 The Greek word means either *life* or *soul*; also in verses 36 and 37.

8:22 *Bethsaida.* See note on 6:45.
8:23 *spit on the man's eyes.* See note on 7:33.
8:27 *Caesarea Philippi.* A Gentile city at the northern boundary of ancient Israel, some 25 miles (40 kilometers) north of the Sea of Galilee. Its earlier name was Paneas, in honor of the pagan god Pan, and Herod the Great built a temple for worshiping Caesar here. Herod's son Philip expanded the city and renamed it Caesarea in the emperor's honor. Like most other cities, Caesarea Philippi depended in part on its many surrounding villages for produce.
8:28 *others say Elijah.* Many people expected Elijah's return before the end (cf. Mal 4:5). This return was also predicted in Sirach and appears commonly in subsequent Jewish literature.
8:29 *Messiah.* Jewish people held a range of opinions about the Messiah, or "anointed one." In general, however, most expected a coming king from the house of David (see, e.g., Isa 9:6 – 7; 11:1 – 5; Jer 23:5 – 6; Psalms of Solomon 17:21). To establish the Davidic kingdom in Israel such a ruler would need military power to overthrow the oppressive kingdom of Rome (for the expectation of oppressive kingdoms' fall, cf. Da 2:44), and many expected such a ruler (cf. Psalms of Solomon 17). In this period they did not normally expect the Messiah to be martyred (v. 31).
8:30 Some evidence suggests that Messianic figures were not expected to accept the title until they succeeded in their mission. Certainly ancient culture frowned on boasting unjustifiably, though leaders were often ready for their followers to do so on their behalf. To accept the title, however, was to publicly (and in this case prematurely) challenge Rome, for even a ruler such as Herod Antipas could not acquire the title of "king" without the emperor's approval. *not to tell.* Some commands to silence (e.g., 1:44; 5:43) may have been to reduce the heavy crowds Jesus faced (2:2; 3:7 – 10), but a direct Messianic claim would bring Jesus into conflict with the authorities even faster than his growing following would. It was not yet the appropriate time (cf. 12:6 – 8; 14:61 – 62).
8:31 *must suffer.* Although perhaps as early as the second century some sources spoke of a suffering Messiah (Messiah ben Joseph), there is no evidence for such a concept in this period (see note on v. 29). Jesus' disciples expected to follow him to the kingdom — not to martyrdom. *the elders, the chief priests and the teachers of the law.* Presumably these together represent members of the Sanhedrin — the municipal senate of Jerusalem. These were aristocrats who in some ways had more in common with Greek or Roman aristocrats than with Galilean peasants or artisans such as Jesus and his followers.
8:32 *Peter … began to rebuke him.* Although Peter may have meant well, openly challenging one's teacher was a serious breach of protocol.
8:33 *Jesus turned.* Disciples were expected to walk behind their teachers. *he rebuked Peter.* Given standard expectations, followers of a Messiah expected to triumph rather than face martyrdom (vv. 34 – 38).
8:34 *take up their cross.* See note on Mt 16:24.
8:35 *to save their life will lose it.* See note on Mt 16:25 – 26.
8:38 *the Son of Man … comes in his Father's glory with the holy angels.* Most Jewish people in the Holy Land

ashamed of them[g] when he comes[h] in his
Father's glory with the holy angels."

9 And he said to them, "Truly I tell you,
some who are standing here will not
taste death before they see that the kingdom of God has come[i] with power."[j]

The Transfiguration

9:2-8pp — Lk 9:28-36
9:2-13pp — Mt 17:1-13

2After six days Jesus took Peter, James
and John[k] with him and led them up a
high mountain, where they were all alone.
There he was transfigured before them. 3His
clothes became dazzling white,[l] whiter than
anyone in the world could bleach them.
4And there appeared before them Elijah and
Moses, who were talking with Jesus.
5Peter said to Jesus, "Rabbi,[m] it is good
for us to be here. Let us put up three shelters — one for you, one for Moses and one
for Elijah." 6(He did not know what to say,
they were so frightened.)
7Then a cloud appeared and covered
them, and a voice came from the cloud:[n]
"This is my Son, whom I love. Listen to
him!"[o]
8Suddenly, when they looked around,
they no longer saw anyone with them except Jesus.
9As they were coming down the mountain, Jesus gave them orders not to tell
anyone[p] what they had seen until the Son
of Man[q] had risen from the dead. 10They
kept the matter to themselves, discussing
what "rising from the dead" meant.
11And they asked him, "Why do the
teachers of the law say that Elijah must
come first?"
12Jesus replied, "To be sure, Elijah does
come first, and restores all things. Why
then is it written that the Son of Man[r]
must suffer much[s] and be rejected?[t] 13But
I tell you, Elijah has come,[u] and they have
done to him everything they wished, just
as it is written about him."

Jesus Heals a Boy Possessed by an Impure Spirit

9:14-28; 30-32pp — Mt 17:14-19; 22,23; Lk 9:37-45

14When they came to the other disciples,
they saw a large crowd around them and
the teachers of the law arguing with them.
15As soon as all the people saw Jesus, they
were overwhelmed with wonder and ran
to greet him.
16"What are you arguing with them
about?" he asked.
17A man in the crowd answered, "Teacher, I brought you my son, who is possessed
by a spirit that has robbed him of speech.
18Whenever it seizes him, it throws him
to the ground. He foams at the mouth,
gnashes his teeth and becomes rigid. I
asked your disciples to drive out the spirit, but they could not."
19"You unbelieving generation," Jesus
replied, "how long shall I stay with you?
How long shall I put up with you? Bring
the boy to me."
20So they brought him. When the spirit
saw Jesus, it immediately threw the boy
into a convulsion. He fell to the ground
and rolled around, foaming at the mouth.[v]
21Jesus asked the boy's father, "How
long has he been like this?"
"From childhood," he answered. 22"It
has often thrown him into fire or water to
kill him. But if you can do anything, take
pity on us and help us."
23" 'If you can'?" said Jesus. "Everything
is possible for one who believes."[w]

8:38 [g] Mt 10:33; Lk 12:9 [h] 1Th 2:19 **9:1** [i] Mk 13:30; Lk 22:18 [j] Mt 24:30; 25:31 **9:2** [k] Mt 4:21 **9:3** [l] Mt 28:3 **9:5** [m] Mt 23:7 **9:7** [n] Ex 24:16 [o] Mt 3:17 **9:9** [p] Mk 8:30 [q] Mt 8:20 **9:12** [r] Mt 8:20 [s] Mt 16:21 [t] Lk 23:11 **9:13** [u] Mt 11:14 **9:20** [v] Mk 1:26 **9:23** [w] Mt 21:21; Mk 11:23; Jn 11:40

expected a future day of judgment. Scripture had promised that God would come with his holy ones (Zec 14:5); here Jesus fills this divine role. He alludes also to the coming Son of man in Da 7:13, at the time that he would receive the kingdom.

9:1 Jewish people believed that God reigned in the present but looked for his kingdom, or reign, in a special way in the world to come. Although Jesus speaks in this context about the ultimate future (8:38), here he probably predicts an event that would foreshadow that future (v. 2).

9:2 *transfigured.* Although ancient literature, including Jewish literature, had various stories of people or other beings who were transformed or transfigured with light, the most widely known, pre-Jesus transfiguration story for early Christians was the story of Moses. Exposed to God's glory on Mount Sinai, Moses reflected that glory (Ex 34:29 – 35); Jesus probably also waits six days here in order to evoke Ex 24:16. Yet Jesus is greater here than Moses (vv. 4 – 7).

9:3 *bleach.* Refers to one of the activities of cloth refiners, who used chemicals to bleach white cloth and tried to remove stains. Jewish sources often depicted heavenly beings in gleaming white.

9:4 *Elijah and Moses.* Elijah was taken to heaven alive (2Ki 2:11); God buried Moses (Dt 34:6), although some Jewish traditions nevertheless said that he was also preserved alive. Jewish people expected the return of Elijah (Mal 4:5 – 6) and the coming of a prophet like Moses (Dt 18:15 – 18).

9:7 *cloud appeared and covered them.* The cloud of God's glory overshadowed Mount Sinai (Ex 24:15 – 16), from which also God spoke from heaven (Ex 20:22). *voice.* See note on 1:11. Jesus is exalted above Elijah and Moses here. *Listen to him!* Some scholars think this statement evokes the command regarding the prophet like Moses in Dt 18:15.

9:11 *come first.* Elijah would prepare the way for God's coming (Mal 4:5 – 6; Sirach 48:10). Jesus applies the prophecy figuratively to John the Baptist (see notes on 1:2 – 3,6).

9:14 *arguing.* If we may judge by the traditions of later rabbis, teachers of the law were skilled in argumentation.

9:22 *thrown him into fire.* Similar experiences are reported in various cultures: some people believed to be controlled by evil spirits inflict physical injury on themselves. Some others perform potentially painful or injurious activities without pain or injury. (But cf. note on Mt 17:15.)

[24]Immediately the boy's father exclaimed, "I do believe; help me overcome my unbelief!"

[25]When Jesus saw that a crowd was running to the scene,[x] he rebuked the impure spirit. "You deaf and mute spirit," he said, "I command you, come out of him and never enter him again."

[26]The spirit shrieked, convulsed him violently and came out. The boy looked so much like a corpse that many said, "He's dead." [27]But Jesus took him by the hand and lifted him to his feet, and he stood up.

[28]After Jesus had gone indoors, his disciples asked him privately,[y] "Why couldn't we drive it out?"

[29]He replied, "This kind can come out only by prayer.[a]"

Jesus Predicts His Death a Second Time

9:33-37pp — Mt 18:1-5; Lk 9:46-48

[30]They left that place and passed through Galilee. Jesus did not want anyone to know where they were, [31]because he was teaching his disciples. He said to them, "The Son of Man[z] is going to be delivered into the hands of men. They will kill him,[a] and after three days[b] he will rise."[c] [32]But they did not understand what he meant[d] and were afraid to ask him about it.

[33]They came to Capernaum.[e] When he was in the house,[f] he asked them, "What were you arguing about on the road?" [34]But they kept quiet because on the way they had argued about who was the greatest.[g]

[35]Sitting down, Jesus called the Twelve and said, "Anyone who wants to be first must be the very last, and the servant of all."[h]

[36]He took a little child whom he placed among them. Taking the child in his arms,[i] he said to them, [37]"Whoever welcomes one of these little children in my name welcomes me; and whoever welcomes me does not welcome me but the one who sent me."[j]

Whoever Is Not Against Us Is for Us

9:38-40pp — Lk 9:49,50

[38]"Teacher," said John, "we saw someone driving out demons in your name and we told him to stop, because he was not one of us."[k]

[39]"Do not stop him," Jesus said. "For no one who does a miracle in my name can in the next moment say anything bad about me, [40]for whoever is not against us is for us.[l] [41]Truly I tell you, anyone who gives you a cup of water in my name because you belong to the Messiah will certainly not lose their reward.[m]

Causing to Stumble

[42]"If anyone causes one of these little ones—those who believe in me—to stumble,[n] it would be better for them if a large millstone were hung around their neck and they were thrown into the sea.[o]

9:25 [x]ver 15 **9:28** [y]Mk 7:17 **9:31** [z]Mt 8:20 [a]ver 12; Ac 2:23; 3:13 [b]Mt 16:21 [c]Mt 16:21 **9:32** [d]Lk 2:50; 9:45; 18:34; Jn 12:16 **9:33** [e]Mt 4:13 [f]Mk 1:29

9:34 [g]Lk 22:24 **9:35** [h]Mt 18:4; 20:26; Mk 10:43; Lk 22:26 **9:36** [i]Mk 10:16 **9:37** [j]Mt 10:40 **9:38** [k]Nu 11:27-29 **9:40** [l]Mt 12:30; Lk 11:23 **9:41** [m]Mt 10:42 **9:42** [n]Mt 5:29 [o]Mt 18:6; Lk 17:2

[a] 29 Some manuscripts *prayer and fasting*

9:25 *deaf and mute spirit.* Although various afflictions and problems could happen without being caused by spirits, spirits could also cause these.
9:26 *convulsed him violently.* Spirits often were believed to depart very demonstratively, as this one does.
9:28 *asked him privately.* Given the public emphasis on honor and shame in the wider culture, disciples would probably not want to draw further public attention to their failure to be able to carry on the activities that their teacher modeled for them. But they would view their teacher as a superior and could ask him privately.
9:32 *afraid to ask him.* In a society where honor was highly valued, people were often reluctant to admit ignorance. In this case, the disciples will also remember Jesus' strong response to Peter's resistance after a previous announcement of Jesus' suffering (8:31–33).
9:34 *argued about who was the greatest.* Rivalry for greater honor was common among ancient Mediterranean men. This practice ranged from playful competition among friends to deadly competition among enemies; Jesus' disciples here are not enemies, but it is probable that they have gone beyond playful banter.
9:35 Jesus' instructions here run completely counter to antiquity's normal public male culture of seeking honor.
9:36 *little child.* Somewhat in contrast to modern Western culture, where children are often objects of consumer marketing and the subjects of greater psychological and educational concern, children in Jesus' culture were normally powerless, expected to be obedient and dependent. They were, however, usually objects of their parents' love. *in his arms.* The culture was more tactile than the modern West, and non-family members holding children was safer and more common.
9:38 *in your name.* That the man would cast demons out in the name of Jesus rather than invoking a spirit or using stinky substances reveals his faith in Jesus (on ancient practices of casting out demons, see note on Mt 8:16). Some exorcists did try to drive out demons by invoking the name of Solomon, who was reputed to be a great exorcist (Josephus, *Antiquities* 8.47), but this man may act in Jesus' name in a different way (cf. v. 37).
9:40 The idea that a person must choose one side or the other was widely circulated in antiquity and would have been familiar to Jesus' disciples. At least in urban politics, networks of alliances typically meant that one was friends with a friend's friends and enemies of a friend's enemies, though such alliances could be adjusted when useful.
9:41 *cup of water.* The poorest person might have only water to offer, but hospitality obligations demanded sharing with a visitor what one had. *not lose their reward.* God would reward hospitable treatment of his prophets (e.g., 1Ki 17:12–16; 2Ki 4:8–17). Jewish people often spoke of reward in relation to the day of judgment.
9:42 *to stumble.* Jewish sources often used "stumble" figuratively for sin or apostasy (e.g., Eze 14:3,7; Sirach 9:5). *large millstone.* See note on Mt 18:6.

43 If your hand causes you to stumble,[p]
cut it off. It is better for you to enter life
maimed than with two hands to go into
hell,[q] where the fire never goes out.[r] [44][a]
45 And if your foot causes you to stumble,[s] cut it off. It is better for you to enter
life crippled than to have two feet and be
thrown into hell.[t] [46][a] 47 And if your eye
causes you to stumble,[u] pluck it out. It is
better for you to enter the kingdom of God
with one eye than to have two eyes and be
thrown into hell,[v] 48 where

"'the worms that eat them do not die,
and the fire is not quenched.'[b][w]

49 Everyone will be salted[x] with fire.
50 "Salt is good, but if it loses its saltiness, how can you make it salty again?[y]
Have salt among yourselves,[z] and be at
peace with each other."[a]

Divorce

10:1-12pp — Mt 19:1-9

10 Jesus then left that place and went
into the region of Judea and across
the Jordan.[b] Again crowds of people came
to him, and as was his custom, he taught
them.[c]

2 Some Pharisees[d] came and tested him
by asking, "Is it lawful for a man to divorce his wife?"
3 "What did Moses command you?" he
replied.
4 They said, "Moses permitted a man to
write a certificate of divorce and send her
away."[e]
5 "It was because your hearts were hard[f]
that Moses wrote you this law," Jesus replied. 6 "But at the beginning of creation
God 'made them male and female.'[c][g] 7 'For
this reason a man will leave his father and
mother and be united to his wife,[d] 8 and
the two will become one flesh.'[e][h] So they
are no longer two, but one flesh. 9 Therefore what God has joined together, let no
one separate."
10 When they were in the house again,
the disciples asked Jesus about this. 11 He
answered, "Anyone who divorces his wife
and marries another woman commits
adultery against her.[i] 12 And if she divorces her husband and marries another man,
she commits adultery."[j]

9:43 [p] Mt 5:29 [q] Mt 5:30; 18:8 [r] Mt 25:41 **9:45** [s] Mt 5:29 [t] Mt 18:8 **9:47** [u] Mt 5:29 [v] Mt 5:29; 18:9 **9:48** [w] Isa 66:24; Mt 25:41 **9:49** [x] Lev 2:13 **9:50** [y] Mt 5:13; Lk 14:34, 35 [z] Col 4:6 [a] Ro 12:18; 2Co 13:11; 1Th 5:13 **10:1** [b] Mk 1:5; Jn 10:40; 11:7 [c] Mt 4:23; Mk 2:13; 4:2; 6:6, 34 **10:2** [d] Mk 2:16 **10:4** [e] Dt 24:1-4; Mt 5:31 **10:5** [f] Ps 95:8; Heb 3:15 **10:6** [g] Ge 1:27; 5:2 **10:8** [h] Ge 2:24; 1Co 6:16 **10:11** [i] Mt 5:32; Lk 16:18 **10:12** [j] Ro 7:3; 1Co 7:10, 11

[a] *44,46* Some manuscripts include here the words of verse 48. [b] *48* Isaiah 66:24 [c] *6* Gen. 1:27 [d] *7* Some early manuscripts do not have *and be united to his wife.* [e] *8* Gen. 2:24

9:43–47 *cut it off ... cut it off ... pluck it out.* Corporal punishment, the removal of a limb (e.g., Ex 21:24), was less serious than capital punishment; Jewish teachers often employed hyperbole, rhetorical overstatement to make a point. See note on Mt 5:30.
9:43,45,47 *hell. Gehinnom* (see note on Mt 3:12). Jewish thinkers sometimes expected God to raise the dead in the form in which they died before healing them (e.g., 2 Baruch 50:2–4).
9:48 Jesus uses the closing verse of Isaiah (Isa 66:24), where the corpses of those who defied God serve as a warning to others. The context is the time of the new creation and deliverance of God's people (Isa 66:22–23).
9:49 *salted with fire.* Priests salted some sacrifices as well as cooked them (Lev 2:13; Eze 43:24). *fire.* Cf. perhaps v. 48.
9:50 *Salt ... loses its saltiness.* Teachers sometimes spoke in riddles. Genuine salt could not lose its saltiness (though some impure salt deposits that Judeans knew could), but if (hypothetically) it did, it was worthless, as one later rabbi noted; one could not make it salty except by salting it (see note on Mt 5:13). Salt was sometimes used in covenants (e.g., Nu 18:19; 2Ch 13:5).
10:1 *across the Jordan.* The region of Perea.
10:2 *divorce.* In Jesus' generation Pharisees were debating among themselves the proper grounds for divorce. See note on Mt 19:3.
10:4 The Pharisees cite the allowance of divorce in Dt 24:1–4.
10:5 *because your hearts were hard.* Ancient teachers of the law sometimes recognized that some of Moses' laws were written as concessions to human weakness. Civil laws don't necessarily represent God's ideals; typically they merely place limits on human sin (see notes on Mt 5:22,28). Thus, e.g., the Law of Moses forbade marrying a wife's sister (Lev 18:18) but not polygamy per se; it limited the abuse of slaves (Ex 21:26–27) but did not outlaw slavery per se. Jesus appeals to a divine ethic more complete than Israel's civil law.
10:6 Teachers sometimes challenged other teachers' interpretations of verses (here some Pharisees' understanding of Dt 24:1) by appealing to other texts that contradicted those interpretations. *at the beginning.* For many Jewish people, the ideals of the "beginning" foreshadowed the future kingdom. God paired the man and woman in Ge 1:27 so that husband and wife could reproduce (Ge 1:28). Others cited the passage for restoring divine ideals; e.g., the people who composed the Dead Sea Scrolls used Ge 1:27 (cited here) to prohibit kings marrying multiple wives.
10:8 *one flesh.* Continuing his reference to the Genesis creation narrative, Jesus cites Ge 2:24. In the OT, members of the same family unit were "one flesh," so marriage created a new family unit.
10:10 *the disciples asked.* Teachers sometimes explained matters privately to their disciples.
10:11 Treating marriage as indissoluble leaves any remarriage adulterous; yet v. 9 prohibits divorce rather than treating it as impossible. Because Jesus often used graphic hyperbole (see note on Mt 5:30), offered general statements that might be qualified in some cases (see note on 1Co 7:15), and elsewhere treated the dissolution of marriage as possible (though wrong; Mk 10:9; Jn 4:18), a number of interpreters view the present statement as hyperbole. Hyperbole was meant to graphically reinforce the point, here the context's warning against breaking one's marriage.
10:12 *if she divorces.* Only men could divorce under the traditional practice in Israel and the custom recognized by the Pharisees (cf. v. 2). But women with means did sometimes divorce their husbands, as was more common in the Greek and Roman world (see notes on 1Co 7:10–11); e.g., Herodias (Mk 6:17) had divorced her husband to marry Antipas (Josephus, *Antiquities* 18.136, though noting his disapproval).

The Little Children and Jesus

10:13-16pp — Mt 19:13-15; Lk 18:15-17

13People were bringing little children to
Jesus for him to place his hands on them,
but the disciples rebuked them. 14When
Jesus saw this, he was indignant. He said
to them, "Let the little children come to
me, and do not hinder them, for the kingdom of God belongs to such as these.[k]
15Truly I tell you, anyone who will not receive the kingdom of God like a little child
will never enter it."[l] 16And he took the
children in his arms,[m] placed his hands
on them and blessed them.

The Rich and the Kingdom of God

10:17-31pp — Mt 19:16-30; Lk 18:18-30

17As Jesus started on his way, a man
ran up to him and fell on his knees[n] before him. "Good teacher," he asked, "what
must I do to inherit eternal life?"[o]
18"Why do you call me good?" Jesus
answered. "No one is good—except God
alone. 19You know the commandments:
'You shall not murder, you shall not commit adultery, you shall not steal, you shall
not give false testimony, you shall not defraud, honor your father and mother.'[a]"[p]
20"Teacher," he declared, "all these I
have kept since I was a boy."
21Jesus looked at him and loved him.
"One thing you lack," he said. "Go, sell
everything you have and give to the poor,[q]
and you will have treasure in heaven.[r]
Then come, follow me."[s]
22At this the man's face fell. He went
away sad, because he had great wealth.

10:14 [k]Mt 25:34 **10:15** [l]Mt 18:3 **10:16** [m]Mk 9:36 **10:17** [n]Mk 1:40 [o]Lk 10:25; Ac 20:32 **10:19** [p]Ex 20:12-16; Dt 5:16-20 **10:21** [q]Ac 2:45 [r]Mt 6:20; Lk 12:33 [s]Mt 4:19

10:23 [t]Ps 52:7; 62:10; 1Ti 6:9, 10, 17 **10:24** [u]Mt 7:13, 14 **10:25** [v]Lk 12:16-20 **10:27** [w]Mt 19:26 **10:28** [x]Mt 4:19 **10:30** [y]Mt 6:33 [z]Mt 12:32 [a]Mt 25:46 **10:31** [b]Mt 19:30 **10:32** [c]Mk 3:16-19

23Jesus looked around and said to his
disciples, "How hard it is for the rich[t] to
enter the kingdom of God!"
24The disciples were amazed at his words.
But Jesus said again, "Children, how hard
it is[b] to enter the kingdom of God![u] 25It is
easier for a camel to go through the eye of
a needle than for someone who is rich to
enter the kingdom of God."[v]
26The disciples were even more amazed,
and said to each other, "Who then can be
saved?"
27Jesus looked at them and said, "With
man this is impossible, but not with God;
all things are possible with God."[w]
28Then Peter spoke up, "We have left everything to follow you!"[x]
29"Truly I tell you," Jesus replied, "no
one who has left home or brothers or sisters or mother or father or children or
fields for me and the gospel 30will fail
to receive a hundred times as much[y] in
this present age: homes, brothers, sisters,
mothers, children and fields—along with
persecutions—and in the age to come[z]
eternal life.[a] 31But many who are first will
be last, and the last first."[b]

Jesus Predicts His Death a Third Time

10:32-34pp — Mt 20:17-19; Lk 18:31-33

32They were on their way up to Jerusalem, with Jesus leading the way, and
the disciples were astonished, while those
who followed were afraid. Again he took
the Twelve[c] aside and told them what was

[a] *19* Exodus 20:12-16; Deut. 5:16-20 [b] *24* Some manuscripts *is for those who trust in riches*

10:13 *to place his hands on them.* Laying hands on someone to bless them was an ancient, Biblical practice (Ge 48:9,14). Like Elisha's disciple Gehazi (2Ki 4:27), Jesus' disciples try to protect him by keeping a suppliant away from him, and like Elisha, Jesus welcomes the petitioner.
10:14 *kingdom ... belongs to such as these.* Some expected warriors to establish the kingdom; few associated it with children (though cf. Isa 11:8).
10:15 *like a little child.* Young children were dependent on their fathers (see note on Mt 6:8).
10:17 *Good teacher.* Praising or even flattering teachers was common. *what must I do to inherit eternal life?* Some Jewish people asked Jewish teachers how to have eternal life. *inherit eternal life.* A common expression; eternal life meant the life of the coming age. Jewish people envisioned this life in various ways, often as a restoration of paradise, as well as living together in peace, joy and justice.
10:18 *Why ... call me good?* People often respected teachers who deflected praise; this was considered honorable behavior. In this case it may also challenge the inquirer's self-certainty (v. 20).
10:20 *since I was a boy.* At least according to later Jewish tradition, a boy became fully responsible for the commandments at his coming-of-age to become a young man, around age 13.
10:21 *sell everything ... give to the poor.* Although very few teachers made demands like the one Jesus makes here, on occasion some radical teachers weeded out uncommitted disciples with such demands. *treasure in heaven.* Jewish people sometimes spoke of heavenly rewards in this way. The brief allusions in the earliest sources usually do not specify what they meant by it, except that it means being rewarded in the coming world. *follow me.* Be his disciple; disciples followed behind their teachers.
10:23 *the rich.* Although some believed that the poor were especially godly, many believed the wealthy were specially blessed by God.
10:25 *camel ... needle.* Camels were the largest animals in the Holy Land; the eye of a needle was proverbially small (it was a small opening at the top of a needle, then as now, not, as some have argued, a gate in Jerusalem). A camel getting through the eye of a needle was apparently a figure of speech for accomplishing what was impossible (like the analogous Babylonian Jewish figure of speech about an elephant getting through a needle's eye). Jewish teachers often used hyperbole to emphasize their points.
10:27 Cf. Ge 18:14.
10:30 *a hundred times as much in this present age ... and in the age to come.* Jewish people expected reward in the world to come, in particular eternal life (see v. 17). Reaping a hundred times what one sowed was an extraordinary yield (Ge 26:12). The rewards in the present to which Jesus refers might be the benefits of believers being one family and sharing their means with those in need.

going to happen to him. 33"We are going up to Jerusalem,"[d] he said, "and the Son of Man[e] will be delivered over to the chief priests and the teachers of the law.[f] They will condemn him to death and will hand him over to the Gentiles, 34who will mock him and spit on him, flog him[g] and kill him.[h] Three days later[i] he will rise."[j]

The Request of James and John

10:35-45pp — Mt 20:20-28

35Then James and John, the sons of Zebedee, came to him. "Teacher," they said, "we want you to do for us whatever we ask."

36"What do you want me to do for you?" he asked.

37They replied, "Let one of us sit at your right and the other at your left in your glory."[k]

38"You don't know what you are asking,"[l] Jesus said. "Can you drink the cup[m] I drink or be baptized with the baptism I am baptized with?"[n]

39"We can," they answered.

Jesus said to them, "You will drink the cup I drink and be baptized with the baptism I am baptized with,[o] 40but to sit at my right or left is not for me to grant. These places belong to those for whom they have been prepared."

41When the ten heard about this, they became indignant with James and John. 42Jesus called them together and said, "You know that those who are regarded as rulers of the Gentiles lord it over them, and their high officials exercise authority over them. 43Not so with you. Instead, whoever wants to become great among you must be your servant,[p] 44and whoever wants to be first must be slave of all. 45For even the Son of Man did not come to be served, but to serve,[q] and to give his life as a ransom for many."[r]

Blind Bartimaeus Receives His Sight

10:46-52pp — Mt 20:29-34; Lk 18:35-43

46Then they came to Jericho. As Jesus and his disciples, together with a large crowd, were leaving the city, a blind man, Bartimaeus (which means "son of Timaeus"), was sitting by the roadside begging. 47When he heard that it was Jesus of Nazareth,[s] he began to shout, "Jesus, Son of David,[t] have mercy on me!"

48Many rebuked him and told him to be quiet, but he shouted all the more, "Son of David, have mercy on me!"

49Jesus stopped and said, "Call him."

So they called to the blind man, "Cheer up! On your feet! He's calling you." 50Throwing his cloak aside, he jumped to his feet and came to Jesus.

51"What do you want me to do for you?" Jesus asked him.

The blind man said, "Rabbi,[u] I want to see."

52"Go," said Jesus, "your faith has healed you."[v] Immediately he received his sight and followed[w] Jesus along the road.

Jesus Comes to Jerusalem as King

11:1-10pp — Mt 21:1-9; Lk 19:29-38
11:7-10pp — Jn 12:12-15

11 As they approached Jerusalem and came to Bethphage and Bethany[x] at the Mount of Olives,[y] Jesus sent two of his disciples, 2saying to them, "Go to the

10:33 [d] Lk 9:51 [e] Mt 8:20 [f] Mt 27:1,2 **10:34** [g] Mt 16:21 [h] Ac 2:23; 3:13 [i] Mt 16:21 [j] Mt 16:21 **10:37** [k] Mt 19:28 **10:38** [l] Job 38:2 [m] Mt 20:22 [n] Lk 12:50 **10:39** [o] Ac 12:2; Rev 1:9 **10:43** [p] Mk 9:35 **10:45** [q] Mt 20:28 [r] Mt 20:28 **10:47** [s] Mk 1:24 [t] Mt 9:27 **10:51** [u] Mt 23:7 **10:52** [v] Mt 9:22 [w] Mt 4:19 **11:1** [x] Mt 21:17 [y] Mt 21:1

10:33 *the chief priests and the teachers of the law.* The powerful elite in Jerusalem; crossing them would make them mortal enemies, but the sort of Messiah (8:29) most people expected would have to deal with them somehow, whether by persuasion or by force. *hand him over.* Because only Rome exercised the right to execute people, hostile members of Jerusalem's elite would have to hand Jesus over to the Roman governor.
10:34 *flog him.* Flogging was standard before execution; abuse of prisoners, including mocking, was common.
10:35–37 James and John expect Jesus to establish his kingdom, perhaps soon in Jerusalem (cf. v. 32). Loyal friends and followers who shared a future ruler's dangers often earned the right to ask him special favors (cf. also expectations engendered by vv. 29–31). Seats beside a ruler were the highest in a kingdom.
10:38,39 *cup.* See note on 14:36. *baptism.* Cf. Lk 12:49–50. James suffered martyrdom before any of the other members of the 12 did (Ac 12:2), but tradition claims that John outlived all the others.
10:42 *Gentiles lord it over.* Jesus accurately depicts the pursuit of power in the ancient Mediterranean world, from the emperor down. Jewish teachers usually used Gentiles as negative examples.
10:44 *first must be slave of all.* As in 9:35, Jesus' teaching here violated expectations for honor in ancient society.
10:45 *serve ... give his life.* The Son of Man was expected to reign (Da 7:13–14), but he came as a servant who would give his life for others (cf. the suffering servant of Isa 53:4,11–12).
10:46 *Jericho.* About 12 miles (20 kilometers)—less than a day's walk—from Jerusalem, although the journey would be uphill from here. In this period Jericho was wealthy, with residences of aristocratic priests and with winter palaces once held by Herod the Great; especially during this time of pilgrimage for the festival, a beggar on the roadside might acquire ample provision. The ruins of the original Jericho lay south of the current city; some scholars thus think that the Jericho mentioned here is a different site than the one in Lk 18:35. *Bartimaeus.* "Bar" (as here in *Bartimaeus*) is Aramaic for "son of."
10:47 *Son of David.* Implies he believes Jesus is the Messianic king.
10:48 *he shouted all the more.* Refusing to be deterred expresses faith (cf., e.g., 2Ki 4:27–28).
11:1 *Bethphage.* An apparently walled suburb of Jerusalem, outside the capital's city walls and about three quarters of a mile (one kilometer) east of the peak of Mount Olivet; it was probably closer to Jerusalem than Bethany, to its east. Bethany was some two miles (three kilometers) east of Jerusalem, on the eastern side of Mount Olivet.
11:2 *no one has ever ridden.* Animals never before ridden

village ahead of you, and just as you enter
it, you will find a colt tied there, which no
one has ever ridden.[z] Untie it and bring it
here. 3If anyone asks you, 'Why are you
doing this?' say, 'The Lord needs it and
will send it back here shortly.'"

4They went and found a colt outside in
the street, tied at a doorway.[a] As they untied it, 5some people standing there asked,
"What are you doing, untying that colt?"
6They answered as Jesus had told them to,
and the people let them go. 7When they
brought the colt to Jesus and threw their
cloaks over it, he sat on it. 8Many people
spread their cloaks on the road, while others spread branches they had cut in the
fields. 9Those who went ahead and those
who followed shouted,

"Hosanna![a]"

"Blessed is he who comes in the name
of the Lord!"[b][b]

10"Blessed is the coming kingdom of our
father David!"

"Hosanna in the highest heaven!"[c]

11Jesus entered Jerusalem and went into
the temple courts. He looked around at
everything, but since it was already late,
he went out to Bethany with the Twelve.[d]

11:2 [z] Nu 19:2; Dt 21:3; 1Sa 6:7 **11:4** [a] Mk 14:16 **11:9** [b] Ps 118:25, 26; Mt 23:39 **11:10** [c] Lk 2:14 **11:11** [d] Mt 21:12, 17 **11:13** [e] Lk 13:6-9

Jesus Curses a Fig Tree and Clears the Temple Courts

11:12-14pp — Mt 21:18-22
11:15-18pp — Mt 21:12-16; Lk 19:45-47; Jn 2:13-16
11:20-24pp — Mt 21:19-22

12The next day as they were leaving Bethany, Jesus was hungry. 13Seeing in the distance a fig tree in leaf, he went to find out
if it had any fruit. When he reached it, he
found nothing but leaves, because it was not
the season for figs.[e] 14Then he said to the
tree, "May no one ever eat fruit from you
again." And his disciples heard him say it.

15On reaching Jerusalem, Jesus entered
the temple courts and began driving out
those who were buying and selling there.
He overturned the tables of the money
changers and the benches of those selling doves, 16and would not allow anyone
to carry merchandise through the temple
courts. 17And as he taught them, he said,
"Is it not written: 'My house will be called

[a] *9* A Hebrew expression meaning "Save!" which became an exclamation of praise; also in verse 10
[b] *9* Psalm 118:25,26

or yoked were often those preferred for dedication to God (Nu 19:2; Dt 21:3; 1Sa 6:7).
11:3 *The Lord needs it.* Roman soldiers could commandeer animals for their use; more to the point here, so could kings, such as the Lord.
11:7 *colt.* Although Mark does not specify Jesus' allusion to Scripture, Jesus entering Jerusalem on a colt evokes Zec 9:9 — the humble king.
11:8 *spread their cloaks.* Casting garments for a ruler to walk on was a way of hailing him king (2Ki 9:13). *spread branches.* People would also wave branches to celebrate triumphs (cf. 1 Maccabees 13:51; 2 Maccabees 10:7).
11:9–10 Pilgrims already present often welcomed the newcomers. The crowds would know Ps 118:25–26 by heart; cf. note on v. 9.
11:9 *Hosanna.* A request for salvation or deliverance, as in Ps 118:25. It was part of the Hallel, consisting of Ps 113–118, which was sung at the Passover season (see also Mt 26:30). Mark's audience may not have known this detail, but it reflects accurately Jesus' original setting. Hopes for a new act of redemption also ran high at Passover; the expectation of the Davidic kingdom here may be provoked by knowledge of Jesus' proclamation of the kingdom and the way he was entering (see v. 7 and note).
11:11 *went into the temple courts.* The temple mount consumed more than a quarter of Jerusalem and constituted the focal point of activity for festal pilgrims, from early morning until late afternoon. (The temple's "evening offering" was about 3:00 p.m.) *Bethany.* On the Mount of Olives, located two miles (three kilometers) to the east, within walking distance from Jerusalem (v. 1), but returning to that village before dark was important. Because Jerusalem was crowded for the festival, it made sense to find lodging outside the holy city until the Passover night itself; Jesus apparently lodged with Simon (14:3; cf. Jn 11:1).
11:13 *fig tree in leaf.* On the eastern side of the Mount of Olives, fig trees could already have leaves at Passover season (late March or early April). They did not yet, however, have ripe figs; they had only green early figs, which did not taste good. They could ripen in June, but often fell off beforehand, so that only leaves remained. If a tree had leaves but produced no early figs, it would remain fruitless that year. *it was not the season for figs.* Jesus would know this but may here be offering an acted parable like the prophets: his judgment against the fig tree (vv. 14,19–20) frames his prophetic protest against the fruitless temple establishment (vv. 15–18).
11:15 *those who were buying and selling.* Jerusalem needed markets and bazaars to supply the massive influx of pilgrims; although most of these may have been outside the temple there was little room immediately outside it, so sacred items (such as animals for sacrifice; cf. pigeons in Lev 1:14; 5:7; 12:8) would likely be purchased on site. (The temple mount offered Jerusalem's largest space and could accommodate an estimated 75,000 people at one time.) *money changers.* Because each local region had its own currencies, moneychangers performed a service by changing local money into standardized currency so people could buy what they needed. Perhaps Jesus objects to the misplaced emphasis. But this site, the massive outer court, was also the only place of worship for the Gentiles (see note on v. 17).
11:16 *temple courts.* The OT temple segregated priests from people, but did not separate Gentiles from the people (1Ki 8:41–43). By contrast, for purity reasons, the current temple, constructed mostly under Herod the Great, divided the outer court into the court of Israel, for Jewish men; on a lower level outside of that the court of (Jewish) women; and on a lower level outside of that a third court that can be referred to as the court of the Gentiles. Posted signs warned that any Gentile going beyond the court of the Gentiles would be killed.
11:17 Isa 56:7 (quoted here) shows God's ideal for the temple: Gentiles were to be welcome (Isa 56:3–6). This

a house of prayer for all nations'[a]?[f] But
you have made it 'a den of robbers.'[b]"[g]
18 The chief priests and the teachers of
the law heard this and began looking for
a way to kill him, for they feared him,[h]
because the whole crowd was amazed at
his teaching.[i]
19 When evening came, Jesus and his
disciples[c] went out of the city.[j]
20 In the morning, as they went along,
they saw the fig tree withered from the
roots. 21 Peter remembered and said to
Jesus, "Rabbi,[k] look! The fig tree you
cursed has withered!"
22 "Have faith in God," Jesus answered.
23 "Truly[d] I tell you, if anyone says to this
mountain, 'Go, throw yourself into the
sea,' and does not doubt in their heart but
believes that what they say will happen,
it will be done for them.[l] 24 Therefore I tell
you, whatever you ask for in prayer, believe that you have received it, and it will
be yours.[m] 25 And when you stand praying,
if you hold anything against anyone, forgive them, so that your Father in heaven
may forgive you your sins."[n] [26][e]

The Authority of Jesus Questioned

11:27-33pp — Mt 21:23-27; Lk 20:1-8

27 They arrived again in Jerusalem,
and while Jesus was walking in the temple courts, the chief priests, the teachers
of the law and the elders came to him.
28 "By what authority are you doing these
things?" they asked. "And who gave you
authority to do this?"
29 Jesus replied, "I will ask you one
question. Answer me, and I will tell you
by what authority I am doing these things.
30 John's baptism — was it from heaven, or
of human origin? Tell me!"
31 They discussed it among themselves
and said, "If we say, 'From heaven,' he will
ask, 'Then why didn't you believe him?'
32 But if we say, 'Of human origin' . . ."
(They feared the people, for everyone held
that John really was a prophet.)[o]
33 So they answered Jesus, "We don't
know."
Jesus said, "Neither will I tell you by
what authority I am doing these things."

The Parable of the Tenants

12:1-12pp — Mt 21:33-46; Lk 20:9-19

12 Jesus then began to speak to them
in parables: "A man planted a vineyard.[p] He put a wall around it, dug a pit
for the winepress and built a watchtower.
Then he rented the vineyard to some farmers and moved to another place. 2 At harvest time he sent a servant to the tenants
to collect from them some of the fruit of

11:17 [f] Isa 56:7 [g] Jer 7:11 **11:18** [h] Mt 21:46; Mk 12:12; Lk 20:19 [i] Mt 7:28 **11:19** [j] Lk 21:37 **11:21** [k] Mt 23:7 **11:23** [l] Mt 21:21 **11:24** [m] Mt 7:7 **11:25** [n] Mt 6:14 **11:32** [o] Mt 11:9 **12:1** [p] Isa 5:1-7

[a] *17* Isaiah 56:7 [b] *17* Jer. 7:11 [c] *19* Some early manuscripts *came, Jesus* [d] *22,23* Some early manuscripts *"If you have faith in God," Jesus answered, 23"truly* [e] *26* Some manuscripts include here words similar to Matt. 6:15.

ideal may contrast with the current arrangement of the temple (see note on v. 16). *den of robbers.* Evokes Jer 7:11; in that context people believe that the temple will protect them from God's judgment, but God warns that he will judge the temple (see 13:2).

11:18 *began looking for a way to kill him.* Any challenge to practices legally conducted in the temple constituted a challenge to the priestly authorities who controlled the temple. Unlike Pharisees, who earlier plotted against Jesus fruitlessly (3:6), the chief priests held significant political power and could swiftly deal with affronts to their honor.

11:19 *out of the city.* Because the festival had swelled Jerusalem's population, it was easiest for those who knew people in the vicinity to find accommodation outside the city walls (vv. 11 – 12).

11:23 "Moving mountains" became a figure of speech for a task that was considered virtually impossible. Some scholars think that "this mountain" refers to the Mount of Olives, which at this point was within sight for the disciples (cf. Zec 14:4); others believe that the temple mount is in view (cf. Zec 4:6 – 9). Neither application would alter the principle here.

11:27 *the chief priests, the teachers of the law and the elders.* The three groups mentioned here are the most powerful elements of Judean society, the elite groups represented in the Sanhedrin. They recognized that Jesus' actions challenged their authority (cf. v. 28).

11:29 Sages often met questions with counter-questions.

11:30 *from heaven.* Jews commonly used "heaven" as a circumlocution for "God" (e.g., Da 4:26; 1QM 12.5).

11:32 *feared the people.* Although the Pharisees were popular with the people, Jesus was more popular. The Sadducees, whose chief priests dominate the alliance against Jesus here (v. 27), held political power but were less popular with the people than were the Pharisees. They were responsible for the temple and could not afford unrest during the crowded conditions of the festival (14:2).

12:1 *parables.* Teaching in parables allows Jesus to speak truth in riddles (see the article "Parables," p. 1692); the meaning is transparent (v. 12) but not directly indictable. *wall . . . winepress . . . watchtower.* See note on Mt 21:33 – 34. *rented the vineyard to some farmers.* Jesus draws the details here from the parable in Isa 5:1 – 2, in which the vineyard was Israel (5:7). The "tenants" here in vv. 1 – 9 must thus represent the temporary caretakers of Israel — the chief priests, the teachers of the law and the elders (v. 12; 11:27). Although many Galileans owned their own plots of land, many landless peasants found work on larger estates. Wealthy absentee landowners were common; they usually either contracted laborers or rented their land to tenant farmers (serfs).

12:2 *some of the fruit.* Tenant farmers lived and worked their estates and merely paid the landowners a portion of the harvest. Because tenants did not own the land they worked, they sometimes had to pay the landowners half the harvest. Profits from vineyards usually did not begin to be realized until four years after planting; the owner in this story is wealthy enough to be able to afford the delay. Contracts specified the tenants' obligations; owners were advised not to be too lenient lest the tenants default on what they owed.

MARK 11

HEROD'S TEMPLE

For hundreds of years the Jerusalem temple was the center of Jewish life. However, in the centuries leading up to the New Testament era, the postexilic edifice rebuilt by Zerubbabel suffered serious damage. The renovation and expansion of this dilapidated structure gave Herod the Great the opportunity to construct the greatest of his numerous building projects and perhaps the most impressive structure Jerusalem has ever seen.

Work on Herod's temple began in 20–19 BC, and though most of it was finished within ten years, adornment continued until AD 63. Herod faced a significant challenge: The size of the temple was limited by the Biblical precedent of Solomon's temple, a fairly modest structure. But pagan temples of the New Testament era were becoming increasingly mammoth, and the Jerusalem temple if confined to Biblical standards would have seemed puny in comparison. Therefore, although the temple proper was left fairly small, the temple precincts in Herod's scheme were enormous. Zerubbabel's temple had to be torn down and the three surrounding valleys filled in. Massive retaining walls helped to support the platform of the temple precinct (the western retaining wall is the familiar "Wailing Wall"). The temple and its surrounding courtyards created a rhomboid shape, measuring 1,590 feet (484.6 meters) on its western side, 1,536 feet (468.2 meters) on the eastern side, 1,035 feet (315.5 meters) on the northern side and 912 feet (278 meters) on the southern side.

The temple area was essentially a series of concentric courts, each of increasing holiness as one proceeded closer to the temple proper.

The first courtyard, the court of the Gentiles, was open to Jews and God-fearing Gentiles. This area contained the merchant and money-changing areas, and here the blind and lame begged and children were present (Mt 21:14–15).

Only Jewish men and women could enter the court of women, which contained chests for tithes that contributed to temple expenses and was the location of the poor widow's contribution (Mk 12:44).

Only ritually clean Jewish men were permitted to proceed beyond into the court of Israel. When Jesus came to the temple and "looked around at everything" (11:11), he was surveying this area.

Only priests could move farther into the temple area. The approach included an altar of uncut stones, the porch and finally the temple itself. Constructed of marble and gold, the temple was built to the same specifications as Solomon's earlier counterpart. Golden spikes lined the roof to prevent birds from alighting there and defiling the structure.

continued on next page

the vineyard. 3But they seized him, beat
him and sent him away empty-handed.
4Then he sent another servant to them;
they struck this man on the head and
treated him shamefully. 5He sent still another, and that one they killed. He sent
many others; some of them they beat, others they killed.

6"He had one left to send, a son, whom
he loved. He sent him last of all,[q] saying,
'They will respect my son.'
7"But the tenants said to one another,
'This is the heir. Come, let's kill him, and
the inheritance will be ours.' 8So they took
him and killed him, and threw him out of
the vineyard.

12:6 [q] Heb 1:1-3

12:5 *killed.* See note on Mt 21:35.
12:6 *son, whom he loved.* See note on Mt 21:37.
12:7 *inheritance will be ours.* See note on Mt 21:38. To the people listening to Jesus' story, this would make the behavior of the tenants appear even more deluded and ridiculous.

Entering the temple proper, one first came to the Holy Place, which contained the lampstand, the table for the bread of the Presence and the incense altar, all cast in pure gold.

Separated by a heavy, embroidered curtain, the Most Holy Place contained only a single rock, upon which the high priest offered incense and sprinkled blood once annually on the Day of Atonement (the ark of the covenant had long since been lost). Some surmise that the Most Holy Place was located where the Islamic holy place, the Dome of the Rock (some prefer Dome of Spirits), now stands.

Other important structures were within the vicinity of the temple. The Fortress of Antonia, north of the temple vicinity, was the barracks for Roman troops in Jerusalem. Soldiers from the fortress could enter the temple area quickly if needed, as when a riot broke out during Paul's visit there (Ac 21:31 – 32). On the south side of the temple was the house for the Sanhedrin and a bathhouse for ritual immersion (a requirement for entering the temple area). As a social center, the temple was the most important locale for education and debate in Judea (Lk 2:46), as well as the backdrop for many events recorded in the Gospels, most notably Jesus' ejection of the merchants. Jesus' actions and words upon that occasion created an "enacted parable." He was angry not only at the extortion (if this was happening) but also at the moneychangers' occupation of the court of the Gentiles, which effectively limited access to this area.

For all its glory, this temple had a short life. Completed in AD 63, it was destroyed in AD 70 by the Romans. Jesus' words to his disciples in this regard were fulfilled: Not one stone was left upon another (Mt 24:2). ◆

A model of Herod's temple and surrounding courtyards.

Berthold Werner/Wikimedia Commons

9"What then will the owner of the
vineyard do? He will come and kill those
tenants and give the vineyard to others.
10Haven't you read this passage of Scripture:

"'The stone the builders rejected
has become the cornerstone;[r]
11the Lord has done this,
and it is marvelous in our eyes'[a]?"[s]

12Then the chief priests, the teachers of
the law and the elders looked for a way
to arrest him because they knew he had
spoken the parable against them. But they

12:10 [r] Ac 4:11
12:11 [s] Ps 118:22,23

[a] *11* Psalm 118:22,23

12:10 – 11 This passage (Ps 118:22 – 23) would resonate with Jesus' hearers — it had been recently sung by these people as part of the Passover. It comes from the Hallel, which consists of Ps 113 – 118 (see notes on 11:9 – 10).

12:12 See note on 11:32.

were afraid of the crowd;[t] so they left him and went away.[u]

Paying the Imperial Tax to Caesar

12:13-17pp — Mt 22:15-22; Lk 20:20-26

13 Later they sent some of the Pharisees and Herodians[v] to Jesus to catch him[w] in his words. 14 They came to him and said, "Teacher, we know that you are a man of integrity. You aren't swayed by others, because you pay no attention to who they are; but you teach the way of God in accordance with the truth. Is it right to pay the imperial tax[a] to Caesar or not? 15 Should we pay or shouldn't we?"

But Jesus knew their hypocrisy. "Why are you trying to trap me?" he asked. "Bring me a denarius and let me look at it." 16 They brought the coin, and he asked them, "Whose image is this? And whose inscription?"

"Caesar's," they replied.

17 Then Jesus said to them, "Give back to Caesar what is Caesar's and to God what is God's."[x]

And they were amazed at him.

Marriage at the Resurrection

12:18-27pp — Mt 22:23-33; Lk 20:27-38

18 Then the Sadducees,[y] who say there is no resurrection,[z] came to him with a question. 19 "Teacher," they said, "Moses wrote for us that if a man's brother dies and leaves a wife but no children, the man must marry the widow and raise up offspring for his brother.[a] 20 Now there were seven brothers. The first one married and died without leaving any children. 21 The second one married the widow, but he also died, leaving no child. It was the same with the third. 22 In fact, none of the seven left any children. Last of all, the woman died too. 23 At the resurrection[b] whose wife will she be, since the seven were married to her?"

24 Jesus replied, "Are you not in error because you do not know the Scriptures[b] or the power of God? 25 When the dead rise, they will neither marry nor be given in marriage; they will be like the angels in heaven.[c] 26 Now about the dead rising—have you not read in the Book of Moses, in the account of the burning bush, how God said to him, 'I am the God of Abraham, the God of Isaac, and the God of Jacob'[c]?[d] 27 He is not the God of the dead, but of the living. You are badly mistaken!"

The Greatest Commandment

12:28-34pp — Mt 22:34-40

28 One of the teachers of the law[e] came and heard them debating. Noticing that Jesus had given them a good answer, he asked him, "Of all the commandments, which is the most important?"

29 "The most important one," answered Jesus, "is this: 'Hear, O Israel: The Lord our God, the Lord is one.[d] 30 Love the Lord your God with all your heart and with all your soul and with all your mind and with all your strength.'[ef] 31 The second is this: 'Love your neighbor as yourself.'[fg] There is no commandment greater than these."

32 "Well said, teacher," the man replied. "You are right in saying that God is one

12:12 [t] Mk 11:18 [u] Mt 22:22 **12:13** [v] Mt 22:16; Mk 3:6 [w] Mt 12:10 **12:17** [x] Ro 13:7 **12:18** [y] Ac 4:1 [z] Ac 23:8; 1Co 15:12 **12:19** [a] Dt 25:5 **12:24** [b] 2Ti 3:15-17 **12:25** [c] 1Co 15:42, 49,52 **12:26** [d] Ex 3:6 **12:28** [e] Lk 10:25-28; 20:39 **12:30** [f] Dt 6:4,5 **12:31** [g] Lev 19:18; Mt 5:43

a 14 A special tax levied on subject peoples, not on Roman citizens *b* 23 Some manuscripts *resurrection, when people rise from the dead,* *c* 26 Exodus 3:6 *d* 29 Or *The Lord our God is one Lord* *e* 30 Deut. 6:4,5 *f* 31 Lev. 19:18

12:13 *Pharisees and Herodians.* Pharisees, some of whom supported older, nationalistic traditions, and Herodians, probably clients or political partisans of Herod Antipas, worked together only in exceptional circumstances—such as these.
12:14 *Is it right to pay the imperial tax ...?* They may expect the leader of a Messianic movement to oppose Roman taxes, like an earlier Galilean revolutionary movement; if Jesus speaks against such taxes, they have public witnesses for arresting him and handing him over to Pilate on the charge of treason (cf. Lk 23:2).
12:16 *coin.* See notes on Mt 22:19–20.
12:17 *Give ... to God what is God's.* See note on Mt 22:21.
12:18 Challenging teachers in public was common. *Sadducees, who say there is no resurrection.* See note on Mt 22:23.
12:19 *a man's brother.* Because widows could be left destitute, the extended families into which they married were supposed to provide for them by a brother of the deceased marrying the widow (Dt 25:5–6).
12:20–22 See note on Lk 20:29–31.
12:23 *At the resurrection.* Sadducees were known to pose conundrums such as this to the Pharisees, seeking to illustrate what they believed were the absurd implications of belief in the resurrection.
12:24 *you do not know the Scriptures.* The highly educated and literate Sadducees would hear this statement as an insult. *power of God.* A common Jewish prayer associated God's power with the resurrection of the righteous at the end of the age.
12:25 *neither marry nor be given in marriage.* Grooms married; fathers gave their daughters in marriage. *like the angels.* Most Jewish people agreed that angels, who are immortal, did not propagate; the same then would be true of those resurrected to immortality.
12:26 *in the Book of Moses.* See note on Mt 22:29. *the God of Abraham, the God of Isaac, and the God of Jacob.* See note on Mt 22:32.
12:28 *Of all the commandments, which is the most important?* This question was one of the issues commonly debated among Pharisaic teachers in the first century. Many, e.g., felt that the greatest was honoring one's parents. Rabbi Akiba, a later rabbi, came closer to Jesus' view here when he asserted that "Love your neighbor" is the greatest commandment.
12:29–30 Dt 6:4 (noted in v. 29) was the cornerstone of Jewish faith, the *Shema.* Jewish people regularly recited this passage (Dt 6:4–5).
12:31 *Love your neighbor as yourself.* See note on Mt 22:39.
12:32 *Well said.* This teacher of the law rightly recognizes

and there is no other but him.[h] 33 To love
him with all your heart, with all your understanding and with all your strength,
and to love your neighbor as yourself is
more important than all burnt offerings
and sacrifices."[i]
34 When Jesus saw that he had answered
wisely, he said to him, "You are not far from
the kingdom of God."[j] And from then on
no one dared ask him any more questions.[k]

Whose Son Is the Messiah?

12:35-37pp — Mt 22:41-46; Lk 20:41-44
12:38-40pp — Mt 23:1-7; Lk 20:45-47

35 While Jesus was teaching in the temple courts,[l] he asked, "Why do the teachers of the law say that the Messiah is the
son of David?[m] 36 David himself, speaking
by the Holy Spirit,[n] declared:

"'The Lord said to my Lord:
"Sit at my right hand
until I put your enemies
under your feet."'[a][o]

37 David himself calls him 'Lord.' How then
can he be his son?"
The large crowd[p] listened to him with
delight.

Warning Against the Teachers of the Law

38 As he taught, Jesus said, "Watch out
for the teachers of the law. They like to
walk around in flowing robes and be greeted with respect in the marketplaces, 39 and
have the most important seats in the synagogues and the places of honor at banquets.[q] 40 They devour widows' houses and
for a show make lengthy prayers. These
men will be punished most severely."

The Widow's Offering

12:41-44pp — Lk 21:1-4

41 Jesus sat down opposite the place
where the offerings were put[r] and watched
the crowd putting their money into the
temple treasury. Many rich people threw
in large amounts. 42 But a poor widow
came and put in two very small copper
coins, worth only a few cents.
43 Calling his disciples to him, Jesus
said, "Truly I tell you, this poor widow
has put more into the treasury than all the
others. 44 They all gave out of their wealth;
but she, out of her poverty, put in everything—all she had to live on."[s]

The Destruction of the Temple and Signs of the End Times

13:1-37pp — Mt 24:1-51; Lk 21:5-36

13 As Jesus was leaving the temple,
one of his disciples said to him,
"Look, Teacher! What massive stones!
What magnificent buildings!"

[a] *36* Psalm 110:1

12:32 [h] Dt 4:35, 39; Isa 45:6, 14; 46:9
12:33 [i] 1Sa 15:22; Hos 6:6; Mic 6:6-8; Heb 10:8
12:34 [j] Mt 3:2 [k] Mt 22:46; Lk 20:40
12:35 [l] Mt 26:55 [m] Mt 9:27
12:36 [n] 2Sa 23:2 [o] Ps 110:1; Mt 22:44
12:37 [p] Jn 12:9
12:39 [q] Lk 11:43
12:41 [r] 2Ki 12:9; Jn 8:20
12:44 [s] 2Co 8:12

Jesus' words as consistent with Scripture; they were also compatible with Jewish tradition.
12:34 *no one dared ask him any more questions.* People often raised questions and objections to publicly challenge or even shame a teacher; the best speakers could silence and shame their opponents, because such teachers could make hostile questions themselves look foolish.
12:36 *speaking by the Holy Spirit.* In traditional Jewish parlance, this is another way of saying "speaking by divine inspiration." See note on Mt 22:44. *under your feet.* In ancient artistic renderings, defeated enemies are often shown as being under their conqueror's feet (cf. Jos 10:24).
12:37 See note on Mt 22:45.
12:38 *be greeted.* Social convention stipulated that social inferiors should greet superiors first; later rabbis believed that the superiors included rabbis. *marketplaces.* Because in villages and towns people congregated especially in marketplaces, this location would provide opportunity for many greetings.
12:39 *most important seats in the synagogues and the places of honor at banquets.* See note on Mt 23:6.
12:40 *devour widows' houses.* Widows often had debt and normally lacked influential advocates; people of status could thus seize their property more readily, often through legal means (e.g., 2Ki 4:1). Scripture demanded special consideration for the defenseless, including widows (Ex 22:22; Dt 10:18; Isa 1:17,23; 10:2; Jer 7:6; 22:3). (In that social system, most women lacked sufficient means to support themselves.) *lengthy prayers.* On lengthy prayers among Gentiles, see note on Mt 6:7; the Jewish temptation would have been similar.
12:41 *money into the temple treasury.* Temples in the ancient world doubled as banks, since they were considered the safest place to deposit money. The temple treasury (where money was stored) was adjacent to the court of women, which was the court between the outer court (where the events of 11:15 – 17 took place) and the court of Israel.
12:42 *copper coins.* Each of these coins was worth only 1/128 of a denarius. *few cents.* This is the smallest Roman coin, a quadrans, worth 1/64 of a denarius—thus perhaps less than ten minutes' wages for an average male worker.
12:44 *poverty.* On the vulnerability of widows, see note on v. 40. For the woman's access to the treasury, see note on v. 41.
13:1 *As Jesus was leaving.* Although teachers normally lectured while sitting (v. 3), some also discoursed while walking. *What magnificent buildings!* Throughout the Mediterranean world the beauty of Jerusalem's temple was well known. It was the largest of all the temples in the ancient world (partly because Jews had only one God and one temple to support). It was even larger than the famous temple of the Ephesian Artemis, which was ranked as one of the seven wonders of the ancient world. Even those Jews who resented Herod, its builder, considered it sacred. It included various courts and outer porches; although laypersons could not pass beyond the court of Israel, the sanctuary's height made it visible from far away. Gates of bronze and a vine made of gold decorated the temple. Although the majority of Jews lived outside of the holy land, they demonstrated their loyalty to the temple by paying the temple tax (see note on Mt 17:24).

[2]"Do you see all these great buildings?"
replied Jesus. "Not one stone here will be
left on another; every one will be thrown
down."[t]
[3]As Jesus was sitting on the Mount of
Olives[u] opposite the temple, Peter, James,
John[v] and Andrew asked him privately,
[4]"Tell us, when will these things happen?
And what will be the sign that they are all
about to be fulfilled?"

13:2 [t]Lk 19:44
13:3 [u]Mt 21:1 [v]Mt 4:21

13:2 *Not one stone here will be left.* See note on Mt 24:2.
13:3 – 4 Disciples sometimes asked their teachers for special information in private. The disciples ask two questions here: When will the temple be destroyed (v. 4), and what sign will portend it? (Unlike Mark, Matthew, probably writing later, specifies the sign as the sign of the end.) This fits a prophetic pattern often found in earlier Biblical prophets, in which events are grouped more by the kind of event than by chronological proximity (Joel, e.g., seems to blend a nearer locust plague with an invasion in the later day of the Lord).

MARK 13

Josephus and the Fall of Jerusalem

The Jewish historian Josephus is our primary source of information about the fall of Jerusalem. During the Jewish revolt of AD 66 – 70 Josephus began as a rebel leader, but midway he switched his allegiance to the Roman side of the conflict. He accompanied the Roman general Titus to the siege of Jerusalem and was thus an eyewitness of the harrowing events of the city's fall.

The Arch of Titus in Rome.

continued on next page

[5]Jesus said to them: "Watch out that no
one deceives you.[w] [6]Many will come in
my name, claiming, 'I am he,' and will deceive many. [7]When you hear of wars and
rumors of wars, do not be alarmed. Such
things must happen, but the end is still to
come. [8]Nation will rise against nation, and
kingdom against kingdom. There will be

13:5 [w] ver 22; Jer 29:8; Eph 5:6; 2Th 2:3, 10-12; 1Ti 4:1; 2Ti 3:13; 1Jn 4:6

13:6 *Many will ... deceive many.* The Jewish historian Josephus reports a number of "false prophets" who tried to emulate Moses or Joshua, who probably viewed themselves as Messianic in some sense, even in the decades between Jesus' resurrection and AD 70 (see notes on Ac 5:36 – 37; 21:38).

13:7 – 8 See note on Mt 24:6 – 14.

13:7 *rumors of wars.* Like other fearful news, rumors of wars spread quickly. Ancient sources report this rapid spread for both true and false news, of both defeats and victories, sometimes spurring premature panic or hope.

Interior of arch, depicting troops carrying away plunder from the temple in Jerusalem.

As the Romans slowly crushed the revolt in outlying areas, refugees flooded into Jerusalem for the climactic battle of the war. The Jews inside the city were torn by internal dissent, with various rebel groups vying for control. There was horrendous loss of life, and conditions worsened as the Romans laid siege to Jerusalem in the spring of AD 70. Titus's troops took the outer wall around May and captured the strategic Fortress of Antonia. The destruction of the temple was imminent, but many of the Jewish defenders likely believed that God would defend them and his temple at the last. Nonetheless, at the end of August the Romans successfully attacked the temple, setting fire to its gates and overwhelming its defenders. With the sanctuary fallen, the Jews lost hope, and carnage ensued.

Josephus described it thus: "No pity was shown on account of age or out of respect for anyone's dignity — children and elderly, lay people and priests alike were slain. The battle surged ahead and surrounded everybody, including both those who begged for mercy and those who resisted. The flames spread out to a great distance and its noise mixed with the groans of the perishing; and such was the height of the ridge and the magnitude of the burning that one would have imagined the whole city was aflame" (*Wars* 6.5.1). Thus was Jesus' prophecy regarding the destruction of the temple fulfilled (Mk 13:2). ◆

earthquakes in various places, and famines.
These are the beginning of birth pains.
9 "You must be on your guard. You will
be handed over to the local councils and
flogged in the synagogues.[x] On account of
me you will stand before governors and
kings as witnesses to them. 10 And the gospel must first be preached to all nations.
11 Whenever you are arrested and brought
to trial, do not worry beforehand about
what to say. Just say whatever is given
you at the time, for it is not you speaking,
but the Holy Spirit.[y]
12 "Brother will betray brother to death,
and a father his child. Children will rebel
against their parents and have them put to
death.[z] 13 Everyone will hate you because
of me,[a] but the one who stands firm to the
end will be saved.[b]
14 "When you see 'the abomination that
causes desolation'[a][c] standing where it[b]
does not belong—let the reader understand—then let those who are in Judea
flee to the mountains. 15 Let no one on the
housetop go down or enter the house to
take anything out. 16 Let no one in the field
go back to get their cloak. 17 How dreadful
it will be in those days for pregnant women
and nursing mothers![d] 18 Pray that this will
not take place in winter, 19 because those
will be days of distress unequaled from the
beginning, when God created the world,[e]
until now—and never to be equaled again.[f]
20 "If the Lord had not cut short those
days, no one would survive. But for the
sake of the elect, whom he has chosen,
he has shortened them. 21 At that time if
anyone says to you, 'Look, here is the
Messiah!' or, 'Look, there he is!' do not
believe it.[g] 22 For false messiahs and false
prophets[h] will appear and perform signs
and wonders[i] to deceive, if possible, even
the elect. 23 So be on your guard;[j] I have
told you everything ahead of time.
24 "But in those days, following that distress,

"'the sun will be darkened,
and the moon will not give its light;
25 the stars will fall from the sky,
and the heavenly bodies will be
shaken.'[c][k]

26 "At that time people will see the Son
of Man coming in clouds[l] with great power and glory. 27 And he will send his angels
and gather his elect from the four winds,
from the ends of the earth to the ends of
the heavens.[m]

13:9 [x] Mt 10:17 **13:11** [y] Mt 10:19, 20; Lk 12:11, 12 **13:12** [z] Mic 7:6; Mt 10:21; Lk 12:51-53 **13:13** [a] Jn 15:21 [b] Mt 10:22 **13:14** [c] Da 9:27; 11:31; 12:11 **13:17** [d] Lk 23:29 **13:19** [e] Mk 10:6 [f] Da 9:26; 12:1; Joel 2:2 **13:21** [g] Lk 17:23; 21:8 **13:22** [h] Mt 7:15 [i] Jn 4:48; 2Th 2:9, 10 **13:23** [j] 2Pe 3:17 **13:25** [k] Isa 13:10; 34:4; Mt 24:29 **13:26** [l] Da 7:13; Mt 16:27; Rev 1:7 **13:27** [m] Zec 2:6

[a] *14* Daniel 9:27; 11:31; 12:11 [b] *14* Or *he*
[c] *25* Isaiah 13:10; 34:4

13:9 *local councils ... synagogues.* Priests and other elders normally judged local councils. Local synagogues doubled as community centers, and disciplines could be meted out there. *flogged.* If beatings were carried out in a way similar to how they appear in somewhat later, idealized tradition, the condemned person would be tied to a post, then given 26 lashes with a calf-leather whip across the back and 13 across the chest. The number of lashes (39; cf. 2Co 11:24) was to prevent accidentally exceeding the Biblical limit of 40 (Dt 25:3). *governors and kings.* See note on Mt 10:18.
13:11 *the Holy Spirit.* Jewish tradition particularly emphasized the OT idea that God's Spirit inspired prophetic speech.
13:12 Betrayal of family members was considered particularly heinous and unusual.
13:14 *abomination that causes desolation.* See note on Mt 24:15. *flee to the mountains.* See note on Mt 24:16.
13:15 *housetop.* See note on Mt 24:17.
13:16 *go back to get their cloak.* See note on Mt 24:18.
13:17 *pregnant women and nursing mothers.* See note on Mt 24:19.
13:18 *winter.* See note on Mt 24:20.
13:19 *unequaled from the beginning.* See note on Mt 4:21.
13:20 *cut short.* Might mean that the period of tribulation would not fill the full expected number of days (cf. Da 12:11–13). *sake of the elect.* Jewish people regarded themselves as the elect, the chosen people (e.g., Ps 105:43; Wisdom of Solomon 4:15); early Christians especially applied the term to Jesus' followers (Ro 8:33; Col 3:12).
13:21–22 See note on v. 6.
13:22 *false prophets will ... perform signs.* Cf., e.g., Ex 7:11,22; 8:7; predictive signs in Dt 13:1–2.
13:23 *ahead of time.* God sometimes provided advance warning so that when words came to pass people would continue to trust him (e.g., Isa 41:26; 48:5).
13:24 Jesus uses Isa 13:10, originally part of a prophecy against Babylon but probably also portending the world's judgment (Isa 13:11) in the ultimate day of the Lord (Isa 13:6–9). The day of the Lord was God's day of reckoning, so it could blend nearer judgments with more ultimate ones (see, e.g., Joel 1:15; 2:1,11,31; 3:14; see also note on Mk 13:3–4).
13:25 Jesus uses Isa 34:4, a judgment against the nations (Isa 34:1–2) with a focus on Edom (Isa 34:5). Jewish people saw the quoted passages in Isaiah as presaging global judgments. People in antiquity expected that they would see cosmic signs before catastrophic events such as Jerusalem's fall; Jewish apocalyptic literature featured expectations of such signs especially before the end.
13:26 *the Son of Man coming in the clouds.* Jesus quotes Da 7:13; the son of man was given "authority, glory and sovereign power" in Da 7:14. Daniel refers to the son of man receiving authority, something that may have happened at Jesus' exaltation. Because Daniel does not foresee two comings, however, he does not distinguish between what we experience as present and future phases of Jesus' reign. Some scholars associate Jesus' coming here strictly with his exaltation, others with his coming in judgment in AD 70, and a larger number with his second coming. On either of the latter views, Jesus' description presupposes the image from Da 7:13–14 already initiated at his exaltation.
13:27 *gather his elect from the four winds.* Jewish people realized that they were scattered among the nations, but believed that God would gather them back to their land at the time of the end (Isa 11:12; 27:12; 40:11; 43:5; 49:5; Jer 29:14; 31:8,10; 32:27; Eze 11:17; 34:13; 36:24; 37:21); Jesus' followers likewise expected to be gathered (1Th 4:17; 2Th 2:1; cf. Gentiles gathered in Isa 56:6–8).

28“Now learn this lesson from the fig
tree: As soon as its twigs get tender and its
leaves come out, you know that summer is
near. 29Even so, when you see these things
happening, you know that it[a] is near, right
at the door. 30Truly I tell you, this generation[n] will certainly not pass away until
all these things have happened.[o] 31Heaven
and earth will pass away, but my words
will never pass away.[p]

The Day and Hour Unknown

32“But about that day or hour no one
knows, not even the angels in heaven, nor
the Son, but only the Father.[q] 33Be on guard!
Be alert[b]![r] You do not know when that time
will come. 34It’s like a man going away: He
leaves his house and puts his servants[s] in
charge, each with their assigned task, and
tells the one at the door to keep watch.
35“Therefore keep watch because you
do not know when the owner of the house
will come back—whether in the evening,
or at midnight, or when the rooster crows,
or at dawn. 36If he comes suddenly, do not
let him find you sleeping. 37What I say to
you, I say to everyone: ‘Watch!’ ”[t]

Jesus Anointed at Bethany

14:1-11pp — Mt 26:2-16
14:1,2,10,11pp — Lk 22:1-6
14:3-8Ref — Jn 12:1-8

14 Now the Passover[u] and the Festival of Unleavened Bread were only
two days away, and the chief priests and
the teachers of the law were scheming to
arrest Jesus secretly and kill him.[v] 2“But
not during the festival,” they said, “or the
people may riot.”
3While he was in Bethany,[w] reclining at
the table in the home of Simon the Leper, a woman came with an alabaster jar
of very expensive perfume, made of pure
nard. She broke the jar and poured the
perfume on his head.[x]
4Some of those present were saying indig-
nantly to one another, “Why this waste of
perfume? 5It could have been sold for more
than a year’s wages[c] and the money given
to the poor.” And they rebuked her harshly.
6“Leave her alone,” said Jesus. “Why
are you bothering her? She has done a
beautiful thing to me. 7The poor you will
always have with you,[d] and you can help
them any time you want.[y] But you will not
always have me. 8She did what she could.
She poured perfume on my body beforehand to prepare for my burial.[z] 9Truly I
tell you, wherever the gospel is preached
throughout the world,[a] what she has done
will also be told, in memory of her.”
10Then Judas Iscariot, one of the
Twelve,[b] went to the chief priests to betray Jesus to them.[c] 11They were delighted to hear this and promised to give him
money. So he watched for an opportunity
to hand him over.

13:30 [n]Lk 17:25 [o]Mk 9:1 **13:31** [p]Mt 5:18 **13:32** [q]Ac 1:7; 1Th 5:1,2 **13:33** [r]1Th 5:6 **13:34** [s]Mt 25:14 **13:37** [t]Lk 12:35-40 **14:1** [u]Jn 11:55; 13:1 [v]Mt 12:14 **14:3** [w]Mt 21:17 [x]Lk 7:37-39 **14:7** [y]Dt 15:11 **14:8** [z]Jn 19:40 **14:9** [a]Mt 24:14; Mk 16:15 **14:10** [b]Mk 3:16-19 [c]Mt 10:4

[a] *29* Or *he* [b] *33* Some manuscripts *alert and pray* [c] *5* Greek *than three hundred denarii* [d] *7* See Deut. 15:11.

13:28 *fig tree.* Unlike most Judean trees, fig trees lost their leaves each year; they produced new leaves (see note on 11:13) before the wheat harvest and well before the grape vintage. Once the signs mentioned in this context were fulfilled, no further barriers would remain to the coming of the end (v. 29).
13:30 *this generation.* The temple was destroyed about 40 years (the rough figure often used as a Biblical generation) after Jesus promised this. The distinction between the specified timing here and unknown timing of v. 32 might relate to the two distinct questions asked in v. 4.
13:31 *my words will never pass away.* Significantly, Jesus here equates his words with God’s (Isa 40:8; Zec 1:5–6; cf. Mt 5:18).
13:32 *only the Father.* See note on Mt 24:36.
13:34–36 Ancient people often told stories of masters returning home unexpectedly to find servants unprepared, or husbands returning to find wives unfaithful. Night guards were supposed to stay awake and ready.
14:1—15:46 Even though writing materials were expensive, biographers in antiquity generally devoted significant space to relating the story of a person’s death, especially when that death was significant (e.g., when writing about a martyr).
14:1 *scheming to … kill him.* The hostile portrayal of the chief priests here is not limited to the Gospels; most surviving Jewish sources from the period (the Dead Sea Scrolls, rabbis’ memories from the Pharisees, and reports in Josephus) depict members of this group exploiting their power against others.
14:2 *riot.* Festivals in Jerusalem were crowded—Jerusalem’s population increased fivefold during Passover. These conditions sometimes led to riots with many deaths, sometimes by trampling.
14:3 *Bethany.* See notes on 11:1,11; because Jerusalem was crowded, it made sense to lodge outside the city until the Passover meal. *reclining.* The normal posture at banquets. *Leper.* Because lepers were unclean, contact with them was discouraged (see Lev 13:45–46; see also note on Mk 1:41), so Simon may have been healed. *alabaster jar of very expensive perfume.* See note on Mt 26:7. *poured … on his head.* Providing a guest with oil to anoint his head could be simple courtesy, but one could also anoint a king on his head (2Ki 9:6).
14:7 *poor you will always have.* Jesus alludes to Dt 15:11, the context of which requires caring for the poor (Dt 15:1–10). Jesus is not minimizing care for the poor but recognizing that honoring him should come before everything else.
14:8 *prepare for my burial.* For the use of flasks of perfume to honor the bodies of the deceased, see note on v. 3.
14:9 *throughout the world.* Other ancient writers used similar hyperbole to speak of the hope or expectation of widespread fame. In this case, of course, the woman’s story is told today throughout the world (though not literally in every recounting of the gospel story), unlike the case of other such claims from antiquity.
14:10 *betray.* See note on v. 18.

PASSION WEEK BETHANY, THE MOUNT OF OLIVES AND JERUSALEM

The Roman road climbed steeply to the crest of the Mount of Olives, affording spectacular views of the Desert of Judea to the east and of Jerusalem across the Kidron Valley to the west.

1 Arrival in Bethany

FRIDAY (Jn 12:1)

Jesus arrived in Bethany six days before the Passover to spend some time with his friends, Mary, Martha and Lazarus. On the following Tuesday evening, while Jesus was still in Bethany, Mary anointed his feet with costly perfume as an act of humility. This tender expression indicated Mary's devotion to Jesus and her willingness to serve him.

2 Sabbath—day of rest

SATURDAY

Not mentioned in the Gospels.

The Lord presumably spent the Sabbath day in traditional fashion with his friends.

3 The "Triumphal" Entry

SUNDAY (Mt 21:1–11; Mk 11:1–11; Lk 19:28–44; Jn 12:12–19)

On the first day of the week Jesus rode into Jerusalem on a donkey, fulfilling an ancient prophecy (Zec 9:9). The crowd welcomed him with the words of Ps 118:25–26, thus ascribing to him a Messianic title as the agent of the Lord, the coming King of Israel.

4 Clearing of the temple

MONDAY (Mt 21:12–17; Mk 11:15–18; Lk 19:45–48)

Jesus returned to the temple and found the court of the Gentiles full of traders and money changers making a large profit. Jesus drove them out and overturned their benches and tables.

5 Day of controversy and parables

TUESDAY (Mt 21:23—24:51; Mk 11:27—13:37; Lk 20:1—21:36)

IN JERUSALEM

Jesus evaded the traps set by the priests.

ON THE MOUNT OF OLIVES OVERLOOKING JERUSALEM

(Tuesday afternoon, exact location unknown)

Jesus taught in parables and warned the people against the Pharisees. He predicted the destruction of Herod's great temple and told his disciples about future events, including his own return.

Day of rest

WEDNESDAY

Although the Gospels do not mention this day, the counting of the days (Mk 14:1; Jn 12:1) seems to indicate that there was another day about which the Gospels record nothing.

6 **Passover, Last Supper**

THURSDAY (Mt 26:17–30; Mk 14:12–26; Lk 22:7–23)

In an upper room Jesus prepared both himself and his disciples for his death. He gave the Passover meal a new meaning. The loaf of bread and cup of wine represented his body soon to be sacrificed and his blood soon to be shed. And so he instituted the "Lord's Supper." After singing a hymn they went to Gethsemane, where Jesus prayed in agony, knowing what lay ahead for him.

7 **Crucifixion**

FRIDAY (Mt 27; Mk 15; Lk 22:66—23:56; Jn 18:28—19:37)

Following betrayal, arrest, desertion, false trials, denial, condemnation, beatings and mockery, Jesus was required to carry his cross to "the place of the skull" (Mt 27:33), where he was crucified with two other prisoners.

8 **In the tomb**

Jesus' body was placed in the tomb before 6:00 p.m. Friday evening, when the Sabbath began and all work stopped, and it lay in the tomb throughout the Sabbath.

9 **Resurrection**

SUNDAY (Mt 28:1–10; Mk 16:1–8; Lk 24:1–49; Jn 20)

Early in the morning, women went to the tomb and found that the stone closing the tomb's entrance had been rolled back. An angel told them Jesus was alive and gave them a message. Jesus appeared to Mary Magdalene in the garden, to Peter, to two disciples on the road to Emmaus and later that day to all the disciples but Thomas.

The Last Supper

14:12-26pp — Mt 26:17-30; Lk 22:7-23
14:22-25pp — 1Co 11:23-25

12 On the first day of the Festival of Unleavened Bread, when it was customary
to sacrifice the Passover lamb,[d] Jesus' disciples asked him, "Where do you want us
to go and make preparations for you to eat
the Passover?"
13 So he sent two of his disciples, telling
them, "Go into the city, and a man carrying a jar of water will meet you. Follow
him. 14 Say to the owner of the house he
enters, 'The Teacher asks: Where is my
guest room, where I may eat the Passover
with my disciples?' 15 He will show you a
large room upstairs,[e] furnished and ready.
Make preparations for us there."
16 The disciples left, went into the city
and found things just as Jesus had told
them. So they prepared the Passover.
17 When evening came, Jesus arrived
with the Twelve. 18 While they were reclining at the table eating, he said, "Truly I tell
you, one of you will betray me — one who
is eating with me."
19 They were saddened, and one by one
they said to him, "Surely you don't mean
me?"
20 "It is one of the Twelve," he replied,
"one who dips bread into the bowl with
me.[f] 21 The Son of Man[g] will go just as it
is written about him. But woe to that man
who betrays the Son of Man! It would be
better for him if he had not been born."

14:12 [d] Ex 12:1-11; Dt 16:1-4; 1Co 5:7 **14:15** [e] Ac 1:13 **14:20** [f] Jn 13:18-27 **14:21** [g] Mt 8:20 **14:22** [h] Mt 14:19 **14:23** [i] 1Co 10:16 **14:24** [j] Mt 26:28 **14:25** [k] Mt 3:2 **14:26** [l] Mt 21:1 **14:27** [m] Zec 13:7 **14:28** [n] Mk 16:7 **14:30** [o] ver 66-72; Lk 22:34; Jn 13:38 **14:31** [p] Lk 22:33; Jn 13:37

22 While they were eating, Jesus took
bread, and when he had given thanks, he
broke it[h] and gave it to his disciples, saying, "Take it; this is my body."
23 Then he took a cup, and when he had
given thanks, he gave it to them, and they
all drank from it.[i]
24 "This is my blood of the[a] covenant,[j]
which is poured out for many," he said to
them. 25 "Truly I tell you, I will not drink
again from the fruit of the vine until that
day when I drink it new in the kingdom
of God."[k]
26 When they had sung a hymn, they
went out to the Mount of Olives.[l]

Jesus Predicts Peter's Denial

14:27-31pp — Mt 26:31-35

27 "You will all fall away," Jesus told
them, "for it is written:

> " 'I will strike the shepherd,
> and the sheep will be scattered.'[b][m]

28 But after I have risen, I will go ahead of
you into Galilee."[n]
29 Peter declared, "Even if all fall away,
I will not."
30 "Truly I tell you," Jesus answered,
"today — yes, tonight — before the rooster
crows twice[c] you yourself will disown me
three times."[o]
31 But Peter insisted emphatically, "Even
if I have to die with you,[p] I will never disown you." And all the others said the same.

[a] *24* Some manuscripts *the new* [b] *27* Zech. 13:7
[c] *30* Some early manuscripts do not have *twice.*

14:12 *the Festival of Unleavened Bread ... Passover.* By this period, these were often treated together as parts of a single festival (e.g., Josephus *Antiquites* 14.21; 17.213; 18.29; 20.106; *Wars* 2.10). *sacrifice the Passover lamb.* During the day, priests in the temple would slaughter the lambs brought by the people. *Where ... ?* See note on Mt 26:17.
14:13 *two of his disciples.* Messengers were often sent two by two. *man carrying a jar of water.* Women usually carried water jars, but well-to-do homes would have servants, and servants of either gender could carry them. In many cities, people would gather water from public fountains, since most individual homes lacked running water. Some bottom-story homes in cities such as Rome did receive water from city pipes. In-house water in the wealthy upper city of Jerusalem also included cisterns that collected rainwater. Most urban residents in antiquity lacked either. In Roman-style cities, apartment buildings of several stories predominated; most apartments could not collect rainwater, but certainly most lacked running water, a special luxury. Even homes with cisterns might want additional water for the festival.
14:15 *a large room upstairs.* A home with a room that would hold all the disciples was presumably in the wealthier upper city of Jerusalem; more people lived in the poorer and more crowded lower city.
14:17 *evening.* See note on Mt 26:20.
14:18 *reclining at the table.* Although Jewish people could sit for other meals, for banquets the men reclined, like Greeks. Men supported themselves on their left elbow, leaving the right hand free to take food from the table. *will betray me.* Betrayal by a close friend was not only painful and dangerous but also brought dishonor to the person betrayed. Likewise, a disciple's behavior reflected on the teacher, and a follower's betrayal would shame a leader. *eating with me.* Eating together established a covenant relationship, so one who betrayed a table companion was counted particularly despicable.
14:20 *dips ... with me.* See note on Mt 26:23.
14:21 Although some Jewish people focused more on God's sovereignty, and others more on human choice, most accepted both without viewing them as contradictory. *better for him if he had not been born.* This woe was widely used by both Jews and Greeks, and appears in earlier Scripture (Job 3:3 – 26; Jer 20:14 – 18).
14:22 See note on Lk 22:19.
14:23 *took a cup.* See note on Mt 26:27.
14:24 *blood of the covenant.* See note on Mt 26:28. The thought of consuming blood revolted Jewish people (e.g., Lev 17:14), but sages sometimes spoke figuratively (see note on Lk 22:19).
14:25 *I will not drink again ... until that day.* See note on Mt 26:29.
14:26 *sung a hymn.* See note on Mt 26:30.
14:27 In its context Zec 13:7 speaks of false prophets, but the principle of sheep scattering without a shepherd is a much wider one (see note on Mt 26:31).
14:30 *before the rooster crows twice.* Roosters crow often, including during what Romans considered the third watch of the night which they characterized as the crow-

Gethsemane

14:32-42pp — Mt 26:36-46; Lk 22:40-46

32 They went to a place called Gethsemane, and Jesus said to his disciples, "Sit
here while I pray." 33 He took Peter, James
and John[q] along with him, and he began to be deeply distressed and troubled.
34 "My soul is overwhelmed with sorrow to
the point of death,"[r] he said to them. "Stay
here and keep watch."

35 Going a little farther, he fell to the
ground and prayed that if possible the
hour[s] might pass from him. 36 "*Abba*,[a] Father,"[t] he said, "everything is possible for
you. Take this cup[u] from me. Yet not what
I will, but what you will."[v]

37 Then he returned to his disciples and
found them sleeping. "Simon," he said
to Peter, "are you asleep? Couldn't you
keep watch for one hour? 38 Watch and
pray so that you will not fall into temptation.[w] The spirit is willing, but the flesh
is weak."[x]

39 Once more he went away and prayed
the same thing. 40 When he came back, he
again found them sleeping, because their
eyes were heavy. They did not know what
to say to him.

41 Returning the third time, he said to
them, "Are you still sleeping and resting?
Enough! The hour[y] has come. Look, the
Son of Man is delivered into the hands of
sinners. 42 Rise! Let us go! Here comes my
betrayer!"

Jesus Arrested

14:43-50pp — Mt 26:47-56; Lk 22:47-50; Jn 18:3-11

43 Just as he was speaking, Judas,[z] one
of the Twelve, appeared. With him was a
crowd armed with swords and clubs, sent
from the chief priests, the teachers of the
law, and the elders.

44 Now the betrayer had arranged a
signal with them: "The one I kiss is the
man; arrest him and lead him away under guard." 45 Going at once to Jesus, Judas
said, "Rabbi!"[a] and kissed him. 46 The men
seized Jesus and arrested him. 47 Then one
of those standing near drew his sword and
struck the servant of the high priest, cutting off his ear.

48 "Am I leading a rebellion," said Jesus,
"that you have come out with swords and
clubs to capture me? 49 Every day I was
with you, teaching in the temple courts,[b]
and you did not arrest me. But the Scriptures must be fulfilled."[c] 50 Then everyone
deserted him and fled.[d]

51 A young man, wearing nothing but a
linen garment, was following Jesus. When
they seized him, 52 he fled naked, leaving
his garment behind.

Jesus Before the Sanhedrin

14:53-65pp — Mt 26:57-68; Jn 18:12,13,19-24
14:61-63pp — Lk 22:67-71

53 They took Jesus to the high priest,
and all the chief priests, the elders and the
teachers of the law came together. 54 Peter followed him at a distance, right into
the courtyard of the high priest.[e] There he
sat with the guards and warmed himself
at the fire.[f]

55 The chief priests and the whole Sanhedrin[g] were looking for evidence against
Jesus so that they could put him to death,
but they did not find any. 56 Many testified

14:33 [q] Mt 4:21
14:34 [r] Jn 12:27
14:35 [s] ver 41; Mt 26:18
14:36 [t] Ro 8:15; Gal 4:6 [u] Mt 20:22 [v] Mt 26:39
14:38 [w] Mt 6:13 [x] Ro 7:22,23
14:41 [y] ver 35; Mt 26:18
14:43 [z] Mt 10:4
14:45 [a] Mt 23:7
14:49 [b] Mt 26:55 [c] Isa 53:7-12; Mt 1:22
14:50 [d] ver 27
14:54 [e] Mt 26:3 [f] Jn 18:18
14:55 [g] Mt 5:22

a 36 Aramaic for *father*

---

ing (some suggest c. 12:30, 1:30 and 2:30 a.m.). Because most people fell asleep at or soon after sundown, however, these are not the most widely considered crowings. Ancient sources mention most often roosters crowing at or shortly before dawn. Jesus thus probably at least warns Peter here that before the night is over he will have denied Jesus three times. Cf. 8:38; Mt 10:33. The crowing at 14:72 suggests even closer precision for his words.

14:36 *Abba.* A respectful but intimate way to address one's father. Although a few parables in much later sources compare God with an *"abba,"* it does not appear in Jewish prayers (unlike "Father"). To our knowledge, this way of directly addressing God seems to have been unique to Jesus (until adopted by his followers; Ro 8:15; Gal 4:6). *this cup.* Biblical prophets used a cup to symbolize sufferings, normally as divine judgment (Isa 51:17; Jer 25:15 – 17; 51:7; Hab 2:16; Zec 12:2); here it applies to Jesus' painful death (vv. 23 – 24; 10:38 – 39).

14:41 *still sleeping.* Passover custom directed that participants stay awake late recounting of God's redemptive acts. The disciples, familiar with this tradition, still fall asleep on this one.

14:43 *swords and clubs.* See note on Mt 26:47.

14:44 *The one I kiss.* See note on Lk 22:47.

14:45 *Rabbi.* Although probably not yet a technical term for an ordained scholar, Rabbi was a respectful Aramaic title, including for (but not limited to) one's teacher, "my master."

14:50 *everyone deserted him.* Abandonment by one's disciples would be a cause for shame.

14:52 *he fled naked.* Jewish people normally abhorred nakedness; one might flee naked only in a time of panic (Am 2:16). Normally one would supplement the undergarment with a heavier outer garment, especially in the cool of the night; one would abandon the outer garment only in the severest of emergencies (see note on Mt 24:18). Underdressed already (whether from poverty, or likelier here, negligence or haste), this youth is so desperate to escape that he abandons his only cloak in the hands of his pursuers.

14:53 *high priest.* Caiaphas; see note on Mt 26:3. Meeting for legal decisions in the private home of the high priest violated conventional legal ethics. The upper city of Jerusalem included homes of the wealthy and even palaces with courtyards inside their gated walls. Some palaces in Jerusalem also had large receiving rooms in the front.

14:55 *Sanhedrin.* See the article "Jesus' Trial," p. 1672; see also Sanhedrin.

falsely against him, but their statements
did not agree.
57Then some stood up and gave this false
testimony against him: 58"We heard him
say, 'I will destroy this temple made with
human hands and in three days will build
another,[h] not made with hands.'" 59Yet
even then their testimony did not agree.
60Then the high priest stood up before
them and asked Jesus, "Are you not going to answer? What is this testimony that
these men are bringing against you?" 61But
Jesus remained silent and gave no answer.[i]
Again the high priest asked him, "Are
you the Messiah, the Son of the Blessed
One?"[j]
62"I am," said Jesus. "And you will see
the Son of Man sitting at the right hand of
the Mighty One and coming on the clouds
of heaven."[k]
63The high priest tore his clothes.[l] "Why
do we need any more witnesses?" he
asked. 64"You have heard the blasphemy.
What do you think?"
They all condemned him as worthy of
death.[m] 65Then some began to spit at him;
they blindfolded him, struck him with
their fists, and said, "Prophesy!" And the
guards took him and beat him.[n]

Peter Disowns Jesus

14:66-72pp — Mt 26:69-75; Lk 22:56-62; Jn 18:16-18,25-27

66While Peter was below in the courtyard,[o] one of the servant girls of the high
priest came by. 67When she saw Peter warming himself,[p] she looked closely at him.
"You also were with that Nazarene,
Jesus,"[q] she said.
68But he denied it. "I don't know or understand what you're talking about,"[r] he
said, and went out into the entryway.[a]
69When the servant girl saw him there,
she said again to those standing around,
"This fellow is one of them." 70Again he
denied it.[s]
After a little while, those standing near
said to Peter, "Surely you are one of them,
for you are a Galilean."[t]
71He began to call down curses, and he
swore to them, "I don't know this man
you're talking about."[u]
72Immediately the rooster crowed the second time.[b] Then Peter remembered the word
Jesus had spoken to him: "Before the rooster crows twice[c] you will disown me three
times."[v] And he broke down and wept.

Jesus Before Pilate

15:2-15pp — Mt 27:11-26; Lk 23:2,3,18-25; Jn 18:29 – 19:16

15 Very early in the morning, the chief
priests, with the elders, the teachers of the law[w] and the whole Sanhedrin,[x]
made their plans. So they bound Jesus, led
him away and handed him over to Pilate.[y]
2"Are you the king of the Jews?"[z] asked
Pilate.
"You have said so," Jesus replied.
3The chief priests accused him of many
things. 4So again Pilate asked him, "Aren't
you going to answer? See how many
things they are accusing you of."
5But Jesus still made no reply,[a] and Pilate was amazed.
6Now it was the custom at the festival

14:58 [h] Mk 15:29; Jn 2:19 **14:61** [i] Isa 53:7; Mt 27:12, 14; Mk 15:5; Lk 23:9; Jn 19:9 [j] Mt 16:16; Jn 4:25,26 **14:62** [k] Rev 1:7 **14:63** [l] Lev 10:6; 21:10; Nu 14:6; Ac 14:14 **14:64** [m] Lev 24:16 **14:65** [n] Mt 16:21 **14:66** [o] ver 54 **14:67** [p] ver 54 [q] Mk 1:24

14:68 [r] ver 30, 72 **14:70** [s] ver 30, 68, 72 [t] Ac 2:7 **14:71** [u] ver 30, 72 **14:72** [v] ver 30, 68 **15:1** [w] Mt 27:1; Lk 22:66 [x] Mt 5:22 [y] Mt 27:2 **15:2** [z] ver 9, 12, 18, 26; Mt 2:2 **15:5** [a] Mk 14:61

[a] 68 Some early manuscripts *entryway and the rooster crowed* [b] 72 Some early manuscripts do not have *the second time.* [c] 72 Some early manuscripts do not have *twice.*

14:58 *destroy this temple.* Some Jewish people expected God to provide a new temple. It is clear, however, that the testimony here rests on a misinterpretation of Jesus (see Jn 2:19). **14:59** *their testimony did not agree.* See note on Mt 26:60. **14:61** *Blessed One.* A familiar Jewish title for God. Although the Dead Sea Scrolls use "Son of God" for the Messiah, one would not expect this usage from the high priest unless he is echoing claims about Jesus, perhaps based on 12:6 (or information from Judas). **14:62** See note on Mt 26:64. **14:63–64** *tore his clothes ... blasphemy.* See note on Mt 26:65. **14:65** This behavior violated all ancient legal ethics, though abuse of prisoners was common in antiquity. *spit.* Spittle was normally deemed ritually impure and disgusting. *Prophesy!* While Jesus' abusers mock him as a false prophet, i.e., for a capital offense (Dt 13:5), Jesus' prophecy about Peter is being fulfilled (vv. 66–72), as one would expect for a true prophet (Dt 18:22). **14:67** *When she saw Peter.* Even in large households servants normally would know who belonged to the household. The high priest's palace was in the part of Jerusalem near the temple, so this servant may have also seen Jesus and his disciples earlier in the week. **14:68** *I don't know.* Used as a legal formula for denial. **14:70** *for you are a Galilean.* See note on Mt 26:73. The high priest's aristocratic household would have regarded Jesus' entire movement as primarily consisting of uneducated Galilean peasants. **14:71** *call down curses ... swore to them.* Peter here escalates his earlier denials. When someone in antiquity swore an oath, one invoked a deity as witness, expecting the deity to avenge his or her honor by punishing any oath offered falsely. Denying knowledge of a person would insult the person (see note on Mt 25:12). **15:1** A night meeting in the high priest's home was not a legal hearing, but in the morning, once the charge is formulated the Sanhedrin could offer an official charge for Pilate. *Very early in the morning.* See note on Mt 27:1. *Pilate.* See note on Mt 27:2. **15:2** *king of the Jews.* The Messianic claim of 14:61–62 now proves useful. For Romans, the charge "king of the Jews" meant treason, as this was a title only the emperor could grant. In the provinces, crucifixion was the usual penalty for treason. **15:5** *no reply.* Ancient Jewish writings about martyrs also included the accused refusing to respond; cf. Isa 53:7. **15:6** *it was the custom.* Customs similar to this one existed in various locations; although governors were not bound

to release a prisoner whom the people requested. 7A man called Barabbas was in
prison with the insurrectionists who had
committed murder in the uprising. 8The
crowd came up and asked Pilate to do for
them what he usually did.
9"Do you want me to release to you the
king of the Jews?"[b] asked Pilate, 10know-
ing it was out of self-interest that the chief
priests had handed Jesus over to him.
11But the chief priests stirred up the crowd
to have Pilate release Barabbas[c] instead.
12"What shall I do, then, with the one you
call the king of the Jews?" Pilate asked them.
13"Crucify him!" they shouted.
14"Why? What crime has he committed?" asked Pilate.
But they shouted all the louder, "Crucify him!"
15Wanting to satisfy the crowd, Pilate
released Barabbas to them. He had Jesus
flogged,[d] and handed him over to be crucified.

The Soldiers Mock Jesus

15:16-20pp — Mt 27:27-31

16The soldiers led Jesus away into the
palace[e] (that is, the Praetorium) and
called together the whole company of soldiers. 17They put a purple robe on him,
then twisted together a crown of thorns
and set it on him. 18And they began to
call out to him, "Hail, king of the Jews!"[f]
19Again and again they struck him on the
head with a staff and spit on him. Falling
on their knees, they paid homage to him.
20And when they had mocked him, they
took off the purple robe and put his own
clothes on him. Then they led him out[g] to
crucify him.

The Crucifixion of Jesus

15:22-32pp — Mt 27:33-44; Lk 23:33-43; Jn 19:17-24

21A certain man from Cyrene,[h] Simon,
the father of Alexander and Rufus,[i] was
passing by on his way in from the country, and they forced him to carry the cross.[j]
22They brought Jesus to the place called
Golgotha (which means "the place of the
skull"). 23Then they offered him wine
mixed with myrrh,[k] but he did not take it.
24And they crucified him. Dividing up his
clothes, they cast lots[l] to see what each
would get.
25It was nine in the morning when they

15:9 [b] ver 2
15:11 [c] Ac 3:14
15:15 [d] Isa 53:6
15:16 [e] Jn 18:28,33; 19:9
15:18 [f] ver 2
15:20 [g] Heb 13:12
15:21 [h] Mt 27:32 [i] Ro 16:13 [j] Mt 27:32; Lk 23:26
15:23 [k] ver 36; Ps 69:21; Pr 31:6
15:24 [l] Ps 22:18

by law to follow these customs, they often chose to honor the precedents set by their predecessors.
15:7–9 See note on Mt 27:17.
15:10 Because Jesus was popular and because male rivalry dominated much of ancient Mediterranean urban life, this statement about the chief priests makes sense. *out of self-interest.* With good reason, ancient politics and biographies often attributed enmity to envy.
15:11 *stirred up the crowd.* Most of Jesus' followers were Galileans; Judean crowds would be more readily swayed by the chief priests. Ancient literature often reports leaders swaying fickle crowds.
15:15 *Wanting to satisfy the crowd.* Jerusalemites had forced Pilate to back down earlier; when Pilate first became governor, under cover of night he brought into Jerusalem the Roman standards that Jewish people regarded as idols. The crowds forced him to back down. *flogged.* See note on Mt 27:26. *handed him over to be crucified.* A governor pronouncing sentence would typically say something like, "You will mount the cross."
15:16 *the Praetorium.* See note on Mt 27:27.
15:17 Naked crucifixion was intended to shame the victim, and was only part of the mockery and ridicule that commonly accompanied execution. Ridiculing and abusing prisoners was common. *purple robe.* The range of the term translated "purple" (here; Jn 19:2) sometimes included scarlet (Mt 27:28). Roman soldiers wore red cloaks, but if a cloak had faded it could resemble what one might call "purple," like the cloaks of Hellenistic princes. *crown of thorns.* Hellenistic vassal princes wore garlands; soldiers may have used an available shrub such as acanthus to weave a wreath for Jesus. Imitating Hellenistic garlands, the soldiers may have intended the thorns to point especially outward, but some of the thorns would nevertheless turn inward, scraping the scalp. Scalp wounds bleed particularly profusely.
15:18 *Hail.* Equivalent to the Latin *Ave,* "Hail!" was a common address to rulers; those hailing a ruler would usually kneel. *king of the Jews.* In ridiculing the "king of the Jews," the soldiers probably also mock Jewish people more generally and further infuriate the crowd.
15:19 *struck him … with a staff.* Some historians suggest that the staff was made of bamboo, which would have been typically used for military floggings. *spit on him.* See note on Mt 27:30. *Falling on their knees.* People typically prostrated themselves before rulers.
15:21 *Cyrene.* See note on Mt 27:32.
15:22 *place of the skull.* The location may have earned this name because so many died there. See note on Mt 15:33.
15:23 *wine.* Had pain-alleviating properties (Pr 31:6–7). *myrrh.* Many think that myrrh also had pain-alleviating properties, although this is disputed. *did not take it.* On our behalf, Jesus chose to embrace the pain fully.
15:24 *Dividing up his clothes.* Jewish people regarded nakedness as a special shame, but men were typically executed nude. Whether tied with ropes or nailed to the cross, those who hung there could not chase away birds or flies from their wounds, could not restrain their bodily wastes for the hours or days it normally took them to finish dying, and could not protect themselves from heat or cold. Because of their position on the cross, some may have died from asphyxiation, but people usually died more quickly from shock (due to blood loss) or dehydration. Crosses could vary somewhat in height, but they were often low enough that dogs could try to eat crucified persons' feet. This also gave the crowd the opportunity to observe the spectacle from close range and served to further humiliate the victim. Divided clothing recalls Ps 22:18, but also fits historical practice. Roman execution squads (typically about four men; in this region most Roman military recruits would be ethnically Syrian) had rights to clothing or other effects that had remained on the prisoner. *cast lots.* Soldiers used dice and other means to gamble (see note on Ac 1:26).

MARK 15

THE SHROUD OF TURIN CONTROVERSY

No artifact in the history of scholarship has been the subject of as much debate and study as the Shroud of Turin. This piece of linen cloth is said to bear the front and rear images of a man apparently crucified in Roman fashion. His injuries correspond to those suffered by Jesus, in that he appears to have had his hands (and possibly feet) pierced, as well as his side wounded. In addition, his legs were not broken. Proponents argue that this is the actual burial cloth of Christ, while opponents refer to it as a clever hoax.

The History of the Shroud

Even the history of the shroud is mysterious. The basic details, as we know them, are as follows:

Its first known appearance was in France in the 1350s. The original owner died in 1356 without revealing where or how he had acquired the cloth.

A fire in 1532 damaged the cloth, and repair patches were added.

It has been housed in Turin since 1578.

Some theorize that the shroud is the same as the Mandylion, a sacred relic of Constantinople that was said to have borne the divine and miraculous imprint of Jesus' face.

The Mandylion is said to have been discovered in 525 in Edessa, an early Christian city in eastern Turkey. It found its way to the Byzantine capital in AD 944.

The shroud disappeared from Constantinople in 1204, when a crusader army looted the city. The leaders of the expedition were French, which could explain the shroud's westward journey.

Basic Facts About the Shroud

The shroud is a swath of linen cloth measuring 14 feet 3 inches (4.34 meters) by 3 feet 7 inches (1.09 meters). The figure on the cloth is naked, with hands folded across the pelvic area. He is bearded and between 5 feet 10 inches (1.78 meters) and 6 feet 1 inch (1.85 meters) in height. The cloth bears a number of extraordinary features:

- Purple stains on it may have originated from blood.
- Potsherds or coins may have covered the eyes. Some argue that the outline of a coin from the time of Pontius Pilate is present, but the fabric is so coarse and the image so unclear that many doubt this claim can be substantiated.
- The image is barely visible up close, and only a rough outline can be discerned by standing farther away. However, when photographed and viewed in negative, the shroud reveals a clear image, formed in such a way that a three-dimensional reconstruction of the man's appearance is possible.
- The image, on the very surface of the cloth only, is said to be no more than two fibrils (filaments or fibers) deep.
- It was not painted on. Rather, some of the threads were themselves changed to produce the image. Adherents suggest that at the moment of the resurrection Jesus' body radiated energy and fixed his image upon the shroud.

continued on next page

- The traces of flogging on the body are said to accurately depict Roman scourging. The Romans used a flagrum with two or three leather thongs with a pair of barbed lead balls or sheep bones at the end of each. During whipping, the scourge would tear out pieces of flesh. The 100-plus lash marks evident on the image have a dumbbell shape, conceivably reflecting the use of a flagrum.
- The shoulders of the individual are said to exhibit abrasions that could have been the result of his having carried the crossbar of a cross.
- Studies on the soil and pollen preserved in the fibers suggest that the cloth originated in or near Jerusalem.

Recent Developments

Supporters of the shroud's authenticity argue that no individual in the Middle Ages could have had the expertise to deliberately create such a piece. In 1988, however, British scientists released the results of carbon 14 testing that dated the cloth to between 1260–1390. The shroud was judged to have been proven a fraud, yet subsequent researchers have argued that the sample for the carbon 14 test was taken from a part of the shroud that had been repaired and not from the original fabric.

In 2002 the shroud underwent substantial restoration, including the removal of the repair patches from 1532. Some researchers fear that this process will limit or invalidate any further testing. The enigma of the shroud continues. It remains either the most significant archaeological artifact ever found or one of the most ingenious forgeries in history. ◆

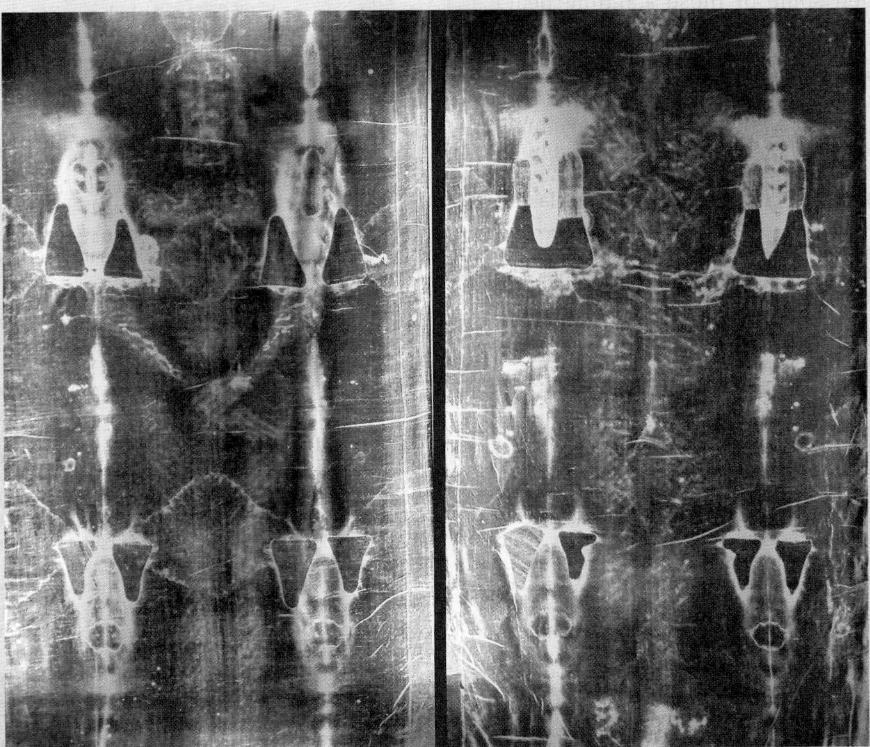

Full-length negatives of the Shroud of Turin.

Wikimedia Commons

crucified him. 26The written notice of the
charge against him read: THE KING OF THE
JEWS.[m]
27They crucified two rebels with him, one
on his right and one on his left. [28][a] 29Those
who passed by hurled insults at him, shaking their heads[n] and saying, "So! You who
are going to destroy the temple and build it
in three days,[o] 30come down from the cross
and save yourself!" 31In the same way the
chief priests and the teachers of the law
mocked him[p] among themselves. "He saved
others," they said, "but he can't save himself! 32Let this Messiah,[q] this king of Israel,[r]
come down now from the cross, that we
may see and believe." Those crucified with
him also heaped insults on him.

The Death of Jesus

15:33-41pp — Mt 27:45-56; Lk 23:44-49; Jn 19:29-30

33At noon, darkness came over the
whole land until three in the afternoon.[s]
34And at three in the afternoon Jesus cried
out in a loud voice, *"Eloi, Eloi, lema sabachthani?"* (which means "My God, my
God, why have you forsaken me?").[b][t]
35When some of those standing near
heard this, they said, "Listen, he's calling
Elijah."
36Someone ran, filled a sponge with
wine vinegar,[u] put it on a staff, and offered it to Jesus to drink. "Now leave him
alone. Let's see if Elijah comes to take him
down," he said.
37With a loud cry, Jesus breathed his last.[v]
38The curtain of the temple was torn in
two from top to bottom.[w] 39And when the
centurion,[x] who stood there in front of
Jesus, saw how he died,[c] he said, "Surely
this man was the Son of God!"[y]
40Some women were watching from a
distance.[z] Among them were Mary Magdalene, Mary the mother of James the younger and of Joseph,[d] and Salome.[a] 41In Galilee these women had followed him and
cared for his needs. Many other women
who had come up with him to Jerusalem
were also there.[b]

The Burial of Jesus

15:42-47pp — Mt 27:57-61; Lk 23:50-56; Jn 19:38-42

42It was Preparation Day (that is, the
day before the Sabbath).[c] So as evening
approached, 43Joseph of Arimathea, a
prominent member of the Council,[d] who
was himself waiting for the kingdom of
God,[e] went boldly to Pilate and asked for
Jesus' body. 44Pilate was surprised to hear
that he was already dead. Summoning the
centurion, he asked him if Jesus had already died. 45When he learned from the
centurion[f] that it was so, he gave the body
to Joseph. 46So Joseph bought some lin-
en cloth, took down the body, wrapped it
in the linen, and placed it in a tomb cut
out of rock. Then he rolled a stone against
the entrance of the tomb.[g] 47Mary Magda-

15:26 [m] ver 2
15:29 [n] Ps 22:7; 109:25 [o] Mk 14:58; Jn 2:19
15:31 [p] Ps 22:7
15:32 [q] Mk 14:61 [r] ver 2
15:33 [s] Am 8:9
15:34 [t] Ps 22:1
15:36 [u] ver 23; Ps 69:21
15:37 [v] Jn 19:30
15:38 [w] Heb 10:19,20
15:39 [x] ver 45 [y] Mk 1:1,11; 9:7; Mt 4:3
15:40 [z] Ps 38:11 [a] Mk 16:1; Lk 24:10; Jn 19:25
15:41 [b] Mt 27:55,56; Lk 8:2,3
15:42 [c] Mt 27:62; Jn 19:31
15:43 [d] Mt 5:22 [e] Mt 3:2; Lk 2:25,38
15:45 [f] ver 39
15:46 [g] Mk 16:3

[a] *28* Some manuscripts include here words similar to Luke 22:37. [b] *34* Psalm 22:1 [c] *39* Some manuscripts *saw that he died with such a cry* [d] *40* Greek *Joses,* a variant of *Joseph;* also in verse 47

15:26 *written notice.* As part of the execution process, sometimes a person would carry a tablet indicating the charge against the prisoner. *THE KING OF THE JEWS.* A treason charge—yet, ironically, Mark's audience knows that Jesus really is king, and this charge climaxes the preaching of the kingdom (1:15). Early Christians would not have dared invent this charge or claim to be followers of someone executed for treason.
15:29 *hurled insults.* Romans preferred to crucify offenders in public places, often on major roads, where passersby would learn the danger of resisting Rome. *shaking their heads.* Recalls Ps 22:7. *destroy the temple.* See note on 14:58.
15:30 *save yourself.* Ancient audiences liked irony, and ironically, Jesus' mockers speak inverted truth: in order to save others, Jesus must choose not to save himself.
15:33 *darkness came over the whole land.* See note on Mt 27:45.
15:34 *Eloi, Eloi, lema sabachthani?* Jesus quotes Ps 22:1, a prayer of a righteous sufferer that begins by expressing abandonment but goes on to celebrate God's vindication (Ps 22:22–24). Mark uses the vernacular Aramaic *Eloi* instead of the psalm's original Hebrew *Eli.*
15:35 *Elijah.* Elijah was expected to appear before the Lord's coming (Mal 4:5–6), but other rabbinic traditions testified that he was also believed to act like an angel who helped rabbis in need.
15:36 *wine vinegar.* See note on Mt 27:48.
15:38 *curtain of the temple.* See note on Mt 27:51. One Jewish tradition mentions a similar event a generation before the temple's destruction; if the tradition is authentic, it would fit this time.
15:39 *Son of God.* Gentiles viewed many figures, especially heroes and the emperor, as sons of gods; recognizing Jesus as Jewish, the centurion recognizes him as the son of the one true God of Israel.
15:40 The presence of at least two women named Mary here is not surprising; sources show that it was by far the most common name for Jewish women in this era.
15:41 *these women had followed him and cared for his needs.* Women providing financial patronage was not unusual, although it could be criticized by a movement's detractors. That the women "followed him," however, may have been viewed by many outsiders as scandalous (see note on Lk 8:2–3). Women were not usually viewed as threats for sedition the way that men were. Nevertheless, men usually viewed as exceptional any women who exhibited courage (which these women, by contrast to most of Jesus' male disciples, did).
15:43 *Joseph . . . asked for Jesus' body.* See note on Mt 27:58.
15:46 *wrapped it in the linen.* Linen shrouds were common for Jewish burials. *placed it in a tomb.* When the condemned were buried at all, they normally received dishonorable burials (see note on Mt 27:60), but Joseph insists on providing Jesus an honorable burial. Because the tomb is immediately available, a reader may presume that it was his own (cf. 1Ki 13:30–31; Isa 53:9), as Matthew makes explicit (Mt 27:60). See note on Mt. 27:60.

lene and Mary the mother of Joseph[h] saw
where he was laid.

Jesus Has Risen

16:1-8pp — Mt 28:1-8; Lk 24:1-10

16 When the Sabbath was over, Mary
Magdalene, Mary the mother of
James, and Salome bought spices[i] so that
they might go to anoint Jesus' body. 2Very
early on the first day of the week, just after sunrise, they were on their way to the
tomb 3and they asked each other, "Who
will roll the stone away from the entrance
of the tomb?"[j]

4But when they looked up, they saw
that the stone, which was very large, had
been rolled away. 5As they entered the
tomb, they saw a young man dressed in a
white robe[k] sitting on the right side, and
they were alarmed.

6"Don't be alarmed," he said. "You are
looking for Jesus the Nazarene,[l] who was
crucified. He has risen! He is not here. See
the place where they laid him. 7But go,
tell his disciples and Peter, 'He is going
ahead of you into Galilee. There you will
see him,[m] just as he told you.' "[n]

8Trembling and bewildered, the wom-
en went out and fled from the tomb. They
said nothing to anyone, because they were
afraid.[a]

[The earliest manuscripts and some other ancient witnesses do not have verses 9–20.]

15:47 [h] ver 40 **16:1** [i] Lk 23:56; Jn 19:39,40 **16:3** [j] Mk 15:46 **16:5** [k] Jn 20:12 **16:6** [l] Mk 1:24 **16:7** [m] Jn 21:1-23 [n] Mk 14:28

16:9 [o] Jn 20:11-18 **16:11** [p] ver 13, 14; Lk 24:11 **16:12** [q] Lk 24:13-32 **16:14** [r] Lk 24:36-43 **16:15** [s] Mt 28:18-20; Lk 24:47,48 **16:16** [t] Jn 3:16, 18,36; Ac 16:31 **16:17** [u] Mk 9:38; Lk 10:17; Ac 5:16; 8:7; 16:18; 19:13-16 [v] Ac 2:4; 10:46; 19:6; 1Co 12:10, 28,30 **16:18** [w] Lk 10:19; Ac 28:3-5 [x] Ac 6:6 **16:19** [y] Lk 24:50,51; Jn 6:62; Ac 1:9-11; 1Ti 3:16 [z] Ps 110:1; Ro 8:34; Col 3:1; Heb 1:3; 12:2

9When Jesus rose early on the first day of the
week, he appeared first to Mary Magdalene,[o]
out of whom he had driven seven demons. 10She
went and told those who had been with him
and who were mourning and weeping. 11When
they heard that Jesus was alive and that she
had seen him, they did not believe it.[p]

12Afterward Jesus appeared in a different
form to two of them while they were walking in
the country.[q] 13These returned and reported it
to the rest; but they did not believe them either.

14Later Jesus appeared to the Eleven as they
were eating; he rebuked them for their lack of
faith and their stubborn refusal to believe those
who had seen him after he had risen.[r]

15He said to them, "Go into all the world and
preach the gospel to all creation.[s] 16Whoever be-
lieves and is baptized will be saved, but whoev-
er does not believe will be condemned.[t] 17And
these signs will accompany those who believe:
In my name they will drive out demons;[u] they
will speak in new tongues;[v] 18they will pick up
snakes[w] with their hands; and when they drink
deadly poison, it will not hurt them at all; they
will place their hands on[x] sick people, and they
will get well."

19After the Lord Jesus had spoken to them,
he was taken up into heaven[y] and he sat at the
right hand of God.[z] 20Then the disciples went
out and preached everywhere, and the Lord
worked with them and confirmed his word by
the signs that accompanied it.

[a] 8 Some manuscripts have the following ending between verses 8 and 9, and one manuscript has it after verse 8 (omitting verses 9-20): *Then they quickly reported all these instructions to those around Peter. After this, Jesus himself also sent out through them from east to west the sacred and imperishable proclamation of eternal salvation. Amen.*

16:1 *Sabbath was over.* Jewish tradition allowed washing and anointing corpses even on the Sabbath, but spices for optimal anointing could not be purchased until after the Sabbath.
16:2 *Very early on the first day.* The Sabbath technically ends at sundown (around 6:00 p.m.) on Saturday evening, when the women could buy spices, but they would not easily and safely find the tomb before first light on Sunday morning (perhaps 5:00 a.m.). Because it was only April, because Jerusalem is over 2,000 feet (610 meters) above sea level, and because the tomb was sealed, they could hope that Jesus' body would still be approachable.
16:3 *roll the stone away.* The disk-shaped stone used to seal a tomb's entrance was large and heavy, normally requiring several men to move it in the groove.
16:5 *young man dressed in a white robe.* People could mistake angels for humans (cf., e.g., Ge 19:15) but often angels were dressed in white (e.g., Da 10:5 ["dressed in linen"]; 2 Maccabees 11:8).
16:7 *tell his disciples.* See note on Mt 28:7.
16:8 *They said nothing to anyone.* Ancient audiences appreciated irony. Sometimes in Mark's Gospel, Jesus warns witnesses of miracles not to tell anyone, yet the witnesses proclaim it widely (1:45; 7:36); here, when finally some people are commanded to tell (v. 7), they remain silent!
16:9–20 This passage is missing in the earliest manuscripts and is not in Mark's style. Many ancient sources, including speeches and biographies, ended abruptly, as Mark does in v. 8. Although vv. 9–20 were probably not written by Mark, they were apparently added very early and probably draw on various early traditions about Jesus (apparently including some from the other Gospels).
16:11 *they did not believe it.* On the usual skepticism about women's testimony in antiquity, see note on Mt 28:7.
16:12 *in a different form.* Greeks had stories of supernatural beings who could change form; Jewish people had similar accounts about angels. Ancient hearers would recognize the supernatural character of Jesus' resurrected body here.
16:17 *speak in new tongues.* This may refer to the healing of mute persons (Isa 35:6), but because the other examples involve doing signs rather than receiving them, it more likely refers to speaking in tongues (as in 1Co 12:10).
16:19 *sat at the right hand of God.* See note on 12:36.

MAJOR ARCHAEOLOGICAL FINDS RELATING TO THE NEW TESTAMENT

SITE OR ARTIFACT	LOCATION — ISRAEL	RELATING SCRIPTURE
Caiaphas ossuary	Jerusalem	Mt 26:3
Herod's temple	Jerusalem	Lk 1:9
Herod's winter palace	Jericho	Mt 2:4
The Herodium (site of Herod's tomb)	Near Bethlehem	Mt 2:19
Masada	Near western shore of Dead Sea	Compare Lk 21:20
Early synagogue	Capernaum	Mt 4:13; Mk 1:21
Pool of Siloam	Jerusalem	Jn 9:7
Pool of Bethesda	Jerusalem	Jn 5:2
Pilate inscription	Caesarea	Lk 3:1
Inscription: Gentile entrance to temple sanctuary	Jerusalem	Ac 21:27–29
Skeletal remains of crucified man	Jerusalem	Mk 15:24
Peter's house	Capernaum	Mt 4:13; Lk 4:38
Jacob's well	Nablus	Jn 4:5–6

Heel bone of crucified man from the first century, found in an ossuary in Jerusalem in 1968.

Z. Radovan/www.BibleLandPictures.com

Masada, located near the western shore of the Dead Sea. Herod the Great fortified Masada c. 37–31 BC as a refuge in the event of a revolt. The fortress became the last holdout of the Jewish zealots in the war against the Romans (AD 66–73).

© Michael Melford/National Geographic Stock

MAJOR ARCHAEOLOGICAL FINDS (CONT.)

SITE OR ARTIFACT	LOCATION — ASIA MINOR	RELATING SCRIPTURE
Derbe inscription	Kerti Hüyük	Ac 14:20
Sergius Paulus inscription	Kythraia, Cyprus	Ac 13:6–7
Zeus altar (Satan's throne?)	Pergamum	Rev 2:13
Fourth-century BC walls	Assos	Ac 20:13–14
Artemis temple and altar	Ephesus	Ac 19:27–28
Ephesian theater	Ephesus	Ac 19:29
Silversmith shops	Ephesus	Ac 19:24
Artemis statues	Ephesus	Ac 19:35

Zeus altar at Pergamum, the third city mentioned in the book of Revelation (1:11; 2:12–17). The altar has been identified as the throne of Satan (2:13) and was perhaps related to emperor worship.

www.HolyLandPhotos.org

The theater at Ephesus.

MAJOR ARCHAEOLOGICAL FINDS (CONT.)

SITE OR ARTIFACT	LOCATION — GREECE	RELATING SCRIPTURE
Erastus inscription	Corinth	Ro 16:23
Synagogue inscription	Corinth	Ac 18:4
Meat market inscription	Corinth	1Co 10:25
Cult dining rooms (in Asclepius and Demeter temples)	Corinth	1Co 8:10; 10:14
Court (bema)	Corinth	Ac 18:12
Marketplace (bema)	Philippi	Ac 16:19
Starting gate for races	Isthmia	1Co 9:24,26
Gallio inscription	Delphi	Ac 18:12
Egnatian Way	Neapolis (Kavalla), Philippi, Amphipolis, Apollonia, Thessalonica	Compare Ac 16:11–12; 17:1
Politarch inscription	Thessalonica	Ac 17:6

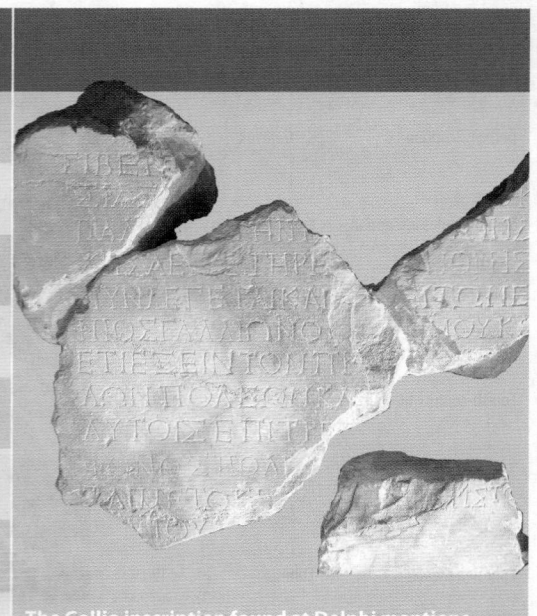

The Gallio inscription found at Delphi mentions Lucius Junius Gallio and indicates that he was the proconsul of Achaia. He is also listed as a "friend of Caesar," which dates his governorship to AD 51/52. He is the same Gallio mentioned in Acts 18:12: "While Gallio was proconsul of Achaia, the Jews of Corinth made a united attack on Paul and brought him to the place of judgment."

Todd Bolen/www.BiblePlaces.com

The Corinthian court (bema) may have been the "place of judgment" (Ac 18:12) where Paul was brought before Gallio in AD 51/52.

MAJOR ARCHAEOLOGICAL FINDS (CONT.)

SITE OR ARTIFACT	LOCATION — ITALY	RELATING SCRIPTURE
Tomb of Augustus	Rome	Lk 2:1
Mamertine Prison	Rome	2Ti 1:16–17; 2:9; 4:6–8
Appian Way	Puteoli to Rome	Ac 28:13–16
Golden House of Nero	Rome	Compare Ac 25:10; 1Pe 2:13
Arch of Titus	Rome	Compare Lk 19:43–44; 21:6,20

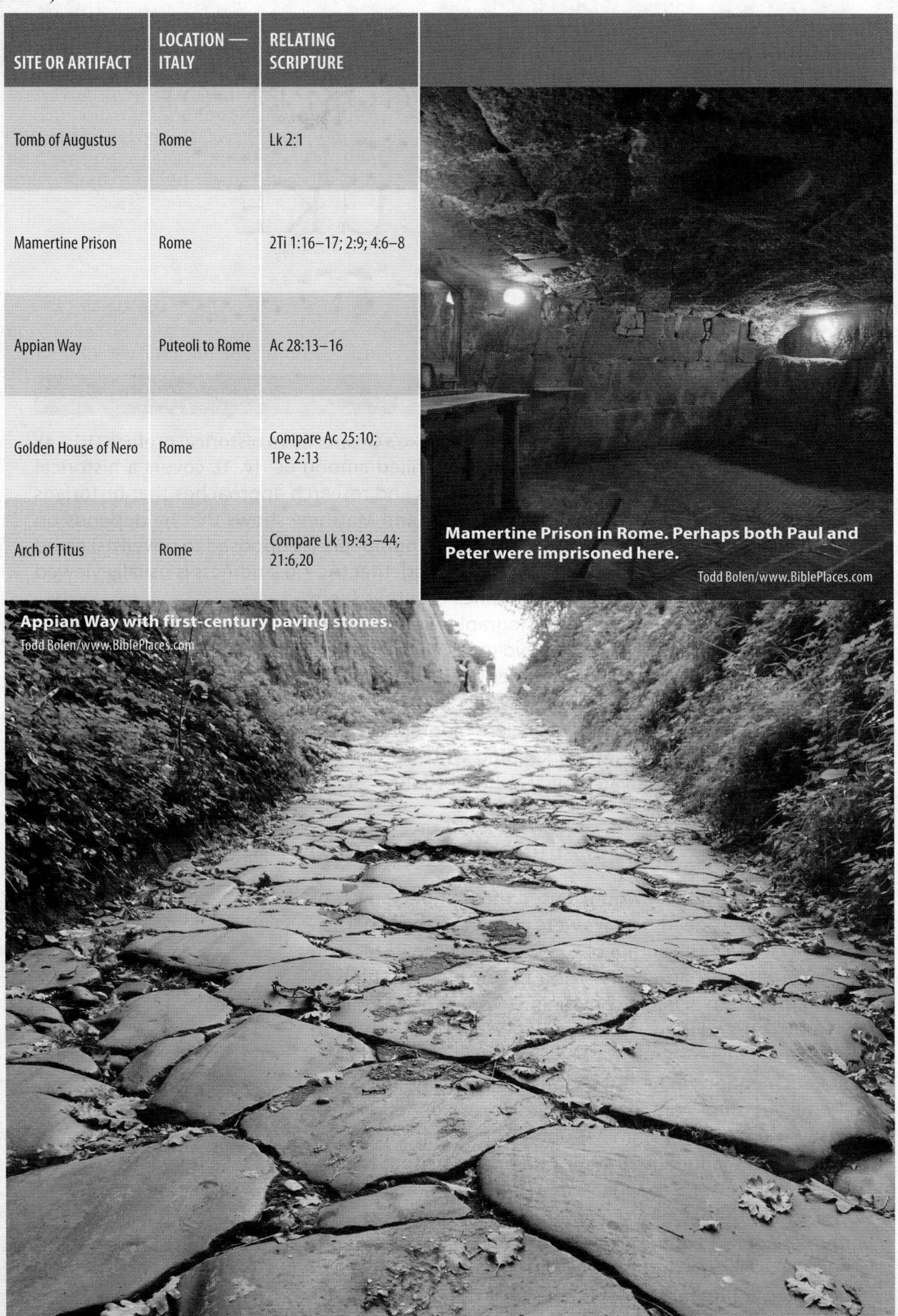

Mamertine Prison in Rome. Perhaps both Paul and Peter were imprisoned here.
Todd Bolen/www.BiblePlaces.com

Appian Way with first-century paving stones.
Todd Bolen/www.BiblePlaces.com

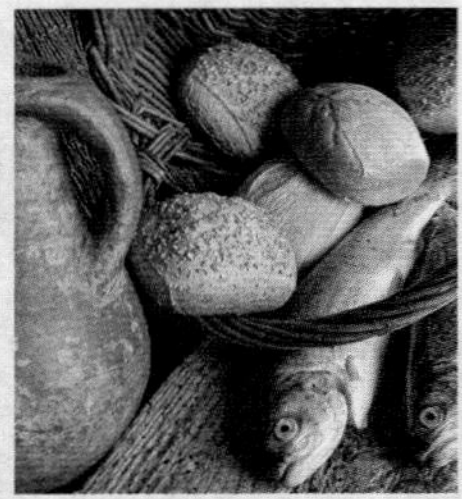

THE GOSPEL OF LUKE

Genre

See Introduction to the Gospels, p. 1598. Luke's Gospel has a historical preface (1:1 – 4), recounts "the things that have been fulfilled among us" (v. 1), covers a historical topic, and mentions the types of sources and research approaches that historians used (vv. 1 – 3). Luke's overlap with Mark and Matthew shows that he depends on prior information, which is what historians and biographers (as opposed to novelists) cared about. Because Luke's Gospel and Acts belong together (Ac 1:1), and Acts is usually viewed as a historical monograph, the two volumes together seem to function as a work of ancient historiography. Some ancient multivolume histories had individual volumes about particular persons, however, and those volumes were biographic in character. Luke's Gospel is a biography, like Matthew, Mark and John, but in the wide range of ancient biographic works Luke's Gospel is written more in keeping with the rules of Greek historiography than are, say, Matthew or John.

QUICK GLANCE

AUTHOR:
Luke, a Gentile physician and missionary companion of Paul

AUDIENCE:
Addressed to Theophilus, but intended for all believers

DATE:
Between the 60s and the 80s AD

THEME:
Luke presents Jesus as the Messiah and Lord whose life, death and resurrection make salvation available to all people everywhere.

Authorship

When ancient historical writings used the first person ("I" or "we"), the writers nearly always were claiming to have participated personally. The author of Luke-Acts plays down his own presence rather than emphasizing it, but includes himself among the group of Paul's companions from Troas to Philippi (Ac 16:10 – 17), and then years later from Philippi to Judea and on to Rome (20:5 — 28:16). Among the traveling companions that Paul mentions in his letters, one who accompanied him to Rome yet is not named in the third person in Acts is Luke the physician (Col 4:14; Phm 24). Contrary to what some have argued, Luke's language does not demonstrate that he was a physician; contrary to what some *others* have assumed, however, his language is quite consistent with that view. Early Christian tradition was also unanimous that Luke was the author of Acts and of the Gospel that now bears Luke's name. Further, early Christians who credited Luke as the author had little reason to choose Luke, who was not a major figure, if they lacked concrete tradition that he was the author. When scholars examine sources from the Greco-Roman world, they usually start with external evidence (in this case, tradition in second-century Christian writers) and then check internal evidence. The tradition of Luke's authorship passes both tests.

Provenance and Date

Given Luke's special interest (in his second volume, Acts) in the northern Aegean region — as well as perhaps his own lengthy sojourn in Philippi (compare Ac 16:10 – 17 with Ac 20:5 – 6) — the center of Luke's target audience may be Macedonia, with a wider circulation in the Aegean region as a whole (including Greece and western Asia Minor). This is, however, uncertain. A range of dates has been proposed, from as early as the closing scene of Acts (perhaps AD 62) to the early second century. Some evidence favors the earlier decades of this range. First, a physician who traveled with Paul to Philippi before AD 50 (see Authorship, above) likelier than not wrote earlier in the range rather than later. Moreover, one theme in the second half of the book of Acts is to defend Paul against the charge of having started riots — the capital charge of sedition (Ac 24:5). This is important because Paul was the most prominent leader of the mission to the Gentiles (Gal 2:8), so charges against him would bring shame on all the churches in the Diaspora (cf. shame about his chains in 2Ti 1:16). Luke narrates many riots associated with Paul, showing that he was not at fault in any of these cases. Yet if Luke wants to defend Paul, why even mention the riots unless they were an issue? Luke probably writes at a time when Paul's legacy remains in question and strong memories remain of the riots in various cities where the book of Acts might travel. It is therefore likely that Luke-Acts dates to a time soon after the final events narrated in Acts. This would allow a time in the 60s (when Acts closes) or 70s. Scholars who believe that Luke has in mind the traumatic conquest of Jerusalem (see Lk 19:43 – 44; 21:6,24) naturally date Luke-Acts sometime after (or occasionally just before) AD 70. Luke, who adapts Mark's grammar for a somewhat more educated Greek audience, also writes after Mark. ◆

Introduction

1:1-4Ref — Ac 1:1

1 Many have undertaken to draw up an
account of the things that have been
fulfilled[a] among us, 2just as they were
handed down to us by those who from
the first[a] were eyewitnesses[b] and servants
of the word.[c] 3With this in mind, since I
myself have carefully investigated everything from the beginning, I too decided to
write an orderly account[d] for you, most
excellent[e] Theophilus,[f] 4so that you may
know the certainty of the things you have
been taught.[g]

The Birth of John the Baptist Foretold

5In the time of Herod king of Judea[h]
there was a priest named Zechariah, who
belonged to the priestly division of Abijah;[i] his wife Elizabeth was also a descendant of Aaron. 6Both of them were righteous in the sight of God, observing all the
Lord's commands and decrees blamelessly.[j] 7But they were childless because Elizabeth was not able to conceive, and they
were both very old.
8Once when Zechariah's division was
on duty and he was serving as priest before God,[k] 9he was chosen by lot, according to the custom of the priesthood, to go
into the temple of the Lord and burn incense.[l] 10And when the time for the burning of incense came, all the assembled
worshipers were praying outside.[m]
11Then an angel[n] of the Lord appeared
to him, standing at the right side of the
altar of incense.[o] 12When Zechariah saw

1:2 [a] Mk 1:1; Jn 15:27; Ac 1:21,22 [b] Heb 2:3; 1Pe 5:1; 2Pe 1:16; 1Jn 1:1 [c] Mk 4:14
1:3 [d] Ac 11:4 [e] Ac 24:3; 26:25 [f] Ac 1:1
1:4 [g] Jn 20:31
1:5 [h] Mt 2:1 [i] 1Ch 24:10
1:6 [j] Ge 7:1; 1Ki 9:4
1:8 [k] 1Ch 24:19; 2Ch 8:14
1:9 [l] Ex 30:7, 8; 1Ch 23:13; 2Ch 29:11
1:10 [m] Lev 16:17
1:11 [n] Ac 5:19 [o] Ex 30:1-10

[a] *1* Or *been surely believed*

1:1 *draw up an account.* In the Mediterranean world, disciples of teachers often committed the teacher's lectures to writing; otherwise, others often did so (especially if the disciples were not very literate). Most scholars agree that at least one of the written works by Luke's day was Mark; one of the many other sources might be a collection of material shared by Matthew and Luke (perhaps a collection of mostly sayings reported by Matthew). Sometimes students published their teacher's sayings in ways that even reflected the teacher's distinctive style. *things that have been fulfilled among us.* Reflects the kind of subject noted by ancient historians (rather than by other kinds of writers) in their prefaces.
1:2 *eyewitnesses.* Historians in the eastern Mediterranean world normally consulted eyewitnesses whenever possible. Oral transmission could be very accurate, especially among disciples of teachers in the east. Ancient memories were carefully trained, both among the educated and among uneducated reciters, and disciples of teachers ordinarily saw one of their chief roles as accurately communicating their teachers' message. See Introduction to the Gospels (p. 1598).
1:3 *carefully investigated everything.* Historians in the eastern Mediterranean valued careful investigation, including travel to sites where events occurred and interviewing witnesses there. Luke could have done this during his extended time in Judea (see Ac 21:8 – 18; 24:27; 27:1). Thus Luke could have "thorough knowledge" (as the term could also be translated), confirming the traditions widely circulated in the church (Lk 1:4). *most excellent Theophilus.* The title "most excellent" suggests that Theophilus was a person of status (cf. Ac 23:26; 24:3; 26:25). Writers often dedicated works, as here, to a person of prominence, which helped promote the book and might secure the dedicatee's help in promoting it. (Sometimes, though not always, the dedicatee was the book's sponsor. The dedicatee was rarely the book's sole intended audience.) Although some have suggested that "Theophilus" is used as a symbolic name, it was a common name, including among Jews in the Diaspora. There is no record of symbolically named dedicatees in ancient sources.
1:5 *Herod king of Judea.* See the article "Herod the Great," p. 1610. *division of Abijah.* There were 24 divisions of priests; the division of Abijah appears in 1Ch 24:10. Priests could marry any fellow Israelite, but they often preferred to marry daughters from priestly families, as here.
1:6 *blamelessly.* Scripture sometimes spoke of people as blameless (Ge 6:9; 17:1; Job 1:1); this did not necessarily mean absolute perfection (cf. Ge 9:21) but meant that they did not break explicit Biblical commandments. Because some people supposed that those unable to bear children (v. 7) were cursed, it is important for Luke to counter that this family was blameless.
1:7 *childless … not able to conceive … very old.* Jewish people often contemplated God's covenant with Abraham (v. 55,73). Luke here evokes the story of Abraham and Sarah; in Ge 11:30 Sarah was also "not able to conceive" (the same Greek term in the Septuagint, the pre-Christian Greek translation of the OT) and the couple was "very old" (Ge 18:11). Childless parents lacked support in their old age, and many people assumed that such a condition reflected divine punishment for sin. Likewise, custom in many Judean circles demanded that if for many years a wife of childbearing age did not bear children, the husband should divorce her so he could father children with a different wife. Zechariah and Elizabeth did not do so.
1:8 Some estimate that there were some 18,000 priests and Levites. Each of the 24 divisions of priests (v. 5) would serve in the temple during major festivals and also one week every half year.
1:9 *chosen by lot.* Because there were so many priests (see note on v. 8), special duties had to be assigned by lot (see note on Ac 1:26). Jewish people believed that God supervised the result of the lot (cf. 1Ch 24:31; 25:8; Ne 10:34). This occasion was likely Zechariah's only opportunity to perform this service during his lifetime.
1:10 *time for the burning of incense.* Priests offered incense in connection with the morning and evening sacrifices; cf. the "time of prayer" in Ac 3:1.
1:11 God often sent the angel of the Lord in the OT to announce tidings, sometimes including about special births (Ge 16:11; Jdg 13:3). Satan had once appeared at the high priest's right side, but the angel of the Lord defended and delivered God's message to the high priest (Zec 3:1 – 7).
1:12 *gripped with fear.* Fear was a common response to an angelic revelation (Da 10:7 – 9). Ancient narrators liked to parallel various characters (see the article "Answered Charges and Parallel Figures in Acts 7," p. 1881). Luke here compares the respected priest Zechariah in Jerusalem's temple (vv. 12 – 22) and the lowly girl Mary in a Galilean village (vv. 26 – 38), with a comparison similar to that between the high priest Eli and the lowly Hannah

him, he was startled and was gripped with
fear.[p] 13 But the angel said to him: "Do not
be afraid,[q] Zechariah; your prayer has
been heard. Your wife Elizabeth will bear
you a son, and you are to call him John.[r]
14 He will be a joy and delight to you, and
many will rejoice because of his birth,[s]
15 for he will be great in the sight of the
Lord. He is never to take wine or other fermented drink,[t] and he will be filled with
the Holy Spirit even before he is born.[u]
16 He will bring back many of the people
of Israel to the Lord their God. 17 And he
will go on before the Lord,[v] in the spirit
and power of Elijah,[w] to turn the hearts
of the parents to their children[x] and the
disobedient to the wisdom of the righteous — to make ready a people prepared
for the Lord."
18 Zechariah asked the angel, "How can
I be sure of this? I am an old man and my
wife is well along in years."[y]
19 The angel said to him, "I am Gabriel.[z]
I stand in the presence of God, and I have
been sent to speak to you and to tell you
this good news. 20 And now you will be silent and not able to speak[a] until the day
this happens, because you did not believe
my words, which will come true at their
appointed time."
21 Meanwhile, the people were waiting for Zechariah and wondering why he
stayed so long in the temple. 22 When he
came out, he could not speak to them.
They realized he had seen a vision in the
temple, for he kept making signs[b] to them
but remained unable to speak.
23 When his time of service was completed, he returned home. 24 After this his
wife Elizabeth became pregnant and for
five months remained in seclusion. 25 "The
Lord has done this for me," she said. "In
these days he has shown his favor and tak-
en away my disgrace[c] among the people."

The Birth of Jesus Foretold

26 In the sixth month of Elizabeth's pregnancy, God sent the angel Gabriel[d] to

1:12 [p] Jdg 6:22, 23; 13:22 **1:13** [q] ver 30; Mt 14:27 [r] ver 60,63 **1:14** [s] ver 58 **1:15** [t] Nu 6:3; Jdg 13:4; Lk 7:33 [u] Jer 1:5; Gal 1:15 **1:17** [v] ver 76 [w] Mt 11:14 [x] Mal 4:5,6 **1:18** [y] ver 34; Ge 17:17 **1:19** [z] ver 26; Da 8:16; 9:21; Mt 18:10 **1:20** [a] Eze 3:26 **1:22** [b] ver 62 **1:25** [c] Ge 30:23; Isa 4:1 **1:26** [d] ver 19

in 1Sa 1:9–20. Rhetorical handbooks show that ancient writers not only contrasted good and bad role models but also good (Zechariah) and better (Mary).

Zechariah (Lk 1:12–22)	Mary (Lk 1:26–38)
Zechariah is "startled" (v. 12)	Mary is "troubled" (v. 29)
"Do not be afraid" (v. 13)	"Do not be afraid" (v. 30)
"You are to call him John" (v. 13)	"You are to call him Jesus" (v. 31)
"He will be great in the sight of the Lord" (v. 15)	"He will be great" (v. 32)
"He will be filled with the Holy Spirit even before he is born" (v. 15)	"The Holy Spirit will come on you" (v. 35)
He will turn people back to God (vv. 16–17)	"He will reign" (vv. 32–33)
"How can I be sure ...?" (v. 18)	"How will this be ...?" (v. 34)
Proof or explanation (vv. 19–20)	Proof or explanation (vv. 35–37)
"You did not believe my words" (v. 20)	"Blessed is she who has believed" (v. 45)

1:13 *Do not be afraid.* In Scripture God repeatedly commands his people, "Do not be afraid," including during revelations (Ge 15:1; 26:24; 46:3; Jos 8:1); the angel of the Lord sometimes offers this command (Ge 21:17; 2Ki 1:15), including when people are afraid because of the revelation (Jdg 6:23; Da 10:12,19). For announcements of births in the OT, see, e.g., Jdg 13:3; Isa 7:14. *Your wife ... will bear you a son, and you are to call him.* Closely echoes Ge 17:19; commands to name a child appear also in Ge 16:11; 1Ch 22:9; Isa 7:14.
1:15 *wine or other fermented drink.* The prohibition of strong drink fits consecrated Nazirites (Nu 6:3), and the language echoes the angel of the Lord's birth announcement to Samson's mother: while pregnant she, and presumably later the Nazirite Samson, must not drink "wine or other fermented drink" (Jdg 13:4,7,14). *filled with the Holy Spirit.* The Spirit of the Lord also came on Samson, but for a different mission (Jdg 13:25; 14:6,19; 15:14).
1:16 *bring back.* The prophets called Israel to return to the Lord.
1:17 *turn the hearts.* Scripture promised that Elijah would "turn the hearts of the parents to their children" (Mal 4:6) before the coming of the day of the Lord (Mal 4:5). John's mission was to prepare the way for God himself, thus for Jesus (see 3:4,16). Preparing people for the Lord was also the mission of the forerunner in Isa 40:3 (quoted in Lk 3:4).
1:18 *How can I be sure of this?* Confronted with astonishing revelations, many earlier hearers requested explanations or signs (Ge 15:8; Jdg 6:17,36–39; 2Ki 20:8) or even openly doubted (Ge 17:17; 18:12). The standards here are higher.
1:19 *Gabriel.* Although Jewish tradition had elaborated the names of many angels, the only two named in Scripture are Gabriel (Da 8:16; 9:21) and Michael (Da 10:13,21; 12:1). Jewish tradition included Gabriel among archangels who stood before God's throne.
1:21 It did not take long to cast incense on the altar. Failure to emerge quickly might suggest that God had punished him or the people for irreverence.
1:22 *could not speak.* Sometimes God blinded the wicked (Ge 19:11) or a revelation could leave one momentarily speechless (Da 10:15); more important, as a sign God had once required a prophet to be silent for a period of time (Eze 24:27; 29:21; 33:22).
1:23 *returned home.* Priests were not supposed to own their own lands, but because of economic necessity (including exploitation by the wealthier priests) some even farmed plots of land.
1:25 *disgrace.* Shame was attached to the inability to have children in Elizabeth's culture (see note on v. 7). Scripture often records the celebration of women who became able to bear children (Ge 21:6–7; 1Sa 2:1–11), including the removal of shame (Ge 30:23).
1:26 *Gabriel.* See note on v. 19. *Nazareth.* In contrast to Jerusalem, with its massive building projects, Nazareth was a lowly village (cf. Jn 1:46).

Nazareth,[e] a town in Galilee, 27 to a virgin
pledged to be married to a man named
Joseph,[f] a descendant of David. The virgin's name was Mary. 28 The angel went
to her and said, "Greetings, you who are
highly favored! The Lord is with you."
29 Mary was greatly troubled at his
words and wondered what kind of greeting this might be. 30 But the angel said to
her, "Do not be afraid,[g] Mary; you have
found favor with God. 31 You will conceive
and give birth to a son, and you are to call
him Jesus.[h] 32 He will be great and will be
called the Son of the Most High.[i] The Lord
God will give him the throne of his father
David, 33 and he will reign over Jacob's descendants forever; his kingdom[j] will never
end."[k]
34 "How will this be," Mary asked the
angel, "since I am a virgin?"
35 The angel answered, "The Holy Spirit
will come on you,[l] and the power of the
Most High[m] will overshadow you. So the
holy one[n] to be born will be called[a] the
Son of God.[o] 36 Even Elizabeth your relative is going to have a child in her old age,
and she who was said to be unable to conceive is in her sixth month. 37 For no word
from God will ever fail."[p]
38 "I am the Lord's servant," Mary answered. "May your word to me be fulfilled." Then the angel left her.

Mary Visits Elizabeth

39 At that time Mary got ready and hurried to a town in the hill country of Judea,[q] 40 where she entered Zechariah's
home and greeted Elizabeth. 41 When Elizabeth heard Mary's greeting, the baby
leaped in her womb, and Elizabeth was
filled with the Holy Spirit. 42 In a loud
voice she exclaimed: "Blessed are you
among women,[r] and blessed is the child
you will bear! 43 But why am I so favored,
that the mother of my Lord should come
to me? 44 As soon as the sound of your
greeting reached my ears, the baby in my
womb leaped for joy. 45 Blessed is she who
has believed that the Lord would fulfill his
promises to her!"

1:26 [e] Mt 2:23 **1:27** [f] Mt 1:16, 18, 20; Lk 2:4 **1:30** [g] ver 13; Mt 14:27 **1:31** [h] Isa 7:14; Mt 1:21, 25; Lk 2:21 **1:32** [i] ver 35, 76; Mk 5:7 **1:33** [j] Mt 28:18 [k] Da 2:44; 7:14, 27; Mic 4:7; Heb 1:8 **1:35** [l] Mt 1:18 [m] ver 32, 76 [n] Mk 1:24 [o] Mt 4:3 **1:37** [p] Mt 19:26 **1:39** [q] ver 65 **1:42** [r] Jdg 5:24

[a] 35 Or *So the child to be born will be called holy,*

1:27 *pledged to be married.* The betrothal period was often a year, and Jewish tradition suggests that couples in Galilee were not left unchaperoned during that time. Betrothal involved a financial agreement between families, and it could be ended only by divorce or death. It concluded with the wedding night, at which point the marriage could finally be consummated sexually. *descendant of David.* Because the royal line was through the father, any legal son of Joseph would belong to David's line. Legal lines mattered more for this purpose than did genetic ones; thus, e.g., the Roman emperors during this period were *adopted* rather than biological sons of their predecessors.

1:28 *highly favored.* The greeting is unusual, especially to a person of low status. Given the usual age of marriage for Galilean virgins, Mary may have been in her midteens; her age, her gender and her being a Galilean villager together would have given her little social standing. *The Lord is with you.* Divine announcements often included the assurance that God was "with" the hearer, including when God was calling someone to a difficult task (e.g., Ge 31:3; Ex 3:12; Jos 1:5; 3:7; Jdg 6:12,16; Jer 1:8,19).

1:30 *Do not be afraid.* See note on v. 13. *favor with God.* Others called by God found favor with him (Ge 6:8; Ex 33:12).

1:31 *will conceive and give birth to a son, and … call him.* The announcement echoes Isa 7:14; this passage appears particularly pertinent for a virgin (v. 34), especially in the Greek translation of Isaiah. For further detail on how early Christians read Isa 7:14, see note on Mt 1:22–23.

1:32 *throne of his father David.* In 2Sa 7:12–16, God promised David an eternal lineage and being adopted as God's children, but David's royal line no longer ruled. From the stump of this line, however, would come an eternal ruler (Isa 11:1), the one who would reign on David's throne eternally (Isa 9:7). This would also be the Mighty God (Isa 9:6; a divine title in Isa 10:21).

1:33 *kingdom will never end.* The eternal kingdom also belonged to the son of man in Da 7:13–14; Jewish people expected this kingdom to come in the time of the fourth empire (Da 2:44), which Jewish people in Jesus' day believed was the Roman Empire.

1:34 *virgin.* Given the usual age of marriage in Judea and Galilee, Mary was probably in her teens. Girls could marry as young as 12, but 13 to 16 was more common, and some were even past 20; apparently most Jewish men married around the ages of 18 to 20, perhaps a decade younger than most Greek men.

1:35 *overshadow.* The language here evokes the image of God's glory (as in 9:34), as when God's glory filled the tabernacle (Ex 40:35; cf. also the Septuagint, the pre-Christian Greek translation of the OT, in Ps 91:4).

1:36–37 Although Sarah doubted that she could have a child in her old age, God reminded her that nothing was impossible with him (Ge 18:14).

1:38 *servant.* Calling oneself the other's servant expressed compliance or gratitude (Ge 33:5; 1Sa 1:18; 25:41; 2Sa 7:25; 9:6,11; 2Ki 4:2), including in addressing God or angels (Ge 19:19; 32:10).

1:39 Presumably Mary's family arranged for her to travel with others journeying in that direction, since it would not have been safe for a young woman to travel several days alone.

1:40 *greeted Elizabeth.* Greetings were important and the most basic Jewish greeting was *shalom,* "Peace" (meaning "May God cause all to be well with you").

1:41 *leaped in her womb.* Many people in antiquity recognized that children could be active even in the womb. The common Greek version of the OT uses the same Greek verb here translated "leaped" for the babies jostling inside Rebekah in Ge 25:22, after God ended her childlessness. Nevertheless, as often in antiquity more widely used as here, leaping is an expression of joy (see v. 44; cf. 6:23).

1:42 *Blessed.* Sometimes one could implicitly bless one person by explicitly blessing another (e.g., 11:27). *the child you will bear.* Lit. "the fruit of your womb," a common Hebrew figure of speech (e.g., Ge 30:2 [NIV "having children"]; Dt 7:13).

Mary's Song

1:46-53pp — 1Sa 2:1-10

46And Mary said:

"My soul glorifies the Lord[s]
47 and my spirit rejoices in God my Savior,[t]
48 for he has been mindful
of the humble state of his servant.[u]
From now on all generations will call
me blessed,[v]
49 for the Mighty One has done great
things[w] for me—
holy is his name.[x]
50 His mercy extends to those who fear
him,
from generation to generation.[y]

1:46 [s] Ps 34:2,3 **1:47** [t] 1Ti 1:1; 2:3 **1:48** [u] Ps 138:6 [v] Lk 11:27 **1:49** [w] Ps 71:19 [x] Ps 111:9 **1:50** [y] Ex 20:6; Ps 103:17

1:46 *My soul.* A poetic way to speak of oneself during worship (Ps 35:9; 103:1; 104:1,35). *glorifies the Lord.* Another way of saying "praises him" (Ps 34:3).
1:47 *rejoices.* The Psalms speak of joy or rejoicing, usually in the context of worship, close to 100 times. As in the Psalms, a second line of praise (here) repeats or develops the thought of the previous line (v. 46). *God my Savior.* A common expression (e.g., Ps 25:5; 27:9; cf. Hab 3:18 for being "joyful in God my Savior").
1:48 *he has been mindful.* Reflects common language in the Septuagint (the pre-Christian Greek translation of the OT) of the Psalms (e.g., Ps 33:13–14; 66:7). *all generations … blessed.* For perpetual honor, see note on Mk 14:9.
1:49 *the Mighty One.* A common Biblical title for God (e.g., Jos 22:22; Ps 50:1; Isa 1:24). *holy.* That God's name is holy is even more pervasive in Scripture (e.g., Lev 20:3; 22:2,32; 1Ch 16:10,35). Cf. "holy … is his name" (Ps 111:9).
1:50 *from generation to generation.* A common Biblical

LUKE 1:46–55

Mary's Allusions to Hannah's Song

If Elizabeth's pregnancy evokes that of aged Sarah in Genesis (see notes on 1:7,36–37), Mary's evokes a wider range of miraculous births in the OT, though of course her virgin birth is unique. Mary's song has special resonances with Hannah's song in 1Sa 2:1–10, when Hannah celebrates the birth of her son Samuel. Just as Hannah's humility and faith bring her greater blessing than the aged priest Eli in 1Sa 1, Mary's humility and faith bring greater blessing than Zechariah's in Lk 1:11–38 (though Zechariah is a less disobedient character than Eli).

Following are some possible connections between the song of Mary and that of Hannah, though Mary's song also draws on a much wider range of Biblical language:

1SA 2:1–10	LK 1:46–55
God exalts the lowly (2:1,4–5,8)	God exalts the lowly (vv. 48,52–53)
"My heart rejoices . . . in your deliverance" (v. 1)	"My spirit rejoices in God my Savior" (v. 47)
"No one holy like the LORD" (v. 2)	"Holy is his name" (v. 49)
Celebrating the exaltation of the humble exalted and bringing down of the proud (vv. 3–9)	Celebrating the exaltation of the humble and bringing down of the proud (vv. 51–53)
The poor versus the rich (vv. 7–8)	The rich leave emptyhanded (v. 53)
The hungry versus the full (v. 5)	God has filled the hungry (v. 53)
The poor displacing nobles (v. 8)	Rulers brought down (v. 52) (using the same term as the Septuagint of 1Sa 2:8)
The shift from personal deliverance to God's anointed king (v. 10)	The shift from personal deliverance to Israel's deliverance (v. 54)

This chart is adapted from Craig S. Keener, *Acts: An Exegetical Commentary* (4 vols.; Grand Rapids: Baker Academic, 2012–2014), 1:557.

51 He has performed mighty deeds with
his arm;[z]
he has scattered those who are
proud in their inmost thoughts.
52 He has brought down rulers from their
thrones
but has lifted up the humble.
53 He has filled the hungry with good
things[a]
but has sent the rich away empty.
54 He has helped his servant Israel,
remembering to be merciful[b]
55 to Abraham and his descendants[c]
forever,
just as he promised our ancestors."

56 Mary stayed with Elizabeth for about
three months and then returned home.

The Birth of John the Baptist

57 When it was time for Elizabeth to
have her baby, she gave birth to a son.
58 Her neighbors and relatives heard that
the Lord had shown her great mercy, and
they shared her joy.
59 On the eighth day they came to circumcise[d] the child, and they were going to
name him after his father Zechariah, 60 but
his mother spoke up and said, "No! He is
to be called John."[e]
61 They said to her, "There is no one
among your relatives who has that name."
62 Then they made signs[f] to his father,
to find out what he would like to name
the child. 63 He asked for a writing tablet, and to everyone's astonishment he
wrote, "His name is John."[g] 64 Immediately his mouth was opened and his tongue
set free, and he began to speak,[h] praising
God. 65 All the neighbors were filled with
awe, and throughout the hill country of
Judea[i] people were talking about all these
things. 66 Everyone who heard this wondered about it, asking, "What then is this
child going to be?" For the Lord's hand
was with him.[j]

Zechariah's Song

67 His father Zechariah was filled with
the Holy Spirit and prophesied:[k]

68 "Praise be to the Lord, the God of
Israel,[l]
because he has come to his people
and redeemed them.[m]
69 He has raised up a horn[a][n] of salvation
for us
in the house of his servant David[o]
70 (as he said through his holy prophets
of long ago),[p]
71 salvation from our enemies
and from the hand of all who hate
us —
72 to show mercy to our ancestors[q]
and to remember his holy covenant,[r]

1:51 [z] Ps 98:1; Isa 40:10 **1:53** [a] Ps 107:9 **1:54** [b] Ps 98:3 **1:55** [c] Ge 17:19; Ps 132:11; Gal 3:16 **1:59** [d] Ge 17:12; Lev 12:3; Lk 2:21; Php 3:5 **1:60** [e] ver 13, 63 **1:62** [f] ver 22
1:63 [g] ver 13, 60 **1:64** [h] ver 20 **1:65** [i] ver 39 **1:66** [j] Ge 39:2; Ac 11:21 **1:67** [k] Joel 2:28 **1:68** [l] Ps 72:18 [m] Ps 111:9; Lk 7:16 **1:69** [n] 1Sa 2:1, 10; Ps 18:2; 89:17; 132:17; Eze 29:21 [o] Mt 1:1 **1:70** [p] Jer 23:5 **1:72** [q] Mic 7:20 [r] Ps 105:8, 9; 106:45; Eze 16:60

[a] 69 *Horn* here symbolizes a strong king.

expression (e.g., Ex 3:15; 17:16; Ps 79:13). Mary knew that God's love was forever with those who loved him (Ps 103:17).

1:51 *mighty deeds with his arm.* Evokes frequent Biblical language; God scattered his enemies with his mighty arm in Ps 89:10.

1:52 God exalts the lowly and casts down the proud (Pr 3:34; Isa 2:11 – 12,17).

1:53 *He has filled the hungry with good things.* The general language about God's generosity in Ps 107:9 is here applied to Mary's experience.

1:54 *his servant Israel.* For God's blessing to Israel, see, e.g., Ps 136:22. *remembering.* For prayers that God will remember mercy, see Ps 25:6; Hab 3:2.

1:56 Some ancient sources speak of ten-month pregnancies, but many recognized that nine was normal. This suggests that Mary remained until John was born (see v. 36).

1:58 *shared her joy.* Neighbors normally shared in celebrating special events such as the births of children.

1:59 *circumcise.* Jewish people circumcised on the eighth day (Ge 17:12; 21:4); in this period the father often performed the ritual.

1:62 In this period, the father had more say than the mother in a child's naming; a child was often named for grandfathers and sometimes for fathers.

1:63 *writing tablet.* A wooden board with a wax surface. *he wrote ... John.* Priests were often educated; writing the name would probably be basic for them.

1:64 For restoration of speech as a prophetic sign, see note on v. 22.

1:66 *the Lord's hand was with him.* Reflects a Biblical idiom regarding God's hand (2Ki 3:15; 2Ch 30:12; Ezr 7:6,28; Eze 1:3; 3:22).

1:67 *filled with the Holy Spirit.* The Holy Spirit was often associated with prophecy in the OT (Nu 11:25 – 26; 1Sa 10:6,10; 19:20,23; Joel 2:28 – 29); early Jewish circles emphasized this prophetic role of the Spirit even more consistently, although often with regard to the prophets of the past era. (The primary exception is in works from specifically Essene circles, which included but did not focus as narrowly on the Spirit's role in inspiration or prophetic empowerment.)

1:68 *Praise be to the Lord.* Pervasive in the OT (e.g., Ge 9:26; Ps 28:6), often more fully, "Praise be to the LORD, the God of Israel" (e.g., 1Sa 25:32; 1Ki 1:48; 8:15), e.g., in praise for fulfilling his promise to David (2Ch 6:4). *redeemed them.* The emphasis on God redeeming his people (including liberating them from slavery) is also pervasive (e.g., Ex 6:6); some texts also speak of God "visiting" his people (here, "has come to his people") when he would help them (the same Greek term in Ge 50:24 – 25; Ps 106:4; Zec 10:3).

1:69 *horn of salvation.* Cf. 2Sa 22:3; Ps 18:2. For the connection between "horn" and "deliverance" (or "salvation") in Hannah's song, see 1Sa 2:1. Because animals could use horns in battle, the horn was a natural figure for strength. *his servant David.* Scripture often speaks of his servant David (1Ki 8:66; 2Ki 8:19; 1Ch 17:24; Ps 78:70; 132:10; 144:10). The OT speaks roughly 24 times of the "house of David."

1:71 The prophets promised Israel future deliverance from their enemies, sometimes connected with the coming of the ultimate Davidic king (e.g., Isa 9:4 – 7; 11:1 – 16). Cf. Ps 106:10.

1:72 – 73 *to our ancestors ... to our father Abraham.* When God acted to redeem his people in the past, he did so in remembrance of his covenant with Abraham, Isaac and

73 the oath he swore to our father
Abraham:[s]
74 to rescue us from the hand of our
enemies,
and to enable us to serve him[t]
without fear
75 in holiness and righteousness[u]
before him all our days.

76 And you, my child, will be called a
prophet[v] of the Most High;[w]
for you will go on before the Lord to
prepare the way for him,[x]
77 to give his people the knowledge of
salvation
through the forgiveness of their
sins,[y]
78 because of the tender mercy of our
God,
by which the rising sun[z] will come
to us from heaven
79 to shine on those living in darkness
and in the shadow of death,[a]
to guide our feet into the path of
peace."

1:73 [s] Ge 22:16-18
1:74 [t] Heb 9:14
1:75 [u] Eph 4:24
1:76 [v] Mt 11:9
[w] ver 32, 35
[x] ver 17; Mal 3:1
1:77 [y] Jer 31:34; Mk 1:4
1:78 [z] Mal 4:2
1:79 [a] Isa 9:2; 59:9; Mt 4:16; Ac 26:18
1:80 [b] Lk 2:40, 52
2:1 [c] Mt 22:17; Lk 3:1
[d] Mt 24:14
2:2 [e] Mt 4:24
2:4 [f] Jn 7:42

80 And the child grew and became strong
in spirit[a];[b] and he lived in the wilderness
until he appeared publicly to Israel.

The Birth of Jesus

2 In those days Caesar Augustus[c] issued
a decree that a census should be taken
of the entire Roman world.[d] 2 (This was the
first census that took place while[b] Quirinius was governor of Syria.)[e] 3 And everyone
went to their own town to register.
4 So Joseph also went up from the town
of Nazareth in Galilee to Judea, to Bethlehem[f] the town of David, because he belonged to the house and line of David. 5 He
went there to register with Mary, who was
pledged to be married to him and was expecting a child. 6 While they were there,
the time came for the baby to be born,
7 and she gave birth to her firstborn, a son.
She wrapped him in cloths and placed him
in a manger, because there was no guest
room available for them.

[a] 80 Or *in the Spirit* [b] 2 Or *This census took place before*

Jacob (Ex 2:24). He had also promised to do so whenever Israel turned to him (Lev 26:42). This showed his grace (2Ki 13:23; 1Ch 16:16; Ps 105:9). Scripture often speaks of God's oath to the patriarchs (see especially Ge 22:16–18).
1:74 *serve him without fear.* This phrase does not mean "without fear of (reverence for) the Lord" (cf. Dt 10:12,20; 13:4; 1Sa 12:14,24), but without reason to fear their enemies (Lev 26:36).
1:76 *prepare the way for him.* Recalls Isa 40:3; Mal 3:1 (as in Mk 1:2–3; Lk 7:27), perhaps especially the former (in view of salvation in v. 77; 3:4–6).
1:77 *forgiveness of their sins.* God had promised to forgive his people (Jer 31:34; 33:8; 50:20).
1:78 *sun will come.* Might evoke Mal 4:2 (in the context of Elijah being the preparer for the Lord, Mal 4:5–6). Some also suggest a connection with "the Branch" of Zech 3:8 and 6:12, which the Septuagint, the pre-Christian Greek translation of the OT, translates with the same expression translated *rising sun* here.
1:79 *to shine on those living in darkness.* Evokes Isa 9:2. *shadow of death.* Also evokes Isa 9:2; appears in the Greek version of Isaiah's passage (though the phrase also appears in three psalms), a Messianic passage (Isa 9:6–7). *path of peace.* Also Biblical language (e.g., Isa 59:8).
1:80 In view of 2:52, this verse continues the comparison between John and the greater Jesus. Ancient comparison not only contrasted bad and good, but also great and greater, as here (see also 7:28). Comparing good and better honored the better all the more. *lived in the wilderness.* Normally only the most radical people (such as one later radical teacher named Bannus, or many Essenes) lived in the wilderness.
2:1 *Caesar Augustus.* Augustus was the most powerful ruler ever known in the Mediterranean world. *the entire Roman world.* This summation need not mean that the census was carried out in every place at the same time. The census was to assess taxes; Romans practiced this irregularly until Augustus. The intervals were originally shorter, but starting at some point, in some locations large censuses probably took place about every 14 years.
2:2 *Quirinius.* Syria's governor during the famous, contentious census of AD 6, but our incomplete historical records do not name Syria's governor during the time of Jesus' birth. Some suggest that Luke confused the two censuses or periods; others, that he deliberately conflated the census here with the later, better-known one. Others suggest that Quirinius was already an official at this time (we lack evidence at this point to say that he was not), in which case Luke may mean, "the first census under Quirinius" (see NIV text). Still others prefer the translation, "before Quirinius was governor." In any case, the region that Romans came to call Palestine belonged to the Roman province of Syria and historians dated events in connection with officials, so it was appropriate to name Syria's governor whether or not he administered the census directly.
2:3 *own town.* The limited surviving evidence suggests that people had to return not to where they were born but to where they owned property; evidence also suggests that such a census may not have affected property in Galilee. Some thus suggest that Joseph still held property in Bethlehem for which he had to register regardless of property in Nazareth. (If so, v. 7 suggests that the property was either in use or had no house.)
2:4 *Bethlehem.* About six miles (nine and a half kilometers) beyond Jerusalem, to its south. The promised ruler would be from David's line (e.g., Isa 9:7).
2:5 *with Mary.* For a woman who was betrothed but not yet married to be pregnant violated social standards.
2:7 *cloths.* Parents and midwives wrapped an infant's limbs in long strips of cloth to help them to grow straight. They could be used until the infant's limbs became firm or for as long as two months. *manger.* A feeding trough for domestic animals; people sometimes kept animals in caves by the house. Gentiles had a few stories of deities born in caves (though also stories of deities born elsewhere). Luke does not specify a cave as the place of the manger, but the tradition that Jesus was born in a cave is early, information apparently already circulating in Bethlehem by the early second century.

LUKE 2:1 – 7

Caesar and Christ

Caesar appears the dominant cause of movement in this narrative, but ultimately God plans his purposes for Christ, whose coming and kingdom differ starkly from that of Caesar. As Scripture says elsewhere, God is near the broken but far from the proud.

Contrasts between Caesar and Christ implied in Lk 2:

AUGUSTUS	JESUS
Augustus (v. 1) ruled from a palace	Jesus was placed in an animal feeding trough shortly after birth (v. 7)
Earthly choirs in imperial temples praised Augustus, celebrating his birthday	Heavenly choirs praised Jesus at his birth (v. 13)
Augustus was hailed as bringer of the *Pax Romana*, the Roman peace	Heaven's choirs praised Jesus as bringer of true peace (v. 14)
Augustus was hailed as savior and lord	The angel of the Lord announces Jesus as Savior and Lord (v. 11)
Augustus enjoyed the praise of the powerful	Angels announced Jesus' birth to shepherds, who were considered lowly and often despised (vv. 8 – 9)

8And there were shepherds living out in
the fields nearby, keeping watch over their
flocks at night. 9An angel[g] of the Lord appeared to them, and the glory of the Lord
shone around them, and they were terrified. 10But the angel said to them, "Do not
be afraid.[h] I bring you good news that will
cause great joy for all the people. 11Today
in the town of David a Savior[i] has been
born to you; he is the Messiah,[j] the Lord.
12This will be a sign[k] to you: You will find
a baby wrapped in cloths and lying in a
manger."
13Suddenly a great company of the
heavenly host appeared with the angel,
praising God and saying,

14"Glory to God in the highest heaven,
and on earth peace[l] to those on
whom his favor rests."

15When the angels had left them and
gone into heaven, the shepherds said to
one another, "Let's go to Bethlehem and
see this thing that has happened, which
the Lord has told us about."
16So they hurried off and found Mary
and Joseph, and the baby, who was lying
in the manger. 17When they had seen him,
they spread the word concerning what had
been told them about this child, 18and all
who heard it were amazed at what the
shepherds said to them. 19But Mary trea-

2:9 [g] Lk 1:11; Ac 5:19
2:10 [h] Mt 14:27
2:11 [i] Mt 1:21; Jn 4:42; Ac 5:31 [j] Mt 1:16; 16:16, 20; Jn 11:27; Ac 2:36
2:12 [k] 1Sa 2:34; 2Ki 19:29; Isa 7:14
2:14 [l] Lk 1:79; Ro 5:1; Eph 2:14, 17

2:8 *shepherds.* Despite Biblical traditions about Moses and David, most people of status throughout the empire viewed shepherds as lowly and sometimes as rough, unclean or even dangerous. That shepherds were watching their flocks outside at night, rather than having them in pens, suggests that the season was warm. (The date of Dec. 25 was selected later, probably to fit a Roman festival.)
2:9 *terrified.* See note on 1:12.
2:10 *Do not be afraid.* See note on 1:13.
2:11 *Savior ... Lord.* Inscriptions hailed Caesar as the empire's savior and lord; Scripture, of course, recognized God as the true Savior (Isa 43:11; 45:21). *born to you.* Probably echoes Isa 9:6.
2:12 *sign to you.* Prophets sometimes offered signs from God to confirm their message (see, e.g., Eze 4:3; perhaps especially relevant in this context is Isa 7:14).
2:14 *peace.* Augustus (v. 1) boasted that he had established peace by conquering Rome's neighbors; in fact, Parthia remained Rome's feared enemy and Augustus's boast was largely propaganda. Jesus, however, was God's agent of a different kind of peace (cf. also 19:38).
2:15 Bethlehem was a small enough town that searching animal mangers for the one with the baby may not have taken long.
2:19 *pondered ... in her heart.* Cf. Ge 37:11.

sured up all these things and pondered them in her heart.[m] 20The shepherds returned, glorifying and praising God[n] for all the things they had heard and seen, which were just as they had been told.

21On the eighth day, when it was time to circumcise the child,[o] he was named Jesus, the name the angel had given him before he was conceived.[p]

Jesus Presented in the Temple

22When the time came for the purification rites required by the Law of Moses,[q] Joseph and Mary took him to Jerusalem to present him to the Lord 23(as it is written in the Law of the Lord, "Every firstborn male is to be consecrated to the Lord"[a]),[r] 24and to offer a sacrifice in keeping with what is said in the Law of the Lord: "a pair of doves or two young pigeons."[b][s]

25Now there was a man in Jerusalem called Simeon, who was righteous and devout.[t] He was waiting for the consolation of Israel,[u] and the Holy Spirit was on him. 26It had been revealed to him by the Holy Spirit that he would not die before he had seen the Lord's Messiah. 27Moved by the Spirit, he went into the temple courts. When the parents brought in the child Jesus to do for him what the custom of the Law required,[v] 28Simeon took him in his arms and praised God, saying:

29"Sovereign Lord, as you have
  promised,[w]
 you may now dismiss[c] your servant
  in peace.[x]
30For my eyes have seen your salvation,[y]
31 which you have prepared in the
  sight of all nations:
32a light for revelation to the Gentiles,
  and the glory of your people Israel."[z]

33The child's father and mother marveled at what was said about him. 34Then Simeon blessed them and said to Mary, his mother:[a] "This child is destined to cause the falling[b] and rising of many in Israel, and to be a sign that will be spoken against, 35so that the thoughts of many hearts will be revealed. And a sword will pierce your own soul too."

36There was also a prophet,[c] Anna, the daughter of Penuel, of the tribe of Asher. She was very old; she had lived with her husband seven years after her marriage, 37and then was a widow until she was eighty-four.[d][d] She never left the temple but worshiped night and day, fasting and praying.[e] 38Coming up to them at that very moment, she gave thanks to God and spoke about the child to all who were looking forward to the redemption of Jerusalem.[f]

39When Joseph and Mary had done everything required by the Law of the Lord, they returned to Galilee to their own town of Nazareth.[g] 40And the child grew and became strong; he was filled with wisdom, and the grace of God was on him.[h]

The Boy Jesus at the Temple

41Every year Jesus' parents went to Jerusalem for the Festival of the Passover.[i] 42When he was twelve years old, they went up to the festival, according to the custom. 43After the festival was over, while his parents were returning home, the boy Jesus

2:19 [m] ver 51 **2:20** [n] Mt 9:8 **2:21** [o] Lk 1:59 [p] Lk 1:31 **2:22** [q] Lev 12:2-8 **2:23** [r] Ex 13:2, 12, 15; Nu 3:13 **2:24** [s] Lev 12:8 **2:25** [t] Lk 1:6 [u] ver 38; Isa 52:9; Lk 23:51 **2:27** [v] ver 22 **2:29** [w] ver 26 [x] Ac 2:24 **2:30** [y] Isa 52:10; Lk 3:6 **2:32** [z] Isa 42:6; 49:6; Ac 13:47; 26:23 **2:34** [a] Mt 12:46 [b] Isa 8:14; Mt 21:44; 1Co 1:23; 2Co 2:16; 1Pe 2:7,8 **2:36** [c] Ac 21:9 **2:37** [d] 1Ti 5:9 [e] Ac 13:3; 14:23; 1Ti 5:5 **2:38** [f] ver 25; Isa 40:2; Lk 1:68; 24:21 **2:39** [g] ver 51; Mt 2:23 **2:40** [h] ver 52; Lk 1:80 **2:41** [i] Ex 23:15; Dt 16:1-8

[a] *23* Exodus 13:2,12 [b] *24* Lev. 12:8 [c] *29* Or *promised, / now dismiss* [d] *37* Or *then had been a widow for eighty-four years.*

2:22–23 *present him … consecrated to the Lord.* See Ex 13:2,12.

2:24 *pair of doves or two young pigeons.* Lev 12:8 allowed poor couples to sacrifice pigeons, which were inexpensive. Possible evidence of a structure for raising pigeons has been found in Jerusalem. Jerusalem was only six miles (nine and a half kilometers) from Bethlehem.

2:25 *consolation of Israel.* God had promised to bring consolation or "comfort" to Israel in the time of the end (Isa 49:13; 51:3; 52:9; 66:13).

2:26 *revealed … by the Holy Spirit.* Scripture spoke of God's Spirit in various ways, but prophetic revelation would be a particularly obvious way, especially to first-century hearers, since early Judaism associated the Spirit especially with prophets and their activities.

2:29 *dismiss your servant.* One might express willingness to die after experiencing a climactic blessing (Ge 46:30; Tobit 11:9).

2:32 *light … to the Gentiles.* See Israel's mission in Isa 42:6; 49:6; recognizing that Israel does not fulfill the task sufficiently (Isa 42:18–19), Isaiah suggests that one within Israel ultimately fulfills Israel's mission (see Isa 52:13—53:12). *glory of … Israel.* In the time of their restoration, see Isa 60:1–2.

2:34 *falling.* May allude to Isa 8:14–15.

2:37 *eighty-four.* Many people in antiquity respected a widow who remained faithful to the memory of her husband by not remarrying. Cf. the Jewish story about the widow Judith, who remained unmarried after widowhood until age 105 (Judith 16:22–23). In this period, even 84 was exceptionally old.

2:38 *redemption of Jerusalem.* God had promised to bring redemption for his people (Isa 52:3; 62:12; Jer 31:11; Hos 13:14; Zec 10:8).

2:40 The language reflects 1Sa 2:26; 3:19 (there are also two comments about Jesus growing as there were about Samuel; see v. 52). See note on 1:80.

2:41 *went to Jerusalem.* Scripture commanded three major festivals (Ex 23:14) that required pilgrimage to Jerusalem every year (Dt 16:16); one of these was Passover (Dt 16:6). Although Jerusalem was too far for most Jews in the Diaspora to travel annually, Galilee was closer. The journey might take three days, but Josephus testifies that entire villages journeyed to Jerusalem.

2:42 *twelve years old.* Jewish boys came of age and became men once they achieved puberty, typically around age 13 (later the age for *bar mitzvah*).

2:43 *unaware.* In a large nuclear family, some children (especially older ones) might be with extended family;

stayed behind in Jerusalem, but they were
unaware of it. 44 Thinking he was in their
company, they traveled on for a day. Then
they began looking for him among their
relatives and friends. 45 When they did not
find him, they went back to Jerusalem to
look for him. 46 After three days they found
him in the temple courts, sitting among
the teachers, listening to them and asking
them questions. 47 Everyone who heard
him was amazed[j] at his understanding
and his answers. 48 When his parents saw
him, they were astonished. His mother[k]
said to him, "Son, why have you treated
us like this? Your father[l] and I have been
anxiously searching for you."

49 "Why were you searching for me?" he
asked. "Didn't you know I had to be in
my Father's house?"[a][m] 50 But they did not
understand what he was saying to them.[n]

51 Then he went down to Nazareth with
them[o] and was obedient to them. But his
mother treasured all these things in her
heart.[p] 52 And Jesus grew in wisdom and
stature, and in favor with God and man.[q]

John the Baptist Prepares the Way

3:2-10pp — Mt 3:1-10; Mk 1:3-5
3:16,17pp — Mt 3:11,12; Mk 1:7,8

3 In the fifteenth year of the reign of Tiberius Caesar — when Pontius Pilate[r]
was governor of Judea, Herod[s] tetrarch of
Galilee, his brother Philip tetrarch of Iturea and Traconitis, and Lysanias tetrarch
of Abilene — 2 during the high-priesthood
of Annas and Caiaphas,[t] the word of God
came to John[u] son of Zechariah[v] in the
wilderness. 3 He went into all the country
around the Jordan, preaching a baptism
of repentance for the forgiveness of sins.[w]
4 As it is written in the book of the words
of Isaiah the prophet:

> "A voice of one calling in the wilderness,
> 'Prepare the way for the Lord,
> make straight paths for him.
> 5 Every valley shall be filled in,
> every mountain and hill made low.
> The crooked roads shall become
> straight,
> the rough ways smooth.
> 6 And all people will see God's
> salvation.'"[b][x]

7 John said to the crowds coming out to
be baptized by him, "You brood of vipers![y]
Who warned you to flee from the coming
wrath?[z] 8 Produce fruit in keeping with repentance. And do not begin to say to yourselves, 'We have Abraham as our father.'[a]
For I tell you that out of these stones God
can raise up children for Abraham. 9 The ax
is already at the root of the trees, and every

2:47 [j] Mt 7:28 **2:48** [k] Mt 12:46 [l] Lk 3:23; 4:22 **2:49** [m] Jn 2:16 **2:50** [n] Mk 9:32 **2:51** [o] ver 39; Mt 2:23 [p] ver 19 **2:52** [q] ver 40; 1Sa 2:26; Lk 1:80 **3:1** [r] Mt 27:2 [s] Mt 14:1 **3:2** [t] Mt 26:3; Jn 18:13; Ac 4:6 [u] Mt 3:1 [v] Lk 1:13 **3:3** [w] ver 16; Mk 1:4 **3:6** [x] Ps 98:2; Isa 40:3-5; 42:16; 52:10; Lk 2:30 **3:7** [y] Mt 12:34; 23:33 [z] Ro 1:18 **3:8** [a] Isa 51:2; Lk 19:9; Jn 8:33, 39; Ac 13:26; Ro 4:1, 11, 12, 16, 17; Gal 3:7

[a] *49* Or *be about my Father's business* [b] *6* Isaiah 40:3-5

often entire villages traveled together from Galilee for pilgrimage festivals.
2:46 *After three days.* Older estimates of Jerusalem's population (25,000 – 30,000) are too low; it may have been closer to 70,000 or 80,000. The population swelled to as high as 500,000 during festivals; although the festival was over, some pilgrims in the Diaspora may have stayed for Pentecost or to visit relatives there, so the city might have remained slightly more crowded than usual. Nazareth was at least three days' journey from Jerusalem, so the rest of the relatives would likely be home by the time Mary and Joseph located Jesus. *sitting … asking them questions.* Disciples would sit at the feet of teachers, both listening and asking questions. Young men could enter this phase even in their early teens; nevertheless, Jesus' preoccupation with Scripture at age 12 marks him as a prodigy. Ancient biographers liked to report any incidents that marked their subjects as prodigies.
2:51 *obedient to them.* Antiquity heavily emphasized children's obedience (especially when they were minors) as an expression of honoring parents, which Scripture commanded (Ex 20:12; Dt 5:16; 21:18).
2:52 Even more clearly than in v. 40, this verse echoes the growth of Samuel "in stature and in favor with the LORD and with people" (1Sa 2:26).
3:1 *fifteenth year.* When Greek historians knew what year events happened, they often dated the events according to a ruler's years in office (cf. also OT historians' practice, e.g., 2Ki 16:1; 17:1). Tiberius reigned from AD 14 until 37, but achieved some equality with his predecessor Augustus already in AD 13; scholars often date the time specified in this verse to between Sept. of AD 27 and Oct. of AD 28. *Pontius Pilate.* Judea's prefect from AD 26 to 36; although well attested in Jewish sources and an inscription, Pilate's only notoriety in the works of any extant Roman historians was a single mention in connection with his execution of Jesus. *Herod.* Herod Antipas, son of Herod the Great and a Samaritan wife (see note on Mk 6:14), remained tetrarch (governor of a territory) of Galilee from 4 BC — after his father's death — until AD 39, when he unwisely petitioned for greater authority. *Philip.* Tetrarch of Traconitis; he was a son of Herod the Great. Josephus attests all of these figures.
3:2 *Annas and Caiaphas.* Annas was the high priest from AD 6 to 15, when the Roman governor Gratus deposed him. Nevertheless, Annas retained thereafter both title and influence, and five of the succeeding high priests were his sons. Gratus soon elevated Joseph Caiaphas, probably also his son-in-law, to this role (AD 18 – 36). Jewish writers such as Josephus in this period used the title "high priest" not only for the highest priestly officer (as in the OT) but for leading members of the aristocratic priestly families in general. *wilderness.* See note on Mk 1:4.
3:3 *the Jordan.* See note on Mk 1:5. *baptism.* See the article "Baptism," p. 1686. *repentance.* See note on Mk 1:4; see also repentance.
3:4 – 6 On the use of Isa 40:3, see note on Mk 1:2 – 3; Luke, however, extends the quotation to Isa 40:5, so he may speak of salvation extending to "all people" (Lk 3:6); as in Ac 2:17, Luke undoubtedly sees here a foretaste of Gentiles' conversion.
3:4 *straight paths.* Roads would be improved before a great king traveled; Isaiah prophesied a new exodus (e.g., Isa 11:11, 16; 52:4, 12; see previous note).
3:6 *see God's salvation.* Cf. 2:30.
3:7 See note on Mt 3:7.
3:8 See note on Mt 3:9.
3:9 See note on Mt 3:10.

tree that does not produce good fruit will
be cut down and thrown into the fire."[b]
10 "What should we do then?"[c] the
crowd asked.
11 John answered, "Anyone who has two
shirts should share with the one who has
none, and anyone who has food should do
the same."[d]
12 Even tax collectors came to be baptized.[e] "Teacher," they asked, "what
should we do?"
13 "Don't collect any more than you are
required to,"[f] he told them.
14 Then some soldiers asked him, "And
what should we do?"
He replied, "Don't extort money and
don't accuse people falsely[g]—be content
with your pay."
15 The people were waiting expectantly and were all wondering in their hearts
if John[h] might possibly be the Messiah.[i]
16 John answered them all, "I baptize you
with[a] water.[j] But one who is more powerful than I will come, the straps of whose
sandals I am not worthy to untie. He will
baptize you with[a] the Holy Spirit and fire.[k]
17 His winnowing fork[l] is in his hand to
clear his threshing floor and to gather the
wheat into his barn, but he will burn up
the chaff with unquenchable fire."[m] 18 And
with many other words John exhorted the
people and proclaimed the good news to
them.
19 But when John rebuked Herod[n] the tetrarch because of his marriage to Herodias, his brother's wife, and all the other evil
things he had done, 20 Herod added this to
them all: He locked John up in prison.[o]

The Baptism and Genealogy of Jesus

3:21,22pp — Mt 3:13-17; Mk 1:9-11
3:23-38pp — Mt 1:1-17

21 When all the people were being baptized, Jesus was baptized too. And as he
was praying,[p] heaven was opened 22 and
the Holy Spirit descended on him[q] in bodily form like a dove. And a voice came from
heaven: "You are my Son,[r] whom I love;
with you I am well pleased."[s]
23 Now Jesus himself was about thirty

3:9 [b] Mt 3:10 **3:10** [c] ver 12, 14; Ac 2:37; 16:30 **3:11** [d] Isa 58:7 **3:12** [e] Lk 7:29 **3:13** [f] Lk 19:8 **3:14** [g] Ex 23:1; Lev 19:11 **3:15** [h] Mt 3:1 [i] Jn 1:19,20; Ac 13:25 **3:16** [j] ver 3; Mk 1:4 [k] Jn 1:26, 33; Ac 1:5; 11:16; 19:4 **3:17** [l] Isa 30:24 [m] Mt 13:30; 25:41 **3:19** [n] ver 1 **3:20** [o] Mt 14:3, 4; Mk 6:17-18 **3:21** [p] Mt 14:23; Mk 1:35; 6:46; Lk 5:16; 6:12; 9:18,28; 11:1 **3:22** [q] Isa 42:1; Jn 1:32,33; Ac 10:38 [r] Mt 3:17 [s] Mt 3:17

[a] 16 Or *in*

3:10 For the question—exploring what repentance (v. 3) involves—see note on Mk 1:4; cf. note on 18:18.
3:11 *two shirts.* Some peasants in impoverished Egypt had only one cloak. Most people in Galilee probably had more, but still not many.
3:12 *tax collectors.* The tax collectors in the Gospels are probably subordinates who worked for the officials responsible for collection. Most people in the Roman Empire did not like tax collectors; Jewish people viewed them as traitors. For assessment purposes, tax collectors were allowed to search anything except the person of a Roman lady; any property not properly declared was subject to seizure. In Egypt, tax collectors were sometimes so brutal that they were known to beat up an aged woman to try to learn where her tax-owing relatives were hiding. When harvests were bad, on occasion an entire village, hearing that a tax collector was coming, would leave town and start a village somewhere else. People sometimes paid tax collectors bribes to reduce higher fees being extorted.
3:14 *be content with your pay.* Soldiers had sometimes demanded higher wages (or even mutinied); sometimes they also used violence or threats to extort things from local people, or legally requisitioned items for personal use. Most soldiers in Judea were Syrian auxiliary troops working for Rome.
3:16 *sandals ... untie.* Carrying or tying another's sandals was the sort of menial work a slave would do; although the prophets were servants of the Lord (e.g., 2Ki 9:7; 17:13; Jer 7:25), John counts himself unworthy to be the coming one's servant. *baptize you with the Holy Spirit.* Most Jewish baptisms were immersions in water, but Jewish people also expected a future pouring out of the Spirit (Isa 32:15; 44:3; Eze 39:29; Joel 2:28–29). Since in Scripture only God could pour out God's Spirit, John regards the coming one as divine. *fire.* In contrast to the promised Spirit, the "fire" here presumably signals end-time judgment (see notes on Mt 3:10,12). (Some people in antiquity thought of the cosmos as consisting of four elements: earth, water, wind and fire.)
3:17 See note on Mt 3:12.
3:18 Summary statements were common in ancient historiography (see, e.g., Ac 2:40).
3:19 *marriage to Herodias.* Taking a brother's wife violated God's law (Lev 18:16; 20:21), but for Herod Antipas the issue was also politically sensitive. For political reasons, Antipas had married the daughter of the powerful Nabatean king Aretas IV (mentioned in 2Co 11:32). When Antipas wanted to take Herodias, his brother's wife, however, Herodias insisted that she would not marry a polygamist, so Antipas determined to divorce the Nabatean princess. She fled to her father, and the resulting feud stirred political trouble for Antipas; many of his Perean subjects were ethnically Nabatean, with loyalties to their people. Eventually, after the events narrated here, Aretas IV vanquished Herod Antipas in battle, and Antipas's own people attributed his loss to divine judgment for Herod's wicked execution of John the Baptist. See note on Mk 6:17.
3:20 *prison.* Josephus (*Antiquities* 18.119) says that Antipas imprisoned John in his Perean fortress Machaerus, which included a dungeon. (Perea was on the east side of the Jordan.) As messengers of God, prophets were supposed to have immunity to speak freely; the entire Mediterranean world regarded the abuse of messengers or heralds as a terrible offense.
3:21 *heaven was opened.* The heavens could be opened for revelations (Eze 1:1); see notes on Mt 3:16; Mk 1:10.
3:22 *like a dove ... a voice.* See notes on Mt 3:16,17; Mk 1:10,11.
3:23–38 When information was available, ancient biographies often listed ancestors, especially well-known ones. Jewish genealogies started with earlier ancestors and culminated with the descendant in question (as in Mt 1); Greek genealogies were much likelier, as here, to start with the descendant and trace back to earlier ancestors. Scholars explain the differences between the genealogies in Matthew and Luke (or their sources) in various ways, such as levirate-related adoptions (Dt 25:5–10) or Matthew midrashically introducing elements to make spiritual points.
3:23 *thirty.* Generally considered a minimum age for entering public service.

years old when he began his ministry.[t]
He was the son, so it was thought, of Joseph,[u]

the son of Heli, 24the son of Matthat,
the son of Levi, the son of Melki,
the son of Jannai, the son of Joseph,
25the son of Mattathias, the son of Amos,
the son of Nahum, the son of Esli,
the son of Naggai, 26the son of Maath,
the son of Mattathias, the son of Semein,
the son of Josek, the son of Joda,
27the son of Joanan, the son of Rhesa,
the son of Zerubbabel,[v] the son of Shealtiel,
the son of Neri, 28the son of Melki,
the son of Addi, the son of Cosam,
the son of Elmadam, the son of Er,
29the son of Joshua, the son of Eliezer,
the son of Jorim, the son of Matthat,
the son of Levi, 30the son of Simeon,
the son of Judah, the son of Joseph,
the son of Jonam, the son of Eliakim,
31the son of Melea, the son of Menna,
the son of Mattatha, the son of Nathan,[w]
the son of David, 32the son of Jesse,
the son of Obed, the son of Boaz,
the son of Salmon,[a] the son of Nahshon,
33the son of Amminadab, the son of Ram,[b]
the son of Hezron, the son of Perez,[x]
the son of Judah, 34the son of Jacob,
the son of Isaac, the son of Abraham,
the son of Terah, the son of Nahor,[y]
35the son of Serug, the son of Reu,
the son of Peleg, the son of Eber,
the son of Shelah, 36the son of Cainan,
the son of Arphaxad,[z] the son of Shem,
the son of Noah, the son of Lamech,[a]
37the son of Methuselah, the son of Enoch,
the son of Jared, the son of Mahalalel,
the son of Kenan, 38the son of Enosh,
the son of Seth, the son of Adam,
the son of God.[b]

3:23 [t]Mt 4:17; Ac 1:1 [u]Lk 1:27 **3:27** [v]Mt 1:12 **3:31** [w]2Sa 5:14; 1Ch 3:5 **3:33** [x]Ru 4:18-22; 1Ch 2:10-12 **3:34** [y]Ge 11:24, 26 **3:36** [z]Ge 11:12 [a]Ge 5:28-32 **3:38** [b]Ge 5:1, 2,6-9

Jesus Is Tested in the Wilderness

4:1-13pp — Mt 4:1-11; Mk 1:12,13

4 Jesus, full of the Holy Spirit,[c] left the
Jordan[d] and was led by the Spirit[e] into
the wilderness, 2where for forty days[f] he
was tempted[c] by the devil. He ate nothing
during those days, and at the end of them
he was hungry.

3The devil said to him, "If you are the Son
of God, tell this stone to become bread."

4Jesus answered, "It is written: 'Man
shall not live on bread alone.'[d]"[g]

5The devil led him up to a high place
and showed him in an instant all the kingdoms of the world.[h] 6And he said to him,
"I will give you all their authority and
splendor; it has been given to me,[i] and I
can give it to anyone I want to. 7If you
worship me, it will all be yours."

8Jesus answered, "It is written: 'Worship
the Lord your God and serve him only.'[e]"[j]

9The devil led him to Jerusalem and had
him stand on the highest point of the temple. "If you are the Son of God," he said,
"throw yourself down from here. 10For it
is written:

"'He will command his angels
concerning you
to guard you carefully;
11they will lift you up in their hands,
so that you will not strike your foot
against a stone.'[f]"[k]

12Jesus answered, "It is said: 'Do not
put the Lord your God to the test.'[g]"[l]
13When the devil had finished all this
tempting,[m] he left him[n] until an opportune
time.

Jesus Rejected at Nazareth

14Jesus returned to Galilee[o] in the power
of the Spirit, and news about him spread
through the whole countryside.[p] 15He was
teaching in their synagogues,[q] and everyone praised him.

16He went to Nazareth,[r] where he had

4:1 [c]ver 14, 18 [d]Lk 3:3, 21 [e]Lk 2:27 **4:2** [f]Ex 34:28; 1Ki 19:8 **4:4** [g]Dt 8:3 **4:5** [h]Mt 24:14 **4:6** [i]Jn 12:31; 14:30; 1Jn 5:19 **4:8** [j]Dt 6:13 **4:11** [k]Ps 91:11, 12 **4:12** [l]Dt 6:16 **4:13** [m]Heb 4:15 [n]Jn 14:30 **4:14** [o]Mt 4:12 [p]Mt 9:26 **4:15** [q]Mt 4:23 **4:16** [r]Mt 2:23

[a] *32* Some early manuscripts *Sala* [b] *33* Some manuscripts *Amminadab, the son of Admin, the son of Arni*; other manuscripts vary widely. [c] *2* The Greek for *tempted* can also mean *tested.* [d] *4* Deut. 8:3 [e] *8* Deut. 6:13 [f] *11* Psalm 91:11,12 [g] *12* Deut. 6:16

4:1–2 *led … into the wilderness … for forty days he was tempted.* Forty periods of time probably evokes Israel's experience, summarized in Dt 8:2; Jesus quotes from the next verse (Dt 8:3) in v. 4. See notes on Mt 4:1,2.

4:3 *stone to become bread.* Magicians sometimes claimed the power to change one substance into another (see note on Mt 4:3).

4:4 The context of Dt 8:3 addressed Israel as God's "son" (Dt 8:5); see notes on vv. 1–2; Mt 4:4. All of Jesus' quotations in this narrative come from this section of Deuteronomy.

4:6 *authority … given to me.* The devil's claim to possess delegated authority over the world fits Jewish ideas prevalent in Jesus' day about the devil's rule over the wicked nations (cf. also Jn 14:30; Eph 2:2; 1Jn 5:19; cf. the spirit of falsehood noted in the Dead Sea Scrolls). Nevertheless, the devil's authority was limited; authority to delegate ultimately belongs to God (Da 4:32).

4:8 The context of Dt 6:13 prohibits idolatry (Dt 6:14), recognizing the one true God (Dt 6:4–5,12).

4:9 See note on Mt 4:5.

4:10–11 See note on Mt 4:6.

4:12 See note on Mt 4:7.

4:16 *synagogue.* Many scholars believe that Nazareth proper had only a few hundred residents. Its synagogue

been brought up, and on the Sabbath day
he went into the synagogue,[s] as was his
custom. He stood up to read, 17and the
scroll of the prophet Isaiah was handed
to him. Unrolling it, he found the place
where it is written:

18 "The Spirit of the Lord is on me,[t]
because he has anointed me
to proclaim good news to the poor.
He has sent me to proclaim freedom
for the prisoners
and recovery of sight for the blind,
to set the oppressed free,
19 to proclaim the year of the Lord's
favor."[a][u]

20Then he rolled up the scroll, gave it
back to the attendant and sat down.[v] The
eyes of everyone in the synagogue were
fastened on him. 21He began by saying to
them, "Today this scripture is fulfilled in
your hearing."

22All spoke well of him and were
amazed at the gracious words that came
from his lips. "Isn't this Joseph's son?"
they asked.[w]

23Jesus said to them, "Surely you will
quote this proverb to me: 'Physician, heal
yourself!' And you will tell me, 'Do here in
your hometown[x] what we have heard that
you did in Capernaum.' "[y]

24"Truly I tell you," he continued, "no
prophet is accepted in his hometown.[z]
25I assure you that there were many widows in Israel in Elijah's time, when the sky
was shut for three and a half years and
there was a severe famine throughout the
land.[a] 26Yet Elijah was not sent to any of
them, but to a widow in Zarephath in the
region of Sidon.[b] 27And there were many
in Israel with leprosy[b] in the time of Elisha the prophet, yet not one of them was
cleansed — only Naaman the Syrian."[c]

28All the people in the synagogue were
furious when they heard this. 29They got
up, drove him out of the town,[d] and took
him to the brow of the hill on which the
town was built, in order to throw him off
the cliff. 30But he walked right through the
crowd and went on his way.[e]

Jesus Drives Out an Impure Spirit

4:31-37pp — Mk 1:21-28

31Then he went down to Capernaum,[f]
a town in Galilee, and on the Sabbath he
taught the people. 32They were amazed at
his teaching,[g] because his words had authority.[h]

33In the synagogue there was a man
possessed by a demon, an impure spirit.
He cried out at the top of his voice, 34"Go
away! What do you want with us,[i] Jesus
of Nazareth?[j] Have you come to destroy

4:16 [s] Mt 13:54 **4:18** [t] Jn 3:34 **4:19** [u] Lev 25:10; Isa 61:1,2 **4:20** [v] ver 17; Mt 26:55 **4:22** [w] Mt 13:54,55; Jn 6:42; 7:15 **4:23** [x] ver 16 [y] Mk 1:21-28; 2:1-12 **4:24** [z] Mt 13:57; Jn 4:44 **4:25** [a] 1Ki 17:1; 18:1; Jas 5:17,18 **4:26** [b] 1Ki 17:8-16; Mt 11:21 **4:27** [c] 2Ki 5:1-14 **4:29** [d] Nu 15:35; Ac 7:58; Heb 13:12 **4:30** [e] Jn 8:59; 10:39 **4:31** [f] ver 23; Mt 4:13 **4:32** [g] Mt 7:28 [h] ver 36; Mt 7:29 **4:34** [i] Mt 8:29 [j] Mk 1:24

a *19* Isaiah 61:1,2 (see Septuagint); Isaiah 58:6
b *27* The Greek word traditionally translated *leprosy* was used for various diseases affecting the skin.

thus may have been small, though probably nearly all residents attended, including those from the surrounding countryside. *stood up to read.* It was customary to stand to read the Scriptures.

4:17 *Isaiah was handed to him.* In this period, there were probably no assigned readings in the Prophets; readers or local leaders would choose their own. The community leader who handed Jesus the scroll (cf. also v. 20) filled the role of what probably came to be known as the *chazan. Unrolling it.* One would unroll (and read) a Hebrew scroll from right to left.

4:18 – 19 Jesus reads Isa 61:1 – 2, with an added line from Isa 58:6 (tradition suggests that synagogue readers were allowed to "skip" material when reading the Prophets). Isa 61:1 – 2 probably evokes the Year of Jubilee (Lev 25), in which all slaves were to be released. Although Jesus' reading ends with salvation, his audience would know that the passage goes on to announce also judgment.

4:20 *sat down.* After standing to read Scripture, the most advanced teachers would sit to explain it.

4:21 *fulfilled in your hearing.* People rightly expected this text to be fulfilled only in the Messianic era, the time of God's coming kingdom. This geographic area may have been sensitive about premature kingdom claims; Nazareth was just four miles (six kilometers) from the major Galilean city of Sepphoris, which had been destroyed after a revolt against Rome about two decades earlier (AD 6). Sepphoris later refused to participate in the revolt of AD 66 – 73, but it maintained some Jewish traditions. Excavations show that the first-century city maintained Jewish law: they did not eat pork, they used ritual pools for purification, and they used stone pottery that did not contract impurity.

4:23 *Physician, heal yourself!* This proverb is attested both in Greek and Jewish circles.

4:24 *no prophet ... hometown.* Scripture noted prophets being rejected, even in their hometowns (Jer 1:1; 11:21); Jewish traditions about the prophets amplified this pattern even further.

4:25 – 27 *Elijah ... Elisha.* Jesus' ministry, like that of Elijah and Elisha, will include raising the dead and curing leprosy. Jesus here highlights their ministry to foreigners (and by implication the resistance of their own people as in v. 24).

4:29 *throw him off the cliff.* Nazareth is on a hill. Jewish custom suggested hurling a person from a cliff before stoning him, but it forbade execution without trial and would also forbid it on the Sabbath. Roman law forbade executions without the governor's permission; this group functions like a lynch mob.

4:31 *Capernaum.* Situated on the Sea of Galilee, Capernaum was larger than Nazareth; some estimate 1000 – 2000 residents in the city proper. By Greco-Roman standards it was a small and obscure town and, like Nazareth, not a location for Jesus that anyone would conceivably have fabricated. Archaeologists have found the site of Capernaum's synagogue, and later rabbis attest that by the second century, Capernaum was a known center for Jewish Christianity.

4:32 *words had authority.* Most teachers did not want to speak on their own authority; when possible, they cited earlier authorities that supported their teaching.

4:33 *possessed by a demon.* See note on Mk 1:23.

4:34 *Have you come to destroy us? I know who you are.* See note on Mk 1:24.

THE CAPERNAUM SYNAGOGUE

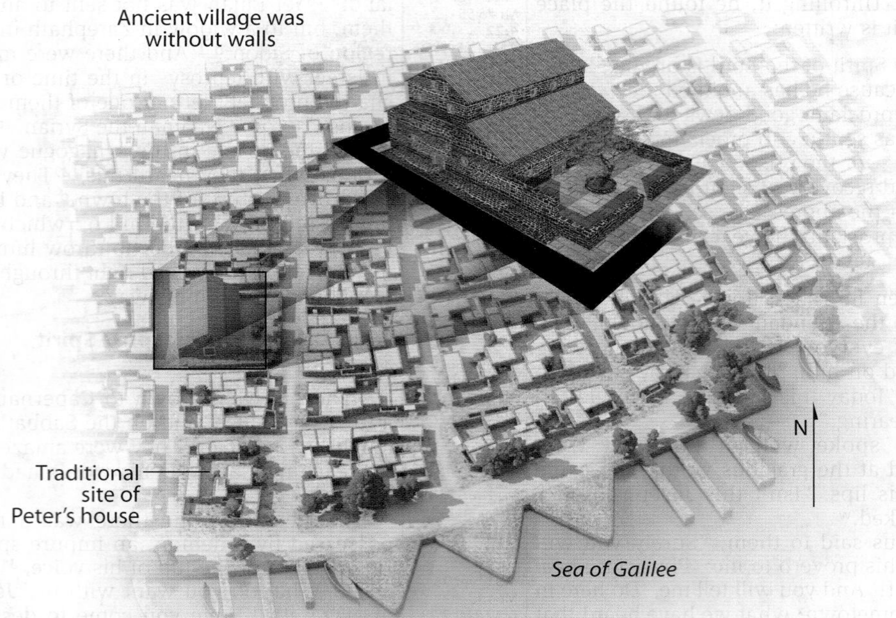

Capernaum was more than a seaside fishing village in the days of Jesus. It was the place that Jesus chose to be the center of his ministry to the entire region of Galilee, and it possessed ideal characteristics as a point of dissemination for the gospel.

There were good reasons for this. The town itself was named Kephar Nahum, "village of [perhaps the prophet] Nahum," and was the centerpiece of a densely populated region having a bicultural flavor. On the one hand, there were numerous synagogues in Galilee (in addition to the one in Capernaum), where the ferment of Jewish religious life was profound. On the other hand, there was Hellenism, a pervasive culture already centuries old and potent in its paganism—a lifestyle that influenced manners, dress, architecture and political institutions as well.

Archaeological work at Capernaum has revealed a section of the pavement of a first-century synagogue below the still-existing ruins of the fourth-century one on the site. A private house later made into a church and a place of pilgrimage has yielded some evidence that may link it to the site of Simon Peter's house (Lk 4:38).

us? I know who you are[k]—the Holy One
of God!"
35"Be quiet!" Jesus said sternly.[m] "Come
out of him!" Then the demon threw the
man down before them all and came out
without injuring him.
36All the people were amazed[n] and said
to each other, "What words these are!
With authority[o] and power he gives orders to impure spirits and they come out!"
37And the news about him spread throughout the surrounding area.[p]

4:34 [k] Jas 2:19 ver 41; Mk 1:24 **4:35** [m] ver 39, 41; Mt 8:26; Lk 8:24 **4:36** [n] Mt 7:28 [o] ver 32; Mt 7:29; Mt 10:1 **4:37** [p] ver 14; Mt 9:26 **4:39** [q] ver 35, 41

Jesus Heals Many

4:38-41pp — Mt 8:14-17
4:38-43pp — Mk 1:29-38

38Jesus left the synagogue and went to
the home of Simon. Now Simon's mother-in-law was suffering from a high fever,
and they asked Jesus to help her. 39So he
bent over her and rebuked[q] the fever, and
it left her. She got up at once and began to
wait on them.
40At sunset, the people brought to Jesus
all who had various kinds of sickness,

4:35 *Come out of him!* See note on Mk 1:26.
4:37 *news ... spread.* Villages were often close together and rumors spread rapidly.
4:38 *home of Simon.* See note on Mk 1:29. *fever.* See note on Mk 1:30.
4:40 *At sunset.* Assuming that Jesus' synagogue visit (v. 38) was on the Sabbath, when people most often gathered there (cf. Mk 1:21), people waiting to bring others to Jesus fits Jewish practice (see note on Mk 1:32).

and laying his hands on each one,[r] he
healed them.[s] [41]Moreover, demons came
out of many people, shouting, "You are the
Son of God!"[t] But he rebuked[u] them and
would not allow them to speak,[v] because
they knew he was the Messiah.
[42]At daybreak, Jesus went out to a solitary place. The people were looking for
him and when they came to where he
was, they tried to keep him from leaving
them. [43]But he said, "I must proclaim the
good news of the kingdom of God[w] to the
other towns also, because that is why I
was sent." [44]And he kept on preaching in
the synagogues of Judea.[x]

Jesus Calls His First Disciples

5:1-11pp — Mt 4:18-22; Mk 1:16-20; Jn 1:40-42

5 One day as Jesus was standing by the
Lake of Gennesaret,[a] the people were
crowding around him and listening to the
word of God.[y] [2]He saw at the water's edge
two boats, left there by the fishermen,
who were washing their nets. [3]He got into
one of the boats, the one belonging to
Simon, and asked him to put out a little
from shore. Then he sat down and taught
the people from the boat.[z]
[4]When he had finished speaking, he
said to Simon, "Put out into deep water,
and let down the nets for a catch."[a]
[5]Simon answered, "Master,[b] we've
worked hard all night and haven't caught
anything.[c] But because you say so, I will
let down the nets."
[6]When they had done so, they caught
such a large number of fish that their nets
began to break.[d] [7]So they signaled their
partners in the other boat to come and
help them, and they came and filled both
boats so full that they began to sink.
[8]When Simon Peter saw this, he fell at
Jesus' knees and said, "Go away from me,
Lord; I am a sinful man!"[e] [9]For he and
all his companions were astonished at the
catch of fish they had taken, [10]and so were
James and John, the sons of Zebedee, Simon's partners.
Then Jesus said to Simon, "Don't be
afraid;[f] from now on you will fish for people." [11]So they pulled their boats up on
shore, left everything and followed him.[g]

Jesus Heals a Man With Leprosy

5:12-14pp — Mt 8:2-4; Mk 1:40-44

[12]While Jesus was in one of the towns,
a man came along who was covered with
leprosy.[b][h] When he saw Jesus, he fell with
his face to the ground and begged him,
"Lord, if you are willing, you can make
me clean."
[13]Jesus reached out his hand and
touched the man. "I am willing," he said.
"Be clean!" And immediately the leprosy
left him.
[14]Then Jesus ordered him, "Don't tell
anyone,[i] but go, show yourself to the
priest and offer the sacrifices that Moses
commanded[j] for your cleansing, as a testimony to them."
[15]Yet the news about him spread all
the more,[k] so that crowds of people came
to hear him and to be healed of their

4:40 [r] Mk 5:23 [s] Mt 4:23 **4:41** [t] Mt 4:3 [u] ver 35 [v] Mt 8:4 **4:43** [w] Mt 3:2 **4:44** [x] Mt 4:23 **5:1** [y] Mk 4:14; Heb 4:12 **5:3** [z] Mt 13:2 **5:4** [a] Jn 21:6 **5:5** [b] Lk 8:24, 45; 9:33, 49; 17:13 [c] Jn 21:3 **5:6** [d] Jn 21:11

5:8 [e] Ge 18:27; Job 42:6; Isa 6:5 **5:10** [f] Mt 14:27 **5:11** [g] ver 28; Mt 4:19 **5:12** [h] Mt 8:2 **5:14** [i] Mt 8:4 [j] Lev 14:2-32 **5:15** [k] Mt 9:26

[a] *1* That is, the Sea of Galilee [b] *12* The Greek word traditionally translated *leprosy* was used for various diseases affecting the skin.

4:42 *solitary place.* See note on Mk 1:35.
5:1 *Lake of Gennesaret.* The name used for the Sea of Galilee especially in this region.
5:2 *washing their nets.* This task would include removing things gathered in the nets other than edible fish.
5:3 *put out a little from shore.* Pushing out from shore provided sufficient distance for Jesus' voice to carry. Galilee had many helpful acoustic settings, including a cove near Capernaum that could allow one's voice to carry to vast numbers of hearers.
5:5 *all night.* Although fishermen also worked during the day and were believed able to endure the hot sun, many felt it was easier to catch fish before sunrise. (During the day many fish stayed in the depths to avoid the hot sun.) *nets.* Fishermen often cast a circular net of mesh, about 15 feet (4.5 meters) wide, into the water to catch fish; lead sinkers pulled most of the net down so it did not all float, and once it had trapped fish it could be hauled in. This method worked in shallow water, but for deeper water fishermen used a dragnet (see note on Mt 13:47).
5:6 *large number of fish.* The lake had several kinds of fish; today these include carp. The OT provided precedent for multiplying food (2Ki 4:1–7,42–44) and animals (Ex 8:6,17,24; 10:13), including to eat (Nu 11:31–32). *nets began to break.* Fishermen would have to repair ruptured nets before they could fish again; for those with less means, sometimes this even required a loan.
5:7 *partners.* Sometimes commercial fishermen partnered together in profitable fishing cooperatives (see also v. 10).
5:8 *I am a sinful man!* In a similar way, God's holiness also made Isaiah aware of his own sinfulness at his calling (Isa 6:5; cf. Job 42:6; cf. also Ex 4:10; Jdg 6:15; Jer 1:6).
5:11 *left everything.* Many believe that commercial fishermen, although not elite, were usually better off economically than the peasants who comprised the majority of Galileans. Peasants' work was also more seasonal than that of fishermen. Leaving behind the fishing business was an economic sacrifice.
5:12 *leprosy.* See note on Mk 1:40.
5:13 *touched the man.* Because lepers were unclean (Lev 13:45–46), anyone who touched them contracted temporary ritual impurity. For one Biblical precedent for healing a leper, see 2Ki 5:10–14; Jesus himself had recently highlighted this precedent during his Nazareth speech (Lk 4:27).
5:14 *Don't tell anyone.* Ancients respected people who did not seek their own honor. *show … the priest.* A priest was required to inspect a leper who believed that he or she was cleansed, and an offering in the temple should follow (Lev 14:1–9).

LUKE 4

DISEASE AND MEDICINE IN THE ANCIENT WORLD

Ancient medical tradition included a mixture of genuinely observed cures and superstitious folk medicine. Various schools of medicine existed, and because there was no standard for certification, not all doctors were competent even by ancient standards. In the first century, Greeks comprised a disproportionate share of doctors in the Roman Empire; many were also well-educated slaves in the service of wealthy estates. Many physicians were women, although the majority of these worked as midwives.

Temples to Asclepius, the Greco-Roman god of healing, were found all over the Mediterranean world. These temples were somewhat like the spas of today; therapy consisted more of rest, massage and a modified diet than of what we would call medicine. Religion also played a major role. A common healing method was "incubation," whereby the sick person would sleep in the confines of the temple of Asclepius in the hope of receiving a dream-revelation from the god. Those who had been healed made special contributions to the temples, which often included plaster reproductions of whatever parts of their bodies had been healed. These were set on display as testimonies to the healing power of the god.

The second-century orator and chronic invalid Aelius Aristides, in his *Sacred Tales*, gives us an insight into the need people had for healing and the methods employed to that end. After falling ill on a journey to Rome and enduring brutal surgery at the hands of Roman doctors, Aristides became a devotee of Asclepius. The cures prescribed for him in the dreams included bathing in a churning river during winter, pouring mud on himself before sitting in the courtyard of the temple, walking about without shoes all winter and blood-letting from various parts of his body.

It was in such a world that Jesus performed his ministry of healing. Unlike many doctors connected to temples, Jesus healed without charge or fanfare. Also, he did not follow any specific ritual that might have been regarded as the key to tapping into

continued on next page

sicknesses. 16But Jesus often withdrew to
lonely places and prayed.[l]

Jesus Forgives and Heals a Paralyzed Man

5:18-26pp — Mt 9:2-8; Mk 2:3-12

17One day Jesus was teaching, and
Pharisees and teachers of the law[m] were sitting there. They had come from every village of Galilee and from Judea and Jerusalem. And the power of the Lord was with Jesus to heal the sick.[n] 18Some men
came carrying a paralyzed man on a mat and tried to take him into the house to lay him before Jesus. 19When they could not
find a way to do this because of the crowd, they went up on the roof and lowered him on his mat through the tiles into the middle of the crowd, right in front of Jesus.
20When Jesus saw their faith, he said, "Friend, your sins are forgiven."[o]
21The Pharisees and the teachers of the

5:16 [l] Mt 14:23; Lk 3:21 **5:17** [m] Mt 15:1; Lk 2:46 [n] Mk 5:30; Lk 6:19 **5:20** [o] Lk 7:48, 49

5:17 *Pharisees and teachers of the law.* In Galilee, teachers of the law may have been more common than Pharisees; cf. Mk 2:6. *teachers of the law.* Can refer even to executors of legal documents in villages, but in the Gospels usually refers to those who were literate and formally trained in the Law of Moses. (In the villages, some may have done both.)

5:19 *roof.* Logs used as roof beams supported most Galilean roofs; reeds or branches were laid across these logs, then the whole was overlaid with packed mud or clay. Luke, however, depicts instead the sort of tile roof familiar to his northern Mediterranean, probably Aegean, audience.

5:21 *blasphemy.* See note on Mk 2:7.

magical, healing power. Sometimes he would touch a person; other times he might place a daub of mud on a blind man's eyes (Jn 9:6) or simply speak a word (Mt 8:13). In short, Jesus' healings pointed to the power of God that dwelled within him; they did not encourage people to seek out rituals for magical healing but were part of his proclamation of the kingdom. Physical healing pointed always to the restoration of creation. ◆

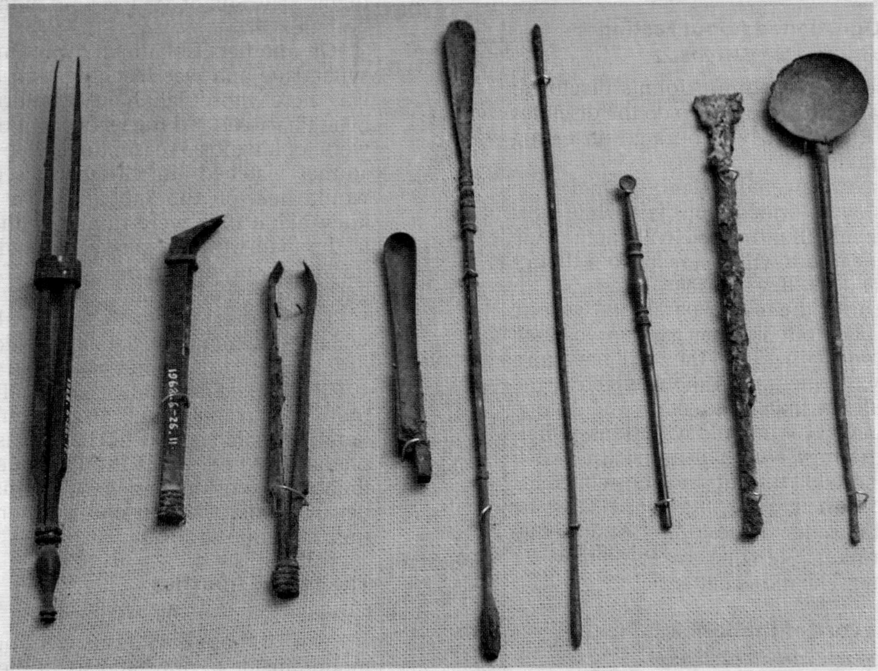

Ancient surgical instruments, Roman, first century AD, Italy.

law began thinking to themselves, "Who
is this fellow who speaks blasphemy?
Who can forgive sins but God alone?"[p]
22 Jesus knew what they were thinking
and asked, "Why are you thinking these
things in your hearts? 23 Which is easier: to
say, 'Your sins are forgiven,' or to say, 'Get
up and walk'? 24 But I want you to know
that the Son of Man[q] has authority on earth
to forgive sins." So he said to the paralyzed
man, "I tell you, get up, take your mat and
go home." 25 Immediately he stood up in
front of them, took what he had been lying
on and went home praising God. 26 Everyone was amazed and gave praise to God.[r]
They were filled with awe and said, "We
have seen remarkable things today."

5:21 [p] Isa 43:25
5:24 [q] Mt 8:20
5:26 [r] Mt 9:8
5:27 [s] Mt 4:19
5:28 [t] ver 11; Mt 4:19

Jesus Calls Levi and Eats With Sinners

5:27-32pp — Mt 9:9-13; Mk 2:14-17

27 After this, Jesus went out and saw a
tax collector by the name of Levi sitting at
his tax booth. "Follow me,"[s] Jesus said to
him, 28 and Levi got up, left everything and
followed him.[t]
29 Then Levi held a great banquet for

5:22 *Jesus knew what they were thinking.* See note on Mk 2:8.
5:24 *Son of Man has authority.* See note on Mk 2:10.
5:27 *tax collector.* Most people disliked tax collectors; see note on Mk 2:14.
5:29 – 30 One might throw a banquet in another's honor; table fellowship established a covenant relationship, hence it could be perceived as connoting acceptance. See note on Mk 2:16.

Jesus at his house, and a large crowd of
tax collectors[u] and others were eating with
them. 30But the Pharisees and the teachers
of the law who belonged to their sect[v] complained to his disciples, "Why do you eat
and drink with tax collectors and sinners?"[w]
31Jesus answered them, "It is not the
healthy who need a doctor, but the sick.
32I have not come to call the righteous, but
sinners to repentance."[x]

Jesus Questioned About Fasting

5:33-39pp — Mt 9:14-17; Mk 2:18-22

33They said to him, "John's disciples[y]
often fast and pray, and so do the disciples
of the Pharisees, but yours go on eating
and drinking."
34Jesus answered, "Can you make the
friends of the bridegroom[z] fast while he is
with them? 35But the time will come when
the bridegroom will be taken from them;[a]
in those days they will fast."
36He told them this parable: "No one
tears a piece out of a new garment to patch
an old one. Otherwise, they will have torn
the new garment, and the patch from the
new will not match the old. 37And no one
pours new wine into old wineskins. Otherwise, the new wine will burst the skins;
the wine will run out and the wineskins
will be ruined. 38No, new wine must be
poured into new wineskins. 39And no one
after drinking old wine wants the new, for
they say, 'The old is better.' "

Jesus Is Lord of the Sabbath

6:1-11pp — Mt 12:1-14; Mk 2:23 – 3:6

6 One Sabbath Jesus was going through
the grainfields, and his disciples began
to pick some heads of grain, rub them in
their hands and eat the kernels.[b] 2Some of
the Pharisees asked, "Why are you doing
what is unlawful on the Sabbath?"[c]
3Jesus answered them, "Have you never read what David did when he and his
companions were hungry?[d] 4He entered
the house of God, and taking the consecrated bread, he ate what is lawful only
for priests to eat.[e] And he also gave some
to his companions." 5Then Jesus said to
them, "The Son of Man[f] is Lord of the Sabbath."
6On another Sabbath[g] he went into the
synagogue and was teaching, and a man
was there whose right hand was shriveled.
7The Pharisees and the teachers of the law
were looking for a reason to accuse Jesus,
so they watched him closely[h] to see if he
would heal on the Sabbath.[i] 8But Jesus
knew what they were thinking[j] and said
to the man with the shriveled hand, "Get
up and stand in front of everyone." So he
got up and stood there.
9Then Jesus said to them, "I ask you,
which is lawful on the Sabbath: to do good
or to do evil, to save life or to destroy it?"
10He looked around at them all, and
then said to the man, "Stretch out your
hand." He did so, and his hand was completely restored. 11But the Pharisees and
the teachers of the law were furious[k] and
began to discuss with one another what
they might do to Jesus.

The Twelve Apostles

6:13-16pp — Mt 10:2-4; Mk 3:16-19; Ac 1:13

12One of those days Jesus went out to a
mountainside to pray, and spent the night
praying to God.[l] 13When morning came,
he called his disciples to him and chose
twelve of them, whom he also designat-

5:29 [u] Lk 15:1
5:30 [v] Ac 23:9 [w] Mt 9:11
5:32 [x] Jn 3:17
5:33 [y] Lk 7:18; Jn 1:35; 3:25,26
5:34 [z] Jn 3:29
5:35 [a] Lk 9:22; 17:22; Jn 16:5-7

6:1 [b] Dt 23:25
6:2 [c] Mt 12:2
6:3 [d] 1Sa 21:6
6:4 [e] Lev 24:5,9
6:5 [f] Mt 8:20
6:6 [g] ver 1
6:7 [h] Mt 12:10 [i] Mt 12:2
6:8 [j] Mt 9:4
6:11 [k] Jn 5:18
6:12 [l] Lk 3:21

5:31 *healthy . . . sick.* Ancient speakers and writers often used sickness and physicians in moral or intellectual analogies.
5:33 *but yours go on eating and drinking.* See note on Mk 2:18.
5:34,35 *fast.* Fasting was often linked with mourning, whereas weddings were the supreme time for rejoicing. In fact, rabbis taught that weddings even took priority over many religious obligations. To fast during a wedding would reject hospitality, fail to participate in festivities, and so prove offensive to the host.
5:37 *new wine into old wineskins.* People employed animal skins, most often goatskins, as containers for fluids. Wine expands as it ferments; fermenting wine had already expanded old wineskins to their limit, so still-expanding new wine would rupture them. Jesus' new order demanded a new approach.
5:39 *The old is better.* This saying evokes a similar Jewish proverb (cf. Sirach 9:10).
6:1 *pick some heads of grain.* Israelite law permitted those who were hungry to pick heads of grain when passing through a field (Dt 23:25; Ru 2:2). The complication here, in the eyes of their detractors, is doing so on the Sabbath (Ex 34:21; cf. reaping in the Mishnah, in *Shabbat* 7:2).
6:2 *Pharisees.* See note on Mk 2:24.
6:3 *Have you never read . . . ?* See note on Mk 2:25.
6:4 *for priests.* Like Matthew (Mt 12:4), Luke omits Mark's more confusing reference to Abiathar (Mk 2:26).
6:5 *Son of Man.* See note on Mk 2:28.
6:7 *heal on the Sabbath.* In general, Jewish teachers felt that whatever one could do before the Sabbath should not be done on the Sabbath. Life-saving procedures were acceptable; other medical treatments on the Sabbath were debated.
6:8 For healing a withered hand, cf. 1Ki 13:6. Technically Jesus does not apply medical treatment or even lay hands on the man; no one considered a command to stretch out one's hand as work!
6:11 These Pharisees are inconsistent with usual Pharisaic traditions. The Pharisaic school of Hillel permitted prayer for the sick on the Sabbath; the dominant Pharisaic school, the Shammaites, rejected this without persecuting Hillelites for it. Jesus, however, may have appeared a more direct threat to their beliefs. See note on Mk 3:6.
6:12 *mountainside to pray.* Praying on a mountainside may follow some OT examples (e.g., Ex 19:20; 24:13,18; Dt 9:9; 1Ki 19:8,11).
6:13 *twelve.* See note on Mk 3:14.

ed apostles:[m] 14 Simon (whom he named
Peter), his brother Andrew, James, John,
Philip, Bartholomew, 15 Matthew,[n] Thomas, James son of Alphaeus, Simon who
was called the Zealot, 16 Judas son of
James, and Judas Iscariot, who became a
traitor.

Blessings and Woes

6:20-23pp — Mt 5:3-12

17 He went down with them and stood
on a level place. A large crowd of his disciples was there and a great number of people from all over Judea, from Jerusalem,
and from the coastal region around Tyre
and Sidon,[o] 18 who had come to hear him
and to be healed of their diseases. Those
troubled by impure spirits were cured,
19 and the people all tried to touch him,[p]
because power was coming from him and
healing them all.[q]
20 Looking at his disciples, he said:

"Blessed are you who are poor,
for yours is the kingdom of God.[r]
21 Blessed are you who hunger now,
for you will be satisfied.[s]
Blessed are you who weep now,
for you will laugh.[t]
22 Blessed are you when people hate you,
when they exclude you[u] and insult
you[v]
and reject your name as evil,
because of the Son of Man.[w]

23 "Rejoice in that day and leap for joy,[x]
because great is your reward in heaven.
For that is how their ancestors treated the
prophets.[y]

24 "But woe to you who are rich,[z]
for you have already received your
comfort.[a]
25 Woe to you who are well fed now,
for you will go hungry.[b]
Woe to you who laugh now,
for you will mourn and weep.[c]
26 Woe to you when everyone speaks well
of you,
for that is how their ancestors
treated the false prophets.[d]

Love for Enemies

6:29,30pp — Mt 5:39-42

27 "But to you who are listening I say:
Love your enemies, do good to those who
hate you,[e] 28 bless those who curse you,
pray for those who mistreat you.[f] 29 If
someone slaps you on one cheek, turn
to them the other also. If someone takes
your coat, do not withhold your shirt from
them. 30 Give to everyone who asks you,
and if anyone takes what belongs to you,
do not demand it back.[g] 31 Do to others as
you would have them do to you.[h]
32 "If you love those who love you, what
credit is that to you?[i] Even sinners love
those who love them. 33 And if you do
good to those who are good to you, what

6:13 [m] Mk 6:30 **6:15** [n] Mt 9:9 **6:17** [o] Mt 4:25; 11:21; Mk 3:7,8 **6:19** [p] Mt 9:20 [q] Mt 14:36; Mk 5:30; Lk 5:17 **6:20** [r] Mt 25:34 **6:21** [s] Isa 55:1, 2; Mt 5:6 [t] Isa 61:2, 3; Mt 5:4; Rev 7:17 **6:22** [u] Jn 9:22; 16:2 [v] Isa 51:7 [w] Jn 15:21

6:23 [x] Mt 5:12 [y] Mt 5:12 **6:24** [z] Jas 5:1 [a] Lk 16:25 **6:25** [b] Isa 65:13 [c] Pr 14:13 **6:26** [d] Mt 7:15 **6:27** [e] ver 35; Mt 5:44; Ro 12:20 **6:28** [f] Mt 5:44 **6:30** [g] Dt 15:7, 8, 10; Pr 21:26 **6:31** [h] Mt 7:12 **6:32** [i] Mt 5:46

6:14 – 16 Second names were common, thus there are some differences in the apostolic lists. Nicknames and being identified by one's father or place of origin was also common, so the apostles who bear the same names (such as Simon and Judas) receive a second identifier. The names Simon, Judas, James and John were very common in this period. See notes on Mk 3:16 – 19.
6:17 *level place.* Can mean either a low area or a flat one; in the hill country (cf. v. 12) it could be a plateau. *Tyre and Sidon.* Phoenician cities to the north, although some Jews lived there.
6:20 *Blessed.* Biblical and ancient Jewish beatitudes, or blessings, declared that it was well with a person who behaved in a particular way (e.g., Ps 1:1; 32:1 – 2; 119:1). *poor.* Many Jewish traditions associated piety with the "poor," which was also often associated with being poor in spirit (Mt 5:3; some scholars suggest that the same Aramaic word stands behind both of these expressions). *kingdom of God.* See the article "Kingdom," p. 1616.
6:21 Many Jewish people expected a reversal of current status in the time of the end, when the lowly would be exalted and the exalted brought low (already in the OT, e.g., Isa 2:11 – 12).
6:22 *because of the Son of Man.* Jewish people spoke of suffering for God's name; here it is because of Jesus.
6:23 Jewish tradition emphasized the persecution faced by the Biblical prophets (e.g., Jer 26:20 – 23).
6:24 – 25 Some have compared the pairing of blessings (vv. 20 – 23) and woes (vv. 24 – 26) with the contrasted pairing of blessings and curses in the OT (e.g., Dt 27:15 — 28:19). "Woes" were laments; prophets often pronounced them as a way of announcing judgments (sometimes sincerely mourning, at other times more mockingly).
6:24 *comfort.* See note on 2:25.
6:26 *false prophets.* Those who promised blessing even when a nation merited judgment were often more popular than true prophets (e.g., 1Ki 22:11 – 28).
6:27 *Love your enemies.* Some ancient thinkers advocated nonresistance, often on the grounds that anything that could be taken away did not really matter; some Jewish sages advocated it because of confidence in God's ultimate vindication. Jesus agrees with God's ultimate vindication, but his words go even deeper than nonretaliation: to love one's enemies.
6:29 *slaps you on one cheek.* The backhanded blow on the right cheek was meant primarily as an insult, a challenge to one's honor. The striker could be taken to court and fined for this offense. *coat.* The one possession that a creditor could not legally seize from a debtor (Ex 22:26 – 27; Dt 24:12 – 13). The very poor might have only a single coat; in such cases, surrendering both the inner and outer garments might leave one naked. In this case, an element of hyperbole might be involved. Some also suggest that such extensive cooperation might shame one's aggressor.
6:30 Antiquity hosted many beggars and also robbers and exploiters ready to take the possessions of those who would not fight back. Although Jesus may use hyperbole, he emphasizes trust in God's provision and devalues desire for possessions.
6:31 Some earlier Jewish teachers offered this principle of wisdom, recognized in many cultures, though often in the negative form (see note on Mt 7:12).

LUKE 6

Qumran and the New Testament

The Dead Sea Scrolls (found at Qumran) are the texts of a Jewish religious community now called the Qumran community. Numerous scholars have pointed out that there are similarities between the beliefs and practices of the Qumran community and those of New Testament Christians. Some have gone so far as to view Christianity as an offshoot of the Qumran community. There is no doubt that the Dead Sea Scrolls provide a unique window into the world of early Judaism and that their value for understanding the New Testament is great, but it is possible to exaggerate the similarities and overlook the differences between the Qumran community and the early Christians.

To be sure, we can find significant examples of how the Qumran community parallels the New Testament church:

- The Qumran community saw itself as the remnant of Israel that had entered into a new covenant with God in the end times.
- The community relied on revelations given to the "Teacher of Righteousness," who had been persecuted by the Jerusalem authorities for his unorthodox beliefs.
- Community members made a sustained effort to read the Old Testament Scriptures in light of the realities of the "last days" that had now come upon Israel.

But these similarities should not be allowed to mask some crucial differences:

- Unlike the Qumran community, the early Christians did not withdraw into the desert. Instead, they remained within the Jewish communities in the Holy Land and in the Diaspora.

The Great Isaiah Scroll.
Wikimedia Commons

continued on next page

View of some of the caves at Qumran, where the Dead Sea Scrolls were found.
© SeanPavonePhoto/Shutterstock

- Even more radical was the willingness of the early Christians to bring the Good News to the Gentiles, an idea completely absent from Qumran.
- The Qumran community abandoned the Jewish mainstream largely because of perceived defects in their calendar and in their interpretation of purity laws. The early Christians, meanwhile, made it clear that such matters should not be allowed to become sources of division (cf. Mk 7:18 – 19; Col 2:20 – 23).
- Finally, while the instruction of the Teacher of Righteousness remained foundational for the Qumran community, this concept pales beside the Christian belief that Jesus has risen from the dead and sits exalted to reign at the right hand of God.

In sum, the Dead Sea Scrolls give us information on the kinds of issues of concern to Jews during the New Testament era: the identity of God's true people, questions of ritual and purity, and the search for a fresh word of revelation in troubled times. But the community that emerged from Jesus' teaching was radically different from that of Qumran. In many ways Qumran depicts for us "the road not taken" by the early Christians. ◆

credit is that to you? Even sinners do that. 34And if you lend to those from whom you expect repayment, what credit is that to you?[j] Even sinners lend to sinners, expecting to be repaid in full. 35But love your enemies, do good to them,[k] and lend to them without expecting to get anything back. Then your reward will be great, and you will be children[l] of the Most High,[m] because he is kind to the ungrateful and wicked. 36Be merciful,[n] just as your Father[o] is merciful.

Judging Others

6:37-42pp — Mt 7:1-5

37"Do not judge, and you will not be judged.[p] Do not condemn, and you will not be condemned. Forgive, and you will be forgiven.[q] 38Give, and it will be given to you. A good measure, pressed down, shaken together and running over, will be poured into your lap.[r] For with the measure you use, it will be measured to you."[s]

39He also told them this parable: "Can the blind lead the blind? Will they not both fall into a pit?[t] 40The student is not above the teacher, but everyone who is fully trained will be like their teacher.[u]

41"Why do you look at the speck of sawdust in your brother's eye and pay no attention to the plank in your own eye? 42How can you say to your brother, 'Brother, let me take the speck out of your eye,' when you yourself fail to see the plank in your own eye? You hypocrite, first take the plank out of your eye, and then you will see clearly to remove the speck from your brother's eye.

6:34 [j] Mt 5:42
6:35 [k] ver 27 [l] Ro 8:14 [m] Mk 5:7
6:36 [n] Jas 2:13 [o] Mt 5:48; 6:1; Lk 11:2; 12:32; Ro 8:15; Eph 4:6; 1Pe 1:17; 1Jn 1:3; 3:1
6:37 [p] Mt 7:1 [q] Mt 6:14
6:38 [r] Ps 79:12; Isa 65:6, 7 [s] Mt 7:2; Mk 4:24
6:39 [t] Mt 15:14
6:40 [u] Mt 10:24; Jn 13:16
6:44 [v] Mt 12:33
6:45 [w] Pr 4:23; Mt 12:34,35; Mk 7:20
6:46 [x] Jn 13:13 [y] Mal 1:6; Mt 7:21
6:47 [z] Lk 8:21; 11:28; Jas 1:22-25
7:1 [a] Mt 7:28

A Tree and Its Fruit

6:43,44pp — Mt 7:16,18,20

43"No good tree bears bad fruit, nor does a bad tree bear good fruit. 44Each tree is recognized by its own fruit.[v] People do not pick figs from thornbushes, or grapes from briers. 45A good man brings good things out of the good stored up in his heart, and an evil man brings evil things out of the evil stored up in his heart. For the mouth speaks what the heart is full of.[w]

The Wise and Foolish Builders

6:47-49pp — Mt 7:24-27

46"Why do you call me, 'Lord, Lord,'[x] and do not do what I say?[y] 47As for everyone who comes to me and hears my words and puts them into practice,[z] I will show you what they are like. 48They are like a man building a house, who dug down deep and laid the foundation on rock. When a flood came, the torrent struck that house but could not shake it, because it was well built. 49But the one who hears my words and does not put them into practice is like a man who built a house on the ground without a foundation. The moment the torrent struck that house, it collapsed and its destruction was complete."

The Faith of the Centurion

7:1-10pp — Mt 8:5-13

7 When Jesus had finished saying all this[a] to the people who were listening, he entered Capernaum. 2There a centurion's servant, whom his master valued highly, was sick and about to die. 3The

---

6:34 In contrast to Gentiles, Jewish people were supposed to lend without charging interest (Ex 22:25; Lev 25:36–37); they also had to release debts in the sabbath (seventh) year and the Year of Jubilee. Toward those years, lenders became less ready to lend, fearing that the poor, who might need to borrow money to sow their crops, could not repay (Lev 25:15,28; Dt 15:9).
6:36 *merciful.* Some have suggested a particular Aramaic word, which can contain nuances of both "merciful" and "perfect," that may stand behind the terms in Mt 5:48 and here in v. 36.
6:37–38 *Do not judge … Do not condemn … Forgive … Give.* In principle, many Jewish sages (and even some Greek thinkers) would have agreed with Jesus (see Sirach 28:1–3). Nevertheless, not all people practiced what these sages taught, and even today, following Jesus in practice requires more than agreeing with him in principle.
6:38 *the measure you use.* "Measuring" appropriately was a familiar image from contemporary marketplaces. "It is measured to one according to the measure by which one measures" was also a Jewish maxim.
6:39 *Can the blind …?* Those who were literally blind often had someone sighted who could guide them. *pit.* For the prevalence of pits, see note on Mt 12:11; for falling into a pit as a metaphor of judgment, see, e.g., Ps 7:15; Pr 26:27; Isa 24:18; Jer 48:43–44; Eze 19:4.
6:40 *The student is not above the teacher.* Ancient protocol mandated that disciples must always respect their teacher; on completing training, however, an advanced disciple could become a teacher.
6:41,42 *speck … plank.* This graphic, hyperbolic image would likely draw laughter—and provoke thought. If a splinter risked blinding one, how much more a roof beam? Ancient eye surgery, meanwhile, was a delicate art that could result in blindness.
6:43 *good tree … bad fruit … bad tree … good fruit.* This was an agricultural principle understood by everyone.
6:44 *figs … grapes.* Like olives, figs and vines were pervasive in the Mediterranean world.
6:48 *rock.* Some other Jewish teachers told a parable similar to vv. 46–49, with a major difference: in their story, the foundational rock was the Torah, God's law. Here Jesus' teaching holds the same role as God's message in the traditional parable.
7:1 *Capernaum.* See note on 4:31.
7:2 *centurion's servant.* Centurions commanded roughly 80 troops; often they worked their way up through the ranks to achieve their position. Roman military units were stationed in Caesarea and in Jerusalem; they consisted of auxiliary troops, mostly recruited from Syria. Servants could be viewed as members of households (see note on Mt 8:6).

centurion heard of Jesus and sent some
elders of the Jews to him, asking him to
come and heal his servant. 4When they
came to Jesus, they pleaded earnestly with
him, "This man deserves to have you do
this, 5because he loves our nation and has
built our synagogue." 6So Jesus went with
them.

He was not far from the house when
the centurion sent friends to say to him:
"Lord, don't trouble yourself, for I do not
deserve to have you come under my roof.
7That is why I did not even consider myself worthy to come to you. But say the
word, and my servant will be healed.[b] 8For
I myself am a man under authority, with
soldiers under me. I tell this one, 'Go,'
and he goes; and that one, 'Come,' and he
comes. I say to my servant, 'Do this,' and
he does it."

9When Jesus heard this, he was amazed
at him, and turning to the crowd following
him, he said, "I tell you, I have not found
such great faith even in Israel." 10Then the
men who had been sent returned to the
house and found the servant well.

Jesus Raises a Widow's Son

7:11-16Ref — 1Ki 17:17-24; 2Ki 4:32-37; Mk 5:21-24, 35-43; Jn 11:1-44

11Soon afterward, Jesus went to a town
called Nain, and his disciples and a large
crowd went along with him. 12As he approached the town gate, a dead person
was being carried out — the only son of
his mother, and she was a widow. And a
large crowd from the town was with her.
13When the Lord[c] saw her, his heart went
out to her and he said, "Don't cry."

14Then he went up and touched the
bier they were carrying him on, and the
bearers stood still. He said, "Young man, I
say to you, get up!"[d] 15The dead man sat
up and began to talk, and Jesus gave him
back to his mother.

16They were all filled with awe[e] and
praised God.[f] "A great prophet[g] has appeared among us," they said. "God has
come to help his people."[h] 17This news
about Jesus spread throughout Judea and
the surrounding country.[i]

Jesus and John the Baptist

7:18-35pp — Mt 11:2-19

18John's[j] disciples[k] told him about all
these things. Calling two of them, 19he
sent them to the Lord to ask, "Are you the
one who is to come, or should we expect
someone else?"

20When the men came to Jesus, they
said, "John the Baptist sent us to you to
ask, 'Are you the one who is to come, or
should we expect someone else?' "

21At that very time Jesus cured many
who had diseases, sicknesses[l] and evil
spirits, and gave sight to many who were
blind. 22So he replied to the messengers,
"Go back and report to John what you
have seen and heard: The blind receive
sight, the lame walk, those who have
leprosy[a] are cleansed, the deaf hear, the
dead are raised, and the good news is proclaimed to the poor.[m] 23Blessed is anyone
who does not stumble on account of me."

24After John's messengers left, Jesus
began to speak to the crowd about John:

7:7 [b] Ps 107:20 **7:13** [c] ver 19; Lk 10:1; 13:15; 17:5; 22:61; 24:34; Jn 11:2

7:14 [d] Mt 9:25; Mk 1:31; Lk 8:54; Jn 11:43; Ac 9:40 **7:16** [e] Lk 1:65 [f] Mt 9:8 [g] ver 39; Mt 21:11 [h] Lk 1:68 **7:17** [i] Mt 9:26 **7:18** [j] Mt 3:1 [k] Lk 5:33 **7:21** [l] Mt 4:23 **7:22** [m] Isa 29:18, 19; 35:5,6; 61:1,2; Lk 4:18

[a] 22 The Greek word traditionally translated *leprosy* was used for various diseases affecting the skin.

7:5 Jewish people appreciated God-fearing Gentiles. Some Gentiles (such as this centurion) became benefactors of local synagogues, although this was much more common in the Diaspora.

7:6 *come under my roof.* Strict Jews considered Gentile homes unclean and would not enter there. The elders may ask for an exception in the centurion's case (v. 4) if they know there is no idolatry there (the main source of uncleanness).

7:8 The centurion understands how authority works: just as soldiers obey the centurion because he is backed by the authority of the empire, every earthly harm, including disease, must submit to Jesus because he is backed by God's authority (cf. 4:32,36; 5:24).

7:12 *dead person was being carried out.* Because bodies had to be buried outside a community, the procession is exiting the town. *widow.* Because women ordinarily could not earn an adequate income in that society, this widow would depend on her son's support in her old age.

7:13 By custom, the widow or the mother of the deceased would lead the procession. Members of a community who heard a funeral procession normally joined it from behind; because Jesus addresses the widow, however, it is clear that he approaches from the front. He was not planning to simply join in mourning.

7:14 *bier.* More like an open stretcher than a coffin; after a person's death, the body was quickly washed and anointed and then carried out to the tomb. Contact with a corpse communicated the severest form of impurity (Nu 19:11 – 20); Jesus' touching the bier shows that he values mercy over purity (cf. 5:13).

7:16 Prophets such as Elijah and Elisha had raised the dead (1Ki 17:23; 2Ki 4:36). *God has come to help his people.* See note on 1:68.

7:18 *two of them.* It was common to send messengers in pairs.

7:19 – 20 Jesus' reported acts (v. 18) were praiseworthy, but differed from the expected baptizing in fire (3:16).

7:22 Jesus depicts his current mission of restoring the disabled and preaching to the poor as foretastes of the promised coming era of restoration. He does so by borrowing language from Isa 35:5 – 6; 61:1 (he cites Isa 61:1 – 2 also in Lk 4:18 – 19).

7:23 *Blessed is.* On beatitudes, see note on Mt 5:3. *stumble.* Often used as a metaphor for sin or falling away.

7:24 *reed.* The emblem on the coins of Herod Antipas, who imprisoned John, was a reed. John's hearers would be familiar with reeds, since they grew as tall as 16 feet (5 meters) high around the Jordan, where John had baptized. *swayed by the wind.* Reeds were used figuratively

"What did you go out into the wilderness
to see? A reed swayed by the wind? 25 If
not, what did you go out to see? A man
dressed in fine clothes? No, those who
wear expensive clothes and indulge in
luxury are in palaces. 26 But what did you
go out to see? A prophet?[n] Yes, I tell you,
and more than a prophet. 27 This is the one
about whom it is written:

> " 'I will send my messenger ahead of
> you,
> who will prepare your way before
> you.'[a][o]

28 I tell you, among those born of women
there is no one greater than John; yet the
one who is least in the kingdom of God[p]
is greater than he."
29 (All the people, even the tax collectors, when they heard Jesus' words, acknowledged that God's way was right, because they had been baptized by John.[q]
30 But the Pharisees and the experts in the
law[r] rejected God's purpose for themselves, because they had not been baptized by John.)
31 Jesus went on to say, "To what, then,
can I compare the people of this generation? What are they like? 32 They are like
children sitting in the marketplace and
calling out to each other:

> " 'We played the pipe for you,
> and you did not dance;
> we sang a dirge,
> and you did not cry.'

33 For John the Baptist came neither eating bread nor drinking wine,[s] and you say,
'He has a demon.' 34 The Son of Man came
eating and drinking, and you say, 'Here is
a glutton and a drunkard, a friend of tax
collectors and sinners.'[t] 35 But wisdom is
proved right by all her children."

Jesus Anointed by a Sinful Woman

7:37-39Ref — Mt 26:6-13; Mk 14:3-9; Jn 12:1-8
7:41,42Ref — Mt 18:23-34

36 When one of the Pharisees invited
Jesus to have dinner with him, he went
to the Pharisee's house and reclined at the
table. 37 A woman in that town who lived
a sinful life learned that Jesus was eating
at the Pharisee's house, so she came there
with an alabaster jar of perfume. 38 As she
stood behind him at his feet weeping, she
began to wet his feet with her tears. Then
she wiped them with her hair, kissed them
and poured perfume on them.
39 When the Pharisee who had invited
him saw this, he said to himself, "If this
man were a prophet,[u] he would know who
is touching him and what kind of woman
she is — that she is a sinner."
40 Jesus answered him, "Simon, I have
something to tell you."
"Tell me, teacher," he said.
41 "Two people owed money to a certain
moneylender. One owed him five hundred
denarii,[b] and the other fifty. 42 Neither of
them had the money to pay him back, so
he forgave the debts of both. Now which
of them will love him more?"
43 Simon replied, "I suppose the one
who had the bigger debt forgiven."
"You have judged correctly," Jesus said.
44 Then he turned toward the woman and said to Simon, "Do you see this
woman? I came into your house. You did
not give me any water for my feet,[v] but
she wet my feet with her tears and wiped

7:26 [n] Mt 11:9 **7:27** [o] Mal 3:1; Mt 11:10; Mk 1:2 **7:28** [p] Mt 3:2 **7:29** [q] Mt 21:32; Mk 1:5; Lk 3:12 **7:30** [r] Mt 22:35 **7:33** [s] Lk 1:15 **7:34** [t] Lk 5:29, 30; 15:1, 2 **7:39** [u] ver 16; Mt 21:11 **7:44** [v] Ge 18:4; 19:2; 43:24; Jdg 19:21; Jn 13:4-14; 1Ti 5:10

[a] *27* Mal. 3:1 [b] *41* A denarius was the usual daily wage of a day laborer (see Matt. 20:2).

---

for what was weak and undependable in time of trouble (1Ki 14:15; 2Ki 18:21; 3 Maccabees 2:22).
7:25 *fine clothes ... palaces.* Antipas was only a tetrarch but was a king's son and the closest to a king with palaces that Jesus' Galilean hearers might ordinarily see.
7:27 *messenger.* The promised messenger of Mal 3:1 may be one like Elijah (see Mal 4:5).
7:28 *least in the kingdom ... is greater than he.* See note on Mt 11:11.
7:31 *To what ... can I compare ...?* Rabbis often began parables with phrases such as this.
7:32 *children.* They sometimes played games of weddings or funerals (e.g., burying a grasshopper). *dance ... cry.* Dancing was appropriate for the celebrations of weddings, and mourning for funerals. Both were community events; as funeral processions passed, e.g., bystanders were often expected to join in the procession. Here Jesus envisions spoiled children who argue inconsistently so long as they get their way.
7:33 *He has a demon.* A prophet with a demon would be assumed a false prophet — for which the penalty was death (Dt 13:5).
7:34 *eating and drinking.* Like a false prophet, a habitual glutton and a drunkard were deemed worthy of death (Dt 21:20 – 21).
7:36 *invited Jesus.* Inviting a traveling teacher for dinner would be viewed as virtuous (but cf. vv. 44 – 46). *reclined.* Reclining as opposed to merely sitting indicates that it was a banquet, perhaps in Jesus' honor.
7:37 *alabaster jar of perfume.* See note on Mt 26:7.
7:38 *behind him.* Banqueters reclining on couches would face the tables with their feet pointed away from the tables; one approaching Jesus' feet thus would stand behind him. *wiped ... with her hair.* Most adult Jewish women in Judea and Galilee were married, and Jewish custom considered it shameful for a married woman to have her hair uncovered, as it must be here.
7:40 *I have something to tell you.* This was sometimes a way of introducing a stern message.
7:41 *owed money.* Those in debt could lose their property or even be reduced to temporary servitude. *five hundred denarii.* More than a year's wages for an average worker.
7:44 Only servants or persons of low rank normally washed feet, but all good hosts would supply water for the guest to wash his feet. Setting aside normal protocols, Jesus openly exposes his host's inhospitality. If intentional,

them with her hair. 45You did not give me
a kiss,[w] but this woman, from the time I
entered, has not stopped kissing my feet.
46You did not put oil on my head,[x] but she
has poured perfume on my feet. 47There-
fore, I tell you, her many sins have been
forgiven — as her great love has shown.
But whoever has been forgiven little loves
little."

48Then Jesus said to her, "Your sins are
forgiven."[y]

49The other guests began to say among
themselves, "Who is this who even forgives sins?"

50Jesus said to the woman, "Your faith
has saved you;[z] go in peace."[a]

The Parable of the Sower

8:4-15pp — Mt 13:2-23; Mk 4:1-20

8 After this, Jesus traveled about from
one town and village to another, proclaiming the good news of the kingdom
of God.[b] The Twelve were with him, 2and
also some women who had been cured
of evil spirits and diseases: Mary (called
Magdalene)[c] from whom seven demons
had come out; 3Joanna the wife of Chu-
za, the manager of Herod's[d] household;
Susanna; and many others. These women
were helping to support them out of their
own means.

4While a large crowd was gathering and
people were coming to Jesus from town
after town, he told this parable: 5"A farmer went out to sow his seed. As he was
scattering the seed, some fell along the
path; it was trampled on, and the birds
ate it up. 6Some fell on rocky ground, and
when it came up, the plants withered because they had no moisture. 7Other seed
fell among thorns, which grew up with it
and choked the plants. 8Still other seed
fell on good soil. It came up and yielded
a crop, a hundred times more than was
sown."

When he said this, he called out, "Whoever has ears to hear, let them hear."[e]

9His disciples asked him what this parable meant. 10He said, "The knowledge
of the secrets of the kingdom of God has
been given to you,[f] but to others I speak in
parables, so that,

> " 'though seeing, they may not see;
> though hearing, they may not
> understand.'[a][g]

11"This is the meaning of the parable:
The seed is the word of God.[h] 12Those
along the path are the ones who hear, and
then the devil comes and takes away the
word from their hearts, so that they may
not believe and be saved. 13Those on the
rocky ground are the ones who receive the
word with joy when they hear it, but they
have no root. They believe for a while,
but in the time of testing they fall away.[i]
14The seed that fell among thorns stands
for those who hear, but as they go on their
way they are choked by life's worries,
riches[j] and pleasures, and they do not mature. 15But the seed on good soil stands for
those with a noble and good heart, who
hear the word, retain it, and by persevering produce a crop.

7:45 [w] Lk 22:47, 48; Ro 16:16 **7:46** [x] Ps 23:5; Ecc 9:8 **7:48** [y] Mt 9:2 **7:50** [z] Mt 9:22; Mk 5:34; Lk 8:48 [a] Ac 15:33 **8:1** [b] Mt 4:23 **8:2** [c] Mt 27:55, 56 **8:3** [d] Mt 14:1

8:8 [e] Mt 11:15 **8:10** [f] Mt 13:11 [g] Isa 6:9; Mt 13:13, 14 **8:11** [h] Heb 4:12 **8:13** [i] Mt 11:6 **8:14** [j] Mt 19:23; 1Ti 6:9, 10, 17

[a] *10* Isaiah 6:9

Simon's actions were conspicuously rude and demeaning toward Jesus.

7:45–46 Greeting a teacher with a kiss and providing a guest oil for him to anoint his head were basic courtesies. Again (see v. 44), the host may have conspicuously insulted Jesus, or at least treated him as being of low rank (which most teachers would have viewed as insulting).

7:49 *Who is this who even forgives sins?* Although priests might pronounce God's forgiveness, only God could forgive sins (Mic 7:18).

8:2–3 Although women in general had fewer resources than men, some were wealthy, and some scholars estimate that a tenth of all patrons in antiquity were women. Women benefactors were normally acceptable (cf. 2Ki 4:8–10), but enemies sometimes used one's support by such benefactors as a grounds for criticism. Married women traveling with men other than their husbands, however, as here, could occasion much more criticism (cf. note on Jn 4:27). Although a few philosophic schools had or permitted some women disciples, they are almost unknown among Jewish schools for the study of the Torah. (Persian and other cultures to the east of the Roman Empire had some strict protocols for women, but even Roman philosophic teachers who welcomed women students, such as Musonius Rufus, sometimes felt compelled to explain that intellectual training would aid women in domestic pursuits. Over the centuries, however, a handful of women in the Roman Empire did become famous philosophers in their own right.)

8:3 *Herod's household.* On Herod Antipas, see notes on Mk 6:14,17.

8:4 *parable.* Parables were normally sermon illustrations; see the article "Parables," p. 1686.

8:5 Many ancient sources speak of plowing before sowing (which would have prevented the farmer from wasting some seed in this case!), but others clearly speak of sowing before plowing. See note on Mk 13:4.

8:6 *rocky ground.* Much of the soil in the Holy Land is rocky.

8:7 *thorns.* A kind of thistle is common around roads and can reach more than three feet (a meter) in April.

8:8 *a hundred times.* The average yield of seed was probably between seven and a half to tenfold. A hundredfold was a remarkably good harvest (Ge 26:12). *Whoever has ears to hear.* A phrase common to the language of a sage's riddles, Jesus invites the wise to consider the meaning.

8:10 *secrets of the kingdom.* See note on Mk 4:11. For the quotation from Isa 6:9, see note on Mk 4:12.

8:11 *the meaning.* Jewish teachers often gave interpretations with their parables, especially to their disciples.

8:12–13 See notes on Mk 4:14,17.

A Lamp on a Stand

16“No one lights a lamp and hides it in a
clay jar or puts it under a bed. Instead, they
put it on a stand, so that those who come
in can see the light.[k] 17For there is nothing hidden that will not be disclosed, and
nothing concealed that will not be known
or brought out into the open.[l] 18Therefore
consider carefully how you listen. Whoever has will be given more; whoever does
not have, even what they think they have
will be taken from them.”[m]

Jesus’ Mother and Brothers

8:19-21pp — Mt 12:46-50; Mk 3:31-35

19Now Jesus’ mother and brothers came
to see him, but they were not able to get
near him because of the crowd. 20Some-
one told him, “Your mother and brothers[n]
are standing outside, wanting to see you.”
21He replied, “My mother and brothers
are those who hear God’s word and put it
into practice.”[o]

Jesus Calms the Storm

8:22-25pp — Mt 8:23-27; Mk 4:36-41
8:22-25Ref — Mk 6:47-52; Jn 6:16-21

22One day Jesus said to his disciples,
“Let us go over to the other side of the
lake.” So they got into a boat and set out.
23As they sailed, he fell asleep. A squall
came down on the lake, so that the boat
was being swamped, and they were in
great danger.
24The disciples went and woke him,
saying, “Master, Master,[p] we’re going to
drown!”
He got up and rebuked[q] the wind and
the raging waters; the storm subsided, and
all was calm.[r] 25“Where is your faith?” he
asked his disciples.
In fear and amazement they asked one
another, “Who is this? He commands even
the winds and the water, and they obey
him.”

8:16 [k] Mt 5:15; Mk 4:21; Lk 11:33 **8:17** [l] Mt 10:26; Mk 4:22; Lk 12:2 **8:18** [m] Mt 13:12; 25:29; Lk 19:26 **8:20** [n] Jn 7:5 **8:21** [o] Lk 6:47; 11:28; Jn 14:21 **8:24** [p] Lk 5:5 [q] Lk 4:35,39,41 [r] Ps 107:29; Jnh 1:15 **8:28** [s] Mt 8:29 [t] Mk 5:7 **8:31** [u] Rev 9:1, 2, 11; 11:7; 17:8; 20:1,3

Jesus Restores a Demon-Possessed Man

8:26-37pp — Mt 8:28-34
8:26-39pp — Mk 5:1-20

26They sailed to the region of the Gerasenes,[a] which is across the lake from Galilee. 27When Jesus stepped ashore, he was
met by a demon-possessed man from the
town. For a long time this man had not
worn clothes or lived in a house, but had
lived in the tombs. 28When he saw Jesus,
he cried out and fell at his feet, shouting
at the top of his voice, “What do you want
with me,[s] Jesus, Son of the Most High
God?[t] I beg you, don’t torture me!” 29For
Jesus had commanded the impure spirit to
come out of the man. Many times it had
seized him, and though he was chained
hand and foot and kept under guard, he
had broken his chains and had been driv-
en by the demon into solitary places.
30Jesus asked him, “What is your
name?”
“Legion,” he replied, because many
demons had gone into him. 31And they
begged Jesus repeatedly not to order them
to go into the Abyss.[u]
32A large herd of pigs was feeding there
on the hillside. The demons begged Jesus
to let them go into the pigs, and he gave
them permission. 33When the demons
came out of the man, they went into the

[a] *26* Some manuscripts *Gadarenes*; other manuscripts *Gergesenes*; also in verse 37

8:16 *lights a lamp.* The most common oil lamps of this period were small enough to hold in the hand.
8:18 *Whoever has… taken from them.* Jesus illustrates with a fairly common observation characteristic of ancient economics (see note on Mt 25:16).
8:21 *My mother and brothers.* Figurative kinship language was common in antiquity; e.g., one could call a respected older woman “mother” and call comrades or fellow members of one’s ethnic group “brothers.” Nevertheless, refusal to give higher priority to one’s physical family would appear offensive in ancient Mediterranean culture.
8:22 *boat.* Galilean fishing boats were usually fairly small; the surviving example is 27 feet (8.2 meters) long, 7.5 feet (2.3 meters) wide and possibly 4.3 feet (1.3 meters) deep. It was built especially of cedar planks (but supplemented with other wood, even scrap wood) with joints and nails. In addition to a mast, it had four places spread out for rowers.
8:23 *squall.* The shape of the hills surrounding the Sea of Galilee can funnel storms onto the lake; they can be sudden and devastating to small boats out in the midst of the lake. Rental contracts stipulated that boats were to be returned unharmed barring an act of God, such as a storm.
8:25 *Where is your faith?* Jewish people understood that God controls the wind and waves (Ps 65:7; 89:9; 107:29).
8:26 *region of the Gerasenes.* See note on Mk 5:1.
8:27 *lived in the tombs.* Jewish people regarded tombs and anything associated with the dead as impure; some associated spirits with such sites.
8:28 *What do you want with me . . . ?* Lit. “What (is there between) us and you?” (cf. Mk 5:7) — a phrase that emphasizes distance and often hostility between the speaker and the one addressed. *Most High God.* See note on Ac 16:17.
8:29 *broken his chains.* Superhuman strength appears in some reports of spirit possession in various cultures, occasionally even to the point of breaking restraints.
8:30 *What is your name?* See note on Mk 5:9.
8:31 *the Abyss.* Various Jewish sources depict spirits being imprisoned, or bound, in various places, including beneath the earth. Although Jewish sources apply “abyss” more widely, the Septuagint, the pre-Christian Greek translation of the OT, apparently applies “abyss” to “the watery depths” (Pr 3:20; 8:24), possibly relevant here (v. 33).
8:32 *pigs.* Jewish people considered pigs unclean (Lev 11:7 – 8).
8:33 *herd … was drowned.* Pigs can typically swim, but not indefinitely, probably especially after plunging over a steep bank, presumably many on top of each other. In

pigs, and the herd rushed down the steep
bank into the lake[v] and was drowned.
34 When those tending the pigs saw
what had happened, they ran off and reported this in the town and countryside,
35 and the people went out to see what
had happened. When they came to Jesus,
they found the man from whom the demons had gone out, sitting at Jesus' feet,[w]
dressed and in his right mind; and they
were afraid. 36 Those who had seen it told
the people how the demon-possessed[x] man
had been cured. 37 Then all the people of
the region of the Gerasenes asked Jesus to
leave them,[y] because they were overcome
with fear. So he got into the boat and left.
38 The man from whom the demons had
gone out begged to go with him, but Jesus
sent him away, saying, 39 "Return home
and tell how much God has done for you."
So the man went away and told all over
town how much Jesus had done for him.

Jesus Raises a Dead Girl and Heals a Sick Woman

8:40-56pp — Mt 9:18-26; Mk 5:22-43

40 Now when Jesus returned, a crowd
welcomed him, for they were all expecting
him. 41 Then a man named Jairus, a synagogue leader,[z] came and fell at Jesus' feet,
pleading with him to come to his house
42 because his only daughter, a girl of about
twelve, was dying.
As Jesus was on his way, the crowds
almost crushed him. 43 And a woman was
there who had been subject to bleeding[a] for twelve years,[a] but no one could
heal her. 44 She came up behind him and
touched the edge of his cloak,[b] and immediately her bleeding stopped.
45 "Who touched me?" Jesus asked.
When they all denied it, Peter said,
"Master,[c] the people are crowding and
pressing against you."

8:33 [v] ver 22, 23
8:35 [w] Lk 10:39
8:36 [x] Mt 4:24
8:37 [y] Ac 16:39
8:41 [z] ver 49; Mk 5:22
8:43 [a] Lev 15:25-30
8:44 [b] Mt 9:20
8:45 [c] Lk 5:5
8:46 [d] Mt 14:36; Mk 3:10 [e] Lk 5:17; 6:19
8:48 [f] Mt 9:22 [g] Ac 15:33
8:49 [h] ver 41
8:51 [i] Mt 4:21
8:52 [j] Lk 23:27 [k] Mt 9:24; Jn 11:11, 13
8:54 [l] Lk 7:14
8:56 [m] Mt 8:4
9:1 [n] Mt 10:1 [o] Mt 4:23; Lk 5:17
9:2 [p] Mt 3:2

46 But Jesus said, "Someone touched
me;[d] I know that power has gone out
from me."[e]
47 Then the woman, seeing that she
could not go unnoticed, came trembling
and fell at his feet. In the presence of all
the people, she told why she had touched
him and how she had been instantly
healed. 48 Then he said to her, "Daughter,
your faith has healed you.[f] Go in peace."[g]
49 While Jesus was still speaking, someone came from the house of Jairus, the
synagogue leader.[h] "Your daughter is
dead," he said. "Don't bother the teacher
anymore."
50 Hearing this, Jesus said to Jairus,
"Don't be afraid; just believe, and she will
be healed."
51 When he arrived at the house of Jairus, he did not let anyone go in with him
except Peter, John and James,[i] and the
child's father and mother. 52 Meanwhile,
all the people were wailing and mourning[j]
for her. "Stop wailing," Jesus said. "She is
not dead but asleep."[k]
53 They laughed at him, knowing that
she was dead. 54 But he took her by the
hand and said, "My child, get up!"[l] 55 Her
spirit returned, and at once she stood up.
Then Jesus told them to give her something to eat. 56 Her parents were astonished, but he ordered them not to tell anyone what had happened.[m]

Jesus Sends Out the Twelve

9:3-5pp — Mt 10:9-15; Mk 6:8-11
9:7-9pp — Mt 14:1,2; Mk 6:14-16

9 When Jesus had called the Twelve together, he gave them power and authority to drive out all demons[n] and to
cure diseases,[o] 2 and he sent them out to
proclaim the kingdom of God[p] and to heal

[a] 43 Many manuscripts *years, and she had spent all she had on doctors*

---

some Jewish traditions demons could be destroyed or could be bound under bodies of water.
8:34 *those tending the pigs.* Pigs require little oversight, but even if the herders were few, they were responsible to the owners for the pigs' welfare.
8:37 *asked Jesus to leave ... they were overcome with fear.* Unfamiliar with the Jewish tradition of Biblical prophets, Gentiles may have thought of Jesus as a dangerous magician, whose power destroyed their herds of pigs.
8:39 The predominantly Gentile residents of the area (see note on v. 37) would not have misunderstood a Messianic claim, but would have viewed him as a magician; thus Jesus urges clarification.
8:41 *synagogue leader.* This was nearly always a person of status and usually wealth; see note on Mk 5:22.
8:43 *bleeding for twelve years.* Under Jewish law, vaginal bleeding made a woman impure (Lev 15:20 – 27, especially vv. 25 – 27); see note on Mk 5:25.
8:44 *touched the edge of his cloak.* Even contact between an unclean person and another's clothes rendered ritually impure the person whose clothes were thus contaminated (Lev 15:26 – 27). Here the effect is the opposite: she is cleansed. See note on Mk 5:27.
8:52 *wailing and mourning.* As soon as a person's death was announced, professional mourners would gather to help facilitate the family's and community's grief. *not dead but asleep.* "Sleep" was a frequent metaphor for death. See note on Mk 5:39.
8:54 *took her by the hand.* Contact with a bleeding person (see notes on vv. 43,44) could render a person impure until evening (Lev 15:21 – 23,27), but touching a corpse rendered one impure for a week (Nu 19:14,16).
9:1 *the Twelve.* In antiquity, groups were sometimes named by the number of members originally in the group. This group was called not only the "Eleven" (Lk 24:9) but also the "Twelve" (1Co 15:5) even after one of the twelve original members fell away.

the sick. 3He told them: "Take nothing for the journey—no staff, no bag, no bread, no money, no extra shirt.[q] 4Whatever house you enter, stay there until you leave that town. 5If people do not welcome you, leave their town and shake the dust off your feet as a testimony against them."[r] 6So they set out and went from village to village, proclaiming the good news and healing people everywhere.

7Now Herod[s] the tetrarch heard about all that was going on. And he was perplexed because some were saying that John[t] had been raised from the dead,[u] 8others that Elijah had appeared,[v] and still others that one of the prophets of long ago had come back to life.[w] 9But Herod said, "I beheaded John. Who, then, is this I hear such things about?" And he tried to see him.[x]

Jesus Feeds the Five Thousand

9:10-17pp — Mt 14:13-21; Mk 6:32-44; Jn 6:5-13
9:13-17Ref — 2Ki 4:42-44

10When the apostles[y] returned, they reported to Jesus what they had done. Then he took them with him and they withdrew by themselves to a town called Bethsaida,[z] 11but the crowds learned about it and followed him. He welcomed them and spoke to them about the kingdom of God,[a] and healed those who needed healing.

12Late in the afternoon the Twelve came to him and said, "Send the crowd away so they can go to the surrounding villages and countryside and find food and lodging, because we are in a remote place here."

13He replied, "You give them something to eat."

They answered, "We have only five loaves of bread and two fish—unless we go and buy food for all this crowd." 14(About five thousand men were there.)

But he said to his disciples, "Have them sit down in groups of about fifty each." 15The disciples did so, and everyone sat down. 16Taking the five loaves and the two fish and looking up to heaven, he gave thanks and broke them.[b] Then he gave them to the disciples to distribute to the people. 17They all ate and were satisfied, and the disciples picked up twelve basketfuls of broken pieces that were left over.

Peter Declares That Jesus Is the Messiah

9:18-20pp — Mt 16:13-16; Mk 8:27-29
9:22-27pp — Mt 16:21-28; Mk 8:31 – 9:1

18Once when Jesus was praying[c] in private and his disciples were with him, he asked them, "Who do the crowds say I am?"

19They replied, "Some say John the Baptist;[d] others say Elijah; and still others, that one of the prophets of long ago has come back to life."[e]

20"But what about you?" he asked. "Who do you say I am?"

Peter answered, "God's Messiah."[f]

Jesus Predicts His Death

21Jesus strictly warned them not to tell this to anyone.[g] 22And he said, "The Son of Man[h] must suffer many things[i] and be rejected by the elders, the chief priests and the teachers of the law,[j] and he must be killed[k] and on the third day[l] be raised to life."[m]

23Then he said to them all: "Whoever wants to be my disciple must deny themselves and take up their cross daily and

9:3 [q] Lk 10:4; 22:35
9:5 [r] Mt 10:14
9:7 [s] Mt 14:1 [t] Mt 3:1 [u] ver 19
9:8 [v] Mt 11:14 [w] ver 19; Jn 1:21
9:9 [x] Lk 23:8
9:10 [y] Mk 6:30 [z] Mt 11:21
9:11 [a] ver 2; Mt 3:2
9:16 [b] Mt 14:19
9:18 [c] Lk 3:21
9:19 [d] Mt 3:1 [e] ver 7,8
9:20 [f] Jn 1:49; 6:66-69; 11:27
9:21 [g] Mt 16:20; Mk 8:30
9:22 [h] Mt 8:20 [i] Mt 16:21 [j] Mt 27:1,2 [k] Ac 2:23; 3:13 [l] Mt 16:21 [m] Mt 16:21

9:3 *Take nothing.* In the poorest areas, many peasants had only a single cloak. Biblical prophets also had to live simply in times of widespread apostasy. See notes on Mk 6:8, 9.
9:4 *Whatever house.* Hospitality was one of the chief virtues in Mediterranean antiquity, and Jewish travelers could normally count on Jewish hospitality even in cities in the Diaspora.
9:5 *shake the dust off your feet.* Proper hospitality included offering water for guests to wash their feet; here the travelers' feet remain conspicuously unwashed. Jewish people sometimes shook profane dust from their feet when entering a more holy place (cf. Ex 3:5); some are said to have done so when leaving pagan territory to enter the Holy Land. Cf. the actions in Ac 18:6; 22:23 (see notes there).
9:7 *Herod the tetrarch.* Herod Antipas—son of Herod the Great (Mt 2:1) by a Samaritan wife named Malthace, and full brother of Archelaus (Josephus, *Wars* 1.562; cf. Mt 2:22)—was a tetrarch, i.e., governor of a territory (in his case, Galilee and Perea).
9:8 *Elijah.* People expected Elijah to prepare the way for the end (Mal 4:5 – 6). Some Jewish people believed that prophets in the ancient sense had ceased, though many other Jews did follow the promises of those who acted like end-time prophets.
9:9 *beheaded John.* Josephus (*Antiquities* 18.119) says that Antipas imprisoned John the Baptist in his Perean fortress Machaerus, which included a dungeon, and executed him. Aretas IV, king of Nabatea, later vanquished Herod Antipas in battle, and Antipas's own people attributed Herod's loss to divine judgment for his wicked execution of John the Baptist. See note on Mk 6:17.
9:10 *Bethsaida.* A town in Herod Philip's territory; it was on the Sea of Galilee's northeastern shore near the Jordan River.
9:12 *villages.* Few towns had more than 3,000 residents; most villages had only a few hundred. Visitors might normally hope for hospitality, but the region could not support 5,000 visitors (v. 14).
9:16 *looking up to heaven, he gave thanks.* The Jewish custom was to thank God before one's meal. See note on Mk 6:41.
9:17 *twelve basketfuls.* See note on Mk 6:43.
9:19 *others say Elijah.* Many Jewish people expected Elijah's return (Mal 4:5).
9:20 *Messiah.* See note on Mk 8:29.
9:21 *not to tell this to anyone.* See note on Mk 8:30.
9:22 *must suffer.* See note on Mk 8:31. *the elders, the chief priests and the teachers of the law.* See note on Mk 8:31.
9:23 *take up their cross.* Disciples were to honor their teachers but were not expected to die for following them. Those condemned to execution would often carry

follow me.[n] 24 For whoever wants to save their life will lose it, but whoever loses their life for me will save it.[o] 25 What good is it for someone to gain the whole world, and yet lose or forfeit their very self? 26 Whoever is ashamed of me and my words, the Son of Man will be ashamed of them[p] when he comes in his glory and in the glory of the Father and of the holy angels.[q]

27 "Truly I tell you, some who are standing here will not taste death before they see the kingdom of God."

The Transfiguration

9:28-36pp — Mt 17:1-8; Mk 9:2-8

28 About eight days after Jesus said this, he took Peter, John and James[r] with him and went up onto a mountain to pray.[s] 29 As he was praying, the appearance of his face changed, and his clothes became as bright as a flash of lightning. 30 Two men, Moses and Elijah, appeared in glorious splendor, talking with Jesus. 31 They spoke about his departure,[a][t] which he was about to bring to fulfillment at Jerusalem. 32 Peter and his companions were very sleepy,[u] but when they became fully awake, they saw his glory and the two men standing with him. 33 As the men were leaving Jesus, Peter said to him, "Master,[v] it is good for us to be here. Let us put up three shelters — one for you, one for Moses and one for Elijah." (He did not know what he was saying.)

34 While he was speaking, a cloud appeared and covered them, and they were afraid as they entered the cloud. 35 A voice came from the cloud, saying, "This is my Son, whom I have chosen;[w] listen to him."[x] 36 When the voice had spoken, they found that Jesus was alone. The disciples kept this to themselves and did not tell anyone at that time what they had seen.[y]

9:23 [n] Mt 10:38; Lk 14:27
9:24 [o] Jn 12:25
9:26 [p] Mt 10:33; Lk 12:9; 2Ti 2:12 [q] Mt 16:27
9:28 [r] Mt 4:21 [s] Lk 3:21
9:31 [t] 2Pe 1:15
9:32 [u] Mt 26:43
9:33 [v] Lk 5:5
9:35 [w] Isa 42:1 [x] Mt 3:17
9:36 [y] Mt 17:9

Jesus Heals a Demon-Possessed Boy

9:37-42,43-45pp — Mt 17:14-18,22,23; Mk 9:14-27,30-32

37 The next day, when they came down from the mountain, a large crowd met him. 38 A man in the crowd called out, "Teacher, I beg you to look at my son, for he is my only child. 39 A spirit seizes him and he suddenly screams; it throws him into convulsions so that he foams at the mouth. It scarcely ever leaves him and is destroying him. 40 I begged your disciples to drive it out, but they could not."

41 "You unbelieving and perverse generation,"[z] Jesus replied, "how long shall I stay with you and put up with you? Bring your son here."

42 Even while the boy was coming, the demon threw him to the ground in a convulsion. But Jesus rebuked the impure spirit, healed the boy and gave him back to his father. 43 And they were all amazed at the greatness of God.

Jesus Predicts His Death a Second Time

While everyone was marveling at all that Jesus did, he said to his disciples, 44 "Listen carefully to what I am about to tell you: The Son of Man is going to be delivered into the hands of men."[a] 45 But they did not understand what this meant. It was hidden from them, so that they did not grasp it,[b] and they were afraid to ask him about it.

46 An argument started among the disciples as to which of them would be the greatest.[c] 47 Jesus, knowing their thoughts,[d] took a little child and had him stand beside him. 48 Then he said to them, "Whoever welcomes this little child in my name welcomes me; and whoever welcomes me welcomes the one who sent me.[e] For it is the one who is least among you all who is the greatest."[f]

9:41 [z] Dt 32:5
9:44 [a] ver 22
9:45 [b] Mk 9:32
9:46 [c] Lk 22:24
9:47 [d] Mt 9:4
9:48 [e] Mt 10:40 [f] Mk 9:35

[a] *31* Greek *exodos*

the horizontal beam of their cross (the *patibulum*) out to the site of their execution, through an often hostile and mocking mob.

9:24 *to save their life will lose it.* See note on Mt 16:25 – 26.

9:26 *the Son of Man ... comes in his glory ... holy angels.* Scripture had promised that God would come with his holy ones (Zec 14:5); here Jesus fills this divine role. He alludes also to the coming son of man in Da 7:13, at the time that he would receive the kingdom.

9:27 See note on Mk 9:1.

9:29 *face changed ... flash of lightning.* Moses talked with God on a mountain and Moses' face reflected God's glory. See note on Mk 9:2.

9:30 *Moses and Elijah.* Elijah was taken to heaven alive (2Ki 2:11); God buried Moses (Dt 34:6), although some Jewish traditions said that he was also preserved alive. Jewish people expected the return of Elijah (Mal 4:5 – 6) and the coming of a prophet like Moses (Dt 18:15 – 18).

9:33 *Let us put up three shelters.* Peter knew how to construct such shelters; Jewish men built them annually for the Festival of Tabernacles.

9:34 *cloud ... covered them.* The cloud of God's glory overshadowed Mount Sinai (Ex 24:15 – 16), from which also God spoke from heaven (Ex 20:22).

9:35 *A voice came from the cloud.* See note on Mk 1:11. Jesus is exalted above Elijah and Moses here. *listen to him.* Some scholars think this evokes the command regarding the prophet like Moses in Dt 18:15.

9:39 See note on Mk 9:22.

9:46 *An argument ... as to which ... would be the greatest.* Rivalry for greater honor was common among ancient Mediterranean men. This practice ranged from playful competition among friends to deadly competition among enemies; Jesus' disciples here were not enemies, but it is possible that they went beyond playful banter.

9:48 *little child.* Children in Jesus' culture were normally powerless, expected to be obedient, and dependent. They were, however, usually objects of their parents' love.

49"Master,"[g] said John, "we saw someone driving out demons in your name and we tried to stop him, because he is not one of us."

50"Do not stop him," Jesus said, "for whoever is not against you is for you."[h]

Samaritan Opposition

51As the time approached for him to be taken up to heaven,[i] Jesus resolutely set out for Jerusalem.[j] 52And he sent messengers on ahead, who went into a Samaritan[k] village to get things ready for him; 53but the people there did not welcome him, because he was heading for Jerusalem. 54When the disciples James and John[l] saw this, they asked, "Lord, do you want us to call fire down from heaven to destroy them[a]?"[m] 55But Jesus turned and rebuked them. 56Then he and his disciples went to another village.

The Cost of Following Jesus

9:57-60pp — Mt 8:19-22

57As they were walking along the road,[n] a man said to him, "I will follow you wherever you go."

58Jesus replied, "Foxes have dens and birds have nests, but the Son of Man[o] has no place to lay his head."

59He said to another man, "Follow me."[p]

But he replied, "Lord, first let me go and bury my father."

60Jesus said to him, "Let the dead bury their own dead, but you go and proclaim the kingdom of God."[q]

61Still another said, "I will follow you, Lord; but first let me go back and say goodbye to my family."[r]

62Jesus replied, "No one who puts a hand to the plow and looks back is fit for service in the kingdom of God."

Jesus Sends Out the Seventy-Two

10:4-12pp — Lk 9:3-5
10:13-15,21,22pp — Mt 11:21-23,25-27
10:23,24pp — Mt 13:16,17

10 After this the Lord[s] appointed seventy-two[b] others[t] and sent them two by two[u] ahead of him to every town and place where he was about to go.[v] 2He

9:49 [g] Lk 5:5 **9:50** [h] Mt 12:30; Lk 11:23 **9:51** [i] Mk 16:19 [j] Lk 13:22; 17:11; 18:31; 19:28 **9:52** [k] Mt 10:5 **9:54** [l] Mt 4:21 [m] 2Ki 1:10, 12 **9:57** [n] ver 51 **9:58** [o] Mt 8:20 **9:59** [p] Mt 4:19 **9:60** [q] Mt 3:2 **9:61** [r] 1Ki 19:20 **10:1** [s] Lk 7:13 [t] Lk 9:1, 2, 51, 52 [u] Mk 6:7 [v] Mt 10:1

[a] 54 Some manuscripts *them, just as Elijah did*
[b] 1 Some manuscripts *seventy*; also in verse 17

9:49 *in your name.* That the man would cast demons out in the name of Jesus rather than invoking a spirit or using strong-smelling substances reveals his faith in Jesus. On ancient practices of casting out demons, see note on Mt 8:16.
9:50 See note on Mk 9:40.
9:51 *resolutely set out.* Sometimes this phrase (lit. "set [one's] face") involved prophetic determination (e.g., Eze 13:17; 20:46). *set out.* Ancient works sometimes signaled a shift in the action of a narrative's plot, as here (cf. Ac 18:23; 19:21–22).
9:52–53 *Samaritan village ... did not welcome him.* Rome ruled both Jews and Samaritans, but the groups mostly hated each other, each circulating stories of the other's atrocities. Samaritans believed in the one God of Israel and claimed to be true heirs of his promises. Samaritans rejected the history of Israel after Joshua, and changed the Ten Commandments to include the requirement to worship on Mount Gerizim. Judeans had destroyed the Samaritan temple on Mount Gerizim; Samaritans likewise hated Jerusalem's temple and often heckled Galilean pilgrims who passed through Samaria on their way to the festival, sometimes even causing bloodshed. See the article "Samaria and Samaritans," p. 1812.
9:54 *call fire down from heaven.* They want to emulate Elijah (2Ki 1:10,12; cf. Elisha in 2Ki 2:24), whom three of them had seen in Lk 9:30–33. Jesus followed the pattern of Elijah in some respects (cf. vv. 16–17,19,61–62), but not in this one.
9:57 *I will follow you.* Disciples normally chose their own teachers, volunteering to follow them. Although some radical Greek teachers called some disciples (as Jesus did with some of his disciples, and as Elijah did with Elisha, 1Ki 19:19), most teachers depended on pupils who came to them. Jewish teachers likewise taught students who enrolled in their schools.
9:58 The proper response to a warning about difficulty (e.g., 2Sa 15:19–20) was to follow anyway (2Sa 15:21–22).
9:59 *bury my father.* Many considered honoring parents a son's greatest obligation (e.g., Josephus, *Against Apion* 2.206), and burying them was the greatest expression of that obligation (e.g., Tobit 4:3–4; 6:15; 4 Maccabees 16:11). The obligation fell most heavily on the eldest son. To neglect this duty was unthinkable; it would make one an outcast from the extended family and dishonored in one's village, normally for the rest of one's life. But a son whose father had just died would not normally be out talking with a rabbi; on receiving the news, he would immediately see to the father's burial. Some scholars note that, "I must first bury my father" sometimes functions as a polite request for delay until the father dies — sometimes a delay of years — so the son can continue with filial obligations in the meantime. Others suggest that this son refers to secondary burial — the custom of reburying the father's bones a year after the initial burial. On either of these views, the son could be requesting a considerable delay.
9:60 *Let the dead bury their own dead.* Even if the son is asking for a considerable delay (see note on v. 59), Jesus' response would be shocking; burying one's father was one of society's greatest obligations (see note on v. 59). In mainstream Jewish society, only God could claim honor above parents. Ancient sources sometimes refer to the spiritually (or socially) dead; alternatively, Jesus could refer to the literal dead, using shocking, graphic language to make his point, as he often did.
9:61–62 *say goodbye to my family ... hand to the plow.* When Elijah called Elisha to follow him, Elisha was plowing. He requested a delay so he could bid farewell to his family; in that case, it included organizing a farewell party. Elijah permitted this (1Ki 19:19–21). Given Elisha's 12 yoke of oxen, he was a wealthy man sacrificing much to adopt the rugged lifestyle of an Israelite prophet. Service in God's kingdom, however, is even more demanding than being an OT prophet.
10:1 *seventy-two others.* God multiplied the prophetic empowerment on Moses by inspiring 72 of Israel's elders (70 plus Eldad and Medad; Nu 11:24–26); Moses wished for

told them, "The harvest is plentiful, but
the workers are few. Ask the Lord of the
harvest, therefore, to send out workers
into his harvest field.[w] 3Go! I am sending
you out like lambs among wolves.[x] 4Do
not take a purse or bag or sandals; and do
not greet anyone on the road.
5"When you enter a house, first say,
'Peace to this house.' 6If someone who
promotes peace is there, your peace will
rest on them; if not, it will return to you.
7Stay there, eating and drinking whatever
they give you, for the worker deserves his
wages.[y] Do not move around from house
to house.
8"When you enter a town and are welcomed, eat what is offered to you.[z] 9Heal
the sick who are there and tell them, 'The
kingdom of God[a] has come near to you.'
10But when you enter a town and are not
welcomed, go into its streets and say,
11'Even the dust of your town we wipe from
our feet as a warning to you.[b] Yet be sure of
this: The kingdom of God has come near.'[c]
12I tell you, it will be more bearable on that
day for Sodom[d] than for that town.[e]
13"Woe to you,[f] Chorazin! Woe to you,
Bethsaida! For if the miracles that were
performed in you had been performed in
Tyre and Sidon, they would have repented
long ago, sitting in sackcloth[g] and ashes.
14But it will be more bearable for Tyre and
Sidon at the judgment than for you. 15And
you, Capernaum,[h] will you be lifted to the
heavens? No, you will go down to Hades.[a]
16"Whoever listens to you listens to me;
whoever rejects you rejects me; but whoever rejects me rejects him who sent me."[i]
17The seventy-two[j] returned with joy
and said, "Lord, even the demons submit
to us in your name."[k]
18He replied, "I saw Satan[l] fall like lightning from heaven.[m] 19I have given you authority to trample on snakes[n] and scorpions and to overcome all the power of the
enemy; nothing will harm you. 20However,
do not rejoice that the spirits submit to
you, but rejoice that your names are written in heaven."[o]
21At that time Jesus, full of joy through
the Holy Spirit, said, "I praise you, Father,
Lord of heaven and earth, because you
have hidden these things from the wise
and learned, and revealed them to little
children.[p] Yes, Father, for this is what you
were pleased to do.
22"All things have been committed to
me by my Father.[q] No one knows who

10:2 [w] Mt 9:37, 38; Jn 4:35 **10:3** [x] Mt 10:16 **10:7** [y] Mt 10:10; 1Co 9:14; 1Ti 5:18 **10:8** [z] 1Co 10:27 **10:9** [a] Mt 3:2; 10:7 **10:11** [b] Mt 10:14; Mk 6:11 [c] ver 9 **10:12** [d] Mt 10:15 [e] Mt 11:24 **10:13** [f] Lk 6:24-26

[g] Rev 11:3 **10:15** [h] Mt 4:13 **10:16** [i] Mt 10:40; Jn 13:20 **10:17** [j] ver 1 [k] Mk 16:17 **10:18** [l] Mt 4:10 [m] Isa 14:12; Rev 9:1; 12:8,9 **10:19** [n] Mk 16:18; Ac 28:3-5 **10:20** [o] Ex 32:32; Ps 69:28; Da 12:1; Php 4:3; Heb 12:23; Rev 13:8; 20:12; 21:27 **10:21** [p] 1Co 1:26-29 **10:22** [q] Mt 28:18

[a] *15* That is, the realm of the dead

this inspiration to extend to all of God's people (Nu 11:29). Jesus chose 12 apostles to lead renewal in Israel (which had 12 tribes; 22:30); Jewish people reckoned that there were 70 (or sometimes 72) nations. *two by two.* Messengers were often sent in pairs.

10:2 *send out workers.* Once grain was ripe, gathering it in quickly before it could spoil was an urgent task. Landowners would hire extra labor.

10:3 *lambs among wolves.* Ancients viewed sheep as helpless against wolves, and some Jewish teachers viewed Israel as such sheep (though not normally, as here, *sent* among wolves). *lambs.* The most helpless of sheep.

10:4 *bag ... sandals.* See notes on Mk 6:8,9. *greet.* Greetings were socially mandatory, except on an urgent prophetic errand or mission as in 2Ki 4:29.

10:5 *Peace to this house.* Greetings were important and the most basic Jewish greeting was *shalom*, "Peace" (meaning "May God cause all to be well with you"). This was a blessing, i.e., an implicit prayer to God.

10:6 *return to you.* A curse was fulfilled only among those meriting it (Pr 26:2); the blessing here works similarly.

10:7 Hospitality was one of the chief virtues in Mediterranean antiquity, and Jewish travelers could normally count on Jewish hospitality even in cities in the Diaspora. When Essenes (members of a strict Jewish sect) traveled, they carried little baggage with them, depending on hospitality from other Essenes.

10:8 *eat what is offered.* It was essential etiquette to welcome hospitality (see note on v. 7).

10:11 *dust ... we wipe from our feet.* Jewish people sometimes shook profane dust from their feet when entering a more holy place; some did so when leaving pagan territory to enter the Holy Land (see vv. 12–14).

10:12 *Sodom.* Sodom rejected God's messengers (Ge 19:4–5). Biblical prophets used Sodom as the epitome of wickedness, and often applied this image to Israel (Dt 32:32; Isa 1:10; 3:9; Jer 23:14; Eze 16:46–49).

10:13 *Woe to you.* See note on Mt 11:21.

10:14 *Tyre and Sidon.* See note on Mt 11:21.

10:15 *Capernaum.* Jesus applies to Capernaum an image from the prophecy against Babylon in Isa 14:11–12.

10:16 However one treated an agent or ambassador reflected one's feelings toward the sender; one's treatment of a prophet reflected one's treatment of God (Ex 16:8; 1Sa 8:7).

10:17 *seventy-two.* In antiquity, groups were sometimes named after their original number. *in your name.* Ancient exorcists coaxed and threatened spirits, and used incantations or applied odorous roots to expel them; by contrast, Jesus' name (presumably indicating his authorization of his disciples) was instantly effective.

10:18 *Satan fall like lightning.* Jewish tradition spoke of Satan's primeval fall in sin (though the Greek verb tense here might mean that Jesus watched Satan fleeing before them). The language of falling from heaven could be used figuratively (see v. 15; La 2:1).

10:19 *snakes and scorpions.* These were among the creatures from which divine protection was valued (Dt 8:15; Ps 91:13).

10:20 *written in heaven.* Jesus here probably appeals to the ancient Jewish image of the book of life (Da 12:1; Mal 3:16; and often in ancient Jewish literature).

10:21 Jesus' prayer here fits earlier Biblical expectations about God discrediting the foolish wisdom of those who thought themselves "wise" (e.g., Isa 19:11–12; 29:14; Jer 8:8–9; Eze 28:6–10).

10:22 *No one knows.* In the Jewish wisdom tradition, God alone knew (Baruch 3:31–32) and could share wisdom with humanity (Wisdom of Solomon 9:16–17).

the Son is except the Father, and no one knows who the Father is except the Son and those to whom the Son chooses to reveal him."[r]

23Then he turned to his disciples and said privately, "Blessed are the eyes that see what you see. 24For I tell you that many prophets and kings wanted to see what you see but did not see it, and to hear what you hear but did not hear it."[s]

The Parable of the Good Samaritan

10:25-28pp — Mt 22:34-40; Mk 12:28-31

25On one occasion an expert in the law stood up to test Jesus. "Teacher," he asked, "what must I do to inherit eternal life?"[t]

26"What is written in the Law?" he replied. "How do you read it?"

27He answered, "'Love the Lord your God with all your heart and with all your soul and with all your strength and with all your mind'[a];[u] and, 'Love your neighbor as yourself.'[b]"[v]

28"You have answered correctly," Jesus replied. "Do this and you will live."[w]

29But he wanted to justify himself,[x] so he asked Jesus, "And who is my neighbor?"

30In reply Jesus said: "A man was going down from Jerusalem to Jericho, when he was attacked by robbers. They stripped him of his clothes, beat him and went away, leaving him half dead. 31A priest happened to be going down the same road, and when he saw the man, he passed by on the other side.[y] 32So too, a Levite, when he came to the place and saw him, passed by on the other side. 33But a Samaritan,[z] as he traveled, came where the man was; and when he saw him, he took pity on him. 34He went to him and bandaged his wounds, pouring on oil and wine. Then he put the man on his own donkey, brought him to an inn and took care of him. 35The next day he took out two denarii[c] and gave them to the innkeeper. 'Look after him,' he said, 'and when I return, I will reimburse you for any extra expense you may have.'

36"Which of these three do you think was a neighbor to the man who fell into the hands of robbers?"

37The expert in the law replied, "The one who had mercy on him."

Jesus told him, "Go and do likewise."

At the Home of Martha and Mary

38As Jesus and his disciples were on their way, he came to a village where a woman named Martha[a] opened her home to him. 39She had a sister called Mary,[b] who sat at the Lord's feet[c] listening to what he said.

10:22 [r] Jn 1:18 **10:24** [s] 1Pe 1:10-12 **10:25** [t] Mt 19:16; Lk 18:18 **10:27** [u] Dt 6:5 [v] Lev 19:18; Mt 5:43 **10:28** [w] Lev 18:5; Ro 7:10 **10:29** [x] Lk 16:15 **10:31** [y] Lev 21:1-3 **10:33** [z] Mt 10:5 **10:38** [a] Jn 11:1; 12:2 **10:39** [b] Jn 11:1; 12:3 [c] Lk 8:35

[a] *27* Deut. 6:5 [b] *27* Lev. 19:18 [c] *35* A denarius was the usual daily wage of a day laborer (see Matt. 20:2).

10:23 *Blessed ... see.* Jewish people often praised one person by uttering a beatitude over someone who knew them; the disciples are blessed because they receive revelation about Jesus and his kingdom (cf. 1Ki 10:8).
10:25 *what must I do to inherit eternal life?* If later Jewish sources are representative, questioning Jewish teachers about how to have eternal life was relatively common. Eternal life was the life of the coming age (Da 12:2), thus of the kingdom (cf. Mt 19:23).
10:26 Jewish teachers asked their disciples and other teachers, "How do you read it?" (i.e., understand the teaching of Scripture) as a way to gauge their understanding and to foster conversation and deeper study; they also often responded to questions with questions.
10:27 It was common to link texts based on a common key word or phrase; Lev 19:18 (quoted at the end of this verse) begins with the same Hebrew phrase as the verse cited at the beginning of this verse (Dt 6:5): *we'ahavta*, "you shall love."
10:28 *Do this and you will live.* Echoes the Torah's promise of life for obeying God's covenant (e.g., Lev 18:5; Dt 8:1).
10:29 *neighbor.* Although Lev 19:18 ("Love your neighbor") applies most directly to loving fellow Israelites (Lev 19:17), the context (Lev 19:34) also addresses loving the "foreigner residing among you."
10:30 *going down.* Jerusalem's elevation was higher than Jericho's. *attacked by robbers.* Jericho was a wealthy community and robbers in the hills could readily accost solitary travelers. *stripped him.* Clothing was often a valuable commodity. *leaving him half dead.* Ancient sources employ "half dead" for one who was, to all appearances, dead.
10:31,32 *passed by on the other side.* People would contract ritual impurity by touching a dead body (which the wounded man may appear to be; v. 30). According to Jewish tradition, they contracted this if so much as their shadow touched the body—thus they passed by on the other side! Priests and Levites avoided impurity when possible (though the priest, also "going down," has completed any duties he may have had in Jerusalem). Many wealthy priests lived in Jericho, so this story rang true to Jesus' listeners.
10:33 *a Samaritan ... took pity on him.* Jews and Samaritans generally hated each other (see note on 9:52–53); while one would not expect most Samaritans to accost Jews (especially on a road largely traveled by Jews), neither would one expect him to help, especially with robbers possibly still around. Some scholars suggest that the Samaritan would not know that the beaten man was Jewish, since he had been stripped of his clothing. On this road, however, the vast majority of travelers would be Jewish, so the wounded man's Jewishness could probably be assumed.
10:34 *oil and wine.* Sometimes used medicinally in wounds; wine might disinfect. *on his own donkey.* Leading a donkey for someone else adopted what was often a servile position; though cf. 2Ch 28:15.
10:35 *I will reimburse you for any extra expense.* Innkeepers generally had a reputation as being untrustworthy, so the Samaritan provides financial incentive for the innkeeper to care for the man.
10:38 *opened her home.* The opportunity to offer hospitality to a famous teacher was considered an honor.
10:39 *sat at the Lord's feet.* People with larger homes (as this one must be to host Jesus and his disciples) could sit on chairs or recline. To sit at a teacher's feet, however, was to take the posture of a disciple (Ac 22:3; Mishnah *'Abot* 1:4).

40 But Martha was distracted by all the preparations that had to be made. She came to
him and asked, "Lord, don't you care[d] that
my sister has left me to do the work by myself? Tell her to help me!"
41 "Martha, Martha," the Lord answered,
"you are worried[e] and upset about many
things, 42 but few things are needed—or
indeed only one.[a][f] Mary has chosen what
is better, and it will not be taken away
from her."

Jesus' Teaching on Prayer

11:2-4pp — Mt 6:9-13
11:9-13pp — Mt 7:7-11

11 One day Jesus was praying[g] in a
certain place. When he finished,
one of his disciples said to him, "Lord,[h]
teach us to pray, just as John taught his
disciples."
2 He said to them, "When you pray, say:

"'Father,[b]
hallowed be your name,
your kingdom[i] come.[c]
3 Give us each day our daily bread.
4 Forgive us our sins,
for we also forgive everyone who
sins against us.[d][j]
And lead us not into temptation.[e]'"[k]

5 Then Jesus said to them, "Suppose
you have a friend, and you go to him at
midnight and say, 'Friend, lend me three
loaves of bread; 6 a friend of mine on a
journey has come to me, and I have no
food to offer him.' 7 And suppose the one
inside answers, 'Don't bother me. The
door is already locked, and my children
and I are in bed. I can't get up and give
you anything.' 8 I tell you, even though he
will not get up and give you the bread because of friendship, yet because of your
shameless audacity[f] he will surely get up
and give you as much as you need.[l]
9 "So I say to you: Ask and it will be giv-
en to you;[m] seek and you will find; knock
and the door will be opened to you. 10 For
everyone who asks receives; the one who
seeks finds; and to the one who knocks,
the door will be opened.
11 "Which of you fathers, if your son asks
for[g] a fish, will give him a snake instead?
12 Or if he asks for an egg, will give him

10:40 [d] Mk 4:38
10:41 [e] Mt 6:25-34; Lk 12:11,22
10:42 [f] Ps 27:4
11:1 [g] Lk 3:21 [h] Jn 13:13
11:2 [i] Mt 3:2
11:4 [j] Mt 18:35; Mk 11:25 [k] Mt 26:41; Jas 1:13
11:8 [l] Lk 18:1-6
11:9 [m] Mt 7:7

[a] 42 Some manuscripts *but only one thing is needed*
[b] 2 Some manuscripts *Our Father in heaven*
[c] 2 Some manuscripts *come. May your will be done on earth as it is in heaven.*
[d] 4 Greek *everyone who is indebted to us*
[e] 4 Some manuscripts *temptation, but deliver us from the evil one*
[f] 8 Or *yet to preserve his good name*
[g] 11 Some manuscripts *for bread, will give him a stone? Or if he asks for*

Although women could hear Torah taught in the synagogue or occasionally even listen in to a teacher's lectures, they were not taught by rabbis in their schools. Boys were schooled in reciting Torah; girls were not (despite some rare, exceptional women who learned Torah in a family setting).
10:40 *distracted by all the preparations.* Because women were expected to fulfill domestic responsibilities, Martha's behavior fits the cultural expectations, while Mary's violates it.
10:41 *Mary has chosen what is better.* Against cultural expectations (see note on v. 40), Jesus affirms Mary's choice more highly: a believer can have no greater role than being Jesus' disciple.
11:1 *When he finished.* Jewish custom prohibited interrupting a person during prayer. Various Jewish circles could use their own prayers, though some prayers (see note on v. 2) were widely used.
11:2 *Father.* Jewish prayers often began by addressing God as Father (already in Isa 63:16; 64:8; Sirach 23:1,4; 51:10). *hallowed be your name.* Jesus here also adapts the opening of the common Jewish prayer called the *Kaddish* (see note on Mt 6:9–10; the prayer in turn reflects motifs common to many ancient Jewish prayers). In its early form, the *Kaddish* began, "Exalted and hallowed be his great name, in the world that he created according to his will; may he cause his kingdom to reign ..." Jewish people expected the hallowing of God's name—i.e., showing it to be sacred, divine and unique—at the time of promised restoration (Eze 36:23; 38:23; 39:27), the time of the promised kingdom.
11:3 *daily bread.* Prayer for food was one of the most common prayers in antiquity. God, who supplied daily bread to his people for 40 years in the wilderness (Dt 8:2–3), could be trusted for sustenance, and the prompt for daily reliance on him reminds hearers of how God provided for his people after bringing them out of Egypt.
11:4 *Forgive us our sins.* The sixth benediction in a regularly prayed Jewish prayer, the Amidah, included a prayer for forgiveness. Some other Jewish sages also emphasized that one who wants to seek God's forgiveness must also forgive other mortals (Sirach 28:1–8). *lead us not into temptation.* A Jewish evening prayer similar to Jesus' prayer about testing here meant not "Do not let us be tempted" but "Do not let us fail when we are tested" (cf. Lk 22:40, 46).
11:5–6 Hospitality obligations demanded that one feed a visitor; indeed, the honor of the village would be at stake should hospitality fail to be extended. Since travel after dark was dangerous, a visitor arriving at midnight was an unusual situation.
11:5 *three loaves of bread.* Since local women often baked bread together, they would know which family might still have bread left over.
11:7 *already locked.* The door may be bolted, so one could not open it without potentially waking the children. Homes often had a single room. The poorest might sleep on mats or together on a large mat, and those who had beds did not always have enough for all family members, so some members might share. Ultimately, however, a villager would not be able to refuse bread under these circumstances; friendship obligations were important, but even more than this, the honor of the village was at stake. Cf. the Jewish tradition of holy men, following the model of Elijah, who persisted with certainty that God would answer (cf., e.g., 1Ki 18:43–46).
11:9 *Ask and it will be given.* See note on Mt 7:7. *the door.* Fits the preceding parable (vv. 5–8).
11:11 *you fathers.* Even if they were poor, as a majority of Galilee's agricultural laborers presumably were, most Jewish fathers would above all else work to provide food for their children. *fish.* Like bread, fish was a basic staple of the Galilean diet.

a scorpion? 13 If you then, though you are
evil, know how to give good gifts to your
children, how much more will your Father
in heaven give the Holy Spirit to those
who ask him!"

Jesus and Beelzebul

11:14,15,17-22,24-26pp — Mt 12:22,24-29,43-45
11:17-22pp — Mk 3:23-27

14 Jesus was driving out a demon that
was mute. When the demon left, the man
who had been mute spoke, and the crowd
was amazed.[n] 15 But some of them said,
"By Beelzebul,[o] the prince of demons, he
is driving out demons."[p] 16 Others tested
him by asking for a sign from heaven.[q]
17 Jesus knew their thoughts[r] and said
to them: "Any kingdom divided against
itself will be ruined, and a house divided
against itself will fall. 18 If Satan[s] is divided against himself, how can his kingdom
stand? I say this because you claim that
I drive out demons by Beelzebul. 19 Now
if I drive out demons by Beelzebul, by
whom do your followers drive them out?
So then, they will be your judges. 20 But if
I drive out demons by the finger of God,[t]
then the kingdom of God[u] has come upon
you.
21 "When a strong man, fully armed,
guards his own house, his possessions are
safe. 22 But when someone stronger attacks
and overpowers him, he takes away the
armor in which the man trusted and divides up his plunder.
23 "Whoever is not with me is against
me, and whoever does not gather with me
scatters.[v]
24 "When an impure spirit comes out of a
person, it goes through arid places seeking
rest and does not find it. Then it says, 'I will
return to the house I left.' 25 When it arrives,
it finds the house swept clean and put in
order. 26 Then it goes and takes seven other
spirits more wicked than itself, and they go
in and live there. And the final condition of
that person is worse than the first."[w]
27 As Jesus was saying these things, a
woman in the crowd called out, "Blessed
is the mother who gave you birth and
nursed you."[x]
28 He replied, "Blessed rather are those
who hear the word of God[y] and obey it."[z]

The Sign of Jonah

11:29-32pp — Mt 12:39-42

29 As the crowds increased, Jesus said,
"This is a wicked generation. It asks for
a sign,[a] but none will be given it except
the sign of Jonah.[b] 30 For as Jonah was a
sign to the Ninevites, so also will the Son
of Man be to this generation. 31 The Queen
of the South will rise at the judgment with
the people of this generation and condemn
them, for she came from the ends of the
earth to listen to Solomon's wisdom;[c] and
now something greater than Solomon is
here. 32 The men of Nineveh will stand
up at the judgment with this generation
and condemn it, for they repented at the
preaching of Jonah;[d] and now something
greater than Jonah is here.

11:14 [n] Mt 9:32, 33
11:15 [o] Mk 3:22 [p] Mt 9:34
11:16 [q] Mt 12:38
11:17 [r] Mt 9:4
11:18 [s] Mt 4:10
11:20 [t] Ex 8:19 [u] Mt 3:2
11:23 [v] Mt 12:30; Mk 9:40; Lk 9:50
11:26 [w] 2Pe 2:20
11:27 [x] Lk 23:29
11:28 [y] Heb 4:12 [z] Pr 8:32; Lk 6:47; 8:21; Jn 14:21
11:29 [a] ver 16; Mt 12:38 [b] Jnh 1:17; Mt 16:4
11:31 [c] 1Ki 10:1; 2Ch 9:1
11:32 [d] Jnh 3:5

11:13 *how much more . . . !* Jewish teachers (and some Gentiles) often used analogy arguments from lesser to greater. *give the Holy Spirit to those who ask.* Most Jewish people in this period believed that the Spirit, if available, rested on only the holiest people; Jesus promises the Spirit's availability to all who ask the Father. Cf. Ac 1:14; 4:29 – 31; 8:15.
11:15 *By . . . the prince of demons, he is driving out demons.* Those accused of sorcery could be accused of dependence on spirits. In antiquity, magical formulas often tried to manipulate spirits. *Beelzebul.* See note on Mt 10:25.
11:16 *sign from heaven.* The crowds could simply be asking for a sign from God (Jewish idiom sometimes used "heaven" as a euphemism for God) or for Jesus to predict a heavenly sign such as an eclipse or other phenomenon.
11:19 *by whom do your followers drive them out?* Other Jewish people engaged in exorcism. *your followers.* Lit. "your sons," a phrase that could refer to disciples or apprentices.
11:20 Jesus' ministry of deliverance is effective far beyond that of others (v. 19). *finger of God.* This may be an allusion to the admission by Pharaoh's magicians that the power in Moses' signs far exceeded their own (Ex 8:19).
11:21 Magicians sought to "bind" spirits to secure their service, but Jesus is not invoking magic. His parable shows his opposition to Satan. Delivering the strong man's (the devil's) possessions from his grasp alludes to God's promise in Isa 49:25: God would defend and deliver his people from the powerful one.
11:22 This is an image of conquest and triumph; conquerors ordinarily divided among their followers the possessions they had seized from the enemy. (The point of the parable, however, is triumph, and we should not press the details so as to envision literal followers gaining these possessions.)
11:23 See note on Mk 9:40.
11:24 – 26 See note on Mt 12:43 – 45.
11:27 *Blessed is the mother who gave you birth.* One could praise a person indirectly by blessing his mother. Jesus uses the praise as an opportunity to teach (v. 28).
11:30 *Ninevites.* The people of Nineveh apparently did not witness the sign of Jonah in the fish's belly; they repented instead through his preaching. One Jewish tradition claims that Jonah tried to avoid preaching to Ninevites lest their repentance shame Israel for failing to do likewise.
11:31 *Queen of the South.* The queen respected Solomon's wisdom (1Ki 10:1 – 13); some Jewish traditions from this period identify her as the queen of Ethiopia.
11:32 In some Jewish traditions, God would render the unrepentant without excuse on the day of judgment; he would do this by having those who repented despite better excuses testify. Although Jewish people expected God to vindicate Israel against the nations in the day of judgment, some later rabbinic traditions claim that repentant Gentiles would testify against unrepentant Israelites at that time.

LUKE 11:14–28

Healing Miracles in the New Testament

In addition to Jesus, other exorcists (Mt 12:27; Lk 11:19; Ac 19:13) and occasionally magical miracle-workers (Ac 8:9–11) existed. Josephus recounts an exorcist who invoked the name of Solomon to cast out spirits, and Gentiles noted Jewish fortune-tellers and practitioners of magic. Later rabbis also recount two pious Jewish sages, at least one from pre-Christian times, who were known for answered prayer, especially the stopping of rain. (Traditions further embellished the details, but these come from several centuries later.) The closest earlier models for Jesus' ministry of healing and exorcism, though, are the Biblical miracles reported about Elijah and Elisha and, to some extent, Moses. Some other Jewish prophetic figures after Jesus tried to imitate Moses or Joshua, but failed.

Gentile stories about miracle-working figures are further from the example of Jesus than are Jewish accounts. The closest stories are those about Apollonius of Tyana, a first-century Pythagorean sage. The stories about Apollonius's purported miracles, however, derive from a much later, third-century writer — from a time when the Gospels were already in wide circulation. Philostratus, the writer, probably took over some stories about Jesus as well as developed his own. In contrast to Philostratus's stories about Apollonius, the canonical Gospels stem from within living memory of Jesus, while some eyewitnesses remained alive.

No other ancient figure comes close to having the sorts of healings and exorcisms attributed to Jesus, except among his own followers acting in his name. Myths about gods and heroes, such as Asclepius, were written centuries after such figures putatively existed. By contrast, Jesus' miracles appear widely already in Mark's Gospel, within a generation of the events and easily within memory of survivors who had experienced them. They also appear in every other layer of Gospel tradition (including material shared by Matthew and Luke in Mt 11:4–6; 12:28; Lk 7:22; 11:20).

Miracles appear in Acts, and Paul recognizes that recipients of his letters had witnessed miracles through him (2Co 12:12). Even critics of Jesus, such as later rabbis and some pagan authors, recognized that Jesus performed dramatic signs, even though they attribute these to sorcery. In the first century, the Jewish historian Josephus describes Jesus as a miracle-working sage in the same language he used for Elisha. ◆

The Lamp of the Body

11:34,35pp — Mt 6:22,23

33"No one lights a lamp and puts it in
a place where it will be hidden, or under
a bowl. Instead they put it on its stand,
so that those who come in may see the
light.[e] 34Your eye is the lamp of your
body. When your eyes are healthy,[a] your
whole body also is full of light. But when
they are unhealthy,[b] your body also is
full of darkness. 35See to it, then, that the
light within you is not darkness. 36Therefore,
if your whole body is full of light,
and no part of it dark, it will be just as
full of light as when a lamp shines its
light on you."

11:33 [e] Mt 5:15; Mk 4:21; Lk 8:16

[a] 34 The Greek for *healthy* here implies *generous*.
[b] 34 The Greek for *unhealthy* here implies *stingy*.

11:33 *lights a lamp.* See note on 8:16.
11:34 *eyes are healthy ... unhealthy.* Jewish people sometimes spoke of a "good" eye as a generous one, and an "evil" (lit. "unhealthy") eye as a stingy one.
11:35 *light ... not darkness.* Because light cannot be darkness, Jesus again uses shocking language to hold his listeners' attention.

Woes on the Pharisees and the Experts in the Law

[37]When Jesus had finished speaking, a
Pharisee invited him to eat with him; so
he went in and reclined at the table.[f] [38]But
the Pharisee was surprised when he noticed that Jesus did not first wash before
the meal.[g]

[39]Then the Lord[h] said to him, "Now
then, you Pharisees clean the outside of
the cup and dish, but inside you are full
of greed and wickedness.[i] [40]You foolish
people![j] Did not the one who made the
outside make the inside also? [41]But now
as for what is inside you—be generous
to the poor,[k] and everything will be clean
for you.[l]

[42]"Woe to you Pharisees, because you
give God a tenth[m] of your mint, rue and
all other kinds of garden herbs, but you
neglect justice and the love of God.[n] You
should have practiced the latter without
leaving the former undone.[o]

[43]"Woe to you Pharisees, because you
love the most important seats in the synagogues and respectful greetings in the
marketplaces.[p]

[44]"Woe to you, because you are like unmarked graves,[q] which people walk over
without knowing it."

[45]One of the experts in the law[r] answered him, "Teacher, when you say these
things, you insult us also."

[46]Jesus replied, "And you experts in the
law, woe to you, because you load people
down with burdens they can hardly carry,
and you yourselves will not lift one finger
to help them.[s]

[47]"Woe to you, because you build tombs
for the prophets, and it was your ancestors who killed them. [48]So you testify that
you approve of what your ancestors did;
they killed the prophets, and you build
their tombs.[t] [49]Because of this, God in his
wisdom[u] said, 'I will send them prophets
and apostles, some of whom they will kill
and others they will persecute.'[v] [50]There-
fore this generation will be held responsible for the blood of all the prophets that
has been shed since the beginning of the
world, [51]from the blood of Abel[w] to the
blood of Zechariah,[x] who was killed between the altar and the sanctuary. Yes, I
tell you, this generation will be held responsible for it all.[y]

[52]"Woe to you experts in the law, because you have taken away the key to
knowledge. You yourselves have not entered, and you have hindered those who
were entering."[z]

11:37 [f]Lk 7:36; 14:1
11:38 [g]Mk 7:3,4
11:39 [h]Lk 7:13 [i]Mt 23:25,26; Mk 7:20-23
11:40 [j]Lk 12:20; 1Co 15:36
11:41 [k]Lk 12:33 [l]Ac 10:15
11:42 [m]Lk 18:12 [n]Dt 6:5; Mic 6:8 [o]Mt 23:23
11:43 [p]Mt 23:6,7; Mk 12:38-39; Lk 14:7; 20:46
11:44 [q]Mt 23:27
11:45 [r]Mt 22:35
11:46 [s]Mt 23:4
11:48 [t]Mt 23:29-32; Ac 7:51-53
11:49 [u]1Co 1:24, 30; Col 2:3 [v]Mt 23:34
11:51 [w]Ge 4:8 [x]2Ch 24:20,21 [y]Mt 23:35,36
11:52 [z]Mt 23:13

11:37 *Pharisee invited him to eat.* As often urban residents with some education, Pharisees were better off economically than Galilean peasants. It was considered an honor to host a famous teacher for a meal.
11:38 *wash.* Pharisees were scrupulous about their customs, including that of washing hands (see note on Mk 7:3).
11:39 *clean the outside.* First-century Pharisees debated whether to cleanse the inside or outside of a cup first. Shammaites doubted that it mattered either way, but Hillelites required cleaning the inside first. Jesus appears to agree with the Hillelites here (v. 40), but unlike the Pharisaic debate he speaks figuratively about the human heart.
11:41 *be generous to the poor.* Here Luke differs from Matthew's "clean" in the parallel text (Mt 23:26), but it is possible that Jesus said something of both in Aramaic and offered a wordplay: Luke's version reflects the Aramaic *zakkau*, and Matthew's the similar-sounding *dakkau*.
11:42 *Woe.* "Woes" could function as laments or mourning, but prophets often used "woes" as creative ways to pronounce impending judgment (cf. 18:7; Isa 5:18–23; cf. mocking laments in Isa 15:5; 16:11; Jer 48:36; 51:8). *a tenth of your mint.* Pharisees were known for their scrupulousness on tithing (see note on Mt 23:23). Because tithes were on food, however, Pharisees in this period debated whether spices such as mint counted (later rabbis decided they did not). Jesus here speaks of a hyperbolic Pharisee, even more scrupulous than normal. Fixated on details, they missed the heart of the law (for earlier summaries, see Dt 10:12–13; Mic 6:8).
11:43 *most important seats.* Throughout the Mediterranean world, people were usually seated according to their social rank; prominent members of the community thus received honor (see note on Mt 23:6). *respectful greetings in the marketplaces.* Social convention stipulated that social inferiors should greet superiors first; because in villages and towns people congregated especially in marketplaces, this location would provide opportunity for many greetings.
11:44 *unmarked graves … walk over.* According to Jewish tradition, if so much as one's shadow touched even a tomb, one incurred ritual impurity. Tombs were marked to warn, e.g., Passover pilgrims coming to Jerusalem for the festival, lest the pilgrims incur ritual impurity by touching the tombs.
11:45 *experts in the law.* Not all were Pharisees, though because Pharisees were scrupulous in the law many of them held this role.
11:46 *not lift one finger.* The idea of offering a mere finger to help with a heavy burden is hyperbole.
11:47,48 *ancestors.* In this period Jerusalem was building many tombs to honor prophetic figures. People employed the phrase "descendants of" literally, but also figuratively for those who acted like their ancestors; Jesus plays on these two senses here.
11:50 *blood of all the prophets.* Jewish tradition acknowledged and even amplified the OT record of persecuted prophets.
11:51 *blood of Abel to the blood of Zechariah.* According to a common Jewish arrangement of the Scriptures, Abel would have been the first martyr in the OT and Zechariah the last in the OT. Abel's blood cried out for vengeance against his killer (Ge 4:10; contrast Heb 11:4; 12:24). As Zechariah was being murdered, he cried out for vengeance (2Ch 24:22). In one Jewish tradition, a fountain of blood spurted up from the site of his murder, inviting judgment for generations until the Babylonians conquered Jerusalem. Only then did the people plead with God to forgive them for the blood of Zechariah, and only then did the fountain stop.

53When Jesus went outside, the Pharisees and the teachers of the law began
to oppose him fiercely and to besiege him
with questions, 54waiting to catch him in
something he might say.[a]

Warnings and Encouragements

12:2-9pp — Mt 10:26-33

12 Meanwhile, when a crowd of many
thousands had gathered, so that
they were trampling on one another, Jesus
began to speak first to his disciples, saying: "Be[a] on your guard against the yeast
of the Pharisees, which is hypocrisy.[b]
2There is nothing concealed that will not
be disclosed, or hidden that will not be
made known.[c] 3What you have said in
the dark will be heard in the daylight, and
what you have whispered in the ear in the
inner rooms will be proclaimed from the
roofs.
4"I tell you, my friends,[d] do not be
afraid of those who kill the body and after
that can do no more. 5But I will show you
whom you should fear: Fear him who, after your body has been killed, has authority to throw you into hell. Yes, I tell you,
fear him.[e] 6Are not five sparrows sold for
two pennies? Yet not one of them is forgotten by God. 7Indeed, the very hairs of
your head are all numbered.[f] Don't be
afraid; you are worth more than many
sparrows.[g]
8"I tell you, whoever publicly acknowledges me before others, the Son of Man
will also acknowledge before the angels
of God.[h] 9But whoever disowns me before
others will be disowned[i] before the angels
of God. 10And everyone who speaks a word
against the Son of Man[j] will be forgiven,
but anyone who blasphemes against the
Holy Spirit will not be forgiven.[k]
11"When you are brought before synagogues, rulers and authorities, do not
worry about how you will defend yourselves or what you will say,[l] 12for the Holy
Spirit will teach you at that time what you
should say."[m]

The Parable of the Rich Fool

13Someone in the crowd said to him,
"Teacher, tell my brother to divide the inheritance with me."
14Jesus replied, "Man, who appointed
me a judge or an arbiter between you?"
15Then he said to them, "Watch out! Be
on your guard against all kinds of greed;
life does not consist in an abundance of
possessions."[n]
16And he told them this parable: "The
ground of a certain rich man yielded an
abundant harvest. 17He thought to himself, 'What shall I do? I have no place to
store my crops.'
18"Then he said, 'This is what I'll do.
I will tear down my barns and build bigger ones, and there I will store my surplus
grain. 19And I'll say to myself, "You have
plenty of grain laid up for many years.
Take life easy; eat, drink and be merry." '
20"But God said to him, 'You fool![o] This
very night your life will be demanded
from you.[p] Then who will get what you
have prepared for yourself?'[q]
21"This is how it will be with whoever
stores up things for themselves but is not
rich toward God."[r]

11:54 [a] Mt 12:10; Mk 12:13
12:1 [b] Mt 16:6, 11, 12; Mk 8:15
12:2 [c] Mk 4:22; Lk 8:17
12:4 [d] Jn 15:14, 15
12:5 [e] Heb 10:31
12:7 [f] Mt 10:30 [g] Mt 12:12
12:8 [h] Lk 15:10
12:9 [i] Mk 8:38; 2Ti 2:12
12:10 [j] Mt 8:20 [k] Mt 12:31, 32; Mk 3:28-29; 1Jn 5:16
12:11 [l] Mt 10:17, 19; Mk 13:11; Lk 21:12, 14
12:12 [m] Ex 4:12; Mt 10:20; Mk 13:11; Lk 21:15
12:15 [n] Job 20:20; 31:24; Ps 62:10
12:20 [o] Jer 17:11; Lk 11:40 [p] Job 27:8 [q] Ps 39:6; 49:10
12:21 [r] ver 33

[a] 1 Or *speak to his disciples, saying: "First of all, be*

11:54 *waiting to catch him in something he might say.* In a culture emphasizing honor, those who were publicly insulted could recoup honor only by humiliating the one who dishonored them.
12:1 *many thousands.* Few towns had more than 3,000 residents; most villages had only a few hundred. *yeast.* Known for spreading and pervading its sphere of influence.
12:3 *from the roofs.* The roofs of Galilean homes were flat, and people could work or rest there. There one's voice could carry above the street unobstructed by buildings.
12:5 *hell.* Often envisioned by Jewish people as a place of fiery torment (see note on Mt 3:12; see also Gehinnom).
12:6 *five sparrows sold for two pennies.* The poor could purchase sparrows, probably the cheapest meat in the market. *pennies.* The penny is an *assarion,* worth less than an hour's wage for the average worker; probably one received a slight discount for purchasing a larger quantity (hence the price is very close in Mt 10:29).
12:7 *hairs of your head.* A promise that not a hair would fall meant that one would be completely protected (1Sa 14:45; 2Sa 14:11; 1Ki 1:52); here, God knows and cares about every detail.
12:8 *before the angels of God.* May suggest "on the day of judgment," or in the heavenly court.
12:11 *before synagogues.* As community centers, synagogues also hosted local legal proceedings and punishments.
12:12 *Holy Spirit will teach you.* Often the OT and even more commonly early Judaism associated the Holy Spirit with prophetic enablement or divine revelation.
12:13 – 15 Inheritance disputes were common (though far more among Gentiles) and they sometimes divided families. Although in Jewish teaching the eldest son received a double portion (Dt 21:17), disputes still arose and rabbis, as experts in the law, were sometimes called to resolve them. For Jesus to treat a normally legitimate legal recourse here as a sign of greed seems to radically value relationships over property (see 6:29 – 30).
12:18 Wealthy landowners often lived in cities or on estates while impoverished tenant farmers worked their land. Excavations show that the landowners often built large silos to hold excess grain. Scripture warned against merely storing grain when others were hungry (Pr 11:26).
12:19 *eat, drink and be merry.* Echoes Isa 22:13, where one celebrates today, deliberately neglecting the impending reckoning with death that is coming tomorrow. Epicurean philosophers were criticized as advocating this lifestyle, but it characterized many people who could afford it.

Do Not Worry

12:22-31pp — Mt 6:25-33

22 Then Jesus said to his disciples:
"Therefore I tell you, do not worry about
your life, what you will eat; or about your
body, what you will wear. 23 For life is
more than food, and the body more than
clothes. 24 Consider the ravens: They do
not sow or reap, they have no storeroom
or barn; yet God feeds them.[s] And how
much more valuable you are than birds!
25 Who of you by worrying can add a single hour to your life[a]? 26 Since you cannot
do this very little thing, why do you worry
about the rest?

27 "Consider how the wild flowers grow.
They do not labor or spin. Yet I tell you,
not even Solomon in all his splendor[t] was
dressed like one of these. 28 If that is how
God clothes the grass of the field, which is
here today, and tomorrow is thrown into
the fire, how much more will he clothe
you — you of little faith![u] 29 And do not set
your heart on what you will eat or drink;
do not worry about it. 30 For the pagan
world runs after all such things, and your
Father[v] knows that you need them.[w] 31 But
seek his kingdom,[x] and these things will
be given to you as well.[y]

32 "Do not be afraid,[z] little flock, for your
Father has been pleased to give you the
kingdom.[a] 33 Sell your possessions and
give to the poor.[b] Provide purses for yourselves that will not wear out, a treasure in
heaven[c] that will never fail, where no thief
comes near and no moth destroys.[d] 34 For
where your treasure is, there your heart
will be also.[e]

12:24 [s] Job 38:41; Ps 147:9 **12:27** [t] 1Ki 10:4-7 **12:28** [u] Mt 6:30 **12:30** [v] Lk 6:36 [w] Mt 6:8 **12:31** [x] Mt 3:2 [y] Mt 19:29 **12:32** [z] Mt 14:27 [a] Mt 25:34 **12:33** [b] Mt 19:21; Ac 2:45 [c] Mt 6:20 [d] Jas 5:2 **12:34** [e] Mt 6:21

12:37 [f] Mt 24:42, 46; 25:13 [g] Mt 20:28 **12:39** [h] Mt 6:19; 1Th 5:2; 2Pe 3:10; Rev 3:3; 16:15 **12:40** [i] Mk 13:33; Lk 21:36 **12:42** [j] Lk 7:13

Watchfulness

12:35,36pp — Mt 25:1-13; Mk 13:33-37
12:39,40; 42-46pp — Mt 24:43-51

35 "Be dressed ready for service and
keep your lamps burning, 36 like servants
waiting for their master to return from a
wedding banquet, so that when he comes
and knocks they can immediately open
the door for him. 37 It will be good for
those servants whose master finds them
watching when he comes.[f] Truly I tell you,
he will dress himself to serve, will have
them recline at the table and will come
and wait on them.[g] 38 It will be good for
those servants whose master finds them
ready, even if he comes in the middle of
the night or toward daybreak. 39 But understand this: If the owner of the house
had known at what hour the thief[h] was
coming, he would not have let his house
be broken into. 40 You also must be ready,[i]
because the Son of Man will come at an
hour when you do not expect him."

41 Peter asked, "Lord, are you telling this
parable to us, or to everyone?"

42 The Lord[j] answered, "Who then is
the faithful and wise manager, whom
the master puts in charge of his servants
to give them their food allowance at the
proper time? 43 It will be good for that
servant whom the master finds doing so
when he returns. 44 Truly I tell you, he will
put him in charge of all his possessions.
45 But suppose the servant says to himself,
'My master is taking a long time in coming,' and he then begins to beat the other

[a] 25 Or *single cubit to your height*

12:24 *Consider the ravens.* Nature had long been an interest of wise teachers (1Ki 4:33), and both Greek and Jewish sages often illustrated points from nature. Jewish people recognized God's providential rule over all of nature. Cf. the permanence of God's Word versus the transitory nature of grass and flowers in Isa 40:6 – 8.

12:31 *seek his kingdom.* Most people in the ancient world were poor, dependent on harvests for food. Some estimate that roughly half lacked resources beyond the subsistence level and so were at risk of potential starvation in times of famine. Naturally, people sought basic necessities; Jesus invited them to trust their heavenly Father enough to seek instead his kingdom. (Jesus is not against working but in his graphic way underlines the great priority of the kingdom; cf. 9:3.) Various opinions circulated regarding how to bring about God's kingdom; some urged violence, others radical obedience, still others passive waiting for God's time. Jesus says to seek it but with confidence in God, because God will give it (v. 32).

12:32 *little flock.* God's people were referred to as his flock (Ps 78:52; Isa 40:11; Mic 2:12; 5:4).

12:33 *treasure in heaven.* Used by Jewish people to speak of divine rewards, normally in the world to come.

12:35 *Be dressed ready.* Lit. "Let your waist be girded up"; long outer robes would have to be tucked up to allow legs to move quickly. Jesus borrows the language of Israel preparing for deliverance in Ex 12:11. *lamps.* Cf. perhaps Mt 25:2 – 4 (see note on Mt 25:4).

12:36 *return from a wedding banquet.* Wedding celebrations could start after dark and last late into the night. *open the door.* Homeowners who could afford outer gates often would have servants assigned to guard the gates.

12:37 *he will dress himself to serve.* Jesus' image here (and in 22:27) is jarring. Apart from one Roman festival that deliberately and temporarily inverted the social order, slaves always served slaveholders, never the reverse.

12:40 *when you do not expect him.* Many believed that God alone knew the time planned for the Messiah's coming.

12:42 *faithful and wise manager.* Slaves could sometimes be entrusted with great authority; household managers were often high-level slaves.

12:45 *beat the other servants … eat and drink and get drunk.* A common story line, appearing also in some Jewish parables, was the temptation posed when a ruler, master or husband went on a long journey. In the stories, the person often returned and caught someone unprepared. Gluttony and drunkenness were often associated with squandering. A slave exploiting fellow slaves and carousing with the master's resources would be punished harshly.

servants, both men and women, and to eat and drink and get drunk. 46The master of that servant will come on a day when he does not expect him and at an hour he is not aware of.[k] He will cut him to pieces and assign him a place with the unbelievers.

47"The servant who knows the master's will and does not get ready or does not do what the master wants will be beaten with many blows.[l] 48But the one who does not know and does things deserving punishment will be beaten with few blows.[m] From everyone who has been given much, much will be demanded; and from the one who has been entrusted with much, much more will be asked.

Not Peace but Division

12:51-53pp — Mt 10:34-36

49"I have come to bring fire on the earth, and how I wish it were already kindled! 50But I have a baptism[n] to undergo, and what constraint I am under until it is completed![o] 51Do you think I came to bring peace on earth? No, I tell you, but division. 52From now on there will be five in one family divided against each other, three against two and two against three. 53They will be divided, father against son and son against father, mother against daughter and daughter against mother, mother-in-law against daughter-in-law and daughter-in-law against mother-in-law."[p]

12:46 [k]ver 40 **12:47** [l]Dt 25:2 **12:48** [m]Lev 5:17; Nu 15:27-30 **12:50** [n]Mk 10:38 [o]Jn 19:30 **12:53** [p]Mic 7:6; Mt 10:21

Interpreting the Times

54He said to the crowd: "When you see a cloud rising in the west, immediately you say, 'It's going to rain,' and it does.[q] 55And when the south wind blows, you say, 'It's going to be hot,' and it is. 56Hypocrites! You know how to interpret the appearance of the earth and the sky. How is it that you don't know how to interpret this present time?[r]

57"Why don't you judge for yourselves what is right? 58As you are going with your adversary to the magistrate, try hard to be reconciled on the way, or your adversary may drag you off to the judge, and the judge turn you over to the officer, and the officer throw you into prison.[s] 59I tell you, you will not get out until you have paid the last penny."[t]

Repent or Perish

13 Now there were some present at that time who told Jesus about the Galileans whose blood Pilate[u] had mixed with their sacrifices. 2Jesus answered, "Do you think that these Galileans were worse sinners than all the other Galileans because they suffered this way?[v] 3I tell you, no! But unless you repent, you too will all perish. 4Or those eighteen who died when the tower in Siloam[w] fell on them — do you think they were more guilty than all the others living in Jerusalem? 5I tell you, no! But unless you repent,[x] you too will all perish."

12:54 [q]Mt 16:2 **12:56** [r]Mt 16:3 **12:58** [s]Mt 5:25 **12:59** [t]Mt 5:26; Mk 12:42 **13:1** [u]Mt 27:2 **13:2** [v]Jn 9:2,3 **13:4** [w]Jn 9:7,11 **13:5** [x]Mt 3:2; Ac 2:38

12:46 *cut him to pieces.* People regarded dismemberment as a terrible punishment, often inflicted just before (for partial dismemberment) or during or after execution.
12:49 *fire.* May connote the promised day of judgment (cf. Isa 66:15 – 16,24), or Jesus' experience of this on others' behalf (cf. v. 50).
12:50 *baptism.* If Jesus refers here to the "baptism" with fire (3:16; cf. v. 49) he may be suggesting that he will first experience the judgment in others' place.
12:51 *division.* Many Jewish people expected the Messiah to bring war against the Gentiles, but Jesus here warns instead that his requirements would bring division within households.
12:52 – 53 Because Mic 7:6 addresses grievous sins that were characteristic of Israel before he announces Israel's restoration, Jewish tradition sometimes applied the same image of familial division to the final tribulation.
12:53 *mother-in-law against daughter-in-law.* Because newly married couples sometimes lived with the groom's family, daughter-in-law and mother-in-law are natural examples of familial strife (more than, e.g., son-in-law). Cf., however, note on 1:17.
12:54 *cloud rising in the west.* In Judea, rain came from the Mediterranean Sea in the west.
12:55 *south wind.* Hot air came from the desert regions to the south of Judea (and especially from the southeast). Through much of the Mediterranean world, winds from the south bring heat.
12:56 *Hypocrites!* Some scholars note that "hypocrite" means "play-actor"; by this period, though, it meant anyone acting in pretense, including for insincere religious activity (Sirach 1:29; 32:15; 33:2).
12:57 *Why don't you judge ...?* It was common for a speaker to challenge his audience to decide for themselves, after the speaker made clear what the right decision should be.
12:58 – 59 Some think this parable uses the image of debt imprisonment, a Gentile custom normally forbidden in Jewish circles in this period. (The term for "officer" here sometimes refers to one who runs a debtor's prison.)
12:59 *penny.* Here the Greek *lepton*; it took 128 of these to amount to a denarius, roughly a day's wage. A *lepton* was thus only a few minutes' wage for an average male worker. It was half of a quadrans (see Mt 5:26 and note), but the thought is the same in both passages: without forgiveness, one will not escape until all is paid.
13:1 *Galileans whose blood Pilate had mixed with their sacrifices.* Pilate was known for his brutality and had massacred people in Jerusalem on other occasions (Josephus, *Antiquities* 18.60 – 62). Crowds were heavy and sometimes out of control at festivals and both Pilate and Galileans were present then. *sacrifices.* People brought lambs for sacrifice at Passover.
13:2 *worse sinners.* People often assumed that, at least in many cases, those who suffered were being punished for sin.
13:4 *tower in Siloam.* Probably on the wall near the Pool of Siloam (Ne 3:15; cf. Jn 9:7,11).

6Then he told this parable: "A man had
a fig tree growing in his vineyard, and he
went to look for fruit on it but did not find
any.[y] 7So he said to the man who took care
of the vineyard, 'For three years now I've
been coming to look for fruit on this fig
tree and haven't found any. Cut it down![z]
Why should it use up the soil?'
8"'Sir,' the man replied, 'leave it alone
for one more year, and I'll dig around it
and fertilize it. 9If it bears fruit next year,
fine! If not, then cut it down.'"

Jesus Heals a Crippled Woman on the Sabbath

10On a Sabbath Jesus was teaching in
one of the synagogues,[a] 11and a woman
was there who had been crippled by a
spirit for eighteen years.[b] She was bent
over and could not straighten up at all.
12When Jesus saw her, he called her forward and said to her, "Woman, you are set
free from your infirmity." 13Then he put
his hands on her,[c] and immediately she
straightened up and praised God.
14Indignant because Jesus had healed
on the Sabbath,[d] the synagogue leader[e]
said to the people, "There are six days for
work.[f] So come and be healed on those
days, not on the Sabbath."
15The Lord answered him, "You hypocrites! Doesn't each of you on the Sabbath
untie your ox or donkey from the stall and
lead it out to give it water?[g] 16Then should
not this woman, a daughter of Abraham,[h]
whom Satan[i] has kept bound for eighteen
long years, be set free on the Sabbath day
from what bound her?"
17When he said this, all his opponents
were humiliated,[j] but the people were delighted with all the wonderful things he
was doing.

The Parables of the Mustard Seed and the Yeast

13:18,19pp — Mk 4:30-32
13:18-21pp — Mt 13:31-33

18Then Jesus asked, "What is the kingdom of God[k] like?[l] What shall I compare
it to? 19It is like a mustard seed, which a
man took and planted in his garden. It
grew and became a tree,[m] and the birds
perched in its branches."[n]
20Again he asked, "What shall I compare
the kingdom of God to? 21It is like yeast
that a woman took and mixed into about
sixty pounds[a] of flour until it worked all
through the dough."[o]

The Narrow Door

22Then Jesus went through the towns and
villages, teaching as he made his way to Jerusalem.[p] 23Someone asked him, "Lord, are
only a few people going to be saved?"
He said to them, 24"Make every effort to
enter through the narrow door,[q] because
many, I tell you, will try to enter and will
not be able to. 25Once the owner of the
house gets up and closes the door, you
will stand outside knocking and pleading,
'Sir, open the door for us.'

13:6 [y] Isa 5:2; Jer 8:13; Mt 21:19 **13:7** [z] Mt 3:10 **13:10** [a] Mt 4:23 **13:11** [b] ver 16 **13:13** [c] Mk 5:23 **13:14** [d] Mt 12:2; Lk 14:3 [e] Mk 5:22 [f] Ex 20:9 **13:15** [g] Lk 14:5 **13:16** [h] Lk 3:8; 19:9 [i] Mt 4:10 **13:17** [j] Isa 66:5 **13:18** [k] Mt 3:2 [l] Mt 13:24 **13:19** [m] Lk 17:6 [n] Mt 13:32 **13:21** [o] 1Co 5:6 **13:22** [p] Lk 9:51 **13:24** [q] Mt 7:13

[a] *21* Or about 27 kilograms

13:6 Fig trees were sometimes planted in Judean and Galilean vineyards.
13:7 *three years.* Fig trees sometimes took four or five years to yield fruit. *Cut it down!* The cutting probably also implies uprooting, commonly done to allow other plants (here perhaps more vines) to grow.
13:8 *fertilize it.* Manuring was common but not usually needed for fig trees; the worker does everything possible to ensure the tree's survival.
13:10 Local synagogues commonly invited respected teachers to lecture.
13:14 *healed on the Sabbath.* In general, Jewish teachers felt that whatever one could do before the Sabbath should not be done on the Sabbath. Life-saving procedures were acceptable; other medical treatments on the Sabbath were debated. Jesus does not apply medicine, but some objected to laying on of hands (v. 13) on the Sabbath. The Pharisaic school of Hillel permitted prayer for the sick on the Sabbath; the dominant Pharisaic school, the Shammaites, rejected this (but did not persecute Hillelites).
13:15 *untie your ox or donkey.* Even strict observers of the Torah, such as the Pharisees, who normally forbade tying or releasing knots on the Sabbath, permitted this for taking animals out to let them drink on the Sabbath.
13:17 *humiliated.* Those who were publicly shamed would normally seek to recoup their honor by, if possible, humiliating the one who embarrassed them.
13:18 *What shall I compare it to?* Rabbis often began parables with such phrases.
13:19 *mustard seed.* Scholars do not all agree about which plant is in view here, but ancient sources agree in describing the mustard seed as proverbially small. Some argue that this shrub often grew eight to ten feet (two and a half to three meters) high around the Sea of Galilee; others argue that the likeliest shrub in view rarely grew to more than five feet (one and a half meters) high. If so, birds could only perch in its branches (not literally "nest," as the Greek term typically implies); the incongruity of the literal image highlights the background that Jesus evokes here. His language evokes a great kingdom of old that would be supplanted by God's kingdom (Da 4:12), and thus is appropriate for the greatest kingdom of all, namely God's. The glorious future kingdom was already active in a hidden way in Jesus' ministry.
13:21 *yeast.* Some Jewish texts used yeast to symbolize evil, but it did not always mean that (Ge 19:3; Ex 12:11,39; Lev 23:17) and does not mean that here. Although bakeries might prepare large amounts of bread, Jesus refers to a Galilean housewife. The amount here is thus exorbitant: her labor would produce enough bread to feed more than 100 people.
13:24 *through the narrow door.* Many mainstream Jews felt that most Jews would be saved, but some, like Jesus, warned that most people would be lost (e.g., the later apocalyptic author of 4 Ezra). See note on Mt 7:13 – 14.

"But he will answer, 'I don't know you
or where you come from.'[r]
26"Then you will say, 'We ate and drank
with you, and you taught in our streets.'
27"But he will reply, 'I don't know you
or where you come from. Away from me,
all you evildoers!'[s]
28"There will be weeping there, and
gnashing of teeth,[t] when you see Abraham, Isaac and Jacob and all the prophets
in the kingdom of God, but you yourselves
thrown out. 29People will come from east
and west[u] and north and south, and will
take their places at the feast in the kingdom of God. 30Indeed there are those who
are last who will be first, and first who
will be last."[v]

Jesus' Sorrow for Jerusalem

13:34,35pp — Mt 23:37-39
13:34,35Ref — Lk 19:41

31At that time some Pharisees came to
Jesus and said to him, "Leave this place
and go somewhere else. Herod[w] wants to
kill you."
32He replied, "Go tell that fox, 'I will
keep on driving out demons and healing
people today and tomorrow, and on the
third day I will reach my goal.'[x] 33In any
case, I must press on today and tomorrow
and the next day — for surely no prophet[y]
can die outside Jerusalem!

13:25 [r] Mt 7:23; 25:10-12
13:27 [s] Mt 7:23; 25:41
13:28 [t] Mt 8:12
13:29 [u] Mt 8:11
13:30 [v] Mt 19:30
13:31 [w] Mt 14:1
13:32 [x] Heb 2:10
13:33 [y] Mt 21:11
13:34 [z] Mt 23:37
13:35 [a] Jer 12:17; 22:5 [b] Ps 118:26; Mt 21:9; Lk 19:38
14:1 [c] Lk 7:36; 11:37 [d] Mt 12:10
14:3 [e] Mt 22:35 [f] Mt 12:2
14:5 [g] Lk 13:15
14:7 [h] Lk 11:43

34"Jerusalem, Jerusalem, you who kill
the prophets and stone those sent to you,
how often I have longed to gather your
children together, as a hen gathers her
chicks under her wings,[z] and you were
not willing. 35Look, your house is left to
you desolate.[a] I tell you, you will not see
me again until you say, 'Blessed is he who
comes in the name of the Lord.'[a]"[b]

Jesus at a Pharisee's House

14:8-10Ref — Pr 25:6,7

14 One Sabbath, when Jesus went
to eat in the house of a prominent Pharisee,[c] he was being carefully
watched.[d] 2There in front of him was a
man suffering from abnormal swelling of
his body. 3Jesus asked the Pharisees and
experts in the law,[e] "Is it lawful to heal
on the Sabbath or not?"[f] 4But they remained silent. So taking hold of the man,
he healed him and sent him on his way.
5Then he asked them, "If one of you has
a child[b] or an ox that falls into a well on
the Sabbath day, will you not immediately pull it out?"[g] 6And they had nothing to
say.
7When he noticed how the guests
picked the places of honor at the table,[h] he
told them this parable: 8"When someone

[a] *35* Psalm 118:26 [b] *5* Some manuscripts *donkey*

13:26 *We ate and drank with you.* Eating with people produced a covenant relationship of friendship. In this case, however, it is those protesting who betrayed this relationship (see "evildoers" in v. 27).
13:27 *I don't know you.* To deny knowing a person or where they are from was a recognized formula of repudiation and rejection.
13:28 *weeping.* People would weep over their damnation (Judith 16:17). *gnashing of teeth.* Can depict anger (Job 16:9; Ps 35:16; 37:12; 112:10) but here may reflect anguish. *when you see Abraham … but you yourselves thrown out.* Many believed that descent from Abraham (3:8) ensured their admittance to the banquet (v. 29); they expected to be with the patriarchs and prophets.
13:29 Jewish people expected a banquet for the righteous in God's end-time kingdom (cf. Isa 25:6). *east … west … north … south.* Could include Jews in the Diaspora (Isa 43:5) but presumably includes Gentiles also (Isa 25:6 – 7; 56:3 – 8).
13:30 *last … first.* Many Jewish thinkers expected the coming age to reverse current fortunes: the lowly would be exalted and the exalted brought low. Most Jewish people expected that God would exalt Israel and punish their Gentile oppressors.
13:31 *Herod wants to kill you.* The Sanhedrin in Jerusalem could not legally execute anyone without Roman permission; Herod Antipas, however, was a tetrarch and could execute whom he chose (9:9). Pharisees supported justice and leniency and they rejected extrajudicial executions; these Pharisees are trying to help Jesus.
13:32 *Go tell that fox.* Foxes were considered cunning, shrewd, and often treacherous and deceitful; most importantly here, they were destructive and were a threat to small domestic livestock (v. 34).
13:33 *no prophet can die outside Jerusalem.* This is hyperbole, but the holy city had a record of killing prophets (e.g., 2Ch 24:21; Jer 26:23), amplified further in Jewish tradition.
13:34 *under her wings.* In the OT and Jewish tradition, God sheltered his people under his wings (Ps 17:8; 36:7; 57:1; 61:4; 63:7; 91:4); some Jewish traditions even spoke of Gentile converts as coming "under the wings of God's presence." Jesus here assumes that divine role.
13:35 *your house is … desolate.* Jesus refers here to the temple's desolation (fulfilled roughly 40 years later, in AD 70) brought about by its desecration. *Blessed is he.* Ps 118:26 was familiar as one of the psalms (Ps 113 – 118) sung during festival season.
14:1 *house of a prominent Pharisee.* It was an honor to host a famous teacher for a meal; Jesus probably lectured in the local synagogue.
14:2 *in front of him.* If the meal has begun, this suggests that he was a guest reclining on a nearby couch (though cf. "sent him on his way" in v. 4). *abnormal swelling of his body.* Ancient physicians knew of this condition, which is called edema.
14:3 *heal on the Sabbath.* See note on 13:14.
14:5 *falls into a well.* People often dug pits to secure ground water or to capture predators, but sometimes their own animals fell into them. Unlike Essenes, who were stricter, Pharisees and most other people did try to help their animals out of pits on the Sabbath, sometimes using a rope.
14:7 *picked the places of honor.* Teachers sometimes lectured or dialogued with disciples or others in banquet settings. People were usually seated according to social rank at banquets; their seating affected others' perceptions of their honor.

invites you to a wedding feast, do not take
the place of honor, for a person more distinguished than you may have been invited. 9If so, the host who invited both of
you will come and say to you, 'Give this
person your seat.' Then, humiliated, you
will have to take the least important place.
10But when you are invited, take the lowest place, so that when your host comes,
he will say to you, 'Friend, move up to a
better place.' Then you will be honored in
the presence of all the other guests. 11For
all those who exalt themselves will be
humbled, and those who humble themselves will be exalted."[i]

12Then Jesus said to his host, "When
you give a luncheon or dinner, do not invite your friends, your brothers or sisters,
your relatives, or your rich neighbors; if
you do, they may invite you back and so
you will be repaid. 13But when you give a
banquet, invite the poor, the crippled, the
lame, the blind,[j] 14and you will be blessed.
Although they cannot repay you, you will
be repaid at the resurrection of the righteous."[k]

The Parable of the Great Banquet

14:16-24Ref — Mt 22:2-14

15When one of those at the table with
him heard this, he said to Jesus, "Blessed
is the one who will eat at the feast[l] in the
kingdom of God."[m]

16Jesus replied: "A certain man was preparing a great banquet and invited many
guests. 17At the time of the banquet he sent
his servant to tell those who had been invited, 'Come, for everything is now ready.'

18"But they all alike began to make excuses. The first said, 'I have just bought
a field, and I must go and see it. Please
excuse me.'

19"Another said, 'I have just bought five
yoke of oxen, and I'm on my way to try
them out. Please excuse me.'

20"Still another said, 'I just got married,
so I can't come.'

21"The servant came back and reported
this to his master. Then the owner of the
house became angry and ordered his servant, 'Go out quickly into the streets and
alleys of the town and bring in the poor,
the crippled, the blind and the lame.'[n]

22" 'Sir,' the servant said, 'what you
ordered has been done, but there is still
room.'

23"Then the master told his servant, 'Go
out to the roads and country lanes and
compel them to come in, so that my house
will be full. 24I tell you, not one of those
who were invited will get a taste of my
banquet.' "[o]

The Cost of Being a Disciple

25Large crowds were traveling with
Jesus, and turning to them he said: 26"If
anyone comes to me and does not hate father and mother, wife and children, brothers and sisters — yes, even their own life —
such a person cannot be my disciple.[p]
27And whoever does not carry their cross
and follow me cannot be my disciple.[q]

14:11 [i] Mt 23:12; Lk 18:14
14:13 [j] ver 21
14:14 [k] Ac 24:15
14:15 [l] Isa 25:6; Mt 26:29; Lk 13:29; Rev 19:9 [m] Mt 3:2
14:21 [n] ver 13
14:24 [o] Mt 21:43; Ac 13:46
14:26 [p] Mt 10:37; Jn 12:25
14:27 [q] Mt 10:38; Lk 9:23

14:10 Jesus uses the same principle from Pr 25:6 – 7 (especially v. 7, "Come up here"), already well-known (if not always observed) among his contemporaries.
14:11 *those who exalt themselves will be humbled.* Many Jewish people expected a reversal of current status in the time of the end, when the lowly would be exalted and the exalted brought low (already in the OT, e.g., Isa 2:11 – 12).
14:12 *do not invite your friends.* Peers would be offended not to be invited and given the best places to recline. People of status often invited to their banquets people of somewhat lower status (such as clients), but not the destitute and those who made a living by begging (v. 13).
14:14 *resurrection.* See the article "Resurrection," p. 2012.
14:15 *the feast in the kingdom.* Many Jewish people expected a banquet in the kingdom (cf. already Isa 25:6, in the context of swallowing up death in Isa 25:8).
14:16 *many guests.* A person of status could increase his honor by inviting many guests to a banquet — provided they showed up. The more respectable the guests, the greater the host's honor (though no one of higher rank than his peers would normally come).
14:17 *everything is now ready.* Invitees would have responded to the first invitation already; it was common for such invitations to require a response in advance. The message sent now simply informs the guests that the banquet, which has required much preparation, is now ready for them.
14:18 *field … see it.* One normally would inspect a field before buying it.
14:19 *five yoke of oxen.* Only a person of wealth with many fields would buy five yoke of oxen. *try them out.* One normally tested oxen *before* buying them.
14:20 *just got married.* Weddings were planned far in advance, so the new husband knew about the conflict before he agreed to come (see note on v. 17). Each of the excuses in vv. 18 – 20 is so weak that it would insult the host; together, it is clear that the excuses constitute deliberate dishonor.
14:21 *alleys.* Poorer areas of a city usually had very narrow alleys. *bring in the poor, the crippled, the blind and the lame.* The refusals would publicly embarrass the host and waste the prepared banquet. The attendance of people of significantly lower status might not compensate fully, but he would recoup some of his lost honor, gaining a reputation for generosity in the community. People of status virtually never invited people who were beggars to banquets; people who were disabled often were forced to make their living as beggars.
14:26 *hate.* Given the emphasis on family in the culture, Jesus' demands would be very offensive, even though hearers would probably understand "hate" as hyperbole (cf. Matt 10:37).
14:27 *carry their cross.* Those condemned to execution would often carry the horizontal beam of their cross (the *patibulum*) out to the site of their execution, through an

28“Suppose one of you wants to build
a tower. Won’t you first sit down and estimate the cost to see if you have enough
money to complete it? 29For if you lay the
foundation and are not able to finish it,
everyone who sees it will ridicule you,
30saying, ‘This person began to build and
wasn’t able to finish.’

31“Or suppose a king is about to go to
war against another king. Won’t he first
sit down and consider whether he is able
with ten thousand men to oppose the one
coming against him with twenty thousand? 32If he is not able, he will send a
delegation while the other is still a long
way off and will ask for terms of peace.
33In the same way, those of you who do
not give up everything you have cannot
be my disciples.[r]

34“Salt is good, but if it loses its saltiness, how can it be made salty again?[s] 35It
is fit neither for the soil nor for the manure
pile; it is thrown out.[t]

“Whoever has ears to hear, let them
hear.”[u]

The Parable of the Lost Sheep

15:4-7pp — Mt 18:12-14

15 Now the tax collectors[v] and sinners
were all gathering around to hear
Jesus. 2But the Pharisees and the teachers
of the law muttered, “This man welcomes
sinners and eats with them.”[w]

3Then Jesus told them this parable:[x]
4“Suppose one of you has a hundred
sheep and loses one of them. Doesn’t he
leave the ninety-nine in the open country
and go after the lost sheep until he finds
it?[y] 5And when he finds it, he joyfully puts
it on his shoulders 6and goes home. Then
he calls his friends and neighbors together
and says, ‘Rejoice with me; I have found
my lost sheep.’[z] 7I tell you that in the same
way there will be more rejoicing in heav-
en over one sinner who repents than over
ninety-nine righteous persons who do not
need to repent.[a]

The Parable of the Lost Coin

8“Or suppose a woman has ten silver
coins[a] and loses one. Doesn’t she light a
lamp, sweep the house and search carefully until she finds it? 9And when she finds
it, she calls her friends and neighbors together and says, ‘Rejoice with me; I have
found my lost coin.’[b] 10In the same way, I
tell you, there is rejoicing in the presence
of the angels of God over one sinner who
repents.”[c]

The Parable of the Lost Son

11Jesus continued: “There was a man
who had two sons.[d] 12The younger one
said to his father, ‘Father, give me my
share of the estate.’[e] So he divided his
property[f] between them.

13“Not long after that, the younger son
got together all he had, set off for a distant
country and there squandered his wealth[g]

14:33 [r] Php 3:7,8 **14:34** [s] Mk 9:50 **14:35** [t] Mt 5:13 [u] Mt 11:15 **15:1** [v] Lk 5:29 **15:2** [w] Mt 9:11 **15:3** [x] Mt 13:3

15:4 [y] Ps 23; 119:176; Jer 31:10; Eze 34:11-16; Lk 5:32; 19:10 **15:6** [z] ver 9 **15:7** [a] ver 10 **15:9** [b] ver 6 **15:10** [c] ver 7 **15:11** [d] Mt 21:28 **15:12** [e] Dt 21:17 [f] ver 30 **15:13** [g] ver 30; Lk 16:1

[a] 8 Greek *ten drachmas*, each worth about a day’s wages

often hostile and mocking mob. Ironically, Jesus’ disciples fail even in carrying Jesus’ cross, so that his executioners have to draft a bystander to carry it (23:26).

14:29 – 30 People gained honor by building, including supporting public works. Unfinished works, however, became embarrassing monuments to the builders’ folly.

14:31 – 32 Sometimes armies defeated those with superior numbers, but whenever feasible they avoided engaging those who outnumbered them.

14:33 *give up everything.* Only the most radical groups (such as the Essenes) expected the surrender of all resources (though for what Jesus’ instructions mean in practice, cf. Ac 2:44 – 45). The analogies for counting the cost (vv. 28 – 32) apply to being Jesus’ disciple: one must recognize that Jesus is worth everything and unreservedly commit oneself to him (vv. 27,33).

14:34 – 35 See note on Mt 5:13.

14:35 *manure pile.* Manure was used as fertilizer (13:8); some believe that salt was used to slow its fermentation.

15:1 *tax collectors.* Those employed as tax collectors were despised and often viewed as collaborators with the occupying empire (see note on Mk 2:14).

15:2 *eats with them.* Table fellowship created a covenant relationship of friendship. Scripture warned against intimate fellowship with sinners (Ps 1:1; Pr 1:15; 13:20; 14:7), but it should be noted that here the influence is going the other direction. The religious critics’ complaint occasions the three parables of vv. 3 – 32. Nevertheless, their values would not allow them to identify easily with the main characters: a shepherd (vv. 4 – 7), a woman (vv. 8 – 10), and an indulgent father (vv. 11 – 32). Urban people in this period often looked down on shepherds; courts mistrusted the testimony of both shepherds and women. Those who love God celebrate with him when what was lost to him is restored (vv. 7,10); the critics here, by contrast, reject the celebration.

15:4 *a hundred sheep.* Many flocks were roughly this size. *leave the ninety-nine.* Shepherds and other herders often watched over their animals together (2:8), so the shepherd here could leave his flock with the other herders while searching for the lost sheep.

15:8 *loses one.* As archaeology shows, people often lost coins between loosely fitted stones in the floor. *light a lamp, sweep.* Oil lamps from this period were small and fit in the palm of the hand, so she supplements the light and sweeps to try to hear the coin.

15:12 *give me my share.* Demanding one’s share of the inheritance before the father died was tantamount to saying, “I wish you were dead”; an ancient audience might have expected the father to discipline the son, perhaps by beating him. Instead, the father here divides the estate; the elder brother would also be told his share (see v. 31). The younger of two sons would normally receive one-third of the inheritance, but the sons would inherit only after the father died.

15:13 *set off . . . squandered.* A father could divide his estate before death, announcing which son would inherit which parts of the property (sheep, trees, etc.), but the father

Silver Greek drachma, 300 – 270 BC. The coins in the parable of the lost coin (Lk 15:8 – 10) were drachmas, each worth about a day's wage.

A.D. Riddle/BiblePlaces.com. Taken at the Ashmolean Museum.

in wild living. 14 After he had spent everything, there was a severe famine in that whole country, and he began to be in need. 15 So he went and hired himself out to a citizen of that country, who sent him to his fields to feed pigs.[h] 16 He longed to fill his stomach with the pods that the pigs were eating, but no one gave him anything.

17 "When he came to his senses, he said, 'How many of my father's hired servants have food to spare, and here I am starving to death! 18 I will set out and go back to my father and say to him: Father, I have sinned[i] against heaven and against you. 19 I am no longer worthy to be called your son; make me like one of your hired servants.' 20 So he got up and went to his father.

"But while he was still a long way off, his father saw him and was filled with compassion for him; he ran to his son, threw his arms around him and kissed him.[j]

21 "The son said to him, 'Father, I have sinned against heaven and against you.[k] I am no longer worthy to be called your son.'

22 "But the father said to his servants, 'Quick! Bring the best robe[l] and put it on him. Put a ring on his finger[m] and sandals on his feet. 23 Bring the fattened calf and kill it. Let's have a feast and celebrate. 24 For this son of mine was dead and is alive again;[n] he was lost and is found.' So they began to celebrate.[o]

25 "Meanwhile, the older son was in the field. When he came near the house, he heard music and dancing. 26 So he called one of the servants and asked him what was going on. 27 'Your brother has come,' he replied, 'and your father has killed the fattened calf because he has him back safe and sound.'

28 "The older brother became angry[p] and refused to go in. So his father went out

15:15 [h] Lev 11:7
15:18 [i] Lev 26:40; Mt 3:2
15:20 [j] Ge 45:14, 15; 46:29; Ac 20:37
15:21 [k] Ps 51:4
15:22 [l] Zec 3:4; Rev 6:11 [m] Ge 41:42
15:24 [n] Eph 2:1, 5; 5:14; 1Ti 5:6 [o] ver 32
15:28 [p] Jnh 4:1

was able to live off the fruit of the land until he died. That meant that the son could not legally sell his share while the father lived. This son, however, emigrates to a distant country, as a number of Judeans seeking fortune did. All moralists in antiquity condemned squandering inherited wealth, but that is what this son does (cf. also v. 30).

15:14 *severe famine.* Famines were common, but the son had kept nothing in reserve.

15:15 *hired himself out to … feed pigs.* For a Jewish hearer, being reduced to the point of feeding pigs, which were considered unclean, would be the ultimate humiliation; in this unclean state, it is likely the young man would not even want to approach a synagogue for help.

15:16 *pods.* Animals ate these carob pods raw; people ate them roasted, but depended on them for sustenance only in times of famine. (Some later rabbis remarked that whenever Israel was reduced to eating carob pods, they repented.) *no one gave him anything.* Moralists commonly observed that those who were friends only for the sake of pleasure would abandon one when the money ran out. A normal ancient story might have ended here, with an obvious moral for listeners: don't disrespect and abandon your father, or you might end up like this! Yet Jesus' story continues.

15:17 *hired servants.* This could refer to rented slaves but likelier to free field hands working for daily wages.

15:18 *heaven.* Sometimes a surrogate name for God (Da 4:26).

15:20 *he ran to his son.* It was considered undignified for an older man to run, but dramatic reunions took precedence over dignity. *kissed him.* A light kiss on the lips (as opposed to romantic kisses) was a common family greeting.

15:22 The father's actions reject the son's proposal in v. 21. *best robe … ring.* This robe would be the father's; the ring would likely be a family signet ring, showing that the father receives him as his son and restoring the son's authority within the family. *sandals.* Poorer people often could not afford sandals, but the father will not receive the son as a servant. Cf. Ge 41:42.

15:23 *fattened calf.* Would feed the entire village. Calves would be fattened with a special occasion in mind, such as a wedding, a son's coming of age, or some other celebration beyond the purview of the parable. A fattened calf offered more meat than a young goat (v. 29). *have a feast.* A person of means invited as many people as possible to a major celebration.

15:24 *dead … alive again … lost … found.* Ancient narratives sometimes bracketed off a special section by framing it with repeated wording. The father's words of v. 32 repeat the words here, setting off the account of the elder brother, which supplements the conclusion of celebration in the previous parables. *dead.* Sometimes used figuratively.

15:25 *older son was in the field.* Normally an elder brother would be expected to help reconcile a father and a younger brother. That the entire village would attend the party and the elder brother alone would be unaware of it is unlikely in real life but this incongruity further drives home the point: the self-righteous critic alone fails to join the party (cf. vv. 1 – 2,6 – 7,9 – 10). *music and dancing.* Characterized most celebrations (e.g., weddings).

15:28 *refused to go in.* Refusing to enter the home during

and pleaded with him. 29But he answered
his father, 'Look! All these years I've been
slaving for you and never disobeyed your
orders. Yet you never gave me even a
young goat so I could celebrate with my
friends. 30But when this son of yours who
has squandered your property[q] with prostitutes[r] comes home, you kill the fattened
calf for him!'
31"'My son,' the father said, 'you are always with me, and everything I have is
yours. 32But we had to celebrate and be
glad, because this brother of yours was
dead and is alive again; he was lost and
is found.'"[s]

15:30 [q] ver 12, 13 [r] Pr 29:3 **15:32** [s] ver 24; Mal 3:17

16:1 [t] Lk 15:13, 30

The Parable of the Shrewd Manager

16 Jesus told his disciples: "There was
a rich man whose manager was
accused of wasting his possessions.[t] 2So
he called him in and asked him, 'What is
this I hear about you? Give an account of
your management, because you cannot be
manager any longer.'
3"The manager said to himself, 'What
shall I do now? My master is taking away
my job. I'm not strong enough to dig, and
I'm ashamed to beg— 4I know what I'll
do so that, when I lose my job here, people will welcome me into their houses.'

---

a village-wide celebration made an intrafamily dispute public gossip and shamed the father in the midst of celebration. Ancient hearers might have expected the father to discipline this son (cf. v. 12). That the father is reduced to going outside to entreat him reinforces the humiliation.
15:29 *Look!* Failure to greet his father with a title ("Father" or "Sir") was offensive. *slaving.* The elder son's language suggests that he related to his father in a way that the father did not accept (see v. 22, rejecting the proposal of v. 21). *young goat.* Fed far fewer people than did a fattened calf (v. 23).
15:30 *this son of yours.* The elder son denies the fraternal bond; the father replies in v. 32 with "this brother of yours." (For one somewhat analogous example of shifting attachment, cf. the exchange between Moses and the Lord regarding "your people" in Ex 32:7,11 – 12.)
15:31 *My son.* The father reaffirms his love for the elder brother; the way is open for him — and for Jesus' religious critics in vv. 1 – 2 — if they are willing.
16:1 *manager.* Wealthy people had managers to run their estates; some of these were slaves (see 1Co 4:1), but this one is free (vv. 2 – 4).
16:2 *Give an account.* The manager must provide his account books but knows he will be fired.
16:3 *dig . . . beg.* Digging (an arduous task sometimes relegated to prisoners of war) and begging were considered shameful, and might yield only subsistence income.
16:4 Ancient culture emphasized reciprocity, returning

PARABLES OF JESUS

PARABLE	MATTHEW	MARK	LUKE
Lamp under a bowl	5:14–15	4:21–22	8:16; 11:33
Wise and foolish builders	7:24–27		6:47–49
New cloth on an old coat	9:16	2:21	5:36
New wine in old wineskins	9:17	2:22	5:37–38
Sower and the soils	13:3–8,18–23	4:3–8,14–20	8:5–8,11–15
Weeds	13:24–30,36–43		
Mustard seed	13:31–32	4:30–32	13:18–19
Yeast	13:33		13:20–21
Hidden treasure	13:44		
Valuable pearl	13:45–46		
Net	13:47–50		
Owner of a house	13:52		
Lost sheep	18:12–14		15:4–7
Unmerciful servant	18:23–34		
Workers in the vineyard	20:1–16		
Two sons	21:28–32		
Tenants	21:33–44	12:1–11	20:9–18
Wedding banquet	22:2–14		
Fig tree	24:32–35	13:28–29	21:29–31
Faithful and wise servant	24:45-51		12:42–48

PARABLE	MATTHEW	MARK	LUKE
Ten virgins	25:1–13		
Bags of gold (minas)	25:14–30		19:12–27
Sheep and goats	25:31–46		
Growing seed		4:26–29	
Watchful servants		13:35–37	12:35–40
Moneylender			7:41–43
Good Samaritan			10:30–37
Friend in need			11:5–8
Rich fool			12:16–21
Unfruitful fig tree			13:6–9
Lowest seat at the feast			14:7–14
Great banquet			14:16–24
Cost of discipleship			14:28–33
Lost coin			15:8–10
Lost (prodigal) son			15:11–32
Shrewd manager			16:1–8
Rich man and Lazarus			16:19–31
Master and his servant			17:7–10
Persistent widow			18:2–8
Pharisee and tax collector			18:10–14

5“So he called in each one of his master’s debtors. He asked the first, ‘How
much do you owe my master?’
6“ ‘Nine hundred gallons[a] of olive oil,’
he replied.
“The manager told him, ‘Take your bill,
sit down quickly, and make it four hundred and fifty.’
7“Then he asked the second, ‘And how
much do you owe?’
“ ‘A thousand bushels[b] of wheat,’ he replied.
“He told him, ‘Take your bill and make
it eight hundred.’
8“The master commended the dishonest manager because he had acted shrewdly. For the people of this world[u] are more
shrewd[v] in dealing with their own kind
than are the people of the light.[w] 9I tell
you, use worldly wealth[x] to gain friends
for yourselves, so that when it is gone, you
will be welcomed into eternal dwellings.[y]
10“Whoever can be trusted with very little can also be trusted with much,[z] and
whoever is dishonest with very little will
also be dishonest with much. 11So if you
have not been trustworthy in handling
worldly wealth,[a] who will trust you with
true riches? 12And if you have not been
trustworthy with someone else’s property,
who will give you property of your own?

16:8 [u] Ps 17:14 [v] Ps 18:26 [w] Jn 12:36; Eph 5:8; 1Th 5:5 **16:9** [x] ver 11, 13 [y] Mt 19:21; Lk 12:33 **16:10** [z] Mt 25:21, 23; Lk 19:17 **16:11** [a] ver 9, 13
16:13 [b] ver 9, 11; Mt 6:24 **16:14** [c] 1Ti 3:3 [d] Lk 23:35 **16:15** [e] Lk 10:29 [f] 1Sa 16:7; Rev 2:23 **16:16** [g] Mt 11:12, 13 [h] Mt 4:23 **16:17** [i] Mt 5:18 **16:18** [j] Mt 5:31, 32; 19:9; Mk 10:11; Ro 7:2, 3; 1Co 7:10, 11 **16:19** [k] Eze 16:49

13“No one can serve two masters. Either
you will hate the one and love the other,
or you will be devoted to the one and despise the other. You cannot serve both God
and money.”[b]
14The Pharisees, who loved money,[c]
heard all this and were sneering at Jesus.[d]
15He said to them, “You are the ones who
justify yourselves[e] in the eyes of others,
but God knows your hearts.[f] What people
value highly is detestable in God’s sight.

Additional Teachings

16“The Law and the Prophets were proclaimed until John.[g] Since that time, the
good news of the kingdom of God is being
preached,[h] and everyone is forcing their
way into it. 17It is easier for heaven and
earth to disappear than for the least stroke
of a pen to drop out of the Law.[i]
18“Anyone who divorces his wife and
marries another woman commits adultery, and the man who marries a divorced
woman commits adultery.[j]

The Rich Man and Lazarus

19“There was a rich man who was
dressed in purple and fine linen and lived
in luxury every day.[k] 20At his gate was laid

[a] *6* Or about 3,000 liters [b] *7* Or about 30 tons

favors. The families dealing with the produce noted in vv. 6–7 are themselves wealthy, and might welcome a manager with business experience who had already supported their interests.

16:5 *How much do you owe . . . ?* Contracts specified what they would owe at harvest time; the manager, however, is able to change the contract. Rather than extorting more money, the manager does the opposite.

16:6 *Nine hundred gallons of olive oil.* That is, more than 3,000 liters; the fruit of some 150 olive trees.

16:7 *A thousand bushels of wheat.* That is, about 30 tons (27 metric tons); the harvest of some 100 acres (40 hectares). Scholars suggest that he forgives about 500 denarii in each case (the olive oil in v. 6 was worth about 1,000 denarii, and the wheat in v. 7 was worth about 2,500). *Take . . . make it.* By having the debtors change the bill in their own handwriting, the manager avoids being held accountable.

16:8 Landowners sometimes forgave or reduced debts in times of famine or other crises; those forgiven normally praised the creditor as benevolent in return. The landowner now recognizes his manager’s shrewdness: if the owner protests that the manager acted on his own, the debtors will be angry with the owner and generous toward the manager. For the sake of his honor, the owner is not likely to try to exact more from the debtors than what his manager promised. As far as the account books, the apparent lower income (v. 1) will now be attributed to generosity rather than to the manager’s mismanagement, honoring the owner. *people of this world.* Lit. “children of this age,” a phrase that would probably communicate to a Jewish audience that these people have no share in the world to come. *the light.* Lit. “children of light,” a phrase the Dead Sea Scrolls use to describe those who truly follow God.

16:9 *use worldly wealth to gain friends.* The point seems to be that one should use money for people rather than as an end in itself. *wealth.* Lit. “mammon” (see note on v. 13).

16:13 *two masters.* Two people sharing a slave was a rare situation; it arose, e.g., when two siblings inherited one slave. When it did occur, the slave normally preferred one master to the other. *money.* Lit. “mammon”; it was an Aramaic designation for money or property, but here Jesus apparently personifies it graphically.

16:14 *Pharisees, who loved money.* Although most Pharisees valued caring for the poor and did not belong to the elite, neither were many poor. The majority came from families with the means to allow them to be educated as Pharisees.

16:15 Jesus may echo 1Sa 16:7. The prophets often warned that God cared more about justice than about religious cultic practices (Isa 1:11–17; 58:3–7; Jer 6:20; Hos 6:6; Am 5:22–24).

16:16 *The Law and the Prophets.* Jewish people often used this phrase to summarize all of Scripture, and here perhaps the era treated in those works. *forcing their way into it.* Some of Jesus’ contemporaries wanted to use force (e.g., fighting against Rome) to bring about God’s kingdom; Jesus may speak here instead, parabolically, of spiritual zeal.

16:17 *least stroke of a pen.* See note on Mt 5:18.

16:18 *Anyone who divorces . . . and marries another . . . commits adultery.* See notes on Mt 5:31,32.

16:19 *purple.* Although imitation purple dye existed, the dominant source of the dye came from crushing murex shellfish around Tyre. It was necessarily expensive; one source estimates 10,000 shellfish to produce a single gram of the dye. Robes so dyed not surprisingly carried a strong odor, but purple’s expense made it a status symbol.

a beggar[l] named Lazarus, covered with
sores 21 and longing to eat what fell from
the rich man's table.[m] Even the dogs came
and licked his sores.

22 "The time came when the beggar died
and the angels carried him to Abraham's
side. The rich man also died and was buried. 23 In Hades, where he was in torment,
he looked up and saw Abraham far away,
with Lazarus by his side. 24 So he called to
him, 'Father Abraham,[n] have pity on me
and send Lazarus to dip the tip of his finger in water and cool my tongue, because
I am in agony in this fire.'[o]

25 "But Abraham replied, 'Son, remember that in your lifetime you received your
good things, while Lazarus received bad
things,[p] but now he is comforted here and
you are in agony.[q] 26 And besides all this,
between us and you a great chasm has
been set in place, so that those who want
to go from here to you cannot, nor can
anyone cross over from there to us.'

27 "He answered, 'Then I beg you, father,
send Lazarus to my family, 28 for I have
five brothers. Let him warn them,[r] so that
they will not also come to this place of
torment.'

29 "Abraham replied, 'They have Moses[s]
and the Prophets;[t] let them listen to them.'

30 " 'No, father Abraham,'[u] he said, 'but
if someone from the dead goes to them,
they will repent.'

31 "He said to him, 'If they do not listen
to Moses and the Prophets, they will not
be convinced even if someone rises from
the dead.' "

16:20 [l] Ac 3:2 **16:21** [m] Mt 15:27 **16:24** [n] ver 30; Lk 3:8 [o] Mt 5:22 **16:25** [p] Ps 17:14 [q] Lk 6:21, 24, 25 **16:28** [r] Ac 2:40; 20:23; 1Th 4:6 **16:29** [s] Lk 24:27, 44; Jn 5:45-47; Ac 15:21 [t] Lk 4:17; Jn 1:45 **16:30** [u] ver 24; Lk 3:8

Sin, Faith, Duty

17 Jesus said to his disciples: "Things
that cause people to stumble[v]
are bound to come, but woe to anyone
through whom they come.[w] 2 It would be
better for them to be thrown into the sea
with a millstone tied around their neck
than to cause one of these little ones[x] to
stumble.[y] 3 So watch yourselves.

"If your brother or sister[a] sins against
you, rebuke them;[z] and if they repent,
forgive them.[a] 4 Even if they sin against
you seven times in a day and seven times
come back to you saying 'I repent,' you
must forgive them."[b]

5 The apostles[c] said to the Lord,[d] "Increase our faith!"

6 He replied, "If you have faith as small
as a mustard seed,[e] you can say to this
mulberry tree, 'Be uprooted and planted
in the sea,' and it will obey you.[f]

7 "Suppose one of you has a servant
plowing or looking after the sheep. Will he
say to the servant when he comes in from
the field, 'Come along now and sit down

[a] 3 The Greek word for *brother or sister* (*adelphos*) refers here to a fellow disciple, whether man or woman.

17:1 [v] Mt 5:29 [w] Mt 18:7 **17:2** [x] Mk 10:24; Lk 10:21 [y] Mt 5:29 **17:3** [z] Mt 18:15 [a] Eph 4:32; Col 3:13 **17:4** [b] Mt 18:21, 22 **17:5** [c] Mk 6:30 [d] Lk 7:13 **17:6** [e] Mt 13:31; 17:20; Lk 13:19 [f] Mt 21:21; Mk 9:23

16:20 *Lazarus.* Greek for Eleazar. Parables occasionally named a character; the surprise for ancient hearers would be that Jesus names the beggar rather than the rich man.
16:21 *what fell from the rich man's table.* In wealthy homes, dogs might eat the scraps from the tables. *dogs … licked his sores.* Although some Gentile homes had dogs as pets, Jewish people considered them unclean scavengers, and would have found their contact with Lazarus's open sores revolting.
16:22 *angels carried him to Abraham's side.* Jewish stories and artwork depicted angels escorting the righteous to paradise and (sometimes) demons dragging the wicked to hell. *Abraham's side.* See note on 13:28. *buried.* The wealthy received lavish burials; Jewish custom required at least a simple burial for even the poorest person, but the parable's silence about Lazarus's burial contrasts starkly with that of the rich man.
16:23 In a similar rabbinic parable the rich sinner went to paradise because he did one good deed; here, however, he is damned, apparently for letting Lazarus starve. *Hades.* Simply specifies the realm of the dead (hence that the rich man died), but the "torment" (here) and "fire" (v. 24) indicate that he is in what Jewish tradition specified as Gehinnom (which was conceived as fiery torment) or at least something like it.
16:24 *fire.* See note on Mt 3:12; see also Gehinnom.
16:25 *he is comforted here and you are in agony.* Many Jewish people expected an inversion of status in the end time (cf. Isa 2:11 – 12; 1 Enoch 96:8; Wisdom of Solomon 5:3 – 5); in particular, God would exalt oppressed Israel and judge the Gentiles. Many believed that they belonged to God, as part of the chosen people, by virtue of their descent from Abraham (see note on Mt 3:9). *comforted.* See note on 2:25.
16:29 *Moses and the Prophets.* Like "the Law and the Prophets" (v. 16), this phrase refers to the entire OT Scripture (the Torah could be referred to as "[the books of] Moses").
16:31 *even if someone rises from the dead.* Ancient writers could prepare their audiences for later plot developments; here the warning portends the later failure to believe Jesus' resurrection.
17:1,2 *stumble.* A common ancient metaphor for sin or apostasy (e.g., Sirach 9:5; 23:8; 32:15); here the stumbling block merits a millstone.
17:2 *thrown into the sea with a millstone tied around their neck.* See note on Mt 18:6.
17:3 *rebuke them.* Jewish custom required private reproof before exposing someone before a Jewish judicial assembly. *forgive them.* Jewish tradition valued forgiveness, though genuine repentance should include restitution and no plans to sin again.
17:6 *mustard seed.* Scholars do not all agree about which plant is meant by the mustard plant, but ancient sources agree in describing the mustard seed as proverbially small. *mulberry tree.* Scholars usually identify the tree here as the black mulberry; its wide root system reportedly made it hard to uproot.
17:7 – 8 *sit down to eat … Prepare my supper.* Masters virtually never ate with slaves, least of all field slaves; one who was reported to do so (Cato) did so because he saved money by sharing the less expensive food served to his slaves, whom he often mistreated. Even a Roman aristocrat who ate even with his freedmen was considered unusual. A home with just one multitasking slave, as here,

to eat'? 8 Won't he rather say, 'Prepare my supper, get yourself ready and wait on me[g] while I eat and drink; after that you may eat and drink'? 9 Will he thank the servant because he did what he was told to do? 10 So you also, when you have done everything you were told to do, should say, 'We are unworthy servants; we have only done our duty.' "[h]

Jesus Heals Ten Men With Leprosy

11 Now on his way to Jerusalem,[i] Jesus traveled along the border between Samaria and Galilee.[j] 12 As he was going into a village, ten men who had leprosy[a][k] met him. They stood at a distance[l] 13 and called out in a loud voice, "Jesus, Master,[m] have pity on us!"

14 When he saw them, he said, "Go, show yourselves to the priests."[n] And as they went, they were cleansed.

15 One of them, when he saw he was healed, came back, praising God[o] in a loud voice. 16 He threw himself at Jesus' feet and thanked him — and he was a Samaritan.[p]

17 Jesus asked, "Were not all ten cleansed? Where are the other nine? 18 Has no one returned to give praise to God except this foreigner?" 19 Then he said to him, "Rise and go; your faith has made you well."[q]

The Coming of the Kingdom of God

17:26,27pp — Mt 24:37-39

20 Once, on being asked by the Pharisees when the kingdom of God would come,[r] Jesus replied, "The coming of the kingdom of God is not something that can be observed, 21 nor will people say, 'Here it is,' or 'There it is,'[s] because the kingdom of God is in your midst."[b]

22 Then he said to his disciples, "The time is coming when you will long to see one of the days of the Son of Man,[t] but you will not see it.[u] 23 People will tell you, 'There he is!' or 'Here he is!' Do not go running off after them.[v] 24 For the Son of Man in his day[c] will be like the lightning,[w] which flashes and lights up the sky from one end to the other. 25 But first he must suffer many things[x] and be rejected[y] by this generation.[z]

26 "Just as it was in the days of Noah,[a] so also will it be in the days of the Son of Man. 27 People were eating, drinking, marrying and being given in marriage up to the day Noah entered the ark. Then the flood came and destroyed them all.

28 "It was the same in the days of Lot.[b] People were eating and drinking, buying and selling, planting and building. 29 But the day Lot left Sodom, fire and sulfur rained down from heaven and destroyed them all.

30 "It will be just like this on the day the Son of Man is revealed.[c] 31 On that day no one who is on the housetop, with possessions inside, should go down to get them. Likewise, no one in the field should go back for anything.[d] 32 Remember Lot's wife![e] 33 Whoever tries to keep their life will lose it, and whoever loses their life will preserve it.[f] 34 I tell you, on that night two people will be in one bed; one will be taken and the other left. 35 Two women

17:8 [g] Lk 12:37 **17:10** [h] 1Co 9:16 **17:11** [i] Lk 9:51 [j] Lk 9:51,52; Jn 4:3,4 **17:12** [k] Mt 8:2 [l] Lev 13:45,46 **17:13** [m] Lk 5:5 **17:14** [n] Lev 14:2; Mt 8:4 **17:15** [o] Mt 9:8 **17:16** [p] Mt 10:5 **17:19** [q] Mt 9:22 **17:20** [r] Mt 3:2 **17:21** [s] ver 23 **17:22** [t] Mt 8:20 [u] Mt 9:15; Lk 5:35 **17:23** [v] Mt 24:23; Mk 13:21; Lk 21:8 **17:24** [w] Mt 24:27 **17:25** [x] Mt 16:21 [y] Lk 9:22; 18:32 [z] Mk 13:30; Lk 21:32 **17:26** [a] Ge 7:6-24 **17:28** [b] Ge 19:1-28 **17:30** [c] Mt 10:23; 16:27; 24:3,27,37,39; 25:31; 1Co 1:7; 1Th 2:19; 2Th 1:7; 2:8; 2Pe 3:4; Rev 1:7 **17:31** [d] Mt 24:17,18; Mk 13:15-16 **17:32** [e] Ge 19:26 **17:33** [f] Jn 12:25

[a] *12* The Greek word traditionally translated *leprosy* was used for various diseases affecting the skin. [b] *21* Or *is within you* [c] *24* Some manuscripts do not have *in his day.*

was far from elite, though this would not likely be the home of a Galilean tenant farmer either. Although field work lasted longer during harvest, during other seasons a slave might finish and be ready to serve an afternoon meal after 3:00 p.m.

17:16 *he was a Samaritan.* In this border region (v. 11), the common condition of leprosy apparently surmounted the normal prejudice between Jews and Samaritans (see note on 9:52 – 53), uniting the lepers (v. 12). Ironically, lepers in ancient Samaria (2Ki 7:3), then the capital of the northern kingdom of Israel, were among those not cleansed in Elisha's day (Lk 4:27).

17:20 – 21 Jewish people prayed regularly for the coming of God's kingdom, or reign (see note on 11:2). They expected it to include Israel's (and usually creation's) restoration. Many debated what signs would portend its coming and some developed schemes to predict when it would come (usually specifying a date in the near future). Although Jewish people recognized that God also reigns in the present, Jesus' answer might appear to the Pharisees like a riddle. Because Jesus was the promised king, his presence indicated that the kingdom had come among them.

17:22 *days of the Son of Man.* Some Jewish teachers spoke of a future era they called "the days of the Messiah." Later rabbis spoke of this as an era when the Messiah would rule, between the present world and the glorious age to come.

17:23 Even in the decades immediately following Jesus' ministry, some figures envisioning themselves as being like Moses or Joshua gained followers to try (unsuccessfully) to bring about God's kingdom.

17:26 – 29 *days of Noah ... days of Lot ... Sodom.* Ancient Jewish sources depicted Noah's generation (Ge 6:11 – 13) and Sodom (Ge 18:20; 19:4 – 9), sometimes together, as the epitome of evil. The point here is that they thought only of life as usual, and sudden judgment took them by surprise (Ge 7:21 – 23; 19:24 – 25).

17:31 *housetop.* Rooftops in this region were flat, and people engaged in various activities on their roofs, such as drying vegetables, chatting with neighbors, praying, and the like. The roof was approached by an outside staircase or ladder, so it would take extra time to enter the house after descending. *field.* See, e.g., Mt 24:18 (see note there).

17:32 *Remember Lot's wife!* Because Lot's wife could not let go of her life in Sodom, she looked back and perished, becoming a pillar of salt (Ge 19:26).

17:35 *grinding grain together.* Many Galilean homes shared a common courtyard with other families, and

will be grinding grain together; one will be
taken and the other left.”[g] [36][a]
37“Where, Lord?” they asked.
He replied, “Where there is a dead body,
there the vultures will gather.”[h]

The Parable of the Persistent Widow

18 Then Jesus told his disciples a parable to show them that they should
always pray and not give up.[i] 2He said: “In a
certain town there was a judge who neither
feared God nor cared what people thought.
3And there was a widow in that town who
kept coming to him with the plea, ‘Grant
me justice[j] against my adversary.’
4“For some time he refused. But finally
he said to himself, ‘Even though I don’t
fear God or care what people think, 5yet
because this widow keeps bothering me,
I will see that she gets justice, so that she
won’t eventually come and attack me!’ ”[k]
6And the Lord[l] said, “Listen to what the
unjust judge says. 7And will not God bring
about justice for his chosen ones, who cry
out[m] to him day and night? Will he keep
putting them off? 8I tell you, he will see
that they get justice, and quickly. However, when the Son of Man[n] comes,[o] will he
find faith on the earth?”

The Parable of the Pharisee and the Tax Collector

9To some who were confident of their
own righteousness[p] and looked down
on everyone else,[q] Jesus told this parable: 10“Two men went up to the temple to
pray,[r] one a Pharisee and the other a tax
collector. 11The Pharisee stood by himself[s]
and prayed: ‘God, I thank you that I am
not like other people — robbers, evildoers,
adulterers — or even like this tax collector.
12I fast[t] twice a week and give a tenth[u] of
all I get.’
13“But the tax collector stood at a distance. He would not even look up to heav-
en, but beat his breast[v] and said, ‘God,
have mercy on me, a sinner.’[w]
14“I tell you that this man, rather than
the other, went home justified before God.
For all those who exalt themselves will be
humbled, and those who humble themselves will be exalted.”[x]

The Little Children and Jesus

18:15-17pp — Mt 19:13-15; Mk 10:13-16

15People were also bringing babies to
Jesus for him to place his hands on them.
When the disciples saw this, they rebuked
them. 16But Jesus called the children to
him and said, “Let the little children come
to me, and do not hinder them, for the
kingdom of God belongs to such as these.
17Truly I tell you, anyone who will not
receive the kingdom of God like a little
child[y] will never enter it.”

[a] 36 Some manuscripts include here words similar to Matt. 24:40.

17:35 [g] Mt 24:41 **17:37** [h] Mt 24:28 **18:1** [i] Isa 40:31; Lk 11:5-8; Ac 1:14; Ro 12:12; Eph 6:18; Col 4:2; 1Th 5:17 **18:3** [j] Isa 1:17 **18:5** [k] Lk 11:8 **18:6** [l] Lk 7:13 **18:7** [m] Ex 22:23; Ps 88:1; Rev 6:10 **18:8** [n] Mt 8:20 [o] Mt 16:27 **18:9** [p] Lk 16:15 [q] Isa 65:5 **18:10** [r] Ac 3:1 **18:11** [s] Mt 6:5; Mk 11:25 **18:12** [t] Isa 58:3; Mt 9:14 [u] Mal 3:8; Lk 11:42 **18:13** [v] Isa 66:2; Jer 31:19; Lk 23:48 [w] Lk 5:32; 1Ti 1:15 **18:14** [x] Mt 23:12; Lk 14:11 **18:17** [y] Mt 11:25; 18:3

---

housewives worked together at a common millstone. Here one is taken to judgment (v. 37) but the other is spared despite their close association.

17:37 *vultures will gather.* Ancient sources often depicted corpses strewn on battlefields or after other slaughter being eaten by carrion birds such as vultures (see, e.g., Eze 32:4; 39:17 – 20).

18:2 *neither feared God nor cared what people thought.* The law required judges to be fair and just (Lev 19:15; Dt 16:18); corruption was forbidden (Ex 23:8; Dt 10:17). As in this case, however, it certainly did happen (1Sa 8:3).

18:3 *widow.* Because men controlled judicial settings and advocacy, widows were easily exploited; the law commanded that they be defended (Ex 22:22; Dt 24:17; Isa 1:17).

18:5 *because this widow keeps bothering me.* Usually only men pleaded cases in court, but when women did speak men considered them courageous and, insofar as we can tell from ancient records, usually granted their requests. In this case, however, the judge gives in just to make her stop harassing him (which was her only means of securing justice).

18:6 – 7 Parables are analogies, and not every point in the story is meant for comparison. Here Jesus reasons (as often in ancient Jewish argument) from lesser to greater: if an unjust judge would grant justice, how much more will the perfectly just God?

18:8 *will he find faith on the earth?* Jewish people often expected a period of intense suffering, leading some to apostasy, before the day of God’s judgment and vindication of his people. Cf. teaching regarding endurance in 21:19,36; 22:32,40.

18:10 *Pharisee … tax collector.* Later rabbis sometimes contrasted Pharisees and tax collectors as the epitomes of piety and sin, respectively.

18:11 Among Jesus’ contemporaries, thanking God for one’s piety, rather than taking credit for it, was considered pious and humble. Yet this Pharisee also “looked down on everyone else” (v. 9).

18:12 *fast twice a week.* Particularly devout Jews fasted without water on Mondays and Thursdays (later Christians, seeking to avoid their example, fasted instead on Wednesdays and Fridays! — *Didache* 8.1) *tenth of all I get.* Pharisees were known to be meticulous in tithing on agricultural produce; so rigorous were they that if they could not be certain that farmers had already tithed the produce, Pharisees would tithe it again. See note on Mt 23:23.

18:13 *look up to heaven.* People often looked to heaven when they prayed. *beat his breast.* An act of mourning, in this case for one’s sin. The tax collector here recognizes that he can depend only on God’s mercy, not his own righteousness.

18:14 The exaltation of the humble and humbling of those who exalt themselves recalls an OT principle of judgment (Isa 2:11 – 12; Eze 21:26), here applied to the religiously proud.

18:15 *bringing babies to Jesus.* A person blessed by God could lay hands on someone to pray for a blessing on them (Ge 48:14). *rebuked them.* Because they were concerned that others respect the time and physical space around their teachers, disciples sometimes tried to protect their teachers from distractions (2Ki 4:27).

18:16 *little children.* See note on Mt 18:3. *do not hinder*

The Rich and the Kingdom of God

18:18-30pp — Mt 19:16-29; Mk 10:17-30

18A certain ruler asked him, "Good
teacher, what must I do to inherit eternal
life?"[z]
19"Why do you call me good?" Jesus
answered. "No one is good — except God
alone. 20You know the commandments:
'You shall not commit adultery, you shall
not murder, you shall not steal, you shall
not give false testimony, honor your father
and mother.'[a][a]
21"All these I have kept since I was a
boy," he said.
22When Jesus heard this, he said to him,
"You still lack one thing. Sell everything
you have and give to the poor,[b] and you
will have treasure in heaven.[c] Then come,
follow me."
23When he heard this, he became very
sad, because he was very wealthy. 24Jesus
looked at him and said, "How hard it is
for the rich to enter the kingdom of God![d]
25Indeed, it is easier for a camel to go
through the eye of a needle than for someone who is rich to enter the kingdom of
God."
26Those who heard this asked, "Who
then can be saved?"
27Jesus replied, "What is impossible
with man is possible with God."[e]
28Peter said to him, "We have left all we
had to follow you!"[f]
29"Truly I tell you," Jesus said to them,
"no one who has left home or wife or
brothers or sisters or parents or children
for the sake of the kingdom of God 30will
fail to receive many times as much in
this age, and in the age to come[g] eternal
life."[h]

Jesus Predicts His Death a Third Time

18:31-33pp — Mt 20:17-19; Mk 10:32-34

31Jesus took the Twelve aside and told
them, "We are going up to Jerusalem,[i] and
everything that is written by the prophets[j] about the Son of Man[k] will be fulfilled. 32He will be delivered over to the
Gentiles.[l] They will mock him, insult him
and spit on him; 33they will flog him[m] and
kill him.[n] On the third day[o] he will rise
again."[p]
34The disciples did not understand any
of this. Its meaning was hidden from
them, and they did not know what he was
talking about.[q]

A Blind Beggar Receives His Sight

18:35-43pp — Mt 20:29-34; Mk 10:46-52

35As Jesus approached Jericho,[r] a blind
man was sitting by the roadside begging.
36When he heard the crowd going by, he
asked what was happening. 37They told
him, "Jesus of Nazareth is passing by."[s]
38He called out, "Jesus, Son of David,[t]
have mercy[u] on me!"
39Those who led the way rebuked him
and told him to be quiet, but he shouted
all the more, "Son of David, have mercy
on me!"[v]
40Jesus stopped and ordered the man to
be brought to him. When he came near,

18:18 [z]Lk 10:25 **18:20** [a]Ex 20:12-16; Dt 5:16-20; Ro 13:9 **18:22** [b]Ac 2:45 [c]Mt 6:20 **18:24** [d]Pr 11:28 **18:27** [e]Mt 19:26 **18:28** [f]Mt 4:19 **18:30** [g]Mt 12:32 [h]Mt 25:46 **18:31** [i]Lk 9:51 [j]Ps 22; Isa 53 [k]Mt 8:20 **18:32** [l]Lk 23:1 **18:33** [m]Mt 16:21 [n]Ac 2:23 [o]Mt 16:21 [p]Mt 16:21 **18:34** [q]Mk 9:32; Lk 9:45 **18:35** [r]Lk 19:1 **18:37** [s]Lk 19:4 **18:38** [t]ver 39; Mt 9:27 [u]Mt 17:15; Lk 18:13 **18:39** [v]ver 38

[a] *20* Exodus 20:12-16; Deut. 5:16-20

them. A man of God could overrule his disciple from keeping a supplicant away; Jesus might here follow the honorable example of Elisha (2Ki 4:27). Perhaps the disciples, eager for Jesus' kingdom in Jerusalem, failed to understand what his kingdom was really about, in caring for others.

18:18 Later surviving sources record that non-disciples sometimes asked Jewish teachers how to have eternal life. This man thus asks a somewhat natural question, but he is not prepared for Jesus' extraordinary answer.

18:20 See notes on Mt 19:17,18 – 19.

18:22 *Sell everything you have.* See note on Mt 19:22.

18:25 *camel … through the eye of a needle.* Against some popular but mistaken notions that the "needle's eye" was the name of a gate in first-century Jerusalem, a needle's eye back then meant what it means today — a very tiny opening. It provided a graphic contrast for a camel. In Babylonia, where the largest animal was an elephant, Jewish teachers could speak of what was nearly impossible as "an elephant passing through the eye of a needle." In Judea and Galilee, the largest animal was a camel; getting it through a needle's eye provided an apt metaphor for what was virtually impossible.

18:27 See note on Mt 19:26.

18:29 *left home or … children.* For the disciples and the Galilean villagers whom Jesus often addressed, loyalty to family was paramount in their culture. Jesus comes before everything else, even the otherwise most important matters.

18:30 *many times as much in this age.* Perhaps this is true because Jesus' followers together are meant to care for one another as family.

18:31 *everything … will be fulfilled.* See note on Mt 16:21.

18:32 *spit on him.* Spitting on someone was a form of malice, and Jewish people deemed the spittle of Gentiles impure.

18:33 *flog him.* Flogging the accused after stripping him naked normally preceded execution.

18:35 *Jericho.* About 17 miles (27 kilometers) — less than a day's walk — from Jerusalem, although the journey would be uphill from here. In this period Jericho was wealthy, with residences of aristocratic priests and with winter palaces once held by Herod the Great. The ruins of the original Jericho lay south of the current city; some scholars thus think that this verse and Mk 10:46 speak of different sites. *begging.* Especially during this time of pilgrimage for the festival, a beggar on the roadside might acquire ample provision.

18:38,39 *Son of David.* An implication that he believes Jesus to be the Messianic king.

18:39 *shouted all the more.* Refusing to be deterred expresses faith (cf., e.g., 2Ki 4:27 – 28).

Jesus asked him, 41“What do you want me
to do for you?”
“Lord, I want to see,” he replied.
42Jesus said to him, “Receive your sight;
your faith has healed you.”[w] 43Immedi-
ately he received his sight and followed
Jesus, praising God. When all the people
saw it, they also praised God.[x]

Zacchaeus the Tax Collector

19 Jesus entered Jericho[y] and was
passing through. 2A man was there
by the name of Zacchaeus; he was a chief
tax collector and was wealthy. 3He wanted
to see who Jesus was, but because he was
short he could not see over the crowd. 4So
he ran ahead and climbed a sycamore-fig[z]
tree to see him, since Jesus was coming
that way.[a]
5When Jesus reached the spot, he
looked up and said to him, “Zacchaeus,
come down immediately. I must stay at
your house today.” 6So he came down at
once and welcomed him gladly.
7All the people saw this and began to
mutter, “He has gone to be the guest of a
sinner.”[b]
8But Zacchaeus stood up and said to the
Lord,[c] “Look, Lord! Here and now I give
half of my possessions to the poor, and if
I have cheated anybody out of anything,[d]
I will pay back four times the amount.”[e]
9Jesus said to him, “Today salvation has
come to this house, because this man, too,
is a son of Abraham.[f] 10For the Son of Man
came to seek and to save the lost.”[g]

The Parable of the Ten Minas

19:12-27Ref — Mt 25:14-30

11While they were listening to this, he
went on to tell them a parable, because
he was near Jerusalem and the people
thought that the kingdom of God[h] was going to appear at once.[i] 12He said: “A man
of noble birth went to a distant country to
have himself appointed king and then to
return. 13So he called ten of his servants[j]
and gave them ten minas.[a] ‘Put this money to work,’ he said, ‘until I come back.’
14“But his subjects hated him and sent
a delegation after him to say, ‘We don’t
want this man to be our king.’
15“He was made king, however, and

18:42 [w]Mt 9:22
18:43 [x]Mt 9:8; Lk 13:17
19:1 [y]Lk 18:35
19:4 [z]1Ki 10:27; 1Ch 27:28; Isa 9:10 [a]Lk 18:37
19:7 [b]Mt 9:11
19:8 [c]Lk 7:13 [d]Lk 3:12, 13 [e]Ex 22:1; Lev 6:4, 5; Nu 5:7; 2Sa 12:6
19:9 [f]Lk 3:8; 13:16; Ro 4:16; Gal 3:7
19:10 [g]Eze 34:12, 16; Jn 3:17
19:11 [h]Mt 3:2 [i]Lk 17:20; Ac 1:6
19:13 [j]Mk 13:34

[a] *13* A mina was about three months’ wages.

19:2 Jericho was fertile and wealthy; many wealthy priests lived there, and because of its strategic border location (between Judea and Antipas’s Perea) customs duties would also be significant. *chief tax collector.* Zacchaeus would hire those who collected taxes and would set collection policies. These factors would have made him wealthy even had he behaved ethically — but he had not (v. 8).
19:3 *short.* People often gave greater attention to those who were tall, but everyone locally would know Zacchaeus (mostly negatively; v. 7). In his case, his height is an issue only because he could not see. For average height in this period, see note on Jn 7:25.
19:4 *sycamore-fig tree. Ficus sycomorus* did bear figs but it was less desirable than the fruit of normal fig trees, and the tree was used especially for wood. Major limbs of the tree spread out close to the ground, making it easier to climb (certainly high enough to see above the crowd).
19:5 *I must stay.* Offers of hospitality were valued, and providing hospitality to a renowned teacher would be considered an honor. Nevertheless, respectable people did not normally *request* hospitality — and especially from someone deemed sinful. Jerusalem remained 17 uphill miles (27 kilometers) farther down the road, so Jesus and his disciples would need to spend the night somewhere and resume the journey the next morning.
19:7 *guest of a sinner.* Zacchaeus would have a home large enough to host Jesus and his disciples. For the poor reputation of tax collectors, see note on Mk 2:14. Zacchaeus also had developed a reputation for lack of integrity (v. 8). Table fellowship created bonds of friendship; Pharisees would also likely doubt that the food had been tithed, and thus question whether it would be acceptable to eat it in that condition.
19:8 *cheated.* People sometimes paid tax collectors bribes to prevent higher fees being extorted. Zacchaeus’s position would have also allowed him to make false accusations that could lead even to people being imprisoned; people would have to cooperate with him, even if reluctantly. *four times the amount.* Normally one made restitution when seeking forgiveness; Zacchaeus offers it in response to the gift of forgiveness. Pharisees demanded four- or fivefold restitution only for the offenses specified in Ex 22:1, but Zacchaeus recognizes that his activity of cheating people is equivalent to theft and promises to make fourfold restitution.
19:9 *son of Abraham.* See note on Mt 3:9.
19:10 *to seek and to save the lost.* God had promised to seek the lost members of his people (Eze 34:4,11 – 12,16).
19:11 *kingdom ... was going to appear at once.* Expecting that the Messiah would establish his kingdom in Jerusalem, Jesus’ followers anticipated imminent military victory. After all, Jesus had been speaking about the kingdom (17:20 – 21; 18:16 – 17,24 – 25) and of salvation “today” (v. 9).
19:12 *A man of noble birth went ... to have himself appointed king.* Because Rome conferred on any subordinate rulers the right to rule, Herod the Great and his son Archelaus (Mt 2:22) both had to travel to Rome to be appointed ruler and then return to Judea. The image was thus intelligible; Jesus was warning his disciples that he would depart before returning.
19:13 *ten minas.* Roughly the wages an average worker could earn in 100 days or (see NIV text note) three months. Although Jewish people were not supposed to charge interest directly to fellow Jews, everyone knew what interest was. Moneylending was common in antiquity, often through temples, which normally doubled as banks because deposits were trusted there.
19:14 *his subjects hated him and sent a delegation.* Historically, Archelaus’s subjects (cf. v. 12) in fact had sent a delegation after him asking that he not be allowed to rule.
19:15 – 19 Because few people had capital, those who had it could lend money at significant interest. Investors thus could receive five or even ten times their investment, or at least double it. Rulers could delegate authority over cities to their own servants. Roman law allowed slaves not only to manage estates, but also to earn and hold money

returned home. Then he sent for the servants to whom he had given the money,
in order to find out what they had gained
with it.
16"The first one came and said, 'Sir,
your mina has earned ten more.'
17" 'Well done, my good servant!'[k] his
master replied. 'Because you have been
trustworthy in a very small matter, take
charge of ten cities.'[l]
18"The second came and said, 'Sir, your
mina has earned five more.'
19"His master answered, 'You take
charge of five cities.'
20"Then another servant came and said,
'Sir, here is your mina; I have kept it laid
away in a piece of cloth. 21I was afraid of
you, because you are a hard man. You take
out what you did not put in and reap what
you did not sow.'[m]
22"His master replied, 'I will judge you
by your own words,[n] you wicked servant! You knew, did you, that I am a hard
man, taking out what I did not put in, and
reaping what I did not sow?[o] 23Why then
didn't you put my money on deposit, so
that when I came back, I could have collected it with interest?'
24"Then he said to those standing by,
'Take his mina away from him and give it
to the one who has ten minas.'
25" 'Sir,' they said, 'he already has ten!'
26"He replied, 'I tell you that to everyone who has, more will be given, but as
for the one who has nothing, even what
they have will be taken away.[p] 27But those
enemies of mine who did not want me to
be king over them — bring them here and
kill them in front of me.' "

19:17 [k]Pr 27:18 [l]Lk 16:10 **19:21** [m]Mt 25:24 **19:22** [n]2Sa 1:16; Job 15:6 [o]Mt 25:26 **19:26** [p]Mt 13:12; 25:29; Lk 8:18

Jesus Comes to Jerusalem as King

19:29-38pp — Mt 21:1-9; Mk 11:1-10
19:35-38pp — Jn 12:12-15

28After Jesus had said this, he went on
ahead, going up to Jerusalem.[q] 29As he approached Bethphage and Bethany[r] at the
hill called the Mount of Olives,[s] he sent
two of his disciples, saying to them, 30"Go
to the village ahead of you, and as you enter it, you will find a colt tied there, which
no one has ever ridden. Untie it and bring
it here. 31If anyone asks you, 'Why are you
untying it?' say, 'The Lord needs it.' "
32Those who were sent ahead went and
found it just as he had told them.[t] 33As they
were untying the colt, its owners asked
them, "Why are you untying the colt?"
34They replied, "The Lord needs it."
35They brought it to Jesus, threw their
cloaks on the colt and put Jesus on it. 36As
he went along, people spread their cloaks[u]
on the road.
37When he came near the place where
the road goes down the Mount of Olives,[v]
the whole crowd of disciples began joyfully to praise God in loud voices for all the
miracles they had seen:

38"Blessed is the king who comes in the
name of the Lord!"[a][w]

"Peace in heaven and glory in the
highest!"[x]

39Some of the Pharisees in the crowd
said to Jesus, "Teacher, rebuke your disciples!"[y]
40"I tell you," he replied, "if they keep
quiet, the stones will cry out."[z]

19:28 [q]Mk 10:32; Lk 9:51 **19:29** [r]Mt 21:17 [s]Mt 21:1 **19:32** [t]Lk 22:13 **19:36** [u]2Ki 9:13 **19:37** [v]Mt 21:1 **19:38** [w]Ps 118:26; Lk 13:35 [x]Lk 2:14 **19:39** [y]Mt 21:15,16 **19:40** [z]Hab 2:11

[a] *38* Psalm 118:26

and receive bonuses. Some imperial freedmen even wielded more power than most aristocrats.
19:20 *laid away in a piece of cloth.* People often buried money in a strongbox to keep it safe, but it would have been safe with the bankers and also increased (in contrast to vv. 16 – 17). To bury it in a piece of cloth, however, was not even safe; it was considered careless. The money did not belong to the servant, and presumably for this reason he did not care what happened to it.
19:21 *hard man.* In a manner that would have shocked ancient audiences, the servant insults the master, essentially blaming his harsh character for why the servant did not increase his investment.
19:22 *by your own words.* Rulers sometimes punished people according to their own answers (e.g., 1Ki 20:40).
19:27 *kill them in front of me.* Herod, Archelaus, and other rulers often dealt harshly with their political opponents.
19:29 *Bethphage.* Apparently a walled suburb of Jerusalem, outside the capital's city walls and about three quarters of a mile (one kilometer) east of the peak of Mount Olivet; it was probably closer to Jerusalem than Bethany, to its east. *Bethany.* Some two miles (three kilometers) east of Jerusalem, on the eastern side of Mount Olivet. *two.* Messengers were often sent in pairs.
19:30 *colt . . . no one has ever ridden.* Animals never before ridden or yoked were often those preferred for dedication to God (Nu 19:2; Dt 21:3; 1Sa 6:7).
19:31 *The Lord needs it.* Roman soldiers could commandeer animals for their use; more to the point here, so could kings, such as the Lord (vv. 34,38).
19:35 Jesus entering Jerusalem on a colt evokes Zec 9:9 — the humble king. A conqueror might enter on a horse; peaceful processions like this one could use donkeys (Jdg 10:4; 12:14; 2Sa 13:29; 1Ki 1:38).
19:36 *spread their cloaks.* Casting garments for a ruler to walk on was a way of hailing him king (2Ki 9:13).
19:38 *the king who comes.* Pilgrims already present often welcomed the newcomers. The crowds would know Ps 118:26 (quoted here) by heart. It was part of the Hallel, consisting of Ps 113 – 118, which was sung at the Passover season. Hopes for a new act of redemption also ran high at Passover; the expectation of the Davidic kingdom here may have been provoked by knowledge of Jesus' proclamation of the kingdom and the way he was entering (see v. 35 and note). *Peace.* See note on 2:14.
19:39 *rebuke your disciples.* As leader, Jesus would be held responsible for the crowd's acclamations unless he corrected them. Public opinion often held teachers accountable for their disciples' behavior.
19:40 *stones will cry out.* Greeks had stories of stones

41 As he approached Jerusalem and saw
the city, he wept over it[a] 42 and said, "If
you, even you, had only known on this
day what would bring you peace—but
now it is hidden from your eyes. 43 The
days will come upon you when your enemies will build an embankment against
you and encircle you and hem you in on
every side.[b] 44 They will dash you to the
ground, you and the children within your
walls.[c] They will not leave one stone on
another,[d] because you did not recognize
the time of God's coming[e] to you."

Jesus at the Temple

19:45,46pp — Mt 21:12-16; Mk 11:15-18; Jn 2:13-16

45 When Jesus entered the temple courts,
he began to drive out those who were
selling. 46 "It is written," he said to them,
" 'My house will be a house of prayer'[a];[f]
but you have made it 'a den of robbers.'[b]"[g]

47 Every day he was teaching at the temple.[h] But the chief priests, the teachers of
the law and the leaders among the people
were trying to kill him.[i] 48 Yet they could
not find any way to do it, because all the
people hung on his words.

The Authority of Jesus Questioned

20:1-8pp — Mt 21:23-27; Mk 11:27-33

20 One day as Jesus was teaching the
people in the temple courts[j] and proclaiming the good news,[k] the chief priests
and the teachers of the law, together with
the elders, came up to him. 2 "Tell us by
what authority you are doing these things,"
they said. "Who gave you this authority?"[l]

3 He replied, "I will also ask you a question. Tell me: 4 John's baptism[m]—was it
from heaven, or of human origin?"

5 They discussed it among themselves
and said, "If we say, 'From heaven,' he
will ask, 'Why didn't you believe him?'
6 But if we say, 'Of human origin,' all the
people[n] will stone us, because they are
persuaded that John was a prophet."[o]

7 So they answered, "We don't know
where it was from."

8 Jesus said, "Neither will I tell you by
what authority I am doing these things."

The Parable of the Tenants

20:9-19pp — Mt 21:33-46; Mk 12:1-12

9 He went on to tell the people this parable: "A man planted a vineyard,[p] rented
it to some farmers and went away for a
long time.[q] 10 At harvest time he sent a servant to the tenants so they would give him
some of the fruit of the vineyard. But the
tenants beat him and sent him away empty-handed. 11 He sent another servant, but
that one also they beat and treated shamefully and sent away empty-handed. 12 He
sent still a third, and they wounded him
and threw him out.

19:41 [a] Isa 22:4; Lk 13:34,35 **19:43** [b] Isa 29:3; Jer 6:6; Eze 4:2; 26:8; Lk 21:20 **19:44** [c] Ps 137:9 [d] Mt 24:2; Mk 13:2; Lk 21:6 [e] 1Pe 2:12 **19:46** [f] Isa 56:7 [g] Jer 7:11 **19:47** [h] Mt 26:55 [i] Mt 12:14; Mk 11:18 **20:1** [j] Mt 26:55 [k] Lk 8:1

20:2 [l] Jn 2:18; Ac 4:7; 7:27 **20:4** [m] Mk 1:4 **20:6** [n] Lk 7:29 [o] Mt 11:9 **20:9** [p] Isa 5:1-7 [q] Mt 25:14

[a] *46* Isaiah 56:7 [b] *46* Jer. 7:11

becoming people (and vice versa), but see note on Mt 3:9. God's creation could be envisioned as celebrating his acts (Isa 55:12).

19:42–44 Within a generation, Rome's army would surround Jerusalem and then destroy it in the year AD 70. The survivors would be slaughtered or enslaved.

19:44 *not leave one stone on another.* This may be hyperbole, but it did underline the traumatic devastation (and makes a verbal connection with v. 40). Ironically, the people in Jerusalem could have averted this fate had they embraced the vision of the kingdom Jesus offered (cf. v. 35).

19:45 See notes on Mk 11:15,16.

19:46 Isa 56:7, quoted here, shows God's ideal for the temple, fitting also Luke's emphasis on prayer. This ideal may contrast with the current arrangement of the temple (see notes on Mk 11:15,16,17). *den of robbers.* Evokes Jer 7:11; in that context people wrongly believe that the temple will protect them from God's judgment, but God warns that he will judge the temple (see vv. 42–44 and note).

19:47 *were trying to kill him.* Any challenge to practices legally conducted in the temple constituted a challenge to the priestly authorities who controlled the temple. The chief priests held significant political power and could deal with affronts to their honor swiftly.

20:1 *teaching the people in the temple courts.* Temples were public places often used for lectures and also suitable for public confrontations. The more public a confrontation, the more each side would feel that its honor was at stake.

20:2 *authority.* Ancient elites saw their own authority as natural (invested by heredity, wealth, or politics) and viewed populist leaders as demagogues who led the unlearned masses astray.

20:3 *also ask you a question.* Questions given in response to questions were common.

20:5–6 *If we say … But if we say.* Without questioning the rightness of their own position, the priestly aristocracy had reason to take into account public opinion before answering in public. In contrast to the Pharisees, the chief priests held minority opinions on many issues, requiring extra sensitivity or Pharisaic help when trying to persuade the people.

20:9 *planted … rented.* Parables allow Jesus to speak truth in riddles (see the article "Parables," p. 1692; see also parables); the meaning is transparent (20:19) but not directly indictable. Although many Galileans owned their own plots of land, many landless peasants worked on larger estates. Wealthy absentee landowners were common; they usually either contracted laborers or rented their land to tenant farmers (serfs).

20:10 Tenant farmers lived and worked landowners' estates and merely paid the landowners a portion of the harvest. Because tenants did not own the land they worked, they sometimes had to pay the landowners half the harvest. Profits from vineyards usually did not begin to be realized until four years after planting; the owner is wealthy enough to be able to afford the delay. Contracts specified the tenants' obligations; owners were advised not to be too lenient lest the tenants default on what they owe.

20:11–12 *beat and treated shamefully … sent away … wounded him … threw him out.* Jewish people hearing the

13“Then the owner of the vineyard said, ‘What shall I do? I will send my son, whom I love;[r] perhaps they will respect him.’

14“But when the tenants saw him, they talked the matter over. ‘This is the heir,’ they said. ‘Let’s kill him, and the inheritance will be ours.’ 15So they threw him out of the vineyard and killed him.

“What then will the owner of the vineyard do to them? 16He will come and kill those tenants[s] and give the vineyard to others.”

When the people heard this, they said, “God forbid!”

17Jesus looked directly at them and asked, “Then what is the meaning of that which is written:

> “ ‘The stone the builders rejected
> has become the cornerstone’[a]?[t]

18Everyone who falls on that stone will be broken to pieces; anyone on whom it falls will be crushed.”[u]

19The teachers of the law and the chief priests looked for a way to arrest him[v] immediately, because they knew he had spoken this parable against them. But they were afraid of the people.[w]

20:13 [r] Mt 3:17
20:16 [s] Lk 19:27
20:17 [t] Ps 118:22; Ac 4:11
20:18 [u] Isa 8:14, 15
20:19 [v] Lk 19:47 [w] Mk 11:18
20:20 [x] Mt 12:10 [y] Mt 27:2

Paying Taxes to Caesar

20:20-26pp — Mt 22:15-22; Mk 12:13-17

20Keeping a close watch on him, they sent spies, who pretended to be sincere. They hoped to catch Jesus in something he said,[x] so that they might hand him over to the power and authority of the governor.[y] 21So the spies questioned him: “Teacher, we know that you speak and teach what is right, and that you do not show partiality but teach the way of God in accordance with the truth.[z] 22Is it right for us to pay taxes to Caesar or not?”

23He saw through their duplicity and said to them, 24“Show me a denarius. Whose image and inscription are on it?”

“Caesar’s,” they replied.

25He said to them, “Then give back to Caesar what is Caesar’s,[a] and to God what is God’s.”

26They were unable to trap him in what he had said there in public. And astonished by his answer, they became silent.

The Resurrection and Marriage

20:27-40pp — Mt 22:23-33; Mk 12:18-27

27Some of the Sadducees,[b] who say there is no resurrection,[c] came to Jesus with a question. 28“Teacher,” they said, “Moses wrote for us that if a man’s brother dies and leaves a wife but no children, the man must marry the widow and raise up offspring for his brother.[d] 29Now there were seven brothers. The first one married a woman and died childless. 30The second 31and then the third married her, and in the same way the seven died, leaving no children. 32Finally, the woman died too. 33Now then, at the resurrection whose wife will she be, since the seven were married to her?”

34Jesus replied, “The people of this age marry and are given in marriage. 35But those who are considered worthy of taking part in the age to come[e] and in the resurrection from the dead will neither marry nor be given in marriage, 36and they can no longer die; for they are like the angels. They are God’s children,[f] since they are children of the resurrection. 37But in the account of the burning bush, even Moses showed that the dead rise, for he calls the

20:21 [z] Jn 3:2
20:25 [a] Lk 23:2; Ro 13:7
20:27 [b] Ac 4:1 [c] Ac 23:8; 1Co 15:12
20:28 [d] Dt 25:5
20:35 [e] Mt 12:32
20:36 [f] Jn 1:12; 1Jn 3:1-2

[a] *17* Psalm 118:22

parable would think of the tradition of Israel persecuting God’s prophets (cf. 13:33 – 34; Ac 7:52).

20:13 – 14,16 See note on Mt 21:37.

20:17 Ps 118:22 (quoted here) is from the Hallel, which consists of Ps 113 – 118 and was sung during Passover season; it would be fresh on everyone’s minds at this time (see note on Mk 11:9).

20:18 See note on Mt 21:44.

20:19 See note on vv. 5 – 6.

20:20 *hand him over.* Roman governors, who had very few people working with them, did not normally seek out people to prosecute but depended on local officials to do this for them.

20:24 *denarius … Whose image and inscription …?* See note on Mt 22:19 – 20.

20:25 *what is Caesar’s … what is God’s.* See note on Mt 22:21.

20:26 *became silent.* In ancient settings where honor was challenged, those who were silenced were also shamed. They may have been unprepared to try to counter Jesus’ answer in part because they had not expected him to be learned enough to debate them.

20:27 *no resurrection.* See note on Mt 22:23.

20:28 *man must marry … raise up offspring.* Because widows could be left destitute, the extended families into which they married were supposed to provide for them by having a brother of the deceased marry the widow (Dt 25:5 – 6).

20:29 – 31 The story line of a widow having seven husbands (though not brothers) evokes a popular Jewish story in Tobit 3:8. In antiquity, many men would assume (even after the second or third husband) that the woman was dangerous or cursed (though this was not correct; Ge 38:11,27).

20:33 Sadducees were known to pose conundrums such as this to the Pharisees, seeking to illustrate what they believed were the absurd implications of belief in the resurrection.

20:34 *marry … given in marriage.* Grooms married; fathers gave their daughters in marriage.

20:36 *like the angels.* Most Jewish people agreed that angels, who were immortal, did not propagate; the same then would be true of those resurrected to immortality.

20:37 *account of the burning bush.* The account of Ex 3.

Lord 'the God of Abraham, and the God of
Isaac, and the God of Jacob.'[a][g] 38He is not
the God of the dead, but of the living, for
to him all are alive."

39Some of the teachers of the law responded, "Well said, teacher!" 40And no
one dared to ask him any more questions.[h]

Whose Son Is the Messiah?

20:41-47pp — Mt 22:41 – 23:7; Mk 12:35-40

41Then Jesus said to them, "Why is it
said that the Messiah is the son of David?[i]
42David himself declares in the Book of
Psalms:

"'The Lord said to my Lord:
"Sit at my right hand
43until I make your enemies
a footstool for your feet."'[b][j]

44David calls him 'Lord.' How then can he
be his son?"

Warning Against the Teachers of the Law

45While all the people were listening,
Jesus said to his disciples, 46"Beware of
the teachers of the law. They like to walk
around in flowing robes and love to be
greeted with respect in the marketplaces and have the most important seats in
the synagogues and the places of hon-
or at banquets.[k] 47They devour widows'
houses and for a show make lengthy
prayers. These men will be punished most
severely."

The Widow's Offering

21:1-4pp — Mk 12:41-44

21 As Jesus looked up, he saw the rich
putting their gifts into the temple
treasury.[l] 2He also saw a poor widow put
in two very small copper coins. 3"Truly I
tell you," he said, "this poor widow has
put in more than all the others. 4All these
people gave their gifts out of their wealth;
but she out of her poverty put in all she
had to live on."[m]

The Destruction of the Temple and Signs of the End Times

21:5-36pp — Mt 24; Mk 13
21:12-17pp — Mt 10:17-22

5Some of his disciples were remarking
about how the temple was adorned with
beautiful stones and with gifts dedicated
to God. But Jesus said, 6"As for what you
see here, the time will come when not one
stone will be left on another;[n] every one of
them will be thrown down."

7"Teacher," they asked, "when will
these things happen? And what will be
the sign that they are about to take place?"
8He replied: "Watch out that you are not

20:37 [g] Ex 3:6 **20:40** [h] Mt 22:46; Mk 12:34 **20:41** [i] Mt 1:1 **20:43** [j] Ps 110:1; Mt 22:44 **20:46** [k] Lk 11:43 **21:1** [l] Mt 27:6; Jn 8:20 **21:4** [m] 2Co 8:12 **21:6** [n] Lk 19:44

[a] 37 Exodus 3:6 [b] 43 Psalm 110:1

Although the most obvious Biblical text to which Jesus would allude to prove his case for the resurrection could be Da 12:2, Jesus here proves his case from the Pentateuch (the first five books of the Bible). When arguing against Sadducees, Pharisees also made a case from the Pentateuch, because that was what Sadducees would readily accept. *the God of Abraham, and the God of Isaac, and the God of Jacob.* See note on Mt 22:32.

20:39 *teachers of the law.* Pharisaic teachers of the law would have actually agreed with Jesus' response (see note on v. 37).

20:40 See note on v. 26.

20:41 *son of David.* Jewish people who expected a royal Messiah expected him to be a descendant of David.

20:42 – 44 See notes on Mt 22:44,45.

20:46 *important seats.* See note on Mk 12:39. *places of honor.* See note on Mt 23:6.

20:47 *devour widows' houses.* Widows often had debt and normally lacked influential advocates; people of status, if unscrupulous, could thus seize their property more readily, often through legal means. Scripture demanded special consideration for the defenseless, including widows (Ex 22:22; Dt 10:18; Isa 1:17,23; 10:2; Jer 7:6; 22:3). (In that social system, most women lacked sufficient means to support themselves.)

21:1 *temple treasury.* Temples in the ancient world doubled as banks, since they were considered the safest place to deposit money; few people were sacrilegious enough to risk offending a deity by robbing a temple. Jewish people also donated money to the temple; indeed, every male Jewish adult paid an annual tax for its upkeep. The temple treasury (where money was stored) was adjacent to the court of women, which was the court between the outer court (where the events of 19:45 – 46 took place) and the court of Israel.

21:2 *copper coins.* Each of the two coins was worth only 1/128 of a denarius. For the woman's access to the treasury, see note on v. 1.

21:4 On the poverty and vulnerability of widows, see note on 20:47.

21:5 *adorned with beautiful stones.* The beauty of Jerusalem's temple was famous throughout the Mediterranean world. It was the largest of ancient temples and considered sacred even to most of those who resented its builder, Herod. It included various courts and outer porches; although laypersons could not pass beyond the court of Israel, the sanctuary's height made it visible. Gates of bronze and a vine made of gold decorated the temple. The majority of Jews lived outside of Israel, but the temple tax (see note on Mt 17:24) shows that they also remained loyal to the temple.

21:6 *not one stone will be left on another.* See note on Mt 24:2.

21:7 *when will these things happen?* Many ancient Jewish thinkers were interested in the timing of events that they associated with the end time and the signs that would accompany them. In the OT, prophecy often linked events according to their topic more than according to their timing; thus scholars debate the relationship between the temple's destruction here and Jesus' future coming (cf. v. 27).

21:8 The Jewish historian Josephus reports a number of "false prophets" who tried to emulate Moses or Joshua, and hence probably viewed themselves as messianic,

deceived. For many will come in my name,
claiming, 'I am he,' and, 'The time is near.'
Do not follow them.[o] 9When you hear of
wars and uprisings, do not be frightened.
These things must happen first, but the
end will not come right away."

10Then he said to them: "Nation will rise
against nation, and kingdom against kingdom.[p] 11There will be great earthquakes,
famines and pestilences in various places, and fearful events and great signs from
heaven.[q]

12"But before all this, they will seize
you and persecute you. They will hand
you over to synagogues and put you in
prison, and you will be brought before
kings and governors, and all on account
of my name. 13And so you will bear testimony to me.[r] 14But make up your mind
not to worry beforehand how you will
defend yourselves.[s] 15For I will give you[t]
words and wisdom that none of your adversaries will be able to resist or contradict. 16You will be betrayed even by parents, brothers and sisters, relatives and
friends,[u] and they will put some of you to
death. 17Everyone will hate you because
of me.[v] 18But not a hair of your head will
perish.[w] 19Stand firm, and you will win
life.[x]

20"When you see Jerusalem being surrounded by armies,[y] you will know that
its desolation is near. 21Then let those who
are in Judea flee to the mountains, let
those in the city get out, and let those in
the country not enter the city.[z] 22For this is
the time of punishment[a] in fulfillment[b] of
all that has been written. 23How dreadful it
will be in those days for pregnant women
and nursing mothers! There will be great
distress in the land and wrath against this
people. 24They will fall by the sword and
will be taken as prisoners to all the nations. Jerusalem will be trampled[c] on by
the Gentiles until the times of the Gentiles
are fulfilled.

25"There will be signs in the sun, moon
and stars. On the earth, nations will be in
anguish and perplexity at the roaring and
tossing of the sea.[d] 26People will faint from
terror, apprehensive of what is coming on
the world, for the heavenly bodies will be
shaken.[e] 27At that time they will see the
Son of Man[f] coming in a cloud[g] with power and great glory. 28When these things
begin to take place, stand up and lift up
your heads, because your redemption is
drawing near."[h]

29He told them this parable: "Look at
the fig tree and all the trees. 30When they
sprout leaves, you can see for yourselves
and know that summer is near. 31Even so,

21:8 [o] Lk 17:23
21:10 [p] 2Ch 15:6; Isa 19:2
21:11 [q] Isa 29:6; Joel 2:30
21:13 [r] Php 1:12
21:14 [s] Lk 12:11
21:15 [t] Lk 12:12
21:16 [u] Lk 12:52,53
21:17 [v] Jn 15:21
21:18 [w] Mt 10:30
21:19 [x] Mt 10:22
21:20 [y] Lk 19:43
21:21 [z] Lk 17:31
21:22 [a] Isa 63:4; Da 9:24-27; Hos 9:7 [b] Mt 1:22
21:24 [c] Isa 5:5; 63:18; Da 8:13; Rev 11:2
21:25 [d] 2Pe 3:10,12
21:26 [e] Mt 24:29
21:27 [f] Mt 8:20 [g] Rev 1:7
21:28 [h] Lk 18:7

---

even in the decades between Jesus' resurrection and AD 70 (see notes on Ac 5:36–37; 21:38).

21:9–11 Many Jewish thinkers offered lists of sufferings that would precede the end of the age. Although these sufferings include those mentioned here, they also include some more unusual phenomena such as mutant infants. In contrast to many other Jewish thinkers, Jesus identifies at least some of the events listed here as not yet the end (v. 9). Wars, earthquakes, and famines happened before AD 70 (as well as afterward).

21:12 *hand you over to synagogues.* Priests and other elders normally judged local councils. Synagogues doubled as community centers, and disciplines could be meted out there. *put you in prison.* Courts used prisons as places of (sometimes lengthy) detention until trial or execution more often than as punishment per se, but prison conditions were usually deplorable: crowded, little food except what was brought from outside, often little light, and no toilet facilities or means of washing.

21:16 *betrayed even by … relatives and friends.* Betrayal by family members and close friends was considered particularly heinous and unusual. Sometimes those so betrayed were also criticized for their poor judgment in choosing friends, unless discernment was clearly impossible. According to many ancient ideals, true friends were supposed to be ready to die for and with one another.

21:18 See note on 12:7.

21:20 *surrounded by armies.* Shortly after Jewish revolutionaries killed the Roman garrison in Jerusalem and took over the city in AD 66, Rome's armies surrounded the city. Initially some fugitives escaped the revolutionaries' control and surrendered to the Romans, but eventually safe surrender became impossible. Syrian auxiliaries working for Rome, hearing that Judean fugitives swallowed jewels in hopes of maintaining resources after their escape, intercepted the fugitives and sliced them open.

21:21 *flee to the mountains.* See note on Mt 24:16.

21:22 *time of punishment.* For similar OT expressions, see Jer 46:10; Hos 9:7.

21:23 *pregnant women and nursing mothers.* See note on Mt 24:19.

21:24 *taken as prisoners to all the nations.* Those who survived Jerusalem's siege were enslaved when Jerusalem fell in AD 70. *Jerusalem will be trampled.* This happened after AD 70. Moreover, after a later revolt, Romans rebuilt Jerusalem as a Roman city, Aelia Capitolina, in AD 135. *until the times of the Gentiles are fulfilled.* Jewish people believed that God had permitted four empires to rule the world (in this period, they believed Rome the final of those four) before God would establish his own kingdom.

21:25 Cf., e.g., Isa 13:10; Joel 2:31. Jewish people expected heavenly signs to precede the kingdom. Josephus also noted reports of heavenly signs before the fall of Jerusalem (*Wars* 6.298).

21:27 *the Son of Man coming in a cloud.* Alludes to Da 7:13; the son of man was given "authority, glory and sovereign power" in Da 7:14.

21:28 *redemption is drawing near.* Some Jewish people spoke of their coming liberation and deliverance as "redemption."

21:29–30 Unlike most Judean trees, fig trees lost their leaves each year; they produced new leaves (see note on Mk 11:13) when summer was coming, before the wheat harvest and well before the grape vintage. Once the signs mentioned in this context were fulfilled, no further predicted barriers would remain to the coming of the kingdom.

when you see these things happening, you
know that the kingdom of God[i] is near.
32“Truly I tell you, this generation[j] will
certainly not pass away until all these
things have happened. 33Heaven and earth
will pass away, but my words will never
pass away.[k]
34“Be careful, or your hearts will be
weighed down with carousing, drunkenness and the anxieties of life,[l] and that day
will close on you suddenly[m] like a trap.
35For it will come on all those who live on
the face of the whole earth. 36Be always
on the watch, and pray[n] that you may be
able to escape all that is about to happen,
and that you may be able to stand before
the Son of Man.”
37Each day Jesus was teaching at the
temple,[o] and each evening he went out[p]
to spend the night on the hill called the
Mount of Olives,[q] 38and all the people
came early in the morning to hear him at
the temple.[r]

Judas Agrees to Betray Jesus

22:1,2pp — Mt 26:2-5; Mk 14:1,2,10,11

22 Now the Festival of Unleavened
Bread, called the Passover, was
approaching,[s] 2and the chief priests and
the teachers of the law were looking for
some way to get rid of Jesus,[t] for they
were afraid of the people. 3Then Satan[u]
entered Judas, called Iscariot,[v] one of
the Twelve. 4And Judas went to the chief
priests and the officers of the temple
guard[w] and discussed with them how he
might betray Jesus. 5They were delighted and agreed to give him money.[x] 6He
consented, and watched for an opportunity to hand Jesus over to them when no
crowd was present.

21:31 [i] Mt 3:2
21:32 [j] Lk 11:50; 17:25
21:33 [k] Mt 5:18
21:34 [l] Mk 4:19 [m] Lk 12:40,46; 1Th 5:2-7
21:36 [n] Mt 26:41
21:37 [o] Mt 26:55 [p] Mk 11:19 [q] Mt 21:1
21:38 [r] Jn 8:2
22:1 [s] Jn 11:55
22:2 [t] Mt 12:14
22:3 [u] Mt 4:10; Jn 13:2 [v] Mt 10:4
22:4 [w] ver 52; Ac 4:1; 5:24
22:5 [x] Zec 11:12
22:7 [y] Ex 12:18-20; Dt 16:5-8; Mk 14:12
22:8 [z] Ac 3:1, 11; 4:13, 19; 8:14
22:13 [a] Lk 19:32
22:14 [b] Mk 6:30 [c] Mt 26:20; Mk 14:17, 18
22:15 [d] Mt 16:21
22:16 [e] Lk 14:15; Rev 19:9

The Last Supper

22:7-13pp — Mt 26:17-19; Mk 14:12-16
22:17-20pp — Mt 26:26-29; Mk 14:22-25; 1Co 11:23-25
22:21-23pp — Mt 26:21-24; Mk 14:18-21; Jn 13:21-30
22:25-27pp — Mt 20:25-28; Mk 10:42-45
22:33,34pp — Mt 26:33-35; Mk 14:29-31; Jn 13:37,38

7Then came the day of Unleavened
Bread on which the Passover lamb had to
be sacrificed.[y] 8Jesus sent Peter and John,[z]
saying, “Go and make preparations for us
to eat the Passover.”
9“Where do you want us to prepare for
it?” they asked.
10He replied, “As you enter the city, a
man carrying a jar of water will meet you.
Follow him to the house that he enters,
11and say to the owner of the house, ‘The
Teacher asks: Where is the guest room,
where I may eat the Passover with my disciples?’ 12He will show you a large room
upstairs, all furnished. Make preparations
there.”
13They left and found things just as
Jesus had told them.[a] So they prepared
the Passover.
14When the hour came, Jesus and his
apostles[b] reclined at the table.[c] 15And he
said to them, “I have eagerly desired to
eat this Passover with you before I suffer.[d]
16For I tell you, I will not eat it again until it finds fulfillment in the kingdom of
God.”[e]
17After taking the cup, he gave thanks
and said, “Take this and divide it among
you. 18For I tell you I will not drink again

21:32 *this generation.* In Luke, this refers to the generation then living (11:50–51; 17:25).
21:33 God's words are more permanent than heaven and earth (Jer 31:35–37; on the permanence of God's word, cf. Isa 40:6–8; Zec 1:5–6).
21:34 *Be careful … suddenly.* The prophets sometimes spoke of judgment as a trap that would catch the unprepared (Isa 8:14; 24:17; Jer 50:24; Eze 12:13; 17:20).
21:36 *escape.* This term can mean "to flee or avoid danger"; cf. perhaps v. 21.
21:37 Because Jerusalem was crowded, it made sense to lodge outside the city until the Passover meal. Jesus was staying in Bethany, on the Mount of Olives, about two miles (three kilometers) east of Jerusalem (see note on Mk 11:1).
21:38 *early in the morning.* Artificial lighting was limited, so most people rose at sunrise.
22:1 *Festival of Unleavened Bread … Passover.* By this period, Passover and the Festival of Unleavened Bread were often treated together as parts of a single festival (e.g., Josephus, *Antiquities* 14.21; 17.213; 18.29; 20.106).
22:2 *some way to get rid of Jesus.* The hostile portrayal of the chief priests here is not limited to the Gospels; most surviving Jewish sources from the period (the Dead Sea Scrolls, rabbis' memories from the Pharisees, and reports in Josephus) depict members of this group exploiting their power against others.
22:3 *Satan entered Judas.* Jewish people understood that Satan could move people to do evil things, though God could still be sovereignly at work (e.g., compare 1Ch 21:1 with 2Sa 24:1).
22:4 *officers of the temple guard.* See note on Ac 4:1.
22:7 See note on v. 1.
22:10 *a man carrying a jar of water.* Although male servants could carry water, more often one would see women carrying water. Because most homes lacked their own running water, urban residents would typically have to go to public fountains to procure water.
22:11–12 See note on Mt 26:17.
22:14 *hour came … reclined.* For banquets, such as Passover, Jews adopted the Greek custom of reclining. The Passover began at sundown, around 6:00 p.m.
22:17 *the cup.* Jewish meals regularly included opening thanks for the wine and the bread. Like the father of a family at a Passover meal, Jesus would lift the cup as he spoke about it. Tradition suggests that the wine used for Passover was red.
22:18 *will not drink again … until.* Jewish people often offered vows of abstinence, promising not to partake of a particular food or drink until such-and-such a matter occurred.

from the fruit of the vine until the kingdom of God comes."
19And he took bread, gave thanks and
broke it,[f] and gave it to them, saying,
"This is my body given for you; do this in
remembrance of me."
20In the same way, after the supper he
took the cup, saying, "This cup is the new
covenant[g] in my blood, which is poured
out for you.[a] 21But the hand of him who
is going to betray me is with mine on the
table.[h] 22The Son of Man[i] will go as it has
been decreed.[j] But woe to that man who
betrays him!" 23They began to question
among themselves which of them it might
be who would do this.
24A dispute also arose among them
as to which of them was considered to
be greatest.[k] 25Jesus said to them, "The
kings of the Gentiles lord it over them;
and those who exercise authority over
them call themselves Benefactors. 26But
you are not to be like that. Instead, the
greatest among you should be like the
youngest,[l] and the one who rules like the
one who serves.[m] 27For who is greater,
the one who is at the table or the one
who serves? Is it not the one who is at the
table? But I am among you as one who
serves.[n] 28You are those who have stood
by me in my trials. 29And I confer on you
a kingdom,[o] just as my Father conferred
one on me, 30so that you may eat and
drink at my table in my kingdom[p] and
sit on thrones, judging the twelve tribes
of Israel.[q]
31"Simon, Simon, Satan has asked[r]
to sift all of you as wheat.[s] 32But I have
prayed for you,[t] Simon, that your faith
may not fail. And when you have turned
back, strengthen your brothers."[u]
33But he replied, "Lord, I am ready to go
with you to prison and to death."[v]
34Jesus answered, "I tell you, Peter, before the rooster crows today, you will deny
three times that you know me."
35Then Jesus asked them, "When I sent
you without purse, bag or sandals,[w] did
you lack anything?"
"Nothing," they answered.
36He said to them, "But now if you have
a purse, take it, and also a bag; and if you
don't have a sword, sell your cloak and buy
one. 37It is written: 'And he was numbered
with the transgressors'[b];[x] and I tell you that
this must be fulfilled in me. Yes, what is
written about me is reaching its fulfillment."
38The disciples said, "See, Lord, here are
two swords."
"That's enough!" he replied.

Jesus Prays on the Mount of Olives

22:40-46pp — Mt 26:36-46; Mk 14:32-42

39Jesus went out as usual[y] to the Mount
of Olives,[z] and his disciples followed him.

22:19 [f] Mt 14:19 **22:20** [g] Ex 24:8; Isa 42:6; Jer 31:31-34; Zec 9:11; 2Co 3:6; Heb 8:6; 9:15 **22:21** [h] Ps 41:9 **22:22** [i] Mt 8:20 [j] Ac 2:23; 4:28 **22:24** [k] Mk 9:34; Lk 9:46 **22:26** [l] 1Pe 5:5 [m] Mk 9:35; Lk 9:48 **22:27** [n] Mt 20:28; Lk 12:37 **22:29** [o] Mt 25:34; 2Ti 2:12 **22:30** [p] Lk 14:15 [q] Mt 19:28 **22:31** [r] Job 1:6-12 [s] Am 9:9 **22:32** [t] Jn 17:9, 15; Ro 8:34 [u] Jn 21:15-17 **22:33** [v] Jn 11:16 **22:35** [w] Mt 10:9, 10; Lk 9:3; 10:4 **22:37** [x] Isa 53:12 **22:39** [y] Lk 21:37 [z] Mt 21:1

[a] 19,20 Some manuscripts do not have *given for you . . . poured out for you.* [b] 37 Isaiah 53:12

22:19 *This is my body given for you.* Passover recalled deliverance from slavery in Egypt. Even at everyday meals, the father could give thanks for the bread, break it and then distribute it. If later tradition reflects first-century practice, however, the household head gave thanks at normal meals for wine first and then bread, whereas at Passover he would give thanks for the bread first, as here. At Passover he would give thanks for the unleavened bread and explain its significance for Passover: "This is the bread of affliction that our ancestors ate when they came from Egypt" (cf. Dt 16:3). No one believed that it was literally the *same* bread eaten by their ancestors; instead, they reenacted their ancestors' experience, participating by faith as their descendants. Tradition suggests that the head of the household would sit up and lift the bread as he spoke about it. Here Jesus shockingly offers a different meaning for the bread, as he speaks of a new act of redemption. *remembrance.* Probably also evokes a Passover context: at Passover, God's people remembered by reenacting the original Passover meal (Ex 12:14; 13:3; Dt 16:2 – 3).
22:20 *new covenant in my blood.* See note on Mt 26:28.
22:21 *with mine on the table.* Jesus might mean that the betrayer shares the same table, hence the same couch or setting with three or four persons. Cf. Mt 26:23, Mk 14:20, Jn 13:28 (see notes there).
22:22 *The Son of Man will go as it has been decreed.* In Da 7:13 – 14,21 – 22, the son of Man apparently is connected with the holy people who suffer as well as reign. *woe.* See note on 6:24 – 25.
22:24 See note on 9:46.
22:25 *Benefactors.* Throughout the empire, inscriptions honored as "benefactors" rulers and other powerful people who gave favors to the public. Traditionally eastern rulers even claimed to be divine, and deceased Caesars were honored in the same way.
22:26 *greatest ... like the youngest.* In general, honor increased with age in ancient culture.
22:30 *judging the twelve tribes of Israel.* Most Jewish people expected God to restore the 12 tribes of Israel at the time of the end. Qumran documents even speak of a group of 12 leaders, apparently because of their expectation that God would restore the 12 tribes.
22:31 *Satan has asked to sift all of you as wheat.* Satan raises charges, accusing and trying God's servants (Job 1:9 – 12; 2:4 – 7). Grain was sifted to remove the elements other than wheat (cf. Am 9:9).
22:34 *before the rooster crows.* Roosters crow often during the night, but ancient literature associates them most often with dawn.
22:36 *if you don't have a sword ... buy one.* Jesus' enemies wanted to charge him with leading a revolutionary movement (23:2); Jesus accommodates this expectation sufficiently (two swords being enough, v. 38) to allow him to be convicted (v. 37), fulfilling Isa 53:12. (On the application to Jesus of Isaiah's servant passages, see note on Mt 12:18 – 21.) *sword.* Here can refer to either a dagger or short sword. Some have even suggested that knives used for cutting the food could be in view in v. 38, though that is not the usual literal sense of the term.
22:39 *went out ... to the Mount of Olives.* See note on Mt 26:30.

40 On reaching the place, he said to them,
"Pray that you will not fall into temptation."[a] 41 He withdrew about a stone's
throw beyond them, knelt down[b] and
prayed, 42 "Father, if you are willing, take
this cup[c] from me; yet not my will, but
yours be done."[d] 43 An angel from heaven
appeared to him and strengthened him.[e]
44 And being in anguish, he prayed more
earnestly, and his sweat was like drops of
blood falling to the ground.[a]

45 When he rose from prayer and went
back to the disciples, he found them
asleep, exhausted from sorrow. 46 "Why
are you sleeping?" he asked them. "Get
up and pray so that you will not fall into
temptation."[f]

Jesus Arrested

22:47-53pp — Mt 26:47-56; Mk 14:43-50; Jn 18:3-11

47 While he was still speaking a crowd
came up, and the man who was called Judas, one of the Twelve, was leading them.
He approached Jesus to kiss him, 48 but
Jesus asked him, "Judas, are you betraying the Son of Man with a kiss?"

49 When Jesus' followers saw what was
going to happen, they said, "Lord, should
we strike with our swords?"[g] 50 And one of
them struck the servant of the high priest,
cutting off his right ear.

51 But Jesus answered, "No more of
this!" And he touched the man's ear and
healed him.

52 Then Jesus said to the chief priests,
the officers of the temple guard,[h] and the
elders, who had come for him, "Am I leading a rebellion, that you have come with
swords and clubs? 53 Every day I was with
you in the temple courts,[i] and you did not
lay a hand on me. But this is your hour[j] —
when darkness reigns."[k]

Peter Disowns Jesus

22:55-62pp — Mt 26:69-75; Mk 14:66-72; Jn 18:16-18,25-27

54 Then seizing him, they led him away
and took him into the house of the high
priest.[l] Peter followed at a distance.[m]
55 And when some there had kindled a fire
in the middle of the courtyard and had sat
down together, Peter sat down with them.
56 A servant girl saw him seated there in
the firelight. She looked closely at him and
said, "This man was with him."

57 But he denied it. "Woman, I don't
know him," he said.

58 A little later someone else saw him
and said, "You also are one of them."

"Man, I am not!" Peter replied.

59 About an hour later another asserted,
"Certainly this fellow was with him, for he
is a Galilean."[n]

60 Peter replied, "Man, I don't know
what you're talking about!" Just as he was
speaking, the rooster crowed. 61 The Lord[o]
turned and looked straight at Peter. Then
Peter remembered the word the Lord had
spoken to him: "Before the rooster crows
today, you will disown me three times."[p]
62 And he went outside and wept bitterly.

The Guards Mock Jesus

22:63-65pp — Mt 26:67,68; Mk 14:65; Jn 18:22,23

63 The men who were guarding Jesus
began mocking and beating him. 64 They
blindfolded him and demanded, "Prophesy!

22:40 [a] Mt 6:13 **22:41** [b] Lk 18:11 **22:42** [c] Mt 20:22 [d] Mt 26:39 **22:43** [e] Mt 4:11; Mk 1:13 **22:46** [f] ver 40 **22:49** [g] ver 38 **22:52** [h] ver 4 **22:53** [i] Mt 26:55 [j] Jn 12:27 [k] Mt 8:12; Jn 1:5; 3:20 **22:54** [l] Mt 26:57; Mk 14:53 [m] Mt 26:58; Mk 14:54; Jn 18:15 **22:59** [n] Lk 23:6 **22:61** [o] Lk 7:13 [p] ver 34

[a] *43,44* Many early manuscripts do not have verses 43 and 44.

22:40 *Pray ... temptation.* In context, one common ancient Jewish prayer against temptation is a prayer that the petitioners would not succumb to temptation; that is probably the meaning in this context as well (vv. 46–47).
22:42 *take this cup.* Biblical prophets used a cup to symbolize sufferings, normally as divine judgment (Isa 51:17; Jer 25:15–17; 51:7; Hab 2:16; Zec 12:2); here it applies to Jesus' painful death (v. 20).
22:45 *exhausted from sorrow.* It was customary to stay awake on Passover and talk of God's acts of redemption, despite the heavy meal. On many Passovers, the disciples had probably stayed awake late — but not this time.
22:47 *approached Jesus to kiss him.* Using a disciple to approach the group would delay resistance or flight and allow the leaders to identify Jesus quickly despite the cover of night. *kiss.* Kisses were used in friendly greetings, including respectful greetings to one's teacher. Betrayal with a kiss (v. 48) was thus particularly heinous (2Sa 20:9–10; Pr 27:6). Typical kisses of greeting were light kisses on the lips, although for superiors one could kiss the cheek or even their finger ring.
22:52 *with swords and clubs.* Some later Jewish traditions complained that the servants of the high priest in this period used clubs when abusing people.
22:53 *your hour — when darkness reigns.* Darkness was viewed as the time when people could commit acts that they would not commit if people could see them. Authorities generally suspected those who acted only at night of being subversive and seeking to hide their activity; here it is the authorities who act this way.
22:54 *house of the high priest.* Trying someone in the high priest's home at night (or even interrogating them there in preparation for a morning hearing) violated ancient judicial ethics, which required unbiased public hearings.
22:55 *courtyard.* Can refer to, among other things, the gated, walled area open to the sky in front of the actual dwelling.
22:59 *he is a Galilean.* See note on Mt 26:73.
22:63 *mocking and beating him.* This behavior violated all official ancient legal ethics, though in practice abuse of prisoners was common in antiquity.
22:64 *Prophesy!* While Jesus' abusers mock him as a false prophet, i.e., for a capital offense (Dt 13:5), Jesus' prophecy about Peter has just been fulfilled (Lk 22:54–62), as one would expect for a true prophet (Dt 18:22).

Who hit you?" [65]And they said many other insulting things to him.[q]

Jesus Before Pilate and Herod

22:67-71pp — Mt 26:63-66; Mk 14:61-63; Jn 18:19-21
23:2,3pp — Mt 27:11-14; Mk 15:2-5; Jn 18:29-37
23:18-25pp — Mt 27:15-26; Mk 15:6-15; Jn 18:39 – 19:16

[66]At daybreak the council[r] of the elders of the people, both the chief priests and the teachers of the law, met together,[s] and Jesus was led before them. [67]"If you are the Messiah," they said, "tell us."

Jesus answered, "If I tell you, you will not believe me, [68]and if I asked you, you would not answer.[t] [69]But from now on, the Son of Man will be seated at the right hand of the mighty God."[u]

[70]They all asked, "Are you then the Son of God?"[v]

He replied, "You say that I am."[w]

[71]Then they said, "Why do we need any more testimony? We have heard it from his own lips."

23 Then the whole assembly rose and led him off to Pilate.[x] [2]And they began to accuse him, saying, "We have found this man subverting our nation.[y] He opposes payment of taxes to Caesar[z] and claims to be Messiah, a king."[a]

[3]So Pilate asked Jesus, "Are you the king of the Jews?"

"You have said so," Jesus replied.

[4]Then Pilate announced to the chief priests and the crowd, "I find no basis for a charge against this man."[b]

[5]But they insisted, "He stirs up the people all over Judea by his teaching. He started in Galilee[c] and has come all the way here."

[6]On hearing this, Pilate asked if the man was a Galilean.[d] [7]When he learned that Jesus was under Herod's jurisdiction, he sent him to Herod,[e] who was also in Jerusalem at that time.

[8]When Herod saw Jesus, he was greatly pleased, because for a long time he had been wanting to see him.[f] From what he had heard about him, he hoped to see him perform a sign of some sort. [9]He plied him with many questions, but Jesus gave him no answer.[g] [10]The chief priests and the teachers of the law were standing there, vehemently accusing him. [11]Then Herod and his soldiers ridiculed and mocked him. Dressing him in an elegant robe,[h] they sent him back to Pilate. [12]That day Herod and Pilate became friends[i] — before this they had been enemies.

[13]Pilate called together the chief priests, the rulers and the people, [14]and said to them, "You brought me this man as one who was inciting the people to rebellion. I have examined him in your presence and have found no basis for your charges against him.[j] [15]Neither has Herod, for he sent him back to us; as you can see, he has done nothing to deserve death. [16]Therefore, I will punish him[k] and then release him." [17][a]

[18]But the whole crowd shouted, "Away with this man! Release Barabbas to us!"[l] [19](Barabbas had been thrown into prison for an insurrection in the city, and for murder.)

[20]Wanting to release Jesus, Pilate appealed to them again. [21]But they kept shouting, "Crucify him! Crucify him!"

[22]For the third time he spoke to them: "Why? What crime has this man committed? I have found in him no grounds for the death penalty. Therefore I will have him punished and then release him."[m]

[23]But with loud shouts they insistently demanded that he be crucified, and their shouts prevailed. [24]So Pilate decided to

[a] *17* Some manuscripts include here words similar to Matt. 27:15 and Mark 15:6.

22:65 [q]Mt 16:21
22:66 [r]Mt 5:22 [s]Mt 27:1; Mk 15:1
22:68 [t]Lk 20:3-8
22:69 [u]Mk 16:19
22:70 [v]Mt 4:3 [w]Mt 27:11; Lk 23:3
23:1 [x]Mt 27:2; Mk 15:1; Jn 18:28
23:2 [y]ver 14 [z]Lk 20:22 [a]Jn 19:12
23:4 [b]ver 14, 22,41; Mt 27:23; Jn 18:38; 1Ti 6:13; 2Co 5:21
23:5 [c]Mk 1:14
23:6 [d]Lk 22:59
23:7 [e]Mt 14:1; Lk 3:1
23:8 [f]Lk 9:9
23:9 [g]Mk 14:61
23:11 [h]Mk 15:17-19; Jn 19:2,3
23:12 [i]Ac 4:27
23:14 [j]ver 4
23:16 [k]ver 22; Mt 27:26; Jn 19:1; Ac 16:37; 2Co 11:23,24
23:18 [l]Ac 3:13, 14
23:22 [m]ver 16

22:66 *At daybreak.* Night hearings lacked even a semblance of legality, but at dawn members of the Sanhedrin (translated here as "council"), Jerusalem's senate, could formulate an official charge for Pilate. The current Sanhedrin was dominated by families originally approved as supporters of Herod the Great; he had reportedly executed more independent-minded members of the previous Sanhedrin (see the article "Herod the Great," p. 1610). **22:69** *Son of Man ... right hand of the mighty God.* Jesus' response combines Daniel's son of man (Da 7:13 – 14) with the psalmist's "Lord" (Ps 110:1). **22:70** *Are you then the Son of God?* The Dead Sea Scrolls attest that some understood the Messiah as Son of God. The Sadducees, whose authority depended on continuing Roman favor and who did not believe in a future resurrection, may not have been convinced about a future Messiah either, but they would be familiar with contemporary views. **23:1** See note on Mt 27:1. *Pilate.* See note on Mt 27:2. **23:2** *opposes payment of taxes to Caesar and claims to be ... a king.* Protests against taxes had led to a disastrous revolt a generation earlier; both (1) inciting people not to pay taxes and (2) claiming to be a king constituted acts of treason, punishable by death. Cf. 20:22 – 25. **23:3** *king of the Jews.* See note on Mt 27:11. **23:4** Pilate was known for not cooperating voluntarily with the local authorities. He may see Jesus as not a political threat but an impractical sage (see note on Jn 18:36). **23:7** *sent him to Herod.* Although Pilate had authority to try Jesus, he could delegate the case to Herod Antipas, who would be in town for Passover. This would free Pilate of the responsibility. **23:11** *elegant robe.* Could also be translated "bright robe," applied especially to white ones; Jewish kings often wore white robes. **23:12** *became friends.* Pilate and Herod Antipas had clashed before. Acts of cooperation could transcend political enmity and create political alliances, which ancients often called "friendship." **23:24** *grant their demand.* For pragmatic Roman gover-

grant their demand. 25He released the man
who had been thrown into prison for insurrection and murder, the one they asked
for, and surrendered Jesus to their will.

The Crucifixion of Jesus

23:33-43pp — Mt 27:33-44; Mk 15:22-32; Jn 19:17-24

26As the soldiers led him away, they
seized Simon from Cyrene,[n] who was
on his way in from the country, and put
the cross on him and made him carry it
behind Jesus.[o] 27A large number of people followed him, including women who
mourned and wailed[p] for him. 28Jesus
turned and said to them, "Daughters of
Jerusalem, do not weep for me; weep
for yourselves and for your children.[q]
29For the time will come when you will
say, 'Blessed are the childless women, the
wombs that never bore and the breasts
that never nursed!'[r] 30Then

"'they will say to the mountains, "Fall
on us!"
and to the hills, "Cover us!"'[a][s]

31For if people do these things when the
tree is green, what will happen when it
is dry?"[t]

32Two other men, both criminals, were
also led out with him to be executed.[u]
33When they came to the place called the
Skull, they crucified him there, along with
the criminals — one on his right, the other
on his left. 34Jesus said, "Father,[v] forgive
them, for they do not know what they are
doing."[b][w] And they divided up his clothes
by casting lots.[x]

35The people stood watching, and the
rulers even sneered at him.[y] They said,
"He saved others; let him save himself if
he is God's Messiah, the Chosen One."[z]

36The soldiers also came up and mocked
him.[a] They offered him wine vinegar[b]
37and said, "If you are the king of the
Jews,[c] save yourself."

38There was a written notice above him,
which read: THIS IS THE KING OF THE JEWS.[d]

39One of the criminals who hung there
hurled insults at him: "Aren't you the Messiah? Save yourself and us!"[e]

40But the other criminal rebuked him.
"Don't you fear God," he said, "since you
are under the same sentence? 41We are
punished justly, for we are getting what
our deeds deserve. But this man has done
nothing wrong."[f]

42Then he said, "Jesus, remember me
when you come into your kingdom.[c]"[g]

43Jesus answered him, "Truly I tell you,
today you will be with me in paradise."[h]

The Death of Jesus

23:44-49pp — Mt 27:45-56; Mk 15:33-41; Jn 19:29-30

44It was now about noon, and darkness
came over the whole land until three in
the afternoon,[i] 45for the sun stopped shining. And the curtain of the temple[j] was

23:26 [n]Mt 27:32 [o]Mk 15:21; Jn 19:17
23:27 [p]Lk 8:52
23:28 [q]Lk 19:41-44; 21:23,24
23:29 [r]Mt 24:19
23:30 [s]Isa 2:19; Hos 10:8; Rev 6:16
23:31 [t]Eze 20:47
23:32 [u]Isa 53:12; Mt 27:38; Mk 15:27; Jn 19:18
23:34 [v]Mt 11:25 [w]Mt 5:44 [x]Ps 22:18
23:35 [y]Ps 22:17 [z]Isa 42:1
23:36 [a]Ps 22:7 [b]Ps 69:21; Mt 27:48
23:37 [c]Lk 4:3,9
23:38 [d]Mt 2:2
23:39 [e]ver 35, 37
23:41 [f]ver 4
23:42 [g]Mt 16:27
23:43 [h]2Co 12:3,4; Rev 2:7
23:44 [i]Am 8:9
23:45 [j]Ex 26:31-33; Heb 9:3,8

[a] *30* Hosea 10:8 [b] *34* Some early manuscripts do not have this sentence. [c] *42* Some manuscripts *come with your kingly power*

nors, the politics of crowd control sometimes took precedence over ideals of justice.

23:26 *Simon.* See note on Mt 27:32.

23:27 *women who mourned and wailed for him.* Later sources suggest that Jerusalem's women mercifully mourned those being led to execution, giving them a pain-killing drink. Throughout ancient Mediterranean culture, women were expected to grieve more passionately than men (also in the OT; cf., e.g., Jer 9:17, 20; 49:3).

23:28 *Daughters of Jerusalem.* This Biblical phrase was natural for Jerusalemite women but in this context might evoke judgment prophecies (Isa 3:16 – 17; 4:4).

23:29 *Blessed are the childless.* See note on 21:23 (unlike Isa 54:1, the idea here involves judgment).

23:30 Jesus quotes (with slight changes) Hos 10:8: judgment would be so terrible that people would want to find cover from it by any means necessary.

23:31 *tree is green … dry.* Dry wood burns faster than green wood; Jesus was unjustly executed, but wider bloodshed was imminent.

23:32 *Two other men.* Executing the condemned at festivals, when the crowds were larger, was thought to send a wider warning against defying Roman power.

23:33 *place called the Skull.* See note on Mt 27:33. *crucified.* See note on Mt 27:35.

23:34 *forgive them.* A person being executed was supposed to confess his sins, but Jesus instead confesses that of his unjust judges. Prayers for judgment against persecutors were common in the OT (see 2Ch 24:22; Ps 137:7 – 9; Jer 15:15; 17:18; 18:23; 20:12); Jesus exemplifies his own teaching here (Lk 6:28). *divided up his clothes … casting lots.* See note on Mt 27:35. *lots.* See note on Ac 1:26.

23:36 *wine vinegar.* Cheaper than normal wine, it assuaged thirst more readily than water; it was widely used by the nonelite, including workers and soldiers.

23:38 *written notice.* Sometimes someone would carry a tablet indicating the *titulus,* or charge, against the prisoner, to the site of the execution. *KING OF THE JEWS.* A treason charge — yet, ironically, Luke's audience knows that Jesus really is king.

23:42 *remember me.* A person achieving rank might "remember" someone else, i.e., help them at some point in the future (Ge 40:14,23; 1Sa 25:31).

23:43 *paradise.* Jewish pictures of the afterlife often contrasted Gehinnom (hell) with the Garden of Eden, paradise (see the article "Paul's Experience of the 'Third Heaven,'" p. 2039). (Jesus going to paradise that day might contrast with some later Christian traditions about him preaching in hell.)

23:44 *about noon … darkness came over the whole land.* Darkness often appears as a judgment in the OT (e.g., Ex 10:21 – 23), including darkness at noon (Am 8:9). Although a minority of intellectuals found natural explanations for eclipses, the majority of people in antiquity found in eclipses omens of impending disaster. The timing here seems hardly coincidental.

23:45 *curtain … torn in two.* The curtain's tearing probably implies the departure of God's presence from the

torn in two.[k] 46Jesus called out with a loud
voice,[l] "Father, into your hands I commit
my spirit."[a][m] When he had said this, he
breathed his last.[n]

47The centurion, seeing what had happened, praised God[o] and said, "Surely
this was a righteous man." 48When all the
people who had gathered to witness this
sight saw what took place, they beat their
breasts[p] and went away. 49But all those
who knew him, including the women who
had followed him from Galilee,[q] stood at a
distance,[r] watching these things.

The Burial of Jesus

23:50-56pp — Mt 27:57-61; Mk 15:42-47; Jn 19:38-42

50Now there was a man named Joseph,
a member of the Council, a good and upright man, 51who had not consented to
their decision and action. He came from
the Judean town of Arimathea, and he
himself was waiting for the kingdom of
God.[s] 52Going to Pilate, he asked for Jesus'
body. 53Then he took it down, wrapped it
in linen cloth and placed it in a tomb cut
in the rock, one in which no one had yet
been laid. 54It was Preparation Day,[t] and
the Sabbath was about to begin.

55The women who had come with Jesus
from Galilee[u] followed Joseph and saw
the tomb and how his body was laid in it.
56Then they went home and prepared spices
and perfumes.[v] But they rested on the Sabbath in obedience to the commandment.[w]

Jesus Has Risen

24:1-10pp — Mt 28:1-8; Mk 16:1-8; Jn 20:1-8

24 On the first day of the week, very
early in the morning, the women took the spices they had prepared[x]
and went to the tomb. 2They found the
stone rolled away from the tomb, 3but
when they entered, they did not find
the body of the Lord Jesus.[y] 4While they
were wondering about this, suddenly two
men in clothes that gleamed like lightning[z] stood beside them. 5In their fright
the women bowed down with their faces
to the ground, but the men said to them,
"Why do you look for the living among
the dead? 6He is not here; he has risen!
Remember how he told you, while he
was still with you in Galilee:[a] 7'The Son
of Man[b] must be delivered over to the
hands of sinners, be crucified and on the
third day be raised again.' "[c] 8Then they
remembered his words.[d]

9When they came back from the tomb,
they told all these things to the Eleven and to all the others. 10It was Mary
Magdalene, Joanna, Mary the mother of
James, and the others with them[e] who
told this to the apostles.[f] 11But they did
not believe[g] the women, because their
words seemed to them like nonsense.
12Peter, however, got up and ran to the
tomb. Bending over, he saw the strips of
linen lying by themselves,[h] and he went
away,[i] wondering to himself what had
happened.

On the Road to Emmaus

13Now that same day two of them were
going to a village called Emmaus, about
seven miles[b] from Jerusalem.[j] 14They were
talking with each other about everything
that had happened. 15As they talked and
discussed these things with each other,

23:45 [k]Heb 10:19,20 **23:46** [l]Mt 27:50 [m]Ps 31:5; 1Pe 2:23 [n]Jn 19:30 **23:47** [o]Mt 9:8 **23:48** [p]Lk 18:13 **23:49** [q]Lk 8:2 [r]Ps 38:11 **23:51** [s]Lk 2:25, 38 **23:54** [t]Mt 27:62 **23:55** [u]ver 49 **23:56** [v]Mk 16:1; Lk 24:1 [w]Ex 12:16; 20:10 **24:1** [x]Lk 23:56 **24:3** [y]ver 23, 24 **24:4** [z]Jn 20:12 **24:6** [a]Mt 17:22, 23; Mk 9:30-31; Lk 9:22; 24:44 **24:7** [b]Mt 8:20 [c]Mt 16:21 **24:8** [d]Jn 2:22 **24:10** [e]Lk 8:1-3 [f]Mk 6:30 **24:11** [g]Mk 16:11 **24:12** [h]Jn 20:3-7 [i]Jn 20:10 **24:13** [j]Mk 16:12

[a] 46 Psalm 31:5 [b] 13 Or about 11 kilometers

temple, prefiguring its destruction (cf. Eze 9:3; 10:4–18), and perhaps also new access to the Most Holy Place (cf. Heb 6:19–20; 9:3; 10:19–20). See note on Mt 27:51.

23:46 Jesus echoes Ps 31:5; a Jewish tradition says that this prayer was recited during the evening offering, roughly the time that Jesus died. Jesus, however, has special reason to use the prayer at this time.

23:48 *beat their breasts.* Expressed mourning (18:13; Isa 32:12; Eze 21:12).

23:49 *women who had followed him.* See note on 8:2–3. Women followers and family members present to mourn faced a lower risk of arrest than did men.

23:51 *Arimathea.* Virtually unknown outside Judea; no one would have invented the idea of Joseph being from Arimathea.

23:52 *asked for Jesus' body.* See note on Mt 27:58.

23:53 *linen cloth.* Linen shrouds were common for Jewish burials. See note on Mk 15:46. *tomb.* Because the tomb is immediately available, a reader may presume that it was Joseph's own (cf. 1Ki 13:30–31; Isa 53:12), as Matthew makes explicit (Mt 27:60). Because his family tomb was likely in Arimathea (cf. v. 51), but he now held a position on Jerusalem's ruling council, this was a new tomb "in which no one had yet been laid." See note on Mt 27:60.

23:56 *rested on the Sabbath.* Jewish tradition allowed washing and anointing corpses even on the Sabbath, but these women plan to honor Jesus' body more fully after the Sabbath ends.

24:1 *very early in the morning.* The Sabbath (23:56) ended at sundown the previous evening, but it would not be safe for these Galilean women to try to relocate this tomb outside the city before morning light. *spices.* Spices diminished the odor of a decomposing corpse and offered a costly way of showing appreciation (or, for wealthy people, status).

24:2 *stone rolled away.* The disk-shaped stone used to seal a tomb's entrance was large and heavy, normally requiring several men to move it in the groove. See note on Mt 27:60.

24:4 *clothes that gleamed like lightning.* Different biblical accounts demonstrate that people could mistake angels for humans (see note on Mk 16:5) but they also could appear dressed in white (Da 10:5) or even as if made of fire (2Ki 6:17; Da 10:6).

24:11 *their words seemed ... like nonsense.* See note on Mt 28:7.

24:13 *Emmaus.* Scholars differ as to the modern site for ancient Emmaus. *seven miles.* Lit. 60 stadia; i.e., 11 kilometers, thus Emmaus is still in Judea.

RESURRECTION APPEARANCES

APPEARANCE	PLACE	TIME	MATTHEW	MARK	LUKE	JOHN	ACTS	1 CO
[The empty tomb]	Jerusalem	Resurrection Sunday	28:1–10	16:1–8	24:1–12	20:1–9]		
To Mary Magdalene in the garden	Jerusalem	Resurrection Sunday		16:9–11		20:11–18		
To other women	Jerusalem	Resurrection Sunday	28:9–10					
To two people going to Emmaus	Road to Emmaus	Resurrection Sunday		16:12–13	24:13–32			
To Peter	Jerusalem	Resurrection Sunday			24:34			15:5
To the ten disciples in the upper room	Jerusalem	Resurrection Sunday			24:36–43	20:19–25		
To the 11 disciples in the upper room	Jerusalem	Following Sunday		16:14		20:26–29		15:5
To seven disciples fishing	Sea of Galilee	Some time later				21:1–23		
To the 11 disciples on a mountain	Galilee	Some time later	28:16–20	16:15–18				
To more than 500	Unknown	Some time later						15:6
To James	Unknown	Some time later						15:7
To his disciples at his ascension	Mount of Olives	40 days after Jesus' resurrection			24:44–49		1:3–8	
To Paul	Damascus	Several years later					9:1–19 22:3–16 26:9–18	9:1

Jesus himself came up and walked along
with them;[k] 16 but they were kept from recognizing him.[l]
17 He asked them, "What are you discussing together as you walk along?"
They stood still, their faces downcast.
18 One of them, named Cleopas,[m] asked
him, "Are you the only one visiting Jerusalem who does not know the things that
have happened there in these days?"
19 "What things?" he asked.
"About Jesus of Nazareth,"[n] they replied. "He was a prophet,[o] powerful in
word and deed before God and all the
people. 20 The chief priests and our rulers[p]
handed him over to be sentenced to death,
and they crucified him; 21 but we had
hoped that he was the one who was going
to redeem Israel.[q] And what is more, it is
the third day[r] since all this took place. 22 In
addition, some of our women amazed us.[s]
They went to the tomb early this morning
23 but didn't find his body. They came and
told us that they had seen a vision of angels, who said he was alive. 24 Then some
of our companions went to the tomb and
found it just as the women had said, but
they did not see Jesus."[t]
25 He said to them, "How foolish you
are, and how slow to believe all that
the prophets have spoken! 26 Did not the
Messiah have to suffer these things and

24:15 [k] ver 36 **24:16** [l] Jn 20:14; 21:4 **24:18** [m] Jn 19:25 **24:19** [n] Mk 1:24 [o] Mt 21:11 **24:20** [p] Lk 23:13 **24:21** [q] Lk 1:68; 2:38; 21:28 [r] Mt 16:21 **24:22** [s] ver 1-10 **24:24** [t] ver 12

24:19 *a prophet.* Many of Jesus' actions (such as speaking God's message, raising the dead, cleansing lepers, and feeding crowds) resembled the actions of Biblical prophets (such as Moses, Elijah and Elisha).
24:21 *hoped that he was ... going to redeem Israel.* Many expected the Messiah to be a liberator, i.e., to "redeem Israel."
24:26 *Did not the Messiah have to suffer ...?* The Biblical prophets spoke of a servant (on behalf of the larger servant Israel) who would both suffer and be exalted

then enter his glory?"[u] 27 And beginning with Moses[v] and all the Prophets,[w] he explained to them what was said in all the Scriptures concerning himself.[x]

28 As they approached the village to which they were going, Jesus continued on as if he were going farther. 29 But they urged him strongly, "Stay with us, for it is nearly evening; the day is almost over." So he went in to stay with them.

30 When he was at the table with them, he took bread, gave thanks, broke it[y] and began to give it to them. 31 Then their eyes were opened and they recognized him,[z] and he disappeared from their sight. 32 They asked each other, "Were not our hearts burning within us[a] while he talked with us on the road and opened the Scriptures[b] to us?"

33 They got up and returned at once to Jerusalem. There they found the Eleven and those with them, assembled together 34 and saying, "It is true! The Lord has risen and has appeared to Simon."[c] 35 Then the two told what had happened on the way, and how Jesus was recognized by them when he broke the bread.[d]

Jesus Appears to the Disciples

36 While they were still talking about this, Jesus himself stood among them and said to them, "Peace be with you."[e]

37 They were startled and frightened, thinking they saw a ghost.[f] 38 He said to them, "Why are you troubled, and why do doubts rise in your minds? 39 Look at my hands and my feet. It is I myself! Touch me and see;[g] a ghost does not have flesh and bones, as you see I have."

40 When he had said this, he showed them his hands and feet. 41 And while they still did not believe it because of joy and amazement, he asked them, "Do you have anything here to eat?" 42 They gave him a piece of broiled fish, 43 and he took it and ate it in their presence.[h]

44 He said to them, "This is what I told you while I was still with you:[i] Everything must be fulfilled[j] that is written about me in the Law of Moses,[k] the Prophets and the Psalms."[l]

45 Then he opened their minds so they could understand the Scriptures. 46 He told them, "This is what is written: The Messiah will suffer and rise from the dead on the third day, 47 and repentance for the forgiveness of sins will be preached in his name[m] to all nations,[n] beginning at Jerusalem. 48 You are witnesses[o] of these things. 49 I am going to send you what my Father has promised;[p] but stay in the city until you have been clothed with power from on high."

24:26 [u] Heb 2:10; 1Pe 1:11
24:27 [v] Ge 3:15; Nu 21:9; Dt 18:15 [w] Isa 7:14; 9:6; 40:10, 11; 53; Eze 34:23; Da 9:24; Mic 7:20; Mal 3:1 [x] Jn 1:45
24:30 [y] Mt 14:19
24:31 [z] ver 16
24:32 [a] Ps 39:3 [b] ver 27, 45
24:34 [c] 1Co 15:5
24:35 [d] ver 30, 31
24:36 [e] Jn 20:19, 21, 26; 14:27
24:37 [f] Mk 6:49
24:39 [g] Jn 20:27; 1Jn 1:1
24:43 [h] Ac 10:41
24:44 [i] Lk 9:45; 18:34 [j] Mt 16:21; Lk 9:22, 44; 18:31-33; 22:37 [k] ver 27 [l] Ps 2; 16; 22; 69; 72; 110; 118
24:47 [m] Ac 5:31; 10:43; 13:38 [n] Mt 28:19
24:48 [o] Ac 1:8; 2:32; 5:32; 13:31; 1Pe 5:1
24:49 [p] Jn 14:16; Ac 1:4

(Isa 52:13; 53:12). Scripture also revealed God's way of raising up deliverers: they often suffered before being exalted (e.g., Joseph, Moses, and David, as well as psalms of the righteous sufferer; cf. Ac 7).

24:27 *all the Scriptures.* Based on other texts in Luke-Acts, we may infer that the passages would have included Dt 18:15 – 18 and royal psalms (e.g., Ps 2) and Ps 110.

24:29 *Stay ... it is nearly evening.* People usually avoided traveling at night because of darkness and robbers; toward evening they would normally lodge in the nearest safe community. In a polite Middle Eastern way, Jesus refuses to impose; he may even test hospitality (as in Ge 19:2). The appropriate, polite Middle Eastern response, however, was to insist on showing hospitality (cf. Ge 19:3; Jdg 19:5 – 9). Showing hospitality was honorable and most people desired to do it.

24:30 *he took bread.* Often the head of the household would break bread. Jesus assumes this role, although the others have in a sense invited him as their guest.

24:31 *eyes were opened and they recognized him.* Jewish people told stories of angels who came disguised and were initially unrecognized. Jesus' resurrection body differs from usual human existence (cf. Php 3:21). For spiritual perception, cf. 2Ki 6:17.

24:36 *Peace be with you.* The conventional Jewish greeting was *shalom*, i.e., "Peace be with you." This greeting constituted an implicit prayer to God for the well-being of the person addressed.

24:37 *ghost.* Even some Jewish people who believed in heaven and hell inconsistently believed in ghosts or other kinds of spirits associated with the dead. People often believed that they saw apparitions of the dead, often in dreams or soon after the appearing person's death; Jesus, however, proves to be no mere apparition (v. 39).

24:39 *Look at my hands and my feet.* Along with the head, the hands and feet were the most exposed parts of the body, not covered by the outer garment. Although some prisoners were simply tied to crosses, executioners sometimes nailed victims there, as they did in Jesus' case. *Touch me.* Many ancients believed in a shadowy afterlife; such shadows could not be grasped with the hands.

24:43 *he took it and ate it.* Many Jewish sources doubted that angels ate human food.

24:44 *the Law of Moses, the Prophets and the Psalms.* Usually Jewish sources summarized the OT as "the Law and the Prophets" (e.g., 16:16), but sometimes distinguished the Writings ("the Psalms") as a third division distinct from the Prophets. The focus on the Psalms here could include both royal psalms (e.g., Ps 2) and the psalms of the righteous sufferer (e.g., Ps 22; 69).

24:46 *This is what is written.* See note on v. 27. *the third day.* If this is included in the references to "the Scriptures" (v. 45), this might evoke the reviving of Israel on the third day in Hos 6:2 or the model of Jonah's reviving after three days (Jnh 1:17; 2:2). By Jewish reckoning, part of a day counted as a day.

24:47 *to all nations.* In Isaiah, God promised that his people would be witnesses before the nations (Isa 43:10,12; 44:8); although this could include testifying against their idolatry, Isaiah also envisions nations acknowledging Israel and Israel's God (Isa 2:2; 11:10; 56:3 – 8; 60:3 – 14), partly through God's people (Isa 42:6; 49:6).

24:49 *clothed with power from on high.* In Isaiah, God would empower his people with his Spirit (Isa 42:1; 44:3; 48:16; 59:21). Other Jewish people employed the expres-

The Ascension of Jesus

50 When he had led them out to the vicinity of Bethany,[q] he lifted up his hands and
blessed them. 51 While he was blessing them,
he left them and was taken up into heaven.[r]
52 Then they worshiped him and returned to
Jerusalem with great joy. 53 And they stayed
continually at the temple,[s] praising God.

24:50 [q] Mt 21:17
24:51 [r] 2Ki 2:11
24:53 [s] Ac 2:46

---

sion "clothed" to refer to qualities (e.g., the Spirit "clothing" a prophet in the Greek translation of 1Ch 12:18 – 19). *on high.* Might echo Isa 32:15.

24:50 *lifted up his hands.* In Jewish tradition, priests would lift their hands when they blessed the people.

24:51 *taken up into heaven.* When Elijah ascended, Elisha was empowered (see note on Ac 1:9; see also the article "Ascensions," p. 1868).

24:53 *at the temple, praising God.* Judeans in the temple prayed and worshiped God. The Gospel of Luke thus closes where it opened (1:8 – 10). It was common to frame a passage by beginning and ending the passage the same way; Luke frames his entire Gospel with this worship in the temple.

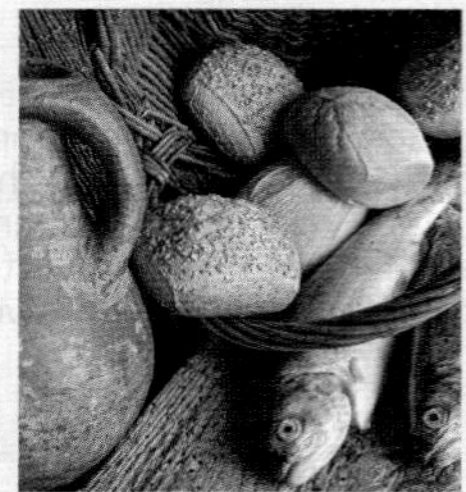

THE GOSPEL OF JOHN

Genre

John, like the other three canonical Gospels, is a biography of Jesus (see the Introduction to the Gospels, p. 1598). Ancient biographies took different forms, however, and most scholars believe that John is more directly interpretive than the other Gospels. This Gospel's narratives resemble theirs, but historians often used speeches to help interpret events, and Jesus' discourses in John's Gospel certainly do that. Moreover, especially in the passion narrative, many scholars believe that John focuses on the symbolic dimension in some details (compare Jn 13:26 with Mk 14:20; Jn 19:17 with Mk 15:21; Jn 19:14 with Mk 15:25, and see notes on these passages in John; see also the article "The Synoptic Passover Meal Versus John's Passover Lamb," p. 1849).

Nevertheless, even though the entire Gospel is written in John's own style, we frequently find elements confirmed by the other Gospels, showing that John is interpreting rather than inventing his material. Indeed, some distinctive elements of John, such as the Sanhedrin's reason to want Jesus executed (Jn 11:48 – 50), Pilate's reason for hesitating to execute him (18:33 – 38), and Jesus carrying his own cross (19:17), fit what is known of the milieu even better than the Synoptic accounts. Many details, such as Jesus citing traditional tabernacle readings at that festival (7:2,37 – 39) and perhaps even his "I am" claim there (see note on 8:58) fit aspects of Jesus' milieu in ways even better than even most Christians in John's day would have realized.

QUICK GLANCE

AUTHOR:
The apostle John

AUDIENCE:
Primarily Jewish believers

DATE:
Probably in the AD 90s

THEME:
John presents Jesus as the Word, the Messiah and the incarnate Son of God, who has come to reveal the Father and bring eternal life to all who believe in him.

Authorship

Why does John feel free to report a different aspect of Jesus' ministry than the one reported by Matthew and Luke, both of whom follow Mark's outline? To some degree, it may be because the material comes from what most scholars believe was an independent eyewitness of Jesus' Judean ministry (19:35; 21:24) — the "disciple whom Jesus loved" (13:23; 21:20). Scholars differ on this witness's identity, but he is among Jesus' very closest disciples (13:23), in a role that can virtually rival that of Peter (13:23 – 25; 20:2 – 8), suggesting to many scholars that he was a prominent disciple, likely among the Twelve. Thus although scholars differ on his precise identity (and how much of the Gospel stems from him), conservative scholars generally prefer the author whose name was preserved by the second-century church: John. Classical scholars normally start with external evidence when considering authorship, and the earliest external evidence in this case firmly favors John.

Scholars today again differ as to which John was in view (though the earliest Christian tradition did not), but the Synoptic Gospels show us that John son of Zebedee was one of Jesus' most intimate disciples. A majority of conservative scholars therefore believe that this John is the author of this Gospel. (A minority of scholars hold to a different author, Judean John the Elder, or to a school developing the apostle John's teaching, or occasionally even to a different figure such as Lazarus, whom Jesus loved in 11:3.) He may have shaped and reshaped it orally over the decades as he continued to recount Jesus' story, inspired by the Spirit (14:26), but the heart of his Gospel reflects his memory of Jesus.

Date

Tradition holds that the Gospel was written in the 90s of the first century. Since disciples were often in their teens, John had years to learn how to communicate Jesus' character best; he was possibly in his 80s at the time of writing. Ancient sources show that, in antiquity as today, some people did remain active in their 80s. (Writing a work usually meant dictating it to a scribe, and a long work like this Gospel would usually be revised at least once before wide publication.) The tradition fits the Gospel's apparent response to a setting that would fit in the 90s.

Situation

The Jewish-Roman war of AD 66 – 70 scattered many Jewish followers of Jesus into more stable regions of the Greek east, including the cities in Asia Minor. After the temple's destruction in 70, the center of Sadducean power vanished, and educated Pharisees competed with other groups, such as the populist followers of Jesus, for the people's allegiance. (Note the heavy focus on Pharisees in John's Gospel. Note also Jesus and the Spirit, rather than the temple, as the true holy place, in 1:14; 2:21; 4:21 – 24; 7:37 – 39; 10:36 and note; 14:2 – 6; 15:4.) In at least some places, this rivalry for control led to efforts to make Jewish believers unwelcome in synagogues (cf. 9:22; 12:42; 16:2; earlier, cf. Lk 6:22); later Jewish sources speak of rabbis' conflicts with followers of Jesus, and indicate that some added a curse against schismatics — which normally included Jewish believers in Jesus — to their regular prayers. These tensions arose not only in Judea, but also apparently in some synagogues in Smyrna and Philadelphia (Rev 2:9 – 10; 3:7 – 9). In the 90s, cities in Asia Minor increasingly accommodated the veneration of the Emperor Domitian as divine. Jews were exempt from the imperial cult, but if Christians were disbarred from some synagogues, their refusal to participate in civic acts honoring the emperor may have been viewed as disloyal. Against considerable social pressure, then, John urges his audience to stand firm in recognizing Christ as both the fulfillment of Jewish hopes and the ultimate Lord. ◆

The Word Became Flesh

1 In the beginning was the Word,[a] and
the Word was with God,[b] and the
Word was God.[c] 2He was with God in the
beginning.[d] 3Through him all things were
made; without him nothing was made that
has been made.[e] 4In him was life,[f] and that
life was the light[g] of all mankind. 5The
light shines in the darkness, and the darkness has not overcome[a] it.[h]
6There was a man sent from God whose
name was John.[i] 7He came as a witness
to testify[j] concerning that light, so that
through him all might believe.[k] 8He himself was not the light; he came only as a
witness to the light.
9The true light[l] that gives light to everyone[m] was coming into the world. 10He was
in the world, and though the world was
made through him,[n] the world did not recognize him. 11He came to that which was
his own, but his own did not receive him.
12Yet to all who did receive him, to those
who believed[o] in his name,[p] he gave the
right to become children of God[q] — 13chil-
dren born not of natural descent, nor of
human decision or a husband's will, but
born of God.[r]

1:1 [a] Rev 19:13 [b] Jn 17:5; 1Jn 1:2 [c] Php 2:6 **1:2** [d] Ge 1:1 **1:3** [e] 1Co 8:6; Col 1:16; Heb 1:2 **1:4** [f] Jn 5:26; 11:25; 14:6 [g] Jn 8:12 **1:5** [h] Jn 3:19 **1:6** [i] Mt 3:1 **1:7** [j] ver 15, 19, 32 [k] ver 12 **1:9** [l] 1Jn 2:8 [m] Isa 49:6 **1:10** [n] Heb 1:2 **1:12** [o] ver 7 [p] 1Jn 3:23 [q] Gal 3:26 **1:13** [r] Jn 3:6; Jas 1:18; 1Pe 1:23; 1Jn 3:9 **1:14** [s] Gal 4:4; Php 2:7, 8; 1Ti 3:16; Heb 2:14 [t] Jn 14:6 **1:15** [u] ver 7 [v] ver 30; Mt 3:11 **1:16** [w] Eph 1:23; Col 1:19 **1:17** [x] Jn 7:19 [y] ver 14 **1:18** [z] Ex 33:20; Jn 6:46; Col 1:15; 1Ti 6:16

14The Word became flesh[s] and made his
dwelling among us. We have seen his glory,
the glory of the one and only Son, who came
from the Father, full of grace and truth.[t]
15(John testified[u] concerning him. He
cried out, saying, "This is the one I spoke
about when I said, 'He who comes after
me has surpassed me because he was before me.' ")[v] 16Out of his fullness[w] we have
all received grace in place of grace already
given. 17For the law was given through Moses;[x] grace and truth came through Jesus
Christ.[y] 18No one has ever seen God,[z] but
the one and only Son, who is himself God
and[b][a] is in closest relationship with the Father, has made him known.

John the Baptist Denies Being the Messiah

19Now this was John's testimony when
the Jewish leaders[c][b] in Jerusalem sent
priests and Levites to ask him who he

[a] 5 Or *understood* [b] 18 Some manuscripts *but the only Son, who* [c] 19 The Greek term traditionally translated *the Jews* (*hoi Ioudaioi*) refers here and elsewhere in John's Gospel to those Jewish leaders who opposed Jesus; also in 5:10, 15, 16; 7:1, 11, 13; 9:22; 18:14, 28, 36; 19:7, 12, 31, 38; 20:19.

[a] Jn 3:16, 18; 1Jn 4:9 **1:19** [b] Jn 2:18; 5:10, 16; 6:41, 52

1:1 *In the beginning.* Echoes especially Ge 1:1, which spoke of God's creative activity, here shared with Jesus. Wisdom was the first of God's creation "at the very beginning" (Pr 8:22 – 23), but Jesus here transcends wisdom, for in the beginning, he already was. *the Word.* Philosophers employed *logos*, or "word," for divine reason that orders the universe; the Jewish philosopher Philo combines that idea with a more traditional Jewish sense. Jewish people sometimes coalesced the ideas of God's word, his wisdom, and his law (see, e.g., Sirach 24:1,23; Baruch 3:28 — 4:1; cf. Sirach 21:11; 34:8). Jewish people sometimes personified these concepts, especially Wisdom. Educated Jewish critics of Jesus' movement accused his followers of not knowing the Scriptures; John replies that believers know the full embodiment of God's revelation: the Word made flesh, Jesus Christ (see note on vv. 14 – 18).
1:3 *all things were made.* God spoke the world into being (Ge 1:3 – 29; the rabbis counted ten commands here), and this powerful creative word was associated with his word to his people (Ps 33:4,6,9). Jewish teachers also said that God created through Wisdom linked with God's word (Wisdom of Solomon 7:22; 9:1 – 3). Some Jewish people in this period envisioned creation organizing chaos; like some other Jewish thinkers, however, John probably means the creation of the universe from nothing.
1:4 – 5 *In him was life ... light.* Scripture and Jewish tradition recognized that God's word offered life (Dt 8:1; 11:9; Baruch 4:1) and also light (Ps 119:105; Baruch 4:2; cf. Wisdom in Wisdom of Solomon 7:26). (Jewish people used "light" as a symbol at times for holy persons, for Israel, and for God; cf. 2Sa 21:17; 22:29; Isa 42:6; 49:6; Mic 7:8.) The Dead Sea Scrolls also divided the world morally into those who follow God's light and those who belong to darkness.
1:10 – 11 *the world did not recognize him ... his own did not receive him.* Jewish tradition declared that the nations rejected God's law at Sinai, leaving it for Israel alone. But Jewish people also had a tradition that they themselves had rejected the prophets (amplifying the existing Biblical tradition on that subject).
1:12 In the OT, God made his chosen people his children (Ex 4:22; Dt 8:5; 32:5).
1:13 *born of God.* See notes on 3:3,5.
1:14 – 18 For philosophers, the *logos* and what was truly divine did not become material. The narrative here echoes the giving of God's Word, the law, through Moses:

Ex 33 – 34	Jn 1:14 – 18
The revelation of God's Word, the Torah	The revelation of God's Word, Jesus
God dwelt among his people in the tabernacle (33:10); Moses pleaded that God would continue to dwell with them (33:14 – 16)	The Word "made his dwelling" [lit. "tabernacled"] among people (1:14)
Moses beheld God's glory (33:12 – 23)	The disciples beheld Jesus' glory (1:14)
The glory was full of grace and truth (34:6)	The glory was full of grace and truth (1:14)
The law was given through Moses (34:1 – 28)	The law was given through Moses (1:17)
No one could see all of God's glory (33:20)	No one could see all of God's glory (1:18a), but it is fully revealed in Jesus (1:18b)

This is one of John's several references to God's servants in the OT experiencing a foretaste of Christ's glory (8:56; 12:41). Thus in Jesus, the fullness of God's glory, God's loving character — in today's terms, his "heart" — is finally revealed. The rest of John's Gospel suggests

was. 20He did not fail to confess, but confessed freely, "I am not the Messiah."[c]
21They asked him, "Then who are you?
Are you Elijah?"[d]
He said, "I am not."
"Are you the Prophet?"[e]
He answered, "No."
22Finally they said, "Who are you? Give
us an answer to take back to those who
sent us. What do you say about yourself?"
23John replied in the words of Isaiah the
prophet, "I am the voice of one calling in
the wilderness,[f] 'Make straight the way for
the Lord.'"[a][g]
24Now the Pharisees who had been sent
25questioned him, "Why then do you baptize if you are not the Messiah, nor Elijah,
nor the Prophet?"
26"I baptize with[b] water," John replied,
"but among you stands one you do not
know. 27He is the one who comes after
me,[h] the straps of whose sandals I am not
worthy to untie."
28This all happened at Bethany on the
other side of the Jordan,[i] where John was
baptizing.

John Testifies About Jesus

29The next day John saw Jesus coming
toward him and said, "Look, the Lamb of
God,[j] who takes away the sin of the world!
30This is the one I meant when I said, 'A
man who comes after me has surpassed
me because he was before me.'[k] 31I myself
did not know him, but the reason I came
baptizing with water was that he might be
revealed to Israel."
32Then John gave this testimony: "I saw
the Spirit come down from heaven as a
dove and remain on him.[l] 33And I myself
did not know him, but the one who sent
me to baptize with water[m] told me, 'The
man on whom you see the Spirit come
down and remain is the one who will baptize with the Holy Spirit.'[n] 34I have seen and
I testify that this is God's Chosen One."[c][o]

John's Disciples Follow Jesus

1:40-42pp — Mt 4:18-22; Mk 1:16-20; Lk 5:2-11

35The next day John[p] was there again
with two of his disciples. 36When he saw
Jesus passing by, he said, "Look, the
Lamb of God!"[q]
37When the two disciples heard him
say this, they followed Jesus. 38Turning
around, Jesus saw them following and
asked, "What do you want?"
They said, "Rabbi"[r] (which means
"Teacher"), "where are you staying?"
39"Come," he replied, "and you will see."
So they went and saw where he was
staying, and they spent that day with him.
It was about four in the afternoon.

1:20 [c] Jn 3:28; Lk 3:15,16 **1:21** [d] Mt 11:14 [e] Dt 18:15 **1:23** [f] Mt 3:1 [g] Isa 40:3 **1:27** [h] ver 15, 30 **1:28** [i] Jn 3:26; 10:40 **1:29** [j] ver 36; Isa 53:7; 1Pe 1:19; Rev 5:6 **1:30** [k] ver 15,27 **1:32** [l] Mt 3:16; Mk 1:10 **1:33** [m] Mk 1:4 [n] Mt 3:11; Mk 1:8 **1:34** [o] ver 49; Mt 4:3 **1:35** [p] Mt 3:1 **1:36** [q] ver 29 **1:38** [r] ver 49; Mt 23:7

[a] 23 Isaiah 40:3 [b] 26 Or *in*; also in verses 31 and 33 (twice) [c] 34 See Isaiah 42:1; many manuscripts *is the Son of God*.

that this revelation of God's glory climaxes in the cross (12:23 – 24). God demonstrated his love in the incarnation and ultimately the scandalous death of his Son.

1:21 *Are you Elijah?… the Prophet?* The Jewish people expected a return of the prophet Elijah (Mal 4:5 – 6) and the prophet who would be like Moses (Dt 18:15 – 18) to precede the coming of the Messiah.

1:23 *voice of one calling in the wilderness.* The Qumran community also used this verse to justify its location in the wilderness; John's use of it authentically fits his time and location. *Make straight the way.* Most importantly, John's use of the the text points to the new era of divine restoration. Roads would be improved before a king traveled; using this imagery, Isaiah prophesied a new exodus: a new era of salvation and restoration for God's people (Isa 11:16; 19:23; 43:16 – 21; 51:10 – 11; cf. Isa 49:8 – 12; 57:14). (The "wilderness" sometimes recalls the time of the exodus elsewhere in this Gospel: Jn 3:14; 6:31, 49.)

1:24 *the Pharisees.* See note on 7:32.

1:25 *Why then do you baptize . . . ?* Jewish washings took various forms, but a one-time immersion for conversion characterized Gentiles turning to Judaism. To baptize Jewish people in a radical turning could be viewed as treating them almost like Gentiles. John's interlocutors wonder why he is requiring this radical commitment unless he sees himself as one of the major promised figures.

1:27 *sandals I am not worthy to untie.* Handling sandals was the sort of task that only a servant would normally perform; the prophets were servants of God (2Ki 9:7; Jer 7:25; 26:5; 29:19; 35:15; 44:4), but John considers himself unworthy even for this role. Clearly he envisions himself as preparing the way for someone divine who was to come.

1:28 *on the other side of the Jordan.* John was baptizing especially beyond the Jordan, i.e., in Perea. Josephus reports that John was later imprisoned in this same region.

1:29 *Lamb of God.* Scholars suggest various possible backgrounds for the title here: sacrificial lambs, Passover lambs, and being like a lamb in Isa 53:7. By this period, Passover was sometimes viewed as sacrificial, so Jesus could be the Passover lamb (cf. Jn 6:4,51 – 56; 19:36) and also a sacrifice.

1:32 *dove.* Doves had various symbolic functions in ancient sources; perhaps the most widespread and relevant for Jewish hearers, if any, would be the dove's role as harbinger of a new world in Ge 8:8 – 12.

1:33 *Spirit come down and remain . . . will baptize with the Holy Spirit.* Biblically, only God could pour out his own Spirit, as he promised to do at the time of the coming restoration (Isa 32:15; 44:3; Eze 39:29; Joel 2:28); as the Spirit-baptizer, Jesus is divine. In the OT, the Spirit often came "on" people without remaining on them (e.g., Nu 11:25; 24:2; 1Sa 11:6).

1:35 – 37 Ancient schools of teachers were sometimes competitive; only rarely were teachers so impressed with another teacher as to refer their students to them. John refers his own disciples to Jesus.

1:36 *Lamb of God.* See note on v. 29.

1:38 *Rabbi . . . where are you staying?* The disciples' inquiry about where Jesus stays is a polite, indirect way of saying that they would like to visit with him. Jesus invites them over in the same indirect way (v. 39).

1:39 *four in the afternoon.* It might be too late to walk home if they lived far away.

40 Andrew, Simon Peter's brother, was
one of the two who heard what John had
said and who had followed Jesus. 41 The
first thing Andrew did was to find his
brother Simon and tell him, "We have
found the Messiah" (that is, the Christ).[s]
42 And he brought him to Jesus.
Jesus looked at him and said, "You are
Simon son of John. You will be called[t]
Cephas" (which, when translated, is Peter[a]).[u]

Jesus Calls Philip and Nathanael

43 The next day Jesus decided to leave
for Galilee. Finding Philip,[v] he said to him,
"Follow me."[w]
44 Philip, like Andrew and Peter, was from
the town of Bethsaida.[x] 45 Philip found Nathanael[y] and told him, "We have found the
one Moses wrote about in the Law,[z] and
about whom the prophets also wrote[a]—
Jesus of Nazareth,[b] the son of Joseph."[c]
46 "Nazareth! Can anything good come
from there?"[d] Nathanael asked.
"Come and see," said Philip.

1:41 [s] Jn 4:25
1:42 [t] Ge 17:5, 15 [u] Mt 16:18
1:43 [v] Mt 10:3; Jn 6:5-7; 12:21, 22; 14:8,9 [w] Mt 4:19
1:44 [x] Mt 11:21; Jn 12:21
1:45 [y] Jn 21:2 [z] Lk 24:27 [a] Lk 24:27 [b] Mt 2:23; Mk 1:24 [c] Lk 3:23
1:46 [d] Jn 7:41, 42,52
1:47 [e] Ro 9:4,6 [f] Ps 32:2
1:49 [g] ver 38; Mt 23:7 [h] ver 34; Mt 4:3 [i] Mt 2:2; 27:42; Jn 12:13
1:51 [j] Mt 3:16 [k] Ge 28:12 [l] Mt 8:20
2:1 [m] Jn 4:46; 21:2 [n] Mt 12:46

47 When Jesus saw Nathanael approaching, he said of him, "Here truly is an Israelite[e] in whom there is no deceit."[f]
48 "How do you know me?" Nathanael
asked.
Jesus answered, "I saw you while you
were still under the fig tree before Philip
called you."
49 Then Nathanael declared, "Rabbi,[g]
you are the Son of God;[h] you are the king
of Israel."[i]
50 Jesus said, "You believe[b] because I
told you I saw you under the fig tree. You
will see greater things than that." 51 He
then added, "Very truly I tell you,[c] you[c]
will see 'heaven open,[j] and the angels of
God ascending and descending[k] on'[d] the
Son of Man."[l]

Jesus Changes Water Into Wine

2 On the third day a wedding took place
at Cana in Galilee.[m] Jesus' mother[n]
was there, 2 and Jesus and his disciples

[a] *42* *Cephas* (Aramaic) and *Peter* (Greek) both mean *rock.* [b] *50* Or *Do you believe . . . ?* [c] *51* The Greek is plural. [d] *51* Gen. 28:12

1:41 *We have found the Messiah.* See Messiah. John translates "Messiah" into Greek; probably most hearers in the Mediterranean Diaspora, including some Jewish ones, did not know the Hebrew title. Because of fraternal loyalty, people usually took seriously reports from their brothers. For a people who actively looked for the appearance of the Messiah, this was a joyful and serious message.
1:42 *Simon son of John.* People were often identified by their name and their father's name. *Cephas.* Means "rock" in Aramaic, as "Peter" does in Greek. (*Cephas* is pronounced *kay-fas*; the "s" ending, however, was added for Greek pronunciation—since Greeks often ended male names with "s"—and was not part of the original Aramaic term.) Many people had nicknames, which usually communicated something about the person. God sometimes gave prophets special knowledge, but see also note on 2:25.
1:43 *Follow me.* Honorable teachers usually expected prospective disciples to ask if they could follow the teacher; only the most radical directly summoned people to "follow me," i.e., "become my disciple." This reality shows that Jesus carefully selected the disciples he wanted to become part of the Twelve, and also reflects the radical nature of what being his disciple means, and thus of our own personal commitment to follow him. We cannot know whether Philip already knew of Jesus, although the connection of Andrew and Peter with Bethsaida (1:44) leaves open this possibility.
1:44 *Bethsaida.* Because Capernaum and Bethsaida were both fishing villages, it is not impossible that the family maintained property in both places or had moved from one to the other (Mk 1:21,29; 2:1). Some suggest that probably soon after Jesus' ministry, around the year 30, Bethsaida more often began to be called Julia; although Josephus later uses both names, the Gospels use only the earlier, local name, indicating that the Gospels report very early and surely authentic memories about Jesus.
1:45 *the one Moses wrote about.* Philip would have in mind texts such as Dt 18:15–18; Isa 9:6–7; 11:1–5; and the like.
1:46 *Nazareth! Can anything good come from there?* Village rivalry was common; it could involve the honor accruing to superior buildings, people, or other matters. If such rivalry is in view, this statement reveals Nathanael's personal perception rather than a commentary on the quality of individuals who lived in or came from the village of Nazareth. Great people also were expected to come from famous places, such as Jerusalem, not from small villages, so that could also be a factor in this statement. Some recent estimates for the population of Nazareth proper are below 500 residents. We as John's readers know what Nathanael could not: the most important place that Jesus is from is heaven (v. 10; 3:13, 31). *Come and see.* Teachers sometimes invited hearers to "come and see," even when explaining Scripture; Philip invites Nathanael to experience Jesus for himself (cf. v. 39; 4:29).
1:47 *an Israelite … no deceit.* Jacob was known for using deception (Ge 27:35), but his descendant here is genuine (cf. Ps 32:2).
1:48 *under the fig tree.* Because of the sunny and warm climate, people frequently studied Scripture, discussed, and rested in the shade of trees; this was a relaxing location (cf., e.g., Mic 4:4; Zech 3:10; 1 Maccabees 14:12). Whatever Nathanael was doing there, presumably acting as a genuine Israelite (v. 47), Nathanael did not expect the rabbi to have known who he was apart from divine revelation (v. 49). His experience allows him to understand Philip's testimony concerning Jesus' Biblical identity (v. 45).
1:51 *you will see … the Son of Man.* Jacob (cf. v. 47 and note) witnessed angels "ascending and descending on" a ladder connecting heaven and earth at Bethel, the "house of God" (Ge 28:12,17,19); Jesus is Jacob's ladder, the connection between heaven and earth (cf. Jn 14:6).
2:1 *third day.* Jewish weddings did not begin on the third day of the week; this simply means the third day after the last event mentioned (as often, e.g., Ge 22:4; 31:22; some see it also as foreshadowing Jn 2:19–20). *Cana.* The village was, depending on the precise site, over 3 miles (5 kilometers) or (likelier) over 8 miles (13 kilometers) from Nazareth; it was a long walk but close enough to know some people.
2:2 Hosts normally invited as many people as possible to weddings and other events.

JOHN 2

Cana of Galilee

John is the only New Testament writer who mentions Cana of Galilee, and he only hints at its location. The fact that Jesus' family had friends or relatives and were able to attend a wedding there suggests that Cana was not too far from Nazareth. In addition, Jn 4:46 – 54 implies that the trip from Cana to Capernaum required somewhat more than a half-day's journey.

Christian pilgrims have long associated Cana with the village of Kefr Kenna, located about four miles northeast of Nazareth. This is probably incorrect, notwithstanding the presence there of churches claiming to preserve the tradition of the miracle at the wedding. Today most scholars agree that Khirbet Qana, located about nine miles north of Nazareth and just north of the Beit Netofa Valley, is the more likely candidate (although both Kefr Kenna and Khirbet Qana meet the requirements of John's Gospel).

Excavation at Khirbet Qana began in 1998. Remains have been found from the Neolithic period through to the modern period, but most physical evidence (pottery, coins and housing remains) dates from the Roman through the Byzantine periods. Remains of what could have been a first-century synagogue (although this has not yet been firmly established) have also been found, along with a *miqveh* (a pool for Jewish ritual cleansing). Cisterns held water for the village since there appears to have been no aqueduct. Jn 2:6 mentions that water was stored in large stone jars. Archaeology is not likely to provide decisive proof that Khirbet Qana was Cana of Galilee, but even the prospect of uncovering artifacts there that existed when Jesus worked his first miracle is suggestive. ◆

Large storage containers similar to those Jesus would have used in his miracle at Cana, first century AD, Jerusalem.

Kim Walton. The Israel Museum, Jerusalem.

MIRACLES OF JESUS

HEALING MIRACLES	MATTHEW	MARK	LUKE	JOHN
Man with leprosy	8:2–4	1:40–42	5:12–13	
Roman centurion's servant	8:5–13		7:1–10	
Peter's mother-in-law	8:14–15	1:30–31	4:38–39	
Two men from Gadara	8:28–34	5:1–15	8:27–35	
Paralyzed man	9:2–7	2:3–12	5:18–25	
Woman with bleeding	9:20–22	5:25–29	8:43–48	
Two blind men	9:27–31			
Mute, demon-possessed man	9:32–33			
Man with a shriveled hand	12:10–13	3:1–5	6:6–10	
Blind, mute, demon-possessed man	12:22		11:14	
Canaanite woman's daughter	15:21–28	7:24–30		
Demon-possessed boy	17:14–18	9:17–29	9:38–43	
Two blind men (including Bartimaeus)	20:29–34	10:46–52	18:35–43	
Deaf mute		7:31–37		
Demon-possessed man in synagogue		1:23–26	4:33–35	
Blind man at Bethsaida		8:22–26		
Crippled woman			13:11–13	
Man with abnormal swelling			14:1–4	
Ten men with leprosy			17:11–19	
The high priest's servant			22:50–51	
Official's son at Capernaum				4:46–54
Sick man at pool of Bethesda				5:1–9
Man born blind				9:1–7
MIRACLES SHOWING POWER OVER NATURE				
Calming the storm	8:23–27	4:37–41	8:22–25	
Walking on water	14:25	6:48–51		6:19–21
Feeding the 5,000	14:15–21	6:35–44	9:12–17	6:6–13
Feeding the 4,000	15:32–38	8:1–9		
Coin in fish's mouth	17:24–27			
Fig tree withered	21:18–22	11:12–14,20–25		
Large catch of fish			5:4–11	
Water turned into wine				2:1–11
Another large catch of fish				21:1–11
MIRACLES OF RAISING THE DEAD				
Jairus's daughter	9:18–19,23–25	5:22–24,38–42	8:41–42,49–56	
Widow's son at Nain			7:11–15	
Lazarus				11:1–44

had also been invited to the wedding. 3When the wine was gone, Jesus' mother said to him, "They have no more wine."

4"Woman,[a][o] why do you involve me?"[p] Jesus replied. "My hour[q] has not yet come."

5His mother said to the servants, "Do whatever he tells you."[r]

6Nearby stood six stone water jars, the kind used by the Jews for ceremonial washing,[s] each holding from twenty to thirty gallons.[b]

7Jesus said to the servants, "Fill the jars with water"; so they filled them to the brim.

8Then he told them, "Now draw some out and take it to the master of the banquet."

They did so, 9and the master of the banquet tasted the water that had been turned into wine.[t] He did not realize where it had come from, though the servants who had drawn the water knew. Then he called the bridegroom aside 10and said, "Everyone brings out the choice wine first and then the cheaper wine after the guests have had too much to drink; but you have saved the best till now."

11What Jesus did here in Cana of Galilee was the first of the signs[u] through which he revealed his glory;[v] and his disciples believed in him.[w]

12After this he went down to Capernaum[x] with his mother and brothers[y] and his disciples. There they stayed for a few days.

Jesus Clears the Temple Courts

2:14-16pp — Mt 21:12,13; Mk 11:15-17; Lk 19:45,46

13When it was almost time for the Jewish Passover,[z] Jesus went up to Jerusalem.[a] 14In the temple courts he found people selling cattle, sheep and doves, and others sitting at tables exchanging money. 15So he made a whip out of cords, and drove all from the temple courts, both sheep and cattle; he scattered the coins of the money changers and overturned their tables. 16To those who sold doves he said, "Get these out of here! Stop turning my Father's house[b] into a market!" 17His disciples remembered that it is written: "Zeal for your house will consume me."[c][c]

18The Jews then responded to him, "What sign can you show us to prove your authority to do all this?"[d]

19Jesus answered them, "Destroy this temple, and I will raise it again in three days."[e]

2:4 [o] Jn 19:26 [p] Mt 8:29 [q] Mt 26:18; Jn 7:6
2:5 [r] Ge 41:55
2:6 [s] Mk 7:3,4; Jn 3:25
2:9 [t] Jn 4:46
2:11 [u] ver 23; Jn 3:2; 4:48; 6:2,14,26,30; 12:37; 20:30 [v] Jn 1:14 [w] Ex 14:31
2:12 [x] Mt 4:13 [y] Mt 12:46
2:13 [z] Jn 11:55 [a] Dt 16:1-6; Lk 2:41
2:16 [b] Lk 2:49
2:17 [c] Ps 69:9
2:18 [d] Mt 12:38
2:19 [e] Mt 26:61; 27:40; Mk 14:58; 15:29

[a] *4* The Greek for *Woman* does not denote any disrespect. [b] *6* Or from about 75 to about 115 liters [c] *17* Psalm 69:9

2:3 *no more wine.* Wedding feasts sometimes lasted seven days. Inviting as many people as possible would bring honor to the family, but because of this culture's emphasis on hospitality, running out of wine would bring grave shame. Women, who were involved in food preparation, might be the first to know about any lack in the essential aspects of the banquet. Jesus' mother's words may be a polite, indirect request.
2:4 *Woman.* To address a woman as such indicated no disrespect; it was similar to the English "Ma'am." Nevertheless, it was not a normal address for one's mother. *why do you involve me?* Lit. "What (is there between) me and you?"—a phrase that emphasizes distance and often hostility between the speaker and the one addressed (see the Septuagint, the pre-Christian Greek translation of the OT, of Jdg 11:12; 1Ki 17:18; 2Ki 3:13; 2Ch 35:21). Jesus may be protesting his mother's implied insistence, since she does not know what the beginning of his ministry will cost him. *hour.* Jesus probably refers here to his impending death (7:30; 8:20; 12:23,27); other ancient sources sometimes also spoke of one's appointed "hour" or "time" to die (cf., e.g., 1Sa 26:10; Mt 26:18; Suetonius, *Nero* 49.2).
2:5 *Do whatever he tells you.* The mother's command might echo Pharaoh's words concerning Joseph's authority for provision in Ge 41:55. Her faith resembles that of Biblical predecessors who would not give up (e.g., 1Ki 18:36–37; 2Ki 2:2,4,6; 4:28).
2:6 *six stone water jars.* Jewish people preferred stone jars because they did not easily contract ritual impurity. Together these pots held sufficient water for a pool for ritual immersion, though such pools were not supposed to use water from pots. Water could also be stored in them for later pouring over hands for washing. (For the custom of hand washing, see notes on Mk 7:3,4. For the issue of ritual purity in this Gospel, see also Jn 3:26; 11:55; cf. also the water motif in 1:33; 3:5; 4:10–14; 5:7; 7:37–39; 9:7; 13:5; 19:34.)
2:7 Ignoring the purpose for which the pots were consecrated, Jesus values more highly his friend's honor (see note on v. 3).
2:8 *the master of the banquet.* An honorary office involving overseeing entertainment and distribution of wine.
2:10 *saved the best till now.* Wedding feasts could last seven days; guests' tastes became dulled through much drinking (though guests could come and go). It was difficult to prevent wine from fermenting, but people often watered wine down two parts water to every part wine. (It was served undiluted only when people deliberately wanted to get drunk, behavior that most Jewish people considered unacceptable.)
2:11 *first of the signs.* For seeing God's glory in signs, see, e.g., Ex 16:7. Contrast here Moses' first public sign, turning water to blood (Ex 7:20–21).
2:13 *Passover... went up to Jerusalem.* Most Galileans went up to Jerusalem for major festivals such as Passover; Josephus reports that entire villages traveled.
2:14 *cattle, sheep and doves.* All these animals were needed for some sacrifices (e.g., Lev 1:5,10; 4:3; 5:7; 22:19). *exchanging money.* Because each local region had its own currencies, money changers performed a service by changing local money into standardized currency so people could buy what they needed.
2:17 *Zeal for your house will consume me.* Ps 69:9 belongs to a psalm of the righteous sufferer (cf. Ps 69:4 in Jn 15:25; possibly Ps 69:21 in Jn 19:29). Early Christians believed that these psalms applied to Jesus as the righteous sufferer *par excellence.*
2:19 *Destroy this temple.* Already in Jesus' day some Jews expected God to replace the current temple with a purer one. By the time John wrote this gospel, after the temple

JOHN 2:6

THE "JEWS" AND "JEWISH LEADERS" IN JOHN'S GOSPEL

John's Gospel sometimes uses "Jews" in a neutral (e.g., 2:6; 4:9) or a positive (4:22; 11:19) way, but sometimes it applies to those hostile toward Jesus (e.g., 6:41,52). Often it means "Judeans" (e.g., 11:8), and most of the negative uses apply to the Judean leaders (the NIV rightly renders many of these instances as "Jewish leaders," e.g., 7:1,11). The negative use of the term "Jews" seems odd in a work in which most of the main protagonists, Jesus and his disciples, are Jewish. Yet within the narrative only a Samaritan (4:9,20) and a Gentile (18:35) call Jesus a "Jew."

One possible reason for John's usage is the setting that John addresses. Most scholars believe that John's audience includes, or even especially includes, Jewish believers in Jesus who have been made unwelcome in their synagogues (cf. 9:22; 12:42; 16:2). Their synagogue leaders have thus treated them as if they no longer belong to Israel, as if the synagogue leaders have the right to decide who belongs and who does not (see note on 10:1–18). To a similar situation in the synagogues of Smyrna and Philadelphia, the book of Revelation apparently denounces those leaders as those who claim to be Jews but are not (see Rev 2:9; 3:9 and notes there). John's Gospel may adopt the opposite rhetorical strategy to make the same kind of point: the hostile leaders get the title "Jews," yet the Gospel depicts Jesus' followers rather than their enemies as those truly faithful to Israel's heritage. Throughout the Gospel, Jesus fulfills key motifs in Jewish festivals and other Biblical images. Meanwhile, his disciples are sheep (Jn 10:26–28), branches on the vine (15:5), and other images related to Israel in earlier Scripture (cf., e.g., Ps 100:3; Isa 5:7). ◆

20They replied, "It has taken forty-six
years to build this temple, and you are
going to raise it in three days?" 21But the
temple he had spoken of was his body.[f]
22After he was raised from the dead, his
disciples recalled what he had said.[g] Then
they believed the scripture and the words
that Jesus had spoken.

23Now while he was in Jerusalem at the
Passover Festival,[h] many people saw the
signs he was performing and believed in his
name.[a] 24But Jesus would not entrust himself to them, for he knew all people. 25He
did not need any testimony about mankind,
for he knew what was in each person.[i]

2:21 [f] 1Co 6:19
2:22 [g] Lk 24:5-8; Jn 12:16; 14:26
2:23 [h] ver 13
2:25 [i] Mt 9:4; Jn 6:61,64; 13:11

3:1 [j] Jn 7:50; 19:39 [k] Lk 23:13
3:2 [l] Jn 9:16, 33 [m] Ac 2:22; 10:38
3:3 [n] Jn 1:13; 1Pe 1:23

Jesus Teaches Nicodemus

3 Now there was a Pharisee, a man
named Nicodemus[j] who was a member of the Jewish ruling council.[k] 2He
came to Jesus at night and said, "Rabbi,
we know that you are a teacher who has
come from God. For no one could perform
the signs[l] you are doing if God were not
with him."[m]

3Jesus replied, "Very truly I tell you, no
one can see the kingdom of God unless
they are born again.[b]"[n]

[a] 23 Or *in him* [b] 3 The Greek for *again* also means *from above*; also in verse 7.

was destroyed in AD 70, Jewish people prayed regularly for its restoration.

2:20 *forty-six years.* Many scholars note that this figure suggests a date of about AD 27.

2:22 *After he was raised from the dead.* Many people in antiquity believed that many prophecies were understood only in retrospect.

2:25 *he knew.* Although Jewish people recognized that prophets sometimes knew some thoughts, they spoke of God as the one who knew all people's hearts. This is just one of the subtle ways that John appealed to his audience to believe in Jesus as divine.

3:1 *Nicodemus.* Ancient Jewish sources report a wealthy Naqdimon (Nicodemus) from this period (e.g., *Sipre Dt* 305.2.1).

3:3 *born again.* As "heaven" was a surrogate title for God, occasionally Jewish sources used "above" in the same way. "Born from above" (the likeliest literal sense here) can

4“How can someone be born when
they are old?” Nicodemus asked. “Surely
they cannot enter a second time into their
mother’s womb to be born!”
5Jesus answered, “Very truly I tell you,
no one can enter the kingdom of God unless they are born of water and the Spirit.[o]
6Flesh gives birth to flesh, but the Spirit[a]
gives birth to spirit.[p] 7You should not be
surprised at my saying, ‘You[b] must be born
again.’ 8The wind blows wherever it pleases. You hear its sound, but you cannot tell
where it comes from or where it is going.
So it is with everyone born of the Spirit.”[c]
9“How can this be?”[q] Nicodemus asked.
10“You are Israel’s teacher,”[r] said Jesus,
“and do you not understand these things?
11Very truly I tell you, we speak of what
we know,[s] and we testify to what we have
seen, but still you people do not accept
our testimony.[t] 12I have spoken to you of
earthly things and you do not believe; how
then will you believe if I speak of heavenly
things? 13No one has ever gone into heav-
en[u] except the one who came from heav-
en[v]—the Son of Man.[d] 14Just as Moses
lifted up the snake in the wilderness,[w] so
the Son of Man must be lifted up,[e][x] 15that
everyone who believes[y] may have eternal
life in him.”[f]

16For God so loved[z] the world that he
gave his one and only Son, that whoever believes in him shall not perish but
have eternal life.[a] 17For God did not send
his Son into the world[b] to condemn the
world, but to save the world through him.[c]
18Whoever believes in him is not condemned,[d] but whoever does not believe
stands condemned already because they
have not believed in the name of God’s
one and only Son.[e] 19This is the verdict:
Light[f] has come into the world, but people loved darkness instead of light because their deeds were evil. 20Everyone
who does evil hates the light, and will not
come into the light for fear that their deeds
will be exposed.[g] 21But whoever lives by
the truth comes into the light, so that it
may be seen plainly that what they have
done has been done in the sight of God.

John Testifies Again About Jesus

22After this, Jesus and his disciples went
out into the Judean countryside, where he
spent some time with them, and baptized.[h]
23Now John also was baptizing at Aenon

3:5 [o] Titus 3:5
3:6 [p] Jn 1:13; 1Co 15:50
3:9 [q] Jn 6:52,60
3:10 [r] Lk 2:46
3:11 [s] Jn 1:18; 7:16,17 [t] ver 32
3:13 [u] Pr 30:4; Ac 2:34; Eph 4:8-10 [v] Jn 6:38,42
3:14 [w] Nu 21:8,9 [x] Jn 8:28; 12:32
3:15 [y] ver 16,36
3:16 [z] Ro 5:8; Eph 2:4; 1Jn 4:9,10 [a] ver 36; Jn 6:29,40; 11:25,26
3:17 [b] Jn 6:29,57; 10:36; 11:42; 17:8,21; 20:21 [c] Jn 12:47; 1Jn 4:14
3:18 [d] Jn 5:24 [e] 1Jn 4:9
3:19 [f] Jn 1:4; 8:12
3:20 [g] Eph 5:11,13
3:22 [h] Jn 4:2

[a] *6* Or *but spirit* [b] *7* The Greek is plural.
[c] *8* The Greek for *Spirit* is the same as that for *wind.*
[d] *13* Some manuscripts *Man, who is in heaven*
[e] *14* The Greek for *lifted up* also means *exalted.*
[f] *15* Some interpreters end the quotation with verse 21.

mean “born from God.” Plays on words were common in antiquity and are also present in many places in John’s Gospel (cf. v. 8).

3:4 *How can … ?* Wise sages in both Greece and the Middle East sometimes spoke in riddles hard for others to understand. Throughout John’s Gospel, outsiders misunderstand Jesus’ riddles and fail to perceive his plays on words. Ancient writers sometimes highlighted the wisdom of a protagonist by providing foils who misunderstand.

3:5 *born of water and the Spirit.* Some Jewish teachers allowed that Gentiles could be “reborn” into Judaism through conversion, which included immersion in water. Some understand the Greek construction here as a hendiadys, which is a two-idea expression designed to more thoroughly describe one idea, hence “born of water, i.e., the Spirit” (cf. 7:39). In the time of restoration, God would use water to purify his people from the impurity of idolatry (Eze 36:25), give them a new spirit (Eze 36:26) and put his Spirit in them (Eze 36:27).

3:6 *Spirit gives birth to spirit.* God would put a new spirit in his people (Eze 36:26) when he put his Spirit in them; then they would obey his laws (Eze 36:27). Ancients accepted the principle that living things produced things that reflected characteristics consistent with their progenitors (e.g., Ge 1:11).

3:8 *wind … sound.* John is fond of wordplays (v. 3). Both in Hebrew and in Greek, the “sound” of the “wind” can also mean the “voice” of the “Spirit.” In the chapter immediately following Eze 36 (see notes on Jn 3:5,6), God’s Spirit comes like a wind to revive and restore his people (Eze 37:1–14).

3:12 Nicodemus should be able to recognize Jesus’ point, which draws on a familiar principle. Some Jewish people already recognized that humans, with limited knowledge even of earthly things, could not understand the heavens (noted in the widely circulated Wisdom of Solomon 9:16)—at least not without the Spirit sent from above (Wisdom of Solomon 9:17). In John, “earthly” analogies for “heavenly things” here might refer to “above” (see NIV text note on v. 3), “water” (v. 5) and “wind” (v. 8).

3:13 *gone into heaven except the one who came from heaven.* Although some Jewish tradition spoke of Moses ascending to heaven or even mystics reaching God’s throne, the description of Jesus here resembles Jewish texts about divine Wisdom that came down from heaven.

3:14 Moses lifted up the snake so whoever looked on it would live (Nu 21:6–9); cf. Jn 6:40.

3:16 *God so loved the world.* Lit., “in this way God loved the world.” Jewish teachers emphasized God’s extraordinary love for Israel; self-sacrificing love for the world, however, exceeds that love. God’s loving character here fits the OT (e.g., Ex 34:6–7; Hos 11:8).

3:17–18 *not … to condemn … but to save … Whoever believes in him is not condemned.* Jewish people anticipated salvation, eternal life, and condemnation in the day of judgment at the end of the age; in Jesus, the future promises have begun to be fulfilled. (This new life begins with the spiritual birth noted in vv. 3,5.)

3:19–21 *Light … darkness … light.* This passage’s language would have been understandable to John’s readers; the Dead Sea Scrolls contrast the people of light (Israel’s chosen remnant) with the people of darkness (everyone else).

3:22 *baptized.* Jewish teachers viewed Jewish groups that had special baptisms for other Jews as movements distinct from the mainstream.

3:23 *Aenon.* The location is debated, but scholars’ best guess so far places it in the vicinity of Samaria (cf. 4:4).

near Salim, because there was plenty of
water, and people were coming and being baptized. 24(This was before John was
put in prison.)[i] 25An argument developed
between some of John's disciples and a
certain Jew over the matter of ceremonial
washing.[j] 26They came to John and said to
him, "Rabbi,[k] that man who was with you
on the other side of the Jordan — the one
you testified[l] about — look, he is baptizing,
and everyone is going to him."
27To this John replied, "A person can receive only what is given them from heaven.
28You yourselves can testify that I said, 'I am
not the Messiah but am sent ahead of him.'[m]
29The bride belongs to the bridegroom.[n] The
friend who attends the bridegroom waits
and listens for him, and is full of joy when
he hears the bridegroom's voice. That joy is
mine, and it is now complete.[o] 30He must
become greater; I must become less."[a]
31The one who comes from above[p] is

3:24 [i] Mt 4:12; 14:3
3:25 [j] Jn 2:6
3:26 [k] Mt 23:7 [l] Jn 1:7
3:28 [m] Jn 1:20, 23
3:29 [n] Mt 9:15 [o] Jn 16:24; 17:13; Php 2:2; 1Jn 1:4; 2Jn 12
3:31 [p] ver 13

[a] *30* Some interpreters end the quotation with verse 36.

3:24 *before John was put in prison.* Josephus notes that Herod Antipas imprisoned John in his fortress Machaerus in Perea, which was on the other side of the Jordan (cf. John's ministry there in v. 26; 1:28; 10:40; see note on Mk 6:17). The verse here might echo Jer 37:4.
3:25 *the matter of ceremonial washing.* Jewish groups differed on opinions about ceremonial washing. For ritual purity, see note on 2:6.
3:26 *everyone is going to him.* Ancient teachers often competed for disciples; on occasion teachers could be friends, yet their students still wished to be rivals.
3:29 When ancient Jewish sources pictured joy, they often pictured weddings. *The friend who attends the bridegroom.* This friend would offer a congratulatory speech and in various other ways support the groom. He would be best honored for honoring the groom, not for seeking his own honor.
3:31 *one who comes from above.* On wisdom from above, see note on v. 13.

JOHN 4

Samaria and Samaritans

From the time of King Ahab's father Omri, Samaria was the capital of the northern kingdom of Israel (1Ki 16:24). Scripture says that when Israel was exiled, foreigners settled in the land, mixed with remaining residents, and mixed their foreign gods with the true God of Israel (2Ki 17:23 – 35; cf. Ezr 4:9 – 10). Nehemiah reports Samaritan opposition to his plan to strengthen Jerusalem (Ne 4:2).

After the exile, the Jewish king John Hyrcanus conquered the country of Samaria and destroyed the capital city of Samaria. Roman rule under the general Pompey, which started in Judea in 63 BC, freed Samaria again from Jewish control. Herod the Great expanded the old city of Samaria, now predominantly a Greek city, and in honor of his patron Augustus, the emperor, named it Sebaste (Greek for Augustus). The Samaritan people, however, lived in the countryside, especially around the old city of Shechem (cf. Josephus, *Antiquities* 11.340).

Samaritans and Jews were hostile toward each other's holy sites. Jews insisted that Jerusalem was the proper place for the temple; Samaritans insisted that it was Mount Gerizim (Josephus, *Antiquities* 13.74); the extant form of the Samaritan Pentateuch even includes the demand to worship at Gerizim in the Ten Commandments! John Hyrcanus had destroyed the Samaritan temple on Mount Gerizim in 128 BC; in the first century AD, a group of Samaritans entered the Jerusalem temple secretly and desecrated it with corpses, leading to Samaritans' permanent exclusion from Jerusalem's temple (Josephus, *Antiquities* 18.30). Galileans usually journeyed through Samaria for festivals in Jerusalem, but Samaritans sometimes heckled them, and sometimes this conflict led to violence (Josephus, *Antiquities* 20.118; *Wars* 2.232).

Josephus claims that Samaritans identified with the more numerous Judeans when it was advantageous but distinguished themselves from Judeans when Judea was in trouble (*Antiquities* 11.340 – 41; 12.257). Later Jewish tradition tried to sort out the ways that Samaritans were like Gentiles and the ways they were not quite as bad. Later

continued on next page

above all; the one who is from the earth
belongs to the earth, and speaks as one
from the earth.[q] The one who comes
from heaven is above all. 32He testifies to
what he has seen and heard,[r] but no one
accepts his testimony.[s] 33Whoever has accepted it has certified that God is truthful. 34For the one whom God has sent[t]
speaks the words of God, for God[a] gives
the Spirit[u] without limit. 35The Father
loves the Son and has placed everything
in his hands.[v] 36Whoever believes in the
Son has eternal life,[w] but whoever rejects
the Son will not see life, for God's wrath
remains on them.

Jesus Talks With a Samaritan Woman

4 Now Jesus learned that the Pharisees
had heard that he was gaining and
baptizing more disciples than John[x]—2al-
though in fact it was not Jesus who baptized, but his disciples. 3So he left Judea[y]
and went back once more to Galilee.
4Now he had to go through Samaria.
5So he came to a town in Samaria called

3:31 [q] Jn 8:23; 1Jn 4:5 **3:32** [r] Jn 8:26; 15:15 [s] ver 11 **3:34** [t] ver 17 [u] Mt 12:18; Lk 4:18; Ac 10:38 **3:35** [v] Mt 28:18; Jn 5:20,22; 17:2 **3:36** [w] ver 15; Jn 5:24; 6:47

4:1 [x] Jn 3:22,26 **4:3** [y] Jn 3:22

[a] 34 Greek *he*

3:33 *certified.* "Sealed"; among the various uses of wax seals in antiquity, one was when witnesses would attest to the truth or content of something. They would seal a document shut with a wad of hot wax, into which they would impress their distinctive signet (often on a ring); the mark would remain when the wax dried, and remained intact until the document or container was opened (see the article "Sealing Documents and Revelation 5," p. 2232).
3:35 *placed everything in his hands.* Jewish teachers reserved such language for divine Wisdom.
3:36 *has eternal life.* The promised future has begun in Jesus; see note on vv. 17–18.
4:4 *had to go through Samaria.* Jews traveling between Judea and Galilee could circumvent Samaria, but most

Samaritan tradition exhibits a conservative piety similar to that of ancient Judaism, but rejected Biblical history after the Pentateuch. Samaritans argued that Moses was the last prophet until a future restorer like Moses (Dt 18:15–18) would arise. Josephus reports a false prophet who persuaded the Samaritans to follow him (*Antiquities* 18.85); if the later Samaritan traditions about a single restorer reflect this early period, Samaritans may have thought that this prophet was the promised one. ◆

View looking west at the well-preserved staircase (c. 200 BC) on the top of the eastern slope of Mt. Gerizim that leads up to the "sacred area" on Mt. Gerizim.

www.HolyLandPhotos.com

Sychar, near the plot of ground Jacob had
given to his son Joseph.[z] 6Jacob's well
was there, and Jesus, tired as he was from
the journey, sat down by the well. It was
about noon.
7When a Samaritan woman came to
draw water, Jesus said to her, "Will you
give me a drink?" 8(His disciples had gone
into the town[a] to buy food.)
9The Samaritan woman said to him,
"You are a Jew and I am a Samaritan[b]
woman. How can you ask me for a drink?"
(For Jews do not associate with Samaritans.[a])
10Jesus answered her, "If you knew the
gift of God and who it is that asks you for
a drink, you would have asked him and he
would have given you living water."[c]
11"Sir," the woman said, "you have
nothing to draw with and the well is deep.
Where can you get this living water?
12Are you greater than our father Jacob,
who gave us the well[d] and drank from it
himself, as did also his sons and his livestock?"
13Jesus answered, "Everyone who
drinks this water will be thirsty again,
14but whoever drinks the water I give
them will never thirst.[e] Indeed, the water
I give them will become in them a spring
of water[f] welling up to eternal life."[g]
15The woman said to him, "Sir, give me
this water so that I won't get thirsty[h] and
have to keep coming here to draw water."
16He told her, "Go, call your husband
and come back."
17"I have no husband," she replied.
Jesus said to her, "You are right when
you say you have no husband. 18The fact
is, you have had five husbands, and the
man you now have is not your husband.
What you have just said is quite true."
19"Sir," the woman said, "I can see
that you are a prophet.[i] 20Our ancestors

4:5 [z]Ge 33:19; 48:22; Jos 24:32 **4:8** [a]ver 5,39 **4:9** [b]Mt 10:5; Lk 9:52,53 **4:10** [c]Isa 44:3; Jer 2:13; Zec 14:8; Jn 7:37,38; Rev 21:6; 22:1,17 **4:12** [d]ver 6 **4:14** [e]Jn 6:35 [f]Jn 7:38 [g]Mt 25:46 **4:15** [h]Jn 6:34 **4:19** [i]Mt 21:11

[a] 9 Or *do not use dishes Samaritans have used*

commonly they took the shortest route through Samaria (Josephus, *Antiquities* 20.118; *Wars* 2.232). This route yielded a three-day journey (Josephus, *Life*, 269). Nevertheless, the words "had to" may reflect the Father's will (especially if Jesus was near John the Baptist in 3:22–23; that region may have been closer to the route that avoided Samaria altogether).

4:5 *Sychar.* Might be Shechem (near Jacob's well), but is more often identified with today's village of Askar. Askar was nearly a mile (about 1.5 kilometers) from the well.

4:6 *Jacob's well.* This well remains today; Mount Gerizim (v. 20) is visible from this site. *noon.* Considered the beginning of the hottest hour; during this hour, people would seek shade, sometimes eat a light meal and often take a siesta. That the woman comes, alone, at this hour suggests that she was not welcome with the other women, since women usually came to draw water together. The passage about the well in the wilderness in Nu 21:16–18 almost immediately follows the passage about Moses lifting the snake there (see note on Jn 3:14).

4:7–26 Conservative ancient practice looked down on men speaking at any length with women who were not relatives; this was all the more the case in rural areas such as this one (see note on v. 27).

4:7 *Will you give me a drink?* Hospitality demanded giving drink to a visitor; more relevant here (see note on v. 16), Isaac's representative asked Rebekah for a drink (Ge 24:17). Most relevant here was the status of Samaritan vessels (see note on v. 9).

4:8 *gone … to buy food.* Teachers sometimes had disciples get food for the group; but the strictest Jews considered some Samaritan foods unclean.

4:9 *How can you ask me for a drink?* Although Jews did not literally reject all dealings with Samaritans, association was limited. According to Jewish tradition, a Samaritan woman was continually unclean; it was therefore impure to drink from her vessel.

4:10 *living water.* An idiom for flowing water (Jer 17:13), which was superior to normal well water. But "living water" can also be a wordplay (see note on Jn 3:3) for the water of life.

4:11 *deep.* The well's ancient depth is uncertain, but it may be similar to its modern depth of 100 feet (30 meters).

4:12 *our father Jacob.* Jews denied Samaritans' descent from Jacob, whereas Samaritans affirmed it. Judeans denied it because Assyrians had mixed other peoples with the descendants of the northern kingdom, and they had originally mixed conflicting beliefs (2Ki 17:24–34,41). By this period, though, Samaritans were monotheists.

4:14 *will never thirst.* A widely circulated work of Jewish wisdom claimed that whoever tasted of Wisdom would thirst for more of her (Sirach 24:21); Jesus claims to offer even better water (see eternal life).

4:15 *have to keep coming here.* The well could be nearly a mile (about 1.5 kilometers) from her village; she might carry the vessel back on her head.

4:16 *call your husband.* Like Jesus in v. 6, Moses sat down by a well before he met Zipporah (Ex 2:15; Jewish tradition claims that he sat there at noon). Isaac's representative, Jacob, and Moses all met future wives at wells, and Jewish sources reveal that people still sometimes hoped to find mates at wells. That the woman is alone is conspicuous (see note on Jn 4:6); male strangers did not normally engage in extensive conversation with women unless they had ulterior motives (see note on v. 27). Possibly she lacked a head covering, which would signal her singleness (see the article "Head Coverings in Antiquity," p. 2003). The woman, then, might interpret Jesus' words as probing whether she was available, possibly infusing her denial of being married (v. 17) with another level of meaning.

4:18 *had five husbands … not your husband.* Nearly all ancient hearers would look negatively on her situation. Given their cultural beliefs, most would assume that she had done something wrong to be deprived of so many husbands; this was true if she was widowed (see note on Lk 20:29–31) and even more significant if she was divorced. That she was living with a man who was not her husband would be even more directly problematic for both Jews and Samaritans. Yet it is to her that Jesus reveals his identity (v. 26).

4:19 *prophet.* Later tradition suggests that Samaritans did not believe in prophets after Moses until the final restorer like Moses (Dt 18:15–18) would come. Thus she sees him either as the final prophet or (more likely at this point) recognizes that her Samaritan tradition is wrong—which leads to her dilemma stated in v. 20.

JESUS IN JUDEA AND SAMARIA

1 The most important port in the Holy Land in NT times

2 The birthplace of Jesus (Mt 2:1; Lk 2:4)

3 John the Baptist baptized here (Jn 3:23). Aenon was also the probable location of John's ministry.

4 Here Jesus talked with a Samaritan woman at Jacob's well (Jn 4:5).

5 The mountain referred to by the Samaritan woman at the well as the worship center for the Samaritans (Jn 4:20–23)

6 Jesus raised Lazarus from the dead (Jn 11:43–44). Here at Bethany Jesus was anointed in the house of Simon the Leper (Mt 26:6). It was also the scene of the ascension (Lk 24:50–51).

7 Jesus healed a blind man here at Jericho (Mt 20:29) and called Zacchaeus down from a tree (Lk 19:1). The Good Samaritan helped a traveler en route here (Lk 10:30).

8 Most important Biblical city. Jesus was crucified at Jerusalem as predicted (Mt 16:21; Mk 10:33; Lk 18:31).

9 The resurrected Jesus appeared to two people walking to Emmaus, and he ate with them there (Lk 24:13).

worshiped on this mountain,[j] but you
Jews claim that the place where we must
worship is in Jerusalem."[k]
21 "Woman," Jesus replied, "believe me, a
time is coming[l] when you will worship the
Father neither on this mountain nor in Jerusalem.[m] 22 You Samaritans worship what
you do not know;[n] we worship what we do
know, for salvation is from the Jews.[o] 23 Yet
a time is coming and has now come[p] when
the true worshipers will worship the Father
in the Spirit[q] and in truth, for they are the
kind of worshipers the Father seeks. 24 God
is spirit,[r] and his worshipers must worship
in the Spirit and in truth."
25 The woman said, "I know that Messiah" (called Christ)[s] "is coming. When he
comes, he will explain everything to us."
26 Then Jesus declared, "I, the one
speaking to you—I am he."[t]

The Disciples Rejoin Jesus

27 Just then his disciples returned[u] and
were surprised to find him talking with a
woman. But no one asked, "What do you
want?" or "Why are you talking with her?"
28 Then, leaving her water jar, the woman went back to the town and said to the
people, 29 "Come, see a man who told me
everything I ever did.[v] Could this be the
Messiah?"[w] 30 They came out of the town
and made their way toward him.
31 Meanwhile his disciples urged him,
"Rabbi,[x] eat something."
32 But he said to them, "I have food to
eat[y] that you know nothing about."
33 Then his disciples said to each other, "Could someone have brought him
food?"
34 "My food," said Jesus, "is to do the
will[z] of him who sent me and to finish his
work.[a] 35 Don't you have a saying, 'It's still
four months until harvest'? I tell you, open
your eyes and look at the fields! They are
ripe for harvest.[b] 36 Even now the one who
reaps draws a wage and harvests[c] a crop
for eternal life,[d] so that the sower and the
reaper may be glad together. 37 Thus the
saying 'One sows and another reaps'[e] is
true. 38 I sent you to reap what you have
not worked for. Others have done the hard
work, and you have reaped the benefits of
their labor."

Many Samaritans Believe

39 Many of the Samaritans from that
town[f] believed in him because of the
woman's testimony, "He told me everything I ever did."[g] 40 So when the Samaritans came to him, they urged him to stay
with them, and he stayed two days. 41 And
because of his words many more became
believers.
42 They said to the woman, "We no longer believe just because of what you said;
now we have heard for ourselves, and we
know that this man really is the Savior of
the world."[h]

4:20 [j] Dt 11:29; Jos 8:33 [k] Lk 9:53 **4:21** [l] Jn 5:28; 16:2 [m] Mal 1:11; 1Ti 2:8 **4:22** [n] 2Ki 17:28-41 [o] Isa 2:3; Ro 3:1, 2; 9:4,5 **4:23** [p] Jn 5:25; 16:32 [q] Php 3:3 **4:24** [r] Php 3:3 **4:25** [s] Mt 1:16 **4:26** [t] Jn 8:24; 9:35-37 **4:27** [u] ver 8 **4:29** [v] ver 17, 18 [w] Mt 12:23; Jn 7:26,31 **4:31** [x] Mt 23:7 **4:32** [y] Job 23:12; Mt 4:4; Jn 6:27 **4:34** [z] Mt 26:39; Jn 6:38; 17:4; 19:30 [a] Jn 19:30 **4:35** [b] Mt 9:37; Lk 10:2 **4:36** [c] Ro 1:13 [d] Mt 25:46 **4:37** [e] Job 31:8; Mic 6:15 **4:39** [f] ver 5 [g] ver 29 **4:42** [h] Lk 2:11; 1Jn 4:14

4:20 *worshiped.* She uses the past tense for Samaritan worship on Mount Gerizim, probably to highlight the fact that, over a century and a half earlier, a Jewish king had destroyed the Samaritans' temple. *in Jerusalem.* Many Jewish synagogues were apparently oriented toward Jerusalem, the rightful place of worship. Yet Samaritans were not welcome in Jerusalem's temple. So if Jesus is a prophet and the Jews are right about religion (vv. 19,22), she has a religious dilemma. She is excluded from the true worship of God.
4:21 *neither on this mountain nor in Jerusalem.* Without denying that the Jewish way was more accurate (v. 22), Jesus transcends the historic ethnic barrier that excluded Samaritans from worship (see note on v. 20).
4:24 *worship in the Spirit and in truth.* The true place of worship is neither in Jerusalem nor on Mount Gerizim, but in Spirit and truth (if this is a hendiadys, perhaps "the Spirit of truth"). Jewish people associated the Spirit especially with prophetic inspiration; the OT offers some preliminary models for prophetic or Spirit-inspired worship (e.g., 1Sa 10:5; 1Ch 25:1–3).
4:25 *Messiah.* Samaritans expected not a Messiah in the Jewish sense, but a prophet like Moses (Dt 18:15–18) who would restore them; Jesus fulfills this hope (Jn 4:26).
4:27 *surprised ... talking with a woman.* Most ancient Mediterranean culture disapproved of men speaking with women in private; Jewish sages warned against it repeatedly. Nevertheless, good disciples were supposed to trust their teacher and not question his motives.
4:29 *Come, see.* Most of ancient Mediterranean culture minimized the value of women's testimony (Josephus, e.g., rejected it as unstable); the woman's reputation (cf. note on v. 18) would make her testimony even more problematic. Her witness, however, is parallel to Philip's (1:46). Like ones impressed with women's testimony in Ge 24:28–32; 29:11–13, Samaritans come out to meet Jesus (v. 30).
4:34 *My food.* For God's message or mission as spiritual food, see, e.g., Ps 19:10; 119:103; Jer 15:16; Eze 3:3.
4:35 *It's still four months until harvest.* Barley harvest fell in March, with wheat in the latter half of April and all of May. Because harvest followed sowing by four or five months, the proverb cited here might encourage sowers that their labor would have its reward.
4:38 *reaped the benefits of their labor.* Sometimes one would reap what another sowed (cf. Ecc 2:18); one should be glad to reap so freely (cf. Dt 6:11).
4:40 *stayed two days.* Ancient Mediterranean culture highly emphasized the virtue of hospitality, but often this was applied only to members of one's ethnic group, and virtually never extended voluntarily and freely between Jews and Samaritans. For Jesus and his disciples to remain there two more days meant eating Samaritan food, dwelling in Samaritan dwellings and continuing to teach Samaritans, all of which would be offensive to most Jews (cf. 8:48).
4:42 *Savior of the world.* Scripture presented God as Israel's true Savior but sometimes spoke also of human saviors or deliverers that God raised up. That the Samaritans regard Jesus as Savior not merely of Israel but of the world is significant. The emperor claimed to be savior and benefactor of the world, but his mission differed starkly from that of Jesus.

Jesus Heals an Official's Son

43 After the two days[i] he left for Galilee.
44 (Now Jesus himself had pointed out that
a prophet has no honor in his own country.)[j] 45 When he arrived in Galilee, the Galileans welcomed him. They had seen all
that he had done in Jerusalem at the Passover Festival,[k] for they also had been there.
46 Once more he visited Cana in Galilee, where he had turned the water into
wine.[l] And there was a certain royal official whose son lay sick at Capernaum.
47 When this man heard that Jesus had arrived in Galilee from Judea,[m] he went to
him and begged him to come and heal his
son, who was close to death.
48 "Unless you people see signs and
wonders,"[n] Jesus told him, "you will never believe."
49 The royal official said, "Sir, come
down before my child dies."
50 "Go," Jesus replied, "your son will
live."
The man took Jesus at his word and departed. 51 While he was still on the way,
his servants met him with the news that
his boy was living. 52 When he inquired as
to the time when his son got better, they
said to him, "Yesterday, at one in the afternoon, the fever left him."
53 Then the father realized that this was
the exact time at which Jesus had said to
him, "Your son will live." So he and his
whole household[o] believed.
54 This was the second sign[p] Jesus performed after coming from Judea to Galilee.

The Healing at the Pool

5 Some time later, Jesus went up to Jerusalem for one of the Jewish festivals. 2 Now there is in Jerusalem near the
Sheep Gate[q] a pool, which in Aramaic[r] is
called Bethesda[a] and which is surrounded by five covered colonnades. 3 Here a
great number of disabled people used to
lie—the blind, the lame, the paralyzed.
[4][b] 5 One who was there had been an invalid for thirty-eight years. 6 When Jesus
saw him lying there and learned that he
had been in this condition for a long time,
he asked him, "Do you want to get well?"
7 "Sir," the invalid replied, "I have no
one to help me into the pool when the
water is stirred. While I am trying to get
in, someone else goes down ahead of me."
8 Then Jesus said to him, "Get up! Pick up
your mat and walk."[s] 9 At once the man was
cured; he picked up his mat and walked.
The day on which this took place was
a Sabbath,[t] 10 and so the Jewish leaders[u]
said to the man who had been healed, "It
is the Sabbath; the law forbids you to carry your mat."[v]
11 But he replied, "The man who made
me well said to me, 'Pick up your mat and
walk.' "
12 So they asked him, "Who is this fellow
who told you to pick it up and walk?"
13 The man who was healed had no idea
who it was, for Jesus had slipped away
into the crowd that was there.
14 Later Jesus found him at the temple
and said to him, "See, you are well again.
Stop sinning[w] or something worse may
happen to you." 15 The man went away
and told the Jewish leaders[x] that it was
Jesus who had made him well.

4:43 [i] ver 40 **4:44** [j] Mt 13:57; Lk 4:24 **4:45** [k] Jn 2:23 **4:46** [l] Jn 2:1-11 **4:47** [m] ver 3, 54 **4:48** [n] Da 4:2, 3; Jn 2:11; Ac 2:43; 14:3; Ro 15:19; 2Co 12:12; Heb 2:4 **4:53** [o] Ac 11:14 **4:54** [p] ver 48; Jn 2:11

5:2 [q] Ne 3:1; 12:39 [r] Jn 19:13, 17, 20; 20:16; Ac 21:40; 22:2; 26:14 **5:8** [s] Mt 9:5, 6; Mk 2:11; Lk 5:24 **5:9** [t] Jn 9:14 **5:10** [u] ver 16 [v] Ne 13:15-22; Jer 17:21; Mt 12:2 **5:14** [w] Mk 2:5; Jn 8:11 **5:15** [x] Jn 1:19

[a] 2 Some manuscripts *Bethzatha;* other manuscripts *Bethsaida* [b] 3,4 Some manuscripts include here, wholly or in part, *paralyzed—and they waited for the moving of the waters. 4From time to time an angel of the Lord would come down and stir up the waters. The first one into the pool after each such disturbance would be cured of whatever disease they had.*

4:44 *no honor in his own country.* Scripture noted prophets being rejected, even in their hometowns (Jer 1:1; 11:21); Jewish traditions about the prophets amplified this pattern even further. Some scholars think that the "country" here is Judea (cf. Jn 1:11).
4:45 *They had seen.* Entire Galilean villages often journeyed to Jerusalem together for festivals.
4:46 *royal official ... Capernaum.* Given the likeliest site for Cana, Capernaum was almost a day's walk away. The royal official works for Herod Antipas; he may be a Hellenized Galilean aristocrat or possibly even a Gentile (though John would probably mention the latter if he knew it to be the case).
4:48 *signs and wonders.* Disbelief despite signs was blameworthy (Nu 14:11), but Jesus invites faith even beyond signs.
4:50 *took Jesus at his word.* Most miracle accounts in antiquity required the miracle worker to be present.
4:52 *Yesterday.* Because Cana was nearly a day's walk from Capernaum, and travelers normally left in the morning, the official had undoubtedly lodged somewhere for the night before journeying back to Capernaum.
5:1 *one of the Jewish festivals.* Although the festival explains why Jesus is in Jerusalem, John does not specify which festival is in view here; the crucial point is the Sabbath (vv. 9–10).
5:2 *pool ... called Bethesda.* People often gathered and conversed near public baths and pools. This particular pool is mentioned in the Dead Sea Scrolls, and archaeologists have discovered a Jerusalem pool with five porches (one on each side and one through the middle, creating twin pools). The pools were about 20 feet (6 meters) deep and together were as large as a football field.
5:3 *disabled people used to lie.* Gentile healing shrines dedicated to Asclepius often included pools; archaeology suggests that this site was used for such purposes in later centuries.
5:10 *the law forbids you to carry your mat.* Working on the Sabbath (v. 9) was in principle a capital offense (Nu 15:32–36). Jewish tradition specified carrying a load as a form of work, and the man's critics here view him as violating that interpretation of the law.
5:14 *Stop sinning or something worse may happen.* Though often suffering had nothing to do with personal sin, both Scripture and Jewish tradition sometimes linked them.

The Authority of the Son

[16]So, because Jesus was doing these things on the Sabbath, the Jewish leaders began to persecute him. [17]In his defense Jesus said to them, "My Father is always at his work[y] to this very day, and I too am working." [18]For this reason they tried all the more to kill him;[z] not only was he breaking the Sabbath, but he was even calling God his own Father, making himself equal with God.[a]

[19]Jesus gave them this answer: "Very truly I tell you, the Son can do nothing by himself;[b] he can do only what he sees his Father doing, because whatever the Father does the Son also does. [20]For the Father loves the Son[c] and shows him all he does. Yes, and he will show him even greater works than these,[d] so that you will be amazed. [21]For just as the Father raises the dead and gives them life,[e] even so the Son gives life[f] to whom he is pleased to give it. [22]Moreover, the Father judges no one, but has entrusted all judgment to the Son,[g] [23]that all may honor the Son just as they honor the Father. Whoever does not honor the Son does not honor the Father, who sent him.[h]

[24]"Very truly I tell you, whoever hears my word and believes him who sent me has eternal life and will not be judged[i] but has crossed over from death to life.[j] [25]Very truly I tell you, a time is coming and has now come[k] when the dead will hear[l] the voice of the Son of God and those who hear will live. [26]For as the Father has life in himself, so he has granted the Son also to have life in himself. [27]And he has given him authority to judge[m] because he is the Son of Man.

[28]"Do not be amazed at this, for a time is coming[n] when all who are in their graves will hear his voice [29]and come out — those who have done what is good will rise to live, and those who have done what is evil will rise to be condemned.[o] [30]By myself I can do nothing;[p] I judge only as I hear, and my judgment is just,[q] for I seek not to please myself but him who sent me.[r]

Testimonies About Jesus

[31]"If I testify about myself, my testimony is not true.[s] [32]There is another who testifies in my favor,[t] and I know that his testimony about me is true.

[33]"You have sent to John and he has testified[u] to the truth. [34]Not that I accept human testimony;[v] but I mention it that you may be saved. [35]John was a lamp that burned and gave light,[w] and you chose for a time to enjoy his light.

[36]"I have testimony weightier than that of John.[x] For the works that the Father has given me to finish — the very works that I am doing[y] — testify that the Father has sent me.[z] [37]And the Father who sent me has himself testified concerning me.[a] You have never heard his voice nor seen his form,[b] [38]nor does his word dwell in you,[c] for you do not believe the one he sent.[d]

5:17 [y] Jn 9:4; 14:10
5:18 [z] Jn 7:1 [a] Jn 10:30, 33; 19:7
5:19 [b] ver 30; Jn 8:28
5:20 [c] Jn 3:35 [d] Jn 14:12
5:21 [e] Ro 4:17; 8:11 [f] Jn 11:25
5:22 [g] ver 27; Jn 9:39; Ac 10:42; 17:31
5:23 [h] Lk 10:16; 1Jn 2:23
5:24 [i] Jn 3:18 [j] 1Jn 3:14
5:25 [k] Jn 4:23 [l] Jn 8:43, 47
5:27 [m] ver 22; Ac 10:42; 17:31
5:28 [n] Jn 4:21
5:29 [o] Da 12:2; Mt 25:46
5:30 [p] ver 19 [q] Jn 8:16 [r] Mt 26:39; Jn 4:34; 6:38
5:31 [s] Jn 8:14
5:32 [t] ver 37; Jn 8:18
5:33 [u] Jn 1:7
5:34 [v] 1Jn 5:9
5:35 [w] 2Pe 1:19
5:36 [x] 1Jn 5:9 [y] Jn 14:11; 15:24 [z] Jn 3:17; 10:25
5:37 [a] Jn 8:18 [b] Dt 4:12; 1Ti 1:17; Jn 1:18
5:38 [c] 1Jn 2:14 [d] Jn 3:17

5:17 *My Father is always at his work.* Jewish tradition recognized that God worked even on the Sabbath, sustaining creation.

5:18 *they tried all the more to kill him.* Jewish teachers believed that rejecting obedience to any law meant rejection of the entire law. *his own Father.* Jewish people addressed God as Father in prayer, but Jesus' implicit claim that he should do whatever his Father did was different. *making himself equal with God.* Even Gentiles normally despised the arrogance of mortals who claimed to be gods; for Jews, it was blasphemy (cf., e.g., Ge 3:5; Isa 14:14). Though Jesus challenges their misunderstanding (Jn 5:19 – 20), later rabbis believed that Christians worshiped two gods.

5:19 *can do only what he sees his Father doing.* It was natural for sons to imitate and obey their fathers. Yet not even a prophet with visions could be said to see and imitate God continually. On what Jesus and the Father do, see note on 7:23.

5:21 – 22 *Father raises the dead … Father judges no one.* Only God could raise the dead, and only God would be humanity's ultimate judge. A daily prayer praised God who raises the dead.

5:23 *honor the Son … honor the Father.* The way one received an ambassador, a commissioned agent, or a son reflected one's attitude toward the sender or father.

5:26 *the Father has life in himself.* Greek-speaking Jews spoke of God as without beginning or source. Thus Jesus' hearers might hear him as stating that the Father has given him the right to claim that he too is eternal and divine.

5:27 Da 7:13 – 14 declared that the Son of Man would rule forever.

5:29 *rise to live … rise to be condemned.* Da 12:2 announced that God would raise both the righteous and the wicked; cf. Isa 26:19. Sadducees rejected belief in the resurrection; most other Judean and Galilean Jews believed in the resurrection of the righteous for eternal life, but not all believed that the wicked would be raised for eternal punishment.

5:30 *By myself I can do nothing.* In Jewish (and more generally, ancient Mediterranean) thought, an agent was to faithfully represent the sender, and to the extent that the agent did so he was fully backed by the sender's authority.

5:31 – 32 *I testify … another who testifies.* Scripture required a minimum of two or three witnesses (Dt 17:6; 19:15).

5:35 *John was a lamp.* Jewish teachers would sometimes speak of important Biblical characters or rabbis as lamps. Most lamps were small enough to hold in the hand; they differ from the much brighter "light of the world" (8:12; cf. 1:4 – 5).

5:37 – 38 *You have never heard … nor seen … nor does his word dwell in you.* In a sense Israel "saw" God and heard his voice at Sinai (Ex 24:10 – 11; Sirach 17:13); ideally God's law, his word, was in their hearts (Dt 30:14). By rejecting God's agent who accurately represented him, however, these critics showed that they did not know God.

39 You study[a] the Scriptures[e] diligently because you think that in them you have eternal life. These are the very Scriptures that testify about me,[f] 40 yet you refuse to come to me to have life.

41 "I do not accept glory from human beings,[g] 42 but I know you. I know that you do not have the love of God in your hearts. 43 I have come in my Father's name, and you do not accept me; but if someone else comes in his own name, you will accept him. 44 How can you believe since you accept glory from one another but do not seek the glory that comes from the only God[b]?[h]

45 "But do not think I will accuse you before the Father. Your accuser is Moses,[i] on whom your hopes are set.[j] 46 If you believed Moses, you would believe me, for he wrote about me.[k] 47 But since you do not believe what he wrote, how are you going to believe what I say?"[l]

Jesus Feeds the Five Thousand

6:1-13pp — Mt 14:13-21; Mk 6:32-44; Lk 9:10-17

6 Some time after this, Jesus crossed to the far shore of the Sea of Galilee (that is, the Sea of Tiberias), 2 and a great crowd of people followed him because they saw the signs[m] he had performed by healing the sick. 3 Then Jesus went up on a mountainside[n] and sat down with his disciples. 4 The Jewish Passover Festival[o] was near.

5 When Jesus looked up and saw a great crowd coming toward him, he said to Philip,[p] "Where shall we buy bread for these people to eat?" 6 He asked this only to test him, for he already had in mind what he was going to do.

7 Philip answered him, "It would take more than half a year's wages[c] to buy enough bread for each one to have a bite!"

8 Another of his disciples, Andrew, Simon Peter's brother,[q] spoke up, 9 "Here is a boy with five small barley loaves and two small fish, but how far will they go among so many?"[r]

10 Jesus said, "Have the people sit down." There was plenty of grass in that place, and they sat down (about five thousand men were there). 11 Jesus then took the loaves, gave thanks,[s] and distributed to those who were seated as much as they wanted. He did the same with the fish.

12 When they had all had enough to eat, he said to his disciples, "Gather the pieces that are left over. Let nothing be wasted." 13 So they gathered them and filled twelve baskets with the pieces of the five barley loaves left over by those who had eaten.

14 After the people saw the sign[t] Jesus performed, they began to say, "Surely this is the Prophet who is to come into the world."[u] 15 Jesus, knowing that they intended to come and make him king[v] by

5:39 [e] Ro 2:17, 18 [f] Lk 24:27, 44; Ac 13:27
5:41 [g] ver 44
5:44 [h] Ro 2:29
5:45 [i] Jn 9:28 [j] Ro 2:17
5:46 [k] Ge 3:15; Lk 24:27, 44; Ac 26:22
5:47 [l] Lk 16:29, 31
6:2 [m] Jn 2:11
6:3 [n] ver 15
6:4 [o] Jn 2:13; 11:55
6:5 [p] Jn 1:43
6:8 [q] Jn 1:40
6:9 [r] 2Ki 4:43
6:11 [s] ver 23; Mt 14:19
6:14 [t] Jn 2:11 [u] Dt 18:15, 18; Mt 11:3; 21:11
6:15 [v] Jn 18:36

[a] 39 Or *39Study* [b] 44 Some early manuscripts *the Only One* [c] 7 Greek *take two hundred denarii*

5:39–40 *you think that in them you have eternal life ... yet you refuse to come to me to have life.* Jewish teachers emphasized that their people would have life by obeying Scripture (cf., e.g., Dt 4:40); Pharisees and many others studied Scripture diligently. By rejecting the one to whom the Scriptures testified, however, they showed that they missed the heart of Scripture.

5:45 *Your accuser is Moses.* Jewish tradition viewed Moses as an intercessor for Israel. Jesus is the prophet of whom Moses wrote (Dt 18:15–18) but also the one whose glory he witnessed (Ex 33:19—34:7; see note on Jn 1:14–18). Jesus will soon offer a sign that both recalls and transcends Moses (6:11–13,32).

6:1 *Sea of Tiberias.* For the city of Tiberias (for which the lake is here named), see note on v. 23.

6:2 Many people in antiquity flocked to healing shrines, to hot springs for health (where available), and to prophetic figures who promised deliverance.

6:3 *sat down.* Grass could be green at Passover (Mk 6:39).

6:4 *Passover Festival.* Commemorated the deliverance through Moses. The feeding of 5,000 in the wilderness will show that the God of Moses remains active (cf. vv. 31–32).

6:7 *more than half a year's wages ... for each one to have a bite.* This might be a reasonable estimate in view of the crowd's size (v. 10); but it is unlikely that surrounding villages had enough bread even had there been money to pay for it. Many villages had only a few hundred residents; a town might have a few thousand, but they would not be expecting so many buyers. Even if barley had already been harvested (see note on 4:35), bread still had to be prepared.

6:9 *barley loaves.* Recalls the loaves Elisha multiplied in 2Ki 4:42–44, even though there it was just 20 loaves for 200 people. Ironically, Andrew does not realize that his protest echoes that of Elisha's servant in that passage, where he asked, "How can I set this before a hundred men?" (2Ki 4:43). Cf. Moses' astonishment in Nu 11:21–22. Barley harvest fell in March, so barley was probably plentiful at this time.

6:10 *plenty of grass.* Fits Passover season (v. 4). *five thousand men.* Often ancient figures included only "men" (as with the Greek term here), so the total number present exceeds 5,000—far more than the average Galilean town. Even the theater at Sepphoris, one of Galilee's two major cities, seated only 3,000 (though it is thought that theaters sometimes seated only 10 percent of a city's residents).

6:11 *gave thanks.* If somewhat later tradition is an indication, a typical blessing before meals was something like, "Blessed are you, Lord our God, king of the universe, who brings forth bread from the earth." *as much as they wanted.* God had multiplied food for prophets (1Ki 17:16; 2Ki 4:42–44) and provided manna for 40 years in the wilderness.

6:12 *left over.* Gracious hosts served more than enough. This demonstrates the generous hospitality of God in the face of need. Sometimes food was left over after a miraculous feeding (2Ki 4:44).

6:13 *twelve baskets.* They filled as many baskets as the 12 could carry—all leftovers from an original five loaves!

6:14 *the Prophet.* The promised prophet like Moses (Dt 18:15–18) who, not coincidentally, also was associated with miraculously feeding crowds.

6:15 *make him king.* Various Jewish writers viewed Moses as a king. At Passover season (v. 4), when Jewish

force, withdrew again to a mountain by himself.[w]

Jesus Walks on the Water

6:16-21pp — Mt 14:22-33; Mk 6:47-51

16When evening came, his disciples went down to the lake, 17where they got into a boat and set off across the lake for Capernaum. By now it was dark, and Jesus had not yet joined them. 18A strong wind was blowing and the waters grew rough. 19When they had rowed about three or four miles,[a] they saw Jesus approaching the boat, walking on the water;[x] and they were frightened. 20But he said to them, "It is I; don't be afraid."[y] 21Then they were

6:15 [w] Mt 14:23; Mk 6:46
6:19 [x] Job 9:8
6:20 [y] Mt 14:27

[a] *19* Or about 5 or 6 kilometers

people commemorated deliverance from oppression, the crowd's reaction is not surprising. During the first century some prophetic figures who promised deliverance drew thousands of Jewish or Samaritan followers; most of these movements ended disastrously, with Romans slaughtering many of the followers.

6:18 Wind rushing down from the mountains can create unexpected squalls on this lake.

6:19 *rowed.* Fishing boats normally had oars. *about three or four miles.* About 5 or 6 kilometers, nearly half the east-west distance across the widest part of the lake (though perhaps a quarter of the north-south distance); probably it was more than half the distance from the place of the feeding to Capernaum.

6:20 *It is I.* Lit. "I am." Although this can mean "It is I," the activity in the context supports an allusion to Jesus' deity (cf. Ex 3:14), especially given John's usage elsewhere (Jn 8:58). In the OT God used prophets to part waters, but

JESUS IN GALILEE

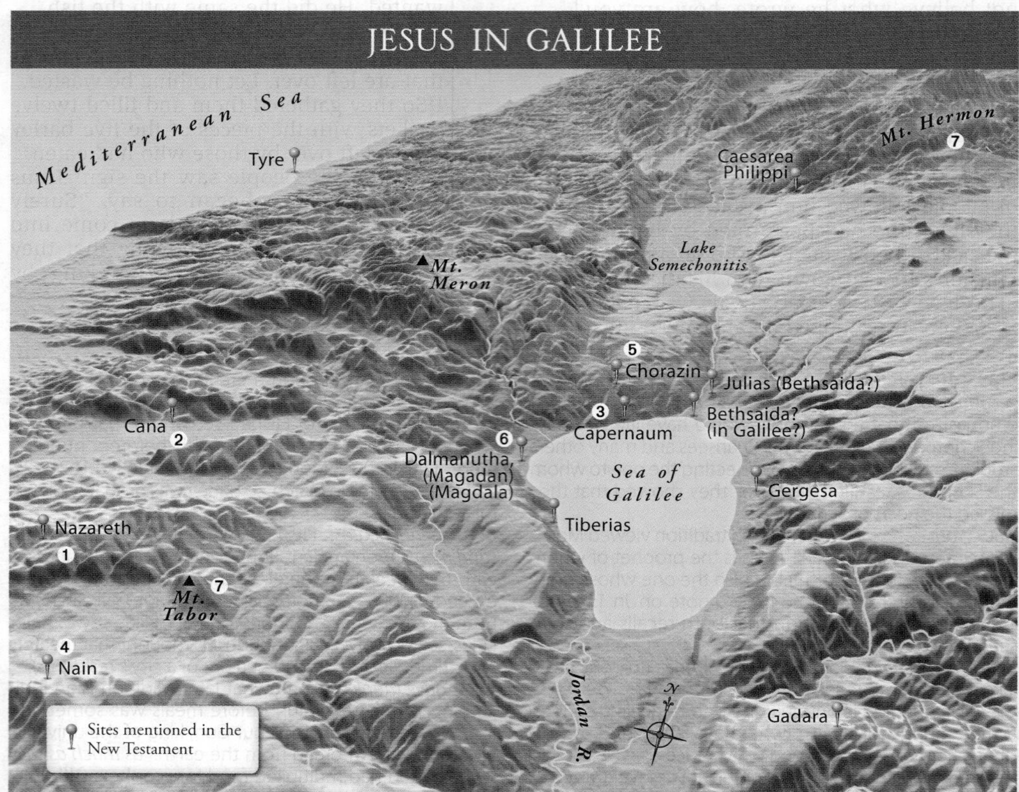

1 Town where Jesus grew up. He was rejected in the synagogue here and people sought to kill him (Lk 4:16).

2 Here at Cana Jesus performed his first miracle by turning water into wine at a wedding feast (Jn 2:1,11). Home of Nathanael (Jn 21:2).

3 Site of many miracles of Jesus (Mt 8:5; Mk 2:1 and Lk 7:1; Mt 17:24; Mk 1:21 and Lk 4:31; Jn 4:46; 6:17). Jesus taught in the synagogue here at Capernaum (Jn 6:59).

4 Here at Nain Jesus raised a widow's son from the dead (Lk 7:11).

5 One of the cities against which Jesus pronounced a woe (Mt 11:21; Lk 10:13).

6 Fishing town and home of Mary Magdalene (Mt 15:39; Mk 8:10).

7 Mount Tabor, the traditional Mount of Transfiguration (Mt 17:1–8; Mk 9:2–8; Lk 9:28–36). However, many scholars identify Mount Hermon as the most likely site of the transfiguration.

willing to take him into the boat, and
immediately the boat reached the shore
where they were heading.
22The next day the crowd that had
stayed on the opposite shore of the lake[z]
realized that only one boat had been there,
and that Jesus had not entered it with his
disciples, but that they had gone away
alone.[a] 23Then some boats from Tiberias[b]
landed near the place where the people
had eaten the bread after the Lord had giv-
en thanks.[c] 24Once the crowd realized that
neither Jesus nor his disciples were there,
they got into the boats and went to Capernaum in search of Jesus.

Jesus the Bread of Life

25When they found him on the other
side of the lake, they asked him, "Rabbi,[d]
when did you get here?"
26Jesus answered, "Very truly I tell you,
you are looking for me,[e] not because you
saw the signs[f] I performed but because
you ate the loaves and had your fill. 27Do
not work for food that spoils, but for food
that endures[g] to eternal life,[h] which the
Son of Man[i] will give you. For on him God
the Father has placed his seal[j] of approval."
28Then they asked him, "What must we
do to do the works God requires?"
29Jesus answered, "The work of God is
this: to believe[k] in the one he has sent."[l]

6:22 [z] ver 2 [a] ver 15-21 **6:23** [b] ver 1 [c] ver 11 **6:25** [d] Mt 23:7 **6:26** [e] ver 24 [f] ver 30; Jn 2:11 **6:27** [g] Isa 55:2 [h] ver 54; Mt 25:46; Jn 4:14 [i] Mt 8:20 [j] Ro 4:11; 1Co 9:2; 2Co 1:22; Eph 1:13; 4:30; 2Ti 2:19; Rev 7:3 **6:29** [k] 1Jn 3:23 [l] Jn 3:17

6:30 [m] Jn 2:11 [n] Mt 12:38 **6:31** [o] Nu 11:7-9 [p] Ex 16:4, 15; Ne 9:15; Ps 78:24; 105:40 **6:33** [q] ver 50 **6:34** [r] Jn 4:15 **6:35** [s] ver 48, 51 [t] Jn 4:14 **6:37** [u] ver 39; Jn 17:2, 6, 9, 24 **6:38** [v] Jn 4:34; 5:30 **6:39** [w] Jn 10:28; 17:12; 18:9 [x] ver 40, 44, 54 **6:40** [y] Jn 3:15, 16

30So they asked him, "What sign[m] then
will you give that we may see it and believe you?[n] What will you do? 31Our ancestors ate the manna[o] in the wilderness;
as it is written: 'He gave them bread from
heaven to eat.'[a]"[p]
32Jesus said to them, "Very truly I tell
you, it is not Moses who has given you
the bread from heaven, but it is my Father
who gives you the true bread from heav-
en. 33For the bread of God is the bread that
comes down from heaven[q] and gives life
to the world."
34"Sir," they said, "always give us this
bread."[r]
35Then Jesus declared, "I am the bread
of life.[s] Whoever comes to me will never
go hungry, and whoever believes in me will
never be thirsty.[t] 36But as I told you, you
have seen me and still you do not believe.
37All those the Father gives me[u] will come
to me, and whoever comes to me I will never drive away. 38For I have come down from
heaven not to do my will but to do the will
of him who sent me.[v] 39And this is the will
of him who sent me, that I shall lose none
of all those he has given me,[w] but raise
them up at the last day.[x] 40For my Father's
will is that everyone who looks to the Son
and believes in him shall have eternal life,[y]
and I will raise them up at the last day."

[a] *31* Exodus 16:4; Neh. 9:15; Psalm 78:24,25

only God walked on them (Job 9:8; cf. Ps 77:19; see notes on Mk 6:48,50).

6:23 *Tiberias.* Tiberias was one of the two sizeable cities in Galilee. Herod Antipas had named it after the emperor and had it constructed over a cemetery. Because Jewish people deemed grave areas impure, religiously strict Jews stayed away (as Antipas undoubtedly wished) and the city was heavily Hellenized. Nevertheless, Josephus shows that Jewish residents strictly observed the Sabbath. Given the Gospels' reports of Jesus' travels in Galilee it appears that he, like most Galileans, spent little or no time in Tiberias. He apparently spent little time or (so far as we can be certain) no time in the other major Galilean city, Sepphoris, though it was not far from Nazareth.

6:24 *went to Capernaum.* Capernaum was fewer than 10 miles (16 kilometers) from Tiberias. Nevertheless, those wishing to voyage in the boats would presumably need to pay for their fare even if the boats had deposited their cargo and might need to stop near Capernaum for other merchandise.

6:26 Israel ate the manna in the wilderness without always obeying God. Emperors kept Rome pacified with free food and entertainment; Jesus had a different mission.

6:30 *What sign then will you give . . . ?* People were expecting a new prophet like Moses; several prophetic figures arose in this period (slightly after Jesus) promising (though failing to produce) signs like Moses or Joshua. Disbelief despite signs was blameworthy (Nu 14:11), but Jesus invites faith even beyond signs.

6:31 The crowd (presumably through its leading spokespersons) quotes Ex 16:4, Ne 9:15 or Ps 78:24 or a blending of these passages. Jewish debate and exposition often paraphrased and elaborated on the cited text, and this is what happens in the following discourse.

6:32 *not Moses . . . but it is my Father.* Rabbis often corrected misinterpretations by returning to the wording of the text in question. The Biblical texts attribute the manna directly to God, not to Moses.

6:34 *give us this bread.* Like many of Jesus' other interlocutors in this Gospel, the crowd misunderstands Jesus' point. In ancient sources, such misunderstandings allowed the main speaker to clarify the point.

6:35 *never go hungry . . . never be thirsty.* A range of ancient Jewish sources compared both manna and water to God's provision of spiritual nourishment, depicted as wisdom, word, or the law. Wisdom invited her hearers to come and eat of her (Sirach 24:19) and promised that those who ate and drank of her would yearn for still more (Sirach 24:21). As the Word (Jn 1:1 – 18), Jesus portrays himself as like divine Wisdom — what Jewish literature presented as closest to God without being the Father. Jesus, however, promises that those who consume him will be satisfied.

6:37 *those the Father gives me.* Jewish people believed that God was sovereign; a regular Jewish prayer acknowledged that God grants repentance. Most accepted both the idea that God controlled the essentials of the future and that God had provided humans choice and responsibility. See note on v. 44.

6:39 *raise them up at the last day.* Many Palestinian Jews believed in a resurrection at the end of the age (explicit in Da 12:2 and many other Jewish sources).

6:40 This verse repeats and elaborates much of the thought of v. 39; repetition in different words was a common ancient way of emphasizing a point.

41 At this the Jews there began to grumble about him because he said, "I am
the bread that came down from heav-
en." 42 They said, "Is this not Jesus, the
son of Joseph,[z] whose father and mother
we know?[a] How can he now say, 'I came
down from heaven'?"[b]
43 "Stop grumbling among yourselves,"
Jesus answered. 44 "No one can come to
me unless the Father who sent me draws
them,[c] and I will raise them up at the last
day. 45 It is written in the Prophets: 'They
will all be taught by God.'[a][d] Everyone who
has heard the Father and learned from him
comes to me. 46 No one has seen the Father
except the one who is from God;[e] only he
has seen the Father. 47 Very truly I tell you,
the one who believes has eternal life. 48 I
am the bread of life.[f] 49 Your ancestors ate
the manna in the wilderness, yet they
died.[g] 50 But here is the bread that comes
down from heaven,[h] which anyone may
eat and not die. 51 I am the living bread that
came down from heaven. Whoever eats
this bread will live forever. This bread is
my flesh, which I will give for the life of
the world."[i]
52 Then the Jews began to argue sharply among themselves,[j] "How can this man
give us his flesh to eat?"
53 Jesus said to them, "Very truly I tell
you, unless you eat the flesh of the Son
of Man[k] and drink his blood, you have
no life in you. 54 Whoever eats my flesh
and drinks my blood has eternal life, and
I will raise them up at the last day.[l] 55 For
my flesh is real food and my blood is real
drink. 56 Whoever eats my flesh and drinks
my blood remains in me, and I in them.[m]
57 Just as the living Father sent me[n] and I
live because of the Father, so the one who
feeds on me will live because of me. 58 This
is the bread that came down from heaven.
Your ancestors ate manna and died, but
whoever feeds on this bread will live forever."[o] 59 He said this while teaching in the
synagogue in Capernaum.

Many Disciples Desert Jesus

60 On hearing it, many of his disciples[p]
said, "This is a hard teaching. Who can
accept it?"
61 Aware that his disciples were grumbling about this, Jesus said to them, "Does
this offend you?[q] 62 Then what if you see
the Son of Man ascend to where he was
before![r] 63 The Spirit gives life;[s] the flesh
counts for nothing. The words I have spoken to you — they are full of the Spirit[b]
and life. 64 Yet there are some of you who
do not believe." For Jesus had known[t]
from the beginning which of them did not
believe and who would betray him. 65 He
went on to say, "This is why I told you
that no one can come to me unless the
Father has enabled them."[u]
66 From this time many of his disciples[v]
turned back and no longer followed him.
67 "You do not want to leave too, do
you?" Jesus asked the Twelve.[w]
68 Simon Peter answered him,[x] "Lord, to
whom shall we go? You have the words
of eternal life. 69 We have come to believe
and to know that you are the Holy One
of God."[y]

6:42 [z] Lk 4:22 [a] Jn 7:27,28 [b] ver 38,62 **6:44** [c] ver 65; Jer 31:3; Jn 12:32 **6:45** [d] Isa 54:13; Jer 31:33,34; Heb 8:10,11; 10:16 **6:46** [e] Jn 1:18; 5:37; 7:29 **6:48** [f] ver 35,51 **6:49** [g] ver 31, 58 **6:50** [h] ver 33 **6:51** [i] Heb 10:10 **6:52** [j] Jn 7:43; 9:16; 10:19 **6:53** [k] Mt 8:20 **6:54** [l] ver 39 **6:56** [m] Jn 15:4-7; 1Jn 3:24; 4:15 **6:57** [n] Jn 3:17 **6:58** [o] ver 49-51; Jn 3:36 **6:60** [p] ver 66 **6:61** [q] Mt 11:6 **6:62** [r] Mk 16:19; Jn 3:13; 17:5 **6:63** [s] 2Co 3:6 **6:64** [t] Jn 2:25 **6:65** [u] ver 37, 44 **6:66** [v] ver 60 **6:67** [w] Mt 10:2 **6:68** [x] Mt 16:16 **6:69** [y] Mk 8:29; Lk 9:20

[a] *45* Isaiah 54:13 [b] *63* Or *are Spirit;* or *are spirit*

6:41 *Jews there began to grumble.* In the wilderness Israel grumbled about their hunger, so God provided manna (Ex 16:2–4); they continued to grumble afterward (Ex 17:3; Nu 14:2; 16:41), leading to judgment (Nu 14:29; Ps 106:24–27). Here they grumble about God's provision of spiritual manna.
6:44 *unless the Father ... draws them.* See note on v. 37. In the OT, God is said to have "drawn" his people to himself (Jer 31:3). The language expresses God's love and that human desire for him comes from God.
6:45 Jesus cites Isa 54:13; it was common to cite a passage from the Prophets when explaining a passage from the Pentateuch.
6:46 *No one has seen the Father.* Moses recognized that no mere human could see all of God's glory (Ex 33:20). See note on Jn 1:14–18.
6:52 *How can this man give us his flesh to eat?* Mediterranean peoples found cannibalism revolting (but see note on v. 53).
6:53 *eat the flesh ... drink his blood.* Figuratively, Jesus could be identified with the Passover lamb (cf. v. 4; Ex 12:8; see note on Jn 1:29). Because the law forbade drinking blood, including that of the Passover lamb (Lev 17:10), a stronger analogy is with divine Wisdom (see note on Jn 6:35).
6:54 *raise them up at the last day.* See note on v. 39. Throughout this context Jesus speaks in riddles, as sages often did (e.g., Pr 1:6; 30:4). He also repeats some points at length; ancients often repeated and elaborated points where they wished to place heavy emphasis.
6:59 *synagogue in Capernaum.* Capernaum was a fishing town; some estimate its population at about 1,500. Archaeologists have found some of this synagogue beneath a later one constructed on the same site. Jewish people gathered in synagogues on the Sabbath to pray and study Scripture; the building could be used for other community purposes during the week.
6:61 *grumbling.* See note on v. 41. *Does this offend you?* Some radical teachers used heavy demands or difficult sayings to weed out less committed disciples.
6:62 *see the Son of Man ascend.* See notes on 20:17; Ac 1:9; see also the article "Ascensions," p. 1868.
6:63 *Spirit gives life.* The Spirit gives resurrection life in Eze 37:14; cf. note on Jn 20:22. For the Spirit teaching truth about God, cf. Ne 9:20; the Spirit was associated most commonly with prophetic inspiration, including of Scripture. *the flesh counts for nothing.* Jesus explains that he is not endorsing literal cannibalism (v. 52), but speaking of imbibing the Spirit.
6:66 *turned back.* Disciples' loyalty brought honor to teachers (but cf. note on v. 61).

70 Then Jesus replied, "Have I not chosen you,[z] the Twelve? Yet one of you is a devil!"[a] 71 (He meant Judas, the son of Simon Iscariot, who, though one of the Twelve, was later to betray him.)

Jesus Goes to the Festival of Tabernacles

7 After this, Jesus went around in Galilee. He did not want[a] to go about in Judea because the Jewish leaders[b] there were looking for a way to kill him.[c] 2 But when the Jewish Festival of Tabernacles[d] was near, 3 Jesus' brothers[e] said to him, "Leave Galilee and go to Judea, so that your disciples there may see the works you do. 4 No one who wants to become a public figure acts in secret. Since you are doing these things, show yourself to the world." 5 For even his own brothers did not believe in him.[f]

6 Therefore Jesus told them, "My time[g] is not yet here; for you any time will do. 7 The world cannot hate you, but it hates me[h] because I testify that its works are evil.[i] 8 You go to the festival. I am not[b] going up to this festival, because my time[j] has not yet fully come." 9 After he had said this, he stayed in Galilee.

10 However, after his brothers had left for the festival, he went also, not publicly, but in secret. 11 Now at the festival the Jewish leaders were watching for Jesus[k] and asking, "Where is he?"

12 Among the crowds there was widespread whispering about him. Some said, "He is a good man."

Others replied, "No, he deceives the people."[l] 13 But no one would say anything publicly about him for fear of the leaders.[m]

Jesus Teaches at the Festival

14 Not until halfway through the festival did Jesus go up to the temple courts and begin to teach.[n] 15 The Jews[o] there were amazed and asked, "How did this man get such learning[p] without having been taught?"[q]

16 Jesus answered, "My teaching is not my own. It comes from the one who sent me.[r] 17 Anyone who chooses to do the will of God will find out[s] whether my teaching comes from God or whether I speak on my own. 18 Whoever speaks on their own does so to gain personal glory,[t] but he who seeks the glory of the one who sent him is a man of truth; there is nothing false about him. 19 Has not Moses given you the law?[u] Yet not one of you keeps the law. Why are you trying to kill me?"[v]

20 "You are demon-possessed,"[w] the crowd answered. "Who is trying to kill you?"

21 Jesus said to them, "I did one miracle, and you are all amazed. 22 Yet, because Moses gave you circumcision[x] (though actually it did not come from Moses, but from the patriarchs),[y] you circumcise a boy on the Sabbath. 23 Now if a boy can be circumcised on the Sabbath so that the law of Moses

6:70 [z] Jn 15:16, 19 [a] Jn 13:27
7:1 [b] Jn 1:19 [c] Jn 5:18
7:2 [d] Lev 23:34; Dt 16:16
7:3 [e] Mt 12:46
7:5 [f] Mk 3:21
7:6 [g] Mt 26:18
7:7 [h] Jn 15:18, 19 [i] Jn 3:19, 20
7:8 [j] ver 6
7:11 [k] Jn 11:56
7:12 [l] ver 40, 43
7:13 [m] Jn 9:22; 12:42; 19:38
7:14 [n] ver 28; Mt 26:55
7:15 [o] Jn 1:19 [p] Ac 26:24 [q] Mt 13:54
7:16 [r] Jn 3:11; 14:24
7:17 [s] Ps 25:14; Jn 8:43
7:18 [t] Jn 5:41; 8:50, 54
7:19 [u] Jn 1:17 [v] ver 1; Mt 12:14
7:20 [w] Jn 8:48; 10:20
7:22 [x] Lev 12:3 [y] Ge 17:10-14

[a] 1 Some manuscripts *not have authority* [b] 8 Some manuscripts *not yet*

6:70 *Yet one of you is a devil!* Very rarely some Jewish sources spoke of "satans" (plural; 1 Enoch 40:7; 65:6); Jesus here speaks figuratively, however (cf. Jn 8:44).
6:71 *Iscariot.* May simply mean "man from Kerioth" (cf. Jos 15:25).
7:1 *Galilee ... Judea.* Galilee and Judea had distinct administrations. Herod Antipas governed Galilee; the Judean ruling class, especially its members in the Sanhedrin, exercised oversight in Judea, under the governance of Pilate.
7:2 *Festival of Tabernacles.* Scripture prescribed two pilgrimage festivals in the spring (Passover and Pentecost) and one in the fall (Tabernacles). The joyful eight-day Festival of Tabernacles commemorated Israel's experience in the wilderness. During this time Jewish men would build and spend time in booths or shelters built with branches, sometimes on their homes' flat roofs.
7:3 *go to Judea.* Often entire Galilean villages would travel to Jerusalem together for major festivals; families often traveled together. Certainly a prominent religious figure would be expected to attend the festival.
7:5 *his own brothers did not believe in him.* Although sibling rivalry was common, brothers ideally were supposed to be united against criticism from outside the family. Unfortunately, in this case they apparently were not.
7:6 *My time.* Jewish wisdom emphasized appropriate timing (cf., e.g., Pr 15:23; perhaps Ecc 3:1 – 8).
7:7 *hates me because I testify that its works are evil.* In Jewish wisdom, those who hated reproof were foolish (Pr 12:1; 23:9; Sirach 21:6; 32:17).
7:10 *in secret.* At times God permitted misleading impressions in order to protect the person's life (see, e.g., 1Sa 16:2 – 4).
7:12 *widespread whispering.* Jewish views in the first century were diverse (so much so that some scholars have even spoken of first-century "Judaisms" to drive home the point). More generally, divisions were rife in ancient public discourse. *deceives the people.* Such a person might be subject to a death sentence (Dt 13:5).
7:14 *temple courts ... to teach.* In antiquity people lectured in public places, including the porticoes of temples. In Jerusalem the temple consumed most public space, so many teachers lectured there.
7:15 *such learning.* Most people in antiquity, especially in rural areas, could neither read nor write; in urban areas a greater number of men could at least read inscriptions. Jewish boys were often taught how to read or recite Torah but were not taught how to write. More advanced education, often in the mid-teens, included writing (for scribes) and studying under a more advanced Torah teacher.
7:16 *not my own.* At least in the Pharisaic tradition, teachers were praised not for their originality but for faithfully reproducing respected, time-tested traditions.
7:20 *demon-possessed.* Sometimes prophets were viewed as possessed, confusing the basis of their inspiration. In view of this passage, it is ironic that false prophets inspired by demons were thought to merit death.
7:23 *circumcised ... healing a man's whole body.* Some rabbis argued from lesser to greater: the requirement

may not be broken, why are you angry with me for healing a man's whole body on the Sabbath? 24 Stop judging by mere appearances, but instead judge correctly."[z]

Division Over Who Jesus Is

25 At that point some of the people of Jerusalem began to ask, "Isn't this the man they are trying to kill? 26 Here he is, speaking publicly, and they are not saying a word to him. Have the authorities[a] really concluded that he is the Messiah? 27 But we know where this man is from;[b] when the Messiah comes, no one will know where he is from."

28 Then Jesus, still teaching in the temple courts,[c] cried out, "Yes, you know me, and you know where I am from.[d] I am not here on my own authority, but he who sent me is true.[e] You do not know him, 29 but I know him[f] because I am from him and he sent me."

30 At this they tried to seize him, but no one laid a hand on him,[g] because his hour had not yet come. 31 Still, many in the crowd believed in him.[h] They said, "When the Messiah comes, will he perform more signs[i] than this man?"

32 The Pharisees heard the crowd whispering such things about him. Then the chief priests and the Pharisees sent temple guards to arrest him.

33 Jesus said, "I am with you for only a short time,[j] and then I am going to the one who sent me.[k] 34 You will look for me, but you will not find me; and where I am, you cannot come."[l]

35 The Jews said to one another, "Where does this man intend to go that we cannot find him? Will he go where our people live scattered[m] among the Greeks,[n] and teach the Greeks? 36 What did he mean when he said, 'You will look for me, but you will not find me,' and 'Where I am, you cannot come'?"

37 On the last and greatest day of the festival,[o] Jesus stood and said in a loud voice, "Let anyone who is thirsty come to me and drink.[p] 38 Whoever believes in me, as Scripture has said,[q] rivers of living water[r] will flow from within them."[a][s] 39 By this he meant the Spirit,[t] whom those who believed in him were later to receive.[u] Up to that time the Spirit had not been given, since Jesus had not yet been glorified.[v]

40 On hearing his words, some of the people said, "Surely this man is the Prophet."[w]

7:24 [z] Isa 11:3, 4; Jn 8:15
7:26 [a] ver 48
7:27 [b] Mt 13:55; Lk 4:22
7:28 [c] ver 14 [d] Jn 8:14 [e] Jn 8:26,42
7:29 [f] Mt 11:27
7:30 [g] ver 32, 44; Jn 10:39
7:31 [h] Jn 8:30 [i] Jn 2:11
7:33 [j] Jn 13:33; 16:16 [k] Jn 16:5, 10,17,28
7:34 [l] Jn 8:21; 13:33
7:35 [m] Jas 1:1 [n] Jn 12:20; 1Pe 1:1
7:37 [o] Lev 23:36 [p] Isa 55:1; Rev 22:17
7:38 [q] Isa 58:11 [r] Jn 4:10 [s] Jn 4:14
7:39 [t] Joel 2:28; Ac 2:17,33 [u] Jn 20:22 [v] Jn 12:23; 13:31,32
7:40 [w] Mt 21:11; Jn 1:21

[a] *37,38* Or *me. And let anyone drink* 38 *who believes in me." As Scripture has said, "Out of him* (or *them*) *will flow rivers of living water."*

to circumcise, hence wound, a boy on the eighth day takes priority over the prohibition of work on the Sabbath; therefore saving a person's life also takes priority. Jesus offers a similar argument, though some rabbis would have insisted that one could defer healing until after the Sabbath. The Pharisaic school of Hillel permitted prayer for the sick on the Sabbath; the dominant Pharisaic school, the Shammaites, rejected this practice. Jesus does what the Father does (5:19); indeed, Jesus "made a person" whole, like God "made humanity" (using forms of the same Greek words) in "our image" (Ge 1:26 – 27).

7:24 *mere appearances.* God evaluates not by appearance but by truth (1Sa 16:7). Many people in antiquity were so invested in judging by appearance that they even developed physiognomy, the association of personality traits with particular physical features.

7:25 *Isn't this the man . . . ?* That the crowds do not know him by sight may suggest that Jesus physically resembled most other Jewish men of his day, with an olive complexion and dark or black hair. Some argue that average height was about five feet one inch (about 155 centimeters), and others about five foot seven inches (about 170 centimeters); because a range of appearances existed, however, these guesses do not inform us very securely about Jesus. Especially in Judea, few people had seen Jesus often and up close.

7:27 *no one will know where he is from.* Some Jewish sources report this "hidden Messiah" tradition.

7:28 – 29 *you know me . . . You do not know him . . . I know him.* When Israel obeyed the covenant they could be said to "know" God; when they disobeyed, they did not know him (Jdg 2:10; Hos 5:4); they would know him when God restored them (Jer 31:33; Eze 37:27; Hos 2:20; Zec 8:8).

7:28 *not here on my own authority.* To the extent that an agent accurately represented his commission he was backed by the sender's authority.

7:32 *The Pharisees.* Pharisees likely constituted only a minority in the Sanhedrin in this period (although rarely poor, probably most Pharisees did not belong to the economic elite), but they and the dominant Sadducees cooperated on issues of public order. *sent temple guards to arrest him.* The chief priests could use Levite temple guards to address trouble in the temple.

7:33 – 34 Sages often taught in riddles; only those committed to the teaching would contemplate it until they came to understand it.

7:35 *Greeks.* Includes descendants of Greeks and Macedonians and those who fully adopted their culture in many cities of the eastern Mediterranean. The majority of Jewish people (sometimes estimated even at 80 percent) lived outside of the Holy Land, and the majority of the Jewish people in the Diaspora in the Mediterranean world (as opposed to Parthia and Babylonia) lived among Greeks in cities such as Alexandria, Antioch and Sardis.

7:37 *come to me and drink.* Jesus speaks on the climactic eighth day of the Festival of Tabernacles (see note on v. 2). He probably echoes divine Wisdom, who invited people to come and drink (Sirach 24:19,21).

7:38 *rivers of living water will flow from within them.* See the article "Tabernacles and the Promise of Living Water," p. 1825.

7:39 Jewish sources often use water as an analogy for wisdom or the Torah, but John's use of the analogy for the Spirit evokes an image available in the Prophets (Isa 44:3 and especially Eze 36:25 – 27). The OT prophets promised a greater outpouring of the Spirit for the coming age (e.g., Eze 37:14; 39:29; Joel 2:28 – 29). See Jn 1:33; 3:5; 4:10,14; cf. also Jn 2:6,9; 5:7 – 8; 9:7; 13:5; 19:34.

7:40 *the Prophet.* The promised prophet like Moses (Dt 18:15 – 18).

JOHN 7:37 – 39

TABERNACLES AND THE PROMISE OF LIVING WATER

A highlight of the Festival of Tabernacles was the water-drawing ceremony; priests would draw water from the Pool of Siloam (see note on 9:7) and lead a procession to the temple, where they would pour out the water at the altar. Before Jerusalem's destruction in AD 70, pilgrims from the Diaspora who visited Jerusalem for the festival knew about this ceremony; indeed, some scholars point to souvenirs from as far away as Cyprus that may depict the ceremony.

Priests poured water at the altar to signify the biblical promise that in the time of restoration, rivers of living water would flow from the temple. This promise was supported from Scriptures read on the last day of the festival: Eze 47, about rivers of water flowing from the temple, and Zec 14, about waters flowing from Jerusalem. (Zec 14 is also the only passage in the Prophets addressing the Festival of Tabernacles.)

Jesus' paraphrase of the Scripture as water flowing from (literally) "his belly" (the NIV renders this "from within them") may evoke the Jewish tradition of Jerusalem and the temple as the navel of the earth. Thus his wording would refer to the Biblically promised waters flowing from Jerusalem. But Jesus refers to the Spirit rather than to literal water (Jn 7:39), and perhaps refers to the temple of his body (2:21; cf. 19:34). Since in 7:39 believers "receive" the Spirit, Jesus seems to be the Spirit's source (with the NIV text note on 7:37,38). Nevertheless, even if one reads with the NIV's main text in 7:37 – 39 and envisions believers as the temple, 7:39 suggests that Jesus remains its foundation and ultimate source (cf. 19:34; the Spirit in the note on 19:30). ◆

41Others said, "He is the Messiah."
Still others asked, "How can the Messiah come from Galilee?[x] 42Does not Scripture say that the Messiah will come from
David's descendants[y] and from Bethlehem,[z] the town where David lived?"
43Thus the people were divided[a] because
of Jesus. 44Some wanted to seize him, but
no one laid a hand on him.[b]

Unbelief of the Jewish Leaders

45Finally the temple guards went back
to the chief priests and the Pharisees,
who asked them, "Why didn't you bring
him in?"
46"No one ever spoke the way this man
does,"[c] the guards replied.
47"You mean he has deceived you
also?"[d] the Pharisees retorted. 48"Have any
of the rulers or of the Pharisees believed in
him?[e] 49No! But this mob that knows nothing of the law — there is a curse on them."
50Nicodemus,[f] who had gone to Jesus
earlier and who was one of their own
number, asked, 51"Does our law condemn
a man without first hearing him to find
out what he has been doing?"
52They replied, "Are you from Galilee,
too? Look into it, and you will find that a
prophet does not come out of Galilee."[g]

7:41 [x] ver 52; Jn 1:46 **7:42** [y] Mt 1:1 [z] Mic 5:2; Mt 2:5,6; Lk 2:4 **7:43** [a] Jn 9:16; 10:19 **7:44** [b] ver 30 **7:46** [c] Mt 7:28 **7:47** [d] ver 12 **7:48** [e] Jn 12:42 **7:50** [f] Jn 3:1; 19:39 **7:52** [g] ver 41

7:42 *from David's descendants ... where David lived.* Although various conceptions of the Messiah circulated, the dominant view was an anointed king from David's line. Mic 5:2 promised a ruler from Bethlehem.
7:43 *people were divided.* See note on v. 12.
7:49 *this mob that knows nothing of the law.* Educated elites in antiquity looked down on the masses. Those who could persuade only people of lower socioeconomic rank were condemned by the elite as demagogues. Some later rabbinic sources share this disdain for those uneducated in the law; we might expect this attitude even more from many aristocratic members of the Sanhedrin.
7:51 *Does our law ...?* Ironically, those insisting on their superior knowledge are here neglecting basic judicial protocol (cf., e.g., Dt 1:16), as Nicodemus points out.
7:52 *a prophet does not come out of Galilee.* Regional prejudices remained prominent in the ancient Mediterranean world. Urban residents often looked down on

---

[The earliest manuscripts and many other ancient witnesses do not have John 7:53—8:11. A few manuscripts include these verses, wholly or in part, after John 7:36, John 21:25, Luke 21:38 or Luke 24:53.]

8 *53 Then they all went home, 1 but Jesus went to the Mount of Olives.*[h]

2 At dawn he appeared again in the temple courts, where all the people gathered around him, and he sat down to teach them.[i] *3 The teachers of the law and the Pharisees brought in a woman caught in adultery. They made her stand before the group 4 and said to Jesus, "Teacher, this woman was caught in the act of adultery. 5 In the Law Moses commanded us to stone such women.*[j] *Now what do you say?" 6 They were using this question as a trap,*[k] *in order to have a basis for accusing him.*[l]

But Jesus bent down and started to write on the ground with his finger. 7 When they kept on questioning him, he straightened up and said to them, "Let any one of you who is without sin be the first to throw a stone[m] *at her."*[n] *8 Again he stooped down and wrote on the ground.*

9 At this, those who heard began to go away one at a time, the older ones first, until only Jesus was left, with the woman still standing there. 10 Jesus straightened up and asked her, "Woman, where are they? Has no one condemned you?"

11 "No one, sir," she said.

"Then neither do I condemn you,"[o] *Jesus declared. "Go now and leave your life of sin."*[p]

8:1 [h] Mt 21:1 **8:2** [i] ver 20; Mt 26:55 **8:5** [j] Lev 20:10; Dt 22:22 **8:6** [k] Mt 22:15, 18 [l] Mt 12:10 **8:7** [m] Dt 17:7 [n] Ro 2:1,22

8:11 [o] Jn 3:17 [p] Jn 5:14 **8:12** [q] Jn 6:35 [r] Jn 1:4; 12:35 [s] Pr 4:18; Mt 5:14 **8:13** [t] Jn 5:31 **8:14** [u] Jn 13:3; 16:28 [v] Jn 7:28; 9:29 **8:15** [w] Jn 7:24 [x] Jn 3:17 **8:16** [y] Jn 5:30 **8:17** [z] Dt 17:6; Mt 18:16 **8:18** [a] Jn 5:37 **8:19** [b] Jn 16:3 [c] Jn 14:7; 1Jn 2:23

Dispute Over Jesus' Testimony

12 When Jesus spoke again to the people, he said, "I am[q] the light of the world.[r] Whoever follows me will never walk in darkness, but will have the light of life."[s]

13 The Pharisees challenged him, "Here you are, appearing as your own witness; your testimony is not valid."[t]

14 Jesus answered, "Even if I testify on my own behalf, my testimony is valid, for I know where I came from and where I am going.[u] But you have no idea where I come from[v] or where I am going. 15 You judge by human standards;[w] I pass judgment on no one.[x] 16 But if I do judge, my decisions are true, because I am not alone. I stand with the Father, who sent me.[y] 17 In your own Law it is written that the testimony of two witnesses is true.[z] 18 I am one who testifies for myself; my other witness is the Father, who sent me."[a]

19 Then they asked him, "Where is your father?"

"You do not know me or my Father,"[b] Jesus replied. "If you knew me, you would know my Father also."[c] 20 He spoke these

---

rural peasants, such as most Galileans were; Jerusalemites often viewed Galilee as backward. Ironically, these experts in the law are mistaken about no prophet coming from Galilee (2Ki 14:25; Gath Hepher was in Galilee).

7:53—8:11 As noted in the bracketed NIV text, this passage is missing in most of the oldest manuscripts. It also interrupts the flow of this Gospel's thought and uses language missing in the rest of the Gospel (such as "the teachers of the law," a phrase common in the Synoptics but absent in John). Because the story fits the character of Jesus, however, many consider it an authentic story about him that is simply out of place where it stands.

8:1 *Mount of Olives.* See notes on Mk 11:1,11.

8:5 *such women.* The law did command stoning adulterers, but this included men and not just "such women" (Lev 20:10; Dt 22:22). One cannot evade the oft-observed point that if the woman was caught in the act of adultery, a male adulterer must have also been present when they caught her.

8:6 *a trap … a basis for accusing him.* Roman law forbade executing anyone without the governor's permission, making death sentences for adultery impossible to carry out. If Jesus as a prophet of restoration insists on following Biblical teaching about stoning, as his critics may expect him to, he can be accused to the authorities as undermining Roman order. *write on the ground.* Apart from scribes, most people in antiquity did not manually write much; in rural areas, many could barely write their own names. What is written here is probably brief, however. Speculations about what Jesus writes abound: For example, before announcing sentences, Roman judges would write them down (the Greek term for writing used here is appropriate for that function). A text such as Ex 20:17 ("You shall not covet … your neighbor's wife") might have drawn attention to their own sin (cf. Ex 31:18). Perhaps he wrote what he also said, or perhaps he was conspicuously ignoring them. Perhaps he wrote nothing but simply (as the Greek term can also mean) drew figures; e.g., one could draw a circle in making an ultimatum (though no such ultimatum is expressed here). Since the narrator offers few clues, the content of the writing might be beside the narrative's point.

8:7 *any one of you who is without sin.* Although some writers made exceptions for a few earlier figures such as Abraham, for the most part Jewish thinkers acknowledged that everyone sinned.

8:12 *light of the world.* Jerusalem was lit up at night most prominently during the Festivals of Tabernacles and Dedication (10:22); the lighting ceremony and dancing were key elements in celebrating Tabernacles. Jewish teachers applied the metaphor of light, including the "light of the world," to many positive people and things. A more specific allusion here could be to the "light to the nations" (NIV "a light for the Gentiles") in Isa 42:6 and Isa 49:6, where it refers to the mission of God's servant (see note on Mt 12:18–21). Cf. Jn 1:9 and note on 1:4–5.

8:15 See note on 7:24.

8:17 *two witnesses.* The law mandated a minimum of two or three witnesses (Dt 17:6; especially Dt 19:15). Pharisaic tradition made this requirement even more strict (for the purpose of making conviction more difficult).

8:19 *Where is your father?* The point of Jesus' critics may be that one cannot appeal to a witness who cannot be questioned in court. Cf. also note on v. 41. Jesus' point, however, may be that God's testimony is available to all who truly listen to him.

words while teaching[d] in the temple
courts near the place where the offerings
were put.[e] Yet no one seized him, because
his hour had not yet come.[f]

Dispute Over Who Jesus Is

21 Once more Jesus said to them, "I am
going away, and you will look for me, and
you will die[g] in your sin. Where I go, you
cannot come."[h]
22 This made the Jews ask, "Will he kill
himself? Is that why he says, 'Where I go,
you cannot come'?"
23 But he continued, "You are from below; I am from above. You are of this
world; I am not of this world.[i] 24 I told you
that you would die in your sins; if you do
not believe that I am he,[j] you will indeed
die in your sins."
25 "Who are you?" they asked.
"Just what I have been telling you from
the beginning," Jesus replied. 26 "I have
much to say in judgment of you. But he
who sent me is trustworthy,[k] and what I
have heard from him I tell the world."[l]
27 They did not understand that he was
telling them about his Father. 28 So Jesus
said, "When you have lifted up[a] the Son
of Man,[m] then you will know that I am
he and that I do nothing on my own but
speak just what the Father has taught me.
29 The one who sent me is with me; he has
not left me alone,[n] for I always do what
pleases him."[o] 30 Even as he spoke, many
believed in him.[p]

Dispute Over Whose Children Jesus' Opponents Are

31 To the Jews who had believed him,
Jesus said, "If you hold to my teaching,[q]
you are really my disciples. 32 Then you
will know the truth, and the truth will set
you free."[r]
33 They answered him, "We are Abraham's descendants[s] and have never been
slaves of anyone. How can you say that we
shall be set free?"
34 Jesus replied, "Very truly I tell you, everyone who sins is a slave to sin.[t] 35 Now a
slave has no permanent place in the family, but a son belongs to it forever.[u] 36 So
if the Son sets you free, you will be free
indeed. 37 I know that you are Abraham's
descendants. Yet you are looking for a way
to kill me,[v] because you have no room for
my word. 38 I am telling you what I have
seen in the Father's presence,[w] and you
are doing what you have heard from your
father.[b]"
39 "Abraham is our father," they answered.
"If you were Abraham's children,"[x] said
Jesus, "then you would[c] do what Abraham

8:20 [d] Mt 26:55 [e] Mk 12:41 [f] Mt 26:18; Jn 7:30 **8:21** [g] Eze 3:18 [h] Jn 7:34; 13:33 **8:23** [i] Jn 3:31; 17:14 **8:24** [j] Jn 4:26; 13:19 **8:26** [k] Jn 7:28 [l] Jn 3:32; 15:15 **8:28** [m] Jn 3:14; 5:19; 12:32 **8:29** [n] ver 16; Jn 16:32 [o] Jn 4:34; 5:30; 6:38 **8:30** [p] Jn 7:31 **8:31** [q] Jn 15:7; 2Jn 9 **8:32** [r] Ro 8:2; Jas 2:12 **8:33** [s] ver 37, 39; Mt 3:9 **8:34** [t] Ro 6:16; 2Pe 2:19 **8:35** [u] Gal 4:30 **8:37** [v] ver 39, 40 **8:38** [w] Jn 5:19, 30; 14:10,24 **8:39** [x] ver 37; Ro 9:7; Gal 3:7

[a] 28 The Greek for *lifted up* also means *exalted.*
[b] 38 Or *presence. Therefore do what you have heard from the Father.* [c] 39 Some early manuscripts *"If you are Abraham's children," said Jesus, "then*

8:20 *in the temple courts … where the offerings were put.* Temples in the ancient world doubled as banks, since they were considered the safest place to deposit money because their ground was sacred. People also dedicated sacrifices and, with regard to Jerusalem's temple, donated resources. The temple treasury (where money was stored) was adjacent to the court of women. Most of the festivities of the Festival of Tabernacles (see note on v. 12) occurred in the court of women.
8:22 *Will he kill himself?* Because in v. 21 Jesus' "going" contrasts with them dying in sin, they rightly understand him speaking of death, but ironically (and perhaps somewhat maliciously) misunderstand how (cf. 10:18; 12:32–33; 13:1; 16:17). Romans and Greek thinkers approved of suicide under some circumstances, but conservative Jewish tradition more commonly disapproved of the practice.
8:23 *I am from above.* Jewish apocalypses contrasted heavenly and earthly spheres, but no mere human would claim to be "from above." Such language did, however, suit divine Wisdom (see note on 3:13).
8:24 *die in your sins.* Jewish tradition often recognized that people could repent of sins only until death. Sages sometimes employed riddles and wordplays. *I am he.* The phrase here can also mean simply "I am" (cf. the Septuagint, the pre-Christian Greek translation, of Isa 43:10: "that you may know and believe … that I am"). See note on v. 58.
8:28 *lifted up.* Also in 3:14; 12:32. This may echo Isa 52:13, a passage quickly followed by Isa 53, a passage that describes Christ as the suffering servant (on early Christian application of Isaiah's servant to Jesus, see note on Mt 12:18–21).
8:31 *If you hold to my teaching.* For conversion to Judaism, for joining individual Jewish movements (such as the Qumran community), and for ancient schools of thought in general, joining without persevering in the teaching was pointless.
8:32 *the truth will set you free.* Ancient thinkers regularly applied the concept of freedom figuratively, e.g., to freedom from false ideologies or from dependence on others.
8:33 *never been slaves of anyone.* For free persons, the title "slave" functioned as an insult, and so could generate resentment. Yet Jewish tradition recognized that Israel had been subject to (hence, in Jewish parlance, enslaved to) multiple empires: Babylon, Persia, Greece and now Rome (based on the usual first-century understanding of Da 7:17).
8:34 *a slave to sin.* Philosophers spoke of freedom from passion, and Jewish teachers of freedom from sin. In general, Jewish teachers acknowledged that everyone sinned sometimes, but they believed that study of the Torah could give power to overcome sin.
8:35 *a slave has no permanent place … but a son belongs … forever.* Slaves were sometimes sold; more often, they were set free, which was common, e.g., in Rome and was required under certain circumstances in Jewish law. Sons remained part of a household unless (and this was rare) they were disinherited.
8:37 *Abraham's descendants.* Jewish tradition emphasized Abraham's righteousness—in contrast to their current behavior.
8:39 *Abraham's children … do what Abraham did.* One could speak of a genetic ancestor (as in v. 37) or a figurative ancestor whose ways one imitated and whose character one exemplified (as in vv. 38,40).

did. 40 As it is, you are looking for a way to kill me, a man who has told you the truth that I heard from God.[y] Abraham did not do such things. 41 You are doing the works of your own father."[z]

"We are not illegitimate children," they protested. "The only Father we have is God himself."[a]

42 Jesus said to them, "If God were your Father, you would love me,[b] for I have come here from God.[c] I have not come on my own;[d] God sent me.[e] 43 Why is my language not clear to you? Because you are unable to hear what I say. 44 You belong to your father, the devil,[f] and you want to carry out your father's desires.[g] He was a murderer from the beginning, not holding to the truth, for there is no truth in him. When he lies, he speaks his native language, for he is a liar and the father of lies.[h] 45 Yet because I tell the truth,[i] you do not believe me! 46 Can any of you prove me guilty of sin? If I am telling the truth, why don't you believe me? 47 Whoever belongs to God hears what God says.[j] The reason you do not hear is that you do not belong to God."

Jesus' Claims About Himself

48 The Jews answered him, "Aren't we right in saying that you are a Samaritan[k] and demon-possessed?"[l]

49 "I am not possessed by a demon," said Jesus, "but I honor my Father and you dishonor me. 50 I am not seeking glory for myself;[m] but there is one who seeks it, and he is the judge. 51 Very truly I tell you, whoever obeys my word will never see death."[n]

52 At this they exclaimed, "Now we know that you are demon-possessed! Abraham died and so did the prophets, yet you say that whoever obeys your word will never taste death. 53 Are you greater than our father Abraham?[o] He died, and so did the prophets. Who do you think you are?"

54 Jesus replied, "If I glorify myself,[p] my glory means nothing. My Father, whom you claim as your God, is the one who glorifies me.[q] 55 Though you do not know him,[r] I know him.[s] If I said I did not, I would be a liar like you, but I do know him and obey his word.[t] 56 Your father Abraham[u] rejoiced at the thought of seeing my day; he saw it[v] and was glad."

57 "You are not yet fifty years old," they said to him, "and you have seen Abraham!"

58 "Very truly I tell you," Jesus answered, "before Abraham was born,[w] I am!"[x] 59 At this, they picked up stones to stone him,[y] but Jesus hid himself,[z] slipping away from the temple grounds.

8:40 [y] ver 26
8:41 [z] ver 38, 44 [a] Isa 63:16; 64:8
8:42 [b] 1Jn 5:1 [c] Jn 16:27; 17:8 [d] Jn 7:28 [e] Jn 3:17
8:44 [f] 1Jn 3:8 [g] ver 38, 41 [h] Ge 3:4
8:45 [i] Jn 18:37
8:47 [j] Jn 18:37; 1Jn 4:6
8:48 [k] Mt 10:5 [l] ver 52; Jn 7:20
8:50 [m] ver 54; Jn 5:41
8:51 [n] Jn 11:26
8:53 [o] Jn 4:12
8:54 [p] ver 50 [q] Jn 16:14; 17:1,5
8:55 [r] ver 19 [s] Jn 7:28,29 [t] Jn 15:10
8:56 [u] ver 37, 39 [v] Mt 13:17; Heb 11:13
8:58 [w] Jn 1:2; 17:5,24 [x] Ex 3:14
8:59 [y] Lev 24:16; Jn 10:31; 11:8 [z] Jn 12:36

8:41 *We are not illegitimate children.* Jewish people recognized that they were children of Abraham through Jacob's line (already in the OT, see, e.g., Ex 4:22; Hos 11:1). To be children of another father could imply that their mother was sexually immoral. Some think that they are taunting Jesus here with a charge of uncertain parentage (cf. Mt 1:23).

8:42 *If God were your Father.* Not only do they not reflect the ancestral character of Abraham (vv. 39 – 40), but they do not reflect God's character either. Rather, they reflect someone else's character (v. 44).

8:44 *He was a murderer from the beginning.* Jewish tradition depicted the devil as a liar who deceived Eve, and therefore also as the first murderer, who brought death on the human race. (Cf. note on 1Jn 3:12.) In ancient legal debates, the accused often returned the charges against the accuser (cf. Jn 7:20), thus challenging their motives for the lawsuit.

8:46 *Can any of you prove me guilty of sin?* In judicial rhetoric, the accused often charged that the accusers had failed to prove their case. The defense also emphasized that the character of the accused was beyond reproach, so the accusations were inconsistent with what was known of the accused.

8:48 In heated courtroom rhetoric, opposing sides often traded the same charges against each other (see note on v. 44). *Samaritan.* Jewish people would consider the label "Samaritan" an insult (see the article "Samaria and Samaritans," p. 1812); they denied that Samaritans were full descendants of Abraham (see note on v. 41). *demon-possessed.* See note on 7:20.

8:51 *whoever obeys my word will never see death.* God's word endures forever (Isa 40:8), further identifying Jesus' "word" with God's (Jn 8:47).

8:52 *Are you greater than our father Abraham?* While exalting Abraham and the prophets, Jewish tradition acknowledged their mortality (unlike what Greeks did with some of their heroes). Yet no mere descendant of Abraham would be expected to be greater than Abraham himself, since descendants could not exist without their ancestors.

8:54 *If I glorify myself … My Father … glorifies me.* Despite the frequency of male ambition and rivalry in the ancient Mediterranean world, explicit boasting was often considered inappropriate; appealing to someone else's approval, however, was acceptable. Because God does not share his glory (Isa 42:8; 48:11), appealing to God's approval could imply Jesus' deity if other factors in the context (such as Jn 8:58) support this implication. A central component of God's covenant promise was that he would be Israel's God (e.g., Ex 6:7; Jer 11:4; 30:22; Eze 36:28); failure to "know" him, however, meant that they had breached the covenant (cf. Jer 31:31 – 34; see note on Jn 7:28 – 29).

8:56 *Abraham rejoiced at … seeing my day.* Jewish tradition elaborated Abraham's vision in Ge 15:13 – 21, contending that he foresaw not only the captivity in Egypt but other future kingdoms and finally God's kingdom. John's Gospel alludes also to the Biblical visions of Moses (see note on 1:14 – 18) and Isaiah (see note on 12:41).

8:57 *not yet fifty.* Jesus' critics imply that he was nowhere near old enough for Abraham to have seen him, but might also implicitly question his credibility; age was respected more than youth. Cf. Lk 3:23.

8:58 *I am!* Jesus claims more than that he *was* before Abraham; "I am" is a divine title (Ex 3:14). A later Jewish source claims that during this festival, the Festival of Tabernacles (Jn 7:2), priests recited God's claim in Isa 43:10,13. In the Septuagint, the pre-Christian Greek translation, of Isa 43:10, God declares, "I am." Jesus' critics would not miss his point (see their response in Jn 8:59).

8:59 *picked up stones to stone him.* Stoning was a standard

Jesus Heals a Man Born Blind

9 As he went along, he saw a man blind
from birth. 2His disciples asked him,
"Rabbi,[a] who sinned,[b] this man[c] or his
parents,[d] that he was born blind?"
3"Neither this man nor his parents
sinned," said Jesus, "but this happened so
that the works of God might be displayed in
him.[e] 4As long as it is day,[f] we must do the
works of him who sent me. Night is coming, when no one can work. 5While I am
in the world, I am the light of the world."[g]
6After saying this, he spit[h] on the
ground, made some mud with the saliva,
and put it on the man's eyes. 7"Go," he
told him, "wash in the Pool of Siloam"[i]
(this word means "Sent"). So the man
went and washed, and came home seeing.[j]
8His neighbors and those who had formerly seen him begging asked, "Isn't this
the same man who used to sit and beg?"[k]
9Some claimed that he was.

Others said, "No, he only looks like
him."

But he himself insisted, "I am the man."
10"How then were your eyes opened?"
they asked.
11He replied, "The man they call Jesus
made some mud and put it on my eyes.
He told me to go to Siloam and wash. So I
went and washed, and then I could see."[l]
12"Where is this man?" they asked him.
"I don't know," he said.

The Pharisees Investigate the Healing

13They brought to the Pharisees the
man who had been blind. 14Now the day
on which Jesus had made the mud and
opened the man's eyes was a Sabbath.[m]
15Therefore the Pharisees also asked him
how he had received his sight.[n] "He put
mud on my eyes," the man replied, "and I
washed, and now I see."
16Some of the Pharisees said, "This man
is not from God, for he does not keep the
Sabbath."[o]

But others asked, "How can a sinner perform such signs?" So they were divided.[p]
17Then they turned again to the blind
man, "What have you to say about him? It
was your eyes he opened."

The man replied, "He is a prophet."[q]
18They[r] still did not believe that he had
been blind and had received his sight until

9:2 [a] Mt 23:7 [b] ver 34; Lk 13:2; Ac 28:4 [c] Eze 18:20 [d] Ex 20:5; Job 21:19 **9:3** [e] Jn 11:4 **9:4** [f] Jn 11:9; 12:35 **9:5** [g] Jn 1:4; 8:12; 12:46 **9:6** [h] Mk 7:33; 8:23 **9:7** [i] ver 11; 2Ki 5:10; Lk 13:4 [j] Isa 35:5; Jn 11:37 **9:8** [k] Ac 3:2, 10 **9:11** [l] ver 7 **9:14** [m] Jn 5:9 **9:15** [n] ver 10 **9:16** [o] Mt 12:2 [p] Jn 6:52; 7:43; 10:19 **9:17** [q] Mt 21:11 **9:18** [r] Jn 1:19

expression of mob violence in the ancient Mediterranean world; even inside cities or near buildings, ancient sources show us that mobs usually found stones to throw. Stoning was appropriate for blasphemy (Lev 24:16,23), which is how Jesus' hearers here understand him. Yet John's audience might recall that God's disobedient people had previously threatened to stone God's servants (Ex 17:4; Nu 14:10). *hid himself.* Greek myths and pagan magic often spoke of invisibility, but that idea is unlikely here. The temple was large and thronged with people, making blending into a crowd easy (cf. Josephus, *Antiquities* 20.164 – 165; *Wars* 2.255). For Jesus' escape, cf. perhaps Jer 36:26 (implying divine action).

9:1 *went along.* Jesus is still likely in the vicinity of the temple (8:59); the Pool of Siloam (v. 7) was in this area. *blind.* Blind people had few options for support other than begging (cf. v. 8), and begging was most profitable in well-traversed public areas.

9:2 *who sinned . . . that he was born blind?* Most people in antiquity believed that unusual sufferings came as a result of someone's sin. Jewish tradition affirmed that people sometimes suffered because of their ancestors' sins, but at least occasionally also allowed the possibility of a person sinning before birth.

9:4 *As long as it is day.* Lacking adequate lighting, most people worked only during the day.

9:5 *light of the world.* See note on 8:12.

9:6 *he spit on the ground, made some mud.* People usually considered spittle disgusting, but it was sometimes associated with healing. Some believe that the action evokes Ge 2:7 (see note on Jn 20:22).

9:7 *the Pool of Siloam.* The pool had four porches and its water was used in the sacred water-drawing ceremony of the Festival of Tabernacles. It is now the final day of that festival (see 7:2; see also the article "Tabernacles and the Promise of Living Water," p. 1825), since 7:53 — 8:11 was added to this Gospel later (see note on 7:53 — 8:11). *means "Sent."* Ancient writers often used wordplays, as here (though John may "stretch" the meaning of Siloam). John makes a contrast with the cure at another pool in 5:3 – 9; Gentile healing shrines often included pools. Compare Elisha's seemingly nonsensical command for Naaman to bathe in the Jordan (2Ki 5:10 – 14).

9:8 Sources show that beggars had to learn to endure being refused and looked down on. Although Judaism deeply valued charity, making the plight of Jewish beggars better than their Gentile counterparts, it was nevertheless a humiliating profession. "Death is better than begging," opined one sage (Sirach 40:28).

9:15 *the Pharisees also asked.* Local elders decided cases that came up in their communities; in Jerusalem, probably most elders would be priests, but some might also be Pharisees (whether priests or not), who were known for their careful study of the law. Pharisees were highly influential with the people, especially around Jerusalem.

9:16 *they were divided.* Pharisees did not all share the same views; in Jesus' day, Pharisaic teachers divided especially between the school of Shammai and the school of Hillel. The Pharisaic school of Hillel permitted prayer for the sick on the Sabbath; the dominant Pharisaic school, the Shammaites, rejected this practice but did not persecute Hillelites for it. Pharisaic rabbis advanced their study of the Torah partly by debating it and examining a range of opinions, though ultimately all were bound to respect the majority view (in a given generation). Later opinion hardened; by the second century, rabbis attributed to sorcery the works of Jesus and his followers.

9:17 *He is a prophet.* Although popular movements still followed prophetic figures, most of the elite believed that prophets ceased with the last of the OT writing prophets. (This was true even for some who allowed continuing prophecy; they still reserved the title "prophet" for those who lived during the earlier era.)

9:18 *sent for the man's parents.* Courts could require witnesses to testify.

they sent for the man's parents. 19"Is this
your son?" they asked. "Is this the one you
say was born blind? How is it that now he
can see?"
20"We know he is our son," the parents answered, "and we know he was
born blind. 21But how he can see now, or
who opened his eyes, we don't know. Ask
him. He is of age; he will speak for himself." 22His parents said this because they
were afraid of the Jewish leaders,[s] who
already had decided that anyone who

9:22 [s] Jn 7:13

9:21 *He is of age.* After reaching puberty, about the age of 13 (the age of the later *bar mitzvah* ceremony), a youth was considered a man and assumed responsibility for obeying the Torah.

9:22 *would be put out of the synagogue.* Various forms of discipline existed in Jewish communities, e.g., beatings (see note on Mt 10:17). One could also be banished from participation in the community for a short time or for a

JOHN 9

THE POOL OF SILOAM

The water of the Pool of Siloam in Jerusalem was regarded as sacred. According to early rabbinic tradition, during the celebration of the Festival of Tabernacles water was drawn from the pool into a golden vessel and carried in procession to the temple (cf. Jn 7). Jesus instructed the man born blind to wash in this same pool (9:1 – 7), although it was Jesus — the source of "living water" (7:38) — who did the healing.

The question of where the Pool of Siloam was located has been examined on the basis of reports from the Bible, Josephus, ancient pilgrims, and archaeological findings. There were actually two pools. The first, the "Lower" or older "Pool of Shiloah" (cf. Isa 8:6; 22:9 – 11) collected water from the Gihon Spring, east of the city, via a short channel. The second, the "Upper" Pool, also received water from the Gihon Spring, but it came through an underground tunnel that was cut into rock by King Hezekiah around 701 BC. Hezekiah strategically situated the Upper Pool within the city walls to serve as a secure water supply. The Lower Pool would have been located outside the city of his day. There is some dispute about which pool, the Upper or the Lower, was the "Siloam Pool" of Jesus' day, although probably it was the Upper Pool. Today, the Upper Pool is known as the Siloam Pool; the Lower Pool is dry. ◆

Steps of the Pool of Siloam, discovered in 2004.

Wikimedia Commons

acknowledged that Jesus was the Messiah would be put out[t] of the synagogue.[u]
23That was why his parents said, "He is of
age; ask him."[v]
24A second time they summoned the
man who had been blind. "Give glory to
God by telling the truth,"[w] they said. "We
know this man is a sinner."[x]
25He replied, "Whether he is a sinner or
not, I don't know. One thing I do know. I
was blind but now I see!"
26Then they asked him, "What did he
do to you? How did he open your eyes?"
27He answered, "I have told you already[y] and you did not listen. Why do you
want to hear it again? Do you want to become his disciples too?"
28Then they hurled insults at him and
said, "You are this fellow's disciple! We are
disciples of Moses![z] 29We know that God
spoke to Moses, but as for this fellow, we
don't even know where he comes from."[a]
30The man answered, "Now that is remarkable! You don't know where he
comes from, yet he opened my eyes. 31We
know that God does not listen to sinners.
He listens to the godly person who does
his will.[b] 32Nobody has ever heard of
opening the eyes of a man born blind. 33If
this man were not from God,[c] he could do
nothing."

34To this they replied, "You were steeped
in sin at birth;[d] how dare you lecture us!"
And they threw him out.[e]

Spiritual Blindness

35Jesus heard that they had thrown him
out, and when he found him, he said, "Do
you believe in the Son of Man?"
36"Who is he, sir?" the man asked. "Tell
me so that I may believe in him."[f]
37Jesus said, "You have now seen him;
in fact, he is the one speaking with you."[g]
38Then the man said, "Lord, I believe,"
and he worshiped him.[h]
39Jesus said,[a] "For judgment[i] I have
come into this world,[j] so that the blind
will see[k] and those who see will become
blind."[l]
40Some Pharisees who were with him
heard him say this and asked, "What? Are
we blind too?"[m]
41Jesus said, "If you were blind, you
would not be guilty of sin; but now that
you claim you can see, your guilt remains.[n]

The Good Shepherd and His Sheep

10 "Very truly I tell you Pharisees, anyone who does not enter the sheep
pen by the gate, but climbs in by some

9:22 [t] ver 34; Lk 6:22 [u] Jn 12:42; 16:2 **9:23** [v] ver 21 **9:24** [w] Jos 7:19 [x] ver 16 **9:27** [y] ver 15 **9:28** [z] Jn 5:45 **9:29** [a] Jn 8:14 **9:31** [b] Ge 18:23-32; Ps 34:15, 16; 66:18; 145:19, 20; Pr 15:29; Isa 1:15; 59:1, 2; Jn 15:7; Jas 5:16-18; 1Jn 5:14, 15 **9:33** [c] ver 16; Jn 3:2 **9:34** [d] ver 2 [e] ver 22, 35; Isa 66:5 **9:36** [f] Ro 10:14 **9:37** [g] Jn 4:26 **9:38** [h] Mt 28:9 **9:39** [i] Jn 5:22 [j] Jn 3:19 [k] Lk 4:18 [l] Mt 13:13 **9:40** [m] Ro 2:19 **9:41** [n] Jn 15:22, 24

[a] *38,39* Some early manuscripts do not have *Then the man said . . . 39Jesus said.*

longer or even a permanent time; these forms of being "put out" appear not only in later rabbinic sources but also in the earlier Dead Sea Scrolls (1QS 6.24—7.25; still earlier, cf. Ezr 10:8).

9:24 *Give glory to God by telling the truth.* Lit. "Give glory to God," but the NIV understands the phrase correctly. When questioning someone for wrongdoing, the command is a call for confession (Jos 7:19; 1 Esdras 9:8). Yet ancient audiences sometimes laughed at characters who were too sure of themselves, as the interrogators are here.

9:25–26 Later rabbis accepted the testimony of miracles only when this testimony supported their opinions based on Torah study. They were also concerned about magic tricks (illusions) and especially genuine sorcery performed through demons.

9:26 Pharisees emphasized fair cross-examination of witnesses. The man's questioners here do not act according to the highest ideal of Pharisaic ethics.

9:28 *We are disciples of Moses!* Those who taught the Torah sometimes called themselves Moses' disciples; but cf. 5:45–47.

9:29 *this fellow, we don't even know where he comes from.* Critics sometimes insulted their opponents by refusing to name them; denying knowledge of where someone was from was a way of repudiating connection with them or denying their importance.

9:31 *God does not listen to sinners.* The man cites a general principle that God listens to the godly rather than to the ungodly (Ps 34:15; Pr 15:8,29; 28:9).

9:32 *Nobody has ever heard.* Such claims in antiquity are very rare, especially for one born blind.

9:34 *they threw him out.* Many scholars believe that at least some of John's audience consisted of Jewish Christians (Messianic Jews) expelled from their synagogues (cf. Rev 2:9; 3:9). This story would feel particularly relevant to their situation, one reason for John selecting this (out of many possible accounts; cf. Jn 20:30; 21:25).

9:35 *Son of Man.* Can simply mean "human being," but here probably evokes Da 7:13–14. Some other Jewish traditions about this "Son of Man," probably in circulation by Jesus' day, also depict the "Son of Man" as a supernatural being.

9:38 Jewish people usually resented bowing down (as the Greek text here suggests), and so expressing such adoration to, humans.

9:39 *so that the blind will see and those who see will become blind.* Many ancient writers spoke of spiritual or moral blindness (e.g., Isa 6:9–10; 42:18–19); some also spoke of those who were physically blind yet had great spiritual insight.

10:1–18 By identifying Jesus' hearers as Pharisees, the NIV rightly recognizes that Jesus is continuing to speak to those whom he addressed in 9:40–41. In this context, the healed man is one of the sheep who hears Jesus' voice; those who expelled him from the synagogue are compared to thieves, robbers and wolves; and Jesus is the good shepherd. By putting the man out of the synagogue, Israel's leaders treated him as not part of Israel. In light of OT background, however, Jesus as the good shepherd (corresponding to Yahweh in the OT, e.g., Ps 23:1; 28:9; Isa 40:11) affirms that the man really is one of his sheep, i.e., does belong to God's people (Ps 74:1; 78:52; 79:13; 100:3). Meanwhile, Jesus portrays some of Israel's leaders in his day as being like the leaders of Israel who were condemned as exploitive shepherds in the OT (Jer 23:1–2; Eze 34:2–6,8).

10:1 *sheep pen.* Used during winter nights to protect against lions, wolves (cf. v. 12) and other dangers to the

other way, is a thief and a robber. 2The
one who enters by the gate is the shepherd of the sheep.[o] 3The gatekeeper opens
the gate for him, and the sheep listen
to his voice.[p] He calls his own sheep by
name and leads them out. 4When he has
brought out all his own, he goes on ahead
of them, and his sheep follow him because
they know his voice. 5But they will never follow a stranger; in fact, they will run
away from him because they do not recognize a stranger's voice." 6Jesus used this
figure of speech,[q] but the Pharisees did
not understand what he was telling them.
7Therefore Jesus said again, "Very truly
I tell you, I am the gate for the sheep. 8All
who have come before me[r] are thieves and
robbers, but the sheep have not listened
to them. 9I am the gate; whoever enters
through me will be saved.[a] They will come
in and go out, and find pasture. 10The thief
comes only to steal and kill and destroy;
I have come that they may have life, and
have it to the full.
11"I am the good shepherd.[s] The good
shepherd lays down his life for the sheep.[t]
12The hired hand is not the shepherd and
does not own the sheep. So when he sees
the wolf coming, he abandons the sheep
and runs away.[u] Then the wolf attacks the
flock and scatters it. 13The man runs away
because he is a hired hand and cares nothing for the sheep.
14"I am the good shepherd;[v] I know my
sheep[w] and my sheep know me — 15just
as the Father knows me and I know the
Father[x] — and I lay down my life for the
sheep. 16I have other sheep[y] that are not
of this sheep pen. I must bring them also.
They too will listen to my voice, and there
shall be one flock[z] and one shepherd.[a]
17The reason my Father loves me is that
I lay down my life[b] — only to take it up
again. 18No one takes it from me, but I lay
it down of my own accord.[c] I have authority to lay it down and authority to take it
up again. This command I received from
my Father."[d]
19The Jews who heard these words were
again divided.[e] 20Many of them said, "He

10:2 [o] ver 11, 14 **10:3** [p] ver 4, 5, 14, 16, 27 **10:6** [q] Jn 16:25 **10:8** [r] Jer 23:1, 2 **10:11** [s] ver 14; Isa 40:11; Eze 34:11-16, 23; Heb 13:20; 1Pe 5:4; Rev 7:17 [t] Jn 15:13; 1Jn 3:16 **10:12** [u] Zec 11:16, 17 **10:14** [v] ver 11 [w] ver 27 **10:15** [x] Mt 11:27 **10:16** [y] Isa 56:8 [z] Jn 11:52; Eph 2:11-19 [a] Eze 37:24; 1Pe 2:25 **10:17** [b] ver 11, 15, 18 **10:18** [c] Mt 26:53 [d] Jn 15:10; Php 2:8; Heb 5:8 **10:19** [e] Jn 7:43; 9:16

[a] 9 Or *kept safe*

sheep. Wolves normally had trouble penetrating a well-built pen. Shepherds could construct makeshift shelters using thornbushes, more enduring shelters with stone walls near a cave or adjoining homes, or even a roofed shelter. The "door" and climbing thieves here may suggest a walled enclosure; some modern villages have these structures higher than six feet (1.8 meters) in family courtyards. *a thief and a robber.* See note on v. 8.

10:3 – 4 *the sheep listen to his voice. He calls his own sheep by name … they know his voice.* Shepherds could separate their sheep from others grazing with them simply by calling them (or apparently in some cases by distinctive flute melodies); sheep recognized their shepherd's voice and were known for their obedience. Shepherds also could have names for various sheep. In the OT, hearing God's voice meant heeding his message (including both the law and what God was saying through the prophets); in this context, the healed man heeds Jesus. Also in the OT, God knew his people by name (Isa 43:1; 45:3), especially those most intimate with him (Ex 33:12,17). Jesus goes on to speak of this experience for his followers in terms of a personal relationship with him (Jn 10:14 – 15).

10:5 *never follow a stranger.* It is true that sheep mistrust strangers.

10:7 *I am the gate.* Because the hill country was cool during winter, shepherds kept sheep in pens close to home; during pasturing season, however, they used temporary shelters. Although ancient writers did not mind mixed metaphors, some scholars have even suggested that the shepherd here *is* the gate. They note, drawing on some modern Middle Eastern shepherding practices, that some shepherds sleep across the entrance to a temporary shelter, guarding it themselves.

10:8 *thieves and robbers.* Robbers typically accosted travelers whereas thieves broke into homes, but here they are paired more generally as dangerous threats to the sheep's welfare (like wolves in v. 12). Those who attacked at night were considered most dangerous and faced serious penalties if caught.

10:9 *come in and go out.* Jesus may here refer to the sheep pen, but he also evokes OT language. Shepherds God had appointed over his people had led them "out and … in" (Nu 27:17; a literal rendering of 2Sa 5:2). Sheep would start grazing at dawn, take shelter from heat starting around noon, and then would graze until, in the evening, they would return to their night shelter.

10:10 *steal and kill and destroy … that they may have life.* Robbers desire to exploit the sheep (see vv. 1, 8), but shepherds watch for the sheep's welfare.

10:11 *I am the good shepherd.* Although Moses and David were shepherds of Israel, Israel's chief shepherd in a greater number of OT passages was God himself, an observation that fits John's message about Jesus. Because the human shepherds of Israel failed to care for the sheep properly, God himself promised to shepherd his people (Eze 34:11 – 17). The good shepherd lays down his life to protect the sheep — thus suffering at the hands of the thieves, robbers, and wolves mentioned in the context.

10:12 *hired hand.* Other ancient writers noted that a hired hand often did not watch over the animals as carefully as an owner would; on leaders who failed to care for the sheep, cf. Jer 23:1 – 2; Eze 34:2 – 10. *when he sees the wolf coming.* Writers often depicted wolves as sheep's enemies.

10:14 – 15 *my sheep know me — just as the Father knows me and I know the Father.* In the promised new covenant (Jer 31:31), God's people would know him (Jer 31:34), perhaps as intimately as a wife ideally knows her husband (cf. Jer 31:32; Hos 2:19 – 20). Exceeding the context's metaphor of sheep knowing the shepherd's voice, the intimate relationship between the Father and the Son depicted elsewhere in this Gospel is here shared with believers (cf. Jn 15:15; 16:13 – 15).

10:16 *other sheep … one flock and one shepherd.* In the Prophets, uniting sheep from different folds represented gathering God's scattered people (Eze 37:21 – 24; Mic 2:12), though Jesus may include here Gentiles grafted in through loyalty to him. The new king from the house of David would be the "one shepherd" (Eze 34:23; 37:24).

10:20 *demon-possessed.* See note on 7:20. *raving mad.*

is demon-possessed[f] and raving mad.[g]
Why listen to him?"
21 But others said, "These are not the
sayings of a man possessed by a demon.[h]
Can a demon open the eyes of the blind?"[i]

Further Conflict Over Jesus' Claims

22 Then came the Festival of Dedication[a]
at Jerusalem. It was winter, 23 and Jesus
was in the temple courts walking in Solomon's Colonnade.[j] 24 The Jews[k] who were
there gathered around him, saying, "How
long will you keep us in suspense? If you
are the Messiah, tell us plainly."[l]
25 Jesus answered, "I did tell you,[m] but
you do not believe. The works I do in my
Father's name testify about me,[n] 26 but you
do not believe because you are not my
sheep.[o] 27 My sheep listen to my voice; I
know them,[p] and they follow me.[q] 28 I give
them eternal life, and they shall never perish; no one will snatch them out of my
hand.[r] 29 My Father, who has given them
to me,[s] is greater than all[b];[t] no one can
snatch them out of my Father's hand. 30 I
and the Father are one."[u]
31 Again his Jewish opponents picked
up stones to stone him,[v] 32 but Jesus said
to them, "I have shown you many good
works from the Father. For which of these
do you stone me?"
33 "We are not stoning you for any good
work," they replied, "but for blasphemy,
because you, a mere man, claim to be
God."[w]
34 Jesus answered them, "Is it not written in your Law,[x] 'I have said you are
"gods" '[c]?[y] 35 If he called them 'gods,' to
whom the word of God came — and Scripture cannot be set aside — 36 what about
the one whom the Father set apart[z] as his
very own[a] and sent into the world?[b] Why
then do you accuse me of blasphemy because I said, 'I am God's Son'?[c] 37 Do not
believe me unless I do the works of my
Father.[d] 38 But if I do them, even though
you do not believe me, believe the works,
that you may know and understand that
the Father is in me, and I in the Father."[e]
39 Again they tried to seize him,[f] but he escaped their grasp.[g]
40 Then Jesus went back across the Jordan[h] to the place where John had been
baptizing in the early days. There he
stayed, 41 and many people came to him.
They said, "Though John never performed
a sign,[i] all that John said about this man
was true."[j] 42 And in that place many believed in Jesus.[k]

The Death of Lazarus

11 Now a man named Lazarus was
sick. He was from Bethany,[l] the
village of Mary and her sister Martha.[m]
2 (This Mary, whose brother Lazarus now
lay sick, was the same one who poured
perfume on the Lord and wiped his feet
with her hair.)[n] 3 So the sisters sent word
to Jesus, "Lord, the one you love[o] is sick."

[a] *22* That is, Hanukkah [b] *29* Many early manuscripts *What my Father has given me is greater than all* [c] *34* Psalm 82:6

10:20 [f] Jn 7:20 [g] Mk 3:21 **10:21** [h] Mt 4:24 [i] Ex 4:11; Jn 9:32,33 **10:23** [j] Ac 3:11; 5:12 **10:24** [k] Jn 1:19 [l] Jn 16:25,29 **10:25** [m] Jn 8:58 [n] Jn 5:36 **10:26** [o] Jn 8:47 **10:27** [p] ver 14 [q] ver 4 **10:28** [r] Jn 6:39 **10:29** [s] Jn 17:2, 6,24 [t] Jn 14:28 **10:30** [u] Jn 17:21-23 **10:31** [v] Jn 8:59 **10:33** [w] Lev 24:16; Jn 5:18 **10:34** [x] Jn 8:17; Ro 3:19 [y] Ps 82:6 **10:36** [z] Jer 1:5 [a] Jn 6:69 [b] Jn 3:17 [c] Jn 5:17,18 **10:37** [d] ver 25; Jn 15:24 **10:38** [e] Jn 14:10,11, 20; 17:21 **10:39** [f] Jn 7:30 [g] Lk 4:30; Jn 8:59 **10:40** [h] Jn 1:28 **10:41** [i] Jn 2:11; 3:30 [j] Jn 1:26, 27,30,34 **10:42** [k] Jn 7:31 **11:1** [l] Mt 21:17 [m] Lk 10:38 **11:2** [n] Mk 14:3; Lk 7:38; Jn 12:3 **11:3** [o] ver 5,36

Prophets were sometimes deemed mad by others (2Ki 9:11; Jer 29:26); see notes on Ac 26:24,25.

10:22 *Festival of Dedication.* Hanukkah lasted eight days; less well attended (and less expected for Galileans) than the recent Festival of Tabernacles, it nevertheless drew many pilgrims from Galilee and even from the Diaspora. This festival celebrated Israel's deliverance and the temple's rededication in the time of the Maccabees. Allusions to the festival are possible in this passage even if not completely clear: unknown to Jesus' hearers at this festival, he is Israel's new deliverer, himself consecrated like the temple (v. 36).

10:23 *Solomon's Colonnade.* Because the outdoor colonnades of Greek temples offered shelter from the elements, people often congregated there. The same was true of the porticoes in the Jerusalem temple; they offered shelter during winter (v. 22). Solomon's Colonnade, a long outside hallway framed by two rows of pillars, lay along the eastern end of the temple's outer court. In Jesus' day, many people believed that the colonnade's pre-Herodian stonework went back to Solomon's time.

10:27 *My sheep listen to my voice.* Cf. perhaps Ps 95:7, which speaks of hearing God's voice and being "the flock under his care," or (lit.) "the sheep of his hand" (thus the "hand" in Jn 10:28 – 29).

10:31 *picked up stones to stone him.* See note on 8:59. Stoning was the conventional punishment for blasphemy, showing that Jesus' hearers understand v. 30 as a claim to divinity. The Festival of Dedication partly commemorated liberation from Antiochus IV Epiphanes, a man who claimed to be divine; but Jesus, though divine, became human (1:14).

10:32 *I have shown you many good works from the Father.* In antiquity, one way to shame opponents was to remind them that the speaker had been kind and generous to them.

10:34,35 *"gods."* Ps 82:6, quoted here in v. 34, probably mocks ancient Near Eastern rulers who saw themselves as divine (cf. Ps 82:7), an issue appropriate to the memory enshrined in this festival (see note on Jn 10:31). Some ancient Jewish interpreters, however, applied this passage to Israel receiving the law at Mount Sinai. Possibly Jesus appeals to his contemporaries' interpretation; or possibly he simply leaves the matter ambiguous, offering another riddle (see notes on 6:54; 7:33 – 34; 8:24).

10:36 *the one whom the Father set apart.* The Festival of Dedication celebrated the setting apart of the temple after it was purified from its desecration. Some think that Jesus, who mentions being "set apart" here, alludes to himself as the new temple (cf. 2:21).

10:40 *across the Jordan.* In Perea, governed by Herod Antipas. The ruling class in Jerusalem, from whom Jesus faced danger (cf. v. 39), lacked authority in Perea.

11:1 *Bethany.* See notes on Mk 11:1,11.

11:2 *Mary.* The most common woman's name in Judea in this period; John thus specifies which one he means.

11:3 *So the sisters sent word to Jesus.* It was the custom for people to visit the sick when informed of their sickness;

4When he heard this, Jesus said, "This sickness will not end in death. No, it is for God's glory[p] so that God's Son may be glorified through it." 5Now Jesus loved Martha and her sister and Lazarus. 6So when he heard that Lazarus was sick, he stayed where he was two more days, 7and then he said to his disciples, "Let us go back to Judea."[q]

8"But Rabbi,"[r] they said, "a short while ago the Jews there tried to stone you,[s] and yet you are going back?"

9Jesus answered, "Are there not twelve hours of daylight? Anyone who walks in the daytime will not stumble, for they see by this world's light.[t] 10It is when a person walks at night that they stumble, for they have no light."

11After he had said this, he went on to tell them, "Our friend[u] Lazarus has fallen asleep;[v] but I am going there to wake him up."

12His disciples replied, "Lord, if he sleeps, he will get better." 13Jesus had been speaking of his death, but his disciples thought he meant natural sleep.[w]

14So then he told them plainly, "Lazarus is dead, 15and for your sake I am glad I was not there, so that you may believe. But let us go to him."

16Then Thomas[x] (also known as Didymus[a]) said to the rest of the disciples, "Let us also go, that we may die with him."

Jesus Comforts the Sisters of Lazarus

17On his arrival, Jesus found that Lazarus had already been in the tomb for four days.[y] 18Now Bethany[z] was less than two miles[b] from Jerusalem, 19and many Jews had come to Martha and Mary to comfort them in the loss of their brother.[a] 20When Martha heard that Jesus was coming, she went out to meet him, but Mary stayed at home.[b]

21"Lord," Martha said to Jesus, "if you had been here, my brother would not have died.[c] 22But I know that even now God will give you whatever you ask."[d]

23Jesus said to her, "Your brother will rise again."

24Martha answered, "I know he will rise again in the resurrection[e] at the last day."

25Jesus said to her, "I am the resurrection and the life.[f] The one who believes in me will live, even though they die; 26and whoever lives by believing in me will never die. Do you believe this?"

27"Yes, Lord," she replied, "I believe that you are the Messiah,[g] the Son of God,[h] who is to come into the world."[i]

28After she had said this, she went back and called her sister Mary aside. "The Teacher[j] is here," she said, "and is asking for you." 29When Mary heard this, she got up quickly and went to him. 30Now Jesus had not yet entered the village, but was still at the place where Martha had met him.[k] 31When the Jews who had been with Mary in the house, comforting her,[l] noticed how quickly she got up and went out, they followed her, supposing she was going to the tomb to mourn there.

32When Mary reached the place where Jesus was and saw him, she fell at his feet and said, "Lord, if you had been here, my brother would not have died."[m]

33When Jesus saw her weeping, and the Jews who had come along with her also weeping, he was deeply moved[n] in spirit and troubled.[o] 34"Where have you laid him?" he asked.

"Come and see, Lord," they replied.

11:4 [p] ver 40; Jn 9:3 **11:7** [q] Jn 10:40 **11:8** [r] Mt 23:7 [s] Jn 8:59; 10:31 **11:9** [t] Jn 9:4; 12:35 **11:11** [u] ver 3 [v] Ac 7:60 **11:13** [w] Mt 9:24 **11:16** [x] Mt 10:3; Jn 14:5; 20:24-28; 21:2; Ac 1:13 **11:17** [y] ver 6, 39 **11:18** [z] ver 1 **11:19** [a] ver 31; Job 2:11

11:20 [b] Lk 10:38-42 **11:21** [c] ver 32, 37 **11:22** [d] ver 41, 42; Jn 9:31 **11:24** [e] Da 12:2; Jn 5:28, 29; Ac 24:15 **11:25** [f] Jn 1:4 **11:27** [g] Lk 2:11 [h] Mt 16:16 [i] Jn 6:14 **11:28** [j] Mt 26:18; Jn 13:13 **11:30** [k] ver 20 **11:31** [l] ver 19 **11:32** [m] ver 21 **11:33** [n] ver 38 [o] Jn 12:27

[a] *16* *Thomas* (Aramaic) and *Didymus* (Greek) both mean *twin.* [b] *18* Or about 3 kilometers

the sisters have special reason for Jesus to come, however, because he is a healer.

11:6 *stayed … two more days.* Bethany was about a day's journey, so even had Jesus not delayed, Lazarus may have already been deceased before the messengers could have brought Jesus back there (cf. v. 17).

11:8 *the Jews there tried to stone you.* Galilee was in the jurisdiction of Herod Antipas; once Jesus entered Judea, his enemies among Jerusalem's elite would have authority to arrest him.

11:9–10 *daylight … light … night.* Without lighting, a traveler easily could stumble on paths at night. Yet Jesus uses this analogy to illustrate the wisdom of following the Father's will and timing; Jewish sources often associate light figuratively with God (see notes on 1:4–5; 3:19–21; 8:12).

11:11 *Lazarus has fallen asleep.* People in the Mediterranean world widely used "sleep" as a euphemism for death.

11:13 *thought he meant natural sleep.* For misunderstanding, see note on 3:4.

11:19 *many Jews had come … to comfort them.* It was the custom for people to visit the bereaved and care for them (including providing meals for them), especially in the week immediately following their loved one's death.

11:20 *Martha … went out to meet him.* The bereaved were to stay at home and mourn for the first week after their loved one's death; Martha might slip out unnoticed for a while, but someone must stay at home with the guests who had come to mourn with the family.

11:22 *even now God will give you whatever you ask.* This is likely a polite but indirect request (see note on 2:3).

11:24 *resurrection at the last day.* With some exceptions such as the Sadducees, most Judeans and Galileans seem to have believed in the resurrection at the end of the age, especially the resurrection for the righteous.

11:28 Martha speaks with Mary privately, whether to protect Jesus or because members of the family were not supposed to go out during the mourning period (though cf. v. 31).

11:31 *supposing she was going to the tomb.* Since the immediate family's first week was to be spent in mourning, the guests assume that she must be going to the tomb.

35 Jesus wept.[p]
36 Then the Jews said, "See how he
loved him!"[q]
37 But some of them said, "Could not he
who opened the eyes of the blind man[r]
have kept this man from dying?"[s]

Jesus Raises Lazarus From the Dead

38 Jesus, once more deeply moved,[t]
came to the tomb. It was a cave with a
stone laid across the entrance.[u] 39 "Take
away the stone," he said.
"But, Lord," said Martha, the sister of
the dead man, "by this time there is a bad
odor, for he has been there four days."[v]
40 Then Jesus said, "Did I not tell you
that if you believe,[w] you will see the glory
of God?"[x]
41 So they took away the stone. Then
Jesus looked up[y] and said, "Father,[z] I thank
you that you have heard me. 42 I knew that
you always hear me, but I said this for the
benefit of the people standing here,[a] that
they may believe that you sent me."[b]
43 When he had said this, Jesus called in
a loud voice, "Lazarus, come out!"[c] 44 The
dead man came out, his hands and feet
wrapped with strips of linen,[d] and a cloth
around his face.[e]
Jesus said to them, "Take off the grave
clothes and let him go."

The Plot to Kill Jesus

45 Therefore many of the Jews who had
come to visit Mary,[f] and had seen what
Jesus did,[g] believed in him.[h] 46 But some of
them went to the Pharisees and told them
what Jesus had done. 47 Then the chief
priests and the Pharisees[i] called a meeting[j] of the Sanhedrin.[k]
"What are we accomplishing?" they
asked. "Here is this man performing many
signs.[l] 48 If we let him go on like this, everyone will believe in him, and then the
Romans will come and take away both our
temple and our nation."
49 Then one of them, named Caiaphas,[m]
who was high priest that year,[n] spoke up,
"You know nothing at all! 50 You do not realize that it is better for you that one man
die for the people than that the whole nation perish."[o]
51 He did not say this on his own, but as
high priest that year he prophesied that
Jesus would die for the Jewish nation,
52 and not only for that nation but also
for the scattered children of God, to bring
them together and make them one.[p] 53 So

11:35 [p] Lk 19:41 **11:36** [q] ver 3 **11:37** [r] Jn 9:6,7 [s] ver 21,32 **11:38** [t] ver 33 [u] Mt 27:60; Lk 24:2; Jn 20:1 **11:39** [v] ver 17 **11:40** [w] ver 23-25 [x] ver 4 **11:41** [y] Jn 17:1 [z] Mt 11:25 **11:42** [a] Jn 12:30 [b] Jn 3:17 **11:43** [c] Lk 7:14 **11:44** [d] Jn 19:40 [e] Jn 20:7
11:45 [f] ver 19 [g] Jn 2:23 [h] Ex 14:31; Jn 7:31 **11:47** [i] ver 57 [j] Mt 26:3 [k] Mt 5:22 [l] Jn 2:11 **11:49** [m] Mt 26:3 [n] ver 51; Jn 18:13, 14 **11:50** [o] Jn 18:14 **11:52** [p] Isa 49:6; Jn 10:16

11:35 *Jesus wept.* Mourning with the bereaved was considered virtuous; those present would see not only how Jesus loved his friend (v. 36) but would also regard his concern as virtuous (cf. their view of him as a holy man with power in v. 37).
11:38 *It was a cave.* Caves were often used as tombs; large stones often closed the entrance to a tomb (see note on Mt 27:60).
11:39 *by this time there is a bad odor.* In this period, Jewish families would allow the body to decompose inside the tomb for one year; at the end of the year, the bones would be placed in a container that could then be stored in a slot in the tomb wall. Sometimes people left spices with the body, but after "four days" one would smell the decomposition. A Jewish tradition later claimed that the soul abandoned the body after three days; if this tradition circulated in the first century, no one expected even a miracle worker to be able to bring Lazarus back from death.
11:40 *see the glory of God.* A sign could reveal God's glory (Ex 16:7).
11:41 *looked up.* Jewish people sometimes looked skyward (toward heaven) when they prayed.
11:42 Cf. 1Ki 18:36.
11:44 *Take off the grave clothes and let him go.* John's audience presumably knew that Lazarus would be tightly wrapped in linen cloths to keep his members straight and his mouth closed. If so, they would understand that it would take a miracle for Lazarus not only to be raised but even to emerge from the tomb. Sometimes face cloths were much larger than the head. Lazarus needs to be released by others from these wrappings — unlike Jesus at his resurrection.
11:47 *Sanhedrin.* The Sanhedrin was Jerusalem's ruling senate or council; Josephus repeatedly illustrates their concern for public order and attempts to prevent hostile Roman intervention. Somewhat later than Jesus' ministry, some Jewish prophetic figures promised (though failed to perform) major signs, drawing large followings; Roman soldiers intervened against them and their followers.
11:48 *take away both our temple and our nation.* Ancient writers expected their audiences to catch irony. A generation after Jesus' execution, the Romans destroyed Jerusalem's temple and enslaved its people.
11:49 *Caiaphas.* Joseph Caiaphas maintained his office of high priest longer than any other first-century priest (AD 18 – 36), presumably because he was politically astute. John's audience might also catch the ironic truth (cf. note on v. 48) in Caiaphas's "You know nothing at all!" *high priest that year.* The office of high priesthood was to be for life (in contrast to some annual Greek priesthoods possibly known to John's audience). In the first century, however, Roman governors withdrew it and bestowed it at will; John may simply be saying that Caiaphas was high priest at that time.
11:50 *better for you that one man die.* Later rabbis insisted that Israel should not betray any of its members to death even to save everyone else. Many of Jerusalem's priestly aristocrats, however, engaged in political machinations like Roman and other elites; Josephus records some of their plots to eliminate potential troublemakers. Further, Rome's governing infrastructure in the provinces was kept deliberately light; governors depended on local elites to locate and bring rabble-rousers to the governors' attention. Failure to do so until matters got out of hand risked allowing the local leaders to appear sympathetic with the agitators.
11:51 – 52 On ironic truth, see notes on vv. 48,49.
11:52 *scattered children of God.* A central Jewish expectation for the future time when God would restore his people was that he would gather the scattered 12 tribes in the Diaspora all back to the promised land. Because the Greek expression for "nation" would normally include

from that day on they plotted to take his
life.[q]
54Therefore Jesus no longer moved
about publicly among the people of Judea.[r] Instead he withdrew to a region near
the wilderness, to a village called Ephraim, where he stayed with his disciples.
55When it was almost time for the Jewish Passover,[s] many went up from the
country to Jerusalem for their ceremonial
cleansing[t] before the Passover. 56They kept
looking for Jesus,[u] and as they stood in
the temple courts they asked one another,
"What do you think? Isn't he coming to
the festival at all?" 57But the chief priests
and the Pharisees had given orders that
anyone who found out where Jesus was
should report it so that they might arrest
him.

Jesus Anointed at Bethany

12:1-8Ref — Mt 26:6-13; Mk 14:3-9; Lk 7:37-39

12 Six days before the Passover,[v] Jesus
came to Bethany,[w] where Lazarus
lived, whom Jesus had raised from the
dead. 2Here a dinner was given in Jesus'
honor. Martha served,[x] while Lazarus was
among those reclining at the table with
him. 3Then Mary took about a pint[a] of
pure nard, an expensive perfume;[y] she
poured it on Jesus' feet and wiped his feet
with her hair.[z] And the house was filled
with the fragrance of the perfume.
4But one of his disciples, Judas Iscariot,
who was later to betray him,[a] objected,
5"Why wasn't this perfume sold and the
money given to the poor? It was worth a
year's wages.[b]" 6He did not say this because he cared about the poor but because
he was a thief; as keeper of the money
bag,[b] he used to help himself to what was
put into it.
7"Leave her alone," Jesus replied. "It
was intended that she should save this
perfume for the day of my burial.[c] 8You
will always have the poor among you,[cd]
but you will not always have me."
9Meanwhile a large crowd of Jews found
out that Jesus was there and came, not
only because of him but also to see Lazarus, whom he had raised from the dead.[e]
10So the chief priests made plans to kill
Lazarus as well, 11for on account of him[f]
many of the Jews were going over to Jesus
and believing in him.[g]

Jesus Comes to Jerusalem as King

12:12-15pp — Mt 21:4-9; Mk 11:7-10; Lk 19:35-38

12The next day the great crowd that
had come for the festival heard that Jesus
was on his way to Jerusalem. 13They took
palm branches and went out to meet him,
shouting,

"Hosanna![d]"

"Blessed is he who comes in the name
of the Lord!"[eh]

"Blessed is the king of Israel!"[i]

11:53 [q]Mt 12:14
11:54 [r]Jn 7:1
11:55 [s]Ex 12:13,23,27; Mt 26:1,2; Mk 14:1; Jn 13:1 [t]2Ch 30:17,18
11:56 [u]Jn 7:11
12:1 [v]Jn 11:55 [w]Mt 21:17
12:2 [x]Lk 10:38-42
12:3 [y]Mk 14:3 [z]Jn 11:2
12:4 [a]Mt 10:4
12:6 [b]Jn 13:29
12:7 [c]Jn 19:40
12:8 [d]Dt 15:11
12:9 [e]Jn 11:43,44
12:11 [f]ver 17,18; Jn 11:45 [g]Jn 7:31
12:13 [h]Ps 118:25,26 [i]Jn 1:49

[a] 3 Or about 0.5 liter
[b] 5 Greek *three hundred denarii*
[c] 8 See Deut. 15:11.
[d] 13 A Hebrew expression meaning "Save!" which became an exclamation of praise
[e] 13 Psalm 118:25,26

Jews in the Diaspora as well, however, John may include here also Gentile believers who have become God's children (1:11 – 13; 3:5). *make them one.* See note on 10:16.

11:55 *ceremonial cleansing.* Since Jewish pilgrims from the Diaspora had to travel long distances, they could not be certain of their precise time of arrival. Because they wanted to be ready for the festival, many would arrive early. Those impure from contact with dead bodies would need seven days to become pure. For the many purification pools on the temple mount, see note on Ac 2:41.

12:1 Bethany was some two miles (three kilometers) east of Jerusalem, on the eastern side of the Mount of Olives. Because the number of pilgrims would swell Jerusalem's population even "six days before the Passover," it makes sense for Jesus to stay with friends in Bethany.

12:2 *reclining at the table with him.* Normally guests would recline, with about three or four per table; Lazarus and Jesus were apparently at the same table.

12:3 *a pint of pure nard.* Spikenard was a costly oil with a sweet smell, imported from northern India. Scholars estimate that the pint referred to here (a Roman pound) was nearly 12 ounces, at about 324 grams. Many flasks contained only a single ounce, so Mary's flask is a large one. *poured it on Jesus' feet.* Hosts would normally provide water for the feet, anointing only the head; Mary is shockingly extravagant. Moreover, only servants normally handled a person's feet. *wiped his feet with her hair.* Women's hair was normally covered (see the article "Head Coverings in Antiquity," p. 2003), although it would not be required in the case of a single woman, as Mary probably was at this time, or alone in her home.

12:6 *he was a thief.* A group's trusted treasurer stealing money was scandalous; outsiders would criticize the entire group.

12:7 *perfume for the day of my burial.* Men could wash only men's corpses; women could wash either men's or women's corpses. After anointing and washing the body, spices (as in v. 3) could be applied to reduce the smell of the body decomposing.

12:8 *You will always have the poor.* Dt 15:11 warns that the poor will always be in the land; the context uses this point to encourage generosity toward them, promising Israel that if they cared for the poor God would supply the nation's needs. Jesus' point is to prioritize devotion to him, not to diminish the importance of serving the poor.

12:12 *great crowd ... had come for the festival.* This group would include many Galileans who already knew Jesus' works. Those present in Jerusalem during festivals often hailed new pilgrims, but Jesus is hailed in a special manner.

12:13 *took palm branches.* People waved palm branches to celebrate victories, including for Judeans (1 Maccabees 13:51; 2 Maccabees 10:7). *Hosanna!* Lit. "Save!" *Blessed is he who comes in the name of the Lord!* A quote from Ps 118:25 – 26; these lines belong to the Hallel (Ps 113 – 118), sung during Passover. Hopes for redemption ran high at Passover. *the king of Israel!* Suggests hope that Jesus may

14 Jesus found a young donkey and sat on
it, as it is written:

15 "Do not be afraid, Daughter Zion;
see, your king is coming,
seated on a donkey's colt."[aj]

16 At first his disciples did not understand all this.[k] Only after Jesus was glorified[l] did they realize that these things had
been written about him and that these
things had been done to him.
17 Now the crowd that was with him[m]
when he called Lazarus from the tomb
and raised him from the dead continued to
spread the word. 18 Many people, because
they had heard that he had performed
this sign,[n] went out to meet him. 19 So the
Pharisees said to one another, "See, this is
getting us nowhere. Look how the whole
world has gone after him!"[o]

Jesus Predicts His Death

20 Now there were some Greeks[p] among
those who went up to worship at the festival. 21 They came to Philip, who was from
Bethsaida[q] in Galilee, with a request. "Sir,"
they said, "we would like to see Jesus."
22 Philip went to tell Andrew; Andrew and
Philip in turn told Jesus.
23 Jesus replied, "The hour has come for
the Son of Man to be glorified.[r] 24 Very truly I tell you, unless a kernel of wheat falls
to the ground and dies,[s] it remains only
a single seed. But if it dies, it produces
many seeds. 25 Anyone who loves their life
will lose it, while anyone who hates their
life in this world will keep it[t] for eternal
life. 26 Whoever serves me must follow
me; and where I am, my servant also will
be.[u] My Father will honor the one who
serves me.
27 "Now my soul is troubled,[v] and what
shall I say? 'Father,[w] save me from this
hour'?[x] No, it was for this very reason I
came to this hour. 28 Father, glorify your
name!"
Then a voice came from heaven,[y] "I
have glorified it, and will glorify it again."
29 The crowd that was there and heard it
said it had thundered; others said an angel
had spoken to him.
30 Jesus said, "This voice was for your
benefit,[z] not mine. 31 Now is the time for
judgment on this world;[a] now the prince
of this world[b] will be driven out. 32 And I,
when I am lifted up[b] from the earth,[c] will
draw all people to myself."[d] 33 He said this
to show the kind of death he was going
to die.[e]
34 The crowd spoke up, "We have heard
from the Law that the Messiah will remain
forever,[f] so how can you say, 'The Son of
Man[g] must be lifted up'?[h] Who is this 'Son
of Man'?"

12:15 [j] Zec 9:9 **12:16** [k] Mk 9:32 [l] Jn 2:22; 7:39; 14:26 **12:17** [m] Jn 11:42 **12:18** [n] ver 11 **12:19** [o] Jn 11:47, 48 **12:20** [p] Jn 7:35; Ac 11:20 **12:21** [q] Mt 11:21; Jn 1:44 **12:23** [r] Jn 13:32; 17:1 **12:24** [s] 1Co 15:36 **12:25** [t] Mt 10:39; Mk 8:35; Lk 14:26 **12:26** [u] Jn 14:3; 17:24; 2Co 5:8; 1Th 4:17 **12:27** [v] Mt 26:38, 39; Jn 11:33, 38; 13:21 [w] Mt 11:25 [x] ver 23 **12:28** [y] Mt 3:17 **12:30** [z] Jn 11:42 **12:31** [a] Jn 16:11 [b] Jn 14:30; 16:11; 2Co 4:4; Eph 2:2; 1Jn 4:4 **12:32** [c] ver 34; Jn 3:14; 8:28 [d] Jn 6:44 **12:33** [e] Jn 18:32 **12:34** [f] Ps 110:4; Isa 9:7; Eze 37:25; Da 7:14 [g] Mt 8:20 [h] Jn 3:14

[a] *15* Zech. 9:9 [b] *32* The Greek for *lifted up* also means *exalted.*

---

be the Messiah. The context immediately qualifies the character of his kingship (vv. 14–15).

12:15 *seated on a donkey's colt.* Zec 9:9 speaks of a "gentle" king (when applied to rulers the description meant gracious and merciful). Most scholars believe this means that he comes as a king, but not as a warrior-conqueror (who would normally ride a horse or be drawn in a chariot).

12:19 *the whole world has gone after him!* Ancient texts often used irony meant to be caught by the reader but not by the speakers within the narrative. Here, ironically, immediately after they mention "the whole world" Greeks approach Jesus (vv. 20–21).

12:20 *Greeks.* Probably refers to citizens of eastern Mediterranean cities who were counted as descendants of those who self-identified as culturally Greek. This group of people often clashed with Jews, but because these Greeks have come to the temple for the festival they are presumably God-fearers (see note on Ac 10:2).

12:21 *They came to Philip.* That the Greeks (v. 20) sought out Philip first makes sense. Most of the Twelve had traditional Jewish names, but Philip's name is Greek; he came from the region governed by Herod Philip. *Bethsaida.* Its location made natural connections with the Decapolis, which consisted of ten cities that were Greek in character.

12:23 *hour has come … to be glorified.* Because Jesus was to draw "all people" (v. 32; cf. 3:16; 4:42), the coming of the Greeks (v. 20) precipitates Jesus' destined "hour" (also, e.g., 7:30; 8:20; 13:1). Both Gentile and Jewish literature spoke of a person's appointed time, day, or "hour" to die. *glorified.* Although the Roman world viewed crucifixion as humiliating torture, Jesus associates it with his glory (which also means "honor").

12:24 Even in cities, ancient Mediterranean people often used and normally understood agrarian images.

12:25 *hates their life … eternal life.* Jewish apocalyptic writers agreed that eternal life was well worth losing one's life in this age.

12:27 *my soul is troubled.* Greek thinkers praised the state of being untroubled. Cf. Mk 14:33.

12:28 *voice came from heaven.* Sometimes God spoke with a voice from heaven (e.g., Ge 22:15–18). Later Jewish teachers recognized this means of God speaking, calling it a *bat qol.*

12:29 *said it had thundered.* Scripture sometimes compares God's voice to thunder (2Sa 22:14; Job 37:2,5; 40:9; Ps 18:13; 29:3–7). Thunder also accompanied some revelations of God (Ex 19:16; 20:18).

12:31 *time for judgment.* Judgment was normally associated with the final day, but in Jesus it has begun (cf. 3:18–19). *prince of this world.* Jewish texts recognized Satan's dominion over the world, though there is no record of them using this title for him.

12:32 *lifted up.* Lifting can be a wordplay: it can refer to either figurative exaltation or to literal hoisting of a body on a tree or cross (cf. Ge 40:13,19). Here it certainly refers to Jesus' death (v. 33), as implied in 3:14 and 8:28 ("when you have lifted up the Son of Man" is addressed to Jesus' enemies in 8:28). The phrase undoubtedly echoes Isa 52:13, which in its Greek translation also mentions the servant being "glorified" (see Jn 12:23,31–32). Some other ancient writers spoke of being "lifted up" on a cross.

12:34 *the Messiah will remain forever … The Son of Man.* Scripture promised that the Messiah (Isa 9:6–7) and Son of Man (Da 7:13–14) would reign forever.

35Then Jesus told them, "You are going
to have the light[i] just a little while longer. Walk while you have the light,[j] before
darkness overtakes you.[k] Whoever walks
in the dark does not know where they are
going. 36Believe in the light while you have
the light, so that you may become children
of light."[l] When he had finished speaking,
Jesus left and hid himself from them.[m]

Belief and Unbelief Among the Jews

37Even after Jesus had performed so
many signs[n] in their presence, they still
would not believe in him. 38This was to
fulfill the word of Isaiah the prophet:

"Lord, who has believed our message
and to whom has the arm of the
Lord been revealed?"[a][o]

39For this reason they could not believe,
because, as Isaiah says elsewhere:

40"He has blinded their eyes
and hardened their hearts,
so they can neither see with their eyes,
nor understand with their hearts,
nor turn—and I would heal them."[b][p]

41Isaiah said this because he saw Jesus'
glory[q] and spoke about him.[r]
42Yet at the same time many even
among the leaders believed in him.[s] But
because of the Pharisees[t] they would not
openly acknowledge their faith for fear
they would be put out of the synagogue;[u]
43for they loved human praise more than
praise from God.[v]
44Then Jesus cried out, "Whoever believes in me does not believe in me only,
but in the one who sent me.[w] 45The one
who looks at me is seeing the one who
sent me.[x] 46I have come into the world as
a light,[y] so that no one who believes in me
should stay in darkness.
47"If anyone hears my words but does
not keep them, I do not judge that person.
For I did not come to judge the world, but
to save the world.[z] 48There is a judge for
the one who rejects me and does not accept my words; the very words I have spoken will condemn them[a] at the last day.
49For I did not speak on my own, but the
Father who sent me commanded me[b] to
say all that I have spoken. 50I know that
his command leads to eternal life. So
whatever I say is just what the Father has
told me to say."

Jesus Washes His Disciples' Feet

13 It was just before the Passover Festival.[c] Jesus knew that the hour had
come[d] for him to leave this world and go to
the Father.[e] Having loved his own who were
in the world, he loved them to the end.
2The evening meal was in progress,
and the devil had already prompted Judas, the son of Simon Iscariot, to betray
Jesus. 3Jesus knew that the Father had put
all things under his power,[f] and that he
had come from God[g] and was returning to
God; 4so he got up from the meal, took off
his outer clothing, and wrapped a towel
around his waist. 5After that, he poured
water into a basin and began to wash his
disciples' feet,[h] drying them with the towel that was wrapped around him.

12:35 [i] ver 46 [j] Eph 5:8 [k] 1Jn 2:11 **12:36** [l] Lk 16:8 [m] Jn 8:59 **12:37** [n] Jn 2:11 **12:38** [o] Isa 53:1; Ro 10:16 **12:40** [p] Isa 6:10; Mt 13:13, 15 **12:41** [q] Isa 6:1-4 [r] Lk 24:27 **12:42** [s] ver 11; Jn 7:48 [t] Jn 7:13 [u] Jn 9:22 **12:43** [v] Jn 5:44 **12:44** [w] Mt 10:40; Jn 5:24 **12:45** [x] Jn 14:9 **12:46** [y] Jn 1:4; 3:19; 8:12; 9:5 **12:47** [z] Jn 3:17 **12:48** [a] Jn 5:45 **12:49** [b] Jn 14:31 **13:1** [c] Jn 11:55 [d] Jn 12:23 [e] Jn 16:28 **13:3** [f] Mt 28:18 [g] Jn 8:42; 16:27, 28, 30 **13:5** [h] Lk 7:44

[a] 38 Isaiah 53:1 [b] 40 Isaiah 6:10

12:35–36 *light ... darkness ... children of light.* First-century Judeans would readily grasp Jesus' image of day and night here. The Dead Sea Scrolls contrasted the children of light who walked in the light with the children of darkness.
12:38 The unbelief of Jesus' contemporaries (v. 37) fulfilled Scripture. John quotes Isa 53:1, following the very context alluded to earlier (Isa 52:13 in Jn 12:23,32).
12:40 John quotes Isa 6:10, apparently adjusting the Septuagint, the pre-Christian Greek version of the OT, in light of the Hebrew original. See note on Mk 4:12.
12:41 *Jesus' glory.* The verse just quoted in v. 40 (Isa 6:10) comes from a context in which Isaiah saw God's glory (Isa 6:1–5). (For other OT visions related to Jesus, cf. notes on Jn 1:14–18; 8:56.) Jewish interpreters naturally connected texts that shared common key terms, and this Isaiah context links readily with the one quoted in v. 38 (Isa 53:1). Both Isa 6:1 and Isa 52:13 use "high" or "exalted" and "lifted up"; the former applies the terms to God (cf. also Isa 57:15) and the latter to the suffering servant, further linking God and Jesus.
12:42 *put out of the synagogue.* See note on 9:34.
12:43 *loved human praise.* Ancient Mediterranean men vied for honor and abhorred shame. The Greek term that the NIV translates here as "praise" is the same Greek word for "glory" in v. 41.
12:44–50 Summaries of key themes were common at the end of sections or works; many scholars view vv. 44–50 as such a summary.
12:45 *seeing the one who sent me.* Divine Wisdom (see notes on 1:1,3,4–5) appears as God's image in Wisdom of Solomon 7:26.
12:48 *the very words I have spoken.* Other teachers affirmed that God's law would judge at the end; Jesus equates his own words here with those of God (because he speaks God's words, v. 49).
12:50 *what the Father has told me to say.* An agent or messenger was supposed to communicate the sender's message without introducing their own ideas.
13:1 *just before the Passover Festival.* See the article "The Synoptic Passover Meal Versus John's Passover Lamb," p. 1849.
13:2 *The evening meal.* Although many ancient banquets included music, ancient rabbis preferred lectures and especially Torah discussions; no lecture appears here, but Jesus teaches his disciples by example. *the devil ... prompted Judas.* See note on Lk 22:3.
13:5 *he ... began to wash his disciples' feet.* Washing others' feet was normally a servile task. Dirt roads made feet dusty; urban streets sometimes included refuse from chamber pots dumped from windows (though probably not in the well-to-do upper city where Jesus dined this night).

6He came to Simon Peter, who said to
him, "Lord, are you going to wash my feet?"
7Jesus replied, "You do not realize now
what I am doing, but later you will understand."[i]
8"No," said Peter, "you shall never wash
my feet."
Jesus answered, "Unless I wash you,
you have no part with me."
9"Then, Lord," Simon Peter replied,
"not just my feet but my hands and my
head as well!"
10Jesus answered, "Those who have had
a bath need only to wash their feet; their
whole body is clean. And you are clean,[j]
though not every one of you." 11For he
knew who was going to betray him, and
that was why he said not every one was
clean.
12When he had finished washing their
feet, he put on his clothes and returned to
his place. "Do you understand what I have
done for you?" he asked them. 13"You
call me 'Teacher'[k] and 'Lord,'[l] and rightly so, for that is what I am. 14Now that I,
your Lord and Teacher, have washed your
feet, you also should wash one another's
feet.[m] 15I have set you an example that
you should do as I have done for you.[n]
16Very truly I tell you, no servant is greater than his master,[o] nor is a messenger
greater than the one who sent him. 17Now
that you know these things, you will be
blessed if you do them.[p]

Jesus Predicts His Betrayal

18"I am not referring to all of you;[q] I
know those I have chosen.[r] But this is to
fulfill this passage of Scripture: 'He who
shared my bread[s] has turned[a][t] against
me.'[b][u]
19"I am telling you now before it happens, so that when it does happen you
will believe[v] that I am who I am.[w] 20Very
truly I tell you, whoever accepts anyone I
send accepts me; and whoever accepts me
accepts the one who sent me."[x]
21After he had said this, Jesus was troubled in spirit[y] and testified, "Very truly I
tell you, one of you is going to betray me."[z]
22His disciples stared at one another, at
a loss to know which of them he meant.
23One of them, the disciple whom Jesus
loved,[a] was reclining next to him. 24Simon
Peter motioned to this disciple and said,
"Ask him which one he means."
25Leaning back against Jesus, he asked
him, "Lord, who is it?"[b]
26Jesus answered, "It is the one to whom
I will give this piece of bread when I have
dipped it in the dish." Then, dipping the

13:7 [i] ver 12
13:10 [j] Jn 15:3
13:13 [k] Jn 11:28 [l] Lk 6:46; 1Co 12:3; Php 2:11
13:14 [m] 1Pe 5:5
13:15 [n] Mt 11:29
13:16 [o] Mt 10:24; Lk 6:40; Jn 15:20
13:17 [p] Mt 7:24, 25; Lk 11:28; Jas 1:25
13:18 [q] ver 10 [r] Jn 15:16, 19 [s] Mt 26:23 [t] Jn 6:70 [u] Ps 41:9
13:19 [v] Jn 14:29; 16:4 [w] Jn 8:24
13:20 [x] Mt 10:40; Lk 10:16
13:21 [y] Jn 12:27 [z] Mt 26:21
13:23 [a] Jn 19:26; 20:2; 21:7, 20
13:25 [b] Jn 21:20

[a] 18 Greek *has lifted up his heel*   [b] 18 Psalm 41:9

Because people would wash the right hand before the appetizers and both hands before the main course, a basin and towel may have been readily available. It appears that one would wash feet by pouring water over them into the basin.

13:10 *bath.* Might refer to ritual purification for the festival (11:55).

13:11 Ancient hearers would not be troubled that John repeats Jesus' statement in different words. As can also be illustrated by differences noted when comparing the Gospels, ancients practiced and appreciated paraphrase. Ancient biographers did not trifle over minor differences in wording.

13:14 *I, your Lord and Teacher, have washed your feet.* Although later rabbis emphasized teachers' humility, they continued to value social rank. Disciples served teachers rather than the reverse, and the one act of service specifically not expected even of them was dealing with the master's feet. (The context indicates that Jesus' service deliberately prefigures his death for others.)

13:15 *set you an example.* Disciples were supposed to follow their teacher's example. Later rabbis even used earlier rabbis' behavior as legal precedent!

13:16 Jesus' statement accurately summarizes this aspect of ancient culture. Only subordinates served and were sent as agents or messengers.

13:17 *you will be blessed.* For beatitudes, see note on Mt 5:3.

13:18 *turned against me.* People viewed table fellowship as establishing a covenant of friendship; betrayal of such a bond was considered heinous. (For a stark example: in one ancient epic, two warriors, discovering that their fathers had shared table fellowship a generation earlier, realized that they could not fight each other.) Lifting one's heel toward another was an insult. The voice of Ps 41:9, like that of some other psalms, is that of a righteous sufferer (cf. notes on Jn 15:25; 19:28).

13:19 *telling you now before it happens.* God declared beforehand what he would do so that after the fact people would recognize that he had acted (cf. Isa 41:26; 43:9–10; 44:7; 48:3–7).

13:20 *whoever accepts … the one who sent me.* Agents, messengers and ambassadors represented their sender, to the extent that they accurately conveyed the sender's message; how one treated them reflected one's attitude toward the sender.

13:21 *one of you is going to betray me.* Some ancient critics viewed a person who was betrayed as a poor judge of character; Jesus, however, warns that he knows about the betrayal in advance.

13:23 *reclining next to him.* At banquets, three or four people (in the eastern Mediterranean world, usually men) would recline on each couch (or, in the possible absence of couches here, they could recline on mats, rugs, or cloaks). Each would lean on the left elbow with the right hand free to collect food (already sliced) from the table in front of the couch. The diner's feet would point away from the table. Each diner to the right of another on the couch would be ranged somewhat further back, so the diner to the right of another could lean back his head on the other's chest (v. 25).

13:24 *Peter motioned to this disciple.* Simon Peter is apparently at a different table, and so motions to the "disciple whom Jesus loved" (v. 23).

13:25 *Leaning back against Jesus.* Because this disciple is able to lean back against Jesus, he is apparently to his right, a position of honor.

13:26 *the one to whom I will give this piece of bread.* In a Passover context (but cf. v. 1), Jesus probably would dip

JOHN 13

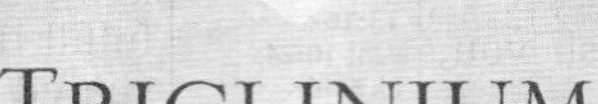

TRICLINIUM

The *triclinium* (plural *triclinia*) was the dining room in a Roman house. Some of the finest examples of *triclinia* have been excavated at Pompeii in the so-called houses of Menander, Pansa, Castor and Pollux and the Golden Cupids. In wealthier homes the walls of triclinia were often adorned with ornate frescoes of mythological or pastoral scenes. The room was typically placed such that it afforded a view of the garden, creating a scenic backdrop for the dining experience. It had an oblong shape and featured long couches placed along three of its walls; hence its name. The couch frames were usually made of wood with bronze adornments. Leather straps crisscrossed the open bottoms of the frames and supported stuffed cushions. The diners reclined on their left sides, freeing their right hands to take food from the low table in the center of the room.

First-century fresco depicting a triclinium scene from Pompeii, Italy.

De Agostini Picture Library/R. Pedicini/Bridgeman Images

The traditional Roman dinner party (*convivium*) involved nine guests, with three persons apiece on each of three couches. These would be arranged in three sides of a square, with entertainment taking place in the open space. Since several diners occupied each couch, each person would place his or her head close to the table and then angle the rest of the body away. The bodies of the diners, then, overlapped, with the head of one diner situated next to the chest of the adjacent guest (their feet were angled back and away from the table). For this reason, according to the historian Pliny, one diner was said to lie "in the bosom" of the other. The historian Livy records that a type of hierarchy developed in this reclining system. The inferior person's head lay near the torso of the superior.

By New Testament times many Jews had adopted the Roman style of dining. The account of the Last Supper in John 13 suggests that Jesus and the disciples were following this custom in a modified form. The Last Supper was not a *convivium* meal but a Passover, and there had to be room for all of Jesus' inner circle of twelve. There was, of course, no entertainment, and so it may have been the case that four couches were arranged around a central table unless, as could happen, four persons reclined per couch or mat. The thirteen diners were reclining as they ate, and John is said to have been leaning against the breast of Jesus, who was naturally in the position of a superior. John's position next to Jesus suggests that he was Jesus' closest friend, which is indeed implied in the narrative (v. 23). ◆

piece of bread, he gave it to Judas, the son of Simon Iscariot. 27As soon as Judas took the bread, Satan entered into him.[c]

So Jesus told him, “What you are about to do, do quickly.” 28But no one at the meal understood why Jesus said this to him. 29Since Judas had charge of the money,[d] some thought Jesus was telling him to buy what was needed for the festival, or to give something to the poor. 30As soon as Judas had taken the bread, he went out. And it was night.[e]

Jesus Predicts Peter’s Denial

13:37,38pp — Mt 26:33-35; Mk 14:29-31; Lk 22:33,34

31When he was gone, Jesus said, “Now the Son of Man is glorified[f] and God is glorified in him.[g] 32If God is glorified in him,[a] God will glorify the Son in himself,[h] and will glorify him at once.

33“My children, I will be with you only a little longer. You will look for me, and just as I told the Jews, so I tell you now: Where I am going, you cannot come.[i]

34“A new command[j] I give you: Love one another.[k] As I have loved you, so you must love one another.[l] 35By this everyone will know that you are my disciples, if you love one another.”[m]

36Simon Peter asked him, “Lord, where are you going?”

13:27 [c] Lk 22:3
13:29 [d] Jn 12:6
13:30 [e] Lk 22:53
13:31 [f] Jn 7:39 [g] Jn 14:13; 17:4; 1Pe 4:11
13:32 [h] Jn 17:1
13:33 [i] Jn 7:33, 34
13:34 [j] 1Jn 2:7-11; 3:11 [k] Lev 19:18; 1Th 4:9; 1Pe 1:22 [l] Jn 15:12; Eph 5:2; 1Jn 4:10, 11
13:35 [m] 1Jn 3:14; 4:20
13:36 [n] ver 33; Jn 14:2 [o] Jn 21:18, 19; 2Pe 1:14
13:38 [p] Jn 18:27
14:1 [q] ver 27
14:2 [r] Jn 13:33, 36
14:3 [s] Jn 12:26
14:5 [t] Jn 11:16
14:6 [u] Jn 10:9 [v] Jn 11:25

Jesus replied, “Where I am going, you cannot follow now,[n] but you will follow later.”[o]

37Peter asked, “Lord, why can’t I follow you now? I will lay down my life for you.”

38Then Jesus answered, “Will you really lay down your life for me? Very truly I tell you, before the rooster crows, you will disown me three times![p]

Jesus Comforts His Disciples

14 “Do not let your hearts be troubled.[q] You believe in God[b]; believe also in me. 2My Father’s house has many rooms; if that were not so, would I have told you that I am going there[r] to prepare a place for you? 3And if I go and prepare a place for you, I will come back and take you to be with me that you also may be where I am.[s] 4You know the way to the place where I am going.”

Jesus the Way to the Father

5Thomas[t] said to him, “Lord, we don’t know where you are going, so how can we know the way?”

6Jesus answered, “I am the way[u] and the truth and the life.[v] No one comes to the Father except through me. 7If you

[a] 32 Many early manuscripts do not have *If God is glorified in him.* [b] 1 Or *Believe in God*

---

the unleavened bread in bitter herbs along with a mixture that later rabbis called *charoset,* which probably included nuts and spices. For Jesus as head of the gathering to dip and hand it to Judas openly honors Judas. Because Jesus is able to dip the piece of bread and hand it to Judas, Judas apparently shares the same table with Jesus, and is presumably to Jesus’ left. In banquets, a position to one’s left was a position of special honor. Whereas Mark emphasizes Judas’ own role in dipping bread (Mk 14:20), John here emphasizes Jesus’ role (cf. Jn 10:18).

13:29 *Judas had charge of the money.* A teacher would sometimes delegate care for the group’s money to a disciple. Some sources that suggest that festivals were also sometimes special occasions for generosity toward the poor. On the night of Passover, markets would be closed (cf. Ex 12:22), but see the article “The Synoptic Passover Meal Versus John’s Passover Lamb,” p. 1849.

13:31,32 *glorified.* See note on 12:23. In the OT God sometimes revealed his glory in theophanies (especially Ex 33:18,22), but the deepest revelation of glory in this context is the cross.

13:33 *children.* Disciples sometimes called their teachers “Father” (cf. note on Mt 23:9), and sages could refer to their disciples as their “children.” Although some could be older, most mature disciples were in their teens.

13:34 *As I have loved you, so you must love one another.* Scripture commanded love of neighbor (Lev 19:18); Jewish tradition valued love, and one later rabbi, Rabbi Akiba, even named this as the greatest commandment. Yet Jesus’ emphasis on the priority of love distinctively pervaded his movement in a way shared by no other ancient movement (e.g., Ro 13:8 – 10; Gal 5:14). What makes the command “new” here is the example that Jesus cites: his example of laying down his life for others.

13:35 *my disciples.* Disciples were expected to imitate their teachers.

13:38 *before the rooster crows.* Roosters crow often, but ancient sources mention most often their crowing at dawn. Jesus thus probably warns Peter here that before the night is over he will have denied Jesus three times.

14:1 *believe in God; believe also in me.* God’s people were to trust in God and in his prophets (as in Ex 14:31; 2Ch 20:20); in the context of John’s Gospel, however, the pairing of the Father and Jesus as objects of faith implies not simply Jesus’ prophethood but his deity (cf. 10:30).

14:2 *rooms.* Cf. v. 23, where the same Greek term is translated “home.”

14:3 *I will come back.* Cf. v. 18; 20:19 – 23. *take you to be with me.* Although other Jewish stories circulated of heroes (especially of Elijah and Enoch) being caught up to God, only here does one going to the Father bring all his followers into the Father’s presence with him.

14:4 *the way.* In Jewish literature, God’s true path of righteousness could be called “the way.” (For its exclusivity, cf. note on Mt 7:13 – 14.) Some scholars also think of the way of salvation in Jn 1:23.

14:5 *how . . . ?* As here and in vv. 8,22, disciples often asked their teachers questions for clarification or requested knowledge.

14:6 *the way.* See note on v. 4. *except through me.* Gentiles complained about Jews’ “intolerance” because Jews insisted on only one God. Some Jewish groups, however, notably the Qumran community, were even more exclusive; they believed that they followed the only path to God and that other Jewish groups were lost. Jesus goes beyond such groups; he does not teach a way to God, but rather *is* the way to God.

really know me, you will know[a] my Father as well.[w] From now on, you do know
him and have seen him."
8Philip said, "Lord, show us the Father
and that will be enough for us."
9Jesus answered: "Don't you know me,
Philip, even after I have been among you
such a long time? Anyone who has seen
me has seen the Father.[x] How can you say,
'Show us the Father'? 10Don't you believe
that I am in the Father, and that the Father
is in me?[y] The words I say to you I do not
speak on my own authority.[z] Rather, it is
the Father, living in me, who is doing his
work. 11Believe me when I say that I am
in the Father and the Father is in me; or at
least believe on the evidence of the works
themselves.[a] 12Very truly I tell you, whoever believes[b] in me will do the works I
have been doing,[c] and they will do even
greater things than these, because I am going to the Father. 13And I will do whatever
you ask[d] in my name, so that the Father
may be glorified in the Son. 14You may ask
me for anything in my name, and I will
do it.

Jesus Promises the Holy Spirit

15"If you love me, keep my commands.[e]
16And I will ask the Father, and he will
give you another advocate[f] to help you
and be with you forever— 17the Spirit of
truth.[g] The world cannot accept him,[h] because it neither sees him nor knows him.
But you know him, for he lives with you
and will be[b] in you. 18I will not leave you
as orphans; I will come to you.[i] 19Before
long, the world will not see me anymore,
but you will see me.[j] Because I live, you
also will live.[k] 20On that day you will realize that I am in my Father,[l] and you are
in me, and I am in you. 21Whoever has my
commands and keeps them is the one who
loves me.[m] The one who loves me will be
loved by my Father,[n] and I too will love
them and show myself to them."
22Then Judas[o] (not Judas Iscariot) said,
"But, Lord, why do you intend to show
yourself to us and not to the world?"[p]
23Jesus replied, "Anyone who loves me
will obey my teaching.[q] My Father will
love them, and we will come to them and
make our home with them.[r] 24Anyone
who does not love me will not obey my
teaching. These words you hear are not
my own; they belong to the Father who
sent me.[s]
25"All this I have spoken while still with
you. 26But the Advocate,[t] the Holy Spirit,
whom the Father will send in my name,[u]
will teach you all things[v] and will remind
you of everything I have said to you.[w]
27Peace I leave with you; my peace I give
you.[x] I do not give to you as the world

14:7 [w] Jn 8:19
14:9 [x] Jn 12:45; Col 1:15; Heb 1:3
14:10 [y] Jn 10:38 [z] Jn 5:19
14:11 [a] Jn 5:36; 10:38
14:12 [b] Mt 21:21 [c] Lk 10:17
14:13 [d] Mt 7:7
14:15 [e] ver 21, 23; Jn 15:10; 1Jn 5:3
14:16 [f] Jn 15:26; 16:7
14:17 [g] Jn 15:26; 16:13; 1Jn 4:6 [h] 1Co 2:14
14:18 [i] ver 3,28
14:19 [j] Jn 7:33, 34; 16:16 [k] Jn 6:57
14:20 [l] Jn 10:38
14:21 [m] 1Jn 5:3 [n] 1Jn 2:5
14:22 [o] Lk 6:16; Ac 1:13 [p] Ac 10:41
14:23 [q] ver 15 [r] 1Jn 2:24; Rev 3:20
14:24 [s] Jn 7:16
14:26 [t] Jn 15:26; 16:7 [u] Ac 2:33 [v] Jn 16:13; 1Jn 2:20,27 [w] Jn 2:22
14:27 [x] Jn 16:33; Php 4:7; Col 3:15

[a] 7 Some manuscripts *If you really knew me, you would know* [b] 17 Some early manuscripts *and is*

14:8 *show us the Father.* Philip's request might echo Moses' prayer to see God's glory in Ex 33:18 (using the same verb in both). Thus Jesus is the one who Moses saw (see notes on Jn 1:14–18; 8:56; 12:41).

14:9 *Anyone who has seen me has seen the Father.* Divine Wisdom (see notes on 1:1,3,4–5) appears as God's image in Wisdom of Solomon 7:26.

14:11 *believe on the evidence of the works themselves.* Faith was the proper response to signs (e.g., Ex 4:4–9; 19:9; Nu 14:11).

14:12–14 *they will do even greater things than these ... I will do whatever you ask in my name ... ask ... and I will do it.* General statements of principle were sometimes qualified for particular circumstances (cf., e.g., 1 Jn 5:14). Nevertheless, few if any other teachers offered promises from God as radical as this (see Mt 7:7–8 and note on Mt 7:7), and none dared offer such radical promises about their own name.

14:13,14 *name.* Although a range of meaning for "name" existed, the idea here may be that they ask based on their relationship with, and as agents of, Jesus (acting as Jesus would and through his privilege).

14:15 *If you love me, keep my commands.* The OT already closely connected love for God with obeying his commandments (Ex 20:6; Dt 5:10; 6:5–6; 11:1,13,22; 13:3–4; 19:9).

14:16 *advocate.* The term translated "advocate" did not always carry, but sometimes carried, legal connotations (cf. 16:8–11).

14:17 *the Spirit of truth.* The Dead Sea Scrolls also spoke of "the Spirit of truth" that worked in God's chosen remnant, contrasting this spirit with the spirit of falsehood at work in the world (cf. 1 Jn 4:6). Judaism treated the Spirit as a divine aspect rather than as a distinct person; this passage treats the Spirit as a distinct person like Jesus. *will be in you.* In Scripture, God's Spirit sometimes filled his agents (e.g., Ex 31:3; 35:31; Dt 34:9; Mic 3:8), was often upon them (Nu 11:17,25–26; 24:2; Jdg 3:10; Eze 11:5), and was sometimes said to be in them (Nu 27:18; cf. Ge 41:38). In the promised time of restoration, however, God would pour his Spirit on all his people (Joel 2:28) and the Spirit would remain in them (Eze 36:27).

14:18 *orphans.* Orphans needed others to speak on their behalf (Dt 10:18; 24:17; Isa 1:17,23). Ancient writers sometimes used "orphan" to refer to those bereaved of others besides a father (in this case, their special teacher). In this context, Jesus' coming may refer to his coming to impart the Spirit (Jn 14:16–17), which occurs in 20:19–23.

14:21 *show myself to them.* Divine revelation was sometimes selective: thus Balaam's donkey saw the angel before Balaam did (Nu 22:23,27–28), only Elisha and his servant witnessed the heavenly armies (2Ki 6:16–17), others felt terror but only Daniel saw a vision (Da 10:7), and so forth.

14:23 *loves ... obey.* See note on v. 15. *our home with them.* God's presence with all his people was always the ideal even in this age (Ex 25:8; 29:46; Lev 26:11–12) and was the promise for the future era (Eze 37:27–28; 43:9); through the Spirit (see note on Jn 14:17) God's people experience his presence on a much more personal level than before (as suggested in Eze 36:27).

14:27 *Peace I leave with you.* Many Jewish teachers valued peace, especially in the wake of the Jewish-Roman war. The "Roman peace" promised by the empire was a

gives. Do not let your hearts be troubled
and do not be afraid.
28“You heard me say, ‘I am going away
and I am coming back to you.’[y] If you
loved me, you would be glad that I am
going to the Father,[z] for the Father is greater than I.[a] 29I have told you now before
it happens, so that when it does happen
you will believe.[b] 30I will not say much
more to you, for the prince of this world[c]
is coming. He has no hold over me, 31but
he comes so that the world may learn that
I love the Father and do exactly what my
Father has commanded me.[d]
“Come now; let us leave.

The Vine and the Branches

15 “I am the true vine,[e] and my Father
is the gardener. 2He cuts off every
branch in me that bears no fruit, while every branch that does bear fruit he prunes[a]
so that it will be even more fruitful. 3You
are already clean because of the word I
have spoken to you.[f] 4Remain in me, as I
also remain in you.[g] No branch can bear
fruit by itself; it must remain in the vine.
Neither can you bear fruit unless you remain in me.
5“I am the vine; you are the branches.
If you remain in me and I in you, you will
bear much fruit;[h] apart from me you can
do nothing. 6If you do not remain in me,
you are like a branch that is thrown away
and withers; such branches are picked up,
thrown into the fire and burned.[i] 7If you
remain in me and my words remain in
you, ask whatever you wish, and it will
be done for you.[j] 8This is to my Father’s
glory,[k] that you bear much fruit, showing
yourselves to be my disciples.[l]
9“As the Father has loved me,[m] so have
I loved you. Now remain in my love. 10If
you keep my commands,[n] you will remain
in my love, just as I have kept my Father’s
commands and remain in his love. 11I have
told you this so that my joy may be in
you and that your joy may be complete.[o]
12My command is this: Love each other
as I have loved you.[p] 13Greater love has
no one than this: to lay down one’s life
for one’s friends.[q] 14You are my friends[r]
if you do what I command.[s] 15I no longer
call you servants, because a servant does
not know his master’s business. Instead,
I have called you friends, for everything
that I learned from my Father I have made
known to you.[t] 16You did not choose me,
but I chose you and appointed you[u] so
that you might go and bear fruit — fruit
that will last — and so that whatever you

14:28 [y] ver 2-4, 18 [z] Jn 5:18 [a] Jn 10:29; Php 2:6 **14:29** [b] Jn 13:19; 16:4 **14:30** [c] Jn 12:31 **14:31** [d] Jn 10:18; 12:49 **15:1** [e] Isa 5:1-7 **15:3** [f] Jn 13:10; 17:17; Eph 5:26 **15:4** [g] Jn 6:56; 1Jn 2:6 **15:5** [h] ver 16 **15:6** [i] ver 2 **15:7** [j] Mt 7:7 **15:8** [k] Mt 5:16 [l] Jn 8:31 **15:9** [m] Jn 17:23, 24,26 **15:10** [n] Jn 14:15 **15:11** [o] Jn 17:13 **15:12** [p] Jn 13:34 **15:13** [q] Jn 10:11; Ro 5:7,8 **15:14** [r] Lk 12:4 [s] Mt 12:50 **15:15** [t] Jn 8:26 **15:16** [u] Jn 6:70; 13:18

[a] 2 The Greek for *he prunes* also means *he cleans.*

hollow fiction in practice, at least in regions where Rome remained at war or in danger of it.

14:29 See note on 13:19.

14:30 *prince of this world.* See note on 12:31.

15:1 *I am the true vine.* In the OT God’s people sometimes appear as a vine (Ps 80:8; Hos 10:1) or vineyard (Isa 5:7). Jesus reapplies the image in a more personal and organic way (e.g., Jn 15:4 – 5). *vine.* Farmers in Palestine, Asia Minor, Greece and elsewhere frequently grew vines; some specialized in this.

15:2 For the metaphor of God’s people bearing fruit when God restores them, cf. Isa 27:6; Hos 14:4 – 8. Vines, normally tied to posts or sometimes trees, required more detailed attention than did most other plants. *cuts off every branch . . . that bears no fruit . . . every branch that does bear fruit he prunes.* The farmer would prune away fruitless branches so that the vine’s strength would go into the fruitful branches. One pruned the weakest vines most thoroughly, for the sake of bearing greater fruit in the long run. Most of the prunings during the year trimmed fruitful branches to strengthen them, but the severest annual pruning cut off the completely fruitless branches (as in v. 6; cf. Isa 18:5 – 6).

15:4 *Neither can you bear fruit.* Branches no longer attached to the vine obviously could not bear fruit; without being supplied by the life of the vine, they would quickly die if they were not already dead.

15:6 *thrown into the fire.* Worthless for building, fruitless vine branches were burned; the image recalls the Jewish belief in the fire of Gehinnom (see note on Mt 3:12).

15:10 *commands . . . love.* See note on 14:15.

15:12 *Love each other.* See note on 13:34.

15:13 *lay down one’s life for one’s friends.* Later rabbis, perhaps reflecting wider Jewish custom, did not place a special value on laying down one’s life for one’s friends. By contrast, Greeks treasured this act as the greatest expression of friendship, and would have appreciated this message. Loyalty was one of the highest ideals of ancient friendship.

15:14 *friends.* Although friendship that emphasized loyalty (v. 13) and intimacy (v. 15) usually involved equality, ancients were aware of forms of friendship between social superiors and inferiors (e.g., the language of friendship was applied to patron-client relationships, in which patrons supplied some needs of clients).

15:15 *I have called you friends.* Many ancient hearers could have related to some of Jesus’ ideas here. Ancient ideals of friendship included intimacy and the sharing of the secrets of one’s heart in confidence. The Jewish philosopher Philo spoke of friendship with God; at times he contrasts this status with being mere servants. Wisdom also was said to make holy persons “friends of God, and prophets” (Wisdom of Solomon 7:27). Scripture called Abraham God’s friend (2Ch 20:7; Isa 41:8), perhaps partly because God would not keep relevant matters from him (Ge 18:17). God also treated Moses as a friend, speaking with him “face to face” (Ex 33:11); cf. the possible allusion to Ex 33:18 in Jn 14:8 (see note there).

15:16 *I chose you and appointed you.* Most Jewish teachers welcomed prospective disciples; although Jesus apparently did the same, the Gospels emphasize that he chose his own core disciples. In the OT God chose his people by his grace (Dt 7:6 – 7; 9:5); the Israelites were the only people to experience that privilege (Dt 14:2). God started by choosing Abram (Ne 9:7); other individuals were chosen for various tasks (e.g., Ex 35:30). Being chosen can give the disciples confidence in their fruitfulness. *ask in my name.* See note on 14:12 – 14.

ask in my name the Father will give you.
17 This is my command: Love each other.[v]

The World Hates the Disciples

18 "If the world hates you,[w] keep in mind
that it hated me first. 19 If you belonged to
the world, it would love you as its own. As
it is, you do not belong to the world, but
I have chosen you[x] out of the world. That
is why the world hates you.[y] 20 Remember
what I told you: 'A servant is not greater than his master.'[a][z] If they persecuted
me, they will persecute you also.[a] If they
obeyed my teaching, they will obey yours
also. 21 They will treat you this way because of my name,[b] for they do not know
the one who sent me.[c] 22 If I had not come
and spoken to them, they would not be
guilty of sin; but now they have no excuse
for their sin.[d] 23 Whoever hates me hates
my Father as well. 24 If I had not done
among them the works no one else did,[e]
they would not be guilty of sin. As it is,
they have seen, and yet they have hated
both me and my Father. 25 But this is to
fulfill what is written in their Law: 'They
hated me without reason.'[b][f]

The Work of the Holy Spirit

26 "When the Advocate[g] comes, whom
I will send to you from the Father[h] — the
Spirit of truth[i] who goes out from the Father — he will testify about me.[j] 27 And you
also must testify,[k] for you have been with
me from the beginning.[l]

15:17 [v] ver 12
15:18 [w] 1Jn 3:13
15:19 [x] ver 16 [y] Jn 17:14
15:20 [z] Jn 13:16 [a] 2Ti 3:12
15:21 [b] Mt 10:22 [c] Jn 16:3
15:22 [d] Jn 9:41; Ro 1:20
15:24 [e] Jn 5:36
15:25 [f] Ps 35:19; 69:4
15:26 [g] Jn 14:16 [h] Jn 14:26 [i] Jn 14:17 [j] 1Jn 5:7
15:27 [k] Lk 24:48; 1Jn 1:2; 4:14 [l] Lk 1:2
16:1 [m] Jn 15:18-27 [n] Mt 11:6
16:2 [o] Jn 9:22 [p] Isa 66:5; Ac 26:9, 10; Rev 6:9
16:3 [q] Jn 15:21; 17:25; 1Jn 3:1
16:4 [r] Jn 13:19
16:5 [s] Jn 7:33 [t] Jn 13:36; 14:5
16:7 [u] Jn 14:16, 26; 15:26 [v] Jn 7:39
16:9 [w] Jn 15:22
16:10 [x] Ac 3:14; 7:52; 1Pe 3:18
16:11 [y] Jn 12:31
16:12 [z] Mk 4:33
16:13 [a] Jn 14:17 [b] Jn 14:26

16 "All this[m] I have told you so that
you will not fall away.[n] 2 They will
put you out of the synagogue;[o] in fact, the
time is coming when anyone who kills you
will think they are offering a service to
God.[p] 3 They will do such things because
they have not known the Father or me.[q] 4 I
have told you this, so that when their time
comes you will remember[r] that I warned
you about them. I did not tell you this
from the beginning because I was with
you, 5 but now I am going to him who sent
me.[s] None of you asks me, 'Where are you
going?'[t] 6 Rather, you are filled with grief
because I have said these things. 7 But very
truly I tell you, it is for your good that I
am going away. Unless I go away, the Advocate[u] will not come to you; but if I go,
I will send him to you.[v] 8 When he comes,
he will prove the world to be in the wrong
about sin and righteousness and judgment: 9 about sin,[w] because people do not
believe in me; 10 about righteousness,[x] because I am going to the Father, where you
can see me no longer; 11 and about judgment, because the prince of this world[y]
now stands condemned.
12 "I have much more to say to you,
more than you can now bear.[z] 13 But when
he, the Spirit of truth,[a] comes, he will
guide you into all the truth.[b] He will not
speak on his own; he will speak only what
he hears, and he will tell you what is yet
to come. 14 He will glorify me because it is

a 20 John 13:16 *b 25* Psalms 35:19; 69:4

15:18 *it hated me first.* Comparison was a major feature of ancient elaboration; Jesus turns from the subject of love in God's community to that of hatred in the world's. In the Mediterranean world, friendship (vv. 13 – 15) normally entailed also being an enemy to a friend's enemies. Jesus does not imply that we should hate the world or treat it as an enemy; the point instead is the world's enmity toward Jesus: those who hate him will also hate his friends.
15:22 *now they have no excuse.* Jewish teachers recognized that knowing the truth increased one's moral responsibility.
15:25 *They hated me without reason.* Quoted from Ps 69:4. The context, as in some other psalms, addresses the righteous who suffer (cf. Jn 2:17).
15:26 *the Advocate ... will testify about me.* The term "testify" was by now used beyond judicial settings, but a judicial image here would fit "Advocate" (see note on 14:16) and a possible image of prosecution in 16:8 – 11.
15:27 Empowerment by the Spirit (v. 26) and testifying are also linked in Isaiah (Isa 42:1; 43:10 – 12; 44:3,8).
16:2 *put you out of the synagogue ... kills you.* Other sources confirm that Jesus did envision ostracism for his name's sake (Lk 6:22), but John's repeated emphasis on this point was probably relevant to his original audience (cf. Jn 12:42; see note on 9:34). Jewish persecutors may have modeled their persecution of Jesus' followers on Phinehas's zeal to appease God's anger (Nu 25:7 – 11; Ps 106:30 – 31); some Jewish groups had earlier persecuted other Jewish groups (reported by Josephus, in the Dead Sea Scrolls, and by later rabbis). Although we read of some deadly violence against Jesus' followers from fellow Jews (Ac 7:58 – 60; cf. Ac 9:1; 1Th 2:14 – 15), it was not the norm. Some scholars think, however, that the expulsion of Jewish believers in Jesus from local synagogues may have sometimes generated the same effect (cf. Rev 2:9 – 10). Without the protection of being recognized as part of the Jewish community, believers in Jesus, on this view, could lose their exemption from the imperial cult and (in some communities) be subject to charges of disloyalty to the state. Direct fatal persecution probably came and was expected to come especially from Gentiles (Rev 2:13; 13:15).
16:7 *Advocate.* See note on 14:16. Here the Spirit comes to believers, and thus in vv. 8 – 11 may work through the believers' proclamation of Jesus as the Spirit had once worked through the prophets (Ne 9:30).
16:8 *he will prove.* Ancient speakers and writers could lay out the points they would cover, as here, before elaborating them (as in vv. 7 – 11). Those who view the context as forensic (see notes on 14:17; 15:26) can view the conviction here as a sort of prosecution. The OT occasionally depicts God as Advocate for his people and consequently the one who enacts justice against their enemies (Jer 50:34; 51:36; La 3:58 – 59,64).
16:13 *the Spirit of truth.* See note on 14:17. *guide you into all the truth.* Lit., "in all the truth"; the psalmist prayed for God to lead him in truth (Ps 25:5), probably meaning God's faithfulness (Ps 86:11), though "truth" here in Jn 16:13 undoubtedly relates to Jesus (14:6). *only what he*

from me that he will receive what he will
make known to you. 15All that belongs to
the Father is mine.[c] That is why I said the
Spirit will receive from me what he will
make known to you."

The Disciples' Grief Will Turn to Joy

16Jesus went on to say, "In a little while[d]
you will see me no more, and then after a
little while you will see me."[e]
17At this, some of his disciples said to
one another, "What does he mean by saying, 'In a little while you will see me no
more, and then after a little while you will
see me,'[f] and 'Because I am going to the
Father'?"[g] 18They kept asking, "What does
he mean by 'a little while'? We don't understand what he is saying."
19Jesus saw that they wanted to ask him
about this, so he said to them, "Are you
asking one another what I meant when I
said, 'In a little while you will see me no
more, and then after a little while you will
see me'? 20Very truly I tell you, you will
weep and mourn[h] while the world rejoices. You will grieve, but your grief will turn
to joy.[i] 21A woman giving birth to a child
has pain[j] because her time has come; but
when her baby is born she forgets the anguish because of her joy that a child is born
into the world. 22So with you: Now is your
time of grief,[k] but I will see you again[l] and
you will rejoice, and no one will take away
your joy. 23In that day you will no longer
ask me anything. Very truly I tell you, my
Father will give you whatever you ask in
my name.[m] 24Until now you have not asked
for anything in my name. Ask and you will
receive, and your joy will be complete.[n]
25"Though I have been speaking figuratively,[o] a time is coming[p] when I will no
longer use this kind of language but will
tell you plainly about my Father. 26In that
day you will ask in my name.[q] I am not
saying that I will ask the Father on your
behalf. 27No, the Father himself loves you
because you have loved me[r] and have believed that I came from God. 28I came from
the Father and entered the world; now I
am leaving the world and going back to
the Father."[s]
29Then Jesus' disciples said, "Now you
are speaking clearly and without figures of
speech.[t] 30Now we can see that you know
all things and that you do not even need
to have anyone ask you questions. This
makes us believe that you came from God."
31"Do you now believe?" Jesus replied.
32"A time is coming[u] and in fact has come
when you will be scattered,[v] each to your
own home. You will leave me all alone. Yet
I am not alone, for my Father is with me.[w]
33"I have told you these things, so that
in me you may have peace.[x] In this world
you will have trouble.[y] But take heart! I
have overcome[z] the world."

Jesus Prays to Be Glorified

17 After Jesus said this, he looked toward heaven[a] and prayed:
"Father, the hour has come. Glorify
your Son, that your Son may glorify
you.[b] 2For you granted him authority over all people that he might give
eternal life to all those you have given
him.[c] 3Now this is eternal life: that
they know you, the only true God,
and Jesus Christ, whom you have
sent.[d] 4I have brought you glory[e] on

16:15 [c] Jn 17:10 **16:16** [d] Jn 7:33 [e] Jn 14:18-24 **16:17** [f] ver 16 [g] ver 5 **16:20** [h] Lk 23:27 [i] Jn 20:20 **16:21** [j] Isa 26:17; 1Th 5:3 **16:22** [k] ver 6 [l] ver 16 **16:23** [m] Mt 7:7; Jn 15:16 **16:24** [n] Jn 3:29; 15:11

16:25 [o] Mt 13:34; Jn 10:6 [p] ver 2 **16:26** [q] ver 23, 24 **16:27** [r] Jn 14:21,23 **16:28** [s] Jn 13:3 **16:29** [t] ver 25 **16:32** [u] ver 2, 25 [v] Mt 26:31 [w] Jn 8:16,29 **16:33** [x] Jn 14:27 [y] Jn 15:18-21 [z] Ro 8:37; 1Jn 4:4 **17:1** [a] Jn 11:41 [b] Jn 12:23; 13:31,32 **17:2** [c] ver 6, 9,24; Da 7:14; Jn 6:37,39 **17:3** [d] ver 8, 18,21,23,25; Jn 3:17 **17:4** [e] Jn 13:31

---

hears. Probably involves speaking what is on the Lord's heart, as Jesus did regarding the Father (see note on 15:15); the Spirit was often connected with prophetic inspiration, so this presumably involves enabling believers to continue to hear the Lord's voice. *what is yet to come.* Might involve the prophetic dimension of the Spirit's work (e.g., Nu 11:25–26; 1Sa 10:6,10); among others, Jewish apocalyptic writers were interested in matters to come.

16:15 *All that belongs to the Father is mine.* One commonly cited ideal in antiquity was that "friends share all things in common"; friends also shared their hearts (cf. v. 13; 15:15).

16:16,17,18 *a little while.* In Isaiah, "a little while" (Isa 26:20) appears in the context of figurative childbirth (Isa 26:17–18) and the raising of the dead (Isa 26:19), as here (Jn 16:21).

16:21 *giving birth ... has pain.* Everyone recognized that birth pangs were severe; it was one of the most common Biblical images for suffering (e.g., Isa 13:8), applied even to ancient Jewish images of the end time. See also note on Jn 16:16,17,18.

16:22 *I will see you again and you will rejoice.* Possibly Jesus alludes to an image in Isaiah: Zion births the restored Jerusalem (Isa 66:8), and they "see" and "will rejoice" (Isa 66:14).

16:23–24 See notes on 14:12–14.

16:25 *I have been speaking figuratively.* Like many sages, Jesus often speaks in riddles.

16:32 *you will be scattered.* When their leader died or failed to shepherd God's people, the people were often scattered (1Ki 22:17; Eze 34:5–6; Zec 13:7).

17:1–26 Writers and speakers often summarized key themes at the end of a section or work; Jewish sources often report a dying figure's final advice to his children or followers; and in genuine farewell speeches people in general could emphasize key advice before dying or departing. This prayer of Jesus to the Father pulls together many important themes from Jesus' teaching found throughout John's Gospel.

17:1 *toward heaven.* Looking up was a common posture in prayer. *hour.* See note on 12:23. *Glorify.* See notes on 12:23,41,43.

17:2 *authority ... eternal life.* Both eternal life and eternal authority belonged to the future age (cf. Da 7:13–14; 12:2). Those who believe in Jesus recognize that the climactic future era of promise has already begun (cf. Ps 110:1–2).

17:3 *that they know you, the only true God, and Jesus Christ.* For knowing God in a covenant relationship, see note on 10:14–15; for life dependent on divine life, cf. note on 15:4.

earth by finishing the work you gave me to do.[f] 5And now, Father, glorify me in your presence with the glory I had with you[g] before the world began.[h]

Jesus Prays for His Disciples

6"I have revealed you[a][i] to those whom you gave me[j] out of the world. They were yours; you gave them to me and they have obeyed your word. 7Now they know that everything you have given me comes from you. 8For I gave them the words you gave me[k] and they accepted them. They knew with certainty that I came from you,[l] and they believed that you sent me.[m] 9I pray for them.[n] I am not praying for the world, but for those you have given me, for they are yours. 10All I have is yours, and all you have is mine.[o] And glory has come to me through them. 11I will remain in the world no longer, but they are still in the world,[p] and I am coming to you.[q] Holy Father, protect them by the power of[b] your name, the name you gave me, so that they may be one[r] as we are one.[s] 12While I was with them, I protected them and kept them safe by[c] that name you gave me. None has been lost[t] except the one doomed to destruction[u] so that Scripture would be fulfilled.

13"I am coming to you now, but I say these things while I am still in the world, so that they may have the full measure of my joy[v] within them. 14I have given them your word and the world has hated them,[w] for they are not of the world any more than I am of the world.[x] 15My prayer is not that you take them out of the world but that you protect them from the evil one.[y] 16They are not of the world, even as I am not of it.[z] 17Sanctify them by[d] the truth; your word is truth.[a] 18As you sent me into the world,[b] I have sent them into the world.[c] 19For them I sanctify myself, that they too may be truly sanctified.

Jesus Prays for All Believers

20"My prayer is not for them alone. I pray also for those who will believe in me through their message, 21that all of them may be one, Father, just as you are in me and I am in you.[d] May they also be in us so that the world may believe that you have sent me.[e] 22I have given them the glory that you gave me, that they may be one as we are one[f]— 23I in them and you in me—so that they may be brought to complete unity. Then the world will know that you sent me[g] and have loved them[h] even as you have loved me.

24"Father, I want those you have given me to be with me where I am,[i] and to see my glory,[j] the glory you have given me because you loved me before the creation of the world.[k]

25"Righteous Father, though the world does not know you,[l] I know you, and they know that you have sent me.[m] 26I have made you[a] known to them,[n] and will continue to make you known in order that the love you have for me may be in them[o] and that I myself may be in them."

17:4 [f] Jn 4:34 **17:5** [g] Php 2:6 [h] Jn 1:2 **17:6** [i] ver 26 [j] ver 2; Jn 6:37, 39 **17:8** [k] ver 14, 26 [l] Jn 16:27 [m] ver 3, 18, 21, 23, 25; Jn 3:17 **17:9** [n] Lk 22:32 **17:10** [o] Jn 16:15 **17:11** [p] Jn 13:1 [q] Jn 7:33 [r] ver 21-23 [s] Jn 10:30 **17:12** [t] Jn 6:39 [u] Jn 6:70 **17:13** [v] Jn 3:29 **17:14** [w] Jn 15:19 [x] Jn 8:23 **17:15** [y] Mt 5:37 **17:16** [z] ver 14 **17:17** [a] Jn 15:3 **17:18** [b] ver 3, 8, 21, 23, 25 [c] Jn 20:21 **17:21** [d] Jn 10:38 [e] ver 3, 8, 18, 23, 25; Jn 3:17 **17:22** [f] Jn 14:20 **17:23** [g] Jn 3:17 [h] Jn 16:27 **17:24** [i] Jn 12:26 [j] Jn 1:14 [k] ver 5; Mt 25:34 **17:25** [l] Jn 15:21; 16:3 [m] ver 3, 8, 18, 21, 23; Jn 3:17; 7:29; 16:27 **17:26** [n] ver 6 [o] Jn 15:9

[a] 6,26 Greek *your name* [b] 11 Or *Father, keep them faithful to* [c] 12 Or *kept them faithful to* [d] 17 Or *them to live in accordance with*

17:5 *glorify me in your presence.* Moses reflected God's glory (Ex 34:29–35), but Jesus reflects God's glory in a greater sense, closer to the way that Jewish thought often applied to divine Wisdom (cf. Wisdom of Solomon 7:25–27). He shared the Father's glory before the world began. On Jesus' preexistence, see notes on Jn 1:1; 8:58. Wisdom was held to exist before the world, but because God does not share his glory with another (Isa 42:8; 48:11), such language implies Jesus' deity.
17:6 *I have revealed you.* Lit. "I have revealed your name," but the sense is close to what appears in the NIV. Revealing God's name included revealing his character (Ex 33:19; 34:5,14). Many Jewish people prayed daily for God's name to be shown holy in all the world and thus honored, as the prophets had promised.
17:8 *I gave them the words you gave me.* Some Jewish hearers might think of how Moses revealed God's words; but Jesus is greater than Moses (cf. note on v. 5).
17:10 *All I have is yours.* Ideally those who were intimate shared everything; it also expressed commitment to act in concert (1Ki 22:4; 2Ki 3:7).
17:12 *the one doomed to destruction.* Lit., "the son of destruction," but the NIV correctly renders this idiom. The Psalms often speak of the enemies of the righteous sufferer perishing (e.g., Ps 9:3; 37:20); the betraying friend of Ps 41:9 would also not triumph (Ps 41:11).
17:15 *not that you take them out of the world.* Some groups, such as some Essenes, probably the group responsible for the major Dead Sea Scrolls, physically withdrew from the world into the wilderness. Jesus instead prays for protection for his people (as Jewish people often did).
17:17 *Sanctify...your word is truth.* God's word is truth (Ps 119:142,160), and Jewish tradition declared that God had consecrated (sanctified) Israel, separating them from the rest of the world, by giving them his law.
17:22 *I have given them the glory.* God was glorified or honored by his glory or honor among his people (Isa 44:23; 46:13; 49:3; 55:5; 60:1–2).
17:23 *complete unity.* Division was common in ancient politics and life; unity was a common exhortation. *loved them.* Jewish people celebrated God's special love for his people, a love here applied to all believers (v. 20).

Jesus Arrested

18:3-11pp — Mt 26:47-56; Mk 14:43-50; Lk 22:47-53

18 When he had finished praying, Jesus left with his disciples and crossed the Kidron Valley.[p] On the other side there was a garden,[q] and he and his disciples went into it.[r]

2Now Judas, who betrayed him, knew the place, because Jesus had often met there with his disciples.[s] 3So Judas came to the garden, guiding[t] a detachment of soldiers and some officials from the chief priests and the Pharisees.[u] They were carrying torches, lanterns and weapons.

4Jesus, knowing all that was going to happen to him,[v] went out and asked them, "Who is it you want?"[w]

5"Jesus of Nazareth," they replied.

"I am he," Jesus said. (And Judas the traitor was standing there with them.) 6When Jesus said, "I am he," they drew back and fell to the ground.

7Again he asked them, "Who is it you want?"[x]

"Jesus of Nazareth," they said.

8Jesus answered, "I told you that I am he. If you are looking for me, then let these men go." 9This happened so that the words he had spoken would be fulfilled: "I have not lost one of those you gave me."[a][y]

10Then Simon Peter, who had a sword, drew it and struck the high priest's servant, cutting off his right ear. (The servant's name was Malchus.)

11Jesus commanded Peter, "Put your sword away! Shall I not drink the cup[z] the Father has given me?"

12Then the detachment of soldiers with its commander and the Jewish officials[a] arrested Jesus. They bound him 13and brought him first to Annas, who was the father-in-law of Caiaphas,[b] the high priest that year. 14Caiaphas was the one who had advised the Jewish leaders that it would be good if one man died for the people.[c]

Peter's First Denial

18:16-18pp — Mt 26:69,70; Mk 14:66-68; Lk 22:55-57

15Simon Peter and another disciple were following Jesus. Because this disciple was known to the high priest,[d] he went with Jesus into the high priest's courtyard,[e] 16but Peter had to wait outside at the door. The other disciple, who was known to the high priest, came back, spoke to the servant girl on duty there and brought Peter in.

17"You aren't one of this man's disciples too, are you?" she asked Peter.

18:1 [p] 2Sa 15:23 [q] ver 26 [r] Mt 26:36 **18:2** [s] Lk 21:37; 22:39 **18:3** [t] Ac 1:16 [u] ver 12 **18:4** [v] Jn 6:64; 13:1,11 [w] ver 7 **18:7** [x] ver 4 **18:9** [y] Jn 17:12 **18:11** [z] Mt 20:22 **18:12** [a] ver 3 **18:13** [b] ver 24; Mt 26:3 **18:14** [c] Jn 11:49-51 **18:15** [d] Mt 26:3 [e] Mt 26:58; Mk 14:54; Lk 22:54

[a] 9 John 6:39

18:1 — 19:42 When ancient biographers wrote about a person whose death was significant (e.g., a martyr), they generally devoted significant space to recounting the person's death.
18:1 *crossed the Kidron Valley.* Rainy season filled the Kidron brook, but at this time of year it was merely an easily crossed ravine.
18:3 *detachment of soldiers and some officials.* Because the military terminology in this context (e.g., the Greek term translated "detachment" here) was often used for Roman military units, some scholars believe that the arrest force is Roman. Others counter that the same terminology appears for Jewish units; that the group is led by chief priests and Pharisees; that Roman soldiers would not have escorted Jesus for interrogation by Annas (v. 13), whom a Roman governor had deposed from office; and that Pilate seems initially unfamiliar with the charges and arrest (vv. 29,31). On this latter view, these are probably members of the Levite police, as in the other Gospels (see note on Mk 14:43). *torches, lanterns and weapons.* Groups traveling at night carried torches or lanterns, but not everyone in the group would need to carry them.
18:5 *I am he.* The Greek phrase used here can also be rendered, "I am" (see note on 8:24), which declares Jesus' deity (Ex 3:14; see note on Jn 8:58).
18:6 *drew back and fell to the ground.* If the guards had heard of Jesus' power and thought of him as a dangerous sorcerer, they may have fallen back in fear; they might know the Jewish tradition that Pharaoh fell when Moses pronounced the divine name. Beyond this, both Scripture (1Sa 19:24; Eze 1:28; Da 10:9) and subsequent history offer examples of people overwhelmed by God's majesty or whose nervous systems were so overcome, often with terror at God's presence, that they fell down.
18:8 *let these men go.* If followers were unarmed, authorities sometimes chose to stop movements by arresting the leader; disillusioned followers would normally scatter afterward, as here.
18:10 *high priest's servant.* A personal servant of the high priest could wield much authority, including over the temple police if this was included in his instructions.
18:11 *the cup.* See note on Mk 14:36.
18:12 – 24 On the trial narratives, see the article "Jesus' Trial," p. 1672.
18:12 *commander.* If over the temple guard, cf. note on Ac 4:1.
18:13 *Annas ... father-in-law of Caiaphas.* Annas was not only the father-in-law of Caiaphas but also the father of five sons, all of whom became high priests in the first century. Annas had held the office himself from AD 6 through 15, when the Roman governor replaced him (against Jewish custom), but through his family he continued to influence local politics until he died in AD 35. Surviving sources from other Jewish circles view him negatively. Ancient legal ethics looked down on interrogating a prisoner in one's home, but the hearing for more official purposes will come later (v. 24). *that year.* On Caiaphas and his priesthood "that year," see note on 11:49.
18:15 *courtyard.* See note on Lk 22:55. Servants guarded the gates in outer walls of ample homes; the wealthiest, such as eminent members of the high priestly family, would have servants whose regular duties included watching the gate. Visitors unfamiliar to the gatekeeper would arouse more suspicion, particularly at night and if their clothing showed that they did not belong to the Levite guards or to households of the elite. Guards would normally screen out visitors of lower social station from this prominent home, and those of lower social station would normally not expect to be admitted.

He replied, "I am not."[f]
18 It was cold, and the servants and officials stood around a fire[g] they had made
to keep warm. Peter also was standing
with them, warming himself.[h]

The High Priest Questions Jesus

18:19-24pp — Mt 26:59-68; Mk 14:55-65; Lk 22:63-71

19 Meanwhile, the high priest questioned
Jesus about his disciples and his teaching.
20 "I have spoken openly to the world,"
Jesus replied. "I always taught in synagogues[i] or at the temple,[j] where all the
Jews come together. I said nothing in secret.[k] 21 Why question me? Ask those who
heard me. Surely they know what I said."
22 When Jesus said this, one of the officials[l] nearby slapped him in the face.[m] "Is
this the way you answer the high priest?"
he demanded.
23 "If I said something wrong," Jesus replied, "testify as to what is wrong. But if I
spoke the truth, why did you strike me?"[n]
24 Then Annas sent him bound to Caiaphas[o] the high priest.

Peter's Second and Third Denials

18:25-27pp — Mt 26:71-75; Mk 14:69-72; Lk 22:58-62

25 Meanwhile, Simon Peter was still
standing there warming himself.[p] So they
asked him, "You aren't one of his disciples
too, are you?"
He denied it, saying, "I am not."[q]
26 One of the high priest's servants, a
relative of the man whose ear Peter had
cut off,[r] challenged him, "Didn't I see you
with him in the garden?"[s] 27 Again Peter
denied it, and at that moment a rooster
began to crow.[t]

Jesus Before Pilate

18:29-40pp — Mt 27:11-18,20-23; Mk 15:2-15; Lk 23:2,3,18-25

28 Then the Jewish leaders took Jesus
from Caiaphas to the palace of the Roman
governor.[u] By now it was early morning,
and to avoid ceremonial uncleanness they
did not enter the palace,[v] because they
wanted to be able to eat the Passover.[w]
29 So Pilate came out to them and asked,
"What charges are you bringing against
this man?"
30 "If he were not a criminal," they replied, "we would not have handed him
over to you."
31 Pilate said, "Take him yourselves and
judge him by your own law."
"But we have no right to execute anyone," they objected. 32 This took place to
fulfill what Jesus had said about the kind
of death he was going to die.[x]

18:17 [f] ver 25 **18:18** [g] Jn 21:9 [h] Mk 14:54,67 **18:20** [i] Mt 4:23 [j] Mt 26:55 [k] Jn 7:26 **18:22** [l] ver 3 [m] Mt 16:21; Jn 19:3 **18:23** [n] Mt 5:39; Ac 23:2-5 **18:24** [o] ver 13; Mt 26:3 **18:25** [p] ver 18 [q] ver 17 **18:26** [r] ver 10 [s] ver 1 **18:27** [t] Jn 13:38 **18:28** [u] Mt 27:2; Mk 15:1; Lk 23:1 [v] ver 33; Jn 19:9 [w] Jn 11:55 **18:32** [x] Mt 20:19; 26:2; Jn 3:14; 8:28; 12:32,33

18:18 *It was cold.* Given its elevation, Jerusalem can be cool at night in April.
18:20 *said nothing in secret.* Those whose teachings were secretive were considered subversive. Teachings of those who taught in public were also easily verifiable by numerous witnesses (a key issue in the much later debate between Gnostics, who claimed unverifiable secret traditions from the first apostles, and mainstream Christians, who appealed to early and public attestation for their beliefs).
18:22 *slapped him in the face.* A blow to the cheek functioned as a severe insult in antiquity. God's servants sometimes experienced this (1Ki 22:24; 2Ch 18:23).
18:23 *But if I spoke the truth, why did you strike me?* By all ancient official approaches to legal ethics, it is Jesus' captors, not Jesus himself, who are transgressing, as Jesus points out. Interrogation in a private home at night without prior notice of a hearing violated legal ideals; striking an unconvicted prisoner was even more problematic.
18:25 *He denied it.* A disciple's denial would shame the teacher. Because many ancient hearers would feel that such behavior reflected badly not only on this important disciple but also on Jesus who chose him, nearly all scholars agree that ancient Christians would never have invented such a story.
18:27 *rooster began to crow.* See note on 13:38.
18:28 *palace.* The splendid palace of Herod the Great, used by governors when they came to Jerusalem during festivals to prevent unrest. *early morning.* See note on Mt 27:1. *to avoid ceremonial uncleanness they did not enter the palace.* Because worshipers of other gods were deemed ritually unclean, religiously strict Judeans would not enter their homes; to do so would render the Judeans themselves too impure to eat the Passover (or to eat unleavened bread the next day, on a different chronology; by this period many people blended Passover with the Festival of Unleavened Bread; see the article "The Synoptic Passover Meal Versus John's Passover Lamb," p. 1849). Archaeology demonstrates that the chief priests were indeed scrupulous about ritual purity.
18:29 *Pilate came out to them.* See note on v. 28. An urgent threat to peace invited the governor to intervene directly and militarily, but under normal circumstances the governor would wait for accusers to bring charges. Discovering and charging those who subverted public order was especially the duty of local elites.
18:31 *judge him by your own law.* Governors normally refused jurisdiction over charges that were not offenses under Roman law, including violation of local religious customs. Such offenses were to be tried by local courts. The governor's decision was necessary in capital cases, however; throughout the provinces, Rome normally reserved for its own officials the right to pronounce death sentences, thereby preventing locals from harming those possibly loyal to Rome. Pilate, who was governor of Judea from AD 26 to 36, was known for not cooperating with the Judean elite except in cases where the fallout from not cooperating would be too great (as in 19:12 – 15). At about this time, e.g., Pilate minted a coin with a pagan image that offended Judea's Jewish residents. Many scholars suggest that Sejanus, the praetorian prefect who ran Rome for Tiberius, was Pilate's patron; if this surmise is true, Pilate's position was relatively secure until Sejanus's disgrace and execution in AD 31. After that Pilate would have needed to act more cautiously.
18:32 *the kind of death.* Ancient Jewish law decreed stoning for blasphemy, but a Roman execution for treason warranted the slow public death involved in crucifixion. Cf. note on 12:32.

JOHN 18

The Synoptic Passover Meal Versus John's Passover Lamb

In the Synoptic Gospels, the Last Supper is a Passover meal that Jesus uses to explain the meaning of his death on the coming afternoon. In John, Jesus apparently dies during the sacrificing of lambs in the temple, before the Passover meal at sundown (Jn 13:1,29; 18:28). Scholars have connected the chronologies of John and the Synoptics at this point in different ways. Some suggest that Jesus held a Passover meal with his disciples one evening early, whether because he would be dead by the next evening or because they followed an existing sectarian calendar, or for both reasons. Various Jewish sects did differ from one another regarding the correct dates of festivals, although lambs would be available in the temple only on the day leading up to Passover evening.

Others suggest that John is more interested in narrative symbolism than are the Synoptics, and thus skips Jesus' symbolic interpretation about Passover (John omits almost all description of the Last Supper; cf. also 6:53) and narrates Jesus' death directly as the Passover lamb (cf. 1:29; 1Co 5:7). Although the latter approach is not typical in ancient biographies, it might fit a pattern in how John relates specifically to the widely known passion narrative. Here Jesus gives Judas the bread (Jn 13:26), rather than Judas simply dipping with him (Mk 14:20); here Jesus carries his own cross (Jn 19:17), rather than Simon carrying it for him (Mk 15:21). Jesus lays down his life; no one takes it from him (Jn 10:18). Because early Christians already heard one approach to the passion story, John might deliberately focus on another approach that highlighted more of the story's meaning. Biographers were allowed to rearrange and conflate events. In Jewish usage in John's day, the entire festival of unleavened bread that followed the Passover proper remained the "Passover," but John might frame his wording in such a way as to make a powerful point, reemphasizing that Jesus is truly the lamb who takes away the sin of the world (1:29,36). ◆

33Pilate then went back inside the palace,[y] summoned Jesus and asked him,
"Are you the king of the Jews?"[z]
34"Is that your own idea," Jesus asked,
"or did others talk to you about me?"
35"Am I a Jew?" Pilate replied. "Your
own people and chief priests handed you
over to me. What is it you have done?"
36Jesus said, "My kingdom[a] is not of
this world. If it were, my servants would
fight to prevent my arrest by the Jewish
leaders.[b] But now my kingdom is from another place."[c]
37"You are a king, then!" said Pilate.
Jesus answered, "You say that I am a
king. In fact, the reason I was born and
came into the world is to testify to the
truth.[d] Everyone on the side of truth listens to me."[e]
38"What is truth?" retorted Pilate. With
this he went out again to the Jews gathered there and said, "I find no basis for a

18:33 [y] ver 28, 29; Jn 19:9 [z] Lk 23:3; Mt 2:2 **18:36** [a] Mt 3:2 [b] Mt 26:53 [c] Lk 17:21; Jn 6:15 **18:37** [d] Jn 3:32 [e] Jn 8:47; 1Jn 4:6

18:33 *Are you the king of the Jews?* As governor, Pilate had complete freedom in the case, but proper procedure was normally to inquire into the charges. The charge in this case is that Jesus claimed to be "king of the Jews"—a title that, if not bestowed by the emperor, constituted treason, a capital offense.

18:35 *Your own people and chief priests handed you over.* Roman infrastructure in the provinces was limited; Rome depended on local elites to charge subversives.

18:36 *My kingdom is not of this world.* Rome's concern was with military and political threats—not with idealistic sages. From Rome, Pilate undoubtedly knew of the many apolitical sages (especially Cynics) who taught their followers how to "reign" in life as if "kings" yet were deemed by the elite as curiosities or laughable rather than relevant to the political order. They spoke about truth but proved harmless. To Pilate, Jesus must have seemed such a sage.

charge against him.[f] 39But it is your custom for me to release to you one prisoner
at the time of the Passover. Do you want
me to release 'the king of the Jews'?"
40They shouted back, "No, not him!
Give us Barabbas!" Now Barabbas had
taken part in an uprising.[g]

Jesus Sentenced to Be Crucified

19:1-16pp — Mt 27:27-31; Mk 15:16-20

19 Then Pilate took Jesus and had him
flogged.[h] 2The soldiers twisted together a crown of thorns and put it on his
head. They clothed him in a purple robe
3and went up to him again and again, saying, "Hail, king of the Jews!"[i] And they
slapped him in the face.[j]
4Once more Pilate came out and said
to the Jews gathered there, "Look, I am
bringing him out[k] to you to let you know
that I find no basis for a charge against
him."[l] 5When Jesus came out wearing the
crown of thorns and the purple robe,[m] Pilate said to them, "Here is the man!"
6As soon as the chief priests and their
officials saw him, they shouted, "Crucify!
Crucify!"
But Pilate answered, "You take him and
crucify him.[n] As for me, I find no basis for
a charge against him."[o]
7The Jewish leaders insisted, "We have
a law, and according to that law he must
die,[p] because he claimed to be the Son of
God."[q]
8When Pilate heard this, he was even
more afraid, 9and he went back inside the
palace.[r] "Where do you come from?" he
asked Jesus, but Jesus gave him no answer.[s] 10"Do you refuse to speak to me?"
Pilate said. "Don't you realize I have power either to free you or to crucify you?"
11Jesus answered, "You would have no
power over me if it were not given to you
from above.[t] Therefore the one who handed me over to you[u] is guilty of a greater
sin."
12From then on, Pilate tried to set Jesus
free, but the Jewish leaders kept shouting, "If you let this man go, you are no
friend of Caesar. Anyone who claims to be
a king[v] opposes Caesar."

18:38 [f] Lk 23:4; Jn 19:4,6 **18:40** [g] Ac 3:14 **19:1** [h] Dt 25:3; Isa 50:6; 53:5; Mt 27:26 **19:3** [i] Mt 27:29 [j] Jn 18:22 **19:4** [k] Jn 18:38 [l] ver 6; Lk 23:4 **19:5** [m] ver 2

19:6 [n] Ac 3:13 [o] ver 4; Lk 23:4 **19:7** [p] Lev 24:16 [q] Mt 26:63-66; Jn 5:18; 10:33 **19:9** [r] Jn 18:33 [s] Mk 14:61 **19:11** [t] Ro 13:1 [u] Jn 18:28-30; Ac 3:13 **19:12** [v] Lk 23:2

18:39 *it is your custom.* Governors were free to follow or disregard precedent, but they often retained popular precedents. Most provincial customs, including this one, are unattested, but this custom is not at all unlikely; similar customs are attested elsewhere. Given Jesus' title, Pilate probably expects him to prove more popular than the other prisoners.
18:40 *had taken part in an uprising.* This phrase reflects a Greek term that can mean simply "robber" (as in 10:1) or can mean, as often in Josephus, a revolutionary (Mk 15:7). Some scholars suggest that some robbers may have been both — part of a marauding band in the countryside that also resisted oppressive elites.
19:1 *had him flogged.* Although flogging was sometimes a punishment by itself, it also normally preceded execution. First, the victim would be stripped naked and tied to a post; then soldiers would beat the victim, sometimes until bones or internal organs were visible. For provincials such as Jesus, the soldiers would probably use a leather whip with sharp metal or bone woven into the ends.
19:2 Ridiculing and abusing prisoners was common. *crown of thorns.* Imitating Hellenistic garlands, the soldiers may have intended the thorns to point especially outward, but some of the thorns would nevertheless turn inward, scraping the scalp. *clothed him in a purple robe.* Soldiers wore red cloaks, but when faded the cloak could resemble "purple," like the cloaks of Hellenistic princes. See note on Mk 15:17.
19:3 *Hail.* A common address to rulers and equivalent to the Latin *Ave.* Most of Rome's soldiers in Jerusalem were Syrian auxiliaries; in many locations, Syrians and Jews often clashed. In ridiculing the "king of the Jews," the soldiers probably also mock Jewish people more generally.
19:4 *I find no basis for a charge.* A governor's verdict would be final — unless political considerations demanded otherwise (v. 12).
19:5 *Here is the man!* Ironically, Pilate unwittingly echoes how God introduced Israel's first king to Samuel (1Sa 9:17).
19:6 *I find no basis for a charge against him.* Pilate was not known for cooperating with Judeans, for whose customs he had little patience. Everyone knew that only Pilate could legally give the death sentence (18:31).
19:7 *We have a law … he must die.* False prophets could be executed under Biblical law (Dt 18:20), and this should have included false claims to be the Messiah; but Rome did not permit Jewish courts to execute capital punishment. Ultimately neither Scripture nor Jewish tradition made Messianic claims a capital offense, since someone might in fact prove to be the Messiah someday (Pharisees and most people hoped for a Messiah, although the Sadducean priests may not have done so). Roman concerns about order, however, made any royal claims a capital offense (cf. vv. 12,15). Ironically, Biblical law supported Jesus rather than demanding his death (5:45 – 46; 15:25). *claimed to be the Son of God.* God called Israel his children (e.g., Ex 4:22); he also called members of David's line his son (2Sa 7:14), particularly with regard to the ultimate Davidic ruler, the Messiah (cf. Ps 2:7).
19:8 *he was even more afraid.* Ironically, Pilate the polytheist takes the claim of Jesus' divine origin more seriously than do Jesus' accusers.
19:9 *Jesus gave him no answer.* Jewish people often respected martyrs who refused to answer their accusers.
19:10 *I have power … to free … or to crucify.* Under Roman law, Pilate could make whatever decision concerning Jesus he thought best.
19:11 *from above.* Often a Jewish way of speaking about God (cf. 3:3). Jesus seems to imply that Caiaphas, "who handed [Jesus] over to [Pilate]" (see 18:28), had illegitimate authority. In fact, Caiaphas did not inherit his office the Biblically-prescribed way, but was installed in his office by the Roman governor Gratus, because Gratus believed Caiaphas would work well with Rome.
19:12 *no friend of Caesar.* Subordinate "friends" of patrons owed them honor in return for favors. "Friend of the emperor" was an especially desirable title sometimes given in this period also to clients of Sejanus, though it could also be used figuratively here. The most dangerous charge under the current emperor, the paranoid Tiberius, was treason.

13When Pilate heard this, he brought
Jesus out and sat down on the judge's
seat[w] at a place known as the Stone Pavement (which in Aramaic[x] is Gabbatha).
14It was the day of Preparation[y] of the
Passover; it was about noon.[z]
"Here is your king,"[a] Pilate said to the
Jews.
15But they shouted, "Take him away!
Take him away! Crucify him!"
"Shall I crucify your king?" Pilate asked.
"We have no king but Caesar," the chief
priests answered.
16Finally Pilate handed him over to
them to be crucified.[b]

The Crucifixion of Jesus

19:17-24pp — Mt 27:33-44; Mk 15:22-32; Lk 23:33-43

So the soldiers took charge of Jesus.
17Carrying his own cross,[c] he went out to
the place of the Skull[d] (which in Aramaic[e]
is called Golgotha). 18There they crucified
him, and with him two others[f] — one on
each side and Jesus in the middle.
19Pilate had a notice prepared and
fastened to the cross. It read: JESUS OF
NAZARETH,[g] THE KING OF THE JEWS.[h] 20Many
of the Jews read this sign, for the place
where Jesus was crucified was near the
city,[i] and the sign was written in Aramaic, Latin and Greek. 21The chief priests of
the Jews protested to Pilate, "Do not write
'The King of the Jews,' but that this man
claimed to be king of the Jews."[j]
22Pilate answered, "What I have written, I have written."
23When the soldiers crucified Jesus,
they took his clothes, dividing them into
four shares, one for each of them, with the
undergarment remaining. This garment
was seamless, woven in one piece from
top to bottom.
24"Let's not tear it," they said to one another. "Let's decide by lot who will get it."
This happened that the scripture might
be fulfilled[k] that said,

> "They divided my clothes among them
> and cast lots for my garment."[a][l]

So this is what the soldiers did.

19:13 [w] Mt 27:19 [x] Jn 5:2 **19:14** [y] Mt 27:62 [z] Mk 15:25 [a] ver 19,21 **19:16** [b] Mt 27:26; Mk 15:15; Lk 23:25 **19:17** [c] Ge 22:6; Lk 14:27; 23:26 [d] Lk 23:33 [e] Jn 5:2 **19:18** [f] Lk 23:32 **19:19** [g] Mk 1:24 [h] ver 14,21 **19:20** [i] Heb 13:12 **19:21** [j] ver 14 **19:24** [k] ver 28, 36,37; Mt 1:22 [l] Ps 22:18

[a] *24* Psalm 22:18

19:13 *judge's seat.* A governor would issue a capital verdict from the judgment seat (see note on Ro 14:10). *Stone Pavement.* Against some earlier proposals, this refers to the elevated paved area near Herod's palace; Pilate spoke to hearers from the platform there also on other occasions.
19:14 *the day of Preparation of the Passover.* The day that lambs were slaughtered in the temple; they would then be eaten during the Passover meal after sundown. John appears to report Jesus delivered and executed when the paschal lambs were being sacrificed, rather than (as in the Synoptics) the day before (see the article "The Synoptic Passover Meal Versus John's Passover Lamb," p. 1849). Some contend that John means simply the day of preparation for the Passover week's Sabbath (which it also was; v. 31; Mk 15:42). *about noon.* Some find in "noon" a connection with 4:6 or an allusion to the alleged time of the Passover offering (though probably the offerings required the full day). Ancient hearers often connected noon especially with bright light and strong heat. *Here is your king.* Ironically, Pilate echoes the acclamation of Zec 9:9 cited in Jn 12:15.
19:15 *We have no king but Caesar.* A daily Jewish prayer requested that God send the Messiah, and another prayer later used in the Passover liturgy affirms that God alone is king. Even aside from the speakers' possible sarcasm here, many Sadducean elite priests probably were more concerned about their future with Rome, which also buttressed their own status, than with the messianic aspirations of a larger segment of their people.
19:16 *Finally Pilate handed him over.* Insistent Judean demands had forced Pilate to give in on other known occasions, such as when Jerusalemites' willingness to die as martyrs compelled him to withdraw the idolatrous Roman standards that he had brought into Jerusalem. He did not take further political risks in those matters in which he had firmer convictions; he would hardly do so for a prisoner. If he followed common procedure, he may have announced, "You will mount the cross."
19:17 *Carrying his own cross.* Normally the condemned person was forced to publicly carry the horizontal beam (the *patibulum*) of his own cross out to the site of his execution. Whereas other Gospels emphasize the failure of Jesus' disciples to help him with the cross, perhaps after he falters, John emphasizes Jesus' own role in carrying his cross (cf. 10:18). *the place of the Skull.* See note on Mk 15:22. The soldiers would have led Jesus from Herod's palace and through the Garden Gate (not following the route enshrined in later tradition). Executions, like burials, were outside the city walls.
19:18 People were crucified naked, on humiliating display as a warning to others. For further details on crucifixion, see note on Mk 15:24.
19:19 *notice.* Sometimes someone would carry a tablet indicating the *titulus*, or charge, against the prisoner, to the site of the execution. *KING OF THE JEWS.* A treason charge — yet, ironically, John's audience knows that Jesus really is king.
19:20 *Many of the Jews read this sign.* Roman executions, like traditional Jewish ones (cf. Lev 24:14, 23; Nu 15:35 – 36; at the city gate, where many would see it, Dt 17:5; 22:24), were outside the city. *Aramaic, Latin and Greek.* Both Aramaic and Greek were in common usage in Israel (the former dominant, e.g., in upper Galilee [northern Galilee], the latter among Jerusalem's elite); Latin was used in the western part of the empire, but also (relevant for Judea) for military inscriptions in the east. (Some key inscriptions even in Jerusalem were in both Latin and Greek.)
19:22 *What I have written, I have written.* Now that the threat of unrest has passed, Pilate is no longer ready to accommodate the local leaders' demands.
19:23 *took his clothes, dividing them.* Divided clothing recalls Ps 22:18 (cited in Jn 19:24; see note there), but also fits historical practice. Roman execution squads (typically about four men) had rights to whatever clothing or other effects remained on the prisoner. *undergarment ... was seamless.* The inner tunic was normally formed by sewing two cloths together; a seamless tunic was thus specially made and valuable.
19:24 *They divided my clothes.* Ps 22:18 also mentions casting lots for one's garment; soldiers used dice and other means to gamble. *lots.* See note on Ac 1:26.

JOHN 19

THE CRUCIFIXION

In the ancient world crucifixion was seen as a particularly disgraceful and grievous form of execution. Assyrian battle reliefs depict a precursor to crucifixion — impaling victims on poles outside the walls of conquered cities. The Persians made widespread use of crucifixion, although sometimes the crucifixion took place only after the victim had been executed by other means (Herodotus, *Histories* 3.125.2 – 3). There are also reports that crucifixion was used by peoples as varied as the Assyrians, Scythians, Celts, Germans, Britons and inhabitants of India, although the reliability of some of these accounts is questionable. Common to most of these cultures was the perspective that crucifixion was a form of execution reserved for the worst offenders, as well as for slaves.

The practice of crucifixion became widespread under Alexander the Great (356 – 323 BC). It became the common form of execution for traitors, defeated armies and rebellious slaves. Later, under the Roman Empire, only non-citizens, lower-class Romans and violent offenders could be crucified. The only possible exceptions were in cases of high treason or desertion during wartime. Slaves were particularly vulnerable to the imposition of crucifixion. Latin literature reflects the dread slaves felt at the prospect of this fate. It was officially accepted as the most painful and disgraceful form of capital punishment, more so than decapitation, being thrown to wild animals or even being burned alive. For these reasons this heinous penalty was often imposed upon foreigners who were seen as threats to Roman rule.

There are also accounts of crucifixion being practiced among Jews. Josephus wrote that the Sadducean high priest Alexander Janneus (in office from 103 to 76 BC) committed the following atrocity against his enemies, the Pharisees: "While dining in a conspicuous place with his concubines, he commanded that about 800 of them be crucified, and while they were still alive before their eyes he had the throats of their children and wives cut" (Josephus, *Antiquities* 13:380).

Victims were often scourged or otherwise tortured prior to crucifixion. Crucifixions were carried out on either a single vertical stake or on a vertical stake with a crossbeam near or on its top. Sometimes blocks were attached to the stake as a seat, footrest or both. Depending upon the presence of these blocks, the victim might linger, alive, for up to three days. The blocks allowed a victim to rest some of his weight, increasing the chance of breathing and proper circulation. Without the blocks a victim's weight would rest totally upon his arms, which were attached to the crosspiece by ropes, nails or both. This would prohibit breathing and circulation and lead to both brain and heart failure. To end the torture, a victim's legs could be broken, after which death would quickly follow. Oftentimes the charge against the guilty party would be written out and nailed to the cross above his head. As a deterrent to would-be rebels and criminals, crucifixions were usually carried out in highly visible locations.

During Jesus' lifetime crucifixion was used by the Romans to exercise and gruesomely display their authority over others. This tortuous execution was viewed by the Jews as a cursed form of death. Dt 21:23 states that "anyone who is hung on a pole is under God's curse." Documents discovered at Qumran reveal that many Jews of Jesus' time applied this text to Roman crucifixion. This perspective of crucifixion demonstrates why the apostle Paul wrote that the cross of Christ was "a stumbling block to Jews and foolishness to Gentiles" (1Co 1:23). Who would have imagined that the Holy One of God would voluntarily take upon himself the curse that should have been ours? This emblem of shame has thus become the symbol of our salvation. ◆

25 Near the cross[m] of Jesus stood his
mother,[n] his mother's sister, Mary the wife
of Clopas, and Mary Magdalene.[o] 26 When
Jesus saw his mother[p] there, and the disciple whom he loved[q] standing nearby, he
said to her, "Woman,[a] here is your son,"
27 and to the disciple, "Here is your mother." From that time on, this disciple took
her into his home.

The Death of Jesus

19:29,30pp — Mt 27:48,50; Mk 15:36,37; Lk 23:36

28 Later, knowing that everything had
now been finished,[r] and so that Scripture would be fulfilled,[s] Jesus said, "I
am thirsty." 29 A jar of wine vinegar[t] was
there, so they soaked a sponge in it, put
the sponge on a stalk of the hyssop plant,
and lifted it to Jesus' lips. 30 When he had
received the drink, Jesus said, "It is finished."[u] With that, he bowed his head and
gave up his spirit.
31 Now it was the day of Preparation,[v]
and the next day was to be a special Sabbath. Because the Jewish leaders did
not want the bodies left on the crosses[w]
during the Sabbath, they asked Pilate to
have the legs broken and the bodies tak-
en down. 32 The soldiers therefore came
and broke the legs of the first man who
had been crucified with Jesus, and then
those of the other.[x] 33 But when they came
to Jesus and found that he was already
dead, they did not break his legs. 34 Instead, one of the soldiers pierced[y] Jesus'
side with a spear, bringing a sudden flow
of blood and water.[z] 35 The man who saw
it[a] has given testimony, and his testimony
is true.[b] He knows that he tells the truth,
and he testifies so that you also may believe. 36 These things happened so that the
scripture would be fulfilled:[c] "Not one of
his bones will be broken,"[bd] 37 and, as another scripture says, "They will look on
the one they have pierced."[ce]

19:25 [m] Mt 27:55, 56; Mk 15:40, 41; Lk 23:49 [n] Mt 12:46 [o] Lk 24:18 **19:26** [p] Mt 12:46 [q] Jn 13:23 **19:28** [r] ver 30; Jn 13:1 [s] ver 24, 36, 37 **19:29** [t] Ps 69:21 **19:30** [u] Lk 12:50; Jn 17:4 **19:31** [v] ver 14, 42 [w] Dt 21:23; Jos 8:29; 10:26, 27 **19:32** [x] ver 18 **19:34** [y] Zec 12:10 [z] 1Jn 5:6, 8 **19:35** [a] Lk 24:48 [b] Jn 15:27; 21:24 **19:36** [c] ver 24, 28, 37; Mt 1:22 [d] Ex 12:46; Nu 9:12; Ps 34:20 **19:37** [e] Zec 12:10; Rev 1:7

The Burial of Jesus

19:38-42pp — Mt 27:57-61; Mk 15:42-47; Lk 23:50-56

38 Later, Joseph of Arimathea asked Pilate for the body of Jesus. Now Joseph

[a] *26* The Greek for *Woman* does not denote any disrespect. [b] *36* Exodus 12:46; Num. 9:12; Psalm 34:20 [c] *37* Zech. 12:10

19:25 Women were expected to mourn and were considered a low risk for acting violently. Soldiers might allow them to come near a dying prisoner even if the soldiers wanted to keep others away.

19:26 *Woman, here is your son.* Jesus' mother might be a widow in her mid-40s; because men controlled most legal proceedings, having a male advocate was vital. Since Jesus as the eldest son was responsible for his mother's care, entrusting this responsibility to another before he died was important. Jesus had younger brothers (7:3 – 5), who would normally take the responsibility, but Jesus entrusts her care to a disciple, treating him as a member of the family (cf. Mk 3:32 – 35). Testaments could entrust care for a family member to a designated person, and one who was dying could assign property or duties verbally. In contrast to many subsequent portrayals, Jesus' cross left him close enough to the ground (like many other ancient crosses) for his mother and disciple to hear him.

19:28 *I am thirsty.* Since Jesus cited Ps 22:1 on the cross (Mk 15:34), some scholars suggest that Jesus' words here evoke the thirst in Ps 22:15.

19:29 *wine vinegar.* May evoke Ps 69:21. Made of watered-down wine vinegar, it was cheap and appealed to ordinary laborers and soldiers, and hence, would have been available. *a stalk of the hyssop plant.* Might have been available on the premises because hyssop was used for Passover (Ex 12:22), an association John's earliest Jewish hearers may have noticed.

19:30 *gave up his spirit.* Could also be translated "gave the Spirit" (cf. 7:39). For wordplays in John's Gospel, see note on 3:8.

19:31 – 32 *did not want the bodies left on the crosses ... came and broke the legs.* Some crucifixion victims may have died from asphyxiation, but they usually died more quickly from shock (due to blood loss from scourging and sometimes from being nailed to the cross) or dehydration. Those who did not die from blood loss could linger for several days, dying a slow and agonizing death. Deferring asphyxiation, a victim could sometimes rest himself on a seat in the cross, allowing himself to pull up his frame and keep breathing. When Romans wished to hasten someone's death, they would break the victim's legs, so that he could not hold himself up. Romans often left corpses on crosses to be picked clean by vultures, but in Jewish territory they would defer to unobjectionable local customs. Jewish law (Dt 21:23), followed in this period, required burial before nightfall.

19:34 *pierced Jesus' side.* A soldier normally carried a lance (*pilum*), roughly 3.5 feet (a meter) long and consisting of a wood shaft with an iron head. Thrust with sufficient force, the lance could pierce the pericardial sac around heart and release its fairly clear fluid along with blood. The limited evidence we have suggests that soldiers sometimes pierced other executed people to make sure they were dead.

19:35 *his testimony ... he testifies.* Ancient eyewitness authors often mentioned themselves in the third person ("he"), though the same author sometimes could mention himself elsewhere in the first person (as "I" or part of "we"; cf. 1:14).

19:36 *Not one of his bones will be broken.* The wording fits Ps 34:20, but also the proscription against breaking the Passover lamb's bones (Ex 12:46; Nu 9:12), relevant in this context. Some suggest that John mixes both texts; ancient Jewish teachers often linked or blended texts.

19:37 John here cites Zec 12:10; some later rabbis construed the text as Messianic, but its immediate context in Zechariah probably refers to God.

19:38 – 42 The early Christian tradition of the site of the tomb is at least as old as the decade following Jesus' interment. Tradition is unanimous — and custom required — that Jesus be buried outside the city walls, but the site is *within* the expanded walls of Jerusalem from the time of AD 41 – 43, so the tradition clearly points to a period before 41 – 43. The tombs on this site (the Catholic and Orthodox site of the Holy Sepulchre) date to the period in question; by the second century, a pagan emperor sought to deliberately desecrate the site because of its reputation

was a disciple of Jesus, but secretly because he feared the Jewish leaders. With
Pilate's permission, he came and took the
body away. 39He was accompanied by Nicodemus,[f] the man who earlier had visited Jesus at night. Nicodemus brought a
mixture of myrrh and aloes, about seventy-five pounds.[a] 40Taking Jesus' body, the
two of them wrapped it, with the spices,
in strips of linen.[g] This was in accordance
with Jewish burial customs.[h] 41At the
place where Jesus was crucified, there was
a garden, and in the garden a new tomb,
in which no one had ever been laid. 42Be-
cause it was the Jewish day of Preparation[i]
and since the tomb was nearby,[j] they laid
Jesus there.

The Empty Tomb

20:1-8pp — Mt 28:1-8; Mk 16:1-8; Lk 24:1-10

20 Early on the first day of the week,
while it was still dark, Mary Magdalene[k] went to the tomb and saw that
the stone had been removed from the entrance.[l] 2So she came running to Simon
Peter and the other disciple, the one Jesus
loved,[m] and said, "They have taken the
Lord out of the tomb, and we don't know
where they have put him!"[n]

3So Peter and the other disciple started
for the tomb.[o] 4Both were running, but the
other disciple outran Peter and reached the
tomb first. 5He bent over and looked in[p] at
the strips of linen[q] lying there but did not
go in. 6Then Simon Peter came along behind him and went straight into the tomb.
He saw the strips of linen lying there, 7as
well as the cloth that had been wrapped
around Jesus' head.[r] The cloth was still
lying in its place, separate from the lin-
en. 8Finally the other disciple, who had
reached the tomb first,[s] also went inside.
He saw and believed. 9(They still did not
understand from Scripture[t] that Jesus had
to rise from the dead.)[u] 10Then the disciples went back to where they were staying.

Jesus Appears to Mary Magdalene

11Now Mary stood outside the tomb crying. As she wept, she bent over to look into
the tomb[v] 12and saw two angels in white,[w]
seated where Jesus' body had been, one at
the head and the other at the foot.

13They asked her, "Woman, why are you
crying?"[x]

"They have taken my Lord away," she
said, "and I don't know where they have
put him."[y] 14At this, she turned around
and saw Jesus standing there,[z] but she did
not realize that it was Jesus.[a]

19:39 [f] Jn 3:1; 7:50 **19:40** [g] Lk 24:12; Jn 11:44; 20:5,7 [h] Mt 26:12 **19:42** [i] ver 14, 31 [j] ver 20,41 **20:1** [k] ver 18; Jn 19:25 [l] Mt 27:60,66 **20:2** [m] Jn 13:23 [n] ver 13 **20:3** [o] Lk 24:12 **20:5** [p] ver 11 [q] Jn 19:40 **20:7** [r] Jn 11:44 **20:8** [s] ver 4 **20:9** [t] Mt 22:29; Jn 2:22 [u] Lk 24:26,46 **20:11** [v] ver 5 **20:12** [w] Mt 28:2, 3; Mk 16:5; Lk 24:4; Ac 5:19 **20:13** [x] ver 15 [y] ver 2 **20:14** [z] Mt 28:9; Mk 16:9 [a] Lk 24:16; Jn 21:4

[a] *39* Or about 34 kilograms

as a local holy site. (By contrast, the Garden Tomb was a recent historical guess, belongs to the wrong period, and lacks any claim to authenticity.)

19:38 *Joseph ... asked Pilate for the body.* Joseph shows courage. Family members would not be punished for requesting the body. For a member of the elite to request the body, however, was to take a significant risk: unless acting officially at the behest of the Sanhedrin, he could be associated with Jesus' alleged treason, risking his own execution. Moreover, officials sometimes liked to pin such charges specifically on members of the elite so that they could confiscate their property. Although Pilate does not act against Joseph, Joseph could not know that in advance, and his request is courageous.

19:39 *mixture of myrrh and aloes.* After the Sabbath, those caring for the body would embalm it with the myrrh and perfume it with the aloes. Although higher figures are known (reportedly 70 pounds, or 32 kilograms, for Gamaliel, and incomparably more for Herod the Great), the spices here are expensive. By way of comparison, this extravagant act of devotion may have cost a hundred times that reported in 12:3 (see note there). In this case, however, no funeral would follow; those executed by the state could not receive public funerals.

19:40 *wrapped ... in strips of linen.* Linen shrouds were common for Jewish burials (see note on Mk 15:46). The person being buried would be tightly wrapped in linen cloths to keep his or her members straight and the mouth closed.

19:41 *in the garden a new tomb.* A tomb so quickly accessible probably already belonged to Joseph (Mt 27:60). Because Joseph was originally from Arimathea rather than Jerusalem, his family tomb here had not yet been used. For other tombs in or near gardens, cf. 2Ki 21:18,26.

19:42 Jewish tradition allowed washing and anointing corpses even on the Sabbath, but for the moment the body and spices are deposited. A body would be allowed to decompose for one year before its bones were placed in an ossuary (a stone box with a lid used to hold bones).

20:1 *Early on the first day.* The Sabbath ended Saturday at sundown, and so is no longer a deterrent. Mary's travel to the tomb in the dark, even though she is not from the environs of Jerusalem, requires serious commitment. *stone had been removed.* In this area a tomb entrance was often covered by a disk-shaped rock, a yard/meter in diameter, requiring multiple people to move it. Such a stone lay in a groove but could not be moved from inside; the practice is common enough for John to take for granted here that his audience understands it.

20:2 *taken the Lord out of the tomb.* The authorities would have sometimes deposited the bodies of the executed in group graves designated for criminals, handing them over only after a year.

20:3 Aside from it being dark when Mary headed for the tomb, men in the ancient Mediterranean world often viewed women as undependable in their testimony. Even if they trusted her fully, however, they would want to discover where the body was.

20:4 *the other disciple outran Peter.* Ancient writers compared not only good and bad figures, but good and better ones. Athletic young men (as these fishermen likely were) sometimes competed with one another as friends; the beloved disciple's strength expresses devotion to the Lord, as does Peter's in 21:7,11.

20:5 *bent over.* Some tombs had a low entrance (see also v. 11).

20:14 *did not realize that it was Jesus.* Jewish people told stories of angels who came disguised and initially unrecognized, and sometimes of God disguising some people's

15He asked her, "Woman, why are you
crying?[b] Who is it you are looking for?"
Thinking he was the gardener, she said,
"Sir, if you have carried him away, tell me
where you have put him, and I will get
him."
16Jesus said to her, "Mary."
She turned toward him and cried out
in Aramaic,[c] "Rabboni!"[d] (which means
"Teacher").
17Jesus said, "Do not hold on to me, for
I have not yet ascended to the Father. Go
instead to my brothers[e] and tell them, 'I
am ascending to my Father[f] and your Father, to my God and your God.'"
18Mary Magdalene[g] went to the disciples[h] with the news: "I have seen the
Lord!" And she told them that he had said
these things to her.

Jesus Appears to His Disciples

19On the evening of that first day of the
week, when the disciples were together,
with the doors locked for fear of the Jewish leaders,[i] Jesus came and stood among
them and said, "Peace[j] be with you!"[k]
20After he said this, he showed them his
hands and side.[l] The disciples were overjoyed[m] when they saw the Lord.
21Again Jesus said, "Peace be with you![n]
As the Father has sent me,[o] I am sending you."[p] 22And with that he breathed on
them and said, "Receive the Holy Spirit.[q]
23If you forgive anyone's sins, their sins
are forgiven; if you do not forgive them,
they are not forgiven."[r]

Jesus Appears to Thomas

24Now Thomas[s] (also known as Didymus[a]), one of the Twelve, was not with
the disciples when Jesus came. 25So the
other disciples told him, "We have seen
the Lord!"
But he said to them, "Unless I see the
nail marks in his hands and put my finger
where the nails were, and put my hand
into his side,[t] I will not believe."[u]
26A week later his disciples were in the
house again, and Thomas was with them.
Though the doors were locked, Jesus came
and stood among them and said, "Peace[v]
be with you!"[w] 27Then he said to Thomas, "Put your finger here; see my hands.
Reach out your hand and put it into my
side. Stop doubting and believe."[x]
28Thomas said to him, "My Lord and my
God!"
29Then Jesus told him, "Because you
have seen me, you have believed;[y] blessed
are those who have not seen and yet have
believed."[z]

The Purpose of John's Gospel

30Jesus performed many other signs[a] in
the presence of his disciples, which are

20:15 [b] ver 13 **20:16** [c] Jn 5:2 [d] Mt 23:7 **20:17** [e] Mt 28:10 [f] Jn 7:33 **20:18** [g] ver 1 [h] Lk 24:10, 22,23 **20:19** [i] Jn 7:13 [j] Jn 14:27 [k] ver 21,26; Lk 24:36-39 **20:20** [l] Lk 24:39, 40; Jn 19:34 [m] Jn 16:20,22 **20:21** [n] ver 19 [o] Jn 3:17 [p] Mt 28:19; Jn 17:18 **20:22** [q] Jn 7:39; Ac 2:38; 8:15-17; 19:2; Gal 3:2 **20:23** [r] Mt 16:19; 18:18 **20:24** [s] Jn 11:16 **20:25** [t] ver 20 [u] Mk 16:11 **20:26** [v] Jn 14:27 [w] ver 21 **20:27** [x] ver 25; Lk 24:40 **20:29** [y] Jn 3:15 [z] 1Pe 1:8 **20:30** [a] Jn 2:11

[a] 24 *Thomas* (Aramaic) and *Didymus* (Greek) both mean *twin*.

appearances. Jesus' resurrection body differs from usual human bodies in this age (cf. Php 3:21).

20:15 *Thinking he was the gardener.* Gardeners were of low social station.

20:16 *Rabboni!* Being from Galilee, Mary's mother tongue would be Aramaic; "Rabboni" means something like "my master."

20:17 *not yet ascended to the Father.* Gentiles had many stories of spiritual ascensions; Jewish people had stories of bodily ascensions, including the explicit Biblical example of Elijah. Ancient writers sometimes reported predictions that would be fulfilled only after the work's conclusion. *Go.* Jesus sending Mary is striking, given the wider culture: both Jewish and Roman law normally regarded women's testimony as of quite limited value. *brothers.* Language suitable for fellow Jews but here means more (see note on Ac 9:17).

20:19 *first day of the week.* The first Sunday evening after the crucifixion the disciples would still be inside in Jerusalem. Not only was the festival continuing, but they were in mourning. The first week of mourning was particularly heavy, making travel unusual (see note on 11:20); so far as they knew, they had several more days left in this week of mourning. *doors locked.* The doors are probably barred or bolted. *Peace be with you!* The conventional Jewish greeting was *shalom*, i.e., "Peace be with you." This greeting constituted an implicit prayer to God for the well-being of the person addressed.

20:20 *showed them his hands and side.* People often displayed wounds to demonstrate their commitment; here Jesus uses them to confirm his identity, just as documents often cited scars as identity markers.

20:21 *I am sending you.* A commissioned agent could act on the authority of the sender to the extent that the agent accurately reflected the commission.

20:22 *breathed on them ... Receive the Holy Spirit.* As God breathed into humanity the breath of life (Ge 2:7), so Jesus here imparts the Spirit. In the OT, God alone could bestow the Holy Spirit, i.e., God's Spirit. Jewish sources, including the OT, often associate the Spirit with prophetic empowerment (relevant for v. 21).

20:25 *nail marks in his hands.* Romans most often tied persons to crosses with rope, but sometimes nailed them, as a sadistic (but often death-hastening) variation on the execution. Unless the person were also tied to the cross, a person could not be simply nailed to it through the palm of the hand, as this would not support his weight (the hand would simply tear open). The Greek term translated "hands" does allow for the nails to be in the forearms.

20:26 See note on v. 19.

20:27 *see my hands.* See note on v. 25.

20:28 *My Lord and my God!* The emperor who reigned when John's Gospel was probably written, Domitian, reportedly desired to be called "Lord God" (Suetonius, *Domitian* 13). Those familiar with the Septuagint, the pre-Christian Greek translation of the OT, however, would already recognize Thomas's confession as a divine title (e.g., Ps 35:23).

20:30–31 Writers often reinforced a major point in a statement concluding a work or section. Jesus affirms Thomas's recognition of Jesus' deity as faith, but greater faith belongs to those who have not seen (vv. 28–29); now, John concludes, this book records the signs so

not recorded in this book.[b] 31But these are
written that you may believe[ac] that Jesus is
the Messiah, the Son of God,[d] and that by
believing you may have life in his name.[e]

Jesus and the Miraculous Catch of Fish

21 Afterward Jesus appeared again to
his disciples,[f] by the Sea of Galilee.[bg] It happened this way: 2Simon Peter,
Thomas[h] (also known as Didymus[c]), Nathanael[i] from Cana in Galilee,[j] the sons of
Zebedee,[k] and two other disciples were together. 3"I'm going out to fish," Simon Peter told them, and they said, "We'll go with
you." So they went out and got into the
boat, but that night they caught nothing.[l]
4Early in the morning, Jesus stood on
the shore, but the disciples did not realize
that it was Jesus.[m]
5He called out to them, "Friends,
haven't you any fish?"
"No," they answered.
6He said, "Throw your net on the right
side of the boat and you will find some."
When they did, they were unable to haul
the net in because of the large number of
fish.[n]
7Then the disciple whom Jesus loved[o]
said to Peter, "It is the Lord!" As soon as
Simon Peter heard him say, "It is the Lord,"
he wrapped his outer garment around him
(for he had taken it off) and jumped into
the water. 8The other disciples followed in
the boat, towing the net full of fish, for
they were not far from shore, about a hundred yards.[d] 9When they landed, they saw
a fire[p] of burning coals there with fish on
it,[q] and some bread.

20:30 [b] Jn 21:25
20:31 [c] Jn 3:15; 19:35 [d] Mt 4:3 [e] Mt 25:46
21:1 [f] Jn 20:19, 26 [g] Jn 6:1
21:2 [h] Jn 11:16 [i] Jn 1:45 [j] Jn 2:1 [k] Mt 4:21
21:3 [l] Lk 5:5
21:4 [m] Lk 24:16; Jn 20:14
21:6 [n] Lk 5:4-7
21:7 [o] Jn 13:23
21:9 [p] Jn 18:18 [q] ver 10, 13
21:13 [r] ver 9
21:14 [s] Jn 20:19, 26
21:15 [t] Mt 26:33, 35; Jn 13:37 [u] Lk 12:32
21:16 [v] Mt 2:6; Ac 20:28; 1Pe 5:2, 3
21:17 [w] Jn 13:38 [x] Jn 16:30 [y] ver 16

10Jesus said to them, "Bring some of
the fish you have just caught." 11So Simon Peter climbed back into the boat and
dragged the net ashore. It was full of large
fish, 153, but even with so many the net
was not torn. 12Jesus said to them, "Come
and have breakfast." None of the disciples dared ask him, "Who are you?" They
knew it was the Lord. 13Jesus came, took
the bread and gave it to them, and did the
same with the fish.[r] 14This was now the
third time Jesus appeared to his disciples[s]
after he was raised from the dead.

Jesus Reinstates Peter

15When they had finished eating, Jesus
said to Simon Peter, "Simon son of John,
do you love me more than these?"
"Yes, Lord," he said, "you know that I
love you."[t]
Jesus said, "Feed my lambs."[u]
16Again Jesus said, "Simon son of John,
do you love me?"
He answered, "Yes, Lord, you know that
I love you."
Jesus said, "Take care of my sheep."[v]
17The third time he said to him, "Simon
son of John, do you love me?"
Peter was hurt because Jesus asked
him the third time, "Do you love me?"[w]
He said, "Lord, you know all things;[x] you
know that I love you."
Jesus said, "Feed my sheep.[y] 18Very
truly I tell you, when you were younger
you dressed yourself and went where you

[a] 31 Or *may continue to believe* [b] 1 Greek *Tiberias*
[c] 2 *Thomas* (Aramaic) and *Didymus* (Greek) both mean *twin.* [d] 8 Or about 90 meters

---

that those who have not seen may believe. Writers often noted, as here, that they could have recounted many other stories (see note on 21:25).

20:30 *this book.* Papyrus was expensive, so only the well-to-do could afford long works; the Gospels, like other ancient biographies, were the appropriate length for circulation.

21:1 – 25 Twentieth-century critical scholars often viewed ch. 21 as a later addition to John's Gospel, noting that it was anticlimactic after the conclusion of 20:30 – 31. While they were correct to note that 20:30 – 31 offers a conclusion to the body of the work, epilogues could continue after such conclusions (and works could end without either). Moreover, Greco-Roman antiquity's most widely circulated work, the *Iliad*, has a closing anticlimactic section (Book 24). Today, noting the shared vocabulary and especially narrative connections with the Gospel's body, an increasing number of scholars treat ch. 21 as an integral part of John's Gospel.

21:3 *going out to fish.* Commercial fishing around the lake was an important part of the local economy, although in this case, it may be simply to provide food for more immediate consumption. *that night.* Galilean fishermen could work with torches at night, farther from the shore; they could catch fish in a dragnet, which had weights around its wider edges so it could drag deep. (In the present account it could not be dragged between two boats, however, as only one boat is involved.)

21:6 *right side of the boat.* Some commentators have suggested that fishermen normally cast nets from the left side of the boat, because the steering oar was on the right side.

21:7 *he had taken it off.* Fishermen were usually considered rugged and strong and accustomed to the rigors of working in the elements. Unless the morning was unusually cold, Peter had probably taken off his outer garment because of the exertion of his work; men often removed their outer garment when working hard. For his athletic prowess, see note on 20:4.

21:11 *153, but … the net was not torn.* People probably wove the nets from hemp or flax ropes; the net's failure to break is itself viewed as miraculous. The large number of fish reinforces the miracle. Scholars suggest a wide range of reasons for the number 153 (e.g., it is a triangular number with a base of 17). Perhaps the disciples, excited about the catch, simply counted afterward.

21:15 – 17 Against those who read great significance into the two Greek terms translated "love" here, writers in John's era (including John) often shifted words with the same meaning for the purpose of literary variation.

21:18 *stretch out your hands.* In his youth Peter, who was strong, girded himself (v. 7), but it would be different

wanted; but when you are old you will
stretch out your hands, and someone else
will dress you and lead you where you do
not want to go." 19 Jesus said this to indicate the kind of death[z] by which Peter
would glorify God.[a] Then he said to him,
"Follow me!"

20 Peter turned and saw that the disciple
whom Jesus loved[b] was following them.
(This was the one who had leaned back
against Jesus at the supper and had said,
"Lord, who is going to betray you?")[c]
21 When Peter saw him, he asked, "Lord,
what about him?"

22 Jesus answered, "If I want him to remain alive until I return,[d] what is that to
you? You must follow me."[e] 23 Because of
this, the rumor spread among the believers[f] that this disciple would not die. But
Jesus did not say that he would not die; he
only said, "If I want him to remain alive
until I return, what is that to you?"

24 This is the disciple who testifies to
these things[g] and who wrote them down.
We know that his testimony is true.[h]

25 Jesus did many other things as well.[i]
If every one of them were written down, I
suppose that even the whole world would
not have room for the books that would
be written.

21:19 [z] Jn 12:33; 18:32 [a] 2Pe 1:14 **21:20** [b] ver 7; Jn 13:23 [c] Jn 13:25 **21:22** [d] Mt 16:27; 1Co 4:5; Rev 2:25 [e] ver 19 **21:23** [f] Ac 1:16 **21:24** [g] Jn 15:27 [h] Jn 19:35 **21:25** [i] Jn 20:30

---

when he was old. One could stretch out hands in prayer or, perhaps here as in some other ancient sources, to have one's hands tied before execution (see note on v. 19).

21:19 *the kind of death by which Peter would glorify God.* Echoes 12:32–33, which predicts Jesus' crucifixion. According to early tradition, the emperor Nero had Peter crucified upside down in Rome, c. AD 64.

21:21–23 For friendly competition, see note on 20:4. Early tradition suggests that the apostle John, unlike most of his colleagues, escaped martyrdom.

21:24 *This is the disciple.* Legal documents often concluded by naming witnesses. *We know that his testimony is true.* Many scholars believe that this line was added by John's own circle, who knew him as the witness. Others suggest that it is similar to 19:35; the witness sometimes says "we" (1 Jn 1:1–3).

21:25 *the whole world would not have room for the books that would be written.* Writers often used similar hyperbole for emphasis, claiming, e.g., that the world could not contain all of someone's exploits, lies, hardships or the like.

ONE SUGGESTED HARMONY OF THE GOSPELS

DATE	EVENT	LOCATION	MATTHEW	MARK	LUKE	JOHN
INTRODUCTIONS TO JESUS CHRIST						
	(1) Luke's introduction				1:1–4	
	(2) Preincarnate Christ					1:1–18
	(3) Genealogy of Jesus Christ		1:1–17		3:23b–38	
BIRTH, INFANCY, AND ADOLESCENCE OF JESUS AND JOHN THE BAPTIST						
7 BC	(1) Announcement of birth of John	Jerusalem (temple)			1:5–25	
7 or 6 BC	(2) Announcement of birth of Jesus to the virgin Mary	Nazareth			1:26–38	
c. 5 BC	(3) Song of Elizabeth to Mary	Hill country of Judea			1:39–45	
	(4) Mary's song of praise				1:46–56	
5 BC	(5) Birth, infancy, and purpose for future of John the Baptist	Judea			1:57–80	
	(6) Announcement of Jesus' birth to Joseph	Nazareth	1:18–25a			
5–4 BC	(7) Birth of Jesus Christ	Bethlehem	1:25b		2:1–7	
	(8) Proclamation by the angels	Near Bethlehem			2:8–14	
	(9) The visit of homage by shepherds	Bethlehem			2:15–20	
	(10) Jesus' circumcision	Bethlehem			2:21	
4 BC	(11) First temple visit with acknowledgments by Simeon and Anna	Jerusalem			2:22–38	
	(12) Visit of the Magi	Jerusalem & Bethlehem	2:1–12			
	(13) Flight into Egypt and massacre of innocents	Bethlehem, Jerusalem & Egypt	2:13–18			
	(14) From Egypt to Nazareth with Jesus		2:19–23		2:39	
Afterward AD 7–8	(15) Childhood of Jesus	Nazareth			2:40	
	(16) Jesus, 12 years old, visits the temple	Jerusalem			2:41–50	
Afterward	(17) 18-year account of Jesus' adolescence and adulthood	Nazareth			2:51–52	
TRUTHS ABOUT JOHN THE BAPTIST						
c. AD 25–27	(1) John's ministry begins	Judean Wilderness	3:1	1:1–4	3:1–2	1:19–28
	(2) Man and message		3:2–12	1:2–8	3:3–14	1:20–23
	(3) His picture of Jesus		3:11–12	1:7–8	3:15–18	1:24–27
	(4) His courage		14:4–12		3:19–20	
BEGINNING OF JESUS' MINISTRY						
c. AD 27	(1) Jesus baptized	Jordan River	3:13–17	1:9–11	3:21–23a	1:29–34
	(2) Jesus tempted	Wilderness	4:1–11	1:12–13	4:1–13	
	(3) Calls first disciples	Beyond Jordan				1:35–51
	(4) The first miracle	Cana in Galilee				2:1–11

ONE SUGGESTED HARMONY OF THE GOSPELS (CONT.)

DATE	EVENT	LOCATION	MATTHEW	MARK	LUKE	JOHN
BEGINNING OF JESUS' MINISTRY (CONT.)						
AD 27	(5) First stay in Capernaum	(Capernaum is "his" city)				2:12
	(6) First cleansing of the temple	Jerusalem				2:13–22
	(7) Received at Jerusalem	Jerusalem				2:23–25
	(8) Teaches Nicodemus about second birth	Jerusalem				3:1–21
	(9) Co-ministry with John	Judea				3:22–36
	(10) Leaves for Galilee	Judea	4:12	1:14	4:14	4:1–4
	(11) Samaritan woman at Jacob's Well	Samaria (town of Sychar)				4:5–42
	(12) Returns to Galilee			1:15	4:15	4:43–45
THE GALILEAN MINISTRY OF JESUS						
AD 27	(1) Healing of the royal official's son	Cana				4:46–54
	(2) Rejected at Nazareth	Nazareth			4:16–30	
	(3) Moved to Capernaum	Capernaum	4:13–17			
	(4) Four become fishers of people	Sea of Galilee	4:18–22	1:16–20	5:1–11	
	(5) Impure spirit driven out on the Sabbath day	Capernaum		1:21–28	4:31–37	
	(6) Peter's mother-in-law cured, plus others	Capernaum	8:14–17	1:29–34	4:38–41	
c. AD 27	(7) First preaching tour of Galilee	Galilee	4:23–25	1:35–39	4:42–44	
	(8) Leper healed and response recorded	Galilee	8:1–4	1:40–45	5:12–16	
	(9) Paralyzed man healed	Capernaum	9:1–8	2:1–12	5:17–26	
	(10) Matthew's call and reception held	Capernaum	9:9–13	2:13–17	5:27–32	
	(11) Disciples defended via a parable	Capernaum	9:14–17	2:18–22	5:33–39	
AD 28	(12) Goes to Jerusalem for second passover; heals lame man	Jerusalem				5:1–47
	(13) Plucked grain precipitates Sabbath controversy	En route to Galilee	12:1–8	2:23–28	6:1–5	
	(14) Shriveled hand healed causes another Sabbath controversy	Galilee	12:9–14	3:1–6	6:6–11	
	(15) Multitudes healed	Sea of Galilee	12:15–21	3:7–12	6:17–19	
	(16) Twelve apostles selected after a night of prayer	Near Capernaum		3:13–19	6:12–16	
	(17) Sermon on the Mount	Near Capernaum	5:1—7:29		6:20–49	
	(18) Centurion's servant healed	Capernaum	8:5–13		7:1–10	
	(19) Raises widow's son from the dead	Nain			7:11–17	

ONE SUGGESTED HARMONY OF THE GOSPELS (CONT.)

DATE	EVENT	LOCATION	MATTHEW	MARK	LUKE	JOHN
THE GALILEAN MINISTRY OF JESUS (CONT.)						
AD 28	(20) Jesus allays John the Baptist's doubts	Galilee	11:2–19		7:18–35	
	(21) Woes upon the privileged		11:20–30			
	(22) A sinful woman anoints Jesus	Simon the Pharisee's house, Capernaum			7:36–50	
	(23) Another tour of Galilee	Galilee			8:1–3	
	(24) Jesus accused of blasphemy	Capernaum	12:22–37	3:20–30	11:14–23	
	(25) Jesus' answer to a demand for a sign	Capernaum	12:38–45		11:24–26, 29–36	
	(26) Mother, brothers seek audience	Capernaum	12:46–50	3:31–35	8:19–21	
	(27) Famous parables of sower, seed, weeds, lamp, mustard seed, yeast, treasure, pearl, net, told	By Sea of Galilee	13:1–52	4:1–34	8:4–18	
	(28) Sea made serene	Sea of Galilee	8:23–27	4:35–41	8:22–25	
	(29) Gadarene (Gerasene) demon-possessed men healed	Eastern shore of Galilee	8:28–34	5:1–20	8:26–39	
	(30) Jairus's daughter raised and woman with hemorrhage healed		9:18–26	5:21–43	8:40–56	
	(31) Two blind men's sight restored		9:27–31			
	(32) Mute demon-possessed man healed		9:32–34			
	(33) Nazareth's second rejection of Christ	Nazareth	13:53–58	6:1–6		
	(34) Twelve sent out		9:35—11:1	6:7–13	9:1–6	
	(35) Fearful Herod beheads John the Baptist	Galilee	14:1–12	6:14–29	9:7–9	
Spring AD 29	(36) Return of 12, Jesus withdraws, 5,000 fed	Near Bethsaida	14:13–21	6:30–44	9:10–17	6:1–15
	(37) Walks on the water	Sea of Galilee	14:22–33	6:45–52		6:16–21
	(38) Sick people healed in Gennesaret	Gennesaret	14:34–36	6:53–56		
	(39) Peak of popularity passes in Galilee	Capernaum				6:22—7:1
AD 29	(40) Traditions attacked		15:1–20	7:1–23		
	(41) Aborted retirement in Tyre: Syrophoenician's daughter healed	Tyre	15:21–28	7:24–30		
	(42) Afflicted healed	Decapolis	15:29–31	7:31–37		
	(43) 4,000 fed	Decapolis	15:32–39	8:1–9		
	(44) Pharisees increase attack	Magadan	16:1–4	8:10–13		

ONE SUGGESTED HARMONY OF THE GOSPELS (CONT.)

DATE	EVENT	LOCATION	MATTHEW	MARK	LUKE	JOHN
THE GALILEAN MINISTRY OF JESUS (CONT.)						
AD 29	(45) Disciples' carelessness condemned; blind man healed		16:5–12	8:14–26		
	(46) Peter confesses Jesus is the Christ	Near Caesarea Philippi	16:13–20	8:27–30	9:18–21	
	(47) Jesus foretells his death	Caesarea Philippi	16:21–26	8:31–38	9:22–25	
	(48) Kingdom promised		16:27–28	9:1	9:26–27	
	(49) The transfiguration	Mountain unnamed	17:1–13	9:2–13	9:28–36	
	(50) Demon-possessed boy healed	Mount of Transfiguration	17:14–21	9:14–29	9:37–42	
	(51) Again tells of death, resurrection	Galilee	17:22–23	9:30–32	9:43–45	
	(52) Taxes paid	Capernaum	17:24–27			
	(53) Disciples contend about greatness; Jesus defines it; also patience, loyalty, forgiveness	Capernaum	18:1–35	9:33–50	9:46–50	
	(54) Jesus rejects his brothers' advice	Galilee				7:2–9
Fall AD 29	(55) Galilee departure and Samaritan rejection		19:1–2		9:51–56	7:10
	(56) Cost of discipleship		8:18–22		9:57–62	
LAST JUDEAN AND PEREAN MINISTRY OF JESUS						
Fall AD 29	(1) Festival of Tabernacles	Jerusalem				7:2,11–52
	(2) Forgiveness of woman caught in the act of adultery	Jerusalem				[7:53— 8:11]
AD 29	(3) Christ—the light of the world	Jerusalem				8:12
	(4) Pharisees dispute the prophet's words and thus try to destroy him	Jerusalem—temple				8:13–59
	(5) Man born blind healed; following consequences	Jerusalem				9:1–41
	(6) Parable of the Good Shepherd	Jerusalem				10:1–21
	(7) The service of the 72	Probably Judea			10:1–24	
	(8) Expert in the law hears the story of the Good Samaritan	Judea (?)			10:25–37	
	(9) The hospitality of Martha and Mary	Bethany			10:38–42	
	(10) Another lesson on prayer	Judea (?)			11:1–13	
	(11) Accused of connection with Beelzebul				11:14–36	
	(12) Judgment against pharisees and experts in the law				11:37–54	

ONE SUGGESTED HARMONY OF THE GOSPELS (CONT.)

DATE	EVENT	LOCATION	MATTHEW	MARK	LUKE	JOHN
LAST JUDEAN AND PEREAN MINISTRY OF JESUS (CONT.)						
AD 29	(13) Jesus deals with hypocrisy, greed, worry, and watchfulness				12:1–59	
	(14) Repent or perish				13:1–5	
	(15) Barren fig tree				13:6–9	
	(16) Crippled woman healed on Sabbath				13:10–17	
	(17) Parables of mustard seed and yeast	Probably Perea			13:18–21	
Winter AD 29	(18) Festival of Dedication	Jerusalem				10:22–39
	(19) Withdrawal beyond Jordan					10:40–42
	(20) Jesus teaches, with special words about Herod	Perea			13:22–35	
	(21) Meal with a Pharisee ruler; heals man with abnormal swelling; parables of ox, best places at the table, and great banquet				14:1–24	
	(22) Demands of discipleship	Perea			14:25–35	
	(23) Parables of lost sheep, coin, son				15:1–32	
	(24) Parables of shrewd manager, rich man and Lazarus				16:1–31	
	(25) Lessons on forgiveness, duty, influence, faith				17:1–10	
	(26) Resurrection of Lazarus	Perea to Bethany				11:1–44
	(27) Reaction to resurrection of Lazarus: withdrawal of Jesus					11:45–54
AD 30	(28) Begins last journey to Jerusalem via Samaria & Galilee	Samaria, Galilee			17:11	
	(29) Heals ten lepers				17:12–19	
	(30) Lessons on the coming kingdom				17:20–37	
	(31) Parables: persistent widow, Pharisee and tax collector				18:1–14	
	(32) Teaching on divorce		19:3–12	10:1–12		
	(33) Jesus blesses children; objections	Perea	19:13–15	10:13–16	18:15–17	
	(34) Rich ruler	Perea	19:16–30	10:17–31	18:18–30	
	(35) Parable of the workers		20:1–16			
	(36) Foretells death and resurrection	Near Jerusalem	20:17–19	10:32–34	18:31–34	
	(37) Ambition of James and John		20:20–28	10:35–45		
	(38) Blind Bartimaeus and his companion healed	Jericho	20:29–34	10:46–52	18:35–43	

ONE SUGGESTED HARMONY OF THE GOSPELS (CONT.)

DATE	EVENT	LOCATION	MATTHEW	MARK	LUKE	JOHN
LAST JUDEAN AND PEREAN MINISTRY OF JESUS (CONT.)						
AD 30	(39) Interview with Zacchaeus	Jericho			19:1–10	
	(40) Parable of the minas	Jericho			19:11–27	
	(41) Returns to home of Mary and Martha	Bethany				11:55—12:1
	(42) Plot to kill Lazarus	Bethany				12:9–11
JESUS' FINAL WEEK AROUND AND IN JERUSALEM						
Spring AD 30						
Sunday	(1) Triumphal Entry	Bethany, Jerusalem, Bethany	21:1–9	11:1–11	19:28–44	12:12–19
Monday	(2) Fig tree cursed and temple cleansed	Bethany to Jerusalem	21:10–19	11:12–18	19:45–48	
	(3) The necessity of sacrifice	Jerusalem				12:20–50
Tuesday	(4) Withered fig tree testifies	Bethany to Jerusalem	21:20–22	11:19–26		
	(5) Sanhedrin challenges Jesus. He answers by parables: two sons, workers in the vineyard and marriage feast	Jerusalem	21:23—22:14	11:27—12:12	20:1–19	
	(6) Tribute to Caesar	Jerusalem	22:15–22	12:13–17	20:20–26	
	(7) Sadducees question the resurrection	Jerusalem	22:23–33	12:18–27	20:27–40	
	(8) Pharisees question commandments	Jerusalem	22:34–40	12:28–34		
	(9) Jesus and David	Jerusalem	22:41–46	12:35–37	20:41–44	
	(10) Jesus' last sermon	Jerusalem	23:1–39	12:38–40	20:45–47	
	(11) Widow's offering	Jerusalem		12:41–44	21:1–4	
	(12) Jesus tells of the future	Mount of Olives	24:1–51	13:1–37	21:5–36	
	(13) Parables: ten virgins, talents, the day of judgment	Mount of Olives	25:1–46			
	(14) Jesus tells date of crucifixion		26:1–5	14:1–2	22:1–2	
	(15) Anointing by Mary at Simon the Leper's feast	Bethany	26:6–13	14:3–9		12:2–8
	(16) Judas contracts the betrayal		26:14–16	14:10–11	22:3–6	
Thursday	(17) Preparation for the Passover	Jerusalem	26:17–19	14:12–16	22:7–13	
Thursday p.m.	(18) Passover eaten, jealousy rebuked	Jerusalem	26:20	14:17	22:14–16, 24–30	
	(19) Feet washed	Upper Room				13:1–20
	(20) Judas revealed, defects	Upper Room	26:21–25	14:18–21	22:21–23	13:21–30
	(21) Jesus warns about further desertion; cries of loyalty	Upper Room	26:31–35	14:27–31	22:31–38	13:31–38
	(22) The last supper	Upper Room	26:26–29	14:22–25	22:17–20	
	(23) Last speech to the apostles and intercessory prayer	Jerusalem				14:1—17:26
Thursday-Friday	(24) The grief of Gethsemane	Mount of Olives	26:30, 36–46	14:26, 32–42	22:39–46	18:1

ONE SUGGESTED HARMONY OF THE GOSPELS (CONT.)

DATE	EVENT	LOCATION	MATTHEW	MARK	LUKE	JOHN
JESUS' FINAL WEEK AROUND AND IN JERUSALEM (CONT.)						
Friday	(25) Betrayal, arrest, desertion	Gethsemane	26:47–56	14:43–52	22:47–53	18:2–12
	(26) First examined by Annas	Jerusalem				18:13–14, 19–23
	(27) Trial by Caiaphas and Sanhedrin; following indignities	Jerusalem	26:57, 59–68	14:53, 55–65	22:54a, 63–65	18:24
Friday	(28) Peter's triple denial	Jerusalem	26:58, 69–75	14:54, 66–72	22:54b–62	18:15–18, 25–27
	(29) Condemnation by the Sanhedrin	Jerusalem	27:1	15:1a	22:66–71	
	(30) Suicide of Judas	Jerusalem	27:3–10			
	(31) First appearance before Pilate	Jerusalem	27:2,11–14	15:1b–5	23:1–6	18:28–38
	(32) Jesus before Herod	Jerusalem			23:7–12	
	(33) Second appearance before Pilate	Jerusalem	27:15–26	15:6–15	23:13–25	18:39—19:16a
	(34) Mockery by Roman soldiers	Jerusalem	27:27–30	15:16–19		
	(35) Led to Golgotha	Jerusalem	27:31–34	15:20–23	23:26–32	19:16b–17
	(36) Events of first three hours on cross	Golgotha	27:35–44	15:24–32	23:33–43	19:18–27
Friday	(37) Last three hours on cross	Golgotha	27:45–50	15:33–37	23:44,46	19:28–30
	(38) Events attending Jesus' death		27:51–56	15:38–41	23:45, 47–49	
	(39) Burial of Jesus	Jerusalem	27:57–61	15:42–46	23:50–54	19:31–42
Friday-Saturday	(40) Tomb sealed	Jerusalem	27:62–66			
	(41) Women watch	Jerusalem		15:47	23:55–56	
THE RESURRECTION THROUGH THE ASCENSION						
AD 30						
Dawn of First Day (Sunday, "Lord's Day")	(1) Women visit the tomb	Near Jerusalem	28:1–8	16:1–8	24:1–11	20:1–2
	(2) Peter and John see the empty tomb				24:12	20:3–10
	(3) Jesus' appearance to Mary Magdalene	Jerusalem		[16:9–11]		20:11–18
	(4) Jesus' appearance to the other women	Jerusalem	28:9–10			
	(5) Guards' report of the resurrection		28:11–15			
Sunday Afternoon	(6) Jesus' appearance to two disciples on way to Emmaus			[16:12–13]	24:13–35	
Late Sunday	(7) Jesus' appearance to ten disciples without Thomas	Jerusalem			24:36–43	20:19–25
One Week Later	(8) Appearance to disciples with Thomas	Jerusalem			24:44–49	20:26–31
During 40 Days until Ascension	(9) Jesus' appearance to seven disciples by Sea of Galilee	Galilee				21:1–25
	(10) Great Commission		28:16–20	[16:14–18]		
	(11) The Ascension	Mount Olivet		[16:19–20]	24:50–53	

THE EARLY CHURCH

ACTS

Genre

Most scholars today agree that Acts is a work of ancient history. Those who view it as history or biography outnumber proponents of all the other views put together. Many details of Acts are confirmed by Paul's letters and (more the focus of this study Bible's notes) external historical information. No nonhistorical work from antiquity exhibits so many correspondences with external information. Corroborating external information, in fact, may be more extensive for Acts than for any other book in the New Testament. As a work of ancient history, it fares well.

There were ways that ancient historical writing in general differed from modern historical writing. Ancient historians, e.g., rather than simply narrating bare information, often developed their scenes. They often developed speeches, using rules of rhetoric, more concerned to make the speech as close to what would have been said than to duplicate their more limited sources. No one expected these speeches to be verbatim. It should be noted, however, that Acts, unlike many of these other ancient histories, was only one volume, and therefore does not expend much space elaborating scenes or expanding its summary speeches. Luke acknowledges that more was said than he can report (Ac 2:40; Lk 3:18).

Ancient historians were also interested in communicating moral, political, or theological lessons; Acts certainly uses its historical information to offer models for the continuing mission to spread the message about Jesus Christ. Further, minority peoples often wrote "apologetic" histories; the political agenda that guided their selection and presentation of material was to show that their peoples merited respect. One of Luke's emphases is that the Christian movement is not a threat to Roman order and that it should therefore be welcomed rather than repressed.

QUICK GLANCE

AUTHOR:
Luke, a Gentile physician and missionary companion of Paul

AUDIENCE:
Addressed to Theophilus, but intended for all believers

DATE:
About AD 63 or later

THEME:
Luke shows how the gospel spread rapidly from Jerusalem to the whole Roman Empire, and from its Jewish roots to the Gentile world.

Authorship

When ancient historical writings used the first person ("I" or "we"), the author was nearly always claiming to have participated personally. The author of Luke-Acts plays down his own presence rather than emphasizing it, but includes himself among the group of Paul's companions from Troas to Philippi (16:10 – 17), and then years later from Philippi to Judea to Rome (20:5 — 28:16). Among the traveling companions that Paul mentions in his letters, one who accompanied him to Rome yet is not named in the third person in Acts is Luke the physician (Col 4:14; Phm 24). Contrary to what some have argued, Luke's language does not demonstrate that he was a physician; his language is, however, quite consistent with that view. Early Christian tradition was also unanimous that Luke was the author of Acts and of the Gospel that now bears his name; Luke was not a major figure for anyone to attribute as author if they lacked concrete reason to focus on him. When scholars examine sources from the Greco-Roman world, they usually start with external evidence (in this case, tradition in second-century Christian writers) and then check internal evidence. The tradition of Luke's authorship passes both tests.

Provenance and Date

Given Luke's special interest in Acts in the northern Aegean region — as well as perhaps his own lengthy sojourn in Philippi (compare 16:10 – 17 with 20:5 – 6) — the center of Luke's target audience may be Macedonia, with a wider circulation in the Aegean region as a whole (including Greece and western Asia Minor). A range of dates have been proposed, from as early as the closing scene of Acts (perhaps AD 62) to the early second century. Some evidence favors a suggestion in the earlier decades of this range. First, a physician who initially traveled with Paul to Philippi before AD 50 likelier than not wrote earlier in the range rather than later. Moreover, one theme in the second half of the book of Acts is to defend Paul against the charge of having started riots — the capital charge of sedition (24:5). This is important because Paul was the most prominent leader of the mission to the Gentiles (Gal 2:8), so charges against him would bring shame on all the Diaspora churches (cf. shame about his chains in 2Ti 1:16). Luke narrates many riots associated with Paul, showing that he was not at fault in any case. Yet if Luke wants to defend Paul, why even mention the riots unless they were an issue? Luke probably writes at a time when Paul's legacy remains in question and strong memories remain of the riots in various cities where the book of Acts might travel. It is therefore likely that Luke-Acts dates to a time soon after the final events narrated in Acts. This would allow a time in the 60s (when Acts closes) or 70s. Scholars who believe that Luke has in mind the traumatic conquest of Jerusalem (see Lk 19:43 – 44; 21:6,24) naturally date Luke-Acts sometime after (or occasionally just before) AD 70. Luke, who adapts Mark's grammar for a somewhat more educated Greek audience, also writes after Mark.

Structure

The structure of Acts follows the basic geographic outline of 1:8, with an emphasis on the ends of the earth (Acts is a history of early Christian mission). One can also note the development of the structure in other ways. Besides these, we may note that whereas Luke's Gospel begins and ends in Jerusalem, Acts begins in Jerusalem but ends in Rome, valuing heritage while pursuing mission. Another structural feature, however, characterizes Luke's two volumes in a special way. Whereas Matthew's Gospel can fit a hierarchical outline, Luke is particularly interested in paralleling figures. Ancient rhetoricians and storytellers often compared and contrasted different figures by narrating about them side by side. Luke parallels similar events in the ministries of Jesus, Peter and Paul (plus Stephen's martyrdom). Greeks looked for such parallels in history, but Luke sees such models in earlier Scripture itself. See "Answered Charges and Parallel Figures in Acts," p. 1881. ◆

Jesus Taken Up Into Heaven

1 In my former book,[a] Theophilus, I
wrote about all that Jesus began to do
and to teach[b] 2until the day he was taken
up to heaven,[c] after giving instructions[d]
through the Holy Spirit to the apostles[e] he
had chosen.[f] 3After his suffering, he presented himself to them and gave many
convincing proofs that he was alive. He
appeared to them[g] over a period of forty
days and spoke about the kingdom of God.
4On one occasion, while he was eating
with them, he gave them this command:
"Do not leave Jerusalem, but wait for the
gift my Father promised, which you have
heard me speak about.[h] 5For John baptized with[a] water, but in a few days you
will be baptized with[a] the Holy Spirit."

6Then they gathered around him and
asked him, "Lord, are you at this time going to restore[i] the kingdom to Israel?"

7He said to them: "It is not for you to
know the times or dates the Father has
set by his own authority.[j] 8But you will
receive power when the Holy Spirit comes
on you;[k] and you will be my witnesses[l] in
Jerusalem, and in all Judea and Samaria,[m]
and to the ends of the earth."[n]

9After he said this, he was taken up[o] before their very eyes, and a cloud hid him
from their sight.

10They were looking intently up into the
sky as he was going, when suddenly two
men dressed in white[p] stood beside them.
11"Men of Galilee,"[q] they said, "why do
you stand here looking into the sky? This
same Jesus, who has been taken from you
into heaven, will come back[r] in the same
way you have seen him go into heaven."

Matthias Chosen to Replace Judas

12Then the apostles returned to Jerusalem[s] from the hill called the Mount of Olives,[t] a Sabbath day's walk[b] from the city.
13When they arrived, they went upstairs to
the room[u] where they were staying. Those

1:1 [a] Lk 1:1-4 [b] Lk 3:23 **1:2** [c] ver 9, 11; Mk 16:19 [d] Mt 28:19, 20 [e] Mk 6:30 [f] Jn 13:18 **1:3** [g] Mt 28:17; Lk 24:34, 36; Jn 20:19, 26; 21:1, 14; 1Co 15:5-7 **1:4** [h] Lk 24:49; Jn 14:16; Ac 2:33 **1:6** [i] Mt 17:11 **1:7** [j] Mt 24:36 **1:8** [k] Ac 2:1-4 [l] Lk 24:48 [m] Ac 8:1-25 [n] Mt 28:19 **1:9** [o] ver 2 **1:10** [p] Lk 24:4; Jn 20:12 **1:11** [q] Ac 2:7 [r] Mt 16:27 **1:12** [s] Lk 24:52 [t] Mt 21:1 **1:13** [u] Ac 9:37; 20:8

[a] *5* Or *in* [b] *12* That is, about 5/8 mile or about 1 kilometer

1:1 *In my former book.* In multivolume works, a new volume would often open by referring to the previous volume. *Theophilus.* Writers often dedicated works, as here, to a person of prominence, which helped promote the book and might secure the dedicatee's help in promoting it. Although some have suggested that Theophilus is used as a symbolic name, it was a common actual name, including among Diaspora Jews. There is no record of symbolically named dedicatees in ancient sources. See note on Lk 1:3.

1:3 A new volume in a series would often open by recapitulating key elements of the previous volume's closing narrative; elements that differed were meant to complement the previous information.

1:5 *baptized with water … baptized with the Holy Spirit.* The analogy with water is often used for God's Spirit in the Prophets (e.g., Isa 44:3; Eze 39:29; Joel 2:28–29). The prophets had associated the Spirit with the promised future era of restoration (Isa 32:15; 44:3; Eze 36:26–27; 37:14; 39:29; Joel 2:28–29; perhaps Zec 12:10). Given talk about the kingdom (v. 3) and the Spirit (vv. 4–5), the disciples then ask the obvious question in v. 6.

1:6 *restore the kingdom to Israel.* A central aspect of ancient Jewish hope was the restoration of Israel, which generally included the return of the "lost" tribes, gathering of the exiles, restoration of the house of David, and restoration of the temple. Jesus' disciples may have shared all these hopes.

1:7 *not for you to know the times or dates the Father has set.* Jewish people debated whether God had fixed the time of restoration beforehand or if it could be adjusted based on Israel's repentance. Many tried to calculate when the end would occur; others argued that the time was unknown.

1:8 *power.* If the term is used here as most often in Luke-Acts, it probably includes occasions of healing and deliverance to draw attention to the message (3:12; 4:7; 6:8; 10:38; Lk 4:36; 5:17; 6:19; 8:46; 9:1); although such experiences were expected for the Messianic era (see Isa 35:5–6; see also note on Lk 7:22), they were not expected as activities of the remnant witnesses. *you will be my witnesses.* In Isaiah, God told the remnant of Israel, "You are my witnesses" (Isa 43:10,12; 44:8); they would affirm the truth about the one true God against the nations' polytheism. The context in Isaiah also may suggest the Spirit prophetically empowering God's servant, i.e., these witnesses (Isa 42:1; 44:3; 48:16; 59:21). Here God's witnesses become Jesus' witnesses. *the ends of the earth.* Echoes many OT passages but most directly Isa 49:6 (cf. Ac 13:47). Ancient works sometimes provided a preliminary outline of subjects they would treat; this verse functions as a very rudimentary (though asymmetric) geographic outline. Jewish people often viewed Jerusalem as the world's center; Luke's first volume begins and ends there, but his second volume progresses from Jerusalem to Rome. Many in Luke's world thought of Spain as the western end of the earth, Ethiopia (8:27; cf. Lk 11:31) as the southern end, and knew of the east as far as China. Although Acts climaxes with the gospel reaching the heart of the empire, Luke's immediate world, "the ends of the earth" looks beyond this to all peoples (e.g., Isa 45:22; 52:10).

1:9 *taken up before their very eyes.* Whether at this time or on further reflection, Jesus' disciples would likely compare his ascension to God's taking up of Elijah (see the article "Ascensions," p. 1868). *cloud.* Fits the announcement that Jesus would "come back in the same way" (v. 11); it probably evokes Da 7:13–14 (cited in Lk 21:27, though Lk 22:69 omits the cloud). It may additionally evoke the cloud of God's glory (Ex 16:10; 40:34–35; 1Ki 8:11).

1:10 *dressed in white.* Cf. note on Lk 24:4.

1:12 *the Mount of Olives.* Relevant to returning "in the same way" (v. 11); the divine Lord had promised to stand on the Mount of Olives (Zec 14:4) in the time of his coming (Zec 14:1), a context to which Luke alludes in Lk 9:26 (Zec 14:5). *a Sabbath day's walk.* This mountain was roughly a half mile (three-quarters of a kilometer) to the temple's east, which was also roughly a Sabbath day's walk by the most common Jewish standards. (A Sabbath day's walk was 2,000 cubits, probably in the general range of some 3,000 feet [900 meters].)

1:13 *upstairs to the room.* Large upper rooms were more available in Jerusalem's wealthy upper city. *Peter … Judas.* Ancient sources often included lists of heroes, leaders, and so forth. See notes on Mk 3:16–19. *Judas son of James.*

ACTS 1:9

ASCENSIONS

The ancient world had many ascension stories, often about humans who were turned into gods at their deaths. Thus, e.g., in one story Heracles (after raping and pillaging) was burned alive on his funeral pyre, and turning into a god, ascended to heaven. These stories, however, normally referred to ascending spirits, not to actual bodily ascensions. They did not envision bodily ascensions because they did not envision bodily resurrections.

A much likelier background, by contrast, is the Biblical account of Elijah's ascension (2Ki 2:1 – 18). This was a bodily ascension and, because it was explicit in the Bible, was the ascension most obvious and widely known to Luke's audience. (Luke cites Greek poets only on rare occasions but cites the Septuagint, the pre-Christian Greek translation of the OT, repeatedly, especially in this section of Acts.) It would also be the background most obvious to Jesus' followers. Just as Elisha was with Elijah when the latter ascended and Elisha received a double portion of the Spirit on Elijah (2Ki 2:9 – 11), so Jesus' followers received the Spirit after Jesus ascended (see note on Ac 1:8). ◆

present were Peter, John, James and Andrew; Philip and Thomas, Bartholomew and Matthew; James son of Alphaeus and Simon the Zealot, and Judas son of James.[v] [14]They all joined together constantly in prayer,[w] along with the women[x] and Mary the mother of Jesus, and with his brothers.[y]

[15]In those days Peter stood up among the believers (a group numbering about a hundred and twenty) [16]and said, "Brothers and sisters,[a] the Scripture had to be fulfilled[z] in which the Holy Spirit spoke long ago through David concerning Judas,[a] who served as guide for those who arrested Jesus. [17]He was one of our number[b] and shared in our ministry."[c]

[18](With the payment[d] he received for his wickedness, Judas bought a field;[e] there he fell headlong, his body burst open and all his intestines spilled out. [19]Everyone in Jerusalem heard about this, so they called that field in their language Akeldama, that is, Field of Blood.)

[20]"For," said Peter, "it is written in the Book of Psalms:

"'May his place be deserted;
let there be no one to dwell in it,'[bf]

and,

"'May another take his place of
leadership.'[cg]

1:13 [v]Mt 10:2-4; Mk 3:16-19; Lk 6:14-16 **1:14** [w]Ac 2:42; 6:4 [x]Lk 23:49, 55 [y]Mt 12:46 **1:16** [z]ver 20 [a]Jn 13:18 **1:17** [b]Jn 6:70, 71 [c]ver 25 **1:18** [d]Mt 26:14, 15 [e]Mt 27:3-10 **1:20** [f]Ps 69:25 [g]Ps 109:8

[a] *16* The Greek word for *brothers and sisters* (*adelphoi*) refers here to believers, both men and women, as part of God's family; also in 6:3; 11:29; 12:17; 16:40; 18:18, 27; 21:7, 17; 28:14, 15. [b] *20* Psalm 69:25 [c] *20* Psalm 109:8

Not Judas Iscariot, but the same person as Thaddaeus (Mt 10:3).

1:14 *constantly in prayer.* Prayer is a key theme in Luke-Acts. Although women were separated from men in later synagogues, there is no evidence for such separation in this period. Nevertheless, it is significant, in view of cultural prejudices, that Luke notes the women's participation in the prayers (so implying also their receiving the Spirit in ch. 2; cf. 2:17 – 18).

1:15 *stood up.* One would normally stand to address a group. *a hundred and twenty.* A large number, especially if all were in an upper room. One Jewish tradition reported that in Ezra's day 120 elders transmitted the Torah; others suggest one priestly leader for every ten members in the Dead Sea Scrolls, and propose that 120 disciples therefore fits a group of about 12 leaders. Apart from the observation that the number is large, none of these proposed parallels is certain.

1:18 – 19 Ancient writers often used digressions. People often expected the wicked to meet a painful end; apostates were deemed among the most wicked. If Judas died by hanging, as in Matthew's account (Mt 27:5), his innards could well have ruptured when the rope was cut and the body fell, if he were far above the ground.

1:19 *in their language.* The local language was Aramaic, though Greek was also widely used in Jerusalem.

1:20 – 21 The texts cited here are Ps 69:25 and Ps 109:8; both verses begin similarly in Greek. Both psalms were laments and prayers for deliverance. Early Christians often applied Ps 69 to Jesus, as it was one of the psalms of a

21Therefore it is necessary to choose one of
the men who have been with us the whole
time the Lord Jesus was living among us,
22beginning from John's baptism[h] to the
time when Jesus was taken up from us.
For one of these must become a witness[i]
with us of his resurrection."
23So they nominated two men: Joseph
called Barsabbas (also known as Justus)
and Matthias. 24Then they prayed,[j] "Lord,
you know everyone's heart.[k] Show us
which of these two you have chosen 25to
take over this apostolic ministry, which
Judas left to go where he belongs." 26Then
they cast lots, and the lot fell to Matthias;
so he was added to the eleven apostles.[l]

The Holy Spirit Comes at Pentecost

2 When the day of Pentecost[m] came,
they were all together[n] in one place.
2Suddenly a sound like the blowing of a
violent wind came from heaven and filled
the whole house where they were sitting.[o]
3They saw what seemed to be tongues of
fire that separated and came to rest on
each of them. 4All of them were filled with
the Holy Spirit and began to speak in other
tongues[a][p] as the Spirit enabled them.
5Now there were staying in Jerusalem God-fearing[q] Jews from every nation under heaven. 6When they heard
this sound, a crowd came together in
bewilderment, because each one heard
their own language being spoken. 7Utter-
ly amazed,[r] they asked: "Aren't all these
who are speaking Galileans?[s] 8Then how
is it that each of us hears them in our
native language? 9Parthians, Medes and
Elamites; residents of Mesopotamia, Judea and Cappadocia,[t] Pontus[u] and Asia,[b][v]
10Phrygia[w] and Pamphylia,[x] Egypt and
the parts of Libya near Cyrene;[y] visitors

1:22 [h] Mk 1:4 [i] ver 8
1:24 [j] Ac 6:6; 14:23 [k] 1Sa 16:7; Jer 17:10; Ac 15:8; Rev 2:23
1:26 [l] Ac 2:14
2:1 [m] Lev 23:15, 16; Ac 20:16 [n] Ac 1:14
2:2 [o] Ac 4:31
2:4 [p] Mk 16:17; 1Co 12:10
2:5 [q] Ac 8:2
2:7 [r] ver 12 [s] Ac 1:11
2:9 [t] 1Pe 1:1 [u] Ac 18:2 [v] Ac 16:6; Ro 16:5; 1Co 16:19; 2Co 1:8
2:10 [w] Ac 16:6; 18:23 [x] Ac 13:13; 15:38 [y] Mt 27:32

[a] 4 Or *languages*; also in verse 11 [b] 9 That is, the Roman province by that name

righteous sufferer. Peter might use the common Jewish "How much more?" approach to applying Scripture: in this case, if something was true of a righteous sufferer's enemies, how much more would it be true of the *most* righteous sufferer's enemies?

1:22 *must become a witness.* Hearers took eyewitness testimony more seriously than other claims. Restoring the original number of chief witnesses was also important. Twelve was the sacred number of Israel's tribes; those who saw themselves as a remnant of or renewal movement within Israel could symbolize this belief by choosing 12 leaders (cf. 1QS 8.1 – 2 in the Dead Sea Scrolls). A group would often be given a title according to the number of its members (e.g., the Four Hundred); in contrast to here ("the eleven" in v. 26; 2:14), the title would sometimes remain even when the number of actual members in the group fluctuated (cf. 1Co 15:5).

1:23 *Joseph called Barsabbas (also known as Justus).* Papyri show that many people had two or even three names or nicknames, especially if one of their names (such as Joseph) was very common. *Barsabbas.* Means "son of the Sabbath"; the name was sometimes given to one born on the Sabbath. *Justus.* Means "the just one"; it was common both as a name and as a nickname.

1:24 *you know everyone's heart.* Judaism widely acknowledged that God knew everyone's heart.

1:26 *they cast lots.* Gentiles cast lots to fill many sorts of leadership positions; Jewish people also did so (e.g., 1Ch 24:5). Because Scripture allowed casting lots, Jewish people did not consider it divination, which was prohibited (although Gentiles treated it like divination). *lots.* People could use various items as lots (often stones or pieces of pottery), often with a particular item designating a particular person; then they could shake the container till a particular lot fell out. At other times, each could pull a random lot.

2:1 *Pentecost.* The Festival of Weeks, about seven weeks or 50 days after Passover (Lev 23:15 – 16). It was here that God's people celebrated the first of the wheat harvest (Ex 34:22; Nu 28:26; Dt 16:9 – 10). Jewish tradition also associated the festival with covenant renewal. Not everyone in the Diaspora could attend the three expected pilgrimage festivals (Dt 16:16; 2Ch 8:13), but local people could, and large numbers of Diaspora Jews would be present for each festival. Jerusalem would thus be crowded at this time.

2:2 – 3 *sound like the blowing of a violent wind … tongues of fire.* Storm phenomena such as wind and fire attended some Biblical theophanies (Ex 19:16; 1Ki 19:11; Eze 1:4). Wind also could evoke God's Spirit raising the dead and restoring God's people, as in Eze 37:5 – 14. Fire similarly could evoke end-time judgment (Isa 29:6; 66:15 – 16,24), as it does elsewhere in Luke's work (Lk 3:16 – 17). Thus the wind and fire may suggest a theophany, the in-breaking of the end-time era, or both.

2:4 *other tongues.* One Jewish tradition suggests that God offered the Torah to all nations at Sinai in their own languages. Most relevant is Luke's connection of the speaking with Joel's promise of prophetic empowerment (vv. 17 – 18); that it is in other languages comports well with Luke's emphasis on the Spirit's power to speak cross-culturally (1:8).

2:5 *staying in Jerusalem God-fearing Jews.* Scholars debate whether these Diaspora Jewish residents had merely stayed over since Passover because the journey was long and their coming would be rare or because they had settled in Jerusalem long-term (such as those noted in 6:1; this fits the usual meaning of the Greek term translated "staying"), or some of both.

2:6 *each one heard their own language.* Diaspora Jews in the Roman Empire mostly spoke Greek; in the east, they spoke especially Aramaic. Yet many Diaspora Jews would also be familiar with local languages and dialects spoken in the areas where they lived. The hearers must have understood at least enough of such dialects to recognize that Jesus' followers were praising God (v. 11).

2:7 – 8 Many scholars see here a reversal of or a parallel with Babel (Ge 11:1 – 9). There God scattered languages to divide the people; here he scatters them to bring people together in Christ.

2:9 – 11 Although updated to reflect the geographic titles of Luke's day, the list of nations here evokes the Bible's first list of nations, Ge 10 — which directly precedes the Biblical account of Babel (Ge 11:1 – 9). Most of the descendants of Israel who had not returned to Judea after the Babylonian exile remained in Parthia and among other eastern peoples listed here. Many Jews in the Mediterranean Diaspora lived in Alexandria in Egypt, Cyrene in

from Rome 11(both Jews and converts to
Judaism); Cretans and Arabs — we hear
them declaring the wonders of God in our
own tongues!" 12Amazed and perplexed,
they asked one another, "What does this
mean?"
13Some, however, made fun of them and
said, "They have had too much wine."[z]

Peter Addresses the Crowd

14Then Peter stood up with the Eleven,
raised his voice and addressed the crowd:
"Fellow Jews and all of you who live in Jerusalem, let me explain this to you; listen
carefully to what I say. 15These people are
not drunk, as you suppose. It's only nine
in the morning![a] 16No, this is what was
spoken by the prophet Joel:

17" 'In the last days, God says,
I will pour out my Spirit on all people.[b]
Your sons and daughters will prophesy,[c]
your young men will see visions,
your old men will dream dreams.
18Even on my servants, both men and women,
I will pour out my Spirit in those days,
and they will prophesy.[d]
19I will show wonders in the heavens above
and signs on the earth below,
blood and fire and billows of smoke.

2:13 [z] 1Co 14:23
2:15 [a] 1Th 5:7
2:17 [b] Isa 44:3; Jn 7:37-39; Ac 10:45 [c] Ac 21:9
2:18 [d] Ac 21:9-12

Libya, Syria, Asia Minor, and Rome. "Arabs" refers especially to the Nabateans, who were common to the east and south of Judea and as far north as Damascus. Nabateans controlled the caravan route from Damascus in the north to the Sinai in the south, and thus also controlled the spice trade from the east; they were known as merchants even in China. Nabatea's capital, Petra, was in a steep and rocky area yet was prosperous and well watered; its king was Aretas IV (see note on 2Co 11:32). They spoke an ancient dialect of Arabic, although Greek was known among them; they were polytheistic, but many Jews settled in their region and some Nabateans converted.

2:13 *made fun.* Heckling speakers was common in public settings, often as a way of making hecklers seem more clever. *had too much wine.* Some ancient writers, especially the Jewish philosopher Philo, depicted divine inspiration as a form of spiritual inebriation.

2:14 *the Eleven.* See note on 1:22, though it could mean "eleven besides himself" (cf. 1:26).

2:15 *nine in the morning!* People who got drunk usually did so at night.

2:17 *In the last days.* Jewish interpreters sometimes adapted the wording of texts to bring out their meaning. Joel says "in those days"; Peter says "in the last days," rightly understanding that Joel's context refers to the end time (Joel 3:1). *prophesy.* Many Jewish people, especially among the educated and the elite, believed that prophets no longer existed in their day in the same manner that they did in the past (though some did allow for accurate prophecy without the prophets). Peter, however, cites the prophetic promise that all God's people would be empowered by the prophetic Spirit to hear from God. *see visions … dream dreams.* Most commonly those who dreamed dreams and saw visions were prophets (e.g., Nu 12:6; 1Sa 3:1; Eze 1:1).

2:18 *and they will prophesy.* Peter adds this to Joel and, in doing so, summarizes Joel's point.

2:19 *wonders … signs.* Although Joel already mentioned wonders, Peter adds "signs," probably to clarify a con-

COUNTRIES OF PEOPLE MENTIONED AT PENTECOST

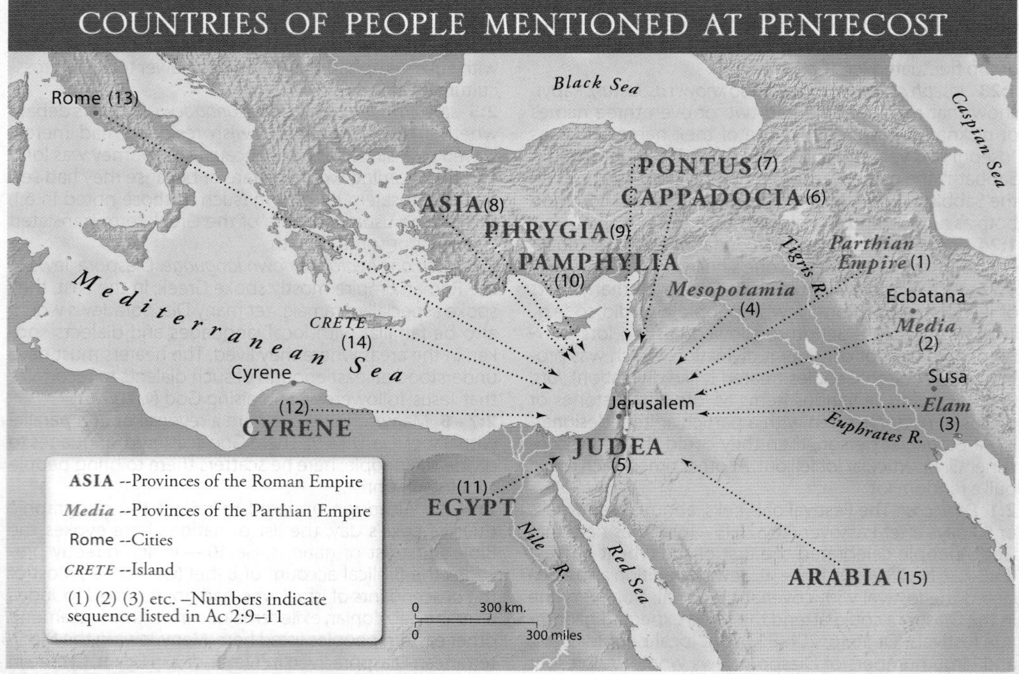

20 The sun will be turned to darkness
and the moon to blood[e]
before the coming of the great and
glorious day of the Lord.
21 And everyone who calls
on the name of the Lord will be
saved.'[a][f]

22 "Fellow Israelites, listen to this: Jesus
of Nazareth was a man accredited by God
to you by miracles, wonders and signs,[g]
which God did among you through him,[h]
as you yourselves know. 23 This man was
handed over to you by God's deliberate
plan and foreknowledge;[i] and you, with
the help of wicked men,[b] put him to death
by nailing him to the cross.[j] 24 But God
raised him from the dead,[k] freeing him
from the agony of death, because it was
impossible for death to keep its hold on
him.[l] 25 David said about him:

"'I saw the Lord always before me.
Because he is at my right hand,
I will not be shaken.
26 Therefore my heart is glad and my
tongue rejoices;
my body also will rest in hope,
27 because you will not abandon me to
the realm of the dead,
you will not let your holy one see
decay.[m]
28 You have made known to me the paths
of life;
you will fill me with joy in your
presence.'[c]

2:20 [e]Mt 24:29
2:21 [f]Ro 10:13
2:22 [g]Jn 4:48; Ac 10:38 [h]Jn 3:2
2:23 [i]Lk 22:22; Ac 3:18; 4:28 [j]Lk 24:20; Ac 3:13
2:24 [k]ver 32; 1Co 6:14; 2Co 4:14; Eph 1:20; Col 2:12; Heb 13:20; 1Pe 1:21 [l]Jn 20:9
2:27 [m]ver 31; Ac 13:35
2:29 [n]Ac 7:8, 9 [o]1Ki 2:10; Ac 13:36 [p]Ne 3:16
2:30 [q]2Sa 7:12; Ps 132:11
2:31 [r]Ps 16:10
2:32 [s]ver 24 [t]Ac 1:8
2:33 [u]Php 2:9 [v]Mk 16:19 [w]Ac 1:4 [x]Jn 7:39; 14:26 [y]Ac 10:45
2:35 [z]Ps 110:1; Mt 22:44
2:36 [a]Lk 2:11
2:37 [b]Lk 3:10, 12, 14
2:38 [c]Ac 8:12, 16, 36, 38; 22:16

29 "Fellow Israelites, I can tell you confidently that the patriarch[n] David died and
was buried,[o] and his tomb is here[p] to this
day. 30 But he was a prophet and knew
that God had promised him on oath that
he would place one of his descendants on
his throne.[q] 31 Seeing what was to come, he
spoke of the resurrection of the Messiah,
that he was not abandoned to the realm
of the dead, nor did his body see decay.[r]
32 God has raised this Jesus to life,[s] and we
are all witnesses[t] of it. 33 Exalted[u] to the
right hand of God,[v] he has received from
the Father[w] the promised Holy Spirit[x] and
has poured out[y] what you now see and
hear. 34 For David did not ascend to heav-
en, and yet he said,

"'The Lord said to my Lord:
"Sit at my right hand
35 until I make your enemies
a footstool for your feet."'[d][z]

36 "Therefore let all Israel be assured of
this: God has made this Jesus, whom you
crucified, both Lord and Messiah."[a]
37 When the people heard this, they
were cut to the heart and said to Peter and
the other apostles, "Brothers, what shall
we do?"[b]
38 Peter replied, "Repent and be baptized,[c] every one of you, in the name of
Jesus Christ for the forgiveness of your

[a] 21 Joel 2:28-32
[b] 23 Or *of those not having the law* (that is, Gentiles)
[c] 28 Psalm 16:8-11 (see Septuagint)
[d] 35 Psalm 110:1

nection with some events that had already taken place. Although aspects of this promise may remain future (Lk 21:25–27), Peter can apply it to the present (v. 22; Lk 23:44–45).

2:21 *will be saved.* Salvation belongs to the same era as the outpoured prophetic Spirit. Peter breaks off his Joel quotation here; Joel goes on to speak of those "whom the LORD calls" (Joel 2:32)—a point to which Peter finally turns in Ac 2:39. In the intervening verses, Peter expounds (as Jewish interpreters often did) the line he has just quoted. In Peter's day, "LORD" (the divine name Yahweh) was read in Hebrew in the same way as "Lord," and the Greek word for "Lord" was used for both, so it is easy for Peter to link the name of "the LORD" in Joel with the exalted "my lord" of Ps 110:1 (see note on Ac 2:34–35).

2:22 *miracles, wonders and signs.* See note on v. 19. The collocation of "wonders" and "signs" recalls the signs that took place when God saved his people in the exodus (e.g., Ex 7:3; Dt 4:34).

2:23 *you … put him to death.* Even if others carried out the direct action, those who designed it shared the guilt (2Sa 12:9). *cross.* Crucifixion was a naked, humiliating death by slow torture.

2:24 *agony of death.* Reflects OT phraseology (cf. the Septuagint, the pre-Christian Greek translation of the OT, for 2Sa 22:6), as do other elements here.

2:29 *his tomb is here to this day.* Tombs dedicated to famous people of the past, including David and Huldah, existed in Jerusalem.

2:30 *one of his descendants.* Many prophecies applied not to David himself but to his line or, in much first-century understanding, his ultimate descendant, the Messiah.

2:33 *he has received … and has poured out.* In the OT, only God could pour out God's Spirit; Peter thus identifies Jesus as divine—God who pours out the Spirit in Joel 2:28–29.

2:34–35 Jewish interpreters commonly linked texts based on a common key word or thought. Ps 110:1, like Ps 16:8–11 (cited in Ac 2:25–28), speaks of exaltation and of a "right hand." Ps 110:1 clearly speaks of one who would rule as God's vizier, and Peter links the Davidic risen one with this ruler at God's right hand.

2:36 *Lord and Messiah.* Ps 16 applied to David's descendant; as the risen one of Ps 16, Jesus is Christ; as the one at God's right hand of Ps 110, he is called "Lord" (as Peter learned from Jesus; Lk 20:42–43).

2:37 *what shall we do?* Ancient writers could examine points from different angles; Luke provides complementary answers for this basic question in different passages (16:30–31; cf. 9:6; Lk 18:18–22).

2:38 *Repent and be baptized.* Peter applies the demand of Joel 2:32, which he quotes in v. 21: "everyone who calls on the name of the Lord will be saved." He has demonstrated that the "Lord's" name (in light of Ps 110:1, Ps 16:8–11, and Jesus' resurrection) is Jesus; people may call on his name by being baptized in it. (Baptism in a "name" made the baptism distinctive.) Jewish people believed in repenting for sins and in various ceremonial washings, but a once-for-all sort of baptism and turning applied especially to

sins.[d] And you will receive the gift of the
Holy Spirit. 39The promise is for you and
your children[e] and for all who are far
off[f]—for all whom the Lord our God will
call."
40With many other words he warned
them; and he pleaded with them, "Save
yourselves from this corrupt generation."[g]
41Those who accepted his message were
baptized, and about three thousand were
added to their number that day.

The Fellowship of the Believers

42They devoted themselves to the apostles' teaching and to fellowship, to the
breaking of bread and to prayer.[h] 43Every-
one was filled with awe at the many wonders and signs performed by the apostles.[i]
44All the believers were together and had
everything in common.[j] 45They sold property and possessions to give to anyone
who had need.[k] 46Every day they continued to meet together in the temple courts.[l]
They broke bread[m] in their homes and ate
together with glad and sincere hearts,
47praising God and enjoying the favor of
all the people.[n] And the Lord added to
their number[o] daily those who were being saved.

Peter Heals a Lame Beggar

3 One day Peter and John[p] were going up to the temple[q] at the time of
prayer—at three in the afternoon.[r] 2Now a
man who was lame from birth[s] was being
carried to the temple gate[t] called Beautiful, where he was put every day to beg[u]
from those going into the temple courts.
3When he saw Peter and John about to
enter, he asked them for money. 4Peter
looked straight at him, as did John. Then
Peter said, "Look at us!" 5So the man gave
them his attention, expecting to get something from them.
6Then Peter said, "Silver or gold I do not
have, but what I do have I give you. In the
name of Jesus Christ of Nazareth,[v] walk."
7Taking him by the right hand, he helped
him up, and instantly the man's feet and
ankles became strong. 8He jumped to his

2:38 [d] Lk 24:47; Ac 3:19
2:39 [e] Isa 44:3 [f] Ac 10:45; Eph 2:13
2:40 [g] Dt 32:5
2:42 [h] Ac 1:14
2:43 [i] Ac 5:12
2:44 [j] Ac 4:32
2:45 [k] Mt 19:21
2:46 [l] Lk 24:53; Ac 5:21,42 [m] Ac 20:7
2:47 [n] Ro 14:18 [o] ver 41; Ac 5:14
3:1 [p] Lk 22:8 [q] Ac 2:46 [r] Ps 55:17
3:2 [s] Ac 14:8 [t] Lk 16:20 [u] Jn 9:8
3:6 [v] ver 16; Ac 4:10

Gentiles converting to Judaism. For Peter, everyone, whether Jewish or Gentile, must acknowledge their need and embrace Christ. *the gift of the Holy Spirit.* Refers to the promise of Joel 2:28–29 (cited in Ac 2:17–18), which most Jewish people believed had been available to at most a few people in their time.

2:39 *for all who are far off.* Probably echoes Isa 57:19. "For all whom the Lord our God will call" completes Peter's quotation of Joel 2:32; from Ac 2:21–36, Peter was explaining an earlier line of Joel 2:32, quoted in Ac 2:21, arguing that Jesus was the Lord's name on which they were to call.

2:40 *With many other words.* Ancient writers lacked means to quote speeches verbatim, except when speakers followed and later published manuscripts of their speeches, but sought to offer their essence. Luke summarizes Peter's urging here in words that echo the Septuagint, the pre-Christian Greek translation of the OT for Dt 32:5 (a "crooked generation").

2:41 *baptized.* Jewish people baptized Gentiles converting to Judaism—for Jewish people to be baptized the same way displays remarkable commitment (see note on v. 38). *three thousand.* So many pools for ritual immersion were on the temple mount that 3,000 could easily be immersed in a few hours. These pools were segregated by gender, and people normally walked down the steps into them naked, immersed themselves (often by bending forward), and then walked back up steps. Against earlier estimates, Jerusalem's population at this time may have been around 70,000 to 80,000 (not including visitors). Nevertheless, 3,000 is no small figure: by way of comparison, Josephus, known to often estimate high, estimates only 6,000 Pharisees in all of Judea.

2:42–47 Summary sections such as this were common in ancient sources.

2:44–45 The language Luke employs here is typical of the language other ancient writers used for ideal, sometimes even utopian, communities; it is, in other words, very positive language. At the same time, the sharing it depicts was very rare. Among exceptions, ancient writers report that the Jewish sect of Essenes (with an estimated 4,000 members) lived without private property, sharing everything in common; the Dead Sea Scrolls confirm this report at least for the community in the desert. Likewise, some Greek idealist sects such as the Pythagoreans rejected private property. By contrast, the early Christians sold property whenever anyone had need (4:34–35); they valued people more than property without rejecting private property altogether. They did not go as far as the Essenes or Pythagoreans, but they went much farther than the vast proportion of ancient society.

2:46 *Every day.* Greek associations typically met once a month. Except for the most radical sects, the daily sharing here is unusual in antiquity and most resembles how people treated members of their own family.

2:47 *enjoying the favor of all the people.* Cf., e.g., Ge 39:4,21; Ex 3:21.

3:1 *the time of prayer—at three in the afternoon.* Coincides with the time of the "evening" offering in the temple.

3:2 *the temple gate called Beautiful.* Some think that this refers to the bronze Nicanor gate, which was renowned for its beauty, although this local name for it (or another of the temple's gates) is not attested elsewhere.

3:3 *about to enter.* Ancient understandings of purity may have kept the disabled from entering the court of Israel, but nothing would have kept them from the outer courts. The temple was a public place, and because Judaism connected piety with generosity, it was probably a more profitable place to beg. The disabled often lacked means of support other than the difficult life of begging (see note on Jn 9:8).

3:6 Ancient observers tried to discern harmful sorcerers from those who worked by divine power. One criterion for distinguishing them was that those who used power for their own material advancement were associated with sorcery; sorcerers also acted secretively. Wonderworkers who lived simply and acted in public, as here, were more respected and trusted. *In the name of Jesus Christ.* Probably means that Peter and John act as his agents, ministering on behalf of Jesus; senders authorized agents to act in their stead.

feet and began to walk. Then he went with
them into the temple courts, walking and
jumping,[w] and praising God. 9When all
the people[x] saw him walking and praising
God, 10they recognized him as the same
man who used to sit begging at the temple
gate called Beautiful,[y] and they were filled
with wonder and amazement at what had
happened to him.

Peter Speaks to the Onlookers

11While the man held on to Peter and
John,[z] all the people were astonished and
came running to them in the place called
Solomon's Colonnade.[a] 12When Peter
saw this, he said to them: "Fellow Israelites, why does this surprise you? Why
do you stare at us as if by our own power
or godliness we had made this man walk?
13The God of Abraham, Isaac and Jacob,
the God of our fathers,[b] has glorified his
servant Jesus. You handed him over to be
killed, and you disowned him before Pilate,[c] though he had decided to let him
go.[d] 14You disowned the Holy[e] and Righteous One[f] and asked that a murderer be
released to you.[g] 15You killed the author
of life, but God raised him from the dead.[h]
We are witnesses of this. 16By faith in the
name of Jesus, this man whom you see
and know was made strong. It is Jesus'
name and the faith that comes through
him that has completely healed him, as
you can all see.
17"Now, fellow Israelites, I know that
you acted in ignorance,[i] as did your leaders.[j] 18But this is how God fulfilled what
he had foretold[k] through all the prophets,[l]
saying that his Messiah would suffer.[m]
19Repent, then, and turn to God, so that
your sins may be wiped out,[n] that times
of refreshing may come from the Lord,
20and that he may send the Messiah, who
has been appointed for you—even Jesus.
21Heaven must receive him[o] until the time
comes for God to restore everything,[p] as
he promised long ago through his holy
prophets.[q] 22For Moses said, 'The Lord
your God will raise up for you a prophet like me from among your own people;
you must listen to everything he tells you.[r]
23Anyone who does not listen to him will
be completely cut off from their people.'[a][s]
24"Indeed, beginning with Samuel, all
the prophets[t] who have spoken have foretold these days. 25And you are heirs[u] of
the prophets and of the covenant[v] God
made with your fathers. He said to Abraham, 'Through your offspring all peoples
on earth will be blessed.'[b][w] 26When God
raised up[x] his servant, he sent him first[y]
to you to bless you by turning each of you
from your wicked ways."

Peter and John Before the Sanhedrin

4 The priests and the captain of the temple guard[z] and the Sadducees[a] came
up to Peter and John while they were
speaking to the people. 2They were greatly disturbed because the apostles were
teaching the people, proclaiming in Jesus

3:8 [w] Ac 14:10 **3:9** [x] Ac 4:16,21 **3:10** [y] ver 2 **3:11** [z] Lk 22:8 [a] Jn 10:23; Ac 5:12 **3:13** [b] Ac 5:30 [c] Mt 27:2 [d] Lk 23:4 **3:14** [e] Mk 1:24; Ac 4:27 [f] Ac 7:52 [g] Mk 15:11; Lk 23:18-25 **3:15** [h] Ac 2:24 **3:17** [i] Lk 23:34 [j] Ac 13:27 **3:18** [k] Ac 2:23 [l] Lk 24:27 [m] Ac 17:2,3; 26:22,23 **3:19** [n] Ac 2:38 **3:21** [o] Ac 1:11 [p] Mt 17:11 [q] Lk 1:70 **3:22** [r] Dt 18:15,18; Ac 7:37 **3:23** [s] Dt 18:19 **3:24** [t] Lk 24:27 **3:25** [u] Ac 2:39 [v] Ro 9:4,5 [w] Ge 12:3; 22:18; 26:4; 28:14 **3:26** [x] ver 22; Ac 2:24 [y] Ac 13:46; Ro 1:16 **4:1** [z] Lk 22:4 [a] Mt 3:7

[a] *23* Deut. 18:15,18,19 [b] *25* Gen. 22:18; 26:4

3:11 *Solomon's Colonnade.* See note on Jn 10:23.
3:12 *as if by our own power or godliness.* Jewish tradition sometimes associated miracle workers with exceptional holiness (as in later rabbinic stories about Honi the Circle-Drawer and Hanina ben Dosa). Peter attributes the power instead to the Lord in whose name he has acted (vv. 6,16).
3:13 *The God of Abraham, Isaac and Jacob.* Jewish prayers regularly referred to God in this way. *glorified his servant Jesus.* In the Septuagint, the pre-Christian Greek translation of the OT, for Isa 52:13, the "servant" (in the passage preceding Isa 53) was "glorified" (cf. also Isa 49:3,5); see notes on Mt 12:18–21; Jn 12:32. *Pilate.* See note on Mt 27:2. *decided to let him go.* Isaiah's servant was "righteous" (Isa 53:11; cf. perhaps Ac 3:14).
3:15 *author of life.* In the Septuagint, the pre-Christian Greek translation of the OT, the term "author" applied to clan leaders, and in the Greek world, to founders of cities, sometimes heroes, and so forth; it had a wide range of meaning, but here some think it refers to the founder who paved the way of life.
3:17 *you acted in ignorance.* In ancient thinking and even law, ignorance reduced culpability.
3:18 *the prophets, saying that his Messiah would suffer.* Some later rabbis suggested (exaggerating for emphasis) that the prophets prophesied only about the Messianic era. Apparently the Christians were the first to recognize biblical teaching about a suffering Messiah, however.
3:20 *that he may send the Messiah.* Later teachers debated whether God had fixed a time for the end (cf. 1:7) or conditioned it on Israel's repentance, or both. Biblical prophets promised restoration when Israel would turn back to the Lord (e.g., Hos 14:1–7; Joel 2:18—3:1; cf. Dt 4:30–31).
3:21 *the time ... to restore everything.* Isaiah promised the restoration of creation—peace and prosperity in the earth (e.g., Isa 11:6–9; 65:17). It was associated with a new Jerusalem (Isa 65:18–19; 66:8–11) and the restoration of God's people (which may be the primary focus here; see Ac 1:6 and note).
3:22–23 Peter cites from Dt 18:15–19; the Dead Sea Scrolls and other sources suggest that many of Peter's contemporaries were expecting a prophet like Moses to arise.
3:25 Peter cites Ge 22:18; cf. Ge 26:4; 28:14; cf. also the wording of Ge 12:3.
4:1 The majority of the ruling elite, especially from aristocratic priestly families, came from the Sadducees. *captain of the temple guard.* Also known as the *sagan*, the captain of the temple guard was a powerful Sadducee and was known for being harsh even to those under his command. *temple guard.* Consisted of Levites designated as the temple's police force, who were tasked with keeping order (cf. 1Ch 9:26–27; 2Ch 35:15).
4:2 *the resurrection of the dead.* Resurrection was the raising and transforming of the body expected at the beginning of the new world. The Sadducees, who rejected future bodily resurrection, tolerated the Pharisees.

the resurrection of the dead.[b] 3They seized Peter and John and, because it was evening, they put them in jail[c] until the next day. 4But many who heard the message believed; so the number of men who believed grew[d] to about five thousand.

5The next day the rulers,[e] the elders and the teachers of the law met in Jerusalem. 6Annas the high priest was there, and so were Caiaphas,[f] John, Alexander and others of the high priest's family. 7They had Peter and John brought before them and began to question them: "By what power or what name did you do this?"

8Then Peter, filled with the Holy Spirit, said to them: "Rulers and elders of the people![g] 9If we are being called to account today for an act of kindness shown to a man who was lame[h] and are being asked how he was healed, 10then know this, you and all the people of Israel: It is by the name of Jesus Christ of Nazareth, whom you crucified but whom God raised from the dead,[i] that this man stands before you healed. 11Jesus is

> " 'the stone you builders rejected,
> which has become the cornerstone.'[a][j]

12Salvation is found in no one else, for there is no other name under heaven given to mankind by which we must be saved."[k]

13When they saw the courage of Peter and John[l] and realized that they were unschooled, ordinary men,[m] they were astonished and they took note that these men had been with Jesus. 14But since they could see the man who had been healed standing there with them, there was nothing they could say. 15So they ordered them to withdraw from the Sanhedrin[n] and then conferred together. 16"What are we going to do with these men?"[o] they asked. "Everyone living in Jerusalem knows they have performed a notable sign,[p] and we cannot deny it. 17But to stop this thing from spreading any further among the people, we must warn them to speak no longer to anyone in this name."

18Then they called them in again and commanded them not to speak or teach at all in the name of Jesus.[q] 19But Peter and John replied, "Which is right in God's eyes: to listen to you, or to him?[r] You be the judges! 20As for us, we cannot help speaking about what we have seen and heard."

21After further threats they let them go. They could not decide how to punish them, because all the people[s] were praising God[t] for what had happened. 22For the man who was miraculously healed was over forty years old.

The Believers Pray

23On their release, Peter and John went back to their own people and reported all that the chief priests and the elders had said to them. 24When they heard this, they raised their voices together in prayer to God. "Sovereign Lord," they said, "you made the heavens and the earth and the

4:2 [b] Ac 17:18
4:3 [c] Ac 5:18
4:4 [d] Ac 2:41
4:5 [e] Lk 23:13
4:6 [f] Mt 26:3; Lk 3:2
4:8 [g] ver 5; Lk 23:13
4:9 [h] Ac 3:6
4:10 [i] Ac 2:24
4:11 [j] Ps 118:22; Isa 28:16; Mt 21:42
4:12 [k] Mt 1:21; Ac 10:43; 1Ti 2:5
4:13 [l] Lk 22:8 [m] Mt 11:25
4:15 [n] Mt 5:22
4:16 [o] Jn 11:47 [p] Ac 3:6-10
4:18 [q] Ac 5:40
4:19 [r] Ac 5:29
4:21 [s] Ac 5:26 [t] Mt 9:8

[a] *11* Psalm 118:22

Evidence suggests that the majority of Judeans and Galileans believed in a future resurrection, and the Sadducees also had to tolerate them. Jesus' witnesses, however, advocated not some theoretical hope for the future but the belief that the first case of the promised resurrection had already occurred.

4:3 *evening.* Most business, including legitimate legal hearings, occurred during daylight; the two apostles had been preaching since late afternoon (3:1).

4:4 *five thousand.* For how extraordinary these numbers are, see note on 2:41. Because no festival was occurring, these converts would be mostly Judeans not already familiar with Jesus' Galilean ministry. The usual ancient practice was to number only the men, as in Luke's source here.

4:5 *the rulers, the elders and the teachers of the law.* Together leading members of these groups constituted the Sanhedrin (v. 15), Jerusalem's municipal senate that oversaw Judean matters.

4:6 *Annas.* See note on Jn 18:13. *Caiaphas.* See note on Mt 26:3. *Alexander.* A common Greek name among the high priests. Other Jewish sources from this era depict the aristocratic priests as abusing their authority.

4:8 *filled with the Holy Spirit.* Jewish sources often associated the Holy Spirit with prophetic inspiration.

4:9 *called to account today for an act of kindness.* The mandatory ancient response to benefaction was gratitude; in ancient legal settings speakers sometimes denounced those who responded to benefaction instead with hostile treatment.

4:10 *whom you crucified.* It was customary to countercharge the accusers with an offense; in this case, one lies ready at hand. Charging one's judges, however, was usually regarded as foolhardy, since it usually led to one's conviction.

4:11 On Ps 118:22, see note on Mk 12:10–11.

4:12 *under heaven.* Everywhere (e.g., for God's future kingdom, Da 7:27).

4:13 *unschooled.* This need not be a comment on their literacy one way or the other; it does indicate that they lacked the sophisticated rhetorical training to which the elite had access. Ancient thinkers appreciated frankness in speaking truth; this behavior characterized most Biblical prophets.

4:17 *to stop this thing from spreading any further.* In a world focused on honor and shame, the elite's public honor is at stake (given the apostles' charge in v. 10).

4:19 *Which is right in God's eyes ...?* Speakers would sometimes offer a choice to their audience, the answer to which was obvious.

4:21 Elites did not normally allow open challenges to their authority from people of lower status (as in vv. 10,20); they thus offered further threats. Elites usually detested those more influential with the people, deriding them as demagogues.

4:24 The prayer may echo Ps 146:6; the context in that psalm emphasizes God helping his needy people.

sea, and everything in them. 25You spoke
by the Holy Spirit through the mouth of
your servant, our father David:[u]

"'Why do the nations rage
and the peoples plot in vain?
26The kings of the earth rise up
and the rulers band together
against the Lord
and against his anointed one.'[a][b][v]

27Indeed Herod[w] and Pontius Pilate[x] met
together with the Gentiles and the people
of Israel in this city to conspire against
your holy servant Jesus,[y] whom you
anointed. 28They did what your power and
will had decided beforehand should happen.[z] 29Now, Lord, consider their threats
and enable your servants to speak your
word with great boldness.[a] 30Stretch out
your hand to heal and perform signs and
wonders[b] through the name of your holy
servant Jesus."[c]
31After they prayed, the place where
they were meeting was shaken.[d] And they
were all filled with the Holy Spirit and
spoke the word of God boldly.[e]

The Believers Share Their Possessions

32All the believers were one in heart
and mind. No one claimed that any of
their possessions was their own, but they
shared everything they had.[f] 33With great
power the apostles continued to testify[g] to
the resurrection[h] of the Lord Jesus. And
God's grace was so powerfully at work in
them all 34that there were no needy persons among them. For from time to time
those who owned land or houses sold
them,[i] brought the money from the sales
35and put it at the apostles' feet,[j] and it
was distributed to anyone who had need.[k]
36Joseph, a Levite from Cyprus, whom
the apostles called Barnabas[l] (which
means "son of encouragement"), 37sold
a field he owned and brought the money
and put it at the apostles' feet.[m]

Ananias and Sapphira

5 Now a man named Ananias, together with his wife Sapphira, also sold
a piece of property. 2With his wife's full
knowledge he kept back part of the money
for himself, but brought the rest and put it
at the apostles' feet.[n]
3Then Peter said, "Ananias, how is it that
Satan[o] has so filled your heart[p] that you
have lied to the Holy Spirit[q] and have kept
for yourself some of the money you received
for the land? 4Didn't it belong to you before
it was sold? And after it was sold, wasn't
the money at your disposal? What made
you think of doing such a thing? You have
not lied just to human beings but to God."
5When Ananias heard this, he fell down
and died.[r] And great fear[s] seized all who
heard what had happened. 6Then some
young men came forward, wrapped up
his body,[t] and carried him out and buried him.

4:25 [u] Ac 1:16
4:26 [v] Ps 2:1, 2; Da 9:25; Lk 4:18; Ac 10:38; Heb 1:9
4:27 [w] Mt 14:1 [x] Mt 27:2; Lk 23:12 [y] ver 30
4:28 [z] Ac 2:23
4:29 [a] ver 13, 31; Ac 9:27; 14:3; Php 1:14
4:30 [b] Jn 4:48 [c] ver 27
4:31 [d] Ac 2:2 [e] ver 29
4:32 [f] Ac 2:44
4:33 [g] Lk 24:48 [h] Ac 1:22
4:34 [i] Mt 19:21; Ac 2:45
4:35 [j] ver 37; Ac 5:2 [k] Ac 2:45; 6:1
4:36 [l] Ac 9:27; 1Co 9:6
4:37 [m] ver 35; Ac 5:2
5:2 [n] Ac 4:35,37
5:3 [o] Mt 4:10 [p] Jn 13:2,27 [q] ver 9
5:5 [r] ver 10 [s] ver 11
5:6 [t] Jn 19:40

[a] *26* That is, Messiah or Christ [b] *26* Psalm 2:1,2

4:25–26 This prayer repeats the familiar Ps 2:1–2, which was understood Messianically in this period.
4:26 *anointed one.* Understood as the Christ (the ultimate royal "anointed one").
4:27 *Herod.* See notes on Mk 6:14,17; on his role, see notes on Lk 23:7,12. *Pilate.* See note on Mt 27:1–2.
4:28 *what your power and will had decided beforehand.* From Scripture, Jewish people recognized that God could establish his purposes sovereignly even through the misdeeds of the wicked.
4:29 In contrast to some OT prayers for vengeance (e.g., 2Ch 24:21–22; Ps 137:9; Jer 15:15), this prayer is for boldness as exhibited in v. 13 (cf. Ps 138:3; 144:1). Here this may be accomplished at least in part through continuing signs (v. 30), as v. 9.
4:31 *shaken.* In some ancient accounts God answered prayers with places shaking or with thunder (cf. 1Sa 12:17–18); most relevant here is Isa 6:4, in the context of Isaiah's calling and empowerment.
4:35 *distributed to anyone who had need.* In many ancient Judean circles, designated leaders distributed group charity funds. See note on 2:44–45.
4:36 Luke offers a specific example of the positive behavior summarized in vv. 34–35. *Joseph … called Barnabas.* Nicknames were common and especially important for those with names as common as Joseph was in Judea. *Cyprus.* Had a large Jewish population.
4:37 *sold a field he owned.* In contrast to OT expectations, some Levites had become fairly wealthy; many of the wealthiest were the Sadducean aristocratic priests in upper-city Jerusalem, with many other wealthy priests in Jericho.
5:1 Ancient writers often paired positive and negative examples; Joseph Barnabas (4:36–37) was a positive example, and (here) Ananias and Sapphira are negative ones. *Sapphira.* Some argue that this rare name appears especially in wealthy circles, so this couple may have had significant monetary resources.
5:2 *he kept back part of the money for himself.* Those who joined the Qumran community had to surrender all their property. Such surrender was voluntary and not always wholesale for early Christians, but it had to be genuine. Ananias and Sapphira wanted the honor without the sacrifice. *kept back.* Can also mean to "steal" or "pilfer"; it likely evokes the Septuagint, the pre-Christian Greek translation of the OT, for Jos 7:1, where Achan took for himself some of the plunder dedicated to God and brought death to himself and his family. (Because the family knew and did not report him, they were counted as accomplices.)
5:3 *Satan has so filled your heart.* The OT and (more abundantly) ancient Jewish literature portrayed Satan as tempter, deceiver and accuser.
5:4 On the voluntary nature of the gift, in contrast to the commitment of members at Qumran, see note on v. 2.
5:5 *he fell down and died.* Occasionally God struck those who violated what was sacred (e.g., Lev 10:2; 2Sa 6:7).
5:6 *wrapped up his body.* People covered the dead, and especially their faces, to protect their honor. Burial was an urgent matter carried out quickly; the action of the

7About three hours later his wife came
in, not knowing what had happened. 8Pe-
ter asked her, "Tell me, is this the price
you and Ananias got for the land?"
"Yes," she said, "that is the price."[u]
9Peter said to her, "How could you conspire to test the Spirit of the Lord?[v] Listen!
The feet of the men who buried your husband are at the door, and they will carry
you out also."
10At that moment she fell down at his
feet and died.[w] Then the young men
came in and, finding her dead, carried her
out and buried her beside her husband.
11Great fear[x] seized the whole church and
all who heard about these events.

The Apostles Heal Many

12The apostles performed many signs and
wonders[y] among the people. And all the believers used to meet together[z] in Solomon's
Colonnade.[a] 13No one else dared join them,
even though they were highly regarded by
the people.[b] 14Nevertheless, more and more
men and women believed in the Lord and
were added to their number. 15As a result,
people brought the sick into the streets and
laid them on beds and mats so that at least
Peter's shadow might fall on some of them
as he passed by.[c] 16Crowds gathered also
from the towns around Jerusalem, bringing
their sick and those tormented by impure
spirits, and all of them were healed.[d]

The Apostles Persecuted

17Then the high priest and all his associates, who were members of the party[e] of
the Sadducees,[f] were filled with jealousy.
18They arrested the apostles and put them
in the public jail.[g] 19But during the night
an angel[h] of the Lord opened the doors
of the jail[i] and brought them out. 20"Go,
stand in the temple courts," he said, "and
tell the people all about this new life."[j]
21At daybreak they entered the temple
courts, as they had been told, and began
to teach the people.
When the high priest and his associates[k]
arrived, they called together the Sanhedrin[l]—the full assembly of the elders of
Israel—and sent to the jail for the apostles. 22But on arriving at the jail, the officers did not find them there. So they went
back and reported, 23"We found the jail securely locked, with the guards standing at
the doors; but when we opened them, we
found no one inside." 24On hearing this report, the captain of the temple guard and
the chief priests[m] were at a loss, wondering what this might lead to.
25Then someone came and said, "Look!
The men you put in jail are standing in
the temple courts teaching the people."
26At that, the captain went with his officers and brought the apostles. They did
not use force, because they feared that the
people[n] would stone them.
27The apostles were brought in and made
to appear before the Sanhedrin[o] to be questioned by the high priest. 28"We gave you
strict orders not to teach in this name,"[p] he
said. "Yet you have filled Jerusalem with
your teaching and are determined to make
us guilty of this man's blood."[q]

5:8 [u] ver 2
5:9 [v] ver 3
5:10 [w] ver 5
5:11 [x] ver 5; Ac 19:17
5:12 [y] Ac 2:43 [z] Ac 4:32 [a] Ac 3:11
5:13 [b] Ac 2:47; 4:21
5:15 [c] Ac 19:12
5:16 [d] Mk 16:17
5:17 [e] Ac 15:5 [f] Ac 4:1
5:18 [g] Ac 4:3
5:19 [h] Mt 1:20; Lk 1:11; Ac 8:26; 27:23 [i] Ac 16:26
5:20 [j] Jn 6:63, 68
5:21 [k] Ac 4:5,6 [l] ver 27,34,41; Mt 5:22
5:24 [m] Ac 4:1
5:26 [n] Ac 4:21
5:27 [o] Mt 5:22
5:28 [p] Ac 4:18 [q] Mt 23:35; 27:25; Ac 2:23, 36; 3:14, 15; 7:52

community here probably evokes Lev 10:4–5. Normally the family would be involved, but here the church acts as family; those who devoted their resources to a community would depend on the community for burial costs.

5:7 *his wife came in.* She may have come looking for her husband. Although values in traditional Athens or Hellenistic Egypt were against wives leaving the home without the husband's permission, in Judea women were free to go to the market or elsewhere in public, though married Judean women covered their hair.

5:10 See notes on vv. 5–6.

5:11 *Great fear seized the whole church.* Judgment miracles generated fear (Nu 16:34; 2Ki 1:13–14); executions were meant to generate fear as a deterrent (Dt 13:11; 17:13; 19:20).

5:12 *signs and wonders.* The ancient world had stories of secretive magicians, but most of its reports of wonderworkers came from many generations after the reputed wonderworkers, in contrast to Acts' reports of the apostles. *Solomon's Colonnade.* See note on Jn 10:23.

5:13 *No one else dared join them.* The fate of Ananias and Sapphira made people fear halfhearted commitment.

5:15 *Peter's shadow might fall on some.* Many people in antiquity believed that one's shadow was attached to a person; some believed, e.g., that injuring the shadow could injure the person, and Jewish tradition suggested that one's shadow touching a corpse made one impure. The crowds may respond to the apostles with elements of superstition, but God touches those who come to Jesus' representatives (cf. 19:12).

5:17 *filled with jealousy.* Caiaphas and other members of the leading aristocratic priestly families were Sadducees. They had theological (see notes on 4:1,2) as well as political (cf. 4:10) reasons for wanting the movement stopped. Considering the warnings given in 4:17–18,21, they probably believe they have been quite patient, but the popularity of Jesus' movement is growing, risking the Jerusalem elite's dishonor. Unlike the Pharisees, Sadducees were not as popular with the people, though the people respected the office of the elite priests. Ancient biographies often note jealousy as a reason for enmity; this is not surprising in view of the ambition and strife that characterized ancient urban politics.

5:18 *public jail.* Imprisonment was sometimes a punishment, but jails were more often used to hold people until the time of their trial or sentence.

5:21 *daybreak.* Most people in antiquity arose at sunrise and people would begin to gather in the temple early.

5:26 *did not use force.* Ancient Jewish sources complain that sometimes these Levite temple police used force at the bidding of the corrupt elite priests. The authorities were not always popular; see note on v. 17.

5:28 *guilty of this man's blood.* Those responsible for murder were "guilty" of the person's "blood" (Dt 21:7–8; 2Sa 21:1; Eze 22:4). Such behavior brought judgment on the

29 Peter and the other apostles replied:
"We must obey God rather than human
beings![r] 30 The God of our ancestors[s] raised
Jesus from the dead[t] — whom you killed
by hanging him on a cross.[u] 31 God exalted
him to his own right hand[v] as Prince and
Savior[w] that he might bring Israel to repentance and forgive their sins.[x] 32 We are
witnesses of these things,[y] and so is the
Holy Spirit,[z] whom God has given to those
who obey him."
33 When they heard this, they were furious[a] and wanted to put them to death.
34 But a Pharisee named Gamaliel,[b] a
teacher of the law,[c] who was honored by
all the people, stood up in the Sanhedrin
and ordered that the men be put outside
for a little while. 35 Then he addressed the
Sanhedrin: "Men of Israel, consider carefully what you intend to do to these men.
36 Some time ago Theudas appeared, claiming to be somebody, and about four hundred men rallied to him. He was killed,
all his followers were dispersed, and it all
came to nothing. 37 After him, Judas the
Galilean appeared in the days of the census[d] and led a band of people in revolt. He
too was killed, and all his followers were
scattered. 38 Therefore, in the present case
I advise you: Leave these men alone! Let
them go! For if their purpose or activity
is of human origin, it will fail.[e] 39 But if it
is from God, you will not be able to stop
these men; you will only find yourselves
fighting against God."[f]
40 His speech persuaded them. They
called the apostles in and had them
flogged.[g] Then they ordered them not
to speak in the name of Jesus, and let
them go.
41 The apostles left the Sanhedrin, rejoicing[h] because they had been counted worthy of suffering disgrace for the Name.[i]
42 Day after day, in the temple courts[j] and
from house to house, they never stopped
teaching and proclaiming the good news
that Jesus is the Messiah.

The Choosing of the Seven

6 In those days when the number of disciples was increasing,[k] the Hellenistic
Jews[a][l] among them complained against

5:29 [r] Ac 4:19 **5:30** [s] Ac 3:13 [t] Ac 2:24 [u] Ac 10:39; 13:29; Gal 3:13; 1Pe 2:24 **5:31** [v] Ac 2:33 [w] Lk 2:11 [x] Mt 1:21; Lk 24:47; Ac 2:38 **5:32** [y] Lk 24:48 [z] Jn 15:26 **5:33** [a] Ac 2:37; 7:54 **5:34** [b] Ac 22:3 [c] Lk 2:46 **5:37** [d] Lk 2:1,2 **5:38** [e] Mt 15:13 **5:39** [f] Pr 21:30; Ac 7:51; 11:17 **5:40** [g] Mt 10:17 **5:41** [h] Mt 5:12 [i] Jn 15:21 **5:42** [j] Ac 2:46 **6:1** [k] Ac 2:41 [l] Ac 9:29

[a] *1* That is, Jews who had adopted the Greek language and culture

land unless the murderers were punished. The apostolic preaching thus threatens the political security of the elite.
5:29 *We must obey God rather than human beings!* Socrates (cf. note on 17:19) was famously reported to have declared that he preferred to obey God rather than people; such boldness helped precipitate his execution. Whether or not Peter would have recognized the similarity with Socrates, the elite priests, many of whom had some Greek education, would have done so.
5:30 *whom you killed.* For secondary guilt, see note on 2:23. *hanging ... on a cross.* Lit. "hanging on wood" or "on a tree"; people normally considered this fate a cursed humiliation (Dt 21:22 – 23), but Peter contrasts God's verdict in v. 31.
5:32 *Holy Spirit, whom God has given to those who obey him.* In some circles, Jewish tradition limited the giving of the Holy Spirit to only a few very pious people in this age; Scripture promised it to all God's people in the era of restoration (see notes on 2:17,18).
5:33 *wanted to put them to death.* The Sanhedrin could not legally execute a person without the Roman governor's permission, and ordinarily would not risk the political repercussions of a public lynching. Other ancient sources, however, reveal that tempers did flare in the Sanhedrin and other senates, sometimes leading to violence.
5:34 *Pharisee named Gamaliel.* Pharisees were known for being much more lenient than Sadducees. Gamaliel I (cf. 22:3) was the best-known Pharisaic sage of his era; he apparently continued the merciful interpretation of the Pharisaic school of Hillel (versus that of Shammai), and was one of the minority Pharisaic members of the elite. (Josephus shows that Gamaliel's son, Simeon ben Gamaliel, was among the highest elite a generation later.)
5:36 – 37 Like most other members of the Sanhedrin, Gamaliel compares Jesus with other leaders of revolutionary movements. Josephus mentions both Judas and Theudas as revolutionary leaders, though his version of the facts differs somewhat from Luke's. Judas the Galilean was the leader in the notorious revolt against the Roman tax census in AD 6; one of Judas's leading supporters was Saddok, a Pharisee like Gamaliel. Josephus's report places Theudas's revolt (a fairly uncommon name) under the governor Fadus, around AD 44 (after Gamaliel's speech). Theudas promised to part the Jordan River, probably trying to emulate Joshua, but Roman soldiers intercepted and killed many of his followers. Theudas was beheaded. Scholars have offered various attempts to harmonize Luke and Josephus, as well as regarding one or the other as mistaken in some details. (No one denies that Josephus was sometimes mistaken.) What would have mattered most to most ancient historians, and what remains undisputed, is the basic point that Gamaliel compares Jesus with revolutionary figures.
5:36 *Theudas appeared, claiming to be somebody.* Cf. 8:9 – 10; Lk 21:8.
5:39 *fighting against God.* Both Greek and Jewish martyr literature often spoke of fighting against God or the gods. One of the first and seminal uses was a passage in the Greek poet Euripides, with the following setting: the god Dionysus delivered his devotees from imprisonment (cf. v. 19; 12:11), and the king who was fighting against him died a terrible death (cf. 12:23). See note on 26:14.
5:40 *flogged.* Public beatings were meant to shame (see v. 41) those so beaten. The person would be stripped and given a maximum of 39 lashes in a public place (see note on Mt 10:17).
5:41 *rejoicing ... counted worthy of suffering disgrace for the Name.* Luke's audience probably knew about and respected philosophers who rejoiced in spite of suffering. Here, however, Jesus' disciples rejoice specifically because of the reason why they suffer (Lk 6:23). Jewish tradition praised suffering for "the Name," meaning that of God; here, however, the name is that of Jesus (cf. Lk 6:22).
6:1 *Hellenistic.* This term was often applied to those who had absorbed much Greek culture. In this passage, it probably refers to foreign (Diaspora) Jews or their descendants for whom Greek remained their mother tongue.

the Hebraic Jews because their widows[m]
were being overlooked in the daily distribution of food.[n] 2So the Twelve gathered all the disciples together and said,
"It would not be right for us to neglect
the ministry of the word of God in order
to wait on tables. 3Brothers and sisters,[o]
choose seven men from among you who
are known to be full of the Spirit and wisdom. We will turn this responsibility over
to them 4and will give our attention to
prayer[p] and the ministry of the word."
5This proposal pleased the whole group.
They chose Stephen,[q] a man full of faith
and of the Holy Spirit;[r] also Philip,[s] Proc-
orus, Nicanor, Timon, Parmenas, and Nicolas from Antioch, a convert to Judaism.
6They presented these men to the apostles, who prayed[t] and laid their hands on
them.[u]
7So the word of God spread.[v] The number of disciples in Jerusalem increased
rapidly, and a large number of priests became obedient to the faith.

Stephen Seized

8Now Stephen, a man full of God's
grace and power, performed great wonders and signs[w] among the people. 9Op-
position arose, however, from members of
the Synagogue of the Freedmen (as it was
called) — Jews of Cyrene[x] and Alexandria
as well as the provinces of Cilicia[y] and
Asia[z] — who began to argue with Stephen.
10But they could not stand up against the
wisdom the Spirit gave him as he spoke.[a]
11Then they secretly[b] persuaded some
men to say, "We have heard Stephen
speak blasphemous words against Moses
and against God."[c]
12So they stirred up the people and the
elders and the teachers of the law. They
seized Stephen and brought him before
the Sanhedrin.[d] 13They produced false witnesses, who testified, "This fellow never
stops speaking against this holy place[e]
and against the law. 14For we have heard
him say that this Jesus of Nazareth will
destroy this place and change the customs
Moses handed down to us."[f]
15All who were sitting in the Sanhedrin[g]
looked intently at Stephen, and they saw
that his face was like the face of an angel.

Stephen's Speech to the Sanhedrin

7 Then the high priest asked Stephen,
"Are these charges true?"
2To this he replied: "Brothers and fathers,[h] listen to me! The God of glory[i] appeared to our father Abraham while he
was still in Mesopotamia, before he lived
in Harran.[j] 3'Leave your country and your

6:1 [m] Ac 9:39, 41 [n] Ac 4:35
6:3 [o] Ac 1:16
6:4 [p] Ac 1:14
6:5 [q] ver 8; Ac 11:19 [r] Ac 11:24 [s] Ac 8:5-40; 21:8
6:6 [t] Ac 1:24; 8:17; 13:3; 2Ti 1:6 [u] Nu 8:10; Ac 9:17; 1Ti 4:14
6:7 [v] Ac 12:24; 19:20
6:8 [w] Jn 4:48
6:9 [x] Mt 27:32 [y] Ac 15:23,41; 22:3; 23:34 [z] Ac 2:9
6:10 [a] Lk 21:15
6:11 [b] 1Ki 21:10 [c] Mt 26:59-61
6:12 [d] Mt 5:22
6:13 [e] Ac 21:28
6:14 [f] Ac 15:1; 21:21; 26:3; 28:17
6:15 [g] Mt 5:22
7:2 [h] Ac 22:1 [i] Ps 29:3 [j] Ge 11:31; 15:7

Hebraic. Probably refers here to traditional Judeans and Galileans, many of whom would have known both Greek and Aramaic. Both groups were Jewish, just as, e.g., American or European Jews today are no less Jewish than are Jews who live in Israel. *distribution of food.* Local synagogues or other circles supported destitute widows within their own circle, but foreign Jews now settled in Jerusalem apparently had a disproportionate number of widows. Many Jews apparently immigrated to the Holy Land in their old age, leaving more widows and fewer younger Hellenists to provide support for them. This wider social problem spilled over into the church.

6:3–4 Moses delegated some of his administrative duties to others who were God-fearing and trustworthy (Ex 18:21), so he could devote himself to prayer for the people and to teaching God's message (Ex 18:19–20). Judaism was already familiar with the common practice of appointing groups of roughly seven leaders (especially as local judges).

6:3 *choose.* This might suggest the Greek and sometimes Jewish practice of voting; for the people choosing someone and the leader ratifying, cf. Dt 1:13. *full of the Spirit and wisdom.* Joshua was filled with the Spirit of wisdom because Moses laid hands on him (Dt 34:9).

6:5 Many Diaspora Jews had Greek names, but most Galileans and Judeans did not. All seven of these men, however, have Greek names; they were not only Hellenists (v. 1), but are very obviously Hellenists. Elites often repressed complaining minorities; here the apostles graciously put trustworthy members of the offended minority into leadership roles. Many Gentile converts to Judaism lived in Antioch.

6:6 *laid their hands on them.* Laying on hands could bring blessing (Ge 48:14) but the more relevant OT model is Moses laying hands on Joshua as his successor (Nu 27:18,23), as a consequence of which Joshua was filled with the Spirit of wisdom (Dt 34:9). (The later rabbinic movement also used laying on hands for ordination.)

6:7 Historians often concluded sections with summary statements. *large number of priests.* Although most of the elite priests were Sadducees, poorer priests held a range of views.

6:11 *blasphemous words.* Words that dishonor are in view here, rather than the later, technical rabbinic sense that involved cursing with God's sacred name. Yet, ironically, false testimony under oath automatically desecrated God's name. False witnesses were so common that a few handbooks of rhetorical instructions even explained how to provide false testimony most effectively (see note on Mt 26:60).

6:14 *destroy this place.* See note on Mk 14:58. Even prophesying the temple's destruction was dangerous (cf. Jer 20:1–2). In the generation following the events of Acts but before the Judean revolt of AD 66, a prophet named Joshua ben Hananiah prophesied the temple's destruction. Members of Jerusalem's elite beat him and handed him over to the governor, who had him scourged until, Josephus reports, some of his bones were visible.

6:15 *face was like the face of an angel.* On transfiguration, see note on Mk 9:2, although some may take the point here as more figurative, given the incomprehension of Stephen's opponents.

7:2 *Abraham.* One of the most respected figures in Jewish history, Abraham was regularly used as a model for righteousness. *still in Mesopotamia.* Some conservative Jewish teachers believed that God revealed himself almost exclusively in the Holy Land (allowing exceptions for pure places near water).

ACTS 6:9

SYNAGOGUE OF THE FREEDMEN

Synagogues functioned as community centers as well as places for studying Torah and praying together on the Sabbath. Many synagogues existed in Jerusalem, including synagogues for settlers from the Diaspora. Archaeology attests that one of the Hellenist synagogues was founded by a man named Vettenos, a freedman; scholars debate whether that is the synagogue in question here. Luke's term for "Freedmen" refers to freed slaves of Roman citizens, who themselves became Roman citizens when they were freed. A century earlier the Roman general Pompey had enslaved thousands of Judeans, but Jews already living in Rome had bought their freedom. Descendants of these freed Jewish slaves remained Roman citizens so long as they married among themselves. Saul of Tarsus (also known as Paul) probably was one of the Cilicians in this synagogue; his ancestors may have become Roman citizens (Ac 22:27–28) as freedpersons and settled in Tarsus. In the eastern Mediterranean, even most civic officials were not Roman citizens, so the founding families of this synagogue could have been proud of their status. Others could join the synagogue, but many of the leading members presumably remained families with a heritage as Roman citizens from the Diaspora. ◆

The Theodotus Inscription, first century BC. The fact that it is in Greek and mentions "those who have need from abroad" suggest the synagogue was used by Jews from the Diaspora. Some identify it with the synagogue of the Freedmen.

Todd Bolen/www.BiblePlaces.com

people,' God said, 'and go to the land I will show you.'[a][k]

4 "So he left the land of the Chaldeans and settled in Harran. After the death of his father, God sent him to this land where you are now living.[l] 5 He gave him no inheritance here, not even enough ground to set his foot on. But God promised him that he and his descendants after him would possess the land,[m] even though at that time Abraham had no child. 6 God spoke to him in this way: 'For four hundred years your descendants will be strangers in a country not their own, and they will be enslaved and mistreated.[n] 7 But I will punish the nation they serve as slaves,' God said, 'and afterward they will come out of that country and worship me in this place.'[b][o] 8 Then he gave Abraham the covenant of circumcision.[p] And Abraham became the father of Isaac and circumcised him eight days after his birth.[q] Later Isaac became the father of Jacob,[r] and Jacob became the father of the twelve patriarchs.[s]

9 "Because the patriarchs were jealous of Joseph,[t] they sold him as a slave into Egypt.[u] But God was with him[v] 10 and rescued him from all his troubles. He gave Joseph wisdom and enabled him to gain the goodwill of Pharaoh king of Egypt. So Pharaoh made him ruler over Egypt and all his palace.[w]

11 "Then a famine struck all Egypt and Canaan, bringing great suffering, and our ancestors could not find food.[x] 12 When Jacob heard that there was grain in Egypt, he sent our forefathers on their first visit.[y] 13 On their second visit, Joseph told his brothers who he was,[z] and Pharaoh learned about Joseph's family. 14 After this, Joseph sent for his father Jacob and his whole family,[a] seventy-five in all.[b] 15 Then Jacob went down to Egypt, where he and our ancestors died.[c] 16 Their bodies were brought back to Shechem and placed in the tomb that Abraham had bought from the sons of Hamor at Shechem for a certain sum of money.[d]

17 "As the time drew near for God to fulfill his promise to Abraham, the number of our people in Egypt had greatly increased.[e] 18 Then 'a new king, to whom Joseph meant nothing, came to power in Egypt.'[c][f] 19 He dealt treacherously with our people and oppressed our ancestors by forcing them to throw out their newborn babies so that they would die.[g]

20 "At that time Moses was born, and he was no ordinary child.[d] For three months he was cared for by his family.[h] 21 When he was placed outside, Pharaoh's daughter took him and brought him up as her own son.[i] 22 Moses was educated in all the wisdom of the Egyptians[j] and was powerful in speech and action.

[a] *3* Gen. 12:1 [b] *7* Gen. 15:13,14 [c] *18* Exodus 1:8
[d] *20* Or *was fair in the sight of God*

7:3 [k] Ge 12:1
7:4 [l] Ge 12:5
7:5 [m] Ge 12:7; 17:8; 26:3
7:6 [n] Ex 12:40
7:7 [o] Ex 3:12
7:8 [p] Ge 17:9-14 [q] Ge 21:2-4 [r] Ge 25:26 [s] Ge 29:31-35; 30:5-13, 17-24; 35:16-18, 22-26
7:9 [t] Ge 37:4, 11 [u] Ge 37:28; Ps 105:17 [v] Ge 39:2, 21, 23
7:10 [w] Ge 41:37-43
7:11 [x] Ge 41:54
7:12 [y] Ge 42:1, 2
7:13 [z] Ge 45:1-4
7:14 [a] Ge 45:9, 10 [b] Ge 46:26, 27; Ex 1:5; Dt 10:22
7:15 [c] Ge 46:5-7; 49:33; Ex 1:6
7:16 [d] Ge 23:16-20; 33:18, 19; 50:13; Jos 24:32
7:17 [e] Ex 1:7; Ps 105:24
7:18 [f] Ex 1:8
7:19 [g] Ex 1:10-22
7:20 [h] Ex 2:2; Heb 11:23
7:21 [i] Ex 2:3-10
7:22 [j] 1Ki 4:30; Isa 19:11

7:4 *After the death of his father.* Some Jewish traditions depict Abraham leaving Harran only after his father's death (cf. Ge 11:31 — 12:1).

7:5 *no inheritance here, not even enough ground to set his foot on.* Besides the clear reference to Ge 17:8, Stephen apparently draws the idea of inheritance from its use in Numbers and Deuteronomy; the phrase "ground to set his foot on" echoes the idiom in Dt 2:5.

7:6 *four hundred years.* This is from Ge 15:13; a more specific estimate was 430 years (Ex 12:40 – 41).

7:9 Defense speeches often returned the charges against the accusers. Stephen begins preparing for that counterattack (vv. 51 – 53) by noting the behavior of the patriarchs against God's chosen deliverer.

7:14 *seventy-five.* Stephen, a Hellenist preaching in Greek to people who understood Greek, takes the count "seventy-five" from the Septuagint, the pre-Christian Greek translation of the OT (although two Qumran Hebrew texts have the same), unlike the reading of the probably dominant Hebrew text, which reads "seventy" (Ge 46:27).

7:16 Because this is only a summary of Biblical history (and perhaps of Stephen's defense), this verse telescopes the story, leaving out some details, as summaries sometimes did. Technically Jacob rather than Abraham bought the land (Ge 33:18 – 19). *Shechem.* The OT has Jacob buried near Hebron and Joseph at Shechem (Jos 24:32); Josephus thinks that Joseph's brothers were buried at Hebron, but they probably died after Jacob and could have been buried at Shechem. Samaritans affirmed that Joseph's brothers were buried with him at Shechem, the center of life for the Samaritan people. Josephus — and Stephen's Judean hearers — would naturally resent such a claim. (Hebron, by contrast, lay in Judea.)

7:19 *forcing them to throw out their newborn babies.* Killing the babies of God's people remained a painful memory for the Jewish people, who had also suffered this oppression (when they circumcised babies) in the time of the evil ruler Antiochus IV Epiphanes. Greeks and many ancient peoples (except Jews and Egyptians) sometimes abandoned babies; usually the babies were either adopted by passersby (as children or slaves) or were eaten by vultures or dogs. Jews strongly opposed such behavior by pagans, so Pharaoh's behavior in Exodus remained a relevant and painful issue for them.

7:20 *no ordinary child.* The Hebrew text of Ex 2:2 notes that Moses was a beautiful child; unlike Stephen here, much Jewish tradition fancifully elaborated this claim, so that Moses shone with brilliant light at his birth. (Ancient writers liked to include special features of their protagonists' births if they were known, but Stephen does not depend on these traditions here.)

7:21 *brought him up as her own son.* In the culture familiar to Luke's audience, the daughter's adoption of Moses made him Egyptian and Pharaoh's grandson.

7:22 *educated in all the wisdom of the Egyptians.* Exodus itself does not specify this, but it is a likely inference; the princes raised in the royal household would be well educated. Egyptian wisdom was famous in the ancient world (though many non-Egyptians in the first century valued Egyptian wisdom especially in the sphere of magic). (Stephen as a Hellenist may appreciate Diaspora education more than did many Judeans.) Jewish writers often

ACTS 7

Answered Charges and Parallel Figures in Acts 7

Defendants were given the opportunity to deny the charges against them — in this case, charges of opposing Moses/the law and the temple (Ac 6:13 – 14). Stephen is clearly not against the law, and makes his case from it. While he is not against the temple per se, he repeatedly challenges his critics' privileging of sacred places. Whereas some traditional Judeans insisted that God revealed himself almost exclusively in the Holy Land, Stephen shows that God reveals himself in places such as Mesopotamia and a mountain in the Sinai desert. Stephen does not remain on the defensive. Defense speeches often sought to turn the accusers' charges against the accusers themselves; Stephen does so here, noting that his opponents continue the tradition of those who opposed Joseph, Moses and the prophets.

Most of Ac 7 directly follows the OT in its most common Greek translation (see NIV text notes for verses). Stephen makes some changes, but most are quite minimal by ancient standards (especially by later rabbinic standards, but also when compared with Josephus or various ancient Jewish retellings of Biblical stories).

Stephen sees patterns in the way that God raised up deliverers; like Joseph and Moses, they could be rejected deliverers. Moreover, God had promised a prophet like Moses (Dt 18:15 – 18), and one aspect of their similarity, Stephen argues, is that both were rejected as leaders by their own people (Ac 7:35,37). Literary critics today regularly find patterns within Biblical narratives; the difference is that Stephen examines aspects of the metanarrative of Biblical history. Following is one example of literary patterns within the Pentateuch:

JOSEPH	MOSES
Brothers sold him into slavery	Family, who were slaves, saved him from slavery
Midianites sold Joseph into Egypt	Midianites welcomed Moses when he fled Egypt
Joseph became Pharaoh's "father" (Ge 45:8)	Moses became a son to Pharaoh's daughter
Joseph was abruptly exalted from slavery, made a prince over Egypt	Moses abruptly lost his Egyptian royalty by defending slaves
Joseph made all Egypt Pharaoh's slaves (47:19)	Through Moses God freed slaves
Through Joseph God delivered Egypt during famine	Through Moses God devastated Egypt's economy
Joseph, exiled in Egypt, marries the daughter of an Egyptian priest	Moses, exiled from Egypt, marries the daughter of a Midianite priest
The name of Joseph's first son (of two named sons) evokes Joseph's sojourn in a foreign land	The name of the first son (of two named sons) evokes Moses' sojourn in a foreign land
Future deliverer's leadership initially rejected by brothers	Future deliverer's leadership initially rejected by his people

Taken from *The IVP Bible Background Commentary: New Testament*; adapted from Keener, *Acts: an Exegetical Commentary* (4 vols.; Grand Rapids: Baker, 2013), 2:1363.

23 “When Moses was forty years old, he
decided to visit his own people, the Israelites. 24 He saw one of them being mistreated by an Egyptian, so he went to his
defense and avenged him by killing the
Egyptian. 25 Moses thought that his own
people would realize that God was using him to rescue them, but they did not.
26 The next day Moses came upon two Israelites who were fighting. He tried to reconcile them by saying, ‘Men, you are brothers; why do you want to hurt each other?’
27 “But the man who was mistreating the
other pushed Moses aside and said, ‘Who
made you ruler and judge over us? 28 Are
you thinking of killing me as you killed
the Egyptian yesterday?’[a] 29 When Moses
heard this, he fled to Midian, where he
settled as a foreigner and had two sons.[k]
30 “After forty years had passed, an angel
appeared to Moses in the flames of a burning bush in the desert near Mount Sinai.
31 When he saw this, he was amazed at the
sight. As he went over to get a closer look,
he heard the Lord say:[l] 32 ‘I am the God of
your fathers, the God of Abraham, Isaac
and Jacob.’[b] Moses trembled with fear and
did not dare to look.[m]
33 “Then the Lord said to him, ‘Take off
your sandals, for the place where you are
standing is holy ground.[n] 34 I have indeed
seen the oppression of my people in Egypt.
I have heard their groaning and have come
down to set them free. Now come, I will
send you back to Egypt.’[c][o]
35 “This is the same Moses they had rejected with the words, ‘Who made you
ruler and judge?’[p] He was sent to be
their ruler and deliverer by God himself,
through the angel who appeared to him in
the bush. 36 He led them out of Egypt[q] and
performed wonders and signs in Egypt, at
the Red Sea[r] and for forty years in the wilderness.
37 “This is the Moses who told the Israelites, ‘God will raise up for you a prophet
like me from your own people.’[d][s] 38 He was
in the assembly in the wilderness, with
the angel[t] who spoke to him on Mount
Sinai, and with our ancestors;[u] and he received living words[v] to pass on to us.[w]
39 “But our ancestors refused to obey
him. Instead, they rejected him and in
their hearts turned back to Egypt.[x] 40 They
told Aaron, ‘Make us gods who will go
before us. As for this fellow Moses who
led us out of Egypt — we don’t know what
has happened to him!’[e][y] 41 That was the
time they made an idol in the form of a
calf. They brought sacrifices to it and reveled in what their own hands had made.[z]
42 But God turned away from them[a] and
gave them over to the worship of the sun,
moon and stars.[b] This agrees with what is
written in the book of the prophets:

“ ‘Did you bring me sacrifices and
offerings
forty years in the wilderness, people
of Israel?
43 You have taken up the tabernacle of
Molek
and the star of your god Rephan,
the idols you made to worship.
Therefore I will send you into exile’[f][c]
beyond Babylon.

7:29 [k] Ex 2:11-15 **7:31** [l] Ex 3:1-4 **7:32** [m] Ex 3:6 **7:33** [n] Ex 3:5; Jos 5:15 **7:34** [o] Ex 3:7-10 **7:35** [p] ver 27 **7:36** [q] Ex 12:41; 33:1 [r] Ex 14:21 **7:37** [s] Dt 18:15, 18; Ac 3:22 **7:38** [t] ver 53 [u] Ex 19:17 [v] Dt 32:45-47; Heb 4:12 [w] Ro 3:2 **7:39** [x] Nu 14:3,4 **7:40** [y] Ex 32:1,23 **7:41** [z] Ex 32:4-6; Ps 106:19,20; Rev 9:20 **7:42** [a] Jos 24:20; Isa 63:10 [b] Jer 19:13 **7:43** [c] Am 5:25-27

[a] *28* Exodus 2:14 [b] *32* Exodus 3:6 [c] *34* Exodus 3:5,7,8,10 [d] *37* Deut. 18:15 [e] *40* Exodus 32:1 [f] *43* Amos 5:25-27 (see Septuagint)

elaborated Moses’ upbringing, e.g., telling stories of his military exploits against Ethiopia; the present speech dispenses with such elaborations.

7:23 *forty.* A round number that may fit some Jewish traditions on this point.

7:25 Although the OT is not clear on this point, Jewish tradition presents Moses’ killing of the Egyptian (Ex 2:12) as a just act of heroism. *rescue them.* This phrase also can be rendered literally “give them salvation,” perhaps recognizing Moses’ mission as foreshadowing the greater rescue by Jesus (cf., e.g., 4:12; Lk 1:69; 19:9 – 10).

7:29 *had two sons.* Mention of Moses’ sons might highlight Moses’ interethnic marriage (Ex 2:21 – 22), furthering Stephen’s emphasis beyond the boundaries of the Holy Land.

7:30 *forty years.* Added to the figure in v. 23, Moses is now 80 in Stephen’s accounting, his age in Ex 7:7.

7:33 *the place … is holy.* Stephen uses the wording of the Law (Ex 3:5) to refute his accusers, for whom only the temple was a fully holy place (6:13).

7:35 – 38 *This is the same Moses … He was … He led … This is the Moses … He was.* In ancient rhetoric, repetition drove home emphasis; in Greek, Stephen repeats “this one” five times. God sent Moses as deliverer and his people rejected him; the expected prophet like Moses (Dt 18:15 – 18) could likewise be rejected.

7:41 *idol in the form of a calf … their own hands had made.* Jewish writers by this period were ashamed of Israel’s calf-idol; Josephus even leaves it out of his retelling of Israel’s history. The Mediterranean world associated the veneration of animals and their images especially with Egypt. Following especially Greek assumptions, most of the Mediterranean world detested this practice, although most Gentiles worshiped more humanlike images. Jewish writers often drew attention to the fact that idols were not divine but were made by human hands.

7:42 *worship of the sun, moon and stars.* Under Mesopotamian influence, veneration of heavenly bodies was growing in popularity in the Roman Empire; most Gentiles viewed stars as divine, whereas Jewish people often viewed them as angels. Stephen’s Jewish hearers, of course, abhorred veneration of stars as idolatry, although even most first-century Jews, following the “science” of their day, believed in astrology’s predictive value.

7:43 *beyond Babylon.* Stephen follows the Greek rendering of Amos, including the names of the deities. The Dead Sea Scrolls also emphasize Am 5:25 – 27. Stephen changes “beyond Damascus” in Am 5:27 to “beyond Babylon,” perhaps foreshadowing other judgments beyond the one that Amos mentioned (cf. Lk 21:24).

44“Our ancestors had the tabernacle of
the covenant law[d] with them in the wilderness. It had been made as God directed Moses, according to the pattern he had
seen.[e] 45After receiving the tabernacle, our
ancestors under Joshua brought it with
them when they took the land from the
nations God drove out before them.[f] It remained in the land until the time of David,
46who enjoyed God’s favor and asked that
he might provide a dwelling place for the
God of Jacob.[a][g] 47But it was Solomon who
built a house for him.

48“However, the Most High does not live
in houses made by human hands.[h] As the
prophet says:

49“ ‘Heaven is my throne,
and the earth is my footstool.[i]
What kind of house will you build for me?
says the Lord.
Or where will my resting place be?
50Has not my hand made all these things?’[b][j]

51“You stiff-necked people![k] Your hearts[l]
and ears are still uncircumcised. You are
just like your ancestors: You always resist
the Holy Spirit! 52Was there ever a prophet
your ancestors did not persecute?[m] They
even killed those who predicted the coming of the Righteous One. And now you
have betrayed and murdered him[n]— 53you
who have received the law that was given
through angels[o] but have not obeyed it.”

The Stoning of Stephen

54When the members of the Sanhedrin heard this, they were furious[p] and
gnashed their teeth at him. 55But Stephen,
full of the Holy Spirit, looked up to heaven
and saw the glory of God, and Jesus standing at the right hand of God.[q] 56“Look,” he
said, “I see heaven open[r] and the Son of
Man[s] standing at the right hand of God.”
57At this they covered their ears and,
yelling at the top of their voices, they all
rushed at him, 58dragged him out of the
city[t] and began to stone him.[u] Meanwhile,
the witnesses laid their coats[v] at the feet
of a young man named Saul.[w]
59While they were stoning him, Stephen

7:44 [d] Ex 38:21 [e] Ex 25:8,9,40 **7:45** [f] Jos 3:14-17; 18:1; 23:9; 24:18; Ps 44:2 **7:46** [g] 2Sa 7:8-16; Ps 132:1-5 **7:48** [h] 1Ki 8:27; 2Ch 2:6 **7:49** [i] Mt 5:34, 35 **7:50** [j] Isa 66:1,2 **7:51** [k] Ex 32:9; 33:3,5 [l] Lev 26:41; Dt 10:16; Jer 4:4; 9:26
7:52 [m] 2Ch 36:16; Mt 5:12 [n] Ac 3:14; 1Th 2:15 **7:53** [o] ver 38; Gal 3:19; Heb 2:2 **7:54** [p] Ac 5:33 **7:55** [q] Mk 16:19 **7:56** [r] Mt 3:16 [s] Mt 8:20 **7:58** [t] Lk 4:29 [u] Lev 24:14,16; Dt 13:9 [v] Ac 22:20 [w] Ac 8:1

[a] *46* Some early manuscripts *the house of Jacob*
[b] *50* Isaiah 66:1,2

7:46 Cf. Ps 132:5.
7:48 *houses made by human hands.* Recalls v. 41 (see note there) and contrasts with what God’s hand has made in v. 50. Some Jewish circles emphasized the five books of the Law to the exclusion of the Prophets; most started with the Law and supplemented with texts from the Prophets. Stephen started with the Law but now moves to the Prophets.
7:49 – 50 Stephen cites Isa 66:1 – 2, a passage that goes on to challenge Israel’s outward ritual as spiritually and morally inadequate (Isa 66:3 – 4).
7:51 *You stiff-necked people!* The most rousing part of a speech was often its conclusion; in a deliberative speech such as this one, the conclusion was meant to stir hearers to change or action. Returning charges against accusers was common; charging one’s judges, by contrast, might provoke one’s own martyrdom. Calling his accusers stiff-necked and uncircumcised in heart evokes various prophetic critiques of Israel, but especially Dt 10:16, where these charges appear together.
7:52 *Was there ever a prophet your ancestors did not persecute?* Jewish tradition emphasized and amplified the persecution faced by the Biblical prophets (e.g., Ne 9:26; Jer 26:20 – 23).
7:53 *the law that was given through angels.* Going beyond the Hebrew text of the OT, ancient Jewish tradition emphasized that angels mediated the law (cf. also Gal 3:19; Heb 2:2). Returning charges was good judicial rhetoric; Stephen returns his accusers’ charge of law breaking (6:13).
7:54 Although gnashing teeth can signify anguish (Ps 112:10; Lk 13:28), it can also depict anger, as here (Job 16:9; Ps 35:16; 37:12).
7:55 *looked up to heaven.* See note on Jn 17:1. By various methods Jewish mystics tried to see God’s glory in heaven as Ezekiel did, but here Stephen experiences this vision spontaneously.
7:56 *Son of Man standing at the right hand of God.* The Son of Man’s coming would vindicate God’s people (Da 7:13 – 14). Ancient writers often paralleled characters, and Stephen follows Jesus’ example of martyrdom. Both declared to the Sanhedrin the Son of Man at God’s right hand (Ac 7:56; Lk 22:69); both entrusted their spirit to God (Ac 7:59; Lk 23:46); and both prayed for their persecutors to be forgiven (Ac 7:60; Lk 23:34). Why is the Son of Man “standing” rather than seated (contrast Lk 22:69)? Witnesses would stand and judges could stand to render their verdict; this may imply that it is Stephen’s accusers and not Stephen who are really on trial before the Lord. (Ancient writers sometimes depicted unjust judges as the ones really on trial before God or the bar of truth.)
7:58 *dragged him out of the city.* Executions and burials needed to be outside cities. *to stone him.* Stoning was the Biblical penalty for blasphemy (Lev 24:16) and some other crimes, but Rome prohibited executions without the governor’s permission. Both Jewish and Gentile texts from antiquity, however, reveal that mobs often stoned people to death. Others had wanted to stone God’s servants (Ex 17:4; Nu 14:10; 2Ch 24:21). If the mob here followed anything like the ideal procedure in some second-century Jewish traditions, Stephen would be thrown from a height, and those above would hurl large stones (requiring both hands), aiming for the chest (though precision was unlikely). The witnesses would strike first (Dt 17:7). *laid their coats.* Because the activity was physically strenuous, they could lay aside their outer garments, as was customary during exercise (especially for Hellenists, as the witnesses here probably are). Ancient practice, however, specified not the stripping of executioners but rather the stripping of the person being executed — Luke may ironically emphasize their stripping themselves to remind the reader who is really on trial (see note on v. 56). *young man.* The term is a general one that can include people in their teens, their 20s (as most often, and as is likely here) and even their 30s. People in antiquity associated youth with both strength and rashness; those who achieved prominent roles in their youth, as here, were generally counted as exceptional.
7:59 *receive my spirit.* Stephen follows Jesus’ example in Lk 23:46; see note on Ac 7:56.

prayed, "Lord Jesus, receive my spirit."[x]
60 Then he fell on his knees[y] and cried out,
"Lord, do not hold this sin against them."[z]
When he had said this, he fell asleep.

8 And Saul[a] approved of their killing
him.

The Church Persecuted and Scattered

On that day a great persecution broke out
against the church in Jerusalem, and all except the apostles were scattered[b] throughout Judea and Samaria.[c] 2 Godly men buried
Stephen and mourned deeply for him. 3 But
Saul[d] began to destroy the church.[e] Going
from house to house, he dragged off both
men and women and put them in prison.

7:59 [x] Ps 31:5; Lk 23:46 **7:60** [y] Ac 9:40 [z] Mt 5:44 **8:1** [a] Ac 7:58 [b] Ac 11:19 [c] Ac 9:31 **8:3** [d] Ac 7:58 [e] Ac 22:4, 19; 26:10, 11; 1Co 15:9; Gal 1:13, 23; Php 3:6; 1Ti 1:13 **8:4** [f] ver 1 [g] Ac 15:35 **8:5** [h] Ac 6:5 **8:7** [i] Mk 16:17 [j] Mt 4:24 **8:9** [k] Ac 13:6

Philip in Samaria

4 Those who had been scattered[f]
preached the word wherever they went.[g]
5 Philip[h] went down to a city in Samaria
and proclaimed the Messiah there. 6 When
the crowds heard Philip and saw the signs
he performed, they all paid close attention
to what he said. 7 For with shrieks, impure
spirits came out of many,[i] and many who
were paralyzed or lame were healed.[j] 8 So
there was great joy in that city.

Simon the Sorcerer

9 Now for some time a man named Simon had practiced sorcery[k] in the city

7:60 *do not hold this sin against them.* Jewish custom insisted that the person being executed confess his sins; instead, Stephen confesses theirs. This fits the reversal of charges in the speech and how Luke depicts the hearers being those really on trial before God (see notes on vv. 56,58). *fell asleep.* Among both Jews and Gentiles, sleep was a common metaphor for being dead.
8:1 *all except the apostles.* Luke depicts the scattering here as affecting more than just the Hellenists, but they were clearly affected (11:19–20).
8:2 *mourned.* Mourning for an executed criminal—which was how Stephen's critics would view his lynching—was typically illegal. Ancient readers respected those who buried and mourned the dead when the prohibition against mourning them was unjust. (Only the most vicious leaders denied their enemies burial.)
8:3 *both men and women.* Only the most severe persecutions targeted women as well as men.
8:5 *a city in Samaria.* This may refer to Neapolis, on the site of ancient Shechem (cf. note on 7:16); Neapolis was the urban center of Samaritan activity. (The OT city of Samaria, now known as Sebaste, no longer had primarily Samaritan residents; Greeks and their religion now dominated it.) Philip was a Hellenist who probably could preach only in Greek, but Greek was widely spoken in Neapolis.
8:9 *sorcery.* Even if Samaritans ignored the nearby Hellenized city of Sebaste, Greek influence was common.

ACTS 8:9

Magic in the New Testament

Magical practices claimed to draw on or manipulate nonhuman spiritual power (usually distinguished from submission to God). Magic was popular in antiquity, including in Judea (see note on Ac 13:6). It is sometimes associated with Ephesus and most fully associated with remnants of ancient religion in Egypt.

In general, people classified as magic whatever was done secretly and for the magician's (rather than the public's) good. They especially classified as magic whatever expressions of spiritual power fit belief systems contrary to their own. Some Jewish teachers regarded some magic as fake but other cases as genuine, dangerous sorcery.

Protective amulets were common, as were magical formulas, instructions, and gestures. One common form was love-magic, sometimes used to try to seduce a person away from their current spouse. Another was to kill rivals, e.g., in chariot races. People sometimes inscribed the names of enemies on pots and then shattered them, cursing them. Magic was thus often viewed as antisocial.

Magic frequently claimed to manipulate spirits, sometimes controlling them by using special knowledge about them bought from others adept in magic. Often magical formulas spoke of "binding" and "loosing" demons to manipulate them to do the bidder's will. Although mostly from later centuries, many magical papyri, replete with various formulas designed to achieve designated ends, have survived from Egypt. ◆

and amazed all the people of Samaria. He
boasted that he was someone great,[l] 10and
all the people, both high and low, gave
him their attention and exclaimed, "This
man is rightly called the Great Power of
God."[m] 11They followed him because he
had amazed them for a long time with his
sorcery. 12But when they believed Philip
as he proclaimed the good news of the
kingdom of God[n] and the name of Jesus
Christ, they were baptized,[o] both men and
women. 13Simon himself believed and was
baptized. And he followed Philip everywhere, astonished by the great signs and
miracles[p] he saw.

14When the apostles in Jerusalem heard
that Samaria[q] had accepted the word of
God, they sent Peter and John[r] to Samaria. 15When they arrived, they prayed for
the new believers there that they might
receive the Holy Spirit,[s] 16because the
Holy Spirit had not yet come on any of
them;[t] they had simply been baptized in
the name of the Lord Jesus.[u] 17Then Peter and John placed their hands on them,[v]
and they received the Holy Spirit.

18When Simon saw that the Spirit was
given at the laying on of the apostles'
hands, he offered them money 19and said,
"Give me also this ability so that everyone
on whom I lay my hands may receive the
Holy Spirit."

20Peter answered: "May your money
perish with you, because you thought you
could buy the gift of God with money![w]
21You have no part or share in this ministry, because your heart is not right[x] before God. 22Repent of this wickedness and
pray to the Lord in the hope that he may
forgive you for having such a thought in
your heart. 23For I see that you are full of
bitterness and captive to sin."

24Then Simon answered, "Pray to the
Lord for me[y] so that nothing you have said
may happen to me."

25After they had further proclaimed the
word of the Lord and testified about Jesus,
Peter and John returned to Jerusalem,
preaching the gospel in many Samaritan
villages.[z]

Philip and the Ethiopian

26Now an angel[a] of the Lord said to
Philip, "Go south to the road—the desert
road—that goes down from Jerusalem to
Gaza." 27So he started out, and on his way
he met an Ethiopian[ab] eunuch,[c] an important official in charge of all the treasury of
the Kandake (which means "queen of the
Ethiopians"). This man had gone to Jerusalem to worship,[d] 28and on his way home
was sitting in his chariot reading the Book
of Isaiah the prophet. 29The Spirit told[e]
Philip, "Go to that chariot and stay near it."

8:9 [l] Ac 5:36
8:10 [m] Ac 14:11; 28:6
8:12 [n] Ac 1:3 [o] Ac 2:38
8:13 [p] ver 6; Ac 19:11
8:14 [q] ver 1 [r] Lk 22:8
8:15 [s] Ac 2:38
8:16 [t] Ac 19:2 [u] Mt 28:19; Ac 2:38
8:17 [v] Ac 6:6
8:20 [w] 2Ki 5:16; Da 5:17; Mt 10:8; Ac 2:38
8:21 [x] Ps 78:37
8:24 [y] Ex 8:8; Nu 21:7; 1Ki 13:6
8:25 [z] ver 40
8:26 [a] Ac 5:19
8:27 [b] Ps 68:31; 87:4; Zep 3:10 [c] Isa 56:3-5 [d] 1Ki 8:41-43; Jn 12:20
8:29 [e] Ac 10:19; 11:12; 13:2; 20:23; 21:11

[a] *27* That is, from the southern Nile region

For magic, see the article "Magic in the New Testament," p. 1884.
8:10 *Great Power of God.* Later tradition, not necessarily dependable, reports that Simon viewed himself and his consort Helena as expressions of the male and female divine principles, respectively. This tradition fits some Greek ideas known in nearby Sebaste, but could depend on subsequent Christian ideas from this area.
8:12 *when they believed ... they were baptized.* Samaritans were already circumcised, but Jewish leaders would not welcome Samaritan "conversions" that did not acknowledge the Jewish way as the right one. Philip's concern, however, is bringing people to Christ.
8:13 *astonished by the great signs and miracles.* Although magic often could emulate God's works, it could not emulate their scale. Divine displays of power can overwhelm rival spiritual powers (Ex 7:11,22; 8:7,18–19; 9:11).
8:17 *placed their hands on them.* See note on 6:6.
8:18 *offered them money.* Magicians sometimes bought magical spells. One common feature of ancient magic was its use for personal purposes rather than the common good.
8:20 *the gift of God.* Most Jewish people viewed the Spirit as a rare or wholly future gift; the Qumran community believed that the Spirit was active among them but as a treasured gift from God. Treating the Spirit like a magic charm was an insult to the Spirit.
8:23 *full of bitterness.* Lit. "gall of bitterness." Gall was bitter. This might evoke the context of idolatry and Gentile sin in the Septuagint, the pre-Christian Greek translation of the OT, for Dt 29:17; 32:32. *captive to sin.* Here Peter reuses language in the Septuagint for Isa 58:6.
8:25 *preaching the gospel in many Samaritan villages.* As a Hellenist, Philip probably could not speak Aramaic well enough to minister in the villages (he could use Greek in the city), but Peter and John knew Aramaic in addition to Greek.
8:26 *south.* Any road to Gaza would lead south, although some take this Greek word to mean "midday" (also one of its meanings), which would make this commission an urgent one (people rarely traveled at midday). *desert road.* Scholars debate whether "desert" belongs with road (as in the NIV) or with "Gaza," since old Gaza lay in deserted ruins near new Gaza.
8:27 *eunuch.* Although the Septuagint, the pre-Christian Greek translation of the OT, sometimes used the term "eunuch" for officials who were not true eunuchs, the emphatic repetition of the term five times in this narrative suggests that this official is a true eunuch. This makes sense because men who served queens in some parts of the world were often eunuchs. As a royal treasurer, the man controlled great wealth (which is obvious also from his chariot and personal Isaiah scroll). Nevertheless, Greeks often derided eunuchs as "half-men," and they were barred from joining the people of Israel (Dt 23:1). Thus, although he worshiped God, he was not a full convert to Judaism (in contrast to the "converts" mentioned in Ac 2:11; 6:5) and is thus the first Gentile Christian, the forerunner of other Gentile believers. *Kandake ... "queen of the Ethiopians."* See the article "The African Empire of Meroë," p. 1886.
8:28 *chariot.* Only a wealthy person would have had access to a four-wheeled, covered carriage such as is likely envisioned here; this official also has servants (v. 38). As noted in the article "The African Empire of Meroë," p. 1886,

ACTS 8:27

The African Empire of Meroë

In Greek, "Ethiopians" were black Africans, and "Ethiopia" referred to all of Africa south of Egypt. Mention of "Kandake" makes clear which African empire is in view here. Nubian empires had existed south of Egypt since about 3000 BC, with Nubians and Egyptians controlling one another in various periods. The Nubian Empire implied here was the kingdom of Meroë, which had flourished since the eighth century BC. Unable to conquer this kingdom, the Romans made a treaty with it instead. It should not be confused with the kingdom of Axum in what is called Ethiopia more narrowly today, though Axum has one of the longest histories of Christianity in the world. (Axum was converted through Syrian Christians' witness in the early fourth century and has maintained a vital Christian presence to this day.)

A treasurer for this kingdom or its queen would control great wealth, since the kingdom was rich. Most of Rome's trade with Africa farther south came through Meroë, and archaeologists have found some of its treasures. The Kandake was a title of many queens of Meroë; Greeks thought it applied to Meroë's ruling queen mother, but Africans probably employed the title more broadly. Luke does not specify whether the queen here was reigning or merely queen mother or the king's wife, but one queen who did reign in this period was Queen Nawidemak. In Meroë's art, queens displayed their wealth with expensive jewels and corpulence. ◆

Queen Amanishakheto tomb treasure, shoulder collar of pearls and amulets, first century BC, found at Meroë.

A.D. Riddle/BiblePlaces.com. Taken at the Berlin Egyptian Museum.

30 Then Philip ran up to the chariot and
heard the man reading Isaiah the prophet.
"Do you understand what you are reading?" Philip asked.
31 "How can I," he said, "unless someone explains it to me?" So he invited Philip to come up and sit with him.
32 This is the passage of Scripture the eunuch was reading:

"He was led like a sheep to the
slaughter,
and as a lamb before its shearer is
silent,
so he did not open his mouth.
33 In his humiliation he was deprived of
justice.
Who can speak of his descendants?
For his life was taken from the
earth."[a][f]

34 The eunuch asked Philip, "Tell me,
please, who is the prophet talking about,
himself or someone else?" 35 Then Philip
began[g] with that very passage of Scripture[h] and told him the good news about
Jesus.
36 As they traveled along the road, they
came to some water and the eunuch said,
"Look, here is water. What can stand
in the way of my being baptized?"[i] [37][b]
38 And he gave orders to stop the chariot.
Then both Philip and the eunuch went
down into the water and Philip baptized
him. 39 When they came up out of the water, the Spirit of the Lord suddenly took
Philip away,[j] and the eunuch did not see
him again, but went on his way rejoicing.
40 Philip, however, appeared at Azotus and
traveled about, preaching the gospel in all
the towns[k] until he reached Caesarea.[l]

Saul's Conversion

9:1-19pp — Ac 22:3-16; 26:9-18

9 Meanwhile, Saul was still breathing out murderous threats against
the Lord's disciples.[m] He went to the
high priest 2 and asked him for letters to
the synagogues in Damascus, so that if
he found any there who belonged to the
Way,[n] whether men or women, he might

8:33 [f] Isa 53:7,8 **8:35** [g] Mt 5:2 [h] Lk 24:27; Ac 17:2; 18:28; 28:23 **8:36** [i] Ac 10:47 **8:39** [j] 1Ki 18:12; 2Ki 2:16; Eze 3:12,14; 8:3; 11:1,24; 43:5; 2Co 12:2 **8:40** [k] ver 25 [l] Ac 10:1,24; 12:19; 21:8,16; 23:23,33; 25:1,4,6,13 **9:1** [m] Ac 8:3 **9:2** [n] Ac 19:9,23; 22:4; 24:14,22

[a] *33* Isaiah 53:7,8 (see Septuagint) [b] *37* Some manuscripts include here *Philip said, "If you believe with all your heart, you may." The eunuch answered, "I believe that Jesus Christ is the Son of God."*

Meroë was a wealthy kingdom. Once reaching Alexandria, the official would probably leave the chariot and sail southward on the Nile. On his reading and the probable language, see note on v. 30.

8:30 *ran up to the chariot.* Some have compared Philip running up to the chariot, which was probably traveling at a leisurely pace, with 1Ki 18:44–46. Ancients praised youthful strength. *heard the man reading.* Reading was normally done aloud, so Philip hears the man, who is probably reading from a Greek translation of the Isaiah scroll. Meroë had a distinct language and script, but the official undoubtedly knows more than one language. Because of trade between Meroë and Egypt, including Alexandria, it is not surprising that the educated Nubian official knows Greek and understands Philip.

8:32–33 This passage uses the Septuagint, the pre-Christian Greek translation of Isa 53:7–8. Jewish teachers often took for granted that their Biblically literate primary hearers knew the context of the passages they cited. A person of means could have easily acquired Septuagint scrolls from Alexandria.

8:34 *who is the prophet talking about . . . ?* Apart from looking back through the passage's fulfillment in Christ, many scholars even today continue to wonder who the servant is in Isaiah. Elsewhere in this section of Isaiah (Isa 41:8; 42:1–4; 44:1–2,21; 45:4; 49:3), the "servant" is Israel; but because the servant fails in his mission (Isa 42:18–19), God raises up one within Israel to fulfill the mission and suffer on behalf of Israel (Isa 49:5–7; 52:13 — 53:12, especially 53:4–6,9). Later in the same context, God declares that he welcomes eunuchs and Gentiles (Isa 56:3–8).

8:36 *What can stand in the way of my being baptized?* As a eunuch the official would not be permitted to enter other forms of Judaism as a convert, hence he would not be allowed to be circumcised (Dt 23:1; see note on Ac 8:27). In addition to circumcision, most converts to Judaism were immersed to wash away their Gentile impurities. Thus the official here understands that, in contrast to his previous inability to convert to other forms of Jewish faith, he is now being welcomed as a member of this new movement.

8:39 *the Lord suddenly took Philip away.* In the OT, prophets could be carried away in visions (Eze 3:12,14), and at least some people expected that prophets could be carried away physically (1Ki 18:12).

8:40 *Azotus.* On the site of OT Ashdod, Azotus was roughly midway between Gaza and Joppa, some 20–25 miles (30–40 kilometers) northeast of Gaza. *Caesarea.* The Roman capital of Judea; it was roughly 50 miles (80 kilometers) north of Azotus. Many Gentiles lived in Gaza, Azotus and Caesarea. Philip anticipates Peter's ministry on the coast and in Caesarea, and Philip's preaching as he traveled fits the pattern in vv. 4,25.

9:1–18 The three accounts of Paul's calling in Acts include different but generally complementary details (9:1–18; 22:4–16; 26:9–18). Ancient hearers liked variation, so including differing elements in the different retellings prevented the narrative from seeming tedious.

9:1 *went to the high priest.* Access to the high priest would be difficult for a young man (7:58) unless he were exceptional (cf. Gal 1:14) and from a prominent family (see the article "Synagogue of Freedmen," p. 1879; see also note on 22:3).

9:2 *letters to the synagogues in Damascus.* Throughout the empire, social superiors provided letters of introduction to their peers or inferiors on behalf of those they recommended. Such recommendations could also aid Jewish travelers in finding lodging with Jews in various areas. Because the high priest in an earlier period had authority to extradite Judean fugitives, Damascus's synagogues would take Saul's commission very seriously. *synagogues.* The plural is not surprising; Damascus had many more than 20,000 Jewish residents. *the Way.* It is also not surprising that a group that believed it preached the true divine path would be called this; the Qumran community called itself this too.

take them as prisoners to Jerusalem. 3 As
he neared Damascus on his journey, suddenly a light from heaven flashed around
him.[o] 4 He fell to the ground and heard a
voice say to him, "Saul, Saul, why do you
persecute me?"
5 "Who are you, Lord?" Saul asked.
"I am Jesus, whom you are persecuting," he replied. 6 "Now get up and go into
the city, and you will be told what you
must do."[p]
7 The men traveling with Saul stood
there speechless; they heard the sound[q]
but did not see anyone.[r] 8 Saul got up from
the ground, but when he opened his eyes
he could see nothing. So they led him by

9:3 [o] 1Co 15:8
9:6 [p] ver 16
9:7 [q] Jn 12:29 [r] Da 10:7; Ac 22:9

9:3 The journey north from Jerusalem to Damascus was about 135 miles (220 kilometers); on foot (cf. v. 8), such a journey could take perhaps six days. *light from heaven.* Sometimes OT theophanies (revelations of God's glory) accompanied a divine call (Ex 3:2 – 10; Isa 6:1 – 8; Eze 1:1 — 2:8), as here (Ac 9:6,15 – 16).
9:4 *fell to the ground.* It was natural to fall when confronted with divine or even angelic glory (Eze 1:28; Da 8:17). Jewish tradition recognized that God sometimes spoke with a heavenly voice, as at times in the OT. *Saul, Saul.* God sometimes doubled the addressee's name, calling special attention to what followed (Ge 22:11; 46:2; Ex 3:4; 1Sa 3:10).
9:5 *Who are you, Lord?* The direct address "Lord" can mean "Sir," but it means more in this context. Saul knows the OT, and, given the theophany and heavenly voice (vv. 3 – 4), he must recognize that God is speaking. But how could he be persecuting (v. 4) God or even an angel? In ancient custom, letters of recommendation (v. 2) often identified the sender with the person recommended; treatment of messengers also reflected the attitude toward their sender. This was also true for God's agents (cf. Ex 16:8; 1Sa 8:7; Lk 10:16).
9:7 Selective and partial revelation appear also in Da 10:7.
9:8 *he could see nothing.* God could strike people blind to stop them from harming others (Ge 19:11), sometimes, as in this case, temporarily (2Ki 6:18 – 20).

ACTS 9:11

TARSUS

Earlier, western Cilicia in southern Asia Minor had a reputation for piracy and violence, but Tarsus in eastern Cilicia was a Hellenized and highly educated urban center. Tarsus was Cilicia's largest city and its prosperity was well known; it was "no ordinary city" (Ac 21:39). Its commercial activities were so widespread that it had official representatives in other strategic cities to protect the interests of its businesspeople there. It controlled land from the Mediterranean coast in the south to the Taurus Mountains in the north. From the sea one could travel inland about 10 miles (16 kilometers) to Tarsus on the Cydnus River, which flowed through the city. Unlike the more rugged and mountainous western part of Cilicia, Tarsus' part was fertile, producing flax. Tarsus' guild of linen workers was prominent; some scholars have connected this background with Paul's trade in Ac 18:3, but others argue that Paul worked leather, not linen.

Tarsus began to experience Hellenization in the fourth century BC and by this period it had fully embraced Greek traditions, though without completely obliterating earlier Asian ones. Public speakers there could assume that many in their audiences were familiar with the full range of Greek poetry and tradition. Rome made its region of Cilicia a Roman province in 64 BC. Rewarding Tarsus' loyalty to him, the emperor Augustus made it a "free city," granting it a degree of autonomy.

Tarsus was a "university town," where education was valued. The Greek geographer Strabo, in fact, deemed Tarsus a greater center of philosophy than even Athens or Alexandria. It was also famous for the study of rhetoric. Students from the rest of the Mediterranean world came to study philosophy and rhetoric there, although most Tarsians who pursued tertiary education chose to do so abroad (cf. perhaps 22:3). Tarsus was one of the few cities that already had its own library. Whatever Paul's age when he left Tarsus (see note on 22:3), at least his earliest years were spent in an environment that valued education.

continued on next page

the hand into Damascus. 9For three days
he was blind, and did not eat or drink anything.
10In Damascus there was a disciple
named Ananias. The Lord called to him in
a vision,[s] "Ananias!"
"Yes, Lord," he answered.
11The Lord told him, "Go to the house
of Judas on Straight Street and ask for a
man from Tarsus[t] named Saul, for he is
praying. 12In a vision he has seen a man
named Ananias come and place his hands
on[u] him to restore his sight."
13"Lord," Ananias answered, "I have
heard many reports about this man and
all the harm he has done to your holy

9:10 [s] Ac 10:3, 17, 19
9:11 [t] ver 30; Ac 21:39; 22:3
9:12 [u] Mk 5:23

9:9 *did not eat or drink anything.* People often used fasting to express mourning, including when repenting from sin. Three days was possible for this kind of fast (Est 4:16), though fasting without water is dangerous if sustained very long.
9:10 *Yes, Lord.* Unlike the carefully trained Saul (v. 5), Ananias offers the natural Biblical response to God's call (Ge 22:11; 46:2; Ex 3:4; 1Sa 3:10; Isa 6:8).
9:11 *Straight Street.* Damascus was a very old city, and old cities tended to have haphazardly winding streets. Much of Damascus's street grid, however, was gradually shifted to the Greco-Roman grid pattern of evenly spaced east-west and north-south streets. Although we cannot be certain, many believe that Straight Street was the colonnaded, major east-west thoroughfare; tradition places Judas's house near its west end. *Tarsus.* See the article "Tarsus," p. 1888.
9:12 Paired visions (here and in the case of Cornelius and Peter in ch. 10) were deemed very convincing, because together they provided independent attestations. Tradition, the reliability of which is uncertain, places Ananias's house north of the eastern end of Straight Street.
9:13 – 14 Even someone who responded with an obedient "Yes, Lord" (v. 10) might voice objections to a calling that made no human sense (cf. 10:14; Ex 3:4,10 – 11; 4:10).

Moralists condemned Tarsus for sexual vice, insolence, and extreme disunity. A traditional eastern deity named Sandan was a major deity there; Greeks identified him with Heracles. The range of deities worshiped there, however, mostly corresponded with the range of deities worshiped elsewhere in the Greek and Roman world.

The Jewish presence in Cilicia was significant (cf., e.g., Ac 6:9; Philo, *Embassy to Gaius* 281). Cilicia had many contacts, including commercial contacts, with Jerusalem, and in general Jewish people found the residents of Cilicia more favorable toward them than were Gentiles in adjoining Syria. ◆

A Roman street in Tarsus.

Cheryl Dunn for Talbot Bible Lands

ROMAN DAMASCUS

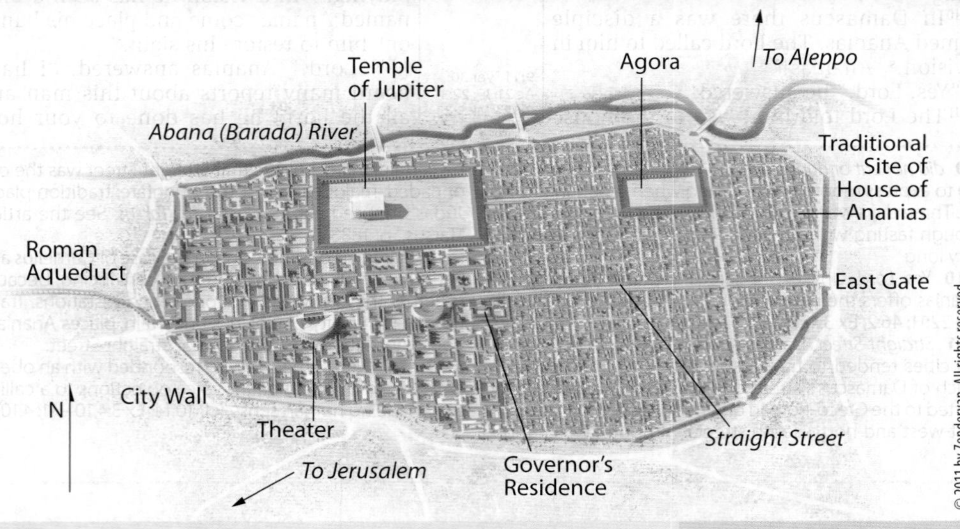

Damascus represented much more to Saul, the strict Pharisee, than any other stop on his campaign of repression. It was the hub of a vast commercial network with far-flung lines of caravan trade reaching into north Syria, Mesopotamia, Anatolia, Persia and Arabia. If the new "Way" of Christianity flourished in Damascus, it would quickly reach all these places. From the viewpoint of the Sanhedrin and of Saul, the archpersecutor, it had to be stopped in Damascus.

The dominant political figure at the time of Paul's escape from Damascus (2Co 11:32-33) was Aretas IV, king of the Nabateans (9 BC–AD 40), though normally the Decapolis cities were attached to the province of Syria and were thus under the influence of Rome.

The city itself was a veritable oasis, situated in a plain watered by the Biblical rivers Abana and Pharpar. Roman architecture overlaid the Hellenistic town plan with a great temple to Jupiter and a mile-long colonnaded street, possibly the "Straight Street" of Ac 9:11. The city gates and a section of the town wall may still be seen today, as well as the lengthy bazaar that runs along the line of the ancient street.

people[v] in Jerusalem.[w] 14And he has come
here with authority from the chief priests[x]
to arrest all who call on your name."
15But the Lord said to Ananias, "Go!
This man is my chosen instrument[y] to proclaim my name to the Gentiles[z] and their
kings[a] and to the people of Israel. 16I will
show him how much he must suffer for
my name."[b]
17Then Ananias went to the house and
entered it. Placing his hands on[c] Saul, he
said, "Brother Saul, the Lord — Jesus, who
appeared to you on the road as you were
coming here — has sent me so that you
may see again and be filled with the Holy
Spirit." 18Immediately, something like
scales fell from Saul's eyes, and he could
see again. He got up and was baptized,

9:13 [v]ver 32; Ro 1:7; 16:2,15 [w]Ac 8:3
9:14 [x]ver 2,21
9:15 [y]Ac 13:2; Ro 1:1; Gal 1:15 [z]Ro 11:13; 15:15,16; Gal 2:7,8; Eph 3:7,8 [a]Ac 25:22,23; 26:1
9:16 [b]Ac 20:23; 21:11; 2Co 11:23-27
9:17 [c]Ac 6:6
9:19 [d]Ac 11:26 [e]Ac 26:20
9:20 [f]Ac 13:5, 14 [g]Mt 4:3
9:21 [h]Ac 8:3 [i]Gal 1:13,23
9:22 [j]Ac 18:5, 28

19and after taking some food, he regained
his strength.

Saul in Damascus and Jerusalem

Saul spent several days with the disciples[d] in Damascus.[e] 20At once he began
to preach in the synagogues[f] that Jesus is
the Son of God.[g] 21All those who heard
him were astonished and asked, "Isn't he
the man who raised havoc in Jerusalem
among those who call on this name?[h] And
hasn't he come here to take them as prisoners to the chief priests?"[i] 22Yet Saul grew
more and more powerful and baffled the
Jews living in Damascus by proving that
Jesus is the Messiah.[j]
23After many days had gone by, there
was a conspiracy among the Jews to kill

9:17 *Brother Saul.* Figurative family terminology was common. People often called members of their own ethnic group, association or other group "brother"; it could also apply, as here, to those who share a common faith.
9:18 *something like scales.* Some of Luke's audience may have recalled the scales or films that fell from Tobit's eyes when he was healed in a traditional Jewish story (Tobit 3:17; 11:11 – 13). *baptized.* Damascus had plenty of water, not least in the Barada River that ran through the city (not far from the traditional location of Straight Street).

him, 24but Saul learned of their plan.[k] Day
and night they kept close watch on the
city gates in order to kill him. 25But his
followers took him by night and lowered
him in a basket through an opening in the
wall.[l]

26When he came to Jerusalem,[m] he tried
to join the disciples, but they were all
afraid of him, not believing that he really
was a disciple. 27But Barnabas[n] took him
and brought him to the apostles. He told
them how Saul on his journey had seen
the Lord and that the Lord had spoken
to him,[o] and how in Damascus he had
preached fearlessly in the name of Jesus.[p]
28So Saul stayed with them and moved
about freely in Jerusalem, speaking boldly
in the name of the Lord. 29He talked and
debated with the Hellenistic Jews,[a][q] but
they tried to kill him.[r] 30When the believers[s] learned of this, they took him down
to Caesarea[t] and sent him off to Tarsus.[u]

31Then the church throughout Judea,
Galilee and Samaria[v] enjoyed a time of
peace and was strengthened. Living in the
fear of the Lord and encouraged by the
Holy Spirit, it increased in numbers.

Aeneas and Dorcas

32As Peter traveled about the country, he
went to visit the Lord's people[w] who lived
in Lydda. 33There he found a man named
Aeneas, who was paralyzed and had been
bedridden for eight years. 34"Aeneas," Peter said to him, "Jesus Christ heals you.[x]
Get up and roll up your mat." Immediately
Aeneas got up. 35All those who lived in
Lydda and Sharon[y] saw him and turned
to the Lord.[z]

36In Joppa[a] there was a disciple named
Tabitha (in Greek her name is Dorcas); she
was always doing good[b] and helping the
poor. 37About that time she became sick
and died, and her body was washed and
placed in an upstairs room.[c] 38Lydda was
near Joppa; so when the disciples[d] heard
that Peter was in Lydda, they sent two
men to him and urged him, "Please come
at once!"

39Peter went with them, and when he
arrived he was taken upstairs to the room.
All the widows[e] stood around him, crying and showing him the robes and other
clothing that Dorcas had made while she
was still with them.

40Peter sent them all out of the room;[f]
then he got down on his knees[g] and
prayed. Turning toward the dead woman, he said, "Tabitha, get up." She opened
her eyes, and seeing Peter she sat up. 41He
took her by the hand and helped her to
her feet. Then he called for the believers,

9:24 [k] Ac 20:3, 19 **9:25** [l] 1Sa 19:12; 2Co 11:32, 33 **9:26** [m] Ac 22:17; 26:20; Gal 1:17, 18 **9:27** [n] Ac 4:36 [o] ver 3-6 [p] ver 20, 22 **9:29** [q] Ac 6:1 [r] 2Co 11:26 **9:30** [s] Ac 1:16 [t] Ac 8:40 [u] ver 11 **9:31** [v] Ac 8:1 **9:32** [w] ver 13 **9:34** [x] Ac 3:6, 16; 4:10 **9:35** [y] 1Ch 5:16; 27:29; Isa 33:9; 35:2; 65:10 [z] Ac 11:21 **9:36** [a] Jos 19:46; 2Ch 2:16; Ezr 3:7; Jnh 1:3; Ac 10:5 [b] 1Ti 2:10; Titus 3:8 **9:37** [c] Ac 1:13 **9:38** [d] Ac 11:26 **9:39** [e] Ac 6:1 **9:40** [f] Mt 9:25 [g] Lk 22:41; Ac 7:60

[a] *29* That is, Jews who had adopted the Greek language and culture

9:24 *learned of their plan.* Both plots and leaks of information were common in antiquity. *kept close watch on the city gates.* Cities closed their gates at night for security, limiting the number of people passing through. Saul's Damascene Jewish opponents were apparently allied with Nabatean opponents as well (see 2Co 11:32–33).
9:25 *lowered him … through an opening in the wall.* Saul and his supporters undoubtedly learned this method of escape from Scripture (Jos 2:15; 1Sa 19:12). Because a very ancient tradition reports that Ananias's house, like a number of ancient houses, was built on the city wall, some suspect that Ananias's house provided the basis for the escape.
9:26–30 Paul's experience in Jerusalem (here) closely follows the pattern of his experience in Damascus (vv. 13–25). By selecting which elements to omit, ancient writers often developed patterns in the way they narrated events.
9:30 Rome used the mixed Jewish and Syrian city of Caesarea, rather than Jerusalem (which was roughly two days' walk inland), as its administrative capital for Judea. Herod the Great had constructed a massive harbor at Caesarea and it was a major hub for maritime commerce. Here Paul could easily find a vessel traveling to southern Asia Minor to return to his childhood home city of Tarsus (v. 11). *Caesarea.* See the article "Caesarea and Its Soldiers," p. 1892.
9:31 On summary statements, see note on 6:7.
9:32 *Lydda.* Roughly 25 miles (40 kilometers) northwest of Jerusalem and 11 miles (17.5 kilometers) from Joppa (v. 36). Joppa and Lydda together were the most important Jewish cities near Judea's coast. (Neither rivaled Caesarea, but Caesarea included a much larger proportion of Gentile residents than these cities did.)
9:33 Visiting the sick was a conventional act of Jewish piety.
9:35 *All those who lived in Lydda and Sharon.* "All" statements such as this tend to be hyperbolic, but at the least indicate massive numbers, probably the majority of people, converting. Second-century sources suggest that Christians continued to flourish in Lydda. *Lydda and Sharon.* Sharon is the coastal plain; Lydda lay on its southern end.
9:36 *Joppa.* Today called Jaffa; it was 11 miles (17.5 kilometers) from Lydda and 30 miles (48 kilometers) south of Caesarea. Though less important than Caesarea, the harbor of which was constructed by Herod the Great, Joppa was wealthy and was the only significant Jewish port. *Dorcas.* Greek for Tabitha, which means "gazelle." In the Mediterranean world many women of means were benefactors, helping sponsor associations; Jewish women were deeply devoted to charity (cf. v. 39).
9:37 *body was washed and placed in an upstairs room.* Women prepared other women's bodies for burial; preparation included washing, as here. Bodies were occasionally kept in upper rooms; Luke might specifically take note of the upper room here to recall the setting of raising stories in 1Ki 17:19,23; 2Ki 4:10,32–35.
9:38 *come at once!* People usually buried bodies before sunset, so the matter is urgent. The 11 miles (17.5 kilometers) between Joppa and Lydda might require four hours' travel each way.
9:39 *All the widows.* Jewish piety emphasized caring for widows, who often lacked other means of support and protection.
9:40 *sent them all out.* For privacy in some prayers for raisings, cf. 1Ki 17:19; 2Ki 4:33.
9:41 *presented her to them alive.* Cf. 1Ki 17:23; 2Ki 4:36.

especially the widows, and presented her
to them alive. 42This became known all
over Joppa, and many people believed in
the Lord. 43Peter stayed in Joppa for some
time with a tanner named Simon.[h]

Cornelius Calls for Peter

10 At Caesarea[i] there was a man
named Cornelius, a centurion in
what was known as the Italian Regiment.
2He and all his family were devout and
God-fearing;[j] he gave generously to those
in need and prayed to God regularly. 3One
day at about three in the afternoon[k] he
had a vision.[l] He distinctly saw an angel[m]
of God, who came to him and said, "Cornelius!"

4Cornelius stared at him in fear. "What
is it, Lord?" he asked.

The angel answered, "Your prayers and
gifts to the poor have come up as a memorial offering[n] before God.[o] 5Now send
men to Joppa[p] to bring back a man named
Simon who is called Peter. 6He is staying

9:43 [h] Ac 10:6
10:1 [i] Ac 8:40
10:2 [j] ver 22, 35; Ac 13:16,26
10:3 [k] Ac 3:1 [l] Ac 9:10 [m] Ac 5:19
10:4 [n] Mt 26:13 [o] Rev 8:4
10:5 [p] Ac 9:36

9:43 Tanners dealt with carcasses and thus with strong odors; they normally had to reside outside the walls of the city. Conservative Jewish pietists would limit involvement with them, since those in contact with carcasses were ritually impure. Like Gentiles, however, Jews were more often concerned with the odors. Later rabbis even ruled that tanners' wives should be permitted to divorce them because of the odors associated with tanning.
10:2 *all his family.* During the typical 20-year span of military service soldiers were officially prohibited marriage. Officers usually looked the other way, however, at liaisons between soldiers and local women, and the government usually recognized these unions as marriages when soldiers retired. Most soldiers remained stationed in particular areas and were unhappy to be moved. Alternatively, they could marry on retirement. By ancient definitions, "family" could also include servants (v. 7), though Cornelius has relatives in the more specific sense (v. 24). *God-fearing.* Diaspora Jews recognized many Gentiles who had not become proselytes (converts) to Judaism and yet were attracted to the synagogues and the one true God.
10:3 *three in the afternoon.* Cornelius was praying at this time (v. 30), which was one of the regular times of prayer,

ACTS 10:1

Caesarea and Its Soldiers

Caesarea Maritima (Caesarea on the Sea, not to be confused with Caesarea Philippi in Mk 8:27) was once the settlement called Strato's Tower. Herod the Great had expanded it and built a massive harbor complex there, described in detail by Josephus and astonishingly confirmed by archaeology. It was now the seat of Judea's Roman governor. The city's theater seated some 4,000 and it had other features of Greek cities, but was divided between the dominant Syrian Gentile population and Jewish residents. Trouble often erupted between these segments, with the Syrian soldiers stationed there siding with the Syrian residents, and in the year AD 66 Josephus estimates that 20,000 Jews were slaughtered in a single wave of genocide. Some other Gentiles, however, were drawn to Judaism.

Judea's governor had five auxiliary infantry cohorts and a cavalry unit. Auxiliaries, unlike legionaries, were generally not Roman citizens; they were local Syrian recruits, many based in this area, but would achieve citizenship when they retired. Centurions commanded centuries, units of about 80 men each. (The traditional, paper strength of a century was, as one would guess from the name, 100 soldiers; in reality, however, a century contained fewer soldiers than this.) Some centurions were aristocrats, but most were common soldiers who climbed their way through the ranks, sometimes over as long as 20 years.

The Italian Regiment (Ac 10:1) means a cohort, one-tenth of a legion, with as many as 600 troops. Five of these cohorts were stationed in Caesarea, with a sixth in the Antonia Fortress in Jerusalem. Cohorts could take their names from the cohort's original location, so there is no reason to expect that the current cohort is Italian rather than (as usual in this region) largely Syrian. Given Cornelius's name, he is probably

continued on next page

with Simon the tanner,[q] whose house is
by the sea."
[7]When the angel who spoke to him had
gone, Cornelius called two of his servants
and a devout soldier who was one of his
attendants. [8]He told them everything that
had happened and sent them to Joppa.[r]

Peter's Vision

10:9-32Ref — Ac 11:5-14

[9]About noon the following day as they
were on their journey and approaching the
city, Peter went up on the roof[s] to pray.
[10]He became hungry and wanted something to eat, and while the meal was being prepared, he fell into a trance.[t] [11]He
saw heaven opened and something like
a large sheet being let down to earth by
its four corners. [12]It contained all kinds
of four-footed animals, as well as reptiles
and birds. [13]Then a voice told him, "Get
up, Peter. Kill and eat."
[14]"Surely not, Lord!"[u] Peter replied. "I
have never eaten anything impure or unclean."[v]
[15]The voice spoke to him a second time,

10:6 [q] Ac 9:43 **10:8** [r] Ac 9:36 **10:9** [s] Mt 24:17 **10:10** [t] Ac 22:17 **10:14** [u] Ac 9:5 [v] Lev 11:4-8, 13-20; 20:25; Dt 14:3-20; Eze 4:14

corresponding with the evening offering in the temple (cf. 3:1). This notice underlines Cornelius's devoutness.
10:9 *About noon.* People normally rested from the day's activities for a period of time around midday. *went up on the roof to pray.* People used their homes' flat roofs for a wide range of activities, from drying flax to sleeping and, here, having a private place to pray. Joppa was some 30 miles (48 kilometers) south of Caesarea; given the time of Cornelius's vision (v. 3), to reach Peter around noon the next day would require hard riding on horses or walking through part of the night. (The return journey is less demanding; vv. 23–24.)
10:10 *became hungry.* Many people in the ancient world would have a light meal around noon.
10:12 *all kinds of four-footed animals, as well as reptiles.* For a strict pietist, the presence of unclean animals such as reptiles would contaminate all the others. During the Maccabean era, Jewish people suffered much for their food laws (the laws appear in Lev 11; Dt 14:3–21), which were a deeply engrained part of their upbringing.
10:14 Peter protests, as did Ezekiel when confronted with an exhortation to eat what appears impure (Eze 4:14; God made a concession in Eze 4:15).

already a citizen, whether as a retired centurion or, perhaps more likely, a citizen lent for this supervisory role from the legion.

In this period young men usually enlisted around age 17 and served 20 years; in difficult areas on the borders of the empire, an average of half are estimated to have survived, but the proportion of survivors was likely higher around Caesarea. Marriage was not officially permitted but having an unofficial concubine was common (see note on Ac 10:2). ◆

Artist's recreation of first-century Caesarea.

"Do not call anything impure that God has
made clean."[w]
16This happened three times, and immediately the sheet was taken back to heaven.
17While Peter was wondering about the
meaning of the vision, the men sent by
Cornelius[x] found out where Simon's house
was and stopped at the gate. 18They called
out, asking if Simon who was known as
Peter was staying there.
19While Peter was still thinking about
the vision, the Spirit said[y] to him, "Simon,
three[a] men are looking for you. 20So get up
and go downstairs. Do not hesitate to go
with them, for I have sent them."[z]
21Peter went down and said to the men,
"I'm the one you're looking for. Why have
you come?"
22The men replied, "We have come from
Cornelius the centurion. He is a righteous
and God-fearing man,[a] who is respected by
all the Jewish people. A holy angel told him
to ask you to come to his house so that he
could hear what you have to say."[b] 23Then
Peter invited the men into the house to be
his guests.

Peter at Cornelius's House

The next day Peter started out with
them, and some of the believers[c] from

10:15 [w] Mt 15:11; Ro 14:14, 17, 20; 1Co 10:25; 1Ti 4:3, 4; Titus 1:15 **10:17** [x] ver 7, 8 **10:19** [y] Ac 8:29 **10:20** [z] Ac 15:7-9 **10:22** [a] ver 2 [b] Ac 11:14 **10:23** [c] Ac 1:16

[a] 19 One early manuscript *two*; other manuscripts do not have the number.

10:17 *vision.* Paired visions (here, those of Cornelius and Peter; cf. also 9:12) were deemed very convincing, because they were independent attestations. *found out.* Tanners (v. 6; see note on 9:43) would generally live in the same neighborhood as other tanners, naturally near water, as here. Once in a neighborhood, visitors normally located homes by asking directions. *the gate.* Homeowners with outer gates possessed more resources than average.
10:19 *the Spirit said to him.* The Spirit was often associated with prophetic insight and speech; Luke emphasizes the Spirit's leading in crossing cultural barriers (1:8; 8:29).
10:23 *invited the men into the house.* Bringing into one's home Gentiles who had probably worshiped idols violated strict Jewish purity protocols; but then, the house already belongs to a tanner (see note on 9:43). Hospitality obligations demanded offering food to the guests; stricter Jewish circles, however, forbade eating with Gentiles. Because Joppa, though predominantly Jew-

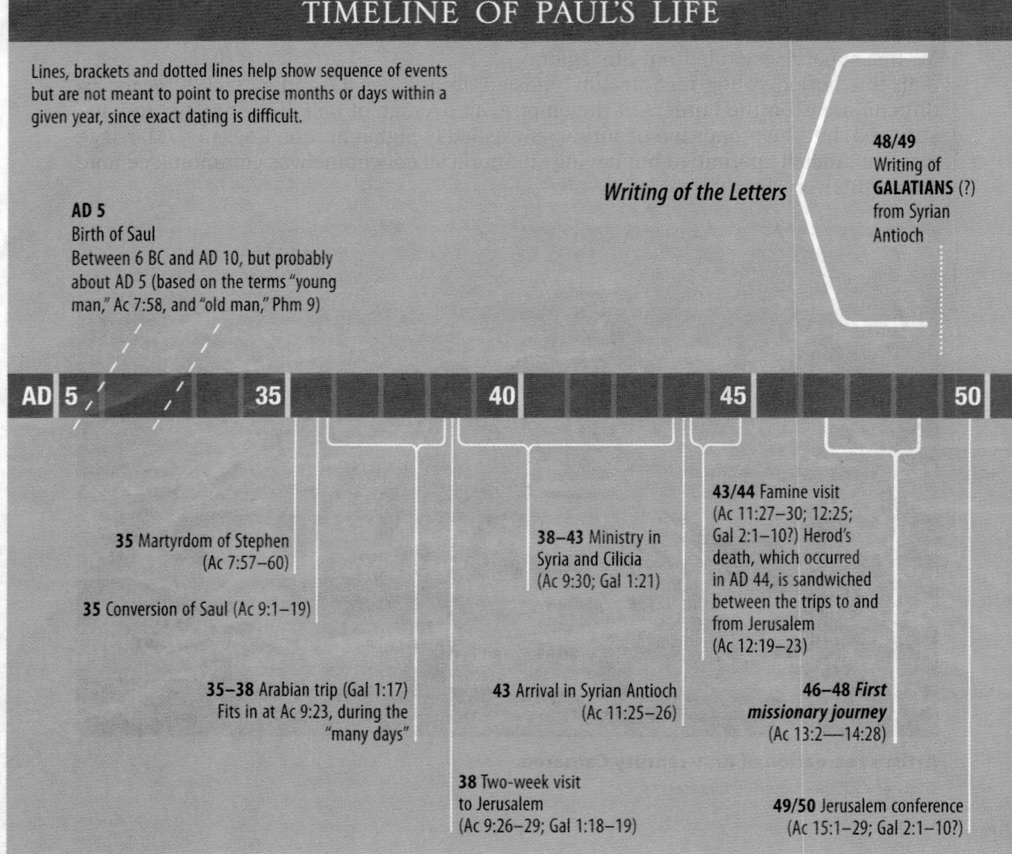

Joppa went along.[d] 24The following day
he arrived in Caesarea.[e] Cornelius was expecting them and had called together his
relatives and close friends. 25As Peter entered the house, Cornelius met him and
fell at his feet in reverence. 26But Peter
made him get up. "Stand up," he said, "I
am only a man myself."[f]
27While talking with him, Peter went
inside and found a large gathering of people. 28He said to them: "You are well aware
that it is against our law for a Jew to associate with or visit a Gentile.[g] But God has
shown me that I should not call anyone
impure or unclean.[h] 29So when I was sent
for, I came without raising any objection.
May I ask why you sent for me?"
30Cornelius answered: "Three days ago
I was in my house praying at this hour, at
three in the afternoon. Suddenly a man in
shining clothes stood before me 31and said,
'Cornelius, God has heard your prayer and
remembered your gifts to the poor. 32Send
to Joppa for Simon who is called Peter. He
is a guest in the home of Simon the tanner,
who lives by the sea.' 33So I sent for you

10:23 [d] ver 45; Ac 11:12
10:24 [e] Ac 8:40
10:26 [f] Ac 14:15; Rev 19:10
10:28 [g] Jn 4:9; 18:28; Ac 11:3 [h] Ac 15:8, 9

ish, included many Gentiles, some Jewish residents may have been less particular about such rules, but the Jerusalem church includes many conservative members (see 11:2–3).

10:24 Caesarea was about 30 miles (48 kilometers) beyond Joppa; they had stayed overnight somewhere, probably lodging in a town that included both Jewish and Gentile residents (cf. v. 30). *called together.* In this period, soldiers were often stationed in the regions where they were recruited; the relatives, probably Syrians, could be relatives of Cornelius or of his wife (whether she was official or unofficial; see note on v. 2).

10:25 *fell at his feet in reverence.* Gentiles prostrated themselves before gods and rulers, or sometimes important persons from whom they needed to beg a favor.

10:26 *I am only a man.* Even Gentiles expected mortals to reject divine honors; Peter (like Paul in 14:11–15; cf. 28:6) behaves honorably here, in contrast to Herod Agrippa I in 12:22–23 (cf. 8:9–10; Lk 21:8).

10:28 Strict Jews avoided eating with Gentiles (cf. 11:3). Ethnic division between Jews and Syrians in Caesarea (11:1) often led to violence; God, however, was working to transcend this barrier.

10:30–33 Ancient literature often repeated events or messages when people recounted them, although by this period they preferred to vary the wording.

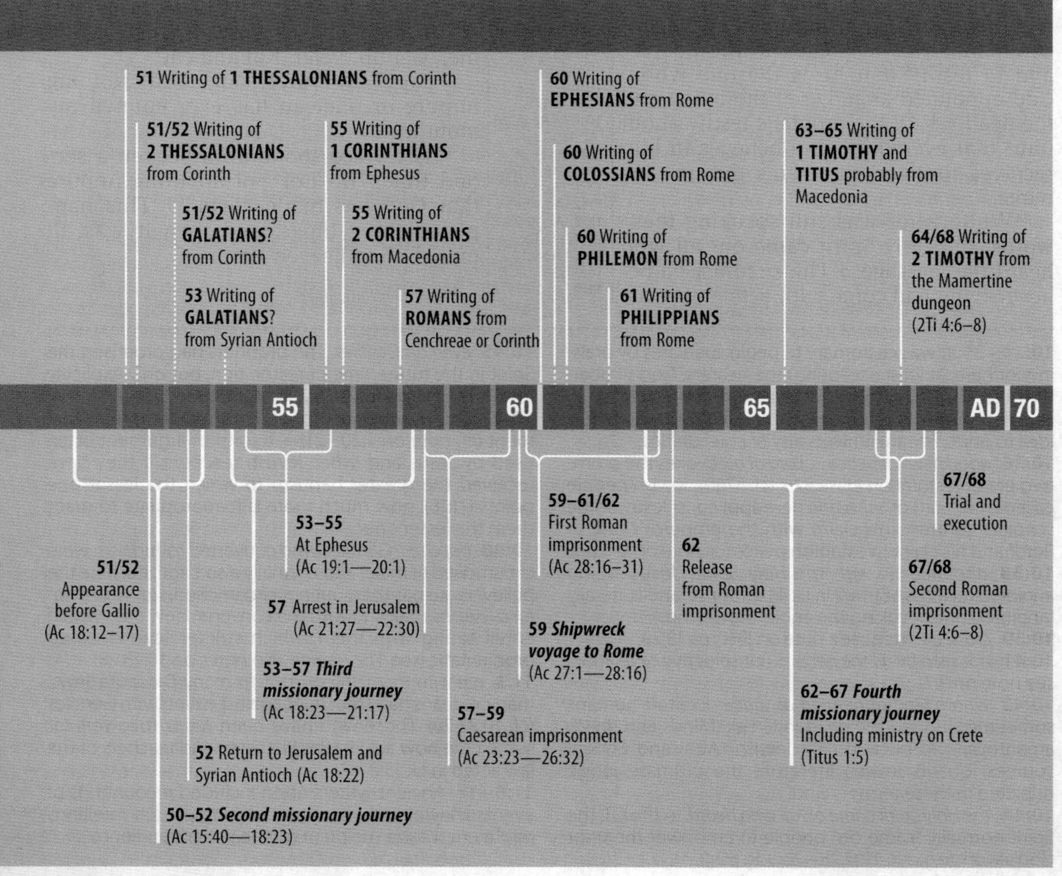

immediately, and it was good of you to
come. Now we are all here in the presence
of God to listen to everything the Lord has
commanded you to tell us."
34Then Peter began to speak: "I now realize how true it is that God does not show
favoritism[i] 35but accepts from every nation
the one who fears him and does what is
right.[j] 36You know the message God sent
to the people of Israel, announcing the
good news[k] of peace[l] through Jesus Christ,
who is Lord of all.[m] 37You know what has
happened throughout the province of Judea, beginning in Galilee after the baptism
that John preached— 38how God anointed[n] Jesus of Nazareth with the Holy Spirit
and power, and how he went around doing good and healing[o] all who were under
the power of the devil, because God was
with him.[p]
39"We are witnesses[q] of everything he
did in the country of the Jews and in Jerusalem. They killed him by hanging him
on a cross,[r] 40but God raised him from the
dead[s] on the third day and caused him to
be seen. 41He was not seen by all the people,[t] but by witnesses whom God had already chosen—by us who ate[u] and drank
with him after he rose from the dead. 42He
commanded us to preach to the people[v]
and to testify that he is the one whom
God appointed as judge of the living and
the dead.[w] 43All the prophets testify about
him[x] that everyone[y] who believes in him
receives forgiveness of sins through his
name."
44While Peter was still speaking these
words, the Holy Spirit came on[z] all who
heard the message. 45The circumcised believers who had come with Peter[a] were astonished that the gift of the Holy Spirit had
been poured out[b] even on Gentiles.[c] 46For
they heard them speaking in tongues[a][d]
and praising God.
Then Peter said, 47"Surely no one can
stand in the way of their being baptized
with water.[e] They have received the Holy
Spirit just as we have."[f] 48So he ordered
that they be baptized in the name of Jesus
Christ.[g] Then they asked Peter to stay with
them for a few days.

Peter Explains His Actions

11 The apostles and the believers[h]
throughout Judea heard that the
Gentiles also had received the word of
God. 2So when Peter went up to Jerusalem, the circumcised believers[i] criticized
him 3and said, "You went into the house of
uncircumcised men and ate with them."[j]
4Starting from the beginning, Peter told
them the whole story: 5"I was in the city
of Joppa praying, and in a trance I saw
a vision.[k] I saw something like a large
sheet being let down from heaven by its
four corners, and it came down to where I
was. 6I looked into it and saw four-footed
animals of the earth, wild beasts, reptiles
and birds. 7Then I heard a voice telling
me, 'Get up, Peter. Kill and eat.'
8"I replied, 'Surely not, Lord! Nothing
impure or unclean has ever entered my
mouth.'
9"The voice spoke from heaven a second time, 'Do not call anything impure
that God has made clean.'[l] 10This happened three times, and then it was all
pulled up to heaven again.

10:34 [i] Dt 10:17; 2Ch 19:7; Job 34:19; Ro 2:11; Gal 2:6; Eph 6:9; Col 3:25; 1Pe 1:17 **10:35** [j] Ac 15:9 **10:36** [k] Ac 13:32 [l] Lk 2:14 [m] Mt 28:18; Ro 10:12 **10:38** [n] Ac 4:26 [o] Mt 4:23 [p] Jn 3:2 **10:39** [q] Lk 24:48 [r] Ac 5:30 **10:40** [s] Ac 2:24 **10:41** [t] Jn 14:17,22 [u] Lk 24:43; Jn 21:13 **10:42** [v] Mt 28:19,20 [w] Jn 5:22; Ac 17:31; Ro 14:9; 2Co 5:10; 2Ti 4:1; 1Pe 4:5 **10:43** [x] Isa 53:11 [y] Ac 15:9 **10:44** [z] Ac 8:15,16; 11:15; 15:8 **10:45** [a] ver 23 [b] Ac 2:33,38 [c] Ac 11:18 **10:46** [d] Mk 16:17 **10:47** [e] Ac 8:36 [f] Ac 11:17 **10:48** [g] Ac 2:38; 8:16 **11:1** [h] Ac 1:16 **11:2** [i] Ac 10:45 **11:3** [j] Ac 10:25,28; Gal 2:12 **11:5** [k] Ac 9:10; 10:9-32 **11:9** [l] Ac 10:15

[a] 46 Or *other languages*

10:34–35 It was customary to begin speeches by praising (or here, at least accepting) the hearers. God's impartiality (cf. Dt 10:17; Ro 2:11) was a common emphasis in Jewish thought. Some Greek writers also appealed to this idea to underline the universality of chief deities.
10:36 *good news of peace ... Lord of all.* Evokes the promised era of restoration in Isa 52:7 (cf. 57:19). Jewish people called God "Lord of all," a title here applied to Jesus. Some scholars contrast this claim with the emperor's title of "lord" and his claim to establish peace (cf. note on Lk 2:14).
10:38 *anointed ... with the Holy Spirit.* Jesus being anointed recalls Isa 61:1–2 in Lk 4:18 ("Christ" also is literally "anointed one," evoking the anointing of kings).
10:39 *cross.* Lit. "tree"; see note on 5:30; cf. 13:29.
10:41 *not seen by all the people.* For selective revelation, see note on 9:7.
10:42 *whom God appointed as judge.* Exalted humans sometimes judged the dead in Greek (Minos and Rhadamanthys) and occasionally Jewish (Abel and Enoch) sources, but in Jewish literature the ultimate judge depicted in these terms is God.
10:44 *the Holy Spirit came on all who heard.* In the OT, the Spirit normally "came on" people to empower them for God's work (e.g., Nu 11:17,25–26; Jdg 6:34).
10:45 *even on Gentiles.* The prophets had promised the Spirit in the future time of restoration, but only explicitly for God's own people (e.g., Isa 44:3; Eze 36:27).
10:47 This may be an implicit "How much more?" argument (cf. note on 1:20–21)—a form of argument often used by Jesus and other Jewish teachers: if they have received the greater baptism to which the lesser one points (11:16), how much more is it appropriate to grant them the lesser one?
10:48 *baptized.* Gentiles who converted to Judaism were circumcised (if male) and normally also baptized; here the believers are baptized but not circumcised. *stay with them for a few days.* Staying with the converts a few days would entail eating with them, which stricter Jews deemed problematic (see 11:2–3; see also notes on 10:23,28).
11:3 *ate with them.* In contrast to many Diaspora Jews, many Judeans had strict rules against eating with Gentiles (cf. 10:23,28). Those who have been Jesus' followers for some time now act like the Pharisees and teachers of the law acted in Lk 15:2.
11:6–17 Ancient writers often included recountings of events they already narrated; including such retellings might emphasize the point for the writer's audience.

11“Right then three men who had been
sent to me from Caesarea stopped at the
house where I was staying. 12The Spirit told[m] me to have no hesitation about
going with them.[n] These six brothers also
went with me, and we entered the man’s
house. 13He told us how he had seen an
angel appear in his house and say, ‘Send
to Joppa for Simon who is called Peter.
14He will bring you a message through
which you and all your household[o] will
be saved.’

15“As I began to speak, the Holy Spirit came on[p] them as he had come on us
at the beginning.[q] 16Then I remembered
what the Lord had said: ‘John baptized
with[a] water, but you will be baptized
with[a] the Holy Spirit.’[r] 17So if God gave
them the same gift he gave us[s] who believed in the Lord Jesus Christ, who was I
to think that I could stand in God’s way?”

18When they heard this, they had no
further objections and praised God, saying, “So then, even to Gentiles God has
granted repentance that leads to life.”[t]

The Church in Antioch

19Now those who had been scattered by
the persecution that broke out when Stephen was killed[u] traveled as far as Phoenicia, Cyprus and Antioch,[v] spreading the
word only among Jews. 20Some of them,
however, men from Cyprus[w] and Cyrene,[x]
went to Antioch and began to speak to
Greeks also, telling them the good news
about the Lord Jesus. 21The Lord’s hand
was with them,[y] and a great number of
people believed and turned to the Lord.[z]

22News of this reached the church in Jerusalem, and they sent Barnabas[a] to Antioch. 23When he arrived and saw what
the grace of God had done,[b] he was glad
and encouraged them all to remain true to
the Lord with all their hearts.[c] 24He was
a good man, full of the Holy Spirit and
faith, and a great number of people were
brought to the Lord.[d]

25Then Barnabas went to Tarsus[e] to
look for Saul, 26and when he found him,
he brought him to Antioch. So for a whole
year Barnabas and Saul met with the
church and taught great numbers of people. The disciples[f] were called Christians
first[g] at Antioch.

27During this time some prophets[h] came
down from Jerusalem to Antioch. 28One
of them, named Agabus,[i] stood up and
through the Spirit predicted that a severe
famine would spread over the entire Roman world.[j] (This happened during the
reign of Claudius.)[k] 29The disciples,[l] as
each one was able, decided to provide

11:12 [m] Ac 8:29 [n] Ac 15:9; Ro 3:22
11:14 [o] Jn 4:53; Ac 16:15,31-34; 1Co 1:11,16
11:15 [p] Ac 10:44 [q] Ac 2:4
11:16 [r] Mk 1:8; Ac 1:5
11:17 [s] Ac 10:45,47
11:18 [t] Ro 10:12,13; 2Co 7:10
11:19 [u] Ac 8:1,4 [v] ver 26,27; Ac 13:1; 18:22; Gal 2:11
11:20 [w] Ac 4:36 [x] Mt 27:32
11:21 [y] Lk 1:66 [z] Ac 2:47
11:22 [a] Ac 4:36
11:23 [b] Ac 13:43; 14:26; 20:24 [c] Ac 14:22
11:24 [d] ver 21; Ac 5:14
11:25 [e] Ac 9:11
11:26 [f] Ac 6:1,2; 13:52 [g] Ac 26:28; 1Pe 4:16
11:27 [h] Ac 13:1; 15:32; 1Co 12:28,29; Eph 4:11
11:28 [i] Ac 21:10 [j] Mt 24:14 [k] Ac 18:2
11:29 [l] ver 26

[a] 16 Or *in*

11:18 *even to Gentiles God has granted repentance that leads to life.* Many Jewish people believed that the small minority of Gentiles who maintained a basic level of decency—no sexual immorality, idolatry or the like—would be saved. More conservative Jewish thinkers, however, demanded conversion, or expected a turning of Gentiles to Israel’s God only in the end time. (The conservative authors of key Qumran documents did not even believe that most Jewish people would be saved.) For the sake of conciseness, Luke may simplify the picture here (cf. 15:1), which was an accepted practice in ancient histories and biographies, and, for that matter, in ordinary speech.
11:19 *Phoenicia, Cyprus and Antioch.* Many Jewish people resided in these locations.
11:20 *Antioch.* Various cities were named Antioch; the Antioch here is Antioch-on-the-Orontes (on the Orontes River), the third or fourth largest city in the empire (with between 100,000 and 600,000 residents). The Roman governor of Syria and his legion resided there; it did not have the status of a Roman colony, but was a “free city” with a measure of autonomy. Antioch and Cyrene had particularly large Jewish populations. Jewish residents may have constituted even a quarter or a third of Cyrene; Antioch’s proportion is unknown (some estimates are close to 10 percent), but many Jews lived there. The status of Jews differed in the two cities: in a time of later strife, many of Cyrene’s Jews were massacred, but after the Judean revolt Antioch spared its Jewish residents. *Greeks.* Lit. “Hellenists,” but this time (in contrast to 6:1) of the Gentile variety (because of the contrast with “Jews” in v. 19); they are cultural Greeks but ethnically could also include Syrians. In contrast to the Syrian countryside, Antioch had many cultural Greeks. It was also a cosmopolitan center with considerable exchange among cultures; many Gentiles converted to Judaism or were God-fearers in Antioch (cf. 6:5). Pagan cults flourished in Antioch as in other Gentile cities; the most famous was the local cult of Apollo.
11:22 *News of this reached . . . Jerusalem.* Antioch was over 300 miles (480 kilometers) north of Jerusalem.
11:25 *Tarsus.* See the article “Tarsus,” p. 1888. The city was roughly 100 miles (160 kilometers) north of Antioch.
11:26 *Christians.* The title seems a political nickname (resembling Pompeiians—members of Pompey’s party—and other titles of political parties). Those who believed that Christ was king could be accused of treason, and the title “Christians” became a legal charge (1Pe 4:16), though it was soon embraced by Jesus’ followers as a welcome title. Here it was probably merely ridicule; Antiochans developed a reputation for mocking people.
11:27 *some prophets.* Although many ancients believed in prophets, no other movement had large numbers of prophets as a norm. Outsiders hearing and believing such reports would be astonished.
11:28 *stood up.* One would stand to address others. *severe famine.* A series of famines struck in the time of the emperor Claudius (AD 41–54), in the mid- to late-40s.
11:29 *provide help for the brothers and sisters.* Trade made Antioch prosperous; nevertheless, their generosity is significant, since the famine is predicted to affect Antioch as well. Cities depended on grain imported from the countryside. Wealthy benefactors were known to contribute to the public good, but all the disciples here share. Given the diverse ethnic composition of the believers in Antioch (v. 20), sharing with Jerusalemites as “brothers and sisters” speaks of spiritual kin ties that transcend even ethnic

help[m] for the brothers and sisters[n] living
in Judea. 30This they did, sending their gift
to the elders[o] by Barnabas and Saul.[p]

Peter's Miraculous Escape From Prison

12 It was about this time that King Herod arrested some who belonged to
the church, intending to persecute them.
2He had James, the brother of John,[q] put
to death with the sword. 3When he saw
that this met with approval among the
Jews,[r] he proceeded to seize Peter also.
This happened during the Festival of Unleavened Bread.[s] 4After arresting him, he
put him in prison, handing him over to
be guarded by four squads of four soldiers
each. Herod intended to bring him out for
public trial after the Passover.

5So Peter was kept in prison, but the
church was earnestly praying to God for
him.[t]

6The night before Herod was to bring
him to trial, Peter was sleeping between
two soldiers, bound with two chains,[u] and
sentries stood guard at the entrance. 7Sud-
denly an angel[v] of the Lord appeared and
a light shone in the cell. He struck Peter
on the side and woke him up. "Quick, get
up!" he said, and the chains fell off Peter's
wrists.[w]

8Then the angel said to him, "Put on
your clothes and sandals." And Peter did
so. "Wrap your cloak around you and follow me," the angel told him. 9Peter followed him out of the prison, but he had
no idea that what the angel was doing was
really happening; he thought he was seeing a vision.[x] 10They passed the first and
second guards and came to the iron gate
leading to the city. It opened for them by
itself,[y] and they went through it. When
they had walked the length of one street,
suddenly the angel left him.

11Then Peter came to himself[z] and
said, "Now I know without a doubt that
the Lord has sent his angel and rescued
me[a] from Herod's clutches and from everything the Jewish people were hoping
would happen."

12When this had dawned on him, he
went to the house of Mary the mother
of John, also called Mark,[b] where many
people had gathered and were praying.[c]
13Peter knocked at the outer entrance, and

11:29 [m] Ro 15:26; 2Co 9:2 [n] Ac 1:16
11:30 [o] Ac 14:23 [p] Ac 12:25
12:2 [q] Mt 4:21
12:3 [r] Ac 24:27 [s] Ex 12:15; 23:15
12:5 [t] Eph 6:18
12:6 [u] Ac 21:33
12:7 [v] Ac 5:19 [w] Ac 16:26
12:9 [x] Ac 9:10
12:10 [y] Ac 5:19; 16:26
12:11 [z] Lk 15:17 [a] Ps 34:7; Da 3:28; 6:22; 2Co 1:10; 2Pe 2:9
12:12 [b] ver 25; Ac 15:37, 39; Col 4:10; Phm 24; 1Pe 5:13 [c] ver 5

---

differences, in a world where such differences were often significant.

11:30 *elders.* Traditionally, elders were the leaders in Jewish communities. Historians often shifted their narration to a different location or series of events only to return to the original subject later (12:25).

12:1 *King Herod.* Herod Agrippa I, the popular grandson of Herod the Great (Mt 2:1) and his favorite wife, the Maccabean princess Mariamne. He was the full brother of Herodias (Mk 6:17), who had to lend him money when he spent his resources too lavishly. During his years in Rome he became close friends with Gaius Caligula, who became emperor; as a result of this connection, Agrippa became the first king of Judea (AD 41 – 44) since his grandfather. After Caligula's death, the new emperor Claudius sent Agrippa to Jerusalem, where he reigned until his death.

12:2 *with the sword.* Decapitation was considered one of the most merciful (because it was swifter) forms of execution. Although the Sanhedrin lacked the right to execute without Roman permission (Jn 18:31), Agrippa as a king approved by Rome could execute at will.

12:3 *met with approval among the Jews.* Agrippa's character here is in keeping with his portrait in Josephus. Agrippa sometimes clashed with the traditional elite in Jerusalem. Despite (or because of) his years living among the elite in Rome, however, he sought to prove his conservative Jewish identity to his people, and often acted to please them, including the Pharisees. This example began a nationalistic resurgence in Judea that continued until the first Judean revolt of AD 66. *during the Festival of Unleavened Bread.* Festival seasons drew large crowds, hence providing optimum warning value for executions (cf. Lk 22:7).

12:4 *four squads of four soldiers each.* The Roman military sometimes delegated special tasks to units of four soldiers. The different "squads" here probably work different shifts. *public trial after the Passover.* Agrippa is known to have sometimes executed condemned persons for public entertainment.

12:6 *between two soldiers, bound with two chains.* Each chain connected Peter to a soldier; this was one of the most secure forms of detention, making escape impossible without collusion.

12:8 *clothes and sandals … cloak.* Prisons did not provide clothes or sandals; these are Peter's own. He may have been using the outer garment as a blanket, as was common.

12:10 *opened … by itself.* In a popular Greek story, the deity Dionysus freed his followers from prison and could make a door open by itself; such features also appear in a traditional Jewish story about Moses. Peter probably did not expect to experience this in his own real life, however. *length of one street.* Possibly Agrippa had kept Peter in the Antonia Fortress on the temple mount; if this is correct (it is not certain), Peter could have followed a major street to Wilson's Arch and from there walked to the wealthy upper city (see vv. 12 – 13).

12:12 *the house of Mary the mother of John.* It is not surprising that in a section of Luke's work addressing first-century Judea (here) and Galilee, we find various women named Mary; Mary was the most common Judean and Galilean female name. In the first three centuries AD, churches met especially in homes, as did some other kinds of associations. This was economically feasible and under some circumstances also safer. A house large enough for many people to gather, with an outer entrance and a servant (v. 13), was wealthier than average and probably located in the upper city of Jerusalem.

12:13 *a servant named Rhoda came to answer the door.* The wealthiest homes had porters to watch the outer gate; in other moneyed homes servants might fill multiple roles. Rhoda was a common slave name. (Meaning "rosebush," "Rhoda" was roughly equivalent to the modern name "Rose.") In socioeconomic terms of education and even social mobility, household slaves often had better advantages than peasants (who comprised the majority of free persons in the empire). Male householders some-

a servant named Rhoda came to answer
the door.[d] 14When she recognized Peter's
voice, she was so overjoyed[e] she ran back
without opening it and exclaimed, "Peter
is at the door!"
15"You're out of your mind," they told
her. When she kept insisting that it was
so, they said, "It must be his angel."[f]
16But Peter kept on knocking, and when
they opened the door and saw him, they
were astonished. 17Peter motioned with
his hand[g] for them to be quiet and described how the Lord had brought him
out of prison. "Tell James[h] and the other
brothers and sisters[i] about this," he said,
and then he left for another place.
18In the morning, there was no small
commotion among the soldiers as to what
had become of Peter. 19After Herod had a
thorough search made for him and did not
find him, he cross-examined the guards
and ordered that they be executed.[j]

Herod's Death

Then Herod went from Judea to Caesarea[k] and stayed there. 20He had been quarreling with the people of Tyre and Sidon;[l]
they now joined together and sought an
audience with him. After securing the support of Blastus, a trusted personal servant
of the king, they asked for peace, because
they depended on the king's country for
their food supply.[m]
21On the appointed day Herod, wearing
his royal robes, sat on his throne and delivered a public address to the people. 22They
shouted, "This is the voice of a god, not
of a man." 23Immediately, because Herod
did not give praise to God, an angel of the
Lord struck him down,[n] and he was eaten
by worms and died.
24But the word of God continued to
spread and flourish.[o]

Barnabas and Saul Sent Off

25When Barnabas[p] and Saul had fin-
ished their mission,[q] they returned from[a]
Jerusalem, taking with them John, also
13 called Mark.[r] 1Now in the church at
Antioch[s] there were prophets[t] and
teachers: Barnabas,[u] Simeon called Niger,
Lucius of Cyrene, Manaen (who had been
brought up with Herod[v] the tetrarch) and
Saul. 2While they were worshiping the
Lord and fasting, the Holy Spirit said,[w]

12:13 [d] Jn 18:16,17 **12:14** [e] Lk 24:41 **12:15** [f] Mt 18:10 **12:17** [g] Ac 13:16; 19:33; 21:40 [h] Ac 15:13 [i] Ac 1:16 **12:19** [j] Ac 16:27 [k] Ac 8:40 **12:20** [l] Mt 11:21 [m] 1Ki 5:9,11; Eze 27:17 **12:23** [n] 1Sa 25:38; 2Sa 24:16,17 **12:24** [o] Ac 6:7; 19:20 **12:25** [p] Ac 4:36 [q] Ac 11:30 [r] ver 12 **13:1** [s] Ac 11:19 [t] Ac 11:27 [u] Ac 4:36; 11:22-26 [v] Mt 14:1 **13:2** [w] Ac 8:29

[a] 25 Some manuscripts *to*

times sexually abused slaves, but this would rarely if ever happen in households headed by women (cf. v. 12).
12:15 *You're out of your mind.* Foolish slave women often constituted the butt of Greek comedy, but here Luke instead makes fun of the foolish people who were praying for Peter (v. 5) yet refused to believe Rhoda (cf. Lk 24:11,37). *his angel.* Jewish sources sometimes compared the righteous deceased with angels.
12:17 *motioned with his hand.* Raising the right hand with the end finger stretched out was a conventional way of calling for silence. *James.* This James, Jesus' half-brother (15:13; 21:18; Gal 1:19), differs from the one executed in v. 2; the name (lit. "Jacob") was common in Judea and Galilee. Known for his conservative piety, this James would invite less hostile attention from the people Agrippa sought to please (v. 3). Indeed, when a high priest martyred him 15 to 20 years later, those most devout in the law, probably Pharisees, led the outcry against the high priest.
12:19 *ordered that they be executed.* Apart from a supernatural explanation, Agrippa could only expect the collusion of the guards on duty for the escape. Romans punished guards who let prisoners escape according to the penalty the prisoners would have received; Agrippa chooses to follow that practice here, executing the squad of four soldiers who had been on duty. *Caesarea.* Judea's capital, easily accessible by sea to representatives from Tyre and Sidon (v. 20).
12:20 *depended on the king's country for their food supply.* Tyre and Sidon were Hellenistic cities dependent on agricultural imports, including from lands under Agrippa's jurisdiction. Agrippa had cut off exports to them, and the limitation of resources (11:28) had made the situation critical.
12:21 *royal robes.* Josephus also comments on the splendor of Agrippa's robes on this occasion, noting that they were woven with silver. *delivered a public address.* He was addressing delegates of Tyre and Sidon in Caesarea's massive theater, where Agrippa often spoke.
12:22 *voice of a god.* Josephus agrees that Agrippa's flatterers called him a god. Although such adulation had a long history in Persia and the eastern Mediterranean world, even Caesar expected non-emperors to reject such honors.
12:23 *struck him down ... eaten by worms and died.* Josephus indicates that Agrippa collapsed and spent the next five days with terrible pain in his stomach before succumbing to death. A range of ancient sources depicts death from bowel troubles or worms as among the most horrible deaths, suitable especially for wicked tyrants.
12:25 *returned from Jerusalem.* Antioch was more than 300 miles (480 kilometers) north of Jerusalem. *taking with them John.* It was safer to travel in groups, and disciples or apprentices could travel with teachers.
13:1 The leadership team has geographic, cultural, and possibly some ethnic diversity. *Simeon.* A common Jewish name. *Niger.* A common Latin name, but here functions as a nickname, meaning "dark." He could be descended from African proselytes, although "dark" was used as a relative term. *Lucius.* A common name; he was from the prosperous North African city of Cyrene, which had a large Jewish population (11:20). *Manaen.* A Greek form of the Jewish name "Menahem." *brought up with Herod the tetrarch.* The Herod in view here is Herod Antipas (see notes on Mk 6:14,17). The designation "brought up with" could mean that Manaen was a slave who used the same wetnurse as Antipas but was later freed and given authority (as sometimes happened for rulers' slave playmates). Conversely, Manaen could have been one of the aristocratic children tutored by the same teacher as Antipas. In any case, he had come from a position of great authority and probably education; he could be in his 60s at this point.
13:2 *fasting.* A primarily Jewish custom, it was often used for mourning, occasionally used to seek revelations, but here, as often, probably linked with prayer.

"Set apart for me Barnabas and Saul for
the work[x] to which I have called them."[y]
3So after they had fasted and prayed, they
placed their hands on them[z] and sent
them off.[a]

On Cyprus

4The two of them, sent on their way by
the Holy Spirit,[b] went down to Seleucia and
sailed from there to Cyprus.[c] 5When they
arrived at Salamis, they proclaimed the
word of God in the Jewish synagogues.[d]
John[e] was with them as their helper.

6They traveled through the whole island until they came to Paphos. There they
met a Jewish sorcerer[f] and false prophet[g]
named Bar-Jesus, 7who was an attendant
of the proconsul,[h] Sergius Paulus. The
proconsul, an intelligent man, sent for
Barnabas and Saul because he wanted to
hear the word of God. 8But Elymas the sorcerer[i] (for that is what his name means)
opposed them and tried to turn the proconsul[j] from the faith.[k] 9Then Saul, who
was also called Paul, filled with the Holy
Spirit,[l] looked straight at Elymas and said,
10"You are a child of the devil[m] and an enemy of everything that is right! You are
full of all kinds of deceit and trickery. Will
you never stop perverting the right ways
of the Lord?[n] 11Now the hand of the Lord
is against you.[o] You are going to be blind
for a time, not even able to see the light
of the sun."

Immediately mist and darkness came
over him, and he groped about, seeking
someone to lead him by the hand. 12When
the proconsul[p] saw what had happened,
he believed, for he was amazed at the
teaching about the Lord.

13:2 [x] Ac 14:26 [y] Ac 22:21 **13:3** [z] Ac 6:6 [a] Ac 14:26 **13:4** [b] ver 2,3 [c] Ac 4:36 **13:5** [d] Ac 9:20 [e] Ac 12:12 **13:6** [f] Ac 8:9 [g] Mt 7:15 **13:7** [h] ver 8, 12; Ac 19:38 **13:8** [i] Ac 8:9 [j] ver 7 [k] Ac 6:7 **13:9** [l] Ac 4:8 **13:10** [m] Mt 13:38; Jn 8:44 [n] Hos 14:9 **13:11** [o] Ex 9:3; 1Sa 5:6,7; Ps 32:4 **13:12** [p] ver 7

13:3 *sent them off.* Probably includes their fare.
13:4 *Seleucia.* A port town on the coast, some 15 miles (24 kilometers) west of Antioch. It was a wealthy and well-fortified mercantile city. From here, Cyprus was just 60 miles (95 kilometers) by sea. *Cyprus.* The island is wealthy and important, and Barnabas already has contacts here (4:36; 11:19–20).
13:5 *Salamis.* The first port that a ship from Seleucia would reach, it was Cyprus's most prominent city and is estimated to have had more than 100,000 residents. A Jewish community is known there, although it was slaughtered during strife in the early second century AD.
13:6 *through the whole island.* The missionaries likelier traveled on the shorter and newer southern road rather than on the northern one; if so, cities where they ministered along the way could have included Citium, Amathus and Curium. *Paphos.* New Paphos on Cyprus's west was the governor's seat, and a fine palace uncovered by archaeologists there may have belonged to the governor. Paphos had a significant harbor and well-known temples, though the most famous shrine, a temple of Aphrodite, lay about seven miles (11 kilometers) to the southeast in old Paphos. *Jewish sorcerer.* Some of the most respected magicians in antiquity were Jewish, and Jewish elements often occurred in magical texts (often alongside pagan elements).
13:7 *attendant of the proconsul.* Rulers and governors sometimes included diviners among their advisors. Inscriptions show that the senatorial family of the Sergii Paulii were established in southern Asia Minor. Growing up in a Roman family in western Asia, Sergius Paulus probably had more eclectic religious tastes than traditional families in Rome. Given what we know of Sergius Paulus's senatorial career and other factors, he was presumably proconsul on Cyprus c. AD 45–46.
13:9 *Paul.* A Roman cognomen, normally only used by Roman citizens (see note on 16:37); Romans had three Roman names, but could go by their cognomen alone. In the eastern Mediterranean, people often had a local name in addition to a Roman name; sometimes, as here, the other name resembled the Roman name in sound (here, Saul) or meaning. (Saul, the name of Israel's only Benjamite ruler, may have been especially favored among Benjamites; cf. Ro 11:1; Php 3:5.)

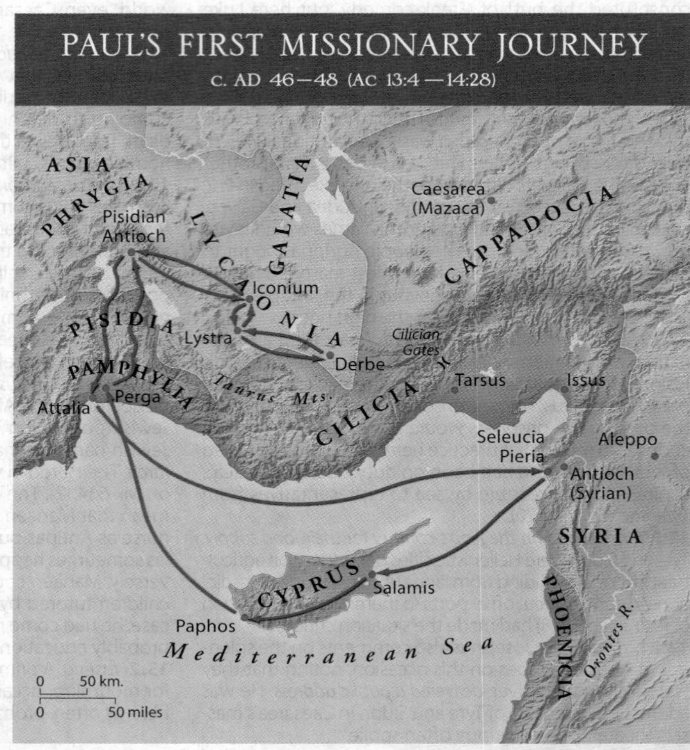

In Pisidian Antioch

13 From Paphos,[q] Paul and his companions sailed to Perga in Pamphylia, where
John[r] left them to return to Jerusalem.
14 From Perga they went on to Pisidian Antioch.[s] On the Sabbath[t] they entered the synagogue[u] and sat down. 15 After the reading
from the Law[v] and the Prophets, the leaders of the synagogue sent word to them,
saying, "Brothers, if you have a word of
exhortation for the people, please speak."
16 Standing up, Paul motioned with his
hand[w] and said: "Fellow Israelites and you
Gentiles who worship God, listen to me!
17 The God of the people of Israel chose
our ancestors; he made the people prosper during their stay in Egypt; with mighty
power he led them out of that country;[x]
18 for about forty years he endured their
conduct[a][y] in the wilderness;[z] 19 and he
overthrew seven nations in Canaan,[a] giving their land to his people[b] as their inheritance. 20 All this took about 450 years.
"After this, God gave them judges[c] until
the time of Samuel the prophet.[d] 21 Then
the people asked for a king,[e] and he gave
them Saul[f] son of Kish, of the tribe of Benjamin,[g] who ruled forty years. 22 After removing Saul,[h] he made David their king.[i]
God testified concerning him: 'I have
found David son of Jesse, a man after my
own heart;[j] he will do everything I want
him to do.'
23 "From this man's descendants[k] God
has brought to Israel the Savior[l] Jesus,[m]
as he promised.[n] 24 Before the coming of
Jesus, John preached repentance and baptism to all the people of Israel.[o] 25 As John
was completing his work,[p] he said: 'Who
do you suppose I am? I am not the one
you are looking for.[q] But there is one coming after me whose sandals I am not worthy to untie.'[r]
26 "Fellow children of Abraham and you
God-fearing Gentiles, it is to us that this
message of salvation[s] has been sent. 27 The
people of Jerusalem and their rulers did
not recognize Jesus,[t] yet in condemning
him they fulfilled the words of the prophets[u] that are read every Sabbath. 28 Though
they found no proper ground for a death
sentence, they asked Pilate to have him
executed.[v] 29 When they had carried out

[a] 18 Some manuscripts *he cared for them*

13:13 [q] ver 6 [r] Ac 12:12
13:14 [s] Ac 14:19, 21 [t] Ac 16:13 [u] Ac 9:20
13:15 [v] Ac 15:21
13:16 [w] Ac 12:17
13:17 [x] Ex 6:6, 7; Dt 7:6-8
13:18 [y] Dt 1:31 [z] Ac 7:36
13:19 [a] Dt 7:1 [b] Jos 19:51
13:20 [c] Jdg 2:16 [d] 1Sa 3:19, 20
13:21 [e] 1Sa 8:5, 19 [f] 1Sa 10:1 [g] 1Sa 9:1, 2
13:22 [h] 1Sa 15:23, 26 [i] 1Sa 16:13; Ps 89:20 [j] 1Sa 13:14
13:23 [k] Mt 1:1 [l] Lk 2:11 [m] Mt 1:21 [n] ver 32
13:24 [o] Mk 1:4
13:25 [p] Ac 20:24 [q] Jn 1:20 [r] Mt 3:11; Jn 1:27
13:26 [s] Ac 4:12
13:27 [t] Ac 3:17 [u] Lk 24:27
13:28 [v] Mt 27:20-25; Ac 3:14

13:13 *Perga in Pamphylia.* On the southern coast of Asia Minor (modern Turkey), Pamphylia was north of Paphos; ships landed especially at Attalia on the coast. A paved road from Attalia led about ten miles (16 kilometers) inland to Perga, one of Pamphylia's two chief cities; some estimate that Perga held over 100,000 residents.

13:14 *went on to Pisidian Antioch.* Three routes northward were possible, but the likeliest is the Via Sebaste (Augustus Highway), which passed through Comama en route to Antioch (and beyond it to Iconium; v. 51). The road from Perga to Antioch was more than 100 miles (160 kilometers) uphill, probably at least a week's journey. Unlike many other cities mentioned in Acts, Pisidian Antioch was not important in the larger scheme of the empire's affairs; it was, however, very important in the interior of Asia Minor. A prosperous Roman colony, it had about 5,000 colonists (a minority of its total population), and had 115 acres (46.5 hectares) inside its walls (plus vast holdings in its larger territory). Technically this Antioch (a common name for cities) lay in Phrygia, but because another Phrygian city also bore the name Antioch, this one was commonly identified by its proximity to Pisidia. Although worshiping many gods, this region was famous especially for its local god called Mên; Antioch's most conspicuous temple, however, honored the emperor. Although this Antioch was strategic as far as the interior of Anatolia went, it could not compete in importance with the coastal megacities. Why did Paul and Barnabas go there? One likely motivation is the connection with Sergius Paulus (vv. 7,12), whose family controlled vast estates in this region. A letter of recommendation from him could be expected to open many doors — at least until local interests shut them (v. 50). *the Sabbath.* When the Jewish community as a whole gathered.

13:15 *reading from the Law and the Prophets.* Scripture was read in synagogues in this period, though probably not yet with specified (lectionary) readings. *leaders of the synagogue.* In many locations an honorary title, but normally belonged to respected people of status who exercised influence on how the synagogue meetings occurred. *if you have a word of exhortation.* Perhaps anyone educated could give public explanations of the readings, especially in the Diaspora.

13:16 *Standing up.* In the Diaspora, a speaker would stand. To secure attention, he might follow the conventional gesture of stretching out his hand with the thumb pointed up. *listen to me!* Speeches normally began by specifying the addressees and often opened with invitations like this one.

13:17 Paul's speech displays thorough knowledge of the OT; on this and the following verses, see the NIV text notes.

13:20 *450 years.* May be a round number blending some 400 years in Egypt (7:6; Ge 15:13) plus 40 years in the wilderness (7:36; Ex 16:35; Dt 2:7); a specific estimate for the former period was 430 years (Ex 12:40 – 41; Gal 3:17).

13:21 *Saul … ruled forty years.* The length of Saul's reign cited here by Paul fits one line of Jewish tradition, though opinions varied.

13:22 See 1Sa 13:14.

13:23 *Savior.* See Savior.

13:25 *sandals I am not worthy to untie.* Carrying or tying another's sandals was the sort of menial work a slave would do; although the prophets were "servants of the LORD" (e.g., 2Ki 9:7; 17:13; Jer 7:25), John counted himself unworthy to be the coming one's servant — even in the most lowly sense of the word.

13:27 *fulfilled the words of the prophets.* In Isa 53:1 – 4, Israel despised their righteous deliverer, fitting a pattern found also in other texts (see note on 7:35 – 38).

13:28 *asked Pilate to have him executed.* The Sanhedrin could not execute anyone without the governor's permission (see note on Jn 18:31). *Pilate.* Pontius Pilate was governor of Judea from AD 26 to 36; he may have remained in

all that was written about him,[w] they took
him down from the cross[x] and laid him in
a tomb.[y] 30But God raised him from the
dead,[z] 31and for many days he was seen
by those who had traveled with him from
Galilee to Jerusalem.[a] They are now his
witnesses[b] to our people.
32"We tell you the good news:[c] What
God promised our ancestors[d] 33he has fulfilled for us, their children, by raising up
Jesus. As it is written in the second Psalm:

" 'You are my son;
today I have become your father.'[ae]

34God raised him from the dead so that
he will never be subject to decay. As God
has said,

" 'I will give you the holy and sure
blessings promised to David.'[bf]

35So it is also stated elsewhere:

" 'You will not let your holy one see
decay.'[cg]

36"Now when David had served God's
purpose in his own generation, he fell
asleep; he was buried with his ancestors[h] and his body decayed. 37But the one
whom God raised from the dead did not
see decay.
38"Therefore, my friends, I want you to
know that through Jesus the forgiveness
of sins is proclaimed to you.[i] 39Through
him everyone who believes is set free from
every sin, a justification you were not able
to obtain under the law of Moses.[j] 40Take
care that what the prophets have said does
not happen to you:

41" 'Look, you scoffers,
wonder and perish,
for I am going to do something in your
days
that you would never believe,
even if someone told you.'[d]"[k]

42As Paul and Barnabas were leaving
the synagogue,[l] the people invited them
to speak further about these things on
the next Sabbath. 43When the congregation was dismissed, many of the Jews and
devout converts to Judaism followed Paul
and Barnabas, who talked with them and
urged them to continue in the grace of
God.[m]
44On the next Sabbath almost the whole
city gathered to hear the word of the Lord.
45When the Jews saw the crowds, they
were filled with jealousy. They began to
contradict what Paul was saying[n] and
heaped abuse[o] on him.
46Then Paul and Barnabas answered
them boldly: "We had to speak the word
of God to you first.[p] Since you reject it and
do not consider yourselves worthy of eternal life, we now turn to the Gentiles.[q] 47For
this is what the Lord has commanded us:

" 'I have made you[e] a light for the
Gentiles,[r]
that you[e] may bring salvation to the
ends of the earth.'[f]"[s]

48When the Gentiles heard this, they
were glad and honored the word of the

13:29 [w] Lk 18:31 [x] Ac 5:30 [y] Lk 23:53 **13:30** [z] Mt 28:6; Ac 2:24 **13:31** [a] Mt 28:16 [b] Lk 24:48 **13:32** [c] Ac 5:42 [d] Ac 26:6; Ro 4:13 **13:33** [e] Ps 2:7 **13:34** [f] Isa 55:3 **13:35** [g] Ps 16:10; Ac 2:27 **13:36** [h] 1Ki 2:10; Ac 2:29 **13:38** [i] Lk 24:47; Ac 2:38 **13:39** [j] Ro 3:28 **13:41** [k] Hab 1:5 **13:42** [l] ver 14 **13:43** [m] Ac 11:23; 14:22 **13:45** [n] 1Th 2:16 [o] Ac 18:6; 1Pe 4:4; Jude 10 **13:46** [p] ver 26; Ac 3:26 [q] Ac 18:6; 22:21; 28:28 **13:47** [r] Lk 2:32 [s] Isa 49:6

[a] *33* Psalm 2:7 [b] *34* Isaiah 55:3 [c] *35* Psalm 16:10 (see Septuagint) [d] *41* Hab. 1:5 [e] *47* The Greek is singular. [f] *47* Isaiah 49:6

power during Jesus' ministry partly because the praetorian prefect Sejanus, who was close to the emperor, may have been his patron. If this was the case, Pilate's position would have become more tenuous, inviting more caution, after Sejanus was executed in AD 31.

13:33 *my son.* Ancient Middle Eastern peoples often cited prophecies confirming that their kings were sons of deities, hence fit to rule. Ps 2 affirms the adoption of David's line. It may look to the ultimate Davidic ruler *par excellence*, and was so applied in early Judaism, after Davidic rule had been cut off. The ruler publicly received the title at his coronation; Jesus' exaltation here is his enthronement.

13:34 *David.* The assumed author of Ps 2 (cited in v. 33), so relevance to the Davidic promise provides a natural connection to the present citation of Isa 55:3 (which goes on to speak also of witness to and ruling other peoples in 55:4).

13:35 Jewish interpreters often connected texts that used the same key word or concept; "holy" appears in Isa 55:3 cited in v. 34 and also in Ps 16:10 cited here. Ancient interpreters assumed that Ps 16 was Davidic, so the theme of the Davidic promise continues in both verses.

13:36 *his body decayed.* Thus the Davidic promise cannot refer to David himself (texts such as Jer 30:9; Eze 34:23–24; 37:24–25 refer not to David literally but to his household; cf. Jer 33:17,21).

13:40–41 Paul cites Hab 1:5 (a text also used in the Dead Sea Scrolls to underline Israel's rejection of God's messengers). Possibly in the original sermon, here condensed, Paul had already explored this context, citing Hab 2:4, in his discussion of justification by faith (summarized in vv. 38–39).

13:44 *almost the whole city.* When a well-known speaker came to town large crowds would gather. Many Gentiles were interested in the Jewish faith but did not wish to be circumcised or become Jewish (which in first-century thought entailed abandoning one's ethnicity to embrace a foreign people as one's own). Most of these Gentiles had also been participating in the local imperial cult and had been worshiping the local god Mên as well as other deities.

13:47 Paul cites Isa 49:6 to support the Gentile mission. Elsewhere in this section of Isaiah (Isa 41:8–9; 44:1–2,21; 45:4; 49:3), the servant who is to carry out God's mission is Israel as a whole; but because the servant fails in his mission (Isa 42:18–19), God raises up one within Israel to fulfill the mission and suffer on behalf of Israel (Isa 49:5–7; 52:13—53:12, especially 53:4–6,9). Jesus fulfills that mission (Ac 8:32–33), and this verse ("commanded us," Ac 13:47) suggests that his agents should follow him in continuing that mission.

13:48 *appointed for eternal life.* Most Jewish people believed that they themselves were the ones appointed to eternal life, but Luke includes here believing Gentiles.

Lord; and all who were appointed for eternal life believed.
49The word of the Lord spread through
the whole region. 50But the Jewish leaders incited the God-fearing women of high
standing and the leading men of the city.
They stirred up persecution against Paul
and Barnabas, and expelled them from
their region.[t] 51So they shook the dust off
their feet[u] as a warning to them and went
to Iconium.[v] 52And the disciples were
filled with joy and with the Holy Spirit.

In Iconium

14 At Iconium[w] Paul and Barnabas
went as usual into the Jewish synagogue. There they spoke so effectively
that a great number of Jews and Greeks
believed. 2But the Jews who refused to
believe stirred up the other Gentiles and
poisoned their minds against the brothers.
3So Paul and Barnabas spent considerable
time there, speaking boldly[x] for the Lord,
who confirmed the message of his grace by
enabling them to perform signs and wonders.[y] 4The people of the city were divided;
some sided with the Jews, others with the
apostles.[z] 5There was a plot afoot among
both Gentiles and Jews, together with their
leaders, to mistreat them and stone them.[a]
6But they found out about it and fled[b] to
the Lycaonian cities of Lystra and Derbe
and to the surrounding country, 7where
they continued to preach[c] the gospel.[d]

In Lystra and Derbe

8In Lystra there sat a man who was
lame. He had been that way from birth[e]
and had never walked. 9He listened to Paul
as he was speaking. Paul looked directly at
him, saw that he had faith to be healed[f]
10and called out, "Stand up on your feet!"
At that, the man jumped up and began to
walk.[g]
11When the crowd saw what Paul had
done, they shouted in the Lycaonian language, "The gods have come down to us
in human form!"[h] 12Barnabas they called
Zeus, and Paul they called Hermes because he was the chief speaker. 13The
priest of Zeus, whose temple was just outside the city, brought bulls and wreaths to
the city gates because he and the crowd
wanted to offer sacrifices to them.

13:50 [t] 1Th 2:16 **13:51** [u] Mt 10:14; Ac 18:6 [v] Ac 14:1, 19, 21; 2Ti 3:11 **14:1** [w] Ac 13:51 **14:3** [x] Ac 4:29 [y] Jn 4:48; Heb 2:4

14:4 [z] Ac 17:4, 5 **14:5** [a] ver 19 **14:6** [b] Mt 10:23 **14:7** [c] Ac 16:10 [d] ver 15, 21 **14:8** [e] Ac 3:2 **14:9** [f] Mt 9:28, 29 **14:10** [g] Ac 3:8 **14:11** [h] Ac 8:10; 28:6

13:50 *God-fearing women.* Many Gentile women, including aristocratic women, were interested in Judaism; inscriptions show that they far outnumbered Gentile men as worshipers of Israel's God. (In addition to considering the pain of circumcision, men would lose considerable social status by following Jewish practices.) The small local elite held much power in a city; in Antioch, the elite were Roman citizens, and the most prominent families were the Caristanii and the relatives of Sergius Paulus.

13:51 *shook the dust off their feet.* Shaking dust from one's feet or even showing one's heel was a sign of repudiation. Because some Jewish people also removed dust of profane, pagan territory when entering the Holy Land, the action may also depict the Jewish opposition as equivalent to pagan behavior (cf. Lk 10:11–12). *Iconium.* A prosperous city, though not comparable to the major coastal cities, it lay over 85 miles (135 kilometers), or over four days' walk, farther east along the Via Sebaste (Augustus Highway) than Pisidian Antioch. Because of the rugged terrain, the Via Sebaste was the only practical route Paul and Barnabas could have taken either to the east or to the west.

14:1 *Iconium.* See note on 13:51. Many people in Iconium spoke a Phrygian dialect but also Greek, and Greek would be the language of the synagogue. Gentiles there worshiped the traditionally Phrygian mother goddess Cybele and the Roman emperor as well as an array of traditional Greek deities.

14:5 *a plot afoot ... to mistreat them and stone them.* Civic leaders could have officially expelled Paul and Barnabas from the city. Stoning exceeded their legal authority, and would constitute a mob action (perhaps designed by some of the Jewish critics because it was the designated penalty for blasphemy).

14:6 *Lycaonian cities.* Ancient writers often included Iconium itself in Lycaonia, but it was culturally Phrygian. The Sergii Paulii owned estates a few days' walk to the north of Iconium, but that area was not well populated, and events in Antioch may have weakened the apostles' assurance of a hospitable reception with more of this family in any case (cf. note on 13:50). They therefore continue south 20–25 miles (32–40 kilometers) on the Via Sebaste to Lystra (see note on v. 8) on the colder Lycaonian Plateau. Derbe lay 60 miles (95 kilometers) farther southeast on another road.

14:8 *Lystra.* A Roman colony that often emphasized its Roman character in ways that connected it more to the more distant Pisidian Antioch (cf. v. 19) than to the Hellenistic towns in its own vicinity. One-third of its inscriptions are in Latin, though the countryside spoke Greek and Lystra was less Romanized than Antioch (see note on v. 11).

14:9 *listened to Paul as he was speaking.* Sages and orators who lacked schools often spoke in markets or other public places to whoever would gather to listen.

14:11 *Lycaonian language.* Most of Lystra's landowners, as Roman colonists, spoke Latin. Lystra, however, also served as a market town for its region, and the other people spoke Greek and the local Lycaonian dialect; local languages persisted in rural Asia Minor long after Greek became the trade language. They would understand Greek even if they spoke with one another in Lycaonian.

14:12 *Zeus ... Hermes.* Zeus was considered king of the gods, and Hermes the messenger of the gods. Although rejecting disguised gods or angels was always deemed dangerous, one regional story in particular may have been most influential on the hearers' behavior here. In this tale, Zeus and Hermes had visited Phrygia but found hospitality with only one couple; the deities had therefore destroyed the rest of the land with a flood. The apostles' hearers determine not to risk the same mistake.

14:13 *temple was just outside the city.* Many temples in Asia Minor were outside their cities. Although only one priest is leading here, Lystra's temple of Zeus may have had multiple priests. *bulls.* Bulls were some of the most expensive sacrifices; possibly these were donated by the priest (in Asia Minor, wealthy benefactors often were rewarded with annual priestly offices). *wreaths.* People

14 But when the apostles Barnabas and
Paul heard of this, they tore their clothes[i]
and rushed out into the crowd, shouting: 15 "Friends, why are you doing this?
We too are only human,[j] like you. We are
bringing you good news,[k] telling you to
turn from these worthless things[l] to the
living God,[m] who made the heavens and
the earth[n] and the sea and everything in
them.[o] 16 In the past, he let[p] all nations
go their own way.[q] 17 Yet he has not left
himself without testimony:[r] He has shown
kindness by giving you rain from heaven
and crops in their seasons;[s] he provides
you with plenty of food and fills your
hearts with joy." 18 Even with these words,
they had difficulty keeping the crowd from
sacrificing to them.

19 Then some Jews[t] came from Antioch
and Iconium[u] and won the crowd over.
They stoned Paul[v] and dragged him outside the city, thinking he was dead. 20 But
after the disciples[w] had gathered around
him, he got up and went back into the
city. The next day he and Barnabas left
for Derbe.

14:14 [i] Mk 14:63 **14:15** [j] Ac 10:26; Jas 5:17 [k] ver 7, 21; Ac 13:32 [l] 1Sa 12:21; 1Co 8:4; 1Th 1:9 [m] Mt 16:16 [n] Ge 1:1; Jer 14:22 [o] Ps 146:6; Rev 14:7 **14:16** [p] Ac 17:30 [q] Ps 81:12; Mic 4:5 **14:17** [r] Ac 17:27; Ro 1:20 [s] Dt 11:14; Job 5:10; Ps 65:10 **14:19** [t] Ac 13:45 [u] Ac 13:51 [v] 2Co 11:25; 2Ti 3:11 **14:20** [w] ver 22, 28; Ac 11:26 **14:21** [x] Ac 13:51 **14:22** [y] Ac 11:23; 13:43 [z] Jn 16:33; 1Th 3:3; 2Ti 3:12 **14:23** [a] Ac 11:30; Titus 1:5 [b] Ac 13:3 [c] Ac 20:32

The Return to Antioch in Syria

21 They preached the gospel in that city
and won a large number of disciples. Then
they returned to Lystra, Iconium[x] and Antioch, 22 strengthening the disciples and encouraging them to remain true to the faith.[y]
"We must go through many hardships[z]
to enter the kingdom of God," they said.
23 Paul and Barnabas appointed elders[a][a] for
them in each church and, with prayer and
fasting,[b] committed them to the Lord,[c] in
whom they had put their trust. 24 After going through Pisidia, they came into Pamphylia, 25 and when they had preached the
word in Perga, they went down to Attalia.

26 From Attalia they sailed back to Antioch,[d] where they had been committed to
the grace of God[e] for the work they had
now completed.[f] 27 On arriving there, they
gathered the church together and reported
all that God had done through them[g] and

[a] *23* Or *Barnabas ordained elders*; or *Barnabas had elders elected*

14:26 [d] Ac 11:19 [e] Ac 15:40 [f] Ac 13:1,3 **14:27** [g] Ac 15:4, 12; 21:19

could wear garlands at festivals; perhaps more relevant, garlands were frequently placed on animals before the animals were sacrificed. *gates.* Could refer to city gates (as the NIV) or to temple gates (since Lystra may have been unwalled).

14:14 *heard of this.* Someone explained to the apostles in Greek what was being said in Lycaonian (see note on v. 11). *tore their clothes.* Jewish tradition mandated tearing one's robes in mourning if one heard blasphemy.

14:15 Although contextualizing the message for their audience (see note on v. 17), the apostles draw on Biblical concepts, such as "worthless things" as a title for idols and "living God" for the true God. The description of the Creator evokes Ps 146:6 and possibly similar texts.

14:17 *rain … crops.* Most of the audience consisted of farmers, and the speech fits their setting; rhetoric emphasized keeping one's speech relevant to one's audience (cf. the very different speeches to different audiences in 13:16–47 and 17:22–31).

14:19 *Jews came from Antioch and Iconium.* Antioch was close to 100 miles (160 kilometers) away and Iconium only 20 miles (32 kilometers), but Antioch would have been influential. As significant colonies in the region, Antioch and Lystra were considered sister cities despite their distance. *won the crowd over.* Mobs were considered extremely fickle, and another explanation is also relevant for why the crowds shift loyalties so quickly: once Paul and Barnabas preach against the people's gods (vv. 15–17), they appear impious rather than divine. Their enemies could thus explain the apostles' superhuman powers as works of magic instead of miracles. *stoned Paul.* Stoning was the conventional punishment for blasphemy (see note on 7:58) but also a frequent action of urban mobs, who sometimes employed tiles and other available objects as well as stones. *dragged him outside the city.* Executions and burials were typically outside cities; even if mob violence killed someone within a city, residents would not want a dead body to remain within the city walls.

14:20 *he and Barnabas left for Derbe.* Decrees from one community (if any decrees in addition to mob actions had occurred) were not binding in another community. That the apostles travel to Derbe—60 miles (95 kilometers), some three days' journey farther southeast on another road, possibly not even paved—shows their eagerness to evade further interference from their opponents. Derbe achieved the status of a Greek city probably in the following decade, but did not yet have even this status.

14:21 *returned to Lystra, Iconium and Antioch.* Returning to the towns where they had preached, instead of crossing the Taurus Mountains south to Paul's familiar land of Cilicia, offers an example of courage for the disciples.

14:22 *go through many hardships.* Most Jewish people expected a time of tribulation that preceded the kingdom, what some later teachers called the "birth pangs of the Messiah" (cf. Mk 13:5–26). The believers must be prepared to suffer.

14:23 *appointed elders.* Because some older men came to be known for wisdom and maturity, select elders ruled OT villages and continued to fill a respected leadership role in this period. Usually they functioned as a group. *fasting.* See note on 13:2.

14:24 *Pisidia … Pamphylia.* These cities were so close geographically that writers sometimes linked them.

14:25 *Perga.* Largely Gentile, and perhaps the missionaries feel more prepared to preach in such a location than they did in 13:13–14. *went down to Attalia.* The paved Via Sebaste did not go beyond Perga, so they took an inferior road to Attalia. Attalia was Pamphylia's main port, and it lay on the mouth of the Catarractes. Most of Attalia lay on a steep elevation just above the sea. That port town included some high-status Roman settlers (notably the Calpurnii). It also had many ships sailing to Syria, being a major port for trade with that region.

14:27 *gathered the church together.* Although most groups in the Mediterranean were informally networked through travelers bringing news, this community has special interest. Its concerted commitment to missions was more formal than comparable expectations in contemporary Judaism.

how he had opened a door[h] of faith to the
Gentiles. 28And they stayed there a long
time with the disciples.

The Council at Jerusalem

15 Certain people[i] came down from
Judea to Antioch and were teaching the believers: "Unless you are circumcised,[j] according to the custom taught
by Moses,[k] you cannot be saved." 2This
brought Paul and Barnabas into sharp dispute and debate with them. So Paul and
Barnabas were appointed, along with
some other believers, to go up to Jerusalem[l] to see the apostles and elders[m] about
this question. 3The church sent them on
their way, and as they traveled through
Phoenicia and Samaria, they told how the
Gentiles had been converted.[n] This news
made all the believers very glad. 4When
they came to Jerusalem, they were welcomed by the church and the apostles and
elders, to whom they reported everything
God had done through them.[o]

5Then some of the believers who belonged to the party of the Pharisees stood
up and said, "The Gentiles must be circumcised and required to keep the law of
Moses."

6The apostles and elders met to consider this question. 7After much discussion, Peter got up and addressed them:
"Brothers, you know that some time ago
God made a choice among you that the
Gentiles might hear from my lips the
message of the gospel and believe. 8God,
who knows the heart,[p] showed that he accepted them by giving the Holy Spirit to
them,[q] just as he did to us. 9He did not
discriminate between us and them,[r] for he
purified their hearts by faith.[s] 10Now then,
why do you try to test God by putting on
the necks of Gentiles a yoke[t] that neither
we nor our ancestors have been able to
bear? 11No! We believe it is through the
grace[u] of our Lord Jesus that we are
saved, just as they are."

12The whole assembly became silent as
they listened to Barnabas and Paul telling
about the signs and wonders[v] God had
done among the Gentiles through them.[w]
13When they finished, James[x] spoke up.
"Brothers," he said, "listen to me. 14Si-
mon[a] has described to us how God first
intervened to choose a people for his
name from the Gentiles. 15The words of
the prophets are in agreement with this,
as it is written:

16" 'After this I will return
and rebuild David's fallen tent.
Its ruins I will rebuild,
and I will restore it,
17that the rest of mankind may seek the
Lord,
even all the Gentiles who bear my
name,

14:27 [h] 1Co 16:9; 2Co 2:12; Col 4:3; Rev 3:8 **15:1** [i] ver 24; Gal 2:12 [j] ver 5; Gal 5:2,3 [k] Ac 6:14 **15:2** [l] Gal 2:2 [m] Ac 11:30 **15:3** [n] Ac 14:27 **15:4** [o] ver 12; Ac 14:27 **15:8** [p] Ac 1:24 [q] Ac 10:44,47 **15:9** [r] Ac 10:28, 34; 11:12 [s] Ac 10:43 **15:10** [t] Mt 23:4; Gal 5:1 **15:11** [u] Ro 3:24; Eph 2:5-8 **15:12** [v] Jn 4:48 [w] Ac 14:27 **15:13** [x] Ac 12:17

[a] 14 Greek *Simeon,* a variant of *Simon;* that is, Peter

15:1 *Unless you are circumcised ... you cannot be saved.* Only the strictest minority of Jews limited salvation to full converts. Most Jewish people believed that righteous Gentiles would be saved (these were Gentiles who were sexually pure and did not worship idols—admittedly a very small proportion of Gentiles). Jewish people did not, however, believe that Gentiles could become members of God's people without conversion (possibly the issue in Paul's letter to the Galatians). From the reign of Agrippa I (AD 41–44) until Jerusalem's fall nationalist attitudes had been growing.

15:2 *go up to Jerusalem to see the apostles and elders.* Local elders led Diaspora synagogues, but until AD 70 Jewish people in the Diaspora nevertheless respected the preeminence of the leaders in Jerusalem; the same principle was likely retained for Jerusalem's role in the early Christian movement.

15:3 *Phoenicia.* Tyre and Sidon (12:19) were among the major cities of Phoenicia.

15:5 *party of the Pharisees.* Josephus similarly applied the term translated here "party" to Pharisees and other groups. After AD 70, the more liberal Hillelite faction prevailed among Pharisees, but the more conservative Shammaites dominated before 70. Hillel reportedly welcomed proselytes diplomatically, but Shammai reportedly insisted on them keeping the entire law from the moment of conversion.

15:6 *met to consider.* Some ideal groups, such as the Essenes, tried to achieve consensus. Jewish sages debated and would settle on a clear majority opinion; consensus was ideal, though on controversial issues rarely achieved. In general, ancient society was heavily divided through political alliances and civic rivalries.

15:7 *Peter ... addressed them.* Speakers often appealed to sources respected by those they needed to persuade; thus, e.g., a more conservative voice carried weight in support of a less conservative opinion, and so forth. The support of Peter and especially James (v. 13) thus carry much weight in the conservative Jerusalem church.

15:8 *giving the Holy Spirit.* The Holy Spirit was an end-time gift for God's people (Isa 44:3; Eze 36:27).

15:10 *a yoke that neither we nor our ancestors have been able to bear.* Jewish teachers spoke favorably of the yoke of God's kingdom and the yoke of his law. They believed that the law's duties freed them from heavier burdens. Jeremiah, however, warned that Israel had failed to keep the law, a situation to be remedied by the new covenant (Jer 31:32–33).

15:13 See note on v. 7.

15:14 *a people for his name from the Gentiles.* Given the wording, James probably already has in mind the Amos quotation that he will offer in v. 17.

15:16 *fallen tent.* In Am 9:11, quoted here, David's house has become a "fallen tent," ("shelter" in Amos) probably like the cut-off stump in Isa 11:1; but God would restore his people and the rule of a Davidic descendant over them. The Qumran scrolls also apply this passage to the promised Davidic king.

15:17 *rest of mankind.* In Am 9:12, quoted here, God's people would "possess the remnant of Edom"; but Jewish teachers often made slight changes in the way they read the Hebrew text to get fuller meaning. The Septuagint,

says the Lord, who does these
things’[a][y]—
18 things known from long ago.[b]

19 “It is my judgment, therefore, that we
should not make it difficult for the Gentiles who are turning to God. 20 Instead we
should write to them, telling them to abstain from food polluted by idols,[z] from
sexual immorality,[a] from the meat of
strangled animals and from blood.[b] 21 For
the law of Moses has been preached in every city from the earliest times and is read
in the synagogues on every Sabbath.”[c]

The Council’s Letter to Gentile Believers

22 Then the apostles and elders, with the
whole church, decided to choose some of
their own men and send them to Antioch
with Paul and Barnabas. They chose Judas
(called Barsabbas) and Silas,[d] men who
were leaders among the believers. 23 With
them they sent the following letter:

The apostles and elders, your brothers,

To the Gentile believers in Antioch,[e]
Syria and Cilicia:[f]

Greetings.[g]

24 We have heard that some went
out from us without our authorization
and disturbed you, troubling your
minds by what they said.[h] 25 So we all
agreed to choose some men and send
them to you with our dear friends
Barnabas and Paul— 26 men who
have risked their lives[i] for the name
of our Lord Jesus Christ. 27 Therefore
we are sending Judas and Silas to
confirm by word of mouth what we
are writing. 28 It seemed good to the
Holy Spirit[j] and to us not to burden
you with anything beyond the following requirements: 29 You are to abstain
from food sacrificed to idols, from
blood, from the meat of strangled animals and from sexual immorality.[k]
You will do well to avoid these things.

Farewell.

30 So the men were sent off and went
down to Antioch, where they gathered the
church together and delivered the letter.
31 The people read it and were glad for its
encouraging message. 32 Judas and Silas,
who themselves were prophets, said much
to encourage and strengthen the believers.
33 After spending some time there, they
were sent off by the believers with the
blessing of peace[l] to return to those who
had sent them. [34][c] 35 But Paul and Barnabas remained in Antioch, where they and
many others taught and preached[m] the
word of the Lord.

15:17 [y] Am 9:11,12 **15:20** [z] 1Co 8:7-13; 10:14-28; Rev 2:14,20 [a] 1Co 10:7,8 [b] ver 29; Ge 9:4; Lev 3:17; Dt 12:16,23 **15:21** [c] Ac 13:15; 2Co 3:14,15 **15:22** [d] ver 27, 32,40 **15:23** [e] ver 1 [f] ver 41 [g] Ac 23:25,26; Jas 1:1 **15:24** [h] ver 1; Gal 1:7; 5:10 **15:26** [i] Ac 9:23-25; 14:19 **15:28** [j] Ac 5:32 **15:29** [k] ver 20; Ac 21:25 **15:33** [l] Mk 5:34; Ac 16:36; 1Co 16:11 **15:35** [m] Ac 8:4

[a] *17* Amos 9:11,12 (see Septuagint) [b] *17,18* Some manuscripts *things’— / [18] the Lord’s work is known to him from long ago* [c] *34* Some manuscripts include here *But Silas decided to remain there.*

---

the pre-Christian Greek translation of the OT, read “Edom” as if it were “Adam,” i.e. “humanity,” and thus translated as “mankind,” as here. (Since his argument will be used by Diaspora Christians, it made sense for James to use the Septuagint, although Luke would have quoted the text in Greek in any case.) Since Edom was simply one example of the nations, the new wording captures the idea; the parallel line already spoke of “all the nations.” *bear my name.* Although having God’s name over them could mean conquest, the phrase also applies to God’s people (Dt 28:10; Isa 63:19; Jer 14:9; Da 9:19). The promised Davidic king would rule the nations (e.g., Isaiah 11:10; 19:25; 56:6).

15:18 *known from long ago.* Might echo Isa 45:21.

15:20 *abstain from … strangled animals and from blood.* Animals that were strangled still had blood in them—and one law given to Noah was the prohibition of eating meat with blood in it (Ge 9:4). These rules applied to foreigners living in Israel in Lev 17—18:16; widespread Jewish tradition applied them to righteous Gentiles who would be saved (what in later rabbinic tradition became known as the Noahide laws, the rules given to all of Noah’s descendants). The list given here maintains a compromise position: Gentile Christians would be treated as righteous Gentiles if they kept these few rules (some of which Biblical morals would demand anyway). The compromise does not address the theological issue on which Paul and many Jerusalem believers would not agree—whether Gentile Christians could be treated as part of God’s people without physical circumcision.

15:21 *preached in every city.* The Jewish Diaspora meant that there were synagogues in most important cities, which could be hyperbolically described as “all.” Gentiles could learn about the law in the synagogues if they wished.

15:23–29 Ancient historians often included letters and decrees in their histories; this letter is of average length. This letter, delivered to many churches, would be well known in the early church.

15:23 *Antioch, Syria and Cilicia.* Antioch was the largest city in the massive Roman province of Syria; in this period Syria’s governor also governed Cilicia (whose chief city was Tarsus). *Greetings.* The standard opening in many ancient letters.

15:24 The Jerusalem leaders honor their Diaspora audience by composing sophisticated Greek (the opening Greek sentence in vv. 24–26 is a Greek “period,” a particularly eloquent Greek literary structure). Ancient writers often denounced those who sowed division.

15:25 *choose some men and send them.* Officials or councils sometimes sent important representatives to bear decrees and/or circular letters to regions.

15:28 *It seemed good.* Often appears in resolutions from councils or senates and in decrees from emperors.

15:29 On these prohibitions, see note on v. 20. *Farewell.* The standard close of letters.

15:30 *delivered the letter.* Would include a public reading of the letter; even in urban areas, most people could not read very well.

15:33 *with the blessing of peace.* Lit., simply “with peace”; to send someone away in peace meant that one had shown them proper hospitality, not doing wrong to them.

Disagreement Between Paul and Barnabas

36 Some time later Paul said to Barnabas, "Let us go back and visit the believers in all the towns[n] where we preached
the word of the Lord and see how they are
doing." 37 Barnabas wanted to take John,
also called Mark,[o] with them, 38 but Paul
did not think it wise to take him, because
he had deserted them[p] in Pamphylia and
had not continued with them in the work.
39 They had such a sharp disagreement that
they parted company. Barnabas took Mark
and sailed for Cyprus, 40 but Paul chose Silas[q] and left, commended by the believers to the grace of the Lord.[r] 41 He went
through Syria[s] and Cilicia,[t] strengthening
the churches.[u]

Timothy Joins Paul and Silas

16 Paul came to Derbe and then to
Lystra,[v] where a disciple named
Timothy[w] lived, whose mother was Jewish and a believer but whose father was a
Greek. 2 The believers[x] at Lystra and Iconium[y] spoke well of him. 3 Paul wanted to
take him along on the journey, so he circumcised him because of the Jews who
lived in that area, for they all knew that
his father was a Greek.[z] 4 As they traveled
from town to town, they delivered the decisions reached by the apostles and elders[a]
in Jerusalem[b] for the people to obey.[c] 5 So
the churches were strengthened[d] in the
faith and grew daily in numbers.

Paul's Vision of the Man of Macedonia

6 Paul and his companions traveled
throughout the region of Phrygia[e] and Galatia,[f] having been kept by the Holy Spirit
from preaching the word in the province
of Asia.[g] 7 When they came to the border
of Mysia, they tried to enter Bithynia, but
the Spirit of Jesus[h] would not allow them
to. 8 So they passed by Mysia and went
down to Troas.[i] 9 During the night Paul had
a vision[j] of a man of Macedonia[k] standing
and begging him, "Come over to Macedonia and help us." 10 After Paul had seen
the vision, we[l] got ready at once to leave
for Macedonia, concluding that God had
called us to preach the gospel[m] to them.

Lydia's Conversion in Philippi

11 From Troas[n] we put out to sea and
sailed straight for Samothrace, and the

15:36 [n] Ac 13:4, 13, 14, 51; 14:1, 6, 24, 25 **15:37** [o] Ac 12:12 **15:38** [p] Ac 13:13 **15:40** [q] ver 22 [r] Ac 11:23 **15:41** [s] ver 23 [t] Ac 6:9 [u] Ac 16:5 **16:1** [v] Ac 14:6 [w] Ac 17:14; 18:5; 19:22; Ro 16:21; 1Co 4:17; 2Co 1:1, 19; 1Th 3:2, 6; 1Ti 1:2, 18; 2Ti 1:2, 5, 6 **16:2** [x] ver 40 [y] Ac 13:51 **16:3** [z] Gal 2:3 **16:4** [a] Ac 11:30 [b] Ac 15:2 [c] Ac 15:28, 29 **16:5** [d] Ac 9:31; 15:41 **16:6** [e] Ac 18:23 [f] Ac 18:23; Gal 1:2; 3:1 [g] Ac 2:9 **16:7** [h] Ro 8:9; Gal 4:6 **16:8** [i] ver 11; 2Co 2:12; 2Ti 4:13 **16:9** [j] Ac 9:10 [k] Ac 20:1, 3 **16:10** [l] ver 10-17 [m] Ac 14:7 **16:11** [n] ver 8

15:39 *such a sharp disagreement that they parted company.* Even ancient biographies favorable to their subjects usually reported negative behavior at times. Given the harmony displayed in v. 28, the conflict here seems negative, although Luke probably expects that God blessed both new ministry teams.
15:40 *chose Silas.* In condensing material, ancient historians sometimes omitted details; here this would include either that Silas had returned or that he was not among those sent off (v. 33).
15:41 *Syria and Cilicia.* See note on v. 23. During warm seasons, travelers could move from Cilicia across the Taurus Mountains in the north to Derbe and Lystra (16:1).
16:1 *Derbe.* See note on 14:20. *Lystra.* See note on 14:8. *mother was Jewish ... father was a Greek.* Although Judeans believed that intermarriage with Gentiles invited God's wrath, the few Jewish residents in a town such as Lystra probably were less strict.
16:2 *Lystra.* See note on 14:8. *Iconium.* See notes on 13:51; 14:6.
16:3 *Paul ... circumcised him.* Timothy's Gentile father apparently forbade his circumcision; Jewish people thus would view Timothy as a Gentile.
16:4 *decisions ... for the people to obey.* See 15:20 and note; 15:29.
16:6 *Phrygia and Galatia.* Much of Phrygia lay in the southern part of the Roman province of Galatia, and Phrygian Galatia is the region likely in view here. (North Galatia was less populated and does not fit a journey from Lystra to Mysia.) *Asia.* An important road led west to the prosperous and heavily populated Roman province of Asia (on the west coast of Asia Minor or today's Turkey); Paul later ministers there (see 19:10; Ephesus was its most prominent city).
16:7 *the border of Mysia.* They may have been at a city on its eastern border in northern Phrygia; there they could turn right to Bithynia in the north (a strategic region), or turn left to Mysia and Asia in the west. They pass northwest through Mysia in v. 8. *Spirit of Jesus.* Identifying the Holy Spirit (v. 6), which Jewish people usually understood as God's Spirit, with the Spirit of Jesus (v. 7) identifies Jesus as divine.
16:8 *Troas.* Alexandria Troas was a large Roman colony in northwestern Mysia, 10–15 miles (16–24 kilometers) south of old Troas, the site of the Trojan War. Romans believed that they descended from the Trojans, so this site commanded great respect for them; it was the historic boundary between Europe and Asia in Greek legend (Homer) and history (Alexander the Great). Some scholars estimate the population of Alexandria Troas at 100,000 people. Geographically, Troas would have been time-consuming for the apostolic team to reach by their travel inland described in 16:7–8, but it was strategically located on the northern trade route between Macedonia (on to Rome) and Asia. Its artificial harbor was the best harbor in the region, and it was consequently prosperous from trade.
16:9 *Macedonia.* Had itself been a powerful empire, especially after the time of Alexander the Great, but Rome defeated it in 167 BC and made it a province in 146 BC. Alexander had invaded Asia with Hellenistic culture, starting with Troas (see note on v. 8); here a different kind of message is about to spread from Asia to Europe. Greeks divided the world into three continents: everything to their east was Asia and everything to the south was Africa. By this definition, now used in the Roman Empire, Judea, like Asia Minor, belonged to Asia.
16:10 *we.* From this point forward, "we" recurs in some parts of the book, usually as a travel notice (vv. 10–17, and on Paul's journeys to Jerusalem and Rome). In ancient historical works, use of the first person almost always indicated the author's action or narration (or in this case, his presence as part of a group).
16:11 *From Troas ... to Neapolis.* More than 150 miles (240 kilometers). *Samothrace.* This island was a rough

next day we went on to Neapolis. 12From
there we traveled to Philippi,[o] a Roman
colony and the leading city of that district[a]
of Macedonia.[p] And we stayed there several days.
13On the Sabbath[q] we went outside the
city gate to the river, where we expected
to find a place of prayer. We sat down and
began to speak to the women who had
gathered there. 14One of those listening
was a woman from the city of Thyatira[r]
named Lydia, a dealer in purple cloth. She
was a worshiper of God. The Lord opened
her heart[s] to respond to Paul's message.

16:12 [o] Ac 20:6; Php 1:1; 1Th 2:2 [p] ver 9
16:13 [q] Ac 13:14
16:14 [r] Rev 1:11 [s] Lk 24:45

[a] *12* The text and meaning of the Greek for *the leading city of that district* are uncertain.

midway point between Troas and Neapolis, and its high mountain made it easy to spot; the best port was in the capital city of the same name, on the island's north shore. *Neapolis.* The port town of Philippi, Macedonia's best port besides Thessalonica. The seasonal winds are more favorable for Paul's voyage here than those in 20:6.

16:12 *Philippi.* Ten miles (16 kilometers) by land from the port of Neapolis (v. 11), Philippi had been a Roman colony since 42 BC; its citizens were therefore citizens of Rome. The city took its colonial status very seriously: e.g., over 80 percent of its inscriptions are in Latin. It was a largely agrarian town and some estimate its population at only 10,000 or even 5,000. Nevertheless, it was prosperous and its location was strategic as the eastern end of the major Via Egnatia, an overland route to the eastern coast of the Adriatic, thus connected to Italy by sea. *leading city.* Thessalonica was Macedonia's capital but Philippi was the most respected city in the first of Macedonia's four districts; Luke may simply call it a "leading city" without implying that no other cities merited the same title.

16:13 *outside the city gate to the river.* The Gangites River was about 1.5 miles (2.4 kilometers) to Philippi's west, reached by means of the Via Egnatia (and outside the city gate); some scholars think that Luke instead means the creek Krenides, closer to Philippi, or an ancient stream on Philippi's east. In any case, Diaspora Jewish ritual included purifying their hands. Thus in a city without a synagogue, one would look for sympathizers with Judaism to gather on the Sabbath near water. A large majority of Gentile sympathizers with Judaism were women, who would lose less status and, in the case of conversion, would not risk the pain of circumcision.

16:14 *a woman.* Macedonian women exercised much more social power, including in religion, than did women in most of traditional Greece to the southwest. *dealer in purple cloth.* Thyatira in western Asia Minor was strong in textiles; it was in the region of ancient Lydia, making Lydia a fitting name for this woman. Some scholars believe that 10,000 crushed shellfish were needed to yield a single gram of the costliest purple dye, the sort from Tyre. Some

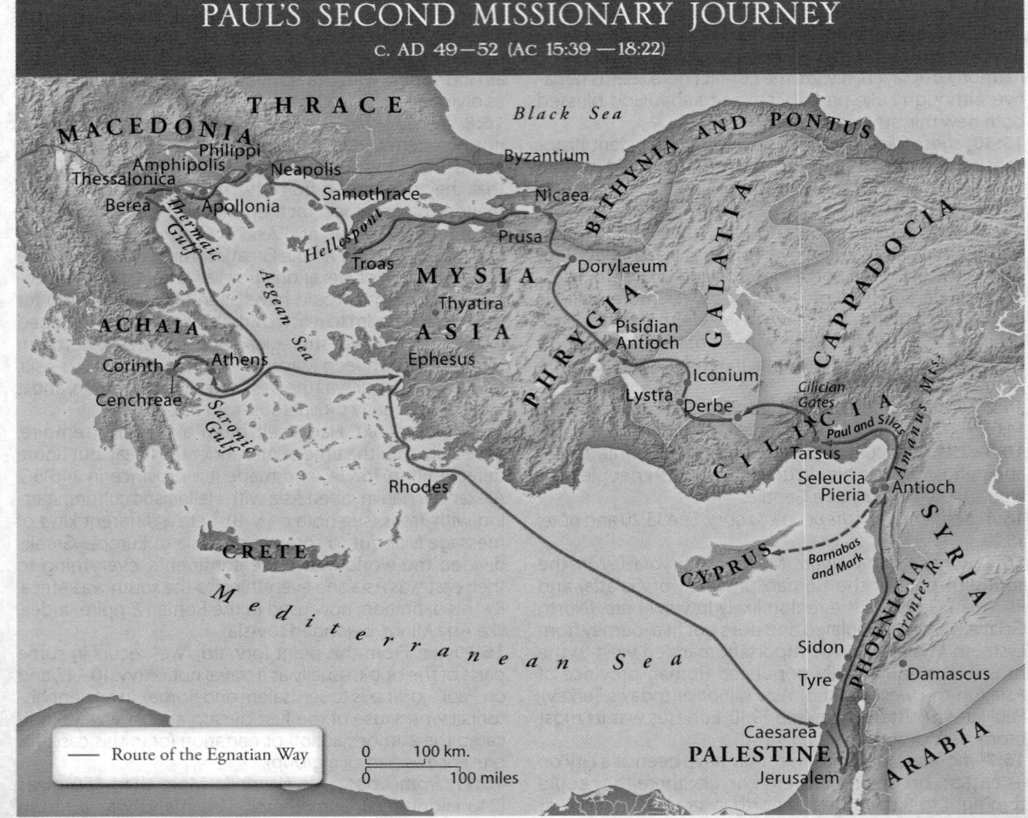

15When she and the members of her
household[t] were baptized, she invited us
to her home. "If you consider me a believer in the Lord," she said, "come and stay
at my house." And she persuaded us.

Paul and Silas in Prison

16Once when we were going to the place
of prayer,[u] we were met by a female slave
who had a spirit[v] by which she predicted
the future. She earned a great deal of money for her owners by fortune-telling. 17She
followed Paul and the rest of us, shouting,
"These men are servants of the Most High
God,[w] who are telling you the way to be
saved." 18She kept this up for many days.
Finally Paul became so annoyed that he
turned around and said to the spirit, "In
the name of Jesus Christ I command you
to come out of her!" At that moment the
spirit left her.[x]
19When her owners realized that their
hope of making money[y] was gone, they
seized Paul and Silas[z] and dragged[a] them
into the marketplace to face the authorities. 20They brought them before the magistrates and said, "These men are Jews,
and are throwing our city into an uproar[b]
21by advocating customs unlawful for us
Romans[c] to accept or practice."[d]
22The crowd joined in the attack against
Paul and Silas, and the magistrates ordered them to be stripped and beaten
with rods.[e] 23After they had been severely

16:15 [t] Ac 11:14 **16:16** [u] ver 13 [v] Dt 18:11; 1Sa 28:3,7 **16:17** [w] Mk 5:7 **16:18** [x] Mk 16:17 **16:19** [y] ver 16; Ac 19:25,26 [z] Ac 15:22 [a] Ac 8:3; 17:6; 21:30; Jas 2:6 **16:20** [b] Ac 17:6 **16:21** [c] ver 12 [d] Est 3:8 **16:22** [e] 2Co 11:25; 1Th 2:2

---

believe that dyers in Thyatira and Macedonia used a less expensive substance (the madder plant, for Thyatira).

16:15 *members of her household.* Who constituted Lydia's household is uncertain; it could have included servants, freedpersons, or workers. She apparently heads her own household, which could mean that she was widowed, divorced, or a prosperous freedwoman. *come and stay at my house.* Dealers in purple could be persons of means, although Lydia is technically a foreigner in the city. Hospitality was a prized virtue in the ancient Mediterranean world, and Lydia would count it an honor for this ministry team to stay with her. It would not be unusual for Jewish people to provide guests lodging for three weeks if they found the guests trustworthy. Inns were notorious for prostitution and other issues that made them less than ideal for Jewish travelers. Perhaps 10 percent of ancient benefactors were women; nevertheless, critics of a movement could attack it for depending on women's financial support.

16:16 *a spirit.* Lit. "the spirit of a Python." Python was an epithet of Apollo, who had slain the dragon named Python; Apollo's most famous temple, at Delphi, had a priestess known as a Pythoness, whose oracles were the most famous in antiquity. She would go into a trance and utter obscure messages that the priests would interpret for the inquirers. This spirit is thus associated with the highest-level pagan prophetic powers.

16:17 *Most High God.* Her utterance may relativize the uniqueness and necessity of faith in Christ by making Paul's God simply the greatest in a pantheon. Jewish people spoke of "the Most High God" (Da 5:18,21), but so did Gentiles, who often applied it to Zeus and/or to the Jewish God. Ancient magic often acknowledged the Jewish God as the strongest because Jews had only one God; magical papyri sometimes tried to replicate and exploit the secret (unpronounced) holy name of YHWH.

16:18 *In the name of Jesus Christ I command you.* One method of exorcism was to invoke more powerful spirits to drive out lower ones (see note on 19:13). Here, however, Paul speaks on the basis of Jesus' delegated authority. On use of the name of Jesus Christ, see notes on 3:6; Mt 7:21–22.

16:19 *the marketplace.* Refers not to Philippi's commercial agora, after the Greek model, but to its nearby central agora, its forum following the Roman model. This large forum — 230 feet by 485 feet (70 meters by 150 meters) was intersected by the Via Egnatia that ran through Philippi and on through Macedonia to the west. *the authorities.* Philippi's two highest officials, the *duoviri.* They would not normally look for criminals but waited for accusers to bring charges, as here. The accusations would be brought to a raised platform close to the forum's north entrance.

16:20 *These men are Jews.* Anti-Judaism was fashionable, and would be especially embraced in this Roman colony at this time if the emperor Claudius had already expelled Jewish people from Rome (18:2). A group of resident aliens (e.g., Egyptians or Judeans), who were neither descendants of the indigenous population or Roman colonists, were allowed to have their own community within a city, but their social situation could be precarious and they dared not challenge the city's traditional customs. Many aristocratic Romans hated Jewish people because the latter proved so effective in winning converts, especially women. Greek anti-Judaism was often even more dangerous, as exemplified in the earlier persecutions by Antiochus Epiphanes and the subsequent massacre of Alexandria's massive Jewish population by that city's Greek residents. Philippi, though a Roman colony, apparently had a very small Jewish population (v. 13) that made an easy target. *throwing our city into an uproar.* Ancient readers disliked demagogues and rabble-rousers, precisely what the missionaries' accusers are here. Because the accusers might not win a case on the grounds of property damage, they charge the missionaries with disturbing the peace, a charge that Roman officials would punish harshly. The accusers, who are probably Roman citizens, can feel assured that their accusation will win in court, because those of higher status could usually prosecute cases successfully against those of lower status. Philippi, proud of its Roman status, gave first preference to citizens of the colony, who were Roman citizens. What the accusers do not imagine is that the accused, who have not flaunted their status, will also turn out to be Roman citizens (v. 37).

16:22 *stripped.* Prisoners were normally stripped naked for punishment; this action was intended to humiliate prisoners, and could be particularly humiliating for Jewish prisoners or other modest peoples from the east. *beaten with rods.* The officials' six lictors carried bundles of rods; these rods were used as an emblem of the officials' authority but also useful for beating prisoners. It was illegal to inflict this punishment on untried Roman citizens, though it sometimes happened where (say, in Jerusalem) officials believed that redress would be difficult. Paul and Silas may not yet understand that in Philippi this illegality will be taken seriously (v. 38).

16:23 *prison.* The filth and lack of good toilet facilities in prisons raised the risk of infection for the missionaries' wounds. Clothing and, apart from subsistence-level sustenance, food had to be supplied from outside, and

flogged, they were thrown into prison, and
the jailer[f] was commanded to guard them
carefully. 24 When he received these orders,
he put them in the inner cell and fastened
their feet in the stocks.[g]
25 About midnight Paul and Silas were
praying and singing hymns[h] to God, and
the other prisoners were listening to them.
26 Suddenly there was such a violent earthquake that the foundations of the prison
were shaken.[i] At once all the prison doors
flew open,[j] and everyone's chains came
loose.[k] 27 The jailer woke up, and when
he saw the prison doors open, he drew
his sword and was about to kill himself
because he thought the prisoners had escaped.[l] 28 But Paul shouted, "Don't harm
yourself! We are all here!"
29 The jailer called for lights, rushed in
and fell trembling before Paul and Silas.
30 He then brought them out and asked,
"Sirs, what must I do to be saved?"[m]
31 They replied, "Believe in the Lord
Jesus, and you will be saved — you and
your household."[n] 32 Then they spoke the
word of the Lord to him and to all the
others in his house. 33 At that hour of the
night[o] the jailer took them and washed
their wounds; then immediately he and all
his household were baptized. 34 The jailer brought them into his house and set a
meal before them; he[p] was filled with joy
because he had come to believe in God —
he and his whole household.
35 When it was daylight, the magistrates
sent their officers to the jailer with the order: "Release those men." 36 The jailer[q]
told Paul, "The magistrates have ordered
that you and Silas be released. Now you
can leave. Go in peace."[r]
37 But Paul said to the officers: "They
beat us publicly without a trial, even
though we are Roman citizens,[s] and threw
us into prison. And now do they want to
get rid of us quietly? No! Let them come
themselves and escort us out."

16:23 [f] ver 27, 36
16:24 [g] Job 13:27; 33:11; Jer 20:2, 3; 29:26
16:25 [h] Eph 5:19
16:26 [i] Ac 4:31 [j] Ac 12:10 [k] Ac 12:7
16:27 [l] Ac 12:19
16:30 [m] Ac 2:37
16:31 [n] Ac 11:14
16:33 [o] ver 25
16:34 [p] Ac 11:14
16:36 [q] ver 23, 27 [r] Ac 15:33
16:37 [s] Ac 22:25-29

those helping prisoners often had to bribe guards to get this help to them. Prisoners normally slept on cold floors with only their outer garment as bedding. *jailer.* Chief jailers tended to be well paid for their harshness.

16:24 *inner cell.* Ordered to "guard them carefully" (v. 23), the chief jailer has them placed in the inner prison. This room was the most poorly ventilated part, and if the jailer detained all the prisoners there for the night (as was sometimes done), it would be crowded. *stocks.* Wood stocks fastened to the floor added both security and a further element of suffering, making movement difficult. These punishments were considered appropriate only for people of low status, and certainly not for untried Roman citizens.

16:25 *midnight.* People usually went to sleep close to sundown or a little later, though the inner cell would lack access to outside light. *praying and singing hymns to God.* Even Gentiles respected sages who, in accordance with their principles, could rejoice in affliction. Cf. Ps 119:61 – 62.

16:26 *violent earthquake.* Most people in antiquity attributed earthquakes to the activity of God or pagan deities. A normal earthquake would not open doors and break everyone's chains while leaving everyone unharmed. For shaking after prayer, cf. 4:31.

16:27 *drew his sword and was about to kill himself.* Although the chief jailer could not be held responsible for the earthquake, he could be deemed negligent for inadequate or sleeping staff. Rather than face execution, Romans often preferred suicide. Although some reasons for or forms of suicide were considered cowardly, Romans considered falling on one's sword in such circumstances noble. (Christian thinkers who addressed the topic in subsequent centuries disagreed, affirming that only God has the right to take life.)

16:28 *We are all here!* Roman law punished harshly those who escaped detention, but some sources suggest that officials might give special treatment to those who refused to flee when they had the opportunity.

16:29 *called for lights.* Given the inner cell's darkness, the chief jailer's subordinates quickly procured torches.

16:30 *Sirs, what must I do to be saved?* His question reflects some knowledge of the original situation behind their charge (v. 17). In a context such as this one, "sirs" could mean "lords," but in v. 31 the missionaries point the jailer to the true Lord (the same Greek term).

16:31 *you and your household.* Ancient households usually followed the religion of the head of the household. (They did not always do so, but it was the norm and it often embarrassed the husband when his wife or children did not.)

16:33 *took them and washed their wounds.* Taking prisoners out of custody without authorization risked severe punishment. *washed.* Jails were often in cities' public areas, where fountains and other water sources existed. Prisoners in jail lacked the means to wash themselves. *baptized.* The jailer washed and, perhaps from the same water source, received washing.

16:34 *brought them into his house.* Fraternizing with prisoners risked severe punishment. *set a meal before them.* Because it is unlikely that the jailer had available food prepared in a kosher manner, Paul and Silas also value the acceptance of hospitality (cf. Lk 10:8) above conventional purity regulations (Lev 11). On the usual diet of prisoners, see note on v. 23; here, however, they would eat the sort of food the jailer had available.

16:35 *daylight.* The rapid release may be because the magistrates recognized the earthquake as a divine sign, but may be simply because the magistrates deemed the previous day's punishment sufficient warning to deter further problems. (That they had so readily accommodated a mob in v. 22 suggests that crowd control was a higher priority for them in the case than individual justice.)

16:37 *we are Roman citizens.* Possibly the jailer informed them that their rights as Roman citizens, violated in v. 22, would actually be taken seriously in Philippi. The name Paul was a cognomen almost always used only by Roman citizens. If Paul did not carry documents attesting his citizenship, it could be verified by records in Tarsus. (A false claim on this matter was not normally expected since it would lead, once checked, to execution.) Paul's ancestors may have acquired citizenship after being freed from slavery in Rome (on the enslavement of Jews by Pompey, and their subsequent release, see the article "Synagogue of the Freedmen," p. 1879).

Citizenship could be acquired by various means: being born to a citizen (as Paul was); under some conditions, being a freed slave of a Roman citizen (as Paul's ancestors may have been); being a citizen of a Roman colony, such

38 The officers reported this to the magistrates, and when they heard that Paul
and Silas were Roman citizens, they were
alarmed.[t] 39 They came to appease them
and escorted them from the prison, requesting them to leave the city.[u] 40 After
Paul and Silas came out of the prison, they
went to Lydia's house,[v] where they met
with the brothers and sisters[w] and encouraged them. Then they left.

In Thessalonica

17 When Paul and his companions had
passed through Amphipolis and Apollonia, they came to Thessalonica,[x] where
there was a Jewish synagogue. 2 As was his
custom, Paul went into the synagogue,[y]
and on three Sabbath[z] days he reasoned
with them from the Scriptures,[a] 3 explaining and proving that the Messiah had to
suffer[b] and rise from the dead.[c] "This Jesus
I am proclaiming to you is the Messiah,"[d]
he said. 4 Some of the Jews were persuaded
and joined Paul and Silas,[e] as did a large
number of God-fearing Greeks and quite a
few prominent women.

16:38 [t] Ac 22:29
16:39 [u] Mt 8:34
16:40 [v] ver 14 [w] ver 2; Ac 1:16
17:1 [x] ver 11, 13; Php 4:16; 1Th 1:1; 2Th 1:1; 2Ti 4:10
17:2 [y] Ac 9:20 [z] Ac 13:14 [a] Ac 8:35
17:3 [b] Lk 24:26; Ac 3:18 [c] Lk 24:46 [d] Ac 9:22; 18:28
17:4 [e] Ac 15:22
17:5 [f] ver 13; 1Th 2:16 [g] Ro 16:21
17:6 [h] Ac 16:19 [i] Mt 24:14 [j] Ac 16:20
17:7 [k] Lk 23:2; Jn 19:12
17:9 [l] ver 5
17:10 [m] ver 13; Ac 20:4

5 But other Jews were jealous; so they
rounded up some bad characters from
the marketplace, formed a mob and started a riot in the city.[f] They rushed to Jason's[g] house in search of Paul and Silas
in order to bring them out to the crowd.[a]
6 But when they did not find them, they
dragged[h] Jason and some other believers
before the city officials, shouting: "These
men who have caused trouble all over
the world[i] have now come here,[j] 7 and Jason has welcomed them into his house.
They are all defying Caesar's decrees, saying that there is another king, one called
Jesus."[k] 8 When they heard this, the crowd
and the city officials were thrown into turmoil. 9 Then they made Jason[l] and the others post bond and let them go.

In Berea

10 As soon as it was night, the believers
sent Paul and Silas away to Berea.[m] On
arriving there, they went to the Jewish
synagogue. 11 Now the Berean Jews were
of more noble character than those in

[a] 5 Or *the assembly of the people*

---

as Philippi or Corinth; being a veteran from the Roman army's auxiliary forces; and, more rarely, an honor granted individuals for special service to Rome. Some also purchased it with bribes (see 22:28).

16:38–39 *they were alarmed … They came to appease them.* The officials could punish many people without trial, but not Roman citizens; the penalty for so treating Roman citizens could include being removed from office, or even trouble for the entire city. While in practice such behavior was overlooked in some places, Philippi was too self-consciously Roman to overlook it. Public honor and shame were important issues in this society; if Paul and Silas left town without some public vindication, it would be more difficult for the church in Philippi. The officials, however, do not want to admit wrong very publicly, so after accompanying Paul and Silas as demanded, they want them and their controversies to leave town.

16:40 *met with the brothers and sisters.* By visiting the believers rather than leaving immediately, Paul and Silas reaffirm their honor; but they quickly comply with the officials' demands rather than risk consequences for the church. *they left.* They leave the city on the Via Egnatia, which will take them to the cities mentioned in 17:1.

17:1 *Amphipolis … Apollonia … Thessalonica.* After traveling 33 miles (more than 50 kilometers) on the Via Egnatia, Paul and Silas would reach Amphipolis. Apollonia was 27 miles (some 40 kilometers) farther west on the same road, and Thessalonica 35 miles (some 55 kilometers) still farther. Amphipolis and Apollonia appear in ancient sources as rest stops on the way to Thessalonica, although they would make for long days' walks, especially considering the preachers' wounds. Unlike the road from Philippi through Apollonia, the trek to Thessalonica was mostly downhill. Thessalonica was a "free" city (i.e., had some autonomy), was the Roman governor's seat for Macedonia, and was massive by ancient standards (estimates range as high as 200,000 inhabitants). It would be their last stop on the Via Egnatia for now (see v. 10).

17:2 *synagogue.* As a port city, Thessalonica hosted not only traditional cults but also foreign ones, such as archaeologically attested Egyptian shrines and a synagogue.

17:4 *prominent women.* Women exercised more freedom in Macedonia. Throughout the empire Gentile women were more drawn to Judaism than were men.

17:5 *marketplace.* The probable location of the Jewish community in Thessalonica is near the forum. Ancient sources note that unemployed idlers in marketplaces were often stirred to mob action; those who stirred them were usually viewed as immoral demagogues. Evidence shows that though Thessalonica was rich, many residents were unemployed, among the many who were impoverished.

17:6 *they dragged Jason and some other believers.* It was normally the responsibility of the accusers to get the accused to court. Although Jason was a traditional Greek name, by this time it was used by many Jews (of whom the Jason here was likely one; cf. Ro 16:21). *city officials.* See note on v. 8. *caused trouble.* In this era Gentiles sometimes accused Jews of causing unrest, a charge here transferred instead to Jesus' followers; the penalty for such a charge of sedition could be death.

17:7 *defying Caesar's decrees.* Thessalonica's devotion to the emperor was evident in its imperial temple and on its coins. *another king.* Speaking of another king is the charge of treason, punishable by death. Some ancient rhetoricians supported inventing any believable charges against one's opponents.

17:8 *city officials.* Lit. "politarchs," a title for officials used in some cities in Macedonia. In this era the number of Thessalonica's politarchs varied from three to seven at various times.

17:9 *post bond.* The politarchs held the host responsible for posting bond, guaranteeing that no more trouble would occur. Such a fine was a small penalty in proportion to the capital charge, suggesting that the politarchs are simply humoring the crowds for the moment. Their virtual ban on Paul could affect only Thessalonica, not any other cities, and would expire once they left office.

17:10 *night.* Night flight could be deemed both cowardly

Thessalonica,[n] for they received the message with great eagerness and examined
the Scriptures[o] every day to see if what Paul
said was true. 12As a result, many of them
believed, as did also a number of prominent Greek women and many Greek men.
13But when the Jews in Thessalonica learned that Paul was preaching the
word of God at Berea, some of them went
there too, agitating the crowds and stirring
them up. 14The believers immediately sent
Paul to the coast, but Silas[p] and Timothy[q]
stayed at Berea. 15Those who escorted
Paul brought him to Athens[r] and then left
with instructions for Silas and Timothy to
join him as soon as possible.[s]

In Athens

16While Paul was waiting for them in
Athens, he was greatly distressed to see
that the city was full of idols. 17So he reasoned in the synagogue[t] with both Jews
and God-fearing Greeks, as well as in the
marketplace day by day with those who
happened to be there. 18A group of Epicurean and Stoic philosophers began to
debate with him. Some of them asked,
"What is this babbler trying to say?" Others remarked, "He seems to be advocating foreign gods." They said this because
Paul was preaching the good news about
Jesus and the resurrection.[u] 19Then they
took him and brought him to a meeting of
the Areopagus,[v] where they said to him,
"May we know what this new teaching[w]
is that you are presenting? 20You are bringing some strange ideas to our ears, and
we would like to know what they mean."
21(All the Athenians and the foreigners
who lived there spent their time doing
nothing but talking about and listening to
the latest ideas.)
22Paul then stood up in the meeting
of the Areopagus and said: "People of

17:11 [n] ver 1 [o] Lk 16:29; Jn 5:39 **17:14** [p] Ac 15:22 [q] Ac 16:1 **17:15** [r] ver 16, 21, 22; Ac 18:1; 1Th 3:1 [s] Ac 18:5 **17:17** [t] Ac 9:20
17:18 [u] ver 31, 32; Ac 4:2 **17:19** [v] ver 22 [w] Mk 1:27

and an admission of guilt, but it was the safest means of escape and the nature of the charges and the opposition made it the only reasonable course. *away to Berea.* Leaving the well-traveled Via Egnatia and avoiding even the coastal road, Paul and his companions veer about 50 miles (80 kilometers) southwest to Berea. *Berea.* After Thessalonica, it was one of Macedonia's chief cities, but it was not the most obvious location for any pursuers to start looking for Paul.
17:12 *prominent Greek women.* See note on v. 4.
17:13 *Jews in Thessalonica ... agitating the crowds.* Public rulings in one city had no effect in another, so Paul's Thessalonian accusers must start over again in Berea.
17:14 *to the coast.* Depending on the route taken, Paul's journey to the coast was between 30 and 50 miles (between 58 and 80 kilometers); he probably traveled to Dion, a coastal city from which Paul could sail south and away from Macedonia.
17:15 *brought him to Athens.* Athens had ports, the best known of which was its port town Piraeus. A visitor would then walk some three miles (five kilometers) inland to Athens. Athens retained fame as the center of philosophy, although some other cities, such as Alexandria and Tarsus, had surpassed it. In 1Th 3:1 – 2, Paul is left at Athens alone because he sends Timothy back to Thessalonica, but Luke reports Silas and Timothy coming from Macedonia only in Acts 18:5. Luke has probably omitted some details unnecessary for his narrative (such as an earlier but temporary reunion in Athens); since Luke's focus remains on Paul, he lacks need to describe the others' coming and going. Ancient historians and biographers frequently omitted such details, focusing on their main character.
17:16 *city was full of idols.* Even before reaching land, the Parthenon, Athena's temple with its huge statue of the goddess, was visible on the Acropolis. Shrines and statues pervaded most public space in ancient Athens, from the agora to the streets and especially on the Acropolis.
17:17 *in the synagogue ... as well as in the marketplace.* The synagogue in Athens is attested in inscriptions. In addition to ministry there, Paul dialogues in the marketplace, where sages and orators without their own schools practiced their skills.
17:18 Paul has much more common ground with Stoics than with Epicureans, as his speech will show (vv. 22 – 26); this is good for Luke's audience, who respected the popular Stoics more than the often criticized Epicureans (cf. the similar alignment with popular Pharisaism as against unpopular Sadducees; 23:6). *babbler.* The term came to apply to those who recycled scraps from other people's opinions rather than offering a coherent and creative synthesis. *Jesus and the resurrection.* Ready as they are to criticize from their own standpoint, these critics are woefully ignorant of Paul's: they think that Paul is "advocating foreign gods," plural, because he preaches "Jesus and the resurrection." That is, they take Resurrection, *Anastasis*, as a feminine name and suppose that Paul preaches a male-female dyad, a common way of viewing deities in this period. Popular religion deemed many philosophers, unlike the Stoics, irreligious for rejecting conventional Greek religion, though most philosophers allowed the value of traditional religion for the masses. The charge against Paul, "advocating foreign gods," evokes one common version of the earlier charge against Socrates (cf. note on v. 19). Athens had arraigned some others on this same charge.
17:19 *Areopagus.* Athens' aristocratic city council and leading court, with roughly a hundred members. Most were not professional philosophers but they were familiar with philosophy. They could investigate foreign cults and determine whether visiting speakers would be granted public lectureships. Centuries earlier they had tried Socrates for "advocating foreign gods" (v. 18) and had him executed; although there is no danger here of Paul being executed, most of Luke's audience would catch the implicit comparison with Socrates and his rejected wisdom.
17:21 *latest ideas.* Athenians were widely known for always seeking what was new.
17:22 – 31 In addition to citing Greek poets (v. 28), Paul's speech here employs high quality literary Greek and rhetorical devices. Especially in vv. 24 – 29, there are many points of contact with the dominant Stoic philosophy; the connections follow a long-standing Jewish intellectual legacy. For more than 300 years Diaspora Jewish intellectuals had selected ideas in Greek philosophy useful for making Judaism respectable among Greeks.
17:22 *I see ... you are very religious.* Speeches customarily opened by praising the audience, including in Athens. Although Paul is not pleased with the city's cults (v. 16), he concedes that they are "very religious." *very religious.* The expression can be either positive or negative; his hearers

Athens! I see that in every way you are
very religious. 23For as I walked around
and looked carefully at your objects of
worship, I even found an altar with this
inscription: TO AN UNKNOWN GOD. So you are
ignorant of the very thing you worship[x]—
and this is what I am going to proclaim
to you.
24"The God who made the world and everything in it[y] is the Lord of heaven and

17:23 [x] Jn 4:22
17:24 [y] Isa 42:5; Ac 14:15

will assume that it is positive, whereas Luke's audience will understand it as at best guarded language. Granted, the Stoic and Epicurean philosophers who brought Paul to the Areopagus (17:18–19) will not be interested in altars (17:23; see notes on 17:24 and 25), though Stoics would consider themselves devout (17:22). By contrast, members of the Areopagus, being civic officials, would be publicly supportive of Athens' civic religion, which was inseparable from civic pride.

17:23 *an altar with this inscription:* TO AN UNKNOWN GOD. Speakers sometimes praised local sites. Paul could have seen any one of Athens' many inscriptions to unknown gods. Athenian tradition declared that during an ancient plague sacrifices to all known deities failed to end the plague. The Cretan Epimenides (cf. v. 28) advised the Athenians, and they built altars to unknown gods wherever the sheep designated for sacrifice rested.

17:24 *does not live in temples.* Epicureans (v. 18) denied the need for temples or sacrifices; although some Stoics (v. 18) accepted such activities, their early tradition was pantheistic and saw no need for them. While relating to philosophers on this point, Paul also evoked Scripture,

ACTS 17:18

Ancient Philosophies

Philosophic schools abounded, with Stoics being dominant in this period (later centuries of Christians engaged more Platonism, which had returned to the fore by that period). Platonism, developing ideas of Socrates' pupil Plato, distinguished the world known through the senses, a world of shadows, from the real world of ideas that stood behind it. Plato emphasized the immortality of the soul. In this period Platonism was adapting some elements of Stoicism; representatives of this period of Middle Platonism are Philo of Alexandria, a Jewish philosopher, and, later, Plutarch. Neo-Pythagoreans shared many views with wider Platonism (e.g., reincarnation) but with distinctive Pythagorean emphasis on numbers, vegetarianism, and the like. Smaller schools also flourished. Peripatetics followed the teaching of Aristotle. Cynics were antisocial. Skeptics emphasized cultural diversity and doubted natural universals.

The philosophic schools noted in Ac 17:18 are Stoics and Epicureans. Only members of the upper classes followed Epicureanism. Epicureanism's "theological" views resemble later deism: deities are not involved in the world and are not relevant to it. Going beyond deists, they denied divine design in nature, against the Stoics and other philosophers who affirmed it. Epicureans believed that whatever deities existed could be known only by means of the senses—thus beings such as stars. Epicureans defined the proper goal of life as pleasure, by which they meant the lack of physical pain and emotional disturbance. It was their view of pleasure that their Stoic rivals opposed most regularly.

Stoicism had socially radical beginnings, but by this period they supported the social status quo and were appreciated by some in power, including the current emperor. They believed that *logos*, or reason, structured the matter of which the universe consisted; the universe would be resolved into periodic fire and even the gods would be recycled. Early Stoicism was monistic, but Stoicism had moved away from that as well as from its radical utopianism. Fate controlled destiny; a person's only defense against it was to control what one genuinely could control, namely, one's own attitude. Calmness rather than negative emotions should rule. Stoics and Epicureans remained rivals, but engaged in more sophisticated dialogue than in earlier periods. Stoics claimed to believe in traditional Greek gods yet allegorized and reinterpreted the myths about such gods, since these myths depicted the gods as immoral and often weak. Stoic ethics overlaps Christian ethics at many points. ◆

earth[z] and does not live in temples built
by human hands.[a] 25 And he is not served
by human hands, as if he needed anything.
Rather, he himself gives everyone life and
breath and everything else.[b] 26 From one
man he made all the nations, that they
should inhabit the whole earth; and he
marked out their appointed times in history and the boundaries of their lands.[c]
27 God did this so that they would seek him
and perhaps reach out for him and find
him, though he is not far from any one of
us.[d] 28 'For in him we live and move and
have our being.'[a][e] As some of your own
poets have said, 'We are his offspring.'[b]
29 "Therefore since we are God's offspring, we should not think that the divine
being is like gold or silver or stone — an
image made by human design and skill.[f]
30 In the past God overlooked[g] such ignorance,[h] but now he commands all people
everywhere to repent.[i] 31 For he has set a
day when he will judge[j] the world with
justice[k] by the man he has appointed.[l] He
has given proof of this to everyone by raising him from the dead."[m]
32 When they heard about the resurrection of the dead,[n] some of them sneered,
but others said, "We want to hear you
again on this subject." 33 At that, Paul left
the Council. 34 Some of the people became
followers of Paul and believed. Among
them was Dionysius, a member of the Areopagus,[o] also a woman named Damaris,
and a number of others.

In Corinth

18 After this, Paul left Athens[p] and
went to Corinth.[q] 2 There he met
a Jew named Aquila, a native of Pontus,
who had recently come from Italy with his
wife Priscilla,[r] because Claudius[s] had ordered all Jews to leave Rome. Paul went

17:24 [z] Dt 10:14; Mt 11:25 [a] Ac 7:48 **17:25** [b] Ps 50:10-12; Isa 42:5 **17:26** [c] Dt 32:8; Job 12:23 **17:27** [d] Dt 4:7; Jer 23:23, 24; Ac 14:17 **17:28** [e] Job 12:10; Da 5:23 **17:29** [f] Isa 40:18-20; Ro 1:23 **17:30** [g] Ac 14:16; Ro 3:25 [h] ver 23; 1Pe 1:14 [i] Lk 24:47; Titus 2:11, 12 **17:31** [j] Mt 10:15 [k] Ps 9:8; 96:13; 98:9 [l] Ac 10:42 [m] Ac 2:24 **17:32** [n] ver 18, 31 **17:34** [o] ver 19, 22

a 28 From the Cretan philosopher Epimenides
b 28 From the Cilician Stoic philosopher Aratus

18:1 [p] Ac 17:15 [q] Ac 19:1; 1Co 1:2; 2Co 1:1, 23; 2Ti 4:20
18:2 [r] Ro 16:3; 1Co 16:19; 2Ti 4:19 [s] Ac 11:28

unknown to them (cf. 7:49). The meeting place of the Areopagus, meanwhile, was surrounded by temples.

17:25 *as if he needed anything.* That God does not need anything was a basic premise of Stoic philosophers and was commonly affirmed in Hellenistic Jewish works. In Scripture, cf., e.g., Ps 50:9 – 13. *he ... gives everyone life and breath.* Cf. Ge 2:7; Isa 42:5.

17:26 *From one man.* Evokes the Biblical account of Adam, although Greeks had some similar traditions. (This does contrast with one Athenian tradition about Athenians springing from the soil, separate from other peoples, though Luke's audience may not have thought of this.) *marked out their appointed times ... and the boundaries.* Biblically, God established the boundaries of nations (Ge 10; many Greeks agreed) and of epochs in history. Jewish thinking about epochs included especially the historical succession of empires, including Rome.

17:27 Stoics taught that God pervaded everything; Jewish thinkers affirmed his omnipresence, though denying (against early Stoics) pantheism.

17:28 *"For in him we live and move and have our being."* This is usually credited to Epimenides (cf. note on v. 23); the same poem is quoted in Titus 1:12. *"We are his offspring."* Since Paul was from Tarsus in Cilicia, he undoubtedly knew of the Cilician poet Aratus, the likeliest author of this statement; Cleanthes, a Stoic, wrote similarly. Although Jewish people regularly prayed to God as Father of his people, they sometimes portrayed him, as Gentiles also sometimes did, as Father of all creation.

17:29 *an image made by human design and skill.* Most philosophers refused to identify gods with their statues; some, however, justified the statues as mere reminders of the gods. Paul and other Jews rejected idols altogether.

17:30 *ignorance.* Speakers on controversial topics built rapport from the beginning of their speeches, reserving the most controversial points for the end. Most of Paul's hearers in the Areopagus, who belonged to the educated elite, would balk at their statue-venerating heritage being called "ignorance," despite admitting their ignorance of the unknown god (v. 23). *repent.* Jewish people welcomed Gentiles to repent, turning to God; philosophers spoke of conversion to philosophy.

17:31 *he has set a day.* Most Jewish views of history included an eschatological climax with a day of judgment; Greeks lacked such a view. *judge the world with justice.* See Ps 96:13; 98:9.

17:32 *resurrection of the dead.* Greeks lacked not only belief in an eschatological climax, but also belief in a bodily resurrection (v. 31); unfamiliar with Jewish understandings of eschatological transformation, some Greeks might even envision such an event as corpses being reconstituted and entering the world of the living. Most who believed in an afterlife believed either that the soul would experience a shadowy netherworld or that it would fly up to the heavens freed from the encumbrance of bodily existence.

17:34 *member of the Areopagus.* The aristocratic Areopagus was Athens' city council and leading court, with roughly a hundred members. *woman named Damaris.* Athens traditionally secluded women (other than high-class prostitutes) from public life, but a minority of philosophic schools had women disciples, of whom Damaris could be one.

18:1 *went to Corinth.* The heavily populated Roman capital of Achaia (Greece) lay 53 miles (85 kilometers) to Athens' west. Because the southern coasts of Greece were dangerous for ships, the sea trade between Italy and the prosperous Roman province of Asia passed through the Isthmus of Corinth, making Corinth wealthy. Rome decimated old Corinth in 146 BC, reestablishing it as a Roman colony in 44 BC. Although some Greeks continued living there in the interim and many Greeks remained in Paul's day, full citizens of Corinth were Roman citizens and Latin was the language of official civic business. Corinth was the best preparation possible for any future ministry of Paul in Rome or the western Mediterranean.

18:2 *Claudius.* Emperor of Rome from AD 41 to 54, he dealt firmly with the Jewish community at various times, and expelled them from the city of Rome, probably in AD 49, shortly before Paul reached Corinth. What provoked the expulsion order was conflict in the Jewish community over one "Chrestus," usually thought to be debates about Jesus as the Christ. Jewish Roman citizens probably

to see them, 3and because he was a tentmaker as they were, he stayed and worked
with them.[t] 4Every Sabbath[u] he reasoned
in the synagogue, trying to persuade Jews
and Greeks.
5When Silas[v] and Timothy[w] came from
Macedonia,[x] Paul devoted himself exclusively to preaching, testifying to the Jews
that Jesus was the Messiah.[y] 6But when
they opposed Paul and became abusive,[z]
he shook out his clothes in protest and
said to them, "Your blood be on your own
heads![a] I am innocent of it.[b] From now on
I will go to the Gentiles."[c]
7Then Paul left the synagogue and went
next door to the house of Titius Justus,
a worshiper of God.[d] 8Crispus,[e] the synagogue leader,[f] and his entire household[g]
believed in the Lord; and many of the Corinthians who heard Paul believed and
were baptized.
9One night the Lord spoke to Paul in a
vision: "Do not be afraid; keep on speaking, do not be silent. 10For I am with
you,[h] and no one is going to attack and
harm you, because I have many people
in this city." 11So Paul stayed in Corinth
for a year and a half, teaching them the
word of God.
12While Gallio was proconsul of Achaia,[i]
the Jews of Corinth made a united attack
on Paul and brought him to the place of
judgment. 13"This man," they charged, "is
persuading the people to worship God in
ways contrary to the law."
14Just as Paul was about to speak, Gallio said to them, "If you Jews were making a complaint about some misdemeanor
or serious crime, it would be reasonable
for me to listen to you. 15But since it involves questions about words and names
and your own law[j]—settle the matter
yourselves. I will not be a judge of such
things." 16So he drove them off. 17Then the
crowd there turned on Sosthenes[k] the synagogue leader and beat him in front of the
proconsul; and Gallio showed no concern
whatever.

18:3 [t] Ac 20:34; 1Co 4:12; 1Th 2:9; 2Th 3:8 **18:4** [u] Ac 13:14 **18:5** [v] Ac 15:22 [w] Ac 16:1 [x] Ac 16:9; 17:14, 15 [y] ver 28; Ac 17:3 **18:6** [z] Ac 13:45 [a] 2Sa 1:16; Eze 18:13; 33:4 [b] Ac 20:26 [c] Ac 13:46 **18:7** [d] Ac 16:14 **18:8** [e] 1Co 1:14 [f] Mk 5:22 [g] Ac 11:14 **18:10** [h] Mt 28:20 **18:12** [i] ver 27 **18:15** [j] Ac 23:29; 25:11, 19 **18:17** [k] 1Co 1:1

would not have left, however, and probably many others also remained; given the controversy, however, leaders of the Jesus movement were probably among those forced to leave.

18:3 *tentmaker as they were.* People of the same trade often lived and ran shops in the same neighborhood with one another, but most Jewish people lived in Jewish enclaves distinct from wider trade connections. Tarsus was known for its textile industry, but many scholars think that the term translated "tentmaker" more often referred generally to leather workers. Certainly tools for leatherworking would have been easier for Paul to carry from one city to the next. *stayed and worked with them.* Despite the importance of hospitality in antiquity, guests were rarely welcomed for more than three weeks. The working arrangement here differs from usual hospitality, however; many workers lived in mezzanine or other apartments attached to their ground-floor shops. Women often worked as artisans or sellers alongside their husbands. Although artisans were often proud of their work, people of status usually despised manual labor, and most Gentile sages avoided it. Some Jewish teachers in this period had another trade besides teaching, often learned from their fathers.

18:4 *synagogue.* Non-Greek religious movements, such as Judaism and the Egyptian cult of Isis and Sarapis, established themselves in and around Corinth. Archaeologists found an inscription in Corinth noting its synagogue.

18:5 *from Macedonia.* Silas and Timothy brought a gift from Macedonian churches (Php 4:15; cf. 2Co 11:8).

18:6 *shook out his clothes in protest.* See Ne 5:13. *Your blood be on your own heads!* One who refused to warn the wicked to turn from their way would be guilty of their blood (Eze 3:18–21; especially 33:4).

18:7 *house of Titius Justus.* The name Titius Justus indicates a Roman citizen; Corinth was a Roman colony whose full citizens were also Roman citizens, mostly descended from Roman settlers and freedpersons. Various associations, sometimes including synagogues, started in homes; churches met mostly there in the earliest centuries. He likely had a large home. Scholars estimate that many of these large homes in Corinth could fit 40 to 50 persons; they did, however, vary considerably in size. *worshiper of God.* See note on 10:2.

18:8 *Crispus.* A Roman name sometimes used by Jewish people; although the name does not prove this, he may have been a Jewish Roman citizen. *synagogue leader.* An influential, high-status member of (or sometimes benefactor for) the local Jewish community. *baptized.* Corinth had many public baths and fountains.

18:12 *Gallio.* Brother of the Stoic philosopher Seneca. An inscription suggests that Gallio became Achaia's proconsul July 1 of AD 51 (or on some views 52); although the normal term of office was two years, Gallio left office early because he was ill. The incident Luke reports here thus probably occurred in late 51 or in 52. *place of judgment.* Probably refers to the fairly new, roofed and elevated platform at the southern end of the city's forum.

18:13 *worship God in ways contrary to the law.* Some scholars believe that the accusers are charging Paul with apostasy from the Jewish community, therefore removing his exemption from being expected to worship the emperor. Others doubt that participation in the emperor cult was legally enforced, although it was certainly wildly popular.

18:15 *settle the matter yourselves.* A judge's first determination was whether to hear a case or not; viewing Paul's faith as Jewish, Gallio views the dispute as an internal Jewish matter. Jewish communities and other groups of resident aliens had freedom to decide their own affairs; Rome did not normally meddle in these matters if they did not affect public order.

18:16 *drove them off.* Gallio's impatience with a local Jewish community in a Roman colony may reflect wider attitudes in the wake of the emperor's recent treatment of Rome's Jewish community (v. 2); on anti-Judaism more generally, see note on 16:20.

18:17 *turned on Sosthenes ... and beat him.* Shouting and tempers were common in ancient legal settings; people could have carried out the beating, however, only if Gallio refused to intervene. Scholars debate whether the abusers are Gentiles hostile toward Jews or members of the Jewish community.

Artist's recreation of the first-century forum at Corinth.

Priscilla, Aquila and Apollos

[18]Paul stayed on in Corinth for some
time. Then he left the brothers and sisters[l]
and sailed for Syria, accompanied by Priscilla and Aquila. Before he sailed, he had
his hair cut off at Cenchreae[m] because of a
vow he had taken.[n] [19]They arrived at Ephesus,[o] where Paul left Priscilla and Aquila. He himself went into the synagogue
and reasoned with the Jews. [20]When they
asked him to spend more time with them,
he declined. [21]But as he left, he promised,
"I will come back if it is God's will."[p]
Then he set sail from Ephesus. [22]When he
landed at Caesarea,[q] he went up to Jerusalem and greeted the church and then went
down to Antioch.[r]

[23]After spending some time in Antioch,
Paul set out from there and traveled from
place to place throughout the region of
Galatia[s] and Phrygia, strengthening all the
disciples.[t]

[24]Meanwhile a Jew named Apollos,[u] a
native of Alexandria, came to Ephesus.
He was a learned man, with a thorough
knowledge of the Scriptures. [25]He had
been instructed in the way of the Lord,
and he spoke with great fervor[a][v] and
taught about Jesus accurately, though he
knew only the baptism of John.[w] [26]He
began to speak boldly in the synagogue.
When Priscilla and Aquila heard him, they

18:18 [l] Ac 1:16 [m] Ro 16:1 [n] Nu 6:2, 5, 18; Ac 21:24
18:19 [o] ver 21, 24; 1Co 15:32
18:21 [p] Ro 1:10; 1Co 4:19; Jas 4:15
18:22 [q] Ac 8:40 [r] Ac 11:19
18:23 [s] Ac 16:6 [t] Ac 14:22; 15:32, 41
18:24 [u] Ac 19:1; 1Co 1:12; 3:5, 6, 22; 4:6; 16:12; Titus 3:13
18:25 [v] Ro 12:11 [w] Ac 19:3

[a] 25 Or *with fervor in the Spirit*

18:18 *Priscilla and Aquila.* Writers normally named husbands before wives unless the wives held higher status. *had his hair cut off.* One normally shaved the head at the completion of a vow, in Jerusalem, but Paul may have shaved before a long vow or perhaps many Diaspora Jews undertook vows without requiring completion in Jerusalem. *Cenchreae.* Corinth had major ports on both sides of the Isthmus of Corinth; Cenchreae was the port on the Aegean side, from which Paul could sail east (cf. note on Ro 16:1).
18:19 *Ephesus.* Asia Minor's most prominent city, with 100,000 or even 200,000 residents. The governor of the Roman province of Asia resided there, and it had a class of newly rich people as well as a Jewish community.
18:21 *I will come back if it is God's will.* Both Jews and (more often) Gentiles often said, "If it is God's will ..." Sometimes Gentiles used the plural (e.g., "if the gods are favorable" or "if the gods will"), but Stoics and others often spoke in this way of "God," usually referring to Fate or the chief deity Zeus.
18:22 *went up to Jerusalem.* The Greek text does not specify "to Jerusalem" but most scholars believe it is strongly implied, given Luke's usual use of "went up." *Antioch.* Over 200 miles (320 kilometers) north of Caesarea, making for an unusually long walk to Antioch unless Paul had other business in Judea.
18:24 *Alexandria.* The chief city of the eastern Mediterranean and the second-largest city in the Roman Empire. Greeks and Macedonians had founded the city in Egypt's delta region, and the dominant Greeks, perhaps a third of the city, referred to their city as "Alexandria *near* Egypt," emphasizing its Greek heritage. Alexandria may have been roughly one-third Jewish. The Jewish elite there had a Hellenistic education, with exposure to rhetoric and philosophy, but Jews, like local Egyptians, were mostly shut out of Alexandrian citizenship.
18:26 *Priscilla and Aquila.* See note on v. 18. Luke uses informal forms of names such as Priscilla and (earlier in Acts) Silas; Paul's letters employ the formal forms Prisca and

invited him to their home and explained
to him the way of God more adequately.
27When Apollos wanted to go to Achaia,[x]
the brothers and sisters[y] encouraged him
and wrote to the disciples there to welcome
him. When he arrived, he was a great help
to those who by grace had believed. 28For
he vigorously refuted his Jewish opponents
in public debate, proving from the Scriptures[z] that Jesus was the Messiah.[a]

Paul in Ephesus

19 While Apollos was at Corinth,[b] Paul
took the road through the interior
and arrived at Ephesus.[c] There he found
some disciples 2and asked them, "Did
you receive the Holy Spirit when[*a*] you believed?"
They answered, "No, we have not even
heard that there is a Holy Spirit."
3So Paul asked, "Then what baptism did
you receive?"
"John's baptism," they replied.
4Paul said, "John's baptism was a baptism of repentance. He told the people to
believe in the one coming after him, that
is, in Jesus."[d] 5On hearing this, they were
baptized in the name of the Lord Jesus.
6When Paul placed his hands on them,[e]
the Holy Spirit came on them,[f] and they
spoke in tongues[*b*g] and prophesied. 7There
were about twelve men in all.
8Paul entered the synagogue[h] and spoke
boldly there for three months, arguing persuasively about the kingdom of God.[i] 9But
some of them[j] became obstinate; they refused to believe and publicly maligned the
Way.[k] So Paul left them. He took the disciples[l] with him and had discussions daily
in the lecture hall of Tyrannus. 10This went
on for two years,[m] so that all the Jews and
Greeks who lived in the province of Asia[n]
heard the word of the Lord.
11God did extraordinary miracles[o]
through Paul, 12so that even handkerchiefs and aprons that had touched him
were taken to the sick, and their illnesses
were cured[p] and the evil spirits left them.
13Some Jews who went around driving
out evil spirits[q] tried to invoke the name
of the Lord Jesus over those who were demon-possessed. They would say, "In the
name of the Jesus[r] whom Paul preaches, I command you to come out." 14Sev-
en sons of Sceva, a Jewish chief priest,
were doing this. 15One day the evil spirit
answered them, "Jesus I know, and Paul
I know about, but who are you?" 16Then
the man who had the evil spirit jumped on
them and overpowered them all. He gave
them such a beating that they ran out of
the house naked and bleeding.
17When this became known to the
Jews and Greeks living in Ephesus,[s] they
were all seized with fear,[t] and the name
of the Lord Jesus was held in high honor.
18Many of those who believed now came
and openly confessed what they had done.

18:27 [x] ver 12 [y] ver 18 **18:28** [z] Ac 17:2 [a] ver 5; Ac 9:22 **19:1** [b] Ac 18:1 [c] Ac 18:19 **19:4** [d] Jn 1:7; Ac 13:24,25 **19:6** [e] Ac 6:6; 8:17 [f] Ac 2:4 [g] Mk 16:17; Ac 10:46 **19:8** [h] Ac 9:20 [i] Ac 1:3; 28:23

19:9 [j] Ac 14:4 [k] ver 23; Ac 9:2 [l] ver 30; Ac 11:26 **19:10** [m] Ac 20:31 [n] ver 22,26,27 **19:11** [o] Ac 8:13 **19:12** [p] Ac 5:15 **19:13** [q] Mt 12:27 [r] Mk 9:38 **19:17** [s] Ac 18:19 [t] Ac 5:5,11

[*a*] 2 Or *after* [*b*] 6 Or *other languages*

Silvanus. *explained to him the way of God more adequately.* By ancient Mediterranean standards, Priscilla's involvement in teaching a man here is unusual, although the less public setting may have mitigated many concerns.

18:27 *Achaia.* Corinth was the capital of the Roman province of Achaia. *wrote to the disciples there to welcome him.* Letters of recommendation were very common and could be carried by the recommendee (see note on 9:2).

18:28 *vigorously refuted his Jewish opponents in public debate.* Corinth highly valued public speaking and displays of knowledge, reinforcing the humiliation of those refuted.

19:2 *have not even heard that there is a Holy Spirit.* Jewish tradition often spoke about the Holy Spirit; they are not claiming that they have not heard the expression, but that they have not heard that the Spirit was already available.

19:5 *baptized in the name of the Lord Jesus.* Besides the nearby Selinus River, Ephesus had numerous fountains and public baths.

19:9 *lecture hall of Tyrannus.* While "Tyrannus" may be a nickname ("tyrant," perhaps for a demanding teacher or landlord), it is a name that appears commonly in Ephesian inscriptions. Possibly Tyrannus—if he was the hall's usual lecturer and not its landlord—lectured in the mornings (lectures often finished by 11:00 a.m.) and Paul rented it for use in the afternoons, perhaps starting during the usual two-hour midday siesta period. From a Greco-Roman perspective, Paul adopts here the role of a philosophic-type sage.

19:10 *all the Jews and Greeks … in the province.* Word spread quickly in and from major urban centers such as Ephesus.

19:12 *handkerchiefs and aprons … cured.* Cf. note on 5:15. Although the matter is debated, many commentators see the handkerchiefs as Paul's sweat cloths wrapped around the head and the aprons as work aprons (cf. 20:34).

19:13 *tried to invoke the name of the Lord Jesus.* Practitioners of magic believed they could control spirits by invoking their names, and they sometimes summoned more powerful spirits to deal with lesser ones. Jewish practitioners of magic were often particularly respected because of their alleged possession of the supreme god's secret name (the name Yahweh was not normally pronounced).

19:14 *Sceva, a Jewish chief priest.* Outsiders would suppose that a chief priest would have access to the sacred name (see note on v. 13), although many scholars think that Sceva's claim is spurious. Some Diaspora Jews had Latin names; Sceva is a Latin name.

19:16 *such a beating that they ran out of the house naked and bleeding.* In some cases of spirit-possession reported in antiquity and in modern anthropological literature, the possessed are violent toward themselves or others, sometimes with what observers regard as superhuman strength.

19:18 *confessed what they had done.* It is possible to translate this phrase "divulging [secret] spells"; such spells were believed effective only if kept secret. (Nevertheless, the phrase could also simply refer to confessing their activities.)

[19]A number who had practiced sorcery
brought their scrolls together and burned
them publicly. When they calculated the
value of the scrolls, the total came to fifty thousand drachmas.[a] [20]In this way the
word of the Lord spread widely and grew
in power.[u]

[21]After all this had happened, Paul
decided[b] to go to Jerusalem,[v] passing
through Macedonia[w] and Achaia.[x] "After
I have been there," he said, "I must visit
Rome also."[y] [22]He sent two of his helpers,[z]
Timothy[a] and Erastus,[b] to Macedonia,
while he stayed in the province of Asia[c]
a little longer.

19:20 [u]Ac 6:7; 12:24 **19:21** [v]Ac 20:16, 22; Ro 15:25 [w]Ac 16:9 [x]Ac 18:12 [y]Ro 15:24, 28 **19:22** [z]Ac 13:5 [a]Ac 16:1 [b]Ro 16:23; 2Ti 4:20 [c]ver 10, 26, 27 **19:23** [d]Ac 9:2 **19:25** [e]Ac 16:16, 19, 20

The Riot in Ephesus

[23]About that time there arose a great
disturbance about the Way.[d] [24]A silversmith named Demetrius, who made silver shrines of Artemis, brought in a lot
of business for the craftsmen there. [25]He
called them together, along with the workers in related trades, and said: "You know,
my friends, that we receive a good income
from this business.[e] [26]And you see and
hear how this fellow Paul has convinced
and led astray large numbers of people

[a] *19* A drachma was a silver coin worth about a day's wages. [b] *21* Or *decided in the Spirit*

19:19 *scrolls.* May here refer to magical papyri. Ephesus was apparently a center of magic; many scholars argue that some magical terms used in smaller charms worn in amulets were called "Ephesian writings." People in the ancient world often burned books to destroy their messages.
19:21 Cf. Lk 9:51; Ro 15:24–26.
19:22 *Erastus.* See note on Ro 16:23 (if the same Erastus is in view).
19:23–41 Rome was concerned above all with order. After anti-Jewish riots, Jewish leaders were keen to prove that their enemies rather than they themselves started the riots. Here, and often, Luke emphasizes that not Paul but his enemies started riots against him (cf. 24:5).
19:24 *silver shrines of Artemis.* An entire month each year, the alleged month of the goddess's birth, was dedicated to Artemis. Many workers in Ephesus made souvenir miniature shrines of Artemis. Most such shrines were of terra cotta; silver shrines were thus particularly expensive and the job accordingly more prestigious. Many other gold and silver workers made statuettes of Artemis weighing between three and seven pounds (between 1.4 and 3.2 kilograms).
19:25 *workers in related trades.* Workers often united to form trade guilds; metalworkers were common, and many silversmiths in Ephesus made statuettes of Artemis. They would gather for guild meetings, but Demetrius could call a special meeting; members of the same guild lived in the same area, and in Ephesus the silversmiths' shops apparently lay on the main street that connected the theater (v. 29) to the harbor. As often in antiquity, so in Ephesus commerce and religion were closely intertwined. Temples served as banks, and the Artemis temple was one of the most famous in antiquity; evidence suggests that it also owned some 70,000 acres (28,350 hectares) of farmland.
19:26 *gods made by human hands are no gods at all.* Demetrius undoubtedly echoes Paul's own echoes of the prophets (see Isa 37:19; Jer 2:11; 16:20). Nevertheless,

Aerial view of the theater at Ephesus and the commercial agora area.

Barry Beitzel/www.BiblePlaces.com

here in Ephesus[f] and in practically the
whole province of Asia. He says that gods
made by human hands are no gods at all.[g]
27There is danger not only that our trade
will lose its good name, but also that the
temple of the great goddess Artemis will
be discredited; and the goddess herself,
who is worshiped throughout the province
of Asia and the world, will be robbed of
her divine majesty."
28When they heard this, they were furious and began shouting: "Great is Artemis of the Ephesians!"[h] 29Soon the whole
city was in an uproar. The people seized
Gaius[i] and Aristarchus,[j] Paul's traveling
companions from Macedonia,[k] and all
of them rushed into the theater together.
30Paul wanted to appear before the crowd,
but the disciples would not let him. 31Even
some of the officials of the province,
friends of Paul, sent him a message begging him not to venture into the theater.
32The assembly was in confusion: Some
were shouting one thing, some another.[l]
Most of the people did not even know
why they were there. 33The Jews in the
crowd pushed Alexander to the front, and
they shouted instructions to him. He motioned[m] for silence in order to make a defense before the people. 34But when they
realized he was a Jew, they all shouted in
unison for about two hours: "Great is Artemis of the Ephesians!"
35The city clerk quieted the crowd and
said: "Fellow Ephesians,[n] doesn't all the
world know that the city of Ephesus is
the guardian of the temple of the great
Artemis and of her image, which fell from
heaven? 36Therefore, since these facts are
undeniable, you ought to calm down and

19:26 [f] Ac 18:19 [g] Dt 4:28; Ps 115:4; Isa 44:10-20; Jer 10:3-5; Ac 17:29; 1Co 8:4; Rev 9:20 **19:28** [h] Ac 18:19 **19:29** [i] Ac 20:4; Ro 16:23; 1Co 1:14 [j] Ac 20:4; 27:2; Col 4:10; Phm 24 [k] Ac 16:9 **19:32** [l] Ac 21:34 **19:33** [m] Ac 12:17 **19:35** [n] Ac 18:19

Demetrius exaggerates Paul's influence; orators in general, but demagogues in particular, used hyperbole to make sweeping denunciations and stir hearers to anger, as here.

19:27 *the temple of the great goddess Artemis.* Ranked among the seven wonders of the ancient world, Artemis's temple was 425 feet by 230 feet (130 meters by 70 meters) — about four times as large as Athens' famous temple for Athena. The temple was just 1.5 miles (2.4 kilometers) northeast of the city, and public processions went there one or two times each month. *discredited.* Despite strong local pride in the Artemis cult, the issue of Artemis's temple being discredited was a potentially live one at this time. A mere decade before Paul's ministry in Ephesus, a scandal involving sacred deposits in the temple's treasury erupted; some of the funds entered private hands. The spread of monotheism genuinely could have economic implications for other cults; in the early second century AD, the governor of Bithynia complained that, through local Christian influence, temples and sacrifices were being neglected. *worshiped throughout ... the world.* That the Ephesian version of Artemis was worshiped throughout the world reflects her renown; cult centers for the Ephesian Artemis have been identified in more than 30 ancient cities.

19:28 *began shouting.* Local loyalty to Artemis was intense; when, e.g., some Sardians in an earlier period allegedly abused worshipers of Artemis, 45 of them were executed. Mobs could chant together, and Ephesians employed acclamations such as the one recorded here.

19:29 *rushed into the theater together.* The theater could hold about 20,000 people and was easily visible even from the harbor; many cultic statues were there. Some information supports the idea that the silversmiths worked near the open-air theater. More importantly, the theater was near the main market, which would be full of people. Many urban riots occurred during this era in Roman Asia. Citizen assemblies were held regularly in the theater, and special emergency assemblies were sometimes called at irregular times.

19:31 *officials of the province.* Only the most elite persons in the Roman province of Asia could become Asiarchs. Several Asiarchs filled the office at a time, but each only for a year, though they kept the title and could be chosen for the office multiple times. Over half of known Asiarchs were somehow associated with Ephesus, the province's most prominent city. Some members of this same elite group also purchased elite priestly roles (the priesthoods were also annual offices), some serving in the imperial cult. Their objective was to achieve honor, not specific commitment to Paul's faith. *friends of Paul.* When applied to people of unequal status, "friends" often meant benefactors; the wealthy sometimes increased their honor by sponsoring popular arts or sages. A sage accused of opposing Artemis, however, would embarrass them. The Asiarchs would want to dissociate Paul from the charge (and perhaps themselves from Paul) as quickly as possible.

19:32 *did not even know why they were there.* Because special emergency assemblies were sometimes called at irregular times, some scholars think that many members of the crowd had wrongly assumed that this was a legal assembly (which it was not; v. 39).

19:33 *pushed Alexander to the front ... shouted instructions to him.* Many polytheists resented Jewish monotheism; Diaspora Jewish communities worked hard not to antagonize their localities, and would not want to be associated with the charges against Paul (vv. 26,37; cf. v. 9). Some cities in antiquity restricted Jewish rights, thereby requiring Jewish people to defend their rights publicly and sometimes even to appeal to Rome.

19:35 *city clerk.* In Ephesus (as opposed to some other cities), the city clerk was the highest official, who represented the city's interests with local Roman officials and announced the decisions of the citizen assembly. He is well informed about the issues behind the riot (vv. 37–38), possibly by Paul's Asiarch friends (see v. 31 and note), members of the clerk's elite social class. *doesn't all the world know ... ?* Orators often began speeches by praising distinctive characteristics of a city; the Artemis temple was renowned (see note on v. 27). *fell from heaven.* Although many other images reportedly fell from heaven, no extant ancient sources make this claim for the Artemis statue in Ephesus, which was carefully carved. Scholars have offered a range of contradictory explanations for the appendages on the front of the Artemis statue's torso, most often that they were a fertility symbol, such as breasts or sometimes bulls' testicles; ancient writers, however, regarded the Ephesian Artemis as a virgin.

19:36 *since these facts are undeniable.* The facts are hardly undeniable; the clerk might even have exaggerated deliberately (e.g., on the image having fallen from heaven) to identify with the crowd's fervor. Luke's better-informed audience surely see the claims as plainly deniable.

not do anything rash. 37You have brought
these men here, though they have neither robbed temples[o] nor blasphemed our
goddess. 38If, then, Demetrius and his fellow craftsmen have a grievance against
anybody, the courts are open and there
are proconsuls.[p] They can press charges.
39If there is anything further you want to
bring up, it must be settled in a legal assembly. 40As it is, we are in danger of being charged with rioting because of what
happened today. In that case we would
not be able to account for this commotion, since there is no reason for it." 41Af-
ter he had said this, he dismissed the assembly.

Through Macedonia and Greece

20 When the uproar had ended, Paul
sent for the disciples[q] and, after encouraging them, said goodbye and set out
for Macedonia.[r] 2He traveled through that
area, speaking many words of encouragement to the people, and finally arrived in
Greece, 3where he stayed three months.
Because some Jews had plotted against
him[s] just as he was about to sail for Syria, he decided to go back through Macedonia.[t] 4He was accompanied by Sopater
son of Pyrrhus from Berea, Aristarchus[u]
and Secundus from Thessalonica,[v] Gaius[w]
from Derbe, Timothy[x] also, and Tychicus[y]
and Trophimus[z] from the province of Asia.
5These men went on ahead and waited for
us[a] at Troas.[b] 6But we sailed from Philippi[c] after the Festival of Unleavened Bread,
and five days later joined the others at Troas,[d] where we stayed seven days.

Eutychus Raised From the Dead at Troas

7On the first day of the week[e] we came
together to break bread. Paul spoke to the
people and, because he intended to leave
the next day, kept on talking until midnight. 8There were many lamps in the
upstairs room[f] where we were meeting.
9Seated in a window was a young man
named Eutychus, who was sinking into a
deep sleep as Paul talked on and on. When
he was sound asleep, he fell to the ground
from the third story and was picked up
dead. 10Paul went down, threw himself on
the young man[g] and put his arms around
him. "Don't be alarmed," he said. "He's
alive!"[h] 11Then he went upstairs again and
broke bread[i] and ate. After talking until
daylight, he left. 12The people took the
young man home alive and were greatly
comforted.

Paul's Farewell to the Ephesian Elders

13We went on ahead to the ship and
sailed for Assos, where we were going to
take Paul aboard. He had made this ar-

19:37 [o] Ro 2:22 **19:38** [p] Ac 13:7, 8, 12 **20:1** [q] Ac 11:26 [r] Ac 16:9 **20:3** [s] ver 19; Ac 9:23, 24; 23:12, 15, 30; 25:3; 2Co 11:26 [t] Ac 16:9 **20:4** [u] Ac 19:29 [v] Ac 17:1 [w] Ac 19:29 [x] Ac 16:1 [y] Eph 6:21; Col 4:7; 2Ti 4:12; Titus 3:12 [z] Ac 21:29; 2Ti 4:20 **20:5** [a] Ac 16:10 [b] Ac 16:8 **20:6** [c] Ac 16:12 [d] Ac 16:8 **20:7** [e] 1Co 16:2; Rev 1:10 **20:8** [f] Ac 1:13 **20:10** [g] 1Ki 17:21; 2Ki 4:34 [h] Mt 9:23, 24 **20:11** [i] ver 7

19:37 *neither robbed temples nor blasphemed our goddess.* Ancients deemed temple robbery one of the most impious acts; they expected deities to avenge this act but they executed the offenders when possible. Jewish apologists disclaimed blaspheming deities, though many Jewish sources ridiculed idols.
19:38 *the courts are open.* Courts normally closed during festivals but were open on the day that the clerk is speaking. Because Asia's proconsul kept a circuit through nine of the province's chief cities, he was not always available in Ephesus, but apparently was present. *there are proconsuls.* Scholars debate whether "proconsuls" is plural as a general reference or because two or three administrators were filling the role until the new proconsul came (if the scene occurred in AD 54).
19:40 *in danger of being charged with rioting.* Ephesus was a "free city," meaning, among other things, that its citizen assembly was granted a measure of autonomy from Roman oversight. Although it never ultimately happened to Ephesus, some cities lost such privileges because of unrest. Rome had little tolerance for riots.
20:1—21:40 Other ancient sources abundantly confirm the travel details in these chapters, even down to the number of days in many locations at the specified time of year. The narrative thus sounds like the work of a genuine traveling companion of Paul on this journey.
20:2 *traveled through that area.* Paul worked partly on the collection for the believers in Jerusalem at this time (Ro 15:26; 1Co 16:1–5; 2Co 8–9).
20:3 *stayed three months.* Paul may have planned his travel so as to stay with the Corinthian believers during the winter, when travel was difficult. Paul composed his letter to the believers in Rome at this time (Ro 15:26; 16:1). *just as he was about to sail for Syria.* Plots were often leaked. Paul presumably prepared to sail for Syria in order to celebrate Passover in Jerusalem; shifting to a land journey requires him to reschedule his arrival for Pentecost instead (v. 16). Journeying to Philippi (v. 6) in Macedonia on foot could take two weeks.
20:4 *He was accompanied.* Travel was safest in groups. Respected representatives from local Jewish communities would carry their communities' temple tax to Jerusalem; Paul adopts a similar approach.
20:5 *us.* See note on 16:10. In Philippi the group adds the narrator (i.e., Luke), who was last reported in Philippi (16:12,16–17).
20:6 *five days.* Prevailing winds slow their voyage to Troas (for contrast, see note on 16:11). The rest of the journey consumes roughly 30 days, so although they have missed Passover, they arrive in time for Pentecost (v. 16).
20:7 *kept on talking until midnight.* This meeting probably runs from Sunday evening through Monday morning and was planned because Paul had to leave on Monday.
20:8 *many lamps.* Such abundant lighting was unusual and facilitated the possibility of a night meeting. Possibly the heat or even odor from the lamps contributed to Eutychus seeking a window seat (v. 9).
20:9 *Seated in a window.* Glass was rare in windows. Some windows could be large, especially above the ground floor. *sinking into a deep sleep.* Teachers roundly criticized those who fell asleep during good teaching.
20:10 *threw himself on the young man.* For physical contact during some resuscitations, cf. 1Ki 17:21; 2Ki 4:34–35.
20:13 *Assos.* This city had the best harbor in its area. The road from Troas to there followed the coast and was about 38 miles (60 kilometers), probably a two-day journey on foot.

PAUL'S THIRD MISSIONARY JOURNEY

c. AD 53–57 (Ac 18:23 — 21:17)

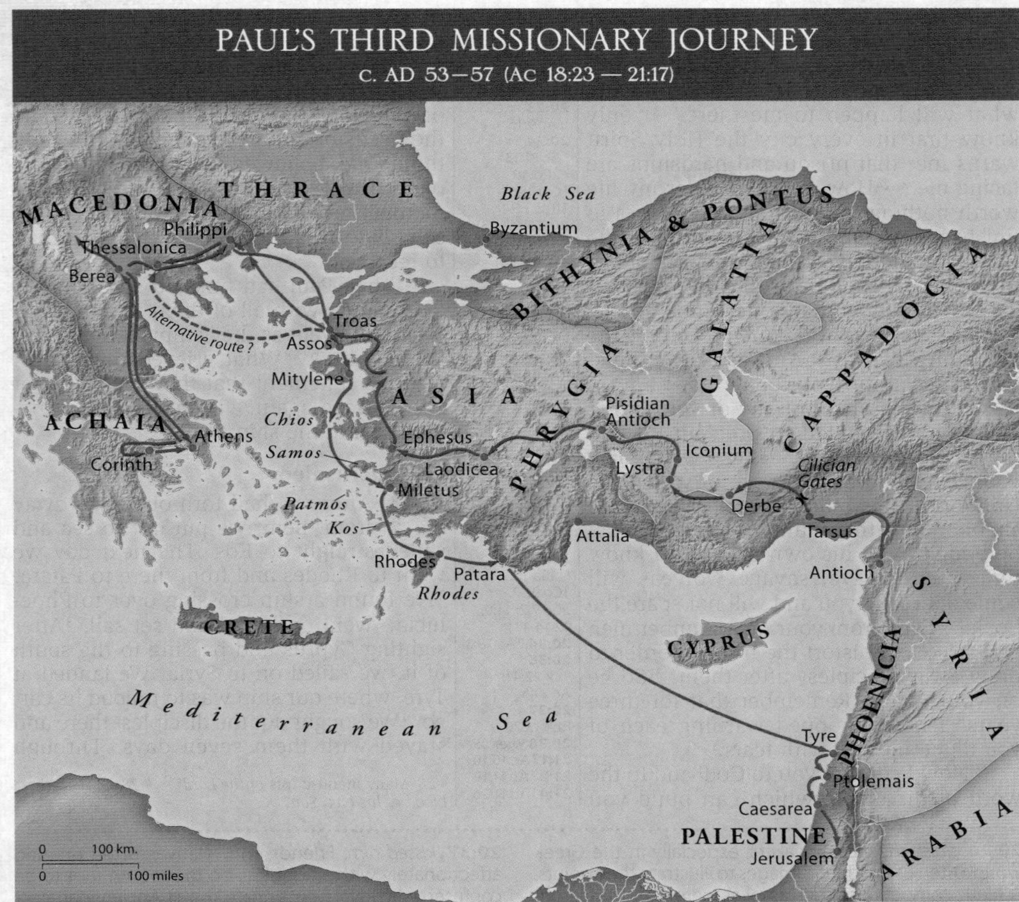

rangement because he was going there
on foot. 14When he met us at Assos, we
took him aboard and went on to Mitylene. 15The next day we set sail from there
and arrived off Chios. The day after that
we crossed over to Samos, and on the following day arrived at Miletus.[j] 16Paul had
decided to sail past Ephesus[k] to avoid
spending time in the province of Asia, for
he was in a hurry to reach Jerusalem,[l] if
possible, by the day of Pentecost.[m]
17From Miletus, Paul sent to Ephesus for
the elders[n] of the church. 18When they arrived, he said to them: "You know how
I lived the whole time I was with you,[o]
from the first day I came into the province
of Asia. 19I served the Lord with great humility and with tears and in the midst of
severe testing by the plots of my Jewish
opponents.[p] 20You know that I have not
hesitated to preach anything[q] that would
be helpful to you but have taught you publicly and from house to house. 21I have declared to both Jews[r] and Greeks that they

20:15 [j] ver 17; 2Ti 4:20
20:16 [k] Ac 18:19 [l] Ac 19:21 [m] Ac 2:1; 1Co 16:8
20:17 [n] Ac 11:30
20:18 [o] Ac 18:19-21; 19:1-41
20:19 [p] ver 3
20:20 [q] ver 27
20:21 [r] Ac 18:5

20:14 *Mitylene.* The chief city of the island of Lesbos, it had two harbors; the group would have sailed to the deeper, northern one.

20:15 Ships not planning to stop in Ephesus often sailed by the Aegean islands of Chios and Samos and then to the massive port city of Miletus, about 30 miles (48 kilometers) south of Ephesus.

20:16 *decided to sail past Ephesus ... to reach Jerusalem.* On the desire to reach Jerusalem by Pentecost, see note on v. 6. Waiting for messengers to reach Ephesus and elders to come from there would have taken at least four days. Scholars debate how Paul's avoiding Ephesus would have saved him time, but one of the likeliest reasons is that ancient obligations to visit friends would have required him to spend time with many people there. A factor not mentioned by Luke is that many considered it better for everyone if Paul stayed away (cf. 19:31,38; 21:27).

20:18–35 Farewell speeches were common and were often an occasion for sorrow (v. 38).

20:19 When speakers appealed to their sufferings on behalf of their audience, the expected response was appreciation and attention.

20:20 *taught you publicly and from house to house.* Houses belonged to the private sphere; like the most respected teachers, Paul labored in the public sphere as well as the private one.

must turn to God in repentance[s] and have
faith in our Lord Jesus.[t]
22“And now, compelled by the Spirit,
I am going to Jerusalem,[u] not knowing
what will happen to me there. 23I only
know that in every city the Holy Spirit
warns me[v] that prison and hardships are
facing me.[w] 24However, I consider my life
worth nothing to me;[x] my only aim is to
finish the race and complete the task[y] the
Lord Jesus has given me[z] — the task of testifying to the good news of God’s grace.
25“Now I know that none of you among
whom I have gone about preaching the
kingdom will ever see me again.[a] 26There-
fore, I declare to you today that I am innocent of the blood of any of you.[b] 27For
I have not hesitated to proclaim to you
the whole will of God.[c] 28Keep watch over
yourselves and all the flock of which the
Holy Spirit has made you overseers.[d] Be
shepherds of the church of God,[a] which
he bought with his own blood.[b] 29I know
that after I leave, savage wolves[e] will
come in among you and will not spare the
flock.[f] 30Even from your own number men
will arise and distort the truth in order to
draw away disciples[g] after them. 31So be
on your guard! Remember that for three
years[h] I never stopped warning each of
you night and day with tears.[i]
32“Now I commit you to God[j] and to the
word of his grace, which can build you
up and give you an inheritance[k] among all
those who are sanctified.[l] 33I have not coveted anyone’s silver or gold or clothing.[m]
34You yourselves know that these hands
of mine have supplied my own needs and
the needs of my companions.[n] 35In everything I did, I showed you that by this kind
of hard work we must help the weak, remembering the words the Lord Jesus himself said: ‘It is more blessed to give than
to receive.’ ”
36When Paul had finished speaking, he
knelt down with all of them and prayed.[o]
37They all wept as they embraced him and
kissed him.[p] 38What grieved them most
was his statement that they would never
see his face again.[q] Then they accompanied him to the ship.

On to Jerusalem

21 After we[r] had torn ourselves away
from them, we put out to sea and
sailed straight to Kos. The next day we
went to Rhodes and from there to Patara.
2We found a ship crossing over to Phoenicia,[s] went on board and set sail. 3After
sighting Cyprus and passing to the south
of it, we sailed on to Syria. We landed at
Tyre, where our ship was to unload its cargo. 4We sought out the disciples[t] there and
stayed with them seven days. Through

20:21 [s] Ac 2:38 [t] Ac 24:24; 26:18; Eph 1:15; Col 2:5; Phm 5 **20:22** [u] ver 16 **20:23** [v] Ac 21:4 [w] Ac 9:16 **20:24** [x] Ac 21:13 [y] 2Co 4:1 [z] Gal 1:1; Titus 1:3 **20:25** [a] ver 38 **20:26** [b] Ac 18:6 **20:27** [c] ver 20 **20:28** [d] 1Pe 5:2 **20:29** [e] Mt 7:15 [f] ver 28 **20:30** [g] Ac 11:26 **20:31** [h] Ac 19:10 [i] ver 19 **20:32** [j] Ac 14:23 [k] Eph 1:14; Col 1:12; 3:24; Heb 9:15; 1Pe 1:4 [l] Ac 26:18 **20:33** [m] 1Sa 12:3; 1Co 9:12; 2Co 7:2; 11:9; 12:14-17 **20:34** [n] Ac 18:3 **20:36** [o] Lk 22:41; Ac 21:5 **20:37** [p] Lk 15:20 **20:38** [q] ver 25 **21:1** [r] Ac 16:10 **21:2** [s] Ac 11:19 **21:4** [t] Ac 11:26

[a] 28 Many manuscripts *of the Lord* [b] 28 Or *with the blood of his own Son.*

20:24 *finish the race.* Speakers, especially in the Greek world, often used athletic images to illustrate their points. Athletic competitions such as races were a central feature of Greek civic life and a point of rivalry among cities, including in the significantly Hellenized culture of western Asia Minor.
20:26 *innocent of the blood.* One who does not warn those facing destruction is morally responsible for their deaths (Eze 3:18 – 20; 33:8 – 9). That Paul mentions “shepherds” in v. 28 may suggest that he goes on from Eze 33 to think of Eze 34.
20:28 *overseers.* A Greek administrative title, “overseer” also appears in the Septuagint, the pre-Christian Greek translation of the OT, and (in Hebrew form) in the Dead Sea Scrolls. *shepherds.* Ancient literature often compared leaders with shepherds, including in the OT (e.g., Isa 56:10 – 11; Jer 3:15; Eze 34:2).
20:29 *savage wolves.* The most obvious and common predators of sheep, wolves were often used to represent humans who would harm others.
20:31 *three years.* In ancient usage, “three years” can mean parts of three years (19:8 – 10). *night and day.* A familiar expression, and could mean parts of night and day.
20:32 *inheritance … sanctified.* Jewish people spoke of their inheritance in the promised future and themselves as sanctified, or consecrated, to God by his covenant. Paul uses this traditional language for Jesus’ followers.
20:33 *I have not coveted.* Because many sages were charlatans, exploiting others for profit, other sages sought to distinguish themselves from the charlatans.
20:35 *In everything I did, I showed you.* Teachers sometimes used themselves as models.
20:37 *kissed him.* Friends and relatives often greeted affectionately with a light kiss on the mouth (not to be confused with lovers’ passionate kisses). Ancient narrators could illustrate a person’s positive character by depicting how others loved the person.
20:38 *accompanied him to the ship.* As is the case in many cultures today, friends saw off those who were leaving, e.g., by going with them to their ship.
21:1 *Kos … Rhodes.* Both islands on the normal route. The city of Rhodes, the capital of the island Rhodes on its northeast coast, had an excellent harbor that faced Patara. *Patara.* One of southern Asia Minor’s leading ports for the Alexandrian grain trade; because of Mediterranean wind conditions, ships sailed north from Alexandria to Asia Minor before turning westward to Rome (cf. 27:5).
21:2 *found a ship.* Many ships moved in and out of Patara (v. 1). Because grain ships typically kept close to the coast, stopping often, the group transfers to a ship navigating the open waters directly to Tyre in Phoenicia, about 350 miles (560 kilometers), which may have taken four or five days.
21:3 Both Phoenicia and Judea belonged to the Roman province of Syria. *unload its cargo.* Unlike this ship (vv. 4 – 6), the largest ships might require a month to unload. Hospitality (v. 4) rather than haste moved them to wait for the ship to finish; it would take only two days to walk from Tyre to Ptolemais (v. 7).
21:4 *stayed with them seven days.* In antiquity people considered it an honor to extend hospitality to traveling members of their social group. *Through the Spirit.* Both the OT and early Jewish writers often associated God’s Spirit with prophecy, which is probably in view here

the Spirit[u] they urged Paul not to go on to Jerusalem. 5When it was time to leave, we left and continued on our way. All of them, including wives and children, accompanied us out of the city, and there on the beach we knelt to pray.[v] 6After saying goodbye to each other, we went aboard the ship, and they returned home.

7We continued our voyage from Tyre[w] and landed at Ptolemais, where we greeted the brothers and sisters[x] and stayed with them for a day. 8Leaving the next day, we reached Caesarea[y] and stayed at the house of Philip[z] the evangelist,[a] one of the Seven. 9He had four unmarried daughters who prophesied.[b]

10After we had been there a number of days, a prophet named Agabus[c] came down from Judea. 11Coming over to us, he took Paul's belt, tied his own hands and feet with it and said, "The Holy Spirit says, 'In this way the Jewish leaders in Jerusalem will bind[d] the owner of this belt and will hand him over to the Gentiles.' "[e]

12When we heard this, we and the people there pleaded with Paul not to go up to Jerusalem. 13Then Paul answered, "Why are you weeping and breaking my heart? I am ready not only to be bound, but also to die[f] in Jerusalem for the name of the Lord Jesus."[g] 14When he would not be dissuaded, we gave up and said, "The Lord's will be done."

15After this, we started on our way up to Jerusalem. 16Some of the disciples from Caesarea[h] accompanied us and brought us to the home of Mnason, where we were to stay. He was a man from Cyprus[i] and one of the early disciples.

Paul's Arrival at Jerusalem

17When we arrived at Jerusalem, the brothers and sisters received us warmly.[j] 18The next day Paul and the rest of us went to see James,[k] and all the elders[l] were present. 19Paul greeted them and reported in detail what God had done among the Gentiles[m] through his ministry.[n]

20When they heard this, they praised God. Then they said to Paul: "You see, brother, how many thousands of Jews have believed, and all of them are zealous[o] for the law.[p] 21They have been informed that you teach all the Jews who live among the Gentiles to turn away from Moses,[q] telling them not to circumcise their children[r] or live according to our customs.[s] 22What shall we do? They will certainly hear that you have come, 23so do what we tell you. There are four men with us who have made a vow.[t] 24Take these men, join in their purification rites[u] and

21:4 [u] ver 11; Ac 20:23 **21:5** [v] Ac 20:36 **21:7** [w] Ac 12:20 [x] Ac 1:16 **21:8** [y] Ac 8:40 [z] Ac 6:5; 8:5-40 [a] Eph 4:11; 2Ti 4:5 **21:9** [b] Lk 2:36; Ac 2:17 **21:10** [c] Ac 11:28 **21:11** [d] ver 33 [e] 1Ki 22:11 **21:13** [f] Ac 20:24 [g] Ac 9:16

21:16 [h] Ac 8:40 [i] ver 3,4 **21:17** [j] Ac 15:4 **21:18** [k] Ac 15:13 [l] Ac 11:30 **21:19** [m] Ac 14:27 [n] Ac 1:17 **21:20** [o] Ac 22:3; Ro 10:2; Gal 1:14 [p] Ac 15:1,5 **21:21** [q] ver 28 [r] Ac 15:19-21; 1Co 7:18,19 [s] Ac 6:14 **21:23** [t] Ac 18:18 **21:24** [u] ver 26; Ac 24:18

---

and in 20:23; but prophetic knowledge was incomplete (2Ki 2:3,5,16; 1Co 13:9), and Paul had a fuller picture of God's leading for him (vv. 13 – 14; 20:22; cf. 2Ki 2:18).

21:5 *on the beach we knelt to pray.* Tyre had famous sandy beaches.

21:7 *Tyre ... Ptolemais.* About 30 miles (48 kilometers) separated the two cities. *greeted ... and stayed with them.* Mediterranean culture highly valued greetings and hospitality (cf. v. 4).

21:8 *Caesarea.* Nearly 40 miles (65 kilometers) from Ptolemais. On Caesarea, including its mixed population, see the article "Caesarea and Its Soldiers," p. 1892.

21:9 *four unmarried daughters.* Philip's daughters being unmarried helps explain why they are at home. Given the usual young age of marriage for women in Mediterranean antiquity, the Greek term (normally translated "virgin") probably also indicates that they are in their teens or younger. *who prophesied.* Many ancient men had prejudice against the wisdom of women and children, although they made exceptions for inspired speech. These young women who regularly prophesied illustrate 2:17 – 18.

21:10 *prophet.* Most Jewish leaders attributed the role of prophets especially to the past; their frequency in early Christianity (e.g., 11:27 – 28) reflects a distinctive ethos (cf. 2:17 – 18). *came down from Judea.* Judea, here, is meant in the narrowest sense; in the Roman administrative sense, Caesarea remained in Judea. One "went down" because Jerusalem was in the hill country and Caesarea on the coast.

21:11 OT prophets often communicated in symbolic actions such as this (e.g., Jer 13:1 – 11); their language was, as here, sometimes more evocative than precise (e.g., Isa 37:29, 36; Jer 4:23 – 27; 46:19 – 20, 25 – 26). *belt.* A cloth that some people wrapped multiple times around their waist; its inside fold could be used as a pocket.

21:12 *pleaded with Paul not to go up.* Prophecies were sometimes conditional warnings that could be evaded (as in Jer 18:7 – 8), and the prophecy's hearers here seem to have understood this prophecy accordingly.

21:15 *started ... up to Jerusalem.* Walking from Caesarea to Jerusalem at a normal pace would require two or three days.

21:16 *brought us to the home of Mnason.* The hospitality of the mixed church of Caesarea, and the reception of Jerusalem believers, for this largely Gentile delegation underlines the ideal of unity; but cf. also (by contrast) vv. 21 – 22. *Cyprus.* An island with a large Jewish population (see 4:36; 11:19); Mnason seems to be a Hellenist (see note on 6:1). Providing lodging for the Gentiles is particularly significant (cf. 10:28).

21:20 *thousands.* Lit. "tens of thousands"; although this might be a small portion of Judea's population (sometimes estimated at half a million), it remains remarkable for a specific movement. Josephus, never known to underestimate numbers, spoke of only 6,000 Pharisees and fewer Essenes. *zealous for the law.* The brief reign of Agrippa I (AD 41 – 44) fanned the flames of Judean nationalism, and many of the believers had been shaped by the political values that surrounded them.

21:21 *you teach all the Jews ... to turn away from Moses.* Even the most tolerant of Judeans normally treated harshly what they deemed as apostasy — which included leading people away from practice of the law. Views of appropriate interpretation of the law varied in the Diaspora, though most Jews supported continuing the practice of Jewish distinctives. Rumor and slander were widespread in antiquity and complicated to counter (cf. Ro 3:8).

21:24 *join in their purification rites and pay their expenses.* Judeans deemed pious those who sponsored Nazirites. By this period, Jewish people expected such vows to

pay their expenses, so that they can have
their heads shaved.[v] Then everyone will
know there is no truth in these reports
about you, but that you yourself are living in obedience to the law. 25 As for the
Gentile believers, we have written to them
our decision that they should abstain from
food sacrificed to idols, from blood, from
the meat of strangled animals and from
sexual immorality."[w]
26 The next day Paul took the men and
purified himself along with them. Then he
went to the temple to give notice of the
date when the days of purification would
end and the offering would be made for
each of them.[x]

Paul Arrested

27 When the seven days were nearly
over, some Jews from the province of Asia
saw Paul at the temple. They stirred up the
whole crowd and seized him,[y] 28 shouting,
"Fellow Israelites, help us! This is the man
who teaches everyone everywhere against
our people and our law and this place.
And besides, he has brought Greeks into
the temple and defiled this holy place."[z]
29 (They had previously seen Trophimus[a]
the Ephesian[b] in the city with Paul and
assumed that Paul had brought him into
the temple.)
30 The whole city was aroused, and the
people came running from all directions.
Seizing Paul,[c] they dragged him[d] from the
temple, and immediately the gates were
shut. 31 While they were trying to kill him,
news reached the commander of the Roman troops that the whole city of Jerusalem was in an uproar. 32 He at once took
some officers and soldiers and ran down
to the crowd. When the rioters saw the
commander and his soldiers, they stopped
beating Paul.[e]
33 The commander came up and arrested him and ordered him to be bound[f]
with two[g] chains.[h] Then he asked who he
was and what he had done. 34 Some in the
crowd shouted one thing and some another,[i] and since the commander could not
get at the truth because of the uproar, he
ordered that Paul be taken into the barracks.[j] 35 When Paul reached the steps,[k] the
violence of the mob was so great he had
to be carried by the soldiers. 36 The crowd
that followed kept shouting, "Get rid of
him!"[l]

21:24 [v] Ac 18:18
21:25 [w] Ac 15:20, 29
21:26 [x] Nu 6:13-20; Ac 24:18
21:27 [y] Ac 24:18; 26:21
21:28 [z] Mt 24:15; Ac 24:5, 6
21:29 [a] Ac 20:4
[b] Ac 18:19
21:30 [c] Ac 26:21 [d] Ac 16:19
21:32 [e] Ac 23:27
21:33 [f] ver 11 [g] Ac 12:6 [h] Ac 20:23; Eph 6:20; 2Ti 2:9
21:34 [i] Ac 19:32 [j] ver 37; Ac 23:10, 16, 32
21:35 [k] ver 40
21:36 [l] Lk 23:18; Jn 19:15; Ac 22:22

cover at least 30 days (but see v. 27). Paul accompanies them but Luke does not specify that Paul himself is undertaking a vow at this time (cf. 18:18).

21:27 *seven days.* Nazirites made impure by contact with corpses offered sacrifices on the seventh day (Nu 6:9–12). Scripture did not specify a minimum length for vows, though Jewish tradition in this period normally required at least 30 days. *province of Asia.* Ephesus was the chief city of the Roman province of Asia and some members of the synagogue there had reason to dislike Paul (19:9,33–34). Larger riots occurred in the temple on a number of occasions and sometimes led to massacres or to thousands being trampled.

21:28 *brought Greeks into the temple.* The OT temple divided the Most Holy Place from the priestly sanctuary, and both from the outer court, but did not segregate Gentiles from Jews in the outer court. Herod's temple, however, divided the outer court into three sections for purity considerations: the court of Israel (which only Jewish men could enter), the court of women outside it (which all Jews could enter), and beyond that the only court where Gentiles could enter. Signs at the entrances to the court of women warned that any Gentiles who entered would be killed; this punishment was approved by Rome.

21:29 *seen Trophimus the Ephesian.* Jewish critics from the Ephesus area (v. 27) would recognize Trophimus. They are mistaken, however, in thinking that Paul brought him into the temple.

21:30 *whole city was aroused.* There is no doubt that a claim that someone desecrated the temple could provoke a riot; it had happened on other occasions, involving thousands of people. *dragged him from the temple.* Bloodshed in a temple could desecrate it, so Paul's assailants remove him from the inner court into the large outer area beyond which Gentiles, who were usually impure, could not pass. *gates were shut.* The Levites who guarded the temple may have closed the gates to the inner courts to keep out other intruders or to secure the area from bloodshed, or may have closed all gates to prevent escape by intruders. Most of the inner gates had two doors, nearly 50 feet (nearly 15 meters) high and over 20 feet (over 6 meters) wide.

21:31 *news reached the commander of the Roman troops.* Four cohorts, probably with between 480 and 600 soldiers each, were stationed in Caesarea, Rome's capital for Judea. One such cohort, however, was stationed in Jerusalem's Antonia Fortress, on the north side of the temple mount adjoining the court of the Gentiles. Guards stationed on its towers quickly noticed unrest, requiring the commander to intervene quickly. The commander here means a Roman tribune, commander of the cohort. The soldiers rushed down the stairs from the fortress into the temple's outer court; Luke correctly depicts the temple's topography.

21:33 *bound with two chains.* A person bound in this way would have each hand chained to a soldier, one on either side; this was primarily to secure the prisoner against opportunity to escape, but chains were also considered humiliating.

21:34 *Some … shouted one thing and some another.* Mobs often acted without accurate information (cf. 19:32). *the barracks.* The Antonia Fortress. It included some lavish facilities, including baths.

21:35 *reached the steps.* Wide steps led from the tall Antonia Fortress down to the outer court of the temple.

21:36 *Get rid of him!* Ancient historians and biographers often linked characters by noting parallels between them; cf. here Lk 23:18 (much closer in Greek than in the NIV). Other parallels will follow (cf. Paul's hearings before two governors and a Herodian prince [Ac 24–26] with Jesus' two hearings before Pilate and one before Herod Antipas in Luke's Gospel [Lk 23:1–25]).

Paul Speaks to the Crowd

22:3-16pp — Ac 9:1-22; 26:9-18

37 As the soldiers were about to take
Paul into the barracks,[m] he asked the commander, "May I say something to you?"
"Do you speak Greek?" he replied.
38 "Aren't you the Egyptian who started a
revolt and led four thousand terrorists out
into the wilderness[n] some time ago?"[o]
39 Paul answered, "I am a Jew, from Tarsus[p] in Cilicia,[q] a citizen of no ordinary
city. Please let me speak to the people."
40 After receiving the commander's permission, Paul stood on the steps and motioned[r] to the crowd. When they were all
22 silent, he said to them in Aramaic[a]:[s]
1 "Brothers and fathers,[t] listen now
to my defense."
2 When they heard him speak to them in
Aramaic,[u] they became very quiet.
Then Paul said: 3 "I am a Jew,[v] born in
Tarsus[w] of Cilicia, but brought up in this
city. I studied under[x] Gamaliel[y] and was
thoroughly trained in the law of our ancestors.[z] I was just as zealous[a] for God as
any of you are today. 4 I persecuted[b] the
followers of this Way to their death, arresting both men and women and throwing
them into prison,[c] 5 as the high priest and
all the Council[d] can themselves testify. I
even obtained letters from them to their
associates[e] in Damascus,[f] and went there
to bring these people as prisoners to Jerusalem to be punished.
6 "About noon as I came near Damascus, suddenly a bright light from heaven
flashed around me.[g] 7 I fell to the ground
and heard a voice say to me, 'Saul! Saul!
Why do you persecute me?'
8 "'Who are you, Lord?' I asked.
"'I am Jesus of Nazareth, whom you are
persecuting,' he replied. 9 My companions
saw the light,[h] but they did not understand
the voice[i] of him who was speaking to me.
10 "'What shall I do, Lord?' I asked.
"'Get up,' the Lord said, 'and go into
Damascus. There you will be told all that

21:37 [m] ver 34 **21:38** [n] Mt 24:26 [o] Ac 5:36 **21:39** [p] Ac 9:11 [q] Ac 22:3 **21:40** [r] Ac 12:17 [s] Jn 5:2 **22:1** [t] Ac 7:2 **22:2** [u] Ac 21:40 **22:3** [v] Ac 21:39 [w] Ac 9:11 [x] Lk 10:39 [y] Ac 5:34 [z] Ac 26:5 [a] Ac 21:20 **22:4** [b] Ac 8:3 [c] ver 19,20 **22:5** [d] Lk 22:66 [e] Ac 13:26 [f] Ac 9:2 **22:6** [g] Ac 9:3 **22:9** [h] Ac 26:13 [i] Ac 9:7

[a] 40 Or possibly *Hebrew*; also in 22:2

21:37 *Do you speak Greek?* Greek was the trade language of the eastern Mediterranean world, including for Egyptian Jews (v. 38). Perhaps the tribune is surprised because he expects a terrorist to prefer Aramaic, the language of the Judean countryside, or perhaps the issue is the quality of Paul's Greek and lack of accent. (People from the northern Mediterranean thought that Egyptians had distinctive accents.) The tribune himself may be Greek (see note on 23:26).

21:38 *the Egyptian who … led four thousand terrorists out into the wilderness.* Many Jewish people hoped for a new exodus in the wilderness, but it was also the only relatively safe place to mobilize without expediting Roman intervention. One of the various prophetic figures who mobilized people in this period was an Egyptian Jew; Josephus, who is known to exaggerate numbers, claimed that he had 30,000 followers. Felix (23:24) intervened militarily, but the Egyptian prophet escaped, and catching him would certainly advance the tribune's career. *terrorists.* Lit. the *sicarii*, some of whom had been assassinating aristocrats in the temple, while others wreaked havoc in rural areas.

21:39 *Tarsus … no ordinary city.* Civic competition and pride characterized much of the eastern Roman Empire. Whereas Greeks and Romans often viewed negatively contemporary Egyptians (v. 38), whom Roman rule had subjugated harshly, Tarsus was a respected Hellenistic city in Roman Asia (see the article "Tarsus," p. 1888). *citizen.* Most Diaspora Jews were considered resident aliens in the cities where they lived, but a minority did become local citizens. Such local citizenship was more common for the more elite families in the Jewish communities, of which Paul's was likely one (see notes on 16:37; 22:3); in this period the privilege was compatible with Roman citizenship.

21:40 Assured that the crowd's outcries about Paul are a case of mistaken identity and that Paul is a person from a respectable class, the tribune permits Paul to quiet the crowd, as outstanding speakers were sometimes able to do (cf. 19:35). *motioned to the crowd.* Ancient rhetoric had special gestures to invite silence or to signal that a speech was beginning. *said to them in Aramaic.* Aramaic had remained the dominant language of the countryside since the time of the Persian Empire; Judean nationalists would favor this language, but Paul's Asian Jewish accusers (v. 27) probably understood little or nothing that he said.

22:2 *Aramaic.* See note on 21:40.

22:3 *born in Tarsus … but brought up in this city.* Like Alexandria and Athens, Tarsus was a leading university center in antiquity; many Tarsians themselves, however, pursued advanced education elsewhere. Jerusalem would have been the ancient center for the study of Torah; Paul's letters reveal particular expertise in Scripture, especially in the Septuagint (the pre-Christian Greek translation of the OT), and such instruction was available in Gamaliel's household in Jerusalem. *brought up.* In light of ancient usage, this probably suggests that Paul spent much of his youth in Jerusalem, though his study with Gamaliel I was at a more advanced level. *studied under.* Lit. "sat at his feet," which was considered the appropriate posture for a disciple. *Gamaliel.* One of the minority of Pharisees who belonged to Jerusalem's elite; he commanded wide respect (see note on 5:34). *zealous for God.* At least by the time of the Judean revolt in AD 66, some Jewish nationalists called themselves "zealous," and hence Zealots; their models for zeal may have included Phinehas and the Maccabees, whose reported "zeal" included violence (Nu 25:10–13; 1 Maccabees 2:26,54).

22:5 *as the high priest and all the Council can themselves testify.* Caiaphas is no longer the high priest (see 23:2) but Paul may presume that some of the elders now leading Jerusalem will remember him.

22:6 *noon.* Considered the beginning of the hottest hour; people would seek shade, sometimes eat a light meal and often take a siesta. Only the most urgent business would require travel at this time.

22:7–11 See notes on 9:4–8. The account is retold slightly differently; ancients appreciated variation. In keeping with ancient rhetorical expectations, Paul highlights the features of his account most relevant to his audience, in this case devout Judeans (see, e.g., v. 12).

you have been assigned to do.'[j] 11My companions led me by the hand into Damascus, because the brilliance of the light had blinded me.[k]

12"A man named Ananias came to see me.[l] He was a devout observer of the law and highly respected by all the Jews living there.[m] 13He stood beside me and said, 'Brother Saul, receive your sight!' And at that very moment I was able to see him.

14"Then he said: 'The God of our ancestors[n] has chosen you to know his will and to see[o] the Righteous One[p] and to hear words from his mouth. 15You will be his witness[q] to all people of what you have seen and heard. 16And now what are you waiting for? Get up, be baptized[r] and wash your sins away,[s] calling on his name.'[t]

17"When I returned to Jerusalem[u] and was praying at the temple, I fell into a trance[v] 18and saw the Lord speaking to me. 'Quick!' he said. 'Leave Jerusalem immediately, because the people here will not accept your testimony about me.'

19"'Lord,' I replied, 'these people know that I went from one synagogue to another to imprison[w] and beat[x] those who believe in you. 20And when the blood of your martyr[a] Stephen was shed, I stood there giving my approval and guarding the clothes of those who were killing him.'[y]

21"Then the Lord said to me, 'Go; I will send you far away to the Gentiles.'"[z]

Paul the Roman Citizen

22The crowd listened to Paul until he said this. Then they raised their voices and shouted, "Rid the earth of him![a] He's not fit to live!"[b]

23As they were shouting and throwing off their cloaks[c] and flinging dust into the air,[d] 24the commander ordered that Paul be taken into the barracks.[e] He directed[f] that he be flogged and interrogated in order to find out why the people were shouting at him like this. 25As they stretched him out to flog him, Paul said to the centurion standing there, "Is it legal for you to flog a Roman citizen who hasn't even been found guilty?"[g]

26When the centurion heard this, he went to the commander and reported it. "What are you going to do?" he asked. "This man is a Roman citizen."

27The commander went to Paul and asked, "Tell me, are you a Roman citizen?"

"Yes, I am," he answered.

28Then the commander said, "I had to pay a lot of money for my citizenship."

"But I was born a citizen," Paul replied.

29Those who were about to interrogate him withdrew immediately. The commander himself was alarmed when he realized that he had put Paul, a Roman citizen,[h] in chains.

Paul Before the Sanhedrin

30The commander wanted to find out exactly why Paul was being accused by the Jews.[i] So the next day he released him[j] and ordered the chief priests and all the members of the Sanhedrin[k] to assemble. Then he brought Paul and had him stand before them.

[a] 20 Or *witness*

22:10 [j] Ac 16:30 **22:11** [k] Ac 9:8 **22:12** [l] Ac 9:17 [m] Ac 10:22 **22:14** [n] Ac 3:13 [o] 1Co 9:1; 15:8 [p] Ac 7:52 **22:15** [q] Ac 23:11; 26:16 **22:16** [r] Ac 2:38 [s] Heb 10:22 [t] Ro 10:13 **22:17** [u] Ac 9:26 [v] Ac 10:10 **22:19** [w] ver 4; Ac 8:3 [x] Mt 10:17 **22:20** [y] Ac 7:57-60; 8:1 **22:21** [z] Ac 9:15; 13:46

22:22 [a] Ac 21:36 [b] Ac 25:24 **22:23** [c] Ac 7:58 [d] 2Sa 16:13 **22:24** [e] Ac 21:34 [f] ver 29 **22:25** [g] Ac 16:37 **22:29** [h] ver 24, 25; Ac 16:38 **22:30** [i] Ac 23:28 [j] Ac 21:33 [k] Mt 5:22

22:14 Cf. perhaps Nu 24:16.
22:16 Cf. perhaps Eze 36:25.
22:17 *at the temple, I fell into a trance.* Most of the ancient world recognized temples as a common place for divine revelations; already in the OT, see, e.g., 1Sa 3:3–4; 1Ki 3:5; Isa 6:1.
22:19 *from one synagogue to another.* Jewish tradition suggests that there were many synagogues in Jerusalem at this time.
22:20 See note on 7:58.
22:21 *to the Gentiles.* Given the rise in Judean nationalism over the previous decade, Paul's mention of ministry to Gentiles rekindles the riot (v. 22), which started over the charge that he had brought a Gentile into the temple (21:27–29).
22:22 *listened ... until he said this.* In a normal speech, the narrative was at the beginning, so Paul may not yet have moved past the early part of his speech, but he is unable to finish. Cf. Lk 23:18; see note on Ac 21:36.
22:23 *throwing off their cloaks.* Cf. note on 7:58. *flinging dust into the air.* May signify Paul's uncleanness (cf. 13:51), repudiating him (cf. 18:6), the desire to stone him (cf. note on 26:10), which must go unfulfilled, or a combination of these possibilities.
22:24 *flogged.* Scourging was used for interrogation, among other purposes. Soldiers working for Rome could use a leather whip with bone, iron, or spikes at the end. This would slice open the flesh, sometimes leaving it in bloody strips or exposing sinews and bones.
22:25 *Is it legal ... to flog a Roman citizen ...?* Roman law prohibited scourging (v. 24) a Roman citizen who had not been legally tried and condemned.
22:26,27 *Roman citizen.* Although Roman citizenship was common in Italy and Roman colonies, at this time it was very rare in the eastern empire outside colonies. Law required that one who claimed citizenship be treated as a citizen even before confirmation was available.
22:28 *money for my citizenship.* Early in Claudius's reign people paid high prices for bribes to become citizens; the cost of the bribes declined toward the end of his reign. The tribune may be trying to assess Paul's citizenship status in hopes that he got his citizenship cheaply. *born a citizen.* See note on 16:37. Being born a Roman citizen made one of higher citizenship status than one who acquired citizenship. Tribunes normally belonged to the Roman class of knights, just below the senatorial class; this tribune was not even born a citizen.
22:29 *alarmed when he realized that he had put Paul, a Roman citizen, in chains.* Even chaining a Roman citizen without trial violated the law; in practice, governors might exercise more flexibility, but a tribune was sometimes politically expendable and could not afford such mistakes.
22:30 *ordered ... the Sanhedrin to assemble.* Members of the Sanhedrin may have met to discuss business regularly,

23 Paul looked straight at the Sanhedrin[l] and said, "My brothers,[m] I
have fulfilled my duty to God in all good
conscience[n] to this day." 2At this the high
priest Ananias[o] ordered those standing
near Paul to strike him on the mouth.[p]
3Then Paul said to him, "God will strike
you, you whitewashed wall![q] You sit there
to judge me according to the law, yet you
yourself violate the law by commanding
that I be struck!"[r]

4Those who were standing near Paul
said, "How dare you insult God's high
priest!"

5Paul replied, "Brothers, I did not realize
that he was the high priest; for it is written: 'Do not speak evil about the ruler of
your people.'[a]"[s]

6Then Paul, knowing that some of them
were Sadducees and the others Pharisees,
called out in the Sanhedrin, "My brothers,[t]
I am a Pharisee,[u] descended from Pharisees. I stand on trial because of the hope
of the resurrection of the dead."[v] 7When
he said this, a dispute broke out between
the Pharisees and the Sadducees, and the
assembly was divided. 8(The Sadducees
say that there is no resurrection,[w] and that
there are neither angels nor spirits, but the
Pharisees believe all these things.)

9There was a great uproar, and some of
the teachers of the law who were Pharisees[x] stood up and argued vigorously. "We
find nothing wrong with this man,"[y] they
said. "What if a spirit or an angel has spoken to him?"[z] 10The dispute became so violent that the commander was afraid Paul
would be torn to pieces by them. He ordered the troops to go down and take him
away from them by force and bring him
into the barracks.[a]

11The following night the Lord stood
near Paul and said, "Take courage![b] As
you have testified about me in Jerusalem,
so you must also testify in Rome."[c]

The Plot to Kill Paul

12The next morning some Jews formed
a conspiracy and bound themselves with
an oath not to eat or drink until they had
killed Paul.[d] 13More than forty men were
involved in this plot. 14They went to the
chief priests and the elders and said, "We

23:1 [l] Ac 22:30 [m] Ac 22:5 [n] Ac 24:16; 1Co 4:4; 2Co 1:12; 2Ti 1:3; Heb 13:18 **23:2** [o] Ac 24:1 [p] Jn 18:22 **23:3** [q] Mt 23:27 [r] Lev 19:15; Dt 25:1, 2; Jn 7:51 **23:5** [s] Ex 22:28 **23:6** [t] Ac 22:5 [u] Ac 26:5; Php 3:5 [v] Ac 24:15, 21; 26:8 **23:8** [w] Mt 22:23 **23:9** [x] Mk 2:16 [y] ver 29; Ac 25:25; 26:31 [z] Ac 22:7, 17, 18 **23:10** [a] Ac 21:34 **23:11** [b] Ac 18:9 [c] Ac 19:21; 28:23 **23:12** [d] ver 14, 21, 30; Ac 25:3

[a] 5 Exodus 22:28

but the tribune now needs from them a competent Jewish opinion of Paul's case; the sanctity of the temple is their business, not his. Releasing Paul would be unwise if he were a political liability, but the governor would want the facts if Paul was sent to him.

23:1 *in all good conscience.* A vital issue raised in legal debates was the character of the accused (as well as that of the accusers).

23:2 *Ananias.* Held the high priesthood from AD 47 to 58 or 59 (i.e., until shortly after the time depicted here). Josephus shows that he, like many members of the priestly aristocracy, abused power to gain more wealth; when Jewish patriots revolted against Rome and the Jerusalem aristocracy, Ananias was among the first officials they assassinated, in AD 66. *strike him on the mouth.* A blow to the cheek was an insult (see note on Jn 18:22). Such abuse of prisoners violated ancient legal ethics.

23:3 *God will strike you, you whitewashed wall!* Walls were whitewashed to conceal their decrepit condition. Most people in antiquity appreciated those who forcefully spoke against tyranny. Paul spoke prophetically (cf. Eze 13:10–15); in a few years Ananias would die a violent death (see note on v. 2). Pointing to the demands of the law would appeal to the Pharisees present (vv. 6–9), who were meticulous about the law and more lenient than Sadducees.

23:5 *I did not realize.* Although Paul was correct in his rebuke (v. 3), he concedes that Scripture disallows speaking evil of a ruler (Ex 22:28). Scholars debate whether Paul actually did not recognize the high priest or (perhaps more likely) Paul answers ironically. Ananias would not be wearing his high priestly apparel (since chairing the Sanhedrin differed from ritual duties), but his role in the meeting would suggest his rank.

23:6 *some of them were Sadducees and the others Pharisees.* One rhetorical strategy witty speakers under duress sometimes used was to divide their audience. *resurrection of the dead.* Belief in the future resurrection of the righteous (Da 12:2) was a key theological division between Pharisees and Sadducees, and one on which Paul's views clearly agreed with Pharisaism (and popular Judean hopes). So great was the division that later rabbinic tradition, based in this regard on Pharisaism, for this reason denied that the Sadducees would share in the world to come.

23:8 *neither angels nor spirits.* Sadducees rejected some other Jews' developed views of angels, and also the belief of many Jews that people became like angels after death and/or after the resurrection. Pharisees affirmed not only the future resurrection but also the survival of one's spirit after death until the resurrection. Thus they could believe that Paul's claim of Jesus appearing to him (22:6–10) was a spirit or an angel (v. 9), something the Sadducees would deny.

23:10 *torn to pieces.* Ancient sources report occasions where victims were torn apart by mob violence. Even august organizations such as the Roman Senate were known to experience division, and Josephus reports that in this period Jerusalem's Sanhedrin once even descended to such a level of indignity that they threw rocks at one another! *bring him into the barracks.* The Antonia Fortress, where the Roman cohort was stationed, was about a third of a mile (half a kilometer) away from the likeliest site of this council chamber. The Antonia Fortress had lavish facilities, including baths.

23:12 *an oath.* The assassins literally placed themselves under a curse; on other occasions in this period revolutionaries offered such vows. Jewish people often offered vows of abstinence, promising not to partake of a particular food or drink until such and such a matter occurred. Under duress they could be released from the vow, but it reveals their strong intention to kill Paul. *until they had killed Paul.* Assassinations in the temple area were common at this time (see note on 21:38).

23:14 Josephus shows that some younger members of the priestly aristocracy sympathized with open revolt against Rome, clashing with their elders.

have taken a solemn oath not to eat anything until we have killed Paul.[e] 15Now
then, you and the Sanhedrin[f] petition the
commander to bring him before you on
the pretext of wanting more accurate information about his case. We are ready to
kill him before he gets here."
16But when the son of Paul's sister heard
of this plot, he went into the barracks[g] and
told Paul.
17Then Paul called one of the centurions and said, "Take this young man to
the commander; he has something to tell
him." 18So he took him to the commander.
The centurion said, "Paul, the prisoner,[h] sent for me and asked me to bring this
young man to you because he has something to tell you."
19The commander took the young man
by the hand, drew him aside and asked,
"What is it you want to tell me?"
20He said: "Some Jews have agreed to ask
you to bring Paul before the Sanhedrin[i] tomorrow on the pretext of wanting more accurate information about him.[j] 21Don't give
in to them, because more than forty[k] of
them are waiting in ambush for him. They
have taken an oath not to eat or drink until
they have killed him.[l] They are ready now,
waiting for your consent to their request."
22The commander dismissed the young
man with this warning: "Don't tell anyone
that you have reported this to me."

23:14 [e] ver 12 **23:15** [f] ver 1; Ac 22:30 **23:16** [g] ver 10; Ac 21:34 **23:18** [h] Eph 3:1 **23:20** [i] ver 1 [j] ver 14, 15 **23:21** [k] ver 13 [l] ver 12, 14

23:23 [m] Ac 8:40 [n] ver 33 **23:24** [o] ver 26, 33; Ac 24:1-3, 10; 25:14 **23:26** [p] Lk 1:3; Ac 24:3; 26:25 [q] Ac 15:23 **23:27** [r] Ac 21:32 [s] Ac 21:33 [t] Ac 22:25-29 **23:28** [u] Ac 22:30 **23:29** [v] Ac 18:15; 25:19 [w] ver 9; Ac 26:31 **23:30** [x] ver 20, 21 [y] Ac 20:3 [z] ver 35; Ac 24:19; 25:16

Paul Transferred to Caesarea

23Then he called two of his centurions
and ordered them, "Get ready a detachment of two hundred soldiers, seventy
horsemen and two hundred spearmen[a] to
go to Caesarea[m] at nine tonight.[n] 24Provide
horses for Paul so that he may be taken
safely to Governor Felix."[o]
25He wrote a letter as follows:

26Claudius Lysias,

To His Excellency,[p] Governor Felix:

Greetings.[q]

27This man was seized by the Jews
and they were about to kill him,[r] but
I came with my troops and rescued
him,[s] for I had learned that he is a
Roman citizen.[t] 28I wanted to know
why they were accusing him, so I
brought him to their Sanhedrin.[u] 29I
found that the accusation had to do
with questions about their law,[v] but
there was no charge against him[w]
that deserved death or imprisonment.
30When I was informed[x] of a plot[y] to
be carried out against the man, I sent
him to you at once. I also ordered his
accusers[z] to present to you their case
against him.

[a] *23* The meaning of the Greek for this word is uncertain.

23:15 *kill him before he gets here.* Only about 1,000–1,500 feet (300–450 meters) lay between the Antonia Fortress and the likeliest site of the Sanhedrin's meeting place; the route adjoined the temple and was fairly narrow, allowing an unexpected attack on the part of the column of soldiers where Paul would be walking.

23:16 *son of Paul's sister heard.* In antiquity, leaks of secret information were common, including from the Sanhedrin and other official bodies, sometimes leading to the foiling of secret plots. *went into the barracks.* Guards could allow visitors if they wished; they often requested bribes, but the case could be different for this family of Roman citizens (Paul's nephew would be a citizen if Paul's sister also married one).

23:17 *one of the centurions.* Centurions were sometimes used to guard high-status prisoners with fairly light custody arrangements.

23:19 *took … by the hand.* Taking someone by the hand communicated assurance or welcome (or even an agreement, as in Gal 2:9).

23:22 *Don't tell anyone.* If it were discovered that Paul's nephew had learned and leaked the plot, his own life would be in danger, because collaborators were among the revolutionaries' chief targets. To prevent having to turn down the local senate's request, which would be politically problematic, the commander must preempt it by acting swiftly and without public knowledge.

23:23 *two hundred soldiers, seventy horsemen and two hundred spearmen.* Some cohorts had 480 foot soldiers and 120 cavalry men; Jerusalem's cohort may have been increased during the recent festival (cf. 20:16), as often happened, but the tribune is sending a large proportion of his force. He does, however, expect most of them to return before Jerusalem knows how many soldiers have gone (v. 32). *Caesarea.* Judea's capital, where the governor normally resided (though governors often visited Jerusalem during festivals). *tonight.* Given the prevalence of night attacks by revolutionaries in the Judean hill country in this period, a strong force would better deter attacks and consequent casualties.

23:24 *taken safely.* Night ambushes in the Judean hills were common in this period. *Governor Felix.* Tiberius Claudius Felix (his most probable full name) was governor of Judea from AD 52 to probably 59. Ancient historians condemn his corruption; a freedman (former slave), he achieved the governor's office only through his freedman brother Pallas, who had favor with the emperor.

23:26–30 The letter contains legal terminology and constitutes a formal referral; it would have been available to Paul (and thus Luke) as part of the trial documentation. Because it would also be available to the prosecution, the tribune words it delicately.

23:26 *Claudius Lysias.* Lysias is a Greek name and Claudius was part of the tribune's Roman name, acquired because he became a citizen under the emperor Claudius (see note on 22:28). *His Excellency.* Although "Excellency" was generally applied to members of the Roman knight class, and Felix was instead a freedman, the title was appropriate for him as a governor. *Greetings.* A standard greeting in letters.

23:27 Lysias paints himself in an ideal light. In view of how benefaction and reciprocal obligations worked in the ancient world, Lysias can expect Paul not to contradict his story.

31So the soldiers, carrying out their orders, took Paul with them during the night
and brought him as far as Antipatris. 32The
next day they let the cavalry[a] go on with
him, while they returned to the barracks.[b]
33When the cavalry[c] arrived in Caesarea,[d]
they delivered the letter to the governor[e]
and handed Paul over to him. 34The governor read the letter and asked what province he was from. Learning that he was
from Cilicia,[f] 35he said, "I will hear your
case when your accusers[g] get here." Then
he ordered that Paul be kept under guard[h]
in Herod's palace.

Paul's Trial Before Felix

24 Five days later the high priest Ananias[i] went down to Caesarea with
some of the elders and a lawyer named
Tertullus, and they brought their charges[j]
against Paul before the governor.[k] 2When
Paul was called in, Tertullus presented his
case before Felix: "We have enjoyed a long
period of peace under you, and your foresight has brought about reforms in this nation. 3Everywhere and in every way, most
excellent[l] Felix, we acknowledge this with
profound gratitude. 4But in order not to
weary you further, I would request that
you be kind enough to hear us briefly.
5"We have found this man to be a troublemaker, stirring up riots[m] among the
Jews[n] all over the world. He is a ringleader
of the Nazarene[o] sect[p] 6and even tried to
desecrate the temple;[q] so we seized him.
[7][a] 8By examining him yourself you will
be able to learn the truth about all these
charges we are bringing against him."
9The other Jews joined in the accusation,[r] asserting that these things were true.
10When the governor[s] motioned for him
to speak, Paul replied: "I know that for a

23:32 [a] ver 23 [b] Ac 21:34 **23:33** [c] ver 23, 24 [d] Ac 8:40 [e] ver 26 **23:34** [f] Ac 6:9; 21:39 **23:35** [g] ver 30; Ac 24:19; 25:16 [h] Ac 24:27 **24:1** [i] Ac 23:2 [j] Ac 23:30, 35 [k] Ac 23:24 **24:3** [l] Lk 1:3; Ac 23:26; 26:25 **24:5** [m] Ac 16:20; 17:6 [n] Ac 21:28 [o] Mk 1:24 [p] ver 14; Ac 26:5; 28:22 **24:6** [q] Ac 21:28 **24:9** [r] 1Th 2:16 **24:10** [s] Ac 23:24

[a] 6-8 Some manuscripts include here *him, and we would have judged him in accordance with our law. 7But the commander Lysias came and took him from us with much violence, 8ordering his accusers to come before you.*

23:31 *as far as Antipatris.* Soldiers were supposed to exercise every day, with periodic forced marches of 20 miles (32 kilometers) in five (or sometimes even four) hours; sometimes they had forced marches of 30 miles (48 kilometers). The Roman road from Jerusalem to Antipatris was longer, 35 to possibly even 45 miles (55 to possibly even 70 kilometers), depending on the exact site, although the journey was downhill. The soldiers would thus need to march from nine that evening until probably well into the morning. Yet ancient sources show that soldiers sometimes made forced marches at a high speed throughout the night.
23:32 *they returned to the barracks.* When they reached Antipatris, they would be at the end of the Judean hill country. The cavalry could continue the mission more safely across the largely Gentile open country by day; they could traverse the 30 miles (48 kilometers) north to Caesarea more quickly without the infantry. The infantry could return to Jerusalem at a less hurried pace during daylight.
23:34 *read the letter.* Reading was usually done out loud (as in 8:30). *province he was from.* If he wished, the governor could defer Paul's case to the governor of Paul's own province, but such deferral was not wise since Paul was from Cilicia. During Paul's specific period, Cilicia was under the governor of Syria, Felix's immediate superior, who would expect Felix to handle the case himself.
23:35 *when your accusers get here.* Roman officials normally waited for accusers to bring charges. Felix stayed in the palace built by Herod the Great in Caesarea. He provides Paul accommodations elsewhere in the same palace; high-status prisoners received better treatment than others.
24:1–21 Courts made summary transcripts of speeches; Paul and his supporters, such as Luke, would have had access to these summaries. The judicial rhetoric in Paul's defense speeches is brilliant, appealing to the best forms of argumentation; if not for political complications (such as the status of his accusers), Paul should have been released immediately.
24:1 *went down to Caesarea.* Unlike Jerusalem in the Judean hill country, Caesarea was on the lower coastal plain. Felix had reason to accommodate Ananias as much as possible; Felix's predecessor was recalled (and the predecessor's assistant executed) because of complaints by Ananias and his colleagues. *brought their charges ... before the governor.* It was not unusual to first summarize the case privately for the governor, but the actual hearing (vv. 2–21) required the defendant's presence (25:16).
24:2 *Tertullus presented his case.* Accusers spoke first. *peace under you ... your foresight.* Speakers normally opened by praising the judges, and often praised officials' commitment to peace and foresight. Felix, however, was corrupt and he badly misadministered Judea; he did not bring about reforms, and his tenure was certainly not peaceful.
24:3 *Everywhere and in every way.* One common rhetorical technique was repeating sounds.
24:4 *in order not to weary you further.* Although public speeches could last two hours, others valued brevity, and provincial officials, who generally had a heavy caseload, would often demand it. It was a common rhetorical technique to note that, for the hearer's sake, one should stop elaborating a point—when in fact the speaker had nothing more to say on the matter anyway.
24:5 *troublemaker ... all over the world.* Resembles a recent accusation from the emperor against some Jewish people; attacking the defendant's character was standard prosecutorial practice. *stirring up riots.* A charge of sedition—a capital offense.
24:6 *tried to desecrate the temple.* Desecrating the temple was a capital offense. That Paul's accusers now charge that he merely tried (rather than that he succeeded) reflects the lack of authentic witnesses, willing to be cross-examined, that Trophimus was actually with Paul in the temple (21:29). Now that the festival (20:16) was over, Paul's accusers have presumably returned to the province of Asia (21:27).
24:8 Speakers often invited judges to examine matters closely, rhetorically implying that the speakers are telling the truth.
24:9 Assertions without evidence were common in trials, making up in quantity what they lacked in quality; speakers also typically asserted that they were giving only facts. Courts took into account not only the content of and evidence for charges, but the social status of the plaintiffs and defendants. Paul's accusers are of high status (v. 1).
24:10 *for a number of years you have been a judge over this nation.* It was customary to praise the judge, but Paul's praise

number of years you have been a judge over
this nation; so I gladly make my defense.
11You can easily verify that no more than
twelve days[t] ago I went up to Jerusalem to
worship. 12My accusers did not find me arguing with anyone at the temple,[u] or stirring
up a crowd[v] in the synagogues or anywhere
else in the city. 13And they cannot prove
to you the charges they are now making
against me.[w] 14However, I admit that I wor-

24:11 [t] Ac 21:27; ver 1
24:12 [u] Ac 25:8; 28:17 [v] ver 18
24:13 [w] Ac 25:7

is more accurate than that of Tertullus in v. 2. Scholars debate when Felix became governor; it may have been as early as AD 52, between four and six years before this hearing; he had also had earlier administrative experience in Judea.
24:11 Speakers would narrate, from their respective perspectives, the events that led up to the present case. *twelve days.* The time given would demonstrate that Paul's coming coincided with a festival (20:16). *went up ... to worship.* Arguments based on a person's character were common; one who came to worship would not desecrate a temple.
24:12 *stirring up a crowd.* A capital charge (v. 5). Speakers often began by stating the charges they were refuting.
24:13 *they cannot prove.* Speakers would commonly point to the other side's lack of proof; in capital cases, accusers bore the burden of proof.
24:14 *I admit.* Speakers in defense speeches sometimes

Aerial view of the theater and coastline at Caesarea. Paul was brought here on trial before Governor Felix (Ac 24:1).

ship the God of our ancestors[x] as a follower
of the Way,[y] which they call a sect.[z] I believe everything that is in accordance with
the Law and that is written in the Prophets,[a] 15and I have the same hope in God as
these men themselves have, that there will
be a resurrection[b] of both the righteous and
the wicked.[c] 16So I strive always to keep my
conscience clear[d] before God and man.

17"After an absence of several years, I
came to Jerusalem to bring my people gifts
for the poor[e] and to present offerings. 18I
was ceremonially clean[f] when they found
me in the temple courts doing this. There
was no crowd with me, nor was I involved
in any disturbance.[g] 19But there are some
Jews from the province of Asia, who ought
to be here before you and bring charges if
they have anything against me.[h] 20Or these
who are here should state what crime they
found in me when I stood before the Sanhedrin — 21unless it was this one thing I
shouted as I stood in their presence: 'It
is concerning the resurrection of the dead
that I am on trial before you today.' "[i]

22Then Felix, who was well acquainted
with the Way, adjourned the proceedings.
"When Lysias the commander comes," he
said, "I will decide your case." 23He ordered the centurion to keep Paul under
guard[j] but to give him some freedom[k]
and permit his friends to take care of his
needs.[l]

24Several days later Felix came with his
wife Drusilla, who was Jewish. He sent for
Paul and listened to him as he spoke about
faith in Christ Jesus.[m] 25As Paul talked
about righteousness, self-control[n] and the
judgment[o] to come, Felix was afraid and
said, "That's enough for now! You may
leave. When I find it convenient, I will send
for you." 26At the same time he was hoping
that Paul would offer him a bribe, so he sent
for him frequently and talked with him.

24:14 [x] Ac 3:13 [y] Ac 9:2 [z] ver 5 [a] Ac 26:6, 22; 28:23
24:15 [b] Ac 23:6; 28:20 [c] Da 12:2; Jn 5:28, 29
24:16 [d] Ac 23:1
24:17 [e] Ac 11:29, 30; Ro 15:25-28, 31; 1Co 16:1-4, 15; 2Co 8:1-4; Gal 2:10
24:18 [f] Ac 21:26 [g] ver 12
24:19 [h] Ac 23:30
24:21 [i] Ac 23:6
24:23 [j] Ac 23:35 [k] Ac 28:16 [l] Ac 23:16; 27:3
24:24 [m] Ac 20:21
24:25 [n] Gal 5:23; 2Pe 1:6 [o] Ac 10:42

confessed what was not a crime, gaining credibility for honesty while admitting nothing that could be prosecuted under law. What Paul confesses is also the issue raised before the Sanhedrin (see note on vv. 20 – 21); Paul knows that Roman officials regard Jewish religious beliefs as an internal Jewish matter outside the Roman purview (cf. 18:14 – 15 and note on 18:15), and thus not punishable by death (cf. note on Jn 18:31).

24:15 *there will be a resurrection.* Sadducees denied the future resurrection (23:8), but Pharisees, who affirmed it, reflected on this point the majority view of Jewish belief in Judea and Galilee. Judaism divided on whether the unrighteous would be raised for eternal judgment (despite Da 12:2). Paul's views (v. 21) are, if anything, closer to the Jewish mainstream than those of his accusers, who would therefore be less inclined to want to make an issue of this point.

24:16 *my conscience clear.* A person's character was a major factor in cases deciding guilt or innocence; Paul offers an example of this character in v. 17.

24:17 *gifts for the poor.* Paul refers to his collection for believers in Jerusalem (Ro 15:26 – 27; 1Co 16:1 – 3; 2Co 8 – 9), though Luke does not expressly elaborate that point. Benefactors were to be honored, not prosecuted; in ancient legal settings speakers sometimes denounced those who responded to benefaction instead with hostile treatment (cf. 4:9).

24:18 *in the temple courts.* Ancients used temples for asylum and protection; attacking someone there was considered a violation of sacred rights.

24:19 *ought to be here before you.* It was standard practice for defendants to reverse charges against their accusers; Paul's incomplete Greek sentence here might leave that implication (cf. more directly 26:21). Paul did not start the riot (v. 18); it was therefore clear that his accusers had. The case's original plaintiffs had apparently not made themselves available for the governor's cross-examination. Under Roman law, therefore, they could be legally charged themselves for abandoning the case. Whenever accusers did not appear, a case was supposed to be thrown out.

24:20 – 21 As in many speeches, Paul's final argument is the most compelling. In ancient courts, changing charges after the beginning of a case invited accusations of fabrication. Paul had maneuvered the debate before the Sanhedrin away from the fabricated charges to the real reason for which some of the leaders wanted to be rid of him (23:6). Official documentation confirmed that the charge was a theological one (23:29). This was not an offense under Roman law, so the case should be immediately dismissed.

24:22 Paul's argument as presented in vv. 10 – 21 should have been sufficient for the case against him to be thrown out; the charge has morphed from a riot caused by his accusers into an opportunity to prosecute him on unrelated matters. For Roman officials, however, political considerations sometimes trumped individual claims to justice. Paul's accusers are of high status (v. 1), but simply handing Paul over for execution could be complicated as well. He was a Roman citizen, and Paul's accusers have already inadvertently informed Felix that Paul is leader in a movement (v. 5) that Felix knows is of significant size (cf. 21:20). Because the case was legally clear-cut, Felix's political motivation for postponing the case would be obvious.

24:23 *under guard.* High-status captives received better custody arrangements, in this case probably still in Herod's palace (23:35), especially given Felix's private hearings with him (vv. 24,26). Centurions were sometimes used to guard high-status prisoners with fairly light custody arrangements (23:17). *permit his friends to take care of his needs.* Normally prisons supplied little food and no clothing; prisoners were dependent on outside help. Felix's orders would prevent the centurion and his soldiers from requiring bribes, as guards often did.

24:24 *Drusilla.* Over the years Felix married three different princesses; the most lasting marriage was with Drusilla, the younger sister of Agrippa II and Bernice, whom Felix had married perhaps four years before this scene. When Drusilla was 16, Felix convinced her to divorce her husband to marry him, even though governors were not supposed to marry women from the provinces they administered. Officials were also not supposed to use prisoners for private ends, as here and in v. 26. *He sent for Paul and listened to him.* Educated people sometimes liked to hear sages lecture; given Felix's lifestyle just mentioned, his discomfort at Paul's lecture topics (v. 25) is not surprising. Ancient readers could respect Paul's courageous speech (see note on 4:13).

24:26 *offer him a bribe.* Josephus shows that, apart from Felix's successor Festus (v. 27), most of Judea's final

27When two years had passed, Felix was succeeded by Porcius Festus,[p] but because Felix wanted to grant a favor to the Jews,[q] he left Paul in prison.[r]

Paul's Trial Before Festus

25 Three days after arriving in the province, Festus went up from Caesarea[s] to Jerusalem, 2where the chief priests and the Jewish leaders appeared before him and presented the charges against Paul.[t] 3They requested Festus, as a favor to them, to have Paul transferred to Jerusalem, for they were preparing an ambush to kill him along the way. 4Festus answered, "Paul is being held[u] at Caesarea, and I myself am going there soon. 5Let some of your leaders come with me, and if the man has done anything wrong, they can press charges against him there."

6After spending eight or ten days with them, Festus went down to Caesarea. The next day he convened the court[v] and ordered that Paul be brought before him. 7When Paul came in, the Jews who had come down from Jerusalem stood around him. They brought many serious charges against him,[w] but they could not prove them.[x]

8Then Paul made his defense: "I have done nothing wrong against the Jewish law or against the temple[y] or against Caesar."

9Festus, wishing to do the Jews a favor,[z] said to Paul, "Are you willing to go up to Jerusalem and stand trial before me there on these charges?"[a]

10Paul answered: "I am now standing before Caesar's court, where I ought to be tried. I have not done any wrong to the Jews, as you yourself know very well. 11If, however, I am guilty of doing anything deserving death, I do not refuse to die. But if the charges brought against me by these Jews are not true, no one has the right to hand me over to them. I appeal to Caesar!"[b]

12After Festus had conferred with his council, he declared: "You have appealed to Caesar. To Caesar you will go!"

Festus Consults King Agrippa

13A few days later King Agrippa and Bernice arrived at Caesarea[c] to pay their re-

24:27 [p] Ac 25:1, 4,9,14 [q] Ac 12:3; 25:9 [r] Ac 23:35; 25:14
25:1 [s] Ac 8:40
25:2 [t] ver 15; Ac 24:1
25:4 [u] Ac 24:23
25:6 [v] ver 17
25:7 [w] Mk 15:3; Lk 23:2, 10; Ac 24:5,6 [x] Ac 24:13
25:8 [y] Ac 6:13; 24:12; 28:17
25:9 [z] Ac 24:27 [a] ver 20
25:11 [b] ver 21, 25; Ac 26:32; 28:19
25:13 [c] Ac 8:40

---

governors before the Judean revolt were corrupt. Many ancient governors, including some in Judea in this period, took bribes, but if it were proved in Rome they could be recalled and prosecuted.

24:27 Felix returned to Rome around the year AD 59 (some prefer 60, and some earlier). At that time, now lacking reason to fear retribution from Felix, some Judeans accused him in Rome. *wanted to grant a favor to the Jews.* Felix's brother Pallas still retained sufficient influence to protect him from punishment, but Felix has reason to want to grant a favor to the Jews when he leaves. A governor of Judea soon after Felix and Festus freed even revolutionaries who paid bribes (cf. v. 26), but governors often lacked incentive to conclude all cases before their departure. Records of Paul's proceedings would remain, but no verdict; the new governor, Porcius Festus (see note on 25:1 – 12), would need to set a new hearing.

25:1 – 12 Like Luke, Josephus depicts Felix as corrupt but his successor Porcius Festus as an effective governor who was more just than other governors of Judea in this period. Festus suppressed disturbances yet was tolerant of Judean customs, including those with which he differed. He died in office, possibly after just two years, and was succeeded by the rapacious Albinus.

25:1 *Three days after arriving.* A new governor's term of office officially began July 1, but because Festus's predecessor was already gone, locals would have looked to him as soon as he arrived. Festus's fairly expeditious meetings after his arrival contrast with Felix's delays and fit Josephus's portraits of these two governors.

25:2 *the chief priests and the Jewish leaders.* The high priest now in charge of Jerusalem's aristocratic leadership is different from Ananias in 23:2; 24:1. Agrippa II had appointed a new high priest, Ishmael son of Phabi, apparently shortly before Felix's departure. The priestly aristocracy had clashed with Felix, but looked for a new start with his successor.

25:3 *have Paul transferred to Jerusalem.* Caesarea, where Paul was already detained, was the capital that Rome had chosen for Judea; moving the venue to Jerusalem would have set a bad precedent of accommodating Judean nationalism.

25:6 *convened the court.* After local accusations (as in v. 2), a governor would hear a case from his tribunal (as here), seeking advice from his consilium if desired (v. 12).

25:7 *could not prove them.* When a case was weak, speakers would make louder assertions, but opposing speakers would draw attention to their lack of evidence.

25:8 *against Caesar.* This probably indicates a new charge (v. 7; contrast 24:5 – 6), though one related to the charge of sedition. In ancient courts, changing charges after the beginning of a case invited the counteraccusation of fabricating charges.

25:9 *wishing to do the Jews a favor.* Although more just than Felix, Festus does not simply dismiss the groundless case. *go up to Jerusalem.* He recognizes the political usefulness of granting them a harmless request, especially considering the bad relations between them and his predecessor (whom they had prosecuted).

25:11 *If, however, I am guilty of doing anything deserving death.* In ancient defense rhetoric, a speaker could affirm that the crime of which he was accused merited death, while protesting that he did not commit it. *I appeal to Caesar!* Evidence suggests that provincials who were Roman citizens (see note on 16:37) could appeal a capital verdict to the emperor. Appealing before a verdict was unusual, however, so Festus consults his council (the consilium of advisors that a governor could rely on if he desired). Dismissing an appeal to the emperor could be politically problematic if criticism were raised. Sending Paul to the emperor, however, was politically useful: Festus escaped the political necessity of condemning someone on weak evidence or of releasing him despite the offense this would cause to the local elite with whom he would have to continue to deal.

25:13 *King Agrippa.* This is Agrippa II, son of Herod Agrippa I (see note on 12:1). Because of Agrippa's youth he ruled only a small area, but he spoke on behalf of his people and also supported Rome. He strongly opposed the Judean revolt and officially celebrated Rome's victory

spects to Festus. 14Since they were spending
many days there, Festus discussed Paul's
case with the king. He said: "There is a man
here whom Felix left as a prisoner.[d] 15When
I went to Jerusalem, the chief priests and the
elders of the Jews brought charges against
him[e] and asked that he be condemned.

16"I told them that it is not the Roman
custom to hand over anyone before they
have faced their accusers and have had an
opportunity to defend themselves against
the charges.[f] 17When they came here with
me, I did not delay the case, but convened
the court the next day and ordered the man
to be brought in.[g] 18When his accusers got
up to speak, they did not charge him with
any of the crimes I had expected. 19Instead,
they had some points of dispute[h] with him
about their own religion[i] and about a dead
man named Jesus who Paul claimed was
alive. 20I was at a loss how to investigate
such matters; so I asked if he would be
willing to go to Jerusalem and stand trial
there on these charges.[j] 21But when Paul
made his appeal to be held over for the
Emperor's decision, I ordered him held until I could send him to Caesar."[k]

22Then Agrippa said to Festus, "I would
like to hear this man myself."

He replied, "Tomorrow you will hear him."[l]

Paul Before Agrippa

26:12-18pp — Ac 9:3-8; 22:6-11

23The next day Agrippa and Bernice[m]
came with great pomp and entered the
audience room with the high-ranking
military officers and the prominent men
of the city. At the command of Festus,
Paul was brought in. 24Festus said: "King
Agrippa, and all who are present with us,
you see this man! The whole Jewish community[n] has petitioned me about him in
Jerusalem and here in Caesarea, shouting that he ought not to live any longer.[o]
25I found he had done nothing deserving
of death,[p] but because he made his appeal to the Emperor[q] I decided to send
him to Rome. 26But I have nothing definite to write to His Majesty about him.
Therefore I have brought him before all
of you, and especially before you, King
Agrippa, so that as a result of this investigation I may have something to write.
27For I think it is unreasonable to send a
prisoner on to Rome without specifying
the charges against him."

26 Then Agrippa said to Paul, "You have
permission to speak for yourself."[r]

So Paul motioned with his hand and
began his defense: 2"King Agrippa, I consider myself fortunate to stand before you
today as I make my defense against all the
accusations of the Jews, 3and especially so
because you are well acquainted with all
the Jewish customs[s] and controversies.[t]
Therefore, I beg you to listen to me patiently.

4"The Jewish people all know the way I
have lived ever since I was a child,[u] from
the beginning of my life in my own country,

25:14 [d] Ac 24:27 **25:15** [e] ver 2; Ac 24:1 **25:16** [f] ver 4, 5; Ac 23:30 **25:17** [g] ver 6, 10 **25:19** [h] Ac 18:15; 23:29 [i] Ac 17:22 **25:20** [j] ver 9 **25:21** [k] ver 11, 12 **25:22** [l] Ac 9:15 **25:23** [m] ver 13; Ac 26:30 **25:24** [n] ver 2, 3, 7 [o] Ac 22:22 **25:25** [p] Ac 23:9 [q] ver 11 **26:1** [r] Ac 9:15; 25:22 **26:3** [s] ver 7; Ac 6:14 [t] Ac 25:19 **26:4** [u] Gal 1:13, 14; Php 3:5

---

many years afterward. Agrippa welcomed and often visited Roman officials. *Bernice.* In its fuller form, the name was Berenike. Bernice was Agrippa's sister, one year younger than he. When Agrippa I died (12:23), Agrippa II was 17 and Bernice 16; the youngest sibling, Drusilla (24:24), was 6. Like Agrippa, Bernice appears favorably in Josephus; she was close to her brother and stayed with him after the collapse of her marriage (the occasional accusation of incest between them was almost certainly slander). Although 15 years older than the future emperor Titus, Bernice later became his mistress when he was besieging Jerusalem. Agrippa and Bernice were both alive when Luke and Josephus were writing their accounts.

25:14 *Festus discussed Paul's case.* Agrippa II could depose and appoint high priests, so if Festus were armed with his advice he would not need to worry about the opinion of the priestly aristocrats. Festus could scarcely send Paul to Rome without some informed advice for Paul's dossier (v. 27).

25:16 *an opportunity to defend themselves against the charges.* Under Roman law, defendants had to be granted a public hearing and have the chance to defend themselves. Festus makes it sound as if the accusers mentioned in v. 15 wished to sidestep this protocol.

25:19 *points of dispute with him about their own religion.* Rome was not interested in settling local religious disputes (cf. 18:14–15).

25:23 *high-ranking military officers.* Lit. "commanders of cohorts"; five military cohorts resided in Caesarea. Thus they include as many as five tribunes, if all were present. Most tribunes were from the Roman class of knights, the class just below senatorial rank, and used the office of tribune as a short step in their political career (though this was not the case with Lysias, 22:28).

25:26 *especially before you, King Agrippa.* Agrippa II was Jewish but also fully Romanized; he was uniquely qualified to offer a respected perspective.

25:27 *specifying the charges.* A dossier (*litterae dimissoriae*, containing at least a cover letter) would be sent to Rome along with a prisoner, since the emperor's tribunal (in which the current emperor, Nero, chose to be largely uninvolved) would need the facts of the case. The tribunal lacked time to be bogged down in research.

26:1 *motioned with his hand.* It was customary to stretch out one's hand at the beginning of a speech, here perhaps (as in the opening of some judicial speeches) sweeping from right to left with the thumb touching the middle finger.

26:2–3 *I consider myself fortunate ... especially so because you.* It was customary to compliment the judge in the opening of one's speech. Though some of the aristocratic priests resented Agrippa and he later sided with Rome during the Judean revolt, he honored the Jewish law and protected his people after the war.

26:3 *I beg you to listen to me patiently.* Ancient speeches often included an appeal to listen patiently.

26:4 *the way I have lived ever since I was a child.* Defense speeches often began with a narrative that would give

and also in Jerusalem. 5They have known
me for a long time[v] and can testify, if they
are willing, that I conformed to the strictest sect of our religion, living as a Pharisee.[w] 6And now it is because of my hope[x]
in what God has promised our ancestors[y]
that I am on trial today. 7This is the promise
our twelve tribes[z] are hoping to see fulfilled
as they earnestly serve God day and night.[a]
King Agrippa, it is because of this hope that
these Jews are accusing me.[b] 8Why should
any of you consider it incredible that God
raises the dead?[c]
9"I too was convinced[d] that I ought to
do all that was possible to oppose[e] the
name of Jesus of Nazareth.[f] 10And that is
just what I did in Jerusalem. On the authority of the chief priests I put many of
the Lord's people[g] in prison,[h] and when
they were put to death, I cast my vote
against them.[i] 11Many a time I went from
one synagogue to another to have them
punished,[j] and I tried to force them to
blaspheme. I was so obsessed with persecuting them that I even hunted them down
in foreign cities.
12"On one of these journeys I was going
to Damascus with the authority and commission of the chief priests. 13About noon,
King Agrippa, as I was on the road, I saw
a light from heaven, brighter than the sun,
blazing around me and my companions.
14We all fell to the ground, and I heard
a voice[k] saying to me in Aramaic,[*a*] 'Saul,
Saul, why do you persecute me? It is hard
for you to kick against the goads.'
15"Then I asked, 'Who are you, Lord?'
" 'I am Jesus, whom you are persecuting,' the Lord replied. 16'Now get up and
stand on your feet.[l] I have appeared to you
to appoint you as a servant and as a witness of what you have seen and will see
of me.[m] 17I will rescue you[n] from your own
people and from the Gentiles.[o] I am sending you to them 18to open their eyes[p] and
turn them from darkness to light,[q] and
from the power of Satan to God, so that
they may receive forgiveness of sins[r] and
a place among those who are sanctified by
faith in me.'[s]
19"So then, King Agrippa, I was not disobedient to the vision from heaven. 20First
to those in Damascus,[t] then to those in
Jerusalem[u] and in all Judea, and then to
the Gentiles,[v] I preached that they should
repent[w] and turn to God and demonstrate
their repentance by their deeds.[x] 21That is
why some Jews seized me[y] in the temple
courts and tried to kill me.[z] 22But God has
helped me to this very day; so I stand here
and testify to small and great alike. I am
saying nothing beyond what the prophets
and Moses said would happen[a]— 23that
the Messiah would suffer and, as the first
to rise from the dead,[b] would bring the
message of light to his own people and to
the Gentiles."[c]
24At this point Festus interrupted Paul's
defense. "You are out of your mind,[d]
Paul!" he shouted. "Your great learning[e]
is driving you insane."

26:5 [v] Ac 22:3 [w] Ac 23:6; Php 3:5 **26:6** [x] Ac 23:6; 24:15; 28:20 [y] Ac 13:32; Ro 15:8 **26:7** [z] Jas 1:1 [a] 1Th 3:10; 1Ti 5:5 [b] ver 2 **26:8** [c] Ac 23:6 **26:9** [d] 1Ti 1:13 [e] Jn 16:2 [f] Jn 15:21 **26:10** [g] Ac 9:13 [h] Ac 8:3; 9:2, 14, 21 [i] Ac 22:20 **26:11** [j] Mt 10:17 **26:14** [k] Ac 9:7 **26:16** [l] Eze 2:1; Da 10:11 [m] Ac 22:14, 15 **26:17** [n] Jer 1:8, 19 [o] Ac 9:15 **26:18** [p] Isa 35:5 [q] Isa 42:7, 16; Eph 5:8; Col 1:13; 1Pe 2:9 [r] Lk 24:47; Ac 2:38 [s] Ac 20:21,32 **26:20** [t] Ac 9:19-25 [u] Ac 9:26-29; 22:17-20 [v] Ac 9:15; 13:46 [w] Ac 3:19 [x] Mt 3:8; Lk 3:8 **26:21** [y] Ac 21:27,30 [z] Ac 21:31 **26:22** [a] Lk 24:27,44; Ac 10:43; 24:14 **26:23** [b] 1Co 15:20, 23; Col 1:18; Rev 1:5 [c] Lk 2:32 **26:24** [d] Jn 10:20; 1Co 4:10 [e] Jn 7:15

a 14 Or *Hebrew*

---

background for the present case (here vv. 4–18 or vv. 4–20). Such narratives also helped establish the person's character, showing that they would not have committed the offense of which they were charged.

26:5 *known me for a long time and can testify.* Speakers often invoked public knowledge. *living as a Pharisee.* Pharisees were considered the most meticulous interpreters of the law that most Judeans would encounter (Essenes were stricter but many lived in the wilderness).

26:8 Arguments from probability figured heavily in ancient courts.

26:9 *convinced that I ought to … oppose the name of Jesus.* Hearers often gave special credence to testimony from unlikely sources—here a persecutor.

26:10 *On the authority of the chief priests … they were put to death.* Since such lynchings as are indicated here violated Roman policy, Paul implicates the class to which his current accusers belong, for he acted on the chief priests' authority. *cast my vote against them.* Against some interpretations, Paul's "vote" does not mean that he was a member of the Sanhedrin. Paul was undoubtedly too young to have been a member (7:58), and "casting a vote" was a frequent figurative expression in Greek for giving approval or making a decision (cf. 22:20). Additionally, because casting a vote could also be translated as casting a "pebble" (as pebbles were traditionally used for voting), there may be a wordplay: others cast stones, and Paul cast his (figurative) pebble.

26:11 Gentile authorities who persecuted Jewish people had found them obstinately unwilling to deny their faith; Christians followed the same model, provoking complaints from persecutors (such as a second-century governor in northern Asia Minor). *tried to force them to blaspheme.* Probably implies that he was unsuccessful in this objective.

26:13 *About noon.* Only the most zealous or desperate people traveled at noon (see note on 22:6).

26:14 In Jewish tradition, the heavenly voice would speak in Hebrew or Aramaic. Agrippa II had a Greek education and, like some of Luke's audience, might also catch Greek allusions here. *kick against the goads.* A Greek proverb that appeared in the same context of the same Greek drama that most prominently highlighted the danger of fighting against God (5:39). A goad was something like a cattle prod, but the image was often used figuratively.

26:16–17 Cf. Jer 1:5–8.

26:18 Cf. Isa 42:6–7,18; 49:6. *sanctified.* See note on 20:32.

26:19 *I was not disobedient to the vision.* Ancient speakers sometimes justified their actions by arguing that their actions were necessary; one form of necessity was compulsion by the orders of a deity.

26:21 *Jews … tried to kill me.* It was standard practice for defendants to reverse charges against their accusers.

26:24 *Festus interrupted.* Judges sometimes interrupted speakers. *out of your mind.* Many people considered philosophers insane (philosophers held the same opinion

25 "I am not insane, most excellent[f] Festus," Paul replied. "What I am saying is
true and reasonable. 26 The king is familiar with these things,[g] and I can speak
freely to him. I am convinced that none
of this has escaped his notice, because it
was not done in a corner. 27 King Agrippa, do you believe the prophets? I know
you do."

28 Then Agrippa said to Paul, "Do you
think that in such a short time you can
persuade me to be a Christian?"[h]

29 Paul replied, "Short time or long — I
pray to God that not only you but all who
are listening to me today may become
what I am, except for these chains."[i]

30 The king rose, and with him the governor and Bernice[j] and those sitting with
them. 31 After they left the room, they began saying to one another, "This man is
not doing anything that deserves death or
imprisonment."[k]

32 Agrippa said to Festus, "This man
could have been set free[l] if he had not appealed to Caesar."[m]

26:25 [f] Ac 23:26
26:26 [g] ver 3
26:28 [h] Ac 11:26
26:29 [i] Ac 21:33
26:30 [j] Ac 25:23
26:31 [k] Ac 23:9
26:32 [l] Ac 28:18 [m] Ac 25:11
27:1 [n] Ac 16:10 [o] Ac 18:2; 25:12, 25 [p] Ac 10:1
27:2 [q] Ac 2:9 [r] Ac 19:29 [s] Ac 16:9 [t] Ac 17:1
27:3 [u] Mt 11:21 [v] ver 43 [w] Ac 24:23; 28:16
27:4 [x] ver 7
27:5 [y] Ac 6:9
27:6 [z] Ac 28:11

Paul Sails for Rome

27 When it was decided that we[n]
would sail for Italy,[o] Paul and some
other prisoners were handed over to a centurion named Julius, who belonged to the
Imperial Regiment.[p] 2 We boarded a ship
from Adramyttium about to sail for ports
along the coast of the province of Asia,[q]
and we put out to sea. Aristarchus,[r] a Macedonian[s] from Thessalonica,[t] was with us.

3 The next day we landed at Sidon;[u] and
Julius, in kindness to Paul,[v] allowed him
to go to his friends so they might provide
for his needs.[w] 4 From there we put out
to sea again and passed to the lee of Cyprus because the winds were against us.[x]
5 When we had sailed across the open sea
off the coast of Cilicia[y] and Pamphylia, we
landed at Myra in Lycia. 6 There the centurion found an Alexandrian ship[z] sailing for

of the masses); those who were inspired were also considered insane (in a positive way). *great learning.* Festus refers to Paul's learning and might additionally think of his visions (vv. 13 – 19).

26:25 *reasonable.* Translates a Greek term often contrasted with "insane" (v. 24); philosophers argued that they were (despite many others' protests) saner than everyone else. Festus might understand Paul's protest in such terms.

26:26 *familiar with these things ... none of this has escaped his notice.* Speakers often invoked public knowledge. Public acts were more trusted than secret ones; Roman officials were anxious about acts performed secretly, which risked subversive behavior. *done in a corner.* A figure of speech for private activity; some used the expression to criticize sages who withdrew from public life.

26:28 Recognizing a rhetorical trap, Agrippa wittily complains that if he answers that he believes the prophets (v. 27), Paul will make him answer as if he is a Christian.

26:29 *except for these chains.* A speech's conclusion often included an emotionally rousing climax, here probably including Paul gesturing with his unjust chains. Given ancient analogies, Paul's right hand may have been chained to a guard's left hand, with an iron shackle weighing 10 or 15 pounds (4.5 or 6.8 kilograms).

26:32 Festus would have Agrippa's expert opinion recorded in the cover letter sent to the emperor's tribunal. *could have been set free.* The appeal to Caesar inhibited Festus from freeing him not legally but politically (see note on 25:11). Sending Paul with Agrippa's support completely freed Festus from repercussions with Paul's elite enemies in Jerusalem.

27:1 – 44 The details of the journey fit the weather conditions and geography so precisely that this account surely reflects an actual voyage under the conditions described.

27:1 *other prisoners.* This might include Roman citizens on appeal like Paul, but the majority were probably condemned criminals being sent to the capital to entertain the Roman people by their public deaths. *a centurion.* Centurions were sometimes used to guard high-status prisoners with fairly light custody arrangements (23:17; 24:23), and were also sometimes given special assignments with small detachments of soldiers (vv. 31 – 32). *the Imperial Regiment.* Lit. "the Augustan Cohort"; the title "Augustan" was borne by various legions and cohorts, including a cohort attested in this region and period.

27:2 *ship.* Apart from the massive ships carrying grain from Alexandria (see note on v. 6), most ships weighed less than 250 tons (225 metric tons). Ships were designed to carry cargo, with transport for passengers on the same vessels being incidental; passengers thus brought their own food and slept on deck. Roman officers could requisition supplies and transport at no cost (cf. Mt 5:41). Caesarea, from which the group sailed, had a renowned harbor complex built by Herod the Great. *Adramyttium.* A city in northwest Asia Minor, Adramyttium had a significant artificial harbor. *Aristarchus ... was with us.* Probably in view of Agrippa's evaluation (26:32), Paul's custody arrangements are light; friends were not always allowed to accompany a prisoner.

27:3 *Sidon.* The voyage begins with making good time; Sidon was nearly 70 nautical miles (110 kilometers) north of Caesarea. *allowed him to go to his friends.* Passengers would not need to remain on board at a port where unloading and reloading freight could require days. Paul's treatment again (as in vv. 1 – 2) shows that his custody is light. At the same time, it is to Julius's advantage to let Paul's friends show Paul hospitality; this allows Julius to requisition fewer supplies from reluctant hosts.

27:4 *passed to the lee of Cyprus.* Although they need to proceed northwest, they must move north before moving west; this was the usual route, but especially important now because winds from the northwest were common late in sailing season. Thus they make their way north partly by using the large island of Cyprus as a shield from the wind.

27:5 *Myra in Lycia.* Land breezes would help them sail west along Asia Minor's coast to Myra's port town, Andriace. This was an even more significant port for the Alexandrian grain ships than was Patara (21:1); finding a larger ship (see v. 6 and note) was therefore not difficult.

27:6 *Alexandrian ship.* Rome imported as much as a third of its grain from Egypt — probably more than 100,000 tons (90,000 metric tons) per year. It doled out grain free to Rome's residents to ensure peace in the capital, while many children in Egypt died of malnutrition and its effects. Many cargo ships, sometimes 180 feet (55 meters)

PAUL'S JOURNEY TO ROME c. AD 59–60 (Ac 27:1—28:16)

Italy[a] and put us on board. 7We made slow
headway for many days and had difficulty
arriving off Cnidus. When the wind did
not allow us to hold our course,[b] we sailed
to the lee of Crete,[c] opposite Salmone. 8We
moved along the coast with difficulty and
came to a place called Fair Havens, near
the town of Lasea.
9Much time had been lost, and sailing
had already become dangerous because by
now it was after the Day of Atonement.[a][d]
So Paul warned them, 10"Men, I can see
that our voyage is going to be disastrous
and bring great loss to ship and cargo, and
to our own lives also."[e] 11But the centurion, instead of listening to what Paul said,

27:6 [a] ver 1
27:7 [b] ver 4 [c] ver 12, 13, 21
27:9 [d] Lev 16:29-31; 23:27-29; Nu 29:7
27:10 [e] ver 21

[a] 9 That is, Yom Kippur

long, plied the waters from Alexandria in Egypt's northern delta to Rome. Persons of means privately owned the ships, but Rome ensured that their investment was economically rewarding. Although the return voyage from Rome was often less than two weeks, because of Mediterranean wind patterns the voyage to Rome ranged from about six weeks to more than two months.

27:7 *arriving off Cnidus ... Salmone.* Cnidus in Asia Minor had two harbors; from there they could sail across the open sea for two or three days to Salmone in northeastern Crete.

27:8 *along the coast.* Because of winds from the northwest, they sail along the southern coast of Crete; few of Crete's good harbors were in its north in any case. *Fair Havens.* A bay two kilometers west of Lasea; sheltered by small islands, it would protect ships from strong winds.

27:9 *become dangerous.* The most dangerous and least sailed season ran from roughly Nov. 10 through early March, but dangers were possible as early as mid-September. Some scholars estimate that 20 percent of long voyages encountered serious dangers; the known remains of over a thousand wrecked ships from antiquity testify how frequently the dangers translated into disasters. Grain ships normally made their first voyage from Alexandria in spring; a second run was economically desirable, but unloading could take 12 days and ships could also face bureaucratic delays in Italy. If a ship returned to Alexandria by late August, they might reload to attempt a second voyage, despite the risks.

27:11 *owner of the ship.* Ship owners were usually wealthy despite their low social status. Current imperial policy offered serious economic benefits to ships bringing Rome grain even in the most dangerous seasons. Ship owners paid high costs for insurance, but the loans they used to fund the cargo would be forgiven if the ship went down. Because sailing was dangerous, most sailors were such from necessity, because they either were very poor or were slaves. Financial considerations normally determined whether ship owners gambled on another voyage. In this case, it is too late to reach Rome

followed the advice of the pilot and of the owner of the ship. 12Since the harbor was unsuitable to winter in, the majority decided that we should sail on, hoping to reach Phoenix and winter there. This was a harbor in Crete, facing both southwest and northwest.

The Storm

13When a gentle south wind began to blow, they saw their opportunity; so they weighed anchor and sailed along the shore of Crete. 14Before very long, a wind of hurricane force,[f] called the Northeaster, swept down from the island. 15The ship was caught by the storm and could not head into the wind; so we gave way to it and were driven along. 16As we passed to the lee of a small island called Cauda, we were hardly able to make the lifeboat secure, 17so the men hoisted it aboard. Then they passed ropes under the ship itself to hold it together. Because they were afraid they would run aground[g] on the sandbars of Syrtis, they lowered the sea anchor[a] and let the ship be driven along. 18We took such a violent battering from the storm that the next day they began to throw the cargo overboard.[h] 19On the third day, they threw the ship's tackle overboard with their own hands. 20When neither sun nor stars appeared for many days and the storm continued raging, we finally gave up all hope of being saved.

21After they had gone a long time without food, Paul stood up before them and said: "Men, you should have taken my advice[i] not to sail from Crete;[j] then you would have spared yourselves this damage and loss. 22But now I urge you to keep up your courage,[k] because not one of you will be lost; only the ship will be destroyed. 23Last night an angel[l] of the God to whom I belong and whom I serve[m] stood beside me[n] 24and said, 'Do not be afraid, Paul. You must stand trial before Caesar;[o] and God has graciously given you the lives of all who sail with you.'[p] 25So keep up your courage,[q] men, for I have faith in God that it will happen just as he told me.[r]

27:14 [f] Mk 4:37 **27:17** [g] ver 26, 39

27:18 [h] ver 19, 38; Jnh 1:5 **27:21** [i] ver 10 [j] ver 7 **27:22** [k] ver 25, 36 **27:23** [l] Ac 5:19 [m] Ro 1:9 [n] Ac 18:9; 23:11; 2Ti 4:17 **27:24** [o] Ac 23:11 [p] ver 44 **27:25** [q] ver 22, 36 [r] Ro 4:20,21

[a] 17 Or *the sails*

before winter, but a better harbor than Fair Havens is available (v. 12).

27:12 *unsuitable to winter in.* Fair Havens (v. 8) was not the ideal harbor, and worse yet few outsiders would want to pass the winter in this small fishing village. *hoping to reach Phoenix.* By contrast, Phoenix, some 40 to 50 miles (65 to 80 kilometers) away, had one of the best harbors in this part of Crete. Reaching Phoenix, however, entailed a degree of risk. A ship could follow Crete's coast four to six miles (6.5 to 9.5 kilometers) past Fair Havens, but at Cape Matala the coast turns north, providing no protection against a wind from the northwest. This would be especially the case if (as is likely) they sailed across open sea (through the bay of Mesará) to reach Phoenix quickly.

27:13 *gentle south wind began to blow.* A wind from the south would help keep them near the coast, preventing risk of being blown out to sea.

27:14 *wind of hurricane force, called the Northeaster.* Unfortunately, mountains immediately north of Fair Havens obscured the visibility of storms coming from the northeast—and in this region, a south wind can suddenly shift to a northeaster. Even if they saw the approaching storm once they reached the bay of Mesará, they did not know local conditions: sandwiched between two mountain ranges, the Platanos Valley could concentrate wind speed and hurl the ship into the open sea.

27:15 *could not head into the wind.* Ancient ships, with their square mainsails, could sail against the wind only by tacking widely; it was impossible for them to sail against a storm.

27:16 *a small island called Cauda.* The northeaster quickly carries them by Cauda, more than 20 miles (32 kilometers) southwest of where the wind struck them. Ominously, it was the southernmost Greek island; the course farther southwest was dangerous (v. 17). *make the lifeboat secure.* The east-northeast side of the island they were passing offered no harbors, but it blocked some of the wind's force long enough for them to salvage the lifeboat, or dinghy. Often it was towed behind the ship, but in this storm it would be lost if not brought aboard.

27:17 *ropes.* Frapping cables used to brace ships' hulls. *sea anchor.* If the NIV is correct in referring to a sea anchor here, it might be used as a drag, but the Greek term's meaning is debated. Some 400 miles (645 kilometers) to the southwest—the direction the storm was driving them—lay the feared Syrtis Major off the Libyan coast. Ships and even fleets had been destroyed there, often grounded in shallow water and then submerged with the onslaught of new waves.

27:18 *throw the cargo overboard.* A common means to try to lighten the ship in drastic conditions. They undoubtedly can discard only a small portion of it here, however (cf. v. 38); the ship was probably transporting far more than 250 tons (225 metric tons) of cargo. Unloading at docks could take 12 days, despite the availability of equipment and manual help needed to move sacks of grain often piled six feet (1.8 meters) deep.

27:19 *threw the ship's tackle overboard.* Many commentators think that the "tackle" refers to the yard, a spar (a long pole made of wood that supported the sails) nearly as high as the ship was long. Workers would need to either secure it or jettison it.

27:20 *neither sun nor stars.* Without stars, sailors could not determine their position or course. In addition to the horror of drowning, ancient beliefs increased their despair. Those who died at sea normally could not obtain burial, and Greek tradition denied the unburied a place in the netherworld; in their belief, the ghost of someone who drowned might hover perpetually over the site of their death.

27:21 *Men.* A customary address in ancient speeches. Some ancient speakers could raise their voices above storms, though it is not clear whether Paul speaks on deck (where passengers remained and even slept during normal conditions) or in one of the larger compartments beneath it. Although the crew would all be male, presumably not all the passengers were.

27:24 *Caesar.* Though Nero himself would not personally take time to judge all the cases, his court would.

27:25 *keep up your courage.* Gentiles respected sages who lived up to their teachings about courage, especially

26 Nevertheless, we must run aground[s] on some island."[t]

The Shipwreck

27 On the fourteenth night we were still being driven across the Adriatic[a] Sea, when about midnight the sailors sensed they were approaching land. 28 They took soundings and found that the water was a hundred and twenty feet[b] deep. A short time later they took soundings again and found it was ninety feet[c] deep. 29 Fearing that we would be dashed against the rocks, they dropped four anchors from the stern and prayed for daylight. 30 In an attempt to escape from the ship, the sailors let the lifeboat[u] down into the sea, pretending they were going to lower some anchors from the bow. 31 Then Paul said to the centurion and the soldiers, "Unless these men stay with the ship, you cannot be saved."[v] 32 So the soldiers cut the ropes that held the lifeboat and let it drift away.

33 Just before dawn Paul urged them all to eat. "For the last fourteen days," he said, "you have been in constant suspense and have gone without food—you haven't eaten anything. 34 Now I urge you to take some food. You need it to survive. Not one of you will lose a single hair from his head."[w] 35 After he said this, he took some bread and gave thanks to God in front of them all. Then he broke it[x] and began to eat. 36 They were all encouraged[y] and ate some food themselves. 37 Altogether there were 276 of us on board. 38 When they had eaten as much as they wanted, they lightened the ship by throwing the grain into the sea.[z]

39 When daylight came, they did not recognize the land, but they saw a bay with a sandy beach,[a] where they decided to run the ship aground if they could. 40 Cutting loose the anchors,[b] they left them in the sea and at the same time untied the ropes

27:26 [s] ver 17, 39 [t] Ac 28:1
27:30 [u] ver 16
27:31 [v] ver 24
27:34 [w] Mt 10:30
27:35 [x] Mt 14:19
27:36 [y] ver 22, 25
27:38 [z] ver 18; Jnh 1:5
27:39 [a] Ac 28:1
27:40 [b] ver 29

[a] *27* In ancient times the name referred to an area extending well south of Italy. [b] *28* Or about 37 meters [c] *28* Or about 27 meters

in storms at sea. *faith in God.* Gentiles believed gods would sometimes rescue ships for the sake of a particularly devout person on board, or sink them because of someone very wicked. Paul's comportment and confidence contrast starkly with the behavior of someone like Jonah (Jnh 1:5–12).

27:27 *On the fourteenth night.* A ship blown southwest from Cauda but attempting to tack north to evade Syrtis (vv. 16–17) would normally reach Malta in roughly 13 days (here it took 14). *Adriatic Sea.* In contrast to the modern definition, the ancient boundaries of the Adriatic Sea included the area as far south as Malta (28:1). *sensed.* The familiar sound of waves pounding land would normally be audible over a mile (1.5 kilometers) from Koura, east of Malta (v. 28).

27:28 *took soundings.* Sailors took soundings by lowering lead weights smeared with grease on a hollow underside, to pick up samples from the sea floor. *a hundred and twenty feet deep.* That is, about 37 meters. This probably indicates that they are within a quarter of a mile (0.4 kilometers) of Koura, east of Malta; they may have passed within 1,500 feet (450 meters) of it. They would reach the second sounding recorded in this verse about half an hour later. *ninety feet deep.* That is, about 27 meters. The rapid decrease in depth means that they are moving swiftly toward being grounded, very possibly on rocks just beneath the sea's surface. This grounding could rupture the ship's hull.

27:29 *dropped four anchors.* To stall for time, probably one after the other. *from the stern.* Usually ships dropped anchors from the bow, the front of the ship, but here sailors drop them from the stern, the back of the ship. Scholars sometimes suggest that they did so to prevent the stern from being driven around into the rocks or because they will resume their course in the morning. *prayed for daylight.* The visibility of daylight is needed to try to ground the ship safely.

27:30 *let the lifeboat down.* The lifeboat, or dinghy, could be used for maneuvers, but sometimes people also tried to use them to escape (as Paul recognizes the case to be here, presumably prophetically). The dinghy would not risk grounding on the rocks ahead, but it held only a handful of people.

27:31 *the centurion and the soldiers.* Though villagers deferred to centurions, the officers mentioned in v. 11 ran the ship under normal circumstances. In the present emergency, however, the soldiers have an advantage: they are armed. *Unless these men stay with the ship.* Without the sailors' skills to navigate the ship closer to land, the others aboard would not survive.

27:34 *Not one … will lose a single hair.* The meaning is obvious enough in any case, but the phrase reflects an OT idiom for protection (1Sa 14:45; 2Sa 14:11; 1Ki 1:52; Lk 21:18).

27:35 *took some bread and gave thanks.* Jewish custom was to offer thanks and then break bread. Passengers on ships had to bring their own food supplies, of which bread was the most common form.

27:37 *276 of us on board.* Alexandrian grain ships such as this one often weighed some 340 tons (300 metric tons). Some grain ships were even larger, a few weighing more than 1,000 tons (900 metric tons) and carrying up to 600 passengers.

27:38 *throwing the grain into the sea.* In an effort to lighten the ship and keep it above subsurface rocks as long as possible, they discard more of the cargo, which consisted especially of sacks of wheat (see note on v. 18). This would be done by forming a chain that would pass the heavy sacks in hold compartments from one person to another until those on the edge of the deck could throw them overboard. They could not have removed all the tons of wheat, but it was important to do what they could. Once wet, the wheat below the deck could expand and even double in size, further rupturing a leaking hull.

27:39 *a bay with a sandy beach.* Although the passage of time has altered the landscape, most scholars agree that the bay here is St. Paul's Bay, on the island's northeast.

27:40 *rudders.* The pair of steering oars at the stern; the pilot used handles to control them and steer the ship. While the anchors held the ship stationary at night the rudders were best kept immobile, but now they were essential for guiding the ship. *foresail.* In addition to the square mainsail (v. 15), they had a smaller, triangular foresail; the latter could be removed when slowing down when coming into a harbor, but now reaching land while they still can is urgent.

that held the rudders. Then they hoisted the foresail to the wind and made for the beach. [41]But the ship struck a sandbar and ran aground. The bow stuck fast and would not move, and the stern was broken to pieces by the pounding of the surf.[c]

[42]The soldiers planned to kill the prisoners to prevent any of them from swimming away and escaping. [43]But the centurion wanted to spare Paul's life[d] and kept them from carrying out their plan. He ordered those who could swim to jump overboard first and get to land. [44]The rest were to get there on planks or on other pieces of the ship. In this way everyone reached land safely.[e]

Paul Ashore on Malta

28 Once safely on shore, we[f] found out that the island[g] was called Malta. [2]The islanders showed us unusual kindness. They built a fire and welcomed us all because it was raining and cold. [3]Paul gathered a pile of brushwood and, as he put it on the fire, a viper, driven out by the heat, fastened itself on his hand. [4]When the islanders saw the snake hanging from his hand,[h] they said to each other, "This man must be a murderer; for though he escaped from the sea, the goddess Justice has not allowed him to live."[i] [5]But Paul shook the snake off into the fire and suffered no ill effects.[j] [6]The people expected him to swell up or suddenly fall dead; but after waiting a long time and seeing nothing unusual happen to him, they changed their minds and said he was a god.[k]

[7]There was an estate nearby that belonged to Publius, the chief official of the island. He welcomed us to his home and showed us generous hospitality for three days. [8]His father was sick in bed, suffering from fever and dysentery. Paul went in to see him and, after prayer,[l] placed his hands on him and healed him.[m] [9]When this had happened, the rest of the sick on the island came and were cured. [10]They honored us in many ways; and when we were ready to sail, they furnished us with the supplies we needed.

Paul's Arrival at Rome

[11]After three months we put out to sea in a ship that had wintered in the island—it was an Alexandrian ship[n] with the figurehead of the twin gods Castor and

27:41 [c]2Co 11:25
27:43 [d]ver 3
27:44 [e]ver 22, 31
28:1 [f]Ac 16:10 [g]Ac 27:26,39
28:4 [h]Mk 16:18 [i]Lk 13:2,4
28:5 [j]Lk 10:19
28:6 [k]Ac 14:11
28:8 [l]Jas 5:14, 15 [m]Ac 9:40
28:11 [n]Ac 27:6

27:41 *sandbar.* May be St. Paul's Bank; it is now about 40 feet (12 meters) underwater, but it would not need to be much higher than that to ground a large ship. *pounding of the surf.* Waves are violent here, so once the ship lodged here and could no longer advance, the waves pounding its stern would soon spell the ship's ruin. Passengers would have to get to shore.

27:42 *planned to kill the prisoners.* Soldiers could be punished if their detainees escaped; shipwreck would normally absolve them, but it was more prudent not to take chances with potentially arbitrary authorities. Most of the prisoners were slated to die to entertain Rome's populace anyway.

27:43 *wanted to spare Paul's life.* But it would be hard to justify treating the prisoners inconsistently, so sparing Paul meant sparing all.

27:44 In these circumstances, no one would expect the survival of all, barring divine intervention. *planks.* Some suggest that the planks were boards used to separate grain in the hold below. Incoming waves near the shore would help propel toward shore both swimmers and those aboard the planks. If Luke's notes were on papyrus, the ink on it would dissolve in water. He would likely have access to a sealable container, however; certainly he had advance notice of the shipwreck (v. 26).

28:1 *Malta.* Ships from Rome heading toward Egypt regularly stopped at Syracuse (v. 12) and then sometimes at Malta. They stopped, however, not at the site Luke depicts here but at the viable harbors farther south on the island; a good harbor seven miles (11 kilometers) south of their landfall was at what is today Valetta, Malta's capital.

28:2 *welcomed us.* Hospitality toward strangers was a valued virtue in antiquity; its importance was particularly recognized toward people who had been shipwrecked. The elite islanders could be conversant in Latin (see v. 7 and note), but most residents of the island spoke Punic, the language of Carthage. *raining and cold.* The temperature on Malta at this time of year averages about 60°F (or about 15°C), but can be cooler after much rain.

28:4 *goddess Justice has not allowed him to live.* Local and Roman culture personified Justice. People often attributed survival at sea to divine favor and hence virtue; one who escaped shipwreck only to die another way was thought cursed by the gods to die one way or another.

28:5 Cf. Nu 21:6–9; Ps 91:13.

28:6 *said he was a god.* Both Jews and Gentiles thought that persons who were exceptionally close to God or gods might experience special protection. Gentiles sometimes venerated such people as partly divine; Gentiles' practice of treating some humans as divine is an issue also elsewhere in Acts (cf. 10:25–26; 12:22–23; 14:11,15).

28:7 *Publius.* A Roman name. Members of the island's elite could be Roman citizens, conversant in Latin and/or Greek. *the chief official of the island.* Inscriptions from Malta sometimes use the term here translated "the chief official" for the governor; at the least he is a leading citizen.

28:8 *suffering from fever and dysentery.* Typhoid and other causes of fever existed, but malaria was the most common cause. Fever also accompanies dysentery.

28:10 *honored us in many ways ... furnished us with the supplies.* Ancient Mediterranean culture emphasized reciprocity; Paul had benefited them, so they honor Paul and supply his needs.

28:11 *After three months.* Sea traffic sometimes became safe again as early as Feb. 7 (see note on 27:9). *put out to sea in a ship.* Roman officers could requisition supplies and transport at no cost (cf. Mt 5:41), in this case on another grain ship from Alexandria that had to stop short of Rome for the winter. *Castor and Pollux.* Sailors commonly invoked the twin brothers Castor and Pollux as their patrons and protectors during storms. In ancient myth, although only Pollux had inherited immortality, he shared it with his

Pollux. [12]We put in at Syracuse and stayed there three days. [13]From there we set sail and arrived at Rhegium. The next day the south wind came up, and on the following day we reached Puteoli. [14]There we found some brothers and sisters[o] who invited us to spend a week with them. And so we came to Rome. [15]The brothers and sisters[p] there had heard that we were coming, and they traveled as far as the Forum of Appius and the Three Taverns to meet us. At the sight of these people Paul thanked God and was encouraged. [16]When we got to Rome, Paul was allowed to live by himself, with a soldier to guard him.[q]

Paul Preaches at Rome Under Guard

[17]Three days later he called together the local Jewish leaders.[r] When they had assembled, Paul said to them: "My brothers,[s] although I have done nothing against our people[t] or against the customs of our ancestors,[u] I was arrested in Jerusalem and handed over to the Romans. [18]They examined me[v] and wanted to release me,[w] because I was not guilty of any crime deserving death.[x] [19]The Jews objected, so I was compelled to make an appeal to Caesar.[y] I certainly did not intend to bring any charge against my own people. [20]For this reason I have asked to see you and talk with you. It is because of the hope of Israel[z] that I am bound with this chain."[a]

[21]They replied, "We have not received any letters from Judea concerning you, and none of our people[b] who have come from there has reported or said anything bad about you. [22]But we want to hear what your views are, for we know that people everywhere are talking against this sect."[c]

[23]They arranged to meet Paul on a certain day, and came in even larger numbers to the place where he was staying. He witnessed to them from morning till evening, explaining about the kingdom of God,[d] and from the Law of Moses and from the Prophets[e] he tried to persuade them about Jesus.[f] [24]Some were convinced by what he said, but others would not believe.[g] [25]They disagreed among themselves and began to leave after Paul had made this final statement: "The Holy Spirit spoke the truth to your ancestors when he said through Isaiah the prophet:

[26]" 'Go to this people and say,
"You will be ever hearing but never
understanding;
you will be ever seeing but never
perceiving."
[27]For this people's heart has become
calloused;[h]

28:14 [o]Ac 1:16 **28:15** [p]Ac 1:16 **28:16** [q]Ac 24:23; 27:3 **28:17** [r]Ac 25:2 [s]Ac 22:5 [t]Ac 25:8 [u]Ac 6:14 **28:18** [v]Ac 22:24 [w]Ac 26:31, 32 [x]Ac 23:9 **28:19** [y]Ac 25:11 **28:20** [z]Ac 26:6, 7 [a]Ac 21:33 **28:21** [b]Ac 22:5 **28:22** [c]Ac 24:5, 14 **28:23** [d]Ac 19:8 [e]Ac 8:35 [f]Ac 17:3 **28:24** [g]Ac 14:4 **28:27** [h]Ps 119:70

brother Castor; in some versions their days among the living alternated.

28:12 *Syracuse.* The voyage from a likely Maltese harbor to Syracuse was nearly 100 miles (160 kilometers). Syracuse was Sicily's leading city, renowned for its beauty, with two harbors. Some estimate its population at this time as high as 250,000 people, making it one of the largest cities of antiquity.

28:13 *Rhegium.* A city in Italy near the strait that separated Sicily from Italy. It was a common stop between Sicily and Rome. *Puteoli.* It had been the chief maritime destination of Alexandrian grain ships until Claudius's recent construction work in Ostia, and it remained a major port.

28:14 *came to Rome.* The inland journey from Puteoli to Rome would cover well over 100 miles (160 kilometers) and could take a week. At Capua, after traveling about 20 miles (32 kilometers), they would walk toward Rome on the famous Appian Way.

28:15 *traveled … to meet us.* Delegations from cities would normally come out to meet and welcome an important public figure. *the Forum of Appius.* Nearly 40 miles (65 kilometers) from Rome on the Appian Way. *Three Taverns.* A town originally named for its smaller way stations, about 30 miles (48 kilometers) from Rome.

28:16 *Rome.* The largest city of the ancient Mediterranean world, boasting close to one million residents. *allowed to live by himself, with a soldier to guard him.* For Paul's accommodations, see note on v. 30. Although being unguarded completely was the lightest form of custody, Paul's is still fairly light. Being chained to only one soldier and living on his own shows that Paul was treated as a high-status person who posed no danger. Presumably the supervisor took the verdict of 26:31 into account. Paul's guard was likely assigned from the Praetorian Guard, the elite units of the Roman military who served in Italy.

28:17 *local Jewish leaders.* Although the massive Alexandrian Jewish community had a top leader, Rome's Jewish community consisted of many autonomous synagogues. A number of Jews in Rome were Roman citizens, but most Jews in Rome were poor and spoke Greek (see the Introduction to Romans: Setting; see also the article "Rome," p. 1948).

28:19 *did not intend to bring any charge against my own people.* The Jewish community in Rome had suffered from scandals in earlier decades, so Paul's assurance that he will not bring any charge against his people is important (on returning charges against accusers, see note on 24:19).

28:21 *have not received any letters.* Paul's ship arrived early in the new sailing season, perhaps before letters could arrive (letters were carried by travelers). If his accusers gave up the case, however, the case would eventually be thrown out.

28:22 *we want to hear what your views are.* Jesus' movement was large in Rome: within probably five years Nero was martyring hundreds of Christians in Rome. Yet the synagogue leaders had little contact with Jesus' followers at this point, although Jewish believers expelled in 18:2 could have returned after Claudius's death in AD 54 (the present scene is probably somewhere near AD 59 – 60). They welcome Paul as an educated person of their own class who can explain about the movement.

28:26 – 27 Lest Paul's dialogue partners suppose that a belief rejected by so many of their own people cannot be true, Paul reminds them from Isa 6:9 – 10 that God's people had often rejected his message.

they hardly hear with their ears,
and they have closed their eyes.
Otherwise they might see with their eyes,
hear with their ears,
understand with their hearts
and turn, and I would heal them.'[a][i]

28 "Therefore I want you to know that
God's salvation[j] has been sent to the Gentiles,[k] and they will listen!" [29][b]

28:27 [i] Isa 6:9, 10
28:28 [j] Lk 2:30 [k] Ac 13:46
28:31 [l] ver 23; Mt 4:23

30 For two whole years Paul stayed there
in his own rented house and welcomed
all who came to see him. 31 He proclaimed
the kingdom of God[l] and taught about the
Lord Jesus Christ — with all boldness and
without hindrance!

[a] *27* Isaiah 6:9,10 (see Septuagint) [b] *29* Some manuscripts include here *After he said this, the Jews left, arguing vigorously among themselves.*

28:30 *two whole years.* Early tradition says that Paul was released but arrested again once Nero began killing Christians in AD 64 (see the Introduction to 1 Peter). As a Roman citizen, Paul was beheaded; Peter was reportedly crucified upside down. *rented house.* The Greek term here simply means "rented quarters." Most of Rome's residents lived in tenement apartments, and Paul may have stayed in one of these. Rome tracked its cases carefully, so if no accusers arrived, Paul eventually would be released.

28:31 *proclaimed ... and taught about the Lord Jesus Christ — with all boldness.* Many ancient works ended abruptly. Acts ends positively, showing how the expansion of the good news repeatedly emphasized earlier in the book continues even in the heart of the empire. In so doing, Acts presumably points to how the good news will continue "to the ends of the earth" (1:8).

NEW TESTAMENT

THE LETTERS & REVELATION

MESSAGES FOR THE GROWING GLOBAL CHURCH

Ancient Letters

In the ancient world, communication was difficult and costly. Writing materials were expensive, and conveying these letters to their intended recipient(s) took time and effort. Although governmental communication was delivered via special courier, no publically or privately funded professional mail service existed, so travelers normally carried letters (cf. Ro 16:1 – 2; Col 4:7).

As a result of these realities, at the time that Paul and other authors in the New Testament composed their letters, a typical letter averaged only 87 words — even more brief than 3 John (about 222 words) or Philemon (about 338 words). Even intellectuals' literary letters to peers were of limited length — e.g., Cicero's averaged about 300 words and Seneca's 1000 words. By contrast, Paul's longest surviving letter, Romans, is more than 7000 words! (In antiquity, the price of a scribe and writing materials meant that producing a letter of this length could cost something like $2000 in early twenty-first century U.S. currency.) Moreover, while some of Paul's correspondence includes personal information, as do most letters, other parts communicate his message as if Paul is preaching to the intended recipients.

Paul's letters contain not only greetings and news, but also persuasive argumentation. Because of this special character of much of Paul's correspondence, many scholars compare his letters more to ancient speeches than to typical letters. Urban Greek and Roman culture honored oratorical skill, or rhetoric, in a speaker's presentation. Rhetoric was pervasive and was highlighted, e.g., in all public assemblies, in courts, and at funerals. Even most letter essays (essays in the form of letters), however, were not arranged as speeches, so scholars debate the degree to which rhetoric shaped Paul's letters. Most scholars at least agree that Paul made use of common forms of argumentation that rhetoric had made popular (or formalized) in his milieu (see the article "Rhetoric and Paul's Letters," p. 1986).

Most of Paul's letters and at least some letters written by other New Testament writers (most obviously 2 and 3 John) address local situations. Because these letters do not all address the same situation, the same writer can argue somewhat differently in different letters (even, e.g., in Romans and Galatians, despite their similarities).

If these New Testament letters address local issues, how can we then reapply their message in our very different contexts today? If we can understand how these writers could address their hearers' settings, we can often find analogous situations in today's world. The principles remain relevant, and the very concreteness of their applications summons us to address the concrete realities of our churches, and of our lives, today as well. (Paul often used the Old Testament the same way, finding examples relevant for his churches; e.g., 1Co 10:11.) Therefore, reading each letter as a whole and trying to hear it in its original context helps us understand better how we can apply it to the most relevant settings today. ◆

THE LETTERS

ROMANS

Setting

Scholars are unanimous that Paul wrote Romans from Corinth or nearby Cenchreae (Ro 16:1) somewhere between AD 55 and 58, but they hold a variety of views concerning the circumstances that form the letter's background. Pious Jews or Gentile converts to Judaism had believed the gospel and then introduced it to Rome (Ac 2:10 – 11), laying the theological foundations for the churches there. This may explain the heavy consideration of Scripture and traditional Jewish themes in Paul's letter to the Romans.

A key issue faced by the Roman church shortly before Paul wrote was the expulsion of Jewish Christians, or at least their most prominent leaders, from Rome probably in AD 49 (Ac 18:1 – 2). Five years later, in AD 54, the edict was repealed and those who wished to return did so. Many scholars believe that this new influx of Jewish believers in Jesus led to some debates with Gentile Christians who may have composed the church's majority in the preceding half decade. Certainly the need for Jewish and Gentile believers to welcome one another figures strategically in Romans (15:7 – 12). Although most of the believers there now appear to be Gentiles (1:6,13; 11:13), some of the leaders of house (or apartment) churches in ch. 16 are Jewish.

QUICK GLANCE

AUTHOR:
The apostle Paul

AUDIENCE:
The church in Rome, predominantly Gentile but including a minority of Jews

DATE:
About AD 57

THEME:
Paul writes to the church in Rome to present his basic statement of the gospel: God's plan of salvation for all peoples, Jew and Gentile alike.

Rome had an estimated population of one million residents; of these, many were slaves and many others were noncitizen immigrants from the provinces, including an estimated 40,000 to 50,000 Jewish residents. Most people lived in multistory apartment buildings. Wealthier residents and businesses occupied the ground floor, which often had access to running water, but most tenants lived in the flimsier and tinier higher stories. Most of the earliest members of the Roman church, both Jewish and Gentile, were predominantly Greek-speaking; many had immigrated from further east. When examining background, readers of Romans and Paul's other letters should keep in mind that Jews in many parts of the empire had absorbed Greek language and elements of Greek culture for centuries. Many Greek ideas and expressions were by this period also found in Judaism. The traditional dichotomy between Jewish and Gentile, then, does not always apply with respect to culture, except for distinctively Jewish practices. Moreover, not all Jews held identical views or practices.

Themes

A primary emphasis in Romans is that both Jew and Gentile are put right with God the same way, through Jesus Christ (1:16 – 17; 3:22,29 – 30; 15:8 – 9). Most Jewish people believed that God had chosen and saved his people Israel because of his love; grace was not, therefore, a foreign concept to them. Nevertheless, in various Jewish movements some views and practices probably mitigated this dependence on grace, as also happens among Christians today. Moreover, to fully convert to Judaism, Gentiles had to be circumcised (if male) and agree to observe the Law of Moses: significant hurdles to those not circumcised as infants or raised with the law as part of their culture. Yet Paul proclaims that God's covenant faithfulness and love declared in the Scriptures has climaxed in Jesus' death and resurrection, and truly embracing God's covenant now must include acknowledging Jesus as the rightful Lord. Reception of the promised, transforming Spirit (Eze 36:26 – 27; Joel 2:28 – 29) takes priority over physical circumcision and laws that merely prepared for this transformation. Gentile followers of Jesus are thus now welcomed into God's covenant on the same terms as Jewish people.

Thus, Paul argues, Jews and Gentiles are equally lost (1:18 — 3:20) but can both be made right with God through Christ and relying on him (1:16 – 17; 3:21 – 30). God values spiritual more than ethnic descent from Abraham (4:1 — 5:11), for all are sinful descendants of Adam (5:12 – 21). The law can teach about righteousness but does not impart it (ch. 7) unless written on the heart by the Spirit (8:2). God is not obligated to choose for salvation based on ethnic descent from Abraham (ch. 9). Gentile Christians, however, should respect Jewish believers and honor their shared heritage (ch. 11). The heart of God's law is loving one another (13:8 – 10). Believers should not look down on one another's food practices or holy days (14:1 — 15:2). Jews and Gentiles should welcome one another in Christ (15:6 – 12), as Jesus came for both (vv. 7 – 9). Paul, a Jewish minister to the Gentiles, was bringing an offering for needy Jewish believers from the Gentile churches, who recognized their shared heritage with the Jewish people (15:25 – 27). Beware, Paul warns, of divisions (16:17), which in Rome probably included divisions over the role of law practice in salvation and in membership among God's people. ◆

1 Paul, a servant of Christ Jesus, called
to be an apostle[a] and set apart[b] for the
gospel of God[c]— 2the gospel he promised
beforehand through his prophets in the
Holy Scriptures[d] 3regarding his Son, who
as to his earthly life[a][e] was a descendant
of David, 4and who through the Spirit of
holiness was appointed the Son of God in
power[b] by his resurrection from the dead:
Jesus Christ our Lord. 5Through him we
received grace and apostleship to call all
the Gentiles[f] to the obedience that comes
from[c] faith[g] for his name's sake. 6And you
also are among those Gentiles who are
called to belong to Jesus Christ.[h]

7To all in Rome who are loved by God[i]
and called to be his holy people:

Grace and peace to you from God our
Father and from the Lord Jesus Christ.[j]

Paul's Longing to Visit Rome

8First, I thank my God through Jesus
Christ for all of you,[k] because your faith is
being reported all over the world.[l] 9God,
whom I serve[m] in my spirit in preaching
the gospel of his Son, is my witness[n] how
constantly I remember you 10in my prayers
at all times; and I pray that now at last by
God's will the way may be opened for me
to come to you.[o]

11I long to see you[p] so that I may impart to you some spiritual gift to make you
strong— 12that is, that you and I may be
mutually encouraged by each other's faith.
13I do not want you to be unaware, brothers and sisters,[d] that I planned many times
to come to you (but have been prevented
from doing so until now)[q] in order that I
might have a harvest among you, just as I
have had among the other Gentiles.

14I am obligated[r] both to Greeks and
non-Greeks, both to the wise and the foolish. 15That is why I am so eager to preach
the gospel also to you who are in Rome.[s]

16For I am not ashamed of the gospel,[t]
because it is the power of God[u] that brings
salvation to everyone who believes: first
to the Jew,[v] then to the Gentile.[w] 17For in
the gospel the righteousness of God is revealed[x]—a righteousness that is by faith
from first to last,[e] just as it is written: "The
righteous will live by faith."[f][y]

1:1 [a] 1Co 1:1 [b] Ac 9:15 [c] 2Co 11:7 **1:2** [d] Gal 3:8 **1:3** [e] Jn 1:14 **1:5** [f] Ac 9:15 [g] Ac 6:7 **1:6** [h] Rev 17:14 **1:7** [i] Ro 8:39 [j] 1Co 1:3 **1:8** [k] 1Co 1:4 [l] Ro 16:19 **1:9** [m] 2Ti 1:3 [n] Php 1:8 **1:10** [o] Ro 15:32 **1:11** [p] Ro 15:23 **1:13** [q] Ro 15:22, 23 **1:14** [r] 1Co 9:16 **1:15** [s] Ro 15:20 **1:16** [t] 2Ti 1:8 [u] 1Co 1:18 [v] Ac 3:26 [w] Ro 2:9, 10 **1:17** [x] Ro 3:21 [y] Hab 2:4; Gal 3:11; Heb 10:38

[a] 3 Or *who according to the flesh* [b] 4 Or *was declared with power to be the Son of God* [c] 5 Or *that is* [d] 13 The Greek word for *brothers and sisters* (*adelphoi*) refers here to believers, both men and women, as part of God's family; also in 7:1, 4; 8:12, 29; 10:1; 11:25; 12:1; 15:14, 30; 16:14, 17. [e] 17 Or *is from faith to faith* [f] 17 Hab. 2:4

1:1 *Paul, a servant of Christ Jesus.* Ancient letters began by naming the sender, then named the intended recipients and offered a greeting (here in v. 7). Sometimes the author could expand on a point (here, about his identity) where it was helpful; although many people in Rome knew Paul (e.g., 16:3 – 15), he had not yet visited the believers there. *Paul.* Most people with the name Paul were Roman citizens. *servant.* Scripture had long called prophets God's "servants" (e.g., Jer 25:4); in the Roman world, leading servants of high-status persons could wield more authority than many free persons.
1:2 *gospel he promised beforehand. Gospel* is "good news," an expression used widely in antiquity. Most relevant is its use in the Septuagint, the pre-Christian Greek translation of the OT: the prophets promised good news of restoration (e.g., Isa 40:9; 52:7), which included the reign of David's descendant (Isa 9:6 – 7; 11:1 – 10); see v. 3.
1:3 *regarding his Son.* Gentiles often spoke of sons of the gods (including the emperor), but Scripture applied the title to David's line (2Sa 7:14; Ps 2:7; 89:27), and some Jewish people recognized that Son of God applied *par excellence* to the Davidic Messiah.
1:4 *by his resurrection.* Regular Jewish prayers celebrated God's power expressed in raising the dead.
1:5 *for his name's sake.* Often applied to God's name (Ps 25:11; 31:3), here applied to Jesus (v. 4).
1:7 *called to be his holy people.* "Holy people" had been applied to God's people in earlier Scripture (e.g., Da 7:18, 22,25). *Grace.* The conventional greeting was *chairein*, "greetings," which early Christians often changed to *charis*, "grace." *peace.* The Jewish greeting (sometimes added to *chairein*) was "peace." Letters frequently included prayers or blessings for their recipients; Jewish people used "peace" as a blessing, meaning that they implicitly asked God to give the recipient well-being. *from God our Father and from the Lord Jesus Christ.* Because Paul invokes the Father as well as Jesus in this blessing, he takes for granted here Jesus' deity.
1:8 *I thank my God ... for all of you.* Ancient letters sometimes offered thanks for the recipient. *your faith is being reported.* News from Rome, the empire's highest-status city, spread quickly throughout its empire.
1:9 – 10 *I remember you in my prayers.* Letters often included a prayer (or here, mention of it) for recipients.
1:9 *God ... is my witness.* See note on Php 1:8.
1:11 *I long to see you.* Letters often included affectionate expressions (presumably usually sincere) of the writer's desire to see the recipient.
1:14 *Greeks and non-Greeks.* Greeks divided the world into Greeks (themselves) and barbarians (non-Greeks).
1:16 – 17 Ancient works sometimes included a thesis statement, which is how a majority of scholars view these two verses.
1:16 *first to the Jew, then to the Gentile.* Jews divided the world into Jews (themselves) and Gentiles (here lit. "Greeks," but used as a metonymy for Gentiles; Greeks were often particularly hostile to Jews).
1:17 *the righteousness of God.* Both Scripture and the Dead Sea Scrolls use this phrase in various ways; one of the ways they use this phrase is to describe God's mercy and his righteous faithfulness to his covenant with his people. *as it is written.* Jewish idiom often introduced Scripture quotations this way (see, e.g., 2:24; 3:4,10; cf., e.g., Ne 10:34; Da 9:13). *The righteous will live by faith.* Paul quotes Hab 2:4; the Hebrew reads "The righteous one will live by his faith," whereas the Greek translation better known to Paul's audience reads "by my faith." Paul, perhaps preferring not to take time to explain the Hebrew text's divergence from the more familiar form, omits the pronoun. The Dead Sea Scrolls apply Hab 2:4 in a similar

ROMANS 1:7

Rome

Against some lower estimates, Rome's population was probably close to a million people, by far the largest city of Mediterranean antiquity. This massive population was sustained by a regular grain dole and heavy imports that included more than 200,000 tons (180,000 metric tons) of grain each year. Nevertheless, most of the residents were poor, living in tenement apartments that grew cheaper but also smaller and less sturdy as the floors went higher.

An estimated 40,000 – 50,000 of Rome's residents were Jewish. Some of these Jewish people were Roman citizens, most of them descended from slaves freed more than a century earlier. Greek was the primary language of Rome's Jewish community, however, and also the language of Paul's letter to the believers in Rome. The majority of Jews were poor, and many worked on the docks by the Tiber River. Sources from the period show that Romans ridiculed some Jewish customs, especially circumcision, the Sabbath and Jewish food laws. Many other Romans were attracted to Judaism, but the conversion of Roman women often provoked aristocratic men to criticize Judaism more harshly.

Because Rome mistrusted meetings that it could not control, the Jewish community in the capitol was not united. In contrast to Alexandria, where one leader spoke for the Jewish community, Rome had many synagogues with separate leaders. Such an environment apparently proved conducive for the spread of Jesus' message in a number of the synagogues.

In the wake of one scandal reportedly involving a single Jewish swindler, the emperor Tiberius (42 BC – AD 37) expelled the Jewish community from Rome. Later, probably in AD 49, the emperor Claudius did the same, although it is not likely in either case that all Jews actually left. Because Claudius's expulsion is believed to have been in response to Jewish divisions about the Messiah, it seems likely that Jewish followers of Jesus (cf. Ac 2:10) were involved. This may explain why Aquila and Priscilla were among those compelled to leave (Ac 18:1 – 2). Many scholars believe that Gentile Christians went their separate way from the synagogues after this, accounting for the limited information about them held by members of the Jewish elite in Ac 28:22.

continued on next page

God's Wrath Against Sinful Humanity

[18]The wrath of God[z] is being revealed
from heaven against all the godlessness
and wickedness of people, who suppress
the truth by their wickedness, [19]since what
may be known about God is plain to them,
because God has made it plain to them.[a]
[20]For since the creation of the world God's
invisible qualities — his eternal power and
divine nature — have been clearly seen,
being understood from what has been
made,[b] so that people are without excuse.

1:18 [z] Eph 5:6; Col 3:6
1:19 [a] Ac 14:17
1:20 [b] Ps 19:1-6

way. Commentators debate whether "faith" here refers to God's/Christ's faithfulness, the faith/faithfulness of the believer, or to both (cf. also Ro 3:22 and NIV text note). The majority of interpreters see here the faith/faithfulness of the believer (note "believes" also in 1:16), although in any case faith in God ultimately entails dependence on his faithfulness (cf. 3:3).

1:18 – 32 In these verses Paul, following an argument similar to the popular Wisdom of Solomon, sets up any Jewish critics to recognize their own need for forgiveness. Jewish people viewed idolatry (vv. 18 – 23) and sexual sin (vv. 24 – 27), especially in its homosexual form (vv. 26 – 27), as reprehensible and almost uniquely characteristic of Gentiles. The vice list in vv. 28 – 32 is more general, however, and in ch. 2 (most clearly 2:17 – 27) Paul denounces especially Jewish sin.

1:18 – 22 Both Jewish people and many Gentile philosophers affirmed that God revealed himself in creation. Stoics and many other thinkers saw traces of divine design in all of nature and especially in the human mind.

Nevertheless, the Christian community in Rome grew exponentially. In AD 54, Claudius's death in effect repealed his earlier expulsion order, so even ringleaders in the previous disputes could return. Paul thus knows personally many of the leaders mentioned in Ro 16. As the heart of the empire, Rome always drew visitors and immigrants, and the visits of Paul and (according to very probable early tradition) Peter undoubtedly encouraged the church's growth there. In AD 64, a fire destroyed much of Rome with its narrow alleys and many flimsy wooden structures. Rumor blamed the emperor, but Nero found a convenient scapegoat in the Christians. Though he burned large numbers of them alive as torches to light his imperial gardens at night and killed some Christians in other ways, the movement remained strong in Rome after Nero's demise. This suggests that by this point, just three and a half decades after Jesus' resurrection in Judea, Jesus had thousands of followers in Rome. ◆

Artist's recreation of the first-century forum at Rome.

21 For although they knew God, they
neither glorified him as God nor gave
thanks to him, but their thinking became futile and their foolish hearts were
darkened.[c] 22 Although they claimed to
be wise, they became fools[d] 23 and exchanged the glory of the immortal God
for images[e] made to look like a mortal
human being and birds and animals and
reptiles.

24 Therefore God gave them over[f] in the
sinful desires of their hearts to sexual impurity for the degrading of their bodies
with one another.[g] 25 They exchanged the
truth about God for a lie,[h] and worshiped

1:21 [c] Jer 2:5; Eph 4:17,18 **1:22** [d] 1Co 1:20,27 **1:23** [e] Ps 106:20; Jer 2:11; Ac 17:29 **1:24** [f] Eph 4:19 [g] 1Pe 4:3 **1:25** [h] Isa 44:20

1:21 *neither glorified ... nor gave thanks.* In a culture obsessed with honor, failure to honor or give thanks to benefactors was deemed reprehensible.

1:23 *made to look like a mortal human being and birds and animals and reptiles.* Greeks and Romans depicted their major deities in human form and ridiculed Egyptians for portraying many deities as animals or part-animals. For Jewish people, idolatry (worship of false images of deity) was one of the worst sins and one specifically characteristic (in this period) of Gentiles. Preparing for his later argument, however, Paul tellingly deploys here language that Scripture had applied to the idolatry of God's own people (Dt 4:16 – 18; especially Ps 106:20; Jer 2:11).

1:24 *gave them over.* God executed his wrath (v. 18) by turning people over to their own sin (vv. 24,26,28), as he had done with Israel (Ps 81:12). *degrading.* See note on 1Th 4:4.

ROMANS 1:24 – 27

Homosexual Activity in Antiquity

Especially among Greeks, adult male homosexual activity was most often, but never exclusively, devoted to boys just entering puberty, and to adolescents (who were deemed young adults). Fathers sometimes protested the courting of their sons, but at other times people viewed such sexual interests as amusing. Although men preferred sexual relationships with younger males, homosexual relationships were not limited to such partners. However, Greek males did not usually exhibit exclusive homosexual attraction; bisexual activity was more common.

Various factors accounted for the prevalence of this behavior among Greeks. One reason was likely the shortage of available wives; census documents of Greeks in Egypt show that they discarded girl babies more often than boy babies, creating a shortage of available wives. Because of this disparity Greek men usually married around age 30, after mortality had thinned out the pool of other men; they often married women about twelve years younger than they were. Until such late marriages, men often had intercourse with slaves, prostitutes and other males. Less frequent but also known were lesbian relationships, celebrated by the Greek poet Sappho.

Greek practice influenced Romans, and urban elite Romans by this period often engaged in homosexual intercourse. Male prostitutes were available in some parts of Rome. Although Nero reportedly married a male lover, he remained married to a woman, and ancient historians treat his reported same-sex marriage as an aberration. Perhaps because marriage was expected to produce heirs, few people in antiquity considered the possibility of same-sex marriage, except occasionally in ridicule.

Some Greek and especially Roman thinkers rejected homosexual intercourse as "against nature," because, unlike heterosexual intercourse in general, it did not fit the design of sexual organs and could not lead to procreation. Greek-speaking Jews adopted the "against nature" charge against homosexual intercourse, blending it with a Biblical argument from God's design in creation. Scripture already prohibited such behavior (Lev 18:22; 20:13), sometimes in lists of major sexual offenses such as incest, adultery, bestiality and child sacrifice (Lev 18:1 – 23; 20:10 – 21). Ancient Jewish sources disparage Jewish adulterers, prostitutes and many other offenders, but seem to regard homosexual intercourse as an exclusively Gentile sin.

Only after establishing common ground with Jewish critics by condemning the stereotypically Gentile sins of venerating deity-images and same-sex intercourse (Ro 1:23 – 27) does Paul turn to a list of sins that pervaded all of humanity (1:28 – 32). Paul ultimately emphasizes that all of humanity has sinned and needs forgiveness in Christ (see 3:19 – 30). ◆

and served created things[i] rather than the Creator — who is forever praised.[j] Amen.

26 Because of this, God gave them over[k] to shameful lusts.[l] Even their women exchanged natural sexual relations for unnatural ones.[m] 27 In the same way the men also abandoned natural relations with women and were inflamed with lust for one another. Men committed shameful acts with other men, and received in themselves the due penalty for their error.[n]

28 Furthermore, just as they did not think it worthwhile to retain the knowledge of God, so God gave them over[o] to a depraved mind, so that they do what ought not to be done. 29 They have become filled with every kind of wickedness, evil, greed and depravity. They are full of envy, murder, strife, deceit and malice. They are gossips,[p] 30 slanderers, God-haters, insolent, arrogant and boastful; they invent ways of doing evil; they disobey their parents;[q] 31 they have no understanding, no fidelity, no love,[r] no mercy. 32 Although they know God's righteous decree that those who do such things deserve death,[s] they not only continue to do these very things but also approve[t] of those who practice them.

God's Righteous Judgment

2 You, therefore, have no excuse,[u] you who pass judgment on someone else, for at whatever point you judge another, you are condemning yourself, because you who pass judgment do the same things.[v] 2 Now we know that God's judgment against those who do such things is based on truth. 3 So when you, a mere human being, pass judgment on them and yet do the same things, do you think you will escape God's judgment? 4 Or do you show contempt for the riches[w] of his kindness,[x] forbearance[y] and patience,[z] not realizing that God's kindness is intended to lead you to repentance?[a]

5 But because of your stubbornness and your unrepentant heart, you are storing up wrath against yourself for the day of God's wrath, when his righteous judgment[b] will be revealed. 6 God "will repay each person according to what they have done."[ac] 7 To those who by persistence in doing good seek glory, honor[d] and immortality,[e] he will give eternal life. 8 But for those who are self-seeking and who reject the truth and follow evil,[f] there will be wrath and anger. 9 There will be trouble and distress for every human being who does evil: first for the Jew, then for the Gentile;[g] 10 but glory, honor and peace for everyone who does good: first for the Jew, then for the Gentile.[h] 11 For God does not show favoritism.[i]

12 All who sin apart from the law will also perish apart from the law, and all who

[a] 6 Psalm 62:12; Prov. 24:12

1:25 [i] Jer 10:14 [j] Ro 9:5 **1:26** [k] ver 24, 28 [l] 1Th 4:5 [m] Lev 18:22,23 **1:27** [n] Lev 18:22; 20:13 **1:28** [o] ver 24, 26 **1:29** [p] 2Co 12:20 **1:30** [q] 2Ti 3:2 **1:31** [r] 2Ti 3:3 **1:32** [s] Ro 6:23 [t] Ps 50:18; Lk 11:48; Ac 8:1; 22:20 **2:1** [u] Ro 1:20 [v] 2Sa 12:5-7; Mt 7:1,2 **2:4** [w] Ro 9:23; Eph 1:7,18; 2:7 [x] Ro 11:22 [y] Ro 3:25 [z] Ex 34:6 [a] 2Pe 3:9 **2:5** [b] Jude 6 **2:6** [c] Ps 62:12; Mt 16:27 **2:7** [d] ver 10 [e] 1Co 15:53,54 **2:8** [f] 2Th 2:12 **2:9** [g] 1Pe 4:17 **2:10** [h] ver 9 **2:11** [i] Ac 10:34

1:26 *natural sexual relations for unnatural ones.* Paul's "unnatural" echoes the critique of homosexual behavior by philosophers and especially Diaspora Jews; he probably connects it to God's design in creation (v. 20). In vv. 26 – 27, Paul employs the same Greek terms for "male" and "female" that are used in the Greek version of Ge 1:27 — which states that God created "male and female" in his image — and thus probably alludes to the Biblical narrative of creation. After distorting God's image through idolatry (Ro 1:23), humanity distorted God's male and female image in themselves through sexual misconduct.

1:27 *men ... were inflamed with lust for one another.* Jewish people believed that most Gentile men were sexually immoral (cf. Lev 18:3,24; 20:23), and Jewish people considered homosexual intercourse an exclusively Gentile vice. Ancient writers frequently described the overpowering experience of *lust* or passion as being *inflamed* (cf. 1Co 7:9).

1:28 – 32 A common literary form in the ancient world consisted of lists of vices, as in vv. 29 – 31. Ancient rhetoric valued repetition and variation. Paul thus condemns the world "filled with" four summary categories of sin and "full of" five specific sins; then he lists eight examples of sinners and concludes with four virtues they lack (each virtue in Greek prefaced with the Greek prefix *a-*, indicating lack). Paul gives examples, not a comprehensive list (compare some different examples in Gal 5:19 – 21); most of his four virtues, e.g., differ from the primary four virtues emphasized by Greek intellectuals. In contrast to the specifically Gentile vices noted in vv. 18 – 27, many of the vices here were also known to be practiced by Jewish people (see ch. 2).

2:1 – 29 In this section and at some other points in Romans, Paul adopts a style that resembles diatribe, a vivid teaching style characterized by rhetorical questions and challenges to an imaginary critic's objections.

2:2 *God's judgment ... is based on truth.* Moralists widely affirmed that people should live by what they taught, and Jewish people affirmed that God would judge sins.

2:3 *you, a mere human being.* To keep audience attention, a speaker would sometimes focus on a single hearer, as here.

2:5 *storing up wrath.* Whereas some Jewish sources urged people to lay up good treasure in heaven, the sinner here stores up wrath. *day of God's wrath.* The prophets warned of the day of God's wrath, sometimes foreshadowed by nearer judgments (Isa 13:9,13; Zep 1:14 – 15,18; 2:2).

2:6 Paul appeals to the words of Scripture (Ps 62:12; Pr 24:12).

2:7 – 10 Paul uses inverted parallelism (what came to be called a chiasm), starting and ending with the same subject: in v. 7 and v. 10, those who do good will be rewarded; in vv. 8 – 9, those who do evil will be punished.

2:11 Jewish people emphasized God's impartiality (Dt 10:17). They did not, however, usually apply the principle to Israel and the Gentiles; they believed that God would ultimately reward Israel's faithfulness and punish the Gentiles for their sin.

2:12 *All who sin.* Although Jewish people recognized that nearly all Gentiles worshiped many gods and most Gentile men were sexually immoral, many Jewish people believed that Gentiles who avoided such obvious sins would be saved. They recognized that God had a higher standard for Israel in the law. Nevertheless, most Jewish

sin under the law[j] will be judged by the
law. 13For it is not those who hear the law
who are righteous in God's sight, but it
is those who obey[k] the law who will be
declared righteous. 14(Indeed, when Gentiles, who do not have the law, do by nature things required by the law,[l] they are a
law for themselves, even though they do
not have the law. 15They show that the requirements of the law are written on their
hearts, their consciences also bearing witness, and their thoughts sometimes accusing them and at other times even defending them.) 16This will take place on the
day when God judges people's secrets[m]
through Jesus Christ,[n] as my gospel[o] declares.

The Jews and the Law

17Now you, if you call yourself a Jew; if
you rely on the law and boast in God;[p] 18if
you know his will and approve of what is
superior because you are instructed by the
law; 19if you are convinced that you are a
guide for the blind, a light for those who
are in the dark, 20an instructor of the foolish, a teacher of little children, because
you have in the law the embodiment of
knowledge and truth— 21you, then, who
teach others, do you not teach yourself?
You who preach against stealing, do you
steal?[q] 22You who say that people should
not commit adultery, do you commit adultery? You who abhor idols, do you rob
temples?[r] 23You who boast in the law,[s] do
you dishonor God by breaking the law?
24As it is written: "God's name is blasphemed among the Gentiles because of
you."[a][t]

25Circumcision has value if you observe the law,[u] but if you break the law,
you have become as though you had not
been circumcised.[v] 26So then, if those
who are not circumcised keep the law's
requirements,[w] will they not be regarded
as though they were circumcised?[x] 27The
one who is not circumcised physically and
yet obeys the law will condemn you[y] who,
even though you have the[b] written code
and circumcision, are a lawbreaker.

28A person is not a Jew who is one only
outwardly,[z] nor is circumcision merely
outward and physical.[a] 29No, a person is
a Jew who is one inwardly; and circumcision is circumcision of the heart, by the
Spirit,[b] not by the written code.[c] Such a

2:12 [j] Ro 3:19; 1Co 9:20,21 **2:13** [k] Jas 1:22, 23,25 **2:14** [l] Ac 10:35 **2:16** [m] Ecc 12:14 [n] Ac 10:42 [o] Ro 16:25 **2:17** [p] ver 23; Mic 3:11; Ro 9:4

2:21 [q] Mt 23:3,4 **2:22** [r] Ac 19:37 **2:23** [s] ver 17 **2:24** [t] Isa 52:5; Eze 36:22 **2:25** [u] Gal 5:3 [v] Jer 4:4 **2:26** [w] Ro 8:4 [x] 1Co 7:19 **2:27** [y] Mt 12:41, 42 **2:28** [z] Mt 3:9; Jn 8:39; Ro 9:6, 7 [a] Gal 6:15 **2:29** [b] Php 3:3; Col 2:11 [c] Ro 7:6

[a] *24* Isaiah 52:5 (see Septuagint); Ezek. 36:20,22
[b] *27* Or *who, by means of a*

people believed that everyone sinned sometimes; Paul argues more strictly that any known sins bring condemnation.

2:13 *those who obey.* Some Jewish teachers debated whether knowing or practicing the law took precedence, but all agreed that it must be practiced.

2:15 *the law ... written on their hearts.* Ancient thinkers often spoke of a universal, natural law that provided people with innate knowledge or decipherable evidence of what is right. Thinkers often connected this natural law with the idea of conscience. Jewish tradition declared that God had already given all humanity some basic commandments (e.g., Ge 9:4–6), which humanity had violated. The point was to emphasize that Gentiles were responsible for their ignorance of God. Many Diaspora Jewish thinkers also spoke of a universal moral law within people. For Paul, the law written on hearts could be obeyed only when it was written as part of the new covenant (Jer 31:32–33).

2:17–24 Diatribe style (see note on vv. 1–29) often lambasted an imaginary opponent; opponents were often caricatured and reduced to the absurd. (Familiar with such a style, neither Jewish nor knowledgeable Gentile readers would take this as typical Jewish behavior. This is a worst-case example.) In these verses, Paul uses an extreme example of hypocrisy to illustrate the evil of hypocrisy. In some respects, his portrait could remind Rome's residents of an actual Jewish false teacher who brought reproach on the entire Jewish community in Rome a generation earlier.

2:17 *Now you.* Ancient speakers drove home points by repetition; Paul attributes to the imaginary critic eleven boasts (vv. 17–20).

2:18 *what is superior.* Jewish people recognized that they alone had the true God and his law. Ancient sources often framed sections with related ideas; boasting in the law frames vv. 17–23, as the meaning of Jewishness frames vv. 17–29.

2:19 *guide ... light.* Jewish people could view themselves as a light for the Gentiles and a guide for helping the blind (Isa 42:6–7).

2:21–23 Paul here epitomizes an ideal hypocrite, with horrendous offenses (theft, adultery and temple robbery—on the last, see note on Ac 19:37) framed more generally with failure to keep God's law. Both diatribe (see note on vv. 1–29) and forensic rhetoric often drove home points with rhetorical questions. Ancient speakers also drove home points by repetition and sometimes by the technique of antithesis, which contrasted points. Paul deploys both antithesis and repetition (here, x ... y / x ... y) with five rhetorical questions.

2:24 *God's name is blasphemed.* In context, Isa 52:5 (cited here) refers to nations blaspheming God through Israel experiencing the judgment of exile; here Gentiles blaspheme God through witnessing a Diaspora Jew's hypocrisy (cf. Eze 36:20–23). If Josephus is correct, one Jewish charlatan, who defrauded people about four decades before Paul wrote the book of Romans, brought such dishonor on his people that the emperor Tiberius expelled the Jewish community from Rome and conscripted thousands of their young men for a deadly war. Jewish people in Rome continued to recall that terrible legacy.

2:25 *Circumcision has value.* Jewish males were circumcised as a sign of the covenant. Male Gentile converts who wished to enter the covenant were circumcised—a painful price for adults—and accepted Jewish laws.

2:26 *regarded as though they were circumcised.* In principle, Jewish teachers often accepted some Gentiles who refrained from idolatry and immorality as righteous even though they had not been circumcised.

2:29 *circumcision of the heart, by the Spirit.* Scripture already warned against God's people being uncircum-

person's praise is not from other people,
but from God.[d]

God's Faithfulness

3 What advantage, then, is there in being a Jew, or what value is there in
circumcision? 2Much in every way! First
of all, the Jews have been entrusted with
the very words of God.[e]
3What if some were unfaithful?[f] Will
their unfaithfulness nullify God's faithfulness?[g] 4Not at all! Let God be true,[h] and
every human being a liar.[i] As it is written:

"So that you may be proved right when
you speak
and prevail when you judge."[a][j]

5But if our unrighteousness brings out
God's righteousness more clearly, what
shall we say? That God is unjust in bringing his wrath on us? (I am using a human
argument.)[k] 6Certainly not! If that were so,
how could God judge the world?[l] 7Some-
one might argue, "If my falsehood enhanc-
es God's truthfulness and so increases his
glory,[m] why am I still condemned as a
sinner?" 8Why not say — as some slanderously claim that we say — "Let us do evil
that good may result"?[n] Their condemnation is just!

No One Is Righteous

9What shall we conclude then? Do we
have any advantage? Not at all! For we
have already made the charge that Jews
and Gentiles alike are all under the power
of sin.[o] 10As it is written:

"There is no one righteous, not even
one;
11 there is no one who understands;
there is no one who seeks God.
12 All have turned away,
they have together become worthless;
there is no one who does good,
not even one."[b][p]
13 "Their throats are open graves;
their tongues practice deceit."[c][q]
"The poison of vipers is on their lips."[d][r]
14 "Their mouths are full of cursing
and bitterness."[e][s]
15 "Their feet are swift to shed blood;
16 ruin and misery mark their ways,
17 and the way of peace they do not know."[f]
18 "There is no fear of God before their
eyes."[g][t]

19Now we know that whatever the law
says,[u] it says to those who are under the
law,[v] so that every mouth may be silenced
and the whole world held accountable to
God. 20Therefore no one will be declared
righteous in God's sight by the works of
the law;[w] rather, through the law we become conscious of our sin.[x]

2:29 [d] Jn 5:44; 1Co 4:5; 2Co 10:18; 1Th 2:4; 1Pe 3:4 **3:2** [e] Dt 4:8; Ps 147:19 **3:3** [f] Heb 4:2 [g] 2Ti 2:13 **3:4** [h] Jn 3:33 [i] Ps 116:11 [j] Ps 51:4 **3:5** [k] Ro 6:19; Gal 3:15 **3:6** [l] Ge 18:25 **3:7** [m] ver 4 **3:8** [n] Ro 6:1

3:9 [o] ver 19,23; Gal 3:22 **3:12** [p] Ps 14:1-3 **3:13** [q] Ps 5:9 [r] Ps 140:3 **3:14** [s] Ps 10:7 **3:18** [t] Ps 36:1 **3:19** [u] Jn 10:34 [v] Ro 2:12 **3:20** [w] Ac 13:39; Gal 2:16 [x] Ro 7:7

[a] *4* Psalm 51:4 [b] *12* Psalms 14:1-3; 53:1-3; Eccles. 7:20 [c] *13* Psalm 5:9 [d] *13* Psalm 140:3 [e] *14* Psalm 10:7 (see Septuagint) [f] *17* Isaiah 59:7,8 [g] *18* Psalm 36:1

cised in heart (Lev 26:41; Jer 4:4; 9:25 – 26), urged them to circumcise their hearts (Dt 10:16), and, most relevant here, promised that God would someday circumcise their hearts (Dt 30:6). For Paul, experiencing the new heart promised in the new covenant, by the Spirit (Jer 31:33; Eze 36:26 – 27), counted more than the mere external sign of the older covenant. *praise … from God.* Paul might play on the Hebrew term behind the name Judah, the ancestor for whom the Jewish people (lit. "Judahites") were named; the name in Hebrew sounds like the Hebrew term for "praise." (Although most of his audience would not know Hebrew, some would know Ge 29:35; see NIV text note on Ge 29:35.)

3:1 – 2 Diatribe (see note on 2:1 – 29) included objections from imaginary opponents, which the speaker could then refute (as Paul does here in v. 2). (Paul may continue the subject in 9:4 – 5.)

3:4 *every human being a liar.* Reflects Ps 116:11, a familiar psalm for some (Ps 113 – 118 were sung at Passover); it paves the way for Paul's claims of universal sinfulness in vv. 10 – 18. More extensively, Paul quotes Ps 51:4, which affirms that God rather than the psalmist is righteous.

3:6 Jewish people recognized that God would judge the world justly.

3:8 *as some slanderously claim.* Slander and misrepresentation of teachings were common; cf. Ac 21:21.

3:10 – 18 Jewish teachers often linked together texts based on common key words or concepts. Here Paul strings together texts, the majority from Psalms (see NIV text notes); after the opening quotation all mention body parts (feet, eyes and especially texts about the mouth); some also mention death. (Paul will address both the body and death later.) Although in their original context only his citation in vv. 15 – 17 refers to all of Israel — most of the others involved the psalmist's enemies — linking the texts in this accepted Jewish manner allows Paul to apply all the passages to the matter at hand.

3:10 – 12 Here Paul cites the Greek version of Ps 14:1 – 3 (cf. Ps 53:1 – 3).

3:10 *no one righteous.* The quoted psalm (see previous note) twice repeats "there is no one who does good" (Ps 14:1,3), so Paul adjusts the first to "there is no one righteous." He may do so by drawing on Ecc 7:20; Jewish teachers often compared and blended texts.

3:13 – 14 Linking texts about the mouth, Paul quotes from the Greek version of Ps 5:9, then Ps 140:3, and then Ps 10:7.

3:15 – 17 In context, Isa 59:7 – 8, quoted here, indicted all of Israel for its sins.

3:15 *Their feet.* The mention of feet in Isa 59:7 brings it into connection with the other quotations mentioning parts of the body in vv. 13 – 18.

3:18 Continuing his connections based on body parts, Paul cites Ps 36:1, which mentions eyes.

3:19 *every mouth … whole world.* Isa 59:7 – 8, cited in vv. 15 – 17, did address all of Israel directly, but Paul invokes the principle that all the OT addressed Israel, who should learn from it. Paul's point is that on the day of judgment (vv. 4,6,8), no one, Jew or Gentile, would be able to voice objections to God's justice (cf. Isa 41:1; Zep 1:7).

3:20 *no one will be declared righteous in God's sight.* Paul's language evokes Ps 143:2: "no one living is righteous

Righteousness Through Faith

21 But now apart from the law the righteousness of God[y] has been made known,
to which the Law and the Prophets testify.[z] 22 This righteousness is given through
faith[a] in[a] Jesus Christ to all who believe.
There is no difference between Jew and
Gentile,[b] 23 for all have sinned and fall
short of the glory of God, 24 and all are
justified freely by his grace[c] through the
redemption[d] that came by Christ Jesus.
25 God presented Christ as a sacrifice of
atonement,[b][e] through the shedding of
his blood[f]—to be received by faith. He
did this to demonstrate his righteousness,
because in his forbearance he had left
the sins committed beforehand unpunished[g]— 26 he did it to demonstrate his
righteousness at the present time, so as
to be just and the one who justifies those
who have faith in Jesus.

27 Where, then, is boasting?[h] It is excluded. Because of what law? The law that requires works? No, because of the law that
requires faith. 28 For we maintain that a
person is justified by faith apart from the
works of the law.[i] 29 Or is God the God of
Jews only? Is he not the God of Gentiles
too? Yes, of Gentiles too,[j] 30 since there is
only one God, who will justify the circumcised by faith and the uncircumcised
through that same faith.[k] 31 Do we, then,
nullify the law by this faith? Not at all!
Rather, we uphold the law.

3:21 [y] Ro 1:17; 9:30 [z] Ac 10:43 **3:22** [a] Ro 9:30 [b] Ro 10:12; Gal 3:28; Col 3:11 **3:24** [c] Ro 4:16; Eph 2:8 [d] Eph 1:7, 14; Col 1:14; Heb 9:12 **3:25** [e] 1Jn 4:10 [f] Heb 9:12, 14 [g] Ac 17:30 **3:27** [h] Ro 2:17, 23; 4:2; 1Co 1:29-31; Eph 2:9 **3:28** [i] ver 20, 21; Ac 13:39; Eph 2:9 **3:29** [j] Ro 9:24 **3:30** [k] Gal 3:8 **4:2** [l] 1Co 1:31 **4:3** [m] ver 5, 9, 22; Ge 15:6; Gal 3:6; Jas 2:23 **4:4** [n] Ro 11:6

Abraham Justified by Faith

4 What then shall we say that Abraham, our forefather according to the
flesh, discovered in this matter? 2 If, in fact,
Abraham was justified by works, he had
something to boast about—but not before
God.[l] 3 What does Scripture say? "Abraham
believed God, and it was credited to him
as righteousness."[c][m]

4 Now to the one who works, wages are
not credited as a gift[n] but as an obligation.
5 However, to the one who does not work
but trusts God who justifies the ungodly,
their faith is credited as righteousness.

[a] *22* Or *through the faithfulness of* [b] *25* The Greek for *sacrifice of atonement* refers to the atonement cover on the ark of the covenant (see Lev. 16:15,16).
[c] *3* Gen. 15:6; also in verse 22

---

before you" (the wording of the Greek version is very similar to Paul's statement). In Ps 143:2 the psalmist admits that he himself could not meet God's holy standard without mercy. *we become conscious.* That greater knowledge yielded greater culpability was widely understood.

3:21 *the righteousness of God.* In Scripture, this idea includes God's mercy and his righteous faithfulness to his covenant with his people. *the Law and the Prophets.* Jewish people often summarized the whole of what we now call the OT, or the Tanakh, in this way.

3:23 *all have sinned.* Whatever their different sins, Gentiles (1:18–32) and Jews (2:1–29) have all sinned. Jewish people understood sin as transgressing God's law, but acknowledged (whether or not they would have agreed with Paul's argument in vv. 10–18) that all have sinned.

3:24 *all are justified freely.* Just as sin affects both Jew and Gentile (see v. 23 and note), so here free justification affects both. *through the redemption.* In the OT, "redemption" (freeing a slave) often required a price to be paid. God "redeemed" Israel, making them his people by grace and liberating them (at the cost of the Passover lamb and the firstborn of Egypt). This was before he gave them his commandments for how to live (cf. Ex 20:2–17). Here their freedom has been secured from sin (v. 9).

3:25 *sacrifice of atonement, through the shedding of his blood.* Paul speaks literally here of the mercy seat, the place of propitiation, annually consecrated to God by sacrificial blood. Both ancient Israel and its milieu understood principles of propitiating, or appeasing, a deity's wrath (cf. 1:18) as well as of cleansing impurity. To emphasize this, atonement through Jesus' shed blood depicts Jesus as a sacrifice (cf. 5:9; 8:3). Some Jewish people already recognized that martyrdom could turn away God's wrath from his people (4 Maccabees 17:22); early Christians regarded Jesus' death as a special category. *left the sins committed beforehand unpunished.* God had graciously "passed over" (cf. Ex 12:13) sins before the time of the cross.

3:26 *demonstrate his righteousness.* Not only Greek but also Biblical conceptions of justice rejected acquitting the guilty (Ex 23:7). Through atonement, however, the sins have been dealt with (v. 25).

3:27 *boasting.* People ridiculed boasting unless it was properly justified as necessary; but of course, no one could boast before God's holy standard (v. 20; 4:2). Paul contrasts two approaches to the law here (and in 8:2; 9:31–32): using it for boasting, or using it to point to the God who gave it (see 3:31—4:1).

3:30 *only one God.* The oneness of God was the most fundamental affirmation of Judaism (Dt 6:4); Jewish people recognized that he was the only God (Isa 45:21–22,25). *by faith … through that same faith.* Likely rhetorical variation for the same point.

3:31 Like other transitions in ancient sources, this verse both concludes what precedes and foreshadows what follows, in this case Paul's argument from the law that follows in ch. 4 (Genesis, expounded in ch. 4, is part of the Torah; see note on 4:1–3).

4:1–3 Because Genesis was considered part of the law, Paul is developing his claim in 3:31 (see note there). As the ancestor of the Jewish people, Abraham was considered the model of righteousness and hospitality. Viewed as a Gentile before his calling, he was also seen as the model for all Gentiles converting to Judaism. In Jewish tradition, he destroyed idols.

4:3 *What does Scripture say?* To fail to take a reliable person (here God) at their word was a great insult. *believed God … credited to him as righteousness.* In context, Ge 15:6 (cited here) refers to dependence on God's promise. Jewish teachers developed the implications of texts they expounded; here Paul highlights the Greek term "credited," which he uses 11 times in ch. 4 ("count" in v. 8), to emphasize God's generosity. Many other Jewish readers, by contrast, understood Abraham's faith here as one of his virtuous works that accrued merit.

4:5 *justifies the ungodly.* Because God as a just judge would not acquit the guilty (Ex 23:7), Paul's dramatic language here would seize attention (see 3:26 and note for the reasoning).

6 David says the same thing when he
speaks of the blessedness of the one to
whom God credits righteousness apart
from works:

7 "Blessed are those
whose transgressions are
forgiven,
whose sins are covered.
8 Blessed is the one
whose sin the Lord will never
count against them."[a][o]

9 Is this blessedness only for the circumcised, or also for the uncircumcised?[p] We
have been saying that Abraham's faith
was credited to him as righteousness.[q]
10 Under what circumstances was it credited? Was it after he was circumcised, or
before? It was not after, but before! 11 And
he received circumcision as a sign, a seal
of the righteousness that he had by faith
while he was still uncircumcised.[r] So then,
he is the father[s] of all who believe[t] but
have not been circumcised, in order that
righteousness might be credited to them.
12 And he is then also the father of the circumcised who not only are circumcised
but who also follow in the footsteps of the
faith that our father Abraham had before
he was circumcised.

13 It was not through the law that Abraham and his offspring received the promise[u] that he would be heir of the world,[v]
but through the righteousness that comes
by faith. 14 For if those who depend on the
law are heirs, faith means nothing and the
promise is worthless,[w] 15 because the law
brings wrath.[x] And where there is no law
there is no transgression.[y]

16 Therefore, the promise comes by
faith, so that it may be by grace[z] and
may be guaranteed[a] to all Abraham's
offspring — not only to those who are
of the law but also to those who have
the faith of Abraham. He is the father of
us all. 17 As it is written: "I have made
you a father of many nations."[b][b] He is
our father in the sight of God, in whom
he believed — the God who gives life[c] to
the dead and calls[d] into being things that
were not.[e]

18 Against all hope, Abraham in hope
believed and so became the father of
many nations,[f] just as it had been said
to him, "So shall your offspring be."[c][g]
19 Without weakening in his faith, he
faced the fact that his body was as good
as dead[h] — since he was about a hundred
years old[i] — and that Sarah's womb was
also dead.[j] 20 Yet he did not waver through
unbelief regarding the promise of God,
but was strengthened in his faith and gave
glory to God,[k] 21 being fully persuaded that
God had power to do what he had promised.[l] 22 This is why "it was credited to him
as righteousness."[m] 23 The words "it was
credited to him" were written not for him
alone, 24 but also for us,[n] to whom God
will credit righteousness — for us who believe in him[o] who raised Jesus our Lord
from the dead.[p] 25 He was delivered over
to death for our sins[q] and was raised to
life for our justification.

4:8 [o] Ps 32:1,2; 2Co 5:19 **4:9** [p] Ro 3:30 [q] ver 3 **4:11** [r] Ge 17:10, 11 [s] ver 16, 17; Lk 19:9 [t] Ro 3:22 **4:13** [u] Gal 3:16, 29 [v] Ge 17:4-6 **4:14** [w] Gal 3:18 **4:15** [x] Ro 7:7-25; 1Co 15:56; 2Co 3:7; Gal 3:10; Ro 7:12 [y] Ro 3:20; 7:7 **4:16** [z] Ro 3:24 [a] Ro 15:8 **4:17** [b] Ge 17:5 [c] Jn 5:21 [d] Isa 48:13 [e] 1Co 1:28 **4:18** [f] ver 17 [g] Ge 15:5 **4:19** [h] Heb 11:11, 12 [i] Ge 17:17 [j] Ge 18:11 **4:20** [k] Mt 9:8 **4:21** [l] Ge 18:14; Heb 11:19 **4:22** [m] ver 3 **4:24** [n] Ro 15:4; 1Co 9:10; 10:11 [o] Ro 10:9 [p] Ac 2:24 **4:25** [q] Isa 53:5, 6; Ro 5:6,8

[a] *8* Psalm 32:1,2 [b] *17* Gen. 17:5 [c] *18* Gen. 15:5

4:6–8 Jewish interpreters often linked texts based on a common key term; they also often expounded a reading in the Torah in connection with a reading elsewhere in Scripture. Paul here explains "credited" in Ge 15:6 (quoted in v. 3) in light of Ps 32:1–2 (quoted in vv. 7–8), which also speaks of what God credits to the righteous (cf. Ps 32:5).
4:10 *before.* Abraham's faith came 13 or more years *before* his circumcision (Ge 15:6; 16:3–4,16; 17:24–25). Abraham's faith grew over the years, climaxing in his offering of Isaac (Ge 22), but God had already counted him righteous with this initial faith in God's promise.
4:11 *circumcision as a sign.* Many Jewish thinkers allowed that exceptional Gentiles who rejected idolatry and immorality could be saved; to become part of God's people, however, they required male Gentiles to be circumcised. Paul agreed that circumcision was a mark of the covenant with Israel, but he shows that the relationship with God it symbolized was a reality long before the mark (v. 10). The inward reality counted more than the sign to which it pointed (2:28–29).
4:13 *heir of the world.* God promised Abraham the "land" (Ge 12:7; 15:7,18), a term that in Hebrew could also mean "earth." Jewish interpreters by this period often spoke of God's people inheriting the world to come (in many views, the wicked would be destroyed).
4:17 *father of many nations.* God announced Abraham as father of many nations (Ge 17:5) even before commanding him and his descendants to be circumcised (Ge 17:10–14). Several peoples descended from him literally (Ge 16:15; 25:2–3; 36:1), but Paul may read the promise together with all the earth's peoples being blessed in Abraham (Ge 12:3; 18:18; 22:18), Isaac (Ge 26:4), and Jacob (Ge 28:14). Spiritual descent mattered more than ethnic descent (Ro 9:6–13,25–29). *gives life to the dead.* Jewish people accepted God's power to create and also (celebrated in prayers) to someday raise the dead; this claim prepares for v. 24.
4:18 *So shall your offspring be.* Paul applies the promise of seed as many as the stars (Ge 15:5) not to Abraham's genetic descendants but to his spiritual descendants, whom Paul expected to someday outnumber ethnic Israel.
4:19 *body was as good as dead.* For Abraham's age, see Ge 17:17. Believing that God could restore their "dead" reproductive functions was like believing that God can raise the dead (Ro 4:24).
4:23–24 *not for him alone, but also for us.* Jewish people understood that the Scriptures did not merely describe the past for antiquarian interest, but that they provided models for the present. (Greek and Roman historians and biographers also applied history similarly, even if not always to the same degree.) In 4:23—5:11, Paul applies the principle of Abraham's faith to those who believe as he did.

Peace and Hope

5 Therefore, since we have been justified through faith,[r] we[a] have peace
with God through our Lord Jesus Christ,
2through whom we have gained access[s]
by faith into this grace in which we now
stand.[t] And we[b] boast in the hope[u] of
the glory of God. 3Not only so, but we[b]
also glory in our sufferings,[v] because
we know that suffering produces perseverance;[w] 4perseverance, character; and
character, hope. 5And hope[x] does not put
us to shame, because God's love has been
poured out into our hearts through the
Holy Spirit,[y] who has been given to us.
6You see, at just the right time,[z] when
we were still powerless, Christ died for the
ungodly.[a] 7Very rarely will anyone die for
a righteous person, though for a good person someone might possibly dare to die.
8But God demonstrates his own love for us
in this: While we were still sinners, Christ
died for us.[b]
9Since we have now been justified by
his blood,[c] how much more shall we be
saved from God's wrath[d] through him!
10For if, while we were God's enemies,[e]
we were reconciled[f] to him through the
death of his Son, how much more, having been reconciled, shall we be saved
through his life![g] 11Not only is this so, but
we also boast in God through our Lord
Jesus Christ, through whom we have now
received reconciliation.

5:1 [r] Ro 3:28
5:2 [s] Eph 2:18 [t] 1Co 15:1 [u] Heb 3:6
5:3 [v] Mt 5:12 [w] Jas 1:2,3
5:5 [x] Php 1:20 [y] Ac 2:33
5:6 [z] Gal 4:4 [a] Ro 4:25
5:8 [b] Jn 15:13; 1Pe 3:18
5:9 [c] Ro 3:25 [d] Ro 1:18
5:10 [e] Ro 11:28; Col 1:21 [f] 2Co 5:18, 19; Col 1:20, 22 [g] Ro 8:34

Death Through Adam, Life Through Christ

12Therefore, just as sin entered the world
through one man,[h] and death through sin,[i]
and in this way death came to all people,
because all sinned—
13To be sure, sin was in the world before
the law was given, but sin is not charged
against anyone's account where there is
no law.[j] 14Nevertheless, death reigned
from the time of Adam to the time of Moses, even over those who did not sin by
breaking a command, as did Adam, who
is a pattern of the one to come.[k]
15But the gift is not like the trespass. For
if the many died by the trespass of the one
man,[l] how much more did God's grace
and the gift that came by the grace of the
one man, Jesus Christ,[m] overflow to the
many! 16Nor can the gift of God be compared with the result of one man's sin: The
judgment followed one sin and brought
condemnation, but the gift followed many
trespasses and brought justification. 17For
if, by the trespass of the one man, death[n]
reigned through that one man, how much
more will those who receive God's abundant provision of grace and of the gift of
righteousness reign in life through the one
man, Jesus Christ!
18Consequently, just as one trespass resulted in condemnation for all people,[o] so

5:12 [h] ver 15, 16, 17; 1Co 15:21, 22 [i] Ge 2:17; 3:19; Ro 6:23
5:13 [j] Ro 4:15
5:14 [k] 1Co 15:22, 45
5:15 [l] ver 12, 18, 19 [m] Ac 15:11
5:17 [n] ver 12
5:18 [o] ver 12

[a] 1 Many manuscripts *let us* [b] 2,3 Or *let us*

5:1 *peace with God.* Although ancients sometimes used "peace" to mean tranquility, more often it applies, as here, to a nonhostile relationship (e.g., through reconciliation ending enmity, as in vv. 10–11). Such peace could be established in various ways, such as through treaties or by a conqueror imposing it (as in the Roman Empire), but the condition of peace was viewed positively.
5:2 *boast in the hope of the glory of God.* Ancient writers often repeated ideas for emphasis, here the Greek term translated as "boast" in vv. 2,11 and as "glory" in v. 3. Philosophers urged courage in the face of sufferings; the OT often illustrates godly persons' weaknesses as well as endurance.
5:3–4 Ancient writers sometimes developed progressive chains of one item leading to another like the chain here. (Such a chain is called *sorites*, concatenation or climax.) For the value of suffering, see note on 1Pe 1:6.
5:5 *the Holy Spirit, who has been given to us.* Many Jewish people believed that the Spirit would be available only in the future time, or that only the most holy people could merit the Spirit in the present. Here the Spirit is a gift, revealing God's love in the cross (vv. 6–10).
5:7 *someone might possibly dare to die.* Greeks valued heroic sacrifice of one's life for a friend, but, apart from war settings, such sacrifice was rare.
5:9 *justified by his blood.* Death by crucifixion did not always entail blood; blood evokes Biblical sacrifices regarding sin (cf. 8:3). Earlier Israelites, contemporary Jews, Greeks and other peoples understood the concept of atoning sacrifices propitiating a god's anger (cf. 5:9).
5:10 *reconciled to him through the death of his Son.* Greeks spoke about reconciliation between persons in conflict, but did not think of deities initiating reconciliation with mortals who had offended them. The idea that God would do so at the cost of his own Son would be shocking.
5:12 *sin entered the world through one man.* Some Jewish traditions emphasized the Biblical idea that Adam's disobedience introduced sin and therefore death to the human race (see the article "Adam in Jewish Tradition," p. 1957).
5:15–21 Speakers in antiquity regularly compared characters, sometimes equals and sometimes very different. They also frequently used antithesis, contrasting claims or (as here) figures. This antithetical repetition here builds to a rousing climax that any ancient orator would have appreciated.
5:15 *trespass.* Paul repeats the Greek term translated "trespass" multiple times in vv. 15–20; speakers used repetition to drive home their points. *how much more.* Jewish and other thinkers often reasoned with "how much more" (also v. 17) arguments: if the lesser was true, how much more the greater?
5:17 *through that one man ... through the one man.* Ancient Israelite thought could envision one person standing for or affecting many. Jewish people thought of corporate identity (e.g., some blessings as Abraham's descendants, provided one walked in his ways); but whereas one is born an heir of Adam, only those who turn to Christ become co-heirs with Christ (6:3–4). Adam's authority (Ge 1:26) will be restored in Christ, most fully in the future age (v. 17).

ROMANS 5:12 – 21

Adam in Jewish Tradition

The OT rarely mentions Adam after Genesis (1Ch 1:1; probably Hos 6:7). Jewish tradition, however, quickly compensated for this seeming deficiency. Many believed that Adam lost his great glory when he sinned but that God's servants would receive this glory again in the future time of restoration. Some later rabbis elaborated on Adam's vast size and other greatness in order to highlight the terrible effects of his fall.

Jewish tradition did not normally speak as if people genetically inherited Adam's sin or automatically inherited his guilt. Rather, the thought was normally that Adam introduced sin and death to humanity, and his descendants then sinned as he did. Jewish tradition usually agreed, however, that everyone had sinned.

Some Diaspora Jews may have thought in ways similar to the Jewish philosopher Philo of Alexandria. Philo believed that the first man God created in his image in Ge 1:26 – 27 was a heavenly man, and contrasted this with the fallen, earthly man of Ge 2 – 3. Paul reverses this sequence in 1Co 15:45 – 47. For Philo, the human of Ge 1:26 – 27 symbolized the pure mind engaging heavenly matters, whereas Adam symbolized a fleshly person whose interests were temporal.

Fourth-century fresco of Adam and Eve, Rome.

Cimitero dei SS. Marcellino e Pietro, Rome, Italy/De Agostini Picture Library/Bridgeman Images

In Scripture, God created humanity in his image (Ge 1:26 – 27). If this image was lost or marred in Adam (in some sense it seems to remain in 1Co 11:7), it seems to be restored in Jesus Christ (1Co 15:49; Col 3:10; cf. also Ro 8:29; 2Co 3:18).

Adam forms a key role in Paul's argument in Ro 5:12 – 21. Because Jewish people could appeal to their descent from Abraham as a supposed basis for merit or (cf. Ro 9:7 – 9) election, Paul reminds his audience that everyone, Jew or Gentile, is descended from the sinner Adam. ◆

also one righteous act resulted in justification[p] and life for all people. 19For just as through the disobedience of the one man[q] the many were made sinners, so also through the obedience[r] of the one man the many will be made righteous.

20The law was brought in so that the trespass might increase.[s] But where sin increased, grace increased all the more,[t] 21so that, just as sin reigned in death,[u] so also grace might reign through righteousness to bring eternal life through Jesus Christ our Lord.

Dead to Sin, Alive in Christ

6 What shall we say, then? Shall we go on sinning so that grace may increase?[v] 2By no means! We are those who have died to sin;[w] how can we live in it any longer? 3Or don't you know that all of us who were baptized[x] into Christ Jesus were baptized into his death? 4We were therefore buried with him through baptism into death in order that, just as Christ was raised from the dead[y] through the glory of the Father, we too may live a new life.[z]

5For if we have been united with him in a death like his, we will certainly also be united with him in a resurrection like his.[a] 6For we know that our old self[b] was crucified with him[c] so that the body ruled by sin[d] might be done away with,[a] that we should no longer be slaves to sin— 7because anyone who has died has been set free from sin.

8Now if we died with Christ, we believe that we will also live with him. 9For we know that since Christ was raised from the dead,[e] he cannot die again; death no longer has mastery over him.[f] 10The death he died, he died to sin[g] once for all; but the life he lives, he lives to God.

11In the same way, count yourselves dead to sin[h] but alive to God in Christ Jesus. 12Therefore do not let sin reign in your mortal body so that you obey its evil desires. 13Do not offer any part of yourself to sin as an instrument of wickedness,[i] but rather offer yourselves to God as those who have been brought from death to life; and offer every part of yourself to him as an instrument of righteousness.[j] 14For sin shall no longer be your master, because you are not under the law,[k] but under grace.[l]

Slaves to Righteousness

15What then? Shall we sin because we are not under the law but under grace? By no means! 16Don't you know that when you offer yourselves to someone as obedient slaves, you are slaves of the one you obey—whether you are slaves to sin,[m] which leads to death,[n] or to obedience, which leads to righteousness? 17But thanks be to God[o] that, though you used to be slaves to sin, you have come to obey from your heart the pattern of teaching[p] that has now claimed your allegiance. 18You have been set free from sin[q] and have become slaves to righteousness.

19I am using an example from everyday life[r] because of your human limitations. Just as you used to offer yourselves as slaves to impurity and to ever-increasing wickedness, so now offer yourselves as slaves to righteousness[s] leading to holiness. 20When you were slaves to sin,[t] you were free from the control of righteousness. 21What benefit did you reap at that time from the things you are now ashamed of? Those things result in death![u] 22But now that you have been set free from sin[v] and have become slaves of God,[w] the benefit you reap leads to holiness, and the

5:18 [p] Ro 4:25
5:19 [q] ver 12 [r] Php 2:8
5:20 [s] Ro 7:7, 8; Gal 3:19 [t] 1Ti 1:13, 14
5:21 [u] ver 12, 14
6:1 [v] ver 15; Ro 3:5, 8
6:2 [w] Col 3:3, 5; 1Pe 2:24
6:3 [x] Mt 28:19
6:4 [y] Col 2:12 [z] Ro 7:6; Gal 6:15; Eph 4:22-24; Col 3:10
6:5 [a] 2Co 4:10; Php 3:10, 11
6:6 [b] Eph 4:22; Col 3:9 [c] Gal 2:20; Col 2:12, 20 [d] Ro 7:24
6:9 [e] Ac 2:24 [f] Rev 1:18
6:10 [g] ver 2
6:11 [h] ver 2
6:13 [i] ver 16, 19; Ro 7:5 [j] Ro 12:1; 1Pe 2:24
6:14 [k] Gal 5:18 [l] Ro 3:24
6:16 [m] Jn 8:34; 2Pe 2:19 [n] ver 23
6:17 [o] Ro 1:8; 2Co 2:14 [p] 2Ti 1:13
6:18 [q] ver 7, 22; Ro 8:2
6:19 [r] Ro 3:5 [s] ver 13
6:20 [t] ver 16
6:21 [u] ver 23
6:22 [v] ver 18 [w] 1Co 7:22; 1Pe 2:16

[a] 6 Or *be rendered powerless*

6:4 *baptism.* The act of conversion to Judaism normally included baptism, seen as washing away the impurities of one's former Gentile life. Gentile converts to Judaism became part of the Jewish people, although their treatment varied in ancient Jewish sources.

6:6 *old self was crucified.* Here those "baptized into Christ" (v. 3) lose their corporate solidarity with the "old self," which could also be translated "old humanity" (in Adam), to find a new identity with Christ instead (see 5:15–21).

6:7 *set free.* Ancient intellectuals combated slavery to wrong ideas, to passions, and sometimes to concerns or dependence on others. Slaveholders often freed slaves, though they retained responsibilities to each other (see notes on 1Co 7:21,22); death, however, ended all obligations (as in Ro 7:2–3).

6:8 *with Christ.* On corporate identity in Christ, see notes on vv. 4,6; 5:17.

6:10 *died to sin once for all.* Jewish people expected the eradication of sin in the time of the end (e.g., Eze 36:26–27; Jubilees 50:5; Dead Sea Scrolls, Community Rule 3.18–19, 23; 4.18–26; 5.5).

6:11 *count yourselves … alive to God.* Ancient philosophers often sought to persuade people to discard wrong beliefs and feelings and recognize the truth about reality. Often this reality included "truths" about the purity of the inner person. Paul believed that people in Adam were sinful (3:23), but that the reality for those in Christ was a new identity (6:1–10). Eleven times in ch. 4 Paul used the term "credited," emphasizing that God counts us as righteous in Christ; using the same Greek term here, Paul urges us to "count" ourselves the way God views us. We can live in a new way to the extent that we embrace by faith our new identity as those united with Christ.

6:14–22 Regarding slavery, see note on v. 7; Jesus also employs the image (Mt 6:24; Lk 16:13). Speakers who wanted to reinforce a point would dwell on it, repeating and developing it in various ways. Rhetorical questions (as in vv. 15–16,21) also reinforced points.

result is eternal life. [23]For the wages of sin
is death,[x] but the gift of God is eternal life[y]
in[a] Christ Jesus our Lord.

Released From the Law, Bound to Christ

7 Do you not know, brothers and sisters[z]—for I am speaking to those who
know the law—that the law has authority over someone only as long as that person lives? [2]For example, by law a married
woman is bound to her husband as long
as he is alive, but if her husband dies, she
is released from the law that binds her to
him.[a] [3]So then, if she has sexual relations
with another man while her husband is
still alive, she is called an adulteress. But if
her husband dies, she is released from that
law and is not an adulteress if she marries
another man.

[4]So, my brothers and sisters, you also
died to the law[b] through the body of
Christ,[c] that you might belong to another, to him who was raised from the dead,
in order that we might bear fruit for God.
[5]For when we were in the realm of the
flesh,[b] the sinful passions aroused by the
law[d] were at work in us,[e] so that we bore
fruit for death. [6]But now, by dying to what
once bound us, we have been released
from the law so that we serve in the new
way of the Spirit, and not in the old way
of the written code.[f]

The Law and Sin

[7]What shall we say, then? Is the law sinful? Certainly not! Nevertheless, I would
not have known what sin was had it not
been for the law.[g] For I would not have
known what coveting really was if the law
had not said, "You shall not covet."[c][h] [8]But
sin, seizing the opportunity afforded by
the commandment,[i] produced in me every
kind of coveting. For apart from the law, sin
was dead.[j] [9]Once I was alive apart from the
law; but when the commandment came,
sin sprang to life and I died. [10]I found that
the very commandment that was intended
to bring life[k] actually brought death. [11]For
sin, seizing the opportunity afforded by the
commandment, deceived me,[l] and through
the commandment put me to death. [12]So
then, the law is holy, and the commandment is holy, righteous and good.[m]

[13]Did that which is good, then, become
death to me? By no means! Nevertheless,
in order that sin might be recognized as
sin, it used what is good to bring about my
death, so that through the commandment
sin might become utterly sinful.

[14]We know that the law is spiritual; but
I am unspiritual,[n] sold[o] as a slave to sin.

6:23 [x] Ge 2:17; Ro 5:12; Gal 6:7, 8; Jas 1:15 [y] Mt 25:46 **7:1** [z] Ro 1:13 **7:2** [a] 1Co 7:39 **7:4** [b] Ro 8:2; Gal 2:19 [c] Col 1:22 **7:5** [d] Ro 7:7-11 [e] Ro 6:13 **7:6** [f] Ro 2:29; 2Co 3:6

7:7 [g] Ro 3:20; 4:15 [h] Ex 20:17; Dt 5:21 **7:8** [i] ver 11 [j] Ro 4:15; 1Co 15:56 **7:10** [k] Lev 18:5; Lk 10:26-28; Ro 10:5; Gal 3:12 **7:11** [l] Ge 3:13 **7:12** [m] 1Ti 1:8 **7:14** [n] 1Co 3:1 [o] 1Ki 21:20, 25; 2Ki 17:17

[a] *23* Or *through* [b] *5* In contexts like this, the Greek word for *flesh* (*sarx*) refers to the sinful state of human beings, often presented as a power in opposition to the Spirit. [c] *7* Exodus 20:17; Deut. 5:21

6:23 *wages of sin ... gift of God.* In antiquity; even slaves could receive "wages"; any sort of wages, however, contrast with a free "gift."

7:2 *by law.* In some Jewish traditions, God's people were married to the law (though in those traditions, the law was the bride). *married woman is bound to her husband.* Possibly Paul also draws on the image of husband and wife becoming one flesh (Ge 2:24), thus here implies marriage to Christ. Perhaps he also substitutes fruit for offspring (vv. 4–5; cf. Dt 7:13), though his use of "fruit" is not unusual.

7:5 *sinful passions aroused by the law.* Philosophers and Diaspora Jewish thinkers often argued that knowledge of truth (for Jewish thinkers, especially knowledge of the law) would subdue the passions. Paul does not share this optimistic view of human ability (see vv. 7–25).

7:6 *new way of the Spirit.* The prophets associated the Spirit especially with the future time of restoration; the Spirit would enable people to fulfill God's commands from the heart (Eze 36:27). This law in the heart (Ro 8:2) would characterize the new covenant, distinguished from the form of the old (Jer 31:32–33).

7:7–24 Both in vv. 7–13 and (even more) in vv. 14–25, scholars debate whether Paul speaks of himself or uses the literary figure *prosopopoiia.* In this figure, one could speak as someone else; suggestions for whom Paul speaks as include Adam, Israel (who was under the law), and more generally simply anyone under the law. (Paul sometimes uses "I" hypothetically for "someone"—e.g., 1Co 10:29–30; 13:1–3; "we" in Ro 6:1). Paul could draw on his own experience as one who had lived under the law. Although the matter is debated, because of tensions with the surrounding context (compare, e.g., v. 14 with 6:18,20,22; 8:9) a majority of scholars believe that the passage cannot refer to Paul's normal present experience. What Paul clearly shows is that the law is good, when used according to its purpose. Yet while it teaches righteousness, knowledge of it does not by itself provide power to change one's thinking.

7:7 *coveting.* Whereas the rest of the Ten Commandments involved outward actions, the prohibition in the tenth commandment—"You shall not covet" (Ex 20:17; Dt 5:21)—involved the heart. It was the law that made clear that even actions of the heart counted as sin—and by drawing attention to these failures magnified the depth of their reach. For bad desire's objects, see Ex 20:17.

7:9 *when the commandment came ... I died.* A Jewish boy was believed to become fully responsible morally at his coming-of-age (about age 13), but Paul probably refers to awareness of sin at an even younger age. Jewish children heard Scripture all their lives, and some began to learn to recite the Torah as early as age five.

7:10 *intended to bring life.* Scripture promised long life to those who obeyed the commandments (e.g., Dt 30:16; 32:47; cf. Pr 4:4).

7:11 *seizing the opportunity afforded by the commandment.* Jewish teachers argued that knowing God's law provided power to overcome sin. Some scholars find here an allusion to Eve in Ge 3:13 (cf. Ro 5:12–21; 2Co 11:3), though the form of the verb in the Greek rendering of Ge 3:13 (translated "deceived") is different and is not distinctive (it occurs some 36 times in the Greek translation of the OT).

7:14 Paul here shifts to the present tense, which ancient writers sometimes used to make their descriptions more vivid. *spiritual.* May mean Spirit-inspired, as Jewish people

15I do not understand what I do. For what I want to do I do not do, but what I hate I do.[p] 16And if I do what I do not want to do, I agree that the law is good.[q] 17As it is, it is no longer I myself who do it, but it is sin living in me.[r] 18For I know that good itself does not dwell in me, that is, in my sinful nature.[a][s] For I have the desire to do what is good, but I cannot carry it out. 19For I do not do the good I want to do, but the evil I do not want to do—this I keep on doing.[t] 20Now if I do what I do not want to do, it is no longer I who do it, but it is sin living in me that does it.[u]

21So I find this law at work:[v] Although I want to do good, evil is right there with me. 22For in my inner being[w] I delight in God's law;[x] 23but I see another law at work in me, waging war[y] against the law of my mind and making me a prisoner of the law of sin at work within me. 24What a wretched man I am! Who will rescue me from this body that is subject to death?[z] 25Thanks be to God, who delivers me through Jesus Christ our Lord!

So then, I myself in my mind am a slave to God's law, but in my sinful nature[b] a slave to the law of sin.

Life Through the Spirit

8 Therefore, there is now no condemnation[a] for those who are in Christ Jesus,[b] 2because through Christ Jesus the law of the Spirit who gives life[c] has set you[c] free[d] from the law of sin[e] and death. 3For what the law was powerless[f] to do because it was weakened by the flesh,[d] God did by sending his own Son in the likeness of sinful flesh[g] to be a sin offering.[e][h] And so he condemned sin in the flesh, 4in order that the righteous requirement of the law might be fully met in us, who do not live according to the flesh but according to the Spirit.[i]

5Those who live according to the flesh have their minds set on what the flesh desires;[j] but those who live in accordance with the Spirit have their minds set on what the Spirit desires.[k] 6The mind governed by the flesh is death, but the mind governed by the Spirit is life[l] and peace. 7The mind governed by the flesh is hostile to God;[m] it does not submit to God's law, nor can it do so. 8Those who are in the realm of the flesh cannot please God.

9You, however, are not in the realm of the flesh but are in the realm of the Spirit, if indeed the Spirit of God lives in you.[n] And if anyone does not have the Spirit of

7:15 [p] ver 19; Gal 5:17
7:16 [q] ver 12
7:17 [r] ver 20
7:18 [s] ver 25
7:19 [t] ver 15
7:20 [u] ver 17
7:21 [v] ver 23, 25
7:22 [w] Eph 3:16 [x] Ps 1:2
7:23 [y] Gal 5:17; Jas 4:1; 1Pe 2:11
7:24 [z] Ro 6:6; 8:2
8:1 [a] ver 34 [b] ver 39; Ro 16:3
8:2 [c] 1Co 15:45 [d] Ro 6:18 [e] Ro 7:4
8:3 [f] Ac 13:39; Heb 7:18 [g] Php 2:7 [h] Heb 2:14, 17
8:4 [i] Gal 5:16
8:5 [j] Gal 5:19-21 [k] Gal 5:22-25
8:6 [l] Gal 6:8
8:7 [m] Jas 4:4
8:9 [n] 1Co 6:19; Gal 4:6

[a] *18* Or *my flesh* [b] *25* Or *in the flesh* [c] *2* The Greek is singular; some manuscripts *me* [d] *3* In contexts like this, the Greek word for *flesh* (*sarx*) refers to the sinful state of human beings, often presented as a power in opposition to the Spirit; also in verses 4-13. [e] *3* Or *flesh, for sin*

agreed Scripture was. *unspiritual.* Lit. "fleshly" (see the article "Flesh and Spirit," p. 1961). *sold as a slave.* The opposite of being redeemed from slavery (cf. 3:24).

7:15–21 Many philosophers, especially Stoics, believed that reason could help one overcome the passions; many believed these were rooted in the body. (Stoics thought that reason could help them eradicate even all negative emotion, which they viewed as unsound belief.) Even most Stoics admitted that they had not personally attained this goal, however. Diaspora Jewish thinkers often claimed that the law, providing moral truth, enabled them to control the passions. Rabbis believed that study of the law cultivated a good impulse that enabled them to overcome the evil impulse. By contrast, Paul's depiction of moral inadequacy here sounds more like ancient portrayals of Medea or others whose passions tragically conquered their reason. For Paul, merely knowing what was right, God's standard in the law, only solidified one's defeat, so that the mind (v. 23) was "governed by the flesh" (8:6). Gentiles sinned because their minds became blind to the truth (1:21–22); Jewish people's minds had the truth in the law yet they sinned anyway (2:12–15).

7:22–23 Philosophers and Diaspora Jewish intellectuals often advocated cultivating the mind, the inner person ("inner being," v. 22), as over against the passions of the body. Sometimes they used war imagery to depict this conflict ("waging war," v. 23). Paul depicts a mind here that has been taken prisoner of war by the members of his body (the NIV translates "my members" in v. 23a simply as "me").

7:24 *What a wretched man I am!* People often used exclamations such as this one; they appeared often in tragedies. *rescue me from this body.* Many Greek thinkers believed that when their perishable bodies died, their immortal souls would ascend freely to the realm of the divine. For Paul, however, who affirmed the resurrection of the body, salvation came not by rejecting the body but by sharing in Christ's finished death (6:3–4; 8:2–4).

7:25 *So then.* Summary statements often concluded sections—here, the inability of mere reason to conquer bodily-based passions.

8:2 *law of the Spirit.* In contrast to the old covenant, the new covenant would write God's law on the hearts of his people (Jer 31:31–34) by the Spirit (Eze 36:27). This had always been God's ideal (Dt 6:6; 30:6,14).

8:3 *to be a sin offering.* A phrase here (lit. "concerning sin") appears in the OT especially for sin offerings; the NIV is thus probably correct to translate "sin offering" here, viewing Jesus' death as a sacrifice (cf. 1Co 5:7; Heb 9:26; 10:10; 1Pe 1:19; cf. also atonement in Ro 3:25; 5:9).

8:5 *minds set on what the Spirit desires.* The wording here probably designates a characteristic disposition of one's mind. Many philosophers urged people to meditate on divine, eternal, heavenly matters instead of the temporal interests of passions generated by the body. For Paul, the mind that depends on God has peace (v. 6).

8:6 Philosophers often associated tranquility with sound thinking, though Paul could think here of peace with God (cf. v. 7; 5:1) and/or might evoke Isa 26:3.

8:8–13 Writers sometimes sustained a contrast between two opposites—here "realm of the flesh" (v. 8) and "realm of the Spirit" (v. 9), as also in vv. 5–7. See the article "Flesh and Spirit," p. 1961. Apart from the Qumran community, few Jewish people seem to have spoken of the Spirit as a present reality available in their communities; this was a blessing the prophets had promised for the period of

ROMANS 8:1 – 17

Flesh and Spirit

The OT describes people and other breathing animals as "flesh," by which it meant bodily, finite, mortal creatures. On two occasions it contrasts "flesh" and "Spirit" (Ge 6:3; Isa 31:3). The more relevant of these is Ge 6:3, where God's Spirit will not contend with flesh (NIV "humans") forever.

The Dead Sea Scrolls, written close to the era of the NT, show that some Jewish people further developed the implications of "flesh" as the finite and mortal state of people in contrast to God. Sometimes in these documents "flesh" connotes not only mortality but moral weakness — susceptibility to sin. The thought was not that the body was an evil part of a person; rather, it was that humans as limited, physical beings were weak.

By contrast, Greek thinkers (especially in the Platonic tradition) often viewed the soul as pure, immortal, and heavenly, but tied down to a body whose interests were mortal. The body would die; philosophy needed to free the soul from dependence on it, often by subduing passions. For followers of Aristotle, this meant controlling passions and keeping them moderate; for Stoics, it meant destroying emotion, or at least negative emotion, altogether (though some excepted initial emotional reflexes as merely "pre-emotion," before cognition could react). Diaspora Jews often embraced some of the intellectual ideas in their milieu, and believed that the mind, informed by the law, could subdue negative bodily passions.

Paul recognizes the mortality and weakness of the flesh; he also sees the connection between passions and bodily existence. But far from believing that the informed mind can necessarily subdue all passions, he recognizes that the mind too can be governed by the flesh (Ro 7:23,25; 8:6 – 7). For Paul the power to live a life that pleases God comes not from humans' finite ability in isolation from God, but by the power of the Spirit. God had promised to provide the Spirit so that his people could fulfill the moral purpose of his law (Eze 36:27; cf. Jer 31:33).

When Paul contrasts Spirit and flesh in Ro 8:4 – 9, he is not contrasting two parts or aspects of the human personality; rather, he is contrasting dependence on God's Spirit (and on Christ's justification that provides the Spirit) with humanity left to its own devices. Nor does Paul assume that only those continuously submitted to the Spirit may belong to the "in the Spirit" category versus the "in the flesh" category. Ancient writers often contrasted groups with ideal types: thus, e.g., Stoics and the book of Proverbs contrasted the wise and the foolish, even though few would be considered infallibly wise. Likewise, Proverbs and the Dead Sea Scrolls contrast the righteous and the wicked, even though no one was assumed virtuous in every respect without exception. The point is that one either belongs to the people who have the Spirit, and therefore their hearts are being transformed by God, or to those who are left to merely the best (or worst) of human effort without dependence on God's gift of the Spirit through faith in Christ. ◆

Christ,[o] they do not belong to Christ. 10But
if Christ is in you,[p] then even though your
body is subject to death because of sin,
the Spirit gives life[a] because of righteousness. 11And if the Spirit of him who raised
Jesus from the dead[q] is living in you, he
who raised Christ from the dead will also
give life to your mortal bodies[r] because of[b]
his Spirit who lives in you.
12Therefore, brothers and sisters, we
have an obligation — but it is not to the
flesh, to live according to it. 13For if you
live according to the flesh, you will die;
but if by the Spirit you put to death the
misdeeds of the body, you will live.[s]
14For those who are led by the Spirit of
God[t] are the children of God.[u] 15The Spirit
you received does not make you slaves,
so that you live in fear again;[v] rather, the
Spirit you received brought about your
adoption to sonship.[c] And by him we cry,
"Abba,[d] Father."[w] 16The Spirit himself testifies with our spirit[x] that we are God's
children. 17Now if we are children, then
we are heirs[y] — heirs of God and co-heirs
with Christ, if indeed we share in his sufferings in order that we may also share in
his glory.[z]

8:9 [o] Jn 14:17; 1Jn 4:13 **8:10** [p] Gal 2:20; Eph 3:17; Col 1:27 **8:11** [q] Ac 2:24 [r] Jn 5:21 **8:13** [s] Gal 6:8 **8:14** [t] Gal 5:18 [u] Jn 1:12; Rev 21:7 **8:15** [v] 2Ti 1:7; Heb 2:15 [w] Mk 14:36; Gal 4:5,6 **8:16** [x] Eph 1:13 **8:17** [y] Ac 20:32; Gal 4:7 [z] 1Pe 4:13

8:18 [a] 2Co 4:17; 1Pe 4:13 **8:20** [b] Ge 3:17-19 **8:21** [c] Ac 3:21; 2Pe 3:13; Rev 21:1 **8:22** [d] Jer 12:4 **8:23** [e] 2Co 5:5 [f] 2Co 5:2,4 [g] Gal 5:5 **8:24** [h] 1Th 5:8

Present Suffering and Future Glory

18I consider that our present sufferings
are not worth comparing with the glory
that will be revealed in us.[a] 19For the creation waits in eager expectation for the
children of God to be revealed. 20For the
creation was subjected to frustration, not
by its own choice, but by the will of the
one who subjected it,[b] in hope 21that[e] the
creation itself will be liberated from its
bondage to decay[c] and brought into the
freedom and glory of the children of God.
22We know that the whole creation has
been groaning[d] as in the pains of childbirth
right up to the present time. 23Not only so,
but we ourselves, who have the firstfruits
of the Spirit,[e] groan[f] inwardly as we wait
eagerly[g] for our adoption to sonship, the
redemption of our bodies. 24For in this
hope we were saved.[h] But hope that is seen
is no hope at all. Who hopes for what they
already have? 25But if we hope for what we
do not yet have, we wait for it patiently.

[a] *10* Or *you, your body is dead because of sin, yet your spirit is alive* [b] *11* Some manuscripts *bodies through* [c] *15* The Greek word for *adoption to sonship* is a term referring to the full legal standing of an adopted male heir in Roman culture; also in verse 23. [d] *15* Aramaic for *father* [e] *20,21* Or *subjected it in hope.* *21For*

restoration that Paul's contemporaries understood as the end time (e.g., Joel 2:28 – 29).

8:11 The image of God's Spirit giving life by resurrecting the dead appears in Eze 37:1 – 14.

8:14 – 17 Ancient sources often contrast a householder's children, who are his heirs (v. 17), with his slaves. The relationship between the two is obviously different. For people in Rome, "adoption" (v. 15) meant a cancellation of old legal relationships, establishing a new relationship as an heir.

8:14 *led by the Spirit of God.* The psalmist could ask for God's Spirit to lead him in God's ways (Ps 143:10). Most often Scripture spoke of God leading his people in the wilderness (e.g., Dt 8:2; Ne 9:19 – 20; Isa 63:14). This image fits other images in this context recalling how God saved his people in the exodus: God called Israel his children (Ex 4:22), redeemed them when they were groaning because of their slavery (Ex 2:23; cf. Ro 8:15,23), and promised them an inheritance in the promised land (cf. "heirs" in 8:17). The prophets had envisioned a new exodus (e.g., Isa 11:16; Jer 16:14 – 15; 23:7 – 8; Hos 2:14 – 15; 11:11; Mic 7:15). The exodus provides a useful image for believers' already/not yet experience: like Israel in the wilderness, Christians have experienced initial redemption but await their full inheritance in the promised land.

8:15 *slaves ... adoption.* See note on vv. 14 – 17. *fear.* Might allude both to the relationship slaves had to masters and to the experience of 7:15 – 25. *Abba.* A respectful but intimate way to address one's father. Although a few parables in much later sources compare God with an *Abba*, it does not appear in Jewish prayers (unlike "Father"); it was apparently learned from Jesus (Mk 14:36).

8:16 *The Spirit himself testifies with our spirit.* Witnesses had to attest to the agreement involved in Roman adoption; God's own Spirit testifies to the believer that this is done. The OT often and subsequent Judaism even more frequently associated the Spirit with prophetic inspiration; God's Spirit here (as in v. 15; 5:5) reminds believers of their relationship with God.

8:18 *present sufferings ... glory.* Jewish thinkers recognized that in the future God would reward his servants for their sufferings in this age. They often contrasted the present age with the age to come, expecting a reversal of present conditions.

8:19 *creation waits in eager expectation.* Many Jewish thinkers agreed that the coming age would transform all creation (Isa 65:17 – 19).

8:21 *liberated from its bondage to decay.* Many Gentiles, though affirming the eternal perfection of the heavens, lamented the continuing decay of the earthly world. Yet as God had liberated his children from slavery in the exodus, leading them by a cloud of glory (see note on v. 14), so God would in the future liberate his children most fully and with them all creation.

8:22 *whole creation has been groaning as in ... childbirth.* When God's people were slaves in Egypt, they "groaned in their slavery" (Ex 2:23), and God heard and delivered them (see note on Ro 8:14). Although possibly evoking such language from Exodus here, Paul further uses the groaning here (also vv. 23,26) another way. In a context emphasizing the bringing forth of God's children (vv. 14 – 17,19,21), birth pangs are significant. Many Jewish people expected a period of intense suffering just before the end of the age, and some spoke of this period as "birth pangs" or even the "birth pangs of the Messiah" or of the new, Messianic era (see note on Mt 24:6 – 14). Paul here portrays the present painful period between the Messiah's comings in these terms: suffering to bring forth a new age.

8:23 *firstfruits.* These were not simply a promise of, but rather the actual beginning of, a harvest. Thus believers already have the initial experience of the Spirit, of redemption, and of being God's children; the fullness awaits their resurrection bodies. The prophets had associated the Spirit with the promised future era of restoration

26 In the same way, the Spirit helps us in
our weakness. We do not know what we
ought to pray for, but the Spirit himself intercedes for us[i] through wordless groans.
27 And he who searches our hearts[j] knows
the mind of the Spirit, because the Spirit
intercedes for God's people in accordance
with the will of God.
28 And we know that in all things God
works for the good of those who love him,
who[a] have been called[k] according to his
purpose. 29 For those God foreknew[l] he
also predestined[m] to be conformed to the
image of his Son,[n] that he might be the
firstborn among many brothers and sisters. 30 And those he predestined,[o] he also
called; those he called, he also justified;[p]
those he justified, he also glorified.[q]

More Than Conquerors

31 What, then, shall we say in response
to these things?[r] If God is for us, who can
be against us?[s] 32 He who did not spare his
own Son,[t] but gave him up for us all —
how will he not also, along with him, graciously give us all things? 33 Who will bring
any charge[u] against those whom God has
chosen? It is God who justifies. 34 Who
then is the one who condemns? No one.
Christ Jesus who died[v] — more than that,
who was raised to life — is at the right
hand of God[w] and is also interceding for
us.[x] 35 Who shall separate us from the love
of Christ? Shall trouble or hardship or persecution or famine or nakedness or danger
or sword?[y] 36 As it is written:

> "For your sake we face death all day
> long;
> we are considered as sheep to be
> slaughtered."[b][z]

37 No, in all these things we are more than
conquerors[a] through him who loved us.[b]
38 For I am convinced that neither death
nor life, neither angels nor demons,[c] neither the present nor the future, nor any
powers,[c] 39 neither height nor depth, nor
anything else in all creation, will be able
to separate us from the love of God[d] that
is in Christ Jesus our Lord.

Paul's Anguish Over Israel

9 I speak the truth in Christ — I am not
lying,[e] my conscience confirms[f] it

8:26 [i] Eph 6:18 **8:27** [j] Rev 2:23 **8:28** [k] 1Co 1:9; 2Ti 1:9 **8:29** [l] Ro 11:2 [m] Eph 1:5, 11 [n] 1Co 15:49; 2Co 3:18; Php 3:21; 1Jn 3:2 **8:30** [o] Eph 1:5, 11 [p] 1Co 6:11 [q] Ro 9:23 **8:31** [r] Ro 4:1 [s] Ps 118:6 **8:32** [t] Jn 3:16; Ro 4:25; 5:8 **8:33** [u] Isa 50:8, 9 **8:34** [v] Ro 5:6-8 [w] Mk 16:19 [x] Heb 7:25; 9:24; 1Jn 2:1 **8:35** [y] 1Co 4:11 **8:36** [z] Ps 44:22; 2Co 4:11 **8:37** [a] 1Co 15:57 [b] Gal 2:20; Rev 1:5; 3:9 **8:38** [c] Eph 1:21; 1Pe 3:22 **8:39** [d] Ro 5:8 **9:1** [e] 2Co 11:10; Gal 1:20; 1Ti 2:7 [f] Ro 1:9

[a] 28 Or *that all things work together for good to those who love God, who*; or *that in all things God works together with those who love him to bring about what is good — with those who* [b] 36 Psalm 44:22 [c] 38 Or *nor heavenly rulers*

(Isa 32:15; 44:3; Eze 36:26 – 27; 37:14; 39:29; Joel 2:28 – 29; perhaps Zec 12:10).

8:26 *intercedes.* See note on v. 34. *groans.* See note on v. 22.

8:27 *he who searches our hearts.* Jewish sources emphasize God's omniscience; some later sources even title him as the one who "searches the hearts" (a description that fits, e.g., 1Ki 8:39; 1Ch 28:9).

8:28 *all things God works for the good.* Stoic philosophers urged the wise not to resist fate; Jewish people affirmed God's sovereignty and his love for his people. Although God often works things for the greater good even in this age (Ge 45:5; 50:20), Paul's primary emphasis here is the ultimate good to come (v. 18), especially the purpose of conformity to Jesus' image (v. 29).

8:29 *foreknew . . . predestined.* Most Jewish people (including the populist Pharisees) believed that God foreknew the future and chose his people (cf. 11:2); as in the OT, however, they also recognized that people disobeyed God. Thus the majority of Jewish thinkers affirmed both that God was sovereign and that humans had responsibility to choose rightly. Paul here encourages his audience, in the face of sufferings, that God is in control and that his promise of the future will succeed (see vv. 31 – 39). *conformed to the image of his Son.* God formed humanity originally in his image (Ge 1:26 – 27); even if sin has marred that image, it is fully restored in Christ. For Christ as God's image, see note on Col 1:15; many Jewish thinkers viewed God's wisdom or his *logos* (see notes on Jn 1:1,3) as his most perfect image.

8:31 *If God is for us.* Paul's language here could echo many Biblical sources, but especially Ps 118:6: "The LORD is with me . . . What can mere mortals do to me?"

8:33 – 34 Paul here echoes Isa 50:8: "He who vindicates me is near. Who then will bring charges against me? . . . Who is my accuser?"

8:34 *right hand of God.* Jesus' position at God's right hand reflects Ps 110:1; cf. perhaps also Ps 110:4, where the Lord is also a priest. *interceding for us.* Some Jewish sources depict angels or even (in later rabbis) God's attribute of mercy interceding before him. Here the intercessor is God's Son, based on his sacrificial death and his resurrection (cf. v. 32); God will certainly grant his requests.

8:35 A writer would sometimes compose a chiasm, an inverted parallel structure: Paul returns to the thought of v. 35a in slightly different terms at the end of v. 39, and the thought of v. 35b in v. 38 and the beginning of v. 39. Ancient speakers sometimes used lists to build to a rhetorical climax. Sages used lists of hardships to demonstrate that they had faced such hardships with integrity. *nakedness.* The Greek term can mean complete nakedness, but can also mean simply inadequate clothing. *sword.* Romans usually beheaded condemned Roman citizens with the sword; for war, see note on Rev 6:4.

8:36 At least by the second century, rabbis applied Ps 44:22 (cited here) to martyrs. Some Roman Christians had recently returned after being expelled from Rome in AD 49; perhaps six years after Paul sent this letter, the emperor began killing hundreds of Christians there (starting in AD 64).

8:38 See note on v. 35. *neither angels nor demons . . . nor any powers.* Given the context, "demons" (lit. "rulers") and "powers" likely refer to the spiritual rulers believed to be guardian angels of the nations, often viewed as hostile toward God's people (attested as early as Da 10:13,20 – 21; also the Greek version of Dt 32:8).

8:39 *neither height nor depth.* Some scholars compare height and depth to astrological terms; many believed that arbitrary Fate ruled the nations through the stars. Paul believed that Christ rather than Fate ruled believers' lives, but he may have simply included the terms as a merism to specify everything from heaven to Hades (Ps 139:8).

through the Holy Spirit— 2 I have great sorrow and unceasing anguish in my heart. 3 For I could wish that I myself[g] were cursed[h] and cut off from Christ for the sake of my people, those of my own race,[i] 4 the people of Israel. Theirs is the adoption to sonship;[j] theirs the divine glory, the covenants,[k] the receiving of the law,[l] the temple worship[m] and the promises.[n] 5 Theirs are the patriarchs, and from them is traced the human ancestry of the Messiah,[o] who is God over all,[p] forever praised![a][q] Amen.

God's Sovereign Choice

6 It is not as though God's word had failed. For not all who are descended from Israel are Israel.[r] 7 Nor because they are his descendants are they all Abraham's children. On the contrary, "It is through Isaac that your offspring will be reckoned."[b][s] 8 In other words, it is not the children by physical descent who are God's children,[t] but it is the children of the promise who are regarded as Abraham's offspring. 9 For this was how the promise was stated: "At the appointed time I will return, and Sarah will have a son."[c][u]

10 Not only that, but Rebekah's children were conceived at the same time by our father Isaac.[v] 11 Yet, before the twins were born or had done anything good or bad—in order that God's purpose[w] in election might stand: 12 not by works but by him who calls—she was told, "The older will serve the younger."[d][x] 13 Just as it is written: "Jacob I loved, but Esau I hated."[e][y]

14 What then shall we say? Is God unjust? Not at all![z] 15 For he says to Moses,

> "I will have mercy on whom I have
> mercy,
> and I will have compassion on
> whom I have compassion."[f][a]

16 It does not, therefore, depend on human desire or effort, but on God's mercy.[b] 17 For Scripture says to Pharaoh: "I raised you up for this very purpose, that I might display my power in you and that my name might be proclaimed in all the earth."[g][c] 18 Therefore God has mercy on whom he wants to have mercy, and he hardens whom he wants to harden.[d]

19 One of you will say to me:[e] "Then why does God still blame us? For who is able to resist his will?"[f] 20 But who are you, a human being, to talk back to God? "Shall what is formed say to the one who formed it,[g] 'Why did you make me like this?'"[h][h] 21 Does not the potter have the right to make out of the same lump of clay some

9:3 [g] Ex 32:32 [h] 1Co 12:3; 16:22 [i] Ro 11:14 **9:4** [j] Ex 4:22 [k] Ge 17:2; Ac 3:25; Eph 2:12 [l] Ps 147:19 [m] Heb 9:1 [n] Ac 13:32 **9:5** [o] Mt 1:1-16 [p] Jn 1:1 [q] Ro 1:25 **9:6** [r] Ro 2:28, 29; Gal 6:16 **9:7** [s] Ge 21:12; Heb 11:18 **9:8** [t] Ro 8:14 **9:9** [u] Ge 18:10, 14 **9:10** [v] Ge 25:21 **9:11** [w] Ro 8:28 **9:12** [x] Ge 25:23 **9:13** [y] Mal 1:2,3 **9:14** [z] 2Ch 19:7 **9:15** [a] Ex 33:19 **9:16** [b] Eph 2:8 **9:17** [c] Ex 9:16 **9:18** [d] Ex 4:21 **9:19** [e] Ro 11:19 [f] 2Ch 20:6; Da 4:35 **9:20** [g] Isa 64:8 [h] Isa 29:16

[a] 5 Or *Messiah, who is over all. God be forever praised!* Or *Messiah. God who is over all be forever praised!*
[b] 7 Gen. 21:12 [c] 9 Gen. 18:10,14 [d] 12 Gen. 25:23
[e] 13 Mal. 1:2,3 [f] 15 Exodus 33:19
[g] 17 Exodus 9:16 [h] 20 Isaiah 29:16; 45:9

9:3 *I could wish that I myself were … cut off … for the sake of my people.* Although nothing could separate Paul from Christ (8:39), he, like Moses, would sacrifice himself for his people (Ex 32:32–34).
9:4 Jewish people celebrated the gifts that Paul lists here. Paul lists these historical claims in a way that would also appeal to his audience rhetorically: in Greek, a series of feminine nouns ending as follows in *-thesia, -a, -ai, -thesia, -a, -ai.*
9:5 *who is God over all.* Jewish doxologies praised only the one true God. Although Paul usually reserves the divine title "God" for the Father and the divine title "Lord" for Jesus, many scholars argue that Paul praises Jesus as God here.
9:6 *not all who are descended from Israel are Israel.* This language would be shocking to a Jewish audience, but Paul uses the examples of Ishmael (vv. 7–9) and Esau (vv. 10–13) to illustrate that ethnic descent, apart from God's promise, does not guarantee covenant relationship (cf. also 1Co 10:1–11).
9:7 *It is through Isaac.* The context of Ge 21:12, cited here, is that the promised line comes not through Ishmael but through Isaac (though God blessed both of them). Mere descent from Abraham, then, was not sufficient even in the OT.
9:9 For faith in God's promise, see also 4:20–21.
9:11–12 *before the twins were born or had done anything good or bad … not by works.* As in vv. 7–8, mere physical descent is not sufficient; the promise specified the (slightly) younger twin, Jacob (Ge 25:23). Offered before their birth, the promise depended solely on God's grace, not on the brothers' prior behavior. Most Jewish people recognized both God's sovereignty and human responsibility without viewing them as contradictory (see note on 8:29). They especially emphasized that God chose Israel as a people; Paul insists here in ch. 9 that God's choice is not limited to Abraham's physical descendants, but more widely can include Gentiles (vv. 24–26).
9:13 *Jacob … Esau.* In Mal 1:2–3, God reminded Israel that he had chosen their ancestor Jacob rather than his brother Esau, and thus would bless them and not the Edomites.
9:14 *Is God unjust?* Israel's sages had sometimes struggled to explain and defend God's justice in a world of suffering and apparent inequity (see, e.g., the book of Job); later rabbis also engaged theodicy (God's justice).
9:15 Ex 33:19, cited here, emphasizes God's mercy and compassion, including toward Moses.
9:17 *I raised you up for this very purpose.* In context, even God raising up this pharaoh involved some mercy: God could have completely destroyed him and his people earlier (Ex 9:15), but God had established him so the world would see God's greatness (Ex 9:16).
9:18 *he hardens whom he wants to harden.* God showed mercy to Moses but hardened Pharaoh (Ex 9:12; 10:27; 11:10). Paul and Exodus celebrate God's sovereignty, but in other contexts they also recognize his justice (cf. v. 14); though God hardened Pharaoh's heart, Pharaoh also initially hardened his own heart (Ex 8:15,32).
9:19 *For who is able to resist his will?* In OT theology, questioning who could resist God's will was a way of praising God's might (2Ch 20:6; Da 4:35), but here the imaginary interlocutor instead questions God's justice. (On imaginary critics, see note on Ro 2:1–29.)
9:21 *the potter.* Paul evokes the potter image of Isa 29:16;

pottery for special purposes and some for
common use?[i]
22 What if God, although choosing to
show his wrath and make his power
known, bore with great patience[j] the objects of his wrath—prepared for destruction? 23 What if he did this to make the
riches of his glory[k] known to the objects of
his mercy, whom he prepared in advance
for glory[l]— 24 even us, whom he also
called,[m] not only from the Jews but also
from the Gentiles?[n] 25 As he says in Hosea:

"I will call them 'my people' who are
not my people;
and I will call her 'my loved one'
who is not my loved one,"[a][o]

26 and,

"In the very place where it was said to
them,
'You are not my people,'
there they will be called 'children of
the living God.'"[b][p]

27 Isaiah cries out concerning Israel:

"Though the number of the Israelites
be like the sand by the sea,[q]
only the remnant will be saved.[r]
28 For the Lord will carry out
his sentence on earth with speed
and finality."[c][s]

29 It is just as Isaiah said previously:

"Unless the Lord Almighty[t]
had left us descendants,
we would have become like Sodom,
we would have been like
Gomorrah."[d][u]

Israel's Unbelief

30 What then shall we say? That the Gentiles, who did not pursue righteousness,
have obtained it, a righteousness that is by
faith;[v] 31 but the people of Israel, who pursued the law as the way of righteousness,[w]
have not attained their goal.[x] 32 Why not?
Because they pursued it not by faith but
as if it were by works. They stumbled over
the stumbling stone.[y] 33 As it is written:

"See, I lay in Zion a stone that causes
people to stumble
and a rock that makes them fall,
and the one who believes in him will
never be put to shame."[e][z]

10 Brothers and sisters, my heart's desire and prayer to God for the Israelites is that they may be saved. 2 For I
can testify about them that they are zealous[a] for God, but their zeal is not based
on knowledge. 3 Since they did not know
the righteousness of God and sought to
establish their own, they did not submit
to God's righteousness.[b] 4 Christ is the culmination of the law[c] so that there may be
righteousness for everyone who believes.[d]
5 Moses writes this about the righteousness that is by the law: "The person who

9:21 [i] 2Ti 2:20 9:22 [j] Ro 2:4 9:23 [k] Ro 2:4 [l] Ro 8:30 9:24 [m] Ro 8:28 [n] Ro 3:29 9:25 [o] Hos 2:23; 1Pe 2:10 9:26 [p] Hos 1:10 9:27 [q] Ge 22:17; Hos 1:10 [r] Ro 11:5 9:28 [s] Isa 10:22, 23 9:29 [t] Jas 5:4 [u] Isa 1:9; Dt 29:23; Isa 13:19; Jer 50:40 9:30 [v] Ro 1:17; 10:6; Gal 2:16; Php 3:9; Heb 11:7 9:31 [w] Isa 51:1; Ro 10:2,3 [x] Gal 5:4 9:32 [y] 1Pe 2:8 9:33 [z] Isa 28:16; Ro 10:11 10:2 [a] Ac 21:20 10:3 [b] Ro 1:17 10:4 [c] Gal 3:24; Ro 7:1-4 [d] Ro 3:22

[a] 25 Hosea 2:23 [b] 26 Hosea 1:10 [c] 28 Isaiah 10:22,23 (see Septuagint) [d] 29 Isaiah 1:9 [e] 33 Isaiah 8:14; 28:16

45:9 (cf. also Isa 64:8; Jer 18:3–6), passages that emphasize God's sovereignty in history and that what he does is just.

9:22 *bore with great patience the objects of his wrath.* For the sake of those who would be saved, God endured those destined for destruction—just as in this context God had endured Pharaoh to make known God's name (v. 17, on Ex 9:16).

9:24 *also from the Gentiles.* God's name would be made known in all the earth (see Ex 9:16 in v. 17).

9:25–26 In support of God calling Gentiles, Paul cites Hos 2:23 and then Hos 1:10. These passages refer to Israel's restoration after a period of rejection for their sin (Hos 1:9). If God could make them his people again from not being his people, he could do the same for Gentiles who also had not been his people.

9:27–28 Jewish teachers often linked texts by a common phrase; Paul undoubtedly knows that Israel in Hos 1:10 (a text just cited in v. 26) is "like the sand on the seashore" (Hos 1:10), facilitating his link here with Isa 10:22–23, cited here in vv. 27–28. (Paul blends some wording of the two texts, a common practice in his day.) In Isa 10:22–23, God punishes his own people, sparing only a remnant.

9:29 Like Isa 10:22–23 (cited in vv. 27–28), Isa 1:9 (cited here in v. 29) refers to only a minority of Israel surviving the judgment; Isa 1:10 compares Israel to Gentiles. These passages in vv. 25–29 show that God does not spare people judgment based on their ancestry (vv. 30–31).

9:31 *pursued the law as the way of righteousness.* On the different ways of approaching the law (also in 10:5–10), see note on 3:27.

9:32,33 *stone.* Again (see vv. 25–29 and notes), Paul in v. 33 shows from Scripture (using Isa 8:14; 28:16) that judgment would come even to Israel; only those who depended on God—who had faith—would be saved. Following common practice, Paul links two texts based on a common word, here blending them into one: in Isa 8:14, Israel would stumble over God as a stone, and in Isa 28:16, whoever trusted in the stone he laid would not be disturbed (in the Greek version, would not be made ashamed). Because Isa 28:16 also depicts this stone as a cornerstone, Paul may have also thought of Ps 118:22, applied by Jesus to himself (Mk 12:10; cf. 1Pe 2:6–7). On the divine stone, see also note on 1Co 10:4.

10:5–10 Many commentators believe that in vv. 5–10 Paul is contrasting two approaches to the law. The first, in v. 5, is to approach the law as a means of achieving righteousness before God (v. 3; 9:31–32); the second, in vv. 6–10, approaches it as a witness to God's saving acts. Some ancient Jewish sources apparently allowed both approaches, but Paul contrasts them as incompatible.

10:5 *righteousness that is by the law ... live by them.* God's people would have long life in the Holy Land if they obeyed God's commands (Lev 18:5; often in Deuteronomy, e.g., Dt 4:1,40). Jewish teachers came to apply this principle also to having eternal life by obeying the commandments. The issue here is not obedience as an expression of faith (which Paul affirms, Ro 1:5) but establishing

does these things will live by them."[a][e]
6 But the righteousness that is by faith[f]
says: "Do not say in your heart, 'Who will
ascend into heaven?' "[b][g] (that is, to bring
Christ down) 7 "or 'Who will descend into
the deep?' "[c] (that is, to bring Christ up
from the dead). 8 But what does it say?
"The word is near you; it is in your mouth
and in your heart,"[d][h] that is, the message
concerning faith that we proclaim: 9 If you
declare[i] with your mouth, "Jesus is Lord,"
and believe in your heart that God raised
him from the dead,[j] you will be saved.
10 For it is with your heart that you believe and are justified, and it is with your
mouth that you profess your faith and
are saved. 11 As Scripture says, "Anyone
who believes in him will never be put to
shame."[e][k] 12 For there is no difference between Jew and Gentile[l] — the same Lord is
Lord of all[m] and richly blesses all who call
on him, 13 for, "Everyone who calls on the
name of the Lord[n] will be saved."[f][o]

14 How, then, can they call on the one
they have not believed in? And how can
they believe in the one of whom they have
not heard? And how can they hear without someone preaching to them? 15 And
how can anyone preach unless they are
sent? As it is written: "How beautiful are
the feet of those who bring good news!"[g][p]

16 But not all the Israelites accepted the
good news. For Isaiah says, "Lord, who
has believed our message?"[h][q] 17 Consequently, faith comes from hearing the message,[r] and the message is heard through
the word about Christ.[s] 18 But I ask: Did
they not hear? Of course they did:

> "Their voice has gone out into all the
> earth,
> their words to the ends of the world."[i][t]

19 Again I ask: Did Israel not understand?
First, Moses says,

> "I will make you envious[u] by those
> who are not a nation;
> I will make you angry by a nation
> that has no understanding."[j][v]

10:5 [e] Lev 18:5; Ne 9:29; Eze 20:11, 13, 21; Ro 7:10 **10:6** [f] Ro 9:30 [g] Dt 30:12 **10:8** [h] Dt 30:14 **10:9** [i] Mt 10:32; Lk 12:8 [j] Ac 2:24 **10:11** [k] Isa 28:16; Ro 9:33 **10:12** [l] Ro 3:22, 29 [m] Ac 10:36 **10:13** [n] Ac 2:21 [o] Joel 2:32 **10:15** [p] Isa 52:7; Na 1:15 **10:16** [q] Isa 53:1; Jn 12:38 **10:17** [r] Gal 3:2, 5 [s] Col 3:16 **10:18** [t] Ps 19:4; Mt 24:14; Col 1:6, 23; 1Th 1:8 **10:19** [u] Ro 11:11, 14 [v] Dt 32:21

[a] *5* Lev. 18:5 [b] *6* Deut. 30:12 [c] *7* Deut. 30:13 [d] *8* Deut. 30:14 [e] *11* Isaiah 28:16 (see Septuagint) [f] *13* Joel 2:32 [g] *15* Isaiah 52:7 [h] *16* Isaiah 53:1 [i] *18* Psalm 19:4 [j] *19* Deut. 32:21

their own righteousness rather than depending on God's saving acts (10:3,6–10).

10:6–10 In vv. 6–8, Paul explains Dt 30:12–14 as midrash—i.e., like a Jewish teacher expounding the text line by line.

10:6 *ascend into heaven.* In Dt 30:12 (cited here), one need not ascend to heaven to receive the law; God already provided it. Jewish tradition also elaborated Moses' ascent on Mount Sinai as an ascent to heaven. Paul applies the principle to a new act of salvation, Christ's coming.

10:7 *descend into the deep.* In Dt 30:13 (cited here), one need not cross the sea to get the law; God had in fact redeemed his people and brought them across the sea. God prefaced his most prominent commandments with this reminder of redemption (Dt 5:6). Ancient expositors sometimes altered some wording to make a point; Paul changes "sea" to "the deep" here (usually the Greek version of the OT applies this Greek term to watery depths), since it bridges better to his analogy of raising Christ from among the dead. One did not need to strive to get God's law, nor to bring about a new act of salvation in Christ's rising.

10:8 *word is near you.* In Dt 30:14 (cited here), the law, God's word, was not too difficult to obey (Dt 30:11); it was in their grasp, insofar as it was in their mouth and their heart. *mouth ... heart.* This presence of God's word probably includes speaking of the law always (Dt 6:7–9), so keeping it in their hearts (Dt 6:6) as an expression of loving God (Dt 6:5; 30:6). This ideal was apparently sometimes fulfilled by believers before the new covenant (Ps 37:31), but the new covenant would establish it among all God's people (Jer 31:33). Paul applies the principle to the divine word spoken in his day as well: the message of faith was also in the heart and mouth (vv. 9–10).

10:11 *Anyone who believes.* Paul revisits (see 9:33) his quotation of Isa 28:16, but underlines its point of "the one who relies" by more explicitly saying, "Anyone who believes." *Anyone.* Translates the Greek term for "all," also used in v. 13 ("everyone") and in the plural in v. 12 ("all").

10:13 *Everyone who calls on the name of the Lord.* Teachers often linked texts with a common key word; Paul links "everyone" in Joel 2:32 with his adapted wording of Isa 28:16 in v. 11 (see previous note). In this way Paul can emphasize that the promise is for Jew and Gentile alike (v. 12). By linking the texts, he shows that never being "put to shame" (v. 11) means being saved (v. 13).

10:14 Ancient speakers and writers appreciated connected chains of thought such as the one in vv. 14–15. *believe.* Taken from the citation in v. 11 (recurs in v. 16); hearing a message in vv. 16–18 (with a supporting citation in v. 16).

10:15 *those who bring good news.* Paul refers to Isa 52:7, where heralds would announce the good news that God was demonstrating his reign by restoring his people.

10:16 *who has believed our message?* Following from the same context he has just cited, Paul refers to Isa 53:1, where God's message and his servant were rejected (Isa 53:1–3). Although Paul's quotation in v. 15 omits the term, he probably knows that a common Greek version of Isa 52:7 included the term in Isa 53:1 translated "message" here in v. 16; i.e., a specific term would point the reader of Isa 53:1 back to the message announced in the earlier verse.

10:18 The point of Paul's appeal to Ps 19:4 (cited here) is debated. Since the psalm's context refers to God's universal witness in creation (Ps 19:1–6; cf. Ps 8:1; 89:37; 97:6; though Ps 19 moves on to the law as special revelation in Ps 19:7–11), it may mean that everyone knows enough to be morally responsible (as in Ro 1:19–20). Alternatively, Paul may make an analogy for the gospel (cf. vv. 6–8), which has spread widely at least in a proleptic way (cf. Col 1:23). Or Paul may be saying that since even Gentiles had some revelation (as in Ps 19:4), how much more Israel, who has heard but (as in v. 16) not believed. Or that the Gentile world, in contrast to Israel (cf. vv. 19–21), received the message; or that Ps 19 shows that God wanted all peoples to have access to the message.

10:19 *by those who are not a nation.* In the context of Dt 32:21 (cited here), God punishes Israel as a perverse generation (Dt 32:20; cf. Php 2:15); they had unfaithfully

[20]And Isaiah boldly says,

"I was found by those who did not
seek me;
I revealed myself to those who did
not ask for me."[aw]

[21]But concerning Israel he says,

"All day long I have held out my hands
to a disobedient and obstinate
people."[bx]

The Remnant of Israel

11 I ask then: Did God reject his people? By no means![y] I am an Israelite myself, a descendant of Abraham,[z]
from the tribe of Benjamin.[a] [2]God did not
reject his people, whom he foreknew.[b]
Don't you know what Scripture says in the
passage about Elijah—how he appealed
to God against Israel: [3]"Lord, they have
killed your prophets and torn down your
altars; I am the only one left, and they are
trying to kill me"[c]?[c] [4]And what was God's
answer to him? "I have reserved for myself seven thousand who have not bowed
the knee to Baal."[dd] [5]So too, at the present
time there is a remnant[e] chosen by grace.
[6]And if by grace, then it cannot be based
on works;[f] if it were, grace would no longer be grace.
[7]What then? What the people of Israel
sought so earnestly they did not obtain.[g]
The elect among them did, but the others
were hardened,[h] [8]as it is written:

"God gave them a spirit of stupor,
eyes that could not see
and ears that could not hear,[i]
to this very day."[ej]

[9]And David says:

"May their table become a snare and a
trap,
a stumbling block and a retribution
for them.
[10]May their eyes be darkened so they
cannot see,
and their backs be bent forever."[fk]

Ingrafted Branches

[11]Again I ask: Did they stumble so as to
fall beyond recovery? Not at all![l] Rather,
because of their transgression, salvation
has come to the Gentiles[m] to make Israel
envious.[n] [12]But if their transgression means
riches for the world, and their loss means
riches for the Gentiles,[o] how much greater
riches will their full inclusion bring!
[13]I am talking to you Gentiles. Inasmuch
as I am the apostle to the Gentiles,[p] I take
pride in my ministry [14]in the hope that I
may somehow arouse my own people to

10:20 [w]Isa 65:1; Ro 9:30 **10:21** [x]Isa 65:2 **11:1** [y]1Sa 12:22; Jer 31:37 [z]2Co 11:22 [a]Php 3:5 **11:2** [b]Ro 8:29 **11:3** [c]1Ki 19:10, 14 **11:4** [d]1Ki 19:18 **11:5** [e]Ro 9:27 **11:6** [f]Ro 4:4 **11:7** [g]Ro 9:31 [h]ver 25; Ro 9:18 **11:8** [i]Mt 13:13-15 [j]Dt 29:4; Isa 29:10 **11:10** [k]Ps 69:22,23 **11:11** [l]ver 1 [m]Ac 13:46 [n]Ro 10:19 **11:12** [o]ver 25 **11:13** [p]Ac 9:15

[a] *20* Isaiah 65:1 [b] *21* Isaiah 65:2 [c] *3* 1 Kings 19:10,14 [d] *4* 1 Kings 19:18 [e] *8* Deut. 29:4; Isaiah 29:10 [f] *10* Psalm 69:22,23

made him jealous with false gods (Dt 32:16,21), so he would make them jealous by blessing a non-people. The same context laments them abandoning God as their rock (Dt 32:15,18), perhaps relevant to Paul's recent citation of stone texts in Ro 9:33 (and the recent allusion to one in 10:11).

10:20 In v. 19, Paul cited Moses (Dt 32) to show that God, judging his disobedient people, welcomed instead another people without understanding. Continuing the same theme, Paul cites Isa 65:1 here; although Paul does not complete that quotation, Isaiah goes on to speak of God revealing himself "to a nation that did not call on my name" (Isa 65:1; cf. Ro 10:13). The sense in Isaiah is debated, although a few chapters earlier in Isaiah God openly welcomed obedient Gentiles (Isa 56:3–8). Paul's linkage of the verse with the previously cited passage from Deuteronomy suggests that Paul applies Isaiah's words to Gentiles here.

10:21 Paul goes on to cite Isa 65:2, which does apply to Israel in the context. *held out my hands.* Stretching out hands can communicate entreaty (Job 11:13; Ps 77:2).

11:2–4 Some early Jewish teachers criticized Elijah for accusing his people to God, but Paul's point here is different. Paul shows that even in a period when Elijah had reason to believe in Israel's wholesale apostasy, God had preserved a remnant faithful to himself (1Ki 19:10,14,18).

11:5 *remnant chosen by grace.* Prophets recognized that after judgment God would deliver the remnant, the survivors (e.g., Isa 10:20–22; 28:5; 37:31–32; Jer 50:20; Mic 5:7–8); see Ro 9:27. Paul speaks of those still faithful to divine truth (11:2–4). God chose his people because of his love (Dt 7:7–8); because Jewish people viewed themselves as the chosen people, Paul's emphasis on the more narrowly chosen remnant challenges their assumptions (cf. Ro 9:6–8).

11:7 *hardened.* See note on 9:18.

11:8 Teachers sometimes blended passages (cf. also 3:10–12; 9:27–28,32,33; see applicable notes there), as Paul does here. He cites Isa 29:10 (what the NIV translates there as "deep sleep" is in the Greek translation of the OT the same wording as the "spirit of stupor" here) with Dt 29:4 ("not … ears that hear" there is roughly the same in Greek as "ears that could not hear" here). In both contexts, Israel had refused to heed God.

11:9–10 Teachers often linked texts with shared words or ideas; eyes that cannot see links the present quotation (Ps 69:22–23) with the composite quotation in v. 8. As a psalm about the mistreatment of a righteous sufferer, Ps 69 often lent itself to early Christian applications to Jesus' suffering (e.g., Ps 69:9 in Ro 15:3).

11:11 *envious.* For Paul's Biblical background for this term here and in v. 14, see note on 10:19.

11:12 *how much greater riches.* Jewish teachers often used "how much more" analogy arguments.

11:13 *I take pride.* In antiquity, public boasting was acceptable only under particular conditions, such as inviting others' emulation to do good.

11:14 *I may somehow arouse my own people … and save some of them.* Paul cited Dt 32:21 in Ro 10:19 and now develops its implications. Some Jewish thinkers expected the conversion of Gentiles in the end time (cf., e.g., Isa 19:24–25; 60:3–12); because this is being fulfilled in Christ, Paul wants his people to see that Jesus' movement is an end-time agent for Israel's God. *envy.* See note on v. 11.

envy[q] and save[r] some of them. 15 For if their rejection brought reconciliation[s] to the world, what will their acceptance be but life from the dead?[t] 16 If the part of the dough offered as firstfruits[u] is holy, then the whole batch is holy; if the root is holy, so are the branches.

17 If some of the branches have been broken off,[v] and you, though a wild olive shoot, have been grafted in among the others[w] and now share in the nourishing sap from the olive root, 18 do not consider yourself to be superior to those other branches. If you do, consider this: You do not support the root, but the root supports you.[x] 19 You will say then, "Branches were broken off so that I could be grafted in." 20 Granted. But they were broken off because of unbelief, and you stand by faith.[y] Do not be arrogant,[z] but tremble.[a] 21 For if God did not spare the natural branches, he will not spare you either.

22 Consider therefore the kindness[b] and sternness of God: sternness to those who fell, but kindness to you, provided that you continue[c] in his kindness. Otherwise, you also will be cut off.[d] 23 And if they do not persist in unbelief, they will be grafted in, for God is able to graft them in again.[e] 24 After all, if you were cut out of an olive tree that is wild by nature, and contrary to nature were grafted into a cultivated olive tree, how much more readily will these, the natural branches, be grafted into their own olive tree!

All Israel Will Be Saved

25 I do not want you to be ignorant[f] of this mystery,[g] brothers and sisters, so that you may not be conceited:[h] Israel has experienced a hardening[i] in part until the full number of the Gentiles has come in,[j] 26 and in this way[a] all Israel will be saved. As it is written:

"The deliverer will come from Zion;
he will turn godlessness away from Jacob.
27 And this is[b] my covenant with them
when I take away their sins."[c][k]

28 As far as the gospel is concerned, they are enemies[l] for your sake; but as far as election is concerned, they are loved on account of the patriarchs,[m] 29 for God's gifts and his call[n] are irrevocable.[o] 30 Just as you who were at one time disobedient[p]

11:14 [q] ver 11; Ro 10:19 [r] 1Co 1:21; 1Ti 2:4; Titus 3:5 **11:15** [s] Ro 5:10 [t] Lk 15:24,32 **11:16** [u] Lev 23:10, 17; Nu 15:18-21 **11:17** [v] Jer 11:16; Jn 15:2 [w] Ac 2:39; Eph 2:11-13 **11:18** [x] Jn 4:22 **11:20** [y] 1Co 10:12; 2Co 1:24 [z] Ro 12:16; 1Ti 6:17 [a] 1Pe 1:17 **11:22** [b] Ro 2:4 [c] 1Co 15:2; Heb 3:6 [d] Jn 15:2 **11:23** [e] 2Co 3:16 **11:25** [f] Ro 1:13 [g] Ro 16:25 [h] Ro 12:16 [i] ver 7; Ro 9:18 [j] Lk 21:24 **11:27** [k] Isa 27:9; Heb 8:10, 12 **11:28** [l] Ro 5:10 [m] Dt 7:8; 10:15; Ro 9:5 **11:29** [n] Ro 8:28 [o] Heb 7:21 **11:30** [p] Eph 2:2

[a] *26* Or *and so* [b] *27* Or *will be* [c] *27* Isaiah 59:20,21; 27:9 (see Septuagint); Jer. 31:33,34

11:15 *life from the dead.* The Jewish people's end-time turning to God was associated with their restoration (cf. Eze 36:24–28; Hos 14:1–7), and their restoration with the resurrection of the dead (Eze 37:1–14).
11:16 *If … the dough offered as firstfruits is holy, then the whole batch is holy.* In Nu 15:20–21, the firstfruits of the dough offering consecrates the "whole batch"; since God had consecrated Israel at the beginning, it remained set aside for his purpose (cf. Jer 2:3). Speakers often used mixed metaphors; in vv. 17–24 Paul will develop his other illustration, about root and branches.
11:17–24 Jewish sources often described Israel as a plant or a tree, whose roots were the patriarchs (Abraham, Isaac and Jacob). (Sometimes they even used the image of an olive tree; indeed, at some point a synagogue in Rome was apparently named the "olive tree.") Contrary to standard Jewish teaching, Paul had argued that uncircumcised Gentiles could become part of that people of God through faith in the Jewish Messiah (ch. 4)—like proselytes, but without physical circumcision. Now he reminds Gentiles to respect the Jewish people, who had brought them their faith. It was easier for Jewish branches to be grafted back into the true form of their own faith than for polytheists who had worshiped idols before their conversion to understand the faith they were now accepting. Like other Jewish teachers of his day, Paul does not regard any particular person's salvation as guaranteed from the human perspective till they have persevered to the end.

Ancient sources often report the grafting of trees—adding a shoot of one tree to another tree. Sometimes shoots from a wild olive tree would be grafted onto a domestic olive tree that was bearing little fruit in an attempt to strengthen or save the life of the tree. The unproductive original branches would be pruned off, and the new graft was considered "contrary to nature" (as in v. 24).

Although some Gentiles joined God's covenant in ancient Israel (e.g., Rahab, Ruth), Jesus' message had now created a new situation: in some places Gentile followers of Israel's God now outnumbered Jewish ones (Gentiles apparently predominated in the Roman church; cf. v. 13; 1:13). Paul warned grafted-in Gentiles not to reverse previous Jewish prejudice by despising the Jewish people—a warning soon neglected in the Roman church and elsewhere, as Gentile Christians in the following centuries boasted that they had replaced Israel.
11:25 *mystery.* Some Jewish writers used "mystery" with regard to a hidden truth, often about the future, now revealed by God (e.g., Da 2:28–30; cf. Ro 16:25–26). *hardening.* See note on 9:18. *until the full number of the Gentiles has come in.* Because Israel's repentance was expected to precipitate the end, God had allowed Israel's resistance (10:16,21) to provide time for the promised witness to Gentiles.
11:26 *all Israel will be saved.* Many Jewish people expected Israel's repentance to precipitate the end (Eze 34:11–31; 36:24–28; Hos 14:4–7; Joel 2:12–32; Am 9:11–15; Jubilees 23:26–27). A significant line of Jewish tradition emphasizes the future salvation of all Israel; while this meant Israel as a whole and not every individual Israelite, only the most notorious sinners were excluded (in the Mishnah see *Sanhedrin* 10:1). Paul supports his case with Isa 59:20–21, a context also mentioning the gift of the Spirit. Ancient writers often paraphrased quotations, as Paul does here (though his quotation is close to the Septuagint, the pre-Christian Greek translation of the OT, form); in the next verse (Ro 11:27) Paul might blend Isa 59:20–21 with Ps 14:7 ("from Zion") and Isa 27:9 ("take away their sins"; only in the Greek version).
11:28 *on account of the patriarchs.* God chose Israel and loved them because of his promise to the patriarchs (Dt 7:6–8; 10:15).
11:30–32 Ancient writers or speakers often summa-

to God have now received mercy as a result of their disobedience, 31 so they too have now become disobedient in order that they too may now[a] receive mercy as a result of God's mercy to you. 32 For God has bound everyone over to disobedience[q] so that he may have mercy on them all.

Doxology

33 Oh, the depth of the riches[r] of the
  wisdom and[b] knowledge of
  God![s]
How unsearchable his judgments,
  and his paths beyond tracing out![t]
34 "Who has known the mind of the
  Lord?
Or who has been his counselor?"[c][u]
35 "Who has ever given to God,
  that God should repay them?"[d][v]
36 For from him and through him and for
  him are all things.[w]
To him be the glory forever! Amen.[x]

A Living Sacrifice

12 Therefore, I urge you,[y] brothers and sisters, in view of God's mercy, to offer your bodies as a living sacrifice,[z] holy and pleasing to God—this is your true and proper worship. 2 Do not conform[a] to the pattern of this world,[b] but be transformed by the renewing of your mind.[c] Then you will be able to test and approve what God's will is[d]—his good, pleasing and perfect will.

Humble Service in the Body of Christ

3 For by the grace given me[e] I say to every one of you: Do not think of yourself more highly than you ought, but rather think of yourself with sober judgment, in accordance with the faith God has distributed to each of you. 4 For just as each of us has one body with many members, and these members do not all have the same function,[f] 5 so in Christ we, though many, form one body,[g] and each member belongs to all the others. 6 We have different gifts,[h] according to the grace given to each of us. If your gift is prophesying, then prophesy in accordance with your[e] faith;[i] 7 if it is serving, then serve; if it is teaching, then teach;[j] 8 if it is to encourage, then give encouragement;[k] if it is giving, then give generously;[l] if it is to lead,[f] do it diligently; if it is to show mercy, do it cheerfully.

Love in Action

9 Love must be sincere.[m] Hate what is

11:32 [q] Ro 3:9 **11:33** [r] Ro 2:4 [s] Ps 92:5 [t] Job 11:7 **11:34** [u] Isa 40:13, 14; Job 15:8; 36:22; 1Co 2:16 **11:35** [v] Job 35:7 **11:36** [w] 1Co 8:6; Col 1:16; Heb 2:10 [x] Ro 16:27 **12:1** [y] Eph 4:1 [z] Ro 6:13, 16, 19; 1Pe 2:5 **12:2** [a] 1Pe 1:14 [b] 1Jn 2:15 [c] Eph 4:23 [d] Eph 5:17 **12:3** [e] Ro 15:15; Gal 2:9; Eph 4:7 **12:4** [f] 1Co 12:12-14; Eph 4:16 **12:5** [g] 1Co 10:17 **12:6** [h] 1Co 7:7; 12:4,8-10 [i] 1Pe 4:10, 11 **12:7** [j] Eph 4:11 **12:8** [k] Ac 15:32 [l] 2Co 9:5-13 **12:9** [m] 1Ti 1:5

[a] 31 Some manuscripts do not have *now.* [b] 33 Or *riches and the wisdom and the* [c] 34 Isaiah 40:13 [d] 35 Job 41:11 [e] 6 Or *the* [f] 8 Or *to provide for others*

rized some themes of a section at its close. Gentiles and Israel exchanging roles of disobedience may allude back to 9:25–26 (cf. 10:21); mercy to 9:15–23. On the common scholarly view today that the Roman church was ethnically divided, this was important news.

11:33–36 Sometimes a writer would conclude a section with rousing rhetoric; discussion of deity, in particular, sometimes invited exalted, almost poetic, rhetoric. Paul praises God for the lavish display of his sovereignty and wisdom in history.

11:34–35 Verse 34 borrows the language of the Greek version of Isa 40:13, and v. 35 might evoke the idea of Job 41:11. For effects on renewed minds, see 12:2; 1Co 2:16.

11:36 *from … through … for.* Philosophers distinguished various levels of causation with terms such as "from," "through," and "for"; all the levels are applicable here.

12:1–3 Some ancient works transitioned from general considerations to practical advice, as here. Nevertheless, the previous demonstration of God's mercy in chs. 9–11 offers the foundation for the present exhortation (v. 1).

12:1 *living sacrifice.* Paul's imagery would be intelligible; both the OT at times and some of his contemporaries could use "sacrifice" figuratively for other expressions of devotion to God (see, e.g., Ps 51:17; Pr 21:3). Because most animal sacrifices were slaughtered, "living" sacrifice might strike hearers as an oxymoron, while stretching the image to cover continued devotion (cf. Ro 6:11). *holy and pleasing to God.* Sacrifices could be holy (e.g., Lev 2:3,10) or pleasing (e.g., Ezr 6:10; Isa 56:7; Jer 6:20) to the Lord. *true and proper.* The Greek can denote what is rational, relevant for vv. 2–3.

12:2 *transformed by the renewing of your mind.* Philosophers wanted hearers to base all decisions on reason; Paul adds an eschatological (end-time) perspective. "This world" is lit. "this age"; the "renewing of your mind," then, includes thinking as citizens of the coming new world. *mind.* See note on 6:11. *good, pleasing and perfect will.* This perspective helps believers to discern God's will—whatever is good, pleasing (cf. v. 1), and perfect in God's sight.

12:3 *Do not think of yourself more highly than you ought.* Many philosophers urged a sound view of oneself based on one's role in the larger universe; Paul urges believers to consider their roles in Christ's body (vv. 4–5).

12:4–5 *many members … form one body.* Earlier Greek and Roman thinkers had compared the state and even the universe to a body of interdependent members. Often ancient writers used the analogy to support hierarchy, but Paul here values the importance of the diverse functions represented.

12:6 *prophesying.* Speaking for God, inspired by God; the OT offers a range of examples, but many include speaking directly in God's name with the prophets functioning as messengers. *in accordance with your faith.* Suggests the faith distributed to each by God (v. 3). Although the OT records many prophecies and the NT records some, clearly most prophecies in those periods never became part of Scripture (cf. 1Co 14:31), and this gift should not be viewed or treated as competing with Scripture or limited to one period.

12:9–21 Ancient writers on moral topics often offered lists of largely unconnected moral exhortations; scholars call such compilations *parenesis.* Paul here offers various exhortations around the theme of treating one another well (an important issue in the Roman church; see Introduction: Setting). Most of Paul's exhortations would be widely acceptable in the culture. Ancients sometimes framed a section with parallel ideas; Paul emphasizes good versus evil in vv. 9,21.

evil; cling to what is good. 10Be devoted to
one another in love.[n] Honor one another
above yourselves.[o] 11Never be lacking in
zeal, but keep your spiritual fervor,[p] serving the Lord. 12Be joyful in hope,[q] patient
in affliction,[r] faithful in prayer. 13Share
with the Lord's people who are in need.
Practice hospitality.[s]

14Bless those who persecute you;[t] bless
and do not curse. 15Rejoice with those who
rejoice; mourn with those who mourn.[u]
16Live in harmony with one another.[v] Do
not be proud, but be willing to associate
with people of low position.[a] Do not be
conceited.[w]

17Do not repay anyone evil for evil.[x] Be
careful to do what is right in the eyes of
everyone.[y] 18If it is possible, as far as it
depends on you, live at peace with everyone.[z] 19Do not take revenge,[a] my dear
friends, but leave room for God's wrath,
for it is written: "It is mine to avenge;
I will repay,"[b][b] says the Lord. 20On the
contrary:

12:10 [n]Heb 13:1 [o]Php 2:3
12:11 [p]Ac 18:25
12:12 [q]Ro 5:2 [r]Heb 10:32,36
12:13 [s]1Ti 3:2
12:14 [t]Mt 5:44
12:15 [u]Job 30:25
12:16 [v]Ro 15:5 [w]Jer 45:5; Ro 11:25
12:17 [x]Pr 20:22 [y]2Co 8:21
12:18 [z]Mk 9:50; Ro 14:19
12:19 [a]Lev 19:18; Pr 20:22; 24:29 [b]Dt 32:35
12:20 [c]Pr 25:21,22; Mt 5:44; Lk 6:27
13:1 [d]Titus 3:1; 1Pe 2:13,14 [e]Da 2:21; Jn 19:11
13:3 [f]1Pe 2:14

"If your enemy is hungry, feed him;
if he is thirsty, give him something
to drink.
In doing this, you will heap burning
coals on his head."[c][c]

21Do not be overcome by evil, but overcome evil with good.

Submission to Governing Authorities

13 Let everyone be subject to the governing authorities,[d] for there is no
authority except that which God has established.[e] The authorities that exist have
been established by God. 2Consequently,
whoever rebels against the authority is rebelling against what God has instituted,
and those who do so will bring judgment
on themselves. 3For rulers hold no terror for those who do right, but for those
who do wrong. Do you want to be free
from fear of the one in authority? Then do
what is right and you will be commended.[f]

[a] *16* Or *willing to do menial work* [b] *19* Deut. 32:35
[c] *20* Prov. 25:21,22

12:10 – 13 Speakers often used repetition at the end of words to hold attention; here in Greek *-oi* concludes three clauses in vv. 10 – 11; *-ontes* or *-ountes* conclude seven clauses in vv. 11 – 13.
12:10 *Honor one another above yourselves.* Competition for honor dominated ancient Mediterranean urban society, particularly Rome; Paul offers a contrary model (here; v. 16).
12:13 *Share with the Lord's people who are in need.* Jewish piety emphasized caring for the needy (following the OT, e.g., Dt 15:7 – 11). *Practice hospitality.* Ancient Mediterranean culture valued hospitality, which could include providing free lodging to travelers; Jewish travelers counted on hospitality from fellow Jews. Sometimes travelers would carry letters of recommendation attesting that they were trustworthy.
12:14 *Bless those who persecute you.* Although some other sages recommended nonretaliation, blessing those who persecute echoes Jesus' teaching (Lk 6:28; cf. Mt 5:44).
12:15 *Rejoice ... mourn.* Ancient ethics expected people to rejoice and mourn with their friends. In Judean and Galilean communities, an entire village could express solidarity by joining in wedding and funeral processions.
12:17 *Do not repay anyone evil for evil.* Stoics and some other philosophers urged nonresistance because they emphasized that the only thing one truly controlled anyway was one's own self; accepting rather than resisting Fate's treatment revealed self-control. Some Jewish sages emphasized nonresistance (already in the OT, see Lev 19:18; Pr 24:29) because one should depend on God's vindication alone (see already Pr 20:22).
12:18 *live at peace with everyone.* Many valued honoring custom; for the sake of society's views of them, minorities, such as Diaspora Jews in the Gentile world, were often careful to honor society's ethical ideals when these did not violate their own beliefs.
12:19 Paul cites Dt 32:35, a context perhaps fresh on his mind, since he cites from Dt 32 in Ro 10:19 (see also 15:10).
12:20 Scholars debate how Paul uses Pr 25:21 – 22, but Paul may still speak of God avenging (v. 19), and hence refer to judgment on an enemy who does not repent despite kindness. In any case, the preferred goal is instead to turn an enemy to a friend (v. 21), a behavior valued both by some Greek and Jewish sages.
13:1 – 7 Ancient thinkers often treated relationship with the state alongside other relationships (cf. 12:17 – 21). Many ancient writers (not least the Stoics) emphasized and even wrote essays on the importance of loyalty to the state. Such writers thought of a general principle, however, not of absolute submission in the case of evil. Thus such exhortations did not mean that one should do evil even at the bidding of the state; philosophers were supposed to maintain their beliefs, and Jews and Christians would not worship the emperor.

Minorities, such as the Jewish community in Rome, tried to avoid scandal and uphold public ideals. Christian witness would be important in Rome, the empire's capital; many had apparently been expelled from Rome over debates about the Messiah less than a decade earlier. Paul's concerns for avoiding scandal would remain important. Within eight years after he sent this letter, the current emperor, Nero, would begin hunting and killing Christians in Rome. Two years after that, Judea would erupt into full-fledged revolt, leading to Jerusalem's destruction.
13:2 *whoever rebels against the authority is rebelling against what God has instituted.* Many Greeks and Jews liked Nero, who at this point had not yet been corrupted by the influence of a future mentor and boyfriend, Tigellinus; he had not yet persecuted Christians. Some Judeans urged revolt against Rome, but many Jews taught submission to civil authorities, arguing that God had established them. Nearly all Jews in Rome emphasized the latter view, which was important for their survival. For God's sovereignty over rulers, see, e.g., Pr 16:10; 21:1; Da 4:32.
13:3 – 5 Paul's warning here reflects conventional moral exhortation. Injustice was rife in the empire, and social status influenced the outcome of trials. Nevertheless, the government was usually a force for order and justice. Rome obviously had interest in suppressing rebellions, such as sometimes erupted in Judea, but following Jesus was not yet deemed a crime at the time Paul wrote.

4For the one in authority is God's servant
for your good. But if you do wrong, be
afraid, for rulers do not bear the sword
for no reason. They are God's servants,
agents of wrath to bring punishment on
the wrongdoer.[g] 5Therefore, it is necessary
to submit to the authorities, not only because of possible punishment but also as
a matter of conscience.
6This is also why you pay taxes, for the
authorities are God's servants, who give
their full time to governing. 7Give to everyone what you owe them: If you owe taxes,
pay taxes;[h] if revenue, then revenue; if respect, then respect; if honor, then honor.

Love Fulfills the Law

8Let no debt remain outstanding, except
the continuing debt to love one another,
for whoever loves others has fulfilled the
law.[i] 9The commandments, "You shall not
commit adultery," "You shall not murder,"
"You shall not steal," "You shall not covet,"[a][j] and whatever other command there
may be, are summed up in this one command: "Love your neighbor as yourself."[b][k]
10Love does no harm to a neighbor. Therefore love is the fulfillment of the law.[l]

The Day Is Near

11And do this, understanding the present
time: The hour has already come[m] for you
to wake up from your slumber,[n] because
our salvation is nearer now than when we
first believed. 12The night is nearly over;
the day is almost here.[o] So let us put aside
the deeds of darkness[p] and put on the armor[q] of light. 13Let us behave decently,
as in the daytime, not in carousing and
drunkenness, not in sexual immorality and
debauchery, not in dissension and jealousy.[r] 14Rather, clothe yourselves with the
Lord Jesus Christ,[s] and do not think about
how to gratify the desires of the flesh.[c]

The Weak and the Strong

14 Accept the one whose faith is weak,[t]
without quarreling over disputable
matters. 2One person's faith allows them
to eat anything, but another, whose faith
is weak, eats only vegetables. 3The one
who eats everything must not treat with
contempt[u] the one who does not, and the
one who does not eat everything must not
judge[v] the one who does, for God has accepted them. 4Who are you to judge someone else's servant?[w] To their own master,
servants stand or fall. And they will stand,
for the Lord is able to make them stand.
5One person considers one day more
sacred than another;[x] another considers
every day alike. Each of them should be

13:4 [g] 1Th 4:6 **13:7** [h] Mt 17:25; 22:17,21; Lk 23:2 **13:8** [i] ver 10; Jn 13:34; Gal 5:14; Col 3:14 **13:9** [j] Ex 20:13-15,17; Dt 5:17-19,21 [k] Lev 19:18; Mt 19:19 **13:10** [l] ver 8; Mt 22:39,40 **13:11** [m] 1Co 7:29-31; 10:11 [n] Eph 5:14; 1Th 5:5,6 **13:12** [o] 1Jn 2:8 [p] Eph 5:11 [q] Eph 6:11,13 **13:13** [r] Gal 5:20,21 **13:14** [s] Gal 3:27; 5:16; Eph 4:24 **14:1** [t] Ro 15:1; 1Co 8:9-12 **14:3** [u] Lk 18:9 [v] Col 2:16 **14:4** [w] Jas 4:12 **14:5** [x] Gal 4:10

[a] *9* Exodus 20:13-15,17; Deut. 5:17-19,21 [b] *9* Lev. 19:18
[c] *14* In contexts like this, the Greek word for *flesh* (*sarx*) refers to the sinful state of human beings, often presented as a power in opposition to the Spirit.

13:4 *sword.* Probably refers to the government's *ius gladii*, "right of the sword," meaning authority to execute; in this period, condemned Roman citizens who were beheaded were normally executed by sword.
13:6–7 The empire as a whole levied a property tax (often about 1 percent) and a head tax; local provinces or kingdoms added further taxes; merchants traveling with goods also paid customs duties. Paul does not ask Christians to pay only for what they approve of; Rome used taxes not only to build roads and support a slender government infrastructure in the provinces but also to finance their armies and build temples for worshiping emperors. Particular taxes became controversial in Rome perhaps just months before Paul wrote this letter; noncitizen Jews who returned to Rome in or after AD 54 may have also been subject to special taxes from which Roman citizens were exempt.
13:7 *if honor, then honor.* Both custom and prudence demanded honoring officials and others of higher social rank. Jews refused to sacrifice to the emperor, but the temple honored him with prayers and sacrifices to God on his behalf. Suspending such offerings in the temple roughly a decade later quickly led to war against Rome (Josephus, *Wars* 2.409).
13:8–10 If believers in Rome were divided over how to treat Biblical law (see Introduction: Setting), Paul's words here would urge them to surmount division. Although Paul refers especially to Biblical law, love would meet even most demands of Roman law (cf. vv. 1–7). Some other Jewish teachers viewed love of neighbor as fulfilling the law, but Paul's ultimate source was believers' ultimate teacher, Jesus (Mt 22:39–40).
13:8 *Let no debt remain.* Teachers of morals often warned against debt (already in the OT, cf. Pr 22:7) and unpaid social obligations. One repaid benefaction with honor, monetary loans with interest. Although Jews were not supposed to charge interest to fellow Jews, interest rates in the Gentile world could be exorbitant. Roman private loans usually involved 12 percent interest, but in one very rare and extreme case, a lender charged an entire city roughly 50 percent interest.
13:9 Paul selects four of the five humanward prohibitions (Ex 20:13–17) in the Ten Commandments; clearly love (Lev 19:18) prevents any of these offenses.
13:11 *wake up from your slumber.* Ancient writers sometimes spoke figuratively of spiritual or other sleep; Paul also thinks of spiritual readiness (Mk 13:36).
13:12 *the day is almost here.* Jewish people anticipated a coming day of judgment. *put on.* Jewish writers could speak of being "clothed" with the Spirit or virtues (e.g., in the familiar Greek translation of Jdg 6:34; 1Ch 12:18; 2Ch 24:20). *armor.* Many Jewish people expected an end-time battle; philosophers often spoke of figurative warfare against passions or false ideologies.
13:13 *as in the daytime.* Drunken parties were normally at night, as were deeds that their perpetrators did not wish to be known.
13:14 *clothe yourselves.* See note on v. 12.
14:2 *eats only vegetables.* Jews avoided only unclean meat, not meat altogether. When they lacked access to kosher-prepared meat, however, they might depend on vegetables (e.g., Da 1:12; 2 Maccabees 5:27).
14:5 *one day more sacred than another.* Rome had numerous festivals, days of ill omen, and (every eight or nine

ROMANS 14:1 – 23

"PURE" AND "UNCLEAN" FOODS

Just before exhorting Jewish and Gentile believers to accept each other (15:7 – 12), Paul addresses the question of "pure" and "unclean" foods (14:14). Sometimes writers saved particularly controversial matters for the end of a speech or letter. After tracing theological (chs. 1 – 11) and moral (parts of chs. 12 – 13) grounds for unity between Jewish and non-Jewish believers, Paul comes to some practical issues that are apparently causing division between Roman Christians (see Introduction: Setting). The three Jewish practices for which non-Jewish Romans especially mocked Jews were circumcision (already addressed in 2:25 – 29; 4:9 – 12), food practices and holy days (though some Gentiles in Rome emulated some Jewish dietary and Sabbath customs); the latter two are addressed in ch. 14.

Most peoples and even some philosophic sects had distinctive food customs. Jewish people, however, attributed their laws to God, and in the Maccabean period many had died as martyrs for refusing to eat pork. (Phoenicians, some Syrians and Egyptian priests also avoided pork; by contrast, Greeks insisted that pork was delicious.) Some educated Jews in Egypt viewed Biblical laws about foods (Lev 11; Dt 14) as merely symbolic, but most Jews insisted on practicing them. Gentiles often mocked Jews for their dietary "separatism."

Jewish people did not expect most Gentiles to observe Jewish food laws or holy days but did expect Gentile converts to Judaism to do so, perhaps including Gentile Christians. (Lev 11:44 – 45 deals with holiness as separation and may suggest that God gave special food laws to Israel particularly to keep it separate from other nations, because most cultures had their own special dietary practices. For Jesus' followers called to reach the world, however, its principle of moral separation could be retained without cultural separation.) ◆

Relief depicting a boar's head at a banquet meal, first century BC. Jews considered pork to be "unclean."

Musee des Antiquites Nationales, St. Germain-en-Laye, France/Bridgeman Images

fully convinced in their own mind. [6]Whoever regards one day as special does so to the Lord. Whoever eats meat does so to the Lord, for they give thanks to God;[y] and whoever abstains does so to the Lord and gives thanks to God. [7]For none of us lives for ourselves alone,[z] and none of us dies for ourselves alone. [8]If we live, we live for the Lord; and if we die, we die for the Lord. So, whether we live or die, we belong to the Lord.[a] [9]For this very reason, Christ died and returned to life[b] so that he might be the Lord of both the dead and the living.[c]

[10]You, then, why do you judge your brother or sister[a]? Or why do you treat them with contempt? For we will all stand before God's judgment seat.[d] [11]It is written:

"'As surely as I live,' says the Lord,
'every knee will bow before me;
every tongue will acknowledge
God.'"[be]

[12]So then, each of us will give an account of ourselves to God.[f]

[13]Therefore let us stop passing judgment[g] on one another. Instead, make up your mind not to put any stumbling block or obstacle in the way of a brother or sister. [14]I am convinced, being fully persuaded in the Lord Jesus, that nothing is unclean in itself.[h] But if anyone regards something as unclean, then for that person it is unclean.[i] [15]If your brother or sister is distressed because of what you eat, you are no longer acting in love.[j] Do not by your eating destroy someone for whom Christ died.[k] [16]Therefore do not let what you know is good be spoken of as evil.[l] [17]For the kingdom of God is not a matter of eating and drinking,[m] but of righteousness, peace and joy in the Holy Spirit,[n] [18]because anyone who serves Christ in this way is pleasing to God and receives human approval.[o]

[19]Let us therefore make every effort to do what leads to peace[p] and to mutual edification.[q] [20]Do not destroy the work of God for the sake of food.[r] All food is clean, but it is wrong for a person to eat anything that causes someone else to stumble.[s] [21]It is better not to eat meat or drink wine or to do anything else that will cause your brother or sister to fall.[t]

[22]So whatever you believe about these things keep between yourself and God. Blessed is the one who does not condemn[u] himself by what he approves. [23]But whoever has doubts[v] is condemned if they eat, because their eating is not from faith; and everything that does not come from faith is sin.[c]

14:6 [y] Mt 14:19; 1Co 10:30,31; 1Ti 4:3,4
14:7 [z] 2Co 5:15; Gal 2:20
14:8 [a] Php 1:20
14:9 [b] Rev 1:18 [c] 2Co 5:15
14:10 [d] 2Co 5:10
14:11 [e] Isa 45:23; Php 2:10,11
14:12 [f] Mt 12:36; 1Pe 4:5
14:13 [g] Mt 7:1
14:14 [h] Ac 10:15 [i] 1Co 8:7
14:15 [j] Eph 5:2 [k] 1Co 8:11
14:16 [l] 1Co 10:30
14:17 [m] 1Co 8:8 [n] Ro 15:13
14:18 [o] 2Co 8:21
14:19 [p] Ps 34:14; Ro 12:18; Heb 12:14 [q] Ro 15:2; 2Co 12:19
14:20 [r] ver 15 [s] 1Co 8:9-12
14:21 [t] 1Co 8:13
14:22 [u] 1Jn 3:21
14:23 [v] ver 5

[a] *10* The Greek word for *brother or sister* (*adelphos*) refers here to a believer, whether man or woman, as part of God's family; also in verses 13, 15 and 21. [b] *11* Isaiah 45:23 [c] *23* Some manuscripts place 16:25-27 here; others after 15:33.

days) regular market days. Romans knew that different peoples and cities in the empire had their own special festivals and holy days. Many Roman Gentiles, however, either specifically respected or detested the Jewish Sabbath; those who detested it considered Jews lazy for taking a day off from work every week. Some Jewish groups divided from other Jews over the precise days on which to celebrate festivals, but all Jews agreed on the weekly Sabbath. Although the Sabbath was ordained from creation (Ge 2:2–3), before its incorporation in the Law of Moses, it was difficult to observe for slaves and those who worked for others. Jews could honor the day within their communities, but many Gentile believers did not have the same options. Fitting 14:2–3, some see fast days here.

14:10 *judgment seat.* A governor could make an official pronouncement from a *bema*, a rostrum, or elevated judgment seat (Jn 19:13; Ac 18:12). Jewish depictions of the end often included God judging everyone.

14:11 In the context of Isa 45:23, cited here, God finally vindicates Israel and summons the nations to acknowledge that he is God.

14:13 *stumbling block.* A frequent metaphor for what could cause a person spiritual harm; "stumble" sometimes meant "sin" or even "fall away from the faith" (e.g., Eze 14:3–7; 18:30; Sirach 9:5; 23:8). *brother or sister.* Figurative family terminology was common. People often called members of their own ethnic group, association or other group "brother"; it could also apply, as here, to those who share a common faith.

14:14 *nothing is unclean in itself.* Jewish people separated "clean" and "unclean" foods, following the OT (Lev 11; Dt 14). Although some elite Diaspora Jews believed that this division was primarily for symbolic purposes, most continued to practice the food laws literally. Although Paul does not discourage his own people from observing kosher rules (i.e., observing the food regulations of Lev 11), his language (here and in v. 20) would shock many of them. He may have found precedent in Jesus' teaching (see the interpretation of that teaching in Mk 7:19).

14:17 *righteousness, peace and joy in the Holy Spirit.* Many Judeans longed for the coming kingdom, when God would reign unchallenged. That would be the era of the outpoured Spirit (Joel 2:32), an era characterized by justice, peace and rejoicing. Because believers already experience the Spirit in the present, we have a foretaste of that coming world. We should therefore live at peace with one another (v. 19).

14:21 *better not to eat meat or drink wine.* Keeping kosher would not normally require abstinence from all meat, provided it was from a clean animal, not sacrificed to idols, and butchered in a kosher manner (i.e., the blood being drained). In Rome and other major urban centers with significant Jewish populations, kosher butchers and meat were available. Wine was likewise acceptable provided no libation had been poured to pagan deities. When under duress, however, Jews might endure a very limited diet (some even subsisting on figs and nuts; Josephus, *Life* 14) rather than eat nonkosher foods.

14:23 *whoever has doubts.* To avoid the possibility of accidentally transgressing the law, Pharisees established a "fence around the law," rules stricter than the law required. Here love for others dictates Paul's concern; he warns believers with sturdy consciences to take into account those whose consciences are more sensitive.

15 We who are strong ought to bear
with the failings of the weak[w] and
not to please ourselves. 2Each of us should
please our neighbors for their good,[x] to
build them up.[y] 3For even Christ did not
please himself[z] but, as it is written: "The
insults of those who insult you have fallen
on me."[a][a] 4For everything that was written
in the past was written to teach us,[b] so
that through the endurance taught in the
Scriptures and the encouragement they
provide we might have hope.
5May the God who gives endurance and
encouragement give you the same attitude
of mind[c] toward each other that Christ
Jesus had, 6so that with one mind and one
voice you may glorify the God and Father[d]
of our Lord Jesus Christ.
7Accept one another,[e] then, just as
Christ accepted you, in order to bring
praise to God. 8For I tell you that Christ
has become a servant of the Jews[b][f] on behalf of God's truth, so that the promises[g]
made to the patriarchs might be confirmed
9and, moreover, that the Gentiles[h] might
glorify God[i] for his mercy. As it is written:

> "Therefore I will praise you among
> the Gentiles;
> I will sing the praises of your
> name."[c][j]

10Again, it says,

> "Rejoice, you Gentiles, with his
> people."[d][k]

11And again,

> "Praise the Lord, all you Gentiles;
> let all the peoples extol him."[e][l]

12And again, Isaiah says,

> "The Root of Jesse[m] will spring up,
> one who will arise to rule over the
> nations;
> in him the Gentiles will hope."[f][n]

13May the God of hope fill you with all
joy and peace[o] as you trust in him, so that
you may overflow with hope by the power
of the Holy Spirit.[p]

Paul the Minister to the Gentiles

14I myself am convinced, my brothers
and sisters, that you yourselves are full
of goodness,[q] filled with knowledge[r] and

15:1 [w] Ro 14:1; Gal 6:1,2; 1Th 5:14
15:2 [x] 1Co 10:33 [y] Ro 14:19
15:3 [z] 2Co 8:9 [a] Ps 69:9
15:4 [b] Ro 4:23,24
15:5 [c] Ro 12:16; 1Co 1:10
15:6 [d] Rev 1:6
15:7 [e] Ro 14:1
15:8 [f] Mt 15:24; Ac 3:25,26 [g] 2Co 1:20
15:9 [h] Ro 3:29 [i] Mt 9:8 [j] 2Sa 22:50; Ps 18:49
15:10 [k] Dt 32:43
15:11 [l] Ps 117:1
15:12 [m] Rev 5:5 [n] Isa 11:10; Mt 12:21
15:13 [o] Ro 14:17 [p] ver 19; 1Co 2:4; 1Th 1:5
15:14 [q] Eph 5:9 [r] 2Pe 1:12

[a] *3* Psalm 69:9 [b] *8* Greek *circumcision* [c] *9* 2 Samuel 22:50; Psalm 18:49 [d] *10* Deut. 32:43 [e] *11* Psalm 117:1 [f] *12* Isaiah 11:10 (see Septuagint)

15:1–2 Ancient speakers and writers would sometimes summarize or provide a climactic exhortation for material that precedes, as these verses do for 14:1–23.
15:3 *even Christ.* Ancient argumentation often appealed to the example of a famous teacher. Paul applies to Jesus' experience of being ridiculed (Mk 14:58,64–65) the language of Ps 69:9 (cited here). Ps 69 emphasizes the anguish of a righteous sufferer, applied by early Christians to Jesus (Mt 27:34; Jn 2:17). Paul looks for present application of both the psalm and Christ's example (v. 4).
15:4 *everything ... was written to teach us.* Some ancient writers, especially some Qumran interpreters, envisioned Scripture as being written especially for their end-time instruction. More relevant here, Jewish people recognized that Scripture was meant to be understood and applied by all generations. God provided the law for his people's instruction (Ex 24:12); for comfort in Scripture, see Ps 119:50,52,76,82; 2 Maccabees 15:9.
15:6 *one mind and one voice.* Harmony was a common emphasis in ancient exhortations because division was very common in society. Like unity of mind, "one voice" signifies unity (as in Ex 24:3); for Paul, unity of love and worship remain possible without unanimity on all details (cf. ch. 14).
15:7–8 Ancient writers often offered moral examples; Paul offers Jesus as the greatest (cf. also v. 3). He then demonstrates this mission of Jesus in light of Scripture (vv. 9–12).
15:9–12 Speakers sometimes reserved their strongest argument for the end. Jewish expositors often linked texts based on a common key word. Linking together texts that specifically mention "Gentiles," Paul shows from the Writings, the Law and the Prophets—the three main sections of Jewish Scripture—that God had always desired Gentiles' worship. These cited OT passages are merely samples of a much wider theme in Scripture.
15:9 Ps 18:49, cited here, was a psalm of David (2Sa 22:1,50) that mentioned the wide reign of David and his descendants (2Sa 22:48–51); Jesus was David's descendant (Ro 1:3).
15:10 Dt 32:43, cited here, invites nations to join with God's people, since God will punish those who oppose him. Paul has recently cited texts from this context—Dt 32:21 in Ro 10:19 and Dt 32:35 in Ro 12:19.
15:11 Paul cites Ps 117:1, inviting all peoples to praise God, from the familiar Hallel (Ps 113–118), a section of psalms some lines from which were already applied to Jesus (see notes on Mk 11:9–10; 12:10–11).
15:12 The context of Isa 11:10, cited here, is clearly Messianic (cf. Isa 11:1) and was so understood by Paul's contemporaries. Although the context indicates the restoration of exiled Israelites among the peoples (Isa 11:11–12,16), its face value sense of nations joining with God's people fits the larger context in Isaiah (Isa 2:2–4; 19:23–25; 56:3–8). Paul's wording follows the Greek version.
15:13 *peace.* See note on v. 33. *that you may overflow with hope by the power of the Holy Spirit.* Paul here applies Isaiah's words about Gentiles hoping in the Davidic king (cited in v. 12) to Paul's audience in Rome. Letters often included prayers. This one is worded as a "wish-prayer" or blessing—grammatically addressed to the hearers but implicitly calling on God.
15:14–33 In a speech's closing, the speaker would often repeat points first advanced in the opening; compare these verses with 1:8–15. The closing often used a personal and affectionate tone. Speakers often reserved the strongest *pathos*, or emotional appeal, for the closing of their speech.
15:14 *you ... are full of goodness, filled with knowledge and competent to instruct.* Those offering letters of advice or speeches of exhortation frequently expressed their confidence in their addressees; this expression helped the readers to listen more favorably to the rest of the letter and sometimes served as a polite way to make a request. *to*

competent to instruct one another. 15 Yet
I have written you quite boldly on some
points to remind you of them again, because of the grace God gave me[s] 16 to be
a minister of Christ Jesus to the Gentiles.[t]
He gave me the priestly duty of proclaiming the gospel of God,[u] so that the Gentiles
might become an offering[v] acceptable to
God, sanctified by the Holy Spirit.
17 Therefore I glory in Christ Jesus[w] in
my service to God.[x] 18 I will not venture
to speak of anything except what Christ
has accomplished through me in leading
the Gentiles[y] to obey God[z] by what I have
said and done — 19 by the power of signs
and wonders,[a] through the power of the
Spirit of God.[b] So from Jerusalem[c] all the
way around to Illyricum, I have fully proclaimed the gospel of Christ. 20 It has always been my ambition to preach the gospel where Christ was not known, so that I
would not be building on someone else's
foundation.[d] 21 Rather, as it is written:

"Those who were not told about him
will see,
and those who have not heard will
understand."[a][e]

22 This is why I have often been hindered
from coming to you.[f]

Paul's Plan to Visit Rome

23 But now that there is no more place
for me to work in these regions, and since
I have been longing for many years to
visit you,[g] 24 I plan to do so when I go
to Spain.[h] I hope to see you while passing through and to have you assist me
on my journey there, after I have enjoyed
your company for a while. 25 Now, however, I am on my way to Jerusalem[i] in the
service[j] of the Lord's people there. 26 For
Macedonia[k] and Achaia[l] were pleased
to make a contribution for the poor
among the Lord's people in Jerusalem.

15:15 [s] Ro 12:3 **15:16** [t] Ac 9:15; Ro 11:13 [u] Ro 1:1 [v] Isa 66:20 **15:17** [w] Php 3:3 [x] Heb 2:17 **15:18** [y] Ac 15:12; 21:19; Ro 1:5 [z] Ro 16:26 **15:19** [a] Jn 4:48; Ac 19:11 [b] ver 13 [c] Ac 22:17-21 **15:20** [d] 2Co 10:15, 16 **15:21** [e] Isa 52:15 **15:22** [f] Ro 1:13 **15:23** [g] Ac 19:21; Ro 1:10, 11 **15:24** [h] ver 28 **15:25** [i] Ac 19:21 [j] Ac 24:17 **15:26** [k] Ac 16:9; 2Co 8:1 [l] Ac 18:12

[a] *21* Isaiah 52:15 (see Septuagint)

instruct. The Greek term can also mean "to admonish"; this was considered gentler than rebuke, and by delegating the task to them Paul avoids appearing to reprove them.
15:15 *I have written you quite boldly.* Ancient thinkers appreciated speaking "boldly" if it was in the audience's interests. *to remind you.* Those who exhorted their hearers often softened the admonition by noting that they were only "reminding" them of what they already knew.
15:16 *priestly duty of proclaiming the gospel of God.* Paul compares his ministry with that of priests offering sacrifice (cf. 12:1; 1Co 9:13 – 14). *an offering acceptable to God.* Many Jewish people expected Israel to someday rule over the Gentiles, so the Gentiles would carry tribute to Jerusalem (e.g., Isa 60:11 – 14). Here the Gentile believers themselves are an offering (cf. Ro 12:1), like the promised role of God's own people to be offered by Gentiles in Isa 66:22. Some Jerusalem Christians may have viewed Paul's collection for the saints in Jerusalem (vv. 25 – 27) as a fulfillment of this vindication of Israel's faith.
15:17 – 18 *I glory in Christ Jesus in my service ... what Christ has accomplished through me.* Although competition for honor characterized ancient urban Mediterranean society, boasting was despised unless properly justified, e.g., as for others' good. Here Paul boasts not in himself but in Christ's work through him.
15:19 *by the power of signs and wonders.* The OT stressed signs and wonders especially in connection with the exodus (Ex 7:3; 11:9 – 10; Dt 4:34; 6:22; 7:19; 11:3; 26:8; 34:11; Jer 32:20 – 21; Wisdom of Solomon 10:15 – 16; Baruch 2:11); early Christians recognized the spreading of the gospel between Jesus' first and second comings as a similar pivotal experience also confirmed by signs and wonders. Acts reports examples of signs and wonders in the ministry of Paul (e.g., Ac 14:3; 15:12; 19:11 – 12) and others (e.g., Ac 6:8; 8:6). *Jerusalem.* Although Paul's ministry began before Jerusalem (Ac 9:20 – 22; cf. Gal 1:17 – 18), Paul starts counting it there; Jewish people treated Jerusalem as the world's center. *Illyricum.* North of Macedonia, across from Italy on the eastern Adriatic coast, on the west of the Yugoslav/Serbo-Croatian region. The Roman province was called Illyricum; Greeks included this region and some more territory farther south (including Dyrrhachium on the Via Egnatia in Macedonia) in what they called Illyria.
15:20 *preach the gospel where Christ was not known.* Thus Paul preached in Illyricum and wished to preach in Spain (vv. 24,28); because Rome was already being evangelized, Paul had not yet come to them (v. 22).
15:21 Paul's mission to those who have not yet heard the good news about Jesus is meant to carry out the mission in Isa 52:15 (cited here), which refers to Gentiles and their kings (in contrast to Israel in Isa 53:1 – 4). This is the mission of the suffering servant (Isa 52:13 — 53:12); early Christians applied this especially to Jesus but also recognized that they shared the servant mission (cf. Ro 10:16; Ac 13:47).
15:22 *hindered from coming to you.* Ancient letters often expressed affection and apologized for not having been able to visit (for Paul's reason, see vv. 19 – 21).
15:23 *longing ... to visit you.* Some ancient letters involved plans for visits.
15:24 *Spain.* In Spain, Paul could not likely start among synagogues (not attested until a later period there) or even among Greek-speakers. Paul or an interpreter could use Latin in the Roman colonies there. Just as ancient geography reckoned Ethiopia as the far south of the world and China as the farthest east, it often reckoned Spain as at the western ends of the earth (see note on Ac 1:8); Paul wishes to bring the gospel to the farthest ends of the world. *to have you assist me on my journey.* Direct requests could cause the requester to lose honor; Paul implies a request for help here. Believers in Rome would, however, count it an honor to show hospitality (which was highly valued in the ancient Mediterranean world) and to provide his expenses for his further voyage to Spain.
15:25 *in the service of the Lord's people.* Ancient writers often cited examples (as in vv. 3,7 – 8), sometimes, as here, of themselves. Like Jesus, Paul is an agent of ethnic reconciliation.
15:26 *Macedonia and Achaia.* Adjoining provinces; since Paul writes this letter from Achaia (16:1), Paul's appeal to the Achaian churches (2Co 8 – 9) was apparently successful. *make a contribution for the poor.* Every year Jewish men throughout the world paid a half-shekel tax for the temple in Jerusalem; trusted messengers would carry it to Jerusalem. As that practice expressed the solidarity of the Jewish people, so this offering from Diaspora churches would demonstrate solidarity among Jewish and Gentile

27They were pleased to do it, and indeed
they owe it to them. For if the Gentiles
have shared in the Jews' spiritual blessings, they owe it to the Jews to share with
them their material blessings.[m] 28So after
I have completed this task and have made
sure that they have received this contribution, I will go to Spain and visit you on
the way. 29I know that when I come to
you,[n] I will come in the full measure of
the blessing of Christ.

30I urge you, brothers and sisters, by our
Lord Jesus Christ and by the love of the
Spirit,[o] to join me in my struggle by praying to God for me.[p] 31Pray that I may be
kept safe[q] from the unbelievers in Judea
and that the contribution I take to Jerusalem may be favorably received by the
Lord's people there, 32so that I may come
to you[r] with joy, by God's will,[s] and in
your company be refreshed.[t] 33The God of
peace[u] be with you all. Amen.

15:27 [m] 1Co 9:11 **15:29** [n] Ro 1:10, 11 **15:30** [o] Gal 5:22 [p] 2Co 1:11; Col 4:12 **15:31** [q] 2Th 3:2 **15:32** [r] Ro 1:10, 13 [s] Ac 18:21 [t] 1Co 16:18 **15:33** [u] Ro 16:20; 2Co 13:11; Php 4:9; 1Th 5:23; Heb 13:20 **16:1** [v] 2Co 3:1 [w] Ac 18:18 **16:2** [x] Php 2:29 **16:3** [y] Ac 18:2 [z] ver 7, 9, 10

Personal Greetings

16 I commend[v] to you our sister Phoebe, a deacon[a,b] of the church in
Cenchreae.[w] 2I ask you to receive her in
the Lord[x] in a way worthy of his people
and to give her any help she may need
from you, for she has been the benefactor
of many people, including me.

3Greet Priscilla[c] and Aquila,[y] my co-
workers in Christ Jesus.[z] 4They risked

[a] *1* Or *servant* [b] *1* The word *deacon* refers here to a Christian designated to serve with the overseers/elders of the church in a variety of ways; similarly in Phil. 1:1 and 1 Tim. 3:8,12. [c] *3* Greek *Prisca*, a variant of *Priscilla*

believers (for the importance of this issue for this letter, see Introduction: Setting).

15:27 *share with them their material blessings.* Some believers in Jerusalem may have envisioned the gift as the firstfruits of the prophetic promise that the nations would bring tribute to Israel (Isa 45:14; 60:6–10; 66:20); Paul may think more broadly of unity in Christ. For Gentiles sharing Jewish blessings, see, e.g., Ro 11:17; Gal 3:14. Social responsibility was corporate as well as personal (e.g., Dt 23:3–4; 2Sa 21:1–9; Ac 11:29).

15:28 *I will go to Spain and visit you on the way.* Friends often announced travel plans in letters. Ships from the east would normally stop in Rome; voyagers to Spain would travel on from there to Tarraco, some 900 miles (nearly 1,500 kilometers). (By road one could also travel from Italy to southern Gaul then across the Pyrenees mountain range.) Travel to Cordoba would be even farther.

15:31 *be kept safe from unbelievers in Judea.* Paul would in fact face the hostility of unbelievers in Judea (Ac 21:27–31). *be favorably received.* Not all believers in Judea were positive toward Paul (Ro 3:8; cf. Ac 21:21), but the leaders probably did welcome his help (cf. Ac 21:17–20; 24:17), since they had requested it (Gal 2:10). To refuse a gift declared that one wished to be the other's enemy, so such a refusal would be rare.

15:32 *in your company be refreshed.* Paul implicitly requests hospitality (in a modest, polite way acceptable in his culture). Hosts normally counted it an honor to lavish hospitality on guests, especially ones respected in their circle.

15:33 As in v. 13 (see note), Paul includes here a "wish-prayer" or blessing—a prayer grammatically addressed to the hearers but implicitly calling on God. *peace.* A standard Jewish blessing, in this case also relevant to the congregation's divisions (see Introduction: Setting).

16:1–2 People of high status wrote letters of recommendation to peers on behalf of those of somewhat lower status. Often such a letter introduced the letter's bearer, praising them and showing why they merited the help requested. The bearer of a document might also be called on to explain the sense of the document, making Phoebe's qualifications important here.

16:1 *Phoebe.* Wealthy benefactors helped their cities or other people, who in turn owed them honor. Most benefactors were male, but a number (some estimate 10 percent) were women. Benefactors of religious associations often allowed the latter to meet in the benefactors' homes. Letters were normally carried by travelers. Phoebe is probably a well-to-do businesswoman traveling on business; Corinth and Rome had close trade ties. *deacon.* If Paul uses the Greek term (*diakonos*) in the way that he most commonly uses it, for ministers of some sort (15:8; 1Co 3:5–6; 2Co 3:6; 6:4; Eph 3:7; 6:20; Col 1:7,23,25; 4:7; 1Ti 4:6), he goes beyond the most common views in his culture (see notes on 1Ti 2:11–12). *Cenchreae.* Corinth had port towns on both sides of the Isthmus of Corinth; Cenchreae was the eastern port.

16:3–16 Letters often closed with greetings to the writer's friends. Because of the close connection between Corinth and Rome, because many people migrated to the capital of the empire, and because any believers expelled from Rome could return there after Claudius's death (compare v. 3 with Ac 18:2), Paul knows many people in Rome. (If there is some truth in the hyperbolic claim that all roads led to Rome, it was because Rome built the roads.)

The church in Rome was large (cf. v. 19; 1:8); less than a decade later, the emperor slaughtered hundreds of Christians in the city, but many escaped. (The letter known as 1 Clement shows that the Roman church remained strong later in the first century.) Many thus suggest that most of those named here are leaders of house churches. Strikingly, of 28 named persons greeted, nearly 40 percent are women. He commends the ministry of more than half the women and roughly one third of the men. Men may have outnumbered women in Rome's population. Women had more freedom in Rome in this period than in many parts of the empire (cf. also Philippi, Php 4:2), but still may have needed special affirmation given their culture.

About half the Jews in Rome bore Latin names, though Greek was their dominant language. Of those with Latin names, many were descended from Jewish slaves of Roman citizens, who became Roman citizens themselves when freed (Philo, *Embassy to Gaius* 155); some argue that a strong majority of Rome's residents were descended from freed slaves from the eastern Mediterranean world. Many names in Paul's greetings, however, are more traditional Greek or Jewish names.

16:3 *Priscilla and Aquila.* Ancient sources normally name the husband before the wife except where the wife held higher status. Given Paul's concerns about worldly status (1Co 1:26–29), he may think of status in the church. *Priscilla.* The Latin name *Prisca* is the formal form of Priscilla.

ROMANS 16

The Erastus Inscription

Erastus was a first-century Christian who worked with Paul. The earliest mention of him is in Ac 19:22: Paul, at Ephesus on his third missionary journey in around AD 53 – 55, "sent two of his helpers, Timothy and Erastus, to Macedonia." Then, in Ro 16:23, Paul wrote (probably from Corinth around the year 57) that "Erastus, who is the city's director of public works," sent greetings. Finally, in 2Ti 4:20, when Paul was writing from prison in Rome toward the end of his life (around the years 66 – 67), he gave a status report on his coworkers, including the statement that "Erastus stayed in Corinth." It appears that Erastus was a resident of Corinth and, if so, most likely became a believer as a result of Paul's 18-month ministry in that city on his second missionary journey, around AD 50 – 52 (Ac 18:1 – 17).

In 1929 an inscription was discovered at Corinth mentioning an Erastus who may have been the same one referred to in the New Testament. Located in a paved area northeast of the theater and dated to the mid-first century AD, it reads, "Erastus in return for his aedileship laid [the pavement] at his own expense." An aedile, an elected official, was a city business manager responsible for such property as streets, public buildings and markets, as well as for the revenue gleaned from them. He was also a judge who decided most of the city's commercial and financial litigation. In addition, an aedile was responsible for the public games taking place within a city.

Thus, Paul's term "director of public works" in Ro 16:23 probably describes Erastus's position as an aedile. Some have argued that since the Greek word Paul used, *oikonomos*, may not have been the exact equivalent of the Latin *aedile*, Erastus may have held a lower position at the time of Paul's writing. On the other hand, it is possible that Paul first encountered Erastus while he was discharging his fiscal responsibilities and thus perceived him primarily in this role. Also, Corinth was distinctive in that the games there were run not by the aedile but by a different set of officials. Thus, the aedile at Corinth basically functioned as a city treasurer (the rendering used in some translations, such as the NASB). ◆

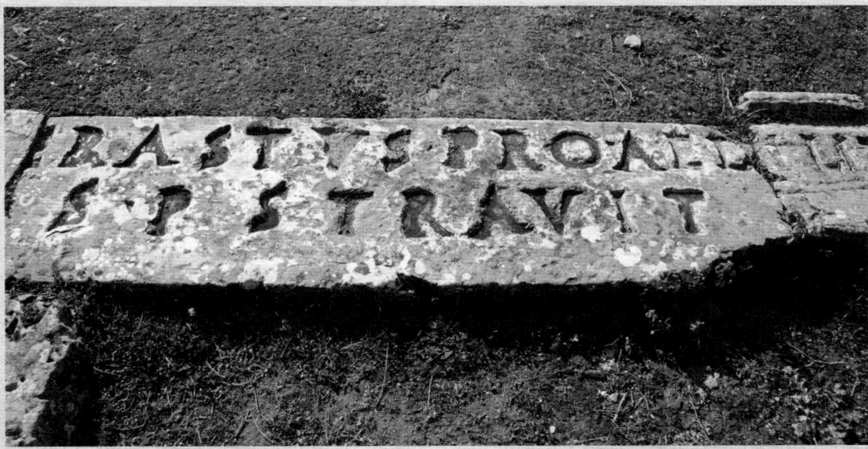

The Erastus Inscription in Corinth.

www.HolyLandPhotos.org

their lives for me. Not only I but all
the churches of the Gentiles are grateful to them.
5 Greet also the church that meets at their
house.[a]
Greet my dear friend Epenetus, who
was the first convert[b] to Christ in the
province of Asia.
6 Greet Mary, who worked very hard for
you.
7 Greet Andronicus and Junia, my fellow
Jews[c] who have been in prison with
me. They are outstanding among[a] the
apostles, and they were in Christ before I was.
8 Greet Ampliatus, my dear friend in the
Lord.
9 Greet Urbanus, our co-worker in Christ,[d]
and my dear friend Stachys.
10 Greet Apelles, whose fidelity to Christ
has stood the test.
Greet those who belong to the household of Aristobulus.
11 Greet Herodion, my fellow Jew.[e]
Greet those in the household of Narcissus who are in the Lord.
12 Greet Tryphena and Tryphosa, those
women who work hard in the Lord.
Greet my dear friend Persis, another
woman who has worked very hard in
the Lord.
13 Greet Rufus, chosen in the Lord, and
his mother, who has been a mother
to me, too.
14 Greet Asyncritus, Phlegon, Hermes, Pat-
robas, Hermas and the other brothers
and sisters with them.
15 Greet Philologus, Julia, Nereus and his
sister, and Olympas and all the Lord's
people[f] who are with them.[g]
16 Greet one another with a holy kiss.[h]
All the churches of Christ send greetings.

17 I urge you, brothers and sisters, to
watch out for those who cause divisions
and put obstacles in your way that are

16:5 [a] 1Co 16:19; Col 4:15; Phm 2 [b] 1Co 16:15 **16:7** [c] ver 11,21 **16:9** [d] ver 3 **16:11** [e] ver 7,21 **16:15** [f] ver 2 [g] ver 14 **16:16** [h] 1Co 16:20; 2Co 13:12; 1Th 5:26

[a] 7 Or *are esteemed by*

16:5 *at their house.* Poorer synagogues and other associations often met in homes until they could afford buildings. For the first three centuries, churches met especially in homes, lavishing resources instead on activities such as caring for the poor and liberating slaves. Most homes in Rome were in apartments. In Rome, many mezzanine apartments existed above ground-floor shops in multistory tenement buildings; Aquila and Priscilla may have lived above their artisan shop. Upper-story apartments were cheaper, smaller and flimsier, with room only to sleep; tall buildings periodically collapsed. Apartment churches could have met in the long hallway connecting small apartments, or on the somewhat more spacious lower floors.

Whereas Jewish communities in Alexandria and other cities of the eastern empire had some overarching leadership, Rome did not allow its synagogues to form a central organization. This lack of organization initially may have allowed the gospel to spread more freely among various synagogues, but it also may have allowed more disunity among the various house churches (see Introduction: Setting).

Churches may have followed models from local synagogues, but Rome in any case did not trust within its walls large gatherings or organizations without government supervision. The Roman house churches might especially be threatened with disunity among themselves, because Rome (unlike the cities of the East) did not allow Jews to assemble on any level larger than local synagogues, and Christians were regarded as Jews.
16:6 *Mary.* Lit. "Maria"; it could be either a Latin name or a Latinized form of the common NT Jewish name Miriam.
16:7 *Andronicus and Junia.* Spouses worked together in some professions, and if a man and woman traveled together without scandal they were presumably married (or siblings, though this is much less likely, given the prevalence of marriage). *Junia.* A feminine Latin name that normally belonged to Roman citizens. (Against some, it cannot be a contraction of the masculine "Junianus"; not only is this contraction not attested, but it does not work for Latin names. Thus ancient interpreters understood her as a woman.) Some Roman citizens were presumably converted before Paul, probably from the Synagogue of the Freedmen in Jerusalem (Ac 6:9).
16:8–9 *Ampliatus ... Urbanus.* Common names for slaves and freedmen in Rome.
16:10 *household.* Could include slaves and former slaves; elite slaves in wealthy households sometimes held considerable power, even among free persons. *Aristobulus.* Although a common Greek name, some think that the Aristobulus here might be the grandson of Herod the Great; this Aristobulus lived in Rome.
16:11 *Herodion.* May be so named because he was a slave or freed person from a Herodian family (see note on v. 10). *household of Narcissus.* May mean the freed persons formerly belonging to Narcissus. If this refers to the well-known Narcissus, he was himself a freedman who was one of the empire's most powerful men under Claudius.
16:12 *Tryphena and Tryphosa.* Greek names, sometimes used also by Jews; the matching names suggest to some scholars that they may have been twins. *Persis.* Free persons used the name Persis, but it was often used also as a name for slaves from Persia.
16:13 *Rufus.* Though some Jews used this Roman name, it was also a common name for slaves. Some suggest that this is the same Rufus as in Mk 15:21, especially since Paul knew his mother. *mother to me, too.* One could affectionately greet older persons as mother or father, including in closing greetings.
16:14 *Phlegon.* A fairly common name among slaves. *Hermes.* Not only Greeks but even Diaspora Jews often adopted names originally belonging to Greek deities, such as Hermes (or Apollo; cf. NT Apollos).
16:15 *Julia, Nereus.* Often slaves and freed persons bore these names.
16:16 *holy kiss.* Occasionally letter writers asked a reader to pass on a kiss to someone else. People regularly showed affection by greeting family members, close friends or some others with a light kiss on the mouth. Although this kiss differed from a passionate lover's kiss, in later centuries the church limited church kisses to one's own gender because of abuses.
16:17 *divisions.* See Introduction: Setting.

contrary to the teaching you have learned.[i]
Keep away from them.[j] 18 For such people
are not serving our Lord Christ, but their
own appetites.[k] By smooth talk and flattery they deceive[l] the minds of naive people. 19 Everyone has heard[m] about your
obedience, so I rejoice because of you; but
I want you to be wise about what is good,
and innocent about what is evil.[n]
20 The God of peace[o] will soon crush[p]
Satan under your feet.
The grace of our Lord Jesus be with
you.[q]
21 Timothy,[r] my co-worker, sends his
greetings to you, as do Lucius,[s] Jason[t] and
Sosipater, my fellow Jews.[u]
22 I, Tertius, who wrote down this letter,
greet you in the Lord.
23 Gaius, whose hospitality I and the
whole church here enjoy, sends you his
greetings.
Erastus,[v] who is the city's director of
public works, and our brother Quartus
send you their greetings. [24][a]

25 Now to him who is able[w] to establish
you in accordance with my gospel,[x] the
message I proclaim about Jesus Christ, in
keeping with the revelation of the mystery[y] hidden for long ages past, 26 but now
revealed and made known through the
prophetic writings by the command of the
eternal God, so that all the Gentiles might
come to the obedience that comes from[b]
faith— 27 to the only wise God be glory
forever through Jesus Christ! Amen.[z]

16:17 [i] Gal 1:8, 9; 1Ti 1:3; 6:3 [j] 2Th 3:6, 14; 2Jn 10 **16:18** [k] Php 3:19 [l] Col 2:4 **16:19** [m] Ro 1:8 [n] Mt 10:16; 1Co 14:20 **16:20** [o] Ro 15:33 [p] Ge 3:15 [q] 1Th 5:28 **16:21** [r] Ac 16:1 [s] Ac 13:1 [t] Ac 17:5 [u] ver 7, 11 **16:23** [v] Ac 19:22 **16:25** [w] Eph 3:20 [x] Ro 2:16 [y] Eph 1:9; Col 1:26,27 **16:27** [z] Ro 11:36

[a] 24 Some manuscripts include here *May the grace of our Lord Jesus Christ be with all of you. Amen.*
[b] 26 Or *that is*

16:18 *appetites.* Ancient intellectuals commonly ridiculed those dominated by their "appetites" (lit. "bellies"). *smooth talk and flattery.* Ancient intellectuals emphasized appropriate reproof, condemning flattery as hurtful to the recipient.
16:19 Cf. Jer 4:22; in light of v. 20, cf. perhaps also Ge 2:9; 3:6.
16:20 *crush Satan under your feet.* The woman's seed would crush the serpent's head (Ge 3:15). Jewish sources often understood the serpent as Satan or a tool of Satan; they sometimes viewed the woman's seed as Israel or the Messiah. Paul applies it to believers (probably in addition to Jesus).
16:21–24 Letter writers sometimes included greetings from people in the senders' location.
16:21 *Lucius.* This name was sometimes abbreviated in Greek as Lucas (Luke; yet the author of Acts, possibly a Gentile Luke [Col 4:11,14], was either not present or returned to Philippi before the others [Ac 20:5–6]). *Sosipater.* A different form of Sopater, so these may be Macedonian colleagues (see Ac 17:6,9; 20:4) who went with Paul to Corinth before traveling as local representatives to bring an offering to Jerusalem (Ro 15:26; 1Co 16:3; 2Co 9:4).
16:22 *Tertius.* Often designated the third-born boy; some Jews used this name, but it would have been common in Corinth (where Paul wrote this letter), with its many Roman citizens. *who wrote down this letter.* Few people were literate enough to write letters; they had to dictate to scribes. Most people with resources also dictated to scribes (sometimes their slaves). A writer who drew attention to his or her signature (as in 1Co 16:21; Gal 6:11; Col 4:18; 2Th 3:17) normally used a scribe for the rest of the letter. Scribes rarely added their own greetings, but Tertius is a fellow believer.
16:23 *Gaius.* Some think that Gaius could be the praenomen for Titius Justus; cf. Ac 18:7. Gaius was an extremely common name. *the whole church.* If Gaius's house accommodated "the whole church" in Corinth, it must have been larger than most of the house churches; but Paul could simply be emphasizing Gaius's great hospitality or that his had been the initial house church. *Erastus … director of public works.* Occasionally such a title indicated a public slave (sometimes a wealthy person taking this role only for a year); often they were public benefactors. An inscription from this period notes a wealthy benefactor named Erastus, probably the one here (this Greek name is not common in Greece). This Erastus was elected *aedile* after promising a major donation to the city. Synagogues and other associations could have patrons who were not members; whether this is the Christian Erastus of Ac 19:22 is debated, but cf. 2Ti 4:20.
16:25–27 Despite much variation in the way that letters concluded, they frequently concluded with a wish for the recipient's health and then "Farewell." Synagogues, however, closed prayers, readings and services with benedictions, and Paul anticipates that his letter will be read publicly in house churches' worship services. Speakers often repeated earlier themes in their conclusions (cf. 1:2–5, especially 1:5; cf. also 1:11,17; 2:16; 3:21; 11:25,33,36).
16:25 *mystery.* In Jewish circles, the Greek term sometimes referred to secret information now revealed only by God (Da 2:28–30,47; Dead Sea Scrolls).
16:26 *now revealed and made known through the prophetic writings.* As Paul notes here, the Scriptures already included this truth (v. 25; see 15:9–12; cf. further Isa 2:2–3; 11:10; 19:18–25; 49:6; 56:3–8; Zec 2:11), but only now was it understood.
16:27 *to … God be glory.* Jewish works often closed with praise to God. *Amen.* Closed prayers and many Jewish works.

THE LETTERS

1 CORINTHIANS

Corinth

In Paul's day, Corinth was the capital of Achaia, a province that included most of what we call Greece; it had been a Roman colony for nearly a century. Rome had destroyed old Corinth in 146 BC; although some local Greeks continued to live on the site, it was Julius Caesar's decree in 44 BC that led to the city's refounding, now as a Roman colony. Roman veterans and freed slaves settled there, so Corinth's citizens were also Roman citizens; the city celebrated its Roman character. Many Greeks who were not officially citizens continued to live in Corinth during this period.

Because most maritime trade between Rome and Asia Minor passed through the Isthmus of Corinth (the rugged southern coast of Greece was dangerous for ships), Corinth was well positioned for trade and wealth. Although wide disparity between rich and poor characterized the Roman Empire more generally, this problem was particularly acute in Corinth. Its mercantile character contributed to the presence of foreign religions and may have accelerated the level of sexual promiscuity, although some promiscuity was characteristic of ancient Greek urban male culture in general. Corinth was known for its prosperity, and the proverbial sexual looseness of earlier Greek Corinth seems to have continued in Roman Corinth as well.

Although Latin was used for official business in Corinth, most people could speak Greek, and this was especially true of settlers from elsewhere in Greece and farther east, including most Jewish immigrants. Clearly the Corinthian Christians, to whom Paul wrote his letters in Greek, understood him. Later in the first century, Clement of Rome also wrote to this church in Greek, which became Corinth's official language again in the early second century.

QUICK GLANCE

AUTHOR:
The apostle Paul

AUDIENCE:
Believers at Corinth whose church was divided by factions and spiritual immaturity

DATE:
AD 55

THEME:
Paul addresses problems in the church and answers questions from the church.

Background of 1 Corinthians

Although the Corinthian Christians had some theological misunderstandings, their culture affected their thinking on many points. The idea of bodily resurrection (6:14; 15:12 – 58) did not make sense to Greeks who thought only the soul (at most) would survive death. Instead of relating it to its Jewish Passover background, Corinthians were treating the Lord's Supper like a typical Corinthian banquet (11:17 – 34). Greek ideologies may have also supported sexual immorality (especially in 6:12 – 20), abstinence from marriage (ch. 7), and certainly issues of food offered to idols (chs. 8 – 10).

Also, although only a small portion of people in the church, and in antiquity more generally, were of high status, those high-status members would wield disproportionate influence in the church. Their social peers would expect better seating and food (11:21), would prefer speakers with elite rhetorical styles and displays of Greek wisdom (1:17 — 2:16; 3:18 – 20), and would be embarrassed by a teacher who was a manual laborer (4:12; cf. 9:12). Even the debate about head coverings might relate to a class issue in the church (11:2 – 16). Their misunderstandings and behavior make more sense to us when we understand their culture. This understanding may in turn help us to see how much many of us or our churches today are like them. ◆

1 Paul, called to be an apostle[a] of Christ
Jesus by the will of God,[b] and our
brother Sosthenes,[c]
2To the church of God in Corinth,[d] to
those sanctified in Christ Jesus and called[e]
to be his holy people, together with all
those everywhere who call on the name of
our Lord Jesus Christ—their Lord and ours:
3Grace and peace to you from God our
Father and the Lord Jesus Christ.[f]

Thanksgiving

4I always thank my God for you[g] because of his grace given you in Christ
Jesus. 5For in him you have been enriched[h] in every way—with all kinds of
speech and with all knowledge[i]— 6God
thus confirming our testimony[j] about
Christ among you. 7Therefore you do not
lack any spiritual gift as you eagerly wait
for our Lord Jesus Christ to be revealed.[k]
8He will also keep you firm to the end, so
that you will be blameless[l] on the day of
our Lord Jesus Christ. 9God is faithful,[m]
who has called you into fellowship with
his Son, Jesus Christ our Lord.[n]

A Church Divided Over Leaders

10I appeal to you, brothers and sisters,[a]
in the name of our Lord Jesus Christ, that
all of you agree with one another in what
you say and that there be no divisions
among you, but that you be perfectly united in mind and thought. 11My brothers
and sisters, some from Chloe's household
have informed me that there are quarrels
among you. 12What I mean is this: One
of you says, "I follow Paul";[o] another, "I
follow Apollos";[p] another, "I follow Cephas[b]";[q] still another, "I follow Christ."
13Is Christ divided? Was Paul crucified
for you? Were you baptized in the name
of Paul?[r] 14I thank God that I did not baptize any of you except Crispus[s] and Gaius,[t]
15so no one can say that you were bap-

1:1 [a] Ro 1:1; Eph 1:1 [b] 2Co 1:1 [c] Ac 18:17 **1:2** [d] Ac 18:1 [e] Ro 1:7 **1:3** [f] Ro 1:7 **1:4** [g] Ro 1:8 **1:5** [h] 2Co 9:11 [i] 2Co 8:7 **1:6** [j] Rev 1:2 **1:7** [k] Php 3:20; Titus 2:13; 2Pe 3:12 **1:8** [l] 1Th 3:13 **1:9** [m] Isa 49:7; 1Th 5:24 [n] 1Jn 1:3 **1:12** [o] 1Co 3:4, 22 [p] Ac 18:24 [q] Jn 1:42 **1:13** [r] Mt 28:19 **1:14** [s] Ac 18:8; Ro 16:23 [t] Ac 19:29

[a] *10* The Greek word for *brothers and sisters* (*adelphoi*) refers here to believers, both men and women, as part of God's family; also in verses 11 and 26; and in 2:1; 3:1; 4:6; 6:8; 7:24, 29; 10:1; 11:33; 12:1; 14:6, 20, 26, 39; 15:1, 6, 50, 58; 16:15, 20. [b] *12* That is, Peter

1:1 *Paul … and our brother Sosthenes.* Ancient writers rarely coauthored letters; sometimes letters that listed secondary authors merely were a special way of the second author sending greetings. Nevertheless, it is not impossible that Sosthenes contributed somehow to the letter. Scholars debate whether this is the Corinthian Sosthenes of Ac 18:17, now (or perhaps even then) a believer.
1:2 *sanctified.* Someone or something that God had consecrated for his own special use. In the OT, God set apart Israel from the nations; here Paul refers to believers in Jesus, consecrated by God for his use.
1:3 *Grace and peace to you.* The conventional greeting was *chairein*, which early Christians often changed to *charis*, "grace." The Jewish greeting (sometimes added to *chairein*) was "peace." Letters frequently included prayers or blessings for their recipients; Jewish people used "peace" as a blessing, meaning that they implicitly asked God to give the recipient well-being. *from God … and the Lord Jesus Christ.* Because Paul invokes Jesus as well as the Father in this blessing, he takes for granted here Jesus' deity.
1:4–8 Speakers usually started with something positive about their audience to secure a more favorable hearing.
1:4 *I always thank my God for you.* Letters sometimes included thanksgivings.
1:5 *all kinds of speech and … knowledge.* Corinthian culture particularly exalted, and even competed in, skills of speech and knowledge, including extemporaneous speeches on random topics. The believers valued especially those spiritual gifts (v. 7; 12:8–10) that were valued, in a more secular form, in their culture.
1:8 *on the day of our Lord Jesus Christ.* Scripture spoke of the day of the Lord (e.g., Isa 13:6,9; Joel 1:15; 2:1,11,31); Paul applies this language to the return of Jesus, who is divine (see note on v. 3). In the Greek world, even Jews often neglected emphasis on God's future promises; this may be one area where the Corinthian believers need correction (see 3:13–15; 4:5; 5:5; 6:14; 11:26; 13:8–12; 15:12–57).
1:10 *that all of you agree with one another in what you say.* Speakers and writers sometimes stated their thesis before arguing it. Here in v. 10 Paul notes that he is appealing for unity (1:10—4:21). Factors in disunity may include the perspectives of different social levels (cf. 11:21) and possibly the different house churches (cf. 16:19), though some argue that these also met together sometimes (cf. Ro 16:23). *divisions.* Division and rivalry were rife in antiquity (in sports and especially speech and politics), and ancient speakers and writers often had to exhort hearers to unity.
1:11 *some from Chloe's household have informed me.* Travelers often carried letters, oral news and their eyewitness testimony; hearers could cite the travelers if the reports were deemed reliable. *Chloe's household.* Chloe may have owned a business in Corinth or Ephesus; trusted servants or freed persons would be considered members of her household, and they would travel between these major mercantile cities on business.
1:12 Urban hearers in places such as Corinth regularly judged and ranked speakers. Students of rival teachers sometimes fought; in one later case slaves of an orator's disciples beat to death a mocker. Disciples sometimes treated teachers as fathers (cf. 4:15). *I follow.* Lit. "I am of"; the phrase was sometimes used as a slogan of ancient political partisans, which Paul caricatures here. Though some disdain Paul for his speaking ability, he here uses anaphora, a type of rhetorical repetition that begins successive phrases in the same way. Many scholars think that the only actual division at this time was between partisans of Paul and those of Apollos, since they are the only groups subsequently addressed (cf. 3:4–6,22; 4:6). *Cephas.* Aramaic; the Greek translation is *Petros*, Peter.
1:13 Speakers sometimes reduced their opponents' arguments to the absurd by how they represented them, often using multiple rhetorical questions to build emotional force.
1:14 *baptize.* Besides the sea, Paul could have baptized in Corinth's many public fountain houses or especially public baths. *Crispus and Gaius.* Corinth's legal citizens were Roman citizens; although the names Crispus (cf. Ac 18:8) and Gaius do not guarantee Roman citizenship, they are Roman names.

tized in my name. 16(Yes, I also baptized the household of Stephanas;[u] beyond that, I don't remember if I baptized anyone else.) 17For Christ did not send me to baptize,[v] but to preach the gospel — not with wisdom[w] and eloquence, lest the cross of Christ be emptied of its power.

Christ Crucified Is God's Power and Wisdom

18For the message of the cross is foolishness to those who are perishing,[x] but to us who are being saved it is the power of God.[y] 19For it is written:

> "I will destroy the wisdom of the wise;
> the intelligence of the intelligent I
> will frustrate."[a][z]

20Where is the wise person?[a] Where is the teacher of the law? Where is the philosopher of this age? Has not God made foolish[b] the wisdom of the world? 21For since in the wisdom of God the world through its wisdom did not know him, God was pleased through the foolishness of what was preached to save those who believe. 22Jews demand signs[c] and Greeks look for wisdom, 23but we preach Christ crucified: a stumbling block[d] to Jews and foolishness[e] to Gentiles, 24but to those whom God has called,[f] both Jews and Greeks, Christ the power of God and the wisdom of God.[g] 25For the foolishness[h] of God is wiser than human wisdom, and the weakness[i] of God is stronger than human strength.

26Brothers and sisters, think of what you were when you were called. Not many of you were wise by human standards; not many were influential; not many were of noble birth. 27But God chose[j] the foolish[k] things of the world to shame the wise; God chose the weak things of the world to shame the strong. 28God chose the lowly things of this world and the despised things — and the things that are not[l] — to nullify the things that are, 29so that no one may boast before him.[m] 30It is because of him that you are in Christ Jesus, who has become for us wisdom from God — that is,

a 19 Isaiah 29:14

1:16 [u] 1Co 16:15 **1:17** [v] Jn 4:2 [w] 1Co 2:1,4,13 **1:18** [x] 2Co 2:15 [y] Ro 1:16 **1:19** [z] Isa 29:14 **1:20** [a] Isa 19:11, 12 [b] Job 12:17; Ro 1:22 **1:22** [c] Mt 12:38 **1:23** [d] Lk 2:34; Gal 5:11 [e] 1Co 2:14 **1:24** [f] Ro 8:28 [g] ver 30; Col 2:3 **1:25** [h] ver 18 [i] 2Co 13:4 **1:27** [j] Jas 2:5 [k] ver 20 **1:28** [l] Ro 4:17 **1:29** [m] Eph 2:9

1:16 Informal letters sometimes included afterthoughts; but speakers also sometimes corrected themselves deliberately to drive home a point. Either interpretation may be possible here. *household.* In matters of religion, Gentiles expected household members to follow the free male household head.
1:17 *Christ did not send me to baptize.* Gentiles who converted to Judaism understood baptism as part of the act of conversion; Jesus' movement adopted the same action. But Paul does not want even this act to detract from emphasis on the cross. *not with wisdom and eloquence.* Corinth highly valued wisdom and speech (see notes on vv. 5,20). Philosophers and moralists often used rhetorical (oratorical) skills, but emphasized that it was the truth, not mere rhetoric, that convinced their hearers. Paul's rhetorical devices in this section could include antithesis (vv. 18,25), paradox (v. 25, also using antithesis), and most clearly, anaphora (vv. 12,20,26) and antistrophe (see note on vv. 27–28).
1:18 *the cross.* A terrifying instrument of execution by slow torture; although rare in Corinth, in Judea it epitomized Roman repression. Romans reserved the punishment especially for slaves and rebel provincials, the antithesis of "savior" benefactors, who could be gods, kings or the wealthy. Jews deemed accursed those who were hanged on stakes (Dt 21:23). *foolishness to those who are perishing.* Corinth valued honor, wealth and social power.
1:19 See Isa 29:14 (part of the context cited by Jesus in Mk 7:6–7).
1:20 The Greco-Roman world's two advanced disciplines were philosophy and (more commonly useful for statesmen) rhetoric. *philosopher of this age.* Lit. "debater of this age" and may refer to rhetoricians, whom philosophers often criticized; "wise person" here may condemn philosophers also. Paul here uses four rhetorical questions to drive home the point, plus anaphora (three times repeating "Where is ...?"); cf. Isa 19:12; 29:14; 33:18; 44:25; Jer 8:9.
1:22 *Greeks look for wisdom.* Others associated Greeks with philosophy, which means "love for wisdom" (cf. Ro 1:14). Various competing philosophic schools, however, promoted different beliefs; see the article "Ancient Philosophies," p. 1913.
1:23 See note on v. 18.
1:24 *the power of God and the wisdom of God.* Jewish tradition sometimes personified divine Wisdom (following Pr 8).
1:25 *foolishness of God ... weakness of God.* In speaking of God's "foolishness" and "weakness" Paul uses the accepted practice of irony. Corinthian culture valued powerful persons (cf. v. 26).
1:26 *Not many of you.* Only a few people in antiquity, fewer than 1 percent, belonged to the truly elite class or the very wealthy; prosperous Corinth would have more people of moderate wealth, but the poor still constituted the majority of the city. In Corinth, even most of the wealthy descended from people of lower class or freed persons, not from a hereditary nobility. Paul three times opens clauses with "not many"; opening repetition, or anaphora, would help hold the attention of rhetorically sensitive Corinthians. Some church members, perhaps especially those who owned the larger homes in which the churches met, may have been of higher status (cf. Ro 16:23). They would be few but disproportionately influential. Many people lived in apartments only large enough for sleeping, but the wealthy could live in larger ground-floor apartments or in separate homes. The wealthiest district in Corinth proper was the Kraneion, or Craneum.
1:27–28 *God chose ... God chose ... God chose.* Paul's threefold repetition is rhetorical antistrophe (repeating a phrase at the end of a line; the phrase appears at the end in Greek, though most translate it at the beginning in English). Paul here develops the three examples from v. 26 — the wise, the powerful and the honored aristocrats.
1:29 *no one may boast.* In vv. 26–29, Paul vaguely echoes Jer 9:23, which warns against the wise, strong and rich boasting in their gifts; this prepares for Paul's explicit quotation of Jer 9:24 in v. 31.
1:30 *who has become for us wisdom.* Greeks and especially Jews sometimes treated wisdom as a personification or

our righteousness,[n] holiness and redemption.[o] 31 Therefore, as it is written: "Let the
one who boasts boast in the Lord."[a][p]

2 And so it was with me, brothers and
sisters. When I came to you, I did
not come with eloquence or human wisdom[q] as I proclaimed to you the testimony about God.[b] 2 For I resolved to know
nothing while I was with you except Jesus
Christ and him crucified.[r] 3 I came to you[s]
in weakness with great fear and trembling.
4 My message and my preaching were not
with wise and persuasive words, but with
a demonstration of the Spirit's power,[t] 5 so
that your faith might not rest on human
wisdom, but on God's power.[u]

God's Wisdom Revealed by the Spirit

6 We do, however, speak a message of
wisdom among the mature,[v] but not the
wisdom of this age[w] or of the rulers of this
age, who are coming to nothing. 7 No, we
declare God's wisdom, a mystery that has
been hidden and that God destined for our
glory before time began. 8 None of the rulers of this age understood it, for if they
had, they would not have crucified the
Lord of glory.[x] 9 However, as it is written:

"What no eye has seen,
what no ear has heard,
and what no human mind has
conceived"[c] —
the things God has prepared for
those who love him —[y]

10 these are the things God has revealed[z] to
us by his Spirit.[a]
The Spirit searches all things, even the
deep things of God. 11 For who knows a
person's thoughts[b] except their own spirit[c] within them? In the same way no one
knows the thoughts of God except the
Spirit of God. 12 What we have received is
not the spirit[d] of the world,[e] but the Spirit
who is from God, so that we may understand what God has freely given us. 13 This
is what we speak, not in words taught us
by human wisdom[f] but in words taught

1:30 [n] Jer 23:5, 6; 2Co 5:21 [o] Ro 3:24; Eph 1:7, 14
1:31 [p] Jer 9:23, 24; 2Co 10:17
2:1 [q] 1Co 1:17
2:2 [r] Gal 6:14; 1Co 1:23
2:3 [s] Ac 18:1-18
2:4 [t] Ro 15:19
2:5 [u] 2Co 4:7; 6:7
2:6 [v] Eph 4:13; Php 3:15; Heb 5:14 [w] 1Co 1:20
2:8 [x] Ac 7:2; Jas 2:1
2:9 [y] Isa 64:4; 65:17
2:10 [z] Mt 13:11; Eph 3:3, 5 [a] Jn 14:26
2:11 [b] Jer 17:9 [c] Pr 20:27
2:12 [d] Ro 8:15 [e] 1Co 1:20, 27
2:13 [f] 1Co 1:17

[a] *31* Jer. 9:24 [b] *1* Some manuscripts *proclaimed to you God's mystery* [c] *9* Isaiah 64:4

even a being; for Jewish people, it was the best way to imagine something divine in character yet distinguished from God the Father (see 8:6; see also note on Jn 1:1). They also viewed God's law as their wisdom and righteousness (Dt 4:6; 6:25).

1:31 Paul here summarizes Jer 9:24 (see note on 1:29).

2:1 *eloquence or human wisdom.* When an orator came to a city, he would often offer a scheduled oration; if this speech brought him enough reputation that he could begin teaching students rhetoric, he would make that city his home. By contrast, Paul sought to honor Christ, not himself (v. 2). Even famous orators frequently began a speech by playing down their speaking abilities, knowing that their skill would quickly become obvious. While many of Paul's letters display brilliant thought, however, his speaking style (cf. v. 3) fell short of his critics' expectations (2Co 10:10; 11:6). Although Josephus, to please his Hellenistic audience, tendentiously presents Moses as a great orator, Paul's rhetorical limitations apparently had some Biblical precedent (Ex 4:10; Jer 1:6).

2:3 *weakness.* Critics complained about speaking skills even if one's arguments were strong but one fell short in appearance or delivery (cf. 2Co 10:10), such as gestures and voice intonation. *fear and trembling.* The OT and Jewish sources applied this phrase in various ways, sometimes emphasizing appropriate reverence for God and sometimes fear of powerful enemies. Against some philosophers, rhetoricians urged speakers to rouse emotion; audiences would often ridicule a speaker who trembled.

2:5 *might not rest on human wisdom, but on God's power.* Criticisms by Socrates and others had led many rhetoricians by this period to admit that rhetoric could be abused — one could market false ideas and persuade people to believe wrong things. Nevertheless, they contended that rhetoric remained essential, for if one had truth one should promote it. Still, speakers also deployed rhetoric in law courts to amplify accusations and commit character assassination.

Philosophers had criticized rhetoric at least since the time of Socrates, valuing truth over skillful speech. By this period, however, philosophers usually used the persuasive devices rhetoricians had identified. Paul would have sided with the philosophers' critique of rhetoric, but like them he was willing to use it. He employed in his letters many rhetorical devices familiar from his milieu, even though he demeaned depending on rhetoric. Despite his deficiencies in critics' eyes (2Co 11:6), he communicated as skillfully as possible in his context while also depending on the Spirit to transform hearts (v. 4). *power.* Rhetoricians sometimes spoke of argumentative "demonstration" (cf. v. 4) and rhetorical "power," but Paul depended instead on the message of the cross (1:18,24; 2Co 13:4), perhaps accompanied by signs (1:22,24; Ro 15:19).

2:6 *mature.* Philosophers could apply this descriptor to those advanced in wisdom — which the Corinthians lack (3:1). But as a Jewish work from this period put it, even one considered "perfect" or "mature" was useless without God's wisdom (Wisdom of Solomon 9:6).

2:7 *before time began.* Jewish tradition emphasized that God formed wisdom before the world, used it to form the world, and that wisdom would endure forever.

2:8 *this age.* Jewish people contrasted this ruined age with the eternal age to come. This age's rulers had human power that would pass away (1:27 – 28); God's wisdom in the cross is eternal (1:18 – 25). *Lord of glory.* Jewish sources normally reserved this title for God; "Lord of glory" can also be translated idiomatically as "glorious Lord."

2:9 Interpreters often slightly adapted the wording of quotations; Paul adapts Isa 64:4 (possibly with wording from Isa 65:17), then qualifies it (v. 10; cf. v. 16).

2:10 *revealed to us by his Spirit.* The prophets promised the Spirit for the coming age; the Spirit's activity now thus provides a foretaste of that age.

2:11 *no one knows the thoughts of God except the Spirit of God.* Jewish thinkers in this period recognized that people could understand God's plans only by the gift of his wisdom and his Spirit (cf. Wisdom of Solomon 9:17; see note on 1Co 2:16).

2:12 *spirit of the world.* The Greek term for "spirit" also means "disposition," and so it need not be personified here.

by the Spirit, explaining spiritual realities with Spirit-taught words.[a] 14The person without the Spirit does not accept the
things that come from the Spirit of God
but considers them foolishness,[g] and cannot understand them because they are
discerned only through the Spirit. 15The
person with the Spirit makes judgments
about all things, but such a person is not
subject to merely human judgments, 16for,

"Who has known the mind of the Lord
so as to instruct him?"[b][h]

But we have the mind of Christ.[i]

The Church and Its Leaders

3 Brothers and sisters, I could not address you as people who live by the
Spirit[j] but as people who are still worldly[k]—mere infants[l] in Christ. 2I gave you
milk, not solid food,[m] for you were not
yet ready for it.[n] Indeed, you are still not
ready. 3You are still worldly. For since there
is jealousy and quarreling[o] among you,
are you not worldly? Are you not acting
like mere humans? 4For when one says, "I
follow Paul," and another, "I follow Apollos,"[p] are you not mere human beings?
5What, after all, is Apollos? And what
is Paul? Only servants, through whom you
came to believe—as the Lord has assigned
to each his task. 6I planted the seed,[q]
Apollos watered it, but God has been making it grow. 7So neither the one who plants
nor the one who waters is anything, but
only God, who makes things grow. 8The
one who plants and the one who waters
have one purpose, and they will each be
rewarded according to their own labor.[r]
9For we are co-workers in God's service;[s]
you are God's field,[t] God's building.[u]
10By the grace God has given me,[v] I laid
a foundation[w] as a wise builder, and someone else is building on it. But each one
should build with care. 11For no one can
lay any foundation other than the one already laid, which is Jesus Christ.[x] 12If anyone builds on this foundation using gold,
silver, costly stones, wood, hay or straw,
13their work will be shown for what it is,[y]
because the Day[z] will bring it to light. It
will be revealed with fire, and the fire will
test the quality of each person's work. 14If
what has been built survives, the builder
will receive a reward. 15If it is burned up,
the builder will suffer loss but yet will be
saved—even though only as one escaping
through the flames.[a]
16Don't you know that you yourselves
are God's temple[b] and that God's Spirit dwells in your midst? 17If anyone destroys God's temple, God will destroy that

2:14 [g] 1Co 1:18
2:16 [h] Isa 40:13 [i] Jn 15:15
3:1 [j] 1Co 2:15 [k] Ro 7:14; 1Co 2:14 [l] Heb 5:13
3:2 [m] Heb 5:12-14; 1Pe 2:2 [n] Jn 16:12
3:3 [o] 1Co 1:11; Gal 5:20
3:4 [p] 1Co 1:12
3:6 [q] Ac 18:4-11
3:8 [r] Ps 62:12
3:9 [s] 2Co 6:1 [t] Isa 61:3 [u] Eph 2:20-22; 1Pe 2:5
3:10 [v] Ro 12:3 [w] Ro 15:20
3:11 [x] Isa 28:16; Eph 2:20
3:13 [y] 1Co 4:5 [z] 2Th 1:7-10
3:15 [a] Jude 23
3:16 [b] 1Co 6:19; 2Co 6:16

[a] 13 Or *Spirit, interpreting spiritual truths to those who are spiritual* [b] 16 Isaiah 40:13

2:14 *without the Spirit.* The Greek term translated thus here (the context does imply the NIV's interpretation) might reflect a Diaspora Jewish interpretation of Ge 2:7 (see discussion at 1Co 15:44–46, where the NIV translates the same term "natural").
2:16 Isa 40:13, cited here, was a rhetorical question denying that humans knew God's Spirit, but because the Spirit has now come (cf. Isa 44:3; Joel 2:28), God's people do have his Spirit. The Greek translation of Isa 40:13 substitutes "mind" for "Spirit"; Paul, who has been writing about God's Spirit in vv. 10–15, draws on both ideas.
3:1 *mere infants in Christ.* Thinkers frequently depicted the unlearned as babies who needed milk (cf. note on 9:7). The image was acceptable for beginning students, but insulting to those who thought themselves mature in wisdom.
3:3 *worldly.* Lit. means more like "resembling what is fleshly"; for the sense, see the article "Flesh and Spirit," p. 1961.
3:4 *mere human beings.* Probably meant as biting irony; for Greeks, the line between human and divine was much thinner than for Jews and equally monotheistic Gentile Christians. Here Paul's hearers are acting like people devoid of God's Spirit (cf. 2:14—3:3).
3:7 Agrarian metaphors were common in antiquity; farmers planted and irrigated but their prayers and offerings confirmed that most of them understood that only God could make plants grow.
3:8 *rewarded according to their own labor.* Farmers' reward was the harvest, when they could pay landowners (on whose estates many of them worked) and the like. Some Jewish sources compared the time of the end with a harvest.
3:9 *God's field, God's building.* Paul uses familiar images: in Scripture, God planted and built up his people (e.g., Jer 18:7; 24:6; 31:28; 45:4).
3:10–11 Paul develops the building image from v. 9 (the temple, vv. 16–17). Believers should not divide over Paul and Apollos (vv. 5–7), whose job was to build them on Christ.
3:13 *the Day.* The day of the Lord (cf. 1:8), associated with the fire of God's judgment (Zep 1:18; cf. Isa 66:15–16). *bring it to light.* Daylight reveals what is hidden (see 4:5). *fire will test the quality of each person's work.* The fire that purified metals destroyed wood and straw. Scripture used metal refining as a metaphor for testing or purifying by judgment (Zec 13:9; Mal 3:2–3), and fire consuming straw to depict the destruction of the wicked (Isa 33:11–12; 47:14).
3:14–15 *builder will receive his reward ... suffer loss.* The metaphor fits: builders do not get paid for shabby construction. The structure here is the church as God's temple (vv. 16–17); judgment day would reveal the degree of builders' (such as Paul's and Apollos's) true effectiveness (vv. 12–13).
3:17 *If anyone destroys God's temple, God will destroy that person.* Almost everyone in antiquity believed that deities avenged any violation of the sanctity of their temples, especially against those who destroyed such temples. Yet those not building but rather tearing down the temple—those sowing division in the church—violated its sanctity. *you together are that temple.* Some thinkers in antiquity envisioned spiritual sacrifices and temples; some passages in the Dead Sea Scrolls apply the image of the temple to God's people.

1 CORINTHIANS 2:1 – 5

Rhetoric and Paul's Letters

Greek and consequently Roman urban culture cherished rhetoric, or oratory, which shaped the speeches in public assemblies as well as oratorical competitions and even public speakers in the market.

Paul's letters are full of rhetorical devices, probably because they contain much more argumentation than the brief, typical papyrus letters that dominate our ancient samples, and even more than appear in most letters of orators such as Cicero, Pliny or Fronto (see "Introduction to the Letters and Revelation: Ancient Letters," p. 1944). Paul's spoken rhetorical skills apparently fell short of those of Apollos and the expectations of educated Corinthian Christians; perhaps his humility, traces of his Judean accent (though contrast perhaps Ac 21:37), or other factors disturbed those accustomed to Attic-style orations. Nevertheless, the argumentation in his letters was more respectable (2Co 10:10).

Because of this special character of much of Paul's correspondence, many scholars compare his letters more to ancient speeches than to typical letters. Of the two advanced disciplines, philosophy and rhetoric, the more popular was rhetoric, or public speaking. Statesmen and orators in Greek and Roman cities employed it in public assemblies, courts, at funerals and so forth; cities with heavy Greek rhetorical influence included Alexandria, Ephesus, probably Antioch, and other cities of the eastern empire. From Josephus it appears that this was often true in Jerusalem as well. Ordinary urban residents would hear speakers in markets and at competitions, and citizens would hear eloquence in citizen assemblies.

From some church fathers to Luther's successor Melanchthon, the rhetorical approach to Paul's letters is a time-honored one. Because even most letter-essays (such as some of Seneca's) were not arranged as speeches, however, some other scholars question this comparison. Scholars usually recognize rhetorical devices in Paul's letters, but many scholars doubt many of the full rhetorical outlines (using speeches as models) that some critics propose. Although the degree to which the comparison with speeches is appropriate is debated, some details about Paul and rhetoric seem clear.

First, the abundance of rhetorical devices reveals that Paul was competent in the dominant rhetorical forms of his day. Scholars debate whether this indicates that he had some academic exposure to rhetoric or whether it merely shows him imbibing these forms after hearing them used by others. Exposure to at least elementary rhetoric occurred early in Greek education; this may have been the case for Greek-speakers even in Jerusalem (Ac 22:3).

Second, by the standards revealed in the papyri, Paul was well educated in Greek. He was not among the highest elite, but his letters abound in rhetorical devices, often

continued on next page

person; for God's temple is sacred, and you together are that temple.

18Do not deceive yourselves. If any of
you think you are wise[c] by the standards of this age, you should become "fools" so that you may become wise.
19For the wisdom of this world is foolishness[d] in God's sight. As it is written: "He catches the wise in their craftiness"[a];[e]
20and again, "The Lord knows that the thoughts of the wise

3:18 [c] Isa 5:21; 1Co 8:2
3:19 [d] 1Co 1:20, 27 [e] Job 5:13

[a] *19* Job 5:13

3:18 *become "fools" ... become wise.* Paul continues arguing that the wisdom of this age is folly; see 1:17 – 31; 2:1 – 16 (especially 2:6 – 8). Paul further demonstrates this point from Scripture in vv. 19 – 20.

3:19 *He catches the wise in their craftiness.* Although Job's accuser Eliphaz uses this wisdom out of context in Job 5:13, the principle remains a wise one.

3:20 In the context of Ps 94:11, cited here, God shows

more than letters by trained rhetoricians (partly because letters were not supposed to use such devices much, and probably partly because he is partially preaching). In some cases, especially in Corinth, this use may respond to criticisms (1Co 2:3; 2Co 11:6); in some cases, it may simply reflect the heavier emphasis on argumentation and persuasion in Paul's letters than in the typical letters of other thinkers. Other thinkers most often published their major ideas in other genres; Paul, being a pastor concerned for congregations, communicated his written counsel especially in pastoral letters.

Third, Paul's primary subject of study seems to have been the OT, especially in its Greek translation. Whereas educated Greeks and Romans revealed their education by peppering their speeches and even their letters with classical quotations and allusions, these are rare in Paul's letters. Instead, he fills many of his letters with Biblical quotations, and does so particularly frequently when he needs to challenge less informed readings of Scripture by others. ◆

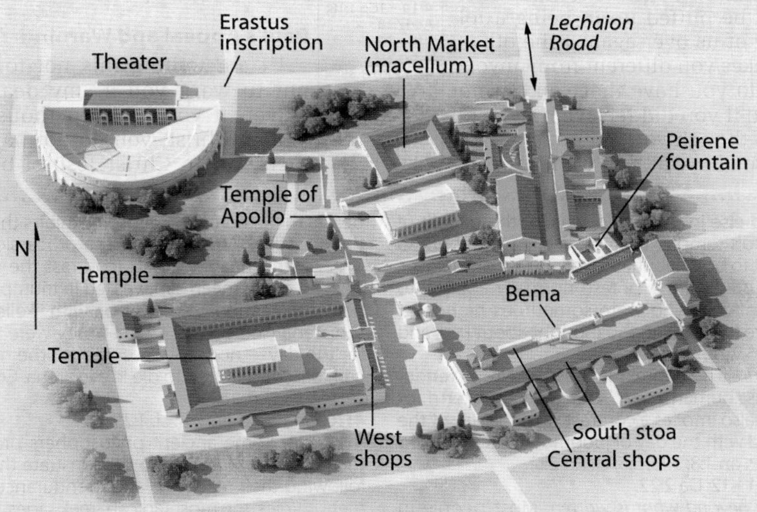

Reconstruction of Corinth, where oratory was very common in Paul's time.

are futile."[a f] 21 So then, no more boasting about human leaders![g] All things are
yours,[h] 22 whether Paul or Apollos or Cephas[b i] or the world or life or death or the
present or the future[j] — all are yours, 23 and
you are of Christ,[k] and Christ is of God.

3:20 [f] Ps 94:11 **3:21** [g] 1Co 4:6 [h] Ro 8:32 **3:22** [i] 1Co 1:12 [j] Ro 8:38 **3:23** [k] 1Co 15:23; 2Co 10:7; Gal 3:29

[a] *20* Psalm 94:11 [b] *22* That is, Peter

the foolishness of the wicked who fail to recognize that the sovereign God sees and will judge their deeds (Ps 94:7 – 10).

3:21 *All things are yours.* Some philosophers claimed that everything belonged to the gods and they were friends of the gods, so everything belonged to them. (By this the most extreme meant that they were free to use anything; they often slept, and sometimes openly excreted, on porches of temples and the like.) Many Jewish people believed that God's people were heirs who would rule the coming world (see note on Ro 4:13). Paul argues that not only apostles who labored to build the church up, but

The Nature of True Apostleship

4 This, then, is how you ought to regard
us: as servants of Christ and as those
entrusted[l] with the mysteries[m] God has revealed. [2]Now it is required that those who
have been given a trust must prove faithful. [3]I care very little if I am judged by you
or by any human court; indeed, I do not
even judge myself. [4]My conscience is clear,
but that does not make me innocent.[n] It is
the Lord who judges me. [5]Therefore judge
nothing[o] before the appointed time; wait
until the Lord comes. He will bring to light
what is hidden in darkness and will expose the motives of the heart. At that time
each will receive their praise from God.[p]
[6]Now, brothers and sisters, I have applied these things to myself and Apollos
for your benefit, so that you may learn
from us the meaning of the saying, "Do
not go beyond what is written."[q] Then
you will not be puffed up in being a follower of one of us over against the other.[r]
[7]For who makes you different from anyone
else? What do you have that you did not
receive?[s] And if you did receive it, why do
you boast as though you did not?
[8]Already you have all you want! Already
you have become rich![t] You have begun
to reign—and that without us! How I
wish that you really had begun to reign so
that we also might reign with you! [9]For it
seems to me that God has put us apostles
on display at the end of the procession,
like those condemned to die[u] in the arena.
We have been made a spectacle[v] to the
whole universe, to angels as well as to human beings. [10]We are fools for Christ,[w] but
you are so wise in Christ![x] We are weak,
but you are strong![y] You are honored, we
are dishonored! [11]To this very hour we go
hungry and thirsty, we are in rags, we are
brutally treated, we are homeless.[z] [12]We
work hard with our own hands.[a] When we
are cursed, we bless;[b] when we are persecuted, we endure it; [13]when we are slandered, we answer kindly. We have become
the scum of the earth, the garbage[c] of the
world—right up to this moment.

Paul's Appeal and Warning

[14]I am writing this not to shame you
but to warn you as my dear children.[d]
[15]Even if you had ten thousand guardians in Christ, you do not have many fathers, for in Christ Jesus I became your

4:1 [l] 1Co 9:17; Titus 1:7 [m] Ro 16:25 **4:4** [n] Ro 2:13 **4:5** [o] Mt 7:1,2; Ro 2:1 [p] Ro 2:29 **4:6** [q] 1Co 1:19, 31; 3:19,20 [r] 1Co 1:12 **4:7** [s] Jn 3:27; Ro 12:3,6 **4:8** [t] Rev 3:17, 18 **4:9** [u] Ro 8:36 [v] Heb 10:33 **4:10** [w] 1Co 1:18; Ac 17:18 [x] 1Co 3:18 [y] 1Co 2:3 **4:11** [z] Ro 8:35; 2Co 11:23-27 **4:12** [a] Ac 18:3 [b] 1Pe 3:9 **4:13** [c] La 3:45 **4:14** [d] 1Th 2:11

also everything else in this world, was for the benefit of the church, God's temple. Their ministers were there to serve them, not to be celebrities to follow and divide over.

4:1 *those entrusted with.* A phrase normally applied to managers of estates, who were sometimes high-level servants, as here (continuing the thought about Paul and Apollos from 3:5,9,22; cf. 4:6).

4:3 *human court.* The context invites the NIV to render "human day" as "human court," but the Greek term for "day" Paul uses also implies a contrast with the day of the Lord, associated with the day of judgment that is implied in v. 5 (see notes on 1:8; 3:13; 5:5; cf. Ro 2:5).

4:5 Cf. Ps 139:11–12; Da 2:22.

4:6 *Do not go beyond what is written.* Most people in antiquity understood that it was inappropriate to boast beyond their proper status in life. Scholars debate the meaning of not exceeding "what is written"; some envisage the background in schoolchildren tracing the writing of their teachers; or people finding harmony by observing an earlier agreement; or most likely, given Paul's usage elsewhere (e.g., 1:19,31; 2:9; 3:19), to not violate Scripture. This would include his earlier warnings in this letter not to rely on mere human wisdom (1:19; 3:19).

4:8 Speakers commonly used irony to drive home a point. Philosophers often claimed to have true wealth, wisdom, power, and the right and wisdom to rule; Paul ironically treats the Corinthian believers as greater sages than himself and Apollos, the Corinthian believers' teachers. Paul's audience, who respected teachers, would surely recognize the irony, in effect challenging their own pretentious claims to wisdom. Corinthian culture boasted in wealth and status. God's people would reign in the future (6:2).

4:9 *on display at the end of the procession.* Some others depicted the wise as exhibited in the theater of the world, but as a matter of honor; here it is an image of shame. The person in charge of games in amphitheaters would exhibit the gladiators who would battle wild beasts there; here God himself exhibits the sufferings of the apostles. "At the end of the procession" is simply a Greek term meaning "last" (contrast the divine view in 12:28); it could mean captives led in triumphal procession before execution (2Co 2:14), or, with likelier reference to the arena (see 1Co 15:32), that they were the final show for the day—normally reserved for the most wretched criminal condemned to die in the arena. Corinth's theater seated 18,000.

4:10 See note on v. 8; cf. 1:25.

4:11–13 Some ancient philosophers provided lists of their hardships, as here, to demonstrate their integrity in following their teachings about endurance and contentment. Cynics, the most radical Greek sages, fit the description in v. 11, as would most people who were homeless. But cf. also the demands of radical mission for Jesus' disciples (Mk 6:8–11).

4:12 *work hard with our own hands.* People of status considered manual labor (Ac 18:3; 20:34) demeaning; with some notable exceptions (such as many Jewish teachers), many sages in antiquity avoided it. (Cynics begged; most other Gentile sages charged tuition or depended on wealthy patrons.)

4:13 *slandered.* Some of the church's more socially respectable members may have counted Paul's work an embarrassment. *answer kindly.* Some philosophers tried to disregard human opinion, ignoring criticism; Cynics, however, often insulted their hearers (and not only those who criticized them). For blessing those who curse, see especially Lk 6:22 (cf. also Pr 15:1; 29:8).

4:14 *as my dear children.* The gentler sages usually warned their students gently, sometimes as their children. Disciples sometimes viewed their teachers as fathers, and teachers viewed them as their children.

4:15 *ten thousand guardians in Christ.* In contrast to v. 14, the Greek term translated "guardians" referred to slaves who ensured the safe transit of boys to and from school.

father through the gospel.[e] 16 Therefore I urge you to imitate me.[f] 17 For this reason I have sent to you Timothy, my son[g] whom I love, who is faithful in the Lord. He will remind you of my way of life in Christ Jesus, which agrees with what I teach everywhere in every church.[h]

18 Some of you have become arrogant, as if I were not coming to you. 19 But I will come to you very soon,[i] if the Lord is willing,[j] and then I will find out not only how these arrogant people are talking, but what power they have. 20 For the kingdom of God is not a matter of talk but of power. 21 What do you prefer? Shall I come to you with a rod of discipline,[k] or shall I come in love and with a gentle spirit?

Dealing With a Case of Incest

5 It is actually reported that there is sexual immorality among you, and of a kind that even pagans do not tolerate: A man is sleeping with his father's wife.[l] 2 And you are proud! Shouldn't you rather have gone into mourning[m] and have put out of your fellowship the man who has been doing this? 3 For my part, even though I am not physically present, I am with you in spirit.[n] As one who is present with you in this way, I have already passed judgment in the name of our Lord Jesus[o] on the one who has been doing this. 4 So when you are assembled and I am with you in spirit, and the power of our Lord Jesus is present, 5 hand this man over[p] to Satan for the destruction of the flesh,[a,b] so that his spirit may be saved on the day of the Lord.

6 Your boasting is not good.[q] Don't you know that a little yeast[r] leavens the whole batch of dough?[s] 7 Get rid of the old yeast, so that you may be a new unleavened batch—as you really are. For Christ, our Passover lamb, has been sacrificed.[t] 8 Therefore let us keep the Festival, not with the old bread leavened with malice and wickedness, but with the unleavened bread[u] of sincerity and truth.

9 I wrote to you in my letter not to associate[v] with sexually immoral people— 10 not at all meaning the people of this world[w] who are immoral, or the greedy and swindlers, or idolaters. In that case you would have to leave this world. 11 But now I am writing to you that you must not associate with anyone who claims to be a brother or sister[c] but is sexually

4:15 [e] 1Co 9:12, 14, 18, 23 **4:16** [f] 1Co 11:1; Php 3:17; 1Th 1:6; 2Th 3:7, 9 **4:17** [g] 1Ti 1:2 [h] 1Co 7:17 **4:19** [i] 2Co 1:15, 16 [j] Ac 18:21 **4:21** [k] 2Co 1:23; 13:2, 10 **5:1** [l] Lev 18:8; Dt 22:30 **5:2** [m] 2Co 7:7-11 **5:3** [n] Col 2:5 [o] 2Th 3:6 **5:5** [p] 1Ti 1:20 **5:6** [q] Jas 4:16 [r] Mt 16:6, 12 [s] Gal 5:9 **5:7** [t] Mk 14:12; 1Pe 1:19 **5:8** [u] Ex 12:14, 15; Dt 16:3 **5:9** [v] Eph 5:11; 2Th 3:6, 14 **5:10** [w] 1Co 10:27

[a] 5 In contexts like this, the Greek word for *flesh* (*sarx*) refers to the sinful state of human beings, often presented as a power in opposition to the Spirit.
[b] 5 Or *of his body*
[c] 11 The Greek word for *brother or sister* (*adelphos*) refers here to a believer, whether man or woman, as part of God's family; also in 8:11, 13.

4:16 *imitate me.* Disciples often learned from their teachers' behavior; children also imitated parents (see note on v. 14).
4:17 *Timothy, my son.* See note on v. 14. *my way of life.* See note on v. 16.
4:19 *if the Lord is willing.* Both Jews and Gentiles sometimes conditioned their plans with phrases such as, "If God wills ..."
4:21 *rod of discipline.* Paul continues the image of ancient fathers (see vv. 15–17), who often used a rod or stick for discipline. Corinthians, influenced by Roman values, would have appreciated gentle and indulgent fathers, but also understood that fathers placed duty first and could be stern.
5:1 *A man is sleeping with his father's wife.* Nearly all ancient Mediterranean cultures (as well as nearly all cultures in history) viewed parent-child incest as unimaginably terrible and divinely punishable. This offense included, as probably here, stepsons with stepmothers (Paul borrows language here from Lev 18:6–8). After divorce or becoming widowers, Greek and Roman men often married wives who were much younger (Greek men did this also at their first marriage), so the stepmother was sometimes closer in age to the eldest son than to the father. (In divorce, children normally went to the father.)
5:2 *you are proud!* Some suggest that the man was a high-status member in whom the congregation took pride; such a man would also have important social connections that could affect the church's standing in the community. *put out of your fellowship.* Cities usually allowed groups of resident aliens to discipline members according to their group's laws, provided they did not exceed Roman law. (Members could refuse the discipline by rejecting their group, but this could leave them socially isolated.) Thus local synagogues could administer various levels of discipline, including beatings (2Co 11:24); their harshest discipline was long-term expulsion from the Jewish community.
5:3,4 *with you in spirit.* Ancient letters used expressions such as this one to communicate intimacy; they were not intended as literal metaphysical presence (or normally even direct spiritual observation, as in 2Ki 5:26).
5:5 *hand this man over to Satan.* On exclusion from the community, see note on v. 2; some Jewish people understood such exclusion as exclusion also from the world to come, unless (as is Paul's hope here) it induced repentance and consequent restoration. *the day of the Lord.* See note on 1:8; cf., e.g., Eze 30:3; Am 5:18,20; Zec 14:1; Mal 4:5.
5:6 *yeast.* Fermented dough (leaven) pervades the dough, hence could apply figuratively to something (here, sin) that infects the whole. Acceptance of sin could contaminate and remove God's blessing from the whole community (Jos 7:5,12–13,25).
5:7 *a new unleavened batch ... our Passover lamb.* Passover commemorated God redeeming Israel from Egypt. When God struck the Egyptian firstborn to make Pharaoh release God's people, he passed over Israelite homes, where he saw the blood of the Passover lamb. The lamb was understood as a sacrifice (Ex 12:27); Jewish people expected a new redemption (cf. Mic 4:10; Zec 10:8). Passover introduced the Festival of Unleavened Bread, which commemorated how Israel left Egypt in haste, without time to leaven their bread.
5:10–11 Speakers and writers commonly listed vices. The lists varied in length; the longest ancient list known to us includes more than 100 vices.
5:11 *sexually immoral.* Most free Roman and especially Greek men had intercourse with slaves or others before

immoral or greedy, an idolater[x] or slanderer, a drunkard or swindler. Do not even eat
with such people.
12 What business is it of mine to judge
those outside[y] the church? Are you not to
judge those inside?[z] 13 God will judge those
outside. "Expel the wicked person from
among you."[a][a]

5:11 [x] 1Co 10:7, 14
5:12 [y] Mk 4:11 [z] ver 3-5; 1Co 6:1-4
5:13 [a] Dt 13:5
6:1 [b] Mt 18:17

Lawsuits Among Believers

6 If any of you has a dispute with another, do you dare to take it before
the ungodly for judgment instead of before the Lord's people?[b] 2 Or do you not
know that the Lord's people will judge the

[a] 13 Deut. 13:5; 17:7; 19:19; 21:21; 22:21,24; 24:7

marriage; Jewish tradition emphasized Gentile sexual immorality. *Do not even eat with such people.* As in Jewish communities, exclusion from the community (vv. 2–5) prohibited members from eating with the excluded person (v. 11).

5:12 *judge those outside the church.* Local groups of resident aliens in cities (such as Diaspora Jews) were normally expected to handle violations of their customs within their communities themselves, provided they did not break Roman laws in doing so (e.g., by executing someone).

5:13 *Expel the wicked person from among you.* For both sexual sins (Dt 22:21,24) and other major transgressions (Dt 13:5; 17:7; 19:19; 21:21; 24:7), Biblical law commanded expelling the wicked from the community by executing them. Romans did not permit subject peoples to execute transgressors, so Jewish people often commuted the punishment to banishment, as here.

6:1 *before the ungodly for judgment.* Roman urban society was rife with lawsuits; in some places court sessions ran from sunrise to sunset, with the numerous cases of poor petitioners each decided swiftly (sometimes in a minute). People of status more often gained a significant hearing, and judges, who came from the elite, favored members of their own social class. Magistrates sometimes assigned criminal cases such as treason, murder and adultery to juries rather than judges. Some people sued others just to inconvenience them; most disputes involved property. Wealthy and influential people sometimes helped arbitrate such cases privately.

6:2 *the Lord's people will judge the world.* Many Jewish people expected God's people to rule in the future era (e.g., Wisdom of Solomon 3:8).

1 CORINTHIANS 6:12–20

Prostitution and Sexual Immorality

A minority of philosophers argued that intercourse with prostitutes to relieve one's appetites was acceptable, so long as one was not "controlled" by it. At the other extreme, many philosophers reasoned that one should have intercourse only for procreation, not pleasure. The views of most people, however, fell between such extremes.

Greek abandonment of more female than male infants led to a shortage of women; Greek men thus often married at about age 30 to women some 12 years their junior. Until marriage, their primary access to intercourse was with prostitutes, slaves or other males. Free Roman men could have intercourse with social inferiors, though not with other respectable free persons (other than free prostitutes). By contrast, Scripture treated intercourse with another person's future spouse as seriously as adultery while married (Dt 22:13–29).

All ancient peoples agreed that adultery (sometimes called "wife-stealing") was immoral, although it was apparently widespread among the Roman elite. Roman law punished adultery, and it affected divorce settlements, though a wronged husband could kill the adulterous pair only if he caught them in the act. Roman law required that a man divorce his wife if he learned that she was committing adultery; one who failed to comply could be charged with "pimping" her, i.e., financially profiting from her behavior. Adultery involved sex with a married woman who was not a prostitute; Gentiles did not punish married men's affairs with unmarried women. By contrast, Paul would have rejected such double standards (cf. 1Co 7:2–5).

continued on next page

world?[c] And if you are to judge the world,
are you not competent to judge trivial cases? 3Do you not know that we will judge
angels? How much more the things of this
life! 4Therefore, if you have disputes about
such matters, do you ask for a ruling from
those whose way of life is scorned in the
church? 5I say this to shame you.[d] Is it
possible that there is nobody among you
wise enough to judge a dispute between
believers?[e] 6But instead, one brother takes
another to court — and this in front of unbelievers![f]
7The very fact that you have lawsuits
among you means you have been completely defeated already. Why not rather
be wronged? Why not rather be cheated?[g]
8Instead, you yourselves cheat and do
wrong, and you do this to your brothers
and sisters.[h] 9Or do you not know that

6:2 [c] Mt 19:28; Lk 22:30 **6:5** [d] 1Co 4:14 [e] Ac 1:15 **6:6** [f] 2Co 6:14, 15 **6:7** [g] Mt 5:39, 40 **6:8** [h] 1Th 4:6

6:6 *one brother takes another to court.* Minority groups within a city were permitted to (and supposed to) settle their own internal affairs. Prejudice against such minorities made more public cases even more damaging to their precarious reputation. Common as lawsuits were between brothers (often over inheritance issues), suing family members was deemed scandalous; Paul applies the same principle to spiritual brothers (his usual meaning for "brother").
6:7 *that you have lawsuits among you.* Many philosophers suggested that one should not sue anyone, since property did not matter. Paul presumably knows Jesus' instruction (Mt 5:39 – 40; Lk 6:29 – 30), but welcomes settling matters within the community of believers (see note on v. 6).
6:9 *wrongdoers will not inherit the kingdom of God.* Paul agrees with Jewish teaching, though this warning would not apply to those who had left such lifestyles. This future for "wrongdoers" contrasts with the promised reign of God's people in vv. 2 – 3. *Do not be deceived.* Ancient writers often warned against being deceived (cf. Mk 13:5). Both Jewish and Gentile writers often included vices in lists (see 5:10 – 11). Jewish people regarded most Gentiles as sexually immoral and based on Scripture also condemned the other sins in 6:9 – 10. *men who have sex with men.* Cf. Lev 20:13; see the article "Homosexual Activity in Antiquity," p. 1950.

Jewish teaching strongly opposed prostitution, although even some Jewish men hired prostitutes against their leaders' beliefs. Some Gentiles, however, even treated it as a deterrent from adultery. The Roman Empire taxed prostitution like any other profession; although prostitutes might be disreputable during their period of service, they were free to marry once they retired. Among Greeks, the most prestigious prostitutes were free women euphemistically titled "friends." Most prostitutes, however, were barmaids at taverns who served differently upstairs; sometimes pictures on the walls advertised them, their prices varying according to their beauty. Most of these prostitutes were slaves, many of them enslaved after being rescued from the trash heaps where some parents abandoned excess children. Then as today, the sex trade exploited many innocent victims. On the prevalence of and reputation for sexual immorality in Corinth in particular, see Introduction to 1 Corinthians: Corinth. ◆

One of the roughly carved stone beds in the Lupanar of Pompeii, the most famous brothel of the Roman city.

wrongdoers will not inherit the kingdom
of God?[i] Do not be deceived:[j] Neither the
sexually immoral nor idolaters nor adulterers nor men who have sex with men[a]
10nor thieves nor the greedy nor drunkards
nor slanderers nor swindlers will inherit
the kingdom of God. 11And that is what
some of you were.[k] But you were washed,[l]
you were sanctified,[m] you were justified in
the name of the Lord Jesus Christ and by
the Spirit of our God.

Sexual Immorality

12"I have the right to do anything," you
say — but not everything is beneficial.[n]
"I have the right to do anything" — but I
will not be mastered by anything. 13You
say, "Food for the stomach and the stomach for food, and God will destroy them
both."[o] The body, however, is not meant
for sexual immorality but for the Lord,
and the Lord for the body. 14By his power
God raised the Lord from the dead, and
he will raise us also.[p] 15Do you not know
that your bodies are members of Christ
himself?[q] Shall I then take the members
of Christ and unite them with a prostitute? Never! 16Do you not know that he
who unites himself with a prostitute is one
with her in body? For it is said, "The two
will become one flesh."[b][r] 17But whoever
is united with the Lord is one with him
in spirit.[c][s]
18Flee from sexual immorality.[t] All
other sins a person commits are outside the body, but whoever sins sexually, sins against their own body.[u] 19Do you
not know that your bodies are temples[v]
of the Holy Spirit, who is in you, whom
you have received from God? You are not
your own;[w] 20you were bought at a price.[x]
Therefore honor God with your bodies.

Concerning Married Life

7 Now for the matters you wrote about:
"It is good for a man not to have sexual relations with a woman."[y] 2But since
sexual immorality is occurring, each man
should have sexual relations with his own
wife, and each woman with her own husband. 3The husband should fulfill his marital duty to his wife,[z] and likewise the wife

6:9 [i] Gal 5:21 [j] 1Co 15:33; Jas 1:16 **6:11** [k] Eph 2:2 [l] Ac 22:16 [m] 1Co 1:2 **6:12** [n] 1Co 10:23 **6:13** [o] Col 2:22 **6:14** [p] Ro 6:5; Eph 1:19,20 **6:15** [q] Ro 12:5 **6:16** [r] Ge 2:24; Mt 19:5; Eph 5:31 **6:17** [s] Jn 17:21-23; Gal 2:20 **6:18** [t] 2Co 12:21; 1Th 4:3,4; Heb 13:4 [u] Ro 6:12 **6:19** [v] Jn 2:21 [w] Ro 14:7,8 **6:20** [x] Ac 20:28; 1Co 7:23; 1Pe 1:18,19; Rev 5:9 **7:1** [y] ver 8,26 **7:3** [z] Ex 21:10; 1Pe 3:7

[a] *9* The words *men who have sex with men* translate two Greek words that refer to the passive and active participants in homosexual acts. [b] *16* Gen. 2:24 [c] *17* Or *in the Spirit*

6:11 *what some of you were.* Because God had consecrated his people to himself, they were to live as holy (consecrated for God; Lev 20:26). Likewise, those transformed by Jesus and the Spirit needed to live accordingly.
6:12 Ancient writers and speakers often cited and then refuted the objections of imaginary interlocutors, as Paul very likely does here (countering alleged rights with what is beneficial); cf. notes on 1:12; 7:1. *right to do anything ... but not everything is beneficial.* Both courts and philosophers reasoned whether actions were permitted and beneficial. *will not be mastered.* Philosophers often warned against being enslaved or controlled by any desire.
6:13 *Food for the stomach.* Ancient moral thinkers commonly depicted pleasures as "the belly" (cf. Ro 16:18; Php 3:19). The imaginary interlocutor here implies that the body is designed for intercourse. Because Greeks viewed the body as temporary (for many, in contrast to the immortal soul), the interlocutor also may object that what one does with the body does not matter.
6:14 *he will raise us also.* Paul appeals to the body's future resurrection, a point he develops in detail in 1Co 15. Those who believed in future judgment often charged that teaching's detractors with greater susceptibility to immorality.
6:15 – 17 Paul appeals not only to Scripture but to the good news that saved them. Because they belong to Christ's body (cf. 12:12 – 13), sleeping with prostitutes was like desecrating Christ's body as well as one's own. Prostitution was common (see the article "Prostitution and Sexual Immorality," p. 1990), and Corinth had a particular and long-standing reputation for it.
6:17 *one with him in spirit.* Ge 2:24 (cited in v. 16) applied to marriage, but Paul applies the principle to all intercourse. Yet Scripture taught that God was married to his people (Isa 54:5 – 6; Hos 2:20), a principle Paul applies to believers' unity with Christ in one body.
6:18 *Flee.* Writers on moral topics frequently urged their hearers to flee vices (cf. 10:14), including sexual ones. *All other sins a person commits are outside the body.* Some attribute this line (the word "other" does not appear here in Greek) to the interlocutor, whom Paul refutes by showing that sexual sin dishonors one's own body.
6:19 *bodies are temples of the Holy Spirit.* Some Jewish people depicted God's people as a spiritual temple (see note on 3:17), an image Paul applies here also to individual believers. Some ancient shrines reportedly practiced sacred prostitution; in old Corinth, prostitutes were reputed to be dedicated to Aphrodite, their patron goddess.
6:20 *bought at a price.* In the OT, God redeemed, or bought, his people (Ex 15:16; Ps 74:2); believers were bought by Christ (1Co 7:23; cf. 5:7). ("Redemption," as in 1:30, means freeing a slave, sometimes by paying ransom.) This price of infinite worth contrasts starkly with the demeaning price paid to hire a prostitute. *honor God with your bodies.* The Greek term for "price" here can also mean "honor," perhaps leading to the play on honoring God with your bodies, though this phrase uses a different verb (cf. 1Th 4:4).
7:1 *Now for.* Sometimes used by ancient writers, as here, to transition to a new subject (the same Greek phrase appears in 7:25; 8:1; 16:1,12; 1Th 4:9; 5:1, where the NIV usually translates "now about"). *It is good for a man not to have sexual relations with a woman.* Many scholars believe that this is a quotation from (or paraphrase of) the Corinthian believers' letter to Paul (cf. 6:12 – 13). To the married, Paul then responds in vv. 2 – 7: avoiding intercourse is not good with one's spouse (cf. Ge 2:18).
7:2 *have sexual relations with.* The NIV correctly interprets a more euphemistic Greek phrase that normally had this meaning. Jewish teachers and even some Gentiles viewed marital intercourse as the best deterrent to extramarital sexual relations (cf. Pr 5:19 – 20).
7:3 *marital duty.* Marriage contracts often stipulated duties; Judean marriage contracts required husbands to grant their wives intercourse. Strong advocates of marital intercourse, rabbis debated whether the maximum period a husband

1 CORINTHIANS 7:1

Celibacy in Antiquity

A small number of Greek sages, mostly Cynics, rejected marriage as a distraction but permitted intercourse with prostitutes as a way of relieving one's passions. The one early Cynic known to have married was Crates, when Hipparchia persuaded him that she could share the radical, homeless Cynic lifestyle. Most philosophers, however, defended marriage as valuable for procreation and childrearing, and thus good for society. Stoics held this view, although they discouraged passion and relegated the purpose of intercourse solely to procreation.

Two small Jewish sects apparently rejected marriage for themselves, and, following Biblical moral teaching, therefore demanded celibacy. There is good reason to believe that Essenes, many of whom lived in the wilderness, were celibate, and the same is said for a more obscure group called Therapeutae.

Most people in antiquity, however, valued marriage as important for society. Concerned about population decline among respectable classes, the emperor Augustus even offered tax incentives for virgins, widows and divorcées of childbearing age to marry quickly and bear children.

Later rabbis, probably reflecting wider Judean opinion, viewed "Be fruitful and increase" (Ge 1:28) as a divine command. Rabbis insisted that men who failed to marry by age 20 were breaking this command; they also generally viewed marriage as a release from the distraction of one's passions (cf. 1Co 7:9). An occasional rabbi protested that love of the Torah so consumed him that marriage would distract him (perhaps closer to Paul's practice, 1Co 7:7), but this was a marginal view. It appears that John the Baptist, Jesus and Paul, like Jeremiah of old, were unmarried, but such a status was exceptional.

Although most people recognized the value of marriage and childbearing for society, lifestyles varied; e.g., divorces and multiple remarriages were extremely common in Roman society. Greeks often abandoned infants when the father deemed that the family could not care for another child; although some of these babies were adopted by others as slaves, others were eaten by vultures and dogs on the trash heaps where they lay. Jews and Egyptians, by contrast, condemned this practice, and Egyptians sometimes rescued abandoned infants. Romans unfortunately taxed more heavily such babies adopted as children than those reared as slaves. Greeks and Romans debated abortion; Jews, the Hippocratic medical tradition and a number of Greco-Roman moral writers condemned it as taking life, but other thinkers defended and/or practiced it. Very early Christian writers, following Jewish values, condemned child abandonment, infanticide and abortion (e.g., *Didache* 2.2; Gospel of Barnabas 19.5). ◆

to her husband. 4The wife does not have
authority over her own body but yields
it to her husband. In the same way, the
husband does not have authority over his
own body but yields it to his wife. 5Do
not deprive each other except perhaps by
mutual consent and for a time,[a] so that
you may devote yourselves to prayer.

7:5 [a] Ex 19:15; 1Sa 21:4,5

could deprive his wife was one week or two (apart from exceptions such as the husband being on a voyage, away to study Torah, and so forth). Paul does not specify a period here, but he clearly advocates marital relations.
7:4 *authority over her own body.* Philosophers sometimes depicted intercourse as submitting to another's power (cf. 6:12); most people were not philosophers, but Romans in general thought of a dominant (masculine) and submissive partner in intercourse. *In the same way.* Many Gentiles expected only the wife to be faithful. Paul's application to both genders here is important.
7:5 *Do not deprive each other.* Like his fellow Judean teachers, Paul urges married couples not to abstain for long periods (see note on v. 3). *tempt.* See notes on vv. 2,9.

Then come together again so that Satan[b]
will not tempt you[c] because of your lack
of self-control. 6I say this as a concession,
not as a command.[d] 7I wish that all of you
were as I am.[e] But each of you has your
own gift from God; one has this gift, another has that.[f]

8Now to the unmarried[a] and the widows
I say: It is good for them to stay unmarried, as I do.[g] 9But if they cannot control
themselves, they should marry,[h] for it is
better to marry than to burn with passion.

10To the married I give this command
(not I, but the Lord): A wife must not separate from her husband.[i] 11But if she does,
she must remain unmarried or else be reconciled to her husband. And a husband
must not divorce his wife.

12To the rest I say this (I, not the Lord):[j]
If any brother has a wife who is not a believer and she is willing to live with him,
he must not divorce her. 13And if a woman has a husband who is not a believer
and he is willing to live with her, she must
not divorce him. 14For the unbelieving
husband has been sanctified through his
wife, and the unbelieving wife has been
sanctified through her believing husband.

7:5 [b] Mt 4:10 [c] 1Th 3:5 **7:6** [d] 2Co 8:8 **7:7** [e] ver 8; 1Co 9:5 [f] Mt 19:11, 12; Ro 12:6; 1Co 12:4, 11 **7:8** [g] ver 1, 26 **7:9** [h] 1Ti 5:14 **7:10** [i] Mal 2:14-16; Mt 5:32; 19:3-9; Mk 10:11; Lk 16:18 **7:12** [j] ver 6, 10; 2Co 11:17

7:14 [k] Mal 2:15 **7:15** [l] Ro 14:19; 1Co 14:33 **7:16** [m] Ro 11:14 [n] 1Pe 3:1 **7:17** [o] Ro 12:3 [p] 1Co 4:17; 14:33; 2Co 8:18; 11:28 **7:18** [q] Ac 15:1, 2 **7:19** [r] Ro 2:25-27; Gal 5:6; 6:15; Col 3:11 **7:20** [s] ver 24

Otherwise your children would be unclean, but as it is, they are holy.[k]

15But if the unbeliever leaves, let it be
so. The brother or the sister is not bound
in such circumstances; God has called us
to live in peace.[l] 16How do you know, wife,
whether you will save[m] your husband?[n]
Or, how do you know, husband, whether
you will save your wife?

Concerning Change of Status

17Nevertheless, each person should live
as a believer in whatever situation the
Lord has assigned to them, just as God
has called them.[o] This is the rule I lay
down in all the churches.[p] 18Was a man
already circumcised when he was called?
He should not become uncircumcised.
Was a man uncircumcised when he was
called? He should not be circumcised.[q]
19Circumcision is nothing and uncircumcision is nothing.[r] Keeping God's commands
is what counts. 20Each person should remain in the situation they were in when
God called them.[s]

21Were you a slave when you were
called? Don't let it trouble you — although

[a] 8 Or *widowers*

7:6 *as a concession.* Jewish law permitted concessions for human weakness; Paul allowing some abstaining in v. 5 ("perhaps by mutual consent") is merely his concession to their wishes (see note on v. 1).

7:9 *better ... than to burn with passion.* Greek sources frequently speak of passion as a wounding or burning fire; whereas Greek romances celebrate such craving, Paul wants believers free from this distraction.

7:10 *A wife must not separate from her husband.* Paul cites Jesus' teaching against divorce (see Mk 10:11 – 12 and notes).

7:11 *a husband must not divorce his wife.* Apart from wealthy households, only men could normally initiate divorce in Judean culture (though if the man were abusive or very negligent, a woman could petition elders to compel her husband to grant a divorce). Greek and Roman practice, relevant for Corinthian society, was very different: remaining married required mutual consent, so either party could divorce the other with little notice. Financial arrangements and relationships between families deterred simply divorcing because of, say, an argument. Nevertheless, divorce was widespread in Corinth, as in many other cities; many believers were likely already remarried before their conversion.

7:12 – 13 Paul must address a situation not specifically envisioned in Jesus' general principle (see vv. 10 – 11 and notes). Many Corinthian Christians were already married to nonbelieving spouses when converted; divorce practice in Corinth allowed either party to unilaterally end the marriage. Paul, however, rejects spiritual incompatibility as grounds for divorce.

7:14 *your children ... are holy.* Roman laws addressed the status of children in marriages between classes or between Roman citizens and provincials; Jewish laws addressed whether the offspring of Jewish-Gentile unions were Jewish; and so forth. In ancient divorces, custody of the children normally went to the father.

7:15 *But if the unbeliever leaves, let it be so.* Paul qualifies here Jesus' general principle (see vv. 10 – 11 and notes), which was not designed as a law covering all situations. In Greek and Roman marriages, either party could dissolve the marriage unilaterally by leaving it. *not bound.* What happens when the marriage is dissolved against the believer's will? In divorce contexts, the meaning of "not bound" is clear; this was the precise language in Jewish divorce contracts for freedom to remarry.

7:17 *live ... in whatever situation the Lord has assigned.* Greek philosophers, especially Stoics, emphasized accepting one's situation (although one was welcome to change it if possible and if the change was beneficial, vv. 21 – 24). But whereas Stoics identified the god who directed their lives with Fate, Paul trusts God as a loving Father.

7:18 *become uncircumcised.* Greeks exercised naked, and when Greek culture invaded Judea two centuries earlier, adherents of its "progressive" culture ridiculed Jews for circumcision. Some Jews therefore submitted to an operation to pull the remains of their foreskin forward and make them appear uncircumcised. Other Jews regarded this procedure as an act of apostasy.

7:21 *if you can gain your freedom, do so.* Even full-scale wars to free slaves had failed, and the small minority of thinkers who rejected slavery in principle lacked means to change the institution. Urban household slaves, the sort addressed here, could face significant hardships, but at other times wielded significant influence and power. In a few cases, slaves of powerful aristocrats wielded more power than some other free aristocrats (see Introduction to Philemon: Situation). Nevertheless, freedom was the better option when possible; slaves who earned money could purchase their freedom. In many other cases, slaveholders freed them to reward their service — or because they did not want to provide for them in their old age.

if you can gain your freedom, do so. 22For
the one who was a slave when called to
faith in the Lord is the Lord's freed person;[t] similarly, the one who was free when
called is Christ's slave.[u] 23You were bought
at a price;[v] do not become slaves of human beings. 24Brothers and sisters, each
person, as responsible to God, should remain in the situation they were in when
God called them.[w]

Concerning the Unmarried

25Now about virgins: I have no command
from the Lord,[x] but I give a judgment as
one who by the Lord's mercy[y] is trustworthy. 26Because of the present crisis, I think
that it is good for a man to remain as he is.[z]
27Are you pledged to a woman? Do not seek
to be released. Are you free from such a
commitment? Do not look for a wife. 28But
if you do marry, you have not sinned; and
if a virgin marries, she has not sinned. But
those who marry will face many troubles in
this life, and I want to spare you this.

29What I mean, brothers and sisters, is
that the time is short.[a] From now on those
who have wives should live as if they do
not; 30those who mourn, as if they did not;
those who are happy, as if they were not;
those who buy something, as if it were not
theirs to keep; 31those who use the things
of the world, as if not engrossed in them.
For this world in its present form is passing away.[b]

32I would like you to be free from concern. An unmarried man is concerned
about the Lord's affairs[c] — how he can
please the Lord. 33But a married man
is concerned about the affairs of this
world — how he can please his wife —
34and his interests are divided. An unmarried woman or virgin is concerned about
the Lord's affairs: Her aim is to be devoted
to the Lord in both body and spirit.[d] But
a married woman is concerned about the
affairs of this world — how she can please
her husband. 35I am saying this for your
own good, not to restrict you, but that you
may live in a right way in undivided[e] devotion to the Lord.

36If anyone is worried that he might not
be acting honorably toward the virgin he
is engaged to, and if his passions are too
strong*[a]* and he feels he ought to marry,
he should do as he wants. He is not sinning.[f] They should get married. 37But the
man who has settled the matter in his own
mind, who is under no compulsion but
has control over his own will, and who
has made up his mind not to marry the
virgin — this man also does the right thing.
38So then, he who marries the virgin does
right,[g] but he who does not marry her
does better.*[b]*

7:22 [t] Jn 8:32, 36; Phm 16 [u] Eph 6:6 **7:23** [v] 1Co 6:20 **7:24** [w] ver 20 **7:25** [x] ver 6; 2Co 8:8 [y] 2Co 4:1; 1Ti 1:13, 16 **7:26** [z] ver 1, 8 **7:29** [a] ver 31; Ro 13:11, 12 **7:31** [b] 1Jn 2:17 **7:32** [c] 1Ti 5:5 **7:34** [d] Lk 2:37 **7:35** [e] Ps 86:11 **7:36** [f] ver 28 **7:38** [g] Heb 13:4

a 36 Or *if she is getting beyond the usual age for marriage* *b* 36-38 Or *36If anyone thinks he is not treating his daughter properly, and if she is getting along in years* (or *if her passions are too strong*), *and he feels she ought to marry, he should do as he wants. He is not sinning. He should let her get married. 37But the man who has settled the matter in his own mind, who is under no compulsion but has control over his own will, and who has made up his mind to keep the virgin unmarried — this man also does the right thing. 38So then, he who gives his virgin in marriage does right, but he who does not give her in marriage does better.*

7:22 *the Lord's freed person.* Under Roman law, a freed slave continued to belong to his or her former holder's extended household and to have some obligations to honor the former holder. Likewise, the former holder was obligated to help the freed person with connections and money; much to the chagrin of some aristocrats, some enterprising freedmen achieved greater wealth than hereditary aristocrats. Many of Corinth's residents were Roman citizens, and slaves they freed normally became Roman citizens themselves. Many of Corinth's residents descended from freed persons.
7:26 *good for a man to remain as he is.* During times of intense hardship (see vv. 29 – 31), including the expected period just before the end, marrying and having children could just make matters more difficult (cf. note on Mk 13:17).
7:27 *pledged . . . free.* The NIV translation of Greek terms here as "pledged" and "free" might make sense if Paul addresses fiancés of virgins (Paul mentions "virgins" in v. 28; see note on v. 36). More likely, Paul simply mentions groups he has already discussed in vv. 12 – 16 (see note there), and adds "virgins" in v. 28 just by way of comparison. The term that the NIV translates as "pledged" here usually means "married"; the term it translates as "a woman" often means "wife," which is how the NIV translates it later in the same verse. The term first translated "released" and then translated "free from such a commitment" later in this verse is literally "freed," hence would normally mean "divorced" (the term could also mean "widowed," but that sense does not fit its first use in this verse). This verse therefore probably addresses marriage and divorce, along with divorce and remarriage, although qualifying the statement in v. 28, presumably at least for the sorts of situations noted in 7:15.
7:29 – 31 These verses describe a time period just before the end times. See note on v. 26.
7:32 – 34 Cynic sages feared that marriage would distract them from the freedom of the Cynic lifestyle, which included no possessions and no responsibilities. Paul acknowledges that family responsibilities can distract from pure focus on the kingdom, although he has also acknowledged that some will be more distracted without marriage (v. 9) and later notes that most apostles were married (9:5).
7:36 – 38 Mothers and especially fathers, normally consulting with their children, arranged their children's marriages. Some scholars believe that Paul addresses virgins' fathers here, translating accordingly (e.g., NASB); although the matter remains debated, the NIV follows the more common interpretation, that Paul addresses virgins' fiancés. Betrothal involved an official agreement between families; breaking betrothals was therefore an official act. Jewish men often married around age 20 and usually married women just a few years younger; Greek men often married around age 30 and married women about 12 years their junior; the ages in Roman marriage generally fell between these ages.

39A woman is bound to her husband as
long as he lives.[h] But if her husband dies,
she is free to marry anyone she wishes,
but he must belong to the Lord.[i] 40In my
judgment,[j] she is happier if she stays as
she is — and I think that I too have the
Spirit of God.

Concerning Food Sacrificed to Idols

8 Now about food sacrificed to idols:[k]
We know that "We all possess knowledge."[l] But knowledge puffs up while love
builds up. 2Those who think they know
something[m] do not yet know as they
ought to know.[n] 3But whoever loves God
is known by God.[a][o]
4So then, about eating food sacrificed to
idols:[p] We know that "An idol is nothing
at all in the world"[q] and that "There is
no God but one."[r] 5For even if there are
so-called gods,[s] whether in heaven or on
earth (as indeed there are many "gods"
and many "lords"), 6yet for us there is
but one God, the Father,[t] from whom
all things came[u] and for whom we live;
and there is but one Lord,[v] Jesus Christ,
through whom all things came[w] and
through whom we live.
7But not everyone possesses this
knowledge. Some people are still so accustomed to idols that when they eat
sacrificial food they think of it as having
been sacrificed to a god, and since their
conscience is weak,[x] it is defiled. 8But
food does not bring us near to God;[y] we
are no worse if we do not eat, and no
better if we do.
9Be careful, however, that the exercise
of your rights does not become a stumbling block[z] to the weak.[a] 10For if someone
with a weak conscience sees you, with all
your knowledge, eating in an idol's temple, won't that person be emboldened to
eat what is sacrificed to idols? 11So this
weak brother or sister, for whom Christ
died, is destroyed[b] by your knowledge.
12When you sin against them[c] in this way
and wound their weak conscience, you sin
against Christ. 13Therefore, if what I eat
causes my brother or sister to fall into sin,
I will never eat meat again, so that I will
not cause them to fall.[d]

Paul's Rights as an Apostle

9 Am I not free? Am I not an apostle?[e]
Have I not seen Jesus our Lord?[f] Are
you not the result of my work in the Lord?[g]
2Even though I may not be an apostle to
others, surely I am to you! For you are the
seal[h] of my apostleship in the Lord.
3This is my defense to those who sit

7:39 [h] Ro 7:2,3 [i] 2Co 6:14 **7:40** [j] ver 25 **8:1** [k] Ac 15:20 [l] Ro 15:14 **8:2** [m] 1Co 3:18 [n] 1Co 13:8,9,12; 1Ti 6:4 **8:3** [o] Ro 8:29; Gal 4:9 **8:4** [p] ver 1,7,10 [q] 1Co 10:19 [r] Dt 6:4; Eph 4:6 **8:5** [s] 2Th 2:4 **8:6** [t] Mal 2:10 [u] Ro 11:36 [v] Eph 4:5 [w] Jn 1:3 **8:7** [x] Ro 14:14; 1Co 10:28 **8:8** [y] Ro 14:17 **8:9** [z] Gal 5:13 [a] Ro 14:1 **8:11** [b] Ro 14:15,20 **8:12** [c] Mt 18:6 **8:13** [d] Ro 14:21 **9:1** [e] 2Co 12:12 [f] 1Co 15:8 [g] 1Co 3:6; 4:15 **9:2** [h] 2Co 3:2,3

[a] *2,3* An early manuscript and another ancient witness *think they have knowledge do not yet know as they ought to know. 3But whoever loves truly knows.*

7:39 *if her husband dies, she is free to marry.* One traditional romantic ideal in antiquity was the widow who never remarried (cf. Lk 2:36–37), but Augustus's tax policy had encouraged younger Roman widows to remarry, and remarriage after a spouse's death was common (cf. 1Ti 5:14).
7:40 *I too have the Spirit of God.* Ancient Jewish circles often associated the Spirit with prophetic inspiration.
8:1 *We all possess knowledge.* Some Corinthian believers may have been making the claim that there is just one God (v. 4), so they can eat sacrificial meat (v. 7). On Paul recounting their views, see notes on 6:12,13; 7:1.
8:4 Idols, or deity statues, were in fact worthless (Isa 44:9–20; 46:5–7), and there is only one God (Isa 45:5–6,18,21–22; 46:9). Unfortunately, some were using this truth to justify eating sacrificial food (v. 7).
8:5 *many "gods" and many "lords."* Like other Gentile cities, Corinth was full of deities. Among the most highly honored deities in mercantile Corinth were Poseidon/Neptune, god of the sea; Aphrodite/Venus, goddess of sexuality; and the emperor.
8:6 *but one God.* Many philosophers spoke similarly of one supreme God over the other deities, as many Diaspora Jews were happy to remind them. The cornerstone of Jewish faith was the confession that there was one God and Lord (Dt 6:4); Paul adapts the wording to apply to both the Father and Jesus. Jewish tradition affirmed that God used personified Wisdom to design and form creation, a role here applied to Jesus (cf. 1Co 1:30). *from … for … through.* Using different prepositions, ancient intellectuals often distinguished kinds of causes, including material ("from"), instrumental ("through"), modal ("in" or "by") and purpose ("for").
8:9 Although Paul's general point is clear, the specific background here is debated. *exercise of your rights.* Some argue that "rights" indicates their citizen rights to eat at festivals. It might simply refer, however, to the authorization to eat sacrificial food being claimed by the "strong." *become a stumbling block to the weak.* Some regard "the weak" as those with less social power, who cannot afford food except at festivals and therefore associate all meat consumption with idols. Paul might simply refer, however, to their weaker conscience, perhaps defined as weaker by the "strong" (vv. 7,10,12; 10:28–29). Philosophers often claimed that "all things" belonged to them (cf. notes on 3:21; 4:8); many despised human opinion, and some despised human custom. Jewish teachers, however, generally warned about doing what could set a bad example for those who misunderstood. For them, nothing was worse than causing another to stumble, i.e., to fall from the right way and be excluded from the world to come.
8:10 *eating in an idol's temple … what is sacrificed.* Although the sacrificial status of food offered in the market was not always clear, food available in the temple had clearly been sacrificed.
9:1 *Am I not free?* Philosophers valued being "free" (cf. v. 19; 10:29) — free from concern about others' opinions of them, free from false ideas and also often free from property concerns and thus being self-sufficient. Freedom was frequently associated with rights (cf. 8:9); thus Paul, who invites the Corinthian believers to sacrifice some of their rights, offers an example of surrendering his own (vv. 4–6,12,18).
9:2 *seal.* Imprints made by signet rings in hot wax could attest or authenticate a document; by extension, a seal could thus mean an authentication.
9:3 *my defense.* Although digressing in ch. 9 to offer himself as an example (as sages sometimes did), Paul

1 CORINTHIANS 8:1 – 13

SACRIFICED FOOD

People in antiquity sacrificed many animals to the gods, but they made it do double duty: after they cooked it in sacrifice, they ate most of it. Most people were poor; they could not afford large animals for sacrifice and probably did not buy much meat. During festivals, however, when many animals were sacrificed, meat was so abundant that it had to be shared with the community before it spoiled.

If one ate in a temple dining hall, one would be certain that the meat one was eating had first been sacrificed. If one purchased meat in the market or ate meat at the home of a friend who lacked scruples about such matters, one could not be sure what had happened to the meat beforehand. Indeed, even normal banquets opened with the pouring of a fluid libation to some god or goddess (just as Jews and Christians gave thanks for their food), so that most meals in Gentile settings were somehow consecrated to a deity.

Food consecrated to other gods had long been a problem for urban Jews in the Diaspora. In cities where many Jews settled, they had their own markets. Judean sages debated what to do in many cases of uncertainty (such as untithed food), but would never have taken a chance on food that might have been offered to an idol. They believed that Jews outside Palestine unwittingly compromised with idolatry when invited to pagans' banquets for their sons, even if they brought their own food. Following such teachings strictly (as some did) would have greatly circumscribed Gentile believers' relationships with pagan colleagues. This issue was an even greater problem for Christians converted from pagan backgrounds: could they meet over lunch with business associates or fellow members of their trade guild, or attend a reception in a temple for a relative's wedding?

Like Jesus in Rev 2:14,20, Paul opposed known sacrificial food on spiritual grounds (1Co 10:1 – 22). Nevertheless, he frames that argument with another one, based on loving fellow believers (1Co 8:1 — 9:27; 10:23 – 33). Poorer believers might rarely have meat except at the pagan festivals; they would have to give up a cherished right, but in 1Co 9 Paul uses his own example to illustrate the principle of surrendering rights. Some wealthier members faced even greater challenges, for they would be served meat at the banquets of their pagan peers. The church's more liberal voices apparently considered themselves "strong" and their more conservative fellow believers "weak." This issue, however, was a fundamental one (1Co 10:20). ◆

in judgment on me. [4]Don't we have the right to food and drink?[i] [5]Don't we have the right to take a believing wife[j] along with us, as do the other apostles and the Lord's brothers[k] and Cephas[a]?

9:4 [i] 1Th 2:6
9:5 [j] 1Co 7:7,8 [k] Mt 12:46

[a] 5 That is, Peter

also offers something of a defense. Defense (and some other) speeches often drove home a point with a series of rhetorical questions (vv. 4 – 8,12 – 13). More elite members may have found Paul's artisan work (4:12) an embarrassment among peers of their own status: in their setting, more respectable sages depended on patrons or tuition. For the elite, manual labor was for those not worthy of support. Probably sometime after this letter, rival teachers play on this concern about Paul (2Co 12:13 – 18).

9:5 *right to take a believing wife along with us.* Most people in antiquity married and took this expectation for granted (see the article "Celibacy in Antiquity," p. 1993). Cynics and other wandering sages, in contrast to stationary teachers, normally could not marry; this was presumably also the case for John the Baptist, Jesus, and earlier, Jeremiah (Jer 16:2). Even disciples who left home to study Torah might be away from their wives for weeks or more at a time. Given the size of Galilee, Jesus' disciples were probably rarely more than two or three days' distance from their families, but those who were married (such as Peter; Mk 1:30) did not bring their wives at that time. (Most men did not marry before 18, and disciples were

6 Or is it only I and Barnabas[l] who lack the
right to not work for a living?
7 Who serves as a soldier at his own expense? Who plants a vineyard[m] and does
not eat its grapes? Who tends a flock and
does not drink the milk? 8 Do I say this
merely on human authority? Doesn't the
Law say the same thing? 9 For it is written in the Law of Moses: "Do not muzzle
an ox while it is treading out the grain."[a][n]
Is it about oxen that God is concerned?[o]
10 Surely he says this for us, doesn't he?
Yes, this was written for us,[p] because
whoever plows and threshes should be
able to do so in the hope of sharing in the
harvest.[q] 11 If we have sown spiritual seed
among you, is it too much if we reap a material harvest from you?[r] 12 If others have
this right of support from you, shouldn't
we have it all the more?

But we did not use this right.[s] On the
contrary, we put up with anything rather
than hinder[t] the gospel of Christ.

13 Don't you know that those who
serve in the temple get their food from
the temple, and that those who serve at
the altar share in what is offered on the
altar?[u] 14 In the same way, the Lord has
commanded that those who preach the
gospel should receive their living from
the gospel.[v]
15 But I have not used any of these
rights.[w] And I am not writing this in the
hope that you will do such things for me,
for I would rather die than allow anyone
to deprive me of this boast.[x] 16 For when
I preach the gospel, I cannot boast, since
I am compelled to preach.[y] Woe to me if
I do not preach the gospel! 17 If I preach
voluntarily, I have a reward;[z] if not voluntarily, I am simply discharging the trust
committed to me.[a] 18 What then is my reward? Just this: that in preaching the gospel I may offer it free of charge,[b] and so
not make full use of my rights as a preacher of the gospel.

Paul's Use of His Freedom

19 Though I am free[c] and belong to no
one, I have made myself a slave to everyone,[d] to win as many as possible.[e] 20 To the
Jews I became like a Jew, to win the Jews.[f]
To those under the law I became like one
under the law (though I myself am not under the law), so as to win those under the
law. 21 To those not having the law I became like one not having the law[g] (though

9:6 [l] Ac 4:36
9:7 [m] Dt 20:6; Pr 27:18
9:9 [n] Dt 25:4; 1Ti 5:18 [o] Dt 22:1-4
9:10 [p] Ro 4:23, 24 [q] 2Ti 2:6
9:11 [r] Ro 15:27
9:12 [s] Ac 18:3 [t] 2Co 11:7-12
9:13 [u] Lev 6:16, 26; Dt 18:1
9:14 [v] Mt 10:10; 1Ti 5:18
9:15 [w] Ac 18:3 [x] 2Co 11:9, 10
9:16 [y] Ro 1:14; Ac 9:15
9:17 [z] 1Co 3:8, 14 [a] Gal 2:7; Col 1:25
9:18 [b] 2Co 11:7; 12:13
9:19 [c] ver 1 [d] Gal 5:13 [e] Mt 18:15; 1Pe 3:1
9:20 [f] Ac 16:3; 21:20-26; Ro 11:14
9:21 [g] Ro 2:12, 14

[a] 9 Deut. 25:4

typically younger than that.) Whether because children were grown or because distances were greater, however, most apostles by the time that Paul writes were married and traveled with their wives.

9:6 *right to not work.* Among Gentiles, the most respectable means of support for sages were dependence on a wealthy patron or charging tuition. Elites despised manual labor, though artisans did not feel the same way. Most people looked down on the other common means of support — begging — but Cynics took pride in how this practice disdained human honor. Many Jewish sages did respect manual labor.

9:7 *soldier at his own expense.* Many common soldiers working for Rome earned about three drachmas a day (far more for centurions; legionaries earned more than auxiliaries); three drachmas amounts to more than three denarii, hence roughly three days wages for an average worker in much of the Roman Empire in this period. Retirement benefits were significant for those who survived the full 20 years of service. *plants ... and does not eat.* Tenant farmers paid landowners a share of the crops but normally retained a significant amount for their own use. *tends a flock and does not drink.* Urban residents had more access to cheese than milk, but sheep and goat milk were more common in the countryside.

9:9 *Do not muzzle an ox while it is treading.* Jewish interpreters often recognized Biblical injunctions regarding kindness toward animals (as in Dt 25:4) as instilling kindness that should also be applied even more fully toward people.

9:11 See note on v. 7.

9:12 *we did not use this right.* In antiquity, many people mistrusted traveling sages as seeking others' money; Cynics even begged on the streets. Other sages worked to counter the stereotype that sages were greedy. If Paul depended on the support of wealthy Corinthian Christians, he could be viewed as their client (see note on v. 6). Patrons expected such dependent sages to please them, but Paul maintains his independence — his "freedom" (see vv. 1,19) — so he can preach truth. *rather than hinder the gospel.* Philosophers often claimed to be unconcerned with others' opinions of them, but some did seek to avoid offending others needlessly; Paul labors to avoid being classified with stereotypical greedy sages.

9:13 *food from the temple.* Priests in most ancient temples (including Israel's, Lev 6:25 – 26,29; 7:5 – 6; Eze 42:13) had the right to eat assigned portions of the sacrificial food (see also the article "Sacrificed Food," p. 1997).

9:14 *the Lord has commanded.* Paul alludes to the Lord's command later recorded in Mt 10:10; Lk 10:7 (cf. 1Ti 5:18).

9:15 *I have not used any of these rights.* Philosophers emphasized being free from concern and free from depending on others; some also appealed to their financial independence to distinguish themselves from greedy charlatans. *I would rather die.* A common verbal contrast with a terrible situation, for both Jews and Gentiles.

9:16 *I am compelled to preach.* Stoics, the most popular philosophic sect in this period, believed that one could not evade Fate, so one should embrace it. More relevant for the personal God of the Bible: God's call was not optional (cf. Ex 4:13 – 14). *Woe to me.* Those lamenting over a situation, both Jews and Gentiles, often cried in this way.

9:19 *I am free.* See notes on vv. 1,12,15. *made myself a slave to everyone.* Rhetoricians recommended adaptation for various audiences; some of the more moderate Pharisees also were ready to accommodate their hearers to bring them to love the Torah. By contrast, many aristocrats despised those who were too flexible as fickle demagogues who tried to please the masses; they sometimes dismissed such demagogues as "slaves." Still, some valued being "slaves" or "pleasing" others if it maintained public order. Paul here serves an even greater purpose.

I am not free from God's law but am under
Christ's law), so as to win those not having the law. 22To the weak I became weak,
to win the weak. I have become all things
to all people[h] so that by all possible means
I might save some.[i] 23I do all this for the
sake of the gospel, that I may share in its
blessings.

The Need for Self-Discipline

24Do you not know that in a race all the
runners run, but only one gets the prize?
Run[j] in such a way as to get the prize.
25Everyone who competes in the games
goes into strict training. They do it to get a
crown that will not last, but we do it to get
a crown that will last forever.[k] 26Therefore
I do not run like someone running aimlessly; I do not fight like a boxer beating
the air. 27No, I strike a blow to my body[l]
and make it my slave so that after I have
preached to others, I myself will not be
disqualified for the prize.

Warnings From Israel's History

10 For I do not want you to be ignorant of the fact, brothers and sisters, that our ancestors were all under the
cloud[m] and that they all passed through
the sea.[n] 2They were all baptized into Moses in the cloud and in the sea. 3They all
ate the same spiritual food 4and drank the
same spiritual drink; for they drank from
the spiritual rock[o] that accompanied them,
and that rock was Christ. 5Nevertheless,
God was not pleased with most of them;
their bodies were scattered in the wilderness.[p]
6Now these things occurred as examples to keep us from setting our hearts
on evil things as they did. 7Do not be
idolaters,[q] as some of them were; as it is
written: "The people sat down to eat and
drink and got up to indulge in revelry."[a][r]
8We should not commit sexual immorality, as some of them did — and in one day
twenty-three thousand of them died.[s] 9We
should not test Christ,[b] as some of them
did — and were killed by snakes.[t] 10And do
not grumble, as some of them did[u] — and
were killed[v] by the destroying angel.[w]
11These things happened to them as examples and were written down as warnings for us, on whom the culmination of
the ages has come.[x] 12So, if you think you
are standing firm,[y] be careful that you
don't fall! 13No temptation[c] has overtaken
you except what is common to mankind.
And God is faithful;[z] he will not let you be
tempted[c] beyond what you can bear.[a] But
when you are tempted,[c] he will also provide a way out so that you can endure it.

Idol Feasts and the Lord's Supper

14Therefore, my dear friends, flee from
idolatry. 15I speak to sensible people; judge

9:22 [h] 1Co 10:33 [i] Ro 11:14
9:24 [j] Gal 2:2; 2Ti 4:7; Heb 12:1
9:25 [k] Jas 1:12; Rev 2:10
9:27 [l] Ro 8:13
10:1 [m] Ex 13:21 [n] Ex 14:22,29
10:4 [o] Ex 17:6; Nu 20:11; Ps 78:15
10:5 [p] Nu 14:29; Heb 3:17
10:7 [q] ver 14 [r] Ex 32:4,6,19
10:8 [s] Nu 25:1-9
10:9 [t] Nu 21:5,6
10:10 [u] Nu 16:41 [v] Nu 16:49 [w] Ex 12:23
10:11 [x] Ro 13:11
10:12 [y] Ro 11:20
10:13 [z] 1Co 1:9 [a] 2Pe 2:9

[a] 7 Exodus 32:6 [b] 9 Some manuscripts *test the Lord*
[c] 13 The Greek for *temptation* and *tempted* can also mean *testing* and *tested*.

9:24 *all the runners run.* Runners and other athletes competing in the Greek games competed on behalf of their cities, following strict rules of training. *the prize.* A garland that would decompose over time. See the article "Athletic Imagery in 1 Corinthians 9," p. 2000.
9:26 – 27 Paul describes the physical training athletes endured to seek a prize. See the article, "Athletic Imagery in 1 Corinthians 9," p. 2000.
10:1 – 2 *under the cloud ... passed through the sea ... baptized ... in the cloud and in the sea.* Jewish people looked back to the exodus as their corporate experience of redemption; Paul makes an analogy with salvation in Christ (cf. 5:7), including baptism (cf. 12:13).
10:3 – 4 *spiritual food ... spiritual drink.* Access to spiritual food and drink did not prevent judgment in the past (vv. 8 – 10), so the present spiritual food and drink (vv. 16 – 17) would not protect those who committed the same sins (vv. 6,11).
10:4 *spiritual rock that accompanied them.* Noticing that Israel drank from a rock in more than one place (Ex 17:6; Nu 20:8), Jewish tradition sometimes suggested that the rock followed them during their journeys. Some Jewish thinkers also compared the rock with personified Wisdom. Paul, who will soon (vv. 20,22) quote from Dt 32, may think also of Dt 32:13, where God is Israel's rock. Paul may use "spiritual" to offer an analogy (cf. Rev 11:8, where "figuratively" translates "spiritually"); or he may mean, "from the Spirit," on which believers must depend. As a source of life, the rock corresponds to Christ.
10:6 *examples.* Speakers regularly exhorted people based on lessons from ancient examples; ancient historians recorded events partly for this purpose (cf. also Nu 16:38; 26:10). *setting our hearts on evil things as they did.* Despising manna, the spiritual food God provided (v. 3), Israel craved something else (Nu 11:4 – 6,18,20), and died (Nu 11:33).
10:7 *idolaters.* Jewish people generally regarded the worship of the golden calf, recalled here (Ex 32:4 – 6), as the most embarrassing incident in their history.
10:8 *sexual immorality.* When Midianite women seduced Israelite men for sexual immorality and then idolatry (Nu 25:1 – 8; 31:16), God judged Israel with a plague that killed 24,000 (Nu 25:9), probably Paul's primary reference here. Paul's slight numerical difference might also recall the three thousand who died in the immediate aftermath of the sin in v. 7 (Ex 32:28), followed by another plague (Ex 32:35).
10:9 *We should not test Christ.* Although God provided food (v. 3) and water (v. 4), Israel complained about these gifts and thus tested God (Ex 17:2,7; Dt 6:16; Ps 78:18). *killed by snakes.* Complaints continued, and finally God sent snakes (Nu 21:5 – 6).
10:10 *grumble.* See note on v. 9. *destroying angel.* Lit. "destroyer"; see Ex 12:23.
10:14 *flee from idolatry.* Writers on moral topics frequently urged their hearers to run from vices (cf. 6:18). Sacrificial food was closely connected with idols (10:14 – 23).
10:15 *judge for yourselves.* Speakers often appealed to hearers in this way.

1 CORINTHIANS 9:24–27

ATHLETIC IMAGERY IN 1 CORINTHIANS 9

Corinth hosted the Isthmian Games every two years (at least once during Paul's stay; Ac 18:11,18); next to the Olympics, this was the most popular of the Greek games. Urban residents were familiar with racing, boxing, and other competitions. (Races were the first event in the Pentathlon, but it did not include boxing.) Preparation for contests involved strict discipline, including, e.g., ten months of training before Olympic competitions.

View of two (modern) wreaths that were used to crown the winners of the games at Isthmia (on the left) and Olympia (on the right).

www.HolyLandPhotos.org

Victors' crowns at Greek competitions were wreaths: wild olive for the Olympics and pine or withered celery for the Isthmian Games. Some other writers spoke of garlands figuratively (occasionally even in the OT; cf. the Greek version of Isa 28:5; 62:3). Ancient writers, including Diaspora Jews, routinely employed athletic illustrations; in 1Co 9:24–27 Paul compares athletes' physical discipline with the deliberate self-discipline needed to persevere.

Boxing (1Co 9:26–27), one of the most popular Greek competitions, was violent. Boxers' leather gloves protected most of their forearms but left the fingers bare. A still more violent version was a form of combat known as the *pankration*, which mixed boxing with wrestling. Its only rules were against gouging the eyes of one's adversary and biting. Shadowboxing, or "beating the air," was insufficient preparation for a real boxing competition; a boxer had to discipline his body better than that to win. In the same way, Paul had to discipline his life to sacrifice what he needed to sacrifice for the sake of the gospel, lest he himself be disqualified from the race and fall short of the wreath of eternal life (1Co 9:25). ◆

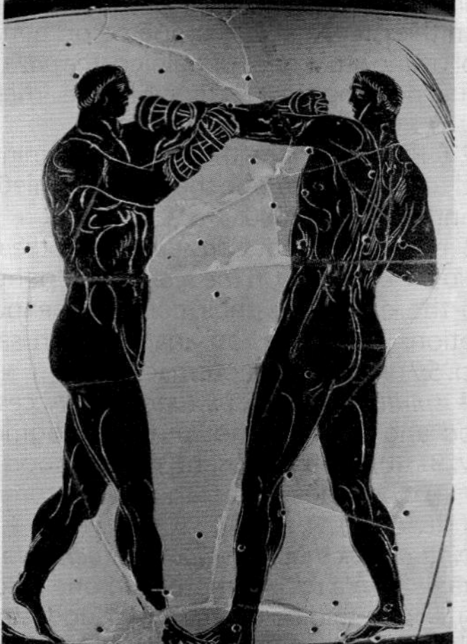

Black-figure Panathenaic amphora depicting a boxing contest, c. 336 BC, Athens.

British Museum, London, UK/Bridgeman Images

for yourselves what I say. 16Is not the cup
of thanksgiving for which we give thanks
a participation in the blood of Christ? And
is not the bread that we break a participation in the body of Christ?[b] 17Because
there is one loaf, we, who are many, are
one body,[c] for we all share the one loaf.
18Consider the people of Israel: Do not
those who eat the sacrifices[d] participate in
the altar? 19Do I mean then that food sacrificed to an idol is anything, or that an idol
is anything?[e] 20No, but the sacrifices of pagans are offered to demons,[f] not to God,
and I do not want you to be participants
with demons. 21You cannot drink the cup
of the Lord and the cup of demons too;
you cannot have a part in both the Lord's
table and the table of demons.[g] 22Are we
trying to arouse the Lord's jealousy?[h] Are
we stronger than he?[i]

The Believer's Freedom

23"I have the right to do anything," you
say—but not everything is beneficial.[j]
"I have the right to do anything"—but
not everything is constructive. 24No one
should seek their own good, but the good
of others.[k]
25Eat anything sold in the meat market
without raising questions of conscience,[l]
26for, "The earth is the Lord's, and everything in it."[a][m]
27If an unbeliever invites you to a meal
and you want to go, eat whatever is put
before you[n] without raising questions of
conscience. 28But if someone says to you,
"This has been offered in sacrifice," then
do not eat it, both for the sake of the one
who told you and for the sake of conscience.[o] 29I am referring to the other person's conscience, not yours. For why is
my freedom[p] being judged by another's
conscience? 30If I take part in the meal
with thankfulness, why am I denounced
because of something I thank God for?[q]
31So whether you eat or drink or whatever you do, do it all for the glory of God.[r]
32Do not cause anyone to stumble,[s] whether Jews, Greeks or the church of God[t]—

10:16 [b] Mt 26:26-28 **10:17** [c] Ro 12:5; 1Co 12:27 **10:18** [d] Lev 7:6, 14,15 **10:19** [e] 1Co 8:4 **10:20** [f] Dt 32:17; Ps 106:37; Rev 9:20 **10:21** [g] 2Co 6:15,16 **10:22** [h] Dt 32:16, 21 [i] Ecc 6:10; Isa 45:9 **10:23** [j] 1Co 6:12 **10:24** [k] ver 33; Ro 15:1,2; 1Co 13:5; Php 2:4,21 **10:25** [l] Ac 10:15; 1Co 8:7 **10:26** [m] Ps 24:1 **10:27** [n] Lk 10:7 **10:28** [o] 1Co 8:7, 10-12 **10:29** [p] Ro 14:16; 1Co 9:1,19 **10:30** [q] Ro 14:6 **10:31** [r] Col 3:17; 1Pe 4:11

[a] *26* Psalm 24:1

10:32 [s] Ac 24:16 [t] Ac 20:28

10:16 *the cup of thanksgiving.* A blessing over wine, thanking God, was normal before Jewish meals, including Passover (see note on 11:25). If the Passover practice in this period was the same as in our somewhat later documents about it, the Passover meal included four cups, as in Greek banquets.

10:17 *one loaf.* Jewish meals also included a blessing over bread. *we, who are many, are one body.* See note on 12:12.

10:18 *those who eat … participate in the altar.* All Israel shared in the Passover offerings (cf. 5:7); priests ate parts of most kinds of sacrifices (see note on 9:13). In antiquity, eating together established relationships, and sacrificial meat was connected with the deity to whom it was offered.

10:19 *that an idol is anything.* Paul agrees with Scripture (e.g., Isa 44:12–20) that idols are nothing themselves (cf. 1Co 8:4); but the demons that are associated with them (see note on v. 20) are the problem.

10:20 *demons.* The Septuagint, the pre-Christian Greek translation of the OT, sometimes renders idols or false gods as "demons" (Dt 32:17, partly quoted here and in Baruch 4:7; see also Ps 96:5; 106:37; Isa 65:3,11). Most early Jewish and Christian sources regard the spirits that Gentiles worshiped as demons, as Paul does here.

10:21 *the Lord's table … table of demons.* Ancient temples had tables for depositing offerings. The OT uses "the Lord's table" similarly (Mal 1:7,12), including for the place of the consecrated bread afterward eaten by the priests (Ex 25:30; 1Sa 21:6). Ancient invitations to dine at a temple often speak of the deity's "table" (e.g., the "table of the lord Serapis").

10:22 Continuing the context evoked in v. 20, Paul here uses the Greek version of Dt 32:21 (echoed also in Baruch 4:7). As in vv. 19,23a, Paul may partly concede their objection, only to refute it afterward.

10:23 *not everything is beneficial.* See note on 6:12. Because others associated sacrificial meat with the demons behind the idols (vv. 28–29), one should abstain.

10:25 *anything sold in the meat market.* Sacrificial meat not used in the temple was sold in Corinth's meat market, without being distinguished from other meat there not brought from this source. To avoid both sacrificial meat and meat that had not been butchered in a kosher manner (draining the blood), Jews in large cities normally had their own meat markets. Probably only people of means could normally afford to purchase meat.

10:26 *The earth is the Lord's.* In reality, everything created belongs to God, not to other spirits. Although documented somewhat later, Jewish tradition associated the verse cited here (Ps 24:1) with blessing (thanking God for) meals.

10:27 *If an unbeliever invites you to a meal.* People invited friends and subordinate clients to banquets; to refuse would insult the host and provoke enmity. *eat whatever is put before you.* One was not obligated to eat all the kinds of food served at a banquet, though meat was expensive and valued.

10:28 *do not eat it.* Because sacrificial food was associated with sacrifices, a polytheistic friend would understand one's willingness to eat explicitly sacrificed food as implied acceptance of sacrifice to the deities in question. (Jewish critics, who refused even to eat pork, would also be scandalized by fellow monotheists eating sacrificial food.)

10:30 *with thankfulness.* Jewish tradition included giving thanks before meals, a practice adopted by early Christians.

10:31 *whether you eat or drink.* God's honor should control one's choices even of food and drink at friends' banquets (vv. 27–29). *for the glory of God.* Jewish teachers emphasized honoring God's name; many philosophers also understood that eternal considerations should take priority over temporal ones.

10:32—11:1 Conclusions of works or, as here, sections within a work often included summarizing statements (cf. 9:19–23).

10:32 *Do not cause anyone to stumble.* Sacrificial meat could confuse Greeks and scandalize both Jews and some fellow Christians.

33 even as I try to please everyone in every way.[u] For I am not seeking my own good but the good of many, so that they may be saved.[v]

11

1 Follow my example,[w] as I follow the example of Christ.

On Covering the Head in Worship

2 I praise you[x] for remembering me in everything[y] and for holding to the traditions just as I passed them on to you.[z] 3 But I want you to realize that the head of every man is Christ,[a] and the head of the woman is man,[a][b] and the head of Christ is God.[c] 4 Every man who prays or prophesies with his head covered dishonors his head. 5 But every woman who prays or prophesies[d] with her head uncovered dishonors her head—it is the same as having her head shaved.[e] 6 For if a woman does not cover her head, she might as well have her hair cut off; but if it is a disgrace for a woman to have her hair cut off or her head shaved, then she should cover her head.

7 A man ought not to cover his head,[b] since he is the image[f] and glory of God; but woman is the glory of man. 8 For man did not come from woman, but woman from man;[g] 9 neither was man created for woman, but woman for man.[h] 10 It is for this reason that a woman ought to have authority over her own[c] head, because of the angels. 11 Nevertheless, in the Lord woman is not independent of man, nor is man independent of woman. 12 For as woman came from man, so also man is born of woman. But everything comes from God.[i]

13 Judge for yourselves: Is it proper for a woman to pray to God with her head uncovered? 14 Does not the very nature of things teach you that if a man has long hair, it is a disgrace to him, 15 but that if a woman has long hair, it is her glory? For

10:33 [u] Ro 15:2; 1Co 9:22 [v] Ro 11:14
11:1 [w] 1Co 4:16
11:2 [x] ver 17, 22 [y] 1Co 4:17 [z] 1Co 15:2, 3; 2Th 2:15
11:3 [a] Eph 1:22 [b] Ge 3:16; Eph 5:23 [c] 1Co 3:23
11:5 [d] Ac 21:9 [e] Dt 21:12
11:7 [f] Ge 1:26; Jas 3:9
11:8 [g] Ge 2:21-23; 1Ti 2:13
11:9 [h] Ge 2:18
11:12 [i] Ro 11:36

[a] 3 Or *of the wife is her husband* [b] 4-7 Or *4Every man who prays or prophesies with long hair dishonors his head. 5But every woman who prays or prophesies with no covering of hair dishonors her head—she is just like one of the "shorn women." 6If a woman has no covering, let her be for now with short hair; but since it is a disgrace for a woman to have her hair shorn or shaved, she should grow it again. 7A man ought not to have long hair* [c] 10 Or *have a sign of authority on her*

11:1 *Follow my example.* As in ch. 9, Paul appeals to his own example; other sages sometimes also did this, and disciples were expected to follow their teachers' example.
11:2 Ancient writers often used digressions; the present one (vv. 2–16), digressing from matters of sacred food, is framed by Paul's praise (v. 2) and lack of it (v. 17). *I praise you for remembering me.* Both letters and (more often) speeches could focus on praise or criticism. *traditions just as I passed them on to you.* Teachers often passed on traditions orally to disciples, expecting them to continue passing them on.
11:3,4 *head.* Besides its literal sense of the top of one's body (cf. vv. 4–6), "head" often signified a position of authority (cf. v. 3; others cite instances also for "source" or "prominent part"). Husbands did hold that role in ancient households, especially Greek and Roman ones. Paul might connect the wife dishonoring her physical head with bringing shame on her family. Ancient writers often argued based on wordplays, and the behavior of one family member was thought to reflect on one's whole family. Romans covered their heads for worship but Greeks uncovered them.
11:5 *woman who prays or prophesies.* Although men normally held the most visible roles in ancient Israel, female prophets were respected (Ex 15:20; Jdg 4:4; 2Ki 22:14; Isa 8:3). Traditional Greeks often frowned on women speaking in the presence of men outside their families, but even they permitted women to speak by a deity's inspiration.
11:6 *she might as well have her hair cut off.* Ancient Mediterranean men often viewed women's hair as sexually appealing; shaving the head had the opposite effect and in that culture was humiliating for a woman (perhaps a factor in Dt 21:12–14). Writers sometimes reduced their opponents' positions to the absurd by showing where they could lead if carried to an extreme.
11:7 *A man … is the image and glory of God; but woman is the glory of man.* Although some ancient Jewish texts (in contrast to others) spoke of only men as God's image, both genders reflect God's image in Ge 1:27 and (especially clearly) Ge 5:1–2. Paul may be emphasizing women's derivation from man (see v. 8 and note).
11:8 *woman from man.* God formed the first woman from the rib of the first man in Ge 2:21–23.
11:9 *woman for man.* In Ge 2:21–23, God created woman because there was no "helper suitable" for the man (Ge 2:18; the Hebrew expression involves the man's need and does not demean the woman).
11:10 *the angels.* Scholars propose various possible meanings. One proposal is that they refer to fallen angels attracted to human women (the most common ancient interpretation of Ge 6:1–2), although this interpretation might suggest the danger of conceiving giants (cf. Ge 6:4). Others, citing a similar idea in the Dead Sea Scrolls, suggest that the angels are simply angels present for worship, offended by immodest apparel. A further possibility is that Paul concisely evokes the angels mentioned earlier in his letter (6:3), implying that because these women will someday judge angels, they should use their authority (the same term translated "right" or "rights" in 8:9; 9:4–6,12,18) responsibly.
11:11–12 Some used arguments similar to vv. 8–9 to subordinate women harshly; Paul warns against extrapolating more from his argument than he intends.
11:12 *woman came from man … man is born of woman.* Everyone knew that men were born through women (Job 14:1; Gal 4:4), though the language here may echo especially the widely-read work 1 Esdras 4:15–17 in the Septuagint, the pre-Christian Greek translation of the OT. Those who argued mutuality of some sort were usually among those ancient writers friendlier toward women. *from … of.* These prepositions translate terms used for different forms of causation (see note on 8:6.)
11:13 *Judge for yourselves.* See note on 10:15.
11:14 *very nature of things.* Many people, and especially philosophers (notably the Stoics), made arguments from nature. Philosophers sometimes argued, e.g., that nature had given men beards to distinguish them from women, so that a shaved man was against nature (though clean-shavenness was the preferred style among honorable men in this region in this generation). *if a man has long hair, it is a disgrace.* Among others, ancient Greek heroes, whose statues abounded, and Biblical Nazirites (Nu 6:5)

1 CORINTHIANS 11:2–16

HEAD COVERINGS IN ANTIQUITY

People in the Mediterranean world covered their heads for various reasons, especially for shame and mourning. Romans covered their heads for worship, and Greeks uncovered them. None of these customs, however, differentiated coverers and non-coverers by gender, as is the case in 1Co 11:2–16.

A practice of head covering associated specifically with women is well attested, however, both in ancient art and in written sources. The farther east one traveled, the more of the head that was normally covered; in Mesopotamia, e.g., women often covered their faces, a practice attested also even among conservative households in Tarsus and Judea. Elsewhere, however, those who covered their heads were especially concerned to shroud their hair from public view.

The reason normally given for the practice was modesty. The custom thus applied especially to married women, not virgins (except in very scrupulous environments). One Spartan gave the reason: virgins must find husbands, whereas wives must keep their husbands. Women's hair was considered a primary visual temptation for young men. In some places, including Judea, a wife who went in public without her hair covered would thus be deemed immodest, dishonoring herself in the eyes of others. Those prone to gossip might consider her promiscuous. Some husbands even considered this an appropriate reason to divorce their wives on grounds of infidelity.

Among earlier Greeks, especially in classical Athens, respectable urban women were at least ideally restricted especially to the home; Corinth in this period had more Roman influence, in which aristocratic women often even banqueted alongside their husbands. Many scholars argue that upper-class women, who had expensive and fashionable hairstyles, were less inclined to cover their hair in public than were other women. That wealthier women were matrons of the sorts of homes in which churches often met may have also made more ambiguous the question of whether they were in "public."

First-century Roman sculpture of a woman wearing a chiton and himation; the latter being worn as a head covering.

Kim Walton. National Archaeological Museum of Athens.

The matter of head coverings, then, could have provoked some tension between church members of different social status. For many, however, probably including most of the congregations' Jewish members, the lack of a head covering would signify the lack of sexual modesty. ◆

1 CORINTHIANS 11:20–21

BANQUETS IN CORINTH

Social status played a large role in Corinthian banquets. People of status could invite peers and/or social subordinates to their banquets, but peers had to receive the "best" places to recline (nearest the host) and the highest quality food and wine. Although private banquets sometimes followed the Greek ideal of equality, often banquets arranged people according to rank. Hosts expected gratitude, but guests who felt their status was slighted (with inferior seating or wine) often felt they had to grovel and complained to others afterward about their treatment. Dinners of private associations, or clubs, were also common; trade guilds, e.g., often met once a month to eat together in the name of their patron deity (e.g., Silvanus for woodcutters, Bacchus for bar owners). People sometimes brought their own food and drink. Such trade guilds would usually include people of the same social class, but they could meet in the home of, or at the sponsorship of, a wealthier patron, or sponsor.

The early churches met primarily in homes (e.g., 1Co 16:19), including in Corinth (Ac 18:7; perhaps Ro 16:23). Many Corinthian residents lived in apartment buildings' rooms large enough only for sleeping; these rooms were too small to host people, unless in the narrow corridor that connected various apartments. Churches thus met in more spacious homes; the largest of these would have been in Corinth's richer residential area, the Kranion. Although more spacious villas existed, an average wealthy home could recline 9–12 people on three large couches in the *triclinium*, an elite dining hall; if needed, more people (even as many as 40) could be accommodated in the larger atrium. Whatever the particulars, the wealthier minority of the congregations (1Co 1:26) probably hosted the rest of the members spatially; perhaps they also provided some or all of the food and wine.

continued on next page

long hair is given to her as a covering. 16If
anyone wants to be contentious about
this, we have no other practice—nor do
the churches of God.[j]

Correcting an Abuse of the Lord's Supper

11:23-25pp — Mt 26:26-28; Mk 14:22-24; Lk 22:17-20

17In the following directives I have no
praise for you,[k] for your meetings do more
harm than good. 18In the first place, I hear
that when you come together as a church,
there are divisions[l] among you, and to
some extent I believe it. 19No doubt there
have to be differences among you to show
which of you have God's approval.[m] 20So
then, when you come together, it is not
the Lord's Supper you eat, 21for when you
are eating, some of you go ahead with
your own private suppers.[n] As a result,
one person remains hungry and another
gets drunk. 22Don't you have homes to

11:16 [j] 1Co 7:17
11:17 [k] ver 2,22
11:18 [l] 1Co 1:10-12; 3:3
11:19 [m] 1Jn 2:19
11:21 [n] 2Pe 2:13; Jude 12

had long hair. Shorter hair was currently in fashion for men, however. Paul would know that peoples outside the empire, e.g., the feared Parthians to the east and Germans to the north, wore their hair very long, but arguments from "nature" were of various kinds, sometimes (as possibly here) from culture.

11:16 *we have no other practice.* Paul has offered various arguments, including from Scripture (vv. 7–9) and nature (vv. 14–15); now he appeals to consensus. Appeal to local or in-group custom was a common form of argument in antiquity. (Indeed, for one skeptical ancient intellectual group called the Skeptics, this was the only persuasive argument.)

11:17 *I have no praise for you.* Paul returns to the matter of sacred food after the digression in vv. 2–16. In contrast to the earlier discussion, the food discussed here is dedicated not to other gods but to the Lord. *praise.* Also in v. 22; see note on v. 2.

11:18 *divisions.* Might include the social divisions in v. 21. *to some extent I believe it.* Some scholars understand Paul's statement here as mock astonishment, a rhetorical device used to drive home the inappropriateness of their behavior.

11:20 *the Lord's Supper.* Cf. note on 10:21; here the phrase contrasts ironically with their own supper (11:21).

11:21 *one person remains hungry.* Some non-aristocrats may have been coming late from work as laborers or slaves

In contrast to typical Corinthian banquets, the Jewish Passover meal (cf. 1Co 5:7) on which the Lord's Supper was modeled was an intimate matter of one or two families. By this period it followed some conventional Mediterranean banquet customs but its focus differed. Its point was not flaunting status but celebrating God's redemption of his people (see notes on Mt 26:17–30). ◆

Fourth-century fresco depicting a banqueting scene, Rome.

Cimitero dei SS. Marcellino e Pietro, Rome, Italy/De Agostini Picture Library/Bridgeman Images

eat and drink in? Or do you despise the
church of God[o] by humiliating those who
have nothing?[p] What shall I say to you?
Shall I praise you?[q] Certainly not in this
matter!
23For I received from the Lord[r] what I
also passed on to you:[s] The Lord Jesus,
on the night he was betrayed, took bread,
24and when he had given thanks, he broke
it and said, "This is my body, which is
for you; do this in remembrance of me."
25In the same way, after supper he took
the cup, saying, "This cup is the new covenant[t] in my blood;[u] do this, whenever

11:22 [o] 1Co 10:32 [p] Jas 2:6 [q] ver 2, 17 **11:23** [r] Gal 1:12 [s] 1Co 15:3 **11:25** [t] Lk 22:20 [u] 1Co 10:16

(cf. v. 33), in contrast to the wealthier hosts who had leisure after their morning appointments. Alternatively, the hosts and any elite guests may want to eat their own high-quality food apart from the more modest meal being shared by the rest of the gathered believers. (This is true whether the guests bring their own food or the host supplies it; hosts were not expected to feed socially subordinate guests at their own social level.) *another gets drunk.* Although people regularly got drunk at banquets, ancient associations had rules for maintaining order at their community meals, barring quarrels. Scripture treated drunkenness as shameful (Pr 20:1; Ecc 10:17). For the contrast between Corinthians' banquet expectations based on local practice and Passover-based expectations for the Lord's Supper, see the article "Banquets in Corinth," p. 2004.

11:23 *received … passed on.* Teachers and others who passed on traditions often used these words together (cf. v. 2). *received from the Lord.* This need not mean that Paul received this directly by revelation, since Jewish teachers often described their traditions as "received from Sinai"—by which they meant only that the traditions went back to Moses. *on the night.* As a Passover meal, the Last Supper occurred at night (Mk 14:16–18).

11:24 *when he had given thanks.* Jewish people gave thanks over bread and wine at the beginning of meals. *This is my body.* At the Passover, the bread was declared to be "the bread of affliction that our ancestors ate" when redeemed from Egypt. No one, of course, considered it literally the same bread from more than a millennium earlier; the point was that they were reenacting Passover, in some way sharing in the experience of their ancestors. As Passover commemorated God's act of redeeming his people (Ex 12:14; 13:3; Dt 16:2–3), so the Lord's Supper commemorates Jesus' act of redemption (cf. 1Co 5:7). Cf. Lk 22:19 and note.

11:25 *This cup is the new covenant in my blood.* See

you drink it, in remembrance of me." 26For whenever you eat this bread and drink this cup, you proclaim the Lord's death until he comes.

27So then, whoever eats the bread or drinks the cup of the Lord in an unworthy manner will be guilty of sinning against the body and blood of the Lord.[v] 28Everyone ought to examine themselves[w] before they eat of the bread and drink from the cup. 29For those who eat and drink without discerning the body of Christ eat and drink judgment on themselves. 30That is why many among you are weak and sick, and a number of you have fallen asleep. 31But if we were more discerning with regard to ourselves, we would not come under such judgment.[x] 32Nevertheless, when we are judged in this way by the Lord, we are being disciplined[y] so that we will not be finally condemned with the world.

33So then, my brothers and sisters, when you gather to eat, you should all eat together. 34Anyone who is hungry[z] should eat something at home,[a] so that when you meet together it may not result in judgment.

And when I come[b] I will give further directions.

11:27 [v] Heb 10:29
11:28 [w] 2Co 13:5
11:31 [x] Ps 32:5; 1Jn 1:9
11:32 [y] Ps 94:12; Heb 12:7-10; Rev 3:19
11:34 [z] ver 21 [a] ver 22 [b] 1Co 4:19

Concerning Spiritual Gifts

12 Now about the gifts of the Spirit,[c] brothers and sisters, I do not want you to be uninformed. 2You know that when you were pagans,[d] somehow or other you were influenced and led astray to mute idols.[e] 3Therefore I want you to know that no one who is speaking by the Spirit of God says, "Jesus be cursed,"[f] and no one can say, "Jesus is Lord,"[g] except by the Holy Spirit.[h]

4There are different kinds of gifts, but the same Spirit[i] distributes them. 5There are different kinds of service, but the same Lord. 6There are different kinds of working, but in all of them and in everyone it is the same God[j] at work.

7Now to each one the manifestation of the Spirit is given for the common good.[k] 8To one there is given through the Spirit a message of wisdom,[l] to another a message of knowledge[m] by means of the same Spirit, 9to another faith[n] by the same Spirit, to another gifts of healing[o] by that one Spirit, 10to another miraculous powers,[p] to another prophecy, to another distinguishing between spirits,[q] to another speaking in different kinds of

12:1 [c] Ro 1:11; 1Co 14:1,37
12:2 [d] Eph 2:11, 12; 1Pe 4:3 [e] Ps 115:5; Jer 10:5; Hab 2:18, 19; 1Th 1:9
12:3 [f] Ro 9:3 [g] Jn 13:13 [h] 1Jn 4:2,3
12:4 [i] Ro 12:4-8; Eph 4:11; Heb 2:4
12:6 [j] Eph 4:6
12:7 [k] Eph 4:12
12:8 [l] 1Co 2:6 [m] 2Co 8:7
12:9 [n] Mt 17:19, 20; 2Co 4:13 [o] ver 28,30
12:10 [p] Gal 3:5 [q] 1Jn 4:1

---

note on v. 24. Jesus' language evokes the blood of the covenant at Sinai (Ex 24:8), but plainly as part of a new covenant (cf. Lk 22:20 and note), promised in Jer 31:31. Cf. Mt 26:27–28 and notes. Because the cup is after supper, it could match the third or possibly fourth cup of the Passover meal (cups divided the banquet into phases). Greeks often had a drinking party with entertainment (or sometimes discussion or lectures) after the meal; for early believers, this may have been the time instead for Scripture exposition. (Pharisees and some other pious Jews insisted that the Torah be the main topic of conversation even during the meal; cf. Dt 6:7; Ps 1:2.)

11:26 *until he comes.* When Jewish people commemorated the Passover, they often also contemplated their future redemption. Many also anticipated an end-time banquet for the righteous (cf. Isa 25:6), which Jesus at the Last Supper also promised (Mk 14:25).

11:27–29 *unworthy manner ... without discerning the body of Christ.* By treating those of lower worldly status as of lesser worth (vv. 21–22), believers in Corinth failed to discern Christ's body in one another (cf. 10:17), and thus demeaned the commemoration of Jesus' sacrificed body.

11:30 *weak and sick.* Possibly Paul implies that demeaning members of Christ's body (see previous note) also inhibits corporate gifts of healings (12:9). *asleep.* A standard euphemism for "dead."

11:32 *so that we will not be finally condemned with the world.* Jewish teachers often emphasized that the righteous suffer in this life to atone for their few sins, whereas the wicked will be tormented in the world to come for their many sins. For Paul, suffering may be a means not of atonement (cf. 1:30; 5:7; 6:11) but of bringing repentance (cf. 5:5).

11:34 *eat something at home.* The urban poor often had limited access to food and cooking in their small rooms; some people cooked on charcoal braziers, but people often ate at cheap neighborhood taverns. Those with more means could eat in their homes before the church gathered. *further directions.* Letters often promised further instructions when the writer would come; speaking face to face was preferred (e.g., 3Jn 10,14).

12:1 *Now about.* Sometimes used by ancient writers (and in the Greek text of 7:1,25; 8:1; 16:1,12) to transition to a new subject.

12:2 *mute idols.* Idols were unable to speak (e.g., Ps 115:5); possibly Paul alludes here also to Greek oracles, where priests or priestesses might speak for a deity. Paul is for prophecy (14:1)—so long as it comes from the true Spirit that honors Jesus (v. 3).

12:4–6 *There are different kinds of ... different kinds of ... different kinds of.* Beginning new clauses the same way is called anaphora. *Spirit ... Lord ... God.* Like a good orator, Paul emphasizes his point here by repeating it in three parallel ways (in this case including the Spirit, Jesus and God the Father).

12:6 *same God at work.* God gets the credit for all the gifts, so no one can boast over their gift versus another's.

12:7 Speakers sometimes emphasized a matter by bracketing it; v. 7 and v. 11 together reinforce the dependence on God's Spirit to empower the activities in vv. 8–10.

12:8–10 Ancient orators liked to use lists (as also in vv. 28–30; 14:26), as well as repetition (here, "to another" seven times, most of them the same Greek term).

12:8 *message of wisdom ... message of knowledge.* Corinthian culture valued speaking (in rhetoric), wisdom (in philosophy) and knowledge.

12:9 *gifts of healing.* Gentiles in Corinth could seek healing at local shrines (especially that of Asclepius), but the Spirit provided healing gifts from the true God among the believers.

12:10 *prophecy.* Prophecy was familiar from the OT (the most common ministry of speaking God's message noted there). *tongues.* Speaking in tongues began at Pentecost, and unlike prophecy, lacked significant pagan parallels at the time.

tongues,[a][r] and to still another the interpretation of tongues.[a] 11All these are the
work of one and the same Spirit,[s] and he
distributes them to each one, just as he
determines.

Unity and Diversity in the Body

12Just as a body, though one, has many
parts, but all its many parts form one
body,[t] so it is with Christ.[u] 13For we were
all baptized by[b] one Spirit[v] so as to form
one body — whether Jews or Gentiles,
slave or free[w] — and we were all given the
one Spirit to drink.[x] 14Even so the body is
not made up of one part but of many.
15Now if the foot should say, "Because
I am not a hand, I do not belong to the
body," it would not for that reason stop
being part of the body. 16And if the ear
should say, "Because I am not an eye, I do
not belong to the body," it would not for
that reason stop being part of the body.
17If the whole body were an eye, where
would the sense of hearing be? If the
whole body were an ear, where would the
sense of smell be? 18But in fact God has
placed[y] the parts in the body, every one of
them, just as he wanted them to be.[z] 19If
they were all one part, where would the
body be? 20As it is, there are many parts,
but one body.[a]
21The eye cannot say to the hand, "I
don't need you!" And the head cannot say
to the feet, "I don't need you!" 22On the
contrary, those parts of the body that seem
to be weaker are indispensable, 23and the
parts that we think are less honorable we
treat with special honor. And the parts
that are unpresentable are treated with
special modesty, 24while our presentable
parts need no special treatment. But God
has put the body together, giving greater
honor to the parts that lacked it, 25so that
there should be no division in the body,
but that its parts should have equal concern for each other. 26If one part suffers,
every part suffers with it; if one part is
honored, every part rejoices with it.
27Now you are the body of Christ,[b] and
each one of you is a part of it.[c] 28And God
has placed in the church[d] first of all apostles,[e] second prophets, third teachers, then
miracles, then gifts of healing,[f] of helping,
of guidance,[g] and of different kinds of
tongues.[h] 29Are all apostles? Are all prophets? Are all teachers? Do all work miracles?
30Do all have gifts of healing? Do all speak
in tongues[c]?[i] Do all interpret? 31Now eagerly desire[j] the greater gifts.

Love Is Indispensable

And yet I will show you the most excellent way.
13 If I speak in the tongues[d][k] of men or
of angels, but do not have love, I am
only a resounding gong or a clanging cym-

12:10 [r] Mk 16:17 **12:11** [s] ver 4 **12:12** [t] Ro 12:5 [u] ver 27 **12:13** [v] Eph 2:18 [w] Gal 3:28; Col 3:11 [x] Jn 7:37-39 **12:18** [y] ver 28 [z] ver 11 **12:20** [a] ver 12, 14 **12:27** [b] Eph 1:23; 4:12; Col 1:18,24 [c] Ro 12:5 **12:28** [d] 1Co 10:32 [e] Eph 4:11 [f] ver 9 [g] Ro 12:6-8 [h] ver 10 **12:30** [i] ver 10 **12:31** [j] 1Co 14:1,39 **13:1** [k] ver 8

[a] 10 Or *languages*; also in verse 28 [b] 13 Or *with*; or *in* [c] 30 Or *other languages* [d] 1 Or *languages*

12:12 *a body, though one, has many parts.* Earlier Greek and Roman thinkers had compared the state and even the universe to a body of interdependent members. Often ancient writers used the analogy to support hierarchy, but Paul here values the importance of the diverse functions represented. Speakers also would elaborate an important point; Paul elaborates the point here in vv. 12 – 27; vv. 12,27 together identify the theme of the section they frame.
12:13 *baptized by one Spirit.* Gentiles who converted to Judaism were immersed in water and Christians had adopted and developed baptism also as a public act of conversion. Most important, however, Christians recognize that God's own Spirit initiates us into this new relationship with God and one another (cf. the promise in Eze 36:25 – 27). *the one Spirit to drink.* Jewish sources speak of drinking from divine Wisdom, but see especially 10:4 and note.
12:14 *not made up of one part but of many.* Speakers sometimes emphasized a matter by bracketing it; v. 14 and v. 20 together stress the value of all the members in the one body in vv. 15 – 19.
12:15 – 16 *if the foot should say ... if the ear should say.* One rhetorical device often used by ancient orators to hold attention was personifying impersonal objects so that they could speak.
12:17 – 19 Rhetorical questions in a series drive home a point. Orators also sometimes would dwell on a point, reiterating it in various ways to drive it home, as in Paul's repeated emphasis throughout this section on the one body with many members.
12:21 *The eye cannot say ... the head cannot say.* See note on vv. 15 – 16. The absurdity of eyes or hands independently speaking reinforce in a graphic, humorous manner the point of our members' interdependence.
12:23 *parts that are unpresentable.* May be the genitals and excretory organs, which people normally covered in public. Exceptions to such coverings included Greek athletics, conventional settings such as public baths and public toilets, and shameful settings such as victims being executed.
12:24 *giving greater honor.* Paul's use of honor and power language may subvert a common ancient use of the body analogy to support hierarchy.
12:28 Orators liked to use lists (see vv. 8 – 10,29 – 30). *first of all.* Numbered examples were usually ranked, although other elements that were not numbered could be randomly arranged.
12:31 *desire the greater gifts.* Speakers sometimes framed a digression with a related thought; desiring the most helpful gifts here and in 14:1 frame a discussion of the gifts and love in ch. 13.
13:1 – 13 Sometimes ancient orators would praise a virtue at length, using exalted prose. Early Christians could elaborate in similar ways on faith (Heb 11) and love (here in ch. 13). Paul's praise of love here is not, however, merely theoretical; it directly challenges the behavior of many of the Corinthian Christians, who are boastful and proud (e.g., compare v. 4 with 3:21; 4:7; 5:2,6).
13:1 *If I ... but do not have love.* Orators often repeated a phrase (vv. 1 – 3) to emphasize a point emotionally. *tongues ... of angels.* Scholars debate whether Paul implies special angelic languages (which some evidence suggests that some ancient Jews may have believed in) or simply uses hyperbole. *gong.* The Greek term indicates an object

bal. 2If I have the gift of prophecy and can
fathom all mysteries[l] and all knowledge, and
if I have a faith[m] that can move mountains,[n]
but do not have love, I am nothing. 3If I give
all I possess to the poor[o] and give over my
body to hardship that I may boast,[a][p] but do
not have love, I gain nothing.
4Love is patient,[q] love is kind. It does
not envy, it does not boast, it is not proud.
5It does not dishonor others, it is not self-
seeking,[r] it is not easily angered, it keeps
no record of wrongs. 6Love does not delight in evil[s] but rejoices with the truth.[t]
7It always protects, always trusts, always
hopes, always perseveres.
8Love never fails. But where there are
prophecies,[u] they will cease; where there
are tongues,[v] they will be stilled; where
there is knowledge, it will pass away.
9For we know in part[w] and we prophesy
in part, 10but when completeness comes,[x]
what is in part disappears. 11When I was a
child, I talked like a child, I thought like a
child, I reasoned like a child. When I became a man, I put the ways of childhood
behind me. 12For now we see only a reflection as in a mirror; then we shall see face
to face.[y] Now I know in part; then I shall
know fully, even as I am fully known.[z]
13And now these three remain: faith,
hope and love.[a] But the greatest of these
is love.[b]

Intelligibility in Worship

14 Follow the way of love[c] and eagerly
desire[d] gifts of the Spirit,[e] especially prophecy. 2For anyone who speaks in
a tongue[b][f] does not speak to people but
to God. Indeed, no one understands them;
they utter mysteries[g] by the Spirit. 3But
the one who prophesies speaks to people
for their strengthening,[h] encouraging and
comfort. 4Anyone who speaks in a tongue[i]
edifies themselves, but the one who
prophesies[j] edifies the church. 5I would
like every one of you to speak in tongues,[c]
but I would rather have you prophesy.[k]
The one who prophesies is greater than
the one who speaks in tongues,[c] unless
someone interprets, so that the church
may be edified.
6Now, brothers and sisters, if I come
to you and speak in tongues, what good
will I be to you, unless I bring you some
revelation[l] or knowledge or prophecy
or word of instruction?[m] 7Even in the
case of lifeless things that make sounds,

13:2 [l] 1Co 14:2 [m] 1Co 12:9 [n] Mt 17:20; 21:21 **13:3** [o] Mt 6:2 [p] Da 3:28 **13:4** [q] 1Th 5:14 **13:5** [r] 1Co 10:24 **13:6** [s] 2Th 2:12 [t] 2Jn 4; 3Jn 3,4 **13:8** [u] ver 2 [v] ver 1 **13:9** [w] ver 12; 1Co 8:2 **13:10** [x] Php 3:12 **13:12** [y] Ge 32:30; 2Co 5:7; 1Jn 3:2 [z] 1Co 8:3 **13:13** [a] Gal 5:5, 6 [b] 1Co 16:14 **14:1** [c] 1Co 16:14 [d] ver 39; 1Co 12:31 [e] 1Co 12:1 **14:2** [f] Mk 16:17 [g] 1Co 13:2 **14:3** [h] ver 4, 5, 12, 17, 26; Ro 14:19 **14:4** [i] Mk 16:17 [j] 1Co 13:2 **14:5** [k] Nu 11:29 **14:6** [l] ver 26; Eph 1:17 [m] Ro 6:17

[a] 3 Some manuscripts *body to the flames* [b] 2 Or *in another language*; also in verses 4, 13, 14, 19, 26 and 27 [c] 5 Or *in other languages*; also in verses 6, 18, 22, 23 and 39

made of bronze, a metal for which Corinth was well known (although scholars often suggest that not all Corinthian bronze was made in Corinth, and some of what circulated under that label may have even been counterfeit).

13:2 *faith that can move mountains.* Cf. Mk 11:23; moving mountains was apparently an ancient figure of speech, also attested in some Jewish sources, for doing what was virtually impossible.

13:4–8a Orators would sometimes develop a point at particular length, here the characteristics of love. Clever repetition of sounds also could sustain attention; every word in v. 4 ends with a vowel sound (the two most common ending sounds here are *-ei* and *-ai*). Three consonantal endings in v. 5 are the only exceptions to vowel-sound endings through v. 8a.

13:8b–13 Valuable as God's present gifts are, they are less permanent, and therefore from a Greek perspective less valuable, than eternal virtues.

13:8b *where there are.* A good preacher, Paul three times repeats this phrase; such opening repetition is anaphora, an ancient rhetorical device that drives home a point and sounds pleasant.

13:9 *prophesy in part.* Prophetic insight, like other knowledge, is often quite limited; see, e.g., 2Sa 7:3–5; 2Ki 2:3,5, 16–18; 4:27; Lk 7:19; Ac 21:4.

13:11 *When I became a man.* Around age 13 (at least in later Jewish tradition) or around age 16 (more often for Romans), boys would enter manhood; at that time a Roman boy would replace his childhood toga for an all-white adult toga.

13:12 *reflection as in a mirror.* Many mirrors were made from bronze, including Corinthian bronze (see note on v. 1), but ancient mirrors offered reflections much less clear than direct sight. *face to face.* Moses saw God "face to face," unlike other prophets (Nu 12:6–8, especially in the Greek version; Dt 34:10), though even he could not see God's glory fully at that time (Ex 33:20). *know fully.* Jeremiah had announced a time when all God's people would know him (Jer 31:33–34).

13:13 *greatest of these is love.* Ancient writers sometimes repeated a point at the beginning and end of a topic, as with love's eternality in v. 8 and here. Ancient thinkers varied in their views of the chief virtue, but Jesus' teaching united his followers around love (Mk 12:29–31).

14:2 *anyone who speaks in a tongue.* Although many ancient peoples claimed to have prophets, speaking in tongues may have been unique to early Christians. Supposed ancient parallels were usually simply a matter of priests editing already basically intelligible speech into a more coherent and eloquent form. *mysteries.* Highly valued—especially when interpreted (cf. Da 2:28–29,47).

14:3 *for their strengthening, encouraging and comfort.* As in the OT, prophecy could include strengthening (building up, as in Jer 1:10), encouraging and comfort (cf. Isa 40:1). That Paul omits specific mention of messages about judgment, despite their frequency in earlier Scripture, may be because he expects this to be less relevant for churches (though cf., e.g., 11:30; Rev 2:5,16).

14:5 *I would like every one of you.* Moses also wanted all God's people to prophesy (Nu 11:29), and Joel promised that God would empower all his people in this way (Joel 2:28). Although some individuals might remain characteristically prophets in contrast to others (1Co 12:28–29), the outpouring at Pentecost democratized prophetically-guided speaking for God far beyond the models in ancient Israel.

14:7–8 Although musical instruments lack language, they could communicate meaning; e.g., flute melodies could give instructions to flocks, and trumpets regularly signaled armies (see note on v. 8).

14:7 *pipe.* A wind instrument that sounded like an oboe;

1 CORINTHIANS 14:1

Prophecy in Antiquity

Peoples in antiquity sought to hear from their gods in various ways. They drew lots, and non-Israelites divined omens, e.g., in the flight of birds, the condition of sacrificial intestines and the like. Hearing from the gods was important when preparing for battles or for other essential matters.

The most important and direct form of guidance for Israelites, however, was prophecy. Most peoples in antiquity, including ancient Israelites, recognized prophecy as speech directly inspired by a deity or spirit. Greeks often associated inspired speech with the frenzy of possession, but could also associate it with music or poetry. Many believed that it could not be controlled, a view that Paul does not share (1Co 14:32). Although most prophecy involved direct inspiration, it could be dictated, written down and delivered on a later occasion (Jer 36:6,32). Some used prophecy as merely a literary device, but most regarded prophecy as directly inspired even if it was afterward edited into a more suitable format, as at Delphi or at times in the prophetic books of Scripture.

By the first century many Jews, perhaps especially among the elite, doubted that prophets flourished in their day the way that they had in ancient Israel. Such skepticism characterized Sadducees, probably most Pharisees (given the views of later rabbis), and more selectively Josephus (who allowed for prophetic speech but apparently not prophets). Apocalyptic writers composed prophetic literary works in the names of earlier figures; scholars debate whether most of them believed themselves inspired. By contrast, some Judeans and Samaritans did follow prophetic figures in the wilderness, often with lethal consequences. Essenes believed that prophecy and God's Spirit remained active among them.

Most prophetic and Spirit-oriented of all, early Christians believed that they lived in a period of the renewal of prophecy (the Christian era, Ac 2:17–18) and prophets (e.g., Ac 21:9–11; 1Co 12:28–29; 14:29,32; Rev 22:9). Just as in the OT, such prophecy needed to be evaluated. Again as in the OT, even when prophecies were true, no one expected very many of them to become canonical, i.e., a standard for the continued guidance of God's people analogous to the law. Although some Scripture included prophecy and a small proportion of prophecies were recorded in Scripture, they were different forms of revelation and never meant to be coextensive. Prophecies seem to have been widespread in the early churches (1Co 14:26–31,39; 1Th 5:20). ◆

such as the pipe or harp, how will anyone know what tune is being played unless there is a distinction in the notes?
8 Again, if the trumpet does not sound a
clear call, who will get ready for battle?[n]
9 So it is with you. Unless you speak intelligible words with your tongue, how
will anyone know what you are saying?
You will just be speaking into the air.
10 Undoubtedly there are all sorts of languages in the world, yet none of them is
without meaning. 11 If then I do not grasp
the meaning of what someone is saying,
I am a foreigner to the speaker, and the
speaker is a foreigner to me. 12 So it is
with you. Since you are eager for gifts of
the Spirit, try to excel in those that build
up the church.

14:8 [n] Nu 10:9; Jer 4:19

common in religious and emotional music, it often had two pipes from the mouthpiece. *harp.* A stringed instrument that often accompanied singing; people regarded it as particularly harmonious.
14:8 *trumpet.* Used to summon troops for battle, to march and so forth; an uncertain trumpeting would confuse the soldiers.
14:11 *foreigner.* Translates a Greek term by which Greeks often designated those who did not speak Greek.

[13]For this reason the one who speaks
in a tongue should pray that they may interpret what they say. [14]For if I pray in a
tongue, my spirit prays, but my mind is
unfruitful. [15]So what shall I do? I will pray
with my spirit, but I will also pray with my
understanding; I will sing[o] with my spirit,
but I will also sing with my understanding.
[16]Otherwise when you are praising God in
the Spirit, how can someone else, who is
now put in the position of an inquirer,[a]
say "Amen"[p] to your thanksgiving,[q] since
they do not know what you are saying?
[17]You are giving thanks well enough, but
no one else is edified.

[18]I thank God that I speak in tongues
more than all of you. [19]But in the church I
would rather speak five intelligible words
to instruct others than ten thousand words
in a tongue.

[20]Brothers and sisters, stop thinking like
children.[r] In regard to evil be infants,[s] but
in your thinking be adults. [21]In the Law[t]
it is written:

"With other tongues
and through the lips of foreigners
I will speak to this people,
but even then they will not listen
to me,[u]
says the Lord."[b]

[22]Tongues, then, are a sign, not for believers but for unbelievers; prophecy,[v]
however, is not for unbelievers but for
believers. [23]So if the whole church comes
together and everyone speaks in tongues,
and inquirers or unbelievers come in,
will they not say that you are out of your
mind?[w] [24]But if an unbeliever or an inquirer comes in while everyone is prophesying, they are convicted of sin and are
brought under judgment by all, [25]as the secrets of their hearts are laid bare. So they
will fall down and worship God, exclaim-
ing, "God is really among you!"[x]

Good Order in Worship

[26]What then shall we say, brothers and
sisters? When you come together, each of
you[y] has a hymn,[z] or a word of instruction,[a] a revelation, a tongue or an interpretation. Everything must be done so that the
church may be built up.[b] [27]If anyone speaks
in a tongue, two—or at the most three—
should speak, one at a time, and someone
must interpret. [28]If there is no interpreter,
the speaker should keep quiet in the church
and speak to himself and to God.

14:15 [o]Eph 5:19; Col 3:16
14:16 [p]Dt 27:15-26; 1Ch 16:36; Ne 8:6; Ps 106:48; Rev 5:14; 7:12 [q]1Co 11:24
14:20 [r]Eph 4:14; Heb 5:12, 13; 1Pe 2:2 [s]Ro 16:19
14:21 [t]Jn 10:34 [u]Isa 28:11, 12
14:22 [v]ver 1
14:23 [w]Ac 2:13
14:25 [x]Isa 45:14; Zec 8:23
14:26 [y]1Co 12:7-10 [z]Eph 5:19 [a]ver 6 [b]Ro 14:19

[a] *16* The Greek word for *inquirer* is a technical term for someone not fully initiated into a religion; also in verses 23 and 24. [b] *21* Isaiah 28:11,12

14:13–15 Many Greeks and some Diaspora Jews believed that prophetic inspiration temporarily possessed and displaced the mind. Paul seems to disagree regarding prophecy (v. 32), and believes that the mind can be used (through interpretation) even in connection with tongues, though tongues appear to focus more on the affective than the cognitive dimension of the human personality. Some in ancient Israel experienced inspired (prophetically guided) worship (e.g., 1Sa 10:5; 1Ch 25:1–3); it became more pervasive in Jesus' movement (cf. Jn 4:24; Eph 5:18–19; Php 3:3).
14:16 *say "Amen."* Jewish prayers typically concluded with "Amen," already used by ancient Israelites to express affirmation (e.g., Ps 41:13; 72:19; 106:48).
14:19 *ten thousand.* The largest Greek number, often thus used hyperbolically.
14:20 *stop thinking like children.* Referring to adults' immaturity in important matters demeaned them (see notes on v. 21; 3:1).
14:21 *other tongues.* In Isa 28, God warns that because Israel acts like immature children (see note on v. 20), refusing to understand his message (Isa 28:9–10), God will speak to them instead by judgment through the unintelligible Assyrians (Isa 28:11).
14:22–25 In light of the quotation in v. 21, the point in v. 22 might be that one of the functions of tongues was to signify that judgment was coming on the disobedient. Some others suppose that Paul cites a Corinthian idea in v. 22 and then refutes it in vv. 23–25. Still others suggest that the point in vv. 23–25 is that tongues can confirm unbelievers and prophecy can invite them to be believers. Or possibly vv. 23–25 shows that even when the situation of v. 22 is reversed, prophecy is more valuable.
14:23 *inquirers or unbelievers come in.* Hosts and members could invite unbelieving friends to the house gatherings. *out of your mind.* Ancient Mediterranean people were familiar with prophecy but not tongues, which lacked close parallels in antiquity. Greeks often were impressed with prophetic madness that would make inspired people out of their mind (this was more common and more relevant to the idea of *inspired* frenzy than the group frenzy of certain cults proposed by a minority of scholars here).
14:25 *secrets of their hearts are laid bare.* Accurate revealing of their hearts' secrets (an eschatological foretaste; cf. 4:5; Ro 2:16), however, would lead to repentance. *fall down and worship.* Outsiders bowing and acknowledging God probably recalls Isa 45:14.
14:26–40 That Paul offers these regulations suggests that he had not provided them earlier during his lengthy stay (Ac 18:11,18). These regulations, then, are probably directed toward a situation of abuses. We also should keep in mind that they applied to house churches, which probably rarely could accommodate 50 or more members. Although principles of order would remain, specifics might differ for larger congregations that could not accommodate all the ministries of v. 26 within one service, and for smaller groups meeting for private prayer without possible unbelievers present.
14:26 *come together.* Synagogues in this period were Jewish community centers used most fully for prayer and corporate study of the Torah on the Sabbath. Many may have been much less formal and allowed wider participation than in a later period. *hymn.* Lit. "psalm"; Jewish people used Biblical and sometimes post-Biblical psalms. By contrast, for anyone to bring a "revelation" or be inspired to speak in a "tongue" they did not know was unlike virtually all other assemblies in antiquity.
14:27 *one at a time.* Ancient assemblies varied in their emphasis on order (those in the Dead Sea Scrolls required strict order), but order would be lost anywhere if multiple

29 Two or three prophets should speak,
and the others should weigh carefully
what is said.[c] 30 And if a revelation comes
to someone who is sitting down, the first
speaker should stop. 31 For you can all
prophesy in turn so that everyone may be
instructed and encouraged. 32 The spirits
of prophets are subject to the control of
prophets.[d] 33 For God is not a God of disorder[e] but of peace — as in all the congregations of the Lord's people.[f]

34 Women[a] should remain silent in the
churches. They are not allowed to speak,
but must be in submission,[g] as the law[h]
says. 35 If they want to inquire about something, they should ask their own husbands
at home; for it is disgraceful for a woman
to speak in the church.[b]

36 Or did the word of God originate
with you? Or are you the only people it
has reached? 37 If anyone thinks they are
a prophet[i] or otherwise gifted by the Spirit, let them acknowledge that what I am
writing to you is the Lord's command.[j]
38 But if anyone ignores this, they will
themselves be ignored.[c]

39 Therefore, my brothers and sisters,
be eager[k] to prophesy, and do not forbid speaking in tongues. 40 But everything
should be done in a fitting and orderly[l]
way.

The Resurrection of Christ

15 Now, brothers and sisters, I want
to remind you of the gospel[m] I
preached to you, which you received and
on which you have taken your stand. 2 By
this gospel you are saved,[n] if you hold
firmly[o] to the word I preached to you. Otherwise, you have believed in vain.

3 For what I received[p] I passed on to
you[q] as of first importance[d]: that Christ

14:29 [c] 1Co 12:10 **14:32** [d] 1Jn 4:1 **14:33** [e] ver 40 [f] Ac 9:13 **14:34** [g] 1Ti 2:11, 12 [h] Ge 3:16 **14:37** [i] 2Co 10:7 [j] 1Jn 4:6 **14:39** [k] 1Co 12:31 **14:40** [l] ver 33 **15:1** [m] Ro 2:16 **15:2** [n] Ro 1:16 [o] Ro 11:22 **15:3** [p] Gal 1:12 [q] 1Co 11:23

[a] *33,34* Or *peace. As in all the congregations of the Lord's people, 34women* [b] *34,35* In a few manuscripts these verses come after verse 40. [c] *38* Some manuscripts *But anyone who is ignorant of this will be ignorant* [d] *3* Or *you at the first*

persons tried to speak at once. Paul disagrees with the Greek view that inspired speech was uncontrollable (v. 32).
14:29 *others should weigh carefully what is said.* In ancient Israel, many junior prophets probably learned especially in small groups under the mentorship of more experienced prophets (cf. 1Sa 19:20; 2Ki 2:3 – 7,15; 6:1 – 7). Most first-generation churches lacked such prophetic mentors, so fellow junior prophets in the congregations would have to help evaluate the extent to which their peers were hearing the Spirit accurately. For the limitations of prophecy, see notes on 13:9; Ac 21:4.
14:30 *someone who is sitting down.* In Diaspora assemblies, one would stand to speak.
14:31 *you can all prophesy in turn.* Paul here depicts house churches more like a school of the prophets (cf. 1Sa 19:20, though Paul requires more order) than like ancient synagogues or other meetings of ancient associations. See the article "Prophecy in Antiquity," p. 2009; see also note on v. 5.
14:32 *subject to the control of prophets.* Paul disagrees with the Greek view that inspired speech was uncontrollable (see note on vv. 13 – 15; cf. Pr 16:32; 25:28).
14:33 *as in all the congregations of the Lord's people.* For a closing appeal to wider consensus, see note on 11:16.
14:34 – 35 Digressions were common, so Paul may digress here to another issue of order.
14:34 *Women should remain silent in the churches.* Although they made an exception for inspired speech (cf. 11:5), Greeks who valued older traditions resented a woman speaking in public where men other than her husband were present. Some may have differed as to whether house churches were, as assemblies, public settings or, as homes, private settings. *the law.* Nowhere does the Torah mandate women's submission, though it depicts it (cf. 1Pe 3:5), especially related to the fall (Ge 3:16); other Jews such as Josephus sometimes made this general statement. Addressing the situation in Corinth, Paul seems to refer to a particular kind of speech (see note on v. 35) rather than all speech (e.g., praying, corporate singing or prophesying; 11:5).
14:35 *inquire about something.* Informed listeners customarily asked questions during lectures, including lectures on Scripture. Ancients deemed unlearned questions to be inappropriate, however; novices were to learn quietly and not to slow down others with inappropriate questions. Whether for this reason or the one noted in the note on v. 34, women's public questions could be offensive. Proportionately, women had far less education than men of the same social classes; Jewish women would hear Scripture explained in synagogues but were virtually never trained as disciples (see note on Lk 10:39) nor even taught to recite Scripture along with boys (see notes on 1Ti 2:11,12). *ask their own husbands at home.* Women often married at age 18 and sometimes much younger; Greek women were an average 12 years younger than their husbands. Because Greek husbands often viewed their wives as being like children, few took an interest in their wives' learning; exceptions were noteworthy. Thus in Paul's culture, encouragement for wives to learn, even privately, would be considered very progressive. Their learning would also counter the reason for these women interrupting lectures with unhelpful questions.
14:37 *what I am writing to you is the Lord's command.* Some Biblical prophets, such as Moses, Deborah, Samuel, Elijah and Elisha, carried special authority recognized by other prophets. Paul expects the truly prophetically gifted to recognize his own inspiration (cf. v. 29).
14:39 – 40 Speakers and writers often concluded a work or a section (here vv. 1 – 38) with a summary statement.
15:1 – 2 Like other skilled speakers and writers of his day, Paul in ch. 15 starts by looking for common ground with his audience. Some of the Corinthian Christians dispute the future resurrection of believers. They cannot, however, dispute the past resurrection of Jesus, because, Paul shows, this is an established fact and the very foundation of their faith. Yet Paul points out that this fact is simply the first installment of the future resurrection of believers, hence cannot be separated from it (vv. 12 – 14,23).
15:3 *what I received I passed on to you.* Those who carefully passed on to others orally what they learned from their teachers often used the terms "received" and "passed on"; they expected those who heard to continue to pass on the information. People in antiquity cultivated skilled memories (see Introduction to the Gospels and Acts: The Gospels' Reliable Sources, p. 1599). The information passed on in vv. 4 – 7 goes back to the earliest experiences

1 CORINTHIANS 15

Resurrection

Resurrection was a holistic Jewish hope that the dead (or at least the righteous dead) would be raised to a new bodily existence of some sort at a future time. Future physical hope was rooted in God's covenant promises to Israel, but came to be applied as a physical hope for individuals most clearly during the Persian period, when new questions were being asked.

Many, probably most, Judeans affirmed an end-time resurrection of the righteous; thus, e.g., Maccabean martyrs expected to receive back their dismembered parts at the resurrection (2 Maccabees 14:46). One is said to have defied his killer with these words: "You are releasing us from the present age, but the world's true king, because we have died on behalf of his laws, will raise us up in an eternal restoration of life" (2 Maccabees 7:9). Scripture itself already noted the resurrection of both the righteous and (for judgment) the wicked at the end of this age (Da 12:2). Views varied on the nature of the resurrection body. Some envisioned it as a heavenly body composed of fire, like the stars (they may have thought also of Da 12:3). Some believed that the body would be raised first in the form in which it died, before healing it, so that no one could question that it was the same person. Later rabbis believed that one bone in the neck was invulnerable and would be the minimal basis for the resurrection. In any case, resurrection was not simply afterlife; it was the restoration of bodily existence in some form.

By contrast, this conception was difficult for Greeks to envision. Many Gentile intellectuals affirmed the soul's immortality without a future for the body; some others denied any afterlife at all. Many tomb inscriptions lamented lack of hope for any afterlife. Even traditional Greek mythology viewed the afterlife as a shadowy semi-existence without a body, perhaps similar to the more ambiguous and perhaps figurative depictions of Sheol in the OT. Sadducees in Judea and undoubtedly many Diaspora Jews influenced by Greek thought did not think in terms of a resurrection, but they would clearly understand that the Galilean apostolic claim meant bodily resurrection.

continued on next page

died for our sins[r] according to the Scriptures,[s] 4that he was buried, that he was
raised[t] on the third day[u] according to
the Scriptures,[v] 5and that he appeared to
Cephas,[a][w] and then to the Twelve.[x] 6Af-
ter that, he appeared to more than five
hundred of the brothers and sisters at the
same time, most of whom are still living,

15:3 [r] Isa 53:5; 1Pe 2:24 [s] Lk 24:27; Ac 26:22,23 **15:4** [t] Ac 2:24 [u] Mt 16:21 [v] Ac 2:25,30,31 **15:5** [w] Lk 24:34 [x] Mk 16:14

[a] 5 That is, Peter

of Jesus' followers. *Christ died for our sins according to the Scriptures.* May evoke the Biblical pattern of God's servants suffering before exaltation, but especially God's servant suffering for sins in Isa 53:4–6,8,11–12.

15:4 *on the third day.* Might simply imply that Jesus was raised before he could "see decay" (Ps 16:10); if Paul thinks of particular texts, they might include Hos 6:2; Jnh 1:17. *according to the Scriptures.* Jewish law required burial even for those executed as criminals (Dt 21:23). Because Jewish thought and the Jewish witnesses understood resurrection as a bodily event, resurrection presupposes an empty tomb (as in Mk 16:6), but Paul focuses on the more important issue of the attesting witnesses (vv. 5–8). Paul's appeal here to the Scriptures likely evokes multiple passages, perhaps including Ps 16:10–11; Isa 53:12.

15:5 *Cephas.* The original Aramaic name for "rock" (pronounced *kay'fa*) that appears in Greek as *Petros*, Peter. *the Twelve.* See note on Ac 1:22. In antiquity, people often named groups according to their initial number, retaining the name even when the number changed; even after Judas's death, then, some would call the group "the Twelve," although not all did (Ac 1:26; 2:14).

15:6 *more than five hundred of the brothers and sisters at the same time.* Ancient writers sometimes appealed to witnesses from whom their hearers could inquire. Because hallucination is nearly always an individual experience, it offers no explanation for the simultaneous, mass experience reported here.

Jewish people expected the resurrection at the end of the age, usually associating it with the time of the Messiah's coming and his kingdom. Greeks and Romans did not envision an end of the age any more than they expected bodily restoration.

Because many people believed in ghosts and an afterlife, a claim that the disciples had seen Jesus as a spirit would not have been very controversial. It is rather the first witnesses' claim that they had seen him bodily that rendered their testimony unique. Supposed ancient parallels that some have proposed with "rising gods" are not very helpful. These accounts mostly involve fertility deities returning each spring and are not bodily, whereas Jesus' resurrection fits the Jewish understanding of bodily resurrection already established in Da 12:2. Accounts of mortals' deification and ascension likewise are not bodily, and in most cases are attested only long after the mortals' deaths (contrast 1Co 15:3 – 8) or were even just primeval myths. ◆

Fourteenth-century coptic icon of Doubting Thomas. It is the first witnesses' claim that they had seen Jesus' resurrected physical body that made their testimony unique.

Gianni Dagli Orti/The Art Archive at Art Resource, NY

though some have fallen asleep. 7Then he
appeared to James, then to all the apostles,[y] 8and last of all he appeared to me
also,[z] as to one abnormally born.
9For I am the least of the apostles[a] and
do not even deserve to be called an apostle, because I persecuted[b] the church of
God. 10But by the grace of God I am what
I am, and his grace to me[c] was not without effect. No, I worked harder than all
of them[d] — yet not I, but the grace of God
that was with me.[e] 11Whether, then, it is I
or they, this is what we preach, and this is
what you believed.

The Resurrection of the Dead

12But if it is preached that Christ has
been raised from the dead, how can some
of you say that there is no resurrection
of the dead?[f] 13If there is no resurrection
of the dead, then not even Christ has
been raised. 14And if Christ has not been

15:7 [y]Lk 24:33, 36,37; Ac 1:3,4 **15:8** [z]Ac 9:3-6, 17; 1Co 9:1 **15:9** [a]Eph 3:8; 1Ti 1:15 [b]Ac 8:3 **15:10** [c]Ro 12:3 [d]2Co 11:23 [e]Php 2:13 **15:12** [f]Ac 17:32; 23:8; 2Ti 2:18

15:7 *James.* The Lord's brother (Gal 1:19). *all the apostles.* Paul uses the designation apostles for others more widely than simply the Twelve (v. 5; cf. 1:1; 4:9; 9:5 – 6; Ro 16:7; 1Th 2:6).
15:12 – 19 Rhetoric used repetition to reinforce points; Paul dwells on an important point here, repeating "if" six times.
15:13 – 14 Speakers often started with common ground; they could also reduce an opponent's case to the absurd, showing that it leads to conclusions that even the opponents would not accept. The Corinthian believers affirm Jesus' resurrection (vv. 1 – 2), but it was a part of the promised future resurrection of the righteous (Da 12:2) and cannot be understood without it.

raised,[g] our preaching is useless and so is
your faith. 15More than that, we are then
found to be false witnesses about God, for
we have testified about God that he raised
Christ from the dead.[h] But he did not raise
him if in fact the dead are not raised. 16For
if the dead are not raised, then Christ has
not been raised either. 17And if Christ has
not been raised, your faith is futile; you are
still in your sins.[i] 18Then those also who
have fallen asleep in Christ are lost. 19If
only for this life we have hope in Christ,
we are of all people most to be pitied.[j]
20But Christ has indeed been raised
from the dead,[k] the firstfruits[l] of those
who have fallen asleep.[m] 21For since death
came through a man,[n] the resurrection of
the dead comes also through a man. 22For
as in Adam all die, so in Christ all will be
made alive.[o] 23But each in turn: Christ, the
firstfruits;[p] then, when he comes,[q] those
who belong to him. 24Then the end will
come, when he hands over the kingdom[r]
to God the Father after he has destroyed
all dominion, authority and power.[s] 25For
he must reign until he has put all his enemies under his feet.[t] 26The last enemy to
be destroyed is death.[u] 27For he "has put
everything under his feet."[a][v] Now when it
says that "everything" has been put under
him, it is clear that this does not include
God himself, who put everything under
Christ.[w] 28When he has done this, then the
Son himself will be made subject to him
who put everything under him,[x] so that
God may be all in all.[y]
29Now if there is no resurrection, what
will those do who are baptized for the
dead? If the dead are not raised at all, why
are people baptized for them? 30And as for
us, why do we endanger ourselves every
hour?[z] 31I face death every day[a]—yes, just
as surely as I boast about you in Christ
Jesus our Lord. 32If I fought wild beasts[b]
in Ephesus[c] with no more than human

15:14 [g] 1Th 4:14
15:15 [h] Ac 2:24
15:17 [i] Ro 4:25
15:19 [j] 1Co 4:9
15:20 [k] 1Pe 1:3 [l] ver 23; Ac 26:23; Rev 1:5 [m] ver 6, 18
15:21 [n] Ro 5:12
15:22 [o] Ro 5:14-18
15:23 [p] ver 20 [q] ver 52
15:24 [r] Da 7:14, 27 [s] Ro 8:38
15:25 [t] Ps 110:1; Mt 22:44
15:26 [u] 2Ti 1:10; Rev 20:14; 21:4
15:27 [v] Ps 8:6 [w] Mt 28:18
15:28 [x] Php 3:21 [y] 1Co 3:23
15:30 [z] 2Co 11:26
15:31 [a] Ro 8:36
15:32 [b] 2Co 1:8 [c] Ac 18:19

[a] *27* Psalm 8:6

15:15 *false witnesses about God.* False witnesses could suffer severe punishment (Dt 19:18–21); testifying falsely about God, like falsely calling on him to attest an oath, invited great punishment (cf. Ex 20:7,16).
15:16–17 See note on vv. 13–14.
15:18 *fallen asleep.* A common ancient metaphor for being dead.
15:19 *If only for this life we have hope.* Gentiles did not expect a bodily resurrection, yet some believed in an afterlife; it appears that in Judea, many people affirmed an afterlife before the promised resurrection. Nevertheless, most Jews in the Holy Land affirmed the importance of physical creation and the body; they would have seen a future without hope of bodily restoration as meaningless.
15:20 *firstfruits.* Gathered at the beginning of the harvest (e.g., Ex 23:16,19); once the harvest had begun, the rest of the harvest was certain.
15:21 *death came through a man.* Death came through Adam (Ge 2:17; 5:5), as Jewish thinkers in the Holy Land often emphasized. See notes on vv. 45,47,48.
15:23 *firstfruits.* See note on v. 20.
15:24 *Then the end will come.* Some Jewish thinkers expected an interim period between this age and the future one. Paul so portrays the period between Christ's comings (vv. 25–27).
15:25 In Ps 110:1, the Lord at the Father's right hand—Jesus (see Mk 12:36–37 and notes)—would reign until his enemies were subdued; he reigns in the present, until the resurrection of the righteous (v. 26). *put all his enemies under his feet.* An ancient image for fully conquering and subjugating one's adversaries.
15:26 *death.* The last of the enemies in v. 25 (from Ps 110), death will end with the resurrection of the righteous (Da 12:1–3).
15:27 Jewish interpreters regularly connected passages that used the same words or phrases; it was therefore natural for Paul to link Ps 8:6 with Ps 110:1. In Ps 8:6, God already put everything under humanity's feet, referring to their original call to govern the earth (Ge 1:26–27). Paul connects Jesus with Adam (v. 22; see notes on vv. 45,47,48). That the psalm in Hebrew speaks of the ruler as "son of man" (see NIV text note on Ps 8:4) strengthens Paul's connection with Jesus.
15:28 *the Son himself will be made subject to him.* The full subjugation of enemies in vv. 25–27 would come when God would raise the righteous at the end of the age. Jesus' reign (v. 25) would then give way to the Father's (v. 24); Jesus being "subject" to the Father might evoke the Hebrew text of Ps 8:5, the context of which Paul has just cited in Greek (v. 27). *God may be all in all.* In contrast to some philosophers, when Jewish thinkers spoke of God being "all" they meant that he ruled everything; "all in all" was a rhetorically emphatic way of speaking.
15:29 *baptized for the dead.* Paul appeals to a practice that the Corinthians affirmed as inconsistent without belief in resurrection (cf. similarly 2 Maccabees 12:43–45). Because Paul does not elaborate, scholars can only guess what Corinthian Christian practice Paul envisions. Some suggest that "baptized for the dead" may mean that another Christian was baptized on behalf of a new convert who had died before being able to be baptized. (Jewish people did sometimes carry out acts posthumously.) Others suggest that Christians were baptizing new converts to fill the ranks of Christians who had died. It might also refer to pre-burial washings of the dead, a standard Jewish custom; religious groups in the ancient Mediterranean supervised the burials of their own members. Sometimes Paul (cf., e.g., 11:10 and note), like other Jewish teachers, used abbreviated ways of communicating a point if he expected his audience to understand. He might use a roundabout way of saying "baptized so as to be able to participate in eternal life with Christians who have already died," hence baptized in the light of their own mortality as well. Or people may be baptized for the sake of their own future resurrection, in view of the sentence of death already in their mortal bodies (cf. Ro 8:10). To whatever practice Paul alludes, it is not clear whether he agrees with the Corinthian practice; even if he does not, however, he can use it to make his point; they are not acting consistently with their own beliefs.
15:30–31 See 4:12–13; 2Co 4:9–12; cf. Ps 44:22 in Ro 8:36.
15:31 *I face death every day.* May also evoke Jesus' teaching regarding suffering for Christ (Mk 8:34; especially Lk 9:23).
15:32 *If I fought wild beasts in Ephesus.* Like many other major cities, both Ephesus and Corinth hosted gladiator battles and wild beast attacks in their outdoor theaters.

hopes, what have I gained? If the dead are
not raised,

"Let us eat and drink,
for tomorrow we die."[a][d]

33Do not be misled: "Bad company corrupts good character."[b] 34Come back to
your senses as you ought, and stop sinning; for there are some who are ignorant
of God — I say this to your shame.

The Resurrection Body

35But someone will ask,[e] "How are the
dead raised? With what kind of body will
they come?"[f] 36How foolish![g] What you
sow does not come to life unless it dies.[h]
37When you sow, you do not plant the
body that will be, but just a seed, perhaps
of wheat or of something else. 38But God
gives it a body as he has determined, and
to each kind of seed he gives its own body.[i]
39Not all flesh is the same: People have
one kind of flesh, animals have another,
birds another and fish another. 40There are
also heavenly bodies and there are earthly
bodies; but the splendor of the heavenly
bodies is one kind, and the splendor of the
earthly bodies is another. 41The sun has
one kind of splendor, the moon another
and the stars another; and star differs from
star in splendor.

42So will it be[j] with the resurrection of
the dead. The body that is sown is perishable, it is raised imperishable; 43it is sown
in dishonor, it is raised in glory;[k] it is sown
in weakness, it is raised in power; 44it is
sown a natural body, it is raised a spiritual body.[l]

If there is a natural body, there is also
a spiritual body. 45So it is written: "The
first man Adam became a living being"[c];[m]
the last Adam,[n] a life-giving spirit.[o] 46The

15:32 [d] Isa 22:13; Lk 12:19
15:35 [e] Ro 9:19 [f] Eze 37:3
15:36 [g] Lk 11:40 [h] Jn 12:24
15:38 [i] Ge 1:11
15:42 [j] Da 12:3; Mt 13:43
15:43 [k] Php 3:21; Col 3:4
15:44 [l] ver 50
15:45 [m] Ge 2:7 [n] Ro 5:14 [o] Jn 5:21; Ro 8:2

[a] *32* Isaiah 22:13 [b] *33* From the Greek poet Menander [c] *45* Gen. 2:7

Observing the mauling deaths of criminals, prisoners of war and sometimes slaves was valued as entertainment; it was one way the emperor pacified the masses of Rome (see note on 4:9). Paul speaks figuratively, however; officials did not execute Roman citizens this way, and Paul had not died. Philosophers depicted the irrational masses as "beasts"; Paul could also draw on Biblical images for oppressors (Ps 22:12 – 13,16,20 – 21; 74:19). *Let us eat ... die.* Paul quotes Isa 22:13; many people who believed in future judgment thought that those who did not (such as Sadducees or Epicureans) lacked reasons to behave morally.
15:33 Paul cites a popular proverb, first attributed to the comic playwright Menander but in common circulation by Paul's day. Both Jewish and Gentile sages urged people to avoid morally inferior company (cf. Ps 1:1; 119:63; Pr 13:20; 14:7; 28:7). Paul believes that others have wrongly influenced the Corinthian Christians' beliefs and values.
15:35 *someone will ask.* Ancient writers often raised rhetorical objections from imaginary opponents. *With what kind of body will they come?* Jewish teachers presented questions like the one Paul raises here as the standard objections nonbelievers raised against the doctrine of the resurrection. (For imaginary interlocutors, see note on 6:12.) For instance, what happened if someone died at sea, or the body was completely destroyed by fire?
15:36 *How foolish!* Speakers often answered ignorant interlocutors with "You fool" (which the NIV translates more gently here).
15:37 *just a seed.* Answering the objection that a destroyed body could not be restored (v. 35), later rabbis claimed that an indestructible bone in the neck would be the basis for the resurrection. Paul's answer is more defensible: regardless of what physical material remains, at least the pattern of the old body persists as the seed for the new body. Many others used and understood analogies from seeds.
15:39 – 41 The raised body will remain a body, but of a different character than the present body. Orators valued repetition; in the original Greek, Paul introduces various categories of bodies with "another" nine times (two of them, in v. 40, with a different Greek term).
15:40 *heavenly bodies.* In ancient thought, heavenly bodies had greater glory (the Greek term is translated "splendor" in vv. 40 – 41, but "glory" in v. 43) than earthly ones.
15:41 *stars.* Most people thought that stars consisted of fire; many Gentiles viewed them as divine, whereas Jews regarded them as angels (sometimes also thought to consist of fire). (Paul's illustration, written in Greek, is designed for ancient cosmology, not to impress modern readers.) Many Gentiles believed that immortal souls ascended into the heavens like stars; many Jewish people compared the resurrection body to angels or stars (Da 12:2 – 3). Cf. Isa 60:1 – 2,19; 62:1.
15:42 – 44 Repetition reinforced a point, often building emotional intensity; here Paul four times begins with "sown" and ends with "raised." Orators also used repeated contrasts to reinforce a point. Some Jewish thinkers expected the body to be resurrected first in the form in which it died so that no one could question that it was the same person. Present "dishonor" and "weakness" (v. 43) may challenge the status-conscious Christians in Corinth (cf. 2Co 12:5,9; 13:4). Many Jewish teachers claimed that Adam had immense glory and authority until he sinned; God would restore these to his people in the world to come.
15:44 *natural ... spiritual.* The Greek term translated "natural" means "of the soul/natural life"; like "spiritual," it prepares for v. 45. Ancient orators sometimes held attention with shocking or paradoxical images; Paul does so here: no one thought of "soulish" or "spiritual" bodies. But as becomes clear in the context, he is contrasting bodies fitted for the present life with future bodies transformed by the Spirit (vv. 45 – 49; cf. Ro 8:11).
15:45 *a living being.* Used in Ge 2:7, it is also the Greek term for "soul" or "life" (see note on v. 44). Some Jewish thinkers outside the Holy Land found in Ge 1:26 – 27 the ideal person, the pure form and model for humanity, but found in the enlivening of Adam in Ge 2:7 a second, inferior type of humanity. If Corinthian Christians knew this tradition, Paul reverses it: the second is greater than the first. Many Jews would have agreed with his sequence: Adam was in the past, but resurrection and the Spirit were promised for the future. *a life-giving spirit.* May also evoke Ge 2:7; the Greek translation for "breath of life" there is "breath of Spirit." Thus Christ, far greater than Adam, corresponds with the very life that animated Adam.

spiritual did not come first, but the natural, and after that the spiritual. 47 The first
man was of the dust of the earth;[p] the
second man is of heaven.[q] 48 As was the
earthly man, so are those who are of the
earth; and as is the heavenly man, so also
are those who are of heaven.[r] 49 And just
as we have borne the image of the earthly
man,[s] so shall we[a] bear the image of the
heavenly man.[t]
50 I declare to you, brothers and sisters,
that flesh and blood[u] cannot inherit the
kingdom of God, nor does the perishable
inherit the imperishable. 51 Listen, I tell
you a mystery:[v] We will not all sleep, but
we will all be changed[w]— 52 in a flash, in
the twinkling of an eye, at the last trumpet. For the trumpet will sound,[x] the dead[y]
will be raised imperishable, and we will
be changed. 53 For the perishable must
clothe itself with the imperishable,[z] and
the mortal with immortality. 54 When the
perishable has been clothed with the imperishable, and the mortal with immortality, then the saying that is written will
come true: "Death has been swallowed up
in victory."[b][a]

15:47 [p] Ge 2:7; 3:19 [q] Jn 3:13, 31
15:48 [r] Php 3:20,21
15:49 [s] Ge 5:3 [t] Ro 8:29
15:50 [u] Jn 3:3,5
15:51 [v] 1Co 13:2 [w] Php 3:21
15:52 [x] Mt 24:31 [y] Jn 5:25
15:53 [z] 2Co 5:2, 4
15:54 [a] Isa 25:8; Rev 20:14
15:55 [b] Hos 13:14
15:56 [c] Ro 5:12 [d] Ro 4:15
15:57 [e] 2Co 2:14 [f] Ro 8:37
15:58 [g] 1Co 16:10
16:1 [h] Ac 24:17 [i] Ac 9:13 [j] Ac 16:6
16:2 [k] Ac 20:7 [l] 2Co 9:4,5
16:3 [m] 2Co 8:18,19

55 "Where, O death, is your victory?
Where, O death, is your sting?"[c][b]

56 The sting of death is sin,[c] and the power
of sin is the law.[d] 57 But thanks be to God![e]
He gives us the victory through our Lord
Jesus Christ.[f]
58 Therefore, my dear brothers and sisters, stand firm. Let nothing move you.
Always give yourselves fully to the work
of the Lord,[g] because you know that your
labor in the Lord is not in vain.

The Collection for the Lord's People

16 Now about the collection[h] for the
Lord's people:[i] Do what I told the
Galatian[j] churches to do. 2 On the first day
of every week,[k] each one of you should
set aside a sum of money in keeping with
your income, saving it up, so that when I
come no collections will have to be made.[l]
3 Then, when I arrive, I will give letters of
introduction to the men you approve[m] and
send them with your gift to Jerusalem. 4 If
it seems advisable for me to go also, they
will accompany me.

[a] 49 Some early manuscripts *so let us* [b] 54 Isaiah 25:8
[c] 55 Hosea 13:14

15:47 *of the dust of the earth.* God formed Adam from the dust of the ground (Ge 2:7).

15:48 Ancients accepted the principle that living things produced things of the same character (cf. Ge 1:11; Jn 3:6). Jewish thinkers in Paul's era emphasized that Adam's sin introduced sin and death on all his descendants.

15:49 *image of the heavenly man.* God created humanity in his image (Ge 1:26–27; 5:1–2). Diaspora Jewish thinkers who distinguished the first man of Ge 1 from the second man of Ge 2 (see note on v. 45) argued that it was the first, heavenly man, not the soulish physical man, that bears God's image; for Paul, God's image has begun to be restored in the heavenly man Christ (2Co 3:18; Ro 8:29; Col 3:10).

15:50 *flesh and blood.* Jewish sources commonly applied this expression to mere humans; Paul applies it to the current, mortal form of humanity in Adam. *inherit the kingdom.* Jewish sources also often used expressions such as this one for the promise of the coming world.

15:51 *I tell you a mystery.* Based on similar language in Daniel (Da 2:28–30,47), some of Paul's Judean contemporaries claimed to reveal mysteries, sometimes related to the end time. *sleep.* See note on v. 18.

15:52 *trumpet will sound.* Trumpets could gather people for war or assemblies. Building on Isa 27:12–13, Jewish tradition spoke of a trumpet gathering God's people in the time of the end. Paul likely draws on Jesus' application of the image (Mt 24:31; see note on 1Th 4:16).

15:53–54 *perishable … imperishable … perishable … imperishable.* Paul continues using rhetorical antithesis. In v. 54 Paul quotes Isa 25:8, which refers to God's triumph over death at the time of the end, at Israel's final restoration; the context fits resurrection in Isa 26:19. *clothe … clothed.* See note on 2Co 5:2–4.

15:55 Jewish interpreters frequently connected texts that shared a common key word; deliverance from death appears not only in Isa 25:8 (which Paul has just cited in v. 54) but also in Hos 13:14 (cited here), which Paul may therefore apply to the resurrection as well (cf. restoration imagery in Hos 14:4–7). "Victory" also occurs in one Greek version of Isaiah (though not in the Septuagint, the pre-Christian Greek translation of the OT); this could be relevant if Paul knew of this variation, since Jewish expositors normally selected whatever translation best suited their needs. This method might allow Paul to make a wordplay, in good Jewish interpretive style, with Hos 13:14, where Paul changes the Greek version's "punishment" (*dikē*) to "victory" (*nikē*).

15:56 Jewish interpreters often explained a text after quoting it (see v. 55).

15:57 Paul's stirring rhetorical devices in vv. 42–56 (see applicable notes) now reach their climax.

15:58 *your labor in the Lord is not in vain.* Speakers and writers often concluded a work or a section with a summary statement (cf. the risk of acting in vain in vv. 2,14,17); conclusions sometimes offered exhortations. Many people who believed in future judgment thought that those who did not (such as Sadducees or Epicureans) lacked reasons to behave morally. In view of the future resurrection of the body, which will last forever, believers should live wholly for Christ (cf. 6:13–14).

16:1–2 Although less dominant in Paul's letters, business was a major reason for many of the brief letters sent in antiquity. In contrast to other ancient associations, which usually required membership dues, gifts among believers were voluntary (cf. Ex 35:5,21–22, 26,29; 36:2), not shaming the body.

16:2 *the first day.* Might reflect the Biblical principle of devoting the first of one's earnings to God (cf. Ex 23:16; Lev 27:26), although payment was by day rather than by week; or it might recall Jesus' resurrection (Mk 16:2). Christians also may have often met on the first day of the week, in honor of Jesus' resurrection, although our first explicit evidence for this role for Sunday comes from the second century, at the earliest from half a century after Paul's letter. *in keeping with your income.* This kind of giving fits Biblical models (Dt 15:14; 16:10,17).

16:3 *letters of introduction.* See note on Ac 9:2. For caution in being above reproach, see notes on 2Co 8:17–24.

Personal Requests

5 After I go through Macedonia, I will
come to you[n] — for I will be going through
Macedonia.[o] 6 Perhaps I will stay with you
for a while, or even spend the winter, so
that you can help me on my journey,[p]
wherever I go. 7 For I do not want to see
you now and make only a passing visit; I
hope to spend some time with you, if the
Lord permits.[q] 8 But I will stay on at Ephesus[r] until Pentecost,[s] 9 because a great door
for effective work has opened to me,[t] and
there are many who oppose me.

10 When Timothy[u] comes, see to it that
he has nothing to fear while he is with
you, for he is carrying on the work of the
Lord,[v] just as I am. 11 No one, then, should
treat him with contempt.[w] Send him on
his way in peace[x] so that he may return
to me. I am expecting him along with the
brothers.

12 Now about our brother Apollos:[y] I
strongly urged him to go to you with the
brothers. He was quite unwilling to go
now, but he will go when he has the opportunity.

13 Be on your guard; stand firm[z] in the
faith; be courageous; be strong.[a] 14 Do everything in love.[b]

15 You know that the household of Stephanas[c] were the first converts[d] in Achaia,[e]
and they have devoted themselves to the
service of the Lord's people. I urge you,
brothers and sisters, 16 to submit[f] to such
people and to everyone who joins in the
work and labors at it. 17 I was glad when
Stephanas, Fortunatus and Achaicus arrived, because they have supplied what
was lacking from you.[g] 18 For they refreshed[h] my spirit and yours also. Such
men deserve recognition.[i]

Final Greetings

19 The churches in the province of Asia
send you greetings. Aquila and Priscilla[a][j]
greet you warmly in the Lord, and so does
the church that meets at their house.[k]
20 All the brothers and sisters here send
you greetings. Greet one another with a
holy kiss.[l]

21 I, Paul, write this greeting in my own
hand.[m]

16:5 [n] 1Co 4:19 [o] Ac 19:21 **16:6** [p] Ro 15:24 **16:7** [q] Ac 18:21 **16:8** [r] Ac 18:19 [s] Ac 2:1 **16:9** [t] Ac 14:27 **16:10** [u] Ac 16:1 [v] 1Co 15:58 **16:11** [w] 1Ti 4:12 [x] Ac 15:33 **16:12** [y] Ac 18:24; 1Co 1:12 **16:13** [z] Gal 5:1; Php 1:27; 1Th 3:8; 2Th 2:15

[a] Eph 6:10 **16:14** [b] 1Co 14:1 **16:15** [c] 1Co 1:16 [d] Ro 16:5 [e] Ac 18:12 **16:16** [f] Heb 13:17 **16:17** [g] 2Co 11:9; Php 2:30 **16:18** [h] Phm 7 [i] Php 2:29 **16:19** [j] Ac 18:2 [k] Ro 16:5 **16:20** [l] Ro 16:16 **16:21** [m] Gal 6:11; Col 4:18

[a] *19* Greek *Prisca*, a variant of *Priscilla*

Similarly, local Jewish communities in the Diaspora would select some of their most respectable representatives to carry their local collections of the annual tax for the support of the Jerusalem temple.

16:5 *I will come to you.* A traveler from Ephesus (v. 8) could sail from Troas to Macedonia, and after traveling along the major Roman road across Macedonia, could head south into Achaia (Greece), to Corinth (Paul earlier traversed this route; Ac 16:11 – 12; 17:1,10,14 – 15; 18:1). Paul later delayed such a planned visit partly to avoid having to confront them forcefully (2Co 1:15 – 23).

16:6 *spend the winter.* Travel became dangerous and difficult during winter, affecting sea traffic in particular. Although not as soon as he had planned, Paul later did apparently spend a winter with them (Ac 20:2 – 3). Friends often wrote about plans to visit, and people in antiquity also felt honored to be able to welcome and provide hospitality to a prominent teacher (cf. note on Ac 16:15), especially the founder of their church. *help me on my journey.* Probably implies financial support for Paul's journey when he would leave them again; this too would be viewed as an honor.

16:7 *if the Lord permits.* Both Jews and Gentiles often qualified their plans with "if God wills" or the like.

16:8 *Ephesus.* Ephesus was the economic center of the Roman province of Asia Minor. *Pentecost.* See note on Ac 2:1; for Paul's and the Corinthians' knowledge of Biblical festivals, see 1Co 5:7; Ac 20:16.

16:9 *a great door … has opened to me.* An open door appears figuratively elsewhere in Greek for free opportunity.

16:10 – 11 For letters of recommendation, see note on Ac 9:2. Such letters often urged their recipients to treat the recommended person as if he were the recommender himself. People in antiquity also recognized the importance of treating one's agent or representative as if he were the person himself.

16:11 *Send him on his way in peace.* A Jewish idiom implying that the sender should treat the person well rather than harm them (e.g., Ge 26:29).

16:12 *Apollos.* Even when their followers competed (1:12; 3:4), leaders were sometimes themselves friends.

16:14 Conclusions sometimes summarized key points in a work; love is one such point (8:1,3; 13:1 – 13).

16:15 – 18 For letters of recommendation, see note on Ac 9:2.

16:15 *first converts.* Lit. "firstfruits," the first part of (and guarantee of) the rest of the harvest; it was an appropriate image near Pentecost (v. 8). *Achaia.* Corinth was the capital and economic center of Achaia, the Roman province of Greece. This verse does not challenge the Athenian converts noted in Ac 17:34, since Athens (as a "free city") was exempted from the province in this period.

16:17 *Stephanas, Fortunatus and Achaicus … have supplied what was lacking.* They may have brought a gift from Corinth for Paul's provision (cf. Php 2:30; 4:10), and Paul probably is sending this letter back with them to Corinth.

16:19 *Asia.* The most prosperous Roman province in Asia Minor, and Ephesus (v. 8) its most prosperous city. *Aquila and Priscilla.* They had relocated with Paul to Ephesus (Ac 18:2 – 3,18,24 – 27); the Corinthians knew them. *church that meets at their house.* Churches, like some other associations with limited resources, met in homes, normally those large enough to host them (see note on Ac 12:12).

16:20 *the brothers and sisters here send you greetings.* People often asked the sender of a letter to convey their greetings. Mail was usually carried by travelers, so messages had to be conveyed especially when such opportunities arose. *holy kiss.* People regularly greeted family members, close friends and some others with a light kiss on the mouth; occasionally letters asked the recipient to pass on a kiss to another (see note on Ro 16:16).

16:21 *I, Paul, write this greeting.* Letters' authors usually dictated them; in such cases letters were written in a scribe's hand. The author, however, could sign it, and the author writing a full greeting showed affection.

[22]If anyone does not love the Lord,[n]
let that person be cursed![o] Come,
Lord[a]![p]
[23]The grace of the Lord Jesus be with
you.[q]
[24]My love to all of you in Christ Jesus.
Amen.[b]

16:22 [n]Eph 6:24 [o]Ro 9:3 [p]Rev 22:20 **16:23** [q]Ro 16:20

[a] 22 The Greek for *Come, Lord* reproduces an Aramaic expression (*Marana tha*) used by early Christians.
[b] 24 Some manuscripts do not have *Amen*.

16:22 *let that person be cursed!* People often pronounced curses; the Greek term here is *anathema*, often used in the Septuagint, the pre-Christian Greek translation of the OT, for what was devoted to God for destruction. *Come, Lord!* The Aramaic *marana tha*. Since the Corinthian believers would not invent an Aramaic prayer, it goes back to the earliest believers in the Holy Land. This suggests that the earliest believers already recognized Jesus as Lord (cf. v. 23; 8:5 – 6) and prayed for his coming (cf. Rev 22:20), giving him a role that Jewish tradition assigned to God.
16:23 For blessings, prayers invoking a deity (here Jesus) but addressed to the persons to be blessed, see note on 1:3.

THE LETTERS

2 CORINTHIANS

Occasion

Some scholars think that this letter sews together more than one letter of Paul; in particular, the shift in tone at 10:1 might point in this direction. But even ancient letter collections usually retained the distinction between one letter and the next. For various reasons, Paul's more controversial tone in chs. 10 – 13 can make sense without us assuming that it represents a separate letter. First, educated writers could vary their tone within a work. Second, orators sometimes reserved the most controversial or emotional material for the final section of their argument; out of sensitivity to the hearers' honor or receptivity, speakers and writers sometimes delayed bringing up the greatest issue of conflict. Paul deals mostly with lesser issues (such as his delay in visiting them, 1:12 — 2:11) first. Third, most elements that predominate earlier in the letter appear at least sometimes later, and vice versa. While the possibility that chs. 10 – 13 are a separate letter is at least defensible, other insertions proposed by some scholars are highly problematic; letters written on papyrus scrolls were not susceptible to modern cutting-and-pasting errors; inserting one letter into the midst of another (with sentences breaking cleanly between them!) was at best infrequent (and only possible in paged books, probably not used for Paul's letters before the second century).

QUICK GLANCE

AUTHOR:
The apostle Paul

AUDIENCE:
The church in Corinth

DATE:
AD 55

THEME:
Paul encourages the Corinthian believers to be reconciled with him and to reject false apostles who are challenging his authority and creating dissension in the church.

Paul challenges opponents most clearly in chs. 10 – 13, but probably provides hints about them earlier (cf. 2:17; 3:1; 4:2; 5:12; 6:14 – 17). These opponents are fellow Jews (11:22), though not necessarily with the same agendas in mind as Paul's opponents in Galatia. They are more rhetorically adept than Paul (11:5 – 6); although they claim to be apostles (vv. 5,13), they are thus not the Jerusalem apostles. They probably entered the picture after 1 Corinthians was written, playing on existing dissatisfaction with some of Paul's behavior.

Whereas Paul came as a servant and refused to accept pay, they are more willing to accept the patronage of the church's more well-to-do members (cf. 11:7 – 12; 12:11,13). Peers who shared their status would be more impressed with a teacher who had the self-respect to let them support him (although this might domesticate what he could say); they would despise a mere artisan, as Paul is (1Co 4:12). Yet Paul needs money for something different —

for the poor in Jerusalem (chs. 8 – 9). So now his critics want to accuse him of exploiting them (12:16 – 18)!

Letters of recommendation for others were common (see note on Ac 9:2), but sometimes one had to defend one's own reputation. Self-defense was one of the limited reasons that ancient hearers accepted for a speaker boasting. In chs. 10 – 13 Paul offers a mock defense, inverting the usual ancient criteria for boasting in view of the cross.

Although scholars have debated the letter's unity, as noted above, they are agreed that Paul is its author. For information on Corinth, see the Introduction to 1 Corinthians and especially the article "Corinth," p. 2022. ◆

1 Paul, an apostle of Christ Jesus by the
will of God,[a] and Timothy our brother,

To the church of God[b] in Corinth, together with all his holy people throughout
Achaia:[c]

2 Grace and peace to you from God our
Father and the Lord Jesus Christ.[d]

Praise to the God of All Comfort

3 Praise be to the God and Father of our
Lord Jesus Christ,[e] the Father of compassion and the God of all comfort, 4 who
comforts us[f] in all our troubles, so that we
can comfort those in any trouble with the
comfort we ourselves receive from God.
5 For just as we share abundantly in the
sufferings of Christ,[g] so also our comfort
abounds through Christ. 6 If we are distressed, it is for your comfort and salvation;[h] if we are comforted, it is for your
comfort, which produces in you patient
endurance of the same sufferings we suffer. 7 And our hope for you is firm, because
we know that just as you share in our sufferings,[i] so also you share in our comfort.

8 We do not want you to be uninformed,
brothers and sisters,[a] about the troubles
we experienced[j] in the province of Asia.
We were under great pressure, far beyond
our ability to endure, so that we despaired
of life itself. 9 Indeed, we felt we had received the sentence of death. But this happened that we might not rely on ourselves
but on God,[k] who raises the dead. 10 He
has delivered us from such a deadly peril,[l] and he will deliver us again. On him
we have set our hope that he will continue to deliver us, 11 as you help us by your
prayers.[m] Then many will give thanks[n] on
our behalf for the gracious favor granted
us in answer to the prayers of many.

Paul's Change of Plans

12 Now this is our boast: Our conscience[o]
testifies that we have conducted ourselves
in the world, and especially in our relations with you, with integrity[b] and godly
sincerity.[p] We have done so, relying not

1:1 [a] 1Co 1:1; Eph 1:1; Col 1:1; 2Ti 1:1 [b] 1Co 10:32 [c] Ac 18:12 **1:2** [d] Ro 1:7 **1:3** [e] Eph 1:3; 1Pe 1:3 **1:4** [f] 2Co 7:6, 7, 13 **1:5** [g] 2Co 4:10; Col 1:24 **1:6** [h] 2Co 4:15 **1:7** [i] Ro 8:17 **1:8** [j] 1Co 15:32 **1:9** [k] Jer 17:5,7 **1:10** [l] Ro 15:31 **1:11** [m] Ro 15:30; Php 1:19 [n] 2Co 4:15 **1:12** [o] Ac 23:1 [p] 2Co 2:17

[a] *8* The Greek word for *brothers and sisters* (*adelphoi*) refers here to believers, both men and women, as part of God's family; also in 8:1; 13:11. [b] *12* Many manuscripts *holiness*

1:1 – 2 *Paul ... To the church of God in Corinth ... Grace and peace to you.* Letters opened with the name of the sender, the recipient, and greetings (see notes on Ro 1:1,7).
1:1 *throughout Achaia.* Corinth was the capital of Achaia, and was surrounded by about 40 settlements (such as Cenchreae).
1:3 *Praise be to the God.* Ancient letters often included a prayer for the recipients. Many Jewish benedictions began with praise for God. *Father of compassion.* Idiomatic for "compassionate Father," a title of God in a frequent Jewish prayer.
1:4 For how God comforted Paul most recently, see 7:4,6 – 7,13.
1:5 *share ... in the sufferings of Christ.* Some commentators stress a connection with the Jewish expectation of end-time suffering as the birth pangs of the Messiah (suffering that would bring deliverance). Others emphasize Paul's theme of unity with Christ (cf. vv. 8 – 10), rooted in the OT perspective of corporate identity (especially the group personified in its leading representative; cf. Ro 5:12 – 21) and believers' experience of the Spirit. Introductions of speeches and written works sometimes introduced important themes; Paul soon revisits this theme of suffering with Christ (e.g., 2Co 2:14 – 16; 4:10 – 12; 11:23; 12:10; 13:4).
1:8 — 2:13 After an introduction, many speeches and some other kinds of works recounted a narrative, tracing the events leading up to the need for the speech or other work.
1:8 *troubles ... in the province of Asia.* Ephesus, where Paul had been ministering (see 1Co 16:8 and note), was the most prominent city in the wealthy Roman province of Asia in western Asia Minor. Paul faced conflicts in Ephesus (see 1Co 15:32 and note), and would soon face the events recounted in Ac 19:23 – 41.
1:9 – 10 *God, who raises the dead ... has delivered us from such a deadly peril.* Scripture could graphically portray divine deliverance from danger (e.g., Ps 18:3 – 19; 30:3). Regular Jewish prayers emphasized that God was the powerful one "who raises the dead." Paul also thinks in terms of unity with Christ (v. 5).
1:11 *gracious favor.* Ancient inscriptions show that the expected response for generous benefaction (such as the "gracious favor" here) was public gratitude. Most ancient cultures also sought to earn deities' favor with sacrifices, but Paul instead simply speaks of God's generosity in answering prayers.
1:12 – 22 Letter writers often affectionately chided their recipients for not visiting or maintaining better contact, but the offense here goes beyond affectionate chiding. Some Corinthian believers feel that Paul has proved unreliable after breaking his word to visit, something he must explain (v. 23; 2:1). They may also feel as if Paul, who has already refused their support (11:7 – 9; 12:13 – 16), has now insulted their hospitality. Showing hospitality was a key virtue in the ancient Mediterranean world, and hosting a respected individual was a great honor. Paul had avoided visiting Corinth only to spare them from needed and direct discipline (v. 23); instead, he sent Titus with a warning (1:23 — 2:11; 7:7 – 12). When Titus did not return to the appointed meeting place in Troas, however, Paul feared for him (given the dangers of traveling in antiquity) and for how the church had responded to his reproof. Paul thus went on into Macedonia (2:12 – 13). There Paul found Titus again, who reported mostly good news about the church (7:5 – 16). But Paul's unfulfilled warnings about discipline (1Co 4:21), because of his gentleness and his wish to spare them, left some doubting whether he could truly act firmly (2Co 10:1 – 2,6,8 – 11). If they forced him, he would need to act firmly now (13:2,10).
1:12 *this is our boast.* Ancient urban audiences accepted self-praise in a justifiable situation, such as defending oneself against criticism, as here. Because charlatans were widespread (2:17), teachers often defended themselves in advance even if no opposition existed (cf. 1Th 2:3 – 7); but some in Corinth were criticizing Paul (e.g., 2Co 3:1; 5:12; 10:10).

2 CORINTHIANS 1

CORINTH

The ancient city of Corinth lay on an isthmus connecting northern Greece, including Athens, and the Peloponnese, the southern part of Greece. The isthmus was about 6,562 yards (6,000 meters) wide at its narrowest point, which led many to consider digging a canal there (a dream not realized until modern times). Two harbors were nearby: Lechaeum to the north, on the Gulf of Corinth, and Cenchrea to the south, on the Saronic Gulf. Corinth's location made the city a site of great strategic and economic importance. Ships often preferred to sail into Corinth and transport their goods overland across the isthmus on the portage track (the *diolkos*) rather than risk the wild seas around the Peloponnese. This brought lively trade to the city—along with the vices often associated with bustling commercial centers. It is not surprising, therefore, that ancient Corinth became a byword for sexual immorality.

Corinth's history may be divided into two distinct periods: its long duration as one of the major cities of classical Greek civilization and its subsequent years after the Roman conquest as a cosmopolitan crossroads. The classical city was at one time a major player in the politics of Greece and was particularly important in the long history of competition between Athens and Sparta (Corinth was usually on the side of Sparta). Later, as head of the Achaean League (a coalition of Greek cities), it led resistance to Roman aggression. Its role as host of the Isthmian games (second only to the Olympic Games in prestige) greatly enhanced Corinth's ancient status. This city, however, was destroyed in 146 BC by the Roman general Lucius Mummius. While some inhabitants stayed in the vicinity of Corinth, the city did not rise to prominence again until 44 BC, when Julius Caesar refounded it as a Roman colony.

The new city was Roman in its administration and architecture, with the majority of its original settlers being freedmen. The natural advantages of the site, coupled with the entrepreneurial vigor of the freedmen, soon led to renewed prosperity. The Corinth of the New Testament era was reputed to be one of the most beautiful cities of the Greco-Roman world. Its importance in trade and its status as a Roman administrative center made Corinth a significant city in Paul's day.

Corinth had a mixed, cosmopolitan populace, as reflected in its many religious shrines:

- Visitors to Corinth can still find archaeological evidence of votive offerings made to Asclepius, the god of medicine, in gratitude for healings. These offerings were

continued on next page

on worldly wisdom[q] but on God's grace.
13For we do not write you anything you
cannot read or understand. And I hope
that, 14as you have understood us in part,
you will come to understand fully that you
can boast of us just as we will boast of you
in the day of the Lord Jesus.[r]

15Because I was confident of this, I
wanted to visit you[s] first so that you might
benefit twice.[t] 16I wanted to visit you on
my way[u] to Macedonia and to come back
to you from Macedonia, and then to have
you send me on my way to Judea. 17Was
I fickle when I intended to do this? Or do

1:12 [q] 1Co 2:1, 4, 13 **1:14** [r] 1Co 1:8 **1:15** [s] 1Co 4:19 [t] Ro 1:11, 13; 15:29 **1:16** [u] 1Co 16:5-7

1:15 *that you might benefit twice.* When the Corinthians hear the Greek term here translated "benefit" (also meaning "grace"), they may think of the gifts benefactors bestowed on communities or persons of somewhat lower status. Paul is their benefactor, not their client (dependent); nevertheless, unlike normal ancient benefactors, he does not seek honor for himself, but only for God (vv. 11,24).

1:16 *on my way to Macedonia.* One could sail directly between Asia and Achaia (cf. Ac 18:18–19) or travel overland via Macedonia (1Co 16:5; Ac 16:11–12; 20:1–3). *send me on my way.* Paul would allow them to provide for his voyage; they would consider this part of the privilege of hospitality.

1:17 *Was I fickle . . . ?* Ancient sources frequently praised

clay models of body parts (often arms, legs or sexual organs) the god had supposedly healed, hung around the temple as tributes to Asclepius.

- Old Corinth was home to a famous temple to Aphrodite that supposedly employed 1,000 temple prostitutes. While this number may be an exaggeration, scholars can hardly doubt that this port city supported a thriving prostitution industry.
- There were also temples to other Greek gods, such as to Poseidon, god of the sea (appropriate for a port city), and to Demeter and Kore, goddesses of an ancient Greek fertility cult.
- The cosmopolitan nature of Corinth is reflected in the fact that it also had numerous places of worship for foreign deities, such as a shrine to the Egyptian goddess Isis — as well as a Jewish synagogue.

With its cultural diversity, wealth, paganism and infamous debauchery, Corinth was perhaps not the place onlookers would have expected the church to flourish. Yet it was precisely here that Paul enjoyed one of his most successful ministries — and also here that he experienced some of his greatest challenges with early converts to Christianity. ◆

Artist's recreation of Corinth, looking south toward Acrocorinth, AD 200.

I make my plans in a worldly manner[v] so
that in the same breath I say both "Yes,
yes" and "No, no"?
[18]But as surely as God is faithful,[w] our
message to you is not "Yes" and "No."
[19]For the Son of God, Jesus Christ, who
was preached among you by us — by me
and Silas[a] and Timothy — was not "Yes"
and "No," but in him it has always[x] been
"Yes." [20]For no matter how many promises[y] God has made, they are "Yes" in
Christ. And so through him the "Amen"[z] is

1:17 [v] 2Co 10:2,3 **1:18** [w] 1Co 1:9 **1:19** [x] Heb 13:8 **1:20** [y] Ro 15:8 [z] 1Co 14:16

[a] 19 Greek *Silvanus,* a variant of *Silas*

people who kept their word despite hardship; these sources also frequently condemn fickleness, especially in leaders. When someone had to change already noted plans, they had to (and sometimes did) supply good reasons and show that they were not fickle. Paul's flexibility may have drawn criticism earlier (cf. 1Co 9:19 – 23), but now he had been unable to fulfill his stated intention.

1:18 – 22 Ancient writers often used digressions; in these verses Paul emphasizes that even if they want to question his integrity regarding his travel plans, his gospel message is reliable.

1:18 For "Yes" being "Yes," see Mt 5:37.

1:20 *Amen.* Concluded and affirmed a prayer; here the risen Christ is the guarantee of all God's promises.

spoken by us to the glory of God. [21]Now it
is God who makes both us and you stand
firm in Christ. He anointed[a] us, [22]set his
seal of ownership on us, and put his Spirit
in our hearts as a deposit, guaranteeing
what is to come.[b]
[23]I call God as my witness[c]—and I stake
my life on it—that it was in order to spare
you[d] that I did not return to Corinth. [24]Not
that we lord it over[e] your faith, but we
work with you for your joy, because it is
2 by faith you stand firm.[f] [1]So I made up
my mind that I would not make anoth-
er painful visit to you.[g] [2]For if I grieve you,[h]
who is left to make me glad but you whom
I have grieved? [3]I wrote as I did,[i] so that
when I came I would not be distressed[j] by
those who should have made me rejoice.
I had confidence[k] in all of you, that you
would all share my joy. [4]For I wrote you[l] out
of great distress and anguish of heart and
with many tears, not to grieve you but to
let you know the depth of my love for you.

Forgiveness for the Offender

[5]If anyone has caused grief,[m] he has
not so much grieved me as he has grieved
all of you to some extent—not to put it
too severely. [6]The punishment[n] inflicted on him by the majority is sufficient.
[7]Now instead, you ought to forgive and
comfort him,[o] so that he will not be overwhelmed by excessive sorrow. [8]I urge
you, therefore, to reaffirm your love for
him. [9]Another reason I wrote you was
to see if you would stand the test and
be obedient in everything.[p] [10]Anyone
you forgive, I also forgive. And what I
have forgiven—if there was anything to
forgive—I have forgiven in the sight of
Christ for your sake, [11]in order that Satan[q] might not outwit us. For we are not
unaware of his schemes.[r]

Ministers of the New Covenant

[12]Now when I went to Troas[s] to preach
the gospel of Christ[t] and found that the
Lord had opened a door[u] for me, [13]I still
had no peace of mind,[v] because I did not
find my brother Titus[w] there. So I said
goodbye to them and went on to Macedonia.

1:21 [a] 1Jn 2:20, 27 **1:22** [b] 2Co 5:5 **1:23** [c] Ro 1:9; Gal 1:20 [d] 1Co 4:21; 2Co 2:1, 3; 13:2, 10 **1:24** [e] 1Pe 5:3 [f] Ro 11:20; 1Co 15:1 **2:1** [g] 2Co 1:23 **2:2** [h] 2Co 7:8 **2:3** [i] 2Co 7:8, 12 [j] 2Co 12:21 [k] 2Co 8:22; Gal 5:10 **2:4** [l] 2Co 7:8, 12 **2:5** [m] 1Co 5:1, 2 **2:6** [n] 1Co 5:4, 5 **2:7** [o] Gal 6:1; Eph 4:32 **2:9** [p] 2Co 10:6 **2:11** [q] Mt 4:10 [r] Lk 22:31; 2Co 4:4; 1Pe 5:8, 9 **2:12** [s] Ac 16:8 [t] Ro 1:1 [u] Ac 14:27 **2:13** [v] 2Co 7:5 [w] 2Co 7:6, 13; 12:18

1:21 *stand firm in Christ.* Paul usually uses "stand firm" generically, but it might be relevant that business documents sometimes used this expression for confirming a sale (see note on "deposit" in v. 22). *He anointed us.* In the OT, anointing with olive oil symbolically consecrated persons or things for special service.

1:22 *seal of ownership.* Documents would be sealed with witnesses' identity markers, and containers of merchandise with those of owners, certifying that no one had tampered with their contents. The stamp of the owner or the person or people witnessing a document would be pressed into hot wax, which then dried over the string tied around the rolled-up document. (Important documents often had about six seals; to open the document one had to break the seals, so a sealed document was one that had not been tampered with.) God himself attested the apostolic message (cf. 3:2–3). *his Spirit.* Judaism especially associated the Spirit with the end of the age (e.g., Eze 39:28–29; Joel 2:28). *deposit.* The Greek term here referred in business documents to the down payment; the Spirit is here the first taste of the life of the coming era when God will reign unchallenged.

1:23 *I call God as my witness.* Since some did not accept Paul's own word, he invokes the most certain witness. Invoking a deity as witness was essentially an oath, which invited the deity's judgment if the person invoked the deity falsely (cf. Ex 20:7). For the way that Paul sought to "spare" them, see 2Cor 2:1.

1:24 *we work with you for your joy.* Patrons and other authorities normally expected praise or even groveling, but like some other more pastorally minded sages in antiquity, Paul offers a different model (cf. especially 4:5).

2:1 *painful visit.* Friendly letters very often protested a friend's failure to visit (or even write frequently); in most cases such protests simply expressed affection, but sometimes they could be serious, as in the case of Corinthian complaints about Paul's failure to visit. Sometimes a letter writer would explain that the only reason for not visiting was out of concern for what was best for the recipient.

2:2–3 In ancient letters between close friends, a writer would sometimes emphasize that he shared the other's grief or other feelings.

2:4 *I wrote you.* The letter to which Paul refers (now lost) admonished the church to discipline a member (vv. 5–10). Paul wrote this letter after 1 Corinthians, although some believe, along with many early church fathers, that the member is also the one addressed in 1Co 5:1–5. *depth of my love for you.* Many ancient letters to friends stressed the depth of the writer's love for the reader. Even orators often showed affection with tears during speeches.

2:6–8 *The punishment … is sufficient. Now … forgive and … reaffirm your love for him.* Most ancient legal settings, including discipline for members in synagogues and in the Qumran community, specified a time of punishment (e.g., for exile or exclusion from the community). Because the man has now genuinely repented, however, he is to be welcomed back fully.

2:11 *Satan … his schemes.* Jewish tradition already recognized Satan as a deceiver (see note on Jn 8:44) as well as tempter and accuser (cf. Job 1:11; Zec 3:1).

2:12–13 Speakers and writers often narrated events leading up to their writing (here; 7:5–16). In antiquity, communication was no faster than travel, so Paul could not be sure how the Corinthian believers had received Titus or Paul's letter (vv. 4–6) via Titus. Paul could sail from Troas to enter Macedonia (v. 13; 7:5) to take the main land route to Corinth, presumably stopping in churches along the way, where Titus would also need to stop. Finally meeting Titus in Macedonia, he receives good news that the Corinthian believers had welcomed him and also obeyed Paul's letter about disciplining the wrongdoer (7:5–16).

2:12 *Troas.* See note on Ac 16:8; it was a strategic place for ministry. *opened a door.* See note on 1Co 16:9.

14But thanks be to God,[x] who always
leads us as captives in Christ's triumphal
procession and uses us to spread the aroma[y] of the knowledge of him everywhere.
15For we are to God the pleasing aroma of
Christ among those who are being saved
and those who are perishing.[z] 16To the
one we are an aroma that brings death;[a]
to the other, an aroma that brings life. And
who is equal to such a task?[b] 17Unlike so
many, we do not peddle the word of God
for profit.[c] On the contrary, in Christ we
speak before God with sincerity,[d] as those
sent from God.[e]

3 Are we beginning to commend ourselves[f] again? Or do we need, like
some people, letters of recommendation[g]
to you or from you? 2You yourselves are
our letter, written on our hearts, known
and read by everyone.[h] 3You show that
you are a letter from Christ, the result of
our ministry, written not with ink but with
the Spirit of the living God, not on tablets
of stone[i] but on tablets of human hearts.[j]
4Such confidence[k] we have through
Christ before God. 5Not that we are competent in ourselves to claim anything for
ourselves, but our competence comes
from God.[l] 6He has made us competent as
ministers of a new covenant[m]—not of the
letter but of the Spirit; for the letter kills,
but the Spirit gives life.[n]

The Greater Glory of the New Covenant

7Now if the ministry that brought
death, which was engraved in letters on
stone, came with glory, so that the Israelites could not look steadily at the face

2:14 [x] Ro 6:17 [y] Eph 5:2; Php 4:18
2:15 [z] 1Co 1:18
2:16 [a] Lk 2:34 [b] 2Co 3:5,6
2:17 [c] 2Co 4:2 [d] 1Co 5:8 [e] 2Co 1:12
3:1 [f] 2Co 5:12; 12:11 [g] Ac 18:27
3:2 [h] 1Co 9:2
3:3 [i] Ex 24:12 [j] Pr 3:3; Jer 31:33; Eze 11:19
3:4 [k] Eph 3:12
3:5 [l] 1Co 15:10
3:6 [m] Lk 22:20 [n] Jn 6:63

2:14—7:4 Ancient writers often used digressions (cf. 1Co 9; 13) that were sometimes quite long. In 2:14—7:4, Paul digresses from his narrative to defend his ministry, as other sages in the Greco-Roman world often did. Some scholars argued instead that 2:14—7:4 is a separate letter accidentally inserted between 1:1—2:13 and 7:5–16. Scrolls, however, did not permit such insertions, and even later codices (paged books) would not be expected to break evenly with sentences closing at the end of pages; therefore, it is far more likely that 2:14—7:4 is a digression.
2:14 *triumphal procession.* Traditionally, Roman generals led their prisoners of war in triumphal procession; by the first century, only the emperor, who did not want competition, could celebrate triumphs. Here Christ as the true ruler leads his captives (Christ's "servants," 4:5); cf. Eph 4:8. Paul would know that most captives were executed afterward; thus Paul, a captive, identifies with Christ's death in 4:8–11; 5:14–15. The Roman senate normally decreed public thanksgivings before the triumphal processions, so they were great celebrations for the victors and great humiliations for the defeated. Here, by contrast, the dying prisoner of war himself offers the thanksgiving!
2:15 *pleasing aroma.* People offered incense during sacrifices, including at triumphs (v. 14); the image of incense could be used figuratively (Ps 141:2; cf. the note on the fragrant offering in Eph 5:2).
2:16 *aroma that brings death ... aroma that brings life.* Those with faith could see life in both Jesus' cross and apostolic sufferings; those without faith could see only death there. *who is equal to such a task?* This rhetorical question is answered in 3:5.
2:17 *Unlike so many.* Paul may think of his antagonists in 11:4–5,13–15,22–23; sometimes people avoided naming the targets of their criticism explicitly, humiliating them with anonymity. *peddle the word of God for profit.* Greedy false teachers were a problem both in ancient Israel (Jer 6:13–14; 8:10–11; Mic 3:5,11) and in the Greco–Roman world. Philosophers and others criticized orators, and many people also criticized philosophers and other sages, for pursuing their work only for the sake of money. Thus many needed to differentiate themselves from charlatans.
3:1 *commend ourselves.* Honorable people in antiquity were not supposed to commend themselves unless they could give good reason for it, such as defending themselves, critiquing others' misplaced arrogance, or setting a positive example (cf. 5:12; 11:12,18; 12:11). *letters of recommendation.* People often wrote letters to their peers or others recommending persons of social status lower than their own, usually carried by the recommended person (cf. Ac 9:2 and note). Philosophers, by contrast, often rejected concern about others' opinions, arguing that their character was already clear.
3:2–3 See note on v. 6. God once wrote his commandments on "tablets of stone" (v. 3; see Ex 24:12; 31:18; Dt 5:22), but he later announced a new law-giving (Isa 2:3), and a covenant that would be inscribed on hearts (Jer 31:31–34), as it was always meant to be (Dt 30:6,11–14). Paul also evokes Ezekiel here: God would replace his people's hearts of stone with hearts of flesh, putting his Spirit in them so they would keep his laws (Eze 36:26–27).
3:5 *competence comes from God.* God more than compensated for human inadequacy (Ex 3:11,14).
3:6 *new covenant.* Paul makes explicit what he implied in vv. 2–3. (Many Jewish people in this era also expected this new or renewed covenant; the sectarians who wrote the Dead Sea Scrolls believed that it applied to their own group, as in the Damascus Document 6.19; 8.21; 19.33; 20.12.) *the letter kills, but the Spirit gives life.* The Law of Moses pronounced death on transgressors; Paul may also think of Ex 20:19. By contrast, the Spirit enables God's people to keep the moral heart of the law (Eze 36:26–27), and brings resurrection life (Eze 37:14).
3:7–18 Orators and interpreters often elaborated comparisons, sometimes between something good and something even better. Paul here elaborates how the new covenant (v. 6) experience is greater than that of the old, and thus apostolic ministry is greater than that of Moses. Some may have exalted Moses and the law over apostolic ministry because God confirmed the old covenant with judgments on Egypt and theophanies on Mount Sinai; the new covenant, while attested with signs and wonders, transforms from within. God's law, always meant to be in the heart (Dt 5:29; 30:14), would finally be there fully (Jer 31:31–34). The new covenant thus offered greater glory than what Moses beheld on Mount Sinai.
3:7 *came with glory.* After Moses received the tablets of stone and beheld God's glory, reflective glory shone from his face (Ex 34:29–30,35). The glory was impermanent and faded over time (cf. v. 13), however. Moreover, the people could not withstand such glory (Ex 34:30), which brought death (Ex 20:19; 33:20; cf. Nu 17:13), unlike the life-giving Spirit (2Co 3:6). The new covenant with the Spirit would produce greater obedience than the first covenant (Jer 31:31–34; Eze 36:26–27).

of Moses because of its glory,[o] transitory
though it was, 8will not the ministry of
the Spirit be even more glorious? 9If the
ministry that brought condemnation[p] was
glorious, how much more glorious is the
ministry that brings righteousness![q] 10For
what was glorious has no glory now in
comparison with the surpassing glory.
11And if what was transitory came with
glory, how much greater is the glory of
that which lasts!

12Therefore, since we have such a hope,
we are very bold.[r] 13We are not like Moses, who would put a veil over his face[s]
to prevent the Israelites from seeing the
end of what was passing away. 14But their
minds were made dull,[t] for to this day
the same veil remains when the old covenant[u] is read.[v] It has not been removed,
because only in Christ is it taken away.
15Even to this day when Moses is read, a
veil covers their hearts. 16But whenever
anyone turns to the Lord,[w] the veil is tak-
en away.[x] 17Now the Lord is the Spirit,[y]
and where the Spirit of the Lord is, there is
freedom.[z] 18And we all, who with unveiled
faces contemplate[a][a] the Lord's glory,[b] are
being transformed into his image[c] with
ever-increasing glory, which comes from
the Lord, who is the Spirit.

Present Weakness and Resurrection Life

4 Therefore, since through God's mercy[d]
we have this ministry, we do not lose
heart. 2Rather, we have renounced secret
and shameful ways;[e] we do not use deception, nor do we distort the word of God.[f]
On the contrary, by setting forth the truth
plainly we commend ourselves to everyone's conscience[g] in the sight of God. 3And
even if our gospel[h] is veiled,[i] it is veiled to
those who are perishing.[j] 4The god[k] of this
age has blinded[l] the minds of unbelievers,
so that they cannot see the light of the gospel that displays the glory of Christ, who is
the image of God. 5For what we preach is
not ourselves,[m] but Jesus Christ as Lord,
and ourselves as your servants[n] for Jesus'
sake. 6For God, who said, "Let light shine
out of darkness,"[b][o] made his light shine
in our hearts[p] to give us the light of the
knowledge of God's glory displayed in the
face of Christ.

[a] 18 Or *reflect* [b] 6 Gen. 1:3

3:7 [o] Ex 34:29-35 **3:9** [p] ver 7 [q] Ro 1:17; 3:21, 22 **3:12** [r] Eph 6:19 **3:13** [s] ver 7; Ex 34:33 **3:14** [t] Ro 11:7, 8 [u] Ac 13:15 [v] ver 6 **3:16** [w] Ro 11:23 [x] Ex 34:34 **3:17** [y] Isa 61:1,2 [z] Jn 8:32 **3:18** [a] 1Co 13:12 [b] 2Co 4:4,6 [c] Ro 8:29 **4:1** [d] 1Co 7:25 **4:2** [e] 1Co 4:5 [f] 2Co 2:17 [g] 2Co 5:11 **4:3** [h] 2Co 2:12 [i] 2Co 3:14 [j] 1Co 1:18 **4:4** [k] Jn 12:31 [l] 2Co 3:14 **4:5** [m] 1Co 1:13 [n] 1Co 9:19 **4:6** [o] Ge 1:3 [p] 2Pe 1:19

3:9 *how much more glorious.* Jewish teachers and others often used "How much more?" reasoning in comparisons. **3:11** *much greater.* Based on Jer 31:31 – 34; Eze 36:26 – 27, the new covenant and its glory must be greater than the old. In vv. 13 – 18, Paul elaborates in what sense this is true. **3:12** *very bold.* Ancient thinkers often used this particular Greek term for being bold (*parrêsia*, "boldness") to emphasize that, unlike flatterers exploiting their hearers, they spoke truth for their hearers' good. Cf. v. 4; 4:1,16. **3:13** *prevent … seeing the end of what was passing away.* Moses had to veil his face because the people could not withstand the glory, which could harm them (Ex 34:30,33 – 35; cf. Ex 33:20). Moses' glory also faded over time. By contrast, Paul and other believers in Jesus experience the Spirit, who dwells in them continually. Far from fading, God's glory in the servants of the new covenant continues to be revealed even in death (cf. 2:15 – 16; 4:6 – 11). **3:14 – 16** Israelites could not witness the full glory revealed with the law (see v. 13 and note); this comes only in the new covenant of the Spirit in the promised Christ. It is only in the new covenant that the Spirit produces full obedience from the heart (Jer 31:31 – 34; Eze 36:26 – 27). Only one intimate with the Lord could experience much of the glory without a veil (Ex 33:11; 34:34), though even Moses could not see all the glory (Ex 33:20,23). **3:17** Jewish interpreters could explain a text by comparing it with a later text that was analogous. *the Lord.* The one who revealed himself to Moses in the Biblical text (Ex 33:9,11,19; 34:5 – 6,34) corresponds to the new covenant experience of the Spirit (cf. v. 18). **3:18** *with unveiled faces … are being transformed.* Although Moses reflected the Lord's glory at the time of the giving of the older covenant (v. 7), the new covenant Spirit provides a fuller experience of the Lord's glory (see vv. 2 – 17). The transformation now, however, is especially within. Many philosophers thought that meditating on divine and heavenly things would transform them toward divinity; yet they deemed their deity emotionless and abstract. By contrast, the God whom Moses saw was full of compassion for his people (Ex 34:6 – 7). *contemplate.* Or "reflect" (see NIV text note; see also 4:4; 1Co 13:12 and notes).

4:2 *we do not use deception.* See note on 2:17. *we commend ourselves.* See note on 3:1. **4:3** *veiled.* See notes on 3:13 – 16. **4:4** *god of this age.* Jewish sources do not call Satan "the god of this age" (cf. Jn 14:30) but did speak of Satan or hostile angels ruling the Gentiles (cf. Eph 2:2). *glory of Christ … the image of God.* Wisdom, which was sometimes personified, provided the best available analogy for Jewish people to understand something divine yet distinct from God the Father. Greek-speaking Jews sometimes described preexistent Wisdom as a mirror reflecting God's image and glory (Wisdom of Solomon 7:26); sometimes they also opined that God stamped his image on people by Wisdom or his *logos*, typically translated as his "word." For Paul the divine image and glory obscured in Adam is restored in Christ. **4:5** *not ourselves.* Some in antiquity complained about teachers who drew attention to themselves rather than to helpful teachings. *servants for Jesus' sake.* See note on Ro 1:1; but slaveholders sometimes had their slaves work for others. **4:6** Although ancient writers often paired contrasts in quick succession (as in 3:7 – 18; 11:22 – 23), they also could do so over a slightly larger span. Contrast believers here with unbelievers in v. 4. *Let light shine out of darkness.* God spoke the light out of darkness in Ge 1:3, but Paul adapts wording from Isa 9:1 – 2, a Messianic context (Isa 9:6 – 7). *light.* Jewish people associated light with God; for various symbolic uses, cf. note on Jn 1:4 – 5. *God's glory displayed in … Christ.* The Spirit would make God's glory in Christ, his image (v. 4), shine greatly through the people of the new covenant (3:7 – 18).

7But we have this treasure in jars of clay[q]
to show that this all-surpassing power is
from God[r] and not from us. 8We are hard
pressed on every side,[s] but not crushed;
perplexed, but not in despair; 9persecut-
ed,[t] but not abandoned;[u] struck down, but
not destroyed.[v] 10We always carry around
in our body the death of Jesus, so that the
life of Jesus may also be revealed in our
body.[w] 11For we who are alive are always
being given over to death for Jesus' sake,[x]
so that his life may also be revealed in our
mortal body. 12So then, death is at work in
us, but life is at work in you.[y]
13It is written: "I believed; therefore I
have spoken."[a][z] Since we have that same
spirit of[b] faith, we also believe and therefore speak, 14because we know that the
one who raised the Lord Jesus from the
dead will also raise us with Jesus[a] and
present us with you to himself.[b] 15All this
is for your benefit, so that the grace that is
reaching more and more people may cause
thanksgiving[c] to overflow to the glory of
God.
16Therefore we do not lose heart.
Though outwardly we are wasting away,
yet inwardly[d] we are being renewed[e] day
by day. 17For our light and momentary
troubles are achieving for us an eternal
glory that far outweighs them all.[f] 18So we
fix our eyes not on what is seen, but on
what is unseen,[g] since what is seen is temporary, but what is unseen is eternal.

Awaiting the New Body

5 For we know that if the earthly[h] tent[i]
we live in is destroyed, we have a
building from God, an eternal house in
heaven, not built by human hands. 2Mean-
while we groan,[j] longing to be clothed
instead with our heavenly dwelling,[k]

4:7 [q] Job 4:19; 2Co 5:1 [r] 1Co 2:5
4:8 [s] 2Co 7:5
4:9 [t] Jn 15:20 [u] Heb 13:5 [v] Ps 37:24
4:10 [w] Ro 6:5
4:11 [x] Ro 8:36
4:12 [y] 2Co 13:9
4:13 [z] Ps 116:10
4:14 [a] 1Th 4:14 [b] Eph 5:27
4:15 [c] 2Co 1:11
4:16 [d] Ro 7:22 [e] Col 3:10
4:17 [f] Ro 8:18; 1Pe 1:6,7
4:18 [g] Ro 8:24; Heb 11:1
5:1 [h] 1Co 15:47 [i] 2Pe 1:13,14
5:2 [j] ver 4; Ro 8:23 [k] 1Co 15:53,54

[a] *13* Psalm 116:10 (see Septuagint) [b] *13* Or *Spirit-given*

4:7 *treasure in jars of clay.* Unlike bronze or other more expensive vessels, jars of clay were inexpensive and thus disposable if they were broken or incurred ceremonial impurity. Corinth produced some of this fragile clay pottery, notably ceramic lamps. Greek sources sometimes depict the body as a vessel containing the soul; Paul instead contrasts humanity's frailty with divine glory. For human vessels, cf. Ps 31:12; Isa 29:16; 30:14; Jer 19:11. For divine treasure, cf., e.g., Ps 119:72,127; Pr 2:4. *power ... not from us.* Gentile sages often emphasized their strength of character in the face of hardship, but Paul depends on God's power.

4:8–12 Orators often offered a series of contrasts, as here, both elaborating and emotionally hammering home a point. Some ancient sages catalogued their sufferings (see 1Co 4:11–13 and note) to demonstrate their integrity in following their teachings about endurance.

4:10–11 On unity with Christ, see note on 1:5.

4:13 Paul uses the most common Greek rendering of Ps 116:10, cited here. In its context in the psalm, the line shows that even a cry of affliction can be spoken in faith concerning God's deliverance, which does come in the end (cf. here vv. 10–11,14).

4:14 *raise us.* Greeks and Romans did not conceive of a future resurrection, an issue that some Corinthian believers had struggled with (see 1Co 15). See the article "Resurrection," p. 2012.

4:15 *grace ... may cause thanksgiving to overflow to the glory of God.* Greeks and Romans praised benefactors; the response deemed appropriate to their generosity (often described as grace) was thanksgiving and the offering of honor (also called, as here, "glory"). Paul is ready to suffer for the sake of enlarging God's people, bringing God honor (cf. 9:13–15).

4:16 *outwardly we are wasting away.* Many intellectuals had long believed that the soul was what mattered, so that people should learn to regard the natural decay of the body as a matter of indifference. Paul adapts this concept in light of God's promises: Christ's resurrection glory is already present ("inwardly") even in those suffering for him (vv. 7–12; cf. 5:5; see note on 5:17).

4:17 *light and momentary troubles ... eternal glory that far outweighs them.* Considering Biblical promises, many Jewish people expected future blessing far outweighing present troubles. For them, the eternal future certainly outweighed the present age. Gentile philosophers also recognized that what was eternal mattered more than anything temporary; many believed that the unseen realm of ideas was more real than physical things, which decay. Paul has already contrasted visible stone tablets and the visible but transitory glory of Moses with the unseen yet unfading glory of the Spirit (3:7–18). Yet Paul also believes in a future for the body (v. 14; 5:4). *eternal glory that far outweighs them all.* Many believed that the heavens were eternal and that what was earthly and physical distracted one from the eternal realm of ideas. Many (including some Hellenistic Jews) had also come to believe that the soul was much lighter than the body, so when the body that weighted it down died, the soul would rise again to the pure heavens from which it came. Paul speaks instead of glory that "outweighs" (lit. is a "weight"). This association is natural; Paul would know that in Hebrew the same term could mean either "heaviness" or "glory."

5:1 *earthly tent ... eternal house.* Greek and some Diaspora Jewish writers described the body as a vessel, a house, or a tent. Whereas some Greek thinkers also envisioned the body as a tomb to be escaped by death, Paul's hope is not for death but for the resurrection body, a thought unintelligible to Greeks. *we have a building from God.* Paul says that a better body awaits (he can use the present tense because of the secure deposit; see v. 5). For the body as a house, see 1Co 6:19 and note.

5:2–4 *longing to be clothed ... clothed ... found naked ... unclothed ... clothed.* Ancient writers sometimes portrayed the present or resurrected body as clothing and death as disrobing. Judeans and other eastern peoples loathed nudity; while Greeks and Romans disliked it in particular situations, both bathed naked in the baths and Greeks exercised naked. For Paul, the image is undesirable—the body's death is not in itself desirable, in contrast to the view of some philosophers (especially Platonists) who viewed positively the soul's release from the body. For the body as clothing, see 1Co 15:53–54.

5:2 *groan.* Evokes anguish and perhaps birth pangs (Jewish tradition expected these preceding the new age; see note on Ro 8:22) and/or groaning for deliverance in Ex 2:23 (the Greek version uses a related noun).

3because when we are clothed, we will not
be found naked. 4For while we are in this
tent, we groan and are burdened, because
we do not wish to be unclothed but to be
clothed instead with our heavenly dwelling,[l] so that what is mortal may be swallowed up by life. 5Now the one who has
fashioned us for this very purpose is God,
who has given us the Spirit as a deposit,
guaranteeing what is to come.[m]
6Therefore we are always confident and
know that as long as we are at home in
the body we are away from the Lord. 7For
we live by faith, not by sight.[n] 8We are
confident, I say, and would prefer to be
away from the body and at home with the
Lord.[o] 9So we make it our goal to please
him,[p] whether we are at home in the body
or away from it. 10For we must all appear
before the judgment seat of Christ, so that
each of us may receive what is due us[q] for
the things done while in the body, whether good or bad.

The Ministry of Reconciliation

11Since, then, we know what it is to fear
the Lord,[r] we try to persuade others. What
we are is plain to God, and I hope it is also
plain to your conscience.[s] 12We are not trying to commend ourselves to you again,[t]
but are giving you an opportunity to take
pride in us,[u] so that you can answer those
who take pride in what is seen rather than
in what is in the heart. 13If we are "out
of our mind,"[v] as some say, it is for God;
if we are in our right mind, it is for you.
14For Christ's love compels us, because we
are convinced that one died for all, and
therefore all died.[w] 15And he died for all,
that those who live should no longer live
for themselves[x] but for him who died for
them and was raised again.
16So from now on we regard no one
from a worldly[y] point of view. Though we
once regarded Christ in this way, we do
so no longer. 17Therefore, if anyone is in
Christ, the new creation[z] has come:[a] The
old has gone, the new is here![a] 18All this
is from God, who reconciled us to himself
through Christ[b] and gave us the ministry
of reconciliation: 19that God was reconciling the world to himself in Christ, not
counting people's sins against them.[c] And
he has committed to us the message of
reconciliation. 20We are therefore Christ's
ambassadors,[d] as though God were making his appeal through us. We implore you

5:4 [l] 1Co 15:53, 54
5:5 [m] Ro 8:23; 2Co 1:22
5:7 [n] 1Co 13:12
5:8 [o] Php 1:23
5:9 [p] Ro 14:18
5:10 [q] Mt 16:27; Ro 14:10; Eph 6:8
5:11 [r] Heb 10:31; Jude 23
[s] 2Co 4:2
5:12 [t] 2Co 3:1
[u] 2Co 1:14
5:13 [v] 2Co 11:1, 16, 17
5:14 [w] Gal 2:20
5:15 [x] Ro 14:7-9
5:16 [y] 2Co 11:18
5:17 [z] Gal 6:15
[a] Isa 65:17; Rev 21:4, 5
5:18 [b] Ro 5:10; Col 1:20
5:19 [c] Ro 4:8
5:20 [d] 2Co 6:1; Eph 6:20

[a] 17 Or *Christ, that person is a new creation.*

5:4 *what is mortal may be swallowed up by life.* See note on 1Co 15:53 – 54.
5:5 Scripture and some Jewish tradition associated the Spirit with the time of the kingdom restoration, which Jewish tradition identified with the world to come (e.g., Isa 44:3; Eze 39:29). *deposit.* The Greek term used here referred in business documents to the first payment; the Spirit is here the first taste of the life of the coming era.
5:8 *away from the body and at home with the Lord.* Pharisees accepted both the immortality of the soul and the future resurrection of the body, and many Jewish writers depicted the experience of heaven after death as a proleptic experience to be completed in paradise after the resurrection. Paul apparently likewise accepted both the soul's continuance after death and bodily resurrection (cf., e.g., Php 1:21 – 23 with Php 3:20 – 21).
5:10 *judgment seat.* In Corinth, the place of judgment was massive. Governors issued decrees and decisions from this raised platform, and Corinthian believers would know of Paul's experience there (Ac 18:12). Nevertheless, Paul particularly recalls the Biblical day of judgment, depicted in early Jewish sources as God judging from his throne (Paul thus depicts Jesus as divine here; cf. Ro 14:10). *while in the body.* See notes on 1Co 6:13,14.
5:11 *fear the Lord.* Because God is judge (v. 10), fearing him offers moral incentive (e.g., Pr 16:6).
5:12 *not trying to commend ourselves.* Honorable people in antiquity were not supposed to commend themselves unless they could give good reason for it, such as defending themselves (v. 12; 3:1) or replying to charges (10:10), for the welfare of one's hearers (v. 12; 10:8), critiquing others' misplaced arrogance (11:12,18), or because of necessity (12:1,11). *what is seen … what is in the heart.* Applying the inward-outward contrast of 4:16 – 18 (cf. also 3:12,18) against his arrogant critics, Paul uses some language from the Greek version of 1Sa 16:7.
5:13 *"out of our mind," … right mind.* Many people considered philosophers out of their minds (philosophers held the same opinion of the masses); more relevantly here, those who were inspired were also deemed out of their mind (in a more positive way). The opposite state was being in one's right mind. Cf. the contrast between Moses when with God and Moses in public in Ex 34:33 – 34; cf. also 2Co 3:7.
5:16 *regard no one from a worldly point of view.* Greek thinkers often challenged outward ways of viewing matters (see notes on 4:16,17). Paul's perspective is informed by the promised new age established in Christ (vv. 15,17).
5:17 *the new creation has come.* Although later teachers sometimes applied it to proselytes, the most common use of new creation language in Jewish sources from this period addresses the age to come. This also fits earlier Biblical usage (Isa 65:16 – 18; 66:22). Paul recognizes that the promised resurrection has begun in Jesus, so that believers have already begun to experience some of the life of the promised age (cf. vv. 5,15; 4:10 – 11).
5:18 – 19 *reconciled … reconciliation … reconciling.* Harmony and thus reconciliation were frequent topics of public discussion.
5:20 *Christ's ambassadors.* An "ambassador" was a representative of one state to another, usually applied in this period to the emperor's legates in the East. How one treated heralds, ambassadors or other representatives, who were supposed to have diplomatic immunity, also honored or shamed the sender (Mk 9:37; Lk 10:16). Like Biblical prophets (Ex 7:1; 1Sa 8:7), apostles were agents authorized as representatives of God — the greatest king. *We implore you on Christ's behalf: Be reconciled to God.* Orators sometimes held attention with startling images — here summoning the Corinthian believers to be reconciled to God (also 6:1). They are alienated from God, it appears, by their alienation from Paul and his coworkers (6:11 – 13; 7:2 – 4; see note on 6:11 — 7:4).

on Christ's behalf: Be reconciled to God.
21 God made him who had no sin[e] to be
sin[a] for us, so that in him we might become the righteousness of God.[f]

6 As God's co-workers[g] we urge you not
to receive God's grace in vain. 2 For he
says,

> "In the time of my favor I heard you,
> and in the day of salvation I helped
> you."[b][h]

I tell you, now is the time of God's favor,
now is the day of salvation.

Paul's Hardships

3 We put no stumbling block in anyone's
path,[i] so that our ministry will not be discredited. 4 Rather, as servants of God we
commend ourselves in every way: in great
endurance; in troubles, hardships and dis-
tresses; 5 in beatings, imprisonments[j] and
riots; in hard work, sleepless nights and
hunger;[k] 6 in purity, understanding, patience and kindness; in the Holy Spirit[l]
and in sincere love; 7 in truthful speech[m]
and in the power of God; with weapons of
righteousness[n] in the right hand and in the
left; 8 through glory and dishonor,[o] bad report and good report; genuine, yet regarded as impostors;[p] 9 known, yet regarded
as unknown; dying,[q] and yet we live on;[r]
beaten, and yet not killed; 10 sorrowful, yet
always rejoicing;[s] poor, yet making many
rich;[t] having nothing, and yet possessing
everything.[u]

11 We have spoken freely to you, Corinthians, and opened wide our hearts to
you.[v] 12 We are not withholding our affection from you, but you are withholding
yours from us. 13 As a fair exchange — I
speak as to my children[w] — open wide
your hearts also.

Warning Against Idolatry

14 Do not be yoked together[x] with unbelievers. For what do righteousness and
wickedness have in common? Or what
fellowship can light have with darkness?[y]
15 What harmony is there between Christ
and Belial[c]? Or what does a believer[z] have

5:21 [e] Heb 4:15; 1Pe 2:22,24; 1Jn 3:5 [f] Ro 1:17 **6:1** [g] 1Co 3:9; 2Co 5:20 **6:2** [h] Isa 49:8 **6:3** [i] Ro 14:13, 20; 1Co 9:12; 10:32 **6:5** [j] 2Co 11:23-25 [k] 1Co 4:11 **6:6** [l] 1Th 1:5 **6:7** [m] 2Co 4:2 [n] 2Co 10:4; Eph 6:10-18 **6:8** [o] 1Co 4:10 [p] Mt 27:63 **6:9** [q] Ro 8:36 [r] 2Co 1:8-10; 4:10,11 **6:10** [s] 2Co 7:4 [t] 2Co 8:9 [u] Ro 8:32; 1Co 3:21 **6:11** [v] 2Co 7:3 **6:13** [w] 1Co 4:14 **6:14** [x] 1Co 5:9, 10 [y] Eph 5:7,11; 1Jn 1:6 **6:15** [z] Ac 5:14

[a] 21 Or *be a sin offering* [b] 2 Isaiah 49:8
[c] 15 Greek *Beliar*, a variant of *Belial*

5:21 *made him who had no sin to be sin for us.* Paul might blend the idea of unblemished sacrifices with that of the scapegoat that embodied the sin of God's people (Lev 1:3; 16:21 – 22). Christ's representatives (v. 20) would represent Christ's righteousness, as Christ represented sin for us.
6:1 See note on 5:20.
6:2 The context of Isa 49:8, cited here, is the promised restoration (Isa 52:7), depicted in cosmic terms (Isa 49:6,13); believers already experience a foretaste of this promise (see 5:17 and note).
6:4 – 10 For sages listing sufferings to verify their character, in contrast with charlatans, see note on 4:8 – 12. Even in court, arguments about one's character affected assessments of guilt or innocence. Orators valued repetition to drive home points, and vv. 4 – 10 would be worthy of any orator: Paul lists nine hardships (vv. 4 – 5) and eight virtues, all prefaced by the Greek *en* ("in"; vv. 6 – 7); then three contrasts regarding weakness prefaced by *dia* (the NIV translates some as "with" and some as "through"; vv. 7 – 8) followed by seven more contrasts divided by "yet" (vv. 8 – 10). One can also read this as three sets of nine elements (cf. nine in 1Co 12:8 – 10; Gal 5:22 – 23; two sets in 2Co 11:23 – 25,26).
6:7 *in the right hand and in the left.* Soldiers normally carried a spear, lance or, after these were discharged, a sword in their right hands and carried a shield in their left.
6:8 – 9 Orators employed antithesis (contrast); orators and sages both liked paradox. The sorts of criticisms noted here were often leveled against sages. Some philosophers ignored criticism, dismissing the value of mortals' opinions; for the sake of the message, others tried to deflect criticism where possible. Society placed considerable pressure on people to seek honor and avoid shame.
6:9 *dying, and yet we live on.* See 4:10 – 12 and the language of Ps 118:17 – 18 (from a group of psalms sung at Jewish festivals and thus particularly familiar; cf. Ps 116:10 in 2Co 4:13 and possibly Ps 119:32 in 2Co 6:11).
6:10 Intellectuals could respect some of Paul's claims here. *having nothing, and yet possessing everything.* Cynic philosophers gave up all possessions to pursue their lifestyle but considered themselves spiritually rich. Cynic and Stoic philosophers claimed that, although they owned little or nothing, all the world belonged to them, because they were friends of the gods.
6:11 — 7:4 Orators often climaxed arguments with an intense emotional appeal, as in 6:11 – 13 and in 7:2 – 4 (letters, which were less formal than speeches, could give even freer play to emotion). Writers often digressed, and often clearly framed the digression by returning to the same point. The appeal to welcome Paul frames his demand to reject some who are evil (6:14 — 7:1), perhaps implying Paul's opponents. In ancient Mediterranean life (and especially in Roman party politics, well known in Corinth), one should be friends with one's friends and enemies to their enemies. By welcoming Paul's opponents, the church was rejecting Paul, and thus the one who sent him (see note on 5:20).
6:12 *We are not withholding our affection ... but you are.* Orators and especially letter writers often expressed deep affection; sometimes they also affectionately protested that the other should reciprocate this love.
6:14 – 16 Hearers accustomed to ancient oratory would have appreciated Paul's emotional climax here: a series of antitheses (contrasts) framed in five rhetorical questions. Jewish sources contrasted the righteous and wicked, the wise and foolish. They also contrasted good and evil as light and darkness; the Dead Sea Scrolls contrasted the people of light and the people of darkness (e.g., War Scroll 1.1, 11).
6:14 *yoked together.* Borrows an image from the Greek text of Lev 19:19 (cf. Dt 22:10). This image would reinforce Biblical prohibitions of intermarriage or close alliances with nonbelievers (e.g., Dt 7:3; Ezr 9:12).
6:15 *Belial.* Jewish sources often called Satan "Belial" or "Beliar" (e.g., Qumran's Manual of Discipline 1.24; 2.5; 10.21). The name derives from a frequent OT Hebrew term meaning "worthlessness" or "wickedness," though by this period it was so commonly used for the devil, especially in Judea (e.g., pervasively in the Dead Sea Scrolls) that hearers may not have thought as directly about the term's original sense.

in common with an unbeliever? 16What
agreement is there between the temple of
God and idols? For we are the temple[a] of
the living God. As God has said:

"I will live with them
and walk among them,
and I will be their God,
and they will be my people."[ab]

17Therefore,

"Come out from them[c]
and be separate,
says the Lord.
Touch no unclean thing,
and I will receive you."[bd]

18And,

"I will be a Father to you,
and you will be my sons and
daughters,[e]
says the Lord Almighty."[c]

7 Therefore, since we have these promises,[f] dear friends, let us purify ourselves from everything that contaminates
body and spirit, perfecting holiness out of
reverence for God.

Paul's Joy Over the Church's Repentance

2Make room for us in your hearts.[g] We
have wronged no one, we have corrupted
no one, we have exploited no one. 3I do
not say this to condemn you; I have said
before that you have such a place in our
hearts[h] that we would live or die with you.
4I have spoken to you with great frankness; I take great pride in you. I am greatly encouraged; in all our troubles my joy
knows no bounds.[i]

5For when we came into Macedonia,[j]
we had no rest, but we were harassed
at every turn[k]—conflicts on the outside,
fears within.[l] 6But God, who comforts the
downcast,[m] comforted us by the coming
of Titus,[n] 7and not only by his coming but
also by the comfort you had given him. He
told us about your longing for me, your
deep sorrow, your ardent concern for me,
so that my joy was greater than ever.

8Even if I caused you sorrow by my letter,[o] I do not regret it. Though I did regret
it—I see that my letter hurt you, but only
for a little while— 9yet now I am happy,
not because you were made sorry, but because your sorrow led you to repentance.
For you became sorrowful as God intended and so were not harmed in any way by
us. 10Godly sorrow brings repentance that
leads to salvation[p] and leaves no regret,
but worldly sorrow brings death. 11See
what this godly sorrow has produced in
you: what earnestness, what eagerness to

6:16 [a] 1Co 3:16 [b] Lev 26:12; Jer 32:38; Eze 37:27 **6:17** [c] Rev 18:4 [d] Isa 52:11 **6:18** [e] Isa 43:6 **7:1** [f] 2Co 6:17, 18 **7:2** [g] 2Co 6:12, 13 **7:3** [h] 2Co 6:11, 12 **7:4** [i] 2Co 6:10 **7:5** [j] 2Co 2:13 [k] 2Co 4:8 [l] Dt 32:25 **7:6** [m] 2Co 1:3, 4 [n] ver 13; 2Co 2:13 **7:8** [o] 2Co 2:2, 4 **7:10** [p] Ac 11:18

[a] *16* Lev. 26:12; Jer. 32:38; Ezek. 37:27 [b] *17* Isaiah 52:11; Ezek. 20:34,41 [c] *18* 2 Samuel 7:14; 7:8

6:16–18 Jewish interpreters sometimes linked or blended Biblical texts, as here (see NIV text notes).
6:16 *idols.* Against Paul's teaching, some may still advocate idol food (see 1Co 8–10; Rev 2:14,20). *we are the temple of the living God.* See note on 1Co 3:17.
6:17 God had consecrated his people to himself (Lev 11:45); the context of Isa 52:11, cited here, is God bringing his people from captivity in Babylon and restoring them (Isa 52:7–15). *I will receive you.* These words follow a Greek translation of God's promise to gather his people in a number of texts, perhaps especially Eze 20:34,41.
6:18 *my sons and daughters.* God's people were his sons and daughters (e.g., Dt 32:19; Jer 3:19), who would be restored to their special relationship with him in the time of the end (Isa 43:6). Paul blends the language of several texts (probably including 2Sa 7:14, in the immediate context of building a temple, 2Co 6:16), as Jewish writers sometimes did; here he may also blend his own prophetic insight (cf. 1Co 14:37–38).
7:1 *we have these promises.* The promises of 6:16–18 are applicable in Christ (1:20).
7:2 *Make room for us in your hearts.* Writers ending a digression (such as 6:14—7:1) often picked up where they left off (see 6:11–13 and note on 6:11—7:4). After arresting hearers' attention with harsh or startling images (as again in 6:14—7:1), speakers also often softened the tone with gentleness. *We have ... we have ... we have.* Orators drove home points with repetition.
7:3 *such a place in our hearts.* Even more than most speakers, friends could show affection in letters. A friend could emphasize that he wrote not to discourage or harm but to demonstrate his love (cf. 2:4; 11:11). *we would live or die with you.* Greeks considered willingness to die for a friend the greatest expression of friendship (cf. Jn 15:13).
7:4 *with great frankness.* Ancient thinkers often used this Greek term for being frank to emphasize that, unlike flatterers exploiting their hearers, they were true friends, speaking the truth for the hearers' good.
7:5–6 Finishing his long digression in 2:14—7:4, Paul picks up where he left off. On narratives, see note on 1:8—2:13; although usually at the beginning, they could be provided where needed. Paul crossed over from Troas to Macedonia to find Titus, whom he had sent to the Corinthians with a harsh letter (2:12–13).
7:6 *God, who comforts the downcast.* See, e.g., Isa 40:1; 49:13; 51:3; 52:9. *comforted ... by the coming of Titus.* Paul was comforted not only by Titus's safety but by the Corinthians' response.
7:7 *your longing for me, your deep sorrow, your ardent concern for me.* Writers of letters were sometimes anxious about how their words would be received. Orators drove home points with repetition, here three affectionate attitudes of the Corinthian believers toward Paul.
7:8–9 *my letter hurt you ... led you to repentance.* A letter writer would sometimes apologize if a recipient felt hurt. Nevertheless, when hearers did not respond to gentleness, moral teachers were ready to speak more harshly, like a doctor inflicting pain to help a patient. Such teachers might not regret frank speech (v. 4) or even rebuke if they proved truly necessary to secure repentance.
7:11 Orators drove home points with repetition; note the multiple repetitions of "what ..." (the Greek term *alla*, which often means "but," separates seven nouns depicting dramatic emotion). Affectionate letters sometimes invited the reader to prove his or her love (cf. 8:24).

clear yourselves, what indignation, what
alarm, what longing, what concern,[q] what
readiness to see justice done. At every
point you have proved yourselves to be
innocent in this matter. 12So even though
I wrote to you,[r] it was neither on account
of the one who did the wrong[s] nor on account of the injured party, but rather that
before God you could see for yourselves
how devoted to us you are. 13By all this
we are encouraged.

In addition to our own encouragement, we were especially delighted to
see how happy Titus[t] was, because his
spirit has been refreshed by all of you.
14I had boasted to him about you,[u] and
you have not embarrassed me. But just
as everything we said to you was true,
so our boasting about you to Titus[v] has
proved to be true as well. 15And his affection for you is all the greater when he
remembers that you were all obedient,[w]
receiving him with fear and trembling.[x]
16I am glad I can have complete confidence in you.[y]

The Collection for the Lord's People

8 And now, brothers and sisters, we
want you to know about the grace that
God has given the Macedonian[z] churches.
2In the midst of a very severe trial, their
overflowing joy and their extreme poverty
welled up in rich generosity. 3For I testify
that they gave as much as they were able,[a]
and even beyond their ability. Entirely on
their own, 4they urgently pleaded with us
for the privilege of sharing in this service[b]
to the Lord's people.[c] 5And they exceeded
our expectations: They gave themselves
first of all to the Lord, and then by the will
of God also to us. 6So we urged[d] Titus,[e]
just as he had earlier made a beginning, to
bring also to completion[f] this act of grace
on your part. 7But since you excel in everything[g]—in faith, in speech, in knowledge,[h] in complete earnestness and in the

7:11 [q] ver 7
7:12 [r] ver 8; 2Co 2:3,9 [s] 1Co 5:1,2
7:13 [t] ver 6; 2Co 2:13
7:14 [u] ver 4 [v] ver 6
7:15 [w] 2Co 2:9 [x] Php 2:12
7:16 [y] 2Co 2:3
8:1 [z] Ac 16:9
8:3 [a] 1Co 16:2
8:4 [b] Ac 24:17 [c] Ro 15:25; 2Co 9:1
8:6 [d] ver 17; 2Co 12:18 [e] ver 16,23 [f] ver 10,11
8:7 [g] 2Co 9:8 [h] 1Co 1:5

7:13 *his spirit has been refreshed by all of you.* Antiquity stressed the virtue of hospitality; e.g., local synagogue communities often accommodated Jewish travelers. How people received one's agent also displayed respect or disdain for the sender.

7:14 *our boasting about you.* People looked down on unjustified boasting in oneself, but boasting about friends was considered honorable.

7:15 *receiving him.* See note on v. 13.

7:16 *I can have complete confidence in you.* Writers sometimes expressed confidence in their audience during or (as here, in chs. 8–9) just before a request.

8:1—9:15 After dealing with minor issues, Paul turns to questions of support (chs. 8–9) before finally addressing the most serious breach (chs. 10–13). Higher-status members of the church felt offended that Paul refused their patronal support (11:7–11; 12:13), and now some criticize his inconsistency. Unwilling to accept support for himself, he asks it on behalf of the poor in Jerusalem, whom the sponsors have never met. Paul uses a range of terms frequent in ancient business documents for funds and benefactors' generosity (such as "sharing" in 8:4, "this matter" in 9:3, an untranslated term for an undertaking in 9:4, and "gift" in 9:5). The Corinthian believers did ultimately provide their contribution (Ro 15:26; cf. Ac 20:2).

A minority of scholars have proposed that because chs. 8–9 address a distinct issue, they must form a separate letter. Although administrative letters were common, business sections within letters that also addressed other topics were no less appropriate. Several scholars want both ch. 8 and ch. 9 to be separate letters, but the dividing chapter break interrupts a continued flow of thought.

8:1 *grace.* When it appears in business documents, the Greek term used here and often in this section, though translated various ways (vv. 1,4 ["privilege"],6–7,19 [no single translated term]; 9:14; cf. v. 9; 9:8 ["bless"],15 ["thanks"]) can mean various things. In addition to divine "grace," it can refer to benefactors' generosity, to the gift or to gratitude (cf. v. 16 ["thanks"]; 9:15 ["thanks"]); God's generosity invites believers' generosity and thanksgiving to God. *the Macedonian churches.* Speakers and writers often appealed to positive models for imitation. They also used comparison with others (v. 8), using rivalry to provoke excellence. Cities competed for honor, and speakers invoked traditional rivalries to spur their hearers on to greater zeal. Corinth, the capital of Achaia, and the province of Macedonia, which included the cities Philippi and Thessalonica, were traditional rivals.

8:2 *extreme poverty.* Although Philippi (where one of Paul's most supportive churches in Macedonia was located, Php 4:15) was prosperous, its prosperity had not filtered down to the poor, who often were unemployed. Despite some exceptions (Ac 16:14; 17:7), the poor may have comprised many of the believers there and in Thessalonica (cf. 1Th 4:11; 2Th 3:8). Further, prejudice against Jesus' followers may have increased their economic disadvantages there (Php 1:30; 1Th 2:14; 3:3–4).

8:3 *as much as they were able … beyond their ability.* Greek and Roman inscriptions often described generous benefaction with expressions such as these. The Macedonian churches gave even beyond the Biblical and early Jewish principle of generosity for the poor in accordance with the giver's resources (Ex 35:24; Dt 15:14).

8:4 *sharing.* Business documents often used the underlying Greek term for economic partnerships. *service.* Jewish sources sometimes used this Greek term for providing for the needy. The Macedonian believers count this activity a privilege.

8:6 *we urged Titus … to bring also to completion.* Titus had raised this issue of support as well as the issue of the harsh letter when he was among them; because Titus has now reported back to him, Paul's concern as to whether the Corinthians' offering would be ready (9:3) probably indicates that they were not. *completion.* Inscriptions often praise benefactors for completing a project to which they had pledged.

8:7 *since you excel in everything.* Orators often accumulated examples in quick succession to drive home a point; Paul here piles up examples of how they excel (faith, speech, etc.; cf. 1Co 1:5–7). Speakers often praised hearers' strengths in order to move them to act beneficially; a letter writer also could appeal to the recipient's affection for the writer to urge some action for the reader's good. *in the love we have kindled in you.* See NIV text note. If Paul refers instead to his love for the Corinthians, superlative claims of love expressed affection.

love we have kindled in you[a]—see that
you also excel in this grace of giving.
8 I am not commanding you,[i] but I want
to test the sincerity of your love by comparing it with the earnestness of others.
9 For you know the grace of our Lord Jesus
Christ,[j] that though he was rich, yet for
your sake he became poor,[k] so that you
through his poverty might become rich.
10 And here is my judgment[l] about what
is best for you in this matter. Last year you
were the first not only to give but also to
have the desire to do so.[m] 11 Now finish the
work, so that your eager willingness[n] to
do it may be matched by your completion
of it, according to your means. 12 For if the
willingness is there, the gift is acceptable
according to what one has,[o] not according
to what one does not have.
13 Our desire is not that others might be
relieved while you are hard pressed, but
that there might be equality. 14 At the present time your plenty will supply what they
need,[p] so that in turn their plenty will
supply what you need. The goal is equality, 15 as it is written: "The one who gathered much did not have too much, and the
one who gathered little did not have too
little."[b][q]

Titus Sent to Receive the Collection

16 Thanks be to God,[r] who put into the
hearts[s] of Titus[t] the same concern I have
for you. 17 For Titus not only welcomed our
appeal, but he is coming to you with much
enthusiasm and on his own initiative.[u]
18 And we are sending along with him the
brother[v] who is praised by all the churches[w] for his service to the gospel.[x] 19 What
is more, he was chosen by the churches to
accompany us[y] as we carry the offering,
which we administer in order to honor the
Lord himself and to show our eagerness
to help.[z] 20 We want to avoid any criticism
of the way we administer this liberal gift.
21 For we are taking pains to do what is
right, not only in the eyes of the Lord but
also in the eyes of man.[a]
22 In addition, we are sending with them
our brother who has often proved to us in
many ways that he is zealous, and now
even more so because of his great con-

8:8 [i] 1Co 7:6 **8:9** [j] 2Co 13:14 [k] Mt 20:28; Php 2:6-8 **8:10** [l] 1Co 7:25, 40 [m] 1Co 16:2, 3; 2Co 9:2 **8:11** [n] 2Co 9:2 **8:12** [o] Mk 12:43,44; Lk 21:3 **8:14** [p] 2Co 9:12 **8:15** [q] Ex 16:18 **8:16** [r] 2Co 2:14 [s] Rev 17:17 [t] 2Co 2:13 **8:17** [u] ver 6 **8:18** [v] 2Co 12:18 [w] 1Co 7:17 [x] 2Co 2:12 **8:19** [y] 1Co 16:3, 4 [z] ver 11, 12 **8:21** [a] Ro 12:17; 14:18

[a] 7 Some manuscripts *and in your love for us*
[b] 15 Exodus 16:18

8:8 *I am not commanding you.* Municipalities sometimes forced wealthy donors to support public works; others thus stressed when donations were voluntary. *test the sincerity of your love.* Sometimes one writing to a friend affectionately explained that he was testing the reader's love by requesting some action (see notes on vv. 7,24).
8:9 *our Lord Jesus Christ ... became poor.* Persuasive speakers often cited examples of figures whose behavior modeled their point; Paul cites the ultimate example. Corinth was a wealthy city, though this wealth was not evenly distributed (see Introduction to 1 Corinthians: Corinth). *become rich.* Paul's use of this phrase might imply that sharing among believers ought to increase until all have enough (v. 14).
8:10 *what is best.* Persuaders often appealed to "what is best" (for reasons for the advantage, see vv. 13 – 15). *Last year.* Could designate any period from 9 to 15 months before; this earlier commitment is evident in 1Co 16:1 – 3.
8:11 *eager willingness.* Cities dedicated inscriptions to honor benefactors who displayed "eager willingness" to help.
8:12 *the gift is acceptable according to what one has.* By Biblical standards, only one's best gift was acceptable to God (see, e.g., Lev 1:3; 22:20 – 21), but what one could give varied according to one's means (see, e.g., Lev 5:11; 14:21 – 22; 27:8).
8:13 *equality.* Corinth was a particularly prosperous city and the church included some members with significant means (cf. Ro 16:23). Central to the Greek conception of friendship were equality and the notion that friends share all things in common. Benefactors who helped sponsor less affluent clients used this language of friendship, but more intimate traditional friendship required fuller sharing. Believers should share so that all their fellow believers have enough.
8:14 *the present time.* The urgent crisis was a famine (cf. Ac 11:28). *their plenty will supply what you need.* In ancient ethics, recipients of benefaction were to pay back the benefactors, though with honor, not money. Food shortages, however, sometimes affected even prosperous Corinth, which depended on trade to pay for sufficient food imports; other believers might someday help them. *equality.* See v. 13 and note.
8:15 The supernatural provision of just the right amount of manna for each household in Ex 16:18, cited here, offered a model for what Paul meant by equality (vv. 13 – 14). Other Diaspora Jewish writers appealed to the same passage to urge equality.
8:16 *Thanks be to God.* Writers sometimes bracketed a section by beginning and ending with the same wording; this is at least possibly the case with this verse and 9:15. Paul, of course, often does stop to praise God (e.g., Ro 1:25; 6:17; 11:36; 1Co 15:57).
8:17 – 18 Throughout the empire, social superiors provided letters of introduction to their peers or inferiors on behalf of those they recommended (see note on 3:1).
8:19 *chosen.* The Greek term can include voting, common in Greek culture; in any case, Paul respects the democratic ideal for local choices valued in Greek culture. *the offering.* Paul and his churches would not have to look far for a model of respectable behavior for a Jerusalem collection. Jewish adult males throughout the world paid a half-shekel tax each year to support the temple; local Diaspora Jewish communities sent respected individuals to carry their local collections to Jerusalem. *to honor the Lord.* Ancients expected generosity to be repaid with honor—here (and in vv. 21,23) to the chief benefactor, God.
8:20 *avoid any criticism.* Mediterranean culture heavily emphasized honor, so qualifications for leaders included that they be respectable and above reproach.
8:21 *taking pains.* Honorary inscriptions used "taking pains" for benefactors' foresight, which sometimes included sending honorable representatives. *do what is right.* Other Jewish teachers also emphasized doing what is right before both God and people. *in the eyes of the Lord.* Paul uses wording from the Greek translation of Pr 3:4.
8:22 *our brother.* If the audience already knew someone, a writer could describe instead of name him. *often proved to us in many ways.* Although class provided ready access

fidence in you. 23As for Titus, he is my
partner[b] and co-worker[c] among you; as
for our brothers,[d] they are representatives
of the churches and an honor to Christ.
24Therefore show these men the proof of
your love and the reason for our pride in
you,[e] so that the churches can see it.

9 There is no need[f] for me to write to
you about this service to the Lord's
people.[g] 2For I know your eagerness to
help, and I have been boasting[h] about
it to the Macedonians, telling them that
since last year[i] you in Achaia[j] were ready
to give; and your enthusiasm has stirred
most of them to action. 3But I am sending the brothers in order that our boasting about you in this matter should not
prove hollow, but that you may be ready,
as I said you would be.[k] 4For if any Macedonians[l] come with me and find you unprepared, we — not to say anything about
you — would be ashamed of having been
so confident. 5So I thought it necessary to
urge the brothers to visit you in advance
and finish the arrangements for the generous gift you had promised. Then it will
be ready as a generous gift,[m] not as one
grudgingly given.[n]

Generosity Encouraged

6Remember this: Whoever sows sparingly will also reap sparingly, and whoever sows generously will also reap generously.[o] 7Each of you should give what
you have decided in your heart to give,[p]
not reluctantly or under compulsion,[q]
for God loves a cheerful giver.[r] 8And God
is able[s] to bless you abundantly, so that
in all things at all times, having all that
you need,[t] you will abound in every good
work. 9As it is written:

> "They have freely scattered their gifts
> to the poor;
> their righteousness endures
> forever."[a][u]

10Now he who supplies seed to the sower
and bread for food[v] will also supply and
increase your store of seed and will enlarge the harvest of your righteousness.[w]
11You will be enriched[x] in every way so
that you can be generous on every occasion, and through us your generosity will
result in thanksgiving to God.[y]

12This service that you perform is not
only supplying the needs[z] of the Lord's
people but is also overflowing in many
expressions of thanks to God.[a] 13Be-
cause of the service[b] by which you have
proved yourselves, others will praise God[c]
for the obedience that accompanies your

[a] 9 Psalm 112:9

8:23 [b] Phm 17 [c] Php 2:25 [d] ver 18,22
8:24 [e] 2Co 7:4, 14; 9:2
9:1 [f] 1Th 4:9 [g] 2Co 8:4
9:2 [h] 2Co 7:4, 14 [i] 2Co 8:10 [j] Ac 18:12
9:3 [k] 1Co 16:2
9:4 [l] Ro 15:26
9:5 [m] Php 4:17 [n] 2Co 12:17, 18
9:6 [o] Pr 11:24, 25; 22:9; Gal 6:7,9
9:7 [p] Ex 25:2; 2Co 8:12 [q] Dt 15:10 [r] Ro 12:8
9:8 [s] Eph 3:20 [t] Php 4:19
9:9 [u] Ps 112:9
9:10 [v] Isa 55:10 [w] Hos 10:12
9:11 [x] 1Co 1:5 [y] 2Co 1:11
9:12 [z] 2Co 8:14 [a] 2Co 1:11
9:13 [b] 2Co 8:4 [c] Mt 9:8

---

to high-status offices, the ancient ideal for leadership was that persons be "proved" before promotion to higher offices. Both Jewish and Greco-Roman moralists recommended that potential leaders be tested in lower positions before achieving public office.

8:23 *representatives of the churches and an honor to Christ.* See note on v. 19.

8:24 *show these men the proof of your love.* Displaying affection, one could ask for proofs of love. Sometimes an influential person writing a letter of recommendation could invite a benefactor to demonstrate to the recommended how effective the recommender's recommendation was. Asking a reader to prove their affection for the writer by granting the latter's request revealed confidence in the friendship.

9:1 Digressions were common in ancient sources; vv. 1 – 2 might be a digression from discussing the delegation (vv. 3 – 5; 8:16 – 23).

9:2 Speakers sometimes used civic pride and rivalry to spur communities to action (see note on 8:1).

9:3 *our boasting about you.* Paul may have boasted about their enthusiasm (v. 2) before the troubles recently aroused by outside critics (11:4 – 15). In boasting, however, he has laid his own honor on the line (see v. 4 and note).

9:4 *having been so confident.* A writer could declare confidence in his readers (e.g., v. 1) even though he has genuine reason for concern (cf. v. 5; 12:16 – 18); he might then urge the readers not to fail his confidence.

9:5 *finish the ... generous gift you had promised.* In antiquity, communities publicly held benefactors to their promises. People often justified by their actions by citing what could be deemed necessary.

9:6 *Whoever sows ... will also reap.* Jewish teachers emphasized God's blessings toward the generous (earlier, see Ps 112:5; Pr 11:24 – 26; 22:9). Sowing as one reaped was a common saying, applied also to stinginess. Appealing to ancient literary and rhetorical tastes, Paul frames his use of the saying with repetition.

9:7 *decided in your heart to give.* Voluntary giving may recall Ex 25:2; 35:5,21 – 22. *not reluctantly.* Recalls the Greek translation of Dt 15:10. *God loves a cheerful giver.* A line added by the Greek translation to Pr 22:8, adapted here, reads: "God blesses a man who is cheerful and a giver."

9:8 *abundantly ... abound.* In ancient business documents the Greek terms related to "abundantly" and "abound" (also in v. 12 ["overflowing"]; 8:2 ["overflowing"]; 8:7 ["excel"]; 8:14 ["plenty"]) could apply to profit margins. *all.* In Greek, Paul uses "all" terms five times, three of them one after the other; such repetition underlined a point as well as verbal skills that Greek hearers honored. *all that you need.* The Greek term meant having enough but also often applied to the virtue of contentment. Some sages insisted that one need have nothing to be content, but most recognized that having enough required meeting at least the fundamental needs of life.

9:9 In context, Ps 112:9, cited here, promises blessings to the righteous.

9:10 *seed to the sower and bread for food.* Closely follows the Greek translation of Isa 55:10, which speaks about God's power and generosity. *harvest of your righteousness.* Evokes the promise just cited in v. 9. Thus God will continue to supply for them to be able to supply others (v. 9; see v. 11). God supplies the corporate need of his people sufficiently so they can share with the needy among them (Dt 15:4 – 11).

9:11 – 13 *thanksgiving ... thanks ... praise.* God is the ultimate supplier (v. 10), and the expected ancient response to benefactors was thanksgiving (here thanks to God).

confession of the gospel of Christ,[d] and for
your generosity in sharing with them and
with everyone else. 14And in their prayers
for you their hearts will go out to you, because of the surpassing grace God has giv-
en you. 15Thanks be to God[e] for his indescribable gift![f]

Paul's Defense of His Ministry

10 By the humility and gentleness[g] of
Christ, I appeal to you—I, Paul,[h]
who am "timid" when face to face with
you, but "bold" toward you when away!
2I beg you that when I come I may not
have to be as bold[i] as I expect to be toward some people who think that we live
by the standards of this world. 3For though
we live in the world, we do not wage war
as the world does. 4The weapons we fight
with[j] are not the weapons of the world.
On the contrary, they have divine power[k]
to demolish strongholds.[l] 5We demolish
arguments and every pretension that sets
itself up against the knowledge of God,[m]
and we take captive every thought to make
it obedient[n] to Christ. 6And we will be
ready to punish every act of disobedience,
once your obedience is complete.[o]
7You are judging by appearances.[a][p] If
anyone is confident that they belong to
Christ,[q] they should consider again that
we belong to Christ just as much as they
do.[r] 8So even if I boast somewhat freely
about the authority the Lord gave us for
building you up rather than tearing you
down,[s] I will not be ashamed of it. 9I do
not want to seem to be trying to frighten
you with my letters. 10For some say, "His
letters are weighty and forceful, but in
person he is unimpressive[t] and his speaking amounts to nothing."[u] 11Such people
should realize that what we are in our letters when we are absent, we will be in our
actions when we are present.
12We do not dare to classify or compare ourselves with some who commend
themselves.[v] When they measure themselves by themselves and compare themselves with themselves, they are not wise.

9:13 [d] 2Co 2:12 **9:15** [e] 2Co 2:14 [f] Ro 5:15, 16 **10:1** [g] Mt 11:29 [h] Gal 5:2 **10:2** [i] 1Co 4:21; 2Co 13:2, 10 **10:4** [j] 2Co 6:7 [k] 1Co 2:5 [l] Jer 1:10; 2Co 13:10 **10:5** [m] Isa 2:11, 12; 1Co 1:19 [n] 2Co 9:13 **10:6** [o] 2Co 2:9; 7:15 **10:7** [p] Jn 7:24 [q] 1Co 1:12; 3:23; 14:37 [r] 2Co 11:23 **10:8** [s] 2Co 13:10 **10:10** [t] 1Co 2:3; Gal 4:13, 14 [u] 1Co 1:17 **10:12** [v] 2Co 3:1

[a] 7 Or *Look at the obvious facts*

9:14 *their prayers for you.* Just as God heeded the cries of the needy against their oppressors (Dt 15:9), he also would hear the prayers of the needy for their benefactors to be blessed.
9:15 *Thanks be to God.* See note on vv. 11–13.
10:1—13:14 As Paul's topic shifts from funds for the poor to responding to his enemies, his tone shifts from gentle to combative (especially toward the enemies). Nevertheless, he offered harsh statements earlier (e.g., 5:12,20; 6:14—7:1) and offers endearing statements now (12:14–15,19; 13:9,11–14). Writers sometimes added material after receiving new information, sometimes composed their work over a span of time, or sometimes included a second letter that would have functioned as an addendum had the first not been sealed. Nevertheless, Paul may have also envisioned this section from the start: speakers and writers often addressed less controversial issues first, building rapport before turning to harsher matters. Likewise, Paul has defended himself earlier in the letter, and after initial considerations defense arguments normally went on the offensive against opponents.
10:1 *humility and gentleness.* Some may have viewed Paul's mercy as weakness (vv. 9–11); high-status culture looked down on humility, except where it meant a leader showing compassion toward the weak—exactly what Paul had done in this case. *of Christ.* Christ's humility and gentleness likely evokes Jesus' claim later recorded in Mt 11:29. *I, Paul, who am "timid."* One sometimes opened a section with the opponent's charge—here that "timid" Paul inconsistently wrote "forceful" letters (v. 10). Letters were supposed to communicate the same persona as one's presence would, but Paul's letter had been harsh (2:4; 7:8). Yet Paul sent this letter rather than coming in person because he wanted to spare them his discipline (1:23—2:4).
10:3 *do not wage war as the world does.* Paul does not show harshness needlessly (vv. 1–2). Speakers often claimed that they were battling false ideas.
10:4 *divine power to demolish strongholds.* In ancient warfare, invaders besieged and sought to demolish strongholds where enemies sought to resist conquest; after succeeding, they took captive and enslaved those who were not killed. Rome had earlier destroyed Corinth in 146 BC; it was rebuilt as a Roman colony in 44 BC.
10:6 *punish every act of disobedience.* When peoples rebelled, ruling powers (most relevant for Paul's audience, Roman armies) wreaked vengeance against them. Paul speaks here figuratively (vv. 3–5).
10:7 *judging by appearances.* Philosophers warned against the common error of judging by mere appearance (cf. also 5:12; 1Sa 16:7).
10:8 *building you up rather than tearing you down.* Although God called some prophets both to build up and to tear down (e.g., Jer 1:10), Paul is called only to build up the Corinthians (2Co 12:19; 13:10).
10:9 *trying to frighten you with my letters.* As noted above (see note on v. 1), letters were supposed to communicate the same persona as one's presence would, but Paul's letter had been harsh (2:4; 7:8).
10:10 *his speaking amounts to nothing.* Although both speaking and writing could reveal one's intellect, some were dissatisfied with Paul's speaking skills in person (11:6). Greeks required respectable speakers to be not only strong in content, but also forceful in tone, having also the appropriate accent, gestures, and even style of clothing and personal grooming.
10:11 *what we are in our letters . . . we will be in our actions.* People in antiquity often emphasized that "actions" mattered more than "words" (a meaning of one of the Greek terms behind "letters" in this verse).
10:12 *compare ourselves with some who commend themselves.* Paul employs satire, refusing to rank himself in the same category as his opponents, whom he further demeans with anonymity. Ancient reasoning often compared persons, but comparing oneself with someone who outclassed one was presumptuous; comparing oneself with oneself, however, was simply stupid. People despised self-commendation unless it was properly justified as necessary or for others' good (as in 12:11). Paul's rivals may have been comparing themselves favorably with him (11:22)—by their own standards (cf. 11:23).

13We, however, will not boast beyond proper limits, but will confine our boasting to
the sphere of service God himself has assigned to us,[w] a sphere that also includes
you. 14We are not going too far in our
boasting, as would be the case if we had
not come to you, for we did get as far as
you[x] with the gospel of Christ.[y] 15Neither
do we go beyond our limits by boasting of
work done by others.[z] Our hope is that, as
your faith continues to grow,[a] our sphere of
activity among you will greatly expand, 16so
that we can preach the gospel in the regions
beyond you.[b] For we do not want to boast
about work already done in someone else's
territory. 17But, "Let the one who boasts
boast in the Lord."[a][c] 18For it is not the one
who commends himself[d] who is approved,
but the one whom the Lord commends.[e]

Paul and the False Apostles

11 I hope you will put up with[f] me in a
little foolishness.[g] Yes, please put up
with me! 2I am jealous for you with a godly
jealousy. I promised you to one husband,[h]
to Christ, so that I might present you[i] as a
pure virgin to him. 3But I am afraid that
just as Eve was deceived by the serpent's
cunning,[j] your minds may somehow be led
astray from your sincere and pure devotion
to Christ. 4For if someone comes to you
and preaches a Jesus other than the Jesus
we preached,[k] or if you receive a different
spirit[l] from the Spirit you received, or a different gospel[m] from the one you accepted,
you put up with it easily enough.
5I do not think I am in the least inferior
to those "super-apostles."[b][n] 6I may indeed
be untrained as a speaker,[o] but I do have
knowledge.[p] We have made this perfectly
clear to you in every way. 7Was it a sin[q]
for me to lower myself in order to elevate
you by preaching the gospel of God to you
free of charge?[r] 8I robbed other churches
by receiving support from them[s] so as to
serve you. 9And when I was with you and
needed something, I was not a burden to
anyone, for the brothers who came from
Macedonia supplied what I needed. I have
kept myself from being a burden to you[t]

[a] 17 Jer. 9:24 [b] 5 Or *to the most eminent apostles*

10:13 [w] ver 15, 16
10:14 [x] 1Co 3:6 [y] 2Co 2:12
10:15 [z] Ro 15:20 [a] 2Th 1:3
10:16 [b] Ac 19:21
10:17 [c] Jer 9:24; 1Co 1:31
10:18 [d] ver 12 [e] Ro 2:29; 1Co 4:5
11:1 [f] ver 4, 19, 20; Mt 17:17 [g] ver 16, 17, 21; 2Co 5:13
11:2 [h] Hos 2:19; Eph 5:26, 27 [i] 2Co 4:14
11:3 [j] Ge 3:1-6, 13; Jn 8:44; 1Ti 2:14; Rev 12:9
11:4 [k] 1Co 3:11 [l] Ro 8:15 [m] Gal 1:6-9
11:5 [n] 2Co 12:11; Gal 2:6
11:6 [o] 1Co 1:17 [p] Eph 3:4
11:7 [q] 2Co 12:13 [r] 1Co 9:18
11:8 [s] Php 4:15, 18 **11:9** [t] 2Co 12:13, 14, 16

10:13 *not boast beyond proper limits.* Ancients despised boasting beyond one's appropriate class, but Paul plainly outclasses his critics (cf. 3:1–2). In antiquity, failure to recognize one's proper place was deemed presumptuous. See the article "Ancient Boasting and 2 Corinthians 11," p. 2037.
10:17 See 1Co 1:31, which also quotes this line from Jer 9:24. Jeremiah's context undercuts typical grounds for human boasting (Jer 9:23).
10:18 For public disdain for self-commendation, see note on v. 12.
11:1 *a little foolishness.* Before launching into something shocking, speakers sometimes offered warnings. Speakers were supposed to be able to vary their styles and sometimes adopt the persona of someone else for rhetorical purposes. Paul here assumes the role of a fool, but only to show that this folly in reality characterizes his rivals, who advance themselves by boasting.
11:2 *godly jealousy.* God was jealous for his people's faithfulness (Ex 34:14; Dt 4:24; 5:9; 6:15) and for his honor (Eze 39:25), and it was honorable to share his zeal (cf. Nu 25:11,13). *I might present you as a pure virgin.* Fathers were responsible to protect their daughters' virginity (Dt 22:15–21) and arrange their marriages (cf Biblical depictions of God marrying Israel or Israel being corrupted, e.g., Isa 54:5; 62:4–5; Jer 2:32; 3:1–2; 31:32; Eze 16:32; Hos 2:19–20). For Paul as the Corinthian believers' father, cf. 1Co 4:14–15 (see note on 1Co 4:14).
11:3 *Eve was deceived by the serpent's cunning.* Fathers were responsible to protect their daughters' chastity (cf. v. 2 and note). Jewish traditions often identified the serpent of Ge 3 with Satan (e.g., Wisdom of Solomon 2:24; 3 Baruch 9:7). In one line of Jewish tradition of uncertain date, Satan, disguised as a good angel (cf. v. 14 and note), deceived Eve sexually (cf. 2 Enoch 31:6; *J Targum Pseudo Jonathan* on Ge 4:1; the serpent in the Mishnah, see *Shabbat* 146a; *Yebamot* 103b). Given the image of the betrothed virgin (v. 2; perhaps betrothed to Christ, the new Adam), Paul could have this tradition partly in view here. More certain is the Biblical allusion to Ge 3, where the serpent deceived Eve. Paul depicts his rivals as adulterers who corrupt betrothed virgins—a crime punishable by banishment under Roman law and death under OT law (Dt 22:23–27).
11:4 *receive a different spirit.* Many Jewish people understood that false prophets could be moved by a spirit other than God's. *you put up with it easily enough.* Ancient writers often used satire (cf. also vv. 19–20).
11:5 *those "super-apostles."* Paul's rivals were better speakers, clearly an advantage in Corinth (see notes on 1Co 1:5; 2:3; 12:8); against some, the "super-apostles" here cannot mean the Jerusalem apostles, who would lack such training.
11:6 *untrained as a speaker, but I do have knowledge.* Paul's letters reveal strong logic and mastery of ancient argumentation, but Greeks expected not only strong content, but also delivery, expressed in forceful tone, the appropriate accent, gestures and so forth. Even the most eloquent orators often demeaned their abilities before displaying them in their orations (see notes on 1Co 2:1,3), but Paul could not compete with his rivals on delivery. The philosophic tradition, however, emphasized that content (here, "knowledge") mattered more than style.
11:7 *free of charge.* In Greco-Roman culture, a rejection of someone's gift was also a rejection of friendship and a declaration of animosity; Paul's rivals thus may have emphasized his refusal to depend on his Corinthian patrons' support. Nevertheless, Paul uses sarcasm: Greco-Roman culture also honored benefactors who provided services freely.

Paul's rivals may claim that they are professionals, in contrast to Paul, a mere amateur who knows that he does not deserve to be paid. Sages on the payroll of patrons, however, had less freedom to challenge the patrons' values, a role Paul rejects. Against normal expectations, especially of the elite, Paul preferred manual labor (1Co 4:12; 9:6) to the usual dependence of teachers on patrons, tuition, or even begging (see notes on 1Co 9:15,19). Paul might also use this practice to distinguish himself clearly from sophists (cf. v. 6), who were accused of speaking and teaching only for money.
11:9 *I was not a burden to anyone.* Patrons sometimes thought of their clients as a burden, and people some-

in any way, and will continue to do so.
10 As surely as the truth of Christ is in me,[u]
nobody in the regions of Achaia[v] will stop
this boasting[w] of mine. 11 Why? Because I
do not love you? God knows I do![x]
12 And I will keep on doing what I am
doing in order to cut the ground from under those who want an opportunity to be
considered equal with us in the things
they boast about. 13 For such people are
false apostles,[y] deceitful[z] workers, mas-
querading as apostles of Christ.[a] 14 And no
wonder, for Satan himself masquerades
as an angel of light. 15 It is not surprising,
then, if his servants also masquerade as
servants of righteousness. Their end will
be what their actions deserve.[b]

Paul Boasts About His Sufferings

16 I repeat: Let no one take me for a
fool.[c] But if you do, then tolerate me just
as you would a fool, so that I may do a little boasting. 17 In this self-confident boasting I am not talking as the Lord would,[d]
but as a fool. 18 Since many are boasting in
the way the world does, I too will boast.[e]
19 You gladly put up with fools since you
are so wise![f] 20 In fact, you even put up
with anyone who enslaves you[g] or exploits you or takes advantage of you or
puts on airs or slaps you in the face. 21 To
my shame I admit that we were too weak[h]
for that!
Whatever anyone else dares to boast
about — I am speaking as a fool — I also
dare to boast about.[i] 22 Are they Hebrews?
So am I.[j] Are they Israelites? So am I.[k] Are
they Abraham's descendants? So am I.
23 Are they servants of Christ? (I am out
of my mind to talk like this.) I am more. I
have worked much harder,[l] been in prison
more frequently,[m] been flogged more severely, and been exposed to death again
and again. 24 Five times I received from the
Jews the forty lashes[n] minus one. 25 Three
times I was beaten with rods,[o] once I was
pelted with stones,[p] three times I was shipwrecked, I spent a night and a day in the
open sea, 26 I have been constantly on the
move. I have been in danger from rivers,
in danger from bandits, in danger from my
fellow Jews,[q] in danger from Gentiles; in
danger in the city,[r] in danger in the country, in danger at sea; and in danger from

11:10 [u] Ro 9:1 [v] Ac 18:12 [w] 1Co 9:15 **11:11** [x] 2Co 12:15 **11:13** [y] 2Pe 2:1 [z] Titus 1:10 [a] Rev 2:2 **11:15** [b] Php 3:19 **11:16** [c] ver 1 **11:17** [d] 1Co 7:12, 25 **11:18** [e] Php 3:3, 4 **11:19** [f] 1Co 4:10 **11:20** [g] Gal 2:4 **11:21** [h] 2Co 10:1, 10 [i] Php 3:4 **11:22** [j] Php 3:5 [k] Ro 9:4 **11:23** [l] 1Co 15:10 [m] Ac 16:23; 2Co 6:4, 5 **11:24** [n] Dt 25:3 **11:25** [o] Ac 16:22 [p] Ac 14:19 **11:26** [q] Ac 9:23; 14:5 [r] Ac 21:31

times expressed their unwillingness to be a burden on another's resources. Philippian believers periodically sent support to Paul (Php 2:25; 4:15 – 16), probably also sending Paul support in Corinth through his colleagues in Ac 18:5.

11:10 *nobody ... will stop this boasting of mine.* Although ancient etiquette prohibited public boasting generally, it was acceptable if one boasted in others or for their sake.

11:11 *Because I do not love you? God knows I do!* Those who wrote letters to friends sometimes emphasized the writers' love.

11:12 *to cut the ground from under.* Boasting was considered appropriate to silence others' inappropriate boasts.

11:14 *masquerades as an angel of light.* Jewish tradition highlighted Satan's role as a deceiver and often depicted him coming in disguises; most interpreted the deceptive serpent in Ge 3 as Satan, and the lustful "sons of God" in Ge 6:2 as fallen angels. In one tradition, Satan even came disguised as a good angel to deceive Eve (see note on v. 3).

11:17 *self-confident boasting.* For Paul's warning of boasting, see note on v. 1. *as the Lord would.* See note on 10:1.

11:19 – 21 Affectionate letters could express the writer's hurt feelings. Ancient writers and speakers commonly used sarcasm to argue a point. Although it was unusual in ordinary polite or friendly letters, it was common in teachers' moral reasoning.

11:20 *slaps you in the face.* See note on Mt 5:39.

11:22 – 23 Ancient speakers sometimes compared two figures, one point after another, as here. *Are they ... Are they?* Orators liked to use repetition for emotional emphasis; here, to ask and answer four rhetorical questions in rapid succession helped drive home a point, even if the sense of the questions overlapped. Speakers could boast in their ancestry or home city.

11:22 *Hebrews ... Israelites ... Abraham's descendants.* Not only Diaspora Jews but also Gentile Christians still recognized that the gospel originated in the Biblical Holy Land, and consequently respected voices from there ("Hebrews" might suggest that they were from there; cf. Php 3:5). Like Paul, however, these rivals were educated and persuasive in a wider Greco-Roman context (cf. 2Co 11:5 – 6).

11:23 *out of my mind to talk like this.* A writer parodying an argument to reduce it to absurdity would naturally be pleased for others to view it as appropriate only to someone out of their mind. *I have worked much harder.* Paul boasts in his weaknesses, beginning with the very low-status labor some of his audience found offensive (see note on v. 7). *been in prison.* People were often embarrassed to be associated with someone imprisoned.

11:24 *forty lashes minus one.* The Jewish community expelled the most extreme offenders, but others could be beaten with up to 39 lashes from a leather whip (Jewish tradition following Dt 25:2 – 3). Someone could evade punishment by renouncing ties with their Jewish community, but Paul, like most other Jews, would not be willing to do so.

11:25 *beaten with rods.* Although the law prohibited beating Roman citizens with rods, provincial officials sometimes did it anyway (see note on Ac 16:22). *pelted with stones.* On Paul's stoning see Ac 14:19. *three times I was shipwrecked.* As all Corinthians knew, given their adjacent ports, shipwrecks were common. Farther away from port survivors were usually a minority; safety mechanisms such as life jackets were nonexistent. For the terror of death at sea, see note on Ac 27:20.

11:26 Few roads were wider than 20 feet (6 meters), but Roman roads remained unmatched in Europe until about 1850. Nevertheless, travel was dangerous and travelers often sought divine protection beforehand. *in danger.* Paul reinforces his point with the familiar rhetorical device of opening repetition, eight times repeating "in danger." *rivers.* Could be especially dangerous to cross, particularly during and soon after the rainy season. *bandits.* Travelers often journeyed together and stopped in towns at night because of robbers in the countryside. *danger at sea.* Rome had suppressed much piracy but sea travel remained dangerous (see v. 25). *false believers.* This includes Paul's rivals (vv. 13 – 15).

2 CORINTHIANS 11:16–21

Ancient Boasting and 2 Corinthians 11

Paul's rivals have demeaned his skill (2Co 11:6), so he rhetorically embraces the role of fool that they have assigned to him; speakers often spoke in the persona of someone else to make a point. Implicitly, however, he attacks his opponents' boasting as foolish (returning charges against opponents was conventional rhetorical custom). He boasts in his weakness, not in his honor. Paul's way of boasting parodies and thus mocks self-boasting, and therefore a central feature of the Greco-Roman valuing of masculine competition and self-promotion. He walks the tightrope of answering fools as their folly deserves without being truly like them (Pr 26:4–5).

Ancient sources show that audiences often resented public boasting. They made exceptions, however, whenever it was done (or pretended to be done) for acceptable reasons — such as a speaker defending himself (as in 2Co 3:1; 5:12), replying to charges (10:10), speaking for his hearers' welfare (5:12; 10:8), critiquing others' misplaced arrogance (11:12,18), or because of necessity (12:1,11).

Sages could boast in how their sufferings demonstrated their endurance (see note on 4:8–12), but many in the Corinthian church probably looked instead to more familiar sources of pride in their culture. Monuments, civic buildings and other sites bore inscriptions praising wealthy donors; civic assemblies featured the voices of the powerful; public culture revolved around power. Boasting in weakness challenged the very values on which most boasts were founded — values antithetical to the good news of a crucified Savior (13:4; cf. 10:17). ◆

Sixth-century Susiya synagogue inscription. The inscription honors the donor, Rabbi Isai, and the scribe, Rabbi Yohannan. Monuments, civic buildings, and other sites often bore inscriptions boasting of wealthy donors.

Z. Radovan/www.BibleLandPictures.com

false believers.[s] 27I have labored and toiled
and have often gone without sleep; I have
known hunger and thirst and have often
gone without food;[t] I have been cold and
naked. 28Besides everything else, I face
daily the pressure of my concern for all
the churches. 29Who is weak, and I do not
feel weak? Who is led into sin, and I do
not inwardly burn?
30If I must boast, I will boast of the
things that show my weakness.[u] 31The
God and Father of the Lord Jesus, who
is to be praised forever,[v] knows that I am
not lying. 32In Damascus the governor under King Aretas had the city of the Dam-
ascenes guarded in order to arrest me.[w]
33But I was lowered in a basket from a
window in the wall and slipped through
his hands.[x]

Paul's Vision and His Thorn

12 I must go on boasting.[y] Although
there is nothing to be gained, I will
go on to visions and revelations[z] from the
Lord. 2I know a man in Christ who fourteen years ago was caught up[a] to the third
heaven.[b] Whether it was in the body or out
of the body I do not know—God knows.[c]
3And I know that this man—whether in
the body or apart from the body I do not
know, but God knows— 4was caught
up to paradise[d] and heard inexpressible
things, things that no one is permitted to
tell. 5I will boast about a man like that,
but I will not boast about myself, except
about my weaknesses. 6Even if I should
choose to boast, I would not be a fool,[e]
because I would be speaking the truth. But
I refrain, so no one will think more of me
than is warranted by what I do or say, 7or
because of these surpassingly great revelations. Therefore, in order to keep me from
becoming conceited, I was given a thorn
in my flesh,[f] a messenger of Satan, to torment me. 8Three times I pleaded with the
Lord to take it away from me.[g] 9But he said
to me, "My grace is sufficient for you, for
my power[h] is made perfect in weakness."
Therefore I will boast all the more gladly about my weaknesses, so that Christ's
power may rest on me. 10That is why, for
Christ's sake, I delight in weaknesses, in
insults, in hardships,[i] in persecutions,[j] in
difficulties. For when I am weak, then I
am strong.[k]

Paul's Concern for the Corinthians

11I have made a fool of myself,[l] but you
drove me to it. I ought to have been commended by you, for I am not in the least

11:26 [s] Gal 2:4
11:27 [t] 1Co 4:11, 12; 2Co 6:5
11:30 [u] 1Co 2:3
11:31 [v] Ro 9:5
11:32 [w] Ac 9:24
11:33 [x] Ac 9:25
12:1 [y] 2Co 11:16, 30 [z] ver 7
12:2 [a] Ac 8:39 [b] Eph 4:10 [c] 2Co 11:11
12:4 [d] Lk 23:43; Rev 2:7
12:6 [e] 2Co 11:16
12:7 [f] Nu 33:55
12:8 [g] Mt 26:39, 44
12:9 [h] Php 4:13
12:10 [i] 2Co 6:4 [j] Ro 5:3; 2Th 1:4 [k] 2Co 13:4
12:11 [l] 2Co 11:1

11:27 *labored.* See note on v. 23. *gone without sleep.* Could refer to the demands of work and ministry together (1Th 2:9), of ministry (Ac 20:7–11,31), of caring for the churches (2Co 11:28–29), or of travel. *I have been cold.* Paul's travels, including in and near Phrygian hill country (Ac 13:14,51; 14:6), would expose him to cold (see also 2Co 11:25), although travelers, including Paul, avoided winter journeys whenever possible (1Co 16:6; 2Ti 4:21). *naked.* Writers used "naked" for being poorly clothed as well as fully naked (though cf. Ac 16:22).

11:30 *boast of ... my weakness.* For the offensiveness of boasting in weakness in a status-conscious culture, see the article "Ancient Boasting and 2 Corinthians 11," p. 2037.

11:32 *Aretas.* Aretas IV ruled Nabatea from 8 or 9 BC until about AD 40. (For his conflict with and defeat of Herod Antipas, see note on Mk 6:17.) Because most of the caravan trade from the east passed through Nabatea, it was the strongest and wealthiest of the minor kingdoms of the Middle East. Some think that Aretas also ruled Damascus for several years, but "governor" here is the term *ethnarch.* An ethnarch might be simply the leader of the Nabatean trading community in and around Damascus. The Syrian city of Damascus (see notes on Ac 9:2,11,18) had a Nabatean quarter, and the Nabatean community in Damascus had its own rights.

11:33 *window in the wall.* Houses were often built along city walls, with windows too high for intruders to penetrate (see also Ac 9:25). Many areas outside city walls would also be inhabited, but because baskets could contain goods, a lowered basket need not appear suspicious. Scripture provided Paul's escape method (Jos 2:15; cf. 1Sa 19:12). Whereas Rome honored the first soldier to scale an enemy wall, Paul boasts in a humiliating night escape from hostile authorities.

12:1 *I must go on boasting.* One of the justifications for which boasting was considered acceptable was that one had been compelled to do so ("must"; cf. v. 11). *visions and revelations from the Lord.* Although Paul rarely spoke about it (cf. 5:13), he had many experiences analogous to Biblical prophets (cf. Nu 12:6; Eze 1:1); of the two he will specify in the coming verses (vv. 2–4,9), the second directly challenges Corinthian boasting (v. 9).

12:5–6 Because pure boasting was offensive, respectable figures found other ways to do it (see the article "Ancient Boasting and 2 Corinthians 11," p. 2037). One way was to say, "I will not elaborate, but you yourselves know," forcing the hearers themselves to remember the speaker's exploits.

12:7 *thorn in my flesh.* Scholars propose a variety of explanations for the "thorn," both physical and psychological. Whatever the thorn is, one cannot infer from the language of "thorn in my flesh" that Paul specifically designates his body, since the wording alludes to how some enemies remained to test Israel (Nu 33:55). As Israel's thorn humbled them and kept them dependent on the Lord, so also Paul's thorn kept him depending on the Lord. Among more specific proposed explanations of the thorn that fit the context, the preceding context could suggest that an evil spirit stirs persecution against him (11:23–33) or could even evoke the human messengers of Satan in 11:13–15. Following Scripture, early Judaism and Christianity recognized that God remained sovereign; Satan needed permission to strike God's servants (cf. Job 1:6—2:6).

12:10 Ancient readers appreciated lists; for Paul boasting in suffering rather than the usual topics of human honor, see the article "Ancient Boasting and 2 Corinthians 11," p. 2037.

12:11 *you drove me to it.* Compulsion was considered an appropriate ground for boasting (see note on v. 1).

2 CORINTHIANS 12:2–4

PAUL'S EXPERIENCE OF THE "THIRD HEAVEN"

Writers could speak of themselves as "a man" (2Co 12:2) in the third person, and context probably suggests that Paul, reluctant to boast, is recounting his own experience (12:1,7). (Even apocalyptic writers adopted the persona of some ancient figure rather than describing their own experiences directly.)

Some Greek thinkers expected the pure and unencumbered soul at death to rise to heaven, and so sought to practice contemplation on the pure heavens beforehand. Some Jewish thinkers tried to mystically cultivate visions of God's heavenly throne, e.g., by depriving themselves of food and sleep, by meditation, and so on. (Some scholars believe that some Jewish mystical experiences stand behind some ancient apocalyptic literature.) Paul here is apparently "caught up" (vv. 2,4) without cultivating it. Some Jewish sources depict the soul being caught up; others assert that the whole person is.

Jewish texts contrasted "paradise" (v. 4), considered the restoration of Eden, with Gehinnom, i.e., hell. Although Jewish thought expected paradise to exist someday on the renewed earth, many also believed that it currently remained in heaven—but which one? Jewish sources diverge as to how many heavens there are (ancient estimates range from 3 to 365!). The most common views were three and seven heavens; the realm of air and the birds was a lower heaven. Paul apparently identified paradise as in the "third heaven" (v. 2), probably meaning the highest heaven, where God is.

Ironically, this vision climaxes with an experience antithetical to boasting: it is too sacred to tell (v. 4). Greek mystery cults had climactic revelations that the initiate was not permitted to tell; Greek-speaking Jewish writers applied the same principle to God's sacred name or greatest wisdom. ◆

inferior to the "super-apostles,"[a][m] even
though I am nothing.[n] 12I persevered in
demonstrating among you the marks of a
true apostle, including signs, wonders and
miracles.[o] 13How were you inferior to the
other churches, except that I was never a
burden to you?[p] Forgive me this wrong![q]
14Now I am ready to visit you for the
third time,[r] and I will not be a burden
to you, because what I want is not your
possessions but you. After all, children
should not have to save up for their parents,[s] but parents for their children.[t] 15So

12:11 [m] 2Co 11:5 [n] 1Co 15:9, 10 **12:12** [o] Jn 4:48 **12:13** [p] 1Co 9:12, 18 [q] 2Co 11:7 **12:14** [r] 2Co 13:1 [s] 1Co 4:14, 15 [t] Pr 19:14

[a] *11* Or *the most eminent apostles*

12:12 *signs, wonders and miracles.* God performed signs and wonders in the plagues against Egypt (Ex 7:3; Dt 4:34) and in subsequent acts (Jer 32:20–21; Da 6:27). Signs and wonders among Jesus and his followers were most commonly healings and exorcisms (e.g., Ac 5:12; 14:3). Paul can avoid boasting here by simply reminding his audience of what they themselves witnessed.

12:13 *Forgive me this wrong!* Irony was common in ancient writing.

12:14 *burden.* See note on 11:9. More well-to-do members of the church may have been embarrassed by Paul's manual labor and dependence on others rather than Paul's depending on them; had Paul allowed them to support him, however, he would have risked assuming the cultural role of a client subordinate to patrons (see note on 11:7). *children … parents.* By speaking of himself as a parent saving for his children, Paul reverses the question of dependence in terms of what matters most. Patrons viewed both their clients and their children as dependent members of their households.

12:15 *will you love me less?* Affectionate letters sometimes pleaded for the receiver to reciprocate the sender's love.

I will very gladly spend for you everything I have and expend myself as well.[u]
If I love you more, will you love me less?
16 Be that as it may, I have not been a burden to you.[v] Yet, crafty fellow that I am, I
caught you by trickery! 17 Did I exploit you
through any of the men I sent to you? 18 I
urged[w] Titus to go to you and I sent our
brother[x] with him. Titus did not exploit
you, did he? Did we not walk in the same
footsteps by the same Spirit?
19 Have you been thinking all along
that we have been defending ourselves
to you? We have been speaking in the
sight of God[y] as those in Christ; and everything we do, dear friends, is for your
strengthening.[z] 20 For I am afraid that
when I come[a] I may not find you as I
want you to be, and you may not find me
as you want me to be.[b] I fear that there
may be discord,[c] jealousy, fits of rage,
selfish ambition,[d] slander, gossip,[e] arrogance and disorder.[f] 21 I am afraid that
when I come again my God will humble me before you, and I will be grieved[g]
over many who have sinned earlier[h] and
have not repented of the impurity, sexual
sin and debauchery in which they have
indulged.

Final Warnings

13 This will be my third visit to you.[i]
"Every matter must be established
by the testimony of two or three witnesses."[a][j] 2 I already gave you a warning when
I was with you the second time. I now repeat it while absent: On my return I will
not spare[k] those who sinned earlier[l] or
any of the others, 3 since you are demanding proof that Christ is speaking through
me.[m] He is not weak in dealing with you,
but is powerful among you. 4 For to be
sure, he was crucified in weakness,[n] yet
he lives by God's power.[o] Likewise, we
are weak[p] in him, yet by God's power
we will live with him in our dealing with
you.
5 Examine yourselves[q] to see whether you are in the faith; test yourselves.[r]
Do you not realize that Christ Jesus is
in you[s] — unless, of course, you fail the
test? 6 And I trust that you will discover
that we have not failed the test. 7 Now
we pray to God that you will not do anything wrong — not so that people will see
that we have stood the test but so that
you will do what is right even though we
may seem to have failed. 8 For we cannot do anything against the truth, but
only for the truth. 9 We are glad whenever we are weak but you are strong; and
our prayer is that you may be fully restored.[t] 10 This is why I write these things
when I am absent, that when I come I
may not have to be harsh in my use of
authority — the authority the Lord gave
me for building you up, not for tearing
you down.[u]

Final Greetings

11 Finally, brothers and sisters,[v] rejoice!
Strive for full restoration, encourage one
another, be of one mind, live in peace.[w]

[a] *1* Deut. 19:15

12:15 [u] Php 2:17; 1Th 2:8 **12:16** [v] 2Co 11:9 **12:18** [w] 2Co 8:6, 16 [x] 2Co 8:18 **12:19** [y] Ro 9:1 [z] 2Co 10:8 **12:20** [a] 2Co 2:1-4 [b] 1Co 4:21 [c] 1Co 1:11; 3:3 [d] Gal 5:20 [e] Ro 1:29 [f] 1Co 14:33 **12:21** [g] 2Co 2:1, 4 [h] 2Co 13:2 **13:1** [i] 2Co 12:14 [j] Dt 19:15; Mt 18:16 **13:2** [k] 2Co 1:23 [l] 2Co 12:21 **13:3** [m] Mt 10:20; 1Co 5:4 **13:4** [n] Php 2:7, 8; 1Pe 3:18 [o] Ro 1:4; 6:4 [p] ver 9 **13:5** [q] 1Co 11:28 [r] Jn 6:6 [s] Ro 8:10 **13:9** [t] ver 11 **13:10** [u] 2Co 10:8 **13:11** [v] 1Th 4:1; 2Th 3:1 [w] Mk 9:50

12:16 For satire, see note on 11:4.

12:17 – 18 Those making a case for themselves sometimes demanded that their hearers show them what they had done wrong to merit such treatment or suspicion (e.g., 1Sa 12:3 – 5). A series of rhetorical questions (vv. 17 – 19) would drive home a point, especially in judicial-type arguments. A writer sometimes reserved a primary point of contention for later in the argument. It is thus possible that Paul's rivals not only heightened criticisms concerning his refusal to accept support, but questioned the integrity of his offering for Jerusalem's poor (see chs. 8 – 9).

12:19 *dear friends.* Letters between friends often expressed affection. *for your strengthening.* Although educated ancients often composed defense speeches, Paul explains that his ironic defense was motivated only by love for the Corinthian believers.

12:20 Lists of vices were common in antiquity. Even Greek and Roman moral writers challenged the vices Paul lists here.

12:21 *sexual sin and debauchery.* Sexual sins, more consistently highlighted as evil in Biblical and early Jewish sources than among Greeks, had been a longstanding problem among believers in Corinth (see 1Co 5:1,9 – 11; 6:9,12 – 20), reflecting values more widely dominant in Corinth (see Introduction to 1 Corinthians: Corinth).

13:1 *third visit to you.* Those who complained that Paul was too meek because he sent them a corrective letter instead of confronting them personally (1:23 — 2:4; 10:1,10 – 11) would now get what they demanded. *testimony … witnesses.* Paul cites legal procedure regarding witnesses (Dt 19:15; cf. 17:6): he will prosecute before God offenders who have not repented.

13:4 *he was crucified in weakness.* The cross of Christ was a challenge to Corinthian values (see note on 1Co 1:18). *by God's power.* Paul will act in the power that they have demanded (for Paul's action, see note on v. 1).

13:5 *test yourselves.* Corinthian culture evaluated speakers (cf. v. 3); Paul turns the question of evaluation back to them.

13:7 – 8 Many other ancient thinkers also disdained mere human opinions about them, yet for the sake of their message sought to prevent misunderstanding.

13:10 *I write … when I am absent.* Letters were often considered a substitute (albeit an inferior one) for one's presence. *for building you up, not for tearing you down.* Although God called some prophets both to build up and to tear down (e.g., Jer 1:10), Paul is called only to build up the Corinthians (2Co 10:8; 12:19).

13:11 Concluding exhortations were common, and often summarized some key themes. Gentiles in Paul's audience could not object to the themes Paul articulates here; they were familiar from orators' public speeches urging harmony and the common good.

And the God of love and peace[x] will be
with you.
[12]Greet one another with a holy kiss.[y]
[13]All God's people here send their greetings.[z]

[14]May the grace of the Lord Jesus
Christ,[a] and the love of God,[b] and the fellowship of the Holy Spirit[c] be with you
all.

13:11 [x]Ro 15:33; Eph 6:23 **13:12** [y]Ro 16:16 **13:13** [z]Php 4:22

13:14 [a]Ro 16:20; 2Co 8:9 [b]Ro 5:5; Jude 21 [c]Php 2:1

13:12 *holy kiss.* See note on Ro 16:16.
13:13 *All God's people here send their greetings.* Means of communication were limited, so when someone was writing a letter and a traveler was available to carry it, others often conveyed their greetings.

13:14 *Jesus Christ … God … the Holy Spirit.* Most Jewish writers treated the Holy Spirit as an aspect of or force from God; Paul links the Spirit here as a divine person alongside Jesus and the Father (cf. 1Co 12:4–6; Eph 4:4–6).

THE LETTERS

GALATIANS

Date and Recipients

Some date this work before the Jerusalem council (Ac 15), partly because Paul does not mention it. Others date it afterward, shortly before Romans, noting that at the time of the council the problem had not yet reached Galatia (Ac 15:23). Some believe that Paul addresses only ethnic Galatians (cf. Gal 3:1), among whom Acts reports no ministry. Most, however, including specialists on Asia Minor, recognize that Paul addresses residents of the Roman province of Galatia, including regions in and near Phrygia reported in Ac 13 – 14. The southern part of the province had many Jewish residents, in contrast to northern Galatia (where ethnic Galatians were concentrated); it was also more accessible for visitors such as Paul's nemeses in this letter.

QUICK GLANCE

AUTHOR:
The apostle Paul

AUDIENCE:
Churches in southern Galatia, and perhaps northern Galatia, founded by Paul during his missionary journey

DATE:
AD 48, or early 50s

THEME:
Paul, a Jewish believer in Jesus, writes to counter the claims of some other Judeans who were telling the Galatian Gentile believers that they must be circumcised and keep the Law of Moses in order to truly belong to God's people.

Situation

Jewish people held a range of views about Gentiles; only the most conservative required circumcision for salvation (as in Ac 15:1; see notes on Ac 15:1,20), but nearly all would expect it for those who wished to become part of God's people, i.e., Jews. In earlier centuries many Jews had died for issues such as circumcision and food laws, and anything that resembled compromise on these issues provoked grave discomfort.

For Paul, the real experience of the Spirit (Gal 3:2,5), the promised reality of the ultimate covenant to which outward circumcision merely pointed, meant that Gentile Christians could join God's people without becoming ethnically Jewish (3:7); through the Spirit, believers would keep the spirit of the law, the law of love to which the Law of Moses always pointed (5:14,18 – 23). It is not surprising, however, that not everyone agreed. Less sensitive to the new believers' culture, other Judean missionaries now wanted to convince Paul's converts to adopt ethnic and cultural Judaism to become fully righteous. Paul suggests that they are more concerned about pressures from other Judeans than about the true gospel (4:29; 5:11; 6:12 – 13). The short-lived reign of Agrippa I (AD 41 – 44) had rekindled Judean nationalism, and judging others by the standards of one's own culture is a common human temptation. ◆

1 Paul, an apostle — sent not from men
nor by a man, but by Jesus Christ[a] and
God the Father, who raised him from the
dead[b] — 2 and all the brothers and sisters[a]
with me,[c]

To the churches in Galatia:[d]

3 Grace and peace to you from God our
Father and the Lord Jesus Christ,[e] 4 who
gave himself for our sins[f] to rescue us
from the present evil age, according to the
will of our God and Father,[g] 5 to whom be
glory for ever and ever. Amen.[h]

No Other Gospel

6 I am astonished that you are so quickly
deserting the one who called[i] you to live in
the grace of Christ and are turning to a different gospel[j] — 7 which is really no gospel
at all. Evidently some people are throwing
you into confusion[k] and are trying to pervert the gospel of Christ. 8 But even if we
or an angel from heaven should preach a
gospel other than the one we preached to
you,[l] let them be under God's curse![m] 9 As
we have already said, so now I say again:
If anybody is preaching to you a gospel
other than what you accepted,[n] let them
be under God's curse!
10 Am I now trying to win the approval
of human beings, or of God? Or am I trying to please people?[o] If I were still trying
to please people, I would not be a servant
of Christ.

Paul Called by God

11 I want you to know, brothers and sisters,[p] that the gospel I preached is not of
human origin. 12 I did not receive it from
any man,[q] nor was I taught it; rather, I received it by revelation[r] from Jesus Christ.
13 For you have heard of my previous
way of life in Judaism,[s] how intensely I
persecuted the church of God and tried
to destroy it.[t] 14 I was advancing in Judaism beyond many of my own age among
my people and was extremely zealous for

1:1 [a] Ac 9:15 [b] Ac 2:24 **1:2** [c] Php 4:21 [d] Ac 16:6; 1Co 16:1 **1:3** [e] Ro 1:7 **1:4** [f] Mt 20:28; Ro 4:25; Gal 2:20 [g] Php 4:20 **1:5** [h] Ro 11:36 **1:6** [i] Gal 5:8 [j] 2Co 11:4 **1:7** [k] Ac 15:24; Gal 5:10 **1:8** [l] 2Co 11:4 [m] Ro 9:3 **1:9** [n] Ro 16:17 **1:10** [o] Ro 2:29; 1Th 2:4 **1:11** [p] 1Co 15:1 **1:12** [q] ver 1 [r] ver 16 **1:13** [s] Ac 26:4,5 [t] Ac 8:3

[a] 2 The Greek word for *brothers and sisters* (*adelphoi*) refers here to believers, both men and women, as part of God's family; also in verse 11; and in 3:15; 4:12, 28, 31; 5:11, 13; 6:1, 18.

1:1 – 3 Letters opened with the sender's name (v. 1), the recipient's name (v. 2), and a blessing (v. 3), expanding on points as needed.
1:1 *sent … by Jesus Christ and God the Father.* Paul's being sent by God (vv. 1,12,16 – 20) may contrast with the proponents of circumcision who want to please their constituency (6:12 – 13).
1:2 *all the brothers and sisters with me.* Writers sometimes named other mutual friends as coauthors even if they did not contribute much to the letter; Paul probably implies at least the backing of other believers. *Galatia.* Refers to the Roman province, which included Pisidian Antioch, Iconium and Lystra (Ac 13 – 14; see Introduction to Galatians: Date and Recipients). Paul often writes in terms of provinces (e.g., Ro 15:26; 16:5; 1Th 1:7 – 8).
1:3 *Grace and peace … from God our Father and the Lord Jesus Christ.* For the fusion of Greek and Jewish greetings, and blessings from both the Father and Jesus as deity, see note on Ro 1:7.
1:4 *present evil age.* Most Judeans expected suffering and evil to characterize the present age but believed that when the Messiah came and the dead were raised, God would establish a new age of righteousness, peace and justice. Because Jesus has come and is yet to come, believers experience now a foretaste of the coming world (cf. 1Co 2:9 – 10; 2Co 5:5; Heb 6:5).
1:6 *I am astonished.* Ancient letters sometimes included a thanksgiving and often a prayer; Paul's other letters to churches include both, so Paul's brusque beginning here (along with the curse that follows in vv. 8 – 9) establishes a harsh tone at the beginning of the letter. Only particularly harsh letters started like this. *deserting.* Members of ancient peoples and movements despised apostates, who were viewed as traitors.
1:7 *which is really no gospel at all.* Speakers sometimes corrected themselves with a starker claim to reinforce the point. *some people.* Leaving the troublemakers anonymous does not necessarily mean that Paul lacks further information; sometimes critics refused to dignify their enemies by naming them. *trying to pervert the gospel.* In the OT those who distorted the divine message were false prophets (e.g., Jer 23:16), for whom the penalty was death (Dt 13:5; 18:20).
1:8 – 9 *let them be under God's curse! … let them be under God's curse!* Repeating a claim reinforced it. People invoked curses on rivals in sports, romance and so forth, but these appear typically in secret magic rather than public letters. The Greek version of Dt 13:15 – 17, however, applies this language to Israelites who follow false gods and thus must be annihilated.
1:8 *if … an angel from heaven should preach.* Some Jewish apocalyptic visionaries and mystics claimed revelations from angels. Perhaps Paul's opponents also claimed them, but Paul might also simply use hyperbole here.
1:10 — 2:21 Various kinds of ancient works often opened (after a preface) with a narration of events leading up to the present situation or case, sometimes even before laying out the case. Sometimes the narration could be autobiographic, especially when defending oneself against critics' complaints; proving one's character was important in such a defense. Themes in ancient argument included divine attestation, examination of character and behavior and comparisons between figures personifying different values or sides of the dispute.
1:10 *approval … of God.* Both prophets and philosophers emphasized seeking divine rather than human approval. *am I trying to please people?* Thinkers despised demagogues who flattered the masses (cf. 6:12 – 13).
1:12 *by revelation from Jesus Christ.* See Ac 9:3 – 6; 22:14 – 16; 26:15 – 18.
1:14 *advancing in Judaism beyond many of my own age.* Usually in cordial ways, members of the same age group often competed during schooling. The most advanced education in Scripture, including for Greek-speakers, was in Jerusalem; whereas the average Judean may have been illiterate, children from wealthy and educated families received more training. Paul apparently had the highest level of training, normally available in the mid to late teens. *zealous.* See note on Ac 22:3. *traditions of my fathers.* Pharisees (cf. Php 3:5) were known for valuing their

the traditions of my fathers.[u] 15 But when
God, who set me apart from my mother's
womb[v] and called me[w] by his grace, was
pleased 16 to reveal his Son in me so that
I might preach him among the Gentiles,[x]
my immediate response was not to consult
any human being.[y] 17 I did not go up to
Jerusalem to see those who were apostles
before I was, but I went into Arabia. Later
I returned to Damascus.

18 Then after three years,[z] I went up to
Jerusalem[a] to get acquainted with Cephas[a]
and stayed with him fifteen days. 19 I saw
none of the other apostles — only James,[b]
the Lord's brother. 20 I assure you before
God that what I am writing you is no lie.[c]
21 Then I went to Syria and Cilicia.[d] 22 I
was personally unknown to the churches
of Judea[e] that are in Christ. 23 They only
heard the report: "The man who formerly persecuted us is now preaching the
faith[f] he once tried to destroy." 24 And they
praised God[g] because of me.

Paul Accepted by the Apostles

2 Then after fourteen years, I went up
again to Jerusalem,[h] this time with
Barnabas. I took Titus along also. 2 I went
in response to a revelation and, meeting
privately with those esteemed as leaders, I
presented to them the gospel that I preach
among the Gentiles.[i] I wanted to be sure
I was not running and had not been running my race[j] in vain. 3 Yet not even Titus,[k]
who was with me, was compelled to be
circumcised, even though he was a Greek.[l]
4 This matter arose because some false believers[m] had infiltrated our ranks to spy
on[n] the freedom[o] we have in Christ Jesus
and to make us slaves. 5 We did not give
in to them for a moment, so that the truth
of the gospel[p] might be preserved for you.

6 As for those who were held in high esteem[q] — whatever they were makes no difference to me; God does not show favoritism[r] — they added nothing to my message.
7 On the contrary, they recognized that I had
been entrusted with the task[s] of preaching the gospel to the uncircumcised,[b][t] just
as Peter[u] had been to the circumcised.[c]
8 For God, who was at work in Peter as
an apostle[v] to the circumcised, was also
at work in me as an apostle to the Gentiles. 9 James, Cephas[d][w] and John, those
esteemed as pillars,[x] gave me and Barnabas[y] the right hand of fellowship when
they recognized the grace given to me.[z]

1:14 u Mt 15:2 **1:15** v Isa 49:1, 5; Jer 1:5 w Ac 9:15 **1:16** x Gal 2:9 y Mt 16:17 **1:18** z Ac 9:22, 23 a Ac 9:26, 27 **1:19** b Mt 13:55 **1:20** c Ro 9:1 **1:21** d Ac 6:9 **1:22** e 1Th 2:14 **1:23** f Ac 6:7 **1:24** g Mt 9:8 **2:1** h Ac 15:2

2:2 i Ac 15:4, 12 j 1Co 9:24; Php 2:16 **2:3** k 2Co 2:13 l Ac 16:3; 1Co 9:21 **2:4** m 2Co 11:26 n Jude 4 o Ac 15:1; Gal 5:1, 13 **2:5** p ver 14 **2:6** q Gal 6:3 r Ac 10:34 **2:7** s 1Th 2:4; 1Ti 1:11 t Ac 9:15 u ver 9, 11, 14 **2:8** v Ac 1:25 **2:9** w ver 7, 11, 14 x 1Ti 3:15 y Ac 4:36 z Ro 12:3

a 18 That is, Peter *b 7* That is, Gentiles *c 7* That is, Jews; also in verses 8 and 9 *d 9* That is, Peter; also in verses 11 and 14

---

ancient traditions. Whereas the two major disciplines in advanced Greek education were rhetoric and philosophy, and elite Greek and Roman writers showed off their learning with lavish classical citations, a chief characteristic of many of Paul's letters is his facility with Scripture. Paul's advanced education focused on Scripture, as was fitting for a Pharisee; although some Greek learning was also available in Jerusalem, in Paul's day it remained the world center of Jewish learning.

1:15 *set me apart from my mother's womb.* Compare especially Jeremiah's prophetic call (Jer 1:5; cf. Isa 49:1).

1:16 *not to consult any human being.* Disciples passed on their teachers' teachings and were their subordinates. Paul was not a disciple of Jesus' disciples.

1:17 *Arabia.* In Paul's day, "Arabia" meant primarily Nabatea, a prosperous kingdom ruled by Aretas IV (see note on 2Co 11:32). Many Nabatean cities were to the east of Galilee, but Nabateans controlled much territory from far south of Judea to nearly as far north as Damascus, and their merchants traveled widely in the east. Most Nabateans spoke their own dialect of Aramaic, although Greek was also known and later (by the early second century) became dominant. Many Jews lived among them, just as some of them lived in Perea (directly east of Judea and Samaria).

1:18 *after three years.* Even part of a year counted as a whole. *Cephas.* Transliterates the Aramaic word for "rock"; the Greek equivalent is Peter. *stayed with him.* The ancient world valued hospitality, and Peter welcomed Paul.

1:20 *assure you before God.* An oath called a deity to witness; breaking the oath therefore invited divine judgment. This recognition deterred most people from swearing falsely.

1:21 *Syria and Cilicia.* Formerly two provinces, they were joined together as a single province at this time. Paul spent time in both Tarsus (in Cilicia) and Antioch (in Syria; Ac 9:30; 11:25 – 26).

1:22 *unknown to the churches of Judea.* Being born in the Diaspora and educated in Jerusalem (Ac 22:3), Paul would have been known to some in Jerusalem but not in wider Judea. Even in Jerusalem, churches knew him more as a persecutor (vv. 13,19,23), and in an era without photographs not all of them would have known him by face. The majority of the Jerusalem church came from a different social class than Paul, and many now estimate Jerusalem's population in this era at 70,000 or higher.

2:1 – 2 *I went up again to Jerusalem ... in response to a revelation.* A majority of scholars believe that in vv. 1 – 10 Paul narrates elements of the Jerusalem council, c. AD 48 (Ac 15), based on key elements shared between them. Others argue that the "revelation" of v. 2 better fits the mission depicted in Ac 11:28 – 30 (though cf. Gal 1:12).

2:1 *after fourteen years.* Parts of a year counted as a whole; the 14 years here probably count from Paul's earlier visit in 1:18 – 19.

2:3 *not even Titus ... was compelled to be circumcised.* Some very conservative Jews required Gentiles to become Jewish (including by circumcision) for salvation; others believed that God accepted sexually pure, nonidolatrous Gentiles (rare as those were), but that one must be circumcised to become part of God's people.

2:4 In Greek, Paul leaves a sentence unfinished; particularly passionate letters and speeches could do this to communicate intensity.

2:6 *God does not show favoritism.* See notes on Ac 10:34 – 35; Ro 2:11.

2:9 *those esteemed as pillars.* Ancient writers often called influential people "pillars." Cf. possibly also Eph 2:20. *the right hand of fellowship.* Taking someone by the hand communicated assurance, welcome or an agreement.

They agreed that we should go to the Gentiles, and they to the circumcised. 10All they asked was that we should continue to remember the poor,[a] the very thing I had been eager to do all along.

Paul Opposes Cephas

11When Cephas[b] came to Antioch,[c] I opposed him to his face, because he stood condemned. 12For before certain men came from James, he used to eat with the Gentiles.[d] But when they arrived, he began to draw back and separate himself from the Gentiles because he was afraid of those who belonged to the circumcision group.[e] 13The other Jews joined him in his hypocrisy, so that by their hypocrisy even Barnabas[f] was led astray.

14When I saw that they were not acting in line with the truth of the gospel,[g] I said to Cephas[h] in front of them all, "You are a Jew, yet you live like a Gentile and not like a Jew.[i] How is it, then, that you force Gentiles to follow Jewish customs?

15"We who are Jews by birth[j] and not sinful Gentiles[k] 16know that a person is not justified by the works of the law, but by faith in Jesus Christ.[l] So we, too, have put our faith in Christ Jesus that we may be justified by faith in[a] Christ and not by the works of the law, because by the works of the law no one will be justified.

17"But if, in seeking to be justified in Christ, we Jews find ourselves also among the sinners,[m] doesn't that mean that Christ promotes sin? Absolutely not![n] 18If I rebuild what I destroyed, then I really would be a lawbreaker.

19"For through the law I died to the law[o] so that I might live for God.[p] 20I have been crucified with Christ[q] and I no longer live, but Christ lives in me.[r] The life I now live in the body, I live by faith in the Son of God,[s] who loved me[t] and gave himself for me.[u] 21I do not set aside the grace of God, for if righteousness could be gained through the law,[v] Christ died for nothing!"[b]

Faith or Works of the Law

3 You foolish Galatians! Who has bewitched you?[w] Before your very eyes Jesus Christ was clearly portrayed as crucified.[x] 2I would like to learn just one thing from you: Did you receive the Spirit by the works of the law, or by believing what you heard?[y] 3Are you so foolish? After beginning by means of the Spirit, are you now trying to finish by means of the flesh?[c] 4Have you experienced[d] so much in

2:10 [a] Ac 24:17 **2:11** [b] ver 7,9,14 [c] Ac 11:19 **2:12** [d] Ac 11:3 [e] Ac 11:2 **2:13** [f] ver 1; Ac 4:36 **2:14** [g] ver 5 [h] ver 7,9,11 [i] Ac 10:28 **2:15** [j] Php 3:4,5 [k] 1Sa 15:18 **2:16** [l] Ac 13:39; Ro 9:30
2:17 [m] ver 15 [n] Gal 3:21 **2:19** [o] Ro 7:4 [p] Ro 6:10,11,14; 2Co 5:15 **2:20** [q] Ro 6:6 [r] 1Pe 4:2 [s] Mt 4:3 [t] Ro 8:37 [u] Gal 1:4 **2:21** [v] Gal 3:21 **3:1** [w] Gal 5:7 [x] 1Co 1:23 **3:2** [y] Ro 10:17

[a] *16* Or *but through the faithfulness of . . . justified on the basis of the faithfulness of* [b] *21* Some interpreters end the quotation after verse 14. [c] *3* In contexts like this, the Greek word for *flesh* (*sarx*) refers to the sinful state of human beings, often presented as a power in opposition to the Spirit. [d] *4* Or *suffered*

2:10 *remember the poor.* Both Scripture and Jewish tradition heavily emphasized care for the poor (e.g., Pr 19:17; 21:13). Cf. examples in Ac 11:30; 24:17.
2:11 *Antioch.* More than 300 miles (480 kilometers) north of Jerusalem, Antioch was the center of the Gentile mission (Ac 11:20), including Paul's mission (Ac 13:1–3; 14:26; 15:35; 18:22–23). *I opposed him to his face.* Conflict between Paul and the proponents of circumcision there had helped precipitate the Jerusalem council (Ac 15:1,22–23). For the confrontation, see note on v. 14.
2:12 *he used to eat with the Gentiles.* Respectable Judean and Galilean Jews did not eat with Gentiles (Ac 10:28; 11:3). The growth of nationalism in Judea (see note on Ac 12:3) pressured moderates (such as Peter and probably James) to avoid offending more conservative voices. Although they probably saw table fellowship with the uncircumcised as secondary to the Jerusalem church's unity (cf. 1Co 9:20–21), Paul saw it as denying the wider unity of God's people. For him, following Christ made a person part of God's people (cf. 3:7,29).
2:14 *in front of them all.* Jewish custom demanded attempts to resolve matters privately before a public rebuke (cf. 6:1; Mt 18:15), except in extraordinary circumstances—such as this one.
2:15 *not sinful Gentiles.* Eating with sinners (see v. 12 and note) might evoke Jesus' ministry (Mk 2:15–17).
2:16 *works of the law.* Some believe these "works" refer to distinctively Jewish customs such as circumcision and food customs, which had become crucial to Jewish people as identity markers. With others, the phrase more likely refers to all Biblical laws; the distinctive markers may well, however, have been those most prominent in people's minds.
2:17 Paul refutes a potential objection (cf. notes on Ro 2:1–29; 1Co 6:12).
2:20 *crucified with Christ.* For crucifixion and its shame, see note on 6:14. *Christ lives in me.* Although the OT spoke of the Spirit empowering God's servants (e.g., Nu 11:25; 27:18), the experience of Christ's life active in believers indicates even fuller identification.
3:1 *foolish.* Only in harsh circumstances, such as answering a rude challenger, did speakers challenge their own hearers with insults such as "Fool!" (cf. 1Co 15:36). *Galatians.* See Introduction: Date and Recipients. *bewitched.* The Greek term sometimes involved someone cursing another by means of a jealous look. *Before your very eyes.* When speakers communicated vividly, hearers said they envisioned the events narrated as if before their very eyes. Paul's life also revealed Christ (2:20).
3:2–5 Ancient argumentation often developed contrasts between opposites, as in vv. 2–3,5.
3:2 *receive the Spirit by the works of the law.* Some Jewish tradition associated the Spirit with special piety, in contrast to here. Scripture associated the Spirit especially with Israel at its restoration (Isa 44:3; Eze 39:29), but here Gentiles received the Spirit through trusting the message.
3:3 *finish by means of the flesh.* Apparently those of the circumcision party want the Galatian believers to "complete" their faith by embracing all the law, just as Jews expected of full converts to Judaism. In Jewish belief, such converts became members of God's people when circumcised in the flesh (6:12–13; the Hebrew of Ge 17:11).
3:4 *if it really was in vain.* One rhetorical technique was making and then correcting a misstatement.

vain—if it really was in vain? [5]So again I
ask, does God give you his Spirit and work
miracles[z] among you by the works of the
law, or by your believing what you heard?
[6]So also Abraham "believed God, and it
was credited to him as righteousness."[a][a]
[7]Understand, then, that those who have
faith[b] are children of Abraham. [8]Scripture
foresaw that God would justify the Gentiles by faith, and announced the gospel
in advance to Abraham: "All nations will
be blessed through you."[bc] [9]So those who
rely on faith[d] are blessed along with Abraham, the man of faith.
[10]For all who rely on the works of the
law are under a curse, as it is written:
"Cursed is everyone who does not continue to do everything written in the Book
of the Law."[ce] [11]Clearly no one who relies
on the law is justified before God, because
"the righteous will live by faith."[df] [12]The
law is not based on faith; on the contrary,
it says, "The person who does these things
will live by them."[eg] [13]Christ redeemed us
from the curse of the law[h] by becoming a
curse for us, for it is written: "Cursed is
everyone who is hung on a pole."[fi] [14]He
redeemed us in order that the blessing giv-
en to Abraham might come to the Gentiles
through Christ Jesus,[j] so that by faith we
might receive the promise of the Spirit.[k]

3:5 [z] 1Co 12:10 **3:6** [a] Ge 15:6; Ro 4:3 **3:7** [b] ver 9 **3:8** [c] Ge 12:3; Ac 3:25 **3:9** [d] ver 7; Ro 4:16 **3:10** [e] Dt 27:26; Jer 11:3 **3:11** [f] Hab 2:4; Gal 2:16; Heb 10:38 **3:12** [g] Lev 18:5; Ro 10:5 **3:13** [h] Gal 4:5 [i] Dt 21:23; Ac 5:30 **3:14** [j] Ro 4:9, 16 [k] ver 2; Joel 2:28; Ac 2:33

The Law and the Promise

[15]Brothers and sisters, let me take an example from everyday life. Just as no one
can set aside or add to a human covenant
that has been duly established, so it is in

[a] *6* Gen. 15:6 [b] *8* Gen. 12:3; 18:18; 22:18
[c] *10* Deut. 27:26 [d] *11* Hab. 2:4 [e] *12* Lev. 18:5
[f] *13* Deut. 21:23

3:5 *work miracles among you.* Although ancients expected healings at shrines of healing deities such as Asclepius, they did not experience them simply in religious gatherings. Early Christians were thus distinctive in experiencing miracles without shrines or wonderworkers.
3:6 *Abraham believed God.* Jewish people praised the righteousness of their ancestor Abraham; his faith in Ge 15:6 was often viewed as one of his important works. Paul points out that Scripture connected his righteousness only with his trust in God's promise. The context of such trust was a relationship with God. At this time when God favored Abram by counting him righteous, Abram's faith was still basic and imperfect (cf. Ge 15:8; 16:2–4); nevertheless, it was developing (Ge 12:1–4; 22:5–10). God saves those he favors because of their trust in him, not because their imperfect good works obligate him to do so.
3:7 *those who have faith are children of Abraham.* Jewish people regarded themselves as Abraham's children and heirs of his covenant. But people also sometimes figuratively labeled those who acted like someone else as that person's children. Paul applies the title spiritually to all who act as Abraham did, following God's promise. (The promise is now more complete in Christ [vv. 14–22,29], so this especially means following Christ.)
3:8 *Scripture foresaw.* As here, Jewish sources sometimes personified Scripture. *announced the gospel in advance to Abraham.* Abraham believed the prototype of the good news already available to him. Jewish teachers connected texts on similar subjects, and Paul draws on a repeated element in the promise to Abraham, namely, the blessing of the nations, or Gentiles (Ge 12:3; 18:18; 22:18). Many Jewish traditions viewed Abraham as the model convert to Judaism, but he was justified (Ge 15:6) years before he was circumcised (Ge 17:24–25).
3:10 *all who rely on the works of the law are under a curse.* Both Ge 12:3 and the blessings of the law in Dt 28 contrast the curses of those who oppose Abraham or those who break the covenant with the blessings of Abraham's descendants or those who keep the covenant. Reasoning by opposites was a frequent method of interpretation. Paul thus argues that imperfect obedience to the works of the law brings a curse (Dt 27:26, the summary of the curses). According to common Jewish teaching, human obedience was always imperfect, so God could not require perfect obedience as a condition for salvation. Like other ancient Jewish teachers, however, Paul interprets a text (here Dt 27:26) for all that he can get from it—after all, God was in a position to demand perfection.
3:11–13 Ancient Jewish teachers often connected texts based on common key words, and Paul provides a string of such linkages in these verses.
3:11 Paul links with Ge 15:6 (cited in v. 6) the only other text that included both "righteous" and faith together—Hab 2:4.
3:12 A shared key term (see note on vv. 11–13) links Hab 2:4 (in v. 11) with Lev 18:5 (and similar texts) here. *The person who does these things will live by them.* One may have life by faith; the law, by contrast, can grant life only to those who live by it. Although Lev 18:5 spoke of long life in the land (e.g., Dt 4:1,40), Jewish teachers also applied such passages to life in the world to come, and the proponents of circumcision (especially if they were as conservative as the teachers in Ac 15:1) may have used these texts to demand that Gentile converts embrace the law. Yet Jewish teachers themselves admitted that virtually everyone sinned. How then could the law grant life? Paul argues that, contrary to the intruders' views, the law was never designed to bring life (v. 21), except perhaps as a way of expressing faith.
3:13 *Cursed is everyone who is hung on a pole.* A shared key term (see note on vv. 11–13) links Dt 27:26 (in v. 10) with Dt 21:23 here. Although Israelites hung only the dead in Dt 21 (cf. Ge 40:19), many peoples in recent centuries had learned to execute people by hanging. Jesus experienced the curse in our place.
3:14 *blessing given to Abraham might come to the Gentiles.* Paul cites the blessing that is for all nations (v. 8). By this period Jewish people applied the promise and blessing given to Abraham not only to the original promised land but to the whole world to come. *the promise of the Spirit.* The Spirit, associated with the world to come, here offers a foretaste (cf. Eph 1:3,13–14). Paul focuses here less on the promise of land, however (cf. Ge 12:1), than the promise of Abraham's seed (Ge 12:2; 15:7) in whom the nations will be blessed (Ge 12:3; 18:18).
3:15 *human covenant.* Greeks usually used Paul's Greek term for "covenant" (*diathēkē*) for a "testament" or "will," a legal document opened at someone's death. By contrast, the Greek version of the Torah used the term to translate a term meaning "covenant." Ancient arguments often used wordplays to advance their case. Paul refers here to the covenant, but he plays on the Greek term's legal nuances;

GALATIANS 3

Paul's Jewish Opponents

Throughout his Christian ministry Paul was dogged by Jewish opponents who sought to undermine his message. Some of these challengers were Jews who rejected the Messianic claims of Jesus and sought to halt the growth of the church by open persecution (1Th 2:14–16), just as Paul himself had once done. On other occasions, however, Paul seems to have been opposed by Jews who were perhaps offended not so much by the fact that Paul preached Christ but that he did not require Gentiles to embrace distinctively Jewish practices (such as circumcision, observance of the Sabbath and avoidance of non-kosher foods). It appears that the Christians in Galatia had been persuaded not to turn away from Christ but to become proselytes. For Paul this was an alarming development because it undercut the core message of the gospel; if salvation could not be attained without adding to faith in Christ, then the death of Christ was insufficient.

Scholars have become vitally interested in understanding Paul's Jewish adversaries, because this issue is key to understanding Paul. The traditional Protestant view is that Paul's Jewish opponents were "legalists" who believed that salvation is not by grace through faith but must be earned by "good works" (which in this case meant adherence to the ritual laws of Judaism).

Against this, some have recently argued that first-century Judaism was not really "legalistic" at all, but that it held to the belief that forgiveness was obtained purely by the mercy of God. These scholars charge that Protestants have judged ancient Jews out of the context of the Protestant Reformation, when Luther faced the legalism of Roman Catholic masses and indulgences, rather than truly listening to the first-century Jews themselves. To the contrary, such critics insist, faithful Jews believed that God had chosen them purely on the basis of his grace and that he required only that they regulate their lives according to the terms of his covenant. The "rules" of Judaism, according to this perspective, helped Jews to preserve their identity and faithfulness but were not a means for acquiring God's favor.

This viewpoint on Judaism has led to an altered perspective on Paul. If the early Jews were not in fact legalistic, then our interpretation of some of Paul's words needs significant revision. On the other hand, many believe that it is valid to claim that many first-century Jews did embrace an excessively moralistic and institutionalized view of religion and that Paul was reacting against this code. Scholars are currently involved in research to try to determine exactly what these early Jews believed about how God's favor was to be obtained.

Even so, it is probably unnecessary to prove that first-century Judaism was formally and theologically legalistic in order to demonstrate that many of Paul's opponents were legalistic in their approach to their religion. When Jesus opposed the Jewish leadership, he was concerned not so much with debating the Pharisees over hypothetical elements of theology as with their unregenerated hearts (e.g., Mt 23). When religious people are unchanged by God's mercy, they often become harsh and judgmental, adhering to a letter-of-the-law code of moral and ethical standards. Their ability to perform religious rites and duties becomes a substitute for an authentic and personal knowledge of God. This is true in Christian communities as well, notwithstanding the fact that no one disputes that Christianity holds to salvation "by grace and not by works" as one of its core teachings. Thus, even though many of Paul's opponents may have formally accepted that forgiveness depends entirely upon the mercy of God, in their practical religious lives they may well have been legalistic. ◆

this case. 16The promises were spoken to
Abraham and to his seed.[l] Scripture does
not say "and to seeds," meaning many
people, but "and to your seed,"[a] meaning one person, who is Christ. 17What
I mean is this: The law, introduced 430
years[m] later, does not set aside the covenant previously established by God and
thus do away with the promise. 18For if the
inheritance depends on the law, then it no
longer depends on the promise;[n] but God
in his grace gave it to Abraham through a
promise.

19Why, then, was the law given at all? It
was added because of transgressions[o] until the Seed[p] to whom the promise referred
had come. The law was given through angels[q] and entrusted to a mediator.[r] 20A mediator,[s] however, implies more than one
party; but God is one.

3:16 [l] Lk 1:55; Ro 4:13,16
3:17 [m] Ge 15:13,14; Ex 12:40
3:18 [n] Ro 4:14
3:19 [o] Ro 5:20 [p] ver 16 [q] Ac 7:53 [r] Ex 20:19
3:20 [s] Heb 8:6; 9:15; 12:24

3:21 [t] Gal 2:17 [u] Gal 2:21
3:22 [v] Ro 3:9-19; 11:32
3:23 [w] Ro 11:32
3:24 [x] Ro 10:4 [y] Gal 2:16

21Is the law, therefore, opposed to the
promises of God? Absolutely not![t] For if
a law had been given that could impart
life, then righteousness would certainly
have come by the law.[u] 22But Scripture has
locked up everything under the control of
sin,[v] so that what was promised, being
given through faith in Jesus Christ, might
be given to those who believe.

Children of God

23Before the coming of this faith,[b] we
were held in custody[w] under the law, locked
up until the faith that was to come would
be revealed. 24So the law was our guardian
until Christ came[x] that we might be justified
by faith.[y] 25Now that this faith has come,
we are no longer under a guardian.

[a] *16* Gen. 12:7; 13:15; 24:7 [b] *22,23* Or *through the faithfulness of Jesus . . .* [23]*Before faith came*

---

that Scripture promised Israel an inheritance in the land (cf. v. 18) reinforced the usefulness of the connection. God's full covenant with Abraham (Ge 17:9–14) foreshadowed the Mosaic covenant, but God deemed Abraham righteous and promised to bless the nations even before this in Ge 12:3; 15:6 (cf. Ro 4:10–11).

A new will could replace an older one, though not after the testator's death. Nevertheless, no one could modify an existing will, since one would have to break the witnesses' seals that guaranteed its validity; it could be validly opened only once, when the testator died. Some may have argued against Paul's idea of a new covenant transforming the Mosaic covenant, but Paul here argues that the covenant introduced by Moses could not abrogate the covenant God made with Abraham to bless all nations (v. 8). If any covenant's stipulations were temporary, then, it was the covenant from Moses' time.

3:16 *does not say "and to seeds" ... but "and to your seed."* As Paul himself knew, the Greek term translated "seed" could apply to a group as well as to an individual (v. 29). Refuting his circumcision-promoting opponents, however, Paul uses a common Jewish argumentative technique of choosing the option (singular or plural) that worked best for the argument. Whereas Jewish interpreters usually applied the inheritance line of Abraham's singular seed to Isaac (cf. 4:28), Paul applies it to Jesus, whom he for other reasons knows to be the climax of Abraham's line and promise. Paul admits Israel as Abraham's seed elsewhere (Ro 9:7; 2Co 11:22), but he has already established those who have faith as being Abraham's offspring in a different way (Gal 3:7; cf. Ro 4:13,16). He also recognizes that Abraham's blessing to the nations (Ge 12:2–3) comes especially through Jesus and his movement.

3:17 *430 years later.* Recalls Ex 12:40. *the covenant previously established by God.* Although some Jewish traditions claimed that the patriarchs observed the law or dated its creation before the world's beginning, everyone acknowledged that Israel accepted the law only at Mount Sinai. If anyone protested that the new covenant (Jer 31:31–34) could not replace the unique stipulations of the prior Sinai covenant, Paul might reply that the new covenant harked back to God's earlier plan exemplified in his promise to Abraham.

3:18 *inheritance ... promise.* Scripture promised Israel an inheritance (e.g., Ex 32:13; Dt 4:21,38), and Jewish tradition spoke often of "inheriting" the coming world. (Naturally, the image never implied God's death.)

3:19 *Why ... was the law given at all?* A civil law was meant to restrain harm, not to save. Paul is aware of the law being written on the heart (cf. 6:2; see note on Ro 8:2), but that was not its public function for Israel as a whole. This external restraining function would not change the earlier covenant or promise of inheritance (v. 15) and was necessary only until the promise's fulfillment (vv. 23–25). Philosophers felt that law was necessary to restrain the masses but that the wise did not need such external direction. *given through angels and entrusted to a mediator.* Moses was mediator of the law (cf. Ex 20:19). Jewish tradition claimed that the law was given through angels; Paul contrasts this with the unmediated promise given by God himself. God is one. No belief was more central to Judaism than this (cf. Dt 6:4).

3:21 *if a law ... could impart life.* Jewish teachers sometimes spoke of eternal life as a reward for observing the law (see note on v. 12). Paul rightly objects, however, that the purpose of civil law was not to bring life (see note on v. 19).

3:22 *under the control of sin.* Although Jewish teachers and traditions sometimes explained away the sins of the patriarchs to which Paul could have pointed, Jewish teachers recognized that virtually everyone sinned.

3:23 *held in custody under the law ... until the faith that was to come would be revealed.* Paul divides history into phases, as Jewish teachers sometimes did. Although transcultural principles in the law might be eternal (e.g., Ex 31:17), its public restraining function was only until the promise. (Some eternal promises also could be revoked temporarily or permanently when their recipients violated the conditions; e.g., 1Sa 2:30; 2Ki 21:7–15.) Paul is getting his hearers' attention; because pious Jewish people loved and praised the law, they would find Paul's strong language shocking.

3:24 *guardian.* The Greek term here refers not even to a teacher but to the slave assigned to watch out for the student on his way to school and help him with his manners and schoolwork. The image is not negative per se; children often grew fond of their slave guardians and later freed them. Guardians were also normally better educated than the free masses. But it would still shock other Jewish thinkers, for whom the law was their teacher.

3:25 *Now that this faith has come.* In most ancient Mediterranean cultures boys came of age as men around age 13 or 14; guardians were no longer needed.

26 So in Christ Jesus you are all children
of God[z] through faith, 27 for all of you who
were baptized into Christ[a] have clothed
yourselves with Christ.[b] 28 There is neither
Jew nor Gentile, neither slave nor free,[c]
nor is there male and female, for you are
all one in Christ Jesus.[d] 29 If you belong to
Christ,[e] then you are Abraham's seed, and
heirs according to the promise.[f]

4 What I am saying is that as long as
an heir is underage, he is no different
from a slave, although he owns the whole
estate. 2 The heir is subject to guardians
and trustees until the time set by his father. 3 So also, when we were underage,
we were in slavery[g] under the elemental
spiritual forces[a] of the world.[h] 4 But when
the set time had fully come,[i] God sent his
Son, born of a woman,[j] born under the
law,[k] 5 to redeem those under the law, that
we might receive adoption[l] to sonship.[b]
6 Because you are his sons, God sent the
Spirit of his Son into our hearts,[m] the Spirit who calls out, *"Abba,*[c] Father."[n] 7 So you
are no longer a slave, but God's child; and
since you are his child, God has made you
also an heir.[o]

Paul's Concern for the Galatians

8 Formerly, when you did not know
God,[p] you were slaves to those who by

3:26 [z] Ro 8:14 **3:27** [a] Mt 28:19; Ro 6:3 [b] Ro 13:14 **3:28** [c] Col 3:11 [d] Jn 10:16; 17:11; Eph 2:14,15 **3:29** [e] 1Co 3:23 [f] ver 16 **4:3** [g] Gal 2:4 [h] Col 2:8,20 **4:4** [i] Mk 1:15; Eph 1:10 [j] Jn 1:14 [k] Lk 2:27 **4:5** [l] Jn 1:12 **4:6** [m] Ro 5:5 [n] Ro 8:15,16 **4:7** [o] Ro 8:17 **4:8** [p] 1Co 1:21; Eph 2:12; 1Th 4:5

[a] 3 Or *under the basic principles* [b] 5 The Greek word for *adoption to sonship* is a legal term referring to the full legal standing of an adopted male heir in Roman culture. [c] 6 Aramaic for *Father*

3:26 *children of God through faith.* God adopted Israel as his children (Dt 14:1), though individual Israelites' participation in this covenant was conditional (cf. Dt 32:5,20). Paul has argued that those who trust God's message as Abraham did are God's true children, i.e., those genuinely in covenant relationship with him (vv. 7,14). They receive the inheritance of v. 18.
3:27 *baptized into Christ ... clothed yourselves with Christ.* Everyone would understand Paul's images. Jewish teachers normally expected Gentiles converting to Judaism to be baptized so they could join God's people; these converts were baptized naked and could then be reclothed after the baptism. Jewish writers could speak of being "clothed" with the Spirit or virtues.
3:28 *all one in Christ Jesus.* Only a minority of groups even claimed to surmount ethnic and class divisions; the Diaspora churches who brought diverse peoples and classes together were thus distinctive. Early Christians formed the fullest bridge between Jews and Gentiles; apart from some comparatively small philosophic groups they proved distinctive in challenging class (slave versus free) and often gender prejudices. Some Greeks thanked the deity for not making them animals, women or non-Greeks; some Jewish teachers thanked God for not making them Gentiles, women or ignorant people (in some versions, slaves).
3:29 *Abraham's seed, and heirs according to the promise.* Jewish people considered themselves "Abraham's seed" and heirs of God's promises; Paul applies this to all who, like Abraham, trust God's promised plan now climaxed in Christ (see v. 16).
4:1 *heir is ... no different from a slave.* Ancient sources often contrast sons and slaves; slaves could be part of the "property" that sons inherited. Laws and philosophic ideals, however, treated minor sons in ways analogous to slaves. The slave here continues the image of the slave guardian (3:24), who was in a way over the minor he guarded.
4:2 *guardians and trustees.* The term translated "guardians" here differs from that in 3:24 and here refers to managers of an estate. Managers and trustees could be relatives, though powerful slaves also were often used to manage estates. *until the time set by his father.* If the father died, the heir could not access his wealth until the will directed or at puberty. The thought was often that he needed to be mature enough to use the resources wisely.
4:3 *in slavery.* Minors could be under a benevolent slave guardian (3:24), but now a more hostile slavery appears. *elemental spiritual forces.* This phrase sometimes referred to anything rudimentary, such as the alphabet. Paul could refer here to calendrical and other rules (cf. v. 10); although their rules differed, both Jews (in the law and its interpretations) and Gentiles had such rules. Alternatively, many scholars believe that the phrase here refers to the elements of the universe treated by many Gentiles as deities (e.g., wind, fire, and other aspects of nature such as the stars and sea; Judaism had demythologized them as angels who ruled over nature). In late antiquity growing numbers feared the personified, power of arbitrary Fate, which was supposed to exercise its will through the astral spirits, the gods who ruled the stars. In contrast to most of his Jewish contemporaries, Paul believes that even the Jewish people were enslaved by such evil spiritual powers apart from Christ (see note on v. 9.
4:4 *set time had fully come.* Paul has divided history into phases (see 3:23 and note), as Jewish teachers sometimes did. Jewish texts often speak of the fulfillment of appointed times in history as a way of recognizing God's perfect wisdom in and sovereignty over history. Here Paul compares this fulfillment to the point at which a boy attains maturity and is considered an adult (typically about 13 or 14 years old; what we now know as the Jewish *bar mitzvah* ceremony is a much later historical development).
4:5 *might receive adoption to sonship.* God had adopted Israel as his child (e.g., Ex 4:22) and promised the nation an inheritance (e.g., Dt 26:1). A frequent reason for adoption in the Greco-Roman world was to have an heir.
4:6 *sent the Spirit.* Developing one OT emphasis about God's Spirit, Jewish people associated the Spirit particularly with inspiration. Here the Spirit inspires believers' assurance of their relationship with God. Abba, *Father.* Jewish people often called God Father, but rarely if ever addressed him as *Abba*, an intimate, vernacular Aramaic title for one's father. Believers in Jesus, most of whom in the Diaspora did not speak Aramaic, undoubtedly borrowed this title from Jesus' use of it (see note on Mk 14:36; Ro 8:15).
4:7 *slave.* Refers to the analogous status of the minor in v. 1 and prepares for v. 8.
4:8 *when you did not know God ... those who by nature are not gods.* Jewish people often said that the Gentiles did not know God, and that their gods were mere creations of the true God. These other gods were not gods at all (Dt 32:17; 2Ki 19:18; 2Ch 13:9; Isa 37:19; Jer 2:11; 5:7; in the Apocrypha, see Epistle of Jeremiah vv. 15,23,29,49,52,65,72). Jews often regarded Gentile gods as nonexistent, though some viewed them as falsely worshiped humans of the

GALATIANS 4

THE GODS OF THE GREEKS AND ROMANS

The "religious marketplace" was extremely crowded during the Hellenistic era. The Olympian deities (and their Roman equivalents) still held a place in popular religion: mighty Zeus and his consort Hera, warlike Ares, erotic Aphrodite, prophetic Apollo, the virgin warrior Athena, Artemis the huntress, Hermes the messenger of the gods, Hephaestus the smith, Poseidon of the sea, Demeter of the field and Hestia of the hearth. Hades (the Roman Pluto), the grim god of the underworld, was not always listed among the "Twelve" but retained a significant place in religious thinking. While these deities were certainly reverenced, they were seldom seen as admirable characters. To the contrary, myths described them as violent and lustful, as well as capricious and conniving in their dealings with humans and with one another (as is seen in Homer's *Iliad* and *Odyssey* and in Ovid's *Metamorphoses*).

It is not surprising, then, that these deities and their stories were later sanitized by the philosophers. In some systems, for example, Zeus was equated with the organizing principle of the universe (examples are Cleanthes' *Hymn to Zeus* and Aratus's *Phaenomena*). This transformation of the idea of Zeus was so thorough that Jews and Christians could sometimes make use of material related to Zeus in their apologetic teaching in the Hellenistic world (as in Paul's reference to a poem by the Stoic Aratus in Ac 17).

Foreign cults also proliferated in Greece and Rome during the Hellenistic age. The worship of the god Sarapis was particularly popular, even though it appears that he was invented as late as the third century BC, drawing characteristics from various Greek and Egyptian deities. Widespread stories of his offering help to his followers (deliverance from shipwreck, healing, etc.) compensated for his lack of a long history. Isis and Osiris, also from Egypt, were popular objects of worship.

Roman statue of the goddess Artemis of Ephesus, a tremendously popular deity (Ac 19:24). At Ephesus, the cult of Artemis the huntress was merged with that of an Anatolian fertility goddess.

Marie-Lan Nguyen/Wikimedia Commons

In addition to these major deities, there remained a host of local spirits and gods that attracted veneration throughout the empire. Household gods, preserving hearth and home, were especially popular among the Romans. Naiads were described as water-nymphs associated with fountains, just as Dryads were associated with trees and Nereids with the sea. Various spirits connected with the earth were thought to bring fertility to crops, as well as to be associated with death and the underworld. The terrifying goddess Hekate became particularly prominent and was frequently invoked in magic spells. Finally, heroes from the past, most notably Heracles (the Roman Hercules), were thought to aid people in distress and sometimes to serve as spiritual mentors. ◆

nature are not gods.[q] 9But now that you
know God — or rather are known by
God[r] — how is it that you are turning back
to those weak and miserable forces[a]? Do
you wish to be enslaved[s] by them all over
again?[t] 10You are observing special days
and months and seasons and years![u] 11I
fear for you, that somehow I have wasted
my efforts on you.[v]
12I plead with you, brothers and sisters,[w]
become like me, for I became like you. You
did me no wrong. 13As you know, it was
because of an illness[x] that I first preached
the gospel to you, 14and even though my
illness was a trial to you, you did not treat
me with contempt or scorn. Instead, you
welcomed me as if I were an angel of God,
as if I were Christ Jesus himself.[y] 15Where,
then, is your blessing of me now? I can
testify that, if you could have done so, you
would have torn out your eyes and given
them to me. 16Have I now become your
enemy by telling you the truth?[z]

4:8 [q] 2Ch 13:9; Isa 37:19 4:9 [r] 1Co 8:3 [s] ver 3 [t] Col 2:20 4:10 [u] Ro 14:5 4:11 [v] 1Th 3:5 4:12 [w] Gal 6:18 4:13 [x] 1Co 2:3 4:14 [y] Mt 10:40 4:16 [z] Am 5:10

17Those people are zealous to win you
over, but for no good. What they want is
to alienate you from us, so that you may
have zeal for them. 18It is fine to be zealous, provided the purpose is good, and
to be so always, not just when I am with
you.[a] 19My dear children,[b] for whom I am
again in the pains of childbirth until Christ
is formed in you,[c] 20how I wish I could be
with you now and change my tone, because I am perplexed about you!

Hagar and Sarah

21Tell me, you who want to be under
the law, are you not aware of what the
law says? 22For it is written that Abraham
had two sons, one by the slave woman[d]
and the other by the free woman.[e] 23His
son by the slave woman was born according to the flesh,[f] but his son by the free
woman was born as the result of a divine
promise.[g]

4:18 [a] ver 13,14 4:19 [b] 1Co 4:15 [c] Eph 4:13 4:22 [d] Ge 16:15 [e] Ge 21:2 4:23 [f] Ro 9:7,8 [g] Ge 18:10-14; Heb 11:11

[a] 9 Or *principles*

past. Most ancient Jewish and all ancient Christian sources regarded the spirits worshiped by Gentiles as actually demons (1Co 10:20; see notes on Gal 4:3,9). *by nature.* Greek thinkers also evaluated beliefs by their correspondence to nature; Jewish thinkers responded that it was against nature to worship what is created. (A minority of Greeks regarded deities other than nature as mere human inventions, but even many of them still venerated forces of nature.)

4:9 *or rather.* Making and then correcting a misstatement was one way to draw attention to one's point. *forces.* See note on v. 3. Some of Phrygia's indigenous cults, such as that of the prominent mother goddess, were closely tied to nature.

4:10 *special days.* Before their conversion, Gentiles observed festivals for their deities and regarded various days as lucky or unlucky. But Judaism also had its own special calendar of holy days, new moons, sabbatical years and so forth. By returning to a ceremonial, calendrical religion regulated by heavenly bodies they once regarded as gods, the Galatians return to pagan bondage under these spiritual forces (cf. vv. 3,9).

4:12 – 20 Unlike the harshest letters of rebuke, Paul includes affectionate elements characteristic of letters between friends. Persuaders often climaxed a section with a deep appeal to emotion as well as reason. The intensity of Paul's expression of love here softens the preceding harsh tone.

4:12 *become like me, for I became like you.* Ancient Mediterranean culture valued reciprocity. Ideally, friends shared everything in common, so what belonged to one belonged to the other (cf. 1Ki 22:4).

4:13 *because of an illness.* Some suggest that Paul's illness was malaria, inviting his work in the higher-elevation Galatian interior (cf. Ac 13:14). *illness.* The Greek term can also mean "weakness," which could also include injuries from persecution. Whatever the case, people often viewed physical problems as divine punishment and viewed physical wholeness and handsomeness as praiseworthy and attractive.

4:14 *as if I were an angel of God.* Receiving someone as an angel of God showed enormous respect (Ge 33:10; 1Sa 29:9; 2Sa 14:17,20; 19:27; Zec 12:8); they received him as the one who sent him (cf. Lk 10:16). It need not mean they actually mistook him for an angel (cf. Ac 14:12).

4:15 *would have torn out your eyes and given them to me.* Although some argue that Galatian believers' willingness to donate their eyes to Paul suggests a vision problem in vv. 13 – 14, giving one's eyes was a known figure of speech for sacrificial love. Sacrificing for a friend expressed one of the highest Greek ideals of friendship. Letter writers sometimes appealed to the recipients' love for them. Likewise, letter writers sometimes affirmed their affection by protesting the recipients' lack of or decline in comparable affection.

4:16 *Have I now become your enemy ...?* A speaker would sometimes challenge hearers as to what crime the speaker has committed, or ask why the hearers have requited his love with enmity. *telling you the truth.* Speakers sometimes protested that they spoke truth firmly for the hearers' good, in contrast to flatterers merely seeking to ingratiate themselves.

4:17 *zealous.* See 1:14; see also note on Ac 22:3.

4:18 *not just when I am with you.* Accusations flourished more when one was not present to defend oneself (e.g., Ac 21:21). Letters were meant to approximate one's presence insofar as possible.

4:19 *dear children.* For Paul addressing them as if unbelievers, see note on 2Co 5:20. *I am again in the pains of childbirth.* Everyone recognized such pain as agonizing; moreover, even with skilled midwives, mothers often died in or soon after childbirth. Writers thus sometimes depicted their hard work as labor pains. Later Jewish teachers said that when one converted someone to their faith, it was as if they had created the person.

4:20 *I am perplexed about you!* In emotionally intense, dismaying situations, skilled speakers and writers could express confusion, as here.

4:21 *Tell me.* Speakers sometimes introduced challenges to imaginary interlocutors in this manner. *what the law says.* Jewish thinkers included Genesis (along with the rest of the Pentateuch) in the law.

4:23 *son by the slave woman.* God blessed Abraham's son Ishmael (Ge 16:10; 17:20; 21:13,18), but this narrative was a digression in Genesis from the narrative of the promised seed (Ge 15:4 – 5; 17:15 – 19,21; 18:14; 21:12). *born according*

[24]These things are being taken figuratively: The women represent two covenants. One covenant is from Mount Sinai
and bears children who are to be slaves:
This is Hagar. [25]Now Hagar stands for
Mount Sinai in Arabia and corresponds to
the present city of Jerusalem, because she
is in slavery with her children. [26]But the
Jerusalem that is above[h] is free, and she is
our mother. [27]For it is written:

"Be glad, barren woman,
you who never bore a child;
shout for joy and cry aloud,
you who were never in labor;
because more are the children of the
desolate woman
than of her who has a husband."[a][i]

[28]Now you, brothers and sisters, like
Isaac, are children of promise. [29]At that
time the son born according to the flesh[j]
persecuted the son born by the power of
the Spirit.[k] It is the same now. [30]But what
does Scripture say? "Get rid of the slave
woman and her son, for the slave woman's son will never share in the inheritance
with the free woman's son."[b][l] [31]Therefore,
brothers and sisters, we are not children of
the slave woman, but of the free woman.

Freedom in Christ

5 It is for freedom that Christ has set us
free.[m] Stand firm,[n] then, and do not let
yourselves be burdened again by a yoke
of slavery.[o]
[2]Mark my words! I, Paul, tell you that if
you let yourselves be circumcised,[p] Christ
will be of no value to you at all. [3]Again I
declare to every man who lets himself be
circumcised that he is obligated to obey
the whole law.[q] [4]You who are trying to be
justified by the law have been alienated
from Christ; you have fallen away from
grace.[r] [5]For through the Spirit we eagerly
await by faith the righteousness for which

4:26 [h]Heb 12:22; Rev 3:12 **4:27** [i]Isa 54:1 **4:29** [j]ver 23 [k]Ge 21:9 **4:30** [l]Ge 21:10 **5:1** [m]Jn 8:32 [n]1Co 16:13 [o]Ac 15:10; Gal 2:4 **5:2** [p]Ac 15:1 **5:3** [q]Gal 3:10 **5:4** [r]Heb 12:15; 2Pe 3:17

[a] *27* Isaiah 54:1 [b] *30* Gen. 21:10

to the flesh. Cf. 3:3 (see note there). Ishmael's birth was according to natural human ways of having children; Isaac's birth was impossible by purely natural means.
4:24 *figuratively.* Writers used this Greek term in various ways; philosophers often used it to deny the literal meaning of a story, but Jewish interpreters usually accepted the literal meaning and simply applied it also in an analogy, as here. (When the Jewish philosopher Philo adds an extra, allegorical meaning to Sarah and Hagar, they represent advanced versus elementary education; Philo clearly addressed a different kind of audience than Paul has in mind here.) *slaves.* Paul continues the slave versus free analogy from 3:24—4:11 and the issue of promise from 3:14–22,29. Because Paul rarely argues allegorically, some think that he is here answering his opponents, who may have compared Gentile God-fearers to Ishmael and those who became members of God's people and kept the law with the line of Isaac. (Both Ishmael and Isaac were circumcised.)
4:25 *Mount Sinai in Arabia.* The region controlled by Nabatean Arabs, to the east, south and northeast of Judea and Galilee (see note on 1:17). Jewish people in this period regarded the Nabatean Arabs as Ishmaelites, Hagar's descendants; this may help to explain why Paul connects Hagar with Sinai "in Arabia." Some scholars believe that Paul answers opponents who connected Sinai and its law with the end-time law going forth from Jerusalem (see v. 26; Isa 2:2–4; 65:17–19).
4:26 *Jerusalem that is above … our mother.* Jewish people celebrated the Biblical promise of a new Jerusalem (Isa 65:17–19), which was sometimes envisioned as a mother (Isa 66:7–10). Both Jews and Gentiles could speak of their ancestral, founding city as a "mother city." Jewish people sometimes also spoke of "Jerusalem above" and envisioned it coming down to earth in the future. (Phrygians worshiped their mother goddess, often identified with earth, but maternal imagery was broader than this; cf. v. 19; Rev 12:2.)
4:27 *barren woman.* Isa 54:1, cited here and following Isa 53, depicts the restoration of God's people in terms of Jerusalem as a mother giving birth (relevant for v. 26). Some later Jewish teachers connected the barren woman giving birth in Isa 54:1 with Sarah in Ge 21:2 (cf. Isa 51:2).
4:28 *children of promise.* Like Isaac, those among the nations blessed in Abraham's seed (3:8) are the humanly impossible children of promise.
4:29 *the son born according to the flesh persecuted the son born by the power of the Spirit.* Comparing the current situation, Paul reintroduces flesh and Spirit (3:3; cf. 5:16–17; 6:8). Circumcision was a sign of the covenant in the flesh (Ge 17:10–14), but a greater proof of the new covenant is the promised end-time gift of the Spirit (Eze 36:24–27), which makes the lesser sign unnecessary. Perhaps someone could construe Ishmael as persecuting Isaac (cf. Ge 21:9), but what is clear is the ancient expectation that the morally inferior persecuted their moral superiors (e.g., interpretations of the Cain and Abel story; Esau and Jacob).
4:30 *Get rid of the slave woman and her son.* Sarah demanded that Hagar's son be sent away to protect Isaac's inheritance (Ge 21:10), and God confirmed this exhortation (21:12). Paul implies that his audience should send away the spiritual Ishmaelites—those trying to tie them to the Sinai covenant rather than the superior promise.
5:1 *freedom … yoke of slavery.* Paul applies his previous analogy regarding freedom and slavery (4:22–31). Jewish teachers honored the yoke of the law (see note on Ac 15:10), but a yoke also symbolized slavery.
5:2 Sometimes one saved the greatest issue of controversy for later in the letter. Although Paul addressed circumcision in his narrative (2:3–12), it is here that he begins to address it as a central issue of conflict with his opponents in Galatia (vv. 2–3,6,11; 6:12–15).
5:3 *obligated to obey the whole law.* Most Jewish teachers believed that God accepted Gentiles who kept the most basic commandments (e.g., against idolatry and sexual immorality). Those who were circumcised and so converted to Judaism, however, became obligated to keep all the laws incumbent on ethnic Israel.
5:4 *alienated from Christ … fallen away from grace.* Jewish people recognized that even Jewish people could fall away (become apostate) if they rejected God's law; Paul here warns of rejecting something greater, God's promise by grace.
5:5 *righteousness for which we hope.* Scripture associated the Spirit with the future restoration (e.g., Eze 37:14). Thus Paul may say that the Spirit provides a foretaste of

we hope.[s] 6For in Christ Jesus neither circumcision nor uncircumcision has any
value.[t] The only thing that counts is faith
expressing itself through love.[u]
7You were running a good race.[v] Who
cut in on you[w] to keep you from obeying
the truth? 8That kind of persuasion does
not come from the one who calls you.[x] 9"A
little yeast works through the whole batch
of dough."[y] 10I am confident[z] in the Lord
that you will take no other view.[a] The
one who is throwing you into confusion,[b]
whoever that may be, will have to pay the
penalty. 11Brothers and sisters, if I am still
preaching circumcision, why am I still being persecuted?[c] In that case the offense[d]
of the cross has been abolished. 12As for
those agitators,[e] I wish they would go the
whole way and emasculate themselves!

5:5 [s] Ro 8:23,24 **5:6** [t] 1Co 7:19 [u] 1Th 1:3 **5:7** [v] 1Co 9:24 [w] Gal 3:1 **5:8** [x] Ro 8:28; Gal 1:6 **5:9** [y] 1Co 5:6 **5:10** [z] 2Co 2:3 [a] Php 3:15 [b] Gal 1:7 **5:11** [c] Gal 4:29; 6:12 [d] 1Co 1:23 **5:12** [e] ver 10 **5:13** [f] 1Co 8:9; 1Pe 2:16

Life by the Spirit

13You, my brothers and sisters, were
called to be free. But do not use your freedom to indulge the flesh[a];[f] rather, serve

[a] *13* In contexts like this, the Greek word for *flesh* (*sarx*) refers to the sinful state of human beings, often presented as a power in opposition to the Spirit; also in verses 16, 17, 19 and 24; and in 6:8.

the perfect righteousness of the future kingdom and/or confirmation that one will be declared righteous in the day of judgment.

5:7 *running a good race.* For athletic metaphors, see the article "Athletic Imagery in 1 Corinthians 9," p. 2000. *cut in.* May continue the athletic metaphor, and supports a wordplay with "emasculate" (lit. "cut off") in v. 12.

5:9 *yeast works through the whole batch.* Fermented dough (leaven; here "yeast") pervades the dough, hence could apply figuratively to something (here sin) that infects the whole.

5:10 *I am confident . . . you will take no other view.* Speakers and writers sometimes expressed confidence that their hearers would respond positively.

5:11 *why am I still being persecuted?* Had Paul required circumcision for conversion, he would not have incurred persecution from his fellow Jews (including in Galatia; cf. Ac 13:43–45,50; 14:2,19). His opponents in Galatia were avoiding this persecution (Gal 6:12–13).

5:12 *go the whole way and emasculate themselves!* Witty insults were conventional in debate. Many Gentiles viewed circumcision as mutilation; castration was, however, horrifying to Jews because it excluded one from the covenant (Dt 23:1). (Others also mocked eunuchs, especially Galli, the self-castrated worshipers of Phrygia's mother goddess.) For the sake of the Galatian believers, Paul wishes that those preaching circumcision would slip with their knives and remove their own male organs.

THE FRUIT OF THE SPIRIT

The aspects of the fruit of the Spirit advocated by Paul in Galatians 5:22–23 occur not only here but also elsewhere in the Scriptures. Most of the attributes are those by which God himself lives.

ASPECT	DEFINITION	ATTRIBUTE OF GOD	ATTRIBUTE FOR CHRISTIANS
love	sacrificial, unmerited deeds to help a needy person	Ex 34:6; Jn 3:16; Ro 5:8; 1Jn 4:8,16	Jn 13:34–35; Ro 12:9,10; 1Pe 1:22; 1Jn 4:7,11–12,21
joy	an inner happiness not dependent on outward circumstances	Ps 104:31; Isa 62:5; Lk 15:7,10	Dt 12:7,12,18; Ps 64:10; Isa 25:9; Php 4:4; 1Pe 1:8
peace	harmony in all relationships	Isa 9:6–7; Eze 34:25; Jn 14:27; Heb 13:20	Isa 26:3; Ro 5:1; 12:18; 14:17; Eph 2:14–17
forbearance	putting up with others, even when one is severely tried	Ro 9:22; 1Ti 1:16; 1Pe 3:20; 2Pe 3:9,15	Eph 4:2; Col 1:11; Heb 6:12; Jas 5:7–8,10
kindness	doing thoughtful deeds for others	Ro 2:4; 11:22; Eph 2:7; Titus 3:4	1Co 13:4; Eph 4:32; Col 3:12
goodness	showing generosity to others	Ne 9:25,35; Ps 31:19; Mk 10:18	Ro 15:14; Eph 5:9; 2Th 1:11
faithfulness	trustworthiness and reliability	Ps 33:4; 1Co 1:9; 10:13; Heb 10:23; 1Jn 1:9	Lk 16:10–12; 2Th 1:4; 2Ti 4:7; Titus 2:10
gentleness	meekness and humility	Zec 9:9; Mt 11:29	Isa 66:2; Mt 5:5; Eph 4:2; Col 3:12
self-control	victory over sinful desires		Pr 16:32; Titus 1:8; 2:12; 1Pe 5:8–9; 2Pe 1:6

one another[g] humbly in love. 14For the entire law is fulfilled in keeping this one command: "Love your neighbor as yourself."[a][h] 15If you bite and devour each other, watch out or you will be destroyed by each other.

16So I say, walk by the Spirit,[i] and you will not gratify the desires of the flesh.[j] 17For the flesh desires what is contrary to the Spirit, and the Spirit what is contrary to the flesh.[k] They are in conflict with each other, so that you are not to do whatever[b] you want.[l] 18But if you are led by the Spirit, you are not under the law.[m]

19The acts of the flesh are obvious: sexual immorality,[n] impurity and debauchery; 20idolatry and witchcraft; hatred, discord, jealousy, fits of rage, selfish ambition, dissensions, factions 21and envy; drunkenness, orgies, and the like.[o] I warn you, as I did before, that those who live like this will not inherit the kingdom of God.

22But the fruit[p] of the Spirit is love,[q] joy, peace, forbearance, kindness, goodness, faithfulness, 23gentleness and self-control.[r] Against such things there is no law. 24Those who belong to Christ Jesus have crucified the flesh[s] with its passions and desires.[t] 25Since we live by the Spirit, let us keep in step with the Spirit. 26Let us not become conceited,[u] provoking and envying each other.

Doing Good to All

6 Brothers and sisters, if someone is caught in a sin, you who live by the Spirit[v] should restore that person gently. But watch yourselves, or you also may be tempted. 2Carry each other's burdens, and in this way you will fulfill the law of Christ.[w] 3If anyone thinks they are something[x] when they are not, they deceive themselves. 4Each one should test their own actions. Then they can take pride in themselves alone, without comparing themselves to someone else, 5for each one should carry their own load. 6Nevertheless, the one who receives instruction in the word should share all good things with their instructor.[y]

5:13 [g] 1Co 9:19; Eph 5:21 **5:14** [h] Lev 19:18; Mt 22:39 **5:16** [i] Ro 8:2, 4-6, 9, 14 [j] ver 24 **5:17** [k] Ro 8:5-8 [l] Ro 7:15-23 **5:18** [m] Ro 6:14; 1Ti 1:9 **5:19** [n] 1Co 6:18 **5:21** [o] Ro 13:13 **5:22** [p] Mt 7:16-20; Eph 5:9 [q] Col 3:12-15 **5:23** [r] Ac 24:25 **5:24** [s] Ro 6:6 [t] ver 16, 17 **5:26** [u] Php 2:3 **6:1** [v] 1Co 2:15 **6:2** [w] Ro 15:1; Jas 2:8 **6:3** [x] Ro 12:3; 1Co 8:2 **6:6** [y] 1Co 9:11, 14

[a] *14* Lev. 19:18 [b] *17* Or *you do not do what*

5:14 *Love your neighbor as yourself.* One of the various texts that Jewish teachers used as summaries of the law was Lev 19:18; this is one of the two that Jesus used (Mk 12:31).

5:15 *devour each other.* Ancient Mediterranean societies abhorred cannibalism, and sometimes used the concept as a metaphor for abusing one another.

5:16 *walk by the Spirit.* Jewish people were supposed to walk in God's law and ways (e.g., Dt 5:33; 26:17). In the promised end time, God would put his Spirit within his people so they would walk in (in the Greek version, "go in") obedience to him (Eze 36:27).

5:17 *flesh desires what is contrary to the Spirit.* One either follows the way of flesh — human desires apart from God — or the way of the Spirit (see the article "Flesh and Spirit," p. 1961). The Dead Sea Scrolls divided humanity into the righteous and wicked and viewed every action as from either God's Spirit or the spirit of error. The members of that community were not claiming to be perfect, but believed that they were on the right side of the divide.

5:18 *led by the Spirit.* Might evoke how God led Israel in the wilderness (see note on Ro 8:14). *not under the law.* Philosophers denied that laws were necessary for the wise, because they would choose what was right. Scripture promised that in the new covenant God would write the law on the hearts of his people (Jer 31:31 – 34), by the Spirit (Eze 36:27). The solution to the flesh is not found in fighting the flesh, but in welcoming the Spirit (vv. 16 – 17).

5:19 – 23 One either follows the way of flesh — human desires apart from God — or the way of the Spirit (see the article "Flesh and Spirit," p. 1961). Some ancient writers included both vice lists (as in vv. 19 – 21) and virtue lists (as in vv. 22 – 23) together.

5:19 – 21 Ancient writers often provided lists of vices.

5:19 *acts.* Lit. "works." Human religion is ineffective without God's Spirit (cf. 3:2 – 3).

5:22 – 23 Ancient writers sometimes provided lists of virtues.

5:22 *fruit of the Spirit.* Both Scripture (see note on Jn 15:2) and the Greek language more generally sometimes used "fruit" figuratively. As Jesus noted, fruit merely reflects the true character of the tree (Mt 7:17 – 18; Lk 6:43 – 44); since people of the Spirit have a new life (Gal 5:24), it is natural for them to reflect the character of the Spirit. "Fruit" thus contrasts with "acts" (i.e., works; v. 19). Some of the positive emotions listed by philosophers correspond to Paul's list here, but Paul's list is moral more than emotional.

5:23 *no law.* For the character of love (v. 22) fulfilling the law, see v. 14; for laws not objecting to right behavior, see note on v. 18.

5:24 *crucified the flesh with its passions and desires.* By using reason, philosophers tried to control or (among Stoics) to eradicate their passions, without pretending that they had achieved this goal. Jewish thinkers claimed that the law gave them rational power to defeat or control passions. Here, however, Paul thinks not of mere human effort but of confidently depending on and acting on Christ's work (vv. 19 – 23; 2:20; 6:14).

5:25 *live by the Spirit.* Cf. Eze 37:1 – 14; Ro 8:8 – 13. *keep in step with the Spirit.* Cf. note on v. 16.

6:1 *restore that person gently.* Many ancient thinkers, and virtually all Jews, valued private and patient correction.

6:2 *Carry each other's burdens.* Carrying burdens was often involuntary (a task required by soldiers or demanded of slaves) but is here offered freely (cf. Mt 5:41). *law of Christ.* In view of Gal 5:14 (see note there), this could evoke Jesus' teaching about love. Paul also believed that the Spirit wrote the heart of the law inside believers (see note on 5:18; cf. Ro 8:2).

6:3 *thinks they are something when they are not.* Philosophers also warned about the ignorant thinking themselves something when they were nothing.

6:5 *each one should carry their own load.* Greeks had similar sayings that meant that one should be self-reliant. Paul might instead emphasize not looking down on others (vv. 1,3).

6:6 *share all good things with their instructor.* Teachers in early Christian communities, unlike many ancient moral teachers, did not normally charge fees or depend on patrons; that model was probably not economically

7Do not be deceived:[z] God cannot be
mocked. A man reaps what he sows.[a]
8Whoever sows to please their flesh, from
the flesh will reap destruction;[b] whoever
sows to please the Spirit, from the Spirit
will reap eternal life.[c] 9Let us not become
weary in doing good,[d] for at the proper
time we will reap a harvest if we do not
give up.[e] 10Therefore, as we have opportunity, let us do good[f] to all people, especially to those who belong to the family[g]
of believers.

Not Circumcision but the New Creation

11See what large letters I use as I write
to you with my own hand![h]
12Those who want to impress people by
means of the flesh are trying to compel
you to be circumcised.[i] The only reason
they do this is to avoid being persecuted[j]
for the cross of Christ. 13Not even those
who are circumcised keep the law,[k] yet
they want you to be circumcised that they
may boast about your circumcision in the
flesh.[l] 14May I never boast except in the
cross of our Lord Jesus Christ, through
which[a] the world has been crucified to
me, and I to the world.[m] 15Neither circumcision nor uncircumcision means anything;[n] what counts is the new creation.[o]
16Peace and mercy to all who follow this
rule—to[b] the Israel of God.
17From now on, let no one cause me
trouble, for I bear on my body the marks[p]
of Jesus.
18The grace of our Lord Jesus Christ[q]
be with your spirit,[r] brothers and sisters.
Amen.

6:7 [z] 1Co 6:9 [a] 2Co 9:6 **6:8** [b] Job 4:8; Hos 8:7 [c] Jas 3:18 **6:9** [d] 1Co 15:58 [e] Rev 2:10 **6:10** [f] Pr 3:27 [g] Eph 2:19 **6:11** [h] 1Co 16:21 **6:12** [i] Ac 15:1 [j] Gal 5:11 **6:13** [k] Ro 2:25 [l] Php 3:3 **6:14** [m] Ro 6:2,6 **6:15** [n] 1Co 7:19 [o] 2Co 5:17 **6:17** [p] Isa 44:5; 2Co 1:5 **6:18** [q] Ro 16:20 [r] 2Ti 4:22

[a] 14 Or *whom* [b] 16 Or *rule and to*

viable for most house congregations, so teachers did not depend on their congregations for their support. Nevertheless, believers should be generous toward them. Some find here also a hint of Paul's collection for Jerusalem (perhaps 2:10; see 1Co 16:1; with Gal 6:7–9, cf. 2Co 9:6–10), although the principle here is probably more general.

6:7 *A man reaps what he sows.* Reaping what one sows became a common proverb in the ancient world (cf., e.g., Pr 11:18; 22:8; Hos 8:7; 10:12). Ancient writers occasionally used sowing as a monetary image.

6:8 *flesh ... Spirit.* See the article "Flesh and Spirit," p. 1961. *Spirit ... life.* The Spirit is associated with resurrection (Eze 37:5–14).

6:10 *do good to all people, especially to those who belong to the family of believers.* Society would view such instructions positively. Most thinkers on moral topics urged work for the common good; a majority also recognized that this work did not preclude special interest in one's group.

6:11 *what large letters ... with my own hand.* Most people did not write letters the length of Galatians, or even short ones, but dictated them to scribes; often they wrote small to finish the task quickly or within the space left on the sheet of papyrus (which could be expensive). Paul, who may be unaccustomed to writing (some even suggest that artisan work in winter weakened his hands), cannot write small and quickly. Some documents also seem to have called attention to especially important points at their beginning or end by using large letters. Whatever the purpose of "large letters" here, the main point is that not a scribe but Paul himself writes this section, as the handwriting shows. Paul's special effort expresses (as it often did in ancient letters) special affection and/or the special importance of what he writes.

6:12 *impress people by means of the flesh.* Circumcision was in the flesh (Ge 17:13–14); Paul's opponents not only sow to the flesh (v. 8) but want to impress their Judean peers with the Galatians' foreskins (one could boast in another; see note on v. 14). *to avoid being persecuted for the cross of Christ.* Some Gentiles viewed circumcision as mutilation, but it was mild compared with the grotesque suffering of crucifixion (see note on v. 14). Paul is unafraid of persecutors (v. 14).

6:14 *May I never boast except in the cross of ... Christ.* Ancients despised boasting for oneself, but boasting in another was acceptable. *cross.* Crucifixion was a shameful death; people did not want to be associated with those executed on crosses.

6:15 *Neither ... means anything.* Circumcision was merely a sign of the covenant, but now the promise is being fulfilled. *new creation.* Points to the widespread Jewish expectation (rooted in Isa 65:17,22) of the new heavens and earth. In Christ, believers begin to experience the foretaste of the new world (cf. 2Co 5:5, 17).

6:16 *Peace and mercy to all who follow this rule.* Jewish people often used the blessing, "Peace (or sometimes mercy) be with" (the person being blessed), and regularly prayed, "Peace ... to Israel."

6:17 *bear on my body the marks of Jesus.* People often displayed their wounds as signs of loyalty or to invite sympathy for their claims. Jesus was whipped and nailed to the cross (cf. Col 2:14), and Paul had also been persecuted (Gal 5:11) and presumably wounded (e.g., Ac 16:22). Sharing in the cross (v. 14; 2:20), Paul's wounds run deeper than circumcision.

6:18 *brothers and sisters.* Jews called fellow Jews brothers and sisters; although various other groups (including religious groups) shared such kinship language, Paul's conclusion of his letter to a mostly Gentile audience (cf. 4:8; 5:2–3) in this way may be significant in view of the preceding arguments (cf. 3:26).

THE LETTERS

EPHESIANS

Authorship

Paul identifies himself as author of the letter (1:1). Many scholars believe that Paul did not write it, or that a disciple compiled Pauline teaching in this letter after his death. Although pseudepigraphic letters did exist, the style is consistent with Paul's undisputed letters, especially when we take into account that, unlike most of Paul's letters, this was probably a circular letter (see note on 1:1). The differences reflect the sorts of variations we find among multiple works by single authors elsewhere in antiquity. Paul probably wrote this letter later in his ministry, using the same sort of Stoic language that often comes to the fore in Philippians, which was probably written in the same period. Such philosophic language accounts for some differences with Paul's earlier letters. Some language might reflect regional philosophic currents or counter the language of false teachers (cf. perhaps 4:14).

Some parts of this letter also elaborate with significant repetition, sometimes with synonyms (e.g., "power" and "strength"). This flowery language characterized a style of oratory known as epideictic, used to praise figures, virtues, and (most relevant here) deities. It also fits the style of rhetoric especially preferred in the province of Asia Minor, where ancient Ephesus was located.

Paul wrote this letter from Roman custody, probably in Rome itself. As believers near Ephesus would have known, Paul was in Roman custody (Ac 28:16) because he had been accused of bringing a Gentile into the temple (Ac 21:28 – 29). Ethnic and cultural differences between Jews and Gentiles became a major issue in the Ephesian church (cf. Ac 19:17); Paul's situation allows him to address it eloquently (Eph 2:12 – 22).

Paul's Roman custody also makes clear to him Roman concerns about religions subverting traditional Roman values related to the household (see notes on 5:21 — 6:9). Paul also takes into account some local converts' background with astrology and magic (in Ephesus, see Ac 19:19; cf. notes on Eph 1:9,21; 3:3). ◆

QUICK GLANCE

AUTHOR:
The apostle Paul

AUDIENCE:
Believers in the church at Ephesus and probably other Christians in western Asia Minor

DATE:
About AD 60

THEME:
Paul seeks to establish unity in the church and in other Christian relationships and envisions both salvation and the church in cosmic terms.

1 Paul, an apostle[a] of Christ Jesus by the
will of God,[b]

To God's holy people in Ephesus,[a] the
faithful[c] in Christ Jesus:

2 Grace and peace to you from God our
Father and the Lord Jesus Christ.[d]

Praise for Spiritual Blessings in Christ

3 Praise be to the God and Father of our
Lord Jesus Christ,[e] who has blessed us in
the heavenly realms[f] with every spiritual
blessing in Christ. 4 For he chose us in him
before the creation of the world to be holy
and blameless[g] in his sight. In love[h] 5 he[b]
predestined[i] us for adoption to sonship[c]
through Jesus Christ, in accordance with
his pleasure[j] and will— 6 to the praise of
his glorious grace, which he has freely giv-
en us in the One he loves.[k] 7 In him we
have redemption[l] through his blood, the
forgiveness of sins, in accordance with the
riches of God's grace 8 that he lavished on
us. With all wisdom and understanding,
9 he[d] made known to us the mystery[m] of
his will according to his good pleasure,
which he purposed in Christ, 10 to be put
into effect when the times reach their fulfillment[n]—to bring unity to all things in
heaven and on earth under Christ.[o]

11 In him we were also chosen,[e] having
been predestined according to the plan of
him who works out everything in conformity with the purpose[p] of his will, 12 in order that we, who were the first to put our
hope in Christ, might be for the praise of
his glory.[q] 13 And you also were included
in Christ when you heard the message of
truth,[r] the gospel of your salvation. When
you believed, you were marked in him
with a seal,[s] the promised Holy Spirit,
14 who is a deposit guaranteeing our inheritance[t] until the redemption of those who
are God's possession—to the praise of his
glory.

Thanksgiving and Prayer

15 For this reason, ever since I heard
about your faith in the Lord Jesus and

1:1 [a] 1Co 1:1 [b] 2Co 1:1 [c] Col 1:2 **1:2** [d] Ro 1:7 **1:3** [e] 2Co 1:3 [f] Eph 2:6; 3:10; 6:12 **1:4** [g] Eph 5:27; Col 1:22 [h] Eph 4:2, 15, 16 **1:5** [i] Ro 8:29, 30 [j] 1Co 1:21 **1:6** [k] Mt 3:17 **1:7** [l] Ro 3:24 **1:9** [m] Ro 16:25 **1:10** [n] Gal 4:4 [o] Col 1:20 **1:11** [p] Eph 3:11; Heb 6:17 **1:12** [q] ver 6, 14 **1:13** [r] Col 1:5 [s] Eph 4:30 **1:14** [t] Ac 20:32

[a] *1* Some early manuscripts do not have *in Ephesus.*
[b] *4,5* Or *sight in love.* [5]*He*
[c] *5* The Greek word for *adoption to sonship* is a legal term referring to the full legal standing of an adopted male heir in Roman culture.
[d] *8,9* Or *us with all wisdom and understanding.* [9]*And he*
[e] *11* Or *were made heirs*

1:1 *holy people.* "Holy people" had been applied to God's people in earlier Scripture (see, e.g., Da 7:18,21–27). *in Ephesus.* Some early manuscripts omit this destination, although others include it. Sometimes emperors, governors, high priests or other leading figures issued circular letters; Ephesians was probably circulated not only in Ephesus but also in the surrounding province of Roman Asia. Ideas would spread quickly from this prominent city to the region around it (cf. Ac 19:10).
1:2 *Grace and peace ... Lord Jesus Christ.* See note on Ro 1:7.
1:3–14 Ancient letters frequently included prayers or blessings, and sometimes thanksgivings.
1:3 *Praise be to the God.* Jewish prayers often opened with "Praise be to God." The Ephesian church included both Jews and Greeks (Ac 19:17; Ephesus was founded by Greeks and Greek culture dominated there). *heavenly realms.* People in the ancient Mediterranean world believed that there were multiple heavens (many envisioned three, others seven, and some many more). They believed that the highest heaven (in view here) was purest; the purest and greatest deity lived there. Nearer the earth, the atmospheric heaven, where birds fly, was also inhabited by many demons or semi-divine spirits (depending on the thinker). Paul thus adapts this language to speak of God's realm and exaltation over other spirits; cf. vv. 20–21; 2:6.
1:4–14 *chose ... predestined ... sonship ... redemption ... inheritance ... possession.* Despite the ethnically mixed character of the church in Ephesus (see note on v. 3), Paul applies to the church significant language that the OT applied to Israel: chose/predestined (Dt 4:37; 7:8), sonship (Dt 14:1), redemption (Isa 41:14), inheritance (Dt 4:21) and possession (Ex 6:8; 19:5).
1:4–5 *chose ... adoption to sonship.* Already in the OT, because of God's great love, he chose his people (Dt 4:37; 10:15) and made them his children (Dt 14:1; 32:19).
1:6 *glorious.* God promised to restore his people at least in part for his glory, or honor (Isa 60:21; 61:3; Jer 13:11).
1:7 *redemption through his blood.* God had redeemed Israel (i.e., freed them from slavery; see, e.g., Dt 7:8; 9:26). *forgiveness of sins.* For sacrifices and God's forgiveness, see, e.g., Lev 4:20,26,31,35.
1:8 *all wisdom and understanding.* Biblical writers sometimes repeated synonyms or related terms such as "wisdom" and "understanding" (e.g., Ex 31:3; 35:31; Pr 1:2,7; Isa 11:2); so did some forms of lavish Greek rhetoric (see Introduction to Ephesians).
1:9 *mystery of his will.* In Jewish circles, a mystery sometimes referred to secret information now revealed only by God (Da 2:28–30,47; Dead Sea Scrolls). The mystery that God purposed includes bringing Gentiles into the fold of God's people (3:6,11).
1:10 *when the times reach their fulfillment.* Jewish people understood that God was sovereignly working to bring history to the promised climax.
1:11 *chosen ... predestined.* For near synonyms, see note on v. 8. *chosen.* See note on vv. 4–5. For the alternate "made heirs" in the NIV text note, see note on v. 14. *plan ... purpose.* For repetition of near-synonyms, see note on v. 8.
1:12 *his glory.* See note on v. 6.
1:13 *message of truth.* This phrase appears in the Greek translation of Ps 119:43, where it refers to God's word (there the law, but here the gospel). In Isa 52:7, the gospel ("good news") is about salvation (as here), peace (as in Eph 6:15), and God's reign, i.e., kingdom (Mk 1:14–15). *seal.* A seal authenticated something (see note on 2Co 1:22). *promised Holy Spirit.* The Holy Spirit was promised by the prophets (e.g., Eze 36:27) and by John the Baptist (Mk 1:8).
1:14 *deposit guaranteeing our inheritance.* Because prophets had promised the Spirit (see note on v. 13) especially for the coming age, at the time of the restoration of God's people (e.g., Eze 39:29; Joel 2:28), the Spirit is here a deposit. *deposit guaranteeing.* Business documents used this Greek term to designate a down payment or first installment. Building on OT promises (e.g., Isa 65:9; Jer 31:11; Mic 4:10), Jewish interpreters spoke of God's people "inheriting" the world to come and they looked for God to redeem them from oppression. *his glory.* Writers

EPHESUS IN THE TIME OF PAUL

The Roman province of Asia with its many splendid cities was one of the jewels on a belt of Roman lands encircling the Mediterranean.

Located on the most direct sea and land route to the eastern provinces of the empire, Ephesus was an emporium that had few equals anywhere in the world. Certainly no city in Asia was more famous or more populous. It ranked with Rome, Corinth, Antioch and Alexandria among the foremost urban centers of the empire.

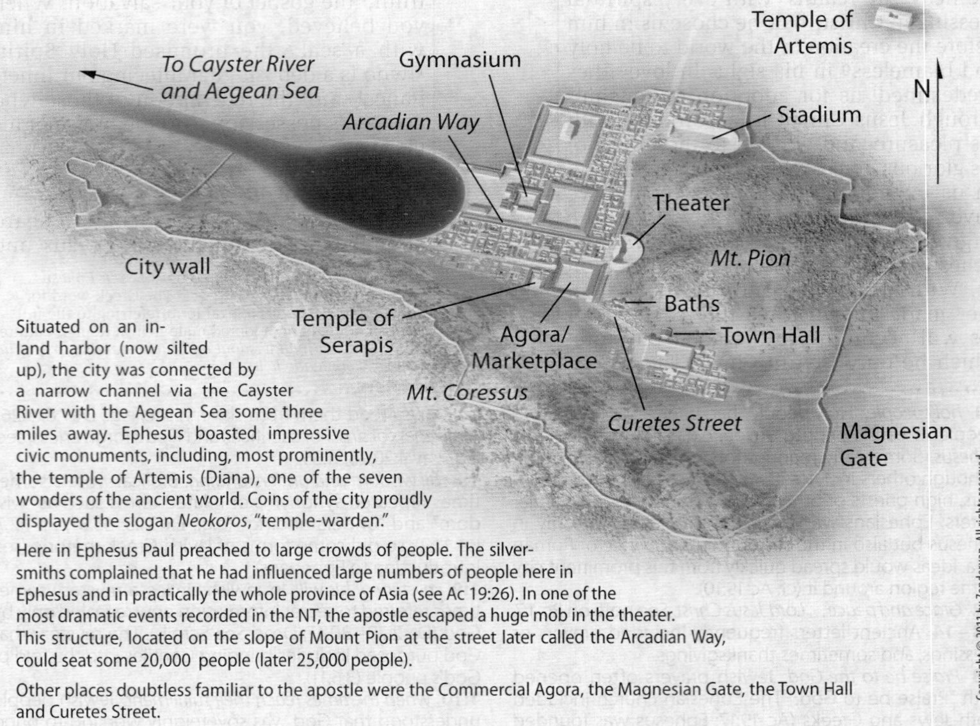

Situated on an inland harbor (now silted up), the city was connected by a narrow channel via the Cayster River with the Aegean Sea some three miles away. Ephesus boasted impressive civic monuments, including, most prominently, the temple of Artemis (Diana), one of the seven wonders of the ancient world. Coins of the city proudly displayed the slogan *Neokoros*, "temple-warden."

Here in Ephesus Paul preached to large crowds of people. The silversmiths complained that he had influenced large numbers of people here in Ephesus and in practically the whole province of Asia (see Ac 19:26). In one of the most dramatic events recorded in the NT, the apostle escaped a huge mob in the theater. This structure, located on the slope of Mount Pion at the street later called the Arcadian Way, could seat some 20,000 people (later 25,000 people).

Other places doubtless familiar to the apostle were the Commercial Agora, the Magnesian Gate, the Town Hall and Curetes Street.

your love for all God's people,[u] 16I have
not stopped giving thanks for you,[v] remembering you in my prayers. 17I keep
asking that the God of our Lord Jesus
Christ, the glorious Father,[w] may give you
the Spirit[a] of wisdom[x] and revelation, so
that you may know him better. 18I pray
that the eyes of your heart may be enlightened[y] in order that you may know the
hope to which he has called you, the riches of his glorious inheritance in his holy
people, 19and his incomparably great power for us who believe. That power[z] is the
same as the mighty strength[a] 20he exerted when he raised Christ from the dead[b]

1:15 [u] Col 1:4 **1:16** [v] Ro 1:8 **1:17** [w] Jn 20:17 [x] Col 1:9 **1:18** [y] Ac 26:18; 2Co 4:6 **1:19** [z] Col 1:29 [a] Eph 6:10 **1:20** [b] Ac 2:24

[a] 17 Or *a spirit*

sometimes reinforced a point by repeating it (cf. vv. 6,12; see note on v. 6).
1:16 *giving thanks for you, remembering you in my prayers.* Letter writers sometimes thanked a deity for the welfare of the letter recipients. They often offered a blessing or prayer for the recipients.
1:17 *Spirit of wisdom.* Following the OT (Ex 31:3; Dt 34:9; Isa 11:2), Jewish writers sometimes emphasized God's Spirit as the Spirit of wisdom.
1:18 *eyes of your heart may be enlightened.* Writers often used vision figuratively for insight. Following OT precedent (Ps 19:8; 119:18), Jewish people sometimes prayed for God to enlighten their eyes to help them understand God's word. *inheritance.* See note on v. 14. *holy people.* See note on v. 1. Just as writers often introduced themes in their introductions, Paul goes on to expound the subjects that, in vv. 18–19, he prays for them to understand.
1:19 *great power ... mighty strength.* The piling up of closely related words (such as "power," "might" and "strength" as in, e.g., 1Ch 29:12; Isa 40:26) fits Jewish praise and also the sort of flowery rhetoric valued for praise in Asia Minor.
1:20 *raised Christ from the dead.* Jewish prayers often celebrated God's power to someday raise the dead. *seated*

and seated him at his right hand in the
heavenly realms, 21 far above all rule and
authority, power and dominion, and every name[c] that is invoked, not only in the
present age but also in the one to come.
22 And God placed all things under his feet[d]
and appointed him to be head[e] over everything for the church, 23 which is his body,
the fullness of him who fills everything in
every way.

Made Alive in Christ

2 As for you, you were dead in your
transgressions and sins,[f] 2 in which
you used to live[g] when you followed the
ways of this world and of the ruler of the
kingdom of the air,[h] the spirit who is now
at work in those who are disobedient.[i] 3 All
of us also lived among them at one time,
gratifying the cravings of our flesh[a][j] and
following its desires and thoughts. Like
the rest, we were by nature deserving of
wrath. 4 But because of his great love for
us, God, who is rich in mercy, 5 made us
alive with Christ even when we were dead
in transgressions[k]—it is by grace you have
been saved.[l] 6 And God raised us up with
Christ and seated us with him[m] in the
heavenly realms[n] in Christ Jesus, 7 in order that in the coming ages he might show
the incomparable riches of his grace, expressed in his kindness[o] to us in Christ
Jesus. 8 For it is by grace you have been
saved,[p] through faith—and this is not
from yourselves, it is the gift of God—
9 not by works,[q] so that no one can boast.[r]
10 For we are God's handiwork, created[s] in
Christ Jesus to do good works,[t] which God
prepared in advance for us to do.

Jew and Gentile Reconciled Through Christ

11 Therefore, remember that formerly
you who are Gentiles by birth and called
"uncircumcised" by those who call themselves "the circumcision" (which is done
in the body by human hands)[u]— 12 remember that at that time you were separate from Christ, excluded from citizenship

1:21 [c] Php 2:9, 10 **1:22** [d] Mt 28:18 [e] Eph 4:15; 5:23 **2:1** [f] ver 5; Col 2:13 **2:2** [g] Col 3:7 [h] Jn 12:31; Eph 6:12 [i] Eph 5:6 **2:3** [j] Gal 5:16 **2:5** [k] ver 1 [l] ver 8; Ac 15:11 **2:6** [m] Eph 1:20 [n] Eph 1:3 **2:7** [o] Titus 3:4 **2:8** [p] ver 5 **2:9** [q] 2Ti 1:9 [r] 1Co 1:29 **2:10** [s] Eph 4:24 [t] Titus 2:14 **2:11** [u] Col 2:11

[a] 3 In contexts like this, the Greek word for *flesh* (*sarx*) refers to the sinful state of human beings, often presented as a power in opposition to the Spirit.

---

him at his right hand. In Ps 110:1 God enthroned the Lord at his right hand until subjugating his enemies beneath his feet. Just as Jesus' resurrection was itself the first installment of a promised future event, so also the ultimate subjugation of all things is already evident in Jesus' present reign (vv. 21–22).

1:21 *all rule and authority, power and dominion.* Jewish people believed that not only human powers but also the angelic ones that worked behind them ruled the nations (see Da 10:13,20); sometimes these guardian angels of the Gentile nations were hostile to God's people. These spiritual rulers, not earthly ones, are the true enemies (6:12; see notes on 1:19–20). *every name that is invoked.* Magicians tried to manipulate powerful spirits by invoking their names, including in Ephesus (see note on Ac 19:13); the supremacy of Jesus' name above all other names shows that he is higher than all the spirit-powers being invoked and cannot be exploited.

1:22 *all things under his feet.* Echoes Ps 8:6; 110:1 (see notes on Eph 1:19–20); Paul, like other Jewish interpreters, often linked passages with similar wording (see note on 1Co 15:27).

1:23 *which is his body.* Ancient philosophers sometimes used the body metaphor (see note on Ro 12:4–5) together with that of the head (as here; v. 22) and sometimes without it. Fitting the image of enthronement (v. 20), if all things are under Jesus' feet (cf. v. 22), they are also under his body here. *fullness … fills everything in every way.* Flowery rhetoric (see Introduction to Ephesians) appreciated repetition such as this (Paul also alliterates in Greek, repeating words beginning with *p*- four times). *fullness.* May mean "what is filled by him."

2:1 *dead in your … sins.* Everyone would understand the image (also in Lk 15:24); some other ancient sources speak of figurative or spiritual death, or being under the sentence of death.

2:2 *ruler of the kingdom of the air.* The air was considered the lowest of the heavens, inhabited by spirits (see 1:20–21). *spirit who is now at work in those who are disobedient.* Jewish people recognized Satan as the ruler of the evil spirits, and many considered demonic influence pervasive, especially among peoples other than themselves. Some very strict Jewish thinkers (whose views appear in the Dead Sea Scrolls) believed that all actions were controlled either by God's spirit or the spirit of error. Paul may envision more indirect influence through the values of the world appealing to biochemical desires.

2:4 *because of his great love for us.* Although God revealed his love in a fuller way in Christ, God's lavish love for his people begins to be evident already in the OT (e.g., Dt 7:6–9).

2:6 *seated us with him in the heavenly realms.* Many Jewish thinkers recognized that the righteous would reign in the coming world (Da 7:22,27; Rev 3:21; 5:10). Here, however, believers have already begun to experience this victory. Specifically, they are enthroned with Christ above spiritual powers (1:20–23), hence are no longer bound by evil compelling them to sin (vv. 1–3). Many people feared spirits as well as the power of Fate through the stars; those exalted with Christ need not fear such powers.

2:8–9 *by grace you have been saved … not by works.* Already in the OT, God did not choose his people because they were righteous (Dt 9:5–6). He redeemed them before instructing them how to live (Ex 20:2); sincere righteousness flows from a transformed heart (Dt 5:29; 30:6,14). Although God's salvation in Christ is greater than this, it clearly reflects the heart of the same God who lavished love on his people from the beginning.

2:11 *uncircumcised.* Though traditionally a negative way to designate many kinds of Gentiles (e.g., Jdg 14:3), sometimes Israel was deemed spiritually uncircumcised (Lev 26:40–42; Jer 9:26). Outward circumcision, a sign of the covenant between God and his people, was meant to point to the more important circumcision of the heart (Dt 10:16; 30:6; Jer 4:4). *by human hands.* Paul's phrase heightens the implicit contrast between physical circumcision and circumcision of the heart; the Greek translation of the OT uses this phrase negatively, especially for idols (e.g., Lev 26:1).

2:12 *excluded from citizenship in Israel.* Although some Gentiles had joined God's people in the OT (e.g.,

in Israel and foreigners to the covenants
of the promise,[v] without hope[w] and without God in the world. 13 But now in Christ
Jesus you who once were far away have
been brought near[x] by the blood of Christ.[y]
14 For he himself is our peace, who has
made the two groups one[z] and has destroyed the barrier, the dividing wall of
hostility, 15 by setting aside in his flesh[a] the
law with its commands and regulations.[b]
His purpose was to create in himself one[c]
new humanity out of the two, thus making peace, 16 and in one body to reconcile
both of them to God through the cross,[d]
by which he put to death their hostility.
17 He came and preached peace to you who
were far away and peace to those who
were near.[e] 18 For through him we both
have access[f] to the Father[g] by one Spirit.[h]
19 Consequently, you are no longer foreigners and strangers,[i] but fellow citizens[j]
with God's people and also members of
his household,[k] 20 built on the foundation[l]
of the apostles and prophets, with Christ
Jesus himself as the chief cornerstone.[m]
21 In him the whole building is joined together and rises to become a holy temple[n]
in the Lord. 22 And in him you too are being built together to become a dwelling in
which God lives by his Spirit.

God's Marvelous Plan for the Gentiles

3 For this reason I, Paul, the prisoner[o] of
Christ Jesus for the sake of you Gentiles—
2 Surely you have heard about the administration of God's grace that was given
to me[p] for you, 3 that is, the mystery[q] made

2:12 [v] Gal 3:17 [w] 1Th 4:13 **2:13** [x] ver 17; Ac 2:39 [y] Col 1:20 **2:14** [z] 1Co 12:13 **2:15** [a] Col 1:21, 22 [b] Col 2:14 [c] Gal 3:28 **2:16** [d] Col 1:20, 22 **2:17** [e] Ps 148:14; Isa 57:19 **2:18** [f] Eph 3:12 [g] Col 1:12 [h] 1Co 12:13 **2:19** [i] ver 12 [j] Php 3:20 [k] Gal 6:10 **2:20** [l] Mt 16:18; Rev 21:14 [m] 1Pe 2:4-8 **2:21** [n] 1Co 3:16, 17 **3:1** [o] Ac 23:18; Eph 4:1 **3:2** [p] Col 1:25 **3:3** [q] Ro 16:25

Ru 1:16; 2Sa 6:10–11; 8:18; 15:18–22; 18:2; 20:23; 24:18–24; 1Ch 11:41,46), they were exceptions. Many more proselytes (who became Jewish and agreed to keep Israel's laws) had joined Israel by this period; males were circumcised when they converted. In the first generation, proselytes were often treated as of lower status than born Israelites. Most other Gentiles remained outside God's covenant, even if they attended synagogue and were considered destined for eternal life; most Jewish people would not consider them as on the same level as full Jews. In Christ, Israel's ultimate king, however, even Gentile followers became full members of God's people and covenant (vv. 13–14).

2:13–14 *you ... were far away ... peace.* "Peace" (v. 14) to those "far away" (v. 13) evokes Isa 57:19 (see note on Eph 2:17).

2:14 *peace.* Cf. Mic 5:5; see previous note. Peace required more than mild feelings. Paul wrote at a time of tension; perhaps as early as half a decade after this letter, Jews and Syrians began massacring each other in Judea and Syria. *dividing wall of hostility.* Although the OT welcomed Gentiles into the temple along with Jews (1Ki 8:41–43), more recent interpretations of purity laws resulted in Gentiles being excluded from the court of Israel (for Jewish men) and even the less pure court of women (for Jewish women). Christians in and around Ephesus would know that Paul was in Roman custody because he had been accused of bringing an Ephesian Gentile beyond the temple's outer court (Ac 21:27–29). Before speaking of one new temple that includes both Jews and Gentiles (vv. 21–22), Paul emphasizes the very dividing wall for which he is now a prisoner (3:1).

2:15 *the law with its commands and regulations.* Interpretations of Biblical purity laws had led to Herod's temple segregating Gentiles from Jews (see note on v. 14). Although the law's principles teach moral truth, its many Israel-specific rules could not be observed by Gentiles. *one new humanity.* See note on 4:24.

2:16 *one body ... through the cross.* Romans executed people naked, by slow torture, on a cross; it epitomized shameful death. Their old humanity (see note on v. 15), with its divisions, died in Jesus' body on the cross; for Jesus' restored body and its implications, see note on 4:4.

2:17 *peace to you who were far away and peace to those who were near.* Paul alludes to Isa 57:19, a promise of restoration for God's people: "Peace, peace, to those far and near." In a typical ancient Jewish interpretive manner, Paul applies one "peace" to those who are "far" and the other to those who are "near." He applies "far" to Gentiles (cf. vv. 13–14). Although one could apply Isa 57:19 to the Jewish Diaspora, Paul knows that not long in Isaiah before this passage God promised that his house would be for foreigners too (Isa 56:3–8). God had planned to save many Gentiles (see Ro 16:25–26 and notes).

2:18 *access to the Father by one Spirit.* God had promised to empower his own people with the Spirit at the time of restoration (Isa 59:21; Eze 36:26–27; 37:14; 39:29; Joel 2:29). For access in the temple, cf. perhaps note on Mk 15:38.

2:19 *fellow citizens with God's people.* In many cities, foreigners who settled could remain "resident aliens" for generations, lacking voting rights and other privileges that belonged to citizens. *members of his household.* Paul can play on the different senses of "house" in Greek: both "household" (as here) and a building (the temple as God's house; see vv. 20–22).

2:20 *chief cornerstone.* Paul follows Jesus' application of Ps 118:22 to Christ himself as the cornerstone or capstone (see notes on Mt 21:44; Lk 20:17).

2:22 *you too are being built together to become a dwelling in which God lives.* Although the OT temple divided only priests from laity, the designers of Herod's temple, standing in Paul's day, had further excluded women and especially Gentiles from the purer court of Jewish men. This new temple would be different. *by his Spirit.* Since God has marked even Gentile followers of Israel's Messiah with the Spirit (see v. 18 and note), they were equally part of God's true, spiritual temple. Some other Jewish writers spoke of God's people as his sacred temple, but they would find revolting this image including Gentiles.

3:1 *Paul, the prisoner of Christ Jesus.* Communicators sometimes emotionally appealed to audience sympathy. Being a Roman prisoner was normally a mark of shame but, like wounds (see note on Gal 6:17), could arouse sympathy or support among loved ones. *for the sake of you Gentiles.* Paul's refusal to compromise the mission to the Gentiles had precipitated his captivity (Ac 22:21–22; cf. Ac 21:28; see note on Eph 2:14).

3:2 Ancient writers often digressed, and sometimes marked the digression. Paul digresses in vv. 2–13, returning only in v. 14 to the point he started in v. 1 (note "For this reason" in both). *administration.* The Greek term was used for management, e.g., of a household (cf. 2:19; see note on 1Co 4:1).

3:3 *mystery made known to me by revelation.* In Daniel (Da 2:18–19,27–30,47) and the Dead Sea Scrolls, "mystery"

known to me by revelation,[r] as I have already written briefly. [4]In reading this, then, you will be able to understand my insight[s] into the mystery of Christ, [5]which was not made known to people in other generations as it has now been revealed by the Spirit to God's holy apostles and prophets.[t] [6]This mystery is that through the gospel the Gentiles are heirs[u] together with Israel, members together of one body,[v] and sharers together in the promise in Christ Jesus.

[7]I became a servant of this gospel[w] by the gift of God's grace given me through the working of his power.[x] [8]Although I am less than the least of all the Lord's people,[y] this grace was given me: to preach to the Gentiles the boundless riches of Christ, [9]and to make plain to everyone the administration of this mystery,[z] which for ages past was kept hidden in God, who created all things. [10]His intent was that now, through the church, the manifold wisdom of God[a] should be made known[b] to the rulers and authorities[c] in the heavenly realms, [11]according to his eternal purpose that he accomplished in Christ Jesus our Lord. [12]In him and through faith in him we may approach God[d] with freedom and confidence.[e] [13]I ask you, therefore, not to be discouraged because of my sufferings for you, which are your glory.

3:3 [r] 1Co 2:10
3:4 [s] 2Co 11:6
3:5 [t] Ro 16:26
3:6 [u] Gal 3:29 [v] Eph 2:15,16
3:7 [w] 1Co 3:5 [x] Eph 1:19
3:8 [y] 1Co 15:9
3:9 [z] Ro 16:25
3:10 [a] 1Co 2:7 [b] 1Pe 1:12 [c] Eph 1:21
3:12 [d] Eph 2:18 [e] Heb 4:16
3:14 [f] Php 2:10
3:16 [g] Col 1:11 [h] Ro 7:22
3:17 [i] Jn 14:23 [j] Col 1:23
3:18 [k] Job 11:8,9
3:19 [l] Col 2:10 [m] Eph 1:23
3:20 [n] Ro 16:25

A Prayer for the Ephesians

[14]For this reason I kneel[f] before the Father, [15]from whom every family[a] in heaven and on earth derives its name. [16]I pray that out of his glorious riches he may strengthen you with power[g] through his Spirit in your inner being,[h] [17]so that Christ may dwell in your hearts[i] through faith. And I pray that you, being rooted[j] and established in love, [18]may have power, together with all the Lord's holy people, to grasp how wide and long and high and deep[k] is the love of Christ, [19]and to know this love that surpasses knowledge—that you may be filled[l] to the measure of all the fullness of God.[m]

[20]Now to him who is able[n] to do immeasurably more than all we ask or imagine, according to his power that is at work

[a] *15* The Greek for *family* (*patria*) is derived from the Greek for *father* (*pater*).

was often used for previously secret information about God's purposes in history that God now revealed.
3:5 *now been revealed by the Spirit to God's holy apostles and prophets.* Many Jewish people, especially the Jewish elite, believed that prophets no longer existed in the OT sense; Paul's claims of current revelation, however, fit the experience of the outpoured Spirit (Ac 2:17–18).
3:6 *through the gospel the Gentiles are heirs together with Israel ... sharers together in the promise.* Gentiles joining God's people appears already in the prophets (e.g., Isa 19:25; Zec 2:11; see Ro 16:25,26 and notes), though Jewish interpreters held a range of views about the Gentiles based on various Biblical passages. (For example, the prophets also expected unrighteous Gentiles to be destroyed.) *heirs ... promise.* Both the inheritance (see notes on 1:14; Gal 3:18,29) and the "promise" (see Gal 3:7,14 and notes) belonged to God's people. *members together of one body.* See 4:4; see also note on Ro 12:4–5.
3:7 *through the working of his power.* God had long empowered his servants for various tasks (e.g., Ex 35:31; Jdg 3:10; 6:34).
3:9 *administration.* See note on v. 2. *mystery.* See note on v. 3.
3:10 *wisdom of God ... made known to the rulers and authorities in the heavenly realms.* Some pre-Christian Jewish texts also speak of God showing the angels his power and glory through his people, and thus God receiving the angels' praise. Insofar as these angelic powers were rulers of the nations (see note on 1:21; see also Da 10:13,20), the church's ethnic unity (cf. vv. 1–8) reveals God's wisdom.
3:12 *freedom.* Means "freedom to enter," presumably because of access into God's house (cf. 2:18, using the same Greek term). *confidence.* Often means "boldness" (e.g., to speak truth; the Greek term recurs in 6:19).
3:13 *my sufferings for you.* See note on v. 1. Roman detention was normally a matter of shame; Paul considers it a matter of honor in view of the reason he is detained. *for ... your glory.* Athletes, soldiers or warriors acted representatively on behalf of their people.
3:14 *I kneel before the Father.* People more often stood for prayer than knelt, but kneeling or prostration (e.g., 1Ki 8:14,22,54) were considered appropriate, especially in extreme circumstances. (Gentiles prostrated themselves before rulers.) Those who knelt in prayer usually stretched out their arms with hands facing the deities being invoked (in heaven, toward statues, etc.).
3:15 *from whom every family in heaven and on earth.* Although Jewish people regularly prayed to God as Father (v. 14) of his people, they also sometimes portrayed him, as Gentiles also sometimes did (cf. Ac 17:28), as Father of all creation. *family.* The Greek term is *patria*, which is derived from *pater*, Father, allowing a play on words in vv. 14–15. The Greek translation of the OT often uses *patria* for a family line descended from a common progenitor. God is thus the originator of all, a notion that further challenges ethnic divisions (vv. 1–13). "Every family in heaven" could imply the same if it signifies or includes guardian angels of the nations (see note on 1:21).
3:16 *in your inner being.* Many Greek thinkers (followed by some Greek-speaking Jews) emphasized the inner being; Paul may use it as equivalent to "heart" (a more common Biblical expression).
3:18 *may have power.* Scripture already associated the Spirit with power (Mic 3:8; Zec 4:6) and moral transformation (Eze 36:27). *how wide and long and high and deep is the love of Christ.* Paul indicates the immeasurable vastness of something, possibly (with the NIV) Christ's love (more explicit in the Greek text of v. 19; cf. also v. 17; Ps 103:11). Whether applied to love or to wisdom, recounting these dimensions could evoke descriptions of God's immeasurable wisdom (e.g., Job 11:5–9), since Paul has just spoken of "manifold wisdom" (v. 10, possibly meaning "many sided"). Others see a comparison (whether of love or of wisdom) with the expanse of creation (cf. Ro 8:39, where God's love transcends it). Much less likely, some find continuing temple imagery (cf. 1Ki 6:20; cf. the new Jerusalem in Rev 21:16).

within us, 21to him be glory in the church
and in Christ Jesus throughout all generations, for ever and ever! Amen.[o]

Unity and Maturity in the Body of Christ

4 As a prisoner[p] for the Lord, then, I
urge you to live a life worthy[q] of the
calling you have received. 2Be completely humble and gentle; be patient, bearing
with one another[r] in love.[s] 3Make every effort to keep the unity[t] of the Spirit through
the bond of peace. 4There is one body and
one Spirit,[u] just as you were called to one
hope when you were called; 5one Lord,
one faith, one baptism; 6one God and Father of all, who is over all and through all
and in all.[v]

7But to each one of us[w] grace has been
given[x] as Christ apportioned it. 8This is
why it[a] says:

> "When he ascended on high,
> he took many captives[y]
> and gave gifts to his people."[b][z]

9(What does "he ascended" mean except
that he also descended to the lower, earthly regions[c]? 10He who descended is the
very one who ascended higher than all
the heavens, in order to fill the whole universe.) 11So Christ himself gave the apostles,[a] the prophets, the evangelists,[b] the
pastors and teachers, 12to equip his people
for works of service, so that the body of
Christ[c] may be built up 13until we all reach
unity[d] in the faith and in the knowledge
of the Son of God and become mature,[e]
attaining to the whole measure of the fullness of Christ.

14Then we will no longer be infants,[f]
tossed back and forth by the waves,[g] and
blown here and there by every wind of
teaching and by the cunning and craftiness of people in their deceitful scheming.[h] 15Instead, speaking the truth in love,
we will grow to become in every respect
the mature body of him who is the head,[i]
that is, Christ. 16From him the whole body,
joined and held together by every supporting ligament, grows[j] and builds itself up in
love, as each part does its work.

Instructions for Christian Living

17So I tell you this, and insist on it in
the Lord, that you must no longer live
as the Gentiles do, in the futility of their
thinking.[k] 18They are darkened in their

3:21 [o] Ro 11:36
4:1 [p] Eph 3:1 [q] Php 1:27; Col 1:10
4:2 [r] Col 3:12, 13 [s] Eph 1:4
4:3 [t] Col 3:14
4:4 [u] 1Co 12:13
4:6 [v] Ro 11:36
4:7 [w] 1Co 12:7, 11 [x] Ro 12:3
4:8 [y] Col 2:15 [z] Ps 68:18
4:11 [a] 1Co 12:28 [b] Ac 21:8
4:12 [c] 1Co 12:27
4:13 [d] ver 3, 5 [e] Col 1:28
4:14 [f] 1Co 14:20 [g] Jas 1:6 [h] Eph 6:11
4:15 [i] Eph 1:22
4:16 [j] Col 2:19
4:17 [k] Ro 1:21

[a] 8 Or *God* [b] 8 Psalm 68:18 [c] 9 Or *the depths of the earth*

3:21 *to him be glory ... for ever and ever!* Jewish prayers often concluded with praise, sometimes ending with "for ever and ever" (cf. 1Ch 16:36; Ps 106:48). *Amen.* Those who prayed or heard prayers frequently concluded in this way (cf. 1Co 14:16).
4:1 *As a prisoner for the Lord.* See note on 3:1. *I urge you.* Much of Paul's letter so far has focused on praise, but now he begins exhorting, a common subject of ancient speeches and intellectual writing.
4:3 *unity.* Especially in the form of harmony, unity was a common subject of ancient exhortation (also in v. 13). *the bond of peace.* Some Jewish sages highly praised peace.
4:4–6 Speakers used repetition to drive home a point; Paul repeats various forms of the Greek term translated "one" seven times in vv. 4–6, and four uses of "all" (three after varied prepositions) in v. 6.
4:4 *one body.* See note on Ro 12:4–5; many used this image for a group, but often in a more hierarchical way than does Paul.
4:8 *it says.* Because Scripture is God's Word, Jewish people often personified it as speaking. Ancient interpreters often paraphrased texts to better suit their point; a later Aramaic paraphrase of Ps 68:18 even adapts it in a manner very similar to Paul's adaptation here. *he ascended on high.* Interpreters applied Ps 68 to God ascending at Mount Sinai; Paul makes an analogy with Jesus' exaltation (on which see notes on 1:20–22). Paul's change of the psalm's wording nevertheless fits its implications: once a conqueror had received tribute and plunder from the defeated (as in Ps 68:18), he distributed most of these spoils to his soldiers (as here). Now exalted, the triumphant Jesus distributes gifts (listed in v. 11) to his people.
4:9 *"he ascended" ... he also descended.* Jewish interpreters analyzed texts (here Ps 68:18) and raised questions; since Jesus came from God (Ro 8:3; 1Co 15:47), he could ascend only because he had first descended. *lower, earthly regions.* Could mean the place of the dead (Ps 63:9; 86:13) or refer to Jesus' incarnation on earth (Ps 139:15; Php 2:7).
4:10 *ascended higher than all the heavens.* God's own throne was "on high" (Ps 7:7; 102:19); in v. 8 Paul applies "on high" in Ps 68:18 to Christ's ascent higher than all the heavens (see 1:20–22).
4:11 Ancient lists were sometimes representative rather than comprehensive, and some elements could overlap. (The Greek grammar links "pastors" and "teachers," probably as dual responsibilities of the same people.) *apostles.* Commissioned messengers or agents; perhaps the closest OT equivalents were the prophetic judges, such as Moses, Deborah and Samuel, and leaders of prophetic or Biblical awakenings, such as Elijah and Elisha. *prophets.* Share messages from God through the Spirit, usually not based exclusively on interpreting Biblical texts (cf. e.g., Ac 11:27–28), in contrast to a primary ministry of teachers. They were apparently quite common in the churches (1Co 14:1, 29, 31, 39), although some may have assumed the role of senior prophets (cf. 1Sa 19:20; Ac 13:1–2; 21:10–11; 1Co 14:37). Although their messages were probably often spontaneous (1Co 14:30), they could also be received before being delivered (2Ch 21:12; Jer 28:12–13; 29:1; 36:4–6; Rev 1:11). *evangelists.* Herald the good news of salvation (e.g., Isa 52:7). *pastors.* Lit. "shepherds," a familiar ancient image of leadership (e.g., Jer 23:4). *teachers.* Presumably expound Scripture (at this time, mostly the OT) and accounts of Jesus. Such proclamatory leaders equip all the church for ministry (vv. 12–13).
4:12 *body.* See also v. 4 (see note on Ro 12:4–5).
4:14 *infants.* Ancient thinkers sometimes contrasted novices (here described as "infants") with the mature (vv. 13,15), those who are wise (see note on 1Co 3:1). *tossed back and forth by the waves.* Others also used seafarers in storms as illustrations.
4:17 *you must no longer live as the Gentiles do.* Having

understanding[l] and separated from the
life of God[m] because of the ignorance that
is in them due to the hardening of their
hearts.[n] 19 Having lost all sensitivity,[o] they
have given themselves over[p] to sensuality[q]
so as to indulge in every kind of impurity,
and they are full of greed.
20 That, however, is not the way of life
you learned 21 when you heard about
Christ and were taught in him in accordance with the truth that is in Jesus. 22 You
were taught, with regard to your former
way of life, to put off[r] your old self,[s] which
is being corrupted by its deceitful desires;
23 to be made new in the attitude of your
minds;[t] 24 and to put on the new self,[u] created to be like God in true righteousness
and holiness.[v]
25 Therefore each of you must put off
falsehood and speak truthfully[w] to your
neighbor, for we are all members of one
body.[x] 26 "In your anger do not sin"[a]: Do
not let the sun go down while you are
still angry, 27 and do not give the devil a
foothold. 28 Anyone who has been stealing must steal no longer, but must work,[y]
doing something useful with their own
hands,[z] that they may have something to
share with those in need.[a]
29 Do not let any unwholesome talk
come out of your mouths,[b] but only what
is helpful for building others up according to their needs, that it may benefit
those who listen. 30 And do not grieve the
Holy Spirit of God,[c] with whom you were
sealed for the day of redemption.[d] 31 Get
rid of all bitterness, rage and anger, brawl-
ing and slander, along with every form of
malice.[e] 32 Be kind and compassionate to
one another, forgiving each other, just as
5 in Christ God forgave you.[f] 1 Follow
God's example,[g] therefore, as dearly
loved children 2 and walk in the way of
love, just as Christ loved us and gave himself up for us[h] as a fragrant offering and
sacrifice to God.[i]
3 But among you there must not be even
a hint of sexual immorality, or of any kind
of impurity, or of greed,[j] because these
are improper for God's holy people. 4 Nor
should there be obscenity, foolish talk or
coarse joking, which are out of place, but

4:18 [l] Ro 1:21 [m] Eph 2:12 [n] 2Co 3:14 **4:19** [o] 1Ti 4:2 [p] Ro 1:24 [q] Col 3:5 **4:22** [r] 1Pe 2:1 [s] Ro 6:6 **4:23** [t] Col 3:10 **4:24** [u] Ro 6:4 [v] Eph 2:10 **4:25** [w] Zec 8:16 [x] Ro 12:5 **4:28** [y] Ac 20:35 [z] 1Th 4:11 [a] Lk 3:11 **4:29** [b] Col 3:8 **4:30** [c] 1Th 5:19 [d] Ro 8:23 **4:31** [e] Col 3:8 **4:32** [f] Mt 6:14, 15 **5:1** [g] Lk 6:36 **5:2** [h] Gal 1:4 [i] 2Co 2:15; Heb 7:27 **5:3** [j] Col 3:5

[a] *26* Psalm 4:4 (see Septuagint)

established that Gentiles in his audience have been admitted to the people of God (2:11–22), Paul summons them to abandon the Gentile lifestyle. Most Jews regarded most Gentiles as worshipers of false deities and (in practice most relevant for males) sexually promiscuous. Converts to Judaism adopted a new lifestyle based on the law (here adapted by the gospel; vv. 20–21). For earlier warnings against God's people acting like Gentiles, see Lev 18:3,24–30; 20:23–24.

4:22–24 *put off your old self ... put on the new self.* Jewish writers could speak of being "clothed" with the Spirit (e.g., three times in the Septuagint, the pre-Christian Greek translation of the OT) or virtues (cf. Job 29:14; Isa 61:3,10; vice in Ps 109:18). *old self ... new self.* Lit. "old person" and "new person."

4:22 *corrupted by its deceitful desires.* Possibly evokes the fall of Adam and Eve (cf. 2Co 11:3).

4:23 *made new in ... your minds.* See note on Ro 12:2.

4:24 *created.* Probably evokes Adam and Eve's creation (see notes on Col 3:9–10), hence new creation in the new Adam.

4:25–31 In contrast to vv. 17–19, which focuses on Gentile vices, Paul in these verses addresses human vices that even Jewish people committed. Both Jewish and Gentile moral teachers warned against these vices.

4:25 *speak truthfully to your neighbor.* Paul quotes fairly closely from the Greek translation of Zec 8:16, where God called his people to "speak the truth to each other."

4:26 *In your anger do not sin.* Paul quotes from the Greek translation of Ps 4:4 (see NIV text note there). *sun go down.* Ps 4:4 also speaks to those "on your beds." Some other ancient thinkers also demanded settling conflicts before sleep (cf. also Dt 24:13, 15).

4:27 *the devil.* Following the OT, Jewish tradition understood the devil (Satan, Belial) as deceiver, tempter and accuser.

4:28 *work ... with their own hands.* Although Jewish sages and probably artisans themselves respected manual labor, people of status generally despised it.

4:29 *only what is helpful for building others up.* Greek, Jewish, and Middle Eastern sages all emphasized wise, appropriate, truthful, and gracious speech (cf. v. 25; 5:3–4). Cf. also, e.g., Pr 10:31–32; 15:2,26,28; 16:24.

4:30 *grieve the Holy Spirit.* A serious offense; God judged Israel after "they rebelled and grieved his Holy Spirit" (Isa 63:10; Paul's wording here is closer to the Hebrew text than to the Greek version). *sealed for the day of redemption.* Implies divine attestation or certification (see note on 2Co 1:22), here needed for the day of judgment (cf. Isa 63:4). This connection may add urgency to Paul's warning not to grieve the Holy Spirit.

4:31 Ancient writers often produced lists of vices; sometimes, as here, they could cluster around a particular topic, underlining the basic point by repetition.

4:32—5:2 *as ... God ... God's example ... as Christ.* Both Jewish and Gentile writers urged imitating God (cf. also Lev 11:44–45; 19:2). *as in Christ God forgave you ... as Christ ... gave himself up for us as a ... sacrifice to God.* Only Christians proclaimed someone who, though divine, sacrificed himself for humanity.

5:2 *fragrant offering.* Scripture sometimes depicted sacrifices that God welcomed as a "pleasing aroma" to him (Ge 8:21; Lev 3:16); God could also describe his acceptance of his people with such language (Eze 20:41).

5:3 Ancient writers often included lists of vices (as, e.g., in Ro 1:29–31; 1Co 6:9–10; Gal 5:19–21; Rev 21:8). *sexual immorality.* On the prevalence of sexual immorality in male Greek culture, see the article "Prostitution and Sexual Immorality," p. 1990.

5:4 *obscenity, foolish talk or coarse joking.* Pornography covered many Greek vase paintings; outside walls of inns (such as one found in Pompeii) could include pictures of the prostitutes inside and the respective prices for their company. People joked about sexual matters, which were also prominent in general entertainment, particularly mimes and some comic novels.

rather thanksgiving.[k] 5For of this you can
be sure: No immoral, impure or greedy
person — such a person is an idolater[l] —
has any inheritance in the kingdom of
Christ and of God.[a m] 6Let no one deceive
you with empty words, for because of
such things God's wrath[n] comes on those
who are disobedient. 7Therefore do not be
partners with them.

8For you were once[o] darkness, but now
you are light in the Lord. Live as children
of light[p] 9(for the fruit[q] of the light consists in all goodness, righteousness and
truth) 10and find out what pleases the
Lord. 11Have nothing to do with the fruitless deeds of darkness, but rather expose

5:4 [k] ver 20 **5:5** [l] Col 3:5 [m] 1Co 6:9 **5:6** [n] Ro 1:18 **5:8** [o] Eph 2:2 [p] Lk 16:8 **5:9** [q] Gal 5:22

[a] 5 Or *kingdom of the Messiah and God*

5:5 *inheritance in the kingdom of Christ and of God.* Jewish people often spoke of "inheriting," or having a future share or place in, God's kingdom (cf., e.g., 1Co 6:9–10).
5:7 *do not be partners.* Some Jews (such as the authors of the Dead Sea Scrolls) demanded total separation; food and other customs often separated other Jews from Gentiles in other respects. Paul does not demand such strict separation or purity rituals, but rather demands moral character (v. 9); their inability to participate in immoral humor or in their culture's pervasive civic religion would have raised criticisms against them. Many Gentiles criticized Jews as antisocial and Christians could face similar criticisms.
5:8 *children of light.* Hearers would likely comprehend this Semitic expression for people of the light. The strict Jewish authors of the Dead Sea Scrolls called their group the "children of light," regarding others as children of darkness (evil).
5:11 *fruitless deeds of darkness.* People who committed acts that they would be ashamed for others to know about often acted secretly, at night. Initiations into Greek mystery cults, some of which had acquired immoral rep-

EPHESIANS 5:21–33

Marriage Roles in Antiquity

Nearly every ancient Mediterranean society expected wives to submit to their husbands, although the particulars of what this looked like varied from one society to another. Elite men in ancient Athens considered the ideal wife obedient, meek and quiet, and someone who would stay at home and away from the gaze of other men. Conservative women were not supposed to speak with other women's husbands. Some Hellenistic marriage contracts stipulated complete obedience for the wife, even to the point of needing the husband's permission to visit her family. Some thinkers, such as Aristotle, attributed women's lower status to their natural inferiority of character.

Actual relationships often produce a love that transcends the narrower views that some people articulate. Nevertheless, many cultures today would view ancient Greek standards as problematic. Probably because female babies were abandoned more frequently, Greek men first married at a much later age than women. A 30-year-old man marrying an 18-year-old woman was a common practice; sometimes the woman could be so young as to have just entered puberty. Most Greek men had sexual experience with slaves, prostitutes, or other males by this point; non-Christian Greek marriage was designed not to constitute men's only acceptable sexual outlet but to bear them legitimate, respectable heirs. Husbands ruled the public sphere; wives normally ran the household.

Many Jewish teachers urged husbands to respect and value their wives; others opined that the only significant purposes of marriage were to protect men from temptation and to provide children. The Jewish sage Joshua ben Sirach suggested that the proper response to a disobedient wife was divorce. Some Jewish authors educated in Greek culture, such as Philo and Josephus, not only expected obedience and service from wives but expressed little respect for women overall. Josephus complains about their character and demeans men who heeded them.

Judean women had some public freedom of movement and respect that Greek women often lacked. Wives cared for household responsibilities such as nursing, mak-

continued on next page

them. 12It is shameful even to mention
what the disobedient do in secret. 13But
everything exposed by the light[r] becomes
visible — and everything that is illuminated becomes a light. 14This is why it is said:

"Wake up, sleeper,[s]
rise from the dead,[t]
and Christ will shine on you."[u]

15Be very careful, then, how you live —
not as unwise but as wise, 16making the
most of every opportunity,[v] because the
days are evil.[w] 17Therefore do not be foolish, but understand what the Lord's will
is.[x] 18Do not get drunk on wine,[y] which
leads to debauchery. Instead, be filled

5:13 [r] Jn 3:20, 21 5:14 [s] Ro 13:11 [t] Jn 5:25 [u] Isa 60:1 5:16 [v] Col 4:5 [w] Eph 6:13 5:17 [x] Ro 12:2; 1Th 4:3 5:18 [y] Pr 20:1

utations in Rome, were normally at night. Travelers who stayed at inns often had prostitutes available especially at night; so did some nocturnal banquets.

5:14 Paul cites lines familiar to his audience but foreign to us today. He may paraphrase Scripture the way Jewish Targums did (Isa 60:1 or perhaps Da 12:2). Others think that Paul cites an early Christian prophecy or song. Perhaps he cites a prophecy or song based on (and summarizing part of the message of) some Biblical texts.

5:18 *Do not get drunk on wine, which leads to debauchery.* Although Jewish wisdom despised drunkenness, it was a common feature of ancient Mediterranean life, especially in Gentile cities. It was common both in the late-night banquets of the rich, often accompanied by sexual immorality, and in the taverns of the poor. (Local taverns provided food and company during the day, but taverns for travelers were part of inns, and those barmaids were typically slaves who functioned as prostitutes at night.) People regularly associated drunkenness with loss of self-control, and occasionally also with a sort of inspiration, madness or possession by Dionysus, god of wine. (These latter cases could also include sexual promiscuity and violence.) *be filled with the Spirit.* God's Spirit provides inspiration for a different way of living (vv. 19 – 21).

ing clothes, washing, grinding grain, and preparing meals. Jewish teachers expected husbands to maintain the standard of living with which their wives had grown up. Judean custom, in contrast to Greek and Roman law, permitted a man to have multiple wives, but in this period the practice was very rare.

Wives had more freedom in some places, such as Macedonia and Rome, than in others, such as Ephesus, where Hellenistic culture dominated. Roman women had gained many new freedoms by the time Paul wrote. Freedoms also may have varied at times by social class; e.g., upper-class Roman women normally had to be treated respectfully. Lower-class families shared many deprivations together.

A minority of writers, such as Xenophon and Musonius Rufus, offered more positive, moderate views toward women and marriage. By ancient standards, Paul's treatment of marriage roles in Eph 5:21 – 33 is clearly among these more moderate approaches (see especially notes on Eph 5:21 – 22,25). ◆

Second-century relief of a married couple and their children, Bulgaria.

National Archaeological Museum, Sofia, Bulgaria/De Agostini Picture Library/A. Dagli Orti/Bridgeman Images

with the Spirit,[z] 19speaking to one another
with psalms, hymns, and songs from the
Spirit.[a] Sing and make music from your
heart to the Lord, 20always giving thanks[b]
to God the Father for everything, in the
name of our Lord Jesus Christ.

Instructions for Christian Households

5:22 – 6:9pp — Col 3:18 – 4:1

21Submit to one another[c] out of reverence for Christ.

22Wives, submit yourselves to your own
husbands[d] as you do to the Lord.[e] 23For
the husband is the head of the wife as
Christ is the head of the church,[f] his body,
of which he is the Savior. 24Now as the
church submits to Christ, so also wives
should submit to their husbands in everything.

25Husbands, love your wives,[g] just as
Christ loved the church and gave himself
up for her[h] 26to make her holy, cleansing[a]
her by the washing[i] with water through
the word, 27and to present her to himself as a radiant church, without stain or
wrinkle or any other blemish, but holy
and blameless.[j] 28In this same way, husbands ought to love their wives[k] as their
own bodies. He who loves his wife loves
himself. 29After all, no one ever hated their
own body, but they feed and care for their
body, just as Christ does the church —
30for we are members of his body.[l] 31"For
this reason a man will leave his father
and mother and be united to his wife, and
the two will become one flesh."[b][m] 32This
is a profound mystery — but I am talking

5:18 [z] Lk 1:15 **5:19** [a] Ac 16:25; Col 3:16 **5:20** [b] Ps 34:1 **5:21** [c] Gal 5:13 **5:22** [d] Ge 3:16; 1Pe 3:1,5,6 [e] Eph 6:5 **5:23** [f] 1Co 11:3; Eph 1:22 **5:25** [g] Col 3:19 [h] ver 2 **5:26** [i] Ac 22:16 **5:27** [j] Eph 1:4; Col 1:22 **5:28** [k] ver 25 **5:30** [l] 1Co 12:27 **5:31** [m] Ge 2:24; Mt 19:5; 1Co 6:16

[a] 26 Or *having cleansed* [b] 31 Gen. 2:24

5:19 – 21 In Greek, all Paul's instructions in vv. 19 – 21 (and thus, by implication, the exposition of v. 21 in 5:22 — 6:9) expound the command in v. 18 to "be filled with the Spirit."
5:19 *psalms, hymns, and songs from the Spirit.* People in antiquity understood that songs could be inspired (cf. v. 18), and this was also the case with the prophetically-inspired worship in the OT temple (1Ch 25:1 – 6) that generated many of the original psalms (2Ch 29:25,30). (Cf. the movement between prophecy and praise in, e.g., 2Sa 23:1 – 2; Ps 46:1,10; 91:2,14.) In Paul's churches this might sometimes include singing in tongues and interpretation (1Co 14:14 – 15). Other ancient worship often used hymns, but not normally spontaneously composed at the time, as may be the case for some worship here (cf. 1Co 14:15).
5:20 *giving thanks … for everything.* Some philosophers emphasized being thankful for everything because they submitted to Fate; some Jewish writers emphasized it because they trusted the personal God who guided events for his people's good.
5:21 — 6:9 Starting at least as early as the fourth-century BC Greek philosopher Aristotle, many thinkers used "household codes" to instruct the male heads of elite homes how to rule their household, specifically their wives, minor children and slaves. (This was the sequence in which Aristotle addressed them.) Male householders ruled these subordinates in different ways; boys, in particular, achieved a different status when they entered manhood.

Because of past incidents, Romans were suspicious that eastern cults (such as the cult of Dionysus, and more recently Judaism and the cult of Isis) undermined Roman family values. Some of these groups therefore emphasized that they did not undermine such values.

Paul, writing from Roman custody, is well aware of Roman suspicions. His instructions offer a lifestyle apologetic, upholding the best in traditional ancient values. At the same time, he adapts these codes. Whereas household codes normally instructed the male householder how to rule, Paul begins and ends with mutual submission (5:21; 6:9), calls for gentleness with children (6:4), and instructs husbands not how to rule their wives but how to love them sacrificially (5:25).
5:21 *Submit to one another.* Household codes instructed male heads of households how to rule wives, children and slaves; while continuing to uphold the call for subordinates to submit, Paul here goes beyond traditional expectations in calling for *mutual* submission (cf. general Christian servanthood to one another in Mk 10:42 – 45; Jn 13:14 – 15; Gal 5:13). This places Paul among the small proportion of ancient thinkers who valued mutual concern and sensitivity. Although Paul specifies only the husband's love (v. 25), he also values mutual love (4:32 — 5:2); in the same way, although specifying the wife's submission in v. 22, he grounds it grammatically in the mutual submission of v. 21.
5:22 — 6:8 Traditional household codes instructed male heads of households how to rule, but Paul also addresses wives (vv. 22 – 24), children (6:1 – 3) and slaves (6:5 – 8).
5:22 *Wives, submit yourselves to your own husbands.* Paul maintains the conventional expectation that wives should submit, but grounds it in more specifically Christian submission (in Greek, the verb "submit" is actually borrowed from v. 21). It should go without saying that this is a general principle not applicable to situations of abuse or participation in sin (cf. e.g., 1Sa 25:18 – 19; Ac 5:2).
5:25 *Husbands, love your wives, just as Christ.* Traditional household codes instructed male heads of households how to rule; Paul instructs husbands here only how to love self-sacrificially (vv. 25 – 31). Thus, although Paul upholds some values in his culture (see note on 5:21 — 6:9), he also goes beyond them (here; see note on v. 21).
5:26 *to make her holy … washing with water through the word.* Paul might cite ancient customs here. Some relate the "washing" to the bride's normal washing before being perfumed, anointed and arrayed in wedding clothes in preparation for the wedding. Perhaps relevant to "make her holy," later Jewish teachers spoke of betrothal as "the sanctification of the bride," meaning setting her apart for her husband.
5:27 *radiant church.* Some suggest that "radiant" might partly recall a similar idea in the description of God's bride in Eze 16:14 (though the Greek term is different).
5:28 *husbands ought to love their wives as their own bodies.* Whereas v. 23 invited the wife to view her husband as "head," perhaps in the sense of authority (v. 22; see note on 1Co 11:3,4), Paul defines headship for the husband in terms of loving and caring for his wife as he would for his own body.
5:30 *members of his body.* On being members of Jesus' body (also in 4:4), see note on Ro 12:4 – 5. Here, however, Paul also connects the image to Scripture (v. 31; cf. also 1Co 6:17).
5:31 *become one flesh.* Paul can speak of the wife in terms of the husband's body in vv. 28 – 30 because of "one flesh" in Ge 2:24, where the language entails a new family unit.

about Christ and the church. 33However, each one of you also must love his wife[n] as he loves himself, and the wife must respect her husband.

6 Children, obey your parents in the Lord, for this is right.[o] 2"Honor your father and mother"—which is the first commandment with a promise— 3"so that it may go well with you and that you may enjoy long life on the earth."[a][p]

4Fathers,[b] do not exasperate your children;[q] instead, bring them up in the training and instruction of the Lord.[r]

5Slaves, obey your earthly masters with respect[s] and fear, and with sincerity of heart,[t] just as you would obey Christ.[u] 6Obey them not only to win their favor when their eye is on you, but as slaves of Christ, doing the will of God from your heart. 7Serve wholeheartedly, as if you were serving the Lord, not people,[v] 8because you know that the Lord will reward each one for whatever good they do,[w] whether they are slave or free.

9And masters, treat your slaves in the same way. Do not threaten them, since you know that he who is both their Master and yours[x] is in heaven, and there is no favoritism with him.

The Armor of God

10Finally, be strong in the Lord[y] and in his mighty power.[z] 11Put on the full armor of God,[a] so that you can take your stand

5:33 [n] ver 25
6:1 [o] Col 3:20
6:3 [p] Ex 20:12
6:4 [q] Col 3:21 [r] Ge 18:19; Dt 6:7
6:5 [s] 1Ti 6:1 [t] Col 3:22 [u] Eph 5:22
6:7 [v] Col 3:23
6:8 [w] Col 3:24
6:9 [x] Job 31:13, 14
6:10 [y] 1Co 16:13 [z] Eph 1:19
6:11 [a] Ro 13:12

[a] 3 Deut. 5:16 [b] 4 Or *Parents*

Paul's point here is the unity of husband and wife (cf. 1Co 7:4).

5:33 *love … respect.* Speakers and writers often concluded material with a summary of what they had stated. Here Paul sums up his main point in vv. 22–32 in terms of husbands loving and wives respecting.

6:1 *Children, obey your parents.* Household codes (see note on 5:21—6:9) instructed fathers (see note on v. 4) how to govern their minor children, but did not normally address the children themselves. Nevertheless, Jewish and Greco-Roman writers unanimously agreed that children needed to honor their parents, and, at least till they grew up, needed to obey them as well. Many Jewish teachers considered the Biblical injunction to honor parents (Ex 20:12; Dt 5:16) the greatest commandment. They also felt this meant not shaming them by one's behavior (cf. Dt 21:18–21). It should go without saying that obedience to parents is a general principle not applicable to participation in sin (cf., e.g., Nu 26:9–11; 1Sa 19:11; 20:32).

6:4 *Fathers, do not exasperate your children.* Household codes instructed fathers how to govern their minor children. Fathers were responsible for their children's education, but this could include beatings (both from the father and from teachers). A minority of teachers, however, warned against beatings and excessive discipline, and Paul here would likely agree. *exasperate.* May suggest deliberate provocation. *bring them up in the training and instruction of the Lord.* Certainly Paul would also share the unanimous sentiments of ancient Jews, Christians and Egyptians against the widespread Greek practices of abandoning babies, aborting them in the womb, or, sometimes when malformed, killing them. Abandoned babies who were not retrieved by others—usually to be reared as slaves—were often eaten by vultures or dogs.

6:5 *Slaves, obey your earthly masters.* Given Christians' tenuous social situation (cf. 1Ti 5:14; 6:1), Paul urges Christian slaves, like wives (see Eph 5:22–24), to submit to the head of the household as if to Christ.

6:7 *Serve wholeheartedly.* The slaveholding class had various stereotypes of slaves, e.g., that they were lazy, especially when no one was looking. In Roman custody, Paul was in no position to liberate slaves physically, and he encourages hard work; yet he also gives slaves a new hope and a different motive for their labor.

6:9 *masters, treat your slaves in the same way.* Paul does invite those in subordinate positions in his culture, including wives and slaves, normally to submit to those in higher positions, but he goes beyond the culture by enjoining mutual submission (5:21)—*all* of Christ's followers must be servants (Mk 10:43–45). Aristotle complained about a small minority of thinkers, presumably especially early Stoics, who believed that slaves were in theory their masters' spiritual equals. Yet so far as we know only Paul goes so far as to suggest that in practice masters treat their slaves in the same way—i.e., serve them (see vv. 5–8). No one in Paul's day was suggesting slavery be abolished (see the article "Slaves and Slaveholders in Ephesians 6," p. 2068), so there was no reason to address it in a series of practical instructions. If the question had been put to Paul, however, v. 9 clearly points more in the direction of its abolitionist interpreters than those who quoted vv. 5–8 out of context to support slavery.

6:10–20 Toward the end of a speech or other persuasive work, one sometimes supplied a rousing conclusion, as Paul does here. Some have even compared it with the much longer speeches generals used to prepare troops psychologically before battle. Philosophers and other speakers sometimes described their conflict with wicked ideas as wrestling in an athletic contest or a war; they also used lists of virtues, the general idea of which Paul incorporates here.

Paul's description of God's armor (v. 11) draws from God's armor in Isa 59:17 (developed also by some other Jewish writers, e.g., Wisdom of Solomon 5:17–20). Nevertheless, most of his audience in Asia Minor would first envision a soldier of the Roman Empire ready for battle. Paul's portrait does not include all the typical elements of Roman armor; e.g., he mentions the sword but omits the lance (the *pilum*) and dagger. (Often soldiers had two *pila*; they could imbed the first into an enemy shield, making it unwieldy, and then strike with the second.) Paul's reason for the omission, however, is clear: Jesus' followers have just one offensive weapon. Paul is not really correlating our specific equipment advantages with specific parts of our bodies (cf. 1Th 5:8); rather, he wants us to know that we need all these advantages to be victorious. All the elements, both defensive and offensive, relate to the truth of the gospel.

6:10 *mighty power.* See note on 1:19.

6:11 *armor of God.* See note on vv. 10–20; may evoke Isa 59:17. *take your stand.* Generals exhorted soldiers to take a stand, viewing retreat and wounds in the back as shameful. Armor did not cover the back, and aggressors easily slaughtered those who were retreating because they could not fight back. Yet as long as they stood together on a flat, open field and did not break ranks, Roman legions were considered virtually invincible.

EPHESIANS 6:5 – 9

Slaves and Slaveholders in Ephesians 6

Household codes (see note on Eph 5:21 — 6:9) instructed elite men how to govern their wives, children and slaves. Of these, slaves more often faced the worst abuses; they could be subject to torture (for purposes of securing judicial information), beatings, sexual abuse and being sold away from family members.

Various moral thinkers did urge fair treatment of slaves (e.g., Stoics; cf. Job 31:13 – 15). Early Stoic philosophers even argued in principle for the equality of all people, although by this period Stoics usually supported the status quo; and even some early Stoics held slaves. The Qumran community rejected slavery but as part of its larger rejection of all private "property."

During this period, virtually no one was calling for the abolition of slavery. In fact, when slaves became free and acquired means, they often bought other slaves for their own use. Rome had repressed three earlier massive slave revolts, ending in bloodbaths without freedom; the purpose of even these revolts was to provide a critical mass of resistance against the slaves' oppressors, but not to abolish slavery in principle. Even if someone wanted to abolish slavery in principle, such an issue would be addressed in a philosophic treatise, not in a letter giving advice to slaves. Indeed, relatively few writers cared to even provide advice directly to slaves.

When household codes addressed the treatment of slaves (as in Eph 6:5 – 9), their interest was specifically in how householders should treat household slaves. Slavery in the mines or gladiatorial combat was a death sentence; in the fields, it was a lifetime of hard labor; but slaves in households were normally in better socioeconomic situations than free peasants. They could earn money on the side and during their lifetimes a large proportion did obtain freedom. (This observation should be balanced, however, with the observation that slaveholders sometimes freed them in midlife to avoid caring for them in old age.) Freedpersons often advanced beyond other free citizens, sometimes provoking the envy of even aristocrats (see notes on

continued on next page

against the devil's schemes. [12]For our
struggle is not against flesh and blood, but
against the rulers, against the authorities,[b]
against the powers[c] of this dark world and
against the spiritual forces of evil in the
heavenly realms.[d] [13]Therefore put on the
full armor of God, so that when the day of
evil comes, you may be able to stand your
ground, and after you have done everything, to stand. [14]Stand firm then, with the
belt of truth buckled around your waist,[e]
with the breastplate of righteousness in

6:12 [b]Eph 1:21 [c]Ro 8:38 [d]Eph 1:3
6:14 [e]Isa 11:5

6:12 *against the rulers ... the spiritual forces of evil in the heavenly realms.* Jewish people believed that not only human powers but also angelic ones behind them ruled the nations (see note on 1:21). The spiritual battle behind the earthly one was always most important; this was fought especially by prayer, worship and earthly activity for God, not by vocally challenging heavenly powers (cf. Ge 32:22 – 32; Ex 12:12; 14:14 – 28; 17:11; 2Sa 5:24; 2Ki 6:16 – 17; 2Ch 20:15 – 24; Da 10:10 – 21). Gentiles called some of their deities "rulers of this world"; Jewish people were also increasingly speaking of high ranks of good and evil angels (e.g., "rulers," "authorities"; cf. already Da 10:13,20 – 21); in Greek, "spiritual forces of evil" means the same thing as "evil spirits," an expression used by Jews and Christians.

6:13 *when the day of evil comes.* Although some scholars also see a hint here of the expected end-time tribulation, "day of evil" could be fairly general; it was a Jewish idiom for a period of trouble or judgment (cf. 5:16).

6:14 *belt of truth.* The "belt" or "girdle" may refer to the leather apron beneath the armor or to the metal belt over the tunic protecting the lower abdomen. *breastplate of righteousness.* The "breastplate" normally consisted of leather overlaid with metal, and it protected the chest in battle; like the helmet (v. 17), it was used only in battle, not for normal wear. Roman soldiers were to face forward in

1Co 7:21,22). Some slaves of Caesar wielded more power and wealth than some senators.

None of this is to deny that even household slavery was an unjust system. Women and girls in particular, though sometimes also boys, were subject to sexual abuse; although slaves used in this way were sometimes given otherwise favored treatment, the abuse must have been devastating. But the differences do mean that we should not read Paul's instructions to slaves in light of typical forms of slavery in the Americas or the traditional Arab world, but in light of the specific forms of servitude that members of his audience experienced.

It also reminds us that, whatever Paul's views about the *institution* of slavery (see note on Eph 6:9), it would be quite unexpected for them to come up directly in his brief instructions to slaves or slaveholders. Further, while the Christian message might appeal more to slaves, free persons did not easily gain direct access to others' slaves without going through the slaveholders. In succeeding generations, slaves sometimes rose even to the position of bishop within the church and Christians often bought the freedom of slaves, including their fellow Christians. Changing the predominantly anti-Christian society, however, could not occur as quickly. ◆

Second-century mosaic at Sepphoris of slaves serving at a banquet.

Kim Walton

place,[f] 15and with your feet fitted with the readiness that comes from the gospel of peace.[g] 16In addition to this, take up the shield of faith,[h] with which you can extinguish all the flaming arrows of the evil one. 17Take the helmet of salvation[i] and the sword of the Spirit, which is the word of God.[j]

6:14 [f] Isa 59:17
6:15 [g] Isa 52:7
6:16 [h] 1Jn 5:4
6:17 [i] Isa 59:17 [j] Heb 4:12

battle, side by side, so the armor needed to protect only their front. In view of Isa 59:17, where it refers to justice, this "breastplate of righteousness" is truly "the armor of God" (v. 13). The Messiah would also figuratively wear righteousness as a belt and faithfulness, or truth, as a sash (Isa 11:5).
6:15 *feet fitted with ... readiness.* Soldiers needed to wear sandals or boots (technically the Roman *caliga*, a half boot) so they could advance toward the enemy undistracted about what they might step on. *the gospel of peace.* Paul's direct source for his language here is the herald of Isa 52:7 who brings the good news (i.e., gospel), announcing peace for God's people. The news in Isaiah declares God's reign (or kingdom), when God delivers and restores his vanquished people.
6:16 *shield of faith ... extinguish all the flaming arrows.* The typical Roman soldier carried a large rectangular wooden shield, four feet (about a meter) high. Its front consisted of leather, which would be wetted before any battle in which the enemy might use flaming arrows, in order to extinguish them. After Roman legionaries closed ranks, the front row holding shields forward and those behind them holding shields above them, they were deemed virtually invulnerable to any attack from flaming arrows. *flaming arrows.* Gentiles applied this image to erotic desire (cf. also note on 1Co 7:9), though Paul probably thinks also of slander and other attacks (cf. Ps 11:2; 57:4; 64:3; Pr 25:18).
6:17 *helmet of salvation.* Part of God's armor (Isa 59:17). A Roman soldier normally wore his helmet only for battle; equipped with cheek pieces and consisting of iron or bronze, it protected the head. *sword of the Spirit.* Soldiers

[18]And pray in the Spirit on all occasions[k] with all kinds of prayers and requests.[l] With this in mind, be alert and
always keep on praying for all the Lord's
people. [19]Pray also for me,[m] that whenever
I speak, words may be given me so that I
will fearlessly[n] make known the mystery
of the gospel, [20]for which I am an ambassador[o] in chains.[p] Pray that I may declare
it fearlessly, as I should.

Final Greetings

[21]Tychicus,[q] the dear brother and faithful servant in the Lord, will tell you everything, so that you also may know how I
am and what I am doing. [22]I am sending
him to you for this very purpose, that you
may know how we are,[r] and that he may
encourage you.

[23]Peace[s] to the brothers and sisters,[a] and
love with faith from God the Father and
the Lord Jesus Christ. [24]Grace to all who
love our Lord Jesus Christ with an undying love.[b]

6:18 [k]Lk 18:1 [l]Mt 26:41; Php 1:4 **6:19** [m]1Th 5:25 [n]Ac 4:29; 2Co 3:12 **6:20** [o]2Co 5:20 [p]Ac 21:33 **6:21** [q]Ac 20:4 **6:22** [r]Col 4:7-9 **6:23** [s]Gal 6:16; 1Pe 5:14

[a] *23* The Greek word for *brothers and sisters* (*adelphoi*) refers here to believers, both men and women, as part of God's family. [b] *24* Or *Grace and immortality to all who love our Lord Jesus Christ.*

carried several weapons (see note on vv. 10–20), but Paul assigns to believers only one: the sword. After soldiers in the front line had hurled their lances, they needed their double-edged sword (*gladius*, 20–24 inches [50–60 centimeters] long) for close combat with the enemy. Whereas other elements of armor protect the believer, the word of God (presumably especially the gospel; see Ro 10:8,17; Eph 1:13) is here the one offensive weapon, the piece that allows believers to take back territory from the enemy (cf. vv. 19–20).

6:18 *pray in the Spirit.* Because Jewish sources often associated the Spirit with inspiration, Paul may think here of Spirit-led prayer. Paul might finish describing the armor in v. 17, but it may be relevant that Roman armor was designed to protect an army marching forward together. Coordinated action with shields helped protect the entire infantry unit. *be alert.* Sentries had to remain alert. Just over a third of the Greek words in v. 18 begin with *p-*; Greek hearers often appreciated alliteration.

6:20 *ambassador in chains.* Most people regarded chains and association with people in chains as humiliating. Kingdoms were careful to treat an ambassador respectfully; chaining or even insulting another country's envoy normally invited war. Indeed, even heralds from hostile nations received diplomatic immunity and were sent back in peace. *fearlessly.* Ancient thinkers respected speaking fearlessly (cf. note on Ac 4:13).

6:21 *Tychicus ... will tell you everything.* Travelers carried most letters; they also delivered news orally. Some news from a prisoner was best delivered orally, since letters could be intercepted and read.

6:23–24 *love with faith from God the Father and the Lord Jesus Christ.* The OT promised God's covenant love to all who loved God (Ex 20:6; Dt 5:10; Ne 1:5; Da 9:4).

THE LETTERS
PHILIPPIANS

For information on the Roman colony of Philippi in Macedonia, see note on Ac 16:12.

Place of Writing

Some scholars think that Paul wrote his captivity letters, including Philippians, from detention in Ephesus. A major reason is that Paul was also a prisoner in Phm 1, which was probably addressed to Asia Minor (compare Phm 2 with Col 4:17); they reason that if Onesimus fled from there and found Paul, Paul was probably nearby, as in Ephesus. Onesimus might well expect that a person of Philemon's status had contacts in Ephesus, however, so fleeing farther, to Rome, is likewise reasonable. Moreover, from Php 2:25 it seems clear that Epaphroditus had traveled a long way from Philippi — a description that fits Rome better than Ephesus. (Epaphroditus may be from Philippi. One Epaphras was originally or partly from Asia Minor [cf. Col 4:12], but this was a common name.)

Although the phrase translated "palace guard" in 1:13 might apply to a governor's residence (note the Greek term in Ac 23:35), the mention of Caesar's household in 4:22 confirms that it likely does refer to the Praetorian Guard stationed around Rome (cf. Ac 28:16). The majority of scholars believe that Paul wrote this letter from Rome.

QUICK GLANCE

AUTHOR:
The apostle Paul

AUDIENCE:
The believers at Philippi, a prosperous Roman colony

DATE:
About AD 61

THEME:
Paul thanks the Christians at Philippi for their unsolicited support, exhorts them to unity and encourages them to live joyfully in every circumstance.

Purpose

Paul wrote this letter partly to thank the Philippian believers for their continued and unsolicited support (4:10 – 20). Writing from Roman custody, however, he is also concerned that the church may well face further persecution (1:30; earlier, cf. Ac 16:22 – 23; 1Th 2:2). He also urges believers to work together (Php 1:27; 2:2,14). Ancient speakers and writers commonly urged civic and other harmony, and Paul has reasons to stress this message in this letter. The Christians in Philippi's house churches loved Paul, but they were not all getting along with each other (4:2 – 3); Paul offers multiple examples of serving others (2:5 – 8,17,20 – 21, 29 – 30). Paul also warns against false teachers who would demand circumcision, though it is not clear whether they have already arrived (3:2 – 21). ◆

1 Paul and Timothy,[a] servants of Christ
Jesus,

To all God's holy people[b] in Christ Jesus
at Philippi,[c] together with the overseers[d]
and deacons[a]:[e]

2Grace and peace to you from God our
Father and the Lord Jesus Christ.[f]

Thanksgiving and Prayer

3I thank my God every time I remember you.[g] 4In all my prayers for all of you,
I always pray[h] with joy 5because of your
partnership[i] in the gospel from the first
day[j] until now, 6being confident of this,
that he who began a good work in you will
carry it on to completion until the day of
Christ Jesus.[k]

7It is right[l] for me to feel this way about
all of you, since I have you in my heart[m]
and, whether I am in chains[n] or defending[o] and confirming the gospel, all of you
share in God's grace with me. 8God can
testify[p] how I long for all of you with the
affection of Christ Jesus.

9And this is my prayer: that your love[q]
may abound more and more in knowledge
and depth of insight, 10so that you may be
able to discern what is best and may be
pure and blameless for the day of Christ,[r]
11filled with the fruit of righteousness[s] that
comes through Jesus Christ—to the glory
and praise of God.

Paul's Chains Advance the Gospel

12Now I want you to know, brothers and
sisters,[b] that what has happened to me has
actually served to advance the gospel. 13As
a result, it has become clear throughout
the whole palace guard[c] and to everyone
else that I am in chains[t] for Christ. 14And
because of my chains,[u] most of the brothers and sisters have become confident in
the Lord and dare all the more to proclaim
the gospel without fear.

15It is true that some preach Christ out
of envy and rivalry, but others out of
goodwill. 16The latter do so out of love,
knowing that I am put here for the defense
of the gospel.[v] 17The former preach Christ
out of selfish ambition,[w] not sincerely,
supposing that they can stir up trouble for
me while I am in chains.[x] 18But what does
it matter? The important thing is that in

1:1 [a] Ac 16:1; 2Co 1:1 [b] Ac 9:13 [c] Ac 16:12 [d] 1Ti 3:1 [e] 1Ti 3:8 **1:2** [f] Ro 1:7 **1:3** [g] Ro 1:8 **1:4** [h] Ro 1:10 **1:5** [i] Ac 2:42; Php 4:15 [j] Ac 16:12-40 **1:6** [k] ver 10; 1Co 1:8 **1:7** [l] 2Pe 1:13 [m] 2Co 7:3 [n] ver 13, 14, 17; Ac 21:33 [o] ver 16 **1:8** [p] Ro 1:9 **1:9** [q] 1Th 3:12 **1:10** [r] ver 6; 1Co 1:8 **1:11** [s] Jas 3:18 **1:13** [t] ver 7, 14, 17 **1:14** [u] ver 7, 13, 17 **1:16** [v] ver 7, 12 **1:17** [w] Php 2:3 [x] ver 7, 13, 14

a *1* The word *deacons* refers here to Christians designated to serve with the overseers/elders of the church in a variety of ways; similarly in Romans 16:1 and 1 Tim. 3:8,12. *b* *12* The Greek word for *brothers and sisters* (*adelphoi*) refers here to believers, both men and women, as part of God's family; also in verse 14; and in 3:1, 13, 17; 4:1, 8, 21. *c* *13* Or *whole palace*

1:1 *Paul and Timothy.* Writers sometimes named other mutual friends as coauthors even if they did not contribute much to the letter. *servants.* Those who served important figures sometimes wielded great influence (see note on Ro 1:1). *holy people.* "Holy people" had been applied to God's people in earlier Scripture (see, e.g., Da 7:18,21 – 27). *overseers.* See note on 1Ti 3:1. *deacons.* see note on 1Ti 3:8.
1:2 *Grace and peace … Lord Jesus Christ.* See note on Ro 1:7.
1:3 *I thank my God.* Affectionate ancient letters sometimes included thanks to a deity for the recipient.
1:4 *I always pray with joy.* Affectionate ancient letters often mentioned the author's joy when receiving news about the recipient.
1:5 *partnership.* People often used the Greek term for financial sharing, relevant here (4:10 – 20).
1:6 *being confident of this.* Affectionate letters often expressed confidence in the receiver. *the day of Christ Jesus.* Recognizing Jesus' deity, Paul looks toward the day of Christ Jesus as OT prophets spoke of the day of the Lord (see note on 1Co 1: 8).
1:7 *I have you in my heart.* Letters between friends often emphasized that each shared the other's sorrows. Paul's defense and vindication for the gospel would also have relevance for their security (see note on v. 25). *I am in chains.* Most people were ashamed to be associated with anyone chained or in custody of the Roman government. This might be particularly the case in Philippi, which emphasized its close ties with Rome, and where Paul had already been publicly charged with undermining order and the Roman customs of which Philippi was particularly proud (Ac 16:20 – 22).
1:8 *God can testify.* Invoking a deity to testify constituted an oath, which invited the deity's judgment if the person invoked the deity falsely (cf. Ex 20:7). *I long for all of you.* Letters to friends often expressed affection and yearning to see and/or hear from the recipient.
1:12 – 26 Letters often filled in readers on recent news. After a basic introduction, many works also traced the events that led to their writing. Many urban people knew the view, commonly articulated by philosophers, that only one's outlook mattered, not secondary issues beyond one's control such as imprisonment and death. People would thus respect Paul's approach, though his reasons are specifically Christian: God uses our suffering for his honor (vv. 12 – 14; a view shared with the OT and ancient Jewish thinkers), and death brings believers a fuller experience of Christ (vv. 21,23).
1:13 *palace guard.* Although Paul was often imprisoned (2Co 11:23) and the Greek term translated "palace guard" could refer to a governor's palace (as in Ac 23:35), it probably does refer to the Praetorian Guard (cf. Ac 28:16; cf. also "Caesar's household" in Php 4:22). To protect the emperor's monopoly on power, policy prohibited armies in Italy. Instead, the emperor's elite guard, commanded by a prefect who was legally barred from becoming emperor, served this function. This Praetorian Guard consisted of several thousand free Italian soldiers in 12 cohorts of as many as a thousand each; although members were deployed elsewhere in Rome, their camp lay in the city's eastern suburbs. They received the best wages of all Roman soldiers and normally had the most secure conditions; moreover, they were treated as clients of the emperor (thus part of his extended household; cf. 4:22). Such factors helped ensure their loyalty.
1:15 *out of envy and rivalry.* Men in ancient Mediterranean urban culture often vied for honor. *others out of goodwill.* Ancient writers and speakers sometimes outlined alternatives before elaborating them (vv. 16 – 17).
1:18 *what does it matter?* Stoic philosophers regarded

every way, whether from false motives or
true, Christ is preached. And because of
this I rejoice.
Yes, and I will continue to rejoice,
19 for I know that through your prayers[y]
and God's provision of the Spirit of Jesus
Christ[z] what has happened to me will
turn out for my deliverance.[a] 20 I eagerly
expect[a] and hope that I will in no way
be ashamed, but will have sufficient courage[b] so that now as always Christ will be
exalted in my body,[c] whether by life or

1:19 [y] 2Co 1:11 [z] Ac 16:7
1:20 [a] Ro 8:19 [b] ver 14 [c] 1Co 6:20

[a] 19 Or *vindication*; or *salvation*

imprisonment and other matters beyond one's control as peripheral issues; what really mattered was one's attitude. *The important thing is that ... Christ is preached.* Although men often competed for honor, Paul's desire is Christ's honor, not his own. *rejoice ... rejoice.* Repeating a word or phrase could be used to emphasize it (cf. 4:4).

1:19 *will turn out for my deliverance.* Paul's phrase here follows the common Greek translation of Job 13:16; Paul sees God as his defender here. *deliverance.* Here means survival and release from custody (vv. 24–26).

1:20–23 *whether by life or by death ... what shall I choose? ... I am torn between the two.* Ancient speakers

PHILIPPI IN THE TIME OF PAUL

The Roman colony of Philippi (*Colonia Augusta Julia Philippensis*) was an important city in Macedonia, located on the main highway leading from the eastern provinces to Rome. This road, the Egnatian Way, ran along the north side of the city's forum and was the chief cause of its prosperity and political importance. Ten miles east on the coast was Neapolis, the place where Paul landed after sailing from Troas in response to the Macedonian vision.

As a prominent city of the gold-producing region of Macedonia, Philippi had a proud history. Named originally after Philip II, the father of Alexander the Great, the city was later honored with the names of Julius Caesar and Augustus. Many Italian settlers from the legions swelled the ranks of citizens and made Philippi vigorous and polyglot. It grew from a small settlement to a city of dignity and privilege. Among its highest honors was the *ius Italicum*, by which it enjoyed rights legally equivalent to those of Italian cities.

Ruins of the theater, the acropolis, the forum, the baths and the commemorative arch (about a mile west of the city) have been found. A little farther beyond the arch at the Gangites River is probably the place where Paul addressed some God-fearing women and where Lydia was converted (see Ac 16:13–15).

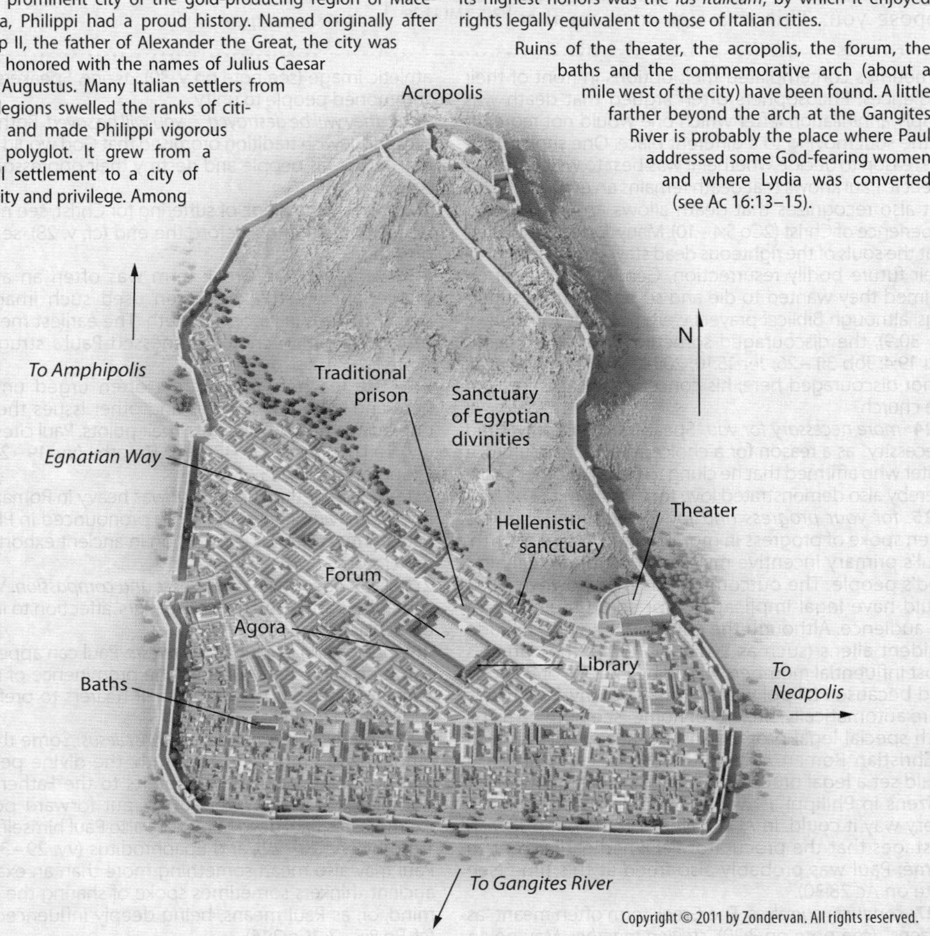

by death.[d] 21For to me, to live is Christ[e]
and to die is gain. 22If I am to go on living
in the body, this will mean fruitful labor
for me. Yet what shall I choose? I do not
know! 23I am torn between the two: I desire to depart[f] and be with Christ,[g] which
is better by far; 24but it is more necessary
for you that I remain in the body. 25Con-
vinced of this, I know that I will remain,
and I will continue with all of you for
your progress and joy in the faith, 26so
that through my being with you again
your boasting in Christ Jesus will abound
on account of me.

Life Worthy of the Gospel

27Whatever happens, conduct yourselves in a manner worthy[h] of the gospel
of Christ. Then, whether I come and see
you or only hear about you in my absence, I will know that you stand firm[i] in
the one Spirit,[a] striving together[j] as one
for the faith of the gospel 28without being frightened in any way by those who
oppose you. This is a sign to them that
they will be destroyed—but that you will
be saved—and that by God. 29For it has
been granted to you[k] on behalf of Christ
not only to believe in him, but also to suffer[l] for him, 30since you are going through
the same struggle[m] you saw[n] I had, and
now hear[o] that I still have.

Imitating Christ's Humility

2 Therefore if you have any encouragement from being united with Christ,
if any comfort from his love, if any common sharing in the Spirit,[p] if any tenderness and compassion,[q] 2then make
my joy complete[r] by being like-minded,[s]
having the same love, being one[t] in spirit and of one mind. 3Do nothing out of
selfish ambition or vain conceit.[u] Rather, in humility value others above yourselves,[v] 4not looking to your own interests but each of you to the interests of
the others.

5In your relationships with one another,
have the same mindset as Christ Jesus:[w]

1:20 [d] Ro 14:8 **1:21** [e] Gal 2:20 **1:23** [f] 2Ti 4:6 [g] Jn 12:26; 2Co 5:8 **1:27** [h] Eph 4:1 [i] 1Co 16:13 [j] Jude 3
1:29 [k] Mt 5:11, 12 [l] Ac 14:22 **1:30** [m] Col 2:1; 1Th 2:2 [n] Ac 16:19-40 [o] ver 13 **2:1** [p] 2Co 13:14 [q] Col 3:12 **2:2** [r] Jn 3:29 [s] Php 4:2 [t] Ro 12:16 **2:3** [u] Gal 5:26 [v] Ro 12:10; 1Pe 5:5 **2:5** [w] Mt 11:29

[a] 27 Or *in one spirit*

sometimes contemplated their options in front of their audiences. Philosophers often argued that death was simply annihilation (after which one would not regret it) or the soul moving to a different place. One should thus use reason to decide whether it was best to welcome it or reject it. Paul knows that death remains an evil (1Co 15:26), but also recognizes that death allows an undistracted experience of Christ (2Co 5:4–10). Many Judeans believed that the souls of the righteous dead stayed in heaven until their future bodily resurrection. Gentile thinkers often claimed they wanted to die and so be free from sufferings; although Biblical prayers were normally for survival (Ps 30:9), the discouraged sometimes lamented living (1Ki 19:4; Job 3:1–26; Jer 15:10; 20:14–18). Paul, however, is not discouraged here; his concern is what is best for the church.

1:24 *more necessary for you.* Speakers commonly cited "necessity" as a reason for a choice; in ancient sources, a writer who affirmed that he clung to life for another's sake thereby also demonstrated love for them.

1:25 *for your progress and joy in the faith.* Thinkers often spoke of progress in moral or intellectual growth. Paul's primary incentive may be to continue teaching God's people. The outcome of his trial, however, also could have legal implications for some members of his audience. Although the church would also include resident aliens (such as Lydia, Ac 16:14), the church's most influential members would be citizens of Philippi. And because Philippi was a Roman colony, its citizens were automatically citizens of Rome (see note on 3:20), with special legal protections. Because Paul was also a Christian Roman citizen, the sentence in his case could set a legal precedent that could be followed for citizens in Philippi as well. Philippi imitated Rome in every way it could. In AD 62 Nero's court freed Jewish hostages that the procurator Felix had earlier sent to Rome; Paul was probably also freed at this time (see note on Ac 28:30).

1:27 *conduct yourselves.* The Greek term often meant "as citizens" (see note on 3:20). *striving together.* May be an athletic image (see note on v. 30). *as one.* Speakers often summoned people to unity.

1:28 *they will be destroyed . . . you will be saved.* Both Scripture and Jewish tradition promised that God would someday deliver his people and destroy their oppressors (e.g., Isa 66:14–16).

1:29 On the privilege of suffering for Christ, see note on Ac 5:41; on suffering before the end (cf. v. 28), see note on 2Th 1:5.

1:30 *struggle.* The Greek term was often an athletic image; ancient thinkers often used such images to depict their own labors for truth. The earliest members of the Philippian church witnessed Paul's struggle in Ac 16:19–39.

2:1–30 Teachers and writers often urged unity (as here and 1:27–30). For this and other issues they also offered examples to illustrate their points. Paul cites Jesus (vv. 5–11), himself (vv. 17–18), Timothy (vv. 19–24) and Epaphroditus (vv. 25–30).

2:1–4 Competition for honor was heavy in Roman society, a behavior if anything more pronounced in Philippi. Paul borrows language common in ancient exhortations to harmony.

2:1 *if you have any . . . tenderness and compassion.* Writers sometimes appealed to their readers' affection to invite a particular course of action.

2:4 *not looking to your own interests.* Paul can appeal to a common value here. Despite the prominence of rivalry, ancient thinkers often urged their hearers to prefer the larger good to one's own.

2:5 *have the same mindset as Christ Jesus.* Some thinkers emphasized embracing the truth, the divine perspective on reality. Jesus here submits to the Father's will, humbling himself. Writers often put forward positive examples, as Paul does here; note also Paul himself (v. 17), Timothy (vv. 20–22), and Epaphroditus (vv. 29–30). Yet Paul may also mean something more than an example; ancient thinkers sometimes spoke of sharing the divine mind, or, as Paul means, being deeply influenced by it (cf. Ro 8:5–7; 1Co 2:16).

6 Who, being in very nature[a] God,[x]
did not consider equality with God[y]
something to be used to his
own advantage;
7 rather, he made himself nothing
by taking the very nature[b] of a
servant,[z]
being made in human likeness.[a]
8 And being found in appearance as a
man,
he humbled himself
by becoming obedient to death[b]—
even death on a cross!

9 Therefore God exalted him[c] to the
highest place
and gave him the name that is above
every name,[d]
10 that at the name of Jesus every knee
should bow,[e]
in heaven and on earth and under
the earth,[f]
11 and every tongue acknowledge that
Jesus Christ is Lord,[g]
to the glory of God the Father.

Do Everything Without Grumbling

12 Therefore, my dear friends, as you
have always obeyed—not only in my
presence, but now much more in my absence—continue to work out your salvation with fear and trembling,[h] 13 for it is
God who works in you[i] to will and to act
in order to fulfill his good purpose.
14 Do everything without grumbling[j] or
arguing, 15 so that you may become blameless and pure, "children of God[k] without
fault in a warped and crooked generation."[c][l] Then you will shine among them
like stars in the sky 16 as you hold firmly
to the word of life. And then I will be able
to boast on the day of Christ that I did
not run or labor in vain.[m] 17 But even if I
am being poured out like a drink offering[n]
on the sacrifice[o] and service coming from
your faith, I am glad and rejoice with all
of you. 18 So you too should be glad and
rejoice with me.

Timothy and Epaphroditus

19 I hope in the Lord Jesus to send Timothy to you soon,[p] that I also may be
cheered when I receive news about you.
20 I have no one else like him,[q] who will
show genuine concern for your welfare. 21 For everyone looks out for their
own interests,[r] not those of Jesus Christ.

2:6 [x] Jn 1:1 [y] Jn 5:18 **2:7** [z] Mt 20:28 [a] Jn 1:14; Heb 2:17 **2:8** [b] Mt 26:39; Jn 10:18; Heb 5:8 **2:9** [c] Ac 2:33; Heb 2:9 [d] Eph 1:20,21 **2:10** [e] Ro 14:11 [f] Mt 28:18 **2:11** [g] Jn 13:13 **2:12** [h] 2Co 7:15 **2:13** [i] Ezr 1:5 **2:14** [j] 1Co 10:10; 1Pe 4:9 **2:15** [k] Mt 5:45, 48; Eph 5:1 [l] Ac 2:40 **2:16** [m] 1Th 2:19 **2:17** [n] 2Ti 4:6 [o] Ro 15:16 **2:19** [p] ver 23 **2:20** [q] 1Co 16:10 **2:21** [r] 1Co 10:24; 13:5

[a] 6 Or *in the form of* [b] 7 Or *the form*
[c] 15 Deut. 32:5

2:6–11 Most scholars believe that Paul here uses an earlier hymn; Greeks often quoted poetry. Nevertheless, the matter remains debated; ancient writers and speakers often used exalted prose, sometimes even with rhythm, to describe deities.
2:6 *did not consider equality with God something to be used to his own advantage.* Scholars often contrast the first Adam who, not content with being made in God's image (Ge 1:26–27), wanted to become divine (Ge 3:5). (For background on Adam, see the article "Adam in Jewish Tradition," p. 1957; see also notes on 1Co 15:45–49.) Likewise, Nero, the emperor before whose court Paul would soon be tried, wanted to be regarded as divine. Scholars also often compare Hellenistic Jewish emphasis on divine Wisdom as God's image (see note on 2Co 4:4).
2:7 *he made himself nothing.* Since this phrase sometimes can also mean "emptied himself" (cf. the image in v. 17), some compare this action with the servant who poured out his life in death in Isa 53:12 (cf. Php 2:8), though Paul's language is different and in this verse he refers to Christ becoming human. The behavior runs contrary to all behavior expected of persons of status in antiquity, who barely ever would eat with their servants, much less act like one of them (cf. Jn 13:5).
2:8 *to death—even death on a cross!* Repeating a word (in this case, "death") could be used to emphasize it. Romans executed people of low status naked, by slow torture, on a cross; the cross epitomized shameful death.
2:10 *bow.* As one did before kings and deities; Paul takes the language here from Isa 45:23. *in heaven and on earth and under the earth.* Paul elaborates those who will bow. Greeks spoke of deities in these three realms (plus the sea). Whatever and wherever beings are, they must ultimately acknowledge the exalted Lord. *in heaven.* Those such as angels (including hostile rulers, see note on Eph 1:21). *under the earth.* Although some thinking had changed, Greek myths located the spirits of most of the dead "under the earth"; they lived only as shadows.
2:11 *every tongue acknowledge.* Paul slightly adjusts his quotation of Isa 45:23 in vv. 10–11, applying directly to Jesus a text about all peoples finally recognizing that Israel's God alone is true. *Lord.* Like the title "God," this was a divine title (cf. 1Co 8:6).
2:12 *not only in my presence, but now much more in my absence.* People often viewed letters as mediating the author's presence (cf. 1Co 5:3–4). *work out your salvation with fear and trembling.* Jewish texts often paired fear and trembling (e.g., Ps 2:11; 55:5).
2:14 *grumbling.* May evoke Israel's rebellious spirit in the wilderness (cf. 1Co 10:10).
2:15 *warped and crooked generation.* Paul cites Dt 32:5, which warns that the Israelites, who acted thus, were not God's children—in contrast to "children of God" in the present verse. *shine among them like stars in the sky.* Jewish sources often compared the righteous with lights; the present passage evokes especially the comparison of the resurrected righteous with stars in Da 12:3. Believers experience a foretaste of the future (cf. 2Co 1:22; Heb 6:5).
2:16 *the day of Christ.* See note on 1:6. *run.* See note on 1:30. *labor in vain.* Others in antiquity also sometimes noted that they feared the possibility of laboring in vain.
2:17 *drink offering.* A familiar image, both in OT libations (e.g., Lev 23:18,37) and those of Gentiles. Gentiles even poured them in memory of the deceased and, most often, at the beginning of banquets. One could pour water or other fluids but wine was most common.
2:19 *send Timothy … receive news about you.* Travelers regularly carried news and letters.
2:20 *I have no one else like him.* Although those who wrote letters of recommendation (see note on Ac 9:2) occasionally offered superlative recommendations for more than one person, they were still very rare and noteworthy.

22But you know that Timothy has proved
himself, because as a son with his father[s]
he has served with me in the work of the
gospel. 23I hope, therefore, to send him
as soon as I see how things go with me.[t]
24And I am confident[u] in the Lord that I
myself will come soon.
25But I think it is necessary to send back
to you Epaphroditus, my brother, co-worker[v] and fellow soldier,[w] who is also your
messenger, whom you sent to take care of
my needs.[x] 26For he longs for all of you[y]
and is distressed because you heard he
was ill. 27Indeed he was ill, and almost
died. But God had mercy on him, and not
on him only but also on me, to spare me
sorrow upon sorrow. 28Therefore I am all
the more eager to send him, so that when
you see him again you may be glad and I
may have less anxiety. 29So then, welcome
him in the Lord with great joy, and honor
people like him,[z] 30because he almost died
for the work of Christ. He risked his life to
make up for the help you yourselves could
not give me.[a]

2:22 [s] 1Co 4:17; 1Ti 1:2 **2:23** [t] ver 19 **2:24** [u] Php 1:25 **2:25** [v] Php 4:3 [w] Phm 2 [x] Php 4:18 **2:26** [y] Php 1:8 **2:29** [z] 1Co 16:18; 1Ti 5:17 **2:30** [a] 1Co 16:17 **3:2** [b] Ps 22:16, 20 **3:3** [c] Ro 2:28, 29; Gal 6:15; Col 2:11

No Confidence in the Flesh

3 Further, my brothers and sisters, rejoice in the Lord! It is no trouble for
me to write the same things to you again,
and it is a safeguard for you. 2Watch out
for those dogs,[b] those evildoers, those
mutilators of the flesh. 3For it is we who
are the circumcision,[c] we who serve God
by his Spirit, who boast in Christ Jesus,
and who put no confidence in the flesh—

2:22 *as a son with his father he has served with me.* The strongest letters of recommendation often said, "Receive this person as you would me"; envoys were to be received that way as well. Teachers often viewed close disciples as their sons, though even among Paul's close associates, his relationship with Timothy was special.

2:23 *I hope … to send him.* Because news was sent with travelers and travel could be hazardous, Paul will not send his next report (after this letter, carried by Epaphroditus) until he has more decisive news.

2:24 *I myself will come soon.* Letters often included travel plans. Affectionate letters often expressed a desire to be together.

2:25 *Epaphroditus.* This may be Epaphras (a short form of the same name), who was also with Paul in Rome for a time (Col 4:12; Phm 23), but Epaphroditus was a very common name. *fellow soldier.* Military images were common (see note on Ro 13:12). *whom you sent to take care of my needs.* It was not safe to send money with people one did not trust; Epaphroditus therefore made the voyage on behalf of the Philippians, bringing their gift to Paul in Rome (4:18).

2:27 *he was ill, and almost died.* Both travelers and letters carried news about health. Travel conditions were hazardous, especially at sea in late fall and early spring, and these conditions decreased one's resistance to antiquity's many diseases. Typhoid fever and especially malaria were common. *God had mercy on him.* Gentiles prayed for healing to Asclepius and other deities; Jewish people regularly prayed to God for this, sometimes describing it as mercy. Scripture often reports healings, but recognizes that they did not always happen (2Ki 13:14; cf. 1Ki 1:1; 14:4).

2:29 *welcome him in the Lord.* A person of status would often write a letter of recommendation for a person who could carry it to another person of status from whom the recommended needed a favor. Although Epaphroditus may not need the recommendation, Paul recommends him anyway in this letter that he sends back with him.

2:30 *risked.* Some interpreters suggest a wordplay: gamblers often used this Greek term and called on the patron goddess of gambling with the term "epaphroditus." "Risked" also appears widely, however, outside gambling contexts.

3:1—4:1 Noting that 3:1—4:1 changes the subject substantially, some earlier scholars supposed that ancient scribes mixed up two ancient letters of Paul, adding 3:1—4:1 inside the rest of Philippians. Even aside from clear literary connections between this section and the rest of Philippians, ancient letter-writing practices render this speculation extremely unlikely. First, the earliest scrolls did not have separate pages allowing such confusion; second, if such confusion occurred in a later codex (paged book), it should not have occurred in all surviving codices; third, if such an error did occur, one would not expect clean sentence breaks from 2:30 to 4:2, since pages were not coordinated with sentences; and finally, digressions are common throughout ancient literature and speeches.

3:1 *to write the same things to you again.* Speakers and writers would often remind hearers of a point and/or repeat it if they thought it needed to be reinforced.

3:2 *Watch out for … those mutilators of the flesh.* In Greek, Paul repeats here "Watch out for" three times; speakers used such repetition to reinforce a point. Philippi's Jewish community was small (Ac 16:13), so those advocating circumcision here (cf. v. 3) are traveling teachers such as those in Gal 1:7; 4:17; 5:12; 6:12–13. Scholars debate whether Paul offers a warning before these false teachers arrive or he has heard of their arrival. *those dogs.* Some Romans posted warnings similar to modern "Beware of dog" signs. People often insulted others by calling them dogs, sometimes implying vulgar public sexual or excretory habits (the way that "Cynic" sages—i.e., "dogs"—got their title). Philosophers considered those ruled by passions "beasts," and Jews could so depict oppressors (Ps 22:16; 59:6). More important in criticism of those promoting circumcision, as some Gentile homes used dogs as pets, Judeans viewed them more like scavenging rodents. Jewish people viewed dogs as unclean and sometimes sexually immoral (cf. male cult prostitutes in Dt 23:17–18). Paul thus depicts these conservative Jewish proponents of circumcision as unclean by Jewish standards. *mutilators.* A wordplay: mutilation (cutting something up) is *katatomê*, and in v. 3 circumcision is *peritomê*; for the idea, see note on Gal 5:12.

3:3 *we who serve God by his Spirit.* Scripture urged God's people to circumcise their hearts (Dt 10:16), and promised that God would someday circumcise their hearts (Dt 30:6). For Paul, experiencing the new heart promised in the new covenant by the Spirit (Jer 31:33; Eze 36:26–27), counted more than the mere external sign of the older covenant. Paul's term translated "serve" here normally means "worship" or serve as in a temple; the Spirit empowers the purest worship (cf. 1Ch 25:1–6; see note on Jn 4:24). Apart from Essenes, ancient Jewish teachers barely ever claimed to experience God's Spirit.

4 though I myself have reasons for such
confidence.

If someone else thinks they have reasons to put confidence in the flesh, I have
more: 5 circumcised[d] on the eighth day, of
the people of Israel,[e] of the tribe of Benjamin,[f] a Hebrew of Hebrews; in regard to
the law, a Pharisee;[g] 6 as for zeal, persecuting the church;[h] as for righteousness
based on the law,[i] faultless.

7 But whatever were gains to me I now
consider loss[j] for the sake of Christ. 8 What
is more, I consider everything a loss because of the surpassing worth of knowing[k] Christ Jesus my Lord, for whose sake
I have lost all things. I consider them
garbage, that I may gain Christ 9 and be
found in him, not having a righteousness
of my own that comes from the law,[l] but
that which is through faith in[a] Christ — the
righteousness that comes from God on the
basis of faith.[m] 10 I want to know Christ —
yes, to know the power of his resurrection and participation in his sufferings,[n]
becoming like him in his death,[o] 11 and so,
somehow, attaining to the resurrection[p]
from the dead.

12 Not that I have already obtained all
this, or have already arrived at my goal,[q]
but I press on to take hold[r] of that for
which Christ Jesus took hold of me.[s]
13 Brothers and sisters, I do not consider
myself yet to have taken hold of it. But one
thing I do: Forgetting what is behind[t] and
straining toward what is ahead, 14 I press
on[u] toward the goal to win the prize for
which God has called[v] me heavenward in
Christ Jesus.

Following Paul's Example

15 All of us, then, who are mature[w]
should take such a view of things.[x] And if
on some point you think differently, that
too God will make clear to you. 16 Only
let us live up to what we have already attained.

17 Join together in following my example,[y] brothers and sisters, and just as you
have us as a model, keep your eyes on
those who live as we do. 18 For, as I have
often told you before and now tell you
again even with tears,[z] many live as enemies of the cross of Christ.[a] 19 Their destiny
is destruction, their god is their stomach,[b]
and their glory is in their shame.[c] Their

3:5 [d] Lk 1:59 [e] 2Co 11:22 [f] Ro 11:1 [g] Ac 23:6 **3:6** [h] Ac 8:3 [i] Ro 10:5 **3:7** [j] Mt 13:44; Lk 14:33 **3:8** [k] Eph 4:13; 2Pe 1:2 **3:9** [l] Ro 10:5 [m] Ro 9:30 **3:10** [n] Ro 8:17 [o] Ro 6:3-5 **3:11** [p] Rev 20:5,6 **3:12** [q] 1Co 13:10 [r] 1Ti 6:12 [s] Ac 9:5,6 **3:13** [t] Lk 9:62 **3:14** [u] Heb 6:1 [v] Ro 8:28 **3:15** [w] 1Co 2:6 [x] Gal 5:10 **3:17** [y] 1Co 4:16; 1Pe 5:3 **3:18** [z] Ac 20:31 [a] Gal 6:12 **3:19** [b] Ro 16:18 [c] Ro 6:21

[a] 9 Or *through the faithfulness of*

3:4 – 6 Lists of virtues and/or advantages were common, including when praising someone. Speakers often reasoned by comparing figures, under appropriate circumstances, even comparing oneself with others. Praising oneself was deemed acceptable if the grounds were justifiable, such as refuting others' grounds for boasting.
3:5 When Gentiles listed praiseworthy features of a person, they often began with the person's background, upbringing, and education (cf. Ac 22:3). *circumcised on the eighth day.* Indicates Paul's birth into the people of Israel. Jewish society ranked converts lower than those born Jewish (Ge 17:12; Lev 12:3). *in regard to the law, a Pharisee.* Pharisees were known for scrupulous interpretation of the law and following their traditions; they lived in the Holy Land, especially near Jerusalem.
3:6 *as for zeal, persecuting the church.* Some common models for Jewish zeal for the law, such as Phinehas and the Maccabees, used violence; one faction of the Judean revolt was known as Zealots (see note on Ac 22:3).
3:8 *garbage.* Somewhat crude, this Greek term refers most commonly to excrement or kitchen scraps — perhaps the sort that dogs might eat (v. 2).
3:9 *righteousness that comes from God on the basis of faith.* The OT sometimes spoke of God's righteousness as including his mercy and faithfulness to his covenant (see note on Ro 1:17); given Paul's arguments elsewhere, he may think here especially of God deeming righteous the one who trusts him (Ge 15:6).
3:10 *I want to know Christ.* In the OT, to know God involved both a covenant relationship (Ex 6:7) and, at its fullest, intimacy with God (e.g., Ex 33:13). The new covenant provides this for all God's people (Jer 31:34; cf. Jer 24:7; Hos 2:20). This language reflects both the covenant relationship (on the corporate level) and intimate fellowship with God (on the personal level experienced by the prophets). But Paul also connects knowing Christ with sharing his sufferings and glory. On the imitation of God, see note on Eph 4:32 — 5:2.
3:12 *arrived at my goal.* Speakers commonly used athletic illustrations figuratively; Paul's goal is the future resurrection in v. 11. Even aged philosophers normally confessed that they were merely making progress toward perfection, though they contrasted the mature (v. 15) with novices.
3:13 *Forgetting what is behind.* Greek runners often ran in a straight line and back, but to win, a runner must keep his eyes ahead, not glancing back to what is behind.
3:14 *God has called me heavenward.* Officials "called" the race's winner (cf. vv. 12 – 13) up for the prize (for prizes in different games, see the article "Athletic Imagery in 1 Corinthians 9," p. 2000). *heavenward.* Lit. "upward"; although winners went up to receive a prize, the literal prize here is indeed in heaven (cf. v. 20; cf. Col 3:1 – 2). Philosophers sometimes contrasted the earthly interests of beasts (cf. v. 2) and the heavenly interests of true thinkers (cf. v. 20).
3:15 *mature.* Philosophic teachers considered their advanced students mature, though not by this implying that any of them had achieved perfection (cf. vv. 12,13).
3:16 *already attained.* See notes on vv. 12 – 13.
3:17 *following my example.* Teachers often used examples, sometimes their own, and disciples often imitated their teachers. Like Paul, the believers should depend on Christ's righteousness alone (v. 9), unlike Paul's adversaries (v. 2), whose destiny is destruction (v. 19).
3:18 *tell you again … with tears.* Good speakers' or writers' tears or (as in v. 2) indignation could move hearers to the same emotions. For love of enemies, see notes on Lk 6:27; Ro 12:14.
3:19 *their god is their stomach.* Ancient moral writers condemned gluttony, but they used "stomach" more broadly than this to include being ruled by one's passions in any kind of way. Many Diaspora Jews emphasized that the

mind is set on earthly things.[d] 20But our
citizenship[e] is in heaven.[f] And we eagerly
await a Savior from there, the Lord Jesus
Christ,[g] 21who, by the power[h] that enables
him to bring everything under his control,
will transform our lowly bodies[i] so that
they will be like his glorious body.[j]

Closing Appeal for Steadfastness and Unity

4 Therefore, my brothers and sisters,
you whom I love and long for,[k] my joy
and crown, stand firm[l] in the Lord in this
way, dear friends!
2I plead with Euodia and I plead with
Syntyche to be of the same mind[m] in the
Lord. 3Yes, and I ask you, my true companion, help these women since they have
contended at my side in the cause of the
gospel, along with Clement and the rest of

3:19 [d] Ro 8:5,6
3:20 [e] Eph 2:19 [f] Col 3:1 [g] 1Co 1:7
3:21 [h] Eph 1:19 [i] 1Co 15:43-53 [j] Col 3:4
4:1 [k] Php 1:8 [l] 1Co 16:13; Php 1:27
4:2 [m] Php 2:2
4:4 [n] Ro 12:12; Php 3:1
4:5 [o] Heb 10:37; Jas 5:8,9
4:6 [p] Mt 6:25-34 [q] Eph 6:18
4:7 [r] Isa 26:3; Jn 14:27; Col 3:15

my co-workers, whose names are in the
book of life.

Final Exhortations

4Rejoice in the Lord always. I will say
it again: Rejoice![n] 5Let your gentleness be
evident to all. The Lord is near.[o] 6Do not
be anxious about anything,[p] but in every
situation, by prayer and petition, with
thanksgiving, present your requests to
God.[q] 7And the peace of God,[r] which transcends all understanding, will guard your
hearts and your minds in Christ Jesus.
8Finally, brothers and sisters, whatever is true, whatever is noble, whatever is
right, whatever is pure, whatever is lovely, whatever is admirable — if anything is
excellent or praiseworthy — think about
such things. 9Whatever you have learned
or received or heard from me, or seen in

law enabled them to master passions; true transformation, however, requires the Spirit (vv. 2 – 3). Philosophers sometimes condemned as "beasts" (cf. v. 2) people whose interests were earthly, focusing almost exclusively on meeting bodily desires.

3:20 *our citizenship is in heaven.* The Philippians understood what it meant to be citizens of a place they had never yet visited. Because Philippi was a Roman colony, its citizens were legally citizens of Rome, with all the privileges that came from that status. Although the Philippian church included resident aliens (cf. Lydia from Thyatira in Ac 16:14), many of its influential members were likely citizens (cf. perhaps Clement in Php 4:3). Philosophers sometimes declared themselves citizens of the world rather than any mere city-state. *Savior.* Like other Gentiles, most Philippians honored the emperor and many other deities as "saviors"; the believers, however, recognize that God is the only Savior (Isa 43:11; 45:21; Hos 13:4).

3:21 *transform our lowly bodies.* For Jewish people, resurrection by definition meant the restoration of the body — a concept foreign to Greeks and Romans. Nevertheless, some Jewish traditions recognized that the resurrected body was of a different, supernatural character (see Da 12:2 – 3). Jewish people also expected resurrection to occur at the time when God would subdue all his enemies (cf. 1Co 15:25 – 28). Paul echoes some of his earlier language in 2:6 – 11.

4:1 *love and long for.* Those who wrote letters to friends frequently emphasized their affection and their desire to see the recipients. *my joy and crown.* As Paul's "crown" the believers in Philippi are part of Paul's prize (see 3:14; 1Th 2:19); such a crown was most often a victor's wreath (see note on 1Co 9:24). *stand firm in the Lord.* Only if they stand firm against the false teachers will Paul receive his reward — their salvation.

4:2 *Euodia ... Syntyche.* Although Philippi was a Roman colony, both women's names here are Greek, possibly suggesting that they were foreign merchants like Lydia; they could have even belonged to her original prayer group (Ac 16:13 – 14), although that can be no more than a guess. Some suggest that the women named here might lead separate house churches; whatever their role, Paul is clear here that they had worked with him (v. 3). This may have proved less controversial than in some other locations. Women in Rome and Macedonia had more freedoms than women in more traditionally Greek areas, and inscriptions show that women played a significant role in Philippi's religious activities.

4:3 *help these women.* Mediators who could reconcile estranged parties played a valuable role in Roman culture. *Clement.* A common Roman name, but tradition suggests that late in the first century this same person wrote from Rome a letter to the Corinthian church called 1 Clement. *whose names are in the book of life.* Jewish tradition often emphasized the OT image of the book of life (e.g., Da 12:1; Mal 3:16).

4:4 *Rejoice ... I will say it again: Rejoice!* Repeating a word could be used to reinforce the point. To rejoice is to express confidence in God, as does "thanksgiving" (v. 6; see note on Eph 5:20).

4:5 *The Lord is near.* May refer to his current presence to help his people (Dt 4:7; Ps 34:18; 119:151; 145:18) or perhaps to his coming (e.g., Joel 1:15; 3:14; Zep 1:7; cf. Php 3:20 – 21).

4:6 *Do not be anxious about anything.* Like philosophers, Paul could speak of an ideal of having no worry; yet love creates concern (2Co 7:5 – 6; 1Th 3:5), and even most philosophers recognized that they had not attained the ideal. (The Greek term translated "concern" in 2Co 11:28 can also mean "worry," as in 1Pe 5:7.) The dominant philosophic school at this time, Stoics, recognized that anxiety was counterproductive; Fate, they thought, could not be resisted. Paul instead emphasizes an active dependence on the benevolent God who hears our cries and takes care of us, if not always the way we expect, always in love.

4:7 *the peace of God.* Philosophers could speak of peace as tranquility in contrast with anxiety (cf. v. 6), but peace could also carry its more common sense of harmony with one another (cf. v. 2; see note on 2:1 – 4). *guard your hearts.* If "guard" carries any of its frequent military sense, it reinforces by means of irony the latter sense of peace. Prayers for peace (e.g., Nu 6:26; Ps 122:8) covered one's full well-being. *minds.* See note on v. 8.

4:8 *whatever is.* The Greek term is repeated seven times (including in the instance translated "if anything is"); hearers appreciated repetition. Philosophers sought to cultivate what they considered realistic and good thinking, working from what they hoped would be a divine (cf. 2:5) or heavenly (cf. Col 3:1 – 2) perspective. Ancient writers often listed virtues. *excellent.* Translates a Greek term for exceptional virtue.

4:9 *Whatever you have learned ... or seen in me.* Disciples were expected to imitate their teachers.

me — put it into practice.[s] And the God of
peace[t] will be with you.

Thanks for Their Gifts

10I rejoiced greatly in the Lord that at
last you renewed your concern for me.[u]
Indeed, you were concerned, but you had
no opportunity to show it. 11I am not saying this because I am in need, for I have
learned to be content[v] whatever the circumstances. 12I know what it is to be in
need, and I know what it is to have plenty.
I have learned the secret of being content
in any and every situation, whether well
fed or hungry,[w] whether living in plenty
or in want.[x] 13I can do all this through him
who gives me strength.[y]
14Yet it was good of you to share[z] in my
troubles. 15Moreover, as you Philippians
know, in the early days[a] of your acquaintance with the gospel, when I set out from
Macedonia, not one church shared with
me in the matter of giving and receiving,
except you only;[b] 16for even when I was
in Thessalonica,[c] you sent me aid more
than once when I was in need.[d] 17Not
that I desire your gifts; what I desire is
that more be credited to your account.[e]
18I have received full payment and have
more than enough. I am amply supplied,
now that I have received from Epaphroditus[f] the gifts you sent. They are a fragrant[g]
offering, an acceptable sacrifice, pleasing
to God. 19And my God will meet all your
needs[h] according to the riches of his glory[i]
in Christ Jesus.
20To our God and Father[j] be glory for
ever and ever. Amen.[k]

Final Greetings

21Greet all God's people in Christ Jesus.
The brothers and sisters who are with me[l]
send greetings. 22All God's people[m] here
send you greetings, especially those who
belong to Caesar's household.
23The grace of the Lord Jesus Christ[n] be
with your spirit. Amen.[a]

4:9 [s] Php 3:17 [t] Ro 15:33
4:10 [u] 2Co 11:9
4:11 [v] 1Ti 6:6,8
4:12 [w] 1Co 4:11 [x] 2Co 11:9
4:13 [y] 2Co 12:9
4:14 [z] Php 1:7
4:15 [a] Php 1:5 [b] 2Co 11:8,9
4:16 [c] Ac 17:1 [d] 1Th 2:9
4:17 [e] 1Co 9:11, 12
4:18 [f] Php 2:25 [g] 2Co 2:14
4:19 [h] Ps 23:1; 2Co 9:8 [i] Ro 2:4
4:20 [j] Gal 1:4 [k] Ro 11:36
4:21 [l] Gal 1:2
4:22 [m] Ac 9:13
4:23 [n] Ro 16:20

[a] 23 Some manuscripts do not have *Amen.*

4:10 – 20 Expressing gratitude to benefactors was an essential virtue in antiquity. At the same time, Paul does not wish to become a client dependent on the church's benefaction; such a position could compromise his ability to speak frankly when needed (see notes on 1Co 9:6,12). Paul must express gratitude without implying that he seeks further gifts; asking for money placed one in a subordinate position. Although Philippi in general was prosperous and some members had significant work (Ac 16:14 – 15; cf. 16:33 – 34), at least some of the Macedonian churches were relatively poor (2Co 8:1 – 3).
4:10 *I rejoiced greatly in the Lord.* A friend responding to another friend's letter often started with a statement of joy about the letter. A writer also often assured the letter's recipients that the writer trusted the readers' intentions.
4:11 – 13 Many Biblical prophets and others had sacrificed for God. Paul borrows language from the Diaspora. Greco-Roman thinkers emphasized the value of being content and thus needing nothing more than oneself. Paul's dependence, however, is on Christ (v. 13) rather than on himself.
4:12 *whether living in plenty or in want.* For an artisan (cf. Ac 18:3), having "plenty" meant having more than enough to eat and wear, not the sort of wealth displayed by ancient elites. (By way of comparison, middle class Westerners who own their own homes and yards have far more resources than some 95 percent of ancients.)
4:14 *share.* Often carried an economic sense; thus Paul might refer to their gift during his troubles.
4:15 – 16 Paul's experiences in Philippi and the rest of Macedonia appear in Ac 16:12 — 17:14. Probably one of the occasions that this church sent help to Paul occurred in Ac 18:5.
4:17 *credited to your account.* Commonly used in financial language.
4:18 *I have received full payment.* Paul figuratively employs this phrase, which was common language in ancient receipts. *fragrant offering, an acceptable sacrifice, pleasing to God.* Writers often used sacrifice language figuratively (see note on Ro 12:1; cf., e.g., Ge 8:21; Lev 1:3,13).
4:19 *God will meet all your needs.* Unable to repay them himself, Paul trusts his God to do so (cf. Dt 15:10; Pr 19:17). *needs.* The Greek term refers to what is necessary, not implying all wants. *riches of his glory.* May be idiomatic for "glorious riches."
4:21 Letter writers sometimes sent greetings to the recipients' location and included greetings from people in the senders' location.
4:22 *especially those who belong to Caesar's household.* Philippi respected and imitated Rome. After an initial hint about his imprisonment advancing the gospel (1:12 – 13), Paul has reserved for the Philippian church a climactic encouragement for his letter's end. Caesar's household could include any of Caesar's dependents, including all his slaves and freedmen. It could also include, and here it very probably refers to, the Praetorian Guard, the elite force of the Roman military (see note on 1:13). Those who guarded Paul would regularly hear his teaching (Ac 28:16,30).
4:23 Blessings invoked a deity; here Paul invokes the Lord Jesus as divine.

THE LETTERS
COLOSSIANS

Author and Date

Although many scholars (probably the majority) believe that Paul wrote Colossians (dictating to a scribe, as in Ro 16:22), some demur. Most of those who do not believe that Paul authored the letter directly suggest that a disciple of Paul wrote the letter in Paul's name (probably with his approval, or posthumously in faithfulness to his teachings).

Against the view that it is a posthumous collection of Paul's ideas, there is good reason to affirm that this letter must have been written during Paul's lifetime (he probably died no earlier than AD 64). Forgers and imitators normally wrote letters in a deceased person's name only long after the person's death, but a date long after Paul's death is unlikely. Colossae was never fully rebuilt after an earthquake devastated the city sometime between AD 60 and 64. Why then would someone writing after the earthquake pretend to direct a letter to Colossae? Meanwhile, it would be difficult to pass off a forgery while Paul and his immediate followers were around to protest it. Such factors reinforce the likelihood of Paul's authorship.

There are some differences in language from Paul's earlier letters, but this is also true for Philippians (from the same period). During his captivity letters, Paul appears to have drawn more on the language of popular philosophy (cf. earlier Ac 19:9). Paul may borrow some language from the false teachers to make his case against them (e.g., "powers" in heavenly places [Col 1:16; 2:15; cf. 2:10]; perhaps "fullness" [1:19; 2:9; cf. 1:25; 2:10]), but even here, most of the language that is used in Colossians has parallels in his undisputed writings (which also differ from one another). Given possible freedoms allowed the scribe and the lapse of several years since Paul's earlier letters, we lack strong reasons to doubt Pauline authorship.

QUICK GLANCE

AUTHOR:
The apostle Paul

AUDIENCE:
The believers at Colossae, a church perhaps planted by Paul's coworker Epaphras

DATE:
About AD 60

THEME:
Paul writes to demonstrate that Christ is supreme over every human philosophy and accomplishment.

The False Teaching in Colossae

Although it is clear that Paul combats false teaching in Colossae, scholars differ in how they reconstruct the error. In light of explicit mention of the New Moon and Sabbath in 2:16 – 18, many believe that the teachers drew on mystical elements in a very Hellenized form of Judaism. (The mysticism may have been something like apocalyptic visions without an emphasis on the future.) Much of the Judaism in Phrygia had assimilated elements of local culture. Some also may have overemphasized angels (2:18) and the authority of such intermediate forces (1:16; 2:8,15,20). ◆

1 Paul, an apostle[a] of Christ
Jesus by the will of God,[b]
and Timothy our brother,
2 To God's holy people in
Colossae, the faithful brothers
and sisters[a] in Christ:

Grace[c] and peace to you
from God our Father.[bd]

Thanksgiving and Prayer

3 We always thank God,[e]
the Father of our Lord Jesus
Christ, when we pray for you,
4 because we have heard of
your faith in Christ Jesus and
of the love[f] you have for all
God's people[g]— 5 the faith
and love that spring from
the hope[h] stored up for you
in heaven[i] and about which
you have already heard in the
true message of the gospel
6 that has come to you. In the same way,
the gospel is bearing fruit[j] and growing
throughout the whole world[k]—just as it
has been doing among you since the day
you heard it and truly understood God's
grace. 7 You learned it from Epaphras,[l] our
dear fellow servant,[c] who is a faithful minister[m] of Christ on our[d] behalf, 8 and who
also told us of your love in the Spirit.[n]
9 For this reason, since the day we heard
about you,[o] we have not stopped praying
for you. We continually ask God to fill you
with the knowledge of his will[p] through
all the wisdom and understanding that the
Spirit gives,[eq] 10 so that you may live a life
worthy[r] of the Lord and please him in every way: bearing fruit in every good work,
growing in the knowledge of God, 11 being
strengthened with all power[s] according to
his glorious might so that you may have
great endurance and patience,[t] 12 and giving joyful thanks to the Father,[u] who has
qualified you[f] to share in the inheritance[v]
of his holy people in the kingdom of light.
13 For he has rescued us from the dominion
of darkness[w] and brought us into the king-

LETTER TO COLOSSAE

ASIA
Aegean Sea
Hierapolis
Laodicea
Colossae
0 300 km.
0 300 miles

1:1 [a] 1Co 1:1 [b] 2Co 1:1 **1:2** [c] Col 4:18 [d] Ro 1:7 **1:3** [e] Ro 1:8 **1:4** [f] Gal 5:6 [g] Eph 1:15 **1:5** [h] 1Th 5:8; Titus 1:2 [i] 1Pe 1:4 **1:6** [j] Jn 15:16 [k] Ro 10:18 **1:7** [l] Phm 23 [m] Col 4:7 **1:8** [n] Ro 15:30 **1:9** [o] Eph 1:15 [p] Eph 5:17 [q] Eph 1:17 **1:10** [r] Eph 4:1 **1:11** [s] Eph 3:16 [t] Eph 4:2 **1:12** [u] Eph 5:20 [v] Ac 20:32 **1:13** [w] Ac 26:18

[a] 2 The Greek word for *brothers and sisters* (*adelphoi*) refers here to believers, both men and women, as part of God's family; also in 4:15. [b] 2 Some manuscripts *Father and the Lord Jesus Christ* [c] 7 Or *slave* [d] 7 Some manuscripts *your* [e] 9 Or *all spiritual wisdom and understanding* [f] 12 Some manuscripts *us*

1:2 *holy people ... Grace and peace.* See note on Ro 1:7.
1:3 *We always thank God.* Letters sometimes included thanksgivings and usually included a prayer, blessing, or at least mention of prayer (cf. also v. 9).
1:4 Speakers and writers often began by praising their audience, thus expressing appreciation and building rapport. *we have heard of.* Paul had heard from Epaphras (v. 7), who was from their region (4:12); when Paul ministered in cosmopolitan Ephesus, many who learned from him probably returned to their home areas to spread the message (cf. Ac 19:10).
1:5 *hope stored up for you in heaven.* Jewish people sometimes spoke of heavenly rewards as treasure in heaven.
1:6 *bearing fruit.* Many Jewish sources used the image of fruit bearing (e.g., Hos 10:1; 14:7–8; Mt 3:8–10; see note on Col 1:10).
1:7 *Epaphras.* This is probably the same Epaphras as in Phm 23, but although Epaphras was a contraction of Epaphroditus, we cannot be certain that this Epaphras is the same Epaphroditus as in Php 2:25. The Epaphroditus of that letter may have been from Philippi in Macedonia, far from Colossae, and Epaphroditus was a common name. See note on Col 1:4.
1:9 *knowledge ... wisdom and understanding.* Both ancient Israelite idiom (Pr 2:6; 9:10) and flowery Asian rhetoric (see Introduction to Ephesians) could pile up related terms such as these. *the Spirit gives.* The Spirit could provide wisdom, knowledge and understanding (Ex 31:3; 35:31; Isa 11:2), whether for (e.g.) artistic skills (Ex 31:3; cf. 1Ki 7:14) or for leadership (Isa 11:2–4).
1:10 *bearing fruit ... growing.* These echo Ge 1:28, the passage that follows humans being created in God's image (cf. Col 3:10). *knowledge of God.* See note on Php 3:10.
1:11 *strengthened with all power ... might.* Both ancient Israelite idiom (2Ch 20:6) and flowery Asian rhetoric could pile up related terms such as these.
1:12 *giving joyful thanks.* See note on Eph 5:20. *inheritance of his holy people.* Scripture and Jewish teaching promised a future inheritance for God's people, which here includes Gentile believers in Jesus as well as Jewish ones (see notes on Eph 1:1,14). *kingdom of light.* This image would be easy for first-century hearers to grasp; e.g., people often contrasted light and darkness as figures for good and evil. (Thus the Jewish sect that composed the Dead Sea Scrolls contrasted themselves as children of light with the rest of humanity, children of darkness under the dominion of Satan.) *kingdom.* See the article "Kingdom," p. 1616.
1:13 *from the dominion of darkness ... into the kingdom of the Son.* Some Jewish people envisioned their deliverance from Egypt as redemption from light to darkness

dom[x] of the Son he loves,[y] 14in whom we
have redemption,[z] the forgiveness of sins.[a]

The Supremacy of the Son of God

15The Son is the image[b] of the invisible
God,[c] the firstborn over all creation. 16For
in him all things were created:[d] things in
heaven and on earth, visible and invisible, whether thrones or powers or rulers
or authorities;[e] all things have been created through him and for him.[f] 17He is before all things,[g] and in him all things hold

1:13 [x] Eph 6:12; 2Pe 1:11 [y] Mt 3:17 **1:14** [z] Ro 3:24 [a] Eph 1:7 **1:15** [b] 2Co 4:4 [c] Jn 1:18 **1:16** [d] Jn 1:3 [e] Eph 1:20,21 [f] Ro 11:36 **1:17** [g] Jn 1:2

and viewed proselytes as adopting a new divine allegiance. Being transferred from one kingdom to another also made sense in a world where people could come under new rulers or some achieved Roman or local citizenship.

1:14 *redemption.* Meant releasing someone from captivity or slavery; the concept often included paying a ransom or price. This image evokes God redeeming his people from Egyptian captivity (cf. v. 13; Dt 7:8; 9:26; 2Sa 7:23). For sacrifices and God's forgiveness, see, e.g., Lev 4:20,26,31,35.

1:15 *image of the invisible God.* Jewish tradition portrayed divine Wisdom as God's archetypal image by which he created the rest of the world (see note on Jn 1:3); some Diaspora Jewish authors so depicted God's *logos*, his reason or word (see note on Jn 1:1). *firstborn over all creation.* In v. 18, "firstborn" applies to Jesus' resurrection as head of a new creation; here, however, the context is the first creation. "Firstborn" designates Jesus not only as God's Son, but also as the preeminent one and heir (Ge 49:3), a title for the Davidic ruler (Ps 89:26–27). (It thus does not imply that the Son was created.) Greeks sometimes called deities firstborn, but more relevantly the Diaspora Jewish author Philo applies the title often to the *logos*. Paul's audience would recognize it as exalted language.

1:16 *in him … through him … for him.* Using different prepositions, ancient intellectuals often distinguished kinds of causation, including the material something was created "from," the agency "through" which something was caused, the mode "in" or "by" which it was caused, and the purpose for which it was created. *all things.* Many philosophers, including Philo, taught that all things derived from and were held together by the *logos*, divine reason. *visible and invisible.* Some Greek and Diaspora Jewish thinkers believed that the Creator used an invisible pattern to shape the visible world. *thrones or powers or rulers or authorities.* Most Gentiles viewed stars as divine, and Jews saw them as angelic; these could be visible created things in heaven. Invisible heavenly beings could include angelic powers and rulers, which were often viewed as angels over the nations (see note on Eph 1:21). (Jewish people also thought of angels ruling various forces of nature; e.g., 1 Enoch 60:12–22; Jubilees 2:2; Dead Sea Scrolls, 1QM 10.11–12; cf. perhaps Ps 148:2–4.) Jewish people recognized God as the Creator of both the visible and invisible, but many, including Philo, gave angels or subordinate divine powers a role in

COLOSSIANS 1:15–20

Background of Colossians 1:15–20

Many Gentiles deemed divine or partly divine a range of spirits, in nature, e.g., or among the deceased. Addressing here some who emphasized intermediate spirits and the forms of rigorous human spirituality found in their culture (see Col 2:16–23 and notes; cf. 2:10,15 and notes), Paul insists that Christ is supreme (cf. 2:6–15). Paul here describes Jesus in the language that Judaism normally reserved for personified Wisdom. This Wisdom tradition, now developed far beyond Pr 8:22–31, was the most exalted image that Judaism had available to depict divine personality distinct from God the Father. Diaspora Jewish sources (such as the essays of Philo, an Alexandrian Jewish philosopher) often depicted this intermediary or power as the *logos*, God's reason or word (see note on Jn 1:1).

Many scholars believe that Paul in Col 1:15–20 incorporates two stanzas of an early Christian hymn (for dividing the stanzas, note the repetition of "firstborn" in vv. 15,18); other ancient sources often quoted poetry unannounced. Nevertheless, the possibility remains that Paul simply waxes poetic here; speakers often shifted to "grand rhetoric," using exalted and even rhythmic prose, especially when praising deities. ◆

together. 18And he is the head[h] of the
body, the church; he is the beginning and
the firstborn from among the dead,[i] so that
in everything he might have the supremacy. 19For God was pleased[j] to have all his
fullness[k] dwell in him, 20and through him
to reconcile[l] to himself all things, whether
things on earth or things in heaven,[m] by
making peace through his blood,[n] shed on
the cross.

21Once you were alienated from God
and were enemies[o] in your minds[p] because of[a] your evil behavior. 22But now
he has reconciled you by Christ's physical
body[q] through death to present you holy
in his sight, without blemish and free from
accusation[r]— 23if you continue in your
faith, established[s] and firm, and do not
move from the hope[t] held out in the gospel. This is the gospel that you heard and
that has been proclaimed to every creature
under heaven,[u] and of which I, Paul, have
become a servant.[v]

Paul's Labor for the Church

24Now I rejoice in what I am suffering
for you, and I fill up in my flesh what is
still lacking in regard to Christ's afflictions,[w] for the sake of his body, which is
the church. 25I have become its servant[x]
by the commission God gave me[y] to present to you the word of God in its fullness— 26the mystery[z] that has been kept
hidden for ages and generations, but is
now disclosed to the Lord's people. 27To
them God has chosen to make known[a]
among the Gentiles the glorious riches of
this mystery, which is Christ in you, the
hope of glory.

28He is the one we proclaim, admon-
ishing[b] and teaching everyone with all
wisdom,[c] so that we may present everyone fully mature[d] in Christ. 29To this end I
strenuously[e] contend[f] with all the energy
Christ so powerfully works in me.[g]

1:18 [h] Eph 1:22 [i] Ac 26:23; Rev 1:5 **1:19** [j] Eph 1:5 [k] Jn 1:16 **1:20** [l] 2Co 5:18 [m] Eph 1:10 [n] Eph 2:13 **1:21** [o] Ro 5:10 [p] Eph 2:3 **1:22** [q] Ro 7:4 [r] Eph 5:27 **1:23** [s] Eph 3:17 [t] ver 5 [u] Ro 10:18 [v] ver 25; 1Co 3:5 **1:24** [w] 2Co 1:5 **1:25** [x] ver 23 [y] Eph 3:2 **1:26** [z] Ro 16:25 **1:27** [a] Mt 13:11 **1:28** [b] Col 3:16 [c] 1Co 2:6,7 [d] Eph 5:27 **1:29** [e] 1Co 15:10 [f] Col 2:1 [g] Eph 1:19

[a] *21* Or *minds, as shown by*

creation. Like some other Jews, Paul here argues against exalting angels too highly (see the article "Background of Colossians 1:15–20," p. 2083). *for him.* Jewish people believed that God created everything through and for God's Word or Wisdom.

1:18 *the body.* See note on Ro 12:4–5; ancient thinkers often combined this image with the head. When used figuratively, "head" most often connoted authority (cf. Col 2:10) but in some contexts could refer to a particularly honored part or even a source (2:19). *the beginning.* In Jewish sources, "the beginning" could be a title for God (as in Rev 21:6), for Wisdom, and for the *logos*; it can naturally apply to the originator of creation (though in this context it applies to the new creation). *firstborn.* See note on v. 15. Because Jesus' resurrection anticipated the promised resurrection of all the righteous, the former was the firstfruits of the latter (1Co 15:23).

1:19 *God was pleased to have all his fullness dwell in him.* In the OT, God was pleased to dwell, e.g., among his people or in Zion (e.g., Ex 25:8; Ps 68:16; Zec 2:10–11), though the verse here goes beyond these examples. *fullness.* Pointing to various Jewish sources (including the OT), some suggest that this may refer to God's wisdom or glory filling the world; others, pointing to other Jewish sources (including Philo) explain it as the fullness of God's presence or attributes (cf. 2:9–10).

1:20 *peace.* Ceasing enmity; this means that heavenly powers (cf. v. 16) will be subjugated, not that they will be saved (2:15). Thus when the emperor's troops subjected his enemies to him, he claimed to have established peace. The powers remain active (2:8) but Christ's kingdom has already triumphed. (Ancient Jewish hearers might have understood well: in some traditions, God sent Enoch to announce to fallen angels under judgment the final doom that awaited them.)

1:23 *proclaimed to every creature under heaven.* May use hyperbole (ancient sources often use such language) or mean that the message has been preached in a representative way among different peoples (cf. Ro 1:8; see note on Ro 10:18). This public proclamation might contrast with merely personal mystic experiences of the false teachers (Col 2:18).

1:24 *I am suffering for you.* Speakers who could point to what they had suffered for their hearers could arouse more respect. Athletes (cf. v. 29) also competed to achieve honor not only for themselves but also for their cities. Many Jewish traditions warned that a requisite amount of affliction would need to precede the end (see note on Rev 6:10–11). Some scholars thus argue that Paul here embraces an extra share of these sufferings, sometimes called "the Messiah's birth pangs" because such sufferings presaged the Messianic era. Others instead or also connect it with sharing Christ's sufferings as part of union with Christ (a concept widespread in Paul's letters, with few strong possible non-Christian parallels). (Paul clearly believes that Christ's own sufferings are sufficient for redemption, however; cf. v. 14; 2:8–10,14.)

1:25 *commission.* This Greek term often meant being a household manager, a role often given to particularly skilled slaves or freedmen (see note on 1Co 4:1).

1:26 *mystery.* See notes on Ro 16:25; Eph 1:9. *now disclosed.* That the mystery has now been revealed would challenge false teachers claiming private revelations that conflicted with it (2:18). Scripture had long noted God's word spreading among Gentiles, but only now was it being proclaimed and increasingly fulfilled (see note on Ro 16:26).

1:27 *Christ in you.* In the OT, God chose to dwell among his people (e.g., Nu 35:34) and promised to do so forever in the future (Eze 43:7,9). Here, however, he dwells even "among the Gentiles" who trust him. Paul may also envision Christ dwelling within them personally (see Col 2:12; 3:4,16; cf. Ro 8:9–10; 2Co 13:5). Some Greek thinkers and the OT occasionally spoke of God dwelling in some special persons (Ge 41:38; Nu 27:18; Da 4:8,18; 5:11,14; cf. 1Pe 1:11), though "filled" and "rested on" were more common OT idioms.

1:28 *everyone.* See note on v. 23; for Gentiles, see note on v. 27. *mature.* Cf. note on 1Co 3:1.

1:29 *strenuously contend.* Cf. 2:1; the Greek term is often an athletic image; teachers often used such images figuratively to make points. *Christ so powerfully works in me.* Paul's experience of Christ empowering him is consistent with God's Spirit working through some people in the OT (e.g., Ex 31:3; Dt 34:9).

2 I want you to know how hard I am
contending[h] for you and for those at
Laodicea,[i] and for all who have not met
me personally. 2 My goal is that they may
be encouraged in heart[j] and united in love,
so that they may have the full riches of
complete understanding, in order that they
may know the mystery of God, namely,
Christ, 3 in whom are hidden all the treasures of wisdom and knowledge.[k] 4 I tell
you this so that no one may deceive you
by fine-sounding arguments.[l] 5 For though
I am absent from you in body, I am present with you in spirit[m] and delight to see
how disciplined[n] you are and how firm[o]
your faith in Christ is.

Spiritual Fullness in Christ

6 So then, just as you received Christ
Jesus as Lord,[p] continue to live your lives
in him, 7 rooted[q] and built up in him,
strengthened in the faith as you were
taught, and overflowing with thankfulness.
8 See to it that no one takes you captive
through hollow and deceptive philosophy,[r] which depends on human tradition
and the elemental spiritual forces[a] of this
world[s] rather than on Christ.
9 For in Christ all the fullness of the Deity lives in bodily form, 10 and in Christ
you have been brought to fullness. He is
the head[t] over every power and authority.
11 In him you were also circumcised[u] with
a circumcision not performed by human
hands. Your whole self ruled by the flesh[b][v]
was put off when you were circumcised
by[c] Christ, 12 having been buried with
him in baptism, in which you were also
raised with him[w] through your faith in the
working of God, who raised him from the
dead.[x]
13 When you were dead in your sins[y] and
in the uncircumcision of your flesh, God
made you[d] alive with Christ. He forgave us

2:1 [h] Col 1:29; 4:12 [i] Rev 1:11 **2:2** [j] Col 4:8 **2:3** [k] Ro 11:33; 1Co 1:24,30 **2:4** [l] Ro 16:18 **2:5** [m] 1Th 2:17 [n] 1Co 14:40 [o] 1Pe 5:9 **2:6** [p] Col 1:10 **2:7** [q] Eph 3:17
2:8 [r] 1Ti 6:20 [s] Gal 4:3 **2:10** [t] Eph 1:22 **2:11** [u] Ro 2:29; Php 3:3 [v] Gal 5:24 **2:12** [w] Ro 6:5 [x] Ac 2:24 **2:13** [y] Eph 2:1,5

[a] 8 Or *the basic principles*; also in verse 20 [b] 11 In contexts like this, the Greek word for *flesh* (*sarx*) refers to the sinful state of human beings, often presented as a power in opposition to the Spirit; also in verse 13. [c] 11 Or *put off in the circumcision of* [d] 13 Some manuscripts *us*

2:1 *for those at Laodicea.* Colossae was in the Lycus Valley and not on an easy route from Ephesus. Like Colossae, Laodicea was in Phrygia; it was roughly ten miles (16 kilometers) west of Colossae.
2:3 *treasures of wisdom and knowledge.* Ancient sages often spoke of wisdom as the true wealth (including in the OT: Job 28:12 – 19; Ps 19:10; 119:14,72,127,162; Pr 3:13 – 15; Isa 33:6).
2:4 *fine-sounding arguments.* The two advanced disciplines were philosophy (v. 8) and, more popular, rhetoric; although even most urban people lacked advanced training of any sort, the public sphere accustomed them to voices shaped by these disciplines. Philosophers sometimes criticized professional speakers for not caring about truth and rhetoricians sometimes criticized philosophers for worthless logic. Rhetorical training valued skill in persuasion irrespective of truth claims.
2:5 *absent from you in body, I am present with you.* Ancient letters used expressions such as these to communicate intimacy (cf. note on 1Co 5:3,4). They are not intended metaphysically.
2:6 *just as you received.* Paul might possibly be preparing a contrast with "tradition" in v. 8 (see note there); teachers passed on teachings and disciples received them to pass on to others.
2:7 *rooted and built up.* Planting and building were among Biblical images used for restoring or strengthening God's people (e.g., Jer 24:6; 42:10). *overflowing with thankfulness.* Gratitude for gifts received was considered a paramount virtue in antiquity.
2:8 *hollow and deceptive philosophy.* Philosophy often addressed cosmology and ethics; outsiders thus sometimes viewed Jews and Christians, whose gatherings discussed ethics, as philosophic schools. Educated Diaspora Jews naturally identified with philosophy, sometimes using it as a vehicle to communicate noble ideas to intelligent Gentiles. Paul uses the language of philosophy (e.g., 1:15 – 20; 3:1 – 2), but only where he deems it compatible with divine wisdom in Christ (2:2 – 3). Some Diaspora Jews (and later Christians) absorbed philosophies less critically, meanwhile sometimes claiming that the philosophers had stolen their ideas from Moses. *human tradition.* Schools passed on their teachings as tradition (cf. note on v. 6); among Jews, Pharisees were particularly known for this, but Jesus critiqued their human tradition (Mk 7:8, using the same Greek expression as here). *elemental spiritual forces.* This phrase may refer to the veneration of nature or perhaps angels over nature (see note on Gal 4:3); this fits the context here (cf. vv. 15,18; 1:16). Alternatively, the phrase may mean what is elementary (e.g., the alphabet), by comparison with Christ's true wisdom.
2:9 *the fullness of the Deity lives in bodily form.* Some philosophers claimed that all things filled the (pantheistic) deity. Some Diaspora Jewish thinkers used "fullness" for all the powers that are agents of God's rule, or to mean that God rules all things. Following the OT, some other Jewish thinkers used such language simply to depict God's Spirit, wisdom or glory filling the world. In any case, Paul claims that Christ is the only full revelation of God, a function that ancient Jewish sources often attributed to divine Wisdom.
2:10 *every power and authority.* May refer to the angelic rulers of the nations (see 1:16; Da 10:13,20; see also note on Eph 1:21).
2:11 *circumcision not performed by human hands.* Many Gentiles despised circumcision as a form of mutilation; conversely, most Jews required Gentiles to embrace it for conversion to Judaism. It was spiritual circumcision, however, that delivered from sin (Dt 10:16; 30:6; see note on Ro 2:29). *by human hands.* See note on Eph 2:11. *the flesh was put off.* Jewish people were circumcised in the "flesh" (see Ge 17:11). Some Greek thinkers complained that the body (*sôma*) was a tomb (*sêma*); Paul says that the old life has been removed in Christ. *flesh.* See the article "Flesh and Spirit," p. 1961.
2:12 *buried with him in baptism.* See notes on Ro 6:4,6.
2:13 *dead in your sins.* Some other ancient sources speak of figurative or spiritual death, or being under the sentence of death. *forgave us all our sins.* Jewish prayers regularly requested God's forgiveness.

all our sins, 14having canceled the charge
of our legal indebtedness,[z] which stood
against us and condemned us; he has tak-
en it away, nailing it to the cross.[a] 15And
having disarmed the powers and authorities,[b] he made a public spectacle of them,
triumphing over them[c] by the cross.[a]

Freedom From Human Rules

16Therefore do not let anyone judge
you[d] by what you eat or drink,[e] or with
regard to a religious festival,[f] a New Moon
celebration[g] or a Sabbath day.[h] 17These are
a shadow of the things that were to come;[i]
the reality, however, is found in Christ.
18Do not let anyone who delights in false
humility[j] and the worship of angels disqualify you.[k] Such a person also goes into
great detail about what they have seen;
they are puffed up with idle notions by
their unspiritual mind. 19They have lost
connection with the head,[l] from whom the
whole body, supported and held together
by its ligaments and sinews, grows as God
causes it to grow.[m]
20Since you died with Christ to the elemental spiritual forces of this world,[n] why,
as though you still belonged to the world,
do you submit to its rules:[o] 21"Do not handle! Do not taste! Do not touch!"? 22These
rules, which have to do with things that
are all destined to perish[p] with use, are
based on merely human commands and
teachings.[q] 23Such regulations indeed have
an appearance of wisdom, with their self-
imposed worship, their false humility and
their harsh treatment of the body, but they
lack any value in restraining sensual indulgence.

Living as Those Made Alive in Christ

3 Since, then, you have been raised with
Christ, set your hearts on things above,
where Christ is, seated at the right hand
of God. 2Set your minds on things above,

2:14 [z] Eph 2:15 [a] 1Pe 2:24 **2:15** [b] Eph 6:12 [c] Lk 10:18 **2:16** [d] Ro 14:3, 4 [e] Ro 14:17 [f] Ro 14:5 [g] 1Ch 23:31 [h] Gal 4:10 **2:17** [i] Heb 8:5 **2:18** [j] ver 23 [k] Php 3:14 **2:19** [l] Eph 1:22 [m] Eph 4:16 **2:20** [n] Gal 4:3,9 [o] ver 14,16 **2:22** [p] 1Co 6:13 [q] Isa 29:13; Mt 15:9; Titus 1:14

[a] *15* Or *them in him*

2:14 *canceled the charge of our legal indebtedness.* Language such as this was used for handwritten notes, usually certificates of debt. Jewish tradition also portrayed sins as "debts" before God; they came to believe that these were canceled on the Day of Atonement. Another Greek term in this phrase was often used for God's laws as his decrees (the same Greek term is translated "regulations" in Eph 2:15); decrees were often posted in public locations. *nailing it to the cross.* Although victims could be hanged on crosses with rope, nails were sometimes used, as for Jesus (Jn 20:25; cf. Ac 2:23).
2:15 *powers and authorities.* Probably refer to the spiritual powers behind the earthly ones (including behind the earthly ones that held Paul in Roman custody!). See notes on 1:16; Eph 1:21. *he made a public spectacle of them.* Whereas in v. 8 Paul warned believers against being taken captive (meaning enslaved as a prisoner of war), here Christ exhibits the hostile powers themselves as captives in his triumphal procession. During a triumph, the emperor, dressed as the ruling god Jupiter, would lead defeated captives behind him, showing them off before their execution (see note on 2Co 2:14). *triumphing over them by the cross.* Because the cross was the most humiliating instrument of execution, Paul inverts the world's wisdom here (cf. v. 8).
2:16 The three Jewish practices for which non-Jewish Romans especially mocked Jews were circumcision (cf. vv. 11 – 13), the prohibition of non-kosher food and drink (see note on Ro 14:21), and holy days (see note on Ro 14:5). Sabbaths are weekly; the New Moon celebration welcomed each month. Jewish people did not expect most Gentiles to observe their food laws or holy days but did expect Gentile converts to Judaism to do so, perhaps including Gentile Christians.
2:17 *the reality, however, is found in Christ.* Developing ideas from earlier philosophers, some, including some Diaspora Jewish thinkers, distinguished the "reality" (lit. "body"; cf. 1:22) that stood behind the visible mere shadows or copies. While recognizing that God inspired OT precepts with true principles in mind, Paul suggests that such principles are fulfilled in Christ (cf. Heb 8:5; 10:1). Those with the reality did not need to depend on the shadows whose function was to point to the reality.
2:18 *false humility.* Jewish people had long used fasting (cf. vv. 21 – 22) to humble themselves (e.g., Ezr 8:21; Ps 35:13), but some also used this to seek revelations. *the worship of angels.* Some think that this refers to worshiping "with" angels, as in some Judean circles. More likely in view, because more clearly problematic, some less educated Diaspora Jews apparently invoked and prayed to angels. Paul counters an excessive emphasis on such spirits (vv. 8,10,15,20; 1:16). *what they have seen.* May imply visions; Jewish apocalyptic visionaries often spoke of what angels had shown them (cf. Gal 1:8 – 9), and both they and other Jewish mystics sought to cultivate visions of God's throne. Some Gentiles and Jews influenced by Plato combined mystic experiences with philosophy (Col 2:8). While appreciating genuine revelations (2Co 12:1 – 4), Paul rejects false ones (cf. Jer 23:32).
2:19 *lost connection with the head.* Ancient medical literature sometimes described the head as the source of life for the rest of the body.
2:20 *elemental spiritual forces.* See note on v. 8. *rules.* The verbal form of the Greek term Paul uses for Jewish "regulations" in Eph 2:15, which also appears in the Greek of v. 14 in this chapter.
2:21 *Do not handle! Do not taste! Do not touch!* Most Diaspora Jews abstained from foods forbidden in Lev 11. They also risked impurity for touching some things (e.g., Lev 11:39; 15:5,21; Nu 19:11; contrast Jesus in Mk 1:41; 5:30 – 34,41). Some Jews extended such rules, e.g., opposing even touching some foods.
2:22 *destined to perish.* Those influenced by philosophical thought recognized that transitory, perishable things were much less valuable than what was eternal. *human commands and teachings.* Evokes the Greek translation of Isa 29:13, a passage cited by Jesus (Mk 7:7).
2:23 *harsh treatment of the body.* In the Diaspora, rules such as those cited in v. 21 sometimes imposed hardships, in extreme situations reducing some to eating just fruits and nuts. Many philosophers taught people to free themselves from bodily pleasures so they could focus on the pure soul. *lack any value in restraining sensual indulgence.* Some Diaspora Jews taught that the Biblical food laws revealed principles for protecting the soul from bad habits.
3:1 – 2 Developing earlier philosophy, many of Paul's contemporaries viewed the heavenly realms as pure and

not on earthly things.[r] 3For you died,[s] and
your life is now hidden with Christ in God.
4When Christ, who is your[a] life, appears,[t]
then you also will appear with him in glory.[u]

5Put to death, therefore, whatever belongs to your earthly nature: sexual immorality, impurity, lust, evil desires and greed,[v]
which is idolatry.[w] 6Because of these, the
wrath of God[x] is coming.[b] 7You used to
walk in these ways, in the life you once
lived.[y] 8But now you must also rid yourselves[z] of all such things as these: anger,
rage, malice, slander,[a] and filthy language
from your lips.[b] 9Do not lie to each other,[c]
since you have taken off your old self with
its practices 10and have put on the new self,
which is being renewed[d] in knowledge in
the image of its Creator.[e] 11Here there is no
Gentile or Jew,[f] circumcised or uncircumcised,[g] barbarian, Scythian, slave or free,[h]
but Christ is all,[i] and is in all.

3:2 [r] Php 3:19, 20
3:3 [s] Ro 6:2; 2Co 5:14
3:4 [t] 1Co 1:7 [u] 1Pe 1:13; 1Jn 3:2
3:5 [v] Eph 5:3 [w] Eph 5:5
3:6 [x] Ro 1:18
3:7 [y] Eph 2:2
3:8 [z] Eph 4:22 [a] Eph 4:31 [b] Eph 4:29
3:9 [c] Eph 4:22, 25
3:10 [d] Ro 12:2; Eph 4:23 [e] Eph 2:10
3:11 [f] Ro 10:12 [g] 1Co 7:19 [h] Gal 3:28 [i] Eph 1:23
3:12 [j] Php 2:3 [k] 2Co 6:6; Gal 5:22, 23
3:13 [l] Eph 4:2 [m] Eph 4:32

12Therefore, as God's chosen people,
holy and dearly loved, clothe yourselves
with compassion, kindness, humility,[j]
gentleness and patience.[k] 13Bear with each
other[l] and forgive one another if any of
you has a grievance against someone. Forgive as the Lord forgave you.[m] 14And over
all these virtues put on love,[n] which binds
them all together in perfect unity.[o]

15Let the peace of Christ[p] rule in your
hearts, since as members of one body you
were called to peace. And be thankful.
16Let the message of Christ[q] dwell among
you richly as you teach and admonish one
another with all wisdom[r] through psalms,
hymns, and songs from the Spirit, singing
to God with gratitude in your hearts.[s]

[a] 4 Some manuscripts *our* [b] 6 Some early manuscripts *coming on those who are disobedient*

3:14 [n] 1Co 13:1-13 [o] Eph 4:3 **3:15** [p] Jn 14:27 **3:16** [q] Ro 10:17 [r] Col 1:28 [s] Eph 5:19

eternal, in contrast to the temporal, perishable world below. Philosophers thus became known for contemplating heavenly things. (Those who made fun of philosophers sometimes depicted them falling into pits because philosophers were always looking at the heavens.) Jewish apocalyptic writers also distinguished between heavenly and earthly realms, emphasizing the purity of God's realm in the upper heavens.

False teachers at Colossae may have been seeking these upper realms through mystical experiences (2:18). Jewish mystics sought especially to envision God's throne; some philosophers sought visions of the ultimate deity, who was pure, emotionless mind and separate from the world of matter. For Paul, by contrast, the object of heavenly contemplation is Christ, who is divine but not detached from humanity. In the context, this includes Christ's character or heavenly values centered on Christ (vv. 10–17), available because those who died and rose with Christ were also exalted with him (cf. vv. 1,5,9–10; 2:20; Eph 2:6). The phrase "heavenly matters" was sometimes used in similar ways.

3:5—4:1 Paul may have sent such instructions to multiple churches (cf. Eph 4:17—6:9). He may have done this directly, or he may have allowed an assistant to draft his basic instructions, which he could then adapt. Scribes were sometimes tasked with drafting material in documents based on already available material.

3:5 *Put to death ... whatever belongs to your earthly nature.* Vice lists were a common literary form in the ancient world, and both Gentile and Diaspora Jewish writers warned against passions. Many also thought that what mattered was the eternal and heavenly soul, not one's perishable, earthly body. For Paul, true heavenly mindedness (vv. 1–2) must shape earthly behaviors. Paul speaks figuratively of killing one's earthly "nature" (lit. "members"), perhaps evoking Jesus' hyperbole (Mk 9:43,45,47). For Paul, one accomplishes this not by literally mistreating or neglecting one's body (Col 2:23), but by embracing by faith one's completed union with Christ (3:3–4).

3:8 Ancient teachers sometimes listed obvious vices first, then offered a second list of less obvious ones. The vices listed in v. 5 were those that Jewish observers believed characterized Gentiles, who abandoned sexual immorality and idolatry if they converted to Judaism. By contrast, here Paul lists vices found even among Jews (cf. note on Ro 1:28–32).

3:9 *old self.* Probably refers to humanity in Adam; Jewish people often spoke of corporate solidarity with Adam (the Hebrew term for "person," here rendered "self").

3:10 *put on.* Jewish writers could speak of being "clothed" with the Spirit or virtues (see note on Eph 4:22–24). *new self.* Indicates the new humanity in solidarity with Christ (see v. 11). *image of its Creator.* As God was Creator of humanity in his image (Ge 1:26–27), so also here for the new creation. God renewed people's hearts even in the OT (Ps 51:10; Eze 18:31), but promised new hearts especially for the age to come (Eze 11:19–20; 36:26–27). Believers have put on the new self; their hearts are renewed as they experience this newness of life.

3:11 *Gentile or Jew.* See note on Ro 1:16. *circumcised or uncircumcised.* Although some other eastern peoples were circumcised, by "circumcised" and "uncircumcised" Jews meant "Jews" and "Gentiles." *barbarian.* See note on Ro 1:14. *Scythian.* The nomadic Scythians lived in much of what is today Russia, the Ukraine, Kazakhstan, and other parts of central Asia. Greeks often deemed Scythians the most cruel and anti-Greek people (although some ancient writers portrayed them as "noble barbarians"). *slave or free.* One major way of dividing humanity socially, although some household slaves wielded more authority and were more advanced socially than many free persons (cf. v. 22).

3:12 *chosen ... holy ... loved.* Paul describes believers using OT language for God's people (e.g., Dt 7:6; 14:2). *clothe yourselves.* See note on v. 10. *compassion ... patience.* Writers commonly listed virtues, sometimes in contrast with vice lists (cf. vv. 5,8; Gal 5:19–23). Sometimes they also listed assorted moral instructions (what scholars call paraenesis).

3:14 *over all these virtues put on love.* Although many ancient thinkers, especially among Jewish teachers, regarded love as an important virtue, Christians were the only movement where it was the chief virtue (following Jesus' teaching, Mk 12:30–31). *perfect unity.* Many thinkers urged unity, i.e., harmony with one another (see note on Ro 15:6); in Greek this may refer to the believers.

3:15 *called to peace.* Many Jewish thinkers praised peace with one another, which also was part of unity (cf. Eph 4:3). *be thankful.* Gratitude was a paramount virtue in antiquity (cf. 2:7).

3:16 *psalms, hymns, and songs from the Spirit.* See notes on 1Co 14:26; Eph 5:19.

COLOSSIANS 3

Mystery Cults

Mystery cults, with their secret rites, flourished during the Roman period and involved the worship of deities from Greece, Egypt and the Near East. Unlike official cults (such as the imperial cult), which sometimes involved primarily pledges of loyalty, these cults provided a sense of belonging to a selective community and sometimes personal salvation. Members participated in rituals and were expected to keep both the rites and the teachings secret; hence the designation "mystery religions." Famous examples are the Greek Eleusinian and Dionysian mysteries, the Mithras mysteries and the Egyptian cult of Isis and Osiris.

Each cult was distinct, but many mystery cults shared a motif of death and afterlife. The Eleusinian mysteries centered upon a myth of the annual descent of Persephone, the daughter of Demeter, into Hades and her subsequent return to the land of the living. The cult of Isis and Osiris was similar. In Egyptian religion Osiris, the lord of the dead, was also believed to be a source of life and renewal. Osiris had been murdered by his brother Set, but his wife/sister, Isis, had located his scattered remains and effected for him a kind of resurrection. Mystery religions that spoke of a deity returning from death normally connected this return with the annual return of life to the world in the spring, in contrast to the Jewish and Christian teaching of a once-for-all bodily resurrection of the righteous (cf. Da 12:2; Ro 1:4).

Some cults focused on cosmic power. The Mithras cult, which became popular with Roman men around the second century AD, involves the Persian deity Mithras, but the mystery cult's teachings were indigenous to the Greco-Roman world. Worship was carried out in a small, cave-like chamber called a Mithraeum, which contained cryptic inscriptions and symbols, the primary clues to the nature of the religion. The central motif centered around a man, Mithras, who had purportedly slain a bull. In the iconography Mithras is accompanied by a dog, a snake, a raven, and a scorpion. All of these

continued on next page

[17]And whatever you do,[t] whether in word or deed, do it all in the name of the Lord Jesus, giving thanks[u] to God the Father through him.

Instructions for Christian Households

3:18 – 4:1pp — Eph 5:22 – 6:9

[18]Wives, submit yourselves to your husbands,[v] as is fitting in the Lord.

[19]Husbands, love your wives and do not be harsh with them.

[20]Children, obey your parents in everything, for this pleases the Lord.

[21]Fathers,[a] do not embitter your children, or they will become discouraged.

[22]Slaves, obey your earthly masters in

3:17 [t] 1Co 10:31 [u] Eph 5:20 **3:18** [v] Eph 5:22

[a] *21* Or *Parents*

3:17 *whatever you do.* Religion pervaded daily life, but for most Gentiles this expressed itself more in rituals than in behavior toward others.
3:18 — 4:1 On household codes, see note on Eph 5:21 — 6:9. Paranoia about minority cults undermining traditional values may provide additional incentive for instructions to household members here (cf. 1Ti 5:14; 6:1).
3:18 *Wives, submit.* On the ways wives were expected to submit in many ancient cultures, see the article "Marriage Roles in Antiquity," p. 2064. Ephesians modifies expectations more than Colossians does here, though ancient ethics often instructed wives not only to submit but to obey (cf. vv. 20,22). Household codes were often elaborated extensively, but they could also be very concise, as here.
3:19 *Husbands, love your wives.* Although the expectation of love was common, it was not commonly expressed in traditional household codes. They instead instructed male heads of households how to rule; Paul instructs husbands here how to love.
3:20 *Children, obey your parents in everything.* See note on Eph 6:1. Normally instructions for sons to obey applied only to minors.
3:21 *Fathers, do not embitter your children.* See note on Eph 6:4. Fathers are addressed rather than "parents" because household codes were normally directed toward fathers (see note on v. 19).
3:22 *Slaves, obey your earthly masters.* See the article "Slaves and Slaveholders in Ephesians 6," p. 2068; see also

creatures equate to constellations (Taurus, Canis Minor, Hydra, Corvus and Scorpio, respectively), and thus the cult may have been astrological in orientation and based upon the belief that Mithras was the ruler of the cosmos. Members of the cult ascended through a hierarchy of seven ranks, corresponding to the seven planets; solar and lunar icons are invariably found in a Mithraeum.

The cults frequently focused upon fertility, were often accompanied by erotic symbolism and included secret rituals that were sometimes either gory or orgiastic. The Dionysian mysteries, which involved a kind of ecstatic madness, were in fact for a time outlawed by the Roman Senate. Popular fear of and fascination with the bacchanalian frenzy is reflected in ancient literary works such as *The Bacchae* by Euripides and the *Metamorphoses* by Ovid. In many mystery religions the initiate underwent a ritual death and rebirth through either ecstatic frenzy or secret ritual. One inscription in a Mithraeum describes the initiate as having been "piously reborn."

Some have suggested that Paul may have been influenced by these cults in his understanding of the "mystery" of the gospel of Christ. It is more likely, however, that the apostle used the term "mystery" to refer to the fact that the Old Testament prophecies, which include much that is mysterious, find their meaning and fulfillment in Christ. The language of revealing mysteries appears in Daniel and in the Dead Sea Scrolls. Converts to Christianity were not sworn to keep its tenets or practices a secret. ◆

Statue of Mithras slaying a bull, accompanied by a dog, snake, raven, and scorpion.

Wikimedia Commons

everything; and do it, not only when their
eye is on you and to curry their favor, but
with sincerity of heart and reverence for
the Lord. 23 Whatever you do, work at it
with all your heart, as working for the
Lord, not for human masters, 24 since you
know that you will receive an inheritance[w]
from the Lord as a reward. It is the Lord
Christ you are serving. 25 Anyone who does
wrong will be repaid for their wrongs, and
there is no favoritism.[x]

3:24 [w] Ac 20:32
3:25 [x] Ac 10:34

4 Masters, provide your slaves with what
is right and fair, because you know
that you also have a Master in heaven.

Further Instructions

2 Devote yourselves to prayer,[y] being
watchful and thankful. 3 And pray for
us, too, that God may open a door[z] for
our message, so that we may proclaim
the mystery of Christ, for which I am
in chains.[a] 4 Pray that I may proclaim it
clearly, as I should. 5 Be wise[b] in the way

4:2 [y] Lk 18:1
4:3 [z] Ac 14:27
[a] Eph 6:19,20
4:5 [b] Eph 5:15

Introduction to Philemon and the article "Ancient Slavery and the Background for Philemon," p. 2134. *not only when their eye is on you.* Slaveholders stereotyped slaves as lazy, especially when no one was looking.
3:23 *work at it with all your heart.* Paul encourages hard work but gives slaves a new hope and a new motive for their labor (v. 24).
4:1 *you also have a Master in heaven.* Aristotle complained about a small minority of thinkers, presumably especially early Stoics, who believed that slaves were in principle equal to their holders; this could be Paul's point here. No one was raising the question of abolishing slavery, so there was no reason to address it in a series of practical instructions. Nevertheless, many thinkers did emphasize right treatment of slaves, and some other Pauline passages reveal more of Paul's views (Eph 6:9; Phm 10–21).
4:3 *open a door.* The concept of an open door appears figuratively elsewhere in Greek for free opportunity. *I am in chains.* Normally those in custody had no means to wash, cut hair, and so forth. Paul's custody is probably lighter, merely chained house arrest (Ac 28:16). People were usually ashamed of chains; cf. further note on Ac 26:29.

you act toward outsiders;[c] make the most
of every opportunity.[d] 6Let your conversation be always full of grace,[e] seasoned
with salt,[f] so that you may know how to
answer everyone.[g]

Final Greetings

7Tychicus[h] will tell you all the news
about me. He is a dear brother, a faithful
minister and fellow servant[a][i] in the Lord.
8I am sending him to you for the express
purpose that you may know about our[b]
circumstances and that he may encourage
your hearts.[j] 9He is coming with Onesimus,[k] our faithful and dear brother, who
is one of you. They will tell you everything
that is happening here.

10My fellow prisoner Aristarchus[l] sends
you his greetings, as does Mark, the cousin
of Barnabas.[m] (You have received instructions about him; if he comes to you, welcome him.) 11Jesus, who is called Justus,
also sends greetings. These are the only
Jews[c] among my co-workers for the kingdom of God, and they have proved a comfort to me. 12Epaphras,[n] who is one of you
and a servant of Christ Jesus, sends greetings. He is always wrestling in prayer for
you,[o] that you may stand firm in all the
will of God, mature[p] and fully assured. 13I
vouch for him that he is working hard for
you and for those at Laodicea[q] and Hierapolis. 14Our dear friend Luke,[r] the doctor, and
Demas[s] send greetings. 15Give my greetings
to the brothers and sisters at Laodicea, and
to Nympha and the church in her house.[t]

16After this letter has been read to you,
see that it is also read[u] in the church of the
Laodiceans and that you in turn read the
letter from Laodicea.

17Tell Archippus:[v] "See to it that you
complete the ministry you have received
in the Lord."[w]

18I, Paul, write this greeting in my own
hand.[x] Remember[y] my chains. Grace be
with you.[z]

4:5 [c] Mk 4:11 [d] Eph 5:16 **4:6** [e] Eph 4:29 [f] Mk 9:50 [g] 1Pe 3:15 **4:7** [h] Ac 20:4 [i] Eph 6:21,22 **4:8** [j] Eph 6:21, 22 **4:9** [k] Phm 10 **4:10** [l] Ac 19:29 [m] Ac 4:36 **4:12** [n] Col 1:7; Phm 23 [o] Ro 15:30 [p] 1Co 2:6 **4:13** [q] Col 2:1 **4:14** [r] 2Ti 4:11; Phm 24 [s] 2Ti 4:10 **4:15** [t] Ro 16:5 **4:16** [u] 2Th 3:14 **4:17** [v] Phm 2 [w] 2Ti 4:5 **4:18** [x] 1Co 16:21 [y] Heb 13:3 [z] 1Ti 6:21; 2Ti 4:22; Titus 3:15; Heb 13:25

[a] *7* Or *slave;* also in verse 12 [b] *8* Some manuscripts *that he may know about your* [c] *11* Greek *only ones of the circumcision group*

4:6 *conversation be always full of grace, seasoned with salt.* The traditional Greek meaning of "grace" included pleasant and graceful speech. Greeks often portrayed pleasant speech as "honeyed." Salt was a preserving and flavoring agent. Cf. Pr 15:1; 16:24.
4:7–8 *Tychicus will tell you ... that you may know about.* Travelers passed on news orally (see note on Eph 6:21).
4:9 *Onesimus.* If Paul wrote Colossians after Philemon granted his implicit request in Phm 10–14,21 (or if Paul sent both letters at the same time), Onesimus here is probably the same person as in Phm 10. An early second-century bishop of Ephesus also bore this name, although identification with the Onesimus here is uncertain.
4:10 *Aristarchus.* Both Aristarchus and, on the likeliest view of Acts' authorship, Luke (v. 14), had accompanied Paul to Rome, where he was a prisoner (Ac 27:2; 28:14). *Mark, the cousin of Barnabas.* Mark's presence in Rome in this period is also suggested by 1Pe 5:13 (though he is absent in 2Ti 4:11).
4:11 *Jesus, who is called Justus.* Many Jewish people bore the name Jesus, which represents the Greek way of pronouncing Joshua's name. Justus is Latin; many Jewish people used a second Greek or Latin name resembling their more traditional Jewish name.
4:12 *Epaphras.* See note on 1:7. *wrestling in prayer.* Athletic metaphors (here, "wrestling"; the same Greek term as in 1:29, where it is translated "strenuously contend") were common in ancient speeches. See the article "Athletic Imagery in 1 Corinthians 9," p. 2000.
4:13 *I vouch for him.* A letter of recommendation sometimes reported the recommendee's appreciation for the letter's receiver; Paul likewise here notes Epaphras's hard work on behalf of (whether for or in the place of) the Phrygian believers. For letters of recommendation, see note on 1Co 16:10–11. *Laodicea and Hierapolis.* The three largest cities of the Lycus Valley in Phrygia were Colossae, Laodicea (ten miles west of Colossae) and Hierapolis (six miles [almost ten kilometers] from Laodicea); of these, Colossae was the least significant in this period. Hierapolis hosted healing cults, a temple to the emperor and the reported entrance to the underworld; it also had a significant Jewish presence in this period. Laodicea was a wealthy commercial center, despite its somewhat remote location (see the article "Laodicea," p. 2228).
4:14 *Luke, the doctor.* Evidence suggests the prominence of medical interests in the Lycus Valley. Doctors were well educated but were often slaves or freedpersons, with relatively low social status. A majority were ethnically Greek. Although most physicians were men, women physicians (most often but not limited to midwives) are known. Empirically valid observations existed alongside folk traditions, superstition, and guesswork; there were no board-accredited physicians, and different schools of medical thought existed. Pagan healing cults allowed for medical practice alongside prayers to a deity; views varied somewhat in Judaism, but later hospitals evolved especially from the eventual Christian practice of caring for the sick in late antiquity. *Demas.* Probably a shortened form for "Demetrius," though he apparently always went by this name.
4:15 *Nympha and the church in her house.* Although men held more wealth and more often sponsored meetings of associations, women could do this as well. As a homeowner and sole named patron of this house church, it is possible that Nympha might be widowed or divorced.
4:16 *the letter from Laodicea.* Paul's letter for the church of the Laodiceans has not survived, unless it was the local Phrygian form of the circular letter that we call Ephesians (see note on Eph 1:1). Most people in antiquity were not very literate, although reading skills ranged higher among urban men. Normally one person would read to a group; even if several could read, it was not easy to transcribe copies for multiple readers. Churches that could afford scrolls read Scripture during their gatherings; by the mid-second century at the latest, apostolic works were regularly read as Scripture there also. *Laodicea.* See note on v. 13; see also the article "Laodicea," p. 2228.
4:17 *Archippus.* May have been Philemon's son or at least a colleague in his house church (Phm 2).
4:18 *write this greeting in my own hand.* Most letters, especially those of any significant length, were dictated to scribes. One could add one's signature at the end of the letter, however (cf. note on Ro 16:22). *Remember my chains.* People were usually embarrassed to associate with prisoners. Paul, however, cites his chains the way soldiers showed their wounds to demonstrate their sacrifices for the people.

THE LETTERS

1 THESSALONIANS

Date and Occasion

Paul probably wrote 1 Thessalonians by AD 50, roughly 20 years after Jesus' execution and resurrection. This may thus be the earliest of Paul's letters (although some scholars date 2 Thessalonians or Galatians earlier). Ac 17:5 – 10 indicates that adversaries charged Paul with illegally announcing Jesus as a royal rival to Caesar (Ac 17:7; cf. "kingdom" in 1Th 2:12; 2Th 1:5). Paul was forced to flee Thessalonica and dared not return until the rulings against him expired (when the politarchs retired). Meanwhile, those who stirred the trouble remained, and the new believers continued to face suffering (1Th 1:6; 3:3 – 4; 2Th 1:4 – 5). Some had died (1Th 4:13), although the cause is not stated. Although many of the believers are Gentiles (1:9), Paul in this early letter draws on Biblical and ancient Jewish end-time imagery, much of it directly from Jesus.

Ancient letters could focus on comfort, thanksgiving, or exhortation; 1 Thessalonians includes elements of all of these. On Thessalonica, see note on Ac 17:1; on religion in Thessalonica, see note on 1Th 1:9. ◆

QUICK GLANCE

AUTHOR:
The apostle Paul

AUDIENCE:
The largely Gentile church in Thessalonica, founded by Paul

DATE:
Close to AD 50, perhaps about AD 51

THEME:
Unable to physically be with the new believers, Paul encourages their faith and strengthens their hope in view of Christ's imminent return.

1 Paul, Silas[a] and Timothy,[a]

To the church of the Thessalonians[b] in
God the Father and the Lord Jesus Christ:

Grace and peace to you.[c]

Thanksgiving for the Thessalonians' Faith

2We always thank God for all of you[d]
and continually mention you in our
prayers. 3We remember before our God
and Father your work produced by faith,[e]
your labor prompted by love, and your
endurance inspired by hope in our Lord
Jesus Christ.

4For we know, brothers and sisters[b]
loved by God, that he has chosen you, 5be-
cause our gospel[f] came to you not simply
with words but also with power, with the
Holy Spirit and deep conviction. You know
how we lived among you for your sake.
6You became imitators of us[g] and of the
Lord, for you welcomed the message in the
midst of severe suffering[h] with the joy giv-
en by the Holy Spirit.[i] 7And so you became
a model to all the believers in Macedonia
and Achaia. 8The Lord's message rang out
from you not only in Macedonia and Achaia — your faith in God has become known
everywhere.[j] Therefore we do not need to
say anything about it, 9for they themselves
report what kind of reception you gave us.
They tell how you turned to God from
idols[k] to serve the living and true God,
10and to wait for his Son from heaven,
whom he raised from the dead[l] — Jesus,
who rescues us from the coming wrath.[m]

Paul's Ministry in Thessalonica

2 You know, brothers and sisters, that
our visit to you[n] was not without results. 2We had previously suffered[o] and
been treated outrageously in Philippi, as
you know, but with the help of our God
we dared to tell you his gospel in the face

1:1 [a] Ac 16:1; 2Th 1:1 [b] Ac 17:1 [c] Ro 1:7 **1:2** [d] Ro 1:8 **1:3** [e] 2Th 1:11 **1:5** [f] 2Th 2:14 **1:6** [g] 1Co 4:16 [h] Ac 17:5-10 [i] Ac 13:52 **1:8** [j] Ro 1:8; 10:18 **1:9** [k] 1Co 12:2; Gal 4:8 **1:10** [l] Ac 2:24 [m] Ro 5:9 **2:1** [n] 1Th 1:5,9 **2:2** [o] Ac 16:22; Php 1:30

[a] *1* Greek *Silvanus*, a variant of *Silas* [b] *4* The Greek word for *brothers and sisters* (*adelphoi*) refers here to believers, both men and women, as part of God's family; also in 2:1, 9, 14, 17; 3:7; 4:1, 10, 13; 5:1, 4, 12, 14, 25, 27.

1:1 *Silas.* The Greek is "Silvanus," a fairly respectable Latin name (consistent with his Roman citizenship in Ac 16:37). In Acts, Luke uses his less formal Jewish name Silas. On coauthors, see note on 1Co 1:1. *Grace and peace.* See note on Ro 1:7, though this earlier Pauline letter is more concise.
1:2–3 Ancient letters sometimes included thanks for the recipients, and prayer or mention of prayer. *God … Lord Jesus.* See note on 1Co 8:6.
1:4 *chosen.* Cf., e.g., Dt 7:6; see note on Col 3:12.
1:5 *You know how.* Persuasive speakers and writers often appealed to what their audience already knew for themselves.
1:6 *imitators of us and of the Lord.* Teachers and writers on moral subjects regularly cited examples; disciples especially imitated their teachers. *suffering.* See Introduction to 1 Thessalonians.
1:7 *Macedonia and Achaia.* Achaia was south of Macedonia; the capital of the former was Corinth, from which Paul writes this letter, and of the latter, Thessalonica. Philippi (2:2) was also in Macedonia.
1:8 *your faith in God has become known everywhere.* News spread through travelers. This would be true especially where they would find hospitality, e.g., Jewish travelers in Jewish homes. Thessalonica lay on the major land route between Asia Minor and anything to Thessalonica's west (and south). *everywhere.* May be an example of the frequent ancient practice of geographic hyperbole (see note on Col 1:23).
1:9 *turned to God from idols.* Most Gentiles venerated statues of deities, although the minority of intellectuals regarded them only as reminders of the deities. Jews and Christians, by contrast, detested them as idols. Such statues and the divinely populated cosmos they implied would have deep sentimental connections for those raised with them; they also represented major social ties with family and society. Respect for civic cults, including that of the emperor, was a social expectation; Thessalonica's temples included a significant one for the worship of the emperor. Converts to Judaism had to abandon all idols; some Gentiles viewed such conversion as betraying one's own family and people to become a Judean. Thessalonica did host a number of foreign cults (e.g., that of Isis), but monotheists' exclusivist insistence on one God appeared more offensive.
1:10 *Jesus, who rescues us from the coming wrath.* Idols (v. 9) would be useless at the time of God's wrath (e.g., Isa 2:19–21; 57:13). Many Jewish people expected a future resurrection of the righteous (Da 12:2); Jesus' resurrection was the foretaste and thus guarantee of that future event. Others, however, would face the wrath from which Jesus rescues believers. The prophets warned of God's wrath for all the earth (e.g., Isa 34:2–4; Zep 3:8; see note on Ro 2:5; cf. the coming wrath in Isa 13:9).
2:1–12 After introductions, ancient speeches and some other kinds of works included a narrative of the events or circumstances leading up to the present matters of discussion. Exhortations and defenses often included a contrast between negative or accused behavior and positive behavior (not/nor … but). Paul is not necessarily answering "opponents" in this passage. Because many people lumped all sages together as charlatans, many sages developed a series of responses to such stock accusations; Paul uses such responses here. Traditional charges sometimes include error, impure motives, and trickery (v. 3), flattery (v. 5), greed (v. 5) or desire for praise (v. 6); a good sage, by contrast, was gentle like a nursing mother (v. 7). Whether or not outsiders had criticized Paul's ministry in Thessalonica (aside from the obvious accusations in Ac 17:7), Paul could expect such criticism and thus equipped the church to be able to answer it (cf. 4:12).
2:2 *treated outrageously in Philippi.* Means being treated in a humiliating manner, which for Jews certainly included public stripping as well as being flogged with rods as if they were criminals (Ac 16:22). These events in Philippi were shortly before their arrival in Thessalonica, and word of their shameful treatment undoubtedly reached Thessalonica quickly. *dared.* Those influenced by philosophy valued those who would speak not with flattery (cf. v. 5) but with boldness (the meaning of the Greek term here; translated "frankness" in 2Co 7:4 [see note there]).

of strong opposition. 3For the appeal we
make does not spring from error or impure motives,[p] nor are we trying to trick
you. 4On the contrary, we speak as those
approved by God to be entrusted with the
gospel.[q] We are not trying to please people[r] but God, who tests our hearts. 5You
know we never used flattery, nor did we
put on a mask to cover up greed[s]—God
is our witness.[t] 6We were not looking
for praise from people, not from you or
anyone else, even though as apostles[u] of
Christ we could have asserted our authority. 7Instead, we were like young children[a]
among you.

Just as a nursing mother cares for her
children,[v] 8so we cared for you. Because
we loved you so much, we were delighted to share with you not only the gospel
of God but our lives as well.[w] 9Surely you
remember, brothers and sisters, our toil
and hardship; we worked[x] night and day
in order not to be a burden to anyone[y]
while we preached the gospel of God to
you. 10You are witnesses,[z] and so is God,
of how holy,[a] righteous and blameless we
were among you who believed. 11For you
know that we dealt with each of you as a
father deals with his own children,[b] 12en-
couraging, comforting and urging you to
live lives worthy[c] of God, who calls you
into his kingdom and glory.

13And we also thank God continually[d]
because, when you received the word of
God,[e] which you heard from us, you accepted it not as a human word, but as it
actually is, the word of God, which is indeed at work in you who believe. 14For
you, brothers and sisters, became imitators of God's churches in Judea,[f] which
are in Christ Jesus: You suffered from
your own people[g] the same things those
churches suffered from the Jews 15who
killed the Lord Jesus[h] and the prophets[i]
and also drove us out. They displease God

2:3 [p] 2Co 2:17
2:4 [q] Gal 2:7
[r] Gal 1:10
2:5 [s] Ac 20:33
[t] Ro 1:9
2:6 [u] 1Co 9:1,2
2:7 [v] ver 11
2:8 [w] 2Co 12:15; 1Jn 3:16
2:9 [x] Ac 18:3
[y] 2Th 3:8
2:10 [z] 1Th 1:5
[a] 2Co 1:12
2:11 [b] ver 7; 1Co 4:14
2:12 [c] Eph 4:1
2:13 [d] 1Th 1:2
[e] Heb 4:12
2:14 [f] Gal 1:22
[g] Ac 17:5; 2Th 1:4
2:15 [h] Ac 2:23
[i] Mt 5:12

[a] 7 Some manuscripts *were gentle*

2:3 *from error or impure motives.* See note on vv. 1–12. Romans suspected eastern cults (in which they included Jews and Christians) of immorality and of seducing women away from their husbands' religions; it is also possible that charges of sexual impurity (cf. 4:7) could have been leveled against them. Critics of movements that had the support of prominent women sometimes included this charge, and women of means sometimes sponsored religious associations. Indigenous residents may have suspected the sponsors of "foreign" cults such as the Egyptian, Jewish and Christian religious associations in Thessalonica (cf. Ac 17:4).
2:4 *not … but.* See the note on vv. 1–12. *tests our hearts.* God tests hearts, knowing what is in them (Pr 17:3; Jer 11:20; 17:10).
2:5 *flattery … greed.* Many denounced greedy sages and flattering speakers who simply told people what they wanted to hear to gain their favor (for demagogues, see note on 1Co 9:19).
2:6 *praise from people.* Competition for honor dominated ancient Mediterranean urban society. Speakers and sages often sought to draw attention to themselves, though the more cultured sought to do it more discreetly.
2:7 *as a nursing mother.* Some harsh sages on the streets berated their hearers, but gentler sages nurtured their disciples. *nursing mother.* The Greek term could apply to anyone who nursed. People of means often used slaves or paid women to care for and nurse their infants. Children often became so fond of such nurses that when the children became adults they often freed the nurses who had been slaves. Most mothers, however, especially in the eastern Mediterranean world where Paul lived, nursed their own children, so the image here probably is that of a caring mother (cf. a different emphasis in 1Co 3:1–3).
2:8 *share with you … our lives.* Greeks considered dying for someone the greatest expression of love; Paul had actually risked his life among them (see Ac 17:7–9).
2:9 *we worked night and day.* Most believers in Thessalonica were poor (cf. 2Co 8:1–2). Philippi's church sent Paul financial support during his time in Thessalonica (Php 4:15–16), but Paul still had to labor as an artisan. For Paul's trade and its background, see note on Ac 18:3; because linen-working required larger equipment that was more difficult to transport, many think that the term for his profession in Ac 18:3 refers to leatherworking. Paul could have done leatherworking in Thessalonica even if his stay was of limited duration (cf. Ac 17:2, although he probably stayed longer than his weeks speaking in the synagogue). *night and day.* Used for extensive work; it often meant parts of the night and parts of the day. A manual laborer began work around sunrise and could talk with visitors while working; but from the early afternoon on Paul might use his time for more direct evangelism.
2:10 *You are witnesses.* Persuaders often appealed to their audience's own knowledge with language such as this.
2:11 *as a father deals with his own children.* People in antiquity usually viewed fathers as loving and often even indulging their children, although fathers might honorably put matters of their country first. Sages sometimes compared themselves with nurses (v. 7) but even more often with fathers; disciples often viewed their teachers as fathers.
2:12 *who calls you into his kingdom and glory.* Accusers had distorted Paul's proclamation of Jesus' kingdom politically, as challenging the earthly emperor (Ac 17:7). Conversion meant that Christians could no longer participate in the civic cult that honored the emperor in Thessalonica (1:9), probably often at great social cost among those who knew them.
2:14–16 Digressions were common in ancient literature, and in these verses Paul digresses to praise the believers' faithfulness in the face of persecution.
2:14 *imitators.* See note on 1:6. *your own people.* Means others in Thessalonica. *from the Jews.* Paul probably digresses to mention his fellow Judeans because the Thessalonian believers knew that Jewish people had incited Gentiles against them in their own city (Ac 17:5–8). Jewish tradition emphasized their ancestors' rejection of the prophets (1Th 2:15; see note on Ac 7:52); some Judeans continued this practice by persecuting Judean churches and driving some people out (see Ac 8:1–3; 12:1–3; Php 3:6). Many Gentiles accused Jews of hating humanity, because they often kept to themselves, ate their own food and could not participate in pagan religious festivals. Paul, however, criticizes only the hostility of many Jews to the spreading of the gospel (v. 16).

and are hostile to everyone 16in their effort to keep us from speaking to the Gentiles[j] so that they may be saved. In this
way they always heap up their sins to the
limit.[k] The wrath of God has come upon
them at last.[a]

Paul's Longing to See the Thessalonians

17But, brothers and sisters, when we
were orphaned by being separated from
you for a short time (in person, not in
thought),[l] out of our intense longing we
made every effort to see you.[m] 18For we
wanted to come to you — certainly I, Paul,
did, again and again — but Satan[n] blocked
our way.[o] 19For what is our hope, our joy,
or the crown[p] in which we will glory[q] in
the presence of our Lord Jesus when he
comes?[r] Is it not you? 20Indeed, you are
our glory[s] and joy.

3 So when we could stand it no longer,[t] we thought it best to be left by
ourselves in Athens.[u] 2We sent Timothy,
who is our brother and co-worker in God's
service in spreading the gospel of Christ,
to strengthen and encourage you in your
faith, 3so that no one would be unsettled
by these trials. For you know quite well
that we are destined for them.[v] 4In fact,
when we were with you, we kept telling
you that we would be persecuted. And it
turned out that way, as you well know.[w]
5For this reason, when I could stand it no
longer,[x] I sent to find out about your faith.
I was afraid that in some way the tempter[y] had tempted you and that our labors
might have been in vain.[z]

Timothy's Encouraging Report

6But Timothy has just now come to us
from you[a] and has brought good news
about your faith and love.[b] He has told us
that you always have pleasant memories
of us and that you long to see us, just as
we also long to see you. 7Therefore, brothers and sisters, in all our distress and persecution we were encouraged about you
because of your faith. 8For now we really
live, since you are standing firm[c] in the
Lord. 9How can we thank God enough for
you[d] in return for all the joy we have in
the presence of our God because of you?
10Night and day we pray[e] most earnestly
that we may see you again[f] and supply
what is lacking in your faith.
11Now may our God and Father himself
and our Lord Jesus clear the way for us to
come to you. 12May the Lord make your

2:16 [j] Ac 13:45, 50 [k] Mt 23:32 **2:17** [l] 1Co 5:3; Col 2:5 [m] 1Th 3:10 **2:18** [n] Mt 4:10 [o] Ro 1:13; 15:22 **2:19** [p] Php 4:1 [q] 2Co 1:14 [r] Mt 16:27; 1Th 3:13 **2:20** [s] 2Co 1:14 **3:1** [t] ver 5 [u] Ac 17:15 **3:3** [v] Ac 9:16; 14:22
3:4 [w] 1Th 2:14 **3:5** [x] ver 1 [y] Mt 4:3 [z] Gal 2:2; Php 2:16 **3:6** [a] Ac 18:5 [b] 1Th 1:3 **3:8** [c] 1Co 16:13 **3:9** [d] 1Th 1:2 **3:10** [e] 2Ti 1:3 [f] 1Th 2:17

[a] 16 Or *them fully*

2:16 *their effort to keep us from speaking to the Gentiles.* Whereas Paul summoned converts to turn from idols (1:9), most Jewish people expected them to be circumcised and accept Jewish customs. They therefore resented Paul's "cheaper" message that undercut their own. *heap up their sins to the limit.* The Greek translation of Ge 15:16 uses wording similar to the words behind this phrase; once sin reached its prescribed limit, judgment would come. Although Jesus had given Jerusalem up to a generation before it would be destroyed, events were already in motion that would lead to Jerusalem's destruction in AD 70 (Mt 23:32 – 38; 24:34). Paul nevertheless expected the eventual repentance and salvation of his people predicted in the Prophets (Ro 11:25 – 27; cf. Mt 23:39).
2:17 *we were orphaned.* Grief-filled separation was often depicted figuratively, including as being orphaned (see note on Jn 14:18). *in person, not in thought.* See note on 1Co 5:3,4.
2:18 *Satan blocked our way.* Paul writes this letter from Corinth, perhaps just two weeks' journey from Thessalonica. Satan may have blocked the way through matters politically indiscreet to mention in a letter that would be read publicly in the house churches — such as the politarchs' decree and the trouble Paul's hosts would face if he returned (see Ac 17:7,8,9 and notes).
2:19 *the crown in which we will glory.* Victors' rewards at Greek competitions were garlands, crowns of interwoven leaves (see the article "Athletic Imagery in 1 Corinthians 9," p. 2000). Jewish people sometimes used such crowns figuratively for their future reward; Paul's reward is the believers' perseverance (v. 20; cf. also 3Jn 4).
3:1 *when we could stand it no longer.* Close friends sometimes shared in letters their sorrow over being apart. *left by ourselves in Athens.* Luke reports Paul's activity in Athens (Ac 17:15 – 34), but omits some details here (such as companions rejoining Paul in Athens and him sending them back to Macedonia). Ancient historians sometimes omitted activities of secondary characters that would require extra explanation (see note on Mt 8:5).
3:3 *these trials ... destined for them.* Some scholars suggest that Paul had taught them about the period of suffering that would precede the promised restoration (cf. Jer 30:7; Da 12:1). Clearly Paul did pass on Jesus' teachings about the end (1Th 4:13 – 18), but many argue that Paul envisioned the entire period between Jesus' comings as end-time tribulation (cf. Ro 8:22). For the specific suffering in Thessalonica, see Introduction to 1 Thessalonians.
3:5 *when I could stand it no longer.* Letters expressing intimate friendship often complained affectionately about not hearing from the recipient; in this case Paul's concern runs even deeper. *the tempter.* Jewish tradition widely recognized Satan's role as tempter, here seeking to turn people from the faith.
3:6 *you long to see us, just as we also long to see you.* Letters expressing intimate friendship protested if they felt the sender's love was not reciprocated, but celebrated reciprocal love.
3:8 *we really live, since you are standing firm.* Letters expressing intimate friendship sometimes declared that the sender was well only if the receiver was. Paul had been ready to give even his life for them (2:8).
3:9 – 10 *we thank God ... we pray most earnestly.* Letter writers usually included a blessing, mention of prayers, and/or thanksgiving for the recipients. Although Paul usually does so early in his letters (1:2), here he does so in response to their faith, the discovery of which he has just narrated (cf. 2:13; 2Co 1:11; 2:12 – 14).
3:11 *Now may our God and Father.* In addition to direct prayers to God, Jewish people also considered as implicit prayers to God blessings addressed to a person or people, as here.

1 THESSALONIANS 3

Travel in the Greco-Roman World

Travelers in the Greco-Roman world could choose to journey either by foot or by sea. Although the opportunities for travel greatly increased under the Roman Empire, journeys continued to be treacherous and slow. The vast expanse of the empire necessarily led to the construction and improvement of an intricate network of roads in order to connect cities from east to west. Major arteries, such as the Via Egnatia (which passed through Thessalonica), conveyed an enormous amount of traffic, and cities along these routes became prosperous and cosmopolitan. These well-developed and maintained roads were necessary for both military operations and trade purposes. Amazingly, the quality of their construction was so high that many of them remain intact to this day.

Voyage by sea put the traveler at the risk of shipwreck and intervention by buccaneers, but the presence of Roman fleets on the seas lessened the fears of piracy. With the exception of the dangerous winter season, running from mid-November until early March, such voyages were significantly less expensive and faster than travel by land. Scholars used to think that ships in classical times hugged the shoreline and never ventured into deep water, but recent research has proved this to be false.

The mobility made possible by the Roman Empire contributed greatly to the spread of Christianity in the Greco-Roman world. Paul and his coworkers traveled extensively, both by foot and by sea, in their efforts to spread the gospel and to maintain contact with the churches they had established (1Th 3:2,6). Reflecting upon his own travels, Paul mentioned three shipwrecks and other dangers that he had faced (2Co 11:25–26). Scholars estimate from the journeys recorded in Acts that Paul must have covered over 10,000 miles during his missionary career. ◆

Ancient Roman road with the citadel of Assos in the top left. Paul may have approached Assos from this road on his third journey (Acts 20:14–15).

www.HolyLandPhotos.org

love increase and overflow for each other[g]
and for everyone else, just as ours does for
you. [13]May he strengthen your hearts so
that you will be blameless[h] and holy in the
presence of our God and Father when our
Lord Jesus comes[i] with all his holy ones.

Living to Please God

4 As for other matters, brothers and sisters,[j] we instructed you how to live in
order to please God,[k] as in fact you are living. Now we ask you and urge you in the
Lord Jesus to do this more and more. [2]For
you know what instructions we gave you
by the authority of the Lord Jesus.
[3]It is God's will that you should be sanctified: that you should avoid sexual immorality;[l] [4]that each of you should learn
to control your own body[a][m] in a way that
is holy and honorable, [5]not in passionate lust[n] like the pagans,[o] who do not
know God; [6]and that in this matter no
one should wrong or take advantage of a
brother or sister.[b][p] The Lord will punish all
those who commit such sins,[q] as we told
you and warned you before. [7]For God did
not call us to be impure, but to live a holy
life.[r] [8]Therefore, anyone who rejects this
instruction does not reject a human being
but God, the very God who gives you his
Holy Spirit.[s]
[9]Now about your love for one another[t] we do not need to write to you,[u] for
you yourselves have been taught by God
to love each other.[v] [10]And in fact, you do
love all of God's family throughout Macedonia.[w] Yet we urge you, brothers and
sisters, to do so more and more,[x] [11]and to
make it your ambition to lead a quiet life:
You should mind your own business and
work with your hands,[y] just as we told
you, [12]so that your daily life may win the
respect of outsiders[z] and so that you will
not be dependent on anybody.

3:12 [g] 1Th 4:9, 10
3:13 [h] 1Co 1:8 [i] 1Th 2:19
4:1 [j] 2Co 13:11 [k] 2Co 5:9
4:3 [l] 1Co 6:18
4:4 [m] 1Co 7:2, 9
4:5 [n] Ro 1:26 [o] Eph 4:17
4:6 [p] 1Co 6:8 [q] Heb 13:4
4:7 [r] Lev 11:44; 1Pe 1:15
4:8 [s] Ro 5:5; Gal 4:6
4:9 [t] Ro 12:10 [u] 1Th 5:1 [v] Jn 13:34
4:10 [w] 1Th 1:7 [x] 1Th 3:12
4:11 [y] Eph 4:28; 2Th 3:10-12
4:12 [z] Mk 4:11

[a] 4 Or *learn to live with your own wife*; or *learn to acquire a wife* [b] 6 The Greek word for *brother or sister* (*adelphos*) refers here to a believer, whether man or woman, as part of God's family.

3:13 *when our Lord Jesus comes with all his holy ones.* Evokes Zec 14:5: "the LORD my God will come, and all the holy ones with him." Paul also applies OT divine texts to Jesus elsewhere (e.g., Php 2:10–11; cf. 1Co 8:6; 2Co 5:10).
4:1 *urge you in the Lord Jesus.* People often urged others in the name of a deity—here Jesus.
4:2 *instructions we gave you by the authority of the Lord Jesus.* Paul probably refers here to passing on some of Jesus' teachings (cf. the article "Jesus' Teachings as Background in 1 Thessalonians 4:13—5:11," p. 2098).
4:3 *sanctified.* Being holy, i.e., consecrated or set apart for God. *sexual immorality.* Common among Greek men, who often married late; Greek culture did not discourage this behavior (see the article "Prostitution and Sexual Immorality," p. 1990). God's holy people were to avoid sexual immorality (see, e.g., Lev 20:7–26).
4:4 *in a way that is holy and honorable.* One's proper sexual behavior was a matter of being honorable, although Gentiles normally shamed primarily women for misbehavior. Outside of marriage, respected Gentile men believed that they maintained honor by sleeping with sexual partners of lower status. For Paul, however, honorable sexual behavior was restricted to marriage. "Body" here is literally "vessel," language that ancient sources sometimes apply to a wife (see NIV note) but much more often apply to the body (NIV text).
4:5 *passionate lust.* Although some more ascetic thinkers viewed passion even in marriage as wrong (while permitting procreation), Paul's concern is only immorality (v. 6; 1Co 7:2,9). Sexual promiscuity was common among male Gentiles (see note on v. 3), and Jewish stereotypes of Gentiles featured it heavily. *pagans.* The same Greek term can be translated "Gentiles." Paul reminds Gentile Thessalonian believers (see 1:9) that, having turned to Israel's God, they are no longer spiritually Gentiles.
4:6 *The Lord will punish all those who commit such sins.* Virtually all societies condemned adultery, sometimes called wife-stealing, although the practice was not uncommon at least among the elite. Biblical law condemned adultery (including intercourse with another's future spouse) as worthy of death (Dt 22:13–24). In this period, however, Jewish people punished adultery with divorce and shame (see note on Mt 1:19; see also the article "Prostitution and Sexual Immorality," p. 1990).
4:7 *impure . . . holy.* Jewish people deemed sexual immorality spiritually defiling, i.e., making one impure rather than holy (cf., e.g., Lev 20:21). See notes on vv. 3,4.
4:8 *Holy Spirit.* God's Spirit (cf. notes on vv. 3,4,7). Although many streams of ancient Jewish thought emphasized the Spirit's Biblical role in inspiring the prophets, some also emphasized the Spirit's Biblical role in purifying God's people (Eze 36:26–27).
4:9 *Now about.* This Greek phrase (also in 5:1) often introduces a change in subject (see note on 1Co 7:1, which uses the same Greek phrase, there translated "now for"). *love for one another.* Those who offered moral advice often emphasized brotherly love, the meaning of the Greek term here (hence, loving God's family in v. 10). *we do not need to write to you.* Those who offered moral advice sometimes noted that their advice was superfluous, since they trusted that their hearers would behave accordingly even without the advice.
4:10 *God's family.* Lit., brothers and sisters; fellow believers are one's spiritual brothers and sisters (see note on Ac 9:17). *throughout Macedonia.* Thessalonica was the capital of and largest port in Macedonia.
4:11 *lead a quiet life.* People often criticized those who sought to remain completely aloof from public life, and Paul does not expect complete withdrawal. Nevertheless, minority groups, such as Jews and Christians, had fewer problems if they remained inconspicuous. *work with your hands.* Although the Thessalonian church may have included a few well-to-do benefactors (Ac 17:4,9), much of the church was probably poor (cf. 2Co 8:1–2), and, like many towns, Thessalonica had its share of unemployed men simply conversing in the marketplace (Ac 17:5). The elite disdained manual labor, but work with the hands was how most people supported themselves (see note on 1Co 4:12).
4:12 *not be dependent on anybody.* Although only the most destitute begged on streets, unemployment was high in Thessalonica (cf. Ac 17:5); some people also depended on wealthier benefactors.

Believers Who Have Died

13Brothers and sisters, we do not want
you to be uninformed about those who
sleep in death, so that you do not grieve
like the rest of mankind, who have no
hope.[a] 14For we believe that Jesus died and
rose again, and so we believe that God will
bring with Jesus those who have fallen
asleep in him.[b] 15According to the Lord's
word, we tell you that we who are still
alive, who are left until the coming of the
Lord, will certainly not precede those who
have fallen asleep.[c] 16For the Lord himself
will come down from heaven, with a loud
command, with the voice of the archangel and with the trumpet call of God,[d] and
the dead in Christ will rise first.[e] 17After
that, we who are still alive and are left[f]
will be caught up together with them in
the clouds[g] to meet the Lord in the air.
And so we will be with the Lord[h] forever.
18Therefore encourage one another with
these words.

The Day of the Lord

5 Now, brothers and sisters, about times
and dates[i] we do not need to write to
you,[j] 2for you know very well that the day
of the Lord[k] will come like a thief in the
night.[l] 3While people are saying, "Peace
and safety," destruction will come on
them suddenly, as labor pains on a pregnant woman, and they will not escape.
4But you, brothers and sisters, are not
in darkness[m] so that this day should surprise you like a thief. 5You are all children
of the light and children of the day. We do
not belong to the night or to the darkness.

4:13 [a] Eph 2:12 **4:14** [b] 1Co 15:18 **4:15** [c] 1Co 15:52 **4:16** [d] Mt 24:31 [e] 1Co 15:23; 2Th 2:1 **4:17** [f] 1Co 15:52 [g] Ac 1:9; Rev 11:12 [h] Jn 12:26 **5:1** [i] Ac 1:7 [j] 1Th 4:9 **5:2** [k] 1Co 1:8 [l] 2Pe 3:10 **5:4** [m] Ac 26:18; 1Jn 2:8

4:13 *those who sleep in death.* "Sleep" was a common euphemism for death. Martyrdom was probably a rare means of death for Christians in this region c. AD 50 and most scholars doubt that it is in view here, though some martyrs are not impossible (in view of persecution noted in 1:6; 2:14–16; 3:3–6; it might not be prudent to elaborate on local executions in a letter). *grieve like the rest of mankind.* Some who consoled others expressed sympathy; some counseled (rather unhelpfully) that grief does no good. *who have no hope.* Although some intellectuals spoke of the disembodied soul rising to heaven, many people envisioned death as annihilation or (as in the old myths) life as shadows in a dreary netherworld. Paul reminds his hearers of a better hope (vv. 14–17).
4:14 *God will bring with Jesus those who have fallen asleep in him.* Many Jewish people who expected the resurrection of the body also affirmed that the righteous soul remained in heaven until the resurrection.
4:15 *According to the Lord's word.* Given the cluster of parallels with Jesus' teaching in this context, "the Lord's word" here presumably means Jesus' teaching. See "Jesus' Teachings as Background in 1 Thessalonians 4:13—5:11," p. 2098. *the coming of the Lord.* Jesus promised his coming (Mt 24:27,37,39); one application of the Greek term (*parousia*) was to the visit of a king or high official, relevant here (cf. note on v. 17).
4:16 *the voice of the archangel.* Jewish tradition mentioned seven archangels, but the chief archangel, the commander of the Lord's hosts and the guardian prince of Israel, was Michael, also mentioned in the OT (Da 10:13,21; 12:1). Jesus had said that he would delegate the gathering of his chosen ones to his angels (Mk 13:27). Cf. the divine battle images in Isa 31:4; 42:13 and especially in Zec 14:3–5. *trumpet call of God.* Trumpets were used to signal armies or summon people to assemble. Often used for gathering, they could be envisioned in the promised gathering of God's people (Isa 27:12–13). Jesus applied this image to his coming to gather his people, coming, as here, with clouds (Mt 24:30–31). In ancient literature, trumpets and shouts were often conjoined in military contexts, in which the shouts were battle cries. *the dead in Christ will rise first.* Most Judeans expected the end-time resurrection, especially for the righteous (here, "the dead in Christ").
4:17 *the clouds.* Recalls Jesus' teaching about his coming (Mk 13:26; 14:62), in turn alluding to Da 7:13. *to meet the Lord.* When used in a context of a royal "coming" (v. 15), "meet" meant that people welcoming him would go to form his escort en route to his destination. *the air.* Considered the lowest of the heavens; thus Jesus "will come down from heaven" (v. 16) and his people will meet him in the air.
4:18 *encourage one another with these words.* Those who wrote letters to console the bereaved sometimes urged their readers to encourage themselves and others. Cf. 5:11; repeating a thought helped reinforce it and often tied together a section.
5:1 *Now ... about.* See note on 4:9. *about times and dates.* Some Jewish contemporaries tried to predict the time of the end; others regarded it as unknown. Paul here echoes the wording of Jesus (later written in Ac 1:7).
5:2 *the day of the Lord will come like a thief in the night.* Paul again echoes Jesus (Mt 24:43; Lk 12:38–39), as do other early Christian writers (2Pe 3:10; Rev 3:3; 16:15). The Biblical prophets warned of the day of the Lord; they also viewed earlier judgments through its prism, but foresaw an ultimate time when God would judge all peoples (e.g., Eze 30:3; Joel 3:14).
5:3 *Peace and safety.* Emperors claimed that their military exploits had brought "peace and safety" to the empire; Paul's critics could interpret Paul as despising such claims here (something interpreted as disrespect to the emperor could stir persecution; cf. Ac 17:7). *destruction will come.* False prophets announcing peace helped lead to Jerusalem's fall to Babylon (Jer 6:14; 8:11; 14:13); false prophets would later predict God's deliverance even immediately before Jerusalem's destruction in AD 70. *as labor pains on a pregnant woman.* Biblical prophets often used labor pains to depict intense suffering (e.g., Isa 26:17–18; 42:14; Jer 4:31; 6:24; 13:21; 22:23), appropriate also for the day of the Lord (Isa 13:6–8). Many Jewish people expected final labor pains as the present order prepared to birth a new age; they often listed various tribulations they expected to characterize it. Here Paul speaks not of gradual tribulations (cf. Mk 13:7–8; Ro 8:22) but of sudden destruction.
5:4 *surprise you like a thief.* Thieves usually broke in at night. Sometimes commentators contrast the unexpected end of the age in vv. 1–2 with preceding signs in 2Th 2:2–4, but the tension exists also in other Jewish texts about the end time. The point here is that the wicked will be caught unprepared (v. 3), but not so the righteous (v. 4).
5:5 *children of the light.* Some radical Jews (see the Dead Sea Scrolls) considered their own group "children of light" and everyone else "children of darkness"; many people used light or day to represent good and night or darkness to represent evil.

1 THESSALONIANS 4:13—5:11

Jesus' Teachings as Background in 1 Thessalonians 4:13—5:11

People often sent letters to console the bereaved, but rarely with the kind of hope Paul offers here. Although some of Paul's images also appear in the OT, the one other place where most of them cluster is in Jesus' teachings, later written down in the Gospels. Some of these were also developed by other Jewish writers at times, whereas others were distinctive or perhaps even unique to Jesus; most important is that nowhere else do they appear with such frequency together in one book, much less in the span of two successive paragraphs. Others appear in 2Th 2:1 – 12; see "Jesus' Teachings as Background in 2 Thessalonians 2:1 – 12," p. 2102. Many other conventional Jewish end-time motifs, such as mutant babies, are omitted by both Jesus and his servant Paul. ◆

MOTIF SHARED BY JESUS AND PAUL	PASSAGE RECORDING JESUS' TEACHING	LOCATION IN 1TH 4:13—5:11	COMMON ELSEWHERE IN EARLIER JEWISH SOURCES?
Coming, using the Greek term *parousia*	Mt 24:3,27,37,39	4:15; cf. 3:13; 5:23; 1Co 15:23; 2Th 2:1,8; Jas 5:7 – 8; 2Pe 3:4,12; 1Jn 2:28	No
Gathering by means of a trumpet	Mt 24:31	4:16; cf. 1Co 15:52	Expected; see Isa 27:12 – 13
Gathering of God's people at the end	Mt 24:31; Mk 13:27	4:16 – 17	Israel's gathering widely expected
Coming on the clouds	Mt 24:30; 26:64; Mk 13:26; 14:62	4:17; cf. Rev 1:7	Da 7:13
Times and dates unknown	Jesus' teaching in Ac 1:7	5:1	No
The time of the end is unknown	Mt 24:36; Mk 13:32	5:1 – 2	Common expectation (balanced against others who tried to predict the time)
Jesus' unexpected return like a thief at night	Mt 24:43; Lk 12:38 – 39	5:2; cf. 2Pe 3:10; Rev 3:3; 16:15	No
Sudden and unexpected destruction of the wicked	Mt 24:38 – 41; Lk 17:26 – 30,34 – 35	5:3	Sources emphasize the destruction of the wicked far more than its unexpected-ness
Birth pangs of end-time sufferings	Mt 24:8 (perhaps applied to the present); Mk 13:8	5:3 (in context perhaps applied to the final pangs)	Common; developed from OT images of suffering caused by judgment
Staying awake (i.e., being prepared) rather than being asleep (i.e., being unprepared)	Mt 24:42; 25:13; Mk 13:33 – 37; Lk 12:37 – 38; 21:36	5:6 – 7	No

6So then, let us not be like others, who are
asleep,[n] but let us be awake and sober.
7For those who sleep, sleep at night, and
those who get drunk, get drunk at night.[o]
8But since we belong to the day, let us
be sober, putting on faith and love as a
breastplate,[p] and the hope of salvation[q]
as a helmet.[r] 9For God did not appoint us
to suffer wrath but to receive salvation
through our Lord Jesus Christ.[s] 10He died
for us so that, whether we are awake or
asleep, we may live together with him.[t]
11Therefore encourage one another and
build each other up, just as in fact you
are doing.

Final Instructions

12Now we ask you, brothers and sisters,
to acknowledge those who work hard
among you, who care for you in the Lord[u]
and who admonish you. 13Hold them in
the highest regard in love because of their
work. Live in peace with each other.[v]
14And we urge you, brothers and sisters,
warn those who are idle[w] and disruptive, encourage the disheartened, help the
weak,[x] be patient with everyone. 15Make
sure that nobody pays back wrong for
wrong,[y] but always strive to do what is
good for each other[z] and for everyone else.
16Rejoice always,[a] 17pray continually,
18give thanks in all circumstances; for this
is God's will for you in Christ Jesus.
19Do not quench the Spirit.[b] 20Do not
treat prophecies[c] with contempt 21but test
them all;[d] hold on to what is good, 22reject
every kind of evil.
23May God himself, the God of peace,[e]
sanctify you through and through. May
your whole spirit, soul and body be kept
blameless at the coming of our Lord Jesus
Christ. 24The one who calls you is faithful,[f]
and he will do it.

25Brothers and sisters, pray for us.[g]
26Greet all God's people with a holy kiss.[h]
27I charge you before the Lord to have this
letter read to all the brothers and sisters.[i]
28The grace of our Lord Jesus Christ be
with you.[j]

5:6 [n] Ro 13:11
5:7 [o] Ac 2:15; 2Pe 2:13
5:8 [p] Eph 6:14 [q] Ro 8:24 [r] Eph 6:17
5:9 [s] 2Th 2:13, 14
5:10 [t] 2Co 5:15
5:12 [u] 1Ti 5:17; Heb 13:17
5:13 [v] Mk 9:50
5:14 [w] 2Th 3:6, 7, 11 [x] Ro 14:1
5:15 [y] 1Pe 3:9 [z] Gal 6:10; Eph 4:32
5:16 [a] Php 4:4
5:19 [b] Eph 4:30
5:20 [c] 1Co 14:1-40
5:21 [d] 1Co 14:29; 1Jn 4:1
5:23 [e] Ro 15:33
5:24 [f] 1Co 1:9
5:25 [g] Eph 6:19
5:26 [h] Ro 16:16
5:27 [i] Col 4:16
5:28 [j] Ro 16:20

5:6–7 Paul may borrow these images from Jesus (cf. Mt 24:45–51; Mk 13:32–37; Lk 12:42–48).
5:8 *a breastplate … a helmet.* Evokes Isa 59:17, which also mentions a breastplate (there, of righteousness; here, of faith and love). Paul developed this image more fully (and slightly differently) later (see notes on Eph 6:10–20). For Roman breastplates, see note on Eph 6:14. For the helmet, see note on Eph 6:17.
5:9 *God did not appoint us to suffer wrath but to receive salvation.* For the expectation of God's end-time wrath destroying the wicked (cf. v. 3), see note on Ro 2:5. *salvation.* End-time salvation presumably refers to the resurrection (cf. 1Th 4:16).
5:11–22 Writers on moral subjects often listed exhortations in a series without directly connecting all of them. Paul's exhortations in this case do apparently exhibit a sort of loose structure, however: honoring leaders (vv. 12–13), helping others (vv. 14–15), prayer and thanksgiving (vv. 16–18) and prophecy (vv. 19–22).
5:12 *acknowledge those who work hard among you.* Ancient leadership was often hierarchical and social rank demanded honor; among Christians leadership was ideally servanthood, but it merited deep appreciation, respect and cooperation.
5:13 *Live in peace with each other.* Harmony was a common subject of ancient exhortation. Some Jewish sages highly praised peace.
5:15 *pays back wrong for wrong.* Some other ancient thinkers emphasized nonretaliation (see notes on Ro 12:17,18,19), including Jesus (Mt 5:39). Many outsiders respected such behavior.
5:16 *Rejoice always.* Rejoicing might be associated with praise (e.g., Ps 9:2; 32:11; 68:4).
5:17 *continually.* Not every moment but constantly, repeatedly (e.g., 1Sa 12:23; Ps 34:1; 35:27; 52:9).
5:18 *give thanks in all circumstances.* See note on Eph 5:20.
5:19 *Do not quench the Spirit.* Scripture (e.g., Nu 11:25,29) and Jewish tradition often associated the Spirit with prophetic inspiration (cf. 1Th 5:20). *quench.* When used most literally, this Greek term usually involved fire; cf. the idea (though not this term) in Jer 20:9.
5:20–21 *prophecies … test them all.* In ancient Israel, many newer prophets learned under the mentorship of senior prophets (e.g., 1Sa 19:20; 2Ki 6:1–3); in early Christianity, those newly moved by the Spirit often lacked senior prophets and often had to work together to evaluate prophecies (1Co 14:29).
5:23 For blessings invoking God yet addressed to people, see note on 3:11. *spirit, soul and body.* Although some ancient Greek thinkers tried to distinguish in detail constituent elements of the soul, Paul here follows more closely the Jewish tradition that could list multiple elements as a way of emphasizing the whole (cf., e.g., Dt 6:5). This is not to deny that Paul distinguished elements for pragmatic reasons, but he does not always employ terms the same way (cf., e.g., 1Co 7:34; 14:14–15).
5:26 *holy kiss.* People regularly showed affection by greeting family members, close friends or some others with a light kiss on the mouth (see note on Ro 16:16).
5:27 *have this letter read to all.* Even in urban areas, a majority of people could read very little (except perhaps for basic inscriptions or graffiti); moreover, even fewer people could write and manually copy Paul's letters. Almost everyone, however, knew how to learn by listening to something read by someone else more literate. Sometimes people read to hearers at banquets; synagogues read Scripture in their assemblies (see note on Col 4:16). For most Jews and Christians, the primary literature they heard read was Scripture.

THE LETTERS

2 THESSALONIANS

Authorship

The majority of commentators on the Thessalonian correspondence accept both letters as genuinely from Paul. Some scholars have questioned the authenticity of 2 Thessalonians because it sometimes features different aspects of the end-time scenario than those found in 1 Thessalonians. These differences, however, are no wider than those found in apocalyptic works that often drew on multiple motifs. In both letters, Paul draws on Jesus' teachings about the end (see "Jesus' Teachings as Background in 2 Thessalonians 2:1 – 12," p. 2102). Moreover, most pseudepigraphic letters were written long after the death of the author they name, but it seems very difficult to date 2 Thessalonians so late. Paul died sometime around AD 64; Jerusalem's temple was destroyed in AD 70, and the entire empire knew of it. It strains credibility to suggest that a forger after that date would be so inept as to pen 2:4, showing no knowledge of the temple's destruction.

Although the matter is debated, 2 Thessalonians was probably written after 1 Thessalonians. Apparently some Thessalonians appreciated Paul's comfort about the coming time of God's kingdom but have reinterpreted it in light of their Greek understanding. Greeks did not expect a future end to the age or a dramatic transformation at some point in the future; consequently some may have understood only the present aspect of the kingdom (2:1 – 2). Although Paul sometimes addressed multiple issues in a letter, some scholars also associate the failure of some to work (3:6 – 12) with such confusion about the end (but cf. 1Th 4:11). ◆

QUICK GLANCE

AUTHOR:
The apostle Paul

AUDIENCE:
The church at Thessalonica

DATE:
About AD 51 or 52

THEME:
Paul writes to correct a misunderstanding concerning the Lord's return and to exhort the Thessalonian believers to be steadfast and to work for a living.

1 Paul, Silas[a] and Timothy,[a]

To the church of the Thessalonians in
God our Father and the Lord Jesus Christ:

2 Grace and peace to you from God the
Father and the Lord Jesus Christ.[b]

Thanksgiving and Prayer

3 We ought always to thank God for
you, brothers and sisters,[b] and rightly so,
because your faith is growing more and
more, and the love all of you have for one
another is increasing.[c] 4 Therefore, among
God's churches we boast[d] about your perseverance and faith[e] in all the persecutions and trials you are enduring.[f]
5 All this is evidence[g] that God's judgment is right, and as a result you will be
counted worthy of the kingdom of God,
for which you are suffering. 6 God is just:
He will pay back trouble to those who
trouble you[h] 7 and give relief to you who
are troubled, and to us as well. This will
happen when the Lord Jesus is revealed
from heaven in blazing fire with his powerful angels.[i] 8 He will punish those who
do not know God[j] and do not obey the
gospel of our Lord Jesus.[k] 9 They will be
punished with everlasting destruction[l] and
shut out from the presence of the Lord and
from the glory of his might[m] 10 on the day[n]
he comes to be glorified[o] in his holy people and to be marveled at among all those
who have believed. This includes you, because you believed our testimony to you.[p]
11 With this in mind, we constantly pray
for you, that our God may make you worthy[q] of his calling, and that by his power
he may bring to fruition your every desire for goodness and your every deed
prompted by faith.[r] 12 We pray this so that
the name of our Lord Jesus may be glorified in you,[s] and you in him, according to
the grace of our God and the Lord Jesus
Christ.[c]

The Man of Lawlessness

2 Concerning the coming of our Lord
Jesus Christ and our being gathered
to him,[t] we ask you, brothers and sisters, 2 not to become easily unsettled or
alarmed by the teaching allegedly from
us — whether by a prophecy or by word
of mouth or by letter[u] — asserting that
the day of the Lord[v] has already come.

1:1 [a] Ac 16:1; 1Th 1:1 **1:2** [b] Ro 1:7 **1:3** [c] 1Th 3:12 **1:4** [d] 2Co 7:14 [e] 1Th 1:3 [f] 1Th 2:14 **1:5** [g] Php 1:28 **1:6** [h] Col 3:25; Rev 6:10 **1:7** [i] 1Th 4:16; Jude 14 **1:8** [j] Gal 4:8 [k] Ro 2:8 **1:9** [l] Php 3:19; 2Pe 3:7

[m] 2Th 2:8 **1:10** [n] 1Co 3:13 [o] Jn 17:10 [p] 1Co 1:6 **1:11** [q] ver 5 [r] 1Th 1:3 **1:12** [s] Php 2:9-11 **2:1** [t] Mk 13:27; 1Th 4:15-17 **2:2** [u] 2Th 3:17 [v] 1Co 1:8

[a] *1* Greek *Silvanus,* a variant of *Silas* [b] *3* The Greek word for *brothers and sisters* (*adelphoi*) refers here to believers, both men and women, as part of God's family; also in 2:1, 13, 15; 3:1, 6, 13. [c] *12* Or *God and Lord, Jesus Christ*

1:1 *Silas.* See note on 1Th 1:1; for coauthors, see note on 1Co 1:1.
1:2 *Grace and peace.* See note on Ro 1:7. *Lord Jesus Christ.* That the blessing is from the Lord Jesus Christ as well as God the Father implies Jesus' divinity.
1:3 *We ought always to thank God for you.* Some ancient letters thanked God or other deities for the letter's recipients.
1:4 *persecutions and trials.* See Introduction to 1 Thessalonians.
1:5 *the kingdom of God, for which you are suffering.* Most Jewish people expected a period of intense suffering and persecution before the end of the age and the coming of the kingdom.
1:6 – 7 *He will pay back trouble … and give relief.* Jewish people expected that the suffering of the righteous would end with the end of the age (cf. Da 12:1 – 2) and that God would reward them for their past sufferings.
1:7 *blazing fire.* Perhaps because Hebrew described wrath as burning and (as well as sometimes a means of judgment, Nu 11:1), fire became a common image of judgment (e.g., Ps 97:3; Isa 26:11), including in passages that were applied to the end (e.g., Isa 66:15 – 16,24). Jewish portraits of the end often included this element, sometimes even for renovation of the cosmos (though end-time pictures varied). The present text probably especially evokes Isa 66:15, from the same context as the new creation (Isa 65:17 – 18; 66:22). *powerful angels.* God's army (cf., e.g., 2Ki 6:17), which some Jewish visionaries also expected to participate at the end.
1:8 *punish those who do not know God.* Jewish people expected God to avenge them against their enemies (Dt 32:41; Isa 35:4; 66:6), especially at the end.
1:9 *everlasting destruction.* Sometimes in ancient Jewish literature this meant complete destruction, sometimes eternal suffering, and sometimes both. *from the presence of the Lord and from the glory of his might.* This verse echoes the Greek translation of Isa 2:10,19,21 (lit. "from the presence of the fear of the LORD and from the glory of his might").
1:10 *glorified in his holy people.* Jewish sources highlighted the Biblical promise of future glory for God's people at their restoration (cf. Isa 46:13; 60:1 – 2; 62:2); in Paul's writings, this happens fully at the resurrection (e.g., 1Co 15:43).
1:11 *we constantly pray for you.* Ancient letters often included the sender's prayers, or the mention of them, for the letter's recipients.
1:12 *glorified in you.* See note on v. 10.
2:1 *the coming of our Lord Jesus Christ.* When used of a king, "coming" (here and v. 8; cf. v. 9) was a powerful, public affair (see notes on 1Th 4:15,17). Some Jewish texts applied it to God's past theophanies and future revelation in glory. *our being gathered to him.* Jesus had spoken of his coming (Mt 24:3,27,37,39) and — what is grammatically connected here — his followers being gathered to him (Mt 24:31; Mk 13:27). Many Biblical and subsequent Jewish sources addressed God gathering Israel; Jesus applied the gathering to his followers.
2:2 Some believers in Thessalonica may have taken too far Paul's teaching on the imminence of Jesus' return (1Th 5:1 – 3). Paul reminds them of his teaching while with them (2Th 2:5,15), showing that some events would in fact precede Jesus' unexpected return (vv. 3 – 4; cf. 1Th 5:4 – 5). The Greek way of thinking did not include a climactic future judgment of the world; given their cultural framework, their misreading of Paul is not surprising. Paul corrects a misinterpretation of his teaching, possibly based on someone's misunderstanding or even on a forgery (2Th 3:17).

3Don't let anyone deceive you[w] in any
way, for that day will not come until the
rebellion occurs and the man of lawlessness[a] is revealed,[x] the man doomed to destruction. 4He will oppose and will exalt
himself over everything that is called God[y]
or is worshiped, so that he sets himself
up in God's temple, proclaiming himself
to be God.[z]
5Don't you remember that when I was
with you I used to tell you these things?
6And now you know what is holding
him back, so that he may be revealed at
the proper time. 7For the secret power of
lawlessness is already at work; but the
one who now holds it back will continue to do so till he is taken out of the
way. 8And then the lawless one will be
revealed, whom the Lord Jesus will overthrow with the breath of his mouth[a] and
destroy by the splendor of his coming.

2:3 [w] Eph 5:6-8 [x] Da 7:25; 8:25; 11:36; Rev 13:5,6 **2:4** [y] 1Co 8:5 [z] Isa 14:13,14; Eze 28:2 **2:8** [a] Isa 11:4; Rev 19:15

[a] 3 Some manuscripts *sin*

2:3–4 *man of lawlessness . . . sets himself up in God's temple, proclaiming himself to be God.* The figure of a general future antichrist figure seems to occur mainly in later Jewish texts, but contemporary Jewish texts do describe some past or present rulers in similar terms (cf. also the evil rulers in Da 9–11); the tradition of pagan kings who made themselves out to be gods is also quite ancient (Isa 14:13–14; Eze 28:2; Da 6:7). Nearly a decade before this letter, Gaius Caligula had tried to set up his image in the Jerusalem temple, almost sparking a Judean revolt. Two decades after this letter, when Titus destroyed the temple, his soldiers desecrated the temple by paying divine honors to the insignia of Emperor Vespasian on the site of the temple.

The imagery used here derives especially from Jesus (cf. Mt 24:15), who took it from Daniel (Da 7:25; 8:11; 9:26–27; 11:31,36). Noting many historical parallels, many scholars conclude that Da 11 describes the abomination caused by Antiochus Epiphanes; yet if read continuously the "end" seems to come at that time (Da 12:1), about two centuries before Jesus, which was not how Jesus' contemporaries understood the prophecy. The way that some in the first century counted the period of Da 9:24–27, the anointed prince (whom some held to be the Messiah) was to be put to death around the time that Jesus in fact died; the destruction of the city followed 40 years later, suggesting a delay of at least 40 years. Christian interpreters differ as to whether (1) a specific future tribulation remains (perhaps vv. 8–9), (2) the Jewish war in AD 66–70 fulfilled it completely (cf. Mt 24:15–21), (3) the whole course of history constitutes this period (cf. note on Rev 12:6) or (4) different passages reuse the language in different useful ways.

2:3 *rebellion.* The Greek term can also mean "apostasy"; both sins appear in Jewish lists of end-time evils, so the sense may depend on whether unbelievers or believers are meant. In context it could signify rebellion against God's law leading to lawlessness.

2:6–7 *what is holding him back . . . the one who now holds it back.* Views of the meaning of the restrainer include: the finished proclamation of the gospel (Mt 24:14); the presence of Christians in Jerusalem (Mt 24:16–21); the ruler preceding the self-deifying emperor or succession of emperors; the Roman Empire (the view of many church fathers); or perhaps likelier, God's restraining hand or presence (Eze 9:3; 11:23), or the archangel Michael, angelic protector of Israel in Jewish tradition (also Da 12:1). Some suggest the church in the world, but this would contradict the context (vv. 1–4). The Thessalonians presumably knew Paul's point (v. 5).

2:8 *breath of his mouth.* Evokes a Messianic passage: Isa 11:4 (cf. Hos 6:5).

JESUS' TEACHINGS AS BACKGROUND IN 2 THESSALONIANS 2:1—12

MOTIF SHARED BY JESUS AND PAUL	PASSAGE RECORDING JESUS' TEACHING	LOCATION IN 2TH 2:1–12	COMMON ELSEWHERE IN EARLIER JEWISH SOURCES?
Coming, using the Greek term *parousia*	Mt 24:3,27,37,39	vv. 1,8; cf. 1Co 15:23; 1Th 3:13; 4:15; 5:23; Jas 5:7–8; 2Pe 3:4,12; 1Jn 2:28	No
Gathering of God's people at the end	Mt 23:31; Mk 13:27	v. 1	Israel's gathering widely expected
Lawlessness	Mt 24:12 (the increase of wickedness, lit. lawlessness)	vv. 3,7–8 ("lawlessness," the "man of lawlessness" and the "lawless one")	Common in Jewish lists of end-time sufferings
People turning from the faith	Mt 24:10,12; Mk 13:12	v. 3 (if "rebellion" includes this)	Apostasy was common in Jewish lists of end-time sufferings
The abomination that causes desolation in the temple	Mt 24:15; Mk 13:14	v. 4 (man of lawlessness in the temple)	Developed from Da 11:31; 12:11
False prophets	Mt 24:5,11,24; Mk 13:6	v. 9	Common in Jewish lists of end-time sufferings
False signs and wonders of false prophets	Mt 24:24; Mk 13:22	v. 9	No

9The coming of the lawless one will be
in accordance with how Satan works.
He will use all sorts of displays of power
through signs and wonders[b] that serve
the lie, 10and all the ways that wickedness deceives those who are perishing.[c]
They perish because they refused to love
the truth and so be saved. 11For this reason God sends them[d] a powerful delusion so that they will believe the lie 12and
so that all will be condemned who have
not believed the truth but have delighted
in wickedness.[e]

Stand Firm

13But we ought always to thank God for
you, brothers and sisters loved by the Lord,
because God chose you as firstfruits[af] to
be saved[g] through the sanctifying work of
the Spirit[h] and through belief in the truth.
14He called you to this through our gospel,
that you might share in the glory of our
Lord Jesus Christ.
15So then, brothers and sisters, stand
firm[i] and hold fast to the teachings[b] we
passed on to you,[j] whether by word of
mouth or by letter.
16May our Lord Jesus Christ himself and
God our Father, who loved us[k] and by his
grace gave us eternal encouragement and
good hope, 17encourage[l] your hearts and
strengthen[m] you in every good deed and
word.

2:9 [b] Mt 24:24; Jn 4:48 **2:10** [c] 1Co 1:18 **2:11** [d] Ro 1:28 **2:12** [e] Ro 1:32 **2:13** [f] Eph 1:4 [g] 1Th 5:9 [h] 1Pe 1:2 **2:15** [i] 1Co 16:13 [j] 1Co 11:2 **2:16** [k] Jn 3:16 **2:17** [l] 1Th 3:2 [m] 2Th 3:3

Request for Prayer

3 As for other matters, brothers and sisters,[n] pray for us[o] that the message
of the Lord[p] may spread rapidly and be
honored, just as it was with you. 2And
pray that we may be delivered from
wicked and evil people,[q] for not everyone has faith. 3But the Lord is faithful,[r]
and he will strengthen you and protect
you from the evil one.[s] 4We have confidence[t] in the Lord that you are doing
and will continue to do the things we
command. 5May the Lord direct your
hearts[u] into God's love and Christ's perseverance.

Warning Against Idleness

6In the name of the Lord Jesus Christ,[v]
we command you, brothers and sisters,
to keep away from[w] every believer who
is idle and disruptive[x] and does not live
according to the teaching[c] you received
from us.[y] 7For you yourselves know how
you ought to follow our example.[z] We
were not idle when we were with you,
8nor did we eat anyone's food without paying for it. On the contrary, we
worked[a] night and day, laboring and toiling so that we would not be a burden to
any of you. 9We did this, not because we
do not have the right to such help,[b] but

3:1 [n] 1Th 4:1 [o] 1Th 5:25 [p] 1Th 1:8 **3:2** [q] Ro 15:31 **3:3** [r] 1Co 1:9 [s] Mt 5:37 **3:4** [t] 2Co 2:3 **3:5** [u] 1Ch 29:18 **3:6** [v] 1Co 5:4 [w] Ro 16:17 [x] ver 7,11 [y] 1Co 11:2 **3:7** [z] 1Co 4:16 **3:8** [a] Ac 18:3; Eph 4:28 **3:9** [b] 1Co 9:4-14

[a] 13 Some manuscripts *because from the beginning God chose you* [b] 15 Or *traditions* [c] 6 Or *tradition*

2:9 *how Satan works ... displays of power through signs and wonders.* Healing shrines and magic were widely used in Paul's day. A generation later people believed that an emperor (whose image was in fact worshiped on the site of the temple in AD 70) worked two miracles, although such claims were rarely made for emperors. False or demonic miracles attempting to replicate divine acts appear earlier (e.g., Ex 7:11), and Paul probably draws especially on Jesus' teaching (cf. Mk 13:22). Jewish tradition associated Satan with deception (sometimes drawing on Ge 3:4–5).
2:10 *wickedness deceives those who are perishing.* God had sometimes brought judgment by handing people over to their own choice to refuse his truth (Isa 29:9–12; cf. Ex 8:15,32; 9:12). *because they refused to love the truth.* Philosophers claimed to love the truth, a behavior viewed as virtuous; Paul sees the truth as the gospel (v. 13).
2:13 *chose.* Cf., e.g., Dt 7:6; see note on Col 3:12. *firstfruits.* See note on 1Co 16:15.
2:14 *glory.* Cf. note on 1:10.
2:15 Many ancient intellectual schools emphasized carefully passing on traditions going back to the school's founders or other earlier teachers; Paul has passed on Jesus' teachings (see "Jesus' Teachings as Background in 2 Thessalonians 2:1–12," p. 2102, and "Jesus' Teachings as Background in 1 Thessalonians 4:13—5:11," p. 2098).
2:16–17 *May our Lord Jesus Christ ... encourage your hearts.* As here, people sometimes invoked, thus implicitly prayed to, God while directly addressing the person or people for whom they wanted God's blessing.
3:1 *that the message of the Lord may spread rapidly.* Probably evokes the Greek version of Ps 147:15, which speaks of God's word running swiftly.
3:2–3 *not everyone has faith. But the Lord is faithful.* Skilled speakers sometimes used antithesis and plays on words; note here the contrast between not having faith (v. 2) and faithfulness (v. 3).
3:2 *pray that we may be delivered from wicked and evil people.* Prayers for deliverance from enemies were common (e.g., Ps 64:1).
3:3 *protect you from the evil one.* Cf. Mt 6:13; Jn 17:15.
3:5 For blessings implicitly addressed to God, see note on 2:16–17.
3:6 *idle and disruptive.* Despite the prosperity of Thessalonica as a whole, many people were unemployed. There, as in many other cities, idle people often sat in the marketplace with nothing better to do (Ac 17:5). Less common were those who refused to work, such as Cynic philosophers or some dependents of the wealthy. Paul was a traveling sage, but unlike Cynics, he worked rather than begged; he distinguishes himself from greedy sages in 1Th 2:1–12.
3:7 *follow our example.* Ancient exhortation frequently appealed to role models; disciples also imitated their teachers.
3:8 *we worked night and day.* For Paul's laboring in Thessalonica, see note on 1Th 2:9. For Paul's work in general, see note on Ac 18:3.

in order to offer ourselves as a model for
you to imitate.[c] 10For even when we were
with you,[d] we gave you this rule: "The
one who is unwilling to work[e] shall not
eat."
11We hear that some among you are idle
and disruptive. They are not busy; they are
busybodies.[f] 12Such people we command
and urge in the Lord Jesus Christ[g] to settle
down and earn the food they eat.[h] 13And
as for you, brothers and sisters, never tire
of doing what is good.[i]
14Take special note of anyone who does
not obey our instruction in this letter. Do
not associate with them,[j] in order that
they may feel ashamed. 15Yet do not regard them as an enemy, but warn them as
you would a fellow believer.[k]

Final Greetings

16Now may the Lord of peace[l] himself
give you peace at all times and in every
way. The Lord be with all of you.[m]
17I, Paul, write this greeting in my own
hand,[n] which is the distinguishing mark in
all my letters. This is how I write.
18The grace of our Lord Jesus Christ be
with you all.[o]

3:9 [c] ver 7
3:10 [d] 1Th 3:4 [e] 1Th 4:11
3:11 [f] ver 6, 7; 1Ti 5:13
3:12 [g] 1Th 4:1 [h] 1Th 4:11; Eph 4:28
3:13 [i] Gal 6:9
3:14 [j] ver 6
3:15 [k] Gal 6:1; 1Th 5:14
3:16 [l] Ro 15:33 [m] Ru 2:4
3:17 [n] 1Co 16:21
3:18 [o] Ro 16:20

3:10 *shall not eat.* As synagogue communities provided for Jews in need, churches presumably did the same. Sometimes people of wealth also sponsored those of somewhat lower station in return for praise. Ancient associations, including churches and (in Judea) probably groups of Pharisees, also had some communal meals. Jewish tradition emphasized generosity, but also hard work (e.g., Pr 12:11; 14:23; 18:9; 21:25).
3:14 *Do not associate with them.* Churches probably borrowed from Jewish communities the model of exercising different levels of discipline. Jewish communities sometimes excluded a person from common meals or fellowship for a period of time, beat them (not attested in early Christianity), or expelled them from the community completely (cf. Mt 18:15 – 20; 1Co 5:5; 1Ti 1:20). The form of discipline here is the lightest.
3:16,18 On blessing-prayers, see note on 2:16 – 17.
3:17 *I, Paul, write this greeting in my own hand.* Sometimes people did forge letters (cf. 2:2). But most letter writers used scribes and signed their names at the end (or sometimes added brief comments), and Paul often follows this practice elsewhere in his letters (e.g., Col 4:18).

THE LETTERS

1 TIMOTHY

Authorship

The style of 1 – 2 Timothy and Titus often differs from that of Paul's earlier letters. Some scholars suggest different authors; others, that Paul gave considerable freedom to his scribe (some even suggest that scribe was Luke, see 2Ti 4:11); others, that the letters or instructions were remembered by Timothy, Titus, and/or others, and then written down in their own words. The many personal allusions in 2 Timothy argue against the work simply being made up by someone later, since such allusions appear only relatively rarely in pseudepigraphic works. Further, the descriptions of elders/overseers and deacons are earlier than those found in the early second-century works of Ignatius. Pseudepigraphic works, by contrast, were usually written long after the claimed author's death.

QUICK GLANCE

AUTHOR:
The apostle Paul

AUDIENCE:
Timothy, one of Paul's closest associates, but no doubt intended also to be read to the whole church in Ephesus

DATE:
About AD 63 – 64

THEME:
Paul writes to instruct Timothy concerning the care of the church at Ephesus.

Setting and Purpose

The letters to Timothy address a setting in Ephesus (1Ti 1:3; cf. 2Ti 1:18; 4:12), where traditional Greek culture was dominant. Paul must correct some errors circulating in this location (1Ti 1:3 – 7,19 – 20; 4:1 – 4; 6:4 – 5; 2Ti 2:14 – 18; 3:6 – 9; 4:3; cf. Titus 1:10 – 11), which include some specifically Jewish issues (1Ti 1:7; cf. Titus 1:10 – 11,14; 3:9). Some teachers advocate asceticism (4:3), deny a future resurrection (2Ti 2:18), misunderstand and dogmatically abuse the law (1Ti 1:7), and follow myths (1:4; 4:7; 2Ti 4:4), apparently Jewish ones (Titus 1:14). Paul thus wants Timothy to teach (1Ti 4:6,16; 2Ti 2:2,14,24 – 26; 3:14 — 4:2) and appoint leaders who can teach soundly and stem the falsehoods (1Ti 3:2,9; 5:17; 2Ti 2:2; cf. Titus 1:5,9). ◆

1 Paul, an apostle of Christ Jesus by the
command of God[a] our Savior and of
Christ Jesus our hope,[b]

2To Timothy[c] my true son[d] in the faith:

Grace, mercy and peace from God the
Father and Christ Jesus our Lord.

Timothy Charged to Oppose False Teachers

3As I urged you when I went into Macedonia, stay there in Ephesus[e] so that you
may command certain people not to teach
false doctrines[f] any longer 4or to devote
themselves to myths[g] and endless genealogies. Such things promote controversial
speculations[h] rather than advancing God's
work — which is by faith. 5The goal of this
command is love, which comes from a
pure heart[i] and a good conscience and a
sincere faith.[j] 6Some have departed from
these and have turned to meaningless talk.
7They want to be teachers of the law, but
they do not know what they are talking
about or what they so confidently affirm.

8We know that the law is good[k] if one
uses it properly. 9We also know that the
law is made not for the righteous but
for lawbreakers and rebels,[l] the ungodly
and sinful, the unholy and irreligious, for
those who kill their fathers or mothers,
for murderers, 10for the sexually immoral, for those practicing homosexuality, for
slave traders and liars and perjurers — and
for whatever else is contrary to the sound
doctrine[m] 11that conforms to the gospel
concerning the glory of the blessed God,
which he entrusted to me.[n]

The Lord's Grace to Paul

12I thank Christ Jesus our Lord, who has
given me strength,[o] that he considered me
trustworthy, appointing me to his service.
13Even though I was once a blasphemer
and a persecutor[p] and a violent man, I
was shown mercy because I acted in ignorance and unbelief.[q] 14The grace of our
Lord was poured out on me abundantly,[r]
along with the faith and love that are in
Christ Jesus.[s]

15Here is a trustworthy saying[t] that deserves full acceptance: Christ Jesus came
into the world to save sinners — of whom
I am the worst. 16But for that very reason
I was shown mercy[u] so that in me, the
worst of sinners, Christ Jesus might display his immense patience as an example
for those who would believe in him and

1:1 [a] Titus 1:3 [b] Col 1:27 **1:2** [c] Ac 16:1 [d] 2Ti 1:2; Titus 1:4 **1:3** [e] Ac 18:19 [f] Gal 1:6,7 **1:4** [g] 1Ti 4:7; Titus 1:14 [h] 1Ti 6:4 **1:5** [i] 2Ti 2:22 [j] 2Ti 1:5 **1:8** [k] Ro 7:12 **1:9** [l] Gal 3:19 **1:10** [m] 2Ti 4:3; Titus 1:9 **1:11** [n] Gal 2:7 **1:12** [o] Php 4:13 **1:13** [p] Ac 8:3 [q] Ac 26:9 **1:14** [r] Ro 5:20 [s] 2Ti 1:13 **1:15** [t] 1Ti 3:1; 2Ti 2:11; Titus 3:8 **1:16** [u] ver 13

1:1 *Paul.* Ancient letters started with the author's name. *God our Savior.* People depicted many gods and even rulers as "saviors," but Jewish texts apply the designation especially to the one true God (e.g., Isa 43:11; 45:21; Hos 13:4).
1:2 *To Timothy.* After naming the designated recipient, letters included greetings. Although most letters were private correspondence, some were written with a wider eventual audience in view (cf. "you all" in 6:21; 2Ti 4:22); Paul addresses Timothy but might also bolster Timothy's public authority through the letter. *my true son in the faith.* See 1Co 4:17 and note on 1Co 4:14. *Grace ... peace.* See note on Ro 1:7.
1:3 *Macedonia ... Ephesus.* One leaving Ephesus for Achaia could travel north to Troas (2Ti 4:13), sail to Macedonia, and then follow the major Roman road through Macedonia until turning south into Achaia, the capital of which was Corinth.
1:4 *myths and endless genealogies.* Philosophers often despised or allegorized myths; they condemned myths and genealogies. Paul probably refers here to Jewish myths and genealogies (Titus 1:14). Jewish people usually denied that Scripture included myths, but many Jewish storytellers expanded on Biblical accounts and some even wrote new "revelations," which they attributed to Biblical persons (see, e.g., note on Jude 14 – 15). Some suggest that "genealogies" here refers to expansions of Biblical genealogies, as in some Jewish works from this period, or perhaps to false post-Biblical attributions of ancestry.
1:5 *a pure heart and a good conscience.* Scripture values a pure heart (Ps 24:4; 51:10; 73:1; Pr 22:11); Greek sources value a good conscience.
1:6 *meaningless talk.* Many ancient sages ridiculed quibbling over trivial matters. Sometimes they also accused teachers of rhetoric of valuing persuasiveness above truth. Some Jewish teachers also quibbled over details or made arguments based on slight changes in spelling or pronunciation.
1:9 – 10 Ancient writers often listed various vices.
1:9 *the law is made not for the righteous but for lawbreakers.* Philosophers believed that wise people did not need laws, because their wise behavior itself modeled the moral truth on which laws were based. Civil law is normally designed to restrain harm, not to transform hearts. *those who kill their fathers or mothers.* Most people in antiquity would have despised sins such as irreligion and regarded murder of parents as among the most heinous conceivable crimes. (The Roman penalty for this crime was drowning.)
1:10 *those practicing homosexuality.* Although the ancient world knew of sexual preferences, it thought in terms of same-sex actions rather than orientation; Greek men often slept with other males as well as with women (see the article "Homosexual Activity in Antiquity," p. 1950). *slave traders.* People sometimes raised for slavery the many babies left to die on trash heaps, but traders also bought and sold people, who often (especially in the case of girls) were raised as prostitutes. (Biblical and ancient Near Eastern law assigned a death penalty for enslaving people who were not prisoners of war; see Ex 21:16; Dt 24:7.) *perjurers.* Deemed impious, since they lied despite invoking the witness of a deity.
1:12 *I thank.* Ancient letters sometimes included a thanksgiving.
1:13 *blasphemer ... persecutor ... violent man.* Paul's past offers hope for others that also need to repent (v. 20). *persecutor.* See Ac 7:58; 8:1 – 3; 9:1 – 2. *I acted in ignorance and unbelief.* Ancient thinkers usually regarded ignorance as mitigating guilt, though not eliminating it.
1:15 *Here is a trustworthy saying.* The Pastoral Letters often cite a "trustworthy saying" (3:1; 4:9; 2Ti 2:11; Titus 3:8).
1:16 *as an example.* Speakers and writers often used people or events as examples or models.

receive eternal life. 17Now to the King[v]
eternal, immortal, invisible,[w] the only
God, be honor and glory for ever and ever.
Amen.[x]

The Charge to Timothy Renewed

18Timothy, my son, I am giving you this
command in keeping with the prophecies
once made about you,[y] so that by recalling them you may fight the battle well,[z]
19holding on to faith and a good conscience, which some have rejected and
so have suffered shipwreck with regard to
the faith.[a] 20Among them are Hymenaeus[b]
and Alexander,[c] whom I have handed over
to Satan[d] to be taught not to blaspheme.

Instructions on Worship

2 I urge, then, first of all, that petitions,
prayers, intercession and thanksgiving
be made for all people— 2for kings and
all those in authority,[e] that we may live
peaceful and quiet lives in all godliness
and holiness. 3This is good, and pleases
God our Savior, 4who wants[f] all people[g] to
be saved and to come to a knowledge of
the truth.[h] 5For there is one God[i] and one
mediator[j] between God and mankind, the
man Christ Jesus, 6who gave himself as a
ransom for all people. This has now been
witnessed to[k] at the proper time.[l] 7And for
this purpose I was appointed a herald and
an apostle—I am telling the truth, I am
not lying—and a true and faithful teacher[m] of the Gentiles.[n]

8Therefore I want the men everywhere
to pray, lifting up holy hands[o] without anger or disputing. 9I also want the wom-
en to dress modestly, with decency and
propriety, adorning themselves, not with
elaborate hairstyles or gold or pearls or expensive clothes,[p] 10but with good deeds,
appropriate for women who profess to
worship God.

11A woman[a] should learn in quietness

1:17 [v] Rev 15:3 [w] Col 1:15 [x] Ro 11:36 **1:18** [y] 1Ti 4:14 [z] 2Ti 2:3 **1:19** [a] 1Ti 6:21 **1:20** [b] 2Ti 2:17 [c] 2Ti 4:14 [d] 1Co 5:5 **2:2** [e] Ezr 6:10; Ro 13:1 **2:4** [f] Eze 18:23, 32 [g] Titus 2:11 [h] 2Ti 2:25 **2:5** [i] Ro 3:29,30 [j] Gal 3:20 **2:6** [k] 1Co 1:6 [l] 1Ti 6:15 **2:7** [m] 2Ti 1:11 [n] Ac 9:15; Eph 3:7,8 **2:8** [o] Ps 134:2; Lk 24:50 **2:9** [p] 1Pe 3:3

[a] *11* Or *wife*; also in verse 12

1:17 *the King eternal, immortal, invisible, the only God.* In praising a deity, Greeks and sometimes Jews would list his or her titles and attributes. Diaspora Jews sometimes spoke like Paul here; even Greek thinkers valued what was eternal and invisible, though to many Gentiles talk of an "only God" (rather than merely a supreme one) sounded intolerant.
1:18 *the prophecies once made about you.* Jewish groups differed as to whether prophecy continued, but no other ancient groups known to us included widespread prophecy to the extent found in early Christianity (1Co 14:31). One or more leaders prophesied to Timothy when they laid hands on him for ministry (1Ti 4:14). *fight the battle well.* Ancient thinkers sometimes depicted their work for spreading truth with military imagery.
1:19 *suffered shipwreck.* Ancient thinkers frequently employed images from sailing (cf. Eph 4:14; Jas 1:6) as well as from battles (see note on v. 18).
1:20 *Hymenaeus.* On Hymenaeus's views (Hymenaeus was not a common name, so this is presumably the same one), see note on 2Ti 2:17–18. *handed over to Satan to be taught not to blaspheme.* Churches probably borrowed the model of different levels of discipline from Jewish communities (attested both in the Dead Sea Scrolls and later rabbis). Jewish communities sometimes excluded a person from common meals or fellowship for a period of time, beat them (not attested in early Christianity), or expelled them from the community completely, for various lengths of time or even permanently. The exclusion here (and in Mt 18:15–20; 1Co 5:5) is to solicit repentance.
2:1–2 *petitions, prayers, intercession and thanksgiving be made … for kings and all those in authority.* Rome allowed the peoples of its empire to worship their own gods, but most also showed their loyalty to Rome by worshiping the goddess Roma and the spirit of the emperor. Because Jewish people rejected all gods but their own (cf. v. 5), Rome allowed them to pray and sacrifice for the emperor's health without praying and sacrificing to him. Synagogues also offered prayers for his welfare. In AD 66, however, when Jewish revolutionaries decided to overthrow Roman rule, they stopped the sacrifices in the temple, thereby declaring war against Rome. Christian prayers for the emperor and provincial and local officials allowed Christians to demonstrate that they were good citizens of the society in which they lived (Jer 29:7). Paul is interested in peace (v. 2) and in the honor of the gospel (vv. 3–4).
2:5 *one God and one mediator between God and mankind.* Although some polytheists identified Israel's God with the supreme God, many considered Jewish people intolerant for believing in only one God. Christians' further limitation to one mediator might seem even more intolerant, though Christians were multiethnic and affirmed that God wanted all to be saved (v. 4). Jewish people viewed Moses as a sort of mediator between God and Israel; Jesus is a fuller mediator between God and all humanity.
2:6 *ransom.* Could be a price for others' freedom (Ex 30:12; Nu 3:12; Mk 10:45).
2:8–15 Paul addresses appropriate conduct in the house churches. He might focus more on women (vv. 9–15) than men (v. 8) because the former outnumber the latter (as was the case among converts to Judaism) or because women are causing more problems in this congregation.
2:8 *lifting up holy hands.* Both Jewish and Gentile worshipers and petitioners of deities lifted or stretched out their hands toward the deities (e.g., Ps 77:2; 134:2). Scripture spoke of hands pure from wrongdoing (Ps 24:4; 73:13), and Diaspora Jews washed their hands before prayers.
2:9–10 *dress modestly … adorning themselves, not with elaborate hairstyles … but with good deeds.* A common topic of moral teachers' warnings, both among Jews and Gentiles, involved excessive adornment, using language similar to what appears here. Jewish teachers were particularly concerned about men being sexually tempted; Gentile writers complained about ostentation. Wealthy women sometimes braided their hair with gold, displaying their extravagance. Because women normally covered much of their body but single women kept their heads bare, men often found hair especially attractive. Wealthier women, in whose homes the churches often met, often kept their heads uncovered, especially in their homes (see the article "Head Coverings in Antiquity," p. 2003). Greco-Roman moralists often stressed that it was inward adornment rather than outward adornment that would please a good husband.
2:11 *quietness and full submission.* Greek culture, predominant in Ephesus, valued women's meekness and quietness. (For behaving respectably in the culture, cf. notes on 5:7; 6:1–2.) More generally, teachers expected

and full submission.[q] 12I do not permit a
woman to teach or to assume authority
over a man;[a] she must be quiet. 13For
Adam was formed first, then Eve.[r] 14And
Adam was not the one deceived; it was the
woman who was deceived and became
a sinner.[s] 15But women[b] will be saved
through childbearing — if they continue
in faith, love[t] and holiness with propriety.

Qualifications for Overseers and Deacons

3 Here is a trustworthy saying:[u] Whoever aspires to be an overseer[v] desires a noble task. 2Now the overseer is to
be above reproach,[w] faithful to his wife,
temperate, self-controlled, respectable,
hospitable,[x] able to teach,[y] 3not given to
drunkenness, not violent but gentle, not
quarrelsome,[z] not a lover of money.[a] 4He
must manage his own family well and see
that his children obey him, and he must
do so in a manner worthy of full[c] respect.[b]
5(If anyone does not know how to manage
his own family, how can he take care of
God's church?)[c] 6He must not be a recent
convert, or he may become conceited[d] and
fall under the same judgment as the devil.
7He must also have a good reputation with
outsiders, so that he will not fall into disgrace and into the devil's trap.[e]
8In the same way, deacons[d][f] are to be
worthy of respect, sincere, not indulging

2:11 [q] 1Co 14:34 **2:13** [r] Ge 2:7, 22; 1Co 11:8 **2:14** [s] Ge 3:1-6, 13; 2Co 11:3 **2:15** [t] 1Ti 1:14 **3:1** [u] 1Ti 1:15 [v] Ac 20:28 **3:2** [w] Titus 1:6-8 [x] Ro 12:13 [y] 2Ti 2:24 **3:3** [z] 2Ti 2:24 [a] Heb 13:5; 1Pe 5:2 **3:4** [b] Titus 1:6 **3:5** [c] 1Co 10:32 **3:6** [d] 1Ti 6:4 **3:7** [e] 2Ti 2:26 **3:8** [f] Php 1:1

[a] *12* Or *over her husband* [b] *15* Greek *she* [c] *4* Or *him with proper* [d] *8* The word *deacons* refers here to Christians designated to serve with the overseers/elders of the church in a variety of ways; similarly in verse 12; and in Romans 16:1 and Phil. 1:1.

---

new students to learn quietly (cf. v. 2) and submissively (see note on 1Co 14:35). In a first-century setting, what might stand out as more unusual here was that, given these conditions, Paul expressly encourages women to learn; see the article "Women's Education in Antiquity," p. 2109. This would be important if some women are being targeted by false teachers (2Ti 3:6).

2:12 *to teach or to assume authority over a man.* Both in Jewish and Gentile cultures, it was extremely rare (in many circles unheard of) for a woman to teach or to assume authority over a man. The present situation would make such a warning even more vital: people were misinterpreting Scripture (1:4–7), women were less trained in Scripture (see the article "Women's Education in Antiquity," p. 2109), and the misinformed were targeting women (who, as noted, were less trained) to spread their teachings (see notes on 5:13; 2Ti 3:6). Paul's warning makes good sense in such a context. If part of the problem is that the women are uninformed, Paul may offer a long-range solution to this deficiency in v. 11 (cf. Ro 16:1–4,7; Php 4:2–3). The matter is, however, debated (see note on v. 14).

2:14 *it was the woman who was deceived.* For the argument from sequence of creation, cf. 1Co 11:7–12 (where Paul urges head coverings), though cf. God often blessing the younger over the older in Genesis, e.g., Ge 25:23; 48:14–19. Jewish tradition elaborated, and sometimes argued women's intellectual inferiority from, Eve's deception in Ge 3:1–6. Paul sometimes applies Scripture in an ad hoc manner (see, e.g., note on Gal 3:16), but he more often employs it universally (see, e.g., Ro 5:12–21 and notes on Ro 15:12,13). Some interpreters thus apply this passage to women universally, suggesting that women should not teach because, being more deceivable, they are apt to mislead others. Other interpreters contend that Paul applies this analogy only to the deceivable, targeted women of Ephesus (for the situation there see notes on vv. 11,12). They cite Paul's support for some ministry of women (Ro 16:1–4,7; Php 4:2–3), and his use of the Eve analogy elsewhere to other groups deceived at the time (especially 2Co 11:3). The matter is thus debated.

2:15 *women will be saved through childbearing.* In Paul, "saved" most often involves deliverance from sin or judgment (as in v. 4; 1:15; 4:16). Some thus understand this passage as suggesting that women have eternal life by following their proper role, including as child-bearers (cf. 5:10), perhaps for the sake of defying the false teachers (cf. 4:3) or for the gospel's respectability (cf. 5:14–15; 6:1; Titus 2:4–5,8,10). Others, noting that the Greek term here translated "saved" usually meant deliverance or safety, especially in a childbearing context, suggest divine protection during childbirth. Both Jewish and Gentile women regularly prayed for this, and some Jewish traditions associated the judgment on Eve with dying in childbirth. On this view, Paul might qualify his analogy with Eve (vv. 13–14), here avoiding association with the judgment of Ge 3:16.

3:1–7 Ancient writers often listed qualifications for offices, and even more often listed virtues appropriate to those holding such offices. Exceptions were not stated in general lists of qualifications but might be made for particular qualifications in extenuating circumstances.

3:1 Some thinkers encouraged anyone qualified for leadership to serve society. *overseer.* A Greek administrative title also appearing in the Greek translation of the OT and (in Hebrew form) in the Dead Sea Scrolls. Cf. note on Titus 1:7.

3:2 *above reproach.* Along with being of "good reputation" (v. 7), expectations of high character frame the list; being honorable in the public view was considered important for leaders, and even more crucial for leading representatives of minority movements, which were sometimes readily slandered. *faithful to his wife.* Cf. 5:9 (see note there). The false teachers shunned marriage (4:3), but adultery and sexual immorality were common (see the article "Prostitution and Sexual Immorality," p. 1990), and some men had multiple concubines or practiced bigamy. (Polygamy, by contrast, was not legal in the Greek and Roman worlds, and thus was not Paul's primary concern here.) *hospitable.* See note on Ac 16:15.

3:4 *must manage his own family well.* Cf. note on v. 15. Many thinkers argued that leaders in society should first prove their leadership skills in the home. (This concern might prove especially important for churches, which at this time met in homes.) *his children obey him.* Family members' behavior could bring honor or shame on the entire household (cf., e.g., Pr 10:1; 27:11; 29:15). Men held considerable authority over their families; all ancient cultures expected minor children to obey (cf. Dt 21:20). In principle, Roman fathers maintained the right of life and death over their children, although this was barely ever exercised in this period except with newborns and would not be relevant in Ephesus. Nevertheless, the principle illustrates the degree of authority that ancient Mediterranean society accorded fathers.

3:6 *not be a recent convert.* See note on v. 10.

3:8 *deacons.* The Greek term here can refer to any kind of minister, or active agent of God's message (e.g., in 2Co 3:6), but here probably refers to a church office (cf. Php 1:1). Perhaps the term involves administration of

1 TIMOTHY 2:11 – 12

Women's Education in Antiquity

Most men considered intellectual activity a predominantly male exercise. This was true even though exceptions were made for elite women, and some intellectuals praised the ability of women (or, more often, of particular women) to learn. Greek men often married women over a decade younger than they were, so it is not surprising that Plutarch observed that most husbands doubted that their wives could learn. By contrast, Plutarch advised a new groom to take an interest in his wife's learning — although warning that, if left to themselves, women are led astray by passion and foolishness.

Women were less likely to be literate than men (sometimes estimated at 10 percent as often as men of the same social class). The two advanced disciplines were philosophy and rhetoric; some philosophers allowed women to be disciples, but throughout Greco-Roman antiquity barely any were trained in rhetoric (i.e., public speaking).

More relevant for the NT was Jewish education in Scripture. Jewish culture reared boys, but not normally girls, to recite Torah (the law). Granted, women listened and learned in synagogues; a few even attended rabbis' lectures. Yet they were not taught to recite Torah, and rabbis did not train them as disciples (see notes on Lk 10:39 – 41). Jews writing for Diaspora audiences (e.g., Josephus and Philo) expressed greater skepticism of women's intellectual abilities than did most rabbis. (Praising the empress as an exceptional woman, Philo concedes that she became virtually "male" intellectually; Philo, *Embassy to Gaius* 320.) Women filled higher roles in synagogues in some Diaspora settings more open to women's leadership, but even there they were rare.

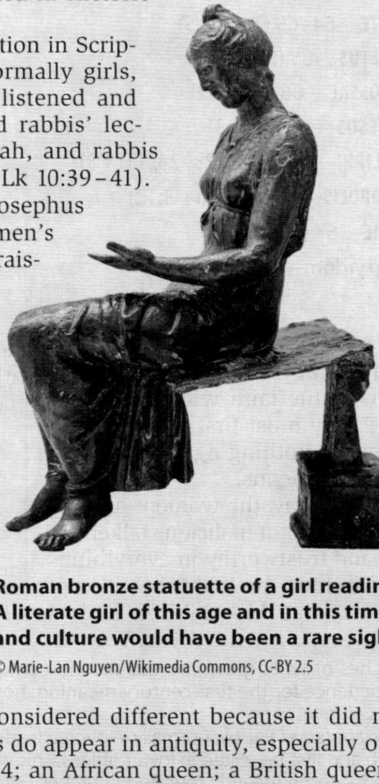

Women were teachers of adult men even more rarely than they were disciples. In all of antiquity, only a tiny proportion of respected sages (such as Aspasia, Sosipatra, and Hypatia) were women who also taught men. In Jewish circles, Beruriah, the second-century wife of Rabbi Meir, was skilled in the law, but she was a rare exception in this period and rabbis often ignored her.

Roman bronze statuette of a girl reading. A literate girl of this age and in this time and culture would have been a rare sight.

Exceptions existed. Inspired speech was considered different because it did not come from the woman herself. Women leaders do appear in antiquity, especially outside the Greek and Roman world (e.g., Jdg 4:4; an African queen; a British queen), but they were considered highly exceptional. Many accused those they believed to be false teachers of targeting women because they were more vulnerable. For gender roles in the first century, see the article "Marriage Roles in Antiquity," p. 2064, and the article "Head Coverings in Antiquity," p. 2003. ◆

PAUL'S FOURTH MISSIONARY JOURNEY c. AD 62–68

It is clear from Ac 13:1—21:17 that Paul went on three long missionary journeys. There is also reason to believe that he made a fourth journey after his release from the Roman imprisonment recorded in Ac 28. The conclusion that such a journey did indeed take place is based on: (1) Paul's declared intention to go to Spain (Ro 15:24,28), (2) Eusebius's implication that Paul was released following his first Roman imprisonment (*Ecclesiastical History* 2.22.2–3) and (3) statements in early Christian literature that he took the gospel as far as Spain (Clement of Rome, *Epistle to the Corinthians*, ch. 5; *Actus Petri Vercellenses*, chs. 1–3; Muratorian Canon, lines 34–39).

The places Paul may have visited after his release from prison are indicated by statements of intention in his earlier writings and by subsequent mention in the Pastoral Letters. The order of his travel cannot be determined with certainty, but the itinerary below seems likely.

1. **ROME**—released from prison in AD 62
2. **SPAIN**—62–64 (Ro 15:24,28)
3. **CRETE**—64–65 (Titus 1:5)
4. **MILETUS**—65 (2Ti 4:20)
5. **COLOSSAE**—66 (Phm 22)
6. **EPHESUS**—66 (1Ti 1:3)
7. **PHILIPPI**—66 (Php 2:23–24; 1Ti 1:3)
8. **NICOPOLIS**—66–67 (Titus 3:12)
9. **ROME**—67 (2Ti 1:17)
10. Martyrdom—67/68 (2Ti 4:6)

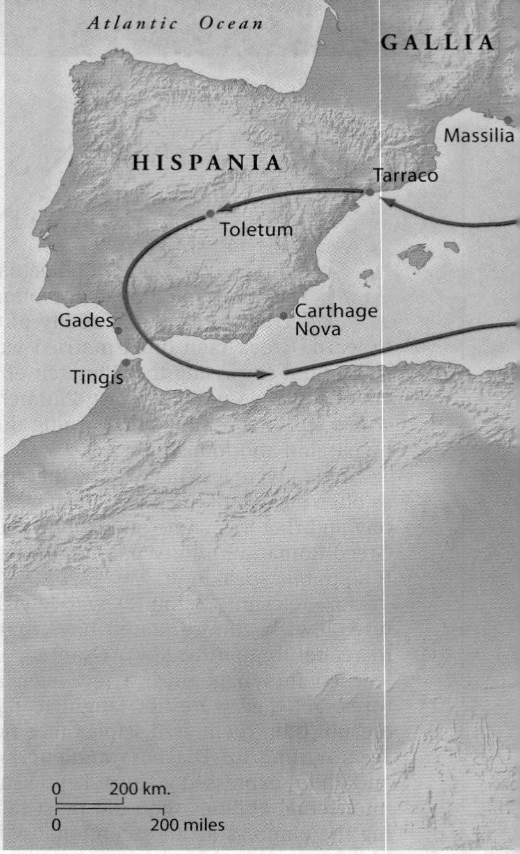

in much wine,[g] and not pursuing dishonest gain. 9They must keep hold of the
deep truths of the faith with a clear conscience.[h] 10They must first be tested; and
then if there is nothing against them, let
them serve as deacons.
11In the same way, the women[a] are to be
worthy of respect, not malicious talkers[i] but
temperate and trustworthy in everything.
12A deacon must be faithful to his wife
and must manage his children and his
household well.[j] 13Those who have served
well gain an excellent standing and great
assurance in their faith in Christ Jesus.

Reasons for Paul's Instructions

14Although I hope to come to you soon,
I am writing you these instructions so that,
15if I am delayed, you will know how people ought to conduct themselves in God's
household, which is the church[k] of the liv-

3:8 [g] Titus 2:3 **3:9** [h] 1Ti 1:19 **3:11** [i] 2Ti 3:3; Titus 2:3 **3:12** [j] ver 4 **3:15** [k] ver 5; Eph 2:21

[a] *11* Possibly deacons' wives or women who are deacons

house churches or what grew into the second-century diaconate; evidence for the first-century meaning, however, remains elusive.
3:10 *must first be tested.* People normally expected leaders to begin with and first be tested in lower offices. This was not possible for some recently founded churches (Titus, e.g., does not mention this requirement), but the church in Ephesus had now existed for more than a decade.
3:11 *the women.* Scholars debate whether "the women" here refers to female deacons or to male deacons' wives (in ancient society, men were sometimes ridiculed for their wives' behavior). By the early second century, a Roman governor in Asia Minor is apparently familiar with female deacons. See the NIV text note. *not malicious talkers.* Women often conversed in their neighborhoods, and custom allowed them to gossip (cf. perhaps 5:13); shaming people in this way served as a form of moral social control, but the scandalous rumors behind it were often false or exaggerated (hence "malicious talkers").
3:12 See notes on vv. 2,4.
3:14 *I hope to come to you soon.* Letters sometimes served as a substitute for one's presence. They also sometimes announced one's coming and often communicated a fond desire to see the recipient in person.
3:15 *God's household, which is the church of the living God.* Ancient political thought treated the household as a micro-

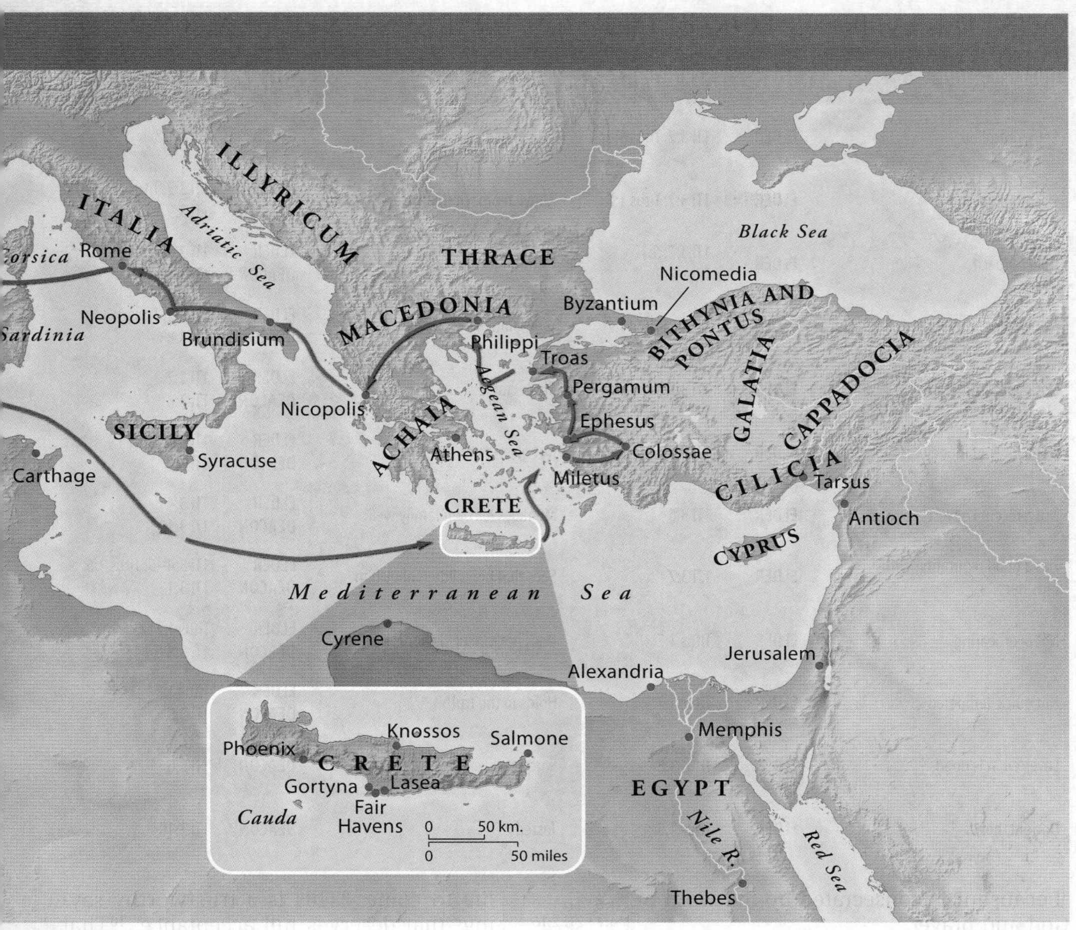

ing God, the pillar and foundation of the
truth. 16Beyond all question, the mystery[l]
from which true godliness springs is great:

He appeared in the flesh,[m]
was vindicated by the Spirit,[a]
was seen by angels,
was preached among the nations,[n]
was believed on in the world,
was taken up in glory.[o]

4 The Spirit[p] clearly says that in later
times[q] some will abandon the faith
and follow deceiving spirits[r] and things
taught by demons. 2Such teachings come
through hypocritical liars, whose consciences have been seared as with a hot
iron.[s] 3They forbid people to marry[t] and
order them to abstain from certain foods,[u]
which God created[v] to be received with
thanksgiving[w] by those who believe and
who know the truth. 4For everything God
created is good,[x] and nothing is to be rejected if it is received with thanksgiving,

[a] 16 Or *vindicated in spirit*

3:16 [l] Ro 16:25 [m] Jn 1:14 [n] Col 1:23 [o] Mk 16:19 **4:1** [p] Jn 16:13 [q] 2Ti 3:1 [r] 2Th 2:3 **4:2** [s] Eph 4:19 **4:3** [t] Heb 13:4 [u] Col 2:16 [v] Ge 1:29 [w] Ro 14:6 **4:4** [x] Ro 14:14-18

cosm for society; some suggest that family-based house churches here might similarly be meant to mirror God's larger household, the church as a whole (cf. vv. 4–5,12).

4:1 *The Spirit clearly says.* Reports a divine message (cf. Ac 21:11). Ancient Jewish thinkers highlighted the Biblical association between the Spirit and prophecy. *later times.* Probably evokes OT passages about the promised future time of restoration (Isa 2:2; Mic 4:1), but applicable to the present era between the Messiah's first and second comings (cf. Ac 2:17). *some will abandon the faith.* Many Jewish thinkers expected widespread apostasy in the period just before the end of the age (cf. note on 2Th 2:3).

4:2 *hypocritical liars, whose consciences have been seared.* Might refer to consciences that no longer function, but might instead refer (in view of "hypocritical") to consciences "branded" with a mark of demonic ownership (cf. v. 1; perhaps Rev 13:16).

4:3 *They forbid people to marry.* Most people in antiquity valued marriage, but some did oppose marriage (see the article "Celibacy in Antiquity," p. 1993). *abstain from certain foods.* See the article "'Pure' and 'Unclean' Foods," p. 1972; see also note on Ro 14:2.

4:4 *everything God created is good . . . received with thanksgiving.* The usual Jewish blessing before a meal praised

QUALIFICATIONS FOR ELDERS/OVERSEERS AND DEACONS

QUALIFICATION	TITLE	SCRIPTURE	QUALIFICATION	TITLE	SCRIPTURE
Self-controlled	**ELDER**	1Ti 3:2; Titus 1:8	Disciplined	**ELDER**	Titus 1:8
Hospitable	**ELDER**	1Ti 3:2; Titus 1:8	Above reproach (blameless)	**ELDER** **DEACON**	1Ti 3:2; Titus 1:6 1Ti 3:9
Able to teach	**ELDER**	1Ti 3:2; 5:17; Titus 1:9	Faithful to his wife	**ELDER** **DEACON**	1Ti 3:2; Titus 1:6 1Ti 3:12
Not violent but gentle	**ELDER**	1Ti 3:3; Titus 1:7	Temperate	**ELDER** **DEACON**	1Ti 3:2; Titus 1:7 1Ti 3:8
Not quarrelsome	**ELDER**	1Ti 3:3	Respectable	**ELDER** **DEACON**	1Ti 3:2 1Ti 3:8
Not a lover of money	**ELDER**	1Ti 3:3	Not given to drunkenness	**ELDER** **DEACON**	1Ti 3:3; Titus 1:7 1Ti 3:8
Not a recent convert	**ELDER**	1Ti 3:6	Manages his own family well	**ELDER** **DEACON**	1Ti 3:4 1Ti 3:12
Has a good reputation with outsiders	**ELDER**	1Ti 3:7	Sees that his children obey him	**ELDER** **DEACON**	1Ti 3:4–5; Titus 1:6 1Ti 3:12
Not overbearing	**ELDER**	Titus 1:7	Does not pursue dishonest gain	**ELDER** **DEACON**	Titus 1:7 1Ti 3:8
Not quick-tempered	**ELDER**	Titus 1:7	Holds to the truth	**ELDER** **DEACON**	Titus 1:9 1Ti 3:9
Loves what is good	**ELDER**	Titus 1:8	Sincere	**DEACON**	1Ti 3:8
Upright, holy	**ELDER**	Titus 1:8	Tested	**DEACON**	1Ti 3:10

5because it is consecrated by the word of God and prayer.
6If you point these things out to the brothers and sisters,[a] you will be a good minister of Christ Jesus, nourished on the truths of the faith[y] and of the good teaching that you have followed.
7Have nothing to do with godless myths and old wives' tales;[z] rather, train yourself to be godly.
8For physical training is of some value, but godliness has value for all things,[a] holding promise for both the present life[b] and the life to come.
9This is a trustworthy saying[c] that deserves full acceptance.
10That is why we labor and strive, because we have put our hope in the living God, who is the Savior of all people, and especially of those who believe.
11Command and teach these things.[d]
12Don't let anyone look down on you because you are young, but set an example[e]

4:6 [y] 1Ti 1:10
4:7 [z] 2Ti 2:16
4:8 [a] 1Ti 6:6 [b] Ps 37:9, 11; Mk 10:29,30
4:9 [c] 1Ti 1:15
4:11 [d] 1Ti 5:7; 6:2
4:12 [e] Titus 2:7; 1Pe 5:3

[a] 6 The Greek word for *brothers and sisters* (*adelphoi*) refers here to believers, both men and women, as part of God's family.

God who created the fruit of the vine; a blessing after the meal, though of uncertain date, announced that "God is good and does good." God had already declared created foods good (Ge 1:12,21,25; 2:9), as also marriage (Ge 2:18).
4:7 *godless myths and old wives' tales.* Women were usually illiterate. Men sometimes ridiculed older women, e.g., for idleness or gossip, and disdained their tales and ideas as fit only for children. Although Paul uses the figure of speech, he commands respect for older women (5:2; though cf. Titus 2:3).
4:8 *physical training is of some value.* Greek men stripped naked for exercise; the gymnasium was the center of civic life in Hellenized towns. Greek and Roman thinkers often used the image of such physical training for moral, intellectual and spiritual discipline. *godliness has value for all things.* Jewish teachers especially praised study of the law, which they deemed profitable for both life in the present age and that of the age to come.
4:12 *because you are young.* Timothy joined Paul before AD 50, and was probably young at that time (Ac 16:1 – 3); society deemed young men adults soon after they reached puberty, and disciples were often in their mid-teens. The narrative date of 1 Timothy may be c. 62 – 64; Timothy thus could be anywhere from his mid-20s to his mid-30s, probably in his 20s. (The term translated "young" here usually applied to someone under age 29, although it could extend up to age 40.) Despite the valuing of youthful vigor, many regarded youth (especially adolescence) as less responsible, more violent, sexually uncontrolled and impetuous. Many ancient leadership

for the believers in speech, in conduct, in
love, in faith[f] and in purity. 13Until I come,
devote yourself to the public reading of
Scripture, to preaching and to teaching.
14Do not neglect your gift, which was giv-
en you through prophecy[g] when the body
of elders laid their hands on you.[h]
15Be diligent in these matters; give yourself wholly to them, so that everyone may
see your progress. 16Watch your life and
doctrine closely. Persevere in them, because if you do, you will save both yourself and your hearers.

Widows, Elders and Slaves

5 Do not rebuke an older man[i] harshly,[j]
but exhort him as if he were your father. Treat younger men[k] as brothers, 2old-
er women as mothers, and younger wom-
en as sisters, with absolute purity.
3Give proper recognition to those widows who are really in need.[l] 4But if a widow has children or grandchildren, these
should learn first of all to put their religion
into practice by caring for their own family
and so repaying their parents and grandparents,[m] for this is pleasing to God.[n] 5The
widow who is really in need[o] and left all
alone puts her hope in God[p] and continues
night and day to pray[q] and to ask God for
help. 6But the widow who lives for pleasure is dead even while she lives.[r] 7Give
the people these instructions,[s] so that no
one may be open to blame. 8Anyone who
does not provide for their relatives, and
especially for their own household, has
denied[t] the faith and is worse than an unbeliever.
9No widow may be put on the list of
widows unless she is over sixty, has
been faithful to her husband, 10and is
well known for her good deeds,[u] such as
bringing up children, showing hospitality, washing the feet[v] of the Lord's people,
helping those in trouble[w] and devoting
herself to all kinds of good deeds.

4:12 [f] 1Ti 1:14
4:14 [g] 1Ti 1:18 [h] Ac 6:6; 2Ti 1:6
5:1 [i] Titus 2:2 [j] Lev 19:32 [k] Titus 2:6
5:3 [l] ver 5, 16
5:4 [m] Eph 6:1, 2 [n] 1Ti 2:3
5:5 [o] ver 3, 16 [p] 1Co 7:34; 1Pe 3:5 [q] Lk 2:37
5:6 [r] Lk 15:24
5:7 [s] 1Ti 4:11
5:8 [t] 2Pe 2:1; Jude 4; Titus 1:16
5:10 [u] Ac 9:36; 1Ti 6:18; 1Pe 2:12 [v] Lk 7:44 [w] ver 16

positions became available only at ages 30 or 40. Some young men did achieve early leadership, however, inviting respect. On "elders," with whom Timothy's youth would be contrasted, see notes on v. 14; 5:1 – 2.

4:13 *public reading of Scripture, to preaching and to teaching.* Jesus' followers followed the synagogues' model of reading Scripture during their gatherings. Most congregations could afford at least a law scroll that someone could read, in many locations in the local Greek language; someone would then explain the section that had been read (cf. already Ne 8:8). By the early to mid-second century, churches were also reading first-century texts from the circle of Jesus' apostles. Ancient thinkers expected letters to convey in some (figurative) sense the writers' presence; Biblical exposition was the next best thing to Paul's direct ministry.

4:14 On Paul's first recorded journey in Timothy's region, Paul appointed elders in Timothy's town of Lystra (Ac 14:21 – 23); after a subsequent visit he took Timothy with him (Ac 16:2 – 3). *through prophecy.* Prophecies to leaders were common in ancient Israel, sometimes including at their calling (e.g., 2Ki 9:6 – 10); see the article "Prophecy in Antiquity," p. 2009. *elders.* Ruled OT villages and continued to fill a respected leadership role in this period, though in the Diaspora the specifics varied from one location to another. Usually they functioned as a group. *laid their hands on you.* Moses laid hands on Joshua (Nu 27:18,23; Dt 34:9); in the early Christian era, mature Jewish teachers often accredited other Jewish teachers by laying hands on them.

4:16 *Watch your … doctrine closely.* Cf. Introduction to 1 Timothy: Setting and Purpose.

5:1 – 2 *father … brothers … mothers … sisters.* Ancient Mediterranean cultures respected elders; some others also advised treating elders like parents and peers like siblings. Some of these elders fill leadership roles (see vv. 17 – 25; 4:14); many Diaspora synagogues also granted an honored person the title of "father" or "mother" of the synagogue. Jewish tradition stressed humbly giving and receiving correction; correction should be done publicly only if private attempts failed.

5:3 – 16 Because Paul addresses elders by age (vv. 1 – 2) and then turns to widows (vv. 3 – 16) and then to the church office of elders (vv. 17 – 22), some suggest that the enrolled widows (vv. 9,11) refer to an order of widows who served the church, as in churches in the second century. Others view them as simply all widows supported by the church; because sufficient wages were far more readily available to men, widows were often destitute without family support. Local synagogues also helped destitute widows among them.

5:4 *if a widow has children.* Widows without resources of their own usually had to depend on relatives, especially adult children. Many emphasized that one should repay aged parents and grandparents for raising one by supporting them in their old age. Jewish tradition also viewed this obligation as part of what it meant to honor parents (cf. also Mk 7:9 – 13). Caring for aged parents was a matter not only of custom but also of law, and was the standard practice even in Western society until recent times.

5:5 *continues night and day to pray.* Jewish tradition valued highly the contribution of prayer offered by older widows dependent on community funds (cf. Lk 2:37).

5:6 *dead even while she lives.* Some used the term "dead" figuratively; here it involves immoral living (cf. Eph 2:1).

5:7 *so that no one may be open to blame.* Mainstream society often suspected members of minority movements of sexual immorality; those exposed in such immorality brought not only blame on themselves but also criticism of their movements (cf. 6:1 – 2).

5:8 *worse than an unbeliever.* Even Gentiles provided for aged parents (cf. note on v. 4).

5:9 – 10 Lists of qualifications were common (see note on 3:1 – 7).

5:9 *over sixty.* Many counted old age from age 60; some discouraged remarriage for widows after age 50 and for widowers after age 60, since procreation after these times was rare. (For younger widows, see note on v. 14.) *faithful to her husband.* The Greek phrase so translated here often appears on ancient inscriptions with the meaning translated thus here; husbands who found their wives faithful and honorable often used this phrase on the deceased wives' tombs.

5:10 *good deeds, such as bringing up children.* Ancient culture respected women especially for bringing up children. *showing hospitality.* Because the wife normally was

11 As for younger widows, do not put
them on such a list. For when their sensual desires overcome their dedication to
Christ, they want to marry. 12 Thus they
bring judgment on themselves, because
they have broken their first pledge. 13 Besides, they get into the habit of being idle
and going about from house to house. And
not only do they become idlers, but also
busybodies[x] who talk nonsense, saying
things they ought not to. 14 So I counsel
younger widows to marry,[y] to have children, to manage their homes and to give
the enemy no opportunity for slander.[z]
15 Some have in fact already turned away
to follow Satan.[a]
16 If any woman who is a believer has
widows in her care, she should continue to
help them and not let the church be burdened with them, so that the church can
help those widows who are really in need.[b]
17 The elders[c] who direct the affairs of
the church well are worthy of double hon-
or,[d] especially those whose work is preaching and teaching. 18 For Scripture says, "Do
not muzzle an ox while it is treading out
the grain,"[a][e] and "The worker deserves his
wages."[b][f] 19 Do not entertain an accusation
against an elder[g] unless it is brought by
two or three witnesses.[h] 20 But those elders
who are sinning you are to reprove[i] before everyone, so that the others may take
warning.[j] 21 I charge you, in the sight of
God and Christ Jesus[k] and the elect angels,
to keep these instructions without partiality, and to do nothing out of favoritism.
22 Do not be hasty in the laying on of
hands,[l] and do not share in the sins of others.[m] Keep yourself pure.
23 Stop drinking only water, and use a
little wine[n] because of your stomach and
your frequent illnesses.
24 The sins of some are obvious, reaching the place of judgment ahead of them;
the sins of others trail behind them. 25 In
the same way, good deeds are obvious,
and even those that are not obvious cannot remain hidden forever.

5:13 [x] 2Th 3:11 **5:14** [y] 1Co 7:9 [z] 1Ti 6:1 **5:15** [a] Mt 4:10 **5:16** [b] ver 3-5 **5:17** [c] Ac 11:30 [d] Php 2:29; 1Th 5:12 **5:18** [e] Dt 25:4; 1Co 9:7-9 [f] Lk 10:7; Lev 19:13; Dt 24:14, 15; Mt 10:10; 1Co 9:14 **5:19** [g] Ac 11:30 [h] Mt 18:16 **5:20** [i] 2Ti 4:2; Titus 1:13 [j] Dt 13:11 **5:21** [k] 1Ti 6:13; 2Ti 4:1 **5:22** [l] Ac 6:6 [m] Eph 5:11 **5:23** [n] 1Ti 3:8

[a] 18 Deut. 25:4 [b] 18 Luke 10:7

in charge of the home and cooking, she also played an important role in hospitality, a highly valued virtue (see v. 2; see also note on Ac 16:15). *washing the feet of the Lord's people.* Although hosts provided guests water for the guests to wash the guests' feet, the hosts did not wash guests' feet themselves. In virtually any setting, those actually washing feet were servants or sometimes others who took such a humble position (cf. 1Sa 25:41; see note on Jn 13:5).

5:11 *sensual desires overcome their dedication to Christ.* People sometimes took vows of commitment when joining a group (here, perhaps, a group of long-term celibate widows supported by the church); breaking such a vow incurred judgment.

5:13 *busybodies who talk nonsense.* Ancient custom expected many uneducated women to indulge in gossip, behavior condemned by ancient moral teachers. The wording here also could apply to those spreading false ideas; the false teachers (cf. 1:6–7) may have targeted widows (cf. 2:11–12; 2Ti 3:6) because (1) women were usually less educated and (2) widows were the women who most often owned their own homes, useful for meeting places for new congregations.

5:14 *younger widows to marry, to have children.* Both Jewish and Gentile cultures valued the rapid remarriage of widows of childbearing age. Moral teachers also urged that wives be sexually pure, modest, meek and obedient to their husbands; they should be devoted to domestic duties, particularly bearing and raising young children. The ideal wife of Pr 31:10–31 works hard, including in public; by contrast, the Greeks' ideal wife stayed largely out of public sight, managing the home. (Greek culture dominated Ephesus.) Although the division of public space from private space was less strict in practice, Greeks treated public space as more the male sphere and private, domestic space as more the female sphere. *slander.* Avoiding grounds for outsiders' slander was essential (see note on v. 7).

5:15 *turned away to follow Satan.* Developing OT teaching, Jewish tradition associated Satan with temptation as well as with deception and accusation. He dominated the unrighteous world.

5:16 *If any woman … has widows in her care.* Although most benefactors were men, a number (some estimate 10 percent) were women. Sometimes they had social dependents, which could include blood relatives, slaves, freedpersons or clients.

5:17 *elders.* See note on 4:14. *double honor.* When "honor" was spoken of, the term sometimes included monetary payment, a sort of "honorarium" (which fits this context, v. 18). Those who performed exceptional service were often given double pay.

5:18 *Do not muzzle an ox.… The worker deserves his wages.* Paul cites the OT (Dt 25:4; cf. 1Co 9:9) and then, apparently as on the same authoritative level, Jesus' teaching (recorded in Lk 10:7).

5:19 *two or three witnesses.* Scripture required a minimum of two or three witnesses for hearings (Dt 17:6; 19:15); the same principle applies to other accusations.

5:20 *reprove before everyone.* Rome allowed Diaspora synagogue communities to discipline members of their own communities; the discipline here is public shaming. Christians normally reproved in private; public rebuke was reserved for the most serious cases.

5:21 *in the sight of God and Christ Jesus and the elect angels.* Ancients often called on deities or their surrogates to attest claims. *keep these instructions without partiality.* Scripture forbade judging with partiality (cf. Lev 19:15; Dt 1:17; 16:19).

5:22 *laying on of hands.* See note on 4:14; leaders must be tested before being commissioned (see note on 3:10).

5:23 *use a little wine.* Most people drank wine with their meals. It was watered down (often about two parts water to one part wine), and not distilled to a higher than natural degree of fermentation. Some have suggested that Timothy was abstaining from wine to avoid the criticism of the false teachers (4:3). *your stomach.* Wine was often used to settle stomachs and was thought to prevent dysentery; it could be used to disinfect water. Some restorative diets recommended water, others wine; wine was also used in some remedies (i.e., medicinally).

5:24–25 On the need to evaluate leaders carefully, see note on v. 22.

6 All who are under the yoke of slavery
should consider their masters worthy of full respect,[o] so that God's name
and our teaching may not be slandered.[p]
2Those who have believing masters should
not show them disrespect just because
they are fellow believers.[q] Instead, they
should serve them even better because
their masters are dear to them as fellow
believers and are devoted to the welfare[a]
of their slaves.

False Teachers and the Love of Money

These are the things you are to teach
and insist on.[r] 3If anyone teaches otherwise[s] and does not agree to the sound
instruction[t] of our Lord Jesus Christ and
to godly teaching, 4they are conceited
and understand nothing. They have an
unhealthy interest in controversies and
quarrels about words[u] that result in envy,
strife, malicious talk, evil suspicions 5and
constant friction between people of corrupt mind, who have been robbed of the
truth[v] and who think that godliness is a
means to financial gain.

6:1 [o] Eph 6:5; Titus 2:9; 1Pe 2:18 [p] Titus 2:5,8
6:2 [q] Phm 16 [r] 1Ti 4:11
6:3 [s] 1Ti 1:3 [t] 1Ti 1:10
6:4 [u] 2Ti 2:14
6:5 [v] Titus 1:15

6But godliness with contentment[w] is
great gain.[x] 7For we brought nothing into
the world, and we can take nothing out
of it.[y] 8But if we have food and clothing,
we will be content with that.[z] 9Those who
want to get rich[a] fall into temptation and
a trap[b] and into many foolish and harmful
desires that plunge people into ruin and
destruction. 10For the love of money[c] is a
root of all kinds of evil. Some people, eager for money, have wandered from the
faith[d] and pierced themselves with many
griefs.

Final Charge to Timothy

11But you, man of God,[e] flee from all
this, and pursue righteousness, godliness,
faith, love,[f] endurance and gentleness.
12Fight the good fight[g] of the faith. Take
hold of[h] the eternal life to which you were
called when you made your good confession in the presence of many witnesses.
13In the sight of God, who gives life to everything, and of Christ Jesus, who while
testifying before Pontius Pilate[i] made the

6:6 [w] Php 4:11; Heb 13:5 [x] 1Ti 4:8
6:7 [y] Job 1:21; Ecc 5:15
6:8 [z] Heb 13:5
6:9 [a] Pr 15:27 [b] 1Ti 3:7
6:10 [c] 1Ti 3:3 [d] Jas 5:19
6:11 [e] 2Ti 3:17 [f] 2Ti 2:22
6:12 [g] 1Co 9:25,26; 1Ti 1:18 [h] Php 3:12
6:13 [i] Jn 18:33-37

[a] 2 Or *and benefit from the service*

6:1–2 Because groups lacking power were easily slandered, their members' behavior was crucial (cf. 5:7 and note). Groups thought to undermine traditional order, including slave-master relations, were particularly suspect (see note on Eph 5:21—6:9).
6:2 *and are devoted to the welfare.* The NIV text note ("and benefit from the service") captures a point that may have surprised ancient hearers: Paul speaks of slaves as benefactors, a term more often applied to wealthy people donating benefactions. Thus Paul, like the philosopher Seneca, might depict slaves as persons free in God's sight who can count their service as an act of generosity toward the slaveholders. For slavery, see Introduction to Philemon; see also the articles "Slaves and Slaveholders in Ephesians 6," p. 2068; "Ancient Slavery and the Background for Philemon," p. 2134.
6:4 *unhealthy interest in controversies.* Pseudointellectuals liked to quibble about detailed nuances of words rather than deal with crucial issues (see note on 1:6).
6:5 *think that godliness is a means to financial gain.* Jewish people often recognized wealth as a sign of God's blessing (e.g., Ge 26:12–13), and many teachers taught that those who served God would become more prosperous. This teaching was, however, meant as a general principle (as in, e.g., Pr 8:18; 10:4,22): the one who works harder earns more. But these teachers also recognized that wealth could be used for good or evil, and many warned of the dangers of being corrupted by wealth, or even linked godliness to poverty. Similarly, many Gentile philosophers allowed that wealth was acceptable if put to good use, whereas others (especially Cynics) thought that it should be rejected altogether as burdensome. Philosophers did not, however, normally see wealth as a reward for doing good. It is debated whether Paul's opponents preach that godliness is a means of gain or simply use religion as a means of gain (cf. Jer 6:13; 8:10; Mic 3:11).
6:6 *godliness with contentment is great gain.* Moralists sometimes used "gain" figuratively, contrasting it with material wealth. Jewish teachers sometimes portrayed present wealth as paltry compared with the true wealth of the world to come. Many philosophers and those influenced by them emphasized contentment; by this philosophers normally meant that people should be self-sufficient, recognizing that they need nothing other than what Nature has given them.
6:7 Here Paul draws on a widely cited principle in antiquity (cf. Job 1:21), sometimes (as in one Roman writer) even with similar wording.
6:8 *if we have food and clothing.* Even the most ascetic thinkers agreed that food and clothing were fundamental needs, though they and the poorest peasants each had just one cloak. *content.* See notes on v. 6; Php 4:11–13.
6:9 *Those who want to get rich fall into temptation.* Ancient writers who warned against seeking to become rich normally addressed those seeking to accumulate wealth (cf. Pr 28:20) rather than those who had already become wealthy through inheritance or industry (v. 17). *rich.* A relative term; the highest elite displayed extravagant opulence, but even artisans would have been astonished at the lifestyle of middle-class Westerners who own their own lot, home and car.
6:10 *the love of money is a root of all kinds of evil.* Paul draws here on a widely cited principle in antiquity that had even become proverbial, with similar wording.
6:11 *man of God.* Scripture applied this title to God's agents, usually prophets (e.g., Dt 33:1; 1Sa 2:27; 9:6–10). Sometimes later Jewish sources kept the OT title; sometimes they changed it to "prophet." *flee from all this.* Writers on moral subjects frequently urged their audience to flee from vices. *righteousness ... gentleness.* Lists of virtues were common.
6:12 *Fight the good fight of the faith.* Ancient writers often used military or, as more likely here, athletic competition images for moral or intellectual battles (cf. 4:7–8; see the article "Athletic Imagery in 1 Corinthians 9," p. 2000).
6:13 *In the sight of God.* A charge with deities as witnesses (cf. also 5:21) could be as binding on the person charged as if that person had sworn an oath.

good confession, I charge you[j] 14 to keep
this command without spot or blame until the appearing of our Lord Jesus Christ,
15 which God will bring about in his own
time — God, the blessed[k] and only Ruler,[l] the King of kings and Lord of lords,[m]
16 who alone is immortal[n] and who lives
in unapproachable light, whom no one
has seen or can see.[o] To him be honor and
might forever. Amen.

17 Command those who are rich in this
present world not to be arrogant nor to put
their hope in wealth,[p] which is so uncertain, but to put their hope in God,[q] who
richly provides us with everything for our
enjoyment.[r] 18 Command them to do good,
to be rich in good deeds,[s] and to be generous and willing to share.[t] 19 In this way
they will lay up treasure for themselves[u]
as a firm foundation for the coming age,
so that they may take hold of the life that
is truly life.

20 Timothy, guard what has been entrusted[v] to your care. Turn away from godless
chatter[w] and the opposing ideas of what
is falsely called knowledge, 21 which some
have professed and in so doing have departed from the faith.[x]

Grace be with you all.[y]

6:13 [j] 1Ti 5:21
6:15 [k] 1Ti 1:11 [l] 1Ti 1:17 [m] Rev 17:14; 19:16
6:16 [n] 1Ti 1:17 [o] Jn 1:18
6:17 [p] Lk 12:20, 21 [q] 1Ti 4:10 [r] Ac 14:17
6:18 [s] 1Ti 5:10 [t] Ro 12:8, 13
6:19 [u] Mt 6:20
6:20 [v] 2Ti 1:12, 14 [w] 2Ti 2:16
6:21 [x] 2Ti 2:18 [y] Col 4:18

6:14 *until the appearing of our Lord Jesus Christ.* Greeks often used "appearing" for a self-revelation of a deity; Jewish sources often apply it to God. The language here thus implies Jesus' deity.
6:15 *King of kings and Lord of lords.* Especially in the east, rulers who claimed to be supreme kings, such as the Babylonian or the Parthian king, called themselves "King of kings and Lord of lords" (cf. Ezr 7:12; Eze 26:7), meaning the greatest ruler over other rulers. Jewish sources apply it to God (cf. Dt 10:17; Ps 136:3); for Jesus, cf. Rev 19:16.
6:16 *alone.* See note on 1:17. *immortal.* Greek-speaking Jews often called God "The Immortal," adapting Greek descriptions of their gods. *unapproachable light.* Kings' great authority made them unapproachable for common people. Jewish traditions described the glory of light around God's throne (cf. Eze 1:27 – 28). Most Jewish sources recognized that no one could witness God's full glory and live (cf. Ex 33:20), though some Jewish mystics claimed to have seen something of God's glory (developing Isa 6:1; Eze 1:26 – 27).
6:17 *those who are rich in this present world.* Most of the wealthy elite profited from renting out inherited land, or from produce that slaves raised on the land. A socially inferior but nonetheless wealthy class of merchants also arose, especially of ship owners; urban Ephesus, with its major harbor, contained more of this latter, newer form of wealth.
6:18 *be generous and willing to share.* Jewish teachers emphasized the Biblical principle (cf., e.g., Pr 14:31; 21:13) of generosity toward those in need.
6:19 *lay up treasure … for the coming age.* Jewish people sometimes spoke of heavenly rewards as treasure in heaven (cf. Mt 6:20 – 21).
6:20 *opposing ideas of what is falsely called knowledge.* Many ancient thinkers claimed to have knowledge; many ancient thinkers also regarded other thinkers' or groups' claims to knowledge as false. The debates were widespread; there is no reason to associate the error here with Gnosticism, which is not clearly attested until the second century.

THE LETTERS

2 TIMOTHY

See Introduction to 1 Timothy: Authorship.

Setting

As early Christian tradition suggests, Paul was probably released after two years of relatively light custody (Ac 28:30 – 31) but some time later rearrested. He was imprisoned under harsher conditions (as in this letter) and ultimately executed under Nero, probably c. AD 64 or shortly thereafter. The church now faces both serious persecution in Rome and, in Ephesus, increasing false teaching (cf. 2Ti 2:15 – 18). If Timothy is going to join Paul, he must do so quickly (4:9, 21); Timothy must also combat erroneous teaching by calling people back to the Scriptures (3:14 — 4:5).

Jewish people greatly valued the final instructions or legacy of a great figure. Like Jeremiah (Jer 43:6 – 7), Paul faced discouraging circumstances toward the end of his life; Jeremiah did not live to see his message fully vindicated in the next generation (2Ch 36:21; Ezr 1:1; Da 9:2). Nevertheless, Paul recognizes that his own destiny is secure and his own work complete (4:6 – 8,18). The rest is in God's hands. ◆

QUICK GLANCE

AUTHOR:
The apostle Paul

AUDIENCE:
Paul's disciple Timothy, who was ministering in Ephesus

DATE:
AD 64 or slightly later

THEME:
Facing imminent death, Paul encourages Timothy to carry on the ministry and faithfully guard the gospel.

1 Paul, an apostle of Christ Jesus by the
will of God,[a] in keeping with the promise of life that is in Christ Jesus,[b]

2 To Timothy,[c] my dear son:[d]

Grace, mercy and peace from God the
Father and Christ Jesus our Lord.

Thanksgiving

3 I thank God,[e] whom I serve, as my ancestors did, with a clear conscience, as
night and day I constantly remember you
in my prayers.[f] 4 Recalling your tears,[g] I
long to see you,[h] so that I may be filled
with joy. 5 I am reminded of your sincere
faith,[i] which first lived in your grandmother Lois and in your mother Eunice[j] and, I
am persuaded, now lives in you also.

Appeal for Loyalty to Paul and the Gospel

6 For this reason I remind you to fan
into flame the gift of God, which is in you
through the laying on of my hands.[k] 7 For
the Spirit God gave us does not make us
timid,[l] but gives us power, love and self-
discipline. 8 So do not be ashamed[m] of the
testimony about our Lord or of me his
prisoner.[n] Rather, join with me in suffering for the gospel,[o] by the power of God.
9 He has saved us and called[p] us to a holy
life — not because of anything we have
done but because of his own purpose and
grace. This grace was given us in Christ
Jesus before the beginning of time, 10 but
it has now been revealed[q] through the appearing of our Savior, Christ Jesus, who
has destroyed death[r] and has brought life
and immortality to light through the gospel. 11 And of this gospel I was appointed
a herald and an apostle and a teacher.[s]
12 That is why I am suffering as I am. Yet
this is no cause for shame, because I know
whom I have believed, and am convinced
that he is able to guard[t] what I have entrusted to him until that day.[u]

13 What you heard from me, keep[v] as the
pattern of sound teaching, with faith and
love in Christ Jesus.[w] 14 Guard the good deposit that was entrusted to you — guard it
with the help of the Holy Spirit who lives
in us.[x]

Examples of Disloyalty and Loyalty

15 You know that everyone in the province of Asia has deserted me,[y] including
Phygelus and Hermogenes.

16 May the Lord show mercy to the
household of Onesiphorus,[z] because he
often refreshed me and was not ashamed

1:1 [a] 2Co 1:1 [b] Eph 3:6; 1Ti 6:19 **1:2** [c] Ac 16:1 [d] 1Ti 1:2 **1:3** [e] Ro 1:8 [f] Ro 1:10 **1:4** [g] Ac 20:37 [h] 2Ti 4:9 **1:5** [i] 1Ti 1:5 [j] Ac 16:1 **1:6** [k] 1Ti 4:14 **1:7** [l] Ro 8:15 **1:8** [m] Mk 8:38; Ro 1:16 [n] Eph 3:1 [o] 2Ti 2:3,9; 4:5

1:9 [p] Ro 8:28 **1:10** [q] Eph 1:9 [r] 1Co 15:26,54 **1:11** [s] 1Ti 2:7 **1:12** [t] 1Ti 6:20 [u] ver 18 **1:13** [v] Titus 1:9 [w] 1Ti 1:14 **1:14** [x] Ro 8:9 **1:15** [y] 2Ti 4:10,11,16 **1:16** [z] 2Ti 4:19

1:2 *To Timothy, my dear son.* See note on 1Ti 1:2.
1:3 *I thank God.* Letters sometimes thanked God or deities, especially for the addressee. *night and day.* A frequent pair in ancient sources, it can include part of the night and part of the day; it does not imply that Paul never slept. *I constantly remember you in my prayers.* Devout Jewish people prayed frequently.
1:4 *I long to see you.* Letters between close friends often noted affectionate longing to see the other and shared deep sorrows and joys.
1:5 *your grandmother Lois ... your mother Eunice.* A boy's primary mentor until age five or seven would be his mother. Although most Jewish mothers would lack advanced knowledge of Scripture (see the article "Women's Education in Antiquity," p. 2109), what they knew from synagogues would be sufficient for young children. (There were also exceptional women, so it is not impossible that Lois was one.) In Jewish homes, fathers held the main responsibility for educating their sons in the law. Because Timothy's father was a Gentile (Ac 16:1), he was dependent on his mother's side of the family for his knowledge of Scripture (2Ti 3:15). Fathers normally determined the religion in which children would be raised, but Timothy's father was apparently unusually tolerant, perhaps as a God-fearer who respected Jewish teaching.
1:6 *gift.* May be the spiritual gift of teaching (1Ti 4:13 – 14), empowered by the Spirit (2Ti 1:7). *laying on of my hands.* See note on 1Ti 4:14.
1:7 *the Spirit God gave us.* Some Jewish people believed spirits specialized in particular vices or problems, but the Greek term for "spirit" can also mean attitude. The OT spoke of God's Spirit empowering people for prophetic or other tasks, and of transforming them. Many Jewish teachers believed that God rarely if ever gave the Spirit to individuals in this era, but early Christians believed that they had experienced the end-time promise of this gift (see v. 14; Ac 2:17 – 18). *timid.* God often encouraged his servants not to be afraid (e.g., Ge 15:1; Jer 1:8).
1:8 *do not be ashamed ... of me his prisoner.* People were often ashamed to be associated with those in Roman custody, withdrawing from them.
1:9 *called.* Biblical and early Jewish language.
1:10 *appearing ... immortality.* Greeks and Greek-speaking Jews spoke of appearing and immortality. *Savior.* The term is both Biblical and Greek. Like many Diaspora Jews, Paul honored Scripture while also communicating intelligibly in their wider culture.
1:12 *shame.* See note on v. 8. *that day.* Presumably the day of the Lord, understood as the day of judgment (cf. Isa 2:11 – 12; Ob 15; Ro 2:5).
1:13 Disciples normally passed on what they learned from their teachers (see 2:2).
1:14 *deposit.* Although already sometimes used figuratively, this Greek term originally applied to property or money entrusted to someone else to guard.
1:15 *everyone.* The Greek term for "everyone" or "all" was often used as hyperbole (for someone who remained faithful in Ephesus, cf. vv. 16 – 18), but error is spreading in the province. *province of Asia.* Ephesus (cf. 1Ti 1:3) was the most prominent city in the Roman province of Asia in western Asia Minor (today western Turkey). *deserted me.* Jewish thinkers often expected widespread apostasy in the end time (cf. 3:1 – 9).
1:16 *household.* Included immediate family and could also include servants or other dependents, where relevant; because family members often shared the faith of the household head, many households became Christian together (e.g., 1Co 16:15), perhaps supplying also meeting homes for churches (e.g., Phm 2). *Onesiphorus.* Scholars debate whether Onesiphorus may have been Onesimus

of my chains. 17On the contrary, when he
was in Rome, he searched hard for me until he found me. 18May the Lord grant that
he will find mercy from the Lord on that
day! You know very well in how many
ways he helped me[a] in Ephesus.

The Appeal Renewed

2 You then, my son, be strong[b] in the
grace that is in Christ Jesus. 2And
the things you have heard me say[c] in the
presence of many witnesses[d] entrust to
reliable people who will also be qualified
to teach others. 3Join with me in suffering, like a good soldier[e] of Christ Jesus.
4No one serving as a soldier gets entangled in civilian affairs, but rather tries to
please his commanding officer. 5Similarly,
anyone who competes as an athlete does
not receive the victor's crown[f] except by
competing according to the rules. 6The
hardworking farmer should be the first to
receive a share of the crops. 7Reflect on
what I am saying, for the Lord will give
you insight into all this.
8Remember Jesus Christ, raised from
the dead,[g] descended from David.[h] This
is my gospel,[i] 9for which I am suffering[j]
even to the point of being chained like a
criminal. But God's word is not chained.
10Therefore I endure everything[k] for the
sake of the elect, that they too may obtain
the salvation that is in Christ Jesus, with
eternal glory.[l]

11Here is a trustworthy saying:

If we died with him,
  we will also live with him;[m]
12if we endure,
  we will also reign with him.[n]
If we disown him,
  he will also disown us;[o]
13if we are faithless,
  he remains faithful,[p]
  for he cannot disown himself.

Dealing With False Teachers

14Keep reminding God's people of these
things. Warn them before God against
quarreling about words;[q] it is of no value, and only ruins those who listen. 15Do
your best to present yourself to God as
one approved, a worker who does not
need to be ashamed and who correctly
handles the word of truth.[r] 16Avoid godless chatter,[s] because those who indulge
in it will become more and more ungodly.
17Their teaching will spread like gangrene.
Among them are Hymenaeus[t] and Phile-
tus, 18who have departed from the truth.
They say that the resurrection has already
taken place, and they destroy the faith of
some.[u] 19Nevertheless, God's solid foundation stands firm,[v] sealed with this inscription: "The Lord knows those who are
his,"[w] and, "Everyone who confesses the
name of the Lord[x] must turn away from
wickedness."

1:18 [a] Heb 6:10
2:1 [b] Eph 6:10
2:2 [c] 2Ti 1:13 [d] 1Ti 6:12
2:3 [e] 1Ti 1:18
2:5 [f] 1Co 9:25
2:8 [g] Ac 2:24 [h] Mt 1:1 [i] Ro 2:16
2:9 [j] Ac 9:16
2:10 [k] Col 1:24 [l] 2Co 4:17
2:11 [m] Ro 6:2-11
2:12 [n] Ro 8:17; 1Pe 4:13 [o] Mt 10:33
2:13 [p] Nu 23:19; Ro 3:3
2:14 [q] 1Ti 6:4
2:15 [r] Eph 1:13; Jas 1:18
2:16 [s] Titus 3:9
2:17 [t] 1Ti 1:20
2:18 [u] 1Ti 1:19
2:19 [v] Isa 28:16 [w] Jn 10:14 [x] 1Co 1:2

(a legitimate contraction of the name; cf. v. 17; Phm 10). They could be different persons, but at least the mention of the former's household here would not necessarily count against the identification; freedpersons did often achieve wealth and honor. *not ashamed of my chains.* See note on v. 8.

1:17 *searched hard for me until he found me.* A benefactor from wealthy Ephesus could well have had means to visit Paul in Rome (although in very different circumstances Onesimus in Phm 10 also may have done so).

2:2 *reliable people who will also be qualified to teach others.* Teachers expected their chief disciples to pass on their teachings to the disciples' disciples.

2:3–5 *like a good soldier ... athlete.* Ancient thinkers often compared their intellectual and moral activities to struggling in a war or athletic competition (see the article "Athletic Imagery in 1 Corinthians 9," p. 2000).

2:4 *No ... soldier gets entangled in civilian affairs.* Soldiers served 20 years; they were not even supposed to marry during that period, although troops stationed in areas for a long time often had unofficial concubines. Except during major wars, probably over half usually survived to retire.

2:5 *competing according to the rules.* Athletes were pledged by oath to ten months of intense discipline preceding their participation in the Olympic games. The winner's prize was a garland (see the article "Athletic Imagery in 1 Corinthians 9," p. 2000).

2:8 Jewish people who expected a royal Messiah expected him to be descended from David (Isa 9:7; 11:1, 10; Jer 23:5; 33:15; Eze 34:23–24; 37:24).

2:9 *chained like a criminal.* Chains were humiliating and could be painful; they were heavy, could cause abrasions on the skin, and the prisoner's sweat sometimes rusted them on the arm. *chained.* Teachers often used examples, and disciples often imitated their teachers.

2:12–13 God's character is unchanging, but he often works with people according to their actions (cf. 2Ch 15:2; Ps 18:25–27).

2:14–16 *quarreling about words ... godless chatter.* See note on 1Ti 1:6.

2:15 *correctly handles the word of truth.* Scripture was called the word of truth (Ps 119:43, regarding the law; cf. 2Ti 3:15–17), though Paul here speaks especially of the true gospel (in contrast with the speech of vv. 14,16).

2:17 *teaching will spread like gangrene.* Ancient writers sometimes compared moral cancers to gangrene, which needed to be cut out of the body. *Hymenaeus.* The name was not common, so this is most likely the false teacher noted in 1Ti 1:20.

2:18 *the resurrection has already taken place.* In contrast to the present experience of the Spirit, believers' future bodily resurrection and a future specific climax to history were barely conceivable in Greek thought. The false teachers modified a key element of the gospel, possibly to fit their cultural perspective.

2:19 *foundation ... sealed with this inscription.* Inscriptions were common on buildings, the securest part of which was the foundation. Foundations could be sealed with the owner's name and could also contain mottos as here.

[20]In a large house there are articles not
only of gold and silver, but also of wood
and clay; some are for special purposes
and some for common use.[y] [21]Those who
cleanse themselves from the latter will be
instruments for special purposes, made
holy, useful to the Master and prepared to
do any good work.[z]
[22]Flee the evil desires of youth and pursue righteousness, faith, love[a] and peace,
along with those who call on the Lord out
of a pure heart.[b] [23]Don't have anything
to do with foolish and stupid arguments,
because you know they produce quarrels.
[24]And the Lord's servant must not be quarrelsome but must be kind to everyone,
able to teach, not resentful.[c] [25]Opponents
must be gently instructed, in the hope that
God will grant them repentance leading
them to a knowledge of the truth,[d] [26]and
that they will come to their senses and escape from the trap of the devil,[e] who has
taken them captive to do his will.
3 But mark this: There will be terrible
times in the last days.[f] [2]People will be
lovers of themselves, lovers of money,[g]
boastful, proud,[h] abusive, disobedient to
their parents,[i] ungrateful, unholy, [3]with-
out love, unforgiving, slanderous, without
self-control, brutal, not lovers of the good,
[4]treacherous, rash, conceited,[j] lovers of
pleasure rather than lovers of God— [5]hav-
ing a form of godliness but denying its power. Have nothing to do with such people.
[6]They are the kind who worm their way[k]
into homes and gain control over gullible
women, who are loaded down with sins
and are swayed by all kinds of evil desires,
[7]always learning but never able to come
to a knowledge of the truth. [8]Just as Jannes and Jambres opposed Moses,[l] so also
these teachers oppose[m] the truth. They are
men of depraved minds,[n] who, as far as
the faith is concerned, are rejected. [9]But
they will not get very far because, as in
the case of those men,[o] their folly will be
clear to everyone.

A Final Charge to Timothy

[10]You, however, know all about my
teaching,[p] my way of life, my purpose,
faith, patience, love, endurance, [11]perse-
cutions, sufferings — what kinds of things
happened to me in Antioch,[q] Iconium and
Lystra, the persecutions I endured.[r] Yet the
Lord rescued me from all of them.[s] [12]In
fact, everyone who wants to live a godly
life in Christ Jesus will be persecuted,[t]

2:20 [y] Ro 9:21 **2:21** [z] 2Ti 3:17 **2:22** [a] 1Ti 1:14; 6:11 [b] 1Ti 1:5 **2:24** [c] 1Ti 3:2,3 **2:25** [d] 1Ti 2:4 **2:26** [e] 1Ti 3:7 **3:1** [f] 1Ti 4:1 **3:2** [g] 1Ti 3:3 [h] Ro 1:30 [i] Ro 1:30
3:4 [j] 1Ti 3:6 **3:6** [k] Jude 4 **3:8** [l] Ex 7:11 [m] Ac 13:8 [n] 1Ti 6:5 **3:9** [o] Ex 7:12 **3:10** [p] 1Ti 4:6 **3:11** [q] Ac 13:14, 50 [r] 2Co 11:23-27 [s] Ps 34:19 **3:12** [t] Ac 14:22

2:22 *Flee.* Writers on moral subjects frequently urged their audience to flee from vices. *evil desires of youth.* On these desires and how Timothy still qualified as young, see note on 1Ti 4:12. Greek writers often thought of young men as more prone to sexual passion and anger. Whereas many excused young men's passionate behavior, Paul respects Timothy's ability to control himself.
2:23 *foolish and stupid arguments.* Cf. note on 1Ti 1:6.
2:24 *the Lord's servant.* Moses was often called the servant of the Lord (e.g., Jos 1:1); the prophets and others were also God's servants (e.g., 2Ki 9:7).
2:25 *Opponents must be gently instructed.* Many moral teachers, both Jewish and Gentile, believed in teaching gently and patiently; they criticized other kinds of teachers (especially some Cynics) who insulted their hearers. Jewish teachers emphasized private reproof, resorting to public rebukes only if all else failed.
3:1 – 5 Many Jewish thinkers expected widespread apostasy and grave suffering in the period just before the end of the age; they sometimes listed the expected sufferings. Ancient writers widely used lists of vices.
3:1 *last days.* See note on 1Ti 4:1.
3:2 *lovers of themselves.* Ancient thinkers warned against such people, by which they meant selfishness or narcissism (not healthy self-esteem). *disobedient to their parents.* A serious offense in all ancient Mediterranean and Middle Eastern cultures (cf. Dt 21:20 – 21). *ungrateful.* In a culture obsessed with honor and expecting those benefitted to repay benefactions with honor, those who were ungrateful were deemed reprehensible (far more often than the proud, though public boasting required appropriate justification).
3:3 – 4 Ancient hearers appreciated clever repetition of sounds; in the Greek text of these verses *a-* prefaces eight words (to negate them, like "un-" or "without" in English).
3:4 *lovers of pleasure.* Except for Epicureans, most ancient thinkers warned against the love of pleasure.
3:5 *having a form of godliness but denying its power.* Nearly everyone criticized false piety.
3:6 *worm their way into homes.* The false teachers here target particular women. They sought access to homes because in the traditional Greek culture of Ephesus most women were less available in public. The women who owned their own homes were most often widows, so widows may have often been targeted (1Ti 5:13) to gain access to homes where the false teachers could establish or influence congregations. (Early Christians usually met in homes.) *gullible women.* In general, women were seen as more gullible than men, with less education or opportunity to exercise critical faculties (see the article "Women's Education in Antiquity," p. 2109; see also notes on 1Ti 2:11,12). *swayed by all kinds of evil desires.* The Greco-Roman cultural expectation for women was that they would be swayed by passion and emotion. They changed beliefs more readily, sometimes positively (in converting to monotheism) but sometimes negatively.
3:7 *always learning.* Some Greek thinkers insisted that moral transformation came from learning truth; but for Paul, it comes through repentance (2:25), and what these women are learning here is not truth in any case (v. 6).
3:8 *Jannes and Jambres.* Jewish tradition named Pharaoh's magicians who opposed Moses (Ex 7:11,22; 8:7). Such Biblical elaborations may have been among the Jewish myths Paul opposed (2Ti 4:4; Titus 1:14). In the end, God's greater power exposed the weakness of Pharaoh's magicians (2Ti 3:9; Ex 8:18 – 19; 9:11).
3:11 *Antioch, Iconium and Lystra.* Paul suffered in these towns in Timothy's region (Ac 13:50 — 14:19) before Timothy joined Paul's mission (Ac 16:1 – 3).
3:12 *persecuted.* Many Jewish people expected false teaching and persecution to flourish in the last days (cf. vv. 1 – 2).

[13]while evildoers and impostors will go from bad to worse,[u] deceiving and being deceived. [14]But as for you, continue in what you have learned and have become convinced of, because you know those from whom you learned it,[v] [15]and how from infancy[w] you have known the Holy Scriptures,[x] which are able to make you wise[y] for salvation through faith in Christ Jesus. [16]All Scripture is God-breathed[z] and is useful for teaching,[a] rebuking, correcting and training in righteousness, [17]so that the servant of God[a][b] may be thoroughly equipped for every good work.[c]

3:13 [u] 2Ti 2:16 **3:14** [v] 2Ti 1:13 **3:15** [w] 2Ti 1:5 [x] Jn 5:39 [y] Ps 119:98,99 **3:16** [z] 2Pe 1:20,21 [a] Ro 4:23,24 **3:17** [b] 1Ti 6:11 [c] 2Ti 2:21 **4:1** [d] Ac 10:42 [e] 1Ti 5:21 **4:2** [f] 1Ti 4:13 [g] Gal 6:6 [h] 1Ti 5:20; Titus 1:13; 2:15

4

In the presence of God and of Christ Jesus, who will judge the living and the dead,[d] and in view of his appearing and his kingdom, I give you this charge:[e] [2]Preach[f] the word;[g] be prepared in season and out of season; correct, rebuke[h] and encourage—with great patience and careful instruction.

[a] 17 Or *that you, a man of God,*

3:13 *imposters.* This Greek term included and often meant "sorcerers" (cf. v. 8), though by this period it also applied more generally to swindlers.

3:15 *from infancy.* Jewish parents taught their children Biblical rules and stories from an early age; for boys, more formal learning in families with means may have begun around age five. Many Gentiles recognized Jewish people's extensive knowledge of their traditions. *the Holy Scriptures.* Most Judeans seem to have accepted the same books of Scripture that we today include as the OT (some sects may have added some books such as Jubilees and 1 Enoch, but others did not view these as Scripture). Most Diaspora Jews also accepted these books (though some focused especially on the Pentateuch). Some Diaspora Jews also apparently included various additional books in Greek that are now part of the Apocrypha, books widely read in the Diaspora but not accepted as canonical by Judeans.

3:16 *God-breathed.* Most people in antiquity believed that deities could inspire prophecies and even poetry; Jewish people recognized that God's Spirit inspired Scripture. Greeks did not all agree regarding the implications of inspiration, but Jewish people argued that the message of their Scriptures was true. Earlier Scripture itself hailed both the law and accurate prophecy as God's word (e.g., 1Sa 15:10,23,26; Ps 119:16,43,172). *teaching, rebuking, correcting and training in righteousness.* Jewish tradition emphasized proper correction and would have agreed with Paul in associating the activities listed here with Scripture.

3:17 *servant of God.* See NIV text note and note on 1Ti 6:11.

4:1 For the authority of a charge that calls deities to witness it, see note on 1Ti 6:13.

4:2 *the word.* When Paul's letters mention "the word," it nearly always means the gospel (e.g., 2:9; 4:15; Titus 2:5); but an appropriate source for this message was Scripture, which was also God's word (see note on 2Ti 3:16) and was useful for the sorts of activities noted here (cf. v. 16). *in season and out of season.* Means both when the audience finds it the right time and when they do not; although Greek sages deliberated the appropriate time for frank criticism (cf. Pr 15:23), God's servants had to speak even when people refused to listen (e.g., Jer 1:17 – 19; 20:8 – 9).

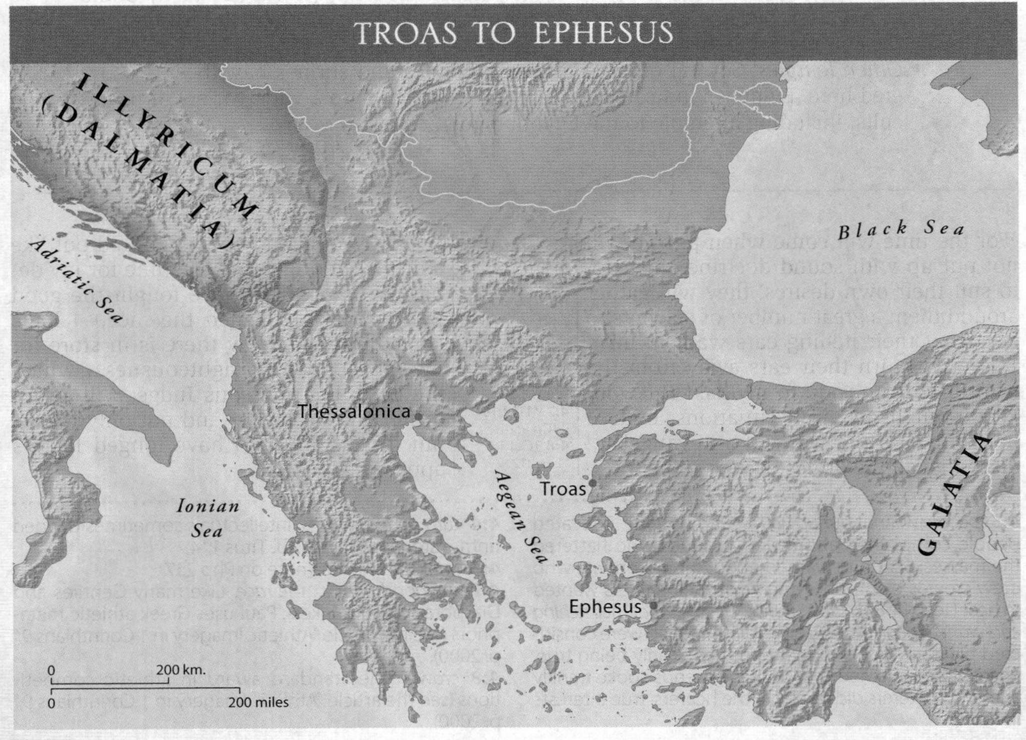

2 TIMOTHY 4

Ephesus During the Time of Paul

By the time of Paul, Ephesus had become enormously wealthy due to its status and position as a major port city of Asia Minor. It boasted a number of major public buildings, including gymnasiums, theaters and a triumphal arch constructed in 3 BC. In addition, the Ephesian temple of Artemis was lauded as one of the seven wonders of the ancient world and was already then a significant source of income (Ac 19:23–27).

Ephesus became a major center of the Christian faith. Although Paul probably wrote Ephesians as a circular letter and not specifically to this congregation, the church of Ephesus was a major focus of his ministry (he stayed there for over two years on his second visit; see Ac 19:1–41). The apostle John also wrote to this church in Revelation 2:1–7, and during the first five centuries AD several church councils were convened there. By the medieval period, however, silt from the Cayster River had extended the coastline so far to the west that Ephesus had ceased to be a port city and was abandoned.

The desertion of Ephesus was a boon for modern archaeology since it meant that the unoccupied city was open for excavation. Today Ephesus exists as one of the most magnificent ruins of the ancient world. Under the direction of Austrian and Turkish archaeologists, the city has reappeared. Important finds include the following:

- *The Temple of Artemis*. Little remains of the temple today (it was sacked by Goths in AD 262), but it was a sacred site for over 1,200 years and was at the center of the controversy between pagans and early Christians.
- *Other Temples*. Several other Roman-era temples and shrines have been discovered here. Evidence indicates that Ephesus was home to a wide variety of pagan cults, including a temple to the Egyptian god Serapis.

continued on next page

3For the time will come when people will
not put up with sound doctrine.[i] Instead,
to suit their own desires, they will gather
around them a great number of teachers to
say what their itching ears want to hear.
4They will turn their ears away from the
truth and turn aside to myths.[j] 5But you,
keep your head in all situations, endure
hardship,[k] do the work of an evangelist,[l]
discharge all the duties of your ministry.

6For I am already being poured out like
a drink offering,[m] and the time for my departure is near.[n] 7I have fought the good
fight,[o] I have finished the race,[p] I have
kept the faith. 8Now there is in store for
me[q] the crown of righteousness, which
the Lord, the righteous Judge, will award
to me on that day[r]—and not only to me,
but also to all who have longed for his
appearing.

4:3 [i] 1Ti 1:10
4:4 [j] 1Ti 1:4
4:5 [k] 2Ti 1:8 [l] Ac 21:8
4:6 [m] Php 2:17 [n] Php 1:23
4:7 [o] 1Ti 1:18 [p] 1Co 9:24
4:8 [q] Col 1:5 [r] 2Ti 1:12

4:3 *people will not put up with sound doctrine.* Educated people complained about demagogues who flattered the masses; Scripture warned about false prophets who drew crowds by prophesying what their hearers wanted to hear (Jer 6:14; 8:11; Eze 13:10,16; Mic 3:5). *what their itching ears want to hear.* Flattery and skillful speech were considered pleasant to the ears without necessarily being true. Philosophers warned that genuine friends spoke frankly and that flatterers did not have the hearers' true interests in mind.

4:4 *turn aside to myths.* Intellectuals sometimes derided untrue stories as myths. Cf. Titus 1:14.

4:6 *drink offering.* See note on Php 2:17.

4:7 *the good fight … the race.* Like many Gentiles and Diaspora Jewish thinkers, Paul uses Greek athletic metaphors (see the article "Athletic Imagery in 1 Corinthians 9," p. 2000).

4:8 *crown.* The standard award in athletic competitions (see the article "Athletic Imagery in 1 Corinthians 9," p. 2000).

- *The Great Theater*. This theater, which eventually would seat 25,000 persons (the full seating was completed after Paul's day), was the location of the tumultuous protest against Paul's preaching in Acts 19. Although Paul wanted to address the crowd gathered there, the disciples restrained him (Ac 19:30). A smaller theater has also been excavated in Ephesus.
- *The Agoras*. Two agoras, or public squares, have been located in Ephesus. One was the Civic Agora (perhaps the location of the temple to Augustus) and the other was the Square or Commercial Agora (near the harbor and the site of numerous shops).
- *The Celsus Library*. One of the great libraries of the ancient world, it was built in AD 115–125 and so was not yet in existence in New Testament times.
- *The Gymnasiums, Baths and Public Latrines*. Several gymnasium and bath complexes have been identified in Ephesus, although a few date to later than the New Testament period. Archaeologists are often able to identify a gymnasium's changing room, exercise room, swimming pool, frigidarium (cold-water bath), caldarium (hot-water bath) and unctorium (oil-massage room). The public latrines also give modern visitors an obvious connection to ordinary life in an ancient city.
- *Private Homes*. Residential areas of Ephesus have been excavated, and several upper-class homes have been unearthed. Frescoes (paintings done on freshly spread, moist lime plaster) have been recovered and kitchens, bathrooms and bedrooms identified.
- *The Basilica of Saint John*. This structure obviously postdates the New Testament, but, according to second-century tradition, the apostle John spent his last years in Ephesus and was buried under what is now the apse of this church, which also features a fine example of an early Christian baptistery. According to tradition Jesus' mother, Mary, may have died in Ephesus; therefore, there is also a church of the Virgin Mary (the site of the ecumenical council of Ephesus in AD 431).

The population of New Testament Ephesus is unknown, but it is clear that the city at that time was a thriving, cosmopolitan center of trade, religion and recreation. Its remains provide a rare look at an ancient city that was also important as a setting for the apostolic mission and the rise of Christianity. Perhaps more than any other archaeological site, Ephesus affords the reader of Acts a sense of context. Since there is no modern city there, the remains of Ephesus distinctively allow visitors to enter vicariously into the ancient world. ◆

Personal Remarks

9 Do your best to come to me quickly, 10 for Demas,[s] because he loved this
world,[t] has deserted me and has gone to
Thessalonica. Crescens has gone to Galatia,[u] and Titus to Dalmatia. 11 Only Luke[v] is
with me.[w] Get Mark[x] and bring him with
you, because he is helpful to me in my
ministry. 12 I sent Tychicus[y] to Ephesus.
13 When you come, bring the cloak that I
left with Carpus at Troas, and my scrolls,
especially the parchments.

4:10 [s] Col 4:14 [t] 1Jn 2:15 [u] Ac 16:6 **4:11** [v] Col 4:14 [w] 2Ti 1:15 [x] Ac 12:12 **4:12** [y] Ac 20:4

4:9 *come to me quickly.* A close friend and especially a son (cf. 1:2) would want to visit a person before the latter's death. For reasons for urgency, see also 4:21 and note.
4:10 *this world.* Many Jewish people contrasted the present "world" (lit. "age"), characterized by the suffering of God's people (cf. Gal 1:4), with the glorious age to come. *deserted me.* Demas had stayed near Paul during his earlier Roman imprisonment, along with Luke and others (Col 4:14; Phm 24), but the danger is now greater. *Dalmatia.* In Illyricum (Ro 15:19) on the Adriatic coast north of Greece; it was near Nicopolis, where Paul had arranged to meet Titus earlier (Titus 3:12). If Timothy traveled north to Troas and overland through Macedonia, and then sailed directly to Italy (2Ti 4:13), he would pass through Thessalonica and Dalmatia, where he could encounter some coworkers.
4:11 *Luke.* The only remaining fellow worker who had come with Paul from the eastern Mediterranean, but there were other believers in Rome (v. 21).
4:12 *I sent Tychicus.* No empire-wide mail service existed; travelers carried letters. Tychicus, whom Timothy knew (Ac 20:4), presumably has brought the letter to Timothy in Ephesus (cf. 1Ti 1:3), and perhaps will fill in for Timothy as he travels to see Paul.
4:13 *bring the cloak … and my scrolls.* Prisoners' friends could supply their needs, but only if permitted by prison officials and guards, who sometimes demanded bribes. *cloak.* The sort of cloak mentioned was like a blanket with a

14 Alexander[z] the metalworker did me
a great deal of harm. The Lord will repay
him for what he has done.[a] 15 You too
should be on your guard against him,
because he strongly opposed our message.
16 At my first defense, no one came to
my support, but everyone deserted me.
May it not be held against them.[b] 17 But
the Lord stood at my side[c] and gave me
strength, so that through me the message
might be fully proclaimed and all the
Gentiles might hear it.[d] And I was delivered from the lion's mouth. 18 The Lord
will rescue me from every evil attack[e]
and will bring me safely to his heavenly
kingdom. To him be glory for ever and
ever. Amen.[f]

4:14 [z] Ac 19:33 [a] Ro 12:19 **4:16** [b] Ac 7:60 **4:17** [c] Ac 23:11 [d] Ac 9:15 **4:18** [e] Ps 121:7 [f] Ro 11:36

Final Greetings

19 Greet Priscilla[a] and Aquila[g] and the
household of Onesiphorus. 20 Erastus[h]
stayed in Corinth, and I left Trophimus[i]
sick in Miletus. 21 Do your best to get here
before winter.[j] Eubulus greets you, and
so do Pudens, Linus, Claudia and all the
brothers and sisters.[b]
22 The Lord be with your spirit.[k] Grace
be with you all.[l]

4:19 [g] Ac 18:2 **4:20** [h] Ac 19:22 [i] Ac 20:4 **4:21** [j] ver 9 **4:22** [k] Gal 6:18; Phm 25 [l] Col 4:18

[a] *19* Greek *Prisca,* a variant of *Priscilla* [b] *21* The Greek word for *brothers and sisters* (*adelphoi*) refers here to believers, both men and women, as part of God's family.

hole for one's head; the ease with which it could be donned probably made it popular with travelers. It was useful only in cold or rainy weather, and Paul had apparently left it at Troas when it was becoming warm enough to travel and had not been able to return for it. Now, imprisoned, Paul is cold and anticipates the approach of winter soon after Timothy's arrival (cf. v. 21). *Troas.* A populous Roman colony north of Ephesus (see note on Ac 16:8). At some point Paul had helped found a church there (2Co 2:12). *scrolls.* Lit. "written works," possibly of Scripture. *parchments.* A Latin loanword for writing materials; if Paul follows the original sense of the term, they were perhaps dried animal skins, which were much more durable than papyrus.

4:14 *Alexander the metalworker.* Some of the metalworkers of Ephesus had opposed Paul (Ac 19:25 – 28), led by Demetrius the silversmith (Ac 19:24). Copper work was a loud trade, and most people of status considered ordinary metalwork demeaning. Alexander could be the false teacher of 1Ti 1:20, or perhaps the local Jewish leader in Ac 19:33; however, Alexander was one of the most common names in antiquity. *The Lord will repay him for what he has done.* Paul's grammar merely predicts Alexander's judgment rather than prays for it (cf., e.g., Ps 63:9 – 10; 73:18 – 20), but Biblical prayers for vindication often did include judgment on enemies (e.g., Ps 17:13 – 14; 55:15).

4:16 *first defense.* Presumably Paul means only his first during this imprisonment (cf. 2Co 6:5; 11:23); this would have been a preliminary hearing, a *prima actio,* before a Roman magistrate. The emperor Nero would not have normally troubled himself personally with such hearings (cf. notes on Ac 25:27; 27:24), but they would appear before his court.

4:17 *delivered from the lion's mouth.* Nero soon after this fed some Christians to animals. Paul may thus evoke deliverances from literal lions (cf. the language of 1Sa 17:37; Da 6:27), but he especially speaks figuratively, as in Ps 7:2; 10:9; 17:12; 22:13,21.

4:19 *Greet.* Letters often closed with greetings. *Priscilla and Aquila.* They earlier relocated from Rome to Corinth (Ac 18:1 – 2), then to Ephesus (Ac 18:18 – 19), and later again to Rome (Ro 16:3), and now, perhaps recently in view of rising pressure and persecution in Rome, had returned to Ephesus. *Onesiphorus.* See note on 1:16.

4:20 *Erastus . . . Trophimus.* Unless this is a different Erastus (possibly Ro 16:23), Erastus and Trophimus were among Timothy's former fellow workers (Ac 19:22; 20:4); letters often mentioned news about people of mutual interest. *sick.* Letters often mentioned news of health; sicknesses such as typhoid fever and especially malaria were common. Because Miletus, like Ephesus, was in Ionia, Timothy may already know about Trophimus. *Miletus.* A major coastal city in Asia Minor; it was about 30 miles (48 kilometers) south of Ephesus.

4:21 *get here before winter.* Usually only the daring and foolish sailed during the heart of winter, even in the narrower stretch of water across the Adriatic (cf. note on v. 10). The period from Nov. 10 to as late as Mar. 10 was considered most dangerous, but even Sept. 15 to Nov. 10 and Mar. 11 to May 26 held dangers as well. If Timothy delayed, he might not be able to come until spring — and that might be too late to see Paul alive. *Pudens, Linus, Claudia.* Although not everyone with a Roman name was Roman, these are all Roman names, a higher proportion than in most of Paul's letters. About half of Roman Jews had Roman names (some because they descended from freed slaves of Roman citizens, and thus were Roman citizens themselves). Still, Greek and Biblical names were also common. Because Paul distinguishes these names from "all the brothers and sisters," they might be leaders or hosts of house churches. *Linus.* Early tradition makes Linus Peter's successor as the second bishop of Rome. *Claudia.* Could have been freed in the emperor Claudius's reign, though the name was not limited to freedwomen.

THE LETTERS

TITUS

See Introduction to 1 Timothy: Authorship.

Setting and Purpose

Paul left Titus behind in Crete to establish church leadership in each city there (Titus 1:5). The errors there (1:10 – 11,14) seem to resemble those addressed in 1 Timothy (see Introduction to 1 Timothy: Setting and Purpose), despite the geographic distance. This similarity seems to suggest that the error was growing. Some advocates of circumcision, possibly related to Paul's old opponents in Galatia (see Introduction to Galatians: Situation), may have continued to try to ensure the proper Jewish conversion of believers in Paul's churches (Titus 1:10,14). Paul's reputation and many of his views eventually prevailed, though he did not live to see it (2Ti 1:15). ◆

QUICK GLANCE

AUTHOR:
The apostle Paul

AUDIENCE:
Titus, a trusted Gentile companion of Paul

DATE:
About AD 63 – 65

THEME:
Paul writes to instruct Titus concerning the care of the church on the island of Crete.

1 Paul, a servant of God[a] and an apostle of Jesus Christ to further the faith
of God's elect and their knowledge of the
truth[b] that leads to godliness— 2in the
hope of eternal life,[c] which God, who does
not lie, promised before the beginning of
time,[d] 3and which now at his appointed
season[e] he has brought to light[f] through
the preaching entrusted to me[g] by the
command of God our Savior,[h]

4To Titus,[i] my true son in our common
faith:

Grace and peace from God the Father
and Christ Jesus our Savior.

Appointing Elders Who Love What Is Good

1:6-8Ref — 1Ti 3:2-4

5The reason I left you in Crete[j] was
that you might put in order what was left
unfinished and appoint[a] elders[k] in every
town, as I directed you. 6An elder must
be blameless,[l] faithful to his wife, a man

1:1 [a] Ro 1:1 [b] 1Ti 2:4 **1:2** [c] 2Ti 1:1 [d] 2Ti 1:9 **1:3** [e] 1Ti 2:6 [f] 2Ti 1:10 [g] 1Ti 1:11 [h] Lk 1:47 **1:4** [i] 2Co 2:13 **1:5** [j] Ac 27:7 [k] Ac 11:30 **1:6** [l] 1Ti 3:2

[a] 5 Or *ordain*

1:1 *servant of God.* A positive title; see note on Ro 1:1. *elect.* Jewish people recognized themselves as chosen (based on Scripture, e.g., Dt 4:37; 7:6; 10:15); Paul regularly applies this to believers in Jesus (e.g., Ro 8:33).
1:2 *hope of eternal life.* The promised resurrection of the righteous would inaugurate eternal life, the life of the coming world (Da 12:2; further developed in early Jewish sources). *God, who does not lie.* In Greek myths, deities lied (newly-born Hermes even killed a man for failing to cover for Hermes' theft), but even Greek philosophers rejected such notions. Scripture (Nu 23:19; 1Sa 15:29) and Jewish tradition recognized that the true God could not lie.
1:4 *To Titus.* See note on 1Ti 1:2. *my true son.* A teacher would often consider a close disciple to be like a son. *Grace and peace.* For letter greetings, see note on Ro 1:7.
1:5 *put in order what was left unfinished.* It was difficult to appoint elders immediately after people's conversion, but now Paul urges the appointing of local leaders among believers in each community. Indigenous leadership was important; it was both efficient for multiplication and more readily able to connect with local culture, issues and people. *elders.* See note on 1Ti 4:14; early Christians borrowed conventional leadership structures that had already proven useful. *in every town.* As elsewhere in the eastern Mediterranean world, in Crete different towns vied with each other for honor.
1:6 *blameless.* See "above reproach" in note on 1Ti 3:2. *faithful to his wife.* See note on 1Ti 3:2. *whose children believe.* See note on 1Ti 3:4. *wild and disobedient.* Youths were considered adults in their mid-teens, and people often applied the Greek term translated "wild" to young men; fathers retained authority over even adult sons (see

TITUS MINISTERED ON THE ISLAND OF CRETE

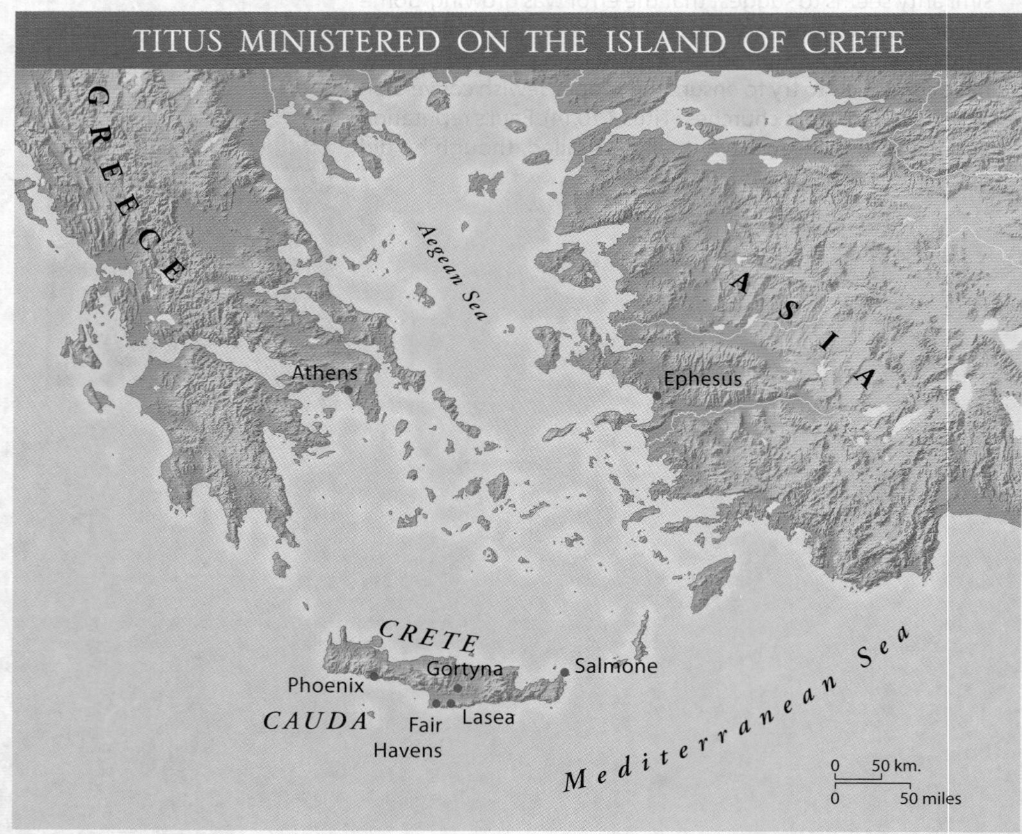

whose children believe[a] and are not open
to the charge of being wild and disobedient. 7Since an overseer[m] manages God's
household,[n] he must be blameless — not
overbearing, not quick-tempered, not giv-
en to drunkenness, not violent, not pursuing dishonest gain.[o] 8Rather, he must be
hospitable,[p] one who loves what is good,[q]
who is self-controlled, upright, holy and
disciplined. 9He must hold firmly[r] to the
trustworthy message as it has been taught,
so that he can encourage others by sound
doctrine[s] and refute those who oppose it.

Rebuking Those Who Fail to Do Good

10For there are many rebellious people,
full of meaningless talk[t] and deception, especially those of the circumcision group.[u]
11They must be silenced, because they are
disrupting whole households[v] by teaching
things they ought not to teach — and that
for the sake of dishonest gain. 12One of
Crete's own prophets[w] has said it: "Cretans[x] are always liars, evil brutes, lazy
gluttons."[b] 13This saying is true. Therefore rebuke[y] them sharply, so that they
will be sound in the faith[z] 14and will pay
no attention to Jewish myths[a] or to the
merely human commands[b] of those who
reject the truth. 15To the pure, all things
are pure, but to those who are corrupted
and do not believe, nothing is pure.[c] In
fact, both their minds and consciences are
corrupted. 16They claim to know God, but
by their actions they deny him.[d] They are
detestable, disobedient and unfit for doing
anything good.

Doing Good for the Sake of the Gospel

2 You, however, must teach what is appropriate to sound doctrine.[e] 2Teach
the older men to be temperate, worthy
of respect, self-controlled, and sound in
faith,[f] in love and in endurance.
3Likewise, teach the older women to
be reverent in the way they live, not to
be slanderers or addicted to much wine,[g]

1:7 m 1Ti 3:1 n 1Co 4:1 o 1Ti 3:3,8 **1:8** p 1Ti 3:2 q 2Ti 3:3 **1:9** r 1Ti 1:19 s 1Ti 1:10 **1:10** t 1Ti 1:6 u Ac 11:2 **1:11** v 2Ti 3:6 **1:12** w Ac 17:28 x Ac 2:11 **1:13** y 2Co 13:10 z Titus 2:2 **1:14** a 1Ti 1:4 b Col 2:22 **1:15** c Ro 14:14, 23 **1:16** d 1Jn 2:4 **2:1** e 1Ti 1:10 **2:2** f Titus 1:13 **2:3** g 1Ti 3:8

[a] 6 Or *children are trustworthy* [b] 12 From the Cretan philosopher Epimenides

note on 1Ti 3:4), though in practice this authority lessened once sons left home.

1:7 *overseer.* Here, this term is used interchangeably with "elder" in v. 6 (as in Ac 20:17,28); see note on 1Ti 3:1. Both were leadership terms in antiquity. *manages God's household.* Well-to-do households often were managed by an educated slave or freedperson accountable to the owner of the house. Greeks also often compared civic or other large-scale management with smaller-scale household management. *drunkenness.* Common in antiquity, and Crete was known for this activity; Scripture treats it as folly (e.g., Dt 21:20; Pr 20:1; 23:21).

1:8 *hospitable.* Included helping travelers, see note on Ac 16:15.

1:10 *meaningless talk.* See note on 1Ti 1:6. *deception.* The local Jewish communities may have been susceptible to being deceived (see also v. 14); other sources reveal that a charlatan was able to take advantage of the large Jewish community in Crete shortly before this period (Josephus, *Antiquities* 17.327; *Wars* 2.103).

1:11 *disrupting whole households.* Some false teachers were disrupting conventional household relationships and consequently also bringing the good news into disrepute (2:4 – 5,8 – 10); for the sensitivity of such matters and its bearing on public views of the gospel, see note on Eph 5:21 — 6:9. If these false teachers are like some others in this period, they may also have ascetic views of marriage (1Ti 4:3), which most people would also view as dishonorable. *for the sake of dishonest gain.* People often charged sages with greed; outsiders also viewed that as a common characteristic of Cretans.

1:12 Outsiders had negative stereotypes of Cretans, some of which Cretans also acknowledged as typical vices among them. *Cretans are always liars.* One of the stereotypes was that Cretans were often deceptive; in support of this view, outsiders cited, e.g., their claim to possess not only the birthplace but also the tomb of Zeus. Although the attribution may be incorrect, Paul would know that the saying cited here was often attributed to the sixth-century BC Cretan thinker Epimenides (cf. Ac 17:28). The attribution was so common that logicians played with it: if Cretans are always liars, then Epimenides was lying, but if he was lying about this, then the saying was untrue and Epimenides need not be lying. *evil brutes, lazy gluttons.* Thinkers called unreasoning people brutes (cf. 2Pe 2:12); gluttons were associated with the base pursuit of pleasure (cf. note on Php 3:19).

1:14 *Jewish myths.* Without changing Scripture itself, Jewish people elaborated many stories about Biblical characters with post-Biblical legends and novels, sometimes also seeking hidden clues to help them amplify or explain Biblical narratives. Those who reapplied Biblical laws for their own era often expanded them with hypothetical rulings and interpretations; Pharisees used these traditions as authoritative guides for interpreting Biblical law. Paul accepts the authority of Scripture but not that of the post-Biblical traditions about it.

1:15 *To the pure, all things are pure.* Whereas Scripture (cf. v. 14) specified which foods were pure (Lev 11:47), Paul's interest is the true spiritual purity to which such laws merely pointed (cf. 1Ti 4:3 – 5; see note on Ro 14:14).

1:16 *They claim to know God.* Those who truly know God are in covenant relationship with him (Isa 19:21; Jer 24:7; Hos 2:20) and must show it by their actions (Jer 22:16).

2:1 – 9 Polytheistic culture was often tolerant of diverse religious views, but many cultures were nevertheless suspicious of foreign cults, especially those they thought undermined traditional household order (see the note on Eph 5:21 — 6:9). Household relationships affected outsiders' perceptions of the movement (Titus 2:5,8,10). Members of minority faiths sometimes used household codes (see again the note on Eph 5:21 — 6:9) to show their allegiance to the social order. Such codes belonged to the wider subject of household management, which included even relations with authorities (Titus 3:1).

2:2 *older men.* Those who acted in the dignified ways Paul lists were respected. *sound in faith, in love and in endurance.* Following appropriate Greek rules of speaking and writing, Paul saves for the end of his descriptors the term ("sound") that will have additional modifiers.

2:3 *older women.* Ancient humor often stereotyped and made fun of older women, especially for their alleged

TITUS 2 

THE BOOKS OF THE APOCRYPHA

The books of the Apocrypha are as follows:

- *Tobit:* Set during the Assyrian exile, Tobit is a historically implausible yet charming narrative about a pious Jew. Tobit, taken into exile in Nineveh, goes blind as a result of sparrow droppings falling into his eyes. He dispatches his son Tobias to Media to retrieve a stash of money, providing a guide, Azariah, who turns out to be the angel Raphael. Raphael instructs Tobias to catch a large fish and to preserve its liver, heart and gall because of their magical powers. The two encounter a lovely Jewess, Sarah, whose seven grooms have died on their respective wedding nights because of the demon Asmodeus. Raphael instructs Tobias in how to thwart Asmodeus through ritual magic. Tobias then marries Sarah, retrieves the money, returns to Nineveh, and heals Tobit with the fish gall.
- *Judith:* This nonhistorical tale describes how a pious Jewish woman effects deliverance for her people. Written during the latter part of the second century BC, it was unaccountably set in the days of "Nebuchadnezzar, king of the Assyrians" (Nebuchadnezzar was king of Babylon).
- *Sirach/Ecclesiasticus:* This book is fundamentally a collection of hymns, prayers and instructions upholding traditional Jewish piety and wisdom. Written in approximately 180 BC, it includes some justly celebrated passages, such as its catalog of heroes of the faith (Sirach/Ecclesiasticus 44:1 — 49:16).
- *Wisdom of Solomon:* Perhaps written in the first century BC and somewhat influenced by Greek philosophy, this work exhorts the reader to pursue wisdom and right behavior.
- *Baruch:* Although purported to have been authored by Baruch, Jeremiah's scribe, the book was probably written long after Baruch's day. Drawing upon diverse

continued on next page

but to teach what is good. [4]Then they can
urge the younger women to love their husbands and children, [5]to be self-controlled
and pure, to be busy at home, to be kind,
and to be subject to their husbands,[h] so
that no one will malign the word of God.[i]

2:5 [h]Eph 5:22 [i]1Ti 6:1

gossip and foolish talk (here, being "slanderers"; see note on 1Ti 4:7). (In more traditional Greek society women talked mainly with other women; on most women's limited education, see the article "Women's Education in Antiquity," p. 2109.) *much wine.* Some caricatured older women as "addicted to much wine" and as sexually desiring younger men. Many men resented drunkenness in women; sadly, some Roman men even praised the severity of much earlier times, when one Roman man reportedly bludgeoned his wife to death for drinking. Some believed that drunkenness in Crete was even worse than elsewhere.

2:4 *they can urge the younger women.* Older women, especially mothers, had long sought to instruct their daughters in the ways of life. This included instruction in how to be a good mother and how to please a good husband. Most younger women were married; they could marry as young as puberty, although marriage in the mid- to late teens was more common. *to love their husbands and children.* Most ancient writers of the subject (normally male) wanted wives to love their husbands and nurture their children; many tomb inscriptions report these characteristics as a woman's crowning virtues.

2:5 *self-controlled.* When moral teachers urged women to be self-controlled, they normally included sexual modesty in this command. *to be busy at home.* Greek culture expected wives to be busy at home. The highest traditional Greek ideal included avoiding being in public, where they could have contact with unrelated men, though this ideal was not always possible in practice. *subject to their husbands.* At least in the ideal, men expected wives to be meek and to obey everything their husbands commanded. *so that no one will malign the word of God.* Paul's concern is that the gospel not be maligned (cf. vv. 9 – 10; see note on vv. 1 – 9).

parts of the Old Testament, it contains prayers, hymns and a passage that praises wisdom and claims it to be the special possession of Israel (Barveh 3:9—4:4).

- *First and Second Maccabees:* These historical texts recount the persecution inflicted upon the Jews by Antiochus IV and the desecration of the temple that ignited the Maccabean revolt. First Maccabees was probably written around 100 BC, while its counterpart may actually have come from a somewhat earlier date. Although the books are propagandistic in nature, they are a vital source for the history and religion of this period.
- *First Esdras:* Written around 100 BC, this is a loose retelling of Biblical history from Josiah's celebration of the Passover to Ezra's reforms. One part not copied from canonical Scripture is 1 Esdras 3:1—5:6, which records how a young Jewish man at the court of Darius solves a riddle about the strongest thing in the world (women are the strongest, but love conquers all). This Jewish man turns out to be Zerubbabel (Ezr 2:2).
- *Second Esdras:* This book is a composite of three writings, the latest of which may have been penned as recently as the third century AD. Apocalyptic in nature, it includes a reaction to the AD 70 destruction of the Jerusalem temple by the Romans. The central portion of the book (2 Esdras 3:1—14:48), dated to about AD 100, is a fictitious series of visions supposedly given by the angel Uriel to Ezra and dealing with such issues as the justice of God. A Christian appendix (2 Esdras 15:1—16:78) was added during the third century AD.
- *Epistle of Jeremiah:* Loosely based on Jer 29, this short, pseudonymous essay denounces the folly of idolatry. The writing most likely came from the third century BC or later.
- *Prayer of Manasseh:* A pseudonymous, penitential prayer beseeching God to cancel Israel's exile, this book claims to be the prayer of Manasseh mentioned in 2Ch 33:12–13; it comes in fact from the second or third century BC. The writing draws upon a number of Biblical texts, especially Psalm 51.
- *Additions to Esther:* This includes six supplements to Esther, adding pious language and motifs in an evident attempt to make up for the fact that the canonical book never mentions God.
- *Additions to Daniel:* These supplements to Daniel include the Prayer of Azariah, the Song of the Three Young Men, Susanna, and Bel and the Dragon (or Serpent). The dates of composition are unknown. ◆

6Similarly, encourage the young men[j] to
be self-controlled. 7In everything set them
an example[k] by doing what is good. In
your teaching show integrity, seriousness
8and soundness of speech that cannot be
condemned, so that those who oppose
you may be ashamed because they have
nothing bad to say about us.[l]
9Teach slaves to be subject to their masters in everything,[m] to try to please them,
not to talk back to them, 10and not to steal
from them, but to show that they can be
fully trusted, so that in every way they will
make the teaching about God our Savior
attractive.[n]
11For the grace of God has appeared that
offers salvation to all people.[o] 12It teaches
us to say "No" to ungodliness and worldly

2:6 [j] 1Ti 5:1 **2:7** [k] 1Ti 4:12 **2:8** [l] 1Pe 2:12 **2:9** [m] Eph 6:5 **2:10** [n] Mt 5:16 **2:11** [o] 1Ti 2:4

2:7 *set them an example.* A teacher's example was recognized as important.
2:9–10 Slaveholders often stereotyped slaves in general as lazy, apt to argue with their masters and liable to steal when they could. (Lower-level slaves, after all, did not always have incentives to perform efficiently.) Given the prejudices and potential persecution that Jesus' followers already faced, they needed to counter stereotypes. See the articles "Slaves and Slaveholders in Ephesians 6," p. 2068; "Ancient Slavery and the Background for Philemon," p. 2134; see also Introduction to Philemon.
2:11 *offers salvation to all people.* Some Jewish people expected salvation only for their own people; others allowed that a small minority of righteous Gentiles would be saved. Paul urges believers to live in a way that commends the gospel (vv. 5,8,10) so that more will be saved.
2:12 *live self-controlled, upright and godly lives.* Philosophers often warned against passions and praised being self-controlled and upright (two of the four cardinal Greek virtues). *in this present age.* Many Jewish thinkers contrasted the present age, under the dominion of evil (cf. Gal 1:4), with the glorious age to come. They expected

SELECTED JEWISH AND CHRISTIAN LITERATURE

Apocrypha	Epistle of Jeremiah (317 BC) Tobit (250–175 BC) Baruch (200 BC–AD 70) Sirach (Ecclesiasticus) (190 BC) Additions of Esther (180–145 BC) Judith (175–110 BC) Song of the Three Young Men (Children) (167–163 BC) 1 Esdras (c. 150 BC)	Bel and the Dragon (150–100 BC) Prayer of Manasseh (150–50 BC) Wisdom of Solomon (150 BC–AD 40) 1 Maccabees (103–63 BC) 2 Maccabees (c. 100 BC) Susanna (c. 100 BC?) 2 Esdras (AD 70–135)
Pseudepigrapha	Enoch (200–63 BC) Letter of Aristeas (170–130 BC) Book of Jubilees (150–100 BC) Testaments of the 12 Patriarchs (c. 130 BC) 3 Maccabees (1st c. BC) 4 Maccabees (?) Sibylline Oracles (c. 80 BC–AD 130)	Psalms of Solomon (c. 40 BC) Life of Adam and Eve (1st c. AD) Lives of the Prophets (1st c. AD) Assumption of Moses (AD 1–30) 2 Baruch (AD 70–100) Martydom and Ascension of Isaiah (2nd c. AD)
Apostolic Fathers	1 Clement (AD 95–96) Ignatius (AD 110–117) The Didache (AD 100–130?)	Shepherd of Hermas (AD 100–140) Epistle of Barnabas (c. AD 132) Polycarp (before 155)

passions,[p] and to live self-controlled, upright and godly lives[q] in this present age,
13 while we wait for the blessed hope — the
appearing of the glory of our great God and
Savior, Jesus Christ,[r] 14 who gave himself
for us to redeem us from all wickedness
and to purify for himself a people that are
his very own,[s] eager to do what is good.[t]
15 These, then, are the things you should
teach. Encourage and rebuke with all authority. Do not let anyone despise you.

Saved in Order to Do Good

3 Remind the people to be subject to rulers and authorities,[u] to be obedient,
to be ready to do whatever is good,[v] 2 to
slander no one,[w] to be peaceable and considerate, and always to be gentle toward
everyone.
3 At one time we too were foolish, disobedient, deceived and enslaved by all
kinds of passions and pleasures. We lived
in malice and envy, being hated and hating one another. 4 But when the kindness[x]
and love of God our Savior appeared,[y]
5 he saved us, not because of righteous
things we had done,[z] but because of his
mercy. He saved us through the washing of rebirth and renewal[a] by the Holy
Spirit, 6 whom he poured out on us[b]

2:12 [p] Titus 3:3 [q] 2Ti 3:12 **2:13** [r] 2Pe 1:1 **2:14** [s] Ex 19:5 [t] Eph 2:10 **3:1** [u] Ro 13:1 [v] 2Ti 2:21 **3:2** [w] Eph 4:31; 2Ti 2:24 **3:4** [x] Eph 2:7 [y] Titus 2:11 **3:5** [z] Eph 2:9 [a] Ro 12:2 **3:6** [b] Ro 5:5

the coming of the Messiah and the resurrection to inaugurate the coming age (cf. v. 13).

2:13 *appearing of … Jesus Christ.* Greeks spoke of the appearing of deities in various ways, but Jewish people spoke of glorious appearings of the true God (2 Maccabees 2:21; 3:24), especially his appearing to inaugurate the future era (cf. Titus 2:12). *great God and Savior.* Diaspora Jews often called their God the great God; he was also the chief Savior (e.g., Isa 43:11; 45:21). Some Jewish thinkers personified Wisdom or sometimes even exalted angels as somewhat divine, but none would have called a human being "our great God and Savior," as Paul apparently does here with Jesus.

2:14 *to redeem … a people that are his very own.* God had "redeemed" his people, i.e., freed them from their slavery (Dt 7:8) (i.e., freed them from slavery in Egypt) to make them "a people that are his very own," which can also be translated "a special people." Paul evokes texts such as Ex 19:5; Dt 7:6; 14:2, where the Greek translation of the OT uses these same words for "treasured possession." *eager.* Also the Greek term for "zealous"; might contrast with the growing zeal of some nationalistic Jews who wished to revolt against Rome (the unrest spread to other Jewish communities), but it probably simply retains its usual, broader sense.

2:15 *These, then, are the things you should teach.* Writers and speakers sometimes summarized their preceding exhortation.

3:1 *be subject to rulers and authorities.* See note on Ro 13:1 – 7. Increasing nationalistic sentiment in Judea had made some prone to revolt (cf. "eager" in note on 2:14); a revolt would break out in AD 66 and lead to Jerusalem's destruction in 70. Paul, however, wants to avoid any association of the young and still-fragile Christian movement with sedition.

3:3 *enslaved by all kinds of passions and pleasures.* Many philosophers complained that humanity was enslaved in this way; they argued that reason alone could deliver one from such enslavement, but Paul speaks instead of rebirth (v. 5).

3:4 *love.* The Greek term is not the usual one; the term praised a person's benevolent and virtuous interest in humanity.

3:5 *not because of righteous things we had done.* Cf. Dt 9:4. *washing of rebirth and renewal by the Holy Spirit.* God had promised to cleanse his people when he would put his Spirit in them and give them new hearts to obey his commands (Eze 36:25 – 27). The image of washing remained natural for conversion; some Jewish teachers allowed that Gentiles could experience rebirth into Judaism through conversion, which included immersion in water. (Some Gentiles also envisioned rebirth in various ways, but not associated with the Holy Spirit.)

3:6 *whom he poured out on us.* The Spirit being poured out echoes the prophets (e.g., Isa 32:15; 44:3; Eze 39:29), and especially (fitting also the Greek version) Joel 2:28 – 29.

generously through Jesus Christ our
Savior, 7so that, having been justified
by his grace,[c] we might become heirs[d]
having the hope[e] of eternal life.[f] 8This is
a trustworthy saying.[g] And I want you
to stress these things, so that those who
have trusted in God may be careful to devote themselves to doing what is good.[h]
These things are excellent and profitable
for everyone.

9But avoid foolish controversies and
genealogies and arguments and quarrels[i]
about the law, because these are unprofitable and useless. 10Warn a divisive person once, and then warn them a second
time. After that, have nothing to do with
them.[j] 11You may be sure that such people
are warped and sinful; they are self-con-
demned.

Final Remarks

12As soon as I send Artemas or Tychicus[k] to you, do your best to come to me at
Nicopolis, because I have decided to winter there.[l] 13Do everything you can to help
Zenas the lawyer and Apollos[m] on their
way and see that they have everything
they need. 14Our people must learn to devote themselves to doing what is good,[n] in
order to provide for urgent needs and not
live unproductive lives.

15Everyone with me sends you greetings. Greet those who love us in the faith.[o]

Grace be with you all.[p]

3:7 [c] Ro 3:24 [d] Ro 8:17 [e] Ro 8:24 [f] Titus 1:2 **3:8** [g] 1Ti 1:15 [h] Titus 2:14 **3:9** [i] 1Ti 1:4; 2Ti 2:14 **3:10** [j] Ro 16:17 **3:12** [k] Ac 20:4 [l] 2Ti 4:9,21 **3:13** [m] Ac 18:24 **3:14** [n] ver 8 **3:15** [o] 1Ti 1:2 [p] Col 4:18

3:7 *heirs ... of eternal life.* Jewish people often used this expression. *eternal life.* The life of the coming age.
3:9 *avoid foolish controversies.* See note on 1Ti 1:6. *genealogies.* See note on 1Ti 1:4.
3:10 Jewish ethics emphasized offering correction appropriately: first privately, then with others, and finally, if necessary, before the assembly. *have nothing to do with them.* The strictest level of discipline in a Jewish community was an offender's expulsion; see note on 1Ti 1:20.
3:12 *Artemas or Tychicus.* Because Paul later sent Tychicus from Rome to Timothy (2Ti 4:12), it was probably Artemas whom he sent to Titus. (The name Artemas derives from the name of the Greek goddess Artemis, popular in Ephesus. By this period, however, in the Diaspora even Jewish names often used the "Artem-" root; cf. the Jewish believer "Apollos" in v. 13, named for the Greek god Apollo, Artemis's brother.) *Nicopolis.* Near the sea and only roughly a century old, it was on the Greek side of the Adriatic coast, about 200 miles (320 kilometers) east of Italy. Apparently wishing to return to Rome, Paul is going to leave Asia, cross Macedonia and wait in Nicopolis for Titus, who is to come up from Crete after receiving Paul's message. Sea travel was not possible during winter (see note on 2Ti 4:21), so Paul would wait there. Titus later walked northward to minister in Dalmatia (2Ti 4:10), where some work had probably been initiated before (Ro 15:19, referring to the same region).
3:13 Letter writers sometimes commended the letter's bearer. *help.* Paul invited the ancient virtue of hospitality, which would include providing for the rest of their voyage (see note on Ac 16:15). Since they are leaving Paul and passing through Crete, where Titus is, they might be returning to Alexandria (Apollos's home city) or possibly traveling to Cyrene. (From Nicopolis, an intended visit to Greece or Rome would not have taken them to Crete.) *Zenas.* The name was used by both Gentiles and Diaspora Jews. *lawyer.* Most cases in Gentile courts were argued by orators (cf. Ac 24:1, where "lawyer" translates a term for "public speaker"); a true lawyer, or law expert, was a jurist, which was far less common. Every other Biblical use of the present Greek term, however, refers to expertise in the Jewish law, including in this context (v. 9). *Apollos.* An Alexandrian Jew learned in Scripture and gifted in speaking (Ac 18:24); he was also an associate of Paul (1Co 16:12).
3:15 *Greet those who love us in the faith.* Writers often appended greetings at the end of a letter.

THE LETTERS
PHILEMON

Genre

This brief letter is much closer to the average length of an ancient letter than are Paul's other letters. It would have required only a single sheet of papyrus.

Situation

For a discussion of slavery relevant to this letter, see the articles "Ancient Slavery and the Background for Philemon," p. 2134; "Slaves and Slaveholders in Ephesians 6," p. 2068. Paul's message to Philemon goes beyond other documents of his time in not only pleading for clemency for an escaped slave (itself considered exceptional) but also suggesting that he be released (to continue working with Paul in ministry) because he is now a Christian. So powerful was this precedent that many of the earliest U.S. slaveholders did not want their slaves to be exposed to Christianity for fear that they would be compelled to free them; the Christian message had to be domesticated (like early Stoicism was by subsequent Stoics) to make it neutral or supportive of slavery.

QUICK GLANCE

AUTHOR:
The apostle Paul

AUDIENCE:
Philemon and the members of the church at Colossae

DATE:
About AD 60

THEME:
Paul urges Philemon to show grace to Onesimus, his runaway slave, and apparently wants him to free Onesimus to allow him to continue in ministry with Paul.

Slaves, especially skilled or educated males, were often sent on errands and trusted as agents with their slaveholders' property. Such slaves could sometimes earn enough money on the side to buy their freedom (although their earnings legally belonged to their slaveholder, slaves were normally permitted to control the money themselves); still, a few took the opportunity of an errand to escape. Because a safe escape required them to get far away from where their slaveholder lived (in the case Paul addresses here, from Phrygia to probably Rome; cf. possibly 2Ti 1:16 – 17), they might take some of their slaveholder's money with them. Recapture normally meant severe punishment.

Such theft may be the point of Phm 18, but Paul might there account for the possibility that Philemon wants repayment for Onesimus himself. From the standpoint of ancient slaveholders, the lost time of an escaped slave was lost money and was legally viewed as stolen property, to which the one harboring him was liable. But more important, slaves themselves were not cheap, and Philemon might have already bought another slave to replace Onesimus. Slaves could cost between 750 sesterces (187.5 denarii) and 700,000 sesterces

(175,000 denarii), with 2,000 as an average. (Keep in mind that a denarius was close to a day's wage for many farmers in this period.)

Biblical law required harboring escaped slaves (Dt 23:15 – 16), but Roman law required Paul to return Onesimus to his master, with serious penalties if he failed to do so. Paul uses his relationship with Philemon to seek Onesimus's release: in a standard "letter of recommendation" one would plead with someone of equal (or sometimes lower) status on behalf of someone of lower status. Paul was not Philemon's equal socially or economically, but as his spiritual father he had grounds to claim the equality that characterized ancient friendship.

Some compare this letter with a letter that Pliny the Younger later wrote to a friend on behalf of an estranged freedman who had pleaded for Pliny's intercession. Despite the similarity of interceding for another, however, Pliny allowed that the slaveholder had a right to be angry, and he spoke merely of a former slave, not a current one. Paul's letter is therefore more countercultural than Pliny's.

Although some have suggested that Paul writes this letter from imprisonment in Ephesus, supposing that Onesimus would not have traveled as far as Rome, Rome remains the likelier site. Paul's custody (v. 10) in this period was likely in Rome (Phil 1:13; 4:22).

Following the usual patterns of persuasion in his day, Paul offers an opening appeal (Phm 4 – 7), a main argument with proofs (vv. 8 – 16), and a summary of his case (vv. 17 – 22). That Philemon preserved the letter suggests that he granted Paul's request. ◆

1 Paul, a prisoner[a] of Christ Jesus, and
Timothy our brother,[b]

To Philemon our dear friend and fellow
worker[c]— 2 also to Apphia our sister and
Archippus[d] our fellow soldier[e]—and to
the church that meets in your home:[f]

3 Grace and peace to you[a] from God our
Father and the Lord Jesus Christ.

Thanksgiving and Prayer

4 I always thank my God[g] as I remember
you in my prayers, 5 because I hear about
your love for all his holy people[h] and your
faith in the Lord Jesus. 6 I pray that your
partnership with us in the faith may be
effective in deepening your understanding
of every good thing we share for the sake
of Christ. 7 Your love has given me great
joy and encouragement,[i] because you,
brother, have refreshed[j] the hearts of the
Lord's people.

1 [a] ver 9, 23; Eph 3:1 [b] 2Co 1:1 [c] Php 2:25 **2** [d] Col 4:17 [e] Php 2:25 [f] Ro 16:5 **4** [g] Ro 1:8 **5** [h] Eph 1:15; Col 1:4 **7** [i] 2Co 7:4, 13 [j] ver 20

[a] 3 The Greek is plural; also in verses 22 and 25; elsewhere in this letter "you" is singular.

1–2 *Philemon … Apphia … Archippus.* These believers live in Phrygia (cf. Col 4:17); if Archippus belongs to the same household, he could be a son, high-ranking slave, or freedman. For discussion of house churches see notes on Ac 12:12; Ro 16:5. Well-to-do owners of homes in which ancient religious groups met were normally granted positions of honor in those groups, as their patrons or benefactors.
2 *fellow soldier.* Ancient thinkers, including Paul, often used such expressions figuratively.
3 *Grace and peace.* See note on Ro 1:7.
4 *I always thank my God.* See note on Ro 1:8. *remember you in my prayers.* See note on Ro 1:9–10.
6 *your partnership with us in the faith.* Friends often expressed appreciation for shared friendship in their letters; sometimes this affirmation also served as a prelude for a request (cf. 8–10).
7 *refreshed the hearts of the Lord's people.* Hospitality was a crucial ancient virtue (see note on Ac 16:15); Philemon also hosted a house church (vv. 1–2).

PHILEMON 8–21

Ancient Slavery and the Background for Philemon

Slavery in the Roman Empire took a wide range of forms, some of which were barely comparable with the forms of slavery later practiced in the Americas or the Arab world. Most doctors, e.g., were Greek slaves; many slaves were educated scribes, and some household slaves in important homes managed estates or wielded more power than most free persons. Slavery in the Roman Empire was not ethnically based; Romans were happy to enslave anyone.

Those observations should not, however, be used to downplay the evils of slavery. Roman law acknowledged that slaves were persons by nature; from an economic standpoint, however, they were treated as property. The head of a household could legally execute his (or sometimes her) slaves (though he had financial incentive not to do so), and they would all be executed if the head of the household were murdered. Slaves composed a large part of the agricultural work force in parts of the empire (e.g., Italy); there they competed with free peasants for the same work. Gladiators and slaves working in the mines had the worst lives, usually dying quickly. Male household slaves generally had life better, though female household slaves (and sometimes boys) were vulnerable to sexual exploitation by slaveholders. Household slaves were the only kind of slaves addressed in Paul's writings addressing urban churches.

In contrast to most slaves in more recent cultures, slaves in the ancient Mediterranean world were able to work for and achieve freedom. Some scholars estimate that even as many as half of household slaves may have had the opportunity to become free at some point in their lives (at least if they lived for an extended time). Some freed household slaves became independently wealthy; at least in Roman custom, their former holders became their patrons and were supposed to help them advance in society.

continued on next page

Paul's Plea for Onesimus

8Therefore, although in Christ I could
be bold and order you to do what you
ought to do, 9yet I prefer to appeal to you
on the basis of love. It is as none other
than Paul — an old man and now also a
prisoner[k] of Christ Jesus — 10that I appeal to you for my son[l] Onesimus,[a m] who
became my son while I was in chains.
11Formerly he was useless to you, but
now he has become useful both to you
and to me.
12I am sending him — who is my very

9 [k] ver 1,23
10 [l] 1Co 4:15 [m] Col 4:9

[a] 10 *Onesimus* means *useful.*

8 *I could be bold and order you.* As a benefactor of the church, Philemon has sufficient means and is probably of higher social status than Paul. Nevertheless, Paul knows that Philemon will recognize Paul's more authoritative role as Christ's agent. Persons of means often hired or invited philosophic teachers who could lecture at banquets and the like and who functioned as the wealthier person's clients. By contrast, Paul is Philemon's benefactor in the faith.
9 *on the basis of love.* Shared friendship could be used as the basis for a request; friends were socially obligated to grant and return favors. *old man.* Respect for age was important in his culture, so Paul appeals to his age. (According to one ancient definition, the Greek term Paul uses here applied to ages 49 to 56; but NT writers often use it loosely for anyone no longer "young." On the basis of other NT evidence, Paul may be around 57, give or take five years.)
10 *my son Onesimus.* Teachers often called disciples "sons." The point of Paul's plea may be that it was unthinkable to hold as a slave the son of one's own spiritual benefactor. *while I was in chains.* Although the lowest slaves might wear chains, it is Paul here who has been chained. Persuaders often appealed to emotions such as pity, as Paul invites here.
11 *he was useless to you.* Many slaveholders stereotyped slaves (among whom they sometimes named Phrygian slaves, as would be the case here) as lazy and ill-disciplined. *he has become useful.* Here Paul plays on Onesimus's name, which means "useful." It was a common slave name, for obvious reasons.

Economically, socially, and with regard to freedom to determine their future, many of these male household slaves were better off than average free persons in the Roman Empire; many scholars contend that most free persons were rural peasants working as tenant farmers on the vast estates of wealthy landowners. See the article "Slaves and Slaveholders in Ephesians 6," p. 2068.

Some philosophers said that slaves were slaveholders' equals as persons, but in this period they did not urge masters to free their slaves. (Earlier Stoics were more radical, but the movement quickly became more mainstream; indeed, even some early Stoics reportedly held slaves. Meanwhile, cynics, like Jewish Essenes, invited prospective followers to abandon everything because they needed nothing, not to free slaves because slavery was wrong.) Nearly everyone took the institution of slavery for granted, except early Stoics who said that it was "against nature." Yet Paul seems to believe that it is against nature in principle (see Eph 6:9), and applies that principle in practice by asking for Philemon to free Onesimus for ministry with Paul, now that Onesimus is a brother in Christ (Phm 8 – 16). ◆

Relief of a Roman gladiator. Slaves were sometimes forced to be gladiators to entertain crowds, which usually led to the slaves' quick death.

Kim Walton. Ephesus Archaeological Museum.

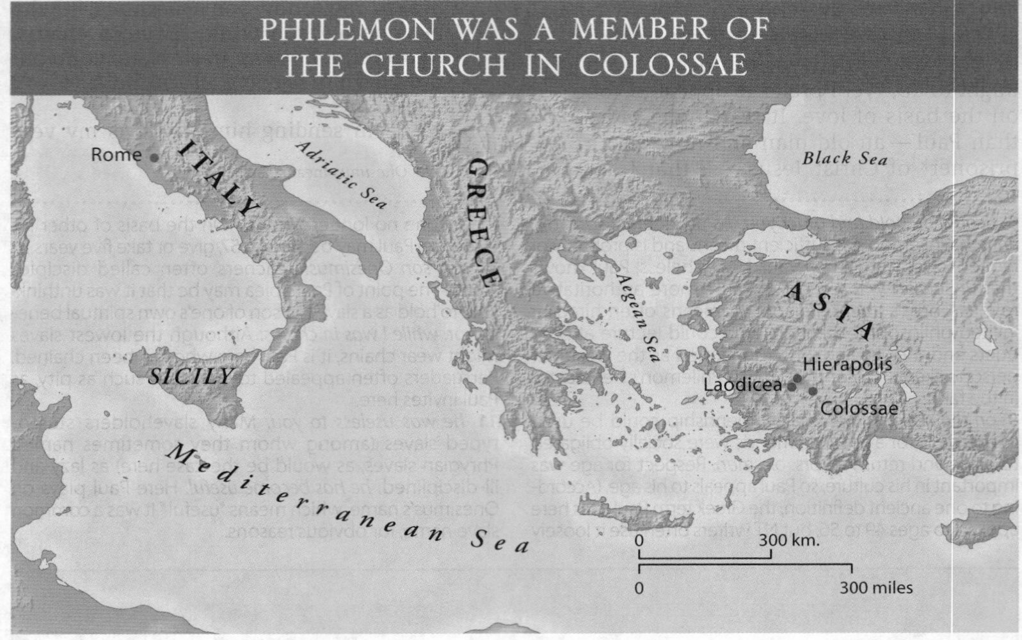

PHILEMON WAS A MEMBER OF THE CHURCH IN COLOSSAE

heart—back to you. 13I would have liked
to keep him with me so that he could take
your place in helping me while I am in
chains for the gospel. 14But I did not want
to do anything without your consent, so
that any favor you do would not seem
forced[n] but would be voluntary. 15Perhaps
the reason he was separated from you for
a little while was that you might have him
back forever— 16no longer as a slave, but
better than a slave, as a dear brother.[o] He
is very dear to me but even dearer to you,
both as a fellow man and as a brother in
the Lord.

17So if you consider me a partner,[p] welcome him as you would welcome me. 18If
he has done you any wrong or owes you
anything, charge it to me. 19I, Paul, am
writing this with my own hand. I will pay
it back—not to mention that you owe me
your very self. 20I do wish, brother, that I
may have some benefit from you in the
Lord; refresh[q] my heart in Christ. 21Con-
fident[r] of your obedience, I write to you,

14 [n] 2Co 9:7; 1Pe 5:2
16 [o] Mt 23:8; 1Ti 6:2
17 [p] 2Co 8:23
20 [q] ver 7
21 [r] 2Co 2:3

13 *I would have liked to keep him.* People of honor often stated their requests indirectly, yet clearly enough to imply what they wanted done. *take your place in helping me.* Masters sometimes freed slaves to become slaves of the temple of some deity; here Paul invites Philemon to free Onesimus for the continued service of the gospel.

14 *any favor you do would not seemed forced but would be voluntary.* Paul appeals not to his own authority but to Philemon's honor as a friend. Runaway slaves were known to be fearful of being captured and taken back to the slaveholders; Paul attempts to use his own relationship with Philemon to establish reconciliation.

15 *separated from you.* Probably implies divine activity arranging this outcome; Jews and Christians both recognized that God sovereignly acted, often for the best interests of his people. *have him back.* This Greek phrase resembles that found in business receipts, but here it is not technically a property transaction in which Philemon receives Onesimus back as a slave, but like welcoming back a family member (v. 16), especially since Paul desires Onesimus' continued work together in the gospel (v. 13).

16 *no longer as a slave, but ... as a dear brother.* Roman law saw slaves as both people and property; but family obligations would not allow one to treat a full brother as property. *brother.* See note on Ac 9:17.

17 *partner.* Cf. v. 6 (see note there); often business terminology, possibly relevant for v. 18. *welcome him as you would welcome me.* Letters of recommendation often urged the receiver, the recommender's friend or peer, to treat the recommended one the way the receiver would treat the recommender.

19 *I will pay it back.* Letters acknowledging debt normally included the promise "I will repay" and were signed by the debtor in his own handwriting. Because it is in writing, this offer would be legally binding in the unlikely event that Philemon would take Paul up on it. *not to mention that you owe me your very self.* Philemon also owes a debt to Paul; persuasive speakers often suggested, "I could remind you of this, but I won't"—thus reminding while pretending not to do so (cf. vv. 8–9). By ancient social custom, friends were bound by the reciprocal obligation of repaying favors; Philemon owes Paul the greatest favor—his very self, his new life in Christ. Letters of recommendation sometimes urged the recipient to count any favor toward the recommended as a favor toward the recommender.

20 On repayment of favors, see note on v. 19. *refresh my heart in Christ.* The one who refreshed God's people with his benefactions (v. 7) should now refresh Paul.

21 *Confident of your obedience.* Professional speakers often sought favors in such terms: "Knowing your good-

knowing that you will do even more than
I ask.
22And one thing more: Prepare a guest
room for me, because I hope to be[s] restored to you in answer to your prayers.[t]

23Epaphras,[u] my fellow prisoner in
Christ Jesus, sends you greetings. 24And so
do Mark,[v] Aristarchus,[w] Demas[x] and Luke,
my fellow workers.
25The grace of the Lord Jesus Christ be
with your spirit.[y]

22 [s] Php 1:25; 2:24 [t] 2Co 1:11 **23** [u] Col 1:7
24 [v] Ac 12:12 [w] Ac 19:29 [x] Col 4:14 **25** [y] 2Ti 4:22

ness, you will gladly hear me" or "grant me such-and-such a request." *even more than I ask.* Paul revisits his indirect request to forgive and free Onesimus and send him back to Paul as his coworker (vv. 12 – 14).

22 *Prepare a guest room for me.* Hospitality was a chief virtue in antiquity, and people counted it an honor to host someone they respected (see note on Ac 16:15).

THE LETTERS

HEBREWS

Authorship

Hebrews is notable for its Greek style, which differs too much from Paul to be attributed to him. Along with sections of Luke-Acts and letters attributed to Peter and James, this document displays more sophisticated Greek than most of the NT; its author probably had rhetorical/literary training and skills (or, less likely given the consistency of skilled argument, a superb editor with a very free hand). The writer is respected in the same circles as Timothy (13:23), probably in the Greek-speaking eastern Mediterranean world. Among the members of this circle who could be proposed as authors, two stand out. Silas was probably in Rome around this time and had literary skills (1Pe 5:12); as a Jewish Roman citizen in the east (cf. Ac 16:37) he probably had a significant level of education. Martin Luther plausibly suggested Apollos, whose Alexandrian education would explain features of the letter (cf. Ac 18:24), though several years earlier he may have been traveling elsewhere, perhaps returning to Alexandria (cf. Titus 3:13). Nevertheless, we cannot eliminate other members of the Pauline circle from consideration, since we lack knowledge about the abilities of most of them.

QUICK GLANCE

AUTHOR:
Unknown; possibly Apollos, Silas or Barnabas

AUDIENCE:
Jewish Christians in the Diaspora

DATE:
About AD 68

THEME:
The author demonstrates that Christ is greater than the old covenant and warns his hearers not to turn back under pressure.

Date

The approximate date of the letter seems clearer than its author. Because Timothy was recently freed (13:23) and the work was apparently written from Italy (13:24), it seems likely that Timothy was arrested in Rome during the Neronian persecution (perhaps shortly after he came to see Paul, 2Ti 4:21) and freed when Nero (and his policy) died in AD 68. The mention of Timothy but not of Paul, who may have died about AD 64 or within a few years after that, also would make sense for a date of approximately AD 68. At this time, when the outcome of the Roman war in Judea would have been assured from Rome's vantage point, one could readily speak of the old temple system as passing away (Heb 8:13), even literally—a process completed in AD 70 with the destruction of the temple. That the writer cannot declare that the temple has been destroyed (although it would have served his argument well to have noted this) also may suggest a date before AD 70.

Recipients

The audience clearly appears to be a Jewish one experiencing some temptation to return to non-Christian Jewish practices. This temptation might come from the synagogue or because Gentiles persecuting Christians might exempt those who claimed to belong to a recognized ancestral faith. Nevertheless, the audience is clearly one at home with the Greek translation of Scripture and forms of thought familiar among Diaspora Jews. Although the Hellenistic Jewish philosopher Philo of Alexandria writes on a higher rhetorical level, his writing offers some of the closest parallels for Hebrews. The seizure of the audience's property in earlier days (10:34) does not fit the situations in Corinth or Ephesus. Heb 13:23 suggests an audience in the Pauline circle (i.e., not in Alexandria, though Apollos was known there too). Heb 13:24 may suggest that the author writes from Italy, probably ruling out an audience in Italy.

Style and Message

The author develops a coherent argument. Although modern readers do not always understand his approach, his interpretive techniques would have made good sense to his ancient Jewish audience. Ancient writers and speakers frequently offered elaborate comparisons between different persons or objects. Christ is greater than the angels (ch. 1) who delivered the law (ch. 2), and thus greater than the law itself. He is greater than Moses and the promised land (3:1 — 4:13). As a priest after the order of Melchizedek (Ps 110:4), he is greater than the OT priesthood (Heb 4:14 — 7:28) because he is attached to a new covenant (ch. 8) and a heavenly temple service (9:1 — 10:18). Therefore, his followers ought to persevere in faith and not return to the earlier order, which merely pointed to the greater promise to follow. They must persevere regardless of the cost (10:19 — 12:13). The writer follows his theoretical discussion, as many letters did, with specific moral exhortations tied into the same theme (13:1 – 17). Interspersed throughout the letter is the repeated warning against apostasy, noting that the penalty for rejecting the new covenant is greater than what the penalty for rejecting the old had been (cf. 2:1 – 4; 3:14; 4:1 – 2,11; 6:1 – 8,11 – 12; 10:26 – 31; 12:14 – 17,25; though cf. expressions of confidence with reasons in 6:9 – 10; 10:39). ◆

God's Final Word: His Son

1 In the past God spoke[a] to our ancestors through the prophets[b] at many
times and in various ways,[c] 2but in these
last days he has spoken to us by his Son,
whom he appointed heir[d] of all things,
and through whom[e] also he made the universe. 3The Son is the radiance of God's
glory[f] and the exact representation of his
being, sustaining all things[g] by his powerful word. After he had provided purification for sins,[h] he sat down at the right
hand of the Majesty in heaven.[i] 4So he became as much superior to the angels as
the name he has inherited is superior to
theirs.[j]

The Son Superior to Angels

5For to which of the angels did God ever
say,

"You are my Son;
today I have become your
Father"[a]?[k]

Or again,

"I will be his Father,
and he will be my Son"[b]?[l]

6And again, when God brings his firstborn
into the world,[m] he says,

"Let all God's angels worship him."[c][n]

7In speaking of the angels he says,

"He makes his angels spirits,
and his servants flames of fire."[d][o]

8But about the Son he says,

"Your throne, O God, will last for ever
and ever;
a scepter of justice will be the
scepter of your kingdom.
9You have loved righteousness and
hated wickedness;
therefore God, your God, has set you
above your companions[p]
by anointing you with the oil[q] of joy."[e]

1:1 [a] Jn 9:29; Heb 2:2, 3 [b] Ac 2:30 [c] Nu 12:6, 8 **1:2** [d] Ps 2:8 [e] Jn 1:3 **1:3** [f] Jn 1:14 [g] Col 1:17 [h] Heb 7:27 [i] Mk 16:19 **1:4** [j] Eph 1:21; Php 2:9, 10 **1:5** [k] Ps 2:7 [l] 2Sa 7:14 **1:6** [m] Heb 10:5 [n] Dt 32:43 (LXX and DSS); Ps 97:7 **1:7** [o] Ps 104:4 **1:9** [p] Php 2:9 [q] Isa 61:1, 3

[a] 5 Psalm 2:7 [b] 5 2 Samuel 7:14; 1 Chron. 17:13
[c] 6 Deut. 32:43 (see Dead Sea Scrolls and Septuagint)
[d] 7 Psalm 104:4 [e] 9 Psalm 45:6,7

1:1–2 These two verses represent perhaps the most articulate Greek prose in the NT, modeled after old Attic Greek (as the most elite works were). One literary device here is alliteration (five Greek words beginning with a *p* sound in v. 1). The author apparently also models some of his language on the opening of the prologue to the popular Jewish Apocryphal book of Sirach. The author here depicts Christ as God's ultimate Word; his Jewish contemporaries identified God's Word with his Wisdom (cf. Sirach 24:1,23; Baruch 3:28—4:1). Jewish tradition developed further the Biblical image of God creating everything through Wisdom or his Word (cf. Ps 33:6; Pr 8:27–30; see note on Jn 1:1). As the fullness of the Word, Christ was superior to the authentic but partial revelation of God in the law.
1:2 *these last days.* The promised end time (Isa 2:2; Eze 38:16; Hos 3:5; Mic 4:1), initiated by the Lord's first coming. *heir.* An heir held title to the property of the one who appointed him heir.
1:3 *radiance.* The Greek term used here evokes the Jewish Apocryphal work Wisdom of Solomon 7:26, in which Wisdom reflects God's light and is a mirror revealing his image. (Philo applies the language to the *Logos*, the Word.) *exact representation of his being.* Jewish authors writing in Greek sometimes said that divine Wisdom was the exact "image" (cf. KJV) of God, the prototypical stamp by which he "imprinted" the seal of his image on the rest of creation (the way an image was stamped on coins). *he had provided purification for sins.* "Purification" of sins was the work of priests; mention of it here anticipates a theme that appears later in the book. *sat down at the right hand of the Majesty.* Sitting down at the right hand of the supreme king was an image of ultimate honor and alludes to Ps 110:1 (see explicitly Heb 1:13).
1:4 *superior to the angels.* Because Christ is greater than the angels who mediated the law (2:2), the punishment for neglecting his salvation is also greater than the punishment for rejecting the law (2:1–4). Some may have also been tempted to reduce Jesus' divine status to the status of a mere angel to better accommodate their synagogue critics; some Diaspora Jews even allowed angels a role in creation. Jesus, however, is greater than angels (2:5–18).
1:5 *to which of the angels did God ever say...?* The author brackets vv. 5–14 by repeating in v. 13 this question from v. 5 (quoting Ps 110:1 in v. 13). *You are my Son ... will be my Son.* The Dead Sea Scrolls show that other Jews also linked Ps 2:7 with 2Sa 7:14 (both cited in this verse) in expectations of the Messiah. *Son ... Son.* Jewish interpreters often linked texts on the basis of a common key word. Like several other Messianic texts, Ps 2 (cited first in this verse) originally celebrated the promise to the Davidic line in 2Sa 7 (cited second in this verse). *become.* This "begetting" (cf. KJV) referred to the royal coronation—in Jesus' case, his exaltation (cf. similarly Ac 13:33).
1:6 *firstborn.* Specified the inheritance rights of the oldest son (Dt 21:17); it is a title of the Davidic king of Ps 89:26–27. *Let all God's angels worship him.* To Jesus' coronation as king and consequent superiority to the angels, the author applies a text from the Greek translation of Dt 32:43, from a context that Diaspora Jews used for worship alongside the Psalms. (The words also appear in some of the early Hebrew manuscripts as well.)
1:7 *spirits ... fire.* Ps 104:4 (cited in this verse) may mean that God uses winds and fire as his messengers; early Jewish thinkers, however, understood it as saying that angels were made of fire. (Many Greeks thought that stars and souls consisted of fire or breath.) Hebrews shows that angels, unlike the Son, are of a lesser nature than God (v. 8).
1:8–9 Ps 45 may have been composed for a royal wedding celebration, but part of it speaks of God's blessing on the king and probably (certainly in the Greek version cited here) addresses God directly. Jewish interpreters read as much literal significance into a passage as they could. Because God is addressed in Ps 45:6 (cited in Heb 1:8), it is natural to assume that he continues to be addressed in Ps 45:7 (cited in v. 9). This allows the author to distinguish the Father ("God" in Ps 45:7, who exalts the one addressed as "God" in Ps 45:6) and the Son (addressed in Ps 45:6).

[10]He also says,

> "In the beginning, Lord, you laid the
> foundations of the earth,
> and the heavens are the work of
> your hands.
> [11]They will perish, but you remain;
> they will all wear out like a
> garment.[r]
> [12]You will roll them up like a robe;
> like a garment they will be changed.
> But you remain the same,[s]
> and your years will never end."[a][t]

[13]To which of the angels did God ever say,

> "Sit at my right hand
> until I make your enemies
> a footstool[u] for your feet"[b]?[v]

[14]Are not all angels ministering spirits[w] sent to serve those who will inherit salvation?[x]

Warning to Pay Attention

2 We must pay the most careful attention, therefore, to what we have
heard, so that we do not drift away. [2]For
since the message spoken[y] through angels[z] was binding, and every violation
and disobedience received its just punishment,[a] [3]how shall we escape if we
ignore so great a salvation?[b] This salvation, which was first announced by the
Lord,[c] was confirmed to us by those who
heard him.[d] [4]God also testified to it by
signs, wonders and various miracles,[e] and
by gifts of the Holy Spirit[f] distributed according to his will.[g]

Jesus Made Fully Human

[5]It is not to angels that he has subjected the world to come, about which we
are speaking. [6]But there is a place where
someone has testified:

> "What is mankind that you are mindful
> of them,
> a son of man that you care for him?[h]
> [7]You made them a little[c] lower than the
> angels;
> you crowned them with glory and
> honor
> [8] and put everything under their
> feet."[d,e][i]

In putting everything under them,[f] God left nothing that is not subject to them.[f] Yet at present we do not see everything

1:11 [r]Isa 34:4 **1:12** [s]Heb 13:8 [t]Ps 102:25-27 **1:13** [u]Jos 10:24; Heb 10:13 [v]Ps 110:1 **1:14** [w]Ps 103:20 [x]Heb 5:9 **2:2** [y]Heb 1:1 [z]Dt 33:2; Ac 7:53 [a]Heb 10:28 **2:3** [b]Heb 10:29 [c]Heb 1:2 [d]Lk 1:2 **2:4** [e]Jn 4:48 [f]1Co 12:4 [g]Eph 1:5 **2:6** [h]Job 7:17 **2:8** [i]Ps 8:4-6; 1Co 15:25

[a] *12* Psalm 102:25-27 [b] *13* Psalm 110:1
[c] *7* Or *them for a little while* [d] *6-8* Psalm 8:4-6
[e] *7,8* Or *[7]You made him a little lower than the angels;/ you crowned him with glory and honor/ [8]and put everything under his feet."* [f] *8* Or *him*

1:12 *your years will never end.* Interpreters frequently connected texts on the basis of a common key word or concept; because God's "throne … will last for ever and ever" (v. 8), the writer cites here Ps 102:25 – 27, where it says that God's faithfulness and "years will never end."
1:13 *Sit at my right hand.* Given links among texts (see note on v. 12), the Son's "throne" (v. 8) shows the Son at the Father's "right hand," as in Ps 110:1. (Jewish people already also spoke of Wisdom being beside God's throne.) In context, the Lord addressed in Ps 110:1 is also the priest-king of Ps 110:4, a text that the author develops starting in Heb 5:6. This is the third citation from the section of Ps 102 – 110 since Heb 1:7, and the sixth citation from Psalms since 1:5.
1:14 *Are not all angels ministering spirits … ?* The author has just suggested from Scripture that "angels" are "spirits" who serve (v. 7). Guardian angels of individuals were already familiar in Jewish tradition.
2:2 *the message spoken through angels.* Jewish tradition held that God had given his law through angels (also Ac 7:53; Gal 3:19; cf. Dt 33:2, especially in the Septuagint, the pre-Christian Greek translation of the OT).
2:3 *ignore so great a salvation.* The law, and therefore Jewish tradition, punished deliberate acts much more harshly than unintentional ones (Nu 15:27 – 31). Some Jewish teachers even viewed deliberate rejection of God's law as unforgivable. Jewish teachers sometimes argued from lesser to greater; here, if neglecting the law mediated through angels (v. 2) merited judgment, how much more does neglecting Christ, who is greater than such angels (vv. 1 – 14)?
2:5 *It is not to angels.* It may be that because some Jewish people criticized Christians' worship of Jesus as the worship of a second god, in the second century some Jewish believers in Jesus argued that he was merely a great angel. If some of Hebrews' audience already found such an approach attractive, however, Hebrews clearly closes off that possibility here.
2:6 *there is a place where someone has testified.* Jewish interpreters sometimes used ambiguous phrases to emphasize that the divine authorship matters more than the human authorship. *son of man.* Although Jesus is the Son of Man in the Gospels, the writer of Hebrews simply follows the standard Greek translation here, referring to human beings.
2:7 *made them a little lower than the angels.* The Greek translation of the passage cited here, Ps 8 interprets the Hebrew "a little lower than God" (the simplest Hebrew sense) as "a little lower than the angels" (certainly a possible translation); the writer of Hebrews uses this translation, which his audience knows.
2:8 *put everything under their feet.* Jewish interpreters often connected texts based on similar language; because God would make Jesus' enemies a "footstool for [his] feet" (1:13), the author can now cite another text about things being put under feet. In Hebrew, Ps 8:4 – 6 (cited in vv. 6 – 8) announces that God generously set people over his creation, a little lower than himself (alluding to Ge 1:26 – 27). *we do not see everything subject to them.* Interpreters often established first what a text could not mean; it was obvious that people were not ruling creation the way God intended in the beginning. Jewish tradition recognized both that angels ruled nature and the nations in the present and that the righteous would reign in the age to come (cf. 1:14). Interpreting Ps 8:4 – 6 in Heb 2:6 – 8a, the writer of Hebrews recognizes that the world is not presently subject to humanity, the way God designed it to be. Yet Jesus is now exalted (v. 9), a forerunner for the future exaltation of all God's children (v. 10). (Cf. the idea of a New Adam in Ro 5:12 – 21 and the article "Adam in Jewish Tradition," p. 1957.)

subject to them.[a] 9But we do see Jesus,
who was made lower than the angels for a
little while, now crowned with glory and
honor[j] because he suffered death,[k] so that
by the grace of God he might taste death
for everyone.[l]
10In bringing many sons and daughters
to glory, it was fitting that God, for whom
and through whom everything exists,[m]
should make the pioneer of their salvation
perfect through what he suffered.[n] 11Both
the one who makes people holy and those
who are made holy[o] are of the same family. So Jesus is not ashamed to call them
brothers and sisters.[bp] 12He says,

"I will declare your name to my
brothers and sisters;
in the assembly I will sing your
praises."[cq]

13And again,

"I will put my trust in him."[dr]

And again he says,

"Here am I, and the children God has
given me."[es]

2:9 [j] Ac 2:33; 3:13; Php 2:9 [k] Php 2:7-9 [l] Jn 3:16; 2Co 5:15 **2:10** [m] Ro 11:36 [n] Lk 24:26; Heb 7:28 **2:11** [o] Heb 10:10 [p] Mt 28:10; Jn 20:17 **2:12** [q] Ps 22:22 **2:13** [r] Isa 8:17 [s] Isa 8:18; Jn 10:29

[a] *8* Or *him* [b] *11* The Greek word for *brothers and sisters* (*adelphoi*) refers here to believers, both men and women, as part of God's family; also in verse 12; and in 3:1, 12; 10:19; 13:22. [c] *12* Psalm 22:22 [d] *13* Isaiah 8:17 [e] *13* Isaiah 8:18

2:9 *lower than the angels.* Fitting the language of the psalm that the author of Hebrews quoted in v. 7, Jesus embraced humanity to restore humanity (cf. v. 14). *crowned with glory.* Now Jesus is exalted, experiencing God's unrealized purpose for humanity, as noted in v. 7.
2:10 *for whom and through whom everything exists.* A phrase used by some philosophers and Diaspora Jews to describe the supreme God (cf. 1Co 8:6). *pioneer.* The Greek term applied to heroes, founders and champions, sometimes to a forerunner who paved the way for others, as here.
2:11 *brothers and sisters.* The author of Hebrews here anticipates his quotation from Isa 8:18 in v. 13; Jesus is there identified as one of "the children."
2:12 *I will declare your name to my brothers and sisters.* Some psalms, including Ps 22 (cited here), depict a righteous sufferer; Jesus fills this role most fully (see quotations and echoes of Ps 22 in, e.g., Mt 27:43; Mk 15:29,34; Jn 19:24). Yet the author of Hebrews, like Jesus, knew that the psalm went on to declare God's deliverance, including in Ps 22:22. There the triumphant psalmist declares God's "name to [his] brothers and sisters" (although the NIV translates differently there in order to capture the meaning).
2:13 The writer may cite Isa 8:17 – 18 here for several reasons. On the most basic level, Jewish interpreters sometimes simply echoed a text that made the point; this one reinforces the point in vv. 11 – 12. More fundamentally for Isa 8:17, the context in Isaiah depicts God as a stone that causes the wicked to stumble (Isa 8:14 – 15); using the Jewish technique of linking texts with similar key terms, early Christians sometimes linked this text with other "stones" and with Jesus (Ps 118:22; Isa 28:16; see Ro 9:32 – 33; 1Pe 2:6 – 8). *and the children God has given me.* Isa 8:18 in context indicates that Isaiah's children have names that communicate God's message to Israel. One of Isaiah's children pointed toward Immanuel, God with us (Isa 7:14; 9:6 – 7; see note on Mt 1:22 – 23), and this text declared the other children brothers.

THE "GREATER THANS" IN HEBREWS

One of the author's main points in Hebrews is that Jesus is greater than all those things associated with the Jewish religion and way of life. Sometimes he actually uses the words "greater than"; sometimes he does not. But in all cases the theme is clear.

THEME	PASSAGE IN HEBREWS
Jesus is greater than the prophets.	1:1–3
Jesus is greater than the angels.	1:4–14; 2:5
Jesus is greater than Moses.	3:1–6
Jesus is greater than Joshua.	4:6–11
Jesus is greater than the Aaronic high priests.	5:1–10; 7:26—8:2
Jesus is greater than the Levitical priests.	6:20—7:25
Jesus as the high priest in the order of Melchizedek is greater than Abraham.	7:1–10
Jesus' ministry is greater than the tabernacle ministry.	8:3–6; 9:1–28
Jesus' new covenant is greater than the old covenant.	8:7–13
Jesus' sacrifice is greater than the OT sacrifices.	10:1–14
Experiencing Jesus is greater than the experience on Mount Sinai.	12:18–24

14Since the children have flesh and
blood, he too shared in their humanity[t] so that by his death he might break
the power[u] of him who holds the power
of death — that is, the devil[v] — 15and free
those who all their lives were held in slavery by their fear[w] of death. 16For surely it
is not angels he helps, but Abraham's descendants. 17For this reason he had to be
made like them,[a][x] fully human in every
way, in order that he might become a merciful[y] and faithful high priest[z] in service
to God,[a] and that he might make atonement for the sins of the people. 18Because
he himself suffered when he was tempted, he is able to help those who are being
tempted.[b]

Jesus Greater Than Moses

3 Therefore, holy brothers and sisters,[c]
who share in the heavenly calling,
fix your thoughts on Jesus, whom we
acknowledge[d] as our apostle and high
priest.[e] 2He was faithful to the one who
appointed him, just as Moses was faithful
in all God's house.[f] 3Jesus has been found
worthy of greater honor than Moses, just
as the builder of a house has greater honor
than the house itself. 4For every house is
built by someone, but God is the builder of
everything. 5"Moses was faithful as a servant[g] in all God's house,"[b][h] bearing witness to what would be spoken by God in
the future. 6But Christ is faithful as the Son[i]
over God's house. And we are his house,[j] if
indeed we hold firmly[k] to our confidence
and the hope[l] in which we glory.

2:14 [t] Jn 1:14 [u] 1Co 15:54-57; 2Ti 1:10 [v] 1Jn 3:8 **2:15** [w] 2Ti 1:7 **2:17** [x] Php 2:7 [y] Heb 5:2 [z] Heb 4:14, 15; 7:26, 28 [a] Heb 5:1 **2:18** [b] Heb 4:15 **3:1** [c] Heb 2:11 [d] Heb 4:14 [e] Heb 2:17 **3:2** [f] Nu 12:7 **3:5** [g] Ex 14:31 [h] ver 2; Nu 12:7 **3:6** [i] Heb 1:2 [j] 1Co 3:16 [k] Ro 11:22 [l] Ro 5:2 **3:7** [m] Heb 9:8 **3:9** [n] Ac 7:36

Warning Against Unbelief

7So, as the Holy Spirit says:[m]

"Today, if you hear his voice,
8 do not harden your hearts
as you did in the rebellion,
during the time of testing in the wilderness,
9where your ancestors tested and tried me,
though for forty years they saw what I did.[n]
10That is why I was angry with that generation;
I said, 'Their hearts are always going astray,
and they have not known my ways.'

[a] 17 Or *like his brothers* [b] 5 Num. 12:7

2:14 *the children.* These children are Jesus' brothers and sisters, as suggested in vv. 11,13; see note on v. 13. *flesh and blood.* A common way of describing humans. *him who holds the power of death ... the devil.* Many Jewish sources recognized the devil as the originator of death (cf. note on Jn 8:44).
2:15 *fear of death.* Philosophers tried to overcome this fear, which they viewed as a fundamental problem; most explained that the fear did not accomplish anything positive, some (such as Epicureans) arguing that death was annihilation and others (such as Stoics) arguing that cooperating with Fate was the most reasonable course. Jesus overcame our enslavement to the fear of death not by assuaging anxiety but by truly overcoming death. Death was not part of God's original design for humanity (vv. 7 – 8), though creation was perishable (cf. divine eternality, 1:8,12).
2:17 *he had to be made like them.* In antiquity, the powerful might show compassion for the weak, but they never made themselves weak to be like them. By contrast, as God chose human high priests as mediators (cf., e.g., Nu 16:44 – 48), Jesus shared our humanity (vv. 9,14).
3:1 *the heavenly calling.* Many ancient thinkers would have appreciated anything "heavenly" (cf. also 6:4; 11:16; 12:22; see notes on 9:23; Col 3:1 – 2). *our apostle and high priest.* Although a few writers viewed Moses as a high priest and some viewed Moses as God's commissioned agent (like an apostle), most recognized that only Aaron and his descendants were high priests; Jesus is thus greater than Moses here.
3:2 *He was faithful ... just as Moses was faithful in all God's house.* In Nu 12:7 – 8, God exalts Moses above other prophets and affirms that "he is faithful in all my house." Jesus is a unique prophet like Moses (Dt 18:15 – 18), but see Heb 3:3 – 6.
3:3 *worthy of greater honor than Moses.* Ancient speakers often compared two honorable figures to show that the greater of these two was great indeed. Many Jewish traditions exalted Moses as the greatest person in history (or second only to Abraham). *the builder ... has greater honor than the house.* Jewish and Christian writers used the argument that the builder was greater than what was made to note that the Creator was greater than his creation (v. 4). This writer identifies Jesus as the Creator. Ancient writers often developed arguments based on wordplays; this writer plays on two senses of house: God's "house" (see vv. 2,5 – 6) and a "builder" (see vv. 3 – 4). (Playing on these senses of "house" occurs already in 2Sa 7:5,11,13,16.)
3:5 *bearing witness to what would be spoken by God in the future.* The author quotes Nu 12:7. Moses prefigured the promised prophet (Dt 18:15 – 18), and Jewish tradition suggested that he foresaw the Messianic era. Other elements of Moses' covenant prefigured heavenly realities (see note on Heb 8:5).
3:6 *faithful as the Son over God's house.* A servant (v. 5) could manage a household, but ancient sources often contrasted a mere servant with a son. An heir owns the household, which in antiquity could include servants.
3:7 — 4:13 Many Jewish people recited psalms in worship; at some point Ps 95 became a significant element in synagogue prayers. The writer comments on Ps 95:7 – 11 (cited in Heb 3:7 – 11) in the way that other Jewish Midrashic writers explained texts. (After this explanation the writer of Hebrews will in 5:6 turn to expounding Ps 110:4.) Ps 95 shows that Israel's wilderness generation rejected God's offer of rest in the promised land (cf. the promise of rest in Ex 33:14; Dt 3:20; 12:10; 25:19; Jos 1:13,15). Moreover, since God was still offering it after Joshua's day, the promise had never yet been completely fulfilled (Heb 4:8); the full promise remained available for a new generation — the time of the promised future restoration of God's people.
3:7 *the Holy Spirit says.* Jewish people recognized that God's Holy Spirit inspired and thus spoke through Scripture.

11 So I declared on oath in my anger,
‘They shall never enter my rest.’ [o]”[a][p]

12 See to it, brothers and sisters, that
none of you has a sinful, unbelieving heart
that turns away from the living God. 13 But
encourage one another daily,[q] as long as it
is called “Today,” so that none of you may
be hardened by sin’s deceitfulness.[r] 14 We
have come to share in Christ, if indeed we
hold[s] our original conviction firmly to the
very end. 15 As has just been said:

“Today, if you hear his voice,
do not harden your hearts
as you did in the rebellion.”[b][t]

16 Who were they who heard and rebelled? Were they not all those Moses
led out of Egypt?[u] 17 And with whom was
he angry for forty years? Was it not with
those who sinned, whose bodies perished
in the wilderness?[v] 18 And to whom did
God swear that they would never enter his
rest[w] if not to those who disobeyed?[x] 19 So
we see that they were not able to enter,
because of their unbelief.[y]

A Sabbath-Rest for the People of God

4 Therefore, since the promise of entering his rest still stands, let us be careful that none of you be found to have fall-
en short of it.[z] 2 For we also have had the
good news proclaimed to us, just as they
did; but the message they heard was of no
value to them, because they did not share
the faith of those who obeyed.[c][a] 3 Now we
who have believed enter that rest, just as
God has said,

“So I declared on oath in my anger,
‘They shall never enter my rest.’ ”[d][b]

And yet his works have been finished
since the creation of the world. 4 For somewhere he has spoken about the seventh
day in these words: “On the seventh day
God rested from all his works.”[e][c] 5 And
again in the passage above he says, “They
shall never enter my rest.”[d]

6 Therefore since it still remains for some
to enter that rest, and since those who formerly had the good news proclaimed to
them did not go in because of their disobedience,[e] 7 God again set a certain day,
calling it “Today.” This he did when a long
time later he spoke through David, as in
the passage already quoted:

“Today, if you hear his voice,
do not harden your hearts.”[b][f]

8 For if Joshua had given them rest,[g] God
would not have spoken[h] later about another day. 9 There remains, then, a Sabbath-
rest for the people of God; 10 for anyone
who enters God’s rest also rests from their
works,[f] just as God did from his.[i] 11 Let us,
therefore, make every effort to enter that
rest, so that no one will perish by following their example of disobedience.[j]

3:11 [o] Heb 4:3, 5 [p] Ps 95:7-11 **3:13** [q] Heb 10:24, 25 [r] Eph 4:22 **3:14** [s] ver 6 **3:15** [t] ver 7, 8; Ps 95:7, 8 **3:16** [u] Nu 14:2 **3:17** [v] Nu 14:29; Ps 106:26 **3:18** [w] Nu 14:20-23 [x] Heb 4:6 **3:19** [y] Jn 3:36 **4:1** [z] Heb 12:15 **4:2** [a] 1Th 2:13
4:3 [b] Ps 95:11; Heb 3:11 **4:4** [c] Ge 2:2, 3; Ex 20:11 **4:5** [d] Ps 95:11 **4:6** [e] Heb 3:18 **4:7** [f] Ps 95:7, 8; Heb 3:7, 8, 15 **4:8** [g] Jos 22:4 [h] Heb 1:1 **4:10** [i] ver 4 **4:11** [j] Heb 3:18

[a] *11* Psalm 95:7-11 [b] *15,7* Psalm 95:7,8 [c] *2* Some manuscripts *because those who heard did not combine it with faith* [d] *3* Psalm 95:11; also in verse 5 [e] *4* Gen. 2:2 [f] *10* Or *labor*

3:11 *They shall never enter my rest.* Some Jewish thinkers debated whether the wilderness generation was excluded from rest only in this age, or also barred from the world to come. Highlighting their rebellion, the writer of Hebrews may see them as barred from both.
3:13 *as long as it is called "Today."* As Jewish interpreters often highlighted a term's applicability for their generation, the writer emphasizes the psalm's continued offer of rest today (v. 7, citing Ps 95:7).
3:14 *if indeed we hold our original conviction.* God's own people, whom he had already redeemed, rebelled rather than persevered (vv. 8 – 10, citing Ps 95:8 – 10) and thus were barred from God's promise (Ps 95:11); perseverance was thus essential.
3:16 – 18 Writers sometimes reinforced a point rhetorically with a series of questions, the answers to which were clear.
3:19 *because of their unbelief.* Scripture was clear that failure to trust God's promise lay behind their failure to obey him (cf. Nu 14:11; Dt 1:32; 9:23; Ps 78:22; 106:24).
4:1 *let us be careful.* The psalmist warned new generations (3:7) not to reject the gift of God's rest (3:11).
4:2 *they did not share the faith of those who obeyed.* Israel in the wilderness lacked faith (3:19) to embrace God's promise of rest (3:8 – 11); the good news about Christ offers a new opportunity for those who will exercise faith (v. 3).
4:3 *believed.* Cf. 3:19 and note. *rest.* See 3:11.
4:4 *somewhere he has spoken about.* For the ambiguity of "somewhere," see note on 2:6. *On the seventh day God rested.* Because in v. 3 the author speaks of people entering God's "rest" (citing Ps 95:11), the author elaborates on the meaning of God's rest. The author notes here in v. 4 that God rested from his work of creating (citing Ge 2:2). (Jewish interpreters often used one text to interpret another on the same subject or with the same wording.) Some Jewish thinkers viewed the coming world as the ultimate Sabbath (cf. v. 9).
4:6 *since it still remains for some to enter that rest.* See notes on v. 2; 3:13. Ps 95:11 shows that the promised rest remained to be fulfilled.
4:8 *if Joshua had given them rest.* Not only did Moses' generation never enter God's rest (vv. 2 – 3,5), but neither was the promise completed in Joshua's day. God gave Israel rest then (Jos 22:4; 23:1), but if it were completed, the author argues, God would not afterward offer it "today." Although Israel had defeated many cities, the local peoples remained and Israel had not yet settled all the land (Jos 13:1 – 5; 23:4; Jdg 1:19,21,27 – 36). Only the generations of David (cf. 2Sa 7:1,11; 8:10), Solomon (1Ch 22:9) and to a lesser extent Josiah (2Ch 34:1 – 7) came close to reaching the boundaries promised to Abraham, and testing and enemies never disappeared for very long. In the author's day, the Jewish people, existing under foreign domination, prayed for God to fulfill his promises and restore the kingdom to Israel.
4:9 *There remains, then, a Sabbath-rest.* The author has already connected God's rest in Ps 95:11 with God's rest from his works in Ge 2:2.

12For the word of God[k] is alive and active.[l] Sharper than any double-edged sword,[m] it penetrates even to dividing soul and spirit, joints and marrow; it judges the thoughts and attitudes of the heart.[n] 13Nothing in all creation is hidden from God's sight.[o] Everything is uncovered and laid bare before the eyes of him to whom we must give account.

Jesus the Great High Priest

14Therefore, since we have a great high priest who has ascended into heaven,[a][p] Jesus the Son of God, let us hold firmly to the faith we profess.[q] 15For we do not have a high priest who is unable to empathize with our weaknesses, but we have one who has been tempted in every way, just as we are[r]—yet he did not sin.[s] 16Let us then approach God's throne of grace with confidence, so that we may receive mercy and find grace to help us in our time of need.

5 Every high priest is selected from among the people and is appointed to represent the people in matters related to God, to offer gifts and sacrifices[t] for sins.[u] 2He is able to deal gently with those who are ignorant and are going astray,[v] since he himself is subject to weakness.[w] 3This is why he has to offer sacrifices for his own sins, as well as for the sins of the people.[x] 4And no one takes this honor on himself, but he receives it when called by God, just as Aaron was.[y]

5In the same way, Christ did not take on himself the glory[z] of becoming a high priest. But God said[a] to him,

"You are my Son;
today I have become your Father."[b][b]

6And he says in another place,

"You are a priest forever,
in the order of Melchizedek."[c][c]

4:12 [k] 1Pe 1:23 [l] Jer 23:29 [m] Eph 6:17; Rev 1:16 [n] 1Co 14:24,25 **4:13** [o] Ps 33:13-15 **4:14** [p] Heb 6:20 [q] Heb 3:1 **4:15** [r] Heb 2:18 [s] 2Co 5:21

5:1 [t] Heb 8:3 [u] Heb 7:27 **5:2** [v] Heb 2:18 [w] Heb 7:28 **5:3** [x] Heb 7:27; 9:7 **5:4** [y] Ex 28:1 **5:5** [z] Jn 8:54 [a] Heb 1:1 [b] Ps 2:7 **5:6** [c] Ps 110:4; Heb 7:17,21

[a] 14 Greek *has gone through the heavens*
[b] 5 Psalm 2:7 [c] 6 Psalm 110:4

4:12 *the word of God is alive and active.* Moses announced the word of God to Israel, and the recipients of this letter encountered it in the good news of Christ (see v. 2). *dividing soul and spirit, joints and marrow.* Jewish tradition, following Scripture, recognized that God could discern even the hidden details of people's hearts (e.g., Ps 139:23). The Alexandrian Jewish philosopher Philo spoke of the power of the universal, divine *Logos*, divine reason, God's word, to divide rational and irrational components of the soul; yet he also sometimes identified spirit and soul, as the NT writers usually do. The point here is not an analysis of human nature, but that God's word searches the heart so deeply that it resembles a sharp sword that divides even what seems almost indivisible, whether soul and spirit or joints and marrow.
4:14–16 The author's argument for Jesus' high priesthood comes especially from Ps 110:4 (cited explicitly in Heb 5:6). At least some Diaspora Jews depicted God's word (v. 12) as high priest but tried to play down the high priest's full humanity when he interceded for Israel. Hebrews' author, by contrast, emphasizes Jesus the high priest identifying with humanity (v. 15; 2:17–18).
4:14 *ascended into heaven.* For the heavenly sanctuary, see note on 8:5.
4:15 *we do not have a high priest who is unable to empathize with our weaknesses.* Although the recipients of Hebrews probably did not know this, many of Jerusalem's priestly elite were corrupt and abusive. The benevolent high priest here offers a stark contrast. *he did not sin.* See note on 5:3.
4:16 *Let us then approach God's throne of grace.* In the temple, the ark of the covenant of the Lord represented God's throne (e.g., 1Sa 4:4; 6:2; Ps 80:1; 99:1). But the ark was unapproachable, secluded in the Most Holy Place, which even the high priest could approach only once a year. Christ has opened full access to God to all his followers (Heb 10:19–20).
5:3 *he has to offer sacrifices for his own sins.* Like other high priests, Christ can sympathize with human weakness; but he is greater than they, since they must first atone for their own sin (Lev 9:7; 16:6), whereas Christ did not sin (Heb 4:15).
5:4 *when called by God, just as Aaron was.* The writer of Hebrews and his Diaspora audience would think of the Biblical high priest, not the political situation in Judea. There Rome or, more recently, Agrippa II, installed and deposed high priests as they deemed fit (cf. note on Jn 19:11).
5:5 *Christ did not take on himself the glory.* The writer of Hebrews shows from Ps 2:7 (cited here and already applied to Jesus in Heb 1:5) that Jesus' royal exaltation was the Father's initiative.
5:6 *a priest forever, in the order of Melchizedek.* If, as in 1:5, Ps 2:7 (the royal verse the author has just cited in Heb 5:5) applied to Jesus, the author can move naturally to another psalm about Jesus' royal exaltation cited in 1:13—namely, Ps 110. The context in that psalm showed clearly that this exalted king was also a special, "priest forever in the order of Melchizedek" (Ps 110:4, cited here in Heb 5:6). (Like Ps 2:7, Ps 110:4 addresses the exalted one; God's "rest" in Ps 95:11 might also recall the "sitting" of Ps 110:1, but that potential connection is less clear here.) Because Ps 110 speaks of a priest-king, it naturally cites the figure of Melchizedek, also a priest-king (Ge 14:18). This image may have evoked nostalgia for some Jews: before full Roman control and Herod's dynasty, Israel had a celebrated dynasty of heroic priest-kings, the Maccabees. Some Jews disliked this combination of kings descended from Levi; the Dead Sea Scrolls, e.g., longed for a future appointed ruler from Judah and a future anointed priest from Levi. But because Melchizedek's priesthood was not Levitical, the promised Davidic king, the Messiah (cf. Heb 7:14), could be a priest-king. Some Jewish circles, including those that produced the Dead Sea Scrolls, exalted Melchizedek as a heavenly figure, perhaps an angel (a view the writer of Hebrews rejects in 2:5–18). The author of Hebrews, however, needs only to cite Ps 110 in order for his audience to recognize that this priest is exalted to heaven (as the Lord beside God's throne in Ps 110:1). The writer's argument was strong enough that later rabbis tried to get around it, claiming (without textual support) that God took the priesthood from Melchizedek and gave it to Abraham (cf. Heb 7:7)!

7During the days of Jesus' life on earth,
he offered up prayers and petitions with
fervent cries and tears[d] to the one who
could save him from death, and he was
heard because of his reverent submission.[e]
8Son though he was, he learned obedience
from what he suffered[f] 9and, once made
perfect,[g] he became the source of eternal
salvation for all who obey him 10and was
designated by God to be high priest[h] in the
order of Melchizedek.[i]

Warning Against Falling Away

6:4-6Ref — Heb 10:26-31

11We have much to say about this, but
it is hard to make it clear to you because
you no longer try to understand. 12In fact,
though by this time you ought to be teachers, you need someone to teach you the
elementary truths[j] of God's word all over
again. You need milk, not solid food![k]
13Anyone who lives on milk, being still an
infant,[l] is not acquainted with the teaching about righteousness. 14But solid food
is for the mature,[m] who by constant use
have trained themselves to distinguish
good from evil.[n]

6

Therefore let us move beyond[o] the elementary teachings[p] about Christ and
be taken forward to maturity, not laying
again the foundation of repentance from
acts that lead to death,[a][q] and of faith in
God, 2instruction about cleansing rites,[b][r]
the laying on of hands,[s] the resurrection
of the dead,[t] and eternal judgment. 3And
God permitting,[u] we will do so.
4It is impossible for those who have
once been enlightened,[v] who have tasted
the heavenly gift,[w] who have shared in the
Holy Spirit,[x] 5who have tasted the goodness of the word of God and the powers
of the coming age 6and who have fallen[c]
away, to be brought back to repentance.[y]
To their loss they are crucifying the Son of
God all over again and subjecting him to
public disgrace. 7Land that drinks in the

5:7 [d] Mt 27:46, 50 [e] Mk 14:36 **5:8** [f] Php 2:8 **5:9** [g] Heb 2:10 **5:10** [h] ver 5 [i] ver 6 **5:12** [j] Heb 6:1 [k] 1Co 3:2; 1Pe 2:2 **5:13** [l] 1Co 14:20

5:14 [m] 1Co 2:6 [n] Isa 7:15 **6:1** [o] Php 3:12-14 [p] Heb 5:12 [q] Heb 9:14 **6:2** [r] Jn 3:25 [s] Ac 6:6 [t] Ac 17:18,32 **6:3** [u] Ac 18:21 **6:4** [v] Heb 10:32 [w] Eph 2:8 [x] Gal 3:2 **6:6** [y] 2Pe 2:21; 1Jn 5:16

[a] *1* Or *from useless rituals* [b] *2* Or *about baptisms* [c] *6* Or *age,* *6if they fall*

5:7 *he offered up prayers … with fervent cries and tears.* At Gethsemane Jesus cried (Mk 14:36; cf. Ps 22:5,24). *he was heard.* The Father answered not by preventing the cross, but by raising Jesus from the dead.
5:8 *he learned obedience from what he suffered.* In Greek, the writer plays on words: "learned" is *emathen*, and "suffered" is *epathen*. Ancient writers sometimes used wordplays to make a point, and this one was common in antiquity. Even aside from wordplays, however, ancient education included children learning through suffering, including physical discipline (cf. also 12:6).
5:9 *made perfect.* The Greek term here (also in 2:10; 7:28) is also the standard Greek way to translate an OT term for ordaining priests (e.g., Ex 29:9,29,33,35; Lev 16:32; Nu 3:3).
5:11—7:28 The author warns that his audience's Biblical knowledge is too basic to understand his entire argument in this section (5:11–14). Nevertheless he plunges into it, warning that they must press beyond these basics (6:1–3) so they can be sure to persevere (6:4–12).
5:11 *We have much to say about this.* Speakers and writers often warned that they were simply offering a portion of the vast evidence that could be offered (cf. 11:32).
5:12 *by this time you ought to be teachers.* Many ancient teachers recognized the value of beginning with the basics. Nevertheless, sages often complained that their students were slow to understand or that by now they should be teachers. *elementary truths.* The Greek term could apply to something as simple as the alphabet; the writer lists such basic teachings in 6:1–2. *You need milk, not solid food!* Teachers spoke of giving milk to elementary students, as if to infants, but solid food to more advanced disciples, whom they considered mature. (Although people used milk from goats, sheep and even cows, the image here is of an infant nursing at their mother's or nurse's breast; cf. note on 1Co 3:1.)
5:14 *trained themselves.* This phrase includes a Greek term meaning "senses" or "sensory faculties." Although the term can apply figuratively to rational sense, many philosophers also discussed the proper use of physical senses (which they often numbered as five). *distinguish good from evil.* Despite limitations of the senses, many thinkers believed that the senses were useful and could be disciplined for moral benefit. Far more widely, the ability to critically "distinguish good from evil," i.e., between truth and falsehood, was valued, including in Scripture (2Sa 14:17; 1Ki 3:9).
6:1 *elementary teachings … maturity.* See note on 5:12. The teachings listed in vv. 1–2 were matters that the Jewish recipients of Hebrews would have understood even before becoming Jesus' followers. *acts that lead to death.* May mean (also in 9:14) simply useless works (cf. similar wording in Jas 2:17,26).
6:2 *instruction about cleansing rites.* Jewish people had many cleansing rites, including washing of hands and immersing new converts. *the laying on of hands.* Probably refers to ordaining teachers (see note on Ac 6:6), though hands were laid also on sacrifices and for blessings. *the resurrection … and eternal judgment.* See, e.g., Da 12:2.
6:4 *once been enlightened.* Jewish people sometimes prayed to be enlightened in understanding Scripture (see note on Eph 1:18), but the experience here refers to conversion (see Heb 10:32). (The Qumran sect also believed that God had enlightened them, making them children of light.) *shared in the Holy Spirit.* Early Christians and (typically in a less dramatic way) Qumranites believed that members of their own groups experienced the Holy Spirit, but most Jewish people believed that only a few worthy people experienced that gift in this age. The Spirit was more widely expected in the coming age (v. 5).
6:5 *tasted the goodness.* Perhaps could evoke the language of Ps 34:8, even though the Greek translation of that passage replaces "good" with "kind." *tasted … the powers of the coming age.* Jewish people expected a coming age of righteousness, justice and peace for their people. Many expected the coming of the Messiah to inaugurate that era of God's reign. Because Jesus the Messiah has already come, his followers experience a foretaste of what will be consummated at his return.
6:6 *to be brought back to repentance.* God held to a higher standard those who should have known better (Nu 14:22–23). Many Jewish circles believed that apostates, or at least the most heinous of them, could never be forgiven. The present text warns of a level of provoking God that makes repentance impossible (cf. 3:8–11; 12:17;

rain often falling on it and that produces a
crop useful to those for whom it is farmed
receives the blessing of God. 8 But land
that produces thorns and thistles is worthless and is in danger of being cursed.[z] In
the end it will be burned.
9 Even though we speak like this,
dear friends,[a] we are convinced of better things in your case — the things that
have to do with salvation. 10 God is not
unjust; he will not forget your work and
the love you have shown him as you
have helped his people and continue
to help them.[b] 11 We want each of you
to show this same diligence to the very
end, so that what you hope[c] for may be
fully realized. 12 We do not want you to
become lazy, but to imitate[d] those who
through faith and patience[e] inherit what
has been promised.[f]

The Certainty of God's Promise

13 When God made his promise to Abraham, since there was no one greater for
him to swear by, he swore by himself,[g]
14 saying, "I will surely bless you and give
you many descendants."[a][h] 15 And so after
waiting patiently, Abraham received what
was promised.[i]
16 People swear by someone greater than
themselves, and the oath confirms what
is said and puts an end to all argument.[j]
17 Because God wanted to make the unchanging[k] nature of his purpose very clear
to the heirs of what was promised,[l] he
confirmed it with an oath. 18 God did this
so that, by two unchangeable things in
which it is impossible for God to lie,[m] we
who have fled to take hold of the hope[n] set
before us may be greatly encouraged. 19 We
have this hope as an anchor for the soul,
firm and secure. It enters the inner sanctuary behind the curtain,[o] 20 where our forerunner, Jesus, has entered on our behalf.[p]
He has become a high priest[q] forever, in
the order of Melchizedek.[r]

Melchizedek the Priest

7 This Melchizedek was king of Salem
and priest of God Most High.[s] He met
Abraham returning from the defeat of the
kings and blessed him,[t] 2 and Abraham
gave him a tenth of everything. First, the

6:8 [z] Ge 3:17, 18; Isa 5:6 **6:9** [a] 1Co 10:14 **6:10** [b] Mt 10:40, 42; 25:40; 1Th 1:3 **6:11** [c] Heb 3:6 **6:12** [d] Heb 13:7 [e] 2Th 1:4; Jas 1:3; Rev 13:10 [f] Heb 10:36 **6:13** [g] Ge 22:16; Lk 1:73 **6:14** [h] Ge 22:17 **6:15** [i] Ge 21:5 **6:16** [j] Ex 22:11 **6:17** [k] Ps 110:4 [l] Heb 11:9 **6:18** [m] Nu 23:19; Titus 1:2 [n] Heb 3:6 **6:19** [o] Lev 16:2; Heb 9:2, 3, 7 **6:20** [p] Heb 4:14 [q] Heb 2:17 [r] Heb 5:6 **7:1** [s] Mk 5:7 [t] Ge 14:18-20

[a] *14* Gen. 22:17

contrast Jas 5:19 – 20). It addresses believers deliberately turning from truth (cf. Heb 2:2 – 3; 12:25), though salvation can be found through no one else but Christ (10:26). *they are crucifying the Son of God all over again.* By willfully embracing the kind of belief that nailed Jesus to the cross, they accept responsibility again for killing him. *subjecting him to public disgrace.* Crucifixion made a public example of its victims, openly killing them by slow and painful torture and disgracing them as they hung naked, their most private parts and bodily functions exposed to passersby.

6:8 *thorns and thistles.* Some other ancient writers used "thorns and thistles" figuratively for moral desolation.

6:9 *we are convinced of better things in your case.* Often a writer would soften warnings by assuring a more trustworthy audience that he was confident that the audience would not fail. For the reason for the writer's assurance here, see v. 10.

6:12 *imitate.* Sages frequently cited models for hearers to imitate (some are listed in ch. 11). *inherit.* Jewish tradition spoke of the righteous inheriting the world to come.

6:13 *he swore by himself.* Interpreters often connected texts based on a common key word or phrase — sometimes even without quoting the phrase. God swore by himself (Ge 22:16) the promise to Abraham (Ge 22:17, cited in Heb 6:14) — just as God swore that the exalted king would be a priest like Melchizedek (Ps 110:4), although the writer has not yet quoted the line about the oath (see Heb 7:21). God had also sworn that the wilderness generation would never enter his rest (see Ps 95:11 in Heb 3:11; 4:3).

6:15 *what was promised.* The writer probably refers to Isaac's birth in Ge 21:1, from whom came countless descendants (Heb 11:12), though some of God's promise remains future (11:10,39).

6:16 *People swear by someone greater than themselves.* Jewish people counted oaths that directly called God to attest their veracity as particularly inviolable; God swore such oaths by himself or his holiness in Ge 22:16; Ps 89:35; Isa 45:23; Jer 22:5; 44:26; 49:13; 51:14; Am 4:2; 6:8; 8:7.

6:17 *unchanging nature of his purpose.* Sometimes God swore oaths that included the assurance that God would not change his mind (Ps 110:4; 132:11; Isa 45:23).

6:18 *impossible for God to lie.* Jewish people recognized that God never lies (Nu 23:19; 1Sa 15:29), but the writer here may focus on the two divine oaths in the passages that he has been mentioning: the oath to Abraham (Ge 22:16) in v. 13 and the oath to the (greater) priest-king like Melchizedek (Ps 110:4; see note on Heb 6:13).

6:19 *anchor for the soul.* This work's original audience would not find this image strange; people in the Diaspora often used the anchor image figuratively. *the inner sanctuary behind the curtain.* Because the writer is still thinking of the exalted priest-king like Melchizedek (cf. note on v. 13; see v. 20), he thinks of the heavenly sanctuary (see 8:1 – 2). *behind the curtain.* Implies inside the temple's Most Holy Place (9:3; Ex 26:33; Lev 16:2). The earthly high priest could enter this place once a year (Heb 9:25), but the writer refers here to the heavenly temple (v. 20; see note on 8:5).

6:20 *forerunner.* Presupposes those who follow (cf. the related idea in the different term "pioneer" in 2:10; 12:2; see note on 2:10). a *high priest forever ... Melchizedek.* Quotes again from Ps 110:4.

7:1 – 10 Ps 110:4, just cited in 6:20, declares that the exalted king is "in the order of Melchizedek"; the author of Hebrews must now examine the psalm's source (Genesis) to elaborate what that comparison entails. The writer uses interpretive techniques common among early Jewish interpreters, and even some conclusions common among them, to show how Jesus the exalted king is a greater priest than those of the Levitical priesthood.

7:1 – 2a The author here summarizes information from Ge 14:17 – 24.

7:1 *Salem.* Jerusalem (see Ps 76:2; cf. also extra-Biblical sources).

7:2 *Abraham gave him a tenth of everything.* Tithing (giving a tenth, Ge 14:20) was practiced both in some ancient

name Melchizedek means "king of righteousness"; then also, "king of Salem"
means "king of peace." 3Without father or
mother, without genealogy,[u] without beginning of days or end of life, resembling the
Son of God,[v] he remains a priest forever.
4Just think how great he was: Even the
patriarch[w] Abraham gave him a tenth of
the plunder![x] 5Now the law requires the
descendants of Levi who become priests to
collect a tenth from the people[y]—that is,
from their fellow Israelites—even though
they also are descended from Abraham.
6This man, however, did not trace his descent from Levi, yet he collected a tenth
from Abraham and blessed[z] him who had
the promises.[a] 7And without doubt the
lesser is blessed by the greater. 8In the one
case, the tenth is collected by people who
die; but in the other case, by him who is
declared to be living.[b] 9One might even
say that Levi, who collects the tenth, paid
the tenth through Abraham, 10because
when Melchizedek met Abraham, Levi
was still in the body of his ancestor.

Jesus Like Melchizedek

11If perfection could have been attained
through the Levitical priesthood—and indeed the law given to the people[c] established that priesthood—why was there
still need for another priest to come,[d] one
in the order of Melchizedek,[e] not in the
order of Aaron? 12For when the priesthood
is changed, the law must be changed also.
13He of whom these things are said belonged to a different tribe,[f] and no one
from that tribe has ever served at the altar.[g] 14For it is clear that our Lord descended from Judah,[h] and in regard to that tribe
Moses said nothing about priests. 15And
what we have said is even more clear if
another priest like Melchizedek appears,
16one who has become a priest not on the
basis of a regulation as to his ancestry but
on the basis of the power of an indestructible life. 17For it is declared:

"You are a priest forever,
in the order of Melchizedek."[a][i]

18The former regulation is set aside because it was weak and useless[j] 19(for the
law made nothing perfect),[k] and a better
hope is introduced, by which we draw
near to God.[l]
20And it was not without an oath! Others became priests without any oath, 21but
he became a priest with an oath when
God said to him:

"The Lord has sworn
and will not change his mind:[m]
'You are a priest forever.' "[a][n]

[a] 17,21 Psalm 110:4

7:3 [u] ver 6 [v] Mt 4:3 **7:4** [w] Ac 2:29 [x] Ge 14:20 **7:5** [y] Nu 18:21, 26 **7:6** [z] Ge 14:19, 20 [a] Ro 4:13 **7:8** [b] Heb 5:6; 6:20 **7:11** [c] ver 18, 19; Heb 8:7 [d] Heb 10:1 [e] ver 17 **7:13** [f] ver 11 [g] ver 14 **7:14** [h] Isa 11:1; Mt 1:3; Lk 3:33 **7:17** [i] Ps 110:4; ver 21; Heb 5:6 **7:18** [j] Ro 8:3 **7:19** [k] Ac 13:39; Ro 3:20; Heb 9:9 [l] Heb 4:16 **7:21** [m] 1Sa 15:29 [n] Ps 110:4

Near Eastern and Greco-Roman settings. *Melchizedek means "king of righteousness"* ... *"king of Salem" means "king of peace."* The author of Hebrews may appeal here to ideas already possibly known to his audience. Greek-speaking Jews often allegorized names, including this one.

7:3 *Without father or mother, without genealogy, without beginning of days or end of life.* When useful, Jewish interpreters would argue from silence that what was not stated did not occur; the author of Hebrews can use this tactic for the sake of elaborating the psalm's comparison. Because the psalmist invites a comparison with the Melchizedek explained in Genesis, Hebrews probes details. Since no parents are mentioned, and since Genesis usually lists parents, the priest like Melchizedek lacks beginning. Since he is a "priest forever" (Ps 110:4), he also lacks ending. Greeks viewed as divine whatever lacked beginning and ending. Some other Jewish interpreters viewed Melchizedek as an exalted, perhaps angelic, figure.

7:4 *Abraham gave him a tenth.* The law assigned tithes to descendants of Levi, who descended from Abraham (e.g., Nu 18:26; 2Ch 31:4–6; Ne 10:37–38; 13:5,12); but Abraham himself tithed to a different, greater priest.

7:7–10 The priesthood like Melchizedek's is "greater" (v. 7) than the Levitical priesthood, for at least two reasons (vv. 8–10). First, whereas the Levites die, the one with the priesthood like Melchizedek would hold this office forever (v. 8; Ps 110:4; cf. Isa 9:7; Da 7:13–14). (Some Diaspora Jews also thought of the perfect priest being eternal.) Second, Melchizedek is greater than Abraham and thus greater than Levi, since Abraham is greater than Levi, who depended on him for existence (vv. 9–10). Seeking to get around this argument, later rabbis said that God withdrew the priesthood from Melchizedek (for blessing Abram before blessing God [Ge 14:19–20]) and gave it to Abraham in Ps 110:4; but Ps 110 clearly refers to the ultimate priest-king who would rule over the nations, not to Abraham.

7:11–28 As the writer's critics would undoubtedly point out, Scripture made the Levitical priesthood permanent (Ex 29:9; 40:15; Nu 25:13; Dt 18:5; Jer 33:21–22). The writer counters by noting that Ps 110:4 promises a different and better kind of priesthood (on its superiority, see Heb 7:7–10 and note). Since it was better, it superseded the need for the lesser priesthood. (Normally, no one complained when God sometimes did more than what he promised rather than less.) The promised priest-king coincided with some other Messianic expectations (see note on 5:6). Soon after Hebrews circulated, the temple was destroyed and the conventional Levitical task became impossible.

7:11–19 Some Diaspora Jews idealized Levi as a model of the perfect priesthood; but most Diaspora thinkers viewed what was perfect as unchanging, since what was perfect did not need to change. What was changeless was also eternal, as was clearly the promised king's priesthood ("a priest forever," v. 17, citing Ps 110:4). Since their Lord, Jesus, was from the tribe of Judah (v. 14), as would be expected for the promised Davidic Messiah (e.g., Isa 9:7; 11:1,10; Jer 23:5–6), the greater priesthood differed from one depending on tribal descent (or genealogy, as in Heb 7:3).

7:20–21 This priesthood is also greater than the Levitical priesthood because, unlike the latter, it is guaranteed with a divine oath (see notes on 6:13–18). God changed some points in the law when such changes were necessary to accomplish his original, eternal purpose in the law (e.g., Jer 3:16; cf. 2Ki 18:4), but in this case he had sworn and promised not to change his mind.

22Because of this oath, Jesus has become
the guarantor of a better covenant.[o]
23Now there have been many of those
priests, since death prevented them from
continuing in office; 24but because Jesus
lives forever, he has a permanent priesthood.[p] 25Therefore he is able to save completely[a] those who come to God[q] through
him, because he always lives to intercede
for them.[r]
26Such a high priest truly meets our
need — one who is holy, blameless, pure,
set apart from sinners,[s] exalted above the
heavens.[t] 27Unlike the other high priests, he
does not need to offer sacrifices[u] day after
day, first for his own sins,[v] and then for the
sins of the people. He sacrificed for their
sins once for all[w] when he offered himself.[x]
28For the law appoints as high priests men
in all their weakness;[y] but the oath, which
came after the law, appointed the Son,[z]
who has been made perfect[a] forever.

The High Priest of a New Covenant

8 Now the main point of what we are
saying is this: We do have such a high
priest,[b] who sat down at the right hand of
the throne of the Majesty in heaven, 2and
who serves in the sanctuary, the true tabernacle[c] set up by the Lord, not by a mere
human being.
3Every high priest is appointed to offer
both gifts and sacrifices,[d] and so it was
necessary for this one also to have something to offer.[e] 4If he were on earth, he
would not be a priest, for there are already
priests who offer the gifts prescribed by
the law.[f] 5They serve at a sanctuary that is
a copy[g] and shadow[h] of what is in heav-
en. This is why Moses was warned[i] when
he was about to build the tabernacle: "See
to it that you make everything according
to the pattern shown you on the mountain."[b][j] 6But in fact the ministry Jesus has
received is as superior to theirs as the covenant[k] of which he is mediator[l] is superior
to the old one, since the new covenant is
established on better promises.
7For if there had been nothing wrong
with that first covenant, no place would
have been sought for another.[m] 8But God
found fault with the people and said[c]:

a 25 Or *forever* *b* 5 Exodus 25:40 *c* 8 Some manuscripts may be translated *fault and said to the people.*

7:22 [o] Heb 8:6 **7:24** [p] ver 28 **7:25** [q] ver 19 [r] Ro 8:34 **7:26** [s] 2Co 5:21 [t] Heb 4:14 **7:27** [u] Heb 5:1 [v] Heb 5:3 [w] Heb 9:12, 26, 28 [x] Eph 5:2; Heb 9:14, 28 **7:28** [y] Heb 5:2 [z] Heb 1:2 [a] Heb 2:10 **8:1** [b] Heb 2:17 **8:2** [c] Heb 9:11, 24 **8:3** [d] Heb 5:1 [e] Heb 9:14 **8:4** [f] Heb 5:1 **8:5** [g] Heb 9:23 [h] Col 2:17; Heb 10:1 [i] Heb 11:7; 12:25 [j] Ex 25:40 **8:6** [k] Lk 22:20 [l] Heb 7:22 **8:7** [m] Heb 7:11, 18

7:22 *guarantor.* Appears often in business documents and entailed a firm obligation.
7:23 *death prevented them from continuing in office.* Even apart from Rome recently deposing high priests at will, priests died; by contrast, Jesus was "a priest forever" (v. 21, citing Ps 110:4).
7:25 *always lives to intercede.* Unlike other priests, Jesus is permanent (v. 24), so he can always intercede.
7:26 *holy, blameless, pure, set apart.* Earthly priests were to be consecrated, separated from ritual impurity during their ministry (later rabbis even thought the high priest should be isolated for a week before the Day of Atonement ritual). *above the heavens.* Separation in heaven from impurity was far greater than separation from it on earth (cf. note on 8:2), and "above the heavens" was where the priest-king was (at God's right hand, Ps 110:1). Many people in antiquity believed that what was in the highest heavens was completely pure and set apart from the corruption of earth.
7:27 *day after day, first for his own sins.* High priests had to atone for themselves before atoning for others (Lev 9:7), relevant primarily to the Day of Atonement (Lev 16:6,11,17,24). Because Jesus' sacrifice is perfect its efficacy is eternal (since what was perfect was changeless and eternal; cf. note on Heb 7:11 – 19). Although the larger argument is clear, the writer of Hebrews may use imprecise wording to make the point; high priests did not directly offer up the daily offerings during the morning and evening sacrifices. Nevertheless, high priests were responsible for the priestly service that did offer them. Also, Jewish tradition (perhaps reflecting recent reality) did speak of Aaron making such daily sacrifices, and others from this period spoke in similar, general terms.
7:28 *perfect forever.* Many believed that what was perfect was eternal; being raised, Jesus certainly qualified as a "priest forever" (Ps 110:4).
8:1 *sat down at the right hand of the throne.* The priest-king of Ps 110:4 was enthroned beside God in Ps 110:1 (see Heb 1:13; 5:6; 7:17). As a priest, then (Ps 110:4), he would have to serve in the sanctuary in heaven, where God was enthroned.
8:2 *the sanctuary, the true tabernacle set up by the Lord.* Although earthly temples invited deities' presence on earth, most people in antiquity believed that many of these deities also resided in heaven. Jewish people affirmed this also for the one true God (cf. 1Ki 8:27; Ps 102:19).
8:5 *copy.* Or pattern; recalls the promised future temple in the Greek translation of Eze 42:15. Many people envisioned a heavenly temple in terms of an earthly one. Both apocalyptic thinkers and Diaspora Jewish ones thought of God's earthly temple as merely a model of the heavenly and/or eternal one. Some, such as Philo of Alexandria, additionally found abundant allegorical significance even in the details. (The earlier Greek philosopher Plato treated the earthly world as shadows of the true realm of ideas above, imagery that was later adapted by Philo.) Some scholars suggest that even God's original instruction to follow the precise model given on the mountain (here, following Ex 25:8 – 9,40) indicated a heavenly temple. Babylonians, Canaanites and others had modeled earthly temples after heavenly ones.

Hebrews finds patterns in the earthly tabernacle that point to the greater, heavenly one. The author's modest suggestions, however, contrast starkly with the wholesale allegorizing of Philo, who explains each detail as a symbol of something that none of Moses' original readers would have guessed (linen as earth, dark red as air, the seven-branched candelabrum as the seven planets, etc.).
8:6 *superior to the old one.* As noted in 7:12, the old priesthood was tied to the old law and its covenant; if the former was superseded or transformed by a greater priesthood guaranteed by God's oath, the latter would also be changed. What was superseded might *point* to eternal principles, yet it was itself imperfect.
8:8 – 12 In one of the author's most extended quotations (cf. also 3:7 – 11), he cites Jer 31:31 – 34 to show Biblically God's plan to improve on or transform the

"The days are coming, declares the Lord,
when I will make a new covenant[n]
with the people of Israel
and with the people of Judah.
9 It will not be like the covenant
I made with their ancestors[o]
when I took them by the hand
to lead them out of Egypt,
because they did not remain faithful to
my covenant,
and I turned away from them,
declares the Lord.
10 This is the covenant I will establish
with the people of Israel
after that time, declares the Lord.
I will put my laws in their minds
and write them on their hearts.[p]
I will be their God,
and they will be my people.[q]
11 No longer will they teach their
neighbor,
or say to one another, 'Know the
Lord,'
because they will all know me,[r]
from the least of them to the
greatest.
12 For I will forgive their wickedness
and will remember their sins no
more.[s]"[a][t]

13 By calling this covenant "new," he has
made the first one obsolete;[u] and what is
obsolete and outdated will soon disappear.

Worship in the Earthly Tabernacle

9 Now the first covenant had regulations for worship and also an earthly sanctuary.[v] 2 A tabernacle[w] was set up.
In its first room were the lampstand[x] and
the table[y] with its consecrated bread;[z]
this was called the Holy Place. 3 Behind
the second curtain was a room called the
Most Holy Place,[a] 4 which had the golden
altar of incense[b] and the gold-covered ark
of the covenant.[c] This ark contained the
gold jar of manna,[d] Aaron's staff that had
budded,[e] and the stone tablets of the covenant. 5 Above the ark were the cherubim
of the Glory,[f] overshadowing the atonement cover. But we cannot discuss these
things in detail now.
6 When everything had been arranged
like this, the priests entered regularly[g] into
the outer room to carry on their ministry.
7 But only the high priest entered[h] the inner room, and that only once a year,[i] and
never without blood, which he offered for
himself[j] and for the sins the people had
committed in ignorance. 8 The Holy Spirit
was showing[k] by this that the way[l] into
the Most Holy Place had not yet been disclosed as long as the first tabernacle was
still functioning. 9 This is an illustration for
the present time, indicating that the gifts
and sacrifices being offered[m] were not
able to clear the conscience of the worshiper. 10 They are only a matter of food[n]
and drink[o] and various ceremonial washings — external regulations[p] applying until
the time of the new order.

The Blood of Christ

11 But when Christ came as high priest[q]
of the good things that are now already

8:8 [n] Jer 31:31 **8:9** [o] Ex 19:5,6 **8:10** [p] 2Co 3:3; Heb 10:16 [q] Zec 8:8 **8:11** [r] Isa 54:13; Jn 6:45 **8:12** [s] Heb 10:17 [t] Ro 11:27 **8:13** [u] 2Co 5:17 **9:1** [v] Ex 25:8 **9:2** [w] Ex 25:8,9 [x] Ex 25:31-39 [y] Ex 25:23-29 [z] Lev 24:5-8 **9:3** [a] Ex 26:31-33 **9:4** [b] Ex 30:1-5 [c] Ex 25:10-22 [d] Ex 16:32,33 [e] Nu 17:10 **9:5** [f] Ex 25:17-19 **9:6** [g] Nu 28:3 **9:7** [h] Lev 16:11-19 [i] Lev 16:34 [j] Heb 5:2,3 **9:8** [k] Heb 3:7 [l] Jn 14:6; Heb 10:19,20 **9:9** [m] Heb 5:1 **9:10** [n] Lev 11:2-23 [o] Col 2:16 [p] Heb 7:16 **9:11** [q] Heb 2:17

[a] 12 Jer. 31:31-34

earlier covenant. The Dead Sea Scrolls also emphasize this passage, but their authors tried to follow the law more strictly. Most understood the new covenant as a renewed covenant with Israel. It differed, however, from the earlier covenant: instead of breaking the covenant (Jer 31:32), all of God's people would now know him, his law written in their hearts (Jer 31:33 – 34). Some had earlier experienced a foretaste of the law being in their hearts (Ps 119:11), which was always God's desire for them (Dt 6:6; 30:14), but this would now be the experience of all God's people, something performed by God himself (Dt 30:6; Eze 36:26 – 27).

8:13 *will soon disappear.* In AD 66 Jewish patriots slaughtered many priests in the temple; in AD 70 the temple was destroyed and Levitical priests could no longer make atonement there. The author probably writes before 70, but had reason to expect judgment on the temple to be completed (cf. Mk 13:14).

9:2 *lampstand.* Ancient Near Eastern temples were to be shrouded from the profane light of the world; lampstands were necessary so that priests could see.

9:4 *the golden altar of incense.* Against some tradition, the altar of incense was not inside the Most Holy Place (Ex 28:43; 40:26), even though (as here) it could be said to belong to it (cf. Ex 40:5; 1Ki 6:20,22; 1Ch 6:49). *gold jar of manna, Aaron's staff.* The writer follows the Biblical description of the tabernacle rather than updating it for Herod's temple or even mentioning the loss of the manna and staff (1Ki 8:9; 2Ki 18:4).

9:5 *cherubim of the Glory.* God was enthroned above the cherubim (1Sa 4:4; 2Sa 6:2); ancient Near Eastern kings sometimes had carved winged creatures on pedestals for thrones. The innermost, most holy place in an ancient Near Eastern temple included a platform or sacred object on top of which sat the image of the deity. God's temple had no image (Ex 20:4), but his glory could appear there.

9:7 *only the high priest entered the inner room, and that only once a year.* The one entrance of the high priest to the Most Holy Place each year was for the Day of Atonement (Lev 16:2,29 – 34).

9:8 *The Holy Spirit was showing.* The single annual entrance to the Most Holy Place illustrated clearly Israel's limited access to God's full presence under the old covenant. This would contrast with the new covenant, in which God would put his laws in his people and they would all know him because he would forgive all their sins (see 8:10 – 12, citing Jer 31:33 – 34). For the understanding that the earthly tabernacle pointed to something greater, see note on Heb 8:5.

9:11 *greater and more perfect tabernacle.* The first covenant (8:9) stipulated rules for "an earthly sanctuary" (9:1); since God would not give a new covenant (8:8) unless it improved over the previous one (8:13), the new covenant not surprisingly has a better tabernacle. *not made*

here,[a][r] he went through the greater and
more perfect tabernacle[s] that is not made
with human hands, that is to say, is not
a part of this creation. 12He did not enter by means of the blood of goats and
calves;[t] but he entered the Most Holy
Place[u] once for all[v] by his own blood,
thus obtaining[b] eternal redemption.
13The blood of goats and bulls and the
ashes of a heifer[w] sprinkled on those
who are ceremonially unclean sanctify
them so that they are outwardly clean.
14How much more, then, will the blood
of Christ, who through the eternal Spirit[x] offered himself unblemished to God,
cleanse our consciences[y] from acts that
lead to death,[c][z] so that we may serve the
living God!

9:11 [r] Heb 10:1 [s] Heb 8:2 **9:12** [t] Heb 10:4 [u] ver 24 [v] Heb 7:27 **9:13** [w] Nu 19:9, 17, 18 **9:14** [x] 1Pe 3:18 [y] Titus 2:14; Heb 10:2, 22 [z] Heb 6:1

[a] 11 Some early manuscripts *are to come* [b] 12 Or *blood, having obtained* [c] 14 Or *from useless rituals*

with human hands. Cf. note on Ac 7:48. A temple built by human beings would be inferior to the heavenly temple; what was heavenly was considered pure and perfect.
9:12 *blood of goats and calves.* The high priest on the annual Day of Atonement brought the blood of a bull for himself and that of a goat for the people (Lev 16:6,11,14–16). *once for all.* Because what was heavenly was understood to be perfect and thus changeless (see notes on 7:11–19,26,27,28), this ultimate sacrifice would not need to be repeated. *eternal redemption.* Some ancient Jewish circles expected perfect and complete redemption, or deliverance, at the time of the end (Dead Sea Scrolls; cf. Da 9:24); the Greek term for redemption sometimes connotes paying a ransom or price (e.g., Nu 18:16), as here.
9:13 *ashes of a heifer.* Alludes to Nu 19:2–10 (and apparently also Nu 19:17–19).
9:14 *How much more.* Jewish interpreters often reasoned in this way; in this case, if the blood of sacrifices on the Day of Atonement can remove sin (hypothetically; cf. 10:4), how much more effective would be the blood of

HEBREWS 9:1–5

FUNCTION OF THE TABERNACLE

The tabernacle was a portable temple. It was enough like other temples to be intelligible to Israelites as a temple, yet it was different enough at key points to teach a distinctive theology. Temples in Egypt, where the Israelites had lived and labored, had an outer court, an inner sanctuary, and, in the back, a most holy place. The building techniques and materials used for the ark of the covenant of the Lord were all found in Egypt. Those who lived in Egypt and served Pharaoh's building projects would have known what such temples looked like. Egyptians also had many portable tent-shrines, and some have cited evidence to support the argument that Midianites, Canaanites and others may have had some as well.

It also appears that the most expensive dyes (blue) and metals (pure gold) were used nearest the ark of the covenant, whereas the least expensive dyes (red) and metals (copper) were used farthest from it. This fits ancient Near Eastern practice; in the ancient Near East, the gradation of materials in relation to the Most Holy Place was meant to emphasize the holiness of the deity. It thus communicated the reverence with which he or she must be approached.

Most ancient temples had a table for offerings, lampstands (because holy places were shrouded from the light of the world), an altar of sacrifice, and (to address the stench of burning sacrifices in closed spaces) an altar of incense. Canaanites had many of the same sorts of offerings the Israelites did. Acacia wood, used to construct the tabernacle, was simply practical: it was the most available wood in the Sinai Desert. (Solomon later used more prestigious cedar wood from Lebanon for his temple.)

Such similarities with surrounding cultures, however, underlined the contrasts all the more graphically. In most ancient temples, the innermost shrine included a platform on which was enthroned the image of the deity. That there is no image in God's tabernacle reinforces the commandment "You shall not make for yourself an image" (Ex 20:4). Many massive Egyptian shrines were flanked with shrines for deities that assisted the major deity. This does not appear in God's tabernacle, for he demanded,

continued on next page

"You shall have no other gods" in my sight (Ex 20:3). Moreover, although some items of furniture (such as altars and a table) parallel other temples, God's tabernacle lacks a bed. Egyptians, Hittites and others would put their deity-images to bed at night, wake them in the morning, provide royal entertainment, and so forth. But the God of Israel "will neither slumber nor sleep" (Ps 121:4).

The forms communicate eternal principles to a particular cultural setting. For the correspondence between heavenly and earthly temples in ancient Near Eastern and Greco-Roman thought, see note on Heb 8:5. ◆

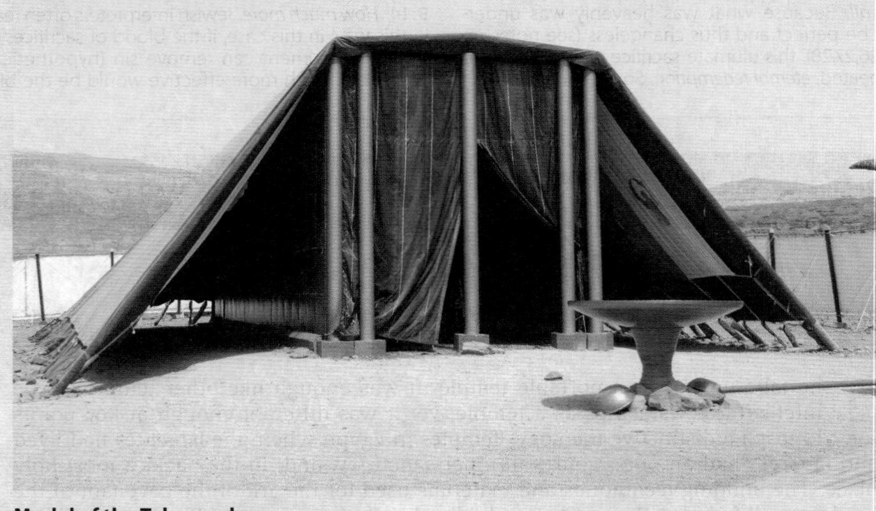

Model of the Tabernacle.
Photo by Heather Biscoe Tarman

[15]For this reason Christ is the mediator[a]
of a new covenant, that those who are
called may receive the promised eternal
inheritance — now that he has died as a
ransom to set them free from the sins committed under the first covenant.[b]
[16]In the case of a will,[a] it is necessary to
prove the death of the one who made it,
[17]because a will is in force only when
somebody has died; it never takes effect
while the one who made it is living. [18]This
is why even the first covenant was not put
into effect without blood.[c] [19]When Moses
had proclaimed every command of the
law to all the people, he took the blood of

9:15 [a] 1Ti 2:5 [b] Heb 7:22
9:18 [c] Ex 24:6-8

[a] *16* Same Greek word as *covenant*; also in verse 17

Christ! The sacrifice of Christ was worth more than any other (cf. Isa 52:15; 53:4 – 6,8 – 12). *eternal Spirit.* Jewish tradition did not understand God's Spirit as *distinct* from God, but it did understand the Spirit as divine and eternal. *offered himself unblemished.* Acceptable sacrifices were to be unblemished, i.e., without defect (Ex 12:5; 29:1; Nu 19:2).
9:15 *Christ is the mediator of a new covenant.* The new covenant provides a better redemption from sin than the old covenant (8:12, citing Jer 31:34). Moses was considered mediator of the first covenant; Jesus was greater than Moses (Heb 3 – 4).
9:16,17 *will.* The writer here plays on the different senses of the same Greek term; the Greek term he has been using for "covenant" (vv. 4,15; 7:22; 8:6 – 10) is also used for "will."
9:16 *necessary to prove the death.* In the case of a will, it was sealed with the seals of witnesses attesting the authenticity of the will; wills were not to be opened until the testator died. In the case of a covenant (v. 15), it was initiated by blood (from a sacrificed animal, Ge 31:54; Ex 24:8), as in v. 18.
9:18 *blood.* For blood and the first covenant, see Ex 24:6 – 8.
9:19 *water, scarlet wool and branches of hyssop.* A significant adaptation, since there is no mention of these ele-

calves, together with water, scarlet wool
and branches of hyssop, and sprinkled the
scroll and all the people.[d] 20He said, "This
is the blood of the covenant, which God
has commanded you to keep."[a][e] 21In the
same way, he sprinkled with the blood
both the tabernacle and everything used in
its ceremonies. 22In fact, the law requires
that nearly everything be cleansed with
blood,[f] and without the shedding of blood
there is no forgiveness.[g]

23It was necessary, then, for the copies[h]
of the heavenly things to be purified with
these sacrifices, but the heavenly things
themselves with better sacrifices than
these. 24For Christ did not enter a sanctuary made with human hands that was
only a copy of the true one;[i] he entered
heaven itself, now to appear for us in
God's presence. 25Nor did he enter heaven
to offer himself again and again, the way
the high priest enters the Most Holy Place[j]
every year with blood that is not his own.[k]
26Otherwise Christ would have had to suffer many times since the creation of the
world.[l] But he has appeared once for all[m]
at the culmination of the ages to do away
with sin by the sacrifice of himself. 27Just
as people are destined to die once,[n] and after that to face judgment,[o] 28so Christ was
sacrificed once to take away the sins of
many; and he will appear a second time,[p]
not to bear sin,[q] but to bring salvation to
those who are waiting for him.[r]

9:19 [d] Ex 24:6-8 **9:20** [e] Ex 24:8; Mt 26:28 **9:22** [f] Lev 8:15 [g] Lev 17:11 **9:23** [h] Heb 8:5 **9:24** [i] Heb 8:2 **9:25** [j] Heb 10:19 [k] ver 7,8 **9:26** [l] Heb 4:3 [m] Heb 7:27 **9:27** [n] Ge 3:19 [o] 2Co 5:10 **9:28** [p] Titus 2:13 [q] 1Pe 2:24 [r] 1Co 1:7 **10:1** [s] Heb 8:5 [t] Heb 9:11 [u] Heb 9:23 [v] Heb 7:19

Christ's Sacrifice Once for All

10 The law is only a shadow[s] of the
good things[t] that are coming — not
the realities themselves.[u] For this reason it
can never, by the same sacrifices repeated endlessly year after year, make perfect[v]
those who draw near to worship. 2Other-
wise, would they not have stopped being
offered? For the worshipers would have
been cleansed once for all, and would no
longer have felt guilty for their sins. 3But
those sacrifices are an annual reminder

[a] 20 Exodus 24:8

ments in Ex 24 (they appear instead in Lev 14:6; Nu 19:6). Perhaps the writer assumes that sprinkled blood was often mixed with this concoction. Jewish interpreters often linked texts; the writer apparently connects Ex 24 (referenced in Heb 9:18 – 21) with Lev 14:6 or Nu 19:6, to emphasize purification — in the latter case, from sin (Nu 19:9).

9:20 *He said.* Cf. Ex 24:8. The author of Hebrews varies the wording slightly, blending in another familiar element from the Pentateuch (Ex 35:1; Lev 9:6; Dt 4:13; 5:15). Ancient interpreters sometimes adapted the wording of the text in ways that clarified the point the writer sought to make. Another ancient source also made one of this writer's minor changes to Moses' words.

9:21 *sprinkled with the blood.* See, e.g., Ex 29:21; Lev 8:30; 16:15; Nu 19:4.

9:22 *nearly everything be cleansed with blood.* Blood did not cleanse physically, but it purified ritually (see, e.g., Lev 14:14; 16:19). Blood was necessary for sin offerings and atonement (e.g., Ex 30:10; Lev 6:30; 16:25,27; 17:11).

9:23 *heavenly things ... with better sacrifices.* The writer returns to the parallel between earthly and heavenly tabernacles (see notes on v. 8; 8:5): if the earthly sanctuary could be dedicated only by blood (vv. 11 – 22), so also the heavenly sanctuary. But a perfect sacrifice was necessary for the perfect sanctuary. Not only Gentile philosophers but even Diaspora Jewish thinkers (such as Philo) sometimes treated earthly things as a shadow of heavenly realities.

9:24 – 26 A heavenly sanctuary (v. 23) made without hands (v. 11) would be perfect and thus changeless (see notes on vv. 11,23; 7:26).

9:26 *once for all.* The eternal priesthood of one like Melchizedek (7:17; "forever" in Ps 110:4) could not depend on annual sacrifices; had the eternal priesthood involved perpetual sacrifices, they would have had no beginning ("since the creation of the world") as well as no ending. Instead it depends on a once-for-all sacrifice of the perfect, unblemished victim. *culmination of the ages.* Jewish people frequently divided history up into many ages (they proposed a number of different schemes), but the most basic was the division between the present age and the age to come. The culmination of all prior ages climaxes in God's reign; in the decisive act of Christ, the writer recognizes that the future age has in some sense invaded history (cf. 6:5).

9:27 *destined to die once, and after that to face judgment.* All people who have sinned need to die once and then face judgment for sin; the sinless Christ died once as a sacrifice for their sins (v. 28).

9:28 *take away the sins of many.* Closely echoes the Greek translation of Isa 53:12 ("bore the sins of many"; cf. Isa 53:11). *he will appear a second time.* Some scholars compare Jesus' reappearance to bring salvation with the reemergence of the high priest from the inner sanctuary that assured the people that God had accepted the sacrifice and forgiven them. Many Jewish people believed that judgment immediately followed death, death being one's final opportunity for repentance (as in Scripture, Eze 18:21 – 32). Some Jewish people did allow for a posthumous purgatory for some Israelites once their judgment was decided.

10:1 – 18 The writer here builds on the argument he began making in 9:23 – 28: only Christ could be a sufficient sacrifice for the heavenly sanctuary.

10:1 *The law is only a shadow.* Some philosophers viewed earthly experience as merely shadows of the real world of ideas, apprehended by reason alone. More relevant, by this period many Diaspora Jewish thinkers viewed the heavens above as pure and perfect. Arguing from even older assumptions (see note on 8:5), the writer views the earthly tabernacle as a shadow of the heavenly one, while also reflecting the perspective of Jewish apocalyptic writers: heaven reveals what the world to come will be like. For this writer, however, the first stage (9:24,28) of that future time had already invaded history (6:5).

10:2 *Otherwise, would they not have stopped being offered?* The author again plays on the idea that what is perfect need not be changed or supplemented. Rhetorical questions were commonly used in ancient reasoning.

10:3 *annual reminder of sins.* Each year the Day of Atonement sacrifices reminded people of their sins that needed to be forgiven (Lev 16:21), perhaps the way Passover reminded them of God's redemptive acts (Ex 12:14). By contrast, the new covenant would deal with sin so that God would "remember their sins no more" (Heb 8:12, citing Jer 31:34).

of sins.[w] 4It is impossible for the blood of
bulls and goats[x] to take away sins.
5Therefore, when Christ came into the
world,[y] he said:

"Sacrifice and offering you did not desire,
but a body you prepared for me;[z]
6with burnt offerings and sin offerings
you were not pleased.
7Then I said, 'Here I am—it is written
about me in the scroll[a]—
I have come to do your will, my
God.' "[a][b]

8First he said, "Sacrifices and offerings,
burnt offerings and sin offerings you did
not desire, nor were you pleased with
them"[c]—though they were offered in
accordance with the law. 9Then he said,
"Here I am, I have come to do your will."[d]
He sets aside the first to establish the second. 10And by that will, we have been
made holy[e] through the sacrifice of the
body[f] of Jesus Christ once for all.[g]
11Day after day every priest stands and
performs his religious duties; again and
again he offers the same sacrifices,[h] which
can never take away sins.[i] 12But when this
priest had offered for all time one sacrifice
for sins, he sat down at the right hand of
God, 13and since that time he waits for his
enemies to be made his footstool.[j] 14For by
one sacrifice he has made perfect[k] forever
those who are being made holy.
15The Holy Spirit also testifies[l] to us
about this. First he says:

16"This is the covenant I will make with
them
after that time, says the Lord.
I will put my laws in their hearts,
and I will write them on their
minds."[b][m]

17Then he adds:

"Their sins and lawless acts
I will remember no more."[c][n]

18And where these have been forgiven,
sacrifice for sin is no longer necessary.

A Call to Persevere in Faith

19Therefore, brothers and sisters, since
we have confidence to enter the Most
Holy Place[o] by the blood of Jesus, 20by
a new and living way[p] opened for us
through the curtain,[q] that is, his body,
21and since we have a great priest[r] over

10:3 [w] Heb 9:7 **10:4** [x] Heb 9:12, 13 **10:5** [y] Heb 1:6 [z] 1Pe 2:24 **10:7** [a] Jer 36:2 [b] Ps 40:6-8 **10:8** [c] ver 5,6; Mk 12:33 **10:9** [d] ver 7 **10:10** [e] Jn 17:19 [f] Heb 2:14; 1Pe 2:24 [g] Heb 7:27 **10:11** [h] Heb 5:1 [i] ver 1,4 **10:13** [j] Heb 1:13 **10:14** [k] ver 1 **10:15** [l] Heb 3:7 **10:16** [m] Jer 31:33; Heb 8:10 **10:17** [n] Heb 8:12 **10:19** [o] Eph 2:18; Heb 9:8, 12, 25 **10:20** [p] Heb 9:8 [q] Heb 9:3 **10:21** [r] Heb 2:17

a *7* Psalm 40:6-8 (see Septuagint) *b* *16* Jer. 31:33
c *17* Jer. 31:34

10:4–5 Animal sacrifices were a standard part of most ancient temples and belong to many religious traditions. Some philosophers rejected the value of blood sacrifice, which they felt was unreasonable in a perfect temple focused on the mind; most people, however, disagreed.

Scripture already relativized the value of animal sacrifices (e.g., 1Sa 15:22; Ps 51:16; Pr 21:3; Isa 1:11; Jer 11:15; Hos 6:6; Am 5:21–27), including in the present citation (Ps 40:6–8), cited here in the Greek version. Before AD 70, many Diaspora Jews and some Jews in the Holy Land emphasized the spiritual, figurative use of sacrificial imagery, but only a few denied the necessity of sacrifices altogether. Later rabbis argued that the Day of Atonement, conjoined with repentance, was necessary for the forgiveness of most violations of the law.

The writer of Hebrews recognizes that blood sacrifice is necessary; yet he deems animal sacrifices inadequate for human redemption in the heavenly sanctuary. He views their past value as symbolic, pointing to the perfect and ultimate sacrifice of Christ (9:23).

10:8 *First he said ... though.* Jewish teachers often explained a text after citing it. From Ps 40:6, the writer points out that God's real interest was not in animal sacrifices.

10:9 *sets aside the first to establish the second.* The writer notes that the psalm distinguishes between sacrifices and God's will, and that the speaker in the psalm came to perform the latter.

10:10 *made holy through the sacrifice of the body of Jesus Christ once for all.* Most Jewish people in the Mediterranean Diaspora heard Scripture in its Greek translation, which is what this writer therefore expounds. Where the surviving Hebrew text reads "my ears you have opened," most Greek versions read "a body you prepared for me" (to do God's will). Jewish interpreters generally chose whichever reading they needed to make their point (some interpreters even changed readings slightly to make their point). Jesus thus offers here not burnt offerings, but his own body.

10:12 *this priest ... sat down at the right hand of God.* The writer returns to what he already established from Ps 110:1,4 (see Heb 1:13; 5:6; 7:17,21 and notes on 1:13; 5:6). *sat down.* The eternal priest like Melchizedek (Ps 110:4) will remain seated until his enemies are put down. Priests stood to offer sacrifices, so the priest-king must have already offered his once-for-all sacrifice.

10:15 *The Holy Spirit also testifies.* Jewish people believed that God's Spirit inspired Scripture as God's word.

10:16–17 Interpreters often returned to earlier texts they had cited (here 8:8–12), comparing passages. See note on 8:8–12.

10:18 *sacrifice for sin is no longer necessary.* If God no longer remembers his people's sins (v. 17), no need remains to atone for them. A Biblical image of the future temple does include sin or guilt offerings (Eze 40:39; 42:13; 43:18–27; 44:29), but no one objected to God doing something even greater than the images with which he conveyed future hopes (here, the removal of sin). Christ's once-for-all offering was greater.

10:19 *confidence to enter the Most Holy Place by the blood of Jesus.* Under the old covenant, access to the Most Holy Place was extremely limited (9:7). By contrast, Jesus offered full access to his followers in the heavenly Most Holy Place (4:16; 6:20).

10:20 *through the curtain.* The curtain (see note on 6:19; cf. Mk 15:38 and note) no longer obstructed the Most Holy Place (Heb 9:3). This new situation fulfilled God's ultimate purpose all along: his people having a personal relationship with the God who dwelled among them (cf. Ex 33:11; Nu 11:29; Jer 31:31–34).

10:21 *over the house of God.* The writer alludes to his earlier citation (in 3:5) of Nu 12:7.

the house of God, 22let us draw near to
God[s] with a sincere heart and with the
full assurance that faith brings, having
our hearts sprinkled to cleanse us from
a guilty conscience[t] and having our bodies washed with pure water. 23Let us hold
unswervingly to the hope[u] we profess, for
he who promised is faithful.[v] 24And let us
consider how we may spur one another
on toward love and good deeds, 25not giving up meeting together,[w] as some are in
the habit of doing, but encouraging one
another[x]—and all the more as you see the
Day approaching.
26If we deliberately keep on sinning[y]
after we have received the knowledge of
the truth, no sacrifice for sins is left, 27but
only a fearful expectation of judgment
and of raging fire[z] that will consume the
enemies of God. 28Anyone who rejected
the law of Moses died without mercy on
the testimony of two or three witnesses.[a] 29How much more severely do you
think someone deserves to be punished
who has trampled the Son of God underfoot,[b] who has treated as an unholy thing
the blood of the covenant[c] that sanctified
them, and who has insulted the Spirit[d] of
grace?[e] 30For we know him who said, "It is
mine to avenge; I will repay,"[a][f] and again,
"The Lord will judge his people."[b][g] 31It is
a dreadful thing to fall into the hands of
the living God.[h]
32Remember those earlier days after
you had received the light,[i] when you endured in a great conflict full of suffering.[j]
33Sometimes you were publicly exposed to
insult and persecution;[k] at other times you
stood side by side with those who were so
treated.[l] 34You suffered along with those in
prison[m] and joyfully accepted the confiscation of your property, because you knew
that you yourselves had better and lasting
possessions.[n] 35So do not throw away your
confidence; it will be richly rewarded.

10:22 [s] Heb 7:19 [t] Eze 36:25; Heb 9:14 **10:23** [u] Heb 3:6 [v] 1Co 1:9 **10:25** [w] Ac 2:42 [x] Heb 3:13 **10:26** [y] Nu 15:30; 2Pe 2:20 **10:27** [z] Isa 26:11; 2Th 1:7; Heb 9:27 **10:28** [a] Dt 17:6, 7; Heb 2:2 **10:29** [b] Heb 6:6 [c] Mt 26:28 [d] Eph 4:30; Heb 6:4 [e] Heb 2:3 **10:30** [f] Dt 32:35; Ro 12:19 [g] Dt 32:36 **10:31** [h] Mt 16:16 **10:32** [i] Heb 6:4 [j] Php 1:29, 30 **10:33** [k] 1Co 4:9 [l] Php 4:14; 1Th 2:14 **10:34** [m] Heb 13:3 [n] Heb 11:16

[a] *30* Deut. 32:35 [b] *30* Deut. 32:36; Psalm 135:14

10:22 *let us draw near to God.* Israel could not draw near the Lord fully (Nu 18:22). Priests sprinkled people for ritual purity, for most rituals using blood (e.g., Ex 24:8, quoted in Heb 9:19–20; cf. 10:29) and for some rituals using water (Nu 8:7; 19:13,18–21); the impure were also supposed to bathe (e.g., Lev 14:8–9; 15:5–27). *having our hearts sprinkled to cleanse us.* The writer envisions the promised spiritual cleansing of hearts in Eze 36:25–27. *having our bodies washed with pure water.* The perfect participle translated "washed" suggests that the washing of "our bodies" refers to the act of baptism, which Judeans already understood as an act of conversion. (Baptism was customary when Gentiles converted to Judaism, and practiced when one joined particular sects, including when one became a follower of Jesus.)
10:23 *Let us hold unswervingly.* The recipients of the letter to the Hebrews face social pressure from the rest of the local Jewish community to return to their previous practices.
10:25 *meeting together.* On average, various groups (such as trade guilds) met together about once a month. Diaspora Jews could use their synagogues at any time, but especially gathered on weekly Sabbaths (e.g., Ac 13:14,42; 16:13). Christians seem to have gathered at least weekly, but persecution (cf. Heb 10:32–39; 12:4) may have dissuaded some people from attending even relatively private house churches. Roman authorities were suspicious of private meetings, although no one would likely investigate them outside Rome unless someone brought an accusation.
10:26 *deliberately keep on sinning.* God judged deliberate sin far more harshly than unintentional sin (Nu 15:29–31). *no sacrifice for sins is left.* Jewish tradition taught that no sacrifice availed for the person who knowingly rejected the authority of God's law. (At Qumran such rebels were expelled; later rabbis thought they could be forgiven only through death.) One who knowingly turned away from life in Christ (v. 29) would not find it anywhere else.
10:27 *fire that will consume the enemies.* Alludes to the future judgment in Isa 26:11.
10:28 *Anyone who rejected the law of Moses.* Jewish teachers recognized that everyone sinned in some ways; but a sin by which a person declared, "I reject the authority of any of God's Word" was considered equivalent to rejecting the whole law and was reckoned as apostasy. *two or three witnesses.* See Dt 17:6–7; 19:15; for apostasy from obedience to God, see Dt 13:6–11; 17:2–7.
10:29 *How much more ...?* Jewish thinkers often used "How much more?" arguments; if rejecting the old covenant merited judgment, how much more for rejecting the new one? *trampled the Son of God underfoot.* Treating as profane what was holy merited judgment (e.g., Lev 10:1–3; Isa 63:18; Eze 22:26). Rebelling against the Spirit (who revealed the truth [Heb 10:15; 9:8] and facilitated Jesus' sacrifice [9:14]) merited judgment (Isa 63:10). *Spirit of grace.* May echo the promise of Zec 12:10.
10:30 The writer uses Dt 32:35–36 to show that God can judge even his own people, reinforcing the warning of Heb 10:26–29. (The NIV translates "judge" as "vindicate" in Dt 32:36, but the author of Hebrews links the phrase with what precedes; although he follows the Hebrew text more closely than the Greek version, the Greek term is the same in both cases.)
10:31 *fall into the hands of the living God.* Scripture often used expressions such as "fall into [someone's] hands" (the Lord's in 2Sa 24:14; the enemy's in, e.g., Jdg 15:18).
10:34 *suffered along with those in prison.* Imprisonment (also 13:3; cf. 11:36) brought shame and exposed one to hunger and disease; prison was normally a holding area until trial or execution, but trials did not always happen quickly. *joyfully accepted the confiscation of your property.* Punishments, including banishment, sometimes included confiscation of property. The emperors Tiberius and Claudius expelled many Jewish residents of Rome in the first century (including Jewish Christian leaders under Claudius, Ac 18:2); in the early second century, Gentiles slaughtered much of Alexandria's Jewish population and seized their goods. The location of the recipients of the letter to the Hebrews is uncertain (see Introduction: Recipients); e.g., at one time believers in Macedonia faced persecution (Php 1:30; 1Th 2:14) and poverty (2Co 8:1–2), as did believers in Judea (Ro 15:26; 1Th 2:14).

36You need to persevere[o] so that when
you have done the will of God, you will
receive what he has promised. 37For,

"In just a little while,
he who is coming[p] will come
and will not delay."[a][q]

38And,

"But my righteous[b] one will live by
faith.[r]
And I take no pleasure
in the one who shrinks back."[c]

39But we do not belong to those who
shrink back and are destroyed, but to
those who have faith and are saved.

Faith in Action

11 Now faith is confidence in what we
hope for and assurance about what
we do not see.[s] 2This is what the ancients
were commended for.[t]
3By faith we understand that the universe was formed at God's command,[u]
so that what is seen was not made out of
what was visible.
4By faith Abel brought God a better offering than Cain did. By faith he was commended as righteous, when God spoke
well of his offerings.[v] And by faith Abel
still speaks, even though he is dead.[w]
5By faith Enoch was taken from this life,
so that he did not experience death: "He
could not be found, because God had tak-
en him away."[d][x] For before he was taken,
he was commended as one who pleased
God. 6And without faith it is impossible to
please God, because anyone who comes to
him[y] must believe that he exists and that
he rewards those who earnestly seek him.
7By faith Noah, when warned about
things not yet seen, in holy fear built an
ark[z] to save his family.[a] By his faith he
condemned the world and became heir of
the righteousness that is in keeping with
faith.
8By faith Abraham, when called to go
to a place he would later receive as his
inheritance,[b] obeyed and went,[c] even
though he did not know where he was going. 9By faith he made his home in the
promised land[d] like a stranger in a foreign
country; he lived in tents,[e] as did Isaac

10:36 [o] Lk 21:19; Heb 12:1 **10:37** [p] Mt 11:3 [q] Rev 22:20 **10:38** [r] Ro 1:17; Gal 3:11 **11:1** [s] Ro 8:24; 2Co 4:18 **11:2** [t] ver 4, 39 **11:3** [u] Ge 1; Jn 1:3; 2Pe 3:5 **11:4** [v] Ge 4:4; 1Jn 3:12 [w] Heb 12:24 **11:5** [x] Ge 5:21-24 **11:6** [y] Heb 7:19 **11:7** [z] Ge 6:13-22 [a] 1Pe 3:20 **11:8** [b] Ge 12:7 [c] Ge 12:1-4; Ac 7:2-4 **11:9** [d] Ac 7:5 [e] Ge 12:8; 18:1,9

[a] *37* Isaiah 26:20; Hab. 2:3 [b] *38* Some early manuscripts *But the righteous* [c] *38* Hab. 2:4 (see Septuagint) [d] *5* Gen. 5:24

10:37 *In just a little while.* The writer here quotes a line from the Greek translation of Hab 2:3, adding "a little while" from the Greek translation of Isa 26:20. The blending is not likely a coincidence; he cited the context of the latter verse in v. 27 (see note there).
10:38 *my righteous one will live by faith.* The writer continues his quotation (v. 37), mostly quoting the Greek version of Hab 2:4 (see note on Ro 1:17). Nevertheless, like Paul elsewhere, this writer omits the Greek version's "my" in front of "faith," in this case joining it instead to "righteous one." Although the common Greek version read "my faith," i.e., God's faithfulness, the Hebrew read "his faith," presumably that of the righteous, as meant here. The writer then elaborates on this persevering faith in 10:39 — 12:3.
10:39 *destroyed ... saved.* In the context of Hab 2:4 (see note on v. 38), the wicked face destruction but the righteous trust God for deliverance.
11:1 – 40 After encouraging his audience regarding persevering faith (10:38 – 39), the author defines this kind of faith (v. 1) and offers a thesis statement (v. 2), an appropriate way to begin a discourse on a subject. Writers sometimes praised a virtue, as here (see note on 1Co 13:1 – 13); orators would often drive home a point by repeating the same opening word or words, as here ("by faith"); and Jewish writers sometimes summarized Jewish history in a way that emphasized a particular element of it (Ac 7; also in works as diverse as 1 Maccabees 2:49 – 69; Sirach 44 – 50). The author climaxes with the ultimate hero of the faith in Heb 12:1 – 3.
11:3 *the universe was formed at God's command.* God spoke existence into being (Ge 1:3 – 24; Ps 33:6; Pr 3:19 – 20). Many cultures believed that the current ordered world was simply the result of arranging already preexistent matter. Jewish people commonly spoke of God creating the universe without prior substance (2 Maccabees 7:28). Some Diaspora Jews believed that God first formed his wisdom, or *Logos*, by which he then designed and created the world (for this belief they combined texts such as Pr 8:22 – 31 with elements of Platonic philosophy).
11:4 *Abel brought God a better offering than Cain.* God preferred Abel's offering (Ge 4:4). *Abel still speaks.* His blood cried from the ground (Ge 4:10), indicating that the legacy of the righteous person remains before God and that vindication will be accomplished. Jewish tradition highlighted Abel as the first martyr and further embellished Cain's wickedness and punishments.
11:5 *Enoch ... did not experience death.* Following the most natural reading of Ge 5:21 – 24, most early Judean sources viewed Enoch as particularly righteous and exempted from death. Some Diaspora Jews identified him with Greek figures such as Atlas. Later rabbis, reacting against the glorifying of Enoch at the expense of more Jewish figures such as Moses, condemned Enoch as shifting between righteousness and wickedness. The writer of Hebrews follows the Biblical account rather than the later traditions some had added to it.
11:6 Writers often cited the example of a person to draw moral lessons from their character; that Enoch pleased God enough to be taken away alive (v. 5) indicates that he had faith. Some other terms in this verse (such as "rewards"; cf. v. 26; 10:35) also fit the author's emphasis.
11:7 *By faith Noah ... condemned the world.* Many early Jewish stories honored Noah. (Later rabbis, emphasizing that most of Noah's descendants were Gentiles, preferred to transfer such stories to Moses.) Jewish teachers sometimes noted that the righteous choices of the righteous would discredit the excuses of the wicked on the day of judgment.
11:8 *By faith Abraham ... obeyed and went.* Jewish tradition highlighted Abraham's faith (already explicit in Scripture, e.g., Ge 15:6) and often used him as a role model. Abraham's obedience to God's call, leaving his home and relatives behind, was an act of faith (Ge 12:1,4).

and Jacob, who were heirs with him of
the same promise.[f] 10For he was looking
forward to the city[g] with foundations,[h]
whose architect and builder is God. 11And
by faith even Sarah, who was past childbearing age,[i] was enabled to bear children[j]
because she[a] considered him faithful who
had made the promise. 12And so from this
one man, and he as good as dead,[k] came
descendants as numerous as the stars in
the sky and as countless as the sand on
the seashore.[l]
13All these people were still living by
faith when they died. They did not receive the things promised;[m] they only
saw them and welcomed them from a
distance,[n] admitting that they were foreigners and strangers on earth.[o] 14People
who say such things show that they are
looking for a country of their own. 15If
they had been thinking of the country
they had left, they would have had opportunity to return.[p] 16Instead, they were
longing for a better country — a heavenly
one.[q] Therefore God is not ashamed[r] to
be called their God,[s] for he has prepared
a city[t] for them.
17By faith Abraham, when God tested him, offered Isaac as a sacrifice.[u] He
who had embraced the promises was
about to sacrifice his one and only son,
18even though God had said to him, "It
is through Isaac that your offspring will
be reckoned."[b][v] 19Abraham reasoned that
God could even raise the dead,[w] and so in
a manner of speaking he did receive Isaac
back from death.
20By faith Isaac blessed Jacob and Esau
in regard to their future.[x]
21By faith Jacob, when he was dying,
blessed each of Joseph's sons,[y] and worshiped as he leaned on the top of his staff.
22By faith Joseph, when his end was
near, spoke about the exodus of the Israelites from Egypt and gave instructions concerning the burial of his bones.[z]
23By faith Moses' parents hid him for
three months after he was born,[a] because
they saw he was no ordinary child, and
they were not afraid of the king's edict.[b]
24By faith Moses, when he had grown
up, refused to be known as the son of
Pharaoh's daughter.[c] 25He chose to be

11:9 [f]Heb 6:17 **11:10** [g]Heb 12:22; 13:14 [h]Rev 21:2, 14 **11:11** [i]Ge 17:17-19; 18:11-14 [j]Ge 21:2 **11:12** [k]Ro 4:19 [l]Ge 22:17 **11:13** [m]ver 39 [n]Mt 13:17 [o]Ge 23:4; Ps 39:12; 1Pe 1:17 **11:15** [p]Ge 24:6-8 **11:16** [q]2Ti 4:18 [r]Mk 8:38 [s]Ex 3:6, 15 [t]Heb 13:14 **11:17** [u]Ge 22:1-10; Jas 2:21 **11:18** [v]Ge 21:12; Ro 9:7 **11:19** [w]Ro 4:21 **11:20** [x]Ge 27:27-29, 39, 40 **11:21** [y]Ge 48:1, 8-22 **11:22** [z]Ge 50:24, 25; Ex 13:19 **11:23** [a]Ex 2:2 [b]Ex 1:16, 22 **11:24** [c]Ex 2:10, 11

[a] 11 Or *By faith Abraham, even though he was too old to have children — and Sarah herself was not able to conceive — was enabled to become a father because he*
[b] 18 Gen. 21:12

11:10 *the city ... whose architect and builder is God.* Many Diaspora Jews viewed God as the world's "architect and builder" (cf. 3:4); some spoke of heaven as the "mother city," designed and constructed by God; one could not look for the heavenly Jerusalem on earth. More often, Judeans and some Diaspora Jews instead saw the new Jerusalem as the city of God for the future age (see note on Gal 4:26). *foundations.* See note on Rev 21:14; cf. also Heb 13:14.
11:11 *Sarah ... was enabled to bear children.* Jewish tradition highlighted and amplified Sarah's faith. Like Abraham, Sarah laughed (Ge 17:17; 18:12); human faith is limited, but God affirmed it and blessed them.
11:12 See Ge 22:17.
11:13 *they were foreigners and strangers on earth.* Jewish residents of Diaspora cities were often counted as resident aliens; Diaspora Jews understood what it meant to be strangers. Abraham was a foreigner and stranger in Canaan (Ge 23:4) and on one level the same was true for Israel, since the land was God's (Lev 25:23).
11:16 *a better country — a heavenly one.* Some Diaspora Jewish thinkers (such as Philo) spoke of heaven rather than earth as the home of the righteous. The author of Hebrews, however, looks for the future experience of the city, i.e., the new Jerusalem (cf. Isa 65:17 – 18; Rev 21:2).
11:17 *By faith Abraham ... offered Isaac as a sacrifice.* God accepted Abraham's faith in Ge 15:6, but it was still limited (Ge 15:8; 16:2); it grew over the years of walking with God. The offering of Isaac, after years of waiting for the promise of this son, was Abraham's ultimate test of faith (Ge 22). Jewish readers rightly recognized this, and presented Abraham's action as a model of faith. Although Jewish tradition also noted Isaac's willingness to be sacrificed, the writer of Hebrews does not add such details to the Biblical narrative. *his one and only son.* Jewish people sometimes used "one and only son" (cf. Ge 22:2) to mean "specially loved," including in the case of Isaac.
11:19 *Abraham reasoned that God could even raise the dead.* Abraham said that he would return with his son (Ge 22:5) and told Isaac that God would provide the offering (Ge 22:8); by now his faith was so strong that he understood that even if he carried out God's instructions, God would restore his son and fulfill the promise. God had, after all, promised that his descendants would be reckoned through Isaac (Ge 21:12).
11:20 *By faith Isaac blessed Jacob and Esau.* Jewish people recognized that Isaac's blessings were inspired and that they included predictions of the future (as divinely led prayers [Ge 27:28 – 29,39 – 40]).
11:21 *By faith Jacob ... blessed each of Joseph's sons.* Jewish people also regarded the blessings of Ge 49 as prophetic. (Jewish storytellers also later expanded on these blessings.)
11:22 *By faith Joseph ... spoke about the exodus.* Joseph knew that the promise of land to Abraham's descendants would be fulfilled, even if not in his own lifetime (see Ge 50:24 – 25).
11:23 *By faith Moses' parents hid him for three months.* The writer follows Ex 2:2 – 3. (Some other Jewish writers expanded the story of Moses' birth, especially his beauty, into reports that glory illumined the room when he was born.)
11:24 *By faith Moses ... refused to be known as the son of Pharaoh's daughter.* Writers often drew lessons from their accounts. This writer does so, but he does not add extra-Biblical tradition. Many Jewish storytellers depicted Moses' Egyptian education (which may be assumed for members of the royal family; cf. Ac 7:22) and Moses himself as an Egyptian military hero. Given common understanding of adoption in the first century, many understood Moses as Pharaoh's heir; whether or not this is in view here (Pharaohs usually had many sons; Moses rejected status to identify with his oppressed people [v. 25]).

mistreated[d] along with the people of God rather than to enjoy the fleeting pleasures of sin. 26He regarded disgrace[e] for the sake of Christ as of greater value than the treasures of Egypt, because he was looking ahead to his reward.[f] 27By faith he left Egypt,[g] not fearing the king's anger; he persevered because he saw him who is invisible. 28By faith he kept the Passover and the application of blood, so that the destroyer of the firstborn would not touch the firstborn of Israel.[h]

29By faith the people passed through the Red Sea as on dry land; but when the Egyptians tried to do so, they were drowned.[i]

30By faith the walls of Jericho fell, after the army had marched around them for seven days.[j]

31By faith the prostitute Rahab, because she welcomed the spies, was not killed with those who were disobedient.[a][k]

32And what more shall I say? I do not have time to tell about Gideon, Barak,[l] Samson and Jephthah, about David[m] and Samuel[n] and the prophets, 33who through faith conquered kingdoms,[o] administered justice, and gained what was promised; who shut the mouths of lions,[p] 34quenched the fury of the flames, and escaped the edge of the sword; whose weakness was turned to strength;[q] and who became powerful in battle and routed foreign armies.[r] 35Women received back their dead, raised to life again.[s] There were others who were tortured, refusing to be released so that they might gain an even better resurrection. 36Some faced jeers and flogging,[t] and even chains and imprisonment.[u] 37They were put to death by stoning;[b][v] they were sawed in two; they were killed by the sword.[w] They went about in sheepskins and goatskins,[x] destitute, persecuted and mistreated — 38the world was not worthy of them. They wandered in deserts and mountains, living in caves[y] and in holes in the ground.

11:25 [d] ver 37
11:26 [e] Heb 13:13 [f] Heb 10:35
11:27 [g] Ex 12:50,51
11:28 [h] Ex 12:21-23
11:29 [i] Ex 14:21-31
11:30 [j] Jos 6:12-20
11:31 [k] Jos 2:1, 9-14; 6:22-25; Jas 2:25
11:32 [l] Jdg 4-5 [m] 1Sa 16:1,13 [n] 1Sa 1:20
11:33 [o] 2Sa 7:11; 8:1-3 [p] Da 6:22
11:34 [q] 2Ki 20:7 [r] Jdg 15:8
11:35 [s] 1Ki 17:22,23
11:36 [t] Jer 20:2 [u] Ge 39:20
11:37 [v] 2Ch 24:21 [w] 1Ki 19:10 [x] 2Ki 1:8
11:38 [y] 1Ki 18:4

[a] *31* Or *unbelieving* [b] *37* Some early manuscripts *stoning; they were put to the test;*

11:26 *the treasures of Egypt.* Although Egypt was repressed under Roman rule, everyone knew of its past grandeur and wealth; it was this region's most powerful empire in Moses' day.
11:27 *not fearing the king's anger.* Many Jewish writers played down Moses' fear. Moses actually did fear the king (Ex 2:14–15), but the writer of Hebrews might mean that Moses was not afraid enough to deny his people; or perhaps that Moses' faith in God surmounted fear; or, perhaps likeliest of all, the writer refers to the exodus, when Moses led his people out of Egypt (cf. their Passover in v. 28). *him who is invisible.* Diaspora Jews emphasized Gods invisibility.
11:28 *By faith he kept the Passover.* The writer alludes to Ex 12. All Israel kept the Passover, though the writer is still emphasizing Moses.
11:29 *By faith the people passed through the Red Sea as on dry land.* Cf. Ex 14:29; Ne 9:11. Exodus reports the completion of Israel's faith after the miracle (Ex 14:31), but Moses exercised faith (Ex 14:13–18), and his people had to act in some faith to enter the basin (cf. Ex 14:22). Some Jewish teachers affirmed Israel's faith but many others attributed the miracle to the faith or merit of their ancestors.
11:30 *By faith the walls of Jericho fell.* See Jos 6.
11:31 *By faith … Rahab … was not killed.* Hebrews follows Jos 2; 6. (By contrast, later rabbis elaborated more extensive stories about Rahab.)
11:32 *I do not have time to tell.* Speakers and writers often noted that they could comment more fully but for the audience's sake would not do so. Sometimes they would introduce the topics that they said they would not cover (cf. Phm 19); in this case, the central audience of Hebrews knew these stories well. *Barak.* Most first-century hearers would consider Barak the official leader in Jdg 4–5 even though Deborah gave the divine instructions.
11:33 *through faith conquered kingdoms.* Alludes to David and many judges (including Gideon, Barak, and Jephthah [v. 32]). *administered justice.* May refer to Samson, among others (see Jdg 15:20, where the NIV text note says Samson "judged" Israel, though this also means, as with the NIV text there, that he led them). *shut the mouths of lions.* Undoubtedly, the writer of Hebrews refers to the faith of Daniel (Da 6:16–24), presumably one of the "prophets" of Heb 11:32.
11:34 *quenched the fury of the flames.* Likely, Daniel's friends are in view here (Da 3:23–27; some Jewish tradition also claimed this for Abraham). *whose weakness was turned to strength.* Could evoke the return of power to Samson (Jdg 16:28–31) but might be more general (1Sa 2:4–5). *routed foreign armies.* Could refer to many leaders, including all those named in v. 32 and the later, renowned Maccabees.
11:35 *Women received back their dead.* See 1Ki 17:17–24; 2Ki 4:18–37. *tortured, refusing to be released.* Nearly all Jews knew the stories of Maccabean martyrs, who were tortured by being scalded to death, having their skin flayed off, and so forth. Common Greek torture practices included fire, thumbscrews and (the activity from which the word translated "tortured" here originally derived) stretching on a wheel to break the person's joints, then beating the victim to death. Jewish people expected martyrs to be rewarded at the resurrection, a hope highlighted, e.g., in 2 Maccabees.
11:36 *flogging.* Scourging, which required first stripping, was a common punishment both by itself and when preceding execution. *chains and imprisonment.* Matters of great shame and deprivation; chains could be heavy and prisoners usually depended on outside help for food to supplement their basic rations.
11:37 *stoning.* Hostile people stoned or considered stoning prophets and other servants of God (Ex 17:4; Nu 14:10; 1Sa 30:6; 2Ch 24:21); some Jewish tradition amplified this, claiming that Jeremiah, e.g., died by stoning. *sawed in two.* Jewish tradition claimed that Isaiah, hiding inside a tree, was sawed in two. *went about in sheepskins and goatskins.* John wore animal skins (Mk 1:6; cf. 2Ki 1:8); he and Elijah sojourned in the wilderness, as did others, including David when fleeing Saul and the Maccabees when fighting guerilla warfare, especially in the hill country.

39 These were all commended[z] for their
faith, yet none of them received what had
been promised,[a] 40 since God had planned
something better for us so that only together with us would they be made perfect.

12 Therefore, since we are surrounded
by such a great cloud of witness-
es, let us throw off everything that hinders
and the sin that so easily entangles. And
let us run[b] with perseverance[c] the race
marked out for us, 2 fixing our eyes on
Jesus, the pioneer and perfecter of faith.
For the joy set before him he endured the
cross,[d] scorning its shame,[e] and sat down
at the right hand of the throne of God.
3 Consider him who endured such opposition from sinners, so that you will not
grow weary[f] and lose heart.

God Disciplines His Children

4 In your struggle against sin, you have
not yet resisted to the point of shedding
your blood.[g] 5 And have you completely
forgotten this word of encouragement that
addresses you as a father addresses his
son? It says,

> "My son, do not make light of the
> Lord's discipline,
> and do not lose heart when he
> rebukes you,
> 6 because the Lord disciplines the one he
> loves,[h]
> and he chastens everyone he accepts
> as his son."[a][i]

7 Endure hardship as discipline; God is
treating you as his children.[j] For what
children are not disciplined by their father? 8 If you are not disciplined — and
everyone undergoes discipline[k] — then
you are not legitimate, not true sons and
daughters at all. 9 Moreover, we have all
had human fathers who disciplined us
and we respected them for it. How much
more should we submit to the Father of
spirits[l] and live![m] 10 They disciplined us
for a little while as they thought best;
but God disciplines us for our good, in
order that we may share in his holiness.[n]
11 No discipline seems pleasant at the
time, but painful. Later on, however, it
produces a harvest of righteousness and
peace[o] for those who have been trained
by it.

12 Therefore, strengthen your feeble arms

11:39 [z] ver 2,4 [a] ver 13
12:1 [b] 1Co 9:24 [c] Heb 10:36
12:2 [d] Php 2:8,9 [e] Heb 13:13
12:3 [f] Gal 6:9
12:4 [g] Heb 10:32-34
12:6 [h] Ps 94:12; Rev 3:19 [i] Pr 3:11,12
12:7 [j] Dt 8:5
12:8 [k] 1Pe 5:9
12:9 [l] Nu 16:22 [m] Isa 38:16
12:10 [n] 2Pe 1:4
12:11 [o] Isa 32:17; Jas 3:17,18

[a] 5,6 Prov. 3:11,12 (see Septuagint)

11:39 – 40 Here the author offers a concluding summary for vv. 3 – 38, part of it rehearsing the author's thesis in v. 2 (though one further example climaxes the list of heroes of the faith in 12:1 – 3). Concluding summaries of one's thesis were very common.

11:40 *perfect.* May refer to the promised future resurrection of the righteous (v. 35); all the righteous would be raised together at the very end of the age (Da 12:2,13).

12:1 *witnesses.* May reflect the image of people watching a race (writers sometimes used "cloud" figuratively for a crowd), but the specific witnesses here may be those who also received God's commendation (lit. "testimony" or "witness") that they were righteous (11:2,4,5,39). (Some Jewish sources thought of a heavenly court; perhaps one could envision faith heroes of the past who would judge those now vying for the same honors.) *throw off everything that hinders.* Could refer to removing artificial weights used in training but not in races, but more likely it simply refers to the Greek custom of stripping off clothes to run unencumbered. (Ancient writers sometimes used "weights" figuratively for vices.). This encouragement is significant, for like Israel in the wilderness, this audience may be tempted to turn back. *let us run with perseverance the race.* The writer here uses the image of runners disciplining themselves for competition (some suggest also in vv. 12 – 13). Greek thinkers often used athletic contests to depict the moral battle waged by the wise person; the Diaspora Jewish writer of 4 Maccabees sometimes applied the image to martyrs.

12:2 *fixing our eyes on Jesus.* One running a race needed to keep one's eyes fixed on the goal (cf. Php 3:14). *pioneer.* See note on 2:10. *pioneer and perfecter of faith.* Jesus climaxes the list of heroes of the faith (11:2 – 40). *endured the cross, scorning its shame.* Jesus suffered in the hope of future reward, as these readers are to do (10:32 – 39). Both Jews (cf. Dt 21:23; Jos 10:26 – 27) and Romans viewed death by crucifixion as shameful. *sat down at the right hand.* Reflects Ps 110:1, cited in Heb 1:13.

12:4 *to the point of shedding your blood.* Although they had suffered (10:32 – 34), they had not yet had to give their lives like some of their esteemed predecessors (v. 2; 11:35 – 37).

12:7 *Endure hardship as discipline; God is treating you as his children.* Some other Jewish thinkers applied Pr 3:11 – 12 (cited in vv. 5 – 6) in similar ways, and the idea that is taught there is even more widespread (cf., e.g., Dt 8:5; Ps 94:12). *disciplined by their father.* Jewish wisdom literature understood appropriate discipline as a sign of a father's concern for his children. Suffering can lead to greater maturity (Ps 119:67,71,75).

12:8 *not legitimate, not true sons and daughters.* In ancient society, not being legitimate was considered shameful and normally meant that one would not inherit; fathers invested more effort in "legitimate" children. (The writer simply draws on a familiar image; he does not genuinely view those born outside marriage as spiritually inferior — compare 11:32 with Jdg 11:1).

12:9 *Father of spirits.* God was often called "Lord of spirits" (1 Enoch 37 – 71 passim; cf. Nu 16:22; 27:16); here he is called "Father of spirits" in contrast to human fathers. Jewish tradition developed the Biblical concept of God as their father (e.g., Ex 4:22), and, as here, understood and often used "How much more?" arguments.

12:10 *God disciplines us for our good.* The audience would easily follow the author's argument. Jewish tradition recognized that God disciplined the righteous for their good and only for a time, and that he would afterward reward them. Jewish people also expected the Lord to punish the wicked more severely, especially in the future.

12:12 *feeble arms and weak knees.* Language such as this sometimes described people's terror in the face of God's judgment, but the language here more closely echoes the encouragement to God's oppressed people

and weak knees.[p] 13“Make level paths for
your feet,”[a][q] so that the lame may not be
disabled, but rather healed.[r]

Warning and Encouragement

14Make every effort to live in peace with
everyone[s] and to be holy;[t] without holiness no one will see the Lord.[u] 15See to
it that no one falls short of the grace of
God[v] and that no bitter root grows up to
cause trouble and defile many. 16See that
no one is sexually immoral, or is godless
like Esau, who for a single meal sold his
inheritance rights as the oldest son.[w] 17Af-
terward, as you know, when he wanted to
inherit this blessing, he was rejected. Even
though he sought the blessing with tears,[x]
he could not change what he had done.

The Mountain of Fear and the Mountain of Joy

18You have not come to a mountain
that can be touched and that is burning
with fire; to darkness, gloom and storm;[y]
19to a trumpet blast[z] or to such a voice
speaking words that those who heard it
begged that no further word be spoken
to them,[a] 20because they could not bear
what was commanded: “If even an animal touches the mountain, it must be
stoned to death.”[b][b] 21The sight was so
terrifying that Moses said, “I am trembling with fear.”[c]
22But you have come to Mount Zion, to
the city[c] of the living God, the heavenly
Jerusalem.[d] You have come to thousands
upon thousands of angels in joyful assembly, 23to the church of the firstborn,
whose names are written in heaven.[e] You
have come to God, the Judge of all,[f] to the
spirits of the righteous made perfect,[g] 24to
Jesus the mediator of a new covenant, and
to the sprinkled blood that speaks a better
word than the blood of Abel.[h]

12:12 [p]Isa 35:3 **12:13** [q]Pr 4:26 [r]Gal 6:1 **12:14** [s]Ro 14:19 [t]Ro 6:22 [u]Mt 5:8 **12:15** [v]Gal 5:4; Heb 3:12 **12:16** [w]Ge 25:29-34 **12:17** [x]Ge 27:30-40 **12:18** [y]Ex 19:12-22; Dt 4:11 **12:19** [z]Ex 20:18 [a]Ex 20:19; Dt 5:5,25 **12:20** [b]Ex 19:12, 13 **12:22** [c]Heb 11:10 [d]Gal 4:26 **12:23** [e]Lk 10:20 [f]Ps 94:2 [g]Php 3:12 **12:24** [h]Ge 4:10; Heb 11:4

[a] *13* Prov. 4:26 [b] *20* Exodus 19:12,13 [c] *21* See Deut. 9:19.

to persevere because they are on the verge of vindication and restoration (Isa 35:3). (Hebrews' major change, a different verb for "strengthen," is related to the verb in the next quotation in v. 13.) Possibly vv. 12 – 13 might revisit the race image of vv. 1 – 3.

12:13 *lame may not be disabled.* The writer echoes Pr 4:26, where this image is a moral one; the healing of the lame may echo the context of the preceding quotation (Isa 35:3), where in the time of restoration God heals the disabled (Isa 35:6).

12:14 – 29 Turning away from Jesus was worse than Esau's shortsighted apostasy (vv. 16 – 17) and more serious than rejecting the revelation of God at Sinai (vv. 18 – 21), for Jesus is greater than Moses and greater than Abel (v. 24). Most of the Jewish people felt embarrassed by the rebellion of many of their ancestors in the wilderness; the writer warns that if his hearers turn their backs on Christ, they are even worse than their ancestors.

12:14 *Make every effort to live in peace.* Echoes the Greek translation of Ps 34:14.

12:15 *no bitter root grows up.* In Dt 29:18, the bitter root of apostasy can spread to infect many.

12:16 *sexually immoral, or ... godless like Esau.* In Ge 25:31 – 34, Esau did not act as if he viewed life from a long-range perspective, much less an eternal one (the rabbis inferred from this text that he denied the future resurrection of the dead). Noting Esau's actions, the Diaspora Jewish writer Philo regarded Esau as enslaved by sensual and temporal desires. Jewish tradition deemed Esau sexually immoral, probably originally based on his initial preference for Gentile wives (Ge 26:34 – 35), which dismayed his parents (Ge 26:35; 28:8).

12:17 *sought the blessing with tears.* Despite his tears (Ge 27:38), it was too late for Esau to regain the blessing, because the first blessing could not be annulled. He was effectively disinherited from the promise (cf. Heb 6:12 – 18).

12:18 God warned of his power in these ways when he gave the law on the mountain (Ex 19:16; 20:18,21; Dt 4:11 – 12). *burning with fire.* Translates similar wording in Dt 4:11; 5:23; 9:15. *darkness.* The Greek term used here appears in the Greek translation of Ex 20:21; Dt 4:11; 5:22. *gloom.* The Greek term for "gloom" rhymes with the Greek term for "darkness." *storm.* The same Greek term appears in the Greek text of Dt 4:11; 5:22.

12:19 *trumpet blast.* See Ex 19:19; 20:18. *begged that no further word be spoken to them.* The people wanted Moses to hear God for them, fearing that if God spoke to them directly, they would die (Ex 20:18 – 21; Dt 5:24 – 27), for he came as a consuming fire (Dt 4:24). But God's purpose was to inspire the fear of God in them to warn them against sin (Ex 20:20).

12:20 *could not bear.* For God's unapproachable holiness here, see Ex 19:12 – 13; cf. Nu 17:13.

12:21 Moses feared for Israel's survival because of their sin (Dt 9:18 – 19).

12:22 *Mount Zion.* A reference to the temple or more broadly, as here, Jerusalem. Jerusalem, as opposed to Mount Sinai, was to be the place of the giving of the new law in the end time (Isa 2:1 – 4). *heavenly Jerusalem.* See note on 11:10. Everyone in antiquity would regard a heavenly place of revelation as superior to an earthly one, regardless of the earthly one's impressiveness (vv. 18 – 21). *thousands upon thousands of angels.* Jewish tradition claimed that vast numbers of angels were present when God gave the law, often citing Ps 68:17; the main source here (probably also for the psalm) is Dt 33:2.

12:23 *the church of the firstborn.* The popular Greek version of the OT already sometimes used the Greek term translated "church" to designate the assembly of God's people; thus the writer of Hebrews here contrasts the congregation led by Jesus with the one led by Moses (v. 19). *firstborn.* See note on 1:6; because the reference to the "firstborn" here is plural in Greek, it may refer to God's people as a whole here — e.g., Ex 4:22. *names are written in heaven.* People's names were often written in ancient citizen registers; the writer probably alludes especially to the widespread Jewish concept of the book of life (see note on Php 4:3). *spirits of the righteous made perfect.* In some Jewish apocalyptic texts, "spirits" could refer to the righteous dead in heaven. Many Diaspora Jews believed that the righteous finally attained perfection in death (or in resurrection, cf. 11:40; some suggest that "the righteous" of 12:23 include the heroes of ch. 11).

12:24 *Jesus the mediator of a new covenant.* Jewish people regarded Moses as the mediator of the first covenant (cf. 8:5 – 6; 9:15), who inaugurated it with sprinkled blood

[25]See to it that you do not refuse him who speaks. If they did not escape when they refused him who warned[i] them on earth, how much less will we, if we turn away from him who warns us from heaven?[j] [26]At that time his voice shook the earth,[k] but now he has promised, "Once more I will shake not only the earth but also the heavens."[a l] [27]The words "once more" indicate the removing of what can be shaken[m]—that is, created things—so that what cannot be shaken may remain.

[28]Therefore, since we are receiving a kingdom that cannot be shaken,[n] let us be thankful, and so worship God acceptably with reverence and awe,[o] [29]for our "God is a consuming fire."[b p]

Concluding Exhortations

13 Keep on loving one another as brothers and sisters.[q] [2]Do not forget to show hospitality to strangers,[r] for by so doing some people have shown hospitality to angels without knowing it.[s] [3]Continue to remember those in prison[t] as if you were together with them in prison, and those who are mistreated as if you yourselves were suffering.

[4]Marriage should be honored by all, and the marriage bed kept pure, for God will judge the adulterer and all the sexually immoral.[u] [5]Keep your lives free from the love of money and be content with what you have,[v] because God has said,

"Never will I leave you;
never will I forsake you."[c w]

[6]So we say with confidence,

"The Lord is my helper; I will not be afraid.
What can mere mortals do to me?"[d]

[7]Remember your leaders,[x] who spoke the word of God to you. Consider the outcome of their way of life and imitate[y] their

12:25 [i]Heb 8:5; 11:7 [j]Heb 2:2,3 **12:26** [k]Ex 19:18 [l]Hag 2:6 **12:27** [m]1Co 7:31; 2Pe 3:10 **12:28** [n]Da 2:44 [o]Heb 13:15 **12:29** [p]Dt 4:24 **13:1** [q]Ro 12:10; 1Pe 1:22 **13:2** [r]Mt 25:35 [s]Ge 18:1-33 **13:3** [t]Mt 25:36; Col 4:18 **13:4** [u]1Co 6:9 **13:5** [v]Php 4:11 [w]Dt 31:6,8; Jos 1:5 **13:7** [x]ver 17,24 [y]Heb 6:12

[a] 26 Haggai 2:6 [b] 29 Deut. 4:24 [c] 5 Deut. 31:6 [d] 6 Psalm 118:6,7

(Ex 24:8). *sprinkled blood ... blood of Abel.* In contrast to Jesus' blood, Abel's blood cried for vengeance (Ge 4:10; cf. Heb 11:4). (Illustrating how seriously Jewish interpreters took that passage in Genesis, later rabbis charged that the blood of all the descendants who would have been born from Abel cried out to God against Cain, and Cain thus had no share in the world to come.) Cf. note on Mt 23:35.

12:25 The heavenly Zion is greater than the earthly Sinai (v. 22), and judgment for rejecting the voice from heaven (Mk 1:11; cf. v. 19) is correspondingly greater. *how much less will we ...?* Reflects a familiar type of "How much more?" argument (cf. v. 9; 9:14; 10:29).

12:26 *shake not only the earth but also the heavens.* Many Jewish people expected a great end-time earthquake, following some OT texts (Isa 13:13; Hag 2:6 [in mind here]; cf. Hag 2:21). The land quaked when God came to give the law on Mount Sinai (Ex 19:18; Ps 68:8); later Jewish tradition amplified this point to say that God shook the whole world.

12:27 *once more.* Might also imply reference to the previous shaking, perhaps referring to Sinai (see v. 26 and note); the future shaking, however, would impact all creation (cf. Rev 6:12). *the removing of what can be shaken.* The author argues that the reason there will be one final shaking is because nothing shakable will remain after it. *what cannot be shaken may remain.* On the permanence of perfect and heavenly things, see note on 7:11–19.

12:28 *kingdom that cannot be shaken.* For God's unshakable reign, cf. the popular Greek translation of Ps 93:1; 96:10; cf. Ps 99:1; for Mount Zion as unshakable, see Ps 46:5; 125:1.

12:29 *God is a consuming fire.* The author quotes Dt 4:24 (cf. Ex 24:17; Dt 9:3; Isa 30:27; 33:14). The context is God's anger against those who broke his covenant by worshiping other deities (Dt 4:23–25).

13:1–17 Ancient moral teachers often provided exhortations loosely fitted together, often after more sustained argumentation (cf., e.g., Ro 12–14; Gal 5–6; Eph 4–6).

13:2 *hospitality to angels.* The highly regarded ancient virtue of hospitality included lodging and feeding trustworthy travelers in one's home. Jewish sources praised as the greatest model of this hospitality Abraham, who welcomed the three visitors (Ge 18)—at least two of whom turned out to be angels. (Some hearers may have also thought of other stories, like an angel in the Jewish story of Tobit or Greek stories about gods visiting people in disguise.)

13:3 *remember those in prison.* Prisoners had to depend on those outside for food beyond basic prison rations, for clothing and other items; guards sometimes required bribes even to grant this much access. Prisons detained people until trial or execution, but prisoners could remain in custody for long periods of time until trial. By the second century, Christians were known for their care for the imprisoned. *those in prison.* Probably refers to some Christians imprisoned for their faith or for practices related to it (as in v. 23; cf. 10:34; 11:36).

13:4 *the marriage bed kept pure.* Many ancient writers spoke of honoring the "(marriage) bed" (the "bed" was a euphemism for intercourse). Most people regarded adultery as wrong, although it is commonly reported. Greek men often married around age 30, before that time fulfilling sexual urges with prostitutes, slaves, or other males. Greek men often had affairs with boys around the age of puberty and young men in their teens. Following Scripture, Jewish circles regarded such behaviors as immoral.

13:5 *Never will I leave you; never will I forsake you.* In Dt 31:6,8 Moses offers this promise to Israel, describing God in the third person, but the writer of Hebrews, who regards all Scripture as God's inspired Word, uses Jos 1:5 (a prophecy of assurance to Joshua as God's servant) to adapt it to God speaking in the first person.

13:6 The author of Hebrews cites the Greek version of Ps 118:6 (cf. Ps 56:11; 118:7). He may add this to the previous quotation of Dt 31:6,8 because Dt 31:6,8 says that the hearers should not be afraid (although the writer of Hebrews does not quote that line). Writers often linked texts based on similar words. (The Judean practice of linking texts in this manner was called *gezerah shevah.*)

13:7 *Remember your leaders.* When teaching on moral subjects, teachers often offered examples as role models.

faith. 8Jesus Christ is the same yesterday
and today and forever.[z]
9Do not be carried away by all kinds
of strange teachings.[a] It is good for our
hearts to be strengthened[b] by grace, not
by eating ceremonial foods,[c] which is
of no benefit to those who do so. 10We
have an altar from which those who
minister at the tabernacle have no right
to eat.[d]
11The high priest carries the blood of
animals into the Most Holy Place as a sin
offering, but the bodies are burned outside the camp.[e] 12And so Jesus also suffered outside the city gate[f] to make the
people holy through his own blood. 13Let
us, then, go to him outside the camp,
bearing the disgrace he bore.[g] 14For here
we do not have an enduring city, but we
are looking for the city that is to come.[h]
15Through Jesus, therefore, let us
continually offer to God a sacrifice[i] of
praise — the fruit of lips[j] that openly profess his name. 16And do not forget to do
good and to share with others,[k] for with
such sacrifices[l] God is pleased.

13:8 [z] Heb 1:12
13:9 [a] Eph 4:14 [b] Col 2:7 [c] Col 2:16
13:10 [d] 1Co 9:13; 10:18
13:11 [e] Ex 29:14; Lev 16:27
13:12 [f] Jn 19:17
13:13 [g] Heb 11:26
13:14 [h] Php 3:20; Heb 12:22
13:15 [i] 1Pe 2:5 [j] Hos 14:2
13:16 [k] Ro 12:13 [l] Php 4:18
13:17 [m] Isa 62:6; Ac 20:28
13:18 [n] 1Th 5:25 [o] Ac 23:1
13:19 [p] Phm 22
13:20 [q] Ro 15:33 [r] Isa 55:3; Eze 37:26; Zec 9:11 [s] Ac 2:24 [t] Jn 10:11
13:21 [u] Php 2:13 [v] 1Jn 3:22 [w] Ro 11:36
13:22 [x] 1Pe 5:12

17Have confidence in your leaders and
submit to their authority, because they
keep watch over you[m] as those who must
give an account. Do this so that their work
will be a joy, not a burden, for that would
be of no benefit to you.
18Pray for us.[n] We are sure that we have
a clear conscience[o] and desire to live honorably in every way. 19I particularly urge
you to pray so that I may be restored to
you soon.[p]

Benediction and Final Greetings

20Now may the God of peace,[q] who
through the blood of the eternal covenant[r]
brought back from the dead[s] our Lord
Jesus, that great Shepherd of the sheep,[t]
21equip you with everything good for doing
his will, and may he work in us[u] what is
pleasing to him,[v] through Jesus Christ, to
whom be glory for ever and ever. Amen.[w]
22Brothers and sisters, I urge you to bear
with my word of exhortation, for in fact I
have written to you quite briefly.[x]

13:8 In part because Greeks often emphasized the value of what was changeless and eternal, many Diaspora Jews emphasized the Biblical picture of God's changelessness (Ps 102:27; Mal 3:6).
13:9 *not by eating ceremonial foods.* Lev 11; Dt 14:3 – 20 listed "unclean" foods that Jewish people were to avoid. Some Diaspora Jews found allegorical significance in these laws, but it appears that the majority still practiced them literally (even those who allegorized them).
13:10 *no right to eat.* Now the author addresses a special kind of pure food (cf. v. 9): the priests' portion of the sacrifice in the tabernacle/temple (see note on 1Co 9:13). Believers, he says, serve as priests (v. 15) at a different kind of altar (cf. 7:13).
13:11 *bodies are burned outside the camp.* Burning sacrifices outside the camp was part of several different rituals (cf. Lev 9:11; Nu 19:3), but the present text refers to the Day of Atonement, when the priest went into the Most Holy Place with the blood of the sacrifice (Lev 16:27). This is the sacrifice Jesus fulfilled for the heavenly altar (Heb 9:12).
13:12 – 13 *outside the city … outside the camp.* That Jesus was crucified and buried outside Jerusalem's walls fits both the Gospel accounts and the ancient requirement that the dead be buried outside the city (so as to avoid contracting ritual impurity caused by contact with graves; cf., e.g., Lev 24:14; Nu 15:35 – 36; Dt 17:5; 22:24). Roman law also required that crucifixions occur outside the city gate. (Although sin offerings on the Day of Atonement were burned outside the camp [Lev 16:27], they were sacrificed in the temple or tabernacle [Lev 16:5 – 19].) For Hebrews' Jewish Christian audience, leaving "the camp" may imply enduring expulsion from their Jewish community, if need be, to follow the God of Abraham wholeheartedly (cf. Heb 11:13 – 16).
13:12 *make the people holy through his own blood.* Blood was sprinkled to purify things or make them holy (9:22).
13:14 *city that is to come.* See note on 11:10.
13:15 *let us continually offer to God a sacrifice of praise.* This passage may reflect Hos 14:2 (cf. also Isa 57:19). Ancient writers often depicted praise as an offering to God; for spiritual sacrifices, cf. Ps 40:6; 50:7 – 15; 51:17; 69:30 – 31; Pr 21:3.
13:16 *do not forget to do good.* Pharisees' belief in piety as a spiritual offering may have helped Pharisaism survive the destruction of the temple in AD 70. Passages such as this one illustrate that, theologically, Christians were even better prepared for that crisis.
13:17 *submit to their authority.* When writing on moral topics, writers often exhorted people how to submit to rulers. The exhortation here might function like a sort of "letter of recommendation" (on these, see note on 2Co 3:1). *submit.* Submission here is general, as often in ancient sources, not the extreme sort found, e.g., in the Dead Sea Scrolls: there leaders of the community would determine members' progress or lack of it, affecting members' standing in the community and before God.
13:19 *that I may be restored to you soon.* Some suspect that the author is imprisoned (cf. v. 23; Phm 22). Some prisoners had access to writing materials, especially in cases of lighter custody or favorable guards.
13:20 *blood of the eternal covenant.* The first covenant was inaugurated by the blood of the covenant (Ex 24:8), which Jewish tradition sometimes called the eternal covenant (a designation Scripture applied more clearly to earlier covenants such as Ge 9:16; 17:7,13; Ps 105:8 – 10; though cf. Lev 24:8; Nu 18:19). But the promised future covenant would also be eternal or everlasting (Isa 55:3; 61:8; Jer 32:40; 50:5; Eze 16:60; 37:26); it is the blood of this new covenant to which the author of Hebrews refers (Heb 9:12 – 22). *great Shepherd of the sheep.* See note on Jn 10:1 – 18. The Greek translation of Isa 63:11 says that God brought up the "shepherd of the sheep" (Moses) from the sea. The prophets had also prophesied a new exodus (cf. note on Ro 10:7).
13:22 *I have written to you quite briefly.* Skilled speakers sometimes claimed that they had spoken only briefly, despite it being obviously untrue, to imply that they could have said much more (cf. 11:32).

[23]I want you to know that our brother Timothy[y] has been released. If he arrives soon, I will come with him to see
you.

[24]Greet all your leaders[z] and all the
Lord's people. Those from Italy[a] send you
their greetings.
[25]Grace be with you all.[b]

13:23 [y] Ac 16:1
13:24 [z] ver 7, 17 [a] Ac 18:2
13:25 [b] Col 4:18

13:23 *Timothy has been released.* Timothy probably traveled to Rome to receive Paul's final instructions (2Ti 4:9,21). It was especially Nero who in this period persecuted Christians in Rome. If, as is likely, Timothy was arrested under Nero in Rome, he may well have been released on Nero's death in AD 68; the Praetorian Guard and the Roman aristocracy had already lost faith in Nero's policies.

13:24 *Those from Italy.* It seems likely that the author writes from Italy. *send you their greetings.* It was common for those in a letter writer's location to convey greetings when they knew the addressees.

THE LETTERS JAMES

Authorship

Although there is debate, the likeliest James who would have the status to address "the twelve tribes" and identify himself only as "James" (1:1) is James the brother of Jesus (Ac 12:17; 15:13 – 21; 21:17 – 26; 1Co 15:7; Gal 2:9,12), as in church tradition. James was a common name, and when one spoke of a less commonly recognized individual with a common name, one usually added a qualifying title. Moreover, it seems unlikely that a letter composed by a relatively unknown James would have achieved sufficiently wide circulation as to survive. Many of the views reflected here (e.g., Jas 2:14 – 26) are also consistent with our knowledge of the James respected by the Jerusalem church (cf. Ac 21:18 – 25; Gal 2:10, 12).

Most Jerusalemites, both Christian and non-Christian, respected James for his devoutness. Nevertheless, his denunciations of the way the elite were oppressing the poor (cf. 5:1 – 6) eventually aroused the aristocratic priesthood's opposition. When the procurator Festus died in office in AD 62, the high priest Ananus II executed James and some other people. The public outcry was so great, however, that when the new procurator Albinus arrived, Ananus was deposed from the high priesthood over the matter.

Some object to James's authorship of this letter-essay by noting its polished Greek style. Yet Greek language and culture did influence lower Galilee, and sons of carpenters had better access to education than the peasants who constituted the majority of Galileans. Over the years, James as leader of the Jerusalem church would also have acquired more skills needed to appeal to even the most Hellenistically-educated members of the Jerusalem church. Still, these advantages do not fully explain the letter's quality. More important, influential Judeans (such as Josephus) often used scribes to improve the quality of their Greek. James, as leader of the mother church, in the one overwhelmingly Jewish city that also provided advanced education in Greek works, surely had access to such editorial help (cf. the Greek in Ac 15:23 – 29).

QUICK GLANCE

AUTHOR:
James, a leader of the Jerusalem church

AUDIENCE:
Jewish Christians, perhaps Jerusalem believers scattered after Stephen's death

DATE:
Perhaps before AD 50

THEME:
James emphasizes vital Christianity characterized by good deeds and faith that works.

Setting

A key situation that James's preaching would have naturally often addressed would be the tensions that within a few years culminated in full-blown war with Rome in AD 66. The material in this letter fits James's lifetime; he was killed about AD 62. Some scholars suggest that James's followers edited his material relevant to the war and re-released some of it (perhaps for a Diaspora audience, 1:1) in collected form after his death, in the wake of the war or tensions leading up to it.

James addresses the pride of the rich (1:9 – 11; 2:1 – 9; 4:13 – 17), prejudice for the rich (2:1 – 4), persecution by the rich (2:6 – 7; 5:6) and pay withheld by the rich (5:4 – 6). He also addresses those tempted to retaliate with violent acts (2:11; 4:2) or words (1:19 – 20,26; 3:1 – 12; 4:11 – 12; 5:9). Denouncing injustice and invoking divine vengeance were appropriate (5:1 – 6), but some may have been instead exhorting people to achieve justice by lethal violence (4:2). James responds with a call to wisdom (1:5; 3:14 – 18), faith (1:6 – 8; 2:14 – 26) and patient endurance (1:3 – 4; 5:7 – 11). Once understood in the context of the situation, his supposedly "disconnected" exhortations all fit together as essential to his argument. ◆

1 James,[a] a servant of God[b] and of the
Lord Jesus Christ,

To the twelve tribes[c] scattered[d] among
the nations:

Greetings.

Trials and Temptations

2 Consider it pure joy, my brothers and
sisters,[a] whenever you face trials of many
kinds,[e] 3 because you know that the testing of your faith produces perseverance.
4 Let perseverance finish its work so that
you may be mature and complete, not
lacking anything. 5 If any of you lacks
wisdom, you should ask God,[f] who
gives generously to all without finding
fault, and it will be given to you.[g] 6 But
when you ask, you must believe and not
doubt,[h] because the one who doubts is
like a wave of the sea, blown and tossed
by the wind. 7 That person should not expect to receive anything from the Lord.
8 Such a person is double-minded[i] and unstable in all they do.
9 Believers in humble circumstances
ought to take pride in their high position.
10 But the rich should take pride in their
humiliation — since they will pass away
like a wild flower.[j] 11 For the sun rises with
scorching heat and withers[k] the plant; its
blossom falls and its beauty is destroyed.[l]
In the same way, the rich will fade away
even while they go about their business.
12 Blessed is the one who perseveres under trial because, having stood the test,
that person will receive the crown of life[m]
that the Lord has promised to those who
love him.[n]
13 When tempted, no one should say,
"God is tempting me." For God cannot be
tempted by evil, nor does he tempt any-

1:1 [a] Ac 15:13 [b] Titus 1:1 [c] Ac 26:7 [d] Dt 32:26; Jn 7:35; 1Pe 1:1 **1:2** [e] Mt 5:12; 1Pe 1:6 **1:5** [f] 1Ki 3:9, 10; Pr 2:3-6 [g] Mt 7:7 **1:6** [h] Mk 11:24 **1:8** [i] Jas 4:8 **1:10** [j] 1Co 7:31; 1Pe 1:24 **1:11** [k] Ps 102:4, 11 [l] Isa 40:6-8 **1:12** [m] 1Co 9:25 [n] Jas 2:5

[a] *2* The Greek word for *brothers and sisters* (*adelphoi*) refers here to believers, both men and women, as part of God's family; also in verses 16 and 19; and in 2:1, 5, 14; 3:10, 12; 4:11; 5:7, 9, 10, 12, 19.

1:1 The three basic elements of a letter's introduction were (1) the author's name; (2) the name of the recipient(s); (3) a greeting (typically the same greeting as here). Although framed as a letter, this work is at most a "general letter" or "letter-essay"; thus, after the introduction it proceeds immediately to the argument, without other features characteristic of letters. *James ... To the twelve tribes scattered.* Because James in the NT is always an English substitution for the original "Jacob," some scholars suggest that the author plays on his own name, addressing the 12 tribes of Israel. Plays on names were common. Jews spoke of themselves as "scattered" or dispersed; this Diaspora included Jews in the Parthian Empire as well as the Roman Empire (although this letter's Greek language and often illustrations probably suggests a more limited primary audience). Most Jewish people believed that 10 of the 12 tribes had been scattered for centuries, and they would be restored only at the end of the age. James's address could, however, simply imply "to all God's people scattered among the nations." Some commentators believe that he means the term symbolically for all Christians as spiritual Israelites (cf. 1Pe 1:1), whereas others think that he addresses specifically Jewish followers of Jesus. Jewish people who did not believe Jesus was the Messiah but appreciated James's piety may have also appreciated the letter's message.
1:2 *trials.* Includes the suffering of the poor (vv. 9 – 11; 2:2 – 7; 5:1 – 6).
1:3 *testing of your faith.* Like some Gentile philosophers, many Jewish thinkers emphasized enduring times of testing, and occasionally even joy in them, due to faith in God's sovereignty (see note on 1Pe 1:6).
1:5 *If any of you lacks wisdom, you should ask God.* Jewish wisdom traditions offered practical advice concerning how to deal with trials. Jewish tradition, following Scripture, also emphasized asking God for wisdom (e.g., 1Ki 3:5,9; Pr 2:3).
1:6 *the one who doubts is like a wave of the sea.* Both Greek and Jewish (Isa 57:20) sources sometimes portrayed the unstable as being blown on the sea, as here, so hearers would relate readily to James's image. In James, a request for wisdom offered in faith (v. 5) must mean that one is prepared to obey whatever God reveals (cf. 2:14 – 26).
1:8 *double-minded.* Jewish wisdom texts condemn the double-minded (cf. 4:8) or double-tongued person; like philosophers, Jewish sages abhorred the hypocrisy of saying one thing and living another way, and speaking or living inconsistently.
1:11 *scorching heat.* Some suggest that James might refer to an especially devastating hot wind blowing into Judea from the southern desert (cf. Ge 41:23; Eze 17:10). But the summer sun by itself also wilted Judean flowers, which were then useless except as fuel. *the rich will fade away.* Wealthy landowners regularly exploited the poor throughout the empire, and Judea and Galilee were no exception. Such economic tensions eventually exploded into a Judean war against Rome, in the course of which many less well-to-do Jewish patriots slaughtered Jewish aristocrats. Both Biblical and post-Biblical Jewish wisdom literature stress that riches fade, that God eventually vindicates the oppressed and the needy, and that God judges persons of means who fail to share their resources with the needy. James's final statement here resembles Isa 40:6 – 7; Ps 102:4,11 — although the idea was by this time common.
1:12 *Blessed is the one who.* A common Jewish literary form, which we call a beatitude. *trial.* The Greek term does not imply that the tester necessarily wants the person to fail; e.g., when God tests he desires perseverance. Specific trials in view in this context (although the principle extends beyond them) include poverty and oppression.
1:13 *tempted.* Testing had a wide semantic range, including but not limited to the sense used in this verse, that of tempting. *God cannot be tempted by evil.* People clearly did "test" God (Nu 14:22; Ps 78:18,41,56; 95:9; Mal 3:15), but more in the sense that they tried his patience, not that they could lead him to succumb to temptation. God also clearly did "test" people (Ge 22:1; Dt 8:2; 13:3; Jdg 2:22), but he never tested them in the sense that is implied here: seeking for them to fail instead of to persevere. Jewish texts distinguished between God's motives in testing people (in love, seeking their good) and Satan's motives in testing them (to make them fall). Although James does not deny Satan's indirect role (4:7), he emphasizes here the human element in succumbing to temptation. In contrast to Greek sources, where people often protested that temptation

one; [14]but each person is tempted when
they are dragged away by their own evil
desire and enticed. [15]Then, after desire has
conceived, it gives birth to sin;[o] and sin,
when it is full-grown, gives birth to death.[p]

[16]Don't be deceived,[q] my dear brothers
and sisters.[r] [17]Every good and perfect gift
is from above,[s] coming down from the Father of the heavenly lights, who does not

1:15 [o] Job 15:35; Ps 7:14 [p] Ro 6:23
1:16 [q] 1Co 6:9 [r] ver 19
1:17 [s] Jn 3:27

was irresistible, Jewish wisdom recognized that people were responsible for their choices if they fell during testing.

1:14 – 15 Skilled speakers sometimes used a rhetorical form in which one point led to another, yielding a list of multiple items (as here; Ro 5:3 – 5; 2Pe 1:5 – 7). James may personify desire as enticing a person, then illegitimately conceiving the child ("sin"), which in turn brings forth "death." Ancient writers sometimes used personification to reinforce a point (Jewish teachers, e.g., occasionally personified the evil impulse and death).

1:17 *Every good and perfect gift is from above ... does not change.* Rather than sending testing to break people (vv. 12 – 16), God sends good gifts, including creation or rebirth (v. 18). That God is the author of everything good was a commonplace idea of Jewish and Greek wisdom. People in antiquity often affirmed that what was in the heavens was perfect and thus changeless, and Jewish writers sometimes used "from above" to mean "from God." *Father of the heavenly lights.* Could mean "Creator of the stars." Many people believed that stars controlled their fate in arbitrary ways, but James instead proclaims that our lives rest in the hands of a loving Father.

JAMES 1:9 – 10

Poverty and Revolt in Judea

Although the Diaspora audience (Jas 1:1) of James's message probably applied it to a variety of situations, his teachings were certainly relevant in his immediate environment of Judea. More than a century before this time, the Roman general Pompey had made many Jewish peasants landless; the exorbitant taxes of Herod the Great probably drove more small farmers out of business. In the first century, many peasants in various parts of the Roman Empire worked as tenants on large, feudal estates. Others became landless day laborers in the marketplaces, finding work only sporadically (more was available during harvest season). Resentment against aristocratic landlords ran high in many parts of the empire, but nonpayment of rent (often a percentage of harvest) to landlords was hardly an option; if landowners found tenants unprofitable, they could simply replace them with harder-working slaves. A few landowners even had their own hit squads of hired assassins to deal with uncooperative tenants.

The situation was less extreme in the towns and cities, where perhaps only 10 percent of the population lived. Nevertheless, even there the divisions were often obvious. For example, the poor in Rome mostly lived in rickety tenements that often caught fire or collapsed; running water was not available above the ground floor, and apartments on the highest floors were large enough only for sleeping. Conditions were also dismal for the poor in Jerusalem. Whereas the aristocracy lived in spacious homes in Jerusalem's upper city, the city's poor lived downwind of that city's sewers. When the aristocratic priests there began to withhold tithe income from the poorer priests, their only means of support, economic tensions increased. (Although this was not always the case everywhere, most Judeans were poor by circumstance, not due to idleness, which Judean culture treated as shameful. The ancient economy did not provide enough resources for everyone to live comfortably, and a vast disparity existed between rich and poor.)

In Rome, grain shortages often led to rioting. Judea and Galilee usually remained more patient, but social and economic tensions simmered and eventually yielded to violence. Pursuing peace with Rome through practical politics, the Jerusalem aristocracy became an object of hatred to Zealots and other elements of resistance, who felt that God alone should rule the land. Various outbreaks of violence eventually

continued on next page

culminated in a revolt in AD 66, followed by a massacre of priests and the Roman garrison on the temple mount. Aristocratic and poor patriots clashed inside the city as Roman armies surrounded it, and in AD 70 Jerusalem fell and its temple was destroyed. The final resistance stronghold at Masada fell in AD 73.

These were years of instability throughout the empire. During the Judean war of 66–70, four new emperors came to power in a single year (AD 69), each following the violent deaths of their predecessors. Immediately after the Judean war, resistance fighters continued to spread their views to Jews in North Africa and Cyprus, ultimately provoking further genocidal actions against local Jewish populations. James's wisdom that had urged peace remained relevant to believers throughout the Roman world, for they might appear suspect as Jewish rebels because of their shared Biblical heritage. ◆

The siege ramp that the Romans built to conquer Masada can still be seen (right-hand side of photo).

change[t] like shifting shadows. 18He chose
to give us birth[u] through the word of truth,
that we might be a kind of firstfruits[v] of all
he created.

Listening and Doing

19My dear brothers and sisters, take note
of this: Everyone should be quick to listen,
slow to speak[w] and slow to become angry,
20because human anger does not produce
the righteousness that God desires. 21Therefore, get rid of[x] all moral filth and the evil
that is so prevalent and humbly accept the
word planted in you,[y] which can save you.

1:17 [t]Nu 23:19; Mal 3:6 **1:18** [u]Jn 1:13 [v]Eph 1:12; Rev 14:4 **1:19** [w]Pr 10:19 **1:21** [x]Eph 4:22 [y]Eph 1:13

1:18 *give us birth through the word of truth.* God's giving birth contrasts with desire's negative bearing in v. 15; scholars dispute whether the issue here is humanity's initial creation by God's word (Ge 1:26) or believers' rebirth through the gospel (cf. v. 21; 1Pe 1:23; for background if the latter view is correct, see notes on Jn 3:3,5).

1:19 These are by far some of the most common admonitions in Jewish wisdom, from Proverbs on (e.g., Pr 14:29; 15:18; 16:32; 19:11); Greeks offered similar wisdom. James contrasts this Biblical and traditional wisdom with the revolutionary fervor sweeping his land.

1:20 Jewish nationalists, having suffered much oppression, were tempted to strike at the Romans and their aristocratic vassals, thinking that such revolt (which broke out fully in AD 66) would serve God's righteous indignation.

22 Do not merely listen to the word, and
so deceive yourselves. Do what it says.
23 Anyone who listens to the word but does
not do what it says is like someone who
looks at his face in a mirror 24 and, after
looking at himself, goes away and immediately forgets what he looks like. 25 But whoever looks intently into the perfect law that
gives freedom,[z] and continues in it—not
forgetting what they have heard, but doing
it—they will be blessed in what they do.[a]
26 Those who consider themselves religious and yet do not keep a tight rein
on their tongues[b] deceive themselves,
and their religion is worthless. 27 Religion
that God our Father accepts as pure and
faultless is this: to look after[c] orphans and
widows[d] in their distress and to keep oneself from being polluted by the world.[e]

Favoritism Forbidden

2 My brothers and sisters, believers in
our glorious[f] Lord Jesus Christ must
not show favoritism.[g] 2 Suppose a man
comes into your meeting wearing a gold
ring and fine clothes, and a poor man in
filthy old clothes also comes in. 3 If you
show special attention to the man wearing fine clothes and say, "Here's a good
seat for you," but say to the poor man,
"You stand there" or "Sit on the floor by
my feet," 4 have you not discriminated
among yourselves and become judges[h]
with evil thoughts?
5 Listen, my dear brothers and sisters:[i]
Has not God chosen those who are
poor in the eyes of the world[j] to be rich
in faith[k] and to inherit the kingdom
he promised those who love him?[l]
6 But you have dishonored the poor.[m]
Is it not the rich who are exploiting
you? Are they not the ones who are
dragging you into court?[n] 7 Are they
not the ones who are blaspheming
the noble name of him to whom you
belong?

1:25 [z] Jas 2:12 [a] Jn 13:17 **1:26** [b] Ps 34:13; 1Pe 3:10 **1:27** [c] Mt 25:36 [d] Isa 1:17,23 [e] Ro 12:2 **2:1** [f] 1Co 2:8 [g] Lev 19:15 **2:4** [h] Jn 7:24 **2:5** [i] Jas 1:16, 19 [j] 1Co 1:26-28 [k] Lk 12:21 [l] Jas 1:12 **2:6** [m] 1Co 11:22 [n] Ac 8:3

But James associates righteousness with peace (3:18) and nonresistance (5:7).

1:22 *Do what it says.* Whatever their personal practice, James's audience would not challenge his point here: Moral teachers widely emphasized the warning that truth must be obeyed and not just studied.

1:23–24 *looks at his face in a mirror … forgets what he looks like.* Some moral teachers recommended use of a mirror for moral reflection. Ancient mirrors rarely produced the more accurate images available today (cf. 1Co 13:12 and note). Those with enough resources to own mirrors used them when fixing their hair; if James alludes to such people, he portrays the forgetful hearer as stupid. Alternatively, he refers to many people who had no mirrors and saw themselves rarely, who might more naturally forget their own appearance. In this case the reference is to the ease with which one loses the memory of the word if one does not work hard to put it into practice.

1:25 *freedom.* See notes on Jn 8:32,34.

1:26 Cf. note on 1:19.

1:27 *look after orphans and widows.* In Scripture, true piety included defending the oppressed and vulnerable (cf. Am 2:6–7; 5:21–24), including widows and orphans (Isa 1:17). In most ancient cultures, fatherless children and widows had neither direct means of support nor automatically dependable legal defenders. God took special interest in defending them (Dt 10:18; Ps 68:5; 146:9), and wanted leaders to defend them (Ps 82:3; Isa 1:23; Jer 5:28) and not exploit them (Ex 22:22–24; Dt 24:17; Ps 94:6; Isa 10:2; Jer 7:6; 22:3; Eze 22:7; Zec 7:10). Traditional Greek society did look out for freeborn orphans, but not other ones. Jewish people valued providing for widows and the fatherless. *the world.* See note on 4:4.

2:1 *believers … must not show favoritism.* Scripture prohibited showing favoritism in legal settings (Ex 23:3; Dt 1:17; 16:19; Pr 18:5; 24:23; 28:21), including toward the powerful (Lev 19:15). *glorious Lord Jesus Christ.* Jewish people normally reserved the title "glorious Lord" for God.

2:2 Many ancient writers ridiculed the extent to which people deferred to the wealthy, often before soliciting their funds. *meeting.* Lit. "synagogue," used either because James addresses the entire Jewish community or because some Jewish-Christian congregations (cf. 5:14) also considered themselves Messianic synagogues. *gold ring.* A mark of great wealth and status. In Rome, it often marked equestrians (the knight class), but throughout the empire it also marked wealth. *fine clothes.* The wealthy often dressed ostentatiously, whereas the poorest peasants had only one cloak.

2:3 *good seat.* Many people in synagogues sat on benches, with the most prestigious seats on the raised platforms (see note on Mt 23:6); given limited seating, however, in some synagogues the poorest may have access only to the floor. *stand … Sit.* Although the setting in vv. 2–3 is not exclusively legal, it may be of interest (cf. vv. 4, 6) that Jewish legal texts condemn judges who make one litigant stand while another is permitted to sit. These hearings often took place in synagogues (v. 2), which doubled as community centers.

2:4 *judges with evil thoughts.* Roman courts favored the rich; in the second century, this preference was even written into laws, as it also was in many other legal collections such as those from the ancient Near East. Judges were of higher social rank and did not ordinarily trust persons of lower class, who were thought to act from economic self-interest when they brought accusations against persons of higher class. Biblical law (Lev 19:15), most Jewish law and traditional Greek philosophers had always rejected such distinctions as immoral. In normal times, the urban public respected the rich as public benefactors.

2:5 *chosen those who are poor.* God heard the cries of the poor, who were the most easily oppressed judicially (Ex 22:27; Dt 15:9).

2:6 *dragging you into court.* Roman courts favored the rich, who could initiate lawsuits against social inferiors, although social inferiors could not hope to win lawsuits against them. In theory, Jewish courts sought to avoid this discrimination, but as in most cultures people of means naturally had legal advantages; e.g., they could hire others to provide articulate defenses.

2:7 *blaspheming the noble name.* Rather than pronouncing the divine name, Jewish people sometimes spoke simply of "the name." In its most technical form, "blaspheming" meant reviling the divine name (Lev 24:16). Some of the poor considered some aristocrats (such as those settled in Tiberias) impious, but the divine name

[8]If you really keep the royal law found
in Scripture, "Love your neighbor as yourself,"[a o] you are doing right. [9]But if you
show favoritism,[p] you sin and are convicted by the law as lawbreakers.[q] [10]For whoever keeps the whole law and yet stumbles
at just one point is guilty of breaking all of

2:8 [o] Lev 19:18
2:9 [p] ver 1
[q] Dt 1:17

[a] 8 Lev. 19:18

here may be that of Jesus (see note on v. 1), which even some Jewish aristocrats who were considered pious might speak against. Sadducean aristocrats were among the main enemies of Jesus' followers in Jerusalem (Ac 4:1; 23:6–10), and not many years later one such aristocrat had James executed.

2:8 *royal law.* Normally meant an imperial edict, which should outweigh prejudices in court (v. 6); Jewish people could envision the divinely given Law of Moses as a king's law. James here cites Lev 19:18. Some Jewish teachers (notably Rabbi Akiba) came to regard this as the chief commandment; James probably thinks of Jesus' use of Lev 19:18 to epitomize the law (cf. Mk 12:29–31).

2:9 *favoritism.* Violated God's law (e.g., Lev 19:15, which might be one element subsumed under loving one's neighbor in Lev 19:18; cf. Jas 2:8).

2:10 *whoever . . . stumbles at just one point is guilty of breaking all.* Some ancient thinkers viewed all sins as equal; while many Jewish teachers distinguished more severe sins from lesser ones, even they usually demanded obedience to even the smallest commandments. To reject the authority of one commandment was to cast off the right-

JAMES 2

Dress and Fashion in the Greco-Roman World

In the Greco-Roman world clothing basically fit into two categories: the tunic and the mantle. The tunic was something like the modern T-shirt, but very long (of knee or ankle length), made of wool or linen, with or without sleeves. In ancient terminology one "entered into" a tunic to put it on. A mantle was something like a large blanket wrapped around a person.

The tunic (or *chiton*) was the basic article of clothing for virtually all people, serving as a linen undergarment worn next to the skin. The only item of clothing the poorest people may have owned, it was often quite dirty.

- The average Roman man added a girdle and an *abolla*, a rectangular woolen mantle worn in a double fold over the right shoulder and fastened with a pin.
- Upper-class men wore a second undergarment over the tunic, in addition to the girdle.
- Prosperous Romans donned the familiar toga, a long, oval-shaped (or semicircular) woolen mantle draped over the body in a series of complicated folds. Although the toga originated among the Romans, it soon found wide acceptance by wealthy citizens throughout the empire and remained the standard formal dress for Roman citizens until the late Roman period.
- Alternative garments for upper-class men included the *himation*, a mantle of a Greek style more popular in the eastern part of the empire, and the *chlamys*, a short, woolen mantle (like a cape), often associated with soldiers.
- Lower-class women often wore only an ankle-length tunic, gathered by a belt across the upper abdomen, while women of higher economic status added a mantle—often either a *himation* or a *peplos*—over the tunic. These garments were held in place by ornate "safety-pins" called *fibula*.
- The *himation* for women was smaller than that for men. It was sometimes dyed in various colors or adorned with a pattern, although coloration and patterning were simple by modern standards. But the patterns and coloring, as well as the size, did distinguish whether a *himation* was intended for a man or a woman. A woman's *himation* was often pleated and could be worn in a wide variety of styles (over

continued on next page

it.[r] [11]For he who said, "You shall not commit adultery,"[a s] also said, "You shall not murder."[b t] If you do not commit adultery but do commit murder, you have become a lawbreaker.
[12]Speak and act as those who are going to be judged by the law that gives freedom,[u] [13]because judgment without mercy will be shown to anyone who has not been merciful.[v] Mercy triumphs over judgment.

2:10 [r] Mt 5:19; Gal 3:10
2:11 [s] Ex 20:14; Dt 5:18 [t] Ex 20:13; Dt 5:17
2:12 [u] Jas 1:25
2:13 [v] Mt 5:7; 18:32-35

[a] *11* Exodus 20:14; Deut. 5:18 [b] *11* Exodus 20:13; Deut. 5:17

ful authority of God's law. In principle rejecting God's law meant apostasy, though in practice these teachers recognized that everyone sinned. *stumbles.* A common Jewish metaphor for sin.

2:11 *You shall not murder.* When James was writing, Judean revolutionaries were periodically murdering aristocrats in the temple. Likewise, careless governors sometimes slaughtered protestors and bystanders indiscriminately, some members of the priestly aristocracy hired assassins, and rich landlords sometimes killed tenants (cf. 5:6). Some of these people, especially the revolutionaries, may have justified their behavior religiously.

2:12 *freedom.* Cf. 1:25; see notes on Jn 8:32,34.

2:13 Whether or not they showed favoritism (v. 9), God would not do so (Dt 10:17; 2Ch 19:7). Jewish tradition similarly warned that the merciless would receive no

the shoulder, as a cape, as a hood, diagonally across the upper body, etc.).

- The *peplos* was a single, large rectangle of cloth, distinguished from the *himation* by its size and especially by the way it was folded: The *peplos* always used a cuff-like overfold called an *apotygma*. A woman's *peplos* was typically as long as the distance from her shoulders to her feet, plus about 12 inches for the *apotygma*. The fold for the *apotygma* was approximately at the shoulders, from which it draped outward and down over the upper body. The fold could be worn as a hood over the head as a sign of modesty when a woman was walking in the streets or taking part in certain religious ceremonies (cf. 1Co 11:6).

Clothes were draped over the body rather than fitted; indeed, this draping effect is part of the classical ideal of dignity and serenity. At night, one's clothing (especially the mantle) could also serve as a blanket. Leather sandals were the standard footwear for all ranks of society.

In ancient sculpture people often appear wearing only a mantle (if anything at all). This is because of the classical ideal of beauty and does not reflect ordinary dress. In fact, people almost always donned tunics under their mantles, and men ordinarily wore loincloth underwear as well. A scene from Pompeii depicts two female athletes wearing garments similar to a modern two-piece swim suit, suggesting that women of means had a fairly wide variety of underwear and outerwear available to them.

Woman wearing Graeco-Roman attire, c. 50 BC, Greece.

Giovanni Dall'Orto/Wikimedia Commons

Upper-class Roman women often sported exotic hairstyles, often with an outlandish display of curls. Dyeing the hair and wearing expensive cosmetics were popular with women (cf. 1Pe 3:3), who also wore decorative tiaras, pins and nets with their hair. The wearing of rings and other jewelry by both men and women contributed to the display of wealth. James (2:1 – 13) warned his readers not to be so dazzled by the finery of the rich that they showed partiality to wealthy believers over their less fortunate Christian brothers and sisters. ◆

Faith and Deeds

14 What good is it, my brothers and sisters, if someone claims to have faith but has no deeds?[w] Can such faith save them?
15 Suppose a brother or a sister is without clothes and daily food.[x] 16 If one of you says to them, "Go in peace; keep warm and well fed," but does nothing about their physical needs, what good is it?[y] 17 In the same way, faith by itself, if it is not accompanied by action, is dead.

18 But someone will say, "You have faith; I have deeds."

Show me your faith without deeds,[z] and I will show you my faith by my deeds.[a]
19 You believe that there is one God.[b] Good! Even the demons believe that[c]—and shudder.

20 You foolish person, do you want evidence that faith without deeds is useless[a]?[d] 21 Was not our father Abraham considered righteous for what he did when he offered his son Isaac on the altar?[e] 22 You see that his faith and his actions were working together,[f] and his faith was made complete by what he did.[g] 23 And the scripture was fulfilled that says, "Abraham believed God, and it was credited to him as righteousness,"[b][h] and he was called God's friend.[i] 24 You see that a person is considered righteous by what they do and not by faith alone.

25 In the same way, was not even Rahab the prostitute considered righteous for what she did when she gave lodging to the spies and sent them off in a different direction?[j] 26 As the body without the spirit is dead, so faith without deeds is dead.[k]

2:14 [w] Mt 7:26; Jas 1:22-25
2:15 [x] Mt 25:35, 36
2:16 [y] 1Jn 3:17, 18
2:18 [z] Ro 3:28 [a] Jas 3:13
2:19 [b] Dt 6:4 [c] Mt 8:29; Lk 4:34
2:20 [d] ver 17, 26
2:21 [e] Ge 22:9, 12
2:22 [f] Heb 11:17 [g] 1Th 1:3
2:23 [h] Ge 15:6; Ro 4:3 [i] 2Ch 20:7; Isa 41:8
2:25 [j] Heb 11:31
2:26 [k] ver 17, 20
3:2 [l] 1Ki 8:46; Jas 2:10 [m] 1Pe 3:10 [n] Mt 12:37 [o] Jas 1:26

Taming the Tongue

3 Not many of you should become teachers, my fellow believers, because you know that we who teach will be judged more strictly. 2 We all stumble[l] in many ways. Anyone who is never at fault in what they say[m] is perfect,[n] able to keep their whole body in check.[o]

[a] *20* Some early manuscripts *dead* [b] *23* Gen. 15:6

---

mercy (cf. also Jesus' teaching in Mt 5:7; 6:15; Lk 6:36–37). Later rabbis emphasized that God's attribute of mercy prevailed over his attribute of judgment when offered even the slightest grounds to do so; Paul indicates that in Christ mercy triumphs without neglecting justice (Ro 3:26).

2:14–26 James could be responding partly to a misinterpretation of Paul's teaching, as some commentators have suggested. More likely, however, he is reacting especially against a strain of Jewish piety that was fueling the revolutionary fervor that was leading toward war (cf. v. 19; 1:26–27). James uses the term "faith" differently here from the way Paul does, but neither writer would disagree with the other's point: *genuine* faith is a reality on which one stakes one's life, not merely passive assent to a doctrine. For James, expressions of faith—like nondiscrimination (vv. 8–9) and nonviolence (vv. 10–12)—must be lived, not merely acknowledged.

2:14–16 Scripture commanded care for the needy (e.g., Dt 15:7–8); such behavior distinguished the righteous from the wicked (e.g., Dt 15:9; Pr 29:7; Jer 22:16).

2:16 *Go in peace.* A Jewish farewell blessing; but Jewish people were expected to show hospitality to other Jewish people in need. They held Abraham as the ultimate example of good hospitality (cf. vv. 21–23). *keep warm.* Alludes to how cold the homeless could become, in Judea relevant especially in Jerusalem and the Judean hill country. Teachers sometimes used absurd examples like this one to point out where faulty thinking can lead.

2:18 *someone will say.* Writers on moral topics often advanced their argument by citing and refuting an imaginary critic's objection. They often introduced the objection with "someone will say." *Show me.* James challenges the imaginary critic; some writers, like the Stoic philosopher Epictetus, also challenged imaginary critics by demanding, "Show me," or, "Demonstrate your case." Here the objection claims that one may have faith, and another deeds; James counters that genuine faith is expressed by deeds.

2:19 *there is one God.* Jewish people daily recited the *Shema*, which consisted of Dt 6:4 (and associated texts), including this line: "the LORD is one." This confession was the cornerstone of Jewish faith, and what Jewish people often meant by faith (*'emuna*). This confession demanded more than empty words, however; if God is one, he must be the supreme object of our love (Dt 6:4–5). Nearly all Jewish teachers would have agreed with James that loyalty to God demanded corresponding behavior. *the demons believe that—and shudder.* Jewish tradition and sometimes even Gentile magical texts recognized that demons trembled at God's name.

2:21–23 Although God accepted Abraham's initial faith (Ge 15:6), it was incomplete (cf. Ge 15:8; 16:2). In the years that followed, Abraham's faith matured as part of his continuing relationship with God; offering Isaac was the ultimate test of his faith. Jewish tradition already had connected Ge 15:6 with the offering of Isaac (Ge 22:1–14), as here. Abraham demonstrated his mature faith (Ge 22:12) and God reaffirmed his promise (Ge 22:16–18).

2:23 *he was called God's friend.* Jewish tradition celebrated Abraham being God's friend, following 2Ch 20:7; Isa 41:8.

2:25 *even Rahab … considered righteous for what she did.* Like Abraham (see note on v. 16), Rahab was known for hospitality; but her act of saving the spies saved her as well (Jos 2:1–21; 6:22–25).

2:26 *the body without the spirit is dead.* Many people used "spirit" and "soul" interchangeably; they recognized that when one's spirit departed, one died.

3:1 *we who teach will be judged more strictly.* Other Jewish sages also warned against teaching error and recognized that teachers would be judged strictly if they led others astray. Some teachers were now advocating a sort of "wisdom" that would soon lead to a failed revolt against Rome and massive suffering (AD 66–70; cf. vv. 13–18).

3:2 *at fault in what they say.* That everyone sinned was standard Jewish doctrine; that one of the most common instruments of sin and harm was the human mouth was also a common Jewish idea (as early as the book of Proverbs; e.g., Pr 11:9; 12:18; 18:21).

3 When we put bits into the mouths of
horses to make them obey us, we can turn
the whole animal.[p] 4 Or take ships as an example. Although they are so large and are
driven by strong winds, they are steered
by a very small rudder wherever the pilot wants to go. 5 Likewise, the tongue is a
small part of the body, but it makes great
boasts.[q] Consider what a great forest is set
on fire by a small spark. 6 The tongue also
is a fire,[r] a world of evil among the parts
of the body. It corrupts the whole body,[s]
sets the whole course of one's life on fire,
and is itself set on fire by hell.

7 All kinds of animals, birds, reptiles and
sea creatures are being tamed and have
been tamed by mankind, 8 but no human
being can tame the tongue. It is a restless
evil, full of deadly poison.[t]

9 With the tongue we praise our Lord
and Father, and with it we curse human
beings, who have been made in God's
likeness.[u] 10 Out of the same mouth come
praise and cursing. My brothers and sisters, this should not be. 11 Can both fresh
water and salt water flow from the same
spring? 12 My brothers and sisters, can a
fig tree bear olives, or a grapevine bear
figs?[v] Neither can a salt spring produce
fresh water.

Two Kinds of Wisdom

13 Who is wise and understanding among
you? Let them show it[w] by their good life,
by deeds done in the humility that comes
from wisdom. 14 But if you harbor bitter
envy and selfish ambition[x] in your hearts,
do not boast about it or deny the truth.[y]
15 Such "wisdom" does not come down
from heaven[z] but is earthly, unspiritual,
demonic.[a] 16 For where you have envy and
selfish ambition, there you find disorder
and every evil practice.

17 But the wisdom that comes from heav-
en[b] is first of all pure; then peace-loving,
considerate, submissive, full of mercy[c] and
good fruit, impartial and sincere.[d] 18 Peacemakers who sow in peace reap a harvest
of righteousness.[e]

Submit Yourselves to God

4 What causes fights and quarrels[f]
among you? Don't they come from
your desires that battle[g] within you?

3:3 [p] Ps 32:9
3:5 [q] Ps 12:3,4
3:6 [r] Pr 16:27 [s] Mt 15:11, 18, 19
3:8 [t] Ps 140:3; Ro 3:13
3:9 [u] Ge 1:26, 27; 1Co 11:7
3:12 [v] Mt 7:16
3:13 [w] Jas 2:18
3:14 [x] ver 16 [y] Jas 5:19
3:15 [z] Jas 1:17 [a] 1Ti 4:1
3:17 [b] 1Co 2:6 [c] Lk 6:36 [d] Ro 12:9
3:18 [e] Pr 11:18; Isa 32:17
4:1 [f] Titus 3:9 [g] Ro 7:23

3:3–4 *bits ... small rudder.* In the ancient Mediterranean world, most people understood the common illustrations of controlling horses with bits and ships with rudders (see note on Ac 27:40). Jewish texts often cast wisdom, reason and God in the role of ideal pilots, but James's point here is not what should control or have power. His point is simply the power of a small instrument (v. 5).
3:5–6 *a great forest is set on fire by a small spark. The tongue also is a fire.* Others also compared the spread of rumors to the igniting of what would rapidly become a forest fire. Here the image is that of a tongue that incites the whole body to violence. Scripture and other sources already warned of the boastful, hostile tongue (Ps 52:1–4) and the tongue as a hurtful fire (Ps 39:1–3; 120:2–4; Pr 16:27; 26:21).
3:6 *set on fire by hell.* That the fire (see vv. 5–6 and note) is sparked by hell suggests where it leads; Jewish pictures of Gehenna typically included flame.
3:7–8 *All kinds of animals ... deadly poison.* Made in God's image (v. 9), people were appointed over all creatures (Ge 1:26). But although other creatures could be subdued as God commanded (Ge 1:28; 9:2), the tongue was like the deadliest snake, full of toxic venom (Ps 58:3–6; 140:3; cf. also Jewish tradition).
3:9 *With the tongue we praise ... and with it we curse.* James's audience would readily grasp his point. Jewish teachers emphasized that however one treated other humans, it was as if one did it to God himself, because people were made in his image. Sometimes they also noted, as here, the specific incongruity of blessing God while cursing other people, who were made in his image. The issue here (as in 1:19–20; 4:11; 5:9) is speech hostile to others—fitting the letter's setting (see Introduction: Setting; see also note on vv. 13–18).
3:12 *can a fig tree bear olives, or a grapevine bear figs?* In vv. 11–12, James produces two other common examples of impossible incongruity. Figs, olives and grapes were the three most common agricultural products of the Judean hills, and alongside wheat and barley they would have constituted the most common crops of the Mediterranean region as a whole. That everything brought forth after its kind was a matter of common observation and became proverbial in Greco-Roman circles (cf. also Ge 1:11–12,21,24–25).
3:13–18 Especially since the era of the Maccabean revolt against Syrian oppressors, many Judeans had valued revolt against oppressors as an act of devotion to God. This time, however, revolt would lead to Judea's devastation, Jerusalem's destruction, and the enslavement of many survivors (AD 66–73). Although some Pharisees emphasized peace, many popular teachers urged that revolt was the only solution to current problems. Instead of this popular course, James counseled waiting on God (5:7–11); cf. Jesus' warning in Mk 13:1–2,14–16.
3:14 *envy.* The Greek term here was also the term for "zeal" used by some who wanted to overthrow Roman rule. The Maccabees and others used Phinehas as their model for violent zeal for God (Nu 25:11, 13; 1 Maccabees 2:26–27,54).
3:15 *does not come down from heaven but is earthly, unspiritual, demonic.* James contrasts divine wisdom with that inspired by evil. Jewish people often used "heaven" and "above" to mean "God." In contrast to heavenly wisdom, violent "wisdom" (cf. v. 14; 4:1–2) was earthly and demonic (cf. Mk 8:33). Some Jewish groups believed that evil spirits inspired all sin; the idea that demons surrounded everyone also grew in folk beliefs. James might suggest a more indirect demonic activity here through people imbibing dominant values of a surrounding culture influenced by evil.
3:17 *wisdom that comes from heaven.* Jewish tradition often envisioned true wisdom as descending "from heaven." *peace-loving ... full of mercy and good fruit.* A description of God's wisdom, in contrast to counsel supporting retaliation.
4:1 *desires that battle within you.* Most Gentile philosophers and many Diaspora Jewish thinkers condemned those ruled by their passions; they described such desires

2You desire but do not have, so you kill.
You covet but you cannot get what you
want, so you quarrel and fight. You do not
have because you do not ask God. 3When
you ask, you do not receive,[h] because you
ask with wrong motives,[i] that you may
spend what you get on your pleasures.
4You adulterous people,[a] don't you
know that friendship with the world[j]
means enmity against God?[k] Therefore,
anyone who chooses to be a friend of the
world becomes an enemy of God.[l] 5Or do
you think Scripture says without reason
that he jealously longs for the spirit he
has caused to dwell in us[b]? 6But he gives
us more grace. That is why Scripture says:

> "God opposes the proud
> but shows favor to the humble."[c][m]

7Submit yourselves, then, to God. Resist
the devil,[n] and he will flee from you. 8Come
near to God and he will come near to
you.[o] Wash your hands,[p] you sinners, and
purify your hearts, you double-minded.[q]
9Grieve, mourn and wail. Change your
laughter to mourning and your joy to
gloom.[r] 10Humble yourselves before the
Lord, and he will lift you up.
11Brothers and sisters, do not slander
one another.[s] Anyone who speaks against
a brother or sister[d] or judges them[t] speaks
against the law and judges it. When you
judge the law, you are not keeping it,[u] but
sitting in judgment on it. 12There is only
one Lawgiver and Judge, the one who is
able to save and destroy.[v] But you — who
are you to judge your neighbor?[w]

Boasting About Tomorrow

13Now listen, you who say, "Today or
tomorrow we will go to this or that city,
spend a year there, carry on business and

4:3 [h] Ps 18:41 [i] 1Jn 3:22; 5:14 **4:4** [j] Jas 1:27 [k] 1Jn 2:15 [l] Jn 15:19 **4:6** [m] Ps 138:6; Pr 3:34; Mt 23:12 **4:7** [n] Eph 4:27; 1Pe 5:6-9 **4:8** [o] 2Ch 15:2 [p] Isa 1:16 [q] Jas 1:8
4:9 [r] Lk 6:25 **4:11** [s] 1Pe 2:1 [t] Mt 7:1 [u] Jas 1:22 **4:12** [v] Mt 10:28 [w] Ro 14:4

[a] *4* An allusion to covenant unfaithfulness; see Hosea 3:1. [b] *5* Or *that the spirit he caused to dwell in us envies intensely;* or *that the Spirit he caused to dwell in us longs jealously* [c] *6* Prov. 3:34 [d] *11* The Greek word for *brother or sister* (*adelphos*) refers here to a believer, whether man or woman, as part of God's family.

for pleasure as battling against reason. Many writers such as Plato, Plutarch and Philo attributed all literal wars to such physically based desires. Judean thinkers also spoke of an evil impulse; later rabbis believed that it influenced every member of the body.

4:2 *so you kill.* Teachers often used hyperbole: graphic, rhetorical exaggeration for effect. Presumably most members of James's original audience had never literally killed anyone, but they were exposed to violent teachers (3:13 – 18) who regarded killing as a satisfactory means of attaining justice and redistribution of wealth. Or James may think of wealthy landowners ready to kill others to achieve their ends (cf. 5:6).

4:3 *you ask with wrong motives.* Prayers for basic needs were common and differ from the seeking condemned here (cf. Pr 30:8 – 9; Mt 6:11).

4:4 *friendship with the world means enmity against God.* When Israel broke covenant with God and pursued idols, God charged her with adultery (e.g., Isa 1:21; Jer 2:20; 3:1 – 3; Eze 16:15 – 17; Hos 1 – 3). *friend of the world . . . enemy of God.* Friends were expected to be friends with their friends' friends and enemies of their friends' enemies. Those who claimed to be God's friends (2:23) but shared the world's values (see note on 3:13 – 18) were unfaithful to God.

4:5 *he jealously longs for the spirit he has caused to dwell in us.* Because no Biblical text says exactly this, and there is more than one way to translate the Greek expression, scholars debate the exact source. Like other Jewish writers, NT authors sometimes blended various texts together; this does not resolve, however, which texts James has in view. Some suggest that James means that "this human spirit jealously longs," as in vv. 1 – 3, perhaps thinking of the Jewish idea of the evil impulse. (Alternatively, but less likely, he could mean that one's spirit or soul ought to long — but for God, as in Ps 42:1 – 2; 63:1; 84:2.) Second, God's Spirit within us could be jealous for our affection (cf. Ge 6:3). A third possibility is that James cites here a maxim that summarizes some Biblical texts (such as Ex 20:5 or Dt 32:21) with the sense that "God is jealous over the spirit he gave us" and will tolerate no competition for its affection (v. 4).

4:6 *God opposes the proud.* James closely follows the common Greek version of Pr 3:34 (cited here), merely changing "the Lord" to "God." Jewish sources often developed this idea. In this context, being humble includes submitting to God (vv. 7,10).

4:7 *he will flee from you.* Ancient magical texts sometimes depicted demons fleeing before incantations, but the idea here is moral, not magical. One must choose between God's values and the world's (v. 4), between God's wisdom and that which is demonic (3:15,17).

4:8 *Wash your hands.* In this period Jewish people washed their hands before prayer; Jewish people also used the language of purity figuratively, so that pure hands could signify not having committed sin with them (Ps 24:3 – 4). Those responsible for bloodshed (Mt 27:24), even if only as representatives of a corporately guilty group (cf. v. 2; Dt 21:6), were to wash their hands. *double-minded.* People disrespected the double-minded, i.e., hypocrites (cf. v. 4).

4:9 – 10 *Grieve, mourn and wail . . . Humble yourselves.* Scripture often connected mourning and humbling oneself with repentance (Lev 23:27 – 29; 26:41), especially when confronted with divine judgment (2Ki 22:11; Joel 1:13 – 14; 2:12 – 13). Biblical prophets also announced the exaltation of the humble (see note on Mt 23:12).

4:11 *do not slander one another.* The issue here (as in 1:19 – 20, 3:9 – 10; 5:9) is speech hostile to others — fitting the letter's setting (see Introduction: Setting; see also note on 3:13 – 18). Part of the law's teaching about loving one's neighbor was avoiding slander (Lev 19:16 – 18).

4:12 *only one Lawgiver and Judge.* Jewish and Christian teachers often recognized that God was the only rightful judge.

4:13 – 17 In the Roman Empire, people acquired wealth in especially two ways: landowners, with high social status, profited from crops raised by tenant farmers or slaves; merchants, by contrast, usually accumulated wealth without the corresponding social status. James addresses both merchants (vv. 13 – 17) and the landed aristocracy (5:1 – 6).

4:13 *Now listen.* Speakers often used expressions such as this, including when making an argument or speaking harshly. *Today or tomorrow.* Many thinkers urged their audi-

make money."[x] [14]Why, you do not even know what will happen tomorrow. What is your life? You are a mist that appears for a little while and then vanishes.[y] [15]Instead, you ought to say, "If it is the Lord's will,[z] we will live and do this or that." [16]As it is, you boast in your arrogant schemes. All such boasting is evil.[a] [17]If anyone, then, knows the good they ought to do and doesn't do it, it is sin for them.[b]

Warning to Rich Oppressors

5 Now listen, you rich people,[c] weep and wail because of the misery that is coming on you. [2]Your wealth has rotted, and moths have eaten your clothes.[d] [3]Your gold and silver are corroded. Their corrosion will testify against you and eat your flesh like fire. You have hoarded wealth in the last days.[e] [4]Look! The wages you failed to pay the workers[f] who mowed your fields are crying out against you. The cries[g] of the harvesters have reached the ears of the Lord Almighty.[h] [5]You have lived on earth in luxury and self-indulgence. You have fattened yourselves[i] in the day of slaughter.[a][j] [6]You have condemned and murdered the innocent one,[k] who was not opposing you.

Patience in Suffering

[7]Be patient, then, brothers and sisters, until the Lord's coming. See how the farmer waits for the land to yield its valuable crop, patiently waiting for the autumn and spring rains.[l] [8]You too, be patient and stand firm, because the Lord's coming is near.[m] [9]Don't grumble against one another, brothers and sisters,[n] or you will be judged. The Judge[o] is standing at the door![p]

[10]Brothers and sisters, as an example of patience in the face of suffering, take the prophets[q] who spoke in the name of

4:13 [x] Pr 27:1
4:14 [y] Job 7:7; Ps 102:3
4:15 [z] Ac 18:21
4:16 [a] 1Co 5:6
4:17 [b] Lk 12:47; Jn 9:41
5:1 [c] Lk 6:24
5:2 [d] Job 13:28; Mt 6:19,20
5:3 [e] ver 7,8
5:4 [f] Lev 19:13 [g] Dt 24:15 [h] Ro 9:29
5:5 [i] Am 6:1 [j] Jer 12:3; 25:34
5:6 [k] Heb 10:38
5:7 [l] Dt 11:14; Jer 5:24
5:8 [m] Ro 13:11; 1Pe 4:7
5:9 [n] Jas 4:11 [o] 1Co 4:5; 1Pe 4:5 [p] Mt 24:33
5:10 [q] Mt 5:12

[a] 5 *Or yourselves as in a day of feasting*

---

ences to remember that one cannot control one's future (cf. Pr 27:1). *this or that city.* Towns and cities offered the primary markets for manufactured goods, where some traders could acquire wealth. Tentatively projecting commitments and profits was prudent. The sin here is not their thinking ahead (cf. Pr 6:8; 20:18; 22:3; 24:27; 27:12; 30:25) but their arrogant presumption—acting as if their lives are in their own hands rather than God's (v. 16; cf., e.g., Am 4:1; 6:1).

4:14 *You are a mist.* For life as but a fleeting breath, see, e.g., Job 7:7; Ps 39:5; for the transitory character of mist, see, e.g., Pr 21:6; Hos 6:4; 13:3.

4:15 *If it is the Lord's will.* Both Jews and Gentiles often qualified plans with "If God wishes" or similar expressions.

5:1–6 See the article "Poverty and Revolt in Judea," p. 2167. James here denounces wealthy exploiters of peasant labor; he does so in a manner resembling Biblical prophets' warnings of judgment, also echoed in other early Jewish sources. James condemns speech that incites human violence (1:19,26; 3:1–12; 4:11), but this does not mean remaining silent about injustice. Like some Jewish visionaries of his day, James appeals to God's judgment rather than to human retribution (4:12; cf. Dt 32:35; Pr 20:22). His prophetic warning proved on the mark; a few years later the Judean aristocracy was mostly obliterated during the revolt against Rome.

5:1 *weep and wail.* Prophets sometimes summoned people to weep and wail as a warning of what was coming (e.g., Isa 13:6; Joel 1:8).

5:2 *clothes.* The poorest peasants might have just a single cloak. Expensive clothing was a sign and form of wealth; a fairly expensive cloak could cost many times the entire property of many poor persons.

5:3 *hoarded wealth.* Various moral teachers in antiquity mocked the vanity of hoarded wealth. *the last days.* Not a wise time to be sinning: God's day of reckoning was coming soon (cf. Isa 2:2; Mic 4:1).

5:4 For this setting, see the article "Poverty and Revolt in Judea," p. 2167. *wages you failed to pay the workers.* Wealthy landowners often lived far away from the estates where their laborers worked. Tenant farmers normally paid the landowner a share of the crops, but landowners could also use slaves or, as in this case, temporary workers. Day laborers—especially in demand during the harvest—made subsistence wages; they depended on these daily wages to feed themselves and their families. *crying out against you.* If an employer withheld a worker's wages (in violation of Lev 19:13; Mal 3:5), the worker would cry out to God and God would avenge him (Dt 24:14–15). *Lord Almighty.* A familiar phrase in the standard Greek translation of the OT, where it translates a phrase suggesting that God had vast hosts, or armies (the phrase here, including God's "ears," recalls the Greek version of Isa 5:9.)

5:5 *fattened yourselves in the day of slaughter.* The rich and their guests consumed much meat in a day of slaughter, i.e., at a feast (e.g., at sheep-shearing or harvest; cf. 1Sa 25:4,36); once an animal was slaughtered, as much as possible was eaten at once, because only drying and salting could preserve the rest. Meat was rarely available to the poor except during public festivals.

Here, however, the picture is of the rich being fattened like cattle for the day of their own slaughter, as in some Jewish apocalyptic works. *day of slaughter.* Recalls Jer 12:3. God regarded as sin not only direct exploitation, as in v. 4, but also living lavishly while others go hungry (cf., e.g., Am 6:4–7).

5:6 *murdered the innocent one.* Murder was increasingly common in the land (see note on 2:11). During a temporary period between Roman governors, the high priest had James himself executed, along with some other innocent people. James was so respected by those who kept the law that their outcry caused this lawless high priest to be deposed.

5:7 *the farmer waits for the land to yield its valuable crop.* Harvest here (cf. v. 4) becomes an image of the day of judgment, as elsewhere in Jewish literature. The chief Judean wheat harvest ran from mid-April through the end of May (earlier than in Greece or Italy). The crop was valuable; farmers' lives depended heavily on good harvests. *autumn and spring rains.* Judea's early, autumn rains fell in October and November; the winter rains (roughly three-quarters of the year's rainfall) fell from December through February. But the late rains of March and April were particularly needed for the main grain harvests.

5:10 *as an example … take the prophets.* In Scripture, prophets sometimes faced persecution; by Jesus' day, Jewish tradition highlighted this point even more.

the Lord. 11As you know, we count as
blessed[r] those who have persevered. You
have heard of Job's perseverance[s] and
have seen what the Lord finally brought
about.[t] The Lord is full of compassion and
mercy.[u]
12Above all, my brothers and sisters, do
not swear — not by heaven or by earth or
by anything else. All you need to say is a
simple "Yes" or "No." Otherwise you will
be condemned.[v]

The Prayer of Faith

13Is anyone among you in trouble? Let
them pray.[w] Is anyone happy? Let them
sing songs of praise.[x] 14Is anyone among
you sick? Let them call the elders of the
church to pray over them and anoint them
with oil[y] in the name of the Lord. 15And
the prayer offered in faith will make the
sick person well; the Lord will raise them
up. If they have sinned, they will be forgiven. 16Therefore confess your sins[z] to
each other and pray for each other so that
you may be healed.[a] The prayer of a righteous person is powerful and effective.[b]
17Elijah was a human being, even as we
are.[c] He prayed earnestly that it would not
rain, and it did not rain on the land for
three and a half years.[d] 18Again he prayed,
and the heavens gave rain, and the earth
produced its crops.[e]
19My brothers and sisters, if one of you
should wander from the truth[f] and someone should bring that person back,[g] 20re-
member this: Whoever turns a sinner from
the error of their way will save[h] them from
death and cover over a multitude of sins.[i]

5:11 [r] Mt 5:10 [s] Job 1:21,22; 2:10 [t] Job 42:10, 12-17 [u] Nu 14:18 **5:12** [v] Mt 5:34-37 **5:13** [w] Ps 50:15 [x] Col 3:16 **5:14** [y] Mk 6:13 **5:16** [z] Mt 3:6 [a] 1Pe 2:24 [b] Jn 9:31 **5:17** [c] Ac 14:15 [d] 1Ki 17:1; Lk 4:25 **5:18** [e] 1Ki 18:41-45 **5:19** [f] Jas 3:14 [g] Mt 18:15 **5:20** [h] Ro 11:14 [i] 1Pe 4:8

5:11 *Job's perseverance.* Although later rabbis debated how faithful Job was, earlier Jewish traditions in the Diaspora praised and even amplified Job's endurance already depicted in Scripture.
5:12 *do not swear.* An oath invoked a deity's witness that one was telling the truth, and hence a curse if one was lying. One of the Ten Commandments prohibited swearing falsely in God's name (Ex 20:7). A few radical sages and sects forbade oaths, demanding that one's integrity be so great that oaths were unnecessary. For swearing by other things besides God's name, see notes on Mt 5:33 – 35. James clearly evokes Jesus' teaching here (Mt 5:33 – 37).
5:13 *Let them sing songs of praise.* Many of the psalms (here translated "songs of praise") are joyful (e.g., Ps 100), although others are more helpful for times of suffering.
5:14 *elders.* The rulers of OT villages, elders continued to fill a respected leadership role in this period. Usually they functioned as a group. *anoint them with oil.* People anointed wounds with oil (cf. Isa 1:6; Lk 10:34) and thought it also had medicinal properties for some ailments; such functions may contribute to its symbolic relevance here. In ancient Israel oil was used to anoint and consecrate priests or rulers (e.g., Ex 30:30; Jdg 9:8). Jesus and his followers may have combined a symbolic medicinal use with a symbol of fresh power from God's Spirit (Mk 6:13; cf. 1Sa 16:13; Isa 61:1).
5:15 *the prayer offered in faith will make the sick person well.* The power for answered prayer that Jewish tradition associated with only the most holy (cf. vv. 17 – 18) James here expects for God's people more widely (having already explained genuine faith and proper asking in 1:3 – 8; 2:22; 4:2 – 3). *they will be forgiven.* Biblical prophets often used healing from sickness as an image for healing from sin (e.g., Isa 6:10), and Jewish literature often associated sin and sickness. Some later rabbis even associated specific afflictions with specific sins. Nevertheless, neither the OT nor James associates every person's sickness with their sin (cf., e.g., 1Ki 14:4; 2Ki 13:14,21).
5:17 – 18 *Elijah … prayed … Again he prayed.* Judeans and Galileans prayed for rain, but only exceptional holy men were thought able to secure it miraculously (and the legends about them securing rain were sometimes told centuries after they lived). These holy men modeled themselves after the prophet Elijah, whom James cites here as a model for all righteous people (v. 16; cf. 1Ki 17:1; 18:41 – 46).
5:17 *a human being, even as we are.* In Scripture, Elijah comes across as fully human (e.g., 1Ki 17:20; 19:4,14). James thus invites all his hearers to use Elijah as a model of a righteous though frail person of prayer.
5:19 – 20 If one abandoned one's former righteousness, it no longer counted in one's favor (Eze 18:24 – 25); yet the repentance of the wicked also canceled their former wickedness (Eze 18:21 – 23). Some Jews regarded some forms of apostasy as unforgivable, but James welcomes the sinner back.
5:20 *cover over a multitude of sins.* The language recalls Pr 10:12, where it probably means keeping quiet about another's wrongs (cf. Pr 17:9). The idea here seems closer to the Jewish use of similar phrases for securing forgiveness. Later rabbis even claimed that when a person converted another to the Jewish faith it was as if the person had created that person. Here one who turns another back to the way rescues them from death.

THE LETTERS

1 PETER

Authorship

There are strong reasons to accept the claim that Peter (1:1) authored this letter. Early Christian writers from the beginning of the second century cite this letter as genuinely from Peter (Papias fragment 21.2). Strong and early tradition supports Peter's martyrdom in Rome, and churches would surely have preserved any letters he wrote from there. Some object to Peter's authorship by noting the letter's polished Greek style. Yet most Galileans could speak Greek, and fishermen had better access to education than the peasants who constituted the majority of Galileans. Peter's Judean ministry may have developed his Greek skills further (including in Ac 9:32 – 43). These factors alone might not explain the letter as it stands, but more important, influential Judeans (such as Josephus) often used scribes to improve the quality of their Greek. Most of Rome's Jewish community and other Christians there could speak Greek, and Peter explicitly notes the assistance of Silas, a Jewish Roman citizen (cf. Ac 16:36 – 37) and thus likely someone well-educated, with this letter (1Pe 5:12). Silas would affect and improve Peter's style.

Peter was martyred during Nero's persecution. Although Peter expects persecution to spread (as it did under some later emperors, see Introduction to Revelation: Setting), under Nero it affected Rome itself most directly. At the time Peter writes, hostility was still more indirect (4:4), perhaps fitting a time shortly before or shortly after Nero's persecution began in AD 64.

QUICK GLANCE

AUTHOR:
The apostle Peter

AUDIENCE:
Gentile and Jewish believers in Pontus, Galatia, Cappadocia, western Asia Minor and Bithynia

DATE:
About AD 60 to 64

THEME:
Peter gives instructions on holy living for those suffering persecution.

Setting

Nero's persecution devastated the Christian community in Rome, although its numbers remained strong afterward. A fire burned much of Rome in AD 64 yet suspiciously left unscathed the estates of Nero and his older boyfriend Tigellinus. Like any good politician, Nero needed a scapegoat for his ills, and what appeared to be a new religious movement, understood as a fanatical form of Judaism begun by a crucified teacher some 35 years before, filled the need perfectly.

Romans viewed Christians, like Jews, as hostile to the rest of society. Certain charges became so common that they were stereotypical by the second century: Christians were "atheists" (for rejecting the gods), "cannibals" (for eating Jesus' "body" and drinking his "blood") and incestuous (for statements like "I love you, brother" or "I love you, sister"). Judaism was a poor target for outright persecution because its adherents were numerous and it was popular in some circles; further, Nero's mistress, Poppaea Sabina, was a patron of Jewish causes. By contrast, Jesus' movement was viewed as a form of Judaism whose support was tenuous even in Jewish circles, and therefore it offered an appropriate political scapegoat.

According to the early second-century historian Tacitus (*Annals*, 15.44), who disliked Christians himself, Nero burned Christians alive as torches to light his gardens at night. Nero killed other Christians in equally severe ways (e.g., feeding them to wild animals for public entertainment). In all, he murdered hundreds, and probably thousands, of Rome's Christians, although many Christians escaped his grasp. (That many survived seems clear from the continuing strong Roman church at the time that Clement sent his letter, *1 Clement*, to Corinth, a few decades later.) Thus, even though the Greek part of the empire loved Nero, Christians saw him as a prototype of the final antichrist. Nero died in disgrace several years later, pursued by fellow Romans who hated him. ◆

PETER WROTE THIS LETTER TO PROVINCES IN ASIA MINOR

1 Peter, an apostle of Jesus
Christ,[a]

To God's elect,[b] exiles scattered throughout the provinces of Pontus, Galatia, Cappadocia, Asia and Bithynia,[c]
2who have been chosen ac-
cording to the foreknowledge[d]
of God the Father, through the
sanctifying work of the Spirit,[e] to be obedient to Jesus
Christ and sprinkled with his
blood:[f]

Grace and peace be yours
in abundance.

Praise to God for a Living Hope

3Praise be to the God and
Father of our Lord Jesus
Christ![g] In his great mercy[h] he
has given us new birth into a
living hope through the resurrection of Jesus Christ from
the dead,[i] 4and into an inheritance that can never perish,
spoil or fade. This inheritance is kept in
heaven for you,[j] 5who through faith are
shielded by God's power[k] until the coming
of the salvation that is ready to be revealed
in the last time. 6In all this you greatly rejoice,[l] though now for a little while[m] you
may have had to suffer grief in all kinds
of trials.[n] 7These have come so that the
proven genuineness[o] of your faith — of
greater worth than gold, which perishes
even though refined by fire[p] — may result
in praise, glory and honor when Jesus
Christ is revealed.[q] 8Though you have not

1:1 [a] 2Pe 1:1 [b] Mt 24:22 [c] Ac 16:7 **1:2** [d] Ro 8:29 [e] 2Th 2:13 [f] Heb 10:22; 12:24 **1:3** [g] 2Co 1:3; Eph 1:3 [h] Titus 3:5; Jas 1:18 [i] 1Co 15:20 **1:4** [j] Col 1:5 **1:5** [k] Jn 10:28 **1:6** [l] Ro 5:2 [m] 1Pe 5:10 [n] Jas 1:2 **1:7** [o] Jas 1:3 [p] Job 23:10; Ps 66:10; Pr 17:3 [q] Ro 2:7

1:1 *To God's elect, exiles scattered.* Jewish people spoke of Jews who lived outside of Judea and Galilee as the Diaspora, or those who were "scattered"; Peter transfers this term to his audience (cf. v. 17; 2:11). *exiles.* This Greek term can also refer to "resident aliens," a status with which Jewish people in Diaspora cities were familiar (see note on v. 17; cf. 2:11). *Pontus, Galatia, Cappadocia, Asia and Bithynia.* These five Roman provinces were geographically connected; Peter omits the southern coastal regions of Asia Minor, some of which (see note on Gal 1:21) could be grouped with Syria in this period instead of as a political part of Asia Minor. (Peter may start in his mind with the province farthest from him and work his way around.) Because this is a circular letter to various regions, it may be something of a general letter, influenced more by the situation in Rome than by the current situation in Asia Minor.
1:2 *who have been chosen.* In Scripture and Jewish tradition, God made promises to the patriarchs and chose their descendants corporately; Peter applies the same language to believers in Jesus. *sprinkled with his blood.* God had set Israel apart and the sprinkling of blood also established the first covenant (Ex 24:7 – 8); for the greater lamb, see v. 19. *Grace and peace.* See note on Ro 1:7.
1:3 – 12 These verses constitute one long sentence in Greek; such long sentences could be viewed as skillful in antiquity, when hearers of lengthy speeches were accustomed to following an extended train of thought.
1:3 *Praise be to the God and Father of our Lord Jesus Christ!* Peter adopts the form of a *berakah*, the Jewish form of blessing that regularly began "Praise be to God." *new birth.* Through which one receives a new nature and identity (see notes on Jn 3:3,5). Scripture and other early Jewish sources speak of receiving a new heart (Eze 36:26) or becoming like a new person (1Sa 10:6). Believers were reborn to a living hope by Jesus' resurrection (here), an inheritance (v. 4) and future salvation (v. 5) — three ideas also naturally connected in Jewish views of the end of the age.
1:4 *inheritance that can never perish.* Jewish people already expected an inheritance in the coming world; some also spoke of a treasure stored up in heaven for the righteous.
1:6 *greatly rejoice … in all kinds of trials.* Both Scripture and Jewish tradition recognized that God sovereignly used trials to strengthen his people's commitment or purify their devotion (see note on Jas 1:13). God's servants could therefore even rejoice in such sufferings, trusting the greater outcome that was God's gift. In many Jewish traditions the end would be preceded by times of great testing. The testing in this case is especially persecution (4:12 – 19).
1:7 *gold … refined by fire.* Both Scripture and subsequent Jewish tradition sometimes depicted the righteous as being tested like precious metals purified in the furnace (Job 23:10; Ps 12:6; 66:10; Pr 17:3; Isa 48:10; perhaps Jer 11:4). Ores of precious metals (the most precious of which was gold) would be melted in a furnace to separate out the impurities and produce purer metal.

seen him, you love him; and even though you do not see him now, you believe in him[r] and are filled with an inexpressible and glorious joy, 9for you are receiving the end result of your faith, the salvation of your souls.[s]

10Concerning this salvation, the prophets, who spoke[t] of the grace that was to come to you, searched intently and with the greatest care,[u] 11trying to find out the time and circumstances to which the Spirit of Christ[v] in them was pointing when he predicted the sufferings of the Messiah and the glories that would follow. 12It was revealed to them that they were not serving themselves but you, when they spoke of the things that have now been told you by those who have preached the gospel to you[w] by the Holy Spirit sent from heaven. Even angels long to look into these things.

Be Holy

13Therefore, with minds that are alert and fully sober, set your hope on the grace to be brought to you when Jesus Christ is revealed at his coming. 14As obedient children, do not conform[x] to the evil desires you had when you lived in ignorance.[y] 15But just as he who called you is holy, so be holy in all you do;[z] 16for it is written: "Be holy, because I am holy."[a][a]

17Since you call on a Father who judges each person's work impartially,[b] live out your time as foreigners here in reverent fear.[c] 18For you know that it was not with perishable things such as silver or gold that you were redeemed[d] from the empty way of life handed down to you from your ancestors, 19but with the precious blood of Christ, a lamb[e] without blemish or defect.[f] 20He was chosen before the creation of the world,[g] but was revealed in these last times[h] for your sake. 21Through him you believe in God,[i] who raised him from the dead and glorified him, and so your faith and hope are in God.

22Now that you have purified[j] yourselves by obeying the truth so that you have sincere love for each other, love one another deeply,[k] from the heart.[b] 23For you have been born again,[l] not of perishable seed, but of imperishable, through the living and enduring word of God.[m] 24For,

"All people are like grass,
and all their glory is like the flowers of the field;
the grass withers and the flowers fall,
25 but the word of the Lord endures forever."[c][n]

And this is the word that was preached to you.

1:8 [r] Jn 20:29
1:9 [s] Ro 6:22
1:10 [t] Mt 26:24 [u] Mt 13:17
1:11 [v] 2Pe 1:21
1:12 [w] ver 25
1:14 [x] Ro 12:2 [y] Eph 4:18
1:15 [z] 2Co 7:1; 1Th 4:7
1:16 [a] Lev 11:44,45
1:17 [b] Ac 10:34 [c] Heb 12:28
1:18 [d] Mt 20:28; 1Co 6:20
1:19 [e] Jn 1:29 [f] Ex 12:5
1:20 [g] Eph 1:4 [h] Heb 9:26
1:21 [i] Ro 4:24
1:22 [j] Jas 4:8 [k] Jn 13:34; Heb 13:1
1:23 [l] Jn 1:13 [m] Heb 4:12
1:25 [n] Isa 40:6-8

[a] *16* Lev. 11:44,45; 19:2 [b] *22* Some early manuscripts *from a pure heart* [c] *25* Isaiah 40:6-8 (see Septuagint)

1:11 *trying to find out the time and circumstances.* Jewish teachers divided over whether God had irrevocably set the time of the end and over whether people could figure out when that would be; Peter recognizes that even the prophets (v. 10) did not know the times, though they predicted the Messiah's suffering and subsequent glory (cf. e.g., Isa 53:12). For the prophets' interest, see also Mt 13:17; Lk 10:24. *Spirit of Christ in them.* Although the OT usually prefers the Hebrew idiom of the Spirit coming "on" people (as in 4:14), the Spirit was also "in" the prophets (Nu 27:18).
1:12 *they were not serving themselves but you.* Some Jewish interpreters, such as those who composed the Dead Sea Scrolls, believed that the Biblical prophets had told especially about the interpreters' own time, and that their end-time meaning had thus remained secret until this new time. By contrast, Peter affirms that the prophets recognized that some of their prophecies applied to the Messiah who would suffer and be exalted (v. 11), and that they knew that many details would make sense to people only once the details happened. *angels long to look into these things.* According to some Jewish traditions, some secrets were so important that God kept them even from angels until the end time (cf. Mk 13:32); in some other traditions, angels envied Israel, who received God's law.
1:13 *with minds that are alert.* Interprets a Greek phrase that means "with the waist of your mind being girded." The meaning of the image—being prepared—would have been obvious to ancient audiences. Especially in much of the east, men wore long robes. Thus they would tuck them into their belt, girding up their waist, so they could move more freely and quickly.
1:14 *obedient children.* All ancient cultures expected minor children to obey their parents; Scripture also required this (Dt 21:18–21), with the obvious exception of sinful commands (e.g., 1Sa 19:11–16; 20:28–34).
1:16 *Be holy, because I am holy.* Children imitated parents. God summoned Israel to be holy as he was, living differently from the nations (Lev 11:44; 19:2; 20:7,26).
1:17 *Father.* Like prayers to God in synagogues, Christians addressed God as "Father." *impartially.* Jewish people emphasized God's impartiality (Dt 10:17). *foreigners.* The Greek term often means "resident aliens"; cities did not treat them as well as they did local citizens, but they were legal residents with greater rights than newcomers. Jewish communities throughout the empire normally held this resident alien status; although some Jews could achieve citizen status, in some places local citizens met their attempts to do so with hostility.
1:19 *a lamb without blemish or defect.* Lambs were sacrificed regularly, including as sin offerings (e.g., Lev 4:32; Nu 6:14). Lambs were especially prominent in large numbers at Passover, which celebrated Israel's redemption from slavery in Egypt. Acceptable sacrifices were to be without blemish or defect (Lev 22:21; Nu 19:2).
1:20 *revealed in these last times.* Jewish people normally thought of the last times as the period after or immediately preceding the end (cf. v. 5); it coincided closely with the coming of the Messiah.
1:23 *born again.* Some thinkers apparently used this image before Christians (see notes on Jn 3:3,5), but it became a much more common image among Christians, for whom conversion entailed transformation. *seed.* Each seed was expected to bring forth according to its own kind (cf. Ge 1:11–12; note on 1Jn 3:9–10).
1:24–25 Peter cites the Greek version of Isa 40:6–8, which contrasts the perishability of people with the

2 Therefore, rid yourselves[o] of all malice and all deceit, hypocrisy, envy, and
slander[p] of every kind. 2Like newborn babies, crave pure spiritual milk,[q] so that
by it you may grow up[r] in your salvation,
3now that you have tasted that the Lord
is good.[s]

The Living Stone and a Chosen People

4As you come to him, the living
Stone[t]—rejected by humans but chosen
by God and precious to him— 5you also,
like living stones, are being built[u] into a
spiritual house[a][v] to be a holy priesthood,[w]
offering spiritual sacrifices acceptable to
God through Jesus Christ.[x] 6For in Scripture it says:

> "See, I lay a stone in Zion,
> a chosen and precious cornerstone,[y]
> and the one who trusts in him
> will never be put to shame."[b][z]

7Now to you who believe, this stone is precious. But to those who do not believe,[a]

> "The stone the builders rejected
> has become the cornerstone,"[c][b]

8and,

> "A stone that causes people to stumble
> and a rock that makes them fall."[d][c]

They stumble because they disobey the
message—which is also what they were
destined for.[d]

9But you are a chosen people,[e] a royal priesthood, a holy nation,[f] God's special possession, that you may declare the
praises of him who called you out of darkness into his wonderful light.[g] 10Once you
were not a people, but now you are the
people of God;[h] once you had not received
mercy, but now you have received mercy.

Living Godly Lives in a Pagan Society

11Dear friends, I urge you, as foreigners
and exiles, to abstain from sinful desires,[i]
which wage war against your soul.[j] 12Live
such good lives among the pagans that,
though they accuse you of doing wrong,
they may see your good deeds[k] and glorify
God[l] on the day he visits us.

2:1 [o] Eph 4:22 [p] Jas 4:11 **2:2** [q] 1Co 3:2 [r] Eph 4:15, 16 **2:3** [s] Heb 6:5 **2:4** [t] ver 7 **2:5** [u] 1Co 3:9 [v] 1Ti 3:15 [w] Isa 61:6 [x] Php 4:18; Heb 13:15 **2:6** [y] Eph 2:20 [z] Isa 28:16 **2:7** [a] 2Co 2:16 [b] Ps 118:22 **2:8** [c] Isa 8:14; 1Co 1:23 [d] Ro 9:22 **2:9** [e] Dt 10:15 [f] Isa 62:12 [g] Ac 26:18 **2:10** [h] Hos 1:9, 10 **2:11** [i] Gal 5:16 [j] Jas 4:1 **2:12** [k] Php 2:15; 1Pe 3:16 [l] Mt 5:16; 9:8

[a] 5 Or *into a temple of the Spirit* [b] 6 Isaiah 28:16 [c] 7 Psalm 118:22 [d] 8 Isaiah 8:14

imperishability of God's word. In Isaiah, this unchangeable "word" is the good news of coming restoration and salvation in the time when God would redeem his people (e.g., Isa 40:9; 52:7–8).

2:1 *rid yourselves of.* "Ridding" oneself of, or "putting aside," the old ways also follows rebirth or new creation in James, Ephesians and Colossians, suggesting a shared early Christian source, perhaps even a teaching by Jesus no longer available to us. See note on Eph 4:22–24.

2:2 *crave pure spiritual milk.* For often two or sometimes even three years after birth (cf. 1:23), infants depended on mothers or nurses to provide breast milk. Business documents used "pure" in connection with food to mean "unadulterated," not mixed with anything else. "Spiritual" is one way to translate the Greek term so rendered (*logikos*); it might thus mean "figurative." The Greek term, however, also often means "rational," and might possibly connect by means of wordplay with the "word" (*logos*) of 1:23.

2:3 *tasted that the Lord is good.* Continuing the image of milk from v. 2, Peter evokes Ps 34:8: "Taste and see that the LORD is good."

2:4 *the living Stone.* Peter soon reveals his sources for speaking of this stone (see vv. 7–8 and note). *rejected.* See v. 7. *chosen … precious.* See v. 6.

2:5 *a spiritual house … offering spiritual sacrifices.* Peter's audience should have understood his image. Both philosophers and Jewish thinkers spoke of spiritual sacrifices, and the Judean group that composed many of the Dead Sea Scrolls saw itself as a spiritual temple. *house.* Could refer to a building, such as the temple, or to a household (cf. 4:17), such as the "house of Israel"; Peter may play on both senses here (as does, e.g., 2Sa 7:5–7,12–16). *holy priesthood.* As becomes clear in v. 9, Peter evokes Ex 19:5–6 (cf. Isa 61:6). As priests (as well as stones) in this new temple, believers offer sacrifices. *spiritual sacrifices.* See notes on Ro 12:1; Heb 13:15).

2:6 Authors of the Dead Sea Scrolls applied Isa 28:16 (cited here) to their own leadership; early Christians applied it to Jesus (Ro 9:33).

2:7–8 Jewish interpreters often linked texts based on shared key terms (Judean teachers called this method *gezerah shevah*); Peter thus adds to Isa 28:16 (cited in v. 6) two other stone texts: Ps 118:22 and Isa 8:14 (as Paul blended Isa 8:14 and Isa 28:16 in Ro 9:33; cf. Mt 21:42,44; Eph 2:20). Jesus taught his followers that the psalm's "cornerstone" image applied especially to himself (Mk 12:10–11).

2:7 Jewish people sang Ps 118 (cited here) during Passover season (see the possible Passover allusion mentioned in note on v. 9).

2:9 *chosen people.* Reflects a wider theme (e.g., Dt 10:15; 14:2; Ps 33:12; the wording is closer to Isa 43:20). *a royal priesthood, a holy nation.* Reflects the Greek version of Ex 19:6. *special possession.* Reflects Ex 19:5. *out of darkness into his wonderful light.* If the tradition is this early, during the Passover celebration some Jewish people described their deliverance from Egypt as a call "from darkness into great light."

2:10 *now you are the people of God … now you have received mercy.* Peter cites Hos 1:10; 2:23, which reverse God's earlier verdict against Israel (Hos 1:6,8–9), promising the ultimate restoration of God's people. Like Paul, Peter believes that Gentile followers of Israel's true king become part of this restored people of God (Ro 9:24–26); cf. Isa 19:24–25; 56:3–8.

2:11 *foreigners.* Often means "resident aliens" (see note on 1:17). The image here is of God's people (vv. 4–10) dispersed among the nations; God's people in the OT were sometimes portrayed in such terms (Lev 25:23), because of their mortality (1Ch 29:15; Ps 39:12), because of zeal for God (Ps 69:8–9) or because of their wanderings (Ge 23:4; 47:9). *wage war against your soul.* Philosophers spoke of heavenly souls as being "strangers" in their bodies, and of fleshly passions as "waging war" against the soul. Whereas philosophers sought to free the soul from earthly distractions, Peter's invitation is to right living (v. 12).

2:12 *pagans.* They often regarded as suspect Jews and their Gentile converts, and would mistrust still more fully Christians, whom they viewed as a smaller Jewish sect. The behavior advocated in the following household

13 Submit yourselves for the Lord's sake
to every human authority:[m] whether to the
emperor, as the supreme authority, 14 or to
governors, who are sent by him to punish those who do wrong[n] and to commend
those who do right.[o] 15 For it is God's will[p]
that by doing good you should silence the
ignorant talk of foolish people.[q] 16 Live as
free people,[r] but do not use your freedom
as a cover-up for evil; live as God's slaves.[s]
17 Show proper respect to everyone, love
the family of believers,[t] fear God, honor
the emperor.[u]

18 Slaves, in reverent fear of God submit yourselves to your masters,[v] not only
to those who are good and considerate,[w]
but also to those who are harsh. 19 For it is
commendable if someone bears up under
the pain of unjust suffering because they
are conscious of God.[x] 20 But how is it to
your credit if you receive a beating for doing wrong and endure it? But if you suffer
for doing good and you endure it, this is
commendable before God.[y] 21 To this[z] you
were called, because Christ suffered for
you, leaving you an example,[a] that you
should follow in his steps.

> 22 "He committed no sin,
> and no deceit was found in his
> mouth."[a b]

23 When they hurled their insults at him,
he did not retaliate; when he suffered, he
made no threats.[c] Instead, he entrusted
himself[d] to him who judges justly. 24 "He
himself bore our sins"[e] in his body on the
cross, so that we might die to sins[f] and
live for righteousness; "by his wounds you
have been healed."[g] 25 For "you were like
sheep going astray,"[b h] but now you have
returned to the Shepherd[i] and Overseer of
your souls.

3 Wives, in the same way submit yourselves[j] to your own husbands[k] so that,
if any of them do not believe the word,
they may be won over[l] without words by

2:13 [m] Ro 13:1 **2:14** [n] Ro 13:4 [o] Ro 13:3 **2:15** [p] 1Pe 3:17 [q] ver 12 **2:16** [r] Jn 8:32 [s] Ro 6:22 **2:17** [t] Ro 12:10 [u] Ro 13:7 **2:18** [v] Eph 6:5 [w] Jas 3:17 **2:19** [x] 1Pe 3:14, 17 **2:20** [y] 1Pe 3:17 **2:21** [z] Ac 14:22

[a] Mt 16:24 **2:22** [b] Isa 53:9 **2:23** [c] Isa 53:7 [d] Lk 23:46 **2:24** [e] Heb 9:28 [f] Ro 6:2 [g] Isa 53:5; Heb 12:13; Jas 5:16 **2:25** [h] Isa 53:6 [i] Jn 10:11 **3:1** [j] 1Pe 2:18 [k] Eph 5:22 [l] 1Co 7:16; 9:19

[a] *22* Isaiah 53:9 [b] *24,25* Isaiah 53:4,5,6 (see Septuagint)

codes (2:13 — 3:12) would undermine one of the most traditional slanders against such faiths — that they subverted the public order and traditional family values (see note on Eph 5:21 — 6:9). *the day he visits us.* Probably evokes the Greek version of Isa 10:3, referring to judgment. Many texts reported that the Gentiles would recognize God's glory in the end time (e.g., Isa 60:1 – 3).

2:13 – 17 Writers often treated household codes (such as in 2:18 — 3:7) when also providing instructions toward the state (as here) or other social obligations.

2:13 *Submit ... to every human authority.* God ultimately directed rulers for his purposes (Ex 9:16; Pr 21:1).

2:14 *governors.* Includes both legates and proconsuls. The former governed imperial provinces as representatives of the emperor (as here, v. 13); the latter governed senatorial provinces.

2:15 *by doing good you ... silence the ignorant talk of foolish people.* Minority groups sometimes used sets of behavioral instructions concerning relationships in the household or society to respond to public suspicions that they would undermine order (see note on Eph 5:21 — 6:9).

2:16 *Live as free people.* Philosophers often treated freedom as freedom to pursue virtue, freedom from desire and freedom to do without, and condemned those who thought that enslavement to passions was freedom. Unlike more radical Cynics, most philosophers who regarded the wise man as the ideal ruler nevertheless urged obedience to the state. For Christians, freedom meant freedom to be God's slaves rather than slaves of sin; it included freedom to honor the state voluntarily (cf. vv. 13 – 15; Mt 5:41; 17:27).

2:17 Other writers also included such brief lists of public duties. Scripture required honoring both God and human rulers (Ex 22:28; Pr 24:21).

2:18 – 25 On slaves and slavery, see the articles "Slaves and Slaveholders in Ephesians 6," p. 2068; "Ancient Slavery and the Background for Philemon," p. 2134. Peter addresses here household slaves, as opposed to slaves working under the harsher conditions of the fields and (worst of all) the mines. Peter does not address the institution of slavery per se — not a practical issue in a pastoral letter, since no one had yet ever succeeded in abolishing it. Nevertheless, he compares slaves' suffering with that of Christ (v. 21), showing where his sympathy clearly lies.

2:19 *bears up under the pain of unjust suffering.* Philosophers — even those who had once been slaves, such as Epictetus — generally counseled that slaves should do their best in the situation in which they found themselves. Achieving freedom was a preferable option, but one over which slaves' own control was extremely limited (see notes on 1Co 7:21 – 22).

2:20 *receive a beating for doing wrong.* Philosophers sometimes contrasted suffering justly with suffering unjustly. Some writers said that when a friend protested that Socrates suffered unjustly, Socrates replied, "So you would rather that I suffer justly?"

2:21 *Christ suffered ... leaving you an example.* Moral teachers often offered examples of people to imitate. Although ancient society valued status and associated power with greatness, Peter identifies Christ with unjustly treated slaves.

2:22 Here Peter quotes Isa 53:9, the first of several allusions to Isa 53 in vv. 22 – 25. Isa 53 describes "the suffering servant," a role fulfilled by Jesus (cf. note on Mt 12:18 – 21).

2:23 *he did not retaliate.* Honor was a central virtue in ancient Mediterranean society, and people guarded their honor by insulting in return those who insulted them. Slaves (v. 18), however, lacked this option. Many philosophers also advocated enduring insults without responding in kind. For the idea here, cf. Isa 53:7, although the wording differs. *to him who judges justly.* Cf., e.g., Ps 96:13; 98:9; Jer 11:20.

2:24 Peter paraphrases lines from Isa 53:4 – 5. *by his wounds you have been healed.* The healing here, as sometimes in other Jewish sources, is probably especially from sin (cf. v. 25; Isa 57:18 – 19).

2:25 *like sheep going astray.* Follows Isa 53:6; for God's people as scattered sheep, cf., e.g., Jer 50:6; Eze 34:6. *Shepherd and Overseer of your souls.* God was Israel's leading shepherd (Isa 40:11); Diaspora Jews also called him "Overseer," the one who watches over and guards. Peter may intend these titles for Jesus (5:4).

3:1 – 7 Although Peter upholds societal norms for the purpose of the church's witness in society (see note on

the behavior of their wives, 2when they
see the purity and reverence of your lives.
3Your beauty should not come from outward adornment, such as elaborate hairstyles and the wearing of gold jewelry or
fine clothes.[m] 4Rather, it should be that of
your inner self,[n] the unfading beauty of a
gentle and quiet spirit, which is of great
worth in God's sight. 5For this is the way
the holy women of the past who put their
hope in God[o] used to adorn themselves.
They submitted themselves to their own
husbands, 6like Sarah, who obeyed Abraham and called him her lord.[p] You are her
daughters if you do what is right and do
not give way to fear.
7Husbands,[q] in the same way be considerate as you live with your wives, and
treat them with respect as the weaker partner and as heirs with you of the gracious
gift of life, so that nothing will hinder your
prayers.

3:3 [m] Isa 3:18-23; 1Ti 2:9 **3:4** [n] Ro 7:22 **3:5** [o] 1Ti 5:5 **3:6** [p] Ge 18:12 **3:7** [q] Eph 5:25-33

3:8 [r] Ro 12:10 [s] 1Pe 5:5 **3:9** [t] Ro 12:17 [u] 1Pe 2:23 [v] 1Pe 2:21 [w] Heb 6:14 **3:12** [x] Ps 34:12-16

Suffering for Doing Good

8Finally, all of you, be like-minded, be
sympathetic, love one another,[r] be compassionate and humble.[s] 9Do not repay
evil with evil[t] or insult with insult.[u] On
the contrary, repay evil with blessing, because to this[v] you were called so that you
may inherit a blessing.[w] 10For,

"Whoever would love life
and see good days
must keep their tongue from evil
and their lips from deceitful speech.
11 They must turn from evil and do good;
they must seek peace and pursue it.
12 For the eyes of the Lord are on the
righteous
and his ears are attentive to their
prayer,
but the face of the Lord is against
those who do evil."[a][x]

[a] 12 Psalm 34:12-16

2:13–17), his sympathy here is with the Christian woman, as it was with the slaves in 2:18–25. He continues to advocate submission to authority, explicitly for the sake of witness (v. 1); husbands were always in the position of authority in that culture. Peter addresses wives at much greater length than husbands. Women converts to Judaism heavily outnumbered male converts; although Christians did not require circumcision, they may have also had more women than men. (Women sympathizers with Judaism also heavily outnumbered male sympathizers who were not full converts.) Husbands had more to lose socially from conversion to an unpopular minority religion than women did.

3:1 *in the same way.* Connects these instructions with those to slaves (see note on 2:18–25). *submit yourselves to your own husbands.* Society expected wives to obey their husbands, including by showing loyalty to their husbands' religions. Romans despised cults that prohibited participation in Roman religious rites, including worship of a family's household gods. *won over without words.* Greek and Roman men valued women's quietness and meekness.

3:2 *purity and reverence.* Ancient culture expected women (but not always men) to remain respectful and sexually pure.

3:3 *outward adornment.* Ancient moral writers regularly condemned such forms of ostentation. (The reference does not necessarily condemn all ornaments any more than it condemns all clothes. It challenges attention-getting, costly excess.) *elaborate hairstyles.* Women of means braided their hair elaborately, following costly fashions. Women of lesser means sometimes tried to imitate them. See note on 1Ti 2:9–10; see also the article "Head Coverings in Antiquity," p. 2003.

3:4 *beauty of a gentle and quiet spirit.* Ancient moral writers praised women who were gentle and quiet, and often contrasted this virtue with dressing fashionably or in other ways seeking to attract men's attention.

3:5 *holy women of the past.* Even Gentile writers often used as examples matrons of the distant past, who were both idealized as and respected for behaving better than current women. Sarah was the ultimate matriarch of Jewish tradition.

3:6 *Sarah, who obeyed Abraham.* Peter does not mention that Abraham also heeded Sarah in Genesis (the Hebrew term translated "agreed" in Ge 16:2 and "listen" in Ge 21:12 can even mean "obeyed"); it is not relevant to his immediate point (v. 1). At least ideally, Greeks and Romans expected wives to obey their husbands. *called him her lord.* Sarah calls Abraham "my lord" in Ge 18:12, fitting expectations for husbands (cf. 1Ki 1:13; cf. also the Hebrew of Hos 2:16), fathers (Ge 31:35), honored brothers (Ge 32:4–5; Nu 12:11), and others addressing someone respectfully (e.g., Ge 18:3; 23:11,15). *You are her daughters.* Jewish people regarded themselves as "children" of Abraham and Sarah; for Christians' fulfilling such a role, cf. 1Pe 2:9–10. *do not give way to fear.* Peter disagrees with moral writers who sometimes urged wives also to fear their husbands (cf. 3:13–14). Husbands displeased with their wives' faith could make life miserable for them. Records of husbands physically abusing their wives in this region and period are rare (in contrast to when Augustine later grew up in North Africa). Nevertheless, husbands could resort to prostitutes, discard newborn infants or simply divorce wives and take the children. In one mid-second-century account, a Christian divorced her husband for his repeated infidelity, so he betrayed her to the authorities as a Christian. Christian wives were limited in their options, but Peter wants them to pursue peace without being intimidated.

3:7 *the weaker partner.* Many writers complained about women's moral, intellectual and sometimes physical weakness. (Peter might apply it mainly to their social position, since he deems women fellow heirs spiritually.) Aristotle earlier argued that women were by nature inferior to men in every way except sexually. Men regarded women's delicacy as an object of both desire and mistrust; even the traditional Roman legal system simply assumed their weakness and inability to make sound decisions on their own. Many, however, cited this weakness as a reason to show them more consideration, which is Peter's reasoning here. *so that nothing will hinder your prayers.* See v. 12.

3:8 *be like-minded.* Ancient moral writers often urged harmony, including between spouses.

3:9 *Do not repay evil with evil or insult with insult.* Jesus' example (2:23) and even teaching (cf. Lk 6:27–29) might inform Peter's counsel here (though it was held more widely, see note on Ro 12:17). *inherit a blessing.* Those who "inherit a blessing" are those God hears in v. 12.

3:10–12 Peter used Ps 34:8 in 2:3; now he quotes from Ps 34:12–16 to confirm his teaching in 2:13—3:9.

13Who is going to harm you if you
are eager to do good?[y] 14But even if you
should suffer for what is right, you are
blessed.[z] "Do not fear their threats[a]; do
not be frightened."[b][a] 15But in your hearts
revere Christ as Lord. Always be prepared
to give an answer[b] to everyone who asks
you to give the reason for the hope that
you have. But do this with gentleness and
respect, 16keeping a clear conscience,[c] so
that those who speak maliciously against
your good behavior in Christ may be
ashamed of their slander.[d] 17For it is better, if it is God's will,[e] to suffer for doing
good[f] than for doing evil. 18For Christ also
suffered once for sins,[g] the righteous for
the unrighteous, to bring you to God. He
was put to death in the body[h] but made
alive in the Spirit.[i] 19After being made
alive,[c] he went and made proclamation
to the imprisoned spirits[j]— 20to those
who were disobedient long ago when
God waited patiently in the days of Noah
while the ark was being built.[k] In it only
a few people, eight in all, were saved[l]
through water, 21and this water symbolizes baptism that now saves you[m] also—
not the removal of dirt from the body but
the pledge of a clear conscience toward
God.[d] It saves you by the resurrection of
Jesus Christ,[n] 22who has gone into heaven
and is at God's right hand[o]—with angels,
authorities and powers in submission to
him.[p]

Living for God

4 Therefore, since Christ suffered in his
body, arm yourselves also with the
same attitude, because whoever suffers in
the body is done with sin. 2As a result,
they do not live the rest of their earthly
lives for evil human desires,[q] but rather
for the will of God. 3For you have spent
enough time in the past[r] doing what pagans choose to do—living in debauchery,
lust, drunkenness, orgies, carousing and
detestable idolatry. 4They are surprised
that you do not join them in their reckless,
wild living, and they heap abuse on you.[s]

3:13 [y] Pr 16:7 **3:14** [z] 1Pe 2:19, 20; 4:15, 16 [a] Isa 8:12, 13 **3:15** [b] Col 4:6 **3:16** [c] Heb 13:18 [d] 1Pe 2:12, 15 **3:17** [e] 1Pe 2:15 [f] 1Pe 2:20 **3:18** [g] 1Pe 2:21 [h] Col 1:22; 1Pe 4:1 [i] 1Pe 4:6 **3:19** [j] 1Pe 4:6 **3:20** [k] Ge 6:3, 5, 13, 14 [l] Heb 11:7
3:21 [m] Titus 3:5 [n] 1Pe 1:3 **3:22** [o] Mk 16:19 [p] Ro 8:38 **4:2** [q] Ro 6:2 **4:3** [r] Eph 2:2 **4:4** [s] 1Pe 3:16

[a] 14 Or *fear what they fear* [b] 14 Isaiah 8:12
[c] 18,19 Or *but made alive in the spirit, [19]in which also*
[d] 21 Or *but an appeal to God for a clear conscience*

3:14 *Do not fear their threats.* See NIV text note. The Lord warned Isaiah not to fear what the people feared (Isa 8:12, the Greek form of which is quoted here) but to only fear the Lord (Isa 8:13).
3:15 *revere Christ as Lord.* The Greek form of Isa 8:13 begins the same way as the Greek text here: "Revere the Lord as holy"—except that Peter expressly applies this divine role to Christ. *answer.* The Greek term normally means a "defense"—something they may eventually need even in court (4:5–6,15–16).
3:16—4:5 Ancient writers sometimes used inverted parallelism, called a chiasm. One such chiasm might occur here, if one may identify the "spirits" of 3:19 with the angels of 3:22, as many scholars do:

A Your slanderers will be ashamed (3:16)
B Suffer though innocent, in God's will (3:17)
C For Christ suffered for the unjust (3:18)
D He triumphed over hostile spirits (3:19)
E Noah was saved through water (3:20)
E′ You are saved through water (3:21)
D′ Christ triumphed over hostile spirits (3:22)
C′ For Christ suffered (4:1a)
B′ Suffer in God's will (4:1b–2)
A′ Your slanderers will be ashamed (4:3–5)

3:16 Cf. note on 2:12.
3:19 *he went and made proclamation to the imprisoned spirits.* The three most common views on this passage are: (1) Between Jesus' death and resurrection, he preached to the dead in Hades, the realm of the dead (the view of many church fathers, citing 4:6). Greeks had myths about heroes such as Heracles or Orpheus descending temporarily to Hades. (2) Christ preached through Noah to people in Noah's day (the view of many Reformers). (3) Before or (more likely) after his resurrection, Jesus proclaimed triumph over the fallen angels (the view of most scholars today, citing v. 22)

Early Christians nearly always used "spirits" for angelic or demonic spirits rather than human ones, except when explicitly stating the latter. The Spirit raised Jesus; by the Spirit (and thus, in this context, presumably after his resurrection) Jesus "made proclamation"; in v. 22, his exaltation declared his triumph over fallen angels. Most ancient Jewish readers believed that Ge 6:1–3 refers to angels who fell in Noah's day (v. 20); after the flood, they were said to be imprisoned (so also 2Pe 2:4; Jude 6), either below the earth or in the atmosphere (cf. v. 22; note on Eph 2:2). Then, according to a well-known Jewish tradition, Enoch was sent to proclaim God's judgment to them; here Christ is the one who proclaims their demise.
3:20 Jewish sources sometimes viewed the flood as a prototype of future judgment, as also in 2Pe 3:6–7. *God waited patiently.* Recalls Ge 6:3 (120 years) and is mentioned in connection with the final judgment in 2Pe 3:9. *only a few people . . . were saved through water.* The salvation of "only a few" could encourage early Christians, who were a persecuted minority.
3:21 *not the removal of dirt from the body.* Baptism mattered as an act of faith, not simply as washing away physical dirt. Jewish teachers used baptism as an act of conversion, but treated it as efficacious only if the repentance it claimed was sincere.
3:22 *angels, authorities and powers in submission to him.* Jewish texts often speak of angelic rulers over the nations (see note on Eph 1:21). Thus even the evil powers behind the rulers who persecuted Christians had been subdued, and no question remained about history's final outcome.
4:3 Banquets often lasted far into the night, with heavy drinking and men often pursuing slave women or boys. Although wine was watered down for ordinary meals, banqueters often sought to become drunk. The worship of false deities pervaded social clubs, household cults and virtually all aspects of Greco-Roman life; hosts poured libations to gods at the beginning of banquets. Although this behavior was not immoral from the general Greco-Roman perspective, Jews and Christians condemned it as immoral. Romans suspected some subversive religious cults of such disorderly behavior.
4:4 *they heap abuse on you.* Although Jewish people did not participate in the lifestyle characterized in v. 3,

5But they will have to give account to him
who is ready to judge the living and the
dead.[t] 6For this is the reason the gospel
was preached even to those who are now
dead,[u] so that they might be judged according to human standards in regard to
the body, but live according to God in regard to the spirit.
7The end of all things is near.[v] Therefore be alert and of sober mind so that
you may pray. 8Above all, love each other
deeply,[w] because love covers over a multitude of sins.[x] 9Offer hospitality to one
another without grumbling.[y] 10Each of
you should use whatever gift you have received to serve others,[z] as faithful[a] stewards of God's grace in its various forms.
11If anyone speaks, they should do so as
one who speaks the very words of God.
If anyone serves, they should do so with
the strength God provides,[b] so that in all
things God may be praised[c] through Jesus
Christ. To him be the glory and the power
for ever and ever. Amen.

Suffering for Being a Christian

12Dear friends, do not be surprised at
the fiery ordeal that has come on you[d]
to test you, as though something strange
were happening to you. 13But rejoice inasmuch as you participate in the sufferings of Christ, so that you may be overjoyed when his glory is revealed.[e] 14If
you are insulted because of the name of
Christ, you are blessed,[f] for the Spirit of
glory and of God rests on you. 15If you
suffer, it should not be as a murderer or
thief or any other kind of criminal, or
even as a meddler. 16However, if you suffer as a Christian, do not be ashamed,
but praise God that you bear that name.[g]
17For it is time for judgment to begin with
God's household;[h] and if it begins with
us, what will the outcome be for those
who do not obey the gospel of God?[i]
18And,

"If it is hard for the righteous to be
saved,
what will become of the ungodly
and the sinner?"[a][j]

19So then, those who suffer according
to God's will should commit themselves
to their faithful Creator and continue to
do good.

4:5 [t] Ac 10:42; 2Ti 4:1 4:6 [u] 1Pe 3:19 4:7 [v] Ro 13:11 4:8 [w] 1Pe 1:22 [x] Pr 10:12 4:9 [y] Php 2:14 4:10 [z] Ro 12:6,7 [a] 1Co 4:2 4:11 [b] Eph 6:10 [c] 1Co 10:31 4:12 [d] 1Pe 1:6,7

4:13 [e] Ro 8:17 4:14 [f] Mt 5:11 4:16 [g] Ac 5:41 4:17 [h] Jer 25:29 [i] 2Th 1:8 4:18 [j] Pr 11:31; Lk 23:31

[a] 18 Prov. 11:31 (see Septuagint)

their pagan neighbors often portrayed them as lawless and subversive because of their alleged antisocial behavior. Many leveled the same charges against Christians, although even interrogation by torture did not produce any supporting evidence. Nero's accusation against the Christians he butchered was that they were "haters of humanity," i.e., antisocial. But rumors of Nero's own base immorality offended even the Roman aristocracy.

4:5 *they will have to give account.* Ultimately it was Christians' accusers who would stand trial; Scripture sometimes depicts God's day of judgment as a trial (cf. Isa 41:1; 43:9).

4:6 *those who are now dead.* Although some commentators regard these dead as souls already dead when the message came (based on their understanding of 3:19–20), from the context more commentators suggest that these were Christians who embraced the gospel before death. Although judged by earthly courts and executed, they would be raised by the Spirit, as in 3:18.

4:7 *be alert.* In many Jewish traditions (including Da 12:1–2), the end of the age would be preceded by a period of great suffering.

4:8 *love covers over a multitude of sins.* Pr 10:12 insists on forgiveness rather than gossip (cf. Pr 17:9; Jas 5:20). Some commentators apply this to believers forgiving one another; other commentators apply this to the principle of those who forgive being forgiven.

4:9 *hospitality.* Included providing lodging and provisions, often for trustworthy travelers; ideally hosts counted this a privilege.

4:11 *the very words of God.* This Greek expression applied to prophecies; early Christians had an emphasis on prophecy that exceeded other Jewish groups' expectations (see the article "Prophecy in Antiquity," p. 2009).

4:12 *fiery ordeal.* Soon after this letter, Nero had Christians burned alive to light his gardens at night (AD 64). The image of fiery testing, of course, is wider than that (e.g., Jer 6:29; Zec 13:9). *to test you.* Peter probably alludes to the image of gold being tried by fire (see note on 1:7). Jewish people expected a period of intense suffering just before the end of the age (cf. also Da 12:1–2).

4:14 *the Spirit of glory and of God rests on you.* Jewish sources, following Scripture, sometimes spoke of the Spirit being "on" God's servants (e.g., Nu 11:17; Eze 11:5); the Spirit "resting on" comes from the Greek version of Isa 11:2, about the Messiah, but Jesus has also empowered his followers with his Spirit.

4:15 Second-century defenders of Christianity argued that the only charge on which true Christians were ever convicted was the charge of being a Christian.

4:16 *Christian.* Probably used here as a legal charge (it was not originally the name believers used for themselves, see note on Ac 11:26). *do not be ashamed.* Greek and Roman male society craved honor, but, as here, many Greek sages noted that it was genuinely honorable to suffer scorn for doing what was right.

4:17 *it is time for judgment to begin with God's household.* Biblical prophets also spoke of judgment beginning with God's household (Eze 9:6; cf. Jer 25:7–29; Am 3:2); cf. also the ominous expression "the time has come!" (Eze 7:7,12). Jewish teachers sometimes viewed even the unjust judgment of earthly courts (v. 6) as God's discipline to refine his people.

4:18 Peter cites the Greek version of Pr 11:31. Some Jewish teachers argued that the righteous suffered in this life, but the wicked in the world to come.

4:19 *commit themselves to their faithful Creator.* Peter probably echoes the familiar language of Jewish prayers developed from Ps 31:5 (cf. Lk 23:46). The final benediction of one regularly uttered Jewish prayer, e.g., included "Our lives are committed to your hand, and our souls are in your care."

To the Elders and the Flock

5 To the elders among you, I appeal
as a fellow elder[k] and a witness[l] of
Christ's sufferings who also will share in
the glory to be revealed:[m] 2Be shepherds
of God's flock[n] that is under your care,
watching over them — not because you
must, but because you are willing, as God
wants you to be; not pursuing dishonest
gain,[o] but eager to serve; 3not lording it
over[p] those entrusted to you, but being
examples[q] to the flock. 4And when the
Chief Shepherd appears, you will receive
the crown of glory[r] that will never fade
away.

5In the same way, you who are younger,
submit yourselves[s] to your elders. All of
you, clothe yourselves with humility toward one another, because,

> "God opposes the proud
> but shows favor to the humble."[a][t]

6Humble yourselves, therefore, under God's
mighty hand, that he may lift you up in
due time.[u] 7Cast all your anxiety on him[v]
because he cares for you.[w]

8Be alert and of sober mind. Your enemy the devil prowls around[x] like a roaring lion looking for someone to devour.
9Resist him,[y] standing firm in the faith,[z]
because you know that the family of believers throughout the world is undergoing
the same kind of sufferings.[a]

10And the God of all grace, who called
you to his eternal glory[b] in Christ, after
you have suffered a little while, will himself restore you and make you strong,[c]
firm and steadfast. 11To him be the power
for ever and ever. Amen.[d]

Final Greetings

12With the help of Silas,[b][e] whom I regard as a faithful brother, I have written

5:1 [k] Ac 11:30 [l] Lk 24:48 [m] 1Pe 1:5,7; Rev 1:9 **5:2** [n] Jn 21:16 [o] 1Ti 3:3 **5:3** [p] Eze 34:4 [q] Php 3:17 **5:4** [r] 1Co 9:25 **5:5** [s] Eph 5:21 [t] Pr 3:34; Jas 4:6 **5:6** [u] Jas 4:10 **5:7** [v] Ps 37:5; Mt 6:25 [w] Heb 13:5 **5:8** [x] Job 1:7 **5:9** [y] Jas 4:7 [z] Col 2:5 [a] Ac 14:22 **5:10** [b] 2Co 4:17 [c] 2Th 2:17 **5:11** [d] Ro 11:36 **5:12** [e] 2Co 1:19

[a] 5 Prov. 3:34 [b] 12 Greek *Silvanus*, a variant of *Silas*

5:1 *elders.* Ruled OT villages and continued to fill a respected leadership role in this period (see note on Ac 14:23).
5:2 *Be shepherds of God's flock.* The ancient world had long used shepherds as an image of leaders; in Scripture, Israel was God's flock and its leaders its shepherds, responsible for serving the flock (Jer 3:15; 23:4). *not pursuing dishonest gain.* Because people often accused teachers of seeking dishonest gain, many of them insisted on being beyond reproach in their behavior. Cf. 2Pe 2:3.
5:3 *being examples to the flock.* Students often imitated teachers. Society valued honor, but Jesus' followers must serve (v. 5; Mk 10:42–45). Israel's shepherds had often abused the flock (e.g., Isa 56:11; Jer 23:1–2; 50:6; Eze 34:2–10), but God had promised better shepherds who would care for his flock (Jer 3:15; 23:4).
5:4 *Chief Shepherd.* Although God had raised up Moses, David, and others as shepherds for Israel, he was the chief shepherd (Ps 23:1; Isa 40:11; Eze 34:11–12), a role here filled by Christ. *the crown of glory that will never fade away.* A winner in an athletic competition would receive a crown, which was a garland that would eventually fade away (see the article "Athletic Imagery in 1 Corinthians 9," p. 2000). Earthly crowns represented glory, or honor and fame, but they would eventually be forgotten.
5:5–9 Similarities with Jas 4:6–10 suggests a common source, but the passages apply the principles to different kinds of tests. In James, the primary test is poverty and oppression, tempting people to retaliate. Here, it appears to be especially persecution, tempting believers to fall away.
5:5 *submit ... to your elders.* All ancient cultures recognized the importance of honoring elders. Such respect normally included deferring to the wisdom of older men and allowing them to speak first. Peter advocates submission to the ruling elders (v. 1), but he also urges — against Greco-Roman society's ideals — mutual humility, citing Pr 3:34 (cf. Jas 4:6).
5:6 *Humble yourselves ... under God's mighty hand.* Peter applies Pr 3:34 (cited in v. 5) to exhort believers. This behavior includes embracing and accepting the suffering until God provides the way out (cf. Jer 27:11); God promised to humble the proud in his day of judgment (Isa 2:11–12,17). The cries of God's people during unjust sufferings had always moved him to act on their behalf (Ex 2:23–25; 3:7–9; Jdg 2:18; 10:16).
5:7 *because he cares for you.* Jewish teachers came to see God's disciplining love in Israel's sufferings, but it made little sense to most Gentiles, who bartered sacrifices to seek benefactions from the gods. The language of God's care might possibly echo Wisdom of Solomon 12:13, but the idea of God's care for his people pervades the OT (e.g., Dt 32:11; Isa 40:11; Eze 34:12).
5:8 *Your enemy the devil prowls around like a roaring lion.* Satan prowled as he traveled around the earth seeking harm in Job 2:2. In Job's Hebrew text, "Satan" appears to have been a title, meaning "enemy" or "accuser"; he may have functioned in Job as a sort of prosecutor. Satan's malevolent character, however, quickly grew clear (cf. Zec 3:1–2), as it was in both Jewish tradition and the NT. *devil.* Originally meant "slanderer." Jewish tradition emphasized Satan's role as accuser, deceiver and tempter, seeking to lead people astray from God; many Jewish people believed that the present age was under the devil's dominion. *like a roaring lion.* An adversary (Ps 22:13) or even exploitive rulers (Pr 28:15; Eze 22:25; Zep 3:3) could be like "roaring lions." Lions were considered the most powerful predators; eventually some Christians were fed to literal ones.
5:9 *the family of believers throughout the world is undergoing the same kind of sufferings.* Christians in Asia (1:1) could take courage from the sufferings of Christians in Rome (see Introduction: Setting) and elsewhere.
5:12 *With the help of Silas.* Rich people dictated to scribes because they could afford to do so; poor people normally dictated to them because they could not write themselves. Early tradition reports that Mark wrote down Peter's recollections about Jesus' ministry; Peter probably depended on help in composing more than did Paul (though Paul also used scribes; cf. Ro 16:22). *Silas.* A Jewish Roman citizen (Ac 16:16–37) who probably had a strong education; he could thus help Peter compose the letter in the most effective way. *I have written to you briefly.* Speeches and letters often closed politely by noting that they had been brief (cf. Heb 13:22), although 1 Peter is much longer than the average ancient letter.

to you briefly,[f] encouraging you and testifying that this is the true grace of God.
Stand fast in it.
13She who is in Babylon, chosen together with you, sends you her greetings, and
so does my son Mark.[g] 14Greet one another with a kiss of love.[h]
Peace[i] to all of you who are in Christ.

5:12 [f] Heb 13:22
5:13 [g] Ac 12:12
5:14 [h] Ro 16:16
[i] Eph 6:23

5:13 *She who is in Babylon.* Jewish people by this period viewed Rome as the fourth of the four kingdoms in Da 7 that would oppress Israel, a successor to Babylon. "Babylon" thus became a fairly common cryptogram for Rome, and even more so after the temple's destruction in AD 70. *my son Mark.* Very early tradition claims that Mark wrote down his Gospel based on anecdotes Peter remembered about Jesus (Papias fragment 3.15).

5:14 *kiss of love.* People often greeted relatives or other people close to them with a light kiss on the lips. See note on Ro 16:16.

THE LETTERS

2 PETER

Authorship

Second Peter may be a general letter intended for a wide range of churches. Of all the NT letters that name their authors, 2 Peter is the most disputed among scholars. In some respects its style differs from 1 Peter; more important, it incorporates much of the letter of Jude. Although one may account for some differences in style because Silas helped draft 1 Peter (1Pe 5:12), 2 Peter is full of Hellenistic Jewish images that would have required considerable learning on the part of someone who spent most of his career in Galilee and Judea.

Some scholars note, however, that just as Peter depended on Silas's help in his first letter, 2 Peter could reflect other editorial help. Others suggest that it could combine genuine material from Peter (e.g., in ch. 1) with material from Jude (especially in ch. 2). (Some have also suggested that Jude himself was the letter's editor.) If Mark wrote down Peter's recollections about Jesus (see Introduction to Mark: Authorship), Peter may have also welcomed some other writers (in this case with greater sophistication in Hellenistic Jewish motifs) to communicate his teachings in other ways.

Although the early church debated the genuineness of 2 Peter, a majority ultimately decided in its favor, and its existence is attested early. The attestation for 2 Peter in early Christian sources is weaker than that for most other NT books but stronger than that of early Christian books that did not become part of the NT, especially those claiming to be Petrine.

QUICK GLANCE

AUTHOR:
The apostle Peter

AUDIENCE:
Christians in western Asia Minor

DATE:
Between AD 65 and 68

THEME:
Peter teaches how to deal with false teachers and evildoers who have come into the church.

Date

Because we do not know the date of Jude, this letter's dependence on Jude does not provide a helpful date range; nor does reference to Paul require a later date, since some of Paul's letters circulated in his lifetime (cf. Col 4:16). Because Gnosticism began to flourish in the second century, some propose that 2 Peter be dated to that time period. But Gnosticism need not be the heresy addressed by Peter (see Opponents). The letter's flowery style also prevailed more in the first century than in the second. Since Peter was martyred during the reign of Nero (AD 54 – 68), Peter's teachings, including those in this letter, must predate Nero's death.

Opponents

Although some have thought that those condemned in the letter were Gnostics, the many allusions to Hellenistic Jewish traditions suggest instead an overly Hellenized Jewish Christian setting. The letter mentions "knowledge" seven times, but philosophers and other thinkers discoursed about knowledge regularly. All the false teachers' and scoffers' ideas mentioned in the letter already existed in Hellenistic Judaism. Ancient sources also widely criticized charlatans. These observations count against any necessary appeal to a later Gnostic background. ◆

1 Simon Peter, a servant[a] and apostle of
Jesus Christ,[b]

To those who through the righteousness[c] of our God and Savior Jesus Christ[d]
have received a faith as precious as ours:

2Grace and peace be yours in abundance through the knowledge of God and
of Jesus our Lord.[e]

Confirming One's Calling and Election

3His divine power[f] has given us everything we need for a godly life through our
knowledge of him who called us[g] by his
own glory and goodness. 4Through these
he has given us his very great and precious promises,[h] so that through them you
may participate in the divine nature,[i] having escaped the corruption in the world
caused by evil desires.[j]

5For this very reason, make every effort
to add to your faith goodness; and to goodness, knowledge;[k] 6and to knowledge, self-
control;[l] and to self-control, perseverance;
and to perseverance, godliness;[m] 7and to
godliness, mutual affection; and to mutual
affection, love.[n] 8For if you possess these
qualities in increasing measure, they will
keep you from being ineffective and unproductive[o] in your knowledge of our Lord
Jesus Christ. 9But whoever does not have
them is nearsighted and blind,[p] forgetting
that they have been cleansed from their
past sins.[q]

10Therefore, my brothers and sisters,[a]
make every effort to confirm your calling
and election. For if you do these things,
you will never stumble,[r] 11and you will
receive a rich welcome into the eternal
kingdom of our Lord and Savior Jesus
Christ.

Prophecy of Scripture

12So I will always remind you of these
things,[s] even though you know them and
are firmly established in the truth you now
have. 13I think it is right to refresh your
memory as long as I live in the tent of this
body,[t] 14because I know that I will soon
put it aside,[u] as our Lord Jesus Christ has
made clear to me.[v] 15And I will make every effort to see that after my departure[w]
you will always be able to remember these
things.

16For we did not follow cleverly devised
stories when we told you about the coming of our Lord Jesus Christ in power, but
we were eyewitnesses of his majesty.[x]
17He received honor and glory from God
the Father when the voice came to him
from the Majestic Glory, saying, "This
is my Son, whom I love; with him I am
well pleased."[b][y] 18We ourselves heard this
voice that came from heaven when we
were with him on the sacred mountain.[z]

1:1 [a] Ro 1:1 [b] 1Pe 1:1 [c] Ro 3:21-26 [d] Titus 2:13 **1:2** [e] Php 3:8 **1:3** [f] 1Pe 1:5 [g] 1Th 2:12 **1:4** [h] 2Co 7:1 [i] Eph 4:24; Heb 12:10; 1Jn 3:2 [j] 2Pe 2:18-20 **1:5** [k] Col 2:3 **1:6** [l] Ac 24:25 [m] ver 3 **1:7** [n] 1Th 3:12 **1:8** [o] Jn 15:2; Titus 3:14 **1:9** [p] 1Jn 2:11 [q] Eph 5:26 **1:10** [r] 2Pe 3:17 **1:12** [s] Php 3:1; 1Jn 2:21 **1:13** [t] 2Co 5:1,4 **1:14** [u] 2Ti 4:6 [v] Jn 21:18, 19 **1:15** [w] Lk 9:31 **1:16** [x] Mt 17:1-8 **1:17** [y] Mt 3:17 **1:18** [z] Mt 17:6

[a] *10* The Greek word for *brothers and sisters* (*adelphoi*) refers here to believers, both men and women, as part of God's family. [b] *17* Matt. 17:5; Mark 9:7; Luke 9:35

1:1 *Simon.* In Greek, the name here is "Simeon," a common Jewish name (cf. Ge 29:33), rather than the usual Greek equivalent "Simon" commonly used in the NT. *our God and Savior Jesus Christ.* Jewish people sometimes used savior as a divine title, an approach inevitable when conjoined with God (cf., e.g., Ps 85:4; Isa 45:15,21; Mic 7:7).
1:2 *Grace and peace.* See note on Ro 1:7.
1:4 *you may participate in the divine nature.* Many Greek thinkers believed that humans could become (or the soul was already) divine; some Diaspora Jews used this language, although they believed in just one God. Most Jews denied that humans could become divine (cf. Ge 3:5). When Diaspora Jews spoke of participating "in the divine nature," they usually referred to becoming immortal. Peter probably evokes especially the early Christian view of God's Spirit transforming believers' moral character in Christ (see note on 1Pe 1:23.) *escaped the corruption in the world caused by evil desires.* Many Greek thinkers in this period wanted to escape the material world of decay around them, believing that their soul was divine and immortal and belonged in the pure and perfect heavens above; some Greek thinkers and cults provided this idea as a hope for the masses. Peter associates the corruption instead with evil desires (cf. 2:14; 3:3).
1:5–7 Both Jews and Gentiles used the literary form of adding one virtue, vice or some other next step to a former one (cf., e.g., Wisdom of Solomon 6:17–20).
1:5 *goodness.* The Greek term (*aretê*) was the catchall Greek virtue, representing nobility of character.
1:7 *love.* The climactic virtue, in accordance with Jesus' teaching (see note on 1Co 13:13).
1:10 *confirm your calling and election.* Jewish tradition applied calling and election to God's people Israel; here Peter applies it to Christian believers.
1:12 *I will always remind you.* Moral teachers would often exhort people, noting that they were simply "reminding" them of truths.
1:13 *the tent of this body.* Many ancient thinkers described the body as a tent (cf. note on 2Co 5:1).
1:14 *I will soon put it aside.* Jewish people and some others paid special attention to the last words of someone expected to die soon. The Greek term here translated "put it aside," along with related terms, had a range of meaning (cf. James 1:21 ["get rid of"]; 1Pe 3:21 ["removal of"]), sometimes including putting off clothing (cf. Ro 13:12; Eph 4:22).
1:15 See note on v. 12.
1:16 *stories.* Lit. "myths"; usually used pejoratively and contrasted with true accounts from eyewitnesses. *coming ... in power.* Here refers to Jesus' transfiguration (Mk 9:1–3), of which Peter was an eyewitness (Mk 9:2,5).
1:17 *from the Majestic Glory.* "The Glory" was sometimes a Jewish circumlocution for God; Peter may use it here to reinforce the transfiguration's allusion to Sinai (see notes on v. 18; Mk 9:2). *my Son ... with him I am well pleased.* The quotation here precisely matches Mt 3:17 (for the heavenly voice, see note there); in terms of Mark's Gospel, it blends the voice at the baptism (Mk 1:11) with the voice at the transfiguration (Mk 9:7).
1:18 *voice that came from heaven ... on the sacred mountain.* God spoke from heaven at the giving of the law (Dt 4:36) and revealed himself to Moses on another sacred mountain, Mount Sinai. He also promised a new and

19We also have the prophetic message
as something completely reliable, and you
will do well to pay attention to it, as to a
light[a] shining in a dark place, until the day
dawns and the morning star[b] rises in your
hearts. 20Above all, you must understand
that no prophecy of Scripture came about
by the prophet's own interpretation of
things. 21For prophecy never had its origin
in the human will, but prophets, though
human, spoke from God[c] as they were carried along by the Holy Spirit.[d]

False Teachers and Their Destruction

2 But there were also false prophets[e]
among the people, just as there will
be false teachers among you.[f] They will
secretly introduce destructive heresies,
even denying the sovereign Lord[g] who
bought them[h] — bringing swift destruction
on themselves. 2Many will follow their depraved conduct and will bring the way of
truth into disrepute. 3In their greed these
teachers will exploit you[i] with fabricated
stories. Their condemnation has long been
hanging over them, and their destruction
has not been sleeping.
4For if God did not spare angels when
they sinned, but sent them to hell,[a] putting them in chains of darkness[b] to be held
for judgment;[j] 5if he did not spare the ancient world[k] when he brought the flood on
its ungodly people, but protected Noah, a
preacher of righteousness, and seven others;[l] 6if he condemned the cities of Sodom
and Gomorrah by burning them to ashes,[m]
and made them an example[n] of what is
going to happen to the ungodly; 7and if he
rescued Lot,[o] a righteous man, who was
distressed by the depraved conduct of the
lawless[p] 8(for that righteous man, living
among them day after day, was tormented

1:19 [a] Ps 119:105 [b] Rev 22:16 **1:21** [c] 2Ti 3:16 [d] 2Sa 23:2; Ac 1:16; 1Pe 1:11 **2:1** [e] Dt 13:1-3 [f] 1Ti 4:1 [g] Jude 4 [h] 1Co 6:20 **2:3** [i] 2Co 2:17; 1Th 2:5 **2:4** [j] Jude 6; Rev 20:1,2 **2:5** [k] 2Pe 3:6 [l] Heb 11:7; 1Pe 3:20 **2:6** [m] Ge 19:24, 25 [n] Nu 26:10; Jude 7 **2:7** [o] Ge 19:16 [p] 2Pe 3:17

[a] 4 Greek *Tartarus* [b] 4 Some manuscripts *in gloomy dungeons*

greater revelation on Mount Zion (Isa 2:2 – 4), what Scripture often called God's holy mountain (the same words in Greek, in, e.g., Ps 2:6; 3:4; 15:1; Joel 3:17). Although the transfiguration was not on Mount Zion per se, the place of his transfiguration became a sacred mountain the same way that Sinai did — the Lord revealed himself there. It thus foreshadowed the future revelation of God on Mount Zion. Jewish tradition recognized that God sometimes spoke from heaven, although later rabbis subordinated the authority of such revelation to Scripture itself.

1:19 *the prophetic message … completely reliable.* Jewish people embraced the Scriptures as God's word; the new revelation in Christ confirmed earlier prophecies and itself was worthy of being regarded as Scripture (cf. also 3:16). *light shining in a dark place, until the day dawns.* Scripture remains the essential light in darkness (Ps 119:105) until the day of the Lord fully dawns (cf. Isa 60:1). *the morning star rises in your hearts.* The day of the Lord would be like a sunrise (Mal 4:2); some ancient Jewish traditions apply the "star" of Nu 24:17 to the Messiah. The morning star (Venus) heralds the advent of dawn; a new age was about to dawn (cf. v. 11; 3:13).

1:20 – 21 *no prophecy … by the prophet's own interpretation of things … but prophets … were carried along by the Holy Spirit.* Ancient thinkers often viewed prophetic inspiration as a divine possession that temporarily displaced the prophet's own mind. The distinctive styles of different Biblical prophets shows that this view oversimplifies the matter; inspiration still used human faculties and vocabulary (cf. 1Pe 1:10 – 12; 1Co 7:40; 14:1 – 2,14 – 19), although there may have been different levels and kinds of ecstasy (cf. 1Sa 10:10 – 11; 19:20 – 24; 1Co 14:2; 2Co 5:13; 12:4). Regardless of particulars, however, ancient thinkers (and especially Jewish thinkers) generally expected inspiration to protect the inspired agents from misrepresenting the divine message (contrast 2:1).

2:1 *false prophets.* In earlier Scripture, false prophets spoke from their own imaginations rather than from divine inspiration (Jer 23:16,18 – 22,25 – 32; Eze 13:3 – 9); they often comforted people in their sin rather than speaking God's true warning of divine judgment (Jer 6:14; 23:17; 28:9; Eze 13:10,16). *bringing swift destruction on themselves.* Prophets who led people away from the Lord merited death (Dt 13:5).

2:2 *bring the way of truth into disrepute.* Just as many people despised all philosophers due to greedy sages, minority faiths suffered when self-proclaimed representatives of their groups generated scandals. (This happened in Rome, e.g., both to Jews and devotees of Isis; cf. note on Ro 2:17 – 24.)

2:3 *exploit you with fabricated stories.* The problem was widespread in the culture; nobler sages often lamented that some other sages or alleged wonderworkers exploited people to gain money. Earlier, see, e.g., Jer 6:13; 8:10; Mic 3:11. Here teachers value their financial gain more than they value the one who once bought *them* (v. 1).

2:4 *did not spare angels when they sinned, but sent them to hell.* Most ancient Jewish traditions understood the "sons of God" in Ge 6:1 – 4 as angels who lusted after women and so fell. *hell.* The Greek term here is from the name Tartarus, a place in Greek mythology where the most wicked (including earlier immortals called the Titans) were tortured in the worst imaginable ways. Some other Jewish sources borrow it to name the place where the fallen angels were imprisoned. Some Jewish people also spoke of the wicked as in hell (*Gehinnom*) until the final judgment, as well as afterward. A widely circulated Jewish source (Sirach 16:7 – 8) spoke of God not "sparing" the offspring of the angels in Noah's day or (later) Sodom (as here in vv. 4 – 6).

2:5 *brought the flood on its ungodly people.* Jewish people usually associated the fallen angels (their understanding of Ge 6:2 – 4) with judgment on Noah's generation (Ge 6:7 – 8). Tradition often elaborated stories about Noah, often depicting Noah as a preacher of repentance. Jewish teachers considered the flood generation as especially wicked and damned, and used the flood story to warn their own generation to repent in view of coming judgment.

2:6 *condemned … Sodom and Gomorrah by burning them.* Jewish teachers often coupled Sodom with the flood generation as examples of just objects of judgment. Biblical prophets earlier warned against acting like Sodom, which exemplified sin and judgment (Dt 32:32; Isa 1:9 – 10; 3:9; 13:19; Jer 23:14; 49:18; La 4:6; Eze 16:46,49; Am 4:11; Zep 2:9).

2:7 – 8 *Lot, a righteous man … tormented in his righteous soul.* Although Jewish thinkers differed over whether Lot was righteous, Scripture portrays him as personally

in his righteous soul by the lawless deeds
he saw and heard) — 9 if this is so, then
the Lord knows how to rescue the godly
from trials[q] and to hold the unrighteous
for punishment on the day of judgment.
10 This is especially true of those who follow the corrupt desire[r] of the flesh[a] and
despise authority.

Bold and arrogant, they are not afraid to
heap abuse on celestial beings;[s] 11 yet even
angels, although they are stronger and
more powerful, do not heap abuse on such
beings when bringing judgment on them
from[b] the Lord.[t] 12 But these people blaspheme in matters they do not understand.
They are like unreasoning animals, creatures of instinct, born only to be caught
and destroyed, and like animals they too
will perish.[u]

13 They will be paid back with harm for
the harm they have done. Their idea of
pleasure is to carouse in broad daylight.[v]
They are blots and blemishes, reveling
in their pleasures while they feast with
you.[c w] 14 With eyes full of adultery, they
never stop sinning; they seduce[x] the unstable; they are experts in greed[y] — an
accursed brood![z] 15 They have left the
straight way and wandered off to follow
the way of Balaam[a] son of Bezer,[d] who
loved the wages of wickedness. 16 But he
was rebuked for his wrongdoing by a donkey — an animal without speech — who
spoke with a human voice and restrained
the prophet's madness.[b]

17 These people are springs without water[c] and mists driven by a storm. Blackest
darkness is reserved for them.[d] 18 For they
mouth empty, boastful words[e] and, by appealing to the lustful desires of the flesh,
they entice people who are just escaping
from those who live in error. 19 They promise them freedom, while they themselves
are slaves of depravity — for "people are
slaves to whatever has mastered them."[f]
20 If they have escaped the corruption of
the world by knowing[g] our Lord and Savior Jesus Christ and are again entangled in
it and are overcome, they are worse off at
the end than they were at the beginning.[h]
21 It would have been better for them not
to have known the way of righteousness,
than to have known it and then to turn

2:9 [q] 1Co 10:13 **2:10** [r] 2Pe 3:3 [s] Jude 8 **2:11** [t] Jude 9 **2:12** [u] Jude 10 **2:13** [v] Ro 13:13 [w] 1Co 11:20,21; Jude 12 **2:14** [x] ver 18 [y] ver 3 [z] Eph 2:3
2:15 [a] Nu 22:4-20; Jude 11 **2:16** [b] Nu 22:21-30 **2:17** [c] Jude 12 [d] Jude 13 **2:18** [e] Jude 16 **2:19** [f] Jn 8:34; Ro 6:16 **2:20** [g] 2Pe 1:2 [h] Mt 12:45

[a] *10* In contexts like this, the Greek word for *flesh* (*sarx*) refers to the sinful state of human beings, often presented as a power in opposition to the Spirit; also in verse 18. [b] *11* Many manuscripts *beings in the presence of* [c] *13* Some manuscripts *in their love feasts* [d] *15* Greek *Bosor*

righteous (Ge 18:25; 19:1 – 16). Lot was less faithful than Abraham (Ge 13:10 – 11; 19:29,32 – 35), but by Sodom's standards he was intolerably righteous (Ge 19:9,15).

2:9 *hold the unrighteous for punishment on the day of judgment.* Jewish traditions often depict the wicked being tortured in Gehenna, whether indefinitely, until the day of judgment, or until their annihilation. In Wisdom of Solomon 10:6, Wisdom "rescued the righteous one," Lot, when the ungodly perished in the fire of Sodom.

2:10 *not afraid to heap abuse on celestial beings.* Some Jewish people (exemplified in the Dead Sea Scrolls and some Jewish teachers) cursed Satan or demons. (By contrast, the Sodomites [v. 6; Ge 19:1 – 29] tried to molest angels but were unaware that they were angels.) They may have insulted both earthly authorities (behavior that readily invited persecution when known) and the angelic authorities behind them (see note on Eph 1:21).

2:12 *animals ... born only to be caught and destroyed.* Ancient writers regarded some animals as existing only to be killed for food; here the animals are objects of the hunt. *creatures of instinct.* Philosophers characterized animals as creatures ruled by instinct as opposed to humans, who were ruled by reason; they considered unreasoning humans to be animals.

2:13 *to carouse in broad daylight.* Because most people who partied did so at night, one who caroused "in broad daylight" was regarded as particularly uncontrolled.

2:14 *eyes full of adultery.* Some Jewish teachers warned about adultery of the eyes (see note on Mt 5:28) or of one looking for adulterous partners (Peter here says lit. "eyes full of an adulteress"). *experts.* The Greek term refers to persons trained or disciplined in something; whereas ancient teachers often spoke of moral training to resist greed, these false teachers have instead developed expertise in greed. *accursed brood!* Could either be a Semitic figure of speech for accursed ones or refer to disinherited children who received curse instead of blessing from parents.

2:15 *the straight way ... the way of Balaam.* The contrast between the two ways may reflect the common ancient image of two paths, one leading the righteous or wise to life, the other leading the foolish to destruction. *the way of Balaam ... who loved the wages of wickedness.* Especially when inspired (cf. 1:20 – 21; Nu 24:4,13,16), Balaam knew that God blessed those who blessed Israel and cursed those who cursed them (Nu 23:20; 24:9). Nevertheless, to gain wealth (Nu 22:7,17; 24:11; Dt 23:4), Balaam showed Israel's enemies how to remove God's protection from Israel — by enticing Israelites into sexual sin (Nu 31:16; cf. Nu 23:21). For his sin Balaam himself reaped death (Nu 31:8; Jos 13:22). Jewish tradition depicted him as the greatest prophet of the Gentiles but also very wicked; he harmed Israel worse than more direct attackers by separating Israel from God's blessing. Thus these teachers also lead others into sexual sin (v. 14), seeking profit (v. 3).

2:16 *rebuked ... by a donkey.* Despite a miraculous warning through an animal that proved wiser than Balaam was (cf. the implications in v. 12), Balaam proceeded with his moral insanity (Nu 22:20 – 35). Jewish thinkers used Balaam as an example for fools who would be damned, and some elaborated the Biblical story further.

2:17 *springs without water.* No springs at all were better than springs without water; the latter raised thirsty travelers' hopes in vain. *Blackest darkness.* Some Jewish sources depicted hell as both darkness and fire.

2:19 *promise them freedom.* Greek and Diaspora Jewish thinkers often spoke of freedom from passion (see note on Jn 8:34). *slaves.* Those defeated in war were often enslaved; ancient thinkers also regarded as slaves those subject to their passion.

2:21 *not to have known the way of righteousness.* Jewish people often spoke of "the way of righteousness" (cf. v. 15).

their backs on the sacred command that
was passed on to them.[i] 22Of them the
proverbs are true: "A dog returns to its
vomit,"[a][j] and, "A sow that is washed returns to her wallowing in the mud."

The Day of the Lord

3 Dear friends, this is now my second
letter to you. I have written both of
them as reminders[k] to stimulate you to
wholesome thinking. 2I want you to recall
the words spoken in the past by the holy
prophets and the command given by our
Lord and Savior through your apostles.

3Above all, you must understand that
in the last days[l] scoffers will come, scoffing and following their own evil desires.[m]
4They will say, "Where is this 'coming'
he promised?[n] Ever since our ancestors
died, everything goes on as it has since
the beginning of creation."[o] 5But they deliberately forget that long ago by God's
word[p] the heavens came into being and
the earth was formed out of water and by
water.[q] 6By these waters also the world of
that time was deluged and destroyed.[r] 7By
the same word the present heavens and
earth are reserved for fire,[s] being kept for
the day of judgment and destruction of the
ungodly.

8But do not forget this one thing, dear
friends: With the Lord a day is like a thousand years, and a thousand years are like
a day.[t] 9The Lord is not slow in keeping
his promise,[u] as some understand slow-
ness. Instead he is patient[v] with you, not
wanting anyone to perish, but everyone to
come to repentance.[w]

10But the day of the Lord will come like
a thief.[x] The heavens will disappear with
a roar; the elements will be destroyed by
fire, and the earth and everything done in
it will be laid bare.[b][y]

2:21 [i] Heb 6:4-6
2:22 [j] Pr 26:11
3:1 [k] 2Pe 1:13
3:3 [l] 1Ti 4:1
[m] 2Pe 2:10; Jude 18
3:4 [n] Isa 5:19; Eze 12:22; Mt 24:48
[o] Mk 10:6
3:5 [p] Ge 1:6, 9; Heb 11:3
[q] Ps 24:2
3:6 [r] Ge 7:21,22
3:7 [s] ver 10, 12; 2Th 1:7
3:8 [t] Ps 90:4
3:9 [u] Hab 2:3; Heb 10:37
[v] Ro 2:4
[w] 1Ti 2:4
3:10 [x] Lk 12:39; 1Th 5:2
[y] Mt 24:35; Rev 21:1

[a] *22* Prov. 26:11 [b] *10* Some manuscripts *be burned up*

2:22 *A dog returns to its vomit.* Pr 26:11 depicts a fool returning to folly as a dog returning to its vomit. *A sow ... returns to her wallowing.* This proverb comes from a version of the well-known story of Ahiqar. Other Jewish people associated dogs and pigs, since both were deemed unclean (cf., e.g., Mt 7:6; Isa 66:3).
3:1–16 Those heavily influenced by the Greek thought of the surrounding culture would not understand a future day of judgment. Like many Jewish teachers, Peter recognizes that minimizing future judgment encouraged immoral behavior or even moral relativism (see note on 2:1).
3:1 *reminders.* See note on 1:12.
3:2 *the command given by our Lord.* May include sayings about readiness such as Mt 24:42–44 (parallel to Lk 12:38–40), which mentions Jesus' return like a thief (cf. 2Pe 3:10).
3:3 *the last days.* The promised future time of restoration (Isa 2:2; Eze 38:16; Hos 3:5; Mic 4:1), but applicable to the present era between the Messiah's first and second comings (cf. Ac 2:17). *scoffers ... following their own evil desires.* Many believed that those who doubted future judgment would behave immorally.
3:4–9 Delays often caused doubts (Eze 12:27–28; Hab 2:3); the authors of the Dead Sea Scrolls also addressed delays in the expected day of judgment. Misunderstanding about the delay began even before Jesus departed (e.g., Mk 10:37; Ac 1:6).
3:4–5 For the promise of Jesus' coming, see Mt 24:27, 37,39.
3:4 *our ancestors.* Although some plausibly argue that this phrase refers to the first generation of Christians looking for Jesus' return, this seems an odd way to refer to those not genetically related. Jewish people might use this language for their ancestors, especially the patriarchs (literally, as here, "the fathers"), as even in early Christian works such as 1 Clement 62.2; Epistle of Barnabas 5.7; 14.1. Gentiles could also think of their ancestors. The point in these cases would be simply that nothing significant changed over the generations. Some Gentiles rejected primeval stories about ancient heroes as myths. *everything goes on as it has since the beginning.* Many thinkers (such as Aristotle) believed that the universe had neither beginning nor ending. Some (such as Epicureans) contended that the basic substance of matter could not be destroyed; some others (such as Stoics) contended that the universe would periodically be resolved into the primeval fire (see note on v. 7) and that eternity was a cycle of ages.
3:5 *by God's word the heavens came into being and the earth was formed.* Even Diaspora Jewish thinkers discussed whether God created the universe from nothing (cf. Jn 1:3) or formed it from preexisting matter. On God creating by his word, see note on Jn 1:3. *out of water and by water.* The Greek philosopher Thales saw water as the primal element (though Peter's wording is much more ambiguous).
3:7 *the present heavens and earth are reserved for fire.* God had promised after Noah's flood (Ge 6–9) never to destroy the earth by water again (Ge 9:15; Isa 54:9), but the prophets did speak of a future fiery judgment and renewal of the present world (cf. Isa 65:17; 66:15,22). Jewish tradition declared that the present world would be destroyed not by water but by fire, and sometimes used the flood as a symbol for the future judgment by fire. (Plato also expected the world to end once by flood and once by fire.) Stoics expected the universe to collapse into primeval fire, be re-created, and the cycle to continue indefinitely. Jewish thought more often envisioned a future day of judgment followed by an eternal new (usually renewed) creation (cf. vv. 10,12–13).
3:8 *a day is like a thousand years.* Peter appeals to Ps 90:4 to make his point, as did many other Jewish writers of his day (who sometimes took "the day as a thousand years" literally and applied it to the days of creation). Some apocalyptic writers lamented that God did not reckon time as mortals do and consequently urged perseverance.
3:9 *promise.* Of Jesus' coming (v. 4). *he is patient.* God's patience may partly allude to the Noah analogy (vv. 5–7; cf. 1Pe 3:20; Ge 6:3). God sometimes delayed judgment to allow opportunity for the wicked to repent (cf. 2Ki 14:26–27). Some ancient Jewish sources emphasized God's patience regarding the day of judgment; once that day arrived, repentance was no longer possible.
3:10 *the day of the Lord.* Biblical prophets warned of the ultimate day of God's judgment as the day of the Lord, his day in court when he settles injustices (e.g., Isa 2:12; Joel 1:15; Am 5:18–20). (In the Prophets, nearer judgments often foreshadowed this ultimate one.) *come like a thief.*

[11]Since everything will be destroyed in this way, what kind of people ought you to be? You ought to live holy and godly lives [12]as you look forward[z] to the day of God and speed its coming.[a][a] That day will bring about the destruction of the heavens

3:12 [z] 1Co 1:7 [a] Ps 50:3 3:12 [b] ver 10

[a] 12 *Or as you wait eagerly for the day of God to come*

Echoes Jesus' words (Mt 24:43; parallel in Lk 12:39). *elements will be destroyed by fire.* Ancient thinkers discussed the elements, usually envisioned as four: earth, water, air and fire. Some Greek thinkers (Stoics) spoke of the entire cosmos being renovated by fire; Jewish apocalyptic thinkers also envisioned the destruction or (more often) purifying renewal of heaven and earth.
3:11 *live holy and godly lives.* Some apocalyptic thinkers shared Peter's interest in moral application; others instead focused on speculating about the future. The sort of future hope often embodied in apocalyptic sources appealed particularly to those who saw themselves as suffering during the present age; hope provided strength to persevere.
3:12 *speed its coming.* Jewish teachers disputed whether God had fixed the time of the end of the age or allowed

2 PETER 3

THE NEW TESTAMENT CANON

The process of determining which texts would comprise the Biblical canon (the standard of authoritative and normative teaching for the church) took place over several centuries. Beginning in the first century AD, Christian communities recognized the authority of texts that they gathered into collections for circulation and use in public worship. Second Peter already suggests a familiarity with multiple letters of Paul and goes so far as to place them on par with the Hebrew Scriptures (3:16). Evidence reveals that during public worship Christians in the earliest centuries read from the texts that would become the New Testament, just as they did from the Hebrew Scriptures.

Scholars often attribute the creation of the New Testament canon to the heretic Marcion, who accepted only the authority of Paul's letters and Luke. In reality, the churches already accepted these texts as authoritative, and Marcion was attempting to exclude the acceptance of any others. The Muratorian Canon (date uncertain), an early attempt to establish a list of canonical books, did not include most of the general epistles. By the fourth century the churches were seeking to compile a definitive list of New Testament books. Eusebius, Athanasius and the Councils of Laodicea (363), Hippo (393) and Carthage (397) created such lists (both of the latter two accepted the 27 books of the New Testament the church now acknowledges). In some sense these lists merely ratified the church's practice by identifying the texts that were already functioning in an authoritative manner. Twenty-seven writings, including the Gospels, Acts and the New Testament letters, formed the New Testament canon and ultimately defined the church's identity.

The selection process considered three key criteria for the acceptance of a particular text as canonical:

- Writings in the canon had to reflect orthodox teaching, i.e., teaching consistent with the undisputed apostolic message. Texts that were determined to contain teaching incongruent with that of the earliest Christians were not to be included.
- The canon sought to include the earliest, most accurate accounts about Jesus and about the early church by selecting texts that had been written either by apostles themselves or by those who were closely associated with them. Texts claiming apostolic authorship were critically inspected, and if the authorship claim was suspect, they were rejected. The Gospels of Mark and Luke received canonical status because they were written by a companion of Peter and a coworker of Paul, respectively. The book of Acts, also written by Luke, was also accepted as canoni-

continued on next page

by fire, and the elements will melt in the
heat.[b] 13But in keeping with his promise we
are looking forward to a new heaven and
a new earth,[c] where righteousness dwells.
14So then, dear friends, since you are
looking forward to this, make every effort to be found spotless, blameless[d] and
at peace with him. 15Bear in mind that
our Lord's patience[e] means salvation,[f]
just as our dear brother Paul also wrote

3:13 [c] Isa 65:17; 66:22; Rev 21:1
3:14 [d] 1Th 3:13
3:15 [e] Ro 2:4 [f] ver 9
3:15 [g] Eph 3:3

it to be speeded by Israel's repentance and obedience. Here, because God has delayed the end to allow more people to repent (vv. 9,15), sharing Christ presumably speeds its coming (cf. Mt 24:14). *elements.* See note on v. 10.

3:13 *a new heaven and a new earth, where righteousness dwells.* Many ancient Jewish writers celebrated the Biblical promise of the new heavens and earth (Isa 65:17; 66:22). They recognized that righteousness would then prevail (Isa 9:7; 11:4–5; 61:11).

3:14 *spotless, blameless.* On moral application, see note on v. 11; this behavior contrasts with the immoral teachers (2:13).

3:15 *our Lord's patience.* Allows more time for repentance

cal. The other two Gospels, the Epistles and the book of Revelation all have clear apostolic connections.

- Texts that were popular in only one region were viewed as doubtful, while those that had found widespread acceptance, both in the east and in Rome, were included in the canon. The writings chosen for the canon were understood to have universal application. For instance, although Paul addressed his letters to specific communities, others quickly acknowledged that his teaching was relevant to them as well.

Other Christian writings circulated alongside the canonical texts. Among these, the Shepherd of Hermas and the Epistle to Barnabas were held in high esteem by some Christians but were eventually rejected from the canon because of their distance from the apostles and the apostolic age. Some works, such as 1 Clement and the Didache, come closer to the apostolic message then do others such as Hermas and Barnabas. Although these texts were not canonized for reading in the public assembly of the church, they were not condemned as heretical. Texts of this sort continued to be used by Christians for personal devotions and reflections but without the same authority as the canonical writings. ◆

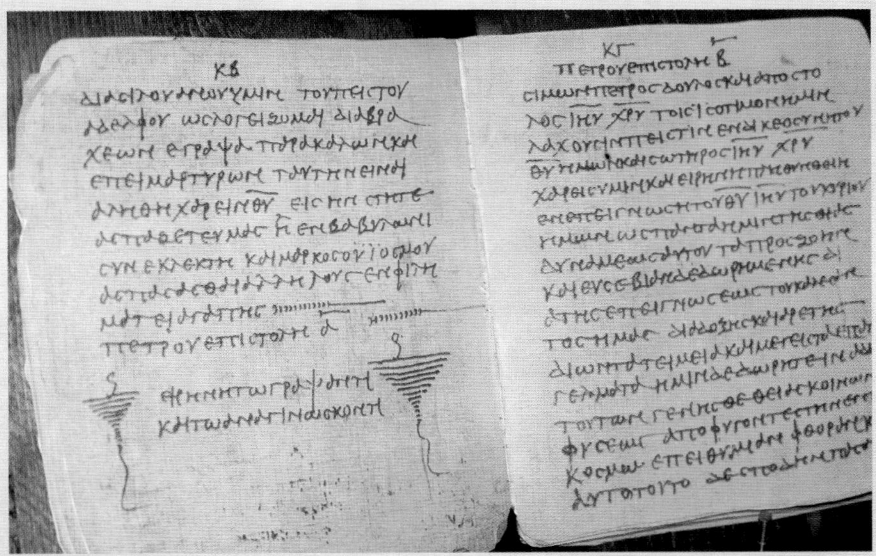

Facsimile leaf of the second letter of Peter on papyrus (P72); c. AD 200.

you with the wisdom that God gave him.[g]
16He writes the same way in all his letters, speaking in them of these matters.
His letters contain some things that are
hard to understand, which ignorant and
unstable[h] people distort, as they do the
other Scriptures,[i] to their own destruction.

17Therefore, dear friends, since you
have been forewarned, be on your guard[j]
so that you may not be carried away by
the error[k] of the lawless and fall from your
secure position.[l] 18But grow in the grace
and knowledge of our Lord and Savior
Jesus Christ.[m] To him be glory both now
and forever! Amen.

3:16 [h] 2Pe 2:14 [i] ver 2
3:17 [j] 1Co 10:12 [k] 2Pe 2:18 [l] Rev 2:5
3:18 [m] 2Pe 1:11

(v. 9), perhaps evoking again the analogy with Noah (vv. 5–7; cf. 1Pe 3:20; Ge 6:3).

3:16 *hard to understand.* In the ancient world, calling something difficult to understand sometimes implied that it was complex and brilliant. *ignorant and unstable people distort.* Many teachers interpreted the Scriptures to say what people wanted to hear, sometimes denying future judgment. *as they do the other Scriptures.* It is very unlikely that all of Paul's letters in our current NT were already collected by the time of Peter's death, but Peter would have known of some of them, such as Romans, from places where he traveled. Others cited some letters of Paul as authoritative (1 Clement 47.1, probably by the end of the first century); no less than prophets, apostles could speak by inspiration. More difficult is Peter calling Paul's letters "Scriptures," which, in the NT, usually meant the OT. But while some Jewish groups in the first century had a closed canon of Scripture, others, including the authors of the Dead Sea Scrolls and many in the Diaspora, had a fluid idea as to where Scripture ended and other edifying literature began.

3:18 *grow in … grace and knowledge.* Even groups that divided humanity plainly between the righteous/wise and the unrighteous/foolish (cf. Stoics) recognized that the righteous or wise needed to progress in their wisdom or righteousness.

THE LETTERS

1 JOHN

Authorship

From a very early period, church fathers identified the apostle John as the author of this letter. Although the matter became more debated in the twentieth century, internal evidence supports this position. The style of this letter closely resembles that of John's Gospel, especially when we allow for differences of genre, subject and possibly a more specific audience for the letter. Individual ancient writers often varied their style far more than the differences between John's Gospel and 1 John. Disciples sometimes imitated their teachers' teachings, but imitating vocabulary and style was far less common. One normally imitated even vocabulary only if one was pretending to be the teacher. In such cases of pretense, however, the writer expressly claims (falsely) to be the teacher. By contrast, no such claim is offered here, since the original audience knew the author's identity.

QUICK GLANCE

AUTHOR:
The apostle John

AUDIENCE:
Believers in western Asia Minor

DATE:
Between AD 85 and 95

THEME:
John writes to assure believers of the certainty of their faith and to refute heretical doctrines teaching that Jesus was not fully human and fully divine.

Genre

Because most of 1 John (except for 2:12 – 14) reads more like a homily than a letter, it might be classified (in later epistolary terms) as a letter-essay.

Background

The letter's situation is somewhat hard to reconstruct. Allusions to material in John's Gospel suggests that hearers of 1 John had also heard the Gospel, or at least the author's teachings provided in that Gospel. Because the audience of John's Gospel may include Jewish believers expelled from their synagogues, it is possible that 1 John at least partly addresses churches where some members have returned to the synagogue by denying Jesus' Messiahship (cf. 2:19,22; 4:2 – 3). This was only one of the problems John addressed in the churches of Asia Minor, however; it was relevant in Smyrna and Philadelphia (Rev 2:9 – 10; 3:7 – 9), but in some locations the primary issue was compromise with idolatry advocated by false prophets (perhaps relevant in 1Jn 4:1; 5:21; cf. Rev 2:14 – 15,20 – 23). One of the challenging forms of idolatry was the imperial cult (cf. Rev 13:14 – 15). Another problem in some churches was that the church needed more love, possibly including love for one another (Rev 2:4). Certainly false apostles and teaching (Rev 2:2,6,14 – 15,20) abounded. Any of these issues, or combinations of these issues, could lie partly in the background.

One often-proposed background for 1 John is the challenge of early Gnosticism. One group, Docetists, believed that Christ was divine but only seemed to become human (cf. 4:2). Another group, followers of one Cerinthus, believed that the Christ-Spirit merely came on Jesus, but they denied that he was actually the one and only Christ (cf. 2:22). Some Gnostics believed that they were incapable of committing real sins, although their bodies could engage in behavior that non-Gnostic Christians considered sinful. Such Gnostic systems are not really attested until decades after 1 John, but it is possible that some thinkers were already moving in these directions.

Whatever the specific background we reconstruct, one point is beyond dispute: the primary troublemakers are clearly "secessionists," people who had been part of the Christian community John addresses but who had rejected the teaching of that community. John advocates testing the spirits by two main criteria: a moral-ethical test (keeping the commandments, especially love of the Christian community) and a faith test (the right view about Jesus). ◆

The Incarnation of the Word of Life

1 That which was from the beginning,[a] which we have heard, which we have seen with our eyes,[b] which we have looked at and our hands have touched[c]—this we proclaim concerning the Word of life. 2 The life appeared;[d] we have seen it and testify to it, and we proclaim to you the eternal life, which was with the Father and has appeared to us. 3 We proclaim to you what we have seen and heard, so that you also may have fellowship with us. And our fellowship is with the Father and with his Son, Jesus Christ.[e] 4 We write this[f] to make our[a] joy complete.[g]

Light and Darkness, Sin and Forgiveness

5 This is the message we have heard[h] from him and declare to you: God is light; in him there is no darkness at all. 6 If we claim to have fellowship with him and yet walk in the darkness,[i] we lie and do not live out the truth.[j] 7 But if we walk in the light, as he is in the light, we have fellowship with one another, and the blood of Jesus, his Son, purifies us from all[b] sin.[k]

8 If we claim to be without sin,[l] we deceive ourselves and the truth is not in us.[m] 9 If we confess our sins, he is faithful and just and will forgive us our sins[n] and purify us from all unrighteousness. 10 If we claim we have not sinned, we make him out to be a liar[o] and his word is not in us.[p]

2 My dear children,[q] I write this to you so that you will not sin. But if anybody does sin, we have an advocate[r] with the Father—Jesus Christ, the Righteous One. 2 He is the atoning sacrifice for our sins,[s] and not only for ours but also for the sins of the whole world.

Love and Hatred for Fellow Believers

3 We know that we have come to know him if we keep his commands.[t] 4 Whoever says, "I know him," but does not do what he commands is a liar, and the truth is not in that person.[u] 5 But if anyone obeys his word,[v] love for God[c] is truly made complete in them.[w] This is how we know we are in him: 6 Whoever claims to live in him must live as Jesus did.[x]

7 Dear friends, I am not writing you a new command but an old one, which you have had since the beginning.[y] This old

1:1 [a] Jn 1:2 [b] Jn 1:14; 2Pe 1:16 [c] Jn 20:27 **1:2** [d] Jn 1:1-4; 1Ti 3:16 **1:3** [e] 1Co 1:9 **1:4** [f] 1Jn 2:1 [g] Jn 3:29 **1:5** [h] 1Jn 3:11 **1:6** [i] 2Co 6:14 [j] Jn 3:19-21 **1:7** [k] Heb 9:14; Rev 1:5 **1:8** [l] Pr 20:9; Jas 3:2 [m] 1Jn 2:4 **1:9** [n] Ps 32:5; 51:2 **1:10** [o] 1Jn 5:10 [p] 1Jn 2:14 **2:1** [q] ver 12, 13, 28 [r] Ro 8:34; Heb 7:25 **2:2** [s] Ro 3:25 **2:3** [t] Jn 14:15 **2:4** [u] 1Jn 1:6,8 **2:5** [v] Jn 14:21, 23 [w] 1Jn 4:12 **2:6** [x] Mt 11:29; 1Pe 2:21 **2:7** [y] 1Jn 3:11, 23; 2Jn 5,6

[a] 4 Some manuscripts *your* [b] 7 Or *every* [c] 5 Or *word, God's love*

1:1 *That which was from the beginning ... the Word.* Alludes to Jn 1:1 (see note there). *we have seen with our eyes.* Probably alludes to the eyewitnesses in Jn 1:14.
1:2 *The life.* Probably evokes Jn 1:4. *eternal life.* The promised life of the coming age (Da 12:2), already available to followers of the promised Messiah. In Johannine literature, the phrase is approximately synonymous with the kingdom of God.
1:5 *light.* See note on Jn 1:4–5. Various Jewish sources (especially the Dead Sea Scrolls) contrasted the followers of light (righteousness) with those of darkness (sin); they recognized from Scripture that God is wholly righteous (cf. Ps 92:15).
1:6 *walk in the darkness.* Suggests the danger of stumbling (2:10–11). Scripture warned against confusing light and darkness, right and wrong (Isa 5:20; cf. Isa 2:5).
1:7 *the blood of Jesus ... purifies us from all sin.* Although water, not blood, cleanses in a physical sense, blood also purified in an OT ritual sense (see note on Heb 9:22). Sacrificial blood set apart what was sacred for God, purifying from sin by making atonement (Lev 16:30).
1:9 *purify.* See note on v. 7; for some of the likely sins of those who withdrew from the believers John first addressed, see note on 3:6.
1:10 *If we claim we have not sinned.* Some scholars think that the false prophets hold errors like those of some later Gnostics, who denied that any of their behavior was sinful no matter what they did. This is possible, but humans are capable of self-deception even without that teaching (e.g., Jer 17:9). Biblical prophets condemned false protestations of innocence as self-deception (e.g., Jer 2:35; Hos 8:2; cf. Pr 30:12); God required instead both admission of the sin and repentance (cf. Lev 5:5; 16:21; Ps 32:1–5; Pr 28:13; Jer 3:13). Jewish tradition continued to recognize these truths.
2:1 *My dear children.* Teachers sometimes addressed their disciples as their "children." *that you will not sin.* In view of 1:8–10, the message here may sound paradoxical. Like riddles, paradox was a common, graphic way for sages to provoke deeper thought; John's Gospel includes many riddles. *we have an advocate.* God sometimes pleaded his people's cause (Jer 50:34; 51:36); Jewish tradition sometimes cited God's mercy as an advocate for Israel. But the greatest advocate before the Father is Jesus (see v. 2).
2:2 *atoning sacrifice.* In Greek culture, such a sacrifice normally appeased or satisfied the wrath of a deity whose standard had been violated. Here it alludes to sacrifices offered for atonement (Nu 5:8; Eze 44:27), especially on the Day of Atonement (Lev 25:9). *but also for the sins of the whole world.* Whereas the OT and Jewish tradition limited the Day of Atonement to Israel, Jesus' sacrifice was offered not only for Christians but even for those who would reject this priceless gift, leaving them without excuse.
2:3 *keep his commands.* Those who are faithful to God's covenant obeyed his commands (e.g., Dt 6:17; 11:1; 13:4; 26:17–18; 30:10,16), especially the most important command of love (1Jn 2:7–11; Lev 19:18; Dt 6:5; 11:13,22; 30:16; Mk 12:29–31; Jn 13:34). Covenant obedience was part of knowing God (Jer 22:16; 31:33–34).
2:5 *obeys his word.* To do so had always been a way of showing love for God (Dt 6:5–6; 10:12; 11:1).
2:6 *live as Jesus did.* Teachers on moral subjects often offered examples as role models, with God as the greatest example. John may here allude to Jesus' example cited also in Jn 13:14–15,34–35; 15:12.
2:7–8 *I am not writing you a new command but an old one ... Yet I am writing you a new command.* Ancient sages used paradox to provoke deeper consideration of their meaning. Jesus had already noted the earlier Biblical command to love (Mk 12:30–31, citing Dt 6:5; Lev 19:18); John's audience knows that Jesus also made it new, based on a new and ultimate example (Jn 13:34). (Even this might not be technically new to John's core audience, as opposed to others, since they had heard it "since the beginning" of the gospel reaching them, v. 7; cf. v. 24; 3:11.)

command is the message you have heard.
8Yet I am writing you a new command;[z] its
truth is seen in him and in you, because
the darkness is passing[a] and the true light[b]
is already shining.[c]
9Anyone who claims to be in the light
but hates a brother or sister[a] is still in the
darkness. 10Anyone who loves their brother and sister[b] lives in the light,[d] and there
is nothing in them to make them stumble.
11But anyone who hates a brother or sister is in the darkness and walks around
in the darkness. They do not know where
they are going, because the darkness has
blinded them.[e]

Reasons for Writing

12I am writing to you, dear children,
because your sins have been
forgiven on account of his
name.
13I am writing to you, fathers,
because you know him who is from
the beginning.
I am writing to you, young men,
because you have overcome the evil
one.[f]

14I write to you, dear children,
because you know the Father.
I write to you, fathers,
because you know him who is from
the beginning.
I write to you, young men,
because you are strong,[g]
and the word of God lives in you,[h]
and you have overcome the evil
one.[i]

On Not Loving the World

15Do not love the world or anything in
the world.[j] If anyone loves the world, love
for the Father[c] is not in them.[k] 16For everything in the world — the lust of the flesh,[l]
the lust of the eyes,[m] and the pride of
life — comes not from the Father but from
the world. 17The world and its desires pass
away,[n] but whoever does the will of God
lives forever.

Warnings Against Denying the Son

18Dear children, this is the last hour;
and as you have heard that the antichrist
is coming,[o] even now many antichrists
have come.[p] This is how we know it is
the last hour. 19They went out from us,[q]
but they did not really belong to us. For if
they had belonged to us, they would have
remained with us; but their going showed
that none of them belonged to us.[r]

2:8 [z] Jn 13:34 [a] Ro 13:12 [b] Jn 1:9 [c] Eph 5:8; 1Th 5:5 **2:10** [d] 1Jn 3:14 **2:11** [e] Jn 12:35 **2:13** [f] ver 14 **2:14** [g] Eph 6:10 [h] Jn 5:38; 1Jn 1:10 [i] ver 13 **2:15** [j] Ro 12:2 [k] Jas 4:4 **2:16** [l] Ro 13:14 [m] Pr 27:20 **2:17** [n] 1Co 7:31 **2:18** [o] ver 22; 1Jn 4:3; 2Jn 7 [p] 1Jn 4:1 **2:19** [q] Ac 20:30 [r] 1Co 11:19

[a] *9* The Greek word for *brother or sister* (*adelphos*) refers here to a believer, whether man or woman, as part of God's family; also in verse 11; and in 3:15, 17; 4:20; 5:16. [b] *10* The Greek word for *brother and sister* (*adelphos*) refers here to a believer, whether man or woman, as part of God's family; also in 3:10; 4:20, 21. [c] *15* Or *world, the Father's love*

2:8 *the darkness is passing and the true light is already shining.* Some Jewish writers (especially in the Dead Sea Scrolls) viewed evil, thus darkness, as prevailing in the present age, but saw themselves as children of light who would inherit the imminent coming age.
2:9–11 Ancient speakers often used antithesis, contrasts between opposites (here hate and love) to emphasize a point.
2:11 *anyone who hates a brother or sister.* Judaism, following Scripture (Lev 19:17), prohibited hatred of a fellow Israelite. John may apply this principle to the secessionists who proved their hatred by withdrawing from the apostolic community (v. 19).
2:12–14 John uses two different tenses for "write" in these verses (in Greek, present and aorist), but refers to his present writing; such differences were common and simply were used for literary variation.
2:12–13 *children ... fathers ... young men.* Ancient writers sometimes addressed different kinds of moral instruction to different age groups. Elders (NIV "fathers," v. 13) were known especially for wisdom; young men for vigor and passion; and children for being dependent.
2:15 *Do not love the world.* God summoned Israel to love him and be consecrated as holy to him, rather than following the pagan values of the nations around them (Lev 20:23–26; Dt 18:9). Likewise, Jesus' followers must avoid any values in their cultures that conflict with his interests.
2:16 *the lust of the flesh.* See, e.g., Nu 11:4; Ps 78:29–30. *flesh.* See the article "Flesh and Spirit," p. 1961. *the lust of the eyes.* This refers not simply to what is pleasant to the sight (e.g., Ge 2:9) but to sinfully grasping for what God prohibits; see, e.g., Ge 3:6 (which also includes three vices); cf. 2Sa 13:1; Pr 6:25.
2:17 *The world ... pass away, but whoever does the will of God lives forever.* Jewish tradition followed the Biblical perspective that the world's people would perish but God's word would remain forever (Isa 40:6–8).
2:18 *the last hour.* Although it could simply characterize the time as part of the final period ("a last hour"; there is no definite article in the Greek phrase here), it may be even more emphatic than "the last days" (see 2Pe 3:3 and note), which the prophets applied to the future era but which Christians understood as overlapping with the present. Jewish tradition emphasized the proliferation of evil in the end time, although Jewish thinkers who considered the length of that period held a range of views (e.g., 40 years, 400 years). *the antichrist ... many antichrists.* At various times Jewish tradition highlighted various evil rulers, such as Antiochus Epiphanes, oppressive Roman emperors or even an oppressive high priest. Early Christians expected such a figure (e.g., 2Th 2:3–4), but John notes that persons opposed to Christ (or possibly seeking to supplant Christ) already flourish (cf. 2Th 2:7).
2:19 *if they had belonged to us, they would have remained.* Many ancient thinkers recognized that commitments that were insincere eventually became evident (cf., e.g., 2Ch 12:14). Some passages (e.g., here; Jn 6:70–71) might also articulate matters from the perspective of God's foreknowledge, whereas others depict human experience (e.g., Gal 5:4; 1Ti 4:1–2; Heb 6:4–5). Jewish theology had no problem accommodating both approaches.

20But you have an anointing[s] from
the Holy One,[t] and all of you know the
truth.[a][u] 21I do not write to you because
you do not know the truth, but because
you do know it[v] and because no lie comes
from the truth. 22Who is the liar? It is whoever denies that Jesus is the Christ. Such a
person is the antichrist—denying the Father and the Son.[w] 23No one who denies
the Son has the Father; whoever acknowledges the Son has the Father also.[x]
24As for you, see that what you have
heard from the beginning remains in you.
If it does, you also will remain in the Son
and in the Father.[y] 25And this is what he
promised us—eternal life.
26I am writing these things to you about
those who are trying to lead you astray.[z]
27As for you, the anointing[a] you received
from him remains in you, and you do
not need anyone to teach you. But as his
anointing teaches you about all things and
as that anointing is real, not counterfeit—
just as it has taught you, remain in him.

God's Children and Sin

28And now, dear children,[b] continue in
him, so that when he appears[c] we may be
confident[d] and unashamed before him at
his coming.[e]
29If you know that he is righteous,[f] you
know that everyone who does what is
right has been born of him.

3 See what great love[g] the Father has
lavished on us, that we should be
called children of God![h] And that is what
we are! The reason the world does not
know us is that it did not know him.[i]
2Dear friends, now we are children of
God, and what we will be has not yet
been made known. But we know that
when Christ appears,[b] we shall be like
him,[j] for we shall see him as he is.[k] 3All
who have this hope in him purify themselves,[l] just as he is pure.
4Everyone who sins breaks the law; in
fact, sin is lawlessness.[m] 5But you know
that he appeared so that he might take
away our sins. And in him is no sin.[n] 6No
one who lives in him keeps on sinning.[o]

2:20 [s] 2Co 1:21 [t] Mk 1:24 [u] Jn 14:26 **2:21** [v] 2Pe 1:12; Jude 5 **2:22** [w] 2Jn 7 **2:23** [x] Jn 8:19; 1Jn 4:15 **2:24** [y] Jn 14:23 **2:26** [z] 2Jn 7 **2:27** [a] ver 20 **2:28** [b] ver 1 [c] 1Jn 3:2 [d] 1Jn 4:17 [e] 1Th 2:19 **2:29** [f] 1Jn 3:7 **3:1** [g] Jn 3:16 [h] Jn 1:12 [i] Jn 16:3 **3:2** [j] Ro 8:29; 2Pe 1:4 [k] 2Co 3:18 **3:3** [l] 2Co 7:1; 2Pe 3:13, 14 **3:4** [m] 1Jn 5:17 **3:5** [n] 2Co 5:21 **3:6** [o] ver 9

[a] 20 Some manuscripts *and you know all things*
[b] 2 Or *when it is made known*

2:20 *anointing from the Holy One.* People were consecrated and anointed with oil for specific tasks, especially for the priesthood (e.g., Ex 29:29; 40:15) or kingship (e.g., 1Sa 10:1; 2Ki 9:6). At least sometimes this physical anointing was associated with the Spirit (1Sa 10:1,6; 16:13; Isa 61:1), probably the point here (cf. 2Co 1:21–22).
2:22 *whoever denies that Jesus is the Christ.* Perhaps as early as AD 100, Cerinthus reportedly taught that the Christ-Spirit came on Jesus but was not identical to him. Jewish believers barred from synagogues may have also been tempted to remain in synagogues by denying that Jesus was the Messiah, the Anointed One.
2:27 *anointing.* See note on v. 20.
2:28 *confident and unashamed ... at his coming.* Although the promised day of judgment would vindicate the righteous, it would terrify the wicked (Isa 2:10–21; Joel 1:15; 2:1,11; Am 5:18–20); on Jesus' appearing, see note on 1Jn 3:2).
2:29 *everyone who does what is right has been born of him.* People in antiquity believed that children inherited much of their character from their father. They also could speak figuratively of one person who was like some person of the distant past as their descendant—though John speaks spiritually here, not figuratively.
3:1 *what great love ... that we should be called children of God!* Jewish teachers spoke of God's special love for Israel (in Scripture, see, e.g., Dt 7:6–9) and recognized that God called Israel his children (in Scripture, e.g., Dt 8:5). The expression of love here is even greater (v. 16).
3:2 *we shall be like him, for we shall see him.* Many Greek thinkers, especially followers of Plato, sought to envision in their minds the highest God, who was pure intellect. (Unlike the Biblical God, however, this god was abstract, without feeling.) They believed that this experience transformed the mediator to be more like the divine, or to recover their innate divinity. Some Diaspora Jewish thinkers held similar views. John expects transformation, but not deification, the language of which he, like other NT authors, avoids. Jewish mystics and apocalyptic visionaries also sought to see God, and some of the latter expected transformation through beholding God's glory through visions or in the end time. John's ultimate model here, however, is the Biblical transformation of Moses through beholding God's glory in Ex 34:29–35 (see note on Jn 1:14–18).
3:4–18 Ancient thinkers often elaborated their argument using antitheses, or contrasting points. In a manner found in Jewish wisdom, some Greek wisdom and in Jewish apocalyptic thought, John contrasts the righteous, who love one another, with the wicked, who hate the righteous.
3:6 *keeps on sinning.* John has already said that Jesus' followers must recognize their sin (1:8–10; cf. 2:1), though paradoxically they are also transformed so as not to sin (1:6–7; 2:3–6). A number of scholars emphasize the verb tense of "sinning" here to mean continuous sin, arguing that John refers to a lifestyle of sin, not normally living righteously but sometimes sinning and then repenting. Some think John depicts potential: one is able to live sinlessly (cf. Jn 8:31–36). Some others think that John challenges the false teachers' claims here (1:8–10): unlike those errorists who merely claim to be sinless, true believers do not regularly live in sin.

With or without reference to the verb tense, John may simply refer to characteristic behavior. Stoics, Essenes and Jewish wisdom literature divided humanity into ideal types: righteous and unrighteous, or wise and foolish. All of these sources, however, recognize the imperfection of the righteous or wise; they might not fit the ideal type in all respects, but their allegiance is clearly decided. Because philosophers and others often spoke in terms of such ideal types, John might claim that one is sinless to the extent that one lives in Christ. Still more likely, he emphasizes that one belongs to one side or the other; one characteristically follows Christ or one does not.

The sins particularly in view here (for this letter's first setting) might be violations of the two basic precepts John emphasizes: the right attitude toward members of

No one who continues to sin has either
seen him[p] or known him.[q]
7 Dear children,[r] do not let anyone lead
you astray.[s] The one who does what is
right is righteous, just as he is righteous.[t]
8 The one who does what is sinful is of the
devil,[u] because the devil has been sinning
from the beginning. The reason the Son
of God appeared was to destroy the devil's work. 9 No one who is born of God[v]
will continue to sin,[w] because God's seed[x]
remains in them; they cannot go on sinning, because they have been born of God.
10 This is how we know who the children
of God are and who the children of the
devil are: Anyone who does not do what is
right is not God's child, nor is anyone who
does not love[y] their brother and sister.

More on Love and Hatred

11 For this is the message you heard[z] from
the beginning: We should love one another.[a] 12 Do not be like Cain, who belonged
to the evil one and murdered his brother.[b]
And why did he murder him? Because his
own actions were evil and his brother's
were righteous. 13 Do not be surprised, my
brothers and sisters,[a] if the world hates
you.[c] 14 We know that we have passed
from death to life,[d] because we love each
other. Anyone who does not love remains
in death.[e] 15 Anyone who hates a brother or sister is a murderer,[f] and you know
that no murderer has eternal life residing
in him.[g]
16 This is how we know what love is:
Jesus Christ laid down his life for us. And
we ought to lay down our lives for our
brothers and sisters.[h] 17 If anyone has material possessions and sees a brother or
sister in need but has no pity on them,[i]
how can the love of God be in that person?[j] 18 Dear children,[k] let us not love with
words or speech but with actions and in
truth.[l]
19 This is how we know that we belong to
the truth and how we set our hearts at rest
in his presence: 20 If our hearts condemn
us, we know that God is greater than our
hearts, and he knows everything. 21 Dear
friends, if our hearts do not condemn us,
we have confidence before God[m] 22 and receive from him anything we ask,[n] because
we keep his commands and do what pleases him.[o] 23 And this is his command: to believe[p] in the name of his Son, Jesus Christ,
and to love one another as he command-

3:6 [p] 3Jn 11 [q] 1Jn 2:4
3:7 [r] 1Jn 2:1 [s] 1Jn 2:26 [t] 1Jn 2:29
3:8 [u] Jn 8:44
3:9 [v] Jn 1:13 [w] 1Jn 5:18 [x] 1Pe 1:23
3:10 [y] 1Jn 4:8
3:11 [z] 1Jn 1:5 [a] Jn 13:34,35; 2Jn 5
3:12 [b] Ge 4:8
3:13 [c] Jn 15:18, 19; 17:14
3:14 [d] Jn 5:24 [e] 1Jn 2:9
3:15 [f] Mt 5:21, 22; Jn 8:44 [g] Gal 5:20,21
3:16 [h] Jn 15:13
3:17 [i] Dt 15:7,8 [j] 1Jn 4:20
3:18 [k] 1Jn 2:1 [l] Eze 33:31; Ro 12:9
3:21 [m] 1Jn 5:14
3:22 [n] Mt 7:7 [o] Jn 8:29
3:23 [p] Jn 6:29

[a] 13 The Greek word for *brothers and sisters* (*adelphoi*) refers here to believers, both men and women, as part of God's family; also in verse 16.

---

the Christian community and the right view about Jesus (v. 24). Thus John may mean that the one who "keeps on sinning" and has never truly known Christ is one who commits the sin that leads to death, i.e., a sin leading out of eternal life (cf. 5:16–17). *No one who continues to sin has either seen him or known him.* Those who have seen him do not live in sin; regarding transforming vision of the Lord, see note on v. 2.

3:8 *of the devil.* In the Dead Sea Scrolls, all sins were influenced by the spirit of error; John need not view the influence as so direct, but he does view the world as in the sphere of the devil and his values (5:19). *from the beginning.* Jewish tradition often understood the serpent of Ge 3 as the devil. On the common view that the devil had introduced sin into the world, and thus, all sins are ultimately the devil's works and reflect his character, see note on Jn 8:44.

3:9–10 *God's seed … God's child.* Some ancient thinkers spoke of divine seed in humans, an idea early Christians could adapt for those born from the Spirit through conversion (see note on 1Pe 1:23; cf. Jas 1:18,21). John plays on this image; children were believed to inherit their father's nature through his seed.

3:9 *they cannot go on sinning, because they have been born of God.* In OT Scripture, having God's word in one's heart enabled righteous living (see, e.g., Dt 30:14; Ps 119:11; Jer 31:32–33). On the claim to sinlessness, see note on v. 6a.

3:12 *Cain … murdered his brother.* John alludes to Ge 4:8; Cain was sinful, whereas God accepted his brother Abel's sacrifice, knowing Abel's motives (Ge 4:3–7). Jewish tradition extensively elaborated and underlined Cain's sinfulness. *belonged to the evil one.* A murderer was a child of the devil (v. 10), for one of the devil's first works had been to bring death to Adam (see note on Jn 8:44). Some later Jewish texts even claim that Cain's father was the devil himself.

3:15 *murderer.* Murder was a capital offense (Ge 9:6; Ex 21:14; Lev 24:17); in Jewish tradition, such offenses deserved damnation in Gehenna. Jesus included as murder the attitude that generated the literal act (cf. Mt 5:21–22).

3:16 *we ought to lay down our lives for our brothers and sisters.* At least some believers in some churches in John's circle had to face martyrdom (Rev 2:10,13). Since slaves were routinely tortured for information, some Christians might have to pay a tremendous price to avoid betraying their fellow Christians to death. Loyalty to the community of believers might also demand refusing compromises that might have preserved them from persecution. In John's day such compromises, perhaps adopted by the secessionists (2:19, 22–23, 26), might include participation in the imperial cult or renouncing faith in Jesus as the Messiah (cf. notes on 2:22; Rev 2:9).

3:17 *sees a brother or sister in need but has no pity.* In some Jewish traditions, withholding goods from someone in need was equivalent to starving them (cf. Jas 2:15). Caring for the needy was part of righteousness (e.g., Dt 15:7–10; Pr 14:21,31; Isa 32:6; 58:7,10; Eze 18:7,16).

3:18 *let us not love with words … but with actions.* Moral writers often condemned those who had merely words but lacked actions.

3:19 *belong to the truth.* The Dead Sea Scrolls sometimes called the righteous "the children of God's truth."

3:20 *he knows everything.* Following Scripture, Jewish tradition recognized that God knew all hearts (e.g., 1Ch 28:9).

3:23 *to believe in the name of his Son … and to love one another.* Those who followed the false teachers and left the community of believers (2:19) violated both of these basic commandments — holding correct belief in Jesus (2:22–24; 4:2–3) and showing love for one another (3:10–15).

ed us.[q] 24The one who keeps God's commands lives in him,[r] and he in them. And
this is how we know that he lives in us: We
know it by the Spirit he gave us.[s]

On Denying the Incarnation

4 Dear friends, do not believe every spirit, but test the spirits to see whether
they are from God, because many false
prophets have gone out into the world.[t]
2This is how you can recognize the Spirit of God: Every spirit that acknowledges
that Jesus Christ has come in the flesh[u] is
from God,[v] 3but every spirit that does not
acknowledge Jesus is not from God. This
is the spirit of the antichrist,[w] which you
have heard is coming and even now is already in the world.

4You, dear children, are from God and
have overcome them, because the one
who is in you[x] is greater than the one who
is in the world.[y] 5They are from the world[z]
and therefore speak from the viewpoint of
the world, and the world listens to them.
6We are from God, and whoever knows
God listens to us; but whoever is not from
God does not listen to us.[a] This is how we
recognize the Spirit[a] of truth[b] and the spirit of falsehood.

God's Love and Ours

7Dear friends, let us love one another,[c]
for love comes from God. Everyone who
loves has been born of God and knows
God.[d] 8Whoever does not love does not
know God, because God is love.[e] 9This is
how God showed his love among us: He
sent his one and only Son into the world
that we might live through him.[f] 10This is
love: not that we loved God, but that he
loved us[g] and sent his Son as an atoning
sacrifice for our sins.[h] 11Dear friends, since
God so loved us,[i] we also ought to love
one another. 12No one has ever seen God;[j]
but if we love one another, God lives in us
and his love is made complete in us.[k]

13This is how we know that we live in
him and he in us: He has given us of his
Spirit.[l] 14And we have seen and testify[m]
that the Father has sent his Son to be the
Savior of the world.[n] 15If anyone acknowledges that Jesus is the Son of God,[o] God
lives in them and they in God. 16And so
we know and rely on the love God has
for us.

God is love.[p] Whoever lives in love lives
in God, and God in them.[q] 17This is how
love is made complete[r] among us so that
we will have confidence on the day of
judgment: In this world we are like Jesus.
18There is no fear in love. But perfect love
drives out fear,[s] because fear has to do
with punishment. The one who fears is
not made perfect in love.

19We love because he first loved us.[t]
20Whoever claims to love God yet hates
a brother or sister[u] is a liar.[v] For whoever does not love their brother and sister, whom they have seen,[w] cannot love

3:23 [q] Jn 13:34 **3:24** [r] 1Jn 2:6 [s] 1Jn 4:13 **4:1** [t] 2Pe 2:1; 1Jn 2:18 **4:2** [u] Jn 1:14; 1Jn 2:23 [v] 1Co 12:3 **4:3** [w] 1Jn 2:22; 2Jn 7 **4:4** [x] Ro 8:31 [y] Jn 12:31 **4:5** [z] Jn 15:19 **4:6** [a] Jn 8:47 [b] Jn 14:17 **4:7** [c] 1Jn 3:11 [d] 1Jn 2:4

4:8 [e] ver 7, 16 **4:9** [f] Jn 3:16, 17; 1Jn 5:11 **4:10** [g] Ro 5:8, 10 [h] 1Jn 2:2 **4:11** [i] Jn 3:16 **4:12** [j] Jn 1:18; 1Ti 6:16 [k] 1Jn 2:5 **4:13** [l] 1Jn 3:24 **4:14** [m] Jn 15:27 [n] Jn 3:17 **4:15** [o] Ro 10:9 **4:16** [p] ver 8 [q] 1Jn 3:24 **4:17** [r] 1Jn 2:5 **4:18** [s] Ro 8:15 **4:19** [t] ver 10 **4:20** [u] 1Jn 2:9 [v] 1Jn 2:4 [w] 1Jn 3:17

[a] 6 Or *spirit*

3:24 *We know it by the Spirit he gave us.* Apart from the Essenes, most Jewish thinkers regarded the Spirit as very rare; early Christians, however, believed that God empowered them with the Spirit (Ac 2:17–18).
4:1 *test the spirits to see whether they are from God.* Jewish tradition usually attributed Biblical prophecy to God's Spirit (often also in the OT, e.g., Nu 11:25). *false prophets have gone out into the world.* Many Jewish circles associated false prophecy with evil spirits (in the OT, cf. prophesying by wrong spirits in 1Sa 18:10; 1Ki 22:22–23; false prophets' own spirits in Eze 13:3). The Greek translation of the OT, which was what most of John's audience would know, uses the label "false prophets" even more often than the Hebrew does (Jer 6:13; 26:7–16; 27:9; 28:1; 29:1,8; Zec 13:2; for the label in the NIV OT, see Isa 44:25; Jer 50:36; Hos 11:6). Some contemporaries, such as apocalyptic Jewish visionaries, pagan oracular priestesses (see note on Ac 16:16) and some within the Christian movement (Rev 2:14,20) falsely claimed to speak God's message.
4:2 *Jesus Christ has come in the flesh.* John announced the Jesus he had known in the flesh (Jn 1:14). The false prophets may deny that Christ was fully human (see Docetism in Introduction: Background). Alternatively, they might treat Jesus as a mere prophet (comparable to John the Baptist), denying that he came as the Christ (2:22), so they could remain in the synagogue.
4:4 *the one who is in you is greater.* That God and his hosts defending his people are greater than human enemies reflects a Biblical principle (2Ki 6:16; 2Ch 32:7–8).
4:6 *the Spirit of truth and the spirit of falsehood.* In a manner similar to John here, the Dead Sea Scrolls contrast God's children and the rest of the world. They go far beyond John, however, in asserting that every individual act is determined by either the spirit of truth or the spirit of error.
4:7 *Everyone who loves has been born of God.* A child was held to reflect the father's nature.
4:10 *atoning sacrifice.* See note on 2:2.
4:12 *No one has ever seen God.* Jewish people agreed that God was invisible (Ex 33:20; see note on Jn 1:14–18), although some sought to see him mystically. *if we love … God lives in us.* God's heart is revealed in love (here; v. 9).
4:13 *He has given us of his Spirit.* See note on 3:24.
4:15 *If anyone acknowledges that Jesus is the Son of God.* Because the Spirit was often associated with prophecy (cf., e.g., 1Sa 19:20,23; Joel 2:28), publicly acknowledging Jesus as God's Son may reflect prophetic inspiration here (v. 2; cf. 1Co 12:3; Rev 19:10).
4:17 *we will have confidence on the day of judgment.* Those who violate God's ways have reason to fear the day of judgment (cf., e.g., 2:28; Isa 13:6,9; Joel 2:31), but agents of Christ's love (1Jn 4:7,12) can face that day with confidence.
4:19 *because he first loved us.* God's people were to imitate his holiness (Lev 11:45); the ultimate expression and example of God's love is Christ (1Jn 4:9–10; cf. Jn 13:34–35).
4:20 *Whoever claims to love God yet hates a brother or sister is a liar.* Some others understood the principle that how one treated people about whom God cared was how one treated God (Pr 19:17).

God, whom they have not seen.[x] 21And he
has given us this command: Anyone who
loves God must also love their brother and
sister.[y]

Faith in the Incarnate Son of God

5 Everyone who believes that Jesus is
the Christ[z] is born of God,[a] and everyone who loves the father loves his
child as well.[b] 2This is how we know
that we love the children of God: by loving God and carrying out his commands.
3In fact, this is love for God: to keep his
commands.[c] And his commands are not
burdensome,[d] 4for everyone born of God
overcomes[e] the world. This is the victory that has overcome the world, even
our faith. 5Who is it that overcomes the
world? Only the one who believes that
Jesus is the Son of God.

6This is the one who came by water and
blood[f] — Jesus Christ. He did not come by
water only, but by water and blood. And
it is the Spirit who testifies, because the
Spirit is the truth.[g] 7For there are three[h]
that testify: 8the[a] Spirit, the water and the
blood; and the three are in agreement. 9We
accept human testimony,[i] but God's testimony is greater because it is the testimony of God,[j] which he has given about his
Son. 10Whoever believes in the Son of God
accepts this testimony.[k] Whoever does
not believe God has made him out to be
a liar,[l] because they have not believed the
testimony God has given about his Son.
11And this is the testimony: God has given
us eternal life, and this life is in his Son.[m]
12Whoever has the Son has life; whoever
does not have the Son of God does not
have life.[n]

Concluding Affirmations

13I write these things to you who believe in the name of the Son of God[o] so
that you may know that you have eternal
life.[p] 14This is the confidence[q] we have in
approaching God: that if we ask anything
according to his will, he hears us.[r] 15And
if we know that he hears us — whatever
we ask — we know[s] that we have what we
asked of him.

16If you see any brother or sister commit a sin that does not lead to death, you
should pray and God will give them life.[t]
I refer to those whose sin does not lead to
death. There is a sin that leads to death.[u] I
am not saying that you should pray about
that.[v] 17All wrongdoing is sin,[w] and there
is sin that does not lead to death.[x]

18We know that anyone born of God
does not continue to sin; the One who
was born of God keeps them safe, and the
evil one cannot harm them.[y] 19We know
that we are children of God,[z] and that the

4:20 [x] ver 12 **4:21** [y] Mt 5:43 **5:1** [z] 1Jn 2:22 [a] Jn 1:13; 1Jn 2:23 [b] Jn 8:42 **5:3** [c] Jn 14:15; 2Jn 6 [d] Mt 11:30 **5:4** [e] Jn 16:33 **5:6** [f] Jn 19:34 [g] Jn 14:17 **5:7** [h] Mt 18:16 **5:9** [i] Jn 5:34 [j] Mt 3:16, 17; Jn 8:17, 18 **5:10** [k] Ro 8:16; Gal 4:6 [l] Jn 3:33 **5:11** [m] Jn 1:4; 1Jn 2:25 **5:12** [n] Jn 3:15, 16, 36 **5:13** [o] 1Jn 3:23 [p] Jn 20:31; 1Jn 1:1, 2 **5:14** [q] 1Jn 3:21 [r] Mt 7:7 **5:15** [s] ver 18, 19, 20 **5:16** [t] Jas 5:15 [u] Heb 6:4-6; 10:26 [v] Jer 7:16 **5:17** [w] 1Jn 3:4 [x] 1Jn 2:1 **5:18** [y] Jn 14:30 **5:19** [z] 1Jn 4:6

[a] 7,8 Late manuscripts of the Vulgate *testify in heaven: the Father, the Word and the Holy Spirit, and these three are one.* 8*And there are three that testify on earth: the* (not found in any Greek manuscript before the fourteenth century)

5:1 *everyone who loves the father loves his child as well.* Although plenty of exceptions existed, people were normally loyal to their families, so love for one member normally entailed love for the family.
5:3 *his commands are not burdensome.* That is, if they are written on one's heart (Dt 30:11 – 14).
5:6 *by water and blood.* Some scholars argue that John opposes specific false ideas in mentioning water and blood; e.g., Cerinthus (see Introduction: Background) reportedly claimed that the Christ-Spirit descended on Jesus at his baptism but departed before his death. Docetists allowed that Jesus was baptized but argued that he was immortal and could not die. Instead of blood Greek gods had ichor, which looked like water; because water as well as blood flowed from Jesus' side (Jn 19:34), some may have thus thought him a demigod. In any case, John reinforces his testimony about Jesus' actual, historical death (Jn 19:34).
5:7 – 8 *there are three that testify: the Spirit, the water and the blood.* Ancient documents often included witnesses' signatures; Scripture required two or three witnesses (Dt 17:6; 19:15), and John offers three. Most clearly, the Spirit's testimony appears in 3:24; 4:6,13. The significance of the other two is debated. Aside from Jn 19:34, Jesus' blood purifies (1:7), as does water (cf. Lev 14:51 – 52); Jesus' blood also reveals his love (1Jn 3:16), as John's baptism testified (Jn 1:29 – 34; for water, see note on Jn 2:6).
5:13 *eternal life.* The promised life of the coming age (Da 12:2), the beginning of which is already available to followers of the promised Messiah.
5:14 – 15 For the general principle here, see note on Jn 14:12 – 14, although John goes on to apply this broader principle to a specific situation in 1Jn 5:15 – 16.
5:16 *a sin that leads to death.* Probably committed by the false teachers; it is presumably one that violates the fundamental commands of believing in Jesus and loving fellow believers (cf. 3:23). In Scripture, atonement was available for unintentional but not defiant sins (Nu 15:27 – 31). Perhaps more relevant, some Jewish circles described offenses for which Scripture prescribed death as "a matter of death," which was normally enforced in their own time by expulsion from the community rather than by literal execution. *I am not saying that you should pray about that.* Those who were sinned against could secure forgiveness for their opponents by prayer (Ge 20:7,17; Job 42:8), but a sin of willful apostasy from God's truth precluded the efficacy of such secondhand prayers for forgiveness (1Sa 2:25; Jer 7:16; 11:14; 14:11). Followers of these severely false teachers cannot be forgiven without their own confession and repentance.
5:18 *the evil one cannot harm them.* Satan cannot harm God's people without God's permission (Job 1:11 – 12; 2:3 – 6). Jewish teachers recognized that God protected his people.
5:19 *the whole world is under the control of the evil one.* Jewish people often recognized that Satan and hostile spiritual forces ruled the world except for God's people.

whole world is under the control of the evil one.[a] 20We know also that the Son of God has come and has given us understanding,[b] so that we may know him who is true.[c] And we are in him who is true by being in his Son Jesus Christ. He is the true God and eternal life.[d]

21Dear children, keep yourselves from idols.[e]

5:19 [a]Gal 1:4 **5:20** [b]Lk 24:45 [c]Jn 17:3 [d]ver 11 **5:21** [e]1Co 10:14; 1Th 1:9

5:21 *keep yourself from idols.* Although Jewish sources sometimes use the term "idols" figuratively, actual idols flourished in John's environment (cf. Ac 19:28; Rev 9:20; 13:12,15); false prophets (1Jn 4:1 – 6) might urge compromise with them (cf. Rev 2:14,20).

THE LETTERS

2 JOHN

See Introduction to 1 John: Authorship.

Authorship

Both 2 John and 3 John are attested later than 1 John because they were too brief to be cited often by early church fathers. Usually letters of this length are too brief for stylistic comparison. Nevertheless, the style (as well as the theology) is close to that of 1 John, and this points to common authorship of the three letters.

QUICK GLANCE

AUTHOR:
The apostle John

AUDIENCE:
The "lady chosen by God," probably a local church in western Asia Minor

DATE:
Between AD 85 and 95

THEME:
John writes to urge discernment in supporting traveling teachers, since false teachers were also traveling and teaching heresy.

Genre

Both 2 John and 3 John are letters. Unlike most NT letters, 2 and 3 John are both the length of most surviving ancient letters. The average ancient letter required only a single sheet of papyrus.

Background

Second John addresses the same central error that 1 John addressed (see Introduction to 1 John: Background). The false teachers may respect Jesus as a great prophet like John the Baptist, but they do not recognize him as the supreme Lord in the flesh (cf. 1Jn 4:1 – 6; Rev 2:14,20). Some scholars think that they may have been affiliated with, or been forerunners of, Cerinthus (who distinguished the divine Christ and the human Jesus) or the Docetists (who claimed that Jesus only appeared to be human). Such beliefs would have made them more acceptable to their culture, but contradicted the eyewitness testimony of those who knew Jesus personally (1Jn 1:1 – 3; 4:2). ◆

1The elder,[a]

To the lady chosen by God[b] and to her children, whom I love in the truth—and not I only, but also all who know the truth[c]— 2because of the truth,[d] which lives in us[e] and will be with us forever:

3Grace, mercy and peace from God the Father and from Jesus Christ,[f] the Father's Son, will be with us in truth and love.

4It has given me great joy to find some of your children walking in the truth,[g] just as the Father commanded us. 5And now, dear lady, I am not writing you a new command but one we have had from the beginning.[h] I ask that we love one another. 6And this is love:[i] that we walk in obedience to his commands. As you have heard from the beginning, his command is that you walk in love.

7I say this because many deceivers, who do not acknowledge Jesus Christ[j] as coming in the flesh, have gone out into the world.[k] Any such person is the deceiver and the antichrist.[l] 8Watch out that you do not lose what we[a] have worked for, but that you may be rewarded fully.[m] 9Anyone who runs ahead and does not continue in the teaching of Christ does not have God; whoever continues in the teaching has both the Father and the Son.[n] 10If anyone comes to you and does not bring this teaching, do not take them into your house or welcome them.[o] 11Anyone who welcomes them shares[p] in their wicked work.

12I have much to write to you, but I do not want to use paper and ink. Instead, I hope to visit you and talk with you face to face,[q] so that our joy may be complete.

13The children of your sister, who is chosen by God,[r] send their greetings.

1 [a] 3Jn 1
[b] Ro 16:13
[c] Jn 8:32
2 [d] 2Pe 1:12
[e] 1Jn 1:8
3 [f] Ro 1:7
4 [g] 3Jn 3,4
5 [h] 1Jn 2:7; 3:11
6 [i] 1Jn 2:5
7 [j] 1Jn 2:22; 4:2,3
[k] 1Jn 4:1
[l] 1Jn 2:18
8 [m] 1Co 3:8
9 [n] 1Jn 2:23
10 [o] Ro 16:17
11 [p] 1Ti 5:22
12 [q] 3Jn 13,14
13 [r] ver 1

[a] 8 Some manuscripts *you*

1 *The elder.* Because some older men came to be known for wisdom and maturity, select elders ruled OT villages and continued to fill a respected leadership role in this period. Some early Christian leaders adopted this title, rather than more prestigious ones, in their later years (Phm 9; 1Pe 5:1). *lady.* Some think she refers to a prophetess/elder (compare v. 4 with 3Jn 4); others that she refers to a local congregation (cf. 2Jn 13). Both Israel and the church were portrayed as women (cf., e.g., Isa 62:5; Rev 12:1; 19:7).
3 *Grace ... peace.* See note on Ro 1:7.
5 *not ... a new command ... love one another.* Earlier Scripture already commanded love (Lev 19:18), but Jesus offered a new model for it (Jn 13:34). See note on 1Jn 2:7–8.
6 *walk in obedience.* See notes on 1Jn 2:3,5.
7 *Jesus Christ as coming in the flesh.* See note on 1Jn 4:2.
10 *do not take them into your house or welcome them.* All ancient Mediterranean and Middle Eastern cultures emphasized hospitality to guests (cf. 3Jn 5–6). Travelers would stay in hosts' homes, sometimes for up to three weeks; Christians were especially eager to supply such hospitality to their visiting workers (cf. Mt 10:9–14). Possibly the homes here also hosted churches. But just as Jewish people would not welcome those they considered impious (such as Samaritans), so Christians needed to show wisdom. The *Didache*, a noncanonical Christian work from this period, reveals that Christians needed to distinguish true visiting prophets and apostles from false ones (*Didache* 11–12).
11 *welcomes.* The Greek term (also in v. 10) indicates greetings. Social custom mandated greetings; the conventional Jewish greeting ("Peace be with you") was intended as a blessing or prayer to impart peace. In the Dead Sea Scrolls, whoever provided for an apostate from the community was deemed an apostate sympathizer and was expelled from the community, as the apostate was.
12 *paper.* Papyrus, made from reeds. *ink.* A compound of charcoal, vegetable gum and water. The pen itself was a reed pointed at the end. *I hope to visit you.* Written letters were considered an inferior substitute for personal presence or a speech, and writers sometimes concluded their letters with the promise to discuss matters further face to face.
13 *The children of your sister ... send their greetings.* It was common to send greetings from those near the sender. *sister.* See note on "lady" in v. 1.

THE LETTERS

3 JOHN

See Introduction to 1 John: Authorship; see also Introduction to 2 John: Authorship.

Genre

See Introduction to 2 John: Genre. This may be a "letter of recommendation" (see note on Ac 9:2) for Demetrius (3Jn 12), who may be a traveling missionary (see vv. 7–8). Such travelers depended on the hospitality of local house churches while evangelizing in their area (cf. notes on Mt 10:11,40,41,42). For the first three centuries of the church's existence, congregations usually met in homes (see note on Ro 16:5).

Situation

In this letter to Gaius, a house-church leader, John is apparently attempting to counter the opposing influences of Diotrephes, a different house-church leader who is asserting his own authority and rejecting emissaries backed by John's apostolic authority. ◆

QUICK GLANCE

AUTHOR:
The apostle John

AUDIENCE:
Gaius, perhaps a leader of one of the churches in western Asia Minor

DATE:
Between AD 85 and 95

THEME:
John writes this letter to commend Gaius for supporting traveling teachers and to rebuke Diotrephes for refusing to welcome them.

[1]The elder,[a]

To my dear friend Gaius, whom I love in the truth.

[2]Dear friend, I pray that you may enjoy good health and that all may go well with you, even as your soul is getting along well. [3]It gave me great joy when some believers[b] came and testified about your faithfulness to the truth, telling how you continue to walk in it.[c] [4]I have no greater joy than to hear that my children[d] are walking in the truth.

[5]Dear friend, you are faithful in what you are doing for the brothers and sisters,[a]

1 [a] 2Jn 1
3 [b] ver 5,10
[c] 2Jn 4
4 [d] 1Co 4:15; 1Jn 2:1

[a] 5 The Greek word for *brothers and sisters* (*adelphoi*) refers here to believers, both men and women, as part of God's family.

1 *Gaius.* There is no need to identify this Gaius with others of the same name; this name was one of the most frequent Roman names.
2 *I pray that you may enjoy good health and that all may go well with you.* This is a standard greeting in many ancient letters, which quite often began with a prayer for the reader's health, frequently including the prayer that all would go well with the person. This greeting might be similar to a modern-day letter writer saying, "I hope you are well," but it represents an actual prayer that all is well with Gaius (see note on 1Th 3:11).
4 *my children.* Teachers sometimes viewed their disciples as their children. John may also speak of them as his converts (cf. note on Gal 4:19).
5 *what you are doing for the brothers and sisters, even though they are strangers to you.* The Mediterranean and Middle East viewed hospitality as a key virtue; Jewish people, in particular, felt obligated to help fellow Jews. Because inns were usually of poor quality and doubled as brothels, Jewish travelers usually preferred to stay with fellow Jews when possible. Letters of recommendation could inform prospective hosts of the guests'

3 JOHN

Writing Materials in the Ancient World

John's statement that he was writing "with pen and ink" (3Jn 13) sounds modern, but in fact ancient people used writing materials that were far removed from what we think of as pen and paper. Ancient texts were written on the following materials:

- *Stone.* This could be ordinary limestone or sandstone, or, for a small inscription, a semiprecious stone such as amethyst, turquoise or opal. The writing tool could be a chisel or metal stylus, but sometimes people wrote on stone with ink. In some instances the stone had a coat of plaster over it, as in Dt 27:2–3. Stone, including marble, was widely used for monumental inscriptions describing the feats of kings, but simple graffiti was also cut into stone.
- *Metal.* This material was primarily used for commemorative and decorative objects, such as for inscriptions on a silver bowl. Two silver amulets inscribed with the text of Nu 6:24–27 were discovered near Jerusalem, while a copper scroll was located at Qumran.
- *Wooden Tablets.* These could be coated with wax or stucco for the writing surface. Wax was especially useful since one could inscribe it with a pointed stylus and then rub out the writing and reuse the tablet.
- *Clay Tablets.* Clay was the medium for cuneiform. While still moist, it would be inscribed with a sharpened stick to create the distinctive wedge-shaped cuneiform script. If baked, tablets became virtually indestructible, and thus many have survived through the centuries.
- *Ostraca.* An ostracon is a common potsherd (a broken piece of pottery). It could be inscribed with a metal stylus or written on with ink. Ostraca were handy for short notes and letters. In Athens voters used them to write down the name of a citizen they wanted to send into exile or to "ostracize" (hence the name).

continued on next page

- *Leather.* Leather pages are often referred to as vellum or parchment. In Israel leather was the medium of choice for writing the books of the Scriptures. The Isaiah scroll from Qumran, e.g., is composed of leather, with the writing done in black ink.
- *Papyrus.* This was the closest thing to paper from the ancient world. The Egyptian papyrus plant was cut into strips and pressed into sheets that were then glued together. This made for a strong, smooth writing surface, and papyrus naturally became very popular in the ancient world. The ink on a papyrus could be erased and the papyrus reused; an erased and reused papyrus document is called a "palimpsest."
- *Scrolls and Codices.* For almost all of Biblical history, papyrus or leather was formed into long strips and rolled up on scrolls. However, around the first century AD people began to stitch together one side of a group of papyrus or leather leaves to create the equivalent of the modern book, called a codex. By the early second century AD, the early Christians adopted the idea of the codex, and thus most early Christian Bibles are in the form of codices rather than scrolls.

Inkwell from the Scriptorium at Qumran, before AD 68.
The Schøyen Collection, Oslo and London, MS 1655, www.schoyencollection.com

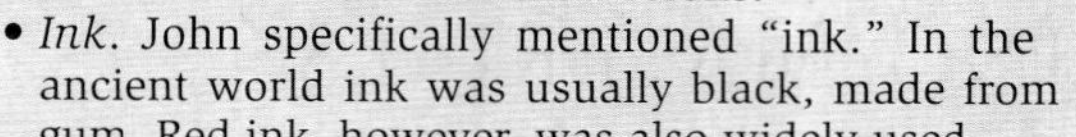

- *Ink.* John specifically mentioned "ink." In the ancient world ink was usually black, made from carbon mixed with a natural gum. Red ink, however, was also widely used.

The literacy rate was especially high in the Greco-Roman world, and writing materials, although difficult to work with by modern standards, were widely available. Letter writing was common, and the relative ease of communication facilitated the missionary and pastoral work of the apostles. ◆

even though they are strangers to you.[e]
6They have told the church about your
love. Please send them on their way in a
manner that honors God. 7It was for the
sake of the Name[f] that they went out, receiving no help from the pagans.[g] 8We
ought therefore to show hospitality to
such people so that we may work together
for the truth.
9I wrote to the church, but Diotrephes,
who loves to be first, will not welcome
us. 10So when I come,[h] I will call attention to what he is doing, spreading malicious nonsense about us. Not satisfied
with that, he even refuses to welcome
other believers.[i] He also stops those who
want to do so and puts them out of the
church.[j]
11Dear friend, do not imitate what is evil
but what is good.[k] Anyone who does what

5 [e] Ro 12:13; Heb 13:2
7 [f] Jn 15:21 [g] Ac 20:33,35
10 [h] 2Jn 12 [i] ver 5 [j] Jn 9:22,34
11 [k] Ps 37:27

trustworthiness. Christians probably adapted such customs.
6 *send them … in a manner that honors God.* Hospitality often included generously providing for the guest as they continued their journey.
7 *for the sake of the Name.* Jewish people sometimes spoke of God's sacred name, *YHWH*, as "the Name"; this may be applied to Jesus here. *receiving no help from the pagans.* Traveling sages and speakers often made their livings from the crowds to whom they spoke, although others took fees or were supported by wealthy patrons. People sometimes suspected as greedy those sages and speakers who depended on their hearers. Evangelists instead depended on the churches.
9 *Diotrephes … will not welcome us.* Apparently Diotrephes was a leader of another house church; he refuses to show hospitality to the missionaries who have letters of recommendation from the elder. To reject a person's representatives or those recommended by a person was to disrespect the person who had written on their behalf.

is good is from God.[l] Anyone who does
what is evil has not seen God.[m] 12Deme-
trius is well spoken of by everyone[n] — and
even by the truth itself. We also speak well
of him, and you know that our testimony
is true.[o]
13I have much to write you, but I do not
want to do so with pen and ink. 14I hope
to see you soon, and we will talk face to
face.[p]

Peace to you. The friends here send
their greetings. Greet the friends there by
name.[q]

11 [l] 1Jn 2:29 [m] 1Jn 3:6,9,10 12 [n] 1Ti 3:7 [o] Jn 21:24 14 [p] 2Jn 12 [q] Jn 10:3

---

12 *Demetrius ... We also speak well of him.* Those influenced by Diotrephes refuse to provide hospitality for Demetrius, so John provides this letter of recommendation for Demetrius (see note on Ac 9:2) so that Gaius's house church will welcome him.

13 *I have much to write you.* Sometimes ancient letters closed as John does here. Most letter writers employed scribes, and if John is writing by hand, he may well wish to close quickly. *pen and ink.* See note on 2Jn 12.

14 *The friends here ... the friends there.* If "friends here" is a title for a group, it probably refers to fellow Christians in the place from which the elder is writing; these Christians may have borrowed the idea from Epicurean philosophers, whose philosophical communities consisted especially of "friends." More likely, it reflects and honors a title given by Jesus (Jn 15:15).

THE LETTERS

JUDE

Authorship

Although a pseudepigrapher would want to clarify which Jude he was (i.e., Jesus' brother) or write in the name of someone more prominent, this author does not specify which Jude he is, making it improbable that the letter was pseudepigraphic. At the same time, his lack of clarification as to which Jude he is and the fact that he seems to be already known to his audience (vv. 3,5) suggest that he is the most prominent Jude, brother of the most prominent James (v. 1) — the younger brother of Jesus (Mk 6:3). This would also help to explain the letter's preservation, despite its brevity and overlap with 2 Peter. Early church tradition varied on which Jude wrote the letter, but this is the only Jude specifically known to us whose brother was called James. His Greek is sophisticated, but the thought world he shares with his readers is that of popular Judaism; for a Galilean Jew's knowledge of Greek, see Introduction to James: Author.

QUICK GLANCE

AUTHOR:
Most likely Jude, the brother of Jesus

AUDIENCE:
Christians who are being threatened by false teachers

DATE:
Between AD 65 and 80

THEME:
Jude writes to warn Christians about false teachers who are trying to convince them that being saved by grace gives them license to sin.

Situation

The letter clearly opposes false teachers whose sexual lifestyles are immoral and who are teaching arrogantly. The thought world of Jude and his readers is popular Judaism; the views of those he opposes may be rooted in the same Jewish-Christian tradition that Jude is, but they have also sought to assimilate many values of immoral pagan culture. Given Jude's heavy use of 1 Enoch, that book may represent a tradition cited by his opponents, who apparently appeal to their own mystical visions as divine revelations, similar to Enoch's (Jude 8). The teachings of 1 Enoch would challenge the immorality practiced by these teachers (cf. Jude 4 – 7). ◆

1 Jude,[a] a servant of Jesus Christ and a
brother of James,

To those who have been called,[b] who
are loved in God the Father and kept for[a]
Jesus Christ:[c]

2 Mercy, peace and love be yours in
abundance.[d]

The Sin and Doom of Ungodly People

3 Dear friends, although I was very eager to write to you about the salvation we
share,[e] I felt compelled to write and urge
you to contend[f] for the faith that was once
for all entrusted to God's holy people. 4 For
certain individuals whose condemnation
was written about[b] long ago have secretly
slipped in among you.[g] They are ungodly
people, who pervert the grace of our God
into a license for immorality and deny
Jesus Christ our only Sovereign and Lord.[h]
5 Though you already know all this, I
want to remind you that the Lord[c] at one
time delivered his people out of Egypt, but
later destroyed those who did not believe.[i]
6 And the angels who did not keep their
positions of authority but abandoned their
proper dwelling—these he has kept in
darkness, bound with everlasting chains
for judgment on the great Day.[j] 7 In a similar way, Sodom and Gomorrah and the
surrounding towns[k] gave themselves up
to sexual immorality and perversion. They
serve as an example of those who suffer
the punishment of eternal fire.[l]
8 In the very same way, on the strength
of their dreams these ungodly people
pollute their own bodies, reject authority and heap abuse on celestial beings.[m]
9 But even the archangel Michael,[n] when
he was disputing with the devil about the
body of Moses, did not himself dare to
condemn him for slander but said, "The
Lord rebuke you!"[d][o] 10 Yet these people
slander whatever they do not understand,
and the very things they do understand by
instinct—as irrational animals do—will
destroy them.[p]

1 [a] Mt 13:55; Ac 1:13 [b] Ro 1:6, 7 [c] Jn 17:12 **2** [d] 2Pe 1:2 **3** [e] Titus 1:4 [f] 1Ti 6:12 **4** [g] Gal 2:4 [h] Titus 1:16; 2Pe 2:1 **5** [i] Nu 14:29; Ps 106:26 **6** [j] 2Pe 2:4,9 **7** [k] Dt 29:23 [l] 2Pe 2:6 **8** [m] 2Pe 2:10 **9** [n] Da 10:13,21 [o] Zec 3:2 **10** [p] 2Pe 2:12

[a] *1* Or *by*; or *in* [b] *4* Or *individuals who were marked out for condemnation* [c] *5* Some early manuscripts *Jesus* [d] *9* Jude is alluding to the Jewish *Testament of Moses* (approximately the first century A.D.).

1 *Jude … a brother of James.* Jude's lack of elaboration on his office suggests that he is the well-known Jude, brother not only of James, current leader of the Jerusalem church, but half-brother of Jesus as well (cf. Mk 6:3; Ac 1:14; 1Co 9:5). Although a son of Joseph and Mary, he now describes his half-brother Jesus as "Lord" (v. 4) rather than as brother. *servant.* See note on Ro 1:1.

4 *whose condemnation was written about long ago.* Earlier false prophets had insisted that because of God's special favor for his people, judgment would not come on them—a teaching that led to sin (Jer 6:14; 8:11; 23:17; Eze 13:10,16; Mic 3:5). *the grace of our God.* Biblical grace means forgiveness and power to overcome sin, not permission to act immorally.

5 *later destroyed those who did not believe.* God redeemed Israel, but many rebelled in the wilderness and were destroyed (e.g., Ex 32:35; Nu 11:33; 14:29; 16:32,35,49; 21:6; 25:9; 26:10).

6 *angels who did not keep their positions of authority.* In most ancient Jewish traditions, the "sons of God" in Ge 6:1–4 were fallen angels who left their assigned positions to have intercourse with women (see note on 2Pe 2:4). *in darkness, bound with everlasting chains.* In the earliest surviving source for these traditions (1 Enoch), the fallen angels were imprisoned and bound; Azazel was thrown into "darkness," which was applied to the realm of the dead in much ancient tradition. *judgment on the great Day.* First Enoch also uses "great Day" for the day of judgment (1 Enoch 22:11; 54:6; 84:4).

7 *In a similar way, Sodom and Gomorrah.* May allude to their pursuit of angels (Ge 19:5), in light of Jude 6; Jude 8 probably mentions disrespect for angels. Yet because Jewish tradition would not call angels "flesh" and the Sodomites did not realize that their prospective victims were angels, many suggest that Jude's point here is their attempt at homosexual rape. Some ancient interpreters emphasized Sodomites' homosexual sin, but more often they focused on their lack of hospitality, an "arrogant" sin (Eze 16:49) or sexual immorality in general, in which Jewish interpreters included homosexual but also nonmarital heterosexual acts. *gave themselves up to sexual immorality and perversion.* In Scripture (e.g., Isa 3:9; Jer 23:14) and still more often in later Jewish tradition, Sodom epitomized sinfulness. *perversion.* Here is lit. "strange" or "other flesh," perhaps meaning "other [than what was natural]." *example of … the punishment of eternal fire.* Sodom and Gomorrah were examples of destruction (e.g., Dt 29:23; Isa 1:9–10).

8 *their dreams.* May imply the activity of false prophets, who prophesy lies based on their dreams (Jer 23:25). *pollute.* In view of v. 7 and mention of "their own bodies," the term could apply to homosexual acts (Lev 18:22,24) or to rape (Ge 34:5,13,27); though by itself it could also apply to a wide range of other activities, including desecration of sacred sites or incurring impurity from touching corpses. *authority.* The Greek term could apply to earthly rulers but could also apply to the angelic rulers behind them (see notes on Eph 1:21; Col 1:16); in any case, earthly authorities could see it as subversive (just as Rome appreciated subject nations honoring Roma, the goddess personifying Rome).

9 *the archangel Michael.* Only two angels are named in the OT: Michael (Da 10:13,21; 12:1) and Gabriel (Da 8:16; 9:21), though the Apocrypha and other sources add others. Michael and Gabriel thus became the two most popular angels in Jewish tradition, with Michael as Israel's guardian and generally the most prominent archangel. *the devil.* Following Scripture (Job 1:9–11; 2:4–5; Zec 3:1), Jewish tradition viewed the devil as an accuser. *the body of Moses.* Jewish traditions about Moses' death (or lack of it, despite Dt 34:5–7) varied widely, and Jude's allusion appears to fit one of these versions, in the Testament of Moses. *did not himself dare to condemn him for slander but said, "The Lord rebuke you!"* Here the great archangel Michael did not challenge the devil's slander against Moses but deferred the issue to God, the supreme judge. This incident follows a principle in Scripture; in Zec 3:2, God's angelic messenger defends the high priest against Satan's accusation by crying, "The LORD rebuke you, Satan!"

10 *these people slander whatever they do not understand.* The false teachers were insulting angelic powers, probably including Satan. Perhaps because Jewish

11 Woe to them! They have taken the
way of Cain;[q] they have rushed for profit
into Balaam's error;[r] they have been destroyed in Korah's rebellion.[s]
12 These people are blemishes at your
love feasts,[t] eating with you without the
slightest qualm — shepherds who feed
only themselves. They are clouds without
rain,[u] blown along by the wind;[v] autumn
trees, without fruit and uprooted[w] — twice
dead. 13 They are wild waves of the sea,[x]
foaming up their shame;[y] wandering stars,
for whom blackest darkness has been reserved forever.[z]
14 Enoch,[a] the seventh from Adam,
prophesied about them: "See, the Lord
is coming with thousands upon thousands of his holy ones[b] 15 to judge[c] everyone, and to convict all of them of all
the ungodly acts they have committed
in their ungodliness, and of all the defiant words ungodly sinners have spoken
against him."[a][d] 16 These people are grumblers and faultfinders; they follow their
own evil desires; they boast[e] about themselves and flatter others for their own advantage.

A Call to Persevere

17 But, dear friends, remember what the
apostles of our Lord Jesus Christ foretold.[f]
18 They said to you, "In the last times[g]
there will be scoffers who will follow
their own ungodly desires."[h] 19 These are
the people who divide you, who follow
mere natural instincts and do not have the
Spirit.[i]
20 But you, dear friends, by building
yourselves up[j] in your most holy faith and
praying in the Holy Spirit,[k] 21 keep yourselves in God's love as you wait[l] for the
mercy of our Lord Jesus Christ to bring
you to eternal life.
22 Be merciful to those who doubt; 23 save
others by snatching them from the fire;[m]
to others show mercy, mixed with fear —

11 [q] Ge 4:3-8; 1Jn 3:12 [r] 2Pe 2:15 [s] Nu 16:1-3, 31-35
12 [t] 2Pe 2:13; 1Co 11:20-22 [u] Pr 25:14; 2Pe 2:17 [v] Eph 4:14 [w] Mt 15:13
13 [x] Isa 57:20 [y] Php 3:19 [z] 2Pe 2:17
14 [a] Ge 5:18, 21-24 [b] Dt 33:2; Da 7:10
15 [c] 2Pe 2:6-9 [d] 1Ti 1:9
16 [e] 2Pe 2:18
17 [f] 2Pe 3:2
18 [g] 1Ti 4:1 [h] 2Pe 2:1
19 [i] 1Co 2:14, 15
20 [j] Col 2:7 [k] Eph 6:18
21 [l] Titus 2:13; 2Pe 3:12
23 [m] Am 4:11; Zec 3:2-5

[a] *14,15* From the Jewish *First Book of Enoch* (approximately the first century B.C.)

---

tradition depicted Enoch as announcing judgment on fallen angels, these teachers seek to emulate Enoch. The Dead Sea Scrolls show that some people cursed Satan (see note on 2Pe 2:10); Jude would reject that practice. Instead, he seems to agree with the moral embodied in a story told by later rabbis: a man named Pelimo went around making fun of the devil until one day the devil showed up and chased him into a bathhouse, whereupon he learned his lesson. Christians also should not speak authoritatively on secret or esoteric matters God has not chosen to reveal (cf. Dt 29:29). *as irrational animals do.* For the comparison with animals, see note on 2Pe 2:12.

11 *the way of Cain … Balaam's error.* Jewish traditions developed the wickedness of Cain and Balaam (see notes on 2Pe 2:15; 1Jn 3:12), using them as symbols of evil. *destroyed in Korah's rebellion.* Jude alludes to Nu 16, where God destroyed Korah and his followers for rejecting Moses' authority. Jewish tradition used Korah as an example of rebellion against God's law.

12 *blemishes.* Scholars debate how to translate this Greek term; "blemishes" fits v. 23 and the interpretation in 2Pe 2:13, yet the following context of problems in nature (Jude 12–13) could suggest the other possible translation of the Greek term — unseen rocks that could tear open the hulls of unsuspecting ships (cf. Ac 27:41). *love feasts.* Just as Jesus' final meal with his disciples was a Passover meal (see notes on Mk 14:12–26), early Christians consumed more during the Lord's Supper than just bread and wine (though these were the particular elements interpreted; cf. 1Co 11:21–34). In ancient Mediterranean values, shared meals created a bond of friendship obligation; love was meant to be a paramount feature of the Christian meal (1Co 11:26). *shepherds who feed only themselves.* Shepherds of God's people who care only for themselves invite judgment on themselves (as in, and perhaps alluding to, Eze 34:8,10). *clouds without rain.* Such clouds offered farmers vain hopes (cf. Pr 25:14). *autumn trees, without fruit and uprooted — twice dead.* Trees that offered no fruit during summer or even as late as autumn were normally dead (on the future second death, see note on Rev 2:11).

13 *wild waves of the sea.* Some Jewish texts used waves to symbolize wickedness (as in Isa 57:20). *foaming up.* The Greek term was sometimes applied figuratively to babbling or exposing secrets. *wandering stars.* In ancient sources they referred to the planets because of their supposedly erratic orbits around the earth. The widely circulated 1 Enoch declared that God imprisoned hostile star-angels. *blackest darkness … forever.* 1 Enoch speaks of judgment as "darkness … forever."

14–15 Jude quotes from 1 Enoch 1:9. The work, normally dated to the second century BC, is not genuinely by Enoch but was widely circulated. The false teachers, who may have believed themselves inspired (cf. v. 8), may have used 1 Enoch while ignoring its message of moral judgment (here and in v. 6). Its message regarding the point quoted may be prophetic; certainly it is consistent with earlier prophets (cf., e.g., Zec 14:1–5).

16 *grumblers.* Might relate to "defiant words" in the citation in v. 15. *flatter others for their own advantage.* Many thinkers denounced greedy sages and flattering speakers who simply told people what they wanted to hear to gain their favor.

17–18 *the apostles … said to you, "In the last times there will be scoffers who will follow their own ungodly desires."* Not all early apostolic teaching has survived, but this warning is certainly consistent with Jesus' warnings about future opposition (e.g., Mk 13:9,12–13). *desires.* Cf. 2Ti 4:3; 1Jn 2:16–17; see the note on 2Pe 3:3.

19 *natural instincts … do not have the Spirit.* See note on 1Co 15:44–46. Those causing division may have claimed inspiration (cf. v. 8), but they lacked the Spirit of true inspiration. (Although the Spirit also performed other activities, Scripture sometimes, and ancient Judaism usually, associated the Spirit with prophetic inspiration.)

20 *praying in the Holy Spirit.* Presumably Spirit-inspired prayer (see note on v. 19); cf., e.g., 1Ch 25:3; see note on Eph 5:19.

23 *snatching them from the fire … clothing stained by corrupted flesh.* In Zec 3:2,4 the high priest is snatched from the fire and delivered from his filthy clothes. (In Zec 3:2 the Lord also rebukes Satan; cf. Jude 9.)

hating even the clothing stained by corrupted flesh.[a][n]

Doxology

[24]To him who is able[o] to keep you from stumbling and to present you before his glorious presence[p] without fault[q] and with great joy— [25]to the only God[r] our Savior be glory, majesty, power and authority, through Jesus Christ our Lord, before all ages, now and forevermore![s] Amen.[t]

23 [n]Rev 3:4
24 [o]Ro 16:25 [p]2Co 4:14 [q]Col 1:22
25 [r]Jn 5:44; 1Ti 1:17 [s]Heb 13:8 [t]Ro 11:36

[a] *22,23* The Greek manuscripts of these verses vary at several points.

24 – 25 Jewish people often closed with a doxology of praise.
24 *To him who is able to keep you from stumbling.* After warning throughout the letter about falling away, Jude praises God's ability to keep Jude's hearers steadfast in the faith.

THE APOCALYPSE

REVELATION

Authorship

The author claims to be John (Rev 1:1,4,9; 22:8); since he does not identify himself more directly, he may be the best-known John, i.e., the apostle. This fits early church tradition. Noting the very different style of the Gospel attributed to the apostle John, however, a third-century elder argued that this author was a different John. Scholars today sometimes support that same position. The stylistic differences between the Gospel and Revelation are real, but many can be explained by the different genres.

Date

Early Christian tradition supports a date of writing in the time of Domitian, probably in the AD 90s; most scholars prefer this date. Some interpreters date Revelation to the time of Nero or his successors in the 60s, given likely echoes of Nero in the book. Against this earlier dating, churches are now established, and some have lost their initial zeal in major cities of the province (1:4); the temple may be already desecrated (cf. 11:2); a return of Nero may be expected (cf. 13:3; 17:10 – 11), and this expectation continued throughout the first century; and the emperor's power appears more stable (cf. 13:7 – 8) than it was among Nero's successors.

QUICK GLANCE

AUTHOR:
The apostle John

AUDIENCE:
Seven churches in western Asia Minor

DATE:
About AD 95

THEME:
John writes to encourage the faithful to stand firm against persecution and compromise in the light of the imminent return of Christ to deliver the righteous and judge the wicked.

Genre

One could explain most individual images in Revelation on the basis of earlier Biblical prophets (with numerous echoes especially of Isaiah, Ezekiel, Daniel and Zechariah). Many of these images that are dominant, however, are the same images popular in post-OT apocalyptic works such as 1 Enoch, 4 Ezra and 2 Baruch. Throughout history, God often communicated with people in ways that were intelligible in their particular cultures, albeit with numerous limitations (e.g., prohibiting divination). Many apocalyptic motifs found in 1 Enoch and these other ancient Jewish works were developed from OT images. Jewish mystics and apocalyptic visionaries sought to cultivate visions of heaven; early Christians clearly experienced visions as well (Ac 2:17; 2Co 12:1 – 4), although they did not regard all revelations as genuine (Rev 2:20; 1Jn 4:1 – 6).

Biblical prophets had often prophesied against the nations. Well before John's day, Daniel's prophecy concerning four kingdoms (Da 2:37 – 45; 7:3 – 12) had become very popular, and Jewish interpreters in this period regarded Rome as the fourth kingdom. Expecting God's imminent kingdom, some apocalyptic seers prophesied Rome's demise, whereas revolutionaries took up arms to try to overthrow Rome, leading to Jerusalem's destruction in AD 70. Even Diaspora Jews in many cities suffered from the resentment that followed, and subsequent revolts by Jews in Egypt and Cyrene also led to the destruction of the Jewish communities there. Works that could be understood as prophesying destruction against Rome were politically sensitive, and the circles that produced such works would be quickly repressed.

Structure

Revelation includes an introduction (ch. 1), letters to seven churches (chs. 2 – 3), and then three sets of seven judgments, with interludes that especially provide a heavenly perspective (chs. 4 – 16). Each of these sets of judgments (seals, trumpets and bowls) apparently climaxes with the end of the age. Prophecies against Rome (chs. 17 – 18) seem to precede prophecies of the end (chs. 19 – 22), although some argue plausibly that the period depicted in 20:1 – 6 rehearses from another perspective the same period surveyed in the sets of judgments in chs. 4 – 16. (This matter remains debated.)

Some view the three series of seven judgments as consecutive; others, noting that each set climaxes in the end of the age (6:12 – 14; 11:15,18; 16:17,20), view them as concurrent. The period in chs. 4 – 16 may be the 1,260 days of 11:3; 12:6,14; 13:5, although the meaning of this period is debated. (Those who view it as symbolic usually interpret it as the period between Jesus' first and second comings [see the article "Time in Revelation," p. 2245]). John may report the visions in the sequence in which he saw them, but every time he notes "And I saw/heard," he is receiving a new image, which need not always follow chronologically what precedes.

Interpreting Revelation

Several major categories of approaches to Revelation exist:

First, the *idealist* approach finds timeless principles in the book of Revelation, though it often ignores specific applicability to first-century situations.

Second, the *historicist* approach argues that Revelation provides a detailed map of history from its own day until Jesus' future return. The connections, however, do not fit very well. This was one of the most popular approaches in church history (especially the nineteenth century), but it is not very popular today.

Third, the *preterist* approach understands Revelation in its first-century setting. The most thoroughgoing preterists, however, apply all of it to *only* the first century, ignoring any future prophecies. Yet a first-century audience, familiar with apocalyptic literature, would likely have understood at least some of Revelation (especially 20:11 — 22:5) as pointing to the future. Ancient apocalyptic literature often did address the future, sometimes partly and sometimes in great detail.

Fourth, the *futurist* approach looks for predictions about the future in Revelation. This approach is much more popular today than it was in most of history. The most thoroughgoing futurists, however, often ignore ways in which the message was contextualized for its original first-century audience.

Many scholars prefer a more eclectic approach, starting with the first-century application (like preterists), looking for enduring principles (like idealists), and recognizing some future elements (like futurists). How much of the book relates specifically to the past (beyond passages such as chs. 2 – 3; 12:5) and how much specifically to the future (beyond passages such as 20:11 — 22:5) remains a matter of debate.

Prophecy miscalculations have littered history. For example, Saint Martin of Tours was certain that the final antichrist was already alive — though Martin died in 397. Others predicted the antichrist's coming for the years 1000, 1184, 1186, 1229, 1345, 1385, and so forth. Thomas Müntzer took part in the Peasant's Revolt of 1524, expecting this to bring about the final judgment; but after 6,000 peasants died he was captured and executed. In those days, end-time miscalculations often died hard — literally.

Similarly, early Baptist leader Thomas Helwys, persecuted by King James I, believed that he and his followers were experiencing the final "great tribulation." Just before the turn of the twentieth century, on Dec. 31, 1899, full-page advertisements in major U.S. newspapers warned that Christ was about to return. Three million copies of a book suggesting that the church might be raptured in 1988 sold that year; the next edition, produced in 1989, failed to sell so many copies. Others predicted the Lord's return for 1993, 1994, 2000, and so forth.

Some popular prophecy teachers have interpreted Revelation based on newspaper headlines, assuming that it addresses only the current generation. Because they have been doing this for more than a century, they have had to reinterpret Revelation and other Biblical prophecies on a regular basis. Thus, e.g., North American interpreters applied "kings from the East" (16:12) to the Turkish Ottoman Empire until the end of World War I — even though the churches of Asia Minor (1:4) would hardly have regarded Turkey as to their east! These Western interpreters applied the phrase to imperial Japan until the end of World War II, to Communist China for much of the rest of the twentieth century, and to Iraq during the first Gulf War with Saddam Hussein. If we pay attention to first-century background for Revelation, as we do for other Biblical books, however, John's image probably had more to do with the ancient Parthians (see the article "Parthia," p. 2239).

John wrote this book in Greek and explicitly addressed churches in Asia Minor (1:4), just as Paul explicitly addressed churches in Philippi, Thessalonica and elsewhere. Thus we should pay attention to what Revelation would have meant in its explicit setting. Reading it this way helps us understand the points the book is making so we can apply them with greater confidence to analogous kinds of situations.

Symbolism was common in OT poetry and thus in preexilic prophecy (e.g., Jdg 5:4; Ps 18:4 – 19; Joel 3:12 – 13), but it is even more common in subsequent Jewish apocalyptic visionary literature. That Revelation recycles in fresh and symbolic ways many OT images is undeniable (e.g., the plagues, the locusts, and the lamb; also 6:13; 12:1); certainly few interpreters think that Revelation was simply commenting about Moses' plagues on Egypt centuries earlier. It is clear that Revelation uses symbols and sometimes even explains them (see 1:20). Consistency with Revelation's most obvious uses of symbolism invites us to be open to symbolism elsewhere in the book. As often in antiquity, Revelation also appears to use some symbolic numbers (seven being a particular favorite).

Setting

Domitian was likely the emperor during the time that Revelation was written (see Date). Domitian expelled astrologers from Rome and also repressed monotheists there, such as Jews and Christians. His example would have allowed those governors who so desired to take similar actions in provinces. Like the earlier emperors Caligula and Nero, Domitian wanted to be worshiped while alive, reportedly with the title "lord and god." No one took down names of people absent from public festivals, but if Christians were accused of subversion, their loyalty could be tested by a demand of worship to Caesar (see the article "The Imperial Cult," p. 2247).

Possibly some members of synagogues in Smyrna and Philadelphia expelled Jewish believers and additionally slandered them to Roman authorities as subversive (cf. 2:9 – 10; 3:9). (In the early second century, synagogue members in Smyrna reportedly favored harsh treatment for the bishop of Smyrna.) In the early second century, a governor ordered those Christians brought before him to offer incense to the emperor's image; those who refused were executed. Such policies, not instituted under Trajan (the emperor at that time), may have started earlier, in the time of Domitian.

Most churches, however, were not facing persecution (apparently Ephesus, Thyatira, Sardis, and Laodicea). Their temptation, by contrast, was to compromise with the same world system that was killing their brothers and sisters elsewhere.

Message

Revelation contrasts Babylon the prostitute, which ultimately embodies the spirit of this age, with new Jerusalem the bride, which embodies the hope of the world to come. One lives either for this age or, with faith, for the greater promise of the world to come. Revelation's description of Babylon fits Rome — a city on seven hills, a maritime power trading in the same goods described, ruling the kings of the part of the earth where John's audience lived. Jewish people often compared Rome with Babylon, the first of Daniel's four empires, which also destroyed the temple and subjugated God's people. But while Rome was the Babylon of John's day, the spirit of Babylon, the ethos of evil empire and the world system, preceded Rome and outlived it. Since John's day empires have risen and fallen, but God's kingdom has been spreading, as John envisioned, among all peoples.

Revelation thus invites its audience to an eternal perspective on the world. It invites us to worship with the hosts in heaven. It invites us to count as triumph our sufferings in this world that will be rewarded in the coming one (e.g., 11:7; 12:11; 13:7; 15:2). The world considered martyrdom folly; in light of eternity, it is a price well paid. Revelation thus comes as a comfort to the suffering churches (such as Smyrna and Philadelphia) but a warning to the compromising and dead churches (such as Thyatira and Sardis). Judgments are warning signs inviting the world to turn from the greater judgment to come (9:20 – 21; 16:9).

Revelation frequently depicts the Lamb, Jesus, in terms that the OT reserved for God. The Father and Son are the book's central figures, and they constitute the foundation for hope throughout the book. The world is clearly in worse condition than it acknowledges, but those who trust Christ's sacrifice for them have the promise of life forever with him in a restored creation. ◆

Prologue

1 The revelation from Jesus Christ,
which God gave him to show his servants what must soon take place. He made
it known by sending his angel[a] to his servant John, [2]who testifies to everything he
saw — that is, the word of God and the
testimony of Jesus Christ.[b] [3]Blessed is the
one who reads aloud the words of this
prophecy, and blessed are those who hear
it and take to heart what is written in it,[c]
because the time is near.

Greetings and Doxology

[4]John,

To the seven churches in the province
of Asia:

Grace and peace to you from him who
is, and who was, and who is to come, and
from the seven spirits[a][d] before his throne,
[5]and from Jesus Christ, who is the faithful
witness,[e] the firstborn from the dead,[f] and
the ruler of the kings of the earth.[g]

To him who loves us and has freed us
from our sins by his blood, [6]and has made
us to be a kingdom and priests[h] to serve
his God and Father — to him be glory and
power for ever and ever! Amen.[i]

[7]"Look, he is coming with the
clouds,"[b][j]
and "every eye will see him,
even those who pierced him";
and all peoples on earth "will
mourn[k] because of him."[c]
So shall it be! Amen.

1:1 [a]Rev 22:16 **1:2** [b]1Co 1:6; Rev 12:17 **1:3** [c]Lk 11:28 **1:4** [d]Rev 3:1; 4:5 **1:5** [e]Rev 3:14 [f]Col 1:18 [g]Rev 17:14 **1:6** [h]1Pe 2:5 [i]Ro 11:36 **1:7** [j]Da 7:13 [k]Zec 12:10

[a] *4* That is, the sevenfold Spirit [b] *7* Daniel 7:13 [c] *7* Zech. 12:10

1:1 *The revelation from Jesus Christ.* Book titles often listed the purported author — here, "the revelation from Jesus Christ." Ancient writers often included titles on the outside of their scrolls, but by the middle of the second century some scribes began transcribing earlier writings into codices, which are essentially the kind of books we use today. Consequently titles that often originally appeared on the outside of documents now often appear in our works as the opening line of the document. *sending his angel.* Apocalyptic literature often reported God sending revelations through angels; this is not surprising, since God had sent some revelations this way in the Bible (Da 9:21 – 22; Zec 1:9,14,19; 2:3; 4:1,4 – 5; 5:5,10; 6:4 – 5). *his servant John.* Authors of most traditional Jewish apocalypses borrowed names from famous Biblical figures who lived centuries earlier, perhaps because some of their contemporaries believed that prophecy was no longer as active in their own day. By contrast, John writes in his own name; early Christians believed that prophecy did remain active. *servant.* See note on Ro 1:1.
1:3 *Blessed is the one who reads aloud the words of this prophecy.* Before printing presses were available, people of means often "published" works especially in public readings, perhaps most often at banquets. But Revelation was read in churches alongside OT Scripture, suggesting its special authority (cf. also 22:18 – 19). Even in urban areas, most people could not read much; thus one person would read the work and others would listen. *blessed are.* Introduces a beatitude, a form common especially in the OT and ancient Jewish sources (see note on Mt 5:3). *near.* Imminent. This means that the book of Revelation makes its demand on the present — not that it specifies a particular time frame (cf., e.g., Dt 32:35; Isa 13:6; Eze 30:3).
1:4 – 8 A work that was not a letter per se could include the same form of introduction as letters because it was sent to someone (cf., e.g., 2 Maccabees 1:1). The preface of a work would often set its tone; expansions on any part often introduce themes in the rest of the work — here the emphasis on God, including Jesus Christ.
1:4 *Asia.* The Roman province of Asia, in western Asia Minor; Christians had multiplied strongly there by this period (cf. Ac 19:10). John names seven of the most prominent and strategic cities in the region, from which word would quickly spread to outlying areas. The leading council of Asiarchs (Ac 19:31) met each year in a succession of seven cities, including six of the seven cities to which John writes. (He replaces Cyzicus, far to the north, with the more centrally located Thyatira.) Ephesus, the first city he mentions, was the most important city in the province, but also the first of the seven cities to which a messenger from Patmos, just 40 – 50 miles (65 – 80 kilometers) away in the Aegean Sea, would have come. *Grace and peace.* See note on Ro 1:7. *him who is, and who was, and who is to come.* A writer would sometimes bracket off a section by starting and finishing on the same phrase (vv. 4,8). This title represents a common Jewish way of understanding the Biblical name "I AM" (Ex 3:14). *seven spirits.* Some take the seven spirits as the seven archangels of Jewish tradition; more often scholars connect them with the sevenfold Spirit of God in Isa 11:2, allowing for a Trinitarian reading of vv. 4 – 5.
1:5 *faithful witness.* Sometimes a divine role (Jer 42:5), although not limited to God (Rev 2:13). *firstborn from the dead.* Most Jewish people expected all the righteous dead to rise at the end of the age (Da 12:2); Jesus' followers believed that he inaugurated that future event in the midst of history, as "firstborn from among the dead" (Col 1:18; see Heb 1:6; cf. Ro 8:29). *ruler of the kings of the earth.* The Roman emperor claimed to rule the earth, ruling subordinate kings, as did the Parthian ruler in his part of the world. In Ps 89:27, however, God's firstborn rules over the other kings of the earth.
1:6 *a kingdom and priests.* John applies to all believers (cf. 5:10; 20:6), who have been grafted into the Biblical heritage of Israel, a title and mission already designated for Israel (Ex 19:6). Yet Exodus's "kingdom of priests" here becomes a kingdom (who will reign, 5:10) and priests (who in Revelation offer the incense of prayer, 5:8). *to him be glory and power for ever and ever!* Whereas traditional Jewish texts praised God the Father, here the praise is directed toward Jesus (cf. Ro 9:5), the one who died for us (v. 5) and made us priests to his Father (v. 6).
1:7 *coming with the clouds ... and all peoples on earth "will mourn because of him."* Jesus' return in the clouds (probably of divine glory) reflects Da 7:13; that those who pierced him would see him and would mourn reflects Zec 12:10. This may echo an earlier saying of Jesus (see Mt 24:30). *peoples.* Lit. "tribes." Might echo the Greek version of Zec 12:12, though "tribes of the earth" appears together elsewhere in the Greek translation of the OT (e.g., Ge 12:3; Zec 14:17). Not only Israel but also many other peoples were organized into tribes; Philadelphia, for instance, had

[8]"I am the Alpha and the Omega,"[l] says
the Lord God, "who is, and who was, and
who is to come, the Almighty."[m]

John's Vision of Christ

[9]I, John, your brother and companion
in the suffering[n] and kingdom and patient
endurance[o] that are ours in Jesus, was on
the island of Patmos because of the word
of God and the testimony of Jesus. [10]On
the Lord's Day I was in the Spirit,[p] and I
heard behind me a loud voice like a trumpet,[q] [11]which said: "Write on a scroll what
you see and send it to the seven churches:[r]
to Ephesus, Smyrna, Pergamum, Thyatira,
Sardis,[s] Philadelphia and Laodicea."

[12]I turned around to see the voice that
was speaking to me. And when I turned
I saw seven golden lampstands,[t] [13]and
among the lampstands was someone like
a son of man,[a][u] dressed in a robe reaching
down to his feet and with a golden sash
around his chest.[v] [14]The hair on his head
was white like wool, as white as snow,
and his eyes were like blazing fire.[w] [15]His
feet were like bronze glowing in a furnace,[x] and his voice was like the sound
of rushing waters.[y] [16]In his right hand he
held seven stars,[z] and coming out of his
mouth was a sharp, double-edged sword.[a]
His face was like the sun shining in all its
brilliance.

[17]When I saw him, I fell at his feet[b] as
though dead. Then he placed his right
hand on me and said: "Do not be afraid. I
am the First and the Last.[c] [18]I am the Living One; I was dead,[d] and now look, I am
alive for ever and ever![e] And I hold the
keys of death and Hades.[f]

[a] *13* See Daniel 7:13.

1:8 [l] Rev 21:6 [m] Rev 4:8 **1:9** [n] Php 4:14 [o] 2Ti 2:12 **1:10** [p] Rev 4:2 [q] Rev 4:1 **1:11** [r] ver 4, 20 [s] Rev 3:1 **1:12** [t] Ex 25:31-40; Zec 4:2 **1:13** [u] Eze 1:26; Da 7:13; 10:16 [v] Da 10:5; Rev 15:6 **1:14** [w] Da 7:9; 10:6; Rev 19:12 **1:15** [x] Da 10:6 [y] Eze 43:2; Rev 14:2 **1:16** [z] Rev 2:1; 3:1 [a] Isa 49:2; Heb 4:12; Rev 2:12, 16 **1:17** [b] Eze 1:28; Da 8:17, 18 [c] Isa 41:4; 44:6; 48:12; Rev 22:13 **1:18** [d] Ro 6:9 [e] Rev 4:9, 10 [f] Rev 20:1

seven, and Persia reportedly had 12. Athens, Rome, and other cities and regions had tribes.

1:8 *the Alpha and the Omega.* Using the first and last letters of the Greek alphabet, John describes God as the first and the last (some Jewish writers did the same with the first and last letters of the Hebrew alphabet). He thus evokes God's title in Isaiah: the first and the last (Isa 41:4; 44:6; 48:12). *the Almighty.* The Greek version of the OT regularly calls the Lord of hosts "Almighty." Although Romans often called various deities "almighty," their gods remained subject to the whims of fate; Israel's God, by contrast, was sovereign over fate.

1:9–20 After completing his letter introduction (vv. 4–8; see note there), John turns to a narrative introduction; narrative introductions were common in speeches, treaties and elsewhere.

1:9 *on the island of Patmos because of the word of God and the testimony of Jesus.* Often people of lower social status were executed, enslaved or banished to the mines or to die in gladiatorial combat. On the likely view of Revelation's authorship, however, John was aged, and sometimes those in authority sentenced persons more lightly on account of their age. Only the emperor could order the harshest form of banishment; it is more likely that John was sentenced by the governor. John probably was thus exiled on Patmos but not sentenced to labor in the mines. Romans often punished people by banishing them, most frequently (to limit opportunity for escape) to islands. They often used two groups of islands in the Aegean Sea near Asia Minor. In one of these island chains, the Sporades, lay Patmos. John thus could easily receive visitors from Ephesus, just 40–50 miles (65–80 kilometers) to the northeast. Patmos had a Greek gymnasium and a cult of Artemis.

1:10 *the Lord's Day.* Some scholars contrast "the Lord's Day" here with the monthly "Lord's day" in some cities of Asia Minor, which was dedicated to venerating the emperor. *in the Spirit.* Probably suggests John's experience of inspiration (cf. Eze 2:2; 3:12–14; 11:5,24).

1:12 *seven golden lampstands.* Throughout the ancient Mediterranean world, including in Asia Minor, the seven-branched lampstand was the most common symbol of Israel and Judaism. It was thus a natural symbol for a congregation of followers of Jesus, the Jewish Messiah.

1:13–16 The goal of many Jewish mystics and apocalyptic seers was to view God on his throne, but Revelation opens with Jesus as the revealer. Here the combination of elements from different Biblical passages does not reduce Jesus to the least of the images (that of an angel). Instead it draws on various Biblical images of splendor to communicate the greatest splendor.

1:13 *someone like a son of man.* Alludes to the figure in Da 7:13–14, who is destined to reign. *robe reaching down to his feet … golden sash.* Some scholars argue that Jesus' robe and sash may recall the Biblical high priest (Ex 28:4; 39:29; Lev 8:7); but cf. also Da 10:5, relevant in this context.

1:14 *hair … white as snow.* Recalls the Ancient of Days before whom the son of man appears in Da 7:9 (the "snow" there described his clothes). *eyes … like blazing fire.* Fire was often used to depict the supernaturally flaming eyes of divine beings or angels, especially the spectacular angel in Da 10:6.

1:15 *feet … like bronze.* Connects with the magnificent angel in Da 10:6, but also the angelic living creatures in Eze 1:7; metal glowing as if in fire, as here, reflects God's own glory in Eze 1:27. *voice … like the sound of rushing waters.* In Da 10:6, the angel's voice sounds like a multitude, but the description here more closely recalls God's voice in Eze 1:24 (and Eze 43:2).

1:16 *seven stars.* See note on v. 20. *out of his mouth was a sharp, double-edged sword.* Evokes the Messianic mouth of judgment in Isa 11:4 and Jewish images of God's Word as a warrior with a sword. *face … like the sun shining in all its brilliance.* Greek texts sometimes portrayed deities shining like the sun or lightning; Jewish texts did the same for angels (cf. Rev 10:1) and others, but also for God himself.

1:17 *I fell at his feet as though dead.* Prophets often fell prostrate before divine and angelic glory (Eze 1:28; 3:23; 43:3; 44:4; Da 8:17; 10:9; also developed in Jewish tradition). *Do not be afraid.* Both in Scripture (Da 10:11–12) and in Jewish tradition, the revealer often raised prostrate people to their feet and/or told them not to be frightened. *I am the First and the Last.* This is precisely the title that identifies deity in the same context (cf. v. 8; Isa 41:4; 44:6; 48:12); Jesus opens his revelation to John by affirming his deity.

1:18 *I hold the keys of death and Hades.* In Greek literature the dead came "to the gates of Hades"; Scripture described them as "the gates of death" (Ps 9:13; 107:18), sometimes translated in the Greek version of the OT as the "gates of Hades" (as in Job 38:17; Isa 38:10). Egyptians

19"Write, therefore, what you have seen,
what is now and what will take place later. 20The mystery of the seven stars that
you saw in my right hand and of the sev-
en golden lampstands[g] is this: The seven
stars are the angels[a] of the seven churches,[h] and the seven lampstands are the sev-
en churches.[i]

To the Church in Ephesus

2 "To the angel[b] of the church in Ephesus write:

These are the words of him who
holds the seven stars in his right
hand[j] and walks among the seven
golden lampstands.[k] 2I know your
deeds,[l] your hard work and your perseverance. I know that you cannot
tolerate wicked people, that you have
tested[m] those who claim to be apostles but are not, and have found them
false.[n] 3You have persevered and have
endured hardships for my name,[o] and
have not grown weary.
4Yet I hold this against you: You
have forsaken the love you had at
first.[p] 5Consider how far you have
fallen! Repent[q] and do the things you
did at first. If you do not repent, I will
come to you and remove your lampstand[r] from its place. 6But you have
this in your favor: You hate the practices of the Nicolaitans,[s] which I also
hate.
7Whoever has ears, let them hear[t]
what the Spirit says to the churches.
To the one who is victorious, I will
give the right to eat from the tree
of life,[u] which is in the paradise[v] of
God.

To the Church in Smyrna

8"To the angel of the church in Smyrna[w]
write:

These are the words of him who
is the First and the Last,[x] who died

1:20 [g] Zec 4:2 [h] ver 4, 11 [i] Mt 5:14, 15 **2:1** [j] Rev 1:16 [k] Rev 1:12, 13 **2:2** [l] Rev 3:1, 8, 15 [m] 1Jn 4:1 [n] 2Co 11:13 **2:3** [o] Jn 15:21 **2:4** [p] Mt 24:12 **2:5** [q] ver 16, 22 [r] Rev 1:20 **2:6** [s] ver 15 **2:7** [t] Mt 11:15; Rev 3:6, 13, 22 [u] Ge 2:9; Rev 22:2, 14, 19 [v] Lk 23:43 **2:8** [w] Rev 1:11 [x] Rev 1:17

[a] 20 Or *messengers* [b] 1 Or *messenger*; also in verses 8, 12 and 18

believed that their afterlife-god Anubis held the keys to this underworld; Greeks assigned control over the house of Hades to their god of that realm, Hades. By contrast, Jewish sources assigned the keys of death and Hades exclusively to the one true God.

1:19 *what is now and what will take place later.* Greeks thought their gods could reveal past, present and future, but in Jewish tradition, only the true God revealed these matters (cf. Isa 42:9; 48:5–7).

1:20 *The mystery … is this.* Both in Scripture (Da 2:27–30,47) and apocalyptic traditions, God often revealed mysteries. *seven stars.* Whereas Gentiles often thought of stars as divine, Jewish observers usually considered them angels. Because of widespread interest in astrology in antiquity, many Gentiles and even many Jews felt that stars controlled the Gentiles' future. Here the stars are in Jesus' hand. Jewish tradition recognized guardian angels of nations (based partly on Da 10:13,20–21) and of individuals; here the idea seems to be guardian angels of churches. *seven lampstands.* See note on 1:12.

2:1 *Ephesus.* The region's most prominent city, more powerful than Pergamum politically and more favored than Smyrna for the imperial cult. It was also the nearest of the seven cities to Patmos (see notes on 1:4,9). Ephesus had a large Jewish community (Ac 19:8–9), but was mostly pagan. The first emperor, Augustus, had allowed Ephesus to build two temples in his honor, and the current ruler, Domitian, had named the city "guardian" of the imperial cult, making it the foremost center of the imperial cult in Roman Asia. Ephesus, in fact, hosted a new cult of the emperors that had opened about five years before Revelation was written. Ephesus was also known for the practice of magic (Ac 19:13–19) and, more than any other religious issue, the worship of Artemis (Ac 19:23–40). *seven stars.* See note on 1:20. *seven golden lampstands.* See note on 1:12.

2:2 *tested those who claim to be apostles but are not.* False teaching posed a major danger in Ephesus in Paul's day (Ac 20:17,29–30; 1Ti 1:3–7; 2Ti 1:15), but their discernment had improved. (Their improved discernment is also reported by Syrian bishop Ignatius in the early second century.)

2:4 *You have forsaken the love you had at first.* If the love is for God, cf. Jer 2:2; if for fellow believers, cf. the contrast with "hate" in v. 6; it might mean for both.

2:5 *I will … remove your lampstand from its place.* Ironically, even the city of Ephesus eventually had to relocate a few miles/kilometers away because the Cayster River kept silting up the harbor. The primary threat expressed in this verse, however, is to the church: the removal of its lampstand would mean that it would cease to exist as a church — whatever else, if anything, it might continue to be.

2:6 *Nicolaitans.* Today we can only guess at their identity. Some nearly a century after Revelation associated them with Nicolas of Antioch (Ac 6:5); others associate them with followers of "Balaam" (Rev 2:14–15).

2:7 *Whoever has ears, let them hear what the Spirit says.* For this invitation to hear, cf. Jesus' words in Mk 4:9,23. Because Jewish tradition associated the Spirit especially with prophetic inspiration (cf. Nu 11:25–26, 29; Ne 9:30; Zec 7:12), it is no surprise that early Christian prophecy was sometimes identified with the speaking of the Spirit (Ac 21:11). *tree of life.* Jewish texts often used it to symbolize various things associated with righteousness. Some texts, however, used it as here — a source of eternal life (Rev 22:2; cf. Ge 3:22). *paradise.* A term used in the common Greek translation of the OT for gardens but especially the Garden of Eden (Ge 2:8–16; 3:1–24). Many Jewish sources portrayed the destiny of the righteous as Eden, and of the wicked as Gehenna. The image of gardens would be familiar in Asia Minor, including in Ephesus, where the garden estates of the Ephesian cult of Artemis included some tree-shrines.

2:8–11 Ancient writers often underlined points through a series of contrasts. In this letter, Jesus is "the First and the Last, who died and came to life again" (v. 8). Those in poverty prove rich; those who slander them "say they are Jews and are not" (v. 9), and if they prove "faithful, even to the point of death" (v. 10), they will receive the crown of life.

2:8 *Smyrna.* Along with Pergamum (v. 12), Smyrna competed (usually unsuccessfully) with Ephesus for preeminence. Smyrna was the second city in Asia permitted to establish an imperial cult. *who died and came to life again.*

and came to life again.[y] 9 I know
your afflictions and your poverty—
yet you are rich![z] I know about the
slander of those who say they are
Jews and are not,[a] but are a synagogue of Satan.[b] 10 Do not be afraid
of what you are about to suffer. I tell
you, the devil will put some of you
in prison to test you,[c] and you will
suffer persecution for ten days.[d] Be
faithful,[e] even to the point of death,
and I will give you life as your victor's crown.
11 Whoever has ears, let them hear
what the Spirit says to the churches.
The one who is victorious will not be
hurt at all by the second death.[f]

To the Church in Pergamum

12 "To the angel of the church in Pergamum[g] write:
These are the words of him who
has the sharp, double-edged sword.[h]
13 I know where you live—where Satan has his throne. Yet you remain
true to my name. You did not renounce your faith in me,[i] not even in
the days of Antipas, my faithful witness, who was put to death in your
city—where Satan lives.[j]
14 Nevertheless, I have a few things
against you:[k] There are some among
you who hold to the teaching of Balaam,[l] who taught Balak to entice the
Israelites to sin so that they ate food
sacrificed to idols and committed sexual immorality.[m] 15 Likewise, you also
have those who hold to the teaching
of the Nicolaitans.[n] 16 Repent therefore! Otherwise, I will soon come to
you and will fight against them with
the sword of my mouth.[o]

2:8 [y] Rev 1:18
2:9 [z] Jas 2:5
[a] Rev 3:9
[b] Mt 4:10
2:10 [c] Rev 3:10
[d] Da 1:12, 14
[e] ver 13
2:11 [f] Rev 20:6, 14; 21:8
2:12 [g] Rev 1:11
[h] Rev 1:16
2:13 [i] Rev 14:12
[j] ver 9, 24
2:14 [k] ver 20
[l] 2Pe 2:15
[m] 1Co 6:13
2:15 [n] ver 6
2:16 [o] 2Th 2:8; Rev 1:16

Some commentators connect the emphasis on resurrection here with Smyrna's recovery centuries earlier, sometimes compared with a sort of resurrection; more important is the relevance to Christians who may soon face death (v. 10).

2:9 *slander of those who say they are Jews and are not.* Jews were exempt from worshiping the emperor; if Jesus' followers became unwelcome in the synagogues, however, they became vulnerable to accusations of disloyalty against Rome. Smyrna's Jewish community apparently remained on good terms with their city, but they could not afford to take chances. The Judean war against Rome two decades earlier resulted in a special tax Jews everywhere in the empire had to pay. Many Asian Jewish leaders thus could have grown uncomfortable with any association with prophetic, Messianic movements like the movement that followed Jesus. (Later, in the early second century, some Jewish accusers participated in denouncing Polycarp, bishop of Smyrna and a disciple of the apostle John, at Polycarp's execution.) Normally Roman officials tried cases only if accusers brought them forward. Such slander could be in view here (cf. earlier accusations in Ac 13:50; 14:2,19; 17:5; 18:12; 24:5; 1Th 2:14–15). Commentators often envision a similar background for the Gospel of John. *a synagogue of Satan.* Some other Jews (especially those who wrote the Dead Sea Scrolls) condemned the rest of Israel as apostate, calling them even "the congregation of Satan." John applies this harsh language only to the believers' direct opponents. This is not a model for how Gentile Christians should address synagogues; this was the sort of intra-Jewish challenge that characterized strong debates about Jewish identity among various competing Jewish groups in this period.

2:10 *put some of you in prison to test you.* People were normally imprisoned until a trial concluded (followed by either release or punishment). *ten days.* People could languish in prison for long periods of time, but here the impending execution sounds swift. Daniel and his colleagues were tested for ten days (Da 1:12–14), and then exalted; the Smyrnean believers will be exalted through martyrdom. *Be faithful, even to the point of death, and I will give you life as your victor's crown.* Jewish traditions sometimes described martyrs as faithful in facing death and promised them eternal life and a crown of victory. *crown.* Jewish tradition also described other eternal rewards as crowns; for the image, borrowed from the garland that was the normal prize for athletic victories, see the article "Athletic Imagery in 1 Corinthians 9," p. 2000. In this passage the "crown" might also have a secondary purpose, a subtle contrast with Smyrna's claims to power: Smyrna's citadel was often compared with a crown, and nearly 20 percent of inscriptions from earlier centuries contain this emblem.

2:11 *second death.* Some other Jewish texts depict the horror of the second death, which could refer to annihilation or resurrection for eternal torment. Revelation apparently depicts the harsher option: the second death (20:6) is the lake of fire (20:14; 21:8), which apparently involves eternal torment (20:10).

2:12 *Pergamum.* A famous and prosperous city with a population often estimated between 100,000 and 200,000 inhabitants. Because they allied themselves with Rome's imperial ambitions in the East early, they had secured special favor with Rome. *sword.* Cf. 1:16; might contrast with the Roman government's "right of the sword," i.e., to execute capital punishment; Jesus, not the governor, holds the power of life and death (cf. 1:18). Because this letter focuses on false teachers, however, the sword refers especially to Jesus battling these teachers (vv. 15–16). The Biblical prophets often used the image for the judgment of war.

2:13 *where Satan has his throne.* Some associate Satan's throne in Pergamum with the healing cult of Asclepius there (symbolized by a serpent); more often scholars think of the famous, massive, throne-like altar of "Zeus the Savior." Likeliest of all suggestions so far is the imperial cult; anyone visiting the city would immediately see the old temple of Augustus on Pergamum's citadel. Among the proposed associations of the throne here, the cult of the emperor would also be the likeliest cause of persecution.

2:14 *Balaam.* Jesus may refer to the original Balaam whose teaching they follow (cf. 2Pe 2:15; Jude 11), or this may be a nickname for a local false prophet (as in v. 20), evoking the Biblical Balaam's gravest offense. He led Israel into sin in order to remove them from God's favor, recognizing that this was the only way to destroy them (Nu 31:16). The sins into which he led Israel were sexual immorality and food offered to idols (Nu 25:1–2), sins that remained temptations in pagan society (1Co 10:7–8). Balaam was ultimately killed for his treachery (Nu 31:8;

17 Whoever has ears, let them hear
what the Spirit says to the churches.
To the one who is victorious, I will
give some of the hidden manna.[p]
I will also give that person a white
stone with a new name[q] written on
it, known only to the one who receives it.[r]

To the Church in Thyatira

18 "To the angel of the church in Thyatira[s]
write:

These are the words of the Son of
God, whose eyes are like blazing fire
and whose feet are like burnished
bronze.[t] 19 I know your deeds,[u] your
love and faith, your service and perseverance, and that you are now doing more than you did at first.
20 Nevertheless, I have this against
you: You tolerate that woman Jezebel,[v] who calls herself a prophet. By
her teaching she misleads my servants
into sexual immorality and the eating
of food sacrificed to idols. 21 I have giv-
en her time[w] to repent of her immorality, but she is unwilling.[x] 22 So I will
cast her on a bed of suffering, and I
will make those who commit adultery[y]
with her suffer intensely, unless they
repent of her ways. 23 I will strike her
children dead. Then all the churches
will know that I am he who searches hearts and minds,[z] and I will repay
each of you according to your deeds.
24 Now I say to the rest of you in
Thyatira, to you who do not hold to
her teaching and have not learned
Satan's so-called deep secrets, 'I will
not impose any other burden on you,[a]
25 except to hold on to what you have[b]
until I come.'

2:17 [p] Jn 6:49, 50 [q] Isa 62:2 [r] Rev 19:12 **2:18** [s] Rev 1:11 [t] Rev 1:14, 15 **2:19** [u] ver 2
2:20 [v] 1Ki 16:31; 21:25; 2Ki 9:7 **2:21** [w] Ro 2:4 [x] Rev 9:20 **2:22** [y] Rev 17:2; 18:9 **2:23** [z] 1Sa 16:7; Jer 11:20; Ac 1:24; Ro 8:27 **2:24** [a] Ac 15:28 **2:25** [b] Rev 3:11

Jos 13:22). *food sacrificed to idols.* By the early second century, Roman officials recognized Christian influence in refusal to eat sacrificial meat, and actively repressed Christians for this. See the article "Sacrificed Food," p. 1997. *sexual immorality.* Rife in Greek-influenced cities in the first century (see the article "Prostitution and Sexual Immorality," p. 1990). Some, however, suggest a figurative use here (cf. 17:1,15–16); Scripture often used the image for spiritual unfaithfulness (e.g., Jer 3:9; 13:27; Eze 16:15–36; 23:7–35; Hos 1:2; 4:12; 5:4).
2:17 *hidden manna.* Alludes to a Jewish tradition that the temple vessels, the ark of the covenant and the manna once deposited in the ark would be restored in the Messianic era (in contrast to Jer 3:16). John thinks not of the earthly ark of the covenant but of the heavenly one (Rev 11:19), and of God's provision in the present world (cf. 12:6,14) and the future one (7:17; 22:2). This promised manna contrasts starkly with food sacrificed to idols (v. 14). Cf. note on Jn 6:35. *white stone with a new name written on it.* The meaning of the white stone is debated, because people used stones in various symbolic ways; often such a *tessera* or small block of stone or ivory would contain inscribed words or symbols. *white.* Often symbolized purity and life; also, though most building materials in Pergamum were of dark brown granite, that city used white marble for its inscriptions. Some scholars contrast here a black stone, the sacred totem of the Phrygian Mother Goddess. Some compare pebbles as admission tokens for public assemblies or festivities (here, manna at the Messianic banquet; cf. 7:9; 19:9). Others compare jurors voting for acquittal with a white stone, implying here promised vindication (cf. v. 13). *new name.* Alludes to Isa 56:5 and especially Isa 62:2, which promise that God will give his people a new name, removing their shame (Isa 62:4). This would fit the time of the new Jerusalem and new creation (Isa 65:15–19).
2:18 *Thyatira.* Like Sardis (3:1), Thyatira was in the region of Lydia. Asia hailed emperors as deities and saviors; an emperor was also considered the son of a god, the previous emperor. (Some scholars further suggest a contrast with Zeus's son Apollo, a patron deity of Thyatira with whom some scholars link deified emperors.) *Son of God.* This is Revelation's only use of this title; still, it was a common title for Jesus (e.g., Jn 20:31; 1Jn 4:15). *burnished bronze.* Jesus also reminds Thyatiran hearers of his feet like bronze (1:15); metalworking was a prominent industry in Thyatira, so its residents would be familiar with the image of glowing bronze.
2:20 *Jezebel.* A nickname for a false prophetess, evoking the Biblical Jezebel's sin of turning Israel away from God. *calls herself a prophet.* The earlier Jezebel was not a prophet, but she sponsored 850 false prophets (1Ki 18:19) and tried to kill God's true prophets (1Ki 18:13; 19:2). *she misleads my servants into sexual immorality.* See note on v. 14. Jezebel is never accused of literal sexual immorality, but she sponsored its spiritual equivalent by leading Israel away from its God (2Ki 9:22, which also compares her activity with witchcraft; cf. Rev 9:21; 18:23). It is debated whether the sexual immorality of Thyatira's Jezebel is literal (cf. 17:2,4,18; 18:3; 19:2; Jer 13:27; Eze 16:25), since the children of v. 23 are undoubtedly not her literal children (see note on v. 23). Certainly literal sexual immorality was widespread in the culture (cf. 9:21; 21:8; 1Co 10:7–8); both elements may be present, but even if the image is wholly figurative, it plays on the moral horror with which Jesus' movement and Judaism viewed literal sexual immorality. *eating of food sacrificed to idols.* See note on v. 14. If believers in Pergamum risked persecution to avoid idolatry, Thyatiran believers may have faced economic risks. Thyatira's economy depended heavily on merchants, craftspeople and their guilds (cf. also Ac 16:14). Refusing to join the guild of one's trade could prove economically disastrous, but guild meetings included a common meal first dedicated to the guild's patron deity. To refuse to share the meal was tantamount to refusing connection with the other members of the guild, whom one needed for economic survival. Aspects of the imperial cult also eventually affected most trade guilds.
2:22 *bed.* Both a place for intercourse and a place where someone very sick remained. God sometimes used sickness as a judgment (e.g., Ex 9:10; 32:35; Dt 28:21–22,27,35; 2Ch 26:19–23).
2:23 *strike her children dead.* Jezebel's children are presumably her disciples, perhaps members of house churches under her influence. *I am he who searches hearts and minds.* In the OT and Jewish tradition, God is the one who searches hearts and minds (e.g., 1Ch 28:9; Ps 7:9). *I will repay each of you according to your deeds.* See note on 22:12.
2:24 *deep secrets.* Language such as this could be used for profound truths associated with divine wisdom and/or revelations; here it is false revelation.

REVELATION 2:1 — 3:22

LETTERS TO THE SEVEN CHURCHES

Like all letters that were not carried by imperial couriers, the book of Revelation would be carried by travelers or (in this case) personal messengers; apart from official business of the empire, no public postal service existed. The letters to the seven churches are "prophetic letters," a sort of writing that appeared earlier in the Bible (2Ch 21:12 – 15; Jer 29), early Jewish literature, and in some ancient Near Eastern sources.

Given the authority of these letters, they resemble in one respect edicts of emperors. Yet they resemble even more closely the Biblical format of prophecies concerning various peoples (Isa 13 – 22; Jer 46 – 51; Eze 25 – 32; Am 1 – 2), here applied more specifically to God's people dispersed in different cities (cf. Mic 1:6 – 16). Each letter is a prophetic message from Jesus (e.g., Rev 2:1) through the Spirit (e.g., Rev 2:7) who is inspiring John (Rev 1:10). The phrase "these are the words" (Rev 2:1) is identical with the standard messenger formula in the Biblical prophets (in the Greek translation of the OT; also Ac 21:11). Each letter follows a similar pattern:

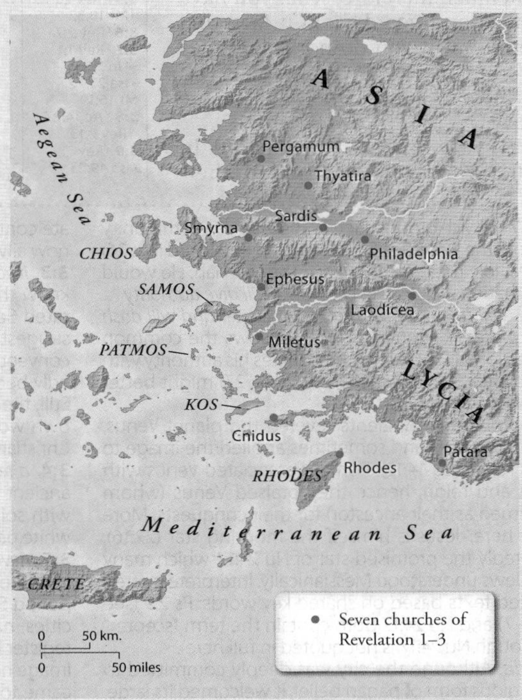

- To the angel of the church in (a city) write
- Jesus (depicted in glory, often in terms from Rev 1:13 – 18) says
- I know (in most instances some praise is offered)
- Yet (where relevant) I hold this against you
- Whoever has ears, let them hear what the Spirit says to the churches
- To the one who is victorious (a promise)

Being victorious was often an athletic image (see "crown" in the note on Rev 2:10) and a military one (as in Rev 13:7; 17:14). That the message is from Jesus, following the same form as earlier Biblical messages from God, plainly implies Jesus' deity. Even Gentiles believed that inspired messages came from gods (or, more commonly in a later period, deified heroes). Indeed, the descriptions of Jesus' glory formally resemble the sort of epithets with which Greeks often addressed their deities. ◆

26To the one who is victorious and
does my will to the end, I will give
authority over the nations[c]— 27that
one 'will rule them with an iron scepter[d] and will dash them to pieces like
pottery'[a][e]—just as I have received
authority from my Father. 28I will
also give that one the morning star.[f]
29Whoever has ears, let them hear[g]
what the Spirit says to the churches.

To the Church in Sardis

3 "To the angel[b] of the church in Sardis
write:

These are the words of him who
holds the seven spirits[c][h] of God and
the seven stars.[i] I know your deeds;[j]
you have a reputation of being
alive, but you are dead.[k] 2Wake up!
Strengthen what remains and is about
to die, for I have found your deeds
unfinished in the sight of my God.
3Remember, therefore, what you have
received and heard; hold it fast, and
repent.[l] But if you do not wake up, I
will come like a thief,[m] and you will
not know at what time I will come
to you.

4Yet you have a few people in
Sardis who have not soiled their
clothes.[n] They will walk with me,
dressed in white,[o] for they are worthy. 5The one who is victorious will,
like them, be dressed in white. I will
never blot out the name of that person from the book of life,[p] but will
acknowledge that name before my
Father[q] and his angels. 6Whoever has
ears, let them hear[r] what the Spirit
says to the churches.

To the Church in Philadelphia

7"To the angel of the church in Philadelphia[s] write:

These are the words of him who is
holy and true,[t] who holds the key of
David.[u] What he opens no one can
shut, and what he shuts no one can
open. 8I know your deeds. See, I have
placed before you an open door[v] that
no one can shut. I know that you
have little strength, yet you have kept
my word and have not denied my
name.[w] 9I will make those who are of
the synagogue of Satan,[x] who claim
to be Jews though they are not, but
are liars—I will make them come and
fall down at your feet[y] and acknowl-

2:26 [c] Ps 2:8; Rev 3:21 **2:27** [d] Rev 12:5 [e] Isa 30:14; Jer 19:11 **2:28** [f] Rev 22:16 **2:29** [g] ver 7 **3:1** [h] Rev 1:4 [i] Rev 1:16 [j] Rev 2:2 [k] 1Ti 5:6 **3:3** [l] Rev 2:5 [m] 2Pe 3:10 **3:4** [n] Jude 23 [o] Rev 4:4; 6:11; 7:9, 13, 14 **3:5** [p] Rev 20:12 [q] Mt 10:32 **3:6** [r] Rev 2:7 **3:7** [s] Rev 1:11 [t] 1Jn 5:20 [u] Isa 22:22; Mt 16:19 **3:8** [v] Ac 14:27 [w] Rev 2:13 **3:9** [x] Rev 2:9 [y] Isa 49:23

[a] *27* Psalm 2:9 [b] *1* Or *messenger*; also in verses 7 and 14 [c] *1* That is, the sevenfold Spirit

2:26–27 Jewish groups such as the Qumran community who wrote the Dead Sea Scrolls applied Ps 2 (cited in v. 26) to the Davidic ruler *par excellence*, the Messiah. He would rule the nations (cf. Ps 2:8; Da 7:14). *I will give authority ... that one 'will rule them with an iron scepter and will dash them to pieces like pottery.'* Closely follows the common Greek version of Ps 2:9. Jesus thus shares his authority with his people (cf. Da 7:13–14,22). "Rule" (v. 27) might better be translated "shepherd."

2:28 *morning star.* Ancients revered the planet Venus, the "morning star," and sometimes applied the image to glorious rulers (Isa 14:12). Romans associated Venus with triumph and reign, hence they praised Venus (whom they claimed as their ancestor) for their conquests. More relevant here, Jesus is himself the morning star (22:16), undoubtedly the promised star of Nu 24:17, which many ancient Jews understood Messianically. Interpreters often connected texts based on shared key words; Ps 2:9 (see Rev 2:6–7) and Nu 24:17 both contain the term "scepter" (even though Nu 24:17 is not quoted in full here).

3:1 *Sardis.* Although the city was deeply committed to its prestigious form of pagan belief, it welcomed its large, monotheistic Jewish community. Local Jews later secured some of the most valued land in the city to build one of the largest synagogues in antiquity, roughly the length of a football field. Apparently Christians too were tolerated here. *seven spirits.* See note on 1:4. *seven stars.* See note on 1:20. *reputation of being alive, but you are dead.* Scholars suggest various backgrounds for this statement: some local religion focused on seasonal renewal of life; Sardians could see both their Acropolis and Necropolis (the latter a burial place for the dead); and, most plausibly, a contrast with their famous past under Croesus. The most important function of the contrast, however, is a deliberate contrast with the Lord himself, who was dead and is now alive (1:18; 2:8).

3:3 *if you do not wake up, I will come like a thief.* Sardians knew their local history. An earthquake at night devastated Sardis about eight decades earlier. Scholars also suggest that conquerors had never overtaken Sardis by conventional war, but had twice conquered it unexpectedly because the guards had failed to watch adequately. Still, the coming "like a thief" most directly evokes Jesus' own words (Mt 24:43; Lk 12:39) often repeated by early Christians (Rev 16:15; 1Th 5:2; 2Pe 3:10).

3:4 *a few people ... who have not soiled their clothes.* In ancient temples, worshipers dared not approach deities with soiled clothes; the normal apparel in temples was white or linen.

3:5 *never blot out the name of that person from the book of life.* Cities in Asia Minor had citizen-registers; in an earlier period Sardis was known for its royal archives. In some cities, names of errant citizens were deleted from the register immediately prior to their execution. *blot out.* The image here most directly stems from Ex 32:32–33, which came to be applied to a heavenly book of life (Ps 69:28; Da 12:1), especially in ancient Jewish writings (cf. also Lk 10:20; Php 4:3).

3:7 *holds the key of David.* Jesus is not only the "root of David" (5:5; 22:16), but also subsumes under his kingship the full role of chief steward of the royal household. This official controlled entrance into the royal palace, a position of the highest authority in the kingdom (Isa 22:15–25, especially v. 22; cf. Is 45:1–2; Eze 44:2). As such Jesus—not the synagogue leaders in v. 9—determines who may enter his household and who may not.

3:9 *synagogue of Satan.* Synagogue leaders in Philadelphia, wrongly claiming that they act for Israel's God, have

edge that I have loved you.[z] [10]Since you have kept my command to endure patiently, I will also keep you[a] from the hour of trial that is going to come on the whole world to test[b] the inhabitants of the earth.[c]

[11]I am coming soon. Hold on to what you have,[d] so that no one will take your crown.[e] [12]The one who is victorious I will make a pillar[f] in the temple of my God. Never again will they leave it. I will write on them the name of my God[g] and the name of the city of my God, the new Jerusalem,[h] which is coming down out of heaven from my God; and I will also write on them my new name. [13]Whoever has ears, let them hear what the Spirit says to the churches.

To the Church in Laodicea

[14]"To the angel of the church in Laodicea write:

These are the words of the Amen, the faithful and true witness, the ruler of God's creation.[i] [15]I know your deeds, that you are neither cold nor hot.[j] I wish you were either one or the other! [16]So, because you are lukewarm—neither hot nor cold—I am about to spit you out of my mouth. [17]You say, 'I am rich; I have acquired wealth and do not need a thing.'[k] But you do not realize that you are wretched, pitiful, poor, blind and naked. [18]I counsel you to buy from me gold refined in the fire, so you can become rich; and white clothes to wear, so you can cover your shameful nakedness;[l] and salve to put on your eyes, so you can see.

[19]Those whom I love I rebuke and discipline.[m] So be earnest and repent.[n] [20]Here I am! I stand at the door[o] and knock. If anyone hears my voice and opens the door,[p] I will come in[q] and eat with that person, and they with me.

[21]To the one who is victorious, I will give the right to sit with me on my throne,[r] just as I was victorious[s] and sat down with my Father on his throne. [22]Whoever has ears, let them hear[t] what the Spirit says to the churches."

3:9 [z] Isa 43:4
3:10 [a] 2Pe 2:9 [b] Rev 2:10 [c] Rev 6:10; 17:8
3:11 [d] Rev 2:25 [e] Rev 2:10
3:12 [f] Gal 2:9 [g] Rev 14:1; 22:4 [h] Rev 21:2, 10
3:14 [i] Col 1:16, 18
3:15 [j] Ro 12:11
3:17 [k] Hos 12:8; 1Co 4:8
3:18 [l] Rev 16:15
3:19 [m] Pr 3:12; Heb 12:5,6 [n] Rev 2:5
3:20 [o] Mt 24:33 [p] Lk 12:36 [q] Jn 14:23
3:21 [r] Mt 19:28 [s] Rev 5:5
3:22 [t] Rev 2:7

marginalized Jewish believers in their synagogue (see note on 2:9). *fall down at your feet.* The Biblical prophets had promised God's people that the Gentiles would bow down to them (Isa 60:14; cf. Isa 45:14; 49:23; others in Isa 45:23; 49:7; 66:23), as Jewish tradition also recognized (but here applied to hostile Jews). *acknowledge that I have loved you.* Here the leaders must recognize that God has chosen these believers among his people (Isa 49:7) and that he has loved them (Isa 43:4; especially Mal 1:2).

3:11 *crown.* See note on 2:10.

3:12 *a pillar in the temple of my God.* Though expelled from a synagogue, the believers remained part of God's temple. This verse recalls Isa 56:5, in which foreigners and eunuchs, excluded from the traditional temple (Dt 23:1; see note on Mk 11:16), would have a place and an eternal name within God's house, better than that of Israelites. Everyone would expect the new temple to include pillars (Eze 40:8—41:3) just as the old one did (Ex 27:9–17; 38:10–28; 1Ki 7:2–6,15–22). Personified pillars specifically functioned as an image of strength or blessing in antiquity, including in Scripture (Ps 144:12; Jer 1:18; Gal 2:9). Ancient pillars often had honorary inscriptions on them. *name of my God and the name of the city of my God ... my new name.* In the first century, Philadelphia adopted two new names, but other factors are more relevant for understanding the promise here. God promised his people a new name (Isa 62:2; see note on Rev 2:17) and emphasized the importance of the new Jerusalem's name (Jer 33:16; Eze 48:35).

3:14 *Laodicea.* See the article "Laodicea," p. 2228. *ruler.* The Greek term also often means "beginning." Both Greek and Jewish religions sometimes describe God or supreme deities as "First" and occasionally called some deities "the firstborn"; the emperor also claimed to be "first" among equals, the "equality" part being a rhetorical fiction. More relevant is the Biblical background; elsewhere in Revelation "beginning" is an explicitly divine title linked with "first" (21:6; 22:13), a clear divine title in Isa 41:4; 44:6; 48:12.

3:15 *neither cold nor hot.* Ancient sources complain that Laodicea's water was full of sediment. (Their nicest comment was simply that it was not as bad as that of Hierapolis; Strabo, *Geography* 13.4.14.) See the article "Laodicea," p. 2228. The water was also lukewarm by the time it arrived in Laodicea, though lukewarm water could always be heated. Mildly hot water was useful for bathing, and waters at hot springs such as those at nearby Hierapolis were considered helpful for relieving ailments. Cold water was useful for drinking, and available in nearby locations like Colossae. Most people preferred cold drinks, but hot drinks were also common at banquets. When speaking of water, both hot and cold are thus useful and pleasant. The point of lukewarm water, by contrast, is simply that it was unpleasant, useless, and disgusting—thus Jesus spits it out (v. 16).

3:17 *I have acquired wealth and do not need a thing.* Laodicea was a prosperous community and banking center. Apparently local believers have absorbed local values, especially pride (cf. Hos 12:8). Ancient writers appreciated irony: in vv. 17–18 the matters in which they pride themselves materially they lack spiritually. *blind.* For spiritual blindness, see, e.g., Isa 6:10; 29:9; 42:19; 43:8; 56:10; Jer 5:21; Eze 12:2.

3:18 *white clothes to wear ... salve to put on your eyes.* The community produced notable textiles, including cloth and carpets woven from black wool. They had a local medical establishment, and eye salve was produced in the region, although they also looked to healing deities for help.

3:19 *Those whom I love I rebuke and discipline.* See Pr 3:12.

3:20 *I stand at the door and knock.* Even an acquaintance would invite in for food a neighbor who was knocking. *I will come in and eat with that person.* Sharing a meal established a covenant relationship. Present fellowship could foreshadow the expected Messianic banquet (19:9; Isa 25:6).

3:21 *sit with me on my throne.* Cf. Da 7:22,27; see note on Eph 2:6.

REVELATION 3:14 – 22

LAODICEA

The city of Laodicea lay in Phrygia's Lycus Valley, ten miles (16 kilometers) west of Colossae (Col 2:1; 4:15 – 16) and six miles (10 kilometers) south of Hierapolis (Col 4:13). Pagan worship, especially of Zeus but also of numerous other deities (such as Dionysus, Helios, Hera, and Athena), flourished there. A significant Jewish community lived in Phrygia (Ac 13:14 – 50; 14:1 – 5,19), but they seem to have blended into Greek culture in many respects.

Laodicea boasted great resources (see notes on Rev 3:17 – 18), but while the Laodicean Christians likely shared their Laodicean neighbors' pride over their self-sufficiency in many respects, they presumably also shared a common dislike for their water supply (Rev 3:15 – 16).

Laodicea was known as a wealthy banking center, and it had flourished especially under the dynasty of emperors ruling in John's day. The city hosted gladiatorial games and boasted a theater. More important, it was the capital of the Cibryatic convention, which included at least 25 towns. Local civic pride grew quite fierce in some cities of Asia, and Laodicea vied for power with its primary rival in Phrygia, namely Antioch. So arrogant was Laodicea about its wealth that when the emperor proposed to help rebuild Laodicea along with other Asian cities destroyed by an earthquake in AD 60, Laodicea refused the funds.

Calcified water pipes in the remains at Laodicea.
Mark Wilson

Laodicea's water was full of sediment. The terra cotta pipes of Laodicea's water tower are full of thick lime deposits; likewise, lime deposits on the waterfall cliff just opposite Laodicea provided a constant visible reminder of their water problems. Laodicea lacked its own water supply, having no direct access to the cold water of the mountains or the hot water of the nearby springs in Hierapolis to the north. In contrast to its claims to self-sufficiency (Rev 3:17), it had to pipe in its water from the south; though much of the aqueduct from the south was underground, nearer the city it came through stone barrel pipes, thus remaining vulnerable to any intended besiegers who wished to cut off the city's water supply. More important for this passage, any water piped into Laodicea had grown lukewarm by the time of its arrival. ◆

The Throne in Heaven

4 After this I looked, and there before
me was a door standing open in heav-
en. And the voice I had first heard speaking to me like a trumpet[u] said, "Come up
here,[v] and I will show you what must take
place after this."[w] 2At once I was in the
Spirit,[x] and there before me was a throne
in heaven[y] with someone sitting on it.
3And the one who sat there had the appearance of jasper and ruby. A rainbow[z]
that shone like an emerald encircled the
throne. 4Surrounding the throne were
twenty-four other thrones, and seated on
them were twenty-four elders.[a] They were
dressed in white[b] and had crowns of gold
on their heads. 5From the throne came
flashes of lightning, rumblings and peals
of thunder.[c] In front of the throne, seven
lamps[d] were blazing. These are the sev-
en spirits[a][e] of God. 6Also in front of the
throne there was what looked like a sea of
glass,[f] clear as crystal.

In the center, around the throne, were
four living creatures,[g] and they were covered with eyes, in front and in back. 7The
first living creature was like a lion, the second was like an ox, the third had a face
like a man, the fourth was like a flying
eagle.[h] 8Each of the four living creatures
had six wings[i] and was covered with eyes
all around, even under its wings. Day and
night they never stop saying:

> " 'Holy, holy, holy
> is the Lord God Almighty,'[b][j]
> who was, and is, and is to come."[k]

4:1 [u] Rev 1:10 [v] Rev 11:12 [w] Rev 1:19 **4:2** [x] Rev 1:10 [y] Isa 6:1; Eze 1:26-28; Da 7:9 **4:3** [z] Eze 1:28 **4:4** [a] Rev 11:16 [b] Rev 3:4,5 **4:5** [c] Rev 8:5; 16:18 [d] Zec 4:2 [e] Rev 1:4 **4:6** [f] Rev 15:2 [g] Eze 1:5 **4:7** [h] Eze 1:10; 10:14 **4:8** [i] Isa 6:2 [j] Isa 6:3; Rev 1:8 [k] Rev 1:4

[a] 5 That is, the sevenfold Spirit [b] 8 Isaiah 6:3

4:1 *I looked.* Ezekiel (e.g., Eze 1:4,15; 2:9; 8:2,7,10; 44:4), Daniel (Da 8:3,15; 10:5; 12:5) and subsequent visionary texts often included phrases such as (lit. here), "I looked, and behold." *a door standing open in heaven.* Open heavens sometimes accompany theophanies and other revelations in Scripture (Eze 1:1) and Jewish apocalyptic sources. *Come up here.* Evokes God's summons to Moses to receive his revelation (Ex 19:20,24; 24:12; 34:2) in the context of Scripture's first throne vision (Ex 24:9 – 12). Jewish tradition elaborated Moses' ascent (all the way to heaven) and spoke of others called to heaven in visions. Cf. John's visionary language in Rev 17:1; 21:9.

4:2 *a throne in heaven with someone sitting on it.* Jewish apocalyptic writings focused on and developed the throne visions of Ezekiel and Isaiah; many mystics regarded such visions as their goal. Most peoples envisioned chief deities as enthroned, and God is enthroned in Biblical visions (1Ki 22:19; Isa 6:1; Eze 1:26; 10:1). Apocalyptic texts often describe the visionary's dangerous journey through various heavenly gates to reach God's throne. By contrast, yet like earlier Biblical prophets, John is simply transported there by God's sovereign summons (v. 1) and the Spirit's inspiration (cf. 17:3; 21:10). Some apocalyptic sources provide angelic help for the ascent, but John ascends simply by the Spirit, as in Ezekiel (Eze 2:2; 3:12,14,24; 8:3; 11:1,5,24; 37:1; 43:5).

4:3 *jasper and ruby ... rainbow that shone like an emerald.* Some ancient apocalypses elaborated in great detail on God's throne, seeking to amplify God's majesty; readier to acknowledge the inadequacy of human images to communicate God's grandeur (cf. 1Co 2:9 – 10), John omits such adornment. The heavenly court nevertheless contrasts starkly with the pretense of merely earthly grandeur of emperors. *jasper.* An opaque gem (including but not limited to modern jasper) that is often reddish but sometimes green or other colors (cf. 21:11,18 – 20). *ruby.* Sardius, translated here as "ruby," was normally red. In Ezekiel God's throne appeared like sapphire (Eze 1:26; 10:1; cf. Rev 21:19), which is often deep blue and was often identified in antiquity with lapis lazuli. *rainbow.* Recalls the radiance of God's throne in Eze 1:28.

4:4 *twenty-four elders.* Some regard these elders as angels; others view them as the OT people of God. Two other common approaches may be more fruitful. First, the doubling of the 12 could represent all the people of God, perhaps OT and NT believers together (see 21:12 – 14). Second, given their function in worship, they may represent the 24 courses of priests in the OT (e.g., 1Ch 24:4), since believers are a kingdom and priests (Rev 1:6; 5:10). In the art of Asia Minor a small number of priests seem to have represented a much larger number of worshipers. *crowns of gold.* Might evoke victories, as in 2:10, but when crowns were of gold they pointed instead to reigning or priestly functions or some sacred competitions.

4:5 *lightning ... thunder.* Ancient Mediterranean peoples often associated them with chief deities, and of course also with the heavens. Here they may evoke especially God's revelation at Mount Sinai (Ex 19:16; 20:18; Ps 77:18). *seven lamps.* An allusion to Zec 4:2 (cf. Zec 4:6).

4:6 *sea of glass.* Vast waters (cf. 1:15) also appear in apocalyptic visions of heaven or paradise, probably developing OT images (Eze 1:24; Ps 104:3; 148:4), and the knowledge that rain and lightning fall from heaven. The most direct source here, however, is the bronze "sea" of Solomon's temple for the priests to wash in (1Ki 7:23 – 44; 1Ch 18:8; 2Ch 4:2,6), because heaven in Revelation appears like a temple (Rev 7:15; 11:19; 14:15,17; 15:5 – 16:1; 16:17). The heavenly worship contrasts starkly with earthly worship of the beast (13:4 – 8,15). Solomon's temple probably included a "sea" for the same reason that ancient Egyptian temples depicted heaven on their ceilings: a symbol of part of the cosmos to testify that their deity ruled the entire cosmos. *glass, clear as crystal.* Evokes the crystalline, heavenly expanse beneath God's throne and above the throne angels in Eze 1:22 (cf. Rev 21:11,18,21). Most glass available in the first century was not very clear. *four living creatures.* Ancient Jewish descriptions of heaven often added to the OT, but they never neglected it. Thus even their more imaginative descriptions usually included Isaiah's fiery "seraphim" (Isa 6:2 – 3) or Ezekiel's cherubim supporting God's throne (Eze 1:4 – 21; 10:1 – 20; 11:22). *covered with eyes.* Might suggest that nothing on earth is hidden from these creatures (Zec 4:10), with the implication, "How much less from God himself?" Cf. Eze 1:18; 10:12.

4:7 The faces reflect those in Eze 1:10; 10:14 (except that in Ezekiel each creature had all four faces). Ezekiel's vision probably employed the most powerful and regal of animals to communicate the majesty of the creatures that carry God's throne.

4:8 *Day and night they never stop.* Ceaseless worship probably suggests both divine empowerment for worship and the worthiness of God (cf. 7:15). Glorious nearly beyond human conception as these creatures are, they serve no other literary function here than to extol God's

REVELATION 4

Heaven as a Temple in Revelation

As in Heb 8:1 – 5, Revelation envisions a heavenly temple. Throughout Revelation God's people in heaven are worshiping (Rev 4:10; 5:14; 7:11; 11:16; 19:4), while on earth God's people are being slaughtered and followers of the beast are worshiping the beast (Rev 13:4,8,12,15; 14:9 – 11). The scenes of worship in heaven are fitting for a heavenly temple.

Heaven's furniture regularly evokes the Biblical temple:

- the ark of the covenant (Ex 25:10; Rev 11:19)
- the tabernacle (Ex 25:9; Rev 15:5)
- the altars of incense and sacrifice (Ex 27:1 – 2; 30:1; Rev 6:9; 8:3 – 5; 9:13)
- the sea (cf. 1Ki 7:23 – 25,39,44; see Rev 4:6; 15:2)
- the lampstands (Ex 25:31; Rev 1:12 – 13; 2:1,5)
- harps (1Ch 25:1,6; Rev 14:2; 15:2)

The church on earth is never closer to heaven than when we are offering God and the Lamb the glory they deserve; it is then that we most fully experience in the Spirit a foretaste of heaven (cf. 1Co 2:9 – 10; 2Co 5:5). A church that suffers in this world will long for heaven, and in turning our hearts toward our heavenly king we will find strength to remember that the future world belongs to us. ◆

9 Whenever the living creatures give glory,
honor and thanks to him who sits on the
throne[l] and who lives for ever and ever,
10 the twenty-four elders[m] fall down before
him[n] who sits on the throne[o] and worship
him who lives for ever and ever. They lay
their crowns before the throne and say:

11 "You are worthy, our Lord and God,
to receive glory and honor and
power,[p]
for you created all things,
and by your will they were created
and have their being."[q]

The Scroll and the Lamb

5 Then I saw in the right hand of him
who sat on the throne[r] a scroll with
writing on both sides[s] and sealed[t] with
seven seals. 2 And I saw a mighty angel proclaiming in a loud voice, "Who
is worthy to break the seals and open
the scroll?" 3 But no one in heaven or on
earth or under the earth could open the

4:9 [l] Ps 47:8
4:10 [m] ver 4 [n] Rev 5:8, 14 [o] ver 2
4:11 [p] Rev 5:12 [q] Rev 10:6
5:1 [r] ver 7, 13 [s] Eze 2:9, 10 [t] Isa 29:11; Da 12:4

holiness. John knows most of their song from Isa 6:3, which had been incorporated into regular Jewish prayers. Even a holy priest among God's holy people would count himself and his people unclean once he witnessed the supreme holiness of God (Isa 6:5).
4:10 *fall down before him.* Nebuchadnezzar demanded that peoples fall down before his image and worship, but only the true God is worthy of such obeisance (Da 3:5 – 15).
4:11 *our Lord and God.* It is said that the current emperor, Domitian, expected worship as "lord and god." Those familiar with the common Greek translation of the OT, however, would already recognize "our Lord and God" as a divine title (e.g., Ps 99:8; 106:47). *glory ... honor ... power.* Praises could heap up related terms, reinforcing the recipient's honor (e.g., Ne 9:5; Ps 66:2; 71:8; 148:13; Da 4:37).
5:1 *a scroll.* Jewish traditions often portray writings in heaven that contained God's heavenly laws or decrees about people's destinies in this life or eternally (for the book of life, see note on 3:5). *writing on both sides.* People usually wrote on only one side of a scroll, its "front" (what was inside as one unrolled it). They usually employed the back only if they ran out of space on the front. The description here evokes Eze 2:9 – 10, a scroll of bad news (see note on 10:10).
5:2 *I saw.* Typical visionary language, not only in the Bible (Eze 1:1; 23:13; Da 8:7) but also in apocalyptic literature. *seals.* See the article "Sealing Documents and Revelation 5," p. 2232.
5:3 *no one ... could open the scroll.* Normally a scroll's seals should be broken only by those to whom it is addressed or by officials; moreover, these seals, on a book in the right hand of the living God (v. 1), are too strong for ordinary mortals to break.

scroll or even look inside it. 4 I wept and
wept because no one was found who was
worthy to open the scroll or look inside.
5 Then one of the elders said to me, "Do
not weep! See, the Lion[u] of the tribe of
Judah, the Root of David,[v] has triumphed.
He is able to open the scroll and its sev-
en seals."

6 Then I saw a Lamb,[w] looking as if it
had been slain, standing at the center of
the throne, encircled by the four living
creatures and the elders. The Lamb had
seven horns and seven eyes,[x] which are
the seven spirits[a] of God sent out into all
the earth. 7 He went and took the scroll
from the right hand of him who sat on the
throne.[y] 8 And when he had taken it, the
four living creatures and the twenty-four
elders fell down before the Lamb. Each
one had a harp[z] and they were holding
golden bowls full of incense, which are the
prayers[a] of God's people. 9 And they sang a
new song, saying:[b]

"You are worthy[c] to take the scroll
and to open its seals,
because you were slain,
and with your blood[d] you
purchased[e] for God
persons from every tribe and
language and people and
nation.
10 You have made them to be a kingdom
and priests[f] to serve our God,
and they will reign[b] on the earth."

11 Then I looked and heard the voice of
many angels, numbering thousands upon
thousands, and ten thousand times ten
thousand.[g] They encircled the throne and
the living creatures and the elders. 12 In a
loud voice they were saying:

"Worthy is the Lamb, who was slain,
to receive power and wealth and
wisdom and strength
and honor and glory and praise!"[h]

13 Then I heard every creature in heaven
and on earth and under the earth[i] and on
the sea, and all that is in them, saying:

"To him who sits on the throne and to
the Lamb[j]
be praise and honor and glory and
power,
for ever and ever!"[k]

5:5 [u] Ge 49:9 [v] Isa 11:1, 10; Ro 15:12; Rev 22:16 **5:6** [w] Jn 1:29 [x] Zec 4:10 **5:7** [y] ver 1 **5:8** [z] Rev 14:2 [a] Ps 141:2 **5:9** [b] Ps 40:3 [c] Rev 4:11 [d] Heb 9:12 [e] 1Co 6:20 **5:10** [f] 1Pe 2:5 **5:11** [g] Da 7:10; Heb 12:22 **5:12** [h] Rev 4:11 **5:13** [i] ver 3; Php 2:10 [j] Rev 6:16 [k] 1Ch 29:11

[a] *6* That is, the sevenfold Spirit [b] *10* Some manuscripts *they reign*

5:5 *Lion of the tribe of Judah, the Root of David.* Ancient literature, including Jewish literature, regularly used lions as images of great strength. Lions were considered the courageous, powerful rulers of the animal kingdom. The specific image of the Lion of the tribe of Judah comes from Ge 49:9–10, which refers to a ruler from Judah who will rule the nations; Jewish tradition naturally applied it to the Davidic Messiah. Revelation links this image with the Root of Jesse (David's father) in Isa 11:10. The ruler described there restores David's truncated line (Isa 11:1), is anointed by the sevenfold Spirit (Isa 11:2) and is appointed to rule all the nations with peace (Isa 11:3–10). Some Jewish sources portrayed him as a mighty warrior prince.
5:6 *Lamb.* In contrast with the lion of v. 5, lambs epitomized helplessness in ancient sources. They were the most vulnerable of sheep, which were in turn portrayed as the weakest of creatures, often victims of lions and other predators. *looking as if it had been slain.* A slain lamb, weakest of all, evokes OT sacrifices (e.g., Ex 29:38; Lev 3:7; 5:6), and especially the Passover lamb, which delivered Israel from the climactic plague (Ex 12:23). *seven horns and seven eyes, which are the seven spirits of God.* Male lambs could have two horns, but not seven. Horns could symbolize kings or power (Da 7:7–24; 8:3–22); here John says that they represent the seven spirits of God—God's power rather than human might (cf. Zec 4:6). John also identifies the horns here with seven eyes, which he might identify with the Spirit (Zec 3:9; 4:10). In Zec 4:10 the seven eyes belong to God himself; Jesus here again appears as divine.
5:8 *harp.* Harps (also 14:2; 15:2) fit the setting of the heavenly temple (cf. 1Ch 15:16; 16:5; 25:1,3,6). *golden bowls full of incense.* Incense offerings were also standard in temples; golden bowls were considered the most exotic. *prayers.* For incense as prayers, see Ps 141:2. Jewish tradition depicted one of the chief angels presenting the prayers of God's people before God; here the heavenly chorus offers them to Jesus.
5:9 *a new song.* May imply a freshly inspired song in addition to the praises already available; in any case, in the OT it is offered to God alone (Ps 33:3; 40:3; 96:1; 98:1; 144:9; 149:1; Isa 42:10). Jewish people often praised God for redeeming Israel (e.g., Dt 9:26). At Passover Jewish people sang hymns to celebrate God's redemption of their people from Egypt. *every tribe and language and people and nation.* Something like this fourfold formula occurs in varying sequences seven times in Revelation (5:9; 7:9; 10:11; 11:9; 13:7; 14:6; 17:15); it matches a threefold formula that occurs six times in Daniel (Da 3:4,7,29; 5:19; 6:25; 7:14). The first of these in Daniel is fourfold in the Greek translation (Da 3:4). Daniel announced that the Son of Man would rule all these peoples (Da 7:14). *every … people.* The Roman Empire conquered as far north as Britain and had trade connections with India, China, and east Africa; educated people knew of much of the world. John's vision of all peoples before God's throne thus would have appeared humanly impossible in his day—though the past two centuries have witnessed a remarkable degree of fulfillment.
5:10 *a kingdom and priests.* See note on 1:6. *they will reign.* God's people would reign with him forever (Da 7:22,27).
5:11 *ten thousand.* The largest number readily available in Greek. The figures come from Da 7:10, a passage often used by Jewish writers to praise God's infinite greatness.
5:12 *Worthy is the Lamb.* Jewish people recognized that God alone merits the praise of all creation (Ps 96:11–13; 148:1–13; Isa 44:23; 55:12). Here the Lamb receives worship alongside God the Father. *power … praise.* On piling up related terms in praise, see note on 4:11. Multiple elements in a list of praises emphasized the subject's greatness (cf., e.g., 1Ch 29:11–12; Da 7:14; for a king, Da 2:37). Long lists of praises appear elsewhere (e.g., Jer 33:9; Da 4:37), sometimes in sets of seven, as here (in the Dead Sea Scrolls, see 4Q403 f1i.2–4; in the Mishnah, see *Pesahim* 10:5). *praise.* Cf., e.g., Ps 72:18–19.
5:13 *in heaven and on earth and under the earth and on the sea.* Greeks divided the rule of their deities among

REVELATION 5:1

SEALING DOCUMENTS AND REVELATION 5

Legal documents normally closed by listing witnesses, usually about six in number. Such documents were normally sealed shut with hot wax over the threads that tied the scroll closed; then witnesses would press their personal seals into the hot wax, making an impression that matched their distinctive seal and attested that they were the witnesses.

No one could open the scroll without breaking the hardened wax seals that held the threads in place, and no one could replace such seals without the witnesses' rings. Thus no one could tamper with the legal document until it was time to publicly open it. Seals reserved the contents of a document for its rightful recipient and authenticated the document with witnesses who attested it.

Some Jewish writers envisioned heavenly scrolls as sealed documents to prevent any accusation of tampering (1 Enoch 89:71). In a later writing, 3 Enoch, these seals could be broken only by high angels before the document was handed to God. A book of judgments could be sealed (Isa 29:11); this was the case with the scroll in Eze 2:9 – 10, which, like the one here in Rev 5, contains writing on both front and back. Here, however, the judgments (or at least the first set of judgments) are not the contents of the book but the attesting witnesses in the seals (6:1 – 17). They show that God will call the world to account. ◆

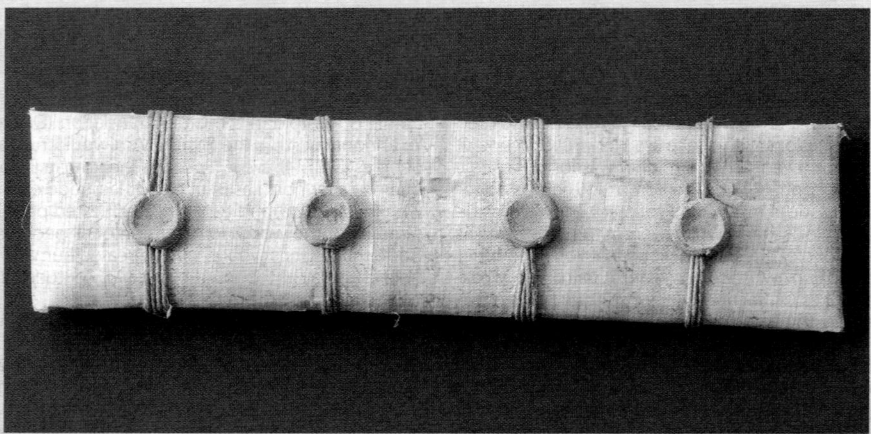

Model of a papyrus document sealed with four clay bulla.

Z. Radovan/www.BibleLandPictures.com

14 The four living creatures said, “Amen,”[l]
and the elders fell down and worshiped.[m]

The Seals

6 I watched as the Lamb[n] opened
the first of the seven seals.[o] Then I
heard one of the four living creatures[p]
say in a voice like thunder,[q] “Come!”
2 I looked, and there before me was a white
horse![r] Its rider held a bow, and he was
given a crown,[s] and he rode out as a conqueror bent on conquest.[t]
3 When the Lamb opened the second
seal, I heard the second living creature[u]
say, “Come!” 4 Then another horse came
out, a fiery red one.[v] Its rider was given
power to take peace from the earth[w] and
to make people kill each other. To him was
given a large sword.
5 When the Lamb opened the third seal,
I heard the third living creature[x] say,
“Come!” I looked, and there before me
was a black horse![y] Its rider was holding
a pair of scales in his hand. 6 Then I heard
what sounded like a voice among the four
living creatures,[z] saying, “Two pounds[a] of
wheat for a day’s wages,[b] and six pounds[c]
of barley for a day’s wages,[b] and do not
damage[a] the oil and the wine!”
7 When the Lamb opened the fourth
seal, I heard the voice of the fourth living creature[b] say, “Come!” 8 I looked, and
there before me was a pale horse![c] Its rider was named Death, and Hades[d] was following close behind him. They were given
power over a fourth of the earth to kill by
sword, famine and plague, and by the wild
beasts of the earth.[e]

5:14 [l] Rev 4:9 [m] Rev 4:10; 19:4
6:1 [n] Rev 5:6 [o] Rev 5:1 [p] Rev 4:6, 7 [q] Rev 14:2; 19:6
6:2 [r] Zec 6:3; Rev 19:11 [s] Zec 6:11; Rev 14:14 [t] Ps 45:4
6:3 [u] Rev 4:7
6:4 [v] Zec 6:2 [w] Mt 10:34
6:5 [x] Rev 4:7 [y] Zec 6:2
6:6 [z] Rev 4:6, 7 [a] Rev 9:4
6:7 [b] Rev 4:7
6:8 [c] Zec 6:3 [d] Hos 13:14 [e] Jer 15:2, 3; Eze 5:12, 17

a 6 Or about 1 kilogram *b* 6 Greek *a denarius*
c 6 Or about 3 kilograms

heaven, earth (and sea) and below the earth (the realm of Hades), or heaven, earth (and Hades) and the sea. Earlier Scripture also sometimes emphasized God’s sovereignty over heaven, earth and sea (Ex 20:11; Ps 96:11; 146:6; Am 9:6; Hag 2:6). *and to the Lamb.* See note on v. 12.

5:14 *Amen.* Closed prayers and many Jewish works. *worshiped.* The Greek word often implies prostration, reinforcing “fell down”; for the meaning, see note on 4:10.

6:1 – 8 Romans listed fearful omens. More important, Biblical prophets often listed together the judgments of war (sword), famine and plague (e.g., Jer 14:12; 21:7 – 9; 27:8; 29:17 – 18; Eze 6:11 – 12; 7:15; 12:16); the present vision makes war emphatic by separating conquest (vv. 2 – 4). Many ancient prophecy teachers catalogued special sufferings they expected in the degenerate time of the end; Jesus listed such sufferings but warned that many occur throughout the present era (Mt 24:6,8; Mk 13:7 – 8).

The four riders most directly recall Zec 1:8, where riders on horses of four different colors represent the Lord’s patrol (Zec 1:8 – 11). Later God sends out four chariots, each drawn by horses of a different color as his patrol (Zec 6:1 – 8); by Revelation’s period cavalry had shifted from chariots to riders. Here they appear with a more active role as angels of judgment.

6:1 *seals.* See the article “Sealing Documents and Revelation 5,” p. 2232. *living creatures.* See note on 4:6.

6:2 *white horse.* White horses were especially prized. *Its rider held a bow.* Biblical prophets used the bow as a frequent image of conquest, though associating it especially with eastern peoples known for their archery. Most fearful to the Roman Empire, Rome’s most formidable enemy, Parthia, was known particularly as mounted archers. They were the only group of mounted archers known in the ancient Mediterranean world. Many Jewish people expected Parthians to play a role in the future war. For the most part, the Euphrates (16:12) divided the Roman and Parthian Empires. See the article “Parthia,” p. 2239.

6:4 *fiery red one.* The much-vaunted “Roman peace” was merely Roman propaganda; the empire’s borders were never fully secure. Later rabbis associated Zechariah’s red horse (Zec 1:8; 6:2) with bloodshed. *large sword.* The “sword” represents the judgment of warfare and violent death more than 100 times in the OT alone. Because Revelation does not mention different nations here, some scholars suggest that people killing each other here might refer to civil war. Rome’s most remembered battles of recent generations were wars within the empire itself, including Rome’s own civil wars. Because it involved bloodshed of one’s own countrymen, many considered civil war the most horrible kind of war.

6:5 – 8 Famine (vv. 5 – 6) and plagues (v. 8) usually closely follow war, killing civilians as well as combatants. In antiquity, fugitives from war often crowded cities, which were soon besieged and sometimes starved into submission. Pestilence sometimes followed from rotting corpses in the water supply. Both Gentiles and Jews recognized that such hardships often represented divine judgments calling for repentance. Biblically, these normally are judgments on societies, not specifically the individuals who suffer them.

6:5 *a pair of scales.* The balance; it was normally used in the marketplace to weigh out the amount of food one could buy for one’s money. Basic Mediterranean staples, depending on one’s location, were barley, wheat and perhaps cheese and olives, plus fish for those near bodies of water.

6:6 *Two pounds of wheat for a day’s wages.* Hired laborers on a farm might be paid as little as two loaves of bread a day (about one pound [0.5 kilograms]), just enough food for themselves. More commonly they were paid in money, and enough to also feed families (on average perhaps two meals a day) in times when employment was available. *six pounds of barley.* Two pounds (one kilogram) of wheat was the amount ancient texts deemed necessary to feed a single worker for a day (though if supplemented with other food, a worker might eat just two-thirds that amount), but if he had a family to support (as most workers did) he would buy instead three times as much barley, which was cheaper. The grain here costs 5 to 15 times what it might in better times. Given the average size household in poorer regions like Egypt, many of the younger children would die or be stunted by malnutrition. *do not damage the oil and the wine!* God’s mercy appears in the midst of judgment. Destroying standing crops in the fields destroyed a year’s produce, but only the most savage enemies destroyed olive trees and vineyards, which would take years to grow back. The imagery would be stark for John’s audience. When Revelation was written, Asia Minor was producing a profitable surplus of wine for export but had to import grain from elsewhere; ordinary people thus paid higher prices for grain.

6:8 *Death, and Hades was following close behind him.* Personified Death and Hades appear together in some Biblical poetry (Ps 49:14; 116:3; Isa 28:15; Hos 13:14; Hab 2:5). *kill by sword, famine and plague, and by the wild beasts.*

9 When he opened the fifth seal, I saw
under the altar[f] the souls of those who had
been slain[g] because of the word of God
and the testimony they had maintained.
10 They called out in a loud voice, "How
long,[h] Sovereign Lord, holy and true,[i] until you judge the inhabitants of the earth
and avenge our blood?"[j] 11 Then each of
them was given a white robe,[k] and they
were told to wait a little longer, until the
full number of their fellow servants, their
brothers and sisters,[a] were killed just as
they had been.[l]

12 I watched as he opened the sixth seal.
There was a great earthquake.[m] The sun
turned black[n] like sackcloth made of goat
hair, the whole moon turned blood red,
13 and the stars in the sky fell to earth,[o]
as figs drop from a fig tree[p] when shaken
by a strong wind. 14 The heavens receded like a scroll being rolled up, and every
mountain and island was removed from
its place.[q]

15 Then the kings of the earth, the princes, the generals, the rich, the mighty, and
everyone else, both slave and free, hid in
caves and among the rocks of the mountains.[r] 16 They called to the mountains and
the rocks, "Fall on us[s] and hide us[b] from
the face of him who sits on the throne
and from the wrath of the Lamb! 17 For the
great day[t] of their[c] wrath has come, and
who can withstand it?"[u]

6:9 [f] Rev 14:18; 16:7 [g] Rev 20:4 **6:10** [h] Zec 1:12 [i] Rev 3:7 [j] Rev 19:2 **6:11** [k] Rev 3:4 [l] Heb 11:40 **6:12** [m] Rev 16:18 [n] Mt 24:29 **6:13** [o] Mt 24:29; Rev 8:10; 9:1 [p] Isa 34:4 **6:14** [q] Jer 4:24; Rev 16:20 **6:15** [r] Isa 2:10, 19,21 **6:16** [s] Hos 10:8; Lk 23:30 **6:17** [t] Zep 1:14, 15; Rev 16:14 [u] Ps 76:7 **7:1** [v] Da 7:2

144,000 Sealed

7 After this I saw four angels standing
at the four corners of the earth, holding back the four winds[v] of the earth to

[a] *11* The Greek word for *brothers and sisters* (*adelphoi*) refers here to believers, both men and women, as part of God's family; also in 12:10; 19:10. [b] *16* See Hosea 10:8. [c] *17* Some manuscripts *his*

The four riders together slay with sword (violent death, as perhaps in the first two riders), famine (the third rider), pestilence (perhaps the fourth), and wild beasts, perhaps added here because it elsewhere appears in Biblical lists of four plagues (Eze 5:17; 14:21).

6:9–11 Earlier Biblical prophets had predicted the witness of God's people to the nations (e.g., Isa 42:1,6; 43:10–12; 44:8; 49:6), the conversion of the nations (Isa 19:19–25; Jer 3:17; Zec 2:11; 8:22–23) and the suffering of God's people in the end time (Da 7:21). Like Mk 13:9–10, this vision connects these themes.

6:9 *under the altar.* Probably recalls the place where priests poured the blood (hence the "life," Lev 17:11) of sacrifices (e.g., Lev 4:7,18,25,34; 5:9; 8:15; 9:9). Jewish tradition by this period recognized martyrs as sacrifices accepted by God.

6:10–11 *How long ...? ... until the full number.* A common Biblical plea for God's swift intervention (e.g., Ps 6:3; 35:17; 79:5; 80:4; Hab 1:2; Zec 1:12). In Jewish apocalyptic traditions, the righteous continued crying for vindication until the judgment; in one source (possibly later than Revelation), the righteous ask, "How long?" and an archangel responds, "Until your number is complete" (4 Ezra 4:33–37). Some other traditions also recognized that the full number of martyrs must be completed before the end. For the very blood of martyrs crying for vindication, cf., e.g., Ge 4:10; Mt 23:35. For martyrs until the end, cf. perhaps Da 11:35.

6:12 *great earthquake.* Such an image might prove particularly graphic and terrifying for Laodicea and other cities devastated by earthquakes within the past generation or two. Jewish writers sometimes used similar poetic language for cataclysmic events within the present age (Jer 4:24; 8:16; Mic 1:4). The description here, however, fits a climactic, eschatological earthquake that truly removes mountains (11:13; 16:18; Eze 38:19–20; Zec 14:5) and which often appears in apocalyptic scenes of the end. *sun turned black ... moon turned blood red.* Both Jews and Gentiles viewed even a mere eclipse of the sun or moon as terrifying, but this is no mere eclipse. Apocalyptic texts place the darkening of sun and moon at the end of the age, the usual Jewish interpretation also of passages on which this vision may draw (Isa 13:9–11; 24:21–23; Joel 2:31).

6:13 *stars ... fell ... as figs drop from a fig tree.* The language evokes Isa 34:4, where the stars would fall "like shriveled figs from the fig tree." The context there is judgment against Edom but also against all nations (Isa 34:1–2).

6:14 *The heavens receded like a scroll being rolled up.* As in v. 13, Revelation continues to draw on Isa 34:4, where "the heavens rolled up like a scroll." One would normally unroll a scroll with the right hand while with the left hand rolling up what one had just finished reading. Other Diaspora Jewish writers associated this image with the entire dome of heaven collapsing on the earth as the universe fell apart.

6:15 *kings ... the mighty, and everyone else.* No marks of status will exempt anyone—even Caesar—from judgment. *both slave and free.* Ancients sometimes summarized humankind by simply contrasting opposites. *hid in caves and among the rocks.* Isa 2:19 mentions hiding in the rocks and caves in the day of God's wrath. Christians in Sardis may have envisioned the cave-tombs of the mountain facing their acropolis. Whereas caves and mountain clefts could hide one from human enemies, nothing could protect mortals from God's wrath (v. 17).

6:16 *Fall on us.* In Hos 10:8 the wicked "say to the mountains, 'Cover us!' and to the hills, 'Fall on us!'" (used also in Lk 23:30). In some apocalyptic scenarios, on the day of judgment it is too late to repent. Thus the unrepentant here entreat mountains for cover rather than God for mercy. *wrath of the Lamb!* A shocking image, since lambs were considered among the most docile creatures (Isa 11:6). The Lamb is again identified here as divine.

6:17 *For the great day of their wrath has come, and who can withstand it?* The question adapts Joel 2:11: "The day of the LORD is great ... Who can endure it?" The preceding verse in Joel speaks of the sun and moon being darkened. Cf. also Mal 3:2: "who can endure the day of his coming?" The question's answer comes in the following vision: the servants of God stand now and thus will stand in that day (7:1–17).

7:1–8 As God protected his own people in Goshen during the plagues, so he would be with them as the world faced his judgments.

7:1 *four angels standing at the four corners of the earth, holding back the four winds of the earth.* Ancients associated the four winds with the four directions (cf. Jer 49:36), though most people viewed the earth as circular or oval, not square (cf. "the four quarters of the earth" in Isa 11:12). In Jewish apocalyptic works, God controls the winds

prevent any wind from blowing on the
land or on the sea or on any tree. [2]Then
I saw another angel coming up from the
east, having the seal of the living God. He
called out in a loud voice to the four angels who had been given power to harm
the land and the sea: [3]"Do not harm[w] the
land or the sea or the trees until we put a
seal on the foreheads[x] of the servants of
our God." [4]Then I heard the number[y] of
those who were sealed: 144,000[z] from all
the tribes of Israel.

[5]From the tribe of Judah 12,000 were sealed,
from the tribe of Reuben 12,000,
from the tribe of Gad 12,000,
[6]from the tribe of Asher 12,000,
from the tribe of Naphtali 12,000,
from the tribe of Manasseh 12,000,
[7]from the tribe of Simeon 12,000,
from the tribe of Levi 12,000,
from the tribe of Issachar 12,000,
[8]from the tribe of Zebulun 12,000,
from the tribe of Joseph 12,000,
from the tribe of Benjamin 12,000.

7:3 [w] Rev 6:6 [x] Eze 9:4; Rev 22:4 **7:4** [y] Rev 9:16 [z] Rev 14:1,3

The Great Multitude in White Robes

[9]After this I looked, and there before
me was a great multitude that no one
could count, from every nation, tribe,
people and language,[a] standing before the
throne[b] and before the Lamb. They were
wearing white robes and were holding
palm branches in their hands. [10]And they
cried out in a loud voice:

"Salvation belongs to our God,[c]
who sits on the throne,
and to the Lamb."

[11]All the angels were standing around the
throne and around the elders[d] and the four
living creatures.[e] They fell down on their
faces[f] before the throne and worshiped
God, [12]saying:

"Amen!
Praise and glory
and wisdom and thanks and honor
and power and strength
be to our God for ever and ever.
Amen!"[g]

7:9 [a] Rev 5:9 [b] ver 15 **7:10** [c] Ps 3:8; Rev 12:10; 19:1 **7:11** [d] Rev 4:4 [e] Rev 4:6 [f] Rev 4:10 **7:12** [g] Rev 5:12-14

---

and delegates them to angels, using them for blessing or judgment. In Zec 6:1–6, God sent out four chariots (cf. Rev 6:1–8); the common Greek translation of Zec 6:5 describes these four heavenly "spirits" as the four "winds" of heaven (see NIV text note on Zec 6:5). *to prevent any wind from blowing.* The blowing of four winds also could announce evil world empires (Da 7:2–3). Here God prevents the winds from blowing in judgment until he has marked his servants for protection (v. 3).

7:2 *another angel ... having the seal of the living God.* A king could delegate his seal to an agent authorized to carry out an activity on his behalf (e.g., Est 3:10; 8:8). Perhaps this angel was one of the witnesses who initially attested the plagues (6:1–7; see the article "Sealing Documents and Revelation 5," p. 2232).

7:3 *seal on the foreheads of the servants of our God.* A seal identifies God's servants here (cf. 3:12; 14:1; 22:4), in contrast to the mark of the wicked (13:16–17; 14:9,11; 16:2; 19:20; 20:4; cf. other visionary labels in 17:5; 19:16). It may attest ownership (cf. Isa 44:5). Views of the background vary. Jewish people showed their fidelity to God's law by wearing phylacteries on the hand or forehead during prayers (see note on Mt 23:5). Some compare the marking of soldiers on the hand, forehead or neck (cf. note on vv. 4–8), though this was not pervasive. Others compare the branding of slaves (cf. "servants" here), though very few ancient slaves were branded. Whatever the case, the most important background is Eze 9:4, where God invisibly marks for protection his own before releasing judgment on others (cf. Ge 4:15; Ex 12:23). In one pre-Christian work, God invisibly marks the righteous with a "sign" to protect them and marks the wicked with a sign for destruction (Psalms of Solomon 15:6–9).

7:4–8 Some compare the form of the list in vv. 5–8 to a military census (Nu 1:3,18,20; 26:2). For some battles Israel's leaders drafted 12 equal contingents from different tribes or regions (Nu 31:4–6; 1Ch 27:1–15); battalions of a thousand were also fairly standard units. Because the only other occasion when John "heard" (v. 4) a number recounts troop strength (9:16), this might be God's people depicted as an army (cf. 12:11; 14:1,4; 15:2; 19:14). Some Jewish people expected an end-time army to wreak judgment on Gentiles (note especially 1QM, War Scroll in the Dead Sea Scrolls). If this imagery is in view here, however, John applies it symbolically; these are God's servants (v. 3), the redeemed (14:3–4). Some apply the image to a nonviolent "army" of martyrs (cf. 5:5–6; see note on v. 9). Although Dan was the first listed to receive his inheritance (Eze 48:1), his tribe is missing in this list. (Jewish sources say some negative things about each of the tribes, so citing their comments about Dan cannot fully explain his omission here.) The numbers 12,000 and 144 both recur together later in Revelation, suggesting that the 144,000 represent new Jerusalemites, the people of the new Jerusalem (21:16–17).

7:4 *144,000.* See note on 14:1.

7:9–17 Although a second vision could add new information, sometimes it presented in a new way the content of a previous vision (as in Ge 41:17–32; Da 7:9–22); sometimes it could also interpret what one had just heard (as in 5:5–6). This vision transforms OT images of God and Israel (Isa 49:10; see note on Rev 7:16–17) to address the Lamb and his people from many nations (v. 9).

7:9 *great multitude that no one could count.* This multitude (in contrast to vv. 4–8) may echo the promise to the patriarchs (Ge 13:16; 15:5; 32:12). By the end of the first century, Christians likely numbered fewer than 144,000, much less an uncountable multitude (which must be no smaller than the numbers in 5:11). John's vision offered a promise well beyond merely human expectation! *every nation, tribe, people and language.* See note on 5:9. *white robes.* Many commentators relate the white robes to those of martyrs (6:9–11). *palm branches.* Often used to hail victors in a military triumph; if vv. 4–8 envision an end-time army (see note on vv. 4–8), this "army" hails the true victor, the Lamb.

7:10 Cf. Ps 3:8; 62:11.

7:11–12 The rest of heaven responds to the multitude's praises as in an antiphonal chorus (cf. Ex 15:21). For the accumulation of praise language, see note on 4:11; for its sevenfold character, see note on 5:12.

13 Then one of the elders asked me,
"These in white robes — who are they, and
where did they come from?"
14 I answered, "Sir, you know."
And he said, "These are they who have
come out of the great tribulation; they have
washed their robes[h] and made them white
in the blood of the Lamb.[i] 15 Therefore,

"they are before the throne of
God[j]
and serve him[k] day and night in
his temple;[l]
and he who sits on the throne
will shelter them with his
presence.[m]
16 'Never again will they hunger;
never again will they thirst.
The sun will not beat down on
them,'[a]
nor any scorching heat.[n]
17 For the Lamb at the center of the
throne
will be their shepherd;[o]
'he will lead them to springs of living
water.'[a]
'And God will wipe away every
tear from their eyes.'[b]"[p]

7:14 [h] Rev 22:14 [i] Heb 9:14; 1Jn 1:7 **7:15** [j] ver 9 [k] Rev 22:3 [l] Rev 11:19 [m] Isa 4:5,6; Rev 21:3 **7:16** [n] Isa 49:10 **7:17** [o] Ps 23:1; Jn 10:11 [p] Isa 25:8; Rev 21:4

The Seventh Seal and the Golden Censer

8 When he opened the seventh seal,[q]
there was silence in heaven for about
half an hour.
2 And I saw the seven angels[r] who stand
before God, and seven trumpets were giv-
en to them.
3 Another angel,[s] who had a golden censer, came and stood at the altar. He was
given much incense to offer, with the
prayers of all God's people,[t] on the golden
altar[u] in front of the throne. 4 The smoke of
the incense, together with the prayers of
God's people, went up before God[v] from
the angel's hand. 5 Then the angel took the
censer, filled it with fire from the altar,[w]
and hurled it on the earth; and there came
peals of thunder,[x] rumblings, flashes of
lightning and an earthquake.[y]

The Trumpets

6 Then the seven angels who had the
seven trumpets[z] prepared to sound them.
7 The first angel sounded his trumpet,
and there came hail and fire[a] mixed with
blood, and it was hurled down on the

8:1 [q] Rev 6:1 **8:2** [r] ver 6-13; Rev 9:1, 13; 11:15 **8:3** [s] Rev 7:2 [t] Rev 5:8 [u] Ex 30:1-6; Heb 9:4; Rev 9:13 **8:4** [v] Ps 141:2 **8:5** [w] Lev 16:12, 13 [x] Rev 4:5 [y] Rev 6:12 **8:6** [z] ver 2 **8:7** [a] Eze 38:22

[a] *16,17* Isaiah 49:10 [b] *17* Isaiah 25:8

7:13 *who ... where ... ?* Jewish sages and also figures in apocalypses sometimes asked questions that their hearers could not answer, provoking attention.
7:14 *you know.* Cf. Eze 37:3. *the great tribulation.* Probably evokes Da 12:1 (cf. also Jesus' language in Mt 24:21, using the same Greek terms). *washed their robes and made them white in the blood of the Lamb.* Some imagery here is meant to shock: blood might purify ritually, but it notoriously stained what was white.
7:15 *serve him day and night in his temple.* Those who resisted the worship of other gods (2:14,20) now serve in God's temple. Various priests and Levites served day and night in God's temple (1Ch 9:33; Ps 134:1); all believers are now priests (Rev 5:10), though many are also sacrifices (6:9). *temple.* For the heavenly temple, see the article "Heaven as a Temple in Revelation," p. 2230. *he ... will shelter them with his presence.* Alludes to the new exodus imagery of Isa 4:5–6.
7:16–17 In Isa 49:10, God promised that in the time of Israel's restoration, his people would "neither hunger nor thirst," nor would "the desert heat or the sun beat down on them." Instead, God as the one with compassion on his people would "lead them beside springs of water." God would shepherd his people (Isa 40:11). In the context of being a "shade from the heat" (Isa 25:4), a "banquet" for all peoples (Isa 25:6), and the one who will "swallow up death forever" (Isa 25:8), God would also "wipe away the tears from all faces" (Isa 25:8). Here Jesus fulfills this divine role, and his followers from all nations (cf. Isa 25:6–7; 49:6) receive promises designated for God's own people.
7:17 *the Lamb ... will be their shepherd.* Lambs were the weakest members of the flock, but here the Lamb leads.
8:1 *silence in heaven.* Interpretations of the silence vary widely. One proposal is that heaven is silenced to allow the prayers of the saints to be heard (vv. 3–5); that, however, belongs to the next vision introduced in v. 2. More compelling, some apocalyptic works use silence to signal a return to the primeval creation, followed by the resurrection. Most relevant, however, is that silence could stem from awe or fear (Job 40:4; cf. Hab 2:20). Indeed, texts that first-century interpreters could apply to the day of judgment refer to the world's silence before God at that time (Isa 41:1; Zep 1:7; Zec 2:13; Ro 3:19; cf. Rev 18:22–23; 20:11–12).
8:2 *the seven angels who stand before God.* In Jewish tradition, these were the seven archangels. *trumpets.* Used to gather people or issue military instructions; given other temple imagery in heaven (e.g., 4:6; 6:9; 7:15; 11:19; 15:5), even more relevant may be the trumpets once used in the temple (2Ch 5:12; 7:6; 29:26; Ezr 3:10).
8:3 *incense ... prayers.* See Ps 141:2. *the prayers of all God's people.* Although full vindication may await the day of judgment (6:9–11), lesser judgments before that day also offer a degree of vindication (vv. 5–6).
8:5 *the altar.* See the article "Heaven as a Temple in Revelation," p. 2230. *thunder ... lightning.* See note on 4:5.
8:7—9:19 Many of the trumpet judgments, like many of the bowls (16:1–17), evoke the plagues against Egypt.

Ex 7–10	Rev 8–9	Rev 16
Water turned to blood (7:20–21)	Water turned to blood, wormwood (8:8–11)	Water turned to blood (16:3–4; cf. 11:6)
Fiery hail (9:22–24)	Fiery hail (8:7)	Hail (16:21)
Locusts (10:12–14)	Locusts (9:3,7)	—
Darkness (10:21–22)	Darkness (8:12)	Darkness (16:10; cf. 16:8)
Frogs (8:2–13)	—	Frogs? (16:13)

Revelation is not simply recounting what happened in Moses' day; it is depicting judgments on the world

earth. A third[b] of the earth was burned
up, a third of the trees were burned up,
and all the green grass was burned up.[c]
8The second angel sounded his trumpet,
and something like a huge mountain,[d] all
ablaze, was thrown into the sea. A third[e]
of the sea turned into blood,[f] 9a third[g] of
the living creatures in the sea died, and a
third of the ships were destroyed.
10The third angel sounded his trumpet,
and a great star, blazing like a torch, fell
from the sky[h] on a third of the rivers and
on the springs of water[i]— 11the name of
the star is Wormwood.[a] A third[j] of the
waters turned bitter, and many people
died from the waters that had become
bitter.[k]
12The fourth angel sounded his trumpet,
and a third of the sun was struck, a third
of the moon, and a third of the stars, so
that a third[l] of them turned dark.[m] A third
of the day was without light, and also a
third of the night.
13As I watched, I heard an eagle that
was flying in midair[n] call out in a loud
voice: "Woe! Woe! Woe[o] to the inhabitants of the earth, because of the trumpet
blasts about to be sounded by the other
three angels!"
9 The fifth angel sounded his trumpet,
and I saw a star that had fallen from
the sky to the earth.[p] The star was given
the key to the shaft of the Abyss.[q] 2When
he opened the Abyss, smoke rose from it
like the smoke from a gigantic furnace.[r]
The sun and sky were darkened[s] by the
smoke from the Abyss. 3And out of the
smoke locusts[t] came down on the earth
and were given power like that of scorpions[u] of the earth. 4They were told not to
harm[v] the grass of the earth or any plant or

8:7 [b] ver 7-12; Rev 9:15,18; 12:4 [c] Rev 9:4 **8:8** [d] Jer 51:25 [e] ver 7 [f] Rev 16:3 **8:9** [g] ver 7 **8:10** [h] Isa 14:12; Rev 6:13; 9:1 [i] Rev 14:7; 16:4 **8:11** [j] ver 7 [k] Jer 9:15; 23:15 **8:12** [l] ver 7 [m] Ex 10:21-23; Rev 6:12,13 **8:13** [n] Rev 14:6; 19:17 [o] Rev 9:12; 11:14 **9:1** [p] Rev 8:10 [q] ver 2,11; Lk 8:31 **9:2** [r] Ge 19:28; Ex 19:18 [s] Joel 2:2,10 **9:3** [t] Ex 10:12-15 [u] ver 5,10 **9:4** [v] Rev 6:6

[a] *11* Wormwood is a bitter substance.

in familiar Biblical terms — on the city figuratively called Sodom and Egypt (11:8). Perhaps most important, the blood of the lamb delivers from the final plague of death (5:9; 7:14; 12:11; cf. Ex 12:12 – 13).

8:7 *hail and fire mixed with blood.* People in the ancient Mediterranean world regarded dangerous hail or hail mixed with other things as a warning of divine judgment. Those who knew Scripture would think of the plague against Egypt in Ex 9:23 – 24. *a third of the trees were burned up.* The destruction of one-third of the trees would cause shortages of fruit, including essential ancient staples such as olives, figs and presumably grapes for wine (vines were often counted as trees). *all the green grass was burned up.* The destruction of all the green grass would mean the impending death of sheep, goats and cattle — hence the end of the world's supply of meat, milk and cheese.

8:8 *huge mountain, all ablaze.* Although a mountain ablaze might evoke Mount Sinai at the giving of the law (Dt 4:11; 5:23; 9:15), in Jewish apocalypses stars sometimes appeared like burning mountains. In one Jewish account, a burning star falls into the sea and burns both the sea and Israel's oppressors; this account and Revelation might both depend on the less obvious image in Jer 51:25,42.

8:9 *a third of the living creatures in the sea died.* This plague recalls Ex 7:20 – 21. Most people ate more fish than meat, so this plague might prove devastating to the food supply faster than its predecessor.

8:10 – 11 *a great star ... fell from the sky on a third of the rivers and on the springs of water — the name of the star is Wormwood.* Like the previous plague, this one contaminates water, yet it adds the severe bitterness associated with the wormwood plant. The probable Hebrew equivalent for this plant was known for its bitterness (Pr 5:4; La 3:15,19) and sometimes was associated with poison (Dt 29:18; Jer 9:15; 23:15).

8:12 *A third of the day was without light, and also a third of the night.* Gentiles feared darkness over the land, but the darkness here probably especially recalls the next-to-last plague against Egypt (Ex 10:21 – 22) and perhaps against its sun-god (Ex 12:12). For partial darkness, cf. perhaps Zec 14:6 – 7.

8:13 *eagle ... call out.* The background of the eagle is debated. People sometimes used eagles to carry messages, but eagles obviously cannot speak. Greeks viewed eagles as omens (whether of good or evil) from Zeus. For this and other reasons the eagle could in some way symbolize judgment. Thus a Roman legion's primary emblem was a silver or gold eagle; this eagle, however, portends a fiercer force than Rome (see 9:7 – 10,14 – 17). Scripture used eagles (as predators) as an image of judgment (Dt 28:49; Jer 48:40; Hos 8:1; Hab 1:8). Indeed, the same Greek term is used for vultures (then considered a type of eagle) devouring dead bodies in Mt 24:28; Lk 17:37 (cf. the image in Eze 39:17; Rev 19:17 – 18). But the eagle here is the messenger, not the judgment itself. The image even applies to God's protection (Ex 19:4; Dt 32:11; cf. Rev 12:14), so it could be simply a majestic heavenly creature (cf. 4:7). *midair.* Could refer to the middle of the heavens or could refer to the highest point of the heavenly dome over the earth, to allow for the message's widest hearing. *Woe! Woe! Woe to the inhabitants of the earth.* Prophets and apocalyptic writers often used woes (laments) to announce judgments (here, the final three trumpet-judgments).

9:1 *the Abyss.* Conventional apocalyptic geography assumed a real location on earth called the abyss. Some also spoke of "the pit" as a place of damnation. Here God is sovereign even over creatures in places of evil (cf. 11:7; 17:8; 20:1,3).

9:2 *sun and sky were darkened by the smoke from the Abyss.* Locusts (v. 3) could cloud the sky (Joel 2:2,10).

9:3 – 11 Like most of the other trumpet judgments, locusts recall a plague against Egypt (Ex 10:13 – 14; see note on Rev 8:7 — 9:19). The specific description of these locusts, however, stems from the book of Joel (Joel 1:6; 2:4), where the locusts are described as an invading army (e.g., Joel 1:4; 2:11,20,25), but an invading eschatological army might be prefigured by the locusts (Joel 3:9 – 12). The locusts here are more than literal locusts (see notes on vv. 4 – 11); they might symbolize either a human army or a demonic one. Revelation might draw on characteristics of Rome's feared enemy in the East, the Parthians (see the article "Parthia," p. 2239). The horses (v. 7; cf. note on 6:2) stem from Joel (2:4), but their long hair (v. 8), characteristic of Parthians, does not come from Joel. Still, specifically Parthian connections here (in contrast with vv. 12 – 19) are few. The locusts here are composite (see note on v. 7).

9:3 *locusts.* See note on vv. 3 – 11. *scorpions.* See note on v. 10.

9:4 *not to harm the grass ... or any plant or tree, but only those people who did not have the seal of God.* Clearly John does not envision normal locusts; locusts target the very

tree,[w] but only those people who did not
have the seal of God on their foreheads.[x]
5They were not allowed to kill them but
only to torture them for five months.[y] And
the agony they suffered was like that of
the sting of a scorpion[z] when it strikes.
6During those days people will seek death
but will not find it; they will long to die,
but death will elude them.[a]
7The locusts looked like horses prepared for battle.[b] On their heads they wore
something like crowns of gold, and their
faces resembled human faces.[c] 8Their hair
was like women's hair, and their teeth
were like lions' teeth.[d] 9They had breastplates like breastplates of iron, and the
sound of their wings was like the thundering of many horses and chariots rushing
into battle.[e] 10They had tails with stingers,
like scorpions, and in their tails they had
power to torment people for five months.[f]
11They had as king over them the angel
of the Abyss,[g] whose name in Hebrew is
Abaddon and in Greek is Apollyon (that
is, Destroyer).
12The first woe is past; two other woes
are yet to come.[h]
13The sixth angel sounded his trumpet, and I heard a voice coming from the
four horns[i] of the golden altar that is before God.[j] 14It said to the sixth angel who
had the trumpet, "Release the four angels who are bound at the great river Euphrates."[k] 15And the four angels who had
been kept ready for this very hour and
day and month and year were released to

9:4 [w] Rev 8:7 [x] Rev 7:2,3
9:5 [y] ver 10 [z] ver 3
9:6 [a] Job 3:21; Jer 8:3; Rev 6:16
9:7 [b] Joel 2:4 [c] Da 7:8
9:8 [d] Joel 1:6
9:9 [e] Joel 2:5
9:10 [f] ver 3, 5,19
9:11 [g] ver 1,2
9:12 [h] Rev 8:13
9:13 [i] Ex 30:1-3 [j] Rev 8:3
9:14 [k] Rev 16:12

sorts of vegetation that these locusts will not harm, but these locusts will harm people.

9:5 *five months.* Although the life span of different kinds of locusts varies significantly, many live roughly three to five months. That God sets limits on their destructiveness, both in intensity (v. 6) and duration (vv. 5,10), may suggest his mercy and again underlines his sovereignty. This limited torment invites repentance (vv. 20–21) to avoid eternal torment (14:10–11; 20:10). *like … the sting of a scorpion.* Scorpions were common in the eastern (and southern) Mediterranean world; their stings were proverbial for causing pain (not usually death in these regions).

9:7 *The locusts looked like horses … their faces resembled human faces.* Ancients often envisioned composite creatures, which they usually deemed superhuman. Griffins mixed eagles and lions; royal Egyptian sphinxes mixed human heads with lions' bodies (turned into monsters among Greeks); the centaurs of Greek myth mixed horses and humans; Babylonians portrayed mixtures of humans with scorpions or horses. Many Greek composites were horrifying, lethal monsters. Those familiar with the Biblical prophets and Jewish apocalyptic literature, however, would recognize that some blending could be metaphor. *horses.* Could recall the Parthians (see note on 6:2), but these already appear in Joel (Joel 2:4; cf. Jer 51:27). *crowns of gold.* If gold crowns suggest royalty or high office (1Ch 20:2; Ps 21:3), they might suggest that each "locust" commands others, implying an army vaster than John can portray. They might also mock the bronze helmets of legionaries. *human faces.* Could indicate the composite design of an angelic creature (Eze 1:10), but may also suggest that this is symbolic of a human army.

9:8 *hair … like women's hair.* Most men in the Roman Empire in this period wore their hair shorter than did women (see note on 1Co 11:14). Everyone knew that the feared Parthians wore their hair long, but ancient portrayals of monstrous or superhuman beings sometimes also included long hair; sometimes Greeks portrayed monsters with snakes as hair, but Revelation spares its audience that image here (though cf. v. 19). *teeth … like lions' teeth.* Reflects Joel 1:6.

9:9 *breastplates of iron.* May compare locusts' scaled bodies with the scales of the armor of eastern soldiers, as in some earlier Jewish texts. *sound of their wings was like the thundering of many horses and chariots.* Might suggest a human army, but the image comes directly from Joel 2:5.

9:10 *tails with stingers, like scorpions.* Everyone knew that scorpions strike with their tails; some connect the tails with the Parthians (see note on v. 19). Jewish people recognized that God used scorpions to execute his judgment.

9:11 *Abaddon.* Scripture regularly linked the Hebrew term *Abaddon* with death and the realm of the dead (e.g., Job 26:6; 28:22; Ps 88:11); the Greek version of the OT sometimes translates this as "Hades" (Job 26:6; Pr 15:11). In Greek, Hades was the sometimes-personified realm of the dead (Rev 6:8), over which God (20:13–14) and Christ (1:18) have ultimate control. But here the control is delegated temporarily to an evil angel who appears to have been imprisoned with the other spirits of the pit. *Apollyon.* The present participle form of the Greek word for "destroy," a noun cognate of which also sometimes translates "Abaddon" (Job 31:12; 28:22; Ps 88:11; cf. Rev 17:8).

9:12–21 Some details of the invasion depicted here derive from the Parthians, Rome's most feared enemy (see the article "Parthia," p. 2239). Whether or not the scene refers to literal Parthians, such details would evoke terror for a Roman audience. (Some prophetic symbolism was intended more to evoke the right response than to predict details.) Literal Parthians obviously did not belch fire like the monsters here do (v. 17). Greeks might envision the horrifying monster called the Chimaera, sometimes depicted as a goat with a fire-breathing lion's head and a dragon's tail. A Diaspora writer envisioned God creating fire-belching monsters specially to execute new judgments. Then again, Jewish apocalyptic sources could depict armies as animals or monsters. Whatever this army represents on a literal level, it is meant to evoke terror—and consequent repentance (vv. 20–21).

9:13 *four horns of the golden altar.* The golden altar represents the incense altar (Ex 30:1–3; Heb 9:4) rather than the sacrificial altar (Ex 35:16); this judgment represents a further response to the prayers of the saints (Rev 8:4–6). Middle Eastern altars normally had four horns.

9:14 *four angels who are bound at the great river Euphrates.* Throughout Mediterranean literature, the Euphrates (also in 16:12) appeared as the traditional boundary between Roman and Parthian territories. *bound.* Pre-Christian apocalyptic writers envisioned evil angels bound in various places, sometimes beneath the earth; other texts portray them as bound in bodies of deep water. Some Jewish prophecies warned of angels stirring the eastern kings of the Parthians and Medes to war and invading the Holy Land. Ancient hearers thus would probably think of the four angels bound in the river Euphrates as evil angels whom God would use as agents of judgment on a wicked world, by stirring the Parthians.

9:15 *for this very hour and day and month and year.* The

REVELATION 9:14

PARTHIA

In the first century BC, Pompey had established the Euphrates River as the boundary between the Roman and Parthian Empires, and that borderline remained in John's day. In Roman sources, when the Parthians crossed the Euphrates, it was to fight the Romans. A later writer observes that only a river separated these two most powerful empires in the world.

The Parthians were the archrivals of the Romans, far more feared than the barbarians on the Roman empire's northern frontier. Early imperial propaganda celebrated Augustus's defeat of Parthia, but the Parthians had sometimes defeated Roman armies since then. Though Rome claimed to subject the north, west and south, Romans admitted that they could not defeat the Parthians to the east. The Parthians were known for their boldness and unpredictability in battle, including the annihilation of some Roman legions with the Parthian riders' backward archery (see note on Rev 9:19).

Earlier, pagan prophecies of an Asian invasion of Rome had terrified the Romans. Some Jewish thinkers expected Nero, whom Christians believed to be an antichrist or at least a precursor to the final antichrist, to cross the Euphrates into Parthia, betraying Rome. They then expected Nero to lead a Parthian invasion of the Roman Empire. As part of the Roman province of Syria, Judea was close to the eastern frontier of the Roman Empire. Thus some first-century Jewish traditions also suggested that God's angels would call together a Parthian invasion of the Holy Land. ◆

Plaque of Parthian archer, first–third century, Syria. Parthian archers were known for being able to ride forward while shooting backward.

kill a third of mankind.[l] 16The number of
the mounted troops was twice ten thousand times ten thousand. I heard their
number.[m]
17The horses and riders I saw in my vision looked like this: Their breastplates were fiery red, dark blue, and yellow as sulfur. The heads of the horses resembled the heads of lions, and out of their mouths[n] came fire, smoke and sulfur.[o]

9:15 [l] ver 18
9:16 [m] Rev 5:11; 7:4
9:17 [n] Rev 11:5 [o] ver 18

designation of specific timing reminds the hearers that God is sovereign. *a third of mankind.* See note on v. 18.
9:16 *twice ten thousand times ten thousand.* Some commentators compare the figure here (200 million) with God's hosts in Ps 68:17; Da 7:10; even this evil army executes God's purposes. The number also outnumbers not only the 144,000 (Rev 7:4–8), but all of Rome's legions—and probably the entire population of the ancient Mediterranean world.
9:17 *horses.* See note on v. 7. *lions.* See v. 8 and note; lions also were considered the most dangerous beasts (cf. 1Ch 12:8; see note on Rev 5:5). *sulfur.* Yellow in substance but burns with a blue flame; sulfur was associated with Sodom's destruction (Ge 19:24; cf. Rev 11:8).

18 A third of mankind was killed[p] by the
three plagues of fire, smoke and sulfur[q]
that came out of their mouths. 19 The power of the horses was in their mouths and in
their tails; for their tails were like snakes,
having heads with which they inflict injury.

20 The rest of mankind who were not
killed by these plagues still did not repent
of the work of their hands;[r] they did not
stop worshiping demons,[s] and idols of
gold, silver, bronze, stone and wood—
idols that cannot see or hear or walk.[t]
21 Nor did they repent[u] of their murders,
their magic arts,[v] their sexual immorality[w]
or their thefts.

The Angel and the Little Scroll

10 Then I saw another mighty angel[x]
coming down from heaven. He was
robed in a cloud, with a rainbow above
his head; his face was like the sun,[y] and
his legs were like fiery pillars.[z] 2 He was
holding a little scroll, which lay open in
his hand. He planted his right foot on the
sea and his left foot on the land, 3 and he
gave a loud shout like the roar of a lion.
When he shouted, the voices of the sev-
en thunders[a] spoke. 4 And when the seven
thunders spoke, I was about to write; but
I heard a voice from heaven say, "Seal up
what the seven thunders have said and do
not write it down."[b]

5 Then the angel I had seen standing on
the sea and on the land raised his right
hand to heaven.[c] 6 And he swore by him
who lives for ever and ever, who created
the heavens and all that is in them, the
earth and all that is in it, and the sea and
all that is in it,[d] and said, "There will be
no more delay![e] 7 But in the days when
the seventh angel is about to sound his
trumpet, the mystery[f] of God will be accomplished, just as he announced to his
servants the prophets."

8 Then the voice that I had heard from
heaven[g] spoke to me once more: "Go, take
the scroll that lies open in the hand of the
angel who is standing on the sea and on
the land."

9 So I went to the angel and asked him
to give me the little scroll. He said to me,
"Take it and eat it. It will turn your stomach sour, but 'in your mouth it will be as
sweet as honey.'[a]"[h] 10 I took the little scroll
from the angel's hand and ate it. It tasted
as sweet as honey in my mouth, but when
I had eaten it, my stomach turned sour.

9:18 [p] ver 15 [q] ver 17 **9:20** [r] Dt 31:29 [s] 1Co 10:20 [t] Ps 115:4-7; 135:15-17; Da 5:23 **9:21** [u] Rev 2:21 [v] Rev 18:23 [w] Rev 17:2,5 **10:1** [x] Rev 5:2 [y] Mt 17:2; Rev 1:16 [z] Rev 1:15 **10:3** [a] Rev 4:5

10:4 [b] Da 8:26; 12:4,9; Rev 22:10 **10:5** [c] Da 12:7 **10:6** [d] Rev 4:11; 14:7 [e] Rev 16:17 **10:7** [f] Ro 16:25 **10:8** [g] ver 4 **10:9** [h] Jer 15:16; Eze 2:8-3:3

[a] 9 Ezek. 3:3

9:18 *A third of mankind was killed.* Though this is judgment, it is also mercy. In some other Jewish traditions, two-thirds of humanity would die from particular judgments. Striking a third (8:7 – 12) or a tenth (11:13) means that the majority still has a chance to repent (vv. 20 – 21).
9:19 *tails … like snakes.* The serpent-like tails may evoke hideous pictures in Greek mythology such as Medusa or various demons with snake hair; cf. also the dragon in 12:3 – 4. Some relate the tails to the Parthians. A devastating Parthian battle tactic was to retreat uphill; when the Romans followed, the Parthian archers, who had perfected the art of riding forward while shooting backward, annihilated them with a hail of arrows.
9:20 *still did not repent.* God mercifully sends judgments to invite repentance (Am 4:6 – 11; Hag 2:17; cf. Ex 8:9 – 10; 9:14,29), as Jewish thinkers recognized. (Many Gentiles agreed, but with different gods, which is part of the problem here.) Despite God's invitations to repentance, the world, like Pharaoh during the plagues on Egypt, refused to repent (Ex 7:22 – 23). *work of their hands.* Following Scripture (e.g., Isa 37:19; 44:19), Jewish writers condemned gods of wood and stone and precious metals. Both early Christians (1Co 10:20) and most Jews believed that the Gentiles' deities were demons.
10:1 – 2 *robed in a cloud … He planted his right foot on the sea and his left foot on the land.* Being robed (cf. 12:1) in a cloud (cf. 11:12; 14:14) and feet straddling land and sea emphasize the angel's heavenly stature. Greeks told of superhuman giants, but Jewish tradition also depicted giant angels, some as high as the heavens. Their magnitude helped hearers to stand in awe of the God who was infinitely greater than such angels.
10:1 *rainbow above his head.* A rainbow surrounds God in Eze 1:28, but in some Jewish traditions it is associated also with some high-ranking angels. *face … like the sun.* Jewish sources often mention shining angels (in Scripture, cf. Da 10:6). *legs … like fiery pillars.* May recall the Greek view of the world supported by pillars (cf. also Job 9:6; Ps 75:3); in Greek myth the giant Atlas supported the world. Appearing right after comparisons with the rainbow and the sun, however, the fiery pillars might evoke especially the heavenly pillar of fire in the wilderness (e.g., Ex 13:21 – 22; 14:24).
10:3 *voices of the seven thunders spoke.* Ancients widely understood that the supreme God ruled thunder (see note on 4:5), and in some ancient traditions thunder could sound like God's voice (cf. Jn 12:29). For a voice from heaven, see note on Mt 3:17.
10:4 *Seal up what the seven thunders have said.* Perhaps the contents of the seven thunders remain mysterious to teach that the hidden things belong to God (19:12; Dt 29:29; cf. 2Co 12:4).
10:5 *raised his right hand to heaven.* People sometimes lifted both hands toward heaven when swearing by heavenly deities; Jewish people lifted at least one hand when swearing an oath (cf. Dt 32:40; Da 12:7).
10:6 *he swore by him who lives for ever and ever.* Recalls Da 12:7; in Daniel the angel announces three and a half more years, but here the angel notes that with the seventh trumpet the end is at hand (v. 7).
10:10 *I took the little scroll from the angel's hand and ate it.* Ezekiel also found a scroll in a heavenly hand (Eze 2:9). God instructed Ezekiel to eat the book (Eze 2:8; 3:1; cf. Rev 10:9). *It tasted as sweet as honey in my mouth, but … my stomach turned sour.* As in Ezekiel (Eze 3:3), the book proved as sweet as honey in his mouth, not surprising for God's words (Ps 19:10; 119:103; Pr 24:13 – 14). That the scroll proves bitter in John's stomach may reflect the message's content: woes (cf. Eze 2:9 – 10).

11Then I was told, "You must prophesy[i]
again about many peoples, nations, languages and kings."

The Two Witnesses

11 I was given a reed like a measuring rod[j] and was told, "Go and
measure the temple of God and the altar, with its worshipers. 2But exclude the
outer court;[k] do not measure it, because
it has been given to the Gentiles.[l] They
will trample on the holy city[m] for 42
months.[n] 3And I will appoint my two witnesses,[o] and they will prophesy for 1,260
days, clothed in sackcloth."[p] 4They are
"the two olive trees"[q] and the two lampstands, and "they stand before the Lord
of the earth."[a r] 5If anyone tries to harm
them, fire comes from their mouths and
devours their enemies.[s] This is how anyone who wants to harm them must die.[t]
6They have power to shut up the heavens so that it will not rain during the time
they are prophesying; and they have power to turn the waters into blood[u] and to
strike the earth with every kind of plague
as often as they want.
7Now when they have finished their testimony, the beast[v] that comes up from the
Abyss will attack them,[w] and overpower
and kill them. 8Their bodies will lie in the
public square of the great city — which is
figuratively called Sodom[x] and Egypt —
where also their Lord was crucified.[y] 9For
three and a half days some from every people, tribe, language and nation will gaze
on their bodies and refuse them burial.[z]

10:11 [i] Eze 37:4,9 **11:1** [j] Eze 40:3; Rev 21:15 **11:2** [k] Eze 40:17, 20 [l] Lk 21:24 [m] Rev 21:2 [n] Da 7:25; Rev 13:5 **11:3** [o] Rev 1:5 [p] Ge 37:34 **11:4** [q] Ps 52:8; Jer 11:16; Zec 4:3,11 [r] Zec 4:14 **11:5** [s] 2Ki 1:10; Jer 5:14 [t] Nu 16:29,35 **11:6** [u] Ex 7:17, 19 **11:7** [v] Rev 13:1-4 [w] Da 7:21 **11:8** [x] Isa 1:9 [y] Heb 13:12 **11:9** [z] Ps 79:2,3

[a] 4 See Zech. 4:3,11,14.

10:11 *prophesy . . . about many peoples, nations, languages and kings.* Whereas Ezekiel was to deliver the message only to the people of Israel (Eze 3:1), John would prophesy to many peoples, like Jeremiah (Jer 1:10) — and the two witnesses (Rev 11:3).

11:1 *measure the temple.* Measuring might symbolize a promise of preservation or greatness, as in the measuring of Jerusalem (Ps 48:12 – 13; Zec 2:1 – 2) or the temple (Eze 40 – 42, especially Eze 40:3); or the spiritual unpreparedness of Israel (Am 7:7 – 9). Whatever the case, some measurements finally appear (only in 21:16) — but for the massive new Jerusalem, which is shaped like the Most Holy Place. This could suggest that the small, persecuted remnant oppressed during this age belongs to the glorious Holy City to come.

11:2 *it has been given to the Gentiles.* Gentiles had been welcome only in the outer court (see note on Mk 11:16). Before the temple's destruction in AD 70, most Jewish tradition considered the temple invulnerable, but some believed that it had been desecrated and would be destroyed (see note on Mt 24:2; for fulfillment, see note on Mt 24:15). Once it was destroyed, the entire temple, not just the outer court, was destroyed. Jerusalem remained under Gentile rule for centuries after AD 70, and especially after AD 135, when it was rebuilt as a Gentile city. Some Jews spoke figuratively of God's people as a temple (in the Dead Sea Scrolls; cf. Rev 3:12; 13:6).

11:3 – 6 Following an ancient Jewish tradition in 4 Ezra, some church fathers (such as Hippolytus, Tertullian and Jerome) believed that because Enoch and Elijah had never died they would return as these witnesses. Many Jewish people expected future prophets who would be like Elijah (Mal 4:5 – 6) and Moses (Dt 18:15 – 18); echoes of these prophets' works appear in v. 6. Because of deviations from these OT models (e.g., in vv. 4 – 5), other interpreters view them as symbolic for God's people more generally as witnesses (see notes on vv. 3 – 4).

11:3 *two witnesses.* Those who take the witnesses symbolically debate the reason for two of them; some think of the need for at least two witnesses (Dt 17:6; 19:15; Mk 6:7), and/or to match the two olive trees or a king and priest (see note on Rev 11:4), and/or the contrast with two evil leaders in 13:11 – 12. *1,260 days.* Equivalent to 42 months of 30 days each, probably adapted from Da 12:11; see the article "Time in Revelation," p. 2245. *sackcloth.* Signified mourning and self-humiliation, often specifically the mourning of repentance.

11:4 *two olive trees.* Recalls the anointed king and priest (Zec 4:11 – 14). In the immediate context in Zechariah, these were Joshua and Zerubbabel, who worked for the good of a city trampled by Gentiles (Zec 3 – 4; cf. Rev 11:2). The lampstand in Zec 4:2 may refer to the source of the Spirit (see Zec 4:6); presumably it burned the same olive oil with which "the two who are anointed to serve the Lord" (Zec 4:14) were anointed. Those who take v. 3 as symbolic may envision here a kingdom and priests (Rev 1:6; 5:10), corresponding to the olive trees of king and priest in Zechariah; this would fit the symbolism elsewhere in Revelation of lampstands as churches (1:20; see note on 1:12).

11:5 *fire comes from their mouths and devours their enemies.* Fire destroying enemies evokes Elijah (2Ki 1:10,12; see note on Rev 11:6), but it coming from the mouth alludes instead to the figurative image regarding Jeremiah in Jer 5:14 (cf. Jer 6:11; 20:9).

11:6 *shut up the heavens.* Evokes Elijah. *turn the waters into blood.* Evokes Moses, as does the ability to strike with other plagues. Jewish people expected future prophets like Elijah (Mal 4:5 – 6) and Moses (Dt 18:15 – 18).

11:7 *beast that comes out from the Abyss will . . . kill them.* The Greek text here suggests that the beast (13:1 – 3) from the Abyss (see 9:11 and note) wages war with them and conquers them. Some Jewish people expected end-time holy war, but the witnesses here have finished their mission and submit to martyrdom (cf. notes on 7:4 – 8,9). Ancient writers valued irony; here the beast conquers the witnesses, but from heaven's perspectives those who resist the beast are truly victorious (2:10 – 11; 3:9,12; 12:11; 15:2).

11:8 *Their bodies will lie in the public square.* Being refused burial was shameful treatment reserved for the worst criminals; the only worse fate was, as here, for the bodies to be publicly displayed. *great city.* Elsewhere in Revelation, the "great city" is Babylon (18:10), but see the end of this note. *figuratively.* The Greek term here may mean "according to insight revealed by the Spirit" (cf. 17:3; 19:10; 21:10). *Sodom.* Fire devoured Sodom (Ge 19:24; cf. Rev 20:9). *Egypt.* Plagues fell on Egypt (see note on 8:7 — 9:19). *where also their Lord was crucified.* Just outside Jerusalem; the witnesses were seen by the world (vv. 9 – 10). In a sense, the city described here may thus symbolize the world system (which could include Judeans, cf. 2:9; 3:9); it contrasts with the Holy City, the new Jerusalem to come (21:2).

11:9 *three and a half days.* May recall the years of their ministry (v. 3), indicating a defeat much briefer than the ministry (cf. v. 11). On the narrative level it also suggests, in

10The inhabitants of the earth[a] will gloat over them and will celebrate by sending each other gifts,[b] because these two prophets had tormented those who live on the earth.

11But after the three and a half days the breath[a] of life from God entered them,[c] and they stood on their feet, and terror struck those who saw them. 12Then they heard a loud voice from heaven saying to them, "Come up here."[d] And they went up to heaven in a cloud,[e] while their enemies looked on.

13At that very hour there was a severe earthquake[f] and a tenth of the city collapsed. Seven thousand people were killed in the earthquake, and the survivors were terrified and gave glory[g] to the God of heaven.[h]

14The second woe has passed; the third woe is coming soon.[i]

The Seventh Trumpet

15The seventh angel sounded his trumpet,[j] and there were loud voices[k] in heaven, which said:

"The kingdom of the world has
    become
  the kingdom of our Lord and of his
    Messiah,[l]
  and he will reign for ever and
    ever."[m]

16And the twenty-four elders,[n] who were seated on their thrones before God, fell on their faces and worshiped God, 17saying:

"We give thanks to you, Lord God
    Almighty,[o]
  the One who is and who was,
because you have taken your great
    power
  and have begun to reign.[p]
18The nations were angry,[q]
  and your wrath has come.
The time has come for judging the
    dead,
  and for rewarding your servants the
    prophets[r]
and your people who revere your name,
  both great and small[s] —
and for destroying those who destroy
    the earth."

19Then God's temple[t] in heaven was opened, and within his temple was seen the ark of his covenant. And there came flashes of lightning, rumblings, peals of thunder, an earthquake and a severe hailstorm.[u]

The Woman and the Dragon

12 A great sign appeared in heaven: a woman clothed with the sun, with the moon under her feet and a crown of twelve stars on her head. 2She was pregnant and cried out in pain[v] as she was

11:10 [a] Rev 3:10 [b] Est 9:19,22 **11:11** [c] Eze 37:5,9, 10,14 **11:12** [d] Rev 4:1 [e] 2Ki 2:11; Ac 1:9 **11:13** [f] Rev 6:12 [g] Rev 14:7 [h] Rev 16:11 **11:14** [i] Rev 8:13 **11:15** [j] Rev 10:7 [k] Rev 16:17; 19:1 [l] Rev 12:10 [m] Da 2:44; 7:14,27 **11:16** [n] Rev 4:4 **11:17** [o] Rev 1:8 [p] Rev 19:6 **11:18** [q] Ps 2:1 [r] Rev 10:7 [s] Rev 19:5 **11:19** [t] Rev 15:5,8 [u] Rev 16:21 **12:2** [v] Gal 4:19

[a] *11* Or *Spirit* (see Ezek. 37:5,14)

---

a Mediterranean setting, that their corpses are rotting; cf. note on Jn 11:39. *every people, tribe, language and nation.* See note on 5:9.

11:10 *celebrate by sending each other gifts.* In Est 9:19, God's people celebrated escape from genocide and the destruction of their enemies. Here, by contrast, the enemies of God's servants exchange gifts after killing them (though cf. later 19:1–7).

11:11 *the breath of life.* May also be translated "the Spirit of life" (see NIV text note), associating the Spirit with resurrection as in Ro 8:2,10–11. This breath evokes Ge 2:7 and contrasts with the false life imparted in Rev 13:15.

11:12 *they went up to heaven in a cloud.* Jewish traditions added some other ascensions, but the best known was the one described in the OT: Elijah (cf. vv. 5–6 and notes) was caught up to heaven (2Ki 2:9–11).

11:13 *a tenth of the city.* Biblical prophets sometimes limited the surviving remnant after judgment to a tenth who would ultimately follow the Lord (Isa 6:13; Am 5:3). *Seven thousand people were killed.* Could epitomize a remnant (1Ki 19:18). Here, however, in God's mercy, it is a tenth (the 7,000) that dies, whereas most of the city turns to God ("gave glory to . . . God" can carry this meaning; cf. 16:9.)

11:15 *seventh angel sounded his trumpet.* Although the final trumpet concludes the series of the seven trumpets, trumpets were also blown at a king's enthronement (1Ki 1:34–41; 2Ki 9:13; 11:14). Many Jewish people prayed daily for the coming of God's kingdom, which would finally supplant the series of world empires (Da 2:44; cf. Da 7:17–18). (For the eternal reign of God, cf. Ps 10:16; 146:10; for that of David's house, cf. Ps 89:29,36; 132:12; for the Davidic prince, cf. Isa 9:7; for the son of man, cf. Da 7:13–14.) *kingdom of our Lord and of his Messiah.* May recall Ps 2:2, where the nations challenged God and the Messiah but would ultimately be crushed (see the nations' anger in note on v. 18).

11:17 *have begun to reign.* Biblical voices already celebrated God's reign (e.g., Ex 15:18; Ps 97:1), but a climactic arrival of the kingdom appears here (see note on v. 15).

11:18 *The nations were angry.* Quoted from the common Greek translation of Ps 2:1; there, God's king would respond angrily by destroying the nations (Ps 2:12). *your servants the prophets.* The OT mentions God's servants the prophets nearly 20 times, though the image here might apply to all God's people (cf. Rev 19:10; Nu 11:29; Joel 2:28–29). *destroying those who destroy the earth.* Echoes the common Greek translation of Jer 51:25, perhaps suggesting that the evil empire, like the earlier Babylon, devastates the whole earth.

11:19 *within his temple was seen the ark of his covenant.* Jewish people often believed that God had hidden the ark, but that it would be restored in the end time (see note on 2:17). Previously the ark of the covenant remained secluded from view in the Most Holy Place (Ex 40:21; Lev 16:2); now it is revealed to the world. Romans displayed edicts in public places, such as temples; God's covenant law was deposited in the ark of the covenant. *lightning . . . thunder.* May evoke God's revelation at Mount Sinai (see note on 4:5).

12:1–2 *a woman . . . about to give birth.* The prophets portrayed righteous Israel as the mother of the restored future remnant of Israel (Isa 26:18–19; 54:1; 66:7–10; Mic 4:9–10; 5:3), and also as the mother of the leader who embodied Israel's restoration (Isa 9:6; cf. Mic 5:2–3). The

REVELATION 12:1 – 6

SYMBOLISM IN REVELATION 12:1–6

John calls both the woman and the dragon "signs" (see 12:1,3; cf. 15:1). This was often the language of prophetic assurances (e.g., Isa 8:18; 20:3; 37:30; Jer 44:29; Eze 4:3; 12:6,12; 24:24,27). Greeks sometimes applied the term to constellations in the heavens, such as Virgo (a woman) and the dragon Draco or the serpent. Images such as those John uses were thus familiar among his Gentile contemporaries. John's signs do not, however, communicate astrological meaning; instead they reapply traditional, and often Biblical, symbols in new ways.

The woman is a mother, somehow the antecedent of the faithful bride of Christ, the new Jerusalem (21:2) and the contrast to Babylon the prostitute (17:5). Although early Christians shared the common experience of the surrounding Greco-Roman world, the one theological resource they shared most was Scripture. There the Prophets portrayed righteous Israel as the mother of the restored future remnant of Israel (e.g., Isa 66:7 – 10), an image they mixed with that of Israel as a bride (Isa 62:5). In Jewish tradition Zion or Jerusalem often appeared as a mother (see note on 12:1 – 2).

Many people in the ancient world believed giant serpents or dragons existed literally in other parts of the world, but John again speaks only of a "sign" (12:3). Serpents were significant in the cult of Asclepius, which was prominent, e.g., in Pergamum. More important was the myth of the dragon opposing a mother in childbirth. In Egyptian mythology, Isis (Hathor), portrayed with the sun on her head, birthed Horus, and the dragon Typhon sought to slay her, but she escaped to an island and her son Horus overthrew the dragon. In the Greek version of the story, the great dragon Python, warned that he would be killed by Leto's son, pursued the pregnant Leto, who was hidden by Poseidon on an island that he then temporarily submerged. After Python had left, Leto birthed the god Apollo, who in four days was strong enough to slay the dragon. Many scholars argue that cities in Asia Minor blended the emperor with Apollo. Here, however, the emperor, like Apollo and Gentiles' other supposed deities, was a pawn of the doomed dragon!

Earlier Scripture provided Revelation precedent by adapting similar mythical images. God's conquest of the primeval dragon Leviathan (Ps 74:14; Isa 27:1) symbolizes especially God's conquest of Egypt (nicknamed "Rahab," Isa 30:7) when God brought his people through the sea (Ps 89:9 – 10; Isa 51:9 – 10). Jewish tradition developed various stories about Leviathan as a literal beast whom God would destroy at the end.

But for John, the dragon is especially the "ancient serpent" (12:9), the one in Genesis who led Adam and Eve to death by enticing them to disobey God (Ge 3:1 – 15) like Balaam later did with the Israelites (Nu 25:1 – 2; 31:16; see note on Rev 2:14). Similarly, Jewish tradition sometimes identified the serpent with the devil or linked him with the devil in other ways. ◆

about to give birth. 3 Then another sign
appeared in heaven: an enormous red
dragon with seven heads and ten horns[w]
and seven crowns[x] on its heads. 4 Its tail
swept a third[y] of the stars out of the sky
and flung them to the earth.[z] The dragon stood in front of the woman who was
about to give birth, so that it might devour her child[a] the moment he was born.
5 She gave birth to a son, a male child, who
"will rule all the nations with an iron scepter."[a][b] And her child was snatched up to
God and to his throne. 6 The woman fled
into the wilderness to a place prepared for
her by God, where she might be taken care
of for 1,260 days.[c]

7 Then war broke out in heaven. Michael and his angels fought against the dragon,[d] and the dragon and his angels fought
back. 8 But he was not strong enough, and
they lost their place in heaven. 9 The great
dragon was hurled down — that ancient
serpent[e] called the devil,[f] or Satan, who
leads the whole world astray.[g] He was
hurled to the earth,[h] and his angels with
him.

10 Then I heard a loud voice in heaven[i]
say:

"Now have come the salvation and the power
and the kingdom of our God,
and the authority of his Messiah.
For the accuser of our brothers and sisters,[j]
who accuses them before our God day and night,
has been hurled down.
11 They triumphed over him
by the blood of the Lamb[k]
and by the word of their testimony;[l]
they did not love their lives so much as to shrink from death.[m]
12 Therefore rejoice, you heavens[n]
and you who dwell in them!
But woe[o] to the earth and the sea,[p]
because the devil has gone down to you!
He is filled with fury,
because he knows that his time is short."

a 5 Psalm 2:9

12:3 [w] Da 7:7, 20; Rev 13:1 [x] Rev 19:12 **12:4** [y] Rev 8:7 [z] Da 8:10 [a] Mt 2:16 **12:5** [b] Ps 2:9; Rev 2:27 **12:6** [c] Rev 11:2 **12:7** [d] ver 3 **12:9** [e] Ge 3:1-7 [f] Mt 25:41 [g] Rev 20:3, 8, 10 [h] Lk 10:18; Jn 12:31

12:10 [i] Rev 11:15 [j] Job 1:9-11; Zec 3:1 **12:11** [k] Rev 7:14 [l] Rev 6:9 [m] Lk 14:26 **12:12** [n] Ps 96:11; Isa 49:13; Rev 18:20 [o] Rev 8:13 [p] Rev 10:6

Dead Sea Scrolls also depict a period of great tribulation as childbirth, possibly to bring forth the righteous remnant. The "sun, with the moon ... and a crown of twelve stars" confirm this vision as symbolizing Israel or its faithful remnant (Ge 37:9). If she symbolizes Israel's righteous remnant before Christ's exaltation (12:1 – 5) — righteous Israelites and Gentile converts — she may also represent God's true followers after Christ's exaltation (12:6 – 17), although this interpretation is debated.

12:3 *an enormous red dragon.* In Isaiah, God promised the suffering, pregnant Israel that she would truly bear new life in the time of the resurrection (Isa 26:17 – 19), the day of God's wrath in which he would slay the serpent (Isa 26:20 — 27:1). In the exodus God crushed this monster when he brought his people through the sea (Isa 51:9 – 10). *red dragon.* In Egyptian myth, the hostile dragon Typhon is red. John connects this dragon with the "ancient serpent" of Ge 3:1 – 15 (see note on Rev 12:9). *seven heads.* In Scripture, the serpent Leviathan had many heads (Ps 74:14), identified in Canaanite tradition as seven.

12:4 *swept a third of the stars out of the sky.* Jewish thinkers often identified stars as angels. Jewish tradition taught that Satan's revolt had long ago led to the fall of many angels (often associated with Ge 6:2), a perspective apparently echoed in 1Pe 3:19 – 22; 2Pe 2:4. Here the image is reapplied (or perhaps reenacted) Christocentrically: the greatest revolt of Satan and the ultimate goal of angelic apostasy was opposition to Jesus' mission on earth. *that it might devour her child.* In ancient myths, a dragon tried to kill a newborn divine child that was destined to slay the dragon if the child survived and grew; see the article "Symbolism in Revelation 12:1 – 6," p. 2243. John's dragon is a Biblical image (see notes on vv. 3,9), but his vision adapts the myth to depict the dragon-slayer as a child.

12:5 *male child, who "will rule all the nations with an iron scepter."* Recalls Ps 2:9; cf. Rev 2:27; 19:15. The emphasis here is not his birth but his enthronement (cf. Ps 2:6 – 7; Ac 13:32 – 33).

12:6 *fled into the wilderness to a place prepared for her by God.* God's deliverance of his people from Egypt, which is portrayed as a dragon (Ps 74:14; 89:10; Isa 51:9 – 10), is now revisited in a new exodus. In Gentile myths about the dragon pursuing a mother, the woman escapes to an island. The distinctly different image here instead recalls Israel's exodus into the wilderness. Because the prophets had promised a new exodus into the wilderness at the time of Israel's future redemption (Isa 40:3; Hos 2:14; see note on Mt 3:3), some Jewish people literally withdrew into the wilderness to await its arrival, and some Messianic claimants arose there. Others sought refuge from oppressors there. *1,260 days.* Adapts Daniel's great tribulation (cf. Da 12:11); working from a 360-day year, 1,260 days would be three and a half years (Da 7:25; 12:7). Some scholars believe that John adapts Daniel's figure with a new meaning here, as he apparently does with the "ten days" in Rev 2:10 (see note there; cf. Da 1:12 – 14). See the article "Time in Revelation," p. 2245.

12:7 – 9 *Michael and his angels fought against the dragon.* Based on Daniel (Da 10:13,21; 12:1), Jewish thinkers recognized Michael as Israel's guardian prince. Although he could ward off the angels of other nations, Michael would be ordered to withdraw when Israel would face its final tribulation (Da 12:1). The Dead Sea Scrolls anticipated an end-time holy war, and Jewish sources elaborate on Michael; here, however, the heavenly victory coincides with Christ's triumph on earth.

12:9 *ancient serpent.* In Genesis, this serpent led Adam and Eve to death by enticing them to disobey God (Ge 3:1 – 15), as Balaam later did with the Israelites (Nu 25:1 – 2; 31:16; see note on Rev 2:14).

12:10 *the accuser ... accuses them before our God day and night.* Jewish tradition elaborated the Biblical picture of Satan as an accuser (Zec 3:1), sometimes directly before God's throne (Job 1:6; 2:1). Some later Jewish sources claimed that he accuses God's people day and night. Christ's exaltation (v. 5) spells Satan's expulsion from his role as heavenly prosecutor (cf. Ro 8:33 – 34).

12:12 *filled with fury.* Cf. 11:18 (see note there).

REVELATION 12:6

Time in Revelation

Following Daniel, writers could envision a final three-and-a-half-year tribulation (Da 9:24–27; 12:1,11). Nevertheless, various Jewish traditions adapted the duration of the final tribulation, suggesting a range of durations (most commonly 40 years). Is it possible that Revelation adapts the period? Although the matter remains debated, the following observations could support the possibility that Revelation adapts this period symbolically:

1. As noted, some of John's contemporaries also symbolically reapplied Daniel's figure for the tribulation.
2. Daniel itself reapplies Jeremiah's 70-years prophecy to a much longer period (Da 9:2,24).
3. Jesus apparently expected Daniel's tribulation to be at least partly fulfilled in the events of AD 66–70, when the temple was desecrated, destroyed and became a site for sacrifices to Caesar (see notes on Mt 24:15,34; Mk 13:30); on the usual date of Revelation, this desolation had already taken place.
4. Revelation rarely takes over Jewish symbols of the end, even from Scripture, without reapplying them in light of Jesus (for symbolic numbers, see note on Rev 7:4–8).
5. More concretely, Rev 12:5–6 sound as if this tribulation period immediately follows Jesus' exaltation (i.e., starting somewhere around AD 30).
6. Satan's expulsion from heaven coincides with "salvation," the "kingdom," and his loss of any right to accuse Jesus' followers before God, now that Jesus is exalted (Rev 12:9–10).

Whether Revelation adapts Daniel's time period will continue to be debated. If it does so, however, it probably does so to tell us about the *kind* of time rather than the length of time, i.e., to use it to depict a period of great, end-time tribulation. If Jesus Christ is king, and if he has come yet will also come again, then Christians are already living in the final era (Ac 2:17; cf. 1Ti 4:1; 2Ti 3:1; Heb 1:2; 1Pe 1:20; 2Pe 3:3–5). Although the consummation remains future, Christ's kingship has inaugurated Satan's expected future defeat. Although interpreters may find in other passages a special end-time tribulation, Revelation might here (most clearly in 12:5–6) apply the image of end-time tribulation to the period between Jesus' comings—giving a Christocentric interpretation of time and a fresh, Christocentric approach to traditional Jewish end-time expectation. ◆

13 When the dragon[q] saw that he had
been hurled to the earth, he pursued the
woman who had given birth to the male
child.[r] 14 The woman was given the two
wings of a great eagle,[s] so that she might
fly to the place prepared for her in the wilderness, where she would be taken care
of for a time, times and half a time,[t] out
of the serpent's reach. 15 Then from his
mouth the serpent spewed water like a

12:13 [q] ver 3 [r] ver 5 **12:14** [s] Ex 19:4 [t] Da 7:25

12:13 *he pursued the woman.* In Jewish tradition, Satan would be unleashed in special fury against Israel in the end time.
12:14 *wings.* Could evoke wings to flee into the wilderness in Ps 55:6–7, or could refer more directly to God's help. In the first exodus, God carried his people on eagles' wings (Ex 19:4; Dt 32:11); in the new exodus God would renew his people to soar like eagles (Isa 40:31). *wilderness.* See note on v. 6. *taken care of.* The miraculous provision in the wilderness here evokes the manna God gave his people in the wilderness. *a time, times and half a time.* Points to the three and a half years of great tribulation, as in Da 7:25; 12:7; see the article "Time in Revelation," p. 2245.
12:15 *the serpent spewed water like a river.* In Greek stories river deities could send floods against their enemies (Homer, *Iliad* 21.248–327); in Scripture, the serpent that God overthrew in the first exodus lived in the waters (Ps 74:13; 89:9–10; Isa 51:9–10; Eze 29:3; 32:2). A flood of water could

river, to overtake the woman and sweep
her away with the torrent. 16But the earth
helped the woman by opening its mouth
and swallowing the river that the dragon
had spewed out of his mouth. 17Then the
dragon was enraged at the woman and
went off to wage war[u] against the rest of
her offspring[v] — those who keep God's
commands[w] and hold fast their testimony
about Jesus.[x]

The Beast out of the Sea

13 The dragon[a] stood on the shore of
the sea. And I saw a beast coming
out of the sea.[y] It had ten horns and sev-
en heads,[z] with ten crowns on its horns,
and on each head a blasphemous name.[a]
2The beast I saw resembled a leopard,[b] but
had feet like those of a bear[c] and a mouth
like that of a lion.[d] The dragon gave the
beast his power and his throne and great
authority.[e] 3One of the heads of the beast
seemed to have had a fatal wound, but
the fatal wound had been healed.[f] The
whole world was filled with wonder[g] and
followed the beast. 4People worshiped the
dragon because he had given authority
to the beast, and they also worshiped the
beast and asked, "Who is like[h] the beast?
Who can wage war against it?"

5The beast was given a mouth to utter
proud words and blasphemies[i] and to exercise its authority for forty-two months.[j]
6It opened its mouth to blaspheme God,
and to slander his name and his dwelling place and those who live in heav-
en.[k] 7It was given power to wage war[l]
against God's holy people and to conquer
them. And it was given authority over every tribe, people, language and nation.[m]

12:17 [u] Rev 11:7 [v] Ge 3:15 [w] Rev 14:12 [x] Rev 1:2 **13:1** [y] Da 7:1-6; Rev 15:2 [z] Rev 12:3 [a] Da 11:36; Rev 17:3 **13:2** [b] Da 7:6 [c] Da 7:5 [d] Da 7:4 [e] Rev 16:10 **13:3** [f] ver 12, 14 [g] Rev 17:8 **13:4** [h] Ex 15:11 **13:5** [i] Da 7:8, 11, 20, 25; 11:36; 2Th 2:4 [j] Rev 11:2 **13:6** [k] Rev 12:12 **13:7** [l] Da 7:21; Rev 11:7 [m] Rev 5:9

[a] *1* Some manuscripts *And I*

represent any sufferings (Ps 32:6; Jer 47:2), including unjust opposition (Ps 18:3–4; 69:1–4,14–15; 124:2–5); serpents' mouths represent slander in Ps 140:1–5. But God would be with his people through the waters (Isa 43:2).

12:16 *the earth helped ... by opening its mouth and swallowing the river.* In the most common form of the Greek myth of the serpent opposing the woman, the serpent was a son of Earth; here, however, the earth, obeying God, helps the woman. (In a different version of the myth, Earth raises up the Aegean island of Delos to help the mother.) Jewish texts portray the earth, at God's command, swallowing sinners, or Sheol swallowing the end-time invaders of the Holy Land. Most relevantly, Scripture poetically depicted the defeat of Israel's pursuers in the sea as the earth swallowing them (Ex 15:10,12).

12:17 *the dragon was enraged.* Cf. v. 12; 11:18; see note on 11:18. *went off to wage war against the rest of her offspring.* Echoes the promise of the woman's seed suffering from and overcoming the serpent (Ge 3:15; see note on Ro 16:20). For how the devil wages war on God's people, see Rev 13:1–8.

13:1 *shore.* Reflects "the nations" over whom the beast rules (20:8). *a beast coming out of the sea.* The beast here recalls Da 7:3–8, where four beasts arise from the "sea" (Da 7:2). *the sea.* Might evoke again the mythical serpent (Ps 74:13–14; 89:9–10; Isa 27:1; see note on Rev 12:15). Judeans, Ephesians and others experienced Rome as coming from "the sea." *ten horns and seven heads.* The ten horns may recall the fourth beast of Da 7:7,24 (see next note). Together with the seven heads the ten horns also look back to another beast, the serpent (12:3). *blasphemous name.* Probably evokes the arrogant boasts of Da 7:8,20; John's churches might think of divine titles — such as "lord," "god" and "son of god" — given to emperors.

13:2 *leopard ... bear ... lion.* Daniel's four beasts are: a winged lion (a griffin) that became somewhat human; a devouring bear; a winged leopard; and finally a ten-horned beast fiercer than its predecessors (Da 7:3–8), preceding the Son of Man's coming (Da 7:9–14). Jewish tradition in this period understood Daniel's fourth beast as Rome, which most Jews believed would be the fourth world empire to subdue Israel. Yet Revelation's beast differs even from Daniel's four-headed fourth beast; Revelation's beast has seven heads and includes features of the leopard, bear and lion. By encompassing all the beasts, this beast embodies the spirit of evil empire — even beyond Rome, the evil empire of John's day.

13:3 *fatal wound had been healed.* The return from death here parodies Jesus' resurrection. The restored head here is probably a Roman ruler (see note on 17:11). This could play on ancient expectations of Nero's return that circulated at the time that Revelation was written (see the article "A New Nero," p. 2248). For persecution of Christians, see note on v. 7. Revelation's primary background for picturing a ruler as a head is in Daniel (Da 7:6); but early Romans also saw a severed head, found buried in the earth during Rome's building, as an omen of Rome's future rule.

13:4 *Who is like the beast?* Parodies the worship properly due to God alone (Ex 15:11). People worshiped the dragon as well as the beast. In John's day, people not only worshiped the emperor, but sacrificed to the gods on behalf of his health.

13:5 *proud words and blasphemies.* Might evoke the boastful speaking of Da 7:8,20, and speaking "against the Most High" in Da 7:25. The dominant ruler of the final beast would persecute God's holy people for three and a half years (Da 7:21,25; cf. Da 9:25–27; 12:7), or about 42 months.

13:6 *to slander his name and his dwelling place and those who live in heaven.* Cf. Da 7:25. The older brother of the current emperor, Domitian, had presided over the burning and desecration of the temple; but John refers to the heavenly temple, in Greek here probably identified with "those who live in heaven" (cf. 3:12).

13:7 *wage war against God's holy people.* Cf. Da 7:21,25. Biblically literate hearers understood that God would vindicate them (Da 7:22), at the time the son of man receives the kingdom (Da 7:13–14). Emperors portrayed themselves in military form and at least claimed to perform a significant military role; but here instead of making war on external threats to the empire's security, the ruler makes war on God's holy people, who do not strike back with violence. *every tribe, people, language and nation.* See note on 5:9. Their submission to the beast was not necessarily initially voluntary (cf. Da 3:4–6). Claims to rule humanity (e.g., Da 3:4,7; 4:1; 5:19) were usually hyperbolic; the emperor Augustus had claimed to rule the entire inhabited world, having even subdued the Parthians (see the article "Parthia," p. 2239). This was, however, merely

REVELATION 13:1

The Imperial Cult

From Egyptians to rulers of empires to the east of Israel, many peoples affirmed that their rulers were divine. When Alexander the Great conquered Persia, he began to accept veneration that was difficult for his Greek and Macedonian followers to accept. Even Greeks, however, had long maintained thin boundaries between deity and humanity: heroes could be deified, and many philosophers spoke of the soul as divine.

The imperial cult took different forms in different locations. Although the Romans did not initially deify their rulers while they lived, they welcomed the desire of many subjects in the eastern empire to worship them; this solidified loyalty to the empire. The Romans deified their rulers only after their death, like Greek heroes; thus the few first-century emperors who demanded worship as gods while they still lived — Caligula, Nero and Domitian — ended up instead widely despised after their deaths.

Massive Roman emperor statue found at Ephesian temple. Only a head and arm were found, but the entire statue was probably 25 feet (eight meters) high.

© William D. Mounce

Ephesus and Smyrna were the first prominent cities of the Roman province of Asia Minor permitted to build temples honoring allegedly divine emperors. In AD 89/90, maybe five or six years before the book of Revelation arrived in the churches of Asia, Ephesus issued a coin that conformed Domitian to the image of the chief deity Zeus. Domitian also dedicated an imperial statue nearly 25 feet (eight meters) high in the imperial temple in Ephesus. Individuals faced social pressure to participate in public cults, but unless they were accused of disloyalty, no one would hunt down nonparticipants to ensure their participation. Judea was exempted from offering sacrifices to the emperor; they instead agreed to offer sacrifices to the one true God on behalf of the emperor's health. (Christians expelled from synagogues might well lose their exemption.) The abolition of these sacrifices in AD 66 constituted a *de facto* declaration of war against Rome. After Jerusalem's destruction, Roman soldiers set up on the site of the temple their standards, which bore the emperor's image, and worshiped the emperor. ◆

Bronze coin of Nero wearing the radiate crown of divinity.

© Baker Publishing Group and Dr. James C. Martin courtesy of the British Museum, London, England

REVELATION 13:3

A New Nero

Nero was the first emperor to declare an official state persecution against Christians. Further, he burned hundreds of Christians alive to light his imperial gardens at night and butchered others in various ways. Nero's local persecution in Rome, however, merely paved the way for many persecutions that followed.

Months of civil war followed Nero's death on June 9, AD 68, as new imperial claimants vied for power. Nevertheless, at the end of the first century, people in the empire still commonly believed that Nero remained alive. Various impostors arose claiming to be Nero, one of them less than a decade before Revelation was written. That most recent false Nero terrified the empire, garnering the support of the feared Parthians (cf. concerns in Rev 9:14; 16:12 [see notes there; see also the article "Parthia," p. 2239]).

Some Jewish visionaries claimed that Nero would return, perhaps from the dead, perhaps leading the Parthians. Some early Christian writers expected a new Nero they called "a great beast." The tradition that Nero would return to persecute Christians became so widespread that in the Armenian language "Nero" actually became the equivalent for Antichrist. Ancient commentators such as Tertullian, Jerome, Augustine, as well as most modern commentators, have seen Nero as a model for the expected evil emperor. See the article "The Mark of the Beast," p. 2249.

None of this means that John expected Nero to return literally. Romans could speak of particular emperors as being like earlier emperors or other figures; e.g., Tiberius was an "Augustus." The evil imperial power came like Nero, just as the figures in Rev 11:3–6 came in the spirit and power of Moses and Elijah. ◆

8 All inhabitants of the earth[n] will worship
the beast — all whose names have not
been written in the Lamb's book of life,[o]
the Lamb who was slain from the creation
of the world.[a p]
9 Whoever has ears, let them hear.[q]

10 "If anyone is to go into captivity,
into captivity they will go.
If anyone is to be killed[b] with the
sword,
with the sword they will be killed."[c r]
This calls for patient endurance and faithfulness[s] on the part of God's people.[t]

The Beast out of the Earth

11 Then I saw a second beast, coming
out of the earth. It had two horns like a
lamb, but it spoke like a dragon. 12 It exercised all the authority[u] of the first beast
on its behalf,[v] and made the earth and
its inhabitants worship the first beast,[w]
whose fatal wound had been healed.[x]
13 And it performed great signs,[y] even
causing fire to come down from heaven[z]
to the earth in full view of the people.
14 Because of the signs[a] it was given power
to perform on behalf of the first beast, it
deceived[b] the inhabitants of the earth. It
ordered them to set up an image in honor of the beast who was wounded by the

13:8 [n] Rev 3:10 [o] Rev 3:5; 20:12 [p] Mt 25:34 **13:9** [q] Rev 2:7 **13:10** [r] Jer 15:2; 43:11 [s] Heb 6:12 [t] Rev 14:12 **13:12** [u] ver 4 [v] ver 14 [w] Rev 14:9, 11 [x] ver 3 **13:13** [y] Mt 24:24 [z] 1Ki 18:38; Rev 20:9 **13:14** [a] 2Th 2:9, 10 [b] Rev 12:9

[a] 8 Or *written from the creation of the world in the book of life belonging to the Lamb who was slain* [b] 10 Some manuscripts *anyone kills* [c] 10 Jer. 15:2

propaganda to impress his empire's subjects (cf. 9:14; 16:12; see notes there).
13:8 *book of life.* Often appears in Jewish tradition (see note on 3:5), but in Revelation it belongs to the Lamb.
13:10 This judgment-prophecy echoes Jer 15:2; 43:11.
13:11 *two horns like a lamb.* May evoke the ram of Da 8:3, but it parodies the seven-horned Lamb of 5:6. *spoke like a dragon.* Its message reveals its true connections.
13:12 *made the earth and its inhabitants worship the first beast.* Some regard this second beast as the priest of the first, royal beast (contrast here the positive king and priest image in the note on 11:4).
13:14 *an image in honor of the beast.* Nebuchadnezzar demanded that all peoples worship the image he set up; Jews and Christians honored Daniel's friends who preferred martyrdom to such worship (Da 3:12–18). But whereas Daniel's friends were divinely rescued (Da 3:23–27), Revelation warns that many faithful Chris-

sword and yet lived. 15The second beast
was given power to give breath to the image of the first beast, so that the image
could speak and cause all who refused to
worship the image to be killed.[c] 16It also
forced all people, great and small,[d] rich
and poor, free and slave, to receive a mark
on their right hands or on their foreheads,[e]

13:15 [c] Da 3:3-6 **13:16** [d] Rev 19:5 [e] Rev 14:9

tians will die (Rev 13:7,15). Christians in Asia Minor had large reason for concern. Shortly before Revelation was written, Domitian dedicated an imperial statue nearly 25 feet (eight meters) high in the imperial temple in Ephesus. Not many years after Revelation was written, a governor in Asia Minor refers to an existing legal tradition of executing Christians who refuse to worship the emperor's image.

13:15 *the image could speak.* Babylonian and Greco-Roman magic included rituals that sought to animate images; an entire branch of magic specialized in animating statues so they could give prophecies. Both traveling charlatans and priests of some cults staged wonders like moving or speaking statues, although it is not clear that this was common. Scripture recognized that false prophets could work (Ex 7:11) or predict signs (Dt 13:1–3); cf. Mt 24:24; 2Th 2:9.

13:16 *a mark on their right hands or on their foreheads.* The mark on the right hands or foreheads may parody the Jewish practice of strapping boxes of Scripture (phylacteries) on the forehead and left hand as a sign of loyalty to God's covenant. Sometimes slaves could be branded, though branding on the forehead was a sign of disgrace

REVELATION 13:16–18

The Mark of the Beast

Whereas the mark on the righteous was to protect them in Eze 9:4–6 and some other texts, a popular first-century BC Jewish work also includes a mark of destruction on the forehead of the wicked (Psalms of Solomon 15:6–9). These marks were symbolic signs visible only to God and his angels, not to people.

The use of a mark to enforce national or empire-wide unity already had a long history that would be known to John's audience. Jewish people in Egypt reported that one ruler of Egypt wanted to brand Jewish people in his realm with an ivy leaf, the symbol of Dionysus.

Ancients, including some Diaspora Jews such as Philo, were adept at using symbolic numbers and calculating special numbers. Scholars offer various connections. The number 666 is a doubly triangular number (there are only four such numbers between 100 and 1,000). Geometers valued triangular numbers just as they valued square numbers. Just as any number with the same number of identical units vertically and horizontally forms a square, a triangular number is one in which the top level has one unit, the next level has two, the next has three, and so forth, so that one can form with it something like an equilateral triangle. The triangular number with a base of 36 units is 666; the triangular number with a base of eight is 36, so that 666 is not only triangular but has a triangular number as its base.

The number 666 is also almost two-thirds of 1,000, and Revelation sometimes calculates judgments in thirds (Rev 8:7–12; 9:15,18). Thinkers as early as the second century suggested that six here might function as an evil parody of seven (a key number in Revelation). Indeed, calculated as a number, the name "Jesus" comes to 888.

Others argue that the invitation to the reader to calculate the number (Rev 13:18) points to a particular name. Both Greek and Hebrew used letters also as numerals, so one could add up the letters in a name as numbers, as many Jewish thinkers did. One Jewish prophecy tradition treated names of various rulers as numbers. People in the empire played on the number of "Nero Caesar" in Greek letters. There are two ways to spell "Nero Caesar" in Hebrew letters; one comes out to 666, and the other to 616. Some manuscripts of Revelation have here 616 instead of 666—as if some knew the riddle's answer but calculated it differently. Transliterated into Hebrew a particular way, the Greek term for "beast" also comes out to 666, and "of the beast" comes out to 616. ◆

17so that they could not buy or sell unless
they had the mark,[f] which is the name of
the beast or the number of its name.[g]
18This calls for wisdom.[h] Let the person
who has insight calculate the number of
the beast, for it is the number of a man.[a][i]
That number is 666.

The Lamb and the 144,000

14 Then I looked, and there before me
was the Lamb,[j] standing on Mount
Zion,[k] and with him 144,000[l] who had his
name and his Father's name[m] written on
their foreheads. 2And I heard a sound from
heaven like the roar of rushing waters[n]
and like a loud peal of thunder. The sound
I heard was like that of harpists playing
their harps.[o] 3And they sang a new song[p]
before the throne and before the four living creatures and the elders. No one could
learn the song except the 144,000[q] who
had been redeemed from the earth. 4These
are those who did not defile themselves
with women, for they remained virgins.[r]
They follow the Lamb wherever he goes.
They were purchased from among mankind[s] and offered as firstfruits[t] to God
and the Lamb. 5No lie was found in their
mouths;[u] they are blameless.[v]

The Three Angels

6Then I saw another angel flying in midair,[w] and he had the eternal gospel to proclaim to those who live on the earth[x]—to
every nation, tribe, language and people.[y]
7He said in a loud voice, "Fear God[z] and
give him glory,[a] because the hour of his
judgment has come. Worship him who
made the heavens, the earth, the sea and
the springs of water."[b]
8A second angel followed and said,
"'Fallen! Fallen is Babylon the Great,'[b][c]
which made all the nations drink the maddening wine of her adulteries."[d]

13:17 [f] Rev 14:9 [g] Rev 14:11; 15:2 **13:18** [h] Rev 17:9 [i] Rev 15:2; 21:17 **14:1** [j] Rev 5:6 [k] Ps 2:6 [l] Rev 7:4 [m] Rev 3:12 **14:2** [n] Rev 1:15 [o] Rev 5:8 **14:3** [p] Rev 5:9 [q] ver 1 **14:4** [r] 2Co 11:2; Rev 3:4 [s] Rev 5:9 [t] Jas 1:18 **14:5** [u] Ps 32:2; Zep 3:13 [v] Eph 5:27 **14:6** [w] Rev 8:13 [x] Rev 3:10 [y] Rev 13:7 **14:7** [z] Rev 15:4 [a] Rev 11:13 [b] Rev 8:10 **14:8** [c] Isa 21:9; Jer 51:8 [d] Rev 17:2,4; 18:3,9

[a] *18* Or *is humanity's number* [b] *8* Isaiah 21:9

rather than loyalty; sometimes soldiers could be branded on the hands as a sign of loyalty. See the article "The Mark of the Beast," p. 2249.

13:17 *could not buy or sell unless they had the mark.* A mid-third-century emperor demanded certificates of sacrifice to the emperor to participate in commerce and escape prosecution. Many Christians bribed officials to get the certificates; some others were executed. There is no evidence for such certificates in John's day; nevertheless, the threat existed. One could not even handle money without involvement in the imperial system, since coins regularly bore the emperor's image. In cities such as Thyatira, trade guilds committed to pagan gods dominated some spheres of commerce.

13:18 *That number is 666.* Enigmatic riddles were common in prophecies. Various meanings have been proposed for 666. One of the most common relates to six as a parody of seven; another is the idea that this evil ruler would be like Nero. See the articles "The Mark of the Beast," p. 2249; "The Imperial Cult," p. 2247.

14:1 *Mount Zion.* The temple mount and, more broadly, Jerusalem. Although Jerusalem after AD 70 lay mostly in shambles and the nations trampled God's sanctuary even symbolically (11:2), the prophets had promised Zion's restoration (Isa 4:5; 51:3; 62:11; Mic 4:2,7). *144,000 who had his name ... on their foreheads.* Ancient writers often emphasized points by stark contrasts; those who have the name of the Lamb and God the Father written on their foreheads contrast starkly with those who bear the number of the beast's name on their hands or foreheads (13:16–18; see the article "The Mark of the Beast," p. 2249). With letters calculated as numbers, the name "Jesus" comes out to 888. Whereas 666 is a doubly triangular number, 144 is a square number (12 x 12), and 144,000 is 144 times the cube of 10 (i.e., 10 x 10 x 10). Because "Mount Zion" is mentioned in this verse, the 144,000 (see notes on 7:4–8,9–17) thus probably represent the new Jerusalemites, the people destined for the city that was 12,000 stadia cubed with a wall of 144 cubits (21:16–17; see note on 21:17; see also the article "Dimensions of the New Jerusalem," p. 2268).

14:2 *rushing waters ... thunder.* These could represent the voice of God (1:15; 4:5; Eze 43:2; see notes on Mt 3:17; Rev 4:5) but in this context probably reflect the sound of the innumerable heavenly multitude (19:6; cf. the sound like a tumult in Eze 1:24; Da 10:6). *harps.* See note on 5:8.

14:3 *new song.* See note on 5:9; for its content here, see note on 15:3–4.

14:4 *they remained virgins.* Some scholars suggest that the 144,000 are celibate because they are dedicated to spiritual holy war (cf. 1Sa 21:5; 2Sa 11:11; Dead Sea Scrolls; see note on 7:4–8). Further, they are the male image corresponding to Christ's pure bride (19:7; 21:2,9), in contrast to Babylon the prostitute (17:1–5). *firstfruits.* The first of the harvest was dedicated to the Lord (Ex 23:19; 34:26; Nu 28:26; Ne 10:35); God had consecrated Israel this way (Jer 2:3). Greek business documents speak specifically of people as "firstfruits" when they were offered to a deity, for instance as temple servants; these spiritual warriors, however, are devoted to the Lamb, who is genuinely divine.

14:5 *No lie ... in their mouths.* Recalls the promise that among the remnant of Israel there would be no lie (Zep 3:13); contrast Rev 21:8.

14:6 *the eternal gospel to proclaim to those who live on the earth.* In the Prophets, the gospel, meaning "good news," is not just the announcement that God is restoring his people (Isa 40:9; 41:27; 52:7; 61:1) but also the announcement of judgment on their enemies (Na 1:15). Judgment is coming on Babylon (vv. 7–8).

14:8 *Fallen! Fallen is Babylon the Great.* The emphatic double "Fallen" (also in 18:2) alludes to idolatrous Babylon's prophesied fall in Isa 21:9. The Romans sometimes poetically called their archenemy, Parthia, (which ruled old Babylonia), "Babylon." Jewish thinkers, however (many of whom lived in Parthia), often called Rome "Babylon"; as Israel once experienced exile under the evil empire Babylon, now they experienced the captivity of a new evil empire in Rome. They normally considered Rome the fourth of Daniel's four kingdoms, and thus Babylon's ultimate evil successor. For churches in Asia Minor, Rome embodied the spirit of Babylon. *drink the maddening wine of her adulteries.* In Jer 51:7, Babylon was a cup in God's hand making the nations of the earth mad with drunkenness from her wine. In context, God warns of Babylon's fall (Jer 51:8); God's people must flee from Babylon, lest they partake of its judgment (Jer 51:6, 9; see Rev 18:4).

9A third angel followed them and said
in a loud voice: "If anyone worships the
beast and its image[e] and receives its mark
on their forehead or on their hand, 10they,
too, will drink the wine of God's fury,[f]
which has been poured full strength into
the cup of his wrath.[g] They will be tormented with burning sulfur in the presence of the holy angels and of the Lamb.
11And the smoke of their torment will rise
for ever and ever.[h] There will be no rest
day or night for those who worship the
beast and its image, or for anyone who receives the mark of its name." 12This calls
for patient endurance on the part of the
people of God[i] who keep his commands
and remain faithful to Jesus.

13Then I heard a voice from heaven say,
"Write this: Blessed are the dead who die
in the Lord[j] from now on."

"Yes," says the Spirit, "they will rest
from their labor, for their deeds will follow them."

Harvesting the Earth and Trampling the Winepress

14I looked, and there before me was a
white cloud, and seated on the cloud was
one like a son of man[a][k] with a crown[l] of
gold on his head and a sharp sickle in his
hand. 15Then another angel came out of
the temple and called in a loud voice to
him who was sitting on the cloud, "Take
your sickle[m] and reap, because the time
to reap has come, for the harvest[n] of the
earth is ripe." 16So he who was seated on
the cloud swung his sickle over the earth,
and the earth was harvested.

17Another angel came out of the temple
in heaven, and he too had a sharp sickle.
18Still another angel, who had charge of
the fire, came from the altar and called in
a loud voice to him who had the sharp
sickle, "Take your sharp sickle and gather the clusters of grapes from the earth's
vine, because its grapes are ripe." 19The
angel swung his sickle on the earth, gathered its grapes and threw them into the
great winepress of God's wrath.[o] 20They
were trampled in the winepress[p] outside
the city,[q] and blood flowed out of the
press, rising as high as the horses' bridles
for a distance of 1,600 stadia.[b]

Seven Angels With Seven Plagues

15 I saw in heaven another great and
marvelous sign:[r] seven angels[s] with
the seven last plagues[t]—last, because with

14:9 [e] Rev 13:14 **14:10** [f] Isa 51:17; Jer 25:15 [g] Rev 18:6 **14:11** [h] Isa 34:10; Rev 19:3 **14:12** [i] Rev 13:10 **14:13** [j] 1Co 15:18; 1Th 4:16 **14:14** [k] Da 7:13; Rev 1:13 [l] Rev 6:2 **14:15** [m] Joel 3:13 [n] Jer 51:33 **14:19** [o] Rev 19:15 **14:20** [p] Isa 63:3 [q] Heb 13:12; Rev 11:8 **15:1** [r] Rev 12:1, 3 [s] Rev 16:1 [t] Lev 26:21

[a] *14* See Daniel 7:13. [b] *20* That is, about 180 miles or about 300 kilometers

14:10 *poured full strength.* On average, ancients diluted wine with two parts water to every part wine, except when they were trying to get drunk. But God has poured his fury in undiluted strength. *the cup of his wrath.* Scripture regularly uses "the cup" as a symbol for God's anger, both temporarily against his people (Isa 51:17,22; Eze 23:31–33) and against the wicked nations (Ps 75:8; Jer 25:15–17,28; 49:12; La 4:21; Hab 2:16; Zec 12:2). *burning sulfur.* Although sulfur here refers to the lake of fire (Rev 19:20; 20:10; 21:8), it also fits the inhabitants of spiritual Sodom (cf. 11:8; Ge 19:24). *in the presence of the holy angels and of the Lamb.* The tormented will be unable to evade the reality of the holy angels and the Lamb whom they once ignored. Nevertheless, Revelation omits a different apocalyptic motif: for some Jewish visionaries, the vindication of God's people included their witnessing the torment of the damned.
14:11 *the smoke … will rise for ever and ever.* Also in 19:3; taken from Isa 34:10, which first-century Jewish hearers would have naturally linked with Isa 66:24.
14:13 *they will rest from their labor.* Most significant is the standard Jewish tradition that also stands behind our traditional "Rest in Peace" (RIP): Jewish sources regularly promised rest for the righteous after death. (One early apocalypse even promises a voice from heaven announcing end-time rest from suffering.)
14:14–20 In Joel 3:13, God calls for the sickle to gather the ripe harvest, and calls for the grapes of the nations' wickedness to be trampled to fill his winepress (against Babylon, cf. Jer 51:33; Jerusalem in La 1:15). The harvest and grape vintage both represent judgment in Joel; scholars debate whether the same is true for the harvest here in vv. 15–16 (cf. v. 4), but the vintage in vv. 17–20 is certainly judgment.
14:18 *angel, who had charge of the fire.* Although this could refer to an angel of nature (see note on Gal 4:3), here it likely means the angel at the incense altar (8:5).
14:19–20 *gathered its grapes and threw them into the great winepress of God's wrath. They were trampled.* Around August or September workers collected ripe grapes in baskets and deposited them in long wooden or stone troughs. There, often to the rhythm of a flutist, workers trampled the grapes into juice with their feet. God had warned that he would go out and trample the blood of the wicked like wine in a winepress, till his garments were stained with their blood (Isa 63:1–6; cf. Jesus in Rev 19:13,15).
14:20 *blood flowed out of the press.* Wine was sometimes called the "blood of grapes" (Ge 49:11; Dt 32:14); here red wine evokes the gruesome image of human blood crushed out of maimed flesh. *rising as high as the horses' bridles.* Ancient descriptions of wars spoke of blood flowing in streams or of rivers flowing with blood when people were slain in them. In poetic depictions the blood obstructed ships, or trees dripped with gore dropped on them when satiated birds grew weary of feasting on corpses. Apocalypses amplified further: in the pre-Christian work 1 Enoch, sinners' blood covers chariots; horses walk up to their chests in the blood. Some later rabbis lament horses drowning in blood and blood rolling huge boulders some 40 miles (65 kilometers) out to the sea. Sometimes the more extreme descriptions were merely figurative ways of expressing the horrific bloodshed (e.g., Eze 32:5–6). *1,600 stadia.* Revelation again rounds to a square number: 1,600 is 40 x 40 (see NIV text note). The figure especially underlines the awful grotesqueness of the image: none of the beast's army will survive. Whereas the river of paradise flows from God's throne (22:1–2) to a significant height (Eze 47:4–5), the wicked would drown in a river of their own blood.
15:1 *seven angels … seven last plagues … completed.* Ancient writers sometimes bracketed units by beginning and ending on the same point. The repetition in v. 8

them God's wrath is completed. 2 And I
saw what looked like a sea of glass[u] glowing with fire and, standing beside the sea,
those who had been victorious over the
beast and its image[v] and over the number
of its name. They held harps given them by
God 3 and sang the song of God's servant
Moses[w] and of the Lamb:

"Great and marvelous are your deeds,[x]
  Lord God Almighty.
Just and true are your ways,[y]
  King of the nations.[a]
4 Who will not fear you, Lord,[z]
  and bring glory to your name?
For you alone are holy.
All nations will come
  and worship before you,[a]
for your righteous acts have been
  revealed."[b]

5 After this I looked, and I saw in heav-
en the temple[b]—that is, the tabernacle of
the covenant law[c]—and it was opened.
6 Out of the temple[d] came the seven angels with the seven plagues.[e] They were
dressed in clean, shining linen and wore
golden sashes around their chests.[f] 7 Then
one of the four living creatures[g] gave to
the seven angels seven golden bowls filled
with the wrath of God, who lives for ever
and ever. 8 And the temple was filled with
smoke[h] from the glory of God and from his
power, and no one could enter the temple[i]
until the seven plagues of the seven angels
were completed.

The Seven Bowls of God's Wrath

16 Then I heard a loud voice from the
temple saying to the seven angels,[j]
"Go, pour out the seven bowls of God's
wrath on the earth."
2 The first angel went and poured out
his bowl on the land,[k] and ugly, festering
sores[l] broke out on the people who had
the mark of the beast and worshiped its
image.[m]
3 The second angel poured out his bowl
on the sea, and it turned into blood like
that of a dead person, and every living
thing in the sea died.[n]
4 The third angel poured out his bowl on
the rivers and springs of water,[o] and they
became blood.[p] 5 Then I heard the angel in
charge of the waters say:

"You are just in these judgments,[q]
  O Holy One,[r]
  you who are and who were;[s]
6 for they have shed the blood of your
  holy people and your prophets,
  and you have given them blood to
  drink[t] as they deserve."

15:2 [u] Rev 4:6 [v] Rev 13:14 **15:3** [w] Ex 15:1; Dt 32:4 [x] Ps 111:2 [y] Ps 145:17 **15:4** [z] Jer 10:7 [a] Isa 66:23 **15:5** [b] Rev 11:19 [c] Nu 1:50 **15:6** [d] Rev 14:15 [e] ver 1 [f] Rev 1:13 **15:7** [g] Rev 4:6 **15:8** [h] Isa 6:4

[i] Ex 40:34, 35; 1Ki 8:10, 11; 2Ch 5:13, 14 **16:1** [j] Rev 15:1 **16:2** [k] Rev 8:7 [l] Ex 9:9-11 [m] Rev 13:15-17 **16:3** [n] Ex 7:17-21; Rev 8:8, 9 **16:4** [o] Rev 8:10 [p] Ex 7:17-21 **16:5** [q] Rev 15:3 [r] Rev 15:4 [s] Rev 1:4 **16:6** [t] Isa 49:26; Rev 17:6

[a] *3* Some manuscripts *ages* [b] *3,4* Phrases in this song are drawn from Psalm 111:2,3; Deut. 32:4; Jer. 10:7; Psalms 86:9; 98:2.

might bracket vv. 1–8 as a unit, elaborating the origin of the plagues in heaven.

15:2 *sea of glass.* Recalls the heavenly temple (see note on 4:6). It might also suggest their new exodus: following the Lamb, they were delivered from the sea monster as Israel was at the exodus (Ps 74:13–14; Isa 51:9–10). *glowing with fire.* Possibly the fire alludes to the fiery hail (Rev 8:7); more likely, it indicates that the victorious ones have overcome the "lake of fire" (20:14–15; cf. 19:20; 20:10; 21:8).

15:3–4 The victorious (v. 2) sing. In Jewish sources, victors celebrated after holy war; here, however, the saints praise God for his deeds of judgment (cf. "great and marvelous" in vv. 1,3), as the Israelites praised God when he overthrew their enemies in the sea (Ex 15:1–21). The "song of ... Moses and of the Lamb" (v. 3) recalls the exodus and the blood of the Passover lamb delivering Israel from the plague of death (Ex 12:21–23). For Moses' songs, see Ex 15:1–18 (Rev 15 evokes some of the same exodus themes found in Ex 15; cf. Ex 15:11: "holiness ... glory ... working wonders") and Dt 31:30—32:43. Cf. Dt 32:4; Ps 22:27–28; 98:2; 145:17.

The words here, however, come especially from Ps 86:9–10 (which evokes Ex 15:11), including "great and ... marvelous deeds" (Ps 86:10), and that the "nations ... will come and worship before you" (Ps 86:9) and "bring glory to your name" (Ps 86:9); and secondarily from Jer 10:7: "Who should not fear you, King of the nations?" (Cf. Zec 14:9. The variant reading to which the NIV text note refers in Rev 15:3, "king of the ages," i.e., "eternal king," would be another way to translate "king of the world," a familiar expression in Hebrew prayers.)

15:5–8 As in apocalyptic thought, heavenly experiences sometimes stand behind earthly ones (cf. 12:5–10); scenes in heaven introduce each of the three major cycles of judgment in Revelation (5:1–2; 8:2; here).

15:5 *I saw in heaven the temple.* See the article "Heaven as a Temple in Revelation," p. 2230.

15:6 *dressed in clean, shining linen and ... golden sashes.* Angels in Jewish tradition normally wore white or linen, but together with golden sashes (cf. Ex 39:8) this apparel suggests that they fulfill priestly acts in the heavenly temple. In some strands of Jewish tradition, destroying angels acted without interest in serving God (though God remained sovereign); here the angels of judgment are God's willing servants.

15:7 *bowls.* The Greek term here often designates bowls used in offerings; they represent urns in the heavenly temple, perhaps for incense (5:8).

15:8 *temple was filled with smoke from the glory of God.* Contrast 14:11; alludes to God's glory filling his house in some Biblical theophanies (Isa 6:4; Eze 10:3–4). Under these circumstances the priests could not minister in the temple (1Ki 8:10–12; 2Ch 7:2) nor could even Moses enter the tabernacle (Ex 40:35).

16:1–11 Most of the bowls, like the trumpets before them, recall the plagues of the exodus: sores (v. 2); water into blood (vv. 3–4); darkness (v. 10; and in this case its antithesis, vv. 8–9).

16:1 *bowls.* See note on 15:7.

16:5 *angel in charge of the waters.* This angel might be an angel with usual jurisdiction over the water (see note on Gal 4:3), though he might simply be the same angel as in v. 4. *You are just in these judgments.* For God's just verdicts, cf. Dt 32:4; Jer 11:20; also the Jewish Apocryphal book of Tobit 3:2.

16:6 *they have shed ... and you have given them blood to drink.* They "shed" (or "poured out") blood, so God

7And I heard the altar[u] respond:

“Yes, Lord God Almighty,
true and just are your judgments.”[v]

8The fourth angel[w] poured out his bowl
on the sun, and the sun was allowed to
scorch people with fire.[x] 9They were
seared by the intense heat and they cursed
the name of God,[y] who had control over
these plagues, but they refused to repent[z]
and glorify him.[a]
10The fifth angel poured out his bowl
on the throne of the beast,[b] and its kingdom was plunged into darkness.[c] People gnawed their tongues in agony 11and
cursed[d] the God of heaven[e] because of
their pains and their sores,[f] but they refused to repent of what they had done.[g]
12The sixth angel poured out his bowl
on the great river Euphrates,[h] and its water was dried up to prepare the way for
the kings from the East.[i] 13Then I saw
three impure spirits that looked like frogs;
they came out of the mouth of the dragon,[j] out of the mouth of the beast[k] and out
of the mouth of the false prophet.[l] 14They
are demonic spirits[m] that perform signs,
and they go out to the kings of the whole
world, to gather them for the battle[n] on
the great day of God Almighty.

15“Look, I come like a thief! Blessed
is the one who stays awake[o] and remains clothed, so as not to go naked
and be shamefully exposed.”

16Then they gathered the kings together to
the place that in Hebrew[p] is called Armageddon.[q]
17The seventh angel poured out his bowl
into the air,[r] and out of the temple[s] came a
loud voice[t] from the throne, saying, “It is
done!”[u] 18Then there came flashes of lightning, rumblings, peals of thunder[v] and a
severe earthquake.[w] No earthquake like it
has ever occurred since mankind has been
on earth,[x] so tremendous was the quake.
19The great city[y] split into three parts, and
the cities of the nations collapsed. God remembered[z] Babylon the Great[a] and gave
her the cup filled with the wine of the fury
of his wrath.[b] 20Every island fled away and
the mountains could not be found.[c] 21From
the sky huge hailstones,[d] each weighing
about a hundred pounds,[a] fell on people.
And they cursed God on account of the
plague of hail,[e] because the plague was
so terrible.

[a] 21 Or about 45 kilograms

16:7 [u] Rev 6:9 [v] Rev 15:3; 19:2 **16:8** [w] Rev 8:12 [x] Rev 14:18 **16:9** [y] ver 11, 21 [z] Rev 2:21 [a] Rev 11:13 **16:10** [b] Rev 13:2 [c] Rev 9:2 **16:11** [d] ver 9, 21 [e] Rev 11:13 [f] ver 2 [g] Rev 2:21 **16:12** [h] Rev 9:14 [i] Isa 41:2 **16:13** [j] Rev 12:3 [k] Rev 13:1 [l] Rev 19:20 **16:14** [m] 1Ti 4:1 [n] Rev 17:14 **16:15** [o] Lk 12:37 **16:16** [p] Rev 9:11 [q] 2Ki 23:29,30 **16:17** [r] Eph 2:2 [s] Rev 14:15 [t] Rev 11:15 [u] Rev 21:6 **16:18** [v] Rev 4:5 [w] Rev 6:12 [x] Da 12:1 **16:19** [y] Rev 17:18 [z] Rev 18:5 [a] Rev 14:8 [b] Rev 14:10 **16:20** [c] Rev 6:14 **16:21** [d] Rev 11:19 [e] Ex 9:23-25

“poured out” judgments (vv. 2,3,4,8,10,12,17), including blood (vv. 3 – 4). The appropriateness of blood for those who shed blood fits the traditional (and likely) Jewish explanation that God turned the Nile bloody to avenge the earlier Egyptian murder of Israelite infants (Wisdom of Solomon 11:6 – 7). (This observation develops a genuine theme in Exodus: In response to Pharaoh drowning Israel's babies in the Nile, God later turned the Nile to blood, struck Egypt's firstborn, and drowned Pharaoh's army.)

16:7 *I heard the altar respond.* The prayers of God's people are associated with both the incense and sacrificial altars (6:9; 8:3,5).

16:10 *People gnawed their tongues in agony.* That the darkness causes agony may evoke the darkness of Moses' day, which could be “felt” (Ex 10:21).

16:12 *Euphrates.* The Euphrates was especially known as the boundary between the Roman and Parthian Empires (see note on 9:14). *its water was dried up.* Unlike some other rivers in the Near East, the massive Euphrates did not dry up during some seasons. But God could dry up waters in judgment (Isa 50:2; Na 1:4); parting the Jordan invited Israel's conquest of Canaan (Jos 3:14 – 17; 4:23 — 5:1). Jewish traditions expected God to part the Euphrates to bring scattered Israelites back to the land (developing Isa 11:15 – 16), or to freeze a river to allow Asia Minor to be invaded.

16:13 *impure spirits that looked like frogs.* If the frogs here recall the OT plague of frogs (Ex 8:2 – 13; Ps 78:45; 105:30), they are transformed (as were the locusts; cf. Ex 10:13 – 14; Rev 9:3).

16:14 *They are demonic spirits.* Some Jewish people expected the release of more demons in the end time (cf. 2Th 2:8 – 9). *to gather them for the battle.* The gathering of the wicked for their own destruction is a common Biblical image of the future (Joel 3:10 – 14; Mic 4:11 – 13; Zep 3:8; Zec 12:3 – 4; 14:2 – 3), sometimes recalled in other early Jewish works.

16:15 *stays awake and remains clothed.* Cf. Jesus' words in Mt 24:43; Lk 12:39; see note on 3:3. Many people did not wear much to bed when it was warm. *be shamefully exposed.* Being stripped or otherwise publicly exposed was considered shameful (cf. 3:18). In the OT God stripped his people (Eze 16:37; Hos 2:3) and Babylon (Isa 47:3) for infidelity, following an ancient Near Eastern custom (see note on Rev 17:16).

16:16 *Armageddon.* Transliterates the Hebrew for “Mount Megiddo.” Although the judgment occurs in a valley in Joel (Joel 3:12,14) and Megiddo lies on a plain (2Ch 35:22; Zec 12:11), apocalyptic geography is flexible. Significant battles were fought in the valley of Megiddo (Jdg 5:19; 2Ki 23:29). The mountain might contrast with Zion (Rev 14:1; 21:10; cf. the negative or neutral uses of mountains in v. 20; 6:14 – 16; 8:8; 17:9), or, less plausibly, the name (*harmagedon*) might pun on the Greek term for chariot (*harma*).

16:18 *lightning … thunder … earthquake.* See notes on 4:5; 6:12.

16:20 *Every island fled … mountains could not be found.* As in 6:14, the image of moving islands and mountains communicates dramatic, cosmic judgment (Isa 42:15; 64:1 – 3; Mic 1:3 – 4; Na 1:5 – 6), appropriate for the end time (Eze 38:19 – 20; Zec 14:4 – 5).

16:21 *huge hailstones, each weighing about a hundred pounds.* The OT plague of hail was severe enough to kill those caught out in it (Ex 9:19). The end-time hailstones here, however, can smash through structures; at about 100 pounds (45 kilograms) each, they are heavier than normal catapult stones.

Babylon, the Prostitute on the Beast

17 One of the seven angels[f] who had
the seven bowls[g] came and said to
me, "Come, I will show you the punishment[h] of the great prostitute,[i] who sits by
many waters.[j] 2 With her the kings of the
earth committed adultery, and the inhabitants of the earth were intoxicated with
the wine of her adulteries."[k]

3 Then the angel carried me away in
the Spirit into a wilderness.[l] There I saw
a woman sitting on a scarlet beast that
was covered with blasphemous names[m]
and had seven heads and ten horns.[n] 4 The
woman was dressed in purple and scarlet, and was glittering with gold, precious
stones and pearls.[o] She held a golden
cup[p] in her hand, filled with abominable things and the filth of her adulteries.
5 The name written on her forehead was
a mystery:

BABYLON THE GREAT[q]
THE MOTHER OF PROSTITUTES
AND OF THE ABOMINATIONS OF THE EARTH.

6 I saw that the woman was drunk with the
blood of God's holy people,[r] the blood of
those who bore testimony to Jesus.

When I saw her, I was greatly astonished. 7 Then the angel said to me: "Why
are you astonished? I will explain to you
the mystery[s] of the woman and of the
beast she rides, which has the seven
heads and ten horns.[t] 8 The beast, which
you saw, once was, now is not, and yet
will come up out of the Abyss and go to its
destruction.[u] The inhabitants of the earth[v]
whose names have not been written in
the book of life[w] from the creation of the
world will be astonished[x] when they see
the beast, because it once was, now is not,
and yet will come.

9 "This calls for a mind with wisdom.[y]
The seven heads are seven hills on which
the woman sits. 10 They are also seven
kings. Five have fallen, one is, the other has not yet come; but when he does
come, he must remain for only a little
while. 11 The beast who once was, and
now is not,[z] is an eighth king. He belongs
to the seven and is going to his destruction.

17:1 [f] Rev 15:1 [g] Rev 21:9 [h] Rev 16:19 [i] Rev 19:2 [j] Jer 51:13 **17:2** [k] Rev 14:8; 18:3 **17:3** [l] Rev 12:6, 14 [m] Rev 13:1 [n] Rev 12:3 **17:4** [o] Rev 18:16 [p] Jer 51:7; Rev 18:6 **17:5** [q] Rev 14:8 **17:6** [r] Rev 18:24 **17:7** [s] ver 5 [t] ver 3 **17:8** [u] Rev 13:10 [v] Rev 3:10 [w] Rev 13:8 [x] Rev 13:3 **17:9** [y] Rev 13:18 **17:11** [z] ver 8

17:1–5 Gentiles often personified their homeland as a woman. Coins and other artwork typically depicted a city as a wealthy goddess enthroned beside a river. Thus, e.g., a bronze coin from the current imperial dynasty included the goddess Roma (who personified Rome's power) sitting on seven hills (cf. v. 9).

Speakers often developed a point by contrasting characters; Revelation contrasts two cities, Jerusalem and Babylon, as a bride (21:2) and prostitute, respectively (17:5). The prophets often portrayed God's people as his faithful bride when pure (e.g., Isa 54:5–6; 62:5; Hos 2:19–20), or a prostitute when unfaithful (e.g., Lev 17:7; Isa 1:21; Jer 3:1; Eze 16:20). In two OT instances, the prostitute is not Israel. Nineveh, the capital of the evil Assyrian empire, seduced the nations with her prostitution and witchcraft (Na 3:4; see note on Rev 18:23). The economic power Tyre acted as a prostitute with all peoples (Isa 23:17). Some Jewish apocalyptic writers contrasted Zion and Babylon, lamenting Babylon's present prosperity but anticipating its judgment.

17:1 *the great prostitute, who sits by many waters.* Babylon lived "by many waters" (Jer 51:13), like most prosperous ancient cities. Rome had its Tiber, but the "waters" represent the nations (v. 15), more like Rome's international power on the seas (cf. note on 13:1).

17:2 *kings.* Includes client-rulers who ruled local kingdoms under Roman authority, as well as allied kings beyond Roman rule. *intoxicated with the wine of her adulteries.* Some, probably pre-Christian, Jewish prophecies complain about Rome's drunken weddings with her many suitors (e.g., Sibylline Oracles 3.356–359), apparently the kings of the East she was seducing.

17:3 *the angel carried me away in the Spirit.* See 21:10 and note; cf. Eze 8:3; 11:1,24. *seven heads and ten horns.* Links the beast with the dragon (12:3) and with Rome (see note on 13:1), as well as with the final evil empire destined to be destroyed by God himself (Da 7:7,20,24). The resemblance to the dragon is certainly deliberate; children were thought to bear the image of their fathers.

17:4 *dressed in purple.* Purple indicates wealth (see note on Ac 16:14). Purple dye was expensive, and among women entirely purple garments were associated with high-class prostitutes. *scarlet … gold, precious stones and pearls.* A personified prostitute might seek to allure lovers with scarlet and jewels (Jer 4:30). Speakers often developed a point by contrasting characters; compare Babylon with the new Jerusalem in 21:18–21 (cf. Isa 54:12; 61:10).

17:5 *name written on her forehead.* Cf. 13:16; 19:13; speakers often developed a point by comparing or contrasting characters. Although headbands were not limited to prostitutes, some commentators suggest that prostitutes in Rome wore headbands with names; perhaps more helpfully, see Jer 3:3. *MOTHER OF PROSTITUTES.* See note on vv. 1–5.

17:6 *drunk with the blood of God's holy people.* Virtually everyone in the Mediterranean world found cannibalism horrifying. Scripture forbade drinking blood (Lev 17:14), but it appears in terrifying prophecies (Dt 32:42; Isa 49:26; Eze 39:19). A generation earlier, Nero had martyred many of God's holy people, and, following Nero's precedent, many subsequent emperors killed them in bloody amusements during festivals and on state occasions.

17:8 *once was, now is not, and yet will come.* Speakers often developed a point by contrasting characters. As the return of the dead evil ruler (v. 11) parodies Christ's resurrection, so the beast parodies "him who is, and who was, and who is to come" (1:4).

17:9 *seven heads are seven hills.* Ancient writers regularly portrayed Rome as a city on seven hills or mountains. Each year Rome celebrated afresh its founding on seven hills with the festival of the seven mountains. Jewish prophecies likewise identified Rome as a city on seven hills (Sibylline Oracles 2.18; 11.109–113).

17:11 *an eighth king … belongs to the seven.* Daniel's beast had ten horns and another horn that cast down three horns, which would then leave seven, not counting the new horn (Da 7:20,24)—though Revelation typically enumerates items in sets of seven in any case. Assuming the correctness of early Christian tradition, the king who *is* must

REVELATION 17:5

Babylon and Rome

Rome does not exhaust the significance of Babylon, but Rome embodied the spirit of Babylon for the first-century churches in Asia Minor. A number of points make clear this connection with Rome.

First, like the earlier empire of Babylon, Rome destroyed the temple and enslaved many of God's people. As Israel once experienced exile under the evil empire of Babylon, now they experienced the captivity of a new evil empire in Rome.

Second, and especially for reasons just noted, Jewish thinkers often compared Rome to Babylon. The connection came partly because of the interpretation of Daniel's prophecies about the four kingdoms (Da 2:36 – 45; 7:3 – 14); Babylon was the first of the kingdoms, and first-century Jewish interpreters understood Rome as the last.

Third, the woman sits on seven mountains (Rev 17:9); ancient writers regularly portrayed Rome in this manner.

Fourth, the leader of Babylon may be a new Nero (Rev 17:8 – 11).

Fifth, this empire rules over the other kings of the earth (Rev 17:18). It rules the nations gathered around the sea because it is a maritime power (Rev 17:15).

Sixth, Rome (and only Rome) traded in the same merchandise noted in Rev 18:12 – 13.

These factors show that Rome was the Babylon, the oppressive empire, of John's day; but many also view Revelation's Babylon as the evil world system that in principle continues beyond Rome's fall. Romans regarded as subversive those who prophesied Rome's fall.

It is easy for modern readers to miss John's audacity: banished to an island, he recounts a funeral dirge over the most powerful empire the Mediterranean world had ever known (Rev 18:2). Rome was close to the height of its power; the church was growing but may have constituted less than 0.1 percent of the empire's population. Yet because John knew that God's people had outlived the earlier, powerful empire of Babylon, just as the prophets had predicted, he had every reason for confidence that the same would happen regarding other powerful empires, including the empire that he lived under. Within five centuries a weakened Rome was sacked. ◆

First-century coin depicting Roma seated on seven hills. John uses this ancient reference to Rome in Rev 17:9.

Sestertius of Vespasian depicting Roma seated on seven hills and Capitoline Wolf, AD 71, verso, Roman coins, first century AD/Palazzo Massimo alle Terme, Rome, Italy/De Agostini Picture Library/A. de Gregorio/Bridgeman Images

12 “The ten horns[a] you saw are ten kings
who have not yet received a kingdom, but
who for one hour[b] will receive authority
as kings along with the beast. 13 They have
one purpose and will give their power and
authority to the beast.[c] 14 They will wage
war[d] against the Lamb, but the Lamb will
triumph over them because he is Lord of
lords and King of kings[e] — and with him
will be his called, chosen[f] and faithful followers.”

15 Then the angel said to me, “The waters[g] you saw, where the prostitute sits,
are peoples, multitudes, nations and languages.[h] 16 The beast and the ten horns
you saw will hate the prostitute. They will
bring her to ruin[i] and leave her naked;[j]
they will eat her flesh[k] and burn her with
fire.[l] 17 For God has put it into their hearts
to accomplish his purpose by agreeing to
hand over to the beast their royal authority, until God’s words are fulfilled.[m] 18 The
woman you saw is the great city[n] that
rules over the kings of the earth.”

17:12 [a] Rev 12:3 [b] Rev 18:10, 17,19
17:13 [c] ver 17
17:14 [d] Rev 16:14 [e] 1Ti 6:15; Rev 19:16 [f] Mt 22:14
17:15 [g] Isa 8:7 [h] Rev 13:7
17:16 [i] Rev 18:17, 19 [j] Eze 16:37, 39 [k] Rev 19:18 [l] Rev 18:8
17:17 [m] Rev 10:7
17:18 [n] Rev 16:19

18:1 [o] Rev 17:1 [p] Rev 10:1 [q] Eze 43:2
18:2 [r] Rev 14:8 [s] Isa 13:21,22; Jer 50:39
18:3 [t] Rev 14:8 [u] Rev 17:2 [v] Eze 27:9-25 [w] ver 7,9

Lament Over Fallen Babylon

18 After this I saw another angel[o] coming down from heaven.[p] He had
great authority, and the earth was illuminated by his splendor.[q] 2 With a mighty
voice he shouted:

“ ‘Fallen! Fallen is Babylon the
Great!’[a][r]
She has become a dwelling for
demons
and a haunt for every impure spirit,
a haunt for every unclean bird,
a haunt for every unclean and
detestable animal.[s]
3 For all the nations have drunk
the maddening wine of her
adulteries.[t]
The kings of the earth committed
adultery with her,[u]
and the merchants of the earth
grew rich[v] from her excessive
luxuries.”[w]

[a] *2* Isaiah 21:9

---

be Domitian; Nero is just three emperors before Domitian if one skips the three interim usurpers who reigned for only a few months between Nero and Vespasian. (By the time of Domitian, in the East apparently counted the three brief rulers only as usurpers.) That the eighth is not the current one but one of the previous seven, all dead, could allude to popular rumors of dastardly Nero’s return (see note on 13:3; see also the article “A New Nero,” p. 2248), or it may be that Julius Caesar, though not truly an emperor, is being counted, and thus Nero is the eighth in line. Such reckoning was not uncommon in the first century.

17:12 *ten horns ... are ten kings.* Cf. Da 7:7,20,24. Probably John would have understood them as Rome-approved rulers of Rome’s client kingdoms; their number varied, but ten fits a rough average.

17:14 *Lord of lords.* A title for God in the OT (Dt 10:17; Ps 136:3), it is here applied to Jesus. *King of kings.* In imperial propaganda, the emperor fancied himself ruler of all the other kings of the earth (v. 18). Babylonian and Persian kings (Ezr 7:12; Eze 26:7; Da 2:37) used the title “King of kings” and it remained the title of the Parthian ruler in John’s day.

17:16 *bring her to ruin and leave her naked.* Rome’s client kingdoms will prove as unfaithful as the prostitute with whom they have had intercourse. The unfaithfulness of a prostitute’s lovers was well-known; a figurative prostitute’s former lovers might betray her (La 1:2), strip her (Eze 16:39; 23:26 – 29) or even kill her (Jer 4:30). In the OT God stripped his people (Jer 13:22,26 – 27; Eze 16:37; Hos 2:3), Nineveh (Na 3:5) and Babylon (Isa 47:3) for infidelity, following an ancient Near Eastern penalty for sexual unfaithfulness. *burn her with fire.* Burning was the normal fate of conquered cities (e.g., Jos 6:24; 8:28) and the promised fate of the beast (Da 7:11); it was also the penalty for what were deemed the most disgraceful acts of promiscuity (Ge 38:24; Lev 20:14; 21:9). Rome’s residents would have taken the threat of fire seriously; most of the city had burned three decades earlier, in AD 64.

17:17 *put it into their hearts to accomplish his purpose.* God often used evil peoples to judge other evil peoples (e.g., Isa 10:5 – 15; Jer 51:11,29; Joel 2:11).

17:18 *great city that rules over the kings of the earth.* Parthians, Nubians, most Germans and many other peoples even near the empire were not subject to Rome, but imperial propaganda claimed authority over all the earth. By this period people in the empire spoke of Rome as the city that ruled land and sea to the ends of the earth (cf. the hyperbole in 2Ch 9:23). In the context of v. 17, however, it is clear that ultimately God rules the kings of the earth (Ps 47:9; 102:15).

18:1 – 24 Ancient sources often contrast the lamentation of funerals with the celebration of weddings. The mourning over Babylon in this section contrasts starkly with rejoicing over its fall that paves the way for the joy of a wedding (19:1 – 9). Laments come from those who profited by sleeping with the prostitute — the client kings whose rule depended on Rome (vv. 9 – 10) and the merchants whose prosperity depended on it (vv. 11 – 19). By contrast, the heaven-dwellers would rejoice (v. 20; 19:1 – 3).

Laments over destroyed cities became a recognized literary form in antiquity. As an artistic way of announcing judgment on cities, the prophets sometimes used reports of laments (Isa 3:26; 16:7 – 11; 19:8; Jer 48:17; Mic 1:10). Like the restoration of Zion (Isa 40:9; 41:27; 52:7), an oppressor’s fall was good news (Na 1:15).

18:2 *Fallen! Fallen is Babylon the Great!* Recalls the dirge over Babylon in Isa 21:9 (cf. Rev 14:8; Jer 51:8). For the double “Fallen,” see note on 14:8. *dwelling for demons.* Some of these prophetic descriptions include creatures that the common Greek version of the OT calls demons (Isa 34:14), including in judgments against Babylon (Isa 13:21). *a haunt for every unclean and detestable animal.* When cities were depopulated no one could prevent animals from taking over. Thus Rome’s population decreased from as much as a million in John’s era to some 30,000 after its fall five centuries later. The prophets had announced such a fate for many powerful cities (Isa 34:11 – 15; Jer 49:33), including Babylon (Isa 13:20 – 22; Jer 50:13; 51:29,37) and (temporarily) Jerusalem (Jer 9:11; 10:22).

18:3 *nations have drunk the maddening wine of her adulteries.* God made Babylon a wine cup to make the nations drunk and drive them mad (Jer 51:7; cf. Zec 12:2), inviting mourning over Babylon (Jer 51:8) and the flight of God’s people (Jer 51:6,45; cf. Zec 2:7). In Rome’s propaganda,

Warning to Escape Babylon's Judgment

[4]Then I heard another voice from heaven say:

"'Come out of her, my people,'[a][x]
so that you will not share in her
sins,
so that you will not receive any of
her plagues;
[5]for her sins are piled up to heaven,[y]
and God has remembered[z] her
crimes.
[6]Give back to her as she has given;
pay her back[a] double for what she
has done.
Pour her a double portion from her
own cup.[b]
[7]Give her as much torment and grief
as the glory and luxury she gave
herself.[c]
In her heart she boasts,
'I sit enthroned as queen.
I am not a widow;[b]
I will never mourn.'[d]
[8]Therefore in one day[e] her plagues will
overtake her:
death, mourning and famine.
She will be consumed by fire,[f]
for mighty is the Lord God who
judges her.

Threefold Woe Over Babylon's Fall

[9]"When the kings of the earth who committed adultery with her[g] and shared her luxury see the smoke of her burning,[h] they will weep and mourn over her.[i] [10]Terrified at her torment, they will stand far off[j] and cry:

"'Woe! Woe to you, great city,[k]
you mighty city of Babylon!
In one hour[l] your doom has come!'

[11]"The merchants[m] of the earth will weep and mourn over her because no one buys their cargoes anymore[n]— [12]cargoes of gold, silver, precious stones and pearls; fine linen, purple, silk and scarlet cloth; every sort of citron wood, and articles of every kind made of ivory, costly wood, bronze, iron and marble;[o] [13]cargoes of cinnamon and spice, of incense, myrrh and frankincense, of wine and olive oil, of fine

18:4 [x]Isa 48:20; Jer 50:8; 2Co 6:17 **18:5** [y]Jer 51:9 [z]Rev 16:19 **18:6** [a]Ps 137:8; Jer 50:15,29 [b]Rev 14:10; 16:19 **18:7** [c]Eze 28:2-8 [d]Isa 47:7,8; Zep 2:15 **18:8** [e]ver 10; Isa 47:9; Jer 50:31,32 [f]Rev 17:16 **18:9** [g]Rev 17:2,4 [h]ver 18; Rev 19:3 [i]Eze 26:17,18 **18:10** [j]ver 15,17 [k]ver 16,19 [l]Rev 17:12 **18:11** [m]Eze 27:27 [n]ver 3 **18:12** [o]Rev 17:4

[a] 4 Jer. 51:45 [b] 7 See Isaiah 47:7,8.

circulated by local elites whose own rank depended on Rome's patronage, Rome brought good to many peoples. Three times, however, the text zeroes in on Babylon's luxuries (vv. 3,7,9). That the nations would mourn her destruction only reveals the extent to which they were "intoxicated" (17:2) and "bewitched" (see 18:23) by her exploitive seduction (14:8). *kings of the earth … merchants of the earth.* Writers sometimes briefly outlined in advance groups they would treat: kings mourn in vv. 9–10, and merchants in vv. 11–19.

18:4 *that you will not share in her sins.* In the same context that mentions that Babylon was an intoxicating cup for the nations and would be mourned (Jer 51:7–8), God warns his people to flee from Babylon, lest they be destroyed because of "her sins" (Jer 51:6; cf. 51:45). (Jeremiah meant these words as a prophecy of future judgment rather than as a present warning, Jer 29:7.)

18:5 *sins are piled up to heaven.* The context that warns God's people to flee from Babylon warns that "her judgment … rises as high as the heavens" (Jer 51:9; cf. 2Ch 28:9; Ezr 9:6). Judgment sometimes waited until sins reached a particular level (Ge 15:16).

18:6 *Give back to her as she has given.* Jewish tradition emphasized that God often punished people in ways that resembled their sin; Revelation might here paraphrase the idea in the last line of Jer 50:15. *pay her back double.* Double payment was exacted from a thief (Ex 22:4,7,9), and from God's people (Isa 40:2; Jer 16:18). Babylon would drink "from her own cup" (cf. Rev 14:8–10; Isa 51:22–23; Jer 50:29; Ob 15).

18:7 *the glory and luxury she gave herself.* Rome glorified itself, encouraging the spread of the worship of the emperor and the goddess Roma, personification of Rome. *queen … not a widow.* Babylon claimed to be an eternal queen (Isa 47:7) and that she would never be a widow (Isa 47:8).

18:8 *Therefore.* Like Babylon in Isaiah, Rome claimed to be an eternal city. Other Jewish visionaries also applied the prophecy of this verse against Rome. *in one day.* Babylon's judgments would come on her all in one day (Isa 47:9). *consumed by fire.* Because most of Rome had burned three decades earlier, in AD 64, the image is a graphic one. *mighty is the Lord God who judges her.* Cf. Jer 50:34.

18:9 *kings of the earth.* Could be Rome's client rulers, those who ruled kingdoms (e.g., earlier Herod the Great and Aretas IV) under Rome's rule. The expression appears at least 15 times in the OT. Jesus is the "ruler of the kings of the earth" (1:5; Ps 89:27), but they would gather against him (Rev 19:19; Ps 2:2); and such rulers once became wealthy through Tyre's trade (Eze 27:33).

18:10 *they will stand far off and cry.* Kings and merchants (v. 15) are terrified at her fall as people were terrified by Tyre's fall (Eze 26:18). *Woe! Woe.* Cf. Eze 16:23.

18:11–19 Rome thrived on trade, especially via the sea; elites praised Rome, but Rome lived luxuriously on the basis of inequitable trade policies toward its provinces. The Roman elite practiced conspicuous consumption (see the article "Rome's Imports," p. 2258). The Roman province of Asia, John's specified audience (1:4), was the empire's richest province. Yet landowners in Asia used so much land for profitable export items such as wine that Asia's cities had to import grain at high prices.

Revelation evokes OT images not only about the political oppressor Babylon but also about the economic power Tyre (especially Eze 26–28), a prostitute (Isa 23:15–17). Alexander the Great captured and brutally slaughtered the people of Tyre, an island city that most observers had previously considered invincible. Merchant kingdoms lamented over Tyre the economic prostitute (Isa 23:5–7,15–17).

Transport was cheaper by sea. Rome's port, Ostia, built roughly half a century before, held a large square full of offices for the merchants. In John's day, pagan symbols were prominent at major Mediterranean ports and on most ships; aspects of the imperial cult affected even shipping lines and merchant guilds.

18:12–13 The list of imports here fits lists of imports to Rome (see the article "Rome's Imports," p. 2258). Some

REVELATION 18:12 – 13 

Rome's Imports

John adapts Ezekiel's list of 40 products in which Tyre traded (Eze 27:2 – 24), but updates it accurately for the trade realities of first-century Rome. Further, whereas Ezekiel's list is arranged geographically, John's is arranged topically, by cargo type. Although he includes some items that were not expensive (oil, though imported in massive quantities), John focuses on and lists many of the most expensive imports, overlapping substantially with the list of expensive items from the first-century Roman writer Pliny the Elder. The overlap is highlighted here, following the sequence of Rev 18:12 – 13. The comments in this article follow especially the research of J. Nelson Kraybill and Richard Bauckham.

Rome's new rich class in this period typically flaunted their gold and silver. Rome imported most of these metals from Spain, where it owned a number of mines, some confiscated from other owners. The slaves who worked such mines rarely lived more than a few years. Rome also imported precious stones, worn in men's rings but especially by women, mainly from India. Many people regarded pearls as the epitome of luxury. They secured some pearls from the Red Sea, better ones from the Persian Gulf, and the most abundant source was India; some regard this as the most lucrative form of trade that Rome had with the East.

Rome imported fine linen from Spain, Asia Minor, and especially Egypt; it had begun to replace wool in Rome by this period. Purple had long been a symbol of affluence, imported especially from Tyre (see note on Ac 16:14); scarlet was also a symbol of luxury, derived mainly from kermes oaks in Asia Minor. Some silk was produced on a Mediterranean island, but Rome imported most of its silk from China. Most came through northwest Indian ports and some came overland through Parthia. Given the distance traveled, it is hardly surprising that it was a symbol of conspicuous consumption available only to the wealthy.

Citron wood originally came westward from the north African coast from Cyrene, but the supply was by this period so depleted that most such wood was imported from Morocco. Tables made of citron wood were so expensive and fashionable that one such table was sold for the price of a large estate.

Trade in ivory had nearly driven the Syrian elephant to extinction and few elephants remained in North Africa. Other costly wood would include maple, cedar and cypress, all of which were used as expensive luxury items. The most famous bronze in the empire was Corinthian bronze; the best iron was imported from the East, though available elsewhere; Rome imported marble from Africa, Egypt and Greece, especially for use in palaces.

Cinnamon bark provided an expensive spice, but trade focused especially on the tree's wood; most probably came from Somalia. Ships involved in the east African trade went as far south as Zanzibar off the Tanzanian coast, in a two-year round trip voyage. The Greek term translated "spice" (Rev 18:13) designates an aromatic spice from southern India; incense was used for rituals and to perfume wealthy homes; myrrh was imported from Yemen and Somalia; frankincense, known as a luxury good, was from south Arabia.

Because the wine trade was more profitable than grain, wealthy Roman owners of large estates in the provinces cultivated vines more than grain. Italy produced some of its own oil but imported more in this period from Africa and Spain. Fine flour (in contrast to wine, oil and wheat) was considered a luxury good; the best was imported from Africa.

continued on next page

Africa and Egypt supplied most of Rome's wheat via thousands of ships run by merchants but regulated by the state. Much of this wheat came from taxes on the provinces; Rome imported an estimated 400,000 tons (363,000 metric tons) of grain each year to keep the people in the capital satisfied. An estimated 200,000 families in Rome received this grain free, while thousands of children in some of the grain-producing areas died from starvation and malnutrition.

Even the rich rarely ate beef; cattle were used especially as work animals. In the first century the rich procured as ranches large estates in Italy and (generally by confiscation or conquest) in the provinces. Some sheep were used for mutton, but Italy mainly imported sheep for rich estates that produced wool. Italy lacked sufficient pasture for many horses but imported them from Africa, Spain, and elsewhere for use in chariot races for public entertainment. Horses also pulled the wealthy's four-wheeled carriages, sometimes plated with silver.

John concludes climactically with the mention of "human beings sold as slaves." Rome no longer fought enough wars to supply many prisoners of war as slaves. Many poor people discarded babies they felt unable to raise, however; while many of these were eaten by dogs or birds, many others were raised by humans for lives of slavery. Asia exported a large quantity of humans to Rome, probably through the port of Ephesus. "Human beings sold as slaves" may evoke the Greek version of Eze 27:13, where Tyre's vicious trade included "human beings," i.e., slaves. ◆

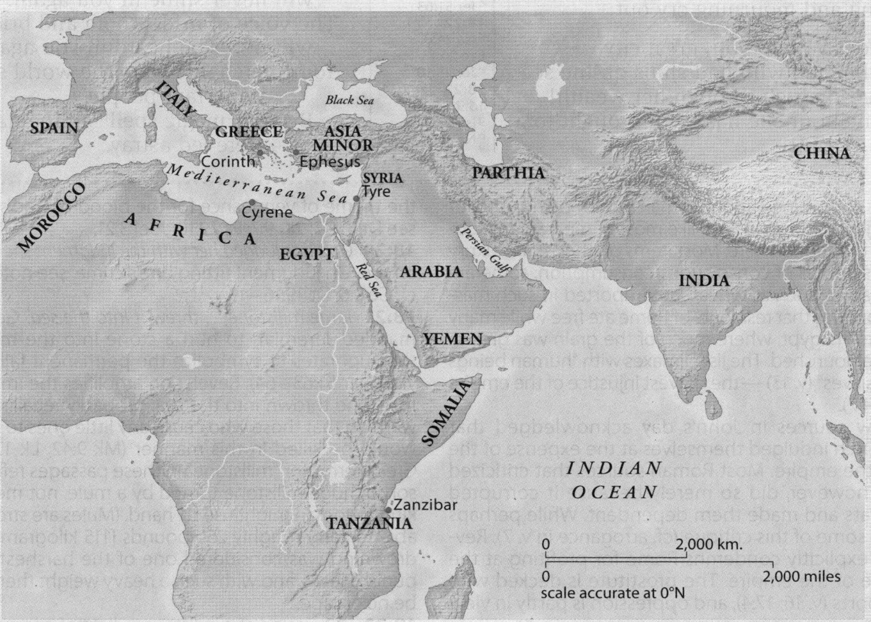

Roman Imports.

flour and wheat; cattle and sheep; horses
and carriages; and human beings sold as
slaves.[p]
14 "They will say, 'The fruit you longed
for is gone from you. All your luxury and
splendor have vanished, never to be recovered.' 15 The merchants who sold these
things and gained their wealth from her[q]
will stand far off, terrified at her torment.
They will weep and mourn[r] 16 and cry out:

"'Woe! Woe to you, great city,
dressed in fine linen, purple and
scarlet,
and glittering with gold, precious
stones and pearls![s]
17 In one hour[t] such great wealth has
been brought to ruin!'[u]

"Every sea captain, and all who travel by ship, the sailors, and all who earn
their living from the sea,[v] will stand far
off. 18 When they see the smoke of her
burning, they will exclaim, 'Was there
ever a city like this great city?'[w] 19 They
will throw dust on their heads,[x] and with
weeping and mourning cry out:

"'Woe! Woe to you, great city,
where all who had ships on the sea
became rich through her wealth!
In one hour she has been brought to
ruin!'[y]

18:13 [p] Eze 27:13; 1Ti 1:10 **18:15** [q] ver 3 [r] Eze 27:31 **18:16** [s] Rev 17:4 **18:17** [t] ver 10 [u] Rev 17:16 [v] Eze 27:28-30 **18:18** [w] Eze 27:32; Rev 13:4 **18:19** [x] Jos 7:6; Eze 27:30 [y] Rev 17:16
18:20 [z] Jer 51:48; Rev 12:12 [a] Rev 19:2 **18:21** [b] Rev 5:2 [c] Jer 51:63 **18:22** [d] Isa 24:8; Eze 26:13 [e] Jer 25:10 **18:23** [f] Jer 7:34; 16:9; 25:10 [g] Isa 23:8 [h] Na 3:4

20 "Rejoice over her, you heavens![z]
Rejoice, you people of God!
Rejoice, apostles and prophets!
For God has judged her
with the judgment she imposed
on you."[a]

The Finality of Babylon's Doom

21 Then a mighty angel[b] picked up a
boulder the size of a large millstone and
threw it into the sea,[c] and said:

"With such violence
the great city of Babylon will be
thrown down,
never to be found again.
22 The music of harpists and
musicians, pipers and
trumpeters,
will never be heard in you again.[d]
No worker of any trade
will ever be found in you again.
The sound of a millstone
will never be heard in you again.[e]
23 The light of a lamp
will never shine in you again.
The voice of bridegroom and bride
will never be heard in you again.[f]
Your merchants were the world's
important people.[g]
By your magic spell[h] all the nations
were led astray.

Romans complained about Roman money being used for luxury goods from the East, like most of the fragrant substances mentioned here. Most items on the list are luxury goods, symbols of conspicuous consumption; some are basic staples, such as wheat, but imported in such massive quantities that residents of Rome ate free while many peasants in Egypt, where much of the grain was grown, were malnourished. The list climaxes with "human beings sold as slaves" (v. 13) — the gravest injustice of the empire (cf. Dt 24:7).

A few sources in John's day acknowledged that Rome's rich indulged themselves at the expense of the rest of the empire. Most Roman sources that criticized luxury, however, did so merely because it corrupted aristocrats and made them dependent. While perhaps sharing some of this critique (cf. arrogance in v. 7), Revelation explicitly condemns Rome for profiting at the expense of the empire. The prostitute is decked with her imports (v. 16; 17:4), and oppression is partly in view (v. 24).

18:14 *luxury and splendor.* Public speakers and some OT prophets used wordplays; in Greek, "luxury" and "splendor" is *lipara* and *lampra.*

18:17 *by ship.* Shipwrecks could ruin ship owners, but some grew wealthy enough to own many ships, reducing the risk. Ship owners grew wealthy especially from the grain trade with Rome; see notes on Ac 27:6, 9, 11. The fall of Rome, however, would put both shipowners and their employees out of business.

18:19 *throw dust on their heads.* A traditional act of mourning by both Greeks and Jews (cf. Jos 7:6; 1Sa 4:12; 2Sa 1:2; 15:32; La 2:10; Eze 27:30).

18:20 – 24 Verses 20 and 24 bracket this literary unit with the theme of vengeance for the blood of God's people; see Dt 32:43; 2Ki 9:7; Ps 79:10; Joel 3:21.

18:20 *God has judged her with the judgment she imposed on you.* On judgment fitting one's crime, see note on v. 6; cf. Ge 9:6; Dt 19:16 – 19.

18:21 *large millstone … threw it into the sea.* God commanded Jeremiah to hurl a stone into the middle of the Euphrates to symbolize the permanent fall of Babylon (Jer 51:63 – 64). Revelation amplifies the image as a millstone thrown into the sea, probably recalling Jesus' warning that those who cause any little ones to stumble would be killed in this manner (Mk 9:42; Lk 17:2). The Greek terms for "millstone" in these passages refer to the sort of huge millstone turned by a mule, not merely the kind a woman might use by hand. (Mules are strong, e.g., able to carry roughly 250 pounds [115 kilograms].) Such drowning was considered one of the harshest Roman punishments, and with such a heavy weight there would be no escape.

18:22 – 23 *sound of a millstone … light of a lamp … voice of bridegroom and bride will never be heard in you again.* When God judged Judah by means of Babylon, Jerusalem became desolate, without lighted lamps or the sounds of millstones or the joyful sound of newlyweds (Jer 25:10; cf. Jer 16:9). Now Babylon, oppressor of God's people, reaps what it sowed. Contrast Rev 19:7; 21:2,9; 21:23 – 24; 22:5,17.

18:23 *By your magic spell all the nations were led astray.* The Biblical prophecy drawn upon in vv. 7 – 8 is also relevant here: once judged, Babylon would no longer protect herself or deceive the people by her magic spells (Isa 47:9). But if Isaiah's prophecy against Babylon supplies the concept, Nahum's prophecy against Nineveh supplies the language: "a prostitute, alluring, the mistress of sorceries,

[24]In her was found the blood of prophets
and of God's holy people,[i]
of all who have been slaughtered on
the earth."[j]

Threefold Hallelujah Over Babylon's Fall

19 After this I heard what sounded like the roar of a great multitude[k] in heaven shouting:

"Hallelujah!
Salvation[l] and glory and power[m]
belong to our God,
[2] for true and just are his judgments.
He has condemned the great prostitute
who corrupted the earth by her
adulteries.
He has avenged on her the blood of his
servants."[n]

[3]And again they shouted:

"Hallelujah!
The smoke from her goes up for ever
and ever."[o]

[4]The twenty-four elders[p] and the four
living creatures[q] fell down[r] and worshiped
God, who was seated on the throne. And
they cried:

"Amen, Hallelujah!"

[5]Then a voice came from the throne,
saying:

"Praise our God,
all you his servants,[s]
you who fear him,
both great and small!"[t]

[6]Then I heard what sounded like a great
multitude,[u] like the roar of rushing waters
and like loud peals of thunder, shouting:

"Hallelujah!
For our Lord God Almighty reigns.
[7]Let us rejoice and be glad
and give him glory!
For the wedding of the Lamb[v] has
come,
and his bride[w] has made herself
ready.
[8]Fine linen, bright and clean,
was given her to wear."
(Fine linen stands for the righteous acts[x]
of God's holy people.)

[9]Then the angel said to me,[y] "Write
this:[z] Blessed are those who are invited to
the wedding supper of the Lamb!"[a] And
he added, "These are the true words of
God."[b]
[10]At this I fell at his feet to worship
him.[c] But he said to me, "Don't do that!
I am a fellow servant with you and with
your brothers and sisters who hold to the
testimony of Jesus. Worship God![d] For it is
the Spirit of prophecy who bears testimony to Jesus."[e]

18:24 [i]Rev 16:6; 17:6 [j]Jer 51:49
19:1 [k]Rev 11:15 [l]Rev 7:10 [m]Rev 4:11
19:2 [n]Dt 32:43; Rev 6:10
19:3 [o]Isa 34:10; Rev 14:11
19:4 [p]Rev 4:4 [q]Rev 4:6 [r]Rev 5:14
19:5 [s]Ps 134:1 [t]Rev 11:18; 20:12
19:6 [u]Rev 11:15
19:7 [v]Mt 22:2; 25:10; Eph 5:32 [w]Rev 21:2,9
19:8 [x]Rev 15:4
19:9 [y]ver 10 [z]Rev 1:19 [a]Lk 14:15 [b]Rev 21:5; 22:6
19:10 [c]Rev 22:8 [d]Ac 10:25, 26; Rev 22:9 [e]Rev 12:17

---

who enslaved nations by her prostitution and peoples by her witchcraft" (Na 3:4).

18:24 *In her was found the blood of prophets and of God's holy people.* Babylon's demise depicted in v. 2 draws on Jer 51:37, where Babylon would fall because of killing God's people, just as Babylon had killed many throughout the earth (Jer 51:49).

19:1 – 10 Ancient writers often developed points by contrasting characters. This passage contrasts the fate of Babylon the prostitute (vv. 1 – 5) with the future of the new Jerusalem, the bride (vv. 6 – 9; cf. 21:2). Both events invite the praises of heaven, reflecting the fulfillment of God's perfect purposes (vv. 1,3 – 7). The prostitute's alienated lovers would kill and burn her (17:16 – 17); by contrast, the Lamb welcomes his bride (vv. 6 – 9).

19:1 *Hallelujah!* Most early Jewish readers, even those who used only Greek, would know that "Hallelujah!" (vv. 1,3,4,6) meant "Praise Yahweh!" in a particularly emphatic form. The expression appears untranslated 23 times in the Septuagint (the pre-Christian Greek translation of the OT), always in Psalms, except for two references in the Apocrypha.

19:3 *smoke from her goes up for ever and ever.* See note on 14:11. Rome's claims to be eternal (see note on 18:7) were as fictitious as those of all other kingdoms.

19:5 The praise here may echo especially Ps 134:1; 115:13.

19:6 *roar of rushing waters.* See note on 1:15.

19:7 *rejoice … For the wedding of the Lamb has come.* Weddings epitomized joy and celebration; guests were obligated to promote the newlyweds' joy. The promise of this banquet appears also as a beatitude, a common literary form ("Blessed are those who …"; cf. v. 9; 1:3; 14:13; 16:15; 20:6; 22:7,14). The wedding banquet was a frequent Jewish figure for the coming Messianic era, based on a promised future banquet (Isa 25:6) when God would destroy death and remove the tears and shame of his people (Isa 25:8). (Some later teachers even decided that Leviathan, the many-headed serpent [Isa 27:1], would be served as the food at the Messianic banquet!) Ancient writers often taught through contrasts; Revelation here contrasts the marriage supper of the Lamb with the great supper of God, in which birds feast on the carcasses of the wicked (vv. 9,17 – 18). *his bride has made herself ready.* The bride would bathe herself and adorn herself in special array (see v. 8).

19:8 *Fine linen.* High-class prostitutes were known for their elaborate garb (18:12,16), but special wedding apparel is beautiful to the groom. *the righteous acts of God's holy people.* May recall the bridal array of righteousness in Isa 61:10.

19:10 *I fell at his feet to worship him.* John may have mistaken the angel for a theophany, since in the OT "the angel of the LORD" sometimes spoke God's message directly or even turned out to be the Lord (Ge 18:10,13,15,17,22,26; 19:1). The angel's explicit prohibition of worshiping him might guard against some syncretistic practices among Jews of Asia Minor, in which some worshiped angels in addition to God. *the Spirit of prophecy who bears testimony to Jesus.* Jewish sources frequently associated the Spirit with prophecy; here all believers are thus potential prophets, inspired to speak the Spirit's central message about Jesus.

The Heavenly Warrior Defeats the Beast

11I saw heaven standing open and there
before me was a white horse, whose rider[f] is called Faithful and True.[g] With justice he judges and wages war.[h] 12His eyes
are like blazing fire,[i] and on his head are
many crowns.[j] He has a name written on
him that no one knows but he himself.[k]
13He is dressed in a robe dipped in blood,[l]
and his name is the Word of God.[m] 14The
armies of heaven were following him, riding on white horses and dressed in fine
linen,[n] white and clean. 15Coming out of
his mouth is a sharp sword[o] with which
to strike down[p] the nations. "He will rule
them with an iron scepter."[a][q] He treads
the winepress[r] of the fury of the wrath of
God Almighty. 16On his robe and on his
thigh he has this name written:[s]

KING OF KINGS AND LORD OF LORDS.[t]

17And I saw an angel standing in the
sun, who cried in a loud voice to all the
birds[u] flying in midair,[v] "Come,[w] gather
together for the great supper of God, 18so
that you may eat the flesh of kings, generals, and the mighty, of horses and their
riders, and the flesh of all people,[x] free
and slave, great and small."

19Then I saw the beast and the kings of
the earth[y] and their armies gathered together to wage war against the rider on the
horse and his army. 20But the beast was
captured, and with it the false prophet[z]
who had performed the signs on its behalf.[a] With these signs he had deluded
those who had received the mark of the
beast and worshiped its image. The two of
them were thrown alive into the fiery lake[b]
of burning sulfur.[c] 21The rest were killed
with the sword[d] coming out of the mouth
of the rider on the horse,[e] and all the birds[f]
gorged themselves on their flesh.

19:11 [f] Rev 6:2 [g] Rev 3:14 [h] Isa 11:4 **19:12** [i] Rev 1:14 [j] Rev 6:2 [k] Rev 2:17 **19:13** [l] Isa 63:2, 3 [m] Jn 1:1 **19:14** [n] ver 8 **19:15** [o] Rev 1:16 [p] Isa 11:4; 2Th 2:8 [q] Ps 2:9; Rev 2:27 [r] Rev 14:20 **19:16** [s] ver 12 [t] Rev 17:14 **19:17** [u] ver 21 [v] Rev 8:13 [w] Eze 39:17 **19:18** [x] Eze 39:18-20 **19:19** [y] Rev 16:14, 16 **19:20** [z] Rev 16:13 [a] Rev 13:12 [b] Da 7:11; Rev 20:10, 14, 15; 21:8 [c] Rev 14:10 **19:21** [d] ver 15 [e] ver 11, 19 [f] ver 17

[a] *15* Psalm 2:9

19:11 – 21 God often sent his people to holy war in the OT, and some Jewish sources expected an end-time battle to throw off the yoke of Rome and other pagan oppressors. But here the armies of heaven (v. 14) do not execute any violence themselves; Jesus is the mighty warrior who strikes the wicked (vv. 11,15,21). Biblical prophets predicted God himself as the ultimate holy warrior (Isa 42:13; Hab 3:11 – 14; Zep 3:17), cloaked for war (Isa 59:17), including the blood of the winepress as here (Rev 19:13,15; cf. Isa 63:3). Jesus here assumes this divine role.
19:11 *white horse.* White horses were often considered the best. Such horses were appropriate mounts for rulers, important officials and conquerors entering Rome in triumph, but the idea of a "King of Kings" (cf. v. 16) mounted on a white horse may draw on the image of the Parthian king. If Rome fears a Parthian invasion, how much more should they fear the true Lord from heaven!
19:12 *eyes are like blazing fire, and on his head are many crowns.* In the context of most ancient sources, Jesus' fiery eyes probably connote divinity and fury; his many crowns (here diadems, not garlands) indicate that he is ruler over all the kings of the world (vv. 12,16). *name … that no one knows but he himself.* Jesus has a hidden name, just like his followers (2:17). Perhaps this name remains a secret, but perhaps it is a secret only to the world, because his "name" is the "Word of God" (v. 13) and "KING OF KINGS AND LORD OF LORDS" (v. 16).
19:13 *robe dipped in blood.* Would represent a terrifying image to the average ancient reader; Gentiles sometimes so portrayed a horrible Fury (an avenging monster). But this verse draws the language specifically from Isa 63: God would go out and trample the blood of the wicked like wine in a winepress, till his garments were stained with their blood (Isa 63:1 – 6; cf. Isa 9:5; 34:3 – 7; 49:26). The blood is from those slain in his wine press, the whole world (v. 15; cf. 14:18 – 20), as in Isa 63:2. *his name is the Word of God.* At his coming, the world will finally realize that Jesus himself is divine.
19:14 *The armies of heaven were following him.* This army may include angels (Zec 14:5), but must include believers (Rev 17:14; cf. the fine linen in v. 8). The army that had overcome the beast by martyrdom (14:1 – 5) now would share Christ's final triumph (cf. the "scepter" in v. 15; 2:27). *white horses.* See note on v. 11; the mounted Parthians were Rome's most feared earthly enemies. Whereas chariots were the elite military units in most of the OT period (cf. 2Ki 2:11; 6:17; Isa 66:15), riders on horses were the elite cavalry of this period.
19:15 *Coming out of his mouth is a sharp sword … "He will rule them with an iron scepter."* As in a widely circulated earlier Jewish work, this verse links Ps 2:9 (ruling with an iron scepter) with Isa 11:4, where the ultimate Davidic ruler strikes the earth with a weapon from his mouth (cf. Rev 1:16; 19:15). *sharp sword.* For many Jewish hearers, the sword might also recall the popular Apocryphal work the Wisdom of Solomon, in which God's word leaped from heaven as a mighty warrior (cf. v. 13), bringing forth God's commandment as a sharp, straight sword to kill the disobedient (Wisdom of Solomon 18:15 – 16). *iron scepter.* See note on 2:26 – 27. *winepress.* See note on v. 13.
19:16 *on his thigh.* Commentators observe that some wrote names on statues in Rome, and Greeks sometimes branded horses on their thighs. *KING OF KINGS.* The Parthian ruler was called the "great king" and the "king of kings." This superlative title had long been a title for eastern monarchs (Ezr 7:12; Eze 26:7; Da 2:37). Scripture applied similar titles to the true suzerain ruler, God (Dt 10:17; Ps 136:3; Da 2:47; Zec 14:9; 1Ti 6:15). Jewish sources subsequent to the OT applied the title almost exclusively to God.
19:17 – 18 *all the birds … may eat the flesh.* Ancients were familiar with the image of carrion birds feasting on the flesh of corpses killed in battle (e.g., in Homer's popular Greek epics; also 1Sa 17:44 – 46; Jer 16:4; Eze 29:5). Such scenes were common in ancient literature, but intended to evoke horror. Given common Greek views of one's image enduring in the realm of departed spirits, the only fate considered worse than death itself was death followed by lack of burial. Lack of burial allowed one's remains to be devoured by animals, and many Gentiles believed that it precluded a place in the realm of the dead. The immediate background is Eze 39:17 – 20: God invited beasts and birds to devour the flesh of the end-time army that opposed him.
19:20 *The two of them were thrown alive into the fiery lake.* In Da 7:11, the beast was slain and thrown into the fire. *burning sulfur.* See note on 14:10. Jewish tradition depicted Gehenna, or hell, as burning.

The Thousand Years

20 And I saw an angel coming down
out of heaven,[g] having the key[h]
to the Abyss and holding in his hand a
great chain. 2He seized the dragon, that
ancient serpent, who is the devil, or Satan,[i] and bound him for a thousand years.[j]
3He threw him into the Abyss, and locked
and sealed[k] it over him, to keep him from
deceiving the nations[l] anymore until the
thousand years were ended. After that, he
must be set free for a short time.

4I saw thrones[m] on which were seated
those who had been given authority to
judge. And I saw the souls of those who
had been beheaded[n] because of their testimony about Jesus and because of the
word of God. They[a] had not worshiped the
beast[o] or its image and had not received its
mark on their foreheads or their hands.[p]
They came to life and reigned with Christ
a thousand years. 5(The rest of the dead
did not come to life until the thousand
years were ended.) This is the first resurrection.[q] 6Blessed[r] and holy are those who
share in the first resurrection. The second
death[s] has no power over them, but they
will be priests[t] of God and of Christ and
will reign with him[u] for a thousand years.

20:1 [g] Rev 10:1 [h] Rev 1:18 **20:2** [i] Rev 12:9 [j] 2Pe 2:4 **20:3** [k] Da 6:17 [l] Rev 12:9 **20:4** [m] Da 7:9 [n] Rev 6:9 [o] Rev 13:12 [p] Rev 13:16 **20:5** [q] Lk 14:14; Php 3:11 **20:6** [r] Rev 14:13 [s] Rev 2:11 [t] Rev 1:6 [u] ver 4

The Judgment of Satan

7When the thousand years are over,[v] Satan will be released from his prison 8and
will go out to deceive the nations[w] in the
four corners of the earth — Gog and Magog[x] — and to gather them for battle.[y] In
number they are like the sand on the seashore.[z] 9They marched across the breadth
of the earth and surrounded[a] the camp of
God's people, the city he loves. But fire
came down from heaven[b] and devoured
them. 10And the devil, who deceived
them,[c] was thrown into the lake of burning sulfur, where the beast and the false
prophet had been thrown. They will be tormented day and night for ever and ever.[d]

The Judgment of the Dead

11Then I saw a great white throne[e] and
him who was seated on it. The earth and
the heavens fled from his presence, and
there was no place for them. 12And I saw
the dead, great and small, standing before the throne, and books were opened.[f]
Another book was opened, which is the
book of life.[g] The dead were judged according to what they had done[h] as re-

20:7 [v] ver 2 **20:8** [w] ver 3, 10 [x] Eze 38:2; 39:1 [y] Rev 16:14 [z] Heb 11:12 **20:9** [a] Eze 38:9, 16 [b] Eze 38:22; 39:6 **20:10** [c] Rev 19:20 [d] Rev 14:10, 11 **20:11** [e] Rev 4:2 **20:12** [f] Da 7:10 [g] Rev 3:5 [h] Jer 17:10; Mt 16:27; Rev 2:23

[a] 4 Or *God; I also saw those who*

20:2–3 *seized the dragon ... bound him ... threw him into the Abyss.* Jewish sources often speak of evil angels being bound, sometimes by good angels, until the day of judgment. In some apocalyptic texts bound angels could also be thrown into the abyss (1 Enoch 88:1).

20:2 *for a thousand years.* See the article "The Millennium," p. 2264.

20:3 *sealed it.* Like a container's seal, sealing Satan in the abyss keeps him inside (cf. Da 6:17).

20:4 *beheaded.* Beheading was the primary method of execution for Roman citizens and was deemed the most merciful (i.e., most swift) means of execution. After being bound to a post, stripped naked and whipped, the victim might be forced to kneel before being decapitated. Earlier Roman executioners often used axes; but by this period, provincial executions employed swords. *reigned with Christ.* See note on 2:26–27.

20:5 Daniel had predicted a resurrection of the damned (Da 12:2), a view followed by some apocalyptic Jewish writers (2 Baruch 51:1–2) and by many early Christian writers (Mt 5:29–30; 10:28; 25:46; Jn 5:29; Ac 24:15).

20:8 *Gog and Magog.* Following Ezekiel, many ancient Jewish comments about the end time mention Gog and Magog. In many Jewish texts Gog serves a mythical function; in some texts, various evil oppressors could fill the role of the final "Gog" if God intended their day as the end time. Jewish writers typically used the invasion of Gog to predict the gathering of all nations against Israel, and Revelation likely employs this image in a similar way. (Many Biblical texts spoke of nations gathering against Israel, cf. Joel 3:11–13; Zec 14:2.)

To some degree Revelation follows the sequence in Eze 36–48: resurrection and kingdom (Eze 37), Gog from Magog (Eze 38–39), and the new temple and city (Eze 40–48). Nevertheless, the correspondence with Ezekiel is not exact or complete by itself; Eze 37 lacks an explicit millennium, and Rev 21–22 lack a physical temple. Whereas in Ezekiel Gog is ruler of Magog, here Gog and Magog together merely symbolize all the nations, "the nations in the four corners of the earth" (see note on 7:1). *like the sand on the seashore.* A common OT hyperbole for an innumerable multitude (e.g., Ge 22:17; Jdg 7:12; 1Sa 13:5).

20:9 *They ... surrounded the camp of God's people ... But fire came down from heaven and devoured them.* The holy city would be unwalled because there would be so many residents (Zec 2:4); thus God himself would be a wall of fire around her (Zec 2:5; cf. Zec 9:8). But "camp" was normally military language; it probably alludes to Israel's experience in the exodus or to a unit of war. If evil is so deeply engrained in humanity that enemies remain even after the thousand years, John might reason, how much more vigilant must God's people remain in the present time.

Fire devouring the enemy host may evoke Sodom (Ge 19:24–25; cf. Rev 11:8). In Ezekiel, God warned that he would cast fire on Magog (Eze 39:6), and that he would cast rain, hailstones and burning sulfur on this army (Eze 38:22). Some other early Jewish texts reflect a similar fate for Israel's final enemies. The point in Ezekiel is that God would be glorified through their destruction (Eze 38:16,23), and that he would defend his people (Eze 38:14–16).

20:11 *great white throne.* Sometimes following Da 7:9, Jewish traditions often describe this day of judgment before a throne. At this point it was considered too late to seek mercy. *The earth ... fled from his presence.* Unrepentant sinners will flee from the one whose face no mortal can see and live (Ex 33:20).

20:12 *books were opened.* Apocalypses and other Jewish works depict heavenly books of judgment reporting people's works, ready to be opened in the day of judgment. The books here, as in some of the other Jewish texts, recall Da 7:10, where books were opened before God's throne.

REVELATION 20:1–6

THE MILLENNIUM

The millennium concerns the 1,000-year period in Rev 20:1–6. The earliest church fathers who addressed the issue (such as Papias and Irenaeus) held premillennial beliefs. They believed that they were either in the final tribulation or about to face it, and that Christ would afterward return and establish a thousand-year kingdom. After Constantine, however, Christians in the Roman Empire felt that tribulation had ended and that Christ was now reigning through his church; by the time of the fourth-century church historian Eusebius, premillennialists were apparently an easily dissuaded minority. This belief that the church was now reigning is usually considered a form of amillennialism, but it also resembles postmillennialism (see below). A thousand years after Constantine, people were expecting the day of judgment that was to follow the millennium.

Biblical amillennialists today hold a more consistent amillennial interpretation. They argue that from heaven's perspective, Christ and his people reign spiritually in the present age (Ps 110:1), even though on earth it is also a period of suffering. Augustine, most medieval interpreters, Luther, Calvin and others held amillennial views.

Various interpreters in history developed a postmillennial view, believing that the church would establish God's kingdom, preparing the world for Christ's return. This optimistic approach prevailed especially at the height of the British Empire, when many English-speaking interpreters believed that God was using righteous governments to spread godliness. Many leaders in the Great Awakenings in the United States, such as Jonathan Edwards and Charles Finney, held this view.

Today the majority of interpreters of Revelation are either premillennialists or amillennialists (though some also remain postmillennialists). One of the strongest arguments favoring premillennialism is that it follows the logic of the narrative.

- Satan does not appear bound (Rev 20:2–3) during the present age in Rev 12:12–13; 13:11–15.
- The beast and false prophet are thrown into the lake of fire in Rev 19:20 and are still there in Rev 20:10.
- Those specified as resurrected in Rev 20:4 are those who have suffered under the beast.

continued on next page

corded in the books. [13]The sea gave up
the dead that were in it, and death and
Hades[i] gave up the dead[j] that were in
them, and each person was judged according to what they had done. [14]Then
death[k] and Hades were thrown into the
lake of fire. The lake of fire is the second death. [15]Anyone whose name was

20:13 [i]Rev 6:8 [j]Isa 26:19 **20:14** [k]1Co 15:26

the book of life. See note on 3:5. *judged according to what they had done.* See note on 22:12.

20:13 *The sea gave up the dead that were in it.* That the sea gave up its dead answers the concern of many people in antiquity concerning the fate of the unburied (cf. note on 1Co 15:35). Many Gentiles believed that those who died at sea were barred from Hades because they were not buried. *Hades.* The realm of the dead; those still dead—those not raised at the first resurrection (vv. 4–6)—were the damned. Some apocalyptic writings expected Hades to return what was entrusted to it when the dead are raised for judgment.

20:14 *death and Hades were thrown into the lake of fire.* An apocalypse consigned the fallen angels, Gentiles, and disobedient Israelites to the abyss of fire (1 Enoch 90:24–27). Revelation goes further; a lake normally contained water, so the image of a lake of fire here is striking. A river of fire flows from God's throne in Da 7:10, an image that is heavily developed in later Jewish tradition; Greeks envisioned a river of fire in the underworld. Most relevant (though not mentioning a body of water) is the Jewish image of fiery Gehenna (Gehinnom), where many Jewish teachers believed that the wicked would be either tortured or consumed. *second death.* See note on 2:11.

- The devil cannot deceive "anymore" suggests a suspension of his deceptive work that transpired from Rev 12:9 onward.
- The resurrection of the righteous is parallel to and contrasted with the rest of the dead returning to life after the thousand years (Rev 20:4–6), suggesting a bodily rather than symbolic resurrection.
- Readers today recognize that the period between Jesus' first and second comings is longer than 1,000 years; in John's own day, however, such a figure for the intermediate period must have seemed too long (Rev 1:3).

Not all premillennialists take the specific figure of 1,000 as literal, but they do insist on an interim period (cf. perhaps Isa 24:22; Da 7:12).

One of the strongest arguments favoring amillennialism is that such an interim period probably does not appear elsewhere in the NT (despite attempts of some to find it in 1Co 15:23–24). Amillennialists also point to the three cycles that repeat judgments earlier in Revelation, and view the millennium in Rev 20 as another such cycle. Some of the cycles do exhibit signs of following earlier cycles in John's narrative, but these are because of the sequence of John's visions, not the events. Moreover, the heavenly perspective in Rev 20 differs from the earthly one; e.g., God's people are slaughtered in Rev 11:7 and Rev 13:7, but from heaven's perspective, it is they who are truly victorious (Rev 12:11). Premillennialists and amillennialists each offer answers for the others' arguments, merely sampled here.

In terms of ancient context: many Jewish views of the future, including visions of the future expressed in many apocalypses, included a future interim period between the beginning and the end of the consummation. Estimated durations of the period, however, vary considerably, such as three generations or 400 years. One rabbi might provide four different estimates of the period's duration based on four different interpretations of Scripture. First Enoch allows so many brief transitional periods that the end appears to come gradually (1 Enoch 91:8–17). One Gentile prophecy predicted Rome's collapse at the end of 6,000 years, followed by a 1,000-year period of peace; at some point at least some Jews envisioned a final thousand years as a Sabbath period.

Premillennialists would point to such beliefs about an intermediate period to argue that John probably did expect a literal interim period. Amillennialists would point to the same beliefs to argue that John transforms an apocalyptic literary device. Some read the millennium as subsequent to the judgments (i.e., as premillennial in the narrative of Revelation), yet argue that to take the millennium literally misreads the nature of Revelation as an apocalypse. Scholars thus remain divided on these questions. ◆

not found written in the book of life[l] was thrown into the lake of fire.

A New Heaven and a New Earth

21 Then I saw "a new heaven and a new earth,"[a][m] for the first heav-
en and the first earth had passed away,
and there was no longer any sea. 2 I saw
the Holy City, the new Jerusalem, coming down out of heaven from God,[n] prepared as a bride beautifully dressed for

20:15 [l] ver 12
21:1 [m] Isa 65:17; 2Pe 3:13
21:2 [n] Heb 11:10; 12:22; Rev 3:12

[a] *1* Isaiah 65:17

21:1 *a new heaven and a new earth.* A new Jerusalem (Isa 65:18) appears in the context of Isaiah's promise of the new heavens and earth (Isa 65:17; 66:22); apocalyptic literature developed both images. *there was no longer any sea.* Some sources spoke of the purification of creation; others, of its transformation; still others, of its destruction and rebirth. Because the sea disappears, Revelation at least evokes transformation, though scholars debate how literally Revelation intends its different images.

Some scholars associate the sea with evil (or chaos, as much earlier in ancient Near Eastern thought), with death (20:13) or with the beast (13:1), but it appears positively in some other passages in Revelation (5:13; 15:2). Perhaps the sea disappears here because Isaiah's new heavens and earth do not specifically mention it. More likely it is replaced with the joyful river of life from God's throne (for the righteous; 22:1) and possibly the lake of fire (for the wicked; 21:8).

21:2 *the Holy City.* Jewish people regularly called Jerusalem by this title, as here (v. 10; 11:2; 22:19); God here renews

her husband. 3 And I heard a loud voice
from the throne saying, "Look! God's
dwelling place is now among the people,
and he will dwell with them. They will be
his people, and God himself will be with
them and be their God.[o] 4 'He will wipe
every tear from their eyes.[p] There will be
no more death'[a][q] or mourning or crying
or pain,[r] for the old order of things has
passed away."

5 He who was seated on the throne[s] said,
"I am making everything new!" Then he
said, "Write this down, for these words are
trustworthy and true."[t]

6 He said to me: "It is done.[u] I am the
Alpha and the Omega,[v] the Beginning and
the End. To the thirsty I will give water
without cost from the spring of the water
of life.[w] 7 Those who are victorious will inherit all this, and I will be their God and
they will be my children. 8 But the cowardly, the unbelieving, the vile, the murderers, the sexually immoral, those who
practice magic arts, the idolaters and all
liars[x]—they will be consigned to the fiery
lake of burning sulfur. This is the second
death."[y]

The New Jerusalem, the Bride of the Lamb

9 One of the seven angels who had the
seven bowls full of the seven last plagues[z]
came and said to me, "Come, I will show
you the bride,[a] the wife of the Lamb."
10 And he carried me away[b] in the Spirit[c] to a mountain great and high, and
showed me the Holy City, Jerusalem,
coming down out of heaven from God.

21:3 [o] 2Co 6:16 **21:4** [p] Rev 7:17 [q] 1Co 15:26; Rev 20:14 [r] Isa 35:10; 65:19 **21:5** [s] Rev 4:9; 20:11 [t] Rev 19:9 **21:6** [u] Rev 16:17 [v] Rev 1:8; 22:13 [w] Jn 4:10
21:8 [x] 1Co 6:9 [y] Rev 2:11 **21:9** [z] Rev 15:1, 6,7 [a] Rev 19:7 **21:10** [b] Rev 17:3 [c] Rev 1:10

[a] 4 Isaiah 25:8

---

a Holy City once defiled (11:2). Some Jewish thinkers envisioned merely a restored and exalted Jerusalem; others thought of a currently hidden city that will ultimately be revealed. In some traditions, God himself would rebuild Jerusalem, possibly the point of its descent from heaven here (cf. 3:12). Jewish people sometimes envisioned the new Jerusalem as heavenly.

Just as Babylon in Revelation represents the people of Rome and not simply its location, and just as "Jerusalem" in the OT usually includes the people and not simply the site, the new Jerusalem undoubtedly includes the people of God. This new Jerusalem is the bride, like God's bride Israel in the OT (e.g., Jer 2:1; Hos 2:19–20) or Christ's bride the church (2Co 11:2; Eph 5:23). Other texts describe Jerusalem's beautiful adornment in the time of her restoration (Isa 52:1; Psalms of Solomon 11:7), including bridal array (Isa 61:10). *beautifully dressed.* See vv. 11–21, especially vv. 19–21 (see note there).

21:3 *God's dwelling place is now among the people.* That God will dwell with his people is a promise of God's covenant with Israel (Ex 25:8; 29:45–46; Lev 26:12; 1Ki 6:13; Eze 37:27; Zec 2:10–11), including in the future temple (Eze 43:7,9). But whereas the restoration of the temple was a standard hope for restored Jerusalem (Eze 37:26–28; 41:1—48:35), in Revelation the entire city is the temple (Rev 21:22), shaped like the Most Holy Place (see note on v. 16; see also the article "Dimensions of the New Jerusalem," p. 2268).

21:4 *wipe every tear from their eyes.* In the time of restoration and resurrection God would "wipe away the tears from all faces" (Isa 25:8). *old order of things has passed away.* "Old order" is lit. "former things"; develops the promise of new creation in Isa 65:16–17, in which "past troubles will be forgotten" and "the former things will not be remembered."

21:6 *the Alpha and the Omega, the Beginning and the End.* See note on 1:8. *I will give water without cost.* Cf. 22:17; probably echoes Isa 55:1, an offer of waters "without cost" at the time of Israel's restoration.

21:7 *I will be their God and they will be my children.* The promise that God would be his people's God and they would be his people was the most basic component of the ancient covenant formula (Ge 17:8; Ex 6:7; 29:45; Lev 26:12,45; Dt 29:13), rehearsed also by the prophets (Jer 7:23; 11:4; 24:7; 30:22; 31:33; Eze 11:20; 14:11; 36:28; 37:23,27; Zec 8:8). But Revelation slightly adapts the formula: the overcomer would be God's child. Israelites were God's children corporately (Ex 4:22; Dt 32:19–20; Hos 1:10; 11:1), but the Greek text here calls each individual believer God's child.

21:8 *the cowardly . . . and all liars.* Vice lists were a common literary form in ancient texts. *those who practice magic arts.* Many people in antiquity, including in Roman Asia, practiced magic arts (cf. Ac 19:13–19). *consigned to the fiery lake of burning sulfur.* Traditional cities kept some groups outside their walls, such as foreigners, traders, and prostitutes, though these groups could work inside the city; outside the new Jerusalem, by contrast, is hell.

21:9–21 Ancient orators often provided stirring descriptions of cities, and valued descriptions so vivid that hearers would virtually "see" the object of their descriptions. Scripture already contained stirring descriptions of present (Ps 48) and future Jerusalem (Isa 2:2–3). Some Jewish writers developed Ezekiel's design for the new Jerusalem and especially the temple mount (Eze 40–48). Some Jewish texts identify the new Jerusalem with paradise. Most such descriptions, however, were meant to praise God for his wonderful plans, rather than to provide a literal blueprint (cf., e.g., streets paved with precious stones in Tobit 13:9–18 in the Apocrypha). Isaiah's crystal gates and walls of precious stones (Isa 54:11–12) also can be depicted as walls of salvation and gates of praise (Isa 26:1; 60:18). Elsewhere in Scripture Jerusalem needs no (material) walls because God himself would be a wall of fire around it (Zec 2:4–5).

Ancient writers often developed their argument by contrasting characters or cities. Both with Babylon and with the new Jerusalem, one of the seven angels who had the seven bowls came and said to John, "Come, I will show you" (the bride in v. 9; the prostitute in 17:1). In each case an angel carries John away in the Spirit (to a great mountain in v. 10; to a wilderness in 17:3). Babylon is decorated with gold and pearls (17:4); the new Jerusalem is built of gold and has gates of pearls (vv. 18,21). Those with faith to wait for the bride will not spoil themselves with the prostitute.

21:10 *he carried me away in the Spirit to a mountain.* God in a vision also set Ezekiel on a mountain, before showing him measurements of a great temple (Eze 40:2). Mount Zion (Rev 14:1) would be the highest mountain (Isa 2:2–3), thus contrasting with the seven mountains/hills on which Babylon sits (17:9). (1 Enoch envisions paradise on seven mountains.)

11It shone with the glory of God,[d] and its
brilliance was like that of a very precious
jewel, like a jasper, clear as crystal.[e] 12It
had a great, high wall with twelve gates,
and with twelve angels at the gates. On
the gates were written the names of the
twelve tribes of Israel.[f] 13There were three
gates on the east, three on the north, three
on the south and three on the west. 14The
wall of the city had twelve foundations,
and on them were the names of the twelve
apostles of the Lamb.

15The angel who talked with me had
a measuring rod[g] of gold to measure the
city, its gates and its walls. 16The city
was laid out like a square, as long as it
was wide. He measured the city with the
rod and found it to be 12,000 stadia[a] in
length, and as wide and high as it is long.
17The angel measured the wall using human measurement, and it was 144 cubits[b]
thick.[c] 18The wall was made of jasper,[h]
and the city of pure gold, as pure as glass.[i]
19The foundations of the city walls were
decorated with every kind of precious
stone.[j] The first foundation was jasper,
the second sapphire, the third agate, the
fourth emerald, 20the fifth onyx, the sixth
ruby,[k] the seventh chrysolite, the eighth
beryl, the ninth topaz, the tenth turquoise,
the eleventh jacinth, and the twelfth amethyst.[d] 21The twelve gates were twelve
pearls, each gate made of a single pearl.
The great street of the city was of gold, as
pure as transparent glass.[l]

21:11 [d] Rev 15:8; 22:5 [e] Rev 4:6 **21:12** [f] Eze 48:30-34 **21:15** [g] Rev 11:1 **21:18** [h] ver 11 [i] ver 21 **21:19** [j] Isa 54:11, 12 **21:20** [k] Rev 4:3 **21:21** [l] ver 18

[a] *16* That is, about 1,400 miles or about 2,200 kilometers
[b] *17* That is, about 200 feet or about 65 meters
[c] *17* Or *high*   [d] *20* The precise identification of some of these precious stones is uncertain.

21:11 *shone with the glory of God ... a very precious jewel.* Until it was destroyed in AD 70, the Jerusalem temple had gates adorned with gold and silver. It could not be compared with God's promised new Jerusalem, however. Some apocalypses expected the end-time Zion to shine with glory (4 Ezra 10:25–27). *jewel.* Gems reflected light; some Jewish traditions even spoke of especially luminous stones. The precious stones here and in vv. 18–21 recall God's promise in Isa 54:11–12, where God would build the walls and gates from precious stones. Many Jewish people felt free to adapt Isaiah's image while preserving the message of incomparable magnificence (Tobit 13:16–17).
21:12 *On the gates were written the names of the twelve tribes of Israel.* Wealthy supporters who funded city building projects often had their names inscribed on them. Yet the honored names on this city are different. The gates here represent instead the 12 tribes of Israel, as in Eze 48:31–34 (and in the Dead Sea Scrolls). The presence of both the 12 tribes (here) and the 12 apostles (v. 14) emphasizes the continuity between God's people through history (vv. 12–14).
21:13 Some Roman towns provided entrance mainly through three gates on one side, but the new Jerusalem provides such access on all sides, implying that it welcomes people from all directions.
21:14 *twelve foundations ... twelve apostles.* Later rabbis typically took literally Isaiah's promise of precious stones for rebuilding Jerusalem (Isa 54:11–12); by contrast, the Dead Sea Scrolls apply the image figuratively to the remnant of Israel and its leaders (12 laymen and three priests). In Biblical tradition 12 stones pointed to 12 tribes (e.g., Jos 4:3–9); the stones in the high priest's breastplate were specifically inscribed with the names of the tribes (Ex 28:17–21). Here, however, they refer to the 12 apostles. Although Jesus is the church's ultimate foundation (1Co 3:11), early Christians emphasized that those who first passed on the message about Jesus were a foundation (Eph 2:20–21; cf. Mt 16:18).
21:15 *measuring rod of gold to measure the city.* The measuring rod reveals the supernatural enormity of the city (v. 16). It recalls the angelic measuring of Jerusalem (Zec 2:1–2) and the temple (Eze 40–41, especially Eze 40:3), and reminds John's oppressed audience that the persecuted remnant whose measuring began in Rev 11:1–2 is the prototype for the glorious future city.
21:16 The size of the city is incomparable; its cubic shape recalls the Most Holy Place, fitting the role of the new Jerusalem as the place of God's dwelling (v. 3). See the article "Dimensions of the New Jerusalem," p. 2268.
21:17 *human measurement.* Recalls Eze 40:5. Some suggest also a contrast: the number of a human who is a beast (13:18) versus the measurements of a human that are also angelic. On this view, the beast's kingdom debases humanity to a beastly level, whereas the new Jerusalem raises it to an angel-like level. *144 cubits thick.* Just as the number 12,000 in v. 16 recalls the uses of the number 12,000 in 7:5–8, the number 144 recalls the use of the number 144,000 in 7:4, who are the people of Zion in 14:1—God's city for God's people (see the article "Dimensions of the New Jerusalem," p. 2268). Why would a city need walls when no enemies remained? One Biblical prophet predicted that Jerusalem would lack walls (Zec 2:4). But others had elaborated on the Holy City's promised magnificence by depicting walls of precious stones (Isa 54:12) or even salvation (Isa 60:18). Ancient cities normally had walls, so lack of walls would require explanation (cf. the lack of a temple in v. 22). When imagery is figurative, it does not need to be harmonized on a literal level.
21:18 *pure as glass.* See note on v. 21; contrast Babylon's impurity in 18:2 and (in Greek) in 17:4.
21:19–21 John lists stones from the priest's breastplate (Ex 28:17–20) and perhaps Tyre's wealthy decorations (Eze 28:16), omitting some of each to arrive at 12 but including 9 stones found in both of those lists. The new Jerusalem is thus a priestly city (cf. 1:6), its gates reflecting the 12 tribes (relevant to the high priest's breastplate stones; see note on v. 14), and a city of plenty that may contrast with exploitive Tyre (see 28:11–19).
21:19 *with every kind of precious stone.* Isaiah had promised walls of precious stones for the restored Jerusalem (Isa 54:12).
21:21 *The twelve gates were twelve pearls.* Isaiah had promised gates of crystal (Isa 54:12); gates of pearls contrast with the mere pearl decorations of Babylon (17:4; 18:12,16). Later rabbis imagined that angels in the sea bottom were currently fashioning such pearls. *great street ... was of gold, as pure as transparent glass.* The capabilities of ancient refining were limited; indeed, in antiquity even glass was rarely fully "clear," much less fully pure. Some of the major north-south and east-west streets of first-century Jerusalem (destroyed probably over two decades earlier) were 30–40 feet (10–13 meters) wide. Even before the city's destruction, however, Jewish people envisioned a greater Jerusalem to come (e.g., streets paved with beryl and

REVELATION 21:15 – 17

DIMENSIONS OF THE NEW JERUSALEM

Ezekiel's new Jerusalem temple was 18,000 cubits all around; John's is nearly 2,000 times larger. At some 1,400 miles (or 2,250 kilometers) by 1,400 miles (2,250 kilometers), the Holy City is larger than any city has ever been. That contrast would have been even clearer in antiquity, where massive cities were smaller than those today. The walls of great cities such as Babylon and Alexandria had a circumference of only nine miles (14.5 kilometers) — not even 1/10,000th the circumference of the New Jerusalem, and less than 1/10,000,000th of its floor plan.

The square shape of the city (Rev 21:16) fits Israel's camp in the wilderness (see "Encampment of the Tribes of Israel," p. 236) and also some ancient city plans. Ancient Israelite towns usually grew randomly, but Greek and Roman cities were carefully planned around the central agora with public works around it. Babylon and Nineveh were thought to be laid out on a square pattern, and Roman settlements often were too. Ezekiel reported that the new Jerusalem would be laid out as a square, with three gates for three tribes of Israel on each of the four sides of the city (Eze 48:16,31 – 35). The square shape (one dimension short of a cube) is also significant in new temple and new Jerusalem imagery (see Eze 40:47; 45:2; 48:20; for the altar, see Ex 27:1; 30:1 – 2; 37:25; 38:1; Eze 43:16; for the ephod, see Ex 28:16; 39:9).

But while this background plays an important part, the new Jerusalem is not merely square; it is cubic, despite the utter incongruity with all human imagination of a city 1,400 miles (2,250 kilometers) high! (Keep in mind that the height of the world's highest mountain today, Mount Everest, is only about 5.5 miles [less than 9 kilometers].) What the world could not accomplish in Babel — a city to the heavens (Ge 11:4) — God grants his people as a gift. The dimensions also seem incongruous for a wall 144 cubits

continued on next page

22I did not see a temple[m] in the city,
because the Lord God Almighty[n] and the
Lamb[o] are its temple. 23The city does not
need the sun or the moon to shine on it,
for the glory of God gives it light,[p] and
the Lamb is its lamp. 24The nations will
walk by its light, and the kings of the

21:22 [m] Jn 4:21, 23 [n] Rev 1:8 [o] Rev 5:6 **21:23** [p] Isa 24:23; 60:19,20; Rev 22:5

streets offering praise in Tobit 13:16 – 17). The city's 12 gates here imply numerous streets; the "great street" here probably is the primary thoroughfare (cf. 11:8; 22:2; the Greek version of Ge 19:2; Jdg 19:15 – 20; Est 6:9 – 11). Roman cities generally organized other streets around a major north-south street and another major east-west street.

21:22 *I did not see a temple.* Following Scripture (Eze 41 – 48), Jewish people expected a splendid end-time temple. A regularly recited prayer, e.g., looked for a renewal of the temple. Indeed, all normal Greek and Roman cities included temples. Revelation does not repudiate Ezekiel's vision, but offers an even greater image: the new city itself is a temple, the dwelling place of God (vv. 3,16). (Cf. perhaps Isa 8:14; Eze 11:16.) Because most prophetic visions of the future were mere images meant to communicate deeper points (cf. 1Co 2:9 – 10), depicting glory greater than what Ezekiel presented does not contradict Ezekiel.

21:23 *The city does not need the sun or the moon ... the glory of God gives it light.* Although one might see a torch-lit city at night against a darkened horizon, most ancient cities were poorly lit at night. The new Jerusalem, by contrast, is full of continual light (cf. v. 25; 22:5). God had promised his people that in the time of their restoration, he himself would be their glory and, better than the sun and moon, would never set or wane (Isa 60:19 – 20; cf. Isa 13:10; 24:23). Other apocalyptic sources recognized that God would shine on his people. See note on 22:5.

21:24 *nations will walk by its light.* Cf. Isa 2:3 – 5; 60:2 – 3. Whereas some texts warned that God would destroy the nations or at least their armies (Jer 30:11; Zep 3:8; Zec 12:9), others depicted the nations serving Israel (Isa 45:14; 49:23; Da 7:14). In contrast to traditions where Gentiles would have no place in Jerusalem (Isa 52:1; Joel 3:17; cf. Zec 14:21), others allowed that some would come to worship God (Isa 2:3; Mic 4:2; Zec 14:16 – 19), as here. Indeed, the nations

(about 200 feet or 65 meters) thick, and especially if the 144 cubits is intended instead as its height or length (the Greek text does not specify "thick"). The dimensions of the city are supernatural (Rev 21:15–16), contrasting starkly with the pretensions of the doomed "great city" Babylon (Rev 18:10,16,18–21).

The astonishing cube shape presumably recalls the Most Holy Place (1Ki 6:20), which only the high priest could enter, and only once each year (Heb 9:7). Not only will God dwell with his people in the new Jerusalem (Rev 21:3), not only will the city need no temple other than God himself (Rev 21:22), but the entire city will be like the Most Holy Place. God's people will experience his presence more fully than ever before.

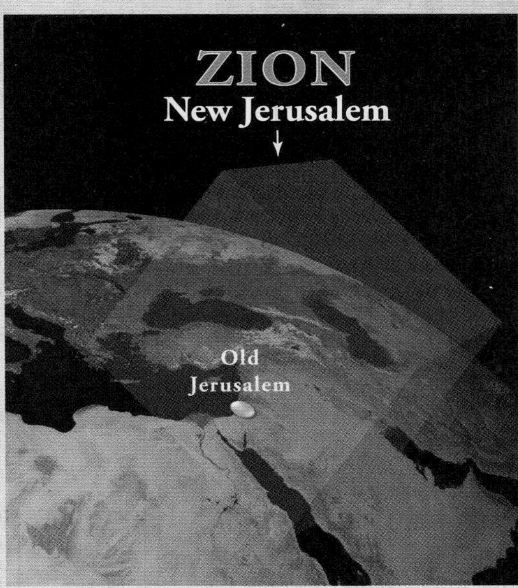

Dimensions of New Jerusalem.

The use of a square number like 144 may offer a vivid contrast with the triangular number 666 (Rev 13:18), like the foundation of a foursquare city versus that of a pyramid. Most important, the numbers in Rev 21:15–17 portray this city as the dwelling of God's people: 12,000 (stadia [see NIV text note on Rev 21:16]) and 144 (cubits [see NIV text note on Rev 21:17]) both recall the number of God's servants (Rev 7:4–8). The new Jerusalem is the city of God for God's people, the new Jerusalemites standing with the Lamb on Mount Zion (Rev 14:1). ◆

earth will bring their splendor into it.[q]
25On no day will its gates ever be shut,[r]
for there will be no night there.[s] 26The
glory and honor of the nations will be
brought into it. 27Nothing impure will
ever enter it, nor will anyone who does
what is shameful or deceitful,[t] but only
those whose names are written in the
Lamb's book of life.

21:24 [q] Isa 60:3, 5 **21:25** [r] Isa 60:11 [s] Zec 14:7; Rev 22:5 **21:27** [t] Isa 52:1; Joel 3:17; Rev 22:14, 15

Eden Restored

22 Then the angel showed me the river of the water of life, as clear as

(or their remnant) are finally converted (15:4; Isa 19:19–25; Jer 3:17; Zec 2:11; 8:22–23). See note on v. 26.

21:25 *On no day will its gates ever be shut.* Isaiah promised that Jerusalem's gates would always stand open so that people could bring in the wealth of the nations (Isa 60:11). To control access and maintain security, Roman cities usually provided entrance on only one side of the city, and city gates were usually shut at night. But the new Jerusalem welcomes all (22:17) and has no enemies to fear.

21:26 In Isaiah, the nations would bring their wealth into Jerusalem (Isa 45:14; 60:5–16; 61:6). But here they bring not simply wealth but also "glory" (cf. Rev 21:24, where the NIV translates the same Greek term as "splendor").

21:27 *nor will anyone who does what is shameful or deceitful.* Ancient sanctuaries often provided refuge for fugitives, but the Bible permitted this only for those whose crimes were unintentional (Ex 21:14; Nu 35:22–25). The new Jerusalem would not harbor any who practice evil; the wicked would be banished (cf. v. 8; Zec 5:3–4).

22:1 *water of life, as clear as crystal, flowing from the throne.* All strong cities must have their own water supply (a deficiency Laodiceans would have keenly felt, see note on 3:15). Present Jerusalem had a water supply that some poetically described as a river (Ps 46:4), and the prophets spoke of water flowing from the future Zion (Eze 47:1–12; Joel 3:18; Zec 14:8). This crystal river flowing directly from God's throne replaces the earlier crystal sea (4:6; 15:2; 21:1). Although evoking especially Ezekiel, the river of life may also evoke the rivers of the first paradise (Ge 2:10), in view of "the tree of life" in v. 2.

crystal,[u] flowing[v] from the throne of God
and of the Lamb 2down the middle of the
great street of the city. On each side of
the river stood the tree of life,[w] bearing
twelve crops of fruit, yielding its fruit every month. And the leaves of the tree are
for the healing of the nations.[x] 3No longer will there be any curse.[y] The throne of
God and of the Lamb will be in the city,
and his servants will serve him.[z] 4They
will see his face,[a] and his name will be on
their foreheads.[b] 5There will be no more
night.[c] They will not need the light of a
lamp or the light of the sun, for the Lord
God will give them light.[d] And they will
reign for ever and ever.[e]

John and the Angel

6The angel said to me,[f] "These words
are trustworthy and true.[g] The Lord, the
God who inspires the prophets,[h] sent his
angel[i] to show his servants the things that
must soon take place."

7"Look, I am coming soon![j] Blessed[k] is
the one who keeps the words of the prophecy written in this scroll."

8I, John, am the one who heard and saw
these things.[l] And when I had heard and
seen them, I fell down to worship at the
feet[m] of the angel who had been showing
them to me. 9But he said to me, "Don't
do that! I am a fellow servant with you
and with your fellow prophets and with all
who keep the words of this scroll.[n] Worship God!"[o]

10Then he told me, "Do not seal up[p] the
words of the prophecy of this scroll, because the time is near.[q] 11Let the one who
does wrong continue to do wrong; let the
vile person continue to be vile; let the one
who does right continue to do right; and
let the holy person continue to be holy."[r]

Epilogue: Invitation and Warning

12"Look, I am coming soon![s] My reward
is with me,[t] and I will give to each person
according to what they have done. 13I am
the Alpha and the Omega,[u] the First and
the Last,[v] the Beginning and the End.[w]

14"Blessed are those who wash their
robes, that they may have the right to the
tree of life[x] and may go through the gates[y]
into the city.[z] 15Outside[a] are the dogs,[b]
those who practice magic arts, the sexu-

22:1 [u] Rev 4:6 [v] Eze 47:1; Zec 14:8 **22:2** [w] Rev 2:7 [x] Eze 47:12 **22:3** [y] Zec 14:11 [z] Rev 7:15 **22:4** [a] Mt 5:8 [b] Rev 14:1 **22:5** [c] Rev 21:25 [d] Rev 21:23 [e] Da 7:27; Rev 20:4 **22:6** [f] Rev 1:1 [g] Rev 19:9; 21:5 [h] Heb 12:9 [i] ver 16 **22:7** [j] Rev 3:11 [k] Rev 1:3 **22:8** [l] Rev 1:1 [m] Rev 19:10 **22:9** [n] ver 10, 18, 19 [o] Rev 19:10 **22:10** [p] Da 8:26; Rev 10:4 [q] Rev 1:3 **22:11** [r] Eze 3:27; Da 12:10 **22:12** [s] ver 7, 20 [t] Isa 40:10 **22:13** [u] Rev 1:8 [v] Rev 1:17 [w] Rev 21:6 **22:14** [x] Rev 2:7 [y] Rev 21:12 [z] Rev 21:27 **22:15** [a] 1Co 6:9, 10; Gal 5:19-21; Col 3:5, 6 [b] Php 3:2

22:2 *On each side of the river stood the tree of life ... the leaves of the tree are for the healing of the nations.* Whereas shops often lined the main streets of ancient cities, Revelation presents a different kind of provision. Eze 47:12 envisioned fruit trees for healing on either side of the temple river; unlike trees whose fruits were seasonal, these trees would bear fruit every month. Some Jewish traditions inferred twelve trees from Eze 47:12, one for each month; Revelation, however, envisions the single tree of life, since there is one source of eternal life, namely, Jesus. To the "healing" of Eze 47:12 Revelation adds "of the nations" (see notes on 5:9; 21:24).

Clarifying Ezekiel's trees as the tree of life is significant. Jewish apocalypses often portray the end time in terms of the primeval Eden. Some writers associated Eden with the new Jerusalem or viewed it as equivalent to the Most Holy Place. Paradise images regularly included rivers and fruitful trees, sometimes including the tree of life mentioned in the original paradise.

22:3 *No longer will there be any curse.* Evokes the Greek translation of Zec 14:11, referring to the restored Jerusalem (cf. Zec 8:13). But in this context about paradise, the abolishing of the curse also evokes a reversal of the fall (Ge 3:14,17).

22:4 *They will see his face.* Traditional Jewish expectation included seeing God's face in the end time or in heaven after death. Whereas seeing God's face banished the old earth and heavens (20:11), requiring a new creation (21:1), God's children would now see his face.

22:5 *the Lord God will give them light.* A wide range of Jewish traditions (some of them following Da 12:3) portrayed the righteous as shining with glory in the future era.

22:6–8 Because ancient writers often bracketed their writings or portions of their writings, the echos of 1:1 in 22:6, of 1:3 in 22:7, and of 1:9 ("I, John") in 22:8 inform the hearers that the book is nearly at an end.

22:10 *Do not seal up the words of the prophecy.* God instructed Daniel to seal up his prophecy (Da 12:4,9), because the time of the end was a long time away (Da 8:26; 9:24; 10:14). By contrast, Revelation must remain unsealed; indeed, some events had already begun (see notes on 12:5–6; see also the article "Time in Revelation," p. 2245).

22:11 *Let the one who does wrong continue to do wrong.* In the end time, the wicked would continue in their wickedness (Da 12:10). In practice, however, God is not inviting anyone to continue in rebellion; rather the language is ironic, serving the rhetorical function of challenging their unrepentance, as sometimes in the Prophets (Isa 29:9; Jer 44:25; Am 4:4; cf. Eze 3:27).

22:12 *I am coming soon! My reward is with me.* In Isa 40:10; 62:11, God comes and his reward is with him; Revelation applies this divine description to the Lord Jesus (cf. v. 20; 3:11). *give to each person according to what they have done.* Fits the expectation of the OT (Ps 62:12; Pr 24:12; Jer 17:10) and Jewish teaching; this divine role is here applied to Jesus.

22:13 Jesus is still speaking here, as in v. 12 (and v. 16); the divine titles here (cf. Isa 41:4; 44:6; 48:12) belong to him (see note on 1:8).

22:14–15 Writers sometimes summarized sections at the end; these verses seems to summarize what precedes.

22:14 *those who wash their robes ... may go through the gates into the city.* Only the pure (21:27) could enter the city's gates (21:25–26).

22:15 See note on 21:8. *dogs.* Calling someone a "dog" was a common insult in Greek, sometimes with sexual connotations; because of the context in Dt 23:17–18, the NIV translates "dog" in the Hebrew (and Greek) text of Dt 23:18 as "male prostitute" (see NIV text note on Dt 23:18). *magic arts.* May refer to a poisoner, but usually relates to occult practices used by people seeking to harm others by sorcery (see the article "Magic in the New Testament," p. 1884).

ally immoral, the murderers, the idolaters
and everyone who loves and practices
falsehood.
16“I, Jesus,[c] have sent my angel to give
you[a] this testimony for the churches.[d] I
am the Root[e] and the Offspring of David,
and the bright Morning Star.”[f]

17The Spirit[g] and the bride say, “Come!”
And let the one who hears say, “Come!”
Let the one who is thirsty come; and let
the one who wishes take the free gift of
the water of life.

18I warn everyone who hears the words
of the prophecy of this scroll: If anyone
adds anything to them,[h] God will add to
that person the plagues described in this
scroll.[i] 19And if anyone takes words away[j]
from this scroll of prophecy, God will take
away from that person any share in the
tree of life and in the Holy City, which are
described in this scroll.
20He who testifies to these things[k] says,
“Yes, I am coming soon.”
Amen. Come, Lord Jesus.[l]
21The grace of the Lord Jesus be with
God’s people.[m] Amen.

22:16 [c] Rev 1:1 [d] Rev 1:4 [e] Rev 5:5 [f] 2Pe 1:19; Rev 2:28 **22:17** [g] Rev 2:7 **22:18** [h] Dt 4:2; Pr 30:6 [i] Rev 15:6-16:21 **22:19** [j] Dt 4:2 **22:20** [k] Rev 1:2 [l] 1Co 16:22 **22:21** [m] Ro 16:20

[a] *16* The Greek is plural.

22:16 *I am the Root and the Offspring of David, and the bright Morning Star.* Jesus is from the root of David (hence of his father Jesse; Isa 11:1). Gentiles viewed the morning star as a deity, but Jesus probably evokes a Messianic title here (Nu 24:17). Jewish interpreters often connected texts based on shared key words or concepts. Here the mention of a star links Nu 24:17, a verse that mentions a scepter, with Isa 11:10, the context of which uses the same Greek term translated “scepter” in Isa 11:1. See notes on Rev 2:26–27,28.
22:17 *The Spirit and the bride say.* Jewish sources often associated the Spirit with prophetic inspiration (as at times in the OT).
22:18–19 Works that claimed to be inspired sometimes included warnings such as these. Moses warned hearers of the law not to add to or subtract from it (Dt 4:2; 12:32); later Jewish writers claimed that the Septuagint, the pre-Christian Greek translation of the OT, was perfect and not to be revised; 1 Enoch threatens with damnation those who alter any prophetic words (1 Enoch 108:6).
22:18 *God will add to that person the plagues described in this scroll.* Fits Biblical and ancient Jewish expectations (Dt 29:19–20,27).
22:20 *Come, Lord Jesus.* Probably a familiar prayer; in Aramaic it is *Marana tha* (1Co 16:22).

Table of Weights and Measures

	Biblical Unit	Approximate American Equivalent	Approximate Metric Equivalent
Weights	talent (60 minas)	75 pounds	34 kilograms
	mina (50 shekels)	$1\frac{1}{4}$ pounds	560 grams
	shekel (2 bekas)	$\frac{2}{5}$ ounce	11.5 grams
	pim ($\frac{2}{3}$ shekel)	$\frac{1}{4}$ ounce	7.8 grams
	beka (10 gerahs)	$\frac{1}{5}$ ounce	5.7 grams
	gerah	$\frac{1}{50}$ ounce	0.6 gram
	daric	$\frac{1}{3}$ ounce	8.4 grams
Length	cubit	18 inches	45 centimeters
	span	9 inches	23 centimeters
	handbreadth	3 inches	7.5 centimeters
	stadion (pl. stadia)	600 feet	183 meters
Capacity			
Dry Measure	cor [homer] (10 ephahs)	6 bushels	220 liters
	lethek (5 ephahs)	3 bushels	110 liters
	ephah (10 omers)	$\frac{3}{5}$ bushel	22 liters
	seah ($\frac{1}{3}$ ephah)	7 quarts	7.5 liters
	omer ($\frac{1}{10}$ ephah)	2 quarts	2 liters
	cab ($\frac{1}{18}$ ephah)	1 quart	1 liter
Liquid Measure	bath (1 ephah)	6 gallons	22 liters
	hin ($\frac{1}{6}$ bath)	1 gallon	3.8 liters
	log ($\frac{1}{72}$ bath)	$\frac{1}{3}$ quart	0.3 liter

The figures of the table are calculated on the basis of a shekel equaling 11.5 grams, a cubit equaling 18 inches and an ephah equaling 22 liters. The quart referred to is either a dry quart (slightly larger than a liter) or a liquid quart (slightly smaller than a liter), whichever is applicable. The ton referred to in the footnotes is the American ton of 2,000 pounds. These weights are calculated relative to the particular commodity involved. Accordingly, the same measure of capacity in the text may be converted into different weights in the footnotes.

This table is based upon the best available information, but it is not intended to be mathematically precise; like the measurement equivalents in the footnotes, it merely gives approximate amounts and distances. Weights and measures differed somewhat at various times and places in the ancient world. There is uncertainty particularly about the ephah and the bath; further discoveries may shed more light on these units of capacity.

Index of Articles in Canonical Order

Index of Articles in Alphabetical Order

CONCORDANCE

The NIV Concordance, created by John R. Kohlenberger III, has been developed specifically for use with the New International Version (NIV). Like all concordances, it is a special index that contains an alphabetical listing of words used in the Bible text.

This concordance contains 2,474 word entries, with more than 10,000 Scripture references. Each word entry is followed by significant Scripture references in which that particular word is found, as well as by a brief excerpt from the surrounding context. In the context, the entry word is abbreviated by its first letter in bold print. Other forms of the entry word and related words indexed in this concordance are in parentheses.

This concordance also contains 155 biographical entries for significant people in the Bible. The descriptive phrases replace the brief context surrounding each occurrence of the name. In those instances where more than one Bible character has the same name, that name is placed under one block entry, and each person is given a number (1), (2), etc.

Two entries are marked with an asterisk (*). LORD* and LORD'S* list occurrences of the proper name of God, *Yahweh,* spelled "LORD" and "LORD's" in the NIV. These entries are distinguished from LORD and LORD's, which list occurrences of the title "Lord" and "Lord's."

The dagger (†) indicates a word that is further examined in the "Hebrew to English Translation Chart" (p. xix). These are Hebrew words that do not have exact equivalents in English; please refer to that chart to further understand the nuances present in the Hebrew term. Two daggers (‡) indicates terms that are further examined in the "Key New Testament Terms" chart that begins on p. 1584.

This concordance is a valuable tool for Bible study. While one of its key purposes is to help the reader find forgotten references to familiar verses, it can also be used to do word studies and to locate and trace biblical themes. Whenever you find a significant context, be sure to read at least the whole verse in the NIV to discover its fuller meaning in its larger context.

AARON

Priesthood of (Ex 28:1; Nu 17; Heb 5:1–4; 7), garments (Ex 28; 39), consecration (Ex 29), ordination (Lev 8).

Spokesman for Moses (Ex 4:14–16, 27–31; 7:1–2). Supported Moses' hands in battle (Ex 17:8–13). Built golden calf (Ex 32; Dt 9:20). Talked against Moses (Nu 12). Priesthood opposed (Nu 16); staff budded (Nu 17). Forbidden to enter land (Nu 20:1–12). Death (Nu 20:22–29; 33:38–39).

ABANDON

Dt 4: 31 he will not **a** or destroy you
1Ti 4: 1 in later times some will **a** the faith

ABBA

Ro 8: 15 And by him we cry, "***A***, Father."
Gal 4: 6 the Spirit who calls out, "***A***,

ABEL

Second son of Adam (Ge 4:2). Offered proper sacrifice (Ge 4:4; Heb 11:4). Murdered by Cain (Ge 4:8; Mt 23:35; Lk 11:51; 1Jn 3:12).

ABIGAIL

Wife of Nabal (1Sa 25:30); pled for his life with David (1Sa 25:14–35). Became David's wife (1Sa 25:36–42).

ABIJAH

Son of Rehoboam; king of Judah (1Ki 14:31—15:8; 2Ch 12:16—14:1).

ABILITY (ABLE)

Ezr 2: 69 According to their **a** they gave
2Co 1: 8 far beyond our **a** to endure,
8: 3 were able, and even beyond their **a**.

ABIMELEK

1. King of Gerar who took Abraham's wife Sarah, believing her to be his sister (Ge 20). Later made a covenant with Abraham (Ge 21:22–33).

2. King of Gerar who took Isaac's wife Rebekah, believing her to be his sister (Ge 26:1–11). Later made a covenant with Isaac (Ge 26:12–31).

ABLE (ABILITY ENABLE ENABLED ENABLES)

Eze 7: 19 gold will not be **a** to deliver them
Da 3: 17 the God we serve is **a** to deliver us
Ro 8: 39 will be **a** to separate us
14: 4 the Lord is **a** to make them stand.
16: 25 to him who is **a** to establish you
2Co 9: 8 God is **a** to bless you abundantly,
Eph 3: 20 him who is **a** to do immeasurably
2Ti 1: 12 that he is **a** to guard what I have
3: 15 which are **a** to make you wise
Heb 7: 25 he is **a** to save completely
Jude : 24 To him who is **a** to keep you
Rev 5: 5 He is **a** to open the scroll and its

ABOLISH

Mt 5: 17 think that I have come to **a** the Law

† ABOMINATION

Da 11: 31 set up the **a** that causes desolation.

ABOUND (ABOUNDING ABOUNDS)

2Co 9: 8 you will **a** in every good work.
Php 1: 9 your love may **a** more and more

ABOUNDING (ABOUND)

Ex 34: 6 to anger, **a** in love and faithfulness,
Ps 86: 5 **a** in love to all who call to you.

ABOUNDS (ABOUND)

2Co 1: 5 also our comfort **a** through Christ.

ABRAHAM

Covenant relation with the LORD (Ge 12:1–3; 13:14–17; 15; 17; 22:15–18; Ex 2:24; Ne 9:8; Ps 105; Mic 7:20; Lk 1:68–75; Ro 4; Heb 6:13–15).

Called from Ur, via Harran, to Canaan (Ge 12:1; Ac 7:2–4; Heb 11:8–10). Moved to Egypt, nearly lost Sarah to Pharoah (Ge 12:10–20). Divided the land with Lot (Ge 13). Saved Lot from four kings (Ge 14:1–16); blessed by Melchizedek (Ge 14:17–20; Heb 7:1–20). Declared righteous by faith (Ge 15:6; Ro 4:3; Gal 3:6–9). Fathered Ishmael by Hagar (Ge 16).

Name changed from Abram (Ge 17:5; Ne 9:7). Circumcised (Ge 17; Ro 4:9–12). Entertained three visitors (Ge 18); promised a son by Sarah (Ge 18:9–15; 17:16). Moved to Gerar; nearly lost Sarah to Abimelek (Ge 20). Fathered Isaac by Sarah (Ge 21:1–7; Ac 7:8; Heb 11:11–12); sent away Hagar and Ishmael (Ge 21:8–21; Gal 4:22–30). Tested by offering Isaac (Ge 22; Heb 11:17–19; Jas 2:21–24). Sarah died; bought field of Ephron for burial (Ge 23). Secured wife for Isaac (Ge 24). Death (Ge 25:7–11).

ABSALOM

Son of David by Maakah (2Sa 3:3; 1Ch 3:2). Killed Amnon for rape of his sister Tamar; banished by David (2Sa 13). Returned to Jerusalem; received by David (2Sa 14). Rebelled against David; seized kingdom (2Sa 15–17). Killed (2Sa 18).

ABSTAIN (ABSTAINS)

1Pe 2: 11 and exiles, to **a** from sinful desires,

ABSTAINS (ABSTAIN)

Ro 14: 6 and whoever **a** does so to the Lord

ABUNDANCE (ABUNDANT)

Lk 12: 15 not consist in an **a** of possessions."
Jude : 2 peace and love be yours in **a**.

† Please see the "Hebrew to English Translation Chart," p. xix.

ABUNDANT (ABUNDANCE)
Dt 28: 11 will grant you **a** prosperity—
Ps 145: 7 They celebrate your **a** goodness
Pr 28: 19 work their land will have **a** food,
Ro 5: 17 who receive God's **a** provision

ABUSE
2Pe 2: 11 do not heap **a** on such beings

ACCEPT (ACCEPTED ACCEPTS)
Ex 23: 8 "Do not **a** a bribe, for a bribe
Pr 10: 8 The wise in heart **a** commands,
19: 20 Listen to advice and **a** discipline,
Ro 15: 7 **A** one another, then, just as Christ
Jas 1: 21 humbly **a** the word planted in you,

ACCEPTED (ACCEPT)
Lk 4: 24 "no prophet is **a** in his hometown.

ACCEPTS (ACCEPT)
Ps 6: 9 the LORD **a** my prayer.
Jn 13: 20 whoever **a** anyone I send **a** me;

ACCOMPANY
Mk 16: 17 *these signs will **a** those who believe:*

ACCOMPLISH
Isa 55: 11 but will **a** what I desire and achieve

ACCORD
Nu 24: 13 not do anything of my own **a**,
Jn 10: 18 me, but I lay it down of my own **a**.

ACCOUNT (ACCOUNTABLE)
Mt 12: 36 will have to give **a** on the day
Ro 14: 12 of us will give an **a** of ourselves
Heb 4: 13 of him to whom we must give **a**.

ACCOUNTABLE (ACCOUNT)
Eze 33: 6 I will hold the watchman **a** for
Ro 3: 19 and the whole world held **a** to God.

ACCUSATION (ACCUSE)
1Ti 5: 19 not entertain an **a** against an elder

ACCUSE (ACCUSATION)
Pr 3: 30 Do not **a** anyone for no reason—
Lk 3: 14 money and don't **a** people falsely—

ACHAN
Sin at Jericho caused defeat at Ai; stoned (Jos 7; 22:20; 1Ch 2:7).

ACHE
Pr 14: 13 Even in laughter the heart may **a**,

ACKNOWLEDGE
Mt 10: 32 also **a** before my Father in heaven.
1Th 5: 12 **a** those who work hard among you,
Php 2: 11 every tongue **a** that Jesus Christ is
1Jn 4: 3 spirit that does not **a** Jesus is not

ACQUIT
Ex 23: 7 to death, for I will not **a** the guilty.

ACTION (ACTIONS ACTIVE ACTS)
Jas 2: 17 if it is not accompanied by **a**,

ACTIONS (ACTION)
Gal 6: 4 Each one should test their own **a**.
Titus 1: 16 God, but by their **a** they deny him.

ACTIVE (ACTION)
Heb 4: 12 For the word of God is alive and **a**.

ACTS (ACTION)
Ps 145: 12 people may know of your mighty **a**
150: 2 Praise him for his **a** of power;
Isa 64: 6 all our righteous **a** are like filthy

ADAM
First man (Ge 1:26—2:25; Ro 5:14; 1Ti 2:13). Sin of (Ge 3; Hos 6:7; Ro 5:12–21). Children of (Ge 4:1—5:5). Death of (Ge 5:5; Ro 5:12–21; 1Co 15:22).

ADD
Dt 12: 32 do not **a** to it or take away from it.
Pr 30: 6 Do not **a** to his words, or he will
Lk 12: 25 by worrying can **a** a single hour
Rev 22: 18 them, God will **a** to that person

ADMIRABLE
Php 4: 8 whatever is lovely, whatever is **a**—

ADMONISH
Col 3: 16 and **a** one another with all wisdom

ADOPTION
Ro 8: 23 wait eagerly for our **a** to sonship,
Eph 1: 5 he predestined us for **a** to sonship

ADORE
SS 1: 4 How right they are to **a** you!

ADORNMENT (ADORNS)
1Pe 3: 3 should not come from outward **a**,

ADORNS (ADORNMENT)
Ps 93: 5 holiness **a** your house for endless

ADULTERY
Ex 20: 14 "You shall not commit **a**.
Mt 5: 27 was said, 'You shall not commit **a**.'
5: 28 lustfully has already committed **a**
5: 32 a divorced woman commits **a**.
15: 19 murder, **a**, sexual immorality, theft,

ADULTS
1Co 14: 20 but in your thinking be **a**.

ADVANCED
Job 32: 7 **a** years should teach wisdom.'

ADVANTAGE
Ex 22: 22 "Do not take **a** of the widow
Dt 24: 14 Do not take **a** of a hired worker
1Th 4: 6 should wrong or take **a** of a brother

ADVERSITY
Pr 17: 17 a brother is born for a time of **a**.

ADVICE
1Ki 12: 8 Rehoboam rejected the **a** the elders
12: 14 he followed the **a** of the young men
Pr 12: 5 but the **a** of the wicked is deceitful.
12: 15 to them, but the wise listen to **a**.
19: 20 Listen to **a** and accept discipline,
20: 18 Plans are established by seeking **a**;

ADVOCATE
Jn 14: 16 he will give you another **a** to help
14: 26 But the **A**, the Holy Spirit,
1Jn 2: 1 sin, we have an **a** with the Father—

AFFECTION
2Pe 1: 7 and to godliness, mutual **a**; and to mutual **a**, love.

AFFLICTION
Ro 12: 12 patient in **a**, faithful in prayer.

AFRAID (FEAR)
Ge 26: 24 Do not be **a**, for I am with you;
Ex 3: 6 because he was **a** to look at God.
Ps 27: 1 of my life—of whom shall I be **a**?
56: 3 When I am **a**, I put my trust in
Pr 3: 24 you lie down, you will not be **a**;
Jer 1: 8 Do not be **a** of them, for I am
Mt 8: 26 of little faith, why are you so **a**?"
10: 28 Do not be **a** of those who kill
10: 31 So don't be **a**; you are worth more
Mk 5: 36 said, Jesus told him, "Don't be **a**;
Jn 14: 27 hearts be troubled and do not be **a**.
Heb 13: 6 Lord is my helper; I will not be **a**.

AGED
Job 12: 12 Is not wisdom found among the **a**?
Pr 17: 6 children are a crown to the **a**,

AGREE
Mt 18: 19 earth **a** about anything they ask for,
Ro 7: 16 want to do, I **a** that the law is good.

AHAB
Son of Omri; king of Israel (1Ki 16:28—22:40), husband of Jezebel (1Ki 16:31). Promoted Baal worship (1Ki 16:31–33); opposed by Elijah (1Ki 17:1; 18; 21), a prophet (1Ki 20:35–43), Micaiah (1Ki 22:1–28). Defeated Ben-Hadad (1Ki 20). Killed for failing to kill Ben-Hadad and for murder of Naboth (1Ki 20:35—21:40).

AHAZ
Son of Jotham; king of Judah, (2Ki 16; 2Ch 28; Isa 7).

AHAZIAH
1. Son of Ahab; king of Israel (1Ki 22:51–2Ki 1:18; 2Ch 20:35–37).
2. Son of Jehoram; king of Judah (2Ki 8:25–29; 9:14–29), also called Jehoahaz (2Ch 21:17—22:9; 25:23).

AIM
1Co 7: 34 Her **a** is to be devoted to the Lord

AIR
1Co 9: 26 not fight like a boxer beating the **a**.
Eph 2: 2 the ruler of the kingdom of the **a**,
1Th 4: 17 clouds to meet the Lord in the **a**.

ALABASTER
Mt 26: 7 him with an **a** jar of very expensive

ALERT
Jos 8: 4 far from it. All of you be on the **a**.
Mk 13: 33 Be **a**! You do not know
Eph 6: 18 be **a** and always keep on praying
1Pe 1: 13 with minds that are **a** and fully

ALIENATED
Gal 5: 4 the law have been **a** from Christ;

ALIVE (LIVE)
Ac 1: 3 convincing proofs that he was **a**.
Ro 6: 11 to sin but **a** to God in Christ Jesus.
1Co 15: 22 die, so in Christ all will be made **a**.
Heb 4: 12 the word of God is **a** and active.

ALMIGHTY (MIGHT)
Ge 17: 1 to him and said, "I am God **A**;
Job 11: 7 Can you probe the limits of the **A**?
33: 4 the breath of the **A** gives me life.
Ps 91: 1 will rest in the shadow of the **A**.
Isa 6: 3 "Holy, holy, holy is the LORD **A**;

ALTAR
Ge 22: 9 Abraham built an **a** there
Ex 27: 1 "Build an **a** of acacia wood,
1Ki 18: 30 he repaired the **a** of the LORD,
2Ch 4: 1 a bronze **a** twenty cubits long,
4: 19 the golden **a**; the tables

ALWAYS
Ps 16: 8 I keep my eyes **a** on the LORD.
26: 3 for I have **a** been mindful of your
51: 3 and my sin is **a** before me.
Mt 26: 11 The poor you will **a** have with you,
28: 20 And surely I am with you **a**,
1Co 13: 7 It **a** protects, **a** trusts, **a** hopes,
Php 4: 4 Rejoice in the Lord **a**. I will say it
1Pe 3: 15 **A** be prepared to give an answer

AMAZIAH
Son of Joash; king of Judah (2Ki 14; 2Ch 25).

AMBASSADORS
2Co 5: 20 We are therefore Christ's **a**,

AMBITION
Ro 15: 20 It has always been my **a** to preach
1Th 4: 11 make it your **a** to lead a quiet life:

AMON
Son of Manasseh; king of Judah (2Ki 21:18–26; 1Ch 3:14; 2Ch 33:21–25).

ANANIAS
1. Husband of Sapphira; died for lying to God (Ac 5:1–11).
2. Disciple who baptized Saul (Ac 9:10–19).
3. High priest at Paul's arrest (Ac 22:30—24:1).

ANCESTORS
Heb 1: 1 spoke to our **a** through the prophets

ANCHOR
Heb 6: 19 We have this hope as an **a**

ANCIENT
Da 7: 9 and the **A** of Days took his seat.

ANDREW
Apostle; brother of Simon Peter (Mt 4:18; 10:2; Mk 1:16–18, 29; 3:18; 13:3; Lk 6:14; Jn 1:35–44; 6:8–9; 12:22; Ac 1:13).

ANGEL (ANGELS ARCHANGEL)
Ps 34: 7 The **a** of the LORD encamps
Ac 6: 15 his face was like the face of an **a**.
2Co 11: 14 Satan himself masquerades as an **a**
Gal 1: 8 or an **a** from heaven should preach

ANGELS (ANGEL)
Ps 8: 5 a little lower than the **a**
91: 11 command his **a** concerning you
Mt 18: 10 that their **a** in heaven always see
25: 41 fire prepared for the devil and his **a**.
Lk 20: 36 for they are like the **a**.
1Co 6: 3 you not know that we will judge **a**?
Heb 1: 4 the **a** as the name he has inherited
1: 14 Are not all **a** ministering spirits
2: 7 them a little lower than the **a**;
13: 2 hospitality to **a** without knowing it.
1Pe 1: 12 Even **a** long to look into these
2Pe 2: 4 if God did not spare **a** when they

ANGER (ANGERED ANGRY)
Ex 32: 10 that my **a** may burn against them
34: 6 slow to **a**, abounding in love
Dt 29: 28 In furious **a** and in great wrath
2Ki 22: 13 Great is the LORD's **a** that burns
Ps 30: 5 For his **a** lasts only a moment,
Pr 15: 1 wrath, but a harsh word stirs up **a**.

ANGERED (ANGER)
Pr 22: 24 do not associate with one easily **a**,
1Co 13: 5 it is not easily **a**, it keeps no record

† Please see the "Hebrew to English Translation Chart," p. xix.
‡ Please see "Key New Testament Terms," p. 1584.

(Nu 22–24; Dt 23:4–5; 2Pe 2:15; Jude 11). Killed (Nu 31:8; Jos 13:22).

BALM
Jer 8: 22 Is there no **b** in Gilead? Is there no

BANISH
Jer 25: 10 will **b** from them the sounds of joy

BANQUET
SS 2: 4 Let him lead me to the **b** hall,
Lk 14: 13 But when you give a **b**,

‡ BAPTIZE (BAPTIZED)
Mt 3: 11 "I **b** you with water for repentance.
3: 11 He will **b** you with the Holy Spirit
Mk 1: 8 I **b** you with water, but he will **b**
1Co 1: 17 For Christ did not send me to **b**,

BAPTIZED (BAPTIZE)
Mt 3: 6 they were **b** by him in the Jordan
Mk 1: 9 and was **b** by John in the Jordan.
10: 38 be **b** with the baptism I am **b** with?"
16: 16 *believes and is **b** will be saved,*
Jn 4: 2 in fact it was not Jesus who **b**,
Ac 1: 5 For John **b** with water, but in a few

BARABBAS
Mt 27: 17 release to you: Jesus **B**, or Jesus

BARBS
Nu 33: 55 remain will become **b** in your eyes

BARE
Heb 4: 13 and laid **b** before the eyes of him

BARNABAS
Disciple, originally Joseph (Ac 4:36), prophet (Ac 13:1), apostle (Ac 14:14). Brought Paul to apostles (Ac 9:27), Antioch (Ac 11:22–29; Gal 2:1–13), on the first missionary journey (Ac 13–14). Together at Jerusalem Council, they separated over John Mark (Ac 15). Later coworkers (1Co 9:6; Col 4:10).

BARTHOLOMEW
Apostle (Mt 10:3; Mk 3:18; Lk 6:14; Ac 1:13). Possibly also known as Nathanael (Jn 1:45–49; 21:2).

BATH
Jn 13: 10 who have had a **b** need only

BATHSHEBA
Wife of Uriah who committed adultery with and became wife of David (2Sa 11), mother of Solomon (2Sa 12:24; 1Ki 1–2; 1Ch 3:5).

BATTLE
2Ch 20: 15 For the **b** is not yours, but God's.
Ps 24: 8 mighty, the LORD mighty in **b**.
Ecc 9: 11 to the swift or the **b** to the strong,

BEAR (BEARING BIRTH BIRTHRIGHT BORE BORN FIRSTBORN NEWBORN)
Ge 4: 13 punishment is more than I can **b**.
Ps 38: 4 me like a burden too heavy to **b**.
Isa 53: 11 many, and he will **b** their iniquities.
Da 7: 5 beast, which looked like a **b**.
Mt 7: 18 A good tree cannot **b** bad fruit,
Jn 15: 2 branch that does **b** fruit he prunes
15: 16 so that you might go and **b** fruit—
Ro 15: 1 We who are strong ought to **b**
1Co 10: 13 tempted beyond what you can **b**.
Col 3: 13 **B** with each other and forgive one

BEARING (BEAR)
Eph 4: 2 patient, **b** with one another in love.
Col 1: 10 **b** fruit in every good work,

BEAST
Rev 13: 18 calculate the number of the **b**, for it

BEAT (BEATING)
Isa 2: 4 They will **b** their swords
Joel 3: 10 **B** your plowshares into swords

BEATING (BEAT)
1Co 9: 26 I do not fight like a boxer **b** the air.
1Pe 2: 20 if you receive a **b** for doing wrong

BEAUTIFUL (BEAUTY)
Ge 6: 2 the daughters of humans were **b**,
12: 11 "I know what a **b** woman you are.
12: 14 saw that Sarai was a very **b** woman.
24: 16 The woman was very **b**, a virgin;
26: 7 of Rebekah, because she is **b**."
29: 17 had a lovely figure and was **b**.
Pr 11: 22 snout is a **b** woman who shows no
Ecc 3: 11 He has made everything **b** in its
Isa 4: 2 the Branch of the LORD will be **b**
52: 7 How **b** on the mountains are the
Eze 20: 6 and honey, the most **b** of all lands.
Zec 9: 17 How attractive and **b** they will be!
Mt 23: 27 which look **b** on the outside
26: 10 She has done a **b** thing to me.
Ro 10: 15 "How **b** are the feet of those who

BEAUTY (BEAUTIFUL)
Ps 27: 4 to gaze on the **b** of the LORD
45: 11 the king be enthralled by your **b**;
Pr 31: 30 is deceptive, and **b** is fleeting;
Isa 33: 17 Your eyes will see the king in his **b**
53: 2 He had no **b** or majesty to attract
61: 3 them a crown of **b** instead of ashes,
Eze 28: 12 full of wisdom and perfect in **b**.
1Pe 3: 4 unfading **b** of a gentle and quiet

BED
Heb 13: 4 and the marriage **b** kept pure,

BEELZEBUL
Lk 11: 15 said, "By **B**, the prince of demons,

BEER
Pr 20: 1 Wine is a mocker and **b** a brawler;

BEERSHEBA
Jdg 20: 1 all Israel from Dan to **B**

BEGINNING
Ge 1: 1 In the **b** God created the heavens
Ps 102: 25 In the **b** you laid the foundations
111: 10 of the LORD is the **b** of wisdom;
Pr 1: 7 the LORD is the **b** of knowledge,
4: 7 The **b** of wisdom is this:
Jn 1: 1 In the **b** was the Word,
1Jn 1: 1 That which was from the **b**,
Rev 21: 6 and the Omega, the **B** and the End.

BEHAVE (BEHAVIOR)
Ro 13: 13 us **b** decently, as in the daytime,

BEHAVIOR (BEHAVE)
Pr 1: 3 receiving instruction in prudent **b**,

† BELIEVE (BELIEVED BELIEVER BELIEVERS BELIEVES BELIEVING)
Pr 14: 15 The simple **b** anything,
Mt 18: 6 those who **b** in me—
21: 22 If you **b**, you will receive whatever
Mk 1: 15 Repent and **b** the good news!"
9: 24 the boy's father exclaimed, "I do **b**;
16: 17 *accompany those who **b**:*
Lk 8: 50 just **b**, and she will be healed."
24: 25 how slow to **b** all that the prophets
Jn 1: 7 so that through him all might **b**.
3: 18 does not **b** stands condemned
6: 29 to **b** in the one he has sent."
10: 38 even though you do not **b** me,
11: 27 "I **b** that you are the Messiah,
14: 1 You **b** in God; **b** also in me.
14: 11 **B** me when I say that I am
16: 30 This makes us **b** that you came
16: 31 "Do you now **b**?" Jesus replied.
17: 21 the world may **b** that you have sent
20: 27 into my side. Stop doubting and **b**."
20: 31 may **b** that Jesus is the Messiah,
Ac 16: 31 They replied, "**B** in the Lord Jesus,
24: 14 I **b** everything that is in accordance
Ro 3: 22 faith in Jesus Christ to all who **b**.
4: 11 he is the father of all who **b**
10: 9 **b** in your heart that God raised
10: 14 how can they **b** in the one of whom
1Th 4: 14 For we **b** that Jesus died and rose
2Th 2: 11 delusion so that they will **b** the lie
1Ti 4: 10 and especially of those who **b**.
Titus 1: 6 a man whose children **b** and are
Heb 11: 6 comes to him must **b** that he exists
Jas 2: 19 You **b** that there is one God. Good! Even the demons **b** that—
1Jn 4: 1 Dear friends, do not **b** every spirit,

BELIEVED (BELIEVE)
Ge 15: 6 Abram **b** the LORD, and he
Jnh 3: 5 The Ninevites **b** God. A fast was
Jn 1: 12 to those who **b** in his name,
2: 22 Then they **b** the scripture
3: 18 already because they have not **b**
20: 8 also went inside. He saw and **b**.
20: 29 who have not seen and yet have **b**."
Ac 13: 48 were appointed for eternal life **b**.
Ro 4: 3 "Abraham **b** God, and it was
10: 14 call on the one they have not **b** in?
1Co 15: 2 Otherwise, you have **b** in vain.
Gal 3: 6 So also Abraham "**b** God, and it
2Ti 1: 12 because I know whom I have **b**,
Jas 2: 23 that says, "Abraham **b** God, and it

BELIEVER (BELIEVE)
1Co 7: 12 brother has a wife who is not a **b**
2Co 6: 15 what does a **b** have in common

BELIEVERS (BELIEVE)
Ac 4: 32 All the **b** were one in heart
5: 12 all the **b** used to meet together
1Co 6: 5 to judge a dispute between **b**?
1Ti 4: 12 set an example for the **b** in speech,
1Pe 2: 17 love the family of **b**, fear God,

BELIEVES (BELIEVE)
Mk 9: 23 is possible for one who **b**."
11: 23 **b** that what they say will happen,
16: 16 *Whoever **b** and is baptized*
Jn 3: 16 whoever **b** in him shall not perish
3: 36 Whoever **b** in the Son has eternal
5: 24 **b** him who sent me has eternal life
6: 35 and whoever **b** in me will never be
6: 40 and **b** in him shall have eternal life,
6: 47 you, the one who **b** has eternal life.
7: 38 Whoever **b** in me, as Scripture has
Ro 1: 16 salvation to everyone who **b**:
9: 33 the one who **b** in him will never be
10: 4 righteousness for everyone who **b**.
1Jn 5: 1 Everyone who **b** that Jesus is
5: 5 Only the one who **b** that Jesus is

BELIEVING (BELIEVE)
Jn 11: 26 whoever lives by **b** in me will never
20: 31 by **b** you may have life in his name.

BELONG (BELONGS)
Dt 29: 29 The secret things **b** to the LORD
Job 25: 2 "Dominion and awe **b** to God;
Ps 47: 9 for the kings of the earth **b** to God;
95: 4 and the mountain peaks **b** to him.
Jn 8: 44 You **b** to your father, the devil,
15: 19 As it is, you do not **b** to the world,
Ro 1: 6 those Gentiles who are called to **b**
7: 4 that you might **b** to another, to him
14: 8 we live or die, we **b** to the Lord.
Gal 5: 24 Those who **b** to Christ Jesus have
1Th 5: 8 But since we **b** to the day, let us be

BELONGS (BELONG)
Job 41: 11 Everything under heaven **b** to me.
Ps 111: 10 To him **b** eternal praise.
Eze 18: 4 For everyone **b** to me, the parent as
Jn 8: 47 Whoever **b** to God hears what God
Ro 12: 5 each member **b** to all the others.

BELOVED (LOVE)
Dt 33: 12 "Let the **b** of the LORD rest
SS 2: 16 My **b** is mine and I am his;
7: 10 I belong to my **b**, and his desire is

BELT
Isa 11: 5 Righteousness will be his **b**
Eph 6: 14 the **b** of truth buckled around your

BENEFICIAL (BENEFIT)
1Co 10: 23 but not everything is **b**.

BENEFIT (BENEFICIAL BENEFITS)
Ro 6: 22 the **b** you reap leads to holiness,
2Co 4: 15 All this is for your **b**,

BENEFITS (BENEFIT)
Ps 103: 2 my soul, and forget not all his **b**—
Jn 4: 38 and you have reaped the **b** of their

BENJAMIN
Twelfth son of Jacob by Rachel (Ge 35:16–24; 46:19–21; 1Ch 2:2). Jacob refused to send him to Egypt, but relented (Ge 42–45).

BEREAN
Ac 17: 11 the **B** Jews were of more noble

BESTOWS
Ps 84: 11 the LORD **b** favor and honor;

BETHLEHEM
Mt 2: 1 After Jesus was born in **B** in Judea,

BETRAY
Pr 25: 9 do not **b** another's confidence,

---

† Please see the "Hebrew to English Translation Chart," p. xix.
‡ Please see "Key New Testament Terms," p. 1584.

BIND (BINDS)
Dt 6: 8 and **b** them on your foreheads.
Pr 6: 21 **B** them always on your heart;
Isa 61: 1 He has sent me to **b**
Mt 16: 19 whatever you **b** on earth will be

BINDS (BIND)
Ps 147: 3 and **b** up their wounds.
Isa 30: 26 when the LORD **b** up the bruises

BIRDS
Mt 8: 20 "Foxes have dens and **b** have nests,

BIRTH (BEAR)
Ps 58: 3 Even from **b** the wicked go astray;
Mt 1: 18 This is how the **b** of Jesus
1Pe 1: 3 great mercy he has given us new **b**

BIRTHRIGHT (BEAR)
Ge 25: 34 up and left. So Esau despised his **b**.

† BLAMELESS
Ge 17: 1 walk before me faithfully and be **b**.
Job 1: 1 This man was **b** and upright;
Ps 84: 11 from those whose walk is **b**.
119: 1 are those whose ways are **b**,
Pr 19: 1 poor whose walk is **b** than a fool
1Co 1: 8 so that you will be **b** on the day
Eph 5: 27 any other blemish, but holy and **b**.
Php 2: 15 that you may become **b** and pure,
1Th 3: 13 your hearts so that you will be **b**
5: 23 body be kept **b** at the coming of
Titus 1: 6 An elder must be **b**, faithful to his
Heb 7: 26 one who is holy, **b**, pure, set apart
2Pe 3: 14 spotless, **b** and at peace with him.

BLASPHEMES
Mk 3: 29 whoever **b** against the Holy Spirit

BLEMISH
1Pe 1: 19 Christ, a lamb without **b** or defect.

BLESS (BLESSED BLESSING BLESSINGS)
Ge 12: 3 I will **b** those who **b** you,
Ro 12: 14 **B** those who persecute you;

BLESSED (BLESS)
Ge 1: 22 God **b** them and said, "Be fruitful
2: 3 Then God **b** the seventh day
22: 18 all nations on earth will be **b**,
Ps 1: 1 **B** is the one who does not walk
2: 12 **B** are all who take refuge in him.
33: 12 **B** is the nation whose God is
41: 1 **B** are those who have regard
84: 5 **B** are those whose strength is
106: 3 **B** are those who act justly,
112: 1 **B** are those who fear the LORD,
118: 26 **B** is he who comes in the name
Pr 29: 18 **b** is the one who heeds wisdom's
31: 28 Her children arise and call her **b**;
Mt 5: 3 "**B** are the poor in spirit, for theirs
5: 4 **B** are those who mourn, for they
5: 5 **B** are the meek, for they will
5: 6 **B** are those who hunger and thirst
5: 7 **B** are the merciful, for they will
5: 8 **B** are the pure in heart, for they
5: 9 **B** are the peacemakers, for they
5: 10 **B** are those who are persecuted
5: 11 "**B** are you when people insult you,
Lk 1: 48 on all generations will call me **b**,
Jn 12: 13 "**B** is he who comes in the name
Ac 20: 35 'It is more **b** to give than
Titus 2: 13 while we wait for the **b** hope—
Jas 1: 12 **B** is the one who perseveres under
Rev 1: 3 **B** is the one who reads aloud
22: 14 "**B** are those who wash their robes,

BLESSING (BLESS)
Eze 34: 26 there will be showers of **b**.

BLESSINGS (BLESS)
Pr 10: 6 **B** crown the head of the righteous,

BLIND
Mt 15: 14 If the **b** lead the **b**, both will fall
23: 16 "Woe to you, **b** guides! You say,
Jn 9: 25 I do know. I was **b** but now I see!"

BLOOD
Ge 9: 6 "Whoever sheds human **b**, by
humans shall their **b** be shed;
Ex 12: 13 The **b** will be a sign for you
24: 8 "This is the **b** of the covenant
Lev 17: 11 For the life of a creature is in the **b**,
17: 11 it is the **b** that makes atonement
Ps 72: 14 for precious is their **b** in his sight.
Pr 6: 17 hands that shed innocent **b**,
Mt 26: 28 This is my **b** of the covenant,
Ro 3: 25 through the shedding of his **b**—
5: 9 have now been justified by his **b**,
1Co 11: 25 cup is the new covenant in my **b**;
Eph 1: 7 we have redemption through his **b**,
2: 13 brought near by the **b** of Christ.
Col 1: 20 by making peace through his **b**,
Heb 9: 12 once for all by his own **b**,
9: 22 everything be cleansed with **b**,
1Pe 1: 19 but with the precious **b** of Christ,
1Jn 1: 7 and the **b** of Jesus, his Son,
Rev 1: 5 has freed us from our sins by his **b**,
5: 9 with your **b** you purchased for God
7: 14 them white in the **b** of the Lamb.
12: 11 over him by the **b** of the Lamb

BLOT (BLOTS)
Ex 32: 32 **b** me out of the book you have
Ps 51: 1 to your great compassion **b** out my
Rev 3: 5 I will never **b** out the name

BLOTS (BLOT)
Isa 43: 25 "I, even I, am he who **b** out your

BLOWN
Eph 4: 14 and **b** here and there by every wind
Jas 1: 6 the sea, **b** and tossed by the wind.

BOAST
1Ki 20: 11 his armor should not **b** like one
Ps 44: 8 In God we make our **b** all day long,
Pr 27: 1 Do not **b** about tomorrow, for you
1Co 1: 31 "Let the one who boasts **b**
Gal 6: 14 May I never **b** except in the cross
Eph 2: 9 not by works, so that no one can **b**.

BOAZ
Wealthy Bethlehemite who showed favor to Ruth (Ru 2), married her (Ru 4). Ancestor of David (Ru 4:18–22; 1Ch 2:12–15), Jesus (Mt 1:5–16; Lk 3:23–32).

BODIES (BODY)
Ro 12: 1 to offer your **b** as a living sacrifice,
1Co 6: 15 not know that your **b** are members
6: 19 not know that your **b** are temples
Eph 5: 28 to love their wives as their own **b**.

BODY (BODIES)
Zec 13: 6 are these wounds on your **b**?'
Mt 10: 28 can destroy both soul and **b** in hell.
10: 28 be afraid of those who kill the **b**
26: 26 "Take and eat; this is my **b**."
Jn 13: 10 their whole **b** is clean.
1Co 11: 24 "This is my **b**, which is for you;
12: 12 Just as a **b**, though one, has many
Eph 5: 30 for we are members of his **b**.

BOLD (BOLDNESS)
Pr 21: 29 The wicked put up a **b** front,
28: 1 but the righteous are as **b** as a lion.

BOLDNESS (BOLD)
Ac 4: 29 to speak your word with great **b**.

BONDAGE
Ezr 9: 9 God has not forsaken us in our **b**.

BOOK (BOOKS)
Jos 1: 8 Keep this **B** of the Law always
Ne 8: 8 They read from the **B** of the Law
Jn 20: 30 which are not recorded in this **b**.
Php 4: 3 whose names are in the **b** of life.
Rev 21: 27 are written in the Lamb's **b** of life.

BOOKS (BOOK)
Ecc 12: 12 Of making many **b** there is no end,

BORE (BEAR)
Isa 53: 4 up our pain and **b** our suffering,

BORN (BEAR)
Isa 9: 6 For to us a child is **b**, to us a son is
Jn 3: 7 my saying, 'You must be **b** again.'
1Pe 1: 23 For you have been **b** again,
1Jn 4: 7 Everyone who loves has been **b**
5: 1 that Jesus is the Christ is **b** of God,

BORROWER
Pr 22: 7 and the **b** is slave to the lender.

BOUGHT
Ac 20: 28 which he **b** with his own blood.
1Co 6: 20 you were **b** at a price.
7: 23 You were **b** at a price;
2Pe 2: 1 the sovereign Lord who **b** them—

BOUNDLESS
Eph 3: 8 the Gentiles the **b** riches of Christ,

† BOW
Ps 95: 6 Come, let us **b** down in worship,
Isa 45: 23 Before me every knee will **b**;
Ro 14: 11 Lord, 'every knee will **b** before me;
Php 2: 10 name of Jesus every knee should **b**,

BRANCH (BRANCHES)
Isa 4: 2 that day the **B** of the LORD will be
Jer 33: 15 I will make a righteous **B** sprout

BRANCHES (BRANCH)
Jn 15: 5 "I am the vine; you are the **b**.

BRAVE
2Sa 2: 7 then, be strong and **b**, for Saul your

BREAD
Dt 8: 3 that man does not live on **b** alone
Pr 30: 8 riches, but give me only my daily **b**.
Isa 55: 2 spend money on what is not **b**,
Mt 4: 4 'Man shall not live on **b** alone,
6: 11 Give us today our daily **b**.
Jn 6: 35 Jesus declared, "I am the **b** of life.
21: 13 took the **b** and gave it to them,
1Co 11: 23 the night he was betrayed, took **b**,

BREAK (BREAKING BROKEN)
Nu 30: 2 he must not **b** his word but must
Jdg 2: 1 'I will never **b** my covenant
Ps 2: 9 You will **b** them with a rod of iron;
Isa 42: 3 A bruised reed he will not **b**,
Mt 12: 20 A bruised reed he will not **b**,

BREAKING (BREAK)
Jas 2: 10 just one point is guilty of **b** all of it.

BREASTPIECE (BREASTPLATE)
Ex 28: 15 "Fashion a **b** for making decisions

BREASTPLATE (BREASTPIECE)
Isa 59: 17 He put on righteousness as his **b**,
Eph 6: 14 the **b** of righteousness in place,
1Th 5: 8 putting on faith and love as a **b**,

BREATHED (GOD-BREATHED)
Ge 2: 7 **b** into his nostrils the breath of life,
Jn 20: 22 with that he **b** on them and said,

BRIBE
Ex 23: 8 "Do not accept a **b**, for a **b** blinds
Pr 6: 35 he will refuse a **b**, however great it

BRIDE
Rev 19: 7 and his **b** has made herself ready.

BRIGHTER (BRIGHTNESS)
Pr 4: 18 shining ever **b** till the full light

BRIGHTNESS (BRIGHTER)
2Sa 22: 13 Out of the **b** of his presence bolts
Da 12: 3 who are wise will shine like the **b**

BROAD
Mt 7: 13 gate and **b** is the road that leads

BROKEN (BREAK)
Ps 51: 17 My sacrifice, O God, is a **b** spirit;
Ecc 4: 12 of three strands is not quickly **b**.

BROKENHEARTED (HEART)
Ps 34: 18 The LORD is close to the **b**
109: 16 the poor and the needy and the **b**.
147: 3 He heals the **b** and binds up their
Isa 61: 1 He has sent me to bind up the **b**,

BROTHER (BROTHER'S BROTHERS)
Pr 17: 17 a **b** is born for a time of adversity.
18: 24 a friend who sticks closer than a **b**.
Mt 18: 15 "If your **b** or sister sins,
Mk 3: 35 Whoever does God's will is my **b**
Lk 17: 3 "If your **b** or sister sins against you,
1Co 8: 13 if what I eat causes my **b** or sister
1Jn 2: 10 who loves their **b** and sister

BROTHER'S (BROTHER)
Ge 4: 9 "Am I my **b** keeper?"

BROTHERS (BROTHER)
Mt 25: 40 did for one of the least of these **b**
Mk 10: 29 "no one who has left home or **b**
Heb 13: 1 Keep on loving one another as **b**

BUILD (BUILDING BUILDS BUILT)
Mt 16: 18 on this rock I will **b** my church,
Ac 20: 32 which can **b** you up and give you
1Co 3: 10 But each one should **b** with care.
14: 12 excel in those that **b** up the church.
1Th 5: 11 one another and **b** each other up,

† Please see the "Hebrew to English Translation Chart," p. xix.

Ro 8: 16 with our spirit that we are God's **c**.
2Co 12: 14 **c** should not have to save for
Eph 6: 1 **C**, obey your parents in the Lord,
6: 4 Fathers, do not exasperate your **c**;
Col 3: 20 **C**, obey your parents in everything,
3: 21 do not embitter your **c**, or they will
1Ti 3: 4 well and see that his **c** obey him,
3: 12 and must manage his **c** and his
5: 10 such as bringing up **c**,
Heb 12: 7 God is treating you as his **c**.
1Jn 3: 1 that we should be called **c** of God!

CHOOSE (CHOOSES CHOSE CHOSEN)
Dt 30: 19 Now **c** life, so that you and your
Jos 24: 15 **c** for yourselves this day whom you
Pr 8: 10 **C** my instruction instead of silver,
Jn 15: 16 You did not **c** me, but I chose you
Ac 15: 14 God first intervened to **c** a people

CHOOSES (CHOOSE)
Jn 7: 17 who **c** to do the will of God

CHOSE (CHOOSE)
Ge 13: 11 Lot **c** for himself the whole plain
Ps 33: 12 the people he **c** for his inheritance.
Jn 15: 16 but I **c** you and appointed you so
1Co 1: 27 But God **c** the foolish things
Eph 1: 4 For he **c** us in him before
2Th 2: 13 because God **c** you as firstfruits

CHOSEN (CHOOSE)
Isa 41: 8 whom I have **c**, you descendants
Mt 22: 14 many are invited, but few are **c**."
Lk 10: 42 Mary has **c** what is better, and it
23: 35 if he is God's Messiah, the **C** One."
Jn 15: 19 but I have **c** you out of the world.
1Pe 1: 20 He was **c** before the creation
2: 9 But you are a **c** people, a royal

‡ **CHRIST** (CHRIST'S CHRISTIAN MESSIAH)
Jn 1: 41 found the Messiah" (that is, the **C**).
Ro 3: 22 faith in Jesus **C** to all who believe.
5: 6 powerless, **C** died for the ungodly.
5: 8 we were still sinners, **C** died for us.
5: 17 life through the one man, Jesus **C**!
6: 4 just as **C** was raised from the dead
8: 1 for those who are in **C** Jesus,
8: 9 does not have the Spirit of **C**, they do not belong to **C**.
8: 35 separate us from the love of **C**?
10: 4 **C** is the culmination of the law so
14: 9 **C** died and returned to life so that
15: 3 even **C** did not please himself but,
1Co 1: 23 but we preach **C** crucified:
2: 2 while I was with you except Jesus **C**
3: 11 one already laid, which is Jesus **C**.
5: 7 For **C**, our Passover lamb, has been
8: 6 Jesus **C**, through whom all things
10: 4 them, and that rock was **C**.
10: 9 We should not test **C**, as some
11: 1 as I follow the example of **C**.
11: 3 that the head of every man is **C**,
11: 3 and the head of **C** is God.
12: 27 Now you are the body of **C**,
15: 3 that **C** died for our sins according
15: 14 And if **C** has not been raised,
15: 22 die, so in **C** all will be made alive.
15: 57 victory through our Lord Jesus **C**.
2Co 3: 3 show that you are a letter from **C**,
4: 5 but Jesus **C** as Lord, and ourselves
5: 10 before the judgment seat of **C**,
5: 17 if anyone is in **C**, the new creation
11: 2 to **C**, so that I might present you as
Gal 2: 20 I have been crucified with **C**
3: 13 **C** redeemed us from the curse
6: 14 in the cross of our Lord Jesus **C**,
Eph 1: 3 and Father of our Lord Jesus **C**,
3: 8 Gentiles the boundless riches of **C**,
4: 13 whole measure of the fullness of **C**.
5: 2 just as **C** loved us and gave himself
5: 23 head of the wife as **C** is the head
5: 25 just as **C** loved the church and gave
Php 1: 21 to live is **C** and to die is gain.
1: 27 manner worthy of the gospel of **C**.
4: 19 to the riches of his glory in **C** Jesus.
Col 1: 27 which is **C** in you, the hope
1: 28 present everyone fully mature in **C**.
2: 6 as you received **C** Jesus as Lord,
2: 17 the reality, however, is found in **C**.
Col 3: 15 Let the peace of **C** rule in your
2Th 2: 1 the coming of our Lord Jesus **C**
1Ti 1: 15 **C** Jesus came into the world to save
2: 5 and mankind, the man **C** Jesus,
2Ti 2: 3 like a good soldier of **C** Jesus.
3: 15 salvation through faith in **C** Jesus.
Titus 2: 13 our great God and Savior, Jesus **C**,
Heb 3: 14 We have come to share in **C**,
9: 14 will the blood of **C**, who through
9: 15 For this reason **C** is the mediator
9: 28 so **C** was sacrificed once to take
10: 10 of the body of Jesus **C** once for all.
13: 8 Jesus **C** is the same yesterday
1Pe 1: 19 but with the precious blood of **C**,
2: 21 called, because **C** suffered for you,
3: 18 For **C** also suffered once for sins,
4: 14 insulted because of the name of **C**,
1Jn 2: 22 whoever denies that Jesus is the **C**.
3: 16 Jesus **C** laid down his life for us.
5: 1 who believes that Jesus is the **C**
Rev 20: 4 reigned with **C** a thousand years.

CHRISTIAN (CHRIST)
1Pe 4: 16 if you suffer as a **C**, do not be

CHRIST'S (CHRIST)
2Co 5: 14 For **C** love compels us, because we
5: 20 We are therefore **C** ambassadors,
12: 9 so that **C** power may rest on me.

‡ **CHURCH**
Mt 16: 18 and on this rock I will build my **c**,
18: 17 if they refuse to listen even to the **c**,
Ac 20: 28 Be shepherds of the **c** of God,
1Co 5: 12 mine to judge those outside the **c**?
14: 4 one who prophesies edifies the **c**.
14: 12 excel in those that build up the **c**.
14: 26 done so that the **c** may be built up.
Eph 5: 23 wife as Christ is the head of the **c**,
Col 1: 24 the sake of his body, which is the **c**.

CIRCUMCISED
Ge 17: 10 Every male among you shall be **c**.
Gal 2: 8 in Peter as an apostle to the **c**,

CIRCUMSTANCES
Php 4: 11 to be content whatever the **c**.
1Th 5: 18 give thanks in all **c**; for this is God's

CITIZENS (CITIZENSHIP)
Eph 2: 19 but fellow **c** with God's people

CITIZENSHIP (CITIZENS)
Php 3: 20 But our **c** is in heaven.

CITY
Heb 13: 14 here we do not have an enduring **c**,

CIVILIAN
2Ti 2: 4 a soldier gets entangled in **c** affairs,

CLAIM (CLAIMS)
Pr 25: 6 do not **c** a place among his great
1Jn 1: 6 If we **c** to have fellowship with him
1: 8 If we **c** to be without sin,
1: 10 If we **c** we have not sinned,

CLAIMS (CLAIM)
Jas 2: 14 if someone **c** to have faith but has
1Jn 2: 6 Whoever **c** to live in him must live
2: 9 Anyone who **c** to be in the light

CLAP
Ps 47: 1 **C** your hands, all you nations;
Isa 55: 12 trees of the field will **c** their hands.

CLAY
Isa 45: 9 Does the **c** say to the potter,
64: 8 We are the **c**, you are the potter;
Jer 18: 6 "Like **c** in the hand of the potter,
La 4: 2 are now considered as pots of **c**,
Da 2: 33 of iron and partly of baked **c**.
Ro 9: 21 the same lump of **c** some pottery
2Co 4: 7 this treasure in jars of **c** to show
2Ti 2: 20 and silver, but also of wood and **c**;

† **CLEAN**
Lev 16: 30 you will be **c** from all your sins.
Ps 24: 4 one who has **c** hands and a pure
Mt 12: 44 swept **c** and put in order.
23: 25 You **c** the outside of the cup
Mk 7: 19 this, Jesus declared all foods **c**.)
Jn 13: 10 you are **c**, though not every one
15: 3 You are already **c** because
Ac 10: 15 impure that God has made **c**."
Ro 14: 20 All food is **c**, but it is wrong

CLING
Ps 63: 8 I **c** to you; your right hand upholds
Ro 12: 9 Hate what is evil; **c** to what is good.

CLOAK
2Ki 4: 29 "Tuck your **c** into your belt,

CLOSE (CLOSER)
Ps 34: 18 The LORD is **c**
Isa 40: 11 and carries them **c** to his heart;
Jer 30: 21 near and he will come **c** to me—

CLOSER (CLOSE)
Ex 3: 5 "Do not come any **c**," God said.
Pr 18: 24 friend who sticks **c** than a brother.

CLOTHE (CLOTHED CLOTHES CLOTHING)
Ps 45: 3 **c** yourself with splendor
Isa 52: 1 Zion, **c** yourself with strength!
Ro 13: 14 **c** yourselves with the Lord Jesus
Col 3: 12 **c** yourselves with compassion,
1Pe 5: 5 **c** yourselves with humility toward

CLOTHED (CLOTHE)
Ps 30: 11 my sackcloth and **c** me with joy,
Pr 31: 25 She is **c** with strength and dignity;
Lk 24: 49 the city until you have been **c**

CLOTHES (CLOTHE)
Mt 6: 25 food, and the body more than **c**?
6: 28 "And why do you worry about **c**?
Jn 11: 44 "Take off the grave **c** and let him

CLOTHING (CLOTHE)
Dt 22: 5 nor a man wear women's **c**,
Mt 7: 15 They come to you in sheep's **c**,

CLOUD (CLOUDS)
Ex 13: 21 them in a pillar of **c** to guide them
Isa 19: 1 the LORD rides on a swift **c** and is
Lk 21: 27 of Man coming in a **c** with power
Heb 12: 1 by such a great **c** of witnesses,

CLOUDS (CLOUD)
Ps 104: 3 He makes the **c** his chariot and
Da 7: 13 man, coming with the **c** of heaven.
Mk 13: 26 Man coming in **c** with great power
1Th 4: 17 them in the **c** to meet the Lord

CO-HEIRS (INHERIT)
Ro 8: 17 heirs of God and **c** with Christ,

COALS
Pr 25: 22 will heap burning **c** on his head,
Ro 12: 20 this, you will heap burning **c** on his

COAT
Lk 6: 29 If someone takes your **c**, do not

COLD
Pr 25: 25 Like **c** water to a weary soul is
Mt 10: 42 anyone gives even a cup of **c** water
24: 12 the love of most will grow **c**,

COMFORT (COMFORTED COMFORTS)
Ps 23: 4 your rod and your staff, they **c** me.
119: 52 ancient laws, and I find **c** in them.
119: 76 May your unfailing love be my **c**,
Zec 1: 17 the LORD will again **c** Zion
1Co 14: 3 strengthening, encouraging and **c**.
2Co 1: 4 that we can **c** those in any trouble
2: 7 you ought to forgive and **c** him,

COMFORTED (COMFORT)
Mt 5: 4 who mourn, for they will be **c**.

COMFORTS (COMFORT)
Job 29: 25 I was like one who **c** mourners.
Isa 49: 13 For the LORD **c** his people
51: 12 "I, even I, am he who **c** you.
66: 13 As a mother **c** her child, so will I
2Co 1: 4 who **c** us in all our troubles,
7: 6 But God, who **c** the downcast,

COMMAND (COMMANDED COMMANDING COMMANDMENT COMMANDMENTS COMMANDS)
Ex 7: 2 You are to say everything I **c** you,
Nu 24: 13 to go beyond the **c** of the LORD—
Dt 4: 2 Do not add to what I **c** you and do
30: 16 For I **c** you today to love
32: 46 so that you may **c** your children
Ps 91: 11 he will **c** his angels concerning you
148: 5 for at his **c** they were created,
Pr 6: 23 For this **c** is a lamp, this teaching is
13: 13 whoever respects a **c** is rewarded.
Ecc 8: 2 Obey the king's **c**, I say,
Joel 2: 11 mighty is the army that obeys his **c**.

† Please see the "Hebrew to English Translation Chart," p. xix.
‡ Please see "Key New Testament Terms," p. 1584.

Jn 13: 34 "A new **c** I give you:
15: 12 My **c** is this: Love each other as I
1Co 14: 37 I am writing to you is the Lord's **c**.
Gal 5: 14 is fulfilled in keeping this one **c**:
1Ti 1: 5 The goal of this **c** is love,
Heb 11: 3 the universe was formed at God's **c**,
1Jn 3: 23 And this is his **c**: to believe
2Jn : 6 his **c** is that you walk in love.

COMMANDED (COMMAND)
Ps 33: 9 came to be; he **c**, and it stood firm.
Mt 28: 20 to obey everything I have **c** you.
1Co 9: 14 way, the Lord has **c** that those who
1Jn 3: 23 and to love one another as he **c** us.

COMMANDING (COMMAND)
2Ti 2: 4 rather tries to please his **c** officer.

COMMANDMENT (COMMAND)
Jos 22: 5 be very careful to keep the **c**
Mt 22: 38 This is the first and greatest **c**.
Ro 7: 12 and the **c** is holy,
Eph 6: 2 is the first **c** with a promise—

COMMANDMENTS (COMMAND)
Ex 20: 6 those who love me and keep my **c**.
34: 28 words of the covenant—the Ten **C**.
Dt 7: 9 those who love him and keep his **c**.
Ecc 12: 13 Fear God and keep his **c**, for this is
Da 9: 4 those who love him and keep his **c**,
Mt 22: 40 the Prophets hang on these two **c**."

COMMANDS (COMMAND)
Dt 11: 27 you obey the **c** of the LORD your
Ps 112: 1 who find great delight in his **c**.
119: 47 in your **c** because I love them.
119: 86 All your **c** are trustworthy;
119: 98 Your **c** are always with me
119:127 I love your **c** more than gold,
119:143 me, but your **c** give me delight.
119:172 word, for all your **c** are righteous.
Pr 3: 1 but keep my **c** in your heart,
10: 8 The wise in heart accept **c**,
Mt 5: 19 teaches these **c** will be called great
Jn 14: 15 "If you love me, keep my **c**.
14: 21 Whoever has my **c** and keeps them
Ac 17: 30 now he **c** all people everywhere
1Co 7: 19 Keeping God's **c** is what counts.
1Jn 5: 3 this is love for God: to keep his **c**.
And his **c** are not burdensome,

COMMEND (COMMENDED COMMENDS)
Ecc 8: 15 So I **c** the enjoyment of life,
1Pe 2: 14 wrong and to **c** those who do right.

COMMENDED (COMMEND)
Ro 13: 3 do what is right and you will be **c**.
Heb 11: 39 These were all **c** for their faith,

COMMENDS (COMMEND)
2Co 10: 18 but the one whom the Lord **c**.

COMMIT (COMMITS COMMITTED)
Ex 20: 14 "You shall not **c** adultery.
Ps 37: 5 **C** your way to the LORD;
Mt 5: 27 was said, 'You shall not **c** adultery.'
Lk 23: 46 into your hands I **c** my spirit."
Ac 20: 32 "Now I **c** you to God
1Co 10: 8 We should not **c** sexual immorality,
1Pe 4: 19 to God's will should **c** themselves

COMMITS (COMMIT)
Pr 6: 32 a man who **c** adultery has no sense;
29: 22 hot-tempered person **c** many sins.
Mt 19: 9 marries another woman **c** adultery."

COMMITTED (COMMIT)
Nu 5: 7 must confess the sin they have **c**.
1Ki 8: 61 may your hearts be fully **c**
2Ch 16: 9 those whose hearts are fully **c**
Mt 5: 28 lustfully has already **c** adultery
2Co 5: 19 And he has **c** to us the message
1Pe 2: 22 "He **c** no sin, and no deceit was

COMMON
Pr 22: 2 Rich and poor have this in **c**:
1Co 10: 13 has overtaken you except what is **c**
2Co 6: 14 and wickedness have in **c**?

COMPANION
Pr 13: 20 for a **c** of fools suffers harm.
28: 7 a **c** of gluttons disgraces his father.
29: 3 but a **c** of prostitutes squanders his

COMPANY
Pr 24: 1 the wicked, do not desire their **c**;
Jer 15: 17 I never sat in the **c** of revelers,
1Co 15: 33 "Bad **c** corrupts good character."

COMPARED (COMPARING)
Eze 31: 2 "'Who can be **c** with you

COMPARING (COMPARED)
Ro 8: 18 present sufferings are not worth **c**
2Co 8: 8 of your love by **c** it
Gal 6: 4 without **c** themselves to someone

COMPASSION (COMPASSIONATE COMPASSIONS)
Ex 33: 19 I will have **c** on whom I will have **c**.
Ne 9: 19 your great **c** you did not abandon
9: 28 in your **c** you delivered them time
Ps 51: 1 to your great **c** blot out my
103: 4 pit and crowns you with love and **c**,
103: 13 As a father has **c** on his children,
145: 9 he has **c** on all he has made.
Isa 49: 13 will have **c** on his afflicted ones.
49: 15 and have no **c** on the child she has
Hos 2: 19 and justice, in love and **c**.
11: 8 all my **c** is aroused.
Jnh 3: 9 with **c** turn from his fierce anger so
Mt 9: 36 saw the crowds, he had **c** on them,
Mk 8: 2 "I have **c** for these people;
Ro 9: 15 I will have **c** on whom I have **c**."
Col 3: 12 clothe yourselves with **c**, kindness,
Jas 5: 11 The Lord is full of **c** and mercy.

COMPASSIONATE (COMPASSION)
Ne 9: 17 gracious and **c**, slow to anger
Ps 103: 8 The LORD is **c** and gracious,
112: 4 for those who are gracious and **c**
Eph 4: 32 Be kind and **c** to one another,
1Pe 3: 8 love one another, be **c** and humble.

COMPASSIONS (COMPASSION)
La 3: 22 not consumed, for his **c** never fail.

COMPEL (COMPELLED COMPELS)
Lk 14: 23 lanes and **c** them to come in,

COMPELLED (COMPEL)
Ac 20: 22 "And now, **c** by the Spirit, I am
1Co 9: 16 boast, since I am **c** to preach.

COMPELS (COMPEL)
2Co 5: 14 For Christ's love **c** us, because we

COMPETENCE (COMPETENT)
2Co 3: 5 but our **c** comes from God.

COMPETENT (COMPETENCE)
Ro 15: 14 and **c** to instruct one another.
1Co 6: 2 are you not **c** to judge trivial cases?
2Co 3: 5 Not that we are **c** in ourselves
3: 6 He has made us **c** as ministers

COMPETES
1Co 9: 25 Everyone who **c** in the games goes
2Ti 2: 5 anyone who **c** as an athlete does

COMPLACENT
Am 6: 1 Woe to you who are **c** in Zion,

COMPLETE
Jn 15: 11 in you and that your joy may be **c**.
16: 24 will receive, and your joy will be **c**.
17: 23 they may be brought to **c** unity.
Ac 20: 24 **c** the task the Lord Jesus has given
Php 2: 2 then make my joy **c** by being
Col 4: 17 it that you **c** the ministry you have
Jas 1: 4 so that you may be mature and **c**,
2: 22 faith was made **c** by what he did.

CONCEAL (CONCEALED CONCEALS)
Ps 40: 10 I do not **c** your love and your
Pr 25: 2 It is the glory of God to **c** a matter;

CONCEALED (CONCEAL)
Jer 16: 17 me, nor is their sin **c** from my eyes.
Mt 10: 26 for there is nothing **c** that will not
Mk 4: 22 whatever is **c** is meant to be

CONCEALS (CONCEAL)
Pr 28: 13 Whoever **c** their sins does not

CONCEITED
Gal 5: 26 Let us not become **c**,
1Ti 6: 4 they are **c** and understand nothing.

CONCEIVE (CONCEIVED)
Isa 7: 14 The virgin will **c** and give birth
Mt 1: 23 "The virgin will **c** and give birth

CONCEIVED (CONCEIVE)
Mt 1: 20 because what is **c** in her is
1Co 2: 9 and what no human mind has **c**"—

CONCERN (CONCERNED)
Eze 36: 21 I had **c** for my holy name,
1Co 7: 32 I would like you to be free from **c**.
1Co 12: 25 that its parts should have equal **c**
2Co 11: 28 of my **c** for all the churches.

CONCERNED (CONCERN)
Jnh 4: 10 "You have been **c** about this plant,
1Co 7: 32 An unmarried man is **c**

CONDEMN (CONDEMNATION CONDEMNED CONDEMNING CONDEMNS)
Job 40: 8 you **c** me to justify yourself?
Isa 50: 9 Who will **c** me? They will all wear
Lk 6: 37 Do not **c**, and you will not be
Jn 3: 17 Son into the world to **c** the world,
12: 48 words I have spoken will **c** them
Ro 2: 27 yet obeys the law will **c** you who,
1Jn 3: 20 If our hearts **c** us, we know that

CONDEMNATION (CONDEMN)
Ro 5: 18 just as one trespass resulted in **c**
8: 1 there is now no **c** for those who are
2Co 3: 9 that brought **c** was glorious,

CONDEMNED (CONDEMN)
Ps 34: 22 who takes refuge in him will be **c**.
Mt 12: 37 and by your words you will be **c**."
23: 33 How will you escape being **c**
Jn 3: 18 Whoever believes in him is not **c**,
16: 11 prince of this world now stands **c**.
Ro 14: 23 whoever has doubts is **c** if they eat,
1Co 11: 32 that we will not be finally **c**
Heb 11: 7 By his faith he **c** the world

CONDEMNING (CONDEMN)
Pr 17: 15 the guilty and **c** the innocent—
Ro 2: 1 you are **c** yourself, because you

CONDEMNS (CONDEMN)
Pr 14: 34 exalts a nation, but sin **c** any people
Ro 8: 34 Who then is the one who **c**?

CONDUCT
Pr 20: 11 is their **c** really pure and upright?
21: 8 but the **c** of the innocent is upright.
Ecc 6: 8 how to **c** themselves before others?
Jer 4: 18 "Your own **c** and actions have
17: 10 each person according to their **c**,
Eze 7: 3 I will judge you according to your **c**
1Ti 3: 15 how people ought to **c** themselves

CONFESS (CONFESSION)
Lev 16: 21 and **c** over it all the wickedness
26: 40 if they will **c** their sins and the sins
Nu 5: 7 **c** the sin they have committed.
Ps 38: 18 I **c** my iniquity; I am troubled by
Jas 5: 16 Therefore **c** your sins to each other
1Jn 1: 9 If we **c** our sins, he is faithful

CONFESSION (CONFESS)
2Co 9: 13 accompanies your **c** of the gospel

CONFIDENCE
Ps 71: 5 LORD, my **c** since my youth.
Pr 11: 13 A gossip betrays a **c**,
25: 9 to court, do not betray another's **c**,
31: 11 Her husband has full **c** in her
Isa 32: 17 will be quietness and **c** forever.
Jer 17: 7 in the LORD, whose **c** is in him.
Php 3: 3 and who put no **c** in the flesh—
Heb 4: 16 God's throne of grace with **c**,
10: 19 since we have **c** to enter the Most
10: 35 So do not throw away your **c**;
11: 1 Now faith is **c** in what we hope
13: 17 Have **c** in your leaders and submit
1Jn 5: 14 This is the **c** we have

CONFIRM
2Pe 1: 10 make every effort to **c** your calling

CONFLICT
Pr 6: 14 his heart—he always stirs up **c**.
6: 19 a person who stirs up **c**
10: 12 Hatred stirs up **c**, but love covers
15: 18 A hot-tempered person stirs up **c**,
16: 28 A perverse person stirs up **c**,
28: 25 The greedy stir up **c**,
29: 22 An angry person stirs up **c**,

CONFORM (CONFORMED)
Ro 12: 2 not **c** to the pattern of this world,
1Pe 1: 14 do not **c** to the evil desires you had

CONFORMED (CONFORM)
Ro 8: 29 predestined to be **c** to the image

CONQUERORS
Ro 8: 37 are more than **c** through him who

CONSCIENCE (CONSCIENCES)
Ro 13: 5 but also as a matter of **c**.

1Co 8: 7 a god, and since their **c** is weak,
8: 12 this way and wound their weak **c**,
10: 25 without raising questions of **c**,
10: 29 being judged by another's **c**?
Heb 10: 22 to cleanse us from a guilty **c**
1Pe 3: 16 keeping a clear **c**, so that those who

CONSCIENCES (CONSCIENCE)
Ro 2: 15 hearts, their **c** also bearing witness,
1Ti 4: 2 whose **c** have been seared as
Titus 1: 15 their minds and **c** are corrupted.
Heb 9: 14 cleanse our **c** from acts that lead

CONSCIOUS
Ro 3: 20 through the law we become **c** of
1Pe 2: 19 unjust suffering because they are **c**

† **CONSECRATE** (CONSECRATED)
Ex 13: 2 "**C** to me every firstborn male.
Lev 20: 7 "'**C** yourselves and be holy,

CONSECRATED (CONSECRATE)
Ex 29: 43 and the place will be **c** by my glory.
1Ti 4: 5 because it is **c** by the word of God

CONSIDER (CONSIDERATE CONSIDERED CONSIDERS)
1Sa 12: 24 **c** what great things he has done
Job 37: 14 stop and **c** God's wonders.
Ps 8: 3 When I **c** your heavens, the work
143: 5 and **c** what your hands have done.
Lk 12: 24 **C** the ravens: They do not sow
12: 27 "**C** how the wild flowers grow.
Php 3: 8 I **c** everything a loss because
Heb 10: 24 And let us **c** how we may spur one
Jas 1: 2 **C** it pure joy, my brothers
1: 26 Those who **c** themselves religious

CONSIDERATE (CONSIDER)
Titus 3: 2 to be peaceable and **c**, and always
Jas 3: 17 then peace-loving, **c**, submissive,
1Pe 2: 18 only to those who are good and **c**,
3: 7 the same way be **c** as you live

CONSIDERED (CONSIDER)
Job 1: 8 "Have you **c** my servant Job?
2: 3 "Have you **c** my servant Job?
Ps 44: 22 we are **c** as sheep to be slaughtered.
Isa 53: 4 yet we **c** him punished by God,
Ro 8: 36 all day long; we are **c** as sheep to be

CONSIDERS (CONSIDER)
Pr 31: 16 She **c** a field and buys it; out of her
Ro 14: 5 One person **c** one day more sacred

CONSIST
Lk 12: 15 life does not **c** in an abundance

CONSOLATION
Ps 94: 19 within me, your **c** brought me joy.

CONSTRUCTIVE
1Co 10: 23 but not everything is **c**.

CONSUME (CONSUMING)
Jn 2: 17 "Zeal for your house will **c** me."

CONSUMING (CONSUME)
Dt 4: 24 For the LORD your God is a **c** fire,
Heb 12: 29 for our "God is a **c** fire."

CONTAIN
1Ki 8: 27 the highest heaven, cannot **c** you.
2Pe 3: 16 His letters **c** some things that are

CONTAMINATES
2Co 7: 1 from everything that **c** body

CONTEMPLATE
2Co 3: 18 unveiled faces **c** the Lord's glory,

CONTEMPT
Pr 14: 31 oppresses the poor shows **c** for
17: 5 Whoever mocks the poor shows **c**
18: 3 so does **c**, and with shame comes
Da 12: 2 others to shame and everlasting **c**.
Ro 2: 4 do you show **c** for the riches of his
Gal 4: 14 did not treat me with **c** or scorn.
1Th 5: 20 Do not treat prophecies with **c**

CONTEND
Jude : 3 urge you to **c** for the faith that was

CONTENT (CONTENTMENT)
Pr 13: 25 The righteous eat to their hearts' **c**,
Php 4: 11 to be **c** whatever the circumstances.
4: 12 learned the secret of being **c** in any
1Ti 6: 8 clothing, we will be **c** with that.
Heb 13: 5 and be **c** with what you have,

CONTENTMENT (CONTENT)
1Ti 6: 6 But godliness with **c** is great gain.

CONTINUAL (CONTINUE)
Pr 15: 15 but the cheerful heart has a **c** feast.

CONTINUE (CONTINUAL)
Php 2: 12 **c** to work out your salvation
2Ti 3: 14 **c** in what you have learned and
1Jn 5: 18 born of God does not **c** to sin;
Rev 22: 11 let the one who does right **c** to do
22: 11 let the holy person **c** to be holy."

CONTRITE
Ps 51: 17 a broken and **c** heart you, God,
Isa 57: 15 and to revive the heart of the **c**.
66: 2 who are humble and **c** in spirit,

CONTROL (CONTROLLED SELF-CONTROL SELF-CONTROLLED)
1Co 7: 9 But if they cannot **c** themselves,
7: 37 but has **c** over his own will,
1Th 4: 4 should learn to **c** your own body

CONTROLLED (CONTROL)
Ps 32: 9 understanding but must be **c** by bit

CONTROVERSIES
Titus 3: 9 But avoid foolish **c** and genealogies

CONVERSATION
Col 4: 6 Let your **c** be always full of grace,

CONVERT
1Ti 3: 6 He must not be a recent **c**, or he

CONVICTION
Heb 3: 14 we hold our original **c** firmly

CONVINCED (CONVINCING)
Ro 8: 38 I am **c** that neither death nor life,
2Ti 1: 12 am **c** that he is able to guard what I
3: 14 have learned and have become **c** of,

CONVINCING (CONVINCED)
Ac 1: 3 and gave many **c** proofs that he was

CORNELIUS
Roman to whom Peter preached; first Gentile Christian (Ac 10).

CORNERSTONE (STONE)
Ps 118: 22 builders rejected has become the **c**;
Isa 28: 16 a precious **c** for a sure foundation;
Eph 2: 20 Christ Jesus himself as the chief **c**.
1Pe 2: 6 a chosen and precious **c**,
2: 7 rejected has become the **c**,"

CORRECT (CORRECTING CORRECTION CORRECTS)
2Ti 4: 2 **c**, rebuke and encourage—

CORRECTING (CORRECT)
2Ti 3: 16 **c** and training in righteousness,

CORRECTION (CORRECT)
Pr 10: 17 but whoever ignores **c** leads others
12: 1 but whoever hates **c** is stupid.
15: 5 whoever heeds **c** shows prudence.
15: 10 the one who hates **c** will die.

CORRECTS (CORRECT)
Job 5: 17 "Blessed is the one whom God **c**;
Pr 9: 7 Whoever **c** a mocker invites insults

CORRUPT (CORRUPTS)
Ge 6: 11 Now the earth was **c** in God's sight

CORRUPTS (CORRUPT)
Ecc 7: 7 into a fool, and a bribe **c** the heart.
1Co 15: 33 "Bad company **c** good character."
Jas 3: 6 It **c** the whole body, sets the whole

COST
Pr 4: 7 Though it **c** all you have,
Isa 55: 1 milk without money and without **c**.
Rev 21: 6 thirsty I will give water without **c**

COUNSEL (COUNSELOR)
1Ki 22: 5 "First seek the **c** of the LORD."
Pr 15: 22 Plans fail for lack of **c**,
Rev 3: 18 I **c** you to buy from me gold

COUNSELOR (COUNSEL)
Isa 9: 6 And he will be called Wonderful **C**,

COUNT (COUNTING COUNTS)
Ro 4: 8 Lord will never **c** against them."
6: 11 **c** yourselves dead to sin but alive

COUNTING (COUNT)
2Co 5: 19 not **c** people's sins against them.

COUNTRY
Jn 4: 44 prophet has no honor in his own **c**.

COUNTS (COUNT)
Jn 6: 63 the flesh **c** for nothing.
1Co 7: 19 God's commands is what **c**.
Gal 5: 6 **c** is faith expressing itself through

COURAGE (COURAGEOUS)
Ac 23: 11 stood near Paul and said, "Take **c**!

COURAGEOUS (COURAGE)
Dt 31: 6 Be strong and **c**. Do not be afraid
Jos 1: 6 Be strong and **c**, because you will
1Co 16: 13 firm in the faith; be **c**; be strong.

COURSE
Ps 19: 5 a champion rejoicing to run his **c**.
Pr 15: 21 understanding keeps a straight **c**.

COURTS
Ps 84: 10 your **c** than a thousand elsewhere;
100: 4 thanksgiving and his **c** with praise;

COVENANT (COVENANTS)
Ge 9: 9 "I now establish my **c** with you
Ex 19: 5 if you obey me fully and keep my **c**,
1Ch 16: 15 He remembers his **c** forever,
Job 31: 1 "I made a **c** with my eyes not
Jer 31: 31 I will make a new **c** with the people
1Co 11: 25 "This cup is the new **c** in my blood;
Gal 4: 24 One **c** is from Mount Sinai
Heb 9: 15 Christ is the mediator of a new **c**,

COVENANTS (COVENANT)
Ro 9: 4 the **c**, the receiving of the law,
Gal 4: 24 The women represent two **c**.

COVER (COVER-UP COVERED COVERS)
Ps 91: 4 He will **c** you with his feathers,
Jas 5: 20 and **c** over a multitude of sins.

COVERED (COVER)
Ps 32: 1 are forgiven, whose sins are **c**.
Isa 6: 2 With two wings they **c** their faces,
Ro 4: 7 are forgiven, whose sins are **c**.
1Co 11: 4 with his head **c** dishonors his head.

COVERS (COVER)
Pr 10: 12 conflict, but love **c** over all wrongs.
1Pe 4: 8 because love **c** over a multitude

COVER-UP (COVER)
1Pe 2: 16 do not use your freedom as a **c**

COVET
Ex 20: 17 "You shall not **c** your neighbor's
Ro 13: 9 "You shall not **c**," and whatever

COWARDLY
Rev 21: 8 But the **c**, the unbelieving, the vile,

CRAFTINESS (CRAFTY)
1Co 3: 19 "He catches the wise in their **c**";

† **CRAFTY** (CRAFTINESS)
Ge 3: 1 the serpent was more **c** than any
2Co 12: 16 Yet, **c** fellow that I am, I caught you

CRAVE
Pr 23: 3 Do not **c** his delicacies, for that
1Pe 2: 2 babies, **c** pure spiritual milk,

† **CREATE** (CREATED CREATION CREATOR)
Ps 51: 10 **C** in me a pure heart, O God,
Isa 45: 18 he did not **c** it to be empty,

CREATED (CREATE)
Ge 1: 1 In the beginning God **c** the heavens
1: 21 So God **c** the great creatures
1: 27 So God **c** mankind in his own
1: 27 male and female he **c** them.
Ps 148: 5 for at his command they were **c**,
Ro 1: 25 and served **c** things rather than
1Co 11: 9 neither was man **c** for woman,
Col 1: 16 For in him all things were **c**:
1Ti 4: 4 For everything God **c** is good,
Rev 10: 6 who **c** the heavens and all that is

CREATION (CREATE)
Mk 16: 15 *preach the gospel to all* **c**.
Jn 17: 24 because you loved me before the **c**
Ro 8: 19 For the **c** waits in eager expectation
8: 39 nor anything else in all **c**, will be
2Co 5: 17 is in Christ, the new **c** has come:
Col 1: 15 God, the firstborn over all **c**.
1Pe 1: 20 He was chosen before the **c**
Rev 13: 8 was slain from the **c** of the world.

† Please see the "Hebrew to English Translation Chart," p. xix.

CREATOR (CREATE)
Ge 14: 22 Most High, **C** of heaven and earth,
Isa 42: 5 LORD says—the **C** of the heavens,
Ro 1: 25 created things rather than the **C**—

CREATURE (CREATURES)
Lev 17: 11 For the life of a **c** is in the blood,

CREATURES (CREATURE)
Ge 6: 19 into the ark two of all living **c**,
Ps 104: 24 the earth is full of your **c**.

CREDIT (CREDITED)
Ro 4: 24 whom God will **c** righteousness—
1Pe 2: 20 it to your **c** if you receive a beating

CREDITED (CREDIT)
Ge 15: 6 and he **c** it to him as righteousness.
Ro 4: 5 their faith is **c** as righteousness.
Gal 3: 6 it was **c** to him as righteousness."
Jas 2: 23 it was **c** to him as righteousness,"

CRIED (CRY)
Ps 18: 6 I **c** to my God for help.

CRIMSON
Isa 1: 18 though they are red as **c**, they shall

CRIPPLED
Mk 9: 45 to enter life **c** than to have two feet

CRITICISM
2Co 8: 20 want to avoid any **c** of the way we

CROOKED
Pr 10: 9 whoever takes **c** paths will be
Php 2: 15 fault in a warped and **c** generation."

CROSS
Mt 10: 38 Whoever does not take up their **c**
Lk 9: 23 take up their **c** daily and follow me.
Ac 2: 23 to death by nailing him to the **c**.
1Co 1: 17 lest the **c** of Christ be emptied of
Gal 6: 14 in the **c** of our Lord Jesus Christ,
Php 2: 8 even death on a **c**!
Col 1: 20 through his blood, shed on the **c**.
2: 14 taken it away, nailing it to the **c**.
2: 15 triumphing over them by the **c**.
Heb 12: 2 joy set before him he endured the **c**,

CROWD
Ex 23: 2 pervert justice by siding with the **c**,

CROWN (CROWNED CROWNS)
Pr 4: 9 and present you with a glorious **c**."
10: 6 Blessings **c** the head
12: 4 noble character is her husband's **c**,
17: 6 Children's children are a **c**
Isa 61: 3 on them a **c** of beauty instead
Zec 9: 16 in his land like jewels in a **c**.
Mt 27: 29 then twisted together a **c** of thorns
1Co 9: 25 to get a **c** that will last forever.
2Ti 4: 8 store for me the **c** of righteousness,
Rev 2: 10 will give you life as your victor's **c**.

CROWNED (CROWN)
Ps 8: 5 the angels and **c** them with glory
Pr 14: 18 the prudent are **c** with knowledge.
Heb 2: 7 you **c** them with glory and honor

CROWNS (CROWN)
Rev 4: 10 They lay their **c** before the throne
19: 12 fire, and on his head are many **c**.

CRUCIFIED (CRUCIFY)
Mt 20: 19 to be mocked and flogged and **c**.
27: 38 Two rebels were **c** with him,
Lk 24: 7 be **c** and on the third day be raised
Jn 19: 18 they **c** him, and with him two
Ac 2: 36 Jesus, whom you **c**, both Lord
Ro 6: 6 that our old self was **c** with him so
1Co 1: 23 but we preach Christ **c**:
2: 2 you except Jesus Christ and him **c**.
Gal 2: 20 I have been **c** with Christ and I no
5: 24 Christ Jesus have **c** the flesh with

CRUCIFY (CRUCIFIED CRUCIFYING)
Mt 27: 22 They all answered, "**C** him!"
27: 31 Then they led him away to **c** him.

CRUCIFYING (CRUCIFY)
Heb 6: 6 their loss they are **c** the Son of God

CRUSH (CRUSHED)
Ge 3: 15 he will **c** your head, and you will
Isa 53: 10 it was the LORD's will to **c** him
Ro 16: 20 peace will soon **c** Satan under your

CRUSHED (CRUSH)
Ps 34: 18 and saves those who are **c** in spirit.
Isa 53: 5 he was **c** for our iniquities;
2Co 4: 8 pressed on every side, but not **c**;

CRY (CRIED)
Ps 34: 15 and his ears are attentive to their **c**;
40: 1 he turned to me and heard my **c**.
130: 1 Out of the depths I **c** to you,

CULMINATION
Ro 10: 4 Christ is the **c** of the law so

CUP
Ps 23: 5 my head with oil; my **c** overflows.
Mt 10: 42 anyone gives even a **c** of cold water
23: 25 You clean the outside of the **c**
26: 39 may this **c** be taken from me.
1Co 11: 25 "This **c** is the new covenant in my

† **CURSE** (CURSED)
Dt 11: 26 you today a blessing and a **c**—
21: 23 is hung on a pole is under God's **c**.
Lk 6: 28 bless those who **c** you,
Gal 1: 8 to you, let them be under God's **c**!
3: 13 redeemed us from the **c** of the law by becoming a **c** for us,
Rev 22: 3 No longer will there be any **c**.

CURSED (CURSE)
Ge 3: 17 "**C** is the ground because of you;
Dt 27: 15 "**C** is anyone who makes an idol—
27: 16 "**C** is anyone who dishonors their
27: 17 "**C** is anyone who moves their
27: 18 "**C** is anyone who leads the blind
27: 19 "**C** is anyone who withholds justice
27: 20 "**C** is anyone who sleeps with his
27: 21 "**C** is anyone who has sexual
27: 22 "**C** is anyone who sleeps with his
27: 23 "**C** is anyone who sleeps with his
27: 24 "**C** is anyone who kills their
27: 25 "**C** is anyone who accepts a bribe
27: 26 "**C** is anyone who does not uphold
Ro 9: 3 I could wish that I myself were **c**
Gal 3: 10 "**C** is everyone who does not

CURTAIN
Ex 26: 33 Hang the **c** from the clasps
26: 33 The **c** will separate the Holy Place
Lk 23: 45 the **c** of the temple was torn in two.
Heb 10: 20 way opened for us through the **c**,

CYMBAL
1Co 13: 1 a resounding gong or a clanging **c**.

DANCE (DANCING)
Ecc 3: 4 a time to mourn and a time to **d**,
Mt 11: 17 the pipe for you, and you did not **d**;

DANCING (DANCE)
Ps 30: 11 You turned my wailing into **d**;
149: 3 Let them praise his name with **d**

DANGER
Pr 27: 12 The prudent see **d** and take refuge,
Ro 8: 35 or nakedness or **d** or sword?

DANIEL
Hebrew exile to Babylon, name changed to Belteshazzar (Da 1:6–7). Refused to eat unclean food (Da 1:8–21). Interpreted Nebuchadnezzar's dreams (Da 2; 4), writing on the wall (Da 5). Thrown into lions' den (Da 6). Visions of (Da 7–12).

DARK (DARKEST DARKNESS)
Ro 2: 19 a light for those who are in the **d**,
2Pe 1: 19 it, as to a light shining in a **d** place,

DARKEST (DARK)
Ps 23: 4 though I walk through the **d** valley,

DARKNESS (DARK)
Ge 1: 4 he separated the light from the **d**.
2Sa 22: 29 the LORD turns my **d** into light.
Job 34: 22 utter **d**, where evildoers can hide.
Jn 3: 19 but people loved **d** instead of light
2Co 6: 14 fellowship can light have with **d**?
Eph 5: 8 For you were once **d**, but now you
1Pe 2: 9 out of **d** into his wonderful light.
1Jn 1: 5 in him there is no **d** at all.
2: 9 a brother or sister is still in the **d**.

DAUGHTERS
Joel 2: 28 Your sons and **d** will prophesy,

DAVID
Son of Jesse (Ru 4:17–22; 1Ch 2:13–15), ancestor of Jesus (Mt 1:1–17; Lk 3:31).
Anointed king by Samuel (1Sa 16:1–13). Musician to Saul (1Sa 16:14–23; 18:10). Killed Goliath (1Sa 17). Relation with Jonathan (1Sa 18:1–4; 19–20; 23:16–18; 2Sa 1). Disfavor of Saul (1Sa 18:6—23:29). Spared Saul's life (1Sa 24; 26). Among Philistines (1Sa 21:10–14; 27–30). Lament for Saul and Jonathan (2Sa 1).
Anointed king of Judah (2Sa 2:1–11); of Israel (2Sa 5:1–4; 1Ch 11:1–3). Promised eternal dynasty (2Sa 7; 1Ch 17; Ps 132). Adultery with Bathsheba (2Sa 11–12). Absalom's revolt (2Sa 14–18). Last words (2Sa 23:1–7). Death (1Ki 2:10–12; 1Ch 29:28).

DAWN
Ps 37: 6 righteous reward shine like the **d**,

DAY (DAYS)
Ge 1: 5 God called the light "**d**,"
Ex 20: 8 "Remember the Sabbath **d**
Lev 23: 28 because it is the **D** of Atonement,
Nu 14: 14 them in a pillar of cloud by **d**
Jos 1: 8 meditate on it **d** and night,
Ps 84: 10 Better is one **d** in your courts than
96: 2 proclaim his salvation **d** after **d**.
118: 24 The LORD has done it this very **d**;
Pr 27: 1 do not know what a **d** may bring.
Joel 2: 31 great and dreadful **d** of the LORD.
Ob : 15 "The **d** of the LORD is near for all
Lk 11: 3 Give us each **d** our daily bread.
Ac 17: 11 examined the Scriptures every **d**
2Co 4: 16 we are being renewed **d** by **d**.
1Th 5: 2 the **d** of the Lord will come like
2Pe 3: 8 With the Lord a **d** is like a thousand

DAYS (DAY)
Dt 17: 19 he is to read it all the **d** of his life so
Ps 23: 6 love will follow me all the **d** of my
90: 10 Our **d** may come to seventy years,
Ecc 12: 1 Creator in the **d** of your youth,
Joel 2: 29 I will pour out my Spirit in those **d**.
Mic 4: 1 In the last **d** the mountain
Heb 1: 2 in these last **d** he has spoken to us
2Pe 3: 3 that in the last **d** scoffers will come,

DEACONS
1Ti 3: 8 way, **d** are to be worthy of respect,

DEAD (DIE)
Dt 18: 11 or spiritist or who consults the **d**.
Mt 28: 7 'He has risen from the **d** and is
Ro 6: 11 count yourselves **d** to sin but alive
Eph 2: 1 you were **d** in your transgressions
1Th 4: 16 and the **d** in Christ will rise first.
Jas 2: 17 is not accompanied by action, is **d**.
2: 26 so faith without deeds is **d**.

DEATH (DIE)
Nu 35: 16 the murderer is to be put to **d**.
Ps 116: 15 of the LORD is the **d** of his faithful
Pr 8: 36 all who hate me love **d**."
14: 12 right, but in the end it leads to **d**.
Ecc 7: 2 for **d** is the destiny of everyone;
Isa 25: 8 he will swallow up **d** forever.
53: 12 he poured out his life unto **d**,
Jn 5: 24 but has crossed over from **d** to life.
Ro 5: 12 **d** through sin, and in this way **d**
6: 23 For the wages of sin is **d**,
8: 13 Spirit you put to **d** the misdeeds
1Co 15: 21 For since **d** came through a man,
15: 31 I face **d** every day—yes, just as
15: 55 "Where, O **d**, is your victory?
1Pe 3: 18 He was put to **d** in the body
Rev 1: 18 I hold the keys of **d** and Hades.
20: 6 The second **d** has no power over
20: 14 The lake of fire is the second **d**.
21: 4 There will be no more **d**'

DEBAUCHERY
Ro 13: 13 not in sexual immorality and **d**,
Eph 5: 18 drunk on wine, which leads to **d**.

DEBORAH
Prophetess who led Israel to victory over Canaanites (Jdg 4–5).

DEBT (DEBTORS DEBTS)
Ro 13: 8 except the continuing **d** to love

DEBTORS (DEBT)
Mt 6: 12 as we also have forgiven our **d**.

DEBTS (DEBT)
Dt 15: 1 seven years you must cancel **d**.
Mt 6: 12 And forgive us our **d**, as we

† Please see the "Hebrew to English Translation Chart," p. xix.

DECAY
Ps 16: 10 will you let your faithful one see **d**.
Ac 2: 27 will not let your holy one see **d**.

DECEIT (DECEIVE)
Mk 7: 22 greed, malice, **d**, lewdness, envy,
1Pe 2: 1 yourselves of all malice and all **d**,
2: 22 and no **d** was found in his mouth."

DECEITFUL (DECEIVE)
Jer 17: 9 The heart is **d** above all things
2Co 11: 13 are false apostles, **d** workers,

DECEITFULNESS (DECEIVE)
Mk 4: 19 the **d** of wealth and the desires
Heb 3: 13 of you may be hardened by sin's **d**.

† DECEIVE (DECEIT DECEITFUL DECEITFULNESS DECEIVED DECEPTIVE)
Lev 19: 11 "'Do not **d** one another.
Pr 14: 5 An honest witness does not **d**,
Mt 24: 5 am the Messiah,' and will **d** many.
Ro 16: 18 flattery they **d** the minds of naive
1Co 3: 18 Do not **d** yourselves. If any of you
Gal 6: 3 they are not, they **d** themselves.
Eph 5: 6 no one **d** you with empty words,
Jas 1: 22 to the word, and so **d** yourselves.
Jas 1: 26 rein on their tongues **d** themselves,
1Jn 1: 8 we **d** ourselves and the truth is not

DECEIVED (DECEIVE)
Ge 3: 13 said, "The serpent **d** me, and I ate."
Gal 6: 7 Do not be **d**: God cannot be
1Ti 2: 14 And Adam was not the one **d**; it was the woman who was **d**
2Ti 3: 13 to worse, deceiving and being **d**.
Jas 1: 16 Don't be **d**, my dear brothers

DECENCY
1Ti 2: 9 modestly, with **d** and propriety,

DECEPTIVE (DECEIVE)
Pr 31: 30 Charm is **d**, and beauty is fleeting;
Col 2: 8 through hollow and **d** philosophy,

DECLARE (DECLARED DECLARING)
1Ch 16: 24 **D** his glory among the nations,
Ps 19: 1 The heavens **d** the glory of God;
96: 3 **D** his glory among the nations,
Isa 42: 9 taken place, and new things I **d**;
Ro 10: 9 If you **d** with your mouth, "Jesus is

DECLARED (DECLARE)
Mk 7: 19 saying this, Jesus **d** all foods clean.)
Ro 2: 13 the law who will be **d** righteous.
3: 20 no one will be **d** righteous

DECLARING (DECLARE)
Ps 71: 8 **d** your splendor all day long.
Ac 2: 11 hear them **d** the wonders of God

DECREED (DECREES)
La 3: 37 it happen if the Lord has not **d** it?
Lk 22: 22 Son of Man will go as it has been **d**.

DECREES (DECREED)
Lev 10: 11 Israelites all the **d** the LORD has
Ps 119:112 on keeping your **d** to the very end.

DEDICATE (DEDICATION)
Pr 20: 25 It is a trap to **d** something rashly

DEDICATION (DEDICATE)
1Ti 5: 11 sensual desires overcome their **d**

DEED (DEEDS)
Col 3: 17 whether in word or **d**, do it all

DEEDS (DEED)
1Sa 2: 3 knows, and by him **d** are weighed.
Ps 65: 5 us with awesome and righteous **d**,
66: 3 to God, "How awesome are your **d**!
78: 4 next generation the praiseworthy **d**
86: 10 you are great and do marvelous **d**;
92: 4 For you make me glad by your **d**,
111: 3 Glorious and majestic are his **d**,
Hab 3: 2 I stand in awe of your **d**, LORD.
Mt 5: 16 that they may see your good **d**
11: 19 wisdom is proved right by her **d**."
Ac 26: 20 their repentance by their **d**.
Jas 2: 14 claims to have faith but has no **d**?
2: 20 that faith without **d** is useless?
1Pe 2: 12 they may see your good **d**

DEEP (DEPTH)
1Co 2: 10 things, even the **d** things of God.
1Ti 3: 9 must keep hold of the **d** truths

DEER
Ps 42: 1 As the **d** pants for streams of water,

DEFEND (DEFENSE)
Ps 74: 22 Rise up, O God, and **d** your cause;
Pr 31: 9 **d** the rights of the poor and needy.
Jer 50: 34 He will vigorously **d** their cause so

DEFENSE (DEFEND)
Ps 35: 23 Awake, and rise to my **d**!
Php 1: 16 put here for the **d** of the gospel.

DEFERRED
Pr 13: 12 Hope **d** makes the heart sick,

DEFILE (DEFILED)
Da 1: 8 Daniel resolved not to **d** himself

DEFILED (DEFILE)
Isa 24: 5 The earth is **d** by its people;

DEFRAUD
Lev 19: 13 "'Do not **d** or rob your neighbor.

DEITY
Col 2: 9 Christ all the fullness of the **D** lives

DELIGHT (DELIGHTS)
1Sa 15: 22 "Does the LORD **d** in burnt
Ps 1: 2 but whose **d** is in the law
16: 3 noble ones in whom is all my **d**."
35: 9 the LORD and **d** in his salvation.
37: 4 Take **d** in the LORD, and he will
43: 4 of God, to God, my joy and my **d**.
51: 16 You do not **d** in sacrifice,
119: 77 I may live, for your law is my **d**.
Isa 42: 1 my chosen one in whom I **d**;
55: 2 you will **d** in the richest of fare.
61: 10 I **d** greatly in the LORD;
Jer 9: 24 earth, for in these I **d**,"
15: 16 they were my joy and my heart's **d**,
Mic 7: 18 angry forever but **d** to show mercy.
Zep 3: 17 He will take great **d** in you;
Mt 12: 18 the one I love, in whom I **d**;
1Co 13: 6 Love does not **d** in evil but rejoices
2Co 12: 10 for Christ's sake, I **d** in weaknesses,

DELIGHTS (DELIGHT)
Ps 22: 8 deliver him, since he **d** in him."
35: 27 who **d** in the well-being of his
36: 8 them drink from your river of **d**.
Pr 3: 12 he loves, as a father the son he **d** in.
12: 22 **d** in people who are trustworthy.
29: 17 will bring you the **d** you desire.

DELILAH
Woman who betrayed Samson (Jdg 16:4–22).

DELIVER (DELIVERANCE DELIVERED DELIVERER DELIVERS)
Ps 72: 12 he will **d** the needy who cry out,
79: 9 **d** us and forgive our sins for your
Da 3: 17 the God we serve is able to **d** us
Mt 6: 13 but **d** us from the evil one.'
2Co 1: 10 that he will continue to **d** us,

DELIVERANCE (DELIVER)
Ps 3: 8 From the LORD comes **d**.
32: 7 and surround me with songs of **d**.
33: 17 A horse is a vain hope for **d**;

DELIVERED (DELIVER)
Ps 34: 4 he **d** me from all my fears.
Ro 4: 25 He was **d** over to death for our sins

DELIVERER (DELIVER)
Ps 18: 2 is my rock, my fortress and my **d**;
40: 17 You are my help and my **d**;
140: 7 my strong **d**, you shield my head
144: 2 stronghold and my **d**, my shield,

DELIVERS (DELIVER)
Ps 34: 17 he **d** them from all their troubles.
34: 19 the LORD **d** him from them all;
37: 40 The LORD helps them and **d** them;

DEMANDED
Lk 12: 20 This very night your life will be **d**
12: 48 been given much, much will be **d**;

‡ DEMONS
Mt 12: 27 And if I drive out **d** by Beelzebul,
Mk 5: 15 been possessed by the legion of **d**,
Ro 8: 38 life, neither angels nor **d**,
Jas 2: 19 Good! Even the **d** believe that—

DEMONSTRATE (DEMONSTRATES)
Ac 26: 20 **d** their repentance by their deeds.
Ro 3: 26 he did it to **d** his righteousness

DEMONSTRATES (DEMONSTRATE)
Ro 5: 8 God **d** his own love for us in this:

DEN
Da 6: 16 and threw him into the lions' **d**.
Mt 21: 13 but you are making it 'a **d**

DENARIUS
Mk 12: 15 "Bring me a **d** and let me look

DENIED (DENY)
1Ti 5: 8 has **d** the faith and is worse than

DENIES (DENY)
1Jn 2: 23 No one who **d** the Son has

DENY (DENIED DENIES DENYING)
Ex 23: 6 "Do not **d** justice to your poor
Job 27: 5 till I die, I will not **d** my integrity.
La 3: 35 **d** people their rights before the
Lk 9: 23 be my disciple must **d** themselves
Titus 1: 16 but by their actions they **d** him.

DENYING (DENY)
Eze 22: 29 the foreigner, **d** them justice.
2Ti 3: 5 a form of godliness but **d** its power.
2Pe 2: 1 even **d** the sovereign Lord who

DEPART (DEPARTED)
Ge 49: 10 The scepter will not **d** from Judah,
Job 1: 21 mother's womb, and naked I will **d**.
Mt 25: 41 to those on his left, '**D** from me,
Php 1: 23 I desire to **d** and be with Christ,

DEPARTED (DEPART)
1Sa 4: 21 "The Glory has **d** from Israel"—
Ps 119:102 I have not **d** from your laws,

DEPOSIT
2Co 1: 22 put his Spirit in our hearts as a **d**,
5: 5 who has given us the Spirit as a **d**,
Eph 1: 14 who is a **d** guaranteeing our
2Ti 1: 14 Guard the good **d** that was entrusted

DEPRAVED (DEPRAVITY)
Ro 1: 28 God gave them over to a **d** mind,
2Pe 2: 7 was distressed by the **d** conduct

DEPRAVITY (DEPRAVED)
Ro 1: 29 of wickedness, evil, greed and **d**.

DEPRIVE
Dt 24: 17 Do not **d** the foreigner
Pr 18: 5 and so **d** the innocent of justice.
Isa 10: 2 to **d** the poor of their rights
29: 21 with false testimony **d** the innocent
1Co 7: 5 Do not **d** each other except

DEPTH (DEEP)
Ro 8: 39 neither height nor **d**, nor anything
11: 33 the **d** of the riches of the wisdom

DESERTED (DESERTS)
Mt 26: 56 all the disciples **d** him and fled.
2Ti 1: 15 in the province of Asia has **d** me,

DESERTING (DESERTS)
Gal 1: 6 you are so quickly **d** the one who

DESERTS (DESERTED DESERTING)
Zec 11: 17 shepherd, who **d** the flock!

DESERVE (DESERVES)
Ps 103: 10 he does not treat us as our sins **d**
Jer 21: 14 I will punish you as your deeds **d**,
Mt 22: 8 those I invited did not **d** to come.
Ro 1: 32 those who do such things **d** death,

DESERVES (DESERVE)
Lk 10: 7 for the worker **d** his wages.
1Ti 5: 18 and "The worker **d** his wages."

DESIRABLE (DESIRE)
Pr 22: 1 name is more **d** than great riches;

† DESIRE (DESIRABLE DESIRES)
Ge 3: 16 Your **d** will be for your husband,
Dt 5: 21 You shall not set your **d** on your
Ps 40: 6 and offering you did not **d**—
40: 8 I **d** to do your will, my God;
73: 25 earth has nothing I **d** besides you.
Pr 3: 15 nothing you **d** can compare
10: 24 what the righteous **d** will be
11: 23 The **d** of the righteous ends only
19: 2 **D** without knowledge is not good

† Please see the "Hebrew to English Translation Chart," p. xix.
‡ Please see "Key New Testament Terms," p. 1584.

Isa 26: 8 and renown are the **d** of our hearts.
53: 2 appearance that we should **d** him.
55: 11 but will accomplish what I **d**
Hos 6: 6 For I **d** mercy, not sacrifice,
Mt 9: 13 'I **d** mercy, not sacrifice.'
Ro 7: 18 For I have the **d** to do what is good,
1Co 12: 31 Now eagerly **d** the greater gifts.
14: 1 and eagerly **d** gifts of the Spirit,
Php 1: 23 I **d** to depart and be with Christ,
Heb 13: 18 **d** to live honorably in every way.
Jas 1: 15 after **d** has conceived, it gives birth

DESIRES (DESIRE)
Ge 4: 7 it **d** to have you, but you must rule
1Ch 29: 18 keep these **d** and thoughts
Ps 34: 12 life and **d** to see many good days,
37: 4 will give you the **d** of your heart.
103: 5 who satisfies your **d** with good
145: 19 He fulfills the **d** of those who fear
Pr 11: 6 the unfaithful are trapped by evil **d**.
19: 22 What a person **d** is unfailing love;
Mk 4: 19 and the **d** for other things come
Ro 8: 5 minds set on what the Spirit **d**.
13: 14 how to gratify the **d** of the flesh.
Gal 5: 16 and you will not gratify the **d**
5: 17 For the flesh **d** what is contrary
1Ti 3: 1 to be an overseer **d** a noble task.
6: 9 harmful **d** that plunge people
2Ti 2: 22 Flee the evil **d** of youth and pursue
Jas 1: 20 the righteousness that God **d**.
4: 1 from your **d** that battle within you?
1Pe 2: 11 to abstain from sinful **d**,
1Jn 2: 17 The world and its **d** pass away,

DESOLATE
Isa 54: 1 the children of the **d** woman than

DESPAIR
Isa 61: 3 of praise instead of a spirit of **d**.
2Co 4: 8 perplexed, but not in **d**;

DESPISE (DESPISED DESPISES)
Job 42: 6 Therefore I **d** myself and repent
Pr 1: 7 fools **d** wisdom and instruction.
3: 11 do not **d** the LORD's discipline,
14: 21 It is a sin to **d** one's neighbor,
15: 32 disregard discipline **d** themselves,
23: 22 do not **d** your mother when she is
Zec 4: 10 "Who dares **d** the day of small
Lk 16: 13 devoted to the one and **d** the other.
Titus 2: 15 Do not let anyone **d** you.

DESPISED (DESPISE)
Ge 25: 34 and left. So Esau **d** his birthright.
Isa 53: 3 He was **d** and rejected by mankind,
1Co 1: 28 of this world and the **d** things—

DESPISES (DESPISE)
Pr 15: 20 but a foolish man **d** his mother.

DESTINED (DESTINY)
Lk 2: 34 "This child is **d** to cause the falling

DESTINY (DESTINED PREDESTINED)
Ps 73: 17 then I understood their final **d**.
Ecc 7: 2 for death is the **d** of everyone;

DESTITUTE
Pr 31: 8 for the rights of all who are **d**.
Heb 11: 37 in sheepskins and goatskins, **d**,

DESTROY (DESTROYED DESTROYS DESTRUCTION)
Pr 1: 32 complacency of fools will **d** them;
11: 9 the godless **d** their neighbors,
Mt 10: 28 of the One who can **d** both soul

DESTROYED (DESTROY)
Job 19: 26 And after my skin has been **d**,
1Co 8: 11 is **d** by your knowledge.
15: 26 The last enemy to be **d** is death.
2Co 5: 1 if the earthly tent we live in is **d**,
Heb 10: 39 those who shrink back and are **d**,
2Pe 3: 10 the elements will be **d** by fire,

DESTROYS (DESTROY)
Pr 6: 32 whoever does so **d** himself.
18: 9 his work is brother to one who **d**.
28: 24 wrong," is partner to one who **d**.
Ecc 9: 18 but one sinner **d** much good.
1Co 3: 17 If anyone **d** God's temple, God will

DESTRUCTION (DESTROY)
Ps 1: 6 the way of the wicked leads to **d**.
Pr 16: 18 Pride goes before **d**, a haughty
Hos 13: 14 Where, O grave, is your **d**?
Mt 7: 13 broad is the road that leads to **d**,
Gal 6: 8 flesh, from the flesh will reap **d**;
2Th 1: 9 will be punished with everlasting **d**
1Ti 6: 9 that plunge people into ruin and **d**.
2Pe 2: 1 bringing swift **d** on themselves.
3: 16 other Scriptures, to their own **d**.

DETERMINED (DETERMINES)
Job 14: 5 A person's days are **d**;
Isa 14: 26 This is the plan **d** for the whole
Da 11: 36 what has been **d** must take place.

DETERMINES (DETERMINED)
Ps 147: 4 He **d** the number of the stars
1Co 12: 11 them to each one, just as he **d**.

DETESTABLE (DETESTS)
Pr 21: 27 The sacrifice of the wicked is **d**—
28: 9 even their prayers are **d**.
Isa 1: 13 Your incense is **d** to me.
Lk 16: 15 What people value highly is **d**
Titus 1: 16 They are **d**, disobedient and unfit

DETESTS (DETESTABLE)
Dt 22: 5 the LORD your God **d** anyone who
23: 18 the LORD your God **d** them both.
25: 16 the LORD your God **d** anyone who
Pr 11: 1 The LORD **d** dishonest scales,
12: 22 The LORD **d** lying lips, but he
15: 8 The LORD **d** the sacrifice
15: 9 The LORD **d** the way
15: 26 The LORD **d** the thoughts
16: 5 The LORD **d** all the proud
17: 15 the LORD **d** them both.
20: 23 The LORD **d** differing weights,

DEVIL (DEVIL'S)
Mt 13: 39 the enemy who sows them is the **d**.
25: 41 the eternal fire prepared for the **d**
Lk 4: 2 forty days he was tempted by the **d**.
8: 12 then the **d** comes and takes away
Eph 4: 27 and do not give the **d** a foothold.
2Ti 2: 26 and escape from the trap of the **d**,
Jas 4: 7 Resist the **d**, and he will flee
1Pe 5: 8 Your enemy the **d** prowls around
1Jn 3: 8 who does what is sinful is of the **d**,
Rev 12: 9 that ancient serpent called the **d**,

DEVIL'S (DEVIL)
Eph 6: 11 your stand against the **d** schemes.
1Ti 3: 7 into disgrace and into the **d** trap.
1Jn 3: 8 was to destroy the **d** work.

DEVISED
2Pe 1: 16 we did not follow cleverly **d** stories

† **DEVOTE** (DEVOTED DEVOTING DEVOTION DEVOUT)
Job 11: 13 "Yet if you **d** your heart to him
Jer 30: 21 who is he who will **d** himself to be
Col 4: 2 **D** yourselves to prayer,
1Ti 4: 13 **d** yourself to the public reading
Titus 3: 8 may be careful to **d** themselves

† **DEVOTED** (DEVOTE)
Ezr 7: 10 For Ezra had **d** himself to the study
Ac 2: 42 They **d** themselves to the apostles'
Ro 12: 10 Be **d** to one another in love.
1Co 7: 34 Her aim is to be **d** to the Lord

DEVOTING (DEVOTE)
1Ti 5: 10 **d** herself to all kinds of good deeds.

DEVOTION (DEVOTE)
1Ch 28: 9 serve him with wholehearted **d**
1Co 7: 35 way in undivided **d** to the Lord.
2Co 11: 3 your sincere and pure **d** to Christ.

DEVOUR
2Sa 2: 26 to Joab, "Must the sword **d** forever?
Mk 12: 40 They **d** widows' houses
1Pe 5: 8 lion looking for someone to **d**.

DEVOUT (DEVOTE)
Lk 2: 25 Simeon, who was righteous and **d**.

DIE (DEAD DEATH DIED DIES)
Ge 2: 17 eat from it you will certainly **d**."
Ex 11: 5 Every firstborn son in Egypt will **d**,
Ru 1: 17 Where you **d** I will **d**, and there I
2Ki 14: 6 each will **d** for their own sin."
Pr 5: 23 For lack of discipline they will **d**,
10: 21 many, but fools **d** for lack of sense.
11: 7 placed in mortals **d** with them;
15: 10 one who hates correction will **d**.
23: 13 them with the rod, they will not **d**.
Ecc 3: 2 a time to be born and a time to **d**,
Isa 66: 24 the worms that eat them will not **d**,
Eze 3: 18 wicked person will **d** for their sin,
18: 4 one who sins is the one who will **d**.
33: 8 wicked person will **d** for their sin,
Mt 26: 52 all who draw the sword will **d**
Jn 11: 25 in me will live, even though they **d**;
11: 26 by believing in me will never **d**.
Ro 5: 7 Very rarely will anyone **d**
14: 8 and if we **d**, we **d** for the Lord.
1Co 15: 22 For as in Adam all **d**, so in Christ
Php 1: 21 to live is Christ and to **d** is gain.
Heb 9: 27 as people are destined to **d** once,
Rev 14: 13 Blessed are the dead who **d**

DIED (DIE)
Ro 5: 6 Christ **d** for the ungodly.
6: 2 We are those who have **d** to sin;
6: 8 Now if we **d** with Christ, we believe
14: 15 someone for whom Christ **d**.
1Co 8: 11 for whom Christ **d**, is destroyed
15: 3 that Christ **d** for our sins according
2Co 5: 14 one **d** for all, and therefore all **d**.
Col 3: 3 For you **d**, and your life is now
1Th 5: 10 He **d** for us so that, whether we are
2Ti 2: 11 If we **d** with him, we will also live
Heb 9: 15 that he has **d** as a ransom to set
Rev 2: 8 Last, who **d** and came to life again.

DIES (DIE)
Job 14: 14 If someone **d**, will they live again?
1Co 15: 36 does not come to life unless it **d**.

DIFFERENCE (DIFFERENT)
Ro 10: 12 For there is no **d** between Jew

DIFFERENT (DIFFERENCE)
1Co 12: 4 There are **d** kinds of gifts,
2Co 11: 4 or a **d** gospel from the one you

DIGNITY
Pr 31: 25 She is clothed with strength and **d**;

DIGS
Pr 26: 27 Whoever **d** a pit will fall into it;

DILIGENCE (DILIGENT)
Heb 6: 11 show this same **d** to the very end,

DILIGENT (DILIGENCE)
Pr 21: 5 The plans of the **d** lead to profit as
1Ti 4: 15 Be **d** in these matters;

DIRECT (DIRECTS)
Ps 119: 35 **D** me in the path of your
119:133 **D** my footsteps according to your
Jer 10: 23 it is not for them to **d** their steps.
2Th 3: 5 May the Lord **d** your hearts

DIRECTS (DIRECT)
Ps 42: 8 By day the LORD **d** his love,
Isa 48: 17 who **d** you in the way you should

DIRGE
Mt 11: 17 we sang a **d**, and you did not

DISAPPEAR
Mt 5: 18 until heaven and earth **d**,
Lk 16: 17 earth to **d** than for the least stroke

DISASTER
Ps 57: 1 your wings until the **d** has passed.
Pr 3: 25 Have no fear of sudden **d**
17: 5 whoever gloats over **d** will not go
Isa 45: 7 I bring prosperity and create **d**;
Eze 7: 5 Unheard-of **d**! See, it comes!

DISCERN (DISCERNING)
Ps 19: 12 But who can **d** their own errors?
139: 3 You **d** my going out and my lying
Php 1: 10 you may be able to **d** what is best

DISCERNING (DISCERN)
Pr 14: 6 knowledge comes easily to the **d**.
15: 14 The **d** heart seeks knowledge,
17: 10 A rebuke impresses a **d** person
17: 24 A **d** person keeps wisdom in view,
17: 28 and **d** if they hold their tongues.
19: 25 rebuke the **d**, and they will gain
28: 11 and **d** sees how deluded they are.

DISCIPLE (DISCIPLES)
Mt 10: 42 of these little ones who is my **d**,
Lk 14: 27 and follow me cannot be my **d**.

‡ **DISCIPLES** (DISCIPLE)
Mt 28: 19 go and make **d** of all nations,
Jn 8: 31 my teaching, you are really my **d**.

† Please see the "Hebrew to English Translation Chart," p. xix.
‡ Please see "Key New Testament Terms," p. 1584.

Jn 13: 35 will know that you are my **d**, if you
Ac 11: 26 The **d** were called Christians first

DISCIPLINE (DISCIPLINED DISCIPLINES)
Ps 38: 1 your anger or **d** me in your wrath.
39: 11 rebuke and **d** anyone for their sin,
94: 12 Blessed is the one you **d**, LORD,
Pr 3: 11 do not despise the LORD's **d**,
5: 12 You will say, "How I hated **d**!
5: 23 For lack of **d** they will die,
10: 17 Whoever heeds **d** shows the way
12: 1 Whoever loves **d** loves knowledge,
13: 18 Whoever disregards **d** comes
13: 24 their children is careful to **d** them.
15: 5 A fool spurns a parent's **d**,
15: 32 disregard **d** despise themselves,
19: 18 **D** your children, for in that there is
19: 20 Listen to advice and accept **d**,
22: 15 the rod of **d** will drive it far away.
23: 13 Do not withhold **d** from a child;
29: 17 **D** your children, and they will give
Heb 12: 5 do not make light of the Lord's **d**,
12: 7 Endure hardship as **d**;
12: 11 No **d** seems pleasant at the time,
Rev 3: 19 Those whom I love I rebuke and **d**.

DISCIPLINED (DISCIPLINE)
Jer 31: 18 'You **d** me like an unruly calf,
1Co 11: 32 we are being **d** so that we will not
Col 2: 5 delight to see how **d** you are
Titus 1: 8 upright, holy and **d**.
Heb 12: 7 For what children are not **d** by

DISCIPLINES (DISCIPLINE)
Dt 8: 5 so the LORD your God **d** you.
Pr 3: 12 because the LORD **d** those he
Heb 12: 6 the Lord **d** the one he loves,
12: 10 but God **d** us for our good,

DISCLOSED
Lk 8: 17 nothing hidden that will not be **d**,

DISCOURAGED
Jos 1: 9 do not be **d**, for the LORD your
10: 25 "Do not be afraid; do not be **d**.
1Ch 28: 20 Do not be afraid or **d**,
Isa 42: 4 or be **d** till he establishes justice
Col 3: 21 children, or they will become **d**.

DISCREDITED
2Co 6: 3 so that our ministry will not be **d**.

DISCRETION
1Ch 22: 12 May the LORD give you **d**
Pr 1: 4 knowledge and **d** to the young—
2: 11 **D** will protect you,
5: 2 that you may maintain **d** and your
8: 12 I possess knowledge and **d**.
11: 22 beautiful woman who shows no **d**.

DISCRIMINATED
Jas 2: 4 have you not **d** among yourselves

DISFIGURED
Isa 52: 14 his appearance was so **d** beyond

DISGRACE (DISGRACEFUL DISGRACES)
Pr 11: 2 then comes **d**, but with humility
19: 26 is a child who brings shame and **d**.
Ac 5: 41 worthy of suffering **d** for the Name.
Heb 13: 13 the camp, bearing the **d** he bore.

DISGRACEFUL (DISGRACE)
Pr 10: 5 sleeps during harvest is a **d** son.
17: 2 servant will rule over a **d** son

DISGRACES (DISGRACE)
Pr 28: 7 companion of gluttons **d** his father.
29: 15 left undisciplined **d** its mother.

DISGUISE
Pr 26: 24 Enemies **d** themselves with their

DISHONEST
Pr 11: 1 The LORD detests **d** scales,
29: 27 The righteous detest the **d**;
Lk 16: 10 whoever is **d** with very little will
1Ti 3: 8 wine, and not pursuing **d** gain.

DISHONOR (DISHONORS)
Lev 18: 7 "'Do not **d** your father by having
Pr 30: 9 and so **d** the name of my God.
1Co 13: 5 It does not **d** others, it is not
15: 43 it is sown in **d**, it is raised in glory;

DISHONORS (DISHONOR)
Dt 27: 16 is anyone who **d** their father

DISMAYED
Isa 41: 10 do not be **d**, for I am your God.

DISOBEDIENCE (DISOBEY)
Ro 5: 19 as through the **d** of the one man
11: 32 has bound everyone over to **d** so
Heb 2: 2 and **d** received its just punishment,
4: 6 did not go in because of their **d**,
4: 11 by following their example of **d**.

DISOBEDIENT (DISOBEY)
2Ti 3: 2 proud, abusive, **d** to their parents,
Titus 1: 6 to the charge of being wild and **d**.
1: 16 **d** and unfit for doing anything

DISOBEY (DISOBEDIENCE DISOBEDIENT)
Dt 11: 28 the curse if you **d** the commands
2Ch 24: 20 'Why do you **d** the LORD's
Ro 1: 30 of doing evil; they **d** their parents;

DISORDER
1Co 14: 33 For God is not a God of **d**
2Co 12: 20 slander, gossip, arrogance and **d**.
Jas 3: 16 there you find **d** and every evil

DISOWN
Pr 30: 9 I may have too much and **d** you
Mt 10: 33 will **d** before my Father in heaven.
26: 35 to die with you, I will never **d** you."
2Ti 2: 12 If we **d** him, he will also **d** us;

DISPLAY (DISPLAYS)
Eze 39: 21 "I will **d** my glory among
1Ti 1: 16 Christ Jesus might **d** his immense

DISPLAYS (DISPLAY)
Isa 44: 23 Jacob, he **d** his glory in Israel.

DISPUTE (DISPUTES)
Pr 17: 14 the matter before a **d** breaks out.
1Co 6: 1 If any of you has a **d** with another,

DISPUTES (DISPUTE)
Pr 18: 18 Casting the lot settles **d** and keeps

DISQUALIFIED
1Co 9: 27 I myself will not be **d** for the prize.

DISREGARD
Pr 15: 32 Those who **d** discipline despise

DISREPUTE
2Pe 2: 2 will bring the way of truth into **d**.

DISSENSION
Ro 13: 13 debauchery, not in **d** and jealousy.

DISTINGUISH
1Ki 3: 9 and to **d** between right and wrong.
Heb 5: 14 have trained themselves to **d** good

DISTORT
2Co 4: 2 nor do we **d** the word of God.
2Pe 3: 16 ignorant and unstable people **d**,

DISTRESS (DISTRESSED)
Ps 18: 6 In my **d** I called to the LORD;
Jnh 2: 2 "In my **d** I called to the LORD,
Jas 1: 27 and widows in their **d** and to keep

DISTRESSED (DISTRESS)
Ro 14: 15 sister is **d** because of what you eat,

DIVIDED (DIVISION)
Mt 12: 25 "Every kingdom **d** against itself
Lk 23: 34 **d** up his clothes by casting lots.
1Co 1: 13 Is Christ **d**? Was Paul crucified

‡ DIVINATION
Lev 19: 26 "'Do not practice **d** or seek

DIVINE
Ro 1: 20 his eternal power and **d** nature—
2Co 10: 4 they have **d** power to demolish
2Pe 1: 4 may participate in the **d** nature,

DIVISION (DIVIDED DIVISIONS DIVISIVE)
Lk 12: 51 peace on earth? No, I tell you, but **d**.
1Co 12: 25 there should be no **d** in the body,

DIVISIONS (DIVISION)
Ro 16: 17 to watch out for those who cause **d**
1Co 1: 10 and that there be no **d** among you,
11: 18 as a church, there are **d** among you,

DIVISIVE (DIVISION)
Titus 3: 10 Warn a **d** person once,

DIVORCE (DIVORCES)
Mt 19: 3 for a man to **d** his wife for any
1Co 7: 11 a husband must not **d** his wife.

DIVORCES (DIVORCE)
Mal 2: 16 man who hates and **d** his wife,"

DOCTOR
Mt 9: 12 "It is not the healthy who need a **d**,

DOCTRINE
1Ti 4: 16 Watch your life and **d** closely.
Titus 2: 1 what is appropriate to sound **d**.

DOMINION
Ps 22: 28 for **d** belongs to the LORD and he

DOOR
Ps 141: 3 keep watch over the **d** of my lips.
Mt 6: 6 close the **d** and pray to your Father,
7: 7 and the **d** will be opened to you.
Rev 3: 20 I stand at the **d** and knock.

DOORKEEPER
Ps 84: 10 I would rather be a **d** in the house

DOUBLE-EDGED
Heb 4: 12 Sharper than any **d** sword,
Rev 1: 16 of his mouth was a sharp, **d** sword.
2: 12 of him who has the sharp, **d** sword.

DOUBLE-MINDED (MIND)
Ps 119:113 I hate **d** people, but I love your law.
Jas 1: 8 Such a person is **d** and unstable

DOUBT
Mt 14: 31 faith," he said, "why did you **d**?"
21: 21 if you have faith and do not **d**,
Mk 11: 23 and does not **d** in their heart
Jas 1: 6 you must believe and not **d**,
Jude : 22 Be merciful to those who **d**;

DOWNCAST
Ps 42: 5 Why, my soul, are you **d**?
2Co 7: 6 who comforts the **d**, comforted us

DRAW (DRAWING DRAWS)
Mt 26: 52 "for all who **d** the sword will die
Jn 12: 32 earth, will **d** all people to myself."
Heb 10: 22 let us **d** near to God with a sincere

DRAWING (DRAW)
Lk 21: 28 your redemption is **d** near."

DRAWS (DRAW)
Jn 6: 44 the Father who sent me **d** them,

DREADFUL
Heb 10: 31 It is a **d** thing to fall into the hands

DRESS
1Ti 2: 9 want the women to **d** modestly,

DRINK (DRUNK DRUNKARDS DRUNKENNESS)
Pr 5: 15 **D** water from your own cistern,
Lk 12: 19 eat, **d** and be merry."'
Jn 7: 37 who is thirsty come to me and **d**.
1Co 12: 13 were all given the one Spirit to **d**.

DRIVES
1Jn 4: 18 But perfect love **d** out fear,

DROP
Pr 17: 14 so **d** the matter before a dispute
Isa 40: 15 Surely the nations are like a **d**

DRUNK (DRINK)
Eph 5: 18 Do not get **d** on wine, which leads

DRUNKARDS (DRINK)
Pr 23: 21 for **d** and gluttons become poor,
1Co 6: 10 the greedy nor **d** nor slanderers

DRUNKENNESS (DRINK)
Lk 21: 34 **d** and the anxieties of life,
Ro 13: 13 not in carousing and **d**,
Gal 5: 21 and envy; **d**, orgies, and the like.
1Pe 4: 3 living in debauchery, lust, **d**, orgies,

DRY
Isa 53: 2 and like a root out of **d** ground.
Eze 37: 4 bones and say to them, '**D** bones,

DUST
Ge 2: 7 a man from the **d** of the ground
Ps 103: 14 he remembers that we are **d**.
Ecc 3: 20 come from **d**, and to **d** all return.

DUTY
Ecc 12: 13 for this is the **d** of all mankind.
Ac 23: 1 I have fulfilled my **d** to God in all
1Co 7: 3 husband should fulfill his marital **d**

DWELL (DWELLING DWELLS)
1Ki 8: 27 "But will God really **d** on earth?
Ps 23: 6 I will **d** in the house of the LORD
Isa 43: 18 do not **d** on the past.
Eph 3: 17 Christ may **d** in your hearts
Col 1: 19 to have all his fullness **d** in him,
3: 16 of Christ **d** among you richly

‡ Please see "Key New Testament Terms," p. 1584.

DWELLING (DWELL)
Eph 2: 22 built together to become a **d**

DWELLS (DWELL)
1Co 3: 16 that God's Spirit **d** in your midst?

EAGER
Pr 31: 13 and flax and works with **e** hands.
1Pe 5: 2 dishonest gain, but **e** to serve;

EAGLE'S (EAGLES)
Ps 103: 5 your youth is renewed like the **e**.

EAGLES (EAGLE'S)
Isa 40: 31 They will soar on wings like **e**;

EAR (EARS)
1Co 2: 9 eye has seen, what no **e** has heard,
12: 16 And if the **e** should say, "Because I

EARS (EAR)
Job 42: 5 My **e** had heard of you but now my
Ps 34: 15 and his **e** are attentive to their cry;
Pr 21: 13 Whoever shuts their **e** to the cry
2Ti 4: 3 to say what their itching **e** want

EARTH (EARTHLY)
Ge 1: 1 God created the heavens and the **e**.
Ps 24: 1 The **e** is the LORD's,
108: 5 let your glory be over all the **e**.
Isa 6: 3 the whole **e** is full of his glory."
51: 6 the **e** will wear out like a garment
55: 9 the heavens are higher than the **e**,
66: 1 throne, and the **e** is my footstool.
Jer 23: 24 "Do not I fill heaven and **e**?"
Hab 2: 20 let all the **e** be silent before him.
Mt 6: 10 will be done, on **e** as it is in heaven.
16: 19 you bind on **e** will be bound
24: 35 Heaven and **e** will pass away,
28: 18 and on **e** has been given to me.
Lk 2: 14 on **e** peace to those on whom his
1Co 10: 26 for, "The **e** is the Lord's,
Php 2: 10 heaven and on **e** and under the **e**,
2Pe 3: 13 to a new heaven and a new **e**,

EARTHLY (EARTH)
Php 3: 19 Their mind is set on **e** things.
Col 3: 2 on things above, not on **e** things.

EAST
Ps 103: 12 as far as the **e** is from the west,

EASY
Mt 11: 30 For my yoke is **e** and my burden is

EAT (EATING)
Ge 2: 17 you must not **e** from the tree
Isa 55: 1 have no money, come, buy and **e**!
65: 25 the lion will **e** straw like the ox,
Mt 26: 26 his disciples, saying, "Take and **e**;
Ro 14: 2 faith allows them to **e** anything,
1Co 8: 13 if what I **e** causes my brother
10: 31 So whether you **e** or drink
2Th 3: 10 is unwilling to work shall not **e**."

EATING (EAT)
Ro 14: 17 kingdom of God is not a matter of **e**

EDICT
Heb 11: 23 they were not afraid of the king's **e**.

EDIFIES
1Co 14: 4 speaks in a tongue **e** themselves,

EFFECT
Isa 32: 17 its **e** will be quietness
Heb 9: 18 was not put into **e** without blood.

EFFORT
Lk 13: 24 "Make every **e** to enter through
Ro 9: 16 depend on human desire or **e**,
14: 19 Let us therefore make every **e** to do
Eph 4: 3 Make every **e** to keep the unity
Heb 4: 11 make every **e** to enter that rest,
12: 14 Make every **e** to live in peace
2Pe 1: 5 make every **e** to add to your faith
3: 14 make every **e** to be found spotless,

ELAH
Son of Baasha; king of Israel (1Ki 16:6–14).

ELDERLY (ELDERS)
Lev 19: 32 show respect for the **e** and revere

ELDERS (ELDERLY)
1Ti 5: 17 The **e** who direct the affairs

ELECTION
Ro 9: 11 God's purpose in **e** might stand:
2Pe 1: 10 to confirm your calling and **e**.

ELI
High priest in youth of Samuel (1Sa 1–4). Blessed Hannah (1Sa 1:12–18); raised Samuel (1Sa 2:11–26).

ELIJAH
Prophet; predicted famine in Israel (1Ki 17:1; Jas 5:17). Fed by ravens (1Ki 17:2–6). Raised Sidonian widow's son (1Ki 17:7–24). Defeated prophets of Baal at Carmel (1Ki 18:16–46). Ran from Jezebel (1Ki 19:1–9). Prophesied death of Azariah (2Ki 1). Succeeded by Elisha (1Ki 19:19–21; 2Ki 2:1–18). Taken to heaven in whirlwind (2Ki 2:11–12).
Return prophesied (Mal 4:5–6); equated with John the Baptist (Mt 17:9–13; Mk 9:9–13; Lk 1:17). Appeared with Moses in transfiguration of Jesus (Mt 17:1–8; Mk 9:1–8).

ELISHA
Prophet; successor of Elijah (1Ki 19:16–21); inherited his cloak (2Ki 2:1–18). Miracles of (2Ki 2–6).

ELIZABETH
Mother of John the Baptist, relative of Mary (Lk 1:5–58).

EMBITTER
Col 3: 21 Fathers, do not **e** your children,

EMPEROR
1Pe 2: 17 of believers, fear God, honor the **e**.

EMPTY
Mt 12: 36 for every **e** word they have spoken.
Eph 5: 6 no one deceive you with **e** words,
1Pe 1: 18 you were redeemed from the **e** way

ENABLE (ABLE)
Lk 1: 74 to **e** us to serve him without fear
Ac 4: 29 **e** your servants to speak your word

ENABLED (ABLE)
Lev 26: 13 **e** you to walk with heads held high.
Jn 6: 65 me unless the Father has **e** them."

ENABLES (ABLE)
Php 3: 21 by the power that **e** him to bring

ENCAMPS
Ps 34: 7 the LORD **e** around those who fear

ENCOURAGE (ENCOURAGEMENT ENCOURAGING)
Ps 10: 17 you **e** them, and you listen to their
Ac 15: 32 said much to **e** and strengthen
Ro 12: 8 if it is to **e**, then give
1Th 4: 18 Therefore **e** one another with these
2Ti 4: 2 correct, rebuke and **e**
Titus 2: 6 Similarly, **e** the young men to be
Heb 3: 13 But **e** one another daily, as long as

ENCOURAGEMENT (ENCOURAGE)
Ac 4: 36 (which means "son of **e**"),
Ro 15: 4 the **e** they provide we might have
15: 5 **e** give you the same attitude of
Heb 12: 5 completely forgotten this word of **e**

ENCOURAGING (ENCOURAGE)
1Co 14: 3 their strengthening, **e** and comfort.
Heb 10: 25 habit of doing, but **e** one another—

END
Ps 119: 33 that I may follow it to the **e**.
Pr 14: 12 right, but in the **e** it leads to death.
19: 20 the **e** you will be counted among
23: 32 In the **e** it bites like a snake
Ecc 12: 12 making many books there is no **e**,
Mt 10: 22 stands firm to the **e** will be saved.
Lk 21: 9 but the **e** will not come right away."
1Co 15: 24 Then the **e** will come, when he

ENDURANCE (ENDURE)
Ro 15: 4 so that through the **e** taught
15: 5 May the God who gives **e**
2Co 1: 6 you patient **e** of the same sufferings
Col 1: 11 might so that you may have great **e**
1Ti 6: 11 faith, love, **e** and gentleness.
Titus 2: 2 and sound in faith, in love and in **e**.

ENDURE (ENDURANCE ENDURES)
Ps 72: 17 May his name **e** forever;
Pr 12: 19 Truthful lips **e** forever, but a lying
27: 24 for riches do not **e** forever,
Ecc 3: 14 everything God does will **e** forever;
Mal 3: 2 who can **e** the day of his coming?
2Ti 2: 12 if we **e**, we will also reign with him.
Heb 12: 7 **E** hardship as discipline;
Rev 3: 10 kept my command to **e** patiently,

ENDURES (ENDURE)
Ps 112: 9 poor, their righteousness **e** forever;
136: 1 *His love **e** forever.*

Da 9: 15 yourself a name that **e** to this day,
1Pe 1: 25 but the word of the Lord **e** forever."

ENEMIES (ENEMY)
Ps 23: 5 before me in the presence of my **e**.
Mic 7: 6 a man's **e** are the members of his
Mt 5: 44 love your **e** and pray for those who
Lk 20: 43 until I make your **e** a footstool

ENEMY (ENEMIES ENMITY)
Pr 24: 17 Do not gloat when your **e** falls;
25: 21 If your **e** is hungry, give him food
27: 6 trusted, but an **e** multiplies kisses.
1Co 15: 26 The last **e** to be destroyed is death.
1Ti 5: 14 and to give the **e** no opportunity
Jas 4: 4 of the world becomes an **e** of God.

ENJOY (JOY)
Dt 6: 2 and so that you may **e** long life.
Eph 6: 3 and that you may **e** long life
Heb 11: 25 than to **e** the fleeting pleasures

ENJOYMENT (JOY)
Ecc 4: 8 why am I depriving myself of **e**?"
1Ti 6: 17 us with everything for our **e**.

ENLIGHTENED (LIGHT)
Eph 1: 18 eyes of your heart may be **e** in
Heb 6: 4 for those who have once been **e**,

ENMITY (ENEMY)
Ge 3: 15 I will put **e** between you

ENOCH
Walked with God and taken by him (Ge 5:18–24; Heb 11:5). Prophet (Jude 14).

ENTANGLED (ENTANGLES)
2Ti 2: 4 soldier gets **e** in civilian affairs,
2Pe 2: 20 Jesus Christ and are again **e** in it

ENTANGLES (ENTANGLED)
Heb 12: 1 hinders and the sin that so easily **e**.

ENTER (ENTERED ENTERS)
Ps 100: 4 **E** his gates with thanksgiving
Mt 5: 20 will certainly not **e** the kingdom
7: 13 "**E** through the narrow gate.
18: 8 It is better for you to **e** life maimed
Mk 10: 15 like a little child will never **e** it."
10: 23 the rich to **e** the kingdom of God!"

ENTERED (ENTER)
Ro 5: 12 just as sin **e** the world through one
Heb 9: 12 he **e** the Most Holy Place once

ENTERS (ENTER)
Mk 7: 18 that nothing that **e** a person
Jn 10: 2 The one who **e** by the gate is

ENTERTAIN
1Ti 5: 19 Do not **e** an accusation against

ENTHRALLED
Ps 45: 11 Let the king be **e** by your beauty;

ENTHRONED (THRONE)
1Sa 4: 4 who is **e** between the cherubim.
Ps 2: 4 The One **e** in heaven laughs;
102: 12 But you, LORD, sit **e** forever;
Isa 40: 22 He sits **e** above the circle

ENTICE
Pr 1: 10 if sinful men **e** you, do not give
2Pe 2: 18 they **e** people who are just escaping

ENTIRE
Gal 5: 14 For the **e** law is fulfilled in keeping

ENTRUSTED (TRUST)
1Ti 6: 20 guard what has been **e** to your care.
2Ti 1: 12 to guard what I have **e** to him until
1: 14 good deposit that was **e** to you—
Jude : 3 once for all **e** to God's holy people.

ENVY
Pr 3: 31 Do not **e** the violent or choose any
14: 30 to the body, but **e** rots the bones.
1Co 13: 4 It does not **e**, it does not boast,

EPHRAIM
1. Second son of Joseph (Ge 41:52; 46:20). Blessed as firstborn by Jacob (Ge 48).
2. Synonymous with Northern Kingdom (Isa 7:17; Hos 5).

EQUAL
Isa 40: 25 Or who is my **e**?" says the Holy
Jn 5: 18 Father, making himself **e** with God.
1Co 12: 25 its parts should have **e** concern

EQUIP (EQUIPPED)
Eph 4: 12 to **e** his people for works of service,
Heb 13: 21 **e** you with everything good

EQUIPPED (EQUIP)
2Ti 3: 17 God may be thoroughly **e** for every

ERROR
Jas 5: 20 the **e** of their way will save them

ESAU
Firstborn of Isaac, twin of Jacob (Ge 25:21–26). Also called Edom (Ge 25:30). Sold Jacob his birthright (Ge 25:29–34); lost blessing (Ge 27). Reconciled to Jacob (Gen 33).

ESCAPE (ESCAPING)
Ro 2: 3 think you will **e** God's judgment?
Heb 2: 3 how shall we **e** if we ignore so great

ESCAPING (ESCAPE)
1Co 3: 15 only as one **e** through the flames.

ESTABLISH (ESTABLISHED ESTABLISHES)
Ge 6: 18 But I will **e** my covenant with you,
1Ch 28: 7 I will **e** his kingdom forever if he is
Ro 10: 3 of God and sought to **e** their own,

ESTABLISHED (ESTABLISH)
Ps 8: 2 infants you have **e** a stronghold

ESTABLISHES (ESTABLISH)
Pr 16: 9 course, but the LORD **e** their steps.

ESTEEM (ESTEEMED)
Isa 53: 3 and we held him in low **e**.

ESTEEMED (ESTEEM)
Pr 22: 1 to be **e** is better than silver or gold.

ESTHER
Jewess who lived in Persia; cousin of Mordecai (Est 2:7). Chosen queen of Xerxes (Est 2:8–18). Foiled Haman's plan to exterminate the Jews (Est 3–4; 7–9).

‡ **ETERNAL** (ETERNITY)
Ps 16: 11 with **e** pleasures at your right hand.
111: 10 To him belongs **e** praise.
119: 89 Your word, LORD, is **e**;
Isa 26: 4 the LORD himself, is the Rock **e**.
Mt 19: 16 good thing must I do to get **e** life?"
25: 41 the **e** fire prepared for the devil
25: 46 but the righteous to **e** life."
Jn 3: 15 who believes may have **e** life
3: 16 him shall not perish but have **e** life.
3: 36 believes in the Son has **e** life,
4: 14 of water welling up to **e** life."
5: 24 believes him who sent me has **e** life
6: 47 the one who believes has **e** life.
6: 68 You have the words of **e** life.
10: 28 I give them **e** life, and they shall
17: 3 Now this is **e** life: that they know
Ro 1: 20 his **e** power and divine nature—
6: 23 of God is **e** life in Christ Jesus our
2Co 4: 17 for us an **e** glory that far outweighs
4: 18 temporary, but what is unseen is **e**.
1Ti 1: 16 believe in him and receive **e** life.
1: 17 Now to the King **e**, immortal,
Heb 9: 12 thus obtaining **e** redemption.
1Jn 5: 11 God has given us **e** life, and this life
5: 13 you may know that you have **e** life.

ETERNITY (ETERNAL)
Ps 93: 2 you are from all **e**.
Ecc 3: 11 has also set **e** in the human heart;

ETHIOPIAN
Jer 13: 23 Can an **E** change his skin

EUNUCHS
Mt 19: 12 choose to live like **e** for the sake

EVANGELIST (EVANGELISTS)
2Ti 4: 5 do the work of an **e**, discharge all

EVANGELISTS (EVANGELIST)
Eph 4: 11 the **e**, the pastors and teachers,

EVE
2Co 11: 3 afraid that just as **E** was deceived
1Ti 2: 13 For Adam was formed first, then **E**.

EVEN-TEMPERED
Pr 17: 27 whoever has understanding is **e**.

EVER (EVERLASTING FOREVER)
Ex 15: 18 "The LORD reigns for **e** and **e**."
Dt 8: 19 you **e** forget the LORD your God
Ps 5: 11 you be glad; let them **e** sing for joy.
10: 16 The LORD is King for **e** and **e**;
25: 3 one who hopes in you will **e** be put
45: 6 throne, O God, will last for **e** and **e**;
52: 8 I trust in God's unfailing love for **e**
89: 33 nor will I **e** betray my faithfulness.
145: 1 I will praise your name for **e** and **e**.
Pr 4: 18 shining **e** brighter till the full light
5: 19 may you **e** be intoxicated with her
Isa 66: 8 Who has **e** heard of such things?
Jer 31: 36 "will Israel **e** cease being a nation
Da 7: 18 possess it forever—yes, for **e** and **e**.'
12: 3 like the stars for **e** and **e**.
Mk 4: 12 "'they may be **e** seeing but never
Jn 1: 18 No one has **e** seen God, but
Rev 1: 18 now look, I am alive for **e** and **e**!
22: 5 And they will reign for **e** and **e**.

EVER-INCREASING (INCREASE)
Ro 6: 19 to impurity and to **e** wickedness,
2Co 3: 18 into his image with **e** glory,

† **EVERLASTING** (EVER)
Dt 33: 27 and underneath are the **e** arms.
Ne 9: 5 your God, who is from **e** to **e**."
Ps 90: 2 world, from **e** to **e** you are God.
139: 24 in me, and lead me in the way **e**.
Isa 9: 6 Mighty God, **E** Father,
33: 14 of us can dwell with **e** burning?"
35: 10 **e** joy will crown their heads.
45: 17 by the LORD with an **e** salvation;
54: 8 **e** kindness I will have compassion
55: 3 I will make an **e** covenant with you,
63: 12 them, to gain for himself **e** renown,
Jer 31: 3 "I have loved you with an **e** love;
Da 9: 24 to bring in **e** righteousness, to seal
12: 2 some to **e** life, others to shame and **e** contempt.
2Th 1: 9 will be punished with **e** destruction
Jude 6 bound with **e** chains for judgment

EVER-PRESENT
Ps 46: 1 and strength, an **e** help in trouble.

EVIDENCE (EVIDENT)
Jn 14: 11 on the **e** of the works themselves.

EVIDENT (EVIDENCE)
Php 4: 5 Let your gentleness be **e** to all.

† **EVIL** (EVILDOER EVILDOERS)
Ge 2: 9 of the knowledge of good and **e**.
Job 1: 1 he feared God and shunned **e**.
1: 8 a man who fears God and shuns **e**."
34: 10 Far be it from God to do **e**,
Ps 23: 4 will fear no **e**, for you are with me;
34: 14 Turn from **e** and do good;
51: 4 and done what is **e** in your sight;
97: 10 those who love the LORD hate **e**,
101: 4 have nothing to do with what is **e**.
Pr 8: 13 To fear the LORD is to hate **e**;
11: 27 **e** comes to one who searches for it.
Isa 5: 20 who call **e** good and good **e**,
13: 11 I will punish the world for its **e**,
Hab 1: 13 Your eyes are too pure to look on **e**;
Mt 5: 45 He causes his sun to rise on the **e**
6: 13 but deliver us from the **e** one.'
7: 11 you are **e**, know how to give
12: 35 an **e** man brings **e** things out of the **e**
Jn 17: 15 you protect them from the **e** one.
Ro 2: 9 for every human being who does **e**:
12: 9 Hate what is **e**; cling to what is
12: 17 Do not repay anyone **e** for **e**.
16: 19 and innocent about what is **e**.
1Co 13: 6 Love does not delight in **e**
14: 20 In regard to **e** be infants, but in
Eph 6: 16 all the flaming arrows of the **e** one.
1Th 5: 22 reject every kind of **e**.
1Ti 6: 10 of money is a root of all kinds of **e**.
2Ti 2: 22 Flee the **e** desires of youth
Jas 1: 13 For God cannot be tempted by **e**,
1Pe 2: 16 your freedom as a cover-up for **e**;
3: 9 Do not repay **e** with **e** or insult
3: 9 the contrary, repay **e** with blessing,

EVILDOER (EVIL)
Pr 24: 20 for the **e** has no future hope,

EVILDOERS (EVIL)
Pr 24: 19 Do not fret because of **e** or be

EXACT
Heb 1: 3 the **e** representation of his being,

EXALT (EXALTED EXALTS)
Ps 30: 1 I will **e** you, LORD, for you lifted
34: 3 let us **e** his name together.
118: 28 you are my God, and I will **e** you.
Isa 24: 15 **e** the name of the LORD, the God
Mt 23: 12 For those who **e** themselves will be

EXALTED (EXALT)
2Sa 22: 47 **E** be my God, the Rock, my Savior!
1Ch 29: 11 you are **e** as head over all.
Ne 9: 5 and may it be **e** above all blessing
Ps 21: 13 Be **e** in your strength, LORD;
46: 10 I will be **e** among the nations,
57: 5 Be **e**, O God, above the heavens;
97: 9 you are **e** far above all gods.
99: 2 he is **e** over all the nations.
108: 5 Be **e**, O God, above the heavens;
148: 13 the LORD, for his name alone is **e**;
Isa 6: 1 high and **e**, seated on a throne;
12: 4 and proclaim that his name is **e**.
33: 5 The LORD is **e**, for he dwells
Eze 21: 26 The lowly will be **e** and the **e** will
Mt 23: 12 who humble themselves will be **e**.
Php 1: 20 now as always Christ will be **e**
2: 9 Therefore God **e** him to the highest

EXALTS (EXALT)
Ps 75: 7 He brings one down, he **e** another.
Pr 14: 34 Righteousness **e** a nation, but sin

EXAMINE (EXAMINED)
Ps 26: 2 try me, **e** my heart and my mind;
Jer 17: 10 search the heart and **e** the mind,
La 3: 40 Let us **e** our ways and test them,
1Co 11: 28 to **e** themselves before they eat
2Co 13: 5 **E** yourselves to see whether you

EXAMINED (EXAMINE)
Ac 17: 11 **e** the Scriptures every day to see

EXAMPLE (EXAMPLES)
Jn 13: 15 I have set you an **e** that you should
1Co 11: 1 Follow my **e**, as I follow the **e**
1Ti 4: 12 set an **e** for the believers in speech,
Titus 2: 7 everything set them an **e** by doing
1Pe 2: 21 leaving you an **e**, that you should

EXAMPLES (EXAMPLE)
1Co 10: 6 Now these things occurred as **e**
10: 11 things happened to them as **e**
1Pe 5: 3 to you, but being **e** to the flock.

EXASPERATE
Eph 6: 4 Fathers, do not **e** your children;

EXCEL (EXCELLENT)
1Co 14: 12 try to **e** in those that build
2Co 8: 7 you also **e** in this grace of giving.

EXCELLENT (EXCEL)
1Co 12: 31 yet I will show you the most **e** way.
Php 4: 8 if anything is **e** or praiseworthy—
1Ti 3: 13 have served well gain an **e** standing
Titus 3: 8 These things are **e** and profitable

EXCHANGED
Ro 1: 23 **e** the glory of the immortal God
1: 25 **e** the truth about God for a lie,

EXCUSE (EXCUSES)
Jn 15: 22 now they have no **e** for their sin.
Ro 1: 20 made, so that people are without **e**.

EXCUSES (EXCUSE)
Lk 14: 18 "But they all alike began to make **e**.

EXISTS
Heb 2: 10 and through whom everything **e**,
11: 6 to him must believe that he **e**

EXPECT (EXPECTATION)
Mt 24: 44 at an hour when you do not **e** him.

EXPECTATION (EXPECT)
Ro 8: 19 waits in eager **e** for the children
Heb 10: 27 but only a fearful **e** of judgment

EXPEL
1Co 5: 13 "**E** the wicked person from among

EXPENSIVE
1Ti 2: 9 or gold or pearls or **e** clothes,

EXPLOIT
Pr 22: 22 Do not **e** the poor because they are
2Co 12: 17 I **e** you through any of the men

EXPOSE
1Co 4: 5 and will **e** the motives of the heart.
Eph 5: 11 of darkness, but rather **e** them.

EXTENDS
Pr 31: 20 poor and **e** her hands to the needy.
Lk 1: 50 His mercy **e** to those who fear him,

---

† Please see the "Hebrew to English Translation Chart," p. xix.
‡ Please see "Key New Testament Terms," p. 1584.

EXTINGUISHED
2Sa 21: 17 the lamp of Israel will not be **e**."

EXTOL
Job 36: 24 Remember to **e** his work,
Ps 34: 1 I will **e** the LORD at all times;
68: 4 **e** him who rides on the clouds;
95: 2 thanksgiving and **e** him with music
109: 30 mouth I will greatly **e** the LORD;
111: 1 I will **e** the LORD with all my
115: 18 it is we who **e** the LORD,
117: 1 **e** him, all you peoples.
145: 2 and **e** your name for ever
145: 10 your faithful people **e** you.
147: 12 **E** the LORD, Jerusalem;

EXTORT
Lk 3: 14 "Don't **e** money and don't accuse

EYE (EYES)
Ex 21: 24 **e** for **e**, tooth for tooth,
Ps 94: 9 Does he who formed the **e** not see?
Mt 5: 29 If your right **e** causes you
5: 38 have heard that it was said, '**E** for **e**,
7: 3 speck of sawdust in your brother's **e**
1Co 2: 9 "What no **e** has seen, what no ear
Col 3: 22 not only when their **e** is on you
Rev 1: 7 and "every **e** will see him,

EYES (EYE)
Nu 33: 55 remain will become barbs in your **e**
Jos 23: 13 your backs and thorns in your **e**,
2Ch 16: 9 For the **e** of the LORD range
Job 31: 1 "I made a covenant with my **e** not
36: 7 not take his **e** off the righteous;
Ps 119: 18 Open my **e** that I may see
121: 1 I lift up my **e** to the mountains—
141: 8 But my **e** are fixed on you,
Pr 3: 7 Do not be wise in your own **e**;
4: 25 Let your **e** look straight ahead;
15: 3 The **e** of the LORD are
Isa 6: 5 and my **e** have seen the King,
Hab 1: 13 Your **e** are too pure to look on evil;
Jn 4: 35 open your **e** and look at the fields!
2Co 4: 18 So we fix our **e** not on what is seen,
Heb 12: 2 fixing our **e** on Jesus, the pioneer
Jas 2: 5 who are poor in the **e** of the world
1Pe 3: 12 For the **e** of the Lord are
Rev 7: 17 away every tear from their **e**."
21: 4 will wipe every tear from their **e**.

EZEKIEL
Priest called to be prophet to the exiles (Eze 1–3).

EZRA
Priest and teacher of the Law who led a return of exiles to Israel to reestablish temple and worship (Ezr 7–8). Corrected intermarriage of priests (Ezr 9–10). Read Law at celebration of Feast of Tabernacles (Neh 8).

FACE (FACES)
Ge 32: 30 "It is because I saw God **f** to **f**,
Ex 34: 29 that his **f** was radiant because he
Nu 6: 25 the LORD make his **f** shine on you
1Ch 16: 11 and his strength; seek his **f** always.
2Ch 7: 14 and seek my **f** and turn from their
Ps 4: 6 Let the light of your **f** shine on us.
27: 8 My heart says of you, "Seek his **f**!"
31: 16 Let your **f** shine on your servant;
105: 4 and his strength; seek his **f** always.
119:135 Make your **f** shine on your servant
Isa 50: 7 Therefore have I set my **f** like flint,
Mt 17: 2 His **f** shone like the sun, and his
1Co 13: 12 in a mirror; then we shall see **f** to **f**.
2Co 4: 6 glory displayed in the **f** of Christ.
1Pe 3: 12 the **f** of the Lord is against those
Rev 1: 16 His **f** was like the sun shining in all

FACES (FACE)
2Co 3: 18 unveiled **f** contemplate the Lord's

FACTIONS
Gal 5: 20 rage, selfish ambition, dissensions, **f**

FADE
1Pe 5: 4 of glory that will never **f** away.

FAIL (FAILING FAILINGS FAILS)
1Ch 28: 20 He will not **f** you or forsake you
2Ch 34: 33 they did not **f** to follow the LORD,
Ps 89: 28 my covenant with him will never **f**.
Pr 15: 22 Plans **f** for lack of counsel,
Isa 51: 6 my righteousness will never **f**.
La 3: 22 for his compassions never **f**.
2Co 13: 5 unless, of course, you **f** the test?

FAILING (FAIL)
1Sa 12: 23 I should sin against the LORD by **f**

FAILINGS (FAIL)
Ro 15: 1 to bear with the **f** of the weak

FAILS (FAIL)
1Co 13: 8 Love never **f**. But where there are

FAINT
Isa 40: 31 weary, they will walk and not be **f**.

FAIR
Pr 1: 3 doing what is right and just and **f**;
Col 4: 1 your slaves with what is right and **f**,

FAITH (FAITHFUL FAITHFULLY FAITHFULNESS FAITHLESS)
2Ch 20: 20 Have **f** in the LORD your God
20: 20 have **f** in his prophets
Mt 9: 29 "According to your **f** let it be done
17: 20 if you have **f** as small as a mustard
24: 10 many will turn away from the **f**
Mk 11: 22 "Have **f** in God," Jesus answered.
Lk 7: 9 I have not found such great **f** even
12: 28 will he clothe you—you of little **f**!
17: 5 said to the Lord, "Increase our **f**!"
18: 8 comes, will he find **f** on the earth?"
Ac 14: 9 him, saw that he had **f** to be healed
14: 27 how he had opened a door of **f**
Ro 1: 12 encouraged by each other's **f**.
1: 17 "The righteous will live by **f**."
1: 17 righteousness that is by **f** from first
3: 22 righteousness is given through **f**
3: 25 of his blood—to be received by **f**.
4: 5 their **f** is credited as righteousness.
5: 1 we have been justified through **f**,
10: 17 **f** comes from hearing the message,
14: 1 Accept the one whose **f** is weak,
14: 23 that does not come from **f** is sin.
16: 26 the obedience that comes from **f**—
1Co 13: 2 have a **f** that can move mountains,
13: 13 three remain: **f**, hope and love.
16: 13 stand firm in the **f**; be courageous;
2Co 5: 7 For we live by **f**, not by sight.
13: 5 to see whether you are in the **f**;
Gal 2: 16 we may be justified by **f** in Christ
2: 20 body, I live by **f** in the Son of God,
3: 11 "the righteous will live by **f**."
3: 24 that we might be justified by **f**.
Eph 2: 8 you have been saved, through **f**—
4: 5 one Lord, one **f**, one baptism;
6: 16 take up the shield of **f**,
Col 1: 23 if you continue in your **f**,
1Th 5: 8 be sober, putting on **f** and love as
1Ti 2: 15 if they continue in **f**,
4: 1 later times some will abandon the **f**
5: 8 has denied the **f** and is worse than
6: 12 Fight the good fight of the **f**.
2Ti 3: 15 salvation through **f** in Christ Jesus.
4: 7 finished the race, I have kept the **f**.
Phm : 6 with us in the **f** may be effective
Heb 10: 38 my righteous one will live by **f**.
11: 1 Now **f** is confidence in what we
11: 3 By **f** we understand that the
11: 5 By **f** Enoch was taken from this
11: 6 without **f** it is impossible to please
11: 7 By **f** Noah, when warned
11: 7 By his **f** he condemned the world
11: 8 By **f** Abraham, when called to go
11: 17 By **f** Abraham, when God tested
11: 20 By **f** Isaac blessed Jacob and Esau
11: 21 By **f** Jacob, when he was dying,
11: 22 By **f** Joseph, when his end was
11: 24 By **f** Moses, when he had grown
11: 31 By **f** the prostitute Rahab,
12: 2 Jesus, the pioneer and perfecter of **f**.
Jas 2: 14 Can such **f** save them?
2: 17 In the same way, **f** by itself, if it is
2: 26 is dead, so **f** without deeds is dead.
2Pe 1: 5 effort to add to your **f** goodness;
1Jn 5: 4 overcome the world, even our **f**.
Jude : 3 contend for the **f** that was once

FAITHFUL (FAITH)
Nu 12: 7 he is **f** in all my house.
Dt 7: 9 he is the **f** God, keeping his
32: 4 A **f** God who does no wrong,
2Sa 22: 26 "To the **f** you show yourself **f**,
Ps 16: 10 will you let your **f** one see decay.
25: 10 and **f** toward those who keep
31: 23 Love the LORD, all his **f** people!
33: 4 right and true; he is **f** in all he does.
37: 28 just and will not forsake his **f** ones.
97: 10 for he guards the lives of his **f** ones
116: 15 is the death of his **f** servants.
145: 13 all he promises and **f** in all he does.
145: 17 in all his ways and **f** in all he does.
146: 6 he remains **f** forever.
Pr 31: 26 and **f** instruction is on her tongue.
Mt 25: 21 'Well done, good and **f** servant!
25: 21 You have been **f** with a few things;
Ro 12: 12 patient in affliction, **f** in prayer.
1Co 4: 2 been given a trust must prove **f**.
10: 13 And God is **f**; he will not let you be
1Th 5: 24 The one who calls you is **f**, and he
1Ti 3: 2 to be above reproach, **f** to his wife,
2Ti 2: 13 he remains **f**, for he cannot disown
Heb 3: 6 Christ is **f** as the Son over God's
10: 23 profess, for he who promised is **f**.
1Pe 4: 10 as **f** stewards of God's grace in its
4: 19 themselves to their **f** Creator
1Jn 1: 9 he is **f** and just and will forgive us
Rev 1: 5 who is the **f** witness, the firstborn
2: 10 Be **f**, even to the point of death,
19: 11 whose rider is called **F** and True.

FAITHFULLY (FAITH)
Dt 11: 13 So if you **f** obey the commands
1Sa 12: 24 and serve him **f** with all your heart;
1Ki 2: 4 if they walk **f** before me with all

FAITHFULNESS (FAITH)
Ps 51: 6 you desired **f** even in the womb;
57: 10 your **f** reaches to the skies.
85: 10 Love and **f** meet together;
86: 15 to anger, abounding in love and **f**.
89: 1 make your **f** known through all
89: 14 love and **f** go before you.
91: 4 his **f** will be your shield
117: 2 the **f** of the LORD endures forever.
119: 75 and that in **f** you have afflicted me.
Pr 3: 3 Let love and **f** never leave you;
Isa 11: 5 and **f** the sash around his waist.
La 3: 23 new every morning; great is your **f**.
Hab 2: 4 righteous person will live by his **f**—
Ro 3: 3 their unfaithfulness nullify God's **f**?
Gal 5: 22 forbearance, kindness, goodness, **f**,

FAITHLESS (FAITH)
Ps 119:158 I look on the **f** with loathing,
Jer 3: 22 "Return, **f** people; I will cure you
2Ti 2: 13 if we are **f**, he remains faithful,

FALL (FALLEN FALLS)
Ps 37: 24 he will not **f**, for the LORD
69: 9 of those who insult you **f** on me.
Pr 11: 28 who trust in their riches will **f**,
Lk 11: 17 a house divided against itself will **f**.
Jn 16: 1 you so that you will not **f** away.
Ro 3: 23 and **f** short of the glory of God,
14: 4 own master, servants stand or **f**.

FALLEN (FALL)
2Sa 1: 19 How the mighty have **f**!
Isa 14: 12 How you have **f** from heaven,
1Co 15: 20 of those who have **f** asleep.
Gal 5: 4 you have **f** away from grace.
1Th 4: 15 precede those who have **f** asleep.
Heb 6: 6 and who have **f** away, to be brought

FALLS (FALL)
Pr 24: 17 Do not gloat when your enemy **f**;
Jn 12: 24 a kernel of wheat **f** to the ground

FALSE (FALSEHOOD FALSELY)
Ex 20: 16 shall not give **f** testimony against
23: 1 "Do not spread **f** reports.
Pr 13: 5 The righteous hate what is **f**,
19: 5 A **f** witness will not go unpunished,
Mt 7: 15 "Watch out for **f** prophets.
19: 18 steal, you shall not give **f** testimony,
24: 11 and many **f** prophets will appear
Php 1: 18 whether from **f** motives or true,
1Ti 1: 3 not to teach **f** doctrines any longer
2Pe 2: 1 there will be **f** teachers among you.

FALSEHOOD (FALSE)
Ps 119:163 and detest **f** but I love your law.
Pr 30: 8 Keep **f** and lies far from me;
Eph 4: 25 each of you must put off **f**

FALSELY (FALSE)
Lev 19: 12 "'Do not swear **f** by my name
Lk 3: 14 money and don't accuse people **f**—
1Ti 6: 20 ideas of what is **f** called knowledge,

FALTER
Pr 24: 10 If you **f** in a time of trouble,
Isa 42: 4 he will not **f** or be discouraged till

FAMILIES (FAMILY)
Ps 68: 6 God sets the lonely in **f**, he leads

FAMILY (FAMILIES)
Pr 31: 15 she provides food for her **f**
Lk 9: 61 go back and say goodbye to my **f**."
12: 52 in one **f** divided against each other,
1Ti 3: 4 He must manage his own **f** well
3: 5 know how to manage his own **f**,
5: 4 practice by caring for their own **f**

FAMINE
Ge 41: 30 seven years of **f** will follow them.
Am 8: 11 I will send a **f** through the land—
Ro 8: 35 or persecution or **f** or nakedness

FAN
2Ti 1: 6 this reason I remind you to **f**

FAST
Dt 13: 4 serve him and hold **f** to him.
Jos 22: 5 to hold **f** to him and to serve him
23: 8 to hold **f** to the LORD your God,
Ps 119: 31 I hold **f** to your statutes, LORD;
139: 10 me, your right hand will hold me **f**.
Mt 6: 16 "When you **f**, do not look somber
1Pe 5: 12 the true grace of God. Stand **f** in it.

FATHER (FATHER'S FATHERLESS FATHERS)
Ge 2: 24 That is why a man leaves his **f**
17: 4 You will be the **f** of many nations.
Ex 20: 12 "Honor your **f** and your mother,
21: 15 "Anyone who attacks their **f**
21: 17 "Anyone who curses their **f**
Lev 18: 7 "'Do not dishonor your **f**
19: 3 must respect your mother and **f**,
Dt 5: 16 "Honor your **f** and your mother,
21: 18 son who does not obey his **f**
Ps 27: 10 Though my **f** and mother forsake
68: 5 A **f** to the fatherless, a defender
Pr 10: 1 A wise son brings joy to his **f**,
23: 22 Listen to your **f**, who gave you life,
23: 24 The **f** of a righteous child has great
28: 7 of gluttons disgraces his **f**.
29: 3 loves wisdom brings joy to his **f**,
Isa 9: 6 Everlasting **F**, Prince of Peace.
Mt 6: 9 "'Our **F** in heaven, hallowed be
10: 37 "Anyone who loves their **f**
15: 4 said, 'Honor your **f** and mother'
19: 5 this reason a man will leave his **f**
Lk 12: 53 **f** against son and son against **f**,
23: 34 Jesus said, "**F**, forgive them,
Jn 6: 44 unless the **F** who sent me draws
6: 46 from God; only he has seen the **F**.
8: 44 You belong to your **f**, the devil,
10: 30 I and the **F** are one."
14: 6 comes to the **F** except through me.
14: 9 who has seen me has seen the **F**.
Ro 4: 11 he is the **f** of all who believe
2Co 6: 18 And, "I will be a **F** to you, and you
Eph 6: 2 "Honor your **f** and mother"—
Heb 12: 7 are not disciplined by their **f**?

FATHER'S (FATHER)
Pr 13: 1 wise son heeds his **f** instruction,
19: 13 A foolish child is a **f** ruin,
Lk 2: 49 know I had to be in my **F** house?"
Jn 2: 16 Stop turning my **F** house
10: 29 can snatch them out of my **F** hand.
14: 2 My **F** house has many rooms;

FATHERLESS (FATHER)
Dt 10: 18 He defends the cause of the **f**
24: 17 the foreigner or the **f** of justice,
24: 19 the foreigner, the **f** and the widow,
Ps 68: 5 A father to the **f**, a defender
Pr 23: 10 or encroach on the fields of the **f**,

FATHERS (FATHER)
Lk 11: 11 "Which of you **f**, if your son asks
Eph 6: 4 **F**, do not exasperate your children;
Col 3: 21 **F**, do not embitter your children,

FATHOM
Job 11: 7 "Can you **f** the mysteries of God?
Ps 145: 3 his greatness no one can **f**.
Ecc 3: 11 no one can **f** what God has done
Isa 40: 28 his understanding no one can **f**.
1Co 13: 2 of prophecy and can **f** all mysteries

FAULT (FAULTS)
Mt 18: 15 sins, go and point out their **f**,
Php 2: 15 of God without **f** in a warped
Jas 1: 5 generously to all without finding **f**,
Jude : 24 his glorious presence without **f**

FAULTFINDERS
Jude : 16 These people are grumblers and **f**;

FAULTS (FAULT)
Ps 19: 12 Forgive my hidden **f**.

FAVORITISM
Ex 23: 3 do not show **f** to a poor person
Lev 19: 15 to the poor or **f** to the great,
Ac 10: 34 true it is that God does not show **f**
Ro 2: 11 For God does not show **f**.
Gal 2: 6 God does not show **f**—
Eph 6: 9 heaven, and there is no **f** with him.
Col 3: 25 for their wrongs, and there is no **f**.
1Ti 5: 21 and to do nothing out of **f**.
Jas 2: 1 Lord Jesus Christ must not show **f**.
2: 9 But if you show **f**, you sin and are

† **FEAR** (AFRAID FEARS)
Dt 6: 13 **F** the LORD your God, serve him
10: 12 you but to **f** the LORD your God,
31: 12 learn to **f** the LORD your God
Ps 19: 9 The **f** of the LORD is pure,
23: 4 the darkest valley, I will **f** no evil,
27: 1 and my salvation—whom shall I **f**?
91: 5 You will not **f** the terror of night,
111: 10 The **f** of the LORD is
Pr 8: 13 To **f** the LORD is to hate evil;
9: 10 The **f** of the LORD is
10: 27 The **f** of the LORD adds length
14: 27 The **f** of the LORD is a fountain
15: 33 instruction is to the **f** the LORD,
16: 6 through the **f** of the LORD evil is
19: 23 The **f** of the LORD leads to life;
29: 25 **F** of man will prove to be a snare,
Ecc 5: 7 Therefore **f** God.
Isa 11: 3 will delight in the **f** of the LORD.
41: 10 So do not **f**, for I am with you;
Lk 12: 5 will show you whom you should **f**:
Php 2: 12 to work out your salvation with **f**
1Jn 4: 18 There is no **f** in love. But perfect love drives out **f**,

FEARS (FEAR)
Job 1: 8 a man who **f** God and shuns evil."
Ps 34: 4 he delivered me from all my **f**.
Pr 31: 30 a woman who **f** the LORD is to be
1Jn 4: 18 The one who **f** is not made perfect

FEED
Jn 21: 15 Jesus said, "**F** my lambs."
21: 17 Jesus said, "**F** my sheep.
Ro 12: 20 "If your enemy is hungry, **f** him;
Jude : 12 shepherds who **f** only themselves.

FEET (FOOT)
Ps 8: 6 you put everything under their **f**:
22: 16 they pierce my hands and my **f**.
40: 2 he set my **f** on a rock and gave me
110: 1 enemies a footstool for your **f**."
119:105 Your word is a lamp to my **f**
Ro 10: 15 "How beautiful are the **f** of those
1Co 12: 21 And the head cannot say to the **f**,
15: 25 has put all his enemies under his **f**.
Heb 12: 13 "Make level paths for your **f**,"

FELLOWSHIP
2Co 6: 14 **f** can light have with darkness?
13: 14 the **f** of the Holy Spirit be with you
1Jn 1: 6 If we claim to have **f** with him
1: 7 light, we have **f** with one another,

FEMALE
Ge 1: 27 male and **f** he created them.
Gal 3: 28 nor is there male and **f**, for you are

FERVOR
Ro 12: 11 but keep your spiritual **f**,

FIDELITY
Ro 1: 31 no understanding, no **f**, no love,

FIELD (FIELDS)
Mt 6: 28 See how the flowers of the **f** grow.
13: 38 The **f** is the world, and the good
1Co 3: 9 you are God's **f**, God's building.

FIELDS (FIELD)
Lk 2: 8 shepherds living out in the **f**
Jn 4: 35 open your eyes and look at the **f**!

FIERY (FIRE)
1Pe 4: 12 do not be surprised at the **f** ordeal

FIG (FIGS)
Ge 3: 7 so they sewed **f** leaves together

FIGHT (FOUGHT)
Ex 14: 14 The LORD will **f** for you;
Dt 1: 30 is going before you, will **f** for you,
3: 22 the LORD your God himself will **f**
Ne 4: 20 Our God will **f** for us!"
Ps 35: 1 **f** against those who **f** against me.
Jn 18: 36 my servants would **f** to prevent my
1Co 9: 26 I do not **f** like a boxer beating
2Co 10: 4 The weapons we **f** with are not
1Ti 1: 18 them you may **f** the battle well,
6: 12 **F** the good **f** of the faith.
2Ti 4: 7 I have fought the good **f**, I have

FIGS (FIG)
Lk 6: 44 People do not pick **f**

FILL (FILLED FILLS FULL FULLNESS FULLY)
Ge 1: 28 **f** the earth and subdue it.
Ps 16: 11 you will **f** me with joy in your
81: 10 wide your mouth and I will **f** it.
Pr 28: 19 chase fantasies will have their **f**
Hag 2: 7 and I will **f** this house with glory,'
Jn 6: 26 you ate the loaves and had your **f**.
Ac 2: 28 you will **f** me with joy in your
Ro 15: 13 May the God of hope **f** you with all

FILLED (FILL)
Ps 72: 19 may the whole earth be **f** with his
119: 64 The earth is **f** with your love,
Isa 11: 9 for the earth will be **f**
Eze 43: 5 glory of the LORD **f** the temple.
Hab 2: 14 For the earth will be **f**
Lk 1: 15 he will be **f** with the Holy Spirit
1: 41 Elizabeth was **f** with the Holy Spirit.
Jn 12: 3 the house was **f** with the fragrance
Ac 2: 4 of them were **f** with the Holy Spirit
4: 8 Then Peter, **f** with the Holy Spirit,
9: 17 and be **f** with the Holy Spirit."
13: 9 called Paul, **f** with the Holy Spirit,
Eph 5: 18 Instead, be **f** with the Spirit,
Php 1: 11 **f** with the fruit of righteousness

FILLS (FILL)
Nu 14: 21 of the LORD **f** the whole earth,
Ps 107: 9 and **f** the hungry with good things.
Eph 1: 23 him who **f** everything in every way.

FILTHY
Isa 64: 6 all our righteous acts are like **f** rags;
Col 3: 8 and **f** language from your lips.

FIND (FINDS FOUND)
Nu 32: 23 be sure that your sin will **f** you out.
Dt 4: 29 you will **f** him if you seek him
1Sa 23: 16 and helped him **f** strength in God.
Ps 91: 4 under his wings you will **f** refuge;
112: 1 LORD, who **f** great delight in his
Pr 14: 22 those who plan what is good **f** love
31: 10 wife of noble character who can **f**?
Jer 6: 16 and you will **f** rest for your souls.
Mt 7: 7 seek and you will **f**;
11: 29 and you will **f** rest for your souls.
16: 25 loses their life for me will **f** it.
Lk 18: 8 will he **f** faith on the earth?"
Jn 10: 9 come in and go out, and **f** pasture.

FINDS (FIND)
Ps 62: 1 Truly my soul **f** rest in God;
119:162 promise like one who **f** great spoil.
Pr 18: 22 He who **f** a wife **f** what is good
Mt 7: 8 the one who seeks **f**; and to the one
10: 39 Whoever **f** their life will lose it,
Lk 12: 37 whose master **f** them watching
15: 4 go after the lost sheep until he **f** it?

FINISH (FINISHED)
Jn 4: 34 him who sent me and to **f** his work.
5: 36 that the Father has given me to **f**—
Ac 20: 24 my only aim is to **f** the race
2Co 8: 11 Now **f** the work, so that your eager
Gal 3: 3 are you now trying to **f** by means
Jas 1: 4 Let perseverance **f** its work so

FINISHED (FINISH)
Ge 2: 2 seventh day God had **f** the work he
Jn 19: 30 the drink, Jesus said, "It is **f**."
2Ti 4: 7 the good fight, I have **f** the race,

FIRE (FIERY)
Ex 13: 21 in a pillar of **f** to give them light,
Lev 6: 12 The **f** on the altar must be kept
Isa 30: 27 and his tongue is a consuming **f**.
Jer 23: 29 "Is not my word like **f**,"
Mt 3: 11 you with the Holy Spirit and **f**.

† Please see the "Hebrew to English Translation Chart," p. xix.

Mt 5: 22 will be in danger of the **f** of hell.
25: 41 the eternal **f** prepared for the devil
Mk 9: 43 hell, where the **f** never goes out.
Ac 2: 3 to be tongues of **f** that separated
1Co 3: 13 It will be revealed with **f**, and the **f**
Heb 12: 29 for our "God is a consuming **f**."
Jas 3: 5 what a great forest is set on **f**
2Pe 3: 10 the elements will be destroyed by **f**,
Jude : 23 by snatching them from the **f**;
Rev 20: 14 **f**. The lake of **f** is the second death.

FIRM
Ex 14: 13 Stand **f** and you will see
2Ch 20: 17 stand **f** and see the deliverance
Ps 33: 11 plans of the LORD stand **f** forever,
37: 23 The LORD makes **f** the steps
40: 2 and gave me a **f** place to stand.
89: 2 that your love stands **f** forever,
119: 89 it stands **f** in the heavens.
Zec 8: 23 nations will take **f** hold of one Jew
Mk 13: 13 the one who stands **f** to the end
1Co 16: 13 on your guard; stand **f** in the faith;
2Co 1: 24 because it is by faith you stand **f**.
Eph 6: 14 Stand **f** then, with the belt of truth
Col 4: 12 that you may stand **f** in all the will
2Th 2: 15 stand **f** and hold fast to the teachings
2Ti 2: 19 God's solid foundation stands **f**,
Heb 6: 19 anchor for the soul, **f** and secure.
1Pe 5: 9 Resist him, standing **f** in the faith,

FIRST
Isa 44: 6 I am the **f** and I am the last;
48: 12 I am the **f** and I am the last.
Mt 5: 24 **F** go and be reconciled to them;
6: 33 But seek **f** his kingdom and his
7: 5 **f** take the plank out of your own
20: 27 wants to be **f** must be your slave—
22: 38 This is the **f** and greatest
23: 26 **F** clean the inside of the cup
Mk 13: 10 the gospel must **f** be preached to all
Ac 11: 26 disciples were called Christians **f**
Ro 1: 16 **f** to the Jew, then to the Gentile.
1Co 12: 28 in the church **f** of all apostles,
2Co 8: 5 They gave themselves **f** of all
1Ti 2: 13 For Adam was formed **f**, then Eve.
Jas 3: 17 comes from heaven is **f** of all pure;
1Jn 4: 19 We love because he **f** loved us.
3Jn : 9 who loves to be **f**, will not welcome
Rev 1: 17 I am the **F** and the Last.
2: 4 have forsaken the love you had at **f**.

FIRSTBORN (BEAR)
Ex 11: 5 Every **f** son in Egypt will die,

FIRSTFRUITS
Ex 23: 19 "Bring the best of the **f** of your soil

FISH
Mk 1: 17 I will send you out to **f** for people."
Lk 5: 10 from now on you will **f** for people."

FITTING
Ps 33: 1 it is **f** for the upright to praise him.
147: 1 how pleasant and **f** to praise him!
Pr 19: 10 It is not **f** for a fool to live
26: 1 in harvest, honor is not **f** for a fool.
1Co 14: 40 everything should be done in a **f**
Col 3: 18 your husbands, as is **f** in the Lord.
Heb 2: 10 to glory, it was **f** that God,

FIX (FIXING)
Dt 11: 18 **F** these words of mine in your
Pr 4: 25 **f** your gaze directly before you.
2Co 4: 18 So we **f** our eyes not on what is
Heb 3: 1 calling, **f** your thoughts on Jesus,

FIXING (FIX)
Heb 12: 2 **f** our eyes on Jesus, the pioneer

FLAME (FLAMES FLAMING)
2Ti 1: 6 you to fan into **f** the gift of God,

FLAMES (FLAME)
1Co 3: 15 only as one escaping through the **f**.

FLAMING (FLAME)
Eph 6: 16 you can extinguish all the **f** arrows

FLASH
1Co 15: 52 in a **f**, in the twinkling of an eye,

FLATTER (FLATTERING FLATTERY)
Ps 12: 2 they **f** with their lips but harbor
Job 32: 21 no partiality, nor will I **f** anyone;
Jude : 16 **f** others for their own advantage.

FLATTERING (FLATTER)
Ps 12: 3 May the LORD silence all **f** lips
Pr 26: 28 it hurts, and a **f** mouth works ruin.

FLATTERY (FLATTER)
Ro 16: 18 **f** they deceive the minds of naive
1Th 2: 5 You know we never used **f**, nor did

FLAWLESS
2Sa 22: 31 The LORD's word is **f**;
Job 11: 4 'My beliefs are **f** and I am pure
Ps 12: 6 And the words of the LORD are **f**,
18: 30 The LORD's word is **f**;
Pr 30: 5 "Every word of God is **f**; he is
SS 5: 2 my darling, my dove, my **f** one.

FLEE
Ps 139: 7 Where can I **f** from your presence?
1Co 6: 18 **F** from sexual immorality.
10: 14 my dear friends, **f** from idolatry.
1Ti 6: 11 man of God, **f** from all this,
2Ti 2: 22 **F** the evil desires of youth
Jas 4: 7 the devil, and he will **f** from you.

FLEETING
Ps 89: 47 Remember how **f** is my life.
Pr 31: 30 is deceptive, and beauty is **f**;

FLESH
Ge 2: 23 bone of my bones and **f** of my **f**;
2: 24 to his wife, and they become one **f**.
Job 19: 26 yet in my **f** I will see God;
Eze 11: 19 of stone and give them a heart of **f**.
36: 26 of stone and give you a heart of **f**.
Mt 26: 41 spirit is willing, but the **f** is weak."
Mk 10: 8 and the two will become one **f**.'
Jn 1: 14 The Word became **f** and made his
6: 51 bread is my **f**, which I will give
Ro 8: 4 do not live according to the **f** but
8: 8 realm of the **f** cannot please God.
1Co 6: 16 said, "The two will become one **f**."
Gal 3: 3 trying to finish by means of the **f**?
5: 19 The acts of the **f** are obvious:
5: 24 crucified the **f** with its passions
Eph 5: 31 and the two will become one **f**."
6: 12 For our struggle is not against **f**

FLOCK (FLOCKS)
Isa 40: 11 He tends his **f** like a shepherd:
Eze 34: 2 not shepherds take care of the **f**?
Zec 11: 17 shepherd, who deserts the **f**!
Mt 26: 31 the sheep of the **f** will be scattered.'
Ac 20: 28 all the **f** of which the Holy Spirit
1Pe 5: 2 of God's **f** that is under your care,

FLOCKS (FLOCK)
Lk 2: 8 keeping watch over their **f** at night.

FLOG
Ac 22: 25 **f** a Roman citizen who hasn't even

FLOODGATES
Mal 3: 10 will not throw open the **f** of heaven

FLOURISHING
Ps 52: 8 am like an olive tree **f** in the house

FLOW (FLOWING)
Nu 13: 27 and it does **f** with milk and honey!
Jn 7: 38 of living water will **f** from within

FLOWERS
Isa 40: 7 The grass withers and the **f** fall,
Lk 12: 27 "Consider how the wild **f** grow.

FLOWING (FLOW)
Ex 3: 8 a land **f** with milk and honey—

FOLDING
Pr 6: 10 a little **f** of the hands to rest—

FOLLOW (FOLLOWS)
Ex 23: 2 "Do not **f** the crowd in doing
Lev 18: 4 laws and be careful to **f** my decrees.
Dt 5: 1 Learn them and be sure to **f** them.
Ps 23: 6 love will **f** me all the days of my
Mt 16: 24 and take up their cross and **f** me.
Jn 10: 4 his sheep **f** him because they know
1Co 14: 1 **F** the way of love and eagerly desire
Eph 5: 1 **F** God's example, therefore,
Rev 14: 4 They **f** the Lamb wherever he goes.

FOLLOWS (FOLLOW)
Jn 8: 12 Whoever **f** me will never walk

FOOD (FOODS)
Pr 20: 13 awake and you will have **f** to spare.
22: 9 for they share their **f** with the poor.
25: 21 enemy is hungry, give him **f** to eat;
31: 15 she provides **f** for her family
Da 1: 8 to defile himself with the royal **f**
Jn 6: 27 Do not work for **f** that spoils, but for **f** that endures to eternal life,
1Co 8: 8 **f** does not bring us near to God;
1Ti 6: 8 But if we have **f** and clothing,
Jas 2: 15 sister is without clothes and daily **f**.

FOODS (FOOD)
Mk 7: 19 this, Jesus declared all **f** clean.)

FOOL (FOOLISH FOOLISHNESS FOOLS)
Ps 14: 1 The **f** says in his heart, "There
Pr 15: 5 A **f** spurns a parent's discipline,
26: 5 Answer a **f** according to his folly,
Mt 5: 22 And anyone who says, 'You **f**!'

FOOLISH (FOOL)
Pr 10: 1 a **f** son brings grief to his mother.
17: 25 A **f** son brings grief to his father
Mt 7: 26 practice is like a **f** man who built
25: 2 Five of them were **f** and five were
1Co 1: 27 God chose the **f** things of the world

FOOLISHNESS (FOOL)
1Co 1: 18 of the cross is **f** to those who are
1: 25 the **f** of God is wiser than human
2: 14 Spirit of God but considers them **f**,
3: 19 of this world is **f** in God's sight.

FOOLS (FOOL)
Pr 14: 9 **F** mock at making amends for sin,
17: 28 Even **f** are thought wise if they
18: 2 **F** find no pleasure in understanding
28: 26 who trust in themselves are **f**,
1Co 4: 10 We are **f** for Christ, but you are so

FOOT (FEET FOOTHOLD)
Jos 1: 3 every place where you set your **f**,
Isa 1: 6 the sole of your **f** to the top of your
1Co 12: 15 Now if the **f** should say, "Because I

FOOTHOLD (FOOT)
Eph 4: 27 and do not give the devil a **f**.

FORBEARANCE
Ro 3: 25 his **f** he had left the sins committed
Gal 5: 22 love, joy, peace, **f**, kindness,

FORBID
1Co 14: 39 and do not **f** speaking in tongues.

FOREIGNER (FOREIGNERS)
Ex 22: 21 "Do not mistreat or oppress a **f**,

FOREIGNERS (FOREIGNER)
1Pe 2: 11 urge you, as **f** and exiles, to abstain

FOREKNEW (KNOW)
Ro 8: 29 those God **f** he also predestined
11: 2 not reject his people, whom he **f**.

† **FOREVER** (EVER)
1Ch 16: 15 He remembers his covenant **f**,
16: 34 for he is good; his love endures **f**.
Ps 9: 7 The LORD reigns **f**;
23: 6 dwell in the house of the LORD **f**.
33: 11 plans of the LORD stand firm **f**,
86: 12 I will glorify your name **f**.
92: 8 But you, LORD, are **f** exalted.
110: 4 "You are a priest **f**, in the order
119:111 Your statutes are my heritage **f**;
Jn 6: 51 Whoever eats this bread will live **f**.
14: 16 to help you and be with you **f**—
1Co 9: 25 do it to get a crown that will last **f**.
1Th 4: 17 And so we will be with the Lord **f**.
Heb 13: 8 the same yesterday and today and **f**.
1Pe 1: 25 the word of the Lord endures **f**."
1Jn 2: 17 does the will of God lives **f**.

FORFEIT
Lk 9: 25 and yet lose or **f** their very self?

† **FORGAVE** (FORGIVE)
Ps 32: 5 And you **f** the guilt of my sin.
Lk 7: 42 him back, so he **f** the debts of both.
Eph 4: 32 other, just as in Christ God **f** you.
Col 2: 13 He **f** us all our sins,
3: 13 Forgive as the Lord **f** you.

FORGET (FORGETS FORGETTING)
Dt 6: 12 that you do not **f** the LORD,
Ps 103: 2 my soul, and **f** not all his benefits—
137: 5 If I **f** you, Jerusalem, may my right
Isa 49: 15 Though she may **f**, I will not **f** you!
Heb 6: 10 will not **f** your work and the love

† Please see the "Hebrew to English Translation Chart," p. xix.

FORGETS (FORGET)
Jn 16: 21 is born she **f** the anguish because
Jas 1: 24 immediately **f** what he looks like.

FORGETTING (FORGET)
Php 3: 13 **F** what is behind and straining

FORGIVE (FORGAVE FORGIVENESS FORGIVING)
2Ch 7: 14 and I will **f** their sin and will heal
Ps 19: 12 **F** my hidden faults.
Mt 6: 12 And **f** us our debts, as we also have
6: 14 if you **f** other people when they sin
18: 21 many times shall I **f** my brother
Mk 11: 25 anything against anyone, **f** them,
Lk 11: 4 **F** us our sins, for we also **f** everyone
23: 34 "Father, **f** them, for they do not
Col 3: 13 **F** as the Lord forgave you.
1Jn 1: 9 and will **f** us our sins and purify

FORGIVENESS (FORGIVE)
Ps 130: 4 But with you there is **f**, so that we
Ac 10: 43 in him receives **f** of sins through
Eph 1: 7 through his blood, the **f** of sins,
Col 1: 14 we have redemption, the **f** of sins.
Heb 9: 22 the shedding of blood there is no **f**.

FORGIVING (FORGIVE)
Ne 9: 17 But you are a **f** God,
Eph 4: 32 to one another, **f** each other, just as

FORMED
Ge 2: 7 the LORD God **f** a man
Ps 103: 14 for he knows how we are **f**,
Isa 45: 18 be empty, but **f** it to be inhabited—
Ro 9: 20 what is **f** say to the one who **f** it,
1Ti 2: 13 For Adam was **f** first, then Eve.
Heb 11: 3 that the universe was **f** at God's

FORSAKE (FORSAKEN)
Jos 1: 5 I will never leave you nor **f** you.
24: 16 us to **f** the LORD to serve other
2Ch 15: 2 you, but if you **f** him, he will **f** you.
Ps 27: 10 Though my father and mother **f** me,
Isa 55: 7 Let the wicked **f** their ways
Heb 13: 5 will I leave you; never will I **f** you."

FORSAKEN (FORSAKE)
Ezr 9: 9 God has not **f** us in our bondage.
Ps 22: 1 God, my God, why have you **f** me?
37: 25 I have never seen the righteous **f**
Mt 27: 46 my God, why have you **f** me?").
Rev 2: 4 You have **f** the love you had at first.

FORTIFIED
Pr 18: 10 name of the LORD is a **f** tower;

FORTRESS
Ps 18: 2 is my rock, my **f** and my deliverer;
71: 3 me, for you are my rock and my **f**.

FOUGHT (FIGHT)
2Ti 4: 7 I have **f** the good fight, I have

FOUND (FIND)
1Ch 28: 9 If you seek him, he will be **f** by you;
Isa 55: 6 Seek the LORD while he may be **f**;
Da 5: 27 on the scales and **f** wanting.
Lk 15: 6 I have **f** my lost sheep.'
15: 9 I have **f** my lost coin.'
Ac 4: 12 Salvation is **f** in no one else,

FOUNDATION
Isa 28: 16 a precious cornerstone for a sure **f**;
1Co 3: 11 can lay any **f** other than the one
Eph 2: 20 built on the **f** of the apostles
2Ti 2: 19 God's solid **f** stands firm,

FOXES
Mt 8: 20 "**F** have dens and birds have nests,

FRANKINCENSE
Mt 2: 11 him with gifts of gold, **f** and myrrh.

FREE (FREED FREEDOM FREELY)
Ps 146: 7 The LORD sets prisoners **f**,
Jn 8: 32 truth, and the truth will set you **f**."
Ro 6: 18 You have been set **f** from sin
Gal 3: 28 neither slave nor **f**, nor is there
1Pe 2: 16 Live as **f** people, but do not use

FREED (FREE)
Rev 1: 5 has **f** us from our sins by his blood,

FREEDOM (FREE)
Ro 8: 21 brought into the **f** and glory
2Co 3: 17 the Spirit of the Lord is, there is **f**.
Gal 5: 13 But do not use your **f** to indulge
1Pe 2: 16 do not use your **f** as

FREELY (FREE)
Isa 55: 7 to our God, for he will **f** pardon.
Mt 10: 8 **F** you have received; **f** give.
Ro 3: 24 and all are justified **f** by his grace
Eph 1: 6 which he has **f** given us in the One

FRIEND (FRIENDS)
Ex 33: 11 face to face, as one speaks to a **f**.
Pr 17: 17 A **f** loves at all times, and a brother
18: 24 there is a **f** who sticks closer than
27: 6 Wounds from a **f** can be trusted,
27: 10 Do not forsake your **f** or a **f** of your
Jas 4: 4 to be a **f** of the world becomes

FRIENDS (FRIEND)
Pr 16: 28 and a gossip separates close **f**.
18: 24 who has unreliable **f** soon comes
Zec 13: 6 I was given at the house of my **f**.'
Jn 15: 13 to lay down one's life for one's **f**.

FRUIT (FRUITFUL)
Ps 1: 3 which yields its **f** in season
Pr 11: 30 The **f** of the righteous is a tree
Mt 7: 16 By their **f** you will recognize them.
Jn 15: 2 branch that does bear **f** he prunes
Gal 5: 22 But the **f** of the Spirit is love, joy,
Rev 22: 2 bearing twelve crops of **f**, yielding its **f** every month.

FRUITFUL (FRUIT)
Ge 1: 22 "Be **f** and increase in number
Ps 128: 3 wife will be like a **f** vine within
Jn 15: 2 so that it will be even more **f**.

FULFILL (FULFILLED FULFILLMENT)
Ps 116: 14 I will **f** my vows to the LORD
Mt 5: 17 to abolish them but to **f** them.
1Co 7: 3 The husband should **f** his marital

FULFILLED (FULFILL)
Pr 13: 19 A longing **f** is sweet to the soul,
Mk 14: 49 But the Scriptures must be **f**."
Ro 13: 8 whoever loves others has **f** the law.

FULFILLMENT (FULFILL)
Ro 13: 10 Therefore love is the **f** of the law.

FULL (FILL)
Ps 127: 5 Blessed is the man whose quiver is **f**
Pr 31: 11 Her husband has **f** confidence in her
Isa 6: 3 the whole earth is **f** of his glory."
Lk 6: 45 speaks what the heart is **f** of.
Jn 10: 10 may have life, and have it to the **f**.
Ac 6: 3 who are known to be **f** of the Spirit

FULLNESS (FILL)
Col 1: 19 to have all his **f** dwell in him,
2: 9 in Christ all the **f** of the Deity lives

FULLY (FILL)
1Ki 8: 61 may your hearts be **f** committed
2Ch 16: 9 whose hearts are **f** committed
Ps 119: 4 precepts that are to be **f** obeyed.
119:138 righteous; they are **f** trustworthy.
1Co 15: 58 Always give yourselves **f**

FUTURE
Ps 37: 37 a **f** awaits those who seek peace.
Pr 23: 18 There is surely a **f** hope for you,
Ro 8: 38 neither the present nor the **f**,

GABRIEL
Angel who interpreted Daniel's visions (Da 8:16–26; 9:20–27); announced births of John (Lk 1:11–20), Jesus (Lk 1:26–38).

GAIN (GAINED)
Ps 60: 12 With God we will **g** the victory,
Mk 8: 36 for someone to **g** the whole world,
1Co 13: 3 but do not have love, I **g** nothing.
Php 1: 21 me, to live is Christ and to die is **g**.
3: 8 them garbage, that I may **g** Christ
1Ti 6: 6 with contentment is great **g**.
1Pe 5: 2 not pursuing dishonest **g**, but eager

GAINED (GAIN)
Ro 5: 2 through whom we have **g** access

GALILEE
Isa 9: 1 in the future he will honor **G**

GALL
Mt 27: 34 Jesus wine to drink, mixed with **g**;

GAP
Eze 22: 30 stand before me in the **g** on behalf

GARBAGE
Php 3: 8 I consider them **g**, that I may gain

GARDENER
Jn 15: 1 true vine, and my Father is the **g**.

GARMENT (GARMENTS)
Ps 102: 26 they will all wear out like a **g**.
Mt 9: 16 the patch will pull away from the **g**,
Jn 19: 23 This **g** was seamless, woven in one
19: 24 them and cast lots for my **g**."

GARMENTS (GARMENT)
Ge 3: 21 The LORD God made **g** of skin
Isa 61: 10 For he has clothed me with **g**
63: 1 with his **g** stained crimson?

GATE (GATES)
Mt 7: 13 "Enter through the narrow **g**.
Jn 10: 9 I am the **g**; whoever enters through

GATES (GATE)
Ps 100: 4 Enter his **g** with thanksgiving
Mt 16: 18 the **g** of Hades will not overcome

GATHER (GATHERS)
Zec 14: 2 I will **g** all the nations to Jerusalem
Mt 12: 30 and whoever does not **g** with me
23: 37 longed to **g** your children together,

GATHERS (GATHER)
Isa 40: 11 He **g** the lambs in his arms
Mt 23: 37 as a hen **g** her chicks under her

GAVE (GIVE)
Ezr 2: 69 their ability they **g** to the treasury
Job 1: 21 The LORD **g** and the LORD has
Jn 3: 16 so loved the world that he **g** his
2Co 8: 5 They **g** themselves first of all
Gal 2: 20 loved me and **g** himself for me.
1Ti 2: 6 who **g** himself as a ransom for all

GAZE
Ps 27: 4 to **g** on the beauty of the LORD
Pr 4: 25 fix your **g** directly before you.

GENEALOGIES
1Ti 1: 4 themselves to myths and endless **g**.

GENERATIONS
Ps 22: 30 **g** will be told about the Lord.
102: 12 renown endures through all **g**.
145: 13 dominion endures through all **g**.
Lk 1: 48 now on all **g** will call me blessed,
Eph 3: 5 other **g** as it has now been revealed

GENEROUS
Ps 112: 5 Good will come to those who are **g**
Pr 22: 9 The **g** will themselves be blessed,
2Co 9: 5 Then it will be ready as a **g** gift,
1Ti 6: 18 and to be **g** and willing to share.

‡ **GENTILE** (GENTILES)
Ro 1: 16 first to the Jew, then to the **G**.
10: 12 no difference between Jew and **G**—

GENTILES (GENTILE)
Isa 42: 6 for the people and a light for the **G**,
Ro 3: 9 **G** alike are all under the power
11: 13 as I am the apostle to the **G**, I take
1Co 1: 23 block to Jews and foolishness to **G**,

GENTLE (GENTLENESS)
Pr 15: 1 A **g** answer turns away wrath,
Mt 11: 29 for I am **g** and humble in heart,
21: 5 to you, **g** and riding on a donkey,
1Co 4: 21 I come in love and with a **g** spirit?
1Pe 3: 4 unfading beauty of a **g** and quiet

GENTLENESS (GENTLE)
2Co 10: 1 By the humility and **g** of Christ,
Gal 5: 23 **g** and self-control.
Php 4: 5 Let your **g** be evident to all.
Col 3: 12 kindness, humility, **g** and patience.
1Ti 6: 11 faith, love, endurance and **g**.
1Pe 3: 15 But do this with **g** and respect,

GETHSEMANE
Mt 26: 36 his disciples to a place called **G**,

GIDEON
Judge, also called Jerub-Baal; freed Israel from Midianites (Jdg 6–8; Heb 11:32). Given sign of fleece (Jdg 6:36–40).

GIFT (GIFTS)
Pr 21: 14 A **g** given in secret soothes anger,
Mt 5: 23 you are offering your **g** at the altar
Ac 2: 38 you will receive the **g** of the Holy
Ro 6: 23 the **g** of God is eternal life in Christ
1Co 7: 7 of you has your own **g** from God;
2Co 8: 12 the **g** is acceptable according
9: 15 be to God for his indescribable **g**!

‡ Please see "Key New Testament Terms," p. 1584.

Eph 2: 8 yourselves, it is the **g** of God—
1Ti 4: 14 Do not neglect your **g**, which was
2Ti 1: 6 you to fan into flame the **g** of God,
Jas 1: 17 good and perfect **g** is from above,
1Pe 4: 10 should use whatever **g** you have

GIFTS (GIFT)
Ro 11: 29 for God's **g** and his call are
12: 6 We have different **g**,
1Co 12: 4 There are different kinds of **g**,
12: 31 Now eagerly desire the greater **g**.
14: 1 and eagerly desire **g** of the Spirit,
14: 12 Since you are eager for **g**

GILEAD
Jer 8: 22 Is there no balm in **G**? Is there no

GIVE (GAVE GIVEN GIVER GIVES GIVING)
Nu 6: 26 toward you and **g** you peace."'
1Sa 1: 11 forget your servant but **g** her a son,
1: 11 I will **g** him to the LORD for all
2Ch 15: 7 be strong and do not **g** up, for your
Pr 21: 26 the righteous **g** without sparing.
23: 26 **g** me your heart and let your eyes
28: 27 Those who **g** to the poor will lack
30: 8 but **g** me only my daily bread.
Eze 36: 26 I will **g** you a new heart and put
Mt 6: 11 **G** us today our daily bread.
10: 8 Freely you have received; freely **g**.
22: 21 them, "So **g** back to Caesar what is
Mk 8: 37 what can anyone **g** in exchange
Lk 6: 38 **G**, and it will be given to you.
11: 13 Father in heaven **g** the Holy Spirit
Jn 10: 28 I **g** them eternal life, and they shall
13: 34 "A new command I **g** you:
Ac 20: 35 'It is more blessed to **g** than
Ro 12: 8 encourage, then **g** encouragement;
12: 8 if it is giving, then **g** generously;
13: 7 **G** to everyone what you owe them:
14: 12 then, each of us will **g** an account
2Co 9: 7 should **g** what you have decided
Rev 14: 7 voice, "Fear God and **g** him glory,

GIVEN (GIVE)
Nu 8: 16 Israelites who are to be **g** wholly
Ps 115: 16 but the earth he has **g** to mankind.
Isa 9: 6 a son is **g**, and the government
Mt 6: 33 all these things will be **g** to you as
7: 7 "Ask and it will be **g** to you;
Lk 22: 19 saying, "This is my body **g** for you;
Jn 3: 27 can receive only what is **g** them
Ro 5: 5 Holy Spirit, who has been **g** to us.
1Co 4: 2 those who have been **g** a trust must
12: 13 and we were all **g** the one Spirit
Eph 4: 7 of us grace has been **g** as Christ

GIVER (GIVE)
Pr 18: 16 ushers the **g** into the presence
2Co 9: 7 for God loves a cheerful **g**.

GIVES (GIVE)
Ps 119:130 unfolding of your words **g** light;
Pr 14: 30 A heart at peace **g** life to the body,
15: 30 good news **g** health to the bones.
Isa 40: 29 He **g** strength to the weary
Mt 10: 42 anyone **g** even a cup of cold water
Jn 6: 63 The Spirit **g** life; the flesh counts
1Co 15: 57 He **g** us the victory through our
2Co 3: 6 the letter kills, but the Spirit **g** life.

GIVING (GIVE)
Ne 8: 8 **g** the meaning so that the people
Ps 19: 8 LORD are right, **g** joy to the heart.
Mt 6: 4 so that your **g** may be in secret.
2Co 8: 7 you also excel in this grace of **g**.

GLAD (GLADNESS)
Ps 31: 7 I will be **g** and rejoice in your love,
46: 4 whose streams make **g** the city
97: 1 LORD reigns, let the earth be **g**;
118: 24 let us rejoice today and be **g**.
Zec 2: 10 "Shout and be **g**, Daughter Zion.
Mt 5: 12 Rejoice and be **g**, because great is

GLADNESS (GLAD)
Ps 45: 15 Led in with joy and **g**, they enter
51: 8 Let me hear joy and **g**;
100: 2 Worship the LORD with **g**;
Jer 31: 13 I will turn their mourning into **g**;

GLORIFIED (GLORY)
Jn 13: 31 "Now the Son of Man is **g** and God
is **g** in him.
Ro 8: 30 those he justified, he also **g**.
2Th 1: 10 he comes to be **g** in his holy people

GLORIFY (GLORY)
Ps 34: 3 **G** the LORD with me; let us exalt
86: 12 I will **g** your name forever.
Mt 5: 16 deeds and **g** your Father in heaven.
Jn 13: 32 God will **g** the Son in himself,
17: 1 **G** your Son, that your Son may **g**

GLORIOUS (GLORY)
Ps 45: 13 All **g** is the princess within her
111: 3 **G** and majestic are his deeds,
145: 5 They speak of the **g** splendor
Isa 4: 2 the LORD will be beautiful and **g**,
12: 5 LORD, for he has done **g** things;
42: 21 to make his law great and **g**.
63: 15 from your lofty throne, holy and **g**.
Mt 19: 28 Son of Man sits on his **g** throne,
Lk 9: 30 and Elijah, appeared in **g** splendor,
Ac 2: 20 of the great and **g** day of the Lord.
2Co 3: 8 of the Spirit be even more **g**?
Php 3: 21 so that they will be like his **g** body.
Jude : 24 you before his **g** presence without

GLORY (GLORIFIED GLORIFY GLORIOUS)
Ex 15: 11 awesome in **g**, working wonders?
33: 18 said, "Now show me your **g**."
1Sa 4: 21 "The **G** has departed from Israel"
1Ch 16: 24 Declare his **g** among the nations,
16: 28 ascribe to the LORD **g**
29: 11 power and the **g** and the majesty
Ps 8: 5 crowned them with **g** and honor.
19: 1 The heavens declare the **g** of God;
24: 7 that the King of **g** may come in.
29: 1 beings, ascribe to the LORD **g**
34: 2 I will **g** in the LORD;
72: 19 the whole earth be filled with his **g**.
96: 3 Declare his **g** among the nations,
Pr 19: 11 is to one's **g** to overlook an offense.
25: 2 It is the **g** of God to conceal
25: 2 a matter is the **g** of kings.
Isa 6: 3 the whole earth is full of his **g**."
42: 8 I will not yield my **g** to another
48: 11 I will not yield my **g** to another.
Eze 43: 2 and I saw the **g** of the God of Israel
Mt 24: 30 of heaven, with power and great **g**.
25: 31 the Son of Man comes in his **g**,
Mk 8: 38 in his Father's **g** with the holy
13: 26 in clouds with great power and **g**.
Lk 2: 9 and the **g** of the Lord shone around
2: 14 "**G** to God in the highest heaven,
Jn 1: 14 have seen his **g**, the **g** of the one
17: 5 your presence with the **g** I had
17: 24 and to see my **g**, the **g** you have
Ac 7: 2 God of **g** appeared to our father
Ro 1: 23 exchanged the **g** of the immortal
3: 23 and fall short of the **g** of God,
8: 18 with the **g** that will be revealed
9: 4 theirs the divine **g**, the covenants,
1Co 10: 31 you do, do it all for the **g** of God.
11: 7 since he is the image and **g** of God;
11: 7 but woman is the **g** of man.
15: 43 sown in dishonor, it is raised in **g**;
2Co 3: 10 what was glorious has no **g** now
3: 18 faces contemplate the Lord's **g**,
4: 17 us an eternal **g** that far outweighs
Php 4: 19 the riches of his **g** in Christ Jesus.
Col 1: 27 is Christ in you, the hope of **g**.
3: 4 you also will appear with him in **g**.
1Ti 3: 16 on in the world, was taken up in **g**.
Titus 2: 13 appearing of the **g** of our great God
Heb 1: 3 The Son is the radiance of God's **g**
2: 7 crowned them with **g** and honor
1Pe 1: 24 all their **g** is like the flowers
Rev 4: 11 to receive **g** and honor and power,
21: 23 for the **g** of God gives it light,

GLUTTONS
Titus 1: 12 always liars, evil brutes, lazy **g**."

GNASHING
Mt 8: 12 will be weeping and **g** of teeth."

GNAT
Mt 23: 24 You strain out a **g** but swallow

GOAL
2Co 5: 9 So we make it our **g** to please him,
Php 3: 14 on toward the **g** to win the prize

GOAT (GOATS SCAPEGOAT)
Isa 11: 6 leopard will lie down with the **g**,

GOATS (GOAT)
Nu 7: 17 five male **g** and five male lambs

GOD (GOD'S GODLINESS GODLY GODS)
Ge 1: 1 beginning **G** created the heavens
1: 2 of **G** was hovering over the waters.
1: 26 Then **G** said, "Let us make
1: 27 So **G** created mankind in his own
1: 31 **G** saw all that he had made, and it
2: 3 Then **G** blessed the seventh day
2: 22 the LORD **G** made a woman
3: 21 The LORD **G** made garments
3: 23 So the LORD **G** banished him
5: 22 walked faithfully with **G** 300 years
6: 2 sons of **G** saw that the daughters
9: 16 everlasting covenant between **G**
17: 1 to him and said, "I am **G** Almighty;
21: 33 name of the LORD, the Eternal **G**.
22: 8 "**G** himself will provide the lamb
28: 12 the angels of **G** were ascending
32: 28 because you have struggled with **G**
32: 30 "It is because I saw **G** face to face,
35: 10 **G** said to him, "Your name is
41: 51 said, "It is because **G** has made me
50: 20 me, but **G** intended it for good
Ex 2: 24 **G** heard their groaning and he
3: 6 he said, "I am the **G** of your father,
3: 6 because he was afraid to look at **G**.
6: 7 know that I am the LORD your **G**,
8: 10 is no one like the LORD our **G**.
13: 18 So **G** led the people around
15: 2 He is my **G**, and I will praise him,
17: 9 with the staff of **G** in my hands."
19: 3 Then Moses went up to **G**,
20: 2 "I am the LORD your **G**,
20: 5 the LORD your **G**, am a jealous **G**,
20: 19 But do not have **G** speak to us
22: 28 "Do not blaspheme **G** or curse
31: 18 stone inscribed by the finger of **G**.
34: 6 the compassionate and gracious **G**,
34: 14 name is Jealous, is a jealous **G**.
Lev 18: 21 not profane the name of your **G**.
19: 2 I, the LORD your **G**, am holy.
26: 12 walk among you and be your **G**,
Nu 22: 38 I must speak only what **G** puts
23: 19 **G** is not human, that he should lie,
Dt 1: 17 anyone, for judgment belongs to **G**.
3: 22 the LORD your **G** himself will
3: 24 For what **g** is there in heaven
4: 24 **G** is a consuming fire, a jealous **G**.
4: 31 the LORD your **G** is a merciful **G**;
4: 39 day that the LORD is **G** in heaven
5: 11 the name of the LORD your **G**,
5: 14 is a sabbath to the LORD your **G**.
5: 26 voice of the living **G** speaking
6: 4 The LORD our **G**, the LORD is
6: 5 Love the LORD your **G** with all
6: 13 Fear the LORD your **G**, serve him
6: 16 Do not put the LORD your **G**
7: 9 is **G**; he is the faithful **G**,
7: 12 the LORD your **G** will keep his
7: 21 is a great and awesome **G**.
8: 5 the LORD your **G** disciplines you.
10: 12 what does the LORD your **G** ask you
but to fear the LORD your **G**,
10: 14 To the LORD your **G** belong
10: 17 For the LORD your **G** is **G** of gods
11: 13 to love the LORD your **G**
13: 3 The LORD your **G** is testing you
13: 4 It is the LORD your **G** you must
15: 6 the LORD your **G** will bless you
19: 9 to love the LORD your **G**
25: 16 the LORD your **G** detests anyone
29: 29 things belong to the LORD our **G**,
30: 2 return to the LORD your **G**
30: 16 today to love the LORD your **G**,
30: 20 you may love the LORD your **G**,
31: 6 the LORD your **G** goes with you;
32: 3 Oh, praise the greatness of our **G**!
32: 4 A faithful **G** who does no wrong,
33: 27 The eternal **G** is your refuge,
Jos 1: 9 the LORD your **G** will be with you
14: 8 the LORD my **G** wholeheartedly.
22: 5 to love the LORD your **G**, to walk
22: 34 that the LORD is **G**.
23: 11 careful to love the LORD your **G**.
23: 14 the LORD your **G** gave you has
Jdg 16: 28 Please, **G**, strengthen me just once
Ru 1: 16 be my people and your **G** my **G**.
1Sa 2: 2 there is no Rock like our **G**.
2: 3 for the LORD is a **G** who knows,
2: 25 **G** may mediate for the offender;
10: 26 men whose hearts **G** had touched.
12: 12 the LORD your **G** was your king.

1Sa 17: 26 defy the armies of the living **G**?"
17: 46 know that there is a **G** in Israel.
30: 6 found strength in the LORD his **G**.
2Sa 14: 14 But that is not what **G** desires;
22: 3 my **G** is my rock, in whom I take
22: 31 "As for **G**, his way is perfect:
1Ki 4: 29 **G** gave Solomon wisdom and very
8: 23 there is no **G** like you in heaven
8: 27 "But will **G** really dwell on earth?
8: 61 committed to the LORD our **G**,
18: 21 If the LORD is **G**, follow him;
18: 37 are **G**, and that you are turning
20: 28 think the LORD is a **g** the hills
2Ki 19: 15 you alone are **G** over all
1Ch 16: 35 Cry out, "Save us, **G** our Savior;
28: 2 for the footstool of our **G**, and I
28: 9 acknowledge the **G** of your father,
29: 10 LORD, the **G** of our father Israel,
29: 17 my **G**, that you test the heart and
2Ch 2: 4 for the Name of the LORD my **G**
5: 14 the LORD filled the temple of **G**.
6: 18 will **G** really dwell on earth
18: 13 can tell him only what my **G** says."
20: 6 you not the **G** who is in heaven?
25: 8 for **G** has the power to help
30: 9 for the LORD your **G** is gracious
33: 12 the favor of the LORD his **G**
Ezr 8: 22 "The gracious hand of our **G** is
9: 6 my **G**, to lift up my face to you,
9: 13 our **G**, you have punished us less
Ne 1: 5 the great and awesome **G**,
8: 8 from the Book of the Law of **G**,
9: 17 But you are a forgiving **G**,
9: 32 "Now therefore, our **G**, the great **G**,
Job 1: 1 he feared **G** and shunned evil.
2: 10 Shall we accept good from **G**,
4: 17 mortal be more righteous than **G**?
5: 17 is the one whom **G** corrects;
11: 7 you fathom the mysteries of **G**?
19: 26 yet in my flesh I will see **G**;
22: 13 Yet you say, 'What does **G** know?
25: 4 a mortal be righteous before **G**?
33: 14 For **G** does speak—now one way,
34: 12 unthinkable that **G** would do wrong,
36: 26 How great is **G**—
37: 22 **G** comes in awesome majesty.
Ps 18: 2 my **G** is my rock, in whom I take
18: 28 my **G** turns my darkness into light.
19: 1 The heavens declare the glory of **G**;
22: 1 My **G**, my **G**, why have you
29: 3 the **G** of glory thunders, the LORD
31: 14 I say, "You are my **G**."
40: 3 mouth, a hymn of praise to our **G**.
40: 8 I desire to do your will, my **G**;
42: 2 My soul thirsts for **G**, for the living
42: 2 When can I go and meet with **G**?
42: 11 Put your hope in **G**, for I will yet
45: 6 O **G**, will last for ever and ever;
46: 1 **G** is our refuge and strength,
46: 10 "Be still, and know that I am **G**;
47: 7 For **G** is the King of all the earth;
50: 3 Our **G** comes and will not be silent
51: 1 O **G**, according to your unfailing
51: 10 O **G**, and renew a steadfast spirit
51: 17 sacrifice, O **G**, is a broken spirit;
62: 7 and my honor depend on **G**;
65: 5 and righteous deeds, **G** our Savior,
66: 1 Shout for joy to **G**, all the earth!
66: 16 Come and hear, all you who fear **G**;
68: 6 **G** sets the lonely in families,
71: 17 my youth, **G**, you have taught
71: 19 Who is like you, **G**?
71: 22 harp for your faithfulness, my **G**;
73: 26 but **G** is the strength of my heart
77: 13 What **g** is as great as our **G**?
78: 19 They spoke against **G**;
81: 1 Sing for joy to **G** our strength;
84: 2 my flesh cry out for the living **G**.
84: 10 the house of my **G** than dwell
86: 12 you, Lord my **G**, with all my heart;
89: 7 of the holy ones **G** is greatly feared;
90: 2 to everlasting you are **G**.
91: 2 fortress, my **G**, in whom I trust."
95: 7 for he is our **G** and we are
100: 3 Know that the LORD is **G**. It is he
108: 1 My heart, O **G**, is steadfast;
113: 5 Who is like the LORD our **G**,
139: 23 Search me, **G**, and know my heart;
Pr 3: 4 a good name in the sight of **G**
Pr 25: 2 It is the glory of **G** to conceal
30: 5 "Every word of **G** is flawless;
Ecc 3: 11 can fathom what **G** has done
11: 5 cannot understand the work of **G**,
12: 13 of the matter: Fear **G** and keep his
Isa 9: 6 Mighty **G**, Everlasting Father,
37: 16 you alone are **G** over all
40: 3 in the desert a highway for our **G**.
40: 8 the word of our **G** endures forever."
40: 28 The LORD is the everlasting **G**,
41: 10 not be dismayed, for I am your **G**.
44: 6 apart from me there is no **G**.
52: 7 who say to Zion, "Your **G** reigns!"
55: 7 and to our **G**, for he will freely
57: 21 says my **G**, "for the wicked."
59: 2 have separated you from your **G**;
61: 10 my soul rejoices in my **G**.
62: 5 so will your **G** rejoice over you.
Jer 23: 23 "Am I only a **G** nearby,"
31: 33 I will be their **G**, and they will be
32: 27 the LORD, the **G** of all mankind.
Eze 28: 13 You were in Eden, the garden of **G**;
Da 3: 17 the **G** we serve is able to deliver us
9: 4 the great and awesome **G**,
Hos 12: 6 But you must return to your **G**;
Joel 2: 13 Return to the LORD your **G**, for he
Am 4: 12 Israel, prepare to meet your **G**."
Mic 6: 8 and to walk humbly with your **G**.
Na 1: 2 is a jealous and avenging **G**;
Zec 14: 5 Then the LORD my **G** will come,
Mal 3: 8 "Will a mere mortal rob **G**?
Mt 1: 23 (which means "**G** with us").
5: 8 pure in heart, for they will see **G**.
6: 24 You cannot serve both **G**
19: 6 Therefore what **G** has joined
19: 26 but with **G** all things are possible."
22: 21 Caesar's, and to **G** what is God's."
22: 37 "'Love the Lord your **G** with all
27: 46 (which means "My **G**, my **G**,
Mk 12: 29 The Lord our **G**, the Lord is one.
16: 19 *at the right hand of* **G**.
Lk 1: 37 For no word from **G** will ever fail."
1: 47 my spirit rejoices in **G** my Savior,
10: 9 'The kingdom of **G** has come near
10: 27 "'Love the Lord your **G** with all
18: 19 "No one is good—except **G** alone.
Jn 1: 1 and the Word was with **G**, and the Word was **G**.
1: 18 No one has ever seen **G**, but
1: 18 who is himself **G** and is in closest
3: 16 For **G** so loved the world that he
4: 24 **G** is spirit, and his worshipers must
7: 17 to do the will of **G** will find
14: 1 You believe in **G**;
20: 28 said to him, "My Lord and my **G**!"
Ac 2: 24 But **G** raised him from the dead,
5: 4 lied just to human beings but to **G**."
5: 29 "We must obey **G** rather than
7: 55 to heaven and saw the glory of **G**,
17: 23 inscription: TO AN UNKNOWN **G**.
20: 27 to you the whole will of **G**.
20: 32 "Now I commit you to **G**
Ro 1: 17 righteousness of **G** is revealed—
2: 11 For **G** does not show favoritism.
3: 4 Let **G** be true, and every human
3: 23 and fall short of the glory of **G**,
4: 24 **G** will credit righteousness—
5: 8 **G** demonstrates his own love for us
6: 23 the gift of **G** is eternal life in Christ
8: 28 in all things **G** works for the good
11: 22 the kindness and sternness of **G**:
14: 12 give an account of ourselves to **G**.
1Co 1: 20 not **G** made foolish the wisdom
2: 9 the things **G** has prepared for those
3: 6 it, but **G** has been making it grow.
6: 20 Therefore honor **G** with your
7: 24 they were in when **G** called them.
8: 8 food does not bring us near to **G**;
10: 13 **G** is faithful; he will not let you
10: 31 you do, do it all for the glory of **G**.
14: 33 For **G** is not a **G** of disorder
15: 28 him, so that **G** may be all in all.
2Co 1: 9 not rely on ourselves but on **G**,
2: 14 But thanks be to **G**, who always
3: 5 our competence comes from **G**.
4: 7 this all-surpassing power is from **G**
5: 19 that **G** was reconciling the world
5: 21 become the righteousness of **G**.
6: 16 we are the temple of the living **G**.
2Co 9: 7 for **G** loves a cheerful giver.
9: 8 **G** is able to bless you abundantly,
Gal 2: 6 **G** does not show favoritism—
6: 7 **G** cannot be mocked.
Eph 2: 10 **G** prepared in advance for us
4: 6 one **G** and Father of all, who is
Php 2: 6 being in very nature **G**, did not consider equality with **G**
4: 19 And my **G** will meet all your needs
1Th 2: 4 not trying to please people but **G**,
4: 7 For **G** did not call us to be impure,
4: 9 yourselves have been taught by **G**
5: 9 For **G** did not appoint us to suffer
1Ti 2: 5 there is one **G** and one mediator
4: 4 For everything **G** created is good,
5: 4 for this is pleasing to **G**.
Titus 2: 13 of the glory of our great **G**
Heb 1: 1 the past **G** spoke to our ancestors
4: 12 For the word of **G** is alive
6: 10 **G** is not unjust; he will not forget
10: 31 fall into the hands of the living **G**.
11: 6 faith it is impossible to please **G**,
12: 10 but **G** disciplines us for our good,
12: 29 for our "**G** is a consuming fire."
13: 15 us continually offer to **G** a sacrifice
Jas 1: 13 For **G** cannot be tempted by evil,
2: 19 You believe that there is one **G**.
2: 23 "Abraham believed **G**, and it was
4: 4 the world becomes an enemy of **G**.
4: 8 Come near to **G** and he will come
1Pe 4: 11 who speaks the very words of **G**.
2Pe 1: 21 from **G** as they were carried along
1Jn 1: 5 him and declare to you: **G** is light;
2: 5 love for **G** is truly made complete
3: 20 that **G** is greater than our hearts,
4: 7 another, for love comes from **G**.
4: 7 has been born of **G** and knows **G**.
4: 9 This is how **G** showed his love
4: 11 Dear friends, since **G** so loved us,
4: 12 No one has ever seen **G**; but if we
4: 16 Whoever lives in love lives in **G**,
Rev 4: 8 holy is the Lord **G** Almighty,'
7: 17 **G** will wipe away every tear
19: 6 For our Lord **G** Almighty reigns.

GOD-BREATHED (BREATHED)
2Ti 3: 16 All Scripture is **G** and is useful

GODLINESS (GOD)
1Ti 2: 2 quiet lives in all **g** and holiness.
4: 8 value, but **g** has value for all things,
6: 6 **g** with contentment is great gain.
6: 11 and pursue righteousness, **g**, faith,

GODLY (GOD)
2Co 7: 10 **G** sorrow brings repentance
11: 2 jealous for you with a **g** jealousy.
2Ti 3: 12 live a **g** life in Christ Jesus will be
2Pe 3: 11 You ought to live holy and **g** lives

GOD'S (GOD)
2Ch 20: 15 For the battle is not yours, but **G**.
Job 37: 14 stop and consider **G** wonders.
Ps 52: 8 I trust in **G** unfailing love for ever
69: 30 I will praise **G** name in song
Mk 3: 35 Whoever does **G** will is my brother
Jn 10: 36 because I said, 'I am **G** Son'?
Ro 2: 3 think you will escape **G** judgment?
2: 4 that **G** kindness is intended
3: 3 nullify **G** faithfulness?
7: 22 my inner being I delight in **G** law;
9: 16 desire or effort, but on **G** mercy.
11: 29 for **G** gifts and his call are
12: 2 test and approve what **G** will is—
13: 6 for the authorities are **G** servants,
1Co 7: 19 Keeping **G** commands is what
2Co 6: 2 now is the time of **G** favor, now is
Eph 1: 7 with the riches of **G** grace
5: 1 Follow **G** example, therefore,
1Th 4: 3 It is **G** will that you should be
5: 18 for this is **G** will for you in Christ
1Ti 6: 1 so that **G** name and our teaching
2Ti 2: 19 **G** solid foundation stands firm,
Titus 1: 7 an overseer manages **G** household,
Heb 1: 3 The Son is the radiance of **G** glory
9: 24 to appear for us in **G** presence.
11: 3 was formed at **G** command,
1Pe 2: 15 For it is **G** will that by doing good
3: 4 which is of great worth in **G** sight.

GODS (GOD)
Ex 20: 3 shall have no other **g** before me.
Ac 19: 26 by human hands are no **g** at all.

GOLD
Job 23: 10 tested me, I will come forth as **g**.
Ps 19: 10 precious than **g**, than much pure **g**;
119:127 love your commands more than **g**,
Pr 22: 1 esteemed is better than silver or **g**.

GOLGOTHA
Jn 19: 17 (which in Aramaic is called **G**).

GOLIATH
Philistine giant killed by David (1Sa 17; 21:9).

† GOOD
Ge 1: 4 God saw that the light was **g**,
1: 31 he had made, and it was very **g**.
2: 18 "It is not **g** for the man to be alone.
50: 20 God intended it for **g**
Job 2: 10 Shall we accept **g** from God,
Ps 14: 1 there is no one who does **g**.
34: 8 Taste and see that the LORD is **g**;
37: 3 Trust in the LORD and do **g**;
84: 11 no **g** thing does he withhold
86: 5 are forgiving and **g**,
103: 5 your desires with **g** things so
119: 68 You are **g**, and what you do is **g**;
133: 1 How **g** and pleasant it is
147: 1 How **g** it is to sing praises to our
Pr 3: 4 and a **g** name in the sight of God
11: 27 Whoever seeks **g** finds favor,
13: 21 are rewarded with **g** things.
17: 22 A cheerful heart is **g** medicine,
18: 22 He who finds a wife finds what is **g**
22: 1 A **g** name is more desirable than
31: 12 She brings him **g**, not harm,
Isa 5: 20 Woe to those who call evil **g** and **g**
52: 7 the feet of those who bring **g** news,
Jer 6: 16 ask where the **g** way is, and walk
Mic 6: 8 shown you, O mortal, what is **g**.
Mt 5: 45 sun to rise on the evil and the **g**,
7: 17 Likewise, every **g** tree bears **g** fruit,
12: 35 A **g** man brings **g** things out of the **g**
19: 17 "There is only One who is **g**.
25: 21 'Well done, **g** and faithful servant!
Mk 3: 4 to do **g** or to do evil, to save life
8: 36 What **g** is it for someone to gain
Lk 6: 27 do **g** to those who hate you,
Jn 10: 11 "I am the **g** shepherd. The **g**
Ro 8: 28 for the **g** of those who love him,
10: 15 feet of those who bring **g** news!"
12: 9 Hate what is evil; cling to what is **g**.
1Co 10: 24 their own **g**, but the **g** of others.
15: 33 company corrupts **g** character."
2Co 9: 8 you will abound in every **g** work.
Gal 6: 9 us not become weary in doing **g**,
6: 10 let us do **g** to all people,
Eph 2: 10 in Christ Jesus to do **g** works,
Php 1: 6 he who began a **g** work in you will
1Th 5: 21 test them all; hold on to what is **g**,
2Th 3: 13 never tire of doing what is **g**.
1Ti 3: 7 have a **g** reputation with outsiders,
4: 4 For everything God created is **g**,
6: 12 Fight the **g** fight of the faith.
6: 18 do **g**, to be rich in **g** deeds,
2Ti 3: 17 equipped for every **g** work.
4: 7 I have fought the **g** fight, I have
Heb 12: 10 but God disciplines us for our **g**,
1Pe 2: 3 you have tasted that the Lord is **g**.
2: 12 Live such **g** lives among the pagans

‡ GOSPEL
Ro 1: 16 For I am not ashamed of the **g**,
15: 16 duty of proclaiming the **g** of God,
1Co 1: 17 to baptize, but to preach the **g**—
9: 16 Woe to me if I do not preach the **g**!
15: 1 to remind you of the **g** I preached
Gal 1: 7 trying to pervert the **g** of Christ.
Php 1: 27 a manner worthy of the **g** of Christ.
1: 27 as one for the faith of the **g**

GOSSIP
Pr 11: 13 A **g** betrays a confidence,
16: 28 and a **g** separates close friends.
18: 8 of a **g** are like choice morsels;
26: 20 without a **g** a quarrel dies down.
2Co 12: 20 slander, **g**, arrogance and disorder.

GOVERNED
Ro 8: 6 the mind **g** by the Spirit is life

‡ GRACE (GRACIOUS)
Ps 45: 2 lips have been anointed with **g**,
Jn 1: 17 **g** and truth came through Jesus
Ac 20: 32 to God and to the word of his **g**,
Ro 3: 24 by his **g** through the redemption
5: 15 that came by the **g** of the one man,
5: 17 God's abundant provision of **g**
5: 20 increased, **g** increased all the more,
6: 14 are not under the law, but under **g**.
11: 6 if it were, **g** would no longer be **g**.
2Co 6: 1 you not to receive God's **g** in vain.
8: 9 you know the **g** of our Lord Jesus
12: 9 to me, "My **g** is sufficient for you,
Gal 2: 21 I do not set aside the **g** of God,
5: 4 you have fallen away from **g**.
Eph 1: 7 with the riches of God's **g**
2: 5 it is by **g** you have been saved.
2: 7 the incomparable riches of his **g**,
2: 8 For it is by **g** you have been saved,
Php 1: 7 all of you share in God's **g** with me.
Col 4: 6 conversation be always full of **g**,
2Th 2: 16 **g** gave us eternal encouragement
2Ti 2: 1 be strong in the **g** that is in Christ
Titus 2: 11 For the **g** of God has appeared
3: 7 having been justified by his **g**,
Heb 2: 9 the **g** of God he might taste death
4: 16 approach God's throne of **g**
4: 16 **g** to help us in our time of need.
Jas 4: 6 But he gives us more **g**. That is why
2Pe 3: 18 grow in the **g** and knowledge of

GRACIOUS (GRACE)
Nu 6: 25 face shine on you and be **g** to you;
Isa 30: 18 the LORD longs to be **g** to you;

GRAIN
Ecc 11: 1 Ship your **g** across the sea;
1Co 9: 9 an ox while it is treading out the **g**."

GRANTED
Php 1: 29 For it has been **g** to you on behalf

GRASS
Ps 103: 15 The life of mortals is like **g**,
1Pe 1: 24 the **g** withers and the flowers fall,

GRAVE (GRAVES)
Pr 7: 27 Her house is a highway to the **g**,
Hos 13: 14 Where, O **g**, is your destruction?

GRAVES (GRAVE)
Jn 5: 28 are in their **g** will hear his voice
Ro 3: 13 "Their throats are open **g**;

GREAT (GREATER GREATEST GREATNESS)
Ge 12: 2 "I will make you into a **g** nation,
Dt 10: 17 gods and Lord of lords, the **g** God,
2Sa 22: 36 your help has made me **g**.
Ps 19: 11 in keeping them there is **g** reward.
89: 1 sing of the LORD's **g** love forever;
103: 11 so **g** is his love for those who fear
108: 4 For **g** is your love, higher than
119:165 **G** peace have those who love your
145: 3 **G** is the LORD and most worthy
Pr 23: 24 father of a righteous child has **g** joy
Isa 42: 21 his righteousness to make his law **g**
La 3: 23 **g** is your faithfulness.
Mk 10: 43 become **g** among you must be your
Lk 21: 27 in a cloud with power and **g** glory.
1Ti 6: 6 with contentment is **g** gain.
Titus 2: 13 appearing of the glory of our **g** God
Heb 2: 3 if we ignore so **g** a salvation?
1Jn 3: 1 See what **g** love the Father has

GREATER (GREAT)
Mk 12: 31 is no commandment **g** than these."
Jn 1: 50 You will see **g** things than that."
15: 13 **G** love has no one than this:
1Co 12: 31 Now eagerly desire the **g** gifts.
Heb 11: 26 as of **g** value than the treasures
1Jn 3: 20 that God is **g** than our hearts,
4: 4 is in you is **g** than the one who is

GREATEST (GREAT)
Mt 22: 38 is the first and **g** commandment.
Lk 9: 48 least among you all who is the **g**."
1Co 13: 13 But the **g** of these is love.

GREATNESS (GREAT)
Ps 145: 3 his **g** no one can fathom.
150: 2 praise him for his surpassing **g**.
Isa 9: 7 the **g** of his government and peace
63: 1 forward in the **g** of his strength?

GREED (GREEDY)
Lk 12: 15 guard against all kinds of **g**;
Ro 1: 29 wickedness, evil, **g** and depravity.
Eph 5: 3 or of **g**, because these are improper
Col 3: 5 desires and **g**, which is idolatry.
2Pe 2: 14 they are experts in **g**—

GREEDY (GREED)
Pr 15: 27 The **g** bring ruin to their
1Co 6: 10 thieves nor the **g** nor drunkards
Eph 5: 5 No immoral, impure or **g** person—

GREEN
Ps 23: 2 makes me lie down in **g** pastures,

GREW (GROW)
Lk 2: 52 And Jesus **g** in wisdom and stature,
Ac 16: 5 in the faith and **g** daily in numbers.

GRIEF (GRIEVE)
Ps 10: 14 you consider their **g** and take it
Pr 14: 13 ache, and rejoicing may end in **g**.
La 3: 32 Though he brings **g**, he will show
Jn 16: 20 grieve, but your **g** will turn to joy.
1Pe 1: 6 have had to suffer **g** in all kinds

GRIEVE (GRIEF)
Eph 4: 30 do not **g** the Holy Spirit of God,
1Th 4: 13 so that you do not **g** like the rest

GROUND
Ge 3: 17 it," Cursed is the **g** because of you;
Ex 3: 5 where you are standing is holy **g**."
Eph 6: 13 you may be able to stand your **g**,

GROW (GREW)
Pr 13: 11 money little by little makes it **g**.
1Co 3: 6 it, but God has been making it **g**.
2Pe 3: 18 But **g** in the grace and knowledge

GRUMBLE (GRUMBLING)
1Co 10: 10 do not **g**, as some of them did—
Jas 5: 9 Don't **g** against one another,

GRUMBLING (GRUMBLE)
Jn 6: 43 "Stop **g** among yourselves,"
1Pe 4: 9 hospitality to one another without **g**.

GUARANTEEING (GUARANTOR)
2Co 1: 22 as a deposit, **g** what is to come.
Eph 1: 14 is a deposit **g** our inheritance until

GUARANTOR (GUARANTEEING)
Heb 7: 22 Jesus has become the **g** of a better

GUARD (GUARDIAN, GUARDIAN-REDEEMER)
Ps 141: 3 Set a **g** over my mouth, LORD;
Pr 4: 23 Above all else, **g** your heart,
13: 3 Those who **g** their lips preserve
21: 23 Those who **g** their mouths and
Isa 52: 12 God of Israel will be your rear **g**.
Mk 13: 33 Be on **g**! Be alert! You do not know
1Co 16: 13 Be on your **g**; stand firm
Php 4: 7 will **g** your hearts and your minds
1Ti 6: 20 **g** what has been entrusted to your

GUARDIAN (GUARD)
Gal 3: 25 come, we are no longer under a **g**.

GUARDIAN-REDEEMER (GUARD)
Ru 3: 9 since you are a **g** of our family."

GUIDE
Ex 13: 21 of cloud to **g** them on their way
15: 13 In your strength you will **g** them
Ne 9: 19 cloud did not fail to **g** them on
Ps 25: 5 **G** me in your truth and teach me,
48: 14 he will be our **g** even to the end.
67: 4 and **g** the nations of the earth.
73: 24 You **g** me with your counsel,
139: 10 even there your hand will **g** me,
Pr 6: 22 When you walk, they will **g** you;
Isa 58: 11 The LORD will **g** you always;
Jn 16: 13 he will **g** you into all the truth.

GUILTY
Ex 34: 7 does not leave the **g** unpunished;
Jn 8: 46 Can any of you prove me **g** of sin?
Heb 10: 22 to cleanse us from a **g** conscience
Jas 2: 10 at just one point is **g** of breaking all

HADES
Mt 16: 18 the gates of **H** will not overcome it.
Lk 16: 23 In **H**, where he was in torment,

HAGAR
Servant of Sarah, wife of Abraham, mother of Ishmael (Ge 16:1–6; 25:12). Driven away by

† Please see the "Hebrew to English Translation Chart," p. xix.
‡ Please see "Key New Testament Terms," p. 1584.

Sarah while pregnant (Ge 16:5–16); after birth of Isaac (Ge 21:9–21; Gal 4:21–31).

HAGGAI

Post-exilic prophet who encouraged rebuilding of the temple (Ezr 5:1; 6:14; Hag 1–2).

HAIR (HAIRS)
Lk 21: 18 not a **h** of your head will perish.
1Co 11: 6 for a woman to have her **h** cut off

HAIRS (HAIR)
Mt 10: 30 even the very **h** of your head are all

HALLELUJAH
Rev 19: 1, multitude in heaven shouting: "**H**!

HALLOWED (HOLY)
Mt 6: 9 Father in heaven, **h** be your name,

HAND (HANDIWORK HANDS)
Ps 16: 8 With him at my right **h**, I will not
37: 24 the LORD upholds him with his **h**.
139: 10 even there your **h** will guide me,
Ecc 9: 10 Whatever your **h** finds to do, do it
Mt 6: 3 not let your left **h** know what your right **h** is doing,
Jn 10: 28 one will snatch them out of my **h**.
1Co 12: 15 say, "Because I am not a **h**, I do not

HANDIWORK (HAND WORK)
Eph 2: 10 For we are God's **h**,

HANDS (HAND)
Ps 22: 16 they pierce my **h** and my feet.
24: 4 one who has clean **h** and a pure
31: 5 Into your **h** I commit my spirit;
31: 15 My times are in your **h**;
Pr 10: 4 but diligent **h** bring wealth.
31: 20 and extends her **h** to the needy.
Isa 55: 12 trees of the field will clap their **h**.
65: 2 out my **h** to an obstinate people,
Lk 23: 46 into your **h** I commit my spirit."
1Th 4: 11 business and work with your **h**,
1Ti 2: 8 lifting up holy **h** without anger
5: 22 not be hasty in the laying on of **h**,

HANNAH

Wife of Elkanah, mother of Samuel (1Sa 1). Prayer at dedication of Samuel (1Sa 2:1–10). Blessed (1Sa 2:18–21).

HAPPY
Ps 68: 3 may they be **h** and joyful.
Pr 15: 13 A **h** heart makes the face cheerful,
Ecc 3: 12 better for people than to be **h**
Jas 5: 13 Is anyone **h**? Let them sing songs

HARD (HARDEN HARDSHIP)
Ge 18: 14 Is anything too **h** for the LORD?
Ps 118: 5 When **h** pressed, I cried
Mt 19: 23 it is **h** for someone who is rich
1Co 4: 12 We work **h** with our own hands.
1Th 5: 12 those who work **h** among you,

HARDEN (HARD)
Ro 9: 18 he hardens whom he wants to **h**.
Heb 3: 8 do not **h** your hearts as you did

HARDHEARTED (HEART)
Dt 15: 7 do not be **h** or tightfisted toward

HARDSHIP (HARD)
Ro 8: 35 Shall trouble or **h** or persecution
2Ti 4: 5 endure **h**, do the work
Heb 12: 7 Endure **h** as discipline;

HARM
Ps 121: 6 the sun will not **h** you by day,
Pr 3: 29 not plot **h** against your neighbor,
31: 12 good, not **h**, all the days of her life.
Ro 13: 10 Love does no **h** to a neighbor.
1Jn 5: 18 and the evil one cannot **h** them.

HARMONY
Ro 12: 16 Live in **h** with one another.
2Co 6: 15 What **h** is there between Christ

HARVEST
Mt 9: 37 "The **h** is plentiful but the workers
Jn 4: 35 at the fields! They are ripe for **h**.
Gal 6: 9 at the proper time we will reap a **h**
Heb 12: 11 it produces a **h** of righteousness

HASTE (HASTY)
Pr 21: 5 lead to profit as surely as **h** leads
29: 20 you see someone who speaks in **h**?

HASTY (HASTE)
Pr 19: 2 how much more will **h** feet miss
Ecc 5: 2 do not be **h** in your heart to utter
1Ti 5: 22 Do not be **h** in the laying

† **HATE** (HATED HATES HATRED)
Lev 19: 17 "'Do not **h** a fellow Israelite
Ps 5: 5 You **h** all who do wrong;
45: 7 righteousness and **h** wickedness;
97: 10 those who love the LORD **h** evil,
139: 21 Do I not **h** those who **h** you,
Pr 8: 13 To fear the LORD is to **h** evil; I **h**
Am 5: 15 **H** evil, love good;
Mt 5: 43 your neighbor and **h** your enemy.'
Lk 6: 27 do good to those who **h** you,
Ro 12: 9 **H** what is evil; cling to what is

HATED (HATE)
Mt 10: 22 be **h** by everyone because of me,
Ro 9: 13 "Jacob I loved, but Esau I **h**."
Eph 5: 29 all, no one ever **h** their own body,
Heb 1: 9 righteousness and **h** wickedness;

HATES (HATE)
Pr 6: 16 There are six things the LORD **h**,
13: 24 spares the rod **h** their children,
Mal 2: 16 "The man who **h** and divorces his
Jn 3: 20 Everyone who does evil **h** the light,
1Jn 2: 9 to be in the light but **h** a brother

HATRED (HATE)
Pr 10: 12 **H** stirs up conflict, but love covers

HAUGHTY
Pr 16: 18 destruction, a **h** spirit before a fall.

HAY
1Co 3: 12 costly stones, wood, **h** or straw,

HEAD (HEADS HOTHEADED)
Ge 3: 15 he will crush your **h**, and you will
Ps 23: 5 You anoint my **h** with oil;
Pr 25: 22 will heap burning coals on his **h**,
Isa 59: 17 the helmet of salvation on his **h**;
Mt 8: 20 of Man has no place to lay his **h**."
Ro 12: 20 will heap burning coals on his **h**."
1Co 11: 3 the **h** of every man is Christ, and the **h** of the woman is man, and the **h** of Christ is God.
12: 21 And the **h** cannot say to the feet,
Eph 5: 23 the husband is the **h** of the wife as Christ is the **h**
2Ti 4: 5 keep your **h** in all situations,
Rev 19: 12 fire, and on his **h** are many crowns.

HEADS (HEAD)
Lev 26: 13 you to walk with **h** held high.
Isa 35: 10 everlasting joy will crown their **h**.

HEAL (HEALED HEALING HEALS)
2Ch 7: 14 their sin and will **h** their land.
Ps 41: 4 **h** me, for I have sinned against
Mt 10: 8 **H** the sick, raise the dead,
Lk 4: 23 'Physician, **h** yourself!'
5: 17 Lord was with Jesus to **h** the sick.

HEALED (HEAL)
Isa 53: 5 him, and by his wounds we are **h**.
Mt 9: 22 he said, "your faith has **h** you."
14: 36 and all who touched it were **h**.
Ac 4: 10 that this man stands before you **h**.
14: 9 saw that he had faith to be **h**
Jas 5: 16 each other so that you may be **h**.
1Pe 2: 24 "by his wounds you have been **h**."

HEALING (HEAL)
Eze 47: 12 for food and their leaves for **h**."
Mal 4: 2 righteousness will rise with **h** in its
1Co 12: 9 to another gifts of **h** by that one
12: 30 Do all have gifts of **h**? Do all speak
Rev 22: 2 the tree are for the **h** of the nations.

HEALS (HEAL)
Ex 15: 26 for I am the LORD, who **h** you."
Ps 103: 3 your sins and **h** all your diseases,
147: 3 He **h** the brokenhearted and binds

HEALTH (HEALTHY)
Pr 3: 8 This will bring **h** to your body
15: 30 good news gives **h** to the bones.

HEALTHY (HEALTH)
Mk 2: 17 "It is not the **h** who need a doctor,

HEAR (HEARD HEARING HEARS)
Dt 6: 4 **H**, O Israel: The LORD our God,
31: 13 law, must **h** it and learn to fear
2Ch 7: 14 then I will **h** from heaven,
Ps 94: 9 he who fashioned the ear not **h**?
Isa 29: 18 day the deaf will **h** the words
65: 24 they are still speaking I will **h**.
Mt 11: 15 Whoever has ears, let them **h**.
Jn 8: 47 The reason you do not **h** is that
2Ti 4: 3 what their itching ears want to **h**.

HEARD (HEAR)
Job 42: 5 My ears had **h** of you but now my
Isa 66: 8 Who has ever **h** of such things?
Mt 5: 21 "You have **h** that it was said
5: 27 "You have **h** that it was said,
5: 33 you have **h** that it was said
5: 38 "You have **h** that it was said,
5: 43 "You have **h** that it was said,
1Co 2: 9 what no ear has **h**, and what no
1Th 2: 13 which you **h** from us, you accepted
2Ti 1: 13 What you **h** from me, keep as
Jas 1: 25 not forgetting what they have **h**,

HEARING (HEAR)
Ro 10: 17 faith comes from **h** the message,

HEARS (HEAR)
Jn 5: 24 whoever **h** my word and believes
1Jn 5: 14 according to his will, he **h** us.
Rev 3: 20 If anyone **h** my voice and opens

HEART (BROKENHEARTED HARDHEARTED HEARTS WHOLEHEARTEDLY)
Ex 25: 2 everyone whose **h** prompts them
Lev 19: 17 not hate a fellow Israelite in your **h**.
Dt 4: 29 him if you seek him with all your **h**
6: 5 LORD your God with all your **h**
10: 12 LORD your God with all your **h**
15: 10 and do so without a grudging **h**;
30: 6 you may love him with all your **h**
30: 10 LORD your God with all your **h**
Jos 22: 5 and to serve him with all your **h**
1Sa 13: 14 sought out a man after his own **h**
16: 7 but the LORD looks at the **h**."
2Ki 23: 3 and decrees with all his **h** and
1Ch 28: 9 for the LORD searches every **h**
2Ch 7: 16 eyes and my **h** will always be there.
Job 22: 22 and lay up his words in your **h**.
37: 1 "At this my **h** pounds and leaps
Ps 14: 1 says in his **h**, "There is no God."
19: 14 this meditation of my **h** be pleasing
37: 4 will give you the desires of your **h**.
45: 1 My **h** is stirred by a noble theme as
51: 10 Create in me a pure **h**, O God,
51: 17 a broken and contrite **h** you, God,
66: 18 If I had cherished sin in my **h**,
86: 11 give me an undivided **h**, that I may
119: 11 in my **h** that I might not sin against
139: 23 Search me, God, and know my **h**;
Pr 3: 5 Trust in the LORD with all your **h**
4: 21 sight, keep them within your **h**;
4: 23 guard your **h**, for everything you
7: 3 write them on the tablet of your **h**.
13: 12 Hope deferred makes the **h** sick,
14: 13 Even in laughter the **h** may ache,
15: 30 eyes brings joy to the **h**, and good
17: 22 A cheerful **h** is good medicine,
24: 17 stumble, do not let your **h** rejoice,
27: 19 the face, so one's life reflects the **h**.
Ecc 3: 11 also set eternity in the human **h**;
8: 5 the wise **h** will know the proper
SS 4: 9 You have stolen my **h**, my sister,
Isa 40: 11 and carries them close to his **h**;
57: 15 and to revive the **h** of the contrite.
Jer 17: 9 The **h** is deceitful above all things
29: 13 when you seek me with all your **h**.
Eze 36: 26 I will give you a new **h** and put
Mt 5: 8 Blessed are the pure in **h**, for they
6: 21 treasure is, there your **h** will be
12: 34 mouth speaks what the **h** is full of.
22: 37 the Lord your God with all your **h**
Lk 6: 45 mouth speaks what the **h** is full of.
Ro 2: 29 is circumcision of the **h**,
10: 10 it is with your **h** that you believe
Eph 5: 19 music from your **h** to the Lord,
6: 6 doing the will of God from your **h**.
Col 3: 23 you do, work at it with all your **h**,
1Pe 1: 22 one another deeply, from the **h**.

HEARTS (HEART)
Dt 11: 18 Fix these words of mine in your **h**
1Ki 8: 39 do, since you know their **h** (for you
8: 61 may your **h** be fully committed
Ps 62: 8 pour out your **h** to him, for God is
Jer 31: 33 their minds and write it on their **h**.
Lk 16: 15 of others, but God knows your **h**.
24: 32 "Were not our **h** burning within us
Jn 14: 1 "Do not let your **h** be troubled.

† Please see the "Hebrew to English Translation Chart," p. xix.

Ac 15: 9 for he purified their **h** by faith.
Ro 2: 15 of the law are written on their **h**,
1Co 14: 25 the secrets of their **h** are laid bare.
2Co 3: 2 written on our **h**, known and read
3: 3 of stone but on tablets of human **h**.
4: 6 shine in our **h** to give us the light
Eph 3: 17 may dwell in your **h** through faith.
Col 3: 1 Christ, set your **h** on things above,
Heb 3: 8 do not harden your **h** as you did
10: 16 I will put my laws in their **h**, and I
1Jn 3: 20 that God is greater than our **h**,

HEAT
2Pe 3: 12 and the elements will melt in the **h**.

HEAVEN (HEAVENLY HEAVENS)
Ge 14: 19 Most High, Creator of **h** and earth.
1Ki 8: 27 even the highest **h**, cannot contain
2Ki 2: 1 take Elijah up to **h** in a whirlwind,
2Ch 7: 14 then I will hear from **h**, and I will
Isa 14: 12 How you have fallen from **h**,
66: 1 "**H** is my throne, and the earth is
Da 7: 13 man, coming with the clouds of **h**.
Mt 6: 9 "'Our Father in **h**, hallowed be
6: 20 up for yourselves treasures in **h**,
16: 19 you the keys of the kingdom of **h**;
16: 19 bind on earth will be bound in **h**,
19: 23 is rich to enter the kingdom of **h**.
24: 35 **H** and earth will pass away, but my
26: 64 and coming on the clouds of **h**."
28: 18 "All authority in **h** and on earth has
Mk 16: 19 *was taken up into* **h**
Lk 15: 7 **h** over one sinner who repents
18: 22 and you will have treasure in **h**.
Ro 10: 6 heart, 'Who will ascend into **h**?'"
2Co 5: 1 an eternal house in **h**, not built
12: 2 ago was caught up to the third **h**.
Php 2: 10 in **h** and on earth and under
3: 20 But our citizenship is in **h**.
1Th 1: 10 and to wait for his Son from **h**,
Heb 8: 5 a copy and shadow of what is in **h**.
9: 24 he entered **h** itself, now to appear
2Pe 3: 13 we are looking forward to a new **h**
Rev 21: 1 I saw "a new **h** and a new earth,"

HEAVENLY (HEAVEN)
2Co 5: 2 clothed instead with our **h** dwelling,
Eph 1: 3 who has blessed us in the **h** realms
1: 20 at his right hand in the **h** realms,
2Ti 4: 18 bring me safely to his **h** kingdom.
Heb 12: 22 of the living God, the **h** Jerusalem.

HEAVENS (HEAVEN)
Ge 1: 1 In the beginning God created the **h**
1Ki 8: 27 The **h**, even the highest heaven,
2Ch 2: 6 since the **h**, even the highest **h**,
Ps 8: 3 When I consider your **h**, the work
19: 1 The **h** declare the glory of God;
102: 25 the **h** are the work of your hands.
108: 4 is your love, higher than the **h**;
119: 89 it stands firm in the **h**.
139: 8 If I go up to the **h**, you are there;
Isa 51: 6 the **h** will vanish like smoke,
55: 9 "As the **h** are higher than the earth,
65: 17 will create new **h** and a new earth.
Joel 2: 30 I will show wonders in the **h**
Eph 4: 10 ascended higher than all the **h**,
2Pe 3: 10 The **h** will disappear with a roar;

HEBREW
Ge 14: 13 and reported this to Abram the **H**.

HEEDS
Pr 13: 1 A wise son **h** his father's
13: 18 whoever **h** correction is honored.
15: 5 but whoever **h** correction shows
15: 32 but the one who **h** correction gains

HEEL
Ge 3: 15 head, and you will strike his **h**."

HEIRS (INHERIT)
Ro 8: 17 **h** of God and co-heirs with Christ,
Gal 3: 29 and **h** according to the promise.
Eph 3: 6 gospel the Gentiles are **h** together
1Pe 3: 7 as **h** with you of the gracious gift

HELL
Mt 5: 22 will be in danger of the fire of **h**.
2Pe 2: 4 but sent them to **h**, putting them

HELMET
Isa 59: 17 and the **h** of salvation on his head;
Eph 6: 17 Take the **h** of salvation
1Th 5: 8 and the hope of salvation as a **h**.

HELP (HELPED HELPER HELPING HELPS)
2Sa 22: 36 You make your saving **h** my shield;
Ps 18: 6 I cried to my God for **h**.
30: 2 called to you for **h**, and you healed
46: 1 an ever-present **h** in trouble.
70: 4 long for your saving **h** always say,
79: 9 **H** us, God our Savior, for the glory
121: 1 where does my **h** come from?
Isa 41: 10 I will strengthen you and **h** you;
Jnh 2: 2 the realm of the dead I called for **h**,
Mk 9: 24 **h** me overcome my unbelief!"
Ac 16: 9 over to Macedonia and **h** us."

HELPED (HELP)
1Sa 7: 12 "Thus far the LORD has **h** us."

HELPER (HELP)
Ge 2: 18 I will make a **h** suitable for him."
Ps 10: 14 you are the **h** of the fatherless.
Heb 13: 6 confidence, "The Lord is my **h**;

HELPING (HELP)
Ac 9: 36 always doing good and **h** the poor.
1Co 12: 28 gifts of healing, of **h**, of guidance,
1Ti 5: 10 **h** those in trouble and devoting

HELPS (HELP)
Ro 8: 26 the Spirit **h** us in our weakness.

HEN
Mt 23: 37 as a **h** gathers her chicks under her

HERITAGE (INHERIT)
Ps 127: 3 Children are a **h** from the LORD,

HEROD
1. King of Judea who tried to kill Jesus (Mt 2; Lk 1:5).
2. Son of 1. Tetrarch of Galilee who arrested and beheaded John the Baptist (Mt 14:1–12; Mk 6:14–29; Lk 3:1, 19–20; 9:7–9); tried Jesus (Lk 23:6–15).
3. Grandson of 1. King of Judea who killed James (Ac 12:2); arrested Peter (Ac 12:3–19). Death (Ac 12:19–23).

HERODIAS
Wife of Herod the Tetrarch who persuaded her daughter to ask for John the Baptist's head (Mt 14:1–12; Mk 6:14–29).

HEZEKIAH
King of Judah. Restored the temple and worship (2Ch 29–31). Sought the LORD for help against Assyria (2Ki 18–19; 2Ch 32:1–23; Isa 36–37). Illness healed (2Ki 20:1–11; 2Ch 32:24–26; Isa 38). Judged for showing Babylonians his treasures (2Ki 20:12–21; 2Ch 32:31; Isa 39).

HID (HIDE)
Ge 3: 8 they **h** from the LORD God among
Ex 2: 2 child, she **h** him for three months.
Jos 6: 17 because she **h** the spies we sent.
Heb 11: 23 faith Moses' parents **h** him for

HIDDEN (HIDE)
Ps 19: 12 Forgive my **h** faults.
119: 11 I have **h** your word in my heart
Pr 2: 4 and search for it as for **h** treasure,
Isa 59: 2 your sins have **h** his face from you,
Mt 5: 14 A town built on a hill cannot be **h**.
13: 44 heaven is like treasure **h** in a field.
Col 1: 26 that has been kept **h** for ages
2: 3 in whom are **h** all the treasures
3: 3 and your life is now **h** with Christ

HIDE (HID HIDDEN)
Ps 17: 8 **h** me in the shadow of your wings
143: 9 LORD, for I **h** myself in you.

HIGH
Isa 57: 15 "I live in a **h** and holy place,

HILL (HILLS)
Mt 5: 14 town built on a **h** cannot be hidden.

HILLS (HILL)
Ps 50: 10 and the cattle on a thousand **h**.

HINDER (HINDERS)
1Sa 14: 6 Nothing can **h** the LORD
Mt 19: 14 do not **h** them, for the kingdom
1Co 9: 12 anything rather than **h** the gospel
1Pe 3: 7 so that nothing will **h** your prayers.

HINDERS (HINDER)
Heb 12: 1 let us throw off everything that **h**

HINT
Eph 5: 3 you there must not be even a **h**

HOLD
Ex 20: 7 LORD will not **h** anyone guiltless
Lev 19: 13 "'Do not **h** back the wages
Jos 22: 5 to **h** fast to him and to serve him
Ps 73: 23 you **h** me by my right hand.
Pr 4: 4 "Take **h** of my words with all your
Isa 54: 2 tent curtains wide, do not **h** back;
Mk 11: 25 if you **h** anything against anyone,
Php 2: 16 as you **h** firmly to the word of life.
3: 12 which Christ Jesus took **h** of me.
Col 1: 17 and in him all things **h** together.
1Th 5: 21 test them all; **h** on to what is good,
1Ti 6: 12 Take **h** of the eternal life
Heb 10: 23 Let us **h** unswervingly to the hope

† HOLINESS (HOLY)
Ex 15: 11 majestic in **h**, awesome in glory,
Ps 29: 2 the LORD in the splendor of his **h**.
96: 9 the LORD in the splendor of his **h**;
Ro 6: 19 to righteousness leading to **h**.
2Co 7: 1 perfecting **h** out of reverence
Eph 4: 24 God in true righteousness and **h**.
Heb 12: 10 in order that we may share in his **h**.
12: 14 without **h** no one will see the Lord.

† HOLY (HALLOWED HOLINESS)
Ex 19: 6 kingdom of priests and a **h** nation.'
20: 8 the Sabbath day by keeping it **h**.
Lev 11: 44 and be **h**, because I am **h**.
20: 7 yourselves and be **h**, because I am
20: 26 You are to be **h** to me because I,
21: 8 LORD am **h**—I who make you **h**.
22: 32 Do not profane my **h** name,
Ps 24: 3 Who may stand in his **h** place?
77: 13 Your ways, God, are **h**. What god is
99: 3 great and awesome name—he is **h**.
99: 5 worship at his footstool; he is **h**.
99: 9 for the LORD our God is **h**.
111: 9 **h** and awesome is his name.
Isa 5: 16 the **h** God will be proved **h** by his
6: 3 "**H**, **h**, **h** is the LORD Almighty;
40: 25 who is my equal?" says the **H** One.
57: 15 who lives forever, whose name is **h**:
Eze 28: 25 I will be proved **h** through them
Da 9: 24 and to anoint the Most **H** Place.
Hab 2: 20 The LORD is in his **h** temple;
Ac 2: 27 will not let your **h** one see decay.
Ro 7: 12 the law is **h**, and the commandment is **h**,
12: 1 sacrifice, **h** and pleasing to God—
2Th 1: 10 to be glorified in his **h** people
2Ti 1: 9 saved us and called us to a **h** life—
3: 15 you have known the **H** Scriptures,
Titus 1: 8 upright, **h** and disciplined.
1Pe 1: 15 is **h**, so be **h** in all you do;
1: 16 "Be **h**, because I am **h**."
2: 9 a royal priesthood, a **h** nation,
2Pe 3: 11 You ought to live **h** and godly lives
Rev 4: 8 "'**H**, **h**, **h** is the Lord God

HOME (HOMES)
Dt 6: 7 Talk about them when you sit at **h**
Ps 84: 3 Even the sparrow has found a **h**,
Pr 3: 33 he blesses the **h** of the righteous.
Mk 10: 29 "no one who has left **h** or brothers
Jn 14: 23 and make our **h** with them.
Titus 2: 5 pure, to be busy at **h**, to be kind,

HOMES (HOME)
Ne 4: 14 daughters, your wives and your **h**."
1Ti 5: 14 to manage their **h** and to give

HOMOSEXUALITY
1Ti 1: 10 for those practicing **h**, for slave

HONEST
Lev 19: 36 **h** weights, an **h** ephah and an **h** hin.
Dt 25: 15 must have accurate and **h** weights
Job 31: 6 let God weigh me in **h** scales and
Pr 12: 17 An **h** witness tells the truth,

HONEY
Ex 3: 8 a land flowing with milk and **h**—
Ps 19: 10 they are sweeter than **h**, than **h**
119:103 taste, sweeter than **h** to my mouth!

HONOR (HONORABLE HONORABLY HONORED HONORS)
Ex 20: 12 "**H** your father and your mother,
Nu 25: 13 he was zealous for the **h** of his God
Dt 5: 16 "**H** your father and your mother,

† Please see the "Hebrew to English Translation Chart," p. xix.

1Sa 2: 30 Those who **h** me I will **h**, but those
Ps 8: 5 crowned them with glory and **h**.
Pr 3: 9 **H** the LORD with your wealth,
11: 16 A kindhearted woman gains **h**,
15: 33 and humility comes before **h**.
20: 3 It is to one's **h** to avoid strife,
31: 31 **H** her for all that her hands have
Mt 15: 4 '**H** your father and mother'
Ro 12: 10 **H** one another above yourselves.
1Co 6: 20 Therefore **h** God with your bodies.
Eph 6: 2 "**H** your father and mother"—
1Ti 5: 17 church well are worthy of double **h**,
Heb 2: 7 crowned them with glory and **h**
Rev 4: 9 **h** and thanks to him who sits

HONORABLE (HONOR)
1Th 4: 4 body in a way that is holy and **h**,

HONORABLY (HONOR)
Heb 13: 18 and desire to live **h** in every way.

HONORED (HONOR)
Ps 12: 8 what is vile is **h** by the human race.
Pr 13: 18 but whoever heeds correction is **h**.
1Co 12: 26 if one part is **h**, every part rejoices
Heb 13: 4 Marriage should be **h** by all,

HONORS (HONOR)
Ps 15: 4 but **h** those who fear the LORD;
Pr 14: 31 is kind to the needy **h** God.
3Jn : 6 their way in a manner that **h** God.

HOOKS
Isa 2: 4 and their spears into pruning **h**.
Joel 3: 10 and your pruning **h** into spears.

HOPE (HOPES)
Job 13: 15 he slay me, yet will I **h** in him;
Ps 42: 5 Put your **h** in God, for I will yet
62: 5 rest in God; my **h** comes from him.
119: 74 for I have put my **h** in your word.
130: 7 Israel, put your **h** in the LORD,
147: 11 put their **h** in his unfailing love.
Pr 13: 12 **H** deferred makes the heart sick,
Isa 40: 31 but those who **h** in the LORD will
Ro 5: 4 and character, **h**.
8: 24 But **h** that is seen is no **h** at all.
12: 12 Be joyful in **h**, patient in affliction,
15: 4 they provide we might have **h**.
1Co 13: 13 three remain: faith, **h** and love.
15: 19 for this life we have **h** in Christ,
Col 1: 27 is Christ in you, the **h** of glory.
1Th 5: 8 and the **h** of salvation as a helmet.
1Ti 6: 17 to put their **h** in God, who richly
Titus 2: 13 while we wait for the blessed **h**—
Heb 6: 19 We have this **h** as an anchor
11: 1 faith is confidence in what we **h**
1Jn 3: 3 All who have this **h** in him purify

HOPES (HOPE)
1Co 13: 7 trusts, always **h**, always perseveres.

HORSE
Ps 147: 10 is not in the strength of the **h**,
Pr 26: 3 A whip for the **h**, a bridle
Zec 1: 8 me was a man mounted on a red **h**.
Rev 6: 2 and there before me was a white **h**!
6: 4 Then another **h** came out, a fiery
6: 5 and there before me was a black **h**!
6: 8 and there before me was a pale **h**!
19: 11 and there before me was a white **h**,

HOSANNA
Mt 21: 9 shouted, "**H** to the Son of David!"

HOSHEA
Last king of Israel (2Ki 15:30; 17:1–6).

HOSPITABLE (HOSPITALITY)
1Ti 3: 2 respectable, **h**, able to teach,
Titus 1: 8 he must be **h**, one who loves what

HOSPITALITY (HOSPITABLE)
Ro 12: 13 people who are in need. Practice **h**.
1Ti 5: 10 showing **h**, washing the feet
Heb 13: 2 shown **h** to angels without knowing
1Pe 4: 9 Offer **h** to one another without

HOSTILE
Ro 8: 7 governed by the flesh is **h** to God;

HOT
1Ti 4: 2 have been seared as with a **h** iron.
Rev 3: 15 that you are neither cold nor **h**.

HOT-TEMPERED
Pr 15: 18 A **h** person stirs up conflict,
19: 19 A **h** person must pay the penalty;
22: 24 not make friends with a **h** person,
29: 22 and a **h** person commits many sins.

HOTHEADED (HEAD)
Pr 14: 16 but a fool is **h** and yet feels secure.

HOUR
Ecc 9: 12 one knows when their **h** will come:
Mt 6: 27 worrying add a single **h** to your life?
Lk 12: 40 an **h** when you do not expect him."
Jn 12: 23 "The **h** has come for the Son
12: 27 this very reason I came to this **h**.

HOUSE (HOUSEHOLD HOUSEHOLDS STOREHOUSE)
Ex 20: 17 shall not covet your neighbor's **h**.
Ps 23: 6 in the **h** of the LORD forever.
84: 10 in the **h** of my God than dwell
122: 1 "Let us go to the **h** of the LORD."
127: 1 Unless the LORD builds the **h**,
Pr 7: 27 Her **h** is a highway to the grave,
21: 9 of the roof than share a **h**
Isa 56: 7 my **h** will be called a **h** of prayer
Zec 13: 6 I was given at the **h** of my friends.'
Mt 7: 24 is like a wise man who built his **h**
12: 29 can anyone enter a strong man's **h**
21: 13 "'My **h** will be called a **h**
Mk 3: 25 If a **h** is divided against itself, that **h**
Lk 11: 17 a **h** divided against itself will fall.
Jn 2: 16 Stop turning my Father's **h**
12: 3 the **h** was filled with the fragrance
14: 2 My Father's **h** has many rooms;
Heb 3: 3 of a **h** has greater honor than the **h**

HOUSEHOLD (HOUSE)
Jos 24: 15 But as for me and my **h**, we will
Mic 7: 6 are the members of his own **h**.
Mt 10: 36 will be the members of his own **h**.'
12: 25 or **h** divided against itself will not
1Ti 3: 12 manage his children and his **h** well.
3: 15 to conduct themselves in God's **h**,

HOUSEHOLDS (HOUSE)
Pr 15: 27 The greedy bring ruin to their **h**,

HUMAN (HUMANITY)
Ge 9: 6 "Whoever sheds **h** blood,
1Sa 15: 29 for he is not a **h** being, that he
Ac 5: 29 obey God rather than **h** beings!
2Pe 1: 21 never had its origin in the **h** will,

HUMANITY (HUMAN)
Heb 2: 14 he too shared in their **h** so

HUMBLE (HUMBLED HUMILIATE HUMILIATING HUMILITY)
2Ch 7: 14 will **h** themselves and pray and
Ps 25: 9 He guides the **h** in what is right
Pr 3: 34 favor to the **h** and oppressed.
Isa 66: 2 those who are **h** and contrite
Mt 11: 29 for I am gentle and **h** in heart,
Eph 4: 2 Be completely **h** and gentle;
Jas 4: 10 **H** yourselves before the Lord,
1Pe 5: 6 **H** yourselves, therefore,

HUMBLED (HUMBLE)
Mt 23: 12 who exalt themselves will be **h**,
Php 2: 8 he **h** himself by becoming obedient

HUMILIATE (HUMBLE)
Pr 25: 7 for him to **h** you before his nobles.

HUMILIATING (HUMBLE)
1Co 11: 22 God by **h** those who have nothing?

HUMILITY (HUMBLE)
Pr 11: 2 but with **h** comes wisdom.
15: 33 LORD, and **h** comes before honor.
2Co 10: 1 the **h** and gentleness of Christ,
Php 2: 3 in **h** value others above yourselves,
1Pe 5: 5 with **h** toward one another,

HUNGRY
Ps 107: 9 and fills the **h** with good things.
146: 7 oppressed and gives food to the **h**.
Pr 25: 21 If your enemy is **h**, give him food
Eze 18: 7 his food to the **h** and provides
Mt 25: 35 For I was **h** and you gave me
Lk 1: 53 has filled the **h** with good things
Jn 6: 35 comes to me will never go **h**,
Ro 12: 20 "If your enemy is **h**, feed him;

HURT (HURTS)
Ecc 8: 9 lords it over others to his own **h**.
Mk 16: 18 *it will not **h** them*
Rev 2: 11 one who is victorious will not be **h**

HURTS (HURT)
Ps 15: 4 who keeps an oath even when it **h**,
Pr 26: 28 A lying tongue hates those it **h**,

HUSBAND (HUSBAND'S HUSBANDS)
1Co 7: 3 The **h** should fulfill his marital
7: 3 and likewise the wife to her **h**.
7: 4 her own body but yields it to her **h**.
7: 4 the **h** does not have authority over
7: 10 wife must not separate from her **h**.
7: 11 And a **h** must not divorce his wife.
7: 13 And if a woman has a **h** who is not
7: 39 But if her **h** dies, she is free
2Co 11: 2 I promised you to one **h**, to Christ,
Eph 5: 23 For the **h** is the head of the wife as
5: 33 and the wife must respect her **h**.

HUSBAND'S (HUSBAND)
Pr 12: 4 of noble character is her **h** crown,

HUSBANDS (HUSBAND)
Eph 5: 22 yourselves to your own **h** as you do
5: 25 **H**, love your wives, just as Christ
Titus 2: 4 the younger women to love their **h**
1Pe 3: 1 yourselves to your own **h** so that,
3: 7 **H**, in the same way be considerate

HYMN
1Co 14: 26 each of you has a **h**, or a word

HYPOCRISY (HYPOCRITE HYPOCRITES)
Mt 23: 28 on the inside you are full of **h**
1Pe 2: 1 of all malice and all deceit, **h**, envy,

HYPOCRITE (HYPOCRISY)
Mt 7: 5 You **h**, first take the plank

HYPOCRITES (HYPOCRISY)
Ps 26: 4 deceitful, nor do I associate with **h**.
Mt 6: 5 do not be like the **h**, for they love

HYSSOP
Ps 51: 7 Cleanse me with **h**, and I will be

IDLE (IDLENESS)
1Th 5: 14 those who are **i** and disruptive,
2Th 3: 6 away from every believer who is **i**
1Ti 5: 13 they get into the habit of being **i**

IDLENESS (IDLE)
Pr 31: 27 and does not eat the bread of **i**.

IDOL (IDOLATRY IDOLS)
Isa 44: 17 From the rest he makes a god, his **i**;
1Co 8: 4 We know that "An **i** is nothing

IDOLATRY (IDOL)
Col 3: 5 evil desires and greed, which is **i**.

IDOLS (IDOL)
1Co 8: 1 Now about food sacrificed to **i**:

IGNORANT (IGNORE)
1Co 15: 34 there are some who are **i** of God—
Heb 5: 2 to deal gently with those who are **i**
1Pe 2: 15 good you should silence the **i** talk
2Pe 3: 16 **i** and unstable people distort,

IGNORE (IGNORANT IGNORES)
Dt 22: 1 not **i** it but be sure to take it back
Ps 9: 12 he does not **i** the cries
Heb 2: 3 escape if we **i** so great a salvation?

IGNORES (IGNORE)
Pr 10: 17 whoever **i** correction leads others

ILLUMINATED
Rev 18: 1 and the earth was **i** by his splendor.

IMAGE
Ge 1: 26 "Let us make mankind in our **i**,
1: 27 God created mankind in his own **i**, in
the **i** of God he created them;
Ro 8: 29 to be conformed to the **i** of his Son,
1Co 11: 7 since he is the **i** and glory of God;
2Co 3: 18 into his **i** with ever-increasing glory,
Col 1: 15 The Son is the **i** of the invisible
3: 10 in knowledge in the **i** of its Creator.

IMAGINE
Eph 3: 20 more than all we ask or **i**,

IMITATE (IMITATORS)
1Co 4: 16 Therefore I urge you to **i** me.
Heb 6: 12 but to **i** those who through faith
13: 7 of their way of life and **i** their faith.
3Jn : 11 do not **i** what is evil but what is

IMITATORS (IMITATE)
1Th 1: 6 You became **i** of us and of the Lord,
2: 14 became **i** of God's churches

IMMANUEL
Isa 7: 14 birth to a son, and will call him **I**.
Mt 1: 23 they will call him **I**" (which means

IMMORAL (IMMORALITY)
1Co 5: 9 to associate with sexually **i** people
5: 10 the people of this world who are **i**,
5: 11 or sister but is sexually **i** or greedy,
6: 9 Neither the sexually **i** nor idolaters

Eph 5: 5 No **i**, impure or greedy person—
Heb 12: 16 See that no one is sexually **i**, or is
13: 4 the adulterer and all the sexually **i**.
Rev 21: 8 the sexually **i**, those who practice
22: 15 arts, the sexually **i**, the murderers,

IMMORALITY (IMMORAL)
Mt 5: 32 except for sexual **i**, makes her
19: 9 except for sexual **i**, and marries
1Co 6: 13 is not meant for sexual **i**
6: 18 Flee from sexual **i**. All other sins
10: 8 We should not commit sexual **i**,
Gal 5: 19 sexual **i**, impurity and debauchery;
Eph 5: 3 must not be even a hint of sexual **i**,
1Th 4: 3 that you should avoid sexual **i**;
Jude : 4 grace of our God into a license for **i**

IMMORTAL (IMMORTALITY)
Ro 1: 23 exchanged the glory of the **i** God
1Ti 1: 17 Now to the King eternal, **i**,
6: 16 who alone is **i** and who lives

IMMORTALITY (IMMORTAL)
Ro 2: 7 and **i**, he will give eternal life.
1Co 15: 53 and the mortal with **i**.
2Ti 1: 10 and **i** to light through the gospel.

IMPERISHABLE
1Pe 1: 23 seed, but of **i**, through the living

IMPORTANCE (IMPORTANT)
1Co 15: 3 I passed on to you as of first **i**:

IMPORTANT (IMPORTANCE)
Mt 23: 23 have neglected the more **i** matters
Mk 12: 29 "The most **i** one," answered Jesus,
12: 33 as yourself is more **i** than all burnt
Php 1: 18 The **i** thing is that in every way,

IMPOSSIBLE
Mt 17: 20 Nothing will be **i** for you."
Lk 18: 27 "What is **i** with man is possible
Heb 6: 18 in which it is **i** for God to lie,
11: 6 without faith it is **i** to please God,

IMPROPER
Eph 5: 3 because these are **i** for God's holy

IMPURE (IMPURITY)
Ac 10: 15 "Do not call anything **i** that God
Eph 5: 5 No immoral, **i** or greedy person—
1Th 4: 7 For God did not call us to be **i**,
Rev 21: 27 Nothing **i** will ever enter it,

IMPURITY (IMPURE)
Ro 1: 24 hearts to sexual **i** for the degrading
Eph 5: 3 or of any kind of **i**, or of greed,

INCENSE
Ex 40: 5 Place the gold altar of **i** in front
Ps 141: 2 my prayer be set before you like **i**;

INCOME
Ecc 5: 10 is never satisfied with their **i**.
1Co 16: 2 of money in keeping with your **i**,

INCOMPARABLE
Eph 2: 7 ages he might show the **i** riches

INCREASE (EVER-INCREASING INCREASED INCREASING)
Ge 1: 22 "Be fruitful and **i** in number and
Ps 62: 10 though your riches **i**, do not set
Lk 17: 5 said to the Lord, "**I** our faith!"
1Th 3: 12 May the Lord make your love **i**

INCREASED (INCREASE)
Ac 6: 7 of disciples in Jerusalem **i** rapidly,
Ro 5: 20 where sin **i**, grace **i** all the more,

INCREASING (INCREASE)
Ac 6: 1 the number of disciples was **i**,
2Th 1: 3 all of you have for one another is **i**.
2Pe 1: 8 these qualities in **i** measure,

INDEPENDENT
1Co 11: 11 in the Lord woman is not **i** of man, nor is man **i** of woman.

INDESCRIBABLE
2Co 9: 15 Thanks be to God for his **i** gift!

INDISPENSABLE
1Co 12: 22 body that seem to be weaker are **i**,

INEFFECTIVE
2Pe 1: 8 they will keep you from being **i**

INEXPRESSIBLE
2Co 12: 4 up to paradise and heard **i** things,
1Pe 1: 8 are filled with an **i** and glorious joy,

INFANTS
Mt 21: 16 the lips of children and **i** you, Lord,
1Co 14: 20 In regard to evil be **i**, but in your

INHERIT (CO-HEIRS HEIRS HERITAGE INHERITANCE)
Ps 37: 11 the meek will **i** the land and enjoy
37: 29 The righteous will **i** the land
Mt 5: 5 the meek, for they will **i** the earth.
Mk 10: 17 "what must I do to **i** eternal life?"
1Co 15: 50 cannot **i** the kingdom of God,

INHERITANCE (INHERIT)
Dt 4: 20 to be the people of his **i**, as you
Pr 13: 22 A good person leaves an **i** for their
Eph 1: 14 deposit guaranteeing our **i** until
5: 5 has any **i** in the kingdom of Christ
Heb 9: 15 receive the promised eternal **i**—
1Pe 1: 4 This **i** is kept in heaven for you,

INIQUITIES (INIQUITY)
Ps 78: 38 he forgave their **i** and did not
103: 10 or repay us according to our **i**.
Isa 59: 2 your **i** have separated you from
Mic 7: 19 hurl all our **i** into the depths

INIQUITY (INIQUITIES)
Ps 51: 2 Wash away all my **i** and cleanse me
Isa 53: 6 has laid on him the **i** of us all.

INJUSTICE
2Ch 19: 7 the LORD our God there is no **i**

INNOCENT
Pr 17: 26 a fine on the **i** is not good,
Mt 10: 16 shrewd as snakes and as **i** as doves.
27: 4 said, "for I have betrayed **i** blood."
1Co 4: 4 clear, but that does not make me **i**.

INSCRIPTION
Mt 22: 20 image is this? And whose **i**?"

INSOLENT
Ro 1: 30 **i**, arrogant and boastful;

INSTITUTED
Ro 13: 2 is rebelling against what God has **i**,

INSTRUCT (INSTRUCTED INSTRUCTION)
Ps 32: 8 I will **i** you and teach you
Pr 9: 9 **I** the wise and they will be wiser
Ro 15: 14 and competent to **i** one another.

INSTRUCTED (INSTRUCT)
2Ti 2: 25 Opponents must be gently **i**,

† **INSTRUCTION** (INSTRUCT)
Pr 1: 3 for receiving **i** in prudent behavior,
1: 7 but fools despise wisdom and **i**.
1: 8 your father's **i** and do not forsake
4: 1 Listen, my sons, to a father's **i**;
4: 13 Hold on to **i**, do not let it go;
6: 23 correction and **i** are the way to life,
8: 10 Choose my **i** instead of silver,
8: 33 Listen to my **i** and be wise;
13: 1 A wise son heeds his father's **i**,
13: 13 Whoever scorns **i** will pay for it,
16: 20 Whoever gives heed to **i** prospers,
16: 21 and gracious words promote **i**.
23: 12 Apply your heart to **i** and your ears
23: 23 wisdom, **i** and insight as well.
Isa 8: 20 Consult God's **i** and the testimony
1Co 14: 6 or prophecy or word of **i**?
14: 26 hymn, or a word of **i**, a revelation,
Eph 6: 4 in the training and **i** of the Lord.
1Th 4: 8 who rejects this **i** does not reject
2Th 3: 14 anyone who does not obey our **i**
1Ti 6: 3 sound **i** of our Lord Jesus Christ
2Ti 4: 2 with great patience and careful **i**.

INSULT (INSULTS)
Pr 12: 16 but the prudent overlook an **i**.
Mt 5: 11 are you when people **i** you,
Lk 6: 22 when they exclude you and **i** you
1Pe 3: 9 not repay evil with evil or **i** with **i**.

INSULTS (INSULT)
Pr 9: 7 corrects a mocker invites **i**;

INTEGRITY
1Ki 9: 4 walk before me faithfully with **i**
Job 2: 3 And he still maintains his **i**,
27: 5 till I die, I will not deny my **i**.
Pr 10: 9 Whoever walks in **i** walks securely,
11: 3 The **i** of the upright guides them,
29: 10 The bloodthirsty hate a person of **i**
Titus 2: 7 In your teaching show **i**,

INTELLIGENCE
Isa 29: 14 the **i** of the intelligent will vanish."
1Co 1: 19 the **i** of the intelligent I will

INTELLIGIBLE
1Co 14: 19 I would rather speak five **i** words

INTERCEDE (INTERCEDES INTERCESSION)
Heb 7: 25 him, because he always lives to **i**

INTERCEDES (INTERCEDE)
Ro 8: 26 the Spirit himself **i** for us through

INTERCESSION (INTERCEDE)
Isa 53: 12 and made **i** for the transgressors.
1Ti 2: 1 **i** and thanksgiving be made for all

INTEREST
Ne 5: 10 But let us stop charging **i**!

INTERESTS
1Co 7: 34 and his **i** are divided.
Php 2: 4 not looking to your own **i** but each of you to the **i** of the others.
2: 21 everyone looks out for their own **i**,

INTERMARRY (MARRY)
Dt 7: 3 Do not **i** with them. Do not give

INVESTIGATED
Lk 1: 3 I myself have carefully **i** everything

INVISIBLE
Ro 1: 20 of the world God's **i** qualities—
Col 1: 15 The Son is the image of the **i** God,
1Ti 1: 17 eternal, immortal, **i**, the only God,

INVITE (INVITED INVITES)
Lk 14: 13 you give a banquet, **i** the poor,

INVITED (INVITE)
Mt 22: 14 "For many are **i**, but few are
25: 35 I was a stranger and you **i** me in,

INVITES (INVITE)
1Co 10: 27 If an unbeliever **i** you to a meal

IRON
1Ti 4: 2 have been seared as with a hot **i**.
Rev 2: 27 'will rule them with an **i** scepter

IRREVOCABLE
Ro 11: 29 for God's gifts and his call are **i**.

ISAAC
Son of Abraham by Sarah (Ge 17:19; 21:1–7; 1Ch 1:28). Offered up by Abraham (Ge 22; Heb 11:17–19). Rebekah taken as wife (Ge 24). Fathered Esau and Jacob (Ge 25:19–26; 1Ch 1:34). Tricked into blessing Jacob (Ge 27). Father of Israel (Ex 3:6; Dt 29:13; Ro 9:10).

ISAIAH
Prophet to Judah (Isa 1:1). Called by the LORD (Isa 6).

ISHMAEL
Son of Abraham by Hagar (Ge 16; 1Ch 1:28). Blessed, but not son of covenant (Ge 17:18–21; Gal 4:21–31). Sent away by Sarah (Ge 21:8–21).

ISRAEL (ISRAELITES)
1. Name given to Jacob (see JACOB).
2. Corporate name of Jacob's descendants; often specifically Northern Kingdom.

Dt 6: 4 Hear, O **I**: The LORD our God,
1Sa 4: 21 "The Glory has departed from **I**"—
Isa 27: 6 **I** will bud and blossom and fill all
Jer 31: 10 'He who scattered **I** will gather
Eze 39: 23 that the people of **I** went into exile
Mk 12: 29 'Hear, O **I**: The Lord our God,
Lk 22: 30 judging the twelve tribes of **I**.
Ro 9: 6 all who are descended from **I** are **I**.
11: 26 and in this way all **I** will be saved.
Eph 3: 6 Gentiles are heirs together with **I**,

ISRAELITES (ISRAEL)
Ex 14: 22 the **I** went through the sea on dry
16: 35 The **I** ate manna forty years,
Hos 1: 10 "Yet the **I** will be like the sand
Ro 9: 27 number of the **I** be like the sand

ITCHING
2Ti 4: 3 say what their **i** ears want to hear.

JACOB
Second son of Isaac, twin of Esau (Ge 25:21–26; 1Ch 1:34). Bought Esau's birthright (Ge 25:29–34); tricked Isaac into blessing him (Ge 27:1–37). Abrahamic covenant perpetu-

† Please see the "Hebrew to English Translation Chart," p. xix.

ated through (Ge 28:13–15; Mal 1:2). Vision at Bethel (Ge 28:10–22). Wives and children (Ge 29:1—30:24; 35:16–26; 1Ch 2–9). Wrestled with God; name changed to Israel (Ge 32:22–32). Sent sons to Egypt during famine (Ge 42–43). Settled in Egypt (Ge 46). Blessed Ephraim and Manasseh (Ge 48). Blessed sons (Ge 49:1–28; Heb 11:21). Death (Ge 49:29–33). Burial (Ge 50:1–14).

JAMES

1. Apostle; brother of John (Mt 4:21–22; 10:2; Mk 3:17; Lk 5:1–10). At transfiguration (Mt 17:1–13; Mk 9:1–13; Lk 9:28–36). Killed by Herod (Ac 12:2).

2. Apostle; son of Alphaeus (Mt 10:3; Mk 3:18; Lk 6:15).

3. Brother of Jesus (Mt 13:55; Mk 6:3; Lk 24:10; Gal 1:19) and Judas (Jude 1). With believers before Pentecost (Ac 1:13). Leader of church at Jerusalem (Ac 12:17; 15; 21:18; Gal 2:9, 12). Author of epistle (Jas 1:1).

JAPHETH

Son of Noah (Ge 5:32; 1Ch 1:4–5). Blessed (Ge 9:18–28).

JARS

2Co 4: 7 we have this treasure in **j** of clay

† JEALOUS (JEALOUSY)

Ex 20: 5 am a **j** God, punishing the children
34: 14 whose name is **J**, is a **j** God.
Dt 4: 24 God is a consuming fire, a **j** God.
Joel 2: 18 Then the LORD was **j** for his land
Zec 1: 14 I am very **j** for Jerusalem and Zion,
2Co 11: 2 am **j** for you with a godly jealousy.

JEALOUSY (JEALOUS)

1Co 3: 3 For since there is **j** and quarreling
2Co 11: 2 I am jealous for you with a godly **j**.
Gal 5: 20 hatred, discord, **j**, fits of rage,

JEHOAHAZ

1. Son of Jehu; king of Israel (2Ki 13:1–9).

2. Son of Josiah; king of Judah (2Ki 23:31–34; 2Ch 36:1–4).

JEHOASH

Son of Jehoahaz; king of Israel (2Ki 13–14; 2Ch 25).

JEHOIACHIN

Son of Jehoiakim; king of Judah exiled by Nebuchadnezzar (2Ki 24:8–17; 2Ch 36:8–10; Jer 22:24–30; 24:1). Raised from prisoner status (2Ki 25:27–30; Jer 52:31–34).

JEHOIAKIM

Son of Josiah; king of Judah (2Ki 23:34—24:6; 2Ch 36:4–8; Jer 22:18–23; 36).

JEHORAM

Son of Jehoshaphat; king of Judah (2Ki 8:16–24).

JEHOSHAPHAT

Son of Asa; king of Judah (1Ki 22:41–50; 2Ki 3; 2Ch 17–20).

JEHU

King of Israel (1Ki 19:16–19; 2Ki 9–10).

JEPHTHAH

Judge from Gilead who delivered Israel from Ammon (Jdg 10:6—12:7). Made rash vow concerning his daughter (Jdg 11:30–40).

JEREMIAH

Prophet to Judah (Jer 1:1–3). Called by the LORD (Jer 1). Put in stocks (Jer 20:1–3). Threatened for prophesying (Jer 11:18–23; 26). Opposed by Hananiah (Jer 28). Scroll burned (Jer 36). Imprisoned (Jer 37). Thrown into cistern (Jer 38). Forced to Egypt with those fleeing Babylonians (Jer 43).

JEROBOAM

1. Official of Solomon; rebelled to become first king of Israel (1Ki 11:26–40; 12:1–20; 2Ch 10). Idolatry (1Ki 12:25–33); judgment for (1Ki 13–14; 2Ch 13).

2. Son of Jehoash; king of Israel (1Ki 14:23–29).

JERUSALEM

2Ki 23: 27 and I will reject **J**, the city I chose,
2Ch 6: 6 now I have chosen **J** for my Name
Ne 2: 17 let us rebuild the wall of **J**,
Ps 122: 6 Pray for the peace of **J**:
125: 2 As the mountains surround **J**,
137: 5 If I forget you, **J**, may my right
Isa 40: 9 You who bring good news to **J**,
65: 18 for I will create **J** to be a delight
Joel 3: 17 **J** will be holy; never again will
Zep 3: 16 On that day they will say to **J**,
Zec 2: 4 man, '**J** will be a city without walls
8: 8 I will bring them back to live in **J**;
14: 8 living water will flow out from **J**,
Mt 23: 37 "**J**, **J**, you who kill the prophets
Lk 13: 34 "**J**, **J**, you who kill the prophets
21: 24 **J** will be trampled
Jn 4: 20 where we must worship is in **J**."
Ac 1: 8 and you will be my witnesses in **J**,
Gal 4: 25 to the present city of **J**,
Rev 21: 2 the new **J**, coming down

JESUS

LIFE: Genealogy (Mt 1:1–17; Lk 3:21–37). Birth announced (Mt 1:18–25; Lk 1:26–45). Birth (Mt 2:1–12; Lk 2:1–40). Escape to Egypt (Mt 2:13–23). As a boy in the temple (Lk 2:41–52). Baptism (Mt 3:13–17; Mk 1:9–11; Lk 3:21–22; Jn 1:32–34). Temptation (Mt 4:1–11; Mk 1:12–13; Lk 4:1–13). Ministry in Galilee (Mt 4:12—18:35; Mk 1:14—9:50; Lk 4:14—13:9; Jn 1:35—2:11; 4; 6), Transfiguration (Mt 17:1–8; Mk 9:2–8; Lk 9:28–36), on the way to Jerusalem (Mt 19–20; Mk 10; Lk 13:10—19:27), in Jerusalem (Mt 21–25; Mk 11–13; Lk 19:28—21:38; Jn 2:12—3:36; 5; 7–12). Last supper (Mt 26:17–35; Mk 14:12–31; Lk 22:1–38; Jn 13–17). Arrest and trial (Mt 26:36—27:31; Mk 14:43—15:20; Lk 22:39—23:25; Jn 18:1—19:16). Crucifixion (Mt 27:32–66; Mk 15:21–47; Lk 23:26–55; Jn 19:28–42). Resurrection and appearances (Mt 28; Mk 16; Lk 24; Jn 20–21; Ac 1:1–11; 7:56; 9:3–6; 1Co 15:1–8; Rev 1:1–20).

MIRACLES. Healings: official's son (Jn 4:43–54), demoniac in Capernaum (Mk 1:23–26; Lk 4:33–35), Peter's mother-in-law (Mt 8:14–17; Mk 1:29–31; Lk 4:38–39), leper (Mt 8:2–4; Mk 1:40–45; Lk 5:12–16), paralytic (Mt 9:1–8; Mk 2:1–12; Lk 5:17–26), cripple (Jn 5:1–9), shriveled hand (Mt 12:10–13; Mk 3:1–5; Lk 6:6–11), centurion's servant (Mt 8:5–13; Lk 7:1–10), widow's son raised (Lk 7:11–17), demoniac (Mt 12:22–23; Lk 11:14), Gadarene demoniacs (Mt 8:28–34; Mk 5:1–20; Lk 8:26–39), woman's bleeding and Jairus' daughter (Mt 9:18–26; Mk 5:21–43; Lk 8:40–56), blind man (Mt 9:27–31), mute man (Mt 9:32–33), Canaanite woman's daughter (Mt 15:21–28; Mk 7:24–30), deaf man (Mk 7:31–37), blind man (Mk 8:22–26), demoniac boy (Mt 17:14–18; Mk 9:14–29; Lk 9:37–43), ten lepers (Lk 17:11–19), man born blind (Jn 9:1–7), Lazarus raised (Jn 11), crippled woman (Lk 13:11–17), man with dropsy (Lk 14:1–6), two blind men (Mt 20:29–34; Mk 10:46–52; Lk 18:35–43), Malchus' ear (Lk 22:50–51). Other Miracles: water to wine (Jn 2:1–11), catch of fish (Lk 5:1–11), storm stilled (Mt 8:23–27; Mk 4:37–41; Lk 8:22–25), 5,000 fed (Mt 14:15–21; Mk 6:35–44; Lk 9:10–17; Jn 6:1–14), walking on water (Mt 14:25–33; Mk 6:48–52; Jn 6:15–21), 4,000 fed (Mt 15:32–39; Mk 8:1–9), money from fish (Mt 17:24–27), fig tree cursed (Mt 21:18–22; Mk 11:12–14), catch of fish (Jn 21:1–14).

MAJOR TEACHING: Sermon on the Mount (Mt 5–7; Lk 6:17–49), to Nicodemus (Jn 3), to Samaritan woman (Jn 4), Bread of Life (Jn 6:22–59), at Feast of Tabernacles (Jn 7–8), woes to Pharisees (Mt 23; Lk 11:37–54), Good Shepherd (Jn 10:1–18), Olivet Discourse (Mt 24–25; Mk 13; Lk 21:5–36), Upper Room Discourse (Jn 13–16).

PARABLES: Sower (Mt 13:3–23; Mk 4:3–25; Lk 8:5–18), seed's growth (Mk 4:26–29), wheat and weeds (Mt 13:24–30, 36–43), mustard seed (Mt 13:31–32; Mk 4:30–32), yeast (Mt 13:33; Lk 13:20–21), hidden treasure (Mt 13:44), valuable pearl (Mt 13:45–46), net (Mt 13:47–51), house owner (Mt 13:52), good Samaritan (Lk 10:25–37), unmerciful servant (Mt 18:15–35), lost sheep (Mt 18:10–14; Lk 15:4–7), lost coin (Lk 15:8–10), prodigal son (Lk 15:11–32), dishonest manager (Lk 16:1–13), rich man and Lazarus (Lk 16:19–31), persistent widow (Lk 18:1–8), Pharisee and tax collector (Lk 18:9–14), payment of workers (Mt 20:1–16), tenants and the vineyard (Mt 21:28–46; Mk 12:1–12; Lk 20:9–19), wedding banquet (Mt 22:1–14), faithful servant (Mt 24:45–51), ten virgins (Mt 25:1–13), talents (Mt 25:1–30; Lk 19:12–27).

DISCIPLES see APOSTLES. Call of (Jn 1:35–51; Mt 4:18–22; 9:9; Mk 1:16–20; 2:13–14; Lk 5:1–11, 27–28). Named Apostles (Mk 3:13–19; Lk 6:12–16). Twelve sent out (Mt 10; Mk 6:7–11; Lk 9:1–5). Seventy sent out (Lk 10:1–24). Defection of (Jn 6:60–71; Mt 26:56; Mk 14:50–52). Final commission (Mt 28:16–20; Jn 21:15–23; Ac 1:3–8).

Ac 2: 32 God has raised this **J** to life, and we
9: 5 Saul asked. "I am **J**, whom you are
15: 11 of our Lord **J** that we are saved,
16: 31 "Believe in the Lord **J**, and you will
Ro 3: 24 redemption that came by Christ **J**.
5: 17 life through the one man, **J** Christ!
8: 1 for those who are in Christ **J**,
1Co 2: 2 I was with you except **J** Christ
8: 6 and there is but one Lord, **J** Christ,
12: 3 and no one can say, "**J** is Lord,"
2Co 4: 5 but **J** Christ as Lord, and ourselves
Gal 2: 16 of the law, but by faith in **J** Christ.
3: 28 for you are all one in Christ **J**.
5: 6 in Christ **J** neither circumcision
Eph 2: 10 in Christ **J** to do good works,
2: 20 with Christ **J** himself as the chief
Php 1: 6 until the day of Christ **J**.
2: 5 have the same mindset as Christ **J**:
2: 10 name of **J** every knee should bow,
Col 3: 17 do it all in the name of the Lord **J**,
2Th 2: 1 the coming of our Lord **J** Christ
1Ti 1: 15 **J** came into the world to save
2Ti 3: 12 life in Christ **J** will be persecuted,
Titus 2: 13 our great God and Savior, **J** Christ,
Heb 2: 9 But we do see **J**, who was made
3: 1 fix your thoughts on **J**, whom we
4: 14 into heaven, **J** the Son of God,
7: 22 **J** has become the guarantor
7: 24 but because **J** lives forever, he has
12: 2 fixing our eyes on **J**, the pioneer
2Pe 1: 16 of our Lord **J** Christ in power,
1Jn 1: 7 and the blood of **J**, his Son,
2: 1 **J** Christ, the Righteous One.
2: 6 to live in him must live as **J** did.
4: 15 acknowledges that **J** is the Son
Rev 22: 20 Amen. Come, Lord **J**.

JEW (JEWS JUDAISM)

Zec 8: 23 take firm hold of one **J** by the hem
Ro 1: 16 first to the **J**, then to the Gentile.
10: 12 there is no difference between **J**
1Co 9: 20 To the Jews I became like a **J**,
Gal 3: 28 There is neither **J** nor Gentile,

JEWELRY (JEWELS)

1Pe 3: 3 wearing of gold **j** or fine clothes.

JEWELS (JEWELRY)

Isa 61: 10 as a bride adorns herself with her **j**.
Zec 9: 16 in his land like **j** in a crown.

JEWS (JEW)

Mt 2: 2 who has been born king of the **J**?
27: 11 him, "Are you the king of the **J**?"
Jn 4: 22 know, for salvation is from the **J**.
Ro 3: 29 Or is God the God of **J** only?
1Co 1: 22 **J** demand signs and Greeks look
9: 20 To the **J** I became like a Jew, to win
12: 13 whether **J** or Gentiles,
Rev 3: 9 claim to be **J** though they are not,

JEZEBEL

Sidonian wife of Ahab (1Ki 16:31). Promoted Baal worship (1Ki 16:32–33). Killed prophets of the LORD (1Ki 18:4, 13). Opposed Elijah (1Ki 19:1–2). Had Naboth killed (1Ki 21). Death prophesied (1Ki 21:17–24). Killed by Jehu (2Ki 9:30–37).

JOASH

Son of Ahaziah; king of Judah. Sheltered from Athaliah by Jehoiada (2Ki 11; 2Ch 22:10—23:21). Repaired temple (2Ki 12; 2Ch 24).

† Please see the "Hebrew to English Translation Chart," p. xix.

JOB

Wealthy man from Uz; feared God (Job 1:1–5). Righteousness tested by disaster (Job 1:6–22), personal affliction (Job 2). Maintained innocence in debate with three friends (Job 3–31), Elihu (Job 32–37). Rebuked by the LORD (Job 38–41). Vindicated and restored to greater stature by the LORD (Job 42). Example of righteousness (Eze 14:14, 20).

JOHN

1. Son of Zechariah and Elizabeth (Lk 1). Called the Baptist (Mt 3:1–12; Mk 1:2–8). Witness to Jesus (Mt 3:11–12; Mk 1:7–8; Lk 3:15–18; Jn 1:6–35; 3:27–30; 5:33–36). Doubts about Jesus (Mt 11:2–6; Lk 7:18–23). Arrest (Mt 4:12; Mk 1:14). Execution (Mt 14:1–12; Mk 6:14–29; Lk 9:7–9). Ministry compared to Elijah (Mt 11:7–19; Mk 9:11–13; Lk 7:24–35).

2. Apostle; brother of James (Mt 4:21–22; 10:2; Mk 3:17; Lk 5:1–10). At transfiguration (Mt 17:1–13; Mk 9:1–13; Lk 9:28–36). Desire to be greatest (Mk 10:35–45). Leader of church at Jerusalem (Ac 4:1–3; Gal 2:9). Elder who wrote epistles (2Jn 1; 3Jn 1). Prophet who wrote Revelation (Rev 1:1; 22:8).

3. Cousin of Barnabas, co-worker with Paul, (Ac 12:12—13:13; 15:37), see MARK.

JOIN (JOINED)

Pr 23: 20 not **j** those who drink too much
24: 21 do not **j** with rebellious officials,
Ro 15: 30 to **j** me in my struggle by praying
2Ti 1: 8 **j** with me in suffering
2Ti 2: 3 **J** with me in suffering, like a good

JOINED (JOIN)

Mt 19: 6 Therefore what God has **j** together,
Mk 10: 9 Therefore what God has **j** together,
Eph 2: 21 the whole building is **j** together
4: 16 body, **j** and held together by every

JOINTS

Heb 4: 12 soul and spirit, **j** and marrow;

JOKING

Eph 5: 4 foolish talk or coarse **j**, which are

JONAH

Prophet in days of Jeroboam II (2Ki 14:25). Called to Nineveh; fled to Tarshish (Jnh 1:1–3). Cause of storm; thrown into sea (Jnh 1:4–16). Swallowed by fish (Jnh 1:17). Prayer (Jnh 2). Preached to Nineveh (Jnh 3). Attitude reproved by the LORD (Jnh 4). Sign of (Mt 12:39–41; Lk 11:29–32).

JONATHAN

Son of Saul (1Sa 13:16; 1Ch 8:33). Valiant warrior (1Sa 13–14). Relation to David (1Sa 18:1–4; 19–20; 23:16–18). Killed at Gilboa (1Sa 31). Mourned by David (2Sa 1).

JORAM

Son of Ahab; king of Israel (2Ki 3; 8–9; 2Ch 22).

JORDAN

Nu 34: 12 boundary will go down along the **J**
Jos 4: 22 'Israel crossed the **J** on dry ground.'
Mt 3: 6 baptized by him in the **J** River.

JOSEPH

1. Son of Jacob by Rachel (Ge 30:24; 1Ch 2:2). Favored by Jacob, hated by brothers (Ge 37:3–4). Dreams (Ge 37:5–11). Sold by brothers (Ge 37:12–36). Served Potiphar; imprisoned by false accusation (Ge 39). Interpreted dreams of Pharaoh's servants (Ge 40), of Pharaoh (Ge 41:4–40). Made greatest in Egypt (Ge 41:41–57). Sold grain to brothers (Ge 42–45). Brought Jacob and sons to Egypt (Ge 46–47). Sons Ephraim and Manasseh blessed (Ge 48). Blessed (Ge 49:22–26; Dt 33:13–17). Death (Ge 50:22–26; Ex 13:19; Heb 11:22). 12,000 from (Rev 7:8).

2. Husband of Mary, mother of Jesus (Mt 1:16–24; 2:13–19; Lk 1:27; 2; Jn 1:45).

3. Disciple from Arimathea, who gave his tomb for Jesus' burial (Mt 27:57–61; Mk 15:43–47; Lk 23:50–53).

4. Original name of Barnabas (Ac 4:36).

JOSHUA

1. Son of Nun; name changed from Hoshea (Nu 13:8, 16; 1Ch 7:27). Fought Amalekites under Moses (Ex 17:9–14). Servant of Moses on Sinai (Ex 24:13; 32:17). Spied Canaan (Nu 13). With Caleb, allowed to enter land (Nu 14:6, 30). Succeeded Moses (Dt 1:38; 31:1–8; 34:9).

Charged Israel to conquer Canaan (Jos 1). Crossed Jordan (Jos 3–4). Circumcised sons of wilderness wanderings (Jos 5). Conquered Jericho (Jos 6), Ai (Jos 7–8), five kings at Gibeon (Jos 10:1–28), southern Canaan (Jos 10:29–43), northern Canaan (Jos 11–12). Defeated at Ai (Jos 7). Deceived by Gibeonites (Jos 9). Renewed covenant (Jos 8:30–35; 24:1–27). Divided land among tribes (Jos 13–22). Last words (Jos 23). Death (Jos 24:28–31).

2. High priest during rebuilding of temple (Hag 1–2; Zec 3:1–9; 6:11).

JOSIAH

Son of Amon; king of Judah (2Ki 22–23; 2Ch 34–35).

JOTHAM

Son of Azariah (Uzziah); king of Judah (2Ki 15:32–38; 2Ch 26:21—27:9).

JOY (ENJOY ENJOYMENT JOYFUL OVERJOYED REJOICE REJOICES REJOICING)

Dt 16: 15 hands, and your **j** will be complete.
1Ch 16: 27 and **j** are in his dwelling place.
Ne 8: 10 for the **j** of the LORD is your
Est 9: 22 their sorrow was turned into **j**
Job 38: 7 and all the angels shouted for **j**?
Ps 4: 7 Fill my heart with **j** when their
21: 6 glad with the **j** of your presence.
30: 11 sackcloth and clothed me with **j**,
43: 4 God, to God, my **j** and my delight.
51: 12 to me the **j** of your salvation
66: 1 Shout for **j** to God, all the earth!
96: 12 all the trees of the forest sing for **j**.
107: 22 tell of his works with songs of **j**.
119:111 forever; they are the **j** of my heart.
Pr 10: 1 A wise son brings **j** to his father,
10: 28 The prospect of the righteous is **j**,
12: 20 those who promote peace have **j**.
15: 30 in a messenger's eyes brings **j**
Isa 35: 10 everlasting **j** will crown their heads
51: 11 Gladness and **j** will overtake them,
55: 12 You will go out in **j** and be led
Lk 1: 44 the baby in my womb leaped for **j**.
2: 10 will cause great **j** for all the people.
Jn 15: 11 and that your **j** may be complete.
16: 20 grieve, but your grief will turn to **j**.
2Co 8: 2 trial, their overflowing **j** and their
Php 2: 2 then make my **j** complete by being
4: 1 love and long for, my **j** and crown,
1Th 2: 19 our **j**, or the crown in which we
Phm : 7 Your love has given me great **j**
Heb 12: 2 the **j** set before him he endured
Jas 1: 2 Consider it pure **j**, my brothers
1Pe 1: 8 an inexpressible and glorious **j**,
2Jn : 4 It has given me great **j** to find some
3Jn : 4 I have no greater **j** than to hear

JOYFUL (JOY)

Ps 100: 2 come before him with **j** songs.
Pr 23: 25 may she who gave you birth be **j**!
Hab 3: 18 I will be **j** in God my Savior.

JUDAH

1. Son of Jacob by Leah (Ge 29:35; 35:23; 1Ch 2:1). Tribe of blessed as ruling tribe (Ge 49:8–12; Dt 33:7).

2. Name used for people and land of Southern Kingdom.

Jer 13: 19 All **J** will be carried into exile,
Zec 10: 4 From **J** will come the cornerstone,
Heb 7: 14 that our Lord descended from **J**,

JUDAISM (JEW)

Gal 1: 13 of my previous way of life in **J**,

JUDAS

1. Apostle (Lk 6:16; Jn 14:22; Ac 1:13). Probably also called Thaddaeus (Mt 10:3; Mk 3:18).

2. Brother of James and Jesus (Mt 13:55; Mk 6:3), also called Jude (Jude 1).

3. Apostle, also called Iscariot, who betrayed Jesus (Mt 10:4; 26:14–56; Mk 3:19; 14:10–50; Lk 6:16; 22:3–53; Jn 6:71; 12:4; 13:2–30; 18:2–11). Suicide of (Mt 27:3–5; Ac 1:16–25).

† JUDGE (JUDGED JUDGES JUDGING JUDGMENT)

Ge 18: 25 Will not the **J** of all the earth do
1Ch 16: 33 LORD, for he comes to **j** the earth.
Joel 3: 12 there I will sit to **j** all the nations
Mt 7: 1 "Do not **j**, or you too will be
Jn 7: 24 but instead **j** correctly."
12: 47 For I did not come to **j** the world,
Ac 17: 31 set a day when he will **j** the world
1Co 4: 3 indeed, I do not even **j** myself.
6: 2 the Lord's people will **j** the world?
2Ti 4: 1 who will **j** the living and the dead,
4: 8 the righteous **J**, will award to me
Jas 4: 12 who are you to **j** your neighbor?
Rev 20: 4 who had been given authority to **j**.

JUDGED (JUDGE)

Mt 7: 1 "Do not judge, or you too will be **j**.
Jn 5: 24 will not be **j** but has crossed over
Jas 3: 1 who teach will be **j** more strictly.
Rev 20: 12 The dead were **j** according to what

JUDGES (JUDGE)

Jdg 2: 16 Then the LORD raised up **j**,
Ps 9: 8 and **j** the peoples with equity.
58: 11 there is a God who **j** the earth."
Ro 2: 16 God **j** people's secrets through Jesus
Heb 4: 12 it **j** the thoughts and attitudes
Rev 19: 11 With justice he **j** and wages war.

JUDGING (JUDGE)

Mt 19: 28 **j** the twelve tribes of Israel.
Jn 7: 24 Stop **j** by mere appearances,
2Co 10: 7 You are **j** by appearances.

JUDGMENT (JUDGE)

Dt 1: 17 of anyone, for **j** belongs to God.
Ps 1: 5 the wicked will not stand in the **j**,
119: 66 Teach me knowledge and good **j**,
Ecc 12: 14 God will bring every deed into **j**,
Isa 66: 16 his sword the LORD will execute **j**
Mt 5: 21 who murders will be subject to **j**.'
10: 15 Gomorrah on the day of **j** than
12: 36 the day of **j** for every empty word
Jn 5: 22 but has entrusted all **j** to the Son,
16: 8 about sin and righteousness and **j**:
Ro 14: 10 will all stand before God's **j** seat.
14: 13 Therefore let us stop passing **j**
1Co 11: 29 eat and drink **j** on themselves.
11: 31 we would not come under such **j**.
2Co 5: 10 we must all appear before the **j** seat
Heb 9: 27 to die once, and after that to face **j**,
10: 27 only a fearful expectation of **j**
1Pe 4: 17 For it is time for **j** to begin
Jude : 6 everlasting chains for **j** on the great

JUST (JUSTICE JUSTIFICATION JUSTIFIED JUSTIFY JUSTLY)

Dt 32: 4 are perfect, and all his ways are **j**.
Ps 37: 28 For the LORD loves the **j** and will
111: 7 of his hands are faithful and **j**;
Pr 1: 3 doing what is right and **j** and fair;
2: 8 for he guards the course of the **j**
Da 4: 37 does is right and all his ways are **j**.
Ro 3: 26 time, so as to be **j** and the one who
Heb 2: 2 received its **j** punishment,
1Jn 1: 9 he is faithful and **j** and will forgive
Rev 16: 7 true and **j** are your judgments."

† JUSTICE (JUST)

Ex 23: 2 do not pervert **j** by siding
23: 6 "Do not deny **j** to your poor people
Job 37: 23 in his **j** and great righteousness,
Ps 9: 16 LORD is known by his acts of **j**;
11: 7 the LORD is righteous, he loves **j**;
45: 6 a scepter of **j** will be the scepter
101: 1 I will sing of your love and **j**;
Pr 21: 15 When **j** is done, it brings joy
29: 4 By **j** a king gives a country stability,
29: 26 is from the LORD that one gets **j**.
Isa 9: 7 and upholding it with **j**
28: 17 I will make **j** the measuring line
30: 18 For the LORD is a God of **j**.
42: 1 and he will bring **j** to the nations.
42: 4 be discouraged till he establishes **j**
56: 1 "Maintain **j** and do what is right,
61: 8 "For I, the LORD, love **j**;
Eze 34: 16 I will shepherd the flock with **j**.
Am 5: 15 maintain **j** in the courts.
5: 24 But let **j** roll on like a river,
Zec 7: 9 'Administer true **j**; show mercy
Lk 11: 42 you neglect **j** and the love of God.

† Please see the "Hebrew to English Translation Chart," p. xix.

JUSTIFICATION (JUST)
Ac 13: 39 sin, a **j** you were not able to obtain
Ro 4: 25 sins and was raised to life for our **j**.
5: 18 one righteous act resulted in **j**

JUSTIFIED (JUST)
Ro 3: 24 all are **j** freely by his grace through
3: 28 that a person is **j** by faith apart
5: 1 since we have been **j** through faith,
5: 9 Since we have now been **j** by his
8: 30 he called, he also **j**; those he **j**,
1Co 6: 11 you were **j** in the name of the Lord
Gal 2: 16 that a person is not **j** by the works
3: 11 relies on the law is **j** before God,
3: 24 came that we might be **j** by faith.

JUSTIFY (JUST)
Gal 3: 8 that God would **j** the Gentiles

JUSTLY (JUST)
Ps 106: 3 Blessed are those who act **j**,
Mic 6: 8 To act **j** and to love mercy

KEEP (KEEPER KEEPING KEEPS KEPT)
Ge 31: 49 "May the LORD **k** watch between
Ex 20: 6 love me and **k** my commandments.
Nu 6: 24 LORD bless you and **k** you;
Ps 18: 28 You, LORD, **k** my lamp burning;
19: 13 **K** your servant also from willful
121: 7 The LORD will **k** you from all
141: 3 **k** watch over the door of my lips.
Pr 4: 24 **K** your mouth free of perversity;
17: 28 are thought wise if they **k** silent,
Isa 26: 3 You will **k** in perfect peace those
Am 5: 13 Therefore the prudent **k** quiet
Mt 10: 10 staff, for the worker is worth his **k**.
Lk 12: 35 service and **k** your lamps burning,
Gal 5: 25 let us **k** in step with the Spirit.
Eph 4: 3 Make every effort to **k** the unity
1Ti 5: 22 the sins of others. **K** yourself pure.
2Ti 4: 5 you, **k** your head in all situations,
Heb 13: 5 **K** your lives free from the love
Jas 1: 26 and yet do not **k** a tight rein on
2: 8 If you really **k** the royal law found
1Jn 5: 3 love for God: to **k** his commands.
Jude : 24 To him who is able to **k** you

KEEPER (KEEP)
Ge 4: 9 "Am I my brother's **k**?"

KEEPING (KEEP)
Ex 20: 8 the Sabbath day by **k** it holy.
Ps 19: 11 in **k** them there is great reward.
Mt 3: 8 Produce fruit in **k** with repentance.
Lk 2: 8 **k** watch over their flocks at night.
1Co 7: 19 **K** God's commands is what counts.
2Pe 3: 9 Lord is not slow in **k** his promise,

KEEPS (KEEP)
1Co 13: 5 angered, it **k** no record of wrongs.
Jas 2: 10 For whoever **k** the whole law

KEPT (KEEP)
Ps 130: 3 LORD, **k** a record of sins, Lord,
2Ti 4: 7 finished the race, I have **k** the faith.
1Pe 1: 4 This inheritance is **k** in heaven

KEYS
Mt 16: 19 will give you the **k** of the kingdom

KILL (KILLS)
Mt 17: 23 will **k** him, and on the third day

KILLS (KILL)
Lev 24: 21 whoever **k** a human being is to be
2Co 3: 6 for the letter **k**, but the Spirit gives

KIND (KINDNESS KINDS)
Ge 1: 24 animals, each according to its **k**."
2Ch 10: 7 "If you will be **k** to these people
Pr 11: 17 Those who are **k** benefit themselves,
12: 25 the heart, but a **k** word cheers it up.
14: 21 blessed is the one who is **k**
14: 31 whoever is **k** to the needy honors
19: 17 Whoever is **k** to the poor lends
Da 4: 27 by being **k** to the oppressed.
Lk 6: 35 because he is **k** to the ungrateful
1Co 13: 4 Love is patient, love is **k**.
15: 35 what **k** of body will they come?"
Eph 4: 32 Be **k** and compassionate to one
2Ti 2: 24 but must be **k** to everyone,
Titus 2: 5 to be **k**, and to be subject to their

† KINDNESS (KIND)
Ac 14: 17 He has shown **k** by giving you rain
Ro 11: 22 but **k** to you, provided that you continue in his **k**.
Gal 5: 22 peace, forbearance, **k**, goodness,
Eph 2: 7 expressed in his **k** to us in Christ

KINDS (KIND)
1Co 12: 4 There are different **k** of gifts,
1Ti 6: 10 of money is a root of all **k** of evil.

† KING (KINGDOM KINGS)

1. Kings of Judah and Israel: see Saul, David, Solomon.

2. Kings of Judah: see Rehoboam, Abijah, Asa, Jehoshaphat, Jehoram, Ahaziah, Athaliah (Queen), Joash, Amaziah, Uzziah, Jotham, Ahaz, Hezekiah, Manasseh, Amon, Josiah, Jehoahaz, Jehoiakim, Jehoiachin, Zedekiah.

3. Kings of Israel: see Jeroboam I, Nadab, Baasha, Elah, Zimri, Tibni, Omri, Ahab, Ahaziah, Joram, Jehu, Jehoahaz, Jehoash, Jeroboam II, Zechariah, Shallum, Menahem, Pekah, Pekahiah, Hoshea.

Jdg 17: 6 In those days Israel had no **k**;
1Sa 12: 12 'No, we want a **k** to rule over us'—
12: 12 the LORD your God was your **k**.
Ps 24: 7 that the **K** of glory may come in.
Isa 32: 1 a **k** will reign in righteousness
Zec 9: 9 See, your **k** comes to you,
1Ti 6: 15 the **K** of kings and Lord of lords,
Rev 19: 16 thigh he has this name written: K

‡ KINGDOM (KING)
Ex 19: 6 you will be for me a **k** of priests
1Ch 29: 11 Yours, LORD, is the **k**;
Ps 45: 6 justice will be the scepter of your **k**.
Da 4: 3 His **k** is an eternal **k**;
Mt 3: 2 for the **k** of heaven has come near."
5: 3 spirit, for theirs is the **k** of heaven.
6: 10 your **k** come, your will be done,
6: 33 But seek first his **k** and his
7: 21 Lord,' will enter the **k** of heaven,
11: 11 the **k** of heaven is greater than he.
13: 24 "The **k** of heaven is like a man who
13: 31 "The **k** of heaven is like a mustard
13: 33 "The **k** of heaven is like yeast
13: 44 "The **k** of heaven is like treasure
13: 45 the **k** of heaven is like a merchant
13: 47 the **k** of heaven is like a net that
16: 19 you the keys of the **k** of heaven;
18: 23 the **k** of heaven is like a king who
19: 24 who is rich to enter the **k** of God."
24: 7 rise against nation, and **k** against **k**.
24: 14 gospel of the **k** will be preached
25: 34 the **k** prepared for you since
Mk 9: 47 you to enter the **k** of God with one
10: 14 for the **k** of God belongs to such as
10: 23 for the rich to enter the **k** of God!"
Lk 10: 9 'The **k** of God has come near
12: 31 But seek his **k**, and these things
17: 21 is,' because the **k** of God is in your
Jn 3: 5 one can enter the **k** of God unless
18: 36 said, "My **k** is not of this world.
1Co 6: 9 wrongdoers will not inherit the **k**
15: 24 when he hands over the **k** to God
Rev 1: 6 has made us to be a **k** and priests
11: 15 "The **k** of the world has become

KINGS (KING)
Ps 2: 2 The **k** of the earth rise
72: 11 May all **k** bow down to him and all
Da 7: 24 ten horns are ten **k** who will come
1Ti 2: 2 for **k** and all those in authority,
Rev 1: 5 and the ruler of the **k** of the earth.

KISS
Ps 2: 12 **K** his son, or he will be angry
Pr 24: 26 An honest answer is like a **k**
Lk 22: 48 the Son of Man with a **k**?"

KNEE (KNEES)
Isa 45: 23 Before me every **k** will bow;
Ro 14: 11 Lord, 'every **k** will bow before me;
Php 2: 10 name of Jesus every **k** should bow,

KNEES (KNEE)
Isa 35: 3 hands, steady the **k** that give way;
Heb 12: 12 your feeble arms and weak **k**.

KNEW (KNOW)
Job 23: 3 If only I **k** where to find him;
Jnh 4: 2 I **k** that you are a gracious
Mt 7: 23 tell them plainly, 'I never **k** you.

KNOCK
Mt 7: 7 **k** and the door will be opened
Rev 3: 20 I stand at the door and **k**.

KNOW (FOREKNEW KNEW KNOWING KNOWLEDGE KNOWN KNOWS)
Dt 18: 21 "How can we **k** when a message
Job 19: 25 I **k** that my redeemer lives,
42: 3 things too wonderful for me to **k**.
Ps 46: 10 says, "Be still, and **k** that I am God;
73: 11 Does the Most High **k** anything?"
139: 1 LORD, and you **k** me.
139: 23 Search me, God, and **k** my heart;
Pr 27: 1 you do not **k** what a day may bring.
Jer 24: 7 I will give them a heart to **k** me,
31: 34 because they will all **k** me,
Mt 6: 3 let your left hand **k** what your right
24: 42 because you do not **k** on what day
Lk 1: 4 so that you may **k** the certainty
Jn 3: 11 you, we speak of what we **k**, and we
4: 22 worship what you do not **k**;
9: 25 One thing I do **k**. I was blind
10: 14 I **k** my sheep and my sheep **k** me—
17: 3 that they **k** you, the only true God,
21: 24 We **k** that his testimony is true.
Ac 1: 7 "It is not for you to **k** the times
Ro 6: 6 we **k** that our old self was crucified
7: 18 I **k** that good itself does not dwell
8: 28 we **k** that in all things God works
1Co 2: 2 I resolved to **k** nothing while I was
6: 15 Do you not **k** that your bodies are
6: 19 Do you not **k** that your bodies are
8: 2 do not yet **k** as they ought to **k**.
13: 12 Now I **k** in part; then I shall **k** fully,
15: 58 because you **k** that your labor
Php 3: 10 I want to **k** Christ—yes, to **k**
2Ti 1: 12 because I **k** whom I have believed,
Jas 4: 14 do not even **k** what will happen
1Jn 2: 4 Whoever says, "I **k** him," but does
3: 14 We **k** that we have passed
3: 16 This is how we **k** what love is:
5: 2 This is how we **k** that we love
5: 13 may **k** that you have eternal life.

KNOWING (KNOW)
Ge 3: 5 will be like God, **k** good and evil."
Php 3: 8 worth of **k** Christ Jesus my Lord,

KNOWLEDGE (KNOW)
Ge 2: 9 the tree of the **k** of good and evil.
Job 42: 3 that obscures my plans without **k**?'
Ps 19: 2 night after night they reveal **k**.
139: 6 Such **k** is too wonderful for me,
Pr 1: 7 of the LORD is the beginning of **k**,
10: 14 The wise store up **k**, but the mouth
12: 1 Whoever loves discipline loves **k**,
13: 16 All who are prudent act with **k**,
19: 2 Desire without **k** is not good—
Isa 11: 9 the **k** of the LORD as the waters
Hab 2: 14 will be filled with the **k** of the glory
Ro 11: 33 riches of the wisdom and **k** of God!
1Co 8: 1 But **k** puffs up while love builds up.
8: 11 Christ died, is destroyed by your **k**.
13: 2 can fathom all mysteries and all **k**,
2Co 2: 14 aroma of the **k** of him everywhere.
4: 6 of the **k** of God's glory displayed
Eph 3: 19 know this love that surpasses **k**—
Col 2: 3 all the treasures of wisdom and **k**.
1Ti 6: 20 ideas of what is falsely called **k**,
2Pe 3: 18 grow in the grace and **k** of our Lord

KNOWN (KNOW)
Ps 16: 11 You make **k** to me the path of life;
105: 1 make **k** among the nations what he
Isa 46: 10 I make **k** the end
Mt 10: 26 or hidden that will not be made **k**.
Ro 1: 19 since what may be **k** about God is
11: 34 "Who has **k** the mind of the Lord?
15: 20 the gospel where Christ was not **k**,
2Co 3: 2 our hearts, **k** and read by everyone.
2Pe 2: 21 than to have **k** it and then to turn

KNOWS (KNOW)
1Sa 2: 3 for the LORD is a God who **k**,
Job 23: 10 But he **k** the way that I take;
Ps 44: 21 since he **k** the secrets of the heart?
94: 11 The LORD **k** all human plans; he **k**
Ecc 8: 7 Since no one **k** the future, who can

† Please see the "Hebrew to English Translation Chart," p. xix.
‡ Please see "Key New Testament Terms," p. 1584.

Mt 6: 8 your Father **k** what you need
24: 36 about that day or hour no one **k**,
Ro 8: 27 searches our hearts **k** the mind
2Ti 2: 19 "The Lord **k** those who are his,"

LABAN

Brother of Rebekah (Ge 24:29–51), father of Rachel and Leah (Ge 29–31).

LABOR

Ex 20: 9 Six days you shall **l** and do all your
Isa 55: 2 your **l** on what does not satisfy?
Mt 6: 28 They do not **l** or spin.
1Co 3: 8 rewarded according to their own **l**.
15: 58 know that your **l** in the Lord is not

LACK (LACKING LACKS)

Pr 15: 22 Plans fail for **l** of counsel,
Col 2: 23 but they **l** any value in restraining

LACKING (LACK)

Ro 12: 11 Never be **l** in zeal, but keep your
Jas 1: 4 and complete, not **l** anything.

LACKS (LACK)

Jas 1: 5 If any of you **l** wisdom, you should

LAID (LAY)

Isa 53: 6 and the LORD has **l** on him
1Co 3: 11 other than the one already **l**,
1Jn 3: 16 Jesus Christ **l** down his life for us.

LAKE

Rev 19: 20 into the fiery **l** of burning sulfur.
20: 14 The **l** of fire is the second death.

LAMB (LAMB'S LAMBS)

Ge 22: 8 "God himself will provide the **l**
Ex 12: 21 and slaughter the Passover **l**.
Isa 11: 6 The wolf will live with the **l**,
53: 7 he was led like a **l** to the slaughter,
Jn 1: 29 "Look, the **L** of God, who takes
1Co 5: 7 our Passover **l**, has been sacrificed.
1Pe 1: 19 a **l** without blemish or defect.
Rev 5: 6 Then I saw a **L**, looking as if it had
5: 12 "Worthy is the **L**, who was slain,
14: 4 as firstfruits to God and the **L**.

LAMB'S (LAMB)

Rev 21: 27 names are written in the **L** book

LAMBS (LAMB)

Lk 10: 3 you out like **l** among wolves.
Jn 21: 15 Jesus said, "Feed my **l**."

LAMENT

2Sa 1: 17 took up this **l** concerning Saul

LAMP (LAMPS)

2Sa 22: 29 You, LORD, are my **l**;
Ps 18: 28 You, LORD, keep my **l** burning;
119:105 Your word is a **l** to my feet
Pr 31: 18 and her **l** does not go out at night.
Lk 8: 16 "No one lights a **l** and hides it
Rev 21: 23 gives it light, and the Lamb is its **l**.

LAMPS (LAMP)

Mt 25: 1 be like ten virgins who took their **l**
Lk 12: 35 service and keep your **l** burning,

LAND

Ge 1: 10 God called the dry ground "**l**,"
1: 11 said, "Let the **l** produce vegetation:
12: 7 your offspring I will give this **l**."
Ex 3: 8 a **l** flowing with milk and honey—
Nu 35: 33 Bloodshed pollutes the **l**,
Dt 34: 1 LORD showed him the whole **l**—
Jos 13: 2 "This is the **l** that remains:
14: 4 Levites received no share of the **l**
2Ch 7: 14 their sin and will heal their **l**.
7: 20 then I will uproot Israel from my **l**,
Eze 36: 24 bring you back into your own **l**.

LANGUAGE

Ge 11: 1 Now the whole world had one **l**
Jn 8: 44 speaks his native **l**, for he is a liar
Ac 2: 6 heard their own **l** being spoken.
Col 3: 8 slander, and filthy **l** from your lips.
Rev 5: 9 God persons from every tribe and **l**

LAST (LASTING LASTS LATTER)

2Sa 23: 1 These are the **l** words of David:
Isa 44: 6 I am the first and I am the **l**;
Mt 19: 30 But many who are first will be **l**,
Mk 10: 31 will be **l**, and the **l** first."
Jn 15: 16 fruit that will **l**—and so
Ro 1: 17 that is by faith from first to **l**,
2Ti 3: 1 will be terrible times in the **l** days.
2Pe 3: 3 in the **l** days scoffers will come,
Rev 1: 17 I am the First and the **L**.
22: 13 the First and the **L**, the Beginning

LASTING (LAST)

Ex 12: 14 to the LORD—a **l** ordinance.
Lev 24: 8 of the Israelites, as a **l** covenant.
Nu 25: 13 have a covenant of a **l** priesthood,
Heb 10: 34 had better and **l** possessions.

LASTS (LAST)

Ps 30: 5 For his anger **l** only a moment,
2Co 3: 11 greater is the glory of that which **l**!

LATTER (LAST)

Job 42: 12 The LORD blessed the **l** part

LAUGH (LAUGHS)

Ecc 3: 4 a time to weep and a time to **l**,

LAUGHS (LAUGH)

Ps 2: 4 The One enthroned in heaven **l**;
37: 13 but the Lord **l** at the wicked, for he

LAVISHED

Eph 1: 8 that he **l** on us. With all wisdom
1Jn 3: 1 See what great love the Father has **l**

†/‡ LAW (LAWS)

Dt 31: 11 you shall read this **l** before them
31: 26 "Take this Book of the **L** and place
Jos 1: 8 Keep this Book of the **L** always
Ne 8: 8 from the Book of the **L** of God,
Ps 1: 2 delight is in the **l** of the LORD,
19: 7 The **l** of the LORD is perfect,
119: 18 may see wonderful things in your **l**.
119: 72 The **l** from your mouth is more
119: 97 Oh, how I love your **l**! I meditate
119:165 peace have those who love your **l**,
Jer 31: 33 "I will put my **l** in their minds
Mt 5: 17 that I have come to abolish the **L**
7: 12 you, for this sums up the **L**
22: 40 All the **L** and the Prophets hang
Lk 16: 17 stroke of a pen to drop out of the **L**.
Jn 1: 17 For the **l** was given through Moses;
Ro 2: 12 All who sin apart from the **l** will
2: 15 requirements of the **l** are written
5: 13 account where there is no **l**.
5: 20 The **l** was brought in so
6: 14 because you are not under the **l**,
7: 6 we have been released from the **l** so
7: 12 So then, the **l** is holy,
8: 3 For what the **l** was powerless to do
10: 4 Christ is the culmination of the **l**
13: 10 love is the fulfillment of the **l**.
Gal 3: 13 curse of the **l** by becoming a curse
3: 24 So the **l** was our guardian until
5: 3 he is obligated to obey the whole **l**.
5: 4 by the **l** have been alienated
5: 14 For the entire **l** is fulfilled
Heb 7: 19 (for the **l** made nothing perfect),
10: 1 The **l** is only a shadow of the good
Jas 1: 25 the perfect **l** that gives freedom,
2: 10 For whoever keeps the whole **l**

LAWLESSNESS

2Th 2: 3 occurs and the man of **l** is revealed,
2: 7 the secret power of **l** is already
1Jn 3: 4 sins breaks the law; in fact, sin is **l**.

LAWS (LAW)

Lev 25: 18 and be careful to obey my **l**,
Ps 119: 30 I have set my heart on your **l**.
119:120 fear of you; I stand in awe of your **l**.
Heb 8: 10 I will put my **l** in their minds
10: 16 I will put my **l** in their hearts, and I

LAY (LAID LAYING)

Job 22: 22 and **l** up his words in your heart.
Isa 28: 16 "See, I **l** a stone in Zion, a tested
Mt 8: 20 of Man has no place to **l** his head."
Jn 10: 15 and I **l** down my life for the sheep.
15: 13 to **l** down one's life for one's
1Co 3: 11 no one can **l** any foundation other
1Jn 3: 16 we ought to **l** down our lives for
Rev 4: 10 They **l** their crowns before

LAYING (LAY)

1Ti 5: 22 not be hasty in the **l** on of hands,
Heb 6: 1 not **l** again the foundation

LAZARUS

1. Poor man in Jesus' parable (Lk 16:19–31).
2. Brother of Mary and Martha whom Jesus raised from the dead (Jn 11:1—12:19).

LAZY

Pr 10: 4 **L** hands make for poverty,
Heb 6: 12 We do not want you to become **l**,

LEAD (LEADERS LEADS LED)

Ex 15: 13 love you will **l** the people you have
Ps 27: 11 **l** me in a straight path because
61: 2 **l** me to the rock that is higher than I.
139: 24 and **l** me in the way everlasting.
143: 10 may your good Spirit **l** me on level
Ecc 5: 6 Do not let your mouth **l** you
Isa 11: 6 and a little child will **l** them.
Da 12: 3 those who **l** many to righteousness,
Mt 6: 13 And **l** us not into temptation,
1Jn 3: 7 do not let anyone **l** you astray.

LEADERS (LEAD)

Heb 13: 7 Remember your **l**, who spoke
13: 17 Have confidence in your **l**

LEADS (LEAD)

Ps 23: 2 he **l** me beside quiet waters,
Pr 19: 23 The fear of the LORD **l** to life;
Isa 40: 11 he gently **l** those that have young.
Mt 7: 13 gate and broad is the road that **l**
Jn 10: 3 sheep by name and **l** them out.
Ro 14: 19 every effort to do what **l** to peace
2Co 2: 14 God, who always **l** us as captives

LEAH

Wife of Jacob (Ge 29:16–30); bore six sons and one daughter (Ge 29:31—30:21; 34:1; 35:23).

LEAN

Pr 3: 5 **l** not on your own understanding;

LEARN (LEARNED LEARNING)

Isa 1: 17 **L** to do right; seek justice.
Mt 11: 29 my yoke upon you and **l** from me,

LEARNED (LEARN)

Php 4: 11 I have **l** to be content whatever
2Ti 3: 14 know those from whom you **l** it,

LEARNING (LEARN)

Pr 1: 5 the wise listen and add to their **l**,
2Ti 3: 7 always **l** but never able to come

LED (LEAD)

Isa 53: 7 he was **l** like a lamb
Am 2: 10 **l** you forty years in the wilderness
Ro 8: 14 For those who are **l** by the Spirit

LEFT

Jos 1: 7 turn from it to the right or to the **l**,
Pr 4: 27 Do not turn to the right or the **l**;
Mt 6: 3 do not let your **l** hand know what
25: 33 on his right and the goats on his **l**.

LEGION

Mk 5: 9 "My name is **L**," he replied,

LEND (LENDS)

Dt 15: 8 freely **l** them whatever they need.
Ps 37: 26 are always generous and **l** freely;
Lk 6: 34 Even sinners **l** to sinners,

LENDS (LEND)

Pr 19: 17 kind to the poor **l** to the LORD,

LENGTH (LONG)

Pr 10: 27 fear of the LORD adds **l** to life,

LEPROSY

2Ki 7: 3 Now there were four men with **l**

LETTER (LETTERS)

Mt 5: 18 not the smallest **l**, not the least
2Co 3: 2 You yourselves are our **l**,
3: 6 not of the **l** but of the Spirit; for the **l** kills,
2Th 3: 14 not obey our instruction in this **l**.

LETTERS (LETTER)

2Co 3: 7 which was engraved in **l** on stone,
10: 10 "His **l** are weighty and forceful,
2Pe 3: 16 He writes the same way in all his **l**,

LEVEL

Ps 143: 10 good Spirit lead me on **l** ground.
Isa 26: 7 The path of the righteous is **l**;
Heb 12: 13 "Make **l** paths for your feet,"

LEVI (LEVITES)

1. Son of Jacob by Leah (Ge 29:34; 46:11; 1Ch 2:1). Tribe of blessed (Ge 49:5–7; Dt 33:8–11), chosen as priests (Nu 3–4), numbered (Nu 3:39; 26:62), allotted cities, but not land

† Please see the "Hebrew to English Translation Chart," p. xix.
‡ Please see "Key New Testament Terms," p. 1584.

(Nu 18; 35; Dt 10:9; Jos 13:14; 21), land (Eze 48:8–22), 12,000 from (Rev 7:7).
2. See MATTHEW.

LEVITES (LEVI)
Nu 1: 53 The **L** are to be responsible
8: 6 "Take the **L** from among all
18: 21 "I give to the **L** all the tithes

LEWDNESS
Mk 7: 22 malice, deceit, **l**, envy, slander,

LIAR (LIE)
Pr 19: 22 better to be poor than a **l**.
Jn 8: 44 for he is a **l** and the father of lies.
Ro 3: 4 be true, and every human being a **l**.

LIBERATED
Ro 8: 21 the creation itself will be **l** from its

LIE (LIAR LIED LIES LYING)
Lev 19: 11 "'Do not **l**. "'Do not deceive
Nu 23: 19 that he should **l**, not a human
Dt 6: 7 when you **l** down and when you
Ps 23: 2 He makes me **l** down in green
Isa 11: 6 the leopard will **l** down
Eze 34: 14 There they will **l** down in good
Ro 1: 25 the truth about God for a **l**,
Col 3: 9 Do not **l** to each other, since you
Heb 6: 18 which it is impossible for God to **l**,

LIED (LIE)
Ac 5: 4 You have not **l** just to human

LIES (LIE)
Ps 34: 13 evil and your lips from telling **l**.
Jn 8: 44 for he is a liar and the father of **l**.

† **LIFE** (LIVE)
Ge 2: 7 into his nostrils the breath of **l**,
2: 9 of the garden were the tree of **l**
9: 11 Never again will all **l** be destroyed
Ex 21: 23 injury, you are to take **l** for **l**,
Lev 17: 14 because the **l** of every creature is its
24: 18 must make restitution—**l** for **l**.
Dt 30: 19 Now choose **l**, so that you and your
Ps 16: 11 make known to me the path of **l**;
23: 6 will follow me all the days of my **l**,
34: 12 Whoever of you loves **l** and desires
39: 4 let me know how fleeting my **l** is.
49: 7 one can redeem the **l** of another
104: 33 I will sing to the LORD all my **l**;
Pr 6: 23 and instruction are the way to **l**,
7: 23 little knowing it will cost him his **l**.
8: 35 For those who find me find **l**
11: 30 fruit of the righteous is a tree of **l**,
21: 21 righteousness and love finds **l**,
Eze 37: 5 enter you, and you will come to **l**.
Da 12: 2 some to everlasting **l**,
Mt 6: 25 do not worry about your **l**,
7: 14 and narrow the road that leads to **l**,
10: 39 whoever loses their **l** for my sake
16: 25 wants to save their **l** will lose it,
20: 28 to give his **l** as a ransom for many."
Mk 10: 45 to give his **l** as a ransom for many."
Lk 12: 15 **l** does not consist in an abundance
12: 22 do not worry about your **l**,
14: 26 yes, even their own **l**—
Jn 1: 4 In him was **l**, and that **l** was the light
3: 15 who believes may have eternal **l**
3: 36 believes in the Son has eternal **l**,
4: 14 of water welling up to eternal **l**."
5: 24 has crossed over from death to **l**.
6: 35 Jesus declared, "I am the bread of **l**.
6: 47 the one who believes has eternal **l**.
6: 68 You have the words of eternal **l**.
10: 10 I have come that they may have **l**,
10: 15 and I lay down my **l** for the sheep.
10: 28 I give them eternal **l**, and they shall
11: 25 "I am the resurrection and the **l**.
14: 6 am the way and the truth and the **l**.
15: 13 lay down one's **l** for one's friends.
20: 31 by believing you may have **l** in his
Ac 13: 48 appointed for eternal **l** believed.
Ro 4: 25 was raised to **l** for our justification.
6: 13 have been brought from death to **l**;
6: 23 God is eternal **l** in Christ Jesus our
8: 38 convinced that neither death nor **l**,
1Co 15: 19 If only for this **l** we have hope
2Co 3: 6 the letter kills, but the Spirit gives **l**.
Gal 2: 20 The **l** I now live in the body, I live
Eph 4: 1 to live a **l** worthy of the calling you
Php 2: 16 as you hold firmly to the word of **l**.
Col 1: 10 you may live a **l** worthy of the Lord
1Th 4: 12 your daily **l** may win the respect
1Ti 4: 8 the present **l** and the **l** to come.
4: 16 Watch your **l** and doctrine closely.
6: 19 take hold of the **l** that is truly **l**.
2Ti 3: 12 live a godly **l** in Christ Jesus will be
Jas 1: 12 person will receive the crown of **l**
3: 13 Let them show it by their good **l**,
1Pe 3: 10 "Whoever would love **l** and see
2Pe 1: 3 a godly **l** through our knowledge
1Jn 3: 14 we have passed from death to **l**,
5: 11 God has given us eternal **l**, and this **l**
Rev 13: 8 written in the Lamb's book of **l**,
20: 12 was opened, which is the book of **l**.
21: 27 are written in the Lamb's book of **l**.
22: 2 side of the river stood the tree of **l**,

LIFT (LIFTED LIFTING)
Ps 121: 1 I **l** up my eyes to the mountains—
134: 2 **L** up your hands in the sanctuary
La 3: 41 Let us **l** up our hearts and our hands

LIFTED (LIFT)
Ps 40: 2 He **l** me out of the slimy pit,
Jn 3: 14 so the Son of Man must be **l** up,
12: 32 I, when I am **l** up from the earth,

LIFTING (LIFT)
1Ti 2: 8 **l** up holy hands without anger

LIGHT (ENLIGHTENED)
Ge 1: 3 "Let there be **l**," and there was **l**.
2Sa 22: 29 LORD turns my darkness into **l**.
Job 38: 19 "What is the way to the abode of **l**?
Ps 4: 6 Let the **l** of your face shine on us.
19: 8 are radiant, giving **l** to the eyes.
27: 1 The LORD is my **l** and my
56: 13 walk before God in the **l** of life.
76: 4 You are radiant with **l**,
104: 2 The LORD wraps himself in **l** as
119:105 lamp to my feet and a **l** for my path.
119:130 unfolding of your words gives **l**;
Isa 2: 5 let us walk in the **l** of the LORD.
9: 2 in darkness have seen a great **l**;
49: 6 also make you a **l** for the Gentiles,
Mt 4: 16 shadow of death a **l** has dawned."
5: 16 way, let your **l** shine before others,
11: 30 yoke is easy and my burden is **l**."
Jn 3: 19 **L** has come into the world,
8: 12 he said, "I am the **l** of the world.
2Co 4: 6 made his **l** shine in our hearts
6: 14 Or what fellowship can **l** have
11: 14 masquerades as an angel of **l**.
1Ti 6: 16 and who lives in unapproachable **l**,
1Pe 2: 9 of darkness into his wonderful **l**.
1Jn 1: 5 God is **l**; in him there is no darkness
1: 7 But if we walk in the **l**, as he is
Rev 21: 23 for the glory of God gives it **l**,

LIGHTNING
Da 10: 6 his face like **l**, his eyes like flaming
Mt 24: 27 For as **l** that comes from the east is
28: 3 His appearance was like **l**, and his

LIKENESS
Ge 1: 26 in our **l**, so that they may rule over
Ps 17: 15 will be satisfied with seeing your **l**.
Isa 52: 14 his form marred beyond human **l**
Ro 8: 3 his own Son in the **l** of sinful flesh
Php 2: 7 a servant, being made in human **l**.
Jas 3: 9 who have been made in God's **l**.

LION
Isa 11: 7 and the **l** will eat straw like the ox.
1Pe 5: 8 around like a roaring **l** looking
Rev 5: 5 See, the **L** of the tribe of Judah,

LIPS
Ps 34: 1 his praise will always be on my **l**.
119:171 May my **l** overflow with praise,
Pr 13: 3 who guard their **l** preserve their
27: 2 an outsider, and not your own **l**.
Isa 6: 5 For I am a man of unclean **l**, and I
Mt 21: 16 read, "'From the **l** of children
Col 3: 8 and filthy language from your **l**.

LISTEN (LISTENING)
Dt 30: 20 LORD your God, **l** to his voice,
Pr 1: 5 let the wise **l** and add to their
12: 15 to them, but the wise **l** to advice.
Jn 10: 27 My sheep **l** to my voice;
Jas 1: 19 Everyone should be quick to **l**,
1: 22 Do not merely **l** to the word,

LISTENING (LISTEN)
1Sa 3: 9 LORD, for your servant is **l**.'"
Pr 18: 13 To answer before **l**—that is folly

LIVE (ALIVE LIFE LIVES LIVING)
Ex 20: 12 that you may **l** long in the land
33: 20 face, for no one may see me and **l**."
Dt 8: 3 that man does not **l** on bread alone
Job 14: 14 If someone dies, will they **l** again?
Ps 119:175 Let me **l** that I may praise you,
Isa 55: 3 come to me; listen, that you may **l**.
Eze 37: 3 "Son of man, can these bones **l**?"
Hab 2: 4 the righteous person will **l** by his
Mt 4: 4 'Man shall not **l** on bread alone,
Ac 17: 24 not **l** in temples built by human
17: 28 'For in him we **l** and move and
Ro 1: 17 "The righteous will **l** by faith."
2Co 5: 7 For we **l** by faith, not by sight.
Gal 2: 20 The life I now **l** in the body,
5: 25 Since we **l** by the Spirit, let us keep
Php 1: 21 me, to **l** is Christ and to die is gain.
1Th 5: 13 **L** in peace with each other.
2Ti 3: 12 who wants to **l** a godly life
Heb 12: 14 Make every effort to **l** in peace
1Pe 1: 17 **l** out your time as foreigners here

LIVES (LIVE)
Job 19: 25 I know that my redeemer **l**,
Pr 11: 30 and the one who is wise saves **l**.
Isa 57: 15 he who **l** forever, whose name is
Da 3: 28 to give up their **l** rather than serve
Jn 14: 17 he **l** with you and will be in you.
Gal 2: 20 I no longer live, but Christ **l** in me.
Heb 13: 5 Keep your **l** free from the love
2Pe 3: 11 You ought to live holy and godly **l**
1Jn 3: 16 to lay down our **l** for our brothers
4: 16 Whoever **l** in love **l** in God,

LIVING (LIVE)
Ge 2: 7 life, and the man became a **l** being.
Jer 2: 13 the spring of **l** water, and have dug
Mt 22: 32 the God of the dead but of the **l**."
Jn 7: 38 said, rivers of **l** water will flow
Ro 12: 1 to offer your bodies as a **l** sacrifice,
Heb 10: 31 to fall into the hands of the **l** God.
Rev 1: 18 I am the **L** One; I was dead,

LOAD
Gal 6: 5 each one should carry their own **l**.

LOCUSTS
Mt 3: 4 His food was **l** and wild honey.

LOFTY
Ps 139: 6 for me, too **l** for me to attain.

LONELY
Ps 68: 6 God sets the **l** in families, he leads

LONG (LENGTH LONGED LONGING LONGS)
1Ki 18: 21 "How **l** will you waver between
Jn 9: 4 As **l** as it is day, we must do
Eph 3: 18 to grasp how wide and **l** and high
1Pe 1: 12 Even angels **l** to look into these

LONGED (LONG)
Mt 13: 17 righteous people **l** to see what you
23: 37 how often I have **l** to gather your
2Ti 4: 8 to all who have **l** for his appearing.

LONGING (LONG)
Pr 13: 19 A **l** fulfilled is sweet to the soul,
2Co 5: 2 **l** to be clothed instead with our

LONGS (LONG)
Isa 30: 18 Yet the LORD **l** to be gracious

LOOK (LOOKING LOOKS)
Job 31: 1 my eyes not to **l** lustfully at a young
Ps 34: 5 Those who **l** to him are radiant;
Pr 4: 25 Let your eyes **l** straight ahead;
Isa 60: 5 Then you will **l** and be radiant,
Hab 1: 13 Your eyes are too pure to **l** on evil;
Zec 12: 10 They will **l** on me, the one they
Mk 13: 21 is the Messiah!' or, '**L**, there he is!'
Lk 24: 39 **L** at my hands and my feet. It is I
Jn 1: 36 by, he said, "**L**, the Lamb of God!"
4: 35 open your eyes and **l** at the fields!
19: 37 "They will **l** on the one they have
Jas 1: 27 to **l** after orphans and widows
1Pe 1: 12 Even angels long to **l** into these

LOOKING (LOOK)
Rev 5: 6 a Lamb, **l** as if it had been slain,

LOOKS (LOOK)
1Sa 16: 7 but the LORD **l** at the heart."

† Please see the "Hebrew to English Translation Chart," p. xix.

Lk 9: 62 puts a hand to the plow and **l** back
Php 2: 21 everyone **l** out for their own interests,

LORD (LORD'S LORDING)
Ne 4: 14 Remember the **L**, who is great
Job 28: 28 human race, "The fear of the **L**—
Ps 54: 4 the **L** is the one who sustains me.
62: 12 and with you, **L**, is unfailing love";
86: 5 You, **L**, are forgiving and good,
110: 1 The LORD says to my **l**:
147: 5 Great is our **L** and mighty in power
Isa 6: 1 died, I saw the **L**, high and exalted,
Da 9: 4 "**L**, the great and awesome God,
Mt 3: 3 'Prepare the way for the **L**,
4: 7 'Do not put the **L** your God
7: 21 "Not everyone who says to me, '**L**,
22: 37 "'Love the **L** your God with all
22: 44 "'The **L** said to my **L**: "Sit at my
Mk 12: 11 the **L** has done this, and it is
12: 29 The **L** our God, the **L** is one.
Lk 2: 9 An angel of the **L** appeared to
6: 46 "Why do you call me, '**L**, **L**,'
10: 27 "'Love the **L** your God with all
Ac 2: 21 on the name of the **L** will be saved.'
16: 31 "Believe in the **L** Jesus, and you
Ro 10: 9 "Jesus is **L**," and believe in your
10: 13 the name of the **L** will be saved."
12: 11 your spiritual fervor, serving the **L**.
14: 8 we live or die, we belong to the **L**.
1Co 1: 31 the one who boasts boast in the **L**."
3: 5 as the **L** has assigned to each his
7: 34 to be devoted to the **L** in both body
11: 23 The **L** Jesus, on the night he was
12: 3 "Jesus is **L**," except by the Holy
15: 57 victory through our **L** Jesus Christ.
16: 22 let that person be cursed! Come, **L**!
2Co 3: 17 Now the **L** is the Spirit, and where
8: 5 gave themselves first of all to the **L**,
10: 17 the one who boasts boast in the **L**."
Gal 6: 14 in the cross of our **L** Jesus Christ,
Eph 4: 5 one **L**, one faith, one baptism;
5: 10 and find out what pleases the **L**.
5: 19 music from your heart to the **L**,
Php 2: 11 acknowledge that Jesus Christ is **L**,
3: 1 and sisters, rejoice in the **L**!
4: 4 Rejoice in the **L** always. I will say it
Col 2: 6 as you received Christ Jesus as **L**,
3: 17 do it all in the name of the **L** Jesus,
3: 23 working for the **L**, not for human
4: 17 you have received in the **L**."
1Th 3: 12 May the **L** make your love increase
5: 2 day of the **L** will come like a thief
5: 23 at the coming of our **L** Jesus Christ.
2Th 2: 1 the coming of our **L** Jesus Christ
2Ti 2: 19 "The **L** knows those who are his,"
Heb 12: 14 holiness no one will see the **L**.
13: 6 confidence, "The **L** is my helper;
Jas 4: 10 Humble yourselves before the **L**,
1Pe 1: 25 the word of the **L** endures forever."
2: 3 you have tasted that the **L** is good.
3: 15 in your hearts revere Christ as **L**.
2Pe 1: 16 the coming of our **L** Jesus Christ
2: 1 sovereign **L** who bought them—
3: 9 The **L** is not slow in keeping his
Jude : 14 the **L** is coming with thousands
Rev 4: 8 holy is the **L** God Almighty,'
4: 11 "You are worthy, our **L** and God,
17: 14 triumph over them because he is **L**
22: 20 Amen. Come, **L** Jesus.

LORD'S (LORD)
Ac 21: 14 up and said, "The **L** will be done."
1Co 10: 26 "The earth is the **L**, and everything
11: 26 you proclaim the **L** death until he
2Co 3: 18 faces contemplate the **L** glory,
2Ti 2: 24 And the **L** servant must not be
Jas 4: 15 "If it is the **L** will, we will live

LORDING (LORD)
1Pe 5: 3 not **l** it over those entrusted to you,

LORD* (LORD'S*; this is the proper name of God, *Yahweh*, spelled "LORD" in the NIV)
Ge 2: 4 when the **L** God made the earth
2: 7 the **L** God formed a man
3: 21 The **L** God made garments of skin
7: 16 Then the **L** shut him in.
15: 6 Abram believed the **L**, and he
18: 14 Is anything too hard for the **L**?
31: 49 "May the **L** keep watch between
Ex 3: 2 There the angel of the **L** appeared
9: 12 But the **L** hardened Pharaoh's heart
14: 30 That day the **L** saved Israel
20: 2 "I am the **L** your God, who
33: 11 The **L** would speak to Moses face
40: 34 glory of the **L** filled the tabernacle.
Lev 19: 2 'Be holy because I, the **L** your God,
Nu 8: 5 The **L** said to Moses:
14: 21 glory of the **L** fills the whole earth,
Dt 2: 7 The **L** your God has blessed you
5: 9 for I, the **L** your God, am a jealous
6: 4 The **L** our God, the **L** is one.
6: 5 Love the **L** your God with all your
6: 16 Do not put the **L** your God
10: 14 **L** your God belong the heavens,
10: 17 For the **L** your God is God of gods
11: 1 Love the **L** your God and keep his
28: 1 If you fully obey the **L** your God
30: 16 you today to love the **L** your God,
30: 20 For the **L** is your life, and he will
31: 6 for the **L** your God goes with you;
Jos 22: 5 to love the **L** your God, to walk
24: 15 household, we will serve the **L**."
1Sa 1: 28 So now I give him to the **L**.
2: 2 "There is no one holy like the **L**;
7: 12 "Thus far the **L** has helped us."
12: 22 his great name the **L** will not reject
15: 22 as much as in obeying the **L**?
2Sa 22: 2 "The **L** is my rock, my fortress
1Ki 2: 3 and observe what the **L** your God
8: 11 the glory of the **L** filled his temple.
8: 61 fully committed to the **L** our God,
18: 21 If the **L** is God, follow him;
2Ki 13: 23 But the **L** was gracious to them
1Ch 16: 8 Give praise to the **L**, proclaim his
16: 23 Sing to the **L**, all the earth;
28: 9 for the **L** searches every heart
29: 11 Yours, **L**, is the kingdom;
2Ch 5: 14 the glory of the **L** filled the temple
16: 9 the **L** range throughout the earth
19: 6 for mere mortals but for the **L**,
30: 9 for the **L** your God is gracious
Ne 1: 5 "**L**, the God of heaven, the great
Job 1: 21 The **L** gave and the **L** has taken
38: 1 the **L** spoke to Job out of the storm.
42: 9 did what the **L** told them;
Ps 1: 2 whose delight is in the law of the **L**,
9: 9 The **L** is a refuge for the oppressed,
12: 6 the words of the **L** are flawless,
16: 8 I keep my eyes always on the **L**.
19: 7 The law of the **L** is perfect,
19: 14 heart be pleasing in your sight, **L**,
23: 1 The **L** is my shepherd, I lack
23: 6 dwell in the house of the **L** forever.
27: 1 The **L** is the stronghold of my life
27: 4 to gaze on the beauty of the **L**
29: 1 ascribe to the **L** glory and strength.
32: 2 one whose sin the **L** does not count
33: 12 is the nation whose God is the **L**,
33: 18 the eyes of the **L** are on those who
34: 3 Glorify the **L** with me; let us exalt
34: 7 of the **L** encamps around those
34: 8 Taste and see that the **L** is good;
34: 18 The **L** is close to the brokenhearted
37: 4 Take delight in the **L**, and he will
40: 1 I waited patiently for the **L**;
47: 2 For the **L** Most High is awesome,
48: 1 Great is the **L**, and most worthy
55: 22 Cast your cares on the **L** and he
75: 8 In the hand of the **L** is a cup full
84: 11 For the **L** God is a sun and shield;
86: 11 Teach me your way, **L**, that I may
89: 5 heavens praise your wonders, **L**,
95: 1 Come, let us sing for joy to the **L**;
96: 1 Sing to the **L** a new song;
98: 4 Shout for joy to the **L**, all the earth,
100: 1 Shout for joy to the **L**, all the earth.
103: 1 Praise the **L**, my soul; all my
103: 8 The **L** is compassionate
104: 1 Praise the **L**, my soul. **L** my God,
107: 8 to the **L** for his unfailing love
110: 1 The **L** says to my lord: "Sit at my
113: 4 The **L** is exalted over all the nations
115: 1 Not to us, **L**, not to us but to your
116: 15 the sight of the **L** is the death of his
118: 1 Give thanks to the **L**, for he is good;
118: 24 The **L** has done it this very day;
121: 2 My help comes from the **L**,
121: 5 The **L** watches over you—the **L** is
125: 2 so the **L** surrounds his people both
Ps 127: 1 Unless the **L** builds the house,
127: 3 Children are a heritage from the **L**,
130: 3 If you, **L**, kept a record of sins,
135: 6 The **L** does whatever pleases him,
136: 1 Give thanks to the **L**, for he is good.
139: 1 You have searched me, **L**, and you
144: 3 **L**, what are human beings that you
145: 3 Great is the **L** and most worthy
145: 18 The **L** is near to all who call on him,
Pr 1: 7 The fear of the **L** is the beginning
3: 5 Trust in the **L** with all your heart
3: 9 Honor the **L** with your wealth,
3: 12 because the **L** disciplines those he
3: 19 By wisdom the **L** laid the earth's
5: 21 your ways are in full view of the **L**,
6: 16 There are six things the **L** hates,
10: 27 The fear of the **L** adds length to life,
11: 1 The **L** detests dishonest scales,
12: 22 The **L** detests lying lips, but he
14: 26 Whoever fears the **L** has a secure
15: 3 The eyes of the **L** are everywhere,
16: 2 but motives are weighed by the **L**.
16: 4 The **L** works out everything to its
16: 9 but the **L** establishes their steps.
16: 33 but its every decision is from the **L**.
18: 10 name of the **L** is a fortified tower;
18: 22 and receives favor from the **L**.
19: 14 but a prudent wife is from the **L**.
19: 17 is kind to the poor lends to the **L**,
21: 3 acceptable to the **L** than sacrifice.
21: 30 plan that can succeed against the **L**.
21: 31 battle, but victory rests with the **L**.
22: 2 The **L** is the Maker of them all.
24: 18 or the **L** will see and disapprove
31: 30 a woman who fears the **L** is to be
Isa 6: 3 holy, holy is the **L** Almighty;
11: 2 The Spirit of the **L** will rest on him
11: 9 of the **L** as the waters cover the sea.
12: 2 The **L**, the **L** himself, is my strength
24: 1 the **L** is going to lay waste the earth
25: 8 The Sovereign **L** will wipe away
29: 15 to hide their plans from the **L**,
33: 6 the fear of the **L** is the key to this
35: 10 those the **L** has rescued will return.
40: 5 For the mouth of the **L** has spoken.
40: 7 because the breath of the **L** blows
40: 10 the Sovereign **L** comes with power,
40: 28 The **L** is the everlasting God,
40: 31 in the **L** will renew their strength.
42: 8 "I am the **L**; that is my name!
43: 11 I am the **L**, and apart from me
44: 24 I am the **L**, the Maker of all things,
45: 5 I am the **L**, and there is no other;
45: 21 Was it not I, the **L**? And there is no
51: 11 Those the **L** has rescued will return
53: 6 the **L** has laid on him the iniquity
53: 10 the will of the **L** will prosper in his
55: 6 Seek the **L** while he may be found;
58: 8 of the **L** will be your rear guard.
58: 11 The **L** will guide you always;
59: 1 the arm of the **L** is not too short
61: 3 a planting of the **L** for the display
61: 10 I delight greatly in the **L**;
Jer 1: 9 Then the **L** reached out his hand
9: 24 in these I delight," declares the **L**.
16: 19 **L**, my strength and my fortress,
17: 7 is the one who trusts in the **L**,
La 3: 40 and let us return to the **L**.
Eze 1: 28 of the likeness of the glory of the **L**.
Hos 1: 7 but I, the **L** their God, will save
3: 5 return and seek the **L** their God
6: 1 "Come, let us return to the **L**.
Joel 2: 1 for the day of the **L** is coming.
2: 11 The day of the **L** is great;
3: 14 day of the **L** is near in the valley
Am 5: 18 you who long for the day of the **L**!
Jnh 1: 3 But Jonah ran away from the **L**
Mic 4: 2 the word of the **L** from Jerusalem.
6: 8 what does the **L** require of you?
Na 1: 2 The **L** is a jealous and avenging
1: 3 The **L** is slow to anger but great
Hab 2: 14 of the **L** as the waters cover the sea.
2: 20 The **L** is in his holy temple;
Zep 3: 17 The **L** your God is with you,
Zec 1: 17 and the **L** will again comfort Zion
9: 16 The **L** their God will save his people
14: 5 Then the **L** my God will come,
14: 9 On that day there will be one **L**,
Mal 4: 5 and dreadful day of the **L** comes.

LORD'S* (LORD*; this is the proper name of God, *Yahweh*, spelled "LORD's" in the NIV)

Ex 34: 34 he entered the **L** presence to speak
Nu 14: 41 you disobeying the **L** command?
Dt 6: 18 is right and good in the **L** sight,
32: 9 For the **L** portion is his people,
Jos 21: 45 all the **L** good promises to Israel
Ps 24: 1 The earth is the **L**,
32: 10 the **L** unfailing love surrounds
89: 1 I will sing of the **L** great love
103: 17 the **L** love is with those who fear
Pr 3: 11 do not despise the **L** discipline,
Isa 24: 14 west they acclaim the **L** majesty.
62: 3 a crown of splendor in the **L** hand,
Jer 48: 10 who is lax in doing the **L** work!
La 3: 22 Because of the **L** great love we are
Mic 4: 1 the mountain of the **L** temple will

LOSE (LOSES LOSS LOST)

1Sa 17: 32 "Let no one **l** heart on account
Mt 10: 39 Whoever finds their life will **l** it,
Lk 9: 25 and yet **l** or forfeit their very self?
Jn 6: 39 that I shall **l** none of all those
Heb 12: 3 will not grow weary and **l** heart.
12: 5 not **l** heart when he rebukes you,

LOSES (LOSE)

Mt 5: 13 But if the salt **l** its saltiness,
Lk 15: 4 a hundred sheep and **l** one of them.
15: 8 has ten silver coins and **l** one.

LOSS (LOSE)

Ro 11: 12 their **l** means riches for the Gentiles,
1Co 3: 15 the builder will suffer **l** but yet will
Php 3: 8 I consider everything a **l** because

LOST (LOSE)

Ps 73: 2 I had nearly **l** my foothold.
Jer 50: 6 "My people have been **l** sheep;
Eze 34: 4 the strays or searched for the **l**.
34: 16 I will search for the **l** and bring
Lk 15: 4 go after the **l** sheep until he finds
15: 6 I have found my **l** sheep.'
15: 9 I have found my **l** coin.'
15: 24 he was **l** and is found.'
19: 10 came to seek and to save the **l**."
Php 3: 8 for whose sake I have **l** all things.

LOT (LOTS)

Nephew of Abraham (Ge 11:27; 12:5). Chose to live in Sodom (Ge 13). Rescued from four kings (Ge 14). Rescued from Sodom (Ge 19:1–29; 2Pe 2:7). Fathered Moab and Ammon by his daughters (Ge 19:30–38).

Est 3: 7 the **l**) was cast in the presence
9: 24 the **l**) for their ruin and destruction.
Pr 16: 33 The **l** is cast into the lap, but its
18: 18 Casting the **l** settles disputes
Ecc 3: 22 their work, because that is their **l**.
Ac 1: 26 cast lots, and the **l** fell to Matthias;

LOTS (LOT)

Ps 22: 18 them and cast **l** for my garment.
Mt 27: 35 divided up his clothes by casting **l**.

† LOVE (BELOVED LOVED LOVELY LOVER LOVERS LOVES LOVING)

Ge 22: 2 son, your only son, whom you **l**—
Ex 15: 13 In your unfailing **l** you will lead
20: 6 showing **l** to a thousand generations
34: 6 abounding in **l** and faithfulness,
Lev 19: 18 but **l** your neighbor as yourself.
19: 34 **L** them as yourself, for you were
Nu 14: 18 abounding in **l** and forgiving sin
Dt 5: 10 showing **l** to a thousand generations
6: 5 **L** the LORD your God with all
7: 13 He will **l** you and bless you
10: 12 to **l** him, to serve the LORD your
11: 13 to **l** the LORD your God
13: 6 or the wife you **l**, or your closest
30: 6 you may **l** him with all your heart
Jos 22: 5 to **l** the LORD your God, to walk
1Ki 3: 3 Solomon showed his **l**
8: 23 you who keep your covenant of **l**
2Ch 5: 13 his **l** endures forever."
Ne 1: 5 covenant of **l** with those who **l** him
Ps 18: 1 I **l** you, LORD, my strength.
23: 6 **l** will follow me all the days of my
25: 6 your great mercy and **l**, for they are
31: 16 save me in your unfailing **l**.
32: 10 LORD's unfailing **l** surrounds
33: 5 the earth is full of his unfailing **l**.
Ps 33: 18 whose hope is in his unfailing **l**,
36: 5 Your **l**, LORD,
36: 7 How priceless is your unfailing **l**,
45: 7 You **l** righteousness and hate
51: 1 God, according to your unfailing **l**;
57: 10 For great is your **l**,
63: 3 Because your **l** is better than life,
66: 20 prayer or withheld his **l** from me!
77: 8 his unfailing **l** vanished forever?
85: 7 Show us your unfailing **l**, LORD,
85: 10 **L** and faithfulness meet together;
86: 13 For great is your **l** toward me;
89: 1 sing of the LORD's great **l** forever;
89: 33 but I will not take my **l** from him,
92: 2 proclaiming your **l** in the morning
94: 18 slipping," your unfailing **l**, LORD,
100: 5 is good and his **l** endures forever;
101: 1 I will sing of your **l** and justice;
103: 4 crowns you with **l** and compassion,
103: 8 slow to anger, abounding in **l**.
103: 11 so great is his **l** for those who fear
107: 8 to the LORD for his unfailing **l**
108: 4 For great is your **l**, higher than
116: 1 I **l** the LORD, for he heard my
118: 1 he is good; his **l** endures forever.
119: 47 your commands because I **l** them.
119: 64 The earth is filled with your **l**,
119: 76 May your unfailing **l** be my
119: 97 Oh, how I **l** your law! I meditate
119:119 dross; therefore I **l** your statutes.
119:124 your servant according to your **l**
119:132 do to those who **l** your name.
119:159 See how I **l** your precepts;
119:163 detest falsehood but I **l** your law.
119:165 peace have those who **l** your law,
122: 6 "May those who **l** you be secure.
130: 7 for with the LORD is unfailing **l**
136: 1 *His **l** endures forever.*
143: 8 bring me word of your unfailing **l**,
145: 8 slow to anger and rich in **l**.
145: 20 LORD watches over all who **l** him,
147: 11 put their hope in his unfailing **l**.
Pr 3: 3 Let **l** and faithfulness never leave
4: 6 **l** her, and she will watch over you.
5: 19 you ever be intoxicated with her **l**.
8: 17 I **l** those who **l** me, and those who
9: 8 rebuke the wise and they will **l** you.
10: 12 but **l** covers over all wrongs.
14: 22 those who plan what is good find **l**
15: 17 with **l** than a fattened calf
17: 9 Whoever would foster **l** covers
19: 22 a person desires is unfailing **l**;
20: 6 Many claim to have unfailing **l**,
20: 13 Do not **l** sleep or you will grow
20: 28 **L** and faithfulness keep a king safe;
21: 21 righteousness and **l** finds life,
27: 5 is open rebuke than hidden **l**.
Ecc 9: 6 Their **l**, their hate and their
9: 9 whom you **l**, all the days of this
SS 2: 4 and let his banner over me be **l**.
8: 6 for **l** is as strong as death,
8: 7 Many waters cannot quench **l**;
Isa 5: 1 sing for the one I **l** a song about his
16: 5 In **l** a throne will be established;
38: 17 In your **l** you kept me from the pit
54: 10 yet my unfailing **l** for you will not
55: 3 my faithful **l** promised to David.
61: 8 "For I, the LORD, **l** justice;
63: 9 In his **l** and mercy he redeemed
Jer 5: 31 and my people **l** it this way.
31: 3 loved you with an everlasting **l**;
32: 18 You show **l** to thousands but bring
33: 11 his **l** endures forever."
La 3: 22 of the LORD's great **l** we are not
3: 32 so great is his unfailing **l**.
Eze 33: 32 more than one who sings **l** songs
Da 9: 4 covenant of **l** with those who **l** him
Hos 2: 19 and justice, in **l** and compassion.
3: 1 **L** her as the LORD loves
11: 4 of human kindness, with ties of **l**.
12: 6 maintain **l** and justice, and wait
Joel 2: 13 slow to anger and abounding in **l**,
Am 5: 15 Hate evil, **l** good; maintain justice
Mic 3: 2 you who hate good and **l** evil;
6: 8 to **l** mercy and to walk humbly
Zep 3: 17 his **l** he will no longer rebuke you,
Zec 8: 19 Therefore **l** truth and peace."
Mt 3: 17 said, "This is my Son, whom I **l**;
5: 44 **l** your enemies and pray for those
6: 24 will hate the one and **l** the other,
17: 5 said, "This is my Son, whom I **l**;
19: 19 '**l** your neighbor as yourself.'"
22: 37 "'**L** the Lord your God with all
Lk 6: 32 "If you **l** those who **l** you,
7: 42 which of them will **l** him more?"
20: 13 I will send my son, whom I **l**;
Jn 13: 34 command I give you: **L** one another.
13: 35 my disciples, if you **l** one another."
14: 15 "If you **l** me, keep my commands.
15: 13 Greater **l** has no one than this:
15: 17 This is my command: **L** each other.
21: 15 do you **l** me more than these?"
Ro 5: 5 because God's **l** has been poured
5: 8 God demonstrates his own **l** for us
8: 28 for the good of those who **l** him,
8: 35 separate us from the **l** of Christ?
8: 39 separate us from the **l** of God that
12: 9 **L** must be sincere. Hate what is
12: 10 Be devoted to one another in **l**.
13: 8 continuing debt to **l** one another,
13: 9 "**L** your neighbor as yourself."
13: 10 Therefore **l** is the fulfillment
1Co 2: 9 prepared for those who **l** him—
8: 1 puffs up while **l** builds up.
13: 1 but do not have **l**, I am only
13: 2 but do not have **l**, I am nothing.
13: 3 but do not have **l**, I gain nothing.
13: 4 **L** is patient, **l** is kind. It does not
13: 6 **L** does not delight in evil
13: 8 **L** never fails. But where there are
13: 13 these three remain: faith, hope and **l**.
But the greatest of these is **l**.
14: 1 Follow the way of **l** and eagerly
16: 14 Do everything in **l**.
2Co 5: 14 For Christ's **l** compels us,
8: 8 sincerity of your **l** by comparing it
8: 24 show these men the proof of your **l**
Gal 5: 6 is faith expressing itself through **l**.
5: 13 serve one another humbly in **l**.
5: 22 But the fruit of the Spirit is **l**, joy,
Eph 1: 4 holy and blameless in his sight. In **l**
2: 4 But because of his great **l** for us,
3: 17 being rooted and established in **l**,
3: 18 high and deep is the **l** of Christ,
3: 19 and to know this **l** that surpasses
4: 2 bearing with one another in **l**.
4: 15 speaking the truth in **l**, we will
5: 2 and walk in the way of **l**, just as
5: 25 Husbands, **l** your wives, just as
5: 28 to **l** their wives as their own bodies.
5: 33 must **l** his wife as he loves himself,
Php 1: 9 that your **l** may abound more
2: 2 having the same **l**, being one
Col 1: 5 **l** that spring from the hope stored
2: 2 in heart and united in **l**,
3: 14 And over all these virtues put on **l**,
3: 19 **l** your wives and do not be harsh
1Th 1: 3 your labor prompted by **l**, and your
4: 9 been taught by God to **l** each other.
5: 8 on faith and **l** as a breastplate,
2Th 3: 5 Lord direct your hearts into God's **l**
1Ti 1: 5 The goal of this command is **l**,
2: 15 faith, **l** and holiness with propriety.
4: 12 conduct, in **l**, in faith and in purity.
6: 10 For the **l** of money is a root of all
6: 11 faith, **l**, endurance and gentleness.
2Ti 1: 7 us power, **l** and self-discipline.
2: 22 faith, **l** and peace, along with those
3: 10 faith, patience, **l**, endurance,
Titus 2: 4 women to **l** their husbands
Phm : 9 to appeal to you on the basis of **l**.
Heb 6: 10 the **l** you have shown him as you
10: 24 may spur one another on toward **l**
13: 5 your lives free from the **l** of money
Jas 1: 12 has promised to those who **l** him.
2: 5 he promised those who **l** him?
2: 8 "**L** your neighbor as yourself,"
1Pe 1: 22 you have sincere **l** for each other,
2: 17 everyone, **l** the family of believers,
3: 8 be sympathetic, **l** one another,
3: 10 For, "Whoever would **l** life and see
4: 8 Above all, **l** each other deeply,
4: 8 because **l** covers over a multitude
5: 14 Greet one another with a kiss of **l**.

† Please see the "Hebrew to English Translation Chart," p. xix.

2Pe 1: 7 and to mutual affection, **l**.
1: 17 saying, "This is my Son, whom I **l**;
1Jn 2: 5 **l** for God is truly made complete
2: 15 Do not **l** the world or anything
3: 1 See what great **l** the Father has
3: 10 who does not **l** their brother
3: 11 We should **l** one another.
3: 14 to life, because we **l** each other.
3: 16 This is how we know what **l** is:
3: 18 let us not **l** with words or speech
3: 23 **l** one another as he commanded
4: 7 one another, for **l** comes from God.
4: 8 not know God, because God is **l**.
4: 9 is how God showed his **l** among us:
4: 10 This is **l**: not that we loved God,
4: 11 us, we also ought to **l** one another.
4: 12 but if we **l** one another, God lives
4: 16 God is **l**. Whoever lives in **l** lives
4: 17 This is how **l** is made complete
4: 18 There is no fear in **l**. But perfect **l**
4: 19 We **l** because he first loved us.
4: 20 whoever does not **l** their brother
4: 21 loves God must also **l** their brother
5: 2 we know that we **l** the children
5: 3 In fact, this is **l** for God: to keep his
2Jn : 5 I ask that we **l** one another.
: 6 his command is that you walk in **l**.
Jude : 12 are blemishes at your **l** feasts,
: 21 yourselves in God's **l** as you wait
Rev 2: 4 You have forsaken the **l** you had
3: 19 Those whom I **l** I rebuke
12: 11 they did not **l** their lives so much

LOVED (LOVE)
Ge 24: 67 she became his wife, and he **l** her;
37: 3 Now Israel **l** Joseph more than any
Dt 7: 8 it was because the LORD **l** you
1Sa 1: 5 a double portion because he **l** her,
20: 17 because he **l** him as he **l** himself.
Ps 44: 3 light of your face, for you **l** them.
Jer 2: 2 youth, how as a bride you **l** me
31: 3 "I have **l** you with an everlasting
Hos 2: 23 to the one I called 'Not my **l** one.'
3: 1 though she is **l** by another man
9: 10 became as vile as the thing they **l**.
11: 1 "When Israel was a child, I **l** him,
Mal 1: 2 "I have **l** you," says the LORD.
Mk 12: 6 one left to send, a son, whom he **l**.
Jn 3: 16 For God so **l** the world that he gave
3: 19 people **l** darkness instead of light
11: 5 Now Jesus **l** Martha and her sister
12: 43 for they **l** human praise more than
13: 1 in the world, he **l** them to the end.
13: 23 the disciple whom Jesus **l**,
13: 34 As I have **l** you, so you must love
14: 21 The one who loves me will be **l**
15: 9 "As the Father has **l** me, so have I **l**
15: 12 Love each other as I have **l** you.
19: 26 disciple whom he **l** standing
Ro 8: 37 conquerors through him who **l** us.
9: 13 "Jacob I **l**, but Esau I hated."
9: 25 'my **l** one' who is not my **l** one,"
11: 28 they are **l** on account
Gal 2: 20 who **l** me and gave himself for me.
Eph 5: 2 just as Christ **l** us and gave himself
5: 25 just as Christ **l** the church and gave
2Th 2: 16 who **l** us and by his grace gave us
2Ti 4: 10 for Demas, because he **l** this world,
Heb 1: 9 You have **l** righteousness and hated
1Jn 4: 10 not that we **l** God, but that he **l** us
4: 11 since God so **l** us, we also ought
4: 19 We love because he first **l** us.

LOVELY (LOVE)
Ps 84: 1 How **l** is your dwelling place,
SS 2: 14 voice is sweet, and your face is **l**.
5: 16 sweetness itself; he is altogether **l**.
Php 4: 8 is pure, whatever is **l**, whatever is

LOVER (LOVE)
1Ti 3: 3 not quarrelsome, not a **l** of money.

LOVERS (LOVE)
2Ti 3: 2 People will be **l** of themselves,
3: 3 brutal, not **l** of the good,
3: 4 **l** of pleasure rather than **l** of God—

LOVES (LOVE)
Ps 11: 7 LORD is righteous, he **l** justice;
33: 5 The LORD **l** righteousness
34: 12 Whoever of you **l** life and desires
127: 2 for he grants sleep to those he **l**.
Pr 3: 12 the LORD disciplines those he **l**,
12: 1 Whoever **l** discipline **l** knowledge,
17: 17 A friend **l** at all times, and
17: 19 Whoever **l** a quarrel **l** sin;
22: 11 One who **l** a pure heart and who
Mt 10: 37 "Anyone who **l** their father
Lk 7: 47 has been forgiven little **l** little."
Jn 3: 35 The Father **l** the Son and has
10: 17 The reason my Father **l** me is that I
14: 21 The one who **l** me will be loved
14: 23 "Anyone who **l** me will obey my
Ro 13: 8 for whoever **l** others has fulfilled
2Co 9: 7 for God **l** a cheerful giver.
Eph 5: 28 He who **l** his wife **l** himself.
5: 33 must love his wife as he **l** himself,
Heb 12: 6 the Lord disciplines the one he **l**,
1Jn 4: 7 Everyone who **l** has been born
5: 1 who **l** the father **l** his child
3Jn : 9 but Diotrephes, who **l** to be first,
Rev 1: 5 To him who **l** us and has freed us

LOVING (LOVE)
Ps 25: 10 All the ways of the LORD are **l**
Heb 13: 1 Keep on **l** one another as brothers
1Jn 5: 2 by **l** God and carrying out his

LOWLY
Job 5: 11 The **l** he sets on high, and those
Pr 29: 23 low, but the **l** in spirit gain honor.
Isa 57: 15 to revive the spirit of the **l**
Eze 21: 26 The **l** will be exalted and
Mt 18: 4 whoever takes the **l** position
1Co 1: 28 God chose the **l** things of this

LUKE
Co-worker with Paul (Col 4:14; 2Ti 4:11; Phm 24).

LUKEWARM
Rev 3: 16 So, because you are **l**—

LUST
Pr 6: 25 Do not **l** in your heart after her
Col 3: 5 impurity, **l**, evil desires and greed,
1Th 4: 5 not in passionate **l** like the pagans,
1Jn 2: 16 the **l** of the flesh, the **l** of the eyes,

LYING (LIE)
Pr 6: 17 haughty eyes, a **l** tongue,
26: 28 A **l** tongue hates those it hurts,

MACEDONIA
Ac 16: 9 a vision of a man of **M** standing

MADE (MAKE)
Ge 1: 16 God **m** two great lights—
1: 25 God **m** the wild animals according
2: 22 the LORD God **m** a woman
2Ki 19: 15 You have **m** heaven and earth.
Ps 95: 5 for he **m** it, and his hands formed
100: 3 It is he who **m** us, and we are his;
139: 14 I am fearfully and wonderfully **m**;
Ecc 3: 11 He has **m** everything beautiful in
Mk 2: 27 "The Sabbath was **m** for man,
Jn 1: 3 Through him all things were **m**;
Ac 17: 24 "The God who **m** the world
Heb 1: 2 whom also he **m** the universe.
Rev 14: 7 Worship him who **m** the heavens,

MAGI
Mt 2: 1 **M** from the east came to Jerusalem

MAGOG
Eze 38: 2 of the land of **M**, the chief prince
39: 6 I will send fire on **M** and on those
Rev 20: 8 Gog and **M**—and to gather them

MAIMED
Mt 18: 8 It is better for you to enter life **m**

MAJESTIC (MAJESTY)
Ex 15: 6 hand, LORD, was **m** in power.
15: 11 **m** in holiness, awesome in glory,
Ps 8: 1 **m** is your name in all the earth!
29: 4 the voice of the LORD is **m**.
111: 3 Glorious and **m** are his deeds,
SS 6: 10 sun, **m** as the stars in procession?
2Pe 1: 17 came to him from the **M** Glory,

MAJESTY (MAJESTIC)
Ex 15: 7 your **m** you threw down those who
Dt 33: 26 and on the clouds in his **m**.
1Ch 16: 27 Splendor and **m** are before him;
Est 1: 4 the splendor and glory of his **m**.
Job 37: 22 God comes in awesome **m**.
40: 10 clothe yourself in honor and **m**.
Ps 45: 4 In your **m** ride forth victoriously
Ps 93: 1 LORD reigns, he is robed in **m**;
145: 5 the glorious splendor of your **m**—
Isa 53: 2 beauty or **m** to attract us to him,
Eze 31: 2 can be compared with you in **m**?
2Pe 1: 16 but we were eyewitnesses of his **m**.
Jude : 25 only God our Savior be glory, **m**,

† MAKE (MADE MAKER MAKES MAKING)
Ge 1: 26 "Let us **m** mankind in our image,
2: 18 I will **m** a helper suitable for him."
12: 2 "I will **m** you into a great nation,
Ex 22: 3 steals must certainly **m** restitution,
Nu 6: 25 the LORD **m** his face shine on you
Ps 108: 1 sing and **m** music with all my soul.
Isa 14: 14 I will **m** myself like the Most
29: 16 formed it, "You did not **m** me"?
Jer 31: 31 "when I will **m** a new covenant
Mt 3: 3 Lord, **m** straight paths for him.'"
28: 19 go and **m** disciples of all nations,
Lk 13: 24 "**M** every effort to enter through
Ro 14: 19 Let us therefore **m** every effort to
2Co 5: 9 So we **m** it our goal to please him,
Eph 4: 3 **M** every effort to keep the unity
Col 4: 5 **m** the most of every opportunity.
1Th 4: 11 **m** it your ambition to lead a quiet
Heb 4: 11 **m** every effort to enter that rest,
12: 14 **M** every effort to live in peace
2Pe 1: 5 **m** every effort to add to your faith
3: 14 **m** every effort to be found spotless,

MAKER (MAKE)
Job 4: 17 man be more pure than his **M**?
36: 3 I will ascribe justice to my **M**.
Ps 95: 6 us kneel before the LORD our **M**;
Pr 22: 2 The LORD is the **M** of them all.
Isa 45: 9 to those who quarrel with their **M**,
54: 5 For your **M** is your husband—
Jer 10: 16 these, for he is the **M** of all things,

MAKES (MAKE)
1Co 3: 7 but only God, who **m** things grow.

MAKING (MAKE)
Ps 19: 7 are trustworthy, **m** wise the simple.
Ecc 12: 12 Of **m** many books there is no end,
Jn 5: 18 Father, **m** himself equal with God.
Eph 5: 16 **m** the most of every opportunity,

MALE
Ge 1: 27 **m** and female he created them.
Gal 3: 28 nor free, nor is there **m** and female,

MALICE (MALICIOUS)
Ro 1: 29 envy, murder, strife, deceit and **m**.
Col 3: 8 anger, rage, **m**, slander, and filthy
1Pe 2: 1 rid yourselves of all **m** and all

MALICIOUS (MALICE)
1Ti 3: 11 not **m** talkers but temperate
6: 4 envy, strife, **m** talk, evil suspicions

MAN (MANKIND MEN WOMAN WOMEN)
Ge 2: 7 the LORD God formed a **m**
2: 18 not good for the **m** to be alone.
2: 23 for she was taken out of **m**."
Dt 8: 3 **m** does not live on bread alone
1Sa 13: 14 sought out a **m** after his own heart
Ps 127: 5 Blessed is the **m** whose quiver is
Pr 30: 19 way of a **m** with a young woman.
Isa 53: 3 by mankind, a **m** of suffering,
Mt 19: 5 this reason a **m** will leave his father
Lk 4: 4 '**M** shall not live on bread alone.'"
Ro 5: 12 entered the world through one **m**,
1Co 7: 2 **m** should have sexual relations
11: 3 that the head of every **m** is Christ,
11: 3 and the head of the woman is **m**,
13: 11 When I became a **m**, I put the ways
Php 2: 8 being found in appearance as a **m**,
1Ti 2: 5 and mankind, the **m** Christ Jesus,
2: 12 or to assume authority over a **m**;

MANAGE
Jer 12: 5 how will you **m** in the thickets
1Ti 3: 4 He must **m** his own family well
3: 12 to his wife and must **m** his children
5: 14 to **m** their homes and to give

MANASSEH
1. Firstborn of Joseph (Ge 41:51; 46:20). Blessed (Ge 48).
2. Son of Hezekiah; king of Judah (2Ki 21:1–18; 2Ch 33:1–20).

MANGER
Lk 2: 12 in cloths and lying in a **m**."

† Please see the "Hebrew to English Translation Chart," p. xix.

MANKIND (MAN)
Ge 1: 26 "Let us make **m** in our image,

MANNA
Ex 16: 31 people of Israel called the bread **m**.
Dt 8: 16 He gave you **m** to eat
Jn 6: 49 Your ancestors ate the **m**
Rev 2: 17 I will give some of the hidden **m**.

MANNER
1Co 11: 27 in an unworthy **m** will be guilty
Php 1: 27 conduct yourselves in a **m** worthy

MARITAL (MARRY)
Ex 21: 10 of her food, clothing and **m** rights.
1Co 7: 3 husband should fulfill his **m** duty

MARK (MARKS)
Cousin of Barnabas (Col 4:10; 2Ti 4:11; Phm 24; 1Pe 5:13), see JOHN.

Ge 4: 15 the LORD put a **m** on Cain so
Rev 13: 16 to receive a **m** on their right hands

MARKS (MARK)
Jn 20: 25 "Unless I see the nail **m** in his
Gal 6: 17 I bear on my body the **m** of Jesus.

MARRED
Isa 52: 14 and his form **m** beyond human

MARRIAGE (MARRY)
Mt 22: 30 neither marry nor be given in **m**;
24: 38 marrying and giving in **m**,
Heb 13: 4 **M** should be honored by all,

MARRIED (MARRY)
Ro 7: 2 by law a **m** woman is bound to her
1Co 7: 33 But a **m** man is concerned
7: 36 is not sinning. They should get **m**.

MARRIES (MARRY)
Mt 5: 32 anyone who **m** a divorced woman
19: 9 and **m** another woman commits
Lk 16: 18 the man who **m** a divorced woman

MARRY (INTERMARRY MARITAL MARRIAGE MARRIED MARRIES)
Mt 22: 30 people will neither **m** nor be given
1Co 7: 9 they should **m**, for it is better to **m**
1Ti 5: 14 So I counsel younger widows to **m**,

MARTHA
Sister of Mary and Lazarus (Lk 10:38–42; Jn 11; 12:2).

MARVELED
Lk 2: 33 mother **m** at what was said

MARY
1. Mother of Jesus (Mt 1:16–25; Lk 1:27–56; 2:1–40). With Jesus at temple (Lk 2:41–52), at the wedding in Cana (Jn 2:1–5), questioning his sanity (Mk 3:21), at the cross (Jn 19:25–27). Among disciples after Ascension (Ac 1:14).
2. Magdalene; former demoniac (Lk 8:2). Helped support Jesus' ministry (Lk 8:1–3). At the cross (Mt 27:56; Mk 15:40; Jn 19:25), burial (Mt 27:61; Mk 15:47). Saw angel after resurrection (Mt 28:1–10; Mk 16:1–9; Lk 24:1–12); also Jesus (Jn 20:1–18).
3. Sister of Martha and Lazarus (Jn 11). Washed Jesus' feet (Jn 12:1–8).

MASQUERADES
2Co 11: 14 for Satan himself **m** as an angel

MASTER (MASTERED MASTERS)
Mt 10: 24 teacher, nor a servant above his **m**.
24: 46 servant whose **m** finds him doing
25: 21 "His **m** replied, 'Well done,
Ro 6: 14 For sin shall no longer be your **m**,
14: 4 To their own **m**, servants stand
2Ti 2: 21 useful to the **M** and prepared to do

MASTERED (MASTER)
1Co 6: 12 but I will not be **m** by anything.
2Pe 2: 19 are slaves to whatever has **m** them."

MASTERS (MASTER)
Mt 6: 24 "No one can serve two **m**.
Eph 6: 5 obey your earthly **m** with respect
6: 9 **m**, treat your slaves in the same
Titus 2: 9 be subject to their **m** in everything,

MATTHEW
Apostle; former tax collector (Mt 9:9–13; 10:3; Mk 3:18; Lk 6:15; Ac 1:13). Also called Levi (Mk 2:14–17; Lk 5:27–32).

MATURE (MATURITY)
Eph 4: 13 of the Son of God and become **m**,
Php 3: 15 who are **m** should take such a view
Heb 5: 14 But solid food is for the **m**,
Jas 1: 4 its work so that you may be **m**

MATURITY (MATURE)
Heb 6: 1 Christ and be taken forward to **m**,

MEAL
1Co 10: 27 If an unbeliever invites you to a **m**
Heb 12: 16 single **m** sold his inheritance rights

MEANING
Ne 8: 8 and giving the **m** so that the people

MEANS
1Co 9: 22 by all possible **m** I might save some.

MEAT
Ro 14: 6 eats **m** does so to the Lord,
14: 21 It is better not to eat **m** or drink

MEDIATOR
1Ti 2: 5 one God and one **m** between God
Heb 8: 6 which he is **m** is superior to the old
9: 15 this reason Christ is the **m** of a new
12: 24 to Jesus the **m** of a new covenant,

MEDICINE
Pr 17: 22 A cheerful heart is good **m**,

MEDITATE (MEDITATES MEDITATION)
Jos 1: 8 **m** on it day and night, so that you
Ps 119: 15 I **m** on your precepts and consider
119: 78 but I will **m** on your precepts.
119: 97 I **m** on it all day long.
145: 5 I will **m** on your wonderful works.

MEDITATES (MEDITATE)
Ps 1: 2 who **m** on his law day and night.

MEDITATION (MEDITATE)
Ps 19: 14 this **m** of my heart be pleasing
104: 34 May my **m** be pleasing to him, as I

MEDIUM
Lev 20: 27 or woman who is a **m** or spiritist

MEEK
Ps 37: 11 But the **m** will inherit the land
Mt 5: 5 Blessed are the **m**, for they will

MEET (MEETING)
Ps 85: 10 Love and faithfulness **m** together;
Am 4: 12 Israel, prepare to **m** your God."
1Th 4: 17 the clouds to **m** the Lord in the air.

MEETING (MEET)
Heb 10: 25 not giving up **m** together, as some

MELCHIZEDEK
Ge 14: 18 **M** king of Salem brought out bread
Ps 110: 4 a priest forever, in the order of **M**."
Heb 7: 11 one in the order of **M**,

MELT
2Pe 3: 12 the elements will **m** in the heat.

MEMBERS
Mic 7: 6 a man's enemies are the **m** of his
Ro 12: 4 of us has one body with many **m**,
1Co 6: 15 your bodies are **m** of Christ
Eph 4: 25 for we are all **m** of one body.
Col 3: 15 since as **m** of one body you were

MEN (MAN)
Ro 1: 27 **M** committed shameful acts with other **m**,
1Ti 2: 8 Therefore I want the **m** everywhere

MENAHEM
King of Israel (2Ki 15:17–22).

MERCIFUL (MERCY)
Dt 4: 31 the LORD your God is a **m** God;
Ne 9: 31 for you are a gracious and **m** God.
Mt 5: 7 Blessed are the **m**, for they will be
Lk 6: 36 Be **m**, just as your Father is **m**.
Heb 2: 17 in order that he might become a **m**
Jude : 22 Be **m** to those who doubt;

† **MERCY** (MERCIFUL)
Ex 33: 19 have **m** on whom I will have **m**,
Ps 25: 6 LORD, your great **m** and love,
Isa 63: 9 his love and **m** he redeemed them;
Hos 6: 6 For I desire **m**, not sacrifice,
Mic 6: 8 to love **m** and to walk humbly
Hab 3: 2 in wrath remember **m**.
Mt 12: 7 mean, 'I desire **m**, not sacrifice,'
23: 23 justice, **m** and faithfulness.
Ro 9: 15 "I will have **m** on whom I have **m**,
Eph 2: 4 love for us, God, who is rich in **m**,
Jas 2: 13 **M** triumphs over judgment.
1Pe 1: 3 In his great **m** he has given us new

MESSAGE
Isa 53: 1 Who has believed our **m**
Jn 12: 38 who has believed our **m**
Ro 10: 17 faith comes from hearing the **m**,
1Co 1: 18 the **m** of the cross is foolishness
2Co 5: 19 to us the **m** of reconciliation.

†/‡ **MESSIAH** (CHRIST MESSIAHS)
Mt 1: 16 of Jesus who is called the **M**.
16: 16 "You are the **M**, the Son
22: 42 "What do you think about the **M**?
Jn 1: 41 "We have found the **M**" (that is,
4: 25 that **M**" (called Christ) "is coming.
20: 31 may believe that Jesus is the **M**,
Ac 2: 36 you crucified, both Lord and **M**."
5: 42 the good news that Jesus is the **M**.
9: 22 by proving that Jesus is the **M**.
17: 3 proving that the **M** had to suffer
18: 28 the Scriptures that Jesus was the **M**.
26: 23 that the **M** would suffer and,

MESSIAHS (MESSIAH)
Mt 24: 24 For false **m** and false prophets will

METHUSELAH
Ge 5: 27 **M** lived a total of 969 years,

MICHAEL
Archangel (Jude 9); warrior in angelic realm, protector of Israel (Da 10:13, 21; 12:1; Rev 12:7).

MIDWIVES
Ex 1: 17 The **m**, however, feared God

MIGHT (ALMIGHTY MIGHTY)
Jdg 16: 30 Then he pushed with all his **m**,
2Sa 6: 14 before the LORD with all his **m**,
Ps 21: 13 we will sing and praise your **m**.
Zec 4: 6 'Not by **m** nor by power, but by my
1Ti 6: 16 To him be honor and **m** forever.

MIGHTY (MIGHT)
Ex 6: 1 of my **m** hand he will let them go;
Dt 7: 8 he brought you out with a **m** hand
2Sa 1: 19 How the **m** have fallen!
23: 8 the names of David's **m** warriors:
Ps 24: 8 and **m**, the LORD **m** in battle.
50: 1 The **M** One, God, the LORD,
89: 8 are **m**, and your faithfulness
136: 12 a **m** hand and outstretched arm;
147: 5 Great is our Lord and **m** in power;
Isa 9: 6 Wonderful Counselor, **M** God,
Zep 3: 17 you, the **M** Warrior who saves.
Eph 6: 10 in the Lord and in his **m** power.

MILE
Mt 5: 41 If anyone forces you to go one **m**,

MILK
Ex 3: 8 a land flowing with **m** and honey—
Isa 55: 1 buy wine and **m** without money
1Co 3: 2 I gave you **m**, not solid food,
Heb 5: 12 You need **m**, not solid food!
1Pe 2: 2 crave pure spiritual **m**, so that by it

MILLSTONE (STONE)
Lk 17: 2 with a **m** tied around their neck

MIND (DOUBLE-MINDED MINDFUL MINDS MINDSET)
1Sa 15: 29 does not lie or change his **m**;
1Ch 28: 9 devotion and with a willing **m**,
Ps 26: 2 me, examine my heart and my **m**;
Mt 22: 37 all your soul and with all your **m**.'
Ac 4: 32 believers were one in heart and **m**.
Ro 7: 25 then, I myself in my **m** am a slave
8: 7 The **m** governed by the flesh is
12: 2 by the renewing of your **m**.
1Co 2: 9 what no human **m** has conceived"
14: 14 spirit prays, but my **m** is unfruitful.
2Co 13: 11 another, be of one **m**, live in peace.
Php 3: 19 Their **m** is set on earthly things.
1Th 4: 11 You should **m** your own business
Heb 7: 21 sworn and will not change his **m**:

MINDFUL (MIND)
Ps 8: 4 is mankind that you are **m** of them,
Lk 1: 48 he has been **m** of the humble state
Heb 2: 6 is mankind that you are **m** of them,

† Please see the "Hebrew to English Translation Chart," p. xix.
‡ Please see "Key New Testament Terms," p. 1584.

MINDS (MIND)
Ps 7: 9 the righteous God who probes **m**
Isa 26: 3 peace those whose **m** are steadfast,
Jer 31: 33 "I will put my law in their **m**
Eph 4: 23 new in the attitude of your **m**;
Col 3: 2 Set your **m** on things above,
Heb 8: 10 I will put my laws in their **m**
Rev 2: 23 he who searches hearts and **m**,

MINDSET (MIND)
Php 2: 5 have the same **m** as Christ Jesus:

MINISTERING (MINISTRY)
Heb 1: 14 Are not all angels **m** spirits sent

MINISTRY (MINISTERING)
Ac 6: 4 to prayer and the **m** of the word."
2Co 5: 18 gave us the **m** of reconciliation:
2Ti 4: 5 discharge all the duties of your **m**.

† MIRACLES
1Ch 16: 12 done, his **m**, and the judgments he
Ps 77: 14 You are the God who performs **m**;
Mt 11: 20 most of his **m** had been performed,
11: 21 the **m** that were performed in you
Mk 6: 2 What are these remarkable **m** he is
Ac 2: 22 accredited by God to you by **m**,
19: 11 did extraordinary **m** through Paul,
1Co 12: 28 then **m**, then gifts of healing,
Heb 2: 4 wonders and various **m**, and by

MIRE
Ps 40: 2 slimy pit, out of the mud and **m**;
Isa 57: 20 whose waves cast up **m** and mud.

MIRIAM
Sister of Moses and Aaron (Nu 26:59). Led dancing at Red Sea (Ex 15:20–21). Struck with leprosy for criticizing Moses (Nu 12). Death (Nu 20:1).

MIRROR
Jas 1: 23 who looks at his face in a **m**

MISERY
Ex 3: 7 "I have indeed seen the **m** of my
Jdg 10: 16 he could bear Israel's **m** no longer.
Hos 5: 15 in their **m** they will earnestly seek
Ro 3: 16 ruin and **m** mark their ways,
Jas 5: 1 because of the **m** that is coming

MISLED
1Co 15: 33 Do not be **m**:

MISS
Pr 19: 2 more will hasty feet **m** the way!

MIST
Hos 6: 4 Your love is like the morning **m**,
Jas 4: 14 You are a **m** that appears for a little

MISUSE
Ex 20: 7 "You shall not **m** the name
Dt 5: 11 "You shall not **m** the name
Ps 139: 20 your adversaries **m** your name.

MOCK (MOCKED MOCKER MOCKERS MOCKING)
Ps 22: 7 All who see me **m** me;
Pr 14: 9 Fools **m** at making amends for sin,
Mk 10: 34 who will **m** him and spit on him,

MOCKED (MOCK)
Mt 27: 29 knelt in front of him and **m** him.
27: 41 of the law and the elders **m** him.
Gal 6: 7 not be deceived: God cannot be **m**.

MOCKER (MOCK)
Pr 9: 7 corrects a **m** invites insults;
9: 12 you are a **m**, you alone will suffer.
20: 1 Wine is a **m** and beer a brawler;
22: 10 Drive out the **m**, and out goes

MOCKERS (MOCK)
Ps 1: 1 take or sit in the company of **m**,

MOCKING (MOCK)
Isa 50: 6 I did not hide my face from **m**

MODEL
1Th 1: 7 And so you became a **m** to all
2Th 3: 9 to offer ourselves as a **m** for you

MOMENT
Job 20: 5 the joy of the godless lasts but a **m**.
Ps 30: 5 For his anger lasts only a **m**, but his
Isa 66: 8 a nation be brought forth in a **m**?
Gal 2: 5 We did not give in to them for a **m**,

MONEY
Ecc 5: 10 loves **m** never has enough;
Isa 55: 1 and you who have no **m**, come,
Mt 6: 24 You cannot serve both God and **m**.
Lk 9: 3 bag, no bread, no **m**, no extra shirt.
1Co 16: 2 you should set aside a sum of **m**
1Ti 3: 3 not quarrelsome, not a lover of **m**.
6: 10 the love of **m** is a root of all kinds
2Ti 3: 2 themselves, lovers of **m**, boastful,
Heb 13: 5 your lives free from the love of **m**

MOON
Ps 121: 6 you by day, nor the **m** by night.
Joel 2: 31 the **m** to blood before the coming
1Co 15: 41 the **m** another and the stars

MORNING
Ge 1: 5 was evening, and there was **m**—
Dt 28: 67 In the **m** you will say, "If only it
Ps 5: 3 In the **m**, LORD, you hear my
2Pe 1: 19 and the **m** star rises in your hearts.
Rev 22: 16 of David, and the bright **M** Star."

MORTAL
1Co 15: 53 and the **m** with immortality.

MOSES
Levite; brother of Aaron (Ex 6:20; 1Ch 6:3). Put in basket into Nile; discovered and raised by Pharaoh's daughter (Ex 2:1–10). Fled to Midian after killing Egyptian (Ex 2:11–15). Married to Zipporah, fathered Gershom (Ex 2:16–22).
Called by the LORD to deliver Israel (Ex 3–4). Pharaoh's resistance (Ex 5). Ten plagues (Ex 7–11). Passover and Exodus (Ex 12–13). Led Israel through Red Sea (Ex 14). Song of deliverance (Ex 15:1–21). Brought water from rock (Ex 17:1–7). Raised hands to defeat Amalekites (Ex 17:8–16). Delegated judges (Ex 18; Dt 1:9–18).
Received Law at Sinai (Ex 19–23; 25–31; Jn 1:17). Announced Law to Israel (Ex 19:7–8; 24; 35). Broke tablets because of golden calf (Ex 32; Dt 9). Saw glory of the LORD (Ex 33–34). Supervised building of tabernacle (Ex 36–40). Set apart Aaron and priests (Lev 8–9). Numbered tribes (Nu 1–4; 26). Opposed by Aaron and Miriam (Nu 12). Sent spies into Canaan (Nu 13). Announced forty years of wandering for failure to enter land (Nu 14). Opposed by Korah (Nu 16). Forbidden to enter land for striking rock (Nu 20:1–13; Dt 1:37). Lifted bronze snake for healing (Nu 21:4–9; Jn 3:14). Final address to Israel (Dt 1–33). Succeeded by Joshua (Nu 27:12–23; Dt 34). Death (Dt 34:5–12).
"Law of Moses" (1Ki 2:3; Ezr 3:2; Mk 12:26; Lk 24:44). "Book of Moses" (2Ch 25:12; Ne 13:1). "Song of Moses" (Ex 15:1–21; Rev 15:3). "Prayer of Moses" (Ps 90).

MOTHER (MOTHER'S)
Ge 2: 24 why a man leaves his father and **m**
3: 20 because she would become the **m**
Ex 20: 12 "Honor your father and your **m**,
Lev 20: 9 they have cursed their father or **m**,
Dt 5: 16 "Honor your father and your **m**,
21: 18 does not obey his father and **m**
27: 16 who dishonors their father or **m**."
1Sa 2: 19 Each year his **m** made him a little
Ps 113: 9 her home as a happy **m** of children.
Pr 23: 25 May your father and **m** rejoice;
29: 15 left undisciplined disgraces its **m**.
31: 1 utterance his **m** taught him.
Isa 49: 15 "Can a **m** forget the baby at her
66: 13 As a **m** comforts her child, so will I
Mt 10: 37 or **m** more than me is not worthy
15: 4 said, 'Honor your father and **m**'
19: 5 a man will leave his father and **m**
Mk 7: 10 'Honor your father and **m**,' and,
10: 19 honor your father and **m**.'"
Jn 19: 27 to the disciple, "Here is your **m**."

MOTHER'S (MOTHER)
Job 1: 21 "Naked I came from my **m** womb,
Pr 1: 8 do not forsake your **m** teaching.

MOTHS
Mt 6: 19 where **m** and vermin destroy,

MOTIVES
Pr 16: 2 but **m** are weighed by the LORD.

1Co 4: 5 and will expose the **m** of the heart.
Php 1: 18 way, whether from false **m** or true,
1Th 2: 3 not spring from error or impure **m**,
Jas 4: 3 because you ask with wrong **m**,

MOUNTAIN (MOUNTAINS)
Mic 4: 2 let us go up to the **m** of the LORD,
Mt 17: 20 you can say to this **m**,

MOUNTAINS (MOUNTAIN)
Isa 52: 7 beautiful on the **m** are the feet
55: 12 the **m** and hills will burst into song
1Co 13: 2 if I have a faith that can move **m**,

MOURN (MOURNING)
Ecc 3: 4 a time to **m** and a time to dance,
Isa 61: 2 of our God, to comfort all who **m**,
Mt 5: 4 Blessed are those who **m**, for they
Ro 12: 15 **m** with those who **m**.

MOURNING (MOURN)
Jer 31: 13 I will turn their **m** into gladness;
Rev 21: 4 There will be no more death' or **m**

MOUTH
Ps 19: 14 May these words of my **m** and this
40: 3 He put a new song in my **m**,
119:103 taste, sweeter than honey to my **m**!
Pr 27: 2 praise you, and not your own **m**;
Isa 51: 16 I have put my words in your **m**
Mt 12: 34 the **m** speaks what the heart is full
15: 11 but what comes out of their **m**,
Ro 10: 9 If you declare with your **m**,

MUD
Ps 40: 2 slimy pit, out of the **m** and mire;
Isa 57: 20 whose waves cast up mire and **m**.
2Pe 2: 22 returns to her wallowing in the **m**."

MULTITUDE (MULTITUDES)
Isa 31: 1 who trust in the **m** of their chariots
1Pe 4: 8 because love covers over a **m**
Rev 7: 9 there before me was a great **m**

MULTITUDES (MULTITUDE)
Joel 3: 14 **M**, **m** in the valley of decision!

MURDER (MURDERER MURDERERS)
Ex 20: 13 "You shall not **m**.
Mt 15: 19 **m**, adultery, sexual immorality,
Ro 13: 9 "You shall not **m**," "You shall not
Jas 2: 11 commit adultery but do commit **m**,

MURDERER (MURDER)
Nu 35: 16 a **m**; the **m** is to be put to death.
Jn 8: 44 He was a **m** from the beginning,
1Jn 3: 15 hates a brother or sister is a **m**,

MURDERERS (MURDER)
1Ti 1: 9 kill their fathers or mothers, for **m**,
Rev 21: 8 vile, the **m**, the sexually immoral,

MUSIC
Ps 27: 6 sing and make **m** to the LORD.
95: 2 and extol him with **m** and song.
98: 4 burst into jubilant song with **m**;
108: 1 sing and make **m** with all my soul.
Eph 5: 19 make **m** from your heart to the Lord,

MUSTARD
Mt 13: 31 kingdom of heaven is like a **m** seed,
17: 20 you have faith as small as a **m** seed,

MUZZLE
Dt 25: 4 Do not **m** an ox while it is treading
Ps 39: 1 I will put a **m** on my mouth while
1Co 9: 9 Do not **m** an ox while it is treading

MYRRH
Mt 2: 11 gifts of gold, frankincense and **m**.
Mk 15: 23 offered him wine mixed with **m**,

‡ MYSTERY
Ro 16: 25 the revelation of the **m** hidden
1Co 15: 51 Listen, I tell you a **m**: We will not
Eph 5: 32 This is a profound **m**—but I am
Col 1: 26 the **m** that has been kept hidden
1Ti 3: 16 the **m** from which true godliness

MYTHS
1Ti 4: 7 Have nothing to do with godless **m**

NADAB
Son of Jeroboam I; king of Israel (1Ki 15:25–32).

NAIL (NAILING)
Jn 20: 25 "Unless I see the **n** marks in his

† Please see the "Hebrew to English Translation Chart," p. xix.
‡ Please see "Key New Testament Terms," p. 1584.

NAILING (NAIL)
Ac 2: 23 him to death by **n** him to the cross.
Col 2: 14 has taken it away, **n** it to the cross.

NAKED
Ge 2: 25 Adam and his wife were both **n**,
Job 1: 21 womb, and **n** I will depart.
Isa 58: 7 you see the **n**, to clothe them,
2Co 5: 3 are clothed, we will not be found **n**.

NAME
Ex 3: 15 "This is my **n** forever, the **n** you
20: 7 "You shall not misuse the **n**
Dt 5: 11 "You shall not misuse the **n**
28: 58 this glorious and awesome **n**—
1Ki 5: 5 will build the temple for my **N**.'
2Ch 7: 14 people, who are called by my **n**,
Ps 34: 3 let us exalt his **n** together.
103: 1 my inmost being, praise his holy **n**.
147: 4 the stars and calls them each by **n**.
Pr 22: 1 A good **n** is more desirable than
30: 4 What is his **n**, and what is the **n**
Isa 40: 26 and calls forth each of them by **n**.
57: 15 who lives forever, whose **n** is holy:
Jer 14: 7 Lord, for the sake of your **n**.
Da 12: 1 everyone whose **n** is found written
Joel 2: 32 the **n** of the Lord will be saved;
Zec 14: 9 one Lord, and his **n** the only **n**.
Mt 1: 21 you are to give him the **n** Jesus,
6: 9 in heaven, hallowed be your **n**,
18: 20 where two or three gather in my **n**,
Jn 10: 3 He calls his own sheep by **n**
16: 24 not asked for anything in my **n**.
Ac 4: 12 is no other **n** under heaven given
Ro 10: 13 on the **n** of the Lord will be saved."
Php 2: 9 the **n** that is above every **n**,
Col 3: 17 do it all in the **n** of the Lord Jesus,
Heb 1: 4 the angels as the **n** he has inherited
Rev 20: 15 whose **n** was not found written

NAOMI
Mother-in-law of Ruth (Ru 1). Advised Ruth to seek marriage with Boaz (Ru 2–4).

NARROW
Mt 7: 13 "Enter through the **n** gate.

NATHANAEL
Apostle (Jn 1:45–49; 21:2). Probably also called Bartholomew (Mt 10:3).

NATION (NATIONS)
Ge 12: 2 "I will make you into a great **n**,
Ps 33: 12 Blessed is the **n** whose God is
Pr 14: 34 Righteousness exalts a **n**, but sin
Isa 65: 1 a **n** that did not call on my name,
1Pe 2: 9 a holy **n**, God's special possession,
Rev 7: 9 could count, from every **n**, tribe,

NATIONS (NATION)
Ge 17: 4 You will be the father of many **n**.
18: 18 and all **n** on earth will be blessed
Ex 19: 5 of all **n** you will be my treasured
Ne 1: 8 I will scatter you among the **n**,
Ps 96: 3 Declare his glory among the **n**,
Isa 40: 15 Surely the **n** are like a drop
Eze 36: 23 has been profaned among the **n**,
Hag 2: 7 what is desired by all **n** will come,
Zec 8: 23 **n** will take firm hold of one Jew
14: 2 I will gather all the **n** to Jerusalem
Mt 28: 19 go and make disciples of all **n**,
Rev 21: 24 The **n** will walk by its light,

NATURAL (NATURE)
1Co 15: 44 it is sown a **n** body, it is raised

NATURE (NATURAL)
Php 2: 6 Who, being in very **n** God, did not

NAZARENE
Mt 2: 23 that he would be called a **N**.

NAZIRITE
Jdg 13: 7 because the boy will be a **N** of God

NECESSARY
Ro 13: 5 it is **n** to submit to the authorities,

NEED (NEEDS NEEDY)
Mt 6: 8 knows what you **n** before you ask
Ro 12: 13 the Lord's people who are in **n**.
1Co 12: 21 say to the hand, "I don't **n** you!"
1Jn 3: 17 sister in **n** but has no pity on them,

NEEDLE
Mt 19: 24 to go through the eye of a **n** than

NEEDS (NEED)
Isa 58: 11 he will satisfy your **n**
Php 4: 19 God will meet all your **n** according

NEEDY (NEED)
Pr 14: 21 is the one who is kind to the **n**.
14: 31 is kind to the **n** honors God.
31: 20 and extends her hands to the **n**.
Mt 6: 2 "So when you give to the **n**, do not

NEGLECT (NEGLECTED)
Ne 10: 39 "We will not **n** the house of our
Ps 119: 16 I will not **n** your word.
Ac 6: 2 for us to **n** the ministry of the word
1Ti 4: 14 not **n** your gift, which was given

NEGLECTED (NEGLECT)
Mt 23: 23 But you have **n** the more important

NEHEMIAH
Cupbearer of Artaxerxes (Ne 2:1); governor of Israel (Ne 8:9). Returned to Jerusalem to rebuild walls (Ne 2–6). With Ezra, reestablished worship (Ne 8). Prayer confessing nation's sin (Ne 9). Dedicated wall (Ne 12).

NEIGHBOR (NEIGHBOR'S)
Ex 20: 16 give false testimony against your **n**.
Lev 19: 18 people, but love your **n** as yourself.
Pr 27: 10 better a **n** nearby than a relative far
Mt 19: 19 and 'love your **n** as yourself.'"
Lk 10: 29 asked Jesus, "And who is my **n**?"
Ro 13: 10 Love does no harm to a **n**.

NEIGHBOR'S (NEIGHBOR)
Ex 20: 17 "You shall not covet your **n** house.
Dt 5: 21 "You shall not covet your **n** wife.
19: 14 not move your **n** boundary stone
Pr 25: 17 Seldom set foot in your **n** house—

NEW
Ps 40: 3 He put a **n** song in my mouth,
Ecc 1: 9 there is nothing **n** under the sun.
Isa 65: 17 I will create **n** heavens and a **n**
Jer 31: 31 I will make a **n** covenant
Eze 36: 26 I will give you a **n** heart and put a **n** spirit in you;
Mt 9: 17 they pour **n** wine into **n** wineskins,
Lk 22: 20 "This cup is the **n** covenant in my
2Co 5: 17 in Christ, the **n** creation has come:
Eph 4: 24 and to put on the **n** self,
2Pe 3: 13 to a **n** heaven and a **n** earth,
1Jn 2: 8 Yet I am writing you a **n** command;

NEWBORN (BEAR)
1Pe 2: 2 Like **n** babies, crave pure spiritual

NEWS
Isa 52: 7 the feet of those who bring good **n**,
Mk 1: 15 Repent and believe the good **n**!"
Lk 2: 10 I bring you good **n** that will cause
Ac 5: 42 proclaiming the good **n** that Jesus
17: 18 Paul was preaching the good **n**
Ro 10: 15 feet of those who bring good **n**!"

NICODEMUS
Pharisee who visited Jesus at night (Jn 3). Argued fair treatment of Jesus (Jn 7:50–52). With Joseph, prepared Jesus for burial (Jn 19:38–42).

NIGHT
Job 35: 10 Maker, who gives songs in the **n**,
Ps 1: 2 meditates on his law day and **n**.
91: 5 You will not fear the terror of **n**,
Jn 3: 2 He came to Jesus at **n** and said,
1Th 5: 2 Lord will come like a thief in the **n**.
5: 5 We do not belong to the **n**
Rev 21: 25 shut, for there will be no **n** there.

NOAH
Righteous man (Eze 14:14, 20) called to build ark (Ge 6–8; Heb 11:7; 1Pe 3:20; 2Pe 2:5). God's covenant with (Ge 9:1–17). Drunkenness of (Ge 9:18–23). Blessed sons, cursed Canaan (Ge 9:24–27).

NOBLE
Ru 3: 11 you are a woman of **n** character.
Ps 45: 1 by a **n** theme as I recite my verses
Pr 12: 4 **n** character is her husband's crown,
31: 10 wife of **n** character who can find?
31: 29 "Many women do **n** things, but
Isa 32: 8 But the **n** make **n** plans, and by **n**
Lk 8: 15 good soil stands for those with a **n**
Php 4: 8 whatever is **n**, whatever is right,

NOTHING
Ne 9: 21 they lacked **n**, their clothes did not
Jer 32: 17 **N** is too hard for you.
Jn 15: 5 apart from me you can do **n**.

NULLIFY
Ro 3: 31 we, then, **n** the law by this faith?

OATH
Dt 7: 8 and kept the **o** he swore to your

OBEDIENCE (OBEY)
2Ch 31: 21 of God's temple and in **o** to the law
Ro 1: 5 all the Gentiles to the **o** that comes
6: 16 to death, or to **o**, which leads
2Jn : 6 that we walk in **o** to his commands.

OBEDIENT (OBEY)
Lk 2: 51 with them and was **o** to them.
Php 2: 8 himself by becoming **o** to death—
1Pe 1: 14 As **o** children, do not conform

OBEY (OBEDIENCE OBEDIENT OBEYED)
Ex 12: 24 "**O** these instructions as a lasting
Dt 6: 3 be careful to **o** so that it may go
13: 4 Keep his commands and **o** him;
21: 18 son who does not **o** his father
30: 2 God and **o** him with all your heart
32: 46 to **o** carefully all the words
1Sa 15: 22 To **o** is better than sacrifice,
Ps 119: 34 your law and **o** it with all my heart.
Mt 28: 20 to **o** everything I have commanded
Jn 14: 23 who loves me will **o** my teaching.
Ac 5: 29 must **o** God rather than human
Ro 6: 16 you are slaves of the one you **o**—
Gal 5: 3 he is obligated to **o** the whole law.
Eph 6: 1 **o** your parents in the Lord, for this
6: 5 heart, just as you would **o** Christ.
Col 3: 20 **o** your parents in everything,
1Ti 3: 4 and see that his children **o** him,

OBEYED (OBEY)
Ps 119: 4 precepts that are to be fully **o**.
Jnh 3: 3 Jonah **o** the word of the Lord
Jn 17: 6 to me and they have **o** your word.
Heb 11: 8 as his inheritance, **o** and went,
1Pe 3: 6 who **o** Abraham and called him

OBLIGATED
Ro 1: 14 I am **o** both to Greeks
Gal 5: 3 that he is **o** to obey the whole law.

OBSCENITY
Eph 5: 4 Nor should there be **o**, foolish talk

OBSOLETE
Heb 8: 13 "new," he has made the first one **o**;

OBTAINED
Ro 9: 30 not pursue righteousness, have **o** it,
Php 3: 12 Not that I have already **o** all this,

OFFENSE (OFFENSIVE)
Pr 17: 9 would foster love covers over an **o**,
19: 11 it is to one's glory to overlook an **o**.

OFFENSIVE (OFFENSE)
Ps 139: 24 See if there is any **o** way in me,

OFFER (OFFERED OFFERING OFFERINGS)
Ro 12: 1 **o** your bodies as a living sacrifice,
Heb 13: 15 let us continually **o** to God

OFFERED (OFFER)
Heb 7: 27 sins once for all when he **o** himself.

† OFFERING (OFFER)
Ge 22: 8 provide the lamb for the burnt **o**,
Ps 40: 6 Sacrifice and **o** you did not desire
Isa 53: 10 the Lord makes his life an **o**
Mt 5: 23 if you are **o** your gift at the altar
Eph 5: 2 himself up for us as a fragrant **o**
Heb 10: 5 "Sacrifice and **o** you did not desire,

OFFERINGS (OFFER)
Mal 3: 8 we robbing you?' "In tithes and **o**.
Mk 12: 33 is more important than all burnt **o**

OFFICER
2Ti 2: 4 tries to please his commanding **o**.

OFFSPRING
Ge 3: 15 and between your **o** and hers;
12: 7 "To your **o** I will give this land."

OIL
Ps 23: 5 You anoint my head with **o**;
Isa 61: 3 the **o** of joy instead of mourning,
Heb 1: 9 by anointing you with the **o** of joy."

† Please see the "Hebrew to English Translation Chart," p. xix.

OLIVE (OLIVES)
Zec 4: 3 Also there are two **o** trees by it,
Ro 11: 17 though a wild **o** shoot, have been
Rev 11: 4 They are "the two **o** trees"

OLIVES (OLIVE)
Jas 3: 12 can a fig tree bear **o**, or a grapevine

OMEGA
Rev 1: 8 "I am the Alpha and the **O**,"

OMRI
King of Israel (1Ki 16:21–26).

OPINIONS
1Ki 18: 21 will you waver between two **o**?
Pr 18: 2 but delight in airing their own **o**.

OPPORTUNITY
Ro 7: 11 sin, seizing the **o** afforded
Gal 6: 10 as we have **o**, let us do good to all
Eph 5: 16 making the most of every **o**,
Col 4: 5 make the most of every **o**.
1Ti 5: 14 to give the enemy no **o** for slander.

OPPOSES
Jas 4: 6 "God **o** the proud but shows favor
1Pe 5: 5 "God **o** the proud but shows favor

OPPRESS (OPPRESSED)
Ex 22: 21 "Do not mistreat or **o** a foreigner,
Zec 7: 10 Do not **o** the widow

OPPRESSED (OPPRESS)
Ps 9: 9 The LORD is a refuge for the **o**,
Isa 53: 7 He was **o** and afflicted, yet he did
Zec 10: 2 the people wander like sheep **o**

ORDERLY
1Co 14: 40 be done in a fitting and **o** way.

ORGIES
Gal 5: 21 drunkenness, **o**, and the like.
1Pe 4: 3 lust, drunkenness, **o**,

ORIGIN
2Pe 1: 21 For prophecy never had its **o**

ORPHANS
Jn 14: 18 I will not leave you as **o**;
Jas 1: 27 to look after **o** and widows in their

OUTCOME
Heb 13: 7 Consider the **o** of their way of life
1Pe 4: 17 what will the **o** be for those who do

OUTSIDERS
Col 4: 5 wise in the way you act toward **o**;
1Th 4: 12 daily life may win the respect of **o**
1Ti 3: 7 also have a good reputation with **o**,

OUTSTANDING
SS 5: 10 and ruddy, **o** among ten thousand.
Ro 13: 8 Let no debt remain **o**,

OUTSTRETCHED
Ex 6: 6 I will redeem you with an **o** arm
Jer 27: 5 power and **o** arm I made the earth
Eze 20: 33 with a mighty hand and an **o** arm

OUTWEIGHS
2Co 4: 17 an eternal glory that far **o** them all.

OVERCOME (OVERCOMES)
Mt 16: 18 and the gates of Hades will not **o** it.
Mk 9: 24 help me **o** my unbelief!"
Jn 16: 33 But take heart! I have **o** the world."
Ro 12: 21 Do not be **o** by evil, but **o** evil
1Jn 5: 4 is the victory that has **o** the world,

OVERCOMES (OVERCOME)
1Jn 5: 4 everyone born of God **o** the world.
5: 5 Who is it that **o** the world?

OVERFLOW (OVERFLOWS)
Ps 119:171 May my lips **o** with praise, for you
Ro 15: 13 so that you may **o** with hope
2Co 4: 15 may cause thanksgiving to **o**
1Th 3: 12 love increase and **o** for each other

OVERFLOWS (OVERFLOW)
Ps 23: 5 anoint my head with oil; my cup **o**.

OVERJOYED (JOY)
Da 6: 23 The king was **o** and gave orders
Mt 2: 10 they saw the star, they were **o**.
Jn 20: 20 disciples were **o** when they saw
Ac 12: 14 she was so **o** she ran back without
1Pe 4: 13 that you may be **o** when his glory

OVERSEER (OVERSEERS)
1Ti 3: 1 to be an **o** desires a noble task.
1Ti 3: 2 Now the **o** is to be above reproach,
Titus 1: 7 Since an **o** manages God's

OVERSEERS (OVERSEER)
Ac 20: 28 the Holy Spirit has made you **o**.
Php 1: 1 together with the **o** and deacons:

OVERWHELMED
Ps 38: 4 My guilt has **o** me like a burden
65: 3 When we were **o** by sins,
Mt 26: 38 "My soul is **o** with sorrow
Mk 7: 37 People were **o** with amazement.

OWE
Ro 13: 7 Give to everyone what you **o** them:
Phm : 19 that you **o** me your very self.

OX
Dt 25: 4 Do not muzzle an **o** while it is
Isa 11: 7 the lion will eat straw like the **o**.
1Co 9: 9 "Do not muzzle an **o** while it is

PAGANS
Mt 5: 47 Do not even **p** do that?
1Pe 2: 12 such good lives among the **p** that,

PAIN (PAINFUL PAINS)
Job 33: 19 on a bed of **p** with constant distress
Jn 16: 21 to a child has **p** because her time

† **PAINFUL** (PAIN)
Ge 3: 17 through **p** toil you will eat food
Heb 12: 11 seems pleasant at the time, but **p**.

† **PAINS** (PAIN)
Ge 3: 16 "I will make your **p** in childbearing

PALMS
Isa 49: 16 engraved you on the **p** of my hands

PANTS
Ps 42: 1 As the deer **p** for streams of water, so my soul **p** for you,

PARADISE
Lk 23: 43 today you will be with me in **p**."
2Co 12: 4 was caught up to **p** and heard
Rev 2: 7 tree of life, which is in the **p** of God.

PARALYZED
Mk 2: 3 bringing to him a **p** man,

PARDON (PARDONS)
Isa 55: 7 and to our God, for he will freely **p**.

PARDONS (PARDON)
Mic 7: 18 like you, who **p** sin and forgives

PARENT (PARENT'S PARENTS)
Pr 17: 21 is no joy for the **p** of a godless fool.

PARENT'S (PARENT)
15: 5 A fool spurns a **p** discipline,

PARENTS (PARENT)
Ex 20: 5 for the sin of the **p** to the third
Pr 17: 6 **p** are the pride of their children.
Lk 18: 29 sisters or **p** or children for the sake
21: 16 You will be betrayed even by **p**,
Ro 1: 30 of doing evil; they disobey their **p**;
2Co 12: 14 not have to save up for their **p**,
Eph 6: 1 Children, obey your **p** in the Lord,
Col 3: 20 obey your **p** in everything,
2Ti 3: 2 disobedient to their **p**, ungrateful,

PARTIALITY
Dt 10: 17 who shows no **p** and accepts no
2Ch 19: 7 our God there is no injustice or **p**
Lk 20: 21 that you do not show **p** but teach

PARTICIPATION
1Co 10: 16 bread that we break a **p** in the body

PASS
Ex 12: 13 I see the blood, I will **p** over you.
La 1: 12 nothing to you, all you who **p** by?
Lk 21: 33 but my words will never **p** away.
1Co 13: 8 there is knowledge, it will **p** away.

PASSION (PASSIONS)
1Co 7: 9 to marry than to burn with **p**.

PASSIONS (PASSION)
Gal 5: 24 have crucified the flesh with its **p**
Titus 2: 12 to ungodliness and worldly **p**,

PASSOVER
Ex 12: 11 Eat it in haste; it is the LORD's **P**.
Dt 16: 1 celebrate the **P** of the LORD your
1Co 5: 7 For Christ, our **P** lamb, has been

PAST
Isa 43: 18 do not dwell on the **p**.
Ro 15: 4 was written in the **p** was written
Heb 1: 1 the **p** God spoke to our ancestors

PASTORS
Eph 4: 11 the evangelists, the **p** and teachers,

PASTURE (PASTURES)
Ps 37: 3 dwell in the land and enjoy safe **p**.
100: 3 are his people, the sheep of his **p**.
Jer 50: 7 their verdant **p**, the LORD,
Eze 34: 13 I will **p** them on the mountains
Jn 10: 9 come in and go out, and find **p**.

PASTURES (PASTURE)
Ps 23: 2 He makes me lie down in green **p**,

PATCH
Mt 9: 16 No one sews a **p** of unshrunk cloth

PATH (PATHS)
Ps 27: 11 me in a straight **p** because of my
119: 9 person stay on the **p** of purity?
119:105 to my feet and a light for my **p**.
Pr 15: 19 the **p** of the upright is a highway.
15: 24 The **p** of life leads upward
Isa 26: 7 The **p** of the righteous is level;
Lk 1: 79 guide our feet into the **p** of peace."
2Co 6: 3 no stumbling block in anyone's **p**,

PATHS (PATH)
Ps 23: 3 He guides me along the right **p**
25: 4 ways, LORD, teach me your **p**.
Pr 3: 6 and he will make your **p** straight.
Ro 11: 33 and his **p** beyond tracing out!
Heb 12: 13 "Make level **p** for your feet,"

PATIENCE (PATIENT)
Pr 19: 11 A person's wisdom yields **p**; it is
2Co 6: 6 understanding, **p** and kindness;
Col 1: 11 may have great endurance and **p**,
3: 12 humility, gentleness and **p**.

PATIENT (PATIENCE PATIENTLY)
Pr 15: 18 the one who is **p** calms a quarrel.
Ro 12: 12 Be joyful in hope, **p** in affliction,
1Co 13: 4 Love is **p**, love is kind. It does not
Eph 4: 2 be **p**, bearing with one another
1Th 5: 14 help the weak, be **p** with everyone.

PATIENTLY (PATIENT)
Ps 40: 1 I waited **p** for the LORD;
Ro 8: 25 we do not yet have, we wait for it **p**.

PATTERN
Ro 5: 14 who is a **p** of the one to come.
12: 2 not conform to the **p** of this world,
2Ti 1: 13 keep as the **p** of sound teaching,

PAUL
Also called Saul (Ac 13:9). Pharisee from Tarsus (Ac 9:11; Php 3:5). Apostle (Gal 1). At stoning of Stephen (Ac 8:1). Persecuted Church (Ac 9:1–2; Gal 1:13). Vision of Jesus on road to Damascus (Ac 9:4–9; 26:12–18). In Arabia (Gal 1:17). Preached in Damascus; escaped death through the wall in a basket (Ac 9:19–25). In Jerusalem; sent back to Tarsus (Ac 9:26–30).

Brought to Antioch by Barnabas (Ac 11:22–26). First missionary journey to Cyprus and Galatia (Ac 13–14). Stoned at Lystra (Ac 14:19–20). At Jerusalem council (Ac 15). Split with Barnabas over Mark (Ac 15:36–41).

Second missionary journey with Silas (Ac 16–20). Called to Macedonia (Ac 16:6–10). Freed from prison in Philippi (Ac 16:16–40). In Thessalonica (Ac 17:1–9). Speech in Athens (Ac 17:16–33). In Corinth (Ac 18). In Ephesus (Ac 19). Return to Jerusalem (Ac 20). Farewell to Ephesian elders (Ac 20:13–38). Arrival in Jerusalem (Ac 21:1–26). Arrested (Ac 21:27–36). Addressed crowds (Ac 22), Sanhedrin (Ac 23:1–11). Transferred to Caesarea (Ac 23:12–35). Trial before Felix (Ac 24), Festus (Ac 25:1–12). Before Agrippa (Ac 25:13—26:32). Voyage to Rome; shipwreck (Ac 27). Arrival in Rome (Ac 28).

PAY (REPAID REPAY)
Lev 26: 43 They will **p** for their sins because
Pr 22: 17 **P** attention and turn your ear
Mt 22: 17 Is it right to **p** the imperial tax
Ro 13: 6 This is also why you **p** taxes,
2Pe 1: 19 you will do well to **p** attention to it,

† Please see the "Hebrew to English Translation Chart," p. xix.

† PEACE (PEACEMAKERS)
Nu 6: 26 toward you and give you **p**.”
Ps 34: 14 and do good; seek **p** and pursue it.
85: 10 righteousness and **p** kiss each
119:165 Great **p** have those who love your
122: 6 Pray for the **p** of Jerusalem:
Pr 14: 30 A heart at **p** gives life to the body,
17: 1 Better a dry crust with **p** and quiet
Isa 9: 6 Everlasting Father, Prince of **P**.
26: 3 in perfect **p** those whose minds are
48: 22 “There is no **p**,” says the LORD,
Zec 9: 10 He will proclaim **p** to the nations.
Mt 10: 34 I did not come to bring **p**,
Lk 2: 14 and on earth **p** to those on whom
Jn 14: 27 **P** I leave with you; my **p** I give you.
16: 33 so that in me you may have **p**.
Ro 5: 1 we have **p** with God through our
1Co 7: 15 God has called us to live in **p**.
14: 33 is not a God of disorder but of **p**—
Gal 5: 22 Spirit is love, joy, **p**, forbearance,
Eph 2: 14 For he himself is our **p**, who has
Php 4: 7 the **p** of God, which transcends
Col 1: 20 by making **p** through his blood,
3: 15 Let the **p** of Christ rule in your
1Th 5: 3 people are saying, “**P** and safety,”
2Th 3: 16 the Lord of **p** himself give you **p**
2Ti 2: 22 love and **p**, along with those who
1Pe 3: 11 they must seek **p** and pursue it.
Rev 6: 4 power to take **p** from the earth

PEACEMAKERS (PEACE)
Mt 5: 9 Blessed are the **p**, for they will be
Jas 3: 18 **P** who sow in peace reap a harvest

PEARL (PEARLS)
Rev 21: 21 each gate made of a single **p**.

PEARLS (PEARL)
Mt 7: 6 do not throw your **p** to pigs.
13: 45 like a merchant looking for fine **p**.
1Ti 2: 9 or gold or **p** or expensive clothes,
Rev 21: 21 The twelve gates were twelve **p**,

PEKAH
King of Israel (2Ki 15:25–31; Isa 7:1).

PEKAHIAH
Son of Menahem; king of Israel (2Ki 15:22–26).

PEN
Mt 5: 18 not the least stroke of a **p**,

PENTECOST
Ac 2: 1 When the day of **P** came, they were

PEOPLE (PEOPLES)
Dt 32: 9 For the LORD's portion is his **p**,
Ru 1: 16 Your **p** will be my **p** and your God
2Ch 7: 14 if my **p**, who are called by my
Ps 133: 1 it is when God's **p** live together
Jer 24: 7 They will be my **p**, and I will be
Zec 2: 11 in that day and will become my **p**.
Mt 4: 19 I will send you out to fish for **p**.”
Lk 2: 10 will cause great joy for all the **p**.
Jn 12: 32 earth, will draw all **p** to myself.”
Ac 15: 14 to choose a **p** for his name
Ro 5: 12 and in this way death came to all **p**,
8: 27 for God's **p** in accordance
1Co 9: 22 I have become all things to all **p** so
2Co 6: 16 their God, and they will be my **p**.”
Eph 1: 18 glorious inheritance in his holy **p**,
6: 18 keep on praying for all the Lord's **p**.
1Ti 2: 4 who wants all **p** to be saved
2Ti 2: 2 entrust to reliable **p** who will also
Titus 2: 14 himself a **p** that are his very own,
Heb 9: 27 Just as **p** are destined to die once,
1Pe 2: 9 But you are a chosen **p**, a royal
Rev 5: 8 which are the prayers of God's **p**.
19: 8 the righteous acts of God's holy **p**.)
21: 3 They will be his **p**, and God

PEOPLES (PEOPLE)
Da 7: 14 **p** of every language worshiped him
Mic 4: 1 the hills, and **p** will stream to it.

PERCEIVING
Isa 6: 9 be ever seeing, but never **p**.’

† PERFECT (PERFECTER PERFECTION)
SS 6: 9 but my dove, my **p** one, is unique,
Isa 26: 3 in **p** peace those whose minds are
Mt 5: 48 Be **p**, therefore, as your heavenly Father is **p**.
Ro 12: 2 his good, pleasing and **p** will.
2Co 12: 9 my power is made **p** in weakness.”
Col 3: 14 binds them all together in **p** unity.
Heb 9: 11 more **p** tabernacle that is not made
10: 14 he has made **p** forever those who
Jas 1: 17 good and **p** gift is from above,
1: 25 looks intently into the **p** law
3: 2 never at fault in what they say is **p**,
1Jn 4: 18 But **p** love drives out fear,

PERFECTER (PERFECT)
Heb 12: 2 on Jesus, the pioneer and **p** of faith.

PERFECTION (PERFECT)
Ps 119: 96 To all **p** I see a limit, but your
Heb 7: 11 If **p** could have been attained

PERFORMS
Ps 77: 14 You are the God who **p** miracles;

PERISH (PERISHABLE)
Ps 102: 26 They will **p**, but you remain;
Lk 13: 3 you repent, you too will all **p**.
Jn 10: 28 eternal life, and they shall never **p**;
Col 2: 22 that are all destined to **p** with use,
Heb 1: 11 They will **p**, but you remain;
2Pe 3: 9 you, not wanting anyone to **p**,

PERISHABLE (PERISH)
1Co 15: 42 The body that is sown is **p**, it is

PERJURERS
1Ti 1: 10 for slave traders and liars and **p**—

PERMIT
1Ti 2: 12 I do not **p** a woman to teach

PERSECUTE (PERSECUTED PERSECUTION)
Mt 5: 11 **p** you and falsely say all kinds
Jn 15: 20 persecuted me, they will **p** you
Ac 9: 4 “Saul, Saul, why do you **p** me?”
Ro 12: 14 Bless those who **p** you; bless and

PERSECUTED (PERSECUTE)
1Co 4: 12 when we are **p**, we endure it;
2Ti 3: 12 godly life in Christ Jesus will be **p**,

PERSECUTION (PERSECUTE)
Ro 8: 35 trouble or hardship or **p** or famine

PERSEVERANCE (PERSEVERE)
Ro 5: 3 we know that suffering produces **p**;
5: 4 **p**, character; and character, hope.
Heb 12: 1 let us run with **p** the race marked
Jas 1: 3 testing of your faith produces **p**.
2Pe 1: 6 and to self-control, **p**; and to **p**,

PERSEVERE (PERSEVERANCE PERSEVERED PERSEVERES)
1Ti 4: 16 **P** in them, because if you do,
Heb 10: 36 You need to **p** so that when you

PERSEVERED (PERSEVERE)
Heb 11: 27 he **p** because he saw him who is
Jas 5: 11 count as blessed those who have **p**.
Rev 2: 3 You have **p** and have endured

PERSEVERES (PERSEVERE)
1Co 13: 7 trusts, always hopes, always **p**.
Jas 1: 12 one who **p** under trial because,

PERSUADE
2Co 5: 11 to fear the Lord, we try to **p** others.

PERVERSION (PERVERT)
Lev 18: 23 sexual relations with it; that is a **p**.
Jude : 7 up to sexual immorality and **p**.

PERVERT (PERVERSION)
Gal 1: 7 are trying to **p** the gospel of Christ.

PESTILENCE
Ps 91: 6 the **p** that stalks in the darkness,

PETER
Apostle, brother of Andrew, also called Simon (Mt 10:2; Mk 3:16; Lk 6:14; Ac 1:13), and Cephas (Jn 1:42). Confession of Christ (Mt 16:13–20; Mk 8:27–30; Lk 9:18–27). At transfiguration (Mt 17:1–8; Mk 9:2–8; Lk 9:28–36; 2Pe 1:16–18). Caught fish with coin (Mt 17:24–27). Denial of Jesus predicted (Mt 26:31–35; Mk 14:27–31; Lk 22:31–34; Jn 13:31–38). Denied Jesus (Mt 26:69–75; Mk 14:66–72; Lk 22:54–62; Jn 18:15–27). Commissioned by Jesus to shepherd his flock (Jn 21:15–23). Speech at Pentecost (Ac 2). Healed beggar (Ac 3:1–10). Speech at temple (Ac 3:11–26), before Sanhedrin (Ac 4:1–22). In Samaria (Ac 8:14–25). Sent by vision to Cornelius (Ac 10). Announced salvation of Gentiles in Jerusalem (Ac 11; 15). Freed from prison (Ac 12). Inconsistency at Antioch (Gal 2:11–21). At Jerusalem Council (Ac 15).

‡ PHARISEES
Mt 5: 20 surpasses that of the **P**

PHILIP
1. Apostle (Mt 10:3; Mk 3:18; Lk 6:14; Jn 1:43–48; 14:8; Ac 1:13).
2. Deacon (Ac 6:1–7); evangelist in Samaria (Ac 8:4–25), to Ethiopian (Ac 8:26–40).

PHILOSOPHY
Col 2: 8 through hollow and deceptive **p**,

PHYLACTERIES
Mt 23: 5 They make their **p** wide

PHYSICAL
1Ti 4: 8 For **p** training is of some value,
Jas 2: 16 does nothing about their **p** needs,

PIECES
Ge 15: 17 and passed between the **p**.
Jer 34: 18 two and then walked between its **p**.

PIERCE (PIERCED)
Ps 22: 16 they **p** my hands and my feet.

PIERCED (PIERCE)
Isa 53: 5 he was **p** for our transgressions,
Zec 12: 10 the one they have **p**, and they will
Jn 19: 37 will look on the one they have **p**.”

PIGS
Mt 7: 6 do not throw your pearls to **p**.

‡ PILATE
Governor of Judea. Questioned Jesus (Mt 27:1–26; Mk 15:15; Lk 22:66—23:25; Jn 18:28—19:16); sent him to Herod (Lk 23:6–12); consented to his crucifixion when crowds chose Barabbas (Mt 27:15–26; Mk 15:6–15; Lk 23:13–25; Jn 19:1–10).

PILLAR
Ge 19: 26 back, and she became a **p** of salt.
Ex 13: 21 by night in a **p** of fire to give them
1Ti 3: 15 the **p** and foundation of the truth.

PIT
Ps 40: 2 He lifted me out of the slimy **p**,
103: 4 who redeems your life from the **p**
Mt 15: 14 the blind, both will fall into a **p**.”

PITIED
1Co 15: 19 we are of all people most to be **p**.

PLAGUE
2Ch 6: 28 famine or **p** comes to the land,

PLAIN
Ro 1: 19 God has made it **p** to them.

PLAN (PLANNED PLANS)
Pr 14: 22 those who **p** what is good find love
Eph 1: 11 to the **p** of him who works

PLANK
Mt 7: 3 attention to the **p** in your own eye?
Lk 6: 41 attention to the **p** in your own eye?

PLANNED (PLAN)
Ps 40: 5 have done, the things you **p** for us.
Isa 46: 11 what I have **p**, that I will do.
Heb 11: 40 since God had **p** something better

PLANS (PLAN)
Ps 20: 4 heart and make all your **p** succeed.
33: 11 But the **p** of the LORD stand firm
Pr 20: 18 **P** are established by seeking advice;
Isa 32: 8 But the noble make noble **p**,

PLANTED (PLANTS)
Ps 1: 3 person is like a tree **p** by streams
Mt 15: 13 Father has not **p** will be pulled
1Co 3: 6 I **p** the seed, Apollos watered it,

PLANTS (PLANTED)
1Co 3: 7 neither the one who **p** nor the one
9: 7 Who **p** a vineyard and does not eat

PLATTER
Mk 6: 25 head of John the Baptist on a **p**.”

† Please see the “Hebrew to English Translation Chart,” p. xix.
‡ Please see “Key New Testament Terms,” p. 1584.

PLAYED
Lk 7: 32 "'We **p** the pipe for you, and you
1Co 14: 7 what tune is being **p** unless there is

PLEADED
2Co 12: 8 Three times I **p** with the Lord

PLEASANT (PLEASE)
Ps 16: 6 lines have fallen for me in **p** places;
133: 1 and **p** it is when God's people live
147: 1 how **p** and fitting to praise him!
Heb 12: 11 No discipline seems **p** at the time,

PLEASE (PLEASANT PLEASED PLEASES PLEASING PLEASURE PLEASURES)
Pr 20: 23 and dishonest scales do not **p** him.
Jer 6: 20 your sacrifices do not **p** me."
Jn 5: 30 for I seek not to **p** myself but him
Ro 8: 8 realm of the flesh cannot **p** God.
15: 2 Each of us should **p** our neighbors
1Co 7: 32 how he can **p** the Lord.
10: 33 even as I try to **p** everyone in every
2Co 5: 9 So we make it our goal to **p** him,
Gal 1: 10 If I were still trying to **p** people,
1Th 4: 1 you how to live in order to **p** God,
2Ti 2: 4 tries to **p** his commanding officer.
Heb 11: 6 faith it is impossible to **p** God,

PLEASED (PLEASE)
Mt 3: 17 with him I am well **p**."
1Co 1: 21 God was **p** through the foolishness
Col 1: 19 God was **p** to have all his fullness
Heb 11: 5 commended as one who **p** God.
2Pe 1: 17 with him I am well **p**."

PLEASES (PLEASE)
Ps 135: 6 The LORD does whatever **p** him,
Pr 15: 8 the prayer of the upright **p** him.
Jn 3: 8 The wind blows wherever it **p**.
8: 29 alone, for I always do what **p** him."
Col 3: 20 in everything, for this **p** the Lord.
1Ti 2: 3 is good, and **p** God our Savior,
1Jn 3: 22 his commands and do what **p** him.

PLEASING (PLEASE)
Ps 104: 34 May my meditation be **p** to him,
Ro 12: 1 living sacrifice, holy and **p** to God
Php 4: 18 an acceptable sacrifice, **p** to God.
Heb 13: 21 he work in us what is **p** to him,

PLEASURE (PLEASE)
Ps 147: 10 His **p** is not in the strength
Pr 21: 17 loves **p** will become poor;
Eze 18: 32 For I take no **p** in the death
Eph 1: 5 in accordance with his **p** and will—
1: 9 of his will according to his good **p**,
2Ti 3: 4 lovers of **p** rather than lovers

PLEASURES (PLEASE)
Ps 16: 11 with eternal **p** at your right hand.
Heb 11: 25 than to enjoy the fleeting **p** of sin.
2Pe 2: 13 reveling in their **p** while they feast

PLENTIFUL
Mt 9: 37 "The harvest is **p** but the workers

PLOW (PLOWSHARES)
Lk 9: 62 "No one who puts a hand to the **p**

PLOWSHARES (PLOW)
Isa 2: 4 They will beat their swords into **p**
Joel 3: 10 Beat your **p** into swords and your

PLUNDER
Ex 3: 22 And so you will **p** the Egyptians."

POINT
Jas 2: 10 yet stumbles at just one **p** is guilty

POISON
Mk 16: 18 *and when they drink deadly* ***p***,
Jas 3: 8 It is a restless evil, full of deadly **p**.

POLLUTE (POLLUTED)
Nu 35: 33 "'Do not **p** the land where you
Jude : 8 these ungodly people **p** their own

POLLUTED (POLLUTE)
Ezr 9: 11 is a land **p** by the corruption
Pr 25: 26 a **p** well are the righteous who give
Ac 15: 20 to abstain from food **p** by idols,
Jas 1: 27 oneself from being **p** by the world.

PONDER
Ps 64: 9 of God and **p** what he has done.
119: 95 me, but I will **p** your statutes.

POOR (POVERTY)
Dt 15: 4 need be no **p** people among you,
15: 11 There will always be **p** people
Ps 34: 6 This **p** man called, and the LORD
82: 3 uphold the cause of the **p**
112: 9 freely scattered their gifts to the **p**,
Pr 13: 7 another pretends to be **p**, yet has
14: 31 oppresses the **p** shows contempt
19: 1 Better the **p** whose walk is
19: 17 Whoever is kind to the **p** lends
22: 2 Rich and **p** have this in common:
22: 9 they share their food with the **p**.
28: 6 Better the **p** whose walk is
31: 20 She opens her arms to the **p**
Isa 61: 1 to proclaim good news to the **p**.
Mt 5: 3 "Blessed are the **p** in spirit,
11: 5 good news is proclaimed to the **p**.
19: 21 your possessions and give to the **p**,
26: 11 The **p** you will always have
Mk 12: 42 a **p** widow came and put in two
Ac 10: 4 and gifts to the **p** have come up as
1Co 13: 3 If I give all I possess to the **p**
2Co 8: 9 yet for your sake he became **p**,
Jas 2: 2 and a **p** man in filthy old clothes

PORTION
Dt 32: 9 For the LORD's **p** is his people,
2Ki 2: 9 "Let me inherit a double **p** of your
La 3: 24 to myself, "The LORD is my **p**;

POSSESS (POSSESSING POSSESSION POSSESSIONS)
Nu 33: 53 for I have given you the land to **p**.

POSSESSING (POSSESS)
2Co 6: 10 nothing, and yet **p** everything.

POSSESSION (POSSESS)
Ge 15: 7 give you this land to take **p** of it."
Nu 13: 30 go up and take **p** of the land,
Eph 1: 14 of those who are God's **p**—

POSSESSIONS (POSSESS)
Lk 12: 15 not consist in an abundance of **p**."
2Co 12: 14 because what I want is not your **p**
1Jn 3: 17 If anyone has material **p** and sees

POSSIBLE
Mt 19: 26 but with God all things are **p**."
Mk 9: 23 "Everything is **p** for one who
10: 27 all things are **p** with God."
Ro 12: 18 If it is **p**, as far as it depends on you
1Co 9: 22 by all **p** means I might save some.

POT (POTSHERDS POTTER POTTERY)
2Ki 4: 40 of God, there is death in the **p**!"
Jer 18: 4 the potter formed it into another **p**,

POTSHERDS (POT)
Isa 45: 9 but **p** among the **p** on the ground.

POTTER (POT)
Isa 29: 16 Can the pot say to the **p**,
45: 9 Does the clay say to the **p**,
64: 8 We are the clay, you are the **p**;
Jer 18: 6 do with you, Israel, as this **p** does?"
Ro 9: 21 Does not the **p** have the right

POTTERY (POT)
Ro 9: 21 of clay some **p** for special purposes

POUR (POURED)
Ps 62: 8 **p** out your hearts to him, for God
Joel 2: 28 I will **p** out my Spirit on all people.
Mal 3: 10 **p** out so much blessing that there
Ac 2: 17 I will **p** out my Spirit on all people.

POURED (POUR)
Ac 10: 45 the Holy Spirit had been **p** out
Ro 5: 5 because God's love has been **p**

POVERTY (POOR)
Pr 14: 23 but mere talk leads only to **p**.
21: 5 profit as surely as haste leads to **p**.
30: 8 give me neither **p** nor riches,
Mk 12: 44 she, out of her **p**, put in everything
2Co 8: 2 their extreme **p** welled up in rich
8: 9 you through his **p** might become

POWER (POWERFUL POWERS)
1Ch 29: 11 greatness and the **p** and the glory
2Ch 32: 7 for there is a greater **p** with us than
Job 36: 22 "God is exalted in his **p**. Who is
Ps 63: 2 and beheld your **p** and your glory.
68: 34 Proclaim the **p** of God,
147: 5 Great is our Lord and mighty in **p**;
Pr 24: 5 The wise prevail through great **p**,
Isa 40: 10 Sovereign LORD comes with **p**,
Zec 4: 6 'Not by might nor by **p**, but by my
Mt 22: 29 the Scriptures or the **p** of God.
24: 30 of heaven, with **p** and great glory.
Ac 1: 8 you will receive **p** when the Holy
4: 33 With great **p** the apostles
10: 38 with the Holy Spirit and **p**,
Ro 1: 16 because it is the **p** of God
1Co 1: 18 us who are being saved it is the **p**
15: 56 is sin, and the **p** of sin is the law.
2Co 12: 9 so that Christ's **p** may rest on me.
Eph 1: 19 his incomparably great **p** for us
Php 3: 10 to know the **p** of his resurrection
Col 1: 11 strengthened with all **p** according
2Ti 1: 7 us timid, but gives us **p**,
Heb 7: 16 of the **p** of an indestructible life.
Rev 4: 11 to receive glory and honor and **p**,
19: 1 glory and **p** belong to our God,
20: 6 second death has no **p** over them,

POWERFUL (POWER)
Ps 29: 4 The voice of the LORD is **p**;
Lk 24: 19 **p** in word and deed before God
2Th 1: 7 in blazing fire with his **p** angels.
Heb 1: 3 sustaining all things by his **p** word.
Jas 5: 16 prayer of a righteous person is **p**

POWERLESS
Ro 5: 6 when we were still **p**, Christ died
8: 3 what the law was **p** to do because it

POWERS (POWER)
Ro 8: 38 present nor the future, nor any **p**,
1Co 12: 10 to another miraculous **p**,
Col 1: 16 whether thrones or **p** or rulers
2: 15 And having disarmed the **p**

PRACTICE
Lev 19: 26 "'Do not **p** divination or seek
Mt 23: 3 for they do not **p** what they preach.
Lk 8: 21 hear God's word and put it into **p**."
Ro 12: 13 who are in need. **P** hospitality.
1Ti 5: 4 put their religion into **p** by caring

PRAISE (PRAISED PRAISES PRAISING)
Ex 15: 2 and I will **p** him, my father's God,
Dt 32: 3 Oh, **p** the greatness of our God!
Ru 4: 14 "**P** be to the LORD, who this day
2Sa 22: 47 **P** be to my Rock!
1Ch 16: 25 the LORD and most worthy of **p**;
2Ch 20: 21 to **p** him for the splendor of his
Ps 8: 2 Through the **p** of children
33: 1 it is fitting for the upright to **p** him.
34: 1 his **p** will always be on my lips.
40: 3 mouth, a hymn of **p** to our God.
48: 1 and most worthy of **p**, in the city
68: 19 **P** be to the Lord, to God our Savior,
89: 5 The heavens **p** your wonders,
100: 4 give thanks to him and **p** his name.
105: 2 Sing to him, sing **p** to him;
106: 1 **P** the LORD. Give thanks
119:175 Let me live that I may **p** you,
139: 14 I **p** you because I am fearfully
145: 21 Let every creature **p** his holy name
146: 1 **P** the LORD. **P** the LORD, my soul.
150: 2 **p** him for his surpassing greatness.
150: 6 Let everything that has breath **p** the LORD. **P** the LORD.
Pr 27: 2 Let someone else **p** you, and not
27: 21 but people are tested by their **p**.
31: 31 let her works bring her **p** at the city
Mt 21: 16 Lord, have called forth your **p**'?"
Jn 12: 43 they loved human **p** more than **p** from God.
Eph 1: 6 to the **p** of his glorious grace,
1: 12 might be for the **p** of his glory.
1: 14 to the **p** of his glory.
Heb 13: 15 offer to God a sacrifice of **p**—
Jas 5: 13 Let them sing songs of **p**.

PRAISED (PRAISE)
1Ch 29: 10 David **p** the LORD in the presence
Ne 8: 6 Ezra **p** the LORD, the great God;
Da 2: 19 Then Daniel **p** the God of heaven
Ro 9: 5 who is God over all, forever **p**!
1Pe 4: 11 God may be **p** through Jesus Christ

PRAISES (PRAISE)
2Sa 22: 50 I will sing the **p** of your name.
Ps 47: 6 Sing **p** to God, sing **p**; sing **p**
147: 1 good it is to sing **p** to our God,
Pr 31: 28 her husband also, and he **p** her:

PRAISING (PRAISE)
Ac 10: 46 speaking in tongues and **p** God.
1Co 14: 16 when you are **p** God in the Spirit,

PRAY (PRAYED PRAYER PRAYERS PRAYING)
Dt 4: 7 our God is near us whenever we **p**

1Sa 12: 23 the LORD by failing to **p** for you.
2Ch 7: 14 will humble themselves and **p**
Job 42: 8 My servant Job will **p** for you,
Ps 122: 6 **P** for the peace of Jerusalem:
Mt 5: 44 and **p** for those who persecute you,
6: 5 for they love to **p** standing
6: 9 "This, then, is how you should **p**:
26: 36 here while I go over there and **p**."
Lk 6: 28 you, **p** for those who mistreat you.
18: 1 them that they should always **p**
22: 40 them, "**P** that you will not fall
Ro 8: 26 not know what we ought to **p** for,
1Co 14: 13 in a tongue should **p** that they may
1Th 5: 17 **p** continually,
Jas 5: 13 Let them **p**. Is anyone happy?
5: 16 **p** for each other so that you may be

PRAYED (PRAY)
1Sa 1: 27 I **p** for this child, and the LORD
Jnh 2: 1 From inside the fish Jonah **p**
Mk 14: 35 and **p** that if possible the hour

PRAYER (PRAY)
2Ch 30: 27 for their **p** reached heaven, his holy
Ezr 8: 23 about this, and he answered our **p**.
Ps 6: 9 the LORD accepts my **p**.
86: 6 Hear my **p**, LORD; listen to my
Pr 15: 8 the **p** of the upright pleases him.
Isa 56: 7 house will be called a house of **p**
Mt 21: 13 house will be called a house of **p**,'
Mk 11: 24 whatever you ask for in **p**,
Jn 17: 15 My **p** is not that you take them
Ac 6: 4 will give our attention to **p**
Php 4: 6 every situation, by **p** and petition,
Jas 5: 15 the **p** offered in faith will make
1Pe 3: 12 and his ears are attentive to their **p**,

PRAYERS (PRAY)
1Ch 5: 20 He answered their **p**, because they
Mk 12: 40 and for a show make lengthy **p**.
1Pe 3: 7 so that nothing will hinder your **p**.
Rev 5: 8 which are the **p** of God's people.

PRAYING (PRAY)
Mk 11: 25 And when you stand **p**, if you hold
Jn 17: 9 I am not **p** for the world,
Ac 16: 25 Silas were **p** and singing hymns
Eph 6: 18 always keep on **p** for all the Lord's

PREACH (PREACHED PREACHING)
Mt 23: 3 they do not practice what they **p**.
Mk 16: 15 *and* **p** *the gospel to all creation.*
Ac 9: 20 At once he began to **p**
Ro 10: 15 how can anyone **p** unless they are
15: 20 to **p** the gospel where Christ was
1Co 1: 17 to baptize, but to **p** the gospel—
1: 23 but we **p** Christ crucified:
9: 14 that those who **p** the gospel should
9: 16 Woe to me if I do not **p** the gospel!
2Co 10: 16 so that we can **p** the gospel
Gal 1: 8 heaven should **p** a gospel other
2Ti 4: 2 **P** the word; be prepared in season

PREACHED (PREACH)
Mk 13: 10 the gospel must first be **p** to all
Ac 8: 4 who had been scattered **p** the word
1Co 9: 27 so that after I have **p** to others,
15: 1 remind you of the gospel I **p** to you
2Co 11: 4 a Jesus other than the Jesus we **p**,
Gal 1: 8 a gospel other than the one we **p**
Php 1: 18 false motives or true, Christ is **p**.
1Ti 3: 16 angels, was **p** among the nations,

PREACHING (PREACH)
Ro 10: 14 can they hear without someone **p**
1Co 9: 18 in **p** the gospel I may offer it free
1Ti 4: 13 of Scripture, to **p** and to teaching.
5: 17 especially those whose work is **p**

PRECEPTS
Ps 19: 8 The **p** of the LORD are right,
111: 7 all his **p** are trustworthy.
111: 10 all who follow his **p** have good
119: 40 How I long for your **p**!
119: 69 I keep your **p** with all my heart.
119:104 I gain understanding from your **p**;
119:159 See how I love your **p**; preserve my

PRECIOUS
Ps 19: 10 They are more **p** than gold,
116: 15 **P** in the sight of the LORD is
Pr 8: 11 for wisdom is more **p** than rubies,

Isa 28: 16 stone, a **p** cornerstone for a sure
1Pe 1: 19 but with the **p** blood of Christ,
2: 6 a chosen and **p** cornerstone,
2Pe 1: 4 us his very great and **p** promises,

PREDESTINED (DESTINY)
Ro 8: 29 **p** to be conformed to the image
8: 30 And those he **p**, he also called;
Eph 1: 5 he **p** us for adoption to sonship
1: 11 been **p** according to the plan

PREDICTION
Jer 28: 9 LORD only if his **p** comes true."

PREPARE (PREPARED)
Ps 23: 5 You **p** a table before me
Am 4: 12 to you, Israel, **p** to meet your God."
Jn 14: 2 that I am going there to **p** a place

PREPARED (PREPARE)
Mt 25: 34 the kingdom **p** for you since
1Co 2: 9 the things God has **p** for those who
Eph 2: 10 which God **p** in advance for us
2Ti 4: 2 be **p** in season and out of season;
1Pe 3: 15 Always be **p** to give an answer

PRESENCE (PRESENT)
Ex 25: 30 Put the bread of the **P** on this table
Ezr 9: 15 not one of us can stand in your **p**."
Ps 31: 20 the shelter of your **p** you hide them
89: 15 who walk in the light of your **p**,
90: 8 secret sins in the light of your **p**.
139: 7 Where can I flee from your **p**?
Jer 5: 22 "Should you not tremble in my **p**?
Heb 9: 24 now to appear for us in God's **p**.
Jude : 24 before his glorious **p** without fault

PRESENT (PRESENCE)
2Co 11: 2 that I might **p** you as a pure virgin
Eph 5: 27 and to **p** her to himself as a radiant
2Ti 2: 15 Do your best to **p** yourself to God

PRESERVES
Ps 119: 50 Your promise **p** my life.

PRESS (PRESSED PRESSURE)
Php 3: 14 I **p** on toward the goal to win

PRESSED (PRESS)
Lk 6: 38 A good measure, **p** down,

PRESSURE (PRESS)
2Co 1: 8 We were under great **p**, far beyond
11: 28 I face daily the **p** of my concern

PREVAILS
1Sa 2: 9 "It is not by strength that one **p**;

PRICE
Job 28: 18 the **p** of wisdom is beyond rubies.
1Co 6: 20 you were bought at a **p**.
7: 23 You were bought at a **p**;

PRIDE (PROUD)
Pr 8: 13 I hate **p** and arrogance,
16: 18 **P** goes before destruction,
Da 4: 37 those who walk in **p** he is able
Gal 6: 4 can take **p** in themselves alone,
Jas 1: 9 to take **p** in their high position.

† **PRIEST** (PRIESTHOOD PRIESTS)
Heb 4: 14 a great high **p** who has ascended
4: 15 do not have a high **p** who is unable
7: 26 Such a high **p** truly meets our need
8: 1 We do have such a high **p**, who sat

PRIESTHOOD (PRIEST)
Heb 7: 24 lives forever, he has a permanent **p**.
1Pe 2: 5 a spiritual house to be a holy **p**,
2: 9 people, a royal **p**, a holy nation,

PRIESTS (PRIEST)
Ex 19: 6 you will be for me a kingdom of **p**
Rev 5: 10 a kingdom and **p** to serve our God,

PRINCE
Isa 9: 6 Everlasting Father, **P** of Peace.
Jn 12: 31 now the **p** of this world will be
Ac 5: 31 him to his own right hand as **P**

PRISON (PRISONER)
Isa 42: 7 blind, to free captives from **p**
Mt 25: 36 I was in **p** and you came to visit
Rev 20: 7 Satan will be released from his **p**

PRISONER (PRISON)
Ro 7: 23 making me a **p** of the law of sin
Eph 3: 1 the **p** of Christ Jesus for the sake

PRIVILEGE
2Co 8: 4 for the **p** of sharing in this service

PRIZE
1Co 9: 24 Run in such a way as to get the **p**.
Php 3: 14 on toward the goal to win the **p**

PROCLAIM (PROCLAIMED)
1Ch 16: 23 **p** his salvation day after day.
Ps 19: 1 the skies **p** the work of his hands.
50: 6 the heavens **p** his righteousness,
68: 34 **P** the power of God, whose majesty
118: 17 will **p** what the LORD has done.
Zec 9: 10 He will **p** peace to the nations.
Ac 20: 27 I have not hesitated to **p** to you
Ro 10: 8 concerning faith that we **p**:
1Co 11: 26 cup, you **p** the Lord's death until

PROCLAIMED (PROCLAIM)
Ro 15: 19 I have fully **p** the gospel of Christ.
Col 1: 23 has been **p** to every creature under

PRODUCE (PRODUCES)
Mt 3: 8 **P** fruit in keeping with repentance.
3: 10 does not **p** good fruit will be cut

PRODUCES (PRODUCE)
Pr 30: 33 so stirring up anger **p** strife."
Ro 5: 3 that suffering **p** perseverance;
Heb 12: 11 it **p** a harvest of righteousness

PROFANE
Lev 22: 32 Do not **p** my holy name, for I must

PROFESS
1Ti 2: 10 for women who **p** to worship God.
Heb 4: 14 let us hold firmly to the faith we **p**.
10: 23 unswervingly to the hope we **p**,

PROMISE (PROMISED PROMISES)
1Ki 8: 20 LORD has kept the **p** he made:
Ac 2: 39 The **p** is for you and your children
Gal 3: 14 faith we might receive the **p**
1Ti 4: 8 holding **p** for both the present life
2Pe 3: 9 Lord is not slow in keeping his **p**,

PROMISED (PROMISE)
Ex 3: 17 I have **p** to bring you up out of
Dt 26: 18 his treasured possession as he **p**,
Ps 119: 57 I have **p** to obey your words.
Ro 4: 21 had power to do what he had **p**.
Heb 10: 23 we profess, for he who **p** is faithful.
2Pe 3: 4 say, "Where is this 'coming' he **p**?

PROMISES (PROMISE)
Jos 21: 45 of all the LORD's good **p** to Israel
Ro 9: 4 law, the temple worship and the **p**.
2Pe 1: 4 us his very great and precious **p**,

PROMPTED
1Th 1: 3 by faith, your labor **p** by love,
2Th 1: 11 and your every deed **p** by faith.

PROPHECIES (PROPHESY)
1Co 13: 8 But where there are **p**, they will
1Th 5: 20 Do not treat **p** with contempt

PROPHECY (PROPHESY)
1Co 14: 1 gifts of the Spirit, especially **p**.
2Pe 1: 20 that no **p** of Scripture came

‡ **PROPHESY** (PROPHECIES PROPHECY PROPHESYING PROPHET PROPHETS)
Joel 2: 28 Your sons and daughters will **p**,
Mt 7: 22 did we not **p** in your name
1Co 14: 39 be eager to **p**, and do not forbid

PROPHESYING (PROPHESY)
Ro 12: 6 If your gift is **p**, then prophesy

† **PROPHET** (PROPHESY)
Dt 18: 18 for them a **p** like you from among
Am 7: 14 neither a **p** nor the son of a **p**,
Mt 10: 41 Whoever welcomes a **p** as a **p** will
Lk 4: 24 "no **p** is accepted in his hometown.

PROPHETS (PROPHESY)
Ps 105: 15 do my **p** no harm."
Mt 5: 17 come to abolish the Law or the **P**;
7: 12 for this sums up the Law and the **P**.
24: 24 messiahs and false **p** will appear
Lk 24: 25 believe all that the **p** have spoken!
Ac 10: 43 All the **p** testify about him
1Co 12: 28 apostles, second **p**, third teachers,
14: 32 The spirits of **p** are subject
Eph 2: 20 foundation of the apostles and **p**,
Heb 1: 1 ancestors through the **p** at many
1Pe 1: 10 the **p**, who spoke of the grace

† Please see the "Hebrew to English Translation Chart," p. xix.
‡ Please see "Key New Testament Terms," p. 1584.

PROSPER (PROSPERITY PROSPERS)
Pr 28: 25 who trust in the LORD will **p**.

PROSPERITY (PROSPER)
Ps 73: 3 when I saw the **p** of the wicked.

PROSPERS (PROSPER)
Ps 1: 3 whatever they do **p**.

PROSTITUTE (PROSTITUTES)
1Co 6: 15 of Christ and unite them with a **p**?

PROSTITUTES (PROSTITUTE)
Mt 21: 31 **p** are entering the kingdom of God
Lk 15: 30 your property with **p** comes home,

PROSTRATE
Dt 9: 18 again I fell **p** before the LORD

PROTECT (PROTECTS)
Ps 32: 7 you will **p** me from trouble
Pr 2: 11 Discretion will **p** you,
Jn 17: 11 **p** them by the power of your name,

PROTECTS (PROTECT)
1Co 13: 7 It always **p**, always trusts,

PROUD (PRIDE)
Pr 16: 5 The LORD detests all the **p**
Ro 12: 16 Do not be **p**, but be willing
1Co 13: 4 envy, it does not boast, it is not **p**.

PROVE
1Co 4: 2 been given a trust must **p** faithful.

PROVIDE (PROVIDED PROVIDES)
Ge 22: 8 "God himself will **p** the lamb
Isa 43: 20 because I **p** water in the wilderness
1Ti 5: 8 Anyone who does not **p** for their

PROVIDED (PROVIDE)
Jnh 1: 17 Now the LORD **p** a huge fish
4: 6 the LORD God **p** a leafy plant
4: 7 dawn the next day God **p** a worm,
4: 8 rose, God **p** a scorching east wind,

PROVIDES (PROVIDE)
1Ti 6: 17 who richly **p** us with everything
1Pe 4: 11 do so with the strength God **p**,

PROVOKED
Ecc 7: 9 Do not be quickly **p** in your spirit,

PRUDENT
Pr 14: 15 the **p** give thought to their steps.
19: 14 but a **p** wife is from the LORD.
Am 5: 13 Therefore the **p** keep quiet in such

PRUNING
Isa 2: 4 and their spears into **p** hooks.
Joel 3: 10 and your **p** hooks into spears.

PSALMS
Eph 5: 19 speaking to one another with **p**,
Col 3: 16 with all wisdom through **p**,

PUBLICLY
Ac 20: 20 have taught you **p** and from house

PUFFS
1Co 8: 1 knowledge **p** up while love builds

PUNISH (PUNISHED)
Ex 32: 34 to **p**, I will **p** them for their sin."
Pr 23: 13 if you **p** them with the rod,
Isa 13: 11 I will **p** the world for its evil,
1Pe 2: 14 by him to **p** those who do wrong

PUNISHED (PUNISH)
La 3: 39 should the living complain when **p**
2Th 1: 9 They will be **p** with everlasting
Heb 10: 29 to be **p** who has trampled the Son

† PURE (PURIFIES PURIFY PURITY)
2Sa 22: 27 to the **p** you show yourself **p**,
Ps 24: 4 who has clean hands and a **p** heart,
51: 10 Create in me a **p** heart, O God,
Pr 20: 9 can say, "I have kept my heart **p**;
Isa 52: 11 Come out from it and be **p**,
Hab 1: 13 Your eyes are too **p** to look on evil;
Mt 5: 8 Blessed are the **p** in heart, for they
2Co 11: 2 I might present you as a **p** virgin
Php 4: 8 whatever is **p**, whatever is lovely,
1Ti 5: 22 the sins of others. Keep yourself **p**.
Titus 1: 15 To the **p**, all things are **p**,
2: 5 to be self-controlled and **p**, to be
Heb 13: 4 all, and the marriage bed kept **p**,
1Jn 3: 3 purify themselves, just as he is **p**.

PURGE
Pr 20: 30 and beatings **p** the inmost being.

PURIFIES (PURE)
1Jn 1: 7 of Jesus, his Son, **p** us from all sin.

PURIFY (PURE)
Titus 2: 14 to **p** for himself a people that are
1Jn 1: 9 and **p** us from all unrighteousness.
3: 3 this hope in him **p** themselves,

PURITY (PURE)
Ps 119: 9 person stay on the path of **p**?
2Co 6: 6 in **p**, understanding,
1Ti 4: 12 conduct, in love, in faith and in **p**.

PURPOSE
Pr 19: 21 it is the LORD's **p** that prevails.
Isa 55: 11 achieve the **p** for which I sent it.
Ro 8: 28 been called according to his **p**.

PURSES
Lk 12: 33 Provide **p** for yourselves that will

PURSUE
Ps 34: 14 and do good; seek peace and **p** it.
2Ti 2: 22 of youth and **p** righteousness, faith,
1Pe 3: 11 they must seek peace and **p** it.

QUALITIES (QUALITY)
2Pe 1: 8 if you possess these **q** in increasing

QUALITY (QUALITIES)
1Co 3: 13 and the fire will test the **q** of each

QUARREL (QUARRELSOME)
Pr 15: 18 the one who is patient calms a **q**.
17: 14 Starting a **q** is like breaching a dam
17: 19 Whoever loves a **q** loves sin;

QUARRELSOME (QUARREL)
Pr 19: 13 **q** wife is like the constant dripping
1Ti 3: 3 gentle, not **q**, not a lover of money.
2Ti 2: 24 the Lord's servant must not be **q**

QUENCH
1Th 5: 19 Do not **q** the Spirit.

QUICK-TEMPERED
Titus 1: 7 not **q**, not given to drunkenness,

QUIET (QUIETNESS)
Ps 23: 2 he leads me beside **q** waters,
Lk 19: 40 "if they keep **q**, the stones will cry
1Ti 2: 2 peaceful and **q** lives in all godliness
1Pe 3: 4 beauty of a gentle and **q** spirit,

QUIETNESS (QUIET)
Isa 30: 15 in **q** and trust is your strength,
32: 17 its effect will be **q** and confidence
1Ti 2: 11 woman should learn in **q** and full

QUIVER
Ps 127: 5 Blessed is the man whose **q** is full

RACE
Ecc 9: 11 The **r** is not to the swift or
1Co 9: 24 that in a **r** all the runners run,
2Ti 4: 7 I have finished the **r**, I have kept
Heb 12: 1 with perseverance the **r** marked

RACHEL
Daughter of Laban (Ge 29:16); wife of Jacob (Ge 29:28); bore two sons (Ge 30:22–24; 35:16–24; 46:19).

RADIANCE (RADIANT)
Heb 1: 3 The Son is the **r** of God's glory

RADIANT (RADIANCE)
Ex 34: 29 that his face was **r** because he had
Ps 34: 5 Those who look to him are **r**;
SS 5: 10 My beloved is **r** and ruddy,
Isa 60: 5 Then you will look and be **r**,
Eph 5: 27 her to himself as a **r** church,

RAIN (RAINBOW)
Mt 5: 45 and sends **r** on the righteous

RAINBOW (RAIN)
Ge 9: 13 I have set my **r** in the clouds, and it

RAISED (RISE)
Ro 4: 25 was **r** to life for our justification.
10: 9 your heart that God **r** him
1Co 15: 4 he was **r** on the third day according

RAN (RUN)
Jnh 1: 3 But Jonah **r** away from the LORD

RANSOM
Mt 20: 28 to give his life as a **r** for many."
Heb 9: 15 he has died as a **r** to set them free

RAVENS
1Ki 17: 6 The **r** brought him bread and meat
Lk 12: 24 Consider the **r**: They do not sow

READ (READS)
Jos 8: 34 Joshua **r** all the words of the law—
Ne 8: 8 understood what was being **r**.
2Co 3: 2 hearts, known and **r** by everyone.

READS (READ)
Rev 1: 3 is the one who **r** aloud the words

REAL (REALITY)
Jn 6: 55 For my flesh is **r** food and my blood is **r** drink.

REALITY (REAL)
Col 2: 17 the **r**, however, is found in Christ.

REAP (REAPS)
Job 4: 8 evil and those who sow trouble **r** it.
2Co 9: 6 generously will also **r** generously.

REAPS (REAP)
Gal 6: 7 A man **r** what he sows.

REASON
1Pe 3: 15 asks you to give the **r** for the hope

REBEKAH
Sister of Laban, secured as bride for Isaac (Ge 24). Mother of Esau and Jacob (Ge 25:19–26). Taken by Abimelek as sister of Isaac; returned (Ge 26:1–11). Encouraged Jacob to trick Isaac out of blessing (Ge 27:1–17).

REBEL
Mt 10: 21 children will **r** against their parents

REBUKE (REBUKING)
Pr 9: 8 **r** the wise and they will love you.
27: 5 Better is open **r** than hidden love.
Lk 17: 3 or sister sins against you, **r** them;
2Ti 4: 2 correct, **r** and encourage—
Rev 3: 19 Those whom I love I **r**

REBUKING (REBUKE)
2Ti 3: 16 and is useful for teaching, **r**,

RECEIVE (RECEIVED RECEIVES)
Ac 1: 8 you will **r** power when the Holy
20: 35 more blessed to give than to **r**.'"
2Co 6: 17 no unclean thing, and I will **r** you."
Rev 4: 11 to **r** glory and honor and power,

RECEIVED (RECEIVE)
Mt 6: 2 they have **r** their reward in full.
10: 8 Freely you have **r**; freely give.
1Co 11: 23 For I **r** from the Lord what I
Col 2: 6 just as you **r** Christ Jesus as Lord,
1Pe 4: 10 should use whatever gift you have **r**

RECEIVES (RECEIVE)
Mt 7: 8 For everyone who asks **r**;
Ac 10: 43 who believes in him **r** forgiveness

RECKONING
Isa 10: 3 What will you do on the day of **r**,

RECOGNIZE (RECOGNIZED)
Mt 7: 16 By their fruit you will **r** them.

RECOGNIZED (RECOGNIZE)
Mt 12: 33 be bad, for a tree is **r** by its fruit.
Ro 7: 13 in order that sin might be **r** as sin,

RECOMPENSE
Isa 40: 10 him, and his **r** accompanies him.

RECONCILE (RECONCILED RECONCILIATION)
Eph 2: 16 and in one body to **r** both of them

RECONCILED (RECONCILE)
Mt 5: 24 First go and be **r** to them;
Ro 5: 10 were **r** to him through the death
2Co 5: 18 who **r** us to himself through Christ

RECONCILIATION (RECONCILE)
Ro 5: 11 whom we have now received **r**.
11: 15 For if their rejection brought **r**
2Co 5: 18 and gave us the ministry of **r**:
5: 19 committed to us the message of **r**.

RECORD
Ps 130: 3 you, LORD, kept a **r** of sins, Lord,

RED
Isa 1: 18 though they are **r** as crimson,

REDEEM (REDEEMED REDEEMER REDEMPTION)
2Sa 7: 23 out to **r** as a people for himself,
Ps 49: 7 No one can **r** the life of another
Gal 4: 5 to **r** those under the law, that we

† Please see the "Hebrew to English Translation Chart," p. xix.

REDEEMED (REDEEM)
Gal 3: 13 Christ **r** us from the curse of the law
1Pe 1: 18 you were **r** from the empty way

† REDEEMER (REDEEM)
Job 19: 25 I know that my **r** lives,

REDEMPTION (REDEEM)
Ps 130: 7 love and with him is full **r**.
Lk 21: 28 because your **r** is drawing near."
Ro 8: 23 to sonship, the **r** of our bodies.
Eph 1: 7 we have **r** through his blood,
Col 1: 14 in whom we have **r**, the forgiveness
Heb 9: 12 blood, thus obtaining eternal **r**.

REFUGE
Nu 35: 11 some towns to be your cities of **r**,
Dt 33: 27 The eternal God is your **r**,
Ru 2: 12 wings you have come to take **r**."
Ps 46: 1 God is our **r** and strength,
91: 2 "He is my **r** and my fortress,

REHOBOAM
Son of Solomon (1Ki 11:43; 1Ch 3:10). Harsh treatment of subjects caused divided kingdom (1Ki 12:1–24; 14:21–31; 2Ch 10–12).

REIGN (REIGNS)
Ro 6: 12 not let sin **r** in your mortal body
1Co 15: 25 he must **r** until he has put all his
2Ti 2: 12 if we endure, we will also **r** with
Rev 20: 6 **r** with him for a thousand years.

REIGNS (REIGN)
Ex 15: 18 "The LORD **r** for ever and ever."

REJECTED (REJECTS)
Ps 118: 22 stone the builders **r** has become
Isa 53: 3 was despised and **r** by mankind,
1Ti 4: 4 nothing is to be **r** if it is received
1Pe 2: 4 **r** by humans but chosen by God
2: 7 stone the builders **r** has become

REJECTS (REJECTED)
Lk 10: 16 whoever **r** me **r** him who sent me."
Jn 3: 36 whoever **r** the Son will not see life,

REJOICE (JOY)
Ps 66: 6 come, let us **r** in him.
118: 24 let us **r** today and be glad.
Pr 5: 18 you **r** in the wife of your youth.
Lk 10: 20 but **r** that your names are written
15: 6 together and says, '**R** with me;
Ro 12: 15 **R** with those who **r**;
Php 4: 4 **R** in the Lord always. I will say it again: **R**!

REJOICES (JOY)
Isa 61: 10 my soul **r** in my God.
Lk 1: 47 and my spirit **r** in God my Savior,
1Co 12: 26 is honored, every part **r** with it.
13: 6 delight in evil but **r** with the truth.

REJOICING (JOY)
Ps 30: 5 night, but **r** comes in the morning.
Lk 15: 7 the same way there will be more **r**
Ac 5: 41 **r** because they had been counted

RELIABLE
2Ti 2: 2 entrust to **r** people who will also be

RELIGION
1Ti 5: 4 of all to put their **r** into practice
Jas 1: 27 **R** that God our Father accepts as

REMAIN (REMAINS)
Nu 33: 55 you allow to **r** will become barbs
Jn 15: 7 If you **r** in me and my words **r**
Ro 13: 8 Let no debt **r** outstanding,
1Co 13: 13 And now these three **r**:

REMAINS (REMAIN)
Ps 146: 6 he **r** faithful forever.
2Ti 2: 13 if we are faithless, he **r** faithful,
Heb 7: 3 Son of God, he **r** a priest forever.

† REMEMBER (REMEMBERS REMEMBRANCE)
Ex 20: 8 "**R** the Sabbath day by keeping it
1Ch 16: 12 **R** the wonders he has done,
Ecc 12: 1 **R** your Creator in the days of your
Jer 31: 34 and will **r** their sins no more."
Gal 2: 10 we should continue to **r** the poor,
Php 1: 3 I thank my God every time I **r** you.
Heb 8: 12 and will **r** their sins no more."

REMEMBERS (REMEMBER)
Ps 103: 14 are formed, he **r** that we are dust.
111: 5 he **r** his covenant forever.
Isa 43: 25 own sake, and **r** your sins no more.

REMEMBRANCE (REMEMBER)
1Co 11: 24 is for you; do this in **r** of me."

REMIND
Jn 14: 26 will **r** you of everything I have said

REMOVED
Ps 30: 11 you **r** my sackcloth and clothed me
103: 12 so far has he **r** our transgressions
Jn 20: 1 that the stone had been **r**

RENEW (RENEWED RENEWING)
Ps 51: 10 and **r** a steadfast spirit within me.
Isa 40: 31 in the LORD will **r** their strength.

RENEWED (RENEW)
Ps 103: 5 that your youth is **r** like the eagle's.
2Co 4: 16 yet inwardly we are being **r** day

RENEWING (RENEW)
Ro 12: 2 transformed by the **r** of your mind.

RENOUNCE (RENOUNCES)
Da 4: 27 **R** your sins by doing what is right,

RENOUNCES (RENOUNCE)
Pr 28: 13 confesses and **r** them finds mercy.

RENOWN
Isa 63: 12 to gain for himself everlasting **r**,
Jer 32: 20 have gained the **r** that is still yours.

REPAID (PAY)
Lk 14: 14 you will be **r** at the resurrection
Col 3: 25 Anyone who does wrong will be **r**

REPAY (PAY)
Dt 32: 35 It is mine to avenge; I will **r**.
Ru 2: 12 May the LORD **r** you for what you
Ro 12: 19 I will **r**," says the Lord.
1Pe 3: 9 the contrary, **r** evil with blessing,

REPENT (REPENTANCE REPENTS)
Job 42: 6 I despise myself and **r** in dust
Jer 15: 19 "If you **r**, I will restore you that you
Mt 4: 17 time on Jesus began to preach, "**R**,
Lk 13: 3 But unless you **r**, you too will all
17: 3 and if they **r**, forgive them.
Ac 2: 38 Peter replied, "**R** and be baptized,
17: 30 all people everywhere to **r**.

‡ REPENTANCE (REPENT)
Lk 3: 8 Produce fruit in keeping with **r**.
5: 32 call the righteous, but sinners to **r**."
Ac 26: 20 demonstrate their **r** by their deeds.
2Co 7: 10 Godly sorrow brings **r** that leads

REPENTS (REPENT)
Lk 15: 10 of God over one sinner who **r**."

REPROACH
1Ti 3: 2 Now the overseer is to be above **r**,

REPUTATION
1Ti 3: 7 also have a good **r** with outsiders,

REQUESTS
Ps 20: 5 May the LORD grant all your **r**.
Php 4: 6 present your **r** to God.

REQUIRE
Mic 6: 8 what does the LORD **r** of you?

RESCUE (RESCUES)
Da 6: 20 been able to **r** you from the lions?"
2Pe 2: 9 the Lord knows how to **r** the godly

RESCUES (RESCUE)
1Th 1: 10 who **r** us from the coming wrath.

RESIST
Jas 4: 7 **R** the devil, and he will flee
1Pe 5: 9 **R** him, standing firm in the faith,

RESOLVED
Da 1: 8 Daniel **r** not to defile himself
1Co 2: 2 For I **r** to know nothing while I

RESPECT (RESPECTABLE)
Lev 19: 3 of you must **r** your mother
19: 32 show **r** for the elderly and revere
Mal 1: 6 a master, where is the **r** due me?"
1Th 4: 12 that your daily life may win the **r**
1Ti 3: 4 do so in a manner worthy of full **r**.
1Pe 2: 17 Show proper **r** to everyone,
3: 7 them with **r** as the weaker partner

RESPECTABLE (RESPECT)
1Ti 3: 2 self-controlled, **r**, hospitable,

† REST
Ex 31: 15 seventh day is a day of sabbath **r**,
Ps 91: 1 the Most High will **r** in the shadow
Jer 6: 16 and you will find **r** for your souls.
Mt 11: 28 burdened, and I will give you **r**.

RESTITUTION
Ex 22: 3 who steals must certainly make **r**,
Lev 6: 5 must make **r** in full, add a fifth

RESTORE
Ps 51: 12 **R** to me the joy of your salvation
Gal 6: 1 by the Spirit should **r** that person

‡ RESURRECTION
Mt 22: 30 the **r** people will neither marry nor
Lk 14: 14 be repaid at the **r** of the righteous."
Jn 11: 25 said to her, "I am the **r** and the life.
Ro 1: 4 in power by his **r** from the dead:
1Co 15: 12 say that there is no **r** of the dead?
Php 3: 10 yes, to know the power of his **r**
Rev 20: 5 This is the first **r**.

RETRIBUTION
Jer 51: 56 For the LORD is a God of **r**;

RETURN
2Ch 30: 9 If you **r** to the LORD, then your
Ne 1: 9 but if you **r** to me and obey my
Isa 55: 11 It will not **r** to me empty, but will
Hos 6: 1 "Come, let us **r** to the LORD.
Joel 2: 12 "**r** to me with all your heart,

REVEALED (REVELATION)
Dt 29: 29 but the things **r** belong to us
Isa 40: 5 the glory of the LORD will be **r**,
Mt 11: 25 and **r** them to little children.
Ro 1: 17 the righteousness of God is **r**—
8: 18 with the glory that will be **r** in us.

REVELATION (REVEALED)
Gal 1: 12 I received it by **r** from Jesus Christ.
Rev 1: 1 The **r** from Jesus Christ,

REVENGE (VENGEANCE)
Lev 19: 18 "'Do not seek **r** or bear a grudge
Ro 12: 19 Do not take **r**, my dear friends,

REVERE (REVERENCE)
Ps 33: 8 all the people of the world **r** him.

REVERENCE (REVERE)
Lev 19: 30 and have **r** for my sanctuary.
Ps 5: 7 in **r** I bow down toward your holy
Col 3: 22 of heart and **r** for the Lord.
1Pe 3: 2 see the purity and **r** of your lives.

REVIVE
Ps 85: 6 Will you not **r** us again, that your
Isa 57: 15 to **r** the spirit of the lowly and to **r**

REWARD (REWARDED)
Ps 19: 11 in keeping them there is great **r**.
127: 3 the LORD, offspring a **r** from him.
Pr 19: 17 he will **r** them for what they have
25: 22 head, and the LORD will **r** you.
Jer 17: 10 to **r** each person according to their
Mt 5: 12 because great is your **r** in heaven,
6: 5 they have received their **r** in full.
16: 27 he will **r** each person according
1Co 3: 14 the builder will receive a **r**.
Rev 22: 12 My **r** is with me, and I will give

REWARDED (REWARD)
Ru 2: 12 May you be richly **r** by the LORD,
Ps 18: 24 The LORD has **r** me according
Pr 14: 14 and the good **r** for theirs.
1Co 3: 8 and they will each be **r** according

RICH (RICHES)
Pr 23: 4 Do not wear yourself out to get **r**;
Jer 9: 23 or the **r** boast of their riches,
Mt 19: 23 for someone who is **r** to enter
2Co 6: 10 poor, yet making many **r**;
8: 9 his poverty might become **r**.
1Ti 6: 17 Command those who are **r** in this

RICHES (RICH)
Ps 119: 14 statutes as one rejoices in great **r**.
Pr 30: 8 give me neither poverty nor **r**,
Isa 10: 3 Where will you leave your **r**?
Ro 9: 23 to make the **r** of his glory known
11: 33 the depth of the **r** of the wisdom

† Please see the "Hebrew to English Translation Chart," p. xix.
‡ Please see "Key New Testament Terms," p. 1584.

Eph 2: 7 he might show the incomparable **r**
3: 8 to the Gentiles the boundless **r**
Col 1: 27 among the Gentiles the glorious **r**

RID
Ge 21: 10 "Get **r** of that slave woman and her
1Co 5: 7 Get **r** of the old yeast, so that you
Gal 4: 30 "Get **r** of the slave woman and her

RIGHT (RIGHTS)
Ge 18: 25 not the Judge of all the earth do **r**?"
Ex 15: 26 God and do what is **r** in his eyes,
Dt 5: 32 do not turn aside to the **r**
Ps 16: 8 With him at my **r** hand, I will not
19: 8 The precepts of the LORD are **r**,
63: 8 your **r** hand upholds me.
110: 1 "Sit at my **r** hand until I make your
Pr 4: 27 Do not turn to the **r** or the left;
14: 12 There is a way that appears to be **r**,
Isa 1: 17 Learn to do **r**; seek justice.
Jer 23: 5 do what is just and **r** in the land.
Hos 14: 9 The ways of the LORD are **r**;
Mt 6: 3 know what your **r** hand is doing,
Jn 1: 12 he gave the **r** to become children
Ro 9: 21 Does not the potter have the **r**
12: 17 careful to do what is **r** in the eyes
Eph 1: 20 and seated him at his **r** hand
Php 4: 8 whatever is **r**, whatever is pure,

† RIGHTEOUS (RIGHTEOUSNESS)
Ps 34: 15 eyes of the LORD are on the **r**,
37: 25 yet I have never seen the **r** forsaken
119:137 You are **r**, LORD, and your laws
143: 2 no one living is **r** before you.
Pr 3: 33 but he blesses the home of the **r**.
11: 30 The fruit of the **r** is a tree of life,
18: 10 the **r** run to it and are safe.
Isa 64: 6 all our **r** acts are like filthy rags;
Hab 2: 4 but the **r** person will live by his
Mt 5: 45 and sends rain on the **r**
9: 13 For I have not come to call the **r**,
13: 49 and separate the wicked from the **r**
25: 46 but the **r** to eternal life."
Ro 1: 17 "The **r** will live by faith."
3: 10 "There is no one **r**, not even one;
1Ti 1: 9 that the law is made not for the **r**
Jas 2: 24 is considered **r** by what they do
1Pe 3: 18 for sins, the **r** for the unrighteous,
1Jn 3: 7 is right is **r**, just as he is **r**.
Rev 19: 8 (Fine linen stands for the **r** acts

† RIGHTEOUSNESS (RIGHTEOUS)
Ge 15: 6 and he credited it to him as **r**.
1Sa 26: 23 rewards everyone for their **r**
Ps 9: 8 He rules the world in **r** and judges
45: 7 You love **r** and hate wickedness;
85: 10 **r** and peace kiss each other.
89: 14 **R** and justice are the foundation
111: 3 deeds, and his **r** endures forever.
Pr 14: 34 **R** exalts a nation, but sin
21: 21 Whoever pursues **r** and love finds
Isa 59: 17 He put on **r** as his breastplate,
Eze 18: 20 The **r** of the righteous will be
Da 9: 24 to bring in everlasting **r**, to seal
12: 3 and those who lead many to **r**,
Mal 4: 2 the sun of **r** will rise with healing
Mt 5: 6 those who hunger and thirst for **r**,
5: 20 you that unless your **r** surpasses
6: 1 practice your **r** in front of others
6: 33 seek first his kingdom and his **r**,
Ro 3: 25 He did this to demonstrate his **r**,
4: 3 and it was credited to him as **r**."
4: 9 faith was credited to him as **r**.
6: 13 to him as an instrument of **r**.
2Co 5: 21 we might become the **r** of God.
Gal 2: 21 **r** could be gained through the law,
3: 6 and it was credited to him as **r**."
Eph 6: 14 with the breastplate of **r** in place,
Php 3: 9 not having a **r** of my own
2Ti 3: 16 correcting and training in **r**,
4: 8 is in store for me the crown of **r**,
Heb 11: 7 and became heir of the **r** that is
2Pe 2: 21 not to have known the way of **r**,

RIGHTS (RIGHT)
La 3: 35 deny people their **r** before the Most

RISE (RAISED)
Isa 26: 19 their bodies will **r**—let those who
Mt 27: 63 'After three days I will **r** again.'
Jn 5: 29 who have done what is good will **r**
1Th 4: 16 and the dead in Christ will **r** first.

ROAD
Mt 7: 13 gate and broad is the **r** that leads

ROBBERS
Jer 7: 11 Name, become a den of **r** to you?
Lk 19: 46 you have made it 'a den of **r**.'"
Jn 10: 8 come before me are thieves and **r**,

ROCK
Ps 18: 2 The LORD is my **r**, my fortress
40: 2 he set my feet on a **r** and gave me
Mt 7: 24 man who built his house on the **r**.
16: 18 on this **r** I will build my church,
Ro 9: 33 and a **r** that makes them fall,
1Co 10: 4 them, and that **r** was Christ.

ROD
Ps 23: 4 your **r** and your staff, they comfort
Pr 13: 24 Whoever spares the **r** hates their
23: 13 if you punish them with the **r**,

ROOM (ROOMS)
Mt 6: 6 go into your **r**, close the door
Lk 2: 7 there was no guest **r** available
Jn 21: 25 the whole world would not have **r**

ROOMS (ROOM)
Jn 14: 2 My Father's house has many **r**;

ROOT
Isa 53: 2 and like a **r** out of dry ground.
1Ti 6: 10 the love of money is a **r** of all kinds

ROYAL
Jas 2: 8 If you really keep the **r** law found
1Pe 2: 9 are a chosen people, a **r** priesthood,

RUIN (RUINS)
Pr 18: 24 unreliable friends soon comes to **r**,
19: 3 person's own folly leads to their **r**,
1Ti 6: 9 desires that plunge people into **r**

RUINS (RUIN)
2Ti 2: 14 value, and only **r** those who listen.

RULE (RULER RULERS RULES)
1Sa 12: 12 'No, we want a king to **r** over us'—
Ps 119:133 to your word; let no sin **r** over me.
Zec 9: 10 His **r** will extend from sea to sea
Col 3: 15 peace of Christ **r** in your hearts,
Rev 2: 27 that one 'will **r** them with an iron

RULER (RULE)
Eph 2: 2 of the **r** of the kingdom of the air,
1Ti 6: 15 the blessed and only **R**, the King

RULERS (RULE)
Ps 2: 2 and the **r** band together against
8: 6 You made them **r** over the works
Col 1: 16 or powers or **r** or authorities;

RULES (RULE)
Ps 103: 19 heaven, and his kingdom **r** over all.
Lk 22: 26 and the one who **r** like the one who
2Ti 2: 5 by competing according to the **r**.

RUMORS
Mt 24: 6 You will hear of wars and **r** of wars,

RUN (RAN)
Isa 40: 31 they will **r** and not grow weary,
1Co 9: 24 **R** in such a way as to get the prize.
Heb 12: 1 let us **r** with perseverance the race

RUTH
Moabitess; widow who went to Bethlehem with mother-in-law Naomi (Ru 1). Gleaned in field of Boaz; shown favor (Ru 2). Proposed marriage to Boaz (Ru 3). Married (Ru 4:1–12); bore Obed, ancestor of David (Ru 4:13–22), Jesus (Mt 1:5).

‡ SABBATH
Ex 20: 8 "Remember the **S** day by keeping it
Dt 5: 12 "Observe the **S** day by keeping it
Col 2: 16 New Moon celebration or a **S** day.

SACKCLOTH
Mt 11: 21 would have repented long ago in **s**

SACRED
Mt 7: 6 "Do not give dogs what is **s**;
1Co 3: 17 for God's temple is **s**, and you

SACRIFICE (SACRIFICED)
Ge 22: 2 **S** him there as a burnt offering
Ex 12: 27 'It is the Passover **s** to the LORD,
1Sa 15: 22 To obey is better than **s**,
Ps 51: 17 My **s**, O God, is a broken spirit;
Hos 6: 6 not **s**, and acknowledgment of God
Mt 9: 13 'I desire mercy, not **s**.'
Ro 12: 1 to offer your bodies as a living **s**,
Heb 9: 26 away with sin by the **s** of himself.
13: 15 offer to God a **s** of praise—
1Jn 2: 2 He is the atoning **s** for our sins,

SACRIFICED (SACRIFICE)
1Co 5: 7 our Passover lamb, has been **s**.
8: 1 Now about food **s** to idols:
Heb 9: 28 so Christ was **s** once to take away

‡ SADDUCEES
Mk 12: 18 Then the **S**, who say there is no

SAFE (SAVE)
Ps 37: 3 in the land and enjoy **s** pasture.
Pr 18: 10 the righteous run to it and are **s**.

SAFETY (SAVE)
Ps 4: 8 alone, LORD, make me dwell in **s**.
1Th 5: 3 "Peace and **s**," destruction will

SAINTS See FAITHFUL, [GOD'S] PEOPLE

SAKE
Ps 44: 22 your **s** we face death all day long;
Php 3: 7 consider loss for the **s** of Christ.
Heb 11: 26 disgrace for the **s** of Christ as

SALT
Ge 19: 26 back, and she became a pillar of **s**.
Mt 5: 13 "You are the **s** of the earth.

SALVATION (SAVE)
Ex 15: 2 he has become my **s**.
1Ch 16: 23 proclaim his **s** day after day.
Ps 27: 1 The LORD is my light and my **s**—
51: 12 Restore to me the joy of your **s**
62: 2 Truly he is my rock and my **s**;
85: 9 Surely his **s** is near those who fear
96: 2 proclaim his **s** day after day.
Isa 25: 9 let us rejoice and be glad in his **s**."
45: 17 the LORD with an everlasting **s**;
51: 6 But my **s** will last forever,
59: 17 and the helmet of **s** on his head;
61: 10 has clothed me with garments of **s**
Jnh 2: 9 '**S** comes from the LORD.'"
Lk 2: 30 For my eyes have seen your **s**,
Jn 4: 22 we do know, for **s** is from the Jews.
Ac 4: 12 **S** is found in no one else, for there
13: 47 that you may bring **s** to the ends
Ro 11: 11 **s** has come to the Gentiles to make
2Co 7: 10 brings repentance that leads to **s**
Eph 6: 17 Take the helmet of **s** and the sword
Php 2: 12 to work out your **s** with fear
1Th 5: 8 and the hope of **s** as a helmet.
2Ti 3: 15 make you wise for **s** through faith
Heb 2: 3 we escape if we ignore so great a **s**?
6: 9 the things that have to do with **s**.
1Pe 1: 10 Concerning this **s**, the prophets,
2: 2 by it you may grow up in your **s**,

‡ SAMARITAN
Lk 10: 33 But a **S**, as he traveled, came where

SAMSON
Danite judge. Birth promised (Jdg 13). Married to Philistine (Jdg 14). Vengeance on Philistines (Jdg 15). Betrayed by Delilah (Jdg 16:1–22). Death (Jdg 16:23–31). Feats of strength: killed lion (Jdg 14:6), 30 Philistines (Jdg 14:19), 1,000 Philistines with jawbone (Jdg 15:13–17), carried off gates of Gaza (Jdg 16:3), pushed down temple of Dagon (Jdg 16:25–30).

SAMUEL
Ephraimite judge and prophet (Heb 11:32). Birth prayed for (1Sa 1:10–18). Dedicated to temple by Hannah (1Sa 1:21–28). Raised by Eli (1Sa 2:11, 18–26). Called as prophet (1Sa 3). Led Israel to victory over Philistines (1Sa 7). Asked by Israel for a king (1Sa 8). Anointed Saul as king (1Sa 9–10). Farewell speech (1Sa 12). Rebuked Saul for sacrifice (1Sa 13). Announced rejection of Saul (1Sa 15). Anointed David as king (1Sa 16). Protected David from Saul (1Sa 19:18–24). Death (1Sa 25:1). Returned from dead to condemn Saul (1Sa 28).

† Please see the "Hebrew to English Translation Chart," p. xix.
‡ Please see "Key New Testament Terms," p. 1584.

SANCTIFIED (SANCTIFY)
Ac 20: 32 among all those who are **s**.
Ro 15: 16 to God, **s** by the Holy Spirit.
1Co 6: 11 you were **s**, you were justified
7: 14 husband has been **s** through his
Heb 10: 29 blood of the covenant that **s** them,

SANCTIFY (SANCTIFIED SANCTIFYING)
1Th 5: 23 peace, **s** you through and through.

SANCTIFYING (SANCTIFY)
2Th 2: 13 be saved through the **s** work

SANCTUARY
Ex 25: 8 "Then have them make a **s** for me,

SAND
Ge 22: 17 sky and as the **s** on the seashore.
Mt 7: 26 man who built his house on **s**.

SANDALS
Ex 3: 5 "Take off your **s**, for the place
Jos 5: 15 "Take off your **s**, for the place

SANG (SING)
Job 38: 7 while the morning stars **s** together
Rev 5: 9 And they **s** a new song, saying:

SARAH
Wife of Abraham, originally named Sarai; barren (Ge 11:29–31; 1Pe 3:6). Taken by Pharaoh as Abraham's sister; returned (Ge 12:10–20). Gave Hagar to Abraham; sent her away in pregnancy (Ge 16). Name changed; Isaac promised (Ge 17:15–21; 18:10–15; Heb 11:11). Taken by Abimelek as Abraham's sister; returned (Ge 20). Isaac born; Hagar and Ishmael sent away (Ge 21:1–21; Gal 4:21–31). Death (Ge 23).

†/‡ SATAN
Job 1: 6 and **S** also came with them.
Zec 3: 2 to **S**, "The LORD rebuke you, **S**!
Mk 4: 15 **S** comes and takes away the word
2Co 11: 14 **S** himself masquerades as an angel
12: 7 a messenger of **S**, to torment me.
Rev 12: 9 or **S**, who leads the whole world
20: 2 **S**, and bound him for a thousand
20: 7 **S** will be released from his prison

SATISFIED (SATISFY)
Isa 53: 11 he will see the light of life and be **s**;

SATISFIES (SATISFY)
Ps 103: 5 **s** your desires with good things

SATISFY (SATISFIED SATISFIES)
Isa 55: 2 and your labor on what does not **s**?

SAUL
1. Benjamite; anointed by Samuel as first king of Israel (1Sa 9–10). Defeated Ammonites (1Sa 11). Rebuked for offering sacrifice (1Sa 13:1–15). Defeated Philistines (1Sa 14). Rejected as king for failing to annihilate Amalekites (1Sa 15). Soothed from evil spirit by David (1Sa 16:14–23). Sent David against Goliath (1Sa 17). Jealousy and attempted murder of David (1Sa 18:1–11). Gave David Michal as wife (1Sa 18:12–30). Second attempt to kill David (1Sa 19). Anger at Jonathan (1Sa 20:26–34). Pursued David: killed priests at Nob (1Sa 22), went to Keilah and Ziph (1Sa 23), life spared by David at En Gedi (1Sa 24) and in his tent (1Sa 26). Rebuked by Samuel's spirit for consulting witch at Endor (1Sa 28). Wounded by Philistines; took his own life (1Sa 31; 1Ch 10).
2. See PAUL

SAVE (SAFE SAFETY SALVATION SAVED SAVIOR)
Isa 63: 1 proclaiming victory, mighty to **s**."
Mt 1: 21 because he will **s** his people
16: 25 wants to **s** their life will lose it,
Lk 19: 10 came to seek and to **s** the lost."
Jn 3: 17 but to **s** the world through him.
1Ti 1: 15 came into the world to **s** sinners—
Jas 5: 20 of their way will **s** them from death

SAVED (SAVE)
Ps 34: 6 he **s** him out of all his troubles.
Isa 45: 22 "Turn to me and be **s**, all you ends
Joel 2: 32 the name of the LORD will be **s**;
Mk 13: 13 stands firm to the end will be **s**.
16: 16 *believes and is baptized will be **s**,*
Jn 10: 9 enters through me will be **s**.
Ac 4: 12 mankind by which we must be **s**."
16: 30 "Sirs, what must I do to be **s**?"
Ro 9: 27 the sea, only the remnant will be **s**.
10: 9 him from the dead, you will be **s**.
1Co 3: 15 will suffer loss but yet will be **s**—
15: 2 By this gospel you are **s**, if you hold
Eph 2: 5 it is by grace you have been **s**.
2: 8 For it is by grace you have been **s**,
1Ti 2: 4 who wants all people to be **s**

‡ SAVIOR (SAVE)
Ps 89: 26 Father, my God, the Rock my **S**.'
Isa 43: 11 and apart from me there is no **s**.
Hos 13: 4 no God but me, no **S** except me.
Lk 1: 47 and my spirit rejoices in God my **S**,
2: 11 town of David a **S** has been born
Jn 4: 42 that this man really is the **S**
Eph 5: 23 his body, of which he is the **S**.
1Ti 4: 10 God, who is the **S** of all people,
Titus 2: 10 about God our **S** attractive.
2: 13 the glory of our great God and **S**,
3: 4 and love of God our **S** appeared,
1Jn 4: 14 his Son to be the **S** of the world.
Jude : 25 to the only God our **S** be glory,

SCALES
Lev 19: 36 Use honest **s** and honest weights,
Da 5: 27 You have been weighed on the **s**

SCAPEGOAT (GOAT)
Lev 16: 10 it into the wilderness as a **s**.

SCARLET
Isa 1: 18 "Though your sins are like **s**,

SCATTERED
Jer 31: 10 'He who **s** Israel will gather them
Ac 8: 4 who had been **s** preached the word

SCEPTER
Rev 19: 15 "He will rule them with an iron **s**."

SCHEMES
2Co 2: 11 For we are not unaware of his **s**.
Eph 6: 11 your stand against the devil's **s**.

SCOFFERS
2Pe 3: 3 that in the last days **s** will come,

SCORPION
Rev 9: 5 of the sting of a **s** when it strikes.

SCRIPTURE (SCRIPTURES)
Jn 10: 35 and **S** cannot be set aside—
1Ti 4: 13 yourself to the public reading of **S**,
2Ti 3: 16 All **S** is God-breathed and is useful
2Pe 1: 20 that no prophecy of **S** came

SCRIPTURES (SCRIPTURE)
Lk 24: 27 in all the **S** concerning himself.
Jn 5: 39 You study the **S** diligently because
Ac 17: 11 examined the **S** every day to see

SCROLL
Eze 3: 1 eat what is before you, eat this **s**;

SEA
Ex 14: 16 the Israelites can go through the **s**
Isa 57: 20 the wicked are like the tossing **s**,
Mic 7: 19 iniquities into the depths of the **s**.
Jas 1: 6 who doubts is like a wave of the **s**,
Rev 13: 1 I saw a beast coming out of the **s**.

SEAL (SEALS)
Jn 6: 27 God the Father has placed his **s**
2Co 1: 22 set his **s** of ownership on us,
Eph 1: 13 you were marked in him with a **s**,

SEALS (SEAL)
Rev 5: 2 "Who is worthy to break the **s**
6: 1 opened the first of the seven **s**.

SEARCH (SEARCHED SEARCHES SEARCHING)
Ps 4: 4 beds, **s** your hearts and be silent.
139: 23 **S** me, God, and know my heart;
Pr 2: 4 and **s** for it as for hidden treasure,
Jer 17: 10 "I the LORD **s** the heart
Eze 34: 16 I will **s** for the lost and bring back
Lk 15: 8 and **s** carefully until she finds it?

SEARCHED (SEARCH)
Ps 139: 1 You have **s** me, LORD, and you

SEARCHES (SEARCH)
Ro 8: 27 who **s** our hearts knows the mind
1Co 2: 10 The Spirit **s** all things, even the

SEARCHING (SEARCH)
Am 8: 12 east, **s** for the word of the LORD,

SEARED
1Ti 4: 2 whose consciences have been **s** as

SEASON
2Ti 4: 2 be prepared in **s** and out of **s**;

SEAT (SEATED SEATS)
Da 7: 9 and the Ancient of Days took his **s**.
2Co 5: 10 all appear before the judgment **s**

SEATED (SEAT)
Ps 47: 8 God is **s** on his holy throne.
Isa 6: 1 high and exalted, **s** on a throne;
Col 3: 1 Christ is, **s** at the right hand of God.

SEATS (SEAT)
Lk 11: 43 you love the most important **s**

SECRET (SECRETS)
Dt 29: 29 The **s** things belong to the LORD
Jdg 16: 6 "Tell me the **s** of your great
Ps 90: 8 you, our **s** sins in the light of your
Pr 11: 13 but a trustworthy person keeps a **s**.
Mt 6: 4 so that your giving may be in **s**.
2Co 4: 2 we have renounced **s** and shameful
Php 4: 12 have learned the **s** of being content

SECRETS (SECRET)
Ps 44: 21 since he knows the **s** of the heart?
1Co 14: 25 as the **s** of their hearts are laid bare.

SECURE (SECURITY)
Ps 112: 8 Their hearts are **s**, they will have
Heb 6: 19 an anchor for the soul, firm and **s**.

SECURITY (SECURE)
Job 31: 24 or said to pure gold, 'You are my **s**,'

SEED (SEEDS)
Lk 8: 11 The **s** is the word of God.
1Co 3: 6 I planted the **s**, Apollos watered it,
2Co 9: 10 he who supplies **s** to the sower
Gal 3: 29 you are Abraham's **s**, and heirs
1Pe 1: 23 again, not of perishable **s**,

SEEDS (SEED)
Jn 12: 24 But if it dies, it produces many **s**.
Gal 3: 16 Scripture does not say "and to **s**,"

SEEK (SEEKS SELF-SEEKING)
Dt 4: 29 you will find him if you **s** him
1Ch 28: 9 If you **s** him, he will be found
2Ch 7: 14 pray and **s** my face and turn
Ps 119: 10 I **s** you with all my heart; do not let
Isa 55: 6 **S** the LORD while he may be
65: 1 found by those who did not **s** me.
Mt 6: 33 But **s** first his kingdom and his
Lk 19: 10 For the Son of Man came to **s**
Ro 10: 20 found by those who did not **s** me;
1Co 7: 27 Do not **s** to be released.

SEEKS (SEEK)
Jn 4: 23 the kind of worshipers the Father **s**.

SEER
1Sa 9: 9 of today used to be called a **s**.)

SELF-CONTROL (CONTROL)
1Co 7: 5 tempt you because of your lack of **s**.
Gal 5: 23 gentleness and **s**.
2Pe 1: 6 and to knowledge, **s**; and to **s**,

SELF-CONTROLLED (CONTROL)
1Ti 3: 2 his wife, temperate, **s**, respectable,
Titus 1: 8 what is good, who is **s**, upright,
2: 2 worthy of respect, **s**, and sound
2: 5 to be **s** and pure, to be busy
2: 6 encourage the young men to be **s**.
2: 12 to live **s**, upright and godly lives

SELF-INDULGENCE
Mt 23: 25 inside they are full of greed and **s**.

SELFISH
Ps 119: 36 statutes and not toward **s** gain.
Pr 18: 1 unfriendly person pursues **s** ends
Gal 5: 20 fits of rage, **s** ambition, dissensions,
Php 1: 17 preach Christ out of **s** ambition,
2: 3 Do nothing out of **s** ambition
Jas 3: 14 envy and **s** ambition in your hearts,
3: 16 you have envy and **s** ambition,

SELF-SEEKING (SEEK)
1Co 13: 5 it is not **s**, it is not easily angered,

SEND (SENDING SENT)
Isa 6: 8 And I said, "Here am I. **S** me!"

† Please see the "Hebrew to English Translation Chart," p. xix.
‡ Please see "Key New Testament Terms," p. 1584.

† Please see the "Hebrew to English Translation Chart," p. xix.

Ro 5: 20 But where **s** increased,
6: 11 count yourselves dead to **s** but alive
6: 23 For the wages of **s** is death,
14: 23 that does not come from faith is **s**.
2Co 5: 21 God made him who had no **s** to be **s**
Gal 6: 1 if someone is caught in a **s**,
Heb 9: 26 to do away with **s** by the sacrifice
11: 25 to enjoy the fleeting pleasures of **s**.
12: 1 and the **s** that so easily entangles.
1Pe 2: 22 "He committed no **s**, and no deceit
1Jn 1: 8 If we claim to be without **s**,
3: 4 in fact, **s** is lawlessness.
3: 5 away our sins. And in him is no **s**.
3: 9 is born of God will continue to **s**,
5: 18 born of God does not continue to **s**;

SINCERE
Ro 12: 9 Love must be **s**. Hate what is evil;
Heb 10: 22 us draw near to God with a **s** heart

SINFUL (SIN)
Ps 51: 5 Surely I was **s** at birth,
Ro 7: 5 the **s** passions aroused by the law
1Pe 2: 11 to abstain from **s** desires,

SINFUL NATURE See FLESH

SING (SANG SINGING SONG SONGS)
Ps 30: 4 **S** the praises of the LORD, you his
47: 6 **S** praises to God, **s** praises; **s** praises
59: 16 in the morning I will **s** of your love
89: 1 I will **s** of the LORD's great love
101: 1 I will **s** of your love and justice;
Eph 5: 19 **S** and make music from your heart

SINGING (SING)
Ps 63: 5 **s** lips my mouth will praise you.
Ac 16: 25 were praying and **s** hymns to God,

SINNED (SIN)
2Sa 12: 13 "I have **s** against the LORD."
Job 1: 5 "Perhaps my children have **s**
Ps 51: 4 have I **s** and done what is evil
Da 9: 5 we have **s** and done wrong.
Mic 7: 9 Because I have **s** against him, I will
Lk 15: 18 I have **s** against heaven and against
Ro 3: 23 for all have **s** and fall short
1Jn 1: 10 If we claim we have not **s**, we make

SINNER (SIN)
Ecc 9: 18 war, but one **s** destroys much good.
Lk 15: 7 heaven over one **s** who repents
18: 13 said, 'God, have mercy on me, a **s**.'
Jas 5: 20 Whoever turns a **s** from the error
1Pe 4: 18 become of the ungodly and the **s**?"

SINNERS (SIN)
Ps 1: 1 stand in the way that **s** take or sit
Pr 23: 17 Do not let your heart envy **s**,
Mt 9: 13 come to call the righteous, but **s**."
Ro 5: 8 While we were still **s**, Christ died
1Ti 1: 15 came into the world to save **s**—

SINNING (SIN)
Ex 20: 20 be with you to keep you from **s**."
1Co 15: 34 senses as you ought, and stop **s**;
Heb 10: 26 If we deliberately keep on **s** after
1Jn 3: 6 one who lives in him keeps on **s**.
3: 9 they cannot go on **s**, because they

SINS (SIN)
Ezr 9: 6 because our **s** are higher than our
Ps 19: 13 your servant also from willful **s**;
32: 1 are forgiven, whose **s** are covered.
103: 3 who forgives all your **s** and heals
130: 3 LORD, kept a record of **s**, Lord,
Pr 28: 13 Whoever conceals their **s** does not
Isa 1: 18 "Though your **s** are like scarlet,
43: 25 and remembers your **s** no more.
59: 2 your **s** have hidden his face
Eze 18: 4 The one who **s** is the one who will
Mt 1: 21 will save his people from their **s**."
18: 15 "If your brother or sister **s**,
Lk 11: 4 Forgive us our **s**, for we also forgive
everyone who **s** against us.
17: 3 your brother or sister **s** against you,
Ac 22: 16 be baptized and wash your **s** away,
1Co 15: 3 Christ died for our **s** according
Eph 2: 1 dead in your transgressions and **s**,
Col 2: 13 He forgave us all our **s**,
Heb 1: 3 he had provided purification for **s**,
7: 27 He sacrificed for their **s** once for all
8: 12 will remember their **s** no more."
Heb 10: 12 for all time one sacrifice for **s**,
Jas 5: 16 Therefore confess your **s** to each
5: 20 and cover over a multitude of **s**.
1Pe 2: 24 so that we might die to **s** and live
3: 18 For Christ also suffered once for **s**,
1Jn 1: 9 If we confess our **s**, he is faithful
1: 9 will forgive us our **s** and purify us
Rev 1: 5 freed us from our **s** by his blood,

SITS
Ps 99: 1 he **s** enthroned between
Isa 40: 22 He **s** enthroned above the circle
Mt 19: 28 Son of Man **s** on his glorious throne,
Rev 4: 9 thanks to him who **s** on the throne

SKIN
Job 19: 20 escaped only by the **s** of my teeth.
19: 26 And after my **s** has been destroyed,
Jer 13: 23 Can an Ethiopian change his **s**

SLAIN (SLAY)
Rev 5: 12 who was **s**, to receive power

SLANDER (SLANDERED SLANDERERS)
Lev 19: 16 spreading **s** among your people.
1Ti 5: 14 the enemy no opportunity for **s**.
Titus 3: 2 to **s** no one, to be peaceable

SLANDERED (SLANDER)
1Co 4: 13 when we are **s**, we answer kindly.

SLANDERERS (SLANDER)
Ro 1: 30 **s**, God-haters, insolent,
1Co 6: 10 nor drunkards nor **s** nor swindlers
Titus 2: 3 not to be **s** or addicted to much

SLAUGHTER
Isa 53: 7 he was led like a lamb to the **s**,

†/‡ SLAVE (SLAVERY SLAVES)
Ge 21: 10 "Get rid of that **s** woman and her
Mt 20: 27 wants to be first must be your **s**—
Jn 8: 34 everyone who sins is a **s** to sin.
1Co 12: 13 whether Jews or Gentiles, **s** or free
Gal 3: 28 Jew nor Gentile, neither **s** nor free,
4: 30 the **s** woman's son will never share

SLAVERY (SLAVE)
Gal 4: 3 in **s** under the elemental spiritual

SLAVES (SLAVE)
Ro 6: 6 we should no longer be **s** to sin—
6: 22 and have become **s** of God,
2Pe 2: 19 for "people are **s** to whatever has

SLAY (SLAIN)
Job 13: 15 Though he **s** me, yet will I hope

SLEEP (SLEEPING)
Ps 121: 4 Israel will neither slumber nor **s**.
1Co 15: 51 We will not all **s**, but we will all be

SLEEPING (SLEEP)
Mk 13: 36 do not let him find you **s**.

SLOW
Ex 34: 6 and gracious God, **s** to anger,
Jas 1: 19 **s** to speak and **s** to become angry,
2Pe 3: 9 The Lord is not **s** in keeping his

SLUGGARD (SLUGGARDS)
Pr 6: 6 Go to the ant, you **s**;

SLUGGARDS (SLUGGARD)
Pr 20: 4 **S** do not plow in season;

SLUMBER
Ps 121: 3 he who watches over you will not **s**;
Pr 6: 10 little **s**, a little folding of the hands
Ro 13: 11 for you to wake up from your **s**,

SNAKE (SNAKES)
Nu 21: 8 "Make a **s** and put it up on a pole;
Pr 23: 32 In the end it bites like a **s**
Jn 3: 14 lifted up the **s** in the wilderness,

SNAKES (SNAKE)
Mt 10: 16 Therefore be as shrewd as **s** and as
Mk 16: 18 *they will pick up* **s**

SNATCH (SNATCHING)
Jn 10: 28 no one will **s** them out of my hand.

SNATCHING (SNATCH)
Jude : 23 save others by **s** them from the fire;

SNOW
Ps 51: 7 me, and I will be whiter than **s**.

SOAR
Isa 40: 31 They will **s** on wings like eagles;

SODOM
Ge 19: 24 rained down burning sulfur on **S**
Ro 9: 29 we would have become like **S**,

SOIL
Ge 4: 2 kept flocks, and Cain worked the **s**.
Mt 13: 23 the seed falling on good **s** refers

SOLDIER
1Co 9: 7 Who serves as a **s** at his own
2Ti 2: 3 like a good **s** of Christ Jesus.

SOLE
Dt 28: 65 resting place for the **s** of your foot.
Isa 1: 6 From the **s** of your foot to the top

SOLID
2Ti 2: 19 God's **s** foundation stands firm,
Heb 5: 12 You need milk, not **s** food!

SOLOMON
Son of David by Bathsheba; king of Judah (2Sa 12:24; 1Ch 3:5, 10). Appointed king by David (1Ki 1); adversaries Adonijah, Joab, Shimei killed by Benaiah (1Ki 2). Asked for wisdom (1Ki 3; 2Ch 1). Judged between two prostitutes (1Ki 3:16–28). Built temple (1Ki 5–7; 2Ch 2–5); prayer of dedication (1Ki 8; 2Ch 6). Visited by Queen of Sheba (1Ki 10; 2Ch 9). Wives turned his heart from God (1Ki 11:1–13). Jeroboam rebelled against (1Ki 11:26–40). Death (1Ki 11:41–43; 2Ch 9:29–31).
Proverbs of (1Ki 4:32; Pr 1:1; 10:1; 25:1); psalms of (Ps 72; 127); song of (SS 1:1).

‡ SON (SONS)
Ge 22: 2 said, "Take your **s**, your only **s**,
Ex 11: 5 Every firstborn **s** in Egypt will die,
Dt 21: 18 rebellious **s** who does not obey his
Ps 2: 7 He said to me, "You are my **s**;
2: 12 Kiss his **s**, or he will be angry
Pr 10: 1 A wise **s** brings joy to his father,
Isa 7: 14 will conceive and give birth to a **s**,
Hos 11: 1 and out of Egypt I called my **s**.
Mt 2: 15 "Out of Egypt I called my **s**."
3: 17 said, "This is my **S**, whom I love;
11: 27 knows the **S** except the Father,
11: 27 knows the Father except the **S**
16: 16 Messiah, the **S** of the living God."
17: 5 said, "This is my **S**, whom I love;
20: 18 the **S** of Man will be delivered over
24: 30 appear the sign of the **S** of Man
24: 44 because the **S** of Man will come
27: 54 "Surely he was the **S** of God!"
28: 19 and of the **S** and of the Holy Spirit,
Mk 10: 45 even the **S** of Man did not come
14: 62 you will see the **S** of Man sitting
Lk 9: 58 the **S** of Man has no place to lay his
18: 8 when the **S** of Man comes, will he
19: 10 For the **S** of Man came to seek
Jn 3: 14 so the **S** of Man must be lifted up,
3: 16 that he gave his one and only **S**,
17: 1 Glorify your **S**, that your **S** may
Ro 8: 29 conformed to the image of his **S**,
8: 32 He who did not spare his own **S**,
1Co 15: 28 the **S** himself will be made subject
Gal 4: 30 for the slave woman's **s** will never
1Th 1: 10 and to wait for his **S** from heaven,
Heb 1: 2 days he has spoken to us by his **S**,
10: 29 punished who has trampled the **S**
1Jn 1: 7 Jesus, his **S**, purifies us from all sin.
4: 9 only **S** into the world that we might
5: 5 believes that Jesus is the **S** of God.
5: 11 eternal life, and this life is in his **S**.

SONG (SING)
Ps 40: 3 He put a new **s** in my mouth,
96: 1 Sing to the LORD a new **s**;
149: 1 Sing to the LORD a new **s**,
Isa 49: 13 burst into **s**, you mountains!
55: 12 hills will burst into **s** before you,
Rev 5: 9 And they sang a new **s**, saying:
15: 3 sang the **s** of God's servant Moses

SONGS (SING)
Job 35: 10 Maker, who gives **s** in the night,
Ps 100: 2 come before him with joyful **s**.
Eph 5: 19 hymns, and **s** from the Spirit.
Jas 5: 13 Let them sing **s** of praise.

† Please see the "Hebrew to English Translation Chart," p. xix.
‡ Please see "Key New Testament Terms," p. 1584.

SONS (SON)
Joel 2: 28 **s** and daughters will prophesy,
2Co 6: 18 you will be my **s** and daughters,

SORROW
Jer 31: 12 garden, and they will **s** no more.
Ro 9: 2 I have great **s** and unceasing
2Co 7: 10 Godly **s** brings repentance that

† SOUL (SOULS)
Dt 6: 5 and with all your **s** and with all
10: 12 all your heart and with all your **s**,
Jos 22: 5 all your heart and with all your **s**."
Ps 23: 3 he refreshes my **s**. He guides me
42: 1 of water, so my **s** pants for you,
42: 11 Why, my **s**, are you downcast?
103: 1 Praise the LORD, my **s**;
Pr 13: 19 A longing fulfilled is sweet to the **s**,
Mt 10: 28 of the One who can destroy both **s**
16: 26 the whole world, yet forfeit their **s**?
22: 37 with all your **s** and with all your
Heb 4: 12 it penetrates even to dividing **s**

SOULS (SOUL)
Jer 6: 16 and you will find rest for your **s**.
Mt 11: 29 and you will find rest for your **s**.

SOUND
1Co 14: 8 the trumpet does not **s** a clear call,
15: 52 the trumpet will **s**, the dead will
2Ti 4: 3 will not put up with **s** doctrine.

SOVEREIGN
Da 4: 25 Most High is **s** over all kingdoms

SOW (SOWS)
Job 4: 8 and those who **s** trouble reap it.
Mt 6: 26 they do not **s** or reap or store away
2Pe 2: 22 "A **s** that is washed returns to her

SOWS (SOW)
2Co 9: 6 and whoever **s** generously will

SPARE (SPARES)
Ro 8: 32 He who did not **s** his own Son,
11: 21 God did not **s** the natural branches,

SPARES (SPARE)
Pr 13: 24 Whoever **s** the rod hates their

SPEARS
Isa 2: 4 and their **s** into pruning hooks.
Joel 3: 10 and your pruning hooks into **s**.
Mic 4: 3 and their **s** into pruning hooks.

SPECTACLE
1Co 4: 9 have been made a **s** to the whole
Col 2: 15 he made a public **s** of them,

SPIN
Mt 6: 28 They do not labor or **s**.

† / ‡ SPIRIT (SPIRITS SPIRITUAL)
Ge 1: 2 the **S** of God was hovering over
6: 3 said, "My **S** will not contend
2Ki 2: 9 inherit a double portion of your **s**,"
Job 33: 4 The **S** of God has made me;
Ps 31: 5 Into your hands I commit my **s**;
51: 10 and renew a steadfast **s** within me.
51: 11 or take your Holy **S** from me.
51: 17 My sacrifice, O God, is a broken **s**;
139: 7 Where can I go from your **S**?
Isa 57: 15 to revive the **s** of the lowly
63: 10 rebelled and grieved his Holy **S**.
Eze 11: 19 heart and put a new **s** in them;
36: 26 a new heart and put a new **s** in you;
Joel 2: 28 I will pour out my **S** on all people.
Zec 4: 6 but by my **S**,' says the LORD
Mt 1: 18 to be pregnant through the Holy **S**.
3: 11 He will baptize you with the Holy **S**
3: 16 he saw the **S** of God descending
4: 1 led by the **S** into the wilderness
5: 3 "Blessed are the poor in **s**, for
26: 41 The **s** is willing, but the flesh is
28: 19 and of the Son and of the Holy **S**,
Lk 1: 80 child grew and became strong in **s**;
11: 13 in heaven give the Holy **S** to those
Jn 4: 24 God is **s**, and his worshipers must worship in the **S**
7: 39 that time the **S** had not been given,
14: 26 the Holy **S**, whom the Father will
16: 13 But when he, the **S** of truth, comes,
20: 22 and said, "Receive the Holy **S**.
Ac 1: 5 will be baptized with the Holy **S**."
2: 4 tongues as the **S** enabled them.
2: 38 will receive the gift of the Holy **S**.
6: 3 who are known to be full of the **S**
19: 2 "Did you receive the Holy **S**
Ro 8: 9 if indeed the **S** of God lives in you.
8: 26 the **S** helps us in our weakness.
1Co 2: 10 God has revealed to us by his **S**.
2: 10 The **S** searches all things,
2: 14 without the **S** does not accept
3: 1 as people who live by the **S** but as
6: 19 bodies are temples of the Holy **S**,
12: 1 Now about the gifts of the **S**,
12: 13 we were all baptized by one **S**
12: 13 and we were all given the one **S**
14: 1 and eagerly desire gifts of the **S**,
2Co 3: 6 the letter kills, but the **S** gives life.
5: 5 who has given us the **S** as a deposit,
Gal 5: 16 say, walk by the **S**, and you will not
5: 22 But the fruit of the **S** is love, joy,
5: 25 Since we live by the **S**, let us keep
Gal 6: 1 who live by the **S** should restore
Eph 1: 13 with a seal, the promised Holy **S**,
4: 30 do not grieve the Holy **S** of God,
5: 18 Instead, be filled with the **S**,
5: 19 hymns, and songs from the **S**.
6: 17 of salvation and the sword of the **S**,
1Th 5: 19 Do not quench the **S**.
2Th 2: 13 the sanctifying work of the **S**
Heb 4: 12 even to dividing soul and **s**,
1Pe 3: 4 beauty of a gentle and quiet **s**,
2Pe 1: 21 were carried along by the Holy **S**.
1Jn 4: 1 do not believe every **s**, but test

SPIRITS (SPIRIT)
1Co 12: 10 another distinguishing between **s**,
14: 32 The **s** of prophets are subject
1Jn 4: 1 but test the **s** to see whether they

SPIRITUAL (SPIRIT)
Ro 12: 11 but keep your **s** fervor,
1Co 2: 13 the Spirit, explaining **s** realities
15: 44 a natural body, it is raised a **s** body.
Eph 1: 3 realms with every **s** blessing
6: 12 against the **s** forces of evil
1Pe 2: 2 crave pure **s** milk, so that by it you
2: 5 offering **s** sacrifices acceptable

SPLENDOR
1Ch 16: 29 the LORD in the **s** of his holiness.
29: 11 glory and the majesty and the **s**,
Job 37: 22 of the north he comes in golden **s**;
Ps 29: 2 the LORD in the **s** of his holiness.
45: 3 clothe yourself with **s** and majesty.
96: 6 **S** and majesty are before him;
96: 9 the LORD in the **s** of his holiness;
104: 1 you are clothed with **s** and majesty.
145: 5 of the glorious **s** of your majesty—
Isa 61: 3 the LORD for the display of his **s**.
63: 1 robed in **s**, striding forward
Lk 9: 30 Elijah, appeared in glorious **s**,
2Th 2: 8 and destroy by the **s** of his coming.

SPOIL
Ps 119:162 promise like one who finds great **s**.

SPOTLESS
2Pe 3: 14 make every effort to be found **s**,

SPREAD (SPREADING)
Ac 12: 24 the word of God continued to **s**
19: 20 way the word of the Lord **s** widely

SPREADING (SPREAD)
1Th 3: 2 in God's service in **s** the gospel

SPRING
Jer 2: 13 forsaken me, the **s** of living water,
Jn 4: 14 in them a **s** of water welling
Jas 3: 12 can a salt **s** produce fresh water.

SPUR
Heb 10: 24 how we may **s** one another

SPURNS
Pr 15: 5 A fool **s** a parent's discipline,

STAFF
Ps 23: 4 your rod and your **s**, they comfort

STAKES
Isa 54: 2 your cords, strengthen your **s**.

STAND (STANDING STANDS)
Ex 14: 13 **S** firm and you will see
2Ch 20: 17 **s** firm and see the deliverance
Ps 1: 5 Therefore the wicked will not **s**
40: 2 rock and gave me a firm place to **s**.
119:120 fear of you; I **s** in awe of your laws.
Eze 22: 30 **s** before me in the gap on behalf
Zec 14: 4 day his feet will **s** on the Mount
Mt 12: 25 divided against itself will not **s**.
Ro 14: 10 we will all **s** before God's judgment
1Co 15: 58 dear brothers and sisters, **s** firm.
Eph 6: 14 **S** firm then, with the belt of truth
2Th 2: 15 firm and hold fast to the teachings
Jas 5: 8 be patient and **s** firm,
Rev 3: 20 I **s** at the door and knock.

STANDING (STAND)
Ex 3: 5 where you are **s** is holy ground."
Jos 5: 15 the place where you are **s** is holy."
1Pe 5: 9 Resist him, **s** firm in the faith,

STANDS (STAND)
Ps 89: 2 that your love **s** firm forever,
119: 89 it **s** firm in the heavens.
2Ti 2: 19 God's solid foundation **s** firm,

STAR (STARS)
Nu 24: 17 A **s** will come out of Jacob;
Rev 22: 16 David, and the bright Morning **S**."

STARS (STAR)
Da 12: 3 like the **s** for ever and ever.
Php 2: 15 you will shine among them like **s**

STEADFAST
Ps 51: 10 and renew a **s** spirit within me.
Isa 26: 3 peace those whose minds are **s**,
1Pe 5: 10 and make you strong, firm and **s**.

STEAL
Ex 20: 15 "You shall not **s**.
Mt 19: 18 you shall not **s**, you shall not give
Eph 4: 28 has been stealing must **s** no longer,

STEP (STEPS)
Gal 5: 25 let us keep in **s** with the Spirit.

STEPS (STEP)
Pr 16: 9 but the LORD establishes their **s**.
Jer 10: 23 it is not for them to direct their **s**.
1Pe 2: 21 that you should follow in his **s**.

STICKS
Pr 18: 24 there is a friend who **s** closer than

STIFF-NECKED
Ex 34: 9 Although this is a **s** people,

STILL
Ps 46: 10 "Be **s**, and know that I am God;
Zec 2: 13 Be **s** before the LORD,

STIRS
Pr 6: 19 a person who **s** up conflict
10: 12 Hatred **s** up conflict, but love
15: 1 wrath, but a harsh word **s** up anger.
29: 22 An angry person **s** up conflict,

STONE (CORNERSTONE MILLSTONE)
1Sa 17: 50 the Philistine with a sling and a **s**;
Isa 8: 14 and Judah he will be a **s** that causes
Eze 11: 19 remove from them their heart of **s**
Mk 16: 3 "Who will roll the **s** away
Lk 4: 3 God, tell this **s** to become bread."
Jn 8: 7 *the first to throw a **s** at her."*
2Co 3: 3 not on tablets of **s** but on tablets

STORE
Pr 10: 14 The wise **s** up knowledge,
Mt 6: 19 "Do not **s** up for yourselves

STOREHOUSE (HOUSE)
Mal 3: 10 Bring the whole tithe into the **s**,

STRAIGHT
Pr 3: 6 and he will make your paths **s**.
4: 25 Let your eyes look **s** ahead;
15: 21 understanding keeps a **s** course.
Jn 1: 23 'Make **s** the way for the Lord.'"

STRAIN
Mt 23: 24 You **s** out a gnat but swallow

STRANGER
Mt 25: 35 I was a **s** and you invited me in,
Jn 10: 5 But they will never follow a **s**;

STRAPS
Mk 1: 7 **s** of whose sandals I am not worthy

† Please see the "Hebrew to English Translation Chart," p. xix.
‡ Please see "Key New Testament Terms," p. 1584.

STREAMS
Ps 1: 3 person is like a tree planted by **s**
46: 4 a river whose **s** make glad the city
Ecc 1: 7 All **s** flow into the sea, yet the sea is

STRENGTH (STRONG)
Ex 15: 2 "The LORD is my **s** and my
Dt 6: 5 all your soul and with all your **s**.
2Sa 22: 33 It is God who arms me with **s**
Ne 8: 10 the joy of the LORD is your **s**."
Ps 28: 7 The LORD is my **s** and my shield;
46: 1 God is our refuge and **s**,
96: 7 ascribe to the LORD glory and **s**.
118: 14 The LORD is my **s** and my
147: 10 pleasure is not in the **s** of the horse,
Isa 40: 31 in the LORD will renew their **s**.
Mk 12: 30 all your mind and with all your **s**.'
1Co 1: 25 of God is stronger than human **s**.
Php 4: 13 this through him who gives me **s**.
1Pe 4: 11 do so with the **s** God provides,

STRENGTHEN (STRONG)
2Ch 16: 9 to **s** those whose hearts are fully
Ps 119: 28 **s** me according to your word.
Isa 35: 3 **S** the feeble hands, steady the
41: 10 I will **s** you and help you;
Eph 3: 16 of his glorious riches he may **s** you
2Th 2: 17 and **s** you in every good deed
Heb 12: 12 **s** your feeble arms and weak knees.

STRIFE
Pr 20: 3 It is to one's honor to avoid **s**,
22: 10 out the mocker, and out goes **s**;

STRIKE
Ge 3: 15 your head, and you will **s** his heel."
Zec 13: 7 "**S** the shepherd, and the sheep will
Mt 26: 31 "'I will **s** the shepherd,

STRONG (STRENGTH STRENGTHEN)
Dt 31: 6 Be **s** and courageous. Do not be
1Ki 2: 2 "So be **s**, act like a man,
Pr 31: 17 her arms are **s** for her tasks.
SS 8: 6 for love is as **s** as death, its jealousy
Lk 2: 40 And the child grew and became **s**;
Ro 15: 1 We who are **s** ought to bear
1Co 1: 27 things of the world to shame the **s**.
16: 13 in the faith; be courageous; be **s**.
2Co 12: 10 For when I am weak, then I am **s**.
Eph 6: 10 be **s** in the Lord and in his mighty

STRUGGLE
Ro 15: 30 join me in my **s** by praying to God
Eph 6: 12 For our **s** is not against flesh
Heb 12: 4 In your **s** against sin, you have not

STUDY
Ezr 7: 10 Ezra had devoted himself to the **s**
Ecc 12: 12 end, and much **s** wearies the body.
Jn 5: 39 You **s** the Scriptures diligently

STUMBLE (STUMBLING)
Ps 37: 24 though he may **s**, he will not fall,
119:165 law, and nothing can make them **s**.
Isa 8: 14 be a stone that causes people to **s**
Jer 31: 9 a level path where they will not **s**,
Eze 7: 19 for it has caused them to **s** into sin.
1Co 10: 32 Do not cause anyone to **s**,
1Pe 2: 8 "A stone that causes people to **s**

STUMBLING (STUMBLE)
Ro 14: 13 your mind not to put any **s** block
1Co 8: 9 rights does not become a **s** block
2Co 6: 3 We put no **s** block in anyone's path,

SUBDUE
Ge 1: 28 fill the earth and **s** it.

SUBJECT (SUBJECTED)
1Co 14: 32 of prophets are **s** to the control
15: 28 the Son himself will be made **s**
Titus 2: 5 and to be **s** to their husbands,
2: 9 slaves to be **s** to their masters
3: 1 Remind the people to be **s** to rulers

SUBJECTED (SUBJECT)
Ro 8: 20 the creation was **s** to frustration,

SUBMISSION (SUBMIT)
1Co 14: 34 but must be in **s**, as the law says.
1Ti 2: 11 learn in quietness and full **s**.

SUBMISSIVE (SUBMIT)
Jas 3: 17 considerate, **s**, full of mercy

SUBMIT (SUBMISSION SUBMISSIVE SUBMITS)
Ro 13: 5 necessary to **s** to the authorities,
1Co 16: 16 to **s** to such people and to everyone
Eph 5: 21 **S** to one another out of reverence
Col 3: 18 **s** yourselves to your husbands, as is
Heb 12: 9 How much more should we **s**
13: 17 leaders and **s** to their authority,
Jas 4: 7 **S** yourselves, then, to God.
1Pe 2: 18 reverent fear of God **s** yourselves

SUBMITS (SUBMIT)
Eph 5: 24 Now as the church **s** to Christ,

SUCCESSFUL
Jos 1: 7 that you may be **s** wherever you go.
2Ki 18: 7 he was **s** in whatever he undertook.
2Ch 20: 20 in his prophets and you will be **s**."

SUFFER (SUFFERED SUFFERING SUFFERINGS SUFFERS)
Isa 53: 10 to crush him and cause him to **s**,
Mk 8: 31 Son of Man must **s** many things
Lk 24: 26 the Messiah have to **s** these things
24: 46 The Messiah will **s** and rise
Php 1: 29 believe in him, but also to **s** for him,
1Pe 4: 16 if you **s** as a Christian, do not be

SUFFERED (SUFFER)
Heb 2: 9 and honor because he **s** death,
2: 18 Because he himself **s** when he was
1Pe 2: 21 called, because Christ **s** for you,

SUFFERING (SUFFER)
Isa 53: 3 a man of **s**, and familiar with pain.
Ac 5: 41 been counted worthy of **s** disgrace
2Ti 1: 8 join with me in **s** for the gospel,

SUFFERINGS (SUFFER)
Ro 8: 17 if indeed we share in his **s** in order
8: 18 that our present **s** are not worth
2Co 1: 5 share abundantly in the **s** of Christ,
Php 3: 10 and participation in his **s**,

SUFFERS (SUFFER)
Pr 13: 20 for a companion of fools **s** harm.
1Co 12: 26 If one part **s**, every part **s** with it;

SUFFICIENT
2Co 12: 9 said to me, "My grace is **s** for you,

SUITABLE
Ge 2: 18 I will make a helper **s** for him."

SUN
Ecc 1: 9 there is nothing new under the **s**.
Mal 4: 2 the **s** of righteousness will rise
Mt 5: 45 He causes his **s** to rise on the evil
17: 2 His face shone like the **s**, and his
Rev 1: 16 His face was like the **s** shining in
21: 23 The city does not need the **s**

SUPERIOR
Heb 1: 4 as the name he has inherited is **s**
8: 6 he is mediator is **s** to the old one,

SUPREMACY
Col 1: 18 in everything he might have the **s**.

SURE
Nu 32: 23 you may be **s** that your sin will find
Dt 6: 17 Be **s** to keep the commands
14: 22 Be **s** to set aside a tenth of all
Isa 28: 16 cornerstone for a **s** foundation;

SURPASS (SURPASSES SURPASSING)
Pr 31: 29 noble things, but you **s** them all."

SURPASSES (SURPASS)
Mt 5: 20 that unless your righteousness **s**
Eph 3: 19 to know this love that **s** knowledge

SURPASSING (SURPASS)
Ps 150: 2 praise him for his **s** greatness.
2Co 3: 10 in comparison with the **s** glory.
9: 14 of the **s** grace God has given you.
Php 3: 8 a loss because of the **s** worth

SURROUNDED
Heb 12: 1 since we are **s** by such a great cloud

SUSPENDS
Job 26: 7 he **s** the earth over nothing.

SUSTAINING (SUSTAINS)
Heb 1: 3 **s** all things by his powerful word.

SUSTAINS (SUSTAINING)
Ps 18: 35 shield, and your right hand **s** me;
146: 9 the foreigner and **s** the fatherless
147: 6 The LORD **s** the humble but casts
Isa 50: 4 to know the word that **s** the weary.

SWALLOWED
1Co 15: 54 "Death has been **s** up in victory."
2Co 5: 4 so that what is mortal may be **s**

SWEAR
Mt 5: 34 I tell you, do not **s** an oath at all:

SWORD (SWORDS)
Ps 45: 3 Gird your **s** on your side,
Mt 10: 34 not come to bring peace, but a **s**.
26: 52 all who draw the **s** will die by the **s**.
Lk 2: 35 a **s** will pierce your own soul too."
Ro 13: 4 for rulers do not bear the **s** for no
Eph 6: 17 of salvation and the **s** of the Spirit,
Heb 4: 12 Sharper than any double-edged **s**,
Rev 1: 16 was a sharp, double-edged **s**.

SWORDS (SWORD)
Pr 12: 18 words of the reckless pierce like **s**,
Isa 2: 4 They will beat their **s**
Joel 3: 10 Beat your plowshares into **s**

SYMPATHETIC
1Pe 3: 8 be **s**, love one another,

‡ SYNAGOGUE
Lk 4: 16 the Sabbath day he went into the **s**,
Ac 17: 2 Paul went into the **s**, and on three

† TABERNACLE
Ex 40: 34 the glory of the LORD filled the **t**.

TABLE (TABLES)
Ps 23: 5 You prepare a **t** before me

TABLES (TABLE)
Ac 6: 2 word of God in order to wait on **t**.

TABLET (TABLETS)
Pr 3: 3 write them on the **t** of your heart.
7: 3 write them on the **t** of your heart.

TABLETS (TABLET)
Ex 31: 18 Sinai, he gave him the two **t**
Dt 10: 5 put the **t** in the ark I had made,
2Co 3: 3 not on **t** of stone but on **t** of human

TAKE (TAKEN TAKES TAKING TOOK)
Dt 12: 32 do not add to it or **t** away from it.
31: 26 "**T** this Book of the Law and place
Job 23: 10 But he knows the way that I **t**;
Ps 49: 17 for they will **t** nothing with them
51: 11 or **t** your Holy Spirit from me.
Mt 10: 38 Whoever does not **t** up their cross
11: 29 **T** my yoke upon you and learn
16: 24 deny themselves and **t** up their cross

TAKEN (TAKE)
Lev 6: 4 they have stolen or **t** by extortion,
Isa 6: 7 your guilt is **t** away and your sin
Mt 24: 40 one will be **t** and the other left.
Mk 16: 19 *them, he was **t** up into heaven*
1Ti 3: 16 on in the world, was **t** up in glory.

TAKES (TAKE)
1Ki 20: 11 not boast like one who **t** it off.'"
Jn 1: 29 who **t** away the sin of the world!
Rev 22: 19 if anyone **t** words away from this

TAKING (TAKE)
Php 2: 7 nothing by **t** the very nature

TALENT See BAGS

TAME
Jas 3: 8 no human being can **t** the tongue.

TASK
Mk 13: 34 each with their assigned **t**, and tells
Ac 20: 24 complete the **t** the Lord Jesus has
1Co 3: 5 the Lord has assigned to each his **t**.
2Co 2: 16 And who is equal to such a **t**?

TASTE (TASTED)
Ps 34: 8 **T** and see that the LORD is good;
Col 2: 21 Do not **t**! Do not touch!"?
Heb 2: 9 God he might **t** death for everyone.

TASTED (TASTE)
1Pe 2: 3 you have **t** that the Lord is good.

TAUGHT (TEACH)
Mt 7: 29 because he **t** as one who had
1Co 2: 13 but in words **t** by the Spirit,
Gal 1: 12 it from any man, nor was I **t** it;

---

† Please see the "Hebrew to English Translation Chart," p. xix.
‡ Please see "Key New Testament Terms," p. 1584.

TAX (TAXES)
Mt 22: 17 to pay the imperial **t** to Caesar
TAXES (TAX)
Ro 13: 7 you owe them: If you owe **t**, pay **t**;
TEACH (TAUGHT TEACHER TEACHERS TEACHES TEACHING)
Ex 33: 13 **t** me your ways so I may know you
Dt 4: 9 **T** them to your children and to
8: 3 to **t** you that man does not live
11: 19 **T** them to your children,
1Sa 12: 23 I will **t** you the way that is good
Ps 32: 8 **t** you in the way you should go;
51: 13 I will **t** transgressors your ways,
90: 12 **T** us to number our days, that we
143: 10 **T** me to do your will, for you are
Jer 31: 34 longer will they **t** their neighbor,
Lk 11: 1 "Lord, **t** us to pray, just as John
Jn 14: 26 will **t** you all things and will
1Ti 2: 12 I do not permit a woman to **t**
3: 2 respectable, hospitable, able to **t**,
Titus 2: 1 **t** what is appropriate to sound
Heb 8: 11 longer will they **t** their neighbor,
Jas 3: 1 that we who **t** will be judged more
1Jn 2: 27 you do not need anyone to **t** you.
TEACHER (TEACH)
Mt 10: 24 "The student is not above the **t**,
23: 8 for you have one **T**, and you are
Jn 13: 14 your Lord and **T**, have washed
TEACHERS (TEACH)
1Co 12: 28 prophets, third **t**, then miracles,
Eph 4: 11 the evangelists, the pastors and **t**,
Heb 5: 12 by this time you ought to be **t**,
TEACHES (TEACH)
1Ti 6: 3 If anyone **t** otherwise and does not
TEACHING (TEACH)
Pr 1: 8 and do not forsake your mother's **t**.
Mt 28: 20 **t** them to obey everything I have
Jn 7: 17 out whether my **t** comes from God
14: 23 who loves me will obey my **t**.
1Ti 4: 13 of Scripture, to preaching and to **t**.
2Ti 3: 16 is God-breathed and is useful for **t**,
Titus 2: 7 In your **t** show integrity,
TEAR (TEARS)
Rev 7: 17 God will wipe away every **t**
TEARS (TEAR)
Ps 126: 5 Those who sow with **t** will reap
Php 3: 18 and now tell you again even with **t**,
TEETH (TOOTH)
Mt 8: 12 will be weeping and gnashing of **t**."
TEMPERATE
1Ti 3: 2 reproach, faithful to his wife, **t**,
3: 11 not malicious talkers but **t**
Titus 2: 2 Teach the older men to be **t**,
TEMPEST
Ps 55: 8 shelter, far from the **t** and storm."
TEMPLE (TEMPLES)
1Ki 8: 27 How much less this **t** I have built!
Hab 2: 20 The LORD is in his holy **t**;
1Co 3: 16 that you yourselves are God's **t**
2Co 6: 16 For we are the **t** of the living God.
TEMPLES (TEMPLE)
Ac 17: 24 does not live in **t** built by human
1Co 6: 19 your bodies are **t** of the Holy Spirit,
TEMPT (TEMPTATION TEMPTED)
1Co 7: 5 Satan will not **t** you because of
TEMPTATION (TEMPT)
Mt 6: 13 lead us not into **t**, but deliver us
26: 41 pray so that you will not fall into **t**.
1Co 10: 13 No **t** has overtaken you except
TEMPTED (TEMPT)
Mt 4: 1 the wilderness to be **t** by the devil.
1Co 10: 13 not let you be **t** beyond what you
Heb 2: 18 he himself suffered when he was **t**,
2: 18 able to help those who are being **t**.
4: 15 but we have one who has been **t**
Jas 1: 13 For God cannot be **t** by evil,
TEN (TENTH TITHE TITHES)
Ex 34: 28 the **T** Commandments.
Ps 91: 7 side, **t** thousand at your right hand,
Mt 25: 28 give it to the one who has **t** bags.
Lk 15: 8 suppose a woman has **t** silver coins
TENTH (TEN)
Dt 14: 22 Be sure to set aside a **t** of all
TERRIBLE (TERROR)
2Ti 3: 1 There will be **t** times in the last
TERROR (TERRIBLE)
Ps 91: 5 You will not fear the **t** of night,
Lk 21: 26 People will faint from **t**,
Ro 13: 3 rulers hold no **t** for those who do
TEST (TESTED TESTS)
Dt 6: 16 your God to the **t** as you did
Ps 139: 23 **t** me and know my anxious
Ro 12: 2 you will be able to **t** and approve
1Co 3: 13 the fire will **t** the quality of each
1Jn 4: 1 **t** the spirits to see whether they are
TESTED (TEST)
Ge 22: 1 Some time later God **t** Abraham.
Job 23: 10 when he has **t** me, I will come forth
Pr 27: 21 but people are **t** by their praise.
1Ti 3: 10 They must first be **t**;
TESTIFY (TESTIMONY)
Jn 5: 39 These are the very Scriptures that **t**
TESTIMONY (TESTIFY)
Isa 8: 20 instruction and the **t** of warning.
Lk 18: 20 you shall not give false **t**,
2Ti 1: 8 be ashamed of the **t** about our Lord
TESTS (TEST)
Pr 17: 3 for gold, but the LORD **t** the heart.
1Th 2: 4 people but God, who **t** our hearts.
THADDAEUS
Apostle (Mt 10:3; Mk 3:18); probably also known as Judas son of James (Lk 6:16; Ac 1:13).
THANKFUL (THANKS)
Heb 12: 28 let us be **t**, and so worship God
THANKS (THANKFUL THANKSGIVING)
Ne 12: 31 assigned two large choirs to give **t**.
Ps 100: 4 give **t** to him and praise his name.
1Co 15: 57 But **t** be to God! He gives us
2Co 2: 14 But **t** be to God, who always leads
9: 15 **T** be to God for his indescribable
1Th 5: 18 give **t** in all circumstances;
THANKSGIVING (THANKS)
Ps 95: 2 Let us come before him with **t**
100: 4 Enter his gates with **t** and his
Php 4: 6 **t**, present your requests to God.
1Ti 4: 3 to be received with **t** by those who
THIEF (THIEVES)
1Th 5: 2 of the Lord will come like a **t**
Rev 16: 15 "Look, I come like a **t**!
THIEVES (THIEF)
1Co 6: 10 nor **t** nor the greedy nor drunkards
THINK (THOUGHT THOUGHTS)
Ro 12: 3 Do not **t** of yourself more highly
Php 4: 8 **t** about such things.
THIRST (THIRSTY)
Ps 69: 21 food and gave me vinegar for my **t**.
Mt 5: 6 hunger and **t** for righteousness,
Jn 4: 14 the water I give them will never **t**.
THIRSTY (THIRST)
Isa 55: 1 all you who are **t**,
Jn 7: 37 "Let anyone who is **t** come to me
Rev 22: 17 Let the one who is **t** come;
THOMAS
Apostle (Mt 10:3; Mk 3:18; Lk 6:15; Jn 11:16; 14:5; 21:2; Ac 1:13). Doubted resurrection (Jn 20:24–28).
THORN (THORNS)
2Co 12: 7 I was given a **t** in my flesh,
THORNS (THORN)
Nu 33: 55 in your eyes and **t** in your sides.
Mt 27: 29 twisted together a crown of **t** and
Heb 6: 8 land that produces **t** and thistles is
THOUGHT (THINK)
Pr 14: 15 the prudent give **t** to their steps.
1Co 13: 11 I talked like a child, I **t** like a child,
THOUGHTS (THINK)
Ps 139: 23 test me and know my anxious **t**.
Isa 55: 8 "For my **t** are not your **t**, neither
Heb 4: 12 it judges the **t** and attitudes
THREE
Ecc 4: 12 of **t** strands is not quickly broken.
Mt 12: 40 the Son of Man will be **t** days and **t** nights in the heart of the earth.
18: 20 where two or **t** gather in my name,
27: 63 said, 'After **t** days I will rise again.'
1Co 13: 13 And now these **t** remain:
14: 27 or at the most **t**—should speak,
2Co 13: 1 testimony of two or **t** witnesses."
THRESHING
2Sa 24: 18 altar to the LORD on the **t** floor
THRONE (ENTHRONED)
2Sa 7: 16 your **t** will be established
Ps 45: 6 Your **t**, O God, will last for ever
47: 8 God is seated on his holy **t**.
Isa 6: 1 high and exalted, seated on a **t**;
66: 1 "Heaven is my **t**, and the earth is
Heb 4: 16 then approach God's **t** of grace
12: 2 at the right hand of the **t** of God.
Rev 4: 10 They lay their crowns before the **t**
20: 11 I saw a great white **t** and him who
22: 3 The **t** of God and of the Lamb will
THROW
Jn 8: 7 *the first to **t** a stone at her."*
Heb 10: 35 So do not **t** away your confidence;
12: 1 let us **t** off everything that hinders
THWART
Isa 14: 27 has purposed, and who can **t** him?
TIBNI
King of Israel (1Ki 16:21–22).
TIME (TIMES)
Est 4: 14 royal position for such a **t** as this?"
Da 7: 25 be delivered into his hands for a **t**, times and half a **t**.
Hos 10: 12 for it is **t** to seek the LORD,
Ro 9: 9 "At the appointed **t** I will return,
Heb 9: 28 and he will appear a second **t**,
10: 12 had offered for all **t** one sacrifice
1Pe 4: 17 For it is **t** for judgment to begin
TIMES (TIME)
Ps 9: 9 a stronghold in **t** of trouble.
31: 15 My **t** are in your hands;
62: 8 Trust in him at all **t**, you people;
Pr 17: 17 A friend loves at all **t**,
Am 5: 13 in such **t**, for the **t** are evil.
Mt 18: 21 sins against me? Up to seven **t**?"
Ac 1: 7 "It is not for you to know the **t**
Rev 12: 14 care of for a time, **t** and half a time,
TIMID
2Ti 1: 7 God gave us does not make us **t**,
TIMOTHY
Believer from Lystra (Ac 16:1). Joined Paul on second missionary journey (Ac 16–20). Sent to settle problems at Corinth (1Co 4:17; 16:10). Led church at Ephesus (1Ti 1:3). Co-writer with Paul (1Th 1:1; 2Th 1:1; Phm 1).
TIRE (TIRED)
2Th 3: 13 never **t** of doing what is good.
TIRED (TIRE)
Ex 17: 12 When Moses' hands grew **t**,
Isa 40: 28 He will not grow **t** or weary,
TITHE (TEN)
Lev 27: 30 "'A **t** of everything
Dt 12: 17 your own towns the **t** of your grain
Mal 3: 10 Bring the whole **t**
TITHES (TEN)
Mal 3: 8 "In **t** and offerings.
TITUS
Gentile co-worker of Paul (Gal 2:1–3; 2Ti 4:10); sent to Corinth (2Co 2:13; 7–8; 12:18), Crete (Titus 1:4–5).
TODAY
Mt 6: 11 Give us **t** our daily bread.
Lk 23: 43 **t** you will be with me in paradise."
Heb 3: 13 as long as it is called "**T**,"
13: 8 Christ is the same yesterday and **t**
† TOIL
Ge 3: 17 through painful **t** you will eat food
TOLERATE
Hab 1: 13 then do you **t** the treacherous?
Rev 2: 2 that you cannot **t** wicked people,

† Please see the "Hebrew to English Translation Chart," p. xix.

† Please see the "Hebrew to English Translation Chart," p. xix.

Isa 53: 6 each of us has **t** to our own way;
Hos 7: 8 Ephraim is a flat loaf not **t** over.
Joel 2: 31 The sun will be **t** to darkness
Ro 3: 12 All have **t** away, they have together

TURNS (TURN)
2Sa 22: 29 the LORD **t** my darkness
Pr 15: 1 A gentle answer **t** away wrath,
Isa 44: 25 of the wise and **t** it into nonsense,
Jas 5: 20 Whoever **t** a sinner from the error

TWELVE
Ge 49: 28 All these are the **t** tribes of Israel,
Mt 10: 1 Jesus called his **t** disciples to him

TWINKLING
1Co 15: 52 a flash, in the **t** of an eye, at the last

UNAPPROACHABLE
1Ti 6: 16 immortal and who lives in **u** light,

UNBELIEF (UNBELIEVER UNBELIEVERS UNBELIEVING)
Mk 9: 24 help me overcome my **u**!"
Ro 11: 20 they were broken off because of **u**,
Heb 3: 19 able to enter, because of their **u**.

UNBELIEVER (UNBELIEF)
1Co 7: 15 But if the **u** leaves, let it be so.
10: 27 If an **u** invites you to a meal
14: 24 if an **u** or an inquirer comes in
2Co 6: 15 have in common with an **u**?
1Ti 5: 8 the faith and is worse than an **u**.

UNBELIEVERS (UNBELIEF)
1Co 6: 6 and this in front of **u**!
2Co 6: 14 Do not be yoked together with **u**.

UNBELIEVING (UNBELIEF)
1Co 7: 14 the **u** husband has been sanctified
7: 14 and the **u** wife has been sanctified
Rev 21: 8 But the cowardly, the **u**, the vile,

UNCERTAIN
1Ti 6: 17 which is so **u**, but to put their hope

UNCHANGEABLE
Heb 6: 18 that, by two **u** things in which it is

UNCIRCUMCISED
1Sa 17: 26 Who is this **u** Philistine that he
Col 3: 11 or Jew, circumcised or **u**,

UNCIRCUMCISION
1Co 7: 19 is nothing and **u** is nothing.
Gal 5: 6 neither circumcision nor **u** has any

† UNCLEAN
Isa 6: 5 For I am a man of **u** lips, and I live
Ro 14: 14 Jesus, that nothing is **u** in itself.
2Co 6: 17 Touch no **u** thing, and I will

UNCONCERNED
Eze 16: 49 were arrogant, overfed and **u**;

UNCOVERED
Heb 4: 13 Everything is **u** and laid bare

UNDERSTAND (UNDERSTANDING UNDERSTANDS)
Job 42: 3 Surely I spoke of things I did not **u**,
Ps 73: 16 When I tried to **u** all this,
119:125 that I may **u** your statutes.
Lk 24: 45 so they could **u** the Scriptures.
Ac 8: 30 "Do you **u** what you are reading?"
Ro 7: 15 I do not **u** what I do. For what I
1Co 2: 14 and cannot **u** them because they
Eph 5: 17 but **u** what the Lord's will is.
2Pe 3: 16 some things that are hard to **u**,

UNDERSTANDING (UNDERSTAND)
Ps 119: 32 for you have broadened my **u**.
119:104 I gain **u** from your precepts;
147: 5 in power; his **u** has no limit.
Pr 3: 5 heart and lean not on your own **u**;
4: 7 Though it cost all you have, get **u**.
10: 23 a person of **u** delights in wisdom.
11: 12 one who has **u** holds their tongue.
15: 21 but whoever has **u** keeps a straight
15: 32 one who heeds correction gains **u**.
Isa 40: 28 and his **u** no one can fathom.
Da 5: 12 a keen mind and knowledge and **u**,
Mk 4: 12 and ever hearing but never **u**;
12: 33 with all your **u** and with all your
Php 4: 7 which transcends all **u**, will guard

UNDERSTANDS (UNDERSTAND)
1Ch 28: 9 every heart and **u** every desire

UNDIVIDED
1Ch 12: 33 to help David with **u** loyalty—
Ps 86: 11 give me an **u** heart, that I may fear
Eze 11: 19 I will give them an **u** heart and put
1Co 7: 35 in a right way in **u** devotion

UNDOING
Pr 18: 7 The mouths of fools are their **u**,

UNDYING
Eph 6: 24 Lord Jesus Christ with an **u** love.

UNFADING
1Pe 3: 4 the **u** beauty of a gentle and quiet

† UNFAILING
Ps 33: 5 the earth is full of his **u** love.
119: 76 May your **u** love be my comfort,
143: 8 bring me word of your **u** love, for I
Pr 19: 22 What a person desires is **u** love;
La 3: 32 compassion, so great is his **u** love.

UNFAITHFUL
Lev 6: 2 is **u** to the LORD by deceiving
1Ch 10: 13 Saul died because he was **u**
Pr 13: 15 but the way of the **u** leads to their

UNFOLDING
Ps 119:130 The **u** of your words gives light;

UNGODLINESS
Titus 2: 12 It teaches us to say "No" to **u**

UNITED (UNITY)
Ro 6: 5 For if we have been **u** with him
Php 2: 1 from being **u** with Christ, if any
Col 2: 2 encouraged in heart and **u** in love,

UNITY (UNITED)
Ps 133: 1 God's people live together in **u**!
Eph 4: 3 keep the **u** of the Spirit through
4: 13 until we all reach **u** in the faith
Col 3: 14 them all together in perfect **u**.

UNIVERSE
Heb 1: 2 through whom also he made the **u**.

UNKNOWN
Ac 17: 23 with this inscription: TO AN **U** GOD.

UNLEAVENED
Ex 12: 17 "Celebrate the Festival of **U** Bread,

UNPROFITABLE
Titus 3: 9 because these are **u** and useless.

UNPUNISHED
Ex 34: 7 Yet he does not leave the guilty **u**;
Pr 19: 5 A false witness will not go **u**,

UNREPENTANT
Ro 2: 5 stubbornness and your **u** heart,

UNRIGHTEOUS
Zep 3: 5 not fail, yet the **u** know no shame.
Mt 5: 45 rain on the righteous and the **u**.
1Pe 3: 18 the righteous for the **u**, to bring
2Pe 2: 9 to hold the **u** for punishment

UNSEARCHABLE
Ro 11: 33 How **u** his judgments, and his

UNSEEN
2Co 4: 18 temporary, but what is **u** is eternal.

UNSTABLE
Jas 1: 8 double-minded and **u** in all they
2Pe 2: 14 they seduce the **u**; they are experts
3: 16 ignorant and **u** people distort,

UNTHINKABLE
Job 34: 12 It is **u** that God would do wrong,

UNVEILED
2Co 3: 18 with **u** faces contemplate the Lord's

UNWORTHY
Job 40: 4 "I am **u**—how can I reply to you?
Lk 17: 10 do, should say, 'We are **u** servants;

UPRIGHT
Job 1: 1 This man was blameless and **u**;
Pr 2: 7 He holds success in store for the **u**,
15: 8 but the prayer of the **u** pleases him.
Titus 1: 8 who is self-controlled, **u**,
2: 12 **u** and godly lives in this present

UPROOTED
Jude : 12 autumn trees, without fruit and **u**

USEFUL
2Ti 2: 21 **u** to the Master and prepared to do
3: 16 God-breathed and is **u** for teaching

USELESS
1Co 15: 14 our preaching is **u** and so is your
Jas 2: 20 that faith without deeds is **u**?

UZZIAH
Son of Amaziah; king of Judah also known as Azariah (2Ki 15:1–7; 1Ch 6:24; 2Ch 26).

VAIN
Ps 33: 17 A horse is a **v** hope for deliverance;
Isa 65: 23 They will not labor in **v**, nor will
1Co 15: 2 Otherwise, you have believed in **v**.
15: 58 your labor in the Lord is not in **v**.
2Co 6: 1 you not to receive God's grace in **v**.

VALLEY
Ps 23: 4 I walk through the darkest **v**,
Isa 40: 4 Every **v** shall be raised up,
Joel 3: 14 LORD is near in the **v** of decision.

VALUABLE (VALUE)
Lk 12: 24 how much more **v** you are than

VALUE (VALUABLE)
Mt 13: 46 When he found one of great **v**,
1Ti 4: 8 For physical training is of some **v**, but godliness has **v** for all things,
Heb 11: 26 as of greater **v** than the treasures

VEIL
Ex 34: 33 to them, he put a **v** over his face.
2Co 3: 14 to this day the same **v** remains

VENGEANCE (AVENGE REVENGE)
Isa 34: 8 For the LORD has a day of **v**,

VICTORIES (VICTORY)
Ps 18: 50 He gives his king great **v**;
21: 1 great is his joy in the **v** you give!

VICTORIOUS (VICTORY)
Zec 9: 9 king comes to you, righteous and **v**,
Rev 2: 7 To the one who is **v**, I will give
2: 11 The one who is **v** will not be hurt
2: 17 To the one who is **v**, I will give
2: 26 To the one who is **v** and does my
3: 5 The one who is **v** will, like them,
3: 12 The one who is **v** I will make
3: 21 To the one who is **v**, I will give
21: 7 Those who are **v** will inherit all

VICTORIOUSLY (VICTORY)
Ps 45: 4 In your majesty ride forth **v**

VICTORY (VICTORIES VICTORIOUS VICTORIOUSLY)
Ps 60: 12 With God we will gain the **v**,
1Co 15: 54 has been swallowed up in **v**."
15: 57 He gives us the **v** through our Lord
1Jn 5: 4 This is the **v** that has overcome

VINDICATED
1Ti 3: 16 in the flesh, was **v** by the Spirit,

VINE
Jn 15: 1 "I am the true **v**, and my Father is

VINEGAR
Mk 15: 36 filled a sponge with wine **v**, put it

VIOLATION
Heb 2: 2 every **v** and disobedience received

VIOLENCE
Isa 60: 18 No longer will **v** be heard in your
Eze 45: 9 Give up your **v** and oppression

VIPERS
Ro 3: 13 "The poison of **v** is on their lips."

† VIRGIN
Isa 7: 14 The **v** will conceive and give birth
Mt 1: 23 "The **v** will conceive and give birth
2Co 11: 2 I might present you as a pure **v**

VIRTUES
Col 3: 14 And over all these **v** put on love,

VISION
Ac 26: 19 disobedient to the **v** from heaven.

VOICE
Ps 95: 7 if only you would hear his **v**,
Isa 30: 21 your ears will hear a **v** behind you,
Jn 5: 28 are in their graves will hear his **v**
10: 3 him, and the sheep listen to his **v**.
Heb 3: 7 "Today, if you hear his **v**,
Rev 3: 20 If anyone hears my **v** and opens

VOMIT
Pr 26: 11 As a dog returns to its **v**, so fools
2Pe 2: 22 "A dog returns to its **v**," and,

---

† Please see the "Hebrew to English Translation Chart," p. xix.

VOW
Nu 30: 2 a man makes a **v** to the LORD
WAGES
Lk 10: 7 you, for the worker deserves his **w**.
Ro 4: 4 **w** are not credited as a gift but as
6: 23 the **w** of sin is death, but the gift
WAILING
Ps 30: 11 You turned my **w** into dancing;
WAIST
2Ki 1: 8 had a leather belt around his **w**."
Mt 3: 4 he had a leather belt around his **w**.
WAIT (WAITED WAITS)
Ps 27: 14 **W** for the LORD; be strong
130: 5 I **w** for the LORD, my whole being
Isa 30: 18 Blessed are all who **w** for him!
Ac 1: 4 **w** for the gift my Father promised,
Ro 8: 23 groan inwardly as we **w** eagerly
1Th 1: 10 and to **w** for his Son from heaven,
Titus 2: 13 while we **w** for the blessed hope—
WAITED (WAIT)
Ps 40: 1 I **w** patiently for the LORD;
WAITS (WAIT)
Ro 8: 19 the creation **w** in eager expectation
WALK (WALKED)
Dt 11: 19 and when you **w** along the road,
Ps 1: 1 Blessed is the one who does not **w**
23: 4 though I **w** through the darkest
89: 15 **w** in the light of your presence,
Isa 2: 5 let us **w** in the light of the LORD.
30: 21 saying, "This is the way; **w** in it."
40: 31 weary, they will **w** and not be faint.
Jer 6: 16 and **w** in it, and you will find rest
Da 4: 37 those who **w** in pride he is able
Am 3: 3 Do two **w** together unless they
Mic 6: 8 and to **w** humbly with your God.
Mk 2: 9 say, 'Get up, take your mat and **w**'?
Jn 8: 12 Whoever follows me will never **w**
1Jn 1: 7 But if we **w** in the light, as he is
2Jn : 6 his command is that you **w** in love.
WALKED (WALK)
Ge 5: 24 Enoch **w** faithfully with God;
Jos 14: 9 which your feet have **w** will be
Mt 14: 29 **w** on the water and came toward
WALL
Jos 6: 20 gave a loud shout, the **w** collapsed;
Ne 2: 17 let us rebuild the **w** of Jerusalem,
Rev 21: 12 a great, high **w** with twelve gates,
WALLOWING
2Pe 2: 22 returns to her **w** in the mud."
WANT (WANTED WANTING WANTS)
1Sa 8: 19 they said. "We **w** a king over us.
Lk 19: 14 say, 'We don't **w** this man to be our
Ro 7: 15 For what I **w** to do I do not do,
Php 3: 10 I **w** to know Christ—yes, to know
WANTED (WANT)
1Co 12: 18 of them, just as he **w** them to be.
WANTING (WANT)
Da 5: 27 weighed on the scales and found **w**.
2Pe 3: 9 with you, not **w** anyone to perish,
WANTS (WANT)
Mt 20: 26 whoever **w** to become great among
Mk 8: 35 For whoever **w** to save their life
Ro 9: 18 on whom he **w** to have mercy,
9: 18 he hardens whom he **w** to harden.
1Ti 2: 4 who **w** all people to be saved
WAR (WARS)
Isa 2: 4 nor will they train for **w** anymore.
Da 9: 26 **W** will continue until the end,
2Co 10: 3 we do not wage **w** as the world
Rev 19: 11 justice he judges and wages **w**.
WARN (WARNED WARNINGS)
Eze 3: 19 if you do **w** the wicked person
33: 9 if you do **w** the wicked person
WARNED (WARN)
Ps 19: 11 By them your servant is **w**;
WARNINGS (WARN)
1Co 10: 11 and were written down as **w** for us,
WARS (WAR)
Ps 46: 9 He makes **w** cease to the ends
Mt 24: 6 will hear of **w** and rumors of **w**,
WASH (WASHED WASHING)
Ps 51: 7 **w** me, and I will be whiter than
Jn 13: 5 and began to **w** his disciples' feet,
Ac 22: 16 be baptized and **w** your sins away,
Rev 22: 14 are those who **w** their robes,
WASHED (WASH)
1Co 6: 11 But you were **w**, you were
Rev 7: 14 they have **w** their robes and made
WASHING (WASH)
Eph 5: 26 the **w** with water through the word,
Titus 3: 5 saved us through the **w** of rebirth
WATCH (WATCHES WATCHING WATCHMAN)
Ge 31: 49 the LORD keep **w** between you
Jer 31: 10 them and will **w** over his flock like
Mt 24: 42 "Therefore keep **w**, because you do
26: 41 "**W** and pray so that you will not
Lk 2: 8 keeping **w** over their flocks at night
1Ti 4: 16 **W** your life and doctrine closely.
WATCHES (WATCH)
Ps 1: 6 For the LORD **w** over the way
121: 3 he who **w** over you will not
WATCHING (WATCH)
Lk 12: 37 servants whose master finds them **w**
WATCHMAN (WATCH)
Eze 3: 17 I have made you a **w** for the people
WATER (WATERED WATERS)
Ps 1: 3 like a tree planted by streams of **w**,
22: 14 I am poured out like **w**, and all my
Pr 25: 21 if he is thirsty, give him **w** to drink.
Isa 49: 10 and lead them beside springs of **w**.
Jer 2: 13 broken cisterns that cannot hold **w**.
Zec 14: 8 On that day living **w** will flow
Mk 9: 41 anyone who gives you a cup of **w**
Jn 4: 10 he would have given you living **w**."
7: 38 rivers of living **w** will flow
Eph 5: 26 washing with **w** through the word,
1Pe 3: 21 this **w** symbolizes baptism that
Rev 21: 6 thirsty I will give **w** without cost
WATERED (WATER)
1Co 3: 6 I planted the seed, Apollos **w** it,
WATERS (WATER)
Ps 23: 2 he leads me beside quiet **w**,
Isa 58: 11 like a spring whose **w** never fail.
1Co 3: 7 nor the one who **w** is anything,
WAVE (WAVES)
Jas 1: 6 the one who doubts is like a **w**
WAVES (WAVE)
Isa 57: 20 whose **w** cast up mire and mud.
Mt 8: 27 the winds and the **w** obey him!"
Eph 4: 14 tossed back and forth by the **w**,
WAY (WAYS)
Dt 1: 33 to show you the **w** you should go.
2Sa 22: 31 "As for God, his **w** is perfect:
Job 23: 10 But he knows the **w** that I take;
Ps 1: 1 stand in the **w** that sinners take
37: 5 Commit your **w** to the LORD;
139: 24 and lead me in the **w** everlasting.
Pr 14: 12 is a **w** that appears to be right,
22: 6 off on the **w** they should go,
Isa 30: 21 behind you, saying, "This is the **w**;
53: 6 of us has turned to our own **w**;
Mt 3: 3 'Prepare the **w** for the Lord,
Jn 14: 6 "I am the **w** and the truth
1Co 10: 13 provide a **w** out so that you can
12: 31 will show you the most excellent **w**.
Heb 4: 15 who has been tempted in every **w**,
9: 8 the **w** into the Most Holy Place had
10: 20 living **w** opened for us through
WAYS (WAY)
Ex 33: 13 teach me your **w** so I may know
Ps 25: 10 All the **w** of the LORD are loving
51: 13 I will teach transgressors your **w**,
Pr 3: 6 in all your **w** submit to him, and he
16: 17 who guard their **w** preserve their
Isa 55: 7 Let the wicked forsake their **w**
55: 8 neither are your **w** my **w**,"
Jas 3: 2 We all stumble in many **w**.
WEAK (WEAKER WEAKNESS)
Mt 26: 41 spirit is willing, but the flesh is **w**."
Ro 14: 1 Accept the one whose faith is **w**,
1Co 1: 27 chose the **w** things of the world
8: 9 a stumbling block to the **w**.
9: 22 To the **w** I became **w**, to win the **w**.
2Co 12: 10 For when I am **w**, then I am strong.
Heb 12: 12 your feeble arms and **w** knees.
WEAKER (WEAK)
1Co 12: 22 seem to be **w** are indispensable,
1Pe 3: 7 them with respect as the **w** partner
WEAKNESS (WEAK)
Ro 8: 26 way, the Spirit helps us in our **w**.
1Co 1: 25 **w** of God is stronger than human
2Co 12: 9 my power is made perfect in **w**."
Heb 5: 2 since he himself is subject to **w**.
WEALTH
Pr 3: 9 Honor the LORD with your **w**,
Mk 10: 22 away sad, because he had great **w**.
Lk 15: 13 and there squandered his **w** in wild
WEAPONS
2Co 10: 4 The **w** we fight with are not the **w**
WEARIES (WEARY)
Ecc 12: 12 and much study **w** the body.
WEARY (WEARIES)
Isa 40: 31 they will run and not grow **w**,
Mt 11: 28 all you who are **w** and burdened,
Gal 6: 9 not become **w** in doing good,
WEDDING
Mt 22: 11 who was not wearing **w** clothes.
Rev 19: 7 For the **w** of the Lamb has come,
WEEP (WEEPING WEPT)
Ecc 3: 4 a time to **w** and a time to laugh,
Lk 6: 21 Blessed are you who **w** now, for
WEEPING (WEEP)
Ps 30: 5 **w** may stay for the night,
126: 6 Those who go out **w**, carrying seed
Mt 8: 12 where there will be **w** and gnashing
WELCOMES
Mt 18: 5 **w** one such child in my name **w** me.
2Jn : 11 Anyone who **w** them shares in
WELL
Lk 17: 19 your faith has made you **w**."
Jas 5: 15 faith will make the sick person **w**;
WEPT (WEEP)
Ps 137: 1 and **w** when we remembered Zion.
Jn 11: 35 Jesus **w**.
WEST
Ps 103: 12 as far as the east is from the **w**,
WHIRLWIND (WIND)
2Ki 2: 1 to take Elijah up to heaven in a **w**,
Hos 8: 7 They sow the wind and reap the **w**.
Na 1: 3 His way is in the **w** and the storm,
WHITE (WHITER)
Isa 1: 18 scarlet, they shall be as **w** as snow;
Da 7: 9 His clothing was as **w** as snow;
Rev 1: 14 hair on his head was **w** like wool,
3: 4 dressed in **w**, for they are worthy.
20: 11 I saw a great **w** throne and him
WHITER (WHITE)
Ps 51: 7 wash me, and I will be **w** than snow.
WHOLE
Mt 16: 26 for someone to gain the **w** world,
24: 14 in the **w** world as a testimony to all
Jn 13: 10 their **w** body is clean.
21: 25 even the **w** world would not have
Ac 20: 27 proclaim to you the **w** will of God.
Ro 3: 19 and the **w** world held accountable
8: 22 the **w** creation has been groaning
Gal 5: 3 he is obligated to obey the **w** law.
Eph 4: 13 attaining to the **w** measure
Jas 2: 10 For whoever keeps the **w** law
1Jn 2: 2 but also for the sins of the **w** world.
WHOLEHEARTEDLY (HEART)
Dt 1: 36 he followed the LORD **w**."
Eph 6: 7 Serve **w**, as if you were serving
WICKED (WICKEDNESS)
Ps 1: 1 does not walk in step with the **w**
1: 5 Therefore the **w** will not stand
73: 3 when I saw the prosperity of the **w**.
Pr 10: 20 the heart of the **w** is of little value.
11: 21 The **w** will not go unpunished,
Isa 53: 9 was assigned a grave with the **w**,
55: 7 Let the **w** forsake their ways
57: 20 But the **w** are like the tossing sea,
Eze 3: 18 that **w** person will die for their sin,
18: 23 any pleasure in the death of the **w**?
33: 14 And if I say to a **w** person,
WICKEDNESS (WICKED)
Eze 28: 15 you were created till **w** was found

WIDE
Isa 54: 2 stretch your tent curtains **w**, do not
Mt 7: 13 For **w** is the gate and broad is
Eph 3: 18 to grasp how **w** and long and high

WIDOW (WIDOWS)
Dt 10: 18 cause of the fatherless and the **w**,
Lk 21: 2 saw a poor **w** put in two very small

WIDOWS (WIDOW)
Jas 1: 27 orphans and **w** in their distress

WIFE (WIVES)
Ge 2: 24 and mother and is united to his **w**,
24: 67 So she became his **w**, and he loved
Ex 20: 17 shall not covet your neighbor's **w**,
Dt 5: 21 shall not covet your neighbor's **w**.
Pr 5: 18 you rejoice in the **w** of your youth.
12: 4 A **w** of noble character is her
18: 22 who finds a **w** finds what is good
19: 13 quarrelsome **w** is like the constant
31: 10 A **w** of noble character who can
Mt 19: 3 for a man to divorce his **w** for any
1Co 7: 2 sexual relations with his own **w**,
7: 33 how he can please his **w**—
Eph 5: 23 head of the **w** as Christ is the head
5: 33 must love his **w** as he loves himself,
5: 33 the **w** must respect her husband.
1Ti 3: 2 faithful to his **w**, temperate,
Rev 21: 9 you the bride, the **w** of the Lamb."

WILD
Lk 15: 13 squandered his wealth in **w** living.
Ro 11: 17 and you, though a **w** olive shoot,

WILL (WILLING WILLINGNESS)
Ps 40: 8 I desire to do your **w**, my God;
143: 10 Teach me to do your **w**, for you are
Isa 53: 10 Yet it was the LORD's **w** to crush
Mt 6: 10 kingdom come, your **w** be done,
26: 39 Yet not as I **w**, but as you **w**."
Jn 7: 17 chooses to do the **w** of God **w** find
Ac 20: 27 to you the whole **w** of God.
Ro 12: 2 test and approve what God's **w** is—
1Co 7: 37 but has control over his own **w**,
Eph 5: 17 understand what the Lord's **w** is.
Php 2: 13 for it is God who works in you to **w**
1Th 4: 3 It is God's **w** that you should be
5: 18 for this is God's **w** for you in Christ
Heb 9: 16 In the case of a **w**, it is necessary
10: 7 I have come to do your **w**,
Jas 4: 15 "If it is the Lord's **w**, we **w** live
1Jn 5: 14 ask anything according to his **w**,
Rev 4: 11 by your **w** they were created

WILLING (WILL)
Ps 51: 12 salvation and grant me a **w** spirit,
Da 3: 28 were **w** to give up their lives rather
Mt 18: 14 Father in heaven is not **w** that any
23: 37 her wings, and you were not **w**.
26: 41 The spirit is **w**, but the flesh is

WILLINGNESS (WILL)
2Co 8: 12 For if the **w** is there, the gift is

WIN
Php 3: 14 on toward the goal to **w** the prize
1Th 4: 12 your daily life may **w** the respect

† WIND (WHIRLWIND)
Jas 1: 6 the sea, blown and tossed by the **w**.

WINE
Pr 20: 1 **W** is a mocker and beer a brawler;
Isa 55: 1 buy **w** and milk without money
Mt 9: 17 Neither do people pour new **w**
Lk 23: 36 They offered him **w** vinegar
Ro 14: 21 drink **w** or to do anything else
Eph 5: 18 Do not get drunk on **w**, which

WINESKINS
Mt 9: 17 people pour new wine into old **w**.

WINGS
Ru 2: 12 under whose **w** you have come
Ps 17: 8 hide me in the shadow of your **w**
Isa 40: 31 They will soar on **w** like eagles;
Lk 13: 34 gathers her chicks under her **w**,

WIPE
Rev 7: 17 God will **w** away every tear

† WISDOM (WISE)
1Ki 4: 29 God gave Solomon **w** and very
Ps 111: 10 the LORD is the beginning of **w**;
Pr 31: 26 She speaks with **w**, and faithful
Jer 10: 12 he founded the world by his **w**
Mt 11: 19 **w** is proved right by her deeds."
Lk 2: 52 And Jesus grew in **w** and stature,
Ro 11: 33 the depth of the riches of the **w**
Col 2: 3 are hidden all the treasures of **w**
Jas 1: 5 If any of you lacks **w**, you should

WISE (WISDOM WISER)
1Ki 3: 12 I will give you a **w** and discerning
Job 5: 13 He catches the **w** in their craftiness,
Ps 19: 7 trustworthy, making **w** the simple.
Pr 3: 7 Do not be **w** in your own eyes;
9: 8 rebuke the **w** and they will love
10: 1 A **w** son brings joy to his father,
11: 30 and the one who is **w** saves lives.
13: 20 Walk with the **w** and become **w**,
17: 28 Even fools are thought **w** if they
Da 12: 3 Those who are **w** will shine like
Mt 11: 25 hidden these things from the **w**
1Co 1: 27 things of the world to shame the **w**;
2Ti 3: 15 make you **w** for salvation through

WISER (WISE)
1Co 1: 25 of God is **w** than human wisdom,

WITHER (WITHERS)
Ps 1: 3 and whose leaf does not **w**—

WITHERS (WITHER)
Isa 40: 7 The grass **w** and the flowers fall,
1Pe 1: 24 the grass **w** and the flowers fall,

WITHHOLD
Ps 84: 11 no good thing does he **w** from
Pr 23: 13 Do not **w** discipline from a child;

WITNESS (WITNESSES)
Jn 1: 8 he came only as a **w** to the light.

WITNESSES (WITNESS)
Dt 19: 15 by the testimony of two or three **w**.
Ac 1: 8 and you will be my **w** in Jerusalem,

WIVES (WIFE)
Eph 5: 22 **W**, submit yourselves to your own
5: 25 love your **w**, just as Christ loved
1Pe 3: 1 **W**, in the same way submit

WOE
Isa 6: 5 "**W** to me!" I cried. "I am ruined!

WOLF
Isa 65: 25 The **w** and the lamb will feed

WOMAN (MAN)
Ge 2: 22 the LORD God made a **w**
3: 15 put enmity between you and the **w**,
Lev 20: 13 with a man as one does with a **w**,
Dt 22: 5 A **w** must not wear men's clothing,
Ru 3: 11 that you are a **w** of noble character.
Pr 31: 30 a **w** who fears the LORD is to be
Mt 5: 28 a **w** lustfully has already committed
Jn 8: 3 *brought in a **w** caught*
Ro 7: 2 by law a married **w** is bound to her
1Co 11: 3 and the head of the **w** is man,
11: 13 Is it proper for a **w** to pray to God
1Ti 2: 11 A **w** should learn in quietness

WOMB
Job 1: 21 I came from my mother's **w**,
Jer 1: 5 I formed you in the **w** I knew you,
Lk 1: 44 the baby in my **w** leaped for joy.

WOMEN (MAN)
Lk 1: 42 "Blessed are you among **w**,
1Co 14: 34 **W** should remain silent
1Ti 2: 9 I also want the **w** to dress modestly,
Titus 2: 3 teach the older **w** to be reverent
1Pe 3: 5 the way the holy **w** of the past

† WONDERFUL (WONDERS)
Job 42: 3 things too **w** for me to know.
Ps 119: 18 that I may see **w** things in your law.
119: 27 I may meditate on your **w** deeds.
119:129 statutes are **w**; therefore I obey
139: 6 Such knowledge is too **w** for me,
Isa 9: 6 he will be called **W** Counselor,
1Pe 2: 9 out of darkness into his **w** light.

WONDERS (WONDERFUL)
Job 37: 14 stop and consider God's **w**.
Ps 17: 7 Show me the **w** of your great love,
31: 21 for he showed me the **w** of his love
Joel 2: 30 I will show **w** in the heavens
Ac 2: 19 I will show **w** in the heavens

WOOD
Isa 44: 19 Shall I bow down to a block of **w**?"
1Co 3: 12 costly stones, **w**, hay or straw,

WORD (WORDS)
Dt 8: 3 but on every **w** that comes
2Sa 22: 31 The LORD's **w** is flawless;
Ps 119: 9 By living according to your **w**.
119: 11 I have hidden your **w** in my heart
119:105 Your **w** is a lamp to my feet
Pr 12: 25 the heart, but a kind **w** cheers it up.
30: 5 "Every **w** of God is flawless; he is
Isa 55: 11 so is my **w** that goes out from my
Jn 1: 1 In the beginning was the **W**, and the **W** was with God, and the **W** was God.
1: 14 The **W** became flesh and made his
2Co 2: 17 we do not peddle the **w** of God
4: 2 nor do we distort the **w** of God.
Eph 6: 17 of the Spirit, which is the **w** of God.
Php 2: 16 as you hold firmly to the **w** of life.
2Ti 2: 15 and who correctly handles the **w**
Heb 4: 12 the **w** of God is alive and active.
Jas 1: 22 Do not merely listen to the **w**,

WORDS (WORD)
Dt 11: 18 Fix these **w** of mine in your hearts
Ps 119:103 How sweet are your **w** to my taste,
119:130 unfolding of your **w** gives light;
119:160 All your **w** are true; all your
Pr 30: 6 Do not add to his **w**, or he will
Jer 15: 16 When your **w** came, I ate them;
Mt 24: 35 but my **w** will never pass away.
Jn 6: 68 You have the **w** of eternal life.
15: 7 in me and my **w** remain in you,
1Co 14: 19 rather speak five intelligible **w**
Rev 22: 19 if anyone takes **w** away from this

WORK (HANDIWORK WORKER WORKERS WORKING WORKS)
Ex 23: 12 but on the seventh day do not **w**,
Nu 8: 11 be ready to do the **w** of the LORD.
Dt 5: 14 On it you shall not do any **w**,
Jer 48: 10 who is lax in doing the LORD's **w**!
Jn 6: 27 Do not **w** for food that spoils,
9: 4 is coming, when no one can **w**.
1Co 3: 13 test the quality of each person's **w**.
Php 1: 6 he who began a good **w** in you will
2: 12 continue to **w** out your salvation
Col 3: 23 you do, **w** at it with all your heart,
1Th 5: 12 those who **w** hard among you,
2Th 3: 10 is unwilling to **w** shall not eat."
2Ti 3: 17 equipped for every good **w**.
Heb 6: 10 he will not forget your **w**

WORKER (WORK)
Lk 10: 7 for the **w** deserves his wages.
1Ti 5: 18 and "The **w** deserves his wages."
2Ti 2: 15 a **w** who does not need to be

WORKERS (WORK)
Mt 9: 37 is plentiful but the **w** are few.
1Co 3: 9 For we are **c** in God's service;

WORKING (WORK)
Col 3: 23 all your heart, as **w** for the Lord,

WORKS (WORK)
Pr 31: 31 her **w** bring her praise at the city
Ro 8: 28 in all things God **w** for the good
Eph 2: 9 not by **w**, so that no one can boast.
4: 12 to equip his people for **w** of service,

WORLD (WORLDLY)
Ps 50: 12 for the **w** is mine, and all that is
Isa 13: 11 I will punish the **w** for its evil,
Mt 5: 14 "You are the light of the **w**.
16: 26 for someone to gain the whole **w**,
Mk 16: 15 *"Go into all the **w** and preach*
Jn 1: 29 who takes away the sin of the **w**!
3: 16 God so loved the **w** that he gave his
8: 12 he said, "I am the light of the **w**.
15: 19 but I have chosen you out of the **w**. That is why the **w** hates you.
16: 33 I have overcome the **w**."
18: 36 said, "My kingdom is not of this **w**.
Ro 3: 19 and the whole **w** held accountable
1Co 3: 19 the wisdom of this **w** is foolishness
2Co 5: 19 that God was reconciling the **w**
10: 3 For though we live in the **w**, we do
1Ti 6: 7 For we brought nothing into the **w**,
1Jn 2: 2 but also for the sins of the whole **w**.
2: 15 not love the **w** or anything in the **w**.
Rev 13: 8 slain from the creation of the **w**.

† Please see the "Hebrew to English Translation Chart," p. xix.

WORLDLY (WORLD)
Titus 2: 12 to ungodliness and **w** passions,

WORMS
Mk 9: 48 where " 'the **w** that eat them do

WORRY (WORRYING)
Mt 6: 25 I tell you, do not **w** about your life,
10: 19 do not **w** about what to say or how

WORRYING (WORRY)
Mt 6: 27 you by **w** add a single hour to your

† WORSHIP
1Ch 16: 29 **W** the LORD in the splendor of his
Ps 95: 6 let us bow down in **w**, let us kneel
Mt 2: 2 it rose and have come to **w** him."
Jn 4: 24 his worshipers must **w** in the Spirit
Ro 12: 1 this is your true and proper **w**.

WORTH (WORTHY)
Job 28: 13 No mortal comprehends its **w**;
Pr 31: 10 She is **w** far more than rubies.
Mt 10: 31 you are **w** more than many
Ro 8: 18 sufferings are not **w** comparing
1Pe 1: 7 of greater **w** than gold,
3: 4 which is of great **w** in God's sight.

WORTHLESS
Pr 11: 4 Wealth is **w** in the day of wrath,
Jas 1: 26 themselves, and their religion is **w**.

WORTHY (WORTH)
1Ch 16: 25 is the LORD and most **w** of praise;
Eph 4: 1 live a life **w** of the calling you have
Php 1: 27 in a manner **w** of the gospel
Rev 5: 2 "Who is **w** to break the seals

WOUNDS
Pr 27: 6 **W** from a friend can be trusted,
Isa 53: 5 and by his **w** we are healed.
Zec 13: 6 'What are these **w** on your body?'
1Pe 2: 24 "by his **w** you have been healed."

WRATH
2Ch 36: 16 at his prophets until the **w**
Ps 2: 5 anger and terrifies them in his **w**,
76: 10 Surely your **w** against mankind
Pr 15: 1 A gentle answer turns away **w**,
Jer 25: 15 cup filled with the wine of my **w**
Ro 1: 18 The **w** of God is being revealed
5: 9 saved from God's **w** through him!
1Th 5: 9 God did not appoint us to suffer **w**
Rev 6: 16 and from the **w** of the Lamb!

WRESTLED
Ge 32: 24 a man **w** with him till daybreak.

WRITE (WRITING WRITTEN)
Dt 6: 9 **W** them on the doorframes of your
Pr 7: 3 **w** them on the tablet of your heart.
Heb 8: 10 minds and **w** them on their hearts.

WRITING (WRITE)
1Co 14: 37 what I am **w** to you is the Lord's

WRITTEN (WRITE)
Jos 1: 8 be careful to do everything **w** in it.
Da 12: 1 everyone whose name is found **w**
Lk 10: 20 that your names are **w** in heaven."
Jn 20: 31 these are **w** that you may believe
1Co 4: 6 "Do not go beyond what is **w**."
2Co 3: 3 **w** not with ink but with the Spirit
Heb 12: 23 whose names are **w** in heaven.

WRONG (WRONGDOING WRONGED WRONGS)
Ex 23: 2 not follow the crowd in doing **w**.
Nu 5: 7 restitution for the **w** they have
Job 34: 12 unthinkable that God would do **w**,
1Th 5: 15 that nobody pays back **w** for **w**,

WRONGDOING (WRONG)
Job 1: 22 not sin by charging God with **w**.

WRONGED (WRONG)
1Co 6: 7 Why not rather be **w**?

WRONGS (WRONG)
Pr 10: 12 conflict, but love covers over all **w**.
1Co 13: 5 angered, it keeps no record of **w**.

YEARS
Ps 90: 4 A thousand **y** in your sight are like
90: 10 Our days may come to seventy **y**,
2Pe 3: 8 the Lord a day is like a thousand **y**,
Rev 20: 2 and bound him for a thousand **y**.

YESTERDAY
Heb 13: 8 Jesus Christ is the same **y** and today

YOKE (YOKED)
Mt 11: 29 Take my **y** upon you and learn

YOKED (YOKE)
2Co 6: 14 Do not be **y** together

YOUNG (YOUTH)
Ps 119: 9 can a **y** person stay on the path
1Ti 4: 12 down on you because you are **y**,

YOUTH (YOUNG)
Ps 103: 5 your **y** is renewed like the eagle's.
Ecc 12: 1 your Creator in the days of your **y**,
2Ti 2: 22 Flee the evil desires of **y** and

ZEAL
Jn 2: 17 **Z** for your house will consume me.
Ro 12: 11 Never be lacking in **z**, but keep

ZECHARIAH
1. Son of Jeroboam II; king of Israel (2Ki 15:8–12).
2. Post-exilic prophet who encouraged rebuilding of temple (Ezr 5:1; 6:14; Zec 1:1).
3. Father of John the Baptist (Lk 1:13; 3:2).

ZEDEKIAH
Mattaniah, son of Josiah (1Ch 3:15), made king of Judah by Nebuchadnezzar (2Ki 24:17—25:7; 2Ch 36:10–14; Jer 37–39; 52:1–11).

ZERUBBABEL
Descendant of David (1Ch 3:19; Mt 1:3). Led return from exile (Ezr 2–3; Ne 7:7; Hag 1–2; Zec 4).

ZIMRI
King of Israel (1Ki 16:9–20).

ZION
Ps 137: 3 "Sing us one of the songs of **Z**!"
Jer 50: 5 They will ask the way to **Z** and
Ro 9: 33 I lay in **Z** a stone that causes people
11: 26 "The deliverer will come from **Z**;

† Please see the "Hebrew to English Translation Chart," p. xix.

INDEX TO MAPS

The Index to Maps will lead you to place-names found on the color maps on pp. 2343 – 2358 at the end of this study Bible. References are to the map number and the margin markings.

Map 1: **WORLD OF THE PATRIARCHS**

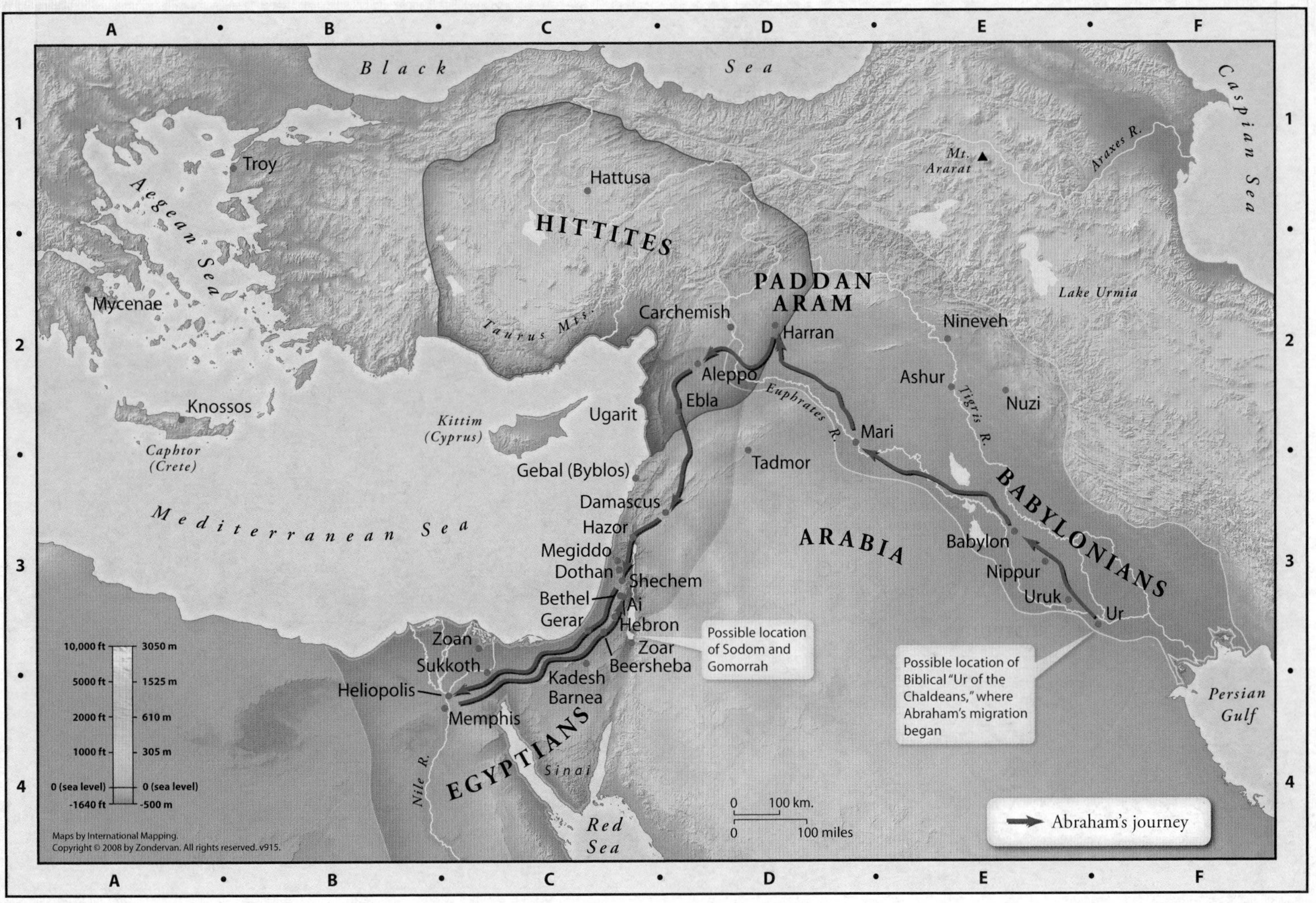
Black Sea
Caspian Sea
Aegean Sea
Mediterranean Sea
Persian Gulf
Red Sea
Araxes R.
Lake Urmia
Mt. Ararat
Tigris R.
Euphrates R.
Nile R.
Taurus Mts.
Sinai
Kittim (Cyprus)
Caphtor (Crete)
HITTITES
PADDAN ARAM
BABYLONIANS
ARABIA
EGYPTIANS
Troy
Mycenae
Knossos
Hattusa
Carchemish
Harran
Aleppo
Ebla
Ugarit
Mari
Tadmor
Nineveh
Ashur
Nuzi
Babylon
Nippur
Uruk
Ur
Gebal (Byblos)
Damascus
Hazor
Megiddo
Dothan
Shechem
Bethel
Ai
Gerar
Hebron
Zoar
Beersheba
Kadesh Barnea
Zoan
Sukkoth
Heliopolis
Memphis
Possible location of Sodom and Gomorrah
Possible location of Biblical "Ur of the Chaldeans," where Abraham's migration began
Abraham's journey
0 100 km.
0 100 miles
10,000 ft 3050 m
5000 ft 1525 m
2000 ft 610 m
1000 ft 305 m
0 (sea level) 0 (sea level)
-1640 ft -500 m
A B C D E F
1 2 3 4
Maps by International Mapping.
Copyright © 2008 by Zondervan. All rights reserved. v915.

Map 2: **HOLY LAND AND SINAI**

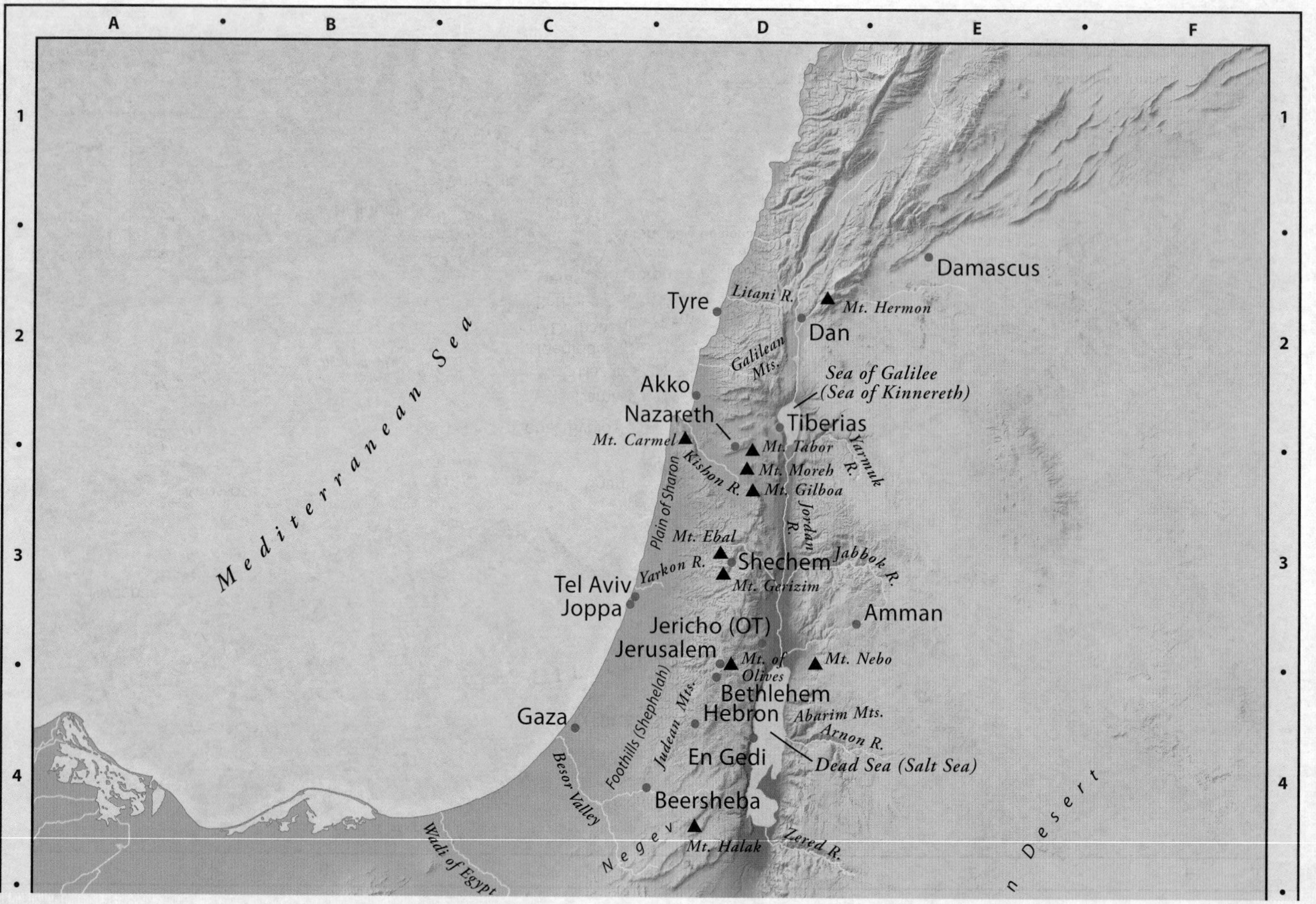

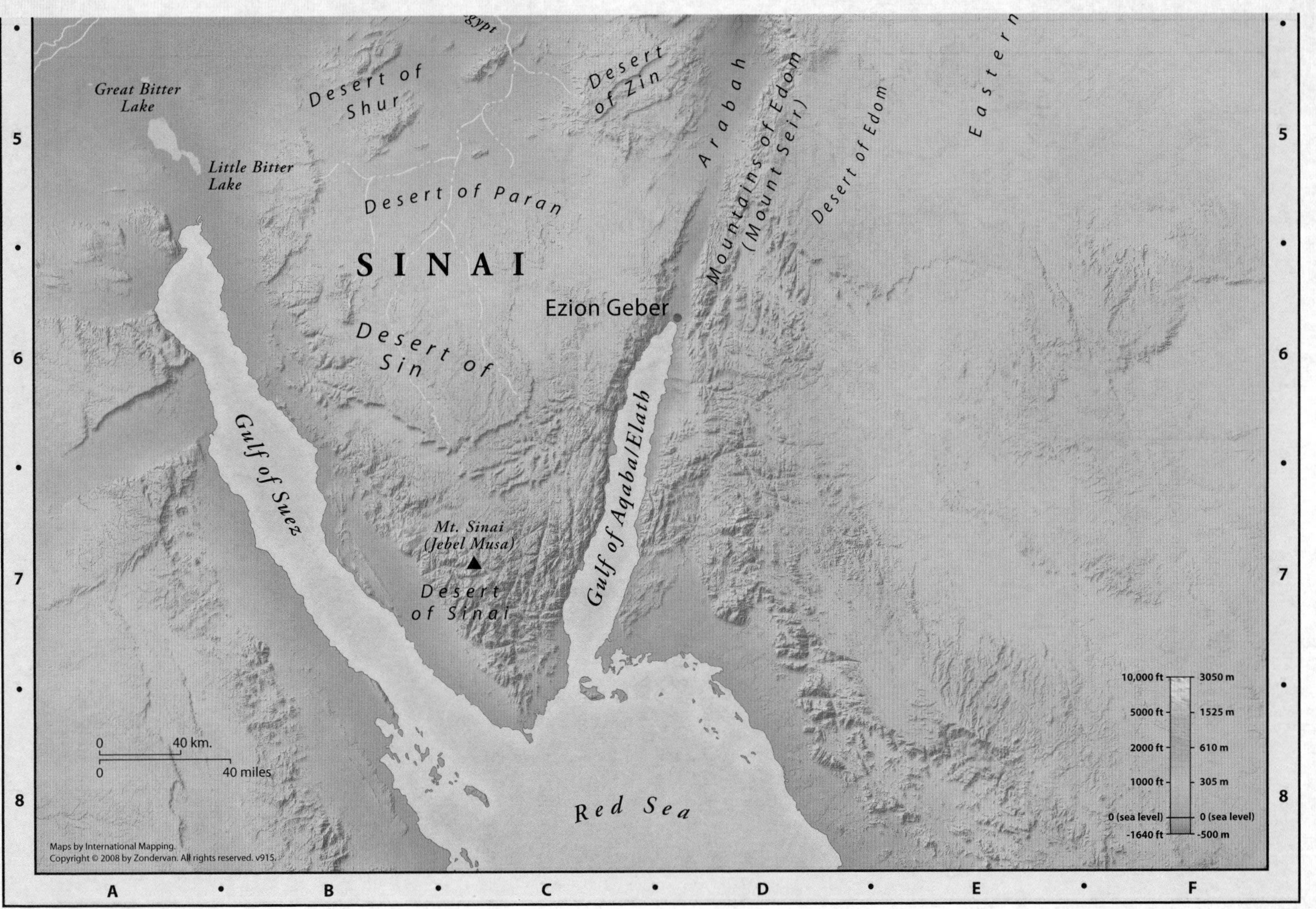
Great Bitter Lake
Little Bitter Lake
Desert of Shur
Desert of Zin
Desert of Paran
SINAI
Ezion Geber
Desert of Sin
Gulf of Suez
Mt. Sinai (Jebel Musa)
Desert of Sinai
Gulf of Aqaba/Elath
Red Sea
Arabah
Mountains of Edom (Mount Seir)
Desert of Edom
Eastern
0 40 km.
0 40 miles
10,000 ft 3050 m
5000 ft 1525 m
2000 ft 610 m
1000 ft 305 m
0 (sea level) 0 (sea level)
-1640 ft -500 m
A B C D E F
5 6 7 8
Maps by International Mapping.
Copyright © 2008 by Zondervan. All rights reserved. v915.

Map 3: **EXODUS AND CONQUEST OF CANAAN**

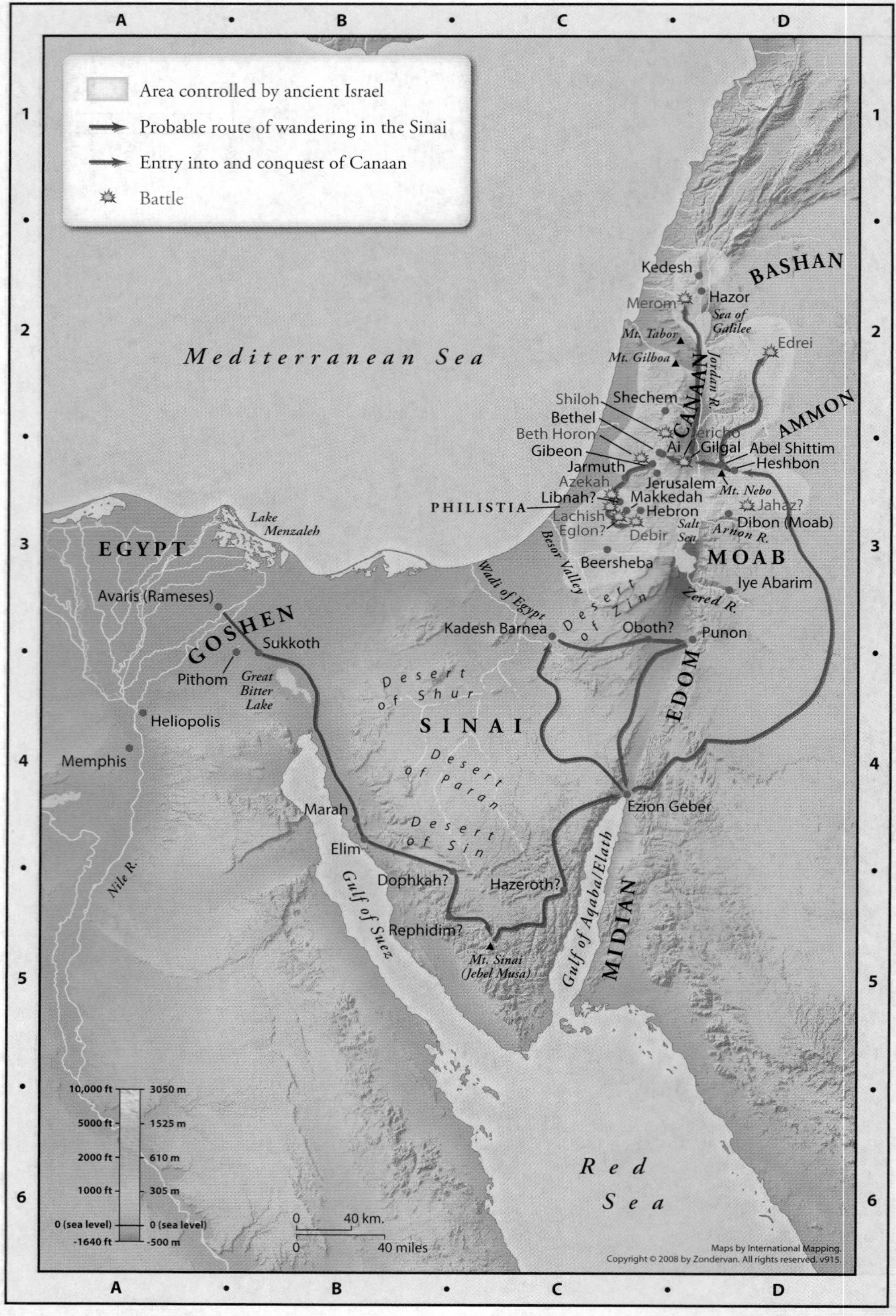

Area controlled by ancient Israel
Probable route of wandering in the Sinai
Entry into and conquest of Canaan
Battle
Mediterranean Sea
EGYPT
Lake Menzaleh
Avaris (Rameses)
GOSHEN
Sukkoth
Pithom
Great Bitter Lake
Heliopolis
Memphis
Nile R.
Marah
Elim
Dophkah?
Rephidim?
Mt. Sinai (Jebel Musa)
Hazeroth?
Gulf of Suez
Gulf of Aqaba/Elath
MIDIAN
Ezion Geber
Desert of Shur
SINAI
Desert of Paran
Desert of Sin
Kadesh Barnea
Desert of Zin
Wadi of Egypt
Besor Valley
Oboth?
Punon
EDOM
MOAB
Iye Abarim
Zered R.
Arnon R.
Dibon (Moab)
Jahaz?
Mt. Nebo
Heshbon
Abel Shittim
AMMON
Edrei
BASHAN
Kedesh
Hazor
Merom
Sea of Galilee
Mt. Tabor
Mt. Gilboa
Jordan R.
CANAAN
Shiloh
Shechem
Bethel
Beth Horon
Gibeon
Jericho
Ai
Gilgal
Jarmuth
Azekah
Jerusalem
Libnah?
Makkedah
Lachish
Hebron
Eglon?
Debir
Salt Sea
PHILISTIA
Beersheba
Red Sea
10,000 ft 3050 m
5000 ft 1525 m
2000 ft 610 m
1000 ft 305 m
0 (sea level) 0 (sea level)
-1640 ft -500 m
0 40 km.
0 40 miles
A B C D
1 2 3 4 5 6

Map 4: **LAND OF THE TWELVE TRIBES**

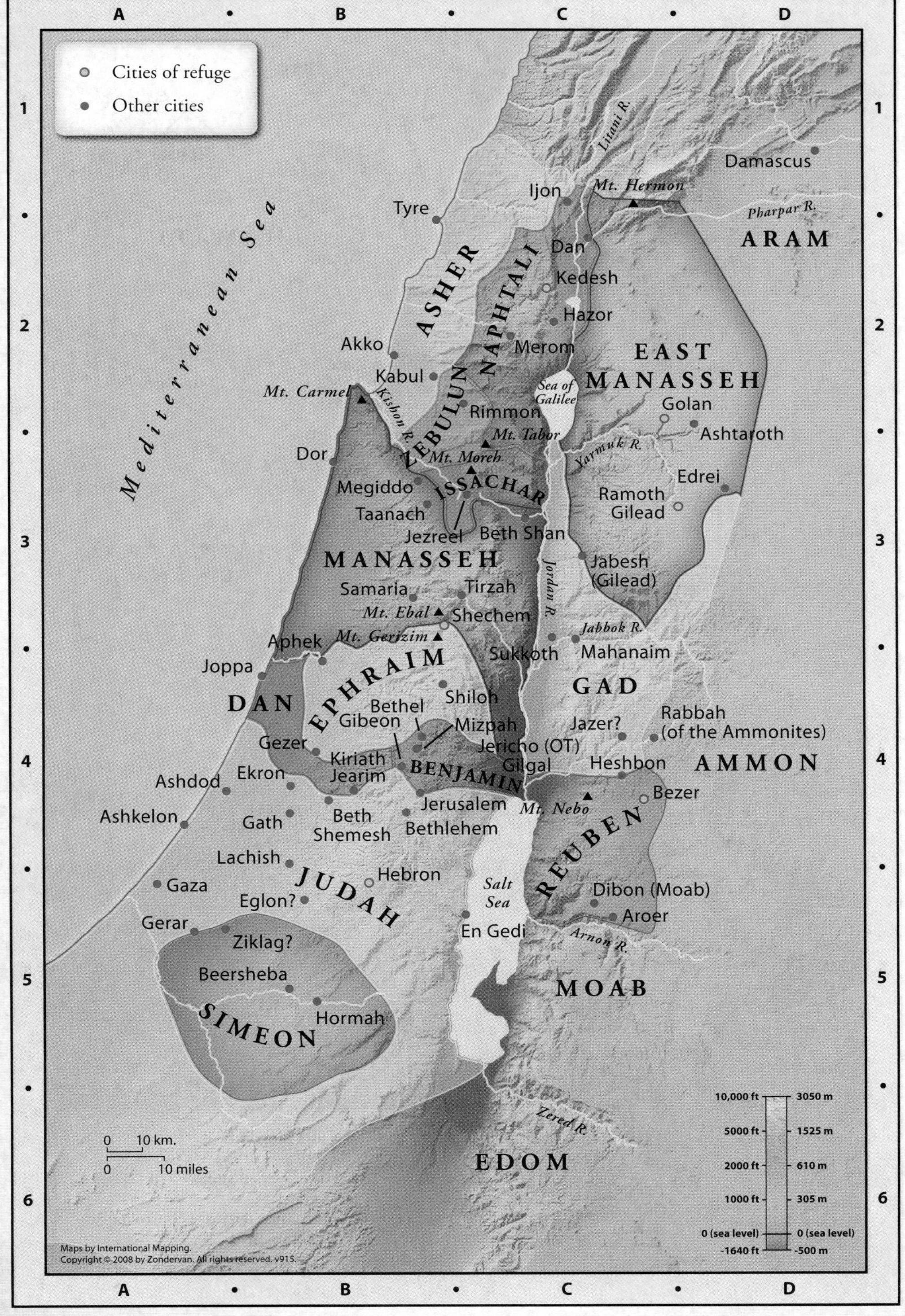
A
B
C
D
1
2
3
4
5
6
Cities of refuge
Other cities
Mediterranean Sea
Litani R.
Damascus
Ijon
Mt. Hermon
Tyre
Pharpar R.
ARAM
Dan
ASHER
NAPHTALI
Kedesh
Hazor
Akko
Merom
EAST
MANASSEH
Kabul
Mt. Carmel
Kishon R.
ZEBULUN
Sea of Galilee
Golan
Rimmon
Ashtaroth
Mt. Tabor
Dor
Mt. Moreh
Yarmuk R.
Edrei
Megiddo
ISSACHAR
Ramoth Gilead
Taanach
Jezreel
Beth Shan
MANASSEH
Jabesh (Gilead)
Samaria
Tirzah
Jordan R.
Mt. Ebal
Shechem
Aphek
Mt. Gerizim
Jabbok R.
Sukkoth
Mahanaim
Joppa
EPHRAIM
GAD
DAN
Shiloh
Bethel
Gibeon
Mizpah
Rabbah (of the Ammonites)
Jazer?
Gezer
Jericho (OT)
Kiriath Jearim
Gilgal
Heshbon
AMMON
Ashdod
Ekron
BENJAMIN
Bezer
Mt. Nebo
Jerusalem
Ashkelon
Gath
Beth Shemesh
Bethlehem
REUBEN
Lachish
Salt Sea
Gaza
JUDAH
Hebron
Dibon (Moab)
Eglon?
Aroer
Gerar
En Gedi
Arnon R.
Ziklag?
Beersheba
MOAB
Hormah
SIMEON
Zered R.
0 10 km.
0 10 miles
EDOM
10,000 ft 3050 m
5000 ft 1525 m
2000 ft 610 m
1000 ft 305 m
0 (sea level) 0 (sea level)
-1640 ft -500 m
Maps by International Mapping.
Copyright © 2008 by Zondervan. All rights reserved. v915.

Map 5: **KINGDOM OF DAVID AND SOLOMON**

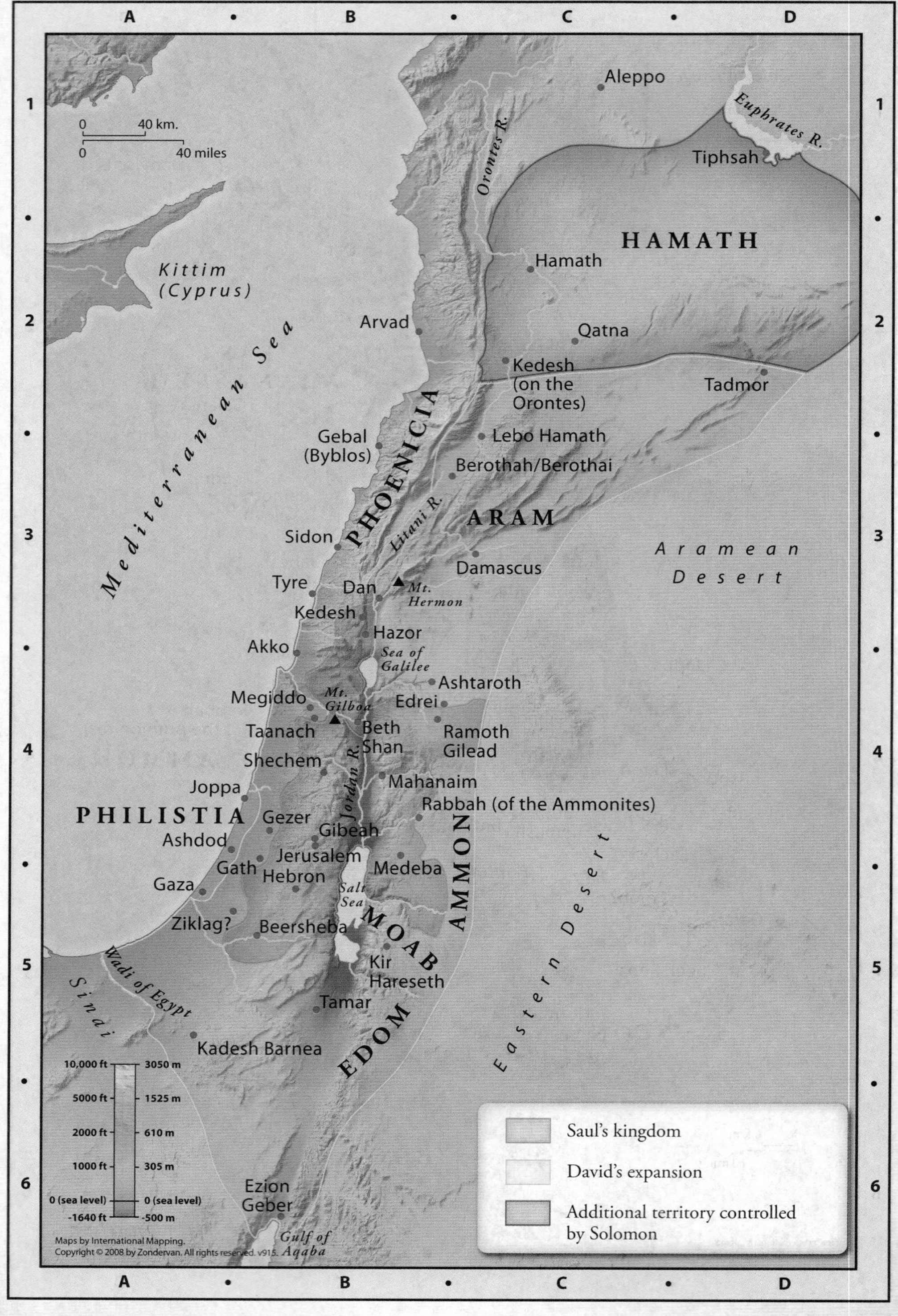

A
B
C
D
1
2
3
4
5
6
0
40 km.
40 miles
Aleppo
Euphrates R.
Tiphsah
Orontes R.
HAMATH
Hamath
Kittim
(Cyprus)
Arvad
Qatna
Mediterranean Sea
Kedesh
(on the
Orontes)
Tadmor
PHOENICIA
Gebal
(Byblos)
Lebo Hamath
Berothah/Berothai
Litani R.
ARAM
Sidon
Aramean
Desert
Damascus
Tyre
Dan
Mt.
Hermon
Kedesh
Hazor
Akko
Sea of
Galilee
Ashtaroth
Megiddo
Mt.
Gilboa
Edrei
Taanach
Beth
Shan
Ramoth
Gilead
Shechem
Jordan R.
Mahanaim
Joppa
Rabbah (of the Ammonites)
PHILISTIA
Gezer
Gibeah
Ashdod
Jerusalem
Gath
Hebron
Medeba
Gaza
Salt
Sea
AMMON
Ziklag?
Beersheba
MOAB
Eastern Desert
Wadi of Egypt
Kir
Hareseth
Sinai
Tamar
EDOM
Kadesh Barnea
10,000 ft
3050 m
5000 ft
1525 m
2000 ft
610 m
1000 ft
305 m
0 (sea level)
0 (sea level)
-1640 ft
-500 m
Saul's kingdom
David's expansion
Additional territory controlled by Solomon
Ezion
Geber
Gulf of
Aqaba

Map 6: **KINGDOMS OF ISRAEL AND JUDAH**

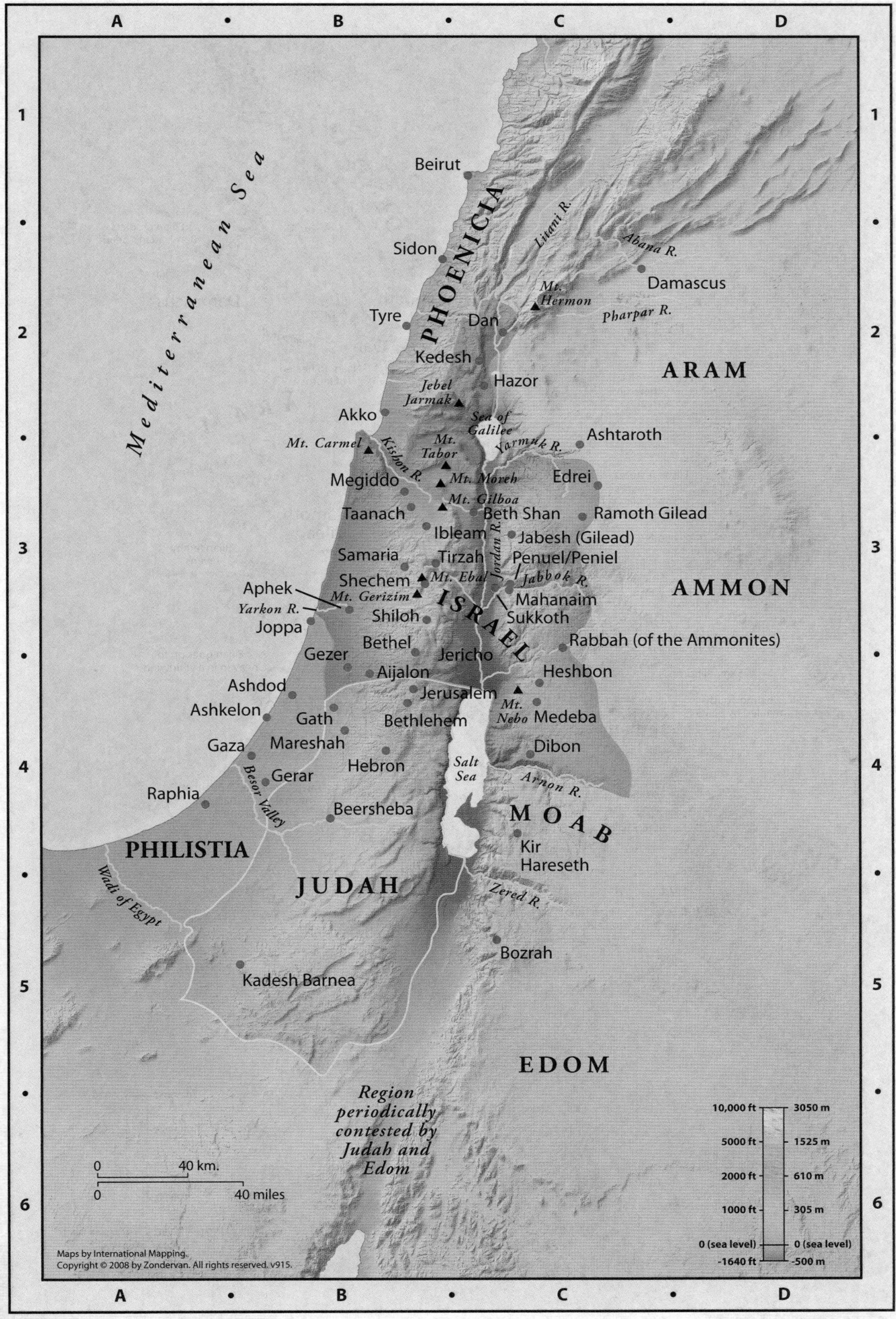
A • B • C • D
1
2
3
4
5
6
Mediterranean Sea
Beirut
PHOENICIA
Sidon
Litani R.
Abana R.
Damascus
Mt. Hermon
Pharpar R.
Tyre
Dan
Kedesh
ARAM
Hazor
Jebel Jarmak
Akko
Sea of Galilee
Ashtaroth
Mt. Carmel
Kishon R.
Mt. Tabor
Yarmuk R.
Mt. Moreh
Edrei
Megiddo
Mt. Gilboa
Taanach
Beth Shan
Ramoth Gilead
Ibleam
Jordan R.
Jabesh (Gilead)
Samaria
Tirzah
Penuel/Peniel
Shechem
Mt. Ebal
Jabbok R.
Aphek
Mt. Gerizim
AMMON
Mahanaim
Yarkon R.
ISRAEL
Shiloh
Sukkoth
Joppa
Bethel
Rabbah (of the Ammonites)
Gezer
Jericho
Aijalon
Heshbon
Ashdod
Jerusalem
Mt. Nebo
Medeba
Ashkelon
Gath
Bethlehem
Gaza
Mareshah
Dibon
Hebron
Salt Sea
Gerar
Besor Valley
Arnon R.
Raphia
Beersheba
MOAB
PHILISTIA
Kir Hareseth
JUDAH
Wadi of Egypt
Zered R.
Bozrah
Kadesh Barnea
EDOM
Region periodically contested by Judah and Edom
0 40 km.
0 40 miles
10,000 ft 3050 m
5000 ft 1525 m
2000 ft 610 m
1000 ft 305 m
0 (sea level) 0 (sea level)
-1640 ft -500 m
Maps by International Mapping.

Map 7: **PROPHETS IN ISRAEL AND JUDAH**

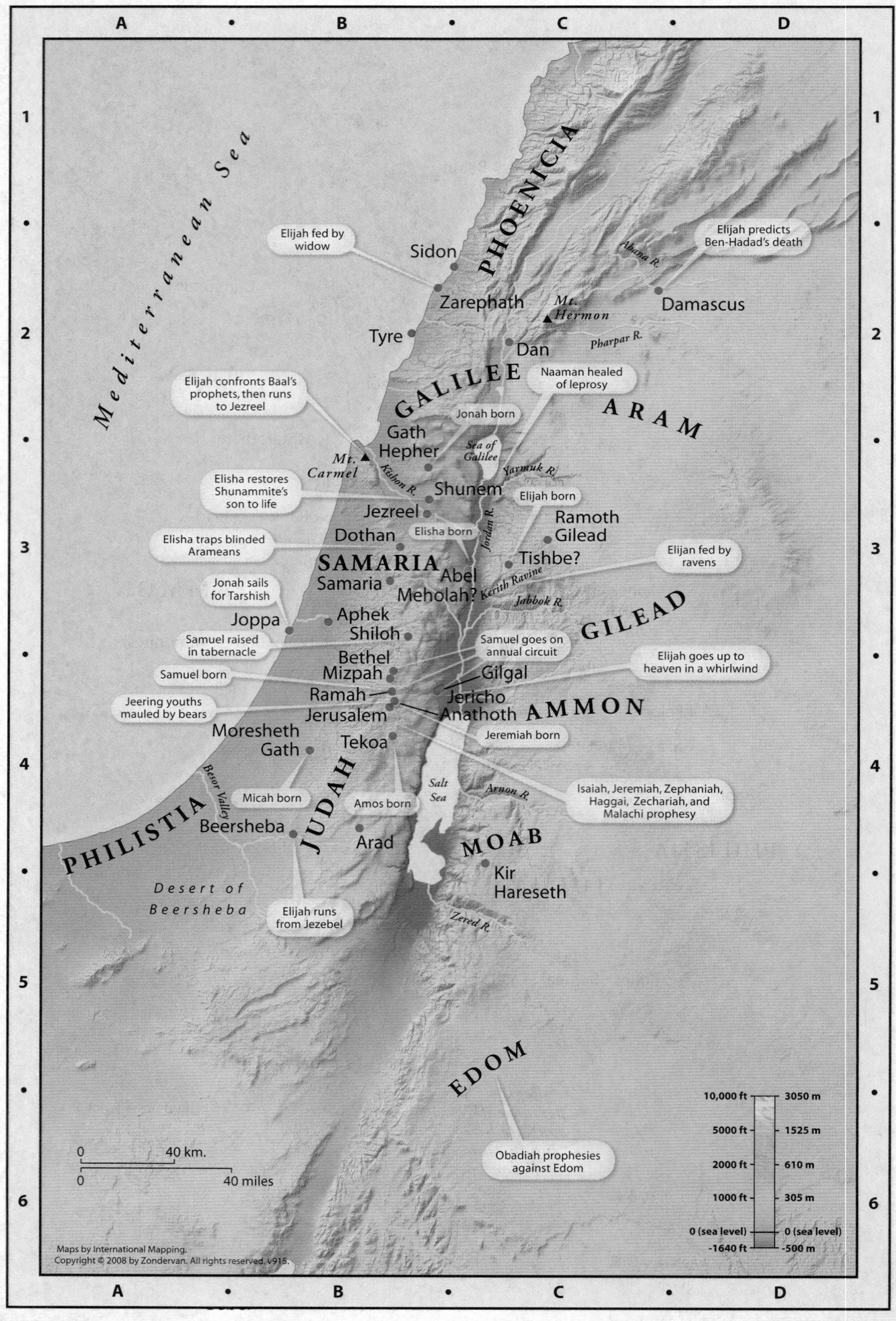
A
B
C
D
1
2
3
4
5
6
Mediterranean Sea
PHOENICIA
Elijah fed by widow
Sidon
Zarephath
Mt. Hermon
Elijah predicts Ben-Hadad's death
Abana R.
Damascus
Tyre
Dan
Pharpar R.
Elijah confronts Baal's prophets, then runs to Jezreel
GALILEE
Naaman healed of leprosy
ARAM
Jonah born
Gath Hepher
Sea of Galilee
Mt. Carmel
Kishon R.
Yarmuk R.
Elisha restores Shunammite's son to life
Shunem
Elijah born
Jezreel
Ramoth Gilead
Elisha traps blinded Arameans
Dothan
Elisha born
Jordan R.
SAMARIA
Tishbe?
Elijan fed by ravens
Jonah sails for Tarshish
Samaria
Abel Meholah?
Kerith Ravine
Jabbok R.
Joppa
Aphek
Shiloh
GILEAD
Samuel raised in tabernacle
Samuel goes on annual circuit
Bethel
Mizpah
Elijah goes up to heaven in a whirlwind
Samuel born
Gilgal
Ramah
Jericho
Jeering youths mauled by bears
Jerusalem
Anathoth
AMMON
Moresheth Gath
Jeremiah born
Tekoa
JUDAH
Besor Valley
Salt Sea
Arnon R.
Isaiah, Jeremiah, Zephaniah, Haggai, Zechariah, and Malachi prophesy
Micah born
Amos born
PHILISTIA
Beersheba
Arad
MOAB
Kir Hareseth
Desert of Beersheba
Elijah runs from Jezebel
Zered R.
EDOM
Obadiah prophesies against Edom
0
40 km.
0
40 miles
10,000 ft
3050 m
5000 ft
1525 m
2000 ft
610 m
1000 ft
305 m
0 (sea level)
0 (sea level)
-1640 ft
-500 m
Maps by International Mapping.
Copyright © 2008 by Zondervan. All rights reserved. v915.

Map 8: ASSYRIAN AND BABYLONIAN EMPIRES

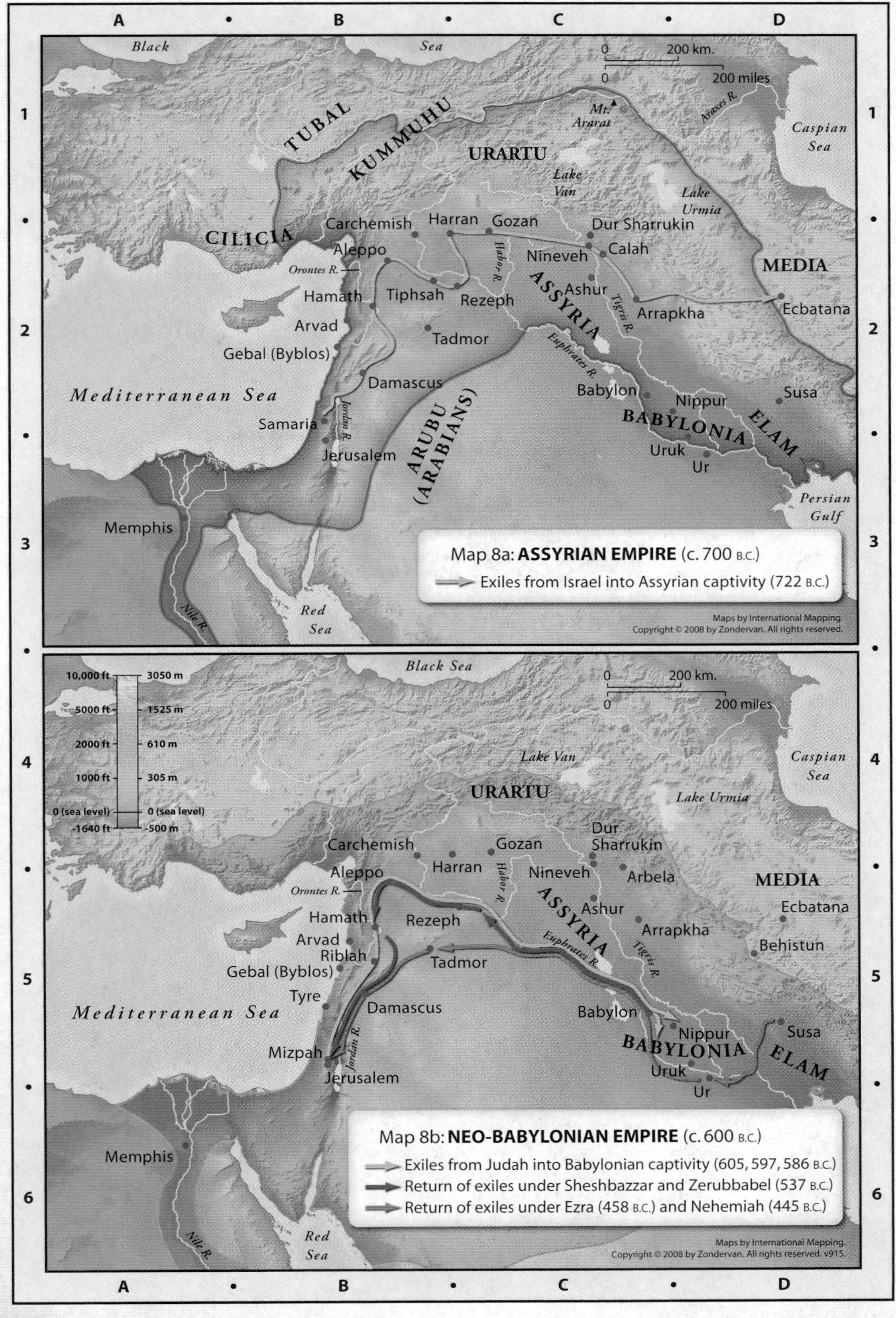
A
B
C
D
1
2
3
4
5
6
Black Sea
Caspian Sea
Mediterranean Sea
Red Sea
Persian Gulf
0 200 km.
0 200 miles
TUBAL
KUMMUHU
URARTU
Mt. Ararat
Araxes R.
Lake Van
Lake Urmia
CILICIA
Carchemish
Harran
Gozan
Dur Sharrukin
Calah
Aleppo
Orontes R.
Habor R.
Nineveh
MEDIA
Hamath
Tiphsah
Rezeph
Ashur
ASSYRIA
Tigris R.
Arrapkha
Ecbatana
Arvad
Tadmor
Gebal (Byblos)
Euphrates R.
Damascus
Babylon
Nippur
Susa
Samaria
Jordan R.
ARUBU (ARABIANS)
BABYLONIA
ELAM
Jerusalem
Uruk
Ur
Memphis
Nile R.
Map 8a: ASSYRIAN EMPIRE (c. 700 B.C.)
Exiles from Israel into Assyrian captivity (722 B.C.)
Maps by International Mapping.
Copyright © 2008 by Zondervan. All rights reserved.
10,000 ft 3050 m
5000 ft 1525 m
2000 ft 610 m
1000 ft 305 m
0 (sea level) 0 (sea level)
-1640 ft -500 m
Lake Van
Lake Urmia
Dur Sharrukin
Arbela
Riblah
Tyre
Mizpah
Behistun
Map 8b: NEO-BABYLONIAN EMPIRE (c. 600 B.C.)
Exiles from Judah into Babylonian captivity (605, 597, 586 B.C.)
Return of exiles under Sheshbazzar and Zerubbabel (537 B.C.)
Return of exiles under Ezra (458 B.C.) and Nehemiah (445 B.C.)
Maps by International Mapping.
Copyright © 2008 by Zondervan. All rights reserved. v915.

Map 9: HOLY LAND IN THE TIME OF JESUS

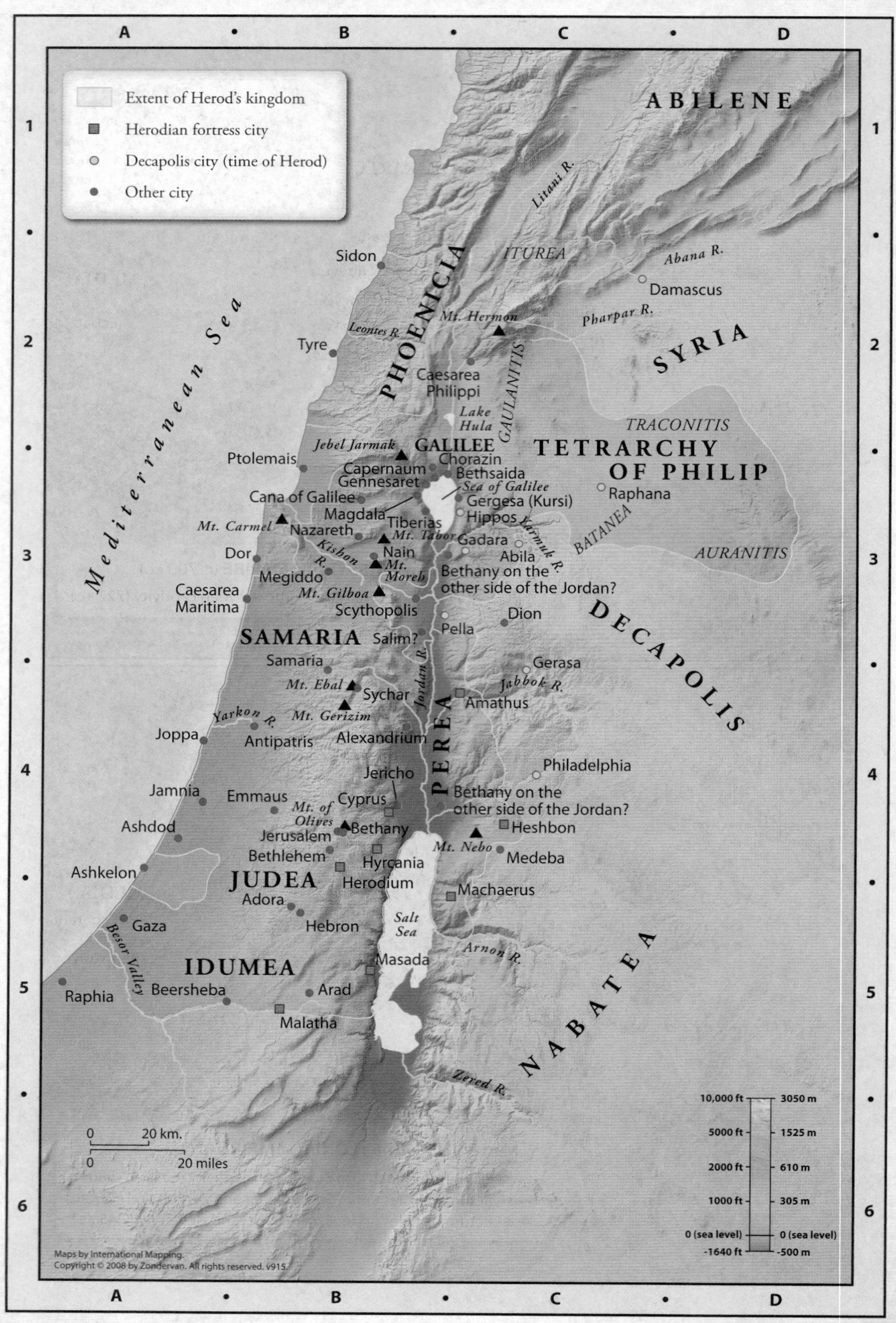
Extent of Herod's kingdom
Herodian fortress city
Decapolis city (time of Herod)
Other city
ABILENE
Litani R.
ITUREA
Abana R.
Damascus
Pharpar R.
SYRIA
Sidon
PHOENICIA
Mt. Hermon
Leontes R.
Tyre
GAULANITIS
Caesarea Philippi
Lake Hula
TRACONITIS
Mediterranean Sea
Jebel Jarmak
GALILEE
TETRARCHY OF PHILIP
Ptolemais
Chorazin
Capernaum
Gennesaret
Bethsaida
Sea of Galilee
Raphana
Cana of Galilee
Gergesa (Kursi)
Magdala
Hippos
Tiberias
Mt. Carmel
Nazareth
Mt. Tabor
Yarmuk R.
BATANEA
Gadara
Dor
Kishon R.
Nain
Abila
AURANITIS
Mt. Moreh
Megiddo
Bethany on the other side of the Jordan?
Caesarea Maritima
Mt. Gilboa
Scythopolis
Dion
DECAPOLIS
Pella
SAMARIA
Salim?
Samaria
Gerasa
Jordan R.
Jabbok R.
Mt. Ebal
Sychar
Amathus
Yarkon R.
Mt. Gerizim
PEREA
Joppa
Antipatris
Alexandrium
Philadelphia
Jericho
Jamnia
Emmaus
Cyprus
Bethany on the other side of the Jordan?
Mt. of Olives
Ashdod
Bethany
Heshbon
Jerusalem
Mt. Nebo
Bethlehem
Medeba
Hyrcania
Ashkelon
JUDEA
Herodium
Machaerus
Adora
Salt Sea
Hebron
Gaza
Besor Valley
Arnon R.
Masada
IDUMEA
NABATEA
Raphia
Beersheba
Arad
Malatha
Zered R.
0 20 km.
0 20 miles
10,000 ft 3050 m
5000 ft 1525 m
2000 ft 610 m
1000 ft 305 m
0 (sea level) 0 (sea level)
-1640 ft -500 m
A B C D
1 2 3 4 5 6

Map 10: **JERUSALEM IN THE TIME OF JESUS**

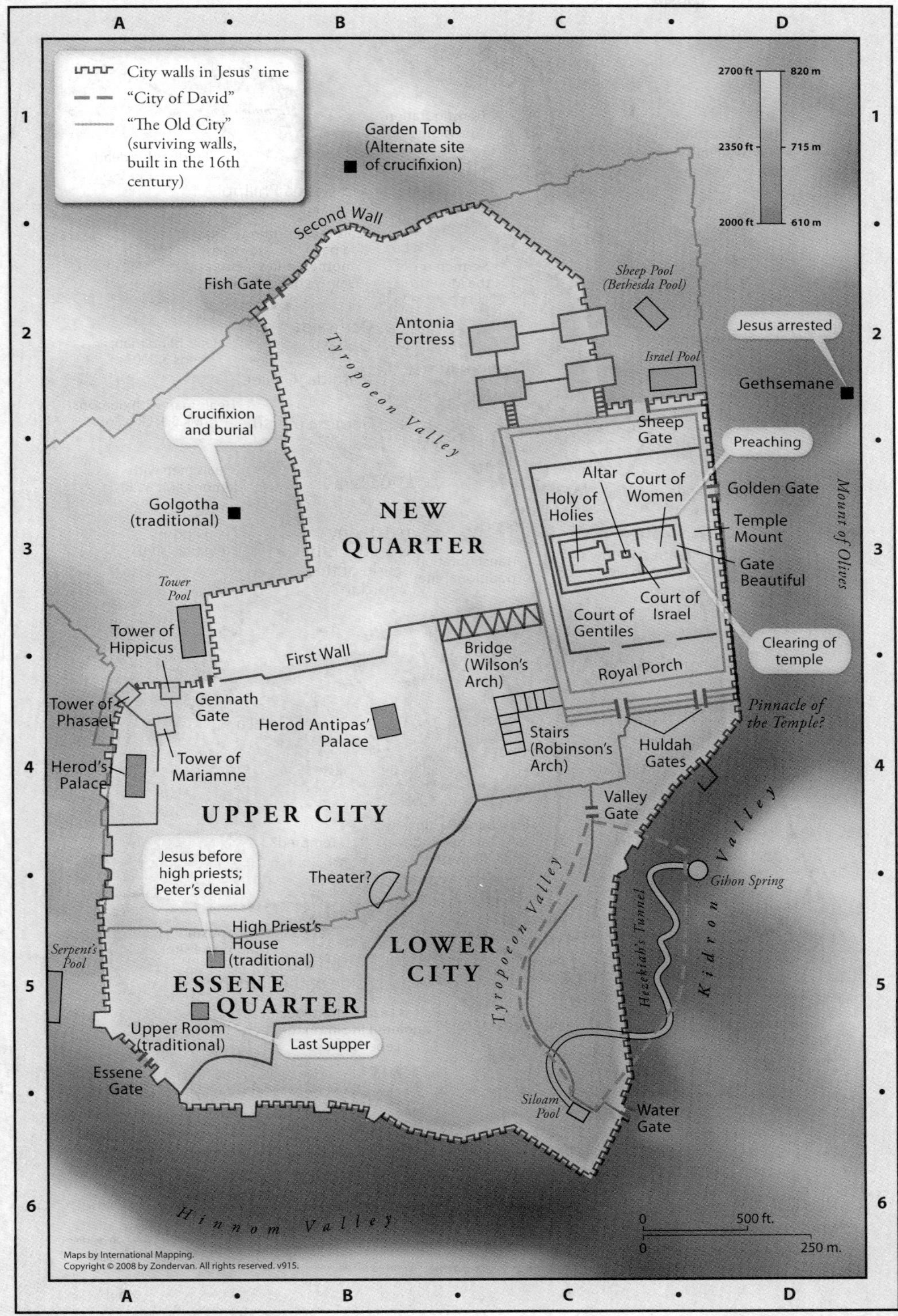
A
B
C
D
1
2
3
4
5
6
City walls in Jesus' time
"City of David"
"The Old City" (surviving walls, built in the 16th century)
Garden Tomb (Alternate site of crucifixion)
2700 ft
820 m
2350 ft
715 m
2000 ft
610 m
Second Wall
Fish Gate
Sheep Pool (Bethesda Pool)
Antonia Fortress
Tyropoeon Valley
Israel Pool
Jesus arrested
Gethsemane
Crucifixion and burial
Sheep Gate
Preaching
Altar
Court of Women
Golden Gate
Holy of Holies
Temple Mount
Mount of Olives
Golgotha (traditional)
NEW QUARTER
Gate Beautiful
Court of Israel
Tower Pool
Court of Gentiles
Tower of Hippicus
First Wall
Bridge (Wilson's Arch)
Clearing of temple
Royal Porch
Tower of Phasael
Gennath Gate
Herod Antipas' Palace
Pinnacle of the Temple?
Stairs (Robinson's Arch)
Huldah Gates
Herod's Palace
Tower of Mariamne
Valley Gate
UPPER CITY
Kidron Valley
Jesus before high priests; Peter's denial
Gihon Spring
Theater?
Hezekiah's Tunnel
Serpent's Pool
High Priest's House (traditional)
LOWER CITY
ESSENE QUARTER
Upper Room (traditional)
Last Supper
Essene Gate
Siloam Pool
Water Gate
Hinnom Valley
0
500 ft.
0
250 m.

Map 11: JESUS' MINISTRY

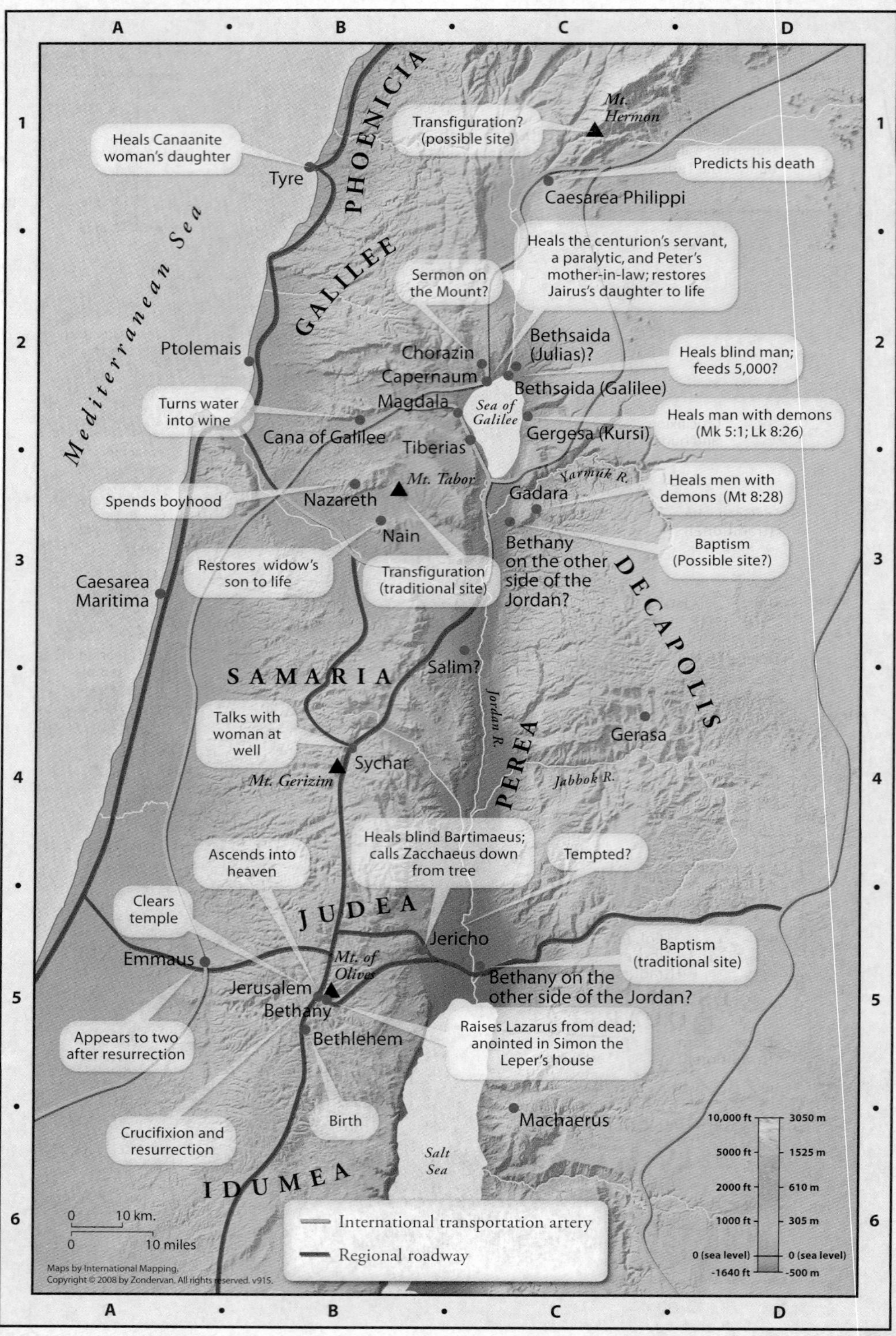

PHOENICIA
GALILEE
Mediterranean Sea
Mt. Hermon
Transfiguration? (possible site)
Heals Canaanite woman's daughter
Tyre
Predicts his death
Caesarea Philippi
Heals the centurion's servant, a paralytic, and Peter's mother-in-law; restores Jairus's daughter to life
Sermon on the Mount?
Ptolemais
Chorazin
Bethsaida (Julias)?
Heals blind man; feeds 5,000?
Capernaum
Bethsaida (Galilee)
Turns water into wine
Magdala
Sea of Galilee
Heals man with demons (Mk 5:1; Lk 8:26)
Cana of Galilee
Gergesa (Kursi)
Tiberias
Mt. Tabor
Yarmuk R.
Heals men with demons (Mt 8:28)
Spends boyhood
Nazareth
Gadara
Nain
Bethany on the other side of the Jordan?
Baptism (Possible site?)
Restores widow's son to life
Transfiguration (traditional site)
Caesarea Maritima
DECAPOLIS
SAMARIA
Salim?
Jordan R.
Gerasa
Talks with woman at well
Sychar
PEREA
Mt. Gerizim
Jabbok R.
Heals blind Bartimaeus; calls Zacchaeus down from tree
Ascends into heaven
Tempted?
Clears temple
JUDEA
Jericho
Baptism (traditional site)
Emmaus
Mt. of Olives
Bethany on the other side of the Jordan?
Jerusalem
Bethany
Appears to two after resurrection
Bethlehem
Raises Lazarus from dead; anointed in Simon the Leper's house
Machaerus
Birth
Crucifixion and resurrection
Salt Sea
IDUMEA
0 10 km.
0 10 miles
International transportation artery
Regional roadway
10,000 ft 3050 m
5000 ft 1525 m
2000 ft 610 m
1000 ft 305 m
0 (sea level) 0 (sea level)
-1640 ft -500 m
A B C D
1 2 3 4 5 6

Map 12: **APOSTLES' EARLY TRAVELS**

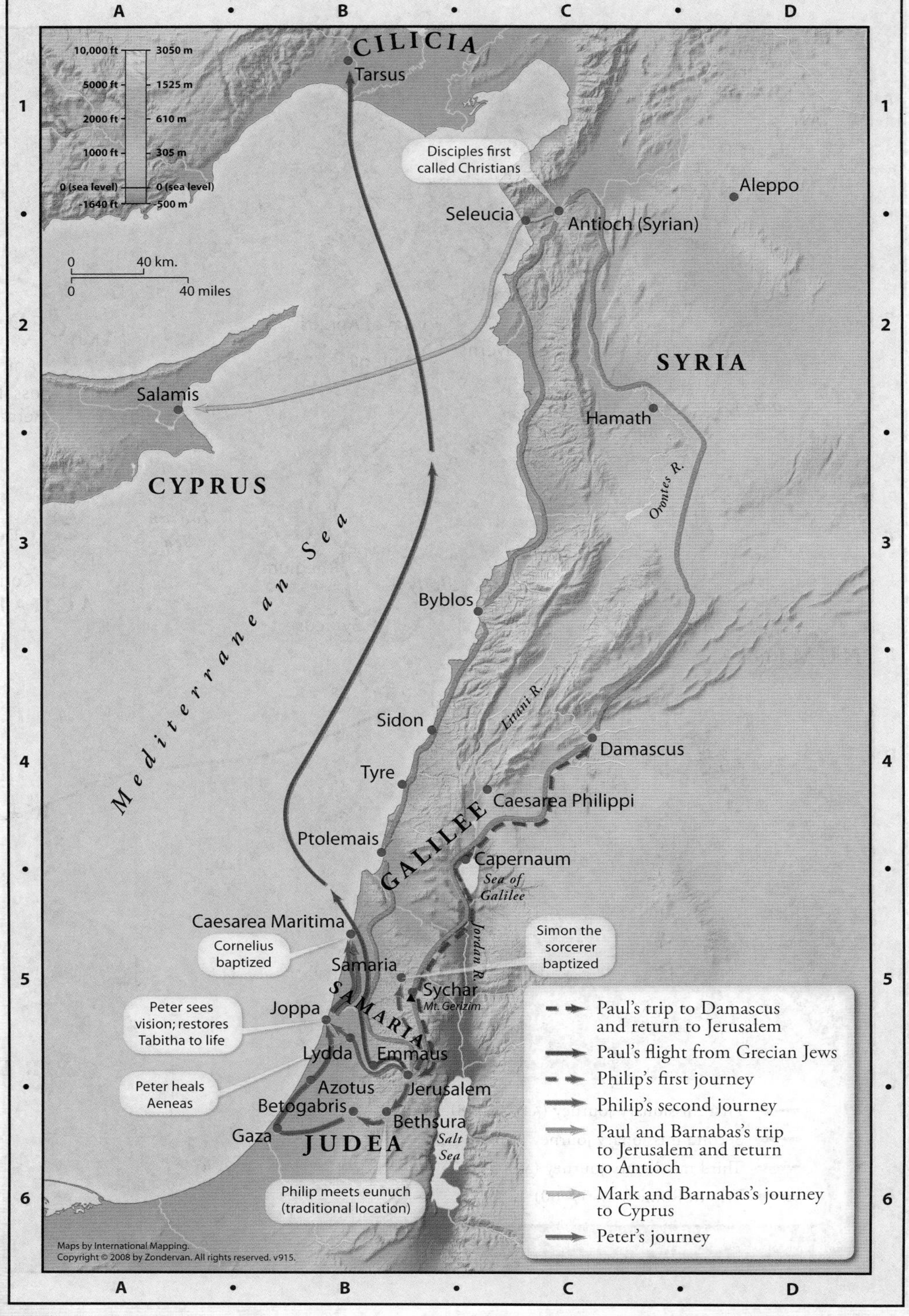
A
B
C
D
1
2
3
4
5
6
10,000 ft
3050 m
5000 ft
1525 m
2000 ft
610 m
1000 ft
305 m
0 (sea level)
0 (sea level)
-1640 ft
-500 m
0
40 km.
0
40 miles
CILICIA
Tarsus
Disciples first called Christians
Seleucia
Antioch (Syrian)
Aleppo
SYRIA
Salamis
Hamath
CYPRUS
Orontes R.
Mediterranean Sea
Byblos
Litani R.
Sidon
Damascus
Tyre
Caesarea Philippi
Ptolemais
GALILEE
Capernaum
Sea of Galilee
Caesarea Maritima
Jordan R.
Simon the sorcerer baptized
Cornelius baptized
Samaria
Sychar
Mt. Gerizim
SAMARIA
Joppa
Peter sees vision; restores Tabitha to life
Lydda
Emmaus
Peter heals Aeneas
Azotus
Jerusalem
Betogabris
Bethsura
Gaza
JUDEA
Salt Sea
Philip meets eunuch (traditional location)
Paul's trip to Damascus and return to Jerusalem
Paul's flight from Grecian Jews
Philip's first journey
Philip's second journey
Paul and Barnabas's trip to Jerusalem and return to Antioch
Mark and Barnabas's journey to Cyprus
Peter's journey
Maps by International Mapping.
Copyright © 2008 by Zondervan. All rights reserved. v915.

Map 13: **PAUL'S MISSIONARY JOURNEYS**

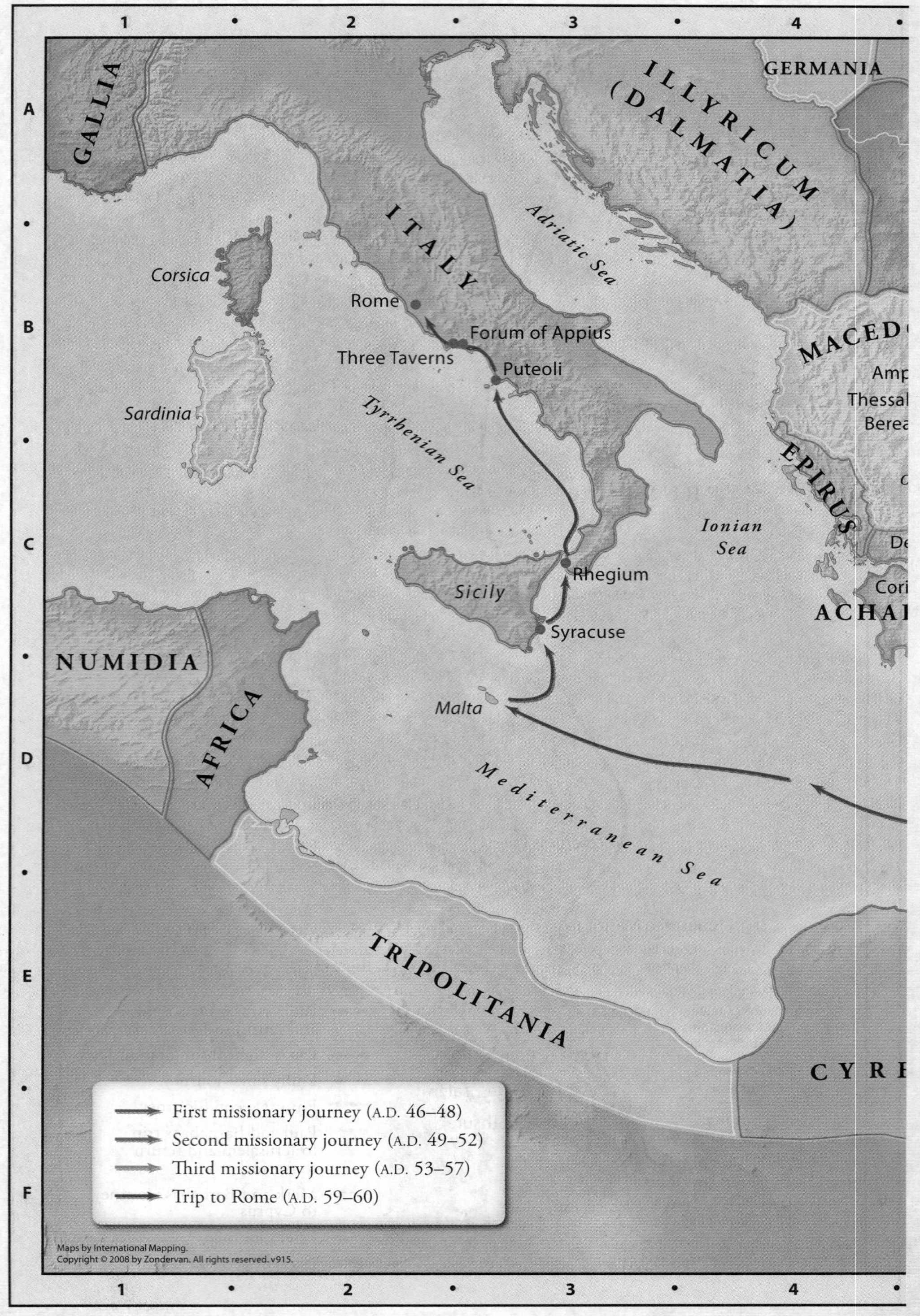

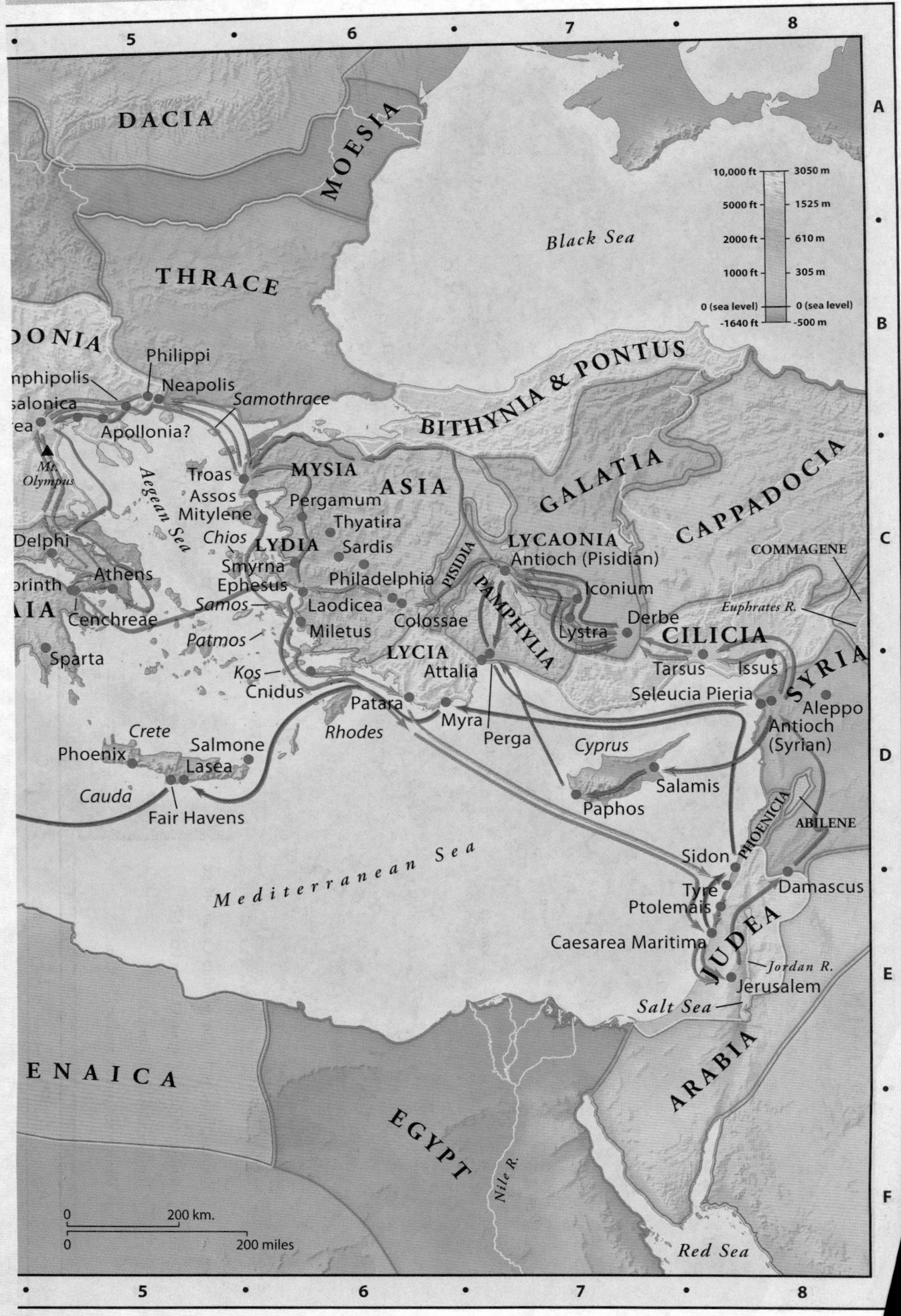
DACIA
MOESIA
THRACE
Black Sea
BITHYNIA & PONTUS
GALATIA
CAPPADOCIA
MYSIA
ASIA
LYDIA
LYCAONIA
PISIDIA
PAMPHYLIA
LYCIA
CILICIA
SYRIA
COMMAGENE
Euphrates R.
PHOENICIA
ABILENE
JUDEA
ARABIA
EGYPT
ENAICA
Philippi
Neapolis
Samothrace
Apollonia?
Mt. Olympus
Aegean Sea
Troas
Assos
Mitylene
Pergamum
Thyatira
Sardis
Chios
Smyrna
Ephesus
Philadelphia
Delphi
Athens
Samos
Laodicea
Colossae
Cenchreae
Miletus
Patmos
Sparta
Kos
Cnidus
Patara
Rhodes
Myra
Attalia
Perga
Antioch (Pisidian)
Iconium
Lystra
Derbe
Tarsus
Issus
Seleucia Pieria
Aleppo
Antioch (Syrian)
Crete
Phoenix
Salmone
Lasea
Cauda
Fair Havens
Cyprus
Salamis
Paphos
Mediterranean Sea
Sidon
Tyre
Ptolemais
Damascus
Caesarea Maritima
Jordan R.
Jerusalem
Salt Sea
Nile R.
Red Sea
10,000 ft 3050 m
5000 ft 1525 m
2000 ft 610 m
1000 ft 305 m
0 (sea level) 0 (sea level)
-1640 ft -500 m
0 200 km.
0 200 miles
5 6 7 8
A B C D E F

Map 14: ROMAN EMPIRE

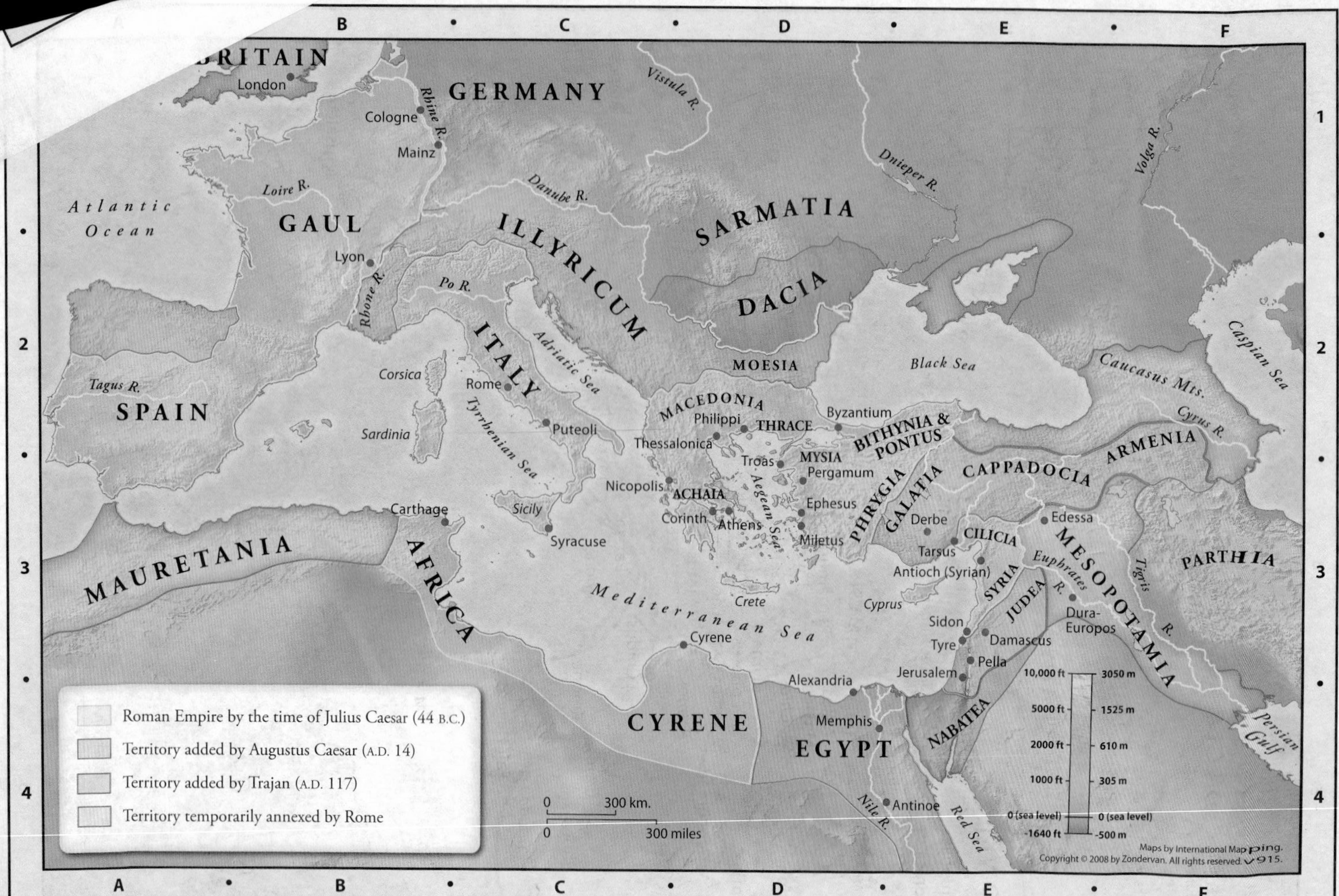

BRITAIN
London
GERMANY
Cologne
Rhine R.
Mainz
Vistula R.
Dnieper R.
Volga R.
Loire R.
Atlantic Ocean
GAUL
Lyon
Danube R.
ILLYRICUM
SARMATIA
DACIA
Rhone R.
Po R.
ITALY
Adriatic Sea
MOESIA
Black Sea
Caspian Sea
Caucasus Mts.
Corsica
Rome
Tagus R.
SPAIN
Sardinia
Tyrrhenian Sea
Puteoli
MACEDONIA
Philippi
THRACE
Byzantium
BITHYNIA & PONTUS
Cyrus R.
ARMENIA
Thessalonica
Troas
MYSIA
Pergamum
CAPPADOCIA
Nicopolis
ACHAIA
Aegean Sea
PHRYGIA
GALATIA
Ephesus
Corinth
Athens
Miletus
Derbe
Edessa
Carthage
Sicily
Syracuse
CILICIA
Tarsus
MESOPOTAMIA
Euphrates R.
Tigris R.
PARTHIA
MAURETANIA
AFRICA
Antioch (Syrian)
SYRIA
JUDEA
Crete
Cyprus
Mediterranean Sea
Sidon
Dura-Europos
Tyre
Damascus
Cyrene
Pella
Jerusalem
Alexandria
Persian Gulf
CYRENE
Memphis
EGYPT
NABATEA
Antinoe
Nile R.
Red Sea
Roman Empire by the time of Julius Caesar (44 B.C.)
Territory added by Augustus Caesar (A.D. 14)
Territory added by Trajan (A.D. 117)
Territory temporarily annexed by Rome
0 300 km.
0 300 miles
10,000 ft 3050 m
5000 ft 1525 m
2000 ft 610 m
1000 ft 305 m
0 (sea level) 0 (sea level)
-1640 ft -500 m
A B C D E F
1 2 3 4
Maps by International Mapping.
Copyright © 2008 by Zondervan. All rights reserved. v915.